The
INTERNATIONAL
WHO'S WHO
of
WOMEN
2002

The INTERNATIONAL WHO'S WHO *of* WOMEN 2002

Third Edition

Third Edition 2002

© **Europa Publications Limited 2001**
11 New Fetter Lane, London, EC4P 4EE, England
(A member of the Taylor & Francis Group)

ISBN: 1-85743-122-7
ISSN: 0965-3775

Editor: Elizabeth Sleeman
Technology Editor: Ian Preston
Freelance Editorial Team: Gerard Delaney,
Suzanne Jones, Susan Leckey, Jenifa Sharif
Editorial Co-ordinator: Mary Hill
Administrative Assistant: Fiona Vas

Typeset by MPG Dataworld and printed by Unwin Brothers Limited,
The Gresham Press, Old Woking, Surrey

FOREWORD

The third edition of THE INTERNATIONAL WHO'S WHO OF WOMEN provides in one volume a library of information on the lives and careers of the most noted women of today.

Women are under-represented generally in who's whos. THE INTERNATIONAL WHO'S WHO OF WOMEN seeks to redress the balance, and reveals that prominent women exist in every profession and on every continent. It remains noteworthy when a woman is appointed to a position such as US National Security Advisor. The book includes heads of state, academics, writers, scientists, economists, United Nations officials, actresses, government ministers and noted politicians, fashion designers, diplomatists, artists, sportswomen, etc, many of whom have reached the pinnacle of their professions. We include details of distinguished women world-wide, from North America, Western and Eastern Europe, Eurasia, Australasia and Japan, to countries as diverse as Mongolia, Panama, Jamaica and Nigeria.

THE INTERNATIONAL WHO'S WHO OF WOMEN contains biographical details of 5,500 women of importance, selected because of the position they have attained within their profession, or because of the authority they wield within their chosen field. Many are household names nationally and internationally, others are noted within their profession for their work. The scope of the book includes women who have only recently achieved prominence, as well as already established figures.

While the main part of the book consists of biographical entries, we have also included an extensive index section, where entrants are listed alphabetically under general career headings. In addition the index states each entrant's nationality and specific profession.

For this edition existing entrants were given an opportunity to make necessary amendments and additions to their entries while potential new entrants were asked to fill out a detailed questionnaire, providing biographical details. Supplementary research has ensured that entries contain accurate and up-to-date information, and that THE INTERNATIONAL WHO'S WHO OF WOMEN provides in one volume an invaluable reference source on the women who are making their mark in the world today.

August 2001

ACKNOWLEDGEMENTS

The Editors are most grateful to all the entrants who completed questionnaires and returned them to us.

We would also like to thank all the people we approached at embassies and national and international organizations who were kind enough to provide us with information on women of note in their country or sphere of interest.

EXPLANATORY NOTES

The list of names is alphabetical, with the entrants listed under surnames.

All names beginning Mc and Mac are treated as though they began Mac. In the case of surnames beginning De, Des, Du, Van or Von the entries are, unless otherwise specified by the entrant, found under the prefix. As a general rule, Chinese names are alphabetized under the first name.

Each biographical entry in THE INTERNATIONAL WHO'S WHO OF WOMEN includes, where appropriate, the following details:

★ Surname

★ Titles and First names

★ Honours, academic degrees and professional qualifications

★ Nationality

★ Profession

★ Date and place of birth

★ Personal details (names of parents and spouse or partner, year of marriage, number of children, etc)

★ Educational establishments attended

★ Career history, including dates. Main career details, in date order, are followed by memberships, directorships, etc. This section also specifies honorary degrees received, and lists general awards and prizes conferred on the entrant. Awards for specific works will be found listed after the particular publication, film or play, etc

★ Titles of major publications, films, plays, recordings, works, etc, with dates

★ Contact addresses with telephone, telex, fax, e-mail and internet numbers. The telephone and fax area codes provided are as required by a reader calling from a foreign country

Supplementary information exists in the following sections of the book:

★ An Index by Career. Entrants are listed under career headings in alphabetical order. The Index gives the Name, First names, Nationality and Profession of the entrants. The index headings, in alphabetical order, are as follows: Academia, Science and Research, Art, Broadcasting and Journalism, Business and Banking, Civil and Public Service, Diplomacy, Fashion, Film and Theatre, Law, Literature, Medicine, Museums, Libraries and Art Galleries, Music, National and International Organizations, Politics and Government, Religion, Sport and Leisure. A Contents list for the various categories will be found before the index.

★ An extensive List of Abbreviations

★ A guide to International Telephone Codes

CONTENTS

LIST OF ABBREVIATIONS

AAAS	American Association for the Advancement of Science
AAF	Army Air Force
AASA	Associate of the Australian Society of Accountants
AB	Aktiebolag; Alberta; Bachelor of Arts
ABA	American Bar Association
AC	Companion of the Order of Australia
ACA	Associate of the Institute of Chartered Accountants
ACCA	Associate of the Association of Certified Accountants
Acad	Academy, Académie
Accad	Accademia
Accred	Accredited
ACIS	Associate of the Chartered Institute of Secretaries
ACP	African, Caribbean and Pacific Group of States; American College of Physicians
ACS	American Chemical Society
ACT	Australian Capital Territory
ADC	Aide-de-camp
Adm	Admiral
Admin	Administration, Administrative, Administrator
AE	Air Efficiency Award
AERE	Atomic Energy Research Establishment
AEU	Amalgamated Engineering Union
AF	Air Force
AFC	Air Force Cross
AFESD	Arab Fund for Economic and Social Development
affil	affiliated
AFL	American Federation of Labor
AFM	Air Force Medal
AG	Aktiengesellschaft (Joint Stock Company)
AGALEV-GROEN	Anders Gaan Leven-Geweldloos, Rechtvaarding, Open Ecologisch Netwerk
Agric	Agriculture
ai	ad interim
AIA	American Institute of Architects; Associate of Institute of Actuaries
AIAA	American Institute of Aeronautics and Astronautics
AIB	Associate of the Institute of Bankers
AICC	All-India Congress Committee
AICE	Associate of the Institute of Civil Engineers
AIChE	American Institute of Chemical Engineers
AID	(US) Agency for International Development
AIDS	Acquired Immune Deficiency Syndrome
AIEE	American Institute of Electrical Engineers
AIME	American Institute of Mining Engineers; Associate of the Institution of Mining Engineers
AIR	All India Radio
AK	Alaska; Knight of the Order of Australia
Akad	Akademie
AL	Alabama
ALS	Associate of the Linnaean Society
Alt	Alternate
AM	Albert Medal; Master of Arts; Member of the Order of Australia
Amb	Ambassador
AMICE	Associate Member of the Institution of Civil Engineers
AMIEE	Associate Member of the Institution of Electrical Engineers
ANU	Australian National University
AO	Officer of the Order of Australia
AP	Andhra Pradesh
Apdo	Apartado
approx	approximately
Apptd	Appointed
Apt	apartment
AR	Arkansas
ARA	Associate of the Royal Academy
ARAM	Associate of the Royal Academy of Music
ARC	Agriculture Research Council; Rainbow Group in the European Parliament
ARCA	Associate of the Royal College of Art
ARCM	Associate of the Royal College of Music
ARCO	Associate of the Royal College of Organists
ARCOB	Verdi Arcobaleno
ARCS	Associate of the Royal College of Science
ARCT	Associate of the Royal Conservatory of Music of Toronto

ARIBA	Associate of the Royal Institute of British Architects
ARSA	Associate of the Royal Scottish Academy; Associate of the Royal Society of Arts
ASEAN	Association of South East Asian Nations
ASLIB	Association of Special Libraries and Information Bureaux
ASME	American Society of Mechanical Engineers
Asoc	Asociación
Ass	Assembly
Asscn	Association
Assoc	Associate
ASSR	Autonomous Soviet Socialist Republic
Asst	Assistant
ATV	Associated Television
AUEW	Amalgamated Union of Engineering Workers
Aug	August
avda	avenida
Ave	Avenue
AZ	Arizona
b	born
B AGR	Bachelor of Agriculture
B AGR SC	Bachelor of Agricultural Science
B ARCH	Bachelor of Architecture
B CH, B CHIR	Bachelor of Surgery
B COM(M)	Bachelor of Commerce
B ECONS	Bachelor of Economics
B ED	Bachelor of Education
B ENG	Bachelor of Engineering
B LIT(T)	Bachelor of Letters
B LL	Bachelor of Laws
B MUS	Bachelor of Music
B PHARM	Bachelor of Pharmacy
B PHIL	Bachelor of Philosophy
B SC	Bachelor of Science
B SC S	Bachelor of Social Science
BA	Bachelor of Arts; British Airways
BAAS	British Association for the Advancement of Science
BAFTA	British Academy of Film and Television Arts
BAO	Bachelor of Obstetrics
BAS	Bachelor in Agricultural Science
BBA	Bachelor of Business Administration
BBC	British Broadcasting Corporation
BC	British Columbia
BCC	British Council of Churches
BCE	Bachelor of Civil Engineering
BCL	Bachelor of Canon Law; Bachelor of Civil Law
BCS	Bachelor of Commercial Sciences
BD	Bachelor of Divinity
Bd	Board
BDS	Bachelor of Dental Surgery
BE	Bachelor of Education; Bachelor of Engineering
BEA	British European Airways
Beds	Bedfordshire
BEE	Bachelor of Electrical Engineering
BEM	British Empire Medal
Berks	Berkshire
BFA	Bachelor of Fine Arts
BFI	British Film Institute
BIM	British Institute of Management
biog	biography
BIS	Bank for International Settlements
BL	Bachelor of Laws
Bldg	Building
BLS	Bachelor in Library Science
blvd	boulevard
BM	Bachelor of Medicine
BMA	British Medical Association
BOAC	British Overseas Airways Corporation
BP	Boîte postale (Post Office Box); British Petroleum
BPA	Bachelor of Public Administration
Br	Branch
Brig	Brigadier
BS	Bachelor of Science; Bachelor of Surgery

BSA	Bachelor of Scientific Agriculture
BT	Baronet
Bucks	Buckinghamshire
c	child, children
c	circa
C CHEM	Chartered Chemist
C ENG	Chartered Engineer
C LIT	Companion of Literature
C PHYS	Chartered Physicist
C SC	Candidate of Sciences
CA	California; Chartered Accountant
CABI	Commonwealth Agricultural Bureaux International
Cad	Caddesi (Street)
Cambs	Cambridgeshire
Cand	Candidate, Candidature
Capt	Captain
CARICOM	Caribbean Community and Common Market
CB	Companion of the (Order of the) Bath
CBC	Canadian Broadcasting Corporation
CBE	Commander of (the Order of) the British Empire
CBI	Confederation of British Industry
CBIM	Companion of British Institute of Management
CBS	Columbia Broadcasting System
CC	Companion of Order of Canada
CCP	Chinese Communist Party
CD	Canadian Forces Decoration; Centrum-Demokraterne
CDA	Christen Democratisch Appèl
Cdre	Commodore
CDS	Centro Democrático y Social; Partido do Centro. Democratico Social
CDU	Christlich-Demokratische Union; Coligação Democratica Unitaria
CE	Chartered Engineer, Civil Engineer
CEAO	Communauté Economique de l'Afrique de l'Ouest
Cen	Central
CENTO	Central Treaty Organization
CEO	Chief Executive Officer
CERN	Conseil (*now* Organisation) Européen(ne) pour la Recherche Nucléaire
CFR	Commander of the Federal Republic of Nigeria
CG	Left Unity
CGM	Conspicuous Gallantry Medal
CGT	Confédération Général du Travail
CH	Companion of Honour
CH B	Bachelor of Surgery
CH M	Master of Surgery
Chair	Chairperson, Chairwoman
Chem	Chemistry
CI	Channel Islands; Imperial Order of the Crown of India
CIA	Central Intelligence Agency
Cia	Compagnia (Company)
Cía	Compañía (Company)
CID	Criminal Investigation Department
CIE	Companion of (the Order of) the Indian Empire
Cie	Compagnie (Company)
CIEE	Companion of the Institution of Electrical Engineers
C-in-C	Commander-in-Chief
CIO	Congress of Industrial Organizations
CiU	Convergència i Unió
CLD	Doctor of Civil Law (USA)
CM	Canada Medal; Master in Surgery
CMEA	Council for Mutual Economic Assistance
CMG	Companion of (the Order of) St Michael and St George
CN	Coalición Nacionalista
CNAA	Council for National Academic Awards
CNI	Centre National des Indépendants et Paysans
CNRS	Centre National de la Recherche Scientifique
Co	Company; County
CO	Colorado; Commanding Officer
Col	Colonel; Colonia
Coll	College
COMECON	Council for Mutual Economic Assistance
Comm	Commission
Commd	Commissioned
Commdg	Commanding
Commdr	Commander, Commandeur
Commdt	Commandant
Commr	Commissioner
Conf	Conference
Confed	Confederation
Cons	Conservative; Conservative and Unionist Party
Contrib	Contribution; Contributor
COO	Chief Operating Officer

Corp	Corporate
Corpn	Corporation
Corresp	Correspondent, Corresponding
CP	Communist Party; Caixa Postal/Case Postale (Post Office Box)
CPA	Certified Public Accountant; Commonwealth Parliamentary Association
CPP	Convention People's Party (Ghana)
CPPCC	Chinese People's Political Consultative Conference
CPRE	Council for the Protection of Rural England
CPSU	Communist Party of the Soviet Union
cr	created
CSCE	Conference on Security and Co-operation in Europe
CSFR	Czech and Slovak Federative Republic
CSI	Companion of (the Order of) the Star of India
CSIRO	Commonwealth Scientific and Industrial Research Organization
CSSR	Czechoslovak Socialist Republic
CStJ	Commander of (the Order of) St John of Jerusalem
CSU	Christlich-Soziale Union
CT	Connecticut
Cttee	Committee
CV	Commanditaire Vennootschap
CVO	Commander of the Royal Victorian Order
CVP	Christelijke Volkspartij
d	daughter(s)
D'66	Democraten 66
D ARCH	Doctor of Architecture
D CL	Doctor of Canon Law
D CN L	Doctor of Canon Law
D COMM	Doctor of Commerce
D ECON	Doctor of Economics
D ED	Doctor of Education
D EN D	Docteur en Droit
D EN MED	Docteur en Medicine
D ENG	Doctor of Engineering
D ÈS L	Docteur ès Lettres
D ÈS SC	Docteur ès Sciences
D HIST	Doctor of History
D HUM LITT	Doctor of Humane Letters
D IUR	Doctor of Law
D IUR UTR	Doctor of both Civil and Canon Law
D JUR	Doctor of Law
D LIT(T)	Doctor of Letters; Doctor of Literature
D(R) MED	Doctor of Medicine
D MIN SCI	Doctor of Municipal Science
D MUS	Doctor of Music
D PHIL	Doctor of Philosophy
D SC	Doctor of Science
D SC S	Doctor of Social Science
D TECH	Doctor of Technology
D THEOL	Doctor of Theology
D UNIV	Doctor of the University
DB	Bachelor of Divinity
DBA	Doctor of Business Administration
DBE	Dame Commander of (the Order of) the British Empire
DC	Democrazia Christiana; District of Columbia
DCB	Dame, Commdr, Order of the Bath
DCL	Doctor of Civil Law
DCM	Distinguished Conduct Medal
DCMG	Dame Commander of (the Order of) St Michael and St George
DCS	Doctor of Commercial Sciences
DCT	Doctor of Christian Theology
DCVO	Dame Commander of the Royal Victorian Order
DD	Doctor of Divinity
DDR	Deutsche Demokratische Republik (German Democratic Republic)
DDS	Doctor of Dental Surgery
DE	Delaware
Dec	December
Del	Delegate, delegation
Dept	Department
DES	Department of Education and Science
Desig	Designate
Devt	Development
DF	Distrito Federal
DFA	Doctor of Fine Arts
DFC	Distinguished Flying Cross
DFM	Distinguished Flying Medal
DH	Doctor of Humanities
DHL	Doctor of Hebrew Literature
DHSS	Department of Health and Social Security

DIANA	Dimograttki Ananeossi
DIC	Diploma of Imperial College
Dip	Diploma
DIP AD	Diploma in Art and Design
DIP AGR	Diploma in Agriculture
DIP ED	Diploma in Education
DIP(L) ENG	Diploma in Engineering
Dir	Director
Dist	District
Div	Division; Divisional
DK	Most Esteemed Family (Malaysia)
DL	Deputy Lieutenant
DLS	Doctor of Library Science
DM	Doctor of Medicine (Oxford)
DMD	Doctor of Dental Medicine
DMS	Director of Medical Services
DMV	Doctor of Veterinary Medicine
DN	Distrito Nacional
DO	Doctor of Ophthalmology
DP	Democrazia Proletaria; Demokratesch Partei
DPH	Diploma in Public Health
DPM	Diploma in Psychological Medicine
Dr	Doctor
DR	Technical Group of the European Right
DR AGR	Doctor of Agriculture
Dr hc	Doctor honoris causa
DR ING	Doctor of Engineering
DR IUR	Doctor of Laws
DR JUR	Doctor of Laws
DR OEC (PUBL)	Doctor of (Public) Economy
DR RER NAT	Doctor of Natural Sciences
DR RER POL	Doctor of Political Science
DR SC	Doctor of Sciences
DR SC NAT	Doctor of Natural Sciences
DS	Doctor of Science
DSC	Distinguished Service Cross
DSM	Distinguished Service Medal
DSO	Companion of the Distinguished Service Order
DSS	Department of Social Security
DST	Doctor of Sacred Theology
DTM(& H)	Diploma in Tropical Medicine (and Hygiene)
DUP	Democratic Unionist Party (Northern Ireland); Diploma of the University of Paris
E	East, Eastern
EBRD	European Bank for Reconstruction and Development
EC	European Communities
ECA	Economic Co-operation Administration; Economic Commission for Africa
ECAFE	Economic Commission for Asia and the Far East
ECE	Economic Commission for Europe
ECLAC	Economic Commission for Latin America and the Caribbean
ÉCOLO-VERTS	Écologistes Confédérés pour l'Organisation de Luttes Originales-Verts Européens pour de Régions Transfrontalières et Solidaires
Econ(s)	Economic(s)
ECOSOC	Economic and Social Council
ECSC	European Coal and Steel Community
ECWA	Economic Commission for Western Asia
ed	edited; editor
Ed	Editor
ED	Doctor of Engineering (USA); Efficiency Decoration
ED D	Doctor of Education
ED M	Master of Education
Edif	Edificio (Building)
Edn	Edition
Educ	Education
EEC	European Economic Community
EFTA	European Free Trade Association
EIB	European Investment Bank
EM	Edward Medal; Master of Engineering (USA)
EMBO	European Molecular Biology Organization
Emer	Emeritus
Eng	Engineering
ENG D	Doctor of Engineering
EP	European Parliament; Coalición por la Europa de los Pueblos Eusko Alkartasuna (EA)
EPP	Group of the European People's Party (Christian-Democratic Group)
ESCAP	Economic and Social Commission for Asia and the Pacific
ESCWA	Economic and Social Commission for Western Asia
esq	esquina (corner)

est	established
etc	et cetera
Éts	Etablissements
EU	European Union
EURATOM	European Atomic Energy Community
Exec	Executive
f	founded
F ENG	Fellow, Fellowship of Engineering
F MED SCI	Fellow of the Academy of Medical Sciences
FAA	Fellow of Australian Academy of Science
FAATS	Fellow Australian Academy of Technological Sciences
FACC	Fellow of the American College of Cardiology
FACCA	Fellow of the Association of Certified and Corporate Accountants
FACE	Fellow of the Australian College of Education
FACP	Fellow of the American College of Physicians
FACS	Fellow of the American College of Surgeons
FAHA	Fellow of the Australian Academy of the Humanities
FAIA	Fellow of the American Institute of Architects
FAIAS	Fellow of the Australian Institute of Agricultural Science
FAIM	Fellow of the Australian Institute of Management
FAO	Food and Agriculture Organization
FASE	Fellow of the Antiquarian Society, Edinburgh
FASSA	Fellow Academy of Social Sciences of Australia
Fax	Facsimile
FBA	Fellow of the British Academy
FBI	Federal Bureau of Investigation
FBIM	Fellow of the British Institute of Management
FBIP	Fellow of the British Institute of Physics
FCA	Fellow of the Institute of Chartered Accountants
FCAE	Fellow Canadian Academy of Engineering
FCGI	Fellow of the City and Guilds of London Institute
FCIA	Fellow Chartered Institute of Arbitrators
FCIB	Fellow Chartered Institute of Bankers
FCIC	Fellow of the Chemical Institute of Canada
FCIS	Fellow of the Chartered Institute of Secretaries
FCO	Foreign and Commonwealth Office
FCSD	Fellow Chartered Society of Designers
FCT	Federal Capital Territory
FCWA	Fellow of the Institute of Cost and Works Accountants
FDGB	Freier Deutscher Gewerkschaftsbund
FDP	Freie Demokratische Partei
Feb	February
Fed	Federal, Federation
FF	Fianna Fail Party
FG	Fine Gael Party
FGS	Fellow of the Geological Society
FGSM	Fellow of the Guildhall School of Music
FIA	Fellow of the Institute of Actuaries
FIAL	Fellow of the International Institute of Arts and Letters
FIAM	Fellow of the International Academy of Management
FIAMS	Fellow of the Indian Academy of Medical Sciences
FIARB	Fellow of the Institute of Arbitrators
FIB	Fellow of the Institute of Bankers
FIBA	Fellow of the Institute of Banking Associations
FIBIOL	Fellow of the Institute of Biologists
FICE	Fellow of the Institution of Civil Engineers
FICHEME	Fellow of the Institute of Chemical Engineers
FID	Fellow of the Institute of Directors
FIE	Fellow of the Institute of Engineers
FIEE	Fellow of the Institution of Electrical Engineers
FIEEE	Fellow of the Institute of Electrical and Electronics Engineers
FIJ	Fellow of the Institute of Journalists
FIL LIC	Licentiate in Philosophy
FIM	Fellow of the Institute of Metallurgists
FIME	Fellow of the Institute of Mining Engineers
FIMECHE	Fellow of the Institute of Mechanical Engineers
FINSTM	Fellow of the Institute of Marketing
FINSTP	Fellow of the Institute of Physics
FIPM	Fellow of the Institute of Personnel Management
FIRE	Fellow of the Institution of Radio Engineers
FITD	Fellow of the Institute of Training and Development
FL	Florida
FLA	Fellow of the Library Association
FLN	Front de Libération Nationale
FLS	Fellow of the Linnaean Society
fmr	former
fmrly	formerly
FN	Front National
FNI	Fellow of the National Institute of Sciences of India
FNZIA	Fellow of the New Zealand Institute of Architects
FNZIC	Fellow of the New Zealand Institute of Chemists

FRACO	Fellow of the Royal Australian College of Ophthalmologists
FRACP	Fellow of the Royal Australasian College of Physicians
FRACS	Fellow of the Royal Australasian College of Surgeons
FRAES	Fellow of the Royal Aeronautical Society
FRAI	Fellow of the Royal Anthropological Institute
FRAIA	Fellow of the Royal Australian Institute of Architects
FRAIC	Fellow of the Royal Architectural Institute of Canada
FRAM	Fellow of the Royal Academy of Music
FRAS	Fellow of the Royal Asiatic Society; Fellow of the Royal Astronomical Society
FRBS	Fellow of the Royal Society of British Sculptors
FRCM	Fellow of the Royal College of Music
FRCO	Fellow of the Royal College of Organists
FRCOG	Fellow of the Royal College of Obstetricians and Gynaecologists
FRCPATH	Fellow of the Royal College of Pathologists
FRCP(E)	Fellow of the Royal College of Physicians (Edinburgh)
FRCPI	Fellow of the Royal College of Physicians of Ireland
FRCP(UK)	Fellow of the Royal College of Physicians (United Kingdom)
FRCPSYCH	Fellow of the Royal College of Psychiatrists
FRCS(E)	Fellow of the Royal College of Surgeons (Edinburgh)
FRECONS	Fellow of the Royal Economic Society
FRES	Fellow of the Royal Entomological Society
FRFPS	Fellow of the Royal Faculty of Physicians and Surgeons
FRG	Federal Republic of Germany
FRGS	Fellow of the Royal Geographical Society
FRHISTS	Fellow of the Royal Historical Society
FRHORTS	Fellow of the Royal Horticultural Society
FRIBA	Fellow of the Royal Institute of British Architects
FRIC	Fellow of the Royal Institute of Chemists
FRICS	Fellow of the Royal Institute of Chartered Surveyors
FRMETSOC	Fellow of the Royal Meteorological Society
FRPS	Fellow of the Royal Photographic Society
FRS	Fellow of the Royal Society
FRSA	Fellow of the Royal Society of Arts
FRSAMD	Fellow of the Royal Scottish Academy of Music and Drama
FRSC	Fellow of the Royal Society of Canada; Fellow of the Royal Society of Chemistry
FRSE	Fellow of the Royal Society of Edinburgh
FRSL	Fellow of the Royal Society of Literature
FRSM	Fellow of the Royal Society of Medicine
FRSNZ	Fellow of the Royal Society of New Zealand
FRSS	Fellow of the Royal Statistical Society
FSA	Fellow of the Society of Antiquaries
FSIAD	Fellow of the Society of Industrial Artists and Designers
FTI	Fellow of the Textile Institute
FTS	Fellow of Technological Sciences
FZS	Fellow of the Zoological Society
GA	Georgia
GATT	General Agreement on Tariffs and Trade
GB	Great Britain
GBE	Knight (or Dame) Grand Cross of (the Order of) the British Empire
GC	George Cross
GCB	Knight Grand Cross of (the Order of) the Bath
GCIE	Knight Grand Commander of (the Order of) the Indian Empire
GCMG	Knight (or Dame) Grand Cross of (the Order of) St Michael and St George
GCSI	Knight Grand Commander of (the Order of) the Star of India
GCVO	Knight (or Dame) Grand Cross of the Royal Victorian Order
GDR	German Democratic Republic
Gen	General
GLA	Greater London Authority
GLC	Greater London Council
Glos	Gloucestershire
GM	George Medal
GmbH	Gesellschaft mit beschränkter Haftung (Limited Liability Company)
Gov	Governor
Govt	Government
GPO	General Post Office
Grad	Graduate
GRSM	Graduate of the Royal School of Music
GRÜNE	Die Grünen
gt	gatan (Street)
GUE	Group for the European Unitarian Left
HABITAT	United Nations Centre for Human Settlements
Hants	Hampshire
hc	honoris causa

HE	His Eminence; Her (or His) Excellency
Herefords	Herefordshire
Herts	Hertfordshire
HH	Her (or His) Highness
HI	Hawaii
HIV	Human immunodeficiency virus
HLD	Doctor of Humane Letters
HM	Her (or His) Majesty
HMS	Her (or His) Majesty's Ship
Hon	Honorary; Honourable
Hosp	Hospital
HQ	Headquarters
HRH	Her (or His) Royal Highness
HSP	Hungarian Socialist Party
HSWP	Hungarian Socialist Workers' Party
Hunts	Huntingdonshire
IA	Iowa
IAEA	International Atomic Energy Agency
IATA	International Air Transport Association
IBA	Independent Broadcasting Authority
IBRD	International Bank for Reconstruction and Development (World Bank)
ICAO	International Civil Aviation Organization
ICC	International Chamber of Commerce; International Computing Centre
ICE	Institution of Civil Engineers
ICEM	Intergovernmental Committee for European Migration
ICFTU	International Confederation of Free Trade Unions
ICI	Imperial Chemical Industries
ICJ	International Court of Justice
ICOM	International Council of Museums
ICS	Indian Civil Service
ICSC	International Civil Service Commission
ICSID	International Centre for Settlement of Investment Disputes
ICSU	International Council of Scientific Unions
ID	Idaho
IDA	International Development Association
IDB	Inter-American Development Bank
IEE	Institution of Electrical Engineers
IEEE	Institution of Electrical and Electronic Engineers
IFAD	International Fund for Agricultural Development
IFC	International Finance Corporation
IIEP	International Institute for Educational Planning
IL	Illinois
ILO	International Labour Organization
IMCO	Inter-Governmental Maritime Consultative Organization
IMECHE	Institution of Mechanical Engineers
IMF	International Monetary Fund
IMO	International Maritime Organization
IN	Indiana
Inc	Incorporated
INCB	International Narcotics Control Board
Ind	Independent
Insp	Inspector
Inst	Institut; Institute; Institution
INSTRAW	International Research and Training Institute for the Advancement of Women
Int	International
INTELSAT	International Telecommunications Satellite Organization
INTERPOL	International Criminal Police Organization
INTUC	Indian National Trades Union Congress
IOC	International Olympic Committee
IP	Izquierda de los Pueblos
IPU	Inter-Parliamentary Union
ISO	Companion of the Imperial Service Order
ITA	Independent Television Authority
ITU	International Telecommunications Union
ITV	Independent Television
IU	Izquierda Unida
IUPAC	International Union of Pure and Applied Chemistry
IUPAP	International Union of Pure and Applied Physics
Jan	January
JCB	Bachelor of Canon Law
JCD	Doctor of Canon Law
JD	Doctor of Jurisprudence
JMK	Johan Mangku Negara (Malaysia)
JP	Justice of the Peace
Jr	Junior
JSD	Doctor of Juristic Science
Jt	Joint
JU D	Doctor of Law

JU DR	Doctor of Law, Juris utriusque Doctor (Doctor of both Civil and Canon Law)	Math(s)	Mathematical, Mathematics
JUD	Juris utriusque Doctor (Doctor of both Civil and Canon Law)	MB	Bachelor of Medicine; Manitoba
		MBA	Master of Business Administration
		MBE	Member of (the Order of) the British Empire
KBE	Knight Commander of (the Order of) the British Empire	MC	Military Cross
KCB	Knight Commander of (the Order of) the Bath	MCE	Master of Civil Engineering
KCIE	Knight Commander of (the Order of) the Indian Empire	MCL	Master of Civil Law
KCMG	Knight Commander of (the Order of) St Michael and St George	MD	Doctor of Medicine; Maryland
		MDS	Master of Dental Surgery
KCSI	Knight Commander of (the Order of) the Star of India	ME	Maine; Myalgic Encephalitis
KCVO	Knight Commander of the Royal Victorian Order	mem	member
KF	Det Konservative Folkeparti	MEP	Member of the European Parliament
KG	Knight of (the Order of) the Garter	MFA	Master of Fine Arts
KGB	Committee of State Security (USSR)	Mfg	Manufacturing
KK	Kaien Kaisha	Mfrs	Manufacturers
KLM	Koninklijke Luchtvaart Maatschappij (Royal Dutch Airlines)	Mgr	Monsignor
		MI	Marshall Islands; Michigan
KP	Knight of (the Order of) St Patrick	MIA	Master of International Affairs
KS	Kansas	MICE	Member of the Institution of Civil Engineers
KSTJ	Knight of (the Order of) St John of Jerusalem	MICHEME	Member of the Institution of Chemical Engineers
KT	Knight; Knight of (the Order of) the Thistle	Middx	Middlesex
kv	kvartira (apartment)	MIEE	Member of the Institution of Electrical Engineers
KY	Kentucky	Mil	Military
		MIMARE	Member of the Institute of Marine Engineers
L A DROGA	Lega Antiproibizionisti Droga	MIMECHE	Member of the Institution of Mechanical Engineers
L EN D	Licencié en Droit	MIMINE	Member of the Institution of Mining Engineers
L ÈS L	Licencié ès Lettres	MINSTT	Member of the Institute of Transport
L ÈS SC	Licencié ès Sciences	MISTRUCTE	Member of the Institution of Structural Engineers
L PH	Licentiate of Philosophy	MIT	Massachusetts Institute of Technology
L TH	Licentiate in Theology	MJ	Master of Jurisprudence
LA	Los Angeles; Louisiana	MLS	Member of Library Science
Lab	Laboratory; Labour; Labour Party	MM	Military Medal
Lancs	Lancashire	MN	Minnesota
LDR	Liberal, Democratic and Reformist Group	MO	Missouri
LDS	Licentiate in Dental Surgery	MOH	Medical Officer of Health
Le Centre	Le Centre pour l'Europe	Mon	Monmouthshire
Legis	Legislative	Movt	Movement
Leics	Leicestershire	MP	Madhya Pradesh (India); Member of Parliament
Les Verts	Les Verts-Europe-Écologie	MPA	Master of Public Administration (Harvard)
LHD	Doctor of Humane Letters	MPP	Member of Provincial Parliament (Canada)
LI	Long Island	MRAS	Member of the Royal Asiatic Society
Lib Dem	Liberal Democrat	MRC	Medical Research Council
LIC EN BIOL	Licenciada en Biologia	MRCP(E)	Member of the Royal College of Physicians (Edinburgh)
LIC EN DER	Licenciada en Derecho	MRCP(UK)	Member of the Royal College of Physicians (United Kingdom)
LIC EN FIL	Licenciada en Filosofia		
LIC EN HIST	Licenciada en Historia	MRCS(E)	Member of the Royal College of Surgeons (Edinburgh)
LIC MED	Licentiate in Medicine	MRCVS	Member of the Royal College of Veterinary Surgeons
Lieut	Lieutenant	MRI	Member of the Royal Institution
Lincs	Lincolnshire	MRIA	Member of the Royal Irish Academy
LITT D	Doctor of Letters	MRIC	Member of the Royal Institute of Chemistry
LL	Lega Lombarda	MRP	Mouvement Républicain Populaire
LL-AN	Lega Lombarda, Lega Nord	MS	Master of Science; Master of Surgery; Mississippi
LL B	Bachelor of Laws	MSI-DN	Movimento Sociale Italiano–Destra Nazionale
LL D	Doctor of Laws	MT	Montana; Mount
LL L	Licentiate of Laws	MTS	Master of Theological Studies
LL M	Master of Laws	MU DR	Doctor of Medicine
LM	Licentiate of Medicine, or Midwifery	MUS BAC or B	Bachelor of Music
LORCS	League of Red Cross and Crescent Societies	MUS DOC or D	Doctor of Music
LRAM	Licentiate of the Royal Academy of Music	MUS M	Master of Music (Cambridge)
LRCP	Licentiate of the Royal College of Physicians	MVD	Master of Veterinary Medicine
LSE	London School of Economics	MVO	Member of the Royal Victorian Order
Ltd(a)	Limited; Limitada	MW	Master of Wine
LVO	Lieutenant, Royal Victorian Order		
		N	North, Northern
m	married; metre(s)	NAS	National Academy of Sciences (USA)
M AGR	Master of Agriculture (USA)	NASA	National Aeronautical and Space Administration
M ARCH	Master of Architecture	Nat	National
M CH	Master of Surgery	NATO	North Atlantic Treaty Organization
M CH D	Master of Dental Surgery	NB	New Brunswick
M CHEM ENG	Master of Chemical Engineering	NBC	National Broadcasting Corporation (USA)
M COM(M)	Master of Commerce	NC	North Carolina
M DIV	Master of Divinity	ND	Nea Dimokratia; North Dakota
M ECON SC	Master of Economic Science	NE	Nebraska; North East
M ED	Master of Education	NEDC	National Economic Development Council
M ENG	Master of Engineering (Dublin)	NF	Newfoundland
M MUS	Master of Music	NGO	Non-governmental Organization
M PH	Master of Philosophy (USA)	NH	New Hampshire
M PHIL	Master of Philosophy	NIH	National Institute of Health
M SC	Master of Science	NJ	New Jersey
M SC S	Master of Social Science	NM	New Mexico
MA	Massachusetts; Master of Arts	no	number, numero
Maj	Major	Northants	Northamptonshire
Man	Management, Manager, Managing		

Notts	Nottinghamshire		PS	Parti Socialiste; Partido Socialista
Nov	November		PSC	Parti Social Chrétien
NPC	National People's Congress		PSD	Partido Social Democrata
nr	near		PSDI	Partito Socialista Democratico Italiano
NRC	Nuclear Research Council		PSE	Party of European Socialists
NS	Nova Scotia		PSI	Partito Socialista Italiano
NSF	National Science Foundation		PSM	Panglima Setia Mahota
NSW	New South Wales		PSOE	Partido Socialista Obrero Español
NT	Northern Territory		Pty	Proprietary
NV	Naamloze Vennootschap; Nevada		Publ(s)	Publication(s)
NW	North West		Publr	Publisher
NWT	North West Territories		PvdA	Partij van de Arbeid
NY	New York (State)		Pvt	Private
NZ	New Zealand		PVV	Partij voor Vrijheid en Vooruitgang
NZIC	New Zealand Institute of Chemistry		PZPR	Polish United Workers' Party
OAS	Organization of American States		QC	Queen's Counsel
OAU	Organization of African Unity		Qld	Queensland
OBE	Officer of (the Order of) the British Empire		QPM	Queen's Police Medal
OC	Officer of the Order of Canada		QSM	Queen's Service Medal
Oct	October		QSO	Queen's Service Order
OECD	Organization for Economic Co-operation and Development		qv	*quod vide*
OEEC	Organization for European Economic Co-operation		qqv	*quae vide*
OH	Ohio			
OK	Oklahoma		RA	Royal Academy; Royal Academician; Royal Artillery
OM	Member of the Order of Merit		RAAF	Royal Australian Air Force
ON	Ontario		RAC	Royal Armoured Corps
ONZ	Order of New Zealand		RACP	Royal Australasian College of Physicians
OPEC	Organization of the Petroleum Exporting Countries		RAF	Royal Air Force
OPM	Office of Production Management		RAFVR	Royal Air Force Volunteer Reserve
OR	Oregon		RAM	Royal Academy of Music
Org	Organization		RAMC	Royal Army Medical Corps
OSCE	Organization for Security and Co-operation in Europe		RAOC	Royal Army Ordnance Corps
Oxon	Oxfordshire		RC	Roman Catholic
			RCA	Radio Corporation of America; Royal Canadian Academy; Royal College of Art
PA	Pennsylvania; Partido Andalucista		RCAF	Royal Canadian Air Force
Parl	Parliament; Parliamentary		RCP	Romanian Communist Party
PASOK	Panellinio Socialistiko Kinima		Rd	Road
PC	Privy Councillor		RDE	Group of the European Democratic Alliance
PCC	Provincial Congress Committee		Regenboog/CPN	Regenboog/Communistische Partij Nederland
PCE	Partido Comunista de España		Regenboog/PPR	Regenboog/Politieke Partij Radikalen
PCF	Parti Communiste Français		Regt	Regiment
PCI	Partito Comunista Italiano		REME	Royal Electric and Mechanical Engineers
PCP	Partido Comunista Português		Rep	Representative; Represented
PCS	Parti Chrétien Social		REP	Die Republikaner
PD	Progressive Democrats		Repub	Republic
PD B	Bachelor of Pedagogy		resgnd	resigned
PD D	Doctor of Pedagogy		retd	retired
PD M	Master of Pedagogy		Rev	Reverend
PDS	Partei des Demokratischen Sozialismus		RI	Rhode Island
PEI	Prince Edward Island		RIBA	Royal Institute of British Architects
Pembs	Pembrokeshire		Rm	Room
PEN	Poets, Playwright, Essayists, Editors and Novelists (Club)		RMA	Royal Military Academy
Perm	Permanent		RN	Royal Navy
PH B	Bachelor of Philosophy		RNR	Royal Naval Reserve
PH D	Doctor of Philosophy		RNVR	Royal Naval Volunteer Reserve
PH DR	Doctor of Philosophy		RNZAF	Royal New Zealand Air Force
PH L	Licentiate of Philosophy		RP	Member Royal Society of Portrait Painters
PHARM D	Docteur en Pharmacie		RPR	Rassemblement pour la République
pl	ploschad (square)		RS DR	Doctor of Social Sciences
PLA	People's Liberation Army; Port of London Authority		RSA	Royal Scottish Academy; Royal Society of Arts
PLC	Public Limited Company		RSC	Royal Shakespeare Company
PMB	Private Mail Bag		RSFSR	Russian Soviet Federative Socialist Republic
POB	Post Office Box		RSL	Royal Society of Literature
POSL	Parti Ouvrier Socialiste Luxembourgeois		Rt Hon	Right Honourable
PP	Partido Popular		Rt Rev	Right Reverend
PPR	Polish Workers' Party		RVO	Royal Victorian Order
PQ	Province of Quebec		RWA	Royal West of England Academy
Pref	Prefecture		RWS	Royal Society of Painters in Water Colours
Prep	Preparatory			
Pres	President		s	son(s)
PRI	President of the Royal Institute (of Painters in Water Colours)		S	South, Southern; Socialdemokratiet
Prin	Principal		SA	Sociedad Anónima, Sociéte Anonyme; South Africa; South Australia
Priv Doz	Privat Dozent (recognized teacher not on the regular staff)		SAE	Society of Aeronautical Engineers
PRL	Parti Réformateur Libéral		Salop	Shropshire
PRO	Public Relations Officer		SALT	Strategic Arms Limitation Treaty
Prof	Professor		SB	Bachelor of Science (USA)
Propr	Proprietor		SC	South Carolina; Senior Counsel
Prov	Province, Provincial		SC B	Bachelor of Science
PRS	President of the Royal Society		SC D	Doctor of Science
PRSA	President of the Royal Scottish Academy		SCAP	Supreme Command Allied Powers

SD	South Dakota
SDLP	Social and Democratic Liberal Party; Social Democratic and Labour Party (Northern Ireland)
SDP	Social Democratic Party
SE	South East
SEATO	South East Asia Treaty Organization
Sec	Secretary
SEC	Securities and Exchange Commission
Secr	Secretariat
SED	Sozialistische Einheitspartei Deutschlands (Socialist Unity Party of the German Democratic Republic)
Sept	September
SF	Socialistisk Folkeparti
SGP	Staatkundig Gereformeerde Partij
SHAPE	Supreme Headquarters Allied Powers in Europe
SIPRI	Stockholm International Peace Research Institute
SJD	Doctor of Juristic Science
SK	Saskatchewan
SLD	Social and Liberal Democrats
SM	Master of Science
SNP	Scottish National Party
SOAS	School of Oriental and African Studies
Soc	Société, Society
SP	Socialistische Partij
SpA	Società per Azioni
SPD	Sozialdemokratische Partei Deutschlands
Sr	Senior
SRC	Science Research Council
SSM	Seria Seta Mahkota (Malaysia)
SSR	Soviet Socialist Republic
St	Saint; Street
Staffs	Staffordshire
STB	Bachelor of Sacred Theology
STD	Doctor of Sacred Theology
STL	Licentiate of Sacred Theology
STM	Master of Sacred Theology
str	strae
Supt	Superintendent
SVP	Südtiroler Volkspartei (Partito Popolare Sudtirolese)
SW	South West
SWET	Society of West End Theatres
TA	Territorial Army
Tas	Tasmania
TD	Territorial Decoration; Teachta Dála (member of the Dáil)
Tech	Technical, Technology
Temp	Temporary
TH B	Bachelor of Theology
TH D	Doctor of Theology
TH DR	Doctor of Theology
TH M	Master of Theology
TN	Tennessee
Trans	Translation, Translator
Treas	Treasurer
TU(C)	Trades Union (Congress)
TV	Television
TX	Texas
u(t)	útca (Street)
UAE	United Arab Emirates
UAR	United Arab Republic
UDEAC	L'Union Douanière et Économique de l'Afrique Centrale
UDF	Union pour la démocratie française
UDR	Union des Démocrates pour la République
UED	University Education Diploma
UK	United Kingdom (of Great Britain and Northern Ireland)
UKAEA	United Kingdom Atomic Energy Authority
ul	ulitsa (Street)
UMIST	University of Manchester Institute of Science and Technology
UMNO	United Malays National Organization
UN(O)	United Nations (Organization)
UNA	United Nations Association
UNCITRAL	United Nations Commission on International Trade Law

UNCTAD	United Nations Conference on Trade and Development
UNDOF	United Nations Disengagement Observer Force
UNDP	United Nations Development Programme
UNDRO	United Nations Disaster Relief Office
UNEF	United Nations Emergency Force
UNEP	United Nations Environment Programme
UNESCO	United Nations Educational, Scientific and Cultural Organisation
UNFPA	United Nations Fund for Population Activities
UNHCR	United Nations High Commissioner for Refugees
UNICEF	United Nations International Children's Emergency Fund
UNIDIR	United Nations Institute for Disarmament Research
UNIDO	United Nations Industrial Development Organization
UNIFEM	United Nations Development Fund for Women
UNITAR	United Nations Institute for Training and Research
Univ	University
UNPF	United Nations Population Fund
UNRISD	United Nations Research Institute for Social Development
UNRRA	United Nations Relief and Rehabilitation Administration
UNRWA	United Nations Relief and Works Agency
UNSCEAR	Secretariat of the United Nations Scientific Committee on the Effects of Atomic Radiation
UNSDRI	United Nations Social Defence Research Institute
UNTAG	United Nations Transition Assistance Group
UNTSO	United Nations Truce Supervision Organization
UNU	United Nations University
UNV	United Nations Volunteers
UP	United Provinces, Uttar Pradesh (India)
UPU	Universal Postal Union
US(A)	United States (of America)
USAAF	United States Army Air Force
USAF	United States Air Force
USN	United States Navy
USNR	United States Navy Reserve
USS	United States Ship
USSR	Union of Soviet Socialist Republics
UT	Utah
UUP	Ulster Unionist Party
UV-PSdA	Unione Valdostana-Partito Sardo d'Azione
V	The Green Group in the European Parliament; Venstre
VA	Virginia
VC	Victoria Cross
Vic	Victoria
Vol(s)	Volume(s)
VT	Vermont
VVD	Volkspartij voor Vrijheid en Democratie
W	West, Western
WA	Washington (State); Western Australia
Warwicks	Warwickshire
WCC	World Council of Churches
WCT	World Championship Tennis
WEU	Western European Union
WFC	World Food Council
WFP	World Food Programme
WFTU	World Federation of Trade Unions
WHO	World Health Organization
WI	Wisconsin
WIDER	World Institute for Development Economics Research
Wilts	Wiltshire
WIPO	World Intellectual Property Organization
WMO	World Meteorological Organization
Worcs	Worcestershire
WP	Workers' Party
WRAC	Women's Royal Army Corps
WRNS	Women's Royal Naval Service
WTO	World Tourism Organization
WV	West Virginia
WY	Wyoming
YMCA	Young Men's Christian Association
Yorks	Yorkshire
YT	Yukon Territory
YWCA	Young Women's Christian Association

INTERNATIONAL TELEPHONE CODES

To make international calls to telephone and fax numbers listed in *The International Who's Who of Women*, dial the international code of the country from which you are calling, followed by the appropriate country code for the organization you wish to call (listed below), followed by the area code (if applicable) and telephone or fax number listed in the entry.

	Country code	+ or – GMT*
Afghanistan	93	+4½
Albania	355	+1
Algeria	213	+1
Andorra	376	+1
Angola	244	+1
Antigua and Barbuda	1 268	–4
Argentina	54	–3
Armenia	374	+4
Australia	61	+7 to +10
Australian External Territories:		
Christmas Island	61	+10
Cocos (Keeling) Islands	61	+10
Norfolk Island	672	+11½
Austria	43	+1
Azerbaijan	994	+5
The Bahamas	1 242	–5
Bahrain	973	+3
Bangladesh	880	+6
Barbados	1 246	–4
Belarus	375	+2
Belgium	32	+1
Belize	501	–6
Benin	229	+1
Bhutan	975	+6
Bolivia	591	–4
Bosnia and Herzegovina	387	+1
Botswana	267	+2
Brazil	55	–3 to –4
Brunei	673	+8
Bulgaria	359	+2
Burkina Faso	226	0
Burundi	257	+2
Cambodia	855	+7
Cameroon	237	+1
Canada	1	–3 to –8
Cape Verde	238	–1
The Central African Republic	236	+1
Chad	235	+1
Chile	56	–4
China, People's Republic	86	+8
Special Administrative Regions:		
Hong Kong	852	+8
Macau	853	+8
China (Taiwan)	886	+8
Colombia	57	–5
The Comoros	269	+3
Congo, Democratic Republic	243	+1
Congo, Republic	242	+1
Costa Rica	506	–6
Côte d'Ivoire	225	0
Croatia	385	+1
Cuba	53	–5
Cyprus	357	+2
'Turkish Republic of Northern Cyprus'	90 392	+2
Czech Republic	420	+1
Denmark	45	+1
Danish External Territories:		
Faroe Islands	298	0
Greenland	299	–1 to –4
Djibouti	253	+3
Dominica	1 767	–4
The Dominican Republic	1 809	–4
East Timor	670	+8
Ecuador	593	–5
Egypt	20	+2
El Salvador	503	–6
Equatorial Guinea	240	+1
Eritrea	291	+3
Estonia	372	+2
Ethiopia	251	+3
Fiji	679	+12
Finland	358	+2
Finnish External Territory:		
Åland Islands	358	+2
France	33	+1
French Overseas Departments:		
French Guiana	594	–3
Guadeloupe	590	–4
Martinique	596	–4
Réunion	262	+4
French Overseas Collectivités Territoriales:		
Mayotte	269	+3
Saint Pierre and Miquelon	508	–3
French Overseas Territories:		
French Polynesia	689	–10
Wallis and Futuna Islands	681	+12
French Overseas Country:		
New Caledonia	687	+11
Gabon	241	+1
The Gambia	220	0
Georgia	995	+4
Germany	49	+1
Ghana	233	0
Greece	30	+2
Grenada	1 473	–4
Guatemala	502	–6
Guinea	224	0
Guinea-Bissau	245	0
Guyana	592	–4
Haiti	509	–5
Honduras	504	–6
Hungary	36	+1
Iceland	354	0
India	91	+5½
Indonesia	62	+7 to +8
Iran	98	+3½
Iraq	964	+3
Ireland	353	0
Israel	972	+2
Italy	39	+1
Jamaica	1 876	–5
Japan	81	+9
Jordan	962	+2
Kazakhstan	7	+6
Kenya	254	+3
Kiribati	686	+12
Korea, Democratic People's Republic (North Korea)	850	+9
Korea, Republic (South Korea)	82	+9
Kuwait	965	+3
Kyrgyzstan	996	+5
Laos	856	+7
Latvia	371	+2

	Country code	+ or – GMT*
Lebanon	961	+2
Lesotho	266	+2
Liberia	231	0
Libya	218	+1
Liechtenstein	423	+1
Lithuania	370	+2
Luxembourg	352	+1
Macedonia, former Yugoslav Republic	389	+1
Madagascar	261	+3
Malawi	265	+2
Malaysia	60	+8
Maldives	960	+5
Mali	223	0
Malta	356	+1
The Marshall Islands	692	+12
Mauritania	222	0
Mauritius	230	+4
Mexico	52	–6 to –7
Micronesia, Federated States	691	+10 to +11
Moldova	373	+2
Monaco	377	+1
Mongolia	976	+8
Morocco	212	0
Mozambique	258	+2
Myanmar	95	+6½
Namibia	264	+2
Nauru	674	+12
Nepal	977	+5½
The Netherlands	31	+1
Netherlands Dependencies:		
Aruba	297	–4
Netherlands Antilles	599	–4
New Zealand	64	+12
New Zealand's Dependent and Associated Territories:		
Cook Islands	682	–10½
Niue	683	–11
Nicaragua	505	–6
Niger	227	+1
Nigeria	234	+1
Norway	47	+1
Norwegian External Territory:		
Svalbard	47	+1
Oman	968	+4
Pakistan	92	+5
Palau	680	+9
Panama	507	–5
Papua New Guinea	675	+10
Paraguay	595	–4
Peru	51	–5
The Philippines	63	+8
Poland	48	+1
Portugal	351	0
Qatar	974	+3
Romania	40	+2
The Russian Federation	7	+2 to +12
Rwanda	250	+2
Saint Christopher and Nevis	1 869	–4
Saint Lucia	1 758	–4
Saint Vincent and the Grenadines	1 784	–4
Samoa	685	–11
San Marino	378	+1
São Tomé and Príncipe	239	0
Saudi Arabia	966	+3
Senegal	221	0
Seychelles	248	+4
Sierra Leone	232	0
Singapore	65	+8

	Country code	+ or – GMT*
Slovakia	421	+1
Slovenia	386	+1
Solomon Islands	677	+11
Somalia	252	+3
South Africa	27	+2
Spain	34	+1
Sri Lanka	94	+5½
Sudan	249	+2
Suriname	597	–3
Swaziland	268	+2
Sweden	46	+1
Switzerland	41	+1
Syria	963	+2
Tajikistan	992	+5
Tanzania	255	+3
Thailand	66	+7
Togo	228	0
Tonga	676	+13
Trinidad and Tobago	1 868	–4
Tunisia	216	+1
Turkey	90	+2
Turkmenistan	993	+5
Tuvalu	688	+12
Uganda	256	+3
Ukraine	380	+2
United Arab Emirates	971	+4
United Kingdom	44	0
United Kingdom Crown Dependencies	44	0
United Kingdom Overseas Territories:		
Anguilla	1 264	–4
Ascension Island	247	0
Bermuda	1 441	–4
British Virgin Islands	1 284	–4
Cayman Islands	1 345	–5
Diego Garcia (British Indian Ocean Territory)	246	+5
Falkland Islands	500	–4
Gibraltar	350	+1
Montserrat	1 664	–4
Saint Helena	290	0
Tristan da Cunha	2 897	0
Turks and Caicos Islands	1 649	–5
United States of America	1	–5 to –10
United States Commonwealth Territories:		
Northern Mariana Islands	1 670	+10
Puerto Rico	1 787	–4
United States External Territories:		
American Samoa	684	–11
Guam	1 671	+10
United States Virgin Islands	1 340	–4
Uruguay	598	–3
Uzbekistan	998	+5
Vanuatu	678	+11
Vatican City	39	+1
Venezuela	58	–4
Viet Nam	84	+7
Yemen	967	+3
Yugoslavia	381	+1
Zambia	260	+2
Zimbabwe	263	+2

* Time difference in hours + or – Greenwich Mean Time (GMT). The times listed compare the standard (winter) times in the various countries. Some countries adopt Summer (Daylight Saving) Time—i.e. +1 hour—for part of the year.

A

ABAKANOWICZ, Magdalena; Polish artist, weaver and sculptor; b 20 June 1930, Falenty, nr Warsaw; d of Konstanty and Helena Abakanowicz; m Jan Kosmowski 1956. *Education:* Warsaw Acad of Fine Arts. *Career:* Mem ZAIKS Asscn of Authors; work includes monumental space forms of woven fibres, cycles of figurative sculptures of burlap, wood and clay, cast metal, stone, drawings, paintings with collage and gouache; Head of Weaving Studio Acad of Fine Arts, Poznań 1965, Prof 1979–90; mem Presidential Council for Culture 1992–95; solo exhibitions include Zachęta State Gallery (Warsaw) 1965, 1975, Kunsthaus Zürich (Switzerland) 1968, Nat Museum Stockholm 1970, Whitechapel Art Gallery (London) 1975, Art Gallery of New S Wales (Sydney) and Nat Gallery of Victoria (Melbourne, Australia) 1976, Henie-Onstad Foundation (Sweden) 1977, Muzeum Sztuki (Łódź) 1978, Musée d'Art Moderne de la Ville de Paris 1982, Museum of Contemporary Art (Chicago, USA) 1982, Musée d'Art Moderne (Montréal, Canada) 1983, Xavier Fourcade Gallery (New York) 1985, Muku Gallery (Hiroshima, Japan) 1987, Mücsarnok Palace of Exhibitions (Budapest) 1988, Städel Kunstinstitut (Frankfurt, Germany) 1989, Marlborough Gallery (New York) 1989, 1992, 1993, 1997, Marlborough Gallery (London) 1990, Sezon Museum of Art (Tokyo) 1991, Museum of Modern Art (Shiga, Japan) 1991, Art Tower (Mito, Japan) 1991, Hiroshima City Art Museum 1991, Walker Art (MN, USA) 1992, PS1 Museum (New York) 1993, BWH (Kraków) 1993, Marlborough Gallery (Madrid) 1994, Centre of Polish Sculpture (Oronsko) 1995, Manchester City Art Galleries (UK) 1995, Yorkshire Sculpture Park (Wakefield, UK) 1995, Ujazdowski Castle (Poland) 1995, Galerie Marwan Hoss (Paris) 1996, Charlottenborg Exhibition Hall (Denmark) 1996, Doris Freedman Plaza (NY) 1996–97, Miami Art Museum 1997, Galeria Starmacha (Cracow) 1998, Galeria Kordegarda (Warsaw) 1999, Metropolitan Museum of Art (NY) 1999, Les Jardins du Palais Royal (Paris) 1999; group exhibitions at Biennales in Lausanne (Switzerland) 1962–79, São Paulo (Brazil) 1965, 1979, Venice (Italy) 1968, 1980, Middelheim (Antwerp, Belgium) 1983, Sydney 1986, and at galleries and museums in Berlin 1982, Helsinki 1983, New York 1987, Washington (DC) 1988, Bonn, Warsaw, Santiago de Compostela 1994, London 1995, Paris, Atlanta 1996, Guggenheim Museum (Bilbao) 1997–98; represented in numerous collections; Hon mem American Acad of Arts and Letters 1996; Dr hc (RCA, London) 1974, (RI School of Design) 1992; Chevalier des Arts et des Lettres 1985; Commdr's Cross with Star, Order of Polonia Restituta 1998; other awards include Minister of Culture and Art Prize (1st Class) 1965, Gold Medal VIII Int Biennale of Arts (São Paulo, Brazil) 1965, State Prize 1972, Gottfried von Herder Prize 1979, Alfred Jurzykowski Foundation Prize 1982, NY Sculpture Centre Award 1993, Leonardo da Vinci World Award of Arts 1997. *Works include:* Sculpture for Elblag, Relief woven composition for N Brabant Prov Bldg (Netherlands); Three-dimensional Woven Forms: Abakans, Figurative Sculptures, Seated Figures, Backs, Incarnations, War Games, Crowd; Large Outdoor Installations: Katarsis (Italy), Neger (Israel), Space of Dragon (Repub of Korea), Space of Nine Figures (Germany), Becalmed Beings (Japan), Sarcophagi in Glass Houses (USA), Manus (USA), Magnus (Italy), The Space of Unknown Growth (Lithuania), Standing Figures (USA), Bronze Crowd (USA). *Leisure interests:* swimming, walking in the countryside, forests. *Address:* ul Bzowa 1, 02-708 Warsaw, Poland (Home); c/o Marlborough Gallery Inc, 40 W 57th St, New York, NY 10019, USA. *Telephone:* (22) 848-6379 (Home); *Fax:* (22) 848-6379 (Home).

ABBASSI BAMIEH, Mayada, BA; Palestinian organization executive; b 25 July 1945, Jaffa; d of Youssef Bamieh and Princess Najat Al Jazaery; m Said Abbassi 1977; one d. *Education:* American Univ of Beirut. *Career:* Asst Research Prof American Univ of Beirut 1969–70; mem Leading Cttee Gen Union of Palestinian Women (Lebanon) 1970–74; Founder and Head Int Relations Dept, Palestinian Red Crescent 1973–75; responsible for social, economic and political advancement of Palestinian women in refugee camps in S Lebanon 1974–77; First Sec Embassy of Palestine Liberation Org, Guinea 1977–78, Angola 1979–85; Co-ordinator Palestinian Women Asscns, Venezuela, Peru and Chile 1978; Dir 'Voice of Palestine', Radio Luanda, Angola 1979–85; mem Palestinian Nat Council (Parl) 1985–; Head of Int Relations, Palestinian Women Mov 1985–, mem Tech Cttee 1991–; mem Gen-Secr Gen Union of Palestinian Women 1985–; Co-Founder Jerusalem Link project 1991; Vice-Pres Women Int Democratic Fed 1994–; mem Palestinian Human Rights Cttee; has attended numerous confs on women's issues and human rights. *Leisure interests:* reading, swimming, writing, painting on silk. *Address:* 25 rue du Charolais, 75012 Paris, France. *Fax:* (1) 40-01-90-81.

ABBOTT, Diane Julie; British politician; b 27 Sept 1953; one s. *Education:* Harrow Co Grammar School and Newnham Coll (Cambridge). *Career:* Fmrly Admin Trainee Home Office, Race Relations Officer Nat Council for Civil Liberties, Researcher Thames TV, Reporter TV-AM, Equality Officer Asscn of Cinematograph, TV and Allied Technicians, Press and Public Relations Officer Greater London Council, Prin Press Officer Lambeth Borough Council; mem Westminster City Council 1982–86; MP (Lab) for Hackney N and Stoke Newington 1987–, mem Treasury Select Cttee; mem Lab Party Nat Exec Cttee 1994–; mem responsible for equality and women's issues, Mayor of London's Cabinet 2000–. *Leisure interest:* cricket. *Address:* House of Commons, London SW1A 0AA, UK. *Telephone:* (20) 7219-3000; *E-mail:* hcinfo@parliament.co.uk.

ABBOTT, Elizabeth, MA, PH D; Canadian historian; b 27 Sept 1942, Ottawa, ON; d of William Richard and Margaret Langley (née Griggs) Abbott; one s. *Education:* Sir George Williams and McGill Univs. *Career:* Research Asst Royal Comm on Bilingualism and Biculturalism 1964–66; Research Dir Centre d'Etude du Québec, Concordia Univ 1966–84; Prof of History Dawson Coll, Montréal 1972–84; Reporter Reuters, Haiti 1986–88; Ed-in-Chief Chronicle Publications (Canada) 1989–91; currently Dean of Women Students, Trinity Coll and Dean of St Hilda's Coll, Univ of Toronto; mem Ed Bd Canadian Human Rights Foundation; Dir St Patrick's Benevolent Soc; Lieut Gov's Silver Medal for History, Sir George Williams Univ 1963; Nat Magazine Award for Environmental Writing 1991. *Publications include:* Racism or Responsible Government? The French Canadian Dilemma of the 1840s (ed) 1967, Debates of the Legislative Assembly of United Canada 1841–1854 (vols I–XIX, ed) 1970–83, Tropical Observation (play) 1986, Haiti: The Duvaliers and Their Legacy 1988, Chronicle of Canada 1990, A History of Celibacy 1999. *Leisure interests:* skating, cycling, swimming. *Address:* St Hilda's College, 44 Devonshire Place, Toronto, ON M5S 2E2, Canada. *Telephone:* (416) 978-2254; *Fax:* (416) 971-2797; *E-mail:* abbott@trinity.utoronto.ca.

ABDEL-RAHMAN, Aisha (pen name **Bint el-Shati**), PH D; Egyptian writer and university professor. *Education:* Cairo Univ. *Career:* Asst Lecturer Cairo Univ 1939; Literary Critic Al Ahram 1942; Insp in Arabic Languages and Literature, Ministry of Educ 1942; Lecturer in Arabic, Ain Shams Univ 1950–57, Asst Prof 1957–62, Prof of Arabic Literature and Chair Univ Coll for Women 1962–; mem Higher Council of Arts and Letters 1960–; State Prize 1936; Acad of Arabic Language Award for Textual Studies 1950, for Short Story 1954. *Publications include:* Rissalet el Ghofram by Abul Ala'a 1950, New Values in Arabic Literature 1961, The Koran: Literary Interpretation 1962, Ibn Seeda's

Arabic Dictionary 1962, Contemporary Arab Women Poets 1963; six books on illustrious women of Islam; two novels; four vols of short stories. *Address:* 13 Agam St, Heliopolis, Cairo, Egypt.

ABDELA, Lesley Julia, MBE, FRSA, FRGS; British writer and consultant; b 17 Nov 1945; d of the late Frederick Abdela and Henrietta (née Hardy) Abdela; m 1972 (divorced); one s. *Education:* Queen Anne's School, Caversham, Châtelard School Les Avants (Switzerland), Queen's Coll Harley St, Hammersmith Coll of Art and London School of Printing. *Career:* Advertising exec; researcher House of Commons 1976–77; Parl Can (Lib) for Herts E 1979; f All-Party 300 Group 1980; UK Consultant Project Liberty, Kennedy School of Govt, Harvard Univ (PA, USA) 1992–98; f Project Parity (UK based equivalent of Project Liberty) 1996, CEO 1996–; Sr Partner Eyecatcher Assocs 1986–, Shevolution Assocs 1998–; OSCE Deputy Dir for Democracy, UN Interim Admin in Kosovo 1999; Political Ed Cosmopolitan 1993–96; consultant BBC TV series 'Breaking Glass' 1994; tutor to dels from Central Europe and Turkey on Beijing Express, train travelling from Warsaw (Poland) to Beijing (People's Republic of China) for the 4th UN World Conf on Women 1995; mem Bd Int Inst for Environment and Devt (IIED) 1992–96, British Council 1995–; Hon D LITT (Nottingham Trent Univ) 1996; UK Woman of Europe 1996. *Publications:* Women With X Appeal, Breaking Through the Glass Ceilings, Do It!–Walk The Talk, What Women Want. *Address:* Project Parity, 46 Portland Place, London W1N 3DG, UK (Office); Harper's Marsh, King's Saltern Rd, Lymington, Hants SO41 9QG, UK. *Telephone:* (1380) 840594; *Fax:* (1380) 840028; *E-mail:* lesley.abdela@shevolution.com.

ABDELLAH, Faye Glenn, BS, MA, ED D; American nurse and psychologist. *Education:* Columbia Univ (NY). *Career:* First woman to be apptd Deputy Surgeon General, US Public Health Service 1981–89; Dean (acting) Univ of Health Sciences 1993–96, Dean, Prof Grad School of Nursing, Uniformed Services Univ of Health Sciences 1993–; 36 academic and professional awards including six hon degrees. *Publications:* Better Patient Care Through Nursing Research (jtly) 1986; more than 135 publs in books and journals. *Leisure interests:* piano, swimming. *Address:* 3713 Chanel Rd, Annandale, VA 22003, USA. *Telephone:* (301) 443-4000.

ABDUL, Paula; American singer and choreographer; b 19 June 1962, Los Angeles, CA; d of Harry and Lorraine Abdul; m 1st Emilio Estevez 1992 (divorced 1994); m 2nd Brad Beckerman 1996. *Education:* Van Nuys High School and California State Univ. *Career:* Has choreographed work for several bands including Duran Duran, Toto, The Pointer Sisters and ZZ Top. *Choreography includes:* Videos: Torture, Control, When I Think of You and Nasty (all for Janet Jackson), City of Crime (from film Dragnet); TV programmes: Dolly Parton Christmas Special and Tracy Ullman Show; Films: Coming to America, Bull Durham, The Doors; *Recordings include:* Straight Up, Forever Your Girl 1988, Spellbound 1991, Will You Marry Me 1992, Head Over Heels 1995. *Address:* c/o Third Rail Entertainment, Tri-Star Bldg, 10202 W Washington Ave, Suite 26, Culver City, CA 90232, USA.

ABDUL MAJID, Mimi Kamariah, PH D; Malaysian professor of law; b 5 Dec 1952, Kuantan; m Abdul Hadi Zakaria 1977; three d. *Education:* Univ of Malaya and Monash Univ (Australia). *Career:* Tutor Faculty of Law, Univ of Malaya 1976–79, Lecturer 1979–87, Assoc Prof 1987–92, Prof 1992–, Dean Faculty of Law 1992–94, 1998–2000, Head of Legal and Man Services Unit 1996–. *Publications:* Pentadbiran Keadilan Jenayah di Malaysia (admin of criminal justice) 1991, Undang-Undang Keluarga di Malaysia (family law) 1992, Dangerous Drugs Laws 1995, Criminal Procedure in Malaysia 1995, Family Law in Malaysia 1999. *Leisure interests:* music, reading. *Address:* Faculty of Law, University of Malaya, 50603 Kuala Lumpur, Malaysia. *Telephone:* (603) 7593903; *Fax:* (603) 7573239.

ABDULLAHI, Rosemary Alewo, MD; Nigerian medical practitioner; b 3 March 1949, Egume, Kogi State; d of David Ikani Ogohi and Alugbe Odawn; m Sam I. Abdullahi 1973; four s one d. *Education:* Govt Girls' Coll (Kano), Ahmadu Bello Univ (Zaria) and Makerere Univ (Kampala, Uganda). *Career:* Intern Gen Hosp, Ilorin 1975–76, Makurdi 1976–78; Chief Health Officer Ministry of Health, Benue State 1979–86, Dir Public Health Services 1986–91; Chair Olamaboro Local Govt, Benue

State 1990–91; Consultant to Fed Ministry of Health and WHO 1989–90; apptd Special Adviser on Agriculture to Kogi State Gov 1992; Gen Sec Nat Council of Women's Socs, Benue State 1986–91; Title Holder Igala Chieftaincy. *Publications:* A Plan for Malaria Control in Benue State 1988, Situation of Women and Children in Benue State 1989. *Leisure interests:* tennis, reading, travel. *Address:* Ministry of Agriculture, Lokoja, Kogi State, Nigeria (Office); 172 Ahmadu Bello Way, POB 452, Lokoja, Kogi State, Nigeria (Home). *Telephone:* (58) 220146.

ABEIDERRAHMANE, Nancy, MBE, BE; Mauritanian (b British) business executive; b 4 Jan 1947, Orsett, Essex; d of Norman S. Jones and Lucia R. Moody; m Mustapha Ould Abeiderrahmane 1969; three s one d. *Education:* Escuela Tecnica Superior de Ingenieros Industriales (Spain). *Career:* Founder and Man Tiviski (camel, cow and goat milk pasturizing dairy), world's first producer of camel cheese; Rolex Award for Enterprise 1993; FAO 50th Anniversary Medal 1995; Slow Food Award 2000; Chevalier de l'Ordre Nat du Mérite 2001. *Leisure interests:* painting, music, reading. *Address:* Tiviski, Nouakchott, Mauritania. *Telephone:* 529 20 53; *Fax:* 525 71 92; *E-mail:* tiviski@mauritel.mr; *Internet:* www.tiviski.com.

ABELLA, Rosalie Silberman, BA, LL B, LL D; Canadian lawyer; b 1 July 1946, Stuttgart, Germany; d of Jacob Sumer and Fanny (née Krongold) Silberman; m Irving Martin Abella 1968; two s. *Education:* Bathurst Heights School and Univ of Toronto. *Career:* Called to the Bar, ON 1972; pvt practice 1972–76; Commr Ontario Human Rights Comm 1975–80; Judge Ontario Family Court Tribunal 1975–76; Chair Study on Access to Legal Services by Disabled 1982–83; Commr Royal Comm on Equality in Employment 1983–84; Chair Ontario Labour Relations Bd 1984–89; Maxwell Boulton Visiting Prof, McGill Univ 1988; Sr Fellow Massey Coll 1989–92, Continuing Fellow 1992–; Chair Ontario Law Reform Comm 1989–92; Justice Ontario Court of Appeal 1992–; Rosalie S. Abella Lecture Series, Univ of Guelph 1989; Programme Chair Gov-Gen's Canadian Study Conf 1990–91; Chief Rapporteur (Halifax), Co-Chair (Vancouver) Canadian Constitutional Confs; Dir Int Comm of Jurists, Inst for Research on Public Policy, Canadian Council of Christians and Jews; mem Bd of Trustees McGill Inst for the Study of Canada 1993–; Hon LL D (Dalhousie) 1985, (Queen's) 1985, (McMaster) 1986, (Windsor) 1988, (Ottawa) 1989, (Mt St Vincent) 1989, (New Brunswick) 1989, (Calgary) 1990, (British Columbia) 1990, (Toronto) 1990, (Waterloo) 1990, (Concordia, York, W Ontario) 1991, (Victoria) 1992, (Mt Allison) 1994; awards include Canadian Bar Asscn (ON) Distinguished Service Award 1992. *Publications:* Family Law: Dimension of Justice (co-ed) 1983, Justice Beyond Orwell (co-ed) 1985; articles in professional journals. *Leisure interests:* reading, music. *Address:* 130 Queen St W, Toronto, ON M5H 2N5, Canada (Office); 375 Glengrove Ave W, Toronto, ON, M5N 1W4, Canada (Home).

ABERDEEN AND TEMAIR, June Marchioness of, (Beatrice Mary) June Gordon, CBE, ARCM, GRSM, FRSE, FRSAMD; British music director and conductor; b 29 Dec 1913, Isle of Wight; d of Arthur Paul and Dorothy C. L. (née Smith) Boissier; m David G. I. A. Gordon (later Marquess of Aberdeen and Temair) 1939 (died 1974); two s two d. *Education:* Southlands School (London) and Royal Coll of Music (London). *Career:* Musical Dir and Conductor Haddo House Choral and Operatic Soc 1945–; Chair Scottish Children's League 1969–94, NE Scotland School of Music 1975–, Advisory Council Scottish Opera 1979–92; Chair Advisory Cttee, Aberdeen Int Festival of Music and the Performing Arts 1980–96; Gov Gordonstoun School 1971–86, Royal Scottish Acad of Music and Drama 1979–82; contribs to univ publs; Dame Order of St John; Hon LL D (Aberdeen) 1968, Hon D MUS. *Leisure interests:* walking, gardening. *Address:* Haddo House, Aberdeen AB41 7EQ, UK. *Telephone:* (1651) 851216.

ABOVA, Tamara Yevgenyevna, D JUR; Russian professor; b 11 Nov 1927; m; one s. *Education:* Moscow Inst of Law. *Career:* Sr Consultant USSR Ministry of Transport 1954–64; Sr Researcher, then Head of Sector, then Head Centre of Civil Research, Inst of State and Law, Russian Acad of Sciences 1964–; Prof Moscow Inst of Int Relations 1973–; arbiter Commercial Arbitrary Court and Marine Arbitrary Comm, Chamber of Trade and Commerce; mem Scientific-Consultative Council, Higher Arbitrary Court, Expert Council Cttee on Industry, Construction, Transport and Energy, Women of Russia Movt.

Publications: over 130 scientific works. *Address:* Centre for Civilist Studies IGPRAN, Znamenka str 10, 119841 Moscow, Russian Federation. *Telephone:* (095) 291-88-54.

ABRAHAMSON, Shirley Schlanger, D JUR; American judge; b 17 Dec 1933, New York; d of Leo and Ceil (née Sauerteig) Schlanger; m Seymour Abrahamson 1953; one s. *Education:* New York and Indiana Univs and Univ of Wisconsin. *Career:* Called to Indiana Bar 1956, New York Bar 1961, Wisconsin Bar 1962; Partner LaFollette, Sinykin, Anderson and Abrahamson 1962–76; Justice Wisconsin Supreme Court 1976, Chief Justice 1996–; Prof Univ of Wisconsin Law School 1966–; Judicial Scholar-in-Residence Southern Illinois Univ Law School 1991; mem Mayor's Advisory Comm (Madison, WI) 1968–70, Bd Dirs Wisconsin Civil Liberties Union 1968–72, Gov's Study Comm on Judicial Orgs (WI) 1970–72, advisory bd Nat Inst of Justice (US Dept Justice) 1980–82, study group Program of Research on Mental Health and the Law, John D. and Catherine T. MacArthur Foundation 1988, DNA Advisory Bd, US Dept of Justice, FBI 1995–, Court Reform Advisory Panel, Int Human Rights Law Group (Cambodian Project) 1995–, Consortium on Legal Services and the Public, ABA 1995–, ABA, Wisconsin Bar Asscn, Dane Co Bar Asscn, Nat Asscn of Women Judges, American Law Inst; mem bd of visitors Law Schools of Indiana Univ 1972–, Univ of Miami, FL 1982–, Brigham Young Univ, UT 1986–88, Univ of Chicago, IL 1988–, Northwestern Univ, IL 1989–; Hon LL D (Willamette) 1978, (Ripon Coll) 1981, (Beloit Coll) 1982, (Capital) 1983, (John Marshall Law School) 1984, (Northeastern) 1985, (Indiana) 1986, (Hamline, Northland Coll) 1988, (Notre Dame) 1993, (Suffolk) 1994, (DePaul) 1996; Wisconsin Outstanding Communicator Award, Wisconsin Communication Asscn 1992; Distinguished Alumni Award, Univ of Wisconsin-Madison 1994; Margaret Brent Women Lawyers of Achievement Award, ABA 1995. *Publications:* Constitutions of the United States (National and State), Vols I and II (ed) 1962; numerous publs in law journals. *Address:* Wisconsin Supreme Court, POB 1688, Madison, WI 53701, USA (Office); 2012 Waunona Way, Madison, WI 53713, USA (Home). *Telephone:* (608) 266-1885 (Office); (608) 222-9358 (Home); *Fax:* (608) 267-2319 (Office).

ABRAMOVA, Olga M., PH D; Russian politician; b 19 Sept 1953, Minsk; d of Mikhail Abramov and Leyla Tenisheva; m Dmitry Shukayev 1979; one s. *Education:* Belarus State Univ. *Career:* Teacher Belarus Tech Inst 1975–91; Asst Prof Belarus State Univ 1991–95; Dir of Research Programmes Nat Centre for Strategic Initiative 'East–West' 1995–96; Deputy, Supreme Council of the Repub of Belarus 1996; Dir of Research and Educational Programmes of the Analytic Centre 'Stategy' 1996–2000; Deputy, House of Reps, Nat Ass of the Rebub of Belarus 2000–; Council of Ministers Award 1976; Award of Komsomol League of the USSR 1976. *Publications:* Belarus Monitor (ed) 1995, Parliamentary Elections (ed) 1996, Chernobyl: Human Dimension (ed) 1996, Belarus–Russia Integration: Between Simulation and Reality (ed) 1988. *Leisure interests:* poetry, painting, art exhibitions, opera, rock, jazz, fishing. *Address:* Government House, 220010 Minsk, pl Nezavisimosti, Belarus; 220012 Minsk, 80–59 Skorina Ave, Belarus. *Telephone:* (17) 222-43-86; *Fax:* (17) 222-31-74; *E-mail:* adm@abelarus.minsk.by.

ABRAMSKY, Jennifer, CBE, BA; British radio producer and editor; b 7 Oct 1946; d of Chimen and Miriam (née Nirenstein) Abramsky; m Alasdair Liddell 1976; one s one d. *Education:* Holland Park School and Univ of E Anglia. *Career:* Joined BBC Radio as Programme Operations Asst 1969, Producer The World at One 1973, Ed 1981, Jt Producer special programme on Nixon 1974, Ed PM 1978, Producer Radio Four Budget Programmes 1979–86, Ed Today Programme 1986–87, Ed News and Current Affairs Radio 1987–93, est Radio Four News FM 1991, Controller Radio Five Live and Ceefax 1993–96, Dir Continuous News (including Radio Five Live, BBC News 24, BBC World, BBC News Online, Ceefax), Dir BBC Radio 1998–2000, BBC Radio and Music 2000–; mem Econ and Social Research Council (ESRC) 1992–96, Editorial Bd British Journalism Review 1993–; Hon Prof Univ of Thames Valley 1994, Hon MA (Salford) 1997, Royal Acad Fellowship 1998; Woman of Distinction, Jewish Care 1990; Sony Radio Acad Award 1995. *Leisure interests:* theatre, music. *Address:* BBC, Broadcasting House, Portland Place, London W1A 1AA, UK. *Telephone:* (20) 8743-8000.

ABRIL, Victoria Merida Rojas; Spanish actress; b 14 July 1959, Madrid; m; two s. *Career:* Fmr showgirl on Spanish TV; film debut 1976; has made films with Pedro Almodóvar, and has acted in French films. *Films include:* Obsesión 1975, Robin and Marian 1975, Robin Hood 1975, Caperucita Roja 1975, Cambio de sexo 1975, La bien plantada 1976, Doña Perfecta 1976, Esposa y Amante 1977, La muchacha de las bragas de oro 1979, Asesinato en el Comité Central 1981, La Guerrillera 1981, La Colmena 1982, La batalla del porro 1982, Le Bastard 1982, La Lune dans le Caniveau 1982, Sem Sombra de pecado 1982, J'ai Epousé un ombre 1982, Rio Abajo 1982, Bajo el signo de Piscis 1983, Le Voyage 1983, Las bicicletas son para el verano 1983, L'Addition 1983, Rouge George 1983, La noche más hermosa 1984, Padre Nuestro 1984, After Dark 1984, L'Addition 1984, La hora bruja 1985, Tiempo de Silencio 1985, Max mon Amour 1985, Vado e torno 1985, El Lute 1987, El placer de matar 1987, Barrios altos 1987, El juego más divertido 1987, Ada dans la jungle 1988, Baton Rouge 1988, Sandino 1989, Atame 1989, A solas contigo 1990, Amantes 1990, Tie Me Up! Tie Me Down! 1991, High Heels 1992, Lovers 1992 (Silver Bear for Best Actress, Berlin Film Festival), Intruso 1993, Kika 1993, Jimmy Hollywood 1994, Casque bleu 1994, Nadie hablará de nosotras cuandro hayamas muerto (Best Actress, Cannes) 1995, Gazon Maudit 1996, Freedomfighters 1996, La femme du cosmonaute 1998, Between Your Legs 1999, Mon père, ma mère, mes frères et mes sœurs 1999; *Plays include:* Obras de Mihura, Company Tirso de Molina 1977, Viernes, día de libertad, Company L. Prendes 1977, Nuit d'Ivresse, Paris 1986. *Address:* c/o JFPM, 11 rue Chanez, 75781 Paris, France; c/o Alsira García-Maroto, Gran Via 63, 28013 Madrid, Spain. *E-mail:* jfpm@jfpm.fr (Office).

ABU RMEILIEH, Nawal Barakat; Jordanian welfare voluntary worker; b 1937 Amman; m 1956; six d four s. *Career:* Voluntary work, including establishment of schools, playgrounds, road maintenance, devt of job opportunities for young people, etc; UNESCO Rep in Jordan; Pres Sweleh Group of Arts and Theatre 1962, Al Nasser Ladies' Social Welfare Soc (also Founder); Vice-Pres Al Nasser Area Local Devt Centre; mem Eyes Bank, Nat Blood Donation Soc, Nat Educ and Devt of Children, Women's Union of Jordan; participant at int confs including UN ESCWA conf on the disabled; awards include Silver Jubilee Shield for Voluntary and Welfare Work 1987, Compilation Certificates (from HM Queen Noor Al-Hussein 1987, Ministry of Health, Ministry of Labour, etc). *Leisure interests:* music, singing. *Address:* POB 4600, Amman, Jordan. *Telephone:* (6) 896853; *Fax:* (6) 618505.

ACHACH, Danièle Juliette, L ÈS L; French civil servant; b 5 May 1940, Oran, Algeria; d of Henri and Gilberte (née Guigui) Touati; m Charles Achach 1961; one s one d. *Education:* Lycées (Oran) and Molière (Paris), Univ of Paris and Ecole Nat d'Admin. *Career:* Teacher 1961–67; civil servant at Ministry of Econ and Finance 1971–75, seconded to Entreprise de recherches et d'activités pétrolières (ERAP) 1975–77, Head of Office, then Sub-Dir Ministry of Econ and Finance 1977–82, 1985–89; Head Overseas Econ Service, Secr of State for Overseas Depts and Territories 1982–85; Contrôleur d'Etat 1989–; Chef de la Mission de contrôle, commerce, exportation, consommation, Centre Français de Commerce Extérieur; mem Admin Bd Banque Commerciale de Paris 1982–85; Chevalier de l'Ordre Nat du Mérite, Chevalier de la Légion d'Honneur. *Address:* CFCE, 10 ave d'Iéna, 75006 Paris, France. *E-mail:* daniele.achach@cfce.fr.

ACHARYA, Shailaja, MA; Nepalese politician; b 8 May 1944, Biratnagar; d of the late Dr Pinaki Prasad and of Indira Acharya. *Education:* Banaras Hindu Univ (India). *Career:* Imprisoned for political reasons at age 16; Pres Democratic Socialist Youth League 1967–68; Ed Tarun (Youth) political magazine of Nepali Congress while in exile in India 1972–74; convener Nat Social Cttee Nepali Congress 1984–89; mem Cen Action Cttee 1991, which launched People's Movt, culminating in the restoration of multi-party democracy in Nepal; mem House of Reps (Parl) 1991; apptd Minister of Agriculture 1992. *Leisure interests:* yoga, meditation. *Address:* Ward No 9, Biratnagar, Nepal. *Telephone:* (21) 24960.

ACHMEDOWA, Jacqueline; German ballet dancer; b 9 Nov 1961, Munich; d of Murat and Gedja Achmedow; m Günter Czernetzky. *Education:* Ballettschule Roleff-King, Bayerische Staatsoper (Munich) and Bolshoi Theatre (Moscow, Russian Fed). *Career:* Numerous prin roles in ballets; Dancer and Soloist Bayerische Staatsoper, Munich, Hessisches Staatstheater, Wiesbaden, Wiener Staatsoper, Vienna; Guest Dancer in Europe, USA, Canada, etc. *Ballets include:* Giselle, La fille mal gardée, Nuages, Ein Sommernachtstraum, Dream Dances, Eugene Onegin. *Leisure interests:* books, music, painting, swimming, tennis, piano.

ACOGNY, Germaine; Senegalese dancer and choreographer; b Benin State, Nigeria; m Helmut Vogt. *Career:* Founded professional dance school, Dakar; Dir Mudra Africa Int Dance School, Dakar until 1983; dancer and choreographer with Peter Gabriel 1984; debut solo performance Sahel 1984; collaborated with Arona N'Diaye on Ye'ou, the Awakening 1985; performance at World of Music and Dance Festival 1993; London Dance and Performance Award for Ye'ou, the Awakening 1991.

ÁCS, Margit; Hungarian writer and editor; b 11 June 1941, Újpest; d of Ferenc and Margit (née Baracsi) Ács; m Mátyás Domokos 1967; two s. *Education:* Loránd Eötvös Univ. *Career:* Ed Szépirodalmi Publishing 1964–87, Magvető Publishing 1987; Füst Milán Prize 1989; József Attila Prize 1991. *Publications:* Short stories: Only Air and Water 1977, Whip and Alms 1983; Novels: Initiation 1979, Chance 1988, The Unsuspecting Traveller 1988. *Leisure interests:* photography, gardening. *Address:* c/o Magvető Könyvkiadó, 1806 Budapest, Vörösmarty tér 1, Hungary (Office); Budapest 1085, Somogyi Béla u 24, Hungary (Home). *Telephone:* (1) 118-5109 (Office); (1) 114-3610 (Home).

ADAGALA, Esther K., MA; Kenyan civil servant and film production executive; b 17 Dec 1950, W Kenya. *Career:* Head Film Production Dept, Ministry of Information and Broadcasting; formed Audio-Visual Practitioners' Asscn; f African Film Week; mem jury film festivals. *Address:* POB 30025, Nairobi, Kenya.

ADAM-SMITH, Patricia Jean (Patsy), AO, OBE; Australian writer and oral historian; b 31 May 1941, Sunset Country; d of B. B. A. Smith. *Education:* Correspondence School. *Career:* First woman to be articled on Australian merchant ship 1954–60; Educ Officer Adult Educ Bd 1960–66; Visual Aids Officer Educ Dept; Myer Foundation Fellowship 1970–71; Australia Council Grant 1972; est Manuscripts and Oral History Dept for Ministry of Arts 1973; work and study in oral history Univ of California at Los Angeles, Tulane Univ (LA), Univ of Indiana and Bucknell Univ (Lewisburg, PA), USA 1974–75; historian State Library of Victoria 1976, Imperial War Museum (UK) 1977; conducted seminar at Embassy of Australia, Tokyo (Japan) 1980; travelled to USSR on govt-to-govt literary cultural exchange 1980; numerous TV appearances 1966–, seminars and talks 1958–85; has travelled to 65 countries researching oral history and folklore; creator semi-fictional characters and story consultant TV series Anzacs 1978–84, writer and presenter Australia Will Be There 1985–87; Triennial Award OBE Assn 1993. *Publications include:* Hear the Train Blow 1964, Moonbird People 1965, Tiger Country 1968, Port Arthur Sketchbook 1971, No Tribesmen 1971, Romance of Australian Railways 1973, Islands of Bass Strait 1978, The Anzacs (Book of the Year 1978) 1978, Romance of Victorian Railways 1980, Outback Heroes 1981, The Shearers 1982, When We Rode The Rails 1983, Australian Women At War 1984, Heart of Exile 1986, Prisoners of War: From Gallipoli to Korea, Goodbye Girlie 1994; over 300 articles in nat and int journals. *Leisure interests:* travel, music. *Address:* Saxton Speakers Bureau, Suite 4/Level 4, 695 Burke Rd, Hawthorn E, Vic 3123, Australia.

ADAMCZEWSKA-WEJCHERT, Hanna, D ARCH; Polish architect and town planner; b 29 Aug 1920, Radom; d of József Wacław and Wanda (née Osińska) Adamczewski; m Kazimierz Wejchert 1962; one d. *Education:* Warsaw Univ of Tech. *Career:* Responsible for town plans of Garwolin, Kolno, Grajewo, Zmbrów 1947–68; working in partnership with Kazimierz Wejchert from 1951; Chief Planner Tychy New Town 1951; Prof Emer and Pres Architecture and Town-Planning Cttee, Polish Acad of Sciences (PAN); Vice-Pres Town Planners' Asscn 1968–72, SARP (Assn of Polish Architects) 1972; numerous prizes for town planning and architecture including First Prize for Town Centre Warsaw 1958, First Prize for Tychy New Town (jtly), State Prize for Planning and Realization of N Tychy 1964. *Publications include:* Domy Atrialne (2nd edn) 1978, Kształtowanie Zespołów Mieszkaniowych

1984, Małe Miasta (jtly) 1985. *Leisure interests:* walking, painting, literature. *Address:* Oręczna 45, 02937 Warsaw, Poland. *Telephone:* (22) 422887.

ADAMS, Victoria (see Beckham, Victoria).

ADANJA-POLAK, Mira, B SC; Yugoslav journalist, producer and broadcaster; b 22 Aug 1942, Budapest, Hungary; d of Solomon and Katarina Adanja; m Martin Polak 1967; one s. *Education:* Privately in Switzerland and at Univs of London and Belgrade. *Career:* Journalist, News Ed and Producer Belgrade TV 1971–, Programme Ed, presenter news programme and monthly documentary programme; reporter 'Royalty' magazine, London, UK; fmrly mem staff NBC TV and ABC TV, USA; has conducted many major interviews; covered civil war in Yugoslavia for Channel Four TV, UK; mem British Union of Journalists; magazine Popularity Awards, USA 1984, 1987, 1993. *TV documentaries include:* Women in Jail, Kidney Transplant, Vatican, Concorde, Solar Energy, The Risk of Love—AIDS, The Berlin Wall, Russian Emigrants, Free Press in Yugoslavia; *Publication:* Amerikanci (The Americans) 1982; articles in foreign press on Yugoslavia. *Leisure interest:* swimming. *Address:* 11000 Belgrade, Dušanova 92, Yugoslavia; 36 Silsoe House, 50 Park Village Estate, London NW1, UK. *Telephone:* (11) 342-576 (Yugoslavia); (20) 7388-5689 (UK); *Fax:* (11) 340-359 (Yugoslavia).

ADCOCK, Fleur, OBE, MA, FRSL; British writer; b 10 Feb 1934, NZ; d of Cyril John Adcock and Irene Robinson; sister of Marylin Duckworth (qv); m 1st Alistair Teariki Campbell 1952 (divorced 1958); two s; m 2nd Barry Crump 1962 (divorced 1966). *Career:* Asst Lecturer Univ of Otago 1958, Asst Librarian 1959–61; with Alexander Turnbull Library 1962; with FCO 1963–79; freelance writer 1979–; Northern Arts Fellowship in Literature Univs of Newcastle-upon-Tyne and Durham 1979–81; Eastern Arts Fellowship Univ of E Anglia 1984; Writer-in-Residence Univ of Adelaide 1986; Buckland Award 1967, 1979; Jessie MacKay Award 1968, 1972; Cholmondeley Award 1976; NZ Book Award 1984. *Publications:* The Eye of the Hurricane 1964, Tigers 1967, High Tide in the Garden 1971, The Scenic Route 1974, The Inner Harbour 1979, Below Loughrigg 1979, The Oxford Book of Contemporary New Zealand Poetry 1982, Selected Poems 1983, The Virgin and the Nightingale: Medieval Latin Poems 1983, Hotspur: A Ballad for Music 1986, The Incident Book 1986, The Faber Book of 20th Century Women's Poetry 1987, Orient Express: Poems by Grete Tartler (translator) 1989, Time Zones 1991, Letters from Darkness: Poems by Daniela Crasnaru (translator) 1991, High Primas and the Archpoet (ed and translator) 1994, The Oxford Book of Creatures (ed with Jacqueline Simms) 1995, Looking Back 1997, Poems 1960–2000 2000. *Address:* 14 Lincoln Rd, London, N2 9DL, UK. *Telephone:* (20) 8444-7881.

ADELAJA, Dupe, LLB, BL, MBA; Nigerian politician and lawyer; b 16 June 1956; d of Chief Abraham Adesanya; m Kofoworola Babatunde Adelaja; two d one s. *Education:* Methodist Girls' High School (Yaba, Lagos), Fed Govt Coll (Odobolu, Ogun State), Univ of Lagos and Univ of Birmingham (UK). *Career:* Fmr Lawyer A. A. Adesanya & Co; fmr Instructor Community Access Centre, Matthew Bolton Coll (Birmingham, UK); fmr researcher on childcare provision, Birmingham (UK); Banking Officer, Fed Mortgage Bank (Lagos); Served Nat Youth Service Corps with Fed Ministry of Housing and Environment 1980–81; Prin State Counsel Minister of Justice 1982–84; Minister of State for Defence (first female in Africa to hold this post); for the Navy; Pres Christ Auxilliary Ladies Soc of St Peters Church Ajele, Lagos. *Leisure interests:* charity work, reading, travelling. *Address:* Ministry of Defence, Ship House, Area 10, Garki, Abuja, Nigeria. *Telephone:* (9) 2348975; *Fax:* (9) 2343371.

ADELMAN, Irma Glicman, PH D; American (b Romanian) professor of economics; b 14 March 1930, Romania; d of the late Jacob Max Glicman and Raissa Etinger; m Frank Louis Adelman 1950 (divorced 1979); one s. *Education:* Univ of California at Berkeley. *Career:* Asst Prof Stanford Univ 1960–62; Assoc Prof Johns Hopkins Univ 1962–66; Prof of Econs Northwestern Univ 1967–72; Sr Economist Devt Research Centre, IBRD 1971–72; Prof of Econs Univ of Maryland 1972–79; Consultant US Dept of State 1963–72, IBRD 1968–, ILO (Geneva, Switzerland) 1973–; Cleveringa Chair Leiden Univ (Netherlands) 1977–78; Prof of Econs and Agric and Resource Econs Univ of

California at Berkeley 1979–94, Emer Prof 1994–; Vice-Pres American Econ Asscn 1979–80; Fellow Netherlands Inst of Advanced Study 1977–78, American Acad of Arts and Sciences, Econometric Soc, Royal Soc for the Encouragement of the Arts, American Agricultural Econs Asscn; Order of the Bronze Tower (Repub of Korea) 1971. *Publications:* Theories of Economic Growth and Development 1964, Society, Politics and Economic Development (jtly) 1967, Economic Growth and Social Equity in Developing Countries (jtly) 1973, Income Distribution Planning (jtly) 1978, Comparative Patterns of Economic Development: 1850–1914 (jtly) 1988, Village Economics (jtly) 1996, Social Effects, The South Korean Miracle: How Replicable Is It? 1999. *Leisure interests:* art, theatre, music. *Address:* Agriculture and Natural Resources Department, 207 Giannini Hall, University of California at Berkeley, 3310 Berkeley, CA 94720, USA (Office); 10 Rosemont Ave, Berkeley, CA 94708, USA (Home). *Telephone:* (510) 642-6417 (Office); (510) 643-8911 (Home).

ADIE, Kathryn (Kate), OBE, BA; British journalist; b 19 Sept 1945; d of John Wilfred and Maud (née Fambely) Adie. *Education:* Sunderland Church High School and Univ of Newcastle upon Tyne. *Career:* Technician and Producer BBC Radio 1969–76; Reporter BBC TV S 1977–78, BBC TV News 1979–81, Corresp 1982–, Chief Corresp 1989–, Hon Prof Sunderland Univ 1995; Hon MA (Bath) 1987, (Newcastle) 1990, Hon D LITT (City) 1989, (Loughborough Univ of Tech) 1991, (Sunderland) 1993, (Robert Gordon) 1996, (Nottingham, Nottingham Trent) 1998; Hon M Univ (Open Univ) 1996; RTS News Award 1981, 1987; Monte Carlo Int News Award 1981, 1990; BAFTA Richard Dimbleby Award 1989; Freeman of Sunderland 1990. *Address:* c/o BBC TV, Wood Lane, London W12 7RJ, UK. *Telephone:* (20) 8576-8830.

ADJANI, Isabelle; French actress; b 27 June 1955; two s. *Education:* Lycée de Courbevoie. *Career:* Pres Comm d'avances sur recettes 1986–88. *Films include:* Faustine ou le bel été 1972, La gifle 1974, L'histoire d'Adèle H. (Best Actress, New York Critics 1976) 1975, Le locataire 1976, Barocco 1977, Violette et François 1977, Driver 1977, Nosferatu 1978, Les Sœurs Brontë 1978, Possession (Best Actress, Cannes 1981) 1980, Clara et les chics types 1980, Quartet (Best Actress, Cannes 1982) 1981, L'année prochaine si tout va bien 1981, Antonieta 1982, L'été meurtrier (Best Actress César 1984) 1983, Mortelle randonnée 1983, Subway 1985, Ishtar 1987, Camille Claudel (Best Actress César 1989, Best Actress Award, Berlin Film Festival 1989) 1988, Damage 1991, La Reine Margot (Best Actress César 1995) 1994, Le Diabolique 1996; *TV appearances include:* Le petit bougnat 1969, Le secret des flamands 1972, L'école des femmes 1973, Top à Sacha Distel 1974, Princesse aux petits pois 1986; *Plays include:* La maison de Bernarda Alba 1970, L'avare 1972–73, L'école des femmes 1973, Port-Royal 1973, Ondine 1974, Mademoiselle Julie 1983. *Address:* c/o Phonogram, 89 blvd Auguste Blanqui, 75013 Paris, France.

ADLER, Freda Schaffer, PH D; American criminologist; b 21 Nov 1934, Philadelphia, PA; d of David and Lucia G. (née de Wolfson) Schaffer; two d one s. *Education:* Univ of Pennsylvania. *Career:* Instructor Dept of Psychiatry, Temple Univ, PA 1971, Research Co-ordinator Addiction Sciences Center 1971–72; Research Dir Medical Coll, PA 1972–74, Asst Prof of Psychiatry 1972–74; Assoc Prof of Criminal Justice Rutgers Univ, NJ 1974–79, Prof 1979–82, Distinguished Prof 1982–, Dean (acting) Grad School of Criminal Justice 1986–87; Consultant Nat Comm on Marijuana and Drug Abuse 1972–73, New York Univ Law School 1972–74, on Female Criminality to UN 1975–; UN Rep Int Prisoner Aid Asscn 1973–75, Centro Nat de Prevenzione e Difesa Sociale 1989–; Sec Bd Dirs Inst for Continuous Study of Man 1974–77; Ed Advances in Criminological Theory 1987–; mem Ed Bd Journal of Criminal Law and Criminology 1982–, Int Scientific and Professional Advisory Council of UN Program on Crime Prevention and Criminal Justice 1994–, Bd Dirs Police Foundation 1996–; Regional Sec-Gen Int Soc of Social Defence 1992–; Pres American Soc of Criminology 1994–95, Fellow 1995–; Herbert Bloch Award (American Soc of Criminology) 1972; Beccaria Medal (jtly, Deutsche Kriminologische Gesellschaft) 1979. *Publications include:* Medical Lollypop, Junkie Insulin, or What? (jtly) 1974, A Systems Approach to Drug Treatment (jtly) 1975, Sisters in Crime 1975, The Criminology of Deviant Women (jtly) 1978, The Incidence of Female Criminality in the Contemporary World 1981, Nations Not Obsessed

with Crime 1983, Outlaws of the Ocean (jtly) 1985, Criminal Justice 1994, Criminology, 2nd edn (jtly) 1995, Criminal Justice: The Core 1996. *Address:* Rutgers University, School of Criminal Justice, 15 Washington St, Newark, NJ 10004, USA (Office); 30 Waterside Plaza, Apt 37, New York, NY 10010, USA (Home).

ADNAN, Etel; Lebanese artist. *Education:* Univ de Paris (Sorbonne) and Univs of Berkeley and Harvard (USA). *Career:* Fmrly Prof of Aesthetics Dominican Coll, San Rafael (CA, USA); Artist c 1960–; Cultural Ed L'Orient-Le Jour.

ADRET, Françoise; French choreographer and ballet director; b 7 Aug 1920, Versailles; d of Alexandre and Jeanne (née Couillaud) Bonnet; m François Guillot de Rode 1940; one d. *Education:* Univ of Paris and with Russian choreographers Rozanne, V. Gsovsky and Nora Kiss. *Career:* Founder, Dir Netherlands Opera Ballet 1951; Choreographer of ballets presented at Festival de Strasbourg 1951, London Festival Ballet (in Nice) 1960, Warsaw Ballet (Poland), Johannesburg Opera (SA); Choreographer for Ballets du Marquis de Cuevas (Festival de Nervi), Ballets de Jean Babilée, Ballets de Roland Petit 1955, 1958, 1964; Ballet Dir Opéra de Nice 1960–63; Dir of Choreography and Educ Ballet Théâtre Contemporain, Maison de la Culture d'Amiens 1969–85; Insp-Gen Dance Div, Ministry of Culture 1982; Dir of Ballet Lyon-Opéra-Ballet 1985; Temporary Artistic Dir Ballet du Nord 1994–95; Chevalier de la Légion d'Honneur; Commdr des Arts et des Lettres; Grand Prix Nat de la Danse 1987. *Ballets include:* Billard 1951, Il Rittorno, Repetto, Le sanctuaire, Apollon Musagète, Les amants, Résurrection, Le Tricorne, Quatre Mouvements 1960, La belle au bois dormant 1966, Cendrillon 1965, La symphonie fantastique 1967, La conjuration (jtly with René Char, Jacques Porte, Georges Braque), Mayerling, Aqua-thème, Requiem (Giorgy Ligeti). *Address:* c/o Patrick Le Levé, 14 rue des Rosiers, 75004 Paris, France; 1 rue Ste-Marie-des-Terreaux, 69001 Lyons, France.

ADYRKHAYEVA, Svetlana Dzantemirovna; Russian ballet dancer; b 12 May 1938, Ordjonikidze; d of Taissya Gougkayeva and Dzantemir Adyrkhayev; m Alexey Zakalinsky 1966; one d. *Education:* Leningrad Choreographic School and Theatre Acad of Russia. *Career:* Danced with Glinka Theatre of Opera and Ballet (Chelyabinsk) 1955–58, with Odessa Opera and Ballet 1958–60, with Bolshoi Theatre 1960–88; Dir Svetlana Adyrkhayeva Ballet Studio, Moscow; USSR People's Artist 1980. *Ballet roles include:* Odette-Odile (Swan Lake), Princess Florine, Woman of the Bronze Mountain (Stone Flower), Zarema (Fountain of Bakhchisaray), Mehmene Banu (Legend of Love), Aegina (Spartacus), Kitri (Don Quixote). *Leisure interests:* reading, travel. *Address:* 121099 Moscow, 1st Smolensky per 9, Apt 74, Russian Federation. *Telephone:* (095) 241-13-62.

AĞAOĞLU, Adalet; Turkish writer; b 1929, Ankara; d of Mustafa and İsmet Sümer; m Halim Ağaoğlu 1954. *Education:* Univ of Ankara. *Career:* Worked for Türkiye Radyo Televizyon Kurumu (TRT) 1953–73; freelance writer 1973–; Sedat Simavi Prize; Orhan Kemal Prize; Madarali Prize. *Publications include (in Turkish):* Novels: Lying Down to Die 1973, The Mince Rose of My Mind 1977, A Wedding Party 1978, Summer's End 1980, Four or Five People 1984, No… 1987, Shiver of Soul 1990; Short stories: High Tension (Sait Faik Prize) 1974, The First Sound of Silence 1978, Come On, Let's Go 1982; Plays: Three Play (Prize of Turkish Language Inst) 1956, Plays 1982, Too Far, Much Closer 1991; works trans to English and German. *Leisure interests:* reading, writing. *Address:* Piyasa Cad, Bülbül Sok, 10/5 Ceviz Apt, Büyükdere, Istanbul, Turkey. *Telephone:* (1) 1422636.

AGARWAL, Bina, PH D; Indian professor of economics; b Jabalpur. *Education:* Univ of Delhi, Univ of Cambridge and Delhi School of Econ. *Career:* Research Assoc Council for Social Devt 1972–74; Visiting Fellow Inst of Devt Studies, Univ of Sussex 1978–79, Research Fellow Science Policy Research Unit 1979–80; Assoc Prof of Econs Inst of Econ Growth, Univ of Delhi 1981–88, Prof 1988–, Head Population Research Center 1996–98; Fellow Bunting Inst, Radcliffe Coll 1989–91; mem and seminar organizer Harvard Center for Population and Devt Studies 1990–91; Visiting Prof Harvard Univ Ctte on Degrees in Women's Studies 1991–92, First Daniel H. H. Ingalls Visiting Prof March–Sept 1999; Visiting Scholar Inst for Advanced Study, Princeton 1995; mem of numerous nat and int editorial bds, advisory cttees and consultancies; K. H. Batheja Award 1995–96, Edgar Graham Book Prize 1996, Ananda Kentish Coomaraswamy Book Prize 1996. *Publications:* Mechanization in Indian Agriculture 1983, Cold Hearths and Barren Slopes: The Woodfuel Crisis in the Third World 1986, A Field of One's Own: Gender and Land Rights in South Asia 1994, Structures of Patriarchy: State, Community and Household in Modernizing Asia (ed) 1988, Women, Poverty and Ideology in Asia (co-ed) 1989, Women and Work in the World Economy 1991; numerous articles on agricultural, environmental, developmental and gender topics in learned journals. *Leisure interests:* writing poetry, reading literature and biography, walking, movies. *Address:* Institute of Economic Growth, University Enclave, University of Delhi, Delhi, 110007, India (Office); 111 Golf Links Rd, New Delhi 110003, India. *Telephone:* (11) 7667101 (Office); (11) 4692203 (Home); *Fax:* (11) 7667410 (Office); *E-mail:* bina@ieg.ernet.in (Office).

AGARWAL, Nirmala, MA; Indian broadcasting executive; b 15 Feb 1941, Delhi; d of P. N. and Lalita Dar; m P. N. Agarwala 1966; three d one s. *Education:* Delhi Univ. *Career:* Prog Exec All India Radio (AIR) 1964, Asst Station Dir 1981, Dir 1985, Sr Dir Int Relations and Drama 1991, Sr Dir of Programmes and Dir-Gen All India Radio 1996; actor in radio soap opera 1986–. *Publications:* Nirjnarni Patthar (Rock and the Mountain Brook—Ministry of Educ Award 1967) 1965, Kashmir Folktales 1975, Vaadi Ki Pukar (Call of the Valley—short stories) 1995. *Leisure interests:* writing, cooking, gardening, social work. *Address:* All India Radio (AIR), Akashvani Bhavan, Rm 113, Parliament St, New Delhi 110 001, India; R71 Greater Kailash Part I, New Delhi 110048, India (Home). *Telephone:* (11) 3714119 (Office); (11) 6410088 (Home).

AGLIETTA, Maria Adelaide; Italian politician; b 4 June 1940, Turin; two d. *Career:* Nat Sec Radical Party 1976–77, Nat Treas 1979, Pres Parl Group 1979, Deputy 1983–86, 1987–89; MEP (Verdi) 1989–, Co-Pres Green Group in European Parl 1991–; mem Chamber of Deputies (Radical Party and Fed Europe group); mem Cttee on Institutional Affairs, Cttee on the Rules of Procedure, the Verification of Credentials and Immunities, Sub-Cttee on Human Rights, Del for Relations with the People's Repub of China. *Address:* European Parliament, rue Wiertz, 1047 Brussels, Belgium; Via Algardi 8, 00157 Rome, Italy. *Telephone:* (2) 2845196 (Office); (6) 5811120 (Italy); *Fax:* (2) 2847837 (Belgium) (Office).

AGNELLI, Susanna, LL B; Italian politician; b 24 April 1922, Turin; 6 c. *Career:* Mayor of Monte Argentario 1974–84; mem Camera dei Deputati (Partito Republicano Italiano) 1976, re-elected 1979, MEP 1978–81, Senator 1983; Under-Sec of State for Foreign Affairs in various govts 1983–91, Sec of State 1995–96; Advisor, Harvard Univ John F. Kennedy School of Govt Council of Women World Leaders 1998–; mem Ind Comm on Int Humanitarian Issues (ONU) 1984–87, Nat Council Republican Party until 1992, Int Comm on Missing Persons 1998–, Bd Dirs of Int Center for Missing and Exploited Children 1999–, Jury of the Conrad Hilton Foundation for the 1999 Humanitarian Prize; Pres Telethon Foundation 1992–, Pres 'Il Faro' Foundation 1997–, Hon Pres AMREF Italy; Hon LL D (Mt Holyoke Coll, MA) 1981. *Publications:* We Always Wore Sailor Suits 1975, Ricordati Gualeguaychù 1982, Addio, addio mio ultimo amore 1985, Questo libro è tuo 1993; numerous articles in magazines and newspapers. *Address:* Fondazione il Faro, Via Virginia Agnelli, 15/21, 00151 Rome, Italy (Office). *E-mail:* ilfaro@ats.it.

AGNÈS B, (see Troublé, Agnès).

AGUIRRE, Esperanza; Spanish politician; b 1952. *Career:* Fmrly mem Madrid City Council, Deputy Mayor; mem Nat Exec Partido Popular (PP—Popular Party) 1996; fmrly Minister for Educ and Culture. *Address:* c/o Ministry of Education, Alcalá 34, 28071 Madrid, Spain.

AGUTTER, Jenny; British actress and dancer; b 20 Dec 1952, Taunton, Somerset; d of Derek and Kit (née Lynam) Agutter; m Johan Tham 1990; one s. *Education:* Elmhurst Ballet School, Surrey. *Career:* Film debut 1964; has appeared in numerous TV films, dramas and series, and on stage with RSC and Nat Theatre; Most Promising Artiste, Variety Club of Great Britain 1971. *Films include:* East of Sudan 1964, Ballerina, Star! 1968, I Start Counting 1969, Walkabout 1969, The Railway

Children 1970, Logan's Run 1975, The Eagle Has Landed 1976, Equus (BAFTA Best Supporting Actress Award 1976), The Man in the Iron Mask 1976, The Riddle of the Sands 1978, Sweet William 1978, The Survivor 1980, Amy 1980, An American Werewolf in London 1981, Secret Places 1983, The Dark Tower 1987, King of the Wind 1989, Child's Play 2 1989, Darkman 1989, Freddie as F.R.O. 7 1993, Blue Juice 1995, English Places, English Faces 1996; *TV appearances include:* The Snow Goose (Emmy for Best Supporting Actress) 1971, A War of Children 1972, Amy 1980, A Dream of Alice 1982, Love's Labour's Lost 1984, Silas Marner 1985, Not a Penny More, Not a Penny Less 1990, Boon 1991, The Good Guys 1991, Puss in Boots 1991, Love Hurts 1994, Heartbeat 1994, September 1995, 1996, The Buccaneers 1995, And The Beat Goes On 1996, A Respectable Trade 1997, Bramwell 1998, The Railway Children 2000; *Plays include:* The Tempest 1974, Spring Awakening 1974, Hedda Gabler 1980, Betrayal 1980, King Lear 1983, The Unified Field 1987, Breaking the Code 1987, Love's Labours Lost, Peter Pan; *Publication:* Snap 1984. *Leisure interest:* photography. *Address:* c/o JY Publicity, 54A Ebury St, London SW1W 9QD, UK. *Telephone:* (20) 7730-2112; *Fax:* (20) 7730-5118.

AHARONI, Ada, PH D; Israeli writer, poet and educationalist; b 30 July 1933; d of Nessim Yadid and Fortunée Hemsi; m Chaim Aharoni 1950; one s one d. *Education:* Hebrew Univ and Univ of London. *Career:* Currently Sr Lecturer in Peace and Conflict Studies Technion–Israel Inst of Tech, Haifa; Pres The Bridge: Jewish and Arab Women for Peace in the Middle East 1978–90, World Congress of Poets XIII 1992; Head IFLA—International Friends of Literature and Writers' and Poets' Asscn 1984–96, PAVE—To Pave a World Beyond War through Literature 1985–96; British Council Poetry Award 1972; World Acad of Arts and Culture, UNESCO Prize 1991. *Publications include:* From the Pyramids to Mount Carmel 1980, The Second Exodus: A Historical Novel 1983, Poems from Israel 1992, Saul Bellow: A Mosaic 1992, Memoirs from Alexandria 1993, From the Nile to the Jordan 1995, The Peace Flower 1996. *Leisure interests:* theatre, gardening, reading, travelling. *Address:* 57 Horev St, Haifa 34343, Israel. *Telephone:* (4) 8243230; *Fax:* (4) 8243230.

AHERN, Nuala; Irish politician and psychologist; b 5 Feb 1949, Belfast, N Ireland; m. *Career:* Currently MEP (Green Group), mem Cttee on Research, Tech Devt and Energy, Cttee on Petitions; anti-nuclear campaigner; Founder Irish Women's Environmental Network. *Address:* European Parliament, rue Wiertz, 1047 Brussels, Belgium. *Telephone:* (2) 284-51-39; *Fax:* (2) 230-91-39; *E-mail:* nahern@europarl.eu.int; *Internet:* www.nualaahern.net.

AHMED, Leila Nadine, PH D; American (b Egyptian) professor of Near Eastern and women's studies; b 29 May 1940, Cairo; d of Abdel Aziz and Ikbul Radi Ahmed. *Education:* Girton Coll (Cambridge, UK). *Career:* Teacher Women's Coll, Al-Azhar Univ, Cairo 1962–65; Cambridge Coll of Arts and Tech and Univ of Cambridge, UK 1971–75, Univ of the United Arab Emirates 1977–79; joined staff Univ of Massachusetts 1980, Asst Prof 1980–86, Assoc Prof 1986–91, Prof 1991–99, Prof of Women's Program, Prof of Near Eastern Studies; Prof of Women's Studies, of Religion Harvard Univ 1999–; British Council Scholar 1966–67; Fellow Nat Humanities Center, NC 1982–83, Bunting Inst, Radcliffe Coll 1985–86. *Publications:* E. W. Lane and British Ideas of the Middle East in the 19th Century 1978, Women and Gender in Islam 1992, A Border Passage 1999. *Address:* Faculty of Arts and Sciences, Harvard University, MA 02138, USA (Office); 15 Gulf Rd, Pelham, MA 01002, USA (Home). *Telephone:* (617) 495-1000 (Office); *Internet:* www.harvard.edu.

AHMED AL-MAHMOUD, Sheikha; Qatari politician. *Career:* Apptd Under-Sec at Ministry of Information and Culture (first woman to hold sr govt post) 1996. *Address:* Ministry of Information and Culture, POB 1836, Doha, Qatar. *Telephone:* 831333; *Fax:* 831518.

AHOOJA-PATEL, Krishna, PH D; Canadian academic and United Nations official; b 15 March 1929, Amritsar, India; m Surendra J. Patel 1950. *Career:* Legal Consultant ECA, Addis Ababa, Ethiopia 1963–65; Research Scholar on Law and Devt, Univ of Addis Ababa 1965; Corresp Econ and Political Weekly 1965–67; Ed Women at Work, Employment and Devt Dept, Office for Women Workers' Questions, and ILO 1976–86, Chief and Deputy Dir Research and Training Dept 1986–89;

fmrly Deputy Dir INSTRAW; Nancy Rowell Jackman Chair, Dept of Women's Studies, Mt St Vincent Univ; currently Dir Int Devt Programme, St Mary's Univ, Nova Scotia. *Publications:* Another Development with Women 1983, Women in Economic Activity: A Global Statistical Survey (ed) 1985, World Economy in Transition (co-ed) 1986, Women's Studies and Women in Development: Bridging the Gap (ed) 1989. *Address:* International Development Programme, St Mary's University, Robie St, Halifax, Nova Scotia B3H BC3, Canada. *Telephone:* (902) 420-5582.

AHRENS, Hanna; German ecclesiastic and writer; b 6 Sept 1938, Heiligenhafen; d of Gustav and Anita Jahnke; m Theodor Ahrens 1965; two s two d. *Education:* Schools in Heiligenhafen and Oldenburg and Univs of Kiel, Zurich (Switzerland), Göttingen and Tübingen. *Career:* Ordination as Lutheran Pastor 1975; mission work, Papua New Guinea 1971–78; freelance writer 1981–; designs cards; gives readings from books, and lectures on peace, stress, joy, etc. *Publications:* Schenk mir einen Regenbogen (trans to English as Who'd be a Mum? 1983), Worte, die den Tag verändern, Und manchmal liegt im Abschied ein Geschenk, Augenblicke des Glücks, Guten Morgen, Frau Pfarrer, Die kleinen Hindernisse, Ein Gefühl von Freiheit und Glück 1988, Und manchmal liegt im Abschied ein Geschenk (2nd edn) 1989, Augenblicke des Glücks 1990. *Leisure interests:* literature, theology, working as pastor on cruise liners, travel, art. *Address:* Süntelstr 85l, 22457 Hamburg, Germany. *Telephone:* (40) 5508811.

AHRLAND, Karin Margareta, LL B; Swedish politician and diplomatist; b 20 July 1931, Torshälla; d of Valfrid and Greta (née Myhlén) Andersson; m 1st Hans F. Petersson 1958 (divorced 1962); m 2nd Nils Ahrland 1964; one s. *Education:* Univ of Lund. *Career:* Chief lawyer Co of Malmöhus 1971–76; mem Riksdag (Parl, Liberal Party) 1976–; Minister for Public Health and Medical Services 1981–82; Del to UN Comm on the Status of Women 1976–79; Amb 1989–90, mem staff Consul, Montréal, Canada 1990–; Chair Nat Cttee for Equality between Men and Women 1979–81; Chair Nat Arts Council 1980. *Address:* c/o Ministry of Foreign Affairs, Gustav Adolfstorg 1, POB 16121, 103 39 Stockholm, Sweden. *Telephone:* (613) 241-8553; *Fax:* (613) 241-2277.

AHRWEILER, Hélène, D ÈS L; French professor; b 28 Aug 1926, Athens, Greece; d of Nicolas Glykatzi and Calliroe Psaltides; m Jacques Ahrweiler 1958; one d. *Education:* Univ of Athens. *Career:* Research worker CNRS 1955–67, Head of Research 1964–67; Prof Univ of Paris I (Panthéon-Sorbonne) 1967–, Pres 1976–81; Rector Acad, Chancellor Univs of Paris 1982–89; Sec-Gen Int Cttee of Historical Sciences 1980–90; Vice-Pres Conseil d'orientation du Centre Nat d'Art et de Culture Georges Pompidou 1975–89, Conseil supérieur de l'Educ Nat 1983–89; Pres Centre Nat d'Art et de Culture Georges Pompidou 1989–91; Pres Univ of Europe (Paris), Comité d'Ethique des Sciences (CNRS) 1994, European Cultural Centre of Delphi (Greece); mem Bd Dirs Lambrakis Research Foundation, Greece; mem Greek, British, Belgian, German and Bulgarian Acads; Dr hc (Univs of London, New York, Belgrade, Harvard (USA), Lima, New Brunswick (Canada), Athens Social Science Univ, American Univ of Paris, Haifa); Officier de la Légion d'Honneur, Officier des Palmes Académiques, Commdr l'Ordre Nat du Mérite, Commdr des Arts et des Lettres, numerous foreign decorations. *Publications include:* Byzance et la mer 1966, Etudes sur les structures administratives et sociales de Byzance 1971, L'idéologie politique de l'empire byzantin 1975, Byzance: les pays et les territoires 1976, Geographica 1981, contribs to numerous books. *Leisure interests:* tennis, swimming. *Address:* Université de Paris I (Panthéon-Sorbonne), 47 rue des Ecoles, 75005 Paris (Office), France (Office); 28 rue Guynemer, 75006 Paris, France (Home).

AHTEE, Liisa, PH D; Finnish professor of pharmacology; b 2 Oct 1937, Turku; d of Aaro and Lyyli Ahtee. *Education:* Helsingin uusi Yhteiskoulu and Univ of Helsinki. *Career:* Lecturer, Dept of Pharmacology, Univ of Helsinki 1962–74, Prof and Chair Div of Pharmacology and Toxicology 1975–; Research Fellow ARC Inst of Animal Physiology, Cambridge, UK 1967–69, Royal Coll of Surgeons of England 1969–70, Univ of Gothenburg, Sweden 1977; mem Advisory Bd several scientific journals. *Publications:* Naunyn-Schmiedeberg Archives of Pharmacology 1989–; numerous articles in journals. *Leisure interests:* walking, reading. *Address:* University of Helsinki, Department of Pharmacy, Division of Pharmacology and Toxicology, Viikinkaari 5, POB 56, Helsinki 00014, Finland; Sepankatu 19A, Helsinki 631988, Finland (Home). *Telephone:* (0) 70859472; *Fax:* (0) 70859471; *E-mail:* liisa.ahtee@helsinki.fi.

AIDOO, Ama Ata; Ghanaian writer; b Ghana; one d. *Career:* Lecturer Univ of Cape Coast 1970–73; consultant at univs, acads and research insts in Africa, USA and Europe; Minister of Educ (Ghana) 1982–83; Chair Africa Regional Panel of the Commonwealth Writers' Prize 1990, 1991; currently living in Zimbabwe. *Publications include:* Novels: Our Sister Killjoy or Reflections from a Black-Eyed Squint 1977, Changes–A Love Story 1991; Poetry: Someone Talking to Sometime 1985, Birds and Other Poems; Plays: The Dilemma of a Ghost 1965, Anowa 1970; Short stories: No Sweetness Here 1970, The Eagle and The Chicken and Other Stories 1987; numerous contribs to magazines and journals; works translated into many languages. *Address:* POB 4930, Harare, Zimbabwe. *Telephone:* (4) 731901.

AÏELLO, Evelyne Josette Nicole; French conductor; b 23 July 1958, Casablanca, Morocco; d of Joseph and Germaine (née Gragnani) Aïello; m M. Candardjis 1984; two d. *Education:* Lycée Jeanne d'Arc (Clermont-Ferrand), Ecole Normale de Musique de Paris, Conservatoire Nat Supérieur de Musique de Paris, Acad Chigiana (Sienna, Italy) and Mozarteum (Salzburg, Austria). *Career:* Conductor in France and abroad; Conductor Orchestre de la Garde Républicaine 1983, Ballets de l'Opéra de Paris 1985, Orchestre Nat d'Ile-de-France 1989, Mozart Concert (Salle Pleyel) 1989, Sofia Orchestra, Hungarian Radio Orchestra (Budapest), New Boston Orchestra (USA), Raanana (Israel) 1995 etc; Artistic Dir and Conductor Festival Lyrique de Gattières 1997–99; Guest Conductor with orchestras including Opéra de Nantes and Opéra de Nancy et de Lorraine playing ballet music, contemporary music, opera, etc; Médaille Maurice Ravel, Ministry of Culture 1976; Médaille d'Honneur de la Ville de Clermont-Ferrand 1976, 1984; First Prize for Conducting, Conservatoire Nat Supérieur de Musique 1983; Laureate Fondation Menuhin 1983; Int Conducting Prize, Salzburg 1984; Laureate, First Concours des jeunes chefs d'orchestre, Ministry of Culture 1986; recorded a compact disc tribute to Marcel Landowski 1995. *Leisure interests:* nature, travel. *Address:* CNR, 22 rue de la Belle Feuille, 92100 Boulogne-Billancourt, France.

AIELLO, Leslie, PH D; British professor of biological chemistry. *Career:* Prof of Biological Chem Dept of Anthropology, Univ Coll, London; field work in the USA, France and the Middle East; Jt Man Ed Journal of Human Evolution. *Publications include:* Discovering the Origins of Mankind 1981, An Introduction to Human Evolutionary Anatomy (jtly) 1990; numerous specialist articles in scientific journals. *Address:* Anthropology Dept, University College, Gower St, London, WC1, UK. *E-mail:* l.aiello@ucl.ac.uk; *Internet:* www.ucl.ac.uk/Anthropology/staff/aiello.htm.

AIG-IMOUKHUEDE, Emily, BA; Nigerian business executive; b 27 Oct 1941, Sabongida-Ora, Owan Edo State; d of the late Mr and of Mrs Meffullhoude; m Frank Abiodun Aig-Imoukhuede 1964; two d two s. *Education:* Anglican Girls' School (Sabongida-Ora), St Anne's School (Ibadan), Nigerian Coll of Arts, Science and Tech and Univ of Ibadan. *Career:* Teacher Aunty Ayo Girls' Secondary School 1964; part-time lecturer in History St Anne's School 1966; Curator Nat Museum, Lagos 1967–73; f pvt art gallery for the promotion of Nigerian art and artists, Lagos 1974; apptd Dir Nat Cargo Handling Co 1987, Warri Refinery and Petrochemical Co, People's Bank of Nigeria Ltd, Nigerian Mining Corpn 1985–86; Nat Pres Nat Council of Women's Socs Nigeria; mem Cttee of Assessors, Nigerian Merit Award Bd, Cabinet Office Child Welfare Cttee, Fed Ministry of Social Devt, Youth and Sports 1980–86, Health Care Finance Cttee, Fed Ministry of Health until 1984, Police Community Relations Cttee until 1984, Bd of Nat Univs Comm 1986, Nigerian Asscn of Univ Women, Int Women's Soc (Lagos), SOS Children's Village Asscn of Nigeria, Museum Educ for Africa Cttee, Int Council of Museums, Standing Cttee on Migration, Int Council of Women; mem Bd Trustees Lambo Foundation, Ikeja, Lagos. *Publication:* The Seven Maidens and other stories 1988. *Leisure interests:* reading, gardening, community services. *Address:* Nat Council of Women's Societies, Nigeria News House, Plot PC 14, Ahmed Onibudo St, Victoria Island, POB 3063, Marina, Lagos, Nigeria. *Telephone:* (1) 612091.

AIKEN, Joan Delano, MBE; British writer; b 4 Sept 1924, Rye, Sussex; d of Conrad Potter and Jessie (née McDonald) Aiken; m 1st Ronald George Brown 1945 (died 1955); one s one d; m 2nd Julius Goldstein 1976. *Education:* Wychwood School, Oxford. *Career:* Librarian UN Info Centre, London 1943–49; Features Ed Argosy 1955–60; Advertising Copywriter J. Walter Thompson 1960–61; writer 1962–; mem Soc of Authors, PEN, Writers' Guild, Mystery Writers of America. *Publications include:* Jr fiction: The Wolves of Willoughby Chase (Guardian Award for Children's Literature, Lewis Carroll Award, USA 1970, also film) 1962, Nightbirds on Nantucket (Guardian Award for Children's Literature) 1966, Black Hearts in Battersea (Guardian Award for Children's Literature) 1964, Nightfall (Mystery Writers of America Award 1972) 1969, Midnight is a Place 1974, Tale of a One-Way Street 1978, The Mystery of Mr Jones's Disappearing Taxi 1982, Fog Hounds, Wind Cat, Sea Mice 1984, Dido and Pa 1986, A Fit of Shivers 1990, Is 1992; Adult fiction: Hate Begins at Home 1967, Died on A Rainy Sunday (also film) 1972, A Touch of Chill 1979, A Whisper in the Night 1982, Deception 1987, The Haunting of Lamb House 1991, Cold Shoulder Road 1995, A Handful of Gold 1995, The Cockatrice Boys 1996, Emma Watson 1996, The Jewel Seed 1997, Mooncake 1998, Limbo Lodge 1999, Lady Catherine's Necklace 2000, In Thunder's Pocket 2000. *Leisure interests:* walking, gardening, reading, listening to music. *Address:* The Hermitage, East St, Petworth, W Sussex GU28 0AB, UK. *Telephone:* (1798) 42279.

AIKEN, Linda H., PH D; American nurse and sociologist; b 29 July 1943, Roanoke, VA; d of William Jordan and Betty Philips (Warner) Harman; one s one d. *Education:* Univs of Florida, Texas and Wisconsin. *Career:* Nurse, Univ of Florida Medical Center 1964–65; instructor, Coll of Nursing, Univ of Florida 1966–67, School of Nursing, Univ of Missouri 1968–70; Clinical Nurse Specialist 1967–70; Lecturer School of Nursing, Univ of Wisconsin 1973–74; Programme Officer Robert Wood Johnson Foundation 1974–76, Dir of Research 1976–79, Asst Vice-Pres 1979–81, Vice-Pres 1981–87; Prof of Nursing and Sociology, Dir Center for Health Services and Policy Research, Univ of PA 1988–; mem Pres Clinton's Nat Health Care Reform Task Force 1993; Commr Physician Payment Review Comm Nat Advisory Council, US Agency for Health Care Policy and Research; Assoc Ed Journal of Health and Social Behavior 1979–81; Jessie M. Scott Award, American Nurses Asscn 1984; Nurse Scientist of the Year 1991; Best of Image Award 1991. *Publications:* Nursing in the 1980s: Crises, Challenges, Opportunities (ed) 1982, Evaluation Studies Review Annual 1985 (co-ed) 1985, Applications of Social Science to Clinical Medicine and Health Policy (jtly) 1986, Charting Nursing's Future: Agenda for the 1990s (co-ed), Hospital Restructuring in North America and Europe 1997, Advances in Hospital Outcomes Research 1998, Accounting for Variation in Hospital Outcomes: Cross-National Study 1999, contribs to professional journals. *Leisure interests:* racquetball, tennis, reading. *Address:* University of Pennsylvania, Center for Health Outcomes and Policy Research, 420 Guardian Drive, NEB 332R, Philadelphia, PA 19104, USA (Office); 2209 Lombard St, Philadelphia, PA 19146, USA (Home). *Telephone:* (215) 898-9759 (Office); (215) 898-5673 (Home); *Fax:* (215) 573-2062 (Office).

AIMÉE, Anouk; French actress; b (Françoise Judith Dreyfus) 27 April 1932, Paris; d of Henry Dreyfus and Geneviève Durand; m 2nd Nico Papatakis 1951; one d; m 3rd Pierre Barouh 1966; m 4th Albert Finney 1970 (divorced 1978). *Education:* Ecole de la rue Milton (Paris), Ecole de Barbezieux, Pensionnat de Bandd, Inst de Megève and Cours Bauer-Therond. *Career:* Film and TV actress 1955–; Commdr des Arts et des Lettres; Golden Globe Award 1968; Prix Féminin, Cannes. *Films include:* Les mauvaises rencontres 1955, Tous peuvent me tuer, Pot bouille and Montparnasse 19 1957, La tête contre les murs 1958, Les dragueurs 1959, La dolce vita, Le farceur, Lola, Les amours de Paris, L'imprévu 1960, Quai Notre Dame 1960, Le jugement dernier 1961, Sodome et Gomorrhe 1961, Les grands chemins 1962, Education sentimentale 1962, Huit et demi 1963, Un homme et une femme 1966, Un soir un train 1967, The Appointment 1968, Model Shop 1968, Justine 1968, Si c'était à refaire 1976, Mon premier amour 1978, Salto nel vuoto 1979, La tragédie d'un homme ridicule 1981, Qu'est-ce qui fait courir David? 1982, Le Général de l'armée morte 1983, Vive la vie and Le succès à tout prix 1984, Un homme et une femme: vingt ans déjà 1986, Dr Norman Bethune 1992, Les Marmottes 1993, Les cent et une nuits 1995, Prêt-à-porter 1995; *Theatre includes:* Sud 1954, Love Letters

1990, 1994; *TV appearances include:* Une page d'amour 1979, Des voix dans le jardin. *Leisure interests:* reading, life, human rights. *Address:* Bureau Georges Beaume, 3 quai Malaquais, 75006 Paris, France; 9 rue Girardon, 75018 Paris, France.

AINARDI, Sylviane; French politician; b 1948. *Career:* Teacher; MEP (PCF) 1989–, mem Cttee on Regional Policy and Regional Planning, Cttee on Econ and Monetary Affairs and Industrial Policy (Substitute mem); mem Midi-Pyrénées Regional Council; Municipal Councillor, Toulouse; Fed First Sec for Haute-Garonne, PCF; Chair French Del Bouge l'Europe GUE/NGL Group 1999–. *Address:* European Parliament, Allée du Printemps, BP 1024/F, 67070 Strasbourg, Cedex, France. *E-mail:* sainardi@europarl.eu.int; *Internet:* www.bouge-leurope .org.

AIREY, Dawn, MA; British television executive; b 15 Nov 1960, Preston, Lancs; partner Martin Pearce. *Education:* Kelly Coll and Girton Coll (Cambridge). *Career:* Man Trainee Central TV 1985, Channel 4 Liaison Officer 1986, Assoc Producer 'Classmates' 1987, Controller of Programme Planning 1988, Dir 1989, mem Central Broadcasting Bd; Controller ITV Network Children's and Daytime Programmes 1993; Controller of Arts and Entertainment Channel 4 1994–96; Dir of Programmes Channel 5 1996–2000, CEO Channel 5 2000–; Fellow Royal TV Soc 1999; Olswang Business Woman of the Year 2000. *Leisure interests:* history, film, theatre, TV, travel. *Address:* Channel 5 Broadcasting Ltd, 22 Long Acre, London WC2E 9LY, UK. *Telephone:* (20) 7550-5549 (Office); *Fax:* (20) 7550-5512 (Office).

AITCHISON, Jean Margaret, MA; British professor of language and communications; b 3 July 1938; d of John Frederick and Joan Eileen Aitchison. *Education:* Wimbledon High School, Girton Coll (Cambridge) and Radcliffe Coll (Harvard, USA). *Career:* Asst Lecturer in Ancient Greek, Bedford Coll, Univ of London 1960–65, Lecturer 1965–82, Sr Lecturer 1982–92, Reader 1992; Reader in Linguistics LSE 1965–92; Rupert Murdoch Prof of Language and Communication, Univ of Oxford and Fellow Worcester Coll, Oxford 1993–; delivered Reith Lecture 1996. *Publications:* The Articulate Mammal: An Introduction to Psycholinguistics (3rd edn) 1989, Language Change: Progress or Decay? (2nd edn) 1991, Linguistics (4th edn) 1992, Introducing Language and Mind 1992, Words in the Mind: An Introduction to the Mental Lexicon (2nd edn) 1994, The Seeds of Speech: Language Origin and Evolution 1996, The Language Web: The Power and Problem of Words (Reith Lectures) 1997. *Leisure interest:* windsurfing. *Address:* Worcester College, Oxford OX1 2HB, UK. *Telephone:* (1865) 278392.

AITKEN-WALKER, Louise, MBE; British racing driver; b 21 Jan 1960, Edinburgh; d of the late James and of Margaret Aitken; m Graham Walker 1984. *Education:* Duns Primary School and Berwickshire High School (Duns). *Career:* Shepherdess until 1979; Rally Driver 1979–; first woman to win nat rally 1983; Coupe des Dames (Monte Carlo) 1983, 1990; Ladies Trophy Lombard RAC Rally 1985, 1986, 1989, 1990, 1991; Ladies European Rally Champion 1989; Ladies World Rally Champion 1990; Segrave Trophy 1991; Jim Clark Trophy 1991; various World Championship awards in Sweden, New Zealand, Australia and Italy 1990. *Leisure interests:* golf, horse-riding, swimming. *Address:* Cairnslaw, Duns, Berwick TD11 3LR, UK. *Telephone:* (1361) 82212; *Fax:* (1361) 83157.

AÏTOFF, Irène; French pianist and singing coach; b 30 July 1904, Saint-Cast; d of David and Catherine (née Alexeïeff) Aïtoff. *Education:* Conservatoire de Paris. *Career:* Pianist accompanying singers; accompanied Yvette Guilbert 1932–39; singing coach Radiodiffusion Française 1930–73, Festival d'Aix-en-Provence 1950–72, Vienna State Opera 1962, 1963, Berlin State Opera 1962, Opéra de Paris 1973–, and Bordeaux, Marseilles, Nice, Munich (Germany), Milan and Florence (Italy) and Brussels Operas; Prof Conservatoire Nat Supérieur de Musique de Paris 1972–, Conservatoire de Lyon and Univ d'Orsay; performed at Chansons 1900 concerts at Les Invalides with Pamina 1999; First Prize for accompaniment, harmony and history of music, Conservatoire de Paris. *Address:* 14 rue de l'Abbé-Rousselot, 75017 Paris, France. *Telephone:* (1) 47-64-98-92.

AKAMATSU, Ryoko; Japanese politician; b 24 Aug 1929, Osaka; d of Rinsaku Asaka Akamatsu; m Tadashi Hanami 1953; one s. *Education:* Tsuda Coll and Univ of Tokyo. *Career:* Ministry of Labour 1953, Dir Women Workers' Div 1970–72; Dir-Gen Yamanashi Labour Standard Bureau 1975–78; Counsellor in charge of Women's Affairs, Prime Minister's Office 1978–79; Minister, Perm Mission to UN 1979–82; Dir-Gen Women's Bureau, Ministry of Labour 1982–85; Amb to Uruguay 1986–89; Pres Japan Inst of Workers' Evolution 1989–93; Prof Bunkyo Women's Coll 1992–93; Minister of Educ, Science, Culture and Sports 1993–94. *Publications:* Girls Be Ambitious (autobiog) 1990, Beautiful Uruguay 1990. *Leisure interests:* reading, swimming, listening to classical music. *Address:* 5-11-22-309, Roppongi, Minato-ku, Tokyo, 106, Japan. *Telephone:* (3) 3423-3534; *Fax:* (3) 3423-3534.

AKHEDJAKOVA, Liya Medjidovna; Russian actress; b 9 June 1938, Dniepropetrovsk; d of Medjid Salekhovich and Yulia Aleksandrovna Akhedjakova; m Vladimir Nikolayevich Persyanov. *Education:* State Inst of Theatre Art. *Career:* Actress Moscow Theatre of Young Spectator 1953–71, Sovremennik Theatre 1971–; leading roles in classical and contemporary plays including Shakespeare, Tennessee Williams; in cinema 1969–; People's Artist of Russia; State Prize, Nike Prize. *Films:* Garage, Office Romance, Blessed Heavens, Twenty Days Without War, Lost Bus. *Leisure interest:* travel. *Address:* Udaltsova str 12, Apt 153, 117415 Moscow, Russian Federation. *Telephone:* (095) 921-63-48 (Office); (095) 131-60-41 (Home).

AKHMADULINA, Bella (Isabella Akhatovna); Russian poet; b 10 April 1937, Moscow; d of Ahat Akhmadulin and Nadya (née Lazareva) Akhmadulina; m 1st Yevgeniy Yevtushenko 1960; m 2nd Yuriy Nagibin; m 3rd Boris Messerer 1974. *Education:* Gorky Inst of Literature. *Career:* Sec USSR (now Russian) Writers' Union 1986–; Hon mem American Acad of Arts and Letters 1977; mem Bd Russian PEN Centre 1989–92; State Prize 1989, Pushkin Prize, Russian President's Prize 1998, Alfred Tepfer Prize. *Poems include:* The String 1962, The Rain 1963, My Ancestry 1964, Summer Leaves 1968, The Lessons of Music 1969, Fever and Other New Poems (trans into English) 1970, Tenerezza 1971, The Rain 1974, Poems 1975, The Dreams about Georgia 1977, The Candle 1978, The Snowstorm 1978, The Mystery 1983, The Garden 1987, The Seaboard 1991, Selected Works (vols 1–3) 1996, The Ancient Style Attracts Me 1997, Beautiful Features of My Friends 1999; numerous translations from Georgian. *Address:* Chernyachovskogo str 4, Apt 37, 125319 Moscow, Russian Federation. *Telephone:* (095) 151-22-00.

AL-AWADHI, Badria A., PH D; Kuwaiti legal and environmental consultant; b 20 April 1944, Kuwait City. *Education:* Cairo Univ (Egypt) and Univ Coll (London). *Career:* Dean Faculty of Law and Sharia, Cairo Univ 1979–83, later Prof of International Law; mem ILO Experts Group on Application of Labour Standards; consultant to Int Red Cross on Application of Int Humanitarian Law. *Publications include:* International Law in Times of Peace and War 1979, The Right of Child in the Legal System of Kuwait 1980, Limitation Clauses of Human Rights in the Constitution of the State of the Gulf Co-operation Council 1984, Legal Status of Women in Kuwait 1985, Protection against Sex Discrimination – International and Comparative Law 1986, Women and the Law 1990. *Leisure interests:* travel, sport, reading. *Address:* Al-Awadhi Towers, Tower 3, 3rd Floor, Ahmed Al-Jaber St, POB 27357 Safat, 13134 Safat, Kuwait City, Kuwait. *Telephone:* 2406882; *Fax:* 2406887.

AL-KHAYYAT, Sana, PH D; Iraqi/British community adviser and teacher; b 25 Dec 1945, Baghdad; m (divorced 1975); one d one s. *Education:* Univs of Baghdad and Keele (UK). *Career:* Teacher in Iraq 1976–78; adviser to Arab Community in London from 1987; teacher Adult Educ Colls 1987; mem Campaign for Women's Rights; f Iraqi Sociological Soc; has given lectures on Middle Eastern and Third World Women at numerous academic confs and seminars 1978–; guest on numerous radio and TV programmes discussing women in society, internal and external family relationships, Arab and Middle Eastern youth in the West, child labour, anger man etc 1998–; campaigner against economic sanctions on Iraq. *Publication:* Honour and Shame (Women in Modern Iraq) 1991. *Leisure interests:* reading, travel, theatre, walking in countryside. *Address:* 1 Helena Court, Eaton Rise, London W5 2RE, UK. *Telephone:* (20) 8991-1721.

AL-NAAMANI, Houda, LL B; Lebanese poet; b Damascus, Syria; two s. *Education:* Lycée-Français, Franciscan School, Univ of Damascus and Cornell Univ (NY, USA). *Career:* Fmrly lawyer; writer 1970–. *Publications include:* Ilayka 1970, Anamili... Laa 1971, Qasidat Hub 1973, Adhkuru Kuntu Nuqtah Kuntu Da'ira 1978, Haa Tatadahraju 'ala al'Thalj 1982, Ru'ya 'ala 'Arsh 1989, Huda... Ana al-Haq 1990.

AL-SABAH, Prof. Rasha H. J., PH D; Kuwaiti politician; b 18 Nov 1950, Kuwait City; d of Sheikh Mamood Al-Jabir Al-Sabah and Ruqaiah Majid Al-Majid. *Education:* Univ of Birmingham (UK) and Yale Univ (USA). *Career:* Vice-Rector Kuwait Univ 1985–91, Prof 1989–; Under-Sec Ministry of Higher Education; Hon D PHIL (Hartford) 1995; Alecso Prize 1985. *Publications:* The Figure of the Arab in Medieval Italian Literature 1977, Studies in Monotheism 1985. *Leisure interests:* squash, fishing, water sports. *Address:* Ministry of Higher Education, POB 27130-Safat, 13132 Safat, Kuwait City, Kuwait. *Telephone:* 2455992; *Fax:* 2400998.

ALAHUHTA, Eila Marjatta, PH D; Finnish university professor; b 23 Sept 1926, Mikkeli; d of Juhani Petäjä and Jenny Rautell; m 1st Matti Savonen 1948; three c (one deceased); m 2nd Kaarlo Alahuhta 1971; two c. *Education:* Univs of Jyväskylä and Helsinki. *Career:* Teacher primary school 1948–53, school for the handicapped 1953–73; Chief Teacher Finnish Coll of Speech 1973–80; Asst Prof of Special Pedagogy Univ of Jyväskylä 1977–83, Academic Docent of Logopedics 1983–91; Prof of Logopedics Univ of Oulu 1983–93, Vice-Dean then Dean, Faculty of Humanities 1988–90; Academic Docent of Special Educ Åbo Akademi 1979–90, Univ of Helsinki 1981–90; Adjunct Prof of Speech Pathology Wayne State Univ, MI, USA 1989–; Prof Emer; Founder Alahuhta Consulting; mem workshops of Bureau Int D'Audiophonologie (BIAP), Council Asscn les Sciences de l'Education (AMSE); Bd Nordic Child Language Asscn, Bd of Advisors Journal Societia Paedagogica Experimentalis; honours and awards include Order of the White Rose of Finland (First Class) 1990, Finnish RA Prize 1991, Corpn of the Union of Finnish Towns Medal of Merit 1993, Int Woman of the Year 1995–96, Int Sash of Academia 1997, Most Admired Woman of the Decade 1998, World Who's Who Hall of Fame 1999, Outstanding Woman of the 21st Century 2000, The First Five Hundred at the New Millennium 2000. *Publications include:* On the Defects of Perception, Reasoning and Spatial Orientation Ability in Linguistically Handicapped Children 1976, The BMA Test 1978, Mother's Treasure–How to Prepare the Child for School 1982, I Play and I Talk, I Move and I Read (2nd edn) 1995; numerous contribs to professional journals. *Leisure interests:* art, literature, cooking. *Address:* Alahuhta Consulting Oy, Tunturikatu 8 A 6, 00100 Helsinki, Finland (Office); Koivuhovintie 6A, 02700 Kauniainen, Finland (Home). *Telephone:* (9) 5054300; *Fax:* (9) 50543012; *E-mail:* alahuhta.consulting@kolumbus .fi.

ALAIN, Marie-Claire; French organist; b 10 Aug 1926, Saint-Germain-en-Laye; d of Albert and Madeleine (née Alberty) Alain; m Jacques Gommier 1950; one s one d. *Education:* Inst Notre Dame (Saint-Germain-en-Laye) and Conservatoire Nat Supérieur de Musique (Paris). *Career:* Hon Organ teacher Conservatoire de Musique de Rueil-Malmaison 1978–94; Lecturer Summer Acad for organists, Haarlem, Netherlands 1956–72; numerous concerts throughout world 1955–; lecturer in field; expert on organology to Minister of Culture; Hon D HUM LITT (Colorado State); Hon D MUS (Southern Methodist); numerous prizes for recordings and performances including Buxtehudepreis (Lübeck, Germany), Prix Léonie Sonning (Copenhagen), Prix Franz Liszt (Budapest); Commdr de la Légion d'Honneur; Commdr de l'Ordre Nat du Mérite; Commdr des Arts et des Lettres. *Recordings:* Complete Works include: Alain, Bach, Balbastre, Böhm, Bruhns, Buxtehude, Clérambault, Couperin, Daquin, Franck, de Grigny, Guilain, Handel, Haydn, Mendelssohn, Vivaldi; over 300 recordings. *Publication:* Notes critiques sur l'œvre d'orgue de Jehan Alain 2001. *Address:* 4 rue Victor Hugo, 78230 Le Pecq, France. *Telephone:* (1) 30-87-08-65; *Fax:* (1) 30-87-08-65.

ALAMA, Fetuao Toia; Western Samoan obstetrician, gynaecologist and civil servant; b 21 May 1940; m Ioane Alama 1966; three d one s. *Education:* Fiji School of Medicine, Univ of Auckland (NZ) and Royal Coll of Gynaecologists (London). *Career:* Head Dept of Obstetrics and Gynaecology, Western Samoa 1982–87, Medical Superintendent

1983–87, pvt practice 1987; Clerk Legis Ass 1988, Chief Electoral Officer 1988, Registrar of Electors 1990; mem Royal Coll of Obstetricians and Gynaecologists 1980, New Zealand Royal Coll of Obstetricians and Gynaecologists 1983. *Publications include:* Compendium of Election Laws of Samoa 1995, Election 1996 (handbook), Manual of Obstetrics for District Health Services 1999, Election 2001 (handbook), Registration of Political Parties 2001, Candidates 2001 (handbook), Department of the Legislative Assembly 2001, Scrutineers 2001 (handbook); contribs to professional journals. *Leisure interests:* reading, weaving. *Address:* POB 921, Apia, Western Samoa. *Telephone:* 21816; *Fax:* 21817; *E-mail:* legislative@ipasifika.net.

ALAOUI, Fatima; Moroccan women's organization official; b 27 March 1947, Marrakech; d of Mohamed and Fatima Zahra Alaoui. *Education:* In Rabat and Univ of Tunis (Tunisia). *Career:* Founder, Dir Ere Nouvelle publrs; Pres Comité des Femmes Marocaines pour le Développement 1987; Founder, Pres Forum Maghrébin pour l'Environnement 1989; Pres Agence de Recherches, d'Information et de Formation pour les Femmes; Rep of S NGOs to UN IFAD; has launched environmental and devt campaigns; Ceres Medal (FAO) 1991. *Publications:* L'arbre sans racines ou je ne suis que journaliste 1981, Le rôle économique de la femme dans le milieu rural 1983, Le rôle et le statut de la femme dans le développement rural 1989, Dettes et crises quelles incidences sur l'environnement et le développement 1990, L'équation: paix droits de l'homme et son incidence sur l'environnement et le développement 1991. *Leisure interests:* tennis, music, walking. *Address:* Comité des Femmes Marocaines pour le Développement, BP 403, 2 rue Zahla, Rabat, Morocco. *Telephone:* (7) 72-74-06; *Fax:* (7) 72-74-06.

ALBECK, Plea Sara, LL M; Israeli lawyer; b 28 Oct 1937; d of Izhak E. and Hildegard Nebenzahl; m Shalom Albeck 1958; three d two s. *Education:* Horev School and Hebrew Univ (Jerusalem). *Career:* Articled clerk Ministry of Justice 1958–60; worked with S. Horowitz & Co 1960–62; called to Israeli Bar 1961; Asst State Attorney 1963–69; Dir Civil Dept, State Attorney's Office 1969–93; f pvt law firm 1993–; lecturer at several univs on land law 1993–; mem and legal adviser of Council for Advancement of Women in Jerusalem 1994–; mem Israeli Forum for Land Policy 1975–; has written several articles on Judaea and Samaria and on the status of women and on land law. *Leisure interest:* knitting. *Address:* 5 Hafzadi St, Jerusalem, Israel (Office); 9 Batey Machase St, Jerusalem 97500, Israel (Home). *Telephone:* (2) 6272333; *Fax:* (2) 627 2333.

ALBEVERIO-MANZONI, Solvejg Giovanna Maria; Swiss artist and writer; b 6 Nov 1939, Arogno; d of Cesco and Madi (née Angioletti) Manzoni; m Sergio Albeverio 1970; one d. *Education:* Textile design (Como, Italy), Kunstgewerbeschule (Zürich, Switzerland) and Statens Handverk og Kunstindustriskole (Oslo, Norway). *Career:* Solo exhibitions include Campione d'Italia, Bielefeld, Bochum, Berlin, and Wilhelmshaven (Germany), Marseille (France), Zürich and Salzburg (Austria); group exhibitions include Fredrikstad (Norway), New York (USA), Bielefeld, Campione d'Italia, Essen (Germany), Maastricht (Netherlands) and Zürich, Ascona, Basel and Lugano (Switzerland); has given poetry readings at int meetings at Ferrara (Italy) 1987, Poesia dell'Europa latina (Fano, Italy) 1987, World Conf for Poets (Crete, Greece) 1991, (Sintra, Portugal) 1995; Premio Ascona for unpublished narrative 1987; Pro Helvetia Scholarship 1995. *Publications:* Da stanze chiuse (poetry and drawings) 1987, Il pensatore con il mantello come meteora (novel) 1990, Controcanto al chiuso (drawings, with poetry by B. M. Frabotta) 1991, Il fiore e il frutto. Triandro donna (poetry, jtly) 1993, Frange di solitudine (novel) 1994, Spiagge confinanti (poetry) 1996, All'ombra delle farfalle in fiore (drawings with poetry by Folco Portinari) 1998, La carcassa color del cielo (novel) 2001; numerous stories, poetry and drawings in magazines, journals and anthologies. *Address:* Liebfrauenweg 5B, Bonn, Germany. *Telephone:* (228) 2599991.

ALBRIGHT, Madeleine Korbel, PH D; American politician and professor of international affairs; b 15 May 1937, Czechoslovakia (now Czech Repub); d of Joseph Korbel and Anna Speeglova; m Joseph Albright (divorced); three d. *Education:* Wellesley Coll and Columbia Univ. *Career:* Prof of Int Affairs Georgetown Univ 1982–83; Vice-Chair Nat Democratic Inst for Int Affairs 1983, Chair 2001–; Head Center for Nat Policy 1985–93; fmrly legis aide to Democratic Senator Edmund

Muskie; fmr mem Nat Security Council staff in Carter Admin; advisor to Democrat cands Geraldine Ferraro 1984 and Michael Dukakis 1988; Perm Rep to UN 1993–97 (first foreign-born holder of this post); Sec of State 1997–2001; mem Council on Foreign Relations, American Political Science Asscn, American Asscn for Advancement of Slavic Studies; Radcliffe Medal 2001. *Publications include:* Poland: the Role of the Press in Political Change 1983, and numerous articles. *Address:* National Democratic Institute for International Affairs, 1717 Massachusetts Ave, NW, Fifth Floor, Washington, DC 20036, USA. *Telephone:* (202) 328-3136; *Fax:* (202)939-3166; *Internet:* www.ndi.org.

ALBUQUERQUE, Lita, BA; American artist and sculptor; b 3 Jan 1946, Santa Monica, CA; d of Mauriceo Yaeche and Ferida (née Hayat) Albuquerque; m Carey P. Peck 1990; two d one s. *Education:* Univ of California at Los Angeles and Otis Art Inst. *Career:* Visiting artist Chicago Art Inst, IL 1984, San Francisco Art Inst, CA 1987; teacher at grad seminars Arizona State Univ 1984, Otis/Parsons School, Los Angeles, CA 1985, 1986, San Francisco Art Inst 1985; Grad Advisor Art Center, Coll of Design, Pasadena, CA 1979–90; one-woman exhibitions include Univ Arts Museum, Univ of California at Santa Barbara 1978, Janus Gallery (Los Angeles, CA) 1979, 1981, 1982, Marianne Deson Gallery (Chicago, IL) 1980, 1984, Lerner-Heller Gallery, (New York) 1981, Robert Cronin Inc (Houston, TX) 1984, Loyola Marymount Univ (Los Angeles, CA) 1984, Saxon-Lee Gallery (Los Angeles, CA) 1986, Works Gallery (Costa Mesa, CA) 1991, 1993, Haines Gallery (San Francisco, CA) 1992; group exhibitions include Smithsonian Inst (Washington, DC) 1981, Museum of Contemporary Art (Los Angeles, CA) 1985, Embassy of USA (Helsinki, Finland) 1986, Fresno Arts Center and Museum (CA) 1987, Wright Art Gallery, Univ of California (Los Angeles, CA) 1987; represented in numerous perm collections; Fellow Nat Endowment of the Arts 1975; Woman of the Year, Palm Springs Museum of Art, FL 1985; Retrospective Fellows Contemporary Art, Santa Monica Museum of Art 1990. *Environmental works include:* Rock and Pigment Installation (Mojave Desert, CA) 1978, Beneath the Black Polished Granite are a Series of Ten Subterranean Islands, Each One Floating on a Copper Plate (Security Pacific Plaza, Los Angeles, CA) 1983, Forbidden City 1983, Sleeping Beauty 1986, Tangency Horizon (Santa Monica, CA) 1986; *Film work includes:* Heartbreakers 1983, The Other Lover 1985, Out On A Limb 1986. *Address:* Annex Gallery, 453 6th Ave, San Diego, CA 92101, USA.

ALCOTT, Amy Strum; American golfer; b 22 Feb 1956, Kansas City, MO; d of Eugene Yale and Leatrice (née Strum) Alcott. *Career:* Professional Golfer 1975–; Asst Coach Univ of California at Los Angeles Women's Golf Team; Dir Women's Golf Devt, Elizabeth Arden Inc, Youth Golf Devt, Sunkist; Host Amy Alcott Golf Classic for Multiple Sclerosis Soc 1980–; has won over 32 professional titles including Canadian Open–Peter Jackson Classic 1979, Women's US Open 1980, Nabisco–Dinah Shore Invitational 1980, 1988, 1991, Tucson Open (AZ) 1985, World Championship of Women's Golf 1985, Ladies Professional Golf Asscn Nat Pro-Am 1986; Rookie of the Year, Ladies Professional Golf Asscn 1975; Player of the Year, Golf Magazine 1980; Jewish Athlete of the Year 1980; Seagrams Seven Crown of Sports Award 1980; Vare Trophy 1980; Founders Cup Award, Ladies Professional Golf Asscn 1986; California Golf Writers' Hall of Fame 1987, World Golf Hall of Fame 1999. *Address:* Ladies Professional Golf Association, POB 956, Pacific Palisades, CA 90272, USA; Ladies Professional Golf Asscn, 100 International Golf Drive, Daytona Beach, FL 32124, USA.

ALDERSON, Margaret Hanne (Maggie), MA; British journalist; b 31 July 1959, London; d of Douglas Arthur and Margaret Dura (née Mackay) Alderson; m Geoffrey Francis Laurence 1991 (divorced 1996). *Education:* St Dominic's Priory and Alleynes School (Stone, Staffs) and Univ of St Andrews. *Career:* Writer and Features Ed several magazines including Honey, You and London Evening Standard 1983–88; Ed ES London Evening Standard Magazine 1988–89, Elle 1989–92, Mode 1994–95; Deputy Ed Cleo 1993–94; journalist and sr writer Sydney Morning Herald 1996–; mem British Soc of Magazine Eds 1988–; Ed of the Year, Colour Supplements (British Soc of Magazine Eds) 1989. *Publications* Shoe Money 1998, Pants On Fire 2000. *Leisure interests:* gardening, reading, painting, travel. *Address:* c/o Sydney Morning Herald, 201 Sussex St, NSW 2000, Australia (Office); 45/2A Ithaca Rd, Elizabeth Bay, Sydney NSW 2011, Australia.

ALDERSON, Matti, BA, FRSA; British organization executive; b 20 Dec 1951. *Education:* Bearsden Acad, Open Univ. *Career:* Legal exec 1970–72; mem staff Advertising Agency Poster Bureau 1972–74, Royd's Advertising 1974–75; Exec Advertising Standards Authority 1975–80, Man 1980–89, Deputy Dir-Gen 1989–90, Dir-Gen 1990–2000; Founder and Vice-Chair European Advertising Standards Alliance (Belgium) 1997–2000; mem Food Advisory Cttee, Ministry of Agric, Food and Fisheries 1997–, Better Regulation Task Force 1998–, Doctors' and Dentists' Remuneration Review Body 1998– (Chair Payroll Review 1999–2000); mem Ed Bd Journal of Regulatory Law and Practice. *Leisure interests:* architecture and design, reading, studying, driving. *Address:* Raglan House, Windsor Rd, Gerrards Cross, Bucks SL9 7ND, UK.

ALDERSON, Sue Ann, MA; American professor of creative writing; b 11 Sept 1940, New York; d of Eugene Leonard and Ruth Edith (née Schuchowsky) Hartley; m Evan Alderson 1965 (divorced); two c. *Education:* Antioch Coll, Ohio State Univ and Univ of California at Berkeley. *Career:* English Instructor Simon Fraser Univ, Canada 1967–71, Capilano Coll 1973–80; Asst Prof Univ of British Columbia, Canada 1980–84, Assoc Prof of Creative Writing 1984–92, Prof 1992– (sole instructor on writing for children); Juror Canadian Council on Children's Literary Prize 1981–83. *Publications include:* For children: Bonnie McSmithers, You're Driving Me Dithers 1974, The Finding Princess 1977, The Adventures of Prince Paul 1977, Hurry Up, Bonnie! 1977, Bonnie McSmithers Is At It Again! 1979, Anne-Marie Maginol tu me rends folle 1981, Ida and the Wool Smugglers 1987; Jr fiction: Comet's Tale 1983, The Not Impossible Summer 1983, The Something in Thurlo Darby's House 1984, Maybe You Had To Be There, By Duncan 1989, Chapter One 1990, Sure as Strawberries 1992, A Ride for Martha 1993, Ten Mondays for Lots of Boxes 1995, Pond Seasons 1997, Wherever Bears Be 1999. *Address:* 4004 West 32 St, Vancouver, BC V6S 1Z6, Canada (Home).

ALDOUS, Lucette; Australian ballet dancer and ballet teacher; b 26 Sept 1938, Auckland, New Zealand; d of Charles Fellows and Marie (née Rutherford) Aldous; m Richard Alder 1972; one d. *Education:* Western Australia Acad of Performing Arts, Royal Ballet School (London) and Kirov Ballet (Leningrad, now St Petersburg, Russian Fed). *Career:* Dancer with London Festival Ballet 1966–71, Royal Ballet 1972, Australian Ballet 1984; Master Teacher Australian Ballet School 1979; Head of Classical Dance Western Australia Acad of Performing Arts 1979–; Guest Teacher Australian Ballet 1988–, New Zealand Ballet Co 1988–, Western Australia Ballet Co 1988–; Guest Kirov Ballet and Ballet School, St Petersburg 1975–76; Guest Dancer in Europe, USA, Australia; Guest Teacher Australia Dance Cos; mem Bd W Australia Ballet Co, Dance Fund Australia; mem Australian Council 1995–97; Patron Australian Cecchetti Soc 1991; Hon D LITT (Edith Cowan Univ) 1999. *Ballets include:* Giselle 1968, Don Quixote 1970, Carmen 1970, The Sleeping Beauty 1970, La Sylphide (for BBC) 1960, The Turning Point (film) 1970; created classical ballet Pastiche 1994; reproduced Paquita 1997, Corsaire 1998; condensed 2 acts of La Bayadère 1998. *Leisure interests:* music, gardening, theatre, opera, breeding Burmese cats. *Address:* c/o Dance Dept, Western Australian Academy of Performing Arts, 2 Bradford St, Mount Lawley, Perth, WA 6050, Australia (Office). *Telephone:* (9) 271 2439 (Home).

ALDOVÁ, Eva, D SC; Czech scientist; b 21 Nov 1922, Prague; d of the late Josef Alda and Františka Aldová; m 1954 (divorced). *Education:* Charles Univ (Prague). *Career:* Joined Nat Inst of Public Health 1941, technician and bacteriologist 1949, bacteriologist at Terezín concentration camp during outbreaks of typhoid and typhus 1944–46, at Czechoslovak hosp in Democratic People's Repub of Korea (N Korea) 1954–55, Consultant to WHO during outbreaks of cholera in Iraq 1966, Guinea 1970, teacher cholera course in Bulgaria 1968, the countries of W Africa including Liberia and Burkina Faso 1970, Yemen 1988; has participated in numerous int confs; has written more than 140 scientific papers; Medal for work during typhus outbreak in Terezín 1945; Anniversary Prize 1975; Pragia Fontium Prize 1989. *Leisure interests:* nature, travel, photography. *Address:* National Institute of Public Health, Šrobárova 48, 100 42 Prague 10, Czech Republic (Office); Patockova 43, 169 00 Prague 6, Czech Republic (Home). *Telephone:* (2) 67082592 (Office); (2) 20510745 (Home).

ALDUY, Dominique, MA; French economist and newspaper executive; b 23 Feb 1944, Paris; d of Maurice and Madeleine (née Colas) Daumas; m Jean-Paul Alduy 1969; one s two d. *Education:* Univ of Paris, Inst d'Etudes Politiques de Paris and Pennsylvania State Univ (USA). *Career:* In charge of local community financial studies, Ministry of Equipment 1972–76; Rep to Secr-Gen for New Towns 1976–78; in charge of Habitat and Environment Comm, Comm Gen du Plan 1979–81; Social Policies Rep to Cabinet of the Prime Minister 1981–83; Dir of Programmes Caisse des Dépôts et Consignations 1983–86, Dir Devt of Deposits-Devt 1986, Pres, Dir-Gen of Communication Devt 1986–89; Dir-Gen Société Nat de Programmes—France Régions 3 (FR3) 1989–93, Dir-Gen Film 3 production 1989–; Dir-Gen Centre Nat d'Art et de Culture Georges Pompidou 1993–94; Dir-Gen Le Monde newspaper 1994–, mem Bd of Dirs Le Monde and Le Monde SA 1995–; Co-Man Cahiers du Cinéma; Chevalier de la Légion d'Honneur. *Address:* Le Monde, 21 bis rue Claude Bernard, 75242 Paris Cedex 05, France (Office); 74A rue Lecourbe, 75015 Paris, France (Home).

ALEANDRO, Norma; Argentine actress; b 6 Dec 1936, Buenos Aires. *Career:* Theatre actress and dir; lived in exile in Uruguay and Spain 1976–82; returned to Argentina 1982. *Plays:* About Love and Other Stories (one-woman show), The Señorita of Tacna (written for her by Mario Vargas Llosa) 1987; *Films include:* La muerte en las calles, Gente conmigo, La tregua (Acad Award nomination), No toquen a la nena, The Official Story (Best Actress Award, Cannes Film Festival, jtly 1986), Gaby: A True Story (Acad Award nomination), Cousins, Vital Signs, The Tombs; *Screenplay:* Los Herederos; also short stories.

ALEGRÍA, Claribel, BA; Salvadorean writer; b 12 May 1924, Estelí, Nicaragua; d of Daniel and Ana Maria (née Vides) Alegría; m Darwin J. Flakoll 1947 (died 1995); three d one s. *Education:* George Washington Univ (DC, USA). *Career:* Extensive travelling in USA, S America and Europe 1943–; writer 1943–; Dr hc (E Conneticut State Univ) 1998. *Publications include:* Poetry: Anillo de Silencio, Sobrevivo (Casa de las Américas, Cuba) 1978; 13 books of poetry, four novellas, one novel, one book of children's stories and several books of memoirs (some jtly with her husband). *Leisure interests:* music, painting. *Address:* Apdo Postal A-36, Managua, Nicaragua. *Telephone:* (2) 774 903; *E-mail:* claribel@ibw.com.ni; *Internet:* www.claribel@ibw.com.ni.

ALEKSEEVA, Tatyana Ivanovna; Russian anthropologist and biologist; b 7 Dec 1928; d of Ivan Shacabrin and Varvara Majorova; m Valery Alekseev. *Education:* Moscow State Univ. *Career:* Jr, Sr then Leading Researcher Research Inst and Museum of Anthropology 1955–; has conducted research on the study of influence of geographical and social medium on aboriginal population; Corresp mem USSR (now Russian) Acad of Sciences 1991, mem 2000; mem World Org of Biologists. *Publications include:* Origin and Ethnic History of Russian People 1965, Ethnogenesis of East Slavs 1973, Geographical Medium and Biology of Man 1977, Adaptive Processes in Populations of Man 1986. *Leisure interests:* riding, pets. *Address:* Research Institute and Museum of Anthropology, Mokhovaya str 11, 103009 Moscow, Russian Federation. *Telephone:* (095) 203-3598 (Office); (095) 331-3273 (Home).

ALEMANY I ROCA, Joaquima; Spanish politician; b 19 May 1942, Barcelona; d of Joan Alemany and Julia Roca; m Jospe M. Sust 1968; three c. *Education:* Univ of Barcelona. *Career:* Mem Dist Council 1983–87; mem Comm for the Advancement of Women 1987–89; Convergència Democràtica de Catalunya (CDC) Senator for Barcelona 1989–; Vice-Pres Women's Inst of Catalonia 1990; mem European Asscn for the Devt and Training of Women 1990; named Leading Lady Liderman Cirt Int 1988; Golden Madrone House of Madrid in Barcelona 1990. *Publications:* Feine de Dones 1989, L'Evolució de la Familia a Catalunya 1989, El Paper de la Dona a Les Forces Armades 1991. *Leisure interests:* music, reading, painting. *Address:* Senado, Plaza de la Marina Española 8, Madrid 13, Spain (Office); Roger de Llúria 117 6è 1A, 08037 Barcelona, Spain (Home). *Telephone:* (1) 4461013 (Office).

ALENIUS, Marianne, PH D; Danish academic; b 17 Oct 1948, Finland; d of Viggo Christensen and Sigyn Alenius; m Niels Ivan Boserup 1980; two s two d. *Education:* Univ of Copenhagen. *Career:* Man Dir Museum Tusculanum Press, Univ of Copenhagen 1988–; Library Consultant on fundraising and academic publishing, Royal Library, Copenhagen

1989–; Pres Kvindelige Akademikere (Danish Asscn of Int Asscn of Univ Women) 1989–. *Publications include:* Doeden og Venskalet. En studie i Senecus breve 1974, Charlotta Dor. Biehl—Mitubetydelige Lernets loeb 1986, Brev Lileftertiden 1987; contribs to books and journals. *Leisure interests:* jogging, walking in the forests. *Address:* Raadhusvej 19, 2920 Charlottenlund, Denmark. *Telephone:* 35-32-91-10; *Fax:* 35-32-91-13; *E-mail:* alenius@coco.ihi.ku.dk.

ALEXANDER, Clare; British literary agent. *Career:* Ed with Penguin Books 1981–97, later Publishing Dir Viking; Ed-in-Chief Macmillan 1997–98; Literary Agent Gillon Aitken Assocs 1998–, agent to Pat Barker (qv) and numerous others. *Address:* 29 Fernshaw Rd, London, SW10 0TG, UK.

ALEXANDER, Elisabeth; German poet and writer; b 21 Aug 1922, Linz/Rhein. *Career:* Freelance writer 1970–; contributor to Feuilleton des Heidelberger Tageblatts magazine 1975–82; publications in newspapers and magazines and for radio and TV, including Frankfurter Rundschau, Basler Zeitung, Frankfurter Hefte, Badische Neueste Nachrichten, Die Zeit, Passagen, Mannheimer Morgen; Visiting Writer Texas Tech Univ, USA 1986; lecture tours of USA, Guest Lecturer Goethe Inst Amsterdam (Netherlands), Paris, Brussels, Montréal (Canada), etc; works translated to English, French and Chinese; First Prize, Poetensitz 1996. *Publications include:* Poetry: Bums 1971, Ich bin kein Pferd 1976, Brotkrumen 1977, Ich hänge mich ans schwarze Brette 1979, Wo bist du Trost 1980, Glückspfennig–Gedichte für das ganze Jahr 1984, Zeitflusen 1986, Die Uhr läuft rückwärts wenn der Schnee fällt 1994; Novels and short stories: Die Frau, die lachte 1975, Fritte Pomm (for children) 1976, Die törichte Jungfrau 1978, Sie hätte ihre Kinder töten sollen 1982, Damengeschichte 1983, Lisas Liebe 1994, Domizil Heidelberg 1995, Bauchschuß; co-writer and ed many other works, works feature in anthologies. *Leisure interests:* languages, writing letters, literature. *Address:* Erwin-Rohde-Str 22, 69120 Heidelberg, Germany.

ALEXANDER, Jane; American actress and government official; b 28 Oct 1939, Boston, MA; d of Thomas Bartlett and Ruth (née Pearson) Quigley; m 1st Robert Alexander 1962 (divorced 1969); one s; m 2nd Edwin Sherin 1975. *Education:* Sarah Lawrence Coll (Bronxville, NY) and Univ of Edinburgh (UK). *Career:* Theatre, TV and film actress 1962–; appeared at Charles Playhouse (Boston) 1964–65, Arena Stage (Washington, DC) 1965–68, 1970, American Shakespeare Festival; Chair Nat Endowment for the Arts 1993–97; mem Bd Dirs Women's Action for Nuclear Disarmament 1981–88, Film Forum 1985–90, Nat Stroke Asscn 1984–91; Hon DFA (The Juillard School) 1994, (NC School of Arts) 1994, Hon PH D (Univ of Pennsylvania) 1995, (Duke Univ) 1996, and numerous other hon degrees; Achievement in Dramatic Arts Award (St Botolph Club) 1979; Israel Cultural Award 1982; Helden Caldicott Leadership Award 1984; Western Heritage Wrangler Award 1985; Living Legacy Award (Women's Int Center) 1988; Lifetime Achievement Award, Americans for Arts 1999; Harry S Truman Award for Public Service 1999, numerous other awards. *Plays include:* Mourning Becomes Electra, The Great White Hope (Tony Award 1969, Drama Desk Award, Theatre World Award) 1968–69, 6 Rms Riv Vu 1972–73, Find Your Way Home 1974, Hamlet 1975, The Heiress 1976, First Monday in October 1978, Goodbye Fidel 1980, Monday After the Miracle 1982, Anthony and Cleopatra 1981, Hedda Gabler 1981, Old Times 1984, Night of the Iguana 1988, Approaching Zanzibar 1989, Mystery of the Rose Bouquet 1989, Shadowlands 1990, The Visit 1992, The Sisters Rosenzweig 1993, Honour 1998; Other stage appearances include: Antony and Cleopatra 1981, Hedda Gabler 1981, Approaching Zanzibar 1989, The Cherry Orchard 2000; *Films include:* The Great White Hope 1970, All the President's Men 1976, Kramer vs Kramer 1979, Brubaker 1980, Night Crossing 1981, Testament 1983, City Heat 1984, Sweet Country 1986, Square Dance 1987, Glory 1989; *TV appearances include:* Eleanor and Franklin 1976, Eleanor and Franklin: The White House Years (TV Critics' Circle Award) 1977, Playing For Time (Emmy Award) 1980, Kennedy's Children 1981, Calamity Jane 1984, Malice in Wonderland 1985, Mountain View 1989, Daughter of the Streets 1990, A Marriage: Georgia O'Keeffe and Alfred Stieglitz 1991, Stay the Night 1992; *Publications:* Ibsen's The Master Builder (trans, jtly) 1978, The Bluefish

Cookbook (jtly, 4th edn) 1990. *Address:* c/o Samuel Liff, William Morris Agency, 1325 Avenue of the Americas, New York, NY 10019, USA. *Telephone:* (202) 682-5400; *Fax:* (202) 682-5798.

ALEXANDER, Susan Mizelle; American artist and sculptor; b 16 Nov 1929, New York, USA; d of Philip Henry and the late Emily Hare Hardie; m Neville Grey Alexander 1951; one s one d. *Education:* Pratt Inst (Brooklyn, NY), Skidmore Coll (Saratoga Springs, NY) and Ecole des Beaux Arts (Lausanne, Switzerland). *Career:* Works in pastel, oil, watercolour and bronze 1947–; mem Jamaica Dance Co 1965–80; organized art classes in maximum security prisons 1970–79; Founder and Dir Upstairs Downstairs Gallery 1980–91; exhibitions include Nat Gallery of Jamaica, Country Art Gallery (New York), Albert White Gallery (Toronto, Canada), Palace of Fine Arts (México), Bolívar Gallery; murals at First Nat City Bank of New York, Aluminum Partners of Jamaica Ltd, Royal Bank Jamaica Ltd, Stacote Paints Ltd; works including murals and altar pieces represented in perm collections; Jamaica Festival Gold Medal 1975; Marcus Garvey Award 1978. *Leisure interests:* dance, travel, opera. *Address:* 108 Harbour St, Kingston, Jamaica (Office); 1 Old Church Rd, Kingston 8, Jamaica (Home). *Telephone:* 922-8260 (Office); 924-2453 (Home).

ALEXANDRA, HRH Princess (see Ogilvy, HRH Princess Alexandra).

ALFTAN, Maija Kyllikki; Finnish magazine editor; b 17 Dec 1948, Alatornio; d of Oskar and Henni Tallgren; m Robert Alftan 1976; two d. *Education:* Sanoma School of Journalism (Helsinki). *Career:* Reporter on Ilta-Sanomat 1969–78, Kotiliesi 1978–83; Man Ed Avotakka 1983–85, Kodin Kuvalehti magazine 1986–89; apptd Ed-in-Chief Kodin Kuvalehti 1989. *Address:* c/o Kodin Kuvalehti, POB 113, 00381 Helsinki, Finland.

ALI, Amina Salum, MBA; Tanzanian politician; b 24 Oct 1956, Zanzibar; d of Salum and Gheda Ali; m Alimarbour Yuai 1982; three d one s. *Education:* Univs of Delhi and Pune (India). *Career:* Asst Dir Ministry of State Planning and Dir Foreign Trade, Ministry of Trade 1981–82; Planning Officer Perm Planning Comm 1984–85; Deputy Minister of Finance, Econ Affairs and Planning 1985–87, Minister of State in charge of Int and Regional Co-operation, Ministry of Foreign Affairs 1987–90; Minister of Finance 1990. *Leisure interest:* reading. *Address:* c/o Ministry of Finance, POB 1154, Zanzibar, Tanzania. *Telephone:* (54) 32853; *Fax:* (54) 32659.

ALIA, Josette (pseudonym of Josette de Benbrahem); French journalist; b 25 Nov 1929, Ferté-Bernard; d of Jack and Germaine (née Legeay) David; m Raouf Benbrahem 1952; one s. *Education:* Inst d'Etudes Politiques de Paris and Univ of Paris (Paris-Sorbonne). *Career:* Journalist Jeune Afrique 1960–62; Corresp Le Monde newspaper 1962–67; Sr Reporter, Ed-in-Chief, Deputy Editorial Dir then Editorial Dir Le Nouvel Observateur magazine 1985–; mem Jury Prix Albert Londres; Echo de la Presse et de la Publicité Best Journalist Award 1980; Personality of the Year 1985; Prix Mumm 1993. *Publication:* Quand le soleil était chaud (Prix des Maisons de la Presse) 1993. *Address:* Le Nouvel Observateur, 10–12 place de la Bourse, 75081 Paris Cedex 02, France (Office); 169 rue de Rennes, 75006 Paris, France (Home).

ALIBHAI-BROWN, Yasmin, MBE, BA, M PHIL; British journalist and broadcaster; b 10 Dec 1949, Kampala, Uganda; m Colin Brown; one s one d. *Education:* Makerene Univ (Kampala) and Univ of Oxford. *Career:* Came to UK from Uganda 1972; adult educ teacher 1975–85; journalist 1985–, regular columnist with The Independent, The Guardian, New Statesman; radio and TV broadcaster; Research Fellow Inst for Public Policy Research 1996–; Sr Research Fellow Foreign Policy Centre June 1999–; mem Home Office Race Forum; Vice-Pres UN Asscn, UK; more than 10 awards for journalism and media including BBC TV ASIA Award 1999, Ethnic Minority Media Achievement Award 2000, BT Emma Award for Media Personality of the Year 2000, Windrush Award; Hon MA (Open Univ). *Publications include:* No Place Like Home, True Colours 1999, Who Do We Think We Are? 2000, After Multiculturalism 2000, Mixed Feelings 2001; numerous pamphlets on race and human rights. *Leisure interest:* theatre. *Address:* 7A Gunnersbury Avenue, London, W5 3NH, UK. *Telephone:* (20) 8932-5673; *Fax:* (20) 8932-5674; *E-mail:* connect.brown@virgin.net.

ALIEVA, Fazu Gamzatovna; Russian poet; b 1932, Ginichutl, Daghestan; d of Ali Alieva and Apipat Gamzatov; m Musa Magomedov 1956; four s. *Education:* Moscow Gorky Literary Inst. *Career:* Chief Ed Woman of Daghestan magazine; Chair Peace Cttee of Daghestan; mem CPSU 1965–91, World Peace Council; People's Poet of Daghestan 1969; Order of the Badge of Honour. *Publications include:* Poetry: Native Village 1959, The Blue Road 1959, On the Sea-Shore 1961, Spring Wind 1962, I Give Out Rainbows 1963, In the Heart of Every Person is Ilyich 1965, The Carving on the Stone 1966, The Eighteenth Spring 1968, The Low of Mountains 1969, The Patrimonial Coat of Arms 1970, The Choice 1976, Curative Words 1981; Novels: Fate 1964, The Wind Won't Carry Away the Clod of Earth 1967, A Basket Full of Ripe Cherry 1983, Tavakal or Why the Men Turn Grey 1988. *Leisure interests:* museums, decorative art. *Address:* Union of Writers, Moscow 121069, ul Vorovskogo 52, Russian Federation.

ALLEMANN, Sabina; American ballet dancer; b Bern, Switzerland. *Education:* Nat Ballet School (Toronto). *Career:* Joined Nat Ballet of Canada, 1980, Second Soloist 1982–84, First Soloist 1984–88, Prin Dancer 1988–89; Prin Guest Artist San Francisco Ballet Co (CA) 1988–89; Prin Dancer 1989–. *Ballets include:* Swan Lake, The Sleeping Beauty, Con Brio, Valses Poeticos, Menuetto, Reflections of Saint Joan, Le Quattro Stagioni, Forevermore, La Pavane Rouge, Tagore, Dark Elegies, Filling Station, La fille man gardée, Job, The End, Nutcracker, Rodeo, Serenade, Glinka, Pas de Trois, The Four Temperaments, Who Cares?, Pulcinella, Seeing Stars, Connotations, Napoli, La Bayadere, Alice, The Merry Widow, Les Sylphides, La Rondel; *Films include:* Onegin 1986, Canciones 1988. *Address:* San Francisco Ballet, 455 Franklin St, San Francisco, CA 94102, USA.

ALLEN, Betty; American opera singer; b Campbell, OH; d of James Corr and Dora Catherine (née Michael) Allen; m Ritten Edward Lee III 1953; two s two d. *Education:* Wilberforce Univ (OH) and Hartford School of Music. *Career:* Opera debut Teatro Colón, Buenos Aires, Argentina 1964; has appeared with San Francisco Opera, Bellas Artes Opera (Mexico), Oslo Opera, Houston Opera, Montréal Opera (Canada), The Hague Opera and at numerous festivals including Marlboro, Helsinki, Saratoga, Caramoor Music, Cincinnati May and Tanglewood Festivals; appearances with major symphony orchestras on concert tours of USA, Europe, N Africa, Caribbean, Canada, S America and Asia; Teacher Teatro Colón 1985–86, Curtis Inst of Music 1987–; Exec Dir Harlem School of the Arts 1979, now also Artistic Dir; recordings for London, Vox, Decca, Deutsche Grammophon, Columbia, RCA and Odeon-Pathe; numerous radio and TV appearances in USA, Canada, Mexico, UK, Germany, Sweden; mem Bd Dirs Arts Alliance, Karl Weigl Foundation, Diller-Quaile School of Music, US Comm for UNICEF, Manhattan School of Music, Theatre Devt Fund, Children's Storefront, Chamber Music Soc of Lincoln Center, New York Housing Authority, Exec Cttee Carnegie Hall, Nat Foundation for Advancement in the Arts; Rep USA to Cultural Olympics (Mexico); John Hay Whitney Fellow 1953–54; numerous hon degrees; Marian Anderson Award 1953–54; Man Award, Nat Music League 1953; Best Singer of Season (Critics' Circle) Argentina and Chile 1959, Uruguay 1961; Duke Ellington Memorial Award, 52nd St American Festival 1989; Bowery Award, Bowery Bank 1989; Harlem School of the Arts Award, Harlem School and Isaac Stern 1990; St Thomas Church Award, St Thomas Catholic Church 1990; Men's Day Celebration Award, St Paul's Church 1990; Martell House of Seagram Award, Avery Fisher Hall 1990. *Address:* Harlem School of the Arts, 645 St Nicholas Ave, New York, NY 10030, USA.

ALLEN, Debbie, BA; American actress, dancer and choreographer; b 16 Jan, Houston, TX; d of Vivian Ayers; m 1st Win Wilford (divorced); m 2nd Norm Nixon; two c. *Education:* Howard Univ (DC). *Career:* Appearances on stage and TV, then choreographer and dir. *Stage appearances include:* Purlie 1972, West Side Story, Guys and Dolls, Raisin, Ain't Misbehavin', Sweet Charity 1985, 1986; Choreographer: Carrie 1988, Acad Awards 1991, 1992, 1993, 1994; *TV includes:* Actress: Dancing in the Wings 1985, Fame (series) 1982, The Debbie Allen Special (also dir, producer, choreographer and co-writer) 1989; Dir: Family Ties (several episodes), A Different World 1988–89, Polly (also choreographer) 1989, Cool Women 2000; *Specials:* Ben Vereen – His Roots, Loretta Lynn in Big Apple Country, Texaco Star Theater – Opening Night, The Kids from Fame, John Schneider's Christmas

Holiday, A Tribute to Martin Luther King Jr – A Celebration of Life, Motown Returns to the Apollo, Sinbad Live (Afros and Bell Bottoms); *Films:* Producer and Dir: The Fish That Saved Pittsburgh 1979, Ragtime 1981, JoJo Dancer Your Life is Calling, Blank Cheque; *Recording:* Special Look 1989. *Address:* c/o William Morris Agency, 151 S El Camino Drive, Beverly Hills, CA 90212, USA.

ALLEN, Dame Ingrid Victoria, DBE, DL, MD, D SC, FRCP, FRCPI, FRCP(E); British professor of neuropathology; b 30 July 1932; d of Rev Robert and Doris V. Allen; m Alan Watson Barnes 1972. *Education:* Cheltenham Ladies Coll and Queen's Univ (Belfast). *Career:* House Officer Royal Victoria Hosp, Belfast 1957–58, Sr Registrar 1964–65; Tutor in Pathology Queen's Univ, Belfast 1958–64, Sr Lecturer and Consultant in Neuropathology, Queen's Univ and Royal Victoria Hosp 1966–78, Reader and Consultant 1978–79, Head N Ireland Regional Neuropathological Service 1979–; mem MRC 1989–; Vice-Pres Int Soc of Neuropathology 1989–92; Emer Prof 1997; Dir of Research and Devt HPSS 1997–2001; Visiting Prof Univ of Ulster 1997–; mem Cttee on Women in Science and Tech, Office of Public Service and Science; Fellow Royal Coll of Physicians and Surgeons of Glasgow; mem Royal Irish Acad; mem numerous editorial bds; contribs to textbooks and professional journals. *Publications include:* Demyelinating Diseases in Greenfield's Neuropathology (5th edn), Pathology of Multiple Sclerosis in McAlpine's Sclerosis (2nd edn) 1980; contribs to journals on neuropathology, demyelinating diseases, neurovirology and neuro-oncology. *Leisure interests:* tennis, history, architecture, reading, sailing. *Address:* Room 113, School of Biology and Biochemistry, Medical Biology Centre, Queen's University of Belfast, 97 Lisburn Rd, Belfast, BT9 7BL, UK (Office); 95 Malone Rd, Belfast BT9 6SP, UK (Home). *Telephone:* (28) 9027-2166.

ALLEN, Joan; American actress; b 1957, Rochelle, IL; m Peter Friedman 1990; one d. *Education:* E Illinois Univ. *Career:* Began acting career with Steppenwolf Theatre, Chicago. *Plays include:* And a Nightingale Sang 1983, Burn This (Tony Award) 1988, The Heidi Chronicles 1988; *Films:* The Ice Storm, Nixon 1996, The Crucible 1997, In Country, Etham Frome, Face/Off, Pleasantville, The Sky is Falling, The Contender (Acad Award nomination for Best Actress) 2001. *Address:* c/o Brian Mann, 8942 Wilshire Blvd, Beverly Hills, CA 90211, USA.

ALLEN, Judy; British writer; b 8 July 1941, Old Sarum, Wilts; d of the late Maj Jack Turner Allen and of Janet Marion Beall. *Education:* Privately. *Career:* Writer 1976–; dramatized The Secret Garden (by Frances Hodgson-Burnett) for BBC Radio 5. *Publications include:* Adult Fiction: December Flower (Christopher Award, USA for TV version 1987) 1982, Bag and Baggage 1988; Jr Fiction: Something Rare and Special 1985, Travelling Hopefully 1987, Awaiting Developments (Children's Section Whitbread Award 1988, Friends of the Earth Earthworm Award 1989) 1988, City Farm series 1990, Endangered Species series 1991–92, Between the Moon and the Rock 1992, Highfliers series 1996; Non fiction: The Last Green Book on Earth 1994; Guide Books: London Arts Guide (Best Specialist Guidebook Award, London Tourist Bd) 1984, The Guide to London by Bus and Tube 1987, London Docklands Street Atlas and Guide 1988; also radio plays. *Leisure interests:* walking, reading, worrying. *Address:* c/o Laurence Fitch Ltd, 483 Southbank House, Black Prince Rd, Albert Embankment, London SE1 7SJ, UK; c/o Rogers, Coleridge & White, 20 Powis Mews, London W11 1JN, UK. *Telephone:* (20) 7735-8171 (Fitch); (20) 7221-3717 (Rogers, Coleridge & White).

ALLEN, Karen Jane; American actress; b 5 Oct 1951, Carrollton, IL; d of Carroll Thompson and Patricia (née Howell) Allen. *Education:* George Washington Univ, Univ of Maryland and with Lee Strasberg at Theatre Inst. *Career:* Mem Washington Theatre Lab, DC 1973–77; numerous film and theatre appearances. *Films:* National Lampoon's Animal House, Manhattan, The Wanderers, Cruising, A Small Circle of Friends, Raiders of the Lost Ark, Shoot the Moon, Split Image, Until September, Starman, The Glass Menagerie, Backfire, Scrooged, Animal Behavior, Secret Places of the Heart, Sweet Talker, Exile, The Sandlot, King of the Hill, Ghost in the Machine; *Plays include:* Monday After the Miracle (Theatre World Award), Extremities, The Glass Menagerie, The Country Girl, Beautiful Bodies, As You Like It. *Address:* The Gersh Agency, 232 N Canon Drive, Beverly Hills, CA 90210, USA.

ALLEN, Mary; British arts administrator and former actress; b 22 Aug 1951, London; d of Fergus Allen and Joan Allen; m 1st Robin Woodhead 1980 (divorced 1990); m 2nd Nigel Pantling 1991. *Career:* Man Waterman Arts Centre, London; Deputy Sec-Gen Arts Council 1992–94, Sec-Gen 1994–97; Chief Exec Royal Opera House, London 1997–98. *Performances include:* Rocky Horror Show; *Publications include:* A House Divided 1998. *Leisure interests:* gardening, cooking, theatre, collecting contemporary art. *Telephone:* (20) 7333-0100.

ALLEN, Mary Darina; Irish cookery writer; b 30 July 1948, Dublin; d of William and Elizabeth O'Connell; m Timothy Allen; two s two d. *Education:* Dominican Convent (Wicklow) and Dublin Coll of Catering. *Career:* Cook at Ballymaloe House Hotel 1968–83; Founder and Prin Ballymaloe Cookery School (with Timothy Allen) 1983; Presenter Radio Telefís Eireann Simply Delicious Series on TV 1989–; featured in BBC Hot Chefs Series 1992; mem Bd BIM (Irish Sea Fisheries Bd) 1989; mem Int Asscn of Culinary Professionals (IACP), Eurotoques; Certified Teacher, Culinary Professional and Food Professional, IACP. *Publications:* Simply Delicious (series of five titles) 1989–92, Darina Allen's Simply Delicious Recipes 1992. *Leisure interests:* gardening, walking, cycling, reading. *Address:* Ballymaloe Cookery School, Shanagarry, Co Cork, Ireland. *Telephone:* (21) 646785; *Fax:* (21) 646909.

ALLEN, Maxine; Antigua and Barbuda broadcasting executive; b 11 Oct 1962, St John's; two s. *Education:* Princess Margaret High School. *Career:* Newsreader Grenville Radio Ltd 1979; Asst Station Man Antigua and Barbuda Broadcasting Service (ABS) 1991, Head of Current Affairs Dept, Radio 1995. *Leisure interests:* playing in a steel band, writing poetry. *Address:* Antigua and Barbuda Broadcasting Service (ABS), POB 590, St John's, Antigua and Barbuda; POB 1906, Whener Rd, St John's, Antigua and Barbuda. *Telephone:* 461-3953; *Fax:* 462-4442.

ALLEN, Roberta L.; American writer and artist; b 6 Oct 1945, New York; d of Sol and Jeanette (née Waldner) Allen. *Education:* Fashion Inst of Tech (New York). *Career:* Lecturer Corcoran School of Art 1975, Kutztown State Coll 1979; Instructor in Creative Writing Parsons School of Design 1986, The Writer's Voice 1992–97, The New School 1993–2001, School of Continuing Education, New York Univ 1993–2000; solo exhibitions include Galerie 845 (Amsterdam, Netherlands) 1967, John Weber Gallery (New York) 1974, 1977, 1979, Galerie Maier-Hahn (Düsseldorf, Germany) 1977, Galleria Primo Piano (Italy) 1981, Galerie Walter Storms (Munich, Germany) 1981, PSI Museums (New York) 1981, Perth Inst of Contemporary Arts (Australia) 1989, Art Resources Transfer (New York) 2001, SUNY, Binghamton (New York) 2001; MacDowell Colony Residency 1971, 1972; Ossabaw Island Project Residency 1972; Creative Artists Public Service Grant 1978–79; Yaddo Residency 1983, 1987, 1993; LINE (NEA and NYS Council) Grant 1985; Virginia Center for Creative Arts Residency 1985, 1994; Artist-in-Residence Fellowship, Art Gallery of Western Australia, Perth 1989; Tennessee Williams Fellow in Creative Writing, Univ of the South (Sewanee, TN) 1998; Fellow Columbia Univ School of the Arts 1998–99, Eugene Long Coll, The New School 2000. *Publications include:* Pointless Arrows 1976, Possibilities 1977, The Traveling Woman 1986, The Daughter 1992, Pointless Acts 1976, Amazon Dream 1993, Certain People 1997, Fast Fiction 1997, The Dreaming Girl 2000, The Playful Way to Serious Writing 2002. *Address:* 5 W 16th St, New York, NY 10011, USA. *Telephone:* (212) 675-0111; *E-mail:* roall@aol.com; *Internet:* hometown.aol.com/roall.

ALLENDE, Isabel; Chilean writer; b 2 Aug 1942, Lima, Peru; d of Tomás Allende Pesce and Francisca Llona Barros; m 1st Miguel Frías 1961 (divorced 1987); one s one d (deceased); m 2nd William Gordon 1988. *Education:* In Chile, Bolivia and Lebanon. *Career:* Journalist for Paula Magazine 1967–74, Mampato Magazine 1969–74, El Nacional (Venezuela) 1975–84; made several TV Shows for Channel 13 and Channel 7 1964–74; teacher Montclair State Coll, NJ 1985, Univ of Virginia 1988, Univ of California at Berkeley, USA 1989; mem Academia de la Lengua, Chile 1988, Academia de Artes y Ciencias, Puerto Rico 1995; Dr hc (New York State at Stonybrook) 1991, (Univ of Chile) 1991, (Bates Coll) 1994, (Dominican Coll) 1994, (Florida Atlantic) 1996, (Columbia Coll) 1996; awards include Chevalier des Arts et des Lettres 1994, Novel of the Year, Panorama Literario (Chile) 1983, Grand Prix Point de Mire (Belgium) 1985, Author of the Year and

Book of the Year (Germany) 1984, Grand Prix d'Evasion (France) 1984, Colima for Best Novel (Mexico) 1985, Author of the Year (Germany) 1986, Mulheres Best Novel (Portugal) 1987, Freedom to Write (PEN Club, USA) 1991, Feminist of the Year Award (Feminist Majority Foundation, USA) 1994, Marin Women's Hall of Fame (USA) 1994, Condecoración Gabriela Mistral (Chile) 1994, Hon Citizen City of Austin (USA) 1995, Read About Me (USA) 1996, Gift of HOPE Award, HOPE Education and Leadership Fund (USA) 1996, Harold Washington Literary Award, Chicago (IL, USA) 1996, Dorothy and Jillian Gish Prize 1998, Sara Lee Frontrunner Award 1998, GEMS Women of the Year Award 1999, Donna Dell'Anno Award (Italy) 1999. *Publications:* Novels: The House of the Spirits 1982, Of Love and Shadows 1984, Eva Luna 1989, Aphrodite 1998, Daughter of Fortune 1999; Plays: El Embajador 1971, La Balada del Medio Pelo 1973, Los Siete Espejos 1974, Paula, Stories of Eva Luna, The House of the Spirits, Eva Luna; Short stories: Tales of Eva Luna 1990, The Infinite Plan 1992, Paula (memoir) 1995, Aphrodite (a memoir of the senses) 1997; Children's story: La Gorda de Porcelana 1984; books trans into 27 languages. *Address:* 116 Caledonia St, Sausalito, CA 94965, USA. *Telephone:* (415) 332-1313; *Fax:* (415) 332-4149.

ALLEY, Kirstie; American actress; b Wichita, KS; m Parker Stevenson (divorced); one s one d. *Education:* Univ of Kansas. *Career:* Has appeared in numerous films and TV series; People's Choice Award 1998. *Films:* Star Trek II, The Wrath of Khan 1982, One More Chance, Blind Date, Champions 1983, Runaway 1984, Summer School 1987, Look Who's Talking 1989, Look Who's Talking Too 1990, Madhouse 1990, Sibling Rivalry, Look Who's Talking Now 1993, Village of the Damned 1995, It Takes Two 1995, Sticks and Stones 1996, Nevada 1996, For Richer or Poorer 1997, Deconstructing Harry 1997, Toothless 1997, Drop Dead Gorgeous 1999, The Mao Game 1999; *Plays include:* Cat on a Hot Tin Roof, Answers; *TV appearances include:* Cheers (series) 1987–93, North and South (mini-series), David's Mother (film) 1994. *Address:* Jason Weinberg and Associates, 122 E 25th St, 2nd Floor, New York, NY 10010, USA; NBC-TV, 30 Rockefeller Plaza, New York, NY 10112, USA.

ALLIALI, Camille Zahakro; Côte d'Ivoire lawyer and politician; b 23 Nov 1926; m; five c. *Education:* Dakar Lycée and Lycée Champolion (Grenoble, France). *Career:* Fmr Advocate, Cour d'Appel, Abidjan; Vice-Pres Nat Ass (Parl) 1957–60, mem 1958–60; Press Sec Parti Démocratique de la Côte d'Ivoire 1959; Senator representing French community 1959–61; Amb to France and Perm Del to UNESCO 1961–63; Minister of Foreign Affairs 1963–66, of Justice 1966–83, of State 1983–89; Commdr de la Légion d'Honneur. *Address:* Office of the Prime Minister, Abidjan, Côte d'Ivoire.

ALLIOT-MARIE, Michèle Yvette Marie-Thérèse, MA, D EN DROIT, D EN SC POL; French politician; b 10 Sept 1946, Villeneuve-le-Roi; d of Bernard Marie and Renée Leyko. *Education:* Faculté de Droit et des Sciences Econ de Paris, Faculté des Lettres de Paris-Sorbonne, Univ de Paris I. *Career:* Asst Lecturer Faculté de Droit et des Sciences Econ de Paris then at Univ de Paris I 1970–84, Sr Lecturer in Econs and Man 1984–; Tech Adviser to Minister of Social Affairs 1972–73, Adviser to Minister of Overseas Territories 1973–74, to Jr Minister for Tourism March–Sept 1974, Tech Adviser to Jr Minister for Univs 1974–76, Chef de Cabinet to Jr Minister for Univs then to Minister for Univs 1976–78; Dir, later Prés-Dir Gén UTA-Indemnité 1979–84; adviser on Admin and Public Service Issues, Rassemblement pour la République (RPR) 1981–84, Asst Sec-Gen Legal Advisory Cttee 1984–, mem Cen Cttee 1984–, Exec Cttee 1985–, Nat Sec for Educ and Research 1985–; Deputy for Pyrénées-Atlantiques (RPR) 1986; Sec of State in charge of schools, Ministry of Educ 1986–88; Nat Sec RPR (Research and Planning) 1988–90, Asst Sec-Gen (Foreign Relations) 1990–92; Municipal Councillor for Ciboure 1983–89, for Biarritz 1989–91; Deputy for Pyrénées-Atlantiques 1988–; MEP (UDF-RPR) 1989; Minister for Youth and Sports 1993–95; mem and First Vice-Pres Regional Council of Pyrénées-Atlantiques 1995–; Mayor of Saint-Jean-de-Luz 1995–; Nat Sec RPR for Social Affairs 1997–, mem Political Cttee 1998–, Nat Sec in charge of elections Aug 1999–, Pres RPR Dec 1999–; mem Political Cttee Alliance pour la France 1998; Pres Comm for Defence of Rights and Freedoms 1980–, Foundation for Voluntary Orgs until 2000, and many current and fmr offices in women's and children's charitable orgs; Commdr de l'Etoile Équatoriale (Gabon),

Commdr de l'Etoile d'Anjouan (Comoros), Commdr du Mérite de l'Educ Nat (Côte d'Ivoire), Commdr l'Ordre de la République (Egypt), Palmes Magistrales (First Class) (Peru). *Publications include:* L'actionnariat des salariés 1975, La décision politique: attention une république peut en cacher une autre 1983, La grande peur des classes moyennes 1996, La république des irresponsables 1999. *Address:* Rassemblement pour la République, 123 rue de Lille, 75007 Paris, France. *Telephone:* (1) 49-55-63-25 (Office); *Fax:* (1) 47-05-54-44 (Office).

ALLMAN-WARD, Michele Ann, BS, MBA; British banking executive; b 27 Aug 1950, Birmingham; d of Keith James and Denise (née Ansay-Robert) Lawley; m Peter Allman-Ward 1973. *Education:* Univ of Southampton and Fordham Univ (NY, USA). *Career:* Man trainee Unilever Corpn 1970–72; Research Exec Market Behavior Ltd 1972–74; Asst Vice-Pres and Man Int Banking Bank of Boston (Luxembourg) 1974–78, (New York) 1978–81; Vice-Pres and Head Int Cash Man, Boston, MA, USA 1981–86; Head Int Marketing Div, Bankers Trust Co, New York 1986–87; apptd Head Corp Marketing Trust and Securities Services, J. P. Morgan and Co Inc, New York 1987; Treas Friends Vieilles Maisons Françaises, New York 1980–84; mem Nat Corp Cash Man Asscn, Nat Asscn of Bank Women; Dean's Award for Academic Excellence, Fordham Univ, NY 1981.

ALLOGGIAMENTO, Nancy Thomas; American business executive; b 23 May 1937, Palos Park, IL; d of Warren Arthur and Ruth Elizabeth (née Martin) Thomas; m Alberto Alloggiamento 1965. *Education:* Univ of Illinois. *Career:* Media Asst Lennen and Newell Advertising, New York 1960–64; Vice-Pres Media, Jameson Advertising, New York 1964–72, Vice-Pres and Dir Account Services Waterman, Getz, Niedelman Advertising, New York 1972–77; Vice-Pres and Account Supervisor DKG Advertising, New York 1977–78, deGarmo Advertising, New York 1978–80, D'Arcy, MacManus and Masius, New York 1980–82; Pres NTA and Co, New York 1982–83, NTA/An Ogilvy and Mather Co, New York 1985; Pres NA Communications, New York 1983–; Pres and CEO Sussman and Sugar/Ogilvy and Mather, New York 1985. *Leisure interests:* reading, music, fashion, travel. *Address:* 60 Sutton Place S, New York, NY 10022, USA.

ALLRED, Gloria, MA, JD; American lawyer; b 3 July 1931, Philadelphia, PA; one d. *Education:* Univ of Pennsylvania, New York Univ and Loyola Univ School of Law (LA). *Career:* Fmr public school teacher and lecturer Univ of S California; Partner Allred, Maroko and Goldberg; Founder-Pres Women's Equal Rights Legal Defense and Educ Fund (WERLDEF); TV Commentator on KABC-TV; Pres's Award, Nat Asscn of Women Lawyers 1985, US Pres's Volunteer Action Award 1986, Public Service Award (Nat Asscn of Fed Investigators) 1986; voted (by leading lawyers) one of the Best Lawyers in America 1987, 1991; Hon JD (Univ of W Los Angeles). *Address:* 6300 Wilshire Blvd, Suite 1500, Los Angeles, CA 90048, USA.

ALOISI DE LARDEREL, Jacqueline, MS, MBA; French United Nations official; b 8 July 1942, Orléans; d of M. Delzenne; m Corso Aloisi de Larderel 1971; one s one d. *Education:* Univ of Paris and European Inst of Business Admin (Fontainebleau). *Career:* Chargé de Mission Ministry of the Environment 1972–77, Head Waste Dept 1977–85, Deputy Dir Directorate for Water, Pollution Prevention and Technological Risks 1985–87; Dir Industry and Environment Office, UNEP 1987, Asst Exec Dir UNEP 2001–, mem French Comm on Sustainable Devt 2000–; Ed Industry and Environment Review. *Address:* Technology, Industry and Economics Office, UNEP, Tour Mirabeau, 39–43 quai André Citroën, 75739 Paris Cedex 15, France. *Telephone:* (1) 44-37-14-41; *Fax:* (1) 44-37-14-74; *E-mail:* unep.tiei@unep.fr.

ALONI, Shulamit, LL B; Israeli politician and lawyer; b 27 Nov 1929, Tel Aviv; d of Polish parents; m Reuven Aloni; three s. *Education:* David Yellin Teachers' Training Coll and Hebrew Univ of Jerusalem. *Career:* Participated in the defence of Jerusalem during the War of Independence; worked as a teacher; columnist for several newspapers; producer of radio programmes dealing with legislation and legal procedures; Founder Israel Consumers' Council, Chair for four years; joined Mapai 1959; MP Knesset (Labour) 1965–69, mem Constitution and Law and Finance Cttees 1965–; Minister without Portfolio 1974; Minister of Educ and Culture 1992, of Communications and the Arts and of Science and Tech 1993–96; Leader Meretz, Democratic Israel

(coalition party); Chair Israeli Council for Consumer Rights 1966; Founder and Chair Ratz (Civil Rights and Peace Movt) 1973; civil rights activist. *Publications:* The Citizen and His/Her Country, The Rights of the Child in Israel, The Arrangement – A State of Law and Not a State of Religion, Women as People. *Leisure interests:* reading, theatre, tennis. *Address:* c/o Ministry of Communications, 23 Yaffo St, Jerusalem 91999, Israel. *E-mail:* intmocil@moc.gov.il.

ALONSO, Alicia; Cuban ballet dancer and choreographer and director; b 21 Dec 1920, Havana; d of Antonio Martínez and Ernestina del Hoyo; m 1st Fernando Alonso 1937; m 2nd Pedro Simón 1975; one s one d. *Education:* Ballet School of Sociedad Pro–Arte Musical, Havana and School of American Ballet, USA. *Career:* Mem American Ballet Caravan 1938–39, American Ballet Theater 1940–41, 1943–48, 1950–55, 1958–60, Ballet Russe, Monte Carlo 1955–59; danced with Greek Theatre, LA, California 1957–59, Washington Ballet 1958; Guest Artist, Teatro Colón, Buenos Aires 1958, Kirov and Bolshoi Ballets 1958, Royal Danish Ballet 1969, Paris Opera 1972, Rome Opera 1987; Founder, Prima Pallerina Assoluta, choreographer and Gen Dir Nat Ballet of Cuba 1948–99; has staged her versions of the maj romantic and classical ballets in Paris, Rome, Milan, Naples, Vienna, Mexico, Sofia and Prague; mem jury several int ballet competitions, Advisory Council, Ministry of Culture and Nat Cttee of Writers, Artists' Union of Cuba, Kennedy Center Artistic Cttee, Washington, DC; numerous awards and honours including Dance Magazine Annual Award 1958, Grand Prix of Paris 1966, 1970, Anna Pavlova Award, Univ of Dance, Paris 1966, Gold Medal of Barcelona Liceo 1971, Annual Award of Gran Teatro de La Habana 1985, Hero of Work, Cuba, Order Félix Varela, Cuba, Order Aguila Azteca, Mexico, Order Isabel la Católica, Spain, Commdr des Arts et des Lettres. *Publication:* Dialogues with the Dance 1988. *Leisure interests:* films, music, scientific discoveries. *Address:* National Ballet of Cuba, Calzada No 510 entre D y E, El Vedado, CP 10400 Havana, Cuba. *Telephone:* (7) 55-2948; *Fax:* (7) 33-3317.

ALP, Rosalind; British environmentalist; b 1973. *Career:* Moved to Sierra Leone 1989, works to save chimpanzees from poachers and to rescue abandoned adult pets; awarded research grant by Nat Geographic Soc of America. *Address:* c/o World Society for the Protection of Animals, POB 34070, Nyali, Mombasa, Kenya.

ALTHER, Lisa, BA; American writer, reviewer and university professor; b 23 July 1944, Kingsport, TN; d of John Shelton and Alice Greene Reed; m Richard Alther 1966 (divorced); one d. *Education:* Wellesley Coll and Radcliffe Coll. *Career:* Editorial Asst Atheneum Publrs (NY) 1967–68; freelance writer 1968–; Lecturer St Michael's Coll (Winooski, VT) 1980–81; Prof and Basler Chair East Tennessee State Univ 1999–. *Publications:* Kinflicks 1975, Original Sins 1980, Other Women 1984, Bedrock 1990, Birdman and the Dancer 1993, Five Minutes in Heaven 1995. *Address:* 1086 Silver St, Hinesburg, VT 05461, USA. *Telephone:* (802) 482-3141; *Fax:* (802) 482-3141.

ALUOCH, Joyce; Kenyan judge; b 22 Oct 1947; m J. Aluoch; three c. *Education:* Limuru Girls' School, Univ of Nairobi and Kenya School of Law. *Career:* Dist Magistrate 1974–76; Resident Magistrate 1976–80; Sr Resident Magistrate, Makadara Law Courts 1980–83; apptd High Court Judge 1983; August Resident Judge in charge of Mombasa High Court 1986, Duty Judge, High Court, Nairobi; Chair Kenya Magistrates Asscn, Kenya Girl Guides Asscn; Trustee YWCA Kenya 1986–91; mem Judicial Service Comm Kenya, Kenya Women Judges Asscn, Task Force Reviewing Laws Relating to Women in Kenya; numerous papers presented at seminars, confs, etc. *Address:* Law Courts Bldg, POB 30041, Nairobi, Kenya.

ALVA, Margaret, BA, LL B; Indian politician; b 14 April 1942, Mangalore; d of P. A. and Elizabeth Nazareth; m Niranhjan Alva; three s one d. *Career:* Sec-Gen All India Catholic Univ Fed 1961; Jt Sec Govt Law Coll Students' Union 1964; State Convenor Congress Women's Front 1972–73, Congress Party Standing Cttee on Information and Broadcasting 1975–76; elected to Rajya Sabha (Council of States) 1974; Minister of State for Parl Affairs 1985, for Youth Affairs, Sports and Child Devt 1985–89; Pres World Women Parliamentarians for Peace 1986–87; mem Indian Del to UN Conf, Mexico 1975, UN Gen Ass 1976; mem All India Congress Cttee, Int Fed of Women Lawyers, Nat

Children's Bd 1977–78, Nat Adult Educ Bd 1978–79. *Address:* 23 Safdarjung Rd, New Delhi, India (Office); 3 Ware Rd, Frazer Town, Bangalore 560005, India (Home).

ALVAREZ, Aida, BA; American politician; b Aguadilla, Puerto Rico. *Education:* Harvard Univ. *Career:* Former news reporter, presenter Metromedia TV, NY; fmr reporter NY Post; fmr mem NY City Charter revision Comm; fmr Vice-Pres NY City Health and Hospitals Corp; investment banker First Boston Corp NY, San Francisco 1986–93; Dir Office Fed Housing Enterprise Oversight 1993–97; Dir Small Business Admin Jan 1997–; fmr mem Bd Dirs Nat Hispanic Leadership Agenda, NY Community Trust, Nat Civic League; fmr Chair Bd Municipal Assistance Corp/Victim Services Agency, NY; NY State Chair Gore Presidential Campaign 1988; Nat Co-Chair Women's Cttee Clinton Presidential Campaign 1992; mem Pres Econ Transition Team 1992; Hon LL D (Iona Coll) 1985; Front Page Award 1982, Assoc Press Award for Excellence 1982. *Address:* Small Business Administration, 409 3rd St, Washington, DC 20416, USA. *Telephone:* (202) 205-6605.

ALVAREZ, Sylvie Françoise Marie; French diplomatist; b 22 July 1942, Saint-Jean-de-Luz; d of Francisco and Jacqueline Alvarez. *Education:* Ecole Nat des Langues Orientales Vivantes and Inst d'Etudes Politiques de Paris. *Career:* Mem staff Europe Dept, Cen Admin, Ministry of Foreign Affairs 1966; Third Sec, Perm Mission of France to UN, New York, USA 1967–70, First Sec 1985–88; Second Sec, Poland 1970–71; seconded to Havas Conseil 1971–72, to Ministry of Cultural Affairs 1972–77, to Directorate-Gen for Cultural, Scientific and Tech Relations 1977–81; Head of information and supervisory service for French people abroad and foreigners in France 1981–85; Consul-Gen, Rabat, Morocco 1988–92; Amb to St Lucia, also accredited to Antigua and Barbuda, Dominica, St Christopher and Nevis, Grenada and St Vincent and the Grenadines 1992–96, to Nicaragua 1997–; Sec Gen to French Presidency of W European Union 1996–97; Chevalier de l'Ordre Nat du Mérite; Chevalier des Arts et des Lettres. *Leisure interests:* cinema, music, swimming, golf, skiing. *Address:* Embajada de Francia, de la Iglesia del Carmen, 1 cuadra y 1/2 abajo, Managua, Nicaragua; 187 rue de Grenelle, 75007 Paris, France.

ALVARIÑO, Angeles, D SC; American biologist and oceanographer; b 3 Oct 1916, El Ferrol, Spain; d of Antonio Alvariño Grimaldos and María del Carmen González Díaz-Saavedra de Alvariño; m Eugenio Leira Manso 1940; one d. *Education:* Universidad Complutense de Madrid and Spanish Inst of Oceanography. *Career:* Prof of Biology, Zoology, Botany and Geology at various colls 1941–48; Fishery Research Biologist Dept of Sea Fisheries, Spain 1948–52; Marine Biologist and Oceanographer Spanish Inst of Oceanography 1950–57; Biologist Scripps Inst of Oceanography, Univ of California at San Diego, USA 1958–69; Research Fishery Biologist Nat Oceanographic and Atmospheric Admin (NOAA), Nat Marine Fisheries Service, CA, USA 1970–87, Research Biologist Emer 1987–; Visiting Prof and Assoc Prof numerous univs 1979–; discovered 22 new animal species; has taken part in many scientific expeditions and cruises in the USA, UK, Spain and Mexico; more than 100 papers published in scientific journals; mem Editorial Comms and Bds of Examiners of several S American Univs; Fellow American Inst of Fishery Research Biologists, American Museum of Natural History, Biological Soc of Washington; Emer Fellow Latin-American Asscn of Researchers on Oceanic Sciences; British Council Fellow 1953–54; Fulbright Fellow 1956–57; Marine Life Research Grants, Office of Naval Research Grants 1958–69; Nat Science Foundation Grants 1961–69; Antarctic Research Grants 1979–82. *Address:* National Marine Fisheries Service, POB 271, La Jolla, CA 92038, USA (Office); 7535 Cabrillo Ave, La Jolla, CA 92037, USA (Home). *Telephone:* (619) 454-1039 (Home).

ALVEAR VALENZUELA, María Soledad; Chilean lawyer and politician; b 17 Sept 1950, Santiago; d of Ernesto Alvear and María Teresa Valenzuela; m Gutenberg Martinez Ocamica 1973; two s one d. *Education:* Univ of Chile. *Career:* Prof Faculty of Law and Social Sciences, Univ of Chile 1973–75; Pvt Practice 1973–90; Consultant to UN 1987–90; Dir Comisión Preparatoria, Servicio Nacional de la Mujer (women's org) 1990; Minister, Dir Servicio Nacional de la Mujer 1991; fmrly Minister of Justice; mem Exec Council Comisión Interamericana de Mujeres (women's org) until 1990; Orden al Mérito Institucional, Consejo Mundial de Educ 1991. *Publications:* Algunas Sugerencias de

modificaciones al Derecho de Familia 1984, Situación de la Mujer Campesina frente a la Legislación 1987, La Mujer Campesina y la Legislación en Colombia 1990. *Leisure interests:* reading, tennis. *Address:* Pasaje Rosa Rodriguez 1375, 6°, Santiago, Chile. *Telephone:* (2) 6973021; *Fax:* (2) 6971082.

AMANPOUR, Christiane; British (Iranian) broadcasting correspondent; b 12 Jan 1958, London; d of Mohammad Amanpour and Patricia Amanpour; m James Rubin 1998; one s. *Education:* Holy Cross Convent, UK, New Hall School, UK and Univ of Rhode Island, USA. *Career:* Radio producer/research asst BBC Radio, London 1980–82; radio reporter, WBRU Brown Univ USA 1981–83; electronic graphics designer, WJAR, Providence, RI 1983; asst CNN int assignment desk, Atlanta, GA 1983; news writer, CNN, Atlanta 1984–86; reporter/producer, CNN, New York 1987–90; Int Corresp CNN 1990, Sr Int Corresp 1994, Chief Int Corresp 1996–; assignments have included coverage of Gulf War 1990–91, break-up of USSR and subsequent war in Tbilisi 1991, extensive reports on conflict in fmr Yugoslavia and coverage of civil unrest and political crises in Haiti, Algeria, Somalia and Rwanda; Fellow, Soc of Professional Journalists; Dr hc (Rhode Island); three Dupont-Columbia Awards 1986–96, two News and Documentary Emmy Awards 1999, George Foster Peabody Award 1999, George Polk Award 1999, Univ of Missouri Honor Award for Distinguished Service to Journalism 1999. *Leisure interests:* reading, riding, tennis, swimming, sky-diving. *Address:* c/o CNN International, CNN House, 19–22 Rathbone Place, London W1P 1DF, UK. *Telephone:* (20) 7637-6800.

AMARA, Lucine; American opera singer; b 1 March 1925, Hartford, CT; d of George and Adrine (née Kazanjian) Armaganian. *Career:* Debut Hollywood Bowl, CA 1948; Soloist San Francisco Symphony 1949–50; performances with Metropolitan Opera (New York), New Orleans Opera (LA), Hartford Opera (CT), Pittsburgh Opera (PA), St Louis Opera (MO), Stockholm Opera, St Petersburg Opera (FL), Venezuela Philharmonic Orchestra and at Glyndebourne and Edinburgh Festivals (UK); opera and concert tours of fmr USSR 1965, Philippines 1968, France 1966, Mexico 1966, Hong Kong and People's Repub of China 1983, Yugoslavia 1988; numerous TV and radio performances; First Prize Atwater-Ken Radio Auditions 1948; Acad of Vocal Arts Hall of Fame. *Operas include:* Aida, Turandot, Tosca, Un Ballo in Maschera; *Recordings include:* Beethoven's Symphony No 9, I Pagliacci, La Bohème, Verdi's Requiem. *Address:* Metropolitan Opera, New York, NY 10023, USA.

AMATHILA, Libertine, MB; Namibian politician; b 10 Dec 1940, Fransfontein; two c. *Education:* Warsaw Medical Acad (Poland), Muhimbili Teaching Hosp (Tanzania), London School of Hygiene and Tropical Medicine (UK), St Goran Medical Clinic (Sweden) and Bamako Medical Faculty (Mali). *Career:* Dir SW Africa People's Org (SWAPO) Women's Council until 1976, Deputy Sec for Health and Welfare and mem Politbureau 1991; mem Nat Ass; Minister-Del of Local Govt and Housing 1987, Minister 1991; Namibian Rep to WHO 1974–89; Dir Children's Centre, Kwanze Norte, Angola 1979–88; SWAPO Ongulambashe Medal for Bravery and Long Service 1987. *Address:* Ministry of Local Government and Housing, Pvt Bag 13289, Windhoek 9000, Namibia (Office); 197 Klein Windhoek Rd, Pvt Bag 13289, Windhoek, Namibia (Home). *Telephone:* (61) 2972911; *Fax:* (61) 2972911.

AMATI, Giovanna; Italian racing driver; b 1963. *Career:* First woman Formula One racing driver since 1981; signed with Brabham 1992; fmrly driver in Int Formula 3000 races.

AMELINE, Nicole, L EN D; French politician; b 4 July 1952, St-Vaasten-Auge; d of André and Anne Ameline. *Education:* Inst d'Etudes Politiques de Paris and Univ of Caen. *Career:* Rep to Minister of the Environment 1978–80; Sec to Mayor of Honfleur 1980–87; Head of Communications, Conseil Général de Calvados 1987–90; Sec-Gen dist of Trouville-Deauville 1991; mem Ass Nat (Parl, UDF) for Calvados 1991–; Sec of State for Decentralization 1995; Vice-Pres Conseil Régional de Basse-Normandie 1998–; Pres Démocratie Libéral 14; Pres Econ Comm, Asscn France–Canada. *Leisure interests:* horse-riding, painting. *Address:* Assemblée Nationale, 126 rue de l'Université, 75007 Paris, France.

AMELING, Elly; Netherlands opera and concert singer; b (Elisabeth Sara Ameling) 1938, Rotterdam; m Arnold W. Beider 1964. *Education:* Studied singing with Jo Bollekamp, Jacoba and Sam Dresden and Bodi Rapp, French art song with Pierre Bernac. *Career:* Has given recitals in Europe, S Africa, Japan; debut in USA 1968, annual tours of USA and Canada 1968–; performances with Concertgebouw Orchestra (Netherlands), New Philharmonic Orchestra, BBC Symphony Orchestra (UK), Berlin Philharmonic (Germany), Cincinnati Symphony (USA), San Francisco Symphony (USA), Toronto Symphony (Canada), Chicago Symphony (USA); has appeared at Mozart Festival (Washington, DC, USA) 1974, Caramoor Festival 1974, Art Song Festival (Princeton, NJ, USA) 1974; First Prize Concours Int de Musique, Geneva, Switzerland; Grand Prix du Disque; Edison Prize; Preis der Deutschen Schallplattenkritik; Stereo Review Record of the Year Award; Knight Order of Orange-Nassau. *Recordings include:* Mozart Concert, Handel Concert, Cantatas (Bach), Mörike Lieder (Wolf), Aimez-vous Handel?, Aimez-vous Mozart?, Christmas Oratorio (Bach), Symphony No 2 (Mahler), Te Deum (Bruckner), Italienisches Liederbuch (Wolf).

AMIEL, Barbara, BA; Canadian journalist and writer; b 4 Dec 1940, Herts, UK; d of Harold Joffre and Vera Isserles (née Barnett) Amiel; m 1st George Jonas 1974; m 2nd Conrad Black 1992. *Education:* N London Collegiate School and Univ of Toronto. *Career:* Columnist Maclean's 1976–, The Times (UK) 1986–90, The Sunday Times 1991–94, The Daily Telegraph 1995–; Vice-Pres Editorial Hollinger Int 1995–; Ed Toronto Sun 1983–85, Assoc Ed 1985–; mem Bd Dirs The Spectator, Jerusalem Post, Saturday Night, Southam Inc, Hollinger Int; Media Club of Canada Award 1976; Periodical Publishers' Asscn Award 1977; Mystery Writers of America Edgar Allan Poe Award; British Press Award 1987; Women of Distinction (UK) 1989. *Publications:* By Person Unknown (jtly) 1977, Confessions 1980. *Address:* c/o The Telegraph, 1 Canary Wharf, Canada Square, London E14 5DT, UK; 10 Toronto St, Toronto, ON, M5C 2B7, Canada.

AMOS, Tori; American singer and songwriter; b 1964, Potomac, MD; d of Edison and Mary Ellen Amos. *Education:* Peabody Conservatory. *Career:* Youngest student ever accepted at Peabody Conservatory, aged 5. *Recordings include:* Y Kant Tori Read 1988, Little Earthquakes 1992, Under the Pink 1994, Boys for Pele 1996, From the Choirgirl Hotel 1998, To Venus & Back 1999. *Address:* c/o Atlantic Records, 1290 Avenue of the Americas, New York, NY 10104, USA.

AMOS, Baroness (Life Peer), cr 1997, of Brondesbury in the London Borough of Brent, **Valerie Ann Amos,** MA; British organization official; b 13 March 1954, Guyana; d of E. Michael and Eunice V. Amos. *Education:* Univs of Warwick, Birmingham and E Anglia. *Career:* Race Relations Adviser London Borough of Lambeth 1981–83; Women's Adviser London Borough of Camden 1983–85; Head of Training and Devt London Borough of Hackney 1985–87, Head of Man Services 1988–89; Chief Exec Equal Opportunities Comm 1989–94; Man Dir Quality and Equality 1994–; Dir Hampstead Theatre 1992–; Deputy Chair Runnymede Trust 1990–; mem Advisory Cttee Centre for Educ Devt Appraisal and Research, Univ of Warwick 1991–, Gen Advisory Council BBC, King's Fund Coll Cttee 1992–, Council Inst of Employment Studies 1993–; Trustee Women's Therapy Centre 1989–; has had various articles on race and gender issues published. *Address:* Summerton Business Centre, 18–24 Middle Way, Oxford OX2 7LG, UK. *Telephone:* (1865) 310651; *Fax:* (1865) 311381.

AMURO, Namie; Japanese pop singer; b 20 Sept 1977, Okinawa; m Sam Maruyama. *Education:* Okinawa Actor's School. *Career:* Mem of group Super Monkeys 1992, leader of group 1994; Japan Records Award 1996. *Music:* Singles include: (with Super Monkeys) Paradise Train, Try Me, Tiayo No Season, (solo) Stop the Music, Body Feels Exit, Chase the Chance, Don't Wanna Cry, You Are My Sunshine, Sweet 19 Blues, Can You Celebrate; Albums include: Sweet 19 Blues, Concentration 20, 181920.

ANAND, Anita, MA; Indian development executive; b 12 Aug 1949; d of Trilok Chand and Vimla Puri Anand; m Mahesh Kumar Uppal 1990; one s. *Education:* Loreto Coll (Calcutta) and Ohio Univ (USA). *Career:* Community organizer, USA 1971–73; Rural Consultant, India 1976–78; Public Policy Analyst, USA 1978–84; on staff of Int News Agency, Italy 1986–90; apptd Dir Women's Feature Service 1990;

Producer audio-visuals on devt 1978–84, a six-part documentary on women and devt 1986; contribs to magazines and newspapers; First Prize Annual Photo Competition, Washington Women's Centre (USA) 1981. *Leisure interests:* film, reading, photography, relaxation. *Address:* Women's Feature Service, 49 (FF) Devence Colony Market, New Delhi 110 024, India (Office); 49 Golf Links, New Delhi 110003, India (Home). *Telephone:* (11) 4629886 (Office); *Fax:* (11) 4626699 (Office).

ANANIASHVILI, Nina Gedevanovna; Georgian ballet dancer; b 28 March 1963, Tbilisi; d of Gedevan Ananiashvili and Lia Gogolashvili; m Gregory Vashadze 1988. *Education:* State Choreographic School of Georgia and Bolshoi Theatre, Moscow Choreographic Inst. *Career:* Joined Bolshoi Ballet 1981, Prima Ballerina 1985–; has performed on tour in USA, Italy, Germany, Switzerland, UK, India and Cuba; guest appearances with New York City Ballet, Boston Ballet (USA), Finnish Nat Ballet, Nat Ballet of Portugal, Ballet de Monte Carlo, Munich Ballet (Germany), Royal Danish Ballet and Royal Ballet (UK); People's Artist of the Georgian Repub; Gold Medal, Varna 1980; Grand Prix Moscow Int Ballet Competition 1981; Grand Prix (Moscow) 1985, (Jackson, MS, USA) 1986; People's Artist State Prize, Repub of Georgia 1992, Russian Fed 1993. *Ballets include:* Swan Lake, Sleeping Beauty, Giselle, Raymonda, Romeo and Juliet, Don Quixote, Nutcracker, La Bayadère, The Golden Age, Chopiniana, Mlada, Apollo, Prince of Pagodas, La fille mal gardée, La Sylphide. *Leisure interests:* antique books on fine arts, modern paintings. *Address:* Frunzenskaya nab 46, Apt 79, 119270 Moscow, Russian Federation. *Telephone:* (095) 242-5864; *Fax:* (095) 476-3470.

ANDERKA, Johanna; German writer; b 12 Jan 1933, Mährisch-Ostrau; d of Leo and Margarete (née Kutschera) Anderka. *Education:* Volksschule and Lyzeum (Mährisch-Ostrau and other towns in E and W Germany) and Handelsschule (Flensburg). *Career:* Office and admin work 1950–; awards include Kulturpreis für Schrifttum (Sudetendeutsche Landsmannschaft) 1988, Hafizpreis Prosa 1988, prize in GEDOK Rhein-Main-Taunus Prose competition 1990, Nikolaus-Lenau-Preis (Künstlergilde Esslingen) 1991, Ehrengabe zum Andreas-Gryphius-Preis 1992, Inge-Czernik-Lyrikpreis 1994, A. Launhardt Lyrikpreis 1998. *Publications include:* Ergebnis eines Tages 1977, Herr, halte meine Hände 1979, Heilige Zeit 1981, Zweierlei Dinge 1983, Für L 1986, Blaue Wolke meiner Träume 1987, Ich werfe meine Fragen aus 1989, Sprachlos mein Schrei 1991, Nachtstadt 1992, Gegen die Fremdheit gesprochen 1994, Vertauschte Gezeiten 1995, Ausgefahren d. Brucken 1997, Bewahrte Landschaft 1999, Silbenhaus 2000; Radio plays: Der Mann im Lift 1983, Beginn einer Freundschaft 1984; numerous publs in anthologies and literary journals. *Leisure interests:* crafts (especially sewing and knitting), photography. *Address:* Tannenäcker 52, 89079 Ulm, Germany. *Telephone:* (731) 42112.

ANDERSEN, Bodil Nyboe, M SC; Danish banking executive; b 9 Oct 1940; d of Poul Nyboe Andersen and Edith (née Raben) Andersen; two c. *Education:* Univ of Copenhagen. *Career:* Asst Prin Ministry of Econ Affairs 1966–68; Assoc Prof (Money and Banking), Univ of Copenhagen 1968–80; Man Dir and mem Man Bd Andelsbanken 1981–90; Group Man Dir Unibank and Unidanmark 1990; mem Bd Govs Danmarks Nationalbank 1990–, Chair 1995–; Gov for Denmark, IMF 1995–; mem Bd Dirs Danish Foreign Policy Inst 1972–78; mem Senate, Univ of Copenhagen 1977–80; Dir Privatinvest 1978–80, CERD 1978–81, Great Belt Ltd 1987–91, Danish Payment Systems Ltd 1988–90, Industrial Mortgage Credit Fund 1991–92, Velux Foundation 1994–; mem Council, European Monetary Inst 1995–98, Danish Foreign Policy Soc 1995–, Gen Council European Cen Bank 1998–; Businesswoman of the Year 1989. *Address:* Danmarks Nationalbank, Havnegade 5, 1093 Copenhagen K, Denmark. *Telephone:* 33 63 60 01; *Fax:* 33 63 71 01; *E-mail:* bna@nationalbanken.dk (Office); *Internet:* www.nationalbanken.dk (Office).

ANDERSEN, Jytte; Danish politician; b 9 Sept 1942, Copenhagen; d of Boye and Inga Johansen; m Andreas Andersen 1965 (divorced 1994). *Career:* Mem Exec Cttee Social Democrat Party (SDP), Vallensbæk 1974–80; mem Municipal Council, Vallensbæk 1975–80; Chair Social Democratic constituency, Glostrup 1974–80; MP 1979–; Minister of Labour 1993–98, of Housing and Urban Affairs 1998–2001, and of Gender Affairs until 2001. *Publications:* The Social Democrat Party and the Future, and numerous articles on labour market issues, educ and training policy, equality and family policy. *Address:* c/o Social Democrat Party, Thorvaldsensvej 2, 1780 Copenhagen V, Denmark. *Telephone:* 35-39-15-22; *Fax:* 35-39-40-30; *E-mail:* socialdemokratiet@net.dialog .dk; *Internet:* www.socialdemokratiet.dk.

ANDERSEN, Lisa; American surfer; b 1969, FL; m (divorced); one d. *Career:* Began surfing at the age of 15, became professional at 18; World Champion 1994, 1995; competitor professional surfing championship, Biarritz, France 1996.

ANDERSON, Annelise Graebner, PH D; American economist; b 19 Nov 1938, Oklahoma City, OK; d of Ellmer and Dorothy (née Zilisch) Graebner; m Martin Anderson 1965. *Education:* Wellesley Coll and Columbia Univ (New York). *Career:* Assoc Ed McKinsey and Co Inc 1963–65; Researcher Nixon Campaign Staff 1968–69; Project Man Dept of Justice 1970–71; Asst Prof of Business Admin, then Assoc Prof California State Univ at Hayward 1975–80; Sr Policy Advisor Reagan Presidential Campaign and Transition, Washington, DC 1980; Assoc Dir of Econs and Govt, Office of Man and Budget, Washington, DC 1981–83; Sr Research Fellow Hoover Institution on War, Revolution and Peace, Stanford Univ, CA 1983–, Assoc Dir 1989–90; mem Bd of Overseers RAND/Univ of California at Los Angeles Center for Soviet Studies 1987–91; mem Nat Science Bd 1985–90. *Publications include:* The Business of Organized Crime: A Cosa Nostra Family 1979, Illegal Aliens and Employer Sanctions: Solving the Wrong Problem 1986, Thinking About America: The United States in the 1990s (co-ed) 1988; numerous contribs to professional journals. *Address:* Stanford University, Hoover Institution on War, Revolution and Peace, Stanford, CA 94305, USA.

ANDERSON, Beverly Jean, BA, FRSA; British educationalist; b 9 Dec 1940; d of Arthur Benjamin and Sylvia Tomlinson Philpotts; m 1st Angus Walker 1968 (divorced 1976); m 2nd Andrew Anderson 1976 (divorced 1986); one s. *Education:* Wellesley Coll (MA, USA) and Univ of London. *Career:* Primary school teacher, then 1968–81; Headteacher Berwood First School, Oxford 1981–83; Sr Lecturer in Educ Oxford Polytechnic 1985–89; Lecturer in Educ Univ of Warwick, educ consultant 1989–93; Chief Exec Book Trust 1993–94; Dir Railtrack 1993–94; Middle School Prin, Trinity School, NY 1999–; Chair Equal Opportunities Working Group, Nat Advisory Body for Public Sector Higher Educ 1987–88; Steering Cttee on Access Courses to HE Framework, Campaign for Nat Academic Awards 1988–89, Council Charter '88 1989–93; Gov BFI 1985–93, Oxford Stage Co Bd 1986–96; mem Nuffield Council on Bioethics 1991–94; Columnist TES 1989–93. *TV includes:* Presenter: Black on Black 1982–83, Nothing but the Best, Sixty Minutes, After Dark 1989–90, Behind the Headlines 1990–91; *Publications:* Learning with Logo: a teacher's guide 1985; numerous articles on educ and social issues. *Leisure interests:* plays, paintings, poems, movies, dancing. *Address:* Trinity School, 139 W 91st St, New York, NY 10024, USA.

ANDERSON, Gillian; American actress; b 9 Aug 1968, Chicago; d of Edward and Gillian Anderson; m Errol Clyde Klotz; one d. *Education:* DePaul Univ and Goodman Theater School (Chicago, USA). *Career:* Worked at Nat Theatre, London; appeared in two off-Broadway productions; best known for role as Special Agent Dana Scully in TV series The X-Files (feature film 1998); Golden Globe Awards 1995, 1997, Screen Actors Guild Awards 1996, 1997, Emmy Award 1997. *TV includes:* films: Home Fire Burning 1992, When Planes, Go Down 1996; presenter: Future Fantastic, BBC TV; *Film:* The House of Mirth 2000. *Address:* William Morris Agency, 151 El Camino Drive, Beverly Hills, CA 90212, USA.

ANDERSON, June, BA; American opera singer (soprano) and concert and oratorio vocalist; b Boston, MA. *Education:* Yale Univ. *Career:* Performances at Metropolitan Opera (New York), New York City Opera, Milwaukee Florentine Opera, San Diego Opera, Seattle Opera, Royal Opera (Covent Garden, London), La Scala (Milan, Italy), and with orchestras including Chicago Pops Orchestra, Denver Symphony Orchestra, St Louis Symphony Orchestra, Cincinnati Orchestra, Maracaibo Symphony Orchestra (Venezuela); *Opera roles include:* Queen of the Night in The Magic Flute, NY City Opera 1978, title role in Lucia di Lammermoor, Milwaukee Florentine Opera 1982 and Chicago 1990, Gulnara in Il Corsaro, San Diego Opera Verdi Festival 1982, I Puritani,

Edmonton Opera 1982–83, title role in Semiramide, Rome Opera 1982–83 and Metropolitan Opera 1990, Rosina in The Barber of Seville, Seattle Opera and Teatro Massimo 1982–83, Cunigande in Candide 1989, Metropolitan Opera debut as Gilda in Rigoletto 1989. *Address:* c/o Columbia Artists, 165 W 57th St, New York, NY 10019, USA.

ANDERSON, Lauren; American ballet dancer. *Education:* Houston Ballet Acad. *Career:* Joined Houston Ballet 1983, Soloist 1986–, Prin Dancer 1990–. *Repertoire includes:* Sleeping Beauty, Swan Lake, The Snow Maiden, La Sylphide, Dracula, The Nutcracker, The Two Pigeons, Giselle, Etudes, Prodigal Son, Simple Gifts 1999, Cleopatra. *Address:* 1916 West Gray, Houston, TX 77019, USA. *Internet:* www .houstonballet.org/Anderson/Anderson.htm.

ANDERSON, Laurie, MFA; American performance artist; b 1947, Wayne, IL; d of Arthur T. and Mary Louise (née Rowland) Anderson. *Education:* Columbia Univ (New York). *Career:* Instructor in Art History, City Coll of New York 1973–75; freelance critic Art News, Art Forum; composer and performer multi-media exhibitions; wrote, directed and performed in film Home of the Brave 1986; one-woman shows include Barnard Coll 1970, Harold Rivkin Gallery (Washington, DC) 1973, Artists' Space (New York) 1974, Holly Solomon Gallery (New York) 1977, 1980–81, Museum of Modern Art 1978, Queen's Museum (NY) 1984, Sadler's Wells Theatre (London, UK) 1994; numerous group exhibitions 1972–; Artist-in-Residence, ZBS Media 1974; several recordings; Guggenheim Fellow 1983. *Recordings include:* O Superman (single) 1981, United States (five album set) 1985, Bright Red 1994; *Publications:* The Package 1971, October 1972, Transportation, Transportation 1973, The Rose and the Stone 1974, Notebook 1976, Artifacts at The End of a Decade 1981, Typisch Frac 1981, United States 1984, Laurie Anderson's Postcard Book 1990, Empty Places: A Performance 1991, Stories from the Nerve Bible 1993.

ANDERSON, Olive Ruth, MA, B LITT, FRHISTS; British historian; b 27 March 1926, Edinburgh; d of Donald H. F. and Ruth Winifred (née Clackson) Gee; m Matthew Smith Anderson 1954; two d. *Education:* King Edward VI Grammar School (Louth, Lincs) and St Hugh's Coll (Oxford). *Career:* Asst Lecturer in History, Westfield Coll, Univ of London 1949–56, Lecturer 1958–69, Reader 1969–86, Prof and Head of Dept 1986–89; Prof and Deputy Head Dept of History, Queen Mary and Westfield Coll, Univ of London 1989–91, Prof Emer 1991–, Hon Research Fellow 1991–, Fellow 1995–; James Ford Special Lecturer, Oxford Univ 1992; Assoc Royal Historical Soc 1953, Fellow 1968, Councillor 1986–91, Vice-Pres 1991–95; mem Academic Council Univ of London 1989–91, Exec Cttee 1990–91; Trustee Theodora Bosanquet Trust 1995–98; mem Finance Cttee British Fed of Women Grads Charitable Foundation 1996–99, Grants Cttee 1998–(Vice-Chair 2000–). *Publications:* A Liberal State at War 1967, Suicide in Victorian and Edwardian England 1987. *Address:* 45 Cholmeley Crescent, London N6 5EX, UK (Home); History Dept, Queen Mary & Westfield College, University of London, London E1 4NS, UK (Office). *Telephone:* (20) 7975-5016 (Office).

ANDERSON, Rachel; British football agent; b 1960; m; two c. *Career:* Worked for Int Award for Valour In Sport; Dir Rachel Anderson Management (RAM) Corpn; only woman soccer agent registered with FIFA (Féderation Internationale de Football Asscn); represents 30 soccer players; launched Islington Community Legal Service (CLS) Sept 2000. *Address:* c/o Community Legal Service Division, Lord Chancellor's Department, 54–60 Victoria St, London SW1E 6QW, UK.

ANDERSON LEE, Pamela; Canadian actress; m Tommy Lee; one s. *Career:* Made commercials for Labatt's Beer. *Films:* Snap-dragon, Good Cop, Bad Cop, Barb Wire; *TV appearances include:* Home Improvements, Baywatch (series). *Address:* c/o Baywatch Production Company, 5433 Beethoven St, Los Angeles, CA 90066, USA. *Telephone:* (310) 302-9189.

ANDERSSON, Bibi; Swedish actress; b 11 Nov 1935; d of Josef and Karin Andersson; m 1st Kjell Grede 1960; one d; m 2nd Per Ahlmark 1979 (divorced). *Education:* Terserus Drama School and Royal Dramatic Theatre School (Stockholm). *Career:* Actress Malmö Theatre 1956–59, Royal Dramatic Theatre (Stockholm) 1959–, Uppsala

Theatre 1962–. *Films include:* Sjunde inseglet (Seventh Seal) 1956, Smultronstället (Wild Strawberries) 1957, Nära livet (The Brink of Life) 1958, Sommarnöje Sökes (Summer House Wanted) 1958, Djävulens öga (Eye of the Devil) 1961, Älskarinnen (The Mistress) 1962, För att inte tala om alla dessa kvinnor (All Those Women) 1964, Juninatt (June Night) 1965, Ön (The Island) 1965, Syskonbädd (My Sister, My Love) 1966, Persona 1966, Duel at Diablo 1966, Story of a Woman 1968, The Girls 1969, The Kremlin Letter 1970, A Passion, The Touch 1971, Scenes from a Marriage 1974, I Never Promised you a Rose Garden, La rivale 1976, An Enemy of the People 1976, Quintet 1979, Svarte Fugler 1982, Berget på månens baksida 1982, Babette's Feast, Litt et Art 1989, The Hill on the Other Side of the Moon, Manika, Fordringsagare; *Plays include:* Erik XIV 1956, King John 1961, Le balcon 1961, La grotte 1962, Uncle Vanya 1962, Who's Afraid of Virginia Woolf? 1963, As You Like It 1964, After the Fall 1964–65, The Full Circle 1973, Twelfth Night 1975, 1980, The Night of the Tribades 1977, Antigone 1981, A Streetcar Named Desire 1981, 1983, L'oiseau bleu 1981, Prisoners of Altona 1982, The Creditors 1984–85, Ett gästabud i Pestens tid 1986, Loner 1994. *Address:* c/o Royal Dramatic Theatre, Stockholm, Sweden; Tykövägen 28, Lidingö 18161, Sweden. *Telephone:* (8) 766 46 16.

ANDERSSON, Harriet; Swedish actress; b 1932, Stockholm. *Career:* Appeared at Oscars Theatre and Malmö City Theatre 1953; now appears regularly at Kunigliga Dramatiska Teatern, Stockholm; Swedish Film Asscn plaque. *Films include:* Summer with Monica 1953, Sawdust and Tinsel 1953, Women's Dreams 1955, Dreams of a Summer Night 1955, Through a Glass Darkly (Grand Prize, German Film Critics) 1961, Siska 1962, One Sunday in September 1963, Dream of Happiness 1963, Loving Couples 1964, All Those Women 1964, To Love (Best Actress Award, Venice Film Festival) 1964, Adventure Starts Here 1965, Stimulantia 1965–66, For the Sake of Friendship 1965, Vine Bridge 1965, The Serpent 1966, Rooftree 1966, The Deadly Affair 1967, The Girls 1968, The Stake, Anna 1970, Cries and Whispers 1973; *Plays include:* The Diary of Anne Frank, Hamlet, The Beggar's Opera and plays by Chekhov. *Address:* c/o Sandrew Film & Theater AB, Box 5612, 114 86 Stockholm, Sweden.

ANDRÉ, Michèle; French politician; b 6 Feb 1947, Saint-Jacques-d'Ambur; m Max André 1968. *Career:* Regional Del for the Rights of Women 1981–83; Deputy Mayor of Clermont-Ferrand, responsible for entertainment, youth and sports 1983–; mem Bd of Dirs PS 1985–; Sec of State for Women's Rights 1988–91; Councillor-Gen Clermont-Ferrand-NE 1989–. *Address:* Conseil Général du Puy-de-Dôme, 24 rue Saint Esprit, 63033 Clermont-Ferrand Cedex, France.

ANDRÉ, Valérie Marie, MD; French air force medical practitioner; b 21 April 1922, Strasbourg; d of Philibert and Valérie André; m Alexis Santini 1963. *Education:* Univ of Paris. *Career:* Army physician in Indo-China 1948; helicopter pilot in territorial army 1953; flying doctor, Brétigny-sur-Orge aviation test centre 1953–58; physician and pilot in Algeria 1959–62; Chief Medical Officer air force bases 1960, 1962; Physician Lieut Col 1965, Col 1970; Tech Medical Adviser to Military Air Transport Command 1971; Physician-Gen (first woman) 1976; Dir of Health Service, 4th Air Region 1976–, 2nd Air Region 1980–81; Physician Insp-Gen (with rank of Maj-Gen) 1981; Founder-mem Acad Nat de l'Air et de l'Espace 1983; Grand-Officier de la Légion d'Honneur; Grand-Croix de l'Ordre Nat du Mérite; Croix du Combattant; Médaille de l'Aéronautique; Legion of Merit; Grande Médaille d'Or de l'Aéro-Club de France. *Publications:* Ici ventilateur 1954, Madame le Général 1988. *Address:* 27 rue Lasserre, 92130 Issy-les-Moulineaux, France.

ANDREOLI, Kathleen Gainor; American university administrator; b 22 Sept 1935, Albany, NY; d of John Edward and Edmunda (née Ringelmann) Gainor; m Thomas Eugene Andreoli 1960; two d one s. *Education:* Georgetown Univ and Vanderbilt Schools of Nursing and Univ of Alabama School of Nursing (Birmingham, AL). *Career:* Staff Nurse Albany Hosp Medical Center, NY 1957; Instructor various schools of nursing 1957–70; Educational Dir Physician Asst Program, Dept of Medicine, School of Medicine, Univ of Alabama 1970–75, Asst then Assoc of Nursing 1970–79, Prof of Nursing 1979; various admin positions Univ of Texas Health Science Center, Houston 1979–87, Prof of Nursing 1982–87, Vice-Pres for Educational Services, Interprofessional Educ and Int Programs 1984–87; Vice-Pres Nursing Affairs and

John L. and Helen Kellogg Dean, Coll of Nursing, Rush Univ, Chicago, IL 1987–; ed Heart and Lung, Journal of Total Care 1971; mem Bd of Dirs American Asscn of Colleges of Nursing 1998–2000; mem Nat Advisory Nursing Council VHA 1992, Advisory Bd Robert Wood Johnson Clinic Nursing School Program, Visiting Cttee Vanderbilt Univ School of Nursing, Editorial/Advisory Bd The Nursing Spectrum 1996–, Advisory Bd Managing Major Diseases: Diabetes Mellitus and Hypertension 1999, numerous other bodies; Fellow American Acad of Nursing; Founders Award, NC Heart Asscn 1970 and numerous other awards. *Publication:* Comprehensive Cardiac Care (jtly)1983; contrib articles in professional journals. *Leisure interests:* music, art, reading, cycling, travelling. *Address:* Rush Presbyterian–St Luke's Medical Center, 600 S Paulina St, Suite 1080, Chicago, IL 60612, USA (Office); 1212 South Lake Shore Drive, Chicago, IL, 60605, USA (Home). *Telephone:* (312) 942-7117 (Office); (312) 266-8338 (Home); *Fax:* (312) 942-3043 (Office); *E-mail:* kandreoli@rushu.rush.edu (Office); *Internet:* www.rushu.rush.edu/nursing (Office).

ANDREW, Ludmilla; Canadian opera singer (soprano); b Canada of Russian parentage. *Career:* Debut in Vancouver as Donna Elvira in Don Giovanni, British debut as Madam Butterfly with Sadler's Wells Opera; has given many broadcasts of French, German and Russian song repertoire with Geoffrey Parsons; numerous recital tours; now appears regularly at leading opera houses and major int music festivals. *Operas include:* Turandot, Aida, Leonore, Norma, Der Fliegende Holländer, Die Walküre, Fidelio.

ANDREWS, Dame Julie, DBE; British actress and singer; b 1 Oct 1935, Walton-on-Thames, Surrey; m 1st Tony Walton 1959 (divorced 1968); one d; m 2nd Blake Edwards 1969; three d (one step, two adopted) one step-s. *Career:* Debut London Hippodrome 1947; played in revues and concert tours; appeared at London Palladium and in New York; work for UN Devt Fund for Women; several Golden Globe Awards, Emmy Award 1987, BAFTA Award 1989. *Plays include:* Cinderella, The Boy Friend 1954, My Fair Lady 1959–60, Camelot 1960–62, Victor/Victoria 1995; *Films include:* Mary Poppins (Acad Award) 1964, The Americanization of Emily, The Sound of Music, Hawaii, Torn Curtain, Thoroughly Modern Millie, Star!, Darling Lili, The Tamarind Seed, 10, S.O.B., Victor/Victoria, The Man Who Loved Women, That's Life, Duet for One, Tchin-Tchin, The Sound of Christmas (TV) 1987, Relative Values 2000; *TV appearances include:* High Tor, Julie and Carol at Carnegie Hall, The Julie Andrews Show, An Evening with Julie Andrews and Harry Belafonte, The World of Walt Disney, Julie and Carol at Lincoln Center, Julie on Sesame Street, Julie Andrews' Christmas Special, Julie Andrews–My Favorite Things, The Julie Andrews Hour (Best Variety Series Emmy Award) 1972–73, Great Performances Live in Concert 1990, Our Sons 1991, The Julie Show 1992; *Publications:* Mandy 1972, Last of the Really Great Wangdoogles 1973. *Address:* Triad Artists, 10100 Santa Monica Blvd, 16th Floor, Los Angeles, CA 90067, USA. *Telephone:* (252) 716-7000.

ANDRIKIENE, Laima Liucija, B SC; Lithuanian economist and politician; b 1 Jan 1958, Druskininkai; d of Marcelinas Galdikas and Ona Galdikienė; m Rimvydas Andrikis 1980 (deceased); one s. *Education:* Secondary school (Druskininkai), Vilnius Univ and Univ of Manchester. *Career:* Scientist Lithuanian Research Inst of Agricultural Econs 1980–89; Researcher UMIST 1988–89; Adviser to Lithuanian Deputy Prime Minister 1989–90; elected to Supreme Council (Parl) 1990, Deputy Minister of Trade 1991, Deputy Speaker 1992; mem Lithuanian Del to negotiate with Russia 1990; mem Independence Party 1990–92; mem Seimas (Parl) 1992–; mem Homeland Union Party (Lithuanian Conservatives) 1993–; Minister of Trade and Industry 1996–98, of European Affairs 1998–2000; has written over 15 papers on agricultural econs. *Leisure interests:* literature, theatre. *Address:* R. Seimas, Gedimino pr 53, 2002 Vilnius, Lithuania; 2026 Vilnius, Gedimino 53, Lithuania. *Telephone:* (2) 618-291; (2) 743-407; *Fax:* (2) 614-544.

ANÉMONE, (pseudonym of Anne Madeleine Louise Bourguignon); French actress; b 9 Aug 1950, Paris; d of André and Claire (née Justin-Besançon) Bourguignon; one s one d. *Education:* Univs of Paris III (Sorbonne-Nouvelle) and Paris X (Paris-Nanterre). *Career:* Actress in films and on stage 1967–; mem Troupe de la Veuve Pichard, then Troupe du Splendid. *Films include:* Anémone 1967, Ultraviolet 1968, Je toi elle 1968, La maison 1969, Attention les yeux 1975, Cours après moi que je t'attrape 1976, Vous n'aurez pas l'Alsace et la Lorraine 1977, Va voir Maman, Papa travaille 1978, Rien ne va plus 1979, Je vais craquer 1979, Viens chez moi, j'habite chez une copine 1981, La gueule du loup 1981, Quand tu seras débloqué, fais-moi signe 1981, Ma femme s'appelle reviens 1981, Pour cent briques, t'as plus rien 1982, Le Père Noël est une ordure 1982, Un homme à ma taille 1982, Le grand chemin (César for Best Actress) 1987, Sans peur et sans reproche 1988, Les baisers de secours 1989, Maman 1989, La belle histoire (Prix Louis Delluc) 1992, Posson-lune 1993, Aux petits bonheurs 1993, Pas très catholique 1994, La cible 1996, Enfants de salaud 1996, Marquise 1997, Lautrec 1998, L'homme de ma vie 1999, Passeurs de rêves 2000; *Plays include:* Baby Boom 1988, Deux femmes pour un fantôme, La baby sitter 1990, Personne d'autre 1992. *Leisure interests:* music, dancing. *Address:* 82 rue Bonaparte, 75006 Paris, France.

ANFINOGENTOVA, Anna Antonovna; Russian scientist; b 29 Dec 1938; m; two c. *Education:* Saratov Inst Econs. *Career:* Economist Lenin's factory, Saratov 1957–62; teacher Inst of Econs 1964–80; Head of sector and Deputy Dir Inst of Social Problems of Devt of Agric-Industrial Complex, USSR Acad of Sciences 1980–90, Dir 1990–; main research on theory and practice of man of many-field agric complexes; Corresp mem Russian Acad of Sciences 1999, mem 2000; Corresp mem Russian Acad of Agric Sciences; mem Scientific Council on Regional Policy and Legal Problems of Agric-Industrial Complex, European Assn of Econ-Agrarians. *Publications:* monographs and numerous articles on problems of agric devt. *Address:* Institute of Social-Economic Problems of Development of Agricultural-Industrial Complex, Moscow str 94, 410600 Saratov, Russian Federation. *Telephone:* (8452) 24 24 26.

ANGEL, Heather Hazel, M SC, FRPS; British photographer, writer and lecturer; b 21 July 1941, Fulmer, Bucks; d of Stanley Paul and Hazel Marie (née Sherwood) Le Rougetel; m Martin Vivian Angel 1964; one s. *Education:* Univ of Bristol. *Career:* Columnist Amateur Photographer 1990–97, The Natural World 1998, Nikon Owner 2001–; Visiting Prof Dept of Life Science, Univ of Nottingham 1994–; exhibitions include The Natural History of Britain and Ireland, Science Museum (London) 1981, Nature in Focus, Natural History Museum (London) 1987, The Art of Wildlife Photography, Nature in Art (Gloucester) 1989, Dimbola Lodge (Isle of Wight) 2000, The Yard Gallery (Nottingham) 2000, Edinburgh Botanic Garden 2001, Aberystwyth Arts Centre (Wales) 2001; Kodak Calendar on The Thames 1987; in Japanese TV documentary, filmed in UK and Sri Lanka 1983; led British Photographic Del to China 1985; Pres The Royal Photographic Soc (RPS) 1984–86; Fellow British Inst of Professional Photography; Hon D SC (Bath) 1986; Hood Medal, RPS 1975; Médaille de Salverte, Société Française de photographie 1984; Louis Schmidt Laureate, Biocommunications Asscn 1998. *TV appearances include:* Me and My Camera 1981, 1983, Gardener's World 1983, Nature 1984, Nocon on Photography 1988; *Publications:* Nature Photography: Its Art and Techniques 1972, Natural History of Britain and Ireland (jtly) 1982, The Family Water Naturalist 1982, The Book of Nature Photography 1982, The Book of Close-up Photography 1983, Heather Angel's Countryside 1983, A Camera in the Garden 1984, A View from a Window 1988, Nature in Focus 1988, Landscape Photography 1989, Animal Photography 1991, Kew: A World of Plants 1992, Photographing the Natural World 1994, Outdoor Photography: 101 Tips and Hints 1997, How to Photograph Flowers 1998, Pandas 1998, How to Photograph Water 1999, Natural Visions 2000. *Leisure interest:* travelling to remote parts of the world to photograph wilderness areas and unusual aspects of animal behaviour. *Address:* Highways, 6 Vicarage Hill, Farnham, Surrey GU9 8HJ, UK. *Fax:* (1252) 727464; *E-mail:* hangel@naturalvisions.co.uk (Office); *Internet:* www.naturalvisions.co.uk (Office).

ANGELICA, Mother M.; American Franciscan nun and business executive; b (Rita Francis Rizzo) 20 April 1923, Canton, OH; d of John and Mae Helen Gianfrancisco Rizzo. *Career:* Entered Franciscan Nuns of the Most Blessed Sacrament, Cleveland, OH 1944; f Our Lady of Angels Monastery, Birmingham, AL 1962 (Major Superior 1962–), Missionaries of the Eternal Word (inst of brothers and priests) 1987, Lay Missionaries of the Eternal Word 1990; f book Apostolate (distributed to 38 countries) 1973; f Eternal Word Television Network (EWTN – first Roman Catholic satellite cable network) 1981, CEO and Chair Bd

1981–, launched in 42 countries in Cen and S America, E and W Europe and Africa 1995, Pacific Rim 1996; Founder-Pres WEWN (world's largest pvtly owned worldwide shortwave radio station) 1992–; numerous awards including The John Paul II Religion Freedom Award (Catholic League for Religion and Civil Rights) 1983, Citizen of the Year (Alabama Cable TV Asscn) 1985, Communicator of the Year (Int Asscn of Business Communicators, Alabama Chapter) 1986, Compostela Award (Cathedral of St James, Brooklyn, New York) 1988, Faith and Family Award (Women for Faith and Family, St Louis, Missouri) 1991, Pro Fidelitate et Virtute Award (Inst on Religious Life) 1995; several honorary degrees. *Publications:* Answers Not Promises, Dawn on the Mountain, Ad Lib with the Lord, The Father's Splendor, Knowing God's Will, Healing Power of Suffering, His Pain Like Mine, Living Prayer; *TV appearances include:* Living the Scripture with Mother Angelica, Mother Angelica Talks It Over, Mother Angelica Presents, Feed My Lambs, Our Hermitage, In His Sandals, Mother Angelica Live. *Address:* 5817 Old Leeds Rd, Birmingham, AL 35210, USA. *Telephone:* (205) 956-9537; *Fax:* (205) 951-0142.

ANGELIDOU, Claire, BA; Cypriot politician; b 1932, Famagusta; m Nicos Angelides (deceased); three s. *Education:* Univ of Athens (Greece). *Career:* School teacher Dist of Famagusta 1956–74, Limassol 1974–91; mem House of Reps from 1991; mem PEN Club, Nat Socs of Writers of Greece and Cyprus; Pres Cyprus Br, Professional Business Women; has published five collections of poetry; contribs to magazines. *Address:* House of Representatives, Nicosia, Cyprus.

ANGELILLI, Roberta; Italian politician; b 1 Feb 1965, Rome. *Career:* MEP (non-aligned), mem Cttee on Social Affairs and Employment, Del to EU–Cyprus Jt Parl Cttee, Del to EU–Hungary Jt Parliamentary Cttee. *Address:* European Parliament, rue Wiertz, 1047 Brussels, Belgium.

ANGELOU, Maya; American writer; b (Marguerite Johnson) 4 April 1928, St Louis, MO; d of Bailey Johnson and Vivian Baxter; one s. *Career:* Assoc Ed Arab Observer 1961–62; Asst Admin, teacher School of Music and Drama, Univ of Ghana 1963–66; Feature Ed African Review, Accra, Ghana 1964–66; Reynolds Prof Wake Forest Univ, NC 1981–; teacher of modern dance Rome Opera House, Italy and Hambina Theatre, Tel Aviv, Israel; wrote poem for the inauguration of President Clinton 1993; Hon Amb to UNICEF 1996–; Dir Down in the Delta (film) 1998; mem Bd of Govs Maya Angelou Inst for the Improvement of Child and Family Educ, Winston-Salem State Univ, NC 1998–; Distinguished Visiting Prof at several univs; mem various arts orgs; more than 50 hon degrees; Woman of Year in Communications 1976; Horatio Alger Award 1992, Grammy Award Best Spoken Word or Non-Traditional Album 1994, Lifetime Achievement Award for Literature 1999, Nat Medal of Arts, numerous other awards. *Publications include:* I Know Why the Caged Bird Sings 1970, Just Give Me A Cool Drink of Water 'Fore I Die 1971, Georgia, Georgia 1972, Gather Together In My Name 1974, Oh Pray My Wings Are Gonna Fit Me Well 1975, Singin' and Swingin' and Gettin' Merry Like Christmas 1976, And Still I Rise 1976, The Heart of a Woman 1986, All God's Children Need Travelling Shoes 1987, Now Sheba Sings the Song 1987, I Shall Not Be Moved 1990, Gathered Together in My Name 1991, Wouldn't Take Nothing for my Journey Now 1993, Life Doesn't Frighten Me 1993, Collected Poems 1994, My Painted House, My Friendly Chicken and Me 1994, Phenomenal Woman 1995, Kofi and His Magic 1996, Even the Stars Look Lonesome 1997, Making Magic in the World 1998; *Plays include:* Cabaret for Freedom 1960, The Least of These 1966, Gettin' Up Stayed On My Mind 1967, Ajax 1974, And Still I Rise 1976, Moon On a Rainbow Shawl (producer) 1988; has written several screenplays and film scores; contrib to Black Scholar, Essence, California Living, Ghanaian Times, Redbook, Ebony, Mademoiselle, Chicago Daily News, Harper's Bazaar, Cosmopolitan, Life, Sunday New York Times. *Theatre appearances include:* Porgy and Bess 1954–55, Calypso 1957, The Blacks 1960, Mother Courage 1964, Look Away 1973, Roots 1977, How To Make an American Quilt 1995; *TV appearances include:* The Richard Pryor Special, Roots; *Producer:* Moon on a Rainbow Shawl 1988; *Film:* How to Make an American Quilt 1996. *Address:* c/o Dave La Camera, Lordly and Dame Inc, 51 Church St, Boston, MA 02116, USA. *Telephone:* (617) 482-3593; *Fax:* (617) 426-8019.

ANGERVO, Helja, BA; Finnish opera singer; b 3 June 1940, Helsinki; d of Prof Kyösti and Piipra Angervo; m Antero Karttunen 1963; one s. *Education:* Sibelius Acad (Helsinki) and Helsinki Univ. *Career:* Debut Helsinki 1964; debut with Finnish Nat Opera 1964, performances with Finnish Nat Opera 1965–, Asst Dir 1992–, Artistic Co-ordinator 1994–; performances with Hamburg State Opera 1974–75; guest appearances with Berlin Philharmonic Orchestra, BBC Symphony Orchestra and numerous other orchestras and at Bayreut festival 1972, Salzburg Festival 1972–77; mem jury of several international competitions; numerous recordings. *Address:* Laajalahden Tie 19A, Helsinki 00330, Finland.

ANGIER, Natalie; American journalist; b 16 Feb 1958, New York; d of Keith and Adele Angier; m Richard S. Weiss 1991. *Education:* Univ of Michigan and Barnard Coll (NY). *Career:* Writer on Discover Magazine, New York 1980–83, Time magazine, New York 1984–86; Ed Savvy Magazine, New York 1983–84; teacher of journalism New York Univ 1987–89; joined New York Times as Reporter 1990, currently Science Corresp, Washington, DC; Pulitzer Prize for Reporting 1991; Journalism Award, GM Ind Bd 1991; Lewis Thomas Award, Marine Biology Labs 1990; Journalism Award, AAAS 1992; Distinguished Alumna Award, Barnard Coll 1993. *Publications:* Natural Obsessions 1988, The Beauty of the Beastly 1995. *Address:* New York Times, Washington Bureau, 1627 I St, NW, 7th Floor, Washington, DC 20006, USA.

ANGLESEY, Marchioness of, (Elizabeth) Shirley Vaughan Paget, LVO, DBE; British public servant; b 4 Dec 1924; d of the late Charles Morgan and Hilda Vaughan; m George C. H. V. Paget, Marquess of Anglesey 1948; three d two s. *Education:* Francis Holland School (London), St James' (W Malvern) and Kent Place School (USA). *Career:* Personal Sec at FCO until 1948; Deputy Chair Prince of Wales Cttee 1970–80; mem Civic Trust for Wales 1967–76, Arts Council 1972–81, Royal Comm on Environmental Pollution 1973–79, IBA 1976–82, Radioactive Waste Man Advisory Cttee 1981–92, Bd British Council 1985–95; Vice-Chair Museums and Galleries Comm 1989–96, C&G 1998–; Chair Nat Fed of Women's Insts 1966–69, Welsh Arts Council 1975–81, Broadcasting Complaints Comm 1987–91; Trustee Pilgrim Trust 1982–; Hon Fellow Univ Coll of N Wales, Bangor 1990; Hon LL D (Wales) 1977. *Address:* Plâs-Newydd, Llanfairpwll, Gwynedd LL61 6DZ, UK. *Telephone:* (1248) 714330.

ANISTON, Jennifer; American actress; b 11 Feb 1969, Sherman Oaks, CA; d of John Aniston; m Brad Pitt 2000. *Education:* New York High School of the Performing Arts. *Films include:* Leprechaun 1993, She's the One 1996, Dream for an Insomniac 1996, 'Til There Was You 1996, Picture Perfect 1997, The Object of My Affection 1998, Office Space 1999; *Plays include:* For Dear Life, Dancing on Checker's Grave; *TV includes:* Molloy (series) 1989, The Edge, Ferris Bueller, Herman's Head, Friends 1994–. *Address:* c/o CAA, 9830 Wilshire Blvd, Beverly Hills, CA 90212, USA.

ANN-MARGRET; American actress, singer and dancer; b Ann-Margret Olsson 1941, Stockholm, Sweden; m Roger Smith 1967. *Career:* Film debut 1961; five Golden Globe Awards, three Female Star of the Year Awards. *Films include:* Pocketful of Miracles, State Fair, Bye Bye Birdie, Once A Thief, The Cincinnati Kid, Stagecoach, Murderer's Row, CC & Co, Carnal Knowledge, RPM, The Train Robbers, Tommy, The Twist, Joseph Andrews, Last Remake of Beau Geste, Magic, Middle Age Crazy, Return of the Soldier, I Ought to Be in Pictures, Looking to Get Out, Twice in a Lifetime, 52 Pick-Up 1987, New Life 1988, Something More, Newsies 1992, Grumpy Old Men 1993, Grumpier Old Men 1995, Any Given Sunday 1999, The Last Producer 2000, A Woman's a Helluva Thing 2000; *TV appearances include:* Who Will Love My Children? 1983, A Streetcar Named Desire 1984, The Two Mrs Grenvilles 1987, Our Sons 1991, Nobody's Children 1994, Following her Heart, Seduced by Madness: The Diane Borchardt Story 1996, Blue Rodeo 1996, Pamela Hanniman 1999, Happy Face Murders 1999, Perfect Murder, Perfect Town 2000, The Tenth Kingdom 2000; *Publications:* (jtly) Ann-Margret: My Story 1994. *Address:* William Morris Agency, 151 El Camino Drive, Beverly Hills, CA 90212.

ANNE, HRH The Princess (see Royal, HRH The Princess).

ANNIS, Francesca; British actress; d of Anthony and Mariquita Annis; two d one s with Patrick Wiseman. *Career:* Actress with RSC 1975–78. *Films include:* Cleopatra, Saturday Night Out, Murder Most Foul, The Pleasure Girls, Run With the Wind, The Sky Pirates, The Walking Stick, Penny Gold, Macbeth, Krull, Dune, Under the Cherry Moon, Golden River, El Rio de Oro, The Debt Collector, The End of the Affair; *Plays include:* The Tempest, The Passion Flower Hotel, Hamlet, Troilus and Cressida, Comedy of Errors, The Heretic, Mrs Klein, Rosmersholm, Lady Windermere's Fan, Hamlet; *TV appearances include:* Great Expectations, Children in Uniform, Love Story, Danger Man, The Human Jungle, Lily Langtry, Madame Bovary, Partners in Crime, Coming Out of Ice, Why Didn't They Ask Evans?, Magnum PI, Inside Story, Onassis–The Richest Man in the World 1990, Parnell and the Englishwoman 1991, Absolute Hell 1991, The Gravy Train 1991, Weep No More My Lady 1991, Between the Lines 1993, Reckless 1997, Deadly Summer 1997, Wives and Daughters 1999, Milk 1999, Deceit 2000. *Address:* c/o ICM, 76 Oxford St, London W1N 0AX, UK.

ANNUNZIATA, Lucia; Italian television presenter and journalist; b 1951. *Career:* Journalist Corriere della Serra; presenter Line 3 TV programme, Radiotelevisione Italiana (RAI-TV). *Address:* Radiotelevisione Italiana (RAI-TV), Viale Mazzini 14, 00195 Rome, Italy.

ANSELL, Barbara Mary, CBE, MD, FRCS, FRCP; British medical practitioner; b 30 Aug 1923, Warwick; d of Herbert Joseph and Annie Olivia Ansell; m Angus Harold Weston (deceased). *Education:* King's High School for Girls (Warwick) and Birmingham Medical School. *Career:* Research Fellow Research and Educ Hosp, Chicago, IL, USA 1953–54; Consultant Physician (Rheumatology) Canadian Red Cross Memorial Hosp, Taplow 1962, Wexham Park Hosp, Slough 1985–88; Head Div of Rheumatology, Clinical Research Centre, Northwick Park Hosp, Harrow 1976–88; Chair or mem of several medical cttees and orgs; Hon FRSM 1989; Hon Fellow Royal Coll of Paediatrics and Child Health 1996; Queen's Prize Birmingham Univ 1944. *Publications:* Surgical Management of Juvenile Chronic Polyarthritis (jtly) 1978, Rheumatic Disorders in Childhood 1980, Inflammatory Disorders in Muscle: in Clinics in Rheumatic Diseases 1984, Paediatric Rheumatology Update (jt-ed) 1991, Colour Atlas of Rheumatology (jt-ed) 1992. *Leisure interests:* opera, travel, cooking, entertaining. *Address:* 9 Beaumont Rd, Windsor, Berks SL4 1HY, UK (Office); Dumgoyne, Templewood Lane, Stoke Poges, Bucks, SL2 4BG, UK (Home). *Telephone:* (1753) 662321 (Office); (1753) 662321 (Home); *Fax:* (1753) 850128 (Office).

ANSTEE, Dame Margaret Joan, DCMG, MA, B SC (ECON); British United Nations official, lecturer, consultant and author; b 25 June 1926, Writtle, Essex; d of Edward C. Anstee and Anne A. Mills. *Education:* Chelmsford Co High School for Girls, Newnham Coll (Cambridge) and Univ of London. *Career:* Lecturer in Spanish, Queen's Univ Belfast 1947–48; Third Sec Foreign Office 1948–52; UN Tech Assistance Bd, Philippines 1952–54, Colombia 1956–57, Uruguay 1957–59, Bolivia 1960–65; Spanish Supervisor Univ of Cambridge 1955–56; Resident Rep UNDP, Ethiopia and UNDP Liaison Officer with ECA 1965–67; Sr Econ Adviser Office of Prime Minister, London 1967–68; Sr Asst to Commr in charge of study of Capacity of UN Devt System 1968–69; Resident Rep UNDP, Morocco 1969–72, Chile (also UNDP Liaison Officer with ECLA) 1972–74; Deputy to UN Under Sec-Gen in charge of Relief Operation to Bangladesh and Deputy Co-ordinator of UN Emergency Assistance to Zambia 1973; with UNDP, New York 1974–78; Asst Sec-Gen of UN (Dept of Tech Co-operation for Devt) 1978–87; Under Sec-Gen, Dir-Gen of UN office at Vienna, Head of Centre for Social Devt and Humanitarian Affairs 1987–92; Special Rep of Sec-Gen to Bolivia 1982–92, for co-ordination of earthquake relief assistance to Mexico 1985–87, to Peru 1990–91, to Kuwait 1991–92, to Angola and Head of UN Angola Verification Mission (peace-keeping and supervising of elections) 1992–93; Co-ordinator UN Drug Control Related Activities 1987–90, Int Co-operation for Chernobyl 1991–92; Sec-Gen 8th UN Congress on Prevention of Crime and Treatment of Offenders 1987–1990; writer, lecturer, consultant and Adviser (ad honorem) to Bolivian Govt 1993–; mem Advisory Bd UN Studies at Yale Univ 1996–, Advisory Council Oxford Research Group 1997–, Advisory Bd UN Intellectual History Project 1999–; Trustee Helpage Int 1994–97; Patron and Bd mem British Angola Forum 1998–; Hon Fellow Newnham Coll Cambridge 1991; Dr hc (Essex) 1994; Hon LL

D (Westminster) 1996, Hon D SC (Econ) (London) 1998; Reves Peace Prize, William and Mary Coll (USA) 1993, Commdr Ouissam Alaouite (Morocco) 1972, Dama Gran Cruz Condor of the Andes (Bolivia) 1986, Grosse Goldene Ehrenzeichen am Bande (Austria) 1993. *Publications:* The Administration of International Development Aid 1969, Gate of the Sun: A Prospect of Bolivia 1970, Africa and the World (co-ed) 1970, Orphan of the Cold War: The Inside Story of the Collapse of the Angolan Peace Process 1992–93 1996. *Leisure interests:* writing, gardening, hill-walking (preferably in the Andes), bird-watching, swimming. *Address:* c/o PNUD, Casilla 9072, La Paz, Bolivia; c/o The Walled Garden, Knill, nr Presteigne, Powys LD8 2PR, UK (Home). *Telephone:* (1544) 267411 (Wales); *Fax:* (2) 391379 (Bolivia Office).

ANTHONY, Evelyn; British writer; b 3 July 1928; d of Henry Christian and Elizabeth (née Sharkey) Stephens; m Michael Ward-Thomas 1955; four s two d (and one d deceased). *Education:* Convent of the Sacred Heart (Roehampton). *Publications include:* Imperial Highness 1953, Curse Not the King 1954, Far Fly the Eagles 1955, Anne Boleyn (US Literary Guild Award) 1956, Victoria (US Literary Guild Award) 1957, Elizabeth 1959, Charles the King 1961, The Heiress 1964, The Assassin 1970, The Tamarind Seed 1971, The Occupying Power 1973, The Persian Ransom 1975, The Silver Falcon 1977, The Grave of Truth 1979, The Defector 1980, The Avenue of the Dead 1981, Albatross 1982, The Company of Saints 1983, Voices on the Wind 1985, No Enemy But Time 1987, The House of Vandekar 1988, The Scarlet Thread 1989, The Doll's Home 1990, Exposure 1992, Bloodstones 1994, The Legacy 1997. *Leisure interests:* horse-racing, gardening, sales. *Address:* Horham Hall, Thaxted, Essex CM6 2NN, UK.

ANTHONY, Julie, OBE, AM; Australian actress and singer; b 24 Aug 1949; d of D. L. and B. Lush; m E. Natt 1976; two d. *Career:* Lead singer The Seekers group 1989–91; appearance in The Sound of Music, Adelaide, Melbourne, Sydney 1983; Gov St George Foundation 1990–; numerous awards including Australian Variety Club Awards for Best Female Vocalist 1976, 1977, 1978, 1980, 1982, 1986, 1988, Entertainer of the Year 1977, 1978, 1982, Most Popular Female Entertainer 1988, Best TV Variety Entertainer (Female) 1978, Best Newcomer, Plays and Players (London) 1976, Female Vocal Variety Performer of the Year (MO Awards) 1994, 1996. *Leisure interests:* tennis, sailing, gardening, music, football. *Address:* c/o ATA Allstar Artists, Locked Bag 5, Haymarket, NSW 1240, Australia.

ANTO, Maria; Polish painter; b 15 Dec 1938, Warsaw; d of Tadeusz and Aniela (née Egiersdorff) Czarnecki; m Roman Cieslak 1979; two s two d. *Education:* Acad of Fine Arts (Warsaw). *Career:* Forty solo and 200 group exhibitions; major solo exhibitions include Warsaw 1966, 1971, 1978, 1992, Caracas 1967, Stockholm 1968, Milan (Italy) 1971, 1973, 1975, Vienna 1981, London 1989; VIII Biennale São Paulo (Brazil) 1963, Vicenza (Italy) 1996; Grand Prix Monte Carlo 1964, Łódź 1976; First Prize Płcok 1966. *Leisure interests:* playing the piano, poetry. *Address:* ul Karpinskiego 12, 01-609 Warsaw, Poland. *Telephone:* (22) 397353.

ANTON-LAMPRECHT, Ingrun, DR RER NAT; German scientific researcher (retd); b 18 June 1932, Dortmund; d of Wilhelm and Edith (née Stephan) Lamprecht. *Education:* Univs of Münster and Innsbruck (Austria). *Career:* At Max-Planck-Inst, Cologne 1959–68; Head Dept for Structure Research, Univ of Heidelberg Dermatology Clinic 1968, Lecturer Univ of Heidelberg 1974, Prof and Dir Inst for Dermatological Structure Research 1976–98; has written over 157 scientific papers and numerous monographs; Hans-Nachtsheim-Preis 1981; Gottron-Just-Preis 1987. *Address:* c/o Voßstr 2, 69115 Heidelberg, Germany.

ANTONAKAKIS, Suzana Maria; Greek architect; b 25 June 1935, Athens; m Dimitris Antonakakis 1961; one s one d. *Education:* Nat Tech Univ of Athens. *Career:* Partnership with Dimitris Antonakakis 1959–, Founder and Co-Prin Atelier 66 1965–; mem Admin Cttee Greek Architects Asscn 1971–72; Pres Dept of Architecture, Tech Chamber of Greece 1982–83; mem Int Design Seminar Delft Univ of Tech (Netherlands) 1987, Univ of Split (Yugoslavia) 1988; numerous awards and prizes. *Works include:* Archaeological Museum (Chios) 1965–66, Hotel Hydra Beach (Hermionis) 1965–69, vertical additions House in Port Phaliron 1967–72, miners' housing complex Distomo 1969, apartment bldg Em Benaki 118 (Athens) 1973–74, holiday house Sparta

1973–75, Hotel Lyttos (Heraclion, Crete) 1973–82, Zannas House, Philopapos Hill (Athens) 1980–82, Ionian Bank (Heraclion, Crete) 1987, Centre of Traditional Mfrs (Ioannina) 1990, Museum of Acropolis (Athens) 1990; *Publication:* Entretien–Le Corbusier (trans) 1971; numerous contribs to professional journals. *Address:* Atelier 66, Em Benaki 118, Athens 114-73, Greece. *Telephone:* (1) 3300323; *Fax:* (1) 330322.

ANTONICHEVA, Anna; Russian ballet dancer; b Baku, Azerbaijan. *Education:* Moscow Academic School of Choreography. *Career:* Leading ballet dancer Bolshoi Theatre; Merited Artist of Russia. *Leading and solo parts in ballets include:* Shirin (Legend of Love), Swan-Princess (Swan Lake), Nikiya (Bayadera), Mirta (Giselle), Juliet (Romeo and Juliet), Frigia (Spartacus), Princess Aurora (Sleeping Beauty), Kitry, Dulcinea (Don Quixote). *Address:* Bolshoi Theatre, Teatralnaya pl 1, Moscow, 103009, Russian Federation.

ANTONOVA, Irina Aleksandrovna; Russian arts administrator; b 20 March 1922, Moscow. *Education:* Moscow State Univ. *Career:* Mem staff Moscow Pushkin Museum of Fine Arts 1945–, Sr Researcher 1945–61, Dir 1962–; Co-Founder with Sviatoslav Richter December Nights Festival of Arts and art shows 1981; organizer of numerous exhibitions and exchanges with museums in Europe and the USA; Vice-Pres Int Council of Museums 1980–92, Hon mem 1992–; mem Russian Acad of Educ 1989; Corresp mem San-Fernando Acad (Madrid, Spain); State Prize 1995, Commdr des Arts et des Lettres. *Publications:* more than 60 articles on problems of museum man, art of Italian Renaissance, contemporary painting. *Leisure interests:* swimming, cars, music, ballet. *Address:* A. S. Pushkin Museum of Fine Arts, Volkhonka str 12, Moscow, Russian Federation. *Telephone:* (095) 230 46 76 (Office).

ANTONSSON, Birgit Anna Katarina, PH D; Swedish library director; b 23 April 1942, Hudiksvall; d of Birger and Anna-Lisa (née Hanson) Antonsson. *Education:* Uppsala Univ and Swedish Library Coll (Borås). *Career:* Librarian Linköping Univ Library 1975–81; First Librarian Uppsala Univ Library 1981–85; Library Dir Stockholm School of Econs 1985–87; Deputy Librarian Royal Library, Nat Library of Sweden 1987–88, Dir 1988–95; Pres Swedish Asscn of Univ and Research Librarians 1984–89; Chair Swedish Council for Research in the Humanities and Social Sciences 1989. *Publications:* Efterkland och särprägel 1972, Tove Jansson på svenska 1976, Biblioteksutbildning för innehavare av doktorsexamen 1984, Pliktleveranslagen 1978 (ed) 1986. *Leisure interest:* literature. *Address:* c/o Royal Library, National Library of Sweden, Box 5039, 102 41 Stockholm, Sweden.

ANTTILA, Sirkka-Liisa; Finnish politician; b 20 Dec 1943, Marttila; d of Paavo Artturi and Ellen Sofia (née Jalonen) Ojala; m Risto Anttila 1967; two d. *Career:* Clerical Asst at Loimaa Tax Office 1965; Admin Notary 1967 and farmstead housewife; mem Centre Party 1967, Parl Constituency of South Häme Prov, Vice-Chair 1994–2000, Chair Women of the Centre Party 1994–; Sec to Sr Physician and Storekeeper, S-W Häme Psychiatric Hosp 1969–72; Finance Dir Kankaanpää Vocational Training Centre 1972–73; Clerical Officer Urjala Municipal Council 1973–74; Deputy Office Man Forssa Health Centre 1974–82; mem Forssa City Council 1977–, Vice-Chair 1991–92, mem City Exec Bd 1977–79, 1982–83, 1988–90; mem Parl Consumer Affairs Council 1979–90, Consumer Policy Comm 1990–99; mem Eduskunta (Parl) 1983–, mem Constitutional Cttee 1983–89, Chair Agric and Forestry Cttee 1991–95, First Deputy Speaker 1995–96, 1999–; substitute mem Finnish Del to Council of Europe 1989–95, mem 1995–96, Vice-Chair 1995, mem Agric Cttee 1989–96, Chair Sub-cttee 1994–96; MEP 1996–99, mem Cttee on Agric and Rural Devt, substitute mem Cttee on Econ and Monetary Affairs and Industrial Policy, substitute mem of Del to EU–Latvia Jt Parl Cttee; mem Supervisory Bd Neste Ltd 1993–97. *Address:* Eduskunta, 00102 Helsinki, Finland. *Telephone:* (0) 4321; *Fax:* (0) 4322703.

ANTUNES, Xana; British newspaper editor; b 1965. *Career:* Began career in journalism with The Independent business section 1988; TV journalist on Business Daily (Channel 4); Business News Ed, Evening Standard 1992–93; Deputy Business Ed, then Business Ed New York Post 1993–2000, Ed New York Post 2000–. *Address:* 1211 Ave of the Americas, New York, NY 10036, USA. *Internet:* www.nypost.com.

ANYANWU, Christina, BA, M SC; Nigerian journalist; b 29 Oct 1950, Mbaise; m; one s one d. *Education:* Univs of Missouri and Florida (USA). *Career:* Journalist; Newsweek Corresp at Nat Ass 1979; journalist Nat TV Authority 1979, Producer Newsline magazine 1986; Commr of Information, Imo State 1989; Founder, Dir and Ed-in-Chief The Sunday Magazine 1989–; sentenced by special military tribunal in camera to life imprisonment for 'spreading false news' July 1995, sentence reduced to 15 years' imprisonment Oct 1995, released June 1998; Nat Nigerian Award for Women Journalists; Garnet Award, Ford Foundation; Prize for Courage, Int Women's Media Foundation 1995; Reporters sans Frontières Award 1995; UNESCO/Guillermo Cano World Press Freedom Prize 1998. *Address:* c/o Reporters sans Frontières, 5 rue Geoffroy Marie, 75009 Paris, France.

APOSTOL, Eugenia (Eggie) Duran; Philippine journalist; b 1926; m Peping Apostol; one s. *Education:* Univ of Santo Tomas. *Career:* Founder and Chair The Weekly Inquirer; produced video documentary Batas Militar 1994; f The Pinoy Times 1999; Eugenia Duran Apostol Hon Collection held at Ateneo Library of Women's Writings (ALIWW) 2000. *Address:* c/o Dept of Education, Culture and Sports, Ultra Complex, Meralco Ave, Pasig City, 1600 Metro Manila, Philippines.

APPEL, Bluma, CM; Canadian business executive; b Montréal, PQ; d of Jack and Dora (née Blitz) Levitt; m A. Bram Appel 1940; two s. *Career:* Designer Chester Reed Clothes 1948–52, New York theatres (USA) 1957–65; Rep to Sec of State 1970–72; Liaison to Minister Responsible for the Status of Women 1975–79; Chair Appel Consultants Inc 1977–; Dir Canmont Investment Corpn Ltd, Canmont Realty Corpn; Dir McMichael Art Gallery 1986–90, mem Bd of Dirs Canadian Centre for Advanced Film Studies 1986–92, Founder and Exec Dir American Friends of Canada Cttee; Dir Brock Univ 1988–94; Dir Ontario Crafts Council 1987, Toronto Arts Awards 1987, Partners in Research 1988; Chair Canadian Foundation for AIDS Research 1989; f Necessary Angel Theatre Co 1987; Bd of Trustees Royal Ontario Museum 1990; Dir Niagara-on-the-Lake Historical Museum 1996, Opera Atelier 1996, Dora Mavor Moore Awards 1997, Telefilm Canada 1998, Council for Canadian Unity 1999; Univ of Toronto Arbour Award 1995, Order of Ontario 1997. *Leisure interests:* swimming, walking, cross-country skiing. *Address:* 18A Hazelton Ave, Apt 406, Toronto, ON M5R 2E2, Canada (Home).

AQUINO, (Maria) Corazon (Cory), BA; Philippine politician; b 25 Jan 1933, Tarlac Prov; d of José Cojuangco, Sr; m Benigno S. Aquino, Jr 1954 (assassinated 1983); four d one s. *Education:* Raven Hill Acad (PA, USA), Notre Dame School (NY, USA) and Mount St Vincent Coll (NY, USA). *Career:* In exile in USA with her husband 1980–83; mem United Nationalist Democratic Org (UNIDO) 1985–; Pres of the Philippines 1986–92; William Fulbright Prize for Int Peace 1996; Ramon Magsaysay Award for Int Understanding 1998. *Address:* 25 Times St, Quezon City, Philippines.

ARABIAN, Ghislaine; French chef; b 3 Aug 1948; m 1st Jean Wevaux 1970 (deceased); m 2nd J. P. Arabian 1986; three s one d. *Career:* Trainee chef, then chef at Restaurant, Lille 1983–92; Kitchen Dir at Pavillion Ledoyen 1992–; awarded two Michelin stars (only female two-star chef in France); has published two books of recipes (1991, 1995). *Leisure interests:* reading, museums, antiques. *Address:* 1 ave Dutuit, 75008 Paris, France; 39 rue du Bac, 92600 Asnières, France (Home). *Telephone:* (1) 47-42-23-23 (Office); (2) 47-91-41-04 (Home); *Fax:* (1) 47-42-55-01 (Office).

ARBATOVA, Maria Ivanovna; Russian writer; b (Maria Ivanova Gavrilina) 17 July 1957, Murom, Vladimir region; d of Ivan Gavrilovich Gavrilin and Ludmila Ilyinichna Aisenstadt; m 2nd Oleg Tumayevich Vitte; two s. *Education:* Moscow State Univ and Moscow Literary Inst (workshop of Victor Rozov). *Career:* Poet 1975–; playwright and prose writer; active participant in Feminist Movt and other political activities 1991–; took part in election campaign of Pres B. Yeltsin 1996; Founder Psychological Club Garmonia 1991–96; Dir Women Interfering with Politics Club 1996–; Cand for State Duma 1999. *TV:* I-Myself (regular appearances); *Publications include:* Plays: Victoria Vassilyeva in the Eye of Strangers (USSR Competition of Young Dramatists Prize 1985), Dreams on the Bank of Dniepr (Festival of Young Dramatists Prize 1990), Detailed Interview on the Subject of Freedom (Bonn Theatre

Festival Prize, Germany), Late Crew (radio-drama); Books: I am 40 (autobiographical novel), I am a Woman (stories); numerous articles and essays. *Address:* EKSMO Publishers, Narognogo Opolcheniya str 38, 1232298 Moscow, Russian Federation (Office). *Telephone:* (095) 246-81-55 (Home); *E-mail:* arbatova@cityline.ru.

ARBOUR, Hon Justice Louise, BA, LL L; Canadian judge; b 10 Feb 1947, Montréal. *Education:* Univ de Montréal. *Career:* Teacher Osgoode Hall Law School, Toronto; called to bar Ontario 1977; fmrly Vice-Pres Canadian Civil Liberties Union; Judge Supreme Court of Ontario 1987–90, Ontario Court of Appeal 1990–99 (on leave 1996–99; Chief Prosecutor, Int War Crimes Tribunals on fmr Yugoslavia and Rwanda, The Hague 1996–99; Judge, Supreme Court of Canada 1999–; Dr hc (Glasgow 2000). *Address:* The Supreme Court of Canada, Supreme Court Building, 301 Wellington St, Ottawa, ON K1A 0J1, Canada (Office); 130 Queen Street W, Toronto, ON M5H 2N5, Canada (Home). *Telephone:* (613) 995-4330 (Office); *Fax:* (613) 996-3063 (Office); *E-mail:* reception@scc-csc.gov.ca (Office).

ARCHER, Anne; American actress; b 25 Aug 1947, Los Angeles, CA; d of John Archer and Marjorie Lord; m Terry Jastrow; two s. *Education:* Claremont Coll. *Career:* Numerous theatre, film and TV appearances. *Plays include:* A Coupla White Chicks Sitting Around Talking 1981, Les Liaisons Dangereuses 1988; *Films include:* Honkers, The All-American Boy, Paradise Alley, Good Guys Wear Black, Raise the Titanic, Green Ice, Waltz Across Texas, Too Scared to Scream, The Check is in the Mail, Fatal Attraction, Love at Large, Narrow Margin, Eminent Domain, Patriot Games, Body of Evidence, Family Prayers, Short Cuts, Clear and Present Danger, There Goes My Baby (narrator); *TV appearances include:* Bob and Carol and Ted and Alice, Falcon Crest, The Man in the Attic, Jake's Women. *Address:* Ilene Feldman Agency, 8730 W Sunset Blvd, Suite 490, Los Angeles, CA 90069, USA.

ARCHER, Mary Doreen, MA, PH D, FRSC; British chemist and business executive; b 22 Dec 1944; d of the late Harold Norman and of Doreen (née Cox) Weeden; m Jeffrey Howard Archer 1966; two s. *Education:* Cheltenham Ladies' Coll, St Anne's Coll (Oxford) and Imperial Coll (London). *Career:* Jr Research Fellow St Hilda's Coll, Oxford 1968–71; Lecturer in Chemistry Somerville Coll, Oxford 1971–72; Research Fellow Royal Inst of GB 1972–76; Reader in Chemistry, Trinity Coll, Cambridge 1976–86; Fellow and Lecturer in Chemistry, Newnham Coll, Cambridge 1976–86, Bye Fellow 1987–; Visiting Prof Leicester Polytechnic (now De Montfort Univ) 1990–, Imperial Coll, London 1991–; Trustee Science Museum 1990–; Visitor Univ of Herts 1993–; mem Council, Royal Inst 1984–85, Lloyds 1989–92, Cheltenham Ladies' Coll 1991–, Founder and Chair Hardship Cttee 1989; mem Cttee on the Public Understanding of Science 1995–; Dir Fitzwilliam Museum Trust 1984, Anglia TV Group 1987–95, Mid Anglia Radio 1988–94, Cambridge and Newmarket FM Radio (now Q103) 1988–97, Addenbrooke's Hosp NHS Trust 1992–; Pres Guild of Church Musicians 1989–; Trustee Science Museum 1990–; Chair Nat Energy Foundation 1990–; Hon D Sc (Herts) 1994; Mistress Grantchester Village Choir. *Publications:* Rupert Brooke and the Old Vicarage, Grantchester 1989, Clean Electricity from Photovoltaics 2001; numerous articles in scientific journals. *Leisure interests:* theatre, cats, tennis. *Address:* The Old Vicarage, Grantchester, Cambridge CB3 9ND, UK. *Telephone:* (1223) 840213; *Fax:* (1223) 842882.

ARCHER, Patricia Dawn, B SC; Australian medical scientist; b 18 Aug 1935, Melbourne; d of the late Maj Henri J. Archer and Stella (née Coller) Archer. *Education:* Fintona Girls' School (Melbourne) and Univ of Melbourne. *Career:* Research Asst CSIRO, Univ of Melbourne 1956; Cytotechnologist Royal Women's Hosp, Melbourne 1959; Sr Cytotechnologist Westminster Hosp, London, UK 1960–61; Sr Cytotechnologist Prince Henry's Hosp, Melbourne 1961–, Educational Co-ordinator Prince Henry's School of Cytotech 1976–82, Sr Research Scientist Cytology Dept, Prince Henry's Hosp 1982–90; Lecturer and Demonstrator in Cytology, Royal Melbourne Inst of Tech 1970–91; Sr Research Scientist Victorian Cytology Service 1990–91; Proxime Accessit (Fintona Girls' School) 1953; Commonwealth Scholar 1953; John Funder Travel Award (Prince Henry's Hosp) 1978; Int Cytotechnologist of the Year (Int Acad of Cytology) 1992. *Leisure interests:*

music, drama, opera, ballet, watercolour painting, photography, travel, exhibiting and breeding Siamese and Oriental cats. *Address:* 4 Highland Ave, Balwyn, Vic 3103, Australia. *Telephone:* (3) 859 1348.

ARCHER, Robyn, BA, DIP ED; Australian performer, songwriter, writer and director; b 18 June 1948, Adelaide; d of Clifford Charles Smith and Mary Louisa Wohling. *Education:* Enfield High School and Adelaide Univ. *Career:* Singer 1952–; recorded 10 albums including Brecht, Weill and Eisler repertoire; has toured world-wide in recital, concert and cabaret performances; has sung with Australian and Adelaide Chamber Orchestras, Adelaide, Melbourne and Tasmanian Symphony Orchestras; numerous TV appearances in Australia and UK; has written over 100 songs; Artistic Dir Nat Festival of Australian Theatre 1993–95, Adelaide Festival 1998, 2000; Creative Consultant Melbourne Museum 1995–; Chair Community Cultural Devt Bd, Australia Council 1992–94; Patron Nat Affiliation of Arts Educators; Hon D UNIV (Flinders), Sydney Critics' Circle Award 1980, Henry Lawson Award 1980, Australian Creative Fellowship 1991–93, Australian Record Industry Award for best soundtrack for Pack of Women 1986, for best children's album for Mrs Bottle 1989, Exec Woman of the Year, Australian Women's Network 1998, and other awards. *Writing includes:* for theatre: Songs from Sideshow Alley, The Pack of Women (also dir), Cut & Thrust Cabaret (also dir), Café Fledermaus, See Ya Next Century, Ningali, A Start is Torn, Comes a Cropper; *Directing for theatre includes:* Accidental Death of an Anarchist; *Publications:* The Robyn Archer Songbook 1980, Mrs Bottle Burps 1983, The Pack of Women 1986, A Star is Torn 1986; contrib to books, magazines and newspapers. *Address:* c/o Rick Raftos Management, POB 445, Paddington, NSW 2021, Australia. *Telephone:* (2) 9360-5311; *Fax:* (2) 9360-5267.

ARCHER, Violet Balesteri, CM, D MUS; Canadian composer; b 24 April 1913, Montréal, PQ; d of Cesar Balestreri Archer and Beatrice Azzi. *Education:* McGill Univ and with Béla Barfók, Richard Donovan and Paul Hindemith at Yale Univ (USA). *Career:* Instructor in Music McGill Univ 1943–47; Composer-in-Residence N Texas State Univ, USA 1950–53, Banff School of Fine Arts 1978, 1979; Asst Prof Univ of Oklahoma 1953–61; Assoc Prof Univ of Alberta 1962, Chair Div of Theory and Composition 1962–78, Prof 1970–78, Prof Emer 1978–; mem Advisory Bd Celebration of Women in the Arts, Edmonton, AB 1988; works performed in countries throughout the world; also pianist, organist, percussionist and adjudicator; numerous articles on music; mem Canadian League of Composers, Canadian Folk Music Soc, Canadian Fed of Music Teachers, Asscn of Canadian Women Composers; Violet Archer Festival held Edmonton 1985; Life mem Accad Tiberina of Rome 1979; Hon Life mem Soc of Artists 1983; Hon D MUS (McGill) 1971, (Windsor) 1986, (Mt Allison) 1992; Hon LL D (Calgary) 1989, (Alberta) 1993; numerous awards and honours including Queen's Silver Jubilee Medal 1978, Award for Outstanding Music 1981, Performing Rights Org of Canada Award for Outstanding Success in the Concert Music Fields 1981, Sir Frederick Haultain Prize, Govt of Alberta 1987, Achievement Award CBC and Prov of Alberta 1990, Commemorative Medal for 125th Anniversary of Canadian Confed 1992, Violet Archer Fellowship named (Dept of Music, Univ of Alberta) 1992. *Compositions include:* Prelude and Allegro for Violin and Piano 1954, Fanfare and Passacaglia for Orchestra 1949, Three Sketches for Orchestra 1961, Sonata for Horn and Piano 1965, Sganarelle 1973, Piano Sonata No 2 1979, String Quartet No 3 1981, The Meal 1983, Improvisations on a Name 1987, Evocations 1988, Four Dialogues for Classical Guitar and Chamber Orchestra 1989; *Film scores:* Someone Cares 1977, Whatsoever Things Are True 1980. *Leisure interests:* reading historical books, biographies and poetry, theatre, art, good films, walking. *Address:* c/o 10805 85th Ave, Edmonton, AB T6E 2L2, Canada.

ARDAILLON-POIRIER, Elisabeth Marie, MA; French business executive; b 17 April 1950, Laxou; d of Jean and Renée (née Goulard de Lacam) Ardaillon; m Jean-Marie Poirier 1990. *Education:* Lycée de Fort-de France and La Bruyère (Versailles), Univs of Strasbourg, Paris X (Paris-Nanterre) and Paris IV (Sorbonne). *Career:* Graduate of Centre d'Etudes Littéraires et Scientifiques Appliquées 1976; Deputy to Dir of Int Relations at Inst Nat de la Santé et de la Recherche Médicale (INSERM) 1977–78; Special Adviser, Pvt Office of Minister for External Trade (later for Administrative Reforms) 1978–81; Dir of Operations Bernard Krief Consulting Group 1982–83, Devt Dir 1984;

Vice-Pres of Corp Communications Saint Gobain Group 1984–86; Vice-Pres of Corp Communications, Hachette Group, mem Exec and Strategic Cttee 1986–93, Exec Dir Fondation Hachette 1989–93, Vice-Pres Corp Communications, mem Corp Man Cttee Hachette-Filipacchi Group (following merger of Matra and Hachette Groups) 1993–94; mem Gov Body Centre de Formation et de Perfectionnement des Journalistes (CFPJ) 1987–91, mem Educ Cttee 1991–94; Dir of Press and Communications Banque de France 1994–; mem External Relations Cttee Cen European Bank 1998–; Chevalier de l'Ordre Nat du Mérite. *Leisure interests:* cinema, travel, reading, swimming. *Address:* Banque de France, 48 rue Croix des Petits Champs, 75049 Paris, France. *Telephone:* (1) 42-92-44-44; *Fax:* (1) 42-92-44-67; *E-mail:* eardaillon@banque-france.fr.

ARDANT, Fanny; French actress; b 22 March 1949, Monte Carlo; d of Lieut-Col Jean Ardant and Jacqueline Lecoq; three c. *Career:* Worked in theatre, then with film dir François Truffaut; Grand Prix National (Ministry of Culture). *Plays include:* Polyeucte, Esther, The Mayor of Santiago, Electra, Tete d'Or; *Films include:* Les Chiens, Les uns et les autres, The Woman Next Door, The Ins and Outs, Life is a Novel, Confidentially Yours, Benevenuta, Desire, Swann in Love, Love Unto Death, Les enragés, L'été prochain, Family Business, Affabulazione, Mélo, The Family, La Paltoquet, Three Sisters, Australia, Pleure pas My Love, Adventure of Catherine C., Afraid of the Dark, Rien que des mensonges, La femme du déserteur, Amok, Colonel Chabert, Beyond the Clouds, Ridicule, Elizabeth. *Address:* Artmédia, 10 avenue George V, 75008 Paris, France (Office).

ARDEN, Rt Hon Lady Justice Arden, Dame Mary (Howarth), DBE, QC, PC, MA, LL M; British high court judge; b 23 Jan 1947; d of the late Lieut-Col E. C. Arden and of M. M. (née Smith) Arden; m Sir Jonathan Mance; two d one s. *Education:* Huyton Coll (Liverpool), Girton Coll (Cambridge) and Harvard Law School (MA, USA). *Career:* Called to the bar Gray's Inn 1971; admitted to Lincoln's Inn 1973, Bencher 1993; QC 1986; DTI Insp Rotaprint PLC 1988–91; Attorney Gen Duchy of Lancaster 1991–93; Judge of High Court of Justice, Chancery Div 1993–2000; Chair Law Comm 1996–99; Lord Justice of Appeal 2000–; bar mem Law Soc's Standing Cttee on Co Law 1976–; Hon D UNIV (Essex) 1997; Hon LL D (Liverpool) 1998, (Warwick) 1999. *Publications:* contrib to numerous books, articles in legal journals. *Leisure interests:* family activities, reading, swimming. *Address:* Royal Courts of Justice, Strand, London WC2A 2LL, UK.

AREEN, Judith Carol, AB, JD; American professor of law; b 2 Aug 1944; d of Gordon Eric and Pauline Jeanette Arren; m Richard M. Cooper 1979; two s. *Education:* Cornell and Yale Univs. *Career:* Called to the Bar, MA 1970, DC 1972; Programme Planner, Higher Educ, Office of the Mayor, New York 1969–70; Dir Educ Voucher Study, Centre for the Study of Public Policy, Cambridge, MA 1970–72; mem staff Georgetown Univ, Washington, DC 1971–, Assoc Prof of Law 1972–76, Prof 1976–, Prof of Community and Family Medicine 1980–89, Assoc Dean Law Centre 1984–87, Dean and Exec Vice-Pres for Law Affairs 1989–; Gen Counsel and Co-ordinator of Domestic Reorganization, Office of Man and Budget, Washington, DC 1977–80; Special Counsel White House Task Force on Regulatory Reform 1978–80; Exec Vice-Pres for Law Affairs, MCI Communications Corpn, Washington, DC; Consultant to NIH 1984, NRC 1985; Sr Research Fellow Kennedy Inst of Ethics 1982–. *Publications include:* Youth Service Agencies 1977, Cases and Materials on Family Law 1978 (4th edn 1999). *Address:* Georgetown University Law Centre, 1507 Isherwood St, NE, No 1, Washington, DC 20002, USA.

ARENAL, Julie; American choreographer; m Barry Primus. *Career:* Teacher and Choreographer Herbert Berghof Studio; Training Programme Asst Lincoln Center Repertory Theatre; Dancer with Cos of Anna Sokolow, Sophie Maslow, John Butler, Jack Cole, Jose Limon; Choreographer for Theatre Co of Boston, Ballet Hispanico, San Francisco Ballet, Cuban Nat Ballet; Dir New York Express Break and Boogie Dance Co; Nat Educ Asscn Grantee for Oregon Shakespeare Festival 1997, Porgy and Bess City Opera, NYC Opera 2000. *Choreography includes:* Hair (New York, then Stockholm—Most Original Choreography of the Year 1968, Best Dir-Choreographer of the Year, Sweden 1969), Indians, Isabel's a Jezebel (also Dir), Fiesta 1972, 20008 $^{1}/_{2}$, Boccaccio 1975, A Private Circus 1975, Free to Be You and Me

1976, The Referee 1976, El Arbito 1978, King of the Gypsies (film), Funny Girl (film, also Dir) 1979–80, Four Friends (film) 1980, Mistress 1991, Great Expectations 1997. *Address:* 205 E Tenth St, New York, NY 10003, USA.

ARGERICH, Martha; Argentine pianist; b 5 June 1941, Buenos Aires. *Education:* Studied with V. Scaramuzzo, Friedrich Gulda, Nikita Magaloff, Madeleine Lipatti and Arturo Benedetto Michaelangeli. *Career:* Debut Buenos Aires 1949, London 1964; soloist with world's leading orchestras; First Prize Busoni Contest, Geneva Int Music Competition (Switzerland) 1957, Int Chopin Competition (Warsaw) 1965; Officier des Arts et des Lettres 1996, Accademica di Santa Cecilia di Roma 1997. *Address:* c/o Jacques Thelen Agence Artistique, 15 Avenue Montaigne, 75008 Paris, France.

ARGI, Raya (née Belahovsky); French artist; b Jerusalem, Israel; m Clément Argi; one s. *Education:* Self-taught. *Career:* Conceptual and expressionist artist working with paints, pastels and tapestry; exhibitions include Musée d l'Art Int, Carnac 1996; Guest of Hon, winner Médaille d'Or Galerie Ferron du Roy, St Galmier, Loire 1984; awards include Médaille d'Argent (Prix de la Côte d'Azur, Casino Municipal, Cannes) 1974, Leon d'Or 1980 and Perseo d'Oro 1981 (Accad Signoria di Firenze, Florence, Italy), Etoile d'Or (Int des Arts, Marseilles) 1981, Médaille d'Or (Acad Toscana Il Machiavello, Rome) 1981, Palmes d'Or Académiques (Acad Int Leonardo da Vinci, Rome) 1984, Premio Palma d'Oro d'Europa (Accad Europea, Italy) 1987, Médaille Vermeil (Acad Arts Sciences Lettres, Paris) 1988, Gold Medal (Accad Leonardo da Vinci, Rome) 1989, Médaille d'Argent with Special Mention for Portrait (Acad Int de Lutèce, Paris) 1991, Médaille d'Or (Paris) 1994, Médaille d'Or (Acad Arts Sciences Lettres) 1995, Medal of Excellence (for two portraits exhibited at 23rd Int Congress on Arts and Communications, Fairmont Hotel, San Francisco, CA, USA) 1996. *Leisure interests:* painting, tapestry, decorative arts, reading, walking, travel, music, golf. *Address:* c/o 9 rue Chevalier Martin, Le Sainte Luce, 06800 Cagnes-sur-mer, France.

ARIAS, Susana, BFA; Panamanian sculptor; b 1953, Panamá. *Education:* Newcomb Coll, Tulane Univ of Louisiana (USA). *Career:* Solo exhibitions include Arteconsult, Panamá 1982, 1986, Museum of Contemporary Art, Panamá 1984, Santa Cruz Art Center 1985, San José Inst of Contemporary Art, San José State Univ, CA, USA 1988, Gallery of Fine Arts, Santa Cruz, CA 1989, Galería Habitante, Panamá 1990, Galería Arteconsult, Panamá 1991; group exhibitions include Artconsult Int, Boston, MA 1984, Barbara Singer Gallery, Cambridge, MA 1985, Laguna Art Gallery, CA 1986, Museum of Contemporary Art, Panamá 1987, Cuenca, Ecuador 1987, Virginia Miller Gallery, Coral Gables, FL 1990, Eloise Pickard Smith Gallery, Santa Cruz, CA 1990, Raymond Gallery, Panamá 1991, Museo de Arte Contemporáneo de Caracas 1992, Long Beach Arts, Long Beach, CA 1995, San Francisco, CA 1995, Centro de Arte de Maracaibo Lía Bermudez, Venezuela 1995; works acquired by perm collections including Museum of Contemporary Art, Panamá, Museum of History, Panamá, Deutsch-Südamerikanische Bank, Panamá, Museum of Modern Art, Santo Domingo, Dominican Repub, Nat Museum of Fine Arts, Havana, Cuba 1986, Bolivarian Museum of Contemporary Art, Santa Marta, Colombia 1986, Museum of Modern Art of Latin America, Washington, DC 1987, Coast Commercial Bank, Aptos, CA 1990, Museo del Barro, Caracas, Venezuela 1994; numerous commissions and grants. *Works include:* Bird 1981, Gallina 1982, Cactus 1984, Shadowed Time 1985, Anna's Wall 1985, Isla 1985, Man and Nature 1986, Portrait of 175 Children 1990, The Park Alive 1993, Findings of the Past 1994. *Address:* POB 2497, Aptos, CA 95001, USA. *Telephone:* (408) 684-0488; *Fax:* (408) 722-0575.

ARJONA PÉREZ, Marta María; Cuban sculptor and ceramic artist; b 3 May 1923, Havana; d of Ernesto and Norak Arjona Pérez. *Education:* San Alejandro Nat School of Beaux Arts and Paris. *Career:* Numerous exhibitions in Cuba and overseas 1945–52; Dir Nuestro Tiempo Soc Gallery 1953–59; Nat Dir of Plastic Arts, then of Museums and Monuments 1959–77; Dir of Cultural Heritage 1977–; Pres Cuban Cttee, Int Council of Museums; contribs to professional journals; Medal of Raúl Gómez 1975, Order of Raúl Gómez 1982. *Works include:* Ceramic Murals at the Palacio de la Revolución (jtly), Escuela V. I.

Lenin (jtly). *Address:* Calle A, No 608 entre 25 y 27, Vedado, Havana, Cuba (Office); Quinta B, No 8605 entre 86 y 88, Miramar, Playa, Cuba (Home). *Telephone:* (7) 2-8155 (Home).

ARKHIPOVA, Irina Konstantinovna; Russian opera singer (mezzo-soprano); b 2 Jan 1925, Moscow; d of Vetoschkin Konstantin and Galda Evdokija; m Plavkò Vladislav; one s. *Education:* Inst of Architecture (Moscow) and Moscow Conservatoire. *Career:* Debut with Sverdlovsk Opera; joined Bolshoi Theatre 1956, opera performances and song recitals since 1956 in Milan, Vienna, Paris, London and in USA performing Russian, French and Italian repertoire, leading soloist until 1988; mem CPSU 1963–91, Supreme Soviet 1962–66; People's Deputy 1989–91; Prof at Moscow Conservatoire 1982–; Pres Int Union of Musicians, Irina Arkhipova Foundation; mem Acad of Creative Endeavours 1991, Int Acad of Sciences 1994; People's Artist of the USSR 1966, Lenin Prize 1978, Hero of Socialist Labour 1984, People's Artist of Kyrgyzstan 1993, State Prize 1997. *Operas include:* Aida, War and Peace, Don Carlos, Carmen; *Publications:* My Muses 1992, Music of Life 1997. *Address:* Bryusov per 2/14, Apt 27, 103009 Moscow, Russian Federation. *Telephone:* (095) 229-60-29 (Office); (095) 229-43-07 (Home).

ARMATAGE, Elizabeth Kay, PH D; Canadian educationalist and film maker; b 15 Jan 1943, SK; d of Trenholm and Elizabeth Armatage; one d. *Education:* Queen's Univ and Univ of Toronto. *Career:* Univ teacher 1972; completed first film 1977; Programmer Toronto Festival of Festivals 1982; Dir of Women's Studies Programme, Univ of Toronto 1987–92, Assoc Prof of Cinema and Women's Studies, Dir Grad Collaborative Programme in Women's Studies 1994–; mem Ontario Arts Council 1991–; has exhibited films at many int festivals in N America and Europe; awards include YWCA Woman of Distinction 1989, Toronto Women in Film Special Merit Award 1988. *Films include:* Jill Johnston 1977, Gertrude and Alice in Passing 1978, Bed and Sofa 1979, Speak Body 1979, Striptease 1980, Storytelling 1983, Artist on Fire 1987; *Publications include:* Gendering the Nation: Canadian Woman's Cinema (co-ed) 1999, Equity & How to Get It (ed) 1999. *Leisure interests:* cinema, arts, gardening. *Address:* University of Toronto, Cinema Studies, Innis Coll, Toronto, ON M5S 1A1, Canada (Office); 53 Brunswick Ave, Toronto, ON M5S 2L8, Canada (Home). *Telephone:* (416) 978-2011 (Office); (416) 978-8572 (Home); *Fax:* (416) 978-5702 (Office); (416) 978-5503 (Home); *Internet:* www.utoronto.ca/womens/kaybio.htm (Office).

ARMATRADING, Joan; British singer and songwriter; b 9 Dec 1950, Saint Christopher and Nevis (St Kitts); d of Amos Ezekiel Armatrading and Beryl Madge Benjamin. *Career:* Moved to Birmingham, UK 1958; began professional career in collaboration with lyric-writer Pam Nestor 1972; world tour 1995–96; Hon Fellow John Moores Univ, Liverpool; awarded three Silver, 28 Gold and six Platinum Discs. *Recordings include:* Whatever's For Us 1973, Back To The Night 1975, Joan Armatrading 1976, Show Some Emotion 1977, Me, Myself, I 1980, Walk Under Ladders 1981, The Key 1983, Secret Secrets 1985, The Shouting Stage 1988, Hearts and Flowers 1990, The Very Best of 1991, Square the Circle 1992, What's Inside (album) 1995. *Leisure interests:* British comics, vintage cars. *Address:* c/o F. Winter & Co, Ramilies House, 2 Ramilies St, London W1V 1DF, UK.

ARMFIELD, Diana Maxwell, RA, RCA, RWA, RWS; British artist; b 11 June 1920, Ringwood, Hants; d of Joseph Harold and Gertude Mary (née Uttley) Armfield; m Bernard Dunstan 1949; three s. *Education:* Bedales School, Bournemouth Art School, Cen School of Arts and Crafts, Slade School of Fine Art (London). *Career:* Textile and wallpaper designer 1949–65; teacher Byam Shaw School of Art 1959–80; Artist-in-Residence Perth, Australia 1985, Jackson Hole, USA 1989; comms from Reuters 1986–87, HRH The Prince of Wales 1989, Nat Trust 1989, Lancaster Co Museum; mem New English Art Club, Royal W of England Acad, Royal Cambrian Acad; Hon mem Pastel Soc; Consultant to Pocket Art Book series, Leisure Painter (also contrib); Finalist, Hunting Prize 1981, 1982, 1983. *Exhibitions include:* Festival of Britain 1951, Royal Acad (London) 1965–, Tegfryn Art Gallery (Anglesey) 1975, 1978, Browse & Darby (London) 1979–2000, Stremmel Gallery (NV, USA) 1981, Perth 1985, Albany Gallery (Cardiff) 1987, 1989, 1995, Glyn y Weddw (Pwlhelli) 1995, Bala (N Wales) 1996, Royal Cambrian Acad 2001, also USA, Australia and

Netherlands; works included in public collections: Victoria and Albert Museum (Textiles), RWA Talbot Collection, Farringdon Collection, British Museum, Yale Centre for British Art, Govt Picture Collection, Mercury Asset Mgmt Collection, Royal Acad Diploma Collection, HRH Prince of Wales Collection; *Publications:* Painting in Oils, Drawing. *Leisure interests:* music, gardening. *Address:* 10 High Park Rd, Kew, Richmond, Surrey TW9 4BH, UK; Llwynhir, Parc, Bala, Gwynedd, N Wales LL23 7YU, UK. *Telephone:* (20) 8876-6633; *Fax:* (20) 8876-6633.

ARMIJOS, Ana Lucía; Ecuadorean economist and politician; b 13 Oct 1949, Quito. *Education:* Pontifical Catholic Univ of Quito, Univ of Illinois and Univ of Mississippi. *Career:* Co-ordinator of Faculty of Econ, Pontifical Catholic Univ of Quito 1976–80; analyst, Dir of Financial Planning, Cen Bank 1976–80, Dir of Monetary Policy 1980–82, Vice-Chair Monetary Policy 1982–87, Dir of Tech Div 1987–88, Dir 1992–93; Macroeconomist on W African team, World Bank 1990–92; econ advisor to Govt of Sixto Durán Ballén; Pres of Monetary Comm 1993–96; Exec Pres of Asscn of Pvt Banks of Ecuador 1996–97; imprisoned 1997–98; Govt Minister 1998–99, of Finance 1999; arrested in Bogotá 1999; faced five charges 1999. *Publications include:* The Theoretical Considerations of External Debt 1981, Interest Rate Policy in Ecuador, 1979–1980, 1993. *Address:* Junta Monetaria Nacional (National Monetary Board), Quito, Ecuador.

ARMITAGE, Karole; American ballet dancer and choreographer; b 3 March 1954, Madison, WI. *Education:* N Carolina School of the Arts and Univ of Utah. *Career:* Dancer Geneva Opera Ballet (Switzerland) 1972–75, Merce Cunningham Dance Co 1976–80; freelance choreographer, NY 1980–1995, 1999–; Founder and Artistic Dir The Armitage Ballet, New York 1980–90; has choreographed for Paris Opera Ballet Co, Extempory Dance Co (London), Tasmanian Dance Co (Australia), Nureyev's Paris Opera Ballet, Baryshnikov's American Ballet Theatre; Dir MaggioDanza di Firenze (Italy) 1995–98; currently Choreographer-in-Residence Ballet de Lorraine (Nancy, France); Guggenheim Fellow 1986; Chevalier des Arts et des Lettres 1992. *Choreography includes:* Do We Could 1979, Objectstacle 1980, The The 1980, Vertige 1980, Drastic Classism 1981, Slaughter 1982, The Last Gone Dance 1983, Paradise 1983, The Watteau Duets 1985, The South Bank Show 1985, The Mollino Room 1986, The Elizabethan Phrasing of the Late Albert Ayler 1986, The Tarnished Angels 1987, Duck Dance/Crucifixus/Oh My God 1988, Kammerdisco 1988, GoGo Ballerina 1988, Without You I'm Nothing (film) 1989, Contempt 1989, Quickstep 1991, Renegade Dance Wave 1991, Overboard 1991, Segunda Piel 1992, Happy Birthday Rossini 1992, Hall of Mirrors (film, also writer and dir) 1992, Hucksters of the Soul 1993, I Had A Dream 1993, Hovering at the Edge of Chaos 1994, Tattoo and Tutu 1994, The Dog Is Us 1994, The Return of Rasputin 1995, Search and Destroy 1994, The Golden Bowl (film) 2000, Rave 2001; *Music videos include:* Vogue (for Madonna) 1990, Love School (for the Dyvinals) 1990, In The Closet (for Michael Jackson) 1992. *Address:* Armitage Foundation, 3 N Moore St, Suite 4, New York, NY 10013, USA.

ARMSTRONG, Anne Legendre, BA; American politician, company director and diplomatist; b 27 Dec 1927, New Orleans, LA; d of Armant and Olive Legendre; m Tobin Armstrong 1950; three s two d. *Education:* Foxcroft School (Middleburg, VA) and Vassar Coll (NY). *Career:* Republican Nat Cttee-woman from Texas 1968–73, Nat Comm Co-Chair 1971–73; Counsellor (with cabinet rank) to Pres Nixon 1973–74, to Pres Ford 1974; resigned from govt service 1974; Amb to UK 1976–77; Lecturer in Diplomacy Georgetown Univ, Washington, DC 1977; Dir Halliburton, Gen Motors, Boise Cascade, American Express Co, Glaxo Holdings; Chair English-Speaking Union of US 1977–80, Pres's Foreign Intelligence Advisory Bd 1981–90, Texas Women's Alliance 1985–89; Chair Bd of Trustees Center for Strategic and Int Studies, Washington, DC 1987–99, Chair Exec Cttee 1999–; Co-Chair Reagan–Bush Campaign 1980; Chair Texas Women's Alliance 1985–89; mem Bd of Regents, Smithsonian Inst 1978–93; mem Visiting Cttee JFK School of Govt, Harvard Univ, Cambridge, MA 1978–82, Comm on Integrated Long-Term Strategy 1987, Gen Motors Corpn Advisory Council; Trustee American Assocs of RA, of TRUST 1985–, Vice-Chair 1996; Pres Blair House Restoration Fund 1985–91, Nat Thanksgiving Comm 1986–94; Hon LL D (Bristol, UK) 1976, (Washington and Lee) 1976, (Williams Coll) 1977, (St Mary's) 1978,

(Tulane) 1978; Republican Woman of the Year Award 1979; Texan of the Year Award 1981; Texas Women's Hall of Fame 1986; Presidential Medal of Freedom 1987; Golden Plate Award, American Acad of Achievement 1989. *Address:* Armstrong Ranch, Armstrong, TX 78338, USA. *Telephone:* (361) 595-5551 (Office); *Fax:* (361) 595-7050; *E-mail:* armranch@intcomm.net.

ARMSTRONG, Dido; British singer; b 1973, London. *Career:* Entered Guildhall School of Music (London) at age six; toured with brother Rollo's band Faithless; signed solo deal with Arista Records, New York. *Recordings:* No Angel (album). *Address:* c/o Arista, 423 New King's Rd, London, SW6, UK. *Internet:* www.dido.co.uk.

ARMSTRONG, Gillian May, AM; Australian film director; b 18 Dec 1950, Melbourne; m; two d. *Education:* Swinburne Coll of Advanced Educ and Australian Film and Television School (Sydney). *Career:* Screenwriter and Dir 1970–; films presented at Houston, USA, New York, USA, Berlin and Cannes, France Film Festivals; mem Dirs Guild of America, Acad of Motion Picture Arts and Sciences. *Films include:* The Roof Needs Mowing 1970, One Hundred a Day 1973, Gretel 1973, The Singer and the Dancer 1976, My Brilliant Career (Australian Film Inst Award, British Film Critics Award for Best First Feature, Christopher Humanitarian Award) 1978, Starstruck 1982, Mrs Soffel 1984, Hard to Handle, High Tide 1987, Fires Within 1991, The Last Days of Chez Nous 1991, Little Women (Christopher Humanitarian Award) 1995, Oscar and Lucinda 1997; *Documentaries include:* Smokes and Lollies 1975, Not Just a Pretty Face 1983, Fourteen's Good, Eighteen's Better 1983, Having a Go 1983. *Address:* c/o Hilary Linstead Associates Pty Ltd, 87 Pitt St, Redfern, NSW 2016, Australia (Office).

ARMSTRONG, Rt Hon Hilary Jane, PC, B SC; British politician; b 30 Nov 1945; d of Ernest Armstrong and Hannah P. Lamb. *Education:* Monkwearmouth Comprehensive School (Sunderland), West Ham Coll of Tech and Univ of Birmingham. *Career:* Social worker Newcastle City Social Services Dept 1970–73; commmunity worker Southwark Neighbourhood Action Project, Sunderland 1973–75; Lecturer on Community and Youth Work, Sunderland Polytechnic 1975–86; MP (Lab) for Durham NW 1987–; Frontbench Spokesperson on Educ 1988–92, on Treasury Affairs 1994–95; Parl Pvt Sec to Leader of the Opposition 1992–94; Minister of State, Depts of the Environment, Transport and the Regions 1997–2001; Chief Whip 2001–. *Leisure interest:* reading. *Address:* House of Commons, London SW1A 0AA, UK. *Telephone:* (20) 7219-5076.

ARMSTRONG, Karen, MA, M LITT; British writer; b Nov 14 1944, Stourbridg, W Midlands; d of John O. S. Armstrong and Eileen H. Machale. *Education:* Convent of the Holy Child Jesus (Birmingham), St Anne's Coll (Oxford). *Career:* Nun 1962–69; Research Fellow, Bedford Coll, London 1973–76; Head of English, James Allen's Girls' School, London 1976–82; writer and broadcaster 1982–. *Publications:* Through the Narrow Gate 1981, The Gospel According to Woman 1996, Holy War 1988, Muhammad, A Biography of the Prophet 1991, A History of God 1993, Jerusalem: One City, Three Faiths 1996, In the Beginning – A New Interpretation of Genesis 1996. *Leisure interests:* music, theatre, literature. *Address:* c/o Felicity Bryan, 2a North Parade, Banbury Rd, Oxford OX2 6PE, UK. *Telephone:* (1865) 513816; *Fax:* (1865) 310055.

ARMSTRONG, Sheila Ann, FRAM; British opera and concert singer (soprano) (retd); b 13 Aug 1942, Northumberland; d of William Robert and Janet (née Thirlwell) Armstrong; m David E. Cooper 1980 (divorced 1999). *Education:* Hirst Park Girls' School (Ashington) and Royal Acad of Music (London). *Career:* Since 1965 has appeared in opera at Glyndebourne, Scottish Nat Opera, Sadlers Wells, English Nat Opera, Opera North and Royal Opera House (Covent Garden, London) as well as giving recitals around the world with most of the major orchestras; numerous TV appearances; has made extensive recordings; Pres Kathleen Ferrier Soc; Trustee Kathleen Ferrier Award; Mozart Prize 1965, Kathleen Ferrier Memorial Award 1965; Fellow Hatfield Coll, Univ of Durham 1992; Hon MA (Newcastle), Hon D MUS (Durham) 1991. *Leisure interests:* collecting keys, interior decoration and design, flower-arranging, sewing, gardening and garden design. *Address:* Harvesters, Tilford Rd, Hindhead, Surrey GU26 6SQ, UK.

ARMYTAGE, Gee; British jockey (retd); b 10 Sept 1965; d of Roddy and Susan Armytage. *Education:* St Gabriel's School (Newbury, Berks). *Career:* Jr show-jumping champion, winner Hickstead Championships 1980, 1981; leading lady jockey 1985–89; first woman to win major prizes at Cheltenham Festival 1986, 1987; rode in Grand National 1988; freelance National Hunt jockey until 1996, retired Oct 1996; awards include Amateur of the Year, A. T. Cross Award, Lanson Lady of the Month, Daily Telegraph Jockey Award, Piper Champagne Horseman of the Year 1986–87; leading lady jump jockey for five seasons; currently Personal Asst to A. P. McCoy (champion jockey). *Publication:*Gee: The Diary of a National Hunt Jockey 1990. *Leisure interests:* keep fit, squash, skiing, walking the dog. *Address:* Edgeside, East Ilsley, Newbury, Berks RG20 7LJ, UK. *Telephone:* (7970) 375503; *Fax:* (1672) 540 826; *E-mail:* ap.mccoy@talk21.com.

ARNDT, Angelica, BA; Chilean journalist; b 19 Aug 1937, Santiago; d of Eduardo and Eleonora (née Garay) Arndt; m Georges de Bourguignon 1958; two s. *Education:* Dunalastair School (Santiago), Catholic Univ of Santiago and Colegio de Periodistas de Chile. *Career:* Ed El Mercurio, Santiago 1974–76; int relations columnist La Tercera 1976–77; int relations reporter Ercilla 1977–80, Revista Negocios 1980–81, Paula 1980–81, Chilean nat TV 1980–81; Dir, Producer and Ed political and cultural programmes, Chilean Nat TV 1980–83; political interviewer Cosas int magazine 1982–; Research Archive Asst Hoover Inst (Stanford, CA, USA) 1991, 1994; freelance political analyst, interviewer and journalist; contribs to int journals. *Address:* Arnex, Casilia 19039, Correo 19, Lo Castillo, Santiago, Chile.

ARNOLD, Eve; American photographer; b Philadelphia, PA, USA; m Arnold Arnold (divorced); one s. *Education:* New School for Social Research. *Career:* With Magnum Photographic Agency since about 1952; moved to the UK in 1961; produced work for the Sunday Times, Time, Life, etc; worked in the UK, USA, S Africa, People's Repub of China, fmr USSR; has photographed Marilyn Monroe, Joan Crawford, John and Anjelica Huston, Francis Bacon, Yves Montand, Margot Fonteyn, Rudolph Nureyev, Malcolm X, photographs examining the status of women, and numerous other topics; numerous exhibitions including Eve Arnold: In Retrospect, premièred Int Center for Photography, NY, retrospective at Nat Museum of Photography, Bradford 1996. *Publications:* The Unretouched Woman, In China, In America, The Great British, Eve Arnold: In Retrospect 1996. *Address:* c/o Magnum Photographic Agency, Moreland Bldgs, 2nd Floor, 5 Old St, London EC1V 9HL, UK; 26 Mount St, London W1Y 5RB, UK (Home). *Telephone:* (20) 7490-1771.

ARNOLD, Roseanne (see Roseanne).

ARNOTHY, Christine; French writer and journalist; b 20 Nov 1934, Budapest, Hungary; d of Mr and Mrs Kovach de Szendrö; m Claude Bellanger 1964 (died 1978); one s one d. *Education:* Lycée français (Austria) and Univ of Paris (Sorbonne). *Career:* Literary critic Le Parisien Libéré, Paris 1961–, Head Literary Column 1978–; literary column in La Suisse, Geneva, Switzerland 1983–; contribs to other newspapers and magazines; Chevalier de la Légion d'Honneur; Commdr des Arts et des Lettres; Chevalier de l'Ordre Nat du Mérite. *Publications:* J'ai quinze ans et je ne veux pas mourir (autobiog, awarded Grand Prix Vérité) 1954, Dieu est en retard 1955, Il n'est pas si facile de vivre (autobiog) 1957, Le Cardinal prisonnier (Gold Cross of Merit, Hungary 1991) 1962, La Saison des Américains 1964, Le jardin noir 1966, Aviva 1968, Chiche! 1970, Un type merveilleux 1972, Lettre ouverte aux rois nus 1974, Le Cavalier mongol (Grand Prix de la Nouvelle, Acad Française) 1976, J'aime la vie 1976, Le bonheur d'une manière ou d'une autre 1977, Toutes les chances plus une (Prix Interallié) 1980, Jeux de mémoire 1981, Un paradis sur mesure 1983, L'ami de la famille 1984, Les Trouble-fête 1986, Vent Africain (Prix des Maisons de la Presse, Prix Bernanos-Artois, Lacouture) 1989, Une affaire d'héritage 1991, Désert brûlant 1992, Voyage de noces 1994, Une question de chance 1995, La piste africaine 1997, Malins plaisirs 1999, Complot de femmes 2000; Clodomir Free ou le grand complot (cartoon text) 1975; also short stories in numerous magazines, and plays for TV and radio; works have been translated into many languages. *Leisure interests:* swimming, walking, music, friendship. *Address:* c/o Fayard, 75 rue des Saints-Pères, 75278 Paris, Cedex 6, France (Office); 2 rue Pedro Meylan, 1208 Genève, Switzerland (Home).

ARNOUL, Françoise (pseudonym of Françoise Gautsch); French actress; b 9 June 1931, Constantine, Algeria; d of Gen Arnoul Gautsch and Jeanne Gradwohl; m Georges Cravenne (divorced). *Education:* Lycée de Rabat, Lycée Molière (Paris) and Paris Conservatoire. *Career:* Numerous TV appearances, films and plays; Chevalier de la Légion d'Honneur, Officier des Arts et des Lettres. *Films include:* Nous irons à Paris, La maison Bonnadieu, Le désir et l'amour, La plus belle fille du monde, Les compagnons de la nuit, Les amants du Tage, French-Cancan, Des gens sans importance, Thérèse Etienne, La chatte, Asphalte, La bête à l'affût, Le bal des espions, La chatte sort ses griffes, La morte-saison des amours, Le testament d'Orphée, Les Parisiennes, Dimanche de la vie, Le Congrès s'amuse, Españolas en Paris 1970, Van der Valk 1972, Dialogue d'exiles 1975, Dernière sortie avant Roissy 1977, Ronde de Nuit 1984, Nuit Docile 1987, Voir L'Éléphant 1990; numerous TV roles; theatre debut in Les Justes (Camus), Versailles 1966. *Leisure interest:* dancing. *Address:* 53 rue Censier, 75005 Paris, France (Home).

ARON-ROSA, Danièle Sylvie, MD; French professor of medicine; b 15 Oct 1934, Tunis, Tunisia; d of André and Renée (née Valensi) Rosa; m Jean-Jacques Aron 1958; two s. *Education:* Univ of Paris. *Career:* Intern, Paris Hosps 1958, Head of Clinic 1962, Head of Ophthalmology Dept 1972–; Prof Univ of Paris VII 1972–; Chair Fondation A. de Rothschild and Robert Debré Hosp 1974–; Visiting Prof Presbyterian Hosp, New York, USA 1981; Sec-Gen Société Française d'Implants Intraoculaires; mem Int Symposium on Neuroradiology 1964–, American Soc of Intra-Ocular Implants, Bd of American Hosp in Paris; inventor and holder of patents for lasers used in opthalmology 1978–; Fellow Univ of Columbia, New York, USA; Chevalier de la Légion d'Honneur 1983; Paleolopos Award 1982; Grand Prize of Science, Arts and Letters 1985; Innovator Award, ASCRS, USA 1987; Scientific Medical Personality of the Year, Science, Arts and Letters 1989; Honor Award, AAO, USA 1990. *Publications:* Pulsed YAG Laser Surgery 1983, Excimer Lasers Re-refractive Surgery 1985–92; numerous publs on ocular surgery. *Leisure interests:* golf, skiing, sailing, painting. *Address:* 28 ave Raphael, 75016 Paris, France. *Telephone:* (1) 45-25-24-59 (Office); *Fax:* (1) 40-50-04-05 (Office); (1) 40-50-04-05 (Home); *E-mail:* aronrosa@aol.com.

ARQUETTE, Patricia; American actress; b 8 April 1968, New York; d of Lewis and Mardi Arquette; m Nicolas Cage 1995. *Career:* Numerous film and TV appearances; *Films include:* A Nightmare on Elm Street 3 1987, Dream Warriors 1987, Pretty Smart 1987, Far North 1988, Prayer of the Rollerboys 1991, The Indian Runner 1991, Ethan Frome 1993, Trouble Bound 1993, Inside Monkey Zetterland 1993, True Romance 1993, Holy Matrimony 1994, Ed Wood 1994, Beyond Rangoon, Infinity 1995, Flirting with Disaster 1996, Nightwatch 1998, In the Boom Boom Room 1999, Goodbye Lover 1999, Stigmata 1999, Bringing out the Dead 1999, Little Nicky 2000; *Films for TV include:* Daddy 1987, Dillinger 1991, Wildflower 1991, Betrayed by Love 1994, Lost Highway 1996, The Secret Agent 1996, Toby's Story 1998, The Hilo Country 1998. *Address:* c/o UTA, 9560 Wilshire Blvd, 5th Floor, Beverly Hills, CA 90212, USA (Office).

ARQUETTE, Rosanna; American actress; b 10 Aug 1959, New York; d of Lewis and Mardi Arquette; m 1st (divorced); m 2nd James N. Howard (divorced); m 3rd John Sidel 1993. *Career:* Numerous film and TV appearances; f Flower Child Productions. *Films include:* Gorp, Off the Wall, S.O.B., The Aviator, Desperately Seeking Susan, 8 Million Ways to Die, After Hours, Nobody's Tool, The Big Blue, Life Lessons, Black Rainbow 1989, Wendy Cracked a Walnut 1989, Sweet Revenge 1990, Baby, It's You 1990, Flight of the Intruder 1990, The Linguini Incident 1992, Fathers and Sons 1992, Nowhere to Run 1993, Pulp Fiction 1994, Beyond Rangoon 1995, Search and Destroy 1995, Crash 1996, Liar 1997, Gone Fishin' 1997, Buffalo '66 1997, Palmer's Pick Up 1998, I'm Losing You 1998, Homeslice 1998, Floating Away 1998, Hope Floats 1998, Fait Accompli 1998, Sugar Town 1999, Palmer's Pick Up 1999; *TV appearances include:* Harvest Home, The Wall, The Long Way Home, The Executioner's Song, One Cooks, the Other Doesn't, The Parade, Survival Guide, A Family Tree, Promised a Miracle, Sweet Revenge, Separation, Son of the Morning Star, The Wrong Man, Nowhere to Hide, I Know What You Did. *Address:* 8033 West Sunset Blvd, #16, Los Angeles, CA 90046, USA (Office).

ARQUETTE COX, Courtney; American actress; b 15 June 1964, Birmingham AL, d of Richard Lewis and Courteney (Bass-Copland) Cox; m David Arquette 1999. *Career:* Modelling career New York; appeared in Bruce Springsteen music video Dancing in the Dark 1984. *Films include:* Down Twisted 1986, Masters of the Universe 1987, Cocoon: The Return 1988, Mr Destiny 1990, Blue Desert 1990, Shaking the Tree 1992, The Opposite Sex 1993, Ace Ventura, Pet Detective 1994, Scream 1996, Commandments 1996, Scream 2 1997, The Runner 1999, Alien Love Triangle 1999, Scream 3 1999; *Television films include:* Roxanne: The Prize Pulitzer 1989, Till We Meet Again 1989, Curiosity Kills 1990, Morton and Hays 1991, Topper 1992, Sketch Artist II: Hands That See 1995; *TV:* Misfits of Science 1985–86, Family Ties 1987–88, The Trouble with Larry 1993, Friends 1994–. *Address:* c/o Creative Artists Agency, 9830 Wilshire Blvd, Beverly Hills, CA 90212, USA.

ARREDONDO, Fabiola; American business executive. *Education:* Stanford Univ and Harvard Business School. *Career:* Began career as investment banker JP Morgan & Co and Furman Selz Mager Dietz and Birney (NY); fmr Dir of Strategic Planning for USA and Europe, later Vice Pres, BMG Entertainment; fmr Dir of Int Distribution and Dir for Europe, Middle East and Africa, also mem Exec Bd BBC Worldwide; Man Dir Yahoo! Europe; mem US Council on Foreign Relations, Foresight Panel on Information, Communications and Media, UK Dept of Trade and Industry. *Address:* Consejero, Bankinter, Paseo de la Castellana 29, 28046 Madrid, Spain.

ARROWSMITH, Sue Louise, BA, D JUR; British professor of law; b 19 April 1962, Northampton; d of Leonard and Mary Rose Arrowsmith. *Education:* Wimbledon High School, Rosebery School (Epsom) and Univ of Oxford. *Career:* Tutor in Law Univ Coll of Wales, Aberystwyth 1987–88, Lecturer 1988–91, Prof of Law 1991–98; Prof of Law, Univ of Nottingham 1998–; Ed Public Procurement Law Review; Commonwealth Scholarship 1984–87; Gibbs Prize, Univ of Oxford 1982. *Publications:* Government Procurement and Judicial Review 1988, Civil Liability and Public Authorities 1992, A Guide to the Procurement Cases of the Court of Justice 1992, The Law of Public and Utilities Procurement 1996, Regulating Public Procurement: National and International Perspectives (with J. Linarelli and D. Wallace Jr) 2000. *Leisure interests:* triathlon, swimming, cross-country skiing, walking, soccer. *Address:* School of Law, University of Nottingham, University Park, Nottingham, NG12 4ZD, UK. *Telephone:* (115) 951-5072; *E-mail:* sue.arrowsmith@nottingham.ac.uk.

ARROYO, Martina, BA; American opera singer; b New York; d of Demetrio and Lucille (née Washington) Arroyo. *Education:* City Univ of New York, Hunter Coll and Metropolitan Opera (New York). *Career:* Visiting Prof Louisiana State Univ, Baton Rouge; debut Carnegie Hall (New York) 1958; Leading Soprano Metropolitan Opera (New York); appearances at all major US Opera Houses and La Scala (Milan, Italy), Munich Staatsoper and Berlin Deutsche Oper (Germany), Rome Opera, Vienna State Opera, Royal Opera House, Covent Garden (London), Teatro Colon (Argentina) and Edinburgh, Tanglewood, Vienna, Berlin and Helsinki Festivals; has performed with all major orchestras in USA and Europe; recordings for London, Philips, EMI, RCA, Angel and Columbia; fmr mem Nat Endowment of the Arts, Washington, DC; Trustee Carnegie Hall, New York; Outstanding Alumna, Hunter Coll. *Address:* School of Music, IU - Bloomington, Bloomington, IN 47405, USA.

ARTEAGA, Rosalía, PH D; Ecuadorean politician; b 5 Dec 1956, Cuerca; m Pedro Fernández de Córdova 1978; three c. *Career:* fmr Minister of Education; fmr Vice-Pres of Ecuador. *Address:* c/o Office of the President, Quito, Ecuador.

ARTHAUD, Florence Monique; French yachtswoman; b 28 Oct 1957, Boulogne-sur-Seine; d of Jacques and Anne-Marie Arthaud; one d. *Education:* Univ of Paris. *Career:* First in women's section Route du Rhum yacht race (St Malo to Pointe-à-Pitre, Guadeloupe) 1978, 19th 1982, 11th 1986, First 1990; First skipper, women's section of Transatlantic double crossing competition 1978, Sixth 1981; First woman in the world to cross the Atlantic single-handed on a trimaran 1982; came second in trimaran section Québec (Canada) to St Malo competition 1984; came seventh in solo Atlantic crossing 1988; fastest crossing of the Atlantic (solo, on trimaran) 1990; came first in Multicup, Mediterranean 1991; fastest crossing of the Mediterranean under sail 1991; Pres Round the World in 80 Days Asscn and creator Jules Verne Trophy 1990–. *Leisure interest:* skiing. *Address:* 28 rue de la Tour, 75016 Paris, France.

ARTHUR, Beatrice; American actress; b 13 May 1926, New York; d of Philip and Rebecca Frankel; m Gene Saks 1950 (divorced); two s. *Education:* Blackstone Coll and Franklin Inst of Science and Arts, New School of Social Research. *Career:* Mem Actors' Equity Asscn, Screen Actors' Guild. *Plays and musicals include:* Lysistrata 1947, Dog Beneath the Skin 1947, Gas 1947, Yerma 1947, No Exit 1948, The Taming of the Shrew 1948, Six Characters in Search of An Author 1948, The Owl and the Pussycat 1948, Le Bourgeois Gentilhomme 1949, Yes Is for a Very Young Man 1949, Creditors 1949, Heartbreak House 1949, Three Penny Orchestra 1954, 1955, Shoestring Revue 1955, Seventh Heaven 1955, The Ziegfeld Follies 1956, What's the Rush? 1956, Mistress of the Inn 1957, Nature's Way 1957, Ulysses in Nighttown 1958, Chic 1959, Gay Divorcee 1960, A Matter of Position 1962, Fiddler on the Roof 1964, Mame (Best Supporting Actress, Tony Award) 1966; *Films include:* That Kind of Woman 1959, Lovers and Others Strangers 1970, Mame 1974, History of the World Part I 1981, Stranger Things 1995; *TV appearances include:* All in the Family 1971, Maude (Best Actress in a Comedy Series, Emmy Award 1977) 1972–78, The Golden Girls (Best Actress in a Comedy Series, Emmy Award 1988) 1985–92, My First Love 1988, The Beatrice Arthur Special, 30 Years of TV Comedy's Greatest Hits.

ARTMANE, Alida-Vija; Latvian actress; b 21 Aug 1929; d of Fritz and Anna Artmane; m Arturs Dimiters 1954 (died 1986); one s one d. *Education:* Middle school and Theatre Studio. *Career:* Actress Rainis Art Theatre 1949–; has acted in over 64 films and over 100 stage productions; mem Soviet Peace Movt 1975; Vice-Pres Soviet Peace Cttee, Moscow 1979–89; Deputy 1980–90; Pres Latvian Theatre Asscn 1983–87; Order of Lenin; Order of the Red Flag; Actress of the Year 1965, 1969; Prize of the Latvian Repub 1979. *Leisure interests:* knitting, gardening, classical music, theatre, cinema. *Address:* Rainis Art Theatre, Rīga, Latvia (Work); Bruninieku Str 67-9, Rīga 226001, Latvia (Home). *Telephone:* (2) 271700 (Home).

ARTZT, Alice Josephine, BA; American classical guitarist, writer and teacher; b 16 March 1943, Philadelphia, PA; d of Harriett Green and Maurice G. Artzt; m Bruce B. Lawton, Jr. *Education:* Columbia Univ (NY), studied composition with Darius Milhaud and guitar with Julian Bream, Ida Presti and Alexandre Lagoya. *Career:* Guitar teacher Mannes Coll of Music, New York 1966–69, Trenton State Univ 1977–80; world-wide tours 1969–; f (jtly) Alice Artzt Guitar Trio 1989; tours in duo with R. Burley; mem Bd of Dirs Guitar Foundation of America, Chair 1986–89; several Critics' Choice Awards. *Recordings include:* The Glory of the Guitar, Virtuoso Romantic Guitar, Tributes, Variations, Passacaglias and Chaconnes; *Publications:* The Art of Practicing, The International GFA Guitarists' Cookbook (ed), Rhythmic Mastery 1997; numerous articles in guitar and music periodicals. *Leisure interests:* hi-fi, travel, Chaplin movies. *Address:* 51 Hawthorne Avenue, Princeton, NJ 08540, USA. *Telephone:* (609) 921-6629; *Fax:* (609) 924-0091; *E-mail:* guitartzt@aol.com (Office); guitartzt@aol.com (Home).

ARYSTANBEKOVA, Akmaral Khaudarovna, PH D; Kazakhstan politician and diplomatist; b 12 May 1948, Alma-Ata (now Almaty); d of Khaidar Arystanbvekov and Sharbanu Bekmanovna Nurmuhamedova. *Education:* Kazak State Univ. *Career:* Mem Staff Dept of Chem, Kazak State Univ 1975–78; Chief of Dept and Sec Cen State Cttee, Kazak Komsomol 1978–83; mem Supreme Council Kazakstan 1985–90, Praesidium 1987–90; Minister of Foreign Affairs 1989–91; Perm Rep and Amb, Perm Mission of Kazakstan to UN 1992–; Deputy Chair Kazak Friendship Soc 1983–84, Chair 1984–89; numerous contribs to periodicals; Medal of Supreme Soviet of USSR 1970, 1981. *Leisure interests:* classical music, piano. *Address:* Permanent Mission of Kazakhstan to the UN, 866 UN Plaza, Room 586, New York, NY 10017, USA. *Telephone:* (212) 472-5947; *Fax:* (212) 737-6035.

ÅS, Berit, PH D; Norwegian feminist and psychologist; b 10 April 1928, Fredrikstad; d of Knut and Ingebjørg Skarpaas; m Dagfinn Ås 1950; three s one d. *Education:* Trara and Fredrikstad secondary schools,

Stabekk Coll and Univs of Oslo and Michigan (USA). *Career:* Research Fellow Norwegian Research Council 1960–66; teacher Univ of Oslo 1967–, Asst Prof 1982–, Prof 1988–; Visiting Prof USA 1966–67, Canada 1981–87, Sweden 1989–; Nat Female Party Leader Democratic Socialist Party (became Socialist Left Party 1975) 1973, Leader Socialist Left Party 1975; mem Storting (Parl) 1973–81; Chair Feminist Univ Bd 1991; mem Bd Women's World Banking 1988, Community Council 1991, several peace orgs; appeared in biographical Swedish TV show A Woman Who is Big and Strong 1976; Hon D HUM LITT (Mount St Vincent) 1991; Hon D SC D (Copenhagen) 1991; Danish Ingrid Pedersen Prize 1972; Bernardijn Ten Zelden Prize 1988. *Publications include:* Consumer in Modern Society 1966, A Theory on Female Culture 1975, Women of all Countries 1980–83, The 5 Master Suppression Techniques: A Woman's Liberation Theory 1979. *Leisure interests:* women's rights, political activity, patchwork, ice bathing (swimming in very cold water). *Address:* University of Oslo, Inst of Psychology, POB 1094, Blindern, 0317 Oslo, Norway (Office); Jørnstadveien 30, 1360 Nesbru, Norway (Home). *Telephone:* 22-85-55-33 (Office); 22-84-61-65 (Home).

ASHBY, Alison Mary, PH D; British molecular plant pathologist; b 25 April 1964, Staffs; d of Barry and Maureen Ashby; m Andrew John McGlashan Richards 1990. *Education:* Pool Hayes School (Willenhall) and Univs of East Anglia and Durham. *Career:* Research Fellow Jesus Coll, Cambridge 1989–; researching into molecular and biochemical analysis of pathogenicity and sexual devt in fungal plant pathogens; over 20 scientific publs in professional journals including New Scientist Magazine 1986–. *Leisure interests:* walking, sports, food, wine, entertaining, amateur mycology, cats. *Address:* University of Cambridge, Dept of Plant Sciences, Downing St, Cambridge, UK (Office); 26 Aldreth Rd, Haddenham, Ely, Cambs CB6 3PW, UK (Home). *Telephone:* (353) 741211 (Home); *Fax:* (223) 333953 (Office).

ASHCROFT, Frances Mary, PH D, FRS, F MED SCI; British professor of physiology; b 15 Feb 1952; d of John and Kathleen Ashcroft. *Education:* Talbot Heath School, Bournemouth and Girton Coll (Cambridge). *Career:* MRC training fellow in Physiology, Leicester Univ 1978–82; demonstrator in Physiology, Oxford Univ 1982–85, EPA Cephalosporin jr research fellow, Linacre Coll 1983–85, Royal Soc Univ research fellow in Physiology 1985–90, Lecturer in Physiology, Christ Church 1986–87, Trinity Coll 1988–89 (sr research fellow 1992–); Tutorial Fellow in Medicine, St Hilda's Coll 1990–91; Univ Lecturer in Physiology 1990–96, Prof of Physiology 1996–; G. L. Brown Prize Lecturer 1997, Peter Curran Lecturer, Yale Univ 1999; Frank Smart Prize, Cambridge Univ 1974, Andrew Culworth Memorial Prize 1990, G. B. Morgagni Young Investigator Award 1991. *Publications include:* Insulin – Molecular Biology to Pathology (jtly) 1992, Ion Channels and Disease 2000, Life at the Extremes 2000, and numerous articles in scientific journals. *Leisure interests:* reading, walking, writing, sailing. *Address:* University Laboratory of Physiology, Parks Rd, Oxford, OX1 3PT, UK.

ASHER, Jane, RSA; British actress, writer and business executive; b 5 April 1946, London; d of the late Dr Richard A. J. Asher and of Maragret (née Eliot) Asher; m Gerald Scarfe; two s one d. *Education:* North Bridge House School and Miss Lambert's PNEU (London). *Career:* Has appeared in numerous films, on TV and the London stage, and has written several best-selling books; f Jane Asher Party Cakes Shop and Tea Room, London 1990; consultant to J. Sainsbury PLC, McVities 1993; mem BBC Gen Advisory Council, BAFTA; Assoc of RADA; Trustee World Wide Fund for Nature (UK), Child Accident Prevention Trust, Ford Martin Trust for Cancer in Children; Pres Nat Autistic Soc; Most Promising Newcomer to Broadway 1971; Actress of the Year, Sony Radio Awards 1987. *Films include:* Greengage Summer, Masque of the Red Death, Alfie, Deep End, Henry the Eighth and his Six Wives, Success is the Best Revenge, Dreamchild, Paris By Night; *Plays include:* Will You Walk a Little Faster 1960, Cleo, Great Expectations, The Happiest Days of Your Life, Romeo and Juliet 1967, Look Back in Anger 1969, The Philanthropist 1970, Strawberry Fields 1976, To Those Born Later 1976, Whose Life is it Anyway 1978, Henceforward..., School for Scandal 1990, Making it Better 1992, The Shallow End 1997, Things We Do for Love 1998; *TV appearances include:* The Mill on the Floss, Brideshead Revisited, Love is Old, Love is New, Voyage Round My Father, The Mistress, Murder Most Horrid,

Closing Numbers 1993, The Choir 1995, Good Living 1997; *Publications include:* Jane Asher's Party Cakes 1982, Silent Nights for You and Your Baby 1984, Easy Entertaining 1987, The Moppy Stories 1987, Keep Your Baby Safe 1988, Children's Parties 1988, Calendar of Cakes 1989, Eats for Treats 1990, Jane Asher's Complete Book of Cake Decorating Ideas 1993, Round the World Cookbook 1994, Rhymes for All Seasons 1995, Time to Play 1995, The Longing (novel) 1996, 101 Things I wish I'd Known 1996, The Question (novel) 1998, Things We Do for Love (play) 1998, Trying to Get Out 2000. *Leisure interests:* reading, Times crossword. *Address:* c/o ICM, Oxford House, 76 Oxford St, London W1R 1RB, UK; Jane Asher Party Cakes Ltd, 24 Cale St, London SW3 3QU, UK (Office).

ASHER, Lila Oliver; American artist; b 15 Nov 1921, Philadelphia, PA; d of Benjamin and Mollie F. Oliver; m 1st Sydney S. Asher 1946 (deceased); m 2nd Kenneth P. Crawford; one s (deceased) one d. *Education:* Univ of the Arts (PA) and student of Frank B. A. Linton. *Career:* Instructor Wilson Teachers' Coll Washington DC 1953–59; Instructor Howard Univ, Washington DC 1947–51, 1961–64, Asst Prof 1964–66, Assoc Prof 1966–71, Prof 1971–91, Prof Emer; solo exhibitions include Univ of Virginia 1970, 1987, Tokyo 1973, Govt Coll of Arts and Crafts (India) 1974, Turkey 1976, Howard Univ 1978, 1991, Nat Museum of History (China–Taiwan) 1982, Kastrupgårdsamlingen (Denmark) 1982, UCLA 1986, Cosmos Club, Washington DC 1992, Nat Inst of Health Bethesda (Maryland) 1993, 1997, Goldman Gallery, Rockville (Maryland) 1997; represented in major museum collections in USA and abroad. *Major works include:* Art in Washington 1970, American Prints from Wood (Smithsonian Inst) 1975; *TV series:* Montgommery County Md, Lila Ashen Printmaker, Artist 1993 and 1999. *Leisure interests:* crafts, cooking. *Address:* 4100 Thornapple St, Chevy Chase, MD 20815, USA. *Telephone:* (301) 654-3371.

ASHLEY, Grace Ann, B SC, FIEE; Jamaican electrical engineer and business executive; b 23 Sept 1954; d of Wilton S. and Curdelle May Ashley. *Education:* Univ of the West Indies. *Career:* Jr Engineer Jamaica Broadcasting Corpn 1976–77; Lecturer Coll of Arts and Tech 1977–81; Project Supervisor and Design Engineer Y. P. Seaton and Assocs 1981–82; Consulting Engineer ADeB Consultants Ltd 1982–87; Man Dir Edames Engineering Services Ltd 1986–88, Ashley and Assocs Ltd 1988; Dir Jamaica Public Service Co Ltd 1990; Sr mem Soc of Women Engineers; Pres Jamaica Inst of Engineers; Chair Nat Advisory Cttee on Energy Conservation. *Leisure interests:* sport, music. *Address:* 22 Norwood Ave, Kingston 5, Jamaica. *Telephone:* 927-6300 (Office); *Fax:* 927-6229 (Office).

ASHRAWI, Hanan, PH D; Palestinian politician and academic; b 1946; m Emile Ashrawi; two d. *Education:* American Univ of Beirut and Univ of Virginia. *Career:* Fmr Spokesperson Gen Union of Palestinian Students; Prof of English Literature Birzeit Univ (West Bank) 1973–90; Spokesperson for Palestine Liberation Org (PLO) until 1993; mem Advisory Cttee Palestinian Del and Chief Palestinian Spokesperson, Madrid Peace Conf on Middle East 1991; mem Palestinian Independent Comm for Palestinian Repub (fmr Head); Founder, Commr Gen Palestinian Ind Comm for Citizens' Rights 1993–95; mem Palestinian Legis Council 1996–; Minister of Higher Educ 1996–98; currently Human Rights Commr (semi-official ombudsman) Palestine and mem Palestinian Council; Media Dir and Spokesperson Arab League 2001–; activist Palestinian Women's Movt 1974–. *Publications:* A Passion for Peace 1994, This Side of Peace 1995. *Address:* Arab League, POB 11642, Arab League Building, Tahrir Square, Cairo, Egypt; Birzeit University, Dept of English Literature, POB 14, Birzeit, via Israel. *Telephone:* (2) 5750511; *Fax:* (2) 5775726.

ASK, Beatrice; Swedish politician; b 20 April 1956, Sveg; d of the late Sven Ask and Anne Marie Mattson; two s. *Education:* Upper Secondary School (Sveg), Akron (OH, USA) and Uppsala Univ. *Career:* Ombudsman for Youth Section of Moderata Samlingspartiet (MS—Moderate Party) 1975–78, Nat Chair Youth Section 1984–88; Asst Sec to Stockholm City Commr 1982–84; Deputy Mayor of Stockholm 1988–91; Minister for Schools and Adult Educ 1991–94, mem Riksdag (Parl) 1994–, Vice-Chair Standing Cttee on Educ. *Address:* Kungsgatan 75, 112 27 Stockholm, Sweden. *Telephone:* (8) 652 55 69.

ASKONAS, Brigitte Alice, PH D, FRS, F MED SCI; Canadian immunologist; b 1 April 1923; d of the late Charles F. and Rose Askonas. *Education:* McGill Univ (Canada) and Univ of Cambridge. *Career:* Research Student School of Biochemistry, Univ of Cambridge 1949–52; mem staff Immunology Div, Nat Inst for Medical Research 1953–88, Head 1977–88; Dept of Bacteriology and Immunology, Harvard Medical School, USA 1961–62, Basel Inst for Immunology, Switzerland 1971–72; attached to Molecular Immunology Group, Inst of Molecular Medicine, John Radcliffe Hosp, Oxford 1989–; Visiting Prof Dept of Medicine, St Mary's Hosp Medical School, London 1988–95, attached to Dept of Immunology 1992–96; Visiting Prof Dept of Biology, Imperial Coll, London 1995–, Fellow 2000; Hon mem American Soc of Immunology, Société Française d'Immunologie, British Soc of Immunology, German Soc of Immunology; mem EMBO; has published scientific papers in various biochemical and immunological journals and books; Hon D SC (McGill Univ) 1987. *Leisure interests:* art, travel. *Address:* Infection and Immunity Section, Dept of Biology, Imperial College of Science, Technology and Medicine, Sir Alexander Fleming Building, London, SW7 2AZ, UK (Office); 23 Hillside Gardens, London N6 5SU, UK (Home). *Telephone:* (20) 7594-5404/5 (Office); (20) 8348-6792 (Home); *Fax:* (20) 7584-2056; *E-mail:* b.askonas@ic.ac.uk (Office).

ASPIOTOU, Koula; Greek shipping executive; b 19 July 1946, Athens; d of John Aspiotou and Ana (née Beni-Psalti) Seimenis; m Nikitas Harhalakis 1981; two c. *Education:* Univ of Athens. *Career:* Jr Clerk Nat Bank of Greece 1965–69; Asst to Prof of Constitutional Law, Univ of Athens 1969; Asst Vice-Pres, Sr Credit Officer, Bank of America 1969–85; mem Bd of Dirs Seastar Navigation Ltd (London), Seastar Chartering Ltd (Piraeus), and Man Dir Seastar Group of Cos (Athens). *Address:* Seastar Group of Cos, 6 Rizariou St, 15233 Athens, Greece (Office); 1 Kithiron St, 14562 Athens, Greece (Home).

ASSAYESH, Shahin, M PHIL; Iranian publishing executive; b 11 March 1939, Mashhad; d of Zabihollah and Afsaneh Shamlou Assayesh; m Nasser Meh 1959 (divorced 1987); two s. *Education:* Univ of London (UK) and Teheran and Mashhad Univs. *Career:* Secondary School Teacher, Teheran 1964–76; moved to UK 1976, to Canada 1983; f Iranian Women's Quarterly Journal 1986, then Ed and Publisher; Pres Iranian Women's Publications 1991–. *Leisure interests:* reading, swimming, yoga, gardening, travel, volunteer work with Iranian refugees and immigrant women. *Address:* 278 Bloor St, Suite 809, Toronto, ON M4W 3M4, Canada. *Telephone:* (416) 920-5228; *Fax:* (416) 920-2265.

ASTUDILLO LOOR, Lucía, LIC EN HIST; Ecuadorean museum executive and international organization official; b 5 March 1948, Portoviejo; d of Alberto Astudillo and Elisa Loor; m 1st Augustín Cueva 1968 (died 1979); m 2nd Holger Parra 1984. *Education:* Univ of Cuenca, Pontificia Univ Católica del Ecuador (Cuenca) and Smithsonian Inst (Washington, DC, USA). *Career:* Fmr Dir Museum of Folk Arts, Inter-American Centre for Folk Arts and Crafts; organized creation of a Museum of Metallurgy in S Ecuador; Chair ICOM (Ecuador) from 1987; Chair ICOM (Latin America and the Caribbean Region) 1989–92; mem Bd ICOM/CECA; involved in setting up women's museum, Casa Cumbe, and in civic and social welfare campaigns for better health care of women and children; Hon Mention, Nat Short Stories Contest 1974; Third Prize, Nat Short Stories of the Sea Contest 1975. *Publications:* The Museum as a Teaching Device (trans to English and French) 1988; articles on museums in int journals. *Leisure interests:* walking, writing, travel, representing her region. *Address:* Calle Sucre 6-83, Cuenca, Ecuador. *Telephone:* (7) 842333; *Fax:* (7) 831636.

ASYLMURATOVA, Altynai; Kazakhstan ballet dancer; b 1962, Alma-Ata (now Almaty); m Konstantin Zaklinsky; one d. *Education:* Vaganova Ballet School (Leningrad, now St Petersburg). *Career:* Dancer with Kirov (now Mariinsky) Ballet 1980, currently Prima Ballerina; numerous foreign tours including Paris 1982, USA and Canada 1987. *Roles include:* Odette/Odile in Swan Lake Shirin, in Legend of Love, Kitzi in Don Quixote, Aurora in Sleeping Beauty, Nike in Boyaderka, Giselle, A Month in the Country 1991. *Address:* Mariinsky Theatre, Teatralnaya 1, St Petersburg, Russian Federation. *Telephone:* (812) 116-41-64 (Office); (812) 315-57-24 (Home).

ASZYK, Urszula, PH D; Polish professor of languages; b 26 Sept 1944, Jedrzejów, Kielce; d of Feliks and Helena (née Sutor) Aszyk. *Education:* Univ of Łódź. *Career:* Asst Prof of Theory, Literature, Theatre and Cinema, Theatre Dept, Univ of Łódź 1968–74, Adjunct Prof 1974–76; Prof of Polish Language and Literature Univ Autónoma, Madrid 1976–81; Adjunct Prof of Spanish Literature, Univ of Warsaw 1981–87, Dir Section on Spanish Language and Literature, Dept of Iberic Studies 1984–, Prof 1988, 2000–; Adjunct Prof State Univ of New York at Stony Brook 1987–88; Visiting Prof Univ of Mainz (Germany) 1991–92, Univ of São Paulo (Brazil) 1993–, Univ of Stockholm 1996–; Sr Research Fellow Univ of Bristol (UK) 1996–; Prof Univ of Silesia 1998–2000; mem Int Inst of Theater, UNESCO 1981–, Int Asscn of Hispanistas, Polish Asscn Polaca de Hispanistas. *Publications:* Iwo Gall's Theatre Searching (Ministry of Educ and Science Award 1979) 1978, Spanish Contemporary Theatre (Ministry of Culture and Theatre Club awards 1989) 1988, Iwo Gall's Works about Theatre 1993, Entre la crisis y la vanguardia. Estudios sobre el teatro español del siglo XX 1995, Federico García Lorca and the Theatre of his Time (in Polish) 1997, Federico García Lorca, Unfinished Theatre, Open Theatre 1998; numerous contribs to professional journals including articles on Calderon's Theatre and Spanish Golden Age 2000. *Address:* University of Warsaw, Dept of Iberic Studies, ul Obozna 8, 00 332 Warsaw, Poland; 2 Kenton Close, Bracknell RG12 9AZ, UK. *Telephone:* (1344) 429307 (UK); *Fax:* (1344) 302788 (UK); *E-mail:* uaszyk@cs.com; *Internet:* ourworld.compuserve.co.uk.

ATAEVA, Aksoltan Toreevna; Turkmenistan diplomatist, politician and medical practitioner; b 6 Nov 1944, Ashgabat; m Tchary Pirmoukhamedov 1969; one s one d. *Education:* Turkmenistan State Medical Inst (Ashgabat). *Career:* Doctor, Hosp No 1 (Ashgabat) 1968–79, Asst to Chief Dr 1979–80; Vice-Dir Regional Health Dept (Ashgabat) 1980–85; Vice Minister of Health 1985–90, Minister 1990–94; Minister of Social Security 1994–95; Amb Extraordinary and Plenipotentiary, Perm Rep to UN 1995–; mem Democratic Party 1992–, Khalk Maslakhaty (Supreme People's Council of Turkmenistan) 1993–; Pres Trade Unions of Turkmenistan 1994–95; Cand of Science, Soviet Union Scientific Research Inst for Social Hygiene and Health Care Man (Moscow) 1985–89; Hon Assoc of Int Acad of Computer Sciences and Systems (Kiev, Ukraine) 1993; Gairat Medal 1992. *Publications:* 108 publs and 2 monographs on health and maternity care. *Leisure interests:* books, arts, sports. *Address:* Permanent Mission of Turkmenistan to UN, 866 UN Plaza, Suite 424, New York, NY 10017, USA. *Telephone:* (212) 486-8908.

ATANASSOVA, Galina Georgieva; Bulgarian economist; b 25 Aug 1953, Belogradchik; d of Goyu and Maria (née Ivanova) Georgiev; m 1st Plamen Bonev 1976; m 2nd Svetlozar Atanassov 1985; one s one d. *Education:* Inst of Econs (Sofia). *Career:* Vice-Pres Union of Disabled People in Bulgaria 1989–90, Pres 1990–; Pres Courage Foundation 1991–; mem Disabled Section, Bulgarian Fed of Sport 1982. *Leisure interests:* reading science-fiction, cooking. *Address:* Union of the Disabled in Bulgaria, 1000 Sofia, 21 Gavril Genov Str, Bulgaria (Office); Sofia 1373, Suhodolska 2 Str, Bldg 42, A, apt 25, Bulgaria (Home). *Telephone:* (2) 65-84-35 (Office); *Fax:* (2) 65-85-07 (Office).

ATKINS, Eileen, CBE; British actress; b 16 June 1934; d of Arthur Thomas and the late Annie Ellen (née Elkins) Atkins; m 1st Julian Glover 1955 (divorced 1962); m 2nd Bill Shepherd 1978. *Education:* Latymer Grammar School, Edmonton and Guildhall School of Music and Drama (London). *Career:* Appearances include Bristol Old Vic and the Old Vic, Duke of York's and Haymarket Theatres (London), and New York; Co-Creator (with Jean Marsh, qv) TV series Upstairs, Downstairs and The House of Elliot 1991; BAFTA Award 1985. *Plays include:* Twelfth Night 1962, Richard III, The Tempest, The Killing of Sister George (Best Actress, London Evening Standard Awards) 1965, The Cocktail Party 1968, Vivat! Vivat Regina! 1970, Suzanne Adler 1973, As You Like It 1973, St Joan 1977, Passion Play 1981, Medea 1986, The Winter's Tale 1988, A Room of One's Own 1989, The Night of the Iguana 1992, Vita and Virginia 1994, Indiscretions 1995, John Gabriel Borkman 1996, A Delicate Balance 1997 (Evening Standard Award), The Unexpected Man 1998 (Olivier Award); *Films include:* Equus 1974, The Dresser 1984, Let Him Have It 1990, Wolf 1994, Cold Comfort Farm; *TV appearances include:* The Duchess of Malfi, Sons and Lovers, Smiley's People, Nelly's Version, The Burston

Rebellion, Breaking Up, The Vision, Mrs Pankhurst in In My Defence (series) 1990, The Lost Language of Cranes 1992, The Maitlands 1993, Cold Comfort Farm 1995, Talking Heads 2 1998, Madame Bovary 2000; *Radio work includes:* adaptation of To The Lighthouse 2000; *Achievements:* adaptation of Mrs Dalloway (Evening Standard Film Award) 1999. *Address:* c/o Paul Lyon Maris, ICM, Oxford House, 76 Oxford St, London, W1N 0AX, UK (Office).

ATKINSON, Kate, BA; British writer; b 1952, York; m (divorced); two c. *Education:* Univ of Dundee. *Career:* Fmrly home help, teacher and short story writer for women's magazines; writer 1988–. *Publication:* Behind the Scences at the Museum (Whitbread Book of the Year 1996, Boeker Prize, SA, Livre Book of the Year, France) 1995, Human Croquet 1998, Emotionally Weird 2001; *Plays include:* Nice 1996, Abandonment 2000. *Address:* c/o Transworld Publishers Ltd, 61–63 Uxbridge Rd, London W5 5SA, UK.

ATKINSON, Sallyanne, AO, BA, FAIM; Australian public servant; b 23 July 1942; d of C. T. Kerr; m Leigh Atkinson 1964 (divorced 1995); four d one s. *Education:* Royal Naval School (Ceylon), St Hilda's School (Qld) and Univ of Queensland. *Career:* Journalist; Research Asst Ministry of Defence 1975–78; Alderman 1979–82; Leader of Opposition, Brisbane City Council 1983–85; Lord Mayor and Leader Brisbane City Council 1985–91; Chair Sustainable Devt Australia Org 1991; Austrade Sr Trade Commr to France 1994; Dir Australian Elizabethan Theatre Trust; Hon Life mem Nat Trust of Qld; Vice-Pres Australian Commonwealth Games Asscn, Australian Paralympic Fed 1990–93; mem Exec Cttee Int Council for Local Environmental Initiatives (UN); Foundation Chair Australian Olympic Cttees Sports for All Comm; Chair Australian Olympic Sport for All Comm 1990, Drought Fund Co-ordinating Cttee 1993; mem Sydney Organizing Cttee for 2000 Olympics 1993–94; Chair Qld Tourist and Travel Corp 1998; Dir Abigroup Ltd; mem Advisory Bd Fujitsu Australia Ltd. *Publications:* Around Brisbane 1978, Sallyanne Atkinson's Brisbane Guide 1985. *Leisure interests:* reading, walking, theatre. *Address:* Abigroup Ltd, 1st Floor, 25-29 Bridge St, Pymble, NSW 2073, Australia.

ATTAH, Judith Sefi, BA; Nigerian diplomatist and politician; b 14 July 1933, Okene; m Christopher Okigbo 1962 (deceased); three d. *Education:* St Theresa's Coll (Ibadan), Univ Coll, Dublin (Ireland) and Univ of Reading (UK). *Career:* School Prin 1960–63; Chief Women's Educ Officer, N Nigeria 1964–68; Asst Dir of Teacher Educ, Fed Ministry of Educ 1971–76, Dir of Higher Educ 1976–82; Perm Del to UNESCO 1982–86; Perm Sec Fed Ministry of Science and Tech 1986–87; Dir-Gen Ministry of External Affairs 1987–91; apptd Amb to Italy, Greece and Cyprus 1991; fmr Minister of Women's Affairs; Ind mem UN Sub-Comm on Human Rights 1988; Order of the Fed Repub (OFR) 1983. *Leisure interests:* reading, music. *Address:* c/o Ministry of Women's Affairs, Abuja, Nigeria.

ATTRIDGE, Elizabeth Ann Johnston, MA; British civil servant; b 26 Jan 1934, Belfast; d of Rev John Worthington Johnston and Mary Isobel McFadden; m John Attridge 1956; one s. *Education:* Univ of St Andrews. *Career:* Joined Ministry of Educ (Northern Ireland) 1955; joined Ministry of Agric, Fisheries and Food 1956, assisted on Agric Acts 1957 and 1958, Head Plant Health Br 1963–66, Finance 1966–69, External Relations Br (GATT, UNCTAD and EC) 1969–72, Asst Sec Animal Health I 1972–75, Marketing Policy and Potatoes 1975–78, Tropical Foods Div 1978–83, Under-Sec EC Group 1983–85, Emergencies, Food Quality and Pest Control 1985–89, Animal Health Group 1989–91, Under-Sec Agricultural Inputs, Plant Protection and Emergencies Group 1991–94; Sr Clerk/Advisor European Legislation Cttee, House of Commons 1994–98; Chair Int Coffee Council 1982–83. *Leisure interests:* collecting fabrics, opera. *Address:* Croxley East, The Heath, Weybridge, Surrey KT13 0UA, UK. *Telephone:* (1932) 846218; *Fax:* (1932) 846218.

ATWOOD, Margaret, CC, AM, FRSC; Canadian writer; b 18 Nov 1939, Ottawa; m Graeme Gibson; one d. *Education:* Univ of Toronto and Harvard Univ (USA). *Career:* Lecturer Univ of British Columbia 1964–65, Sir George Williams Univ 1967–68, Univ of Alberta 1969–70; Asst Prof York Univ 1971; Writer-in-Residence Univ of Toronto 1972–73, Univ of Alabama (USA) 1985; Berg Prof New York Univ 1986, Macquarie Univ (Australia) 1987, Trinity Univ (TX, USA) 1989;

Berg Prof New York Univ (USA) 1986; Guggenheim Fellow 1981; Hon D LITT (Trent) 1973, (Concordia) 1980, (Smith Coll) 1982, (Toronto) 1983, (Mount Holyoke Coll) 1985, (Waterloo) 1985, (Guelph) 1985, (Victoria Coll) 1987, (Montréal) 1991, (Oxford) 1998; Hon LL D (Queen's) 1974; numerous awards including Bess Hoskins Poetry Prize (USA) 1974, Molson Award 1981, Ms Magazine Woman of the Year 1986, Commonwealth Literary Prize 1987, City of Toronto Book Awards, Coles Book of the Year, Canadian Booksellers Author of the Year 1989, Order of Ontario 1990, Centennial Medal (Harvard Univ) 1990, Govt of ON Trillium Award (with Jane Urquhart, qv) 1993. *Publications include:*Novels: The Edible Woman 1969, Surfacing 1972, Lady Oracle 1976, Dancing Girls 1977, Life Before Man 1979, Bodily Harm 1981, Encounters With the Element Man 1982, Murder in the Dark 1983, Unearthing Suite 1983, The Handmaid's Tale (Gov-Gen's Award) 1985, Cat's Eye (City of Toronto Book Award, Coles Book of the Year, Canadian Booksellers Author of the Year, shortlisted for Booker Prize, UK 1989) 1988, The Robber Bride 1993, Bones and Murder 1995, The Labrador Fiasco 1996, Alias Grace (shortlisted for Booker Prize 1996) 1996, The Blind Assassin 2000 (Booker Prize 2000); Poetry: The Circle Game 1966, The Animals in that Country 1969, The Journals of Susanna Moodie 1970, Procedures for Underground 1970, Power Politics 1971, You Are Happy 1974, Selected Poems 1976, Two Headed Poems 1978, True Stories 1981, Snake Poems 1983, Interlunar 1984, Selected Poems II 1986, Selected Poems 1966–1984 1990, Margaret Atwood Poems 1965–1975 1991, Morning in the Burned House 1995; Short stories: Bluebeard's Egg 1983, Wilderness Tips 1991; Children's Fiction: Up in the Tree 1978, Anna's Pet 1980, For the Birds 1990, Princess Prunella and the Purple Peanut 1995; Non-fiction: Survival: a Thematic Guide to Canadian Literature 1972, Second Words: Selected Critical Prose 1982, The Oxford Book of Canadian Verse in English (ed) 1982, The Oxford Book of Canadian Short Stories in English (ed) 1986, The New Oxford Book of Canadian Short Stories in English 1995; reviews and critical articles. *Address:* c/o McClelland & Stewart, 481 University Avenue, 9th Floor, Toronto, ON M5G 2E9, Canada (Office); Oxford University Press, 70 Wynford Drive, Don Mills, ON M3C 1J9, Canada (Office).

AUBRY, Cécile (pseudonym of Anne-José Madeleine Henriette Bénard); French writer and scriptwriter; b 3 Aug 1928, Paris; d of Lucien and Marguerite (née Candelier) Bénard; m prince Si Brahim El Glaoui 1951 (divorced); one s. *Education:* Lycée Janson-de-Sailly (Paris) and Lycée Jean de la Fontaine (Paris). *Career:* Actress 1948–51; writer and scriptwriter 1961–72; adapted series of children's books (Poly, Sébastien and Le jeune Fabre) into ten series for TV; Officier des Arts et des Lettres 1985. *Publications:* Children's books: Poly 1961, Les vacances de Poly, Poly au Portugal, Poly et le secret des sept étoiles, Belle et Sébastien, Sébastien parmi les hommes, Sébastien et la Mary Morgan, Un été pour Sébastien, Séverine Belle et Sébastien, David et Prisca, Hervé et l'anneau d'émeraude, Hervé au château, Le jeune Fabre; Novels: Je n'avais pas pensé à toi 1977, La Grande Bastide 1979, Le bonheur volé 1982. *Leisure interests:* horse-riding, swimming, ballet, painting, drawing. *Address:* Le Moulin Bleu, 6 chemin du Moulin Bleu, 91410 Saint-Cyr-sous-Dourdan, France. *Telephone:* (1) 64-59-01-06.

AUBRY, Geneviève; Swiss politician and journalist; b 4 March 1928; d of Virgile Moine; m Paul Aubry 1949. *Career:* Fmrly mem Nat Council (Parl); mem Econ Cttee of Interparl Union; Pres World Anti-Communist League 1988–90; mem Albert Einstein Foundation, Nat Swiss Foundation. *Publications:* Jura: le temps des imposteurs, Mon aïeule derrière ses fourneaux, Sous la coupole, pas sous la coupe, toques et politique. *Address:* 4 Niesenweg 3012, Berne, Switzerland.

AUBRY, Martine Louise Marie; French politician, civil servant and business executive; b 8 Aug 1950, Paris; d of Jacques Delors and Marie Lephaille; m Xavier Aubry; one d. *Education:* Inst Saint-Pierre-Fourier, Lycée Paul-Valéry, Univ of Paris, Inst des Sciences Sociales du Travail, Inst d'Etudes Politiques and Ecole Nat d'Admin. *Career:* Civil servant Ministry of Labour 1975–79; Instructor Ecole Nat d'Admin 1978–; Dir of preparations for admin econ competition, Univ of Paris IX (Paris-Dauphine) 1978–; civil servant seconded to Conseil d'Etat (Council of State) 1980–81; Maître des Requêtes (Counsel) 1987; Deputy Dir Cabinet of Minister of Labour 1981, Dir of Labour Relations Ministry of Labour 1984–87, Minister of Labour 1991–93; special assignment for Minister of Social Affairs and Nat Solidarity 1983–84; Deputy Dir-Gen for Labour Relations and Nuclear Affairs, Pechiney group 1989–91; Pres FACE 1993–97; First Asst Mayor of Lille 1995–; Vice-Pres Lille Urban Council 1995–; mem Nat Ass for Nord region 1997– (Socialist Party); Minister of Employment and Social Affairs 1997–; fmr Chair Study Group on European Social Policy. *Publication:* Le Choix d'Agir 1994, Petit dictionnaire pour lutter contre l'extrême droite (jtly) 1995, Il est grand temps… 1997. *Leisure interests:* opera, cooking. *Address:* Ministry of Employment and Social Affairs, 127 rue de Grenelle, 75700 Paris, France; FACE, 91 bis rue du Cherche Midi, 75006 Paris, France; Mairie de Lille, 59001 Lille, France.

AUDERSKA, Halina; Polish writer; b 3 July 1904, Odessa, Ukraine; d of Roman and Helena Auderska. *Education:* Warsaw Univ. *Career:* School teacher 1926–39; underground teaching activity during German occupation, soldier in Home Army, ed Operation 'N', military press corresp in Warsaw Rising 1944; Head Publishing House Trzaska, Evert i Michalski 1946–50; Head Lexicographical Dept, co-ordinator, Deputy Ed-in-Chief Dictionary of Polish Language (11 vols), Polish Acad of Sciences 1950–69; Co-Founder, Sec of Dialog 1956–59; mem Sejm (Parl) 1980–89; Pres Polish Writers' Asscn 1983–86, Hon Pres 1986–; mem Editorial Bd Concise Dictionary of Polish Language 1969, Editoral Cttee Encyclopedia of Warsaw, Polish PEN Club, Nat Council of Culture; awards include The City of Warsaw Prize 1971, Prime Minister Prize 1975, Minister of Culture and Art Prize 1977, Homo Varsoviensis 1986, Meritorious Order for Nat Culture 1986; Commdr's, Officer's and KT's Cross Order of Polonia Restituta, Order of Banner of Labour (1st and 2nd Class), Cross of Valour (twice), Cross of Warsaw Rising. *Publications include:* Novels: Poczwarki wielkiej parady 1935, Jabłko granatu 1971, Ptasi gościniec 1973, Babie Lato 1974, Zwyczajnie człowiek 1980, Miecz Syreny 1980, Smok w herbie: Królowa Bona 1983, Zabic strach 1985; Plays: Zbiegowie 1952, Rzeczpospolita zapłaci 1954, Spotkanie w ciemnościach 1961; Stories: Szmaragdowe oczy 1977, Bratek 1977, Koän, 1985; Memoirs: Pisane okupacyjną nocą in: Akcja 'N' Wspomnienia 1941–1944 1972; Kwartet wokalny (radio plays) 1977. *Leisure interest:* gardening. *Address:* ul Kopernika 11 m 11, 00-359 Warsaw, Poland. *Telephone:* (22) 26-35-14.

AUDRAN, Stéphane (see Colette Dacheville).

AUFFARTH, Susanne; German writer; b 8 Sept 1920, Gr Malchau. *Education:* Secondary school in Uelzen. *Career:* Prizes include Herta-Bläschke Gedächtnispreis (Klagenfurt) 1983 and Edition L. Lyrikpreis (Bayreuth) 1988. *Publications:* Lofoten (poems to Else Winter's watercolours) 1985, Der Knabe mit der Geige (fairy tales) 1989, Unvergessenes Leben (poetry) 1990, Acht Märchen, Vier Erzählungen, Dorfchronik, Zwölf Märchen, Olympias. *Leisure interests:* literature, painting, psychology. *Address:* Gr Malchau, 29597 Stoetze, Germany.

AUGUSZTINOVICS, Maria, D ECON SC; Hungarian professor; b 12 Feb 1930, Budapest; m Gabor Fekecs; one s. *Education:* Budapest Univ of Economics. *Career:* At Ministry of Finance 1955–61; at Nat Planning Bureau 1961–84; Sr Research Adviser, Hungarian Acad of Sciences 1984–86, Prof of Econs 1986–. *Address:* Institute of Economics, Hungarian Academy of Sciences, POB 262, 1502 Budapest, Hungary. *Telephone:* (1) 309-2645 (Office); (23) 344-226 (Home); *Fax:* (1) 319-3136 (Office); (23) 344-226 (Home); *E-mail:* auguszti@econ.core.hu (Office); auguszti@mail.matav.hu (Home).

AULAGNON, Maryse; French civil servant and business executive; b 19 April 1949, Oran, Algeria; d of César and Paule Bettan; m Thierry Aulagnon 1974; one d one s. *Education:* Univs of Montpellier and Paris I (Panthéon), Inst d'Etudes Politiques de Paris and Ecole Nationale d'Administration (ENA). *Career:* Auditor Conseil d'Etat (Council of State) 1975, Maître des Requêtes (Counsel) 1979; Del to Financial Counsellor, Washington, DC (USA) 1979–81; Tech Adviser to Cabinet of the Minister-Del for Econ and Finance 1982–83; Tech Adviser then Rep to Minister of Industry and Research 1983–84; Deputy Dir Compagnie Générale d'Electricité (CGE) 1984, Dir 1985–87; Dir-Gen, mem Bd Compagnie Européenne d'Investissements (EURIS) 1987–90; Pres Affine 1990–, Promaffine 1991–96, Imaffine 1992–; Pres Sovabail 1994–; Pres-Dir-Gen Immobail 1999–; Officier de l'Ordre Nat du Mérite. *Leisure interests:* water-skiing, tennis. *Address:* Affine, 65 rue d'Anjou, 75008 Paris, France.

AULENTI, Gae; Italian architect and designer; b 4 Dec 1927, Palazzolo dello Stella, Udine; d of Aldo Aulenti and Virginia Gioia; one d. *Education:* Milan Polytechnic. *Career:* Mem ed staff Casabella-Continuità review 1955–65; Asst, Venice Faculty of Architecture 1960–62, Milan Faculty of Architecture 1964–67; own architecture, exhibition design, interior design, industrial design, stage design practice, Milan 1956–; solo exhibition, Padiglione d'Arte Contemporanea (PAC), Milan 1979; group exhibition Museum of Modern Art, NY 1972; Hon mem American Soc Interior Designers; Hon Fellow American Inst of Architects; Int Prize for Italian Pavilion, Milan Triennale 1964, Praemium Imperiale for Architecture, Japan Art Asscn, Tokyo 1991; Chevalier de la Légion d'Honneur, Cavaliere di Gran Croce, Rome 1995. *Stage designs:* Elektra, La Scala, Milan 1994, King Lear, Teatro Lirico, Milan 1995, Viaggio a Reims, Rossini Opera Festival, Pesaro 1999; *Major works:* conversion of Gare d'Orsay into museum, Paris 1980–86; interior design of Musée Nat d'Art Moderne, Centre Georges Pompidou, Paris 1982–85; restoration of Palazzo Grassi, Venice 1986; conversion of Palau Nacional into Museu Nacional d'Art de Catalunya, Barcelona 1987–2001; new access ramp to Santa Maria Novella railway station, Florence 1990; Italian Pavilion at EXPO '92, Seville 1992; new gallery for temporary exhibitions at Triennale, Milan 1994; conversion of fmr Leopolda railway station into venue for temp exhibitions, Florence 1996–; conversion of San Francisco Old Main Library into Asian Art Museum 1996–; Spazio Oberdan (new HQ of Nat Film Hall), Milan 1999; renovation of former Papal Stables at Quirinale as temp exhibition gallery, Rome 1999; redevt of Piazza Cadorna, Milan 2000; in progress: extension of Mt Zion Hotel, Jerusalem, renovation of Venaria Royal Palace nr Turin, redevt of Piazza Cavour and Piazza Dante, Naples; *Installations:* Futurism 1986, Renaissance, Venice and the North: crosscurrents in the time of Bellini, Dürer, Titian 1999, and other exhibitions at Palazzo Grassi, Venice, The Italian Metamorphosis 1943–1968, Guggenheim Museum, New York and Kunstmuseum, Wolfsburg, Germany 1994–95; *Industrial design:* furniture, lamps, objects for Kartell, Knoll, Fontana Arte, Louis Vuitton, Tecno, Venini, Zanotta. *Leisure interest:* collecting paintings and sculptures. *Address:* 4 piazza San Marco, 20121 Milan, Italy. *Telephone:* (2) 8692613; *Fax:* (2) 874125; *E-mail:* aulenti@tin.it.

AUNG SAN SUU KYI, B SC S; Myanma politician; b 19 June 1945; d of the late Gen Aung San; m Michael Aris 1972 (died 1999); two s. *Education:* St Francis Convent, Methodist English High School, Lady Shri Ram Coll, Delhi Univ, St Hugh's Coll (Oxford, UK). *Career:* Asst Sec Advisory Cttee on Admin and Budgetary Questions, UN Secr, NY 1969–71; Resident Officer Ministry of Foreign Affairs, Bhutan 1972; Visiting Scholar Kyoto Univ, Japan 1972–74, 1985–86; Fellow Indian Inst of Advanced Studies 1987; returned from UK 1988 and placed under house arrest 1989–95, placed under de facto house arrest Sept 2000; Co-Founder Nat League for Democracy, Leader 1989–91, Gen Sec 1995–; Sakharov Prize 1990, European Parl Human Rights Prize 1991; Nobel Peace Prize 1991; Simón Bolívar Prize 1992, Liberal Int Prize for Freedom 1995, Jawaharlal Nehru Award for Int Understanding 1995, Freedom Award of Int Rescue Cttee 1995; numerous hon degrees. *Publications:* Aung San 1984, Burma and India: some aspects of colonial life under colonialism 1990, Freedom from Fear 1991, Towards a True Refuge 1993, Freedom from Fear and Other Writings 1995. *Address:* c/o National League for Democracy, 97B W Shwegondine Rd, Bahan Township, Yangon, Myanmar.

AURE, Aud Inger, CAND, JUR; Norwegian politician; b 12 Nov 1942, Avcrøy; m; three c. *Career:* Mem Kristiansund Municipal Council 1979–83, Møre og Romsdal Co Council 1984–95, Cen Exec Cttee Women's Org Christian Democratic Party 1982– (Deputy Chair 1986–88, Chair 1988–94); Deputy mem Storting for Møre og Romsdal Co 1985–93, mem 1989–90; mem Standing Cttee on Justice; Regional Employment Officer 1992–95; Mayor of Kristiansund 1995–; mem Cen Exec Cttee Christian Democratic Party 1995–; Minister of Justice 1997–99. *Address:* c/o Ministry of Justice and Police, Akersgt 42, POB 8005 Dep, Oslo, Norway.

AUSTIN, Hon Margaret Elizabeth, B SC; New Zealand politician; b 1 April 1933; d of Thomas and Margaret (née Brady) Leonard; m John Maurice Austin 1955; two d one s. *Education:* Univ of Canterbury. *Career:* Teacher several schools, Christchurch 1954–65; temp lecturer in Science Christchurch Teachers' Coll 1975; Sr Mistress Riccarton High

School 1977–84; Chair Avonhead Br, Yaldhurst Electorate Cttee 1983–84; mem House of Reps (Parl, Lab) for Yaldhurst 1984–, Sr Govt Whip 1987, Chair Educ and Science Select Cttee 1988–89; Minister of Research, Science and Tech, Arts and Culture, Internal Affairs, Civil Defence, Responsible for New Zealand Symphony Orchestra 1990; Shadow Minister of Educ 1990; fmr mem Canterbury Regional Devt Council, Canterbury Medical Research Council; exec mem Life Educ New Zealand; Teaching Fellow Univ of Canterbury 1970; Commonwealth Trust Fellow Inst of Educ, London 1980–81, Trustee Nat Library; mem Council Music Centre, Osteoporosis Soc, International Volunteer Asscn. *Leisure interests:* classical music, walking, theatre, New Zealand flora and bird life. *Address:* Parliament House, Wellington, New Zealand. *Telephone:* (4) 719-117; *Fax:* (4) 724-143.

AUTISSIER, Isabelle; French yachtswoman; b 18 Oct 1956, Paris; d of J. and Marie-Thérèse Schneider. *Education:* Ecole Nat Supérieure Agronomique (Rennes). *Career:* Teacher and Researcher in Agronomy 1978–87; solo yachtswoman in races 1987, 1988, 1989; first woman to complete BOC Challenge solo round-the-world voyage (came sixth) 1990–91; set record New York to San Francisco (USA) 1994; winner first stage of BOC Challenge on Ecureuil Poitou-Charentes II 1994–95. *Publication:* Isabelle Autissier, une solitaire autour du monde (jtly) 1997. *Leisure interests:* flute, reading. *Address:* c/o Seven Seas, 32 rue du Temple, 75004 Paris, France.

AUTRY, Carolyn, MFA; American artist; b 12 Dec 1940, Dubuque, IA; d of William Tilden and Vela Laseman Autry; m Peter Elloian 1966; one d. *Education:* Univ of Iowa. *Career:* Instructor of Art and Art History Baldwin-Wallace Coll 1965–66; Assoc Prof of Art History Univ of Toledo 1966–; Adjunct Instructor of Printmaking Lacoste School of the Arts, France 1987; exhibitions include San Fancisco Museum of Art 1973, Santa Barbara Museum 1975, Ljubljana Int Biennial (Yugoslavia) 1975, 1981, 1987, Biella (Italy) 1976, Visual Arts Centre, Anchorage, AK 1980, American Embassy Cultural Centre (Yugoslavia) 1983, Museu Arte Contemporaneo (Spain) 1984, Inter-Grafik (Germany) 1984, 1987, Seoul and Korean Cultural Service (France) 1989, Barbican Centre (UK) 1989, Fine Arts Assoc Gallery (Vietnam) 1991, Fondation Mona Bismarch (France) 1991, International Impact Art Festival, Kyoto City Museum (Japan) 1990, 1991, 1992, 1993, 1994, Taejon Expo of Graphic Art (Repub of Korea) 1993, Taipei Fine Arts Museum (Taiwan) 1983, 1985, 1987, 1991, 1995, Philadelphia Museum of Art 1997, Hill Country Arts Foundation 1998, 1999, Univ of Hawaii, Hilo 2000, Baton Rouge Gallery 2000; represented in numerous perm collections including Library of Congress; recipient of many awards including Yale-Norfolk Summer School of Art and Music Fellowship 1962, Ford Foundation Grant 1961–64, Ohio Arts Council Grant 1979, 1990. *Address:* 26114 W River Rd, Perrysburg, OH 43551-9786, USA. *Telephone:* (419) 872-9558.

AVERY, Mary Ellen, AB, MD; American physician; b 6 May 1927, NJ; d of William Clarence Avery and Mary Catherine Miller. *Education:* Wheaton Coll (MA) and Johns Hopkins School of Medicine. *Career:* Eudowood Assoc Prof of Paediatrics, Johns Hopkins Univ 1966–69; Prof and Chair of Paediatrics, Faculty of Medicine, McGill Univ, concurrently Physician-in-Chief, Montréal Children's Hosp, Canada 1969–74; Thomas Morgan Rotch Prof of Paediatrics, Harvard Medical School 1974–96, Distinguished Emer Prof 1996–; Physician-in-Chief Children's Hosp, Boston, MA 1974–85; John and Mary Markle Scholar 1961–66; mem Council Inst of Medicine; Dir AAAS; mem NAS 1994–, mem Council 1997–; Pres American Paediatric Soc 1990; numerous hon degrees; Trudeau Medal, American Thoracic Soc, Nat Medal of Science 1991, Marta Philipson Award, Karolinska Inst, Stockholm 1998. *Publications:* The Lung and its Disorders in the Newborn Infant 1981, Born Early 1983, Diseases of the Newborn 1984, Pediatric Medicine 1989. *Address:* Children's Hospital, 221 Longwood Ave, Boston, MA 02115, USA (Office). *Telephone:* (617) 355-8330 (Office); *Fax:* (617) 732-4151 (Office).

AVICE, Edwige, L ÈS L; French politician; b 13 April 1945, Nevers; d of Edmond Bertrand and Hélène Guyot; m Etienne Avice 1970. *Education:* Cours Fénelon (Nevers), Lycée Pothier (Orléans), Univ de Paris, Inst d'Etudes Politiques and Inst du Commerce Int (Paris). *Career:* Mem staff Nat Cttee for Housing Improvement 1970, Int Dept, Crédit Lyonnais 1970–73; worked for Dir-Gen of Paris Hosps 1973–78;

mem Parti Socialiste (PS) 1972, mem Exec Bureau 1977, Nat Secr 1987–94, Nat Del for Nat Service; mem Nat Ass (Parl) 1978–81, 1986–88; Minister-Del for Free Time, Youth and Sports 1981–84, State Sec attached to Minister of Defence 1984–86, attached to the Minister for Foreign Affairs 1988–91, Minister of Co-operation and Devt 1991–93; Paris Councillor 1983–88; Pres Asscn Démocratique des Français de l'Etranger 1991–93, Financière de Brienne 1993–, Brienne Council and Finance 1996–; Pres Econ Defence Council 1999–. *Publication:* Terre d'élection 1993. *Leisure interests:* travel, music, swimming, walking, fencing. *Address:* Financière de Brienne, 2 place Rio de Janeiro, 75008 Paris, France (Office).

AVRAMOV, Smilja, PH D; Yugoslav (Serbian) lawyer; b 15 Feb 1918, Pakrac; d of Mihailo and Danica Blagojević; m Dušan Avramov 1939; two d. *Education:* Zagreb, Belgrade, Vienna, Paris, London and New York. *Career:* Legal Adviser to Attorney-Gen 1945–49; Asst Prof, Faculty of Law, Belgrade Univ 1949–55, then Lecturer in Int Law, Prof of Int Law 1960–87; Ed Medj javno pravo 1958–96; Dositej Obradović 1994. *Publications:* Revizija medj ugovora 1956, Kontrola spolj politike 1987, Genocid v Jugoslaviji 1991. *Leisure interest:* piano. *Address:* 11000 Belgrade, Sv Save 22a, Yugoslavia. *Telephone:* (11) 434-329.

AW SIAN, Sally; Hong Kong business executive; b 1931, Rangoon, Burma (now Myanmar). *Career:* Joined Sing Tao 1952, Chair 1957–, published first overseas edn of Sing Tao (Chinese language newspaper), San Francisco, CA, USA 1969, publishes newspaper in six cities in the USA, in London, Sydney, and Wellington, publishes Singguang Monthly magazine, in collaboration with People's Daily (People's Repub of China newspaper) 1992–, South China Economic Daily (business newspaper) 1993–. *Address:* Sing Tao Bldg, 3rd Floor, Wang Kwong Rd, Kowloon Bay, Kowloon, Hong Kong. *Telephone:* 27982575; *Fax:* 27953022.

AYCOCK, Alice, MA; American artist; b 1946 Harrisburg, PA; d of Jesse N. and Alyce F. (née Haskins) Alcock; one s. *Education:* Douglas Coll (New Brunswick, NJ) and Hunter Coll (New York). *Career:* Artist-in-Residence Williams Coll, MA 1974; Visiting Sculptor and teacher Rhode Island School of Design 1977, School of Visual Arts, NY 1977–78, 1979–82, Princeton Univ, NJ 1979, San Francisco Art Inst, CA 1979; Fine Arts Instructor School of Visual Arts, Yale Univ 1977–82, 1991–92, Sr Critic 1988–90, Dir of Grad Sculpture Studies 1991–92; Asst Prof Hunter Coll, NY 1982–85; Teaching Residency Kansas City Art Inst 1987, Atlantic Centre for the Arts, FL 1989, Ecole Nat Supérieure des Beaux-Arts (Paris); numerous lectures 1979–; one-woman and group exhibitions in USA, Europe and Japan 1974–, including Sun/Glass 1971, Studies For A Town 1977, Studies in Mesmerism 1979, The Game of Flyers 1980, The Nets of Solomon Phase II 1983, The Chart of Magnetic Forces 1985, The Tower of Babel 1986, Universe Wheel 1988, Concrete Water Works 1989, Fantasy Sculpture II 1990, project at New 107th Police Precinct, New York 1992, project at Medical Center, Univ of Nebraska 1993; awards include Nat Endowment for the Arts Fellowship 1975, 1976, 1980, 1986, La Fondation Cartier (residency) 1991. *Address:* John Weber Gallery, 142 Greene St, New York, NY 10012-3236, USA.

AYOT, Theodora Olunga, PH D; Kenyan lecturer in history; b 7 Jan 1946, Rusinga Island; d of Kiliopa and Priscila Orwa; m Henry Okello Ayot; two d two s. *Education:* Union Endicott High School (Endicott, NY, USA), Hiram Coll (OH, USA), Univ of Nairobi, Georgetown Univ (Washington, DC, USA) and Kenyatta Univ. *Career:* History Teacher various Kenyan high schools 1970–80; Sr Lecturer Kenya Polytechnic 1980–85; Lecturer Dept of History, Kenyatta Univ 1986–; Prin Researcher Women's Studies Project, Inst of African Studies, Univ of Nairobi 1989–; US AID Scholarship Award 1979–80; Ford Foundation Scholarship 1981–82. *Publications include:* The Luo Settlement in South Nyanza District 1987, A History of the Luo of Western Kenya 1590–1930 1987, The Position of Women in the Luo Societies, Case Study of Jok'Onyango 1750–1920. *Leisure interests:* reading, classical music, travel. *Address:* Kenyatta University, Dept of History, POB 43844, Nairobi, Kenya (Office); POB 21144, Nairobi, Kenya (Home). *Telephone:* (2) 567834.

AYRES, Gillian, OBE, ARA; British artist; b 3 Feb 1930; d of Stephen and Florence Ayres; m Henry Mundy (divorced); two s. *Education:* St Paul's Girls' School and Camberwell School of Art. *Career:* Art teacher 1959–81; Sr Lecturer St Martin's School of Art and Head of Painting Winchester School of Art 1978–81; Sr Fellow Royal Coll of Art 1996; fmr RA, London, resgnd 1997, rejoined 2000; One-woman exhibitions include Gallery One 1956, Redfern Gallery 1958, Moulton Gallery 1960, 1962, Kasmin Gallery 1965, 1966, 1969, William Darby Gallery 1976, Women's Int Centre (New York, USA) 1976, Knoedler Gallery 1979, 1982, 1987, Museum of Modern Art (Oxford) 1981, Sackler Gallery at Royal Acad, London 1997; retrospective exhibition Serpentine Gallery 1983; works have also appeared in group exhibitions in London, New York and Paris, and in public collections at Tate Gallery (London), Museum of Modern Art (New York) and Gulbenkian Foundation (Lisbon); Hon D LITT (London); prizewinner, Tokyo Biennale 1963, Major Arts Council Bursary 1979; Charles A. Wolaston RA Award 1989; Gold Medal, Indian Triennale 1991. *Leisure interest:* wildlife and nature conservation. *Address:* c/o Gimpel Fils Gallery, 30 Davies St, London, W1, UK (Office); Tall Trees, Gooseham, near Bude, Cornwall, UK. *Telephone:* (1288) 83206.

AYRES, Pamela; British writer and broadcaster; b 19 March 1947; d of Stanley William Ayres and Phyllis Evelyn Loder; m Dudley Russell 1982; two s. *Education:* Faringdon Secondary Modern School (Berks). *Career:* Served Women's RAF 1965–69; writer and performer. *TV:* Opportunity Knocks 1975, The World of Pam Ayres 1977, numerous specials in UK, Hong Kong and Canada; *Radio:* Pam Ayres Radio Show 1995, Pam Ayres on Sunday 1996–99; *Publications include:* Some of Me Poetry 1976, Some More of Me Poetry 1976, Thoughts of a Late-Night Knitter 1978, All Pam's Poems 1978, Bertha and the Racing Pigeon 1979, The Ballad of Bill Spinks' Bedstead and Other Poems 1981, Dear Mum 1985, Guess Who? 1987, Guess What? 1987, When Dad fills in the Garden Pond 1988, When Dad cuts down the Chestnut Tree 1988, Piggo and the Nosebag 1990, Piggo has a Train Ride 1990, The Bear who was Left Behind 1991, Pam Ayres: The Works 1992, Guess Why? 1994, With These Hands: a Collection of Work 1997, The Nubbler 1997. *Leisure interests:* gardening, bee-keeping, drawing wildlife. *Address:* POB 64, Cirencester GL7 5YD, UK. *Telephone:* (1285) 644622.

AZIZ, Paduka Rafidah, M ECONS; Malaysian politician; b 4 Nov 1943, Selama Perak; m Mohammed Basir bin Ahmad; three c. *Education:* Univ of Malaya. *Career:* Tutor, Asst Lecturer, Lecturer and Chair Rural Devt Div, Faculty of Econs, Univ of Malaya 1966–76; mem Parl 1978–; Deputy Minister of Finance 1977–80; Minister of Public Enterprise 1980–88, of Int Trade and Industry March 1988–; mem UMNO Supreme Council 1975–; holds many other public offices and del to numerous int confs; Ahli Mangku Negara, Datuk Paduka Mahkota Selangor. *Leisure interests:* reading, decoration, music, squash. *Address:* Ministry of Trade and Industry, Block 10, Govt Offices Complex, Jalan Duta, 50622 Kuala Lumpur, Malaysia. *Telephone:* (3) 6510033; *Fax:* (3) 6512306; *E-mail:* mitiweb@miti.gov.my; *Internet:* www.miti.gov.my.

AZIZAH, Wan Ismail; Malaysian politician and surgeon; b 1952; m Datuk Seri Anwar Ibrahim; six c. *Education:* St Nicholas Convent (Alor Setar), Tunku Kurshiah Coll (Negeri Sembilan) and Royal Coll of Surgeons & Physicians (Ireland). *Career:* Ophthalmologist and Lecturer Univ Hosp Malaya (Kuala Lumpur); Founder and Leader Parti Keadilan Nasional (PKN, Nat Justice Party) 1999–; MP (Permatang Pauh) 1999–. *Address:* Parti Keadilan Nasional, Menaro Dato' Onn, 38th Floor, Jalan Tun, 50480 Kuala Lumpur, Malaysia.

AZMI, Shabana, BA; Indian actress and politician; b 18 Sept 1950, Hyderabad; d of Kaifi and Shaukat Kaifi Azmi; m Javed Akhtar 1984. *Education:* St Xavier's Coll (Bombay) and Film Inst, Pune. *Career:* Pres Jury Montréal Film Festival (Canada) 1990; Retrospectives of films held in Washington, DC (USA), Paris and Nantes (France) and Oslo; fmrly Chair Children's Film Soc of India, Anti-Dowry Cttee; Jt Convenor Rights of Slum Dwellers of Bombay; mem Nat Integration Council; Pres Cairo Film Festival 1995; mem Rajya Sabha 1997; speaker on women's rights and communication in USA; active campaigner on social justice issues; Chair Nivara Hakk Suraksha Samiti (campaigning org for upgrading of slum dwellings); mem Nat Integration Council, Advisory Council Endowment Campaign for Chair in Indian Studies, Columbia Univ; numerous awards for films including Best Actress, Filmfare Award, BFJA Award and Gold Medal for Best Student (Film Inst of India) 1973, Soviet Land Nehru Award 1985, Padma Shri (Govt of India) 1988, Int Human Rights Award (presented by Pres Mitterrand, France) 1989, Rajiv Gandhi Award for Excellence in Secularism 1994, Yash Bhartiya Award for promoting women's issues, Govt of Uttar Pradesh. *Films include:* Ankur (Nat Award Best Actress) 1974, Shatranj ke Khiladi 1976, Arth (Nat Award) 1983, Mandi 1983, Paar (Nat Award) 1985, Khandar (Nat Award) 1984, Madame Sousatzka 1988, City of Joy 1992, Libaas (Int Best Actress Award, N Korea 1993), Patang (Best Actress Award, Taormina Art Festival 1994), Swami, Bhavna (Filmfare Award), Junoon, Shatranj Ke Khilan, Parinay, Amardeep, Sparsh, Massom, Doosri Dulhan, Madame Sousatzka, Bengali Night, In Custody, The Journey, Son of the Pink Panther, City of Joy, Fire (Best Actress Award, Chicago Int Film Festival) 1996. *Leisure interests:* reading, singing. *Address:* 23 Ashoka Rd, New Delhi, 110001, India (Office); 702 Sagar Samrat, Green Fields, Juhu, Mumbai 400049, India (Home). *Telephone:* (11) 3366874 (Office); (22) 6200066 (Home); *Fax:* (11) 3347017 (Office); *E-mail:* shabana@bom3.vsnl.net .in.

B

BABBITT, Harriet, JD; American diplomatist; b 13 Nov 1947, Charleston, WV; d of Henry B. Coons, II and Harriet Edmunds Coons; m Bruce Edward Babbitt; two s. *Education:* Arizona State Univ. *Career:* Dir Nat Democratic Inst for Int Affairs 1988–93; Amb and Perm Rep of USA to OAS 1993, Chair OAS Cttee monitoring embargo against Haiti 1993–94, Special Co-ordinating Cttee, Summit of the Americas, Implementation of Initiatives of 1994 meeting in Miami, FL. *Leisure interests:* back-packing, skiing. *Address:* Department of State, ARA/USOAS, 2201 C St, NW, Washington, DC 20520-6263, USA. *Telephone:* (202) 647-9430; *Fax:* (202) 647-0911.

BABI, Parveen, BA; Indian actress and interior decorator; b 4 April 1954, Junagiarh; d of Valimohamad Khan and Jamalbakht Babi. *Education:* St Xavier's Coll (Ahmedabad). *Career:* Fashion model 1972–73; actress 1973–83; has appeared in 60 feature films and received several awards; interior designer and decorator 1991–; numerous contribs to newspapers and magazines 1973–92. *Leisure interests:* music, piano, painting, architecture, literature, writing, cultural and archaeological study, politics, photography, sculpture, human rights issues. *Address:* 702 Riviera, Giandhigiram Rd, Juhu, Mumbai 400049, India. *Telephone:* (22) 6200075.

BABOOLAL, Linda; Trinidad and Tobago politician. *Career:* Minister of Social Welfare and Consumer Affairs 1991–95, of Health 1996; Chair Gen Council People's Nat Movt Party 1997–. *Address:* People's National Movement, 1 Tranquility St, Port of Spain, Trinidad and Tobago. *Telephone:* 625-1533; *E-mail:* pnm@carib-link.net; *Internet:* www.pnm.org.tt.

BACA, Susana; Peruvian popular singer; b Chortillos, Lima; m Ricardo Pereira. *Career:* Formed experimental group combining poetry and song; took part in Int Agua Dulce Festival, Lima; with husband f Instituto Negrocontinuo; first US performance in Brooklyn 1995; one US and six European tours. *Albums include:* Susana Baca 1997, Del Fuego y del Agua 1999, Eco de Sombras 2000; *Publication:* The Cultural Importance of Black Peruvians (co-author with Richard Pereira) 1992. *Address:* c/o Iris Musique, 5 Passage St Sebastien, 75011 Paris, France.

BACALL, Lauren (pseudonym of Betty Joan Perske); American actress; b 16 Sept 1924; m 1st Humphrey Bogart 1945 (died 1957); one s one d; m 2nd Jason Robards 1961 (divorced 1969); one s. *Career:* Fmr model; Commdr des Arts et des Lettres 1995. *Films include:* To Have and Have Not 1944, Confidential Agent 1945, The Big Sleep 1946, Two Guys from Milwaukee 1946, Dark Passage 1947, Key Largo 1948, Young Man with a Horn 1950, Bright Leaf 1950, How to Marry a Millionaire 1953, Woman's World 1954, The Cobweb 1955, Blood Alley 1955, Written on the Wind 1956, Designing Woman 1957, The Gift of Love 1958, Flame over India 1959, Sex and the Single Girl 1964, Shock Treatment 1964, Harper 1966, Murder on the Orient Express 1974, The Shootist 1976, Health 1980, The Fan 1981, Appointment with Death 1988, Mr North 1988, Tree of Hands 1989, A Star for Two 1990, Misery 1990, All I Want for Christmas 1991, A Foreign Field, The Portrait, Prêt à Porter 1995, The Mirror has Two Faces, Le jour et la nuit 1996; *Plays:* Goodbye Charlie 1960, Cactus Flower 1966, Applause! (Tony Award, Best Actress in a Musical) 1970, Wonderful Town 1977, Woman of the Year (Tony Award) 1981, Sweet Bird of Youth 1985, The Visit 1995, Waiting in the Wings; *TV appearances include:* The Petrified Forest 1955, Applause! 1973, The Rockford Files, Perfect Gentleman 1977, A Little Piece of Sunshine 1989, Dinner At Eight 1990, Painting Churches 1992; *Publications:* Lauren Bacall By Myself (Nat Book Award 1980) 1979, Lauren Bacall Now 1994.

Address: c/o Johnnie Planco, William Morris Agency, 1325 Ave of the Americas, New York, NY 10019, USA (Agent); Dakota, Central Park W, New York, NY, USA (Home).

BACHMANN-ARNOLD, Ulrike; German pianist and music teacher; b 14 June 1961. *Education:* Musikhochschule (Lübeck). *Career:* Concert pianist in duo with Silvia Zenker (qv) 1984–89; has given concerts in Germany and abroad, and performances on radio and TV; numerous recordings of works for piano (duets); First Prize in Music, Possehlstiftung Lübeck 1984; Hansekulturpreis, Stadt Lübeck 1987; First Prize Int Piano Duet Competition, Italy 1988. *Leisure interests:* literature, sport. *Address:* Zaunkönigsweg 1, 55765 Birkenfeld, Germany.

BACON, Jennifer Helen, CB, BA; British civil servant; b 16 April 1945, Birmingham; d of the late L. J. and Joyce Bacon. *Education:* New Hall (Cambridge). *Career:* Mem staff Ministry of Labour 1967–86, Prin Pvt Sec to Sec of State 1978–91, Dept of Employment and Manpower Services Comm 1981–82; mem staff Department of Educ, Nat Curriculum Assessment Legislation 1986–89; Prin Finance Officer then Dir of Resources and Strategy, Dept of Employment 1989–92; Deputy Dir-Gen Health and Safety Exec 1992–95, Dir-Gen 1995–; Visiting Fellow Nuffield Coll, Oxford 1989. *Leisure interests:* classical music, travel, walking. *Address:* Health and Safety Executive, Rose Court, 2 Southwark Bridge, London SE1, UK; 87 Northchurch Rd, London N1 3NU, UK (Home). *Telephone:* (20) 7717-6633 (Office); *Fax:* (20) 7717-6616 (Office).

BADAWI, Zeinab Mohammed-Khair, MA; Sudanese broadcaster and journalist; b 3 Oct 1959, Sudan; d of Mohammed-Khair el Badawi and Asia Malik; m David Crook 1991; two d one s. *Education:* Hornsey School for Girls, St Hilda's Coll (Oxford) and Univ of London. *Career:* TV researcher, reporter and presenter; journalist and presenter Yorkshire TV 1982–86, reporter BBC TV 1986–87, news presenter ITN (Independent TV News) 1988–, Channel 4 News 1989, BBC World Service 2001–; mem Advisory Council Foreign Policy Centre 1988–; Vice-Pres UN Int Asscn; mem Panel 2000. *Leisure interests:* languages, opera, yoga, reading. *Address:* BBC World Service, Bush House, Strand, London WC2B 4PH, UK (Office). *Telephone:* (20) 7240-3456 (Office); *Fax:* (20) 7557-1258 (Office); *E-mail:* worldservice.letters@bbc.co.uk (Office).

BADDOUR, Anne Bridge; American pilot; b 1930, Royal Oak, MI; d of William George and Esther Rose (née Pfiester) Bridge; m Raymond F. Baddour 1954; two d one s. *Education:* Detroit Business School (MI). *Career:* Air stewardess, Boston, MA 1952–54; Instructor Aeronautics Powers School, Boston 1958; Co-pilot and flight attendant Raytheon Co, Bedford, MA 1958–63; Flight Dispatcher, Ferry Pilot Comerford Flight School, Bedford 1974–76; Admin Asst, Ferry Pilot Jenney Beachcraft, Bedford 1976; Man, Pilot Baltimore Airways Inc, Bedford 1976–77; Pilot Lincoln Lab Flight Test Facility, MIT 1977–97; Aviation Consultant and Corpn Pilot Energy Resources Inc, Cambridge, MA 1974–84; Commr Commonwealth of Massachusetts, Massachusetts Aeronautics Comm; Chair Regional Council, Fed Aviation Admin 1984–88; holder World Class Speed Records for single-engine aircraft (all in 1985) Boston–Goose Bay (Canada), Boston–Reykjavík (Iceland), Portland (ME)–Goose Bay, Portland (ME)–Reykjavík, Goose Bay–Reykjavík, Records for twin-engine aircraft (1988) Sept Isles (Canada)–Goose Bay, Mont Joll–Goose Bay, Presque Isle–Goose Bay, Millinocket–Goose Bay, Bedford–Goose Bay, Goose Bay–Narssassrag (Greenland), Narssassrag–Klevelevic (Iceland), Narssassrag – Reykjavík, Bedford–Narssassrag, Millinochet–Narssassrag, Presque Isle–Narssassrag, (1991) Bedford–St John, Bedford–Charlottetown,

Charlottetown–Kennebunk, Charlottetown–Portsmouth, Muncton – Bedford, St John–Kennebunk, St John–Bedford; Winner Pennsylvania Transcontinental Air Race 1954, New England Air Race 1957; Clifford B. Harmon Trophy Int Aviatrix 1988; Special Recognition Award, Fed Aviation Admin 1990; Hon Int Aviation Forest of Friendship, Atchison, KS 1991; Pilot of the Year, New England section, Int Women Pilots Org/The Ninety-Nines Inc 1992. *Address:* c/o MIT, Lincoln Lab, 224 Wood St, Lexington, MA 02173-6499, USA (Office); 96 Fletcher Rd, Belmont, MA 02178, USA (Home).

BAEZ, Joan Chandos; American folk singer; b 9 Jan 1941, Staten Island, NY; d of Albert V. and Joan (née Bridge) Baez; m David Harris 1968 (divorced 1973); one s. *Education:* School of Fine and Applied Arts, Boston Univ. *Career:* Began career as singer in coffee-houses; appeared at Ballad Room, Club 47 1958–68, Gate of Horn, Chicago 1958, Newport Folk Festival, RI 1959–69, Town Hall and Carnegie Hall, New York 1962, 1967, 1968; gave concerts in colls in S USA 1963; toured Europe and USA 1960s–, Vietnam 1972, Australia 1985; began refusing payment of war taxes 1964, detained for civil disobedience opposing conscription 1967, speaking tour of USA and Canada for draft resistance 1967–68; Founder, Vice-Pres Inst for Study of Non-Violence (now Resource Center for Non-Violence) 1965, Humanitas Int Human Rights Comm 1979–92; mem Nat Advisory Council Amnesty Int 1974–; many TV appearances; recordings with Vanguard Records 1960–72, A & M Record Co 1972–76, Portrait Records 1977–80, Gold Castle Records 1987–89, Virgin Records 1990–93, Guardian Records 1995–, Grapevine Label Records 1995–; Founder, Vice-Pres Inst for Study of Non-Violence (now called Resource Center for Non-violence) 1965; f Humanitas Int Human Rights Comm 1979–92; Dr hc (Rutgers, Antioch Univ); awarded eight gold albums, one gold single, three Bay Area Music (BAMMY) Awards 1978, 1979, 1996; Gandhi Memorial Int Foundation Award 1988; Chevalier de la Légion d'Honneur. *Publications include:* Joan Baez Songbook 1964, Daybreak 1968, Coming Out (with David Harris) 1971, And then I wrote... (songbook) 1979, And a Voice to Sing With 1987; *Albums include:* Rare, Live and Classic 1993, Gone From Danger 1997. *Address:* Diamonds and Rust Productions, POB 1026, Menlo Park, CA 94026, USA. *Telephone:* (650) 328-0266; *Internet:* www.joanbaez.com.

BAGLANOVA, Rosa; Kazakhstan actress; b 1 Jan 1927, Kazalinsk, Kzil-Orda Dist; m Zhadbayev Satibaldy Hierushevich; one s. *Education:* Kazakh State Conservatoire and Opera Studio (Alma). *Career:* Active in World War II 1941–45; now actress; Pres Moslem Women's League, Traditions of Centuries Union; Chair Int Cttee for People's Rules, Cttee for Disabled Workers and Soldiers; Medal for Service in Battle, Warsaw, Poland 1945; Order of Lenin 1958; Order of Labour Red Banner 1970; Order of Friendship 1982; People's Artist of the USSR. *Leisure interests:* cooking, reading. *Address:* 480064 Alma, Rm 23, 165 Furmanov Str, Kazakhstan. *Telephone:* (327) 69-66-24; *Fax:* (327) 24-86-33.

BAHL, Kamlesh, CBE, LL B, FRSA; British solicitor and administrator; b 28 May 1956, Kenya; d of the late Swinder Nath and of Leela Wati Bahl; m Nitin Lakhani 1986. *Education:* Univ of Birmingham. *Career:* Solicitor GLC 1978–81, British Steel Corpn 1981–84, Texaco 1984–87; Co Sec and Man Legal Services Data Logic Ltd 1987–93; Chair Equal Opportunities Comm 1993–98; Chair Law Soc, Commerce and Industry Group 1988–89, mem Law Soc Council 1990, Deputy Vice-Pres 1998–99, Vice-Pres 1999–2000; Non-Exec Dir Parkside Health Authority 1990–93; mem Justice Sub-Cttee on Judiciary 1991–92, Ethnic Minorities Advisory Cttee and Tribunals Cttee 1991–94, Council and Standing Cttee on Health Authorities, Nat Asscn of Health Authorities and Trusts 1993–94, Council of Justice 1993–94; independent mem Diplomatic Service Appeal Bd, FCO 1993–; EC Rep EC Consultative Comm on Racism and Xenophobia 1994–; Hon MA (N London) 1997, Hon LL D (De Montfort) 1998, Dr hc (Birmingham) 1999. *Publication:* Managing Legal Practice in Business (ed) 1989. *Leisure interests:* travelling, swimming, theatre, fund-raising for charity. *Address:* The Law Society, 113 Chancery Lane, London WC2A 1PL, UK.

BAHL-DHALL, Sudesh, MD, FRCOG, FRCSE; Indian medical practitioner; b 10 Feb, Peshawar; d of A. R. Dhall; m R. K. Bahl 1965; two s. *Education:* Elizabeth High School (Peshawar), Isabella Thoburn Coll (Lucknow) and Lady Harding Medical Coll (Delhi). *Career:* Mem staff Obstetrics and Gynaecology Dept, Hadinge Hosp 1956–57, Surgery Dept Safdaiping Hosp 1957–58; mem Anatomy Dept All-India Inst of Medical Sciences 1959; mem staff Royal Samaritan and Royal Maternity Hosps, Glasgow, UK 1960–61; mem staff Obstetrics and Gynaecology Dept, Crumpsall Hosp, Manchester, UK 1961–62; Sr Consultant Gynaecologist and Obstetrician, and Dir Ganga Ram Hosp, Dhall Hosp; mem Action Cttee Social and Welfare Ministry, Quota Int of Noida 2001–; contribs to professional journals; Haskar Prize 1956; B. L. Kapoor Award Delhi Medical Asscn. *Leisure interests:* trees, the environment, farming, boating, family planning, population control. *Address:* Quota International of Noida, F-14, Sector 40, Noida, UP 201 303, India. *Telephone:* (91) 4577116 (Home); *E-mail:* drsbahldhall@usa.net.

BAI SHUXIANG; Chinese ballet dancer; b 1939. *Education:* Beijing Coll of Dancing. *Career:* Prin Dancer Cen Ballet 1958, Deputy Dir Cen Ballet 1972, Dir 1984–90; mem Nat Cttee 5th CPPCC 1978–82, 6th Prin Dancer Cen Ballet Co 1958, Dir 1984–90; mem 5th Nat Cttee CPPCC 1978–82, 6th 1983–87, 7th 1988–92, 8th 1993–; Perm mem China Dancers' Asscn, now Chair; First Grade Dancer of the Nation (award). *Ballets include:* Swan Lake, Giselle, The Foundation of Bakhchisarai, The Emerald, Sylvia, Red Women Army, Song of Yimeng, Song of Jiaoyang. *Address:* Chinese Dancers' Association, Di An Men Dong Dajie, Beijing 100009, People's Republic of China.

BAILAR, Barbara Ann, PH D; American statistician; b 24 Nov 1935, Monroe, MI; d of Malcolm and Clara (née Parent) Dezendorf; m 1st John F. Powell 1958 (divorced); m 2nd John C. Bailar 1966; two d. *Education:* State Univ of New York, Virginia Polytechnic Inst and the American Univ. *Career:* Statistician Census Bureau 1958, Chief Center for Research Methods 1973, Assoc Dir for Statistical Standards and Methodology 1979; Exec Dir American Statistical Asscn (ASA) 1988–95; Vice-Pres Survey Research, Nat Opinion Research Centre, Chicago, IL 1995–; teacher George Washington Univ 1984–85; mem AAAS (Chair Statistics Section 1984–85), Int Asscn of Survey Statisticians (Pres 1989–91), Int Statistics Inst (Vice-Pres 1993–95); contribs to statistical journals. *Leisure interests:* reading, travel. *Address:* National Opinion Research Centre, 1155 E 60th St, Chicago, IL 60637, USA.

BAILES, Alyson Judith Kirtley, MA; British diplomatist; b 6 April 1949; d of John-Lloyd and Barbara (née Martin) Bailes. *Education:* The Belvedere School (Liverpool) and Somerville Coll (Oxford). *Career:* Mem staff British Embassy, Hungary 1970–74, Germany 1981–84, People's Repub of China 1987–89; mem UK Del to NATO 1974–76; mem staff FCO 1976–79, 1984–86, 1994–96; Asst to EC Study Group 1979; seconded to Ministry of Defence 1979–81; Deputy Head of Mission, Norway 1990–93; on attachment to Royal Inst of Int Affairs 1990; Vice-Pres Inst for East West Studies, New York, USA 1996–97; Political Dir, WEU, Brussels 1997–2000; Amb to Finland 2000–. *Leisure interests:* music, travel, nature. *Address:* Embassy of the UK, Itäinen puistotie 17, 00140 Helsinki, Finland. *Telephone:* (9) 22865100; *Fax:* (9) 22865262; *E-mail:* info@ukembassy.fi; *Internet:* www.ukembassy.fi.

BAILEY, Adetoun Olabowale; Nigerian nurse. *Education:* Various hosps in the UK and Gen Nursing Councils of England and Wales and Scotland. *Career:* Staff Nurse, Student Midwife and Nursing Sister, UK and Nigeria 1950–55; Ward Admin and Teaching Sister Gen Hosp, Limbe, Cameroon 1956–58; Operating Theatre Sister Gen Hosp, Lagos 1958–61; Nursing Sister Fed Ministry of Health, Lagos 1961; Sec Midwives Bd of Nigeria 1962–72, Nursing Council of Nigeria 1962–77; Visiting Nurse Examiner to Schools of Nursing, Sierra Leone 1973–77; responsible for review of Nurses and Midwives Acts (Nigeria) 1966, introduced new standards in nursing training and practice, organized workshops and nat seminars 1966–75; mem Governing Council Lagos State Health Man Bd 1984–86; f Theatre Nurses Asscn of Nigeria; Pres Nat Council of Soroptimist Int Clubs in Nigeria 1985–87; mem Exec Cttee Lagos State Br, Nat Asscn of Nurses and Midwives; Rockefeller Grantee 1964; Foundation Fellow West Africa Coll of Nursing. *Publications include:* Macmillan Tropical Health Science and Nursing Series (co-ordinating ed) 1974–; numerous conf papers and contribs to professional journals. *Address:* 73 Coker Rd, Ilupeju, Lagos, Nigeria.

BAILEY, Glenda Adrianne, MA; British magazine editor; b 16 Nov 1958, Derby; d of John Ernest and Constance (née Groome) Bailey; partner Steve Sumner. *Education:* Noel Baker Grammar School (Derby) and Kingston Polytechnic. *Career:* Fmrly consultant Fashion Forecast, Design Direction; fmr Ed Honey; Ed Marie Claire (UK) 1988–1996, Marie Claire (USA) 1996–; Women's Magazine Ed of the Year, British Soc of Magazine Eds 1990; Media Week Press Award, Consumer Magazine of the Year 1991; Periodical Publishers Award, Consumer Magazine of the Year 1991. *Leisure interest:* indulgence. *Address:* c/o Marie Claire Magazine, 1790 Broadway, 3rd Floor, New York, NY 10019, USA. *Telephone:* (212) 649-4450.

BAILEY, Rhea, BA; Cypriot artist; b 26 Aug 1946, Nicosia; d of Vassos Athanassiades and Haritini Kalispera; m David Bailey 1967 (divorced 1981); one d. *Education:* Pancyprian Gymnasium (Nicosia), Sir John Cass School of Art (London) and Liverpool Coll of Art (UK). *Career:* Dip in Art and Design 1969; Artist 1971–; Rep Cyprus at Int Competition of Contemporary Art (Monaco) 1979, Paris Young Artists Biennale 1980, Plein-air (Bulgaria) 1989; one-woman exhibitions in Cyprus, Greece, Spain, USA and UK 1971–99; group exhibitions in France, UK, Greece, Belgium, Italy, Ireland, fmr USSR, fmr E and W Germany, Australia, People's Repub of China, Cuba, Romania, Kuwait, Yugoslavia, Bulgaria, Hungary, Czechoslovakia, Jordan and Tunisia; has given lectures at Rathbone Gallery (Albany, NY, USA) 1977, Ledra Hotel (Nicosia) 1990, Mahares (Tunisia) 1995; Medallist Golden Nightingale Int Art Competition 1973; Grand Gold Prix for Int Quality, Madrid 1998; Twentieth Century Achievement Award, 'Five Hundred Leaders of Influence', American Biographical Inst 1999; '2000 Outstanding Artists and Designers of the 20th Century' Medal, Int Biographical Centre, Cambridge (UK) 1999; '2000 Outstanding Scholars of the 20th Century' 2000. *Leisure interests:* music, sewing, swimming, reading, yoga, meditation. *Address:* 14 Diogenous St, Nicosia 2122, Cyprus. *Telephone:* (2) 330850; *Fax:* (2) 330850.

BAINBRIDGE, Dame Beryl, DBE, FRSL; British writer and actress; b 21 Nov 1934, Liverpool; d of Richard and Winifred (née Baines) Bainbridge; m Austin Davies 1954 (divorced); two d one s. *Education:* Merchant Taylor's School (Liverpool) and Arts Educational Schools (Tring). *Career:* columnist Evening Standard 1987–93; Hon D LITT (Liverpool) 1988; James Tait Black Fiction Prize 1996. *Plays:* Tiptoe Through the Tulips 1976, The Warriors Return 1977, It's a Lovely Day Tomorrow 1977, Journal of Bridget Hitler 1981, Somewhere More Central (TV) 1981, Evensong (TV) 1986; *Publications:* Novels: A Weekend with Claude 1967, Another Part of the Wood 1968, Harriet Said... 1972, The Dressmaker 1973, The Bottle Factory Outing (Guardian Fiction Award) 1974, Sweet William 1975 (film 1980), A Quiet Life 1976, Injury Time (Whitbread Award) 1977, Young Adolf 1978, Winter Garden 1980, English Journey (TV series) 1984, Watson's Apology 1984, Mum and Mr Armitage 1985, Forever England (TV series 1986) 1986, Filthy Lucre 1986, An Awfully Big Adventure 1989, The Birthday Boys 1991, Something Happened Yesterday 1993, Collected Stories 1994, Northern Stories (Vol 5, co-ed), Kiss Me Hardy 1996, Every Man for Himself (Whitbread Novel Prize) 1996, Master Georgie 1998. *Leisure interests:* reading, smoking. *Address:* 42 Albert St, London NW1 7NU, UK. *Telephone:* (20) 7387-3113 (Home).

BAINS, Leslie Elizabeth, BA; American banking executive; b 28 July 1943, Glen Ridge, NJ; d of Pliny Otto and Dorothy Ethel Tawney; m Harrison Mackellar Bains, Jr. *Education:* American Univ (DC). *Career:* Asst Treas Citicorp, New York 1965–73; Vice-Pres Manufacturers Hanover NY 1973–80; Vice-Pres, Division Exec Chase Manhattan Bank NY 1980–86, Vice-Pres Group Exec 1986–87, Sr Vice-Pres Group Exec 1987–91; Man Dir Citibank NY 1991–93; Exec Vice-Pres Repub Nat Bank NY 1993–2000; Sr Exec Vice-Pres HSBC Bank USA, NY 2000–; mem Bd Dirs Interplast 1990 (Chair 1991), Bankers Lawyers Cttee 1983–; Chair Educ Cable Consortium Summit, NJ 1987–91; mem Corp Advisory Panel, NJ Council of Churches 1990, Bd of Visitors Kogod School of Business, American Univ 1992–, Bd of Visitors NY Philharmonic Relations 1991, American Bankers Asscn; one of Top 100 Women in Corp America, Business Monthly 1989. *Address:* HSBC Bank USA, 452 Fifth Ave, New York, NY 10018, USA.

BAIRD, Patricia Ann, OC, B SC, MD, CM; Canadian geneticist; b Lancs, UK; d of Harold and Winifred Cainen Holt; m Robert Merrifield Baird 1964; two s one d. *Education:* McGill Univ (Montréal). *Career:* Resident in Paediatrics, Vancouver Gen Hosp 1964–68; Instructor in Paediatrics, Div of Medical Genetics, Univ of British Columbia 1968, Asst Prof 1972, Assoc Prof 1977, Head of Dept 1979–89, Prof of Medical Genetics 1982–94, Univ Dist Prof 1994–, Acting Dir Centre for Molecular Genetics 1982–87, mem Bd of Govs 1984–90; Head Dept of Medical Genetics, Grace Hosp and Children's Hosp of British Columbia 1981–89, Univ Hosp 1986–89; Medical Consultant Health Surveillance Registry of British Columbia 1977–90; Chair Royal Comm on New Reproductive Techs 1989–93, Bd British Columbia Medical Services Foundation 1984–90; Co-Chair Nat Forum of Science and Tech Councils 1991; Vice-Pres Canadian Inst for Advanced Research 1991–; Temp Advisor to WHO 1999, 2000, 2001; mem Nat Advisory Bd on Science and Tech to Fed Govt 1987–91, Medical Research Council of Canada 1987–90, Ethics Panel of Int Paediatric Asscn, Royal Coll of Physicians and Surgeons of Canada, American Soc of Human Genetics, W Soc for Pediatric Research, Genetics Soc of Canada; Fellow Royal Coll of Physicians of Canada, Fellow Royal Soc of Canada, Order of BC, Hon DU (Ottawa), Hon D SC (McMaster Univ), Hon LL D (Wilfred Laurier Univ). *Publications include:* Proceed With Care: Final Report of the Royal Commission on New Reproductive Technologies 1993, numerous papers in medical literature. *Leisure interests:* gardening, skiing. *Address:* 226-6174 University Blvd, Vancouver, BC V6T 1Z3, Canada. *Telephone:* (604) 822-6115; *Fax:* (604) 822-3565; *E-mail:* pbaird@interchange.ubc.ca.

BAIRD, Zoe, JD; American lawyer; b 20 June 1952, New York; d of Ralph Louis and Naomi (née Allen) Baird; m Paul Gewirtz 1986; one s. *Education:* Univ of California at Berkeley. *Career:* Called to the Bar CA 1977, DC 1979, CT 1989; Law Clerk to Hon Albert Wollenberg, San Francisco, CA 1977–78; Attorney and Adviser Office of Legal Counsel, Dept of Justice, Washington, DC 1979–80; Assoc Counsel to the Pres 1980–81; Assoc then Partner O'Melveny and Myers, Washington, DC 1981–86; Counsellor and Staff Exec Gen Electric (GE), Fairfield, CT 1986–90; Vice-Pres and Gen Counsel Aetna Life and Casualty, Hartford, CT 1990–93, Sr Vice-Pres 1993–96; Pres John and Mary Markle Foundation, NY 1998–. *Address:* John and Mary Markle Foundation, 10 Rockefeller Plaza, 16th Floor, New York, NY 10020, USA.

BAIYANG, (YANG CHENGFANG); Chinese actress; b 22 April 1920, Beijing; d of the late Yang Zhenghua and Ding Fengyi; m Jiang Junchao 1950 (died 1991); one s one d. *Education:* Beijing Lianhua Co Film School. *Career:* Actress Bolyba Dramatic Group, Beijing 1932–33, Chinese Travelling Troupe and Stagecraft Soc of China, Nanjing 1934–36, Star Mingxing Film Studio, Shanghai 1936–37, Kuhlun Film Co, Shanghai 1946–48, Shanghai Film Studio 1950–90; active in Resistance Theatre Movt (Chongqing and Chendu) 1937–45; Deputy to 1st NPC 1954–58, 2nd NPC 1959–63, 3rd NPC 1964–66; mem 5th CPPCC 1978–82, 6th CPPCC 1983–87; Standing mem Culture Cttee, 7th CPPCC 1988–92; criticized during Cultural Revolution 1966–76, rehabilitated 1978; Vice-Chair Shanghai Film Art Cttee 1981; Vice-Pres Asscn of Chinese Filmworkers 1985–; visited Moscow (USSR, now Russian Fed) 1949, USA 1981–; Best Film Actress Award 1957, 1990; Special Award from Int Festival in Czechoslovakia 1957; Hon Greatest Star in the History of Chinese Cinema 1989; Eighth TV Golden Eagle Award 1990; Flying Apsarasa Award 1990. *Appearances include:* Crisscross Streets 1936, Chu Yuan 1942, 1953, The Spring River Flows East 1947–48, Zhu Fu (New Year's Sacrifice) 1957, Madame Sun Soong Chingling 1989; *Publication:* In Pursuit of Film Acting. *Leisure interests:* poetry, music, painting, reading. *Address:* 978 Huashan Rd, Shanghai 200050, People's Republic of China. *Telephone:* (21) 2510371.

BAKER, Anita; American singer and songwriter; b 26 Jan 1958, Toledo, OH; m Walter Bridgeforth, Jr 1988; one s. *Career:* Mem Chapter 8 (funk band) 1978–80; Receptionist Quin and Budajh, Detroit, MI 1980–82; singer-songwriter 1982–; Image Award, Best Female Vocalist and Best Album of the Year, Nat Asscn for the Advancement of Colored People (NAACP), Best Female Vocalist and Best Album of the Year. *Recordings include:* Albums: I Just Wanna Be Your Girl (with Chapter 8) 1980, The Songstress 1983, Rapture (Best Rhythm and Blues Vocal Performance

Grammy Award 1987) 1986, Giving You the Best That I Got 1988, Compositions (Best Rhythm and Blues Performance Grammy Award 1990) 1990, Rhythm of Love (Best Female Vocal Grammy Award and Best Song Grammy Award 1995) 1994; Singles: No More Tears, Angel, Caught Up in the Rapture, Love, You Bring Me Joy, Been So Long, No One in the World. *Address:* c/o All Baker's Music, 345 N Maple Drive, Beverly Hills, CA 90210, USA.

BAKER, Carroll; American actress; b 28 May 1931, Johnstown, PA; d of William W. Baker and Virginia Duffy; m 1st Jack Garfein 1955 (divorced); one s one d; m 2nd Donald Burton 1982. *Education:* St Petersburg Jr Coll (FL). *Career:* Has appeared in several Broadway shows and numerous films; toured Vietnam with Bob Hope 1966; mem Acad of Motion Picture Arts and Sciences; several acting awards. *Films include:* Giant 1956, Baby Doll 1957, The Big Country 1958, But Not for Me 1959, The Miracle 1959, Bridge to the Sun 1960, Something Wild 1961, How the West Was Won 1962, Station Six Sahara 1962, Carpetbaggers 1963, Cheyenne Autumn 1963, Mr Moses 1964, Sylvia 1964, Harlow 1965, The Harem 1967, Honeymoon 1968, The Sweet Body of Deborah 1968, Captain Apache 1971, Bad 1977, Watcher in the Woods 1980, Red Monarch 1983, The Secret Diary of Sigmund Freud 1983, Star 80 1983, Ironweed 1987, Native Son, Red Monarch, Kindergarten Cop, Blonde Fist, Cybereden, Undercurrent, Skeletons, Just Your Luck, The Game, Nowhere to Go; *Broadway appearances include:* All Summer Long 1954, Come on Strong 1962; *Publications:* Baby Doll (autobiog), A Roman Tale.

BAKER, Dame Janet Abbott, CH, DBE, FRSA; British opera singer (mezzo-soprano); b 21 Aug 1933, Hatfield, Yorks; d of Robert Abbott and May (née Pollard) Baker; m James Keith Shelley 1957. *Education:* York Coll for Girls and Wintringham School (Grimsby). *Career:* Int career as concert, opera and Lieder singer and recording artist with major conductors and orchestras; Pres London Sinfonia 1986–; Chancellor Univ of York 1991–; mem Opera Bd, Royal Opera House 1994–; Trustee Countess of Munster Trust, Kathleen Ferrier Memorial Prize, Emmie Tillett Memorial Trust, Foundation for Sport and the Arts 1991–; numerous recordings; Hon Fellow St Anne's Coll, Oxford 1975, Downing Coll, Cambridge 1985; Hon D MUS (Birmingham) 1968, (Leicester) 1974, (London) 1974, (Hull) 1975, (Oxford) 1975, (Leeds) 1980, (Lancaster) 1983, (York) 1984, (Cambridge) 1984; Hon LL D (Aberdeen) 1980; Hon D LITT (Bradford) 1983; Kathleen Ferrier Memorial Prize 1956; Queen's Prize 1959; Shakespeare Prize (Hamburg) 1971; Grand Prix French Nat Acad of Lyric Recordings 1975; Leonie Sonning Prize (Denmark) 1979; Gold Medal of the Royal Philharmonic Soc 1990; Commdr des Arts et des Lettres. *Publication:* Full Circle (autobiog) 1982. *Leisure interests:* enjoying life, reading. *Address:* c/o Transart (UK) Ltd, 8 Bristol Gardens, London W9 2JG, UK.

BAKEWELL, Joan Dawson, CBE, BA; British broadcaster and writer; b 16 April, Stockport; d of John Rowlands and Rose Bland; m 1st Micheal Bakewell 1955 (divorced 1972); one s one d; m 2nd Jack Emery 1975. *Education:* Stockport High School for Girls and Newnham Coll (Cambridge). *Career:* TV Critic The Times 1978–81; Columnist Sunday Times 1988–90; Assoc Newnham Coll, Cambridge 1980–91, Assoc Fellow 1984–87; Gov BFI 1994–99, Chair 1999–; Pres Soc of Arts Publicists 1984–90; Dimbleby Award, BAFTA 1995. *TV includes:* Sunday Break 1962, Home at 4.30 (writer and producer) 1964, Meeting Point 1964, The Second Sex 1964, Late Night Line Up 1965–72, The Youthful Eye 1968, Moviemakers at the National Film Theatre 1971, Film 72, Film 73, For the Sake of Appearance, Where is Your God?, Who Cares?, The Affirimative Way (series) 1973, Thank You, Ron 1974, Fairest Fortune 1974, Edinburgh Festival Report 1974, Holiday '74, '75, '76, '77, '78 (series), What's it all About? (series), Time Running Out (series) 1974, The Shakespeare Business, The Brontë Business, Generation to Generation (series) 1976, Reports Action (series) 1976–78, My Day with the Children 1977, The Moving Line 1979, Arts UK: OK? 1980, The Heart of the Matter 1988–90, My Generation 2000; *Radio includes:* Artist of the Week 1998–99, The Brains Trust 1999–, Belief 2000; *Publications:* The New Priesthood: British Television Today (jtly) 1970, A Fine and Private Place (jtly) 1977, The Complete Traveller 1977, The Heart of the Heart of the Matter 1996; contribs to journals. *Leisure interests:* theatre, travel,

cinema. *Address:* Knight Ayton Management, 10 Argyll St, London W1V 1AB, UK. *Telephone:* Telephone: (20) 7722-2839 (Office); *Fax:* (20) 7586-7112 (Office).

BAKHTEARI, Quratul Ain, PH D; Pakistani development consultant and environmentalist; b 25 Dec 1949, Multan; d of H. and K. Bakhteari; three s. *Education:* St Joseph's School (Karachi), Univ of Karachi and Loughborough Univ of Tech (UK). *Career:* Devt Worker UNICEF, Karachi 1979–84, Project Officer, Urban Devt 1984–86, Programme Officer 1987–88; mem IBRD/Canadian Int Devt Agency (CIDA) Rural Water Supply, Health and Sanitation Mission for Pakistan 1987, Deputy Project Man 1987; Resource Consultant Workshop and Nat Policy Conf, Water and Health Sector 1988; Consultant, trainer Pakistan-Canada Small Projects Office 1991; Co-ordinator Female Community Social Organization, UNICEF 1991; Founding Dir Inst for Devt Studies and Practices (IDSP); involved in USAID Primary Educ Project, Baluchistan 1992; Consultant Cowater Int 1988, Inst of Social Welfare (Karachi), Family Planning Asscn of Pakistan, numerous other orgs; has taken part in many workshops; mem Fed of Univ Women, Pakistan Council for S Asian Partnership, Centre of Excellence Univ of Karachi Women's Study Cell; contribs to professional journals; Pakistan Jaycees Award; Women's Devt Award 1986; Matushita Memorial Award for Int Year of Shelter for the Homeless, Tokyo 1987. *Leisure interests:* travel, being with people, reading. *Address:* St 26, House 43, Phase V, Defense Soc, Karachi, Pakistan. *Telephone:* (21) 534037; *Fax:* (21) 534037.

BAKOYANNIS, Dora; Greek politician; b May 1954, Athens; d of Konstantinos Mitsotakis and Mari Ka Yannoukou; m Pavlos Bakoyannis 1974 (died 1989); two c. *Education:* German School in Paris (France), Germany and Univ of Athens. *Career:* In Paris 1968–74; Sec to Minister of Econ Co-ordination 1978–80, to Minister of Foreign Affairs 1980–81; Chef de Cabinet to Pres of Nea Demokratia (New Democratic) Party 1984–89, Int Sec 1991; mem Vouli (Parl) for Euritania 1989; Under-Sec of State to Prime Minister 1990–91, 1992; Minister of Cultural Affairs 1992; Int Leadership Award, Women's Int Center 1992; Fontana di Roma Award, 14th Int Symposium 1993. *Leisure interests:* travel, music, reading. *Address:* 3 Dion Areopagitou St, 107 42 Athens, Greece; 1 P Aravantinou St, 106 74 Athens, Greece (Home). *Telephone:* (1) 9249487; *Fax:* (1) 9249426.

BALASKO, Josie; French actress and film producer; b (Josiane Balaskovic) 15 April 1950, Paris; d of Ivan and Fernande (née Gattechaud) Balaskovic; m Philippe Berry 1980; two c. *Education:* Lycée Lamartine, Ecole Supérieure des Arts Graphiques and acting lessons with Tania Balachova (Paris). *Career:* Actress with La Troupe du Splendid; film producer and scriptwriter; Chevalier de l'Ordre Nat du Mérite; Chevalier des Arts et des Lettres; César d'Honneur for Lifetime Achievement 2000. *Plays include:* Writer and Actress: Amours, coquillages et crustacés, Le pot de terre contre le pot de vin, Les bronzés, Les bronzés font du ski, Le Père Noël est une ordure, Bunny's bar ou Les hommes préfèrent les grosses, Nuit d'ivresse, L'ex-femme de ma vie; *Films include:* Actress: Les bronzés, Les bronzés font du ski, Le Père Noël est une ordure, Les petits câlins, Clara et les chics types, Les hommes préfèrent les grosses, Signes extérieurs de richesse, Hôtel des Amériques, La Smala, Nuit d'ivresse 1986, Trop belle pour toi 1988, Tout le monde n'a pas eu la chance d'avoir des parents communistes 1993, Arlette 1997; Producer, Scriptwriter and Actress: Sac de nœuds 1985, Les Keufs 1987, Ma vie est un enfer 1991, Gazon maudit 1995 (César for Best Original Screenplay 1996, Prix Pierre Bellan for Best Screenplay 1996, Lumières de Paris Best Screenplay Prize 1996), Un grand cri d'amour 1998. *Address:* JFPM, 11 rue Chanez, 75016 Paris, France.

BALAYÉ, Simone, D ÈS L; French librarian; b 14 March 1925, Versailles; d of Fernand and Denise (née Fromont) Balayé. *Education:* Lycées Victor Duruy and Camille Sée (Paris), Lycée Jeanne d'Arc (Orléans) and Univ of Paris (Sorbonne). *Career:* Curator Bibliothèque Nat, Paris 1951–90, Hon Curator 1990–; Visiting Prof Univ of Ottawa, Canada 1970, Hebrew Univ of Jerusalem, Israel 1971; Pres Soc des études staëliennes 1984–; Vice-Pres Soc française d'études du 18ème siècle, Paris 1985–97; delivered Zaharoff Lecture, Univ of Oxford 1995; mem Bd Soc des études romantiques, Paris; mem Bd of Dirs Asscn Benjamin Constant, Lausanne and other literary cttees; mem Admin Council Int Asscn of French Studies 1994; Hon mem Cttee

Chateaubriand Soc 1997; corresp mem Soc d'histoire et d'archéologie de Genève; Chevalier des Arts et des Lettres; Chevalier des palmes académiques. *Publications include:* Lettres de Madame de Staël à Ribbing 1960, Les Carnets de voyages de Madame de Staël, contribution à la genèse de ses oeuvres (Broquette-Gonin Prize, Acad Française) 1971, Madame de Staël: Lumières et liberté (Alfred Née Prize, Acad Française) 1979, La Bibliothèque nationale des origines à 1800 (Prix Roland de Jouvenel, Acad Française 1990) 1988, Madame de Staël: écrire, lutter, vivre 1994, Dix années d'exil de Mme de Staël 1996 (Louis Barthou Prize, Acad Française); numerous articles in literary journals and conf papers. *Address:* 44 rue Vaneau, 75007 Paris, France. *Telephone:* (1) 45-49-30-03.

BALÁZS, Éva H., DR SC; Hungarian professor of modern history; b 20 Dec 1915, Székelyudvarhely; d of Sándor Balázs and Judit Beczássy; m Lajos Hunyady 1941; one s. *Education:* Univ of Budapest. *Career:* Asst Inst of Political Science, Ministry of Foreign Affairs 1939–41; Lecturer Dept of Medieval History, Univ of Budapest 1945–54, Dept of Medieval and Modern World History 1961–77, Prof 1978–87, Head of Dept 1982–87, Prof Emer 1987–; Head Dept of History, Coll of Pedagogy 1947; responsible for historians' affairs Office of Prime Minister 1947–49; Fellow Inst of History, Hungarian Acad of Sciences 1949–61; Vice-Pres jt cttee of French and Hungarian historians; mem History Cttee Hungarian Acad of Sciences, Comm of Austrian-Hungarian Historians; First Prize of Renovanda Hungariae Cultura Foundation 1996; Officier des Palmes Académiques Françaises, Laureate of Hungarian Acad, Officer's Cross of the Repub of Hungary, Chevalier de la Légion d'Honneur 1997. *Publications:* The Age of Enlightenment 1964, Gergely Berzeviczy, the Reform Politician 1967, Paysannerie française-paysannerie hongroise (ed and contrib) 1973, Beförderer der Aufklärung in Mittel-und Osteuropa 1979, Noblesse 1981, Intellectuels 1985, Absolutisme éclairé 1985, Vienna and Pest-Buda 1765–1800 1988, Magyarország történet 1989, Hungary and the Habsburgs 1765–1800. An Experiment in Enlightened Absolutism 1997. *Leisure interests:* music, swimming. *Address:* Eötvös Loránd Tudomány Egyetem, BTK, Múzeum krt 6-8, Budapest, 1088 (Office), Hungary (Office); 11 Érmelléki u 7, Budapest, 1026, Hungary (Home). *Telephone:* (1) 213-8986.

BALDAUF, Sari Maritta; Finnish business executive; b 10 Aug 1955, Kotka. *Education:* Helsinki Business School. *Career:* Began career with Finnish Export Inst 1979–81; with Falcon Communications (Abu Dhabi) 1981–83; Planning Man Nokia 1983–89, Man Cellular Networks 1990–95, Dir Nokia Asia-Pacific 1996–98, Pres Nokia Networks July 1998–; mem Bd Int Youth Foundation. *Leisure interest:* skiing. *Address:* c/o Nokia Group Corporate Communications, Keilalahdentie 4, 02150 Espoo, Finland.

BALDI, Monica Stefanie; Italian politician; b 26 April 1959, Pistoia. *Career:* Fmrly MEP (Union for Europe Group, Forza Italia), mem Cttee on the Environment, Public Health and Consumer Protection, Cttee on Devt and Co-operation. *Address:* European Parliament, rue Wiertz, 1047 Brussels, Belgium.

BALIUNAS, Sallie; American scientist. *Career:* Chair Harvard-Smithsonian Center for Astrophysics; mem Science Advisory Bd George C. Marshall Institute. *Address:* Harvard-Smithsonian Center for Astrophysics, c/o Smithsonian Astrophysical Observatory, 60 Garden St, Cambridge, MA 02138, USA.

BALLETBO PUIG, Anna Maria, BA; Spanish politician and journalist; b 15 Dec 1943, Barcelona; d of Joan and Antonia Balletbo Puig; three s one d. *Education:* Univ of Barcelona and Autonomous Univ of Barcelona. *Career:* Mem Congress of Deputies (Parl, PSOE) for Barcelona 1979, mem Cttees on Control of RTVE—Radiotelevisión Española, Foreign Affairs 1979; Prof of Information Science Autonomous Univ of Barcelona; Pres World Women Parliamentarians for Peace; mem Comm on Global Governance; Woodrow Wilson Center Scholar. *Publication:* Propuesta de Paz para el Próximo Oriente 1991, Condicionamientos de la Paz y Estabilidad en el Proximo Oriente 1992, Consolidación Democrática en América Latina 1994, Naciones Unideas y la seguridad Global 1996. *Address:* Calle Nicaragua 75, 08029 Barcelona, Spain. *Telephone:* (3) 3210100.

BALTSA, Agnes; Greek opera singer (mezzo-soprano); b Lefkas. *Education:* Acad of Music (Athens) and in Munich (Germany). *Career:* Debut Frankfurt 1968, at Vienna State Opera 1970, Salzburg Festival 1970, La Scala (Milan, Italy) 1976, Paris Opera and Royal Opera House (Covent Garden, London) 1976, Metropolitan Opera (New York, USA) 1980; mem Deutsche Oper, Berlin 1973–; performs at all major opera houses and has given concerts in Europe, USA and Japan with Karajan, Böhm, Abbado, Marriner, Levine, Patané, Bernstein, Muti; Maria Callas Scholarship; title Österreichische Kammersängerin conferred 1980; Deutscher Schallplattenpreis 1983; Prix Prestige Lyrique (French Ministry of Culture) 1984. *Recordings include:* Carmen, der Rosenkavalier, Aida, Don Carlos, Salome, Verdi's Requiem, Mozart's Requiem, Maria Stuarda, Cavalleria Rusticana, Samson and Delila, Greek Songs. *Leisure interests:* swimming, fashion. *Address:* c/o Management Rita Schültz, Rütistr 52, 8044 Zurich-Gockhausen, Switzerland.

BALZAN, Rena, B PHARM, PH D; Maltese writer and molecular biologist; b 5 Nov 1946, Siggiewi; d of Carmelo and Nicholina Aquilina Balzan. *Education:* Univ of Malta, Univ of Milan (Italy) and Cranfield Univ (UK). *Career:* Part-time Lecturer Biology Dept, Univ of Malta 1977–89, Asst Lecturer 1989–94, Lecturer Dept of Physiology and Biochemistry 1994–1999, Sr Lecturer 1999–; Asst Head Upper Lyceum Msida 1981–89; Dir Lombard Bank 1984–87; Chair Malta Council for Science and Tech 1997–98. *Publications include:* (In Maltese): Hidden Colours 1973, Choice in Separation 1981, The Sold Dream 1982, Steps (jtly) 1983, Bonds Beyond Time 1987, In Tune with City Life 1995, Alfa (jtly) 2000. *Leisure interests:* reading, swimming, travel. *Address:* University of Malta, Dept of Physiology and Biochemistry, Msida MSD 06, Malta (Office); Miraġġ, 64 Fawwara Rd, Siggiewi QRM 13, Malta (Home). *Telephone:* 316655 (Office); 466691 (Home); *E-mail:* rbal1@ um.edu.mt.

BAMBRICK, Susan Caroline, OBE, B ECON, PH D; Australian educationalist; b 20 Oct 1941, Brisbane. *Education:* Univ of Queensland and Australian Nat Univ. *Career:* Course Dir, Lecturer Australian Mineral Foundation, Adelaide 1977–; Visiting Fellow Resource Systems Inst, E/W Center, HI, USA 1981–82, Centre for Resource and Environmental Studies, Australian Nat Univ; fmr Dean of Students, Sr Lecturer in Econs and Acad Asst to Vice-Chancellor, Australian Nat Univ; Dir of Studies Australian Public Service Bd 1982; Dir ANUTECH 1984–91; fmrly Dir Univ of New England-Coffs Harbour Centre; Pro-Vice-Chancellor La Trobe Univ 1997–99; Deputy Vice Chancellor (Academic), Univ of S Queensland 1999–; mem Uranium Advisory Council 1978–82; Exec mem Trade Devt Council (TDC) 1979–85, TDC Rep Industrial Consultative Cttee to GATT; mem Advisory Council, Commonwealth Scientific and Industrial Research Orgs (CSIRO) 1980–86, Panel Defence Industry Cttee 1983–85, Bd Australian Centre for Maritime Studies 1986–87; mem Ministerial Working Party on Gas Regulation, ACT 1989–91, Bd of Enquiry into Gas Regulation, ACT 1990–91; Exec mem Australian Acad of Sciences 1986–; Life mem Australian Inst of Bankers; Fellow Australian Inst of Energy; First Fulbright Australian Scholar-in-Residence to the US 1982. *Publications:* The Economics of the World's Mineral Industries (jtly) 1978, Australian Minerals and Energy Policy 1979, Cambridge Encyclopedia of Australia (ed); contribs to books. *Address:* University of Southern Queensland, Toowoomba, Qld 4350, Australia. *Telephone:* (7) 4631-2189; *Fax:* (7) 4631-2782.

BANCROFT, Anne; American actress; b 17 Sept 1931, New York; d of Michael and Mildred (née DiNapoli) Italiano; m 2nd Mel Brooks 1964; one s. *Education:* Christopher Columbus High School (New York). *Career:* Has appeared in numerous films, TV and Broadway shows; Broadway debut 1958; Golden Globe Award 1968, Lifetime Achievement in Comedy Award, American Comedy Awards 1996. *Plays include:* Two for the Seesaw 1958, The Miracle Worker 1959–60, The Devils 1965, 1977, The Little Foxes 1967, A Cry of Players 1968, Golda 1977, Mystery of the Rose Bouquet 1989; *Films include:* The Miracle Worker (Acad Award) 1962, Don't Bother to Knock, Tonight We Sing, Demetrius and the Gladiators, The Pumpkin Eater, Seven Women, The Graduate 1968, Young Winston 1971, The Prisoner of Second Avenue 1974, The Hindenburg 1975, Lipstick 1976, Silent Movie 1976, The Turning Point 1977, Golda 1977, The Elephant Man 1980, Fatso (also writer and director) 1980, To Be or Not to Be 1984, Agnes of God 1985, 84 Charing Cross Road 1986, 'Night Mother 1986, Torch Song Trilogy

1989, Bert Rigby You're a Fool 1989, Broadway Bound 1992, The Assassin, How to Make and American Quilt, Home for the Holidays 1995, The Homecoming 1996, Sunchasers 1997, GI Jane 1997, Critical Care 1997, Great Expectations 1998, Antz 1998 (voice only), Twain's America in 3D 1998, Up at the Villa 1999; *TV appearances include:* Mother Courage and her Children, Annie, the Woman in the Life of a Man (Emmy Award) 1970, Jesus of Nazareth 1977, Marco Polo 1981. *Address:* c/o The Culver Studios, 9336 W Washington Blvd, Culver City, CA 90232, USA (Office).

BANDLER, Vivica Aina Fanny; Finnish theatre director; b 5 Feb 1917, Helsinki; d of Erik von Frenckell and Ester Margaret Lindberg; m Kurt Bandler 1943. *Education:* Univ of Helsinki. *Career:* Mem Helsingfors Student Theatre 1939; asst film dir France 1939, Sweden 1945–46; war service 1939–40, 1941–43; Dir Swedish Theatre, Helsinki 1948; Head theatre section Helsinki's 400th anniversary festival 1948; f Peasants' Theatre Group 1951; Man and Prin Dir Lilla Teatern, Helsinki 1955–67, mem Bd 1983; Man and Dir Oslo Nye Teater, Norway 1967–69; Head Stockholm City Theatre 1969–80; theatre dir Sweden and Finland 1980–; Artistic Dir Tampere Int Theatre Festival, Finland 1989–95; theatre dir Eri dance theatre (Finland) 1989; Pres Bd Swedish Theatre Union/Swedish Int Theatre Inst (ITI) 1978–92, mem Exec Cttee 1981–86, mem Drama Cttee 1990–92; mem Bd Nordic Theatre Union 1986–88; Pres Theatre Acad of Sweden 1992–2000; Patron Hangö Theatre Festival 1996–97; Hon mem Swedish Authors' Asscn in Finland, Union of Theatre Dirs; Golden Boot award, Dagens Nyheter; Medal of City of Stockholm; Medal of Swedish Parl; August Award; Swedish Dramatists' Asscn; Medal for Nordic Co-operation, Letterstedt Foundation; Thalia Award, Swedish Actors' Asscn; Memory Medal of War 1939–40; Commdr Finnish Lion, Northern Star of Sweden; Pro Finlandis. *Publications:* Adressaten okänd (Addressee Unknown, jtly) 1992; numerous articles about theatre, translations of plays, and several dramatizations of novels, film scripts and musicals. *Leisure interest:* mice and men. *Address:* Villagatan 1B, 00150 Helsinki, Finland; Upplandsgatan 28, 113 28 Stockholm, Sweden. *Telephone:* (0) 635483 (Finland); (8) 314322 (Sweden).

BANERJEE, Kumari Mamata, B ED, LL B, MA; Indian politician; b 5 Jan 1955, Calcutta (now Kolkata); d of Shri Promileswar and Gyitri Banerjee. *Education:* Univ of Calcutta. *Career:* Gen Sec Mahila Congress (I), W Bengal 1970–80; Sec Dist Congress Cttee (Calcutta S) 1978–81; mem Lok Sabha (House of the People, Parl) 1984, 1991–; mem numerous Parl Cttees 1985–; Gen Sec and mem Nat Council, All India Youth Congress (I) Cttee 1985–87; mem Consultative Cttee, Ministry of Human Resource Devt 1987–93, of Home Affairs 1987–88, 1993–96, 1996–97, 1998–99; mem Exec Cttee, Congress Parl Party 1988–, Pradesh Congress Cttee 1989–; Pres Youth Congress (W Bengal) 1990; Union Minister of State, Human Resource Devt, Dept of Youth Affairs and Sports, and Women and Child Devt 1991–93, of Railways Oct 1999–; Chair Cttee on Railways 1998–99; mem Gen Purposes Cttee 1998–99, March 2001–; Leader All India Trinamool Congress Parl Party 1999–. *Publications include:* Upalabdhi, Janatar Darbare, Maa, Pallabi, Manabik, Struggle for Existence, Motherland, Crocodile Island, Trinamool. *Leisure interest:* music and writing. *Address:* 30-B Harish Chatterjee St, Kolkata, 700 026, West Bengal, India; C-4, M.S. Flats, B.K.S. Marg, New Delhi 110 001, India. *Telephone:* (22) 4753000.

BANERJI, Sara Ann; British writer; b 6 June 1932, Bucks; d of Sir Basil and Anita Mostyn; m Ranjit Banerji 1951; three d. *Education:* Schools and Convents in UK and S Rhodesia (now Zimbabwe). *Career:* Fmrly teacher, jockey, waitress, gardener and riding instructor; now writer; Arts Council Award for Literature; Write Out Loud Award for radio writing. *Publications include:* Cobwebwalking 1987, The Wedding of Mayanthi Mandel 1988, The Teaplanter's Daughter 1989, Shining Agnes 1990, Absolute Hush 1991, Shining Hero 2002. *Leisure interests:* transcendental meditation, gardening, painting, cooking, crafts, interior decorating, entertaining, family gatherings. *Address:* 7 London Place, Oxford OX4 1BD, UK. *Telephone:* (1865) 251250; *E-mail:* sara .banerji@ntlworld.com.

BANFIELD, Jillian Fiona, PH D; Australian professor of geology and geophysics; b 18 Aug 1959, Armidale, NSW; d of James E and Eve Banfield; m Perry Smith; two s one d. *Education:* Australian Nat Univ, Johns Hopkins Univ, USA. *Career:* Exploration geologist W Mining Corpn 1982–83; Asst Prof Dept of Geology and Geophysics, Univ of Wisconsin–, Madison 1990–95, Assoc Prof 1995–99, Prof 1999–2001, Dept of Chem 1998–2001; Prof Dept of Earth and Planetary Science, Univ of California at Berkeley 2001–, Prof Dept of Environmental Science, Policy and Man 2001–; Assoc Prof Mineralogical Inst, Univ of Tokyo 1996–97, Prof 1998; Distinguished Lecturer, Mineralogical Soc of America 1994–95, Fellow 1997–; Gast Lecturer, Geochemical Soc 2000; NSF Earth Science Week Lecturer (Inaugural) 2000; John Simon Guggenheim Foundation Fellowship 2000; Honours include Geological Soc of Australia Prize 1978, Award for Outstanding Research, Dept of Energy, USA 1995, Mineralogical Soc of America Award 1997, D. A. Brown Medal, ANU 1999 and several other prizes and awards. *Publications:* numerous scientific papers. *Address:* University of Wisconsin, 315 Lewis G. Weeks Hall for Geological Science, 1215 W Dayton St, Madison, WI 53706, USA (Office); 5214 Raymond Rd, Madison, WI 53711, USA (Home). *Telephone:* (608) 265-9528 (Office); (608) 276-9381 (Home); *Fax:* (608) 262-0693 (Office); *E-mail:* jill@ geology.wisc.edu (Office); *Internet:* www.geology.wisc.edu/~jill/banfield .html (Office).

BANKS, Lynne Reid (see Reid Banks, Lynne).

BANNISTER, Ivy, PH D; American writer; b 11 July 1951; d of Richard and Hortense Eberhart; m Frank Bannister 1976; two s. *Education:* Smith Coll (MA) and Trinity Coll (Dublin). *Career:* Writer 1988–; has given lectures on literature and writing; columnist Image magazine 1995–; contrib Sunday Miscellany; Hennessy Award 1988; Mobil Ireland Playwriting Award 1993; Francis McManus Award; An Chomhairle Ealaion Bursary 1994. *Publications:* The Wilde Circus Show 1990, Magician 1997. *Leisure interests:* exercise, reading. *Address:* 76 Stillorgan Wood, Stillorgan, Co Dublin, Ireland. *Telephone:* (1) 288-4037.

BANOTTI, Mary; Irish politician; b 29 May 1939, Dublin. *Career:* Fmr nurse, social worker and broadcaster; nurse and Welfare Officer Irish Distillers 1972–84; MEP (Bureau of EPP, FG) 1984–, Quaestor 1999–; mem Cttees on Citizen's Freedoms and Rights, Justice and Home Affairs; Special mediator on Transnationally Abducted Children 1995–; mem Int Centre for Missing and Exploited Children; co-f hostel for battered wives; Pres Irish Centre for Parentally Abducted Children; Hon UN Goodwill Ambassador on Population and Maternal Health; European of the Year 1997. *Address:* c/o European Parliament, 43 Molesworth St, Dublin, 2, Ireland; 8 Cambridge Ave, Ringsend, Dublin 4, Ireland; European Parliament, rue Wiertz, 1047 Brussels, Belgium.

BAPPOO, Sheilabai; Mauritian politician; b June 1947; m Dayanan Bappoo; two d. *Education:* Henry Boswell and Queen Elizabeth Coll. *Career:* Teacher 1966–83; joined Mouvement Militant Mauricien (MMM) 1970, Pres 1973; Municipal Councillor for MMM 1977–78; joined Mouvement Socialiste Mauricien (MSM) 1983; mem Legis Ass 1983–; Minister for Women's Rights and Family Welfare 1983–86, of Labour and Industrial Relations, Women's Rights and Family Welfare 1986–91, of Women's Rights, Child Devt and Family Welfare 1991–95. *Leisure interests:* reading, cooking, music. *Address:* c/o Mouvement Socialiste Mauricien, Sun Trust Building, 31 Edith Cavell St, Port Louis, Mauritius.

BARAD, Jill Elikann, BA; American business executive; b 23 May 1951, New York; d of Lawrence Stanley and Corinne Elikann; m Thomas K. Barad 1979; two s. *Education:* Queens Coll. *Career:* Asst Marketing Man Coty Cosmetics, New York 1976–77, Product Marketing Man 1977; Account Exec Wells Rich Greene Advertising Agency, Los Angeles, CA 1978–79; Product Marketing Man Mattel Toys, Inc, Los Angeles 1981–82, Dir of Marketing 1982–83, Vice-Pres Marketing 1983–85, Sr Vice-Pres Marketing 1985–86, Sr Vice-Pres Product Devt 1986, Exec Vice-Pres Product Design and Devt, Exec Vice-Pres Marketing and Worldwide Product Devt 1988–89, Pres Girls' and Activity Toys Div 1989–, Pres Bd of Dirs Mattel USA, El Segundo, CA 1990–, Pres and COO Mattel, Inc 1992–97, Pres and CEO 1997, Chair and CEO 1997–2000; mem Bd of Dirs Arco Toys, Reebok Int Ltd 1992–, Microsoft 1996–; Chair Exec Advisory Bd Children Affected by AIDS Foundation, Mattel Foundation. *Address:* Mattel Inc, 333 Continental Blvd, El Segundo, CA 90245, USA.

BARBARA, Agatha; Maltese politician; b 11 March 1923, Zabbar; d of the late Joseph and Antonia (née Agius) Barbara. *Education:* Govt Grammar School (Valletta). *Career:* School teacher; mem Lab Party 1946–; First woman elected to Maltese Parl 1947–82; Minister of Educ 1955–58, 1971–73, of Lab, Culture and Welfare 1974–82; Pres of Malta 1982–1987; Chancellor Univ of Malta 1982–87; fmr mem ARP (World War II), later supervisor Victory Kitchens and Army Munitions Depot; fmr Man Freedom Press; Pres Malta Lab Party Women's Club, Founder and Chair Exec Cttee Malta Lab Party Women's Movt; Chair The Samaritans 1989; mem St John Alliance (UK), Int Social Democratic Women; Patron St Michael's Band Club, Zabbar Maltese Settlers' Club (Australia); Hon mem of several int acads; Hon PH D (Beijing); Queen Elizabeth II Coronation Medal 1953; Stara Planina (First Class with Ribbon, Bulgaria) 1983; Order of Nat Flag (First Class, Democratic People's Repub of Korea); Hishan-E-Pakistan; Companion of Hon, Nat Order of Merit (Malta); 50th Anniversary George Cross Medal 1995, 50th Anniversary of Responsible Govt Medal 1996; Re-Introduction of the Malta Self-Government 75th Anniversary Medal 1996; Grand Dame (Grand Cordon) Sovereign Order of St John of Jerusalem, Knights Hospitaller 1996; Sceptre of Authority (Peru); awarded keys and freedom of Lahore, Buenos Aires, Lima, San José, Santa Fe de Bogotá, Montevideo, Aden. *Leisure interests:* philately, classical and modern music. *Address:* 'Il-Kenn Taghna', Wied Il-Ghajn St, Zabbar, Malta (Home). *Telephone:* 825208.

BARBER, Frances; British actress; b 13 May 1957, Wolverhampton; d of S.W. Brooks and late Gladys Simpson. *Education:* Univ of Bangor and Univ of Cardiff. *Career:* Fmrly with Hull Truck Theatre Co, Glasgow Citizens Theatre, Tricycle Theatre, RSC. *Films include:* The Missionary 1982, A Zed and Two Noughts, White City, Castaway, Prick Up Your Ears, Sammy and Rosie Get Laid, We Think the World of You, The Grasscutter, Separate Bedrooms, Young Soul Rebels, Secret Friends, The Lake, Soft Top, Hard Shoulder, The Fish Tale, Three Steps to Heaven, Photographing Fairies; *Plays include:* Night of the Iguana, Pygmalion, Closer, Uncle Vanya; *TV:* Clem, Jackie's Story, Home Sweet Home, Flame to the Phoenix, Reilly, Ace of Spies, Those Glory Glory Days, Hard Feelings, Behaving Badly, The Nightmare Year, Real Women, Just in Time, The Ice House. *Leisure interests:* poetry, reading, swimming.

BARBIERI, Fedora; Italian opera singer; b 4 June 1919. *Education:* Trieste High School and Conservatoire. *Career:* Scholarship to Teatro Lirico, Florence 1940; debut in The Secret Marriage (Cimarosa), Teatro Comunale, Florence 1940; has appeared in leading roles at La Scala (Milan) 1942–, Teatro Colón (Buenos Aires, Argentina) 1947–, Metropolitan Opera House (New York, USA) and Royal Opera House, Covent Garden (London, UK) 1950–; has also appeared at numerous int festivals and opera seasons in Italy, Germany, USA, France, Spain, Portugal, Brazil, and Austria. *Recordings include:* Aida, Il Trovatore, Requiem, Falstaff, Un Ballo in Maschera, La Gioconda, La Favorita, Linda di Chamonix, Suor Angelica. *Address:* Viale Belfiore 9, Florence, Italy.

BARBIERI, Margaret Elizabeth; South African ballet mistress; b 2 March 1947; d of Ettore and Lea Barbieri; m Iain Webb 1983; one s. *Education:* Convent High School (Durban), under Iris Manning and Brownie Sutton (SA) and Royal Ballet Sr School (London). *Career:* Dancer Royal Ballet, London 1968, Prin 1970–74; Sr Prin Sadler's Wells Royal Ballet (now Birmingham Royal Ballet) 1974–89; teacher and coach Royal Ballet School; Dir Classical Graduate Course, London Studio Centre 1990–; appearances include Covent Garden (London) 1968–, Leeds (UK) 1969, Frankfurt (Germany) 1977; Guest dancer Birmingham Royal Ballet (UK) 1990–91, Guest teacher 1991–92; Gov Royal Ballet (London) 1991–; tours with Royal Ballet world-wide; several TV appearances. *Ballets include:* Sleeping Beauty, Swan Lake, Romeo and Juliet, La fille mal gardée, Two Pigeons, The Dream, Wedding Bouquet, Pineapple Poll, The Invitation, Solitaire, The Four Seasons, Checkmate, The Rake's Progress, Summer Garden, Cinderella, Papillon, The Taming of the Shrew, Coppelia, Les Sylphides, Spectre de la Rose, Petrushka, Sacred Circles and the Sword, Summertide, Metamorphosis, Flowers of the Forest. *Leisure interests:* theatre, music, gardening. *Address:* c/o Royal Ballet School, 155 Talgarth Rd, London W14 9DE, UK. *Telephone:* (20) 8748-8964.

BARBIZET, Patricia Marie Marguerite; French business executive; b 17 April 1955, Paris; m Jean Barbizet 1979; one d. *Education:* Ecole Supérieure de Commerce de Paris. *Career:* Man Asst Renault Véhicules Industriels 1977–79, Int Treas 1979–82, Group Treas 1977–84; Financial Dir Renault Crédit Int 1984–89; Financial Dir Groupe Pinault 1988–90, Deputy Dir-Gen in charge of Finance and Communication 1990–92, Dir-Gen Financière Pinault 1992–; Admin, Dir-Gen Artémis 1992–; Pres French Asscn for Co Treasurers 1989–92; mem Ed Cttee Marchés et Techniques Financières; Chevalier de l'Ordre Nat du Mérite; Chevalier de la Légion d'Honneur. *Address:* Artémis, 5 blvd de Latour Maubourg, 75007 Paris, France (Office); 10 rue du Dragon, 75006 Paris, France (Home). *Telephone:* (1) 44-11-20-52; *Fax:* (1) 44-11-20-18.

BARDOT, Brigitte; French actress and environmentalist; b 28 Sept 1934, Paris; d of Louis and Anne-Marie (née Mücel) Bardot; m 1st Roger Vadim (died 2000); m 2nd Jacques Charrier; m 3rd Gunther Sachs 1966 (divorced 1969); one s. *Education:* Paris Conservatoire. *Career:* Stage and film career 1952–; Founding Pres Brigitte Bardot Foundation; involved in animal welfare campaigns; Etoile de Cristal Acad of Cinema 1966; Chevalier de la Légion d'Honneur 1985; Global 500 Award, UNEP 1992. *Films include:* Manina: la fille sans voile, Le fils de Caroline chérie, Futures vedettes, Les grandes manoeuvres, La lumière d'en face, Cette sacrée gamine, La mariée est trop belle, Et Dieu créa la femme, En effeuillant la marguerite, Une parisienne, Les bijoutiers du clair de lune, en cas de malheur, La femme et le pantin, Babette s'en va-t-en guerre, Voulez-vous danser avec moi?, La vérité, Please not now?, Le mépris, Le repos du guerrier, Une ravissante idiote, Viva Maria, A cœur joie 1967, Two Weeks in September 1967, Shalako 1968, Les femmes 1969, Les novices 1970, Boulevard du rhum 1971, Les pétroleuses 1971, Don Juan 1973, L'Histoire très bonne et très joyeuse de Colinot trousse-chemise 1973; *Publication:* Initiales BB (autobiog, Prix Paul Léautaud 1996) 1996, Le Carré de Pluton 1999. *Leisure interest:* swimming. *Address:* Fondation Brigitte Bardot, 45 rue Vineuse, 75016 Paris, France (Office); 45 rue Vineuse, 75116 Paris, France. *Telephone:* (1) 45-05-14-60 (Office); *Fax:* (1) 45-05-14-80 (Office); *E-mail:* f-b-bardot@calva.net (Office); *Internet:* www.fondationbrigittebardot.fr (Office).

BARFOOT, Joan, BA; Canadian novelist and journalist; b 17 May 1946, Owen Sound, Ontario;. *Education:* Univ of W Ontario. *Career:* Reporter, Religion Ed Windsor Star 1967–69; feature and news writer Mirror Publications, Toronto 1969–73, Toronto Sunday Sun 1973–75; with London Free Press 1976–79, 1980–94; has taught journalism and creative writing at School of Journalism, Univ of W Ontario 1987–; Canadian del First Int Feminist Book Fair and Festival, UK 1983; juror Books in Canada First Novel Award 1987, Gov-Gen's Award for English Language Canadian Fiction 1995, Trillium Literary Award 1996; mem Writers' Union of Canada, PEN Canada; Books in Canada First Novel Award 1978, Marian Engel Award 1992. *Publications:* Abra 1978, Dancing in the Dark 1982, Duet for Three 1985, Family News 1989, Plain Jane 1992, Charlotte and Claudia Keeping in Touch 1994, Some Things About Flying 1997, Getting Over Edgar 1999. *Address:* 286 Cheapside St, London, ON N6A 2A2, Canada. *E-mail:* jbarfoot@sympatico.ca.

BARKER, Audrey Lilian, FRSL; British writer; b 13 April 1918, Kent; d of the late Harry and Elsie Annie Barker. *Education:* Surrey and Kent. *Career:* Journalist 1940; Publisher's Reader Cresset Press 1946; Sec and Sub-Ed, BBC 1949–78; writer 1947–; Atlantic Award in Literature 1946; Somerset Maugham Award 1947; Arts Council Award 1970; Soc of Authors Travelling Scholarship 1988; Macmillan Silver Pen Award for Fiction 1986, 1989. *Publications include:* Short Stories: Innocents 1947, Lost Upon the Roundabouts 1964, Femina Real 1971, Life Stories 1981, No Word for Love 1985, Any Excuse for a Party 1991, Element of Doubt: ghost stories 1992; Novels: The Joy Ride 1963, John Brown's Body (shortlisted for the Booker Prize) 1969, A Source of Embarrassment 1974, A Heavy Feather 1978, Relative Successes 1984, The Gooseboy 1987, The Woman Who Talked to Herself 1989, Zeph 1992, The Haunt 1999. *Telephone:* (20) 8642-4530.

BARKER, Kate, BA; British economist; b 1958; m; two c. *Education:* Univ of Oxford. *Career:* Mem staff Nat Inst of Econ and Social Research; joined Ford (Europe) 1985, Head of Econs; Chief Econ Adviser CBI

1994–; mem Treasury panel of industrial economists, Guardian panel of women economists; mem Monetary Policy Cttee Bank of England 2001–. *Address:* Bank of England, Threadneedle St, London EC2R 8AH, UK.

BARKER, Pat, CBE, B ECONS; British writer; b 8 May 1943, Thornaby-on-Tees; d of Moira Drake; m David Faubert Barker 1978; one s one d. *Education:* LSE and Univ of Durham. *Career:* Fmrly teacher at colls of further educ, currently writer; Hon M LITT (Teesside) 1994; Hon D LITT (Napier) 1996, (Durham) 1998, (Herts) 1998; Dr hc (Open Univ) 1997; Hon Fellow LSE 1998; Fawcett Prize 1983; Northern Electric Special Arts Award 1993; Guardian Fiction Prize 1994; Booksellers Author of the Year Award 1996. *Publications:* Union Street (film version Stanley and Iris 1985) 1982, Blow your House Down (adapted for theatre 1994) 1984, The Century's Daughter (re-titled Liza's England 1996) 1986, The Man Who Wasn't There 1989, The Regeneration Trilogy: Regeneration 1991, The Eye in the Door 1993, The Ghost Road (Booker Prize 1995) 1995, Another World 1998, Border Crossing 2001. *Leisure interests:* walking, reading. *Address:* c/o Gillon Aitken Associates, 29 Fernshaw Rd, London, SW10 0TG, UK. *Telephone:* (20) 7351-7561; *Fax:* (20) 7376-3594; *E-mail:* reception@aitkenassoc.demon.co.uk.

BARKER, Sarah Evans, JD; American judge; b 10 June 1943, Mishawaka, IN; d of James McCall and Sarah (née Yarbrough) Evans; m Kenneth R. Barker 1972. *Education:* Indiana and American (Washington, DC) Univs. *Career:* Called to Bar, IN 1969, US Court of Appeals (7th Circuit) 1973, US Supreme Court 1978; Legal Asst to Senator 1969–71; Dir Research, Scheduling and Advance, Senator Percy Re-election Campaign 1972; First Asst US Attorney 1976–77; US Attorney 1981–84; Judge US Dist Court, IN 1984–94, Chief Judge 1994–; Assoc then Partner Bose, McKinney and Evans, Indianapolis 1977–81; mem Exec Cttee Judicial Conf of USA; mem Indiana Historical Soc, ABA, Fed Judges' Asscn, Nat Asscn of Former US Attorneys; mem Bd Dirs Methodist Hosp (IN) Inc, Conner Prairie. *Address:* US District Court, 210 US Courthouse, 46 E Ohio St, Indianapolis, IN 46204, USA.

BARKETT, Rosemary, JD; American judge; b 29 Aug 1939, Ciudad Victoria, Mexico; d of Maria and Assad Barkett. *Education:* Spring Hill Coll and Univ of Florida. *Career:* Pvt Law Practice 1971–79; Circuit Court Judge, Palm Beach, FL 1979, Judge Court of Appeal, W Palm Beach 1984–; apptd to Florida Supreme Court 1985 (first woman apptd), Chief Justice 1992–94; Judge US Court of Appeal (11th circuit), Miami, FL 1994–; Lecturer in Continuing Legal Educ, Florida Bar; Trustee Palm Beach Marine Inst Inc; Chair Study Comm on Guardianship Law; mem Editorial Bd The Florida Judges Manual; Fellow Acad of Matrimonial Lawyers; mem Florida Bar Asscn, Nat Asscn of Women Judges, ABA; Achievement Award, Acad of Florida Trial Lawyers 1988; Florida Women's Hall of Fame 1986; Judicial Achievement Award Asscn of Trial Lawyers of America 1986; Woman of Achievement Award, Palm Beach Co Comm on the Status of Women 1985; Award American Acad of Matrimonial Lawyers 1984. *Leisure interests:* jogging, tennis, travel. *Address:* US Court of Appeals, NE 4th St, Room 1223, Miami, FL 33132, USA.

BARKIN, Ellen; American actress; b 16 April 1954, Bronx, NY; m Gabriel Byrne 1988; one s. *Education:* City Univ of New York and Hunter Coll. *Career:* Numerous stage, film and TV appearances. *Films include:* Diner 1982, Tender Mercies 1983, Daniel 1983, Eddie and the Cruisers 1983, Harry and Son 1984, Terminal Choice, Desert Bloom 1986, Down By Law 1986, The Big Easy 1987, Siesta 1987, Sea of Love 1989, Johnny Handsome 1989, Switch 1991, Man Trouble 1992, Mac 1993, This Boy's Life 1993, Into the West 1993, Bad Company 1995, Wild Bill 1995, Mad Dog Time 1996, The Fan 1996, Fear and Loathing in Las Vegas, Popcorn, Drop Dead Gorgeous; *Plays include:* Shout Across the River 1980, Killings on the Last Line 1980, Extremities 1982, Eden Court, Bad Company; *TV includes:* Search for Tomorrow, Kent State 1981, We're Fighting Back 1981, Terrible Joe Moran 1984, Before Women Had Wings 1998 (Emmy Award). *Address:* c/o CAA, 9830 Wilshire Blvd, Beverly Hills, CA 90212, USA (Office).

BARLINSKA, Izabela, MA; Polish international organization official; b 10 Sept 1955, Gdańsk. *Education:* Univ of Warsaw. *Career:* Asst Polish Acad of Sciences, Inst of Philosophy and Sociology, Warsaw 1978–82; Asst Int Sociological Asscn, Montréal, Canada 1982, Deputy Exec Sec, Amsterdam, Netherlands 1983–86, Exec Sec, Madrid 1987–. *Address:* International Sociological Association, Faculdade de Ciências Políticas e Sociologica, Sala 3.205, Universidade Complutense, Campus de Somosaguas, 28223 Madrid, Spain. *Telephone:* (1) 3527650; *Fax:* (1) 3524945; *E-mail:* isa@sis.ucm.es; *Internet:* www.ucm.es/info/isa.

BARNES, Jhane Elizabeth; American fashion designer; b 4 March 1954, Baltimore, MD; d of Richard Amos and Muriel Florence (née Chase) Barnes; m 1st Howard Ralph Feinberg 1981 (divorced); m 2nd Katsuhiko Kawasaki 1988. *Career:* Pres and Designer Jhane Barnes for ME, New York 1976–78, Jhane Barnes Inc, New York 1978–; numerous awards including Menswear Award (Coty American Fashion Critics) 1980, Most Promising Designer Cutty Sark 1980, Outstanding Designer 1982, Outstanding Menswear Designer (Council of Fashion Designers of America) 1982, Contract Textile Award (American Soc of Interior Designers) 1983, 1984, Product Design Award (Inst of Business Designers and Contract Magazine) 1983, 1984, 1986, 1989. *Address:* Jhane Barnes Inc, 119 W 40th St, 20th Floor, New York, NY 10018, USA.

BARNES, Rosemary (Rosie) Susan, BA; British politician; b 16 May 1946, Nottingham; d of Alan and Kathleen Allen; m Graham Barnes 1967; two s one d. *Education:* Bilborough Grammar School (Nottingham) and Univ of Birmingham. *Career:* Management Trainee Unilever 1967–69; Marketing Exec Yardley of London Ltd 1969–72; primary school teacher 1973; freelance researcher 1973–87; MP for Greenwich, London (SDP 1987–92) 1987–92; Dir WellBeing (fmrly known as Birthright) 1992–96; CEO Cystic Fibrosis Trust 1996–. *Leisure interests:* gardening, walking, travel, cooking, reading, yoga. *Address:* 11 London Rd, Bromley, Kent, BR1 1BY, UK.

BARNETT, Vivian Endicott, MA; American curator; b 8 July 1944, Putnam, CT; d of George and Vivian (née Wood) Endicott; m Peter Herbert Barnett 1967; two d. *Education:* Vassar Coll (NY), New York Univ and City Univ of New York. *Career:* Research Asst Solomon R. Guggenheim Museum, NY 1973–77, Curatorial Assoc 1978–79, Assoc Curator 1980–81, Research Curator 1981–82, Curator 1982–91, Dir Hans K. Rothel and Jean K. Benjamin Archives 1991–; mem American Asscn of Museums, Int Council of Museums, Coll Art Asscn of America; John Simon Guggenheim Fellow 1990. *Publications include:* The Guggenheim Museum: Justin K. Thannhauser Collection 1978, The Guggenheim Museum Collection 1900–1980, Kandinsky Watercolors 1981, Kandinsky at the Guggenheim 1983, 100 Works by Modern Masters from the Guggenheim Museum 1984, Kandinsky Watercolours: Catalogue Raisonné, Vol I 1900–21 1992, Vol II 1922–44 1994, Das bunte Leben: Kandinsky in Lenbachhaus 1995. *Address:* Solomon R. Guggenheim Museum, 1071 Fifth Ave, New York, NY 10128, USA. *Telephone:* (212) 423-3612; *Fax:* (212) 410-7889.

BARNEVA, Margarita, PH D; Bulgarian scientist; b 8 Aug 1935, Lovetch; d of Radoi Kolev and Stefka Nikolova Doshev; m Peter Christov Barnev 1958; two d. *Education:* Univ of Sofia. *Career:* Computer scientist in USSR 1961–63; Research Assoc Inst of Maths and Informatics, Bulgarian Acad of Sciences 1964–78, Sr Research Assoc 1978–; Visiting Prof Univ of Sofia 1968–90, Paisij Hilendarski Univ of Plovdiv 1981–; 38 scientific papers and one textbook published; has taken part in many int workshops on computer sciences; awarded Sign of Honour of Bulgarian Cttee of Science 1975. *Leisure interests:* lace making, embroidery. *Address:* Bulgarian Academy of Sciences, 1112 Sofia, Mladost 3, Bl 307, vh 8, Bulgaria. *Telephone:* (2) 97-93-02; *E-mail:* barneva@math.bas.bg.

BARR, Roseanne (see Roseanne).

BARRAULT, Marie-Christine; French actress; b 21 March 1944, Paris; d of Max-Henri and Marthe (née Valmier) Barrault; m 1st Daniel Toscan du Plantier (divorced); one d one s; m 2nd Roger Vadim 1990 (died 2000). *Education:* Conservatoire Nat d'Art Dramatique. *Career:* Numerous appearances in films and on stage and TV; Officier des Arts et des Lettres. *Plays include:* Andorra 1965, Un couple pour l'hiver 1975, Travail à domicile 1976, Conversation chez les Stein sur Monsieur de Goethe absent 1978, Dylan, Cet animal étrange 1983, 1985, L'étrange intermède 1987, Même heure l'année prochaine 1991, Enfin seuls! 1991, La cerisaie 1993, Le bonheur des autres 1995; *Films include:* Ma nuit chez Maud 1966, Le Distrait 1970, Cousin cousine (Acad Award nomination, Prix Louis Delluc) 1975, Du côté des tennis 1976, L'Etat sauvage 1978, Femme entre chien et loup 1978, Ma chérie 1979, Même les mômes ont du vague à l'âme 1980, Stardust Memories 1980, L'amour trop fort 1981, Un amur en allemagne 1983, Les mots pour le dire 1983, Un amour de Swann 1984, Le pouvoir du mal 1985, Pianoforte 1985, Vaudeville 1986, Le jupon rouge 1987, Adieu je t'aime 1988, Sanguines 1988, Prisonnières 1988, Un été d'orages 1989, Dames galantes 1990, L'amour nécessaire 1991, Bonsoir 1994, C'est la tangente que je préfère 1998, la Dilettante 1999, Berlin Niagara 2000, Obsession; *TV appearances include:* Petit déjeuner compris (series) 1980, Point de rencontre 1981, Marie Curie (series, Nymphe d'Argent, Monte Carlo Television Festival, 7 d'Or for Best Actress) 1991, La Nouvelle Tribu 1996, Le Grande Batre 1997, Maison de Famille 1999; *Publications:* Souffler n'est pas jouer 1984, Le Cheval dans la pierre 1999. *Address:* Agence Cinéart, 36 rue de Ponthieu, 75008 Paris, France.

BARRÉ-SINOUSSI, Françoise Claire, D ÈS SC; French research scientist; b 30 July 1947, Paris; d of Roger and Jeanine (née Fau) Sinoussi; m Jean-Claude Barré 1978. *Education:* Lycée Bergson, Univs of Paris VII and VI. *Career:* Researcher Inst Nat de la Santé et de la Recherche Médicale (INSERM) 1975–86, Dir of Research 1986–; Head of Lab Unité de Biologie des Rétrovirus, Inst Pasteur 1988–92, Head of Unit 1993–; works on origin and evolution of HIV virus and its role in AIDS; Körber Foundation Prize for the Promotion of European Science 1986; Prix de l'Acad de Médecine 1988; Prix Roi Fayçal de Médecine (Saudi Arabia) 1993; Chevalier de la Légion d'Honneur; Chevalier de l'Ordre Nat du Mérite. *Leisure interests:* theatre, reading. *Address:* Institut Pasteur, Unité de Biologie des Rétrovirus, 25 rue du Dr Roux, 75724 Paris, France.

BARRETTE-JONCAS, Hon Justice Claire, BA, LL L; Canadian judge; b 18 May 1933, Montréal, PQ; d of the late Jean and of Cécile (née Guindon) Barrette; m Claude Joncas 1963; one s one d. *Education:* Jésus-Marie Coll and Univ of Montréal. *Career:* Called to the Bar, Montréal 1957; first woman to preside Jr Bar of Montréal 1961–62; first woman to sit on Bar Councils of Montréal and of the Prov of Québec 1962–63; Lecturer in Criminal Law Univ of Montréal 1962–64, McGill Univ 1967–70; QC 1971; Justice Superior Court of Québec 1975–; Judge in charge of Criminal Assizes, Dist of Montréal 1984–99; part-time mem Law Reform Comm of Canada 1971–75; Treas Inst Philippe Pinel de Montréal until 1975; fmr Dir John Howard Soc of Montréal; fmr Sec Legal Aid Bureau, Bar of Montréal; mem Bd of Dirs Univ of Montréal 1985–89. *Leisure interests:* reading, genealogy, travel. *Address:* Court House, 1 Notre-Dame St E, Montréal, PQ H2Y 1B6, Canada (Office). *Telephone:* (514) 393-2134 (Office); *Fax:* (514) 873-6815 (Office).

BARRIOS DE CHAMORRO, Violeta; Nicaraguan politician; b 18 Oct 1929, Rivas; m Pedro Joaquín Chamorro (died 1978); two s two d. *Education:* Our Lady of the Lake Catholic School (San Antonio) and Blackstone Coll (USA). *Career:* Pres and Dir-Gen La Prensa; Minister of Nat Defence 1990; Nat Opposition Union Presidential Cand 1989–90, Pres of Nicaragua 1990–97. *Publication:* Dreams of the Heart (autobiography) 1996.

BARROW, Dame Jocelyn (Anita), DBE, FRSA; British public servant; b 15 April 1929; d of Charles Newton and Olive Irene (née Pierre) Barrow; m Henderson Downer 1970. *Education:* Univ of London. *Career:* Fmr mem Taylor Cttee on School Govs; Sec-Gen, later Vice-Chair Campaign Against Racial Discrimination 1964–69; Vice-Chair Cttee, Int Human Rights Year 1968; mem Community Relations Council 1968–72, Parole Bd 1983–87, Econ and Soc Cttee, EC 1990; a Gov BBC 1981–88; Deputy Chair Broadcasting Standards Council 1989–95; Chair Independent Cttee of Man, Optical Consumer Complaints Service 1992–; Ind Equal Opportunities Inquiry into Ethnicity and Training and Assessment on Bar Vocational Course 1993–94; Non-Exec Dir Whittington Hosp, NHS Trust 1993–; Devt

Dir Focus Consultancy Ltd 1996–; Nat Vice-Pres Nat Townswomen's Guilds 1978–80, 1987–; Founder, Pres Community Housing Asscn, Camden; mem Econ and Social Cttee, EC 1990–; Gov Farnham Castle 1977–93, BDI 1991–, Gov and Patron Goldsmiths Coll; Hon D LITT (E London) 1992. *Leisure interests:* cooking, reading, music, theatre. *Address:* c/o Focus Consultancy Ltd, Elmsgate House, Steeple Ashton, Trowbridge, BA14 6HP, UK.

BARROW, Ursula Helen (Viscountess Waverley), MA, LL M, PH D; Belizean diplomatist; b 31 Oct 1955; d of Raymond Hugh and Rita Helen Barrow; m Viscount Waverley 1994; one s. *Education:* Newnham Coll (Cambridge). *Career:* Econ Devt Planner Planning Unit, Govt of Belize 1978; Consultant for small business affairs, urban planning and marketing, Frazier & Assocs 1979–85; Counsellor and Deputy High Commr in London 1988–89, High Commr 1993–98; Perm Rep to UN 1989–91; Asst Dir (Pol), Commonwealth Secr 1991–93; Amb to the EU, Belgium, France, Germany and the Holy See; Belize Open Scholarship 1974; Cambridge Commonwealth Trust Scholarship 1985. *Address:* c/o Ministry of Foreign Affairs, Economic Development and Education, POB 174, Belmopan, Belize.

BARRYMORE, Drew; American film actress; b 22 Feb 1975, Los Angeles; d of John, Jr and Jaid Barrymore; m 1st Jeremy Thomas 1994 (divorced); m 2nd Tom Green 2001. *Career:* Appeared in dog food commercial 1976; film debut in TV movie Suddenly Love 1978. *Films include:* Altered States 1980, E.T.: The Extra-Terrestrial 1982, Irreconcilable Differences 1984, Firestarter 1984, Cat's Eye 1985, See You In The Morning 1988, Guncrazy 1992, Poison Ivy 1992, Beyond Control: The Amy Fisher Story 1992, Wayne's World 2 1993, Bad Girls 1994, Boys On The Side 1995, Batman Forever 1995, Mad Love 1995, Scream 1996, Everyone Says I Love You 1996, All She Wanted 1997, Best Men 1997, Never Been Kissed (also producer) 1998, Home Fries 1998, The Wedding Singer 1998, Ever After 1998, Charlie's Angels 2000. *Address:* 1122 South Robertson Blvd, #15, Los Angeles, CA 90035, USA.

BARSHEFSKY, Charlene, BA, JD; American government official and lawyer. *Education:* Univ of Wisconsin. *Career:* Fmrly int trade lawyer; partner, Steptoe & Johnson (law firm), Washington, DC 1975–93; Deputy US Trade Rep 1993–96, Acting US Trade Rep April–Nov 1996, US Trade Rep March 1997–. *Address:* Office of the United States Trade Representative, Executive Office of the President, 600 17th St, NW, Washington, DC 20508, USA (Office).

BARSTOW, Dame Josephine Clare, DBE, BA; British opera singer; b 27 Sept 1940, Sheffield; d of Harold and Clara (née Shaw) Barstow; m 1st Terry Hands 1964 (divorced 1968); m 2nd Ande Anderson 1969 (died 1996). *Education:* Univ of Birmingham. *Career:* Debut 1964; Contract Artist Welsh Nat Opera; now freelance singer; performs in all major opera houses in UK, France, Italy, Austria, Germany, fmr USSR, USA, Switzerland; Hon D MUS (Birmingham, Kingston, Sheffield Hallam); Fidelio Medal. *Opera roles include:* Violetta (Traviata), Leonora (Forza del Destino), Elisabeth (Don Carlos), Lady Macbeth, Leonore (Fidelio), Sieglinde, Arabella, Salome, Chrysothemis, Amelia, The Marschallin, Tosca, Mimi, Minnie, Manon Lescaut, Emilia Marty, Jenufa, Katya Kabanova, Medea, Renata (The Fiery Angel), Katerina Ismailova, Kostelnicka (Jenufa), Marie (Wozzeck), Gloriana; world premières of Tippet, Henze and Penderecki; *Recordings include:* Verdi Recital Record with English Nat Opera Orchestra and Mark Elder, Un Ballo in Maschera with Herbert von Karajan, The Knot Garden, Oliver, Kiss Me Kate, Street Scene, Four Finales. *Leisure interest:* farming (cattle) and breeding Arabian horses. *Address:* c/o Askonas Holt, Lonsdale Chambers, 27 Chancery Lane, London WC2A 1PF, UK (Office). *Telephone:* (20) 7400-1700.

BARTH, Else M.; Norwegian/Netherlands professor of logic and analytical philosophy; b 3 Aug 1928, Strinda, Norway; m Hendrik A. J. F. Misset 1953. *Education:* Univs of Oslo, Trondheim, Amsterdam and Leiden. *Career:* Reader in Logic Utrecht Univ, Netherlands 1971–77; Prof of Analytical Philosophy Groningen Univ, Netherlands 1977–87, of Logic and Analytical Philosophy 1987–; Pres Evert Willem Beth Foundation 1976–; mem Royal Netherlands Soc of Sciences, Norwegian Soc of Sciences. *Publications:* The Logic of the Articles in Traditional Philosophy, A Contribution to the Study of Conceptual

Structures 1974, From Axiom to Dialogue – A Philosophical Study of Logics and Argumentation (jtly) 1982, Argumentation: Approaches to Theory Formation, Problems, Functions, and Semantic Roles – A Pragmatist's Analysis of Montague's Theory of Sentence Meaning (jtly) 1986; numerous contribs to learned journals and has published lectures. *Leisure interests:* music, cultural and political philosophy, literature, skiing. *Address:* Filosofisch Instituut, University of Groningen, Westersingel 19, 9718 CA Groningen, Netherlands (Office); Kamperfoelieweg 16, 9765 HK Paterswolde, Netherlands (Home); Nachtegaallaan 26, 2224 JH Katwijk aan Zee, Netherlands (Home). *Telephone:* (50) 636146 (Office); (5907) 4315 (Paterswolde); (1718) 13353 (Katwijk aan Zee).

BARTHET-MAYER, Christine; French politician; b 22 Dec 1948, Munster. *Career:* Chargée de mission Préfet du Haut-Rhin 1992–94; Municipal Councillor for Colmar 1983–MEP (Energie Radicale, Group of the European Radical Alliance), mem Cttee on Agric and Rural Devt, Del to EU-Malta Jt Parl Cttee 1994–99; f Association Nationale Pain Contre la Faim. *Address:* Hôtel de ville, 2 place de la Mairie, 68000 Colmar, France; 10 Petite rue des Tanneur, 68000 Colmar, France. *Telephone:* (2) 284-21-11; *Fax:* (2) 230-69-43.

BARTLETT, Jennifer, MFA; American artist; b 14 March 1941, Long Beach, CA; m 1st Edward Bartlett 1964 (divorced 1972); m 2nd Mathieu Carrière 1983. *Education:* Mills Coll (Oakland, CA) and Yale Univ School of Art and Architecture. *Career:* Art teacher Univ of Connecticut 1964–72, School of Visual Arts, New York 1972; numerous one-woman and group exhibitions including Alan Saret's SoHo Gallery (NY) 1970, Documenta (Kassel, Germany) 1977, Venice Biennale (Italy) 1980; represented in numerous collections including Museum of Modern Art, Metropolitan Museum of Art, Whitney Museum of American Art (NY), Art Gallery of S Australia (Adelaide), Rhode Island School of Design, Yale Univ Art Gallery and Walker Art Center (Minneapolis, MN); Harris Prize Art Inst of Chicago 1976, Award of American Acad, Award of Inst of Arts and Letters 1983. *Works include:* Large-scale murals and other works: Rhapsody 1976, Swimmers Atlanta (Richard B. Russel Fed Bldg, Atlanta, GA) 1979, 270 steel plates for Inst for Scientific Information (PA), murals for AT&T Bldg (NY), sculpture and other objects for Volvo Corpn HQ (Göteborg, Sweden). *Address:* c/o Robert Miller Gallery, 526 West 26th St, New York, NY 10001, USA. *Telephone:* (212) 366-4774; *Fax:* (212) 366-4454; *E-mail:* rmg@robertmillergallery.com; *Internet:* www.robertmillergallery.com.

BARTLEY, Luella; British fashion designer; b 1974, Stratford upon Avon. *Education:* St Martin's School of Art. *Career:* Began career as fashion writer with the Evening Standard and Vogue; freelance corresp, The Face, Dazed and Confused; launched first two collections with boutiques Whistles and Henri Bendel; fourth collection launched at Milano Moda Donna (Milan Fashion show) May 2001; Elle Fashion Award. *Address:* c/o Bottega Veneta, Viale Piceno 15/17, 20129 Milan, Italy.

BARTOLI, Cecilia; Italian opera singer (mezzo-soprano) and recitalist; b 4 June 1966, Rome; d of Pietro Angelo Bartoli and Silvana Bazzoni. *Education:* Acad of Santa Cecilia (Rome). *Career:* Debut on TV 1985; debut in USA at Mostly Mozart Festival, New York 1990, in France at Opéra de Paris Bastille 1990, in Italy at La Scala, Milan 1990, in Austria at Salzburg Festival 1992; has performed with Montréal Symphony Orchestra, PQ, Canada, Philadelphia Orchestra, PA, USA 1990, with András Schiff 1990–, at Rossini bicentenary celebration, Lincoln Center, New York, NY, USA 1992, in Florence 1991, and in Chicago, IL, USA 1992; Grammy Award for Best Classical Vocal 1994. *Operas include:* The Marriage of Figaro, Le Comte Ory, Così fan tutte; *Albums include:* Rossini Recitals, Mozart Arias, Rossini Heroines, If You Love Me 1992, Mozart Portraits 1995, An Italian Songbook 1997, Vivaldi Album 1999. *Address:* c/o Edgar Vincent, 157 W 57th St, Suite 502, New York, NY 10019, USA (Office).

BARTON, (Barbara) Anne, PH D, FBA; British professor of English; b 9 May 1933; d of Oscar Charles Roesen and Blanche Godfrey Williams; m 1st William Harvey Righter 1957; m 2nd John Adie Barton 1969. *Education:* Bryn Mawr Coll (PA) and Univ of Cambridge (UK). *Career:* Lecturer History of Art Ithaca Coll, NY 1958–59; Rosalind Carlisle

Research Fellow Girton Coll, Cambridge 1960–62, Official Fellow in English 1962–72, Asst Lecturer Univ of Cambridge 1962–64, Lecturer 1964–72, Prof of English 1984–2000, Fellow Trinity Coll 1986–; Hildred Carlile Prof of English and Head Dept of English, Bedford Coll, Univ of London 1972–74; Fellow and Tutor in English New Coll, Oxford and Common Univ Fund Lecturer 1974–84; mem Editorial Bds Shakespeare Survey 1972–, Shakespeare Quarterly 1981–, Studies in English Literature 1976–, Romanticism 1995–; Hon Fellow Shakespeare Inst, Univ of Birmingham, New Coll, Oxford 1991; mem Academia Europaea; Crawshay Prize of the British Acad 1991. *Publications:* Shakespeare and the Idea of the Play 1962, Ben Jonson, Dramatist 1984, The Names of Comedy 1990, Byron: Don Juan 1992, Essays, Mainly Shakesperean 1994; numerous essays in journals. *Leisure interests:* opera, travel, fine arts. *Address:* University of Cambridge, Trinity College, Cambridge CB2 1TQ, UK (Office). *Telephone:* (1223) 338466 (Office); (1223) 338466 (Home); *E-mail:* ab10004@hermes.cam.ac.uk (Home).

BARTON, Glenys, MA, RCA; British artist; b 24 Jan 1944, Stoke on Trent; d of Alexander James and Gertrude Elizabeth (née Farmer) Barton; m Martin Hunt; one s. *Education:* Royal Coll of Art. *Career:* Part-time lecturer Portsmouth Polytechnic 1971–74, Camberwell School of Arts & Crafts 1971–87; numerous solo and group exhibitions, UK and abroad 1980–; works in numerous public collections including: Nat Portrait Gallery, London, Royal Scottish Museum, Edinburgh, Scottish Nat Portrait Gallery, Edinburgh, Victoria and Albert Museum, London, Potteries Museum, Stoke On Trent, Wedgwood Museum, Barlaston, and in Birmingham, Leeds, Leicester, Manchester, Norwich, Portsmouth, Reading, Southampton, Rotterdam, Melbourne, Pennsylvania, Leeuwarden and Stockholm. *Exhibitions:* solo: Museum of Decorative Art, Copenhagen 1973, Oxford Gallery, Oxford 1973, Angela Flowers Gallery, London 1974, 1981, 1983, 1986, 1994, Gallery Het Kapelhuis, Amersfoort, Netherlands 1976, Germeenttelijkmuseum, Leeuwarden, Netherlands 1976, Crafts Council Gallery, London 1977, Wedgwood New York 1978, Flowers East, London 1990, 1993, 1996, 1997, Nat Portrait Gallery, London 1997, Manchester City Art Gallery 1997, City Museum and Art Gallery, Stoke On Trent 1998, Flowers West, Santa Monica 2000. *Leisure interest:* gardening. *Address:* c/o Flowers East Contemporary Gallery, 199–205 Richmond Rd, London E8 3NJ, UK.

BARTON, Nelda Ann Lambert; American political activist and business executive; b 12 May 1929, Providence, KY; d of Eulis Grant and Rubie Lois (née West) Lambert; m Harold Bryan Barton 1951 (died 1977); three s (one deceased) two d. *Education:* Providence High School (KY), Western Kentucky Univ and Norton Memorial Infirmary School of Medical Tech. *Career:* Medical Technologist 1950–52; Nursing Home Admin 1979; Dir Corbin Deposit Bank Bd 1980–84, mem Exec Comm 1983–84; Chair of Bd and Organizer Tri-Co Nat Bank 1985, Williamsburg Nat Bank 1989, Campbellsville Nat Bank 1990; Pres Tri-County Bancorp Inc, Corbin, KY 1987; Chair Green Co Banshares Inc 1987; Dir and mem Exec Cttee Greensburg Deposit Bank 1987; Pres, Chair Health Systems Inc (Corbin) 1978, Barton & Assocs Inc, Hazard Nursing Home Inc, Williamsburg Nursing Home Inc, Corbin Nursing Home Inc, Barbourville Nursing Home Inc, Harlan Nursing Home Inc, Knott Co Nursing Home Inc, Wolfe Co Health Care Center, The Whitley Whiz Inc, Institutional Pharmacy Inc; Dir and Organizer McCreary Nat Bank 1994; Republican Nat Ctteewoman for Kentucky 1968–96; Vice-Chair Republican Nat Cttee 1984–93, Sec 1993; mem Republican Nat Cttee President's Club 1981, Nat Steering Cttee Bush–Quayle Campaign 1987–88; mem numerous civic and political cttees and orgs; Hon D JUR (Cumberland Coll) 1991. *Address:* Health Systems Inc, PO Drawer 1450, Corbin, KY 40702, USA (Office); 1311 Seventh St Rd, Corbin, KY 40701-2207, USA (Home).

BARTOŞ, Daniela; Romanian politician. *Career:* Sec of State Ministry of Health until 1996, Minister 1996–, Minister of Health and Family 2000–. *Address:* Ministry of Health, 70109 Bucharest, Str Ministerului 1–3, Romania. *Telephone:* (1) 6141526; *Fax:* (1) 3124883.

BARTOS-HÖPPNER, Barbara; German writer; b 4 Nov 1923, Eckersdorf, Kreis Bunzlau/Schleswig. *Career:* Freelance writer of novels and children's books 1956–; Bundesverdienstkreuz; other awards include First Prize New York Herald Tribune 1963, Hans Christian

Andersen Prize 1968, European Children's Book Prize 1976, Großer Preis, Deutsche Akad für Kinder- und Jugendliteratur 1982. *Publications include:* Kosaken gegen Kutschum-Kahn 1959, Sturm über den Kaukasus 1963, Aljoscha und die Bärenmütze 1968, Schnüpperle (8 vols) 1969–91, Ein Ticket nach Moskau 1970, Auf dem Rücken der Pferde 1975, Tiermärchen, Wintermärchen 1977, Silvermoon (3 vols) 1977, 1979, 1981, Das große Bartos-Höppner-Buch 1981, Elbsaga 1985, Das Osterbuch 1987, Norddeutsche Feste und Bräuche 1987, Kommst du mit, Kolja? 1989, Von Aachener Printen bei Zürcher Leckerli 1989, Kinderreime 1990, Muz, kleiner Muz 1990, Zaubertopf und Zauberkugel 1991, Maria 1991, Rebekka 1991, Rübezahl 1992, Die Schuld der Grete Minde 1993, Vom Himmel hoch 1999, Osterfest und Frühlingszeit 2000.

BÁRTOVÁ, Daniela; Czech athlete; b 6 May 1974, Ostrava, d of Alois Bárta and Marie Bártová. *Education:* Charles Univ, Prague. *Career:* Gymnast 1983–92, competed in European Championships 1989, World Championships 1991, Olympic Games, Barcelona, Spain 1992, Champion of Czechoslovakia (now Czech Repub) 1989, 1990; Pole-vaulter 1993–, holder of World Record 1995–96, competed in European Championships. *Leisure interests:* astronomy, history. *Address:* Charvátova str 640/5, 71500 Ostrava 2, Czech Republic.

BARTZ, Carol; American business executive; b 1949; one d. *Education:* Univ of Wisconsin. *Career:* various roles with Sun Microsystems rising to Exec Officer 1983–92; CEO Autodesk Inc 1992–. *Address:* Autodesk Inc, 111 McInnis Parkway, San Rafael, CA 94903, USA.

BASINGER, Kim; American actress; b 8 Dec 1953, Athens, GA; d of Don Basinger; m 1st Ron Britton 1980 (divorced 1990); m 2nd Alec Baldwin 1993. *Education:* Neighbourhood Playhouse (NY). *Career:* Fashion model 1971–76; actress 1976–. *Films include:* Hard Country 1981, Mother Lode 1982, Never Say Never Again 1982, The Man Who Loved Women 1983, The Natural 1984, 9½ Weeks 1985, Fool for Love 1985, No Mercy 1986, Blind Date 1987, My Stepmother is an Alien 1988, Batman 1989, The Marrying Man 1990, Too Hot To Handle 1991, Final Analysis 1992, Cool World 1992, The Real McCoy 1993, Getaway 1994, Wayne's World II 1994, Prêt-à-Porter 1994, LA Confidential 1997 (Acad Award and Golden Globe for Best Supporting Actress), Bless the Child 2000, Dreamed of Africa 2000; *TV appearances include:* Dog and Cat 1977, Katie – Portrait of a Centerfold 1978, The Ghost of Flight 401 1979, From Here to Eternity 1979. *Address:* c/o Rick Nicita, CAA, 9830 Wilshire Blvd, Beverly Hills, CA 90212, USA; c/o Judy Hofflund, Hofflund Polone, 9465 Wilshire Blvd, Suite 820, Beverly Hills, CA 90212, USA.

BASSETT, Angela; American actress; b 16 Aug 1958, New York. *Education:* Yale School of Drama. *Films:* F/X 1986, Kindergarten Cop 1990, Boyz N the Hood 1991, City of Hope 1991, Critters 4, Innocent Blood 1992, Malcolm X 1992, Passion Fish 1992, What's Love Got to Do with It 1993 (Golden Globe Award Best Actress 1994), Strange Days 1995, Panther 1995, Waiting to Exhale 1995, A Vampire in Brooklyn 1995, Contact 1997, How Stella Got Her Groove Back 1998, Music of the Heart 1999, Supernova 2000; *Plays:* Colored People's Time 1982, Antigone, Black Girl, The Mystery Plays 1984–85, The Painful Adventures of Pericles, Prince of Tyre 1986–87, Joe Turner's Come and Gone 1986–87, Ma Rainey's Black Bottom, King Henry IV (Part I) 1987; *TV:* Line of Fire: The Morris Dees Story 1991, The Jacksons: An American Dream 1992, A Century of Women 1994. *Address:* c/o ICM, 8942 Wilshire Blvd, Beverly Hills, CA 90211, USA.

BASSETT, Isabel Glenthorne, MA; Canadian journalist and broad-caster; d of Ranald and Janet (née MacKinnon) Macdonald; m John White Hughes 1967; two d one s. *Education:* Queen's Univ, Ontario Coll of Educ and York Univ. *Career:* Teacher 1961–64; reporter Toronto Telegram 1964–67; Lecturer York Univ 1974–75; Reporter W5 CTV Television Network 1976–77; Reporter, Presenter and Producer CFTO-TV 1977–84, Producer and Reporter Documentaries 1984–93; elected to Ontario Legis 1995, Minister of Citizenship, Culture and Recreation, Govt of Ont 1997–99; Chair and CEO TVONTARIO 1999–; Dir Toronto Women in Film and Television 1994; numerous awards including awards for documentaries. *TV includes:* Hourlong 1977–84, Survival 2000 1982, Children Take Care (assoc producer, Canada Pro Awards Gold Medal 1984) 1983, No Place to Hide

(Canada Pro Awards Gold Medal, Canadian TV and Film Asscn Gold Medal 1986) 1985, Missing 1986, Growing Up in the '80s 1987, Quebec Today 1987, No Fixed Address 1988, Beyond the Blues 1989, Kids in Turmoil 1989, The Dark Society 1991, Dead Time 1991; *Publications:* The Parlour Rebellion 1975, The Bassett Report: Career Success of Canadian Women 1985. *Leisure interests:* jogging, riding, reading. *Address:* 76 Binscarth Rd, Toronto, ON M4W 1Y4, Canada (Office); 76 Binscarth Rd, Toronto, ON M4W 1Y4, Canada (Home).

BASSEY, Dame Shirley, DBE; British popular singer; b 8 Jan 1937, Tiger Bay, Cardiff; d of the late Eliza Mendi; m 1st Kenneth Hume; m 2nd Sergio Novak; four c (one deceased). *Career:* Appearances at Astor Club (London), with impresario Jack Hylton 1955, in New York 1961, at Royal Festival Hall, London 1994, 1995; numerous awards include 20 Gold Discs and 14 Silver Discs for int record sales, Best Female Singer (TV Times) 1972, 1973, (Music Week) 1974, Britannia Award 1977, Best Female Entertainer (American Guild of Variety Artists) 1976. *Film:* La Passione 1996; *Recordings include:* Singles: Banana Boat Song, As I Love You, Kiss Me Honey Honey Kiss Me, As Long As He Needs Me, theme song for film Goldfinger 1964, Diamonds Are Forever 1971; Albums: Born to Sing the Blues 1958, And I Love You So 1972, Magic is You 1978, Sassy Bassy 1985, I Am What I Am 1984, New York, New York 1991, Great Shirley Bassey 1999. *Address:* c/o IMG Artists, 616 Chiswick High Rd, London, W4 5RX, UK (Office).

BÁSTI, Juli; Hungarian actress; b 10 Aug 1957, Budapest; d of Lajos Básti and Zsuzsa Zolnay; m Péter Gotmár 1981 (divorced 1986); one s. *Education:* Acad of Dramatic Arts (Budapest). *Career:* Mem Csiky Gergely Theatre Co (Kaposvár) 1980–85, Katona József Theatre Co 1985–; Best Actress Award (San Remo, Italy) 1982, (Moscow, Russian Fed) 1985; Award for Best Acting in Theatre (Budapest) 1985; Jászay Marit Prize 1985; Kossuth Prize 1993. *Stage roles include:* Beatrice (The Changeling), Ophelia (Hamlet), Helena (Midsummer Night's Dream), Lady Anne (Richard III), Mother Ubu (King Ubu), Masha (Three Sisters), Anna Andrejevna (The Government Inspector), Anna Petrovna (Platonov), Velma Kelly in Chicago (musical), Sally in Cabaret (musical) 1993; *Films include:* Wasted Lives 1980, The Red Countess 1983, The Followers 1983, Laura 1986, The Horoscope of Jesus Christ 1988, The Bride of Stalin 1990, The Holidaymaker 1990. *Leisure interest:* forests. *Address:* Krecsányi utca 6, 1025 Budapest, Hungary. *Telephone:* 2742219 (Home).

BASYSTIUK, Olga, BA; Ukrainian soprano; b 18 Aug 1951, Poliana; d of the late Ivan and of Maria Basystiuk; m Vladimir Gaptar 1986; one s. *Education:* State Lysenko Musical Conservatory (Lvov). *Career:* Soloist Franko Opera and Ballet Theatre, Lvov 1974, State Organ Hall, Kiev 1981–; Grand Prix, 7th Int Singers' Competition, Rio de Janiero, Brazil 1975; Gold Medal, 10th Int Popova Singers' Festival, Pleven, Bulgaria 1975; Hon Artist of Ukraine 1976; Laureate, UNESCO Int Records Competition, Bratislava, Czechosovakia 1978; People's Artist of Ukraine 1985; UN Peace Medal 1985; Laureate, State Taras Shevchenko Prize 1987; Gold Medal and Prize, Mikhailo Dem'yaniv Int Foundation 1993; Order of King Yaroslav the Wise 1995. *Recordings include:* 7 Concurson Int de Canto 1975, O. Basystiuk 1978. *Leisure interests:* collecting art, reading, walking. *Address:* ul Lysenko 4, kv 20, Kiev 252034, Ukraine. *Telephone:* (44) 2256791.

BATE, Jennifer Lucy, BA, FRCO, LRAM, ARCM; British organist; b 11 Nov 1944, London; d of Horace Alfred and Dorothy Marjorie (née Hunt) Bate. *Education:* Univ of Bristol. *Career:* Shaw Librarian, LSE 1966–69; int concert career 1969–, has performed in over 20 countries; organizer several teaching programmes; collaboration with Olivier Messiaen 1975–92; designed portable pipe organ with N. P. Mander Ltd 1984, prototype computer organ 1987; numerous TV appearances, including La Nativité du Seigneur at Norwich Cathedral, shown on Channel Four; Contrib to Grove's Dictionary of Music and Musicians; F. J. Read Prize, Royal Coll of Organists; Young Musician 1972; Personnalité de l'Année (France) 1989; one of the Women of the Year (UK) 1990–97, Hon Italian Citizenship in the Prov of Alessandria for services to Music 1996; Grand Prix du Disque (Messiaen), Diapason d'Or, Prix de Répertoire (France), Preis der Deutschen Schallplatten Kritik (Germany) and MRA Award for 18th century series From Stanley to Wesley. *Compositions:* Toccata on a Theme of Martin Shaw, Introduction and Variations on an Old French Carol, Four Reflections,

Homage to 1685, The Spinning Wheel, Lament, An English Canon, Variations on a Gregorian Theme; *Recordings include:* Olivier Messiaen: Complete Organ Works, The Great Organ Works of César Franck, Peter Dickinson: Organ Concerto, From Stanley to Wesley (series of recordings), Reflections – the Organ (music of Jennifer Bate played by the composer). *Leisure interests:* cooking, theatre, philately, gardening. *Address:* 35 Collingwood Ave, Muswell Hill, London N10 3EH, UK. *Telephone:* (20) 8883-3811; *Fax:* (20) 8444-3695; *E-mail:* jenniferbate@ pva.co.uk (Office); jenniferbate@classical-artists.com (Home); *Internet:* www.classical-artists.com/jbate (Home).

BATES, Kathy; American actress; b 28 June 1948, Memphis, TN; d of Langdon Doyle and Bertye Kathleen (née Talbot) Bates; m Tony Campisi 1991. *Education:* White Station High School and S Methodist Univ. *Career:* Singing waitress Catskill mountains, cashier Museum of Modern Art, Manhattan; numerous stage appearances before film debut in 1971. *Plays include:* Varieties 1976, Crimes of the Heart (Pulitzer Prize 1981) 1979, The Art of Dining 1979, Goodbye Fidel 1980, Chocolate Cake 1980, Extremities 1980, The Fifth of July 1981, Come Back to the 5 and Dime Jimmy Dean Jimmy Dean 1982, 'night Mother (Outer Critics Circle Award) 1983, Days and Nights Within 1985, Rain of Terror 1985, Deadfall 1985, Curse of the Starving Class 1985, Frankie and Johnny in the Clair de Lune (Obie Award, Los Angeles Drama Critics Award) 1987, The Road to Mecca 1988; *Films include:* Taking Off 1971, Straight Time 1978, Arthur 2 on the Rocks 1988, Signs of Life, High Stakes 1989, Dick Tracy 1990, White Palace 1990, Misery (Acad Award for Best Actress, Golden Globe, Chicago Film Critics Award) 1990, At Play in the Fields of the Lord, The Road to Mecca, Prelude to a Kiss 1991, Fried Green Tomatoes at the Whistle Stop Cafe 1991, Used People 1992, A Home of Our Own 1993, North 1994, Curse of the Starving Class 1994, Angus 1996, Diabolique 1996, The War at Home 1996, Primary Colors 1998, Swept from the Sea 1998, Titanic 1998, A Civil Action 1999, Dash and Lilly 1999, My Life as a Dog 1999; *TV appearances include:* Films: Johnny Bull, Uncommon Knowledge, Roe vs Wade, No Place like Home, One for Sorrow—Two for Joy, Signs of Life, Murder Ordained, Straight Time, Hostages, The West Side Waltz 1995, The Late Shift 1996; Guest: St Elsewhere, Cagney and Lacey, LA Law, China Beach, All My Children; Murder Ordained (mini-series). *Address:* c/o Susan Smith, 121 N San Vincente Blvd, Beverly Hills, CA 90211, USA.

BATTAGLIA, Letizia; Italian photographer and politician; b 1936, Palermo; m; three d. *Career:* Worked as photographer in Milan; Photographic Dir, L'Ora, Palermo; elected as Green candidate to Palermo Council 1985–90; Co-Founder Rete (Network, anti-Mafia party); Eugene Smith Prize for Social Photography. *Publication:* Passion, Justice, Freedom. *Address:* c/o Aperture, 20 E 23rd St, New York, NY 10010, USA.

BATTLE, Kathleen, M MUS; American opera singer; b Portsmouth, OH; d of Ollie Layne and Grady Battle. *Education:* Univ of Cincinnati. *Career:* Debut New York 1977; regular guest with orchestras of New York, Chicago, Boston, Philadelphia, Cleveland, Los Angeles, San Francisco, Vienna, Paris and Berlin; appearances at Salzburg (Austria), Tanglewood, Spoleto (Italy) and Cincinnati May Festivals and at major opera houses in UK, USA, France, Austria and Italy; recitals in USA, France, UK, Austria and Japan; Dr hc (Cincinnati and Westminster Choir Coll, Princeton); Grammy Award 1987, 1988. *Operas include:* Tannhäuser, Der Rosenkavalier, The Marriage of Figaro, St Francis of Assisi, Ariadne auf Naxos, L'Elisir d'amore; *Recordings include:* Brahms' Requiem and Songs, Mozart's Requiem, Don Giovanni, The Abduction from the Seraglio and Concert Arias, Verdi's Un Ballo in Maschera and Berg's Lulu Suite, New Year's Eve Gala (Vienna), Fauré's Requiem. *Leisure interests:* gardening, cooking, sewing, piano, dance. *Address:* c/o Columbia Artist Management Inc, 165 W 57th St, New York, NY 10019, USA.

BAUCHET, Jacqueline (née Griffon); French civil servant; b 21 Feb 1927, Paris; m Pierre Bauchet 1953; two s one d. *Education:* Lycée Camille Sée (Paris), Inst d'Etudes Politiques de Paris and Ecole Nat d'Admin (Paris). *Career:* Auditor then Counsel, Conseil d'Etat (Council of State) 1953–73, Conseiller d'Etat 1977, Deputy Pres Legal Service 1987–, mem Court of Budgetary and Financial Discipline 1987–96, Vice-Pres Tribunal for Disputes 1990–93, Pres Comm des Sondages

1996–99; Officier de la Légion d'Honneur; Commdr de l'Ordre Nat du Mérite. *Leisure interests:* drawing, reading. *Address:* Conseil d'Etat, Palais Royal, 75100 Paris, France (Office); 12 rue Pestalozzi, 75005 Paris, France (Home). *Telephone:* (1) 45-87-34-41 (Home).

BAUDRIER, Jacqueline; French journalist and diplomatist; b 16 March 1922, Beaufai; m 1st Maurice Baudrier (divorced); m 2nd Roger Perriard 1957. *Education:* Univ of Paris. *Career:* Political reporter Actualités de Paris, Foreign News reporter and presenter of various news programmes Office de Radiodiffusion-Télévision Française (ORTF) 1950–60, Ed-in-Chief of news programmes 1963–66, in charge of main news programme 1966–68, Asst Dir of Radio Broadcasting in charge of Information 1968–69, Dir of Information A2 TV channel 1969–72, Dir TF1 TV channel network (TF1) 1972–74; Chair Société Nationale de Radiodiffusion (Radio-France) 1975–81; Perm Rep of France to UNESCO 1981–85; mem Exec Cttee UNESCO 1984–85, Comm nat de la Communication et des Libertés 1986–89; columnist Quotidien de Paris 1989; columnist and mem Ed Bd L'Observatoire de la Télévision 1993–; mem Bd of Dirs Télédiffusion de France (TDF) 1975–81; Pres Communauté radiophonique des programmes de langue française 1977–79, Cosmo Communications 1989–95, Channel 5 TV Programming Comm 1995; Vice-Pres Nat Comm for UNESCO 1996; Vice-Chair Programming Comm Union européenne de radiodiffusion 1978, 1980; Prix Maurice Bourdet 1960; Prix Ondes 1969; Chevalier de la Légion d'Honneur; Officier de l'Ordre Nat du Mérite, numerous other awards. *Address:* La Cinquième, 8 rue Marceau, 92136 Issy-les-Moulineaux, Cedex, France (Office); 60 quai Louis Blériot, 75016 Paris, France (Home).

BAUSCH, Pina; German dancer and choreographer; b 27 July 1940, Solingen; one s. *Education:* Folkwang School (Essen) and Juilliard School (NY). *Career:* Mem Paul Sanasardo and Donya Feuer Dance Co, danced at Metropolitan Opera, New York 1960–62; soloist Folkwang-Ballett 1962, choreographer 1968–73, Dir 1968–73; f Tanztheater Wuppertal 1973; Head Dance Dept Folkwang Hoschschule (Essen) 1983–89; Artistic Dir Folkwang-Tanzstudio 1983–; numerous awards including Commdr des Arts et des Lettres, Cruz da Ordem Militar de Santiago de Espada, Portugal, Pour le Mérite Orden, Bundesverdienstkreuz mit Stern, Praemium Imperiale 1999. *Choreography includes:* Fritz, Iphigenie auf Tauris, Adagio–Fünf Lieder von Gustaf Mahler 1974, Orpheus und Eurydice, Die Sieben Todsünden 1976, Café Muller Kontakthof 1978, Walzer, Nelken 1982, Two Cigarettes in the Dark 1985, Viktor 1986, Ahnen 1987, Die klage der Kaiserin, Palermo 1989, Tanzabend II 1991, Das Stück mit dem Schiff 1993, Ein Trauerspiel 1994, Danzón 1995, Nur Du 1996, Der Fensterputzer 1997, Masurca 1998, Lissabon-Projekt 1998. *Address:* Tanztheater Wuppertal, Spinnstrasse 4, 42283 Wuppertal, Germany. *Telephone:* (202) 5634253; *Fax:* (202) 5638171.

BAVADRA, Adi Kuini Teimumu Vuikaba, BA; Fijian politician; b 23 Dec 1949, Ba; d of late Senator Ratu Qoro and of Lanieta Vuni Latianara; m 1st Dr Timoci Bavadra fmr Prime Minister of Fiji (died 1989); m 2nd Clive Speed 1991; two s two d eight step-c. *Education:* Suva Grammar School, Univ of the S Pacific and Australian Nat Univ. *Career:* Rep Fiji Public Service Asscn Women at world conf org by Public Service Int 1984; Pres Fiji Labour Party (FLP) 1989–91; All Nationals Congress Party (ANC) cand in gen election 1994; Pres ANC (now merged with Fijian Asscn–FA) 1994–; Head Fiji Del to World Conf on UN End of Decade for Women, Nairobi, Kenya 1985; fmrly Pres Women's Wing, Fiji Public Servants' Asscn, Univ of the S Pacific Alumni Asscn. *Leisure interests:* reading, bible study, political debates, biographical documentaries of world leaders and literary figures. *Address:* General Post Office 633, Suva, Fiji. *Telephone:* 320 533; *Fax:* 320 533.

BAWDEN, Nina Mary, CBE, MA, JP, FRSL; British writer; b 19 Jan 1925, London; d of Charles and Ellalaine Ursula May Mabey; m 1st H. W. Bawden 1947; two s (one deceased) one d; m 2nd Austen S. Kark 1954; one d two step-d. *Education:* Ilford Co High School and Somerville Coll (Oxford). *Career:* Asst Town and Country Planning Asscn 1946–47; apptd JP Surrey 1968; Pres Soc of Women Writers and Journalists 1981–; Hon Fellow Somerville Coll (Oxford) 2000; Guardian Prize for Children's Literature 1975; Yorkshire Post Novel of the Year Award 1976; Phoenix Award; The Children's Literature Award 1993.

Publications: The Birds on the Trees 1970, Anna Apparent 1972, George Beneath a Paper Moon 1974, Afternoon of a Good Woman 1976, Familiar Passions 1979, Walking Naked 1981, The Ice House 1983, Circles of Deceit 1987, Family Money 1992, A Nice Change 1998, Ruffian on the Stair 2001; Children's books: Carrie's War (Phoenix Award 1993), The Peppermint Pig, The Runaway Summer, The Finding 1985, Princess Alice 1985, Keeping Henry 1988, The Outside Child, Family Money 1991, Humbug 1992, The Real Plato Jones 1993, Granny the Pag 1995, Devil By The Sea 1997, Off the Road 1999. *Leisure interests:* theatre, cinema, travel, croquet. *Address:* 22 Noel Rd, London N1 8HA, UK; 19 Kapodistriou, Nauplion 21100, Greece. *Telephone:* (20) 7226-2839 (Office).

BAXENDALE, Presiley Lamorna, BA; British barrister; b 31 Jan 1951; d of Geoffrey Arthur and the late Elizabeth Baxendale; m Richard Kieran FitzGerald 1978; one s one d. *Education:* St Anne's Coll (Oxford). *Career:* Called to the Bar, Lincoln's Inn 1974, Bencher 1999; Jr Counsel to Crown, Common Law 1991; QC 1992; mem Ind Cttee for Supervision of Telephone Information Services 1986–90; Counsel to Scott Inquiry 1992–95; mem Council of Justice 1994–, Vice-Chair Exec Cttee 1994–96; mem Court of Govs LSE 1988–. *Address:* Blackstone Chambers, Blackstone House, Temple, London EC4Y 9BW, UK. *Telephone:* (20) 7583-1770; *Fax:* (20) 7822-7350.

BAXTER GRILLO, Dorothea, LM, PH D; Jamaican professor of anatomy; b 1931, Kingston; d of George and Lilian Fredrick Baxter; m Prof T. A. I. Grillo 1955. *Education:* St Andrew's High School for Girls (Kingston) and Royal Coll of Surgeons (Dublin). *Career:* Fellow in Paediatrics, Stanford Univ, CA, USA 1960; WHO Fellow, Univ of Khartoum 1969; Visiting Hon Research Assoc Tokyo Medical and Dental Univ 1968; Exchange Visitor, Japan 1975; Prof of Anatomy, Univs of Ife and Maiduguri, Nigeria 1978–85; Visiting Scholar New Hall, Cambridge, UK 1989; Prof of Anatomy Univ of the West Indies, Kingston 1985–; numerous publs. *Leisure interests:* music, archaeology, art, bird-watching. *Address:* University of the West Indies, Faculty of Medicine, Dept of Anatomy, Mona, Kingston 7, Jamaica.

BAYE, Nathalie; French actress; b 6 July 1948, Mainneville; d of Claude Baye and Denise Coustet; one d by Johnny Hallyday. *Education:* Conservatoire Nat d'Art Dramatique de Paris. *Plays include:* Galapages 1972, Liola 1973, Les trois sœurs 1978, Adriana Monti 1986, Les fausses confidences 1993, La parisienne 1995; *Films include:* Two People 1972, La nuit américaine 1973, La gueule ouverte 1974, La gifle 1974, Un jour la fête 1974, Le voyage de noces 1975, Le plein de super 1976, Mado 1976, L'homme qui aimait les femmes 1977, Monsieur Papa 1977, la Communion solennelle 1977, La chambre verte 1978, Mon premier amour 1978, La mémoire courte 1978, Sauve qui peut 1979, Je vais craquer 1979, Une semaine de vacances 1980, Provinciale 1980, Beau-père, Une étrange affaire, L'Ombre rouge 1981, Le retour de Martin Guerre 1981, La Balance (César for Best Actress 1983) 1982, J'ai épousé une ombre 1982, Notre histoire 1983, Rive droite, rive Gauche 1984, Détective 1984, Le neveu de Beethoven 1985, Lune de miel 1985, De guerre lasse 1987, En toute innocence 1988, La Baule-les-Pins 1990, Un week-end sur deux 1990, The Man Inside 1990, L'Affaire Wallraff 1991, La Voix 1992, Mensonges 1993, La Machine 1994, Les Soldats de L'Espérance 1994, Enfants de salaud 1996, Si je t'aime... prends garde à toi 1998, Food of Love 1998, Paparazzi 1998, Vénus beauté 1999, Une liaison pornographique 1999 (Prix d'interprétation féminine, Venice Film Festival 1999). *Address:* c/o Artmédia, ave Georges V, 75008 Paris, France.

BAYEFSKY, Anne Fruma, MA, LL B, M LITT; Canadian professor of law; b 8 Nov 1953, Toronto; d of Aba and Evelyn Bayefsky; m Raj Anand 1986 (divorced); three d. *Education:* Univs of Toronto and Oxford (UK) and Int Inst of Human Rights (Strasbourg). *Career:* Prof of Law Univ of Ottawa 1981–96; Stagiaire European Comm of Human Rights, Strasbourg 1981; called to the Bar, ON 1983; Special Adviser Canadian Del to UN Gen Ass 1984, Special Observer 1989, Observer to Human Rights Comm 1993–97; Fellow Centre for the Study of Human Rights, Columbia Univ, NY, USA 1985; Visiting Researcher Faculty of Law, Univ of Toronto 1986–87; Visiting Fellow Osgoode Hall Law School, York Univ 1988–89, Visiting Prof 1989–90; Chair Bds of Inquiry under Ontario Human Rights Code (Govt of Ontario) 1986–98; Prof Dept of Political Science and Dir Centre for Refugee

Studies, York Univ 1996–99; Visiting Prof Columbia Univ Law School 2001–02; mem Advisory Council Interights—Int Centre for Legal Protection of Human Rights, London, UK 1986–96, Cttee on Human Rights Law and Practice (Int Law Asscn) 1993–, Cttee on Int Law in Municipal Courts, Int Law Asscn 1989–98, External Research Advisory Cttee UN High Comm for Refugees 1996–98; Commonwealth Scholarship 1980–81; Bora Laskin Nat Fellowship in Human Rights Research 1992; MacArthur Foundation Research Grant 1995–96. *Publications include:* Canada's Constitution Act 1982 and Amendments: A Documentary History 1989, Canadian Yearbook of Human Rights (vols 1–4, ed) 1983–87, Equality Rights and the Canadian Charter of Rights and Freedoms (co-ed) 1985, International Human Rights Law: Use in Canadian Charter of Rights and Freedoms Litigation 1992, Human Rights and Forced Displacement (co-ed) 2000, The UN Human Rights Treaty System in the 21st Century (ed) 2000, The UN Human Rights Treaty System: Universality at the Crossroads 2001; numerous contribs to professional journals. *Address:* York University, Department of Political Science, 4700 Keele St, North York, ON M3J 1P3, Canada. *Telephone:* (416) 736-5663; *E-mail:* bayefsky@yorku.ca.

BAYER, Fern Patricia, MA; Canadian curator; b 23 Oct 1949, Montréal, PQ; d of George and Catherine (née Boucher) Bayer. *Education:* McGill Univ, Univ Int dell'Arte (Italy) and Univ of Toronto. *Career:* Curator of art exhibitions in the Middle East, Asia, Europe, Canada and Brazil; Teaching Asst Univ of Toronto 1975–76; freelance art consultant 1975–77; Chief Curator Art Collection, Govt of Ontario 1977–95; now ind art curator of int exhibitions of contemporary art in Canada, USA, Japan, Middle East and Europe. *Publications:* The Ontario Collection 1984; articles and contribs to books and catalogues. *Address:* 131 Bloor St W, Suite 1017, Toronto, ON M5S 1S3, Canada. *Telephone:* (416) 921-6602; *Fax:* (416) 921-2800; *E-mail:* fpbayer@aol .com.

BAYNES, Pauline Diana; British designer and illustrator; b 9 Sept 1922; d of Frederick William Wilberforce Baynes and Jessie Harriet Maud Cunningham; m Fritz Otto Gasch 1961 (died 1988). *Education:* Beaufront School (Camberley), Farnham School of Art and Slade School of Art (London). *Career:* Voluntary Worker Camouflage Devt and Training Centre, Royal Engineers 1940–42, Hydrographic Dept, Admiralty 1942–45; Designer world's largest crewel embroidery, Plymouth Congregational Church, MN, USA 1970; mem Women's Int Art Club 1938–; Kate Greenaway Medal, Library Asscn 1968. *Publications include:* Writer and illustrator: Victoria and the Golden Bird 1948, How Dog Began 1985, King Wenceslas 1987; Illustrator: Farmer Giles of Ham 1949 and subsequent books by J. R. R. Tolkien, The Lion, the Witch and the Wardrobe 1950 and subsequent books by C. S. Lewis, The Arabian Nights 1957, The Puffin Book of Nursery Rhymes 1963, Recipes from an Old Farmhouse 1966, Dictionary of Chivalry 1968, Snail and Caterpillar 1972, A Companion to World Mythology 1979, The Enchanted Horse 1981, Frog and Shrew 1981, All Things Bright and Beautiful 1986, The Story of Daniel 1986, Noah and the Ark 1988. *Leisure interest:* walking the dogs. *Address:* Rock Barn Cottage, Dockenfield, Farnham, Surrey GU10 4HH, UK. *Telephone:* (1428) 713306.

BEACHAM, Stephanie; British actress; b 28 Feb 1949, Herts; two d. *Education:* Royal Acad of Dramatic Art (London). *Career:* Seasons at Liverpool Everyman, Bristol Old Vic, Nottingham Playhouse, Oxford Playhouse and Sheffield Crucible; numerous plays and TV and film appearances; Distinguished Service Award (American Speech and Hearing Asscn) 1991. *Plays include:* Monsieur Barnett, The Basement, Tea Party, On Approval, London Cuckolds, Can You Hear Me At The Back?, Happy Family, The Singular Life of Albert Nobbs, An Audience Called Edward, The Rover, Venice Preserved, Twelfth Night; *Films include:* The Nightcomers, Tam Lyn, The Games, Movie Blackmail, The Confessional, The Old and The Young, Troop Beverly Hills, The Wolves of Willoughby Chase, A Girl Called Harry, The Lilac Bus; *TV appearances include:* The Picnic, The Silent Preacher, Ego Hugo, Sentimental Education, Sorrell And Son, All The World's A Stage, Tenko, Napoleon and Josephine, Lucky, To Be The Best, Marked Personal, Connie, The Colbys, Dynasty, Sister Kate, Secrets, Foreign Affairs, Jane Eyre, A Sentimental Education. *Leisure interests:* drawing, cycling, hiking, gardening. *Address:* c/o PFD, Drury House, 34-43 Russell St, London, WC2B 5HA, UK.

BEAMISH, Sally; British composer; b 26 Aug 1956, London; d of Anthony Beamish and Ursula Snow-Beamish; m Robert Irvine 1988; two d one s. *Education:* Royal Northern Coll of Music (Manchester) and Staatliche Hochschule für Musik (Detmold, Germany). *Career:* Viola player, Raphael Ensemble, Acad of St Martin-in-the-Fields, London Sinfonietta, Lontano 1979–1990; Composer 1990–; Composer-in-Residence Swedish Chamber Orchestra 1998–, Scottish Chamber Orchestra 1998–; performed première of her Viola Concerto at BBC Henry Wood Promenade Concert, London 1995; comms from the City of Reykjavík, BBC TV, English Nat Opera, Brighton Festival, etc; Paul Hamlyn Award for Outstanding Achievement in Composition 1993. *Compositions include:* Tuscan Lullaby 1989, Symphony 1992, Violin Concerto 1994, Viola Concerto 1995, Piano Sonata 1996; *Recordings include:* River (Cello, Viola and Oboe Concertos), Sun on Stone (Saxophone Concertos). *Leisure interests:* drawing, painting, gardening. *Address:* Scottish Music Information Centre, 1 Bowmont Gardens, Glasgow G12 9LR, UK. *Telephone:* (141) 334-6393; *Fax:* (141) 337-1161.

BEAR, Isabel Joy, AM, D SC; Australian research scientist; b 4 Jan 1927, Camperdown, Vic; d of Rolfe W. and Isabel H. Bear. *Education:* Hampton High School, Melbourne Tech Coll and Royal Melbourne Inst of Tech. *Career:* Experimental Scientist Atomic Energy Research Establishment, Harwell, UK 1950–51; Research Asst Birmingham Univ, UK 1951–53; Experimental Officer Div of Mineral Chem, CSIRO, Melbourne 1953–67, Sr Research Scientist 1967–72, Prin Research Scientist 1972–78, Sr Prin Research Scientist 1978–92, Hon Fellow 1992–; part-time Commr Victoria Post-Secondary Educ Comm 1986–91; Chair Advisory Cttee on Technological Research and Devt in Colls of Advanced Educ, Victoria 1987–91; Fellow Australasian Inst of Mining and Metallurgy, Royal Australian Chemical Inst; mem Order of Australia 1986; Leighton Memorial Medal (Royal Australian Chemical Inst) 1988. *Publications:* Alumina to Zirconia - The History of the Csiro Division of Mineral Chemistry (jtly); numerous contribs to professional journals. *Address:* Unit 2, 750 Waverley Rd, Glen Waverley, Vic 3150, Australia. *Telephone:* (3) 9561-7304 (Home).

BEARD, Mary, PH D; British lecturer in classics and writer; b 1 Jan 1955, Much Wenlock, Shropshire; d of Roy Whitbread and Joyce Emily Beard; m Robin Sinclair Cormack 1985; one d one s. *Education:* Shrewsbury High School and Newnham Coll (Cambridge). *Career:* Research in Roman History 1977–79; Lecturer in Classics King's Coll, London 1979–83; Univ Lecturer in Classics, Dir of Studies and Fellow, Newnham Coll, Cambridge 1984–, Reader in Classics 1999–. *Publications include:* Rome in the Late Republic (jtly) 1985, The Good Working Mother's Guide 1988, Pagan Priests (jtly) 1990, A Very Short Introduction to Classics (jtly) 1995, The Invention of Jane Harrison 2000, Classical Art: From Greece to Rome (jtly) 2001. *Address:* University of Cambridge, Newnham College, Cambridge CB3 9DF, UK. *Telephone:* (1223) 335712; *Fax:* (1223) 335110; *E-mail:* mb127@hermes.cam.ac.uk.

BÉART, Emmanuelle; French actress; b 14 Aug 1965, St Tropez; d of Guy and Nelly Béart; one d. *Career:* Began acting career with appearance as a child in Demain les Mômes 1978. *Film appearances include:* Les amants interdits 1984, Femme de sa vie 1986, Manon des Sources (César Award for Best Supporting Actress) 1986, Date with an Angel 1987, La belle noiseuse 1991, J'embrasse pas 1991, Un coeur en hiver 1991, Ruptures 1992, L'enfer 1993, Mission Impossible 1995, Nelly and Mr Arnaud 1995, Time Regained 1999, Les destinées sentimentales 2000, La répétition 2001.

BEATRIX, (Beatrix Wilhelmina Armgard); Netherlands Queen of the Netherlands; b 31 Jan 1938, Baarn; d of Queen Juliana (qv) and Bernhard, Prince of the Netherlands; m Claus George Willem Otto Frederik Geert von Amsberg 10 March 1966; three s: Prince Willem-Alexander Claus Georg Ferdinand, Prince of Orange; b 27 April 1967; Prince Johan Friso Bernhard Christiaan David, b 25 Sept 1968; Prince Constantijn Christof Frederik Aschwin, b 11 Oct 1969. *Education:* Baarn Grammar School and Leiden State Univ. *Career:* Succeeded to the throne on abdication of her mother 30 April 1980; Hon KG. *Address:* c/o Government Information Service, Press and Publicity Dept, Binnenhof 19, 2513 AA The Hague, Netherlands. *Telephone:* (70) 356-4136.

BEATTIE, Ann, MA; American writer; b 8 Sept 1947, Washington; d of James Beattie and Charlotte Crosby; m Lincoln Perry. *Education:* American Univ and Univ of Connecticut. *Career:* Visiting Asst Prof Univ of Virginia 1976–77, Visiting Writer 1980; Briggs Copeland Lecturer in English, Harvard Univ 1977; Guggenheim Fellow 1977; mem American Acad and Inst of Arts and Letters, PEN, Authors' Guild; Hon LHD (American Univ); Literature Award, American Acad and Inst of Arts and Letters 1980. *Publications:* Chilly Scenes of Winter 1976, Distortion 1976, Secrets and Suprises 1979, Falling in Place 1980, Jacklighting 1981, The Burning House 1982, Love Always 1985, Where You'll Find Me 1986, Alex Katz 1987 (art criticism), Picturing Will 1990, What Was Mine (story collection) 1991, My Life Starring Dara Falcon 1997, Park City: New and Selected Stories 1998. *Address:* c/o Janklow and Nesbit, 445 Park Avenue, New York, NY 10022, USA (Office).

BEAUCHEMIN, Micheline, OC, FRSC, RCA; Canadian tapestry weaver; b Longueuil, PQ. *Education:* Ecole des Beaux Arts (Montréal) and under Ossip Zadkine. *Career:* Worked on stained glass windows, Chartres, France, later with tapestry and embroidery, Greece 1955; wardrobe mistress and designer Canadian Broadcasting Corpn; exhibitions in Canada, Mexico, Japan, France; exhibited at Centre des arts contemporains du Québec, Montréal 2000; tours to People's Repub of China and India; research with Andean and jungle Indians, S America; Centennial Medal 1967. *Address:* 22 chemin du Roy, Les Grondines, PQ G0A 1WO, Canada.

BEAUDOIN, Louise, BA; Canadian politician and historian; b 26 Sept 1945, Québec, PQ; d of Jean-Robert and Louise (née Des Rivières) Beaudoin; m François Dorlot 1973. *Education:* Univs of Laval and Paris (Sorbonne). *Career:* Admin Vie Optimum, Paris, Théâtre expérimental des femmes, Montréal, Domaine Forget de Charlevoix Inc; Asst Dir of Studies Public Admin School, Univ of Québec 1971–76; Dir Cabinet of Minister of Intergovt Affairs, PQ 1976–81; Dir of French Affairs, Minister of Int Affairs, PQ 1981–84; Rep to Lavalin and Canadair 1986–87; Dir of Distribution, Marketing and Int Affairs, Telefilm Canada 1987–90; Dir-Gen Société du Palais de la Civilisation 1990–94; Deputy for Chambly 1994; Minister-Del for Intergovernmental Canadian Affairs, PQ 1994; Minister Responsible for the Application of the French Language Charter, Govt of Quebec 1995–, Minister for Int Relations, for Francophonie 1998–; Officier de la Légion d'Honneur. *Address:* Hôtel du Parlement, Québec PQ G1A 1A4, Canada. *Internet:* www.mri.gouv.qc.ca.

BEAUMAN, Sally, MA; British writer; b 25 July 1944; d of Ronald and Gabrielle (née Robinson) Kinsey-Miles; m 1st Christopher Beauman 1966 (divorced 1973); m 2nd Alan Howard; one s. *Education:* Redland High School (Bristol) and Girton Coll (Cambridge). *Career:* Contributing Ed New York Magazine, USA 1967; Features Ed Vogue 1968–69, Harper's Bazaar 1969–70; Ed Queen 1970; Arts Ed Telegraph Magazine 1971–79; writer 1980–; Catherine Pakenham Memorial Prize for Journalism 1970. *Publications include:* The Royal Shakespeare Company: A History of Ten Decades 1982, Destiny 1987, Dark Angel 1990, Lovers and Liars 1994, Danger Zones 1996; contribs to numerous publs in UK and USA. *Leisure interests:* shrub roses, Rhone wines. *Address:* c/o PFD, Drury House, 34-43 Russell St, London, WC2B 5HA, UK.

BEAUMONT, Lady Mary Rose, BA; British art historian; b 6 June 1932, Petersfield; d of Charles Edward Wauchope and Elaine Margaret Armstrong-Jones; m Lord Beaumont of Whiley, The Rev Timothy Wentworth Beaumont 1955; one s (one s deceased) two d. *Education:* Prior's Field School (Godalming, Surrey), Courtauld Inst of Fine Art and Univ of London. *Career:* Art critic for Art Review 1978–96; Lecturer in Modern Art for Christies' Educ 1978–; exhibition curator for British Council in E Europe and Far E 1983–87, for The Human Touch, Fischer Fine Art Gallery 1986, The Dark Side of the Moon, Rhodes Gallery 1990, Three Scottish Artists, Pamela Auchincloss Gallery, New York 1990; Picker Fellow Kingston Polytechnic 1986–87; Lecturer in Humanities Dept City & Guilds School of Art 1996–; mem Exec Cttee of Contemporary Art Soc 1979–89. *Publications:* An American Passion: The Susan Kasen Summer and Robert D. Summer Collection of Contemporary British Painting (contrib artists' profiles) 1995, Open Studio: Derek Healey 1997, Jean MacAlpine: Intervals in Light 1998,

Carole Hodgson 1999, George Kyriacou 1999. *Leisure interests:* reading novels, listening to opera. *Address:* 40 Elms Rd, London, SW4 9EX, UK. *Telephone:* (20) 7498-8664; *Fax:* (20) 7498-8664.

BEAUPRE, Odette; Canadian opera singer; b 5 April 1952, Rivière-du-Loup, PQ; d of Maurice and Eméline (née Pelletier) Beaupre. *Education:* Music Conservatory of Québec. *Career:* Mem Canadian Opera Co Ensemble 1983–85; performances with Opera of Québec, Montréal Opera, Edmonton Opera, Canadian Opera Co, Québec Symphony Orchestra, Montréal Symphony Orchestra, Les Jeunesses Musicales du Canada; First Prize Int Festival of Toronto; First Prize Chalmer's Foundation, Ontario Arts Council. *Operas include:* Così fan tutte, Faust, Madam Butterfly, The Merry Widow, The Beggar's Opera, Carmen, Cavalleria Rusticana, Roméo et Juliette, Rigoletto.

BEAUX, Gilberte Yvonne Andrée; French business executive; b 12 July 1929, Paris; d of Paul and Germaine Lovisi; m Edouard Beaux 1951; one d. *Education:* Lycée de jeunes filles (Marseilles), Lycée Racine (Paris) and Inst Tech de Banque. *Career:* Bank Rep 1946–56; Dir financial cos 1956–68; Admin Société de Gestion Hôtelière 1961–; Pres, Dir-Gen numerous cos, including Banque Occidentale pour l'Industrie et le Commerce 1976–79 (Pres Bd 1979–81); Dir-Gen Générale Occidentale 1969–87, Admin 1987–; Pres Basic Resources Int Ltd (Bahamas) 1982–97; Pres, Dir-Gen Gen Oriental Ltd (Hong Kong) 1980–82, Vice-Pres, Dir-Gen 1982–85; Pres Basic Petroleum Int Ltd 1982–97; Vice-Pres, Admin Presses de la Cité 1987–88; Admin many insts and cos, including Ecole Nat d'Admin 1976–83, Application des Gaz 1979–82, Edper Holding Ltd and Edper Equities Ltd (Canada) 1982–84, Compagnie Occidentale Forestière (also Pres) 1984–88, Express group 1986–88, Fiat-France 1989–98, Imétal 1991–98, Banque Française de Service et de Crédit 1994, Scott Paper Co 1995–97; Pres, Pres-Dir Gen, later Admin-Dir Gen Efficacité Finance Conseil 1998–; Pres-Dir Gen Cogestel SA 1997–, Basic Holdings Ltd 1997–; Vice-Pres Bernard Tapie Finance (Germany) 1990–93; Vice-Pres Convention Libéral européenne et sociale 1988–98; mem supervisory council Adidas 1990–93 (Pres 1993–94), Pres Bd of Dirs 1992–93; involved in cos in France, the Netherlands, Cayman Islands, UK, Canada, etc; mem Conseil Economique et Social 1989–94; Commdr de la Légion d'Honneur, Commdr de l'Ordre Nat du Mérite; Businesswoman of the Year 1987. *Leisure interests:* skiing, hunting. *Address:* Efficacité Finance Conseil, 1 Rond-Point des Champs-Elysées, 75008 Paris, France (Office).

BECCHI, Ada, B ECONS; Italian politician; b 30 May 1937, Torino; d of Carlo and M. Costamagna Becchi; m Antonio Collidá 1961 (divorced 1973); two c. *Education:* Liceo Classico and Univ of Genova. *Career:* Asst to Chair of Econ History, Univ of Genova 1959–61; research on devt policies, Rome 1962–68; Research Dept Metalworkers' Union, Rome 1969–77; teacher Faculty of Econs, Univ of Ancona 1973–79; Assoc Prof of Urban and Regional Econs, Univ of Venice 1977–87, Prof 1987–94, Prof of Econs and Politics 1993–; teacher Scuola Superiore della Pubblica Amministra 1997–98; elected to Chamber of Deputies 1987, mem Post Earthquake Comm 1989–91, Anti-Mafia Comm 1988–92; Pres Equal Opportunities Cttee (IUAV). *Publications include:* Sviluppo economico e crescita urbana 1968, Politiche del lavoro e garanzia del reddito 1978, La ristrutturazione industriale: il caso Fiat 1986, Le Politiche per il Mezzogiorno 1998, Il riciclaggio nel contesto dei rapporti tra economia criminale ed economia legale 1999. *Leisure interest:* gardening. *Address:* IUAV, S Croce 1957, 30135 Venice, Italy (Office); via Dandolo 74, 00153 Rome, Italy (Home). *Telephone:* (041) 2572153; *Fax:* (041) 5240403; *E-mail:* ada@iuav.it; *Internet:* www.iuav.it.

BECHTEL, Marie Françoise; French educationalist; b 19 March 1946, Coarraze, Basses Pyrénées; d of Gaston and Marie Cassiau (née Sahores); one s one d. *Education:* Univ de Paris-Sorbonne; student at Ecole Nat d'Admin 1978–80. *Career:* Secondary school teacher 1972–75; Officer Council of State 1980–84, Counsel 1984–85, Sr mem 1996; Dir Ecole Nat d'Admin 2000–; Tech Advisor to Minister of Nat Educ 1984–86; Sr Lecturer, Inst d'Etudes Politiques 1983–87. *Address:* L'Ecole Nationale d'Administration, 13 rue de l'Université, 75343 Paris, Cedex, France; 29 bd Edgard Quinet, 75014 Paris, France (Home). *E-mail:* bechtel@ena.fr; *Internet:* www.ena.fr.

BECK, Béatrix Marie; Swiss writer; b 30 July 1914. *Education:* Lycée de St Germain-en-Laye and Univ de Grenoble. *Career:* Fmr sec to André Gide; journalist; mem Jury Prix Fémina; Prix Félix Fénéon; Prix Fondation Delmas 1979. *Publications:* Barny, Une mort irrégulière, Léon Morin, prêtre (Prix Goncourt), Des accommodements avec le ciel, Le premier mai, Abram Krol, Le muet, Cou coupé court toujours, Confidences de Gorgoulle 1999. *Address:* Editions Bernard Grasset Editions Bernard Grasset, 75006 Paris, France (Office), 61 rue des Saints-Pères, 75006 Paris, France (Office).

BECK-COULTER, Eva Maria Barbara, B SC; British (b German) journalist; b 14 Oct 1941, Berlin, Germany; d of Wilhelm and Ursula Beck; m Ian Coulter 1971; two s one d. *Education:* Victoria-Luise Gymnasium (Hamelin, Germany), Univ of Munich and Univ of London. *Career:* Mem Editorial Staff The Economist 1965–74, European Ed 1974–80, Asst Ed 1980–81, Surveys Ed 1995–; Sec-Gen Anglo-German Foundation for the Study of Industrial Soc 1981–91; Ed International Management (monthly European business magazine) 1991–94; Head of Communications (Europe) Andersen Consulting 1994; broadcaster, writer and lecturer on current affairs in English and German; Chair Reform Club 1991; mem Steering Cttee Anglo-German Koenigswinter Conf 1982–91, Council Royal Inst of Int Affairs 1984–90, Academic Council Wilton Park (conf centre) 1984–91, Int Council Science Centre Berlin 1990–95; Fellow Royal Soc for the Encouragement of Arts, Manufactures and Commerce 1990. *Publications:* regular articles published in The Economist and other publs over the past three decades. *Leisure interests:* family life, food, classical music, gardening. *Address:* 9 Paget St, London, EC1V 7PA, UK; The Economist, 25 St James's St, London SW1A 1HG, UK. *Telephone:* (20) 7830-7168; *E-mail:* barbarabeck@economist.com.

BECKER, Mary Louise, PH D; American political scientist and advisor; b St Louis, MO; d of W. R. and Evelyn (née Thompson) Becker; two s. *Education:* Washington Univ (DC), Radcliffe Coll (MA) and Univ of Karachi (Pakistan). *Career:* Lecturer on Int Relations 1954–; Intelligence Research Analyst Dept of State, Washington, DC 1957–59; Int Relations Officer Agency for Int Devt, Washington, DC 1959–64, Community Relations Officer 1964–66, Science Research Officer 1966–71, UN Relations Officer 1971; Pres Int Devt Enterprises, Washington, DC 1992–; Advisor to Dels to several Governing Council Sessions, UN Devt Programme, US Dels to Exec Bd Sessions, UNICEF 1987–89, US Del third preparatory cttee meeting, World Conf UN Decade for Women; mem American Political Science Asscn, Soc of Int Devt, Asscn of Asian Studies, Asia Soc, American Soc of Public Admin; Blewett Fellow, Washington Univ 1951; Resident Fellow Radcliffe Coll, New York 1952–56; Fulbright Scholar Univ of Karachi 1953–54. *Publications include:* Muhammed Iqbal 1965, Concise Encyclopedia of Middle East (ed) 1973. *Address:* North Bldg, Suite 700, 601 Pennsylvania Ave, NW, Washington, DC 20004, USA.

BECKETT, Rt Hon Margaret Mary, PC; British politician; b 15 Jan 1943, Ashton-under-Lyne, Lancs; d of Cyril and Winifred Jackson; m Leo Beckett 1979; two step-s. *Education:* Notre Dame High School (Norwich), Manchester Coll of Science and Tech and John Dalton Polytechnic. *Career:* Metallurgy Eng apprentice Associated Electrical Industries, Manchester; Experimental Officer Univ of Manchester; Prin Researcher Granada TV 1979–83; Industrial Policy Researcher, Lab Party HQ; MP for Lincoln 1974–79, for Derby South 1983–; Parl Pvt Sec to Minister for Overseas Devt 1974–75, Asst Govt Whip 1975–76, Minister Dept of Educ 1976–79; mem Lab Party Nat Exec Cttee 1980–81, 1985–86, 1988–, Deputy Leader Lab Party 1992–94, Leader 1994; Opposition Spokesperson with responsibility for Social Security 1984–89, Shadow Chief Sec to the Treasury 1989–92, Shadow Leader of the House and campaign co-ordinator 1992–94; Shadow Sec of State for Health 1994–95, Shadow Pres of Bd of Trade 1995–97; Pres of Bd of Trade and Sec of State for Trade and Industry 1997–98; Pres of Council and Leader of the House of Commons 1998; Sec of State for the Environment, Food and Rural Affairs 2001–; apptd to Privy Council 1993; mem Campaign for Nuclear Disarmament (CND), Amnesty Int, Anti-Apartheid Movt and numerous other orgs. *Leisure interests:* cooking, reading, caravanning. *Address:* House of Commons, London SW1A 0AA, UK. *Telephone:* (20) 7219-5135 (Office).

BECKETT, Sister Wendy, MA; British nun and art historian; b 25 Feb 1930, Johannesburg, S Africa. *Education:* Univ of Oxford. *Career:* Moved to UK 1946, joined Sisters of Notre Dame, Carmelite Order, Sussex; fmrly teacher; contrib to Modern Painters. *Publications:* Song of Songs (trans from Latin), Contemporary Women Artists, Art and the Sacred, A Thousand Masterpieces, The Story of Painting, Meditations, My Favourite Things, Sister Wendy's American Collection 2000; *TV includes:* several series for BBC and Public Broadcasting Service (US) including Sister Wendy's Odyssey (six-part series on art) 1992, Sister Wendy's Grand Tour, Sister Wendy's Story of Painting. *Address:* Carmelite Monastery, Quindenham, Norfolk, UK.

BECKHAM, Victoria; British singer; b 7 April 1975; d of Tony and Jackie Adams; m David Beckham 1999; one s. *Education:* Jason Theatre School, Laine Arts Theatre Coll. *Career:* Mem group The Spice Girls 1993–, signed to Virgin 1995; awards include Best Video (for Say You'll Be There), Best Single (for Wannabe) Brit Awards 1997; two Ivor Novello song writing awards 1997; Best Band Smash Hits Awards 1997; three American Music Awards 1998; Special Award for Int Sales Brit Awards 1998. *Albums and singles include:* Spice 1996 (UK number 1), Spiceworld 1997 (UK number 1, platinum UK, double platinum USA, number 1 in numerous countries, Forever 2000; Singles from album Spice include: Wannabe 1996 (number 1 in 31 countries including UK and USA), Say You'll Be There 1996 (UK number 1), 2 Become 1 (UK number 1) 1996, Mama/Who Do You Think You Are 1997 (UK number 1, first band to go to number 1 in UK with first four singles); from album Spiceworld: Spice Up Your Life 1997 (UK number 1), Too Much 1997 (UK number 1), Stop 1998, Viva Forever 1998 (UK number 1), Goodbye 1998 (UK number 1); from album Forever: Holler/Let Love Lead The Way 2000 (UK number 1); solo single: Out of Your Mind (jtly) 2000; *Films:* Spiceworld: The Movie 1997; *Publications:* Learning to Fly (autobiography) 2001. *Leisure interest:* shopping. *Address:* c/o Lee & Thompson, Green Garden House, 15-22 St Christopher's Place, London W1M 5HE, UK. *Telephone:* (20) 7935-4665; *Fax:* (20) 7486 -2391; *Internet:* c3.vmg.co.uk/spicegirls.

BECKINSALE, Kate; British actress; b 26 July 1973; d of Richard Beckinsale and Judy Loe; partner Michael Sheen; one d. *Education:* New Coll (Oxford). *Films:* Much Ado about Nothing 1993, Prince of Jutland 1994, Uncovered 1994, Haunted 1995, Shooting Fish 1997, The Last Days of Disco 1998, Brokedown Palace 1999, The Golden Bowl 2000, Serendipity 2001, Pearl Harbor 2001; *TV:* One Against the Wind 1991, Rachel's Dream 1992, Cold Comfort Farm 1996, Emma 1997, Alice Through The Looking Glass 1999, Unforgettable Richard Beckinsale 2000. *Address:* c/o ICM, Oxford House, 76 Oxford St, London W1D 1BS, UK.

BEDDINGTON, Rosa, D PHIL, FRS; British geneticist; b 23 March 1956, d of the late Roy Julian and Anna Dorothy Beddington; m Rev Robin Alastair Denniston 1987. *Education:* Brasenose Coll (Oxford). *Career:* Research fellow Lister Inst for Preventive Medicine, Oxford 1983–88; research scientist Imperial Cancer Research Fund, Oxford 1988–91; sr research fellow Centre for Genome Research, Edinburgh 1991–93; int scholar Howard Hughes Medical Inst 1993–98; Head Div of Mammalian Devt, Nat Inst of Medical Research 1993–; Visiting Prof Miller Inst, Berkeley, California 1996; mem numerous scientific advisory bds. *Publications:* Manipulating the Mouse Embryo (jtly) 1994, and numerous articles in scientific journals. *Leisure interests:* gardening, painting. *Address:* MRC National Institute of Medical Research, The Ridgeway, Mill Hill, London NW7 1AA, UK. *Telephone:* (20) 8959-3666.

BEDFORD, Sybille, OBE, C LIT; British writer; b 16 March 1911, Berlin; d of Maximilian von Schoenebeck and Elizabeth Bernhard; m Walter Bedford 1935. *Education:* pvt schools in France and England. *Career:* Literary journalist 1930s–; Vice-Pres English PEN. *Publications:* A Visit to Don Otavio 1953, A Legacy 1956, The Best We Can Do 1958, The Faces of Justice 1961, A Favourite of the Gods 1968, A Compass Error 1968, Aldous Huxley: A Biography (Vol I) 1973, (Vol II) 1974, Jigsaw 1989, As It Was 1990. *Leisure interests:* wine, food, reading, travel, history, politics. *Address:* c/o Lutyens & Rubinstein, 231 Westbourne Park Rd, London W11 1EB, UK. *Telephone:* (20) 7792-4855.

BEECROFT, Norma Marian; Canadian composer; b 11 April 1934, Oshawa, ON; d of Julian and Eleanor (née Norton) Beecroft. *Education:* Toronto Royal Conservatory of Music, Berks Music Centre, Acad of St Cecilia (Rome) and in Germany and UK. *Career:* Freelance commentator on modern music 1969–; Dir Workshops York Univ 1984–87; numerous TV and radio appearances; producer programmes on TV and radio, including programmes on Murray Adaskin 1993 and Violet Archer (qv) 1994; mem Composers', Authors' and Publishers' Asscn of Canada; numerous commissions; Armstrong Award for Excellence in FM Broadcasting, Victor M Lynch–Staunton Award 1978–79, 1989–90; Dr hc (York Univ) 1996. *Compositions include:* Tre Pezzi Brevi 1961, From Dreams of Brass 1964, Elegy and Two Went to Sleep 1967, Undersea Fantasy 1967, The Living Flame of Love 1967, Three Impressions From Sweetgrass 1973, Piece for Bob 1975, Consequences for Five 1977, Quaprice 1980, Cantorum Vitae 1981, Troissants 1982, Macbeth (score) 1983, Midsummer Night's Dream (score) 1984, Jeu de Bach 1985, Images 1987, The Dissipation of Purely Sound 1988, Accordion Play 1988, Hemispherics 1990, Evocations: Images of Canada 1991, Amplified String Quartet 1991–92, Esprit Eternel 1994, Face à Face 1994. *Address:* 1866 Glendale Drive, Pickering, ON L1V 1V5, Canada.

BEER, Dame Gillian Patricia Kempster, DBE, LITT D, FBA; British professor of English literature and college president; b 27 Jan 1935; d of Owen Kempster Thomas and Ruth Winifred Bell; m John Bernard Beer 1962; three s. *Education:* St Anne's Coll (Oxford). *Career:* Asst Lecturer Bedford Coll, London 1959–62; part-time Lecturer Univ of Liverpool 1962–64; Asst Lecturer Univ of Cambridge 1966–71, Lecturer, then Reader in Literature and Narrative 1971–89, Prof of English 1989–94, King Edward VII Prof of English Literature and Pres Clare Hall 1994–; Fellow Girton Coll 1965–94; Vice-Pres British Acad 1994–96; Trustee British Museum 1992–; Chair Poetry Book Soc 1992–96; Pres History of Science Section, British Asscn for the Advancement of Science; Chair Judges, Booker Prize 1997; Hon mem American Acad of Arts and Sciences; Hon Fellow Univ of Wales (Cardiff) 1996, St Anne's Coll (Oxford); Hon D LITT (Liverpool) 1995; Hon doctorates from Leicester, APU, Sorbonne (Paris); Medals from MIT, Nat Autonomous Univ (Mexico). *Publications:* Meredith: a change of masks 1970, The Romance 1970, Darwin's Plots 1983, George Eliot 1986, Arguing with the Past 1989, Open Fields 1996, Virginia Woolf: The Common Ground 1996. *Leisure interests:* singing, travel, conversation. *Address:* Clare Hall, Herschel Rd, Cambridge CB3 9AL, UK; 6 Belvoir Terrace, Cambridge CB2 2AA, UK. *Telephone:* (1223) 332360; (1223) 356384; *Fax:* (1223) 332333; *E-mail:* gpb1000@cam.ac.uk.

BEERLI, Christine; Swiss politician and lawyer; b 26 Mar 1953, Biel. *Education:* Univ of Bern. *Career:* Leader Parliamentary Group, Free Democratic Party of Switzerland; mem Bd Dirs New Medical Tech, Annuity Bank; Pres Bd Dirs Dynamic Test Centre (Vauffelin); Pres Alcohol Comm; Dir of Univ of Tech and Architecture. *Address:* Postfach 6136, 3001 Bern, Switzerland (Office); Heightway 84, 2502 Biel, Route Struck 84, 2502 Bienne, Switzerland (Home). *Telephone:* (31) 3203535 (Office); *Fax:* (31) 3203508 (Office); *E-mail:* christine.beerli@hta-bi .bfh.ch (Office); *Internet:* www.christine.beerli.ch.

BEERS, Charlotte Leonore, BS; American business executive; b 26 July 1935, Beaumont, TX; d of Glen and Frances (née Bolt) Rice; m Donald C. Beers 1971; one d. *Education:* Baylor Univ (Waco, TX). *Career:* Group Product Man Uncle Ben's Inc 1959–69; Sr Vice-Pres and Dir of Client Services J. Walter Thompson 1969–79; COO Tatham, Laird & Kudner, Chicago, IL 1979, then Man Partner, Chair and CEO; Vice-Chair RSCG Group Roux Seguela, Cayzac & Goudard, France; Chair and CEO Ogilvy & Mather Worldwide, New York, Ogilvy Group Inc, New York 1992–97, Chair Emer 1997–99; Chair J. Walter Thompson 1999–2000; mem American Asscn of Advertising Agencies, Women's Advertising Club, Chicago, IL; Nat Advertising Woman of the Year, American Advertising Fed 1975. *Address:* c/o J. Walter Thompson, 466 Lexington Ave, Floor 2, New York, NY 10017, USA (Office).

BEEVI, M. S. Fathima (see Fathima Beevi, M. S.).

BEGGS, Jean Duthie, PH D, FRS, FRSE; British molecular biologist; b 16 April 1950; d of William Renfrew and Jean Crawford (née Duthie) Lancaster; m Ian Beggs 1972; two s. *Education:* Univ of Glasgow. *Career:*

Postdoctoral Fellow Dept of Molecular Biology, Univ of Edinburgh 1974–77; Plant Breeding Inst, Cambridge 1977–79; Beit Memorial Fellow for Medical Research 1976–79; Lecturer in Biochemistry Imperial Coll, Univ of London 1979–85; Univ Research Fellow Dept of Molecular Biology, Univ of Edinburgh 1985–89, Professorial Research Fellow 1994–99, Prof of Molecular Biology 1999–. *Address:* Institute of Cell and Molecular Biology, University of Edinburgh, King's Buildings, Mayfield Rd, Edinburgh, EH9 3JR, UK. *Telephone:* (131) 650-5351; *E-mail:* j.beggs@ed.ac.uk.

BÉGIN, Rt Hon Monique, PC, OC, MA, FRSC; Canadian politician and educationalist; b 1 March 1936, Rome, Italy; d of Lucien and Marie-Louise (née Vanhavre) Bégin. *Education:* Teachers' Coll (Rigaud) and Univs of Montréal and Paris. *Career:* Teacher, Montréal 1955–61; sociologist, consultant, Montréal 1963–67; Exec Dir Royal Comm on Status of Women in Canada, Ottawa 1967–70; Asst Dir of Research, Canadian Radio and TV Comm 1970–72; mem House of Commons for Montréal (first Quebec woman to be elected to Fed Parl) 1972–84; Parl Sec to Sec of State for External Affairs 1975–76; Minister of Nat Revenue 1976–77; Minister of Nat Health and Welfare 1977–84; fmr Prof Notre Dame (IN, USA) and McGill Univs; Jt Chair Women's Studies, Carleton and Ottawa Univs 1986–90; Dean of Health Sciences, Univ of Ottawa 1990–97, Prof Emer 1997–; mem McGill-Queen's Univ Press 1986–93; mem Bd of Govs McGill Univ 1986–90, Advisory Council, Kellogg Inst for Int Studies, Univ of Notre Dame 1987–91; Chair Royal Comm on Learning 1993–95; Canadian Breast Cancer Research Initiative 1995–; mem International Independent Comm on Population and Quality of Life 1993–96; Ryerson Polytechnical Inst Fellow, Toronto 1992; Hon PH D (St Thomas) 1977; Dr hc (Mt St Vincent) 1982; Hon LL D (Dalhousie, Queen's) 1987, (Laurentian) 1988, (Toronto, Alberta) 1989, (McGill) 1991, (McMaster) 1993, (York) 1995, (Newfoundland) 2000; Dr Brock Chisholm Medal, Medical Soc of WHO, Geneva 1984. *Publications:* L'assurance-santé: plaidoyer pour le modèle canadien 1987, Medicare: Canada's Right to Health 1988, Re-designing Health Care for Women 1989, Annotated Bibliography on Women and Aging, Canada 1975–89. *Leisure interests:* nature and gardening, travel, music. *Address:* 125 University Priv (MNT 335), Ottawa, ON K1N 6N5, Canada. *Telephone:* (613) 787-6705; *Fax:* (613) 787-6725.

BEHAL, Monisha, PH D; Indian social scientist and development worker; b 15 Sept 1951, Shillong; d of Hriday and Padma Agarwala; m Rana Behal 1977; one s one d. *Education:* Loreto Convent (Darjeeling), Indraprastha Coll (Univ of Delhi) and Gauhati Univ (Assam). *Career:* Social researcher in Assam 1978–87, Uttar Pradesh 1984; Co-ordinator women's devt project, Women in Agriculture, Assam from 1988; documentalist of women's life histories and econ status 1989–; consultant to charities, evaluating women's devt projects; contribs on women of rural India to Economic and Political Weekly and other publs. *Leisure interests:* music, especially jazz. *Address:* Deshbandhu Society, Flat 42, 15 Patparganj, Delhi 110 092, India. *Telephone:* (11) 2216679.

BEHRENS, Hildegard; German opera singer; b 1937, Oldenburg; m Seth Schneidmann. *Education:* Freiburg Music Conservatory. *Career:* Debut Freiburg 1971; resident mem Deutsche Oper am Rhein, Düsseldorf; Soloist with Chicago Symphony Orchestra (USA) 1984; has appeared with Frankfurt Opera, Teatro Nacional de San Carlo (Lisbon, Portugal), Vienna State Opera (Austria) and Metropolitan Opera (New York, USA). *Address:* c/o Herbert H. Breslin Inc, W 57th St, New York, NY 10019, USA.

BEHRENS, Katja; German writer; b 18 Dec 1942, Berlin; m Peter Behrens 1960 (divorced 1971). *Career:* Trans of contemporary American literature (including William S. Burroughs and Henry Miller) 1960–73; Ed, publishing house 1973–78; writer 1978–; Writer-in-Residence, Stadt Mainz 1992; Förderpreis zum Ingeborg Bachmann Preis 1978; Förderpreis der Märkische Kulturkonferenz 1978; Thaddäus Troll Preis 1985; Premio Internazionale 'Lo Stellato' 2000. *Publications include:* Die Weiße Frau 1978, Die Dreizehnte Fee 1983, Im Wasser tanzen 1990, Salomo und die anderen 1992, Die Vagantin 1997, Zorro 1999, Alles Sehen Kommt von der Seele–Die Lebensgeschichte der Helen Keller 2001. *Leisure interests:* music, horse-riding. *Address:* 6 Park Rosenhöhe 23, 64287 Dormstadt, Germany. *Telephone:* (6151) 54762; *Fax:* (6151) 54762.

BEKHTEREVA, Natalya Petrovna, D MED SCI; Russian physiologist; b 7 July 1924, Leningrad (now St Petersburg); d of Pyotr Vladimirovich Bekhterev and Zinaida Vasilievna Bekhtereva; m 1st Vsevolod Medvedev 1948 (divorced 1973); one s; m 2nd Ivan Kastelian 1973 (died 1990). *Education:* Leningrad Medical Inst. *Career:* Jr Researcher USSR Acad of Medical Sciences, Inst of Experimental Medicine 1950–54, Head of Lab then Deputy Dir 1962–70, Dir 1970–90; mem staff Neurosurgical Inst, Ministry of Health 1954–62; Scientific Dir Bekhterev Inst for Research into the Brain, Russian Acad of Sciences 1990–; mem CPSU 1959–91; USSR People's Deputy 1970–74, 1989–91; Corresp mem Australian Acad of Sciences; Foreign mem Cuban Physiological Soc; Hon mem Czechoslovakian Neurochirurgical Soc J. E. Purkyne, Hungarian Electrophysiological Soc; mem USSR (now Russian) Acad of Sciences 1981–, USSR (now Russian) Acad of Medical Sciences 1975; Fellow Academia Medicina et Psychiatria (USA); USSR State Prize Winner 1985; McCulloch Medal, USA Cybernetics Soc; Hans Berger Medal, GDR Electrophysiological Soc; Medal of Bulgarian Union of Research Workers, Bechterev's Gold Medal, Russian Acad of Sciences, Century Award of the Int Org of Psychophysiology 1998. *Publications:* over 300 publs in Russian and English on physiology of mental activity, structural and functional org of physiological activity of brain, incl The Healthy and Diseased Human Brain 1985. *Leisure interests:* music, fine art. *Address:* Institute of the Human Brain, Pavlova St 9, St Petersburg, 197376, Russian Federation (Office). *Telephone:* 234-22-21 (Office); *Fax:* 234-32-47 (Office).

BEKOVA, Alfia; Kazakhstan cellist; b Karaganda. *Education:* Cen Music School for Children (Moscow, Russian Fed), with Rostropovich. *Career:* Moved to London 1981; London debut, with sisters Elvira (qv) and Eleanora (qv), Royal Festival Hall 1989; tours to Canada, Australia and Far East 1996; concert performances include Moscow, Russian Fed 1995, Lebanon Festival, Lincoln Center, New York, NY, USA, and Queen Elizabeth Hall, London, UK 1996.

BEKOVA, Eleanora; Kazakhstan pianist; b Karaganda; one s. *Education:* Music Conservatory (Moscow, Russian Fed), with Gilels. *Career:* Moved to London 1989; London debut, with sisters Elvira (qv) and Alfia (qv), Royal Festival Hall 1989; tours to Canada, Australia and Far East 1996; concert performances include Moscow, Russian Fed 1995, Lebanon Festival, Lincoln Center, New York, USA and Queen Elizabeth Hall, London, UK 1996.

BEKOVA, Elvira; Kazakhstan violinist; b Karaganda; one d. *Education:* Music Conservatory (Moscow, Russian Fed), with David Oistrakh. *Career:* Moved to London 1989; London debut, with sisters Eleanora (qv) and Alfia (qv), Royal Festival Hall 1989; tours to Canada, Australia and the Far East 1996; concert performances include Moscow, Russian Fed 1995, Lebanon Festival, Lincoln Center, New York, NY, USA and Queen Elizabeth Hall, London, UK 1996.

BELILLO, Katia; Italian politician; b 1952. *Career:* Mem Italian Communist Party, began career as provincial women's rights official, Umbria 1973; Deputy Head Prov of Perugia 1995–; Minister for Regional Affairs 1998–2000, for Equal Opportunities 2000–. *Address:* Ministry of Equal Opportunities, Palazzo Chigi, Piazza Colonna 370, 00187 Rome, Italy.

BELL, Eileen, BA; British political party official and representative; b 15 Aug 1943, Dromara, Co Down, N Ireland; d of Joseph and Mary Neeson; m Derek Bell 1968. *Education:* Dominican Coll (Belfast) and Univ of Ulster. *Career:* Spokesperson Alliance Party of N Ireland, Sec-Gen 1986–90, Spokeswoman on Educ 1993–, Chair 1997–99, Pres 1999–; Alliance Party Del to Stormont Talks 1991, Brooke-Mayhew Talks 1991–92, to N Ireland Peace Talks 1996–98; mem Peace People, Sec-Gen 1991–92; Admin Peace Train Org 1990–95; mem N Down Borough Council for Bangor W 1993–, New N Ireland Ass (for N Down) 1998–; mem Dublin Forum for Peace and Reconciliation 1994–96, N Ireland Forum for Political Dialogue 1996, Good Friday Agreement Talks 1998, N Ireland Probation Bd; involved in civil liberties, non-violence and women's issues in N Ireland. *Leisure interests:* voluntary work with prisoners and families, justice and civil liberties issues, community relations work. *Address:* Alliance Party of Northern

Ireland, Rm 328, Parliaments Bldgs, Belfast, BT4 3XX, UK (Office); 27 Maryville Rd, Bangor, Co Down, UK (Home). *Telephone:* (28) 9052-0352; *Fax:* (28) 9145-2321; *E-mail:* eileen.bell@niassembly.gov.uk.

BELL, Hon Justice Judith Miriam, QC, LL B; Canadian judge; b 7 Feb 1940, Ottawa; d of the late Hon Richard Albert and Winnifred O. (née Sinclair) Bell. *Education:* Nepean High School and Dalhousie Univ. *Career:* Jr Lawyer Fraser and Beatty 1964–65; Assoc and Partner Bell, Baker 1965–86; QC 1975; Bencher Law Soc of Upper Canada 1983–86; Lecturer in Community Planning and Land Use, Ottawa Univ Law School 1976–83, in Municipal Law, Algonquin Coll 1986; Judge Supreme Court of Ontario 1986–; mem Ontario Court of Justice, Gen Div (fmrly High Court of Justice for Ontario) 1986–; fmr mem Bd of Govs Carleton Univ, Heart Inst Advisory Bd Univ of Ottawa. *Address:* Ontario Court of Justice (Gen Div), 161 Elgin St, Rm 6040, ON K2P 2K1, Canada. *Telephone:* (613) 239-1400.

BELL, Judy; American sporting organization executive; b 1937, KS. *Career:* Professional golfer, rep USA in the Curtis Cup 1960, 1962, 1986, 1988; Sec United States Golf Asscn (USGA)1992–93, Vice-Pres 1994–95, Pres 1996–98; *Awards include:* Ike Grainger Award 1995, Metropolitan Golf Writers Ascn Lifetime Achievement Award 1998, Herb Graffis Award, Nat Golf Foundation 1999, Professional Golf Asscn (PGA) of America's First Lady of Golf Award 2001, elected to World Golf Hall of Fame 2001. *Address:* c/o United States Golf Asscn, Golf House, POB 708, Far Hills, NJ 07931, USA.

BELL BURNELL, S(usan) Jocelyn, CBE, PH D, FRAS, FINSTP; British astronomer and professor of physics; b 15 July 1943; d of (George) Philip and (Margaret) Allison (née Kennedy) Bell; m Martin Burnell 1968 (separated 1989); one s. *Education:* The Mount School (York), and Univs of Glasgow and Cambridge. *Career:* Discovered first four pulsars (neutron stars) 1967–68; Research and Teaching Fellowship Univ of Southampton 1968–73; Programmer and Fellow Mullard Space Science Lab, Univ Coll, London 1974–82; Sr Scientific Officer and Fellow Royal Observatory, Edinburgh 1982–91; Prof of Physics The Open Univ 1991–2001, mem Council 1997; Dean of Science, Univ of Bath 2001–; Vice-Pres Royal Astronomical Soc 1995–97; Visiting Prof for Distinguished Teaching, Princeton Univ 1999–2000; mem Int Astronomical Union 1979–; Foreign mem Onsala Telescope Bd, Sweden 1996–; frequent radio and TV broadcaster on science, on being a woman in science and on science and religion; Hon Fellow New Hall (Cambridge) 1996; Hon D SC 1993, 1995 (twice), 1996, 1997 (twice), 1999 (twice), 2001 (three times); Hon D UNIV 1994; awards include Michelson Medal 1973, J. Robert Oppenheimer Memorial Prize 1978, Tinsley Prize 1987, Herschel Medal, Royal Astronomical Soc, London 1989, Edinburgh Medal 1999, Giuseppi Piazzi Prize (Italy) 1999, Magellanic Premium 2000. *Publications:* Broken for Life 1989, Next Generation Infrared Space Observatory (jt ed) 1992, and more than 70 scientific papers and 35 Quaker publs. *Leisure interests:* popularising astronomy, walking, Quaker and ecumenical activities, listening to choral music. *Address:* Dean of Science, University of Bath, Bath, BA2 7AY, UK. *Telephone:* (1225) 826772; *Fax:* (1225) 323353.

BELLAMY, Carol, JD; American international organization executive; b 1942, Plainfield, NJ. *Education:* Gettysburg Coll and New York Univ. *Career:* Assoc Cravath, Swaine and Moore 1968–71; Prin Morgan Stanley & Co 1986–90; Man Dir Public Finance Dept, Bear Stearns & Co 1990–93; Dir Peace Corps 1993–95; Exec Dir and Under-Sec-Gen UNICEF 1995–; Senator State Senate of NY 1973–77; Pres New York City Counil 1978–85; Chair New York City Task Force on Adolescent Pregnancy; mem State-wide Coalition to Fight Infant Mortality, NY State Comm on Judicial Nomination, New York City Comm to Review Health and Hosps Corpn, NY State Blue Ribbon Comm on State Legis Practices and Ethics, Exec Cttee of the Citizens Budget Comm; Fellow Inst of Politics, Kennedy School of Govt, Harvard Univ. *Address:* UNICEF, 3 United Nations Plaza, New York, NY 10017, USA (Office). *Telephone:* (212) 326-7028 (Office); *Fax:* (212) 326-7758 (Office); *Internet:* www.unicef.org (Office).

BELLANGER, Françoise Marie; French civil servant and communications executive; b 13 April 1943, Brussels, Belgium; d of François Duchatel and Suzanne Marsaud; m Maurice Bellanger 1965; one s one d. *Education:* Lycée Français de Bruxelles and Univs of Lille and Paris.

Career: Researcher Inst de Recherches Scientifiques sur le Cancer, Villejuif 1968–72; Founder Press Service, Inst National de la Santé et de la Recherche Médicale (INSERM) 1973–81; Rep for Scientific and Tech Press and Information, Cabinet of the Minister for Research and Tech 1981–83; Dir of Information and Regional Cultural Activities Agence Nat de Valorisation de la Recherche (ANVAR), and Deputy Gen Commr of Festival de l'Industrie et de la Technologie 1983–87; Dir of Communication and Promotion Cité des Sciences et de l'Industrie 1988–96, Dir of Scientific Film and Television 1996–2000, responsibility for Scientific Affairs 2000–; Chevalier de la Légion d'Honneur, Officier de l'Ordre Nat du Mérite 1991. *Leisure interests:* reading, theatre, cinema. *Address:* Cité des Sciences et de l'Industrie, 30 ave Corentin Cariou, 75019 Paris, France. *Telephone:* (1) 40-05-70-40; *Fax:* (1) 40-05-73-44.

BELLERSEN, Monique Maria, PH D; Netherlands management consultant; b 4 May 1956. *Education:* Univ of Utrecht. *Career:* Public Health Information Officer, Information Campaign on AIDS, Ministry of Welfare, Health and Cultural Affairs 1984–87, Project Leader Personnel Information System and Head Information Policy Dept 1987–89; Accounts Man L & T Informatica Ltd 1989–91; Man Consultant, City of Rotterdam 1991–95; Man Partner Organisatie Adviesgroep Rotterdam 1995–. *Leisure interests:* tennis, skiing, squash. *Address:* Bentinklaan 55C, 3039 KY Rotterdam, Netherlands. *Telephone:* (10) 46-56-621; *Fax:* (10) 41-72-220.

BENAKIS, Anna, DR JUR; Greek politician and professor of criminal law; b 12 Dec 1934, Athens; m Linos Benakis 1957. *Education:* Pierce Coll of Athens and Univs of Athens and Bonn (Germany). *Career:* Asst, Asst Prof Univ of Athens, Univ of Bonn, Max-Planck Inst for Int Criminal Law, Freiburg, Germany 1962–78; Consultant on Higher Educ to Ministry of Educ 1975–77, 1980–81; mem Legal Comms of Ministry of Justice 1977–81; mem foreign teaching staff Temple Univ Philadelphia, PA, USA 1981–85; currently Prof of Criminal Law, Univ of Athens; mem Parl 1981; Speaker on legal and educ matters, Nea Democratia Party 1981–89; Alt Minister of Educ 1989, of Culture 1991; Minister of Culture 1991–92, of Justice 1992–93; Vice-Pres Greek Soc for Criminal Law 1988. *Publications:* four books and several articles on criminal matters; political articles. *Leisure interests:* water-skiing, swimming, classical music, literature. *Address:* Skoufa 75, 10680 Athens, Greece (Office); Sina 58, 10672 Athens, Greece (Home). *Telephone:* (1) 3602634 (Office); (1) 3636818 (Home); *Fax:* (1) 3602633 (Office); (1) 3645179 (Home).

BENATAR, Pat; American singer; b (Pat Andrejewski) 1953, Brooklyn, NY; m Neil Geraldo; one c. *Career:* Grammy Awards for Best Female Rock Vocal Performance 1981, 1982, 1983, 1984. *Recordings include:* Albums: In the Heat of the Night 1979, Crimes of Passion 1980, Precious Time 1981, Get Nervous 1982, Live From Earth 1983, Tropico 1984, Seven the Hard Way 1985, Wide Awake in Dreamland 1988, Best Shots 1989, True Love 1991, Gravity's Rainbow 1993, All Fired Up: The Very Best of Pat Benatar 1994; Singles: Treat Me Right, Hit Me With Your Best Shot, Love is a Battlefield, Hell is for Children. *Address:* c/o Tom Ross Creative Artists Agency Inc, 9830 Wilshire Blvd, Beverly Hills, CA 90212, USA.

BENESOVÁ, Libuse, D PHIL, PH D; Czech politician; b 5 July 1948, Benesov; m Jiří Benes; one d. *Education:* Charles Univ (Prague). *Career:* Mayor of Lesany 1990–92; Head Dist Council, Prague-West 1993–94; Vice-Minister of Finance 1995–97; Senator 1996–, Pres of Senate 1998–. *Publication:* Handbook of Municipal Administration 1994. *Leisure interests:* cooking, gardening, knitting, reading, sewing. *Address:* The Senate, Valdstejnské nám 4, 118 11 Prague, 1, Czech Republic. *Telephone:* (2) 57072513; *Fax:* (2) 24249024; *E-mail:* benesoval@senat.cz.

BENGLIS, Lynda, BFA; American artist; b 1941, Lake Charles, LA. *Education:* Newcomb Coll. *Career:* Asst Prof of Sculpture Univ of Rochester, NY 1970–72; Asst Prof Hunter Coll, NY 1972–73; Visiting Prof California Inst of Arts 1974, 1976, Princeton Univ 1975, Univ of Arizona 1982, School of Visual Arts 1985–87; Visiting Artist Kent State Univ 1977, Skowhegan School of Painting and Sculpture 1979; one-woman exhibitions include Univ of Rhode Island 1969, Kansas State Univ 1971, Paula Cooper Gallery (NY) 1973, 1975, 1978, 1980, 1982,

1987, 1990, Margo Leavin Gallery (LA) 1977, 1985, Real Art Ways (CT) 1979, David Heath Gallery (GA) 1980, Dart Gallery (IL) 1983, Linda Farris Gallery (WA) 1990, travelling exhibition to Georgia, California and Louisiana 1991; jt (two-person) exhibitions in USA, Germany and Japan 1970–89; group exhibitions in USA, Germany and Sweden; Guggenheim Fellowship 1975, Artpark Grant 1976, Australian Art Council Award 1976, Nat Endowment for Arts 1979, 1990, Minos Beach Art Symposium 1988, Olympiad of Art, Sculpture Park (Korea) 1988, Nat Council of Art Administration Award 1989. *Leisure interest:* travel. *Address:* Cheim and Read Gallery, 521 W 23rd St, New York, NY 10011, USA.

BENING, Annette; American actress; b 29 May 1958, Topeka, KS; m 1st Steven White (divorced); m 2nd Warren Beatty 1992; three c. *Education:* San Francisco State Univ. *Career:* Stage appearances in works by Ibsen, Chekhov and Shakespeare in San Diego and San Francisco; European Achievement in World Cinema Award 2000. *Films:* The Great Outdoors 1988, Valmont, Postcards from the Edge, The Grifters (Nat Soc of Film Critics Award, Acad Award nomination) 1990, Guilty by Suspicion, Regarding Henry, Bugsy, Love Affair, The American President, Richard III, Blue Vision, Mars Attacks! 1996, Against All Enemies, The Siege, In Dreams, American Beauty 1999, What Planet Are You From?; *Plays include:* Coastal Disturbances (Theatre World Award), The Great Outdoors, Spoils of War. *Address:* c/o Kevin Huvane, CAA, 9830 Wilshire Blvd, Beverly Hills, CA 90212, USA (Office).

BENNASAR TOUS, Francisca; Spanish politician; b 11 Dec 1943, Palma de Mallorca. *Career:* MEP (EPP, Partido Popular) 1994–99, mem Cttee on Women's Rights, Del to the EU–Malta Jt Parl Cttee; Vice-Pres EPP 2000–. *Address:* c/o EPP, 67 rue d'Arlon, 1047 Brussels, Belgium. *Telephone:* (2) 285-41-40; *Fax:* (2) 285-41-41.

BENNETT, Enid Maude; Jamaican politician; b Linstead, St Catherine; d of the late James Bennett and Margaret Gordon. *Education:* St Helen's Commercial School (Linstead). *Career:* Mem Parl from 1967; Minister of State, Ministry of Local Govt 1980–84, Ministry of Social Security 1984–89; Deputy Leader Jamaica Lab Party (JLP) 1978–. *Leisure interest:* reading. *Address:* Begonia Lodge, Linstead PO 14, Jamaica (Office).

BENNETT, Hazel Eloise, PH D, M SC, FLA; Jamaican librarian; b 1924, Portland, Jamaica; d of Mortimer and Catherine Gray; m Wycliffe Bennett 1957; one s one d. *Education:* Southern Connecticut Coll and Univ of Chicago (USA) and Univ of Loughborough (UK). *Career:* Deputy Dir Jamaica Library Service 1957–67; librarian, Documentalist Univ of the West Indies School of Educ 1967–71, Lecturer, then Sr Lecturer 1971–88; currently conducting research; mem Jamaican Nat Comm for UNESCO, Nat Council on Libraries; Inst of Jamaica Centenary Medal; Shortwood Coll Distinguished Service Award. *Publication:* History of Libraries in Jamaica. *Leisure interests:* gardening, performing arts. *Address:* 7 Earls Court, Kingston 8, Jamaica. *Telephone:* 925-8246.

BENNETT, Jana Eve, OBE, BA, M SC, FRTS; British broadcasting executive; b 6 Nov 1957, Cooperstown, USA; d of Gordon Willard Bennett and Elizabeth Cushing; m Richard Clemmow 1996; one s one d. *Education:* Bognor Comprehensive, St Anne's Coll (Oxford) and London School of Econs. *Career:* News trainee BBC 1979, fmrly Asst Producer The Money Programme, Producer Newsnight, Producer/Dir Panorama, Series Producer Antenna, Ed Horizon, Head of BBC Science; BBC Dir of Production and Deputy Chief Exec 1997–99; Exec Vice Pres Learning Channel, US Discovery Communications Inc 1999–; Golden Nymph Award (Panorama), BAFTA, Emmy, Prix Italia (Horizon). *Publication:* The Disappeared: Argentina's Dirty War 1986. *Leisure interests:* mountaineering, music, children. *Address:* 7700 Wisconsin Ave, Bethesda, MD 20814, USA.

BENNETT-COVERLEY, Hon Louise Simone, OJ, MBE; Jamaican folklorist and writer; b 7 Sept 1919, Kingston; d of the late Augustus and Kerene Bennett; m Eric Winston Coverley 1954; one s. *Education:* St Simon's Coll, Excelsior Coll, Friends Coll. *Career:* Artiste in Caribbean Carnival, BBC 1945–46, 1950–53; Drama Officer Jamaica Social Welfare Comm 1956–59, Dir 1959–63; lecturer, performer at univs in the Caribbean, N America and Europe; Chair Folklore Cttee, Arts Devt

Council; Patron Nat Dance Co; mem Man Cttee Little Theatre Movt; Hon D LIT; British Council Scholarship to Royal Acad of Dramatic Art (London) 1945; Silver and Gold Musgrave Medals 1964, 1979; Norman Manley Award for Excellence (Folklore and Art) 1972. *Publications:* Humorous Verses in Jamaica Dialect 1942, Jamaican Verses and Folk Stories, Laugh with Louise 1962, Jamaica Labrish 1966, Anancy and Miss Lou 1979; *Recordings include:* Jamaica Folksongs: Folkways 1953, Jamaica Singing Games 1953, Carifesta Ring Ding 1976, The Honorable Miss Lou 1981, Miss Lou Live (London) 1983, Yes Me Dear. *Address:* Enfield House, Gordon Town PO, St Andrew, Jamaica.

BENSON, Susan, RCA; Canadian theatre designer; b 22 April 1942, Bexleyheath, UK; d of John and Nella Benson; m Michael Whitfield. *Education:* Talbot Heath School (Bournemouth) and W of England Coll of Art (Bristol). *Career:* Theatre designer (sets and costumes) 1963–; emigrated to Canada 1966; Designer Stratford Festival Theatre Co 1974–; Asst Prof Univ of Illinois, USA 1970–74; Lecturer Nat Theatre School, Banff School of Fine Arts, York Univ, Univ of Michigan; Resident Designer Krannert Centre for the Performing Arts 1970–74; has designed for Canadian Opera Co, Nat Ballet of Canada, Manitoba Theatre Centre, Australian Opera Co, New York City Opera, Nat Ballet of Finland, San Francisco Opera; Assoc Dir Stratford Festival 1995–; one-woman exhibitions of paintings 1980–84; rep Canada at Prague Quadrennial 1979, 1983, 1987, 1991; mem Assoc Designers of Canada; Art Teachers Dip; 7 Dora Mayor Moore Awards; Ace TV Award for Costume Design, US Acad of Cable TV 1987; Banff Centre Nat Awards for the Arts; Senior Canada Council Arts Award. *Productions include:* A Midsummer Night's Dream 1977, The Mikado 1982, Don Quichotte 1986, The Gondoliers 1989, Cabaret 1990, Guys and Dolls 1990, The Marriage of Figaro 1990, Madame Butterfly 1990, The Taming of the Shrew 1992, Romeo and Juliet 1995, The Golden Ass 1999, The Ballad of Baby Doe 2001. *Leisure interests:* painting, gardening. *Address:* 236 William St, Stratford, ON N5A 4Y3, Canada. *Telephone:* (519) 271-8392.

BENTEL, Maria-Luise Ramona Azzarone, B ARCH; American architect; b 15 June 1928, New York; d of Louis and Maria Teresa (née Massaro) Azzarone; m Frederick R. Bentel 1952; three c. *Education:* MIT and Scuola d'Architettura (Venice, Italy). *Career:* Partner Bentel & Bentel 1956–; Pres Tesstoria Realty Corpn from 1961; Sec, Treas Correlated Designs Inc 1961; apptd Prof of Architecture New York Inst of Tech 1971; Fellow American Inst of Architects 1976; awards for design of St Joseph's Coll Library 1990, Stonybrook Museums 1990, St Stephen's Church 1991. *Publication:* Church Design, Architectural Time Saver Standards 1973. *Leisure interests:* skiing, photography. *Address:* 22 Buckram Rd, Locust Valley, NY 11560, USA (Office); 23 Frost Creek Drive, Locust Valley, NY 11560, USA (Home). *Telephone:* (516) 676-2880.

BENYON, Margaret, MBE, PH D, BFA FRPS; British artist; b 29 April 1940, Birmingham; m William Rodwell 1974; one s one d. *Education:* Kenya High School, Slade School of Fine Art, Univ Coll London and Royal Coll of Art. *Career:* Visiting Tutor Coventry Coll of Art 1966–68, Trent Polytechnic, Nottingham 1968–71, Holography Unit, RCA 1985–89; Fellow in Fine Art, Univ of Nottingham 1968–71; Leverhulme Sr Art Fellow, Univ of Strathclyde 1971–73; Co-ordinator Graphic Investigation, Canberra School of Art, Australia 1977–80; Creative Arts Fellow ANU, Canberra 1978; Artist-in-Residence, Museum of Holography, New York 1981, Center for Holographic Arts, New York 1999; pioneered holography as an art medium; works in public collections including Australian Nat Gallery, Nat Gallery of Vic, Australia, MIT Museum, USA, Calouste Gulbenkian Foundation, Portugal, Victoria and Albert Museum, London; 100 exhibitions to date, including London, Vienna, New York, Frankfurt, Lisbon, Madrid, Nagoya, Liverpool, Bradford, Berlin, Boston, Tokyo; Audrey Mellon Prize 1964, Carnegie Trust Award 1972, Kodak Photographic Bursary 1982, Calouste Gulbenkian Holography Award 1982, Agfa 'Best of Exhibition' Award, USA 1985, Sheerwater Foundation Holography Award, USA 1987, Lifetime Achievement Award, Art in Holography International Symposium, UK 1996. *Works include:* Hot Air 1970, Bird in Box 1973, Solar Markers 1979, White Rainbow 1980, Tiresias 1981, Conjugal Series 1983, Tigirl 1985, Cosmetic Series 1986–93, Cornucopia 1994–. *Address:* 40 Springdale Ave, Broadstone, BH18 9EU, UK. *Telephone:* (1202) 698067; *Fax:* (1202) 698067; *E-mail:* benyon@ holography.demon.co.uk; *Internet:* www.holography.demon.co.uk.

BERARD, Marie-Hélène; French civil servant and banking executive; b 13 Nov 1947, Paris; d of Emmanuel Genstein and Simone Moros; m Jean-Michel Berard 1974; two d one s. *Education:* Lycée Hélène Boucher (Paris), Inst des Etudes Politiques and Ecole Nat d'Admin (Paris). *Career:* Admin Dept of the Budget, Ministry of Finance 1972–76, Head of Office Dept of the Budget 1978–79, Dir 1982–86; Adviser in Cabinet of the Minister of Health and Social Welfare 1976–78; Tech Adviser in Cabinet of the Prime Minister 1979–81, Adviser 1986–88; Del Dir-Gen Marceau Investissement 1988–90; Exec Adviser to the Pres of Crédit Commercial de France 1990–. *Publication:* Dictionnaire de la constitution française (jtly, 2nd edn) 1988. *Address:* Crédit Commercial de France, 103 ave des Champs-Elysées, 75008 Paris, France (Office); 6 rue Cassini, 75014 Paris, France (Home). *Telephone:* (1) 40-70-24-00 (Office); *Fax:* (1) 40-70-71-42 (Office).

BEREK, Katalin; Hungarian actress; b 7 Oct 1930; d of Józset and Karolina (née Rauch) Berek; m Pál Zolhay 1958; one s. *Education:* Acad of Acting (Budapest). *Career:* Actress 1952–, at Nat Theatre (Budapest) 1952–82, Kisfaludy Theatre (Gjör), Gairdohji Theatre (Eger) and Katona József (Kecskemet) 1985–92; recipient of numerous awards. *Address:* Budapest II kev 1023, Harcsa Vica 2, Hungary. *Telephone:* (1) 115-3568.

BERÈS, Pervenche Madeleine Agnès; French politician; b 10 March 1957, Neuilly-sur-Seine; d of Pierre and Annick Berès; two s. *Education:* Ecole Alsacienne (Paris). *Career:* Admin Secr of Nat Ass Del to EC 1981–83; Admin Secr of Comm on Foreign Affairs 1983–88; Rep, later Technical Counsellor to Cabinet of Pres of Nat Ass 1988–92; Nat Sec for Co-operation and Devt, PS 1993–94, 1994–; MEP (PSE) 1994–, mem Cttee on External Econ Relations, Del for Relations with the Mashreq Countries and the Gulf States; Pres French Del European Socialist Group. *Address:* European Parliament, rue Wiertz, 1047 Brussels, Belgium.

BERESFORD, Meg, BA; British peace campaign organizer; b 5 Sept 1937, Birmingham; d of the late John Tristram Beresford and of Anne Isobel (née Stuart Wortley) Northcroft; m William Tanner 1959; two s. *Education:* Sherborne School for Girls (Dorset) and Univ of Warwick. *Career:* Founder-mem, Co-ordinator Campaign Atom, Oxford 1980–81; mem Nat Council, Campaign for Nuclear Disarmament (CND) 1980–, Vice-Chair 1983–85, Gen Sec 1985–90; Organizing Sec European Nuclear Disarmament 1981–83; Staff Co-ordinator The Iona Community 1991–94; Asst Dir Wiston Lodge YMCA 1994–97, Man 1997–. *Publication:* Into the Twenty First Century 1989. *Leisure interests:* walking, the environment, reading, art. *Address:* The Sheiling, Wiston Lodge, Wiston, Biggar ML12 6HT, UK. *Telephone:* (18995) 228.

BERGANZA, Teresa; Spanish opera singer (mezzo-soprano); b 16 March 1935, Madrid; d of Guillermo and Ascensión Berganza; m 1st Felix Lavilla 1957; one s two d; m 2nd José Rifa 1978. *Education:* Real Conservatorio (Madrid). *Career:* Debut Aix-en-Provence, France 1957; has appeared at La Scala (Milan) and Opera Roma (Italy), Metropolitan Opera (New York), Chicago Opera House and San Francisco Opera (USA), Royal Opera House (Covent Garden, London), and at festivals in Edinburgh (UK), Netherlands and Glyndebourne (UK); performances at concerts in France, Belgium, Netherlands, Italy, Germany, Spain, Austria, Portugal, Scandinavia, Israel, Mexico, Argentina, USA and Canada; performed at opening ceremony of Expo 92, Seville, Spain, also at opening ceremonies Barcelona Olympics 1992, mem Real Academia de Bellas Artes de San Fernando, Spanish Royal Acad of Arts 1994; has made over 200 recordings; Premio Lucrezia Arana; Premio extraordinario del Conservatorio de Madrid; Grande Cruz Isabel la Católica; Harriet Cohen Award; Int Critic Award 1988; Commdr des Arts et des Lettres. *Publication:* Flor de Soledad y Silencio 1984; *Films:* Don Giovanni; two further films of operas. *Leisure interests:* art, music, reading. *Address:* c/o Lies Askonas, 19A Air St, Regent St, London W1, UK; La Rossiniana, Archanda 5, Apdo 137, 28200 San Lorenzo del Escorial, Madrid, Spain. *Telephone:* (20) 7734-5459 (UK); (1) 8960941 (Madrid); *Fax:* (1) 8960816 (Madrid).

BERGÉ-LAVIGNE, Maryse; French politician; b 29 Jan 1941, Pamiers, Ariège; d of Jean and Alice (née Durrieu) Bergé; m Paul Lavigne; two s. *Career:* Fmr teacher; Regional Councillor Midi-Pyrénées 1986–92; PS Senator for Haute-Garonne 1989–; Sec Sénat 1993–; Vice-Chair Parl Group for Space, Parl Group for Civil Aviation, Parl Friendships for Tibet Asscn; mem League for Human Rights, Regional Agency for the Environment. *Leisure interests:* walking, reading. *Address:* Sénat, Palais du Luxembourg, 75291 Paris Cedex 06, France (Office); 195 rue de Muret, 31300 Toulouse, France (Home). *Telephone:* (1) 42-34-29-15 (Office); *Fax:* (1) 42-34-42-36 (Office).

BERGEN, Candice Patricia; American actress and photo-journalist; b 9 May 1946, Beverly Hills, CA; d of Edgar and Frances (née Westerman) Bergen; m Louis Malle 1980 (died 1995); one d. *Education:* Westlake School for Girls and Univ of Philadelphia. *Career:* Photographic work has appeared in Vogue, Cosmopolitan, Life and Esquire magazines. *Appearances include:* The Group 1966, The Sand Pebbles 1966, The Day the Fish Came Out 1967, Vivre Pour Vivre 1967, The Magus 1968, Getting Straight 1970, Soldier Blue 1970, The Adventurers 1970, Carnal Knowledge 1971, The Hunting Party 1971, T. R. Baskin 1972, 11 Harrowhouse 1974, Bite the Bullet 1975, The Wind and the Lion 1976, The Domino Principle 1977, A Night Full of Rain 1977, Oliver's Story 1978, Starting Over 1979, Rich and Famous 1981, Gandhi 1982, Stick 1985, Murphy Brown 1989; *Publications:* The Freezer (in Best Short Plays of 1968), Knock Wood (autobiog) 1984. *Address:* c/o William Morris Agency, 151 El Camino, Beverly Hills, CA 90212, USA.

BERGEON, Ségolène France Marie Nelly, L ÈS SC; French civil servant and curator; b 1 Dec 1942, Montpellier. *Education:* Univ of Lyons, Ecole du Louvre and Ecole Nat d'Admin (Paris). *Career:* Curator Nat Museums 1969; at Acad de France, Villa Médicis, Rome 1971–72; Curator Painting Restoration Service 1972–88; apptd Chief Curator 1988; Head Dept of Libraries and Man of the Louvre, Ministry of Culture 1989, Rep 1990; Rep to Dept of Nat Heritage (Archaeology) 1990–92; Dir Inst Français de Restauration d'Oeuvres d'Art (IFROA) 1992–95; Rep to Dept of Architecture and Heritage 1995–; mem Conseil Int des Musées, Int Inst for Conservation; Officier des Arts et des Lettres. *Publications:* Comprendre Sauver Restaurer 1976, La restauration des peintures 1980, Science et patience ou la restauration des peintures 1990. *Leisure interests:* sailing, reading, swimming. *Address:* Ministère de la Culture, 10 rue du Parc Royal, 75003 Paris, France (Office); 42 rue Molitor, 75016 Paris, France (Home).

BERGER, Geneviève, PH D; French research scientist; b 1955, Moselle. *Education:* Ecole normale supérieure, Cachan. *Career:* Founder Parametric Imaging Lab 1991; Pres Treatment and Drugs: Design and Resources Section, Nat Cttee for Scientific Research 1995–98; Dir of Tech, Ministry of Research 1998–2000; Dir-Gen CNRS 2000–; Honours include CNRS Silver Medal, Yves Rocard Prize 1997, Chevalier des Palmes Académiques, Chevalier de la Légion d'Honneur 1988. *Address:* Centre National de la Recherche Scientifique, 3–5 rue Michel-Ange, 75794 Paris, Cedex 16, France. *Telephone:* (1) 44-96-40-00 (Office); (1) 44-96-50-00 (Home).

BERGER, Juliane-Helene; German artist; b 18 Sept 1952, Uelzen; d of Julius and Helene (née Meyer) Berger; one s. *Education:* Art School (Alsterdam), Hochschule für Bildende Künste (Hamburg) and Akad der Freien Künste (Berlin). *Career:* Exhibitions in Hamburg, Hanover, Frankfurt/Main, Miami (FL, USA), Osaka (Japan), Museum of Modern Art, New York, Barcelona and Granada (Spain), Washington (DC, USA), Chicago (IL, USA), Paris, Antwerp (Belgium), Düsseldorf, Basel (Switzerland), Bonn, Neûchatel (Switzerland), Koblenz and Montreux (Switzerland), Brazil, etc; Participant Salon, Tokyo 1991; Exhibition at Expo Hannover 2000; mem GEDOK (Hamburg) 1989, Fed Int Culturelle Féminine; awards include First Prize (Fani Fine Art Acad, Italy) 1993, First Prize (Pesaro Fine Art Acad, Italy) 1994, Gold Rembrandtmedaille 1994, Gold Euro-Prize 1995. *Leisure interests:* piano, cooking, gardening. *Address:* Bohldamm 21, 29525 Uelzen, Germany. *Telephone:* (581) 17473; *Fax:* (581) 71574.

BERGER, Senta; German/Austrian actress; b 13 May 1941, Vienna; d of Josef Berger and Therese Jany; m Michael Verhoeven 1966; two s. *Education:* Max Reinhardt–Seminar and Academy of Arts (Vienna).

Career: Actress in films 1957–, in theatre 1958–; has performed in Austria, Germany, Italy, France, UK and USA; has won numerous acting and production awards including Max–Ophüls-Prize 1998, Karl Valentin Order 1998. *Appearances include:* Major Dundee, Quiller Memorandum, Diaboliquement Votre, Scarlett Letter, Kir Royal, Die schnelle Gerdi; *Productions include:* The White Rose (Bundesfilmpreis) 1983, The Nasty Girl (Das schreckliche Mädchen—BAFTA Award for Best Foreign Film 1992, New York Film Critics' Award, nominated for Oscar) 1991. *Address:* Sentana Film Productions, Gebsattelstr 30, 8000 Munich, Germany. *Telephone:* (89) 4485266; *Fax:* (89) 4801968.

BERGERON-DE VILLIERS, Louise, B SC S; Canadian civil servant; b Ottawa; m; two s two d. *Education:* Univ of Ottawa. *Career:* Mem staff Status of Women Canada 1983, Deputy Co-ordinator 1987, Co-ordinator 1994; fmr mem staff Depts of Nat Health and Welfare, External Affairs and Office of the Sec of State; rep of Canada at int governmental confs; Pres Ottawa YMCA-YWCA 1992–93; mem Bd Govs Carleton Univ until 2002, Man Cttee Commonwealth Sports Devt Programme 2000–. *Address:* c/o Commonwealth Games Association of Canada, 720 Belfast Rd, Suite 216, Ottawa, ON K1G 0Z5, Canada; 420 chemin Crégheur, Luskville, PQ J0X 2G0, Canada. *Internet:* www.commonwealthgames.ca.

BERGET, Grete Anni; Norwegian politician and journalist; b 25 March 1954, Vinstra; d of Bjarne and Gudrun Berget; m Per Ritzler 1989; one d. *Education:* Oppland Dist Coll, Norwegian School of Journalism and Crafts School. *Career:* Journalist on local radio and newspapers 1978–82; Ed Lab Youth org newspaper 1982–84; journalist on Arbeiderbladet (Lab newspaper), Oslo 1984–88; Information Dir Office of the Prime Minister 1988–89, Political Adviser to the Prime Minister 1989–91; Minister of Children and Family Affairs 1991. *Leisure interests:* spending time with husband and daughter, mountain tours, skiing, football, music. *Address:* c/o Ministry of Children and Family Affairs, Akersgt 59, Postboks 8036 Dep, 0030 Oslo, Norway. *Telephone:* 22-34-90-90; *Fax:* 22-34-95-15.

BERGHOFER-WEICHNER, Mathilde, DR JUR; German politician; b 1931; m Robert Berghofer 1969 (died 1973). *Career:* Mem CSU; mem Communal Councils of Gauting and Starnberg; fmr Minister of Justice, Fed State of Bavaria, State Sec for Educ and Culture until 1986, mem Landtag (regional Parl), Minister of Justice, Deputy Minister-Pres, Fed State of Bavaria 1986–93. *Address:* Justizpalast, Prielmayerstr 7, 80335 Munich, Germany. *Telephone:* (89) 55971.

BERGLIN, Eva Elisabet, BM, BS; Swedish surgeon; b 2 Jan 1947, Gothenburg; d of Tore and Ingrid (née Cederberg) Berglin; m Göran William-Olsson 1976; one s. *Education:* Univ of Gothenburg. *Career:* Intern Sahlgren's Hosp 1975–76, Resident in Cardiothoracic Surgery 1976–81, mem Organ Transplantation Staff 1981–83, Specialist in Cardiothoracic Surgery 1982–88, Consultant 1988–, Head of Cardiac Transplantation 1988–97; Research Fellow Univ of Gothenburg 1972–76; lecturer in field; numerous articles in scientific journals; mem Swedish Transplant Soc, European Soc of Heart Transplantation, Nordic Circle of Cardiac Surgeons. *Address:* Sahlgren's Hospital, Department of Cardiothoracic Surgery, 41345 Gothenburg, Sweden. *Telephone:* (31) 3421000; *Fax:* (31) 417991; *E-mail:* eva.berglin@ vgregion.se.

BERGMAN, Stephenie Jane, DIP AD; British artist; b 18 April 1946, London; d of Jack 'Kid' Berg and Morya Bergman. *Education:* St Paul's Girls' School and St Martin's School of Art. *Career:* One-woman exhibitions in UK at Garage Art Ltd (London) 1973, 1975, Nottingham 1976, Cambridge 1977, Chester 1978, Anthony Stokes (London) 1978, 1980, Riverside Studios (London) 1980, Crafts Council Gallery 1984 and Butler's House (Kilkenny, Ireland) 1984; has participated in group exhibitions in UK, France, Belgium, Australia, Zimbabwe; Gulbenkian Award 1975. *Leisure interest:* horse-racing.

BERGMANN, Barbara Rose, PH D; American professor of economics; b 20 July 1927, New York; d of Martin and Nellie (née Wallenstein) Bergman; m Fred H. Bergmann 1965; one s one d. *Education:* Cornell and Harvard Univs. *Career:* Economist US Bureau of Labor Statistics, NY 1949–53; Econs Instructor Harvard Univ 1958–61; Sr Staff Economist Council of Econ Advisors, Exec Office of the Pres 1961–62; Assoc Prof of Econs Brandeis Univ 1962–64; Sr mem staff The Brookings Inst 1963–65; Sr Econ Advisor AID, US Dept of State 1966–67; Assoc Prof of Econs Univ of Maryland 1965–71, Prof 1971–88; Distinguished Prof of Econs American Univ, Washington, DC 1988–97, Prof Emer 1997–; Vice-Pres American Econ Asscn 1976; Columnist on econ affairs NY Times 1981–82, LA Times 1983; Pres American Asscn of Univ Profs 1990–92, Int Asscn for Feminist Economists 1999; mem Ed Bd American Econ Review, Women and Politics, Academe, Challenge, Signs; Columnist on Econs New York Times 1981–82, Los Angeles Times 1984–. *Publications include:* Projection of a Metropolis (jtly) 1961, The Impact of Highway Investment on Development (jtly) 1966, Structural Unemployment in the US (jtly) 1967, Micro Simulation – Models, Methods and Application (co-ed) 1977, A Microsimulated Transactions Model of the US Economy (jtly) 1985, Women's Work in the World Economy (co-ed), The Economic Emergence of Women 1986, Saving Children from Poverty: What the United States Can Learn From France 1995, In Defense of Affirmative Action 1996, Is Social Security Broke? A Cartoon Guide to the Issues 1999; numerous articles and contribs to professional books and journals. *Address:* Department of Economics, American University, Washington, DC 20016, USA (Office); 5430 41st Place, NW, Washington, DC 20015, USA (Home). *Telephone:* (202) 885-2725 (Office); (202) 537-3036 (Home); *Fax:* (202) 885-3790 (Office).

BERGMANN, Christine, DR RER NAT; German politician; b 7 Sept 1937, Dresden; m Volker Bergmann 1963; one s one d. *Education:* Leipzig Univ. *Career:* Fmrly worked as apothecary; freelance work then full-time employee in pharmaceutics propagation Berlin Pharmaceutical Inst 1967–77, Head of Dept 1977; mem Social Democratic Party of Germany (SPD) 1989–, State Chair Berlin 1989, mem Party Exec Cttee and Presidium 1995–; Fed Minister of Family Affairs, Sr Citizens, Women and Youth 1998–; Pres Berlin Ass of City Councillors 1990–91, Mayoress of Berlin and Senator 1991–98. *Address:* Ministry of Family Affairs, Senior Citizens, Women and Youth, Taubenstrasse 42–43, 10117 Berlin, Germany. *Telephone:* (228) 9300; *Fax:* (228) 930-22-21.

BERGQUIST, Dame Patricia Rose, DBE, PH D, D SC, FRSNZ; New Zealand professor of zoology; b 10 March 1933, Auckland; d of William and Bertha E. Smyth; m Peter L. Bergquist 1958; one d. *Education:* Takapuna Grammar School and Univ of Auckland. *Career:* Lecturer in Zoology, Auckland Univ 1958, Prof of Zoology (Personal Chair) 1981–99, Head of Dept 1986–99, Prof Emer 1999–; Post-doctoral research Yale Univ 1961–64; career concentrated on sponge biology, chemistry, chemo-taxonomy; pioneered application of chem and pharmacology of marine sponges to resolving major questions of sponge phylogeny and relationships; Int Consultant in marine sponge taxonomy and marine ecology; Prof of Zoology (Personal Chair), Univ of Auckland 1981–, Head of Dept 1986–, Asst Vice-Chancellor (Academic) 1989–96, Deputy Vice-Chancellor 1996, Special Asst to Vice-Chancellor 1997–98; Hector Medal, Royal Soc of NZ 1988. *Publications:* more than 150 articles in professional journals. *Leisure interests:* fishing, stamp collecting, classical music. *Address:* Department of Anatomy, University of Auckland, Private Bag 92019, Auckland, 1, New Zealand; 3A Pukerangi Crescent, Ellersie, Auckland 5, New Zealand (Home). *Telephone:* (9) 3737599 (Office); (9) 5796291 (Home); *Fax:* (9) 3737484; *E-mail:* pr.bergquist@auckland.ac.nz (Office).

BERKOVÁ, Alexandra, PH D; Czech writer; b 2 July 1949; m Vladimir Novák; one s one d. *Education:* Charles Univ (Prague). *Career:* Freelance writer 1985–; f New Humanity feminist org 1992; mem PEN Club 1989–. *Publications include:* Red Cover Book (short stories) 1986, 1988, Majorie (novel, Egon Hostorský Prize) 1991, The Sufferings of Devoted Lousehead 1993; has written 12 radio and TV Plays. *Address:* Uvodárny 4, 13000 Prague 3, Czech Republic. *Telephone:* (2) 24257528.

BERMAN, Brigitte (Ursula), BA, B ED; Canadian film producer, director and writer; b 15 Jan, Frankfurt, Germany. *Education:* York Mills Coll Inst (Toronto), Queen's Univ and McArthur Coll. *Career:* Researcher Canadian Broadcasting Corpn 1973–75, Producer 1975–84; Pres Bridge Film Productions Inc 1979–; Dir Canadian Centre for Advanced Film Studies 1988–89; mem American Acad of Motion Picture Arts and Sciences, Toronto Women in Film and Video; numerous awards including Acad Award for Best Documentary Feature 1987. *TV includes:* Artie Shaw: Time Is All You've Got, The Many Faces of Black 1977, Elmira 1975, The Osbornes: A Very Special Family 1982, Judy Chicago 1982, The Circle Game 1993–94. *Leisure interests:* music, films, theatre, the arts. *Address:* 44 Charles St W, Toronto, ON M4Y 1R7, Canada.

BERMAN, Jennifer, MD, BA; American urologist; b 1965; m; one c. *Education:* Hollins College (Roanoke, VA), Univ of Maryland and Univ of Boston. *Career:* Jt Dir Women's Sexual Health Clinic Boston 1998–2001; Co-Founder Female Sexual Medicine Center UCLA 2001–; mem Editorial Bd Health Gate Inc, Sexual Health Capsule and Comment; mem American Medical Asscn, American Urological Asscn, New England Urological Section, Soc for the Study of Impotence Research. *Publications:* For Women Only (co-author with sister Laura (qv)), numerous publications in academic journals and chapters in textbooks. *Address:* Female Sexual Medicine Center, University of California at Los Angeles, Los Angeles, CA 90024, USA.

BERMAN, Laura, PH D; American sexologist; b 1969; m (divorced); one s. *Education:* Univ of New York. *Career:* Jt Dir Women's Sexual Health Clinic Boston 1998–2001; Co-Founder Female Sexual Medicine Center UCLA 2001–, Network for Excellence in Women's Sexual Health (NEWSHE); mem Bd Soc for the Scientific Study of Sexuality (SSSS); mem American Asscn of Sex Educators Counselors and Therapists (AASECT), Nat Asscn of Social Workers (NASW). *Publications:* For Women Only (co-author with sister Jennifer (qv)), numerous publications in academic journals and popular publications. *Address:* Female Sexual Medicine Center, University of California at Los Angeles, Los Angeles, CA 90024, USA.

BERNARD, Claire Marie Anne; French violinist; b 31 March 1947, Rouen; d of Yvan Bernard and Marie Chouquet. *Education:* Conservatoire Régional de Musique (Rouen) and Conservatoire Nat Supérieur de Musique (Paris). *Career:* Professional solo violinist 1965–; Prof of Violin at numerous conservatoires and music schools; mem jury Tchaikovsky Int Competition, Moscow, USSR (now Russian Fed) 1974; Prof Ecole de Musique, Asnières 1975; Prof of Violin at state-run conservatoires and music schools in France; Asst Conservatoire national supérieur de musique, Lyon 1990–; Chevalier de l'Ordre Nat du Mérite; numerous other awards and prizes. *Recordings include:* Works of: Khatchaturian, Prokofiev, Barber, Milhaud, Mozart, Haydn, Sarasate, Leclair, Telemann. *Leisure interests:* painting, gymnastics, swimming. *Address:* 53 rue Rabelais, 69003 Lyon, France (Home).

BERNHARD, Sandra; American actress, comedienne and singer; b 6 June 1955, Flint, MI; d of Jerome and Jeanette Bernhard. *Career:* Fmr pedicurist; stand-up comedienne in nightclubs in Beverly Hills 1974–78; own stage shows as stand-up comedian Without You I'm Nothing, USA 1988, Giving Till It Hurts, USA 1992, in London and on tour in the UK 1992, Excuses for Bad Behaviour, Royal Festival Hall, London, UK 1994; debut album 1985; Model for Comme Des Garçons fashion show, Paris 1992; has written articles for magazines including Vanity Fair. *Films include:* Cheech and Chong's Nice Dreams 1981, The King of Comedy 1983 (Nat Soc Film Critics Award), Sesame Street Presents: Follow That Bird 1985, The Whoopee Boys, Casual Sex, Track 29 1988, Without You I'm Nothing 1990, Hudson Hawk 1991, Truth or Dare 1991, Inside Monkey Zetterland 1993, Dallas Doll 1994, Unzipped 1995, Catwalk 1995, Somewhere in the City 1997, Lover Girl 1997, The Apocalypse 1997, Exposé 1998, Wrongfully Accused 1998; *TV appearances include:* Living in America (host) 1990, Roseanne (series); *Plays include:* Without You I'm Nothing 1988, Giving Till It Hurts 1992; *Recordings include:* I'm Your Woman 1985, Without You I'm Nothing 1989, Excuses for Bad Behavior Part I 1994; Confessions of a Pretty Lady 1988, Love, Love and Love 1993. *Address:* Noe-Man Management, 26500 West Agoura Rd, Suite 575, Calabasas, CA 91302, USA (Office); c/o Susan DuBow, 9171 Wilshire Blvd, Beverly Hills, CA 90210, USA.

BERTELL, Rosalie, PH D; American scientist and environmentalist; b 1925. *Career:* Dir, Int Medical Comms on Bhopal and Chernobyl; Ed-in-Chief International Perspectives in Public Health; mem Ecosystem Study Group (Canada), US Science Advisory Bd; mem Grey Nuns of the Sacred Heart; Pres Asscn of Contemplative Sisters for N America and Canada, Int Inst of Concern for Public Health; Right Livelihood Award 1986; World Federalist Peace Award 1988; Health Innovator

Award (Ontario, Canada) 1991; Marguerite D'Youville Humanitarian Award (Lexington, MA) 1992. *Publications include:* Handbook for Estimating the Health Effects of Ionizing Radiation 1984, 1986, No Immediate Danger, Planet Earth, The Latest Weapon of War 2000. *Address:* c/o The Women's Press, 34 Great Sutton St, London, EC1, UK. *Internet:* www.ccnr.org/bertell_bio.html.

BERTINI, Catherine, BA; American United Nations official; b 30 March 1950, Syracuse, NY; d of Fulvio and Ann Vino Bertini; m Thomas Haskell 1988. *Education:* Cortland High School and State Univ of New York at Albany. *Career:* Youth Dir, New York Republican State Cttee 1971–74, Republican Nat Cttee 1975–76; Man Public Policy, Container Corpn of America, Chicago, IL 1977–87; Dir Office of Family Assistance, US Dept of Health and Human Services 1987–89, Acting Asst Sec, Dept of Health and Human Services 1989; Asst Sec US Dept of Agric 1989–92; Exec Dir UN World Food Programme, Rome 1992–; Youth Dir New York Republican State Cttee 1971–74, Nat Cttee 1975–76; Commr Illinois State Scholarship Comm 1979–84, Illinois Human Rights Comm 1985–87; mem Del to People's Repub of China 1989; US Expert on Female-headed Households, UN Status of Women Expert Group Meeting on Vulnerable Women 1990, UN Envoy Horn of Africa; Fellow Inst of Politics, John F. Kennedy School of Govt, Harvard Univ 1986; mem UN Sec-Gen's Panel of High-Level Personalities on African Devt 1992–95; Hon D SC (McGill Univ, Montréal) 1997; Hon DHL (State Univ of New York, Cortland) 1999; Leadership in Human Services Award, American Public Welfare Asscn 1989; Excellence in Public Service Award, American Acad of Pediatrics 1991; Leadership Award, Nat Asscn of Women, Infants and Children (WIC) Dirs 1992; Quality of Life Award 1994; Auburn School of Human Sciences Award 1996. *Address:* c/o World Food Programme, Cesare Giulio Viola 68/70, 00148 Rome, Italy (Office).

BERTRAND, Françoise, BA; Canadian broadcasting executive; b 1948, Montréal. *Education:* Collège Ste-Marie, Univ of Montreal and York Univ. *Career:* Dir Soc des jeux du Québec 1976–78; Project Man SORECOM Inc 1978–80; Asst Vice-Pres (Academic and Research) Univ of Quebec, Montréal 1980–82, Asst Dean Research Man 1983–84, Dean 1984–88; CEO Soc de radio-télévision du Québec 1988–95; Sr Dir Communications Practices, KPMG Consulting 1995–96; Chair CRTC 1996–; Chair Bd Théâtre Populaire du Québec 1990–96; mem Bd Asscn for Tele-Educ in Canada (ATEC), (Chair 1993–94), TV5 Quebec Canada 1988–95; Vice-Chair Bd TV5 Latin America 1993–95; one of three Commrs on Fed Water Policy Comm 1984–85; mem Bd of Govs and Exec Cttee Univ of Quebec 1990–96; mem various bds and research orgs involved in educ and social and community orgs. *Address:* Canadian Radio-television and Telecommunications Commission (CRTC), Ottawa, ON K1A 0N2, Canada. *Telephone:* (819) 997-3430; *Fax:* (819) 994-0218; *E-mail:* info@crtc.gc.ca; *Internet:* www.crtc.gc.ca.

BERTRAND, Solange Anne; French artist; b 20 March 1913, Metz; d of Léon and Lucie (née Hermann) Bertrand. *Education:* Ecole des Beaux-Arts (Nancy). *Career:* Nurse with French Red Cross 1939–45; solo exhibitions throughout France and in Luxembourg, Belgium, Italy and the Netherlands; group exhibitions in Cairo, London, New York, Milan (Italy), Düsseldorf (Germany), etc; works in pvt collections in France, Germany, Sweden, Belgium, UK, USA, Italy, Netherlands, Luxembourg, and in museums including Metz, Nancy, Musée Picasso (Antibes), Musée Cheret (Nice), Musée Int de l'Imagerie (Epinal) and the state archives; donated sculpture l'Homme du 3ème Millénaire to Montigny-les-Metz (home town) 1991; Dr hc 1987; Hon Maître de Peinture, Séminaire Int d'Art Contemporain 1982; Maître Académicien 1984; Chevalier des Arts, Acad d'Italie 1985; Senator, Gold Medallist Forum Académique 1987; Monique Corpet Prize, Taylor Foundation 1996; Chevalier des Arts et des Lettres 1996. *Leisure interests:* crosswords, shooting. *Address:* 3 blvd Victor, 75015 Paris, France; 35 rue de Reims, 57158 Metz, France. *Telephone:* (1) 45-54-26-04 (Paris); (3) 87-65-34-32 (Metz).

BESSMERTNOVA, Natalya Igorevna; Russian ballet dancer; b 19 July 1941, Moscow; d of Igor Borisovich Bessmertnov and Antonia Yakovlevna Bessmertnova; m Yury N. Grigorovich. *Education:* Bolshoi Theatre Ballet School. *Career:* Soloist with Bolshoi Theatre Ballet 1961–63; Prima Ballerina 1963–95, Ballet Coach 1993–95; Pres European Dance Acad 1996–; toured USA 1989; appearance at Covent

Garden (London) 1992; gives masterclasses abroad; Gold Medal Second Int Ballet Competition, Varna, Bulgaria 1965, Lenin Prize 1970, 1986, People's Artist, USSR 1976, USSR State Prize 1977, Anna Pavlova Prize, Parisian Dance Acad, France 1970. *Ballet roles include:* Mazurka and 7th Valse (Chopiniana), Pas de trois (Swan Lake), variations (Class-concert), Giselle (Giselle), The Muse (Paganini, music by Rachmaninov), Florin (Sleeping Beauty), Leila (Leila and Medjnun, by Balasanyan), Shirin (Legend of Love), Odette-Odile (Swan Lake), Girl (Le Spectre de la Rose), Maria (The Fountain of Bakhtchisaray), Phrygia (Spartacus), Juliet (Romeo and Juliet), Masha (The Nutcracker), Nikia (The Kingdom of Shades), Rita (Golden Age), Valentina (The Angara), Aurora (Sleeping Beauty), Anasthasia (Ivan the Terrible), Raymonda. *Leisure interests:* reading, politics, TV. *Address:* Sretensy blvd 6/1, kv 9, 101000 Moscow, Russian Federation. *Telephone:* (095) 925-64-31; *Fax:* (095) 925-65-57.

BESSY, Claude (pseudonym of Claude Jeanne Andrée Durand); French ballet dancer and choreographer; b 21 Oct 1932, Paris; d of André and Jeanne Durand; m 1st Albert Sarfati (divorced); m 2nd Claude Gueveler (divorced). *Education:* Ecole du Théâtre de l'Opéra de Paris. *Career:* Petit Rat Théâtre Nat de l'Opéra 1942–46, mem Corps de Ballet 1946, Grand Sujet 1950, Prima Ballerina 1956; Ballet Mistress Opéra de Paris 1970–71, Dir Ecole de Danse, Opéra de Paris 1972–; organizer int ballet classes and exchanges between ballet schools in France, UK, Russian Fed, USA, etc; appearances in films and on TV; Officier de la Légion d'Honneur; Commdr de l'Ordre Nat du Mérite; Grand Prix Nat des Arts et des Lettres (for ballet). *Ballets include:* Dancer: Les noces fantastiques, L'oiseau de feu, Daphnis et Chloé, Phèdre, Pas de dieux, Le lac des cygnes, Casse-Noisette, Studio 60, La fille mal gardée; Choreographer: Les fourmis, Le bourgeois gentilhomme 1972, My Fair Lady 1984; *Publication:* Danseuse étoile 1961. *Leisure interests:* painting, porcelain. *Address:* Ecole de Danse de l'Opéra National de Paris, 20 allée de la Danse, 92000 Nanterre, France. *Telephone:* (1) 40-01-80-33; *Fax:* (1) 40-10-80-50; *Internet:* www.opera-de-paris.fr.

BETHAM, Mere Tuiasosopo, BA; American (American Samoan) judge; b 3 April 1932; d of the late Maiota Tuiasosopo, Sr and Venise Pulefaasisina; m James M. Betham 1955; three s three d. *Education:* Geneva Coll (Beaver Falls, PA), Univ of Southern California at Los Angeles and Univ of Hawaii. *Career:* Dir of Educ, American Samoa; Co-creator Pacific Regional Educational Lab; Educ Consultant 1985–87; Dir of Catholic Educ 1987–89; designer teaching policies, American Samoa; apptd Assoc Judge High Court of American Samoa (first woman) 1991; mem Council, fmr Chair Cttee on Extra-State Jurisdictions; mem Council of Chief State School Officers, American Samoa's Political Status Comms, American Samoa Constitutional Cttee 1972, Review Cttee 1984; numerous awards including Samoa Educator of the Year, Brigham Young Univ Distinguished Service to Educ Award, Distinguished Service to Educ Award (American Samoa Dept of Educ) 1991. *Publication:* Bold Experiment: the story of educational television in American Samoa 1981. *Address:* Supreme Court, Pago Pago, AS 96799, American Samoa; POB 764, Pago Pago, AS 96799-0764, American Samoa. *Telephone:* 633-4600.

BETTENCOURT, Liliane; French business executive; d of Eugene Schueller; one d. *Career:* Chair Man and Remuneration Cttee, L'Oréal. *Leisure interest:* wine. *Address:* L'Oréal, Centre Eugene Schueller, 41 rue Matre, 92110 Clichy, France.

BEUSTES, Annie, M ECON SC; New Caledonian politician; b (Annie Campagne) 1945, Arget, France; two d. *Education:* Faculté de droit et de sciences économiques de Bordeaux (France). *Career:* Personnel Man Société le Nickel (mining co), Nouméa 1970–82; Sec-Gen Fédération Patronale (Employee's Fed) 1982–1998; mem Advisory Bd Caisse d'Epargne; Minister for Economic Affairs and for Relations with the Econ and Social Council until 2001; currently Vice-Pres Congrès, Pres Congrès Comm on Health; Chevalier de l'Ordre Nat du Mérite. *Address:* Conseiller de la Nouvelle Calédonie, BP L1, 98849 Nouméa, Cedex, New Caledonia (Office); 14 ave du Révérend Père Clément, Nouméa, New Caledonia (Home). *Telephone:* 258088 (Office); 273610 (Home); *Fax:* 274900; *E-mail:* beustes@offratel.nc.

BEUTLER, Maja; Swiss writer; b 8 Dec 1936, Berne; m Urs Bentler 1961; two s one d. *Education:* Dolmetscher Schule (Zurich), France, UK and Italy. *Career:* Trans for UNESCO, Rome; radio presenter (Italian and German) for Swiss int radio 1962–70; currently radio presenter and writer; Schillerstiftung Prize for works 1983; Weltpreis für Drama 1985, Literaturpreis, Stadt Berne 1989. *Publications:* Novels: Fuss fassen 1980, Die Wortfalle (2nd edn) 1990, Die Stunde, da wir fliegen Lerhen 1994; Short stories: Flissingen fehlt auf der Karte 1976, Das Bildnis der Doña Quichotte 1989; Plays: Das Blaue Gesetz 1979, Das Marmelspiel 1985, Lady Macbeth Wäscht Sich Die Hände Nicht Mehr 1994; Collected radio contribs: Wärchtig 1986, Beiderlei 1991, Tagwärts 1996. *Address:* Schosshaldenstr 22A, 3006 Berne, Switzerland. *Telephone:* (31) 3523538; *Fax:* (31) 3523538; *E-mail:* maja.beutler@swissonline.ch.

BHARTIA, Shobhana; Indian business executive; b 4 Jan 1957, Calcutta (now Kolkata); d of Birla and Manorama Devi; m Shyam Sunder Bhartia 1974; two s. *Education:* Loreto House (Calcutta). *Career:* Exec Dir The Hindustani Times Ltd 1986–; Dir Press Trust of India Ltd 1987; Dir Indian Airlines, New Delhi 1988–90; Dir Air Travel Bureau Pvt Ltd 1989; Chair and Treas Bd of Govs, Delhi Coll of Arts and Commerce 1988–90; Chair HT Vision Ltd 1990–; Chair Bd of Govs Shyama Prasad Mukherjee Coll (for Women) 1992; mem Sri Mata Vaishnu Devi Shrine Bd, Katra 1991; Pres FICCI women's org, Leader dels to Australia, New Zealand, the Philippines and to World Congress of Women conf (Moscow, fmr USSR) 1987–88; Int Cultural Devt Org Award 1989; Mahila Shiromani Award 1990; Lok Shri Award, Inst of Econ Studies 1990; Vijaya Shri Award, Int Friendship Soc of India 1991. *Leisure interests:* reading, music. *Address:* Hindustani Times House, 18-20 Kasturba Gandhi Marg, New Delhi 110 065, India. *Telephone:* (11) 3317955 (Office); (11) 6830260 (Home); *Fax:* (11) 3319021 (Office).

BHATT, Ela R.; Indian women's organization executive; b 7 Sept 1933, Ahmedabad; m Ramesh M. Bhatt (deceased); two c. *Career:* Currently Sec-Gen Self Employed Women's Asscn (SEWA), Chair SEWA Cooperative Bank, Ahmedabad 1972–; mem Rajya Sabha (Parl) 1986–89; Chair Fed of Voluntary Orgs 1983–91, Women's World Banking (New York, USA) 1985, Nat Comm on Self-Employed Women (New Delhi) 1987–89, Gov Body State Women's Co-operatives Fed 1992, Int Coalition of Women and Credit 1993; mem Governing Body Gandhi Labour Inst 1983–91, Nat Integration Council 1984–, Union Planning Comm 1990–91, Labour Devt Inst 1991, Advisory Cttee Asia Soc 1991, Women's World Summit Foundation (Geneva, Switzerland) 1991–, Exec Cttee International Union of Food and Allied Workers 1992, Nat Integration Foundation 1992, Advisory Cttee McArthur Foundation (Chicago, IL, USA) 1992–95, WHO Global Comm on Women (Geneva, Switzerland) 1994, Advisory Cttee UNFPA 1995, Consultative Group World Bank (Washington, DC, USA) 1995, Governing Body Indian Inst of Man 1995; Hon D LITT (SNDT) 1991; Hon DH (Haverford Coll) 1993, (Temple) 1994; Magasasay Award for Community Leadership 1977; Susan Anthony Award for Nat Integration 1982; Best Entrepreneur Woman 1983; Alternate Nobel (Right Livelihood Prize) 1984; Padmashri 1985; Padmabhusan 1986; Gurjar Ratna 1987; Women in Creation Award, Alliance de Femme (Paris) 1990; Nat Citizen's Award 1993; CARE Humanitarian Award (Washington, DC) 1994. *Publications include:* Gujarat ni Nari 1975, Profiles of Self-Employed Women 1975, Grind of Work 1989, Aapni Shramjivi Baheno 1992, Hum Savita 1995. *Address:* SEWA, Bhadra, Ahmedabad 380 001, India. *Telephone:* (79) 5506444; *Fax:* (79) 5506446; *E-mail:* sewa.mahila@axcess.net.in.

BHATTACHARJI, Sukumari, PH D; Indian former professor of Sanskrit and researcher; b 12 July 1921, Midnapore, W Bengal; d of the late Sarasi K. and Santabala Datta; m Amal Bhattacharji 1948 (deceased); one d. *Education:* Victoria Coll, Univ of Calcutta and Jadavpur Univ. *Career:* Lecturer Lady Brabourne Govt Coll, Calcutta 1945–57; Lecturer in Comparative Literature Jadavpur Univ 1957–58, in Sanskrit 1958–64, Reader 1964–81, Prof 1981–86; Fellow Asiatic Soc 1976–, B. M. Barua Sr Research Fellow 1989–92. *Publications include:* The Indian Theogony 1970, Literature in the Vedic Age (2 vols) 1984, Mrcchakatika (play, trans from Sanskrit, 3rd edn) 1991, Buddhist Hybrid Sanskrit Literature 1992, Classical Sanskrit Literature 1992, Women and Society in Ancient India 1993, Fatalism in Ancient India

1995, Legends of Devi 1996. *Leisure interests:* literature, music, paintings, ancient art works. *Address:* 239a Netaji Subhash Chandra Bose Rd, Kolkata 700 047, India. *Telephone:* (33) 4712352.

BHAVSAR, Veerbala, PH D; Indian artist; b 10 Oct 1941, Banswara, Rajasthan; d of Dhulji Bhai and Vijaya Davi Bhavsar. *Education:* Banswara School, Fine Arts Coll (Ahmedabad), Vikram Univ and Univ of Rajasthan. *Career:* Assoc Prof of Painting and Sculpture Univ of Rajasthan from 1974; solo exhibitions at Ahmedabad, New Delhi, Jaipur, Bombay, Calcutta, Bhopal and Udaipur 1971–90; participated in group exhibitions including Nat Exhibition of Art 1983, 1988, 1989, State Exhibition of Art (Gujarat) 1964, 1973, (Rajasthan) 1975, 1992; works in various govt and pvt collections; numerous TV and radio appearances and contribs to professional journals; awards include Nat Rajasthan Lalit Kala Akademi Award 1982, 1992, TIAS All India Award 1987, Kalidas All India Award 1987, Raipur All India Award 1988. *Address:* University of Rajasthan, Dept of Drawing and Painting, Gandhi Nagar, Jaipur 302 004, India (Office); Viral–Vaatee, 41/36 Viral Path, Mansarovar, Jaipur 302 020, India (Home). *Telephone:* (141) 72063 (Office); (141) 872241 (Home).

BHIMJI, Zarina; British artist and photographer; b 30 Aug 1963. *Education:* Leicester Polytechnic, Goldsmiths' Coll (Univ of London) and Slade School of Fine Art (Univ Coll, London). *Career:* Fmr Artist-in-Residence Plymouth Art Gallery; Community Arts/Photography worker for Horizon Arts, London 1986; Organizer Insights Photography Exhibition and Jagrati exhibition of S Asian women artists (jtly) 1986–87; teacher of photography and art 1987–90; Fine Art Fellow Cardiff School of Art and Design 1990–91; fmr Researcher/Outreach worker for Whitechapel Art Gallery, London; Artist-in-Residence India Dept, Victoria and Albert Museum, Plymouth Art Gallery, Whitechaple Art Gallery 1992, Kettle's Yard, Cambridge 1993; part-time lecturer at numerous art schools 1990–91; Lecturer London Coll of Printing 1992–; solo exhibitions include Slade School of Art (Univ of London) 1989, Tom Allen Community Art Centre (London) 1989, Ikon Gallery (Birmingham) 1992, Kettle's Yard, Univ of Cambridge 1995; group exhibitions include Dislocation (Kettle's Yard, Cambridge) 1987, Black Women Photographers (Camden Arts Centre, London) 1987, Towards a Bigger Picture (Victoria and Albert Museum and tour) 1989, Whitechapel Open (Coopers & Lybrand Award) 1989, Photokina '90 (Cologne, Germany and world tour) 1990, Shocks to the System '90s Political Art (Arts Council Collection) 1990, Whitechapel Open 1992, Critical Decade (Museum of Modern Art, Oxford) 1992, Antwerp '93 (MUHKA Museum, Antwerp, Belgium) 1993, Revir/Territory (Kulturhuset, Stockholm) 1994, INIVA (Inauguration exhibition, London) 1994, The Impossible Science of Being (The Photographers' Gallery, London) 1995, In/Sight (Guggenheim Museum, New York) 1996; works in pvt and public collections; mem Photography Advisory Panel, Arts Council; Advisory mem Autograph; Visiting Fellow Darwin Coll, Cambridge 1993; Judge Selection Panel, South Bank Photo Show; Julian Sullivan Award, Slade School of Art 1989. *Publications:* Ikon Gallery Catalogue 1992, Illuminations Television (CD ROM) 1995. *Address:* 14 Downing Court, Grenville St, London WC1N 1LX, UK.

BHOSLE, Asha; Indian singer and actress; b 8 Sept 1933, Sangli; d of Dinanath and Mai Mangeshkar; m 1st Ganpatrao Bhosle 1947 (deceased); two s one d; m 2nd R. D. Burman 1979. *Career:* Recorded first song for film Chunariya 1946; recorded songs in every Indian language and dialect; Host and Singer TV Series This is Asha 1974; Founder-mem The West India Company, UK-based pop group 1985; has given concerts in USA, UK, Canada, New Zealand, Sweden, Denmark, Singapore, Indonesia, Thailand, Middle East, Mauritius, Hong Kong, fmr USSR, Far East and Australia; Patron Fellowship of the Physically Handicapped; has made numerous recordings (over 10,000 songs) and appeared in films; Hon D LITT (Amravati) 1989; numerous Gold, Platinum and Silver Discs, and other music awards; Govt of India Nat Awards for film performances 1982, 1988; seven Filmfare awards 1967–78; EMI Gold Disc for Three Decades of Outstanding Contribution to Music 1988. *Album:* Ave Maria. *Leisure interests:* music, reading. *Address:* 102 Prabhu Kunj, Pedder Rd, Mumbai 400 026, India. *Telephone:* (22) 4938070; *Fax:* (22) 4938070.

BHREATHNACH, Niamh; Irish politician; b 1945; m; two c. *Career:* Fmrly teacher; councillor Dublin Co and Dun Laoghaire Borough; Chair Lab Party and Spokeswoman on Women's Affairs; mem Dáil (Parl) for Dun Laoghaire 1992–, Minister for Educ 1993–97. *Address:* c/o Labour Party, 17 Ely Place, Dublin, 2, Ireland.

BHUIYAN, Rabia, BCL; Bangladeshi politician and lawyer; b 1 March 1944, Dhaka; m Mozammel Hoque Bhuiyan; one s one d. *Career:* Fmrly Barrister Bangladesh Supreme Court; Minister for Social Welfare and Women's Affairs 1985–87; fmr mem Exec Cttee and Asst Sec, Supreme Court Bar Asscn; Vice-Pres Asian and Pacific Region, Int Fed of Women Lawyers; Pres Bangladesh Mahila Ainjibi Samiti; Dir and Founder-mem Inst of Democratic Rights; mem Faculty of Law Dhaka Univ, Ethical Cttee Bangladesh Medical Research Council, World Asscn Muslim Scholars, UK and American Bar Asscns; mem numerous cttees and councils; contribs to professional journals. *Address:* c/o Ministry of Social Welfare and Women's Affairs, Bangladesh Secretariat, Bhaban 6, New Bldg, Dhaka, Bangladesh.

BHUTTO, Begum Nusrat; Pakistani politician; b 23 March 1929; d of Mirza Mohamed and Fatima Sultana Isphahani; m Zulfikar Ali Bhutto 1951 (died 1979); two s two d (Benazir Bhutto qv). *Education:* Convent of Jesus and Mary (Bombay, India). *Career:* Fmr First Lady of Pakistan; Capt Women's Nat Guard 1947–48; Chair Pakistan Red Crescent Soc 1974–77; elected to Nat Ass 1977; imprisoned 1977–80; Chair Pakistan People's Party (PPP) and involved in the Movt for the Restoration of Democracy in Pakistan 1984–93; mem Nat Ass 1988, fmr Cabinet mem; recipient Red Lion and Sun Award, Iran 1975. *Leisure interest:* reading. *Address:* Pakistan People's Party (PPP), 70 Clifton, Karachi 75600, Pakistan. *Telephone:* (21) 5691151.

BHUTTO, Benazir; Pakistani politician; b 21 June 1953; d of the late Zulfikar Ali Bhutto (died 1979) and of Begum Nusrat Bhutto (qv); m Asif Ali Zardari 1987; one s two d. *Education:* Radcliffe Coll and Harvard Univ (USA) and Lady Margaret Hall (Oxford, UK). *Career:* Under house arrest 1977–84; leader in exile of Pakistan People's Party (PPP) with her mother Nusrat and involved in the Movt for the Restoration of Democracy in Pakistan 1984–; Opposition Leader 1990–93; Chair Pakistan People's Party 1993–; returned to Pakistan 1986; Prime Minister 1988–90, 1993–96 (removed from position by Presidential decree and charged with corruption and abuse of power Aug 1990), and Minister for Finance and Econ Affairs 1993–96; Head Parl Foreign Affairs Cttee 1993–96; dismissed by Presidential decree Nov 1996, dismissal upheld by Supreme Court Jan 1997; charged with corruption and money laundering July 1998; charged with taking bribes Oct 1998; sentenced with Asif Zardari to five years' imprisonment for corruption April 1999, disqualified from politics for five years, sent into exile in Dubai; appeal against conviction for corruption upheld April 2001; Dr hc (Harvard) 1989, (Lady Margaret Hall, Oxford) 1989; numerous int awards including Bruno Kreisty Human Rights Award. *Publications:* Foreign Policy in Perspective 1978, Daughter of The East (autobiog) 1988. *Address:* c/o Bilawal House, Boat Basin Area, Clifton, Karachi, Pakistan (Home).

BIEDERMANN, Julia; German actress; b 15 March 1967, Berlin. *Education:* T. Gsovsky Dance School and Dannhoff Actors Studio. *Career:* Began TV and stage acting career as child in 1973; stage appearances include Schiller Theater and Freie Volksbühne, Berlin 1976–79, Hamburg 1988–89, Theater am Kurfürstendamm, Berlin 1988–89, Renaissance Theatre, Berlin 1989; Ramo di Palma d'Oro, San Remo, Italy 1987. *Plays include:* Die Weber 1976–78, Die Wildente 1979, Das Haus in Montevideo 1988–89, Bunbury 1989, Otello darf nicht platzen; *Films:* The Formula 1980, Die Bleierne Zeit 1981, Ein Schweizer namens Nökli 1988; *TV series include:* Sesame Street 1973–75, Traumschiff 1981, Ein Fall für zwei 1982, Ich heirate eine Familie 1983–86, Praxis Bülowbogen 1986–89, Tatort 1988, The Dirty Dozen 1988, Hotel Paradies 1989, Das Schloß am Wörthersee 1990–91, Der Landarzt 1992, Glückliche Reise, Schwarz greift ein, Blankenese, Marienhof. *Leisure interests:* karate, swimming, French cuisine, baking. *Address:* Agentur B. Kleine, Von-der-Vring Str, 81929 Munich, Germany. *Telephone:* (89) 476081.

BIEN, Ania Franczeska; American artist; b 5 Oct 1946, Cracow, Poland; d of Joseph S. and Carola Bien; m Kees C. Hodde 1974; one c. *Education:* Pratt Inst (New York), Columbia Univ (New York) and Ateliers 63 (Netherlands). *Career:* Lives in the Netherlands; exhibitions include Museum of Modern Art, San Francisco, CA, USA 1987, Amsterdam Historial Museum 1988, Municipal Museum, Arnhem 1988, De Vierde Wand, Amsterdam 1989, 1991, Photobiennale Rotterdam 1990, Jewish Historical Museum, Amsterdam 1990, 1993, Int Photobiennale, Ein Harod, Israel 1991, Municipal Museum, Arnhem 1991, Fodor Museum, Amsterdam 1991, 1992, Laing Art Gallery, Newcastle upon Tyne, UK 1991, Camden Arts Centre, London 1992, Arnolfini, Bristol, UK 1992, Bertha Urdang Gallery, New York 1992, Scottish Int Festival of Photography, Edinburgh, UK 1993, Nederlands Foto Inst, Rotterdam 1994, Victoria and Albert Museum, London 1995, Ludwig Forum, Aachen 1995; works in perm public and pvt collections in Europe and USA including Stedelijk Museum (Amsterdam), Gemeente Museum (Arnhem), Smith Coll Museum, Netherlands Ministry of Culture, Bibliothèque Nat, etc; featured in numerous catalogues and publs. *Publications:* Hotel Polen (ed) 1987, Home (ed) 1993; contribs to several catalogues and books. *Address:* Singel 30, 1015 AA Amsterdam, Netherlands. *Telephone:* (20) 623-01-98.

BIESHU, Mariya Lukyanovna; Moldovan opera singer (soprano); b 3 Aug 1935; d of Luca and Tatiana Bieshu; m Arcady Rodomsky 1965. *Education:* Chişinău (Kishinev) Conservatoire. *Career:* Soloist with Moldovan Folk Orchestra 1958–60; with Moldovan Opera and Ballet 1961–; mem La Scala (Milan, Italy) 1965–67; Prof Chişinău Conservatoire 1980–; awards include First Prize Int Puccini Competition (Japan) 1967, People's Artist of USSR 1970, Lenin Prize 1982. *Opera roles include:* Tosca 1962, Desdemona in Othello 1967, Leonora in Il Trovatore 1969, Zemphira in Aleko 1973, Mimi in La Bohème 1977, Turandot 1979, Iolanta 1979, Elizabeth of Valois in Don Carlos 1985, Amelia in A Masked Ball 1989, Abigail in Nabucco 1991. *Leisure interests:* dogs, open country. *Address:* 24 Pushkin Str, 2012 Chişinău, Moldova.

BIGELOW, Kathryn; American film director; b 1952, San Carlos, CA; m James Cameron 1990 (separated). *Education:* San Francisco Art Inst. *Career:* Worked with Art and Language performance group, UK; awarded Scholarship to Independent Study Programme, Whitney Museum, New York. *Films include:* Set Up (short), The Loveless 1982, Near Dark 1987, Blue Steel 1990, Point Break, Strange Days 1995, Weight of Water 2000. *Address:* c/o Ken Stovitz, CAA, 9830 Wilshire Blvd, Beverly Hills, CA 90210, USA.

BÍLÁ, Lucie (Hana Zanáková); Czech singer; b 7 April 1966, Otvovice; d of Joseph Zanák; partner Petr Kratochvíl (separated 2000); one s. *Career:* Co-owner Theatre Ta Fantastika, Prague; has toured throughout W Europe; has performed in charity concerts in Czech Repub; numerous awards including Czech Grammy Prize 1992–96, Most Popular Singer (Czech Repub) 1994–97, Czech Musical Acad Prize 1997, Czech Nightingale Trophy 1999. *Film:* King Ubu; *Music:* albums include Missariel 1993, Lucie Bílá 1994, Binoculars 1995, Stars as Stars 1998; *Plays include:* Les Misérables 1992, Dracula 1995, Rat-Catcher 1996, Johanka z Arku 2000. *Leisure interest:* family. *Address:* Theatre Ta Fantastika, Karlova ul 8, 110 00 Prague, Czech Republic. *Telephone:* (2) 24-23-25-32.

BILA, Vera; Czech singer; b 22 May 1954, Rokycany, Bohemia; m; one adopted son. *Career:* Sings with Romany band Kale; subject of documentary Cerna a bila v barve (Black and White in Color) 1999. *Recordings include:* Me la na kamav (I Don't Want Her), Ara, more (Go Away), Miro rom hin ternoro (My Husband is Too Young), Ma dara (Don't Be Afraid). *Address:* c/o BMG International (Ariola), Bedford House, 69 Fulham High St, London, SW6, UK.

BILANIUK, Larissa Tetiana, MD; American professor of radiology; b 15 July 1941, Ukraine; d of Jaroslaw and Myroslawa Zubal; m O. M. Bilaniuk 1964; two d. *Education:* Cass Tech High School (Detroit, MI) and Wayne State Univ. *Career:* Resident Radiologist Hosp of the Univ of Pennsylvania 1966–67, 1968–71, Assoc in Radiology School of Medicine 1972–74, Asst Prof 1974–79, Assoc Prof 1979–82, Prof 1982; Visiting Prof of Radiology Univ of Munich, Germany 1988; Fellow Fondation Ophtalmologique Rothschild, Paris 1972, Visiting Radiologist 1980; Reviewer American Journal of Neuroradiology 1981–, Annals of Neurology 1986–; mem Radiology Study Group NIH 1983–86; lecture tours to Brazil, fmr USSR, People's Repub of China, Morocco, France, Mexico, Japan, Sweden, Canada, UK, Netherlands, Italy, Germany 1974–92; Fellow American Coll of Radiology 1982; mem American Soc of Neuroradiology, Ukrainian Medical Asscn of N America, Soc of Magnetic Resonance in Medicine; contribs to professional journals and books. *Leisure interests:* photography, Alpine hiking, downhill skiing, gliding. *Address:* Children's Hospital of Philadelphia, Dept of Radiology, 3401 Civic Centre Blvd, Philadelphia, PA 19104-4302, USA. *Telephone:* (215) 590-4117; *Fax:* (215) 590-4127.

BILLINGHAM, Baroness (Life Peer), cr 2000, of Banbury in the County of Oxfordshire, **Angela Theodora Billingham;** British politician; b 31 July 1939; two d. *Education:* Univ of London. *Career:* Mem Banbury Borough Council 1970–74, Cherwell Dist Council 1974–84, Oxfordshire Co Council 1993–94; Mayor of Banbury 1976; MEP (Lab) Northamptonshire and Blaby 1994–99, Chair Cen Region MEPs 1995; Chief Whip Party of European Socialists 1995–99; JP N Oxfordshire and Bicester 1976. *Leisure interests:* gardening, bridge, cinema. *Address:* 6 Crediton Hill, London NW6 1HP, UK.

BINCHY, Maeve; Irish writer and journalist; b 28 May 1940; d of William Binchy and Maureen Blackmore; m Gordon Snell 1977. *Education:* Univ Coll Dublin. *Career:* Teacher of History and French, Pembroke School (Dublin) 1961–68; columnist The Irish Times 1968–; Hon D LIT (Queen's, Belfast) 1998. *Publications:* short stories: Central Line 1978, Silver Wedding 1979, Victoria Line 1980, Dublin Four 1982, The Lilac Bus 1984, Dear Maeve; novels: Light a Penny Candle 1982, London Transports 1983, Echoes 1985, Firefly Summer 1987, Silver Wedding 1989, Circle of Friends 1990, Copper Beech 1992, The Glass Lake 1994, Evening Class 1996, Tara Road 1999, Scarlet Feather 2000. *Address:* Dalkey, Co Dublin, Ireland.

BINGHAM, Hon Charlotte Mary Thérèse; British writer; b 29 June 1942; d of Baron Clanmorris (John) and Madeleine Mary (née Ebel) Bingham; m Terence Brady 1964; one s one d. *Education:* The Priory (Haywards Heath) and Univ of Paris (Sorbonne). *Career:* Writer of screenplays with Terence Brady. *Stage Plays include:* I Wish, I Wish 1989; *TV includes:* Series: Boy Meets Girl, Take Three Girls, Upstairs Downstairs, Away From it All, No—Honestly, Yes—Honestly, Pig in the Middle, Thomas and Sarah, Father Matthew's Daughter, Oh Madeleine!, Forever Green, The Upper Hand; Films: Love With a Perfect Stranger 1986, Losing Control 1987, The Seventh Raven 1987, The Magic Moment 1988; *Publications include:* Coronet Among the Weeds 1963, Lucinda 1965, Coronet Among the Grass 1972, Victoria (jtly) 1972, Rose's Story (jtly) 1973, Victoria and Company (jtly) 1974, Belgravia 1983, Country Life 1986, At Home 1987, To Hear a Nightingale 1988, The Business 1989, In Sunshine or in Shadow 1991, Stardust 1992, By Invitation 1993, Nanny 1993, Change of Heart 1994, Debutantes 1995, The Nightingale Sings 1996, Grand Affair 1997, Love Song 1998, The Kissing Garden 1999, The Love Knot 2000, The Blue Note 2000. *Address:* c/o United Authors, Garden Studios, 11-15 Betterton St, London WC2H 9BP, UK.

BINNS, Susan May, B SC; British European Union official; b 22 April 1948, Keighley, Yorks; d of John Spencer and the late Mollie (née Summerscales) Binns. *Education:* Keighley Preparatory School, Harrogate Coll and LSE. *Career:* Joined FCO 1968, worked in London 1968–70, 1975–78, Belgium 1970–75, India 1978–80; mem staff European Comm 1981–84, mem Del to Washington, DC, USA 1985–88, to Belgrade, Yugoslavia 1988, Deputy Chief of Cabinet, Cabinet of Bruce Millan (Commr responsible for Regional Policies) 1989, Chief of Cabinet 1991–95, Dir DG XV Internal Market 1995–. *Leisure interests:* tennis, art history, theatre. *Address:* European Commission, 200 rue de la Loi, 1049 Brussels, Belgium. *Telephone:* (2) 296-3285; *Fax:* (2) 299-4745.

BINOCHE, Juliette; French actress; b 9 March 1964, Paris; d of Jean-Marie Binoche and Monique Stalens; one s by André Halle. *Education:* Nat Conservatory of Drama and with Jean-Pierre Martino, Louis Bihoreau and Vera Gregh. *Career:* Film debut 1981. *Films include:* Les nanas, La vie de famille, Rouge baiser, Liberty Belle, Rendez-vous, Boy Meets Girl, Mauvais sang, Mon beau-frère a tué ma soeur, Un tour de manège, Amants du Pont-Neuf, The Unbearable Lightness of Being, Wuthering Heights 1992, Damage 1992, Trois couleurs: bleu 1993, Trois couleurs: blanc, Trois couleurs: rouge, Le hussard sur le toit 1995, The English Patient (Acad Award for Best Supporting Actress 1996, Berlin Film Festival Award 1996, BAFTA Award 1997), Alice et Martin 1999, Les enfants du siècle 1999, La veuve de Saint-Pierre 2000, Chocolat 2001, Code Unknown 2001; *Plays include:* Naked (Almeida, London) 1998. *Address:* c/o UTA, 9560 Wilshire Blvd, Floor 5, Beverly Hills, CA 90212, USA (Office).

BIRCH, Thora; American actress; b 11 Mar 1982, LA; d of Jack and Carol Birch. *Career:* Appeared as child actress in TV commercials; TV acting debut 1988 in Day by Day. *Appearances include:* TV: Day by Day 1988, Parenthood 1990, The Outer Limits 1996, Promised Land 1996, Touched by an Angel 1996; Films: Purple People Eater (Youth in Film Award) 1988, Paradise 1991, All I Want for Christmas 1991, Hocus Pocus 1992, Patriot Games 1992, Clear and Present Danger 1994, Monkey Trouble 1994, Now and Then 1995, Alaska 1996, American Beauty 1999, Anywhere But Here 1999, Dungeons & Dragons 1999, Night Ride Home 1999, Ghost World 2001, The Hole 2001. *Address:* c/o Sam Mendes, Donmar Warehouse, 41 Earlham St, London, WC2H 9LD, UK. *Internet:* www.thora.org.

BIRET, Idil; Turkish pianist; b 1941, Ankara; d of Münir and Leman Biret; m Sefik Büyükyüksel 1976. *Education:* Paris Conservatoire. *Career:* Debut 1957; has given concerts throughout the world with major orchestras including Boston Symphony Orchestra (USA), Leningrad Philharmonic (Russian Fed), Leipzig Gewandhaus (Germany), London Symphony, Tokyo Philharmonic (Japan), Sydney Symphony (Australia), Dresden Staatskapelle (Germany); has performed with major conductors and at int festivals including Montréal (Canada), Athens, Berlin, Dubrovnik (Croatia), Istanbul (performance with Yehudi Menuhin), etc; mem jury Queen Elisabeth Competition (Belgium), Van Cliburn Competition (USA), Busoni (Italy); Lily Boulanger Memorial Fund (Boston) 1954, 1964; Harriet Cohen/Dinu Lipatti Gold Medal (London) 1959; title of State Artist of Turkey conferred 1973; Polish Artistical Merit 1974; Chevalier de l'Ordre Nat du Mérite 1976; Grand Prix du Disque Chopin (Poland) 1995; Golden Diapason Award (France) 1995. *Recordings:* Over 70 recordings including Beethoven, Liszt, Brahms, Chopin, Rachmaninov, Boulez, Ligeti and Stravinsky. *Leisure interests:* collecting antiques, reading, decorating. *Address:* 526 ave Louise, 1050 Brussels, Belgium; 255 Moda cad, Kadiköy, Istanbul, Turkey. *Fax:* (2) 648-40-17 (Belgium); *E-mail:* Sefik.Buyukyuksel.dc .67@aya.yale.edu; *Internet:* www.idilbiret.de.

BIRICH, Tamara A., MD; Belarus ophthalmologist; b 1939; m. *Education:* Minsk Medical Inst. *Career:* Prof Minsk Medical Inst; current specialist area is the structure of morbidity in areas affected by the Chernobyl nuclear disaster; has written more than 100 scientific papers. *Leisure interests:* nature, swimming. *Address:* 220100 Minsk, 15–67 Kulman St, Belarus. *Telephone:* (172) 271165.

BIRKE, Lynda, D PHIL; British scientist; b 20 May 1948, London; d of Albert R. and Yvonne E. Perry. *Education:* Streatham Hill and Clapham High School (London), Parsons Mead School (Ashtead) and Univ of Sussex. *Career:* Researcher in History and Social Studies of Science Univ of Sussex 1978; Educ Officer Royal Soc for the Protection and Care of Animals 1979; Research Biologist in Animal Behaviour Open Univ 1980–87; freelance teacher and science journalist 1987–90; Researcher, Lecturer in Science and Women's Studies, Dept of Continuing Educ, Univ of Warwick from 1989; Founder-mem Brighton Women and Science Group 1976–80, Science for Women 1985–89. *Publications include:* Alice Through The Microscope: The Power of Science Over Women's Lives (co-ed) 1980, Women, Feminism and Biology: The Feminist Challenge 1986, More Than The Parts: Biology and Politics (co-ed) 1984, Tomorrow's Child: Reproductive Technologies in the '90s (jtly) 1990. *Leisure interests:* competitive horse-riding, swimming, gardening. *Address:* University of Warwick, Dept of Continuing Educ, Coventry, CV4 7AL, UK. *Telephone:* (24) 7652-3844.

BIRKIN, Jane; French (b British) actress and singer; b 14 Dec 1946, London; d of David and Judy Birkin; m John Barry (divorced); one d; fmr partner Serge Gainsbourg (deceased); one d (Charlotte Gainsbourg, qv); partner Jacques Doillon; one s. *Career:* Lives in France; singer of songs written by Serge Gainsbourg; concert at Olympia, Paris 1996; Chevalier des Arts et des Lettres; Gold Leaf Award, Canada 1968; Triomphe du Cinéma 1969, 1973; Asscn des Cadres de l'Inst Cinématographique Prize 1975; Best Female Singer, Victoire de la Musique (for best female singer) 1992. *Plays include:* Carving a Statue 1964, Passion Flower Hotel 1965, La fausse suivante 1985, l'Ex-femme de ma vie 1988, Quelque part dans cette vie 1990, L'aide-mémoire 1993, Créatrice et interprète de oh! pardon tu dormais 1999; *Films include:* The Knack 1965, Blow Up 1966, Slogan 1967, Les chemins de Katmandou 1969, Projection privée 1973, Comment réussir quand on est c... et pleurnichard 1974, Catherine et Cie 1975, Je t'aime, moi non plus 1976, Mort sur le Nil 1978, La fille prodigue 1981, Enfer et passion 1983, L'ami de Vincent 1983, Le neveu de Beethoven, Dust 1985, La femme de ma vie 1986, Jane B par Agnès V 1988, Daddy nostalgie (title in English These Foolish Things) 1990, La belle noiseuse 1991, Noir comme le souvenir 1995, La fille d'un soldat ne pleure jamais 1999; *Recordings include:* songs by Serge Gainsbourg: C'est la vie qui veut ça, La baigneuse de Brighton, Je t'aime moi non plus (Le Métier trophy 1970), Di doo dah, Le canari est sur le balcon, Baby Song, Si ça peut te consoler, Tu n'es pas le premier garçon, Lolita Go Home, Love for Sale, La ballade, Ex-fan des sixties, Baby Alone in Babylone (Grand Prix du disque, Acad Charles-Cros). *Address:* c/o VMA, 10 ave George V, 75008 Paris, France (Office).

BIRLEY, Sue, PH D; British academic and banking executive; m 1st Arwyn Hopkins 1964 (divorced 1970); m 2nd David Norburn 1975. *Education:* Nelson Grammar School and Univ Coll, London. *Career:* Lecturer Lanchester Polytechnic 1966–68; Lecturer and Sr Lecturer Polytechnic of Cen London 1968–72; Sr Research Fellow City Univ 1972–74; Sr Research Fellow London Business School 1974–79, Lecturer 1979–82; Adjunct Assoc Prof Univ of Notre Dame, IN, USA 1978–82, Assoc Prof of Strategy and Entrepreneurship 1982–85; Philip and Pauline Harris Prof of Entrepreneurship Cranfield Inst of Technology 1985–90; Academic Dir European Foundation for Entrepreneurship Research 1988–91; Prof of Man, Imperial College, London 1990–; mem Advisory Panel on Deregulation, Dept of Trade and Industry 1989–91; Founder, Dir Guidehouse Group 1980–85, Greyfriars Ltd 1982–85, Newchurch & Co 1986–97; Gov Harris City Technology Coll 1990–92; mem Bd Dirs NatWest Group, mem remuneration, audit and compliance cttees 1996–2000; mem Bd Dirs Process Systems Enterprise Ltd 1997–, Impel Ltd 1997–. *Publications include:* From Private to Public (jtly) 1977, The Small Enterprises 1982, Exit Routes (jtly) 1989, The British Entrepreneur (jtly) 1989, European Entrepreneurship: emerging growth companies (ed) 1989, International Perspectives on Entrepreneurship (co-ed) 1992; numerous contribs to journals. *Leisure interest:* gardening. *Address:* The Management School, Imperial College of Science, Technology and Medicine, 83 Prince's Gate, Exhibition Rd, London SW7 2PG, UK. *Telephone:* (20) 7607-1566.

BIRNIE DANZKER, Jo-Anne, BA, B ED; Canadian arts administrator; b 1945, Brisbane, Australia; d of Colin and Margaret Birnie Danzker; m Otfriedd Zimmermann 1987. *Education:* Univ of Queensland (Australia). *Career:* Curator The Electric Gallery, York Univ, Ontario 1973–74; Vancouver Art Gallery 1977–84, Acting Dir 1984, Dir 1985–87; Visual Arts Consultant, Canada House, UK 1974; Man Ed Flash Art 1975–76; Canadian Commr, art exhibition, Japan 1987; Dir Kultur Inc 1988–91; Dir Museum Villa Stuck, Munich 1992–; Chair Bd of Dirs Wyman Dance Theatre Foundation 1989–90; Dir MBD Assocs 1991; mem Special Council Cttee on the Arts, City of Vancouver 1989–93, Cross-Cultural Subcttee 1989–91, Advisory Council Vancouver Dance Centre 1990–92; Head Moderator for BC, Citizens' Forum on Canada's Future 1991; mem American Asscn of Museums, Asscn Int des Critiques d'Art 1985–90; art columnist Vancouver magazine 1989–; contribs to art journals and catalogues. *Address:* 1477 Fountain Way, Suite 101, Vancouver, BC V6H 3W9, Canada.

BIRTWISTLE, Sue; British TV producer; m Richard Eyre. *Education:* Coventry Coll of Educ. *Career:* Fmrly teacher, actress, theatre dir; currently Dir Chestermead (ind production co). *Productions include:* Hotel du Lac, Pride and Prejudice, Emma; *Publication:* The Making of Jane Austen's Emma (jtly) 1996.

BIRULÉS, Ana, PH D; Spanish politician and business executive. *Education:* Univ of Barcelona and Univ of California at Berkeley. *Career:* Worked for regional govt of Catalonia; with Banco Sabadell 1990–97, negotiated acquisition of Banco NatWest 1996; Man Dir Retevisión 1997–2000; Minister of Science and Tech 2000–. *Address:* Ministry of Science and Technology, Paseo de la Castellana 160, 28071 Madrid, Spain. *Telephone:* (91) 3494976; *Fax:* (91) 4578066; *E-mail:* info@min.es; *Internet:* www.min.es.

BISS, Adele, FRSA; British business and organization executive; b 18 Oct 1944; d of Robert and Bronia Biss; m Roger Oliver Davies 1973; one s. *Education:* Cheltenham Ladies' Coll and Univ Coll, London. *Career:* Fmrly mem staff Unilever 1968, Thomson Holidays 1970; public relations consultant and tour guide; f Biss Lancaster, public relations co, Chief Exec 1978–88; Chair British Tourist Authority and English Tourist Bd 1993–96; Dir Aegis PLC 1985–90, British Railways Bd 1987–92, European Passenger Services 1990–, Bowthorpe 1993–, Harry Ramsden's 1995–; Gov Middx Univ 1995–; mem Council GDST 1996–, UCL 1997–. *Leisure interests:* piano, hiking, skiing. *Address:* A S Biss & Co, 100 Rochester Row, London SW1P 1JP, UK. *Telephone:* (20) 7828-3030; *Fax:* (20) 7828-5505.

BISSET, Jacqueline; British actress; b 13 Sept 1944, Weybridge. *Education:* French Lycée (London). *Career:* Film debut 1965; numerous appearances in films and on TV. *Films include:* The Knack 1965, Two for the Road 1967, Casino Royale 1967, The Sweet Ride 1968, The Detective 1968, Bullitt 1968, The First Time 1969, Airport 1970, The Grasshopper 1970, The Mephisto Waltz 1971, Believe in Me 1971, The Life and Times of Judge Roy Bean 1972, Stand Up and Be Counted 1972, The Thief Who Came to Dinner 1973, Day for Night 1973, Murder on the Orient Express 1974, The Spiral Staircase 1974, End of the Game 1974, St Ives 1975, The Deep 1976, Le Magnifique 1977, Sunday Woman 1977, The Greek Tycoon 1978, Secrets 1978, Too Many Chefs 1978, I Love You, I Love You Not 1979, When Time Ran Out 1980, Rich and Famous 1981, Inchon 1981, Class 1982, Under the Volcano 1983, Forbidden 1986, Choices 1986, High Season 1988, Scenes from the Class Struggle in Beverly Hills 1989, Wild Orchid 1989, The Groundhogs 1993, The Honest Courtesan, La cérémonie 1995, The Maid, A Judgement in Stone, Once You Meet a Stranger 1996, The Honest Courtesan 1996, Let the Devil Wear Black 1998, Dangerous Beauty; *TV includes:* Leave of Absence 1994, September (mini-series). *Address:* c/o William Morris Agency, 151 El Camino Drive, Beverly Hills, CA 90212, USA (Office); VMA, 10 avenue George V, 75008 Paris, France (Office).

BITTOVÁ, Iva; Czech singer and violinist; b 22 July 1958, Bruntál; d of Koloman and Ludmila Bitto; two d. *Education:* State Conservatorium (Brno). *Career:* Actress, singer and violinist 1976–. *Films include:* Růžové Sny (Pink Dreams) 1975, Step Across the Border 1990; *Recordings include:* Bittová–Fajt 1989, Bittová Iva 1991. *Leisure interests:* crafts, family, gardening, music. *Address:* 664 31 Lelekovice 258, Czech Republic. *Telephone:* (5) 784135; *Fax:* (5) 784135.

BJERREGAARD, Ritt; Danish politician; b 19 May 1941, Copenhagen; d of Gudmund and Rita Bjerregaard; m Søren Mørch 1966. *Career:* Mem Folketing (Parl—Social Democratic Party) 1971, Minister for Education 1973, 1975–78, for Social Affairs 1979–81, Chair Parl group Social Democratic Party 1981–82, 1987–92, Chair Parl Cttee on Public Accounts 1990–95; Pres Danish European Movt 1992–94; Vice-Pres Parl Ass of CSCE 1992–95, Socialist International Women 1992–94; EU Environment Commr 1995–99; mem Trilateral Comm, Centre for European Policy Studies. *Publications:* several books on politics in general and the role of women in politics. *Leisure interests:* her apple farm, organic farming, the environment. *Address:* c/o Ministry of Foreign Affairs, 15 rue des Petits Carmes, 1000 Brussels, Belgium.

BJÖRK, Anita; Swedish actress; b 25 April 1923, Tällberg Dalécarlia; m Stig Dagerman (deceased); two d one s. *Education:* Royal Dramatic Theatre School (Stockholm). *Career:* Has toured USA, Canada, UK and France; numerous stage appearances at Royal Dramatic Theatre, Stockholm; O'Neill Prize, Medal of Art, Lisbon, Swedish Critics' Award 1990 and many other Swedish awards. *Plays include:* Miss Julie 1951, Agnes (Brand, Ibsen), Celia (The Cocktail Party, Eliot), Rosalind (As You Like It, Shakespeare), Juliet (Romeo and Juliet, Shakespeare), Eliza (Pygmalion, Shaw), Solange (Les Bonnes, Genet), The girl (Look Back in Anger, Osborne), Johanna (Les séquestrés d'Altona, Sartre), Siri von Essen (Night of The Tribades, P. O. Enquist), Madame Arkadina (The Seagull, Chekhov) 1982–83, Hanna Luise Heiberg (Life of the Rainsnakes, Enquist), Christa Wolf (Kassandra, Wolf), La Marquise de Sade 1989, Autumn and Winter 1990, Love Letters 1992, The Baccaë 1995, Euripides 1995, Celestina 1998, The Image Maker 1999, Copenhagen (Michael Frayn) 2000; *Films include:* Himlaspelet 1942, Räkna de lyckliga stundarna blott (Count Your Blessings) 1944, Hundra dragspel och en flicka (One Hundred Concertinas and a Girl) 1946, Ingen väg tillbaka (No Return) 1947, Kvinna utan ansikte 1947, Det kom en gäst (There Came a Guest) 1947, På dessa skuldror (On these Shoulders) 1948, Människors rike (The Realm of Men and Women) 1949, Fröken Julie (Miss Julie, First Prize Cannes Film Festival 1951) 1950–51, Night People 1953, Die Hexe 1954, Giftas 1955, Der Cornet 1955, Sängen om den eldröda blommen 1956, Mannekäng i rött 1958, Goda vänner trogna grannar 1960, Vita frun 1962, Älskande par 1964, Mme de Monfreuil (The Marchioness of Sade), Mother and Daughter 1990, Euskilda Saintal. *Leisure interest:* reading. *Address:* AB Baggensgatan 9, 111 31 Stockholm, Sweden (Office). *Telephone:* (8) 209747.

BJÖRK, (Björk Guðmundsdóttir); Icelandic singer and songwriter; b 21 Nov 1965, Reykjavik; one s. *Career:* Made first album 'Bjork' 1977; formed several bands including Exodus and Tappi Tikarras; mem The Sugarcubes (fmrly Kukl) 1986–92; solo artist 1992–; Best Int Female Award, MTV European Music awards, Brit Awards 1996. *Recordings include:* With the Sugarcubes: Birthday, Life's Too Good, Here Today, Tomorrow, Next Week!, Stick Around for Joy; Solo recordings: Human Behaviour, Venus As A Boy, Big Time Sensuality, Violently Happy, Play Dead, Army of Me, Blow A Fuse (Oh It's So Quiet), Hyperballad, Debut 1993, Post (platinum disc in UK), Selma Songs 2000; *Film:* Dancer in the Dark 2000. *Address:* One Little Indian Records, 250 York Rd, London, SW11 3SJ, UK (Office). *Telephone:* (20) 7924-1661; *Fax:* (20) 7924-4274.

BJÖRN, Dinna; Danish ballet dancer, director and choreographer; b 14 Feb 1947, Copenhagen; d of Niels Björn Larsen and Elvi Henriksen. *Education:* Edite Feifere Frandsen Ballet School (Copenhagen) and Royal Danish Ballet Aspirant School. *Career:* Joined Royal Danish Ballet 1964, solo debut in L'après-midi d'un faune 1966; Co-Founder Soloists of the Royal Danish Ballet 1976, Artistic Dir 1985–90; teacher Royal Danish Ballet School 1985–90; Artistic Dir Norwegian Nat Ballet, Oslo 1990–; Guest Teacher Boston Ballet (USA), Berlin Opera Ballet, Munich Opera Ballet (Germany), The Israel Ballet, Paris Opera Ballet School, English Nat Ballet School, etc; Bronze Medal and Special Prize Varna Int Ballet Competition (Bulgaria) 1976; Dansk Balletklub Prize of Honour 1990. *Ballets include:* 8+1, Anatomic Safari, The Butterfly Mask, Hat-Trick, The Marriage, Early Spring Dances, Hommage à Jean Cocteau, Cha-Cha-Cha. *Leisure interests:* astrology, occultism, writing, piano playing. *Address:* c/o Den Norske Opera, POB 8800, Youngstorget, 0028 Oslo, Norway. *Telephone:* (2) 42-92-75; *Fax:* (2) 42-05-73.

BLACK, Cathleen P.; American publishing executive; b 1944. *Career:* Fmrly Pres and Publr USA Today; Pres and CEO Newspaper Asscn of America 1991–95; Pres Hearst Magazines 1995–. *Address:* Hearst Magazines, 224 W 57th St, New York, NY 10019-3203, USA.

BLACK, Hon Dame Jill Margaret, DBE, BA (LAW); British judge; b 1 June 1954; d of Dr James Irvine Currie and the late Margaret Yvonne Currie; m David Charles Black 1978; one s one d. *Education:* Penrhos Coll, Colwyn Bay and Univ of Durham. *Career:* Called to the Bar, Inner Temple 1976, QC 1994, Recorder 1998, Justice of the High Court 1999–. *Publications:* Divorce: The Things You Thought You'd Never Need to Know (5th edn) 1997, A Practical Approach to Family Law (5th edn) 1998, The Working Mother's Survival Guide (co-author) 1988, The Family Court Practice (contrib) 2001. *Address:* Royal Courts of Justice, Strand, London, WC2A 2LL, UK.

BLACK, Mary; Irish singer and songwriter; b 1955; m Joe O'Reilly; three c. *Career:* Singer with traditional and contemporary Irish groups; now solo singer; toured USA and Japan 1990; UK tour 1991; Best Irish Solo Artist, IRMA Milk Music Awards 1992. *Album:* Mary Black, Collected, Without the Fanfare, By the Time it Gest Dark, Babes in the Wood, No Frontiers, The Collection, The Holy Ground, Circus 1995.

BLACK, Shirley Temple; American actress and diplomatist; b 23 April 1928, Santa Monica, CA; d of George F. and Gertrude Temple; m 1st John Agar, Jr 1945 (divorced 1949); one d; m 2nd Charles A. Black 1950; one s one d. *Education:* Privately and Westlake School for Girls. *Career:* Career as film actress commenced at 3½ years; Del to UN, New York 1969–70; Amb to Ghana 1974–76, to Czechoslovakia 1989–92; White House Chief of Protocol 1976–77; mem US Comm for UNESCO 1973–; mem US Del on African Refugee Problems, Geneva, Switzerland 1981; Dir Nat Multiple Sclerosis Soc; awards include Dame Order of Knights of Malta 1968, American Exemplar Medal 1979, Gandhi Memorial Int Foundation Award 1988, and numerous state decorations. *Films include:* Stand Up and Cheer, Little Miss Marker, Baby Take a Bow, Bright Eyes, Our Little Girl, The Little Colonel, Curly Top, The Littlest Rebel, Captain January, Poor Little Rich Girl, Dimples, Stowaway, Wee Willie Winkie, Heidi, Rebecca of Sunnybrook Farm, Little Miss Broadway, Just Around the Corner, The Little Princess, Susannah of the Mounties, The Blue Bird, Kathleen, Miss Annie Rooney, Since You Went Away, Kiss and Tell, That Hagen Girl, War Party, The Bachelor and the Bobby-Soxer, Honeymoon; *TV appearances include:* Shirley Temple Storybook 1958, Shirley Temple Show 1960; *Publication:* Child Star (autobiog) 1988. *Address:* c/o Academy of Motion Picture Arts and Sciences, 8949 Wilshire Blvd, Beverly Hills, CA 90211, USA (Office); 115 Lakeside Drive, Woodside, CA 94062, USA (Home).

BLACK, Susan Harrell, BA, JD; American federal judge; b 20 Oct 1943, Valdosta, GA; d of William and Ruth (née Phillips) Harrell; m Louis Eckert Black 1966. *Education:* Florida State Univ and Univ of Florida. *Career:* Called to the Bar, FL 1967; fmr Asst State Attorney, Asst Gen Counsel, Jacksonville, Judge Duval Co Court, Fourth Judicial Circuit Court of Florida; Dist Judge Florida Middle Dist, Jacksonville 1979–90, Chief Judge 1990–92; Judge US Court of Appeals (11th circuit), Jacksonville, FL 1992–; mem American Bar Asscn. *Address:* US District Court, POB 53135 Jacksonville, FL 32202-3135, USA.

BLACKADDER, Elizabeth, OBE, RA, RSA, MA; British artist; b 24 Sept 1931, Falkirk, Scotland; m John Houston 1956. *Education:* Falkirk High School, Univ of Edinburgh and Edinburgh Coll of Art. *Career:* Teacher of art, St Thomas of Aquin's School, Edinburgh 1958–59; librarian, Fine Art Dept, Univ of Edinburgh 1959–61; Lecturer in drawing and painting, Edinburgh Coll of Art 1962–86; one-woman exhibitions include Mercury Gallery (London) 1965–, 57 Gallery 1959, The Scottish Gallery (Edinburgh) 1961, 1966, Vaccarino Gallery (Florence, Italy) 1970, Theo Waddington Gallery (Toronto, Canada) 1981–82, Lillian Heidenberg Gallery (New York) 1986, Scottish Arts Council retrospective exhibition Edinburgh, Sheffield, Aberdeen, Liverpool and Cardiff 1981–82; has participated in numerous group exhibitions in UK, USA and Canada including British Painting 1952–77 (RA, London); stained glass window commissioned by Nat Library of Scotland 1987; Hon D LITT (Herriot Watt) 1989, (Strathclyde) 1998; Dr hc (Edinburgh) 1990; Hon LL D (Aberdeen) 1997; Watercolour Foundation Award, RA Summer Exhibition (jtly) 1988. *Publication:* Favourite Flowers (jtly) 1994. *Address:* 57 Fountainhill Rd, Edinburgh, EH9 2LH, UK; c/o Royal Scottish Academy, The Mound, Edinburgh EH2 2EL, UK.

BLACKBURN, Elizabeth Helen, PH D, FRS; Australian biologist; b 26 Nov 1948, Hobart; d of Harold Stewart Blackburn and Marcia Constance Jack; m John Sedat 1975; one s. *Education:* Univ of Melbourne and Univ of Cambridge (UK). *Career:* Researcher Molecular Biology Lab, Univ of Cambridge 1971–74; Postgrad Researcher Yale Univ, USA 1975–77; mem Faculty Univ of California at Berkeley, USA 1978–90, Prof of Microbiology and Immunology, Prof of Biochem, San

Francisco 1990–; Pres American Soc for Cell Biology 1998; Memorial Sloan-Kettering Cancer Center Katharine Berkan Judd Award Lectureship 2001; Travelling Gowrie Research Scholar 1971–73; Anna Fuller Fund Fellowship 1975–77; Steven and Michele Kirsch Foundation Investigator Fellowship 2000; Fellow American Acad of Arts and Sciences 1991, American Acad of Microbiology 1993, AAAS 2000; mem American Acad of Excellence 2000, Inst of Medicine 2000; numerous articles in scientific journals; Hon D SC (Yale) 1991; awards include Australian Soc for Microbiology Prize 1967, Eli Lilly Research Award for Microbiology and Immunology 1988, Nat Acad of Sciences Award in Molecular Biology 1990, Gairdner Foundation Award 1998, Australia Prize 1998, California Scientist of the Year 1999, Novartis-Drew Award for Biomedical Science 1999, Feodor Lynen Award 2000, Dickson Prize in Medicine 2000, American Cancer Soc Medal of Honor 2000, American Asscn for Cancer Research–Pezcoller Foundation Int Award for Cancer Research 2001, General Motors Cancer Research Foundation Alfred P. Sloan Award 2001. *Leisure interest:* music. *Address:* University of California, Dept of Microbiology and Immunology, San Francisco, CA 94143-0414, USA. *Telephone:* (415) 476-4912; *Fax:* (415) 514-2913.

BLACKBURN, Julia, BA; British writer; b 12 Aug 1948, London; d of Thomas Blackburn and Rosalie de Meric; m Hein Bonger 1978 (divorced); one d one s; m Herman Makkink 1999. *Education:* Univ of York. *Career:* Writer 1979–. *Publications include:* The White Men 1979, Charles Waterton 1989, The Book of Colour 1991, Daisy Bates in the Desert 1994, The Emperor's Last Island 1997, The Leper's Companions 1999, Selected Poems by Thomas Blackburn (ed and introduction) 2000. *Leisure interests:* travel, mountain walking. *Address:* Sandpit, Thorington Rd, Bramfield, Suffolk 1P19 9H2, UK; c/o Toby Eedy, 9 Orme Court, London W2 4RL, UK. *Telephone:* (1986) 784215; *Fax:* (1986) 784665.

BLACKMAN, Honor; British actress; b 1926, London. *Career:* Numerous stage, TV and film appearances 1946–. *Films include:* Fame is the Spur 1947, Green Grow the Rushes 1951, Come Die My Love 1952, The Rainbow Jacket 1953, The Glass Cage 1954, Dead Man's Evidence 1955, A Matter of Who 1961, Goldfinger 1964, Life at the Top 1965, Twist of Sand 1967, The Virgin and the Gipsy 1970, To the Devil a Daughter 1975, Summer Rain 1976, The Cat and the Canary 1977, Talos—The Mummy, To Walk With Lions; *TV appearances include:* Four Just Men 1959, Man of Honour 1960, Ghost Squad 1961, Top Secret 1962, The Avengers 1962–64, The Explorer 1968, Visit from a Stranger 1970, Out Damned Spot 1972, Wind of Change 1977, Robin's Nest 1982, Never the Twain 1982, The Secret Adversary 1983, Lace 1985, The First Modern Olympics 1986, Minder on the Orient Express 1986, Dr Who 1986, William Tell 1986, The Upper Hand (series); *Plays include:* Mademoiselle Colombe 2000. *Address:* c/o Jean Diamond, London Management, 2–4 Noel St, London, W1V 3RB, UK (Office).

BLACKSTONE, Baroness (Life Peer), cr 1987, of Stoke Newington in Greater London, **Tessa Ann Vosper Blackstone,** PC, PH D; British politician and former college principal; b 27 Sept 1942, London; d of the late Geoffrey Vaughan Blackstone and of Joanna Blackstone; m Thomas Evans 1963 (divorced); one s one d. *Education:* Ware Grammar School and LSE. *Career:* Assoc Lecturer Enfield Coll 1965–66; Asst Lecturer, then Lecturer Dept of Social Admin, LSE 1966–75; Adviser Cen Policy Review Staff, Cabinet Office 1975–78; Prof of Educational Admin Univ of London, Inst of Educ 1978–83; Deputy Educ Officer (Resources), then Clerk and Dir of Educ, Inner London Educ Authority (ILEA) 1983–87; Master Birkbeck Coll, Univ of London 1987–97; mem House of Lords 1987–, Opposition Spokesperson on Educ and Science 1990–92, on Foreign Affairs 1992–97; Minister of State in Dept of Educ and Employment 1997–; Fellow Centre for Studies in Social Policy 1972–74; Dir Royal Opera House 1987–97; Chair BBC Gen Advisory Council 1988–91; Chair Bd of Trustees, Inst for Public Policy Research 1988–97; mem Bd of Trustees Natural History Museum 1992–97; Dir Thames TV 1991–92; Fellow Birkbeck Coll, Univ of London 1997–; Hon Fellow Coll of Preceptors 1991, LSE 1995; Hon D LITT (Bradford) 1990, (Bristol Polytechnic) 1991; Hon D UNIV (Middlesex) 1993, (Strathclyde) 1994, (Leeds Metropolitan) 1996; Hon LL D (Aberdeen) 1994, (St Andrews) 1995; Dr hc (Strathclyde) 1996; Hon Dauphine (Sorbonne, Paris) 1998. *Publications:* Students in Conflict (jtly) 1970, A Fair Start 1971, Education and Day Care for Young People in Need 1973, The Academic Labour Market 1974 (jtly), Social Policy and Administration in Britain 1975, Disadvantage and Education (jtly) 1982, Education Policy and Educational Inequality (jtly) 1982, Response to Adversity (jtly) 1983, Testing Children (jtly) 1983, Inside the Think Tank: Advising the Cabinet 1971–83 (jtly) 1988, Prisons and Penal Reform (jtly) 1990, Race Relations in Britain (jtly) 1997. *Leisure interests:* tennis, walking, ballet, opera. *Address:* c/o Department for Education and Employment, Sanctuary Buildings, Great Smith St, London, SW1P 3BT, UK (Office); 2 Gower St, London WC1E 7HX, UK (Home). *Telephone:* (20) 7925-6243; *Fax:* (20) 7925-5011; *E-mail:* blackstone.ps@dfee-gov.uk (Office).

BLACKWELL, Susan Barbara, BA; Australian publishing executive; b 24 May 1957, Sydney, NSW; d of Bruce and Barbara Blackwell. *Education:* PLC Pymble (Sydney) and Univ of Sydney. *Career:* Ed Harper and Row Pty Ltd 1980–81; Asst Dir Australian Book Publishers' Asscn Ltd 1985–88, Exec Dir 1988–; Dir Arts Training Australia 1988–, Australian Copyright Council 1990–, Dante Alighieri Soc 1991–92; mem Commonwealth Govt's Copywright Law Review Cttee 1999–2000. *Leisure interests:* tennis, travel, theatre, reading. *Address:* Australian Book Publishers' Association, 89 Jones St, Ultimo, NSW 2007, Australia. *Telephone:* (2) 281 9788; *Fax:* (2) 281 1073.

BLADES, Ann; Canadian writer and illustrator; b 16 Nov 1947, Vancouver, BC; d of Arthur and Dorothy Sager; m David Morrison 1984; two s. *Education:* Croft House School (Vancouver) and Univ of British Columbia. *Career:* Elementary school teacher 1967–71; Registered Nurse 1974–80; illustrator 1968–; artist 1982–; exhibitions include Vancouver Art Gallery 1971, Biennale of Illustrations (Bratislava, Czechoslovakia) 1977, Art Gallery of Ontario 1977, Master Eagle Gallery (New York) 1980, Dunlop Art Gallery 1982, Bau Xi Galleries (Toronto and Vancouver) 1982–91, Canada at Bologna 1990. *Publications include:* Writer and illustrator: Mary of Mile 18 (Book of the Year Award, CACL—Canadian Asscn of Children's Librarians, Hon List German and Austrian Kinderbuchpreis 1976) 1971, A Boy of Taché (A Child Study Asscn Best Children's Book 1977) 1973, A Cottage at Crescent Beach 1977, By the Sea: An Alphabet Book (Elizabeth Mrazik-Cleaver Canadian Picture Book Award 1986) 1985, Seasons Board Books 1989; Illustrations: Jacques the Woodcutter 1977, A Salmon for Simon (Children's Literature Award for Illustration, Canada Council 1979, Amelia Frances Howard-Gibbon Award, CACL) 1978, Six Darn Cows 1979, Pettranella 1980, A Candle for Christmas 1986, Ida and the Wool Smugglers 1987, A Guide to Authors and Illustrators 1988, Anna's Pet 1989, The Singing Basket 1990, A Dog Came, Too 1992, A Ride for Martha 1993. *Leisure interests:* gardening, garage sales. *Telephone:* (604) 538-5852.

BLAIS, Marie-Claire, CC; Canadian writer; b 5 Oct 1939, Québec City; d of Fernando Blais and Veronique Nolin. *Education:* In Québec, France and USA. *Career:* Guggenheim Fellowship, New York 1963, 1964; Hon Prof Calgary Univ 1978; mem Acad Royale de Langue et de Litterature Française de Belgique 1993; Dr hc (York, Toronto) 1975; Hon D LITT (Victoria, BC) 1990; awards include Prix de la Langue Française 1961, Prix Médicis 1966, Prix Belgique–Canada (Brussels) 1976, Prix de l'Acad Française 1983, Prix Athanase-David 1982, Prix Wessim Habif 1991, 125th Anniversary of Confed of Canada Commemorative Medal 1992, Ordre Nat du Québec 1995, Decree of Int Woman of the Year for Services to Literature and Creative Writing, Int Biog Inst (USA) 1995, 1996, 1997; Chevalier des Arts et des Lettres (France) 1999, Prix Int Union Latine des Literatures Romanes (Italy) 1999, W. A. Mitchell Award 2000. *Publications:* Novels: La belle bête 1959, Tête blanche 1960, Le jour est noir 1962, Une saison dans la vie d'Emmanuel (Prix France–Québec, Paris 1966) 1965, L'insoumise 1966, David Sterne 1967, Les manuscrits de Pauline Archange (Gov-Gen of Canada Prize 1969) 1968, Vivre, Vivre 1969, Les voyageurs sacrés 1966, Les apparences 1971, Le loup 1972, Un Joualonais sa Joualonie 1973, Une liaison parisienne 1975, Les nuits de l'underground 1978, Le sourd dans la ville (Gov-Gen of Canada Prize) 1979, Visions d'Anna 1982, Pierre 1984, L'île 1988, L'Ange de la solitude 1989, Soifs (Gov-Gen of Canada Award for French Language novel 1996) 1995, These Festive Nights 1997, Dans la foudre et la lumière 2001; Plays: L'exécution 1968, Fièvre 1974, La nef des sorcières 1977, L'océan 1977, Sommeil d'hiver 1986, L'île 1988, Un jardin dans la

tempête 1990, Wintersleep 1998; Poetry: Existence, Pays voiles 1964, Oeuvre poétique 1997; Essays: Parcours d'un ecrivain: Notes americaines 1993; Short Stories: L'Exile 1993; Other writings:Theatre (collection) 1998, Radio Texts (collection) 1999. *Leisure interests:* painting and drawing, biking, handwriting analysis. *Address:* c/o John C. Goodwin et Associés, 839 Sherbrooke est, Suite 2, Montréal, PQ H2L 1K6, Canada. *Telephone:* (514) 598-5252; *Fax:* (514) 598-1878; *E-mail:* artistes@goodwin.agent.ca.

BLAKE-HANNAH, Barbara Makeda; Jamaican/British writer, journalist and film-maker; b 5 June 1941; d of Evon Blake and Veronica Stewart; m Deeb Roy Hanna 1984; one s. *Education:* Hampton High School, Wolmers Girls' School and Inst of Public Relations (London). *Career:* TV reporter and interviewer (UK) 1968–72; Organizer Annual Festival of Black and Third World Films 1974–85, Cuban Film Week 1975; Special Asst to Minister of Information and Culture 1976–77; Dir of Public Relations Kingston 1978, Montego Bay 1980; mem Senate (Independent) 1984–87; Founder Jamaica Media Productions Ltd 1982; Man Dir Alpha Beta Productions 1996–; Rep of Jamaica Festival of Palestinian Films (Iraq) 1978, Film Festival of World Festival of Youth and Students (Cuba) 1978; mem Jury XXI Leipzig Film Festival (Germany) 1978; film publicist 1994; columnist and feature writer numerous magazines and newspapers; reporter and interviewer Jamaica Broadcasting Corp, RJR-Radio Jamaica, KLAS-FM, IRIE-FM 1972–96; UN Peace Medal 1974. *Film and TV includes:* Kids Paradise—The Movie, Hotel Kids Paradise—the Great Lost Treasure Hunt, Race, Rhetoric, Rastafari, The Peaceful Gun, By The Land We Live; *Publications:* Rastafari: The New Creation 1981, Joseph: A Rasta Reggae Fable 1992. *Address:* Masquel Ltd, 21 Buttercup Drive, Kingston 6, Jamaica. *Telephone:* 927-1412; *Fax:* 927-1412.

BLANCHET, Lise Marion, L ÈS L; French journalist and broadcaster; b 12 Dec 1956, Lille; d of Louis Blanchet and Laure Crépy; two s one d. *Education:* Univ of Paris IV (Paris-Sorbonne) and CELSA (Paris). *Career:* Journalist Société Nat de Programmes—France Régions 3 (FR3) working on Thalassa 1981–92, Int Reporter 1992–; Prix Albert Londres 1992. *Leisure interests:* reading, boating. *Address:* 97 blvd Magenta, 75010 Paris, France. *Telephone:* (1) 42-47-06-71; *Fax:* (1) 42-89-15-02.

BLANCHETT, Cate; Australian actress; b 1 Jan 1969; m Andrew Lipton 1997. *Education:* Melbourne Univ and Nat Inst of Dramatic Art. *Films include:* Parkland, Paradise Road 1997, Thank God He Met Lizzie 1997, Oscar and Lucinda 1997, Elizabeth 1998 (Golden Globe Award), Dreamtime Alice (also co-producer), The Talented Mr Ripley, An Ideal Husband, Pushing Tin 1999, Lord of the Rings 2000, Bandit 2000, The Man Who Cried 2000, The Gift 2001; *Plays:* Top Girls, Kafka Dances (1993 Newcomer Award), Oleanna (Rosemont Best Actress Award), Hamlet, Sweet Phoebe, The Tempest, The Blind Giant is Dancing, Plenty; *TV:* Heartland 1994, GP, Police Rescue. *Address:* c/o Robyn Gardiner, POB 128, Surry Hills, Sydney, NSW 2010, Australia.

BLANCHETTE, Manon; Canadian art historian and museum curator; b 1 Oct 1952; d of René Blanchette and Gabrielle Malouin; one s. *Education:* Univ of Paris X (Paris-Nanterre) and Univ of Québec. *Career:* Museum and art gallery curator; Chief Curator Musée d'Art Contemporain de Montréal 1986–91, Dir of Communications and Marketing 1993–; Cultural Councillor, Canadian Embassy, Paris 1991–92; speaker at many confs; numerous articles in professional journals; Chevalier des Arts et des Lettres 1992. *Leisure interest:* everything to do with culture and the arts in all disciplines. *Address:* 185 St Catherine St W, Montréal, Québec, H2X 3X5, Canada. *Telephone:* (514) 847-6911; *Fax:* (514) 847-6291; *E-mail:* mablanch@macm.org.

BLANDIANA, Ana, BA; Romanian writer, poet and politician; b 25 March 1942, Timisoara; m Romulus Rusan 1960. *Education:* Univ of Cluj. *Career:* Has given numerous lectures on cultural and civic issues in the UK, France, Netherlands, Norway, Austria and Germany; has participated in international seminars on human rights and multiculturalism in Canada, France, Greece, Germany, USA, Norway and Russian Fed, confs at the Univ of Rome 1991, The German Rectors' Conf, Bonn 1992, Free Univ of Berlin 1992, Univ of Paris, Sorbonne 1993, Univ of Vienna 1994, Univ of Prague 1994, Univ of Heidelberg, Austria 1995, INALCO, Paris 1996, and poetry festivals in Finland, Paris, Romania, USA, Italy, UK, France, Austria and Norway; Pres

Romanian PEN Centre (has participated in several int confs), Academia Civica Foundation; poetry prize, Romanian Writers' Union 1969; poetry prize, Romanian Acad 1970; poetry prize, Asscn of Writers in Bucharest 1980; Int Herder Prize (Austria) 1982. *Publications include:* Poetry: First Person in the Plural 1964, The Vulnerable Heel 1966, The Third Sacrament 1960, 50 Poems 1970, October, November, December 1982, Poems 1974, The Sleep in the Sleep 1977, Events in my Garden 1980, The Eye of the Cricket 1981, The Sand Hour 1984, The Prey Star 1986, Other Events in my Garden 1987, Events on my Street 1988, Poems 1988, The Architecture of the Waves 1990, 100 Poems 1991; Essays: The Witness Quality 1970, I Write, You Write, He/She Writes 1975, The Most Beautiful of the Possible Worlds 1978, Passage of Mirrors 1983, Self-portrait with Palimpsest 1985, City of Syllables 1987; Short Stories: Four Seasons 1977, Projects of the Past 1982, Imitation of a Nightmare 1995; Novel: The Drawer with Applauses 1992. *Leisure interest:* gardening. *Address:* Str Transilvaniei 56, 70778 Bucharest, Romania. *Telephone:* (1) 6595909; *Fax:* (1) 3125854.

BLANZAT, Anne-Marie Eliane; French opera singer (soprano); b 24 Nov 1944, Neuilly-sur-Seine; d of Marius and Paulette (née Delaveau) Blanzat; m Jacques Plas 1965; one s. *Education:* Maîtrise de Radio-France. *Career:* Began singing career in child operatic rôles at the age of 13; int career performing at operas, concerts and festivals including Aix-en-Provence, Glyndebourne and Gulbenkian Festivals, Opéra de Bruxelles, Paris, Geneva, Lyons, Strasbourg, Naples, Palermo, Turin, Lisbon, etc; Oscar for Best Lyric Singer in France 1974; Chevalier des Arts et des Lettres 1984. *Operas include:* Pelleas et Mélisande, Carmen, Le Nozze di Figaro, Falstaff, Les dialogues des Carmélites, Les contes d'Hoffmann, Béatrice et Bénédicte, Les pêcheurs de perles, Les liaisons dangereuses, Manon; *Videos:* Pelleas et Mélisande 1982, Les dialogues des Carmélites 1982, Manon 1984. *Leisure interests:* gardening, gastronomy, crafts. *Address:* 2 square Servan, 75011 Paris, France. *Telephone:* (1) 48-05-37-36.

BLATCH, Baroness (Life Peer), cr 1987, of Hinchingbrooke in the County of Cambridgeshire, **Emily May Blatch,** CBE, FRSA; British politician; b 24 July 1937; d of the late Stephen and Sarah Triggs; m John Blatch 1963; three s (one deceased) one d. *Career:* Air Traffic Controller, Women's Royal Air Force 1955–59; Leader Cambridgeshire Co Council 1981–85; mem Peterborough Devt Corpn 1984–85; mem EC Econ and Social Cttee 1986–87; Cons mem House of Lords 1987–; Baroness-in-Waiting (Govt Whip) 1990; Parl Under-Sec of State for the Environment 1990–91; Minister of State Dept of the Environment 1991–92, Dept of Educ 1992–94, Home Office 1994–97; Shadow Minister for Educ and Employment 1997; Deputy Leader of the Opposition, House of Lords; Privy Councillor 1993–; Hon LL D (Teesside); Paul Harris Fellow (Rotary Award). *Leisure interests:* music, theatre, family. *Address:* House of Lords, Westminster, London SW1A 0AA, UK. *Telephone:* (20) 7219-3000; *Fax:* (20) 7219-6396; *E-mail:* blatche@parliament.uk.

BLEGEN, Judith; American opera and concert singer; b Lexington, KY; d of Halward Martin and Dorothy Mae (née Anderson) Blegen; m 1st Peter Singher 1967 (divorced 1975); one s; m 2nd Raymond Gniewek 1977. *Education:* Curtis Inst of Music (Philadelphia, PA) and Music Acad of the West (Santa Barbara, CA). *Career:* Leading soprano Nuremberg Opera (Germany) 1965–68, Staatsoper (Vienna) 1968–70, Metropolitan Opera (New York) 1970–; appearances at Spoleto (Italy) and Edinburgh (UK) Festivals; Fulbright Scholarship; Grammy Awards. *Opera roles include:* Zerbinetta (Ariadne auf Naxos), Rosina (The Barber of Seville), Aennchen (Der Freischütz), Norina (Don Pasquale), Marzelline (Fidelio), Sophie (Werther), Mélisande (Pelléas et Mélisande), Sophie (Der Rosenkavalier), Adina (L'Elisir d'amore), Juliette (Roméo et Juliette), Susanna (The Marriage of Figaro), title-role in Manon, Gilda (Rigoletto), Despina (Così fan tutte), Blondchen (The Abduction from the Seraglio), Sophie; *Recordings include:* La Bohème (Puccini), Carmina Burana (Orff), Symphony No 4 (Mahler), Harmoniemesse (Haydn), The Marriage of Figaro (Mozart), A Midsummer Night's Dream (Mendelssohn), Nelson Mass (Haydn), Gloria (Poulenc), Peer Gynt Suite (Grieg), Lieder recital (Richard Strauss and Hugo Wolf), Baroque Music recital. *Address:* c/o Thea Dispeker, 59 E 54th St, New York, NY 10022, USA (Office).

BLETHYN, Brenda Anne; British actress; b 20 Feb 1946; d of William Charles and Louisa Kathleen Bottle; partner Michael Mayhew 1977. *Education:* St Augustine's RC School (Ramsgate), Thanet Tech Coll and Guildford School of Acting. *Career:* With Nat Theatre (now Royal Nat Theatre) 1975–90; mem Poetry Soc 1976–; Boston Film Critics 1997, LA Film Critics 1997, Golden Globe 1997, London Film Critics 1997, BAFTA 1997. *Films include:* The Witches, A River Runs Through It 1992, Secrets and Lies (Best Actress Award, Cannes Film Festival) 1996, Remember Me 1996, Music From Another Room 1997, Girls' Night 1997, Little Voice 1999, Saving Grace 1999, Night Train 1999, Daddy and Them 1999, RKO 281 1999; *Plays include:* Mysteries 1979, Steaming 1981, Double Dealer 1982, Benefactors 1984, Dalliance 1987, A Doll's House 1987, Born Yesterday 1988, The Beaux' Stratagem 1989, An Ideal Husband 1992, Wildest Dreams 1993, The Bed Before Yesterday 1994, Habeas Corpus 1996, Absent Friends (New York) 1996; *TV:* Henry VI (Part I) 1981, King Lear 1983, Chance in a Million 1983–85, The Labours of Erica 1987, The Bullion Boys 1993, The Buddha of Suburbia 1993, Sleeping with Mickey 1993, Outside Edge 1994–96, First Signs of Madness 1996. *Leisure interests:* reading, swimming, cryptic crosswords. *Address:* c/o ICM, 76 Oxford St, London W1N 0AX, UK. *Telephone:* (20) 7636-6565.

BLEY, Carla Borg; American jazz composer; b 11 May 1938, Oakland, CA; d of Emil Carl Borg and Arlene Anderson; m 1st Paul Bley 1959 (divorced 1967); m 2nd Michael Mantler 1967 (divorced 1992); one d. *Career:* Freelance composer 1956–; pianist Jazz Composers Orchestra, New York 1964–; European concert tours with Jazz Realities 1965–66; f WATT 1973; toured Europe with Jack Bruce Band 1975, USA and Europe with Carla Bley Band 1977–; Cultural Council Foundation grantee 1971, 1979; Guggenheim Fellow 1972; Nat Endowment for Arts grantee 1973; Winner (eight times) Int Jazz Critics' Poll, Down Beat magazine, Best Composer of Year, Down Beat Readers' Poll 1984, Best in Field Jazz Times Critics' Poll 1990, Composer/Arranger of Year 1985–92, Best Arranger Downbeat Critics' Poll 1993, 1994. *Recordings include:* A Genuine Tong Funeral 1967, Escalator Over the Hill (opera, Oscar du Disque de Jazz 1973) 1970–71, Tropic Appetites 1973, Dinner Music 1976, The Carla Bley Band—European Tour 1977, Music Mecanique 1979, Fictitious Sports 1980, Social Studies 1980, Carla Bley Live! 1981, Heavy Heart 1984, I Hate to Sing 1985, Night Glo 1985, Sextet 1987, Duets 1988, Fleur Carnivore 1989, The Very Big Carla Bley Band (Prix Jazz Moderne 1992) 1991, Go Together 1993, Big Band Theory 1993, Songs with Legs 1995, Goes to Church 1996, Fancy Chamber Music 1998; *Compositions include:* A Genuine Tong Funeral 1967, Tropic Appetites 1973, Chamber Orchestra $3/4$ 1974–75, Mortelle Rautonnée (film score) 1983. *Address:* c/o Watt Works, POB 67, Willow, NY 12495, USA (Office).

BLICK, Freda, LL B; Ugandan diplomatist; b 15 Sept 1946, Namir-embe; d of the late Yusufo Kironde and of Hannah Namuli Lule; m Frederick W. Blick 1970; two s one d. *Education:* Mount St Mary's Namagunga (Lugazi), Makerere Coll School (Kampala) and Makerere Univ. *Career:* Amb to France, Italy, Switzerland, Spain, Portugal, Greece, UNESCO and UN (Geneva agencies) 1986–88, to Germany, Vatican City, Austria and UN (Vienna agencies) 1988–97; Grand Cross Order of Pope Pius IX 1992. *Leisure interest:* sports. *Address:* c/o Ministry of Foreign Affairs, POB 7048, Kampala, Uganda.

BLOCH, Julia Chang, MA; American former diplomatist and banking executive; b 2 March 1942, Chefoo, People's Republic of China; m Stuart Bloch 1968. *Education:* Univ of California at Berkeley and Harvard Univ. *Career:* Mem Voluntary Peace Corps, Sabah, Malaysia 1964–66, Training Officer for E Asia and Pacific Region, Washington, DC 1967–68, Evaluation Officer 1968–70; mem Minority Staff, US Senate Select Cttee on Nutrition and Human Needs 1971–76, Chief Minority Counsel 1976–77; Deputy Dir Office of African Affairs, Int Communications Agency, Washington, DC 1977–80; Fellow Inst of Politics, Harvard Univ 1980–81; Asst Admin Bureau for Food for Peace and Voluntary Assistance, Agency for Int Devt 1981–87, Bureau for Asia and Near E 1987–88; Amb to Nepal 1989–93; Group Exec, Vice-Pres Bank America, San Fransisco 1993–; Dir American West Airlines 1994–; mem US Nat Cttee for Pacific Econ Co-operation 1984–; mem American Refugee Comm Bd 1993–, American Himalayan Foundation Bd 1994; Commr Asian Art Museum, San Francisco 1994; several awards. *Publication:* Chinese Home Cooking (jtly) 1986. *Leisure interests:*

ceramics, collecting art, cooking. *Address:* c/o Bank America Corporate Relations, 8139 555 California St, Suite 4730, San Francisco, CA 94104-1712, USA.

BLOCH VON BLOTTNITZ, Undine-Uta; German politician; b 20 Aug 1936, Berlin. *Career:* MEP (Green Group), mem Cttee on Research, Technological Devt and Energy, Del for Relations with the Countries of S America, Del for Relations with Australia and New Zealand. *Address:* European Parliament, rue Wiertz, 1047 Brussels, Belgium. *Telephone:* (2) 284-21-11; *Fax:* (2) 230-69-43.

BLONDET MONTERO, Cecilia, BA; Peruvian sociologist and historian; b 7 July 1951, Lima; d of Carlos Blondet and Marta Montero; m Luis Peirano Falconi 1972; three s. *Education:* Sacred Heart Sophianum (Lima) and Pontifical Catholic Univ of Peru. *Career:* Mem Exec Cttee Instituto de Estudios Peruanos. *Publications include:* Conquistadores de un Nuevo Mundo (jtly) 1986, Las Mujeres y el Poder: una Historia de villa El Salvador 1991. *Leisure interests:* music, tennis, sports. *Address:* Avda Dos de Mayo 1675, Apt 301, San Isidro, Lima, Peru. *Telephone:* (14) 225854; *Fax:* (14) 324981.

BLONDIN-ANDREW, Ethel, PC, B ED; Canadian politician; b 25 March 1951, Tulita, NWT; d of the late Joseph and of Mary Blondin; m Leon Andrew; two s one d. *Education:* NWT Teacher Educ Program (Fort Smith) and Univ of Alberta. *Career:* Teacher NWT 1974–81, Univ of Calgary and Arctic Coll 1993; program specialist in languages Dept of Educ, Yellowknife (NWT) 1981–84; Man, Acting Dir Public Service Comm of Canada, Ottawa 1984–86; Asst Deputy Minister of Culture and Communication, Yellowknife 1986–88; mem Parl (Western Arctic, first Aboriginal woman elected to Parl) 1988–, Liberal Critic for Aboriginal Affairs, Special Jt Cttee on a Renewed Canada, Standing Cttees on Aboriginal Affairs and Northern Devt 1998–93, Liberal Assoc Critic for Employment Equity 1988–90; Sec of State (Training and Youth 1993–97, 1997–; played leading role in creating Youth Service Canada, in developing the Govt of Canada's Youth Employment Strategy and Aboriginal Head Start Program for Aboriginal children and in the devt of 1.6 billion Aboriginal Human Resource Devt Agreement (AHRDA) 1997; Chair Northern and Western Liberal Caucus 1990–, Co-Chair Liberal Leadership Convention 1990–; Hilroy Scholarship 1982; Hon LL D (Brock Univ) 2001; Outstanding Young Canadian Award 1978; Govt Service Award 1982; MLA Award for Culture and Heritage Preservation 1987. *Address:* Human Resources Development Canada, 140 Promenade du Portage, Hull, QC K1A 0J9, Canada (Office); 175 E Block, House of Commons, Ottawa, ON K1A 0A6, Canada (Office); POB 694, Arthur Laing Bldg, 5003-49th St, Yellowknife, NWT X1A 2N5, Canada (Office). *Telephone:* (613) 992-4587 (Ottawa); (867) 873-6995 (Yellowknife); *Fax:* (613) 992-7411 (Ottawa); (867) 920-4233 (Yellowknife); *E-mail:* blonde@parl.gc.ca; ethel@ssimicro.com.

BLOOM, Claire; British actress; b 15 Feb 1931, London; d of Edward Bloom and Elizabeth Grew; m 1st Rod Steiger 1959 (divorced 1969); one d; m 2nd 1969; m 3rd Philip Roth 1990 (divorced 1995). *Education:* London, Bristol and New York. *Career:* Actress Oxford Repertory Theatre 1946, Stratford-on-Avon 1948; first major stage appearances in The Lady's Not For Burning 1949, Ring Around the Moon 1950; Old Vic 1951–53; performs her one woman shows Enter the Actress and These are Women, A Portrait of Shakespeare's Heroines, throughout the USA; Fellow Guildhall School of Music and Drama 1975. *Plays include:* Duel of Angels 1956, The Trojan Women 1964, Ivanov 1966, A Doll's House 1971, 1973, Hedda Gabler 1971, Vivat, Vivat Regina! 1972, A Streetcar Named Desire (London Evening Standard Drama Award for Best Actress) 1974, The Innocents 1976, Rosmersholm 1977, The Cherry Orchard 1981, 1984, When We Dead Awaken 1990, Long Day's Journey into Night 1996, Electra 1999, Conversations after a Burial 2000, A Little Night Music 2001; *Films include:* Limelight, Man Between, Richard III, Alexander the Great, Brothers Karamazov, Buccaneer, Look Back in Anger, Three Steps to Freedom 1960, The Brothers Grimm, The Chapman Report 1962, The Haunting 1963, 80,000 Suspects 1963, Il Maestro di Vigevano 1963, The Outrage 1964, Spy Who Came in from the Cold 1965, Charly 1966, Three into Two Won't Go 1967, Illustrated Man 1968, Red Sky at Morning 1970, A Doll's House 1973, Islands in the Stream 1975, The Clash of the Titans 1979, Always 1984, Sammy and Rosie Get Laid 1987, Brothers 1988,

Crimes and Misdemeanours 1989, Mighty Aphrodite 1994, Daylight 1995; *TV appearances include:* A Legacy 1975, The Orestea 1978, Henry VIII 1979, Brideshead Revisited 1979, Hamlet 1980, Cymbeline 1982, Separate Tables 1982, King John 1983, Time and the Conways 1984, Ellis Island 1984, Florence Nightingale 1984, Shadowlands (BAFTA Award for Best Actress) 1985, Liberty 1985, Promises to Keep 1985, Oedipus the King 1985, Lightning Always Strikes Twice 1985, Anastasia 1986, Queenie 1986, The Belle of Amherst 1986, Intimate Contact 1987, A Shadow on the Sun 1988, These are Women, A Portrait of Shakespeare's Heroines, The Camomile Lawn 1991, The Mirror Crack'd from Side to Side 1992, Remember 1993, A Village Affair 1994, Family Money 1996; *Publications:* Limelight and After 1982, Leaving a Doll's House 1996. *Leisure interests:* walking, music. *Address:* c/o Jeremy Conway, 18–21 Jermyn St, London, SW1Y 6HB, UK.

BLOOM, Patsy; British business executive; b 20 July 1940, London. *Education:* Paddington and Maida Vale High School for Girls. *Career:* Fmr Marketing Man Oxfam, Mary Quant and Queen Magazine; Marketing Man London Org Cen British Fund 1970–80; CEO Pet Plan Group 1976–96, Dir 1996–; currently Dir Patsy Bloom Enterprises Ltd; Veuve Clicquot Business Woman of the Year 1992. *Publication:* Tails of the Unexpected 1995. *Leisure interests:* bridge, charity work, animals. *Address:* POB 11217, London NW1 4WE, UK. *Telephone:* (20) 7935-4070; *Fax:* (20) 7935-0766.

BLOW, Isabella; English stylist and fashion consultant; b Nantwich, Cheshire; d of Sir Evelyn Delves Broughton and Helen Mary Shore; m Detmar Blow 1989. *Education:* Heathfield School and Ascot and Columbia Univ (New York, USA)). *Career:* Various jobs including domestic cleaner, shop asst, waitress, etc; worked on American Vogue, The Tatler, British Vogue magazines; Fashion Dir The Sunday Times 1997–; contrib to The Face and French Vogue. *Leisure interests:* art, Gloucester Cathedral, rare breeds of agricultural animals and birds, reading, family. *Address:* c/o The Sunday Times Style Magazine, 1 Pennington St, London E1 9XW, UK. *Telephone:* (20) 7782-5437; *Fax:* (20) 7782-5120.

BLOW, Sandra, RA, FRCA; British artist; b 14 Sept 1925; d of Jack and Lily Blow. *Education:* St Martin's School of Art, Royal Acad Schools and Accademia di Belle Arti (Rome). *Career:* Tutor Painting School, RCA 1960–75; one-woman exhibitions include Gimpel Fils 1952, 1954, 1960, 1962, Saidenbury Gallery (New York) 1957, New Art Centre (London) 1966, 1968, 1971, 1973, Francis Graham-Dixon Gallery 1991, Sackler Galleries, London 1994, Tate, St Ives 2001; group exhibitions in UK, USA, Italy, Denmark and France; represented in perm collections of Peter Stuyvesant Foundation, Nuffield Foundation, Arts Council of GB, Arts Council of N Ireland, Walker Art Gallery (Liverpool), Allbright Knox Art Gallery (Buffalo, NY), Museum of Modern Art (New York), Tate Gallery (London), Gulbenkian Foundation, Ministry of Public Bldg and Works, Contemporary Art Soc; silk screen prints in Victoria and Albert Museum (London), Fitzwilliam Museum (Cambridge), City of Leeds Art Gallery, Graves Art Gallery (Sheffield); painting purchased for liner Queen Elizabeth II; British Section Int Guggenheim Award 1960, Second Prize John Moores Liverpool Exhibition 1961, Arts Council Purchase Award 1965–66, Korn/Ferry Picture of the Year Award 1998. *Address:* c/o Royal Academy of Arts, Piccadilly, London W1V 0DS, UK; Bullans Court, Bullans Lane, St Ives, Cornwall TR26 1RB, UK (Home). *Telephone:* (1736) 797279 (Home).

BLUME, Judy, BA; American writer; b 12 Feb 1938, Elizabeth, NJ; d of Rudolph and Esther (née Rosenfeld) Sussman; m 1st John M. Blume 1959 (divorced 1975); one s one d; m 2nd George Cooper 1987; one step-d. *Education:* New York Univ. *Career:* Fr and Trustee The Kids Fund 1981; mem PEN Club, Authors' Guild, Nat Coalition Against Censorship, Soc of Children's Book Writers; Hon LHD (Kean Coll) 1987; Carl Sandburg Freedom to Read Award, Chicago Public Library, IL 1984, Civil Liberties Award, American Civil Liberties Union 1986. *Publications include:* Fiction: Wifey 1977, Smart Women 1984, Wish They Could Tell You 1986, The Judy Blume Memory Book 1988; Jr Fiction: The One in the Middle is the Green Kangaroo 1969, Iggie's House 1970, Are You There God? It's Me, Margaret (Outstanding Children's Book 1970), Freckle Juice 1971, It's Not the End of the

World 1972, Otherwise Known as Sheila the Great 1972, Deenie 1973, Blubber 1974, Forever 1975, Tales of a Fourth Grade Nothing 1976, Starring Sally J. Freedman as Herself 1977, The Pain and the Great One 1984, Just As Long As We're Together 1987, Fudge-A-Mania 1990, Here's to You, Rachel Robinson 1993, Summer Sisters 1998, Places I Never Meant To Be (ed) 1999. *Address:* c/o Harold Ober Associates, 425 Madison Ave, New York, NY 10017-1110, USA.

BLUMHARDT, Suzanne, MA; New Zealand diplomatist; b 28 July 1943; d of George and Jean Madgwick; m Lance David Blumhardt 1969 (divorced 1994). *Education:* Wallington Girls Coll, Victoria Univ of Wellington and Univ of Hawaii (HI, USA). *Career:* Joined Dept of External Affairs 1966, First Sec High Comm, UK 1973–77, mem staff Ministry of Foreign Affairs 1989–95, Amb to Fiji and High Commr to Tuvalu and Nauru 1995; mem staff OXFAM (Oxford, UK) 1978–82, Health and Safety Exec (Liverpool, UK) 1982–88. *Leisure interests:* reading, gardening, beekeeping, photography, the arts. *Address:* Embassy of New Zealand, Reserve Bank of Fiji Bldg, 10th Floor, Pratt St, POB 1378, Suva, Fiji. *Telephone:* 311422; *Fax:* 300842.

BLUNDELL, Pamela; British fashion designer; b 23 Feb 1969. *Education:* Univ of Southampton and Epsom School of Art & Design. *Career:* Fmrly worked on samples, design and marketing with the late John Flett; numerous freelance clients including English Nat Opera, Liberty of London; fmr Lecturer Cen St Martin's School of Art (London); f Copperwheat Blundell with Lee Copperwheat 1993; Visiting Lecturer Cen St Martin's School of Art, Univ of Nottingham, Brighton Polytechnic 1991–95; winner Courtaulds knitwear competition; Smirnoff Fashion Award for Best Young Designer 1987; Young Designer of the Year 1994 (with Lee Copperwheat). *Address:* Copperwheat Blundell, 14 Cheshire St, London E2 6EH, UK. *Telephone:* (20) 7613-0651; *Fax:* (20) 7729-8600.

BLYTH, Myrna, BA; American magazine editor; b 22 March 1939, New York; d of Benjamin and Betty (née Austin) Greenstein; m Jeffrey Blyth 1962; two s. *Education:* Bennington Coll. *Career:* Sr Ed Datebook 1960–62, Ingenue 1963–68; Book Ed Family Health 1968–71; Book and Fiction Ed, then Assoc Ed Family Circle 1972–78, Exec Ed 1978–81; Ed-in-Chief Ladies' Home Journal 1981–, Sr Vice-Pres and Publishing Dir 1987–; mem Exec Bd American Soc of Magazine Eds; mem Bd of Govs Overseas Press Club, Child Care Action Campaign; mem Authors' Guild, Women's Media Group; fmr Pres New York Women in Communications Inc; awards include Matrix Award, New York Women in Communications Inc 1988, Magazine of the Year Award, Clarion Award 1984, 1989, MagazineWeek Publishing Excellence Award 1991. *Publications include:* For Better and For Worse, Cousin Suzanne; contribs to magazines. *Leisure interest:* reading. *Address:* Ladies' Home Journal, 100 Park Ave, New York, NY 10017-5599, USA. *Telephone:* (212) 351-3579; *Fax:* (212) 351-3562.

BOAG, Michelle; New Zealand politician and business executive; b 1954, Auckland. *Career:* Fmr Public Relations Consultant; Prin Michelle Boag and Assocs; Pres NZ Nat Party July 2001–. *Address:* New Zealand National Party, 14th Floor, Willbank House, 57 Willis St, POB 1155, Wellington, 60015, New Zealand. *Telephone:* (4) 472-5211; *Fax:* (4) 478-1622; *E-mail:* hq@national.org.nz; *Internet:* www.national.org .nz.

BOCHNIARZ, Henryka Teodora, PH D; Polish politician and economist; b 29 Oct 1947; m Zbigniew Bochniarz 1969; one d one s. *Education:* Warsaw School of Econs and Foreign Trade Research Inst (Warsaw). *Career:* Research Asst Int Inst of Socialist Econ Systems, Moscow, USSR (now Russian Fed) 1978; Visiting Asst Prof Vienna Inst for Comparative Econ Systems 1983–84; Deputy Head and Asst Agric Div, Foreign Trade Research Inst, Warsaw 1976–80, Asst Prof and Lecturer 1980–84, Dir 1984–90; mem Polish del to UN Cttee on Agric, Econ Comm for Europe, Geneva, Switzerland 1976–85; Visiting Prof Dept of Agricultural and Applied Econs, Univ of Minnesota, USA 1985–87; mem Negotiating Group on Agric, Uruguay Round GATT talks 1987; Minister of Industry and Trade 1991–92; Dir Proexim Ltd 1988–90; Pres Nicom Consulting Ltd 1990–91, 1992–; Pres Asscn of Econ Consultants in Poland 1991–. *Publications:* Polish Agricultural Trade (annual reports) 1975–90, Poland: The Impact of Foreign Trade Policy on Self-Sufficiency in Agriculture 1987; numerous papers and

contribs to professional journals. *Leisure interests:* theatre, skiing, volleyball. *Address:* c/o NICOM Consulting Ltd, 10 Inwalidów Square, 01-552 Warsaw, Poland.

BÖCK, Emmi; German writer and folklorist; b 17 June 1932, Zweibrücken; d of Robert Böck and Klara Heist. *Education:* Gnadenthal Coll (Ingolstadt) and Univ of Munich. *Career:* Freelance book reviewer and writer 1961–; Researcher for Bavarian State Foundation (Bayer Landessiftung on collection of folklore from Oberpfalz 1980, from Middle-Franconia 1989; research on regional collection of folklore, Neuburg/Donau 1988; Bundesverdienstkreuz 1981; Bayerischer Verdienstorden 1987; Kulturpreis der Stadt Ingolstadt 2000. *Publications include:* Ingolstadt. Bildband 1966, Sagen und Legenden aus Ingolstadt und Umgebung 1973, Die Hallertau. Bildband 1973, Sagen aus der Hallertau 1975, Sagen aus Niederbayern 1977, Sagen aus Eichstätt und Umgebung 1977, Regensburger Stadtsagen 1982, Bayerische Legenden 1984, Sagen aus der Oberpfalz, Aus der Literatur 1986, Sitzweil, Oberpfälzer Sagen aus dem Volksmund 1987, Sagen aus dem Neuburg-Schrobenhauser Land 1989, Bayerische Schwänke 1991, Köschinger Sagenbiachl 1993, Sagen aus Mittelfranken. Aus der Literatur 1995, Kleine Regensburger Volkskunde 1996, Legenden und Mirakel aus Ingolstadt und Umgebung 1998, Baustellen des Himmels (co-author) 2001. *Leisure interests:* art, psychology, games, swimming, ping-pong, walking. *Address:* Münchner Str 74, 85051 Ingolstadt/Donau, Germany. *Telephone:* (841) 72433.

BODEN, Margaret Ann, MA, PH D, SC D, FBA; British professor of philosophy and psychology; b 26 Nov 1936, London; d of Leonard F. and Violet D. (née Dawson) Boden; m John R. Spiers 1967 (divorced 1981); one s one d. *Education:* Newnham Coll (Cambridge) and Harvard Grad School (USA). *Career:* Lecturer in Philosophy Univ of Birmingham 1959–65; Lecturer then Reader in Philosophy and Psychology, Univ of Sussex 1965–80, Prof 1980–, Founding Dean School of Cognitive and Computing Sciences 1987; Curator Univ of London Inst for Advanced Study 1995–; co-f Harvester Press Ltd 1970, Dir 1970–85; Vice-Pres British Acad 1989–91, Royal Inst of GB 1993–95, Chair of Council 1993–95, Academia Europaea 1993–, Animal Procedures Cttee 1995–99; mem Advisory Bd for the Research Councils 1989–90; Fellow American Asscn for Artificial Intelligence 1993–; Fellow European Coordinating Cttee for Artificial Intelligence 1999–. *Publications include:* Purposive Explanation in Psychology 1972, Artificial Intelligence and Natural Man 1977, Piaget 1979, Minds and Mechanisms 1981, Computer Models of Mind 1988, Artificial Intelligence in Psychology 1989, The Philosophy of Artificial Intelligence (ed) 1990, The Creative Mind 1990, Dimensions of Creativity (ed) 1994, Artificial Intelligence and the Mind (co-ed) 1994, The Philosophy of Artificial Life (ed) 1996, Artificial Intelligence (ed) 1996. *Leisure interests:* dressmaking, travel. *Address:* c/o School of Cognitive and Computing Sciences, University of Sussex, Falmer, Brighton, BN1 9QH, UK. *Telephone:* (1273) 606755; (1273) 678386; *Fax:* (1273) 671320; *E-mail:* maggieb@cogs.susx.ac.uk.

BOESCHE-ZACHAROW, Tilly; German writer and publisher; b 31 Jan 1928, Elbing; d of Ernst and Maria Großkopf; m Hans Boesche 1950 (divorced 1963); two s two d. *Education:* In Berlin. *Career:* Fmr clerk and bookseller; writer 1950–; Ed and Publr 1980–, Ed of four children's books, fairy tales, books on religious philosophy, feminism, etc; has written 300 romantic thrillers (under various pseudonyms including Eva Trojan, Ilka Korff, Eve Jean, etc); Dr hc 1981; Dip di merito, Dip d'Honore, European Banner of Arts 1984; Studiosis Humanitas 1985. *Publications:* Dream of Jalna 2001, The Small Line Between Sky and Water 2001, The Rabbi 2001, Pintus of Seehausen 2001, O Israel, They Want to Kill You 2001. *Leisure interest:* building bridges between human beings. *Address:* Laurinsteig 14A, 13465 Berlin, Germany. *Telephone:* (30) 4019009.

BOGLE, Ellen Gray, BA; Jamaican diplomatist and government official; b 9 Oct 1941, St Andrew; d of Victor Gray and Eileen Averil (née Rampie) Williams; one s one d. *Education:* St Andrew High School and Univ of the West Indies. *Career:* Dir Foreign Trade Div, Ministry of Foreign Affairs 1978–81; Dir Jamaica Nat Export Corpn; High Commr to Trinidad and Tobago (also accred to Barbados, E Caribbean States, Guyana and non-resident Amb to Suriname) 1981–89, to UK (also non-resident Amb to Denmark, Sweden, Norway and Spain) 1989–94; Amb,

Ministry of Foreign Affairs and Foreign Trade 1996–; Amb and Special Envoy to the Asscn of Caribbean States (ACS) and CARICOM 1997–; has represented Jamaica at numerous int confs; Order of Distinction (Commdr) 1987. *Leisure interests:* gardening, reading, cooking, table-tennis. *Address:* Ministry of Foreign Affairs and Foreign Trade, 21 Dominica Drive, Kingston, 5, Jamaica (Office).

BOGUINSKAYA, Svetlana; Belarus gymnast; b 1973. *Career:* Gold Medallist, Team and Vault Gymnastics, Olymic Games, Seoul, Repub of Korea 1988; Gold Medallist Team Gymnastics, Barcelona, Spain 1992; competitor Olympic Games, Atlanta 1996, Sydney 2000.

BOGUSLAVSKAYA, Zoya Borisovna; Russian writer and critic; b 16 April 1929, Moscow; d of Boris Lvovich Boguslavsky and Emma Iosifovna Boguslavskaya; m Andrei Andreyevich Voznesensky; one s. *Education:* Moscow State Inst of Arts and Inst of History of Art (USSR Acad of Sciences). *Career:* Ed, Sovetsky Pisatel publishing house; Lecturer Moscow Higher School of Theatre Art; Head Div of Literature, USSR State Cttee on Lenin's and State Prizes; critic in various newspapers and magazines; f Festival of Arts Christmas Carousel (Moscow-Paris); mem Asscn of Women-Writers of Russia, Russian Writers' Union 1960, Int Asscn of Women-Writers in Paris; mem Bd Dirs Russian Pen-Centre; winner Russian Ind Triumph and Foundation Prize. *Publications include:* novels and short stories: And Tomorrow 1959, Change, Ghost, Mediators, Defence, By Transit, Races 1981; plays: Windows Overlooking the South, Contact, Promise (banned for political reasons), Leonid Leonov, Vera Panova, American Women Plus; essays: Unthought-Up Stories, Time of Lubimov and Vysotsky, Lisa and Baryshnikov, One Way Ticket. *Leisure interests:* classical music, swimming.. *Address:* Kotelnicheskaya nab 1/15, korpus B, apt 62, 109240 Moscow, Russian Federation. *Telephone:* (095) 227-49-90.

BOHRINGER, Romane; French actress; b 14 Aug 1973, Paris; d of Richard Bohringer. *Career:* Stage debut in The Tempest 1990; Cesar Award for Most Promising New Artist 1992. *Films and Theatre include:* The Tempest 1990, Les Nuits Fauves (Most Promising Actress César Award) 1993, Vigo, L'Accompagnatrice 1993, Passion for Life 1997, Lulu. *Address:* c/o Richard Bohringer, Editions Denoel, 9 rue du Cherche Midi, 75006 Paris, France.

BÖHRK, Gisela; German teacher and politician; b 8 June 1945, Leipzig; one d. *Education:* Ann Arbor High School, in Lübeck and Pädagogische Hochschule (Kiel). *Career:* Programmer 1965–66; teacher 1969–75; mem Landtag (regional Parl) Schleswig-Holstein (SPD) 1975–, Minister for Women 1988; Deputy Chair SPD Schleswig-Holstein 1991–. *Address:* Ministry for Women, Beselerallee 41, 2300 Kiel 1, Germany (Office); Gartenstr 6, 24103 Kiel, Germany (Home). *Telephone:* (431) 5963100 (Office); *Fax:* (431) 5962505 (Office).

BOISARD, Geneviève; French librarian; b 27 Sept 1931, Paris; d of Pierre and Geneviève (née Dubois) Salleron; m Pierre Boisard 1957; two s one d. *Education:* Lycée Camille Sée and Ecole Nat des Chartes (Paris). *Career:* Librarian Bibliothèque centrale de prêt de la Seine-Maritime 1956–57, Inst de recherche et d'histoire des textes (CNRS) 1957–59; Librarian, then Chief Librarian Bibliothèque Nat 1959–86; Dir Bibliothèque Sainte-Geneviève, Paris 1987–95; Curator-Gen, Rep to Inspection Générale des Bibliothèques 1995–; Pres Asscn of Univ Library Dirs 1990–92; has written articles for professional journals; Officier de l'Ordre Nat du Mérite 1982; Chevalier des Arts et des Lettres; Chevalier des Palmes Académiques. *Leisure interests:* reading, cinema, music. *Address:* Inspection Générale des Bibliothèques, 1 rue d'Ulm, 75005 Paris, France (Office); 51 blvd Auguste Blanqui, 75013 Paris, France (Home).

BOLAND, Eavan Aisling, BA; Irish poet; b 24 Sept 1944, Dublin; d of Frederick Boland and Frances Kelly; two d. *Education:* Schools in London, New York (USA) and Dublin, and Trinity Coll (Dublin). *Career:* Chair judging panel Irish Times–Aer Lingus Irish Literature Prizes; mem Irish Acad of Letters; Macaulay Fellowship 1967; Irish-American Foundation award 1983. *Publications:* New Territory 1967, War Horse 1976, In her own Image 1980, Night Feed 1982, The Journey 1987, Outside History 1990, Object Lessons 1995. *Address:* 4 Ailesbury Grove, Dundrum, Dublin 16, Ireland. *Telephone:* (1) 2981073.

BOLAND, Hon Janet Lang, BA, LL B; Canadian judge; b 6 Dec 1924, Kitchener, ON; d of George and Miriam (née Geraghty) Lang; m John Brown Boland 1949; three s. *Education:* Waterloo Coll and Osgoode Hall. *Career:* Called to the Bar, ON 1950; QC 1965; mem staff White, Bristol, Beck and Phipps, Toronto 1959–69; Partner Lang Michener, Toronto 1969–72; York Co Judge, Toronto 1972–76; Judge Trial Div, Supreme Court of Ontario, Toronto 1976–; Co-Chair Jt Cttee, Penal Reform for Women 1956–58; Hon LL D (Wilfrid Laurier) 1976. *Leisure interests:* tennis, travel, skiing. *Address:* Osgoode Hall, Queen St, Toronto, ON M5H 2N7, Canada (Office); 164 Inglewood Drive, Toronto, ON M4T 1H8, Canada (Home).

BONA, Dominique Henriette Marie; French journalist and writer; b 29 July 1953, Perpignan; d of Arthur and Colette Conte; m Philippe Bona 1973; one s one d. *Education:* Cours Dupanloup (Boulogne), Lycée Victor Duruy and Univ of Paris IV (Paris-Sorbonne). *Career:* Journalist on Quotidien de Paris 1980–85, on Figaro 1985–; writer of novels and biographies; mem Jury Prix Renaudot 1999–; Chevalier des Arts et des Lettres. *Publications:* Novels: Les heures volées 1981, Argentina 1984, Malika (Prix Interallié) 1992, Le manuscit de Port-Ebène (Prix Renaudot) 1998; Biographies: Romain Gary (Grand Prix de la Biographie, Acad Française) 1987, Les yeux noirs ou les vies extraordinaires des sœurs Hérédia (Grand Prix de la Femme, Prix Lutèce, Prix de l'Enclave des Papes 1990) 1989, Gala 1994, Stefan Zweig, l'ami blessé 1996, Berthe Morisot (Prix Goncourt de la Biographie) 2000. *Leisure interests:* skiing, golf. *Address:* Editions Grasset, 61 rue des Saints-Pères, 75006 Paris, France.

BONALY, Surya Varuna Claudine; French ice skater; b 15 Dec 1973, Nice; d of Georges and Suzanne Bonaly. *Education:* Correspondence courses. *Career:* Numerous prizes in int competitions, including first prize Trophée Lalique, Paris 1989, 1990, 1992, 1993, Skate Canada 1991, NHK Trophy, Japan 1992, 1993, Goodwill Games, St Petersburg, Russian Fed 1994, Skate America, Pittsburg, USA 1994, Pro-Am, Philadelphia, USA 1994; came third Jr World Championships, Sarajevo, Yugoslavia 1988, second, Colorado Springs, USA 1989, Jr World Champion, Budapest 1991; came first Sr French Championships 1988, 1989, 1991, 1992, 1993, 1994, 1996; came fourth European Championships, Leningrad (now St Petersburg) 1990, European Champion, Sofia 1991, Lausanne, Switzerland 1992, Helsinki 1993, Copenhagen 1994, Dortmund, Germany 1995; came fifth Olympic Games, Albertville, France 1992, fourth Olympic Games, Lillehammer, Norway 1996; came second World Championships, Prague 1993, Japan 1994, Birmingham, UK 1995. *Leisure interests:* travel, animals, films. *Address:* rue de la 16e Olympiade, 73710 Pralognan-la-Vanoise, France (Office); Les Darbelays, 73710 Pralognan, France (Home).

BOND, Victoria Ellen, D MUS; American composer and conductor; b 6 May 1945, Los Angeles, CA; d of Philip and Jane Bond; m Stephan Peskin 1974. *Education:* Univ of Southern California and Juilliard School of Music. *Career:* Musical Dir New Amsterdam Symphony Orchestra, NY 1978–80, Pittsburgh Youth Symphony Orchestra 1978–80, Bel Canto Opera, NY 1983–86, Roanoke Symphony Orchestra 1986–95, Empire State Youth Orchestra 1988–90; Artistic Dir Opera Roanoke 1989–95, Bel Canto Opera 1986–88; Guest Conductor with numerous orchestras including Colorado Philharmonic, Houston Symphony, Buffalo Philharmonic, Pittsburgh Symphony, Anchorage Symphony, Hudson Valley Philharmonic, RTE Symphony (Dublin), Albany Symphony, Des Moines Symphony, Virginia Symphony, Shanghai Symphony; mem Music Panel, New York State Council of Arts 1987–; Bd of Dirs American Music Center 1987–, Conductors Guild; mem American Soc of Composers, Authors and Publishers (ASCAP), American Fed of Musicians, American Symphony Orchestra League; Dr hc (Hollins Coll, Roanoke Coll) 1995; numerous awards from ASCAP 1975–; Victor Hubert Award 1977; named Exxon Arts Endowment Conductor 1978–90, Virginia Woman of the Year 1990. *Commissions include:* Molly Manybloom 1990, Hot Air 1990, Dreams of Flying 1990, Goodbye My Fancy 1992; *Recordings include:* Live from Shanghai, Victoria Bond: Compositions. *Leisure interests:* horse-riding, sailing, hiking. *Address:* American International Artists, 315 E 62nd St, New York, NY 10021, USA (Agent); 265 W 10th St, 3b, New York, NY 10014, USA (Home). *Telephone:* (212) 715-0470 (Agent); (212) 691-6858 (Home); *Fax:* (212) 715-0461 (Agent); (212) 627-4258 (Home).

BONDAR, Roberta Lynn, OC, PH D, FRCP; Canadian former astronaut and medical practitioner; b 4 Dec 1945, Sault-Ste-Marie, ON. *Education:* Univ of Guelph, McMaster Univ and Univs of Western Ontario and Toronto. *Career:* Intern Toronto Gen Hosp 1977–78; resident Toronto W Hosp 1981–82; Asst Prof McMaster Univ 1982–84; Asst Prof Faculties of Medicine and Nursing, Univ of Ottawa 1984–87; Astronaut Canadian Astronaut Prog 1983–92, Astronaut on American Shuttle 1992; Adjunct Prof Dept of Biology, Univ of New Mexico, Albuquerque, USA 1991–93; Distinguished Prof Ryerson Polytechnic Inst 1992–93; Visiting Research Scholar Dept of Neurology, Univ of New Mexico 1993–94; Visiting Distinguished Fellow Faculty of Health Sciences, McMaster Univ 1993–94; Visiting Research Scientist Univs Space Research Asscn, Johnson Space Center, TX, USA 1993–94; Visiting Distinguished Prof Faculty of Kinesiology, Univ of W Ontario 1994; mem Premier's Council for Science and Tech 1986–89; mem Bd of Dirs Int Space Univ 1987–92; mem staff Sunnybrook Medical Centre, Toronto 1988–93; Career Scientist Award, Prov Minister of Health 1982–83; Hon Life mem Canadian Fed of Univ Women 1986–; mem American Acad of Neurology, Canadian Neurological Soc, Canadian Medical Protective Asscn, Canadian Aeronautics and Space Inst, Flying 99s Int Women Pilots' Asscn, Aerospace Medical Asscn; Hon D SC (Mt Allison) 1989, (Lakehead, Algoma Coll, Laurentian) 1991, (St Mary's, McMaster, York) 1992, (Royal Roads Military Coll, Memorial, Laval, Carleton) 1993, (Montréal, Price Edward Island) 1994; Hon D HUM LITT (Mt St Vincent) 1990; Hon PH D (Guelph) 1990; Hon DSL (Wycliffe Coll, Toronto) 1993; numerous awards, including NASA Space Medal 1992, Order of Ontario 1993. *Address:* 530 Balliol St, Toronto, ON M4S 1E3, Canada.

BONDESTAM, Anitha, LL B; Swedish judge; b 1941; one d one s. *Education:* Uppsala Univ. *Career:* Attached to Dist Courts and Stockholm Court of Appeal 1964–74; Sec, Legal Adviser Ministry of Commerce 1972–73; Legal Adviser Ministry of Justice 1974–77; Perm Sec Ministry of Transport and Communications 1977–78; Minister 1978–79; Justice Admin Court of Appeal, Gothenburg 1980–92, Chief Justice and Pres 1998–; Dir-Gen Data Inspection Board 1992–1998; mem Bd Swedish Nat Road Admin, Council of the School of Econs (Gothenburg); Pres Driving Licence 2000 Cttee. *Address:* Vasagatan 36, 41124 Göteborg, Sweden. *Telephone:* (31) 105100; *Fax:* (31) 105138.

BONDURANT, Amy L., BS, JU D; American diplomatist and lawyer; b 20 April 1951, Union City, TN; d of Judge John C. Bondurant; m David E. Dunn III; one s. *Education:* Univ of Kentucky and Washington Coll of Law, American Univ. *Career:* Legis aide to Senator Wendell Ford 1975; Counsel, then Sr Counsel Senate Cttee on Commerce, Science and Transportation, Consumer Sub-cttee 1978–87; Sr Partner (first woman bd mem) Verner, Liipfert, Bernhard, McPherson & Hand Law Firm (Washington, DC) 1987–97; Sr Search Man, Office of the Pres of the US (Washington, DC) 1992–93; mem Bd, Sec-Treas Vice-Pres's Residence Foundation (Washington, DC) 1991–97; Chair Commercial Space Transportation Advisory Cttee (Washington, DC) 1993–97; US Amb, Chief of US Mission (first woman) OECD (Paris) 1997–2001; Sec-Treas and mem Bd Vice-Pres's Residence Foundation 1993–97; mem American, Dist of Columbia and Kentucky Bar Asscns, Founding Cttee of Forum 21 Conf on TransAtlantic Dialogue 2001, Cosmos Club. *Publication:* Physician Heal Thyself: Can International Organizations Reform? 2001. *Address:* 145 ave de Malakoff, 75116 Paris, France. *Telephone:* (1) 45-00-19-44; *Fax:* (1) 45-00-19-56; *E-mail:* albond.attglobal.net; *Internet:* www.state.gov.

BONET, Lisa; American actress; b 16 Nov 1967, Los Angeles, CA. *Career:* Career began at the age of 15, playing in The Cosby Show on TV; Youth in Film Award. *TV appearances include:* The Cosby Show (series), A Different World (series), Tales From the Dark Side, Don't Touch; *Films:* Angel Heart 1987, Dead Connection 1994, Bank Robber 1993, Serpent's Lair 1995, Enemy of the State 1998, High Fidelity 2000. *Address:* 1551 Will Geer Rd, Topanga, CA 90290-4291, USA.

BONHAM CARTER, Helena; British actress; b 26 May 1966, London; d of Hon Raymond and Elena Bonham Carter; (great granddaughter of fmr British Prime Minister Lord Asquith). *Education:* South Hampstead High School and Westminster School. *Career:* Face of Yardley Cosmetics Co. *Films include:* Lady Jane 1986, A Room with a View 1986, Maurice 1987, Francesco, The Mask, Getting it Right 1989, Where

Angels Fear to Tread, Howard's End 1992, Mary Shelley's Frankenstein 1994, The Glace Bay Miners' Museum 1994, A Little Loving 1995, Mighty Aphrodite 1995, Twelfth Night 1996, Margaret's Museum 1996, Parti chinois 1996, The Theory of Flight 1997, Keep the Aspidistra Flying 1997, The Wings of the Dove 1998, The Revengers' Comedies 1998, Woman Talking Dirty 1999, Fight Club 1999, Planet of the Apes 2001; *TV appearances include:* A Pattern of Roses, Miami Vice, A Hazard of Hearts, The Vision, Arms and the Man, Beatrix Potter, A Dark Adapted Eye (film) 1994; *Plays include:* The Barber of Seville 1992, Trelawny of the 'Wells' 1992. *Address:* c/o Conway van Gelder Ltd, 18/21 Jermyn St, London, SW1Y 6HP, UK (Office). *Telephone:* (20) 7287-0077.

BONINO, Emma, PH D; Italian politician; b 9 March 1948, Bra, Turin; d of the late Filippo Bonino and of Catterina Barge. *Education:* Bocconi Univ of Milan. *Career:* Founder Centro Informazione, Sterilizzazione e Aborto (CISA) 1975; mem Camera dei Deputati (Chamber of Deputies—Parl) 1976–83, 1986, 1992, 1994, Deputy Speaker; MEP 1979, 1989–; EC Commr for Consumer Policy, EC Humanitarian Office and Fisheries 1995–99; ; Pres Transnat Radical Party 1991–93, Sec 1993–94; Cand in Presidential elections 1999; presented own list in general elections 2001; awarded Gran Cruz de la Orden de Mayo (Argentina) 1996, Premio Principe de Asturias (Spain) 1998. *Leisure interests:* sailing, diving. *Address:* European Parliament, 60 rue Wiertz, 1047 Brussels, Belgium. *Telephone:* (0332) 284 5288; *Fax:* (0332) 284 9288; *E-mail:* ebonino@visto.com; *Internet:* www.radicalparty.org.

BONNAIRE, Sandrine; French film actress; b 31 May 1967, Gannat, Auvergne; one d. *Career:* Film debut in La Boum 1980; Honours include Venice Film Festival Award 1995. *Films include:* A Nos Amours (César for Best Newcomer) 1983, Sans Toi Sans Loi (also known as Vagabonde, Venice and César Awards) 1985, Blanche et Marie, La Puritaine, Sous le soleil de Satan, Les innocents, Monsieur Hire 1989, La captive du désert, Joan of Arc 1992, La Cérémonie 1995, Judgment in Stone, Circle of Passion 1996, Secret Défense 1998, The Colour of Lies 1999, East–West 2000.

BONNER, Elena Georgievna; Russian human rights activist and writer; b 25 Feb 1923, Moscow; m Andrei Sakharov 1970 (died 1989); one s one d. *Education:* First Leningrad Medical Inst. *Career:* Nurse 1941–45, Lieut 1945; medical practitioner 1953–83; f Moscow group to monitor observation of 1975 Helsinki accords; regular visitor to Sakharov during latter's exile in Gorky 1980–84; sentenced to five years' exile 1984, released 1986; became political activist after husband's death; Chair Comm for perpetuation of Andrei Sakharov's memory. *Publications:* Alone Together (memoirs) 1986, PS (Post Scriptum) 1991.

BONNEY, Barbara; American opera singer (soprano); b 14 April 1956, Montclair, NJ; d of Alfred and Janet (née Gates) Bonney; m Håkan Hagegård 1989; m 2nd Maurice Whittaker. *Education:* Univ of New Hampshire and Mozarteum (Salzburg, Austria). *Career:* Debut Darmstadt Staatstheater, Germany 1979, since then major appearances include Der Rosenkavalier, Covent Garden 1984, Metropolitan Opera, New York 1990, Die Zauberflöte, La Scala 1985, Falstaff, Metropolitan Opera 1990, The Marriage of Figaro, Covent Garden 1995, Zurich Opera, Metropolitan Opera 1998, 1999, Les Boréades, Salzburg Festival 1999, Idomeneo, San Francisco 1999; noted especially for Mozart and Strauss interpretations; appears regularly as recitalist accompanied by Geoffrey Parsons. *Recordings include:* Brahms' Requiem 1985, Giulini 1985, Die Zauberflöte 1986, Harnoncourt 1986; over 40 further recordings of works by Schönberg, Haydn, R. Strauss, Donizetti, Mozart, Mendelssohn, Wolf etc. *Leisure interests:* textiles, interior decorating, calligraphy. *Address:* c/o IMG, 3 Burlington Lane, Chiswick, London W4 2TH, Sweden. *Telephone:* (20) 8233-5000; *Fax:* (20) 8233-5801.

BONREPOS-BAINVILLE, Bernadette Clémence de; French banking executive; b 17 Jan 1951, Washington, DC; d of Ludovic and Cynthia Fax de Bonrepos; m Jacques Bainville 1977; two d. *Education:* Cours Hattemer and Victor Hugo (Paris), Univ of Paris X and Inst d'Etudes Politiques de Paris. *Career:* Mem staff Banque Rivaud 1972–77; Rep, later Dir Industrial Dept, Inst for Industrial Devt 1977–84; Vice-Pres, Dir of Business Banking, Man Dir Chase Investment Bank at Chase Manhattan Bank, Paris, 1984–88; Deputy

Dir-Gen Marceau Investissements, in charge of business bank Trianon Finance 1988; Dir Techpak 1983–, Financière Techpak, Continentale d'Entreprise 1987–, Foncière du Château d'Eau de Paris 1988, Sete, Parmedias, Bolloré technologies 1994, Nord-Est 1998–; Head of Pres's Cabinet Elf Aquitaine 1995–99. *Address:* Continentale d'entreprise, 4 ave Velasquez, 75018 Paris, France. *E-mail:* b.de-bonrepas@wanadoo.fr.

BOODAI, Nejoud, BA; Kuwaiti fashion designer; b 16 Nov 1972. *Education:* The American Coll (London). *Career:* Founder Nejoud Boodai Fashion Design Ltd, London 1995, launced first collection Aug 1995, opened first shop Nov 1996; commissioned by Arab Food Group, Kuwait to design uniforms for restaurant staff 1995; has taken part in design show in aid of Egyptian Flood Victims Appeal, London and travelling exhibition 'Opposites', Rotterdam, Netherlands 1995; Spring/Summer '96 collection shown at Regency Palace Hotel, Kuwait Oct 1995, fashion collection shown at Sheraton Hotel, Kuwait Dec 1996; regular appearances on radio station MBC; Second Prize Fashion Design Competition, Vilene Int 1993; Fashion Future Award for evening wear, Igedo Trade Fair, Dusseldorf, Germany 1994; Outstanding Student Award for fashion design, American Coll, London 1994; Second Prize Golden Thread Award, Łódź. *Address:* c/o 34 Beauchamp Place, London SW1 1NU, UK. *Telephone:* (20) 7581-5989; *Fax:* (20) 7581-5043.

BOOTH, Cherie, QC, LL B, FRSA; British barrister; b Sept 23 1954, Bury, Lancs; d of Anthony and Gale (née Smith) Booth; m Anthony Charles Lynton Blair 1980; three s one d. *Education:* Seafield Convent Grammar School (Crosby, Liverpool) and LSE. *Career:* Called to Bar (Lincoln's Inn) 1976, Bencher 1999; pupillage with Alexander Irvine (now Lord Irvine of Lairg) 1976–77; Tenant New Court Chambers 1977–91, 4/5 Gray's Inn Square, London 1991–2000, Matrix Chambers 2000–; apptd QC April 1995; Asst Recorder 1996–99, Recorder 1999–; Gov LSE 1998–); Fellow John Moores Univ, Liverpool (Chancellor 1998–); Patron Sargent Cancer Care for Children 1998–, Breast Cancer Care 1997–, SHADO (Liverpool) 1998–, Islington Music Centre 1999–; mem Bd Trustees Refuge, the Citizenship Foundation; Kennedy Scholar Lincoln's Inn 1975; Hon D UNIV (Open Univ) 1999, Hon LL D (Westminster). *Leisure interests:* reading, working out, the arts, children. *Address:* Matrix Chambers, Griffin Building, Gray's Inn, London WC1R 5LN, UK (Office); 10 Downing Street London SW1A 2AA, UK (Home). *Telephone:* (20) 7404 3447 (Office); (20) 7980 4433 (Home); *Fax:* (20) 7404 3448 (Office); *E-mail:* cheriebooth@matrixlaw.co.uk (Office); *Internet:* www.matrixlaw.co.uk (Office).

BOOTH, Dame Margaret (Myfanwy Wood), DBE, QC; British high court judge (retd); b 1933; d of the late Alec Wood and of Lillian May Booth; m 1st Joseph Jackson 1982 (died 1987), m 2nd Peter Glucksmann 1993. *Education:* Northwood Coll and Univ Coll London. *Career:* Called to the Bar, Middle Temple 1956; Bencher 1979; QC 1976; High Court Judge, Family Div 1994–94; Visiting Prof of Law 1994–; Chair Family Law Bar Asscn 1976–78, Matrimonial Causes Procedure Cttee 1982–85, Children Act Procedure Cttee 1990, Children Act Advisory Cttee 1991–93, Bd Govs UK Coll of Family Mediators 1996–; Gov Northwood Coll 1975–; mem Council Univ Coll London 1980–84, Univ of Liverpool 1994–; Trustee Joseph Rowntree Foundation 1996–. *Publications:* Rayden on Divorce (co-ed), Clarke Hall and Morrison on Children (co-ed) 1977. *Address:* 15 Wellington House, Eton Rd, London NW3 4SY, UK.

BOOTHROYD, Baroness (Life Peer), cr 2001, of Sandwell in the County of West Midlands, **Rt Hon Betty Boothroyd,** PC; British politician; b 8 Oct 1929, Dewsbury, Yorks; d of Archibald and Mary Boothroyd. *Education:* Dewsbury Coll of Commerce and Art. *Career:* Personal Asst to Lab Ministers; accompanied Parl dels to European Confs 1955–60, USSR, China and Vietnam 1957; del to N Atlantic Ass 1974; MP (Lab, W Bromwich W) 1974–, Asst Govt Whip 1974–75, mem Select Cttee on Foreign Affairs 1979–81, Speaker's Panel of Chairs 1979–87, House of Commons Comm 1983–87, Deputy Chair Ways and Means 1987–92, Deputy Speaker House of Commons 1987–92, Speaker (first woman) 1992–2000; MEP 1975–77; mem Lab Party Nat Exec Cttee 1981–87; Chancellor Open Univ 1994–; several hon degrees

from British univs including Hon LL D (Cambridge) 1994, Hon DCL (Oxford) 1995. *Leisure interests:* dominoes, Scrabble. *Address:* House of Lords, Westminster, London SW1A 0AA, UK.

BORCHERS, Elisabeth; German editor; b 27 Feb 1926, Homberg; d of Rudolf and Claire (née Beck) Sarbin; m (divorced); two s. *Career:* Ed Luchterhand 1960–71, Suhrkamp Verlag and Insel Verlag 1971–98; Vice-Pres Int Erich Fried Soc for Literature and Language, Vienna; mem PEN, Acad of Sciences and Literature (Mainz), Acad of Language and Poetry (Darmstadt); German Industry Culture Prize; Roswitha von Gandersheim-Literaturpreis 1976; Order of Merit of the Federal Republic of Germany 1996. *Publications include:* Poetry: Der Tisch, an dem Wirsitzen (Erzählerpreis, Süddeutscher Rundfunk), Wer lebt (Friedrich Hölderlin-Preis 1986), Von der Grammatik des heutigen Tages 1992, Was ist die Antwort 1998, Alles redet, schweigt und ruft (collected poems) 2001. *Address:* Arndtstrasse 17, 60325 Frankfurt, Germany. *Telephone:* (69) 74 63 91; *Fax:* (69) 74 09 3909.

BORD, Nancy, PH D; American academic. *Education:* MIT. *Career:* Head of Strategic Planning Pacificorp; partner in an investment boutique (buying and selling small and medium-sized enterprises), Washington, DC; Advisor on Regulatory Affairs to the Office of Vice-Pres Dan Quayle; mem staff Hoover Inst on War, Revolution and Peace, Stanford, CA; Dir Liverpool Business School, Liverpool John Moores Univ. *Address:* c/o Liverpool John Moores University, Rodney House, 70 Mount Pleasant, Liverpool L3 5UX, UK.

BORDA, Deborah, BA; American orchestra director; b 15 July 1949, NY; d of William and Helene (née Malloy) Borda. *Education:* Bennington Coll and Royal Coll of Music (London). *Career:* Programme Dir Massachusetts Council of Arts and Humanities, Boston 1974–76; Man Boston Musica Viva 1976–77; Gen Man Handel and Haydn Soc, Boston 1977–79, San Francisco Symphony 1979–86; Pres St Paul Chamber Orchestra 1986–88; Exec Dir Detroit Symphony Orchestra 1988–90, New York Philharmonic Orchestra 1991–; Pres Minnesota Orchestra, Minneapolis 1990–91. *Address:* New York Philharmonic Orchestra, Avery Fisher Hall, 10 Lincoln Center Plaza, New York, NY 10023-6673, USA.

BORDALLO, Madeleine Mary; Guam politician; b 31 May 1933, Graceville, MN; d of Christian Peter and Mary Evelyn (née Roth) Zeien; m Ricardo Jerome Bordallo 1953; one d. *Education:* St Mary's Coll (South Bend, IN). *Career:* Mem Civic Opera Co, St Paul, MN 1952–53; mem staff KUAM radio and tv station, Agaña 1954–63; Nat Democratic Ctteewoman for Guam 1974–94; First Lady of Guam 1974–78, 1981–85; Senator Guam Legislature 1981–82, 1987–88, 1993–94; Lt-Gov Guam 1994, 1995–; mem numerous dels and cttees. *Address:* Office of the Governor, POB 2950, Adelup, Agaña, GU 96910, Guam.

BORGESE, Elisabeth Mann, OC, BA; Canadian professor of political science and writer; b 24 April 1918, Munich, Germany; d of the late Thomas Mann and Katia Pringsheim; m G. A. Borgese 1939; two d. *Education:* Freies Gymnasium and Conservatory of Music (Zurich, Switzerland). *Career:* Research Assoc Univ of Chicago, IL, USA and Ed Common Cause 1946–52; Ed Int Publs 1952–62; Sr Fellow Centre for the Study of Democratic Insts 1964–78; Killam Sr Fellow Dalhousie Univ 1979, Prof of Political Science 1980–, Adjunct Prof School of Law 1996–; Exec Sec Bd of Eds Encyclopaedia Britannica 1964–66; Chair Int Ocean Inst (Malta) 1972; mem Bd of Trustees Nova Scotia Environmental Trust Fund 1990–, Minister's Advisory Council on the Oceans 2000–; Hon PH D (Mount St Vincent) 1985; Cross for High Merit, Govt of Canada 1982; UN Sasakawa Environmental Prize 1987; Order of Merit, Colombia 1992; St Francis of Assisi Int Environment Prize 1993; Bundesverdienstkreutz. *Publications:* The Drama of the Oceans 1975, Sea Farm 1981, The Mines of Neptune 1985, The Future of the Oceans 1986, Ocean Frontiers 1992, Ocean Governance and the United Nations 1995, The Oceanic Circle 1998; also short stories, children's books, plays and essays. *Leisure interests:* music, study of animals, skiing, swimming. *Address:* Dalhousie University, International Ocean Inst, 1226 Le Marchant St, Halifax, NS B3H 3P7, Canada. *Telephone:* (902) 868-2818; *Fax:* (902) 494-2034; *E-mail:* eborgese@compuserve.com.

BORKH, Inge; Swiss opera singer (soprano); b 26 May 1921. *Education:* Drama School (Vienna) and Vienna Acad. *Career:* Dancing, piano and theatre performances in Vienna, Milan and in Switzerland; int career 1951–; appearances at Bayreuth, Paris, Vienna, Edinburgh Festivals, Carnegie Hall (New York) 1958, Metropolitan Opera (New York) 1958, opening of Nationaltheater (Munich, Germany) 1963; gave world première of Irische Legende (Egk) 1955; title of Bayerische Kammersängerin conferred 1963; Reinhard Ring Award 1973. *Operas and recordings include:* The Consul, Salome, Elektra (Grand Prix du Disque), Antigone (Grand Prix du Disque), Schönberg's Gurrelieder (Grand Prix du Disque), Die Frau ohne Schatten 1963. *Address:* Florentinerstr 20, Apt 2018, 7000 Stuttgart, 75, Germany. *Telephone:* (711) 47022018.

BORNHAUSEN-O'CONNOR, Angelica; German ballet dancer; m Martin O'Connor 1982. *Education:* Hamburg Opera, Paris and Bolshoi Theatre (Moscow). *Career:* Soloist, Cologne; Prin Dancer Canadian Nat Ballet; Soloist in Zurich and Hamburg; Dir Summer Acad, Cologne, and courses in France and Switzerland; Ballet Mistress in Freiburg and Kassel; Förderungspreis für junge Künstler 1968. *Ballets include:* Daphnis und Chloë, Allegro Brillante, Concerto barocco, Pas de dix, Feuervogel, Petrushka, Les Sylphides, Dornröschen, Giselle, Transition, Don Quichotte, La Corsaire, La Bayadère, Nutcracker, Schwanensee, Sarenach, La fille mal gardée, Die sieben Todsünden, Don Juan. *Address:* c/o Ahnatalstr 42, 34128 Kassel, Germany.

BORODINA, Olga Vladimirovna; Russian mezzo-soprano; b 29 July 1963, Leningrad (now St Petersburg); d of Vladimir Nikolaevich and Galina Fedorovna Borodins; one s. *Education:* Leningrad Conservatory. *Career:* Debut as Siebel (Faust); on tour with Mariinsky Theatre in most European countries; debut in USA with Mariinsky Theatre 1992, solo recitals 1993–; debut in UK as Delilah, Covent Garden; Metropolitan Opera, debut in Boris Godunov 1997; winner of First Prizes: All-Union Glinka Competition 1987, Int Rosa Poncell Competition (New York) 1987, Int Francisco Vignas Competition (Barcelona) 1989. *Opera roles include:* Olga in Eugene Onegin, Marfa in Khovanshchina, Konchakovna in Prince Igor, Poline in Queen of Spades, Lubava in Sadko, Marina Mnichek in Boris Godunov, Cinderella in La Cenerentola. *Leisure interest:* fishing. *Address:* c/o Askonas Holt, Lonsdale Chambers, 27 Chancery Lane, London, WC2A 1PF, UK (Office). *Telephone:* (20) 7400-1780 (Home); *Fax:* (20) 7400-1799 (Office); *E-mail:* nicola-fee .babl@askonasholt.co.uk (Office).

BORTNIK, Aida; Argentine scriptwriter; b 16 July 1941, Buenos Aires. *Career:* Scriptwriter in Spain and Argentina. *Films include:* La Tregua (Acad Award nomination) 1974, Una mujer 1975, Crecer de golpe 1976, La isla 1979, Un tiro al aire 1980, Volver 1982, The Official Story (jtly, Acad Award for Best Foreign Language Film) 1984, Pobre mariposa 1986, Old Gringo 1987.

BOS, Caroline Elisabeth, BA; Netherlands architect; b 17 June 1959, Rotterdam; d of Peter Bos and Ellen Guibal; m Ben van Berkel; one d. *Education:* Birbeck Coll, Univ of London. *Career:* Freelance journalist 1982–88; Co-Founder and Dir Van Berkel & Bos Architectur Bureau 1988–99; Co-Founder and Dir UN Studio 1999–; British Council Fellowship 1986; winning entry for Police HQ, Berlin 1995, Museum Het Valkof 1995, Music Theatre, Graz 1998, Papendorp Bridge, Utrecht 1998, Ponte Parodi, Genoa 2001; awards include Eileen Gray Award 1983, Charlotte Köhler Prize 1991. *Projects include:* switching substation, Amersfoort 1989–93, Erasmus Bridge, Rotterdam 1990–96, Villa Wilbrink, Amersfoort 1992–94, Möbius House, 't Gooi 1993–98, Rijksmuseum Twente, conversion and extension, Enschede 1992–96, Museum Het Valkhof, Nijmegen 1995–99, Masterplan of station area, Arnhem 1996–(2005), Willemstunnel, Arnhem 1996–99, City Hall and Theatre, Ijsselstein 1996–2000, Lab for NMR facilities, Utrecht 1996–2000, Switching station, Innsbruck 1998–2001, Music Faculty, Graz 1998–2002; *Group Exhibitions include:* Architecture et Utopie, Paris and Berlin 1989–90, Architectural Biennale of Venice 1991–93, 1996, 2000, Crossing Points, Berlin and Zürich 1993, Das Schloss, Berlin, Vienna and Stuttgart 1993–94, Light Construction, Museum of Modern Art, New York 1995, Mobile Forces, UCLA, LA and New York 1997, The Un-Private House, Museum of Modern Art, New York 1999, UCLA, LA 2000–2001. *Address:* UN Studio Van Berkel & Bos,

Stadhouderskade 113, 1073 AX Amsterdam, Netherlands. *Telephone:* (20) 570 2040; *Fax:* (20) 570 2041; *E-mail:* info@unstudio.com; *Internet:* www.unstudio.com.

BOSERUP, Ester Talke, PH D; Danish writer and consultant; b 18 May 1910, Frederiksberg; d of Holger and Talke (née Hansen) Börgesen; m Mogens Boserup 1931 (died 1978); two s one d. *Education:* Univ of Copenhagen. *Career:* Direktorat for Vareforsyning, Danish Govt Service 1935–47; Research Div UN Econ Comm for Europe, Geneva, Switzerland 1947–57; freelance writer and consultant on devt problems 1957–, various assignments have included stays in India 1957–59, Senegal 1964–65; mem UN Expert Cttee of Devt Planning 1971–80; mem Bd Scandinavian Inst of Asian Studies 1978–80, UN Int Research and Training Inst for Advancement of Women 1979–85; Foreign mem NAS; Dr hc (Wageningen) 1978, (Copenhagen) 1979, (Brown) 1983. *Publications:* Conditions of Agricultural Growth 1965, Woman's Role in Economic Development 1970, Population and Technology 1981, Economic and Demographic Relationships in Development 1990. *Address:* Casa Campagnola, Nevedone, 6614 Brissago, Switzerland. *Telephone:* (91) 7931732.

BØSTERUD, Helen; Norwegian politician; b 15 Feb 1940, Oslo. *Career:* Mem Akershus Co Council 1975–79; mem Storting (Parl) 1977, Chair Standing Cttee on Justice 1981–86, on Defence 1989–94; State Sec Ministry of Health and Social Affairs 1980–81; Minister of Justice 1986–89; Dir-Gen Directorate for Civil Defence and Emergency Planning 1993–. *Address:* c/o Directorate for Civil Defence and Emergency Planning, Sandakervn 12, POB 8136, Dep 0033, Oslo, Norway.

BOSTWICK, Janet Gwennett; Bahamian politician; b 30 Oct 1939, Nassau; d of Nick and Lois Musgrove; m J. Henry Bostwick; four c. *Education:* Govt High School (Nassau). *Career:* Pvt Sec to Attorney-Gen 1961–67; Called to the Bar 1971; Crown Counsel 1971–74; Crown Prosecutor 1972–74; Partner Bostwick and Bostwick 1975; mem House of Ass (Parl, first woman) 1982–, Minister for Social Services, Nat Insurance and Housing 1992–93, of Justice and Immigration 1993–94, Attorney-Gen and Minister of Justice 1994, Minister of Foreign Affairs 1995, Attorney-Gen and Minister of Foreign Affairs with responsibility for Women's Affairs 1995–; Pres Caribbean Women for Democracy. *Leisure interests:* fishing, reading, animal farming. *Address:* Ministry of Foreign Affairs, East Hill St, POB N-3746, Nassau, Bahamas. *Telephone:* 322-7624; *Fax:* 328-8212.

BOTÍN, Ana Patricia; Spanish business executive; d of Emilio Botín; three c. *Career:* Jt Pres Banco Santander Central Hispano (BSCH); f Suala Capital Advisers; Chair coverlink.com. *Leisure interest:* golf. *Address:* c/o Emilio Botín, Banco Santander Central Hispano (BSCH), Plaza de Canalejas 1, 28014 Madrid, Spain.

BOTTERBUSCH, Vera; German journalist and film producer; b 10 Feb 1942, Dortmund; m Klaus Konjetzky 1976; two d. *Career:* Freelance contrib to Süddeutsche Zeitung and Bavarian TV, Munich 1975–; publr of poems and short stories. *Films include:* Strukturen, Gewebte Bilder—Textile Objekte 1978, Die Hebriden, Annäherungen an eine Musik von Felix Mendelssohn-Bartholdy 1980, Die Jagd nach dem Glück, Hommage à Stendhal 1982, Die lange Rede der ich bin: der Dichter Louis Aragon 1983, Das Gefühl der vagen Empfindungen: die Schriftstellerin Nathalie Sarraute 1985, Wo die wilden Stiere wohnen: eine Unterwegsgeschichte aus der Camargue 1985, Man muß die Wahrheit sagen: der Schriftsteller Julien Green 1987, Mit dem Esel durch die Cevennen: eine Reise von Robert Louis Stevenson 1988, Ein provencalischer Pan: der Schriftsteller Jean Giono 1989, Jede Straße führt in die Kindheit: der Schriftsteller Horst Bienek 1990, Die Zeit, die wir nicht haben, Carl Amery: ein bayerischer Querdenker 1991, Bäume im Weg: Was wird aus den ostdeutschen Alleen 1992, Den Kopf zwischen die Schultern trägt jeder für sich, Alfred Döblins Polenreise 1992, Und meine Seele spannte weit ihre Flügel aus, Die Malerstraße durch der Sächsischen Schweiz 1993, Im Windschatten der Mauer, Günter de Bruyn: Chronist seiner Zeit 1993, Verloren daheim, Ernst Barlach: Künstler in dunkler Zeit 1994. *Leisure interests:* painting, photography. *Address:* Pilarstr 8, 80638 Munich, Germany. *Telephone:* (89) 175131.

BÖTTIGER, Anneliese, D ENG; German professor of engineering; b 1 June 1936, Berlin; d of Ludwig and Elisabeth Böttiger. *Education:* High School (Fürth), Tech Hochschule Darmstadt and Purdue Univ (IN, USA). *Career:* Electrical Technician Siemens 1955–58; Research Engineer Deutsche Forschungsanstalt für Luft- und Raumfahrt 1963–64, Dornier AG, Friedrichshafen 1968–71; Grad Instructor Purdue Univ, IN, USA 1964–68; Lecturer Eng Coll of Hamburg 1971–75; Prof of Automatic Control, Flight Instructor Univ Flying Group, Univ of Fed Armed Forces, Munich 1975–; Female Motor Flying Champion, Germany 1976; Bronze Medal Rally-Flying World Championships 1978. *Publications include:* Beispiele und Aufgaben zur Regelungstechnik (jtly, 4th edn) 1991, Regelungstechnik, eine Einführung für Ingenieure und Naturwissenschaftler (3rd edn) 1998; contribs to professional journals. *Leisure interests:* playing the piano, flying, cycling. *Address:* Universität der Bundeswehr München, Faculty of Electro-Tech, Inst für Meß~und Automatisierungstechnik, Werner-Heisenberg-Weg 39, 85579 Neubiberg, Germany (Office); Gronsdorfer Str 90, 85540 Haar, Germany (Home). *Telephone:* (89) 60043985 (Office); *Fax:* (89) 60043910 (Office).

BOTTOMLEY, Rt Hon Virginia Hilda Brunette Maxwell, PC, BA, M SC, JP; British politician; b 12 March 1948; d of the late W. John Garett and of Barbara Rutherford-Smith; m Peter Bottomley 1967; two d one s. *Education:* Putney High School (London), Univ of Essex and LSE. *Career:* Researcher Child Poverty Action Group 1971–73, concurrently Lecturer in Further Educ; Psychiatric Social Worker Child Guidance Units, Brixton and Camberwell, London 1973–84; Vice-Chair Nat Council of Carers and their Elderly Dependants 1982–88; MP (Cons) for Surrey SW 1984–, Sec Cons Backbench Employment Cttee 1985; Parl Pvt Sec to Minister of State for Educ and Science 1985–86, to Minister of Overseas Devt 1986–87, to Sec of State for Foreign and Commonwealth Affairs 1987–88; Parl Under Sec of State, Dept of Environment 1988–89; Minister for Health 1989–92, Sec of State for Health 1992–95; Sec of State for Nat Heritage 1995–97; consultant Odgers Int 2000–; Co-Chair Women's Nat Comm 1991–92; Dir Midland S Water Co 1987–88; mem Court of Govs LSE 1985–, Medical Research Council 1987–88, British Council 1997–, House of Commons Select Cttee on Foreign Affairs 1997–; Fellow Industry Parl Trust 1987; JP Inner London 1975, Chair Lambeth Juvenile Court 1981–84; Chair Millenium Comm; Hon LL D (Portsmouth) 1992. *Leisure interest:* family. *Address:* House of Commons, London, SW1A 0AA, UK. *Telephone:* (20) 7219-6499 (Office).

BOUCHARDEAU, Huguette; French politician and writer; b 1 June 1935, Saint-Etienne; d of Marius and Rose (née Noel) Briaut; m Marc Bouchardeau 1955; two d one s. *Career:* Teacher of philosophy Lycée Honoré d'Urfé 1961–70; Lecturer in Educ Sciences Univ of Lyons II 1969–83; Sec-Gen Parti Socialiste Unifié 1979–85; unsuccessful presidential cand 1981; Sec of State for Environment and Quality of Life 1983–84; Minister for the Environment 1984–86; mem Nat Ass (Parl, PS) for Doubs 1986; Ed H. B. Editions 1995–; Mayor Aigues-Vives 1995; Spokesperson for France, Entente européenne pour l'environnement 1988. *Publications:* Pas d'histoire, les femmes 1977, Hélène Brion: La voie feministe 1978, Un coin dans leur monde 1980, Le ministère du possible 1986, Choses dites de profil (novel) 1988, Georges Sand, la Lune et les sabots (essay) 1990, Rose Noël 1990, La grande verrière (novel) 1991, Carnets de Prague 1992, Le Déjeuner 1993, La Famille Renoir 1994, Simone Weil 1995, Les roches rouge 1996, Faute de regard 1997, Agatha Christie 1999, Voyage autour de ma bibliothèque 2000. *Address:* H. B. Editions, 3 Grand Rue, 30670 Aigues-Vives, France (Office); 41 rue de Calvisson, 30670 Aigues-Vives, France (Home). *Telephone:* (1) 40-63-84-36 (Home); *Fax:* (1) 40-63-84-99 (Home); *E-mail:* bouchardeau-hb-editions@wanadoo.fr (Office).

BOULDING, Elise Marie, PH D; American sociologist and international organization executive; b 20 July 1920, Oslo, Norway; d of Joseph and Birgit (née Johnson) Biorn-Hansen; m Kenneth Boulding 1941; four s one d. *Education:* Douglass Coll (NJ), Iowa State Univ and Univ of Michigan. *Career:* Research Assoc Univ of Michigan 1957–60; Prof of Sociology Univ of Colorado 1967–78; Chair Dept of Sociology, Dartmouth Coll 1978–85, Prof Emer and Sr Fellow Dickey Endowment 1985–; Ed Int Peace Research Newsletter 1963–68, 1983–87, Sec-Gen Int Peace Research Asscn 1988–91; Int Chair Women's Int League for Peace and Freedom 1967–70; mem UNU Council 1980–85, Jury

UNESCO Peace Prize 1982–87, Bd of Friends Service Comm 1987–95; mem American Sociological Asscn, World Future Soc, Consortium on Peace Research, Educ and Devt (COPRED); Lentz Int Peace Research Award 1976; Women of Conscience Award 1980; Athens Award 1983; Nat Women's Award 1985, 1990; Inst for Defense and Disarmament Peace and Democracy Award. *Publications:* Women in the 20th Century World 1977, Children's Rights and the Wheel of Life 1979, Building Global Civic Culture 1988, One Small Plot of Heaven 1989, Underside (2nd edn) 1991, Cultures of Peace: The Other Side of History. *Leisure interests:* family, mountains, thinking. *Address:* 624 Pearl St, Apt 206, Boulder, CO 80302, USA.

BOUQUET, Brigitte, D ÈS L; French research centre and museum director; b 29 Oct 1941; m Bernard Bouquet 1969. *Career:* Fmr social worker, univ teacher, Dir of training centre; Dir Centre d'Etudes, de Documentation, d'Information et d'Action Sociales (CÉDIAS—Musée Social) 1988–; co-author two books, numerous articles. *Leisure interest:* dancing. *Address:* Centre d'Etudes, de Documentation, d'Information et d'Action Sociales, 5 rue Las-Cases, 75007 Paris, France (Office); 121 Résidence des Eaux Vives, 91120 Palaiseau, France (Home). *Telephone:* (1) 45-51-66-10 (Office); (3) 60-14-60-47 (Home).

BOUQUET, Carole; French actress and model; b 1958, Neuilly-sur-Seine; m; two s. *Career:* Model for Chanel No 5 perfume 1986–; film debut 1977. *Films include:* Cet obscur objet du désir 1977, Buffet Froid 1979, Le Manteau d'Astrakan 1979, For Your Eyes Only 1981, Le jour des idiots 1981, Bingo Bango 1982, Dream One 1983, Mystère 1983, Dagobert 1984, Rive droite, Rive gauche 1984, Double messieurs 1985, Special Police 1985, Le mal d'aimer 1986, Jenatsch 1986, On se dépêche d'en rire 1987, Bunker Palace Hotel 1988, Trop belle pour toi 1988 (César Award for Best Female Actress 1989), Grosse fatigue, A Business Affair, Lucie Aubrac, In All Innocence, The Bridge 2000.

BOURAOUI, Nina; French writer; b 31 July 1967, Rennes; d of Rachid Bouraoui and Maryvonne Henry-Bouraoui. *Education:* Lycée Français (Algiers, Algeria) and Zurich (Switzerland), Inst Catholique (Paris) and Univ of Paris II (Panthéon-Assas). *Career:* Writer. *Publication:* La voyeuse interdite (Prix Livre Inter) 1991. *Address:* 47 rue Claude Bernard, 75005 Paris, France. *Telephone:* (1) 43-37-54-31.

BOURG, Claude; French business executive; b 19 Dec 1935, Baccarat; d of Maurice and Alphonsine Demeusy; m Roland Bourg 1961; two s one d. *Education:* Maisons d'Educ de la Légion d'Honneur (Ecouen and Saint-Denis). *Career:* Founder, Pres Dir-Gen Permanence Européenne group 1960–; f Claude Bourg Inc, Montréal (Canada) 1975; Founder, Pres Fondation Claude Bourg pour l'Esprit d'Entreprise 1979–; Pres, Dir-Gen Nord-Est Intérim and Assistance No 1 1982; Sr Lecturer Ecole des Hautes Etudes Commericales 1981–84; Pres Alpha Immobilier 1986–; Founder Claude Bourg Développement 1990–; Chevalier de la Légion d'Honneur; Chevalier de l'Ordre Nat du Mérite. *Publications:* Femme et chef d'entreprise (Prix Louis Pergaud) 1975, J'ai créé mon entreprise 1986. *Leisure interest:* horse-riding. *Address:* 68 quai Louis Blériot, 75016 Paris, France.

BOURGEOIS, Louise; French/American artist and sculptor; b 24 Dec 1911, Paris; d of Louis Bourgeois; m Robert Goldwater; three s. *Education:* Lycée Fénelon (Paris), Ecole des Beaux Arts and Ecole du Louvre (Paris). *Career:* Began career as sculptor in New York in the 1940s. *Publications:* He Disappeared Into Complete Silence 1947, Destruction of The Father/Reconstruction of the Father 1998; *Exhibitions include:* Eccentric Abstraction 1966, Retrospective 1982, Museum of Modern Art (MOMA, NY) 1982, Venice Biennale 1993, The Unilever Series: Louise Bourgeois, Tate Modern, London 2000. *Address:* c/o Tate Modern, Bankside, London SE1, UK.

BOURGOIS, Joëlle Marie-Paule; French diplomatist; b 24 June 1945, Thaon-les-Vosges; d of André and Paulette Lombard-Platet; m Olivier Bourgois 1976; two d. *Education:* Inst d'Etudes Politiques de Paris and Ecole Nat d'Admin. *Career:* Sec for Foreign Affairs, Ministry of Foreign Affairs 1970, Counsellor 1977, Rep to Admin and Finance Dir CNRS 1970–71, at European Directorate 1977, Deputy Dir for N Africa and the Middle East 1986–89, Deputy Dir for Econ and Financial Affairs and Head Dept for Int Industrial Relations 1989–91; First Sec French Embassy, Vatican 1976–77; Head Int Relations Div, Hydrocarbons

Directorate, Ministry of Industry 1979–84; First Counsellor, Embassy, Mexico 1984–86; Minister Plenipotentiary, SA 1990, Amb 1991–95, also accredited to Lesotho 1994–95; Amb to Desarmament Conf (Geneva, Switzerland) 1995–99; Amb and Perm Rep to OECD 1999–; Chevalier de la Légion d'Honneur; Chevalier de l'Ordre Nat du Mérite. *Address:* Délégation permanente de la France auprès de l'OCDE, 21 rue Octave Feuillet, 75775 Paris, Cedex 16, France. *E-mail:* dfraocde@ diplomatie.fr.

BOURNE, Margaret Janet, OBE, B SC, FIEE; British civil servant (retd); b 18 Aug 1931; d of Thomas William and Nora Annia (née Pelling) Southcott; m George Bourne 1960. *Education:* Twickenham Grammar School and Royal Holloway Coll (London). *Career:* Staff mem Fairey Engineering 1953–62, Army Operational Research Establishment 1962–65, Defence Operational Analysis Establishment 1965–76; Asst Dir Scientific Advisory Group, Army 1976–80; Head of Assessments Div, Admiralty Surface Weapons Establishment 1980–82, Head of Weapon Dept 1982–84; Deputy Dir Admiralty Research Establishment 1984–87; Asst Chief Scientific Adviser on Capabilities, Ministry of Defence 1987–91, Chair CORDA (BAeSEMA Co) 1992–2001; mem Royal Aeronautical Soc. *Leisure interests:* gardening, natural history, music. *Address:* Tregantle, Kiln Way, Grayshott, Hindhead, Surrey, GU26 6JF, UK. *Telephone:* (1428) 714329.

BOURNE, Vicki Worrall, MS; Australian politician; b 22 Oct 1954, Sydney, NSW; d of Victor and Hazel (née Worrall) Bourne. *Education:* Fort Street Girls' High School (Sydney) and Univ of New South Wales. *Career:* Pvt Sec to Senator Colin Mason 1978–87; Parl Officer to Senator Paul McLean 1987–90; Senator for NSW 1990–. *Leisure interests:* watercolour painting, reading, theatre. *Address:* Senate, Parliament House, Rm M13, Canberra, ACT 2600, Australia (Office); POB 36, Sydney, NSW 2001, Australia (Home). *Telephone:* (62) 77 3820 (Office); *Fax:* (62) 73 1380 (Office).

BOURRET, Caprice; American model, actress and singer; b 1971. *Career:* Signed up with Select Model Management modelling agency 1994; advertising campaigns include Bonjour jeans, Estée Lauder cosmetics; Caprice lingerie range launced at Debenhams; columnist The Mirror. *Films:* Nailing Vienna, Bubbles; *TV includes:* The Dream Team 1999, Caprice Travels; *Music:* singles: Oh Yeah, Once Around The Sun. *Address:* Panic, 2 Mortimer House, Furmage St, London SW18 4DF, UK. *E-mail:* ghislain@panic-uk.com; *Internet:* www .caprice-supermodel.com.

BOURVEN, Monique Jeannine; French banking executive; b 24 Nov 1942, Paris; d of Raymond and Yvonne Bourven. *Education:* Univ of Montpellier and Inst d'Etudes Politiques de Paris. *Career:* Teacher 1961–66; Analyst Caisse Nat de Crédit Agricole 1969–72, Head Financial–Stock Market Research section 1972–77, Head Dept of Transferable Property Man 1977–81, Deputy Head Dept of Financial and Securities Markets 1981–85, Head Dept 1985–87, Dir Dept of Capital Markets 1987–89, Deputy Dir-Gen responsible for Int Activities 1990; Pres Alfi-Gestion 1991–; Pres, Dir-Gen State Street Global Advisors France SA (now State Street Banque SA), Pres, Dir-Gen State Street Vie SA, Admin State Street Global Advisors Inc 1991–; Adviser to Pres of Crédit Nat 1991–; Chevalier du Mérite Agricole. *Leisure interests:* reading, opera, mountain sports, golf. *Address:* State St Banque SA, 21 rue Balzac, 75008 Paris, France.

BOUTIN, Anne Marie; French college administrator and public auditor; b 1 May 1938, Tlemcen, Algeria; d of Paul and Marcelle (née Perrier) Boutin; m Thierry Gaudin 1986; one s. *Education:* Lycées Armand Fallières and Carnot (Tunis), Ecole Normale Supérieure (Paris) and Univ of Paris (Sorbonne). *Career:* Asst (tech mathematics for physics and probability studies) Univ of Paris-Censier 1962–68; Research Eng Soc d'Econ et de Math Appliquées 1963–70; Sr Lecturer in Mathematics and Social Sciences Univ of Paris I (Panthéon-Sorbonne) 1968–70; Scientific Adviser Ecole Nat d'Admin 1971–77, Dir of Studies 1978–79, Rep for Int Relations 1979–81; Public Auditor Cour des Comptes 1979, mem Chamber controlling Ministry of Defence credit man 1979–84, Master Counsellor 1993–; Pres Agence pour la Création Industrielle (APCI) 1983–; Pres and Pres Admin Bd, Ecole Nat Supérieure de Création Industrielle (Les Ateliers), Paris 1985–92; Perm Expert French Design Del to EC; Expert IBRD, mission

to Indonesia to form policy on design 1990; mem Bd Int Council of Socs of Industrial Design; Vice-Pres European Design Expert Asscn; mem French UNESCO Comm, Scientific Council Univ of Industrial Arts (Helsinki), Scientific Council Inst Herstein (Vienna); Chevalier de l'Ordre Nat du Mérite; Officier des Arts et des Lettres. *Leisure interests:* sailing, yoga. *Address:* Cour des Comptes, 13 rue Cambon, 75001 Paris, France. *Telephone:* (1) 49-23-12-12; *Fax:* (1) 43-38-51-36.

BOUYGUES, Corinne Suzanne Marie Edmée; French business executive; b 24 Aug 1947, Laval; d of Francis and Monique Bouygues; m Sergio Gobbi 1995; two s one d. *Career:* Public Relations Officer Compagnie Européenne de Publication 1979–81; Press Attachée Bouygues group 1981, Dir-Gen for Communication 1989–; Deputy Dir-Gen of Communication Télévision Française 1 (TF1) 1987–89, Dir of Communication 1989, Deputy Dir-Gen TF1 Publicité (advertising) 1990–91, Dir-Gen 1991, Admin 1992–97, Admin TF1 1993–1997; Pres, Dir-Gen Une Musique 1994–97; Pres, Dir-Gen Téléshopping SA 1994–97. *Address:* c/o TF1 Publicité, 1 quai du Point-du-Jour, 92656 Boulogne-Billancourt Cedex, France.

BOWDEN, Ruth Elizabeth Mary, OBE, D SC, FRCS, FRSM; British professor of anatomy; b 21 Feb 1915; d of the late Frank and Louise Bowden. *Education:* Westlands School, St Paul's Girls' School and Univ of London. *Career:* House Surgeon, later House Physician Elizabeth Garrett Anderson Hosp 1940–42; House Surgeon Royal Cancer Hosp 1942; Asst Peripheral Nerve Injury Unit, Oxford 1942–45; Asst Lecturer in Anatomy Royal Free Hosp School of Medicine 1945, later Lecturer, then Reader in Human Anatomy 1949, Prof 1951–80, Prof Emer 1980–; Hunterian Prof Royal Coll of Surgeons 1950, Prof 1984–89; WHO Consultant in Anatomy, Univ of Khartoum 1972, 1974, 1977; Hon Research Fellow Inst of Neurology 1980–; mem Exec Cttee Women's Nat Comm 1984–89, and Council N London Hospice Group 1986–; Dame Grand Cross Order of St Lazarus of Jerusalem 1988; Jubilee Medal 1977. *Publications:* Peripheral Nerve Injuries 1958; contribs to medical books and journals. *Leisure interests:* painting, music, walking, carpentry, gardening. *Address:* 6 Hartham Close, Hartham Rd, London N7 9JH, UK. *Telephone:* (20) 7607-3464.

BOWE, Colette, M SC, PH D; British finance executive; b 27 Nov 1946; d of Philip and Norah Bowe. *Education:* Notre Dame High School (Liverpool), Queen Mary Coll (London) and LSE. *Career:* Research Officer LSE 1969–70; Econ Adviser Nat Ports Council 1971–73; Econ Adviser Dept of Industry 1975–78, Prin 1979–81; Asst Sec Dept of Trade and Industry 1981–84, Dir of Information 1984–87; Controller of Public Affairs, Ind Broadcasting Authority 1987–89; Dir Securities and Investment Bd 1989–93; Chief Exec Personal Investment Authority 1994–97; Exec Chair Save & Prosper and Fleming Fund Man (Luxembourg) 1998–; mem Statistics Comm 2000–. *Address:* Fleming Asset Management, Finsbury Dials, 20 Finsbury St, London, EC2Y 9AQ, UK. *Telephone:* (20) 7417-2280.

BOWERING, Marilyn Ruthe, MA; Canadian writer; b 13 April 1949, Winnipeg, MB; d of Herbert James and Elnora May (née Grist) Bowering; m Michael S. Elcock 1982; one d. *Education:* Univs of Victoria, British Columbia and New Brunswick. *Career:* Instructor Continuing Educ Univ of British Columbia 1977; Ed, Writer Gregson/Graham marketing and communications 1978, 1979, 1980; Ed Noel Collins and Blackwells, Edinburgh, UK 1980–82; Lecturer Dept of Creative Writing, Univ of Victoria 1978–80, 1982–86, 1989; Writer-in-Residence Aegean School of Fine Arts, Paros, Greece 1973–74; mem Writers' Union of Canada, League of Canadian Poets, PEN Club; numerous awards including Gov-Gen's Award for Poetry, Canada Council Project Award 1972, 1986, Nat Magazine Award for Poetry 1978, 1988, Canada Council Arts Award 1973, 1977, 1980, 1981, 1984, CBC Literary Prize, Commonwealth Poetry and Photography Prizes. *Publications include:* Fiction: The Visitors Have All Returned 1979, To All Appearances A Lady (4th edn) 1992; Poetry: The Liberation of Newfoundland 1973, One Who Became Lost 1976, Many Voices (co-ed) 1977, Sleeping with Lambs 1980, Giving Back Diamonds 1982, The Sunday Before Winter 1984, Grandfather Was A Soldier 1987, Calling All the World 1989, Anyone Can See I Love You (2nd edn) 1989, The Killing Room (2nd edn) 1990, Love As It Is 1992, Autobiography 1996; Plays: Anyone Can See I Love You, Hajimari-No-Hajimari, Temple of the Stars 1996; *Radio programmes include:*

Grandfather Was a Soldier 1983, Anyone Can See I Love You 1986, Laika and Folchakov 1987, A Cold Departure 1989. *Address:* c/o 3777 Jennifer Rd, Victoria, BC V8P 3X1, Canada.

BOWN, Jane Hope, CBE; British photographer; b 13 March 1925, Ledbury; d of Charles Wentworth Bell and Daisy Bown; m Martin Grenville Moss 1954; two s one d. *Education:* William Gibbs School for Girls (Faversham, Kent). *Career:* Photographer for the Observer 1950–; Hon D LITT (Bradford). *Publications:* The Gentle Eye 1980, Women of Consequence 1985, Men of Consequence 1986, The Singular Cat 1988, Pillars of the Church 1991, Jane Bown: Observer 1996, Faces 2000. *Leisure interests:* animals, the country, antiques. *Address:* Old Mill House, 50 Broad St, Alresford SO24 9AN, UK. *Telephone:* (1962) 732419.

BOWTELL, Dame Ann (Elizabeth), DCB, BA; British civil servant; b 25 April 1938, Geneva, Switzerland; d of John Albert and Olive Rose Kewell; m Michael John Bowtell 1961; two s two d. *Education:* Kendrick Girls' School (Reading, Berks) and Girton Coll (Cambridge). *Career:* Joined Nat Assistance Bd, UK 1960, Prin 1964; mem staff Ministry of Social Security 1966–73; Asst Sec Dept of Health and Social Security 1973–80, Under-Sec 1980–86, Deputy Sec Dept of Social Security 1986–90, Perm Sec 1995–99; Deputy Sec Dept of Health 1990–93; Civil Service Commr 1993–95. *Leisure interests:* cooking, reading, walking, music. *Address:* 26 Sidney Rd, Walton-on-Thames, Surrey KT12 2NA, UK.

BOXER, Barbara, BA; American politician; b 11 Nov 1940, Brooklyn, New York; d of Ira Boxer and Sophie (Silvershein) Levy; m Stewart Boxer 1962; one d one s. *Education:* Brooklyn Coll (New York). *Career:* Stockbroker, New York 1962–65; journalist, Assoc Ed 'Pacific Sun' 1972–74; Congressional Aide Republican 5th Congressional Dist, San Francisco, CA 1974–76; mem (Democratic) 98th–102nd Congresses for 6th CA Dist; Senator from CA 1993–; mem Bd Supervisors Marin Co, San Rafael, CA 1976–82, Pres 1980–81; mem Bd Dirs Golden Gate Bridge Highway and Transport Dist, San Francisco, CA 1978–82; Pres Democratic New Mems Caucus 1983; numerous awards. *Address:* US Senate, 112 Hart Senate Office Bldg, Washington, DC 20510, USA.

BOYCOTT, Rosie; British journalist and author; b 13 May 1951; d of Charles and Betty Boycott; m 1st David Leitch (divorced); one d; m 2nd Charles Howard 1999. *Education:* Cheltenham Ladies' Coll and Univ of Kent. *Career:* Founder Spare Rib magazine 1972, Virago Books 1973; mem staff 'Village Voice' (New York); Features Ed Honey; Deputy Ed Male and Femail pages, Daily Mail; Ed Discount Traveller; commissioning Ed The Sunday Telegraph; Deputy Ed Harpers & Queen 1989; Deputy Ed and Features Ed (British) Esquire 1991, Ed 1992–96, of Independent on Sunday 1996–98, of the Independent 1998, of the Express 1998–2001, of the Express on Sunday 1998–2001; involved in the production of Make A Change magazine. *Publication:* A Nice Girl Like Me: A Story of the Seventies. *Address:* c/o Express Newspapers PLC, Ludgate House, 245 Blackfriars Rd, London SE1 9UX, UK (Office).

BOYD, Liona, OC, CM, B MUS; Canadian classical guitarist and composer; b 11 July 1950, London, UK; d of John and Eileen (née Hancock) Boyd; m John B. Simon 1992. *Education:* Kipling Collegiate, Univ of Toronto and Eli Kassner Guitar Acad under Alexandre Lagoya. *Career:* Composer and guitarist, performs and composes both classical and popular music; ; numerous pvt and command performances; first recording 1975; Pres Liona Boyd Productions Inc, Anoil Ltd; numerous int tours, including USA, UK, Brazil, India, Japan, Cuba, Trinidad, Jamaica, Singapore, Nepal, Canada, Germany, Chile; tour of Europe with Tracy Chapman (qv) 1989; Royal Command performances, Ottawa 1975, Edinburgh 1983; first Canadian to perform in the Kremlin—on last day of existence of the USSR 1991; guest artist with several orchestras; numerous TV specials; mem American Fed of Musicians; Hon Mayor of San Antonio, TX, USA; Hon LL D (Lethbridge) 1982, (Brock) 1990, (Simon Fraser) 1991; Four Juno Awards for Instrumental Artist of the Year; Vanier Award 1979; Order of Ontario 1991; four Gold and one Platinum recordings. *Recordings include:* The Guitar Artistry of Liona Boyd 1976, Miniatures for Guitar 1977, The First Lady of the Guitar 1978, Spanish Fantasy 1980, A Guitar for Christmas 1981, Virtuoso 1983, Live in Tokyo 1984, The

Romantic Guitar 1985, Persona 1986, Encore 1989, Christmas Dreams 1989, Highlights 1989, Paddle to the Sea 1990, Dancing on the Edge 1991; *Publications include:* Folk Songs From Around the World, Meet Liona on the Guitar, Favourite Songs. *Leisure interests:* travel, reading, writing, canoeing. *Address:* 3 Canterbury Rd, Islington, ON M9A 5B2, Canada. *Telephone:* (416) 231-0670.

BOYER, Michèle, L ÈS SC; French business executive; b 11 April 1937, Rennes. *Education:* Univ of Paris. *Career:* Sales officer, Dir of Training pharmaceutical laboratory, Riom 1964–73; Regional Dir Smith Kline and French laboratories 1974–76; Dir of Training Lancaster, then Helena Rubinstein and Elizabeth Arden 1977–80; Commercial Dir Learning Int (Times–Mirror Group) 1980–89, Pres, Dir-Gen Kaset Int (Times–Mirror Group) 1989–92; Founder, Co-Dir, Dir-Gen and Commercial Dir Qualistar 1993–; Regional Pres (Ile-de-France) French Commercial Dirs Asscn 1985. *Leisure interests:* reading, film, cooking, golf. *Address:* Qualistar, 59 ave Victor Hugo, 75116 Paris, France (Office); 5 rue Crevaux, 75116 Paris, France (Home). *Telephone:* (1) 53-70-92-94 (Office); *Fax:* (1) 47-55-67-56 (Office).

BOYES, Kate Emily Tyrrell, MA; British civil servant; b 22 April 1918; d of S. F. Boyes; m Cyril Woods Sanders 1944; three d one s. *Education:* Newnham Coll (Cambridge). *Career:* Admin Home Office 1939; Pvt Sec to Parl Sec 1942–45, Prin 1945; Sec to Council on Prices, Productivity and Incomes 1958–60, Asst Sec 1961; Speechwriter to Pres Bd of Trade 1963–64; Under-Sec Europe, Industry and Tech Div, Dept of Trade and Industry (later Dept of Trade) 1972–78; Chair Civil Service Selection Bds 1978–; mem Council Nat Trust 1969–79, Exec Keep Britain Tidy Group 1980–. *Leisure interests:* skiing, sailing, climbing, archaeology. *Address:* 41 Smith St, London SW3 4EP, UK; Giles Point, Winchelsea, Sussex, UK; Canower, Cashel, Connemara, Ireland. *Telephone:* (20) 7352-8053 (London); (1797) 226431 (Sussex).

BOYLAN, Clare Catherine; Irish writer; b 1948, Dublin; d of the late Patrick and of Evelyn Boylan; m Alan Wilkes 1970. *Education:* St Louis Convent School (Dublin). *Career:* Journalist Evening Press, Dublin 1968; Ed Young Woman Magazine 1969, Image magazine, Dublin 1981–84; also TV and radio journalist; Benson and Hedges Prize for outstanding work in Irish journalism 1974; Spirit of Light Award for Literature 1997. *Publications include:* Holy Pictures 1983, Last Resorts 1984, Black Baby 1988, Home Rule 1992, The Agony and the Ego 1993, The Literary Companion to Cats 1994, Room for a Single Lady 1997, Beloved Stranger 1999; four collections of short stories, two non-fiction anthologies (ed). *Address:* c/o Rogers, Coleridge and White, 20 Powis Mews, London W11 1JN, UK (Agent). *Telephone:* (20) 7221-3171.

BOYNER, Umit, B ECON; Turkish business executive; b 1964; m Cem Boyner; two c. *Education:* Univ of Rochester (USA). *Career:* Chief Financial Officer Boyner Holding (retail group). *Address:* A. S. Eski Buyukdere Caddesi, Park Plaza 22, Kat 15 Maslak, 80670 Istanbul, Turkey.

BOZO, Luljeta, DIP ENG, DS; Albanian civil engineer; b 2 Oct 1942, Tirana; d of Vasil and Panajota Konomi; m Todi Bozo 1964; one s one d. *Education:* Inst of Architecture (Moscow) and Tirana Univ. *Career:* Research into construction materials 1965–68, building clay of Tirana 1976–81; teacher Dept of Construction, Univ of Tirana 1968–76, Head of Dept 1985–; Naim Frasheri Prize second degree 1979, first degree 1986. *Publications include:* Building Materials 1980, Mechanics of Soil and Rocks 1983, The Technique of Foundations 1985, Examples of Calculating Foundations 1989; 11 books for students. *Leisure interests:* sport, mountaineering, walking, the arts. *Address:* Ruga Naim Frasheri Pallati, 60/3 Shkolla 2, Ap 29, Tirana, Albania. *Telephone:* (42) 24970.

BRACEWELL, Hon Dame Joyanne, DBE, LL M; British high court judge; b 5 July 1934; d of Jack and Lilian Bracewell; m Roy Copeland 1963; one s one d. *Education:* Univ of Manchester. *Career:* Called to the Bar, Gray's Inn 1955; mem N Circuit 1956–90; Recorder Crown Court 1975–83; QC 1978; Circuit Judge 1983–90; Family Div Liaison Judge for London, High Court 1990–97; Consulting Ed Butterworth's Family Law Service 1989–; Ed-in-Chief The Family Court Practice; Hon LL D

(Manchester) 1991. *Leisure interests:* cooking, reading, walking, wildlife conservation, antiques. *Address:* Royal Courts of Justice, Strand, London WC2A 2LL, UK.

BRADES, Susan Ferleger, MA; American art historian and gallery director; b 7 July 1954, New York; d of Alvin and Beatrice Ferleger; m Peter Brades 1979; one s. *Education:* Univ of Massachusetts (Amherst), Barnard Coll (Columbia Univ, New York) and Courtauld Inst of Art (London). *Career:* Curatorial Co-ordinator The Solomon R. Guggenheim Museum, New York 1975–79; Researcher in British Sculpture in the Twentieth Century, Whitechapel Art Gallery, London 1979–80; Sr Exhibition Organizer and Deputy Dir Hayward Gallery, London 1980–96, Dir 1996–; Art Programme Co-ordinator S Bank Centre, London 1990; Purchaser Arts Council Collection 1983–84, 1985–86, 1988–89, 1996–; mem ICOM, Visual Arts Advisory Cttee; Trustee IVAM Centro Julio Gonzalez (Valencia, Spain); Patron Artworks (Nat Children's Art Awards) 2001; Nat Endowment for the Arts Fellow 1975–76; recipient Travel Grant for Museum Professionals, Smithsonian Inst 1977. *Leisure interests:* swimming, cooking, reading, walking, trail riding. *Address:* Hayward Gallery, South Bank, London SE1 8XX, UK. *Telephone:* (20) 7921-0873; *Fax:* (20) 7401-2664; *E-mail:* sbrades@hayward.org.uk.

BRADFORD, Barbara Taylor; British writer and journalist; b 10 May 1933, Leeds; d of Winston Taylor and Freda Walker; m Robert Bradford 1963. *Education:* Privately. *Career:* Reporter Yorkshire Evening Post 1949–51, Women's Ed 1951–53; Fashion Ed Woman's Own 1953–54; columnist London Evening News 1955–57; Exec Ed London American 1959–62; Ed Nat Design Centre Magazine 1965–69; syndicated columnist Newsday Specials, Long Island, USA 1968–70; nat syndicated columnist Chicago Tribune-New York (News Syndicate), USA 1970–75, Los Angeles Times Syndicate, USA 1975–81; mem Bd American Heritage Dictionary, Police Athletic League, Author's Guild Foundation, Girls Inc; Hon D LITT (Leeds) 1990, (Bradford) 1995, Hon D HUM LITT (Teikyo Post Univ) 1996; numerous awards and prizes. *Publications include:* Non-Fiction: Complete Encyclopaedia of Homemaking Ideas 1968, How to be the Perfect Wife 1969, Easy Steps to Successful Decorating 1971, Decorating Ideas for Casual Living 1977, How to Solve your Decorating Problems 1976, Making Space Grow 1979, Luxury Designs for Apartment Living 1981; Fiction: A Garland of Children's Verse 1968, A Woman of Substance 1979, Voice of the Heart 1982, Hold the Dream 1984, Act of Will 1986, To Be The Best 1988, The Women in his Life 1990, Remember 1991, Angel 1993, Everything to Gain 1994, Dangerous to Know 1995, Love in Another Town 1995, Her Own Rules 1996, A Secret Affair 1996, Power of a Woman 1997, A Sudden Change of Heart 1998, Where You Belong 2000. *Address:* Bradford Enterprises, 450 Park Ave, New York, NY 10022, USA. *Telephone:* (212) 308-7390; *Fax:* (212) 935-1636.

BRADFORD, Jane Mary, FRSA; British banking executive; b 25 Sept 1946, Derby; d of Eric and Winifred Perry; m 1st Paul Adams 1968 (divorced 1984); m 2nd Geoffrey William Bradford 1984. *Education:* Homelands Grammar School for Girls (Derby). *Career:* Joined Westminster Bank 1964, Equal Opportunities Man 1980–82, Branch Man 1982–86, Product and Marketing Man for Commercial Sectors 1986–89, Strategic and Business Planning Man 1989–91, Head of Small Business Serivces 1991–94, Regional Exec Dir 1994–95, Regional Man Dir, Retail Banking Services 1995–; Founder-mem Women in Banking 1980; mem Consumer Cttee Eastern Electricity 1990–92, CBI Small Firms Council 1992–94, Rural Devt Commr 1993–. *Publication:* National Westminster Code for Business Banking 1991. *Address:* National Westminster Bank Plc, Radford House, Radford Blvd, Nottingham NG7 5QG, UK. *Telephone:* (115) 942-1521; *Fax:* (115) 942-0278.

BRADFORD, Sarah Mary Malet (Viscountess Bangor); British writer; b 3 Sept 1938, Bournemouth; d of the late Brig Hilary Anthony Hayes and Mary Beatrice de Carteret Malet; m 1st Anthony John Bradford 1959; one s one d; m 2nd Viscount Bangor 1976. *Education:* St Mary's Convent (Shaftesbury) and Lady Margaret Hall (Oxford). *Publications:* Portugal and Madeira 1969, Portugal 1973, Cesare Borgia 1976, Disraeli 1982, The Story of Port (2nd edn) 1983, Princess Grace 1984, King George VI 1989, Sacheverell Sitwell 1993, Elizabeth, a Biography of Her Majesty The Queen 1996, America's Queen, The Life of

Jacqueline Kennedy Onassis 2000. *Leisure interests:* reading, biographies, diaries, letters, gardening, travelling, watching Liverpool Football Club. *Address:* c/o Gillon Aitken Associates, 29 Fernshaw Rd, London, SW10 0TG, UK. *Telephone:* (20) 7351-7561; *Fax:* (20) 7376-3594; *E-mail:* reception@aitkenassoc.demon.co.uk.

BRADY, Karren Rita; British business/sports executive; b 4 April 1969; d of T. and R. Brady; m Paul Peschisolido 1995; one d. *Education:* Aldenham School (Herts). *Career:* Mem staff Saatchi and Saatchi 1987–88, LBC Radio 1988, various sports newspapers 1988–93, Birmingham City Football Club 1993–, currently Man Dir. *Publications:* Brady plays the Blues 1996, United 1996, Trophy Wives 1998. *Leisure interests:* business, family, writing. *Address:* Birmingham City Football Club, St Andrew's Stadium, Birmingham B9 4NH, UK. *Telephone:* (121) 772-0101; *Fax:* (121) 766-7269; *E-mail:* karrenbrady@ birminghamfc.fsnet.co.uk; *Internet:* www.bcfc.com.

BRAGA, Sonia; Brazilian actress; b 1951, Maringa, Paraná. *Career:* Acting career began at the age of 14 on Brazilian children's TV. *Films include:* The Main Road, A Moreninha, Captain Bandeira vs Dr Moura Brasil, Mestica, The Indomitable Slave, Dona Flor and Her Two Husbands, Gabriella, I Love You, A Lady in the Bus, Kiss of the Spider Woman, The Milagro Beanfield War, Moon Over Parador, The Rookie, Roosters, Two Deaths, Tiete do Agreste 1996, 1998, From Dusk Till Dawn 3: The Hangman's Daughter 2000, Angel Eyes 2001; *TV appearances include:* The Bill Cosby Show, Sesame Street (producer); many Brazilian soap operas.

BRANDT, Ingeborg, MD; German paediatrician; b 19 Jan 1931, Berlin; d of Johannes and Paulina Kietzmann; m Helmut Brandt 1964. *Education:* Berlin, Tübingen, Bonn and Inst of Child Health (London). *Career:* Head Dept of Developmental Paediatrics, Children's Hosp, Rheinische Friedrich-Wilhelms-Univ, Bonn 1979–; Fellow WHO centres for special training in longitudinal studies, USA 1967–68; numerous publications on developmental neurology and growth of infants and children. *Leisure interests:* gardening, music. *Address:* University Children's Hospital Bonn, Zentrum für Kinderheilkunde, Adenauerallee 119, 53113 Bonn, Germany (Office); Pützbroicher Str 24, 53639 Königswinter-Thomasberg, Germany (Home). *Telephone:* (228) 2873239 (Office); (2244) 2580 (Home); *Fax:* (228) 2873314 (Office).

BRAUN, Carol Moseley (see Moseley-Braun, Carol).

BRAUN, Ewa; Polish interior decorator and art director; b 2 Aug 1944, Kraków. *Education:* Warsaw Univ. *Career:* Costume designer Documentary Film Producers 1967–72, interior decorator, art dir Film Production Agency 1972–; mem History of Art Soc 1971–; mem Polish Film Asscn 1994–. *Works include:* Interior decorations and designs in over 60 films including: Illumination 1972, Jealousy and Medicine 1973, Enchanted Beats 1974, Protective Colouring 1976, Nikodem Dyzma's Career 1979, Queen Bona 1980, C. K. Dezerterzy 1985, Wonderful Child (Gdansk Bronze Lion 1987) 1986, Europe, Europe 1989, Schindler's List (Acad Award 1994) 1993, Les Milles 1994, Holy Week 1995, Bandit 1996, Last Chapter 1996, Brother of Our God 1997, Jacob the Liar 1997, Deserters' Gold 1998. *Leisure interests:* movies, travels, music, literature. *Address:* Agencja Produkcji Filmowej, ul Pulawska 61, 02-295 Warsaw, Poland. *Telephone:* (22) 845 40 41.

BRAYFIELD, Celia Frances; British writer and journalist; b 21 Aug 1945, London; d of the late Felix and Ellen (née Jakeman) Brayfield; one d. *Education:* St Paul's Girls' School and Univ de Grenoble. *Career:* Feature writer Daily Mail 1969–71; TV critic London Evening Standard 1974–82, The Times 1983–88; columnist Sunday Telegraph 1989–90, The Times 1998–; contrib to numerous other media; Dir Nat Acad of Writing; mem Cttee of Man Nat Council for One Parent Families 1990–. *Publications:* Glitter: The Truth About Fame 1985, Pearls 1987, The Prince 1990, White Ice 1993, Harvest 1995, Bestseller 1996, Getting Home 1998, Sunset 1999, Heartswap 2000. *Leisure interests:* family life, the arts. *Address:* c/o Curtis Brown Ltd, Haymarket House, 28/29 Haymarket, London SW1Y 4SP, UK. *Telephone:* (20) 7396-6600; *Fax:* (20) 7396 0110; *Internet:* www.celiabrayfield.com.

BRÉCHIGNAC, Catherine, DR SC; French physicist; b 12 June 1946; d of Jean Tillac and Andrée Kerleguer; m Philippe Bréchignac 1969; two s one d. *Education:* Ecole Normale Supérieure, Fontenay-aux-Roses. *Career:* Research Asst CNRS 1971–78, supervisor 1978–85, Dir of Research 1985–91, Del to the Scientific Dir, Dept of Physical and Math Sciences 1985–89, Dir of Aimé Cotton Lab 1989–95, Scientific Dir Dept of Physical and Math Sciences 1995–97, Dir Gen CNRS 1997–; Corresp mem Acad des Sciences 1997–; mem American Acad of Arts and Sciences; Chevalier da la Légion d'Honneur; Chevalier de l'Ordre Nat du Mérite; Acad des Sciences Prize 1991; CNRS Gold Medal 1994. *Leisure interests:* opera, painting, literature. *Address:* Centre National de la Recherche Scientifique, 3-5 rue Michel-Ange, 75794 Paris, Cedex 16, France. *Telephone:* (1) 44-96-40-00; *Fax:* (1) 44-96-50-00.

BREDIN, Frédérique Marie Denise Colette; French business executive; b 2 Nov 1956, Paris; d of Jean-Denis and Danièle (née Hervier) Bredin; m Jean-Pascal Beaufret 1985; two c. *Education:* Inst des Etudes Politiques (Paris) and Ecole Nat d'Admin. *Career:* Insp Gen of Finance 1980–84; special assignment to Minister of Culture 1984–86, to Pres of Repub 1986–88; Socialist Deputy to Nat Ass for Seine-Maritime 1988–91, 1995–, to European Parl 1994–96; Mayor of Fécamp 1989–95; Minister of Youth and Sport 1993–95; Nat Sec Socialist Party, with responsibility for Culture and Media 1996–; mem Haute-Normandie Regional Parl 1998–; Dir of Strategy and Devt, Lagardère Médias 2000–. *Address:* 4 rue de Presbourg, 75116 Paris, France (Office). *Telephone:* (1) 40-69-18-75; *Fax:* (1) 40-69-16-62.

BREGVADZE, Nani Georgievna; Georgian singer; b 21 July 1936, Tbilisi; m Merab Mamaladze 1951; one d. *Education:* Tbilisi State Conservatoire, studied under Machutadze. *Career:* Asst Polytechnical Univ 1962; Soloist with Georgian State Philharmonic Orchestra 1959–, with Rero (Georgian popular orchestra) 1959–64, with Orera 1964–78; specializes in Georgian music and Russian romances; has toured abroad on numerous occasions; has made several films and numerous recordings; People's Artist of USSR 1983, Hon Citizen of Tbilisi 1995, Order of Honour 1994, People's Artist of Georgia 1996, State Prize of Georgia 1997. *Leisure interests:* yoga, classical opera, women's organization. *Address:* Irakly Abashidze str 18A, Apt 10, 380079 Tbilisi, Georgia; Tbilisi, Barnov St 120A, Flat 10, Georgia (Home). *Telephone:* (32) 22-37-22.

BREIEN, Anja; Norwegian film director. *Education:* Inst des hautes études cinématiques (France). *Films include:* short films: 17. Mai—en film om ritualer 1969, Ansikter 1971, Murer rundt fengslet 1972, Herbergister 1973, Mine Søsken, goddag 1974, Gamle 1975, Solvorn 1997; feature films: Vokse opp (Part 1 of Dager fra 100 år) 1967, Voldtekt (Rape) 1971, Hustruer (Wives) 1975, Den Allvarsamme Leken (Games of Love and Loneliness) 1977 (Silver Hugo Award, Chicago 1977), Arven (Next of Kin/The Inheritance) 1979, Forfølgelsen (Witch Hunt) 1981, Papirfuglen (Paper Bird) 1984 (Silver Hugo Award, Chicago 1984), Hustruer—ti år etter (Wives—Ten Years After) 1985, Smykketyven (Twice upon a Time) 1990, Hustruer III (Wives III) 1996; has also written script for film Trollsyn (Second Sight), dir Ola Solum 1994. *Address:* c/o Norsk Film, Filmparken-Wedel Jarlsbergs vei 36, 1342 Jar, Mellbyedalen 8, 0287 Oslo, Norway. *Telephone:* 67-52-53-00; *Fax:* 67-12-51-08.

BREILLAT, Catherine; French writer, scriptwriter and film director; b 13 July 1948, Bressuire; d of Marcel and Marie-Jeanne Breillat; two s one d. *Films include:* Dracula père et fils 1976, Tapage Nocturne 1979, Police (scriptwriter) 1985, 36 Fillette 1988, Aventure de Catherine C. 1990, Sale comme un ange (Dirty Like An Angel) 1991, Romance 1999; *Publications:* L'homme facile 1968, Le silence, après 1970, Le soupirail 1974, Tapage nocturne 1979, Police 1985, 36 fillette 1987, Les vêtements de mer (poems) 1972.

BRENON, Anne; French archivist and historian; b 14 Nov 1945, Mâcon; d of Georges and Jeanne (née Charpigny) Brenon; m 1st Alain Jolliot 1968 (divorced 1974); m 2nd Michel Rion 1976 (divorced 1983); two s one d. *Education:* Lycées de Pont de Vaux and Henri IV (Paris), Ecole Nat des Chartes and Ecole des Hautes Etudes en Sciences Religieuses (Paris). *Career:* Curator Departmental Archive Services 1970–82; Curator seconded to the Centre Nat d'Etudes Cathares 1982–; Editorial Sec Heresis journal; Prix Notre Histoire 1990;

Chevalier des Palmes Académiques 1991. *Publications:* Le vrai visage du Catharisme 1988, Les femmes Cathares 1992, Les prénoms occitans au temps du Catharisme 1992. *Leisure interests:* classical and folk music, walking in the mountains. *Address:* Centre National d'Etudes Cathares, Carcassonne, France (Office); Le Moulin, 11600 Villegly, France (Home). *Telephone:* (4) 68-77-10-21 (Home).

BRÉTECHER, Claire; French cartoonist; b Nantes; one s. *Career:* Cartoon Strip for Nouvel Observateur. *Publications include:* Les Frustrées (5 vols), Both Mothers, Where's My Baby Now?, The Mother, Agrippina 1988, Mothers 1992, Oxford French Cartoon-Strip Vocabulary Builder (illustrator) 2000; *exhibitions include:* Les Etats d'Art de la Bande Dessinée 2001.

BRETH, Andrea; German theatre director; b 31 Oct 1952, Rieden, Allgau; d of Herbert and Maria (née Noether) Breth. *Education:* Darmstadt and Heidelberg. *Career:* Theatre Dir 1976–, Bernarda Albas Haus, Freiburg 1984, Schauspielhaus, Bochum 1986–90, Burgtheatre, Vienna, Austria 1990, 1991, Schaubuhne, Berlin 1991, 1992, Tschulimsk, Wampilow 1992, Kaiser 1993, 1995; mem Berlin Acad of Arts; Deutscher Kritiker Preis; Nordrhein-Westfalen Forderpreis; Kortner Preis. *Plays include:* Lorca 1984, Le Sud, The Last, Zerbrochener Krug, Kleist, Einsamer Weg, Nachtasyl, End of the Begining, Letzen Sommer, Von morgens bis mitternachts, Hedda Gabler, Orestes, Die Möwe. *Leisure interests:* literature, music, painting. *Address:* c/o Schaubühne am Lehniner Platz, Kurfürstendamm 153, 10709 Berlin, Germany.

BREUEL, Birgit; German business executive and politician; b 1937 Hamburg; d of the late Alwin and of Gertrud (née Nolte) Münchmeyer; m Ernst Breuel 1959; three s. *Education:* Univs of Hamburg, Oxford (UK) and Geneva (Switzerland). *Career:* Mem Hamburg State Parl 1970; Minister of Econs, Niedersachsen (Lower Saxony) 1978, of Finance 1986; mem CDU Fed Bd, Bonn 1986; Chief Exec Treuhandanstalt (formed to manage and/or sell fmrly state-owned cos of fmr GDR), Berlin 1990, Pres 1991–95; Gen Sec, Co-ordinator and Chief Del Expo 2000, Hanover 1995–; Chair Bd Deutsche Messe AG, Hanover; mem Bd Volkswagen AG, Norddeutsche Landesbank AG, Deutsche Bundesbahn AG, Salzgitter AG, PREAG; Adviser Hamburg-Mannheimer Versicherung AG, Zweites Deutsches Fernsehen (ZDF); Senator Max Planck Gesellschaft, Munich; Dr hc (Cologne) 1994. *Publications:* Es gibt kein Butterbrot umsonst 1976, Der Amtsschimmel absatteln 1979, Der Mensch lebt nicht nur von Umsatzzahlen 1987. *Address:* EXPO 2000 Hannover GmbH, EXPO Plaza11-Gelände, 30521 Hanover, Germany (Office).

BREWSTER, Elizabeth Winifred, B LS, MA, PH D; Canadian professor of English and writer; b 26 Aug 1922, Chipman, NB; d of Frederick and Ethel (née Day) Brewster. *Education:* Univ of New Brunswick, Radcliffe Coll, King's Coll (London), Univs of Toronto and Indiana (USA). *Career:* Faculty mem Univ of Saskatchewan 1972–, Prof of English 1980–90, Prof Emer 1990–; staff mem numerous libraries; mem League of Canadian Poets, Writers' Union of Canada, Asscn of Canadian Univ Teachers of English, Canadian Asscn of Commonwealth Literature and Language Studies, PEN Club Int; Hon D LITT (New Brunswick) 1982; Canadian Council of Sr Artists Awards for Poetry 1971–72, 1976, 1978–79, 1985–86; Pres's Medal for Poetry, Univ of Western Ontario 1980; Literary Award, Canadian Broadcasting Corp 1991; Saskatoon Arts Bd Award for Lifetime Excellence in the Arts 1995. *Publications include:* Poetry: East Coast 1951, Passage of Summer 1969, Sunrise North 1972, In Search of Eros 1974, Sometimes I Think of Moving 1977, It's Easy to Fall on the Ice 1977, The Way Home 1982, Digging In 1982, Entertaining Angels 1988, Spring Again 1990, The Invention of Truth 1991, Wheel of Change 1993, Footnotes to the Book of Job 1995, Garden of Sculpture 1998, Burning Bush 2000; Novels: The Sisters 1974, Junction 1982; Short stories: A House Full of Women 1983, Visitations 1987. *Address:* 206 Colony Square, 910 9th St East, Saskatoon, SK S7H 0N1, Canada (Home); University of Saskatchewan, Dept of English, Saskatoon, SK S7N OWO, Canada. *Telephone:* (306) 343-7695.

BREWSTER, Samantha; British yachtswoman; b 5 July 1967. *Career:* Fmr outdoor activities technician Outdoor Pursuits Centre, Ambleside, Cumbria; crew volunteer on yacht Heath Insured in British Steel Challenge Round the World Yacht Race (East–West) 1992–93; First

Mate on Heath Insured Round Britain Tour 1994; First Mate on Heath Insured, Challenge Adventure sailing, Plymouth (UK)–Boston (MA, USA) and back 1994; sailed single-handed and non-stop round the world from East–West on Heath Insured (first woman and youngest person) 1995–96. *Address:* c/o Albemarle Connection, 99 Charterhouse St, London EC1M 6HR, UK.

BREYER, Hiltrud; German politician; b 22 Aug 1957, Saarbrücken. *Career:* MEP (Die Grünen) 1989–, mem Cttee on the Environment, Public Health and Consumer Protection, Del for Relations with the Countries of S Asia and the S Asia Asscn for Regional Co-operation (SAARC); campaigner against pollution, Saarland, Germany, and against nuclear contamination. *Address:* European Parliament, rue Wiertz, ASP 8G265, 1047 Brussels, Belgium; Regionalbüro, Ormesheimer Straße, 66399 Mandelbachtal Saarbrücken, Germany. *Telephone:* (2) 284-52-87 (Belgium); *Fax:* (2) 284-92-87 (Belgium); *E-mail:* hbreyer@europarl.eu.int; *Internet:* www.hiltrud-breyer.de.

BRIDGEMAN, June, CB, BA, FRSA; British public servant; b 26 June 1932, London; d of Gordon and Elsie Forbes; m John Michael Bridgeman 1958; four d one s. *Education:* Westfield Coll (London). *Career:* Civil servant 1954–90, Under-Sec 1974–90; has served at Bd of Trade, Dept of Econ Affairs, Prices and Incomes Bd, Ministry of Housing and Local Govt, Dept of the Environment, Cabinet Office Cen Policy Review Staff 1976–79, Dept of Transport 1979–90; Deputy Chair Equal Opportunities Comm 1991–94; Nat Council for One Parent Families 1994–; Vice-Pres Fawcett Soc 1994–; Bishops Selector, Advisory Council for Church's Ministry 1974–89; mem Council Policy Studies Inst 1984–90, Girls Public Day School Trust 1995–; Fellow Queen Mary and Westfield Coll 1993. *Leisure interest:* feminism. *Address:* Bridge House, Culverden Park Rd, Tunbridge Wells TN4 9QX, UK. *Telephone:* (1892) 525578.

BRIDGEMAN, Victoria Harriet Lucy (Viscountess Bridgeman), MA, FSA; British fine arts specialist and library executive; b 30 March 1942, Co Durham; d of Ralph Meredyth Turton and Mary Blanche (née Chetwynd Stapylton) Turton; m Viscount Bridgeman 1966; four s. *Education:* St Mary's School (Wantage) and Trinity Coll (Dublin). *Career:* Exec Ed The Masters 1965–69; Ed Discovering Antiques 1970–72; est own co producing books and articles on fine and decorative arts; Founder, Man Dir The Bridgeman Art Library; European Woman of the Year (Arts Section) Award 1997. *Publications:* Encyclopaedia of Victoriana, Needlework: An Illustrated History, The British Eccentric 1975, Society Scandals 1977, Beside the Seaside 1977, Guide to the Gardens of Europe 1980, The Last Word 1982 (all jtly with Elizabeth Drury), eight titles in Connoisseur's Library series. *Leisure interests:* reading, family, travel. *Address:* The Bridgeman Art Library, 17–19 Garway Rd, London W2 4PH, UK (Office); The Bridgeman Art Library Int, 65 East 93rd St, NY 10128, USA (Office); The Bridgeman Art Library, 31 rue Etienne Marcel, 75001 Paris, France (Office); 19 Chepstow Rd, London W2 5BP, UK (Home); Watley House, Sparsholt, Nr Winchester, Hants SO21 2LU, UK. *Telephone:* (20) 7727-4065 (London Office); (1962) 776297 (Hants); (20) 7727-5400 (London Home); *Fax:* (20) 7792-8509 (London Office); (1962) 776297 (Hants); (20) 7792-9178 (London Home).

BRIEDIENE, Vanda; Lithuanian folk artist; b 12 Jan 1944, Biržai, d of Alvina Puziniene and Juozapas Puzinas; m Povilas Briedis 1968; three s. *Education:* Nemunelio Radviliškis School. *Career:* Worked on collective farms 1960–80, at a kindergarten 1981–91; folk artist (painting, carving, knitting, weaving, ceramics) 1981–96, numerous group exhibitions; awards include Liongino Šepkos Prize 1994. *Leisure interests:* music, gardening, cooking, baking, sewing, embroidery. *Address:* 5291 Biržu Raj, Apaščios 34, Nemunelio Radviliškis, Lithuania. *Telephone:* (20) 55340.

BRIGGS, Karen Valerie, MBE; British sportswoman; b 11 April 1963, Hull, N Humberside; d of Albert and Elsie May Briggs. *Education:* Bransholme High School (Hull) and Hull Coll of Further Educ. *Career:* Judo Black Belt 1980; mem British Judo Team 1980–; World Judo Champion (under 48kg) 1982, 1984, 1986, 1989; European Champion (under 48kg) 1982–1984, 1986, 1987; Japanese Open Champion (under 48kg) 1983–1986, 1988; Gold Medallist, Commonwealth Games 1990; mem British Olympic Judo Team (under 48kg); currently coaching at Hull School of Judo (Humberside, UK). *Publications:* Blood, Sweat and Tears (play) 1986, Karen Briggs Judo Champion 1987. *Leisure interests:* running, swimming, squash, cycling, weight-training. *Address:* School of Judo, Beverley Rd, Hull, UK. *Telephone:* (1482) 821479.

BRIGHTMAN, Sarah; British actress and singer; d of Grenville and Pauline (née Hall) Brightman; m Andrew Lloyd Webber 1984 (divorced 1990); partner Frank Peterson. *Career:* Fmr singer with Pan's People and Hot Gossip groups; concerts world-wide; has performed in numerous works written by Andrew Lloyd Webber. *Performances include:* Cats, Requiem Mass, Phantom of the Opera, Aspects of Love, I and Albert, The Nightingale, The Merry Widow, Trelawney of the Wells, Relative Values, Dangerous Obsession; *Albums include:* Eden 1999; *Singles:* I Lost My Heart to a Starship Trouper, Pie Jesu, Amigos para siempre (with José Carreras) 1992. *Address:* c/o Sunhand Limited, 63 Grosvenor St, London, W1X 9DA, UK (Office). *Telephone:* (20) 7493-7831 (Office).

BRINDLEY, Lynne Janie, MA, FLA, FRSA; British librarian; b 2 July 1950, London; d of Ivan and Janie (née Williams) Blowers; m Timothy Stuart Brindley 1972. *Education:* Truro High School, Univ of Reading, Univ Coll London. *Career:* Head of Marketing and of Chief Exec's Office, British Library 1979–85, Chief Exec British Library 2000–; Dir of Library and Information Services, also Pro-Vice Chancellor Aston Univ 1985–90; Prin Consultant KPMG 1990–92; Librarian and Dir of Information Services LSE 1992–97; Librarian and Pro-Vice Chancellor Univ of Leeds 1997–2000, Visiting Prof of Knowledge Man 2000–; Visiting Prof of Information Man Leeds Metropolitan Univ 2000–; mem Int Cttee on Social Science Information, UNESCO 1992–97, Lord Chancellor's Advisory Cttee on Public Records 1992–98, Stanford Univ Advisory Council for Libraries and Information Resources 1999; Trustee Thackray Medical Museum, Leeds 1999–; Hon D LITT (Nottingham) 2001; Freeman, City of London 1989; Liveryman, Goldsmiths' Co 1993. *Publications:* numerous articles on electronic libraries and information man. *Leisure interests:* classical music, theatre, modern art, hill walking. *Address:* The British Library, 96 Euston Rd, London, NW1 2DB, UK (Office); 85 New River Head, 173 Rosebery Ave, London EC1R 4UP, UK (Home). *Telephone:* (20) 7412-7273; *Fax:* (20) 7412-7268; *E-mail:* chief-executive@bl.uk; *Internet:* www.bl.uk.

BRINK, Nina; American business executive; b 1955. *Career:* Fmr dir of electronics components distribution co; Founder and Chair World Online Int NV 1997–2000; Co-Founder Renessence Ventures 2000; Business Woman of the Year Telecom Trade Show (Geneva, Switzerland) 1999. *Address:* Charles House, 18B Charles St, London, W1, UK.

BRINKER-GABLER, Gisela, D PHIL; German professor of comparative literature; m Udo H. Brinker; one s. *Education:* Univ of Cologne. *Career:* Asst Prof Univ of Florida, USA 1974–75; Lecturer Univ of Essen 1976–81, Univ of Cologne 1981–88; Ed book series Die Frau in der Gesellschaft for Fischer publrs, Frankfurt/Main 1978–86; Prof of Comparative Literature, State Univ of New York at Binghamton, USA 1989–. *Publications:* Deutsche Dichterinnen vom 16. Jahrhundert bis zur Gegenwart 1978; Ed: Zur Psychologie der Frau 1978, Fanny Lewald: Meine Lebensgeschichte 1980, Toni Sender: Autobiographie einer deutschen Rebellin 1981, Bertha von Suttner: Kämpferin für den Frieden 1983, Deutsche Literatur von Frauen vom 18. Jahrhundert bis zur Gegenwart 1988, Encountering the Other(s) 1995, Writing New Identities: Gender, Nation and Immigration in the Contemporary Europe 1996. *Address:* State University of New York at Binghamton, Comparative Literature, Binghamton, NY 13902-6000, USA. *Telephone:* (607) 777-2890; *Fax:* (607) 777-2892.

BRISEPIERRE, Paulette Louise Fernande Mireille; French politician; b 21 April 1917, Bordeaux; m 1st Baron Lionel de la Fontaine (deceased); five s two d; m 2nd Charles Brisepierre. *Education:* Univ of Michigan (USA). *Career:* Adviser French External Trade 1968–; mem Superior Council, French Nationals Abroad 1968–, Vice-Pres 1974–77; elected RPR Senator for French ex-patriots 1989–; mem Econ and Social Council 1976–78, 1980–82, 1986–88; Chevalier de la Légion d'Honneur; Officier de l'Ordre Nat du Mérite; Chevalier du Mérite

Agricole. *Address:* Sénat, Palais du Luxembourg, 75291, Paris Cedex 06, France (Office); 18 rue de Bourgogne, 75007 Paris, France (Home). *Telephone:* (1) 42-34-20-00 (Office); *Fax:* (1) 43-29-86-47 (Office).

BRITTON, Rita; British fashion executive; b Barnsley; m Geoff Britton 1973; three s. *Education:* Barnsley Lea Secondary Modern and Raley School. *Career:* Mill worker 1959–66; f Pollyanna (Barnsley and Glasgow) 1966–; Advisor to 'New Deal' 1998, Nation Skills Task Force 1998–2000; Gov N Coll 1995–98, Bretton Hall Coll (Leeds) 1999–2001; consultant, advisor and lecturer at numerous colls of Fashion and Design. *Leisure interest:* learning. *Address:* Pollyanna, 16 Market Hill, Barnsley, Yorks S7O 2QE, UK (Office); Hoylandswain, Barnsley, Yorks, UK (Home). *Telephone:* (1226) 291665 (Office); *Fax:* (1226) 206075; *E-mail:* enquiries@pollyanna.com.

BRÖCKER, Marianne G. J., PH D; Netherlands management consultant; b 5 Dec 1956, Ukkel, Belgium. *Education:* Univ of Groningen. *Career:* Man Consultant M D P 1987–; Vice-Pres women's org, Nederlandse Vereniging van Vrouwen met Academische Opleiding (VVAO) 1990–, Pres 1992–. *Publications:* Het vaststellen van werkgedrageffecten van bedrijfsopleidingen, Wetenswaardigheden voor opleiders (jtly) 1988. *Address:* Nederlandsche Vereniging van Vrouwn met Academische Opleiding, POB 13226, 3507 LE Utrecht, Netherlands; Bybaen 12, 8624 TE Uitwellingerga, Netherlands. *Telephone:* (5135) 418; *Fax:* (50) 25-03-67.

BRODIN, Katarina, MA, PH D; Swedish civil servant and diplomatist; b 8 Sept 1934, Örebro; d of Per and Karin (née Krook) Barck; m 1st Ulf Brodin 1961 (divorced 1981); two d; m 2nd P. O.Ahlin 1982. *Education:* Helsinki School of Econs and Univs of Helsinki and Stockholm. *Career:* Mem staff Swedish Inst of International Affairs 1962–74; Research Assoc Swedish Nat Defence Research Inst, Stockholm 1975–76; Head Int Studies Prog, Secr of Nat Security and Long-Term Planning, Ministry of Defence 1976–83, Sr Adviser to Minister 1983–84; Asst Under-Sec for Nat Security Affairs, Political Dept, Ministry of Foreign Affairs 1984–90, Counsellor Embassy, Sweden 1991–95, Amb to Estonia 1995; mem Royal Swedish Acad of Military Sciences; numerous books and articles on int relations. *Address:* c/o Ministry of Foreign Affairs, Box 16121, 10323 Stockholm, Sweden.

BRODY, Jane Ellen, MS; American journalist; b 19 May 1941, Brooklyn, NY; d of Sidney Brody and Lillian Kellner; m Richard Engquist 1966; two s. *Education:* New York State Coll of Agric, Cornell Univ and Univ of Wisconsin. *Career:* Reporter Minnesota Tribune 1963–65; science writer, personal health columnist, New York Times 1965–; mem Advisory Council New York State Coll of Agric 1971–77; numerous awards including Howard Blakeslee Award, American Heart Asscn 1971, Science Writers' Award, ADA 1978, J. C. Penney-Univ of Missouri Journalism Award 1978, Lifeline Award, American Health Foundation 1978. *Publications include:* Secrets of Good Health (jtly) 1970, You Can Fight Cancer and Win (jtly) 1977, Jane Brody's Nutrition Book 1981, Jane Brody's New York Times Guide to Personal Health 1982, Jane Brody's Good Food Book 1985, Jane Brody's Good Food Gourmet 1989, Jane Brody's Good Seafood Book (jtly) 1994, Jane Brody's Cold and Flu Fighter 1995, Jane Brody's Allergy Fighter 1997, The New York Times Book of Health 1997. *Address:* c/o New York Times, 229 W 43rd St, New York, NY 10036, USA.

BROGLIE, Jeanne Marie-Osmonde Dolorès de, L ÈS L; French business executive (retd); b 26 March 1929, Paris; d of Gilles, Duc de Maillé, and Princess Anne-Marie Radziwill; m Prince Guy de Broglie 1949 (divorced 1962); one s one d. *Education:* Privately, Pensionnat des Dominicaines (Asnières-sur-Seine), Inst Sainte-Marie (Neuilly-sur-Seine) and Univ of Paris (Sorbonne). *Career:* Galeries Daniel Cordier, Paris 1956–59; Dir Salons Pierre Cardin 1960–; pvt dealer in modern paintings 1961–68; Dir Christie's France 1968–88, Chair Christie's Europe 1984–88; wrote articles for Connaissance des Arts and Belvédère; mem Conseil des Amis du Musée d'Orsay, Soc des Amis du Musée Nat d'Art Moderne, Asscn pour le Rayonnement de l'Opéra, Conseil des Amis du Louvre. *Leisure interests:* travel, opera, literature, gardening. *Address:* 32 rue Washington, 75008 Paris, France (Home); La Vignerme, 84800 Saumane de Vaucluse, France (Home). *Telephone:* (1) 45-63-80-80 (Paris); *Fax:* (1) 45-63-80-80 (Paris).

BRON, Eleanor, BA; British actress and writer; b 14 March 1938, Stanmore; d of Sydney and Fagah Bron. *Education:* North London Collegiate School and Newnham Coll (Cambridge). *Career:* Started at Establishment Night Club, toured USA 1961; appearances on stage and screen; Dir Actors' Centre 1982–93, Soho Theatre Co 1994–2000. *Plays include:* The Prime of Miss Jean Brodie 1967, 1984, Hedda Gabler 1969, The Merchant of Venice 1975, Private Lives 1976, Uncle Vanya 1977, The Cherry Orchard 1978, On Her Own 1980, The Amusing Spectacle of Cinderella and Her Naughty, Naughty Sisters 1980, Betrayal 1981, Heartbreak House 1981, Duet for One 1982, The Real Inspector Hound 1985, The Duchess of Malfi 1985, Oedipus 1987, The Madwoman of Chaillot 1988, The Chalk Garden 1989, The Miser 1991, The White Devil 1991, Die Glückliche Hand (Opera) 1991, Desdemona – If You Had Only Spoken 1992 (one-woman show), Hamlet 1993, A Delicate Balance 1996, A Perfect Ganesh 1996, Be My Baby, Making Noise Quietly; *Films include:* Help!, Alfie, Two For the Road, Bedazzled, Women in Love, The National Health, Turtle Diary, The Day that Christ Died 1980, Little Dorrit 1987, The Attic 1988, Deadly Advice, Black Beauty, A Little Princess, The House of Mirth 2000; *TV appearances include:* Nina 1978, A Month in the Country 1985, Quatermaine's Terms 1987, The Hour of the Lynx 1990; *Concert appearances (as narrator) include:* Façade, Carnival des Animaux, Peter and the Wolf; *Publications:* Song Cycle (jtly) 1973, verses for Saint-Saëns Carnival of the Animals 1975, Is Your Marriage Really Necessary? (jtly) 1972, Life and Other Punctures 1978, The Pillow Book of Eleanor Bron 1985, Desdemona – If You Had Only Spoken! (translation of original by Christine Brückner (qv)) 1992, Double Take (novel) 1996. *Address:* c/o Rebecca Blond, 69A King's Rd, London, SW3 4NX, UK (Office). *Telephone:* (20) 7351-4100 (Office); *Fax:* (20) 7351-4600 (Office).

BROOKE-ROSE, Christine, PH D; British professor of English, writer and critic. *Education:* Univs of London and Oxford. *Career:* Researcher and critic 1955–; Reviewer Times Literary Supplement, The Times, Observer, The Sunday Times, The Listener, The Spectator, The London Magazine 1956–68; Lecturer Univ of Paris 1969–75, Prof of English Language and Literature 1975–88; Hon D LITT (E Anglia) 1988; James Tait Black Memorial Prize 1966. *Publications:* Novels: The Languages of Love 1957, The Sycamore Tree 1958, The Dear Deceit 1960, The Middlemen 1961, Out 1964, Such 1965, Between 1968, Thru 1975, Amalgamemnon 1984, Xorander 1986, Verbivore 1990, Textermination 1991, Remake 1996, Next 1998, Subscript 1999; Criticism: A Grammar of Metaphor 1958, A ZBC of Ezra Pound 1971, A Rhetoric of the Unreal 1981, Stories, Theories and Things 1991; Short Stories: Go When You See the Green Man Walking 1969. *Leisure interests:* travel, people. *Address:* c/o Cambridge University Press, POB 110, Cambridge CB2 3RL, UK.

BROOKNER, Anita, CBE; British art historian and writer; b 16 July 1928; d of Newson and Maude Brookner. *Education:* James Allen's Girls' School, King's Coll (London), Courtauld Inst (London) and Paris. *Career:* Visiting Lecturer Univ of Reading 1959–64; Lecturer Courtauld Inst of Art 1964, Reader 1977–87; Slade Prof Univ of Cambridge 1967–68; Fellow New Hall, Cambridge, King's Coll, London; Hon D LITT (Loughborough Univ of Tech) 1990, Dr hc (Smith Coll, USA). *Publications:* Watteau 1968, The Genius of the Future 1971, Greuze: the Rise and Fall of an Eighteenth Century Phenomenon 1972, Jacques-Louis David 1980, A Start in Life 1981, Providence 1982, Look at Me 1983, Hôtel du Lac (Booker Prize for Fiction) 1984, Family and Friends 1985, A Misalliance 1986, A Friend from England 1987, Latecomers 1988, The Stories of Edith Wharton (ed) 1988, Lewis Percy 1989, Brief Lives 1990, Fraud 1992, A Family Romance 1993, A Private View 1994, Incidents in the rue Laugier 1995, Altered States 1996, Visitors 1997, Soundings 1997, Falling Slowly 1998; articles in Burlington Magazine etc. *Address:* 68 Elm Park Gardens, London SW10 9PB, UK. *Telephone:* (20) 7352-6894.

BROOKS, Alison, B ARCH; Canadian architect; b 29 Dec 1962; d of Geoffrey F. Brooks and Barbara A. Robinson; m Charles H. Walker 1994; two s. *Education:* Univ of Waterloo (Ontario). *Career:* Partner Ron Arad Assocs 1991–96; f Alison Brooks Architects (ABA) 1996; Speaker Royal Architectural Inst of Canada 2001; mem RIBA 1990–, Architecture Foundation Programme Council; British Steel Young Architect of the Year Award 1999. *Design projects include:* Chalk Farm Studios, London 1991, New Tel Aviv Opera, Israel 1994, Belgo Noord, London

1994, Belgo Centraal, London 1995, Adidas Sports Café, Toulon 1996, Atoll Hotel, Helgoland 1999 (two HotelSpec European Hotel Design and Devt Awards), Street Furniture in Rope Walks, Liverpool; several pvt residential comms. *Address:* 35 Britannia Row, London N1 8QH, UK; 99 Tennyson Rd, London NW6 7RU, UK. *Telephone:* (20) 7704-8808; *Fax:* (20) 7704-8409; *E-mail:* info@abaspace.com.

BROOKS, Diana (Dede), AB; American business executive; b 1950, Glen Cove, NY; m Michael C. Brooks; two c. *Education:* Miss Porter's School (Farmington, CT), Smith Coll and Yale Univ (CT). *Career:* Joined Sotheby's (New York) 1979, Sr Vice-Pres, Chief Finance and Admin Officer 1982–84, Exec Vice-Pres 1984–85, COO 1985–87, Pres 1987–90, Pres and CEO 1990–; Pres and CEO Sotheby's Holdings Inc 1993–; Trustee Yale Univ (CT). *Address:* Sotheby's Inc, 1334 York Ave, New York, NY 10021-4806, USA.

BROOKS, Reva; Canadian photographer; b 10 May 1913, Toronto, ON; d of Morris and Jeannie (née Klein) Silverman; m Leonard Brooks 1935. *Education:* Univ of Toronto. *Career:* Solo exhibitions include Santa Barbara Museum of Art, Anglo-Mexican Inst (México), Witte Museum (TX, USA), Museum of Modern Art (New York), Dartmouth Coll; group exhibitions include Salon Int du Portrait Photographique (Paris) 1961, Versailles (France) 1962, Expo Montréal 1967, Palacio de Bellas Artes (México) 1970, Royal Ontario Museum 1972; works in collections including Bibliothèque Nat de Paris, David Alfaro Siqueiros (México), Rico Lebrum (Los Angeles, USA), John Huston (Ireland), Henry Miller (California); numerous contribs to catalogues; established Leonard and Reva Brooks Foundation 1992. *Address:* Calle Quinta 10, Colonia Guadiana, CP 84, San Miguel de Allende, GTO 37700, Mexico.

BROOME, Claire Veronica, BA, MD; American epidemiologist and researcher; b 24 Aug 1949, Tunbridge Wells, UK; d of Kenneth and Heather (née Platt) Broome; m John Head 1988; one s. *Education:* Harvard Univ. *Career:* Deputy Chief Special Pathogens Br, Centers for Disease Control, Atlanta, GA 1979–80, Chief of Meningitis and Special Pathogens Br 1981–90, Assoc Dir for Science 1991–94, Deputy Dir 1994–; Consultant on Vaccine Devt, Agency for Int Devt 1988–; mem WHO Programme for Vaccine Devt Steering Cttee on Encapsulated Bacteria 1988–91, Chair 1992–; Consultant NIH, numerous univs; mem Advisory Cttee on Vaccines, Food and Drug Admin, Washington, DC 1990–; Fellow Infectious Diseases Soc of America; mem ACP, American Epidemiologic Soc, American Soc of Microbiology; numerous contribs to scientific journals; Rockefeller Fellow 1970–71; awards include Meritorious Service Medal, US Public Health Service 1986, Shephard Award 1986. *Address:* Centers for Disease Control, D-39, Atlanta, GA 30333, USA. *Telephone:* (404) 639-7000; *Fax:* (404) 639-7111.

BROUN, Elizabeth, PH D; American museum director; b 15 Dec 1946, Kansas City, MO; d of Augustine Hughes and Roberta Catherine (née Hayden) Gibson; m Ronald Broun 1968. *Education:* Univs of Missouri and Bordeaux (France). *Career:* Curator of Prints and Drawings Spencer Museum of Art, Kansas 1976–83; Asst Prof Univ of Missouri 1978–83; Asst Dir and Chief Curator Nat Museum of American Art, Washington, DC 1983–88, Dir 1989–; many exhibition catalogues 1979–; Woodrow Wilson Fellow 1968–69, Ford Foundation Fellow 1970–72. *Address:* National Museum of American Art, 8th and G Sts, NW, Washington, DC 20560, USA.

BROUWENSTYN, Gerarda; Netherlands opera singer. *Education:* Amsterdam. *Career:* Joined Amsterdam Opera and became First Soprano; has appeared in UK, Spain, Germany, Belgium, Denmark, Austria and Argentina; Order of Orange-Nassau. *Operas include:* La Forza del Destino, Tosca, Aida, Otello, Un Ballo in Maschera, Tannhäuser, Die Walküre, Die Meistersinger, Le Nozze di Figaro, Jenufa, Troubadour, Cavalleria Rusticana, Don Carlos.

BROWN, Denise (see Scott Brown, Denise).

BROWN, Gillian, CBE, PH D; British professor of English; b 23 Jan 1937; d of Geoffrey Rencher Read and Elsie Chapman; m Edward Brown 1959; three d. *Education:* Girton Coll (Cambridge) and Univ of

Edinburgh. *Career:* Lecturer Univ Coll of Cape Coast, Ghana 1962–64; Lecturer Univ of Edinburgh 1965–81, Reader 1981–83; Prof Univ of Essex 1983–88; Prof of English as Int Language, Univ of Cambridge 1988–; mem numerous editorial bds; mem Educ and Human Devt Cttee, Econ and Social Research Council 1983–87, Chair Research Grants Bd 1987–90; Gov Bell Educational Trust 1987–92; mem Council Philological Soc 1988–93, English Teaching Advisory Cttee, British Council 1989–94, Cttee of Man British Inst in Paris 1990; Curator School of Advanced Studies, Univ of London 1994–; Dr hc (Lyons) 1987. *Publications include:* Phenological Rules and Dialect Variation 1972, Listening to Spoken English 1977, Discourse Analysis (jtly) 1983; articles in professional journals. *Address:* Clare College, Cambridge CB2 1TL, UK.

BROWN, Helen Gurley (see Gurley Brown, Helen).

BROWN, Iona, OBE; British violinist and artistic director; b 7 Jan 1941, Salisbury. *Education:* Studied under Hugh Maguire, Remy Principe and Henryk Szeryng. *Career:* Violinist Nat Youth Orchestra of GB 1955–60, Philharmonic Orchestra of London 1963–66, Acad of St Martin-in-the-Fields, London 1964–, Concertmaster and Dir 1974–; Artistic and Music Dir Norwegian Chamber Orchestra; Guest Dir City of Birmingham Symphony Orchestra 1985–89; Musical Dir Los Angeles Chamber Orchestra, CA, USA 1987; has performed at concert halls and festivals world-wide and with orchestras including the San Francisco Symphony, St Louis Symphony, Nat Symphony Washington, San Diego Symphony, Detroit Symphony (all USA), Vancouver Symphony (Canada), Lausanne Chamber (Switzerland), Oslo Philharmonic (Norway), Stuttgart Chamber, Halle and Leipzig (Germany), Aarhus Symphony (Denmark), Tokyo Symphony (Japan) and Jerusalem Symphony (Israel); Hon mem RAM 1996; Order of Merit (KT, First Class), King Harald of Norway 1991; Instrumentalist of the Year, Royal Philharmonic Soc 1994. *Recordings include:* Vaughan-Williams' Lark Ascending, Beethoven's Violin Concerto, Vivaldi's Four Seasons, Mozart's violin concerti, Handel's Concerti Grossi Op 3 and 6, Bartok's Second Violin Concerto, David Blake's Vioin Concerto. *Address:* Little Misselfore, Bowerchalke, Salisbury, Wilts SP5 5BZ, UK.

BROWN, June Gibbs, MBA, JD, CPA; American former government agency official; b 5 Oct 1933, Cleveland, OH; d of Thomas D. and Lorna Merritt Gibbs; m 1st Victor Janezic 1952 (divorced 1974); m 2nd Ray L. Brown 1975 (divorced 1990); three d one s. *Education:* Cleveland State Univ, Univ of Denver and Harvard Univ. *Career:* Insp-Gen Dept of Interior 1978–81, Insp-Gen NASA 1981–85, Insp-Gen US Dept of Defense 1987–89; Vice-Pres and Chief Financial Officer Systems Devt Corpn 1985–86; Assoc Admin for Man NASA 1986–87; Deputy Insp-Gen US Navy Pacific Fleet 1989–91, Insp-Gen 1991–93; Insp-Gen Dept of Health and Human Services (HHS), Washington, DC 1993–2001; retd 2001; fmrly served at Bureau of Land Man, Bureau of Reclamation and Navy Finance Centre; mem Bd Dirs Hawaii Soc of CPAs 1990–93; Vice-Chair Pres's Council on Integrity and Efficiency; Certified Govt Financial Man; fmr Pres Asscn of Govt Accountants; fmr mem Pres's Council on Integrity and Efficiency, Pres's Council for Man Improvement, Bd of Advisers, Nat Contract Man Asscn, Bd Dirs Fed Law Enforcement Training Center, Interagency Auditor Training Program, Dept of Agric Grad School; Fellow Nat Acad of Public Admin; Grad Advanced Man Program; numerous awards including Financial Management Improvement Award (Jt Financial Man Improvement Program) 1980, Exceptional Service Medal (NASA) 1985, Outstanding Achievement in Aerospace Award (Women in Aerospace) 1987, Robert W. King Memorial Award (Asscn of Govt Accountants) 1988, Distinguished Service Medal (Dept of Defense) 1989; Leadership Award, Govt Exec Magazine and Nat Capital Area Chapter, American Soc of Public Admin 1994. *Leisure interests:* travel, hiking, scuba diving. *Address:* 7306 Bloomsbury Lane, Spotsylvania, VA 22553, USA. *Telephone:* (540) 710-6236; *Fax:* (540) 710-5342; *E-mail:* igjgb@yahoo.com.

BROWN, Kathleen, BA; American state government official and banking executive; d of Edmund and Bernice Brown; m 1st George Rice (divorced 1979); three c; m 2nd Van Gordon Sauter 1980; two step-s. *Education:* Stanford and Fordham Univs. *Career:* Mem Los Angeles Bd of Educ 1975–80; joined O'Melveny and Myers, New York and Los Angeles; Commr Los Angeles Bd of Public Works 1987–; Treas of

California 1990–94; Exec Vice-Pres Bank of America, LA 1994–99; Pres Pvt Bank W 1999–; Co-Chair Capital Budget Comm, Washington 1997—. *Address:* c/o Bank of America, 555 S Flower St, 51th Floor, Los Angeles, USA. *Telephone:* CA 90071.

BROWN, Rebecca; Australian swimmer; b 8 May 1977, Brisbane. *Career:* Australian record holder 100m and 200m breast stroke 1993; World Record Holder for 200m breast stroke 1994; Silver Medallist Commonwealth Games 1994; competed in World Championships 1994; Nat MLC Jr Sports Foundation winner 1994; Channel 7/Coca Cola Jr Sports Star 1994. *Leisure interests:* TV, films, reading, music. *Address:* 14 West St, Highgate Hill, Brisbane, 4101 QLD, Australia. *Telephone:* (7) 3846 1624.

BROWN, Rita Mae, BA, PH D; American writer and scriptwriter; b 28 Nov 1944, Hanover, PA; d of Ralph and Julia Brown. *Education:* Broward Jr Coll, Univ of New York, School of Visual Arts and Inst of Policy Studies. *Career:* Lecturer Fed City Coll 1970–71; mem Faculty Goddard Coll 1973–; Pres American Artists Inc, VA 1980–; mem Bd of Dirs Human Rights Campaign Fund, NY 1986; Award for Best Variety Show, TV Writers' Guild of America 1982. *Publications include:* The Hand that Rocks the Cradle 1971, Rubyfruit Jungle 1973, A Plain Brown Rapper 1976, Six of One 1978, Southern Discomfort 1982, Sudden Death 1983, High Hearts 1986, Starting From Scratch: A Different Kind of Writer's Manual 1988, Bingo 1988, Wish You Were Here 1990, Rest in Pieces 1991, Dolley 1992, Murder at Monticello 1992, Venus Envy 1994, Pay Dirt 1995, Riding Shotgun 1996, Murder, She Meowed 1996; *TV includes:* I Love Liberty (Emmy nomination) 1982, The Long Hot Summer (Emmy nomination) 1985, My Two Loves 1986, The Mists of Avalon 1986, The Girls of Summer 1989, Rich Men, Single Women 1989, Southern Exposure 1990, The Thirty Nine Year Itch 1990, The Woman Who Loved Elvis 1992, A Family Again 1994, Cat on the Scent 1999, Loose Lips 1999, Out Foxed 2000, Pawing Through the Past 2000. *Address:* Teatime Farm, 1295 Greenfield Rd, Afton, VA 22920, USA.

BROWN, Sandra; American writer; b 1948; m Michael Brown 1968; one s one d. *Education:* Texas Christian Univ. *Career:* Fmrly model, feature reporter PM Magazine; has written 57 books since 1981; has had 20 books on New York Times bestseller list since 1990; attended numerous Roman Writers of America confs. *Publications include:* Love's Encore (as Rachel Ryan), Love Beyond Reason, Slow Heat in Heaven 1988, Best Kept Secrets 1989, Mirror Image 1990, Breath of Scandal 1991, French Silk 1992 (also TV film), Where There's Smoke 1993, Charade 1994, The Witness, Exclusive 1996. *Address:* c/o Warner Books Inc, 1271 Ave of the Americas, New York, NY 10020, USA.

BROWN, Sarah Elizabeth, BA; British civil servant; b 30 Dec 1943; d of Sir Maurice and Anne (née Gibson) Dean; m Philip Brown 1976. *Education:* Newnham Coll (Cambridge). *Career:* Asst Prin Bd of Trade 1965, Pvt Sec to Second Perm Sec 1968, Prin 1970, Asst Sec 1978, Sec to Crown Agents' Tribunal 1978–82, Personnel Management Div 1982–84, Head Financial Services Bill group 1984–86, Under-Sec 1986, Head Companies Div, Dept of Trade and Industry 1986–91, Head Small Firms and Business Link Div 1991–94, Dir Company Law 1994–96; mem Competition (fmrly Monopolies and Mergers) Comm 1998–; Commr Friendly Socs Comm 1997–2000. *Leisure interests:* theatre, travel, gardening. *Address:* 32 Cumberland St, London, SW1V 4LX, UK.

BROWN, Tina, CBE, MA; British writer and magazine editor; b 21 Nov 1953, Maidenhead; d of George Hambley and Bettina Iris Mary (née Kohr) Brown; m Harold Evans 1981; one s one d. *Education:* Univ of Oxford. *Career:* Columnist Punch 1978; Ed-in-Chief Tatler 1979–83, Vanity Fair, New York 1984–92, London 1991–92; Ed-in-Chief The New Yorker literary magazine 1992–98, Talk magazine 1999–; Partner and Chair Talk Media 1998–; Most Promising Female Journalist, Katherine Pakenham Prize, Sunday Times 1973; Young Journalist of the Year 1978, USC Distinguished Achievement in Journalism Award 1994. *Plays:* Under the Bamboo Tree (Sunday Times Drama Award) 1973, Happy Yellow 1977; *Novels:* Loose Talk 1979, Life as A Party 1983. *Address:* Miramax/Talk Media, 152 W 57th St, 56th Floor, New York, NY 10019, USA (Office). *Fax:* (212) 830-5838.

BROWN, Trisha, BA; American ballet dancer and choreographer; b Aberdeen, WA. *Education:* Mills Coll (California). *Career:* With Judson Dance Theater 1960s; f The Trisha Brown Dance Co 1970; mem Nat Council on the Arts 1994–97; Hon mem American Acad of Arts and Letters; numerous hon doctorates; Nat Endowment for the Arts Fellowship in Choreography (five times), John Simon Guggenheim Memorial Foundation Fellowship in Choreography (twice), MacArthur Foundation Fellowship Award 1991, Samuel H. Scripps American Dance Festival Award 1994, Prix de la Danse de la Soc des Auteurs et Compositeurs Dramatiques 1996, NY State Gov's Arts Award 1999; Officier des Arts et des Lettres 2000. *Choreography includes:* Walking on the Walls, Roof Piece 1973, Son of Gone Fishin' 1981, Bessie 1984, Lateral Pass 1985, Newark 1987, For M. G.: The Movie 1991, Astral Converted 1991, Another Story: As in Falling 1993, Yet Another Story 1994, Long and Dream 1994, If You Could See Me 1994, You Can See Us 1995, M. O. 1995, Twelve Ton Rose 1996, Canto/Pianto 1997, L'Orfeo (opera) 1998, Five Part Weather Invention 1999, Rapture to Leon James 2000. *Address:* Trisha Brown Dance Company, 211 West 61st St, Floor 4, New York, NY 10023, USA (Office).

BROWNE, Sheila Jeanne, CB, MA; British former college principal; b 25 Dec 1924; d of Edward Elliott and Esmé (née Lush) Browne. *Education:* Lady Margaret Hall (Oxford) and Ecole des Chartes (Paris). *Career:* Asst Lecturer Royal Holloway Coll, Univ of London 1947–51; Tutor, Fellow and Lecturer in French St Hilda's Coll, Oxford 1951–61, Hon Fellow St Hilda's Coll 1978; HM Insp of Schools 1961–70, Staff Insp for Secondary Educ 1970–72, Chief Insp 1972; Deputy Sr Chief Insp, Dept of Educ and Science 1972–74, Sr Chief Insp 1974–83; Prin Newnham Coll, Cambridge 1983–92; mem Franco-British Council 1987–93, Marshall Aid Commemoration Comm 1987–92; Trustee Gladstone Memorial Trust 1991–; Gov Anglia Polytechnic Univ 1987–93; Hon Fellow Lancs Polytech 1989, Polytech of North London 1989; Hon D LITT (Warwick) 1981; Hon LL D (Exeter) 1984, (Birmingham) 1987. *Leisure interests:* bell-ringing, medieval France, mountains. *Address:* 101 Walton St, Oxford, OX2 6EB, UK. *Telephone:* (1865) 511128; *E-mail:* sheila.browne@lmk.ox.ac.uk.

BROWNER, Carol M., JD; American lawyer and politician; b 1956; m Michael Podhorzer; one s. *Education:* Univ of Florida. *Career:* Gen-Counsel Cttee FL Legislature 1979–83; Assoc Dir Citizen Action, Washington, DC 1983–86; mem staff Senator Lawton Chiles 1986–89; mem staff Senate Cttee on Energy and Natural Resources 1989; Legis Dir on staff of Senator Al Gore 1989–90; Head Dept of Environmental Regulation, FL 1990–93; Admin Environmental Protection Agency (EPA) 1993–. *Address:* Environmental Protection Agency, 1200 Penn Avenue NW, Washington, DC 20460, USA (Office).

BRÜCKNER, Christine; German writer; b 10 Dec 1921, Schmilling-hausen, Waldeck; d of Carl and Clotilde (née Schulze) Emde; m 1st Werner Brückner 1948 (divorced); m 2nd Otto H. Kühner 1967 (died 1996). *Education:* Büchereischule (Stuttgart) and Univ of Marburg. *Career:* Compulsory military service 1939–45; Asst Forschungsinst für Kunstgeschichte, Univ of Marburg 1947–50; Ed Frauenwelt, Nurem-berg 1951–52; freelance writer 1954–; production asst State Theatre, Kassel 1960–61; Vice-Pres PEN Club (Germany) 1980–84; f (jtly) Kasseler Literaturpreis für grotesken Humor 1984; First Prize Bertels-mann Verlag 1954; Goetheplakette (State of Hessen) 1982; Hon Citizen, Kassel 1987; Hessischer Verdiensторden 1990; Christian-Rauch-Plakette Arolsen 1990; Bundesverdienstkreuz Erst Klasse 1991; Großes Bundesverdienstkreuz 1996. *Publications include:* Ehe die Spuren verwehen 1954, Die Zeit danach 1961, Der Kokon 1966, Das glückliche Buch der a.p. 1970, Überlebensgeschichten 1971, Jauche und Levkojen 1975, Nirgendwo ist Poenichen 1977, Erfahren und erwandert 1979, Das eine sein, das andere lieben 1981, Mein schwarzes Sofa 1981, Wenn du geredet hättest, Desdemona 1983 (trans to English title Desdemona If You Had Only Spoken 1992), Die Quints 1985, Deine Bilder/Meine Worte (jtly) 1987, Hat der Mensch Wurzeln? (autobiographical essays) 1988, Die Letzte Strophe 1989, Über Christine Brückner 1989, Die Stunde des Rebhuhns 1991, Gesammelte Werke 1992, Früher oder später 1996; novels, stories, children's books, radio plays, etc. *Leisure interests:* modern art, travel – especially on foot. *Address:* c/o Hans-Böckler-Str 5, 34121 Kassel, Germany. *Telephone:* (561) 24304; *Fax:* (561) 2888045; *E-mail:* fwblock@uni-kassel.de.

BRUNDTLAND, Gro Harlem, M PH, MD; Norwegian politician and physician; b 20 April 1939, Oslo; d of Gudmund and Inga Harlem; m Arne Olav Brundtland 1960; three s (one deceased) one d. *Education:* Univ of Oslo and Harvard Univ (USA). *Career:* Consultant Ministry of Health and Social Affairs 1965–67; Medical Officer Oslo City Health Dept 1968–69; Deputy Dir School Health Services, Oslo 1969; Minister of Environment 1974–79; Deputy Leader Lab Party 1975–81, Leader Parl Group 1981–, Chair until 1992; Prime Minister 1981, 1986–89, 1990–96; fmr mem Parl Standing Cttee on Finance, currently mem Cttee on Foreign Affairs; mem of Storting (Parl) 1977–97; Dir-Gen WHO 1998–; Chair UN World Comm on Environment and Devt; fmr Vice-Chair Sr Secondary Schools' Socialist Asscn, Students' Asscn of Lab Party; numerous contribs to professional journals; Dr hc (Oxford) 2001; Third World Prize for Work on Environmental Issues 1989; Indira Gandhi Prize 1990; Onassis Foundation Award 1992. *Publications:* articles on preventive medicine, school health and growth studies. *Leisure interest:* cross-country skiing. *Address:* World Health Organization, Avenue Appia, 1211 Geneva, 27, Switzerland (Office). *Telephone:* (22) 7912111 (Office); *Fax:* (22) 7910746 (Office); *E-mail:* info@who.ch (Office); *Internet:* www.who.int (Office).

BRUNN, Anke; German politician; b 17 Sept 1942, Behlendorf; m Gerhard Brunn 1965; one s. *Education:* Univs of Hamburg, Cologne and Paris. *Career:* SPD mem Landtag (regional Parl) of Nordrhein-Westfalen (N Rhine-Westphalia) 1970–81, 1985–, Minister for Science and Research 1985; Senator for Youth, Family and Sport, Berlin 1981; mem House of Reps, Berlin 1981–83; Man 1983–85; mem Fed Bd SPD 1986–, Dist Chair 1987–. *Leisure interests:* gardening, walking. *Address:* Sielsdorfer Str 29, 50935 Cologne, Germany. *Telephone:* (221) 433686.

BRYAN, Joan Helen, AO, PH D; Australian entomologist; b 2 Aug 1939, Brisbane; d of Wilfred Walter Bryan and Jean Henzell. *Education:* Somerville House (Brisbane), Univs of Queensland and London. *Career:* Research Officer Medical Research Council, Fajara, Gambia 1976–82; Head Entomology Section, Commonwealth Inst of Health, Sydney 1982–87; Assoc Prof, Tropical Health Programme and Reader in Medical Entomology, Univ of Queensland 1987–; has written more than 70 papers on vector-borne diseases, in scientific journals 1973–. *Leisure interest:* bird watching. *Address:* University of Queensland, Medical School, Tropical Health Programme, Herston Rd, Herston, Qld 4006, Australia. *Telephone:* (7) 3365 5407; *Fax:* (7) 3365 5599.

BRYANT, Anne L., ED D; American administrator; b 26 Nov 1949, Jamaica Plain, MA; d of John Winslow and Anne (née Phillips) Bryant; m Peter Harned Ross 1986; two step-c. *Education:* Simmons Coll and Univ of Massachusetts. *Career:* Dir Nat Asscn of Bank Women Educational Foundation, Chicago, IL 1974–86; Vice-Pres P. M. Haeger, Chicago, IL 1978–86; Exec Dir American Asscn of Univ Women, Washington, DC 1986–; Exec Dir Educational Foundation, Legal Advocacy Fund; mem Exec Cttee Simmons Coll, Boston, MA 1971–; Fellow American Soc of Asscn Execs; Woman of the Year for Educ, YWCA 1976; William H. Cosby, Jr Award, Univ of Massachusetts 1983; Key Award, American Soc of Asscn Execs 1992. *Address:* American Asscn of University Women, 1111 16th St, NW, Washington, DC 20036, USA.

BRYCE, Quentin Alice Louise, AO, BA, LLB; Australian lawyer and administrator; b 23 Dec 1942; d of Norman Walter and Naida Edith Strachan; m Michael John Bryce 1964; three s two d. *Education:* Univ of Queensland and Moreton Bay Coll. *Career:* Called to Bar, Qld; Tutor in Law Univ of Queensland 1968–72, Sr Tutor 1972–75, Lecturer 1976–83; Dir Women's Information Service, Qld 1983–86, Human Rights and Equal Opportunity Comm, Qld 1987, Fed Sex Discrimination Commr, Human Rights and Equal Opportunity Comm 1988–93; Chair and Chief Exec Nat Childcare Accreditation Council 1993–; mem Australian Del to UN Human Rights Comm, Geneva, Switzerland 1990–91; Dir Family Planning Council of Queensland 1981–, Australian Children's TV Foundation Bd 1982–; mem Bd Schizophrenia Foundation of Australia 1987–, Australian Bicentennial Authority Unsung Heroes Panel 1987–, Legal Cttee Childhood Accident Prevention Foundation of Australia 1984, Advisory Bd Nat Inst for Law Ethics and Public Affairs 1993–; has written numerous papers on children's rights, equal opportunities and status for women,

civil liberties and women's human rights. *Leisure interests:* gardening, reading, opera. *Address:* 209 Hawken Drive, St Lucia, Qld 4067, Australia.

BRZYSKA SZTEYN, Wanda, PH D; Polish professor of general and inorganic chemistry; b 19 Feb 1931, Grodno; m Leopold Brzyski 1957; one d. *Education:* Marie Curie-Skłodowska Univ. *Career:* Lab Asst Marie Curie-Skłodowska Univ 1955–56, Asst Prof of Chem 1956–65, Adjunct Prof 1965–73, Docent 1973–89, Prof 1989–, Head Dept of Inorganic and General Chem 1977–, Vice-Dean Faculty of Mat Physical Chem 1984–87, Pro-Rector 1980–81; Chair Polish Chem Soc (Lublin) 1983–89, Science Soc of Lublin 1983–90; awards include High Schools Min Prize 1972, 1980, 1989, Gold Cross of Merit 1974, Cavalry Cross of Merit 1979, Hon Citizen of Veigneulles (France) 1982, Medal of the Asscn of French-Polish Friendship 1983. *Publications include:* Lanta-norce i aktynowce 1987; two monographs, over 200 contribs to professional journals. *Leisure interests:* literature, folklore, theatre, tourism, science. *Address:* Marie Curie-Skłodowska University, Dept of Inorganic and General Chemistry, Plac Marii Curie-Skłodowskiej 3, 20-031 Lublin, Poland (Office); ul Raabego 3 m 20, 20-030 Lublin, Poland (Home). *Telephone:* (81) 375760 (Office); (81) 32662 (Home).

BUCHANAN, Isobel; British opera singer (soprano); b 15 March 1954, Glasgow; d of Stewart and Mary Buchanan; m Jonathan King (actor Jonathan Hyde) 1980; two d. *Education:* Cumbernauld Comprehensive High School and Royal Scottish Acad of Music and Drama. *Career:* Debut in Sydney (Australia) with Richard Bonynge and Joan Sutherland 1976–78; appearances at Glyndebourne 1978, Vienna Staatsoper 1978, Royal Opera House (Covent Garden, London) 1979, Paris Opera, USA and Germany 1979, English Nat Opera 1985; has also performed in Munich, Cologne and Hamburg (Germany), Monte Carlo (Monaco) and Chicago (USA); now freelance artist working with all major opera cos and orchestras. *Recordings:* Beethoven's Ninth Symphony, Werther, Mozart Arias and Duets. *Leisure interests:* cooking, reading, gardening, yoga, knitting. *Address:* c/o Marks Management Ltd, 14 New Burlington St, London W1X 1FF, UK.

BUCK, Joan Juliet; American magazine editor and author; b Los Angeles, CA; m John Heilpern (divorced). *Career:* Fmr journalist with numerous magazines including Interview, WWD, The Observer Magazine, Condé Nast, Vogue USA, The New Yorker; Ed-in-Chief French Vogue June 1994–; mem PEN Newsletter Cttee, Best Dressed List Hall of Fame. *Publications include:* The Only Place To Be, Daughter of the Swan; five screenplays. *Address:* French Vogue, 73 rue de Vingirard, 75431 Paris, France.

BUDAI, Ilona; Hungarian singer; b 3 April 1951, Felpéc; d of János Budai and Ilona Tulok; m Jósef Zelnik 1973; one s. *Education:* Ménfőcsanak Coll and Sopron Music Secondary School (Budapest). *Career:* Folk singer 1972–; teacher of folk singing Hungarian Folk Music School 1986–; numerous TV and radio performances, host Let's Sing Together programme; Young Master of Popular Art 1970; Kodály Prize 1984. *Recordings include:* Dancehouse Festival (jtly) 1981, Transylvania rings the bells 1989. *Leisure interests:* excursions, cooking, sewing. *Address:* 1116 Budapest, Abádi u 12, Hungary. *Telephone:* (1) 181-3641.

BUDAL, Livia; Hungarian opera singer; b 23 June 1950; d of Ferenc and Martha (née Koszegi) Budal; m Julian Batky. *Education:* Ferenc Liszt Acad of Music (Budapest). *Career:* Mem Artistic Staff Budapest State Opera 1973–75, Gelsenkirchen Music Theatre, Germany 1977–80, Munich State Opera, Germany 1980–83; appearances in Brussels, Royal Opera House (Covent Garden, London), Paris, Canada, Metropolitan Opera (New York), San Francisco (USA); mem Bd of Dirs J. B. EM Services Inc, St Laurent, Montréal; numerous recordings and TV appearances; Ravel Prize 1974. *Address:* JBS Marketing, 4280 rue Sere, Saint Laurent, PQ H6T 1A6, Canada.

BUDD, Ruth June; Canadian bassist; b 20 June 1924, Winnipeg, MB; one s one d. *Education:* Toronto Conservatory of Music and Univ of Toronto. *Career:* Bassist Vancouver Jr Symphony, later Vancouver Symphony; first woman bassist Toronto Symphony Orchestra 1947–52, 1964–89; bassist Vancouver Opera Orchestra 1992–; Founder Toronto Sr Strings 1993–; Mandola player Shevchenko Mandolin Orchestra 1996–; mem Symphony Six 1952, later CBC Symphony, Stratford

Festival Orchestra; Prin Bass Halifax Symphony Orchestra; Founder, Chair Org of Canadian Symphony Musicians; mem Performing Artists for Nuclear Disarmament; Women of Distinction Award 1983. *Leisure interests:* folk music, pottery, theatre, literature. *Address:* 407 St Clair Ave E, Toronto, ON M4T 1P6, Canada. *Telephone:* (416) 488-9452; *Fax:* (416) 488-7152.

BUDD, Zola; South African sportswoman; b 26 May 1966; m Mike Pieterse 1989 (separated); one d. *Career:* Obtained British citizenship 1984; finished 7th in 3,000m race, Los Angeles Olympic Games, USA 1984; won European Cup for 3,000m 1985; winner World Cross-Country Championships 1985, 1986; winner 3,000m, Women's WAAA Championships 1985, 1,500m 1986; came 4th in 3,000m, European Championships 1986; returned to South Africa 1988; mem South African team for Barcelona Olympic Games, Spain 1992; competitor world half-marathon, Palma, Majorca 1996. *Address:* POB 186, Bloemfontein 9300, South Africa.

BUFFET, Marie-George; French politician; b 7 May 1949, Sceaux (Hauts-de-Seine); d of Paul Kossellek and Raymonde Rayer; m Jean-Pierre Buffet 1972; two c. *Career:* Joined Parti Communiste Français (PCF) 1969, elected to PCF Cen Cttee 1987, mem Nat Bureau 1994, Head Nat Women's Cttee 1996, elected to Nat Secr 1996; municipal councillor, then Deputy Mayor Châtenay-Malabry (Hautes-de-Seine) 1977–83; Nat Ass Deputy for Seine-Saint-Denis 1997–; Minister for Youth and Sport 1997–. *Address:* Ministry for Youth and Sport, 78 rue Olivier de Serres, 75015 Paris, France. *Telephone:* (1) 40-45-90-00; *Fax:* (1) 42-50-42-49.

BUGGE FOUGNER, Else, LL B; Norwegian lawyer and politician; b 9 Nov 1944, Moss; m; three c. *Career:* Supreme Court Advocate 1975; Partner Hjort, Eriksrod & Co 1977–; Minister of Justice and Police 1989–90; Chair Bd Nat Hosp, Small Business Fund; mem Perm Defence Counsel, Oslo City Court until 1989, Perm Comm on Criminal Law, Bd of Dirs Statoil, Bergen Bank. *Address:* c/o Ministry of Justice, Akersgt 42, POB 8005 Dep, 0030 Oslo 1, Norway.

BUJOLD, Geneviève; Canadian actress; b 1 July 1942, Montréal, PQ; d of Firmin and Laurette (née Cavanaugh) Bujold; m Paul Almond 1967 (divorced); one s. *Education:* Montréal Conservatory of Dramatic Art. *Career:* Numerous film, stage and TV appearances; winner Best Actress Award, Carthagenia Film Festival; ACTRA Earle Grey Award for Most Outstanding Performer in Canada 1972. *Films include:* La guerre est finie (Susanne Bianchetti Award) 1966, Saint Joan (Emmy nomination) 1967, Entre la mer et l'eau douce, King of Hearts, The Thief of Paris, Isabel (ETROG Best Actress Award) 1968, Anne of the Thousand Days (Hollywood Golden Globe Award, Acad Award nomination) 1969, The Trojan Women, The Journey, Earthquake, Alex and the Gypsy, Obsession, Another Man Another Chance, Coma, Murder by Decree, Final Assignment, Tightrope, Trouble in Mind, The Moderns, Dead Ringers, False Identity, Secret Places of the Heart, The Paper Wedding 1990, Star Trek: Generations, An Ambush of Ghosts, Mon Ami Max, Dead Innocent, The House of Yes, Last Night, Eye of the Beholder; *Stage appearances include:* The Barber of Seville, A Midsummer Night's Dream, A House... A Day; *TV appearances include:* St Joan, Antony and Cleopatra, Mistress of Paradise, Red Earth, White Earth, Star Trek. *Address:* c/o William Morris Agency, 151 South El Camino Drive, Beverly Hills, CA 90212, USA (Office).

BUKSPAN, Elisabeth Suzanne; French civil servant and business executive; b 14 Sept 1948, Paris; d of Maximilien and Ginette Bukspan. *Education:* Inst d'Etudes Politiques de Paris, Ecole des Hautes Etudes Commerciales de Jeunes Filles and Ecole Nat d'Admin. *Career:* Sr Officer Treasury 1975; Rep to Dir of External Econ Relations, Ministry of Econ 1979; fmr Sr Lecturer Ecole Nat d'Admin and Ecole Polytechnique; Tech Adviser to Cabinet of the Minister of State for Foreign Trade 1981–83; Rep to Minister of Foreign Trade and Tourism 1983; Dir-Gen Agence pour la Coopération Tech Industrielle et Econ 1984–87; Sec-Gen Thomson CSF (finance) 1987–91; Dir of Industrial Agreements Total group 1991–95; Head of Cabinet of the Minister of Industry and Finances 1995–96; French Rep Dir EBRD 1996–97, Gen Inspectorate of Finances 1998–; Chevalier de l'Ordre Nat du Mérite. *Leisure interests:* music, swimming. *Address:* Inspection générale des finances, 139 rue de Bercy, 75012 Paris, France.

BULAJICH, Borjana, MA; Yugoslav United Nations official; b 5 Nov 1961, Belgrade; d of Krsto and Vera Bulajich. *Education:* Gymnasium (Belgrade), Carleton Univ (Ottawa) and Concordia Univ (Montréal, Canada). *Career:* Social Affairs Officer, Liaison Office INSTRAW, New York, USA 1987–; creates training packages on water supply, sanitation, energy and women's affairs for developing countries. *Leisure interests:* tennis, music, theatre, films, arts, reading. *Telephone:* (212) 963-5684 (New York); *Fax:* (212) 963-2978 (New York).

BULARD, Martine, L ÈS L; French newspaper editor; b 12 June 1952. *Career:* Chief Econ Columnist on L'Humanité newspaper (organ of the French Communist Party) 1980–, Ed-in-Chief L'Humanité Dimanche. *Address:* L'Humanité-Dimanche, rue Jean Jaurès, 93528 Saint Denis Cedex, France. *Telephone:* (1) 49-22-72-72; *Fax:* (1) 49-22-73-00.

BULL, Deborah Clare, CBE; British ballet dancer, writer, broadcaster and arts administrator; b 22 March 1963, Derby; d of Rev Michael John Bull and Doreen Audrey Bull (née Plumb). *Education:* Royal Ballet School, London. *Career:* With the Royal Ballet, Covent Garden 1981–2001, promoted Principal 1992; teacher of Nutrition, Royal Ballet School 1996–99; Dir Artists' Devt Initiative, mem Dance Panel, Arts Council 1996–, Arts Council 1998–; Dir Clore Studio Upstairs, Royal Opera House 1999–; Artistic Dir Linbury and Clore Studio Theatres, Royal Opera House 2001–; Gov South Bank Centre 1997–, Royal Opera House, Covent Garden 1998–2001; columnist The Telegraph 1999–; contrib Ed Harpers & Queen magazine 2000–; Patron Nat Osteoporosis Soc, Foundation for Community Dance; Dr hc (Derby) 1998; Prix de Lausanne 1980; Dancer of the Year, Sunday Express and The Ind on Sunday 1996. *Dance:* appearances with Royal Ballet include leading roles in La Bayadère (Gamzatti), Swan Lake (Odette/Odile), The Sleeping Beauty (Aurora), Don Quixote (Kitri), Steptext (cr for her by William Forsythe) 1995; appeared in Harrogate Int Festival 1993, 1995, An Evening of British Ballet, Sintra Festival, Portugal 1994, 1995, Diamonds of World Ballet Gala, Kremlin Palace, Moscow 1996; *TV appearances include:* Dance, Ballerina, Dance (BBC2) 1998, Travels with My Tutu (BBC2) 2000; *Radio work includes:* Breaking the Law (BBC Radio 4) 2000; *Publications include:* The Vitality Plan 1998, Dancing Away 1998; numerous articles and reviews in newspapers and dance magazines. *Leisure interests:* mountain pursuits, writing, reading, arts, kayaking, walking. *Address:* c/o Royal Opera House, Covent Garden, London WC2E 9DD, UK (Office). *Telephone:* (20) 7240-1200 (Office); *Internet:* www.deborahbull.com.

BULL, Tove; Norwegian university rector and professor; b 31 Oct 1945, Alta; d of Kaare and Sonja Bull; m 1st Steinar Jager 1967 (divorced); m 2nd Svein Pedersen 1977; one s. *Education:* Univs of Oslo and Trondheim. *Career:* Lecturer Tromsø Coll 1973–84; Asst Prof Univ of Tromsø 1984, Prof 1990–, Pro-Rector 1990–95, Rector 1996–2001; Norwegian Council of Research Prize (jtly) 1989; has written books and papers on reading and writing, linguistic variation in N Norway, sociolinguistics, language contact, language and gender. *Address:* University of Tromsø, Hovedgården, Breirika, 9037 Tromsø, Norway; Gnistr 5, 9014 Tromsø, Norway. *Telephone:* 77-64-49-88; *Fax:* 77-64-47-60; *E-mail:* tove.bull@adm.uit.no.

BULLOCK, Sandra; American actress; b 26 July 1966; d of John and Helga Bullock. *Education:* E Carolina Univ. *Career:* Appeared on stage in Europe with her mother, an opera singer, and in off-Broadway productions; f Fortis production co; numerous awards. *Films include:* Love Potion 9, The Vanishing, The Thing Called Love, When The Party's Over, Demolition Man, Wrestling Ernest Hemmingway, Speed, While You Were Sleeping, Making Sandwiches (also writer and dir) 1996, In Love and War, A Time To Kill 1996, Stolen Hearts 1996, Practical Magic, Forces of Nature, Gun Shy, Miss Congeniality, Speed 2, Hope Floats (also exec producer) 1998, Prince of Egypt (voice only), 28 Days, Famous 2000; *TV includes:* The Preppy Murder (film), Lucky Chances (mini-series), Working Girl (NBC series). *Address:* UTA, 9560 Wilshire Blvd, Fl 5, Beverly Hills, CA 90212, USA (Office).

BULMAHN, Edelgard; German politician; b 4 March 1951, Minden; m Joachim Wolschke-Bulmahn 1978. *Education:* Univ of Hanover. *Career:* Grammar School teacher 1981–87; mem Hanover-Linden Dist

Council 1981–86; joined SPD 1969; mem Bundestag (Parl) 1987–. *Address:* Bundeshaus, 5300 Bonn 1, Germany. *Telephone:* (228) 1685858; *Fax:* (228) 1686868.

BUMBRY, Grace-Melzia Ann, MA; American opera singer; b 4 Jan 1937, St Louis, MO; d of Benjamin and Melzia Bumbry. *Education:* Boston and Northwestern Univs and Music Acad of the West. *Career:* Debut Paris Opera 1959; has appeared at Basel Opera (Switzerland) 1960–63, Royal Opera (Brussels), Bayreuth Festival (Germany) 1961, 1962, Chicago Lyric (IL, USA) 1962–78, Vienna State Opera 1963, Royal Opera House (Covent Garden, London) 1963, 1968, 1969, 1976, 1978, Salzburg Festival (Austria) 1964, La Scala (Milan, Italy) 1964–79, Metropolitan Opera (New York) 1965–79; has toured Japan; numerous recordings, two Grands Prix du Disque; UNESCO Ambassadorship 1991; Hon DH (St Louis) 1968, (Rust Coll) 1975; Hon D MUS (Rockhurst Coll); Hon D HUM LITT (Missouri) 1980; Marian Anderson Award 1958; Richard Wagner Medal 1963; Grammy Award 1979, Royal Opera House Medal 1988, Commdr des Arts et des Lettres; Hon Citizen of Baltimore, Los Angeles, Philadelphia, St Louis. *Leisure interests:* interior decorating, designing clothes. *Address:* J. F. Mastroianni Associates, 161 W 61st St, New York, NY 10032, USA (Office).

BUNDSGAARD, Lotte; Danish politician; b 20 Jan 1973, Niva; m Sorens Thorsager 1997. *Education:* Sankt Knuds Gymnasium and Odense Teaching Coll. *Career:* Minister for Housing and Urban Affairs and Gender Equality 2000–; Co-Founder Café au Lait (political club). *Address:* Ministry of Housing and Urban Affairs and Gender Equality, Slotsholmsgade 1, 1216 Copenhagen K, Denmark; Tranesyen 26, 5250 Odense, Denmark. *Telephone:* (33) 926100; *Fax:* (33) 926104; *E-mail:* post@lotte.dk; *Internet:* www.bm.dk.

BURBIDGE, (Eleanor) Margaret Peachey, PH D, FRS; American astronomer; b Davenport, England; d of Stanley John and Marjorie (née Stott) Peachey; m Geoffrey Burbidge 1948; one d. *Education:* Frances Holland School (London) and Univ Coll London. *Career:* Second Asst, Asst Dir and Acting Dir Univ of London Observatory 1946–51; Research Fellow Yerkes Observatory, Univ of Chicago 1951–53, California Inst of Tech 1955–57; Research Fellow and Assoc Prof Univ of Chicago 1957–62; Assoc Research Physicist Univ of California at San Diego 1962–64, Prof 1964–82, Univ Prof 1982–90, Research Prof 1990–, Dir Center for Astrophysics and Space Sciences 1979–88, Research Physicist Dept of Physics 1990; Dir Royal Greenwich Observatory 1972–73; Ed Observatory 1948–51; mem Editorial Bd Astronomy and Astrophysics 1969–85; Lindsay Memorial Lecture NASA 1985; mem Royal Astronomical Soc, American Astronomical Soc (Pres 1978), American Acad of Arts and Science, NAS, AAAS (Fellow 1981, Pres 1982), Soc Royale des Sciences de Liège, New York Acad of Sciences; Fellow Univ Coll, London, Lucy Cavendish and Girton Colls, Cambridge, UK, Philosophical Soc; Hon D SC (Smith Coll, Williams Coll, Rensselaer Polytechnic Inst and Univs of Sussex, Leicester, Bristol, Michigan, Massachusetts, Notre Dame, London, Chicago); numerous prizes and awards including Helen B. Warner Prize (jtly with G. Burbidge) 1959, Bruce Gold Medal, Astronomical Soc of the Pacific 1982, Nat Medal of Science 1984, Einstein Medal 1988. *Publications:* Quasi-Stellar Objects (with Geoffrey Burbidge) 1967; numerous contribs to professional journals. *Address:* Center for Astrophysics and Space Sciences, University of California at San Diego, Mail Code #0424, La Jolla, CA 92093, USA. *Telephone:* (619) 534-4477.

BURCHILL, Julie; British journalist and writer; b 1960, Bristol; m 1st Tony Parsons; m 2nd Cosmo Landesman (separated). *Career:* Fmrly journalist NME (Nat Music Express), Sunday Times, Mail on Sunday, Sunday Express, numerous magazines; freelance journalist Sunday Express; f Modern Review; columnist The Guardian 1998–. *Publications:* Ambition 1989, Sex and Sensibility 1992, No Exit 1993, I Knew I Was Right (autobiog) 1998, Diana 1998, Buried Alive 1999; *TV includes:* Prince (film), several plays. *Address:* Simpson Fox, 52 Shaftesbury Ave, London W1V 7OE, UK.

BURDUS, Julia Ann, BA; British business executive; b 4 Sept 1933; d of Gladstone Beaty and Julia Booth; m Ian Robertson 1981. *Education:* Univ of Durham. *Career:* Clinical Psychologist 1956–60; Research Exec

Ogilvy, Benson and Mather 1961–67; Research Dir McCann Erickson 1971–75, Vice-Chair 1975–81; Dir of Strategic Planning and Devt, Interpublic 1981–83, Audits of GB Ltd 1983–86, AGB Research 1986–89; Jt Deputy Chair and mem Health Educ Authority 1987–90; Chair Advertising Educ Authority 1987–90, The Marketing Triangle 1992–; Dir of Communications and Marketing, Olympia and York, Canary Wharf, London (Docklands) 1989–92; Dir Dawson Int 1992–, BEM Ltd 1992–; Non-exec Dir Argyll Group 1993–, Next 1993–, Prudentail Corpn 1996–; mem Council Inst of Dirs 1995–. *Leisure interest:* home-building.

BURGESS, Sally, ARCM; British opera singer; b 9 Oct 1953; d of Douglas Burgess and Edna (née Sharman) Rushton; m Neal Thornton 1988; one s. *Education:* Royal Coll of Music. *Career:* Joined English Nat Opera 1977–; performances at numerous opera houses and festivals including Royal Opera House (Covent Garden, London), Metropolitan Opera (New York), Strasbourg (France), Wiesbaden (Germany), Lausanne (Switzerland), Nancy (France), Glyndebourne (UK), Houston (TX), Israel, Munich (Germany); numerous recordings. *Operas include:* Ariadne, Julius Caesar, Werther, Carmen, Aida, Trojans, Love for Three Oranges, Faust, Rigoletto, Showboat, Orfeo, Fennimore and Gerda, Duke Bluebeard's Castle, La Gioconda, Il Trovatore, Die Walküre, The Voyage, Katya Kabanova, Genovava, the Rake's Progress, Ariodante. *Leisure interests:* cooking, walking, reading, music, family, theatre. *Address:* c/o AOR Management Ltd, Westwood, Lorraine Park, Harrow Weald, Middx HA3 6BY, UK. *Telephone:* (20) 8954-7646; *Fax:* (20) 8420-7499; *E-mail:* jennyrose@ aormanagementuk.com; *Internet:* www.aormanagementuk.com.

BURGOS, Norma, BA, MPA; Puerto Rican politician and city planner; two s. *Education:* Univ of Puerto Rico, Georgia Inst of Tech. *Career:* Various admin posts with San Juan municipality 1976–; Pres and Exec Dir Corpn for Redevt of Old San Juan (CODEVISA) 1986–90; in charge of special project Puerto Rico 2005; Assoc mem and Chair Puerto Rico Planning Cttee; Sec of State 1995–99; Exec Dir Gov's Council for Econ Productivity; Senator 1999–; Dr of Political Science (Caribbean Univ); Eagle Award; Distinguished Citizen of Puerto Rico 1966. *Publications include:* Transnacionalización en la Década del 80 (co-author) 1984, Administración Pública en Puerto Rico ante el Nuevo Siglo (co-author) 1996. *Address:* US Senate, Washington, DC 20510, USA.

BURKE, Kathy; British actress; b London. *Education:* Anna Scher's Theatre School (London). *Films:* Scrubbers, Nil by Mouth (Best Actress, Cannes Film Festival 1997), Elizabeth 1998, This Year's Love 1999, Kevin and Perry Go Large 2000; *Plays include:* Mr Thomas, London, Boom Bang-a-Bang, London (dir); *TV includes:* Harry Enfield and Chums, Absolutely Fabulous, Common as Muck, Mr Woods' Virgins (Royal TV Soc Award), Tom Jones, Gimme Gimme Gimme.

BURN, Jane; British ballet dancer; b 23 May 1973; d of Maureen and Derek Burn. *Education:* Maureen Gardener School (Winchester) and Royal Ballet School (Richmond, Surrey). *Career:* Joined Royal Ballet Co 1991, First Soloist 2000; represented Royal Ballet in the Erik Bruhn Int Ballet Competition 1994; created roles in Tidelines (Dance Bites) 1999, There Where She loves (The New Works) 2000; Professional Level Prize, Prix de Lausanne 1991. *Repertory includes:* Lise, Swanilda, Amour, Flower Girl (Don Quixote), Vera (A Month in the Country), Stephanie (Mayerling), Hunca Munca (Tales of Beatrix Potter), Violente, Princess Florine (Sleeping Beauty), Dora Penney (Enigma Variations), Tatiana (Anastasia). *Address:* c/o Royal Opera House, Covent Garden, London WC2E 9DD, UK. *Telephone:* (20) 7240-1200.

BURNETT, Carol; American actress, comedienne and singer; b 26 April 1936, San Antonio; d of Jody and Louise (née Creighton) Burnett; m Joseph Hamilton 1963 (divorced); three d. *Education:* Univ of California at Los Angeles. *Career:* Debut on Broadway in Once upon a Mattress 1959; numerous TV appearances include own TV show 1966–77, 1990–; numerous awards including eight Golden Globe Awards. *Stage appearances include:* Fade Out-Fade In 1964, Plaza Suite 1970, I Do, I Do 1973, Same Time Next Year 1977; *Films include:* Pete 'n' Tillie 1972, Front Page 1974, A Wedding (San Sebastian Film Festival Award 1978) 1977, Friendly Fire 1978, The Grass is Always Greener Over the Septic Tank 1979, Health 1979, Four Seasons 1981,

Chu Chu and the Philly 1981, Annie 1982, Between Friends 1983, Hostage 1988, Men, Movies & Carol 1994, Happy Birthday Elizabeth: A Celebration of Life 1997, Grace 1998. *Address:* c/o Bill Robinson, ICM, 8942 Wilshire Blvd, 2nd Floor, Los Angeles, CA 90211-1908, USA.

BURNETT, Syringa Marshall, B SC, MA; Jamaican lecturer in nursing; b 11 May 1935, St Mary; d of the late Lionel Frederick and Mildred Malore Marshall; m Jasper Burnett 1974; one d. *Education:* Toronto, New York and Univ of the W Indies. *Career:* Nursing consultant; Sr Lecturer in Nursing, Head Dept of Advanced Nursing Educ, Univ of the W Indies, Mona 1972–; mem Senate, fmr Pres of Senate, mem Jt Select Cttee on the Jamaican Constitution 1993–95; Ed The Jamaican Nurse 1976–; mem WHO Expert Cttee on Nursing 1994–, Panel of Overseas Advisers to Journal of Advanced Nursing (Blackwell Scientific Pubs, UK), Constitutional Comm to Review Jamaican Constitution; Order of Distinction, Commdr Class CD, Govt of Jamaica; Hon Award for Services to Nursing in the Region, Caribbean Nurses Org 1984; ATL Group of Cos 21st Anniversary Award 1989. *Address:* Dept of Advanced Nursing Education, University of the West Indies, Gibralter Camp Rd, Mona, Kingston, Jamaica. *Telephone:* 927-1660.

BURNLEY, Gwendoline Etonde, BA; Cameroonian politician and development consultant; b 29 Feb 1932; d of Ernest Kofele and Hannah Nene Enanga (née Steane) Martin; m R. E. G. Burnley 1960; four s two d. *Education:* Lagos Church Missionary Society Girls' Boarding School (Nigeria), Kings Coll (Lagos, Nigeria) and The Hague (Netherlands). *Career:* Teacher of English, GTT Centre 1959–60, Clerical and Executive Staff Asscn 1963; Sec various govt ministries 1963–65, Public and Police Comms 1965–67; Sr Asst Sec Ministry of the Interior, Sec Local Govt Service then Prin Admin Officer 1967; mem State Parl and Bureau, then Sec 1968–72; mem Nat Ass (Parl) 1973–, mem Cttee of Finance Infrastructure and Econ Planning, Vice-Chair Educ, Social and Cultural Affairs Cttee 1973–88, mem Cen Cttee ruling party 1985–, Sec Cen Cttee Women's Bureau 1985; consultant on women and devt issues, resource person gender seminars and workshops, volunteer worker encouraging small businesses among women's groups; Del UN Women's Year Conf (Mexico) 1975, UN Gen Ass 1975, 1984; Chair Women's Nat Status Bd 1984–; mem Bd Société Nat de Raffinage (SONARA) 1978–; Co-ordinator Trickle Up Programme 1988–, Fako Div of Buea/Guelph (Canadian Int Devt Agency—CIDA) Project 1991–; KT Cameroon Order of Valour 1978, Officer 1981, Commdr 1994; Woman of the Year 1994. *Publications include:* Managing Rural Development in Africa 1963; contribs to professional journals and seminar documents. *Leisure interests:* gardening, walking, care of domestic pets. *Address:* POB 400, Limbe, Fako Division, SW Province, Cameroon.

BURNS, Ellen Bree, BA, LL B; American federal judge; b 13 Dec 1923, New Haven, CN; d of Vincent and Mildred (née Bannon) Bree; m Joseph Burns 1955 (deceased); two s one d. *Education:* Albertus Magnus Coll and Yale Univ. *Career:* Called to the Bar, CN 1947; Dir Legis Legal Services State of Connecticut 1949–73; Judge Connecticut Circuit Court 1973–74, Connecticut Court of Common Pleas 1974–76, Connecticut Superior Court 1976–78, US Dist Court 1978–, Chief Judge 1988–92; Trustee Albertus Magnus Coll 1985–; mem ABA, American Bar Foundation; Hon LL D (Albertus Magnus Coll) 1974, (Yale), (New Haven) 1981, (Sacred Heart) 1986, (Fairfield) 1991; Judiciary Award Connecticut Bar Asscn 1987; Raymond E. Baldwin Public Service Award, Bridgeport Law School 1992. *Address:* US District Court 208, US Courthouse 141, Church St, New Haven, CT 06510, USA.

BURNS, Ikuko Kawai, BA; American (b Japanese) artist; b 1 Jan 1936, Tokyo, Japan; d of Ichiro and Asa Kawai; m Padraic Burns 1959; two d one s. *Education:* Yamagata Univ and School of the Museum of Fine Arts (Boston). *Career:* TV and Radio Announcer Hokkaido Broadcasting Co (Japan) 1958–59; Instructor in Japanese Yale Univ 1960; at Museum of Fine Arts, Boston, MA 1961–63, 1965–66; freelance sculptor 1975–; Foundry Asst David Phillips Bronze Art Casting, MA from 1980; Lecturer Univ of Massachusetts at Boston 1982–83; exhibitions include Wako Gallery (Japan), Duxbury Art Complex Museum (MA); comms and collections include Fisherman's Memorial (Québec, Canada), Prince and Princess Mikasa (Tokyo), Sapporo City

Hall (Japan), Yamagata State House and Yamagata City Hall (Japan) 1980, Pres Hopkins Memorial, Dartmouth Coll (NH); mem Bd Dirs Japan Soc of Boston 1980; awards include Cultural Exchange Grant (Sapporo) 1987, Excellent Maquette Award, Hakone Open Air Museum (Japan) 1988. *Leisure interest:* cultural activities and volunteer work. *Address:* 311 Walnut St, Wellesley Hills, MA 02181, USA (Office); 9 Downing Rd, Brookline, MA 02146, USA (Home). *Telephone:* (617) 232-0109 (Home).

BURNS, Kathryn Anne, PH D; American oceanographer; b 1 Dec 1948, Detroit, MI; d of Edward W. and Mary E. (née Roberts) Ohlert; m Robert Joseph Burns 1969. *Education:* Michigan State Univ, MIT and Woods Hole Oceanographic Inst. *Career:* Researcher Marine Chem Unit, Ministry for Conservation, Vic, Australia 1976–80; Head of Organic Chem Section, Int Lab of Marine Radioactivity (IAEA), Monaco 1980–85; Research Scientist Bermuda Biological Station for Research 1986, concurrently Adjunct Prof Marine Science Center, State Univ of New York; Consultant to Alaska for Valdez Spill Assessment 1989–90; Consultant to UNESCO for Arabian Gulf Assessment Study 1991–92; mem Steering Cttee Intergovernmental Oceanographic Comm—IOC/UNESCO Int Mussel Watch; mem American Soc of Limnology and Oceanography, American Geophysical Union, AAAS, Australian Marine Science Asscn, Asscn of Women in Science, Int Asscn of Official Analytical Chemists; contribs to scientific journals. *Leisure interests:* dance, sailing, gardening. *Address:* Bermuda Biological Station, 35 Biological Station Lane, Saint Georges GEO1, Bermuda.

BURNS, Robin; American business executive. *Education:* Syracuse Univ. *Career:* Fmr mem Staff Bloomingdale's, NY; Vice-Pres Calvin Klein Cosmetics; Pres and CEO Estée Lauder USA, NY 1990–. *Address:* Estée Lauder USA, 767 Fifth Ave, New York, NY 10153, USA.

BUROLLET, Thérèze, L ÈS L; French curator; b 11 Feb 1933, La Tronche; d of André and Marguerite Burollet. *Education:* Univs of Toulouse and Paris (Sorbonne). *Career:* Curator Musée d'Art Moderne de la Ville de Paris 1961–66, Musée Cognacq-Jay, Dépôt des œuvres d'art d'Ivry 1962–82; Chief Curator Musée du Petit Palais, Paris 1983–; Curator-Gen of Nat Heritage 1991; Officier des Palmes Académiques. *Publications:* Catalogue des peintures et dessins du musée Cognacq-Jay 1980, Catalogue des porcelaines du musée Cognacq-Jay 1983; contribs on 19th Century art. *Address:* Musée du Petit Palais, 1 ave Dutuit, 75008 Paris, France.

BURROWES, Norma Elizabeth, BA, FRAM; British opera and concert singer; b Bangor, Co Down; d of Henry and Caroline Burrowes; m 1st Steuart Bedford 1969 (divorced 1980); m 2nd Emile Belcourt 1987; one s one d. *Education:* Queen's Univ (Belfast) and RAM. *Career:* Debut with Glyndebourne Touring Opera 1969; appearances with London orchestras, Glyndebourne Opera, Scottish Opera, Aldeburgh Festival, English Nat Opera, Welsh Nat Opera, in Austria, USA, Canada, Argentina and France and on BBC Radio and TV; numerous recordings; Hon D MUS (Queen's Univ, Belfast) 1979; Order of Worshipful Co of Musicians. *Opera roles include:* Blöndchen in The Abduction from the Seraglio, Oscar (Ballo in Maschera), Despina (Così Fan Tutte), Woodbird (Siegfried), Sophie (Der Rosenkavalier), The Cunning Little Vixen, Manon (Massenet), Titania (Midsummer Night's Dream), Nanetta (Falstaff), Gilda (Rigoletto), Marie (Daughter of the Regiment), Juliet (Romeo and Juliet), Adina (Elisir d'Amore), Susanna (Le Nozze di Figaro), Lauretta (Gianni Schicchi). *Leisure interests:* gardening, embroidery. *Address:* 56 Rochester Rd, London NW1 9JG, UK. *Telephone:* (20) 7485-7322.

BURROWS, Eva, AC, BA, M ED; Australian Salvation Army officer (retd); b 15 Sept 1929, Newcastle, Australia; d of Robert J. Burrows and Ella M. Watson. *Education:* Brisbane High School Univ of Queensland, Univ of London and Univ of Sydney. *Career:* Missionary educator Howard Inst, Zimbabwe (fmrly Rhodesia) 1952–67; Prin Usher Inst, Zimbabwe 1967–69; Vice-Prin Int Coll for Officers, London 1970–73, Prin 1974–75; Leader Women's Social Services in UK and Ireland 1975–77; Territorial Commdr Salvation Army, Sri Lanka 1977–79, Scotland 1979–82, Australia 1982–86; Gen (int leader) of the Salvation Army 1986–93; Hon PH D (Ewha Woman's Univ, Seoul, Repub of Korea) 1988, (Queenstown) 1993; Hon Dr Liberal Arts (Ewha Woman's Univ, Seoul) 1988; Hon D IUR (Asbury Coll, USA) 1988;

Hon D UNIV (Griffith Univ) 1994; Hon LL D (New South Wales) 1996; Hon doctorate (Melbourne Coll of Divinity) 2000; Living Legacy Award (USA) 1996. *Leisure interests:* classical music, reading, travel. *Address:* 102 Domain Park, 193 Domain Rd, South Yarra, Vic 3141, Australia. *Telephone:* (3) 9820 9701; *Fax:* (3) 9866 5240; *E-mail:* eva_burrows@aus.salvationarmy.org.

BURSTYN, Ellen; American actress; b 7 Dec 1932, Detroit, MI; d of John Austin and Coriene Marie (née Hamel) Gillooly; m 1st William C. Alexander; m 2nd Paul Roberts; m 3rd Neil Burstyn; one s. *Education:* Cass Tech High School (Detroit, MI). *Career:* Co-artistic Dir The Actor's Studio, New York 1982–; Pres Actors' Equity Asscn 1982–88. *Plays include:* Acted in: Fair Game 1957, Same Time Next Year 1975, 84 Charing Cross Road, Shirley Valentine 1989–90; Directed: Judgement 1981, Into Thin Air 1985; *Films include:* Goodbye Charlie 1964, For Those Who Think Young 1965, Tropic of Cancer 1969, Alex in Wonderland 1970, The Last Picture Show (Best Supporting Actress, New York Film Critics Award, Nat Soc of Film Critics Award) 1971, The King of Marvin Gardens 1972, The Exorcist 1973, Harry and Tonto 1974, Alice Doesn't Live Here Anymore (Best Actress Acad Award, British Acad Award) 1975, Providence 1976, Dream of Passion 1978, Same Time Next Year (Best Actress, Tony Award, Drama Desk Award, Outer Critics' Circle Award) 1978, Resurrection, Silence of the North 1980, Alamo Bay 1985, Twice in a Lifetime 1985, Hannah's War 1987, The Colour of Evening 1990, Dying Young 1990, The Cemetery Club 1993, How to Make an American Quilt 1995, The Babysitters Club 1995, Deceiver 1997, You Can Thank Me Later 1998, Playing By Heart 1998, Walking Across Egypt 1999, Requiem for a Dream 1999, The Yards 1999; *TV appearances include:* When You Remember Me, Thursday's Game. *Address:* c/o CAA, 9830 Wilshire Blvd, Beverly Hills, CA 90212, USA (Office).

BURTON, Iris Grace; British magazine editor; d of Arthur and the late Alice Burton; m; one s one d. *Education:* Roan Girls' Grammar School and City of London Coll. *Career:* Journalist SE London Mercury until 1966; writer, later Features Ed Woman's Own 1966–78, Ed 1980–86; Asst Ed TV Times 1978–80; Ed-in-Chief Prima magazine 1986–87, Best magazine 1987–88; Editorial Dir G + J of the UK 1988–91; Ed-in-Chief Woman's Realm magazine 1991–, Woman's Weekly magazine 1992–; mem Press Complaints Comm 1993–. *Address:* IPC Magazines, King's Reach Tower, Stamford St, London SE1 9LS, UK.

BUSH, Barbara Pierce; American former First Lady; b 8 June 1925, Rye, NY; d of Marvin and Pauline (née Robinson) Pierce; m George Herbert Walker Bush 1945; four s one d. *Education:* Smith Coll. *Career:* Mem Bd of Dirs Reading is Fundamental, Business Council for Effective Literacy; mem Advisory Council, Soc of Memorial Sloan-Kettering Cancer Center; Hon Chair Advisory Council Literacy Volunteers of America; Pres Ladies of the Senate 1981–88; numerous hon degrees; Outstanding Mother of the Year Award 1984, Free Spirit Award, Freedom Forum 198, Distinguished Leadership Award, United Negro Coll Fund 1986, Distinguished American Woman Award, Coll Mt St Joseph 1987. *Publication:* Barbara Bush: A Memoir 1994. *Address:* 490 E L'Enfant Plaza, SW, Room 6125, Washington, DC 20594, USA (Office).

BUSH, Kate (Katherine); British singer and performer; b 30 July 1958, Welling. *Career:* Contributed to soundtracks of Castaway (Be Kind to My Mistakes) and She's Having a Baby (This Woman's Work); Dir Novercia Ltd; British Phonographic Industry Award for Best Vocalist 1979, 1987. *Recordings include:* Singles: Wuthering Heights, The Man with the Child in His Eyes, Wow, Symphony in Blue, Babooshka, Army Dreamers, Breathing, Sat in Your Lap, The Dreaming, Running Up That Hill, Don't Give Up (with Peter Gabriel), The Sensual World, Be Kind to My Mistakes (from soundtrack of Castaway), This Woman's Work (from soundtrack of She's Having a Baby); Albums: The Kick Inside, Lionheart, Never Forever, The Dreaming, The Single File, Hounds of Love, The Sensual World, The Whole Story, The Red Shoes. *Address:* c/o EMI Records (UK), EMI House, 43 Brook Green, London W6 7EF, UK (Office).

BUSSELL, Darcy Andrea, CBE; British ballet dancer; b 27 April 1969, London; d of Philip Michael and Andrea (née Williams) Pemberton; m Angus Forbes 1997. *Education:* Arts Educational School and Royal Ballet School. *Career:* Joined Sadlers Wells Royal Ballet (now Birmingham Royal Ballet) 1987; Soloist, Royal Ballet (London) 1988, First Soloist 1989, Prin (Royal Ballet's youngest Prin Dancer) 1989–; performed at Queen Mother's 90th Birthday Tribute, London; Prix de Lausanne 1989; Most Promising Newcomer Award Variety Club of Great Britain 1990; Dancer of the Year (Dance and Dancers Magazine) 1990; Award for Dance (London Evening Standard) 1990. *Ballets include:* Royal Ballet: leading roles in The Spirit of Fugue (created for her by David Bintley), first Royal Ballet performances of Balanchine's Rubies and Stravinsky Violin Concerto, Ashley Page's Bloodlines (creator of leading role), Swan Lake (Odette/Odile), The Nutcracker (Sugar Plum Fairy), La Bayadère (Gamzatti), The Prince of the Pagodas (created for her by Kenneth MacMillan), Manon, Cinderella, Sleeping Beauty, Elite Syncopations (MacMillan), Raymonda, Bloodlines, Romeo and Juliet and others; *Publication:* My Life in Dance 1998. *Leisure interests:* sketching/painting, arts. *Address:* Royal Opera House, Covent Garden, London WC2E 9DD, UK (Office); 155 New King's Rd, London SW6 4SJ, UK (Home). *Telephone:* (20) 7240 1200 (Office).

BUTENUTH-GABRIEL, Claudia Gloria; German actress and artist; b Sept, Göttingen; one s. *Education:* Acting in Bochum and Munich, homeopathy in Munich. *Career:* Actress 1965–; has acted in the theatre, in films and in TV films for German, French, Italian, and US TV; appearances in more than 100 TV plays for German TV; exhibition of paintings, Munich 1980; composer I'm Still Crazy About You for German film 1980; created sculpture of Dali 1981; Prize for Best Play for TV of the Month 1979. *Films include:* Silent Night, Brass Target, Ein Mord, den jeder begeht 1983; *TV appearances include:* Schwarzwaldklinik, Hotel Paradies, Glückliche Familie; *Publications:* Begegnungen (autobiog) 1990, Zwei Männer und eine Frau... (short stories) 1992. *Leisure interests:* writing, tennis, painting, psychology. *Address:* Agentur Breilmann, Postfach 1461, 27416 Sittensen, Germany.

BUTLER, Marilyn Speers, D PHIL, FRSL, FRSA; British college rector and academic; b 11 Feb 1937, Kingston-on-Thames, Surrey; d of Sir Trevor and Margaret (née Gribbin) Evans; m David Edgeworth Butler 1962; three s. *Education:* Wimbledon High School (London) and St Hilda's (Oxford). *Career:* Trainee BBC 1960–62; temporary Lecturer ANU 1967; Research Fellow St Hilda's Coll, Oxford 1970–73, Fellow and Lecturer St Hugh's Coll, and Oxford Univ Lecturer 1973–86; Visiting Fellow Caltech 1985, ANU 1986; King Edward II Prof of English Literature, Univ of Cambridge 1986–93; Rector Exeter Coll, Oxford 1993–; Titular Prof of English Language and Literature, Univ of Oxford 1998–; British Acad Reader 1982–85; Visiting Prof Univ of Virginia, USA 1989; Fellow Royal Soc of Literature 1990; Hon LITT D (Leicester) 1992, (Birmingham) 1993, (Oxford Brookes), (Williams Coll, MA) 1995, (Lancaster, Warwick, Surrey) 1997, (Kingston) 1998; British Acad Crawshay Prize 1972. *Publications include:* Maria Edgeworth, A Literary Biography 1972, Jane Austen and the War of Ideas 1975, Peacock Displayed 1979, Romantics, Rebels and Reactionaries 1981, Burke, Paine, Godwin and the Revolution Controversy (ed) 1984, Collected Works of Mary Wollstonecraft (co-ed) 1989, Edgeworth's Castle Rackrent (ed) 1992, Ennui (ed) 1992, Mary Shelley's Frankenstein (ed) 1993, Jane Austen's Northanger Abbey (ed) 1995, Collected Works of Edgeworth (ed with M. Myers) 1999. *Leisure interests:* books, films, gossip, avoiding exercise. *Address:* The Rector's Lodgings, Exeter College, Exeter, OX1 3DP, UK (Office). *Telephone:* (1865) 279647 (Office); (1865) 279644 (Home); *Fax:* (1865) 279674 (Office); *E-mail:* rector@exeter.ox.ac.uk (Office).

BUTLER-SLOSS, Rt Hon Dame (Ann) Elizabeth (Oldfield), DBE, PC, FRSM; British judge; b 10 Aug 1933; d of the late Sir Cecil Havers and Enid Snelling; m Joseph Butler-Sloss 1958; two s one d. *Education:* Wycombe Abbey School. *Career:* Called to Bar, Inner Temple 1955, Bencher 1979; contested Lambeth, Vauxhall as Conservative cand 1959; practising barrister 1955–70; Registrar, Prin Registry of Probate, later Family Div 1970–79; Judge, High Court of Justice, Family Div 1979–87; Lord Justice of Appeal 1988–99; Pres of Family Div 1999–; Chair Cleveland Child Abuse Inquiry 1987–88; Advisory Council, St Paul's Cathedral; Pres Honiton Agricultural Show 1985–86; Treas Inner Temple 1998–; mem Judicial Studies Bd 1985–89; Hon Fellow St Hilda's Coll, Oxford 1988; Fellow Kings Coll, London 1991, mem Council 1992–; Chancellor Univ of W of England 1993–; Hon FRCP, Fellow Royal Soc of Phychiatrists; Hon LL D (Hull) 1989, (Keele)

1991, (Bristol) 1991, (Brunel, Exeter) 1992, (Manchester) 1995, (Greenwich) 2000, (East Anglia) 2001, (Liverpool) 2001; Hon D LITT (Loughborough Univ of Tech) 1993; Hon D UNIV (Univ of Cen England) 1994; Hon FRCP, FRCPSYCH. *Publications:* Phipson on Evidence (co-ed, 10th edn), Corpe on Road Haulage (2nd edn), Supreme Court Practice (ed) 1976, 1979. *Leisure interests:* walking, theatre, music. *Address:* c/o Royal Courts of Justice, Strand, London, WC2A 2LL, UK (Office). *Telephone:* (20) 7947-6084.

BUTTLE, Eileen, PH D; British environmental administrator; b 19 Oct 1937; d of George Ernest and Mary Stewart Linford; m Hugh Langley Buttle 1970. *Education:* Univ of Southampton. *Career:* Research Fellow Univ of Southampton 1963–65; research scientist Nat Inst of Research in Dairying 1965–71; mem staff Cattle Breeding Centre, Ministry of Agriculture and Fisheries 1971–79, Policy Admin 1976–89; fmrly Chief Exec Natural Environment Research Council; mem Scientific Cttee European Environment Agency (EEA) 1994–. *Address:* European Environment Agency, Kongens Nytorv 6, 1050 Copenhagen K, Denmark. *Telephone:* 33-36-71-00; *Fax:* 33-36-71-99.

BUTTROSE, Ita Clare, AO, OBE; Australian editor, broadcaster, writer and publishing executive; b 17 Jan 1942, Sydney; d of Charles Oswald and Mary Clare (née Rodgers) Buttrose; m 1st Alasdair MacDonald 1963 (divorced); m 2nd Peter Sawyer 1979 (divorced); one d one s. *Education:* Sacred Heart Convent (Rose Bay, Sydney) and Dover Heights High School (Sydney). *Career:* Joined Australian Consolidated Press Pty Ltd 1958, Dir 1974–81, Publr Women's Div 1977–80; Founding Ed Cleo 1972–75; Ed Australian Women's Weekly 1975–76, Ed-in-Chief 1976–77, columnist and feature writer 1998–; Sub-Ed Woman's Own (UK) 1967–69; Ed-in-Chief The Daily Telegraph and The Sunday Telegraph (Sydney) 1981–84; Dir News Ltd Australia 1981–84; Ed-in-Chief The Sun-Herald 1988; Publishing Consultant Woman's Day and Portfolio magazines 1983–88; Ed Ita Magazine 1989–94; CEO Capricorn Publishing Pty Ltd 1988–94; Broadcaster Radio 2KY, 2UE (Sydney) 1984–87, Radio 3UZ (Melbourne) 1988–90; TV personality Beauty & the Beast Foxtel and Network TEN 1996–; Dir TV and Telecasters Pty Ltd 1991–93, Prudential Corpn Australia Ltd 1990–96; Dir Hope Town Special School Wyong Ltd 1990–; Chair Nat Advisory Cttee on AIDS (NACAIDS) 1984–88, Chair AIDS Trust of Australia 1990–94; Convenor First Nat Family Summit (Canberra); Communications Strategist World Vision Australia 1995–97; Chair Australian Services Nurses Nat Memorial Fund Cttee 1997–99; Nat Spokesperson Arthritis Foundation of Australia 1997–99, 2001–; Dir Sydney Symphony Council 1996–, The Smith Family 1997; Fellow Australian Inst of Co Dirs, Autralian Inst of Man; Assoc Fellow Professional Marketing Asscn; mem Council Australian Nat Art Gallery 1989–, Australian Soc of Authors, Chief Exec Women; Hartnett Medal (Royal Soc for the Encouragement of Arts, Manufactures and Commerce) 1992; mem Program Reference Group 2001, Australian Govts Women Speak Conf; Amb Melbourne Museum 2001–. *Publications include:* A Guide to Modern Etiquette 1985, Early Edition: My First Forty Years 1985, A Passionate Life 1998, A Word to the Wise 1999, What is Love? 2000. *Leisure interests:* reading, travel, gardening, opera, ballet, theatre. *Address:* POB 648, Double Bay, NSW 1360, Australia. *Telephone:* (2) 9361-6636; *Fax:* (2) 9361-5757.

BUZKOVÁ, Petra, D JUR; Czech politician and lawyer; b 7 Dec 1965, Prague; d of Josef Buzek and Olga Buzková (née Hodráková); m Josef Kotrba 1994. *Education:* Charles Univ. *Career:* Mem Poslanecká sněmovna (Parl) 1982–, Vice-Pres 1996–; Vice-Pres Czech Social Democratic Party 1993–. *Address:* Czech Social Democrat Party, (Ceska strana socialne demokraticka), Lidovy dum, Hybernská 7, 110 00 Prague 1, Czech Republic. *Telephone:* (2) 24592111; *Fax:* (2) 24222749.

BUZOIANU, Cătălina; Romanian theatrical director; b 13 April 1938, Brăila; d of Roman and Elena Buzoianu; m Papil Panduru 1963; one s one d. *Education:* Bucharest Theatrical and Cinematographic Art Inst. *Career:* Started career at Nat Theatre Iaşi with Le Malade Imaginaire (Molière) 1970, Teatrul Tineretului (Youth Theatre) in Piatra Neamţ; Prin Dir Teatrul Mic, Bucharest 1978–85; Prof Theatre and Cinema Institute; Dean of Theatre Dept, Theatre and Film Acad 1990–; directed numerous plays abroad; tours abroad and participation in int festivals; numerous awards including Salvo Randoni Award for whole career, and especially for Pirandello performances, Italy 1995, Prix théâtre vivant, Radio France Int 1994, Prize for Excellence, Int Asscn of Critics, Romanian Section. *Publications:* Novele teatrale (essays), Meridiane (ed) 1987; articles and essays in various periodicals. *Address:* Bulandra Theatre, Bd Schitu Măgureanu 1, 70626 Bucharest, Romania (Office); C A Rosetti Str, Et 7, Ap 19, Sect 1, Bucharest, Romania (Home). *Telephone:* 1.211.00.88 (Home); *Fax:* 1.312.28.97 (Office).

BYATT, Dame Antonia Susan, DBE, BA, FRSL; British writer; b 24 Aug 1936; d of John F. Drabble and the late Kathleen M. Bloor; m 1st Ian C. R. Byatt 1959 (divorced 1969); one s (deceased) one d; m 2nd Peter J. Duffy 1969; two d. *Education:* Sheffield High School, The Mount School (York), Newnham Coll (Cambridge), Bryn Mawr Coll (USA) and Somerville Coll (Oxford). *Career:* Extra-Mural Lecturer Univ of London 1962–71; Lecturer in Literature Cen School of Art and Design 1965–69, in English, Univ Coll London 1972–81, Sr Lecturer 1981–83; Assoc Newnham Coll, Cambridge 1977–82; mem BBC Social Effects of TV Advisory Group 1974–77; mem Bd of Creative and Performing Arts 1985–87, Bd of British Council 1993–98; Kingman Cttee on English Language 1987–88; Man Cttee Soc of Authors 1984–88, Chair 1986–88; mem Literature Advisory Panel of the British Council 1990–98; Hon Fellow Newnham Coll Cambridge, London Inst; broadcaster, reviewer and judge of literary prizes; Hon D LITT (Bradford) 1987, (Durham, York) 1991, (Nottingham) 1992, (Liverpool) 1993, (Portsmouth) 1994, (London) 1995, (Cambridge) 1999, (Sheffield); PEN-Macmillan Silver Pen for Still Life 1986. *Publications include:* Shadow of the Sun 1964, Degrees of Freedom: The Novels of Iris Murdoch 1965, The Game 1967, Wordsworth and Coleridge in Their Time 1970, Iris Murdoch 1976, The Virgin in the Garden 1978, George Eliot: The Mill on the Floss (ed and introduction) 1979, Still Life 1985, Sugar and Other Stories 1987, Possession (Booker Prize, Irish Times–Aer Lingus Int Fiction Prize, Eurasian Regional Award of the Commonwealth Writers' Prize) 1990, George Eliot: Selected Essays and Other Writings 1990, Robert Browning: Dramatic Monologues (ed and introduction) 1990, Passions of the Mind (selected essays) 1991, Art Work 1991, The Shadow of the Sun 1991, Angels and Insects (novellas) 1992, The Matisse Stories (short stories) 1993, Degrees of Freedom: The Early Novels of Iris Murdoch, The Djinn in the Nightingale's Eye 1994, Imagining Characters (jtly) 1995, New Writing 4 (co-ed) 1995, Babel Tower 1996, New Writing 6 (co-ed) 1997, Elementals: Stories of Fire and Ice (short stories) 1998, The Oxford Book of English Short Stories (ed and introduction) 1998, The Biographer's Tale 2000, On Histories and Stories (essays) 2000. *Address:* 37 Rusholme Rd, London SW15, UK. *Telephone:* (20) 7387 7050 (Office); (20) 8789 3109 (Home).

BYNOE, Dame Hilda Louisa, DBE, MB; Grenadian public servant and medical practitioner; b 18 Nov 1921, Grenada; d of T. Joseph and Louisa Gibbs; m Peter Bynoe 1947; two s. *Education:* St Joseph's Convent (Grenada) and Univ of London. *Career:* Teacher St Joseph's Convents, Grenada and Trinidad 1939–44; Public Service Medical Officer, Port-of-Spain, Trinidad 1954–55, Dist Medical Officer 1958–65; Public Service Medical Officer, Georgetown, Guyana 1955–58; pvt medical practice 1965–68, 1974–89; Gov of Grenada 1968–74; Patron Caribbean Women's Asscn 1970–, John Hayes Memorial Kidney Foundation 1979–, Music Foundation of Trinidad and Tobago 1986–. *Leisure interests:* poetry writing, swimming, travel. *Address:* 5A Barcant Ave, Maraval, Trinidad and Tobago. *Telephone:* 628-3342.

C

CABALLÉ, Montserrat; Spanish opera singer (soprano); b Barcelona; m Bernabe Marti 1964; one s one d. *Education:* Conservatorio del Liceo and studied under Eugenia Kemeny, Conchita Badia and Maestro Annovazi. *Career:* Debut with State Opera of Basel (Switzerland); appeared at Glyndebourne Festival 1965, and at opera houses worldwide including Metropolitan Opera (New York), Gran Teatro del Liceo (Barcelona, Spain), La Scala (Milan, Italy), Vienna State Opera, Paris and Rome Operas, Bayerische Staatsoper (Munich, Germany), Royal Opera House (Covent Garden, London) and Teatro Colón (Buenos Aires); numerous hon degrees, awards and medals including Most Excellent and Illustrious Doña and Cross of Isabella la Católica, Commdr des Arts et des Lettres 1986. *Operas include:* La Bohème, Manon 1964, Lucrezia Borgia 1965, Der Rosenkavalier, The Marriage of Figaro 1965, Faust 1965; *Recordings include:* Lucrezia Borgia, La Traviata, Salomé, Aida, Rossini, Donizetti, Verdi, Eternal, Barcelona (with Freddie Mercury). *Address:* c/o RCA, Bedford House, 69/79 Fulham High St, London SW6 3JW, UK.

CACHIN, Françoise; French museum director; b 1936. *Career:* Fmr Dir Musée d'Orsay; Dir Musées de France (34 nat museums and collections at 1,000 other museums in France) 1994–. *Address:* 6 rue des Pyramides, 75041 Paris Cedex 01, France. *Telephone:* (1) 40-15-73-00; *Fax:* (1) 40-15-34-10.

CAFÉ, Maria Mambo, M ÈS SC ECON; Angolan economist and politician; b 6 Feb 1945, Cabinda; d of Zacarias Mendes and Dina Chivela Café; m (divorced); two d. *Education:* Luanda and Plehanov Higher Inst of Economic Science (Moscow). *Career:* Teacher in areas controlled by Movimento Popular de Libertação de Angola (MPLA), Moxico and Kuandu Kubango 1969–73; Deputy Rep of MPLA in Bucharest 1974; Admin Inst of Credit of Angola 1975–77; Vice-Minister of Commerce 1977–78; Sec Cen Cttee MPLA 1979–86, mem Bd of Dirs 1988–90, 1996; Minister of State for Econ and Social Affairs 1986–87; Gov Cabinda 1991; mem Nat Ass (Parl) and Pres Banque de Commerce et Industrie in Nat Ass; three decorations for former soldiers (maximum number of decorations) 1990. *Leisure interest:* gardening. *Address:* Assembleia Nacional, CP 1204, Luanda, Angola; Rua Fernão Mendes Pinto 112/112A, Luanda, Angola. *Telephone:* (2) 321881; *Fax:* (2) 321152.

CAHILL, Teresa Mary, LRAM; British opera and concert singer; b 30 July 1944, Maidenhead, Berks; d of Henry D. and Florence (née Dallimore) Cahill; m John A. Kiernander 1971 (divorced 1978). *Education:* Notre Dame High School (London), Guildhall School of Music and Drama and London Opera Centre. *Career:* Debut at Glyndebourne 1969, Royal Opera House, Covent Garden, London 1970, La Scala (Milan, Italy) 1976, Philadelphia Opera (USA) 1981; Prof Royal Northern Coll of Music and Trinity Coll of Music, London; Vocal Consultant Univ of York; specializes in works of Mozart, Strauss, Mahler, Elgar and Tippett; concert appearances throughout Europe, USA and Far East; Master Classes Dartington Festival 1984, 1986, Oxford Univ 1995–96, Peabody Inst Baltimore 1999; Artistic Adviser Nat Mozart Competition 1997–; Adjudicator Live Music Now 1988– (Musical Adviser 2000–); Gov Royal Soc of Musicians 2000; recordings include works of Elgar, Strauss, Mahler; Worshipful Company of Musicians Silver Medal 1966; John Christie Award 1970. *Leisure interests:* cinema, theatre, photography, travel, reading, and going to sales from car boots to Sotheby's. *Address:* 65 Leyland Rd, London, SE12 8DW, UK.

CAISERMAN-ROTH, Ghitta, BA; Canadian artist; b 1923, Montréal, PQ; d of Hanane and Sarah (née Wittal) Caiserman; m 1st Alfred Pinsky 1945; m 2nd Max W. Roth 1962; one d. *Education:* High School of Montréal (PQ) Ecole des Beaux-Arts (Montréal, PQ) and Parson's School of Design (NY, USA). *Career:* Teacher of Art Concordia Univ (Montréal), Univ de Québec, Saidye Bronfman Centre, Nova Scotia Coll of Art, Arts Sutton; participant travelling show The Canadian Landscape 1983; represented in over 100 public collections in Canada and USA including McMichael Conservatory, Gallery Kleinberg, Montréal Museum of Fine Arts (PQ), Nat Gallery of Canada (Ottawa, ON), Vancouver Art Gallery (BC), Winnipeg Art Gallery (MB), London Public Library and Art Museum (ON), Beaverbrook Art Gallery (Fredericton, NB), Dept of Foreign Affairs (Ottawa); Vice-Chair Status of the Artist Comm; mem Council Royal Canadian Acad; Canada Council Fellow, Grantee 1989; Centennial Medal 1967. *Publications include:* Creativism (jtly) 1980, Pulsions-Pulse (jtly) 1983, Drawing from the Model – A Sensuous Tactile Approach. *Leisure interests:* tennis, cross-country skiing, music, theatre. *Address:* 3475 Jeanne Mance, Montréal, PQ H2X 2J7, Canada. *Telephone:* (514) 844-4722.

CALDER, Elisabeth Nicole, BA; British publisher; b 20 Jan 1938; d of Ivor George and Florence Mary Baber; m Richard Henry Calder 1958 (divorced 1972); one s one d. *Education:* Palmerston North Girls' High School (NZ) and Univ of Canterbury (NZ). *Career:* Reader Metro-Goldwyn-Mayer Story Dept 1969–70; Publicity Man Victor Gollancz 1971–74, Editorial Dir 1975–78; Editorial Dir Jonathan Cape 1979–86; Publishing Dir Bloomsbury Publishing 1986–. *Leisure interests:* junking, thinking about gardening, reading. *Address:* Bloomsbury Publishing, 38 Soho Square, London W1V 5DF, UK (Office). *Telephone:* (20) 7494-2111 (Office).

CALDICOTT, Dame Fiona, DBE, MA, BM, B CH, FRCP(UK), FRCPSYCH, FRCP(I); British psychiatrist; b 12 Jan 1941; d of Joseph Maurice Soesan and Elizabeth Jane Ransley; m Robert Gordon Woodruff Caldicott 1965; one d (one s deceased). *Education:* City of London School for Girls and Oxford Univ. *Career:* House Surgeon and Physician, Coventry Hosps 1966–67; GP, Family Planning and Child Welfare 1968–70; training in psychiatry 1970–76; Sr Registrar in Psychiatry, W Midlands Regional Training Scheme 1977–79; Consultant Psychiatrist, Univ of Warwick 1979–85; Consultant Psychotherapist Uffculme Clinic, Birmingham 1979–96; Sr Clinical Lecturer in Psychotherapy, Univ of Birmingham 1982–96; Unit Gen Man, Mental Health, Central Birmingham 1989–91; Clinical Dir Adult Psychiatric and Psychotherapy Service, Mental Health Unit, S Birmingham 1991–94; Medical Dir S Birmingham Mental Health NHS Trust 1994–96; mem Sec of State's Standing Advisory Cttee on Medical Manpower (now Workforce) Planning 1991–, on Postgrad Medical Ed 1993–; Chair Monospecialist Cttee for Psychiatry 1995– (Sec 1991–95); Sec European Bd of Psychiatry 1992–96; Sub-Dean Royal Coll of Psychiatrists 1987–90, Dean 1990–93, Pres 1993–96; Chair Conf of Medical Royal Colls 1995–96; Prin Somerville Coll Oxford 1996–; mem Union of European Medical Specialists, Broadcasting Standards Council 1996–, Czech Psychiatric Soc 1994; Fellow Acad of Medicine, Singapore 1994; Hon D SC (Warwick) 1997, Hon MD (Birmingham) 1997; Chevalier du Tastevin 1991. *Publications:* contrib to Discussing Doctors' Careers (ed Isobel Allen) 1988; papers in learned journals on psychiatry. *Leisure interests:* family, friends, reading, theatre, wine. *Address:* Somerville College, Oxford OX2 6HD, UK (Office); The Old Rectory, Manor Farm Lane, Balscote, Banbury OX15 6JJ, UK (Home). *Telephone:* (01295) 730293 (Home); *Fax:* (01295) 730293 (Home).

CALISHER, Hortense, AB; American writer; b 20 Dec 1911, New York; d of Joseph H. and Hedwig (née Lichtstern) Calisher; m 1st Heaton Bennet Heffelfiner 1935 (divorced); one s one d; m 2nd Curtis Harnack 1959. *Education:* Hauter Coll High School, Barnard Coll (New York) and Columbia Univ. *Career:* Adjunct Prof of English Barnard Coll, Columbia Univ, NY 1956–57, Adjunct Prof Columbia Univ 1968–70; Visiting Lecturer State Univ of Iowa 1957, 1959–60, Stanford Univ 1958, Sarah Lawrence Coll (New York) 1962, 1967; Adjunct Prof City Coll of New York 1969; Visiting Prof of Literature Brandeis Univ 1963–64, Univ of Philadelphia 1965, State Univ of New York, Purchase 1971–72, Bennington Coll 1978, Washington Univ, St Louis 1979, Brown Univ 1986; Regent's Prof Univ of California 1976; Guggenheim Fellow 1952, 1955; mem American Acad, Inst Arts and Letters (Pres 1987–90), American PEN (Pres 1986–87); Hon LITT D (Skidmore Coll) 1980; Hon LL D (Grinnell) 1986; Acad of Arts and Letters Award 1967; Nat Council Arts Award 1967; Nat Endowment for the Arts Award for Lifetime Achievement 1988. *Publications include:* In the Absence of Angels (short stories) 1951, Tale for the Mirror 1961, False Entry 1961, Extreme Magic 1963, Textures of Life 1963, The Railway Police and The Last Trolley Ride 1965, Journal from Ellipsia 1965, Queenie 1969, The New Yorkers 1969, Standard Dreaming 1971, Herself (autobiog) 1972, Eagle Eye, On Keeping Women 1977, Mysteries of Motion 1984, Saratoga, Hot (short fiction) 1985, The Bobby Soxer (Kafka Prize) 1986, Age 1987, Kissing Cousins (memoir) 1988, The Small Bang (novel) (under pseudonym Jack Fenno) 1992, In The Palace of the Movie King 1993, In the Slammer with Carol Smith 1996; several novellas, articles and reviews. *Leisure interest:* the other arts. *Address:* c/o Marion Boyars Publishers, 237 E 39th St, New York, NY 10016, USA (Office).

CALLAWAY, Mary, B COM, M ECON SC, DIP ED; Australian academic accountant; b 22 Sept 1943, Bacchus Marsh, Vic; d of Wilfred and Iris Rogers; m Barry Callaway 1966; three s. *Education:* Univs of Melbourne and New England and Bendigo Coll of Advanced Educ. *Career:* Teacher (Hamilton, Vic) 1965, (Bendigo, Vic) 1976–79; Educ Officer Papua New Guinea 1966–68, 1971–74; Sr Tutor Bendigo Coll of Advanced Educ 1980, Lecturer 1981–85; Lecturer Mitchell Coll of Advanced Educ (Bathurst, NSW) 1986–87; Sr Lecturer in Accountancy Charles Sturt Univ 1987–; Br Councillor and Deputy Chair Australian Soc of CPAs (Bendigo, Vic) until 1986, Br Councillor and Chair (Aalbury Wodanga) 1988–1993; State Councillor Australian Fed of Business and Professional Women, Vic 1984–85, NSW 1986–87, Nat Treas 1987–90, Pres 1990–93; Treas Int Fed of Business and Professional Women 1993–96. *Publications:* Business in Australia (jtly, 2nd edn) 1996; contribs to books. *Leisure interests:* Church, propagating orchid and cyclamen, walking, family history. *Address:* Charles Sturt University, School of Business, POB 789, Albury, NSW, Australia; 287 Tracy St, Lavington, NSW 2641, Australia. *Telephone:* (60) 418861; (60) 401571; *Fax:* (60) 418878; (60) 401571; *E-mail:* mcallaway@csu.edu.au.

CALLE, Sophie; French photographer; b 1953, Paris. *Career:* Freelance photographer; columnist Libération 1983; solo exhibitions include Centre Nat d'Art et de Culture Georges Pompidou 1980, Gallerie Montenegro (Madrid) 1988, Musée d'Art Moderne de la Ville de Paris 1991, Sala Mendoza, Caracas (Venezuela) 1993, High Museum of Art, Atlanta (Georgia) 1996, The Birthday Ceremony, Tate Gallery (London) 1998, Galerie Matthias Arndt (Berlin) 1999, Museum Fridericianum (Kassel) 2000; group exhibitions include: Une Idée en l'Air (New York) 1980, The Ready Made Boomerang, Biennale de Sydney 1990, Hayward Gallery London 1992, The vision of art in a paradoxical world, 4th Int Biennial of Instanbul (Turkey) 1995, Deep Storage Munich and Berlin 1997, Passage New French Art, Setagaya Art Museum (Tokyo) 1999, L'empire du temps, mythes et création, Musée du Louvre (Paris) 2000. *Films include:* Double Blind (jtly with Greg Shepard); *Publication:* Suite Vénitienne (text and photographs) 1983; *Photographs include:* Les Dormeurs 1979, The Bronx 1980, The Blind 1986, Les Arges 1984, photos taken on Trans-Siberian Railway journey 1984, Les Tombes 1988, Histoire Autobiographique 1988.

CALLIL, Carmen Thérèse, BA, FRSA; Australian publisher; b 15 July 1938, Melbourne; d of Frederick Alfred Louis Callil and Lorraine Claire Allen. *Education:* Star of the Sea Convent (Melbourne), Loreto Convent (Melbourne) and Univ of Melbourne. *Career:* Buyer's Asst Marks and Spencer (UK) 1963–65; Editorial Asst Hutchinson Publishing Co

1965–66, B. T. Batsford 1966–67; Publicity Man Panther Books then Granada Publishing 1967–70, André Deutsch 1971–72; Publicity Officer For Ink Newspaper 1972; f Carmen Callil Ltd, Book Publicity Co and Virago Press 1972; Chair and Man Dir Virago Press 1972–82, Chair 1982–95; Man Dir Chatto and Windus, The Hogarth Press 1982–93; Publr-at-large Random House UK 1993–94; Ed-at-large Knopf, NY, USA 1993–94; mem Exec Cttee Man Bd Random House Group; mem Bd Channel 4 1985–91, Random Century 1989–94; Gov Museum of London 1992–; Chair Booker Prize for Fiction 1996–; Hon D LITT (Sheffield) 1994, (Oxford Brookes) 1995; Hon D UNIV (York) 1995, (Open) 1997; Distinguished Service Award Int Women's Writing Guild. *Publication:* The Modern Library: the 200 best novels in England since 1950 (jtly) 1999. *Leisure interests:* friends, reading, animals, films, gardening. *Address:* 30 Bedford Square, London WC1B 3EG, UK.

CALLUS, Angela, BA; Maltese organization executive; b 23 Oct 1945, Safi; d of Nazarene and Paulina Callus. *Education:* Univ of Malta, Univ Delgi Studi di Siena and Univ Italiana per Stranieri (Perugia, Italy). *Career:* Secondary school teacher 1966–81, Admin 1981–89; mem Nationalist Party 1977, mem Nat Exec Cttee 1989; mem European Cttee for Equality Between Women and Men, Council of Europe 1987, Comm for the Advancement of Women 1989, Nat Comm for UNESCO, Council of Univ of Malta, Public Transport Authority 2000–; Medalja ghall-Qadi tar-Repubblika. *Publications:* (in Maltese): A Study on Sexism in Local Primary School Textbooks 1989, A Book on Women's Rights 1992; Il-Mara Maltija Socjeta'li Qed Tinbidel (ed) 1996, The Maltese Women After 2000 (ed) 1998. *Leisure interests:* reading, gardening. *Address:* Public Transport Authority, Cannon Buildings, Triq il-Kanun, St Venera, Malta (Office); 31A St Paul St, Safi 2RQ 11, Malta (Home). *Telephone:* 250724 (Office); 826892 (Home); *Fax:* 447228 (Office); *E-mail:* pta@maltanet.net; *Internet:* www.maltanet.net/pta.

CALLWOOD, June, OC; Canadian journalist; b 2 June 1924, Chatham; d of Harold Callwood and Gladys LaVoie; m Trent Frayne 1944; two s (one deceased) two d. *Career:* Reporter and Columnist Toronto Globe and Mail 1942–45, 1975–78, 1983–89; TV Host 1975–78, 1991–92; Guest Lecturer on Human Rights, Univ of Ottawa 1984; Founder-mem and Vice-Pres Canadian Civil Liberties Asscn 1965–88, Hon Dir for Life 1988; Pres and Founder Nellie's Hostel for Women 1974–78, Dir 1985–89, 1990–91, Casey House Hospice 1988–89, Hon Dir 1989–, Jessie's Centre for Teenagers 1982–83, 1987–89; Pres and Founder-mem Learnx Foundation 1977–79, Justice for Children 1979–80; Pres Casey House Foundation 1992–93 (Hon Dir 1993–); Pres Maggie's (prostitutes' community service project) 1986–94, Canadian Soc for Prison Improvement; Chair The Writers' Union of Canada 1979–80; mem Council Amnesty Int (Canada) 1978–85; Vice-Pres PEN (Canada) 1987–88, Dir 1988–89, Pres 1989–90; Bencher Law Soc of Upper Canada 1987–91; Vice-Pres Ward's Retreat 1990–91; Dir Canadian Inst for Admin of Justice 1983–84; The Electronic Rights Licensing Agency 1997–99; Judge Gov-Gen's Literary Awards 1983–86; Chair Book and Periodical Council 1995–96; Gov Etobicoke Gen Hosp 1994–98; Co-Chair Campaign Against Poverty 1997–; Duthie Lecture (Simon Fraser Univ) 1990, Margaret Laurence Lecture 1993, Bruce Hutchison Lecture 1998; Writer-in-Residence N York Public Library 1995–96; involved in many public and humanitarian activities; numerous hon degrees including Hon D UNIV (Ottawa) 1987; Hon Dr of Sacred Letters (Trinity Coll) 1988; Hon LL D (Memorial Univ, Toronto) 1988, (Univ of Western Ontario) 1993, (McMaster) 1994, (Law Soc of Upper Canada, Univ of Calgary) 1997; Hon LITT D (Carleton Univ) 1988, (Guelph Univ) 1989, (New Brunswick) 1990; Hon DCL (Acadia Univ) 1993; Hon D HUM LITT (Mount St Vincent Univ) 1993; Canadian Newspaper Hall of Fame 1984; Manitoba Order of the Buffalo Hunt 1984; Order of Ontario 1988; Toronto Arts Foundation Lifetime Achievement Award 1990. *Publications include:* Love, Hate, Fear and Anger 1964, The Law is Not for Women 1973, A Portrait of Canada 1981, Emma 1984, Emotions 1986, Twelve Weeks in Spring 1986, Jim: A Life with AIDS 1988, The Sleepwalker 1990, June Callwood's National Treasurers 1994, Trial Without End 1995, The Man Who Lost Himself 2000, and 16 other books; *Radio work includes:* Court of Opinions 1959–67, Human Senility 1966; *TV work includes:* (Host) Generations 1966, In Touch 1975–78, Callwood's National Treasures 1991–98, Caregivers 1998. *Leisure* *interests:* swimming, books, gliding. *Address:* 21 Hillcroft Drive, Toronto, ON M9B 4X4, Canada. *Telephone:* (416) 231-1923; *Fax:* (416) 231-1923; *E-mail:* callwood@interlog.com.

CAMERON, Averil Millicent, CBE, PH D, FBA, FSA; British historian and academic; b 8 Feb 1940, Leek, Staffs; d of Tom Roy and Millicent (née Drew) Sutton; m Alan D. E. Cameron 1962 (divorced 1980); one s one d. *Education:* Somerville Coll (Oxford) and Univ Coll (London). *Career:* Asst Lecturer in Classics King's Coll, London 1965, Lecturer 1968, Reader in Ancient History 1970, Prof 1978–89, Prof Late Antique and Byzantine Studies 1988–94, Dir Centre for Hellenic Studies 1989–94; Warden of Keble Coll, Oxford 1994–; Prof of Late Antique and Byzantine History, Univ of Oxford 1997–, Pro-Vice-Chancellor 2001–; Summer Fellow Dumbarton Oaks 1980; Sather Prof of Classical Literature, Univ of California, USA 1985–86; Visiting Prof Columbia Univ, New York 1967–68; Visiting Prof Coll de France 1987, Lansdowne Lecturer, Victoria, BC 1992; Visiting mem Inst for Advanced Study, Princeton Univ, USA 1977–78, Distinguished Visitor 1992; Ed Journal of Roman Studies 1985–90; Chair Soc for the Promotion of Byzantine Studies 1983–89, Cathedrals Fabric Comm for England 1999–, Review Group on the Royal Peculiers 1999–; Pres Soc for the Promotion of Roman Studies 1995–98; Hon Fellow Somerville Coll, Oxford; Hon D LITT (Warwick, St Andrews, Queen's Belfast); Hon D THEOL (Lund). *Publications include:* Procopius 1967, Agathias 1970, Corippus, In laudem Iustini minoris libri quattuor 1976, Continuity and Change in Sixth-Century Byzantium 1981, Images of Women in Antiquity (ed) 1983, Constantinople in the Eighth Century (jtly) 1984, Procopius and the Sixth Century 1985, The Greek Renaissance in the Roman Empire (co-ed) 1989, Christianity and the Rhetoric of Empire 1991, The Byzantine and Early Islamic Near East I: Problems in the Literary Sources (ed) 1992, II (ed) 1994, III (ed) 1995, The Later Roman Empire 1993, The Mediterranean World in Late Antiquity AD 395–600 1993, Land Use and Settlement Patterns (ed) 1994, States, Resources and Armies (ed) 1995, Changing Cultures in Early Byzantium 1996, Cambridge Ancient History Vol XIII–The Late Empire (co-ed) 1997, Eusebius, Life of Constantine (jtly) 1999, Cambridge Ancient History Vol XIV–Late Antiquity: Empire and Successors (co-ed) 2000; many articles and chapters in edited books. *Address:* Warden's Lodgings, Keble College, Oxford OX1 3PQ, UK. *Telephone:* (1865) 272700 (Office); *Fax:* (1865) 272785 (Office); *E-mail:* averil.cameron@keb.ox.ac.uk (Home).

CAMPBELL, Bonnie Jean, BA, JD; American lawyer and politician; b 9 April 1948, Norwich, NY; d of Thomas Pierce and Helen Slater; m Edward Campbell 1974. *Education:* Drake Univ (IA). *Career:* Clerk Dept of Housing and Urban Devt, Washington, DC 1965–67, Senate Sub-cttee on Intergovernmental Relations 1967–69; case-worker Harold E. Hughes, Washington, DC 1969–74; Field Rep staff of Senator John C. Culver, Des Moines, IA 1974–80; Legal Clerk Wimer, Hudson, Flynn and Neugent, Des Moines, IA 1983–85, Assoc 1985–89; Called to the Bar, IA 1985; Council Belin, Harris, Helmick, Des Moines, IA 1989–91; Attorney-Gen State of IA 1991–95; Head Agency for Combating Violence Against Women, Dept of Justice 1995–; Chair Iowa State Democratic Nat Cttee 1987. *Address:* Department of Justice, 10th St and Constitutional Ave, Washington 20530, DC, USA (Office); 300 Walnut St No 187, Des Moines, IA 50309, USA (Home).

CAMPBELL, Cheryl Anne; British actress; b 22 May 1949. *Education:* Francis Bacon Grammar School (St Albans) and London Acad of Music and Dramatic Art. *Career:* Frmly Asst Stage Man (acting) Watford Palace Theatre; performed at Glasgow Citizens' Theatre, Watford Repertory Theatre, Birmingham Repertory Theatre, King's Head and Nat Theatre. *Plays include:* A Doll's House (Soc of West End Theatres—SWET Award 1982, 1983), All's Well That Ends Well, Miss Julie 1983, Little Eyolf 1985, Daughter-in-law 1985, The Sneeze 1988, Betrayal 1991, The Merry Wives of Windsor 1992, The Changeling 1992, Misha's Party 1993, Macbeth 1993, The Strip 1995, Some Sunny Day 1996, The Seagull 1997, Passion Play 2000; *Films include:* Chariots of Fire 1981, Greystoke 1983, The Shooting Party 1985; *TV appearances include:* Pennies from Heaven, Testament of Youth (Best Actress Award BAFTA, British Broadcasting Press Guild Award 1979), Malice Aforethought, A Winter Harvest, Centrepoint, The Secret Agent 1992, Monsignor Renard 2000. *Address:* c/o Rebecca Blond Associates, 69A King's Rd, London SW3 4NX, UK. *Telephone:* (20) 7351-4100.

CAMPBELL, Enid Mona, OBE, B ECON, LL B, PH D; Australian professor of law; b 30 Oct 1932; d of Neil and Mona (née Hutton) Campbell. *Education:* Methodist Ladies' Coll (Launceston), Univ of Tasmania and Duke Univ (NC, USA). *Career:* Lecturer in Political Science, Univ of Tasmania 1959; Lecturer, Sr Lecturer, later Assoc Prof of Law Univ of Sydney 1960–67; Sir Isaac Isaacs Prof of Law Monash Univ 1967–97; mem Royal Comm on Australian Govt Admin 1974–76, Australian Constitutional Comm 1985–88; Hon LL D (Tasmania) 1990. *Publications:* Parliamentary Privileges in Australia 1966, Freedom in Australia (2nd edn) 1973, Rules of Court – A Study of Rule-Making Powers and Procedures 1985, Legal Research: Methods and Materials (jtly, 3rd edn) 1988, (jtly, 4th edn) 1996. *Leisure interest:* reading. *Address:* c/o Monash University, Dept of Law, Wellington Rd, Clayton, Vic 3168, Australia.

CAMPBELL, Ffyona; British walker, writer and artist; b 1967, Dartmouth, Devon; one d. *Education:* Aboyne Acad (Scotland) and St Margaret's School for Girls (Aberdeen). *Career:* Walked around the world, through Scotland and England from John O'Groats to Land's End in 49 days 1983, aged 16, across USA 1985–86, across Australia (from Sydney to Perth, 3,200 miles) in 95 days 1988, through Africa (from Cape Town to Tangiers, 10,000 miles) 1991–93, through Europe from Algeciras to John O'Groats 1994. *Publication:* Feet of Clay 1991, On Foot Through Africa 1994, The Whole Story 1997. *Address:* c/o PFD, Drury House, 34-43 Russell St, London WC2B 5HA, UK. *Telephone:* (20) 7344-1000.

CAMPBELL, Juliet Jeanne d'Auvergne, CMG, MA; British former diplomatist and university college head (retd); b 23 May 1935, London; d of Wilfred d'Auvergne Collings and Harriet Nancy Draper Bishop; m Alexander E. Campbell 1983. *Education:* schools in S Africa, Palestine, Lebanon and UK, Lady Margaret Hall (Oxford). *Career:* Foreign Office 1957, 1963, News Dept 1967–70, European Integration Dept 1974–77, Head Training Dept 1984–87; UK Del to Brussels Conf 1961–63; Second then First Sec, Thailand 1964–66; First Sec, Paris—NATO 1966, The Hague, Netherlands 1970; Counsellor, France 1977–80; Royal Coll of Defence Studies 1981; Counsellor and Head of Chancery, Indonesia 1982–83; Amb to Luxembourg 1987–91; Mistress Girton Coll, Cambridge 1992–98, Deputy Vice-Chancellor Univ of Cambridge 1993–98; mem Council Queen's Coll, Harley St 1992–, Gov 1993–; mem Wilton Park Acad Council 1992–2000; Trustee Cambridge European Trust 1994–98, Kurt Hahn Trust 1995–98, Changing Faces (charity) 1992–; Gov Marlborough Coll 1999–; Hon Fellow Lady Margaret Hall (Oxford) 1992. *Address:* 3 Belbroughton Rd, Oxford OX2 6UZ, UK (Home). *Telephone:* (1865) 558685 (Home); *Fax:* (1865) 302912; *E-mail:* JenCampbell@aol.com (Home).

CAMPBELL, Rt Hon Kim (Avril Phaedra), PC, QC, LL B; Canadian former politician; b 10 March 1947, Port Alberni, BC; d of George T. and Phyllis M. Vroom; m 1st Nathan Divinsky (divorced 1982); m 2nd. *Education:* Univs of British Columbia and Oregon (USA) and LSE (UK). *Career:* Lecturer in Science and History, Vancouver Community Coll, in Political Science, Univ of BC, Exec Dir Office of the Premier 1985–86; mem Legis Ass of Vancouver (BC) 1986–88; mem House of Commons 1988–93, mem numerous house cttees 1988–93; Minister of State for Indian Affairs and Northern Devt 1989–90, Minister of Justice and Attorney-Gen 1990–93, Minister of Defence 1993, Prime Minister June–Nov 1993; Lecturer Harvard Univ, MA, USA 1993, Fellow John F. Kennedy School of Govt 1994, mem Advisory Bd Youth Option Program, Visiting Cttee Center for Int Affairs, Harvard Univ 1995–; Hon Dir Volunteer Grandparents Asscn; Hon Fellow LSE 1994. *Publication:* Time and Chance: A Political Memoir of Canada's First Woman Prime Minister 1996. *Leisure interests:* painting, playing the piano and cello. *Address:* 550 South Hope, 9th Floor, Los Angeles, CA 90071, USA.

CAMPBELL, Naomi; British fashion model; b 1970, London; d of Valerie Morris. *Education:* Barbara Speake Stage School and Italia Conti. *Career:* Fashion model 1985–; first black model to appear on the cover of French Vogue; recording artist with Sony Epic; Co-propr Fashion Café, London (with Claudia Schiffer, Christy Turlington and Elle MacPherson, qv) 1996–. *Publication:* Swan (novel) 1994; *Film appearances include:* Ready To Wear 1994, Miami Rhapsody 1995, Catwalk 1995, Invasion of Privacy 1996, Beautopia 1996, Unzipped

1996, Prisoner of Love 1999, Destinazione Verna 2000; *Recordings include:* Albums: Baby Woman 1994, Love and Tears 1994. *Address:* Women Model Agency, 2nd Floor, 107 Greene St, New York, NY 10012, USA (Office).

CAMPBELL, Neve Adrienne; Canadian actress; b 3 Oct 1973, Guelph, Ont; m Jeff Colt 1995 (divorced 1997). *Education:* Nat Ballet School (Canada). *Career:* Various dance television and film roles; awards include Saturn Award for Best Actress 1996 (for Scream), MTV Movie Award for Best Female Performance 1996 (for Scream), 1997 (for Scream 2), Blockbuster Entertainment Award for Favourite Actress – Horror 1997 (for Scream 2). *Dance:* The Phantom of the Opera, The Nutcracker, Sleeping Beauty; *Films:* Paint Cans 1994, The Dark 1994, Love Child 1995, The Craft 1996, Scream 1996, A Time to Kill 1996, Simba's Pride 1997, Scream 2 1997, Wild Things 1998, Hairshirt 1998, 54 1998, Three to Tango 1999, Scream 3 2000; *TV:* Catwalk 1992–93, Web of Deceit 1993, Baree 1994, The Forget-Me-Not Murders 1994, Party of Five 1994–98, The Canterville Ghost 1996. *Address:* Creative Artists Agency, 9830 Wilshire Blvd, Beverly Hills, CA 90212, USA.

CAMPION, Jane, BA; New Zealand film director and writer; b 30 April 1954, Wellington; d of Richard and Edith Campion. *Education:* Victoria Univ, Chelsea School of Arts (London, UK) and Australian Film, TV and Radio School. *Films include:* Peel (Palme d'Or, Cannes Film Festival 1986) 1981, Girls' Own Story (awards at Sydney and Melbourne Film Festivals, Cinestud Amsterdam Film Festival and Australian Film Inst awards) 1983, After Hours 1984, Passionless Moments (also scriptwriter) 1984, Dancing Daze 1986, Sweetie (Georges Sadoul Prize, Australian Critics Award, two awards in USA) 1989, Angel At My Table 1990, The Piano (Palme d'Or, Cannes Film Festival 1994) 1993, Portrait of A Lady 1996, Holy Smoke 1999. *Address:* Hilary Linstead & Associates, 500 Oxford St, Level 18, Plaza II, Bondi Junction, NSW 2022, Australia (Office).

CAN XUE, see Deng Xiaohua.

CANALE NOVELLA, Liliana; Peruvian economist and politician; b 20 May 1953, Lima; m (divorced); two c. *Education:* Catholic Univ (Lima). *Career:* Fmr Gen Man Peruvian Exports Bd and Foreign Trade Inst; Gen Man Peruvian Nat Exporters Asscn 1989–92; Vice-Minister for Tourism 1992–94; Minister of Industry, Tourism, Integration and Int Trade Negotiations 1994; Chair Comm for the Promotion of Peru (PROMPERU); Rep to Andean Group Comm and Andean Devt Corpn. *Address:* Ministry of Industry, Tourism, Integration and International Trade Negotiations, Calle 1 Oeste, Corpac, San Isidro, Lima 27, Peru.

CANAVAGGIO, Perrine Marie Hélène, L ès L; French curator; b 20 Oct 1947; d of Jacques and Geneviève Ramin; m Jean Canavaggio 1977; four c. *Education:* Ecole Nat des Chartes and Inst d'Etudes Politiques (Paris). *Career:* Curator departmental archives of Côte d'Or 1972; Head of Mission, Nat Archives of the Ministry of the Interior 1973–80; Chief Curator, Head of the Archives of the Presidency of the Repub 1974–94; Curator-Gen of National Heritage 1992; at Nat Archives 1994–, Deputy Dir Archives de France 1995–96; Chevalier de la Légion d'Honneur; Chevalier de l'Ordre Nat du Mérite; Chevalier des Arts et des Lettres 1986. *Leisure interests:* skiing, sailing. *Address:* Archives Nationales, 60 rue des Francs-Bourgeois, 75141 Paris Cedex 03, France.

CANNEGIETER, Dorothea Adelheid Sjoerdtje, PH D; Netherlands museum director; b 6 Jan 1943; d of Jan Egens Cannegieter and Suze Titia Leutscher. *Education:* Alexander Hegius Gymnasium (Deventer) and Univ of Groningen. *Career:* Volunteer work 1971–74; Curator Stedelijke Musea Zutphen 1974–79, Dir 1979–86; Dir Rijksmuseum Twenthe, Enschede 1987–. *Address:* Rijksmuseum Enschede, Lasondersingel 129, 7514 BP Enschede, Netherlands (Office). *Telephone:* (53) 435-86-75 (Office); *Fax:* (53) 435-90-02 (Office).

CANOVAS, Isabel Catherine; French fashion designer; b 1 May 1945, Paris; d of Blas and Geneviève (née Le Corre) Canovas; m 1st Olivier Merlin (divorced 1983); one d; m 2nd Michaël Grunelius 1984. *Education:* Insts Maintenon and Notre Dame des Oiseaux and Univ of Paris-Nanterre. *Career:* Designer for Christian Dior 1972–76, 1978–80,

for Louis Vuitton 1976–77; Founder, Pres Calius, Paris 1981, New York 1985–; Founder, Pres Liusca SA, Madrid 1988; Fashion Group Award, New York 1990; T of Telva Award, Spain 1991. *Leisure interests:* gardening, hunting. *Address:* 39 rue de l'Université, 75007 Paris, France. *Telephone:* (1) 47-23-70-05; *Fax:* (1) 40-70-92-10.

CANTIEN, Dominique, L ès L; French broadcasting executive; b 13 March 1953, Rosendaël; d of Pierre and Michelle Sadyn; one s. *Education:* Lycée Fénelon and Univ of Paris IV (Paris-Sorbonne). *Career:* Production Asst Radio-Télé-Luxembourg (RTL) 1976; Producer Télévision Française 1 (TF1) 1983–84, Artistic Dir 1987–94, Creative Dir 1995–; Producer Canal Plus 1984; Head of Variety Programmes Dept, Société Nat de Télévision en Couleur—Antenne 2 (A2) 1985–87; Artistic Dir France Télévision 1994. *Address:* Télévision Française 1 (TF1), 1 quai du Point du Jour, 92656 Boulogne, France.

CAO LEI; Chinese actress and film dubbing director; b 8 July 1940, Ganzhou; d of the late Cao Juren and of Deng Keyun; m Li Deming 1976; one s. *Education:* Shanghai Drama Inst. *Career:* Teacher Shanghai Drama Inst 1962–65; Actress, Asst Dir Shanghai Film Studio 1965–81; Dubbing Actress Shanghai Film Dubbing Studio from 1982, Dubbing Dir 1985–. *Plays include:* A Doll's House 1961–63, A Peach Blossom Fan 1961–63, The Young Generation 1961–63, Passport 1991; *Films include:* Actress: On the Bank of the Jinsha 1963, The Young Generation 1965; Dubbing actress: La Raison d'Etat 1984, Spartacus 1988, Mephisto 1989, The Third Man, Le Dernier Métro; Dubbing Dir: Superman 1985, Spartacus 1987, A Room with a View 1988, War and Peace 1987, Mephisto 1989, Good Morning Babylon 1989, Great Blue 1990, Bix 1991; *TV includes:* Dubbing Dir: Yes, Minister 1988, Full House 1989; Falcon Crest (dubbing actress). *Leisure interest:* writing. *Address:* Shanghai Film Dubbing Studio, (Shanghai Dianying Yizhipian Chang), Shanghai, People's Republic of China (Office); Apt 102, 587 Nanjing Rd W, Shanghai 200041, People's Republic of China (Home). *Telephone:* (21) 2580504.

CAO YI, PH D; Chinese scientist; b 22 July 1930, Shanghai; d of Z. X. Cao and Y. Dong; m Shi Da Zhao 1955; one s one d. *Education:* Jing Ling Univ and Acad of Sciences of the USSR. *Career:* Research Asst Shanghai Inst of Organic Chem, Academia Sinica 1953–56, Research Assoc Inst of Chem 1956–75, Assoc Prof Inst of Photographic Chem 1975–85, Prof 1985–, Deputy Dir of Inst 1978–87, Dir 1987–93, Dir Lab of Photochem 1990–; Chair Comm on Photochem, Chinese Chemical Soc 1987–; mem Council 1990–; mem Council Chinese Material Research Soc 1990–; Nat Rep Photochem IUPAC 1992–; mem Council Chinese Women Scientists and Engineers Soc 1992–; over 100 papers published in nat and int chem journals; Chair numerous int confs including Beijing Int Symposium on Photochem 1985, Sino-Japan Binational Symposia on Photochem 1988, 1991, 1994, China–US Binational Symposia on Photochem 1985, 1992, Ninth Int Conf on Chemical Conversion and Storage of Solar Energy 1992; Second Prize Natural Sciences Award, Academia Sinica 1985, 1992; Special Contrib Prize, State Council of China 1991. *Address:* Academia Sinica, Institute of Photographic Chemistry, Bei Sha Tan, Beijing 100101, People's Republic of China. *Telephone:* (1) 2017061; *Fax:* (1) 2029375.

CAPDEBOSCQ, Géraldine Marie-Laure, M SC; French business executive; b 4 Nov 1944, Paris; d of Francis and Claude Postel-Vinay; m Georges Capdeboscq 1968; two s one d. *Education:* Univ of Paris I (Panthéon-Sorbonne), Inst d'Etudes Politiques de Paris and Ecole Nat d'Admin. *Career:* Civil servant Dept of Budget, Ministry of Econ and Finance 1970–; in charge of Budget, Ministry of Industry, and supervision of public enterprises in the energy sector 1979; Head Finance Dept, Commissariat Gen du Plan 1979–81; Dir Gen Admin, Ministries of Research, Industrial Redeployment and Foreign Trade 1982–86; Contrôleur d'Etat 1986; in charge of public enterprises in the media sector 1986–88; Financial and Admin Dir, Commercial Section, Bull SA 1988–90, Dir of Planning, Finance and Admin Bull-Produits-Systèmes 1991–93, Dir-Gen Bull Emerging Technologies 1994–, Deputy Dir-Gen Technology Strategy 1998–; Pres, Dir-Gen CP8 Transac (subsidiary of Bull Emerging Technologies) 1995–; mem Bd Dirs Internet Corpn for Assigned Names and Numbers (Icann) 1998–. *Leisure interests:* piano, sailing. *Address:* Bull SA, 68 route de Versailles BP 45, 78431 Louveciennes Cedex, France.

CAPELING-ALAKIJA, Sharon, B ED; Canadian United Nations official; b 6 May 1944, Montréal, PQ; m 1985 (husband deceased); three s. *Education:* Univ of Saskatchewan. *Career:* Volunteer then mem staff CUSO (Canadian Univ Service Overseas), has worked in Public Affairs in Barbados and Tanzania, in Funding and Human Resource Devt in Ottawa and as W Africa Regional Dir (based in Lomé, Togo), responsible for programmes in Ghana, Nigeria, Togo, Sierra Leone, Cameroon and The Gambia until 1989; Dir UNIFEM (UNDP for Women) 1989–94; Dir Office of Evaluation and Strategic Planning (UNDP, NY) 1994–97; Exec Co-ordinator UN Volunteers Programme Jan 1998–; exec mem Bd of North/South Inst; Hon LL D (Saskatchewan) 1998. *Leisure interests:* swimming, reading, dancing. *Address:* United Nations Volunteers, Postfach 260111, 53173 Bonn, Germany. *Telephone:* (228) 8152501; *Fax:* (228) 8152952; *Internet:* www.unv.org.

CAPLAN, Elinor; Canadian politician; b 20 May 1944, Toronto, ON; d of Samuel Solomon and Thelma S. (née Goodman) Hershorn; m Wilf Caplan 1963; four c. *Education:* Centennial Coll. *Career:* Admin Leader Publishing Inc 1971–72; Pres Elinor Caplan and Assocs, title searching and conveyancing 1973–78; Alderman City of N York 1978–85; mem Ontario Legislature for Oriole 1985–, Minister of Health 1987–90, of Citizenship and Immigration 1999–; Ontario Official Opposition Critic (Liberal) for the Ministry of Revenue, Treasury Bd and Man Bd 1990–92; fmrly Chair of Man Bd of Cabinet, Minister of Govt Services and Chair Cabinet; Chair Standing Cttee on Social Devt 1990–91; mem Bd N York Inter-Agency and Community Council. *Leisure interests:* music, theatre, bridge. *Address:* Whitney Block, Rm 1307, Parliament Bldgs, Queen's Park, Toronto, ON M7A 1A2, Canada. *Telephone:* (416) 325-3607.

CAPRIATI, Jennifer; American tennis player; b 29 March 1976, New York; d of Stefano and Denise Capriati. *Education:* Saddlebrook High School (FL). *Career:* Professional Tennis Player 1990–; mem Wightman Cup Team 1989, US Fed Cup Team 1990–91; Puerto Rican Open Champion 1990, San Diego Champion 1991, Canadian Open Champion 1991, Italian Open Doubles Champion (with Monica Seleš, qv) 1991; Semifinalist Wimbledon (UK) 1991, US Open 1991, German Open 1991; Gold Medal, Olympics 1992; ranked No 6 (Singles) 1991, 1992, 1993; Gold Medallist Olympic Games, Barcelona, Spain 1992; left women's tour 1993, re-joined 1996; Winner Australian Open 2001, French Open 2001; Athlete of the Year in the Sport of Tennis, US Olympic Cttee 1989; Women's Tennis Asscn Most Impressive Newcomer Award 1990; Kraft Gen Foods Player of the Month Aug 1991. *Leisure interests:* dancing, swimming, golf, music, reading, spending time with friends. *Address:* c/o Barbara Perry, International Management Group, 22 E 71st St, New York, NY 10021, USA (Office).

CARDEN, Joan Maralyn, AO, OBE; Australian opera singer; b Melbourne; d of the late Frank Carden and of Margaret Carden (née Cooke); m William Coyne 1962 (divorced 1980); two d. *Education:* Melbourne, Trinity Coll of Music (London), London Opera Centre and voice studies with Thea Phillips and Henry Portnoj (Melbourne) and Vida Harford (London). *Career:* Debut at Sadler's Wells, London; joined The Australian Opera 1971; appearances at Royal Opera House, Covent Garden (London), Metropolitan Opera (New York), Glyndebourne Festival (UK) and with Sydney Symphony Orchestra and Australian Broadcasting Comm; Dame Joan Hammond Award for Outstanding Service to Opera in Australia 1987, Australia Creative Fellowship 1993. *Opera debuts include:* Our Man in Havana, Rigoletto 1974, Don Giovanni 1977, Tancredi 1977. *Leisure interests:* gardening, theatre, reading. *Address:* c/o The Australian Opera, POB 291, Strawberry Hills, NSW 2012, Australia (Office).

CARDINALE, Claudia; Italian film actress; b 15 April 1938, Tunis, Tunisia; d of Franco and Yolanda Cardinale; m Franco Cristaldi 1966; one c. *Education:* Lycée Carnot and Collège Paul Cambon (Tunis). *Career:* Debut 1958; UNESCO Goodwill Amb; awards include Nastro d'Argento, David di Donatello, Grolla d'Oro. *Films include:* 8½, The Pink Panther, The Leopard, The Professionals, Once Upon a Time in the West, Fury, The Magnificent Showman, La Scoumoune, Fitzcarraldo 1982, Le Ruffian 1982, History, A Man in Love 1988, The French Revolution 1989, Hiver '54, L'abbé Pierre, Mother, 588 Rue Paradis, Son of the Pink Panther 1993, Women Only Have One Thing On Their Minds. *Address:* Vides Piazza, Pitagora 9, Rome, Italy.

CAREY, Mariah; American singer and songwriter; b 1969, Long Island, NY; m Tommy Mottola 1993. *Career:* Fmrly waitress, New York; singer and song-writer 1988–; signed contract with Columbia Records 1989, has sold more than 80 millon records worldwide; f Crave record label 1997; f Camp Mariah holiday project for inner-city children; awards include two Grammy awards (Best New Artist, Best New Pop Vocal, Female) 1990, three Soul Train Music Awards (Best New Artist, Best Album, Female, Best Single, Female) 1990, four American Music Awards 1992–96, eight World Music Awards 1991–95, seven Billboard Awards 1991–96. *Recordings include:* Singles: Fantasy, One Sweet Day (jtly); Albums: Mariah Carey 1990, Emotions 1992, MTV Unplugged 1992, Music Box 1993, Merry Christmas 1994, Daydream 1995, Butterfly 1997, Rainbow 1999. *Address:* c/o LD Publicity Ltd, Fenton House, 55–57 Great Marlborough St, London W1V 1DD, UK (Office).

CARLSON NELSON, Marilyn; American business executive; b 1940; m Glen Nelson; one s. *Education:* Smith Coll (Mass), Sorbonne (Paris, France) and Inst des Hautes Etudes Economiques Politiques (Geneva, Switzerland). *Career:* Began career as Securities Analyst with Paine-Webber; Dir of Community Relations, Carlson Cos Inc 1968–88, Sr Vice-Pres 1988, CEO 1997–, Pres 1998–, Vice-Chair Carlson Holdings Inc; mem Bd Exxon, US West Inc; Co-Founder Minnesota Women's Econ Roundtable; Royal Order of the North Star (Sweden), Order of the White Rose (Finland); Outstanding Business Leader 1996. *Address:* Carlson Parkway, POB 59159, Minneapolis, MN 55459, USA.

CARLYLE, Joan Hildred; British opera singer (soprano); b 6 April 1931; d of the late Edgar J. Carlyle and Margaret M. Carlyle; m Robert Duray Aiyar; two d. *Education:* Howell's School (Denbigh, N Wales). *Career:* Prin Lyric Soprano Royal Opera House, Covent Garden, London 1955; appearances at Salzburg, Metropolitan Opera (New York) and Teatro Colón (Buenos Aires) 1968, also at La Scala Milan, Staats Oper Vienna, Munich, Berlin, San Carlo Naples, Monet Monte Carlo, Nice, Milan, Cape Town, Brussels, Geneva, Zurich, Amsterdam, Boston; currently teaching and advising young opera singers. *Operas include:* Un Ballo in Maschera 1957–58, Der Rosenkavalier 1958–59, 1968, Pagliacci 1959, La Bohème 1960, Midsummer Night's Dream (Britten) 1960, The Magic Flute 1962, 1966, The Marriage of Figaro 1963, Arabella 1964, 1967, Suor Angelica 1965, Otello 1965, Midsummer Marriage 1969, Don Giovanni 1970, Oberon 1970, Adriana Lecouvreur 1970, Don Carlos 1975; Major roles sung abroad include: Oscar, Nedda, Mimi, Pamina, Zdenka, Micaela, Donna Anna, Arabella, Elizabetta and Desdemona; *Recordings include:* Von Karajan's production of Pagliacci as Nedda, Midsummer Marriage as Jenifer, Medea, Pagliacci from Buenos Aires, Mavra, Purcell Anthology. *Leisure interests:* gardening, travel, preservation of the countryside, interior design, cooking. *Address:* Laundry Cottage, Hanmer, Wrexham SY13 4QX, N Wales, UK. *Telephone:* (1948) 830265.

CARMODY, Heather Irene, B SOC SC; Australian administrator; b 16 Nov 1951; d of James and Shirley Carmody; partner Anthony Baird since 1985. *Education:* Curtin Univ of Tech and Royal Melbourne Inst of Tech. *Career:* Man State Electricity Comm of Vic 1984–87; Regional Man Workcare Rehabilitation 1987–89; Exec Dir Council for Equal Opportunity in Employment 1989–93; Vice-Chair Workplace Australia 1991; Dir World Competitive Practices 1993–; Man Ind Consulting Services; mem Ethics Cttee, Alfred Hosp, Nat Children's Services Advisory Council, USA Conf Bd Work and Family Advisory and Research Panel 1991; mem Senate Univ of Western Australia 1982–84; Rotary Foundation Award 1976; Queen Elizabeth II Silver Jubilee Trust Award 1981. *Publications:* Equal Opportunity at Work: 112 Studies of Major Australian Organizations 1990, Families at Work: Practical Examples from 140 Businesses 1991, International Practice: Families at Work 1992. *Leisure interests:* community activity, fishing, travel. *Address:* Level 7, 21 Victoria St, Melbourne, Vic 3000, Australia.

CARNEGY OF LOUR, Baroness (Life Peer), cr 1982, of Lour in the District of Angus, **Elizabeth Patricia Carnegy of Lour,** DL; British politician; b 28 April 1925, London; d of the late Ughtred Elliot Carnegy, 12th of Lour, and of Violet (née Henderson) Carnegy. *Education:* Downham School (Essex). *Career:* Mem staff Cavendish Lab, Cambridge 1943–46, Girl Guides Asscn 1947–89; farmer 1956–89; Local Govt Councillor (Cons) Tayside Region 1974–82; mem Manpower Services Comm and Chair for Scotland 1979–83; Chair

Scottish Council for Community Educ 1981–88; mem House of Lords 1982–, House of Lords Scrutiny Cttees on European Community 1983–97; mem Council Open Univ 1984–96, Court of St Andrews Univ 1991–96; Hon LL D (Dundee) 1991. *Leisure interests:* youth work, countryside, community affairs. *Address:* House of Lords, London SW1A 0PW, UK (Office); Lour, Forfar, Angus DD8 2LR, UK (Home). *Telephone:* (20) 7219-5242 (Office); (1307) 82237 (Home); *Fax:* (20) 7219-6393 (Office).

CARNEY, Rt Hon Patricia, PC, MA; Canadian politician and economist; b 26 May 1935, Shanghai, People's Repub of China; d of James Carney and Dora Sanders; m 1st; one s one d; m 2nd Paul S. White 1998. *Education:* Univ of British Columbia and British Columbia School of Community and Regional Planning. *Career:* Fmrly econ journalist and socio-econ and communications consultant; mem House of Commons 1980–90, fmrly Caucus Spokesperson for Energy, Mines and Resources, for Finance, fmr Minister of State for Finance, Sec of State, fmr mem Standing Cttee on Finance, on Trade and Econ Affairs, on Communications and Culture, on Justice and Legal Affairs; Minister of Energy, Mines and Resources 1984–86, of Int Trade 1986–88; Pres of Treasury Bd 1988; Senator 1990–; fmr Chair Standing Cttee on Energy, the Environment and Natural Resources, Cabinet Cttee on Trade; mem Standing Cttee on Foreign Affairs, on Fisheries, on Aboriginal Peoples; mem Asscn Professional Economists, BC, Canadian Econs Asscn, Inst of Planners, Int Inst of Planners; Hon Fellow Royal Architectural Inst of Canada 1989, BC Yukon Div of the Arthritis Soc 1998; Hon LL D (British Columbia) 1990, (British Columbia Open) 1991. *Publication:* Trade Secrets: A Memoir 2000. *Address:* The Senate, Parliament Bldgs, Wellington St, Ottawa, ON K1A 0A4, Canada (Office). *Telephone:* (613) 995-1900; *Fax:* (613) 995-4998; *E-mail:* carnep@sen.parl.gc.ca; *Internet:* www.sen.parl.gc.ca/pcarney.

CAROLINE, Princess Caroline Louise Marguerite; Monégasque royal; b 23 Jan 1957; d of Prince Rainier III and the late Princess Grace (née Kelly); m 1st Philippe Junot 1978 (divorced 1980, annulled 1992); m 2nd Stefano Casiraghi 1983 (died 1990); two s one d. *Address:* Palais de Monaco, Monte Carlo, Monaco.

CAROLUS, Cheryl, BA; South African organization executive; m Graeme Bloch 1989. *Education:* Univ of the Western Cape. *Career:* Gen Sec Nat Exec Cttee, United Democratic Front (UDF) 1983–87, Fed of S African Women (FedSAW) 1987, UDF Western Cape Region 1983; mem Interim Leadership Group S African Communist Party 1990; mem Interim Leadership Cttee African Nat Congress (ANC) 1990, ANC Rep at talks with Govt at Groote Schurr, Cape Town 1990, Deputy Sec-Gen ANC 1994; High Commr to UK 1998–; UDF Del Int Centre for Swedish Labour Movt 1986; mem Congress of S African Trade Unions, Nat Educ Crisis Cttee 1989, Org of African Unity (Harare); detained under emergency regulations 1986, 1989. *Address:* South Africa House, Trafalgar Square, London WC2N 5DP, UK. *Telephone:* (20) 7451-7299; *Fax:* (20) 7451-7284; *Internet:* www .southafricahouse.com.

CARON, Leslie Claire Margaret; French actress and ballet dancer; b 1 July 1931, Boulogne-Billancourt; m 1st George Hormel; m 2nd Peter Reginald Frederick Hall 1956 (divorced 1965); one s one d; m 3rd Michael Laughlin 1969 (divorced). *Education:* Convent of the Assumption (Paris) and Conservatoire de Danse. *Career:* Dancer Ballet des Champs Elysées 1947–50, Ballet de Paris 1954; stage appearances in France, UK, USA, Germany and Australia; Chevalier de la Légion d'Honneur, Officier de l'Ordre Nat du Mérite. *Theatre includes:* Orvet, La Sauvage, Gigi, 12 rue de l'Amour, Ondine, Carola, La Répetition, On Your Toes, L'Inaccessible, Grand Hotel, George Sand, Le martyre de Saint Sébastien, Nocturne for Lovers, Babar the Elephant; toured France in Apprends-moi Céline 1998–99; *Films include:* An American in Paris, Man with a Cloak, Glory Alley, Story of Three Loves, Lili, Glass Slipper, Daddy Long Legs, Gaby, Gigi, The Doctor's Dilemma, The Man Who Understood Women, The Subterranean, Fanny, Guns of Darkness, The L-Shaped Room, Father Goose, A Very Special Favor, Promise Her Anything, Is Paris Burning?, Head of the Family, Madron, The Contract, The Unapproachable 1982, Deathly Moves 1983, Génie du Faux 1984, The Train 1987, Guerriers et Captives 1988; Courage Mountain 1988, Damage 1992, Funny Bones 1994, Let It Be Me 1994, The Ring 1995, The Reef 1996, The Last of the Blonde Bombshells

1999, Chocolat 2000; *Publication:* Vengeance 1983. *Address:* c/o PFD, Drury House, 34–43 Russell St, London WC2B 5HA, UK (Office); Auberge la Lucarne aux chouattes, 89500 Villeneuve-sur-Yonne, France.

CARR, Glenna, BA; Canadian civil servant; b 1945, SK; d of D. William and Frances (née Close) Carr; m Alan Gordon; three step-c. *Education:* Neuchâtel Jr Coll (Switzerland) and Univ of Toronto. *Career:* Educational adviser to media 1970–75; Govt of Ontario posts include Policy Analyst and Affirmative Action Man 1972–82, Dir in Municipal Affairs, Housing Admin Ontario Women's Directorate 1983–86, Deputy Minister Man Bd of Cabinet (Skills Devt, Consumer and Commercial Relations) 1986–91, Deputy Minister Man Bd of Cabinet and Chair Civil Service Comm 1991–92; Vice Pres Corporate Affairs, Laidlow Inc 1992–95; CEO Carr-Gordon Ltd 1995–. *Address:* 525 University Ave, Suite 1050, Toronto, ON M5G 2L3, Canada; Frost Bldg, S, Queen's Park Circle, Toronto, Canada. *E-mail:* consulting@ carrgordon.ca; *Internet:* www.carrgordon.ca.

CARR, Shirley G. E., OC; Canadian trade union official; b Niagara Falls, ON; d of John James and Mary Geraldine (née Wilson) Boutilier; m W. Bruce 1948; one s. *Education:* Stamford Collegiate Vocational Inst and Niagara Coll of Applied Arts and Tech. *Career:* Various posts at local, provincial and nat levels Canadian Union of Public Employees 1960–74; Exec Vice-Pres Canadian Labour Congress 1974–84, Sec-Treasurer 1984–86, Pres 1986–92, Pres Emer 1992–; Vice-Pres Int Confed of Free Trade Unions (ICTFU); Chair Commonwealth Trade Union Council; Co-Chair Canadian Labour Market Productivity Centre; mem Council Amnesty Int; mem Governing Body Int Labour Org (ILO) 1991, Chair Workers' Group of Governing Body and Vice-Chair Governing Body 1991; mem Bd Govs Labour Coll of Canada; Hon LL D (Brock) 1981, (McMaster) 1988; Hon DCL (Acadia) 1984; Hon PH D (Univ of Western Ontario) 1988; Hon Fellow Ryerson Polytech Inst 1987; Centennial Medal 1980; Gov-Gen Award in Commemoration of the Persons Case 1994. *Leisure interests:* reading, embroidery. *Address:* c/o Canadian Labour Congress, 2841 Riverside Drive, Ottawa, ON K1V 8X7, Canada. *Telephone:* (613) 521-3400; *Fax:* (613) 521-4655.

CARR, Vikki; American singer; b (Florencia Bisenta de Casillas Martinez Cardona) 19 July 1940, El Paso, TX; d of Carlos and Florencia Cardona. *Education:* Rosemead High School (CA). *Career:* Soloist with Pepe Callahan Mexican-Irish band; appeared at Royal Command Performance 1967, Inaugural Celebration, Kennedy Music Center 1973; Host Mrs America Pageant 1981–87, Mrs World Pageant 1984–87, Hispanic World Vision 1989, 1990; appearances on TV shows include Dean Martin, Ed Sullivan, Smothers Brothers, Jerry Lewis, Jonathan Winters, Carol Burnett shows, Bob Hope, Jim Nabors and Johnny Carson specials; toured military bases in Vietnam; numerous awards including Woman of the Year (Los Angeles Times) 1970, Best Mexican-American Performance Grammy Award 1985, Silver Achievement Award (YWCA) 1989, Humanitarian and Golden Eagle Awards (Nosotros) 1981, 1989. *Appearances include:* Musicals: South Pacific, Unsinkable Molly Brown, I'm Getting My Act Together and Taking It on the Road; TV: Mod Squad 1972; *Recordings include:* Albums: Disculpame, Total, Ni Princesa; Singles: Can't Take My Eyes Off You, It Must be Him, With Pen in Hand, Cosas del Amor (Best Latin Pop Album Grammy Award 1991). *Leisure interests:* tennis, off-road racing, photography. *Address:* c/o Dianne Forthman, Vi-Car Enterprises Inc, POB 5126, Beverly Hills, CA 90210, USA.

CARRERE D'ENCAUSSE, Hélène, D ÈS L; French professor specializing in Soviet affairs and politician; b 6 July 1929, Paris; d of Georges Zourabichvili and Nathalie von Pelken; m Louis Carrère 1952; two d one s. *Education:* Univ of Paris (Sorbonne). *Career:* Fmr Prof Univ of Paris IV (Paris-Sorbonne); now Prof Inst d'Etudes Politiques (Paris) and Dir of Research Fondation Nat des Sciences Politiques; mem Bd of Dirs East–West Inst for Security Studies; Visiting Prof at numerous univs in USA; MEP 1994–99; mem Acad Française, Sec for Life 2000–; Assoc mem Acad Royale de Belgique; Dr hc (Montréal); Officier de la Légion d'Honneur; Prix Aujourd'hui 1978, Prix de la Fondation Louis-Weiss 1986. *Publications include:* Le marxisme et l'Asie 1965, Réforme et révolution chez les musulmans de l'Empire russe 1966, L'URSS et la Chine devant les révolutions dans les sociétés pré-industrielles 1970,

L'Empire éclaté 1978, Lénine: la révolution et le pouvoir 1979, Staline: l'ordre par la terreur 1979, Le pouvoir confisqué 1982, Le Grand Frère 1983, La déstalinisation commence 1984, Ni paix ni guerre 1986, Le grand défi: bolcheviks et nations 1917–30 1987, Le malheur russe 1988, La gloire des nations ou la fin de l'Empire soviétique 1991, Victorieuse Russie 1992, Nicholas II: la transition interrompue 1996, Lénine 1998, La Russie inachevée 2000. *Address:* Académie Française, 23 quai Conti, 75006 Paris, France (Office). *Telephone:* (1) 44-41-43-00 (Office); *Fax:* (1) 43-29-47-45 (Office).

CARRINGTON, Leonora; British artist; b 1917, Lancs. *Career:* Artist 1937–; has worked in France, Mexico and USA; exhibitions include Serpentine Gallery, London 1991, Brewster Arts Ltd 1999. *Paintings include:* Rencontre (with Max Ernst), Femme et Oiseau, Self-Portrait, The Inn of the Dawn Horse, Portrait of Max Ernst, Portrait of the late Mrs Partridge, Who art thou, White Face?, Ferret Race, And Then We Saw the Daughter of the Minotaur. *Address:* c/o Brewster Arts Ltd, 41 W 57th St, New York, NY 10019, USA.

CARSEY, Marcia Lee Peterson, BA; American television production executive; b 21 Nov 1944, S Weymouth, MA; d of John Edwin and Rebecca White Peterson; m John Jay Carsey 1969; one d one s. *Education:* Univ of New Hampshire. *Career:* Exec Story Ed Tomorrow Entertainment 1971–74; Sr Vice-Pres Prime Time Series, ABC-TV 1978–81; f Carsey Productions 1981, Co-propr Carsey-Werner Co 1982–. *Productions include:* Oh Madeline 1983, The Cosby Show (exec producer), A Different World 1987–, Roseanne 1988–, Chicken Soup 1989–, Grand 1990, Davis Rules, Frannie's Turn, You Bet Your Life, Grace Under Fire, Cybill, Carol Carl Whoopi and Robin. *Address:* Carsey-Werner Co, 4024 Radford Ave, Studio City, CA 91604, USA.

CARTWRIGHT, Nancy Delaney, PH D, FBA; American professor of philosophy; b 24 June 1944, PA; d of Claudis and Eva Delaney; m 1st Bliss Cartwright 1966 (divorced); m 2nd Ian Hacking 1974 (divorced); m 3rd Sir Stuart Hampshire 1985; two d. *Education:* Univs of Pittsburgh (PA) and Illinois. *Career:* Prof of Philosophy Stanford Univ, CA 1983–91; Prof of Philosophy, Logic and Scientific Method, LSE 1991–; Dir Centre for the Philosophy of the Natural and Social Sciences 1993–; mem American Acad of Arts and Science 2001; Fellow British Acad 1996; MacArthur Foundation Award 1993. *Publications:* How the Laws of Physics Lie 1983, Nature's Capacities and Their Measurement 1989, Otto Neurath: Between Science and Politics (jtly) 1994, The Dappled World: A Study of the Boundaries of Science 1999. *Address:* Centre for the Philosophy of the Natural and Social Sciences, London School of Economics, Houghton St, London WC2A 2AE, UK (Office). *Telephone:* (20) 7955-7330 (Office); *Fax:* (20) 7995-6869 (Office).

CARTWRIGHT, Sally Amanda, OBE; British publishing executive; b May 8 1944, London; d of Dennis Cartwright and Eileen Sargeant Cartwright; m John Brian Hutchings 1980. *Education:* Merton House School (Keymer). *Career:* Worked on numerous magazines until 1990; Publishing Dir Hello! magazine 1990–; mem Bd Periodical Publishers Assccn (Chair 1998–2000), Council Ski Club of GB. *Leisure interests:* skiing, gardening, embroidery, science fiction, theatre, opera. *Address:* Wellington House, 69–71 Upper Ground, London SE1 9PQ, UK. *Telephone:* (20) 7667-8741; *Fax:* (20) 7667-8742.

CARTWRIGHT, Dame Silvia Rose, DBE, LL B; New Zealand Governor-General and judge; b 7 Nov 1943, Dunedin; d of Monteith and Eileen Jane Poulter; m Peter John Cartwright 1969. *Education:* Univ of Otago. *Career:* Partner Harkness, Henry and Co, Hamilton 1971–81; Judge Dist and Family Courts 1981–89; Chief Dist Court Judge 1989–93, NZ High Court Judge 1993–2001; Gov-Gen of NZ 2001–; mem Comm for the Future 1975–80; mem UN CEDAW Cttee 1992; conducted inquiries into Social Science Funding 1986–87, Treatment of Cervical Cancer at Nat Women's Hosp, Auckland 1987–88; Hon LL D (Otago) 1993, (Waikato) 1994. *Leisure interests:* reading, gardening, needlework. *Address:* Government House, Wellington, New Zealand.

CARUANA, Josette; Maltese artist; b 3 April 1959, Pieta, d of Anthony and Catherine Caruana. *Education:* Malta Coll of Arts, Science and Tech and Accademia di Belle Arti (Perugia and Florence, Italy). *Career:* Freelance artist 1973–; numerous group and one-woman exhibitions include Malta 1976, 1982, 1986, 1990, 1994, 1995, 1996, Algiers 1984,

Florence (Italy) 1985, 1987, Rome 1989, Paris 1987, New York 1991, Palermo (Italy) 1991, Landsberg (Germany) 1993. *Leisure interests:* bowling, cycling, swimming. *Address:* 15/2 Sappers St, Valetta 11, Malta. *Telephone:* 343455.

CARVEN, Carmen Marie Louise Jeanne; French fashion designer; b 31 Aug 1909, Châtellerault; d of André and Louise de Tommaso; m 1st Philippe Mallet (deceased); m 2nd René Grog (deceased)1972. *Education:* Ecole des Beaux-Arts (Paris). *Career:* Founder Maison Carven, Paris 1945; has held fashion shows world-wide; Officier de la Légion d'Honneur; Chevalier des Arts et des Lettres; Chevalier du Mérite Commercial; Médaille d'Argent de la Ville de Paris. *Leisure interests:* swimming, antiques. *Address:* Carven, 6 rond point des Champs Elysées, 75008 Paris, France.

CASA-DEBELJEVIC, Lisa Della (Della Casa); Swiss opera singer; b 2 Feb 1919. *Education:* Berne Conservatoire. *Career:* Debut at Zurich Opera House 1943; mem Vienna State Opera Co 1947–, New York Metropolitan Opera Co 1953–; appearances in UK, USA, Italy, Germany and S America at festivals in Salzburg (Austria) 1947, 1948, 1950, 1953–58, Glyndebourne 1951 and Edinburgh (UK) 1952, Zurich and Lucerne (Switzerland), Bayreuth and Munich (Germany) 1951–58; apptd Austrian State Kammersängerin. *Address:* c/o Schloß Gottlieben, Thurgau, Switzerland.

CASDIN-SILVER, Harriet, AB; American artist; b 2 Oct 1925, Worcester, MA; d of Casdin-Cohen and Rose Fanya Ostroff; m Simon Silver 1952; two d. *Education:* Univ of Vermont, Columbia Univ (NY), New School for Social Research (Cambridge, UK) and Goddard Grad School (MA). *Career:* Artist-in-residence American Optical Research Labs, Framingham, MA 1968–73, Ukrainian Inst of Physics, Kiev 1989; Asst Prof of Physics Brown Univ, RI 1974–78; Fellow Center for Advanced Visual Studies, MIT 1976–85; consultant Rockefeller Foundation Arts Program 1980–81; Visiting Lecturer RCA, London 1992, also Univ of Ghent; Prof of Art Massachusetts Coll of Art and Design, Boston 1999–; also independent artist. *Publications:* My First 10 Years as Artist/Holographer 1989, Holographic Installations: Sculpting with Light 1991. *Leisure interest:* reading. *Address:* 51 Melcher St, 5th Floor, Boston, MA 02210, USA (Office); 99 Pond Ave, D403, Brookline, MA 02445 USA (Home). *Telephone:* (617) 423-4717 (Office), (617) 739-6869 (Home); *Fax:* (617) 739-6869 (Home).

CASE, Anthea Fiendley, BA; British civil servant; b 7 Feb 1945; d of Thomas Fiendley and the late Bess Stones; m David Charles Case 1967; two d. *Education:* Christ's Hosp (Hertford) and St Anne's Coll (Oxford). *Career:* Asst Prin HM Treasury 1966–70, Pvt Sec to Financial Sec 1970–71, Prin 1971–79, Asst Sec 1980–88, Under-Sec 1988–95, with Fiscal Policy Group 1993–95, Asst Dir Budget and Public Finances Directorate 1995; Dir Nat Heritage Memorial Fund 1995–. *Address:* National Heritage Memorial Fund, 7 Holbein Place, London SW1W 8NR, UK. *Telephone:* (20) 7591-6000.

ČÁSLAVSKÁ, Věra; Czech gymnast; b 3 May 1942, Prague; d of Václav and Anna Čáslavská; m Josef Odlozil 1968 (divorced 1988); one s one d. *Education:* Charles Univ (Prague). *Career:* Gold Medallist (Overall, Vault and Beam) Olympic Games, Tokyo 1964, (Overall, Floor, Asymmetric Bars and Vault) Olympic Games, Mexico 1968, Silver Medallist (Beam) Olympic Games 1968; First Place (Overall and Vault), Second Place (Beam and Floor) and mem winning team World Championships, Dortmund, Germany 1966; Five First Places, European Championships, Sofia 1965, Amsterdam 1967; signatory The Two Thousand Words 1968, a declaration of the principles of communist rule; coach Sports Centre, Prague 1970–79, Mexico 1979–; Adviser to Pres of CSFR 1990, on Social Policy 1990–91; Pres Czechoslovak Olympic Cttee 1990–92, Czech Olympic Cttee 1992–96; mem Int Olympic Cttee 1995–; Meritorious Master of Sports 1962, Christopher Columbus Prize 1964, Order of the Republic 1968, Pierre de Coubertin Fair Play Prize 1989, Silver Olympic Order 1992, Sievert Prize 1993, Medal for Merit, Czech Repub 1995, Hiranuma Prize 1996. *Publication:* Věra Čáslavská Narrates 1965. *Address:* Czech Olympic Committee, Benesovska 6, 101 00 Prague, 10, Czech Republic (Office). *Telephone:* (2) 7173-4734; *Fax:* (2) 7173-1318.

CASSAB, Judy, AO, CBE, D LITT; Australian artist; b 15 Aug 1920, Vienna, Austria; d of Imre Kaszab and Ilona Kont; m John Kampfner 1939; two s. *Education:* Budapest and Prague. *Career:* Artist 1953–; over 64 exhibitions in Australia, London and Paris, represented in Nat Gallery (Canberra), Nat Portrait Gallery (London), Nat Gallery of Hungary (Budapest) and in numerous galleries in USA, Australia and UK; mem Council for the Hons of Australia 1974–77; Trustee Art Gallery of New South Wales 1980–88; Dr hc (Sydney) 1995; awards include Perth Prize 1955, The Archibald Prize 1961, 1968, Helena Rubinstein Prize 1964, 1965, Sir Charles Lloyd Jones Memorial Prize 1965, 1971–1973, Trustees Watercolour Prize (Art Gallery of NSW) 1994, Foundation for Australian Literary Studies Prize 1996, The Pring Prize (Art Coll of NSW) 1994, 1997, 1998. *Publications:* Ten Australian Portraits (lithographs) 1984, Judy Cassab, Artists and Friends 1988, Judy Cassab Diaries (Nita Kibble Award for Literature 1996) 1995, Judy Cassab, Portraits of Artists and Friends 1998. *Leisure interest:* writing a journal. *Address:* 16A Ocean Ave, Double Bay, Sydney, NSW 2028, Australia. *Telephone:* (9) 326 1348.

CASSANI, Barbara Ann, BA; American business executive; b 10 May 1960, Boston; d of James and Noreen Cassani; m Guy Davis 1985; one s one d. *Education:* Mount Holyoke Coll and Princeton Univ. *Career:* Man Consultant Coopers & Lybrand (now PricewaterhouseCoopers), Washington and London 1984–87; Man British Airways (UK and USA) 1987–97; CEO Go Fly Ltd 1997–. *Leisure interests:* reading, travel. *Address:* Stansted Airport, Stansted, Essex CM24 1SB, UK. *Telephone:* (1279) 666303; *E-mail:* b.cassani@go-fly.com.

CASSELTON, Lorna Ann, MA, PH D, FRS; British professor of genetics; b 18 July 1938; d of William Charles Henry Smith and Cecille Bowman; m 1st Peter John Casselton 1961 (divorced 1978); m 2nd William Joseph Dennis Tollett 1981. *Education:* Univ Coll London. *Career:* Asst Lecturer Royal Holloway Coll 1966–67, Lecturer 1967–76; Reader Queen Mary Coll (now Queen Mary and Westfield Coll) 1976–89, Prof of Genetics 1989–91, Visiting Prof of Genetics 1997; Agricultural and Food Research Council (now Biotech and Biological Sciences Research Council) Postdoctoral Fellow, Univ of Oxford 1991–95, Sr Research Fellow 1995–2001, Prof of Fungal Genetics 1997–; Fellow St Cross Coll, Oxford; Hon Fellow St Hilda's Coll Oxford. *Leisure interests:* classical music, dancing, reading. *Address:* 83 St Bernards Rd, Oxford OX2 6EJ, UK (Home). *Telephone:* (1865) 275109 (Office); (1865) 559997 (Home); *E-mail:* lorna.casselton@plants.ox.ac.uk.

CASSIDY, Sheila Anne, BM, B CH, MA; British medical practitioner and psychotherapist; b 18 Aug 1937, Lincs; d of the late Air Vice-Marshal J. R. Cassidy and of Barbara Margaret Drew. *Education:* Our Lady of Mercy Coll (Parramatta, NSW), Univ of Sydney (Australia) and Univ of Oxford. *Career:* Resident posts Radcliffe Infirmary, Oxford 1963–68; Leicester Royal Infirmary 1968–70; Medical Asst 1970–71; Asst Surgeon Assistencia Pública, Santiago, Chile 1971–75; tortured and imprisoned for treating wounded guerrilla 1975; Human Rights Lecturer 1976–77; studied monastic life Ampleforth Abbey, York 1977–79; Novice in Bernardine Cistercian Convent 1979–80; Sr House Officer in Radiotherapy Plymouth Gen Hosp 1980–82; Medical Dir St Luke's Hospice, Plymouth 1982–93; Palliative Care Physician Plymouth Gen Hosp 1993–96; Specialist in Psychosocial Oncology, Plymouth Oncology Unit, Freedom Fields Hosp 1996–; UK Council for Psychotherapy registered; Hon D SC (Exeter) 1991; Hon D LITT (Council for Nat Academic Awards) 1992; Valiant for Truth Media Award 1978; Freedom of the City of Plymouth 1998. *Publications:* Audacity to Believe (autobiog) 1977, Prayer for Pilgrims 1979, Sharing the Darkness 1988, Good Friday People 1991, Light from the Dark Valley 1994, The Loneliest Journey 1995, Creation Story 1996. *Leisure interests:* writing, broadcasting, drawing, walking, swimming. *Address:* Plymouth Oncology Centre, Derriford Hospital, Plymouth PL6 8DH, UK (Office); 6 The Esplanade, The Hoe, Plymouth PL1 2PJ, UK (Home). *Telephone:* (1752) 763976 (Office); *Fax:* (1752) 763992; *E-mail:* s.a.cassidy@amserve.net.uk.

CASTA, Laetitia; French model and actress; b 11 May 1978, Pont-Audeme; d of Dominique and Line Casta. *Career:* Launched by Yves Saint Laurent; first major advertising campaign for GUESS jeans 1993; model, Victoria's Secret 1996–; appeared in Sports Illustrated 1997, 1998, 1999; contracts with L'Oréal, Galeries Lafayette; has appeared on covers of Vogue, Elle, Cosmopolitan, Rolling Stone; chosen to represent Marianne (French nat symbol). *Films include:* Asterix et Obelix contre Cesar 1999, La Bicyclette Bleue, Les Ames Fortes 2001. *Address:* c/o Artmedia, 10 ave George V, 75008 Paris, France.

CASTANIER-MOTTA, Nicole Suzanne Juliette; French business executive; b June 21 1928, Paris; d of Albert Castanier and of Simone Combre; m Tullio Motta 1970; one d. *Education:* Coll Molière, Ecole supérieure de chimie de Paris. *Career:* Mem staff veterinary research laboratory, Auxerre 1951–60; mem staff Mondial Pratic 1962, Pres Dir-Gen 1968–; Hon Pres Syndicat national des fabricants et constructeurs de bâtiments industriels; Vice-Pres then Hon Vice–Pres Femmes chefs d'entreprises, section Cannes-Côte d'Azur 1986–; mem Council on Foreign Trade 1974. *Leisure interests:* violin, painting. *Address:* les Floridées, 34 blvd Cointet, 06400 Cannes, France. *Telephone:* (4) 93-48-15-01; *Fax:* (4) 93-38-44-20.

CASTELINO, Meher B.; Indian fashion journalist and consultant; b 6 July 1944, Bombay (now Mumbai); d of Rustom and Dinoo Mistry; m Bruno B. Castelino 1977 (deceased); one d one s. *Education:* Lawrence School (Lovedale, Nilgiris). *Career:* Fashion Ed GFQ 1984–88, Flair 1988–89, Discover India 1988; Columnist Mid-Day/Indian Express 1986, Newstime 1984; syndicated fashion column 1990; Fashion Consultant Eve's 1991–; freelance journalist contributing to more than 30 publications in India and abroad including Sunday Mail, Hindustan Times, Khaleej Times-Dubai, Fitnesse, Saturday Times and Apparel; Promoter Indian Fashion Show at Igedo Fashion Fair (Dusseldorf, Germany); Miss India 1964; Miss Airlines 1974; Miss Goldwater 1975. *Publications:* Manstyle 1987, Fashion Kaleidoscope 1994. *Leisure interests:* reading, writing, singing, painting, needle-craft. *Address:* 54 Deepak, 6th Floor, Peddar Rd, Mumbai 400 026, India. *Telephone:* (22) 3869063; *Fax:* (22) 3869216.

CASTELLINA, Luciana, D JUR; Italian journalist and politician; b 9 Aug 1929, Rome; m (divorced); one s one d. *Education:* Univ of Rome. *Career:* Mem PCI 1947–69, 1984–91, mem Cen Cttee 1986–91, Dir 1989–91, later Dir Rifondazione Comunista (Communist Re-establishment) Party; Ed Nuova Generazione 1958–62, Il Manifesto 1971–76, Pace e Guerra 1980–84, Nuova Liberazione; mem Chamber of Deputies (Parl) 1976, 1979, 1983, 1992; MEP 1984, mem Cttee on Culture, Youth, Educ and the Media, Chair 1994–96, fmr Chair External Econ Relations Cttee; Vice-Pres Int League of Rights of Peoples 1987; fmr mem Presidence Italian Women's Union, directorate Italian Communist Party. *Publications include:* Famiglia e società 1972, Che cosa c'è in America 1973; many essays. *Leisure interest:* films. *Address:* c/o European Parliament, rue Wiertz, 1047 Brussels, Belgium; Lega Internazionale Popoli, via della Dogana Vecchia 5, Rome, Italy. *Telephone:* (2) 284-51-51; *Fax:* (2) 284-91-51.

CASTLE OF BLACKBURN, Baroness (Life Peer), cr 1990, of Ibstone in the County of Buckinghamshire, **Barbara Anne Castle,** PC, BA; British politician; b 6 Oct 1910, Chesterfield; d of F. Betts and Annie Rebecca Ferrand; m Edward Castle (later Lord Castle of Islington) 1944 (died 1979). *Education:* Bradford Girls' Grammar School and St Hugh's Coll (Oxford). *Career:* Admin Officer Ministry of Food 1941–44; Housing Corresp and Forces Adviser Daily Mirror 1944–45; mem St Pancras Borough Council, London 1937–45; MP (Lab) for Blackburn 1945–79; Minister of Overseas Devt 1964–65, of Transport 1965–68, First Sec of State for Employment and Productivity 1968–70, Sec of State for Social Services 1974–76; MEP for Greater Manchester N 1979–84, for Greater Manchester W 1984–89, Vice-Pres EP Socialist Group and Leader Britist Lab Group 1979–85; mem House of Lords 1990–; Chair of Lab Party 1958–59; mem Metropolitan Water Bd 1940–45, Nat Exec Cttee of Lab Party 1950–85; Hon Fellow St Hugh's Coll, Oxford 1968, Bradford and Ilkley Community Coll 1985, UMIST 1991, Humberside Polytechnic 1991, York Univ 1992; Hon D TECH (Bradford) 1968, (Loughborough) 1969; Hon D IUR (Lancaster) 1991; Hon LL D (Manchester) 1993, (Cambridge) 1998; Hon D LITT (De Montfort) 1998; Cross of Order of Merit of the Fed Repub of Germany 1990. *Publications:* The Castle Diaries 1974–76 1980, The Castle Diaries 1964–70 1984, Christabel and Sylvia Pankhurst 1987, Fighting all the Way (autobiog) 1993. *Leisure interests:* walking, gardening, reading. *Address:* House of Lords, London SW1A 0AA, UK (Office). *Telephone:* (20) 7219-3000.

CASTRO, Ida, MA, JD; American lawyer and public servant. *Education:* Univ of Puerto Rico and Rutgers Univ of NJ. *Career:* Began career as labour and employment lawyer; Assoc Counsel Eisner, Levy, Pollack & Ratner; Assoc Counsel Giblin & Giblin; Sr Legal Counsel for Legal Affairs, Health and Hosp Corpn, New York; Special Counsel to the Pres and Dir of Labor Relations Hostos Community Coll, City Univ of New York; fmr Assoc Prof Inst for Man and Labor Relations, Rutgers Univ; Deputy Asst Sec and Dir Office of Workers' Compensation Programs, US Dept of Labor (DOL) 1994–96, Acting Dir Women's Bureau, DOL 1996–98; Chair Equal Employment Opportunity Comm (EEOC) Oct 1998–; mem NJ Comm on the Status of Women; Outstanding Leadership Award, Puerto Rican Legal and Educ Fund. *Address:* 1801 L St, NW, Washington, DC 20507, USA.

CASWELL, Tricia, BA; Australian environmentalist and organization executive; b 22 Aug 1948, Brisbane; d of John and Christina Jessie Caswell; partner Brian Boyd. *Education:* Univs of Queensland and Western Australia, LaTrobe Univ and Univ of London. *Career:* Teacher Olsh Coll, Darwin 1968–70, Mercedes Coll 1971; Lecturer Leedersville Tech Coll, Perth 1972–73; Theatre Arts WAIT 1973; Asst Sec Tech Teachers Trades Hall Council 1979–81, Gen Sec 1981–84; Industrial Officer Vic Trades Hall Council 1984–92; Exec Dir Australian Conservation Foundation 1992–95; Nat Exec Dir PLAN Int, Australia 1995–; mem numerous orgs and cttees; numerous papers on industrial relations, women in the workforce, conservation and the environment, literacy, etc. *Leisure interests:* drama, visual and community arts. *Address:* PLAN International Australia, Level 4, 533 Little Lonsdale St, Melbourne, Vic 3000, Australia.

CATALA, Nicole, L ÈS L; French politician, professor of law and judge; b 2 Feb 1936, Millau; one d. *Education:* Secondary school in Millau, Univ of Montpellier, Tulane Law School (LA, USA) and Univ of Paris. *Career:* Prof of Law in Dakar (Senegal) and Dijon 1961–69, Univ of Paris II (Panthéon-Assas) 1969–2000; mem Conseil Economique et Social 1979–84; Regional Councillor, Ile de France 1986–88; Sec of State for Professional Training 1986–88; mem Nat Ass (Parl, RPR) for Paris 1988–, Vice-Pres of Nat Ass 1993–; Councillor, Deputy Mayor of Paris 1989–; Judge High Court of Justice 1993–. *Publications:* numerous publs on civil, labour and European social law. *Leisure interests:* cinema, walking, skiing, swimming. *Address:* Assemblée Nationale, 75355 Paris, France (Office); 66 ave de Breteuil, 75007 Paris, France (Home). *Fax:* (1) 40-63-99-67 (Office); (1) 45-67-86-29 (Home).

CATLEY-CARLSON, Margaret, BA; Canadian international organization official; b 6 Oct 1942, Regina, SK; d of George Lorne and Helen Margaret Catley; m Stanley Frederick Carlson 1970. *Education:* Univ of British Columbia. *Career:* Joined Dept of External Affairs 1966, seconded to Sri Lanka 1968, UK 1975, Asst Under-Sec 1981; Vice-Pres Canadian Int Devt Agency (CIDA) 1978, Sr Vice-Pres/Acting Pres 1979–80, Pres 1983–89; Asst Sec-Gen, UN and Deputy Exec-Dir of Operations, UNICEF 1981; Deputy Minister of Health and Welfare 1989–92; Pres Population Council 1993–99; Chair Water Supply and Sanitation Collaborative Council (WHO) 1992–96; Trustee Women's World Banking 1992–96; several hon degrees. *Leisure interests:* skiing, gardening. *Address:* 1790 Broadway, Suite 800, New York, NY 10019, USA. *E-mail:* mcatleycarlson@ny.hra-inc.com.

CATSELLI, Irene (Rina); Cypriot politician and writer; b 31 March 1938, Kyrenia; m Stelios Catsellis; two d. *Education:* Kyrenia Gymnasium. *Career:* Mem Nat Liberation Struggle 1955–59, imprisoned 1958; mem Democratic Party 1978–, mem Kyrenia Dist Cttee 1981–; mem House of Reps (first woman to win seat) 1981–96, Deputy Chair Foreign Affairs Cttee, mem Refugee and Environment Cttees; numerous publs on the history and traditions of Cyprus; awarded three State Prizes for Literature. *Publications include:* Kyrenia – A Historical Study 1974, 1979, Refugee in My Homeland 1979, 2001, Blue Whale 1983. *Leisure interests:* painting, wood carving. *Address:* 27 Al Papadiamantis Str, Makedonitissa, 2400 Nicosia, Cyprus. *Telephone:* (2) 353929; *E-mail:* rina@spidernet.com.cy.

CATTAUI, Maria Livanos, BA; Swiss foundation executive; b 25 June 1941, New York; d of the late George M. and of Kakia (née Vernicos) Livanos; m Stéphane Cattaui 1969; two s. *Education:* Harvard Univ. *Career:* Fmrly Staff Writer and Researcher then Editorial Supervisor and Planner Encyclopaedia Britannica, Time Life Books then freelance writer 1963–68; joined World Econ Forum 1977, mem Exec Bd, Exec Dir, then Man Dir 1991–96; Sec-Gen International Chamber of Commerce (ICC), Paris 1996–, Dir ICC's 33rd World Congress, Hungary 2000. *Leisure interests:* reading, music. *Address:* International Chamber of Commerce, 38 Cours Albert 1er, 75008 Paris, France. *Telephone:* (1) 49-53-28-18; *Fax:* (1) 49-53-28-35; *E-mail:* sg@iccwbo.org; *Internet:* www.iccwbo.org.

CAUBET, Annie Françoise; French curator; b 20 May 1942, Laon; d of Pierre and Yvette Caubet. *Education:* Ecole du Louvre (Paris) and Univ of Paris. *Career:* Curator Dept of Oriental Antiquities, Musée du Louvre, Paris 1965–88, Curator-Gen 1988–; has taken part in numerous archaeological expeditions, including digs in Cyprus, Syria and the Middle East; Fellow of the Society of Antiquaries (UK); Chevalier des Arts et des Lettres; Chevalier de l'Ordre Nat du Mérite; Prix de l'Inst de France 1967. *Leisure interest:* 19th Century drawings and paintings. *Address:* Palais du Louvre, 75058 Paris Cedex 01, France.

CAUR, Arpana; Indian painter; b 4 Sept 1954, New Delhi; d of Dr Rajinder Singh and Ajeet Cour (qv); m Harinder Singh. *Education:* Univ of Delhi. *Career:* First exhibition 1975; one-woman exhibitions in India, UK, Sweden, Canada, Denmark; group exhibitions in India, Greece, Japan, Algeria, Iraq, Bangladesh, UK, USA, Cuba, Germany, Poland, France and Brazil; represented in public collections including Nat Gallery of Delhi, Chandigarh Museum, Ethnografic Museum (Stockholm), Kunstmuseum (Düsseldorf, Germany), Glenbarre Museum (Japan), Bradford Museum (UK); painting commissioned by Hiroshima Museum of Modern Art (on the 50th anniversary of the nuclear explosion) 1995; mem Purchase Cttee Nat Gallery of Modern Art, Delhi; mem jury Lalit Kala Akademi Award 1989, Republic Day Pageants 1989, 1990, 1991, 1995, 1996; Research Grant Lalit Kala Akademi, Delhi 1984–85; named Eminent Artist, Lalit Kala Akademi; All-India Fine Arts Soc Award 1985; Gold Medal for Painting, Sixth Triennele India; Critics Commendation, Algiers Biennale (Algeria) 1986. *Address:* 166 SFS Flats, Mount Kallash, opp Delhi Public School, New Delhi 110 0651, India.

CAVAGNOUD, Régine; French skier; b 1970. *Career:* First entry in World Ski Championships at age 15, 1985; winner of Super-G title Cortina d'Ampezzo (Italy) 2001, Gold Medal Women's Super-G World Ski Championships, St Anton (Austria) 2001. *Address:* c/o International Ski Federation, Marc Hodler House, Blochstrasse 2, 3653 Oberhofen/Thunersee, Switzerland. *Internet:* www.regine-cavagnoud.com.

CAVAN, Susan G., BA, LL B; Canadian business executive and producer; b 8 June, Toronto, ON; d of Albert and Joyce Cavan. *Education:* Queen's Univ. *Career:* Called to Bar, Ontario 1978; Lawyer Roberts and Drabinsky until 1980; Vice-Pres of Business Affairs Cineplex Corpn; Gen Counsel Int Cinema Corpn (ICC) 1982; Partner, Sr Vice-Pres of Business and Legal Affairs Alliance Entertainment 1985; Partner and Pres Alliance Entertainment Corpn 1987; Chair and CEO Accent Entertainment Corpn 1989–; mem Law Soc of Upper Canada, Toronto Women in Film. *Productions include:* The Bay Boy, Joe's So Mean to Josephine, Mesmer, Sweating Bullets, Magic Hunter; numerous films. *Address:* Accent Entertainment Corporation, 666B Queen St W, 2nd Floor, Toronto, ON M6J 1E5, Canada.

CAVANI, Liliana, PH D; Italian film director; b 12 Jan 1937, Reggio di Emilia, nr Modena. *Education:* Univ of Bologna and Centro Sperimentale de Cinematografia (Rome). *Career:* Worked for Italian TV as documentary dir 1962–66; dir of several operas. *TV includes:* History of the Third Reich, Women in the Resistance, The Age of Stalin, Philippe Pétain: Trial at Vichy (Golden Lion, Venice Festival), Jesus My Brother, Day of Peace, Francis of Assisi; *Films include:* Galileo, I Cannibali, L'Ospite, Night Porter, Beyond Good and Evil, The Skin, The Berlin Affair, Francesco, Sans Pouvoir le Dire, Ripley's Game 2001.

CAWLEY, Evonne Fay Goolagong, AO, MBE; Australian tennis player; b 31 July 1951, Barellan, NSW; d of the late Kenneth Goolagong and of Melinda Goolagong; m Roger Cawley 1975; one s one d. *Education:* Willoughby High School (Sydney). *Career:* Professional tennis player since 1970; Wimbledon Champion 1971, 1980 (singles), 1974 (doubles); Australian Champion 1974, 1975, 1976, 1977; French Champion 1971; S African Champion 1972; Italian Champion 1973; Virginia Slims Circuit Champion 1975, 1976; played Fed Cup for Australia 1971–76; consultant to Indigenous Sports Programme; Sports Amb to Aboriginal and Torres Strait Island Communities 1997–; Amb and Exec Dir Evonne Goolagong Sports Trust; Founder Evonne Goolagong Getting Started Programme for young girls. *Publications:* Evonne Goolagong (jtly) 1975, Home: The Evonne Goolagong Story (jtly) 1993. *Leisure interests:* fishing, reading, researching Aboriginal heritage, movies, soccer. *Address:* c/o IMG, 281 Clarence St, Sydney, NSW 2000, Australia (Office). *Telephone:* (7) 5474 0112; *Fax:* (7) 5474 0113.

CAZENAVE, Anny, D ÈS SC; French scientific researcher; b 3 March 1944, Draveil; d of Henry and Suzanne Boistay; m Michel Cazenave 1965; two s. *Education:* Univ of Paris. *Career:* Engineer Maths Div, Centre Nat d'Etudes Spatiales (CNES) 1969–71, Researcher Groupe de Recherche de Géodésie Spatiale 1971, Science Head Starlette geodesy satellite 1975, Head Dept of Geodesy and Spatial Oceanography 1989–; mem Acad Nat de l'Air et de l'Espace, Academia Europae; corresp mem Acad des Sciences; Fellow American Geophysical Union; numerous publs in professional journals on satellite geodesy, geophysics and planetology; Chevalier de l'Ordre Nat du Mérite; Bronze Medal, CNRS; Prix Doisteau-Blutel, Acad des Sciences 1979, 1990; Prix Kodak-Pathé, Acad des Sciences 1996. *Address:* GRGS-CNES, 18 ave E. Belin, 31400 Toulouse, France.

CEDARBAUM, Miriam Goldman, BA, LL B; American federal judge; b 16 Sept 1929; d of Louis Albert and Sarah (née Shapiro) Goldman; m Bernard Cedarbaum 1957; two s. *Education:* Barnard Coll and Columbia Univ (NY). *Career:* Called to New York Bar 1954; Law Clerk to US Dist Judge, S Dist of New York 1953–54, Asst Dist Attorney S Dist of New York 1954–57; Attorney Dept of Justice, Washington, DC 1958–59; Legal Consultant 1959–62; First Asst Counsel New York Moreland Comm on Alcoholic Beverage Control Law 1963–64; Assoc Counsel Museum of Modern Art, New York 1965–79; Assoc then Sr Attorney, Davis Polk and Wardwell 1979–86; Village Justice, Scarsdale, New York 1978–82 (acting), 1982–86; Judge S Dist, New York 1986–98, Sr Judge 1998–; Co-counsel Scarsdale Open Soc Asscn Inc 1968–86, Scarsdale Bd of Architectural Review 1977–78, Advisory Cttee on Labor Relations, Scarsdale Bd of Educ 1976–77; Trustee Barnard Coll; mem Judicial Conf Cttee on Defender Services 1993–99; mem American Law Inst, New York State Bar Asscn, ABA, Asscn of the Bar of the City of New York, Fed Bar Council, Copyright Soc of USA, Bd Revising Eds Columbia Law Review, Bd of Visitors Columbia Law School; Jane Marx Murphy Prize, Univ of Columbia; Barnard Medal of Distinction 1991. *Address:* US District Court, US Courthouse, 500 Pearl St, New York, NY 10007, USA.

CELLIER, Caroline; French actress; b 7 Aug 1945, Montpellier; d of Hubert and Jacqueline Cellier; m Jean Poiret 1989; one s. *Education:* Lycées de Montpellier and Molière (Paris). *Career:* Numerous appearances on stage, in films and on TV; Prix Marcel Achard 1963; Prix Suzanne Biancetti 1967; Prix Gérard Philipe 1968. *Plays include:* On ne peut jamais dire 1963, Du vent dans les branches de Sassafras 1965, Pygmalion 1967–68, Pourquoi m'avez-vous posée sur le palier? 1970, Trahisons 1982, L'âge de Monsieur est avancé 1985, Les liaisons dangereuses 1988; *Films include:* La vie, l'amour, la mort 1968, Les aveux les plus doux 1970, Mariage 1975, Certaines nouvelles 1980, Surprise party 1983, Femmes de personne 1984, L'année des méduses (César for Best Actress) 1985, Poulet au vinaigre 1985, Grand guignol, Charlie Dingo, Vent de panique 1987, Poker 1988, La contre-allée 1991, Le zèbre 1992, Délit mineur 1993, Farinelli 1994, L'élève 1996, Didier 1996, Le plaisir (et ses petits tracas) 1998; *TV appearances include:* Marie Curie 1965, Molière pour rire et pour pleurer 1973, Danger passion 1986, La disgrace 1996, Les grands enfants 1998. *Leisure interest:* horse-riding. *Address:* c/o Artmédia, 10 ave George V, 75008 Paris, France.

CERVANTES, Lorna Dee; American poet; b 1954, San Jose, CA. *Career:* Prof Univ of Colorado at Boulder; Ed Mango (literary magazine), Red Dirt (poetry journal); Lila-Wallace Reader's Digest Foundation Writers Award 1995. *Publications include:* Emplumada 1981 (American Book Award), From the Cables of Genocide: Poems on Love

and Hunger 1991 (Paterson Prize for Poetry, Latino Literature Award), Bird Ave. *Address:* University of Colorado at Boulder, Boulder, CO 80309, USA. *Telephone:* (303) 492-8908.

CHABRIDON, Jacqueline; French business executive; b 1 Jan 1940, Désertines; d of Aristide and Georgette Chabridon; m 1st Charles Hernu (divorced); m 2nd Alain Fernbach (divorced); one d. *Education:* Univ of Paris. *Career:* Journalist Radio-Télé-Luxembourg (RTL) 1961–63; Journalist on Le Figaro newspaper 1963–76; Head Politics Dept, Ed-in-Chief Radio Monte-Carlo 1976–83; Dir of Communication Crédit Lyonnais 1983–88, 1989–90, Adviser to Bd 1990; Head Press Office and Tech Adviser on Communication, Office of the Prime Minister 1988–89; Dir of Communication Régie Autonome des Transports Parisiens (RATP—Paris public transport) 1990–94; Dir of Communication Air France 1994–98, Groupe d'Hôtellerie et de Casinos Lucien Barrière 1998–; Auditor Inst des Hautes Etudes de Défense Nat 1983–84; Chevalier de l'Ordre Nat du Mérite. *Publication:* Les 180 jours de François Mitterrand (as Philippe de Commines) 1977. *Leisure interests:* music, rugby, golf, cycling. *Address:* Groupe Lucien Barrière, 9 ave de l'Opéra, 75001 Paris, France (Office).

CHADWICK, Whitney, PH D; American art historian; b 28 July 1943, New York; d of Cecil Chadwick and Helen Reichert; m Robert A. Bechtle 1982. *Education:* Middlebury Coll and Pennsylvania State Univ. *Career:* Teacher MIT 1972–78, Univ of California at Berkeley 1977, Stanford Univ 1990; Prof of Art San Francisco State Univ 1978–; mem Bd Dirs Coll of Art Asscn 1989–92; Nat Endowment for the Humanities Fellow 1981; Sr Fellow American Council of Learned Socs 1988. *Publications:* Myth in Surrealist Painting 1929–1939: Dali, Ernst, Masson 1980, Women Artists and the Surrealist Movement 1985, Women, Art and Society 1990, Significant Others: Creativity and Intimate Partnership (co-ed) 1993, Leonora Carrington: La Realidad de la Imaginación 1994. *Address:* 871 DeHaro St, San Francisco, CA 94107, USA. *Telephone:* (415) 824-1353; *Fax:* (415) 285-9828.

CHAHAL, Gurbinder, MA; Indian civil servant; b 13 July 1944, Bhatinda Dist; d of Jangir Singh Sidhu and Parsin Kaur; m Jasbir Singh Chahal 1970; two s one d. *Education:* Univ of Delhi. *Career:* Joined Govt Service, Punjab Region; Sec Punjab State Electricity Bd 1978–81; Jt Sec of Finance 1981–82; Dir Food and Supplies 1982–85; Sec of Tech Educ 1985–87, of Educ 1986–88, of Planning 1988–90, of Labour and Employment 1990–92, of Social, Women's and Children Welfare 1992–93, of Tourism and Cultural Affairs (Govt of Punjab) 1994–. *Leisure interest:* light reading. *Address:* Punjab Mini Secretariat, Kothi No 589, Sector 10 D, Chandigarh, India. *Telephone:* (172) 43691.

CHAKRABORTY, Ajita, MB, BS, DPM, FRCP(E), FRCPSYCH; Indian psychiatrist and medical practitioner; b 31 Oct 1926, Calcutta (now Kolkata); d of the late K. B. and Tamalini Debi Chakraborty. *Education:* Univ of Calcutta, Royal Coll of Physicians (Edinburgh, UK) and Royal Coll of Psychiatrists (London). *Career:* Psychiatrist in UK 1950–60; Postgrad teacher 1960; Prof of Psychiatry and Head of Neurology and Psychiatric Dept, Inst of Postgrad Medical Educ and Research 1976–84, Dir 1983–84; Pvt Practice 1985–; Pres Psychosocial Research and Training Centre; Gen Sec Indian Psychiatric Soc 1967–68, Pres 1976; mem Cttee Transcultural Section, World Psychiatric Asscn 1971–94. *Publications include:* Social Stress and Mental Health: A Social Psychiatric Field Study in Calcutta 1990; numerous contribs to professional journals. *Leisure interests:* golf, growing cacti. *Address:* 84 NE, Block E, New Alipore, Kolkata 700053, India. *Telephone:* (33) 4780302; *E-mail:* ajachak@satyam.net.in.

CHALKER, Baroness (Life Peer), cr 1992, of Wallasey, **Lynda Chalker,** PC; British politician; b 29 April 1942, Hitchin, Herts; d of the late Sidney Henry James and Marjorie Kathleen (née Randell) Bates; m 1st Eric Robert Chalker 1967 (divorced 1973); m 2nd Clive Landa 1981. *Education:* Univs of Heidelberg (Germany) and London. *Career:* Statistician Research Bureau Ltd 1963–69; Deputy Market Research Man Shell Mex & BP Ltd 1969–72; Chief Exec Int Div, Louis Harris Int 1972–74; MP (Cons) for Wallasey 1974–1992, Jt Sec Cons Health and Social Services Cttee 1975–76, Opposition Spokesperson on Social Services 1976–79, Parl Under-Sec of State at DHSS 1979–82, at Dept of Transport Services 1982–83, Minister of State, Dept of Transport 1983–86, FCO 1986–97, Minister for Overseas Devt 1989–97; mem

House of Lords 1992–; ind consultant on Africa and Devt 1997–; Chair Africa Matters Ltd; Advisory Dir Unilever PLC and NV 1998–; Non-exec Dir Capital Shopping Centres 1997–2000, Landell Mills Ltd 1999–, Ashanti Goldfields Co 2000–; Hon Fellow Queen Mary and Westfield Coll; Dr hc (Bradford) 1995. *Publications include:* We are Richer than We Think (jtly) 1978, Africa: Turning the Tide 1989; several pamphlets. *Leisure interests:* cooking, theatre, driving, music. *Address:* 51 Causton St, London SW1P 4AT, UK (Office); House of Lords, London SW1A 0PW, UK (Office). *Telephone:* (20) 7976-6850 (Office); *Fax:* (20) 7976-4997 (Office); (20) 7834-5880 (Office); *E-mail:* lchalker@africamatters.com (Office).

CHAMARETTE, Christabel Marguerite A., M SC; Australian psychologist and politician; b 1 May 1948, Hyderabad, India; d of Arthur William and Aileen Marion Chamarette. *Education:* Univs of Western Australia and Liverpool (UK). *Career:* Psychologist Authority for the Intellectually Handicapped 1970; Clinical Psychologist Fremantle Prison 1971–76, 1980–85, Bandyup Prison 1980–85; Community Worker HEED, Bangladesh 1976–79; Pvt Practice 1985–92; Consultant Psychologist Multiple Sclerosis Soc, WA 1991–; mem Alternative Coalition 1988–89, Cand for S Metro 1989, for Fremantle City Council 1989; mem Greens (WA) Senate team 1990 (Senator 1992–96), Jt Standing Cttee on Foreign Affairs, Defence and Trade, Electoral Matters; mem Anglican Social Responsibilities Comm 1987– (Chair 1991–); Chair Aboriginal Driver Training Programme 1987–91, Christian Justice Asscn 1988–91. *Leisure interests:* cycling, chatting, flowers, markets, coffee shops. *Address:* Suite 1/111, Colin St, W Perth, WA 6005, Australia; POB 137, W Perth 61, Australia. *Telephone:* (9) 481 1244; *Fax:* (9) 322 1048.

CHAMBERLAIN, Lesley, BA, M LITT; British writer; b 26 Sept 1951, Rochford, Essex; one d; m Pavel Seifter 1999. *Education:* Univ of Exeter and Wolfson Coll (Oxford). *Career:* Lecturer Portsmouth Polytechnic 1977–86; Corresp and Sr Sub-Ed Reuters (Moscow) 1978–79; Freelance writer and teacher 1986–, regular contrib to The Times Literary Supplement, Los Angeles Times Book Review, The Independent and other nat publications. *Publications:* The Food and Cooking of Russia 1982, The Food and Cooking of Eastern Europe 1989, In the Communist Mirror 1990, Volga, Volga A Journey Down the Great River 1994, Nietzsche in Turin 1996, In a Place Like That 1998, The Secret Artist – A Close Reading of Sigmund Freud 2000. *Leisure interests:* opera, chamber music, travel, fitness, food and wine. *Address:* c/o Quartet Books, 27 Goodge St, London W1P 2LD, UK (Office). *E-mail:* lesleychamb@aol.com.

CHAN, Anson, CBE, JP, BA; Hong Kong politician and civil servant; b 1940, Shanghai; d of Fang Zhaoling. *Education:* Hong Kong Univ. *Career:* Asst Sec Govt Secr 1963, 1966, Sec 1988; Asst Financial Sec 1970, Prin Financial Sec 1972; Deputy Sec for NT 1975, for Social Services 1976–79; Dir of Social Welfare 1980, 1982–84; Sec for Econ Services 1987–93, Chief Sec 1993–2001. *Leisure interests:* music, reading, cooking. *Address:* E2, 11th Floor, Villa Monte Rosa, 41A Stubbs Rd, Hong Kong Special Administrative Region, People's Republic of China. *Telephone:* 28497766; *Fax:* 28494423; *E-mail:* ajchan@ netvigator.com.

CHAN HENG CHEE, PH D; Singaporean academic and diplomatist; b 19 April 1942, Singapore. *Education:* Nat Univ of Singapore and Cornell Univ (NY, USA). *Career:* Asst Lecturer, Nat Univ of Singapore 1967–70, Lecturer 1970–75, Sr Lecturer 1976–80, Assoc Prof of Political Science 1981–, Head Dept of Political Science 1985–88, Prof 1990; Dir Inst of Policy Studies 1988; Perm Rep to the UN 1989–91; Amb to Mexico and High Commr to Canada 1989–91; Prof Dept of Political Science, Nat Univ of Singapore 1990–; Dir Inst of SE Asian Studies 1993–96; Exec Dir Singapore Int Foundation 1991–; Visiting Lecturer Ohio Univ, USA 1974; Visiting Prof Columbia Univ, NY, USA 1985; Visiting Fellow Yale Univ, CT, USA 1976, Australian Nat Univ 1984; mem Int Council of Asia Soc 1991–, Int Advisory Panel, East–West Center, Honolulu, HI, USA 1993, Bd of Govs Civil Service Coll 1993–, Cttee Singapore, Nat Cttee of the Council for Security Co-operation in Asia-Pacific (CSCAP) 1993–, Council Int Inst for Strategic Studies (IISS), London 1993–, Int Advisory Bd, Council on Foreign Relations 1995, Australian Nat Univ/Australian Research Council Jt Review Team of Inst of Advanced Studies 1995–, Int Inst for Strategic

Studies Council, Hong Kong 1995–; External Specialist Review of Center of Asian Studies, Univ of Hong Kong 1995–; Hon D LIT (Newcastle, Australia) 1994; Rachael Myer Book Prize 1964; Woman of the Year (Singapore) 1991. *Publications include:* Singapore: The Politics of Survival 1965–67 1971, The Dynamics of One Party Dominance: The PAP at the Grassroots (Nat Book Award) 1976, A Sensation of Independence: A Political Biography of David Marshall (Nat Book Award 1986) 1984, Government and Politics of Singapore (co-ed), The Prophetic and the Political: Selected Speeches and Writings of S. Rajaratnam 1987; numerous contribs to books and journals. *Address:* Singapore International Foundation, 111 Somerset Rd, 11-07 Devonshire Wing, Singapore, 238164, Singapore.

CHANET, Christine Simone; French lawyer and civil servant; b 23 Feb 1944, Paris; d of Robert and Marcelle Chanet. *Education:* Lycée La Fontaine (Paris) and Univ of Paris. *Career:* Auditor Ecole Nat de la Magistrature 1968–70; Magistrate Cen Admin, Ministry of Justice 1970–74; Tech Adviser, then Rep to Secr of State for Women's Affairs 1974–76; Rep to Secr of State for Culture 1976–77; Rep to Judicial Affairs Section, Ministry of Foreign Affairs 1981–88; Sub-Dir for Human Rights and Int Civil and Penal Affairs 1983; Tech Adviser Cabinet of the Minister of Justice, Keeper of the Seals 1988–90; Deputy Attorney-Gen Cour d'Appel de Paris (Court of Appeal) 1992–96; Counsel Cour de Cassation 1996–; Pres UN Cttee on Human Rights 1997–99; articles in law journals; Laureate of Law Faculty, Paris 1967; Chevalier de l'Ordre Nat du Mérite 1988. *Leisure interests:* plastic arts, cooking, theatre, opera, reading. *Address:* 4 rue du Laos, 75015 Paris, France; 12350 Lanuéjouls, France (Home). *Telephone:* (1) 47-83-37-02 (Paris).

CHANG, Judy Yukzun, B COMM, CA; Trinidad and Tobago accountant; b 5 Sept 1943, Arima; d of John Albert and Ella (née Fong) Chai; m Leslie Peter Chang 1968; one d one s. *Education:* Bishop Anstey High School, Univ of Toronto (Canada) and Inst of Chartered Accountants of Ontario (Canada). *Career:* Joined Price Waterhouse (Toronto, Canada) 1968, Sr Accountant (Trinidad and Tobago) 1972, Man 1976, Partner 1980; apptd to Bd Dirs Cen Bank of Trinidad and Tobago 1987, Deposit Insurance Corpn 1987; mem Council Inst of Chartered Accountants of Trinidad and Tobago 1983, Vice-Pres 1988–89, Chair Legislation Cttee 1989; Chair Cttee for Co Law Reform from 1990, submitted draft Co Law Act to Cabinet; mem Bd of Man Bishop Anstey High School. *Leisure interests:* reading, gardening, cooking. *Address:* Price Waterhouse, POB 550, 56-58 Richmond St, Port of Spain, Trinidad and Tobago (Office); 3 Bougainvillea Drive, Petit Valley, Trinidad and Tobago (Home). *Telephone:* 623-1361 (Office); *Fax:* 623-6025 (Office).

CHANG, Jung, PH D; British lecturer and writer; b 25 March 1952, Yibin, People's Repub of China; d of the late Shou-Yu Chang and of De-Hong Xia; m Jon Halliday 1991. *Education:* Sichuan Univ (People's Repub of China) and Univ of York. *Career:* Farm labourer 1969–71; 'barefoot doctor' 1970–71; steel worker 1971–72; electrician 1972–73; Asst Lecturer Sichuan Univ 1977–78; moved to UK 1978; Adviser TV Series The Heart of the Dragon 1982–84; Co-ordinator of Chinese Studies for External Services, School of Oriental and African Studies, Univ of London 1986–92; Hon D LITT (Buckingham) 1996, (Warwick, York) 1997, (Open Univ) 1998. *Publication:* Wild Swans: Three Daughters of China (NCR Book Award 1992, UK Writers' Guild Best Non-Fiction 1992, Fawcett Soc Book Award UK 1992, Book of the Year (UK) 1993, Humo's Gouden Bladwijzer (Belgium) 1993, 1994, Best Book of 1993 Award, Humo's Pop Poll (Belgium), Bjørnsonordenen, Den Norske Orden for Literature (Norway) 1995) 1991. *Leisure interests:* travel, gardening, watching old films, reading, tennis. *Address:* c/o Toby Eady Associates, 9 Orme Court, 3rd Floor, London W2 4RL, UK. *Telephone:* (20) 7792-0092; *Fax:* (20) 7792-0879.

CHANG WANG, Sylvia Ai-Chia; American film maker; b 22 July 1953, Repub of China (Taiwan); d of Chang Wen Cheung and Emily Wei; m Billy Wang 1991; one s. *Education:* Int School of the Sacred Heart (Taipei). *Career:* Singer, recorded seven albums; TV Presenter and Producer 1970; Actress 1971–, has appeared in 80 films, now film Producer and Dir. *Films include:* Acted in: The Dream of the Red Chamber 1977, Legend of the Mountain 1978, That Day on the Beach

1983, Shanghai Blues 1984, Jasmine House, My Grandpa (Taiwan Golden House Award), Passion (Best Actress, Hong Kong Film Festival) 1986, Sour Sweet 1988, Queen of Temple Street (Best Actress, Hong Kong Film Festival) 1990, Eight Tales of Gold (Best Actress, Hong Kong Film Festival), Paternity and Perplexity (Best Actress, Asian Film Festival, Taiwan Golden House Award); Directed: Passion (Taiwan Golden House Award), Once Upon a Time 1978, My Way 1981, The Game They Call Sex 1987, Mary From Beijing 1991, Conjugal Affairs 1993, Siao Yu (Best Picture, Best Screenplay, Best Actress, Best Production Design, Best Sound Effects awards, Asian Pacific Film Festival), Tonight Nobody Goes Home 1996; Produced: Sisters of the World Unite 1991. *Leisure interests:* reading, cooking. *Address:* 17 Homantin Hill Rd, Apt 1A Canbury Court, Kowloon, Hong Kong. *Telephone:* 27613975; *Fax:* 27157098.

CHANG XIANGYU; Chinese actress, opera singer and arts administrator; b 15 Sept 1923, Gongxian Co, Henan Prov; d of Zhang Fuxian and Wei Cairong; m Chen Xianzhang 1944; three d two s. *Education:* Drama training, Ministry of Culture. *Career:* Opera debut 1936; est Xiangyu Henan Opera School 1948, Xiangyu Henan Opera Troupe 1949; Pres Henan Opera Acad, Henan Prov 1956; Prin Traditional Opera School, Henan Prov 1978; Hon Prof Henan Univ 1983, Shenyang Conservatory of Music 1985; mem 1st NPC 1954–58, 5th NPC 1978–83, 6th NPC 1983–87, 7th NPC 1988; Vice-Chair Dramatists' Asscn 1979; Chair Henan Prov Dramatists' Asscn 1980; Consultant to Cultural Dept, Henan Prov 1982; Pres Henan School of Traditional Operas 1982; mem 5th Nat Cttee, Fed Literary and Art Circles 1988; attended World Peace Congress of Vienna 1952; Honour Prize 1952; Certificate of Merit, Ministry of Culture 1980; Honour Prize, First Chinese Art Festival 1987; First Golden Gramophone Record Prize 1989. *Films, plays and recordings include:* Random Talk about Art 1980, Chinese Methods of Singing and Performing 1985, Hua Mulan (film), Hong Niang (Red Girl), The Story of the White Snake, Break Through Hongzhou, Huang Guiying Offers a Great Sacrifice to Her Fiancé on the Execution Ground. *Leisure interests:* painting, calligraphy. *Address:* The Dramatists' Association, Beijing, People's Republic of China (Office); 113-16 Chengdong Rd, 450004 Zhengzhou City, Henan Prov, People's Republic of China (Home). *Telephone:* (371) 229006 (Home).

CHANNING, Carol; American actress; b 31 Jan 1921; d of George Channing and Carol Glaser; m 3rd Charles Lowe 1956; one s. *Career:* Has appeared in numerous plays and films; Tony Award 1968, Lifetime Achievement Tony Award 1995. *Plays include:* No for an Answer, Let's Face It, So Proudly We Hail, Lend an Ear (Critics' Circle Award), Gentlemen Prefer Blondes, Wonderful Town, The Vamp, Hello Dolly (Tony Award 1963), Lorelei; *Films include:* The First Traveling Saleslady 1956, Thoroughly Modern Millie (Golden Globe Award for Best Supporting Actress) 1967, Skidoo 1968, Sgt Pepper's Lonely Hearts Club Band 1978, Hans Christian Andersen's Thumbelina 1994 (voice), The Line King: Al Hirschfield 1996, Homo Heights 1998. *Address:* c/o William Morris Agency, 151 S El Camino Blvd, Beverly Hills, CA 90212, USA (Office).

CHANNING, Stockard, BA; American actress; b (Susan Stockard) 13 Feb 1944, New York, NY; m (four times). *Education:* Harvard Univ. *Career:* Mem Theatre Co of Boston (MA) 1967; Stage debut London 1992. *Plays include:* Two Gentlemen of Verona 1972–73, No Hard Feelings 1973, Vanities 1976, As You Like It 1978, They're Playing Our Song, Lady and the Clarinet 1983, The Golden Age 1983, A Day in the Death of Joe Egg (Tony Award for Best Actress) 1985, House of Blue Leaves 1986, Woman in Mind 1988, Love Letters 1989, Six Degrees of Separation 1990, Four Baboons Adoring the Sun 1992; *Films include:* Comforts of the Home 1970, The Fortune 1975, Sweet Revenge 1975, The Big Bus 1976, Grease 1978, The Cheap Detective 1978, Boys Life 1978, Without A Trace 1983, Heartburn 1986, Men's Club 1986, Staying Together 1987, Meet the Applegates 1987, Married to It 1993, Six Degrees of Separation 1993, Smoke 1995, Up Close and Personal 1996, Moll Flanders, Edie and Pen, The Red Door 1999, Other Voices 1999, Isn't She Great 1999, The Venice Project 1999, Where the Heart Is 2000; *TV includes:* The Stockard Channing Show 1979–80 and various TV movies including The West Wing 1999, Batman Beyond 1999. *Address:* ICM, 40 W 57th St, New York, NY 10019, USA (Office).

CHAO, Elaine L., B ECONS, MBA; American politician and banker; b China; d of James S. C. and Ruth (née Chu) Chao; m Mitch McConnell. *Education:* Mount Holyke Coll, Harvard Business School, MIT, Dartmouth Coll and Columbia Univ. *Career:* Banker Citicorp 1979–83; White House Fellow 1983–84; Vice-Pres Syndications BankAmerica Capital Markets Group, San Francisco 1984–86; Deputy Admin Maritime Admin 1986–88, Chair Fed Maritime Comm 1988–89; Deputy Sec Dept of Transportation; Dir Peace Corps, est first Peace Corps in Baltic nations and newly ind states of fmr USSR; Pres and CEO United Way America 1992–96; Sec of Labor (first Asian-American woman apptd to US Pres's Cabinet) Jan 2001–; Distinguished Fellow Heritage Foundation, Washington DC 1996–, Chair Asian Studies Center Advisory Council 1998–; Sr Ed Policy Review: The Journal of American Citizenship; mem Bd Dirs Dole Food Co, Vencor, Protective Life Corpn; Hon doctorates from Villanova Univ, Sacred Heart Univ, St John's Univ, Drexel Univ, Niagra Univ, Thomas More Coll, Bellarmine Coll, Univ of Toledo, Univ of Louisville; Goucher Outstanding Young Achiever Award, Nat Council of Women 1986; Harvard Univ Grad School of Business Alumni Achievement Award 1994. *Leisure interests:* charitable volunteer work, gardening, reading, movies. *Address:* Department of Labor, 200 Constitution Ave, NW, Washington, DC 20210, USA. *Telephone:* (202) 693-6000; *Fax:* (202) 693-6111; *E-mail:* SecretaryElaineChao@dol-gov; *Internet:* www.dol.gov.

CHAPLIN, Geraldine; American actress; b 1944, Santa Monica, CA; d of Charles and Oona (née O'Neill) Chaplin; one s. *Education:* Pvt Schools and Royal Ballet School (London). *Films include:* Doctor Zhivago 1965, Stranger in the House 1967, I Killed Rasputin 1968, The Hawaiians 1970, Innocent Bystanders 1973, Buffalo Bill and the Indians or Sitting Bull's History Lesson, The Three Musketeers 1974, The Four Musketeers, Nashville 1975, Welcome to LA Cria, Roseland 1977, Remember My Name, A Wedding 1978, The Mirror Crack'd 1980, Voyage en Douce 1981, Bolero 1982, Corsican Brothers, The Word, L'Amour Par Terre, White Mischief 1988, The Moderns 1988, The Return of the Musketeers, I Want to Go Home, The Children, Chaplin 1992, Jane Eyre, Gulliver's Travels, The Eyes of Asia, In the Name of God's Poor 1997, Cousin Bette 1998, In the Beginning 2000; *TV includes:* My Cousin Rachel, A Foreign Field 1994, To Walk With Lions 1999. *Address:* c/o Ames Cushing, William Morris Agency, 151 S El Camino Drive, Beverly Hills, CA 90212, USA (Office).

CHAPLINA, Natalya; Russian newspaper editor; b 15 Feb 1957, Leningrad (now St Petersburg); m 2nd 1996; two d. *Education:* St Petersburg State Univ. *Career:* Journalist 1975–; Founder and Editor-in-Chief Chas Pik (first independent newspaper in Russian Fed) 1990–; USSR Journalists' Union award 1991; Russian Journalists' Union award 1994; has written five books. *Address:* Chas Pik, 191040 St Petersburg, Nevsky pr 81, Russian Federation. *Telephone:* (812) 279-25-65; *Fax:* (812) 279-22-70; *E-mail:* news@chaspik.spb.su.

CHAPMAN, Honor; British business executive. *Career:* Partner Jones Lang Wootton; Chief Exec London First Centre 1993–95, later mem Bd; Commr Crown Estate 1997–; Non-Exec Dir Legal & General. *Address:* Crown Estate Commissioners, 16 Carlton House Terrace, London SW1Y 5AH. *Telephone:* (20) 7210-4377; *Fax:* (20) 7930-1295.

CHAPMAN, Jan; Australian film producer and director. *Films include:* Dir: Showtime 1978; Producer: Sweet and Sour 1984, Displaced Persons 1985, Dancing Daze 1986, Last Resort (exec producer) 1988, Last Days of Chez Nous 1991, Love Serenade 1996, Holy Smoke! 2000, Quills 2000.

CHAPMAN, Rhiannon, LL B; British organization executive; b 21 Sept 1946, Pembrokeshire; d of 2nd Viscount St Davids and Doreen Guiness Jowett; m Donald Hudson Chapman 1974 (divorced 1992); two step-s. *Education:* Pvt schools in Australia and England, King's Coll (Univ of London). *Career:* Asst Personnel Man London Weekend TV 1968–70; Divisional Personnel Man Philips Electronics Industries; Personnel Man CPI Data Peripherals; Personnel Dir London Stock Exchange 1980–90; Dir The Industrial Soc 1991–93; mem Welsh Devt Agency 1994–98; Non-exec Dir S. R. Gent PLC 1994–97; Man Dir Plaudit 1994–; Chair Fleming Managed Growth PLC 1999–; mem Employment Appeal Tribunal 1991, Council Policy Studies Inst 1993, Council London Lighthouse 1994; Gov London Guildhall Univ 1992; Chair

Asscn of Financial Service Orgs. *Leisure interests:* tennis, circuit training, handcrafts, theatre, opera, travel. *Address:* 39 Spice Court, Asher Way, London E1 9JD, UK. *Telephone:* (20) 7709-0226.

CHAPMAN, Tracy; American singer and songwriter; b 1964, Cleveland, OH. *Education:* Tufts Univ (MA). *Career:* Composer and performer; Best New Artist, Best Female Pop Vocal Performance and Best Contemporary Folk Performance Grammy Awards 1989, Best Rock Song Grammy Award for Give Me One Reason 1996. *Recordings include:* Tracy Chapman 1988, Crossroads 1989, Matters of the Heart 1992, New Beginnings 1995, Telling Stories 2000. *Address:* Elektra Records, 75 Rockefeller Plaza, New York, NY 10019, USA.

CHARLES, Caroline; British fashion designer; b 18 May 1942, Cairo, Egypt; d of Noel St John Fairhurst and Helen T. Williams; m Malcolm Valentine 1966; one d one s. *Education:* Sacred Heart Convent (Woldingham, Surrey) and Swindon Art School. *Career:* Fashion Designer 1963–; est retail outlet in London selling Caroline Charles Collection 1979; launched first Caroline Charles House of Design (London) 1989, now Man Dir; wholesale business suppliers to leading British shops and exports to USA, Japan, Australia and Europe; awards include Evening Standard Design Award 1983. *Publication:* Weekend Wardrobe. *Leisure interests:* travel, theatre, gardening. *Address:* Caroline Charles, 56–57 Beauchamp Place, London SW3 1NY, UK. *Telephone:* (20) 7225-3197 (Office).

CHARLES, Dame (Mary) Eugenia, DBE, BA; Dominican politician; b 15 May 1919, Pointe Michel; d of John B. and Josephine (née Delauney) Charles. *Education:* Univ of Toronto and LSE. *Career:* Mem Inner Temple, London 1947; legal practice Barbados, Windward and Leeward Islands; political career 1968–; Co-Founder and first Leader Dominica Freedom Party; mem House of Ass (Parl) 1970–95; Leader of the Opposition 1975–79; Prime Minister, Minister of Finance and Devt 1980–95, of Foreign Affairs 1980–90; mem Council Women World Leaders, John F. Kennedy School of Govt, Harvard Univ; fmr Minister of Tourism and Devt; Pres Int Fed of Women Lawyers 1990–; fmr Dir Dominica Co-operative Bank; fmr mem Bd Dominica Infirmary. *Leisure interests:* reading, travel. *Address:* POB 121, 1 Cross Lane, Roseau, Dominica. *Telephone:* 4482855 (Home).

CHARLES-ROUX, Marie-Charlotte Elisabeth Edmonde; French journalist and writer; b 17 April 1920, Neuilly-sur-Seine; d of the late François and Sabine (née Gounelle) Charles-Roux; m Gaston Defferre 1973 (deceased). *Education:* Lycée Chateaubriand (Rome). *Career:* In army 1944–45; Columnist Elle magazine 1947–49; Ed-in-Chief French edn of Vogue magazine 1950–66; Commr Moments de la Mode exhibition, Musée de la Mode et du Costume 1986; mem Acad Goncourt 1983–; Croix de Guerre 1939–45; Chevalier de la Légion d'Honneur 1989; Grand Prix Littéraire de Provence 1977. *Publications;* Oublier Palerme (Prix Goncourt) 1966, Elle Adrienne 1971, L'irrégulière 1974, Le temps Chanel 1979, Stèle pour un bâtard 1980, Un désir d'Orient: La Jeunesse d'Isabelle Eberhardt 1988, Nomade j'étais 1995: Les années africaines d'Isabelle Eberhardt 1995. *Leisure interests:* music, sea and sailing. *Address:* Editions Grasset, 61 rue des Saints-Pères, 75006 Paris, France (Office).

CHARRAT, Janine; French ballet dancer and choreographer; b 24 July 1924, Grenoble; d of Roger and Laura Charrat; m 1st Gérard Bourret 1957; m 2nd Michel Humbert 1969. *Education:* Privately. *Career:* With Ballets Roland Petit 1941–44, 1948, Ballets des Champs-Elysées 1945, Nouveau Ballet de Monte-Carlo 1946, Ballet du Marquis de Cueval 1946–47, 1950, Opéra-Comique 1947, Budapest Opera 1948, 1974, Berlin Opera 1949, Stockholm and Amsterdam Operas 1950, Hanover Opera 1977; f own ballet co 1951; Artistic Dir Ballet, Grand Théâtre de Genève, Switzerland 1962–64; Co-Founder Ballet Int de Paris 1965; Founder Acad de Danse Janine Charrat 1969; Dance Adviser Centre Nat d'Art et de Culture Georges Pompidou, Paris 1979–; worldwide tours with own co; Commdr de la Légion d'Honneur; Commdr des Arts et des Lettres; Oscar for Bravery 1962. *Ballets include:* Dancer and choreographer: Jeu de cartes, Abraxas, Ballet d'Obéron, Le massacre des amazones, Les sept péchés capitaux, Orfeo 1951, Les Algues 1957, Up to date, Electre 1960, 1968, Séquence 1972, Offrandes 1973, Dyacronie 1979, Concerto pour la main gauche 1981, Hécube 1982,

Palais des glaces 1987, Inventaire 1987, La passion 1994–95. *Leisure interests:* sculpture, drawing, horse-riding. *Address:* 11 rue Pasteur, 92500 Rueil-Malmaison, France. *Telephone:* (1) 47-08-60-07.

CHASE, Doris Totten; American sculptor, artist and film maker; b 29 April 1923, Seattle; d of William and Helen (née Feeney) Totten; m Elmo Chase 1943 (divorced 1972); two s. *Education:* Univ of Washington. *Career:* Sculptor, artist, film and video maker 1945–; lecture tours for US Information Agency, India 1972, S America 1975, Europe 1978, Australia 1986, E Europe 1987; one-woman exhibitions in USA, Japan, Thailand, UK, Italy 1962–; represented in perm collections in USA, France, Japan, Canada; mem Actors' Studio; Grantee Nat Endowment for the Arts, American Film Inst 1988, New York State Council for Arts, Seattle Arts Comm, Retirement Research Foundation; Gov's Art Award (WA) 1992; numerous awards at int film festivals. *Productions include:* Doris Chase Dance Series 1973–79, Doris Chase Concept Series 1980–85, The Chelsea 1993, Doris Chase–Artist in Motion (written by Dr Patricia Failing) 1993; By Herself (TV series) 1985–91, Glass Curtain 1984, Table for One 1985, Dear Papa (jtly) 1986, A Dancer (jtly) 1987, Still Frame (jtly) 1988, Sophie (jtly) 1989, The Chelsea 1994. *Address:* Chelsea Hotel, 222 W 23rd St, New York, NY 10011, USA. *Telephone:* (212) 243-3700 (NY); (206) 624-3700 (WA); *Fax:* (212) 243-3700 (NY); (206) 382-3780 (WA); *Internet:* www.911media.org/dorischase.

CHASE-RIBOUD, Barbara Dewayne, MFA; American/French sculptor and writer; b 26 June 1939, Philadelphia, PA; d of Charles Edward and Vivian May Braithwaite West Chase; m 1st Marc Eugene Riboud 1961 (divorced 1981); m 2nd S. G. Tosi 1981; two s. *Education:* Yale Univ. *Career:* One-woman shows include Berkeley Museum (CA) 1973, MIT 1973, Museum of Modern Art (Paris) 1974, Kunstmuseum (Düsseldorf, Germany) 1974, Bronx Museum (NY) 1979, Pasadena Coll (CA) 1990, Metropolitan Museum of Art (NY) 1999, Walters Museum (Washington DC) 2000; has taken part in numerous group exhibitions and is represented in perm collections in USA and France; Fellow John Hay Whitney Foundation 1958, Nat Endowment for Arts 1973; Hon PH D (Temple Univ, Univ of Connecticut, Mullenberg Coll); Kafka Prize 1979; Gold Medal (Acad of Italy) 1979; Carl Sandburg Poetry Prize 1988; US Gen Services Design Award for Best Public Sculpture 1998; KT of French Repub 1996. *Publications include:* From Memphis and Peking, Poems 1974, Sally Hemings, A Novel 1979, Study of a Nude Woman as Cleopatra 1987, Valide 1986, Echo of Lions 1989, The President's Daughter 1995, Roman Egyptian 1995, The Sculpture of Barbara Chase-Riboud, Selz, Jansen A., Abrams. *Address:* 3 rue August Comte, 75006 Paris, France; Palazzo Ricci, 146 via Guilia, 00186 Rome, Italy. *Telephone:* (1) 43-29-69-63; *Fax:* (1) 43-29-47-53; *E-mail:* bchaseriboud@hotmail.com; *Internet:* www .chase-riboud.com.

CHASSAGNE, Yvette Madeleine, L ÈS L; French civil servant and insurance executive; b 28 March 1922, Bordeaux; d of André and Lily Brunetière; m Jean Chassagne (divorced); two c. *Education:* Univ of Bordeaux and Ecole Nat d'Admin. *Career:* Sub-Dir Dept of Assurance, Ministry of Econ and Finance 1966; Dir of Econ Devt Ministry of Co-operation 1974–78; Adviser Cour des Comptes 1979–87; Prefect for Loir-et-Cher dept 1981–83; Pres Union des Assurances de Paris (UAP) 1983–87, Hon Pres 1987–; Deputy Head Crédit foncier de France; Pres Sicau Invesco; Hon Pres Co Camerounaise d'Assurances et de Réassurances 1983, Union Générale des Assurances de Niger 1985; fmr Hon Vice-Pres Société Libano-française d'Assurances; Hon Fmr Admin Banque Worms, Société Lyonnaise des Eaux; Hon mem Econ and Social Council 1984–; Hon Pres Comm d'Evaluation des Entreprises Publiques 1989–, Prévention Routière 1989–, Bd Inst de Protection et de Sûreté Nucléaire 1990–; Hon Pres Mouvement de la Jeunesse Européenne; Commdr de la Légion d'Honneur; Grand Officier de l'Ordre Nat du Mérite; Chevalier des Palmes Académiques; Chevalier du Mérite Agricole; nat decorations from Italy, Gabon, Côte d'Ivoire, Senegal, Cen African Repub, Cameroon, Niger and Mali. *Publication:* Fonctionnaire et patron, les préjugés renversés 1988. *Address:* Domaine de Montjoie, route de Cuxac, 11100 Narbonne, France.

CHATTERJEE, Margaret, PH D; Indian philosopher and writer; b 13 Sept 1925, London; d of Norman Herbert and Edith Gantzer; m Nripendranath Chatterjee 1946; two d one s. *Education:* Parkstone

Grammar School Somerville Coll (Oxford) and Univ of Delhi. *Career:* Moved to India 1946; teacher of Philosophy Univ of Delhi 1956–90, Prof of Comparative Religion 1976–77; Visiting Prof Drew Univ, NJ, USA 1983, Westminster Coll, Oxford, UK 1992–; Dir Indian Inst of Advanced Study, Simla 1986–89; Visiting Fellow Woodbrooke, Birmingham 1990; Spalding Visiting Fellow in Indian Philosophy, Wolfson Coll, Oxford, UK 1991; Commonwealth Visiting Fellow, Univ of Calgary, Canada 1991; Pres Int Soc for Metaphysics 1985–90. *Publications include:* Our Knowledge of Other Selves 1963, Philosophical Enquiries 1968, The Existentialist Outlook 1974, The Language of Philosophy 1981, Gandhi's Religious Thought 1983, The Religious Spectrum 1984, The Concept of Spirituality 1988, The Philosophy of Nikunja Vihari Banerjee 1990, Gandhi and his Jewish Friends 1992; Poetry: The Spring and the Spectacle 1967, Towards the Sun 1970, The Sandalwood Tree 1972, The Sound of Wings 1978, The Rimless World 1987; Short stories: At the Homeopath's 1975. *Leisure interests:* music, travelling, gardening. *Address:* Westminster College, Oxford OX2 9AT, UK; 49 Kala Kunj, A/0 Shalimar Bagh, Delhi 110052, India. *Telephone:* (1865) 247644 (UK); *Fax:* (1865) 251847 (UK).

CHAUVET, Christine Elizabeth Murielle, L ÈS L; French business executive and politician; 19 Sept 1949, Paris; d of Claude and Fay (née Rogers) Chauvet. *Education:* Ecole Supérieure de Publicité, Univ of Paris X (Paris-Nanterre) and Centre Universitaire de Gestion Dauphine. *Career:* Public Relations with Unilever, London 1971; Publicity Asst DIM SA 1972; with Pierre Cardin 1972–73; Dir Chauvet Int RP and Chauvet Int Import Export 1973; Dir-Gen France-Asia Industries SA 1981–; Pres Fondation pour la Reprise d'Entreprises 1985–; Hon Pres Parti Républicain (PR) Seine-Saint-Denis 1989, Nat Del 1990; Nat Pres Asscn des Femmes Chefs d'Entreprises 1992–; Pres World Asscn of Women Execs 1992–; Vice-Pres Econ and Social Cttee of Ile-de-France 1990; Sec of State for External Trade 1995; Dir-Gen Centre Français du Commerce Extérieur 1996–98; CEO Fleishman & Hillard 2001–; Chevalier de la Légion d'Honneur; Officier de l'Ordre Nat du Mérite. *Publications include:* Lettre ouverte aux hommes qui ont peur des femmes en politique 1990, Les femmes dans l'économie française 1995. *Leisure interest:* ballet and tap dancing. *Address:* 9 rue Léo Delibes, 75116 Paris, France. *Telephone:* (1) 47-27-77-49; *Fax:* (1) 45-53-85-01.

CHAUVIRÉ, Yvette; French ballet dancer; b 22 April 1917, Paris; d of Henri Chauviré and Berthe Pinchard. *Education:* Paris Opera Ballet School. *Career:* Joined Paris Opera Ballet 1930, Danseuse Etoile 1942; with Monte Carlo Opera Ballet 1946–47; Artistic and Tech Adviser to Admin of Paris Opera 1963–68; Dir Acad int de danse, Paris 1970–; f French School at Kyoto Acad, Japan; Pres Europa Danse 1999–; Commdr de la Légion d'Honneur; Commdr des Arts et des Lettres; Grand Officier de l'Ordre Nat du Mérite. *Ballets include:* Istar, Les deux pigeons, Sleeping Beauty, David triomphant, Giselle, Les créatures de Prométhée, Roméo et Juliette, L'écuyère, Les suites romantiques, Lac des cygnes, L'oiseau de feu, Petrouchka, Sylvia, La belle Hélène, Casse-Noisette, Les mirages, Le cygne, La dame aux camélias; *Films include:* Carrousel napolitain 1953, Le cygne 1984, Une étoile pour l'exemple; *Publication:* Je suis ballerine. *Leisure interests:* drawings, watercolours, collecting swans. *Address:* 21 Place du Commerce, 75015 Paris, France.

CHÁVEZ DE OCAMPO, Martha, LL M; Peruvian lawyer and politician; b 12 Jan 1953, Callao. *Education:* Pontifical Catholic Univ of Peru and Univ degli Studi di Roma (Italy). *Career:* Lecturer in Labour Legislation, Univ of Lima 1978, in Gen Admin, Univ of Piura 1983, in Fundamentals of Law, Montemar Inst 1983, in Labour Law, Pontifical Catholic Univ of Per 1988, 1990, 1991; lawyer Ministry of Labour and Social Promotion; lawyer Office of Rubio Normand, Hernández and Associates; Sec to Council of Ministers 1992; Spokesperson for Movimiento Político Nueva Mayoría 1992, for Alianza Nueva Mayoría—Cambio 90 1992–; mem Congress (Alianza Nueva Mayoría—Cambio 90) 1992–95, Pres of Congress 1995, mem Permanent Comm and Exec Council of Congress; mem Special Privatization Cttee of Petromar SA 1992, of Petróleos del Perú SA 1992; mem Bd of Dirs Empresa de Telecomunicaciones del Perú SA (Entel Perú) 1992. *Address:* Oficina del Presidente del Congreso, Congreso, Lima, Peru.

CHEBOTAREVA, Anastasia Savelyevna; Russian violinist; b 8 Aug 1972, Odessa; d of Chebotarev Savely Ignatyevich and Chebotareva Varvara Igorevna. *Education:* Moscow State Conservatory (class of I. Bochkova). *Career:* Asst Prof Moscow State Conservatory; Prof of Violin Kurashiki Sakuyo Univ, Japan; soloist Moscow State Philharmonics; performed with maj Russian and European orchestras including Tchaikovsky Big Symphony under V. Fedoseyev, St-Petersburg Philharmonic under Yu. Temirkanov, Vienna Chamber orchestra; won prizes in Paganini Competition (Genoa, Italy) 1990, Int European Juventus Festival 1991; won 1st prize in Rodolfo Lipizer Competition (Italy) 1992, Tchaikovsky Music Competition (Moscow) 1994. *Address:* Vavilov str 72, Apt 38, Moscow, Russian Federation. *Telephone:* (095) 959-30-69 (Office).

CHEDID, Andrée, BA; French writer; b 20 March 1920, Cairo, Egypt; d of Selim Saab and Alice K. Haddad; m Louis A. Chedid 1942; one s one d. *Education:* French Schools (Cairo and Paris) and American Univ in Cairo. *Career:* Has lived in Paris since 1946; Officier de la Légion d'Honneur; Commdr des Arts et des Lettres; Prix Louise Labé 1966; L'aigle d'or de la poésie 1972; Grand Prix des Lettres Françaises de l'Acad Royale de Belgique 1975; Prix de l'Afrique Mediterranéenne 1975; Prix de l'Acad Mallarmé 1976; Prix Goncourt 1979; Prix de Poésie, Soc des Gens de Lettres 1991; Prix PEN Club Int 1992; Prix Paul Morand, Acad Française 1994; Prix Albert Camus 1995. *Publications include:* Novels: Le sommeil délivré 1952, Le sixième jour 1960, L'autre 1969, Nefertiti et le rêve d'Akhnaton 1974, La maison sans racines 1985, L'enfant multiple 1989; Poetry: Fraternité de la parole 1975, Epreuves du vivant 1983, Textes pour un poème 1949–1970 1987, Poèmes pour un texte 1970–91, Par delà les mots 1995; Plays: Bérénice d'Egypte, Les nombres, Le montreur 1981, Echec à la reine 1984, Les saisons de passage 1996; Short Stories: Les corps et le temps 1979, Mondes Miroirs Magies 1988, A la mort, A la vie 1992, La Femme de Job 1993, Les saisons de passage 1996, Le jardin perdu 1997, Territoires du souffle 1999, Le cœur demeure 1999; numerous essays and children's books. *Leisure interest:* collages. *Address:* c/o Flammarion, 26 rue Racine, 75006 Paris, France. *Telephone:* (1) 40-51-31-00.

CHEN AILIAN; Chinese dancer and choreographer; b 24 Nov 1939, Shanghai; d of Chen Xi Kang and Yu Xiu Ying; m Wei Dao-Ning; two d. *Education:* Beijing Dance School. *Career:* Teacher Beijing Coll of Dancing 1959–63; Chief Dancer and Actress China Opera and Dancing House 1963; Prof Arts Dept Nan Kai Univ, Hainan Univ; Head of Chen Ailian Artistic Troupe; mem Exec Cttee Chinese Dancers' Asscn; Chief Dancer Chinese Art del to fmr USSR, USA, France, Spain, Belgium, Denmark, Finland, Sweden, Italy, Norway, Hong Kong and Germany; Founder Chen Ailian Artistic Troupe 1989 (first non-governmental performing org in China); demonstrations and lectures in Shangdong Prov, Shanxi Prov, Beijing Univ, Foreign Languages Inst, Post and Telegraph Inst, Light Industry Inst, and Municipal Dancers' Unions; contribs to magazines and newspapers; Champion Dancer 8th World Youth Festival in Helsinki 1962; Excellent Performance Award First Nat Dance Concert; First Prize Ministry of Culture for Dance Soirée and Princess Wenzhen. *Performances include:* The Peony Pavilion, In the Dusk of Evening, The Oriental Melody, The Lantern Dance, Water, The Sword Dance, Snake Dance, Bow Dance, Mermaid, Moonlight on the Spring River, Ball Dance, The Song of the Serfs, Women Militia in the Grassland, The Red Silk Dance. *Leisure interests:* literature, music, traditional opera, travel, mountain-climbing. *Address:* Room 101/7, 2 Nanhuadong St, Hufang Rd, 100050 Beijing, People's Republic of China. *Telephone:* (1) 3015066; *Fax:* (1) 3011942.

CHEN BAOLIU, BA; Chinese diplomatist; b 24 July 1938; d of the late Chen Gaobiao and Xi Zhilian; m Shi Bingyi 1968; one s. *Education:* Nanjing and Beijing Univs. *Career:* Joined Ministry of Foreign Affairs 1962, Third Sec, then Second Sec, Embassy Burma (now Myanmar) 1979–84, First Sec 1986–89, Amb 1994; Deputy Dir Asian Dept, Ministry of Foreign Affairs 1989; Counsellor Embassy Philippines 1992. *Leisure interests:* reading, swimming, dancing. *Address:* c/o Ministry of Foreign Affairs, 225 Chaoyangmennei Dajie, Dongsi, Beijing, 100701, People's Republic of China.

CHEN LIYING; Chinese public servant; b 1934, Changde Co, Hunan Prov. *Education:* Tianjin textile Inst. *Career:* Joined CCP 1955; Deputy Chief Engineer Yunnan Textile Mill 1981–85; Vice-Gov Yunnan Prov 1989; Vice-Chair Yunnan Prov Cttee, 7th CPPCC 1993. *Address:* c/o Office of the Governor, Kumming City, Yunnan Province, People's Republic of China.

CHEN MUHUA; Chinese politician; b 1921, Zhejiang Prov.. *Education:* Yanan Mil School. *Career:* Chief of Div Communication Bureau, State Planning Comm, Deputy Dir Complete-Plant Bureau, Gen Bureau of Foreign Econ Relations, Vice-Minister then Minister of Foreign Econ Relations, Vice-Premier of State Council, Dir of Cen Patriotic Public Health Campaign Cttee and Dir of State Family Planning Comm, State Councillor and Minister of Foreign Econ Relations and Trade, Pres People's Bank of China, Chair Council and Hon Chair of Bd of Dirs 1949–88; Vice-Chair Standing Cttee Nat People's Congress, Pres All China Women's Fed 1988–, Hon Pres 1998–; Advisor Nat Co-ordination Group for Anti-Illiteracy Work 1994–, Chinese Asscn for Promotion of the Population Culture; Hon Pres Int Econ Co-operation Soc 1983–, Florists' Asscn 1984–; Hon Pres China Asscn of Women Judges 1994–, China Asscn of Women Doctors, Asscn for Import and Export Commodity Inspection. *Address:* All China Women's Federation, 15 Jian Guo Men Nei St, 100130 Beijing, People's Republic of China. *Telephone:* (10) 65225357; *Fax:* (10) 65136044.

CHEN SUZHI; Chinese party official; b 1931, Shengyang City, Liaoning Prov. *Education:* Liaoning Univ. *Career:* Mem CCP 1949–; dir of factory 1978; Vice-Gov Liaoning, in charge of industrial work 1982; alt mem 12th CCP Cen Cttee 1982–87, 13th 1987; mem Standing Cttee Liaoning Prov Cttee, 7th CPC 1985; Rep to CCP 13th Nat Congress; Vice-Gov Liaoning Prov 1988; Deputy 8th NPC Liaoning Prov; Vice-Chair Liaoning Prov 8th People's Congress Standing Cttee 1992. *Address:* Liaoning Trade Union Offices, Shenyang, People's Republic of China.

CHENEY, Lynne Ann, PH D; American public organization administrator and writer; b 14 August 1941, Casper (WY); d of Wayne and Edna (née Lybyer) Vincent; m Richard Bruce Cheney 1964; two d. *Education:* Colorado Coll, Univs of Colorado and Wisconsin. *Career:* Freelance writer 1970–83; Lecturer George Washington Univ (DC) 1972–77, Univ of Wyoming, Mills 1982–83; researcher, writer MD Public Broadcasting, Owing Mills 1982–83; Sr Ed Washington magazine 1983–86; Chair, Nat Endowment for the Humanities 1986–93; W. H. Brady Fellow Int Enterprise Inst 1993–95, Sr Fellow 1996–; Commr US Constitution Bicentennial Comm 1985–87; mem Women's Forum, Washington, DC. *Publications:* Executive Privilege 1978, Sisters 1981, Kings of the Hill (jtly) 1983, The Body Politic 1988, Telling the Truth 1995. *Address:* American Enterprise Institute, 1150 17th St, NW, Washington, DC 20036, USA (Office).

CHENG NAISHAN; Chinese writer; b 14 June 1946, Shanghai; d of Cheng Xueqiao and Pan Zuojun; m Yan Erchun 1969; one d. *Education:* Shanghai Educational Inst. *Career:* Teacher 1965–85; writer 1985–; invited to speak in Germany, USA and Philippines 1986–. *Publications:* The Blue House (also film) 1983, The Clove Villa (also film) 1984, The Poor Street (also film) 1984, Daughters' Tribulations (also film) 1985, The Bankers 1989, The Piano Tuner 1989. *Leisure interest:* music. *Address:* Lane 48, No 36, Yu Yuan Rd, 200040 Shanghai, People's Republic of China. *Telephone:* (21) 2531652.

CHENG YANAN; Chinese sculptor; b 15 Jan 1936, Tianjin; d of Cheng Goliang and Liuo Shijing; m Zhang Zuoming 1962 (died 1989); one s one d. *Education:* Cen Acad of Fine Arts (Beijing). *Career:* Sculptor Beijing Architectural Artistic Sculpture Factory 1961–84, Sculpture Studio, Cen Acad of Fine Arts 1984–; mem China Artists' Asscn; exhibitions include Jia Mei Shi Museum (Aomen) 1986, Hong Kong 1990, and Japan, France, Zaire, Congo and Hungary. *Address:* 452 New Building of Central Institute of Fine Arts, No 5 Shuaifuyan Lane, East District, Beijing, People's Republic of China.

CHER; American actress and singer; b (Cherilyn Lapierre Sarkisian) 20 May 1946, El Centro, CA; d of John Sarkisian and Georgina Holt; m Sonny Bono (divorced 1975; died 1998); one d; m 2nd Gregg Allman (divorced); one s. *Career:* Fmr mem singing duo Sonny and Cher; Sonny and Cher Comedy Hour (TV) 1971–75; own TV variety series and night club act; numerous solo concerts; 11 Gold and three Platinum records. *Recordings include:* I Got You Babe, The Beat Goes On, Bang Bang, You Better Sit Down Kids, We All Sleep Alone, Black Rose (album) 1980, Cher 1987, Heart of Stone 1989, Love Hurts, It's a Man's World 1996, The Casablanca Years 1996, Believe 1998 (Grammy Award for Best Dance Recording), Strong Enough 1999; *Films include:* Good Times, Chastity; Come Back to the Five and Dime, Jimmy Dean, Jimmy Dean; Silkwood, Mask (Best Actress Award, Cannes Film Festival), Witches of Eastwick, Moonstruck (Acad Award) 1987, Suspect, Mermaids, Love and Understanding, If the Walls Could Talk (also a dir); *Plays include:* Come Back to the Five and Dime, Jimmy Dean, Jimmy Dean; *Videos include:* Cher Fitness 1992, A New Attitude 1994. *Address:* c/o ICM, 8942 Wilshire Blvd, Beverly Hills, CA 90211, USA (Office).

CHERNOBROVKINA, Tatyana Anatolyevna; Russian ballet dancer; b 14 Aug 1965. *Education:* Saratov School of Choreography. *Career:* Soloist Saratov Theatre of Opera and Ballet 1983–87; Prima Ballerina Moscow Stanislavsky and Nemirovich-Danchenko Musical Theatre 1987–; prize-winner 5th Moscow Int Competition of Ballet Dancers 1985; Merited Artist of Russia 1994. *Address:* Saratov School of Choreography, Moscow Musical Theatre, B Dmitrovka str 17, 103009 Moscow, Russian Federation. *Telephone:* (095) 229-28-35.

CHERRY, Bridget Katherine, BA, FSA; British architectural historian; b 17 May 1941; d of Norman Stayner and Christiane (née Christinnecke) Marsh; m John Cherry 1966; one s one d. *Education:* Oxford High school for Girls, Lady Margaret Hall (Oxford) and Courtauld Inst (Univ of London). *Career:* Asst Librarian Conway Library, Courtauld Inst 1964–68; Research Asst to Sir Nikolaus Pevsner for Buildings of England series 1968–83, Ed Buildings of England series 1983–, Ed Buildings of Scotland, Ireland and Wales 1991–; mem English Heritage London Advisory Cttee 1985–99, English Heritage Historic Buildings Advisory Cttee 1986—, Royal Comm on Historical Monuments of England 1987–94; Commr English Heritage 1991–; Trustee Sir John Soanes Museum 1995–; Hon FRIBA. *Publications include:* Reviser, co-author or ed Buildings of England Series: London 1 1973, Wiltshire 1975, Hertfordshire 1977, London 2: South 1983, Devon 1989, London 3: North West 1991, London 4: North 1998; various articles and reviews. *Address:* Buildings of England, Penguin Books, 27 Wrights Lane, London W8 5TZ, UK.

CHERRY, Nenah; Swedish singer and song-writer; b 10 March 1964, Stockholm; step-d of the late Don Cherry; m Cameron McVey; three d. *Career:* Vocalist Rip Rig And Panic 1981, later Float-Up CP bands; backing vocalist the Slits and The The; currently solo artist; toured Europe, Australia, New Zealand and UK 1996; has collaborated with Tricky and Youssou N'Dour. *Recordings include:* Albums: Raw Like Sushi, Man; Singles: Buffalo Stance 1989, Manchild, Kisses on the Wind, Seven Seconds (with Youssou N'Dour), Woman, Kootch.

CHEUNG, Maggie; Hong Kong actress; b 1964, Hong Kong. *Career:* Fmrly fashion model; actress 1984–; Miss Hong Kong 1982. *Films include:* Police Story, The Yellow Story, Song of Exile, As Tears Go By, The Actress, Song Dynasty, Irma Vep, In the Mood for Love 2000.

CHEUNG, Man Yee, BA; Hong Kong broadcasting executive; b 25 Dec 1946, Hong Kong. *Education:* Chung Chi Coll and The Chinese Univ of Hong Kong. *Career:* Dir of Broadcasting Radio Television Hong Kong 1986; Pres Commonwealth Broadcasting Asscn 1988–92; mem Henley Asscn 1980, The Outstanding Young Persons' Asscn 1980, The Asia Soc (Hong Kong Center) 1991; mem Advisory Bd Hong Kong AIDS Foundation 1991, Exec Cttee Helping Hand 1993; Ten Outstanding Persons Award 1980; Imperial Service Order 1992. *Leisure interests:* music, bridge, reading. *Address:* Radio Television Hong Kong, Broadcasting House, POB 70200, 30 Broadcast Drive, Kowloon, Hong Kong Special Administrative Region, People's Republic of China. *Telephone:* 23396333; *Fax:* 23372403.

CHIANG KAI-SHEK, Madame (Soong, Mayling), LL D, LHD; Chinese sociologist; b 5 March 1897; m (Pres) Chiang Kai-shek 1927 (died 1975). *Education:* Wellesley Coll (USA). *Career:* First Chinese woman apptd mem of Child Labour Comm; inaugurated Moral Endeavour

Asscn; est schools in Nanking for orphans of revolutionary soldiers; fmr mem Legislative Yuan; fmr Sec-Gen of Chinese Comm on Aeronautical Affairs; Dir-Gen New Life Movt; Founder, Dir Nat Chinese Women's Asscn for War Relief and Nat Asscn for Refugee Children; accompanied husband on mil campaigns; Hon Chair American Bureau for Medical Aid to China and Cttee for the Promotion of the Welfare of the Blind; Patron Int Red Cross Cttee; Hon Chair British United Aid to China Fund and United China Relief; First Hon mem Bill of Rights Commemorative Soc; Hon LHD (John B. Stetson Univ, Bryant Coll, Hobart and William Smith Coll); Hon LL D (Rutgers Univ, Goucher Coll, Wellesley Coll, Loyola Univ, Hahnemann Medical Coll, Wesleyan Coll, Univs of Michigan and Hawaii and Boston Univ); Hon FRCS; Hon mem numerous socs; first Chinese woman to be decorated by Nat Govt of China, awards include Gold Medal of Nat Inst of Social Sciences. *Publications:* Sian: A Coup d'Etat 1937, China in Peace and War 1939, China Shall Rise Again 1939, This is Our China 1940, We Chinese Women 1941, American Tour Speeches 1942–43, Little Sister Su 1943, The Sure Victory 1955, Madame Chiang Kai-shek: Selected Speeches 1958–59, Album of Reproductions of Paintings (vol 1) 1952, (vol 2) 1962, Religious Writings 1963, Madame Chiang Kai-shek: Selected Speeches 1965–66, Album of Chinese Orchid Paintings 1971, Album of Chinese Bamboo Paintings 1972, Album of Chinese Landscape Paintings 1973, Album of Chinese Floral Paintings 1974, Conversations with Mikhail Borodin 1977. *Address:* Lattingtown, Long Island, New York, USA.

CHIARA, Maria; Italian opera singer (soprano); b 24 Nov 1939, Oderzo; m Antonio Cassinelli. *Education:* Conservatorio Benedetto Marcello (Venice) with Maria Carbone. *Career:* Debut Venice 1965; appearances at Rome Opera 1965, La Scala (Milan) 1972, 1985/86, Royal Opera House, Covent Garden (London) 1973, Metropolitan Opera (New York), Lyric Opera (Chicago, USA) 1977, Germany and Austria 1970; performs at all major opera houses in Europe, USA and S America. *Opera débuts include:* Otello 1965, Turandot 1969, La Traviata 1977, Manon Lescaut 1977, Aida 1985; *Recordings include:* Il Segreto di Susanna and a disc of operatic arias (Decca). *Address:* Národní divadlo, Ostrovní 1, Prague 1, Nové Mesto, Czech Republic.

CHIBESAKUNDA, Justice Lombe Phyllis, BL; Zambian lawyer and diplomatist; b 5 May 1944. *Education:* Chipembi Girls' School, Nat Inst of Public Admin (Lusaka). *Career:* Called to the Bar, Gray's Inn, UK; State Advocate Ministry of Legal Affairs 1969–72; pvt legal practice with Jacques and Partners 1972–73; mem Nat Ass (Parl) for Matero 1973; fmr Solicitor-Gen and Minister of State for Legal Affairs; Amb to Japan 1975–77; High Commr in the UK, concurrently Amb to the Netherlands and the Holy See 1977–81; High Court Judge, Lusaka; Chair Industrial Court of Zambia, Perm Human Rights Comm (PHRC) 1998–; Chief Zambian Del, UN Law of the Sea Conf 1975, Rep UN Comm on the Status of Women; Chair Equality Cttee Sub-Cttee UN Independence Party's Women's League; Founder Social Action Charity (Lusaka); Founder-mem Link Voluntary Org; Life mem Commonwealth Parl Asscn; KT Grand Cross of the Order of Pope Pius IX 1979. *Address:* High Court of Zambia, POB 50067, Lusaka, Zambia.

CHIBURDANIDZE, Maiya Grigorevna; Georgian chess player; b 17 Jan 1961, Kutaisi. *Education:* Tbilisi Medical Inst. *Career:* Int Chess Grand Master 1977; Honoured Master of Sport 1978; USSR Champion 1977; World Champion 1978–91; winner of women's int chess tournaments in Brasov (Romania) 1974 and Tbilisi (Georgia) 1976; Capt of winning Soviet team at 8th Women's Chess Olympics 1978, Georgian winning team at Chess Olympics 1994; Oscar Chess Prize 1984–87. *Address:* Georgian Chess Federation, Tbilisi, Georgia.

CHICAGO, Judy, MFA; American artist; b (Judy Cohen) 20 July 1939, Chicago Ill; m 1st Jerry Gerowitz 1961 (died 1962); m 2nd Lloyd Hamrol 1969; m 3rd Donald Woodman. *Education:* Univ of Calif, Los Angeles. *Career:* Taught art at Univ of California Extension, Los Angeles 1963–69, Univ of California Inst Extension, Irvine 1966–69, Californian State Univ, Fresno (f art program for women) 1969–71, California Inst of the Arts, Valencia (f first Feminist Art Program) 1971–73; Co-Founder Feminist Studio Workshop and Woman's Bldg, Los Angeles; Presidential Appt in Art and Gender Studies, Indiana Univ 1999; Robb Lecture, Univ of Auckland 1999; numerous awards. *Art exhibitions:* Womanhouse (with students of Calif Inst of the Arts) 1972,

The Dinner Party (multi-media project) 1974–79, The Birth Project 1980–85 (units now housed in numerous public collections, with core display at Museum of Albuquerque), Powerplay, Holocaust Project: From Darkness into Light 1993, Resolutions: A Stitch in Time 2000; retrospective: Florida State Univ Art Museum 1999; has exhibited throughout USA, Canada, Europe, Australia and Asia; *Publications:* Through the Flower: My Struggle as a Woman Artist 1975, The Dinner Party: A Symbol of Our Heritage 1979, Embroidering Our Heritage: The Dinner Party Needlework 1980, The Birth Project 1985, Holocaust Project: From Darkness into Light 1993, The Dinner Party/Judy Chicago 1996, Beyond the Flower: The Autobiography of a Feminist Artist 1996. *Leisure interest:* cats and exercise. *Address:* Through the Flower, 101 N 2nd St, Belen, NM 87002, USA. *Telephone:* (505) 864-4080; *Fax:* (505) 864-4088; *E-mail:* throughtheflower@compuserve .com; *Internet:* www.judychicago.com.

CHICK, Victoria, MA; American economist; b 8 April 1936, Berkeley, CA; d of the late Humphrey Hyde and Beverley Victoria (née Durbrow) Chick. *Education:* Anna Head School (Berkeley, CA), Univ of California at Berkeley and LSE (UK). *Career:* Asst Lecturer Dept of Econs, Univ Coll London 1963–64, Lecturer 1964–84, Reader 1984–93, Prof 1993–; Research Economist Fed Reserve Bank of New York 1963; Visiting Asst Prof Univ of California at Berkeley 1964; Visiting Economist Reserve Bank of Australia 1975–76; Visiting Lecturer Univ of Southampton 1977; Visiting Prof Univ of California at Santa Cruz, Univ of Aarhus (Denmark) 1980, McGill Univ (Canada) 1981; Research Fellow Catholic Univ of Louvain, Belgium 1986; Deputy Chair Academic Council, Univ of London 1994; Bundesbank Visiting Prof Free Univ of Berlin 2000–2001; mem Editorial Bd Metroeconomica; mem council Royal Econ Soc, American Econ Asscn. *Publications:* The Theory of Monetary Policy (2nd edn) 1977, Macroeconomics After Keynes: A Reconsideration of the General Theory 1983, On Money, Method and Keynes 1992, Recent Developments in Post-Keynesian Economics (co-ed) 1992, Finance, Development and Structural Change (co-ed) 1995; numerous contribs to professional journals. *Leisure interests:* singing, travel, art galleries, theatre. *Address:* University College London, Dept of Economics, Gower St, London WC1E 6BT, UK. *Telephone:* (20) 7679-5250; *Fax:* (20) 7916-2775; *E-mail:* v.chick@ ucl.ac.uk.

CHIEPE, Gaositwe Keagakwa Tibe, MBE, PMS, B SC, MA, FRSA; Botswana diplomatist and politician; b 20 Oct 1922, Serowe; d of the late T. and S. T. (née Sebina) Chiepe. *Education:* Secondary school in Tigerloof and Univs of Fort Hare (S Africa) and Bristol (UK). *Career:* Educ Officer Botswana 1948, Sr Educ Officer 1962, Deputy Dir of Educ 1965, Dir of Educ 1968; High Commr in UK and Nigeria 1970–74, concurrently accredited to Sweden, Norway, Denmark, Germany, France, Belgium and the EC; Minister of Commerce and Industry 1974–77, of Mineral Resources and Water Affairs 1977–84, of External Affairs 1984–95, of Educ 1995–99; Patron Botswana Forestry Soc; Hon Pres Kalahari Conservation Soc; Hon LL D (Bristol); Hon D HUM LITT (De Paul); Hon D LITT (Chicago) 1994; Hon ED D (Fort Hare) 1996; Presidential Order of Honour 1996. *Leisure interests:* music, gardening. *Address:* c/o Ministry of Education, Private Bag 005, Gaborone, Botswana.

CHIGBUE, Irene Nkechi, B SC, LL M, M PHIL; Nigerian lawyer and business consultant; b 7 Dec 1954, Imo State; d of Robert and Eugenia Ndukwe; m Michael Chigbue 1979; two s. *Education:* Queen's Coll (Enugu State), and Univs of Nigeria, Lagos and London. *Career:* Economist Cen Bank of Nigeria and Ministry of External Affairs 1977–79; Lawyer Kehinde Sofola & Co 1983–84; Founder Chigbue & Co 1985; Legal Adviser and Bd Sec Tech Cttee on Privatization and Commercialization 1988–92; Dir of several cos; has written several articles; Chieftaincy Title Adaoha of Umuihi 1990; Distinction Award Ezidi Bu Eze Club of Nigeria 1991. *Leisure interests:* community development and charity related projects, meditation. *Address:* c/o Technical Committee on Privatization and Commercialization, 3rd Floor Wing F, Federal Govt Secretariat, POB 60238, Ikoyi, Lagos, Nigeria; Chigbue and Co, 53 Razaq Balogun St, Surulere, Lagos, Nigeria. *Telephone:* (1) 688722; (1) 603660; *Fax:* (1) 685846.

CHIGUDU, Hope; Zimbabwean organization executive. *Career:* Founder Zimbabwe Women's Resource Center and Network (Harare); Chair Bd Dirs Global Fund for Women (USA); consultant to UNIDO in eight countries in Africa; mem Zimbabwe African Women's Org, Sister Links Harare, Musasa Project, Klemens Action Group. *Address:* Global Fund for Women, Suite 400, 1375 Sutter St, San Francisco, CA 94109, USA. *Telephone:* (415) 212-7640; *Fax:* (415) 212-8604; *E-mail:* gfw@globalfundforwomen.org; *Internet:* www.globalfundforwomen .org.

CHILD, Hon Joan, AO; Australian politician; b 3 Aug 1921, Melbourne; d of Warren Arthur Lilen Olle and Hilda Mary Seedsman; m Han Child 1942; five s. *Education:* Camberwell Girls' Grammar. *Career:* Mem House of Reps (Australian Labour Party) for Henty 1974–75, 1980–90; Deputy Speaker 1984–86, Speaker 1986–90; mem Historical Cttee Nat Museum; Patron Vic-ACW 1999–; Intl Award for Excellence in Communication 1986. *Leisure interests:* reading, gardening, patchwork. *Address:* 237 Grange Rd, Carnegie, Vic 3163, Australia. *Telephone:* (3) 578 2743.

CHINERY-HESSE, Mary, BA; Ghanaian United Nations official; b 29 Oct 1938, Accra; d of R. S. Blay and Marjorie Mould; m Lebrecht James Chinery-Hesse 1963; three d one s. *Education:* Trinity Coll, Univ of Dublin (Ireland), Univ of Ghana and Econ Devt Inst EBRD (USA). *Career:* Asst Econ Officer Planning Comm 1962–66; Sr Econs Officer Ministry of Finance and Econ Planning 1968–72, Prin Econs Officer 1972–74; Resident Rep of UNDP in Sierra Leone 1981–86, Tanzania 1986–88, Uganda 1988–89; fmr Deputy Dir-Gen ILO, Geneva, Switzerland, now Exec Dir Social Protection Section; Chair High-level Panel for the Review of the Implementation of the Programme of Action for the 1990s 2000; mem Global Policy Forum Panel 2000–; Hon Fellow Voltal Hall (Legon, Ghana) 1991; Hon D JUR (Ghana) 1991; Sunday Mirror Award (Ghana) 1963. *Address:* 14 Les Rossanets, 01170 Segny, Gex, France.

CHIRWA, Vera, LL M; Malawi lawyer; b 26 May 1932; d of the late Theodore Kadengende Chirwa and Elizabeth Chibambo; m Orton E. C. Chirwa 1951 (died 1992); five d (three step) three s. *Education:* Domasi, Livingstonia, Blantyre and Univ Coll London. *Career:* Exec mem Nyasaland African Congress 1948–59; Founder League of Malawi Women 1960; called to the Bar 1966; Prosecuting State Attorney in Attorney Gen's Chamber, Tanzania 1967–73; Sr Asst Counsel in the E African Community 1973–77; Lecturer in Law, Univ of Zambia 1977–81; prisoner of conscience (held chained, in solitary confinement) 1981–93; Founder and Exec Dir Malawi CARER (Legal Resources Centre for Advice, Research and Education) 1994–; Organizer Constitutional Symposium 1994; First Chair Nat Comm of Women in Devt 1994; Founder and Pres Women's Voice 1993; Trustee Teachers' Union of Malawi 1997–; Fellow Univ Coll London 1995; Hon DD (Knox Univ, Canada) 1994; Int Woman of the Year (Cambridge Biographical Centre) 1994–95, 1995–96, 1996–97; Geuzen Hero's Medallion (Netherlands) 1998; and numerous other honours and decorations. *Leisure interests:* singing, reading, netball, debate, walking. *Address:* c/o Centre for Advice, Research and Education Rights, POB 30479, Blantyre; Women's Voice, Pvt Bag 231, Blantyre, Malawi. *Telephone:* 636007; *Fax:* 621637; *E-mail:* malawicarer@malawi.net.

CHITTISTER, Joan D., PH D; American social psychologist, writer and lecturer; b 26 April 1936, Dubois, PA; d of Harold C. and Loretta Cuneo Chittister. *Education:* St Benedict Acad and Mercyhurst Coll (Erie), Univ of Notre Dame and Pennsylvania State Univ. *Career:* Teacher elementary schools 1955–59, secondary schools 1959–74, Pennsylvania State Univ 1969–71; Pres Fed of St Scholastica 1971–78; Prioress Benedictine Sisters of Erie 1978–90; nat and int lecture tours 1990–; Pres Conf of American Benedictine Prioresses 1974–90; mem Exec Bd Ecumenical and Cultural Inst, St John's Univ 1976–, Bd of Dirs Nat Catholic Reporter Publs, Bd Corporators, St Vincent Foundation 1986–, Bd of Trustees Global Educ Asscn 1990–; Invited Fellow and Research Assoc Von Hugel Inst, St Edmund's Coll, Cambridge (UK) 1995–1996; mem Exec Bd Ecumenical and Cultural Inst St John's Univ Collegeville 1976–98; Exec Dir Benetvision; mem Bd of Dirs Nat Catholic Reporter; 8 hon degrees and several awards including Pope Paul VI Teacher of Peace Award 1990, Distinguished Daughter of Pennsylvania 1991, Catholic Press Asscn Book Award 1996, Nat Ethics

Award 1996, PA Women's Roll of Honor 1996, Notre Dame Alumni Assoc Women's Award of Achievement 1997. *Publications:* Climb Along the Cutting Edge: An Analysis of Change in Religious Life 1977, Living the Rule Today 1982, Women, Church and Ministry 1983, Faith and Ferment: An Interdisciplinary Study of Christian Beliefs and Practices 1983, Winds of Change: Women Challenge the Church 1986, Wisdom Distilled from the Daily: Living the Rule of Benedict Today 1990, Womanstrength: Modern Women, Modern Church 1990, Job's Daughters: Women and Power 1990, Rule of Benedict: Insights for the Ages 1992, In a High Spiritual Season 1995, There is a Season 1995, Fire in these Ashes 1995, The Psalms: Meditations for Everyday 1996, Beyond Beijing: The Next Step for Women 1996, Passsion for Life: Fragments of the Face of God 1996, Songs of Joy: New Meditations on the Psalms 1997, Light in the Darkness: New Reflections on the Psalms 1998, Heart of Flesh: A Feminist Spirituality for Women and Men 1998, In Search of Belief 1999, Gospel Days: Reflections for Every Day of the Year 1999, The Story of Ruth: Twelve Movements in Every Woman's Life 2000, The Illuminated Life: Monastic Wisdom for Seekers of Light 2000; numerous articles and lectures on religious life, peace and justice issues and women in church and society. *Leisure interests:* computers, music, reading. *Address:* St Scholastica Priory, 355 E 9th St, Erie, PA 16503, USA. *Telephone:* (814) 454-4052; *Fax:* (814) 459-8066.

CHIZEA, Dora Obiajulu, MD; Nigerian medical practitioner; b 7 Sept 1946, Asaba, Delta State; d of Bernard Ricemefuna and Ejima Obielua Chizea; m Rowland O. Abuah 1979; three s. *Education:* Queen's School (Ede), Bryn Mawr Coll and Temple Univ (USA). *Career:* Clinical Instructor Temple Univ 1976–78; Medical Dir Comprehensive Health Services Program, PA 1976–78; Instructor for Grad Students from Third World Countries 1976–78; Consultant Physician Yaba Military Hosp 1978; Pvt Practice, Nigeria from 1978; apptd Dir of Medical Services Bomec Medical Clinic 1979; apptd Consultant Physician Durbar Hotel 1982; Health Consultant and Columnist Daily Times of Nigeria 1989–92; has participated in numerous UN Confs including UN Environment Conf (Stockholm) and Population Conf (Bucharest); Chair Nat Council of Women Task Force on Political Transition 1989; mem Nigerian Inst of Man; Fellow Inst of Admin Man of Nigeria; numerous awards including Most Distinguished Woman of the Decade Award 1981–91 ADSEV 1981 Club of Asaba, Distinguished Int Educ Award Lagos Inst of Man and Tech Studies 1991. *Publications include:* Your Own Health Series: Living with Hypertension 1986, Coping with Stress in Nigeria 1988, Obesity: Nigerian Disease of Tomorrow 1987, Selected Topics on Nigerian National Health 1987, The Nigerian Health Compendium 1991; contribs to professional journals. *Leisure interests:* sports, reading, writing, music. *Address:* Bomec Medical Clinic, 1 Bomec Compound, POB 948, Ikeja, Lagos, Nigeria (Office); 1 Oyedele St, Akiode Village, POB 948, Ikeja, Lagos, Nigeria (Home). *Telephone:* (1) 926467 (Office); *Fax:* (1) 664206 (Office).

CHOJNACKA, Elisabeth, MA; French harpsichordist; b 10 Sept 1939, Warsaw, Poland; d of Tadeusz Chojnacki and Edwarda Chojnacka; m Georges Lesèvre 1966. *Education:* Warsaw Acad of Music, Ecole Supérieure de Musique and with Aimée van de Wiele (Paris). *Career:* First recital of contemporary harpsichord, L'Arc, Paris 1971; interpreter of harpsichord works by many contemporary composers including Xenakis, Ligeti, Halffter, Donatoni, Ferrari, Busotti, Govechi, Takemitsu; Soloist with Orchestre de Paris, Cleveland and Minneapolis Orchestras (USA) 1974, Suisse Romande Orchestra (Switzerland) 1979, Orchestre Nat de France 1981; numerous tours in Europe, USA, Japan and Mexico; Prof of Contemporary Harpsichord, Mozarteum Acad of Music, Salzburg, Austria 1991–; appearances at prin festivals of contemporary music; master classes; collaborates with choreographer Lucinda Childs 1991–; numerous recordings of classical and contemporary music; contribs to professional journals including La Revue Musicale; First Prize, Int Harpsichord Competition (Vercelli, Italy) 1968, Orphée Prize 1981, Grand Prix de la SACEM 1983; Chevalier de la Légion d'Honneur; Officier des Arts et des Lettres; Croix d'Officier Ordre de Mérite pour la Pologne. *Leisure interests:* cinema, literature, dancing, genetics, astrophysics, theatre, ballet, paintings. *Address:* 17 rue Emile Dubois, 75014 Paris, France. *Telephone:* (1) 45-82-52-82; *Fax:* (1) 45-65-31-90 (Office).

CHOJNOWSKA-LISKIEWICZ, Krystyna Danuta; Polish yachtswoman; b 15 July 1936, Warsaw; d of Juliusz Chojnowski and Kazimiera Chojnowska; m Wacław Liskiewicz 1960. *Education:* Tech Univ of Gdańsk. *Career:* Sr Designer Stocznia Gdańsk 1960–75, Shipbuilding Design Centre 1984–; first woman to circumnavigate the world solo 1976–1978, in yacht 'Mazurek'; Commdr Cross of Order Polonia Restituta 1978; awards include Hon Medal Czechoslovakian Women's Union 1978, Prize of Minister of Foreign Affairs 1978, Slocum Award 1978, Médaille d'Argent de la Jeunesse et des Sports (France) 1979 and other decorations. *Publication:* Pierwsza dookoła Świata (The First One Round the World) 1979, Matki chrzestne statków (Good Mothers of Ships) 1998. *Leisure interests:* sailing, skiing, swimming, science-fiction, music, books. *Address:* Ul Norblina 29 m 50, 80-304 Gdańsk Oliwa, Poland. *Telephone:* (58) 556-03-71; *Fax:* (58) 556-03-71; *E-mail:* pz-1898@wp.pl.

CHOTRANI, Mala Arjan, BA; Indian dancer, choreographer and producer; b 11 June 1959, Bombay (now Mumbai); d of the late U. N. and P. U. Raisinghani; m 1948. *Education:* Univ of Bombay and Sophia B. K. Somani Polytechnic. *Career:* Classical Bharata Natyam dancer, performances in India and abroad 1970–85; photographer, fashion model and choreographer 1975–83; Fand Man Natyalaya dance school, Singapore 1985–; promoter of Indian culture at Katong Community Centre 1985–95; Dir Pandu Man Pte Ltd 1994–; numerous performances and productions in Malaysia, India and Singapore 1980–95; Merit Award, Rotary Club of Marina City, Singapore 1986. *Dance Dramas include:* Ekta (also dir) 1985, Rang Rangeeli Holi (also dir) 1986. *Address:* 75 Nepean Sea Rd, Sagar Tarang, Mumbai 400 006, India; 50D Marine Parade Rd, Suite 24–22, Amberville, Singapore 449268.

CHOUCAIR, Saloua Raouda; Lebanese artist; b 1916, Beirut; m; one d. *Education:* American Univ of Beirut and Nat School of Fine Art and Grande Chaumière Acad (Paris). *Career:* Exhibitions 1947–, Paris 1951, Beirut 1951–62, retrospective 1974; awards include Court of Justice Prize 1963, Ministry of Tourism Prize 1966, Alexandria Biennale Prize 1968, Nat Prize of Sculpture 1971, Sursock Museum Prize 1965, 1966, 1967, 1973. *Address:* Rue Sidani, Beirut, Lebanon.

CHOWDHURY, Renuka, MA; Indian politician; b 1954, Visakhapatham, AP; d of K. S. Rao; m Mr Chowdhury 1973; two d. *Education:* Madras and Bangalore Univ. *Career:* Regional Organizer Dept of Women and Child Welfare, Andhra Pradesh; elected to Rajya Sabha (Parl) 1986, mem Cttee on Privileges 1986–87, 1988, Parl Cttee on Public Enterprises, House Cttee; mem Int Airports Authority, Municipal Corpn of Banjara Hills, Hyderabad; adviser and patron various trade unions; numerous publs include short stories, one-act plays and articles; Daily Telegraph Trophy; Mahila Shiromani Award. *Leisure interests:* reading, painting, interior decoration, poetry, benefit shows, organizing. *Address:* Rajya Sabha, Parliament House, New Delhi 110 011, India (Office); 18 Willingdon Crescent, New Delhi 110 001, India (Home). *Telephone:* (11) 389977 (Office); (11) 603399 (Home); *Fax:* (11) 6874242 (Home).

CHOWLA, Damyanti, BA; Indian artist; b 5 April 1920, Punjab; d of the late K. R. and Susheela Batra; m M. L. Chowla 1942; one s one d. *Education:* Govt Coll for Women and Slade School of Art, Univ of London. *Career:* Freelance artist, studios in New Delhi (India) and Orinda (CA, USA); exhibitions include Woodstock Gallery (London) 1960, AIFACS Gallery (New Delhi) 1962, 1963, 1974, 1981, Jehangir Art (Bombay) 1964, Gallery Haus Am Lutzowplatz (Berlin) 1967, Friendship House (Moscow, Russian Fed) 1967, Kunsthaus Fishinger (Stuttgart, Germany) 1970, Centre of Int Co-operation ZAMALEK (Cairo) 1978, Embassy of India (Washington, DC, USA) 1978, India House (New York) 1978, Yugoslavia 1985; represented in perm collections of Punjab Museum (India), Berlin Museum of Modern Art, Ministry of Cultural Affairs (Paris) and many pvt collections; awards from All-India Fine Arts and Crafts and Punjab Lalit Kala Akademi. *Leisure interest:* classical Western and Indian music. *Address:* S-172 Panch-shila Park, New Delhi 110 017, India; 28 Ivy Drive, Orinda, CA 94563, USA. *Telephone:* (11) 6441808 (India); (415) 932-2931 (USA).

CHRAMOSTOVÁ, Vlasta; Czech actress and human rights activist; b 17 Nov 1926, Brno; m Stanislav Milota 1971; one s (died 1963). *Education:* Conservatoire of Music and Performing Arts (Brno). *Career:* Actress Free Theatre (Brno) 1945, Town Theatre (Olomouc) 1945–46, State Theatre (Brno) 1946–49, Theatre in Vinohrady (Prague) 1950–70, Theatre behind the Gate 1970–72, Flat Theatre 1976–80, Nat Theatre Drama Co (Prague) 1991–; banned from acting in public 1973 (banned from appearing on Czechoslovak radio, TV or in films 1969–89); signed Charter 77 1977, activist 1977–89; sentenced to imprisonment for 3 months, sentence suspended on one-year probation 1989; Hon mem Masaryk Democratic Movt 1990–, Nat Theatre Ensemble (Prague) 1990–91; joined Drama Co of Nat Theatre Prague 1991; Merited Artist 1965; Czech Theatre Artists' Award 1967; Peace Prize awarded by Paul Lauritzen Foundation 1989; Order of T. G. Masaryk 1998. *Plays include:* Cyrano de Bergerac 1956, Mary Stuart 1958, The Shoemaker's Wife Beautiful 1960, Taming of the Shrew 1962, Anna Karenina 1963, The Night of the Iguana 1967, All the Beauties of the World 1976, Appleplatz II 1977, Macbeth (broadcast on Austrian TV) 1978, The Report on Funerals in Bohemia (broadcast on Austrian TV) 1978. *Address:* Národní divadlo, Ostrovní 1, Prague, 1, Nové Mesto, Czech Republic. *Telephone:* (2) 2366513.

CHRISTENSEN, Helena; Danish fashion model; b 25 Dec 1968, Copenhagen; d of Flemming and Elsa Christensen. *Education:* Zahles Gymnasium (Copenhagen). *Career:* Fashion model 1987–, has since worked as one of world's leading models in promotions for Versace, Rykiel, Chanel, Lagerfeld, Revlon, Dior, Prada, etc; has appeared on cover of British Vogue and in all maj magazines; has worked with photographers including Herb Ritts, Bruce Weber, Patrick de Marchelier, Penn, Steven Meisel and Helmut Newton. *Films include:* Prêt-a-Porter 1994, Unzipped 1995. *Leisure interests:* photography (black and white), oil/watercolour painting. *Address:* Marilyn's Agency, 4 rue de la Paix, Paris, France. *Telephone:* (1) 53-29-53-53.

CHRISTIE, Julie Frances; British actress; b 14 April 1940, Assam, India; d of Frank St John and Rosemary (née Ramsden) Christie. *Education:* Brighton Tech Coll and Cen School of Speech and Drama (London). *Career:* Dr hc (Warwick) 1994; Motion Picture Laurel Award, Best Dramatic Actress 1967, Motion Picture Herald Award 1967; Fellow BAFTA 1997. *Films include:* Crooks Anonymous 1962, The Fast Lady 1962, Billy Liar 1963, Young Cassidy 1964, Darling (Acad Award 1966) 1964, Doctor Zhivago (Donatello Award) 1965, Fahrenheit 451 1966, Far From the Madding Crowd 1966, Petulia 1967, In Search of Gregory 1969, The Go-Between 1971, McCabe and Mrs Miller 1972, Don't Look Now 1973, Shampoo 1974, Demon Seed, Heaven Can Wait 1978, Memoirs of a Survivor 1980, Gold 1980, The Return of the Soldier 1981, Les quarantièmes rugissants 1981, Heat and Dust 1982, The Gold Diggers 1984, Miss Mary 1986, The Tattooed Memory 1986, Power 1987, Fathers and Sons 1988, Dadah is Death 1988, Fools of Fortune 1989, McCabe and Mrs Miller 1990, The Railway Station 1991, Hamlet 1995, Afterglow 1998; *Plays include:* Old Times 1995, Suzanna Andler 1997, Afterglow 1998. *Address:* c/o International Creative Management, 76 Oxford St, London W1N 0AX, UK (Office).

CHRISTOPHER, Ann, BA, RA, FRBS, RWA; British sculptor; b 4 Dec 1947, Watford, Herts; d of late William and Phyllis Christopher; m Kenneth Cook 1969. *Education:* Watford Girls' Grammar School, Harrow School of Art and West of England Coll of Art. *Career:* Works include bronze sculpture, Castle Park, Bristol 1993, Corten sculpture, Marsh Mills, Plymouth 1996, Bronze Sculpture for offices of Linklaters and Paines solicitors, London 1997; works in Redfern Gallery, London, Adelson Galleries, New York; Royal Soc of British Sculptors Silver Medal for sculpture of outstanding merit 1994. *Leisure interests:* cinema, travel, architecture. *Address:* Stable Block, Hay St, Marshfield, Chippenham, SN14 8PF, UK. *Telephone:* (1225) 891717; *Fax:* (1225) 891717.

CHRISTOPHERSON, Romola Carol Andrea, BA; British civil servant; b 10 Jan 1939; d of Albert Edward and Kathleen (née Marfitt) Christopherson. *Education:* Collegiate School for Girls (Leicester) and St Hugh's Coll (Oxford). *Career:* Dept of Scientific and Industrial Research (now Science and Eng Research Council), Ministry of Tech 1962; Dept of the Environment 1970; Ministry of Agriculture, Fisheries and Food 1978; N Ireland Office 1981; Deputy Press Sec to Prime Minister 1983; Head of Information Dept of Energy 1984; Dir of

Information Dept of Health 1986–98; Assoc Dir Media Strategy 1999–; Non-Exec Dir Primary Care Group Ltd 1999–. *Leisure interests:* amateur dramatics, antiques. *Address:* 28 Wharton St, London WC1X 9PJ, UK.

CHRYSSA; American artist; b 1933, Athens, Greece. *Education:* Acad Grand Shaumière (Paris) and San Francisco School of Fine Arts. *Career:* One-woman exhibitions include Solomon Guggenheim Museum (New York) 1961, Museum of Modern Art (New York) 1963, Walker Art Centre (Minneapolis) 1968, Whitney Museum of Modern Art (New York) 1972, Musée d'Art Contemporain (Montréal, Canada) 1974, Musée d'Art Moderne de la Ville de Paris (France) 1979, Nat Pinacotheque Museum Alexander Soutsos (Athens) 1980, Albright-Knox Gallery (Buffalo) 1982, Leo Castelli Gallery 1988 and at galleries in New York, Boston, San Francisco, Paris, Cologne and Düsseldorf (Germany), Zurich (Switzerland), Turin (Italy) and Athens since 1961; has appeared in many group exhibitions and is represented in numerous public collections in USA and Europe; Guggenheim Fellowship 1973. *Address:* c/o Albright-Knox Art Gallery, 1285 Elmwood Ave, Buffalo, New York NY 14222, USA.

CHUA, Amy, BA; Singaporean broadcasting executive; b 4 May 1950; d of Mr and Mrs Chua Kim Yeow; m Tan Wee Him 1981. *Education:* Nat Univ of Singapore. *Career:* Librarian Nat Library 1971–73; Journalist The Straits Times 1975–77; Documentary Producer Singapore Broad-casting Corpn 1973–75, TV Producer 1977–81, Exec Producer 1981–89, Controller Current Affairs 1989–90, apptd Sr Controller 1990; Rep of Singapore, ASEAN meetings on culture and information 1982–84; Leader Del, ASEAN exchange of journalists programme, visiting ASEAN countries 1983; mem TV Broadcasting in the US project 1991. *Productions include:* Diary of a Nation, Nature in Singapore, Pacesetters, A Home Away From Home (Special TV Prize, Asia Broadcasting Union 1979), Pollution – the Death of a River (Third Prize, Festival of Int Specialized Films and Slides for a Documentary 1977); numerous documentaries on Singapore, Phillippines and ASEAN. *Leisure interests:* nature photography, plays, musicals, TV, films, travel. *Address:* Singapore Broadcasting Corpn, Caldecott Hill, Andrew Rd, Singapore 1129, Singapore. *Telephone:* 3503684; *Fax:* 2504335.

CHUDAKOVA, Marietta Omarovna, D LIT; Russian academic; b 2 Jan 1937, Moscow; m Alexander Pavlovich Chudakov; one d. *Education:* Moscow State Univ. *Career:* Sr Researcher, Head Manuscripts Div, Div of Rare Books and Div of Library Research, All-Union Lenin's Public Library 1965–84; Teacher Inst of Literature 1986–, Prof 1992–; main research on history of Russian Literature (Soviet Period), archives and literary criticism; Visiting Prof Stanford Univ (CA, USA) 1989, Univ of S California (USA) 1990, Ecole Normal Supérieure (Paris) 1991, Geneva Univ (Switzerland) and European Inst (Geneva, Switzerland) 1991; Chair All-Russian Mikhail Bulgakov Fund; mem Acad Europae; Moskovsky Komsomolets Prize 1970. *Publications:* Effendi Kapiev (biog) 1970, Craftsmanship of Yuri Olesha 1972, Talks about Archives 1975, Poetics of Mikhail Zoshchenko 1979, Mikhail Bulgakov 1988; over 200 articles in magazines on literary subjects and political essays. *Leisure interests:* rowing, skiing. *Address:* Miklikha-Maklai str 39, korp 2, Apt 380, 117485 Moscow, Russian Federation. *Telephone:* (095) 202-84-44 (Office); (095) 335-92-57 (Home).

CHULABHORN, HRH Princess, PH D; Thai environmental chemist and royal; b 4 July 1957, Bangkok; d of King Bhumibol Adulyadej and Mom Rajawong Sirikit Kitiyakara; m Squadron Leader Virayuth Didyasarin 1982; two d. *Education:* Kasetsart and Mahidol Univs (Bangkok) and Univ of Ulm (Germany). *Career:* Prof of Organic Chem Mahidol Univ 1985–; Founder and Pres Chulabhorn Research Inst, Bangkok 1987–, Dir of numerous programmes 1989–; Pres Chulabhorn Foundation 1986–; Chair Working Group on the Chem of Natural Products (collaborative project between Japanese Soc for the Promotion of Sciences and Nat Research Council of Thailand) 1987–, Foundation for Promotion of National Conservation and Environmental Protection 1987–; Exec mem Int Org for Chemical Sciences in Devt (IOCD) 1986–; Hon Pres Heritage Trust, UK 1988–90; Special Advisor UNEP 1989–; mem Scientific and Tech Cttee, Int Decade for Natural Disaster Reduction, UN 1990–91, Special High-Level Council 1991–; Patron Int Foundation for Science, Sweden 1987–; mem Selection Cttee UNEP Sasakawa Environment Prize 1992; Goodwill Amb WHO

1989–90; Visiting Prof at numerous univs; contribs to professional journals; numerous honours, awards and prizes including Hon Fellow Royal Soc of Chem, London, Einstein Gold Medal (UNESCO), Tree of Learning Award (World Conservation Union) 1990. *Address:* Chulabhorn Research Institute, 54 Moo 4 Vipavadee-Rangsit Highway, Bangkok 10210, Thailand. *Telephone:* (2) 574-0595; *Fax:* (2) 574-0612.

CHUNG, Fay King, M PHIL; Zimbabwean politician; b 12 March 1941; one d. *Education:* Univs of Zimbabwe and Leeds (UK). *Career:* School teacher 1963–68; lecturer various polytechnics 1968–71, Univ of Zambia 1971–75; Head of Teacher Training and Research, Zimbab-wean Refugee Schools, Mozambique 1976–80; Head of Planning, then Head of Curriculum Devt, later Head of School Admin, Ministry of Educ 1980–87, Minister 1988; Minister of State in the Pres's Office, in charge of Nat Affairs, Employment Creation and Co-operatives until 1994; currently Dir Int Inst for Capacity Building in Africa (UNESCO). *Publications:* Socialism and Education in Zimbabwe 1986, Basic Principles of Administration 1988. *Leisure interests:* reading, writing, drama. *Address:* UNESCO-IICBA, POB 2305, Addis Ababa, Ethiopia. *Telephone:* (1) 557586; *Fax:* (1) 557585; *E-mail:* fchung@unesco-iicba .org.

CHUNG, Kyung-Wha; South Korean violinist; b 26 March 1948, Seoul; m Geoffrey Leggett 1984; two s. *Education:* Juilliard School of Music (USA), studied under Ivan Galamian. *Career:* European debut 1970; has played under numerous conductors including Abbado, Barenboim, Davis, Dorati, Dutoit, Giulini, Haitink, Jochum, Kempe, Kondrashin, Leinsdorf, Levine, Maazel, Mehta, Muti, Previn, Rattle, Rozhdestvensky and Solti, with major orchestras including all London Orchestras, Chicago, Boston and Pittsburgh Symphony Orchestras, New York, Cleveland and Philadelphia (USA), Berlin, Israel and Vienna Philharmonics, Orchestre de Paris, and at Festivals in Salzburg (Austria) 1973, Vienna 1981, 1984 and Edinburgh (UK) 1981, and at eightieth birthday concert of Sir William Walton March 1982; recordings for EMI 1988–; Leventritt Competition Winner 1968. *Leisure interests:* arts, family. *Address:* c/o Harrison Parrott Ltd, 12 Penzance Place, London W11 4PA, UK (Office).

CHURCHER, Elizabeth Ann Dewar (Betty), AO, MA; Australian arts administrator; b 11 Jan 1931; d of William Dewar and Vida Margaret Cameron; m Roy Wilfred Clarence Churcher 1955; four s. *Education:* Royal Coll of Art and Courtauld Inst (London). *Career:* School teacher 1958–70; Sr Lecturer Kelvin Grove Council of Adult Educ 1977–78; Sr Lecturer School of Art and Design, Phillip Inst of Tech 1979–80, Prin Lecturer 1981, Dean 1982–87; Dir Art Gallery of Western Australia 1987–89, Nat Gallery of Australia 1990–97; Chair Visual Arts Bd 1983–87; mem Nat Cttee for UNESCO, Nat Cultural Heritage Cttee; Hon D LITT (Curtin) 1994; Dr hc (Royal Melbourne Inst of Tech) 1995; Hon LL D (ANU) 1996; London Times Award 1974. *Publications include:* Understanding Art 1974, Molvig: The Lost Antipodean 1984. *Address:* c/o National Gallery of Australia, POB 1150, Canberra, ACT 2600, Australia.

CHURCHILL, Caryl Lesley, BA; British playwright; b 3 Sept 1938, London; d of Robert and Jan (née Brown) Churchill; m David Harter 1961; three s. *Education:* Trafalgar School (Montréal, Canada) and Lady Margaret Hall (Oxford). *Career:* Playwright 1958–, Resident Royal Court Theatre, London 1974. *Plays include:* Downstairs 1958, Having a Wonderful Time 1960, Owners 1972, Objections to Sex and Violence 1975, Vinegar Tom 1976, Light Shining in Buckinghamshire 1976, Cloud Nine 1979, Top Girls 1982, Fen (Susan Smith Blackburn Prize) 1983, Softcops 1984, Serious Money (Susan Smith Blackburn Prize) 1987, Ice Cream with Hot Fudge 1988, Mad Forest 1990, Lives of the Great Poisoners 1991, The Striker 1994, Thyestes (trans) 1994, Hotel 1997, This Is A Chair 1997, Blue Heart 1997; Radio: The Ants, Not... Not... not... not enough Oxygen, Abortive Schreiber, Nervous Illness, Identical Twins, Perfect Happiness, Henry's Past; *TV includes:* The Judge's Wife, The After Dinner Joke, The Legion Hall Bombing, Fugue (jtly). *Address:* c/o Casarotto Ramsay Ltd, National House, 60–66 Wardour St, London W1V 3HP, UK. *Telephone:* (20) 7287-4450; *Fax:* (20) 7734-9293.

CHURIKOVA, Inna Mikhailovna; Russian actress and screenwriter; b 5 Oct 1945, Belibey, Bashkiria; d of Mikhail Churikov and Elezabetha Mantrova; m Gleb Panfilov 1974; one s. *Education:* Shchepkin Theatre School. *Career:* With Moscow Youth Theatre 1965–68, Lenkom Theatre (Moscow) 1973–; film debut 1961; awards include: Lenin Komsomol Prize 1976, RSFSR People's Artist 1985, USSR State Prize 1985, USSR People's Artist 1985, Nika Prize 1993, Triumph Prize 1994, Kinotaur Festival Prize 1994, Kamaz Festival First Prize 1994, Russian Fed State Prize 1997, Cristal Turandot Drama Asscn Award (twice). *Acting roles include:* No Ford Through Fire (Panfilov) 1968, The Beginning 1970, May I Speak? 1976, Valentina 1981, Vassa 1983, War-Novel 1984 (Berlin Film Festival Prize), Three Girls in Blue (theatre) 1985, The Theme 1986, Mother 1991, Adam's Rib 1991 (Critics' Prize), Sorry (theatre) 1992, Casanova's Mantle 1992, The Seagull (theatre) 1994, The Year of the Dog 1994; *Plays include:* Three Girls in Blue 1985, Sorry 1992, The Seagull 1994, The Gambler (Stanislavsky Award) 1996, The Sheep 1997, Old Women 1999, City of Millionaires 2000; *Films:* No Ford Through Fire 1968, The Beginning 1970, May I Speak? 1976, Valentina 1981, Vassa 1983, War-Novel (Berlin Film Festival Prize) 1984, The Theme 1986, Mother 1991, Adam's Rib 1991, Casanova's Mantle 1993, The Year of the Dog 1994, Shirly Myrly 1995, Riaba my Chicken 1995. *Leisure interests:* art, reading, music, film, theatre. *Address:* Lenkom Theatre, Malaya Dmitrovka 6, Moscow, Russian Federation. *Telephone:* (095) 137-89-67; *Fax:* (095) 229-67-93; *E-mail:* varadero@mail.ru (Home); *Internet:* www.lenkom.ru (Office).

CHUTIKUL, Saisuree; Thai civil servant; b 2 March 1935, Bangkok; m Kavi Chutikul; one s one d. *Education:* Indiana Univ (USA). *Career:* Consultant in Social Planning, UNICEF 1975–78; Deputy Sec-Gen Nat Educ Comm, Prime Minister's Office 1980–83, Sec-Gen Nat Youth Bureau 1983–89, later Minister, Office of the Prime Minister and Insp-Gen, Office of the Perm Sec; KT Grand Cordon of the Most Noble Order of the Crown of Thailand 1991. *Leisure interest:* music. *Address:* Office of the Permanent Sec, Office of the Prime Minister, Govt House, Nakhon Pathom Rd, Bangkok 10300, Thailand (Office); 118 Ulit Lane, Sukhumvit 4, Bangkok, Thailand (Home). *Telephone:* (2) 252-8343 (Office).

CHÝLKOVÁ, Ivana; Czech actress; b 27 Sept 1963; d of Jaroslav Chýlek and Anna Chýlková; m Karel Roden. *Education:* Acad of Arts (Prague). *Career:* Appearances in numerous films and on TV; many awards and prizes including Most Popular Actress in Czechoslovakia 1990, 1991, Best Actress in Czechoslovakia 1991. *Films include:* Good Light 1986, Papilio 1987, The Animals in the City 1988, Time of the Servants (Stars of the Future Award, Geneva Festival, Best Actress Award, Bratislava) 1989, The Flames of Royal Love 1991, Rama—Dama 1991, Thanks for Every New Morning 1992; *TV appearances include:* Swans (Japan); *Plays include:* Y, Divadlo na Zábradlí. *Leisure interest:* singing. *Address:* Chodská 31, Vinohrady, 120 00 Prague 2, Czech Republic. *Telephone:* (2) 252935.

CICCIOLINA, La (see Staller, Ilona).

ÇIÇEKOĞLU, Feride, PH D; Turkish writer; b 27 Jan 1951, Ankara; d of Hasan and Nihal Çiçekoğlu; m Zafer Aldemir 1986; one d. *Education:* Middle East Tech Univ and Univ of Pennsylvania (USA). *Career:* Teacher 1977–80; political prisoner 1980–84; Ed, writer and Film Consultant 1984–92; apptd Sec-Gen Cultural Foundation for Audio-visual and Cinema, Istanbul 1991. *Publications include:* Don't let Them Shoot the Kite (book) 1986, (screenplay, Golden Orange Award) 1989, The Other Side of the Water (book) 1990, (screenplay) 1991, Did Your Father Ever Die 1990; *Film:* Journey of Hope (Acad Award) 1991. *Address:* TÜRSAK, Fahri Gizden Sok 16/2, Gayrettepe, Istanbul, Turkey. *Telephone:* (1) 2721102; *Fax:* (1) 2728602.

ÇILLER, Tansu, PH D; Turkish economist and politician; b 24 May 1946, Istanbul; d of Muazzer Çiller; m Özer Uçuran Çiller 1963; two s. *Education:* Yale Univ (CT, USA), Univs of Connecticut and New Hampshire (USA) and Bosphorus Univ. *Career:* Lecturer Univ of Connecticut, Assoc Prof Univ of Quinnipiac, Asst Prof Franklin Marshall Coll then Prof of Econs and Head Dept of Econs Bosphorus Univ; mem Doğru Yol Partisi (True Path Party), Asst to Leader 1990, Leader 1993–; elected to Turkish Parl 1991; Minister of State for Econs 1991–93; Prime Minister 1993–96; Deputy Prime Minister and Minister of Foreign Affairs 1996–97. *Publications include:* Import Substitution and Protectionism in Turkish Industry 1974, Reform Proposals 1988, The Cost Increasing Effects of State Economic Enterprises in Economy 1988, Public Deficits and Inflation 1989, Problems in the Turkish Finance Sector and Reform Proposals 1989. *Address:* True Path Party, Selanik Cad 40, Kızılay, Ankara, Turkey. *Telephone:* (312) 4172241; *Fax:* (312)4185657; *Internet:* www.dyp.org.tr.

CISNEROS DE PÉREZ, Imelda, MA; Venezuelan politician and business executive; b 10 Nov 1946, Caracas; d of Juan José and Josefina Alzuru Cisneros; m Francisco Pérez Santana 1974; two c. *Education:* Cen Univ of Venezuela. *Career:* Fmr Dir Inter-American Affairs Dept, Cen Office of Co-ordination and Planning of the Presidency (CORDI-PLAN); Dir-Gen Ministry of State for Int Econ Affairs, Econ Affairs Cttee, Ministry of the Presidency; Dir Consultation and Co-ordination, Latin-American Econ System (SELA); Vice-Minister of Devt 1989, Minister 1990–92; mem several presidental comms; Dir Banco Central de Venezuela; fmr Dir Venezuelan Investment Fund; Pres Nat Council for Foreign Investment. *Address:* c/o Banco Central de Venezuela, Avda Urdaneta esq de las Carmelitas, Caracas 1010, Venezuela. *Telephone:* (2) 801-5111; *Fax:* (2) 861-0048.

CISSE, Awa Evelyne, L ÈS SC; Senegalese scientist and civil servant; b 22 Aug 1957, Dakar; d of Abdourahamne Cisse and Fatma Sankhare; m Abdoulaye Godiane Diane 1981 (divorced 1984). *Education:* Lycées John F. Kennedy and Blaise Diagne and Univ Cheikh Anta Diop de Dakar. *Career:* Researcher Univ Cheikh Anta Diop de Dakar 1986; in charge of application and follow-through of Biotech in Senegal, Direction des Affaires Scientifiques et Techniques (DAST—under Ministry of Modernization of the State and Tech) apptd 1989; Founder-mem Asscn SOS Environnement 1987; Treas Asscn des Chercheurs Sénégalais 1987; mem UNESCO-Senegal Man and Biosphere Cttee 1990, Asscn Amis de la Nature 1992; contribs to scientific journals. *Leisure interests:* cinema, dancing, beach, sport. *Address:* DAST, 23 rue Calmette, BP 218, Dakar, Senegal (Office); Ministry of Modernization of the State, Domicile villa 12, rue 2 J, Cité géographique Castors, BP 21571, Dakar-Ponty, Senegal (Office). *Telephone:* 21-32-60.

CIXOUS, Hélène, D ÈS L; French writer and professor of literature; b 5 June 1937, Oran, Algeria; d of Georges and Eve (née Klein) Cixous; one d one s. *Education:* Lycée d'Alger and Lycée de Sceaux (Sorbonne). *Career:* Mem staff Univ of Bordeaux 1962–65; Asst Lecturer, Sorbonne 1965–67; Lecturer, Univ of Paris X (Nanterre) 1967–68; Co-Founder Univ of Paris VIII (Vincennes à St Denis) 1968, Prof of English Literature 1968–; Founder, Dir Centre d'Etudes Féminines 1974–; Co-Founder Poetique journal 1969; Visiting Lecturer abroad, and has attended numerous int symposia; Dr hc (Queen's Univ, Kingston) 1991, (Edmonton) 1992, (York) 1993, (Georgetown) 1995, (North-western) 1996; Prix Médicis 1969, Officier de la Croix du Sud (Brazil) 1989, Chevalier de la Légion d'Honneur 1994, Prix des critiques 1994, Officier de l'Ordre Nat du Mérite 1998. *Publications:* Novels and poetry: Le prénom de Dieu 1967, Dedans 1969, Le troisième corps, Les commencements 1970, Un vrai jardin 1971, Neutre 1972, Tombe, Portrait du soleil 1973, Révolutions pour plus d'un Faust 1975, Souffles 1975, La 1976, Partie 1976, Angst 1977, Préparatifs de noces au-delà de l'abîme 1978, Vivre l'orange 1979, Anankè 1979, Illa 1980, With ou l'art de l'innocence 1981, Limonade tout était si infini 1982, Le livre de Promethea 1983, Manne 1988, Jours de l'an 1990, L'Ange au secret 1991, Déluge 1992, Beethoven à jamais 1993, La fiancée juive 1995, Messie 1996, Or, les lettres de mon père 1997, Osnabrück 1999, Les rêveries de la femme sauvage 2000, Le jour où je n'étais pas là 2000; Plays: Portrait de Dora 1976, Le nom d'Oedipe 1978, La prise de l'école de Madhubaï 1984, L'Histoire terrible mais inachevée de Norodom Sihanouk, roi du Cambodge 1985, L'Indiade ou l'Inde de leurs rêves 1987, On ne part pas on ne revient pas 1991, Voile noire voile blanche 1994, L'Histoire qu'on ne connaîtra jamais 1994, La ville Parjure le réveil des Erinyes 1994, Tambours sur la digue 1999 (Molière Award 2000); Essays: L'exil de James Joyce 1969, Prénoms de personne 1974, La jeune née 1975, La venue à l'écriture 1977, Entre l'écriture 1986, L'heure de Clarice Lispector 1989, Reading with Clarice Lispector 1990, Readings, the Poetics of Blanchot, Joyce, Kafka, Lispector, Tsvetaeva 1992, Three Steps on the Ladder of Writing 1993, Photos de racines 1994, Stigmata, Escaping Texts 1998. *Address:* Éditions Galilée,

9 rue Linné, 75005 Paris, France (Office); Centre d'études féminines, Université Paris VIII, 2 rue de la Liberté, 93526 Saint-Denis Cedex 2, France (Office).

CLAIBORNE, Liz, DFA; American fashion designer; b 31 March 1929, Brussels, Belgium; d of Omer Villère and Louise Carol Claiborne; m 1st Ben Schultz 1950; m 2nd Arthur Ortenberg 1957; one s. *Education:* Belgium and France. *Career:* Worked with Tina Lesser, Ben Rieg, Omar Kiam, Junior Rite Co, Rhea Manufacturing Co of Milwaukee; Chief Designer Youth Guild 1960–75; Founder Liz Claiborne Inc 1976, Head Designer and Pres 1976–89, currently mem Bd; Dr hc (Rhode Island School of Design) 1991; numerous awards including Entrepreneurial Woman of the Year 1980, Council of Fashion Designers Award 1986, Gordon Grand Fellowship Award (Yale Univ) 1989, Jr Achievement Award (Nat Business Hall of Fame) 1990. *Leisure interests:* environmental issues, running, swimming, photography. *Address:* Liz Claiborne Inc, 1441 Broadway, New York, NY 10018, USA.

CLAPINSON, Mary, MA, FSA, FRHISTS; British librarian; b 19 Dec 1944, Merthyr Tydfil; d of Ralph P. and Mary Cook; m Michael D. Clapinson 1968. *Education:* Queen Victoria High School (Stockton-on-Tees) and St Hugh's Coll (Oxford). *Career:* Teacher St Felix School, Southwold, Suffolk 1966–67; Asst then Sr Asst Librarian Dept of Western Manuscripts Bodleian Library, Oxford 1967–86, Keeper of Western Manuscripts 1986–; Professorial Fellow St Hugh's Coll, Oxford 1986–. *Publications include:* Victorian and Edwardian Oxfordshire from old photographs 1978, Bishop Fell and Nonconformity 1980; Summary Catalogue of Post-Medieval Western Manuscripts in the Bodleian Library. *Leisure interests:* cooking, gardening, visiting France. *Address:* Dept of Western Manuscripts, Bodleian Library, Oxford OX1 3BG, UK. *Telephone:* (1865) 277158; *Fax:* (1865) 277187.

CLARK, Eugenie, PH D; American professor emeritus of zoology; b 4 May 1922, New York; d of Charles and Yumiko Mitomi Clark; m 1st Hideo Umaki 1946; m 2nd Ilias Konstantinou 1950; m 3rd Chandler Brossard 1968; m 4th Igor Klatzo 1971 (divorced); two s two d. *Education:* Hunter Coll and New York Univ. *Career:* Teacher of Zoology, various colls and univs 1953–67; teacher Univ of Maryland, Coll Park 1968–, Prof 1973–, now Prof Emer; Founding Exec Dir Mote Marine Lab, Sarasota, FL 1955–67, now Dir Emer; Course Dir AAAS-NSF Chautaqua-Type Short Course for Coll teachers 1977–84; Grants and Contracts from govt and pvt scientific orgs for the study of fish behaviour, ecology and taxonomy, including Atomic Energy Comm 1949–50 (Fellow 1949), Fulbright Comm (Egypt) 1950–51, NSF 1969–70, Nat Geographic Soc 1969–91, Univ of Maryland Foundation 1984–91; Pacific Science Bd Scholar (Micronesia) 1949; Eugene Saxton Memorial Fellow 1952; Breadloaf Writer's Fellow 1952; four species of fish named for her: *Callogobius clarki, Sticharium clarkae, Enneaptergius clarkae, Atrobucca geniae;* numerous honours and awards include Hon DS (Massachusetts, Dartmouth) 1992, (Guelph, Long Island) 1995; Golden Plate Award (American Acad of Achievement) 1965, Gold Medal (Soc of Women Geographers) 1975, Diver of the Year Award (Boston Sea Rovers) 1978, Ocean Hero 1986, Gov of Red Sea Medal (Egypt) 1988, Woman of Distinction Award (NASPA) 1990, Hon Citizen and Key to City of Sarasota (FL) 1990. *Publications include:* Lady with a Spear 1953, The Lady and the Sharks 1969, Desert Beneath the Sea (jtly) 1991, Adventures of a Shark Scientist 2000; numerous contribs to professional journals; *Films include:* The Sharks 1982, Naturewatch: Ras Mohammed National Marine Park (Best Film Award, Wildscreen Int Film Festival) 1985, Reefwatch, live from the Red Sea 1988. *Leisure interest:* gardening. *Address:* University of Maryland, Dept of Zoology, College Park, MD 20742-4415, USA. *Telephone:* (301) 405-6920; *Fax:* (301) 314-9358.

CLARK, Rt Hon Helen Elizabeth, PC, MA; New Zealand politician; b 26 Feb 1950, Hamilton; m Peter Davis. *Education:* Epsom Girls' Grammar School (Auckland) and Auckland Univ. *Career:* Lecturer Dept of Political Studies, Auckland Univ 1973–75, 1977–81; mem Labour Party 1971–, Party Exec 1978–88, 1989–; MP (Lab) for Mt Albert 1981–96, for Owairaka 1996–, Chair Foreign Affairs and Defence Select Cttee, Disarmament and Arms Control Select Cttee, mem Govt Admin Select Cttee, convenor Govt Caucus Cttee on External Affairs and Security 1984–87; Minister of Housing and of Conservation 1987–89, of Health and of Labour 1989–90, chaired

several Cabinet cttees; Deputy Prime Minister 1989–90, Minister for Arts, Culture and Heritage, responsibility for the NZ Security Intelligence Service and Ministerial Services; Deputy Leader of Opposition and Opposition Spokesperson on Health and Labour 1990–93, Leader of the Opposition 1993–99; Prime Minister of New Zealand 1999–; fmr Pres Labour Youth Council, exec mem Auckland Regional Council, Sec Labour Women's Council, mem Policy Council; Danish Peace Foundation Peace Prize 1985. *Leisure interests:* tennis, films, theatre, classical music, opera, Spanish, cross-country skiing, trekking. *Address:* Department of the Prime Minister and Cabinet, Executive Wing, Parliament Bldgs, Wellington, New Zealand (Office); Labour Party, 160–162 Willis St, Wellington, New Zealand. *Telephone:* (4) 471-9999 (Office); *Fax:* (4) 472-9309 (Office); *Internet:* www.dpmc .govt.nz (Office).

CLARK, Margaret, CMG, PH D; New Zealand professor of political science; b 28 Jan 1941, Wellington; d of John Kyle H. and Florence (née Aitken) Clark; m Bernard V. J. Galvin 1980; three step-s one step-d. *Education:* Victoria Univ of Wellington, Columbia Univ (New York) and Univ of Malaya (Malaysia). *Career:* Lecturer Univ of Melbourne 1964–66, Univ of Malaya 1966–69; Asst Prof City Univ of New York, USA 1972–75; Sr Lecturer Victoria Univ 1976–78, Prof and Head Dept of Political Science 1978–. *Publications:* The Politics of Belonging 1974, Beyond Expectations 1986, The Politics of Education in New Zealand 1981, Godwits Return 1992, Sir Keith Holyoake: Towards a Political Biography 1997, Peter Fraser: Master Politician 1998, Three Labour Leaders: Nordmeyer, Kirk, Rowling 2001. *Leisure interests:* reading, music, walking, gardening. *Address:* Victoria University of Wellington, Department of Politics, POB 600, Wellington, New Zealand (Office); 10 Jellicoe Towers, 189 The Terrace, Wellington 1, New Zealand (Home). *Telephone:* (4) 463-5262 (Office); (4) 472-8143 (Home); *Fax:* (4) 496-5414 (Office); *E-mail:* politics@vuw.ac.nz.

CLARK, Mary Higgins, BA; American writer and business exec; b 24 Dec 1931, New York; d of Luke Higgins and Nora Durkin; m Warren Clark 1949 (died 1964); three d two s. *Education:* Fordham Univ. *Career:* Advertising Asst Remington Rand 1946; stewardess Pan Am 1949–50; radio scriptwriter, producer Robert G. Jennings 1965–70; Vice-Pres, Partner, Creative Dir, Producer of Radio Programming, Aerial Communications, New York 1970–80; Chair Bd and Creative Dir D. J. Clark Enterprises, New York 1980–; mem American Acad of Arts and Sciences, Mystery Writers of America, Authors League; Dr hc (Villanova) 1983, (Rider Coll) 1986; Grand Prix de Littérature Policière, France 1980. *Publications:* Aspire to the Heavens, A Biography of George Washington 1969, Where Are The Children? 1976, A Stranger is Watching 1978, The Cradle Will Fall 1980, A Cry in the Night 1982, Stillwatch 1984, Weep No More, My Lady 1987, While My Pretty One Sleeps 1989, The Anastasia Syndrome 1989, Loves Music, Loves to Dance 1991, All Around the Town 1992, I'll Be Seeing You 1993, Remember Me 1994, The Lottery Winner 1994, Let Me Call You Sweetheart 1995, Silent Night 1996, Moonlight Becomes You 1996, My Gal Sunday 1996, Pretend You Don't See Her 1997, All Through the Night 1998, We'll Meet Again 1999, Before I Say Good-Bye 2000. *Address:* 210 Central Park S, New York, NY 10019, USA.

CLARK, Petula, CBE; British singer and actress; b (Sally Olwen) 15 Nov 1934, Epsom; d of Leslie Norman and Doris Olwen; m Claude Wolff 1961; two d one s. *Career:* Started career as child singer entertaining troops during World War II; early appearances in films under contract to Rank Organization; made numerous recordings and television appearances in both UK and France; success of single Downtown started career in the US; two Grammy Awards, ten Gold Discs. *Stage appearances include:* Sound of Music 1981, Someone Like You (also wrote) 1989, Blood Brothers (Broadway) 1993, Sunset Boulevard 1995–96; nat tour 1994–95, Sunset Boulevard 1995, 1996, New York 1998, USA tour 1998–2000; *Films include:* Medal for the General 1944, Murder in Reverse 1945, London Town 1946, Strawberry Roan 1947, Here Come the Huggetts, Vice Versa, Easy Money 1948, Don't Ever Leave Me 1949, Vote for Huggett 1949, The Huggetts Abroad, Dance Hall, The Romantic Age 1950, White Corridors, Madame Louise 1951, Made in Heaven 1952, The Card 1952, The Runaway Bus 1954, My Gay Dog 1954, The Happiness of Three Women 1955, Track the Man Down 1956, That Woman Opposite 1957, Daggers Drawn 1964,

Finian's Rainbow 1968, Goodbye Mr Chips 1969, Second Star to the Right 1980. *Address:* c/o John Ashby, POB 288, Woking GU22 0YN, UK.

CLARKE, Patricia Hannah, D SC, FRS; British microbial biochemist; b 29 July 1919, Pontypridd; d of David S. Green and Daisy L. A. Willoughby; m Michael Clarke 1940; two s. *Education:* Howells School (Llandaff) and Girton Coll (Cambridge). *Career:* Armament Research Dept, Ministry of Supply 1940–44; Wellcome Research Labs 1944–47; Public Health Research Labs 1951–53; Lecturer Dept of Biochem, Univ Coll London 1953, Reader in Microbial Biochem 1966, Prof 1974–84, Prof Emer 1984–; Hon Research Fellow Chem and Biochem Eng Dept, Univ Coll London 1984–; Hon Professorial Fellow Inst of Science and Tech, Univ of Wales 1984–89; Leverhulme Emer Fellow 1984–87; Kan Tong-Po Prof Chinese Univ of Hong Kong 1986; Vice-Pres Royal Soc 1981–82; Chair Inst for Biotechnological Studies 1986–87; mem Cttee on Women in Science and Tech, Office of Public Service and Science; numerous research papers published in professional journals 1946–91. *Leisure interests:* walking, gardening, reading, education. *Address:* 7 Corinium Gate, Cirencester, Glos GL7 2PX, UK.

CLARKSON, Rt Hon Adrienne, CC, CD; Canadian Governor-General and broadcaster; b 1939, Hong Kong; d of Bill Poy; m John Ralston Saul. *Education:* Univ of Toronto and Sorbonne (Paris, France). *Career:* Broadcaster with CBC TV 1965–82, 1988–98; Ontario's Agent-Gen in Paris 1982–87; Pres McClelland & Stewart Publishing 1987–88; fmr Chair Bd of Trustees, Canadian Museum of Civilization, Hull, Quebec; fmr Pres Exec Bd IMZ, Vienna (int audio-visual asscn of music, dance and cultural programmers); Gov-Gen of Canada Oct 1999–; fmr Bencher of Law Soc of Upper Canada; numerous hon doctorates and academic distinctions. *TV includes:* Take Thirty, Adrienne at Large, The Fifth Estate, Adrienne Clarkson's Summer Festival, Adrienne Clarkson Presents, Something Special; has published three books and numerous magazine and newspaper articles. *Address:* Rideau Hall, 1 Sussex Drive, Ottawa, ON K1A 0A1, Canada. *Telephone:* (613) 993-8200.

CLAY, Dame Marie Mildred, DBE; New Zealand professor of education; b 3 Jan 1926; d of Donald Leolin and Mildred Blanche Irwin; m Warwick Victor Clay 1951; one s one d. *Education:* Wellington Teachers' Coll, Univs of New Zealand, Minnesota (USA) and Auckland. *Career:* Univ Lecturer Univ of Auckland 1960–67, Sr Lecturer 1968–72, Assoc Prof 1973–74, Prof of Educ 1975–91, Prof Emer 1991–, Head Dept of Educ 1975–78, 1986–88; Distinguished Visiting Prof Ohio State Univ, USA 1984–85; Visiting Fellow Wolfson Coll, Oxford, UK 1987–88; George A. Miller Visiting Prof Univ of Illinois, USA 1991; Pres Int Reading Asscn 1991–92; Fulbright Scholar Univ of Minnesota (USA) 1950–51; Fellow NZ Psychological Soc, Royal Soc of New Zealand; Hon Fellow NZ Educational Inst; Mackie Medal (Australian and New Zealand Asscn for the Advancement of Science) 1983; New Zealander of the Year 1994. *Publications include:* What Did I Write 1975, Reading: The Patterning of Complex Behaviour (2nd edn) 1979, Children of Parents Who Separate 1978, Reading Begins at Home 1979, Observing Young Readers 1982, Round About Twelve 1983, The Early Detection of Reading Difficulties (3rd edn) 1985, Writing Begins at Home 1987, Quadruplets and Higher Multiple Births 1989, Becoming Literate: the Construction of Inner Control 1991, An Observation Survey 1993, Reading Recovery 1993, By Different Paths to Common Outcomes 1998. *Address:* Flat 4, 153 Bassett Rd, Auckland 5, New Zealand.

CLAYBURGH, Jill, BA; American actress; b 30 April 1944, New York; d of Albert H. and Julia (née Door) Clayburgh; m David Rabe 1979. *Education:* Sarah Lawrence Coll (Bronxville, NY). *Career:* Broadway debut 1979; Best Actress Award, Cannes Film Festival. *Plays include:* The Rothschilds 1979, In the Boom Boom Room, Design for Living *Films include:* Portnoy's Complaint 1972, The Thief Who Came to Dinner, The Terminal Man 1974, Gable and Lombard 1976, Silver Streak 1976, Semi-Tough 1977, An Unmarried Woman (Golden Apple Award) 1978, La Luna 1979, Starting Over 1979, It's My Turn 1980, I'm Dancing as Fast as I Can 1982, Hannah K 1983, Shy People 1987, Beyond the Ocean, Between the Lines 1990, Rich in Love 1993, Naked in New York 1994, Fools Rush In 1997, Going All the Way 1997; *TV*

film appearances include: Crowned and Dangerous 1998, My Little Assassin 1999. *Address:* 12424 Wilshire Blvd, Suite 1000, Los Angeles, CA 90025, USA (Office).

CLAYTON, Dame Barbara Evelyn, DBE, PH D, MD, FRCP, FRCPE, FRCPATH, FRCPI, F MED SCI; British honorary research professor in metabolism; b 2 Sept 1922, Liverpool; d of William and Constance Clayton; m William Klyne 1949 (died 1977); one d one s. *Education:* Bromley County School for Girls and Univ of Edinburgh. *Career:* Consultant Hosp for Sick Children 1959–78 (mem Bd of Govs 1968–78); Prof of Chemical Pathology, Inst of Child Health, Univ of London 1970–78; Prof of Chemical Pathology and Human Metabolism Univ of Southampton 1979–87, Dean of Medicine 1983–86, Hon Research Prof and Hon Consultant Chemical Pathologist 1987–; Pres Royal Coll of Pathologists 1984–87; Hon Pres British Dietetic Asscn 1989–; mem Royal Comm on Environmental Pollution 1981–86, WHO Expert Advisory Panel on Nutrition 1988–98; Pres Asscn of Clinical Biochemists 1977–78, Soc for Study of Inborn Errors of Metabolism 1981–82 (Hon mem 1988), Royal Coll of Pathologists 1984–87, Nat Soc for Clean Air and Environmental Protection 1995–97; Chair Standing Cttee on Postgrad Medical and Dental Educ 1988–99, Health of the Nation Task Force on Nutrition 1992–95, Medical and Scientific Panel, Leukaemia Research Fund 1988–; mem Gen Medical Council 1983–87; Gov British Nutrition Foundation, Hon Pres 1999; Hon Fellow American Soc of Clinical Pathologists 1987, Hon Fellow Inst of Biology 2000; Hon D SC (Edinburgh) 1987, (Southampton) 1992, (London) 2000; Jessie MacGregor Prize for Medical Science, Royal Coll of Physicians, Edinburgh 1985; Wellcome Prize, Asscn of Clinical Biochemists 1988, Gold Medal for Distinguished Merit (British Medical Asscn) 1999. *Publications:* Clinical Biochemistry and the Sick Child (jtly) 1994; numerous publs on nutrition, pediatrics and the environment. *Leisure interests:* natural history, visiting the Arctic. *Address:* Room AC19, Level C, South Academic Block, Southampton SO16 6YD, UK (Office). *Telephone:* (23) 8079-6800 (Office); (23) 8076-9937 (Home); *Fax:* (23) 8079-4760; *E-mail:* apc@soton.ac.uk.

CLAYTON, Lisa; British yachtswoman and business executive; b 30 Dec 1958, Birmingham; d of Dan Trevor and Gwendoline Syona Clayton; m Rodney Salmon 1978 (divorced 1984). *Education:* Edgbaston Church of England Coll for Girls and N Worcestershire Coll of Further and Higher Educ. *Career:* Trainee Chartered Accountant Kenneth Morris & Co 1977–79; Controller of Accounts Horizon Holidays 1979–86; Chartering Partner Sailaway 1986–92; sailed, in yacht Spirit of Birmingham, around the world unassisted, single-handed and non-stop in 285 days Sept 1994–June 1995; Partner Clayton Harding Assocs 1995–; Amb for The Prince's Trust 1995–; Hon Pres Co Air Ambulance 1996–; Hon DS (Birmingham); awards include Person of the Year 1995, Super Diamond Award 1995, Midlander of the Year 1995, Sportswoman of the Year 1995, BBC Midlands Sports Achievement Award 1995, Freedom of the City of Birmingham 1996. *Publication:* The Mercy of the Sea 1996 (also available on video tape). *Address:* Clayton Harding Assocs, 33 Lionel St, Birmingham B3 1AP, UK. *Telephone:* (121) 233-0550; *Fax:* (121) 233-9923.

CLEAVE, Mary L., PH D; American engineer and astronaut; b 5 Feb 1947, Southampton, NY. *Education:* Colorado and Utah State Univs. *Career:* Research Asst Utah State Univ 1971–80; Astronaut NASA Lyndon B. Johnson Space Center, Houston, TX 1980, mission specialist STS 61-B 1985, STS-30 1989. *Address:* NASA, Johnson Space Center Astronaut Office, Houston, TX 77058, USA.

CLEMENTS, Suzanne; British fashion designer; m Inacio Ribeiro 1992. *Education:* Cen St Martin's Coll of Art and Design (London). *Career:* Produced own range of knitwear; design consultant with husband, Brazil 1991–93; Founder Clements Ribeiro with husband, London 1993; first collections launched Oct 1993, numerous since; first solo show London Fashion Week March 1995; fashion shows since in Paris, Brazil, Japan; consultant to cos in UK and Italy; winner of Designer of the Year New Generation Category 1996. *Address:* Clements Ribeiro Ltd, 48 South Molton St, London W1X 1HE, UK. *Telephone:* (20) 7409-7719; *Fax:* (20) 7409-1741.

CLEMET, Kristin; Norwegian politician; b 20 April 1957, Harstad; m. *Education:* Norwegian School of Econs and Business Admin. *Career:* Pvt Sec to Minister of Industry 1981–83; Group Sec Cons Party Parl Group 1983–84; Information Sec Cons Party HQ 1985, Head Political Affairs Dept 1988–89, Chair Bd of Cons Party Telemarketing Ltd 1988; Pvt Sec and Adviser Prime Minister's Office 1985–86; Deputy Mem Storting (Parl) 1985–89, Mem 1989–93; Minister of Labour and Govt Admin 1989–91; mem Kleppe Cttee 1987–89; fmr Dir-Gen Confed of Business and Industry. *Address:* c/o Confederation of Business and Industry, POB 251, Skøyen, 0213 Oslo, Norway.

CLERIDES, Katherine, MA; Cypriot politician; b 10 May 1949, London, UK; d of Glafcos and Lilla (née Erulkar) Clerides. *Education:* English School (Nicosia), Bedford Coll (Univ of London) and New York Univ. *Career:* Social researcher 1970–74; in charge of briefing foreign journalists on Cyprus question and refugee problems following Turkish invasion 1974–75; Information Officer Int Planned Parenthood Fed (IPPF), London 1975–77; called to the Bar 1978; Legal Adviser Bank of Cyprus 1980–91; mem Nicosia Municipal Council 1986–91; mem House of Reps (Democratic Rally Party) 1991; Sec Women's Section Democratic Rally Party 1991; mem Bd Asscn for Welfare of People with Mental Handicap. *Leisure interest:* running programme to encourage women's participation in politics. *Address:* House of Representatives, Nicosia, Cyprus (Office); 5A John Clerides St, Nicosia, Cyprus (Home). *Telephone:* (2) 403451 (Office); (2) 458914 (Home); *Fax:* (2) 366611 (Office); (2) 449894 (Home).

CLEVERDON, Julia, CBE; British business executive; b 1949; m 1st 1971 (divorced 1976); m 2nd John Garnett 1986; two d. *Education:* Camden School for Girls and Newnham Coll (Cambridge). *Career:* Fmrly mem staff British Leyland, then joined Industrial Soc, Head of Pepperell Unit; CEO Business in the Community (BITC) 1992–. *Address:* BITC, 44 Baker St, London W1M 1DH, UK. *Telephone:* (20) 7224-1600.

CLIJSTERS, Kim; Belgian tennis player; b 8 June 1983, Bilzen; d of Leo and Els Clijsters. *Career:* Began playing tennis at age 5 with her family; Finalist in Junior Singles, Wimbledon 1998; won French Open Junior Doubles Title 1998; winner Sanex World Tennis Asscn (WTA) Tour 1999, 2000; world ranking no 18, Nov 2000; Finalist Indian Wells 2001; Sanex WTA Tour Most Impressive Newcomer Award 1999; Karen Krantzke Sportsmanship Award 2000. *Address:* c/o Bank Lane, Roehampton, London SW15 5XZ, UK.

CLINGAN, Judith Ann, AM, BA; Australian musician and composer; b 19 Jan 1945, Sydney, NSW; d of Victor Lawrence and Marian Dorothy (née Tasker) Clingan; one d. *Education:* Univs of Sydney and New S Wales, ANU and Kodaly School of Music Educ (Hungary). *Career:* Composer for Kodaly Educ Inst 1986, ACT Bicentennial Year 1987, 1988; Founder and Dir Gaudeamus 1983–93; Creative Arts Fellow ANU 1989; Composer-in-Residence Gaudeamus and Young Music Soc 1990; Composer Fellow 1991; Dir Voicebox Youth Opera S Australia; Dir of Music Mt Barker Waldorf School, SA 1994–; mem numerous orgs. *Compositions include:* Francis 1986, Nganbra 1988, Terra Beata—Terra Infirma 1989, Kakadu 1990, The Birds' Noel 1990, Marco 1991, Songs of Solitude 1991, The Grandfather Clock 1992; *Publications include:* The Complete Chorister 1971, So Good a Thing 1981, Music is for Everyone 1984. *Leisure interests:* Anglican Church, new liturgies, new church music, environment, public awareness. *Address:* 1 Flaxley Rd, Mt Barker, SA 5251, Australia.

CLINTON, Hillary Rodham, MA, D JUR; American politician and lawyer; b 26 Oct 1947, Chicago, IL; d of Hugh Ellsworth and Dorothy Howell Rodham; m Bill (William) Jefferson Clinton 1975; one d. *Education:* Wellesley Coll (MA) and Yale Univ (CT). *Career:* Joined Rose Law Firm 1977, now Sr Partner; Lecturer in Law Univ of Arkansas, Little Rock 1979–80, Asst Prof of Law, Fayetteville and Dir Legal Aid Clinic 1974–77; Legal Counsel Nixon impeachment staff, House Judiciary Cttee 1974; Chair Comm on Women in the Profession, ABA 1987–91; Head Pres's Task Force on Nat Health Reform 1993–94; newspaper columnist 1995–; Senator from New York 2001–; Co-Chair Children's Defense Fund 1973–74; fmr Ed Yale Law Review; mem Bd Dirs Southern Devt Bancorpn 1986, Nat Center on Educ and the Economy 1987, Franklin and Eleanor Roosevelt Inst 1988, Children's

TV Workshop 1989, Public/Private Ventures 1990, Arkansas Single Parent Scholarship Fund Program 1990; numerous contribs to professional journals; Hon LL D (Univ of Arkansas, Little Rock) 1985, (Arkansas Coll) 1988, (Hendrix Coll) 1992; Hon DHL (Drew) 1996; numerous awards and prizes including The Best Lawyers in America 1987, 1989–90, 1991–92, One of the 100 Most Influential Lawyers in America (Nat Law Journal) 1988, 1991, Gayle Pettus Pontz Award (Woman's Law Student Asscn, Univ of Arkansas) 1989, Directors' Choice Award (Nat Women's Economic Alliance Foundation) 1991, Arkansas State Press Publishers' Award 1992, ROSE Award (School of Educ, Univ of Southern California) 1992, Outstanding Lawyer-Citizen Award (Arkansas Bar Asscn) 1992, Lewis Hine Award, Nat Child Labor Law Comm 1993, Friend of Family Award, American Home Econs Foundation 1993, Humanitarian Award, Alzheimer's Asscn 1994, Elie Wiesel Foundation 1994, AIDS Awareness Award 1994, Grammy Award 1996. *Publications:* Every Child Needs a Village 1995, It Takes a Village 1996, Dear Socks, Dear Buddy 1998; numerous contribs to professional journals. *Leisure interests:* reading, walking, tennis. *Address:* US Senate, Washington, DC 20510, USA (Office).

CLORE, Melanie, BA; British business executive and auctioneer; b 28 Jan 1960; d of Martin and Cynthia Clore; m Yaron Meshoulam 1994; one s one d. *Education:* Channing School (London) and Univ of Manchester. *Career:* Joined Sotheby's 1981, mem Impressionist and Modern Art Dept 1982, Dir 1988–, Sr Dir 1991–, Auctioneer 1985–, Head of Worldwide Impressionist and Modern Art Dept 1992– (Co-Chair 2000–), mem Bd Sotheby's Europe 1994–, Deputy Chair 1997–. *Leisure interests:* theatre, films, music, art galleries. *Address:* Sotheby's, 34 New Bond St, London W1A 2AA, UK. *Telephone:* (20) 7293-5394; *Fax:* (20) 7293-5932.

CLOSE, Glenn; American actress; b 19 March 1947, Greenwich, CT; d of William and Bettine Close; m 1st Cabot Wade (divorced); m 2nd James Marlas 1984 (divorced); one d by John Starke. *Education:* William and Mary Coll. *Career:* Joined New Phoenix Repertory Co 1974; Co-propr The Leaf and Bean Coffee House, Bozeman 1991–; Woman of the Year, Hasty Puddings Theatricals 1990; Dartmouth Film Soc Award 1990. *Plays include:* Love for Love, The Rules of the Game, The Singular Life of Albert Nobbs, Childhood, Real Thing (Tony Award), A Streetcar Named Desire, King Lear, The Rose Tattoo, Benefactors, Death and the Maiden (Tony Award for Best Actress) 1992, Sunset Boulevard; *Films include:* The World According to Garp 1982, The Big Chill 1983, The Natural 1984, The Stone Boy 1984, Maxie 1985, Jagged Edge 1985, Fatal Attraction 1987, Dangerous Liaisons 1989, Reversal of Fortune 1989, The House of Spirits 1990, Meeting Venus 1990, Hamlet 1990, Immediate Family 1991, The Paper 1994, Mary Reilly 1994, Serving in Silence: The Margaret Cammermeyer Story 1995, 101 Dalmatians 1996, Mars Attacks! 1996, Air Force One 1997, Paradise Road 1997, Tarzan 1999, Cookie's Fortune 1999, 102 Dalmatians 2000; numerous TV film appearances. *Address:* c/o CAA, 9830 Wilshire Blvd, Beverly Hills, CA 90212, USA (Office).

CLWYD, Ann; British politician, journalist and broadcaster; b 21 March 1937; d of Gwilym Henri and Elizabeth Ann Lewis; m Owen Dryhurst Roberts 1963. *Education:* Holywell Grammar School, The Queen's School (Chester), Univ of Wales and Univ Coll of N Wales. *Career:* Welsh Corresp The Guardian and The Observer 1964–79; Vice-Chair Welsh Arts Council 1975–79; MEP (Lab) 1979–84; MP (Lab) for Cynon Valley 1984–, Chair Lab Back-bench Cttee on Health and Social Security 1985–87, Vice-Chair Lab Back-bench Cttee on Defence 1985–87, mem Parl Cttee 1992, Opposition Front-bench Spokesperson on Women 1987–88, on Educ 1987–88, on Overseas Devt and Co-operation 1989–92, on Wales 1992, on Employment 1993–94, on Foreign Affairs 1994–95; Shadow Sec of State for Nat Heritage 1992–93; mem Select Cttee on Int Devt 1997–; Chair All-Party Group on Human Rights 1997–; Chair Cardiff Anti-Racialism Cttee 1978–80, Nat Exec Council of Labour Party 1983–84; mem numerous cttees and orgs; Hon Fellow Univ of N Wales. *Leisure interests:* walking, boating. *Address:* House of Commons, London SW1A 0AA, UK (Office); 6 Deans Court, Deans St, Aberdare, Mid Glamorgan, CF44 7BN, UK (Office). *Telephone:* (20) 7219-3000 (London); (1685) 871394 (Aberdare); *Fax:* (20) 7219-5943 (London).

COAKLEY, Sarah Anne, MA, TH M, PH D; British professor of theology; b 10 Sept 1951, London; d of Frank Robert and Anne Wilson Furber (née McArthur); m James Farwell Coakley 1975; two d. *Education:* Blackheath High School for Girls, New Hall (Cambridge) and Divinity School (Harvard). *Career:* Univ Lecturer in Religious Studies Lancaster Univ 1976–90, Sr Lecturer 1990–91; Tutorial Fellow in Theology Oriel Coll, Oxford and Univ Lecturer 1991–93; Hulsean Lecturer Univ of Cambridge 1991–92; Prof of Christian Theology Harvard Divinity School 1993–95, Edward Mallinckrodt, Jr Prof of Divinity 1995–; Harkness Fellow 1973–75; Select Preacher, Oxford Univ 1991; Hulsean Lecturer, Univ of Cambridge 1991–92, Hulsean Preacher 1996; Samuel Ferguson Lecturer, Univ of Manchester 1997, Riddell Lecturer, Univ of Newcastle 1999, Tate-Wilson Lecturer, South Methodist Univ 1999, Prideaux Lecturer, Univ of Exeter 2000; Hulsean Prize, Univ of Cambridge 1977. *Publications:* Christ Without Absolutes: A Study of the Christology of Ernst Troelysch 1988, The Making and Remaking of Christian Doctrine (co-ed) 1993, Religion and the Body (ed) 1997; contribs to Church of England Doctrine Comm Reports 1987, 1991; articles in theological journals. *Leisure interests:* musical activities, thinking about the garden. *Address:* The Divinity School, Harvard University, 45 Francis Ave, Cambridge, MA 02138, USA (Office). *Telephone:* (617) 495-4518; *Fax:* (617) 495-9489.

COATES, Anne Voase; British film executive and producer; b 12 Dec 1925, Reigate, Surrey; d of Laurence Calvert and Kathleen Voase (née Rank) Coates; m Douglas Hickox 1958 (deceased); two s one d. *Education:* Micklefield School (Reigate), High Trees School (Horley, Surrey) and Bartrum Gables (Broadstairs, Kent). *Career:* American Cinema Eds' Lifetime Achievement Award 1996, Woman in Film Crystal Life Achievement Award 1998, Woman in Film Carlton Life Achievement Award 2000. *Films include:* Pickwick Papers, Grand National Night, Forbidden Cargo, To Paris With Love, The Truth About Women, The Horse's Mouth, Tunes of Glory 1960, Don't Bother to Knock, Lawrence of Arabia (Acad Award 1962) 1961–62, Becket (Acad Award) 1963, Young Cassidy, Those Magnificent Men in their Flying Machines (co-ed) 1964, Hotel Paradiso, Great Catherine, The Bofors Gun, The Adventurers, Friends, The Public Eye, The Nelson Affair, 11 Harrowhouse, The Medusa Touch (producer and ed) 1977, The Elephant Man 1981, Murder on the Orient Express 1982, Man Friday, Aces High, The Eagle Has Landed, The Legacy, The Bushido Blade, Ragtime (co-ed), The Pirates of Penzance, Greystoke: The Legend of Tarzan, Lord of the Apes 1984, Lady Jane, Raw Deal, Masters of the Universe, Farewell to the King (co-ed), Listen to Me, I Love You to Death, What About Bob?, Charlie Chaplin 1992, In the Line of Fire (GBFE Award) 1993, Pontiac Moon, Congo, Striptease, Out to Sea, Out of Sight 1997, Erin Brochovich 1999. *Leisure interests:* cinema, theatre, horse-riding, sailing, skiing, travel. *Address:* c/o The Gersh Agency, 232 North Canon Drive, Beverly Hills, CA 90210, USA (Office). *Telephone:* (213) 654-7282.

COCHRANE, Hon Ethel M., M ED; Canadian politician; b 23 Sept 1937, Lourdes, NF; m James Cochrane 1956; six c. *Education:* Prince of Wales Coll (St John's, NF), Memorial Univ (NF) and St Francis Xavier Univ (NS). *Career:* School teacher for 21 years; Senator 1986–, mem Senate Social Affairs Cttee and Science and Tech Cttee 1995–96, fmrly mem Senate Internal Econ Cttee, Budgets and Admin Cttee, currently mem Energy, Environment and Natural Resources Cttee; mem Salvation Army Advisory Bd (Corner Brook, NF), Canada-Latin American Parl Asscn, Canada-Italy Friendship Group, Canadian NATO Parl Asscn, Canadian-Europe Parl Asscn; Hon mem 2415 Gonzaga Cadet Corps. *Address:* Parliament Bldgs, Wellington St, Ottawa, ON K1A 0A4, Canada (Office); POB 233, Port au Port, NF A0N 1T0, Canada (Home). *Telephone:* (613) 992-1577 (Office); *Fax:* (613) 995-6691 (Office).

COCKE, Ulla, BA; Swedish magazine editor; b 14 April 1947; d of Gert and Lisa Ljungstrom; m Thomas Cocke 1974; one d. *Education:* Stockholm Univ. *Career:* Journalist 1980–; Ed-in-Chief Min Värld 1984, Hemmets Veckotidning weekly magazine 1985. *Address:* Hemmets Veckotidning, Allers Förlag AB, 205 35 Malmö, Sweden. *Telephone:* (40) 385 900.

COGHILL, Joy Dorothy, CM, BA, MFA; Canadian actress, producer, director and writer; b 13 May 1926, Findlater, SK; d of Rev George and Dorothy Coghill; m John Thorne 1955; two s one d. *Education:* Univ of British Columbia and Art Inst of Chicago (Goodman Theatre). *Career:* Has performed in and produced numerous theatre, film and TV performances; Founder and Artistic Dir Holiday Theatre (Canada's first professional theatre for children) 1953–69; Artistic Dir Vancouver Playhouse 1967–69; Dir English Acting Section, Nat Theatre School of Canada 1971–74; mem Nat Council, Canadian Actors' Equity 1983–; Hon mem Asscn for Canadian Theatre History 1983; Canadian Drama Award 1963, Canadian Centennial Medal 1967, Canadian Silver Jubilee Medal 1977, Sam Payne Award (ACTRA) 1986, Woman of Distinction (YWCA) 1986, Gascon-Thomas Award (Nat Theatre School) 1990. *Performances include:* Theatre: Silver Cord (Dominion Drama Festival Award) 1946, Song of This Place (also wrote and produced) 1987, Road to Mecca (Province People's Choice Award) 1990, Curtains for a Crazy Old Lady (Best Performance Community 'Jessie') 1991, Jo Egg, M.S.N.D., Midsummer Night's Dream (Benjamin Britten's Opera), Ma!, My Memories of You, Curtains, Sunrunner, The Raft, Tsymbaly, Memoir II, Forever Yours Marie-Lou, Albertine in Five Times; TV: Ma! 1985, Red Serge Wives 1985; Radio: Sweet Second Summer of Kitty Malone.

COHEN, Abby Joseph, MA; American financial executive; b 29 Feb 1952, New York; d of Raymond and late Shirley (née Silverstein) Joseph; m David M. Cohen 1973; two d. *Education:* Martin Van Buren High School, Cornell Univ and George Washington Univ. *Career:* Jr economist, Fed Reserve Bd, Washington, DC 1973–76; economist/analyst, T. Rowe Price Assocs, Baltimore, Maryland 1976–83; Investment Strategist, Drexel Burnham Lambert, New York 1983–90, BZW, New York 1990, Goldman, Sachs & Co 1990–, Man Dir 1996–, Man Partner 1998–; Chair Inst of Chartered Financial Analysts; mem Bd of Govs Nat Economists Club, New York Soc of Security Analysts; Vice-Chair Asscn for Investment Man Research; mem Nat Asscn of Business Economists; Trustee/Fellow Cornell Univ; Woman Achiever (Woman of the Year) Award, YWCA, New York 1989. *Address:* Goldman, Sachs & Co, 85 Broad St, New York, NY 10004, USA.

COHEN, Lea; Bulgarian musician and diplomatist; b 29 June 1942, Sofia; m 1st Nikola Zidarov 1964; m 2nd Vladimir Bojkov 1984; one s. *Education:* Sofia Conservatory and Univ of Utrecht (Netherlands). *Career:* Writer, TV scriptwriter and Ed cultural review 1967–70; Dir Sofia Philharmonic Orchestra 1976–79; elected to Nat Ass 1990; Amb to Belgium, Head of Mission to the EC 1991. *Publications:* La musique contemporaine bulgare 1971, La musique contemporaine française 1974, Etudes musicales pour le théâtre 1989, Oeuvres critiques de Debussy (in Bulgarian) 1990; also monographs. *Address:* Embassy of Bulgaria, 58 ave Hamoir, 1180 Brussels, Belgium. *Telephone:* (2) 374-59-63; *Fax:* (2) 375-84-94.

COHEN, Myrella, QC, FRSA; British circuit judge; b 16 Dec 1927, Manchester; d of the late Samuel and Sarah Cohen; m Mordaunt Cohen 1953; one s one d. *Education:* Manchester High School for Girls, Colwyn Bay Grammar School and Victoria Univ of Manchester. *Career:* Called to the Bar, Gray's Inn 1950; QC 1970; Recorder Kingston upon Hull 1971; Ciruit Judge (SE Circuit), Deputy Judge of Family Div 1972–95; mem Parole Bd 1983–86; Vice-Pres N England Career Research Co; Deputy Pres Int Asscn of Jewish Lawyers and Jurists, Chair UK Br; Life mem and fmr Pres Sunderland Soroptimist Int; Life mem Council of League of Jewish Women; Patron Suzy Lamplugh Trust; Hon LL D (Sunderland) 1992. *Address:* Crown Court at Harrow, Haisham Drive, Harrow, Middx HA1 4TU, UK. *Telephone:* (20) 8424-2294.

COHEN OF PIMLICO, Baroness (Life Peer), cr 2000, of Pimlico in the City of Westminster, **Janet Cohen,** MA; British banking executive and writer; b 4 July 1940, Oxford; d of George Edric and Mary Isabel Neel; m James Lionel Cohen 1971; two s one d. *Education:* South Hampstead High School (London) and Newnham Coll (Cambridge). *Career:* Man Consultant USA and UK 1966–69; Civil Servant Dept of Trade 1969–81; Asst Dir Charterhouse Bank Ltd 1982–88, Dir 1988–; Non-exec Vice-Chair Yorkshire Bldg Soc 1994–99; Dir John Waddington plc 1994–97, BPP Holdings plc 1994, Defence Logistics Org 1999–; Adviser Ministry of Defence 1999–; Gov BBC 1994–99; mem Bd Sheffield Devt Corpn 1993–97; John Creasey Award for Best First

Crime Novel 1988. *Publications include:* As Janet Neel: Death's Bright Angel 1988, Death on Site 1989, Death of a Partner 1991, Death Among the Dons 1993, A Timely Death 1996, To Die For 1998, O Gentle Death 2000; As Janet Cohen: The Highest Bidder 1992, Children of a Harsh Winter 1994. *Leisure interests:* writing, family. *Address:* Charterhouse Bank Ltd, 1 Paternoster Row, London EC4M 7DH, UK; House of Lords, London SW1A 0PW, UK. *Telephone:* (20) 7248-4000.

COHN, Mildred, MA, PH D; American professor of biochemistry and biophysics; b 12 July 1913, New York City; d of Isidore M. Cohn and Bertha Klein; m Henry Primakoff 1938; two d one s. *Education:* Hunter Coll and Columbia Univ (New York). *Career:* Mem staff Cornell Univ Medical Coll, New York 1938–46, Washington Univ Medical School, St Louis, MO 1946–60; Prof of Biophysics and Biophysical Chem, Univ of Pennsylvania 1961–75, Prof of Biochem and Biophysics 1975–82, Benjamin Rush Prof of Physiological Chem 1978–82, Prof Emer 1982–; Career Investigator American Heart Asscn 1964–78; Sr mem Inst for Cancer Research 1982–85; mem AAAS, NAS, American Philosophical Soc; over 150 contribs to professional journals; Hon DS (Women's Medical Coll of Pennsylvania) 1966, (Radcliffe Coll) 1978, (Washington Univ) 1981, (Brandeis, Hunter Coll, Univ of Pennsylvania) 1984, (N Carolina) 1985, (Miami) 1990; Hon PH D (Weizmann Inst of Science) 1988; awards include Cresson Medal (Franklin Inst) 1975, Garvan Medal (American Chem Soc) 1982, Nat Medal for Science 1982, Chandler Medal (Columbia Univ) 1986, Distinguished Service Award (Coll of Physicians, PA) 1987, Remsen Award (MD Section, American Chemical Soc) 1988, Gov's Award for Excellence in Science, PA 1993, Founders Medal, Magnetic Resonance in Biology 1994, Stein-Moore Award, Protein Soc 1997, Oesper Award, Cincinnati Section American Chemical Soc 2000. *Leisure interests:* travel, writing, history of science. *Address:* Dept of Biochemistry and Biophysics, University of Pennsylvania School of Medicine, 242 Anat-Chem Philadelphia, PA 19104-6059, USA (Office); 226 W Rittenhouse Square #1806, Philadelphia, PA 19103, USA (Home). *Telephone:* (215) 898-8404 (Office); (215) 546-3449 (Home); *Fax:* (215) 898-4217; *E-mail:* cohn@mail.med.upenn.edu.

COJOCARU, Alina; Romanian ballet dancer; b 27 May 1981, Bucharest; d of George and Nina Cojocaru. *Education:* Kiev Ballet School (Ukraine) and Royal Ballet School (London). *Career:* Dancer wih Kiev Ballet 1998–89; joined Royal Ballet Co 1999, First Soloist 2000, Prin April 2001–; 2nd Prize, Moscow Int Ballet Competition; Gold Medal, Japan Int Ballet Competition; Most Promising Newcomer Award, Critics' Circle Dance Section. *Repertoire includes:* Kiev Ballet: Don Quixote, Sleeping Beauty, Cinderella, Nutcracker, Coppélia, Swan Lake; Royal Ballet: Symphonic Variations, Masquerade, Ad Infinitum, There Where She Loves, This House Will Burn, Swan Lake, Ondine, Romeo & Juliet, Giselle. *Leisure interests:* reading, music, shopping, swimming, volleyball. *Address:* Royal Opera House, Covent Garden, London WC2E 9DD, UK. *Telephone:* (20) 7212-9165; *Fax:* (20) 7212-9725.

COK, Lucija, M SC, PH D; Slovenian politician; b 7 April 1941, Lokavec, Ajdovščina; m Vanda Bolko; two s one d. *Education:* Koper High School and Univ of Ljubljana. *Career:* Univ teacher of didactics of early language learning 1986–95; Dir of Science and Research and Sr Research Fellow in bilingualism, language and culture contact phenomena, Centre of Koper 1995–2000; Pres KORIS (nat science co-ordination); co-ordinator of nat projects in curricula reform in Slovenia and of int TEMPUS projects 1992–1997; author of models, methods and text books on early foreign language teaching 1994–2000; piloted Portfolio of Languages in Slovenia 1998–2000; teacher trainer in Slovenia, Italy, Austria and France; Minister of Educ, Science and Sport 2000–; Chevalier des Palmes Académiques. *Publications:* Contributo alla didattica della lingua italiana come lingua seconda 1990, Enseigner une seconde langue 1991, Apprentissage précoce de langues 1992, Education in Bilingual Setting: Linguistic Complementarity as one of the Preconditions for Tolerance in Education 1994, Insegnamento/apprendimento delle lingue seconde nell'Istria slovena 1996, L'enseignement de la langue étrangère au niveau précoce est-il un processus d'apprentissage intégré ou non-intégré? 1997, Foreign Languages at Primary School Level: What Forms of Instruction? (for Council of Europe) 1998, My First Portfolio of Languages 1999. *Leisure interests:* skiing, cycling,

gardening. *Address:* Ministry of Education and Sports, 1000 Ljubljana, Župančičeva 6, Slovenia. *Telephone:* (1) 4784708; *Fax:* (1) 4784723; *E-mail:* lucia.cok@msrs.si; *Internet:* www.mss.edus.si.

COLAVITO, Mauricette; French sportswoman and business executive; b 6 July 1945; d of Maurice and Adeline (née Plantier) Chavinas; m Jean-Pierre Colavito 1965; one d one s. *Education:* Inst Saint-Charles and Cours Pigier (Avignon). *Career:* Clay-Pigeon Shooting Champion of the World five times, of France 13 times; has won 38 Gold Medals; European Vice-Champion 1992; took part in Olympics, Barcelona, Spain 1992; Co-Founder Société Contrôle et Traitement des Charpentes (CTC) 1965, Sec 1965–71, Dir 1971; Médaille d'Or de la Jeunesse et des Sports 1991. *Leisure interest:* films. *Address:* Société Contrôle et Traitement des Charpentes (CTC), 27 ave Pierre Sémard, 84000 Avignon, France (Office).

COLE, Babette, BA; British writer; b 10 Sept 1949, Jersey; d of Frederick and Iris (née Horseford) Cole. *Education:* Convent FCJ (St Helier) and Canterbury Coll of Art. *Career:* Mem staff BBC, Children's TV; lived in Okavango Swamps (Botswana) 1976; writer of children's books; 2nd place Kate Greenaway Prize 1986, 1987, Smarties Prize 1987. *Publications include:* Promise Solves the Problem 1976, Nunqu and the Hippopotamus 1978, Nunqu and the Elephant 1980, Promise and the Monster 1981, Don't Go Out Tonight 1981, Beware of the Vet 1982, Nunqu and the Crocodile 1983, The Trouble with Mum 1983, The Hairy Book 1984, The Trouble with Dad 1985, The Slimey Book 1985, Princess Smartypants 1986, Prince Cinders 1987, The Smelly Book 1987, The Trouble with Grandad 1988, King Change-a-lot 1988, The Silly Book 1989, Three Cheers for Errol 1989, Cupid 1989, Hurrah for Ethelyn 1991, The Trouble with Uncle 1992, Tarzanna 1992, The Bible Beasties 1992, Mummy Laid an Egg (or The Great Egg Race) 1993, Winni Allfours 1995, The Trouble with Gran 1997, Two of Everything 1997, Bad Good Manners Book 1997, King Change-a-lot 1998, Bad Habits!: or the Taming of Lucretzia Crum 1999. *Leisure interests:* breeding and showing horses, sailing. *Address:* c/o Rosemary Sandberg Ltd, 6 Bayley St, London WC1B 3HB, UK (Office); Ivy Cottage, Wingmore Lane, Wingmore, Elham, Nr Canterbury, Kent CT4 6LS, UK (Home). *Telephone:* (20) 7304-4110 (Office); (1303) 840772 (Home).

COLE, Johnnetta Betsch, MA; American academic and university administrator; b 19 Oct 1936, Jacksonville, FL; m 1st Robert Eurgen Cole (divorced); three s; m 2nd Arthur J Robinson, Jr 1988. *Education:* Fisk Univ, Oberlin Coll and Northwestern Univ. *Career:* Began career as Lecturer Washington State Univ; fmr Prof of Anthropology and Afro-American Studies Univ of Mass (Amherst), also Assoc Provost of Undergrad Educ; Prof of Anthropology and Dir, Latin American and Caribbean Studies Program, Hunter Coll 1984–87; Pres Spelman Coll 1987–97; Presidential Distinguished Prof of Anthropology, Women's Studies and African-American Studies, Emory Univ 1998–; Cluster Co-ordinator for Educ, Labor and the Arts for Bill Clinton's transition team 1992; mem Bd of Dirs Home Depot, Merck & Co Inc, NationsBank S, Coca-Cola Enterprises; Fellow American Anthropological Asscn; mem Asscn of Black Anthropologists; numerous honorary degrees. *Publications include:* Anthropology for the Eighties 1982, All American Women 1986, Anthropology for the Nineties 1988, Conversations 1993, Dream the Boldest Dreams 1998. *Address:* Emory University, Atlanta, GA 30322, USA.

COLE, Natalie, BA; American singer; b 6 Feb 1950, Los Angeles, CA; d of the late Nat 'King' and Marie (née Hawkins) Cole; m 1st Marvin J. Yancy 1976 (died 1985); m 2nd André Fischer 1989 (divorced); one s. *Education:* Univ of Massachusetts, Amherst. *Career:* New York debut 1973, since then numerous appearances throughout USA; Best New Artist of the Year Grammy Award and Best Rhythm-and-Blues Vocal Performance by a Female Artist Grammy Award 1976. *Recordings include:* Albums: Inseparable 1975, Natalie 1976, Thankful 1977, Unpredictable 1977, Natalie Live 1978, I Love You So 1979, We're the Best of Friends 1979, Don't Look Back 1980, Happy Love 1981, I'm Ready 1983, Unforgettable – A Tribute to Nat 'King' Cole (with Johnny Mathis) 1983, Dangerous 1985, Everlasting 1987, Good To Be Back 1989, Unforgettable (Seven Grammy Awards) 1991, Too Much Weekend 1992, Take A Look 1993, Holly and Ivy 1994, Stardust (two

Grammy Awards), Magic of Christmas 1999. *Address:* c/o Jennifer Allen, PMK, 995 S Carrillo Drive, Suite 200, Los Angeles, CA 90048, USA (Office).

COLE, Nicky; British business executive and explorer; b 1959; d of Robin Begg; m (divorced); one s. *Career:* First woman to walk, without air-drops and teams of dogs, to the South Pole, 120 miles in seven days 1993.

COLEGATE, Isabel Diana, FRSL; British writer; b 10 Sept 1931; d of Sir Arthur and Winifred Mary Colegate; m Michael Briggs 1953; two s one d. *Education:* Runton Hill School (Norfolk). *Career:* Literary Agent Anthony Blond (London) Ltd 1952–57; Hon MA (Bath) 1988. *Publications:* The Blackmailer 1958, A Man of Power 1960, The Great Occasion 1962 (re-issued as Three Novels 1983), Statues in a Garden 1964, Orlando King 1968, Orlando at the Brazen Threshold 1971, Agatha 1973 (re-issued as the Orlando Trilogy 1984), News from the City of the Sun 1979, The Shooting Party (W. H. Smith Literary Award 1980, filmed 1985) 1980, A Glimpse of Sion's Glory 1985, Deceits of Time 1988, The Summer of the Royal Visit 1991, Winter Journey 1995. *Leisure interest:* walking the dog. *Address:* c/o PFD, Drury House, 34–43 Russell St, London WC2B 5HA, UK (Office). *Telephone:* (20) 7344-1000; *Fax:* (20) 7836-9539.

COLERIDGE, Geraldine Margaret (Gill); British literary agent; b 26 May 1948; d of Antony Duke Coleridge and June Marian Caswell; m David Roger Leeming 1974; two s. *Education:* Queen Anne's School (Caversham) and Marlborough Secretarial Coll (Oxford). *Career:* Mem staff BPC Partworks, Sidgwick & Jackson, Bedford Square Book Bang until 1971; Publicity Man Chatto & Windus 1971–72; Dir and Literary Ageny Anthony Sheil Assocs 1973–88; Partner Rogers, Coleridge & White, Literary Agents 1988–; Pres Assoc of Authors' Agents 1988–91. *Leisure interests:* reading, entertaining, music, sailing. *Address:* 113 Calabria Rd, London N5 1HS, UK. *Telephone:* (20) 7226-5875.

COLES, Anna L. Bailey, PH D; American professor of nursing; b 16 Jan 1925, Kansas City; d of Gordon A. Bailey and Lillie Mai Buchanan; m 1953 (divorced 1980); three d. *Education:* Freedmen's Hosp School of Nursing (Washington, DC), Avila Coll (Kansas City, MO) and Catholic Univ of America. *Career:* Instructor Veterans' Admin Hosp, Topeka, KS 1950–52; Supervisor Veterans' Admin Hosp, Kansas City, KS 1952–58; Asst Dir In-Service Educ, Freedmen's Hosp 1960–61, Admin Asst to Dir 1961–66, Assoc Dir Nursing Service 1966–67, Dir of Nursing 1967–69; Prof and Dean Howard Univ Coll of Nursing 1968–86, Dean Emer 1986–, retd 1986; Dir Minority Devt, Univ of Kansas School of Nursing 1991–95; Pres Societas Docta, Inc 1996–; mem Inst of Medicine; Meritorious Public Service Award (DC) 1968, Distinguished Alumni Award, Howard Univ, Lifetime Achievement Award Asscn of Black Nursing Faculty in Higher Educ 1993 and numerous other awards. *Publications include:* Fundamentals of Stroke Care (contrib) 1976, Nurses, in Encyclopedia of Black America 1981; numerous contribs to professional journals. *Leisure interests:* reading, outdoor cooking, travel. *Address:* 15107 Interlachen Drive, Apt 205, Silver Spring, MD 20906, USA (Office). *Telephone:* (301) 598-3680 (Home); *Fax:* (301) 598-3680 (Home).

COLLETTE, Toni; Australian actress. *Films include:* Muriel's Wedding 1994, Lilian's Story 1995, Cosi 1996, Emma 1996, Pallbearer 1996, Clockwatchers 1997, Diana and Me 1997, The Sixth Sense 1999, Shaft 2000, Hotel Sordide 2000.

COLLEY, Linda Jane, PH D, FRHISTS, FBA; British professor of history; b 13 Sept 1949; d of Roy and Margaret (née Hughes) Colley; m David Nicholas Cannadine 1982 ; one d (deceased). *Education:* Univ of Bristol and Univ of Cambridge. *Career:* Eugenie Strong Research Fellow, Girton Coll, Cambridge 1975–78; Fellow Newnham Coll, Cambridge 1978–79, Christ's Coll, Cambridge 1979–81; Asst Prof of History Yale Univ 1982–85, Assoc Prof 1985–90, Prof of History 1990–92, Richard M. Colgate Prof of History 1992–98, Dir Lewis Walpole Library 1982–96; Prof School of History, LSE 1998–, Leverhulme Personal Research Prof, European Inst 1998–; mem Bd British Library, Advisory Bd Tate Britain, Paul Mellon Centre for British Art; Anstey Lecturer Univ of Kent 1994; William Church Memorial Lecturer, Brown Univ 1994, Distinguished Lecturer in British History, Univ of Texas at Austin

1995, Trevelyan Lecturer Cambridge Univ 1997, Wiles Lecturer, Queen's Univ Belfast, Prime Minister's Millennium Lecture 2000. *Publications:* In Defiance of Oligarchy: The Tory Party 1714–60 1982, Namier 1989, Crown Pictorial: Art and the British Monarchy 1990, Britons: Forging the Nation 1707–1837 1992 (Wolfson Prize 1993); numerous articles and reviews in UK and American learned journals. *Leisure interests:* travel, looking at art. *Address:* European Institute, LSE, Houghton St, London WC2A 2AE, UK; c/o Curtis Brown, Haymarket House, 28–29 Haymarket, London SW1 4SP, UK.

COLLI COMELLI, Ombretta; Italian politician; b 21 Sept 1943, Genova. *Career:* fmrly MEP (Group Union for Europe, Forza Italia), mem Cttee on Social Affairs and Employment, Cttee on Women's Rights, Del for Relations with Russia, Del for Relations with the Countries of Cen America and Mexico. *Address:* c/o European Parliament, rue Wiertz, 1047 Brussels, Belgium.

COLLIER, Lesley Faye, CBE; British ballet dancer; b 13 March 1947; d of Roy and Mavis Collier; twin s. *Education:* Royal Ballet School (London). *Career:* Joined Royal Ballet 1965, Prin Dancer 1972–95, Ballet Mistress 1995–, Répétiteur 2000–; has danced most of the prin roles in the repertoire; London Evening Standard Ballet Award 1987. *Address:* c/o Royal Ballet Company, Royal Opera House, Covent Garden, London WC2E 9DD, UK (Office).

COLLINS, Cardiss; American politician; b 24 Sept 1931, St Louis, MO; m George W. Collins (deceased); one s. *Education:* Northwestern Univ. *Career:* Sec Illinois Dept of Revenue, Accountant then Revenue Auditor; mem Congress (7th Illinois Dist) 1973–97, fmrly mem Govt Operations Cttee, Energy and Commerce Cttee, Oversight and Investigation Cttee, Select Cttee on Narcotics and Substance Abuse, Sub-cttee on Health and Finance; fmrly Majority Whip-at-Large, Chair Congressional Black Caucus; mem Nat Council of Negro Women, Black Women's Agenda. *Address:* 1110 Roundhouse Lane, Alexandria, VA 22314, USA.

COLLINS, Jackie; British writer and novelist; b 4 Oct 1941; d of Joseph William and Elsa (née Bessant) Collins. *Publications include:* The World is Full of Married Men 1968, The Stud 1969, Sunday Simmons and Charlie Brick 1971, Lovehead 1974, The World is Full of Divorced Women 1975, The Hollywood Zoo 1975, Lovers and Gamblers 1977, The Bitch 1979, Chances 1981, Hollywood Wives 1983, Lucky 1985, Hollywood Husbands 1986, Rock Star 1988, Lady Boss 1990, Love and Desire and Hate 1990, American Star 1993, Hollywood Kids 1994, Vendetta–Lucky's Revenge 1996, Thrill 1998, LA Connections (four-part serial novel) 1998, Dangerous Kiss 1999, Hollywood Wives: The New Generation 2001; *Screenplays include:* Yesterday's Hero, The World is Full of Married Men, The Stud; *TV mini-series include:* Hollywood Wives (ABC TV), Lucky Chances (NBC TV), Lady Boss (NBC TV). *Address:* c/o Simon and Schuster, 1230 Avenue of the Americas, New York, NY 10020, USA. *Fax:* (310) 278-6517.

COLLINS, Joan, OBE; British actress; b 23 May 1933, London; d of Joseph William and Elsa (née Bessant) Collins; m 1st Maxwell Reed (divorced); m 2nd Anthony Newley (divorced); one s one d; m 3rd Ronald S. Kass 1972 (divorced); one d; m 4th Peter Holm 1985 (divorced 1987). *Education:* Francis Holland School (London). *Career:* Stage debut 1946, Film debut 1952; Emmy Awards; Golden Globe Awards. *Plays include:* A Doll's House 1946, The Last of Mrs Cheyne, London 1979–80, Private Lives (London 1990, Broadway 1991), Love Letters 1999, USA tour 2000; *Films include:* I Believe in You 1952, Our Girl Friday 1953, The Good Die Young 1954, Land of the Pharaohs 1955, The Virgin Queen 1955, The Girl in the Red Velvet Swing 1955, The Opposite Sex 1956, Island in the Sun 1957, Sea Wife 1957, The Bravados 1958, Seven Thieves 1960, Road to Hong Kong 1962, Warning Shot 1966, The Executioner 1969, Quest for Love 1971, Revenge 1971, Alfie Darling 1974, The Stud 1979, The Bitch 1980, Sunburn 1980, The Big Sleep, The Nutcracker 1984, Decadence 1994, In the Bleak Midwinter 1995, Annie: A Royal Adventure 1995, Clandestine Marriage 1999, The Flintstones: Viva Rock Vegas 1999, Joseph and the Amazing Technicolor Dreamcoat 1999, These Old Broads 2000, Ozzie 2001; *TV appearances include:* Series: The Moneychangers 1976, Dynasty 1981–89, The Cartier Affair 1985, Sins 1986, Monte Carlo 1986, Tonight at 8.30 1991, Pacific Palisades (serial) 1998, Roseanne 1998, Will and Grace (USA) 2000; Films: Tales of the Unexpected 1977, Neck 1983, Georgy Porgy 1983, Cartier Affair 1985, The Making of a Male Model, Her Life as a Man, Paper Dolls, The Wild Women of Chastity, Gulch, Drive Hard Drive Fast, Hart to Hart 1995; *Publications:* Past Imperfect 1978, The Joan Collins Beauty Book 1980, Katy, A Fight for Life 1982, Prime Time 1988, Love, Desire, Hate 1990, My Secrets 1994, Too Damn Famous 1995, Second Act 1996, My Friends' Secrets 1999, Star Quality 2001. *Leisure interests:* cinema, antiques, reading, collecting. *Address:* c/o Paul Keylock, 16 Bulbecks Walk, S Woodham Ferrers, Essex CM3 5ZN, UK. *Telephone:* (1245) 328367; *Fax:* (1245) 328625; *E-mail:* pkeylock@aol.com; *Internet:* joancollins.net.

COLLINS, Judy Marjorie; American singer and songwriter; b 1 May 1939, Seattle; d of Charles T. and Marjorie Collins; m Peter A. Taylor 1958 (divorced); one s. *Career:* Trained as a classical pianist; began folk singing career in clubs in Cen City and Denver 1959; full-time career at Gate of Horn Club, Chicago and Gerde's Club (NY); signed to Elektra Records 1961; has performed concerts at major concert halls around the world; numerous radio and TV appearances; Grammy Award 1968; Silver Medal, Atlanta Film Festival; Blue Ribbon Award, American Film Festival. *Albums include:* Bread & Roses, Colors of the Day, So Early in the Spring, Hard Times for Lovers 1979, Running for my Life 1980, Trust Your Heart 1987, Judy Sings Dylan 1993, Live at Newport 1994, Forever 1997, Both Sides Now 1998; *Publication:* Trust Your Heart (autobiog) 1987. *Address:* c/o Charles Rothschild Productions, 330 E 48th St, New York, NY 10017, USA.

COLLINS, Martha Layne, BS; American politician; b 7 Dec 1936, Shelby Co, KY; d of Everett Larkin and Mary Lorena (Taylor) Hall; m Bill Collins 1959; one s one d. *Education:* Lindenwood Coll and Univ of Kentucky. *Career:* Fmr high school teacher; Clerk Court of Appeals 1975, then Clerk of Supreme Court, KY; fmr Lieut Gov State of Kentucky, Gov 1983–87; Chair Nat Gov's Task Force on Drug and Substance Abuse 1986; Exec-in-Residence Univ of Louisville, School of Business 1988–; Pres Martha Layne Collins & Assocs 1988–; Pres St Catherine Coll, KY 1990–; mem Woodford Co (KY) Democratic Exec Cttee, Democratic Nat Cttee 1972–76, Credentials Cttee, Democratic Nat Cttee, Vice-Presidential Selection Process Comm, Kentucky Democratic Cen Exec Cttee; Sec Kentucky Democratic Party. *Address:* Office of the President, St Catherine College, KY 40061, USA (Office).

COLLINS, Pauline; British actress; b 3 Sept 1940, Exmouth, Devon; d of William Henry Collins and Mary Honora Callanan; m John Alderton; two s one d. *Education:* Cen School of Speech and Drama (London). *Career:* Stage debut 1962. *Plays include:* A Gazelle in Park Lane 1962, Passion Flower Hotel, The Erpingham Camp, The Happy Apple, The Importance of Being Earnest, The Night I Chased the Women with an Eel, Come as You Are, Judies, Engaged, Confusions, Romantic Comedy, Woman in Mind, Shirley Valentine (Olivier Award for Best Actress—London, Tony, Drama Desk and Outer Critics' Circle Awards—New York), Shades 1992; *Films include:* Secrets of a Windmill Girl, Shirley Valentine 1989, City of Joy 1992, My Mother's Courage 1997, Paradise Road 1997; *TV appearances include:* Upstairs, Downstairs, Thomas and Sarah, No—Honestly, Tales of the Unexpected, Knockback, Tropical Moon over Dorking, Forever Green, The Ambassador 1998; *Publication:* Letter to Louise 1992. *Address:* c/o James Sharkey Associates, 15 Golden Square, London W1R 3AG, UK.

COLOMBO SVEVO, Maria Paola; Italian politician; b 21 Jan 1942, Rho. *Career:* fmrly MEP (EPP, Partito Popolare Italiano), mem Cttee on Civil Liberties and Internal Affairs, Cttee on Women's Rights, Del for Relations with the Countries of S Asia and the S Asia Asscn for Regional Co-operation (SAARC). *Address:* c/o European Parliament, rue Wiertz, 1047 Brussels, Belgium.

COLSON, Andrée; French violinist; b 5 Sept 1924, Paris; d of Georges and Blanche Colson; m Charles Meyer 1946; one s one d (deceased). *Education:* Conservatoire Nat Supérieur de Musique (Paris) and Acad Chigiana (Sienna, Italy). *Career:* Founder chamber orchestra Ensemble Instrumental Andrée Colson 1955 (became Nouvel ensemble instrumental Andrée Colson—Vallée des rois 1989), Conductor and First Violin at concerts world-wide; f Disques Vernou 1972, Journées Musicales Internationales de Langeais 1975, also formed recording

studio; has made numerous recordings; Pres Asscn pour la Sauvegarde de la Région de Langeais; Chevalier de la Légion d'Honneur 1994; Officier des Arts et des Lettres 1987; Grands Prix du Disque 1972, 1977. *Leisure interests:* horse-riding, hunting. *Address:* Domaine de Vernou, BP 22, 37130 Langeais, France. *Telephone:* (2) 47-96-80-59; *Fax:* (2) 47-96-64-97; *E-mail:* andree.colson@wanadoo.fr; *Internet:* www.multimania.com/disquesvernou; perso.wanadoo.fr/andreecolson.

COLSON, Elizabeth Florence, PH D; American anthropologist; b 15 June 1917, Hewitt, MN; d of Louis Henry and Metta Damon Colson. *Education:* Wadena Public High School, Univ of Minnesota and Radcliffe Coll. *Career:* Sr Research Officer Rhodes-Livingstone Inst 1946–47, Dir 1948–51; Sr Lecturer Univ of Manchester, UK 1951–53; Assoc Prof Goucher Coll 1954–55; Assoc Prof and Research Assoc Boston Univ 1955–59; Prof Brandeis Univ 1959–63, Univ of California at Berkeley 1964–84, Prof Emer 1984–; Visiting Prof Univ of Zambia 1987; Field Research for Nature America, CA and WA 1939–42, in Zambia 1946; mem NAS, AAAS; Fellow Center for Advanced Study in the Behavioral Sciences, Stanford Univ; Fairchild Fellow California Inst of Tech; Hon Fellow Royal Anthropological Soc (UK); Hon D SC (Brown) 1978, (Rochester) 1985, (Univ of Zambia); Rivers Memorial Medal; Distinguished Lecture, American Anthropological Asscn 1975; Faculty Research Lecture Univ of California, Berkeley 1983; Malinowski Distinguished Lecture, Soc for Applied Anthropology 1984. *Publications:* Seven Tribes of British Central Africa, 1951, The Makah 1953, Marriage and the Family among the Plateau Tonga 1958, Social Organization of the Gwembe Tonga 1962, Social Consequences of Resettlement 1971, Tradition and Contract 1974, Autobiographies of Three Pomo Women 1974; Secondary Education and the Formation of an Elite (jtly) 1980, Voluntary Efforts in Decentralized Management (jtly) 1983, People in Upheaval (jr ed) 1987, For Prayer and Profit (jtly) 1988, The History of Nampeyo 1991. *Leisure interests:* walking, reading. *Address:* Dept of Anthropology, University of California, Berkeley, CA 94720, USA (Office); 840 Arlington Blvd, El Cerrito, CA 94530, USA (Home). *Telephone:* (510) 642-3391 (Office); (510) 526-3743 (Home); *E-mail:* colson@sscl.berkeley.edu.

COLVIN, Marie, BA; American journalist; b New York; d of William Joseph and Rosemarie Colvin; m Patrick Bishop (divorced 1995); m 2nd Juan Carlos Gumucio (divorced 2001). *Education:* Yale Univ. *Career:* Journalist United Press Int, New York 1980, Foreign Desk Editor, Washington 1982, Paris Bureau Chief 1984; Middle East Corresp The Sunday Times (UK) 1986–96, Foreign Affairs Corresp 1996–; Foreign Reporter of the Year, British Press Awards 2000; Journalist of the Year, Foreign Corresps Asscn, London, UK 2000; Courage in Journalism Award, Int Women's Media Foundation, USA 2000. *Address:* c/o Sunday Times Foreign Desk, 1 Pennington St, London E1 9XW, UK. *Telephone:* (20) 7782-5692; *Fax:* (20) 7782-5050; *E-mail:* mariecolvin@ hotmail.com.

COLWELL, Rita Rossi, PH D; American professor of microbiology; b 23 Nov 1934, Beverly, MA; d of Louis and Louise (née DiPalma) Rossi; m Jack H. Colwell 1956; two d. *Education:* Purdue Univ and Univ of Washington. *Career:* Research Asst Univ of Wash 1957–58, Asst Prof Georgetown Univ 1964–66, Assoc Prof 1966–72; Prof Dept of Microbiology, Univ of Maryland 1972–, Vice Pres of Academic Affairs 1983–87, Founding Dir Centre for Marine Biotech 1987–91, Maryland Biotech Inst 1987–91, Pres Maryland Biotech Inst 1991–98; Dir Nat Science Foundation 1998–; Extraordinary Prof Catholic Univ, Valparaíso, Chile 1976; Hon Prof Univ of Queensland, Australia 1988; nine hon doctorates including Hon DS (Heriot-Watt) 1987, (Hood Coll) 1991; numerous awards include Gold Medal, Canterbury (UK) 1990 Purkinje Gold Award (Czechoslovakia) 1991, MD Pate, Civic Award 1991, Barnard Medal, Colorado Univ 1996. *Publications:* Vibrios in the Environment 1984, Biomolecular Data: Research in Transition 1988; 18 books, over 500 articles in journals, book chapters, abstracts; Film: Invisible Seas 1976. *Leisure interests:* gardening, sailing. *Address:* National Science Foundation, 4201 Wilson Blvd, Suite 1205, Arlington, VA 22230, USA (Office); 5010 River Hill Rd, Bethesda, MD 20816, USA (Home). *Telephone:* (703) 306-1000 (Office); (301) 229-5129 (Home); *Fax:* (703) 306-0109 (Home); *E-mail:* rcolwell@nsf.gov (Office); *Internet:* www.nsf.gov (Office).

COMANECI, Nadia; Romanian former gymnast; b 12 Nov 1961, Oneşti, Bacău Co; m Bart Connor 1996. *Education:* Coll of Physical Educ and Sports (Bucharest). *Career:* Overall European Champion (Skien, Norway) 1975, (Prague) 1977, (Copenhagen) 1979; Overall Olympic Champion, (Montréal, Canada) 1976; Overall World Univ Games Champion (Bucharest) 1981; Gold Medals European Championships (Skien) 1975 (vault, asymmetric bars, beam), (Prague) 1977 (bars), (Copenhagen) 1979 (vault, floor exercises), World Championships (Strasbourg, France) 1978 (beam), (Fort Worth, USA) 1979 (team title), Olympic Games, (Montréal) 1976 (bars, beam), (Moscow, now Russian Fed) 1980 (beam, floor), World Cup, (Tokyo) 1979 (vault, floor), World Univ Games (Bucharest) 1981 (vault, bars, floor and team title); Silver Medals European Championships (Skien) 1975 (floor), (Prague) 1977 (vault), World Championships (Strasbourg) 1978 (vault), Olympic Games (Montréal) 1976 (team title), (Moscow) 1980 (individual all-round, team title), World Cup (Tokyo) 1979 (beam); Bronze Medal Olympic Games (Montréal) 1976 (floor); retd 1984; Jr Team Coach 1984–89; granted refugee status in USA 1989; with Bart Connor Gymnastics Acad; promotes commercial products, dancer, gymnastics entertainer; Sportswoman of the Century Prize, Athletic Sports Category 1999.

COMET, Catherine; American conductor; m Michael Aiken; one d. *Education:* Juilliard School of Music. *Career:* Conductor Univ of Wisconsin Symphony and Chamber Orchestras, St Louis (MO) Symphony Orchestra 1981–84; Music Dir St Louis Youth Orchestra, Grand Rapids (MI) Symphony Orchestra 1986–90, 1991, American Symphony Orchestra (NY) 1990–91; guest conductor to several orchestras including San Diego Symphony Orchestra 1998; First Prize Int Young Conductors' Competition (France) 1966; Award at Dmitri Mitroupolos Int Contest 1968. *Address:* c/o Grand Rapids Symphony Orchestra, 220 Lyon St, NW, Suite 415, Grand Rapids, MI 49503, USA.

CONDORI, Ana María; Bolivian campaigner for indigenous rights; b 1953. *Career:* Aymara Indian; worked as maid, later became involved in unions (one of first indigenous women to do so); mem staff co-operative financed by UN NGO, aimed at encouraging women to become more involved in indigenous people's rights; instigated creation of cocoa co-operative El Ceibo, Alto Beni; assisted in launch of UN campaign 'Cultural Diversity, Equal Rights' 1996. *Publication:* Nayan Uñatatavi (My Awakening).

CONLEY, Rosemary Jean Neil; British writer and business executive; b 19 Dec 1946, Leicester; d of Oswald Neil and the late Edith Cicelia Weston; m 1st Philip Conley 1968 (divorced 1983); m 2nd Michael John Rimmington 1986; one d. *Education:* Bushloe High School and Goddards Secretarial Coll. *Career:* Founder Slimming and Good Grooming Club (SAGG) 1972–80; Man Dir Successful Slimming Clubs 1980–85; presented own series BBC 1 TV; Partner Rosemary Conley Enterprises from 1989; Trustee Head Start Trust 1992; Founder Rosemary Conley Diet and Fitness Magazine; Golden Arrow Award 1989. *Publications include:* Rosemary Conley's Hip and Thigh Diet 1988, Rosemary Conley's Complete Hip and Thigh Diet 1989, Hip and Thigh Diet and Cookbook 1989, Rosemary Conley's Inch Loss Plan 1990, Metabolism Booster Diet 1991, Whole Body Programme 1991, Low Fat Cookbook, Low Fat Cookbook 2 2000; *Videos include:* Hip and Thigh Diet and Exercise, Inch Loss Plan Hip and Thigh Cookbook 1990, Whole Body Programme, 7 Day Workout 1991, Whole Body Programme 2, Top to Toe Collection 1992, Fat Attack 2000; *TV series:* Eat Yourself Slim 2001. *Leisure interests:* gardening, flower-arranging, keeping fit. *Telephone:* (1533) 375285; *Fax:* (1533) 376162.

CONNELL, Elizabeth, B MUS; Irish opera singer; b 22 Oct 1946, South Africa; d of the late (Gordon) Raymond and (Maud) Elizabeth (née Scott) Connell. *Education:* Univ of the Witwatersrand, Johannesburg Coll of Educ and London Opera Centre. *Career:* Debut at Wexford Festival, Ireland 1972; with Australian Opera 1973–75, English Nat Opera 1975–80; appearances at Royal Opera House (Covent Garden, London), Bayreuth Festival (Germany), Salzburg Festival (Austria), Metropolitan Opera (New York), Vienna State Opera, Glyndebourne Festival (UK), La Scala (Milan, Italy), Hamburg and Cologne (Germany), Sydney (Australia); tour of Japan 1992; sang full range of dramatic mezzo repertoire until 1983 when moved into dramatic

soprano field; Maggie Teyte Prize 1972. *Operas include:* Katya Kabanova, I Lombardi, Lohengrin, Idomeneo, La Clemenza di Tito, Tannhäuser; *Recordings:* Mahler's Eighth Symphony, Schoenberg's Gurrelieder, Schubert: Lieder (jtly). *Leisure interests:* reading, theatre, concerts, cooking, embroidery, writing and composing. *Address:* c/o IMG Artists, Media House, 3 Burlington Lane, London W4 2TH, UK (Office). *Telephone:* (20) 8233-5800 (Office); *Fax:* (20) 8233-5801 (Office); *E-mail:* jrobinson@imgworld.com.

CONNOR-CRAWFORD, Geraldine Roxanne; British musician; b 22 March 1952, London; d of Edric Eselus and Pearl Cynthia (née Nunez) Connor; m Thorma Anthony Crawford 1989. *Education:* Diego Martin Secondary School (Trinidad), Camden School for Girls (London), Valsayn Teacher Training Coll (Trinidad) and Royal Coll of Music (London). *Career:* Head Dept of Music, Queen's Royal Coll, Trinidad and Tobago 1976–84; Educ Supervisor and Registrar Brent Black Music Co-operative, London 1984–87; apptd Chair Steelband Asscn of Great Britain 1987, apptd Lecturer in Extra-Mural Musical Studies Univ of the W Indies 1987; apptd Dir Nat Steelband Music Co Ltd 1988; Lecturer and Co-ordinator Indo/Afro-Caribbean Music Tutorials, Best Village Folk Programme 1989; apptd Sr Lecturer of Afro-Caribbean Music Studies, City of Leeds Coll of Music 1990; Presenter Trinidad and Tobago TV Co Ltd, TV series Learn to Make Music 1984; Consultant to Birmingham Task Force, Music Survey (UK) 1987, CARIFESTA V 1989; has produced and arranged numerous albums, f several groups and directed many tours. *Recordings with:* Jimmy Cliff, Wilma Reading, Judith Durham, Tom Jones, Gene Lawrence, Sound Revolution, Reggae Sunsplash, Milly Jackson; *Musicals composed/directed include:* O Babylon 1988, From Coffee Beans to Disinfectant 1986, Ah, Pan for Christmas 1983, Ebony Eyes 1991, A Jamaican Airman Foresees His Death 1991, Hiphopera 1991, The Man Who Lit Up The World 1991, Afro-Goth 1991, Pot Pourri 1991. *Address:* Oakland Cottage, 37 Curly Hill, Ilkley, W Yorkshire LS29 0AY, UK; POB 3084 St James Post Office, St James, Port of Spain, Trinidad and Tobago. *Telephone:* (1943) 817015 (UK); 6324367 (Trinidad and Tobago).

CONNORS, Jane Frances, BA, LL M; Australian lecturer in law; b 24 March 1953, Sydney; d of John and Patricia Connors; two d. *Education:* St Clare's Coll (Canberra) and ANU. *Career:* Apptd Lecturer in Law School of Oriental and African Studies, Univ of London 1983; specialist in comparative domestic law relating to women and children, human rights law and violence against women. *Publication:* Violence Against Women in the Family 1989. *Leisure interests:* travel, politics, voluntary work with women and refugees. *Address:* c/o University of London, School of Oriental and African Studies, Dept of Law, Thornaugh St, Russell Square, London WC1H 0XG, UK. *Telephone:* (20) 7637-2388; *Fax:* (20) 7436-3844.

CONRAN, Shirley Ida, RSA; British designer and writer; b 21 Sept 1932; d of Ida and W. Thirlby Pearce; m 1st Sir Terence Conran (divorced 1962); two s; m 2nd John Stephenson; m 3rd. *Education:* St Paul's Girls' School (London), La Chatelainie (Switzerland) and Portsmouth Art Coll. *Career:* Press Officer Asprey Suchy 1953–54; Publicity Adviser to Conran Group Cos 1955, organized and designed several kitchen and design exhibitions; Design and Sales Dir Conran Fabrics Ltd 1957; started Textile Design Studio 1958; Home Ed Daily Mail 1962, Women's Ed 1968; Women's Ed The Observer Colour Magazine 1964, Women's Ed The Observer 1969; contrib to Woman's Own 1964; Columnist Vanity Fair 1970–71, Over 21 1972; numerous TV and radio appearances; Author of the Year (Variety Club of GB) 1984. *Publications include:* Superwoman 1974, Superwoman Yearbook 1975, Superwoman in Action 1977, Futures 1979, Lace 1982, The Magic Garden 1983, Lace 2 1984, Savages (novel)1987, Down with Superwoman 1990, The Amazing Umbrella Shop 1990, Crimson 1992, Tiger Eyes 1994, The Revenge of Mimi Quinn 1998. *Leisure interests:* long-distance swimming, yoga, collecting ethnographic sculptures, modern paintings. *Address:* c/o 39 ave Princess Grace, Monte Carlo, MC 98000, Monaco.

CONSTANT, Paule Michèle, D ÈS L; French writer and academic; b 25 Jan 1944, Gan; d of Yves and Monique (née Tauzin) Constant; m August Bourgeade 1968; one d one s. *Education:* Univs of Bordeaux, Pau and Paris (Sorbonne). *Career:* Asst Lecturer in French Literature Univ

Nat de Côte d'Ivoire, Abidjan 1968–75; Sr Asst 1976–85; Sr Lecturer Inst d'Etudes Françaises pour Etudiants Etrangers, Univ of Aix-Marseille III 1986–95; Prof Aix-Marseilles III Univ 1995–; diarist, Revue des Deux Mondes, Paris; mem Acad des Lettres Pyrénéennes; Chevalier de l'Ordre de l'Educ Nat (Côte d'Ivoire); Prix Valéry Larbaud 1980, Grand Prix de l'Essai, Acad Française 1987, Prix François Mauriac 1990, Grand Prix du Roman, Acad Française 1990, Prix Goncourt 1998. *Publications:* Ourégano (Prix Valéry Larbaud) 1980, Propriété privée 1981, Balta 1983, Un monde à l'usage des demoiselles (Grand Prix de l'Essai, Acad Française) 1987, White Spirit (Prix François Mauriac, Prix du Sud Jean Baumel, Grand Prix du Roman, Acad Française) 1990, Le grand Ghâpal (Prix Gabrielle d'Estrées) 1991, La fille du Gobernator 1994, Confidence pour confidence 1998. *Leisure interests:* swimming, collecting children's books and educational tracts from the 18th and 19th centuries. *Address:* Institut d'études françaises pour étudiants étrangers, 23 rue Gaston de Saporta, 13100 Aix-en-Provence, France (Office); 29 rue Cardinale, 13100 Aix-en-Provence, France. *Telephone:* (4) 42-38-45-08.

COOK, Beryl Frances, OBE; British artist; b 10 Sept 1926, Egham, Surrey; d of Adrian S. Barton-Lansley and Ella M. Farmer-Francis; m John V. Cook 1948; one s. *Education:* Kendrick Girls School (Reading). *Career:* Exhibitions include Plymouth Arts Centre 1975, Whitechapel Art Gallery (London) 1976, Walker Art Gallery (Liverpool) 1979, Grafton Art (London) 1979, Musée de Cahors (France) 1981, Chelmsford Museum 1982, Glasgow 1992, New York 1992, Plymouth Arts Centre (20th anniversary exhibition) 1995; retrospective travelling exhibitions in Plymouth, Stoke-on-Trent, Preston, Nottingham, Edinburgh 1988–89, Drumcroon Arts Centre, Wigan 1994, Blackpool, Durham, Hartlepool, Stoke-on-Trent 1998; Kate Greenaway Medal 1980. *Publications include:* The Works 1978, Private View 1980, Only Seven Years and a Day (illustrations) 1980, One Man Show 1981, Bertie and the Big Red Ball (illustrations) 1982, My Granny (illustrations) 1983, Beryl Cook's New York 1985, Beryl Cook's London 1988, Mr Norris Changes Trains (illustrations) 1990, Bouncers 1991, The Loved One (illustrations) 1993, Happy Days 1995, Folio Soc's edn of The Prime of Miss Jean Brodie (illustrations) 1998, Happy Days 1999, Cruising 1999, Bumper Book 2000. *Leisure interests:* reading, travel. *Address:* The Coach House, 1A Camp Rd, Clifton, Bristol BS8 3LW, UK.

COOK, Frances D., MBA; American diplomatist; b 7 Sept 1945, Charleston, WV; d of Nash and Vivian Cook. *Education:* Mary Washington Coll and Harvard Univ. *Career:* Officer Dept of State, Washington, DC 1967, Personnel Officer for Africa 1975–77, Dir Office of Public Affairs, African Bureau 1978–80, Deputy Asst Sec of State 1986–87, Dir Office of W African Affairs 1987–89, US Co-ordinator for Sudan 1993, Deputy Asst Sec of State 1993; Asst to Amb, France 1968–69; mem USA Del to Paris Peace talks on Vietnam 1970–71; Cultural Affairs Officer, Australia 1971–73, Senegal (also First Sec) 1973–75; Amb to Burundi 1980–83, to Cameroon 1989–93, to Oman 1996–99; mem Policy Council Una Chapman Cox Foundation, Council on Foreign Relations; numerous awards from Dept of State. *Leisure interests:* tennis, museums, antiques, reading. *Address:* 767 NW 18th St, Homestead, FL 33030, USA.

COOK, Rebecca Johnson, MPA, JD; American professor of law; b 2 Dec 1946, Bennington, VT; d of John R. and Helen C. (née Vanderbilt) Cook; m Bernard M. Dickens 1987. *Education:* Columbia (NY), Tufts (MA) and Harvard (MA) Univs. *Career:* Asst Prof Columbia Univ, School of Public Health, NY 1983–87; Asst Prof (Research) Univ of Toronto, Faculties of Law and Medicine, Canada, Assoc Prof (Research) 1990–, Prof 1995–, Dir Int Human Rights Programme, Faculty of Law 1987–98; Dir Law Programme, Int Planned Parenthood Fed 1973–78; Co-Dir Int Programme on Reproductive and Sexual Health Law; mem Expert Advisory Panel on Human Reproduction, WHO 1987–; Ethical and Legal Issues Co-Ed International Journal of Gynecology and Obstetrics; mem Ed Advisory Bd Human Rights Quarterly, Reproductive Health Matters, Third World Legal Studies Journal; Fellow Royal Soc of Canada; Int Fed of Gynaecologists and Obstetricians Certificate of Recognition for Outstanding Contrib to Women's Health; Ludwik and Estelle Jus Memorial Human Rights Prize. *Publications:* Women's Health and Human Rights 1984, Human Rights of Women: National and International Perspectives (ed) 1994, Considerations for Formulating Reproductive Health Laws (co-author,

2nd edn) 2000; numerous contribs to professional journals and chapters in books. *Leisure interest:* gardening. *Address:* University of Toronto, Faculty of Law, 84 Queen's Park, Toronto, ON M5S 2C5, Canada. *Telephone:* (416) 978-4446; *Fax:* (416) 978-7899; *E-mail:* rebecca .cook@law.utoronto.ca.

COOKE, Jean Esme Oregon, RA; British artist; b 18 Feb 1927, Lewisham, London; d of Arthur Oregon Cooke and Dorothy E. Cranefield; m John Bratby 1953 (divorced 1977, died 1992); three s one d. *Education:* Blackheath High School, Cen School of Arts and Crafts, City and Guilds School and Goldsmiths' Coll School of Art and Royal Coll of Art. *Career:* Pottery workshop 1950–53; Lecturer in Painting, Royal Coll of Art 1964–74; mem Council Royal Acad 1983–85, 1992–94, Academic Bd Blackheath School of Art 1986–88, Tertiary Educ Bd (Greenwich, London) 1984–86; Gov Cen School of Art and Design 1984–86; Life Pres Friends of Woodlands Art Gallery 1990–, Pres Blackheath Art Soc 1995–; numerous one-woman exhibitions in UK 1963–, works exhibited annually at Royal Acad and in other group exhibitions. *Publications:* Contemporary British Artists, The Artist 1980, The Artist's Garden 1989, Seeing Ourselves: Women's Self Portraits 1998; *TV film:* Portrait of John Bratby 1978. *Leisure interests:* ungardening, talking, shouting, walking along the beach, reading. *Address:* 7 Hardy Rd, Blackheath, London SE3 7NS, UK. *Telephone:* (20) 8858-6288.

COOLIDGE, Martha; American film director; b 17 Aug 1946, New Haven, CT; m Michael Backes. *Education:* Rhode Island School of Design, School of Visual Arts and Columbia Univ (New York). *Career:* Dir of films, documentaries and children's TV programmes; Co-Founder Asscn of Independent Video and Filmmakers Inc; has won numerous prizes for work. *Documentaries include:* Passing Quietly Through, David: Off and On, Old Fashioned Woman (CINE Golden Eagle Award); *Films include:* Not a Pretty Picture (Blue Ribbon Award, American Film Festival), Bimbo (short), The City Girl, Valley Girl, Joy of Sex, Real Genius, Plain Clothes, The Friendly (short), That's Adequate, Rope Dancing, Rambling Rose 1991, Lost in Yonkers, Angie, Three Wishes, Out to Sea 1997; *TV includes:* Magic Tom (for children) 1968, The Twilight Zone, Sledge Hammer, House and Home, Roughhouse, Trenchcoat in Paradise (film), Bare Essentials (film), Crazy in Love 1992, Introducing Dorothy Dandridge 1999, If These Walls Could Talk II 2000, The Ponder Heart 2000. *Leisure interest:* breeding Paso-Fino horses. *Address:* c/o Beverly Magid Guttman Assocs, 118 S Beverly Drive, Suite 201, Beverly Hills, CA 90212, USA.

COOPER, Imogen; British concert pianist; b 28 Aug 1949, London; d of the late Martin Du Pré Cooper and of Mary Stewart; m John Batten 1982. *Education:* Paris Conservatoire and privately under Alfred Brendel (Vienna). *Career:* TV debut 1975; first British pianist and first woman pianist in South Bank Piano series, Queen Elizabeth Hall (London); regular broadcasts for BBC; appearances at Promenade Concerts (London) and in Australia, Austria, France, Germany, Iceland, Japan, Netherlands, Portugal, S America, Spain, Scandinavia, USA, New Zealand; gives solo recitals worldwide; Premier Prix (Paris Conservatoire) 1967; Mozart Memorial Prize 1969; Hon MUS D (Exon) 1999. *Recordings include:* Schubert's Schwannengesang, Winterreise, Die Schöne Mullerin and Schumann's Heine Lieder and Kerner Lieder (with Wolfgang Holzmair), Mozart's Concerto for two and three pianos (with Alfred Brendel, Acad of St Martin in the Fields, Neville Marriner) 1985, Schubert four-hand piano music with Anne Queffélec and 'The Last Six Years' of Schubert's piano music 1986–90. *Leisure interests:* visual arts, reading, walking, architecture. *Address:* c/o Van Walsum Management Ltd, 26 Wadham Rd, London SW15 2LR; 3 Addison Bridge Place, London W14 8XP, UK (Office). *Telephone:* (20) 7371-4343; *Fax:* (20) 7371-4344.

COOPER, Jilly; British writer; b 21 Feb 1937, Essex; d of Brig W. B. Sallitt and Mary Elaine Whincup; m Leo Cooper 1961; one s one d. *Education:* Godolphin School (Salisbury). *Career:* Fmrly reporter Middx Ind 1957–59; account exec; copy writer; publr's reader; receptionist; puppy fat model; switchboard wrecker; temp typist 1959–69; Columnist Sunday Times 1969–82, Mail on Sunday 1982–87. *Publications include:* How to Stay Married 1969, How to Survive from Nine to Five 1970, Jolly Super 1971, Men and Super Men 1972, Jolly Super Too 1973, Women and Super Women 1974, Jolly Superlative 1975, Emily 1975,

Bella 1976, Harriet 1976, Octavia 1977, Super Jilly 1977, Prudence 1978, Imogen 1978, Class 1979, The British in Love 1980, Violets and Vinegar (jtly) 1980, Supercooper 1980, Love and Other Heart Aches (short stories) 1981, Intelligent and Loyal 1981, Jolly Marsupial (jtly) 1982, Animals in War 1983, The Common Years 1984, Leo and Jilly Cooper on Cricket 1985, Hot Foot to Zabrieskie Point, the Unipart Calendar Book (with Patrick Lichfield) 1985, Riders 1985, How to Survive Christmas 1986, Leo and Jilly Cooper on Horse Mania 1986, Turn Right at the Spotted Dog 1987, Rivals 1988, Angels Rush In 1990, Polo 1991, The Man Who Made Husbands Jealous, Araminta's Wedding 1993, Apassionata 1995, How to Survive Christmas 1996, Score! 1999; Children's fiction: Little Mabel 1980, Little Mabel's Great Escape 1981, Little Mabel Wins 1982, Little Mabel Saves the Day 1985. *Leisure interests:* merry-making, music, wild flowers, mongrels. *Address:* c/o Vivienne Schuster, Curtis Brown, 4th Floor, Haymarket House, 28-29 Haymarket, London SW1Y 4SP, UK (Office). *Telephone:* (20) 7396-6600 (Office); *Fax:* (20) 7396-0110 (Office).

COPE, Wendy Mary, MA FRSL; British writer; b 21 July 1945, Erith; d of Fred Stanley and Alice Mary (née Hand) Cope. *Education:* Farringtons School, St Hilda's Coll (Oxford) and Westminster Coll of Educ (Oxford). *Career:* Primary school teacher, London 1967–86; professional writer 1986–; Hon D LITT (Southampton), Cholmondeley Award for Poetry 1987, Michael Braude Award, American Acad of Arts and Letters 1995. *Publications:* Making Cocoa for Kingsley Amis (poetry) 1986, Serious Concerns (poetry) 1992, If I Don't Know (poetry) 2001. *Leisure interest:* music. *Address:* c/o Faber and Faber, 3 Queen Square, London WC1N 3AU, UK. *Telephone:* (20) 7465-0045.

COPPS, Hon Sheila Maureen, PC, BA; Canadian politician; b 27 Nov 1952, Hamilton, ON; d of Victor Kennedy and Geraldine Florence (Guthro) Copps; one d. *Education:* Univs of Western Ontario and Rouen (France) and McMaster Univ. *Career:* Journalist, Ottawa Citizen 1974–76, Hamilton Spectator 1977; Constituency Asst to Leader Liberal Party, ON 1977–81; mem Parl of ON for Hamilton Centre 1981–84; mem House of Commons (Parl) 1984–, Deputy Leader of Opposition 1991, Deputy Prime Minister 1993–97, Environment Minister 1993–96, Minister of Canadian Heritage 1996–. *Publication:* Nobody's Baby 1986. *Address:* House of Commons, Ottawa, ON K1A 0A6, Canada (Office); Ministry of Canadian Heritage, Immeuble Jules Léger, 25 rue Eddy, Hull, Québec K1A 1K5, Canada (Office). *Telephone:* (819) 997-7788; *E-mail:* min_copps@pch.gc.ca (Office); *Internet:* www.pch.gc.ca (Office).

COQUERY-VIDROVITCH, Catherine Marion, D ÈS L; French professor of history; b 25 Nov 1935, Paris; d of Rémi and Marcelle Vidrovitch; m Michel Coquery 1958; three d one s. *Education:* Univ of Paris and Ecole Normale Supérieure de Jeunes Filles. *Career:* Asst Ecole Pratique des Hautes Etudes 1968–70; Sr Asst Univ of Paris VII 1971, Sr Lecturer 1972, Prof 1975–, Dir Lab for Third-World Studies 1977–; Co-Dir Research Dept on Third-World and Africa (CNRS) 1983–94; Assoc Prof State Univ of New York, USA 1980–; Visiting Lecturer Univs of Montréal and Laval (Canada) 1968, Senegal 1971–95, Chad 1972, Congo 1973, 1980, Gabon 1975, Burkina Faso 1977–78, 1984, Togo 1978–79, Niger 1980, 1988, Côte d'Ivoire 1983, 1995, Rwanda, Botswana, Zimbabwe, Zambia and Kenya 1985, Guinea, Madagascar 1988; Fellow W. Wilson Center for Int Scholars 1987, Shelby Cullom Davis Center, Univ of Princeton, USA 1992, Humanities Research Centre, Canberra 1995; mem Jt Cttee on African Studies, Social Science Research Council (USA) 1984–87, Int Cttee of Historical Science 2000, Int Conf of Historical Studies 2000–; Officier de la Légion d'Honneur; Africanist (ASA) Award, USA 1999. *Publications include:* La découverte de l'Afrique des origines au XVIIIème siècle (2nd edn) 1971, Brazza et la prise de possession du Congo 1883–86 1971, Le Congo au temps des grandes compagnies concessionnaires 1898–1930 1972, Afrique noire, permanences et ruptures (Prix d'Aumale, Acad des Sciences Morales et Politiques 1987) 1985 Histoire des ville d'Afrique noire des origines à la colonisation 1993, Les Africaines, histoire des femmes d'Afrique noire du XIXème au XXème siècle 1994, Femmes d'Afrique (ed) 1997, L'Afrique et les Africains au XIX siècle 1999; numerous contribs to books. *Leisure interests:* hiking, swimming, theatre. *Address:* 2 place Jussieu, 75005 Paris, Cedex 5, France. *Telephone:* (1) 43-35-06-98; *Fax:* (1) 44-27-79-87; *E-mail:* coqueryv@noos.fr.

CORBETT, Hon Marie, BA, LL B; Canadian judge; b 14 July 1943, Avondale, Newfoundland; m C. Alexander Squires 1977; two s. *Education:* McGill Univ, Univ of Toronto and Law Soc of Upper Canada. *Career:* Lawyer Toronto Legal Dept 1970–72; pvt practice 1972–74, 1980–86; mem Ontario Municipal Bd 1974–77; Counsel Royal Comm on the Status of Pensions 1977–80; QC 1982; Judge Dist Court of Ontario 1986–90, Ontario Court of Justice, Gen Div 1990–; Hon Solicitor Prov Council of Women 1983–86; Women of Distinction Special Award, YWCA 1993. *Publications include:* Equal Pension Benefits for Men and Women (jtly) 1985, Pension Benefits Standards Act 1985 1986; numerous contribs to legal journals. *Leisure interests:* golf, skiing. *Address:* Court House, 361 University Ave, Toronto, ON M5G 1T3, Canada. *Telephone:* (416) 327-5417 (Home); (416) 327-5284 (Office).

CORCIULO, Maria Sofia; Italian university professor; b 8 Aug 1941, Squinzano, Lecce. *Education:* Lycée Classique (Lecce). *Career:* Asst Univ of Camerino, then Assoc Prof, now Prof; Vice-Pres Int Comm for the History of Representative and Parl Insts 1985; currently Prof Univ of Rome 'La Sapienza'; mem Arcadia Acad. *Publications include:* La Nascita del Regime Parlamentare in Franca – Prima Restaurazione 1977, Istituzioni Parlamentari in Francia 1979, Dall'Amministrazione alla Costituzione 1992. *Leisure interests:* literature, classical music, films, walking. *Address:* International Commission for the History of Representative and Parliamentary Institutions, via A. Baldassarri 25, 00139 Rome, Italy. *Telephone:* (6) 8863765.

CORDAY, Barbara; American broadcasting executive; b 15 Oct 1944, New York; m Barney Rosenzweig (divorced). *Career:* Publicist, then writer for TV; Vice-Pres for Comedy Series Devt ABC TV 1982–84; Pres Columbia Pictures TV 1984–87; Exec Vice-Pres Primetime Programmes CBS Entertainment 1988–; Co-Creator (with Barney Rosenzweig) of Cagney and Lacey TV series.

CORDERO DE PERALTA, Isabel, BFA; Costa Rican sculptor, painter, decorator and horticulturalist; b 22 July 1930; m 1952. *Education:* Young Ladies' High School, Sacred Heart Coll and Univ of Costa Rica. *Career:* Founder La Guaria Cultural Club and Gardening Club of Greece 1956–64; Head of Public Relations Orchidology Asscn and Greek Women's Club 1980–84; currently Asst Man Juanito Mora Ltd and Lotificación Peralta; Treas Mexican Art and Cultural Inst and Inter-American Comm 1980–82, Professional Women of Costa Rica (also Pres) 1977–90; mem Educ Co-op Cttee and Victoria Garden Club 1953–54; produced training videos for women 1986–90; Aduardo Martina Literature Prize 1946; Artistic Design Award 1980. *Publication:* Bulletin of Diplomatic Association 1974–79. *Leisure interests:* ballet, fencing, folk dancing, gymnastics. *Address:* Condominio Saturno 432, San José 2000, Costa Rica. *Telephone:* 317472 (Home); 317171 (Office).

CORN, Wanda M., PH D; American professor of art history; b 13 Nov 1940, New Haven, CT; d of Keith M. and Lydia M. Jones; m Joseph J. Corn 1963. *Education:* New York Univ. *Career:* Lecturer Univ of California, Berkeley 1970, Visiting Asst Prof 1976; Lecturer Mills Coll, Oakland, CA 1970, Visiting Asst Prof 1971, Asst Prof 1972–77, Assoc Prof 1977–80; Assoc Prof Stanford Univ, CA 1980–89, Robert and Ruth Halperin Prof in Art History 1989–, Chair Dept of Art 1989–; Dir (acting) Stanford Museum, CA 1989–91; Anthony P. Meier Family Dir, Stanford Humanities Center 1992–95; Commr Nat Museum of American Art 1988–95; Fellow Ford Foundation 1966–70, Smithsonian Inst 1978–79, Woodrow Wilson Inst 1979–80, Stanford Humanities Center 1982–83; Regents Fellow Smithsonian Inst 1987; Grave Award 1974–75. *Publications include:* The Color of Mood, American Tonalism 1880–1910 1972, The Art of Andrew Wyeth 1973, Grant Wood: The Regionalist Vision 1983, The Great American Thing: Modern Art and American Identity 1915–35 1999; numerous contribs to professional journals. *Address:* Stanford University, Dept of Art and Art History, Stanford, CA 94305-2018, USA. *Telephone:* (650) 723-6282.

CORNEA, Doina; Romanian philologist, writer and human rights activist; b 30 May 1929, Brasov; m; one d. *Education:* Faculty of Philology, Univ of Cluj. *Career:* Lecturer in French Literature Univ of Cluj; dismissed for writing an open letter to Those Who Have Ceased to Think 1983; held for interrogation for five weeks 1987, under house arrest 1988–89; mem Romanian Nat Salvation Front 1989–90, Memory Foundation; Founder-mem of Social Dialogue Group (GDS) 1989, of Civil Alliance; Co-Founder Antitotalitarian Forum of Romania 1990; Dr hc (Brussels) 1989; numerous int awards for human rights activities; Officier de la Légion d'Honneur 1999; Thorolf Rafto Human Rights Award, Norway 1989. *Publications:* Liberté? 1990, Open Letters and Other Texts 1991, Fata Nevazuta a Lucrurilor 1990–99 1999; several translations from French. *Address:* Str Alba Iulia Nr 16, Cluj-Napoca, 3400, Romania. *Telephone:* (64) 198460; *Fax:* (64) 432571.

CORNING, Joy, BA; American politician; b 7 Sept 1932, Bridgewater, IA; d of Perry and Ethel Marie Sullivan; m Burton Eugene Corning 1955; three d. *Education:* Univ of N Iowa. *Career:* Teacher Greenfield Elementary School 1951–53, Waterloo Community School 1954–55; Iowa State Senator 1984–90; Lieut-Gov of Iowa 1991–99; mem Iowa Housing Finance Authority, Des Moines 1981–84; mem League of Women Voters, American Asscn of Univ Women, Cedar Arts Forum, Iowa Asscn School Bd, The Caring Foundation; Citizen of the Year (Cedar Falls Chamber of Commerce, IA) 1984; Alumni Achievement Award (Univ of N Iowa) 1985; ITAG Distinguished Service to Iowa's Gifted and Talented Students Award 1991; Public Service Award, Iowa Home Econs Asscn 1994; Friend of Mathematics Award, Iowa Council of Teachers of Mathematics 1995. *Address:* 4323 Grand Ave, No 324, Des Moines, IA 50312, USA.

CORNWELL, Patricia D.; American writer; b 1957, Miami, FL. *Education:* Davidson Coll (NC). *Career:* Fmrly reporter Observer; currently mem staff Office of the Chief Medical Examiner (Richmond, VA) and writer. *Publications include:* A Time of Remembering: the Story of Ruth Bell Graham 1983 (re-issued as Ruth: a Portrait 1997), Postmortem (John Creasey Award, British Crime Writers' Asscn 1991, Anthony Award, Boucheron Award, World Mystery Convention, MacAvity Award, Mystery Readers Int) 1990, Body of Evidence, 1991, All That Remains 1992, Cruel and Unusual 1993, The Body Farm 1994, From Potter's Field 1995, Cause of Death 1996, Unnatural Exposure 1997, Point of Origin 1998, Black Notice 1999. *Address:* c/o Little, Brown & Co, Brettenham House, Lancaster Place, London WC2E 7EN, UK; c/o Don Congdon Associates Inc, 156 5th Ave, Suite 625, New York, NY 10010–7002, USA.

CORRIGAN, Maura Denise, BA, JD; American judge; b 14 June 1948, Cleveland, OH; d of Peter J. Corrigan; m Joseph D. Grano 1976; one s one d. *Education:* Univ of Detroit and Marygrove Coll (Detroit). *Career:* Law Clerk Michigan Court of Appeals 1972–74; Asst Prosecutor Wayne Co 1974–79; Asst US Attorney 1979–85, First Asst 1986–89; Shareholder Plunkett and Cooney, PC 1989–92; apptd Judge Michigan Court of Appeals 1992, Chief Judge 1997–98, Justice Michigan Supreme Court 1998–2000, Chief Justice 2000–; Hon LL D (Northern Michigan); Dir's Award, US Dept of Justice 1985; Leonard Gilman Award to Outstanding Practitioner of Criminal Law, Fed Bar Asscn 1989. *Leisure interests:* reading, gardening, music. *Address:* Michigan Supreme Court, 500 Woodward Ave, Floor 20, Detroit, MI 48226-3435, USA.

CORRIGAN-MAGUIRE, Mairead; British human rights activist; b 27 Jan 1944, Belfast; d of Andrew and Margaret Corrigan; m 2nd Jackie Maguire 1981; two s three step-c. *Education:* St Vincent's Primary School (Belfast) and Miss Gordon's Commercial Coll. *Career:* Founder Community of the Peace People (fmrly Northern Ireland Peace Movt) 1976, Chair 1980–81; Hon LL D (Yale) 1976; Nobel Peace Prize (with Betty Williams, qv) 1976; Carl von Ossietzky Medal for Courage (Berlin Section, Int League of Human Rights). *Leisure interests:* swimming, walking. *Address:* Community of the Peace People, 224 Lisburn Rd, Belfast BT9 6GE, UK (Office). *Telephone:* (28) 9066-3465 (Office); *Fax:* (28) 9068-3947 (Office); *E-mail:* peacepeople@gn.apc.org (Office).

CORTANZE, Martine Marie Roero de; French rally driver and sport executive; b 4 Aug 1945, Boulogne-sur-Seine; d of Hervé and Caroline (née Mea) Magny; m Christian Roero de Cortanze 1972 (divorced). *Education:* Ecoles Caroline Louise de Marillac (Paris) and des Cadres (Neuilly). *Career:* Dir Cossutta and Assocs, Paris 1972–80; Press and Public Relations Attaché Agence Energy Int, Paris 1980–82, Courrèges

SA, Courrèges Homme and Courrèges Design 1983–88; automobile journalist Maisons et Jardins magazine 1985–88; Dir of Promotion and Communication Comité Nat Olympique et Sportif Français 1988–96; Paris Liaison Officer Sportel of Monaco 1996–; Vice-Pres Union Nat des Attachés de Presse et Professionnels de la Communication (UNAPC) 1989–; major competition victoires include Coupe des Dames at Monte Carlo Rally, Tour de Corse, Coupe des Alpes, RAC Rally, Rallye du Maroc 1983 car rallies, women's motor-cycling competitions including Paris–Dakar Rally 1979–83, Croisière Verte 1979, 1980, women's speedboat competitions including huit heures de Dunkerque 1985, six heures de Paris 1985, Grand Prix de Monaco (Class III) 1986, Grand Prix de St Tropez (Class III) 1986, Championnat de France d'endurance (Bronze Medal) 1985–87; weightlessness experimenter for Helena Rubinstein Novespace/NASA 1988; Chevalier de l'Ordre Nat du Mérite 2001. *Publications:* Une fille dans le désert 1980, Les raids 1982. *Leisure interest:* golf. *Address:* Sportel Organisation, 19 rue Cognacq-Jay, 75007 Paris, France. *Telephone:* (1) 49-55-02-17; *Fax:* (1) 49-85-02-35; *E-mail:* splparis@club-internet.fr.

CORTES, Maria del Carmen, B ARCH; Chilean architect; b 7 Aug 1952, Salitrera Victoria; d of Celedonio Cortes and Palacida Arce. *Education:* Univs of Chile and Minnesota (USA). *Career:* Chief Architect and Rural Planner Maria Pinto Commune 1981–88; Architect and Community Developer Fundación M. Kast 1988–89; Housing Evaluator Habitacoop 1988–89; pvt practice; Exec Dir FINAM (Women's World Banking in Chile) 1989–91; apptd Co-ordinator US Peace Corps Programme 1991; H. H. Humphrey Fellow 1985–86; Hon Citizen Award (MN, USA) 1988. *Leisure interests:* reading, women's development issues, music. *Address:* Manuel Barrios 4730, Santiago 10, Chile. *Telephone:* (2) 2257160; *Fax:* (2) 2257595.

COSGROVE-SACKS, Carol, M SC, PH D; British international civil servant; b 7 May 1943; d of Thomas and Gaye Cosgrove; m Kenneth Twitchett 1966; two s; m Jeffrey Sacks 1995; two step-s. *Education:* LSE. *Career:* Lecturer School of European Studies, Univ of Reading 1966–69, Univ of Aberdeen 1969–71, Univ of Surrey 1975–79; Information Officer for Educ, Research and Devt, European Comm Office (London) 1972–74; European Business Consultant Overseas Trade and Devt Co 1980–84; Int Business Consultant 1984–94; Dir Trade Division, UN Econ Commr for Europe 1994–; JP 1976–79; Black Well SA Prize 1971; EC Research Prize 1976. *Publications include:* Europe & Africa 1976, a Framework for Development – The EC and the ACP 1981, Trade from Aid 1992, The EU and Developing Countries – Challenges of Globalization 1999, Europe, Diplomacy and Development 2001; more than 50 articles on European trade issues. *Leisure interests:* travelling, children. *Address:* UN/ECE, Palais des Nations, 1211 Geneva 10, Switzerland. *Telephone:* (22) 9172480; *Fax:* (22) 9170037; *E-mail:* carol .cosgrove-sacks@unece.org.

COSTA, Mary; American opera singer; b Knoxville, TN. *Education:* Los Angeles Conservatory of Music. *Career:* Debut at Los Angeles Opera 1958, San Francisco Opera 1959, Metropolitan Opera (New York) 1964, Bolshoi (USSR, now Russian Fed) 1970; appearances at opera houses in UK, Canada, USSR, Portugal; Vice-Pres Hawaiian Fragrances 1972, California Inst of the Arts; Los Angeles Woman of Year 1959; DAR Honour Medal 1974; Tennessee Hall of Fame Award 1987; Women of Achievement Award Nat Women's Bd of Northwood Inst (Palm Beach, FL) 1991. *Operas include:* La Bohème 1959, La Traviata 1964, 1970, Candide 1971; *Films:* Sleeping Beauty (voice of Sleeping Beauty), The Great Waltz 1972. *Address:* c/o California Artists Management, 41 Sutter St, Suite 723, San Francisco, CA 94104-4903, USA.

COSTALL, Brenda, PH D, D SC; British academic; b 12 Sept 1947, York; d of John and Eileen Stella (née Austin) Costall; m Robert John Naylor 1969. *Education:* Kesteven and Grantham Girls' School and Univ of Bradford. *Career:* Medical Research Council Research Fellow, Univ of Bradford 1972–73, Lecturer in Pharmacology 1973–79, Sr Lecturer 1979–83, Reader in Neuropharmacology 1983–85, Prof of Neuropharmacology 1985–, Pro-Vice-Chancellor with responsibility for Planning and Resources 1990–92, Sr Pro-Vice-Chancellor 1992–94, Deputy Vice-Chancellor with responsibility for Research, Planning and Resources 1994–98, Head of Dept Bradford School of Pharmacy 1998–; awarded numerous research grants by orgs including Medical Research

Council, Science and Eng Research Council, Wellcome Trust, Parkinson's Disease Soc, Asscn to Combat Huntington's Chorea, British Technology Group; has written research papers and articles in books and professional journals. *Leisure interests:* managing a large Georgian property, collecting antique furniture and paintings, the arts, fashion. *Address:* University of Bradford, Bradford, West Yorks BD7 1DP, UK. *Telephone:* (1274) 383016; *Fax:* (1274) 395256; *E-mail:* b .costall@bradford.ac.uk.

COTRUBAŞ, Ileana; Romanian opera and concert singer (retd); b 1939, Galaţi; d of Maria and Vasile Cotrubaş; m Manfred Ramin 1972. *Education:* Conservatorul Ciprian Porumbescu (Bucharest). *Career:* Debut at Bucharest Opera 1964; appearances at Frankfurt Opera (Germany) 1968–70, Glyndebourne Festival (UK) 1968, Salzburg Festival (Austria) 1969, Royal Opera House (Covent Garden, London) 1971, Lyric Opera of Chicago (USA) 1973, Paris Opera 1974, La Scala (Milan, Italy) 1975, Metropolitan Opera (New York) 1977; concerts with all major European orchestras; Lieder recitals at Musikverein Vienna, Royal Opera House (London) Carnegie Hall (New York) and La Scala (Milan); First Prize Int Singing Competition (Hertogenbosch, Netherlands) 1965, First Prize Munich Radio Competition 1966; title Austrian Kammersängerin conferred 1981; Grand Officer Order of Sant'Iago da Espada (Portugal) 1990, Hon Citizen of Bucharest 1995. *Operas include:* Pelléas et Mélisande, The Marriage of Figaro, The Magic Flute, Rigoletto, La Traviata, Manon, Tales of Hoffman, Eugene Onegin, La Bohème; *Recordings include:* Bach Cantatas, Mozart Masses, Brahms Requiem, Mahler Symphonies 2, 8; complete operas including Le Nozze di Figaro, Die Zauberflöte, Hänsel und Gretel, Calisto, Louise, L'Elisir d'Amore, Les Pêcheurs de Perles, La Traviata, Rigoletto, Alzira, Manon; *Publication:* Opernwahrheiten 1998.

COTTA, Michèle, L ES L, D ÈS SC; French journalist; b 15 June 1937, Nice; d of Jacques Cotta and Hélène Scoffier; m 1st Claude Tchou (divorced); one s (deceased) one d; m 2nd Phillipe Barret 1992. *Education:* Lycée de Nice, Univ of Nice and Inst d'Etudes Politiques de Paris. *Career:* Journalist L'Express 1963–69, 1971–76, Europe I 1970–71; Political Diarist France-Inter 1976–80; Head of political service Le Point 1977–80, Reporter 1986–; Chief Political Ed RTL 1980–81; Pres Dir-Gen Radio France 1981–82; Pres Haute Autorité de la Communication Audiovisuelle 1982–86; Producer Faits de Société, Télévision Française 1 (TF1) 1987, Dir of Information 1987–92, Pres Sofica Images Investissements 1987; producer and presenter La Revue de presse, France 2 1993–95; political ed Nouvel Economiste 1993–96; producer and presenter Polémiques, France 2 1995–99, Dir-Gen France 2 1999–; editorial writer RTL 1996–99; mem Conseil économique et social; Chevalier de la Légion d'Honneur. *Publications include:* La collaboration 1940–1944, 1964, Les elections présidentielles 1966, Prague, l'été des tanks 1968, La Vième République 1974, Les miroirs de Jupiter 1986, Les secrets d'une victoire 1995. *Address:* France 2, 7 esplanade Henri de France, 75387 Paris Cedex 15, France (Office).

COTTEE, Kay, AO; Australian yachtswoman and business executive; b 25 Jan 1954; d of James J. D. and Joyce Minie McLaren; m Peter Westland Sutton 1989. *Education:* Moorefield Girls' High (Sydney) and Summerhays Business Coll. *Career:* Propr Yacht Charter Business 1980–1985, then professional Boatbuilder and Sailor, now Corp Motivational Speaker and writer; first woman to sail single-handed non-stop and unassisted around the world, in 37-ft yacht which she had built, Nov 1987–June 1988; Chair Australian Nat Maritime Museum; hon mem Cruising Yacht Club of Australia, Royal Yacht Club of Tasmania, Short-Handed Sailing Asscn of Australia, Sydney Maritime Museum; Patron New S Wales Govt Kay Cottee Sailing Encouragement Programme, Bilgola Surf Life Saving Club, Life Educ Programme of New South Wales; numerous awards include Bicentennial Australian of the Year 1988, Cutty Sark Medal, Spirit of Australia Award, Single-Handed Hall of Fame (Newport, RI, USA), Int Navigation Award (NY, USA), Outstanding Personal Achievement Award (Confed of Australian Sport). *Publication:* First Lady 1989, All at Sea on Land 1998. *Leisure interests:* reading, sailing, painting, writing. *Address:* 24 Clarke St, Crows Nest, NSW 2065, Australia. *Telephone:* (2) 9439 1781; *Fax:* (2) 9957 1638; *E-mail:* sailaus@nor.com.au.

COUCH, Jane; British boxer; b Aug 1968, Fleetwood, Lancs. *Career:* First professional fight: beat Sandra Geiger to win WIBF Welterweight Title, Copenhagen, May 1996; won tribunal ruling against British Bd of Boxing Control (BBBC) to gain first British women's professional boxing licence, Aug 1998; won World Boxing Fed Women's Light-weight Title Oct 1999. *Telephone:* (1454) 632448; *E-mail:* jcouch@ globalnet.co.uk.

COUPER, Heather Anita, PH D, FRAS; British science broadcaster and writer; b 2 June 1949; d of George and the late Anita (née Taylor) Couper. *Education:* St Mary's Grammar School (Northwood) and Univs of Leicester and Oxford. *Career:* Man trainee Peter Robinson Ltd 1967–69; Research Asst Cambridge Observatories 1969–70; Lecturer Greenwich Planetarium, Old Royal Observatory 1977–83; Gresham Prof of Astronomy 1993–; Comm Millenium Commission 1994–; Dir Pioneer TV Productions 1988–99; Pres British Astronomy Asscn 1984–86; presenter numerous TV and radio programmes; columnist The Independent; Hon D LITT (Loughborough) 1991; Hon D SC (Hertfordshire) 1994. *TV includes:* Heavens Above 1981, Spacewatch 1983, The Planets 1985, The Stars 1988, The Neptune Encounter 1989, A Close Encounter of the Second Kind 1992, ET – Please Phone Earth 1992, Space Shuttle Discovery 1993, Electric Skies 1994, On Jupiter 1996, Black Holes 1997; *Radio includes:* Science Now 1983, Cosmic Pursuits 1985, Seeing Stars 1991–, ET on Trial 1993, Starwatch 1996, Sun Science 1999, The Essential Guide to the 21st Century 2000; *Publications include:* Exploring Space 1980, Heavens Above (jtly) 1981, Journey into Space 1984, Starfinder (jtly) 1984, The Halley's Comet Pop-Up Book (jtly) 1984, The Universe: A 3-dimensional study (jtly) 1985, Space Scientist (series) 1985–87, Comets and Meteors: The Planets, The Stars, The Sun (jtly), The Moon (jtly), Galaxies and Quasars (jtly), Satellites and Spaceprobes (jtly), Tele-scopes and Observatories (jtly), The Space Atlas (jtly) 1992, Guide to the Galaxy (jtly) 1994, How the Universe Works (jtly) 1994, Black Holes 1996, Big Bang 1997, Is Anybody Out There? 1998, To the Ends of the Universe 1998, Space Encyclopedia 1999, Universe 1999; contribs to magazines, newspapers, etc. *Leisure interests:* travel, the English countryside, classical music. *Address:* David Higham Associates, 5–8 Lower John St, Golden Square, London W1R 4HA, UK.

COUR, Ajeet, M ECONS; Indian writer; b 16 Nov 1934, Lahore, Pakistan; d of M. S. Bajaj and Jaswant Kaur; m Rajinder Singh 1953 (deceased); one d (Arpana Caur, qv). *Education:* Univ of Delhi. *Career:* Writer 1961–, accredited journalist 1961–; Chief Ed Rupee Trade 1963–; Chair Acad of Fine Arts and Literature 1975–; Vice-Chair Indian Council of Poverty Alleviation 1991; Writer-Del Int Women's Congress (Moscow, Russian Fed) 1987; many works have been made into TV films, including Doosra Kewal (13 episodes); numerous awards include Shiromani Sahitkar of the Year (Punjabi Sahitya Samikhta Bd) 1979, one of Nine Distinguished Punjabi Writers and Artists (Punjab Govt) 1979, Sahitya Akademi Award 1986, Bharatiya Bhasha Parishad (Calcutta) Award 1989, Punjabi Sahitya Sabha Award 1989, Dhaliwal Award 1990. *Publications include:* Directory of Indian Women Today (ed), Directory of Trade Between India and East European Countries; Short stories: Gul Bano 1962, Mahik Di Maut, But Shikan, Faltu Aurat, Saviyan Chirian, Maut Ali Babe Dee, Na Maaro, Guari; Novellas: Dhupp Wala Shehar, Post Mortem; Autobiography: Khaana Badosh (Sahitya Akademi Award 1986); Translations and adaptations: Portrait of a Lady (Henry James), Return of the Red Rose (K. A. Abbas), The Scarlet Letter (Hawthorne), The Sikhs (Khushwant Singh). *Leisure interests:* books, films, music, art exhibitions, travel. *Address:* 166 SFS Flats, Mount Kallash, opp Delhi Public School, New Delhi 110 065, India. *Telephone:* (11) 6438070.

COURT, Rev Margaret, MBE; Australian former tennis player; b (Margaret Smith) 16 July 1942, Albury, NSW; d of Lawrence and Maud Smith; m Barry Court 1967; three d one s. *Education:* Albury High School. *Career:* Amateur tennis player 1960–67, professional 1968–77; played Fed Cup for Australia 1963, 1964, 1965, 1966, 1968, 1969, 1971; Australian Champion 1960, 1961, 1962, 1963, 1964, 1965, 1966, 1969, 1970, 1971, 1973; French Champion 1962, 1964, 1969, 1970, 1973; Wimbledon Champion (UK) 1963, 1965, 1970; USA Champion 1962, 1965, 1969, 1970, 1973; holds more major titles in singles, doubles and mixed doubles than any other player in history; won two Grand Slams mixed doubles 1963, singles 1970; played Fed Cup for

Australia 1963, 1964, 1965, 1966, 1968, 1969, 1971. *Publications:* The Margaret Smith Story 1964, Court on Court 1974, Winning Faith (jtly) 1993. *Address:* 21 Lowanna Way, City Beach, Perth, WA 6010, Australia.

COX, Baroness (Life Peer), cr 1982, of Queensbury in Greater London, **Caroline Anne Cox**, MS; British member of the House of Lords; b 6 July 1937; d of Robert John McNeill Love and Dorothy Ida Borland; m Murray Cox 1959; two s one d. *Education:* Univ of London. *Career:* Lecturer, Sr Lecturer then Prin Lecturer Dept of Sociology, Polytechnic of N London 1969–74, Head of Dept 1974–77; Dir Nursing Educ Research Unit, Univ of London, Chelsea Coll 1977–84, Centre for Policy Studies 1983–85; Deputy Speaker House of Lords 1986–; Visiting Prof Faculty of Health and Social Work, Anglia Polytechnic Univ 1990; Co-Dir Educ Research Trust 1980–; Chair Academic Council for Peace and Freedom 1984, Jagiellonian Trust 1984–93, Parental Alliance for Choice in Educ 1985, Health Studies Cttee, CNAA 1987–93; mem Council of Man St Christopher's Hospice 1986; Vice-Pres Royal Coll of Nursing; Pres Incorporated Asscn of Preparatory Schools 1991; Trustee Medical Emergency Relief Int; Patron Medical Aid for Poland Fund; Hon PH D (Polish Univ in London); Commdr's Cross Order of Merit (Poland) 1990. *Publications include:* A Sociology of Medical Practice (co-ed) 1975, Rape of Reason: The Corruption of the Polytechnic of North London (jtly) 1975, The Right to Learn (jtly) 1982, Sociology: A Guide for Nurses, Midwives and Health Visitors 1983, The Insolence of Office (jtly) 1989, Choosing a State Schoool: how to find the best education for your child (jtly) 1989, Trajectories of Despair: misdiagnosis and maltreatment of Soviet orphans (jtly) 1991, Ethnic Cleansing in Progress: war in Nagorno Karabakh 1993, Remorse and Reparation 1998. *Leisure interests:* campanology, squash, hill-walking. *Address:* 1 Arnellan House, 144–146 Slough Lane, Kingsbury, London NW9 8XJ, UK. *Telephone:* (20) 8204-2321.

CRACKNELL, Ruth Winifred, AM; Australian actor and writer; b 6 July 1925, Maitland, NSW; d of Cahrles Cracknell and Winifred Watts; m Eric Charles Harry Phillips 1957 (deceased); one s two d. *Education:* N Sydney Girls' High School. *Career:* Joined John Alden Co 1948; with BBC, London 1953–54; numerous TV and film roles; mem Bd of Dirs Sydney Theatre Co, Christian Children's Fund; Hon D LITT (Sydney Univ, Queensland Univ of Tech). *Theatre includes:* Murder in the Cathedral, A Delicate Balance, The Chalk Garden, King Oedipus, Trelawny of the Wells, Arsenic and Old Lace, The Seagull, Habeas Corpus, School for Scandal, The Cherry Orchard, Bedroom Farce, The Dresser, The Way of the World, Nicholas Nickleby, All's Well that Ends Well, Tom and Viv, Medée (with Australian Opera), The Importance of Being Earnest 1988–89, 1990–91, Lettice and Lovage 1990, Lost in Yonkers 1992, Three Tall Women 1995, A Little Night Music 1996–97, Vita and Virginia 1997–98; *Publication:* A Biased Memoir (autobiog) 1997. *Leisure interest:* peace and quiet. *Address:* c/o International Casting Service and Associates, 147A King St, Sydney, NSW 2000, Australia. *Fax:* 2221 4091.

CRAIG, Mary, MA; British writer; b 2 July 1928, St Helens, Lancs (now Merseyside); d of the late William Joseph and of Anne Mary Clarkson; m Francis John Craig 1952 (died 1995); four s (one deceased). *Education:* Notre Dame Convent (St Helens), Univ of Liverpool and St Anne's Coll (Oxford). *Career:* Market Researcher Unilever 1949–50; taught at various schools 1950–64; NW Organizer Sue Ryder Trust 1962–68, Ed in-house magazine Remembrance; freelance journalist and broadcaster BBC Radio 1969–77, Thames TV, Southern TV 1971–79; TV Critic Catholic Herald 1971–76; mem Soc of Authors, Women of the Year Asscn; Officer's Cross of Order of Polonia Restituta 1987; John Harriott Award 1993 and other awards. *Publications include:* Adult: Longford 1978, Woodruff at Random 1978, Blessings (The Christopher Book Award, USA) 1979, Man from a Far Country 1979, Candles in the Dark 1983, The Crystal Spirit 1986, Spark from Heaven 1991, Tears of Blood: A Cry for Tibet 1992, Kundun: The Family of the Dalai Lama 1997, The Last Freedom: A Journal 1997, Waiting for the Sun: A Peasant Boy in Occupied Tibet 1998, His Holiness the Dalai Lama (anthology) (ed) 2001; Children: Pope John Paul II 1982, Mother Teresa 1984, Lech Wałęsa 1989. *Leisure interests:* travel, playing the piano, crosswords. *Address:* c/o PFD, Drury House, 34–43 Russell St,

London WC2B 5HA, UK (Office); 1 Lodge Gardens, Penwood, Bueghclere, Nr Newbury, Berks RG20 9EF, UK (Home). *Telephone:* (20) 7344-1000 (Office).

CRAMOND, Teresa Rita O'Rourke, MB, BS; Australian professor of anaesthetics; b 22 Feb 1926, Maryborough, Qld; d of William and Jane (née O'Rourke) Brophy; m Humphry Cramond 1985. *Education:* St Ursula's Coll (Toowoomba) and Univ of Queensland. *Career:* Dean Faculty of Anaesthetists, Royal Australasian Coll of Surgeons 1972–74; Foundation Prof of Anaesthetics Univ of Queensland 1978–; Hon Fed Sec Australian Soc of Anaesthetists 1960–64; Chair Medical Advisory Cttee, Surf Life Saving Asscn of Australia 1975–84; Pres Queensland Br Australian Medical Asscn 1981; Vice-Chair Australian Resuscitation Council 1976–88; mem Senate Univ of Queensland 1978–80; Fellow Australian Medical Asscn 1983; numerous contribs to professional journals; awards include Nuffield Prize 1955 and Gold Medal (Royal Coll of Surgeons, England) 1983, Gilbert Brown Prize (Royal Australasian Coll of Surgeons) 1967, Dame Magistral Grace, Sovereign Military Order of Malta 1979, Orton Medal (Royal Australasian Coll of Surgeons) 1980. *Leisure interests:* history, music, gardening. *Address:* c/o Multi-disciplinary Pain Centre, Royal Brisbane Hospital, Herston Rd, Herston, Qld 4029, Australia.

CRAVEN, Gemma; British actress; b 1 June 1950, Dublin, Ireland. *Education:* Loretto Convent and Bush Davies Schools. *Career:* Numerous film, play, musical and TV appearances. *Plays and musicals include:* South Pacific, They're Playing Our Song (Best Actress in a Musical Award), A Chorus of Disapproval, Song and Dance, Songbook, Jacobowsky and the Colonel, The Magistrate, Three Men On a Horse, Loot, London Vertigo 1992, Private Lives 1992, Present Laughter; *Films:* Double X, Wagner, Why Not Stay For Breakfast?, The Slipper and the Rose (Variety Club and Evening News Awards), Words Upon the Windowpane, Still Life; *TV appearances:* Gemma, Pennies From Heaven, Emily, East Lynne, She Loves Me, Robin Of Sherwood, Girls and Gershwin, Must Wear Tights, The Morecambe and Wise Show, The Perry Como Show, The Bruce Forsythe Show, The Harry Secombe Show, The Des O'Connor Show, Child's Play, Treasure Hunt, Gemma Girls and Gershwin, Boon, The Bill, The Marshal. *Address:* Stella Richards Management, 42 Hazlebury Rd, London SW6 2ND, UK. *Telephone:* (20) 7736-7786; *Fax:* (20) 7731-5082.

CRAWFORD, Cindy; American fashion model; b 1966; m 1st Richard Gere 1991 (divorced); m 2nd Rande Gerber 1998; one s. *Career:* Endorses Revlon (cosmetics) and Pepsi Cola; has own fashion show on MTV (cable and satellite); cover-girl on numerous magazines; model for numerous fashion designers; has released several exercise videos; face of Kelloggs Special K 2000; spokesperson for eStyle.com, Omega watches, 24 Hr Fitness. *Films include:* Fair Game 1995, Unzipped 1996; *Publications include:* Cindy Crawford's Basic Face 1996; for children: About Face 2001. *Address:* c/o Wolf-Kasteler, 132 S Rodeo Drive, Suite 300, Beverly Hills, CA 90212, USA (Office).

CRAWFORD, Mary Catherine, BA; Australian politician; b 12 April 1947, Toowoomba; d of John Joseph and Lorna Marjorie Crawford. *Education:* Univ of Queensland. *Career:* Teacher London and Cyprus 1970–74, Alice Springs High School 1974–78; Moderator, English, NT 1981–82; Asst Prin Stuartholme School, Brisbane 1986–87; mem House of Reps (Parl, Australian Lab Party) for Forde, Qld 1987, Chair House Reps Standing Cttee on Employment, Educ, Training, Sec Caucus 1990–93, Parl Sec to Minister for Housing and Regional Devt 1994. *Leisure interests:* reading, swimming, watching football. *Address:* 20 Barcoo St, Runcorn, Qld 4113, Australia.

CRAWLEY, Baroness (Life Peer), cr 1998, of Edgbaston in the County of West Midlands, **Christine Mary Crawley;** British politician; b 9 Jan 1950, Wicklow, Ireland; two d one s. *Career:* Youth Theatre Leader 1977–82; Local Authority Councillor, Didcot and S Oxfordshire Dist Council 1979–84; MEP (Group of the Party of European Socialists, Lab) 1984–99, fmrly mem Cttee on Civil Liberties and Internal Affairs, Cttee on Women's Rights, Del to the EU-Malta Jt Parl Cttee; Chair Women's Nat Comm 1999–. *Address:* House of Lords, London SW1A 0PW.

CRAWLEY, Jacqueline Nina, PH D; American neuroscientist; b 14 June 1950, Philadelphia, PA; d of Samuel and Miriam (née Schultz) Lerner; m 1st Carl B. Crawley 1971 (divorced 1979); m 2nd Barry B. Wolfe 1986; one s. *Education:* Univs of Pennsylvania and Maryland. *Career:* Instructor Univ of Maryland 1975–76, Prince George's Community Coll (Largo, MD) 1976, Yale Univ (New Haven, CT) 1978; Pharmacology Research Assoc Nat Inst of Mental Health, Bethesda, MD 1979–81, apptd Chief Unit of Behavioral Neuropharmacology 1983; Sr Neurobiologist E. I. DuPont de Nemours and Co, Wilmington, DE 1981–83; Co-organizer First Int Conf Neuronal Cholecystokinin, Brussels 1984; Chair Winter Neuropeptide Conf, Breckenridge, CO 1984–89; Guest Lecturer George Washington Univ (DC) 1987, Univ of Maryland 1987, Univ of Pennsylvania 1986, Foundation for the Advancement of Educ Sciences (Bethesda) 1984; Ed Neuronal Cholecystokinin 1985; mem Editorial Bds several journals; mem AAAS, numerous professional orgs; Grantee A. H. Robins Co (Richmond, VA), Pfizer Co (Groton, CT) 1986–90; contribs to professional journals, several TV appearances; Nat Research Scientist Award (NIH) 1985–88; Visiting Scientist Award (Nat Science Foundation) 1988–89. *Address:* National Institute of Mental Health, NIMH Bldg 10, Rm 4N214, Bethesda, MD 20892, USA.

CRAYMER, Judy; British theatre producer; b 1957, London. *Education:* Guildhall School of Music. *Career:* Began career as stage manager on original London production of Cats; Man Dir Three Knights 1984; worked in TV; Co-Founder Little Star Services; Exec Producer Mamma Mia (Prince Edward Theatre). *Address:* 30 Old Compton St, London W1, UK.

CRESPIN, Régine; French opera singer (soprano); b 23 Feb 1927, Marseilles; d of Henri and Marguerite (née Meirone) Crespin; m Lou Bruder 1962. *Education:* Conservatoire Nat d'Art Dramatique. *Career:* With Paris Opera 1951; appeared in prin concert houses in Europe and USA; singing teacher Higher Nat Conservatory of Music 1976–92; Commdr de la Légion d'Honneur, Commdr de l'Ordre Nat du Mérite, Commdr des Arts et des Lettres. *Publication:* A la scène, à la ville (memoirs) 1997. *Address:* 3 ave Frochot, 75009 Paris, France.

CRESSON, Edith; French politician; b 27 Jan 1934, Boulogne-sur-Seine; d of Gabriel and Jacqueline Campion; m Jacques Cresson 1959; two d. *Career:* Nat Sec Parti Socialiste, Youth Organizer 1975, mem Nat Secr 1987; Mayor of Thuré 1977, Châtellerault 1983–97, Deputy Mayor 1997–; MEP 1979; Minister of Agric 1981–83, of Foreign Trade and Tourism 1983–84, of Industrial Redeployment and Foreign Trade 1984–86, of European Affairs 1988–90; Prime Minister 1991–92; mem Nat Ass (Parl) for Vienne 1986–88; Dir-Gen affiliated co of Schneider 1990; European Commr for Educ, Research, Science and Devt 1994–99; Pres Assen Démocratique des Français à l'Étranger 1986, SISE 1992–94; Chevalier de la Légion d'Honneur; Dr hc (Weizmann Inst). *Publications:* Avec le soleil 1976, Innover ou subir 1998. *Address:* Mairie, 86108 Châtellerault Cedex, France.

CROSIO, Hon Janice Ann, OBE; Australian politician; b 3 Jan 1939, Sydney; d of Harry Gustard and Jean Rennerberg; m Ivo Crosio 1957; two d one s. *Education:* Stratfield Girls' High School (Sydney). *Career:* Alderman Fairfield City Council 1971–80, Deputy Mayor 1972–73, Mayor 1974–75, 1977–80; mem NSW Legis Ass for Fairfield 1981–88, for Smithfield 1988–90, Minister for Natural Resources and Minister assisting the Premier on Women's Interests 1984–86, for Water Resources and for Local Govt 1986–88, Asst Minister for Transport 1987–88, Shadow Minister for Local Govt 1988–89; Mem House of Reps (Parl) for Prospect 1990–, Parl Sec to Minister for Arts and Admin Services 1993, to Minister for Environment, Sport and Territories 1993–94, to Minister for Social Security 1994–96; mem Co-ordinating Cttee of Women Parliamentarians of Inter-Parliamentary Union 2000–, Jt Standing Cttee Foreign Affairs Defence Austrade 2000–; Queen Elizabeth Jubilee Medal 1977; Knight Order of Merit of the Italian Repub 1980. *Leisure interests:* reading, family. *Address:* 115 The Crescent, POB 802, Fairfield, NSW 2165, Australia. *Telephone:* (2) 972 64 100; *Fax:* (2) 972 46 115.

CROSLAND, Margaret McQueen, BA; British writer and translator; b 17 June 1920, Bridgnorth, Shropshire; d of Leonard and Beatrice (née Wainwright) Crosland; m Max Denis (divorced); one s. *Education:*

Royal Holloway Coll (London). *Career:* Temp civil servant and researcher, then worked in antiquarian book trade; now writer and translator; Prix de Bourgogne (France) 1973–74; Enid McLeod Literary Prize 1993. *Publications include:* Madame Colette 1953, Jean Cocteau 1955, Louise of Stolberg 1962, Colette, The Difficulty of Loving 1973, Women of Iron and Velvet 1976, Beyond the Lighthouse 1981, Piaf 1985, Simone de Beauvoir 1992, The Enigma of Giorgio de Chirico 1999, Madame de Pompadour 2000. *Leisure interest:* music. *Address:* 25 Thornton Meadow, Wilsborough Green, Billingshurst, W Sussex, RH14 OBW, UK. *Telephone:* (1403) 700652; *E-mail:* crosden@aol.com.

CROSS, K. Patricia, PH D; American professor of education; b 17 March 1926, Normal, IL; d of Clarence L. and Katherine (née Dague) Cross. *Education:* Illinois State Univ and Univ of Illinois. *Career:* Asst Dean of Women Univ of Illinois 1953–59; Dean of Students Cornell Univ 1959–63; Research Scientist Educational Testing Service and Research Educator Univ of California 1963–80, Elizabeth and Edward Conner Prof of Higher Educ, Berkeley 1988–94, David Pierpont Gardner Prof of Higher Educ 1994; Prof Harvard Grad School of Educ 1980–88, Chair Dept of Admin, Planning and Social Policy 1985–88; Regents Medal of Excellence (Bd of Regents of New York) 1984; Distinguished Alumni Award (Illinois State Univ); E. F. Lindquist Award (American Educational Research Asscn) 1986; Nat Leadership Award (American Asscn of Community Jr Colls) 1990. *Publications:* Beyond the Open Door 1971, Accent on Learning 1976, Adults as Learners 1981, Classroom Assessment Techniques (jtly) 1993, Classroom Research (jtly) 1996. *Address:* University of California at Berkeley, School of Educ, 3531 Tolman Hall, CA 94720, USA (Office); 904 Oxford St, Berkeley, CA 94707, USA (Home). *Telephone:* (510) 642-6000 (Office); (510) 526-9020 (Home).

CROW, Sheryl; American singer; b Feb 1962, Kennett, Missouri. *Education:* Univ of Missouri. *Career:* Trained as classical pianist; worked as music teacher and part-time bar singer; fmr backing singer to Rod Stewart, Eric Clapton, Don Henley, Michael Jackson; Grammy Award 2001. *Recordings include:* Tuesday Night Club Music 1994, All I Wanna Do 1995, A Change Would Do You Good, Tomorrow Never Dies 1997, The Globe Sessions 1999. *Address:* c/o A&M Records, 2220 Colorado Ave, Santa Monica, CA 90404, USA. *E-mail:* sheryl@sherylcrow.com; *Internet:* www.sherylcrow.com.

CROWLEY, Hon Rosemary Anne, MB, BS; Australian politician; b 30 July 1938, Melbourne; d of E. J. and M. M. Willis; three s. *Education:* Brigidine Convent and Melbourne Univ. *Career:* Pathology Registrar Royal Children's Hosp, Melbourne 1964; Jr Clinical Asst Paediatrics Medical Dept, Adelaide Children's Hosp 1970–71; Asst in Clinical Haematology, Inst of Medical and Veterinary Sciences 1972–74; Founder-mem S Australia Mental Health Review Tribunal 1979–83; Senator (Australian Labour Party) for S Australia 1983–, Minister for Family Services 1993–96, Minister assisting the Prime Minister for the Status of Women 1993, Leader Parl Del to Argentina and Brazil 1992, Chair Senate Select Cttees on Health Legislation and Health Insurance, Environment, Recreation and the Arts, Educ, Employment and Training References, mem Senate Standing Cttees on Scrutiny of Bills, Econs and Industrial Relations, and numerous other cttees; Dir Australian People for Health Educ and Devt Abroad (APHEDA) 1984–; mem Australian Fed of University Women, Medical Practitioners Against War, Amnesty Int—Parl Group, Campaign Against Racial Exploitation; Patron Australian Netball, Australian Women's Basketball. *Leisure interests:* jogging, theatre, gardening. *Address:* Senate, Parliament House, Canberra, ACT 2600, Australia (Office); 354 King William St, Adelaide, SA 5000, Australia (Home). *Telephone:* (6) 277 5789 (Office); *Fax:* (6) 273 3105 (Office).

CROZIER, Lorna, MA; Canadian poet and lecturer; b 24 May 1948, Saskatchewan, SK; d of Emerson and Peggy (née Ford) Crozier; m Patrick Lane 1978. *Education:* Univs of Saskatchewan, Regina and Alberta. *Career:* English teacher 1966–73; Writer-in-Residence Univ of Toronto, ON until 1990; Assoc Prof Dept of Writing, Univ of Victoria, BC 1992–; Guest at int poetry festivals in Faenza (Italy), Cheltenham (UK), Toronto and Vancouver; Gov-Gen's Award for Poetry 1992; Pat Lowther Award for Poetry 1992, 1996; Award for Poetry, Canadian Authors' Asscn 1992. *Publications include:* Crow's Black Joy 1978,

Human and Other Beasts 1980, The Weather 1983, The Garden Going On Without Us 1985, Angels of Flesh, Angels of Silence 1988, Inventing the Hawk 1992, Everything Arrives at the Light 1996, A Saving Grace 1996, What the Living Won't Let Go (poetry) 1999, Desire in Seven Voices (ed) 1999. *Leisure interests:* reading, walking, gardening, swimming. *Address:* 1886 Cuttra Ave, Saanichton, BC V8M 1L7, Canada. *Telephone:* (604) 652-3956; *Fax:* (604) 652-1430.

CRUZ, Celia; Cuban jazz singer; b 21 Oct. 1929, Havana; d of Simón Cruz and Catalina Alfonso; m Pedro Knight 1962. *Career:* Has performed at concerts and festivals worldwide, including Birmingham and London 1992; performed salsa music with various artists including: La Sonora Matancera, Ray Barretto, Willie Colón and Tito Puente; has made over 70 albums since the 1940s; Grammy award for Latin Tropical Performance (with Ray Barretto) 1974; Nat Medal of Arts 1994. *Recordings include:* Azúcar Negra, Homenaje a los Santos; *Films include:* Salsa 1988, Fires Within 1991, The Mambo Kings 1992, The Perez Family 1995, Damas del Swing, Las 1997, Alma no tiene color, El 1997, Yo Soy, del Son a la Salsa 1997; *TV appearances include:* The 1997, Summer Video Jams 1999. *Address:* c/o Omar Padillo, 568 Broadway, Room 806, New York, NY 10012, USA (Office).

CRUZ, Penélope; Spanish actress. *Films include:* Live Flesh, Belle Epoque 1992, Jamón, Jamón 1992, La Celestina 1996, Open Your Eyes 1997, The Hi-Lo Country 1998, Talk of Angels 1998, The Girl of Your Dreams (Goya Award) 1998, All About My Mother 1999, Woman on Top 1999, All the Pretty Horses 2000, Captain Corelli's Mandolin 2001, Blow 2001. *Address:* c/o Pedro Almodóvar, El Deseo SA, Ruiz Perello 15, Madrid, 28028, Spain.

CSAVLEK, Etelka; Hungarian opera singer and ceramic artist; b 29 May 1947, Budapest; d of Andras and Etelka (née Toth) Csavlek; m Zoltan Nemeth 1970; two d. *Education:* Budapest Acad of Arts. *Career:* Ceramist 1972–82; opera singer with Hungarian Opera House from 1982; concerts in Italy, Spain, Germany, Switzerland, France and USA; Franz Liszt Prize 1988. *Operas include:* La Traviata, Magic Flute, Così fan Tutte, Fidelio, Tales of Hoffmann; *Recordings include:* works of Wagner, Donizetti, Verdi, Mozart, Beethoven, Offenbach. *Leisure interests:* gardening, travel. *Address:* 1117 Budapest, Irinyi József u 28B, Hungary. *Telephone:* (1) 654-174.

CUEVAS DE DOLMETSCH, Angela, LL M; Colombian lawyer; b 1942. *Education:* Univ of London and LSE (UK). *Career:* Lawyer, business executive and Pres Women for Democracy (women's political party); fmr Pres Int Fed of Women Lawyers; mem Women Looking at the World 1998–; has participated in nat and int activites concerning women and the women's movt. *Address:* Women Looking At The World, Apartado Aereo 12, 54 Cali, Colombia. *Fax:* 8842516; *E-mail:* atadol@ aol.com.

CUMMINGS, Constance, CBE; British actress; b (Constance Halverstadt) 15 May 1910, Seattle, USA; m Benn W. Levy 1933 (died 1973); one s one d. *Education:* St Nicholas School (Seattle). *Career:* First appeared on the stage in Sour Grapes, since then in many stage, film and TV roles; performances at Royal Albert Hall and Festival Hall, London; mem Arts Council 1965–70, Chair Arts Council Young People's Theatre Panel 1965–74; mem Royal Soc of Arts 1975, Council English Stage Co 1978–. *Plays include:* Sour Grapes, Emma Bovary, The Taming of the Shrew, Romeo and Juliet, St Joan, Lysistrata, Coriolanus, Long Day's Journey into Night, The Cherry Orchard, The Bacchae, Mrs Warren's Profession, Wings (Antoinette Perry Award for Best Actress) 1978–79, Hay Fever 1980, The Chalk Garden 1982, 1992, The Old Ladies 1983, Eve 1984, The Glass Menagerie 1985, Fanny Kemble at Home 1986, Crown Matrimonial 1987, Tête-à-Tête 1990, Uncle Vanya 1996; *Films include:* Busman's Honeymoon 1940, Blithe Spirit 1945, John and Julie 1955, The Intimate Stranger 1956, The Battle of the Sexes 1959, Sammy Going South 1962, In the Cool of the Day 1963; *Musical performances include:* Peter and the Wolf, St Joan at the Stake (oratorio). *Leisure interests:* needlework, gardening. *Address:* 68 Old Church St, London SW3, UK. *Telephone:* (20) 7352-0437.

CUMMINS, Hyacinth Alissandra, MA; Barbadian museum official; b 30 Oct 1958; d of Gordon T. M. and Hyacinth Cummins. *Education:* Queen's Coll (Bridgetown) and Univs of E Anglia and Leicester (UK).

Career: Deputy Dir Barbados Museum and Historical Soc 1983–85, Dir 1985–, Nat Del to Int and Regional Meetings 1983–; Co-ordinator several regional museum training programmes for Govt of Barbados, UNESCO, OAS, ICOM 1984–; Govt Adviser Nat Museum Devt 1985–; Sec Caribbean Conservation Asscn 1988–90; Pres Museums Asscn of the Caribbean 1989–92, Barbados Nat Cttee of ICOM 1989–96, Int Asscn of Caribbean Archaeology 1991–94; Vice-Chair Commonwealth Asscn of Museums 1992–; mem Steering Cttee CARICOM Museum Devt Project 1990–94; Judge Nat Art Collection Competitions 1985, 1987; mem Peter Moores Barbados Trust; Fellow Museums Asscn (UK) 1993; Euan P. McFarlane Award Island Resources Foundation 1991; numerous contribs to professional journals. *Leisure interests:* sailing, swimming, horse-riding, reading, films, art. *Address:* The Barbados Museum and Historical Society, St Ann's Garrison, St Michael, Barbados. *Telephone:* 426-6459; *Fax:* 429-5946.

CURIE, Parvine; French sculptor; b 3 Feb 1936, Nancy; m 1st Marcel Marti 1958; m 2nd François Stahly 1975; one s. *Education:* Self-taught. *Career:* Numerous solo and group exhibitions in France and abroad including Musée Bourdelle, Musée d'Art Moderne (Troyes), Milan (Italy), Barcelona and Madrid (Spain), Winterthur (Switzerland), Luxembourg and Museum of Dortmund (Germany); works in perm collections of Fonds Nat d'Art Contemporain, Musée d'Art Moderne de la Ville de Paris, Musée de la Sculpture Contemporaine en Plein Air, Centre d'Art Contemporain, and many other nat and int museums; has produced a book, several catalogues and a video; Prix Bourdelle 1979. *Leisure interests:* walking, travel, nature. *Address:* 1 bis rue du Bassin, 92190 Meudon, France. *Telephone:* (5) 45-34-26-04.

CURRIE, Edwina, MA, M SC; British politician and writer; b 13 Oct 1946; m Raymond F. Currie 1972 (separated); two d. *Education:* Liverpool Inst for Girls, St Anne's Coll (Oxford) and LSE. *Career:* Lecturer in Econs, Econ History and Business Studies 1972–81; mem Birmingham City Council 1975–86, Chair Social Services Cttee 1979–80, Housing Cttee 1982–83; MP (Cons) for Derbyshire S 1983–97, mem Select Cttee on Social Services 1983–86; Parl Pvt Sec to Sec of State for Educ and Science 1985–86; Parl Under-Sec of State for Health 1986–88; Chair Cons Group for Europe 1995–97; Vice-Chair European Movt 1995–99; Jt-Chair Future fo Europe Trust 1995–97; Speaker of the Year (Asscn of Speakers' Clubs) 1990; Campaigner of the Year (Spectator/Highland Park Parliamentarian of the Year Award) 1994. *Publications include:* Life Lines 1989, What Women Want 1990, Three Line Quips 1992, A Parliamentary Affair (novel) 1994, A Woman's Place (novel) 1996, She's Leaving Home (novel) 1997, The Ambassador (novel) 1999, Chasing Men (novel) 2000, This Honourable House (novel) 2001; articles and contribs to professional journals; *Radio presenter:* Late Night Currie, BBC 1998–. *Leisure interests:* keeping fit, family, theatre. *Address:* c/o Little, Brown (UK) Ltd, Brettenham House, Lancaster Place, London WC2E 7EN, UK (Office). *Telephone:* (20) 7911-8000.

CURTIS, Jamie Lee; American actress; b 22 Nov 1958, Los Angeles, CA; d of Tony Curtis and Janet Leigh; m Christopher Guest (now Baron Haden Guest of Saling); one s (adopted). *Education:* Choate School (CT) and Univ of the Pacific (CA). *Films include:* Halloween, The Fog, Terror Train, Halloween II, Road Games, Prom Night, Love Letters, Trading Places, The Adventures of Buckaroo Banzai: Across the 8th Dimension, Grandview, USA, Perfect, 8 Million Ways to Die, Amazing Grace and Chuck, A Man in Love, Dominick and Eugene, A Fish Called Wanda, Blue Steel, Queens Logic, My Girl, Forever Young, My Girl 2, True Lies 1994 (Golden Globe Award for Best Actress in a musical or comedy), House Arrest 1996, Fierce Creatures 1996, Halloween H20 1998, Virus 1998; *TV appearances include:* She's In The Army Now, Dorothy Stratten: Death of a Centrefold, Operation Petticoat, The Love Boat, Columbo, Quincy, Charlie's Angels, Anything but Love (Dir), Money on the Side, As Summers Die, Mother's Boys, True Lies, Drowning Mona (Dir) 2000, The Tailor of Panama (Dir) 2000; *Publications include:* When I Was Little 1993, Today I Feel Silly and Other Moods That Make My Day 1999. *Address:* c/o Rick Kurtzmann, CAA, 9830 Wilshire Blvd, Beverly Hills, CA 90212, USA (Office).

CURY, Marta Bittar, MA; Brazilian business executive; b 7 Nov 1941; d of Jorge and Lulu Andraus Bittar; m Lindberg Aziz Cury 1966; two s one d. *Education:* Catholic Univ of São Paulo and Univ of Brasilia.

Career: Fmrly teacher and Univ lecturer; currently business exec; Pres Brazilian Fed of Business and Prof Women 1990–92; mem Fundraising Cttee, Int Fed of Business and Prof Women 1991–93; mem Brazilian Programme of Quality and Productivity 1991–; Outstanding Woman entrepreneur of Brazil 1990; Chevalier des Arts et des Lettres. *Leisure interests:* music, reading, sport. *Address:* SMPW Quadra 26, Conjunto 12 Casa 8, Parkway, Brasilia, 71700-500, Brazil (Home).

CUSACK, Joan; American actress; b 11 Oct 1962, New York; d of Dick Cusack; m Dick Burke; one s. *Films include:* My Bodyguard 1980, Broadcast News 1987, Working Girl 1988 (Oscar nomination), Married to the Mob 1988, Stars and Bars 1988, Addams Family Values 1993, Grosse Point Blank 1997, In and Out 1997, Toy Story 2 (voice) 1999, High Fidelity 2000, Where the Heart Is 2000.

CUSACK, Sinead Mary; Irish actress; b 1948; d of the late Cyril Cusack and Maureen Kiely; m Jeremy Irons 1977; two s. *Career:* Numerous appearances in film and TV drama, theatre performances in the Oxford Festival, Gate Theatre, Dublin, Royal Court and more. *Films:* Alfred the Great, Tamlyn, Hoffman 1969, David Copperfield 1970, Revenge 1971, The Devil's Widow 1971, Horowitz in Dublin Castle, The Last Remake of Beau Geste 1977, Rocket Gibraltar, Venus Peter, Waterland, God on the Rocks 1992, Bad Behaviour 1993, The Cement Garden 1993, The Sparrow, Flemish Board, Stealing Beauty; *Plays include:* Lady Amaranth in Wild Oats, Lisa in Children of the Sun, Isabella in Measure for Measure, Celia in As You Like It, Evadne in The Maid's Tragedy, Lady Anne in Richard III, Portia in The Merchant of Venice, Ingrid in Peer Gynt, Kate in The Taming of the Shrew, Beatrice in Much Ado About Nothing, Lady Macbeth in Macbeth, Roxanne in Cyrano de Bergerac (all for RSC). *Address:* c/o Markham & Froggatt Ltd, 4 Windmill St, London W1P 1HF, UK. *Telephone:* (20) 7636-4412; *Fax:* (20) 7637-5233.

CUSENS, Doris; Maltese tourism executive; b 30 July 1946; d of Joseph Degiorgio and Helena Noto; m Thomas Cusens 1967; three s one d. *Education:* St Joseph High School and Univ of Malta. *Career:* Presenter and Dir several TV programmes 1978–82; Licenced Nat Tourist Guide 1989–; Life Pres and Examiner Keep Fit Movt Malta 1984–; Pres Guardian Angel School for the Handicapped 1996; organized numerous fund-raising activities 1971–96; Life mem Maltese Nat Council of Women; Guest of Honour Nat Keep Fit Festival, Royal Albert Hall, London 1982. *Recording:* Keep Fit and Slim with Doris Cusens (keep fit exercises) 1979. *Leisure interests:* keep fit, sport, travel, reading, history, archaeology. *Address:* Tower Reef Apts 182/3, Tower Rd, Sliema SLM 10, Malta. *Telephone:* 333277; *Fax:* 343952.

CUSK, Rachel, BA; British writer; b 8 Feb 1967, Canada; d of Peter Cusk and of Carolyn Cusk; m Adrian Clarke; two d. *Education:* St Mary's Convent (Cambridge) and New Coll (Oxford). *Career:* Writer 1992–; Whitbread First Novel Award for Saving Agnes 1993. *Publications:* Saving Agnes 1992, The Temporary 1995, The Country Life (Somerset Maugham Award) 1997, A Life's Work 2001. *Leisure interests:* walking, piano. *Address:* The Dower House, Nettlecombe, Williton, Somerset TA4 4HS, UK.

CYWIŃSKA, Izabella, MA; Polish theatre director and director; b 22 March 1935, Kamień Puławski; d of Andrzej Cywiński and Elzbieta Cywińska; m Janusz Michalowski 1968. *Education:* Warsaw Univ, Higher State School of Drama (Warsaw). *Career:* Asst Faculty of Rural Architecture, Warsaw Tech Univ 1956–58; Stage Dir Aleksander Węgierko Theatre (Białystok) 1966–68, Theatre in Cracow-Nowa Huta 1968–69, Polski Theatre (Poznań) 1969–70; Dir and Artistic Man Wojciech Bogusławski Theatre (Kalisz) 1970–73, Nowy Theatre (Poznań) 1973–89; Minister of Culture and Art 1989–91; has directed in USA and fmr USSR; Exec Pres Culture Foundation 1991; Vice-Pres Understanding Cttee of Creative Circles (Poznań) 1980–81; mem Polish Stage Artists' Asscn, Presidential Council for Culture 1992–, Presidential Council for Culture 1992–95, Gen Ass European Cooperation Foundation, Brussels; Artistic Dir 50th Anniversary of the Revolt in the Warsaw Ghetto; has also dir in USA and USSR; All-Poland Drama Festival Award (Kalisz) 1970, 1973, 1980, (Opole) 1976, 1989, (Wrocław) 1976, Minister of Culture and Art Award (2nd class) 1977, Kt's Cross Order of Polonia Restituta, Medal Kalos Kagathos, Gold Cross of Merit, Nat Educ Comm Medal and other decorations. *Plays directed include:* Iphigenie auf Tauris 1968, The Morals of Mrs Dulska 1970, The Death of Tarelkin 1973, I giganti della montagna 1973, Lower Depths 1974, They 1975, Wijuny 1976, Bath-house 1978, Judas from Karioth 1980, The Accused: June '56 1981, Enemy of the People 1982, Virginity 1986, Cementeries 1988, Tartuffe 1989, Antygona in New York 1993; *Publication:* Nagłe Zastępstwo 1992; *TV work includes:* Frédéric's Enchantment (film about Chopin) 1998, Purym's Miracle (film), God's Lining (series) 1997, Beauty (1998–TV theatre, First Prize, Int TV Festival, Plovdiv, Bulgaria 1997), Second Mother 1999. *Leisure interests:* foreign travel, politics. *Address:* ul Piwna 7A M5, 00-265 Warsaw, Poland (Home). *Telephone:* (22) 635 32 33; *Fax:* (22) 635 32 33.

D

DA ROSA AMORIM, Maria Luísa Rodrigues Garcia, MD; Portuguese politician; b 17 March 1946, Lisbon. *Education:* Lisbon Univ. *Career:* Fmrly Medical Pracitioner; mem Partido Comunista Português (PCP, Portuguese Communist Party); elected to Assembléia da República (Parl) 1987; Nat Sec and mem Nat Council and Nat Leadership of the Democratic Movt of Portuguese Women; Vice-Pres Int Democratic Fed of Women. *Address:* c/o Assembléia da República, Largo das Cortes, 1200 Lisbon, Portugal. *Telephone:* (1) 660141.

DA SILVA, Benedita Souza; Brazilian politician; b 26 April 1942, Rio de Janeiro; d of José Tobias and Maria da Conceiçao de Souza; five c. *Career:* Fmrly auxiliary nurse and social services worker; mem Partido dos Trabalhadores (PT, Ind Labour Party); Leader Municipal Chamber of Rio de Janeiro 1983–86, Town Councillor 1983–87; Chair Sub-cttee for Negroes, Indigenous Population, the Disabled and Minorities 1987; Subsitiute Chair Sub-cttee for Nationality, Sovereignty and Int Relations 1987; mem Chamber of Deputies (Parl) for Rio de Janeiro 1987, Chair Cttees for External Relations, Social Welfare and Social Assistance 1989–90, for Social Security and the Family 1990–91, for Justice 1991, Substitute Chair Cttee for Consumer Protection, the Environment and Minorities 1990–91; mem Senado Fed (Fed Senate—Senator); Friend of the City of Los Angeles (CA, USA) 1983; Personality of the Year 1984; Guest of Hon, City of Managua, Nicaragua 1985. *Address:* Senado Federal, Praça dos Três Poderes, Edif Principal, 70.160 Brasília, DF, Brazil.

DABROWA-BAJON, Miroslawa Maria, PH D; Polish academic; b 19 May 1931, Sulejow; d of Antoni and Miroslawa Dabrowa; m Wieslaw Bajon 1955; two d. *Education:* Warsaw Univ of Tech. *Career:* Chair and Head of Traffic Control, Faculty of Transport, Warsaw Univ of Tech 1970, Vice-Dean Faulty of Transport, 1971–72; Dir Transport Inst 1973–78, 1981–84; mem Transport Cttee, Polish Acad of Sciences 1970, Council of the Warsaw Subway 1975–, Transport Acad of Russia 1995, and several scientific councils; 27 hon doctorate degrees; received seven awards for scientific work and handbooks 1970–90. *Publications:* Railway Traffic Control 1970, Design Principles for Systems and Railway Traffic Control 1981, Computer Aided Traffic Supervisory System for Polish Railways 1992, 1998, Principles of Railway Traffic Control (handbook) 2001; over 150 publications on modernization and computerization of traffic control systems. *Leisure interests:* reading, tourism. *Address:* Filtrowa 71 M 6, 02-055 Warsaw, Poland. *Telephone:* (22) 6286492; *Fax:* (22) 6215687; *E-mail:* mdb@it.pw.edu.pl.

DACHEVILLE, Colette (pseudonym Stéphane Audran); French actress; b 8 Nov 1932, Versailles; d of Corneille Dacheville and Jeanne Rossi; m 1st Jean-Louis Trintignant; m 2nd Claude Chabrol 1964; one s. *Education:* Lycée Lamartine (Paris) and Cours Charles Dullin. *Career:* Studied drama under Tania Balachova and Michel Vitold; Commdr de la Légion d'Honneur. *Films include:* Les bonnes femmes 1959, L'œil du malin 1961, Landru 1962, Champagne Murders 1966, Les biches (Best Actress, Berlin) 1968, La femme infidèle 1968, La dame dans l'auto avec les lunettes et un fusil 1969, Le boucher (Best Actress, San Sebastián) 1970, La rupture 1970, Juste avant la nuit 1971, Without Apparent Motive 1971, Un meurtre est un meurtre 1972, Dead Pigeon on Beethoven Street 1972, Discreet Charm of the Bourgeoisie (Best Actress, Soc of Film and TV Arts) 1972, Les noces rouges 1973, Comment réussir dans la vie quand on est con et pleurnichard 1973, Le cri du cœur 1974, Ten Little Indians 1974, B Must Die 1974, The Black Bird 1975, Vincent, François, Paul and Others 1975, Folies bourgeoises 1976, Silver Bears 1976, Devil's Advocate 1976, Violette Nozière 1978, Le Soleil en face 1979, The Big Red One 1980, Coup de Torchon 1981, Boulevard des assassins 1982, Le choc 1982, On ira tous au paradis, Le

sang des autres 1983, Poulet au vinaigre 1984, Babette's Feast (Best Actress, Taormina) 1988, La Cage aux Folles III: The Wedding, Manika: The Girl Who Lived Twice 1989, Quiet Days in Clichy 1989, Betty 1991; *TV appearances include:* Brideshead Revisted 1981, Mistral's Daughter 1984, The Sun Also Rises 1984, Poor Little Rich Girl 1986, Tecx 1989, Cry No More My Lady. *Address:* c/o 2F De Marthod, 11 rue Chanez, Paris 75016, France. *Telephone:* (1) 47-43-13-14.

DADA, Corina, B SC; Romanian business executive; b 1959; one s. *Education:* Univ of Bucharest. *Career:* Granted first export/import licence in post-revolutionary Romania; f Brother's Ltd 1990, exports furniture to Netherlands and Israel, imports computers from USA.

D'AGNESE, Helen Jean De Santis; American artist; b New York; d of Leonardo and Rose (née Redavid) De Santis; m John J. D'Agnese 1942; five d two s. *Education:* City Univ of New York and Atlanta Coll of Art. *Career:* Paints in oils and acrylics, sculpts in bronze and stone; solo exhibitions include the Maude Sullivan Gallery (El Paso) 1964, Karo Manducci Gallery (San Francisco) 1968, Lord & Taylor Gallery (New York) 1969, Atlanta Coll of Art 1976–80, Highland Gallery (Atlanta) 1987; group exhibitions include Benedictine Art Show (New York) 1967, Museo des Artes (Juárez, Mexico) 1968, Nat Judaic Theme Exhibition (Atlanta) 1976, Odyssey Collection Gallery (Michigan) 1988; contributions to perm collections include the Carter Presidential Center (Atlanta), Museo des Artes (Juárez), Vatican Museum (Rome); received Gold Medal Award of Accademia Italia delle Arti 1979, Golden Flame Award 1986; mem Nat Museum of Women in the Arts. *Leisure interests:* swimming, tennis, walking, music, reading. *Address:* D'Agnese Studio and Fine Art Gallery, 14½ N 4th St, Fernandina Beach, FL 32034, USA (Studio); 3240 S Fletcher Ave, Apt 551, Fernandina Beach, FL 32034, USA (Home). *Telephone:* (904) 261-0433 (Studio); (904) 261-6044 (Home); *Fax:* (904) 261-2653 (Studio).

DAGRI DIABATE, Henriette Rose, PH D; Côte D'Ivoire historian and politician; b Bingerville; five c. *Education:* Univ Cheikh Anta Diop of Dakar (Senegal), Univs of Aix-en-Provence and Paris (Sorbonne, France) and Univ of Abidjan. *Career:* Teacher 1959–60; Asst Univ Nat Côte d'Ivoire 1968–76; Dir of Science Houphouet-Boigny Foundation 1976–84; Chief Asst in History Univ of Abidjan, Head of Confs, Dept of History and Prof of History 1984–90; fmr Minister of Culture; founding mem Inst of African History, Art and Archaeology (IHAAA), Asscn of African Historians; Deputy mem Bureau of Asscn of Part or Wholly French-Speaking Univs (AUPELF); mem Asscn of Writers in the French Language; Chevalier des Palmes Académiques; Chevalier de l'Ordre Nat du Merité. *Publications include:* Aniaba, un Assinien à la cour de Louis XIV 1975, Origine du Sannvi 1979, Le Sannvi un royaume akan de la Côte d'Ivoire 1701–1902 1984, Le Sannvin: Sources, oracles et histoire, Mémorial de la Côte d'Ivoire (vol 1) 1987, Toujours plus haut... Notre Abidjan 1991.

DAGWORTHY PREW, Wendy Ann, BA, DIP AD; British fashion designer; b 4 March 1950, Gravesend; d of Arthur S. Dagworthy and Jean A. Stubbs; m Jonathan W. Prew 1973; two s. *Education:* Medway Coll of Design and Hornsey Coll of Art. *Career:* Started own design co, Designer and Dir Wendy Dagworthy Ltd 1972–; Dir London Designer Collections 1982; Consultant to CIYAA Fashion/Textiles Bd 1982–; Course Dir Fashion BA Hons Degree Cen St Martin's Coll of Art and Design 1989–; Prof of Fashion Royal Coll of Art 1998–; Judge Royal Soc of Arts Bd; judge of art and design projects for various manufacturers; participating designer in Fashion Aid and many charity shows; exhibits seasonally in London, Milan, New York and Paris; Lecturer and External Assessor at numerous polytechnics and colls of art and design;

frequent TV appearances; Fil d'Or Int Linen Award 1986. *Leisure interests:* dining out, cooking, reading, painting, horse-racing. *Address:* Royal College of Art, Kensington Gore, London SW7 3EU (Office), UK (Home); 18 Melrose Terrace, London W6, UK (Home). *Telephone:* (20) 7759-4444 (Office); (20) 7602-6676 (Home); *Fax:* (20) 7590-4360 (Office); *E-mail:* w.dagworthy@rca.ac.uk (Office); *Internet:* www.rca.ac.uk (Office).

DAHL, (Rut) Birgitta, BA; Swedish politician; b 20 Sept 1937, Råda, Co of Gothenburg and Bohus; d of Sven Dahl and Anna-Brita Axelsson; m 1st Benat Kettner 1957; m 2nd Enn Kokk; two d one s. *Education:* Univ of Uppsala. *Career:* Teacher 1960–64; Clerical Officer Scandinavian Inst of African Studies (Uppsala) 1964–65, Dag Hammarskjöld Foundation 1965–68; Sr Admin Officer Swedish Int Devt Authority 1965; mem Riksdag (Parl, Social Democratic Party) for Uppsala 1968–; Minister with special responsibility for Energy Issues, Ministry of Industry 1982–86, for the Environment and Energy 1987–90, for the Environment 1990–91, Speaker 1994–; mem Nordic Council 1991–94; Del to UN Gen Ass; Chair Environment Cttee of Socialist Int 1986–93, Confed of Socialist Parties of EC 1990–95; mem Bd Dirs Nat Housing Bd, Exec Cttee Social Democratic Party 1975–95; mem Advisory Council of Foreign Affairs; Vice-Chair Advisory Bd on Sustainable Devt 1993, Chair 1996–97; Sr Advisor Global Environment Facility (GEF) 1998–; numerous contribs to professional journals 1950–. *Leisure interests:* literature, music, nature. *Address:* Riksdag, 100 12 Stockholm, Sweden (Office). *Telephone:* (8) 786-40-00 (Office); *Fax:* (8) 786-61-43 (Office).

DAHL, Sophie; British fashion model; b 1978; granddaughter of Patricia Neal (qv) and the late Roald Dahl. *Career:* Discovered as a model by Isabella Blow (qv) who saw her crying in the street; has worked with fashion photographers Nick Knight, David La Chapelle, Karl Lagerfeld, David Bailey, Enrique Badulescu, Herb Ritts and Ellen Von Unwerth; has appeared in ID, The Face, Arena, Elle, Esquire, Scene magazines and advertising campaigns for Lainey Keogh, Bella Freud (qv), Printemps, Nina Ricci, Karl Lagerfeld, Oil of Ulay, Hennes; music videos for U2, Elton John and Duran Duran; contribs to The Telegraph, The Sunday Times, Tatler and Elle magazine; cameo appearance in films Mad Cows and Best 1999; stage appearance in The Vagina Monologues, The Old Vic 1999. *Address:* c/o Storm Model Management, 5 Jubilee Place, London SW3, UK. *Telephone:* (20) 7352-2278.

DAHLBECK, Eva; Swedish actress and writer; b 8 March 1920, Nacka; d of Edvard Dahlbeck and Greta Österberg; m Sven Lampell 1944; two s. *Education:* Royal Dramatic Theatre School (Stockholm). *Films include:* The Counterfeit Traitor 1961, Biljett till Paradiset 1961, För Att Inte Tala Om Alla Dessa Kvinnor 1964, Alskande Par 1964, Kattorna 1965, Les créatures 1965, Den Röda Kappan 1966; *Plays include:* Candida 1961, Ändå älskar vi varavdra 1963, Tchin-Tchin 1963, The Balcony 1964, Doctors of Philosophy 1964; *Publications:* Play: Dessa mina minsta 1955; Novels: Hem till Kaos 1964, S'ïs'ta Spegeln 1965, Den S'junde Natten 1966, Domen 1967, Med Seende Ögon 1972, Hjrätslagen 1974, Saknadens Dal 1976, Maktspråket 1978, I Våra Tomma Rum 1980. *Leisure interests:* reading, music.

DAI AILIAN; Chinese dancer and choreographer; b 1916, Trinidad, W Indies; m Ye Qianyu (divorced). *Career:* Studied in London 1931; worked with Modern Dance Co of Ernst and Lotte Berk; studied at Jooss-Leeder Dance School, and with Anton Dolin, Margaret Craske, Marie Rambert; went to China 1941; teacher Nat Opera School, Nat Inst of Social Educ and Yucai School; since 1949 has been leader dance team attached to N China Univ, Cen Theatrical Inst, leader Cen Song and Dance Ensemble, Artistic Dir dance drama troupe, Cen Experimental Opera Theatre; Pres Beijing Dancing Acad, China Ballet Soc, China Labanotation Soc; Vice-Chair Chinese Dancers' Asscn; Advisor Cen Ballet; mem Int Jury Int Youth Festival (Bucharest) 1953, (Moscow) 1955, Choreography Competition (Torino, Italy) 1983, 3rd USA Int Ballet Competition (Jackson, MI) 1986, 2nd Int Ballet Competition (New York) 1987, 3rd Int Ballet Competition (Paris) 1988, 3rd Tokyo Ballet Competition for Asia and Pacific 1987, New York Int Ballet Competition 1990; Chair China Nat Ballet Competition 1984, New York 1987; Hon Chair Chinese Dancers' Asscn 1991–; Sr Consultant China Asscn for the Advancement of Int Friendship; Cttee mem Int Dance Council UNESCO, Vice-Chair 1982–86, 1986; lecture

demonstrations on Chinese Ethnic Folk Dance at CEO China Forum, Beijing, UNESCO, Paris, Dartington Coll of Arts, Devon (UK) 1988–89; Consultant London Chinese Cultural Centre 1989–90, Int Folk Arts Org, Mödling, Austria 1990; mem Cttee China Int Cultural Exchange Centre; mem Int Labanotation Council; lecture on Labanotation in China, Laban Centre, London 1988; Patron Language of Dance Centre, London 1992, Laban Inst, Univ of Surrey 1992; mem Standing Cttee CPPCC; mem Presidium 6th CPPCC Nat Comm 1983–, 8th CPPCC Nat Comm 1993–; Fellow Hong Kong Acad of Arts 1996; Guest Lecturer Univs of Toronto, Ottawa and Vancouver, Canada 1997; Hon mem China Fed of Literary and Art Circles 1996. *Works include:* Lotus Dance, The Old Carries the Young, Flying Apsaras, The Women Oil-drillers' Dance, Tears of Pear Blossoms. *Address:* Apt 2-16 Hua Qiao Gong Yu, Hua Yuan Cun, Hai Dian, Beijing 100044, People's Republic of China. *Telephone:* (10) 68414163.

DALAL, Naina, MA; Indian artist; b Aug 1935, Baroda; d of Ramanlal and Ratanben Dalal; m Ratan Parimoo 1960; two d. *Education:* Maharaja Sayajirao Univ of Baroda, Polytechnic of Cen London and Pratt Inst (New York). *Career:* Freelance painter and printmaker; works in permanent collections throughout India and in Univ of Durham Oriental Museum (UK) and Chase Manhattan Bank (New York), Victoria and Albert Museum (London), Museum fur Indische Kunst (Berlin); solo exhibitions include Bombay 1973, 1984, 1986, 1990, Delhi 1982, Calcutta 1989; group exhibitions include Senefelder Group of Artist Lithographers (London) 1961–63, South Asian Artists (Durham/London) 1962, Group 8 (New Delhi) 1975–78, (Chandigarh) 1979–85, Gujarat State, Bombay Art Soc, Lalit Kala Akademi (New Delhi) 1980–84, Exhibition of Women Artists (Bombay) 1976, India Festival (USA) 1985, Graphic Arts in India since 1850 (New Delhi) 1985, 6th India Triennale (New Delhi) 1986, Women Artists (Nat Gallery of Modern Art, New Delhi) 1986, Galaxy of Prints (Chemould Gallery, Bombay) 1987, 8 Baroda Painters (CMC Gallery, New Delhi) 1990, Artists Against Communalism (touring exhibition, Sahmat) 1991–92, Bharat Bhava (Bhopal Biennale) 1992, Wounds (CIMA, Calcutta, New Delhi) 1993 Int Graphics Exhibition (BC, Canada) 1993; Indian Ministry of Educ Fellowship for Printmaking 1982–84; First Prize for Painting (Bombay State Art Exhibition) 1960; Prize for Lithography (Gujarat State Art Exhibition) 1964, 1968; prizes for etching Bombay Art Soc 1975, Group 8 Medal 1980, Gujarat State 1981. *Leisure interests:* folklore, traditional music. *Address:* R4 Sarathi, Pashabhai Patel Park, Race Course Circle, Baroda 390 015, India.

DALLE, Béatrice; French actress; b 19 Dec 1964. *Films include:* 37, 2° Dans le matin (English title Betty Blue) 1986, On a volé Charlie Spencer, La vision du sabbat, Chimère, Night on Earth, Black Out.

DALY, Tyne; American actress; b (Ellen Tyne Daly) 21 Feb 1946, Madison, WI; d of the late James Daly and of Hope Newell; m Georg Stanford Brown (divorced); three d. *Education:* Brandeis Univ (MA). *Plays include:* The Butter and Egg Man 1966, Come Back Little Sheba 1987, Gypsy (Tony Award for Best Actress) 1990, Theatre on The Town 1992; *Films:* John and Mary, Angel Unchained, Play It As It Lays, The Enforcer, Telefon, Speedtrap, Zoot Suit, The Aviator, Movers and Shakers; *TV appearances include:* Cagney and Lacey (series, four Emmy Awards), In Search of America, A Howling in the Woods, The Man Who Could Talk to Kids, The Entertainer, Intimate Strangers, The Women's Room, A Matter of Life or Death, Kids Like These, Stuck With Each Other, The Last to Go 1990, Face of a Stranger 1991, On the Town 1993, Scattered Dreams 1994, Christy 1994, Colombo; Bird in the Hand 1994, Columbo: Undercover 1994, The Forget-Me-Not Murders 1994. *Address:* 272 Lasky Drive, Apt 402, Beverly Hills, CA 90212, USA.

DALZIEL, Lianne Audrey, LL B; New Zealand politician; b 7 June 1960, Christchurch; d of Ronald Paul and Glenys Eileen (née Cusack) Dalziel. *Education:* Univ of Canterbury (Christchurch). *Career:* Solicitor and barrister 1984; Legal Officer Canterbury Hotel and Hosp Workers Union 1984–87, Sec 1987–90; Canterbury Rep New Zealand Council of Trade Unions 1987–90; MP (Lab) for Christchurch Cent 1990–96, List MP 1996–99, MP (Lab) for Christchurch E 1999–; Minister of Immigration, for Accident Insurance, for Sr Citizens; Assoc Minister of

Educ. *Leisure interests:* music, reading, tennis. *Address:* House of Representatives, POB 18041, Wellington, New Zealand. *Telephone:* (4) 471-9999; *Fax:* (4) 495-8463.

DAM-JENSEN, Inger; Danish opera singer; b 13 March 1964, Copenhagen; m Morten Ernst Lassen. *Education:* Royal Danish Acad of Music and Danish Opera School. *Career:* Studied with Kirsten Buhl Møller; started career 1992; concert appearances with numerous orchestras including Danish Radio Symphony, New York Philharmonic, Berlin Philharmonic, Czech Philharmonic and Gabrieli Consort; has performed at BBC Promenade Concerts and Edin Festival. *Operas include:* Arabella, Hamlet, Don Pasquale, Der Rosenkavalier, L'elisir d'amore, Le Nozze di Figaro, La Bohème, Così fan Tutte, Die Entführung aus dem Serail, Mitridate. *Address:* c/o Harrison Parrott Ltd, 12 Penzance Place, London, W11 4PA, UK (office); Hollændervej 4A, 1855 Frederiksberg C, Denmark (Home). *Telephone:* 26 17 4059 (Denmark) (Office); 33 23 4059 (Home); *Fax:* 33 23 4059 (Office); *E-mail:* inger@danlassen.dk.

DAMANAKI, Maria; Greek politician; b 31 May 1952, Aghios Nikolaos, Crete; d of Theodore and Eleftheria Damanaki; m Dimitris Danikas; one s one d. *Education:* Nat Tech Univ of Athens. *Career:* Chemical Engineer; elected to Vouli (Parl), Athens 1977, Vice-Pres Vouli 1989; Pres Left Coalition (Synaspismos) 1991; mem Communist Party of Greece (KKE), Tech Chamber of Greece; mem Ass 2000–; mem Group of the Unified European Left; mem Cttee on Culture, Science and Educ; has published various books and articles. *Leisure interests:* cinema, reading. *Address:* 7 rue Themistocleus, 106 77 Athens, Greece (Home). *Telephone:* (1) 3619232; *Fax:* (1) 3648263.

DAMBRICOURT-MALASSÉ, Anne Brigitte Patricia Marie, D ÈS SC; French palaeontologist; b 14 July 1959, Hauts de Seine; d of the late Xavier Dambricourt and Jacqueline Josse; m Claude Malassé 1982; one s. *Education:* Univ de Paris XI (Paris-Sud) and Musée Nat d'Histoire Naturelle (Paris). *Career:* Gen Sec Fondation Teilhard de Chardin 1990; Researcher Inst de Paléontologie Humaine, CNRS 1990–; Fondation FYSSEN grant 1989. *Publication:* Hominisation et Chaos 1992. *Leisure interests:* tennis, climbing. *Address:* Fondation Teilhard de Chardin, 38 rue Geoffroy-St-Hilaire, 75005 Paris, France; Institut de Paléontologie Humaine (IPH), 1 rue René-Panhard, 75013 Paris, France. *Telephone:* (1) 43-31-62-91 (IPH); *Fax:* (1) 43-31-22-79 (IPH).

DAMON, Dominique, PH D; French business executive; b 1947. *Career:* Joined Alusuisse-Lonza 1988, Chief Operating Officer and Group Chief Exec 1994–95; Pres-Dir Gen Rhône Poulenc Chimie, Dir Gen Chimie Europe 1996–97; Pres-Dir Gen Impress Metal Packaging 1997–; Chevalier de la Légion d'Honneur; Dr hc (Sheffield Hallam, UK). *Address:* Impress Metal Packaging, World Trade Center, Tower C, 8th Floor, Schiphol Blvd 221, 1118 BH, Luchthaven Schiphol, Netherlands.

D'ANCONA, Hedy, D SC; Netherlands politician; b 1 Oct 1937. *Career:* Fmr journalist and broadcaster; mem Partij van de Arbeid (Lab Party); mem Senate 1974; State Sec for Female Emancipation 1981–82; MEP 1984–89; Minister of Welfare, Public Health and Culture 1989–94. *Address:* c/o Partij van de Arbeid, Nicolaas Witsenkade 30, 1017 ZT Amsterdam POB 1310, 1000 BH Amsterdam, Netherlands (Office).

DANCZOWSKA, Kaja; Polish violinist; b 25 March 1949, Cracow; one d. *Education:* State Higher Music School (Cracow) and Moscow Conservatory. *Career:* Studied violin under teachers E. Uminska and David Oistrakh; Prof Acad of Music (Cracow) 1977–; Prof at courses of interpretation in Poland and abroad 1984–; Ordinary Prof 1997; mem of jury int violin competitions in Poznan, Munich, New York and Tokyo 1986–; participation in the greatest violin festivals; co-operation with the greatest conductors and orchestras; recordings for Wifon, Polskie Nagrania, Deutsche Grammophon, Philips; numerous awards include four prizes in Int Violin Competition 1967–75, Queen Elizabeth Prize, Brussels 1976 (Silver Medal), Individual Prize of Minister of Culture and Art 1991, Prize of Minister of Culture and Art 1998, Excellence in Teaching Award, USA 1998, Polish Culture Foundation Award 1998. *Leisure interests:* film, literature. *Address:* Polska Agencja Artystyczna "Pagart", pl Pilsudskiego 9, 00-078 Warsaw, Poland. *Telephone:* (22) 8274463.

DANELLA, Utta (née Denneler); German writer. *Career:* Writer of over 45 novels. *Publications include:* Alle Sterne von Himmel, Die Frauen der Talliens, Alles Töchter aus guter Familie, Die Reise nach Venedig, Stella Termogen oder der Versuch der Jahre, Tanz auf dem Regenbogen, Der Maulbeerbaum, Der Mond im See, Vergiß, wenn du leben willst, Quartett im September, Jovana, Niemandsland, Gestern oder die Stunde nach Mitternacht, Der blaue Vogel, Die Hochzeit auf dem Lande, Zwei Tage im April, Gespräche mit Janos, Familiengeschichten, Jacobs Frauen; Trilogy: Der dunkle Strom, Flutwelle, Der Unbesiegte; Children's books: Tränen vom vergangenen Jahr, Das Hotel im Park, Meine Freundin Elaine. *Address:* c/o Franz-Schneekluth Verlag, Widenmayerstr 34, 80538 Munich, Germany.

DANES, Claire; American actress; b 12 April 1979, New York; d of Chris and Carla Danes. *Education:* Performing arts school (NY) and Lee Strasberg Studio. *Career:* First acting roles in off-Broadway theatre productions: Happiness, Punk Ballet and Kids on Stage. *Films:* Dreams of Love (debut) 1992, Thirty (short) 1993, The Pesky Suitor (short), Little Women 1994, Romeo and Juliet 1996, To Gillian on Her 37th Birthday 1996, Polish Wedding, U-Turn 1997, The Rainmaker 1997, Les Misérables 1998, Brokedown Place 1999; *TV:* My So-Called Life (series), No Room for Opal (film), The Coming Out of Heidi Leiter. *Address:* c/o Susan Geller and Associates, 335 N Maple St, Suite 254, Beverly Hills, CA 90210, USA.

D'ANGELO, Beverley; American actress; b 15 Nov 1954, Columbus, OH. *Career:* Fmrly cartoonist Hanna-Barbera Studios, Hollywood, CA, singer with Elephant rock band; fmrly actress with Charlotte Town Festival Co. *Films include:* The Sentinel 1977, Annie Hall, Every Which Way But Loose, Hair, Coal Miner's Daughter, Honky Tonk Freeway, Paternity, National Lampoon's Vacation, National Lampoon's European Vacation, Trading Hearts, High Spirits, National Lampoon's Christmas Vacation, Pacific Heights, The Miracle, The Pope Must Die, Man Trouble, Lonely Hearts, Lightning Jack, Eye for an Eye, Edie and Pen; *TV appearances include:* A Streetcar Named Desire, Hands of a Stranger, The Switch, Menendez: A Killing in Beverly Hills.

DANITZ, Marilynn Patricia, MS; American dancer and choreographer; b Buffalo, NY. *Education:* Columbia Univ (NY). *Career:* Artistic Dir High Frequency Wavelengths/Danitz Dances world-wide 1976–; Prof Tainan Cheng Chuan Coll (Repub of China, Taiwan) 1984; Dancer Ballet Municipal (Strasbourg, France), Ballet Municipal (Geneva, Switzerland); choreography comms include 11th Int Ballet Competition (Varna, Bulgaria) 1983, Tbilisi Ballet Co, Nat Ballet of Colombia, Nat Cheng Kung Dance Group and Cheng Chuan Dancers (Repub of China, Taiwan); has conducted numerous master choreography workshops in People's Repub of China, Repub of China (Taiwan), Philippines and Australia; works shown on TV in Venezuela and Colombia and performed by Nat Philharmonic Orchestra of Colombia; mem Nat Asscn for Regional Ballet, Performance Project, American Dance Guild, Dance Theater Workshop; Fellow NIH; numerous scholarships; Gold Medal (Conservatoire de Genève, Switzerland); One of Three Outstanding Dance-Theatre Works of 1986 Award (Dance Brew-ATV Cable Manhattan). *Address:* 560 Riverside Drive, Apartment 2E, New York, NY 10027-3202, USA.

DAOUST, Sylvia, MA, RCA; Canadian sculptor; b 24 May 1902, Montréal, PQ. *Education:* Beaux-Arts (Montréal, PQ). *Career:* Created portrait sculptures for Canadian Bar Asscn and Govt of Québec; exhibitions in Canada, USA and Brazil 1946–; sculptures include Edouard Montpetit Monument, Univ of Montréal 1967, Marie-Victorin E. C. Monument, Jardin Botanique de Montréal 1954, Trois Sculpteurs, Museum of the St Joseph Oratory of Mount Royal 1979–80; Québec Scholar to Europe 1929; Scholar Soc Royale de Canada; mem Order of Canada, Sculptors' Soc of Canada; First Prize (jtly) Willingdon Arts Competition 1929; Medal and Allied Arts Award, Sculpture (Royal Architects Inst of Canada); Gold Medal (City of Dorval) 1975; Prix Philippe-Hébert (Société Saint-Jean-Baptiste de Montréal) 1975; Mérite Diocésain (Montréal) 1983; Chevalier de l'Ordre Nat du Québec 1987. *Address:* c/o Jean Famelart, 9178 14th Ave, St Michel, Montréal, H1Z 3N2, Canada.

DAPKUNAITE, Ingeborga; Lithuanian actress; b Vilnius; m Simon Stokes 1993. *Plays include:* Madame Butterfly, Aida, A Slip of the Tongue; *Films include:* Katia Ismailova (Best Actress Award, Russian Film Acad), Burnt by the Sun (Acad Award for Best Foreign Language Film), Mission Impossible, On Dangerous Ground, Intergirl, Autumn in Chertanova, Cynics, Libra. *Address:* c/o Sony Pictures Classics, 550 Madison Ave, 8th Floor, New York, NY 10022, USA.

D'APPARECIDA, Maria; Brazilian opera singer; b 17 Jan 1936, Rio de Janeiro; d of Sylvio and Dulce (née Adelino) Marques. *Education:* Teacher training, Conservatório Brasileiro de Música (Rio de Janeiro) and Conservatoire Nat Supérieur de Musique de Paris. *Career:* Teacher; Radio announcer 1955–58; performed Brazilian songs at Odéon-Théâtre de France 1961; has given recitals and appeared in concerts and at festivals, and has appeared at major opera houses in France; Officier des Arts et des Lettres; Chevalier de la Légion d'Honneur; numerous awards including Médaille d'Argent (Ville de Paris), Orphée d'Or 1969, Grand Prix du Disque Français 1972, Printemps de Suède 1972, Hon Citizen (Rio de Janeiro) 1981, Gold Medal Société d'Encouragement au Progrès, named Gen Rep for Brazil 1992. *Performances include:* Didon et Enée 1962, Carmen (Bordeaux) 1962, (Paris) 1965–68, L'Amérique 1964, Les fiançailles à Saint-Domingue, Lucrèce de Padoue 1967, L'heure espagnole 1972, L'amour sorcier, La voix humaine, Canta o Brazil 1988, Recital au Sénat 1995; *Recordings include:* Brasileirissimo (Grand Prix Int de l'Acad Charles Cros) 1988. *Leisure interest:* collecting paintings. *Address:* 19 rue Auguste Vacquerie, 75116 Paris, France. *Telephone:* (1) 47-20-96-50.

DA'PRATO, Rina Maria, BA; British fashion designer; b 22 May 1957, Irvine; d of Gino and Marjory (née Pettigrew) Da'Prato. *Education:* Douglas Ewart High School, St Dominic's Priory School (Staffs), Manchester and Liverpool Polytechs. *Career:* Designer Charnos Garment Ltd 1980–82; freelance designer and Design Consultant to Design Council 1982–87; est own designer label specializing in knitwear and crochet 1984; showed collections at British designer shows; sold label in UK, Europe and USA; opened first retail outlet at Hyper Hyper, Kensington, London 1991; designs featured on TV in The Clothes Show, Lovejoy, Insp Morse, and in numerous fashion magazines including Vogue, Elle, Harpers and Queen; designs selected by British Design Council (part of Best of British Product Design) 1987. *Leisure interests:* markets, tennis, exhibitions, entertaining, yoga. *Address:* 87 Brewer St, London W1R 3PG, UK. *Telephone:* (20) 7287-4350.

DARBOVEN, Hanne; German artist, writer and musician; b 29 April 1941, Munich. *Education:* Hochschule für Bildende Künste (Hamburg). *Career:* Has participated in numerous group exhibitions of contemporary art in galleries in Europe, USA, Canada, São Paulo Biennale 1973, Venice Biennale 1982. *Art Exhibitions include:* Düsseldorf 1967, 1968, 1970, 1971, 1975, Munich 1969, Cologne 1970, 1980, Amsterdam 1970, 1972, 1974, 1975, 1976, Leo Castelli Gallery, New York 1973, 1974, 1976, 1977, 1978, 1980, 1982, Paris, Brussels, Oxford, Turin, Milan, Bologna, Zürich, Basle, Houston, etc; *Music:* series of pieces for solo instruments, chamber and full orchestra; *Publications include:* El Lissitzky, Hosmann, Hamburg und Yves Gevaert 1974, Atta Troll Kunstmuseum 1975, Baudelaire, Heine, Disecpolo, Maizi, Flores, Kraus: Pour écrire la liberté 1975, New York Diary 1976, Ein Jahrhundert, Vol 1 1971–77, Schreibzeit 1999. *Leisure interest:* keeping goats. *Address:* Am Burgberg 26, D-21, Hamburg 90, Germany. *Telephone:* (40) 763-3033.

DARC, Mireille (pseudonym of Mireille Aigroz); French actress; b 15 May 1938, Toulon; d of Marcel and Gabrielle Aigroz. *Education:* Conservatoire de Toulon and Cours Maurice Escande (Paris). *Career:* Numerous appearances on TV, in plays and in films. *Films include:* Les Barbouzes, Galia (Prize, Festival de Mar-del-Plata) 1966, Du rififi à Paname, La blonde de Pékin, Le week-end 1967, Le rallye de Monte-Carlo, Summit 1968, Elle boit pas, elle fume pas, elle drague pas, mais… elle cause, Madly (also scriptwriter), Il était une fois un flic 1971, Il n'y a pas de fumée sans feu 1972, La valise, Le téléphone rose 1975, Les passagers 1977, Jamais avant le mariage 1982, Si elle dit oui, je ne dis pas non (also co-scriptwriter) 1983, Réveillon chez Bob 1984, La barbare (also co-scriptwriter) 1989; *TV appearances include:* La grande Bretèche, Hauteclaire, L'été en hiver, Les cœurs brûlés 1992, Les yeux

d'Hélène 1994. *Leisure interests:* swimming, climbing trees. *Address:* Agents Associés, 201 rue du Faubourg Saint-Honoré, 75008 Paris, France.

DARCY, Judy; Canadian trade union executive; b 1949, Grinsted, Denmark; m Gary Caroline 1977; one s. *Career:* Active mem Canadian Union of Public Employees (CUPE) 1972–, Regional Vice-Pres 1983–89, Pres CUPE Metro Toronto Council 1984–89, mem Exec Bd Ontario Div 1984–89, Nat Sec-Treas 1989–91, Nat Pres 1991–; Vice-Pres Canadian Labour Congress 1990–91, Gen Vice-Pres 1991–. *Address:* 21 Florence St, Ottawa, ON K2P 0W6, Canada (Office); 750 Eastbourne Ave, Ottawa, ON K1K OH7, Canada (Home). *Telephone:* (613) 237-1590 (Office); *Fax:* (613) 237-5508 (Office); *E-mail:* jdarcy@cupe.ca (Office); *Internet:* www.cupe.ca (Office).

D'ARCY, Margaretta; Irish writer and playwright; m John Arden 1957; five s (one deceased). *Career:* Artistic Dir Corrandulla Arts and Entertainment Club 1973–, Galway Women's Entertainment 1982, Galway Women's Sceal Radio 1986, Radio Pirate-Woman 1990; Chair Women in Media and Entertainment (consultative status at ECOSOC, UN) 1991; elected mem AOSDANA (Irish Poets Soc) 1981, mem Int Women Count Network 1990, Women's Global Strike 1999; Arts Council Playwriting Award (with John Arden) 1972, Women's Int Newsgathering Service, Katherine Davenport Journalist of the Year Award 1998. *Publications:* The Happy Haven 1960, Business of Good Government 1960, Ars Longa Vita Brevis 1964, The Royal Pardon 1966, Friday's Hiding 1967, The Hero Rises Up 1968, Muggins is a Martyr 1968, The Island of the Mighty 1973, The Non-Stop Connolly Show 1975, A Pinprick of History 1977, Vandaleur's Folly 1978, The Little Gray Home in the West 1978, The Making of Muswell Hill 1979, Tell Them Everything (Prison Memoirs) 1981, The Manchester Enthusiasts 1984, Whose Is the Kingdom? 1988, Awkward Corners 1988, A Suburban Suicide 1994 (all with John Arden); A Pinprick of History 1977, Tell Them Everything (prison memoirs) 1981, Galway's Pirate Women, a Global Trawl 1996; *TV documentary:* Profile of Sean O'Casey 1973 (with John Arden); *Radio work includes:* Keep Those People Moving 1972, The Manchester Enthusiasts 1984, Whose Is the Kingdom? 1988, A Suburban Suicide 1994 (all with John Arden). *Address:* c/o Casarotto Ramsay, 60–66 Wardour St, London W1V 3HP, UK; 10 St Bridget's Place, Lower Galway, Ireland. *Telephone:* (20) 7287-4450; *Fax:* (20) 7287-9128; *E-mail:* margaretta@eircom.net.

DARGEL, Olga B., BA; Belarus politician; b 1940. *Education:* Belarusian State Univ. *Career:* School teacher, Dir several school youth orgs; mem Supreme Soviet; currently Minister of Social Welfare. *Leisure interests:* poetry, theatre, art. *Address:* 220010 Minsk, Ministry of Social Welfare, bul Sovetskaya 9, Belarus. *Telephone:* (172) 202764; *Fax:* (172) 226849.

D'ARGY SMITH, Marcelle; British magazine editor; b 1947. *Career:* Fmr Ed Cosmopolitan magazine until 1995; freelance journalist and broadcaster 1995–97; Ed Woman's Journal 1997–; stood as Pro Euro Conservative cand, European elections 1999. *Address:* Kings Reach Tower, Stamford St, London SE1, UK.

DARKES, Maureen Kempston; Canadian organization executive; b 1949; m Lawrence J Darkes. *Career:* Fmrly Vice Pres of Corp Affairs and Legal Counsel Gen Motors; Pres and Gen Man Gen Motors of Canada Ltd 1994–, Vice Pres GM Corpn 1994–; several hon degrees. *Address:* General Motors of Canada Ltd, 1908 Colonel Sam Drive, Ottawa, ON L1H 8P7, Canada.

DARRAS, Danielle; French politician; b 22 Dec 1943, Carency. *Career:* MEP (PSE, PS); mem Cttee on Regional Policy, Transport and Tourism; Del to the EU-Malta Jt Parl Cttee, Del for Relations with Canada; mem Jt Parl Ass APC-EU; mem Pas-de-Calais Departmental Council 1982–, Deputy Chair 1986–; First Deputy Mayor of Liévin 1983–. *Address:* Hôtel de Ville, Rue Basly, 62801 Liévin Cedex, France; European Parliament, rue Wiertz, 1047 Brussels, Belgium. *Telephone:* (2) 284-21-11 (Belgium); *Fax:* (2) 230-69-43 (Belgium).

DARRIEUX, Danielle; French actress; b 1 May 1917, Bordeaux; d of Jean and Marie-Louise (née Witkowski) Darrieux; m 3rd Georges Mitsinkides 1948; one s. *Education:* Univ of Paris. *Career:* First appeared in films 1931, in theatre 1937; Chevalier de la Légion d'Honneur; Commdr des Arts et des Lettres; César d'Honneur 1985; Prix de l'Amicales des Cadres de l'Industrie Cinématographique 1987. *Films include:* Le bal, Mayerling, Un mauvais garçon, Battement de cœur, Premier rendez-vous, Ruy Blas, Le plaisir, Madame de..., Le rouge et le noir, Bonnes à tuer, Le salaire du péché, L'amant de Lady Chatterley, Typhon sur Nagasaki, La ronde, Alexander the Great, Marie Octobre, L'homme à femmes, Les lions sont lâchés, Le crime ne paie pas, Le diable et les dix commandements, Le coup de grâce, Patate, Greengage Summer, Les demoiselles de Rochefort, 24 heures de la vie d'une femme, Divine, L'année sainte, En haut des marches, Le lieu du crime, Corps et biens, Quelques jours avec moi, Bille en tête, Le Jour des rois, Les Mamies; *Plays:* La robe mauve de Valentine 1963, Gillian 1965, Comme un oiseau 1965, Secretissimo 1965, Laurette 1966, CoCo 1970, Ambassador (musical) 1971, Folie douce 1972, Les amants terribles 1973, Boulevard Feydau 1978, L'intoxe 1981, Gigi 1985, Adorable Julia 1987, Adelaïde 90 1990, George et Margaret 1992, Les Maimes 1992, Harold et Maude 1995, Ma petite fille, mon amour 1998, Une douche écossaise 1998. *Address:* Agence Nicole Cann, 1 rue Alfred de Vigny, 75008 Paris, France (Office).

DASHKOVA, Polina Victorovna (pseudonym of Tatyana Polyachenko); Russian writer; b 14 July 1960, Moscow; d of Vitaly Vassiliyevich and Tatyana Leonidovna Polyachenko; m Shishov Alexei Vitalyevich; two d. *Education:* Moscow Literary Inst. *Career:* Freelance writer, began career as poet and trans 1976–; Journalist Selskaya Molodezh magazine 1980–88; Head Div of Lit, Russian-American magazine Russian Courier 1988–93. *Publications include:* Blood of the Unborn 1996, Chechen Puppet 1996, Light Steps of Craziness 1997, No One Will Cry 1997, A Place Under the Sun 1998, Image of the Enemy, Golden Sand 1999, Time on Air 1999, Nursery 2000, Cherub 2001. *Address:* Maly Tishinsky pe 11/12, Apt 10, 123056 Moscow, Russian Federation. *Telephone:* (095) 253-17-39 (Moscow); (22) 144 4254, (22) 1460053 (Agent: Galina Dursthoff, Astrel, Germany).

DASKALAKI, Katerina; Greek politician; b 26 March 1944, Athens. *Career:* Fmr MEP (Group Union for Europe, Politiki Anixi), mem Cttee on Foreign Affairs, Security and Defence Policy, Del for Relations with SE Europe, Del to the EU-Bulgaria Jt Parl Cttee; now journalist; mem Bd Journalists in Europe Fund. *Address:* c/o Journalists in Europe Fund, 4 rue du Faubourg Montmartre, 75009 Paris, France. *Telephone:* (1) 55-77-20-00; *Fax:* (1) 48-24-40-02; *E-mail:* europmag@europmag.com; *Internet:* www.europmag.com.

DATE, Kimiko; Japanese tennis player; b 28 Sept 1970, Kyoto; d of Juichi and Masako Date. *Career:* Professional Tennis Player 1989–; Winner (singles competition) Futures/Matsuyama (Japan), Futures/Kyoto (Japan) 1988, Futures/Sutton (UK), Futures/Lee-on-Solent (UK) 1989, Japan Open 1992, 1993, 1994, Australian Open 1994, Pan Pacific 1994; Finalist Los Angeles (CA, USA) 1991, Osaka, Tokyo-Nichirei 1993, Lipton, Japan Open, Strasbourg (France) 1995; Semi-finalist Pan Pacific 1992, Lipton 1993, Australian Open, Virginia Slims Championship (USA), Strasbourg (France), Canadian Open 1994, Australian Open, French Open (first Japanese woman) 1994; Quarter-finalist Wimbledon, UK 1995; Finalist (doubles competition) Japan Open 1992; mem Japanese Fed Cup Team 1995.

DÄUBLER-GMELIN, Herta, D JUR; German politician and lawyer; b 12 Aug 1943, Bratislava, Czechoslovakia; m Wolfgang Däubler-Gmelin; one s one d. *Education:* Eberhard-Karls-Univ Tübingen and Univ of Berlin. *Career:* Mem Social Democratic Party of Germany (SPD) 1965–, Chair Tübingen Dist br 1971–72, State Chair Asscn of Social Democrat Women Baden-Württemberg 1971–76, mem State Exec Baden-Württemburg, elected to Fed Exec Cttee 1979, Deputy Chair Bundestag Parl Group 1983, 1991–93, elected mem Party Presidium 1984, 1997, Deputy Chair 1988–, legal adviser to Parl Group 1994, elected to Party Exec Cttee 1997; Fed Minister of Justice 1998–; Chair working group on Equality for Women 1983, Bundestag Legal Affairs Cttee 1980–83, Legal Policy Working Group 1994; Dr hc (Free Univ, Berlin). *Publications:* numerous books, articles in political journals and newspapers. *Address:* Ministry of Justice, Heinemannstrasse 6, 53175 Bonn, Germany (Office); Geierweg 2, 72114 Dusslingen, Germany. *Telephone:* (228) 580 (Bonn); *Fax:* (228) 58-45-25 (Bonn).

DAVENPORT, Lindsay; American tennis player; b 8 June 1976, Palos Verdes, California. *Career:* Turned professional 1993; career wins include: Lucerne 1993, 1994, Brisbane 1994, singles and doubles (with Jana Novotná, qv), Bausch & Lomb Championships 1997, Bank of the West 1998, Toshiba Classic 1998, Acura Invitational 1998, US Open 1998, European Championships 1998, Toray Pan Pacific (Doubles) 1999, Sydney Int 1999, Wimbledon 1999, Advanta Championships, Philadelphia 1999, Chase Championships, NY 1999, Australian Open 2000; mem Olympic Team 1996, Gold Medallist Singles. *Address:* US Tennis Asscociation, 70 West Red Oak Lane, White Plains, NY 10604, USA.

DAVID, Baroness (Life Peer), cr 1978, of Romsey in the City of Cambridge, **Nora Ratcliff David,** MA; British politician; b 23 Sept 1913; d of George Blockley Blakesley; m Richard William David 1935; two s two d. *Education:* Ashby de la Zouch Girls' Grammar School, St Felix School (Southwold) and Newnham Coll (Cambridge). *Career:* Mem Cambridge City Council (Lab Party) 1964–67, 1968–74, Cambridgeshire Co Council 1974–78, House of Lords 1978–; Baroness-in-Waiting and Govt Whip 1978–79; Opposition Whip and Educ Spokesperson 1979–85; Opposition Deputy Chief Whip 1983–87; Opposition Front Bench Spokesperson on the Environment 1985–87, on Educ and Science 1987–97; JP 1965–; mem Bd Peterborough Devt Corpn 1976–78; Hon Fellow Newnham Coll, Cambridge 1986, Anglia Polytechnic Univ 1998; Hon D LITT (Staffs). *Leisure interests:* walking, swimming, theatre, travel. *Address:* House of Lords, London SW1A 0PW, UK (Office); 50 Highsett, Cambridge CB2 INZ, UK (Home). *Telephone:* (20) 7219-3107 (Office); *Fax:* (20) 7219-3159 (Office).

DAVIDOVICH, Bella; American (USSR born) pianist; b 16 July 1928, Baku, Azerbaijan (then USSR); m Julian Sitkovetsky 1950 (died 1958); one s. *Education:* Moscow Conservatory with Konstantin Igumnov and Jakob Flier. *Career:* Teacher Moscow Conservatory for 16 years, Juilliard School of Music, New York 1982; soloist with Leningrad (now St Petersburg) Philharmonic for 28 consecutive seasons; emigrated to USA 1978, became US citizen 1984; has performed with world's leading conductors and orchestras in USA, Europe and Japan; Prof, Juilliard School of Music; Judge Queen Elisabeth Int Piano Competition, Brussels 1991; Most Deserving Artist of the Soviet Union; First Prize Chopin Competition, Warsaw 1949. *Recordings include:* Grieg: Concerto in A Minor, Sonatas Nos I–3; Chopin: 24 Preludes, Polonaise in C Minor, Rondeau in E Flat, Barcarolle in F Sharp, Ballades Nos 1–4, Impromptus Nos 1–4; Rachmaninov: Rhapsody on a Theme of Paganini; Scriabin: Sonata Fantasy in G Sharp Minor, Poeme in F Sharp Major, Mazurka in G Flat Major, Waltz in F Minor; Brahms: Three Sonatas for Violin and Piano (with Dmitry Sitkovetsky, violin). *Leisure interests:* opera, reading. *Address:* c/o Columbia Artists Management, Sheldon Division, 165 W 57th St, New York, NY 10019, USA (Office); 8300 Talbot St, Kew Gardens, NY 11415, USA (Home). *Telephone:* (212) 315-2430 (Office).

DAVIDSON, Inger Margareta; Swedish party official; b 2 Dec 1944, Enskede; d of Ernst and Kerstin Winblad; m Hans G. E. Davidson 1968; three c. *Education:* Univ of Stockholm. *Career:* Secondary school teacher 1968–87; mem Kristdemokajerna (Christian Democratic Party) 1966–, Political Sec 1987–88, Sec-Gen 1989–91, mem Bd and Exec Cttee, Vice-Chair County of Stockholm Dist Bd; Minister of Public Admin 1991–94; mem Riksdag (Parl) 1994–, Chair Standing Cttee on Culture 1998–; mem Parochial Church Council. *Leisure interests:* travelling, reading. *Address:* Sveriges Riksdag, 100 12 Stockholm, Sweden (Office). *Telephone:* (8) 786-44-00; *Fax:* (8) 791-75-60.

DAVIDSON, Janet Marjorie, ONZ, MA, D SC, FRSNZ; New Zealand archaeologist and ethnologist; b 23 Aug 1941, Lower Hutt; d of Albert and Christine (née Browne) Davidson; m Bryan Foss Leach 1979; one d. *Education:* Hutt Valley High School, Victoria Univ of Wellington, Univ of Auckland. *Career:* Field Assoc Bernice P. Bishop Museum, Honolulu, HI, USA 1964–66; E. Earle Vaile Archaeological Auckland Inst and Museum 1966–79; Hon Lecturer in Anthropology Univ of Otago 1980–86; Ethnologist Nat Museum of New Zealand 1987–91,

Curator (Pacific) Museum of New Zealand, Te Papa Tongarewa 1991–; extensive archaeological field work in New Zealand and the Pacific; Rhodes Visiting Fellow, Lady Margaret Hall, Oxford, UK 1974–76. *Publications:* Archaeology on Nukuaro Atoll 1971, The Prehistory of New Zealand 1984; numerous articles on the archaeology and prehistory of New Zealand and various Pacific Islands. *Leisure interests:* music, theatre, opera, ballet, cooking. *Address:* Museum of New Zealand, Box 467, Wellington 1, New Zealand (Office); 5 Hillview Crescent, Paparangi, Wellington 4, New Zealand (Home).

DAVIES, Dorothy Irene Blair, BA; British lecturer and international official; b 9 Jan 1942, Glasgow; m Trevor Davies 1965; one s one d. *Education:* Univ of Manchester. *Career:* Probation Officer 1965–68; Lecturer Univ of Birmingham 1968–70, Open Univ 1970–71, adult educ coll, Ain (France) 1972–77; Consultant UN educ training service, Geneva 1977–80; Staff Counsellor WMO, Geneva 1980–88; Sec-Gen Int Fed of Univ Women 1988–95; cttee mem Ecumenical Women's Asscn 1977–79, Pres 1979–82; mem Asscn Suisse des Femmes Diplômées des Univs, European Soc of Asscn Execs. *Leisure interests:* reading, church work, travel. *Address:* c/o 9 ave Riant-Parc, 1209 Geneva, Switzerland.

DAVIES, Kay Elizabeth, CBE, MA, D PHIL, FRCPATH, F MED SCI; British geneticist; b 1 April 1951, Stourbridge; d of Harry and Florence Partridge; m Stephen Davies 1973 (divorced 2000); one s. *Education:* Somerville Coll (Oxford). *Career:* Guy Newton Jr Research Fellow Univ of Oxford 1976–78; Royal Soc European Post-Doctoral Fellow, France 1978–80; Cystic Fibrosis Research Fellow St Mary's Hosp, London 1980–82, MRC Sr Research Fellow 1982–84; MRC Sr Research Fellow John Radcliffe Hosp, Oxford 1984–86, External Staff Nuffield Dept of Clinical Medicine 1986–89, Univ Research Lecturer 1989–92, External Staff Inst of Molecular Medicine 1989–92, Head Molecular Genetics Group 1994–95; Fellow, Green Coll, Oxford 1989–92, 1994–95; MRC Research Dir, MRC Clinical Sciences Centre, Royal Postgraduate Medical School, Hammersmith Hosp and Prof of Molecular Genetics Univ of London 1992–94; Prof of Genetics Univ of Oxford, Assoc Head of External Relations, Dept of Biochemistry and Fellow Keble Coll 1995–98; currently Dr Lee's Prof of Anatomy and Head of Dept of Human Anatomy and Genetics, Univ of Oxford; Hon Dir MRC Functional Genetics Unit, Dept of Human Anatomy and Genetics 1999; Co-Dir Oxford Centre for Gene Function Oct 2000–; Hon Fellow Somerville Coll (Oxford) 1996; Hon D SC (Victoria, Canada) 1990; Hon D UNIV (Milton keynes) 1999; Wellcome Trust Award for Research in Biochem Related to Medicine 1996; S. Mouchly Small Scientific Achievement Award, Muscular Dystrophy Asscn (USA) 1997; Soc of Chemical Industry's Medal 1999; Feldberg Foundation for Anglo-German Scientific Exchange (Germany) 1999. *Publications include:* Molecular Analysis of Inherited Disease (jtly) 1988, The Fragile X Syndrome (ed) 1989, Application of Molecular Genetics to the Diagnosis of Inherited Disease (ed) 1989. *Leisure interests:* music, tennis, reading, general keep-fit. *Address:* University of Oxford, Department of Human Anatomy and Genetics, South Parks Rd, Oxford OX1 3QX, UK. *Telephone:* (1865) 272179; *Fax:* (1865) 272427; *E-mail:* kay .davies@anat.ox.ac.uk; *Internet:* units.ox.ac.uk/departments/anatomy.

DAVIES, Laura, CBE; British golfer; b 5 Oct 1963, Coventry. *Career:* Professional Golfer 1985–; won Belgian Open 1985; Winner British Women's Open 1986, US Women's Open 1987, AGF Biarritz Open 1990, LPGA 1994, 1996, Evian Masters (France) 1995, 1996, Wilkinson Sword English Open 1995, Irish Open 1995, Danish Open 1997; rep England in World Team Championship, Taiwan 1992, Europe in Solheim Cup 1990, 1992, 1994; ranked number one in world 1994; Rookie of the Year 1985; Order of Merit 1985, 1986, 1992. *Publication:* Carefree Golf 1991. *Leisure interest:* fast cars. *Address:* c/o Women's Professional Golf European Tour, The Tytherington Club, Dorchester Way, Tytherington, Macclesfield SK10 2JP, UK (Office).

DAVIES, Sharron, MBE; British swimmer (retd) and broadcaster; b 1962; d of Terry Davies; m John Crisp 1986 (separated 1991). *Career:* Mem British Swimming Team, Olympic Games, Montréal, Canada 1976, Moscow, USSR (now Russian Fed) 1980, Barcelona, Spain 1992; retired 1980, came out of retirement 1988; radio journalist covering Olympic Games, Los Angeles, CA, USA 1984, Seoul, Repub of Korea 1988; Silver Medallist Moscow 1980; Gold Medallist Commonwealth

Games (twice). *TV includes:* The Big Breakfast (presenter, Channel Four) 1996–97, Gladiators (ITV), BBC Sport (presenter). *Address:* c/o BBC Sport, BBC Television Centre, Wood Lane, London W12 7RJ, UK.

DAVIES, Siobhán (Susan), MBE; British dancer and choreographer; b 18 Sept 1950; d of Grahame Henry Wyatt and Tempé Mary (née Wallich) Davies; partner David John Buckland; one s one d. *Education:* Queensgate School for Girls, Hammersmith Coll of Art and Building. *Career:* Dancer and choreographer, London Contemporary Dance Theatre 1967–87, Assoc choreographer 1971, Assoc Dir 1983; f Siobhán Davies Co 1980; Jt Dir Second Stride 1981–86; Dir Siobhán Davies Dance Co 1988–; Assoc Choreographer Rambert Dance Co 1989–93; Digital Dance Award 1988, 1989, 1990, 1992; Laurence Olivier Award for Outstanding Achievement in Dance 1993, 1996; South Bank Award for Dance 2000 and many others. *Choreography includes:* Pilot, Different Trains, Arctic Heart.

DAVIES, Susan Elizabeth, OBE; British gallery director (retd) and photographic consultant; b 14 April 1933, Iran; d of Stanworth Wills and Joan Mary Margaret (née Charlesworth) Adey; m John Ross Twiston Davies 1954; two d. *Education:* Nightingale Bamford School (New York), Eothen School (Caterham, Surrey) and Triangle Secretarial Coll. *Career:* Sec various magazines 1952–54; Artists' Placement Group 1966–67; Inst of Contemporary Arts 1967–70; f Photographers' Gallery 1971, Dir 1971–91; currently freelance photographic consultant and writer; mem (Ind) S Bucks Dist Council 1995–99; Parish Councillor Burnham (Bucks) 1995–; Hon FRPS, Pres's Medal 1982; Photokina Award 1986; Nat Artist Karel Plicka Medal 1989; Kulturpreis, German Photographic Soc 1990. *Leisure interests:* jazz, gardening, grandchildren. *Address:* Walnut Tree Cottage, 53–55 Britwell Rd, Burnham, Bucks SL1 8DH, UK. *Telephone:* (1628) 662677; *Fax:* (1628) 662677; *E-mail:* suedavies@msn.com (Home).

DAVILA, Maria Eugenia; Colombian actress; b 3 May 1949. *Career:* India Catalina Prize for Best Television Actress, Cartagena Film Festival 1985. *Films include:* Esposos en vacaciones 1978, Un angel de la calle 1985, Time To Die 1985, El día que me quieras (Best Film Actress award) 1987, Mariacano, la illuminada. *Address:* Calle 52 No 24-31, Santa Fe de Bogotá, Colombia.

DAVIS, Christine Agnes Murison, CBE, MA; British public servant; b 5 March 1944, Salisbury, Wilts; d of William Russell and Betsy Mary (née Murison) Aitken; m Robin John Davis 1968; two d. *Education:* Univs of St Andrews and Aberdeen. *Career:* Teacher of History and Modern Studies in several schools 1967–, Corton Vale Prison 1979–87; apptd Pres Council of Churches for Britain and Ireland 1990; Clerk London Yearly Meeting (Quaker) 1991; Chair Electricity Consultative Council for N Scotland 1980–90, Scottish Legal Aid Bd 1991–98; Chair Scottish Agricultural Wages Bd 1995–; ind adviser on Public Appointments 1998–; mem numerous Town and Co Councils 1972–75, Public and Ecumenical Bodies 1974, Scottish Econ Council 1987, Scottish Cttee, Council on Tribunals 1989; Trustee Joseph Rowntree Charitable Trust 1996–. *Leisure interests:* Church work, embroidery, the garden, walking. *Address:* 24 Newton Crescent, Dunblane, Perthshire FK15 0DZ, UK. *Telephone:* (1786) 823226; *Fax:* (1786) 825633; *E-mail:* camdavis@gn.apc.org.

DAVIS, Geena, BFA; American actress; b 21 Jan 1957, Wareham, MA; m 1st Richard Emmolo 1981 (divorced 1983); m 2nd Jeff Goldblum (divorced 1990); m 3rd Renny Harlin 1993. *Education:* Boston Univ. *Career:* Mem Mount Washington Repertory Theatre Co; fmrly worked as a model. *Films include:* Tootsie 1982, Fletch 1984, Transylvania 6-5000 1985, The Fly 1986, Beetlejuice 1988, The Accidental Tourist (Acad Award for Best Supporting Actress) 1988, Earth Girls are Easy 1989, Quick Change, The Grifters, Thelma and Louise, A League of Their Own, Hero, Angie, Speechless (also producer), Cutthroat Island, The Long Kiss Goodnight 1996, Stuart Little 2000; *TV appearances include:* Buffalo Bill 1983, Sara 1985, Family Ties, Remington Steele. *Address:* c/o ICM, 8942 Wilshire Blvd, Beverly Hills, CA 90211, USA (Office).

DAVIS, Judy; Australian actress; b 23 April 1956, Perth; m Colin Friels; one s one d. *Education:* W Australia Inst of Tech and Nat Inst of Dramatic Art (Sydney). *Career:* Fmr rock singer; actress with theatre cos in Adelaide, Sydney, London, Los Angeles (USA), etc. *Films include:* My Brilliant Career, High Tide, Kangaroo, A Woman Called Golda, A Passage to India, Impromptu, Alice, Barton Fink, Where Angels Fear to Tread, Naked Lunch, Husbands and Wives, The Ref, The New Age, Children of the Revolution, Blood and Wine, Absolute Power, Deconstructing Harry, Celebrity, Gaudi Afternoon, Me and My Shadows. *Address:* c/o Shanahan Management Pty Ltd, POB 478, Kings Cross, NSW 2011, Australia (Office); Sydney Theatre Co, The Wharf, Pier 4, Hickson Rd, Walsh Bay, NSW 2000, Australia.

DAVIS, Ruth A., BA; American diplomatist; b 28 May 1943, Phoenix, AZ. *Education:* Spelman Coll and Univ of California at Berkeley. *Career:* Consular Officer Kinshasa, Zaire 1969–71, Nairobi, Kenya 1971–73, Tokyo 1973–76, Naples, Italy 1976–80; Special Asst on Int Affairs to Mayor of Washington 1980–82; Sr Watch Officer Operations Centre, Dept of State 1982–84, Chief of Training and Liaison Bureau Personnel 1984–86; Consul-Gen Barcelona, Spain 1987–91; Amb to Benin 1992–96; Prin Dept Asst Sec of State for Consular Affairs, Dept of State 1995–97; Dir Nat Foreign Affairs Training Center 1997–; mem sr seminar Foreign Service Inst 1992. *Address:* Foreign Service Institute, 4000 Arlington Blvd, Arlington, VA 22204, USA.

DAWNAY, Caroline Margaret; British literary agent; b 22 Jan 1950, Reading; d of Oliver Dawnay and Margaret Boyle; one s. *Education:* St Mary's School (Wantage, Oxon), Univ per Stranieri (Florence, Italy) and Alliance Française (Paris). *Career:* Noel Gay Artists 1968–70, Michael Joseph publishers, London 1971–77; Dir A. D. Peters & Co Ltd 1977–88, Peters Fraser & Dunlop Group Ltd 1988–; Dir June Hall Literary Agency; Treas Asscn of Authors' Agents 1991–94, Pres 1994–97. *Address:* c/o PFD, Drury House, 34-43 Russell St, London WC2B 3HA, UK. *Telephone:* (20) 7344-1000.

DAWSON, Marilyn Janice, BA, MPA; American United Nations official; b 1 Aug 1953, Boston, MA; d of James W. and Barbara J. Dawson. *Education:* Winsor School (Boston, MA) and Brown and Princeton Univs. *Career:* Social and Econ Planner PADCO (Planning and Devt Collaborative Int) 1977–80; Social and Econ Planner Urban Project Office, UNICEF (Recife, Brazil) 1980–84, Training Consultant (New York) 1985; Urban Project Officer (Kingston, Jamaica) 1985–86, Head of Jamaica Office 1986–92, Programme Officer Asia and Africa Sections (New York) 1992–2001; UN Fund for Int Partnerships 2001–; Outstanding Young Woman of America 1990. *Leisure interests:* travel, reading. *Address:* c/o UN Fund for International Partnerships, United Nations DC1-1308, New York, NY 10017, USA. *Telephone:* (212) 963-9645; *Fax:* (212) 963-1486.

DAWSON, Sandra Jane Noble, BA; British college principal and professor of management studies; b 4 June 1946; d of Wilfred and Joy (née Noble) Denyer; m Henry R.C. Dawson 1969; two d one s. *Education:* Dr Challoner's Grammar School (Amersham) and Univ of Keele. *Career:* Research Officer Govt Social Survey 1968–69; Research Officer, then Lecturer, Sr Lecturer Industrial Sociology Unit, Dept of Social and Econ Studies, Imperial Coll of Science, Tech and Medicine 1969–90; Prof of Organizational Behaviour, Man School 1990–95; KPMG Prof of Man Studies and Dir Judge Inst of Man Studies, Univ of Cambridge 1995–, also Fellow Jesus Coll 1995–99; Master Sidney Sussex Coll, Cambridge 1999–; Chair Riverside Mental Health Trust 1992–95; Non Exec Dir Riverside Health Authority 1990–92, Cambridge Econometrics 1996–, Fleming Claverhouse Investment Trust 1996–; mem Research Strategy Bd, Offshore Safety Div, Health and Safety Exec 1991–95, Strategic Review Group, Public Health Lab Service 1994–99, Sr Salaries Review Body 1997–, Econ and Social Research Council Research Priorities Bd 2000–; Hon Fellow Jesus Coll, Cambridge; Hon D LITT (Keele) 2000; Anglian Businesswoman of the Year 2000. *Publications:* Analysing Organisations 1986, Safety at Work: The Limits of Self Regulation 1988, Managing the NHS 1995, papers on management in learned journals. *Leisure interests:* music, walking, family. *Address:* Judge Institute of Management Studies, Trumpington St, Cambridge CB2 1AG, UK; Sidney Sussex College, Cambridge CB2 3HU, UK. *Telephone:* (01223) 339700 (Judge Inst); (01223) 338800 (Sidney Sussex Coll); *E-mail:* s.dawson@jims.cam.ac.uk.

DAY, Doris (Doris von Kappelhoff); American actress and singer; b 3 April 1924, Cincinnati, OH; d of Frederick Wilhelm and Alma Sophia von Kappelhoff; m 1st Al Jorden 1941 (divorced 1943); one s; m 2nd George Weilder 1946 (divorced 1949); m 3rd Marty Melcher 1951 (died 1968). *Career:* Professional dancing appearances Doherty and Kappelhoff, Glendale, CA; singer Karlin's Karnival, radio station WCPO; singer with bands Barney Rapp, Bob Crosby, Fred Waring, Les Brown; singer and leading lady Bob Hope radio show (NBC) 1948–50, Doris Day Show (CBS) 1952–53; singer for Columbia Records 1950–; with Warner Bros film studio. *Films include:* Romance on the High Seas 1948, My Dream is Yours 1949, Young Man With a Horn 1950, Tea for Two 1950, West Point Story 1950, Lullaby of Broadway 1951, On Moonlight Bay 1951, I'll See You in My Dreams 1951, April in Paris 1952, By the Light of the Silvery Moon 1953, Calamity Jane 1953, Lucky Me 1954, Young at Heart 1954, Yankee Doodle Girl 1954, Love Me or Leave Me 1955, The Pajama Game 1957, Teacher's Pet 1958, The Tunnel of Love 1958, It Happened to Jane 1959, Pillow Talk 1959, Please Don't Eat the Daisies 1960, Midnight Lace 1960, Lover Come Back 1962, That Touch of Mink 1962, Jumbo 1962, The Thrill of It All 1963, Send Me No Flowers 1964, Do Not Disturb 1965, The Glass Bottom Boat 1966, Caprice 1967, The Ballad of Josie 1968, Where Were You When the Lights Went Out? 1968, With Six You Get Egg Roll 1968, Sleeping Dogs, Hearts and Souls 1993, That's Entertainment III 1994; *TV appearances include:* The Doris Day Show (series) 1968–72, The Pet Set 1972. *Address:* c/o Doris Day Animal League, 227 Massachusetts Avenue, NE, Washington, DC 20002, USA (Office).

DAY, Lucienne; British fabric designer; b 1917; d of Felix Conradi and Dulcie Lilian Duncan-Smith; m Robin Day 1942; one d. *Education:* Croydon School of Art and Royal Coll of Art (London). *Career:* Mem Faculty of Royal Designers for Industry (RSA) 1962, Master 1987–89; teacher Beckenham School of Art 1942–47; Designer Edinburgh Weavers, Heal's Fabrics, Cavendish Textiles, Tomkinsons, Wilton Royal, Thos Somerset and cos in Scandinavia, USA and Germany 1947–, Rosenthal China (Selb, Germany) 1956–68, Barbican Arts Centre 1979; Consultant to John Lewis Partnership 1962–87; represented in numerous perm collections including Victoria and Albert Museum (London), Trondheim Museum (Norway), Cranbrook Museum (MI, USA), Röhsska Museum (Gothenberg, Sweden), Musée des Arts Décoratifs (Montréal, PQ, Canada), Art Inst of Chicago (USA), Whitworth Art Gallery (Manchester); retrospective exhibitions Whitworth Art Gallery, Manchester and RCA 1993, Aberdeen 1994; mem Jury Rosenthal Studio-line 1960–68, Cttee Duke of Edinburgh's Prize for elegant design 1960–63, Council RCA 1962–67, RSA Design Bursaries Juries; First Award (American Inst of Decorators) 1950; Gold Medal (Ninth Triennale di Milano, Italy) 1951; Gran Premio (10th Triennale di Milano, Italy) 1954; Design Council Awards 1957, 1960, 1968. *Leisure interests:* plant collecting in Mediterranean regions, gardening. *Address:* 49 Cheyne Walk, Chelsea, London SW3 5LP, UK. *Telephone:* (20) 7352-1455.

DAYAN, Yael; Israeli politician and writer; b 1939; d of Moshe and Ruth Dayan; m Dov Sion; one s one d. *Career:* Mem (Lab) Knesset (Parl) 1993–. *Publications include:* My Father, His Daughter. *Address:* Knesset, Hakirya, Jerusalem 91000, Israel.

DAYDÉ, Liane; French ballet dancer and choreographer; b 27 Feb 1932, Paris; d of Raoul and Marie (née Roullot) Daydé; m Claude Giraud 1961; one s. *Education:* Lycée Lamartine (Paris). *Career:* Première Danseuse Etoile, Opéra de Paris 1950; Artistic Dir and Première Danseuse Etoile, Grand Ballet Classique de France 1962–; Prof and Dir of Studies Conservatoire Nat Supérieur de Paris 1979–; Pres Ecole Int de Mimodrame de Paris Marcel Marceau 1992–; has toured world-wide; Officier de l'Ordre Nat du Mérite; Chevalier des Arts et des Lettres; Officer of Ouissam Alaouite (Morocco); Officer of Nicham Iftikar (Tunisia); Officer of the Royal Order of Cambodia; Prix Anna Pavlova; Prix de l'Univ de la Danse; Prix Marquis de Cuevas. *Ballets include:* Blanche-Neige, Fourberies, Roméo et Juliette, Le chevalier, La demoiselle, Gisèle, La dame à la licorne, La belle au bois dormant. *Leisure interests:* drawing, embroidery, horse-riding, water sports. *Address:* 233 rue du Faubourg Saint-Honoré, 75008 Paris, France.

DAYIOĞLU, Gülten; Turkish writer; b 15 May 1935, Emet Kütahya; d of Lüftü and Emine Uyan; m Ceudet Dayioğlu 1958; two s. *Education:* Atatürk Girls' School (Istanbul) and Istanbul Univ. *Career:* Primary school teacher 1962–77; Journalist Cumhuriyet 1965–67, Milliyet 1967; writer from 1977, has written TV and radio plays, novels, short stories, travel books for children, series of children's books and research works on Turkish educ system. *Publications (in Turkish) include:* Adult Fiction: The Offspring (short stories, Yunus Nadi Story Award 1964–65), Those Who Were Left Behind (short stories), The Green Cherry (novel); Children's books: They were four Siblings, Suna's Sparrows, When I Grow Up, The Clever Fleas, The Immortal Queen, The Stork in the Snow (Children's Literature Story Award, Arkin Bookstore 1974–75), The Beautiful Lady (Children's Literature Tale Award, Arkin Bookstore 1974–75), Gül The Bride (Story Award, Turkish Family Planning Foundation) 1987, Journey to the Back of the Mountain Kaf (Children's Literature Award, Ministry of Culture and Tourism) 1988, Mystery of the Parbat Mountain (İzmir Metropolitan Municipality Children's Novel Award) 1989, Trip to a Totally Different World: America 1990, Trip to China: The Land of Legends 1990, The Eyes of the Midos Eagle (Altin Kitap Odülü Golden Books Award) 1991. *Address:* Nişantaşi Ihlamuryolu 45, Çatalkaya Apt Daire 9, 80200 Nişantaşi, Istanbul, Turkey. *Telephone:* (1) 1483087; *Fax:* (1) 1483087.

DDUMBA, Margaret M.; Ugandan broadcasting executive; b 21 Dec 1943; d of Benjamin Munya; m Clement Ddumba 1970; five s three d. *Education:* Missionary schools (Kabarole and Kampala) and Trinity Coll (Nabbingo). *Career:* Joined Civil Service 1962; trained by various int radio stations: BBC, Deuch Welle, AACC-Nairobi and Netherlands 1969; Head Current Affairs Programmes, Radio Uganda; Vice-Chair Uganda Media Women's Asscn 1983, Old Girl's Asscn Nabbingo; f Asscn of Retired and Ageing Persons – Uganda (RAPU) 1995; mem NGO Del to UN World Conf for Women, Kenya (contrib paper) 1985; volunteer Rural Outreach Programme for women with Uganda Media Asscn; Leader of married couples – Nsambya Parish 1995–2001; has made radio programmes on emancipation; has written numerous articles for newspapers and women's magazine New Era, press reports on the state of rural women (UMWA). *Leisure interests:* crafts and needlework, int womens org, singing in choir. *Address:* POB 22917, Kampala, Uganda. *Telephone:* (71) 813630; *E-mail:* rapu@cyberworldco.ug.

DÉ, Shobha, BA; Indian writer and journalist; b 7 Jan 1948, Satara; m 1st (divorced); m 2nd Dilip Dé 1984; four d two s. *Education:* Queen Mary's School, Bombay and Univ of Bombay. *Career:* Model 1968–73; copywriter, then freelance columnist 1971–; writer and scriptwriter 1989–; Founder and Ed Stardust, Society and Celebrity magazines. *Publications include:* Socialite Evenings (novel) 1989, Strange Obsession (novel) 1993, Snapshots (novel), Small Betrayals (short stories); articles and columns in newspapers and magazines; *TV includes:* Swabhimaan (daily soap opera) 1995. *Leisure interests:* music, dancing, movies, reading. *Address:* c/o Penguin Books India, 11 Community Centre, Panchsheel, Park, New Delhi 110017, India (Office). *Telephone:* (11) 6494401; *Fax:* (11) 6494403.

DE BEHAR, Lisa Block, PH D; Uruguayan professor of semiotics; b 12 March 1937, Montevideo; d of Juan and Rosa Block; two c. *Education:* Ecole des Hautes Etudes en Sciences Sociales (Paris, France). *Career:* Prof Ministry of Educ and Culture 1961–73, of Linguistics, Inst of Profs 1971–84; apptd Prof of Semiotics, Univ of the Repub 1985; Fulbright Fellow 1984; mem Asscn of Semiotic Studies, Int Semiotic Inst. *Publications include:* Analisis de un lenguaje en crisis 1969, El lenguaje de la publicidad 1973, Una retorica del silencio 1984, Al margen de Borges 1987, Jules Laforgue o las metáforas del desplazamiento 1987, Dos medios entre dos medios 1990. *Address:* Universidad de la República, 18 de Julio y Eduardo Acevedo, Montevideo, Uruguay.

DE CARDI, Beatrice Eileen, OBE, BA; British archaeologist; b 5 June 1914, London; d of Edwin, Count de Cardi and Christine Berbette Wurfflein. *Education:* St Paul's Girls' School and Univ Coll London. *Career:* Sec, then Asst, London Museum 1936–44; Personal Asst to Rep of Allied Supplies Exec of War Cabinet, China 1944–45; Asst UK Trade Commr, Delhi 1946, Karachi and Lahore (Pakistan) 1947–49; Asst Sec, then Sec, Council for British Archaeology 1949–73; retd 1973; Fellow Soc of Antiquaries of London 1950, Vice-Pres 1976–80, Dir 1980–1983; Winston Churchill Memorial Trust Fellowship 1973;

Fellow Univ Coll, London 1996; al-Qasimi Medal (Ras al-Khaimah, UAE) 1989; Burton Memorial Medal (Royal Asiatic Soc) 1992. *Publications:* reports on excavations at Bampūr, Iran (1966) and Kalāt, Pakistan 1970, and surveys in Qatar 1978, Oman 1975, 1977, 1979, UAE 1971, 1985, 1994 and Baluchistan (1948, 1957) 1983. *Leisure interests:* archaeological fieldwork, travel, cooking. *Address:* 1A Douro Place, Victoria Rd, London W8 5PH, UK. *Telephone:* (20) 7937-9740.

DE CHAMPLAIN, Vera Chopak, FRSA; American artist; b 26 Jan 1928, Kulmbach, Germany; d of Nathaniel and Selma Florsheim; m Albert Chopak de Champlain 1948. *Education:* Art Students' League (NY). *Career:* Art Dir and teacher Emanuel Center, New York 1967–; one-woman exhibitions include Fusco Gallery (New York) 1969–70, B. Altman Gallery (New York) 1982; group exhibitions include Rudolph Gallery (New York) 1967, Artists Equity Gallery (New York) 1970–77, Avery Fisher Hall, Cork Gallery (New York) 1970, 1982, 1983, 1984, 1987, 1989, 1994 Fontainebleau Gallery (New York) 1972, 1973, 1974, Lever House (New York) 1974, 1980, 1985, 1988, New York Univ 1978, Metropolitan Museum of Art (New York) 1979, Muriel Karasik Gallery (New York) 1980, Broom St Gallery (New York) 1991, 1992, 1993, 1994, 1995; represented in perm collections Butler Inst of American Art (OH), Georgia Museum of Art, Slater Museum (CT), Webster Coll (MO), Smithsonian Inst (DC), Archives of American Art, Jacobs Javits Fed Bldg (NY); Award for Portrait Painting (Hainsfalls, NY) 1965; First Prize, World Award (Acad Italia, Parma, Italy) 1985, 1987. *Address:* 230 Riverside Drive, New York, NY 10025-6172, USA.

DE ESTEBAN MARTIN, Laura; Spanish politician; b 8 Aug 1962, Madrid. *Career:* MEP (EPP, Partido Popular), mem Cttee on Civil Liberties and Internal Affairs, Del for Relations with the Countries of Cen America and Mexico; spokesperson EPP; mem Cttee on Constitutional Affairs 2001. *Address:* European Parliament, rue Wiertz, 1047 Brussels, Belgium.

DE GRAAFF-NAUTA, Dieuwke Ij. W.; Netherlands politician; b 22 May 1930, Sneek; m C. De Graaf; two c. *Education:* Teacher Training Coll. *Career:* Teacher 1949–54; mem Friesland Prov Council 1966–78; mem Presidium Christian Democratic Alliance 1980–82; mem Friesland Prov Exec with responsibility for admin, inter-prov affairs, planning, co-ordination and information 1982–86; Sec of State for Home Affairs 1986–94; Minister for Home Affairs 1994; Chair Chapter of the Royal Civil Orders 1995. *Address:* Chancery of the Royal Orders, Nassaulaan 18, POB 30436, 2500 GK The Hague, Netherlands. *Telephone:* (70) 30-26-302; *Fax:* (70) 36-39-153.

DE HAVILLAND, Olivia Mary; American (b British) actress; b 1 July 1916, Tokyo, Japan; d of Walter Augustus and Lilian Augusta (née Ruse) de Havilland; m 1st Marcus Aurelius Goodrich 1946 (divorced 1953); one s; m 2nd Pierre Paul Galante 1955 (divorced 1979); one d. *Education:* Saratoga Grammar School, Notre Dame Convent, Los Gatos Union High School. *Career:* Stage debut 1934, film debut 1935; Pres Cannes Film Festival, France 1965; lecture tours in USA 1971–80; mem Bd Trustees American Coll in Paris 1970–71, American Library in Paris 1974–81; mem Altar Guild, Lay Reader American Cathedral in Paris 1971–81; Hon D HUM LITT (American Univ of Paris) 1994; numerous awards including New York Critics Award 1948, 1949, Look Magazine Award 1941, 1946, 1949, Venice Film Festival Award (Italy) 1948, Filmex Tribute 1978, American Acad of Achievement Award 1978, American Exemplar Medal 1980, Golden Globe 1988. *Plays include:* A Midsummer Night's Dream 1934, Romeo and Juliet 1951, Candida 1951–52, A Gift of Time 1962; *Films include:* A Midsummer Night's Dream 1935, Captain Blood 1935, Anthony Adverse 1936, The Adventures of Robin Hood 1938, Gone with the Wind 1939, Hold Back the Dawn 1941, Princess O'Rourke 1942, To Each His Own (Acad Award) 1946, The Dark Mirror 1946, The Snake Pit 1947, The Heiress (Acad Award) 1949, My Cousin Rachel 1952, Not as a Stranger 1954, The Proud Rebel 1957, The Light in the Piazza 1961, Lady in a Cage 1963, Hush Hush Sweet Charlotte 1964, The Adventurers 1968, Airport '77 1976, The Swarm 1978, The Fifth Musketeer; *TV appearances include:* Noon Wine 1966, Screaming Woman 1972, Roots, The Next Generations 1979, Murder is Easy 1981, Charles and Diana: A Royal Romance 1982, North and South II 1986, Anastasia (Golden Globe Award) 1986, The Woman He Loved 1987; *Publications include:* Every Frenchman Has One 1962, Mother and Child (contrib) 1975.

Leisure interests: crossword puzzles, reading tales of mystery and imagination, painting on Sunday. *Address:* BP 156-16, 75764 Paris Cedex 16, France.

DE KEERSMAEKER, Baroness Anne Teresa; Belgian choreographer; b 11 June 1960, Wemmel; d of Maurits de Keersmaeker and Marie-Jeanne Lindemans; one s one d. *Education:* School of Maurice Béjart (Brussels), Tisch School of the Arts and New York Univ. *Career:* Debut Brussels (Belgium) 1980; Founder, Artistic Dir Rosas Dance Co 1983–, resident Théâtre de la Monnaie, Brussels 1992–; appeared at Turning World Festival, London 1992; directed opera Bluebeard (Bartók) 1997; Artistic Dir PARTS School 1995–; has also directed work for video; recipient of numerous int dance awards; Dr hc (Free Univ of Brussels) 1999. *Choreography includes:* Asch 1981, Fase: four movements to music of Steve Reich 1982, Rosas danst Rosas 1983, Elena's Aria 1984, Bartók/Aantekeningen 1986, Verkommenes Ufer/Medeamaterial/Landschaft mit Argonauten 1987, Mikrokosmos-Monument/Selbstporträt mit Reich und Riley (und Chopin ist auch dabei)/Im zart fliessender Bewegung-Quatuor Nr 4 1987, Ottone, Ottone 1988, Stella 1990, Achterland 1990, Erts 1992, Mozart/Concert Arias, un moto di gioia 1992, Toccata 1993, Kinok 1994, Amor Constante más allá de la muerte 1994, Erwartung/Verklärte Nacht 1995, Woud 1996, Just Before 1997, Three Solos for Vincent Dunoyer 1997, Duke Bluebeard's Castle 1998, Drumming 1998, Quartett 1999, I Said I 1999, In Real Time 2000; *Films include:* Hoppla! 1989, Achterland 1994, Rosas danst Rosas 1997. *Address:* Rosas VZW, Van Volxemlaan 164, 1190 Brussels, Belgium (Office). *Telephone:* (2) 344-55-98 (Office); *Fax:* (2) 343-53-52 (Office); *E-mail:* mail@rosas.be (Office); *Internet:* www.rosas.be (Office).

DE KLERK, Nina, MA, D LITT, PH D; South African professor of communications; b 12 Nov 1953, Vereeniging, Transvaal; d of Adrian Jacobus and Catharina Johanna (née Ackermann) Van Rooyen; m Dr Willem de Klerk; one s. *Education:* Rand Afrikaans Univ (Johannesburg, SA). *Career:* Lecturer Rand Afrikaans Univ 1977–82, Sr Lecturer 1982–84, Chair Dept of Communication Science 1982–92, Prof 1984–94; Guest Lecturer Univ of California at Sacramento, USA 1986; Distinguished Visiting Radcliffe Prof, Baylor Univ, Texas, USA 1992; Consultant to various S African cos 1980–89; Ed Communicare (official journal for communication sciences in SA) 1984–92; Exec Dir Asscn of Advertising Agencies 1995; invited by Council on Foreign Relations, New York to testify on the nature, effects and implications of the media restrictions then existing in SA 1988; Del Inst for a Democratic Alternative for S Africa, African Nat Congress (ANC), Harare, Zimbabwe 1989; Guest Speaker Advista Arabia IV Conf, Bahrain 1996; mem Council USA SA Leadership Exchange Prog 1990–94; mem South African Acad of Arts and Science; hosted Int Conf of European Asscn of Communications Agencies, Johannesburg (SA) 2000; numerous contribs to professional books and journals—over 45 scientific pubs and papers nat and int; named in Women We Remember 1886–1986 by Johannesburg City Council 1986; Finalist Boss of the Year 1992. *Address:* Association of Advertising Agencies, POB 2302, Parklands, 2121 Johannesburg, South Africa (Office); 13 Denbigh Rd, Parkwood, 2193 Johannesburg, South Africa (Home). *Telephone:* (11) 781-2772.

DE LA MARTINEZ, Odaline; Cuban composer and conductor; b 31 Oct 1949; d of Julian J. and Odaline M. Martinez. *Education:* In USA. *Career:* Founder, Dir European Women's Orchestra (EWO) 1990–, performances at Chard Festival of Women in Music 1990, in Abbotsbury (Dorset) and St John's Smith Square (London) 1992; Conductor with EWO of works by female composers including Clara Schumann, Grazyna Bacewicz, Eleanor Alberga, Minna Keal, etc; first woman to conduct a Promenade Concert, Royal Albert Hall, London 1984. *Compositions include:* First String Quartet; *Opera:* Sister Aimée: an American Legend 1984; *Publications include:* Mendelssohn's Sister. *Address:* c/o Kantor Concert Management, 67 Teignmouth Rd, London NW2 4EA, UK.

DE LA TOUR, Frances; British actress; b 30 July 1944, Bovingdon, Herts; d of Charles and Moyra (née Fessas) de la Tour; m Tom Kempinski 1972 (divorced 1982); one s one d. *Education:* Lycée français de Londres and Drama Centre (London). *Career:* With the RSC 1965–71. *Plays for the RSC include:* As You Like It 1967, The Relapse

1969, A Midsummer Night's Dream 1971, The Man of Mode 1971, Antony and Cleopatra 1999–2000; *Other plays include:* Small Craft Warnings (Best Supporting Actress, Plays and Players Award) 1973, The Banana Box 1973, The White Devil 1976, Hamlet (title role) 1979, Duet for One (Best Actress, New Standard Award, Best Actress, Critics Award, Best Actress, Soc of West End Theatres—SWET Award) 1980, Skirmishes 1981, Uncle Vanya 1982, Moon for the Misbegotten (Best Actress, SWET Award) 1983, St Joan 1984, Dance of Death 1985, Brighton Beach Memoirs 1986, Lillian 1986, Chekhov's Women 1986, 1990, Façades 1988, King Lear 1989, When She Danced 1991 (Best Performance in a Supporting Role Olivier Award, SWET), The Pope and The Witch 1992, Greasepaint 1993, Les Parents Terribles 1994, Three Tall Women 1995, Blinded by the Sun 1996, The Forest 1999, Fallen Angels (Variety Club Best Actress Award) 2001; *Films include:* Our Miss Fred 1972, To the Devil a Daughter 1976, Rising Damp (Best Actress, Standard Film Award) 1980, Murder with Mirrors 1984, Bejewelled 1990, Genghis Cohn 1994, The Cherry Orchard 1998; *TV appearances include:* Play for Today 1973, Crimes of Passion 1973, Rising Damp 1974, 1976, Cottage to Let 1976, Flickers 1980, Skirmishes 1982, Duet for One 1985, Partners 1986, Clem 1986, A Kind of Living (series) 1987/88, Downwardly Mobile (series) 1994, Cold Lazarus 1996, Tom Jones 1997; Hon Fellow Goldsmith Coll (London) 1999. *Address:* c/o Kate Feast Management, 10 Primrose Hill Studios, Fitzroy Rd, London NW1 8TR, UK (Office). *Telephone:* (20) 7586-5502; *Fax:* (20) 7586-4092.

DE LANDTSHEER-DE WAELE, Rita; Belgian international organization official; b Schellebelle; m Olivier de Landtsheer 1959; two s. *Education:* St Pierre (Ghent), Catholic Univ of Louvain, Univ of Geneva (Switzerland). *Career:* Freelance Press Attaché Nat Tourism Office 1974; f Brussels Convention Bureau 1977; Gen Sec European Fed of Conf Towns 1980–93, Gen Sec then Dir Int Relations 1993; Man Dir Congress Co-ordination Office 1982; f EMILG (European Meeting Industry Liaison Group); rep of business tourism at the insts of the EU; mem Soroptimist Club, Brussels and Sablon 1976–, Pres 1990–92; mem Club L (women's forum) 1985. *Leisure interests:* golf, arts, travel. *Address:* Keiweg 12, 1730 Asse, Belgium (Office). *Telephone:* (2) 452-98-30 (Office); (2) 452-71-44 (Home); *Fax:* (2) 452-21-50 (Office).

DE LOS ANGELES, Victoria; Spanish opera singer (soprano); b (Victoria Gómez Cima) 1 Nov 1923, Barcelona; m Enrique Magriñá 1948 (deceased); two s. *Education:* Univ and Conservatoire of Barcelona. *Career:* Barcelona debut 1945, Paris Opera and La Scala, Milan, Italy 1949, Royal Opera House, Covent Garden, London 1950, Metropolitan Opera House, New York 1951, Vienna State Opera 1957; numerous appearances at other opera houses, concert tours and recordings; Dr hc (Barcelona); First Prize, Geneva Int Competition 1947; Cross of Lazo de Dama of the Order of Isabel la Católica; Condecoración Banda de la Orden Civil de Alfonso X (El Sabio); numerous other orders and decorations. *Address:* Avda de Pedralbes 57, 08034 Barcelona, Spain.

DE MADARIAGA, Isabel, PH D, FBA, FRHISTS; British professor of Russian studies; b 27 Aug 1919, Glasgow; d of Salvador de Madariaga and Constance Archibald; m Leonard B. Schapiro 1943 (divorced 1976). *Education:* Ecole Int (Geneva, Switzerland), Headington School for Girls (Oxford), Instituto Escuela (Madrid) and Univ of London. *Career:* BBC Monitoring Service 1940–43; Cen Office of Information, London 1943–47; Econ Information Unit, Treasury 1947–48; Editorial Asst Slavonic and E European Review 1951–64; Part-time Lecturer in History LSE 1953–66; Lecturer in History Univ of Sussex 1966–68; Sr Lecturer in Russian History Univ of Lancaster 1968–71; Reader in Russian Studies School of Slavonic and E European Studies Univ of London 1971–81, Prof 1981–84, Emer Prof 1984–; Corresp mem Royal Spanish Acad of History, Spain. *Publications include:* Britain, Russia and the Armed Neutrality of 1780 1963, Opposition (jtly) 1965, Russia in the Age of Catherine the Great 1981, Catherine II: A Short History 1990, Politics and Culture in Eighteenth-Century Russia 1998; many scholarly articles. *Leisure interest:* music. *Address:* 25 Southwood Lawn Rd, Highgate, London N6 5SD, UK. *Telephone:* (20) 8341-0862.

DE MOLLER, June Frances; British business executive; b 25 June 1947; m 1967 (divorced 1980). *Education:* Roedean School, Hastings Coll and Univ de Paris (Sorbonne). *Career:* Mem staff Tangent

Industries; Exec Dir Carlton Communications 1983–93, Head of Corp Strategy and Business Devt 1991–93, Man Dir (with direct responsibility for TV equipment businesses) 1993–99; Dir British Telecommunications (BT) Ltd 1999–; Non-Exec Dir Anglian Water 1992–2000, Cookson Group PLC 1999–, Lynx Group PLC 1999–; mem Bd Riverside Mental Health Trust 1992–96. *Leisure interests:* reading, riding, tennis, Rare Breed Soc. *Address:* BT Ltd, 35 Cadogan Square, London SW1X 0HU, UK.

DE MORNAY, Rebecca; American actress; b 29 Aug 1962, Los Angeles, CA; m Bruce Wagner 1989 (divorced). *Education:* In Austria and Lee Strasberg's Los Angeles Inst. *Career:* Apprenticed at Zoetrope Studios. *Plays include:* Born Yesterday 1988, Marat/Sade 1990; *Films include:* One from the Heart 1982, Risky Business 1983, Testament 1983, The Slugger's Wife 1985, Runaway Train 1985, The Trip to Bountiful 1985, Beauty and The Beast 1987, And God Created Woman 1988, Feds 1988, Dealers 1989, Backdraft 1991, The Hand that Rocks the Cradle (Best Actress , Cognac Crime Film Festival 1992), Guilty as Sin 1993, The Three Musketeers 1993, Never Talk to Strangers, The Winner 1996, Thick as Thieves 1998, Table for One 1998, The Right Temptation 1999; *TV appearances include:* The Murders in the Rue Morgue 1986, By Dawn's Early Light 1990, An Inconvenient Woman 1992, Blind Side 1993, Getting Out 1994, The Shining 1996, The Con 1997, Night Ride Home 1999; Dir The Conversion 1996, ER 1999.

DE OBALDIA, Isabel, BFA; Panamanian painter; b 1957. *Education:* Pilchuck School of Glass (WA, USA), Rhode Island School of Design (USA), Ecole des Beaux Arts (Paris) and Univ of Panamá. *Career:* One-woman exhibitions in Panamá include Etcetera Gallery 1977, El Sotano de Panarte 1978, Arteconsult Gallery 1980, 1985, 1990, Museum of Contemporary Art 1981, 1986, 1989, Habitante Gallery 1990; group exhibitions include I Bienal Italo–Latinamerican (Rome) 1978, VI Bienal de San Juan–Latinamerican Etching (PR, USA) 1983, Nohra Haime Gallery (New York) 1985, II Bienal de la Habana (Cuba) 1986, I Bienal Internacional of Contemporary Painting (Cuenca, Ecuador) 1987, Coconut Grove Gallery (Miami, FL, USA) 1988, Juan de Juanes Gallery (Alicante, Spain) 1989, The Drawing Center (New York) 1989, The Emerging Generation (Nagoya, Japan) 1991, La Tertulia Museum (Cali, Colombia) 1991, Opus Gallery (Miami, FL, USA) 1991; John Hauberg Fellow (Pilchuck Glass School, WA, USA) 1990, nominated to Corning Glass Works Foundation 1991; First Prize for Graphic Arts (Panamanian Inst of Culture) 1990; Crystalex Novy Bor (Interglass Symposium, Czechoslovakia) 1991. *Leisure interests:* graphic design, etching in glass, karate. *Address:* Box 6-3125 El Dorado, Panamá, Panama.

DE PALMA, Rossy; Spanish actress; b (Rosa Elena García), Palma de Mallorca. *Career:* Fmrly singer with punk band Peor Imposible; actress in films of Pedro Almodóvar; fashion model for Spanish designers and for Jean Paul Gaultier, Paris. *Films include:* Law of Desire, Women on the Verge of a Nervous Breakdown, Kika, Las Hetairas, Prêt à Porter.

DE PANAFIEU, Françoise Marie-Thérèse; French politician; b 12 Dec 1948, Moyeuvre; d of François and Hélène Moissoffe; m Guy de Panafieu 1970; two s two d. *Education:* Inst de la Tour and Univ of Paris. *Career:* Exec personnel recruitment co 1970–73; Adviser to Deputy for 17th arrondissement of Paris 1974–79; Councillor 17th arrondissement of Paris 1979–80, 1995–, 16th arrondissement 1983–95; Deputy Mayor of Paris responsible for extra-curricular matters 1980–83, responsible for culture 1983–95, responsible for Parks, Gardens and Green Spaces 1995–2000; mem RPR, mem Political Bureau 1998–; mem Nat Ass (Parl) 1986–95, 1997–; apptd Minister of Tourism 1995. *Address:* Assemblée Nationale, 75355 Paris, France (Office); 56 rue Boileau, 75016 Paris, France (Home).

DE PASSE, Suzanne; American record company executive, writer and producer; m Paul Le Mat. *Education:* Manhattan Community Coll (NY). *Career:* Creative Asst to Pres Motown Productions, Los Angeles, CA 1968–81, Pres 1981; acts signed and developed for Motown include The Jackson Five, The Commodores, Frankie Valli and the Four Seasons, Lionel Richie, Thelma Houston, Billy Preston, Teena Marie, Rick James, Stephanie Mills; Chief Exec de Passe Entertainment. *TV and film productions include:* Lady Sings the Blues (co-author screenplay), Lonesome Dove, Motown on Showtime, Nightlife, Motown Revue,

Motown Returns to the Apollo (Emmy Award, Nat Acad for the Advancement of Colored People—NAACP Image Award), Motown 25: Yesterday, Today, Forever (Emmy Award, NAACP Image Award), Happy Endings (writer), Jackson 5 Goin' Back to Indiana (writer), Git on Broadway—Diana Ross and the Supremes and Temptations (creative consultant), TCB—Diana Ross and the Supremes and Temptations. *Address:* de Passe Entertainment, 5750 Wilshire Blvd, Suite 610, Los Angeles, CA 90036, USA.

DE PEDERY-HUNT, Dora, OC, MA; Canadian sculptor; b 16 Nov 1913, Budapest, Hungary; d of Attila and Emilia de Pédery. *Education:* State Lyceum (Budapest) and Royal School of Applied Art. *Career:* Moved to Canada 1948; mem Canada Council 1970–76; exhibitions, public collections include Laing Galleries (Toronto, ON), Int Exhibition of Contemporary Medals (The Hague, Netherlands) 1963, Biennial of Christian Art (Salzburg, Austria), Dorothy Cameron Gallery, Douglas Gallery (Vancouver, BC), Wells Gallery (Ottawa, ON) 1967, Govt of Canada Pavilion Expo '67, Int Sculpture Symposium 1978, Prince Arthur Gallerie 1978, Hamilton Art Gallery 1979, Nat Gallery of Canada, Art Gallery of Ontario, Dept of External Affairs (Ottawa), Museum of Contemporary Crafts, Royal Cabinet of Toronto, Smithsonian Inst (Washington, DC, USA), and Cologne (Germany) 1971, Helsinki 1973, Cracow (Poland) 1975, The Hague, Budapest 1975, Lisbon 1979; awards include Centennial Medal 1967, The Olympic Gold 100 Dollar Coin 1976, Ontario Arts Council Medal, Canada Nat Arts Centre Medal, Queen's Jubilee Medal 1977, Canadian Medal of Service. *Address:* 84 Carlton St, Apartment 613, Toronto, ON M5B 2P4, Canada.

DE PERIO-SANTOS, Rosalinda, BS, LL B; Philippine diplomatist; b 18 Oct 1939; d of José T. de Perio and Soledad M. Molina; m (deceased); one d. *Education:* Univ of the Philippines, Far Eastern Univ, Columbia Univ (New York) and Northwestern Univ (IL, USA). *Career:* Adviser Philippines Mission to the UN, New York 1962–64; Vice-Consul Consulate-Gen, New York 1964–66; Consul Consulate-Gen, Chicago, USA 1966–72; Minister Counsellor and Consul-Gen Brasilia 1981–83; Perm Rep of the Philippines to the UN and other int orgs, Geneva, Switzerland 1986–89; Amb to Israel and Non-Resident Amb to Cyprus and Jordan 1993–; numerous awards include Colombo Plan Fellow 1961, Rockefeller Fellow, Carnegie Endowment for Int Peace, Columbia Univ, NY 1961–62, Northwestern Univ Scholar 1967–68, Hague Acad Int Fellow 1974, Outstanding Zambaleña 1986, Outstanding Woman Lawyer, CIRDA 1987. *Leisure interests:* reading, music, travel. *Address:* Embassy of the Philippines, Textile Centre Bldg, 13th Floor, 2 Rehov Kaufmann, POB 50085, Tel-Aviv, Israel. *Telephone:* (3) 5175263; *Fax:* (3) 5102229; *E-mail:* filembis@netvision .net.il.

DE PIERREBOURG, Muriel, L ÈS L; French press attaché; b (Muriel Morra) 20 Oct 1950, Monaco; m Olivier de Pierrebourg 1970; three s. *Education:* Lycée Albert I (Monaco), Univs of Nice and Paris II (Panthéon-Assas). *Career:* Freelance Journalist 1975–81; Information Officer and External Relations Officer Fondation Delta 7 1980–81; Press Officer Radio Monte-Carlo 1981–84, Head Press Dept 1984–87; Pvt Sec to Chair La Sept (TV station) 1987–88; Official Rep to Presidency of the French Repub 1988–91, Press Attaché 1991–95; Head of Press and Communications, Cour des comptes 1995–2001; Spokesperson Dir-Gen UNESCO Aug 2001–; Chevalier de la Légion d'Honneur. *Address:* UNESCO, 7 place de Fontenoy, 75007 Paris, France. *Telephone:* (1) 45-68-10-00; *E-mail:* m.depierrebourg@unesco .org.

DE POSADAS, Carmen; Uruguayan author; b 13 Aug 1953, Montevideo; d of Luis and Sara de Posadas; m 1st (divorced); two d; m 2nd Mariano Rubio (died 1979). *Education:* British Schools in Uruguay and Madrid and St Julian's Convent (Oxford). *Publications include:* Mr North Wind (Ministry of Culture Prize) 1984, Cinco moscas azules 1996, Liliana Broja 1997 (Special Mention, Bologna Fook Fair), Nada es lo que parece 1997, Pequeñas Infamias (Planeta Prize) 1998, Un verano llamado amor 1999; 20 works for children; 2 screenplays; works translated into 10 languages including Japanese. *Leisure interests:* tennis, travel, reading and writing. *Address:* Jovellanos No 5, 280141 Madrid, Spain. *Telephone:* (91) 5213860; *Fax:* (91) 5217190; *E-mail:* visiortega@hotmail.com.

DE PRÉMONVILLE DE MAISONTHOU, Myrène Sophie Marie; French fashion designer; b 1 April 1949, Hendaye; d of Jean-Marie de Prémonville and Monique Arnault; m Yves Le Floc'h 1968 (divorced); one d. *Education:* Les Oiseaux (Paris). *Career:* Designer Pronostyl 1970–75; freelance designer and designer for Fiorucci (Italy) 1975–83; f Myrène de Prémonville SARL 1983 (Myrène de Prémonville SA 1986–), Gen Man and Designer. *Leisure interests:* art, cinema, travel. *Address:* 180 rue de Grenelle, 75007 Paris, France. *Telephone:* (1) 47-05-44-10.

DE RIVOYRE, Christine Berthe Claude Denis, L ÈS L; French journalist and writer; b 29 Nov 1921, Tarbes; d of François de Rivoyre and Madeleine Ballande. *Education:* Insts du Sacré-Cœur of Bordeaux and Poitiers, Univ of Paris and School of Journalism (Syracuse Univ, NY, USA). *Career:* Journalist with Le Monde 1950–55; Literary Ed Marie-Claire 1955–65; mem Haut comité de la langue française 1969–, Jury of Prix Médicis 1970–; Chevalier de la Légion d'Honneur; Chevalier des Arts et des Lettres; Grand Prix de la ville de Bordeaux 1973; Grand Prix Littéraire Prince Rainier de Monaco 1982; Prix Paul Morand 1984. *Publications:* L'alouette au miroir 1956, La mandarine 1957, La tête en fleurs 1960, La glace à l'ananas 1962, Les sultans 1964, Le petit matin (Prix Interallié) 1968, Le seigneur des chevaux (with Alexander Kalda) 1969, Fleur d'agonie 1970, Boy (Prix des Trois Couronnes) 1973, Le voyage à l'envers 1977, Belle alliance 1982, Reine-mère 1985, Crépuscule taille unique 1989, Racontez-moi les flamboyants 1995, Le petit matin 1998. *Address:* Editions Grasset, 61 rue des Saints-Pères, 75006 Paris (Office), France; Onesse-Laharie, 40110 Morcenx, France.

DE ROMILLY, Jacqueline, D ÈS L; French professor of classics and writer (retd); b 26 March 1913, Chartres; d of Maxime and Jeanne (née Malvoisin) David; m Michel Worms de Romilly (divorced). *Education:* Lycée Molière and Ecole Normale Supérieure (Paris). *Career:* Secondary school teacher 1939–49; Sr Lecturer Univ of Lille 1949–51, Prof 1951–53; Prof Ecole Normale Supérieure de Jeunes Gens 1953–60; Prof of Greek Language and Literature Univ of Paris 1957–73; Prof, Chair of 'Greece and the formation of moral and political thought', Collège de France 1973–84; retd 1984; mem Acad des Inscriptions et Belles-Lettres, Inst de France 1975–, elected to Acad Française 1988; mem Royal Danish Acad of Sciences and Letters; Corresp Fellow British Acad, Austrian Acad of Sciences, Acad of Athens, Bavarian Acad of Sciences (Germany), Royal Netherlands Acad of Arts and Sciences, American Acad of Arts and Sciences; Hon mem Soc for the Promotion of Hellenic Studies; Dr hc (Oxford, Athens, Dublin, Heidelberg, Yale, Montréal); Commdr de la Légion d'Honneur; Grand Officier de l'Ordre Nat du Mérite; Commdr des Palmes Académiques; Commdr des Arts et des Lettres; Commdr Greek Order of the Phoenix; Hon Insignia for Art and Sciences, Austria; Laureate, Acad Française 1974, Grand Prix for life's work 1984; Prix de la Langue de France 1987; Prix Onassis pour la culture 1995. *Publications:* L'enseignement en détresse 1984, Problèmes de la démocratie grecque (2nd edn) 1986, La modernité d'Euripide 1986, Sur les chemins de Sainte-Victoire 1987, Les grands sophistes dans l'Athènes de Périclès 1988, La Grèce antique à la découverte de la liberté 1989, Ouverture à cœur (novel, Prix Littéraire Rotary 1991) 1990; Pourquoi la Grèce? 1992, les Oeufs de Pâques 1993, Lettres aux Parents sur les Choix Scolaires 1993, Tragédies grecques au fil des ans 1995, Rencontres avec la Grèce antique 1995, Alcibiade ou les dangers de l'ambition 1995, Jeux de lumière sur l'Hellade 1996, Hector 1997, Le Trésor des savoirs oubliés 1998, Laisse flotter les rubans 1999, La Grèce antique contre la violence 2000, Héros tragiques, héros lyriques 2001 and about twenty books on classical Greek literature. *Address:* 12 rue Chernoviz, 75016 Paris, France. *Telephone:* (1) 42-24-59-07.

DE SMET, Chantal J. A., MA; Belgian art historian and feminist; b 13 Nov 1945, Ostend; d of André and Jeanne (née Provost) De Smet; m Michel Tanret 1971 (divorced 1978); partner Florent Vandekerckhove (until 1990); one d (adopted). *Education:* State Univ of Ghent, Nice, Budapest and Research Inst of Marxism-Leninism (Moscow). *Career:* Teacher Stedelijk Kunstinstituut 1971–75, Dir 1982–89; Prof of Fine Art and Aesthetics Royal Acad of Fine Arts, Ghent 1975–82, Dir 1989–95; Dean Dept Koninklijke Academie voor Schone Kunsten, Ghent 1995–; Adviser to Minister of Education 1992–94, to the Vice-Pres 1995–; mem Kommunistische Partij van België 1961–83, mem

Cen Cttee and Bureau 1982–83; mem Zal Wel Gaan 1966–69, Left Women's Alliance 1982–85; Co-Founder Studentenvakbeweging 1967, Dolle Mina (feminist group) 1970–75, Vrouwenoverlegkomitee (feminist co-ordination cttee) 1970–78, Masereelfonds 1970–79; Co-Founder and mem Bd RoSa (feminist research centre) 1979–94; f LeF-cahiers (left and feminist publs) 1978–82; Pres Abortion Support Org (Ghent) 1979–91; Vice-Pres Belgian Palestinian Org 1982–85; Pres Time Festival 1990–; mem Bd and Exec Cttee and Chair Programming Cttee European League of Insts of the Arts (ELIA) 1994–; mem Bd Stichting Kunste Naarsmateriaal 1996–. *Publications include:* Red Book of Women 1970, numerous articles on women, educ, culture, art. *Leisure interests:* reading, walking, black and white films. *Address:* KASK, J. Kluyskensstraat 6, 9000 Ghent, Belgium (Office); Nieuwland 48, 9000 Ghent, Belgium (Home). *Telephone:* (9) 266-08-85; *Fax:* (9) 266-08-81.

DE WAARD, Elly; Netherlands poet; b 8 Sept 1940, Bergen. *Education:* Murmellius Gymnasium (Alkmaar) and Univ of Amsterdam. *Career:* Teacher of poetry at Amazone 1983–; Founder-mem Anna Bijns Foundation and Anna Bijns Prijs (prize for women writers) 1985; Founder-mem The New Wild Ones (group of young female poets) 1988. *Publications:* Afstand 1978, Luwte 1979, Furie 1981, Strofen 1984, Een Wildernis van Verbindingen 1986, Onvoltooiing 1988, Eenzang 1992. *Leisure interest:* female friendship. *Address:* Vogelwater, Staringweg, 1935 MZ Egmond-Binnen, Castricum, Netherlands.

DE WACHTER, Marcia, M A (ECONS), PH D; Belgian economist and banker; b 9 Oct 1953, Wilrijk; d of Albert de Wachter and Flor van de Sande; m Leo Steenbergen 1976; two s. *Education:* Univ of Antwerp and Univ of Chicago. *Career:* Research Fellow Universitaire Faculteiten St Ignatius (UFSIA), Univ of Antwerp 1975–77, 1979–86, Lecturer 1984–88; Research Fellow Univ of Amsterdam 1984–85; Econ Advisor Econ Affairs Office of the PM 1986–1988; Co-ordinator Nat Bank of Belgium 1988–90, Spokeswoman 1990–94, Dept Advisor Gov's Office 1991–96, Sec-Gen 1996–99, Vice-Gov March 1999–; Fellow of Belgian–American Educational Foundation 1977; Award of the Socutera Inst 1970, of the Ranstad Inst 1981. *Publications include:* Macroeconomic Indicators for Belgium 1987, Belgium, A Buoyant Economy 1987, Investment in Belgium, Belgium–the Heart of Europe 1987; several specialist articles on employment policies and labour force participation. *Address:* blvd de Berlaimont 14, 1000 Brussels, Belgium; Boslaan 51, 3090 Overijse, Belgium. *Telephone:* (2) 221-21-54; *Fax:* (2) 221-31-21; *E-mail:* marcia.dewachter@bnbb.be; *Internet:* www.bnb.be.

DEAN, Laura; American composer and choreographer; b 3 Dec 1945, Staten Island, NY. *Education:* School of American Ballet and High School of Performing Arts. *Career:* Mem Paul Taylor Dance Co 1965–66; debut Brooklyn Acad of Music (New York) 1975, appearances at Joyce Theater, New York State Theater, Walker Arts Center; f Laura Dean Dancers and Musicians; commissioned by Joffrey Ballet and Ohio Ballet; exhibited paintings at Philadelphia Inst of Contemporary Art, Walker Arts Center, Pratt Inst, Het Muziektheater, Nat Museum of Dance; mem numerous review panels, Nat Endowment for the Arts, Nat Choreographic Project, Business in the Arts Awards; mem Bd Dirs Dance/USA, Nat Advisory Cttee Mid-America Arts Alliance; Guggenheim Fellow; Bessie Award; Brandeis Creative Arts Award; Dancemagazine Award. *Choreography includes:* Song, Dance, Music, Space, Bach Preludes, Stamping Dance, Spiral, Circle Dance, Changing Pattern Steady Pulse, Drumming, Tympani, High Fidelity, Night, Fire, Force Field, Sky Light, Transformer, Impact, For Two, Patterns of Change, Gravity, Dream Collector, Equator.

DEAN OF THORNTON-LE-FYLDE, Baroness (Life Peer), cr 1993, of Eccles in the Metropolitan County of Greater Manchester, **Brenda Dean;** British organization executive; b 29 April 1943, Salford; d of Hugh and Lillian Dean; m Keith Desmond McDowall 1988. *Education:* Stretford High School for Girls. *Career:* Admin Sec Soc of Graphic and Allied Trades (SOGAT, now Graphical Paper and Media Union—GPMU) 1959–72, Asst Sec Manchester Br 1972–76, Sec 1976–83, mem Nat Exec Council 1977–83, Co-Chair Women's Nat Comm 1985–87, Printing and Publishing Training Bd 1974–83, Supplementary Benefits Comm 1976–80, Price Comm 1977–79, Occupational Pensions Bd 1983–87, Pres 1983–85, Gen Sec 1985–91, Deputy Gen Sec 1991–92; Chair Independent Cttee for Supervision of Standards of Telephone Information Services 1993–; Dir Iveresk PLC

1994–; mem BBC Gen Advisory Council 1984–88, TUC Gen Council 1985–92, NEDC 1989–92, Employment Appeal Tribunal 1991–93, Armed Forces Pay Review Body 1993–94, Broadcasting Complaints Comm 1993–94, Press Complaints Comm 1993–98, Nat Cttee of Inquiry into Future of Higher Educ 1996–97, Royal Comm on House of Lords Reform 1999, House of Lords Appointments Comm 2000–; Hon MA (Salford) 1986; Hon DCL (City) 1993. *Leisure interests:* sailing, reading, relaxing, thinking. *Address:* House of Lords, London SW1A 0PW, UK.

DEANE, Phyllis Mary, MA, FBA, FRHISTS; British professor of economic history; b 13 Oct 1918; d of John Edward Deane and Elizabeth Jane Brooks. *Education:* Chatham County School, Hutcheson's Girls' Grammar School (Glasgow) and Univ of Glasgow. *Career:* Carnegie Research Scholar 1940–41; Research Officer Nat Inst of Econ and Social Research 1941–45; Colonial Research Officer 1946–48; Research Officer Colonial Office 1948–49; Dept of Applied Econs, Cambridge Univ 1950–61, Lecturer Faculty of Econs and Politics 1961–71, Reader in Econ History 1971–81, Prof 1981–82, now Prof Emer; Fellow Newnham Coll 1961–83, Hon Fellow 1983; Ed Economic Journal 1968–75; Pres Royal Econ Soc 1980–82; Hon D LITT (Glasgow) 1989. *Publications:* The Future of the Colonies (jtly) 1945, The Measurement of Colonial National Incomes 1948, Colonial Social Accounting 1953, British Economic Growth 1688–1959 (jtly) 1962, The First Industrial Revolution 1965, The Evolution of Economic Ideas 1978, The State and the Economic System 1989, The Life and Times of J. Neville Keynes 2001; papers and reviews in econ journals. *Leisure interest:* walking and gardening. *Address:* 4 Stukeley Close, Cambridge CB3 9LT, UK.

D'EAUBONNE, Françoise (Marie-Thérèse); French writer; b 12 March 1920, Paris; d of Count Etienne Piston and Rosita (née Martinez Franco) d'Eaubonne; m 1st Jacques Aubenque 1943; one d one s; m 2nd Pierre Sanna 1977. *Education:* Inst des Dames de Saint-Maur, Univ of Toulouse and Ecole des Beaux-Arts (Toulouse). *Career:* First book published 1944; 53 novels, essays and poetry collections published in total; journalist, Paris 1946–60; Publr's Reader Julliard 1953–, Calmann-Levy 1960–, Flammarion 1966–; broadcaster on ind local radio 1983–87, radio literary critic 1990–; Gen Sec Asscn SOS Sexisme 1988–; mem Conseil Nat des Ecrivains 1953–. *Publications include:* Comme un vol de gerfauts (Prix des Lecteurs) 1947, Les tricheurs 1960, Mme Germaine de Staël (Prix Chevassu 1967) 1966, La couronne de sable 1970, Les femmes avant le patriarcat 1976, A la limite des ténèbres 1983, Les grandes aventurières 1989, Toutes les sirènes sont mortes 1992, Vingt ans de mensonge ou la baudruche crevée 1994, Féminin et philiosophie 1997, La liseuse et la lyre 1997, Le sexocide des sorcières 1999, La plume et le baîllon 2000, L'homme de demain a-t-il futur? 2001. *Leisure interests:* travel in Europe, USA and N Africa. *Address:* 8 blvd Bonne-Nouvelle, 75010 Paris, France. *Telephone:* (1) 47-70-35-65.

DEBENEST, Jane; French diplomatist; b 21 Jan 1937, Niort; d of Delphin and Simone Debenest. *Education:* Inst d'Etudes Politiques (Paris) and Ecole Nat des Langues Orientales. *Career:* Sec Eastern Dept, Ministry of Foreign Affairs 1961, Asia-Oceania Dept 1962–64, Secr-Gen 1965, Europe Dept 1973–78; Third Sec, Belgium 1965–69, Second Sec, Japan 1969–72, Second Counsellor, USA 1978–84; Amb to Nicaragua 1984–86, to Trinidad, Tobago, Barbados and Guyana 1987; Amb, Perm Observer and Rep to OAS, Washington, DC, USA 1990–93; Minister Plenipotentiary to Lithuania 1991, Amb 1993–96; Amb to Luxembourg 1998–; Chevalier de la Légion d'Honneur; Chevalier de l'Ordre Nat du Mérite. *Address:* Embassy of France, 9 blvd Prince Henri, BP 359, 2013 Luxembourg.

DEBONNEUIL, Michèle; French economist; b 10 July 1948, Fontenay-aux-Roses; m Xavier Debonneuil 1971; one s one d. *Education:* Ecole Nat de la Statistique et des Etudes Economiques. *Career:* Dir INSEE (Inst Nat de la Statistique et des Etudes) 1974–86; Econ Councillor at the Treasury 1987–89; Dir and Economist Banque Indosuez 1990–96; Chef du Service Économique, Financier et Int, Govt Planning Dept 1998–; Adviser to OECD. *Publications:* several specialist papers on econs. *Leisure interests:* piano, running. *Address:* Commissariat général du Plan, 18 rue de Martignac, 75007 Paris, France (Office); 8 rue Feroy, 75006 Paris, France (Home). *Telephone:* (1) 40-46-04-76 (Office); *E-mail:* mdebonneuil@plan.gov.fr (Office).

DEBONO, Giovanna, BA; Maltese politician; b 25 Nov 1956, Gozo; d of the late Coronato Attard and of Anna (née Tabone) Attard; m Anthony Debono 1984; one s one d. *Education:* Victoria Girls' Secondary School and Univ of Malta. *Career:* Teacher Educ Dept 1981–87; MP, Nationalist Party 1987–; Parl Sec Ministry for Social Policy 1995–96; Opposition Spokesperson for Family Welfare 1996–98; Minister for Gozo 1998–. *Address:* Ministry for Gozo, St Francis Square, Victoria, VCT 102, Gozo, Malta. *Telephone:* 561482; *Fax:* 559360; *E-mail:* giovannadebono@magnet.int.

DECKER, Mary (see Slaney, Mary Teresa Decker).

DECROW, Karen, JD; American lawyer, writer, lecturer and feminist; b 18 Dec 1937, Chicago, IL; d of Samuel Meyer and Juliette Lipschultz; m 1st Alexander Allen Kolben 1960 (divorced 1965); m 2nd Roger Edward De Crow 1965 (divorced 1972). *Education:* Northwestern (IL) and Syracuse (NY) Univs. *Career:* Called to Bar, NY; Ed American Soc of Planning Officials 1960–61; writer Center for Study of Liberal Educ for Adults, Chicago, IL 1961–64; Ed Holt, Rhinehart, Winston Inc 1965; Textbook Ed Singer 1965–66; writer E Regional Inst for Educ 1967–69, Public Broadcasting System 1977; teacher Women and Law 1972–74; columnist Syracuse New Times; lecturer on law, gender and int feminism in USA, Canada, Greece, People's Repub of China, Mexico, Finland, USSR (now Russian Fed); Hon Trustee Elizabeth Cady Stanton Foundation; Co-Founder Woman Watch 1988; Nat Pres Nat Org for Women (NOW) 1974–77; mem numerous cttees and orgs; Hon DHL (State Univ of New York) 1994; Ralph E. Kharas Award (American Civil Liberties Union) 1985; Recognition Award for Best Newspaper Column (Syracuse Press Club) 1990; Best Column Award (New York Press Asscn) 1991, 1992, 1995. *Publications include:* with Roger De Crow: University Adult Education: A Selected Bibliography 1967, The Young Woman's Guide to Liberation 1971, Sexist Justice 1974, First Women's State of the Union Message 1977; The Pregnant Teenager (ed) 1968, Corporate wives, Corporate casualties (ed) 1973, Women Who Marry Houses: Panic and Protest in Agoraphobia (jtly) 1983, United States of America vs Sex: How the Meese Commission Lied About Pornography (jtly) 1988, Good Will Toward Men: Women Talk Candidly About the Balance of Power Between the Sexes 1994; numerous contribs to journals and newspapers. *Address:* 7599 Brown Gulf Rd, Jamesville, NY 13078-9636, USA.

DEECH, Ruth Lynn, MA, FRSM; British university administrator and lawyer; b 29 April 1943, London; d of Josef and Dora Fraenkel; m John Stewart Deech 1967; one d. *Education:* Christ's Hosp School, St Anne's Coll (Oxford) and Brandeis Univ (USA). *Career:* Called to the Bar, Inner Temple 1967; Legal Asst Law Comm 1966–67; Asst Prof Law Faculty, Univ of Windsor, Canada 1968–70; Fellow and Tutor in Law, Univ of Oxford 1970–91, Vice-Prin St Anne's Coll 1988–91, Prin 1991–; Common Univ Fund Lecturer in Law 1971–91; Lecturer in Law Hertford Coll 1973–78; Sr Proctor 1985–86; Visiting Prof Osgoode Hall Law School, York Univ, Canada 1978; Gov Carmel Coll 1980–90, Oxford Centre for Hebrew and Jewish Studies 1994–2000; Chair UK Human Fertilisation and Embryology Authority 1994–; mem Human Genetics Comm 2000–; Rhodes Trustee 1997–; Hon Fellow Soc for Advanced Legal Studies 1997; mem Hebdomadal Council 1986–, Exec Council Int Soc on Family Law 1988–; numerous articles on family and property law; Hon Bencher, Inner Temple 1996–. *Publications:* Divorce Dissent 1994; articles on family law, property law. *Leisure interests:* music, entertaining, after-dinner speaking. *Address:* St Anne's Coll, Oxford OX2 6HS, UK. *Telephone:* (1865) 274820 (Office); *Fax:* (1865) 274895; *E-mail:* ruth.deech@st-annes.oxford.ac.uk.

DEFEVER, Mia, D SC S; Belgian professor of medical sociology; b 4 May 1945, Ostend; m Paul Bracke 1967; one s one d. *Education:* Catholic Univ of Leuven. *Career:* Currently Prof School of Public Health, Catholic Univ of Leuven and Dir European Health Policy Forum; Assoc Ed Health Policy journal; numerous contribs to professional journals and lectures on health care trends in Europe, in Europe and USA 1983–; W. K. Kellogg Int Fellow 1986–90. *Leisure interest:* reading. *Address:* European Health Policy Forum, School of Public Health, Kapucijenvoer 35, 3000 Louvain, Belgium (Office); Keibergstraat 41, 8820 Torhout, Belgium (Home). *Telephone:* (16) 33-69-78 (Office); (50) 22-06-95 (Home); *Fax:* (50) 22-05-41 (Office); *E-mail:* mia.defever@med.kuleuven.ac.be.

DEFORGES, Régine Marie Léone; French writer and publisher; b 15 Aug 1935, Montmorillon; d of Clément and Bernadette (née Peyon) Deforges; one s one d; m 2nd Pierre Wiazemsky 1984; one d. *Education:* Inst St-Martial (Montmorillon). *Career:* Bookseller 1960–76; Founder and Chair Editions l'Or du Temps 1968, became Editions Régine Deforges 1984; Rep to Ministry of Culture 1982–83; mem Comité consultatif de la langue française, PEN-Club; mem judging panel Prix Fémina 1984–; Chair Soc des Gens de Lettres de France 1988–; Maisons de la Presse award 1981; Officier de la Légion d'Honneur 1992; Officier de l'Ordre Nat du Mérite. *Publications:* O m'a dit 1975, Blanche et Lucie 1977, Le cahier volé 1978, Contes pervers, Lola et quelques autres 1979, La révolte des nonnes 1981, La bicyclette bleue (three vols) 1982–86, Les enfants de Blanche 1983, Léa aux pays des dragons 1983, 101 avenue Henri Martin 1984, Le diable en rit encore 1985, L'Apocalypse 1985, Pour l'amour de Marie Salat 1986, Le livre du point de croix 1986, Sous le ciel de Novgorod 1988, Ma cuisine 1989, Juliette Gréco 1990, Mais Tango 1990, Rue de la Soie 1994, Roger Stéphane ou la passion d'admirer 1995, La dernière colline 1996, l'orage 1996, Pêle-mêle. Chroniques de l'Humanité 1998, 1999, 2000, Paris Chansons 1998, Cuba libre! 1999, Camilo 1999, Ville Blanche 2001. *Leisure interests:* bookbinding, framing, embroidery, painting, books. *Address:* 58 rue St André des Arts, 75006 Paris, France. *Fax:* (1) 43-54-39-16.

DEFRANTZ, Anita L., BA, JD; American sports administrator; b 4 Oct 1952. *Education:* Connecticut Coll and Univ of Pennsylvania. *Career:* Mem US Rowing Team 1975–80; Bronze Medallist and Team Captain Montréal Olympics 1976; four times finalist and Silver Medallist, World Rowing Championships 1978; mem US Oylmpic Cttee; mem Int Olympic Cttee (IOC) 1986–, mem Exec Bd 1992–, Vice-Pres 1997–, Chair IOC Women and Sport Working Group 1995–, mem numerous IOC Comms; mem Bd of Dirs US Rowing Asscn; Pres S Californian Olympian Soc, Amateur Athletic Foundation of LA 1987–; Vice-Pres Int Rowing Fed (FISA) 1993–; Trustee Women's Sports Foundation. *Address:* Chateau de Vidy, Case Postale 356, 1007 Lausanne, Switzerland.

DEGENERES, Ellen; American actress; b 26 Jan 1958, New Orleans. *Films:* Wisecracks, Coneheads 1993, Mr Wrong, Goodbye Lover, EdTV, If These Walls Could Talk 2000; *TV includes:* (series) Duet 1988–89, Open House 1989, Laurie Hill 1992, Ellen 1994–98 (also producer).

DEKANIĆ-OŽEGOVIĆ, Darinka, MD, PH D; Croatian medical practitioner; b 1 Nov 1943, Samobor; d of Ivan and Marija Dekanić; m Slavko Ožegović 1973; one d one s. *Education:* Univ of Zagreb and MRC Mineral Metabolism Unit (Leeds, UK). *Career:* Head Lab for Human Metabolism, Center for Osteoporosis, Inst for Medical Research and Occupational Health 1984; mem Croatian Soc of Physicians 1970, of Physiologists 1970, of Rheumatologists 1978, of Physical Medicine and Rehabilitation 1978; mem Nat Osteoporosis Soc (UK) 1992; numerous contribs to professional journals 1970–95; Rudjer Bošković Republican Scientific Award 1980. *Leisure interests:* gardening, reading. *Address:* Institute for Medical Research and Occupational Health, 10001 Zagreb, Ksaverska cesta 2, POB 291, Croatia. *Telephone:* (1) 214-460; *Fax:* (1) 274-572.

DEL CASTILLO VERA, Pilar; Spanish politician and academic; b 31 July 1952, Nador (Marruecos); m Guillermo Gortázar; two c. *Education:* Universidad Complutense de Madrid, Univ of Ohio (USA). *Career:* Lecturer in Constitutional Law, subsequently Prof of Political Science and Admin, Universidad Nacional de Educación a Distancia (UNED) 1986–; wrote policy papers for Fundación para el Análisis y los Estudios Sociales (FAES); Tech Adviser Centro de Investigaciones Sociológicas (CIS) 1987–88, Pres 1996–2000; Minister of Educ, Culture and Sport 2000–; fmr Ed Nueva Revista de Política, Cultura y Arte; mem Asociación Nacional e Internacional de Ciencia Política; Fulbright Scholar. *Address:* Ministry of Education, Culture and Sport, Alcala 34, 28071 Madrid, Spain. *Telephone:* (91) 5221100; *Fax:* (91) 5213575; *Internet:* www.mec.es.

DEL DUCA, Simone; French publisher and foundation executive; b 18 July 1912, Saint-Maur-des-Fossés; d of Henri and Gaëtane Nirouet; m Cino Del Duca (deceased). *Career:* Dir Del Duca group 1967–80, Pres

Dir-Gen Del Duca printing and publishing 1967–80; Dir Paris-Jour newspaper 1967–72; Admin La Vie des Métiers and Gallia-Publicité; literary Publr, Publr of Modes de Paris, Nous-Deux, Intimité, Télé-Poche magazines; Pres Industrie Grafiche Cino del Duca, Milan, Italy; Founder, Pres Fondation Simone et Cino del Duca 1975; Corresp mem Inst de France (Acad des Beaux-Arts) 1994–; Dr hc (Paris and Urbino, Italy); Commdr de la Légion d'Honneur; Officier de l'Ordre Nat du Mérite; Chevalier des Arts et des Lettres; Grand Officier du Mérite (Italy); Commdr de la Stella della Solidarieta Italiana (Italy); decorations from Malta and Monaco and numerous awards. *Leisure interest:* horse-racing. *Address:* Fondation Simone et Cino del Duca, 10 rue Alfred de Vigny, 75008 Paris, France.

DEL PAPA, Frankie Sue, JD, BA, LL B; American state official. *Education:* Univ of Nevada, George Washington Univ (DC) and Nat Law Centre. *Career:* Staff Asst Sen Alan Bible 1971–74; Law Clerk for US Dist Judge Bruce Thompson (Reno, NV) 1974–75; Assoc Lesley B. Grey 1975–78; Legis Asst to Sen Howard Cannon (Washington, DC) 1978–79; Partner Thronton and Del Papa (Reno, NV) 1979–84; pvt practice 1984–87; Sec-of-State, Nevada 1987–91; Attorney-Gen 1991–; mem numerous bds and cttees including Democratic Nat Cttee, Sierra Arts Foundation 1980–, Nevada Women's Fund, Univ of Nevada Bd of Regents 1980–86, Advisory Cttee Univ of Nevada, Coll of Arts and Science 1980–81, Truckee Meadows Community Coll 1980–86, Trust for Public Land 1985–, Women Execs in State Gov, Nevada Women's Comm, Nevada Domestic and Family Violence Prevention Council; awards include Humanitarian of the Year, Nat Conf of Christians and Jews 1989, Outstanding Democrat of the Year Award, Paradise Democratic Club of Las Vegas 1990, YWCA Woman of the Year 1994, Golden Pine Cone award for Environmental Excellence 1995, Sr Advocate's Person of the Year 1995, Woman of Distinction Award, Soroptimist International of Carson City 1996, Soroptimist International of the Americas, Sierra Nevada Region 1996. *Address:* Capitol Complex, Carson City, NV 89710, USA. *Telephone:* (702) 687-3510; *Fax:* (702) 687-5798.

DEL PONTE, Carla; Swiss lawyer; b 9 Feb 1947, Lugano. *Career:* Investigating Magistrate, Lugano Dist Attorney's Office 1981–, later Public Prosecutor; Swiss Fed Attorney-Gen 1994–2000; UN Chief War Criminals Prosecutor, UN Int Criminal Tribunal for Rwanda and Fmr Yugoslavia, The Hague, Netherlands Sept 1999–. *Address:* Public Information Unit, POB 13888, 2501 The Hague, Netherlands. *Telephone:* (70) 416-5233; *Fax:* (70) 416-5355.

DELAIR, Suzy; French actress and singer; b (Suzanne Pierrette Delaire) 31 Dec 1917, Paris; d of Clovis-Mathieu and Thérèse (née Nicola) Delaire. *Career:* Toured extensively throughout the world; Commdr des Arts et des Lettres; Chevalier de la Légion d'Honneur 1991. *Plays include:* Deux doux dingues, Adieu Prudence, Croque monsieur, Oscar, Le tube, L'ours, Tricoche et Cacolet, Que les hommes sont bêtes 1968, Nuits de Chine 1973, Le don d'Adèle; *TV appearances:* Hortense Schneider, L'argent par les fenêtres, L'or et la paille, Le manège des amoureux, Le mythomane, L'âge vermeil 1984, Traquenard 1987, Les tableaux qui parlent 1988; *Films:* Le dernier des six 1941, L'assassin habite au 21 1942, Défense d'aimer 1942, La vie de bohème 1942, Copie conforme 1946, Quai des orfèvres 1947, Par la fenêtre 1947, Pattes blanches 1948, Botta e riposta (Je suis de la revue) 1949, Lady Paname 1949, Souvenirs perdus 1950, Atoll K 1951, Le fil à la patte 1954, Gervaise 1955, Le couturier de ces dames 1956, Les régates de San Francisco 1959, Rocco et ses frères 1960, Du mouron pour les petits oiseaux 1962, Les aventures de Rabbi Jacob 1973, Oublie-moi Mandoline 1975; *Operettas:* Ta bouche, Un chien qui rapporte, La chaste Suzanne, Feu d'artifice, Mobylette, La vie parisienne, La Périchole, Boyfriend, Véronique 1980; *Recordings include:* Suzy Delair Chante Offenbach (Grand Prix du Disque 1962), Trois Valses (Prix de l'Acad Charles Cros). *Address:* 46 rue de Varenne, 75007 Paris, France.

DELAMAR SHAWYER, Penny; British make-up artist; b 31 Dec 1943, Denham; d of Mickey and Roma Rice Delamar; m David Shawyer 1977; two d one s. *Education:* Stoodley Knowle Convent (Torquay), Exeter Coll of Art and BBC TV Make-up Training School (London). *Career:* BBC TV Make-up Dept 1963–73, Make-up Designer 1968–73; Freelance TV and film make-up 1973–83; Founder and Dir The Make-up Centre 1986; Prin Delamar Acad of Make-up; Chair film make-up artists' branch of Broadcasting, Entertainment and Cinematograph Technicians' Union (BECTU); Key Rep Working Party on Nat Vocational Qualifications for Make-up and Hair in Broadcast, Film and Video; Trustee British Guild of Screen Make-up Artists. *Publication:* The Complete Makeup Artist Working in Film, Televisison and Theatre 1995; *TV programmes include:* The Scarlet Pimpernel, Wolcott, Nelson, Who Dares Wins, Covington Cross; *Films:* The Silent Witness, Børstene, Overlord, Caleb Williams, Chariots of Fire, Return to Oz, Underworld, Dream Lover, Santa Claus—The Movie, Revolution, Anguish 1986, Hope and Glory 1986, Aria 1987, Who Framed Roger Rabbit? 1987, Willow 1987, Imposter of Baker St 1987, Rainbow, Around the World in 80 Days, Dangerous Love, Indiana Jones and the Last Crusade, Jekyll and Hyde, The Punk 1992. *Leisure interests:* drawing, painting, gardening, reading, riding, skiing. *Address:* c/o The Make-up Centre, 26 Bute St, London SW7 3EX, UK.

DELAMATER, Clara Jeanne; French/American sculptor; b 28 March 1955, Neuilly-sur-Seine; d of Lloyd A. and Marie-Louise (née Viborel) Delamater. *Education:* American School (Paris), Acad Julian, Ecole des Beaux-Arts and Ecole d'Art de Montparnasse (Paris) and with Jacques Gestalder. *Career:* Prof of Sculpture Centre de Formation aux Techniques Artistiques, Paris 1978–80; Prof of Sculpture Parsons School of Design, Paris 1989–; Artistic Adviser and double for Isabelle Adjani's hands on film Camille Claudel 1988; has made programmes for nat and cable TV; solo exhibitions in Paris, Aix-en-Provence and Princeton (USA); numerous group exhibitions include La Nationale des Beaux Arts (Grand Palais, Paris) 1991 and Le Salon de Mars (Galerie Pierre Dumonteil, Paris) 1991, Galerie Mouvance (Paris) 1994, Galerie CCC (Paris) 1994, Musée Despiau Wlerick (Mont-de-Marsan) 1994, Princeton (USA) 1995, Espace Boullée (Hôtel de Ville, Issy-les-Moulineaux) 1995; comms include sculptures for Opéra de Paris 1982, Montparnasse Cemetery (Paris) 1984, Trocadéro (Paris) 1984, busts of Pres François Mitterrand, la Marianne and others for Aix-en-Provence and Marseilles town halls 1987–88, bust of Gen de Gaulle 1995; Assoc mem Acad des Beaux-Arts; Premier Prix des Jeunes Sculpteurs, Grand Palais, Paris; Premier Prix du Portrait P. L. Weiller, Acad des Beaux-Arts; Prix de l'Acad des Beaux-Arts 1990. *Leisure interests:* Brazilian and African dance, travel. *Address:* c/o 83 rue de la Tombe-Issoire, 75014 Paris, France.

DELANEY, Shelagh; British playwright; b 1939, Salford; one d. *Education:* Broughton Secondary School. *Career:* Has written numerous plays, films, radio plays and TV series. *Plays include:* A Taste of Honey (Charles Henry Foyle New Play Award, Arts Council Bursary, New York Drama Critics' Award) 1958, The Lion in Love 1960; *Films include:* A Taste of Honey (BFA Award, Robert Flaherty Award) 1961, The White Bus 1966, Charlie Bubbles (Writers' Guild Award) 1968, Dance with a Stranger (Prix Film Jeunesse-Etranger, Cannes, France) 1985; *TV includes:* Plays: St Martin's Summer 1974, Find Me First 1979; Series: The House that Jack Built 1977; *Radio plays:* So Does the Nightingale 1980, Don't Worry About Matilda 1983; *Publications include:* A Taste of Honey 1959, The Lion in Love 1961, Sweetly Sings the Donkey 1963. *Address:* c/o Tessa Sayle, 11 Jubilee Place, London SW3 3TE, UK.

DELANO SMITH, Catherine, D PHIL; British academic; b 31 March 1940, Wallingford. *Education:* Lady Margaret Hall (Oxford). *Career:* Asst Lecturer Dept of Geography, Univ of Durham 1964–67; Lecturer Dept of Geography, Univ of Nottingham 1967–79, Sr Lecturer 1979–89, Reader in Historical Geography 1989–90; Hon Reader in Historical Geography, Queen Mary and Westfield Coll, London 1990–93; Research Fellow Inst of Historical Research, London 1993–; Ed Imago Mundi, The International Journal for the History of Cartography 1994–. *Publications include:* Western Mediterranean Europe: A Historical Geography of Italy, Spain and Southern France since the Neolithic 1979, Maps in Bibles 1500–1600 (jtly) 1991. *Leisure interests:* gardening, listening to music. *Address:* 285 Nether St, London N3 1PD, UK. *Telephone:* (20) 8346-5112; *Fax:* (20) 8346-5112; *E-mail:* c.delano-smith@qmw.ac.uk.

DELAVAULT, Huguette, D ÈS SC; French mathematician; b 15 Jan 1924, Andilly; d of Franc Gilbert and Léopoldine (née Boeuf) Delavault. *Education:* Ecole Normale d'Institutrices (La Rochelle), Lycée Mondenard (Bordeaux), Ecole Normale Supérieure (Fontenay-aux-Roses) and Univ of Paris. *Career:* Researcher CNRS 1952–58; Prof of Mathematics Univ of Rennes 1958–70; Prin Inst Préparatoire à l'Enseignement Secondaire des Sciences, Rennes 1961–70; Jt Head Centre Pédagogique Régional de Rennes 1968–70; Prof Univ of Caen and Ecole d'Ingénieurs, Caen 1970–76, 1980–84; Deputy Head Ecole Normale Supérieure, Fontenay-aux-Roses 1976–80; retd 1984; Chair Asscn Française des Femmes Diplômées des Univs 1984–86, 1988–94; Prix de l'Acad des Sciences 1958; Officier des Palmes Académiques 1967; Chevalier de l'Ordre Nat du Mérite 1971; Chevalier de la Légion d'Honneur 1995. *Publication:* Les transformations intégrales à plusieurs variables—applications 1961. *Leisure interests:* music, reading. *Address:* 18 rue Juge, 75015 Paris, France. *Telephone:* (1) 45-75-50-24; *E-mail:* huguette.delavault@wanadoo.fr.

DELAY, Florence; French writer and professor of literature; b 19 March 1941, Paris; d of Jean Delay and Marie Madeleine Carrez. *Education:* Lycée Jean de la Fontaine (Paris) and the Sorbonne (Paris). *Career:* Lecturer in Comparative Literature Univ of Paris III 1972–; mem Editorial Bd Critique review 1978–96; theatre critic Nouvelle Revue Française 1978–85; mem Acad Française; mem jury Prix Fémina 1978–81; Officier des Arts et des Lettres; Grand prix de la ville de Paris 1999. *Publications include:* Minuit sur les jeux 1973, Le aie aie de la corne de brume 1975, Graal théâtre 1981, L'insuccès de la fête 1980, Riche et légère (Prix Fémina) 1983, Course d'amour pendant la deuil 1986, Petites formes en prose 1987, Partition rouge et l'Hexameron 1989, Etxemendi (Prix Mauriac) 1990, Semaines de Suzanne 1991, Catalina 1994, La fin des temps ordinaires 1996, La séduction brève 1997, Dit Nerval 1999. *Address:* c/o Gallimard, 5 rue Sebastien Bottin, 75007 Paris, France.

DELGADO MONTALVAN, M. Patricia, BA, MBA; Nicaraguan diplomatist and business executive; b 24 June 1947; d of Dr Tomas Delgado Mayorga and Olivia Montalvan de Delgado; m (divorced); two s one d. *Education:* Cen American Inst for Business Admin, Univ Centroamericana (Managua) and San Francisco Coll for Women (USA). *Career:* Asst to Pres Cen Bank of Nicaragua 1978–80, Deputy Head Org and Method Div 1981, Head Org and Method and Data Processing Divs 1981–83, Gen Sec 1984–86, Adviser to Pres 1986; Project Devt Officer Cen American Inst for Business Admin 1986–88, Assoc Dir for Devt 1988–90; Amb of Nicaragua to Nordic countries (Sweden, Denmark, Finland, Iceland, Norway) 1991. *Publications:* Effects of the Course 'Motivation for Achievement' based on McClelland's Theory of Motivation for Economic Achievement 1974, Central Bank of Nicaragua's Wage and Salary System 1977, Study of Production Units of the Ministry of Social Welfare 1980. *Leisure interests:* cooking, reading, dancing, personal development. *Address:* Embassy of Nicaragua, Sandhamnsgt 40, 115 28 Stockholm, Sweden (Office); Ynglingagatan 17, 4 tr, 113 47 Stockholm, Sweden (Home). *Telephone:* (8) 667 18 57 (Office); *Fax:* (8) 662 41 60 (Office).

DELHANTY, Joy Dorothy Ann, PH D; British geneticist; b 16 March 1937, Edgware; d of Ernest A. and Florence M. Thomson; m James J. Delhanty 1959; two s one d. *Education:* Harrow Co Girls' Grammar School and Univ of London. *Career:* Research Asst Dept of Genetics, Univ Coll London 1961–65, Lecturer 1965–84, Sr Lecturer 1984–92, Reader in Genetics 1992–; papers contributed to medical journals. *Leisure interests:* gardening, walking, cinema, travel. *Address:* University College London, Galton Lab, Human Genetics Group, Wolfson House, 4 Stephenson Way, London NW1 2HE, UK. *Telephone:* (20) 7380-7409; *Fax:* (20) 7387-3496.

DELL, Dame Miriam Patricia, DBE, ONZ, BA; New Zealand teacher and public servant; b 14 June 1924, Hamilton; d of the late Gerald and Ruby (née Crawford) Matthews; m Richard K. Dell 1946; four d. *Education:* Epsom Girls' Grammar School, Auckland Univ and Auckland Teachers' Training Coll. *Career:* Fmr teacher; Del Wellington Br Nat Council of Women 1957, Foundation mem Hutt Valley Br 1958, Pres 1966–68, Vice-Pres Nat Bd of Officers 1967–70, Nat Pres 1970–74, Nat Life mem 1984; Vice-Pres Int Council of Women (ICW) 1976–79, Pres 1979–86, Hon Pres 1986–88, Co-ordinator Devt Programme 1988, mem Cttee of Honour 1988–; NZ Govt Del to UN Int Women's Year Conf (México) 1975, UN Habitat Conf (Vancouver, Canada) 1976, German Marshall Plan Conf on Employment of Women (Paris) 1979, UN Mid-Decade Conf on Women (Copenhagen) 1980,

UN End of Decade Conf on Women (Nairobi) 1985; ICW Rep to UN Conf on Least Developed Countries (Paris) 1981, UN Conf for Non-Govt Orgs on Energy (New York) 1981; Chair numerous ICW Seminars and Workshops in the Middle and Far East, Europe, N America, Africa, etc 1970–90; Chair Cttee on Women 1974–81, 1993 Suffrage Year Centennial Trust 1991–94; Jt-Chair ECO (Environment and Conservation Org of NZ) 1986; mem Nat Devt Council 1969–74, Cttee of Inquiry into Equal Pay 1971–72, Educ Sub-Cttee and Nat Exec, Nat Marriage Guidance Council 1972–76, Social Security Appeal Authority 1974–99, Nat Comm for UNESCO 1974–85, Steering Cttee Nat Comm for Int Year of the Child 1977–79, Nat Advisory Cttee on Women and Educ 1979–82, Nat Museum Council 1989, Wellington Conservation Bd 1990–98; mem Inter-Church Council on Public Affairs 1974, Chair 1981–86, Sec 1986–87; mem Anglican Church Comm on Social Responsibility 1988–91, Convenor Public Affairs Unit 1988–90; Adele Ristori Prize 1976; Queen's Jubilee Medal 1977; Commemorative Medal 1990; NZ Suffrage Medal 1993. *Leisure interests:* gardening, reading, handcrafts, family, friends. *Address:* c/o 98 Waerenga Rd, Otaki, New Zealand.

DELPY, Julie; French actress; b 21 Dec 1969. *Education:* Univ of New York (USA). *Films:* Detective 1985, Mauvais Sang 1986, La Passion Béatrice 1987, L'Autre Nuit 1988, La Noche Oscura 1989, Europa Europa 1991, Voyager 1991, Warszawa 1992, Young and Younger 1993, The Three Musketeers 1993, When Pigs Fly 1993, The Myth of the White Wolf 1994, Killing Zoe 1994, Mesmer 1994, Trois Couleurs Blanc 1994, Trois Couleurs Rouge 1994, Before Sunrise 1995, An American Werewolf in Paris 1997, The Treat, LA Without a Map, Blah, Blah, Blah (Dir).

DELVAUX-STEHRES, Mady, MA; Luxembourg politician; b 11 Oct 1950, Luxembourg; three c. *Education:* Univ of Paris IV (Paris-Sorbonne). *Career:* Teacher Michel-Rodange High School until 1989; mem POSL 1974, mem Man Cttee 1984; Communal Councillor Luxembourg City 1987; Deputy for Centre Constituency, Head of List; Sec of State for Health, Social Security, Sports and Youth 1989–94; Minister for Communication, Transport and Social Security 1994–99. *Address:* c/o Ministry of Social Security, 26 rue Zithe, L-2936, Luxembourg.

DEMEESTER-DE MEYER, Wivina; Belgian politician; b 13 Dec 1943, Aalst; m Paul Demeester 1966; three s one d. *Education:* Koninklijk Atheneum Oudenaarde and State Univ of Ghent. *Career:* Agricultural Engineer; Co-Founder centre for the handicapped, Monnikenheide, Zoersel 1973, Dir 1973–84; elected to Chamber of Reps (CVP) for Antwerp 1974; mem City Council, Zoersel 1982; Sec of State for Nat Health and the Handicapped 1985–88, for Finance 1988; Minister of the Budget 1991; Community Minister for Finance and the Budget, Health Insts, Social Welfare and the Family 1992–1999; mem Parl of Flanders 1999–. *Publications:* Sociale Integratie voor Gehandicapten 1977, Bio-Ethica in de jaren '90 1987, Fiscaliteit 2000 1991, Het glazen plafond 1991. *Address:* Monnikendreef 5, 2980 Zoersel, Belgium. *Telephone:* (3) 312-23-60; *Fax:* (3) 311-77-06; *E-mail:* wivina.demeester@vlaamsparlement.be (Office) wivina.c.demeester@pandora.be (Home); *Internet:* www.demeester.com.

DEMENTIEVA, Elena; Russian/American tennis player; b 15 Oct 1981, Moscow; d of Viatcheslav and Vera Dementiev. *Career:* Began playing tennis at age 7, turned professional 1998; Semifinalist US Open 2000, Miami 2001; Silver medallist 2000 Olympics; reached final Sanex World Tennis Asscn Tour (Acapulco) 2001; world ranking of 12 in 2000. *Leisure interests:* chess, skiing. *Address:* c/o Bank Lane, Roehampton, London SW15 5XZ, UK.

DEMESSINE, Michelle; French politician; b 18 June 1947, Frelinghien (Nord); m; one c. *Education:* Valentine Labbé Tech Lycée (Lille). *Career:* Worked as sec 1964–75; elected a union del 1968, apptd mem Département Exec Cttee of Conféd Générale du Travail 1973; Dept Br Sec Union des Femmes Françaises 1976–90, now Hon Chair; joined Parti Communiste Français (PCF) 1970, elected mem Nord Département Cttee 1977, mem PCF Bureau 1977–; mem Regional Econ and Social Cttee 1983–95; Senator for Nord 1992–97; Vice-Chair Social Affairs Cttee, study group on combating drug trafficking and addiction, fact-finding mission on women in public life; municipal councillor for

Houplines 1995–; Sec of State for Tourism 1997–. *Publication:* Femmes d'ici (jtly) 1985. *Address:* Secretariat d'Etat au Tourisme, 40 rue du Bac, 75700 Paris, France.

DEMETEROVA, Gabriela; Czech violinist; b May 1971, Prague. *Education:* Prague Conservatoire and Acad of Fine Arts (Prague). *Career:* Has performed with leading Czech orchestras in France, Germany, UK, USA; winner Jaroslav Kocián Competition, Yehudi Menuhin Competition 1993. *Music:* recordings include: selection from Biber's Biblical Sonatas 1996, Di Italian Baroque, and numerous recordings for Czech Radio. *Leisure interests:* cycling, computer games, horse riding. *Address:* Ars Koncert sro, Úvoz 39, 602 00 Brno, Czech Republic. *Telephone:* (54) 3233116; *Fax:* (54) 3233358; *E-mail:* ars@arskoncert.cz.

DEMICHEL, Francine Denise; French university president; b 31 Oct 1938, Marseilles; d of Pierre and Françoise Batailler; m André Demichel 1967; one d. *Education:* Univ of Paris and Inst d'Etudes Politiques de Paris. *Career:* Prof Univ of Besançon 1969–70, Univ Lumière Lyon 2 1970–73; Prof Univ of Paris VIII (Vincennes à Saint-Denis) 1984–, Pres of Univ 1987–91; Deputy Dir, responsible for Educ, Directorate of Higher Educ, Ministry of Nat Educ 1992–93; Advisor to Ministry of Educ 1997; Dir of Higher Educ, Ministry of Educ 1998–; mem Council Ordre des Palmes Académiques 1998–. *Publications:* La lutte idéologique en France 1982, Eléments pour une étude des relations internationales 1987. *Address:* University of Paris VIII (Vincennes à Saint-Denis), 2 rue de la Liberté, 93526 Saint-Denis Cedex 02, France.

DEMIDOVA, Alla Sergeyevna; Russian actress; b 29 Sept 1936, Moscow; d of S. Demodov and A. Kharchenko; m Vladimir Valutsky 1961. *Education:* Moscow Univ and Shchukin Theatre School. *Career:* Actress with Taganka Theatre (Moscow) 1964–; f Little Theatre 'A' 1993; USSR State Prize 1977; People's Artist of RSFSR 1984. *Films include:* Day Stars 1968, The Sixth of July 1968, A Degree of Risk 1969, Tchaikovsky 1970, I Come to You 1972, The Seagull 1975, The Mirror 1975, The Little Scarlet Flower 1978, Father Sergius 1978, A Glass of Water 1979, Demons 1993; *Plays include:* The Cherry Orchard, Hamlet, Fedra M. Tsvetaeva, Wooden Horses; also performed Akhmatova's Requiem; *Publications:* The Shadows Behind the Mirrors, works on the art of theatre including The Second Reality, The Running Line of My Memory 2000; numerous articles. *Leisure interests:* philosophy, painting, gardening, her animals (two dogs and a cat). *Address:* 103009 Moscow, ul Tverskaya 8, korp 1, Apt 83, Russian Federation. *Telephone:* (095) 229-04-17.

DEMNEROVÁ, Kateřina, DIP ENG, PH D; Czech microbiologist; b 27 Sept 1947, Prague; d of Hugo Kaldarar and Ludmila Kaldararová; m Jiří Demner 1970 (divorced 1982); one s one d. *Education:* Prague Inst of Chemical Tech, Charles Univ (Prague), Univ of J. E. Purkyne (Brno). *Career:* Asst to Prof of Microbiology Prague Inst of Chemical Tech 1970–73, Research Asst (Microbiology) 1974–85, Assoc Prof of Microbiology (Gen Microbiology, Industrial Microbiology, Special Microbiology for Food Chemists, Microbiology for Students of Pharmacology) 1985–; Visiting UNIDO Research Scholar Univ of Manchester (UK) 1979–80; USIA grantee City Coll, City Univ of New York 1992; PECO grantee Univ of Wales (UK), Univ of Salamanca (Spain) 1992–95; mem Czech Society for Biochemistry and Molecular Biology, Biodeterioration Soc, Czech Biotechnology Soc, Czech Soc of Biology, Czech Chemical Soc, Czechoslovak Soc for Microbiology; 62 papers, 17 patents, seven textbooks published. *Leisure interests:* classical music, books, dance, travel. *Address:* Milady Horákové 63, 170 00 Prague 7, Czech Republic. *Telephone:* (2) 373405.

DEN HERTOG, Johanna Agatha; Canadian politician and trade union official; b 19 Aug 1952, Rijswijk, Netherlands; d of Wim and Ann Maria (née Smits) den Hertog; m Ronald Kirk Johnson 1985; one s one d. *Education:* Strathcona Comprehensive High School and McGill Univ (Montréal). *Career:* Co-Founder Vancouver Rape Relief 1973–75; Ombudsman Vancouver Status of Women 1975–76; Dir of Legislation and Research British Columbia Fed of Labour 1977–79; Asst to Pres and Vice-Pres Telecommunications Workers' Union 1979–92; Fourth Vice-Pres British Columbia New Democratic Party 1982–83, Chair Policy Review Cttee 1983–85, First Vice-Pres 1984–85, Nat Pres 1987–89; Fed election cand (Vancouver Centre) 1984, 1988; Dir of

Trade and Econ Liaison for the Premier of BC 1992–94; Special Adviser Int Relations on Forestry and the Environment, Office of the Premier, BC 1994, Ministry of Forests, BC 1995–; Nat Commr Citizens' Inquiry into Peace and Security 1990–92; mem Bd Canadian Centre for Arms Control 1985; Hon Canadian Scholarship (McGill Univ) 1970, 1971. *Publication:* English Canada Speaks Out (jtly) 1991. *Leisure interests:* music, travel, languages, family. *Address:* 2866 West 15th Ave, Vancouver, BC V6K 2Z9, Canada (Office); 2866 W 15th Ave, Vancouver, BC V6K 2Z9, Canada (Home). *Telephone:* (604) 733-0962 (Home).

DENCH, Dame Judith (Judi) Olivia, DBE; British actress; b 9 Dec 1934, York; d of Reginald Arthur and Eleanora Olave (née Jones) Dench; m Michael Williams 1971; one d. *Education:* The Mount School (York) and Cen School of Speech Training and Dramatic Art. *Career:* Played in Old Vic seasons 1957–61, with Old Vic Co at two Edinburgh Festivals, in Venice (Italy), on tour to Paris, Belgium and Yugoslavia, and on tour to USA and Canada; appearances with RSC 1961–62, Assoc mem 1969–, also on tour with RSC to Japan and Australia 1970, Japan 1972; on tour to W Africa with Nottingham Playhouse 1963; mem Bd Nat Theatre 1988–91; Hon D LITT (Warwick) 1978, (York) 1983, (Keele, Birmingham) 1989, (Loughborough) 1991, (Open Univ) 1994, (London) 1994, (Oxford) 2000; Prin Royal Scottish Acad of Music and Drama 2001–; Hon Fellow Royal Holloway Coll (London); Dr hc (Open Univ, London, Glasgow, Surrey); numerous awards include Paladino d'Argentino (Venice Festival Award for Juliet) 1961, Soc of West End Theatre (SWET) Award (for Lady Macbeth) 1977, BAFTA Award for Best Television Actress 1981. *Plays include:* The Three Sisters 1964–65, The Astrakhan Coat 1965, The Promise (Best Actress of Year, Variety London Critics) 1967, Cabaret 1968, London Assurance 1970, 1972, Major Barbara 1970, The Good Companions 1974, Too True to be Good 1975, 1976, Juno and the Paycock (Best Actress New Standard Drama Awards) 1980–81, The Importance of Being Earnest (Best Actress New Standard Drama Awards) 1982, A Kind of Alaska (Best Actress New Standard Drama Awards 1983) 1982, Pack of Lies 1983, Mother Courage 1984, Waste 1985, Mr and Mrs Nobody 1986, Antony and Cleopatra (Best Actress New Standard Drama Awards, Olivier Award for Best Actress) 1987, Entertaining Strangers 1987, Hamlet 1989, The Cherry Orchard 1989, The Sea 1991, The Plough and the Stars 1991, Coriolanus 1992, The Gift of the Gorgon 1993, The Seagull 1994, The Convent 1995, Absolute Hell 1995, A Little Night Music (Olivier Award for Best Actress in a Musical) 1996, Amy's View 1997, (New York) 1999, Filumena 1998; *Plays directed:* Much Ado About Nothing 1988, Look Back in Anger 1989, The Boys from Syracuse 1991, The Plough and the Stars 1991; *Films include:* A Study in Terror 1965, He Who Rides a Tiger 1966, Four in the Morning (Most Promising Newcomer, British Film Acad) 1966, A Midsummer Night's Dream (RSC Production) 1968, The Third Secret 1978, Dead Cert, Wetherby 1985, A Room with a View (BAFTA Award for Best Supporting Actress 1987) 1986, 84 Charing Cross Road 1987, A Handful of Dust (BAFTA Award for Best Supporting Actress) 1988, Henry V 1989, Jack and Sarah 1995, Goldeneye 1995, Mrs Brown (Golden Globe and BAFTA Best Actress Award) 1996, Tea with Mussolini 1998, Shakespeare in Love (Acad Award for Best Supporting Actress) 1998, The World is Not Enough 1999, Chocolat 2000; *TV appearances include:* Major Barbara, Pink String and Sealing Wax, Talking to a Stranger, The Funambulists, Age of Kings, Jackanory, Hilda Lessways, Luther, Neighbours, Parade's End, Marching Song, On Approval, Days to Come, Emilie, Comedy of Errors, Macbeth, Langrishe Go Down, On Giants Shoulders, Love in a Cold Climate, A Fine Romance, The Cherry Orchard, Going Gently, Saigon – Year of the Cat 1982, Ghosts 1986, Behaving Badly 1989, Absolute Hell, Can You Hear Me Thinking?, As Time Goes By, Last of the Blonde Bombshells (BAFTA Best Actress); *Publications include:* Judi Dench: A Great Deal of Laughter (autobiog), Judi Dench: With a Crack in Her Voice 1998. *Leisure interests:* painting, drawing, swimming, sewing, catching up with letters. *Address:* c/o Julian Belfrage Associates, 46 Albemarle St, London W1X 4PP, UK (Office).

DENES, Agnes (Cecilia); American artist; b 1931, Budapest, Hungary. *Career:* Instructor School of Visual Arts (New York) 1974–79, Skowhegan School of Painting and Sculpture (ME) 1979; Visiting Critic Univ of Pennsylvania 1991; lecturer at numerous univs and colls in USA, Canada, Italy and UK 1977–; one-woman exhibitions include

Columbia Univ (New York) 1965, Ohio State Univ 1974, Corcoran Gallery of Art (Washington, DC) 1974, Univ of Akron (OH) 1976, Newport Harbor Art Museum (CA) 1976, Rutgers Univ (NJ) 1976, Tyler School of Art, Temple Univ (PA) 1977, Centre Culturel Americain (Paris) 1978, Ikon Gallery (Birmingham, UK) 1978, Amerika Haus (Berlin) 1978, Inst of Contemporary Art (London) 1979, Galleriet (Lund, Sweden) 1980, Galerie Aronowitsch (Stockholm) 1980, Elise Meyer Inc (New York) 1980, Hayden Gallery, MIT 1980, Kunsthalle (Nuremberg, Germany) 1982, Northern Illinois Univ Art Gallery (IL) 1985, Univ of Hawaii Art Gallery (Honolulu) 1985, The Arts Club of Chicago 1990, Anselmo Alverez Galeria de Arte (Madrid) 1990, Herbert F. Johnson Museum of Art, Cornell Univ (NY) 1992, Wynn Kramarsky (New York) 1994; group exhibitions in N and S America, Europe, Japan; comms include Stelae—Messages from Another Time (Genova, Italy) 1986, Hypersphere—The Earth in the Shape of the Universe (New York) 1986–87, Bird Project: Visual Investigation of Systems in Motion (American-Scandinavian Foundation) 1988–89, N Waterfront Park Master Plan (Berkeley, CA) 1988–91, The Harold Washington Library Center (Chicago, IL) 1990–91, Bioscapes (Columbus, OH) 1991–; Individual Artist Fellow Nat Endowment for the Arts 1981, 1989; Research Fellow Studio for Creative Inquiry, Carnegie Mellon Univ (PA) 1993–; numerous awards and honours include Ann and Donald McPhail Award (The Print Club, Philadelphia, PA) 1982, Hassam and Speicher Fund Purchase Award (American Acad of Arts and Letters) 1985, Eugene McDermot Achievement Award (MIT Council for the Arts) 1990. *Publications include:* Sculptures of the Mind 1976, Paradox and Essence 1976, Isometric Systems in Isotropic Space: Map Projections 1979, Notes on Visual Philosophy 1986, Book of Dust—the Beginning and the End of Time and Thereafter 1989, The Dream 1990; numerous exhibition catalogues. *Address:* 595 Broadway, New York, NY 10012, USA. *Telephone:* (212) 966-0288; *Fax:* (212) 941-5484.

DENEUVE, Catherine (Catherine Dorléac); French actress; b 22 Oct 1943, Paris; d of Maurice Dorléac and Renée Deneuve; m David Bailey 1965 (divorced); one s (with Roger Vadim) one d (with Marcello Mastroianni). *Education:* Lycée La Fontaine (Paris). *Career:* Film debut in Les petits chats 1959; Pres, Dir-Gen Films de la Citrouille 1971–79; f Société Cardeva 1983; Jt-Chair UNESCO Campaign to protect the World's Film Heritage 1994–; photographic model for Yves Saint Laurent beauty products. *Films include:* Les portes claquent 1960, L'homme à femmes 1960, Le vice et la vertu 1962, Et Satan conduit le bal 1962, Vacances portugaises 1963, Les parapluies de Cherbourg (Palme d'Or, Festival de Cannes 1964) 1963, Les plus belles escroqueries du monde 1963, La chasse à l'homme 1964, Un monsieur de compagnie 1964, La Costanza della Ragione 1964, Repulsion 1964, Le chant du monde 1965, La vie de château 1965, Liebes Karussell 1965, Les créatures 1965, Les demoiselles de Rochefort 1966, Belle de jour (Golden Lion at Venice Festival 1967) 1967, Benjamin 1967, Manon 70 1967, Mayerling 1968, La chamade 1966, Folies d'avril 1969, Belles d'un soir 1969, La sirène du Mississippi 1969, Tristana 1970, Peau d'âne 1971, Ça n'arrive qu'aux autres 1971, Liza 1971, Un flic 1972, L'évènement le plus important depuis que l'homme a marché sur la lune 1973, Touche pas la femme blanche 1974, La femme aux bottes rouges 1975, La grande bourgeoisie 1975, Hustle 1976, March or Die 1977, Coup de foudre 1977, Ecoute, voir... 1978, L'argent des autres 1978, A nous deux 1979, Ils sont grands ces petits 1979, Le dernier métro 1980, Je vous aime 1980, Le choix des armes 1981, Hôtel des Amériques 1981, Le choc 1982, L'africain 1983, The Hunger 1983, Le bon plaisir 1984, Paroles et musiques 1984, Le lieu du crime 1986, Pourvu que ce soit une fille 1986, Drôle d'endroit pour une rencontre 1989, Helmut Newton: Frames from the Edge, La reine blanche 1991, Indochine (César Award for Best Actress 1993) 1992, Ma saison préférée 1993, La partie d'Échecs 1994, Les voleurs, Genéalogie d'un crime 1997, Place Vendôme 1998, Le vent de la nuit 1999, Belle-Maman 1999, Pola x 1999, Time Regained 1999, Dancer in the Dark 2000. *Address:* c/o Artmedia, 10 ave George-V, 75008 Paris, France (Office).

DENG LIN; Chinese artist; b 1941, Hebei Prov; d of Deng Xiaoping. *Career:* Solo exhibition Hong Kong 1993; group exhibition Blunden Oriental, Economist Office, London 1995. *Address:* Ministry of Culture, Jia 83, Donganmen Bei Jie, Dongcheng Qu, Beijing, People's Republic of China.

DENG NAN; Chinese politician; b Oct 1945, Guang'an, Sichuan Prov; d of the late Deng Xiaoping (fmr Gen Sec, CCP; fmr Chair, Gen Mil Comm, CCP) and of Zhuo Lin. *Career:* Joined CCP 1978; Vice-Minister in charge of State Science and Tech Comm 1991–98; Vice-Minister of Science and Tech 1998–. *Address:* Ministry of Science and Technology, 15B Fuxing Lu, Haidian Qu, Beijing 10015, People's Republic of China. *Telephone:* (10) 68515050; *Fax:* (10) 68515006; *Internet:* www.most.gov.cn.

DENG RONG; Chinese politician; b 1950, Chongqing, Sichuan; d of Deng Xiaoping; m He Ping. *Career:* Mem staff Embassy of the People's Repub of China 1976; mem Gen Political Dept, People's Repub of China Army; accompanies Deng Xiaoping on official engagements and expeditions. *Publication:* Deng Xiaoping: My Father 1995. *Address:* c/o Chinese Military Commission, Beijing, People's Republic of China.

DENG XIAOHUA, (pseudonym Can Xue); Chinese writer; b 30 May 1953, Changsha, Hunan; d of Deng Jun Hong and Li Ying; m Lu Rong 1979; one s. *Career:* Factory worker 1970–80; tailor 1980–85; professional writer 1985–. *Publications include:* Soap Bubbles on Dirty Water, Dialogues in Paradise 1989, Yellow Mud Street, Dating, Old Floating Cloud 1989, Apple Tree in the Corridor, The Instant when the Cuckoo Sings 1991, The Embroidered Shoes 1997, Castle of the Soul (essays on Kafka) 1999; works on Borges and Shakespeare. *Address:* c/o Chinese Literature Press, 24 Baiwanzhuang Lu, Beijing 100037, People's Republic of China; c/o 3-3 Bldg, No 904, He Xi, Changsha, Hunan, People's Republic of China.

DENG YAPING; Chinese table tennis player; b Feb 1973, Zhengzhou, He'nan Prov. *Career:* Mem of Chinese Women's Table Tennis Team 1988; winner of over 20 gold medals in various world championships; mem Sports Cttee of IOC. *Address:* c/o State General Bureau for Physical Culture and Sports, 9 Tiyuguan Rd, Chongwen District, Beijing, People's Republic of China.

DENHAM, Susan Gageby, BA, LL M; Irish judge; b 22 Aug 1945, Dublin; d of R. J. D. Gageby and Dorothy Lester; m Brian Denham 1970; three s one d (and one s deceased). *Education:* Alexandra Coll (Dublin), Univ of Dublin Trinity Coll, King's Inns (Dublin) and Columbia Univ (New York). *Career:* Called to the Bar 1971, to the Inner Bar 1987; mem Midland Circuit 1971–91; Sr Counsel 1987; Judge High Court 1991–92, Supreme Court 1992–; Pro-Chancellor Univ of Dublin Trinity Coll 1996–; Chair Cttee on Court Practice and Procedure; mem Courts Service Bd; fmr mem Free Legal Advice Centres, Garda Síochana Complaints Bd, Adoption Bd; fmr Chair Working Group on Courts Comm 1995–98; Hon Sec Cttee on Judicial Conducts and Ethics. *Leisure interests:* horses, gardens. *Address:* Supreme Court, The Four Courts, Morgan Place, Dublin 7, Ireland. *Telephone:* (1) 8725555; *Fax:* (1) 8725451.

DENIZE, Nadine; French opera singer; b 6 Nov 1942; d of Jean and Christiane Denize; m Bernard Bovrer-Lapierre 1971; one s. *Education:* Conservatoire Nat Supérieur de Musique de Paris. *Career:* Singer Opéra and Opéra Comique, Paris 1966–71, Opéra du Rhin, Strasbourg 1974–77, Vienna Opera 1977–79; Guest Singer Opéra de Paris 1974–89, Opéra Bastille, Paris 1989–93 and numerous opera houses in Germany, Italy, Portugal, Hungary, Yugoslavia, Netherlands, USA, Argentina, etc; has performed at the major opera houses and with major orchestras and concert groups in France and world-wide 1974–; appearances at numerous festivals; has performed the works of Wagner, Berlioz, Verdi, Beethoven, Mozart, Schoenberg, Mahler and Mussorgsky; Officier des Arts et des Lettres; Chevalier de l'Ordre Nat du Mérite 1986. *Leisure interest:* painting. *Address:* c/o Jean-Marie Polivé, 16 ave Franklin-Roosevelt, 75016 Paris, France (Agent); 35 rue François Bonvin, 75015 Paris, France (Home). *Telephone:* (1) 47-34-98-59 (Home).

DENNERLEIN, Barbara; Austrian jazz musician and composer; b 25 Sept 1964, Munich; d of Hans and Waltraud Dennerlein. *Education:* Ernst-Mach Gymnasium (Haar). *Career:* Began playing organ 1975; first concerts 1978; professional musician and composer 1983–, concerts and recordings world-wide; Head of Bebab, own record label; Deutsche Schallplattenkritik Award 1985, 1987; Downbeat Critics' Poll

No 1 (organ) 1990, 1991. *Recordings:* Orgelspiele 1984, Bebab 1985, Tribute to Charlie 1987, Barbara Dennerlein Plays Classics 1988, Straight Ahead 1989, Live on Tour 1989, Hot Stuff 1990. *Leisure interests:* music, arts. *Address:* Tsingtauerstr 66, 8000 Munich 82, Germany. *Telephone:* (8106) 31190 (Vaterstetten); (89) 4301500 (Munich); *Fax:* (8106) 1476 (Vaterstetten).

DENNIS, Donna Frances; American sculptor and teacher; b 16 Oct 1942, Springfield, OH; d of Donald P. and Helen Hogue Dennis. *Education:* Carleton Coll (Northfield, MN), Paris and New York. *Career:* Teaching positions at Skowhegan School of Painting and Sculpture (ME) 1982, Boston Museum School (Visiting Artist) 1983, State Univ of New York, Purchase Coll 1984–86, 1988–90, Assoc Prof 1990–96, Prof 1996, School of Visual Arts, New York 1983–90, Princeton Univ (Visiting Artist) 1984; one-woman exhibitions include West Broadway Gallery (New York) 1973, Holly Solomon Gallery (New York) 1976, 1980, 1983, 1998, Contemporary Arts Center, Cincinnati 1979, Locus Solus Gallery (Genova, Italy) 1981, Neuberger Museum (State Univ of New York, Purchase Coll) 1985, Univ Gallery (Univ of Massachusetts at Amherst) 1985, Brooklyn Museum (New York) 1987, Richard Green Gallery (New York) 1987, 112 Greene St (New York) 1987, Delaware Art Museum (Wilmington) 1988, Muhlenberg Coll Center for the Arts (Allentown, PA) 1988, Madison Art Center (WI) 1989, Indianapolis Museum of Art 1991–98, Sculpture Center (New York) 1993; group exhibitions include Walker Art Center (Minneapolis) 1977, Biennial Exhibition Whitney Museum 1979, Hirshhorn Museum (Washington, DC) 1979, 1984, Devts in Recent Sculpture (Whitney Museum) 1981, (Venice Biennale, Italy) 1982, 1984, New Art at the Tate (Tate Gallery, London) 1983, Storm King Art Center (Mountainville, NY) 1991, 42nd St Art Project 1994, Katonah Museum (NY) 1994, Neuberger Museum (State Univ of NY), Purchase Coll 1997, Asheville Art Museum (Asheville, NC) 1998; Fellow Nat Endowment for the Arts 1977, 1980, 1986, 1994; Distinguished Achievement Award, Carleton Coll 1989, Bard Award, City Club of New York 1989, Bessie Award for Set Design 1992. *Permanent commissions include:* Dreaming of Faraway Places: The Ships come to Washington Market, PS 234, New York, Klapper Hall, Queens Coll, City Univ of NY 1995, American Airlines Terminal, JFK Int Airport, NY 1996; *Publication:* 26 Bars (jtly) 1987. *Leisure interests:* exotic cooking, reading fiction, swing dancing. *Address:* 131 Duane St, New York, NY 10013, USA. *Telephone:* (212) 233-0605.

DERN, Laura; American actress; b 10 Feb 1967, Los Angeles; d of Bruce Dern and Diane Ladd. *Education:* Lee Strasberg Inst and Royal Acad of Dramatic Art (London). *Career:* Film debut at age 13 in Foxes 1980. *Films:* Teachers 1984, Mask 1985, Smooth Talk 1985, Blue Velvet 1986, Haunted Summer 1988, Wild at Heart 1990, Rambling Rose 1991, Jurassic Park 1993, A Perfect World 1993, Devil Inside, Citizen Ruth 1996, Bastard Out of Carolina 1996, Ruby Ridge 1996, October Sky; *TV appearances include:* Happy Endings, Three Wishes of Bill Greer, Afterburn 1992 (Golden Globe Award for Best Actress), Down Came a Blackbird, Fallen Angels 1993; The Gift (Dir) 1999; *Stage appearances include:* The Palace of Amateurs 1988, Brooklyn Laundry.

DERNESCH, Helga; Austrian opera singer; b 3 Feb 1939, Vienna; two c. *Career:* Sang many operatic roles in Berne, Switzerland 1961–63, Wiesbaden 1963–66 and Cologne, Germany 1966–69; freelance guest appearances at all major opera houses in Europe 1969–; regular appearances at Bayreuth Festival, Germany 1965–69, at Salzburg Easter Festival, Austria 1969–73; since 1979 has sung as mezzo-soprano; regular appearances at San Francisco Opera, USA 1981–; debut Metropolitan Opera, New York 1985; has sung in operas and concerts throughout Europe, N and S America, Japan; many recordings. *Leisure interests:* films, people, literature. *Address:* Neutorgasse 2/22, 1013 Vienna, Austria.

DERRYCK, Vivian Lowery, MIA; American organization official; b 30 Jan 1945, Cleveland, OH; m Robert Berg 1989; one d one s. *Education:* Columbia Univ (New York). *Career:* Sr Assoc Vice-Pres's Task Force on Youth Employment 1979; Dir US Secr World Conf of UN Decade for Women 1979–80; Deputy Asst Sec Dept of State 1980–82; Exec Vice-Pres and Dir Int Div, Nat Council of Negro Women 1982–84; Consultant Advisory Comm on Voluntary Foreign Aid and Agency for

Int Affairs 1984; Vice-Pres Nat Democratic Inst for Int Affairs 1984–88; Exec Dir Washington Int Center and Vice-Pres Meridian House 1988–89; Chair African-American Inst 1989; mem Int Devt Conf, Washington, DC 1983, Vice-Pres, mem Bd of Dirs 1983–89; Sec Bd, mem Exec Comm InterAction, Washington, DC 1990; fmr Asst Admin for Africa, United States Agency for Int Devt; fmr Sr Vice-Pres and Dir Public Policy Acad for Educ Devt (AED), Sr Vice-Pres and Dir Public/Pvt Partnerships Jan 2001–; Woman of the Year, Freetown, Sierra Leone 1990. *Address:* Academy for Educational Development, 1825 Connecticut Ave, Washington, DC 20009, USA. *Telephone:* (202) 884-8000; *Fax:* (202) 884-8000; *Internet:* www.aed.org.

DES PORTES, Elisabeth Marie Anne; French international organization official; b 21 Aug 1948; m Jean des Portes 1975; two s. *Career:* Teacher of Classics 1972–81; Researcher Marcel Proust work group, Centre d'Analyse des Manuscrits Modernes (attached to CNRS) 1975–80; Rep to Direction des Musées de France 1982–86; Asst Gen Sec ICOM 1986–90, Sec-Gen 1990; has published various articles for Le bulletin d'informations proustiennes, Archéologia, Brise and Museum 1975–80. *Leisure interests:* classical music, theatre, skiing. *Address:* ICOM, UNESCO, 1 rue Miollis, 75015 Paris, France. *Telephone:* (1) 47-34-05-00; *Fax:* (1) 43-06-78-62; *E-mail:* desportes@icom.org.

DESAI, Anita; Indian writer; b 24 June 1937; d of Toni Nimé and D. N. Mazumbar; m Ashvin Desai 1958; two s two d. *Education:* Queen Mary's School (Delhi) and Miranda House, Univ of Delhi. *Career:* Winifred Holtby Prize, Royal Soc of Literature 1978; Sahitya Adad Prize 1978; Hadassah Prize (New York) 1988; Padma Sri 1989; Neil Gunn Award for Int Writing 1994; Alberto Moravia Prize (Italy) 1999. *Publications:* Cry, The Peacock 1963, Voices in the City 1965, Bye-Bye Blackbird 1971, Where Shall We Go This Summer? 1973, Fire on the Mountain 1978, Games at Twilight 1979, Clear Light of Day 1980, The Village by the Sea 1983, In Custody 1984, Baumgartner's Bombay 1988, Journey to Ithaca 1995, Fasting, Feasting 1999, Diamond Dust and Other Stories 2000; *Film screenplay:* In Custody 1994; *TV:* The Village By The Sea (BBC) 1994. *Address:* c/o Deborah Rogers Ltd, 20 Powis Mews, London W11 1JN, UK.

DESCOMBES, Elisabeth; French business executive; b 20 April 1947, Paris; d of Jacques Mouchel-Blaisot and Mrs Barcelo (née Micheline); m 1st Patrick Descombes; one d; m 2nd Claude Limare 1980; one d. *Education:* Univ of Nanterre and Ecole Supérieure de Commerce (Paris). *Career:* French teacher 1968–73; Head of Advertising Jeune Afrique magazine, then Partir magazine 1974–79; Sales Dir Georges Chetochine marketing studies group 1979–80; Advertising Dir Première magazine 1980–85, Le Nouvel Observateur 1985–90; Sales Dir Régie 5 advertising co 1991–92; Man Dir Génération Expertise Média 1992–94, NRJ 1994–97, La Tribune newspaper 1997–2000; Vice Pres Radio Classique 1999–, Dir Gen 2000–. *Leisure interests:* cinema, travel, theatre, water skiing, swimming, collecting art deco objects. *Address:* Radio Classique, 12 bis place Henri Bergson, 75008 Paris, France.

DESHAYS, Claudie-André; French astronaut; b 1957. *Career:* Rheumatologist, expert in neuroscience; spent two weeks studying effects of weightlessness on the human body; returned to Earth from orbiting space station Mir Sept 1996, landed in Kazakhstan.

DESHPANDE, Shashi, BA, MA, BL; Indian writer; b 19 Aug 1938, Dharwood; d of Adya Rangacharya and Sharada Adya; m D. H. Deshpande 1962; two s. *Education:* Univs of Bombay and Mysore. *Career:* Fmrly worked for a law journal and magazine; full-time writer 1970–; mem Sahitya Akademi Bd for English 1989–94; Thirumathi Rangammal Prize; Sahitya Akademi Award for a Novel; Nanjangud Thirumalamba Award. *Film Script:* Drishti; *Publications:* The Dark Holds No Terrors 1980, Roots and Shadows 1983, That Long Silence 1988, The Binding Vine 1993, A Matter of Time 1996, The Intrusion and Other Stories 1994, Small Remedies 2000. *Leisure interests:* reading, music. *Address:* 409 41st Cross, Jayanagar V Block, Bangalore 560041, India. *Telephone:* (80) 6636228; *Fax:* (80) 6641137; *E-mail:* shashid@blr.vsnl.net.in.

DESJARDINS, Hon Justice Alice, BA, LL M; Canadian judge; b 11 Aug 1934, Montréal, PQ; d of Louis and Alexandrina (née Venne) Desjardins. *Education:* Coll Basile-Moreau (Montréal), Univ of Montréal and Harvard Univ (MA, USA). *Career:* Called to Bar, Québec 1958; Asst Lecturer in Law Univ of Montréal 1961–68, first Canadian woman Assoc Prof of Law 1968–69; Legal Counsellor Office of Privy Council, Ottawa 1969–74; Head Consultation and Admin Law Dept, Dept of Justice, Ottawa 1974–81; Justice Superior Court of Québec 1981–87; Judge Fed Court of Canada Appeal Div and *ex officio* mem Dept of First Instance 1987–; Judge Court of Appeal, Courts Martial of Canada 1988–; Cttee mem American Soc of Int Law 1971–72; Pres Ottawa Chapter Inst of Public Admin 1975, Nat Bd mem 1975–78; Pres Ottawa Chapter Canadian branch Int Law Asscn 1977–79, Vice-Pres Canadian Br 1984; Chair Int Section Harvard Law School Asscn 1999–; MacKenzie King Travelling Scholarship 1958–59, Ford Foundation Scholarship 1966; Hon D UNIV (Ottawa). *Address:* Federal Court of Canada, Appeal Div, Supreme Court Bldg, cnr Kent and Wellington Sts, Ottawa, ON K1A 0H9, Canada. *Telephone:* (613) 992-4997; *Fax:* (613) 952-1264.

DESROCHES-NOBLECOURT, Christiane; French curator and archaeologist; b 17 Nov 1913, Paris; d of Louis and Madeleine Desroches; m André Noblecourt 1942; one s. *Education:* Univ of Paris, Ecole du Louvre and Ecole des Hautes Etudes de la Sorbonne. *Career:* Curator, later Chief Curator Egyptian Antiquities at Musée du Louvre; Insp-Gen of Museums; fmr Prof Ecole du Louvre, UNESCO Adviser to Egyptian Govt; retd 1981; Commdr de la Légion d'Honneur; Commdr des Palmes Académiques; Commdr des Arts et des Lettres; Médaille de la Résistance; Grand Officier de l'Ordre de la Libération (Egypt); Silver Medal for Science and Culture (UNESCO); Médaille d'Or du CNRS 1975; Prix Saint-Simon 1992. *Publications:* Le style égyptien, Les religions égyptiennes, L'art égyptien, Toutankhamon, vie et mort d'un Pharaon, Catalogue of Toutankhamon Exhibition (Paris) 1969, Catalogue Ramses II Exhibition (Paris) 1977, Le petit temple d'Abou Simbel (2 vols), La grammaire des formes et des styles: Antiquité, L'univers des formes (jtly), La femme au temps des Pharaons 1987, La grande Nubiade 1992, Amours et fureurs de la lointaine 1995. *Address:* c/o 19 rue du Docteur Blanche, 75116 Paris, France.

DESSAY, Natalie; French soprano. *Education:* Bordeaux Conservatoire and Ecole de l'Art Lyrique. *Career:* Began career with concert of Mozart arias at La Scala (Milan); has since sung with many leading opera houses in France, Switzerland, Austria, USA and UK; Premier Prix de Concours, Les Voix Nouvelles Competition; First Prize, Int Mozart Competition, Vienna Staatsoper. *Operas include:* Die Entführung (Opéra de Lyon), Die Fledermaus (Geneva), Tales of Hoffmann (Opéra Bastille) 1992, Ariadne, Der Rosenkavalier (Vienna Staatsoper) 1993, Die Zauberflöte (Aix-en-Provence) 1994, Arabella (Metropolitan Opera, NY) 1994, Tales of Hoffman (La Scala, Milan) 1994, Die Zauberflöte (Opéra de Lyon 1996, Salzburg Festival 1997), Candide (Glyndebourne Festival) 1997, Alcina (Opera Garnier) 1999, Lulu (Vienna Staatsoper) 2000, Hamlet (Toulouse) 2000. *Address:* c/o EMI Classics, EMI House, Brook Green, London W6, UK.

DESTIVELLE, Catherine Monique Suzanne; French mountaineer; b 24 July 1960, Oran, Algeria; d of Serge and Annie (née Saigot) Destivelle; m Erik Decamp 1996; one s. *Education:* Lycée Corot (Savigny-sur-Orge) and Ecole Necker de kinésithérapie (Paris). *Career:* Physiotherapist 1981–85; mountaineer 1985–; winner World Climbing Championship 1985, 1986; solo ascent of Mt El Puro, Spain, by Chouca route 1988; winner Snowbird Int Competition, USA 1988; First woman to lead climb of Trango Tower (Karakoram Range, Jammu and Kashmir) 1990; First woman solo climber of Pilier Bonatti, Mont Blanc range 1990; First woman to open new solo route, Destivelle route, Mont Blanc 1991; First woman solo ascent N face of the Eiger, Swiss Alps 1992; attempted ascent of W face of Makalu (Nepal) 1993; ascent of Walker, N face of the Grandes Jorasses (France/Italy) 1993, Bonatti route, N face of Cervin (Italy) 1994; ascent of S face of Xixapangma (Tibet) 1994; First woman solo ascent of the N Face of the Cima Grande (Italy) 1999; Chevalier de l'Ordre Nat du Mérite; Prix Paul Deutsch de la Meurthe. *Films:* E pericoloso sporgersi 1985, Séo 1987, Solo Thaî 1989, Nameless Tower 1990, 11 jours dans les Drus 1991, Eiger 1992, Balade à Devil's Tower 1992, Cascade 1996; *Publications:* Danseuse de Roc 1988, Rocs Nature 1991, Annapurna, Duo pour un 8,000 1994,

L'Apprenti alpiniste 1997. *Leisure interests:* skiing, cycling, windsurfing, music, literature. *Address:* 53 rue Grenéta, 75002 Paris, France; Les Chavaux, 74310 Les Houches, France. *Telephone:* (4) 50-54-59-23; *Fax:* (4) 50-54-59-24; *E-mail:* catherine@destivelle.com; *Internet:* www.destivelle.com.

DETIÈGE, Leona Maria, BCS; Belgian politician; b 26 Nov 1942, Antwerp; d of A. Frans and Clementina Detiège; one d. *Education:* Coll of Governmental Commerce. *Career:* Mem SP, Nat Pres Socialist Women; Admin Sec and Asst Councillor Research Service for Ministry of Econ Affairs 1964–77; Special Adviser Cabinet of Econ Affairs 1970–74, assigned to Planning Office 1972–77; Prov Councillor Antwerp 1974–77, Alderman 1977–82; mem Chambre des Représentants/Kamer van Volksvertegenwoordigers (Parl) 1987–92, Hon mem 1995–, mem Sénat/Senaat (Senate) 1992–95, Minister of Employment and Social Affairs for Flanders 1992–95; Mayor of Antwerp 1995; mem Interparl Council of Benelux until 1988; Sec of State for Pensions 1988; Vice-Pres Belgian COOP; Pres OIVO (consumer asscn) until 1988; Pres Flemish Opera. *Address:* Cornelius Broeckxstraat 11, 2030 Antwerp, Belgium.

DEUTEKOM, Cristina; opera singer; b 28 Aug 1938, Amsterdam; one d. *Career:* First major appearance at Munich State Opera, Germany 1966, then at Vienna Festwochen; sang at Metropolitan Opera, New York 1967; has sung in all the major opera houses in Europe, especially Italy, and USA; specializes in bel canto operas by Rossini, Bellini and Donizetti and the Verdi operas; recordings for EMI, Decca and Philips; Grand Prix du Disque 1969, 1972. *Leisure interests:* driving round the world, singing, shopping (especially for shoes).

DEVERS, Gail; American sportswoman; b 19 Nov 1966, Seattle, WA. *Education:* Univ of California, Los Angeles. *Career:* Gold Medallist, 100m Olympic Games, Barcelona, Spain 1992, Atlanta, GA, USA 1996; Competitor World Championships 1994, 1995. *Address:* US Olympic Cttee, 1750 E Boulder St, Colorado Springs, CO 80909, USA.

DEVESON, Anne, AO; Australian writer and film producer; b 19 June 1930, Kuala Lumpur, Malaysia; d of Douglas and Barbara Deveson; m Ellis Blain 1957 (divorced 1978); two s one d. *Education:* Univ of London. *Career:* Broadcaster Macquarie Network 1966–74; mem Royal Comm into Human Relationships 1974–77; mem New S Wales Anti-Discrimination Bd 1977–80; Dir Australian Film, TV and Radio School 1985–88; mem Australian Film Finance Corpn 1990–; Chair SA Film Corpn 1983–85; Chair SA Children's Interest Bureau 1983–85, Ministerial Advisory Cttee on Mental Health 1990–, Centre for Independent Journalism, Univ of Tech, Sydney 1991; Chair Australian Soc of Authors 1995–98, Nat Advisory Cttee on Homelessness 1995–97; Deputy Chair Schizophrenia Australian Foundation 1985; mem NSW Guardianship Bd 1989–90, Advisory Cttee Brotherhood of St Lawrence Child Poverty 1989–90, Australian Writers' Guild, Australian Conservation Foundation; Hon Fellow Univ House ANU; Dr hc (New S Wales) 1994, (S Australia) 1995; UN Special Gold Citation Media Peace Prize 1981, 1983, 1984; Red Ribbon Award (New York Film Festival); Lifetime Achievement Award, Producers' and Dirs' Guild of Australia 1995. *Publications include:* Australians at Risk 1979, Faces of Change 1984, Tell Me I'm Here 1991, 1998, Coming of Age 1994. *Address:* Australian Society of Authors, POB 1566, Strawberry Hills, NSW 2012, Australia.

DEVLIN, Polly, OBE; Irish writer and journalist; b Co Tyrone. *Career:* Features Ed Vogue magazine; Columnist New Statesman, London Evening Standard; journalist with Vogue (American edn), Sunday Times, the Observer; winner Vogue talent competition 1964; mem judging panel Irish Times-Aer Lingus Irish Literature Prizes 1992. *Publications:* The Far Side of the Lough, All of Us There; Novel: Dora 1990.

DEVOY, Susan Elizabeth Ann, MBE; New Zealand squash player; b 4 Jan 1964, Rotorma; d of John Joseph and Tui Mavis Devoy; m John Oakley 1986. *Career:* Began playing squash at age six; NZ Jr Champion at age 11; represented NZ Sr Team at age 17; ranked No 1 in world from 1983; youngest ever winner British Open 1984; winner seven consecutive British Open titles, three World Championships (world record); walked length of NZ to raise money for Muscular Dystrophy charities

1988. *Publication:* Susan Devoy on Squash. *Leisure interest:* golf. *Address:* 122 Kingston Rd, Teddington, Middx TW11 9JA, UK. *Telephone:* (9) 602-353 (NZ); *Fax:* (9) 686-345 (NZ).

DEX, Shirley, BA, M SC, PH D; British economist; b 1 Oct 1950, Rochdale; d of Stanley H. and Alice Dex; m Roger Fane Sewell 1985; one d one s. *Education:* Greenhill Grammar School for Girls (Rochdale), Univs of Keele and Bristol. *Career:* Tutor in Sociology Univ of Exeter 1977–78; Lecturer in Econs Univ of Aston 1978–80, Univ of Keele 1980–89, later Sr Lecturer in Econs; Lecturer Judge Inst of Man Studies, Cambridge. *Publications:* The Sexual Division of Work 1985, British and American Women at Work (jtly) 1986, Women's Occupational Mobility 1987, Women's Attitudes Towards Work 1988, Life and Work History Analyses (ed) 1991.

DHALL, Kamala, MD; Indian professor of medicine; b 16 Sept 1932, Lyallpur; d of the late M. L. and S. D. Dhawan; m Gian Indra Dhall 1964; two c. *Education:* Panjab Univ and Univ of Madras. *Career:* Lecturer then Assoc Prof, Postgrad Inst of Medical Educ and Research until 1982, apptd Prof of Obstetrics and Gynaecology 1982, first Prof of Perinatology (sub-speciality of obstetrics and gynaecology) in India; chief investigator research projects funded by Family Planning Foundation, Indian Council of Medical Research, Nat Inst of Immunology; Del Conf on Role of Women in the Devt of Science and Tech in the Third World 1989; Guest Lecturer Perinatal Soc of Singapore 1990, Fed of Asia Oceania Perinatal Socs (Perth, WA) 1990; Pres Indian Soc of Perinatology and Reproductive Biology 1988–90; mem Asia Oceania Fed of Obstetrics and Gynaecology, Int Fed of Gynaecology and Obstetrics; numerous contribs to professional journals and chapters in textbooks; Population Council Fellow (Univ of Colorado, USA) 1970–71; WHO Fellow 1980; Swaran Kanta Dingley Oration Award (Indian Council of Medical Research) 1988. *Leisure interests:* gardening, cooking, interior decoration. *Address:* Postgraduate Inst of Medical Education and Research, Dept of Obstetrics and Gynaecology, Chandigarh 160012, India. *Telephone:* (172) 43043.

DHAMO, Dhorka, PH D; Albanian art historian; b 2 Dec 1935, Pogradec; d of Fondi Burnazi and Aspasi Gusho; m Kristaq Dhamo 1961; two d. *Education:* Univ Lomonosov (Moscow). *Career:* Medieval Art Section, Inst of History and Linguistics, Tirana 1957–69; Prof, Chair of Art History, Inst of Fine Arts, Tirana 1969–72; apptd Sr Lecturer 1972; Head Art History Section History Inst, Acad of Sciences, Tirana 1972–82, Head Ancient and Medieval Art Section, Centre for Archaeological Research 1982–90, later External Collaborator, Centre for Archaeological Research; External Prof in Gen History, Yugoslavia 1972–75; helped found Albanian Medieval Art Museum, Korça 1980–82 mem Editorial Bd Studime historike review 1980–84; mem Restoration Comm, Inst of Monuments and Culture 1980, Scientific Council Inst of History, Centre for Archaeological Research 1982, Scientific Council Fine Art Gallery 1986; contribs to historical journals. *Publications:* L'art médiéval albanais, L'art antique grecque et byzantin. *Address:* Druga Barrikada Pallati 216, Shkalla 4, Apt 21, Tirana, Albania. *Telephone:* (42) 27410.

D'HARCOURT, Florence; French politician; b 10 March 1929; d of Jean and Elisabeth (née de la Mauvinière) Deville; m 2nd Guillaume d'Harcourt 1955; four s one d. *Education:* Lycée de Charleville and Coll Ste-Marie (Paris). *Career:* Vice-Pres, later Pres Centre Féminin d'Etudes et d'Information—Femme Avenir 1970–75, Ed-in-Chief Femme-Avenir 1970–75; mem UDR, Deputy Sec-Gen 1974; Auditor Inst des Hautes Etudes de Défense Nat 1976; mem Nat Ass (Parl) 1977–88, mem Comm de la Défense Nat et des Forces Armées, currently Hon mem Nat Ass; Regional Councillor for Ile-de-France 1981–87; Municipal Councillor in Neuilly 1983–89; Judge High Court of Justice 1988; currently Vice-Pres Haut Comité Français pour la Défense Civile; numerous articles in newspapers; Médaille de la Famille Française 1975. *Publication:* La loi du clan 1998. *Leisure interests:* skiing, golf, trekking in the Himalayas. *Address:* 2 bis ave Raphaël, 75016 Paris, France. *Telephone:* (1) 45-04-14-88; *Fax:* (1) 45-04-24-35; *E-mail:* flodharcourt@aol.com.

DHARKER, Ayesha; Indian actress; b 1977, Bombay (now Mumbai); d of Anil and Imtiaz Dharker. *Education:* St Xaviers Coll (Bombay). *Career:* Film debut at the age of nine. *Films include:* Manika, Une Vie

Plus Tard 1986, City of Joy, The Terrorist (Best Artistic Contrib by an Actress, Cairo Film Festival), Star Wars Episode II; *TV includes:* Split Wide Open, Arabian Nights 2000; *Theatre includes:* The Ramayana (Royal Nat Theatre, London) 2001. *Address:* c/o ICM, 8942 Wilshire Blvd, Beverly Hills, CA 90211, USA.

D'HERBEZ DE LA TOUR, Solange Pauline Eugénie, B ARCH; French architect; b 8 Sept 1924, Bucharest, Romania; d of Albert and Juliette (née Zamfirolu) d'Herbez de la Tour. *Education:* Polytechnic (Bucharest). *Career:* Founder architectural co, Paris 1952–; architectural and urban planning comms for Ministries of Equipment and Housing, Health, Nat Educ, Youth and Sports; designer of housing units, flats, educ and cultural bldgs, shops, town planning projects, etc; Founder, Pres Union Française des Femmes Architectes (UFFA) 1960–, Union Int des Femmes Architectes (UIFA) 1963–; mem Bd and Council Int Union of Architects (French section) and various professional orgs; Hon Fellow American Inst of Architects 1986; Chevalier de l'Ordre Nat du Mérite 1965; Officier de la Légion d'Honneur 1981. *Leisure interests:* sports, films, paintings. *Address:* 14 rue Dumont d'Urville, 75116 Paris, France. *Telephone:* (1) 47-20-88-82; *Fax:* (1) 47-23-38-64.

DI NOVI, Denise; Canadian film producer; b 1957; two c. *Career:* Fmr journalist, reporter and film critic, Toronto; fmr Unit Publicist; Co-Producer, Assoc Producer and Exec in charge of Production Film Plan production co, Montréal 1980; Exec Vice-Pres of Production New World; Head Tim Burton Productions 1989–92. *Films include:* Visiting Hours, Going Berserk, Videodrome, Heathers, Edward Scissorhands, Meet the Applegates, Batman Returns, The Nightmare Before Christmas, Cabin Boy, Ed Wood, Little Women.

DIAH, Herawati, BA; Indonesian journalist; b 1917; m Burhanudin Mohamad Diah 1942. *Education:* Barnard Coll (Columbia Univ, New York). *Career:* Announcer and feature writer Indonesian Radio 1942; Sec to Minister of Foreign Affairs, Repub of Indonesia Sept–Dec 1945; Reporter daily Merdeka 1946; Ed Indonesian Sunday paper Minggu Merdeka Jan–July 1947 (when it was banned by Dutch authorities); Reporter Merdeka 1947–48; Ed illustrated weekly Madjalah Merdeka 1948–51, of Minggu Merdeka May 1951; Ed women's monthly magazine Keluarga (Family) 1953–59, daily Indonesian Observer 1955–59; Founder, Dir Foundation for Preservation of Indonesian Art and Culture 1967–; mem Int Fund for Cultural Devt (UNESCO) 1977; mem Exec Bd of Inst for Man and Educ Devt. *Address:* Jalan Diponegoro 61, Jakarta, Indonesia.

DIALLO, Aïssatou, M SC; Malian forestry engineer; b 1953, Mamou, Guinea; d of El Hadj Mamadou Tioutou Diallo and the late Hadja Fatou Barry; m Abou Lamine Berthe 1982; one s one d. *Education:* Inst Polytechnique (Conakry, Guinea) and Technical Forestry Acad (Leningrad, now St Petersburg, Russian Fed). *Career:* Apptd civil servant Direction Nat des Eaux et Forêts, Mali 1982, responsible for planning and evaluating econ action in the areas of forestry exploitation and women's employment in rural forestry. *Publications:* Femme et foresterie rurale au Mali 1989, Promotion des foyers améliorés au Mali: une solution aux problèmes 1991, Femme et gestion des ressources naturelles 1991. *Leisure interests:* reading, cinema, theatre, tourism. *Address:* Direction Nationale des Eaux et Forêts, BP 275, Bamako, Mali. *Telephone:* 22-58-50.

DIAMANTOPOULOU, Anna; Greek politician; b 1959, Kozani; m; one c. *Education:* Aristotle Univ of Thessaloniki and Panteion Univ of Athens. *Career:* Civil engineer 1981–85; Lecturer, Inst of Higher Technological Educ 1983–85; Man Dir of regional devt co; Prefect of Kastoria 1985–86; Sec-Gen for Adult Educ 1987–88; Sec-Gen for Youth 1988–89; mem Cen Cttee of PASOK 1991–99; Pres of Hellenic Org of Small and Medium-Sized Enterprises and Handicrafts (EOMMEX); Sec-Gen for Industry 1994–96; mem of Parl for Kozani 1996–99; Deputy Minister for Devt 1996–99; EU Commr for Employment and Social Affairs 1999–; mem Forum for Co-operation of Balkan Peoples, Int Women's Network. *Address:* Commission of the European Communities, 200 rue de la Loi, 1049 Brussels, Belgium. *Telephone:* (2) 298-2000; *Fax:* (2) 298-2099; *Internet:* europa.eu.int.

DIAZ, Cameron; American actress; b 30 Aug 1972, Long Beach Calif; d of Emilio and Billie Diaz. *Career:* Fmr model; Star of Tomorrow, Sho'West (film industry group) 1996. *Films include:* The Mask, The Last Supper, Feeling Minnesota, Head Above Water, She's The One, A Life Less Ordinary, There's Something About Mary 1998, Very Bad Things 1998, Being John Malkovich 1999, Invisible Circus 1999, Any Given Sunday 1999, Gangs of New York 2000, Charlie's Angels 2000, Things You Can Tell Just by Looking at Her 2000, Shrek (voice) 2001. *Address:* c/o International Creative Management, 8942 Wilshire Blvd, Beverley Hills, CA 90211, USA.

DICKINSON, Angie (pseudonym of Angeline Brown); American actress; b 30 Sept 1931, Kulm ND. *Education:* Immaculate Heart Coll and Glendale Coll. *Films:* Lucky Me 1954, Man With the Gun, The Return of Jack Slade, Tennessee's Partner, The Black Whip, Hidden Guns, Tension at Table Rock, Gun the Man Down, Calypso Joe, China Gate, Shoot Out at Medicine Bend, Cry Terror, I Married a Woman, Rio Bravo, The Bramble Bush, Ocean's 11, A Fever in the Blood, The Sins of Rachel Cade, Jessica, Rome Adventure, Captain Newman M. D., The Killers, The Art of Love, Cast a Giant Shadow, The Chase, The Poppy is Also a Flower, The Last Challenge, Point Blank, Sam Whiskey, Some Kind of a Nut, Young Billy Young, Pretty Maids All in a Row, The Resurrection of Zachary Wheeler, The Outside Man, Big Bad Mama, Klondike Fever, Dressed to Kill, Charlie Chan and the Curse of the Dragon Queen, Death Hunt, Big Bad Mama II, Even Cowgirls Get the Blues, The Maddening, Sabrina, The Sun—The Moon and The Stars, Pay It Forward; *TV films:* The Love War, Thief, See the Man Run, The Norliss Tapes, Pray for the Wildcats, A Sensitive Passionate Man, Overboard, The Suicide's Wife, Dial M for Murder, One Shoe Makes it Murder, Jealousy, A Touch of Scandal, Stillwatch, Police Story: The Freeway Killings, Once Upon a Texas Train, Prime Target, Treacherous Crossing, Danielle Steel's Remembrance; TV series: Pearl, Hollywood Wives, Wild Palms Police Woman, Cassie & Co.

DICKSON, Barbara; British singer and actress; b 27 Sept 1947, Dunfermline; d of the late Alastair H. W. and of Ruth (née Malley) Dickson; m Oliver F. Cookson 1984; three s. *Education:* Woodmill High School (Dunfermline). *Career:* Signed recording contract with Robert Stigwood Org 1975, with CBS Records 1978; Scot of the Year; Soc of West End Theatre Award (SWET—Best Actress in a Musical); Platinum, Gold and Silver Discs for album sales. *Musicals include:* John, Paul, George, Ringo and Bert 1974, Blood Brothers 1983; *Recordings include:* Singles: Answer Me 1976, Another Suitcase in Another Hall 1977, Caravans 1980, January February 1980, I Know Him So Well (jtly—UK No 1) 1986; Albums: All For a Song 1982. *Leisure interests:* walking, theatre, antiques, wine, paintings, politics. *Address:* c/o Rostrum House, Cheriton Place, Folkestone, Kent CT20 2DS, UK. *Telephone:* (1303) 850828; *Fax:* (1303) 244174.

DICKSON, Jennifer, CM, RA, LL D; Canadian artist and photographer; b 17 Sept 1936, S Africa; d of the late John L. and Margaret J. (née Turner) Dickson; m Ronald A. Sweetman 1962; one s. *Education:* Goldsmiths' Coll School of Art, Univ of London. *Career:* Assoc Atelier 17 (graphic workshop), Paris 1960–65; teacher Brighton Coll of Art, UK 1961–68, Univ of W Indies, Jamaica 1968, Univ of Wisconsin, USA 1972, Saidye Bronfman Centre, Montréal 1970–71, 1982–83, Ohio Univ, Athens 1973, 1979, Univ of S Illinois 1973, California State Univ, Sacramento 1974 and Denison Univ, USA 1976, Univ of Ottawa 1980–83, Sessional Instructor 1980–85; History of Art Lecturer Montréal Museum of Fine Arts 1988–91; visiting artist at many univs, colls etc; has held more than 55 one-woman exhibitions in six countries and participated in more than 350 group exhibitions; works in numerous public collections including Nat Gallery of Canada, Metropolitan Museum (New York), British Museum (London) and Hermitage Museum (St Petersburg, fmrly Leningrad); Fellow Royal Soc of Painter-Etchers and Engravers; Hon LL D (Alberta) 1988; awards include Prix de Jeunes Artistes pour Gravure (Biennale de Paris) 1963, Special Purchase Award, World Print Competition, San Francisco Museum of Art 1974, Biennale Prize, 5th Norwegian Int Print Biennale 1981. *Publications:* The Hospital for Wounded Angels 1987, The Royal Academy Gardener's Journal 1991, Water Song 1997, Garden Capricci 1999, Sanctuary: A Landscape of the Mind 2000, and suites of original prints and photographs; *Art Exhibitions:* The Last Silence: Pavane for a Dying World, Canadian Museum of Contemporary Photography 1993.

Leisure interests: historic gardens, opera, films. *Address:* 20 Osborne St, Ottawa, ON K1S 4Z9, Canada. *Telephone:* (613) 233-2315 (Studio); (613) 730-2083 (Home); *Fax:* (613) 730-1818 (Home).

DIDION, Joan, BA; American writer; b 5 Dec 1934, Sacramento, CA; d of Frank Reese and Eduene (née Jerrett) Didion; m John Gregory Dunne 1964; one d. *Education:* Univ of California at Berkeley. *Career:* Assoc Features Ed Vogue magazine 1956–63; fmr columnist Saturday Evening Post, Life; now freelance writer; mem American Acad of Arts and Letters, American Acad of Arts and Sciences; First Prize Vogue's Prix de Paris 1956; Morton Dauwen Zabel prize (American Asscn of Arts and Letters) 1978, Edward McDowell Medal 1996. *Publications:* Novels: Run River 1963, Play it as it Lays 1970, A Book of Common Prayer 1977, Democracy 1984, The Last Thing He wanted 1996; Essays: Slouching Towards Bethlehem 1969, The White Album 1979, After Henry 1992; Non-fiction: Salvador 1983, Miami 1987; Screenplays (with John Gregory Dunne): The Panic in Needle Park 1971, Play It as It Lays 1976, A Star is Born 1977, True Confessions 1982, Hill Like White Elephants 1990, Broken Trust 1995, Up Close and Personal 1996. *Address:* c/o Janklow & Nesbit, 445 Park Avenue, Floor 13, New York, NY 10022-2606, USA.

DIDO, (see Armstrong, Dido).

DIEKHAUS, Waltraud; German doctor and international organization executive. *Career:* Sec-Gen Medical Women's Int Asscn. *Address:* Medical Women's International Asscn, Wilhelm-Brand-Str 3, 44141 Dortmund, Germany. *Telephone:* (231) 9432-771; *Fax:* (231) 9432-773; *E-mail:* mwia@aol.com; *Internet:* members.aol.com/mwia/index.htm.

DIEZ DE RIVERA ICAZA, Carmen, LIC; Spanish politician; b 29 Aug 1942, Madrid. *Education:* Univ Complutense de Madrid and Escuela Oficial de Idiomas de Madrid. *Career:* Fmrly worked for Revista de Occidente, for Sociedad de Estudios y Publicaciones; Prof of Higher Educ, Côte d'Ivoire 1964–67; Head Int Relations for Spanish TV; Dir Cabinet of the Pres during transition to parl govt 1976; f Movimiento por el Desarrollo, la Paz y la Libertad (movt for devt, peace and liberty), Entente Ecológica Europea, and other ecological orgs; mem PSOE; MEP for the Balearic Islands and Menorca 1987, mem Socialist Group, Cttee on the Environment, Public Health and Consumer Protection, Interparl Del for Relations with Israel; mem Council Unión Europea de Radiodifusión; has written books on ecological subjects; Prize from Federación Amigos de la Tierra (Friends of the Earth) 1988. *Leisure interests:* swimming, cycling, music, reading. *Address:* European Parliament, rue Wiertz, 1047 Brussels, Belgium (Office); Henares No 10, Portal 3 izquierda, 28002 Madrid, Spain (Home). *Telephone:* (2) 284-58-95 (Office); (1) 4115151 (Home); *Fax:* (2) 284-98-95 (Office); (1) 4115151 (Home).

DIJK, Petronella (Nel) Bernardina Maria van; Netherlands politician; b 22 Oct 1952, Tilburg; one s. *Career:* Mem Communist Party of the Netherlands—CPN (later Rainbow/CPN, now GroenLinks) 1970–; MEP 1987, mem cttee on Social Affairs, Employment and the Working Environment, Chair Cttee on Transport 1991–94, Cttee on Women's Rights 1994. *Address:* European Parliament, 97–113 rue Belliard, 1047 Brussels, Belgium. *Telephone:* (2) 284-21-11; *Fax:* (2) 230-69-43; *E-mail:* nelvdijk@xs4all.nl; *Internet:* www.dds.nl/~groen-l/europa.html.

DILLARD, Annie, MA; American writer; b 30 April 1945, Pittsburgh, PA; d of Frank Doak and Gloria Lambert; m 1st R. H. W. Dillard 1965; m 2nd Gary Clevidence 1979 (divorced); m 3rd Robert D. Richardson, Jr 1988; one d two step-d. *Education:* Hollins Coll. *Career:* Contributing Ed Harper's Magazine 1974–85; Distinguished Visiting Prof Wesleyan Univ 1979–83, Adjunct Prof 1983–, Writer-in-Residence 1987–; mem Bd of Dirs Writers' Conf 1984– (Chair 1991–); mem Nat Cttee on US-China Relations; Nat Endowment for the Arts (Literature) Grant 1981; Guggenheim Memorial Grant 1985; Gov of CT's Award 1993; Campion Award 1994; Milton Prize 1994, American Arts and Letters Award in Literature 1998. *Publications:* Tickets for a Prayer Wheel (poetry), Pilgrim at Tinker Creek (prose, Pulitzer Prize) 1974, Holy the Firm 1978, Living by Fiction 1982, Teaching a Stone to Talk 1982, Encounters with Chinese Writers 1984, An American Childhood 1987, The Writing Life 1989, The Living 1992, The Annie Dillard Reader 1994, Mornings Like This (poetry) 1995, For the Time Being 1999. *Leisure interests:* soup kitchens in Key West, FL, and Chapel Hill, NC. *Address:* c/o Timothy Seldes, Russell and Volkening, 50 W 29th New York, NY 10011, USA (Office).

DIMITROV, Olga, RCA; Canadian costume designer; b 5 Jan 1933, Czechoslovakia; d of Svetoslav and Miskovska Dimitrov; m 1957; one c. *Education:* School of Ceramics (Karlsbad) and Acad of Applied Arts (Prague, Czechoslovakia). *Career:* Resident designer Civic Theatre Kladno and Civic Theatre Presov; guest designer for over 360 plays, operas, ballets and musicals throughout the fmr Czechoslovakia; costume designer for 18 films 1964–68; moved to Canada 1968; resident costume designer Neptune Theatre, Halifax, NS and Theatre London Co; costume designer Opera Dept, Indiana Univ, USA 1971–73; freelance costume designer for film, theatre and TV 1977–. *Designs include:* Films, TV, theatre: Closely Watched Trains, The End of August in Hotel Ozone, Fantastica, In Praise of Older Women, Agency, Silence of the North, Death Hunt, Harry Tracy, Dead Zone, The Boyfriend, One Magic Christmas, Samuel Lount, Man of La Mancha (Best Costumes Dora Mavor Moore Award), Millennium 1990, Bethune: Making of the Hero (Genie Award for Best Costume Design) 1991, Agaguk 1992, Johnny Mnemonic, Shadow of the Wolf (Genie Award for Best Costume Design) 1993, Pocahontas Legend 1993. *Address:* R.R.3, Crowes Line Rd, Bobcaygeon, ON K0M 1A0, Canada.

DIMITROVA, Blaga Nikolova, PH D; Bulgarian writer and politician; b 2 Jan 1922, Biala Slatina; d of Nikola and Maria Dimitrov; m Jordan Assenov Vassilev 1967; one s one d. *Education:* Univ of Sofia, Leningrad (now St Petersburg) State Univ and Moscow State Univ. *Career:* Ed Septemvri, Bulgarski Pissatel, Narodna Kultura 1952–77; mem Narodno Sobraniye (Parl) 1991–; Vice-Pres of Bulgaria 1992; visited Vietnam five times 1966–77; has written 12 books of poetry, four novels, three books on Bulgarian culture (jtly) and one book of political essays; Gotfried Herder Prize 1992. *Leisure interest:* music. *Address:* 1042 Sofia, General Parenssov str 4, Bulgaria.

DIMITROVA, Ghena; Bulgarian opera singer (soprano); b 6 May 1941, Beglej; m Gores Stoykov 1969; one d (adopted). *Education:* Bulgarian State Conservatoire (with Christo Bumbarov). *Career:* Debut Sofia Opera; Singer Laureate, Int Competition, Treviso, Italy 1972; appearances in France, Italy and Spain 1970, at Bolshoi Theatre (Moscow) 1975–78, Vienna State Opera 1978, Verona (Italy) 1980–, Barbican (London) 1983, La Scala (Milan, Italy) 1983, 1985–86, Salzburg Festival (Austria) 1984, Royal Opera House (Covent Garden, London) 1984, in Cen and S America, Germany, USA, Switzerland; Gold Medal and First Prize, Fourth Int Competition for Young Singers, Sofia 1970; People's Artist 1979; Golden Archer Prize (Rome) 1981; Giovanni Zenatello Prize (Verona) 1981; Verdi Prize 1987; Puccini Prize 1989. *Operas include:* Nabucco, Un Ballo in Maschera, Turandot, La Gioconda, Macbeth, Aida, Tosca, Norma, La Forza del Destino, Andrea Chénier, La Fanciulla del West; *Recordings include:* Nabucco, Oberto, Conte di San Bonifacio, Puccini arias. *Address:* Mühlgasse 22, No 21, Vienna 1040, Austria (Home). *Telephone:* (20) 7493-9158 (Agent); (1) 587-53-56 (Home); *Fax:* (20) 7629-0017 (Agent).

DIMMICK, Carolyn Reaber, BA, JD; American federal judge; b 24 Oct 1929, Seattle, WA; d of Maurice C. and Margaret T. Reaber; m Cyrus Allen Dimmick 1955; one d one s. *Education:* Univ of Washington. *Career:* Called to Bar, WA; Asst Attorney-Gen, WA 1953–55; Prosecuting Attorney King Co, WA 1955–59, 1960–62; pvt practice, Seattle, WA 1959–60, 1962–65; Judge NE Dist Court, WA 1965–75; King Co Superior Court 1976–80, US Dist Court (W Dist), Seattle 1985–; Justice Washington Supreme Court 1981–85; mem World Asscn of Judges, ABA, Judges' Asscn, Nat Asscn of Women Judges, American Judicature Soc; Hon LL D (Gonzaga Univ, City Univ of New York); Order of the Coif; Matrix Table Award 1981; World Plan Execs Council Award 1981. *Address:* US District Court 911, US Courthouse, 1010 5th Ave, Seattle, WA 98104, USA.

DINEEN, Molly; British film-maker; b 1959. *Education:* Nat Film School. *Career:* Has made numerous observational documentaries 1985–. *Films include:* Home From the Hill 1985, The Ark (Bafta Award) 1993, In The Company of Men 1995.

DINESCU, Violeta, MA; German (b Romanian) composer and professor of music; b 13 July 1953, Bucharest; d of Alfons and Elena Dinescu; m Nicolae Manolache 1993. *Education:* Ciprian Porumbescu Conservatory of Music. *Career:* Instructor of Theory, Piano, Harmony, Counterpoint and Aesthetics, George Enescu Music School 1987–90, Conservatory for Church Music (Heidelberg, Germany) 1989–91, Conservatory for Music (Frankfurt, Germany) 1989–92, Acad of Church Music, Bayreuth 1990–94; Prof of Composition Univ of Oldenburg (Germany); Special Corresp Music Section Romania Literară, Muzică 1975–82; European Corresp Living Music, CA, USA 1987–; Guest Lecturer univs in Germany, SA and USA; performances and radio recordings in Romania, Germany, France, UK, USA, Italy, Belgium, Switzerland, Austria, El Salvador, SA, Colombia, Finland, Czech Republic, Sweden, Portugal, Mexico, Luxembourg, Canada etc; mem Union of Composers of Romania 1982–, Int Arbeitskreis Frau und Musik (Germany) 1982–, Minnesota Composers' Forum (USA) 1984–, Exec Bd Int league of Women Composers (USA) 1985–; has been awarded numerous int grants, awards and prizes 1972–. *Compositions include:* Chamber music: Echoes I, Parra Quitarra, Din Cimpoiu, Dies Diem Docet, Scherzo da Fantasia III, Sleep Song, Kata, Ichthys, Figuren III, Stringquartet din Terra Lonhdana, Contraste, Alternances, Festspielfanfare, Fragment V, Letitae, Flutesplay II, In Search of Mozart!, Terra Lonhdana; Orchestra music: Transformations, Anna Perenna, Memories, Joc, Fresco, Kybalion; Voice and instrument music: Amont, Quatrain, Psalm 126, Concertino, Fragment I, Euraculos, Arpagic, In my Garden, Spring Song, Latin Sentences, Flower Song, Zori de flori, Bewitch Me into a Silver Bird!, The Play; Operas: Hunger and Thirst, Der 35 Mai, Eréndira, Schachnovelle; Ballet: Der Kreisel, Effi Briest; *Recordings include:* Internationales Festival Heidelberg 1987 1988, Fanny Mendelssohn-Quartet 1988, Internationales Festival Neue Musik 1991, over 40 CDs. *Leisure interests:* literature, travel. *Address:* Presuhn Str 39, 26133 Oldenburg, Germany. *Telephone:* (441) 42979; *Fax:* (441) 94904555; *E-mail:* violetta.dinescu@ uni-oldenburg.de; *Internet:* www.dinescu.net.

DING FENGYING; Chinese party official; b 1943, Luotian Co, Hubei Prov. *Education:* Huazhong Teachers' Coll. *Career:* Joined CCP 1961; Chair Hubei Br Chinese Women's Fed 1973; Vice-Chair Revolutionary Cttee, Hubei Prov 1978–79; Alt mem 12th CCP Cen Cttee 1982–87; First Sec CCP Cttee, Huangguang Pref 1983–; Deputy Sec CCP Cttee, Hubei Prov 1986–, mem 5th CPC Hubie Prov 1988–, Sec Comm for Discipline Inspection, Hubei Prov 1988–; mem CCP Cen Discipline Inspection Comm 1992–. *Address:* Hubei Dangwei, 1 Beihuanlu Rd, Shuiguohu, Wuchang City, Hubei Province, People's Republic of China. *Telephone:* (451) 813351.

DING JIEYIN; Chinese sculptor; b 4 Feb 1926, Yinxian, Zhejiang; d of Ding Yong-sen and Gao Yu-ding; m Hong Bo 1952; one d. *Education:* Cen Acad of Fine Arts (Beijing). *Career:* Asst Researcher Sculpture Studio, Cen Acad of Fine Arts; Ed China Sculpture; Chief Ed supplement Chinese Art, New Evening newspaper, Hong Kong; Vice-Dir Longshan Art Acad, Rizhao 1992–; mem China Artists' Asscn; has created about 60 pieces of sculpture; works in jt exhibition of Women Sculptors, China Art Gallery, Hong Kong 1990, China Art Gallery, Beijing 1991, 1992, and commissioned by various cities. *Publications:* Clay Figures in the Temples of Da Tong 1982, The Art of Colour Clay Sculpture in Jin Ancestral Temple 1988; articles in Meishu, Art Research, People's Daily and Chinese Art supplement, New Evening (Hong Kong). *Leisure interests:* literature, basketball. *Address:* Xiao-Wei-Hu-Tong 68, Beijing 100005, People's Republic of China. *Telephone:* (1) 5136377.

DINKINS, Carol Eggert, D JUR; American lawyer. *Education:* Univs of Houston and Texas. *Career:* Prin Assoc Texas Law Inst of Coastal and Marine Resources and Adjunct Asst Prof of Law Univ of Houston 1971–73; joined Vinson and Elkins 1973, Partner 1980–81, 1983–84, mem Man Cttee 1991–96, Partner 1991–; Asst Attorney-Gen Environment and Natural Resources Div, Dept of Justice, Washington, DC 1981–83, Deputy Attorney-Gen 1984–85; Visiting Prof Univ of Colorado 1986, various other univs 1986–; Del to Japanese-American Environmental Conf (Japan) 1982; Chair Gov's Task force on Coastal Zone 1979, Gov's Flood Control Action Group 1980–81, Pres's Task Force on Legal Equity for Women 1981–83; Commr Native Hawaiians Study Comm 1981–83; Sec Texas Nature Conservancy 1992–, Chair

1996–99; mem Environmental Protection Cttee of Interstate Oil Compact Comm 1979–81, Cttee Fed Judiciary Evaluation 1985–, Texas Legis Jt Select Cttee on Judiciary 1987–89, Policy Cttee of Galveston Bay Nat Estuary Program Man Conf 1988–91; mem numerous co bds including Oryx Energy Co (Dallas, TX) 1990–94, Environmental and Energy Study Inst (Washington, DC) 1986–, Nat Ocean Industries' Asscn 1986–92; mem ABA; Fellow Houston Bar Foundation, American Bar Foundation, Texas Bar Foundation; numerous awards and honours include Outstanding Houston Woman of the Year for Business (YWCA) 1989, One of the Nation's Leading Practitioners of Environmental Law (Nat Law Journal) 1990. *Address:* Vinson & Elkins, 2300 First City Tower, 1001 Fannin St, Houston, TX 77002, USA. *Telephone:* (713) 758-2528.

DION, Celine; Canadian singer; b 30 March 1968, Charlemagne, PQ; d of Adhémar and Thérèse Dion; m Rene Angelil 1995; one s. *Career:* First recordings in French, from the age of 12; became first Canadian to win Gold Disc in France with single D'amour ou d'amitié which sold over 700,000 copies 1983; winner of Eurovision Song Contest, Dublin 1988; tours of Europe 1995, UK 1996, world tour 1996–97; performed anthem The Power of the Dream at opening ceremony of Olympic Games, Atlanta 1996; semi-retd 2000; Officer, Nat Order of Québec; numerous nat and int awards including Gold Medal, Yamaha World Song Festival, Tokyo 1982, Female Vocalist of the Year, Juno Awards 1991, 1992, 1993, Medal of Arts (France) 1996 and many other awards. *Recordings include:* Albums: Unison 1991, Celine Dion 1993, The Colour of My Love 1994, D'Eux (biggest-selling album of all time in France) 1995, Falling Into You 1996, Let's Talk About Love 1997, S'il suffisait d'aimer 1998, These are Special Times 1998 (Grammy and Juno Awards 1999), All the Way ... A Decade of Song 1999; Singles: Beauty and the Beast (jtly) (Acad Award for Best Song Written for a Motion Picture or TV 1992, Grammy Award 1993) 1992, If You Asked Me To 1992, Love Can Move Mountains 1992, When I Fall In Love, Where Does My Heart Beat Now 1993, The Power of Love 1994, Misled 1994, Think Twice 1994, Only One Road 1995, Pour que tu m'aimes encore 1995, Misled 1995, Falling Into You 1996, Because You Loved Me 1996, It's All Coming Back to Me Now 1996, Call the Man 1996, All By Myself 1996, The Reason 1997, Tell Him 1997, My Heart Will Go On (Grammy Award 1999) 1998, Immortality 1998, Treat her Like a Lady 1998, That's the Way It Is 1999, The First Time I Ever Saw Your Face 2000; *Publication:* All the Way 2000. *Leisure interests:* skiing, water-skiing, roller-blading, miniature cups, crystal objects, tea pots, cuddly frogs, looking after son, golf. *Address:* Les Productions Feeling, 2540 Blvd Daniel-Johnson, Porte 755, Laval, Québec H7T 2S3, Canada (Office).

DISNEY, Anthea; British business executive; b 13 Oct 1946, Dunstable; d of Alfred Leslie and Elsie Wale; m Peter Robert Howe 1984. *Education:* Queen's Coll. *Career:* Journalist Daily Sketch, New York 1969; Overseas Corresp Daily Mail, New York 1973–75, Features Ed Daily Mail, London 1975–77, Bureau Chief, New York 1977–79; columnist London Daily Express, New York 1979–84; Man Ed New York Daily News 1984–87; Ed Sunday Daily News 1984–87; Ed US magazine 1987–88; Ed-in-Chief Self magazine 1988–89; magazine developer Murdoch magazines 1989–90; Exec Producer A Current Affair, Fox TV 1990–91; Ed-in-Chief TV Guide magazine 1991–95, Delphi Internet Service; Editorial Dir Murdoch Magazines 1994–95; Pres and CEO HarperCollins Publrs 1996–97; Chair, CEO News America Publishing 1997–; Feature Ed New York Daily News 1984; Ed Us magazine 1987, Self magazine 1988; Ed-in-Chief TV Guide 1991–95, Delphi Internet Service, Exec Producer A Current Affair, News Corpn; Pres and CEO HarperCollins 1996–. *Address:* News America Publishing Group, 1211 Avenue of the Americas, New York, NY 10036, USA (Office).

DISS, Eileen, FRSA; British theatre, film and television designer; b 13 May 1931; d of Thomas and Winifred Diss; m Raymond Everett 1953; two s one d. *Education:* Cen School of Art and Design. *Career:* Designer BBC TV 1952–59; freelance Designer for theatre, film and TV 1959–; BAFTA TV Design Award 1962, 1965, 1974, 1992, 2000. *Plays include:* Butley 1971, The Caretaker 1972, 1980, 1991, Blithe Spirit 1976, Close of Play 1979, When We Are Married 1979, Otherwise Engaged 1980, Translations 1981, Incident at Tulse Hill 1981, Measure for Measure 1981, Rocket to the Moon 1982, The Trojan War Will Not Take Place

1983, The Communication Cord 1983, The Common Pursuit 1984, Other Places 1985, Sweet Bird of Youth 1985, Circe and Bravo 1986, The Deep Blue Sea 1988, Veterans Day 1989, The Mikado 1989, Steel Magnolias 1989, Burn This 1990, The Philanthropist 1991, Private Lives 1992, Oleanna 1993, Cellmates 1995, Taking Sides 1995, The Hothouse 1995, Twelve Angry Men 1996, The Heiress 1997, Ashes to Ashes 1998, Arcadia 1999, The Room 2000, Celebration 2000; *Films include:* A Doll's House 1972, Sweet William 1978, Betrayal 1982, Secret Places 1984, 84 Charing Cross Rd 1986, A Handful of Dust 1988, August 1994; *TV includes:* Series and plays: Maigret 1962–63, The Tea Party 1964, Up the Junction 1965, Somerset Maugham 1969, Uncle Vanya 1970, The Duchess of Malfi 1972, Candide 1972, The Importance of Being Earnest 1973, Pygmalion 1973, Caesar and Cleopatra 1974, Moll Flanders 1975, The Winslow Boy 1976, You Never Can Tell 1977, The Rear Column 1980, The Potting Shed 1981, Porterhouse Blue 1987, Behaving Badly 1989, Jeeves and Wooster 1989, 1990, Love on a Branch Line 1993, A Dance to the Music of Time 1997, Longitude 1999; TV Opera: The Merry Widow 1968, Tales of Hoffmann 1969, Die Fledermaus 1971, Falstaff 1972, The Yeomen of the Guard 1974; Films: Cider with Rosie 1971, Robinson Crusoe 1975. *Leisure interests:* music, cinema. *Address:* 4 Gloucester Walk, London W8 4HZ, UK. *Telephone:* (20) 7937-8794.

DITTRICH VAN WERINGH, Kathinka, PH D; German cultural administrator; b 26 June 1941, Mittenwald; m Jacobus van Weringh. *Education:* Munich and Amsterdam. *Career:* Worked at Goethe-Inst in Germany 1967–69, in Barcelona (Spain) 1975–79, in New York (USA) 1979–86; Head Goethe-Inst, Amsterdam 1986–90; Dept Head Goethe-Inst Cen Admin, Munich 1986–90; Head Culture Centre in Moscow 1990–94; Head Culture Dept, City of Cologne. *Publications:* Der niederländische Spielfilm der dreißiger Jahre und die deutsche Filmemigration 1987; many other publs on European art and culture. *Address:* c/o Department of Culture, Richartzstr 2, 50667 Cologne, Germany.

DIXON, Sharon Pratt (see Kelly, Sharon Pratt).

DJWA, Sandra Ann, B ED, PH D; Canadian professor of English; b 16 April 1939, St John's, NF; d of Walter William and Dora Beatrice Drodge; m 1st Peter Djing Kioe Djwa 1958 (divorced 1987); one s; m 2nd Lalit Srivastava 1991. *Education:* Univ of British Columbia. *Career:* Asst Prof of English Simon Fraser Univ, BC 1968–75, Assoc Prof 1976–80, Prof 1980–, Chair Dept of English 1986–94; Ed Annual Review of Poetry, Letters in Canada, Univ of Toronto Quarterly 1979–84; Sr Killam Family Fellow 1981–82; mem Asscn of Canadian Univ Teachers of English; Fellow Royal Soc of Canada 1994. *Publications include:* E. J. Pratt: The Evolutionary Vision 1974, Saul and Selected Poetry of Charles Heavysege 1976, On F. R. Scott: Essays on his Contributions to Law, Literature and Politics (co-ed) 1983, The Politics of the Imagination: A Life of F. R. Scott 1987, E. J. Pratt: Complete Poems (co-ed), Giving Canada a Literary History: A Memoire (ed) 1991. *Leisure interests:* gardening, writing. *Address:* 2947 Marine Drive W, Vancouver, BC V7V 1M3, Canada.

DLAMINI-ZUMA, Nkosazana C., MB CH B; South African politician and doctor; b 27 Jan 1949; m; four c. *Education:* Amanzintoti Training Coll, Univ of Zululand, Univ of Natal, Univ of Bristol (UK) and Univ of Liverpool (UK). *Career:* Research Technician Medical School, Univ of Natal 1972; Vice-Pres SA Students Org 1975–76; Chair ANC Youth Section GB 1977–78; House Officer Frenchay Hosp Bristol 1978–79; House Officer Canadian Red Cross Memorial Hosp, Berks 1979–80; Medical Officer-Pediatrics Mbabane Govt Hosp Swaziland 1980–85; Pediatric attachment Wittington Hosp 1987–89; Vice Chair Regional Political Cttee of ANC GB 1978–88, Chair 1988–89; ANC Health Dept Lusaka 1989–90; Research Scientist Medical Research Council, Durban 1991–94; Minister of Health 1994–99; Dir Health Refugee Trust, Health and Devt Org, UK 1988–90; Chair S Natal Region Health Cttee of ANC 1990–92; mem Exec Cttee S Natal Region of ANC 1990–93; Chair S Natal Region ANC Women's League 1991–93; mem Steering Cttee National AIDS Coordinating Cttee 1992–; mem Bd Centre for Social Devt Studies Univ of Natal, Durban 1992–; Trustee Health Systems Trust 1992–. *Address:* c/o Ministry of Health, 2027 Civitas Bldg, Cnr Andries and Struben Sts, Pretoria, 0002, South Africa (Office); 602 Stretten Bay, St Andrews St, Durban 4001, South Africa (Home).

DMITRIYEVA, Tatyana Borisovna, MD; Russian politician and professor of medicine; b 21 Dec 1951, Ivanovo; m Aleksander Sergeyevich Dmitriyev. *Education:* Ivanovo State Medical Inst. *Career:* Psychiatrist Ivanovo Region Psychiatric Hosp 1975–76; jr, then sr researcher All-Union Serbsky Research Inst of Gen and Judicial Psychiatry 1976–86, Head of Clinical Dept, Deputy Dir 1986–90; Dir Serbsky State Scientific Centre of Social and Judicial Psychiatry 1990–96, 1998–; concurrently Prof, Head of Chair Moscow Sechenov Acad of Medicine; Minister of Public Health 1996–98; mem State Duma 1999, resgnd; Regional Vice-Pres World Asscn of Social Psychiatrists for E Europe 2000; Corresp mem Russian Acad of Medical Science. *Address:* Serbsky Scientific Centre, Kropotkinsky per 23, 119839 Moscow, Russian Federation (Office). *Telephone:* (095) 201 5262.

DOBBS, Mattiwilda; American opera singer; b 11 July 1925, Atlanta, GA; d of John Wesley and Irene Thompson Dobbs; m 1st Luis Rodríguez García 1953 (died 1954); m 2nd Bengt Janzon 1957 (died 1997). *Education:* Spelman Coll (Atlanta) and Columbia Univ (New York). *Career:* Studied with Lotte Leonard 1946–50; Marian Anderson Scholarship, Soloist at Mexico Univ Festival 1947; studied at Mannes Music School and Berkshire Music Center 1948, with Pierre Bernac, Paris 1950–52; concert tour Netherlands, France and Sweden 1952; debut La Scala (Milan, Italy) in L'Italiana in Algeri 1953; appearances at Glyndebourne (UK) 1953, 1954, 1956, 1961, Royal Opera House, Covent Garden (London) 1954, 1955, 1956, 1959, San Francisco Opera 1955, Metropolitan Opera (New York) 1956–64; Stockholm Royal Opera 1957–71; Hamburg State Opera (Germany) 1961–63; concert appearances in Europe, USA, Mexico, Israel, Australia, New Zealand and fmr USSR; Order of the North Star (Sweden); First Voice Prize, Geneva Int Competition 1951. *Address:* 1101 S Arlington Ridge Rd, Apt 301, Arlington, VA 22202, USA. *Telephone:* (703) 892-5234.

DOBRIANSKY, Paula Jon, MA; American organization executive; b 14 Sept 1955, Alexandria, VA; d of Lev Eugene and Julia Kusy Dobriansky. *Career:* Admin Asst Dept of the Army, Washington, DC 1973–76; Staff Asst Embassy of America, Rome 1976; Research Asst Jt Econ Cttee, House of Reps 1977–78; NATO Analyst Bureau of Intelligence and Research, Dept of State, Washington, DC 1979, mem staff Nat Security Council, White House 1980–83, Deputy Dir European and Soviet Affairs 1983–84, Dir 1984–87, Deputy Asst Sec of State for Human Rights and Humanitarian Affairs 1987–90; Deputy Head US Del to Conf on Security and Co-operation in Europe, Copenhagen 1990; Assoc Dir for Policy and Programs, US Information Agency 1990–93; Co-Chair Int TV Council, Corp Public Broadcasting 1993–94; Sr Int Affairs and Trade Advisor Hunton and Williams, Washington, DC 1994–97; Host Freedom's Challenge, Nat Empowerment TV 1994–96; mem Bd Dirs American Cttee for Aid to Poland 1994–95, Congressional Human Rights Foundation 1994–, Western NIS Enterprise Fund 1994–; mem Bd Visitors George Mason Univ, Fairfax, VA 1994–; mem Int Inst for Strategic Studies, Council on Foreign Relations, American Political Science. *Address:* Council on Foreign Relations, 1779 Massachusetts Ave, NW, Washington, DC 20036, USA.

DOBROVOLSKAYA, Marina Karamanovna, PH D; Russian academic and politician; b 9 Aug 1960, Tianebi, Georgia; d of Tamara V. Striganova; m Valery S. Dobrovolsky. *Education:* Moscow State Inst of Pedagogics. *Career:* Sec Chief Naval Staff 1981–93; Chair Union of Women in the Navy 1992–; Co-Chair Women of Russia movt 1993–; Mem State Duma (Parl), Chair Sub-cttee, Standing Cttee on Defence 1993–95; Advisor Analytical Dept State Duma 1996–; mem Defence Comm, Pres's Politicial Consultations Bd 1996–; Corresp mem Acad of Acmeological Sciences 1995. *Publications:* Social Psychological Concept of Improving Morale Support System in the Russian Armed Forces under the Military Reform 1995, Morale Support System in the Russian Armed Forces: Methodological Principles of it's Social Psychological Fundaments 1995. *Leisure interests:* music, maritime art. *Address:* State Duma, Analytical Dept, 103 256 Moscow, Okhotny Ryad 1, Russian Federation. *Telephone:* (095) 292-74-52; *Fax:* (095) 292-31-26.

DOBSON, Annette Jane, PH D; Australian professor of bio-statistics. *Education:* Chisipite School (Harare, Zimbabwe), Univ of Adelaide and James Cook Univ of N Queensland. *Career:* Prof of Biostatistics/Statistics Univ of Newcastle, NSW 1986–99, Dir Centre of Clinical

Epidemiology and Biostatistics 1993–95, Dean Faculty of Econs and Commerce 1996–98; Prof Biostatistics Univ of Queensland School of Population Health 2000–; Prin Investigator and mem Steering Cttee of WHO MONICA Project (to monitor trends and determinants of cardiovascular disease) 1985–; Project Dir Australian Longitudinal Study of Women's Health 1995–; mem Nat Cttee on Health and Vital Statistics, and numerous nat advisory cttees; Accred Statistician, Statistical Soc of Australia. *Publications include:* Self Paced Introductory Mathematics Modelling (jtly) 1979, Introduction to Generalized Linear Modelling 1990, 2001; numerous contribs to scientific and professional journals. *Leisure interest:* dog-showing and training. *Address:* School of Population Health, University of Queensland, Herston, Qld 4006, Australia (Office); 13 Gleneagles Crescent, Albany Creek, Qld 4035, Australia (Home). *Telephone:* (7) 3365-5346 (Office); *Fax:* (7) 3365-5442 (Office); *E-mail:* a.dobson@sph.uq.edu.au.

DOBSON, Rosemary de Brissac; Australian writer and poet; b 18 June 1920, Sydney; d of A. A. G. and Marjorie (née Caldwell) Dobson; m Alexander Thorley Bolton 1951; two s one d. *Education:* Frensham School (Mittagong, NSW) and Univ of Sydney. *Career:* Teacher of Art; mem Editorial Dept Angus and Robertson Publrs, Sydney; freelance writer 1951–; Hon D LITT (Sydney) 1996; Robert Frost Prize 1979; Sr Literary Fellowship Australia Council 1980; Patrick White Award for Literature 1984; Grace Leven Prize for Poetry 1984; Victoria Premier's Literary Awards for Poetry (jtly) 1985; Officer Order of Australia for Services to Literature 1987. *Publications:* In a Convex Mirror 1944, The Ship of Ice 1948, Child with a Cockatoo 1955, Australian Poets: Rosemary Dobson 1963, Cock Crow 1965, Focus on Ray Crooke (prose) 1971, Moscow Trefoil (jtly) 1975, Greek Coins 1977, Over the Frontier 1978, Seven Russian Poets (jtly) 1979, Selected Poems 1980, The Three Fates (poetry collection) 1984, Summer Press 1987, Collected Poems 1991. *Leisure interests:* all forms of art. *Address:* 61 Stonehaven Crescent, Deakin, ACT 2600, Australia; c/o Curtis Brown Pty Ltd, POB 19, Paddington, NSW 2021, Australia. *Telephone:* (6) 281 1436 (ACT); *Fax:* (6) 281 5842 (ACT).

DOBSON, Sue, BA; British magazine editor; b 31 Jan 1946, Maidstone, Kent; d of Arthur and Nellie Henshaw; m Michael Dobson 1966 (divorced 1974). *Education:* Holy Family Convent and Assumption Convent (Ramsgate), Ursuline Convent (Westgate-on-Sea) and Polytechnic of North-East London. *Career:* Ed Small Trader, London 1964; Fashion, Cookery and Beauty Ed Femina, S Africa 1965–69; Contributing Ed Fair Lady, S Africa 1969–71; Ed S Africa Inst of Race Relations 1972–74, Wedding Day and First Home, London 1978–81, Successful Slimming, London 1981–82, Woman and Home, London 1982–94; Ed-in-Chief Choice magazine 1994. *Publication:* The Wedding Day Book (2nd edn) 1989. *Leisure interests:* travel, photography, reading, opera. *Address:* Kings Chambers, 39-41 Priestgate, Peterborough, PE1 1FR, UK.

DOBSON, Wendy K., PH D; Canadian economist; b 23 Nov 1941, Vernon, BC. *Education:* Univ of British Columbia, Harvard (MA) and Princeton Univs (NJ, USA). *Career:* Special Asst to Pres Int Devt Research Centre, Ottawa, ON 1972–75; Economist C. D. Howe Inst 1979–81, Pres 1981–87; Assoc Deputy Minister of Finance 1987–89; Visiting Fellow Inst of Int Econs, Washington, DC 1989–; Prof Univ of Toronto and Dir Inst for Int Business 1990–; Dir DuPont Canada Inc 1989, IBM Canada Ltd 1989, Toronto Dominion Bank 1990, Trans Canada Pipelines Ltd 1992; mem Bd Univ of Toronto Press 1991, Japan Soc 1993, Toronto Stock Exchange Cttee on Corp Governance 1993–94. *Publications include:* Exports to Developing Countries 1979, Canada's Energy Policy Debate 1980, Shaping Comparative Advantage (jtly) 1987, Canadian-Japanese Economic Relations 1987. *Leisure interests:* tennis, hiking, skiing, photography, music. *Address:* Rotman School of Management, University of Toronto, 105 St George St, Toronto, ON M5S 3E6, Canada.

DODD, Lois; American artist; b 22 April 1927, Montclair, NJ; one s. *Education:* Montclair High School and Cooper Union. *Career:* Founder Tanager Gallery 1952–62 (jt); mem Bd of Govs Skowhegan School of Painting and Sculpture 1980– (Chair 1986–88); mem Nat Acad of Design 1988–, American Acad of Arts and Letters 1998–; American Acad and Inst of Arts and Letters Award 1986, Hassam, Speicher, Betts and Symons Purchase Prize 1991, Nat Acad of Design Leonilda S.

Gervas Award 1987, Henry Ward Ranger Purchase Award 1990. *Art Exhibitions:* Tanager Gallery, New York 1954–62, Green Mountain Gallery, New York 1969–76, Fischbach Gallery, New York 1978–, Caldbeck Gallery, Rockland, Maine 1990–; works in perm collections including: Bryn Mawr Coll (Pa), Dartmouth Coll (NH), Kalamazoo Art Center (Mich), Nat Acad of Design, New York, Wadsworth Atheneum, Hartford, Conn, Whitney Museum, New York, Museo dell'Arte, Udine, Italy. *Address:* c/o American Academy of Arts and Letters, 633 West 155th St, New York, NY 10032, USA (Office); 30 East 2nd St, New York, NY 10003, USA (Home). *Telephone:* (212) 254-7159; *Fax:* (212) 254-7159.

DODWELL, Christina; British traveller, writer and broadcaster; b 1 Feb 1951, Nigeria; m 1991. *Career:* Explorer and travel writer; 3-year journey in Africa by horse 1975–1978, 2 years visiting remote tribes in Papua New Guinea by horse and canoe 1979–81, many other journeys spanning 20 years; f The Dodwell Trust; mem Consulate of Madagascar (London); Mungo Park Medal (Royal Scottish Geographical Soc) 1989. *Publications include:* Travels with Fortune 1979, In Papua New Guinea 1982, An Explorers Handbook 1984, A Traveller in China 1986, A Traveller on Horseback 1987, Travels with Pegasus 1989, Beyond Siberia 1993, Madagascar Travels 1995; *TV includes:* River Journey-Waghi (BBC, BAFTA Award) 1984; *Radio:* over 40 documentary programmes for BBC Radio 4. *Address:* Hodder Headline, 338 Euston Rd, London NW1 3BH, UK.

DOHERTY, Moya; Irish producer and director; b Donegal. *Career:* Fmr actress with Team Educational Theatre Co; worked as TV presenter and journalist in Britain and Ireland; Exec Producer Eurovision Song Contest 1994; commissioned original Riverdance performance; Producer Riverdance – The Show (Point Theatre, Dublin) 1995; Founder and Dir Tyrone Productions (film and TV production co) 1987–; Dir Today FM (Irish nat radio station); Chair Dublin Theatre Festival; Veuve Clicquot Business Woman of the Year 1997; Ernst & Young Entrepreneur of the Year Award 1999. *Address:* 23 Mary St Little, Dublin, 7, Ireland. *Internet:* www.tyroneproductions.com.

DOI, Takako; Japanese politician; b 30 Nov 1928, Kobe. *Education:* Doshisha Univ. *Career:* Fmr univ lecturer on Japanese constitution; mem House of Reps (Parl, Lower House) 1969–, Speaker 1993–96; Leader Japanese Socialist Party (JSP) 1986–91; Chair Social Democrat Party of Japan 1996–. *Leisure interests:* singing, pachinko. *Address:* Social Democratic Party of Japan, 1-8-1 Nagata-cho, Chiyoda-ku, Tokyo 100, Japan. *Telephone:* (3) 3580-1171; *Fax:* (3) 3580-0691.

DOKIC, Jelena; Australian tennis player; b 12 April 1983, Belgrade, Yugoslavia; d of Damir and Liliana Dokic. *Career:* Began playing tennis at age 6, professional player 1998–; ranked World No 1 Junior Player, 1998; mem Australian Fed Cup Team 1999–2000, Australian Olympic Team 2000; Semifinalist, Wimbledon 2001; winner, Hamburg 2001; winner, Italian Open 2001; ranked World No 18 Woman Player 2001; Amb Sydney Olympic Games 2000. *Leisure interest:* cinema. *Address:* Octagon, POB 3297, North Burnley, Vic 3103, Australia.

DOLANSKÁ, Nora, PH D; Czech academic and journalist; b 11 Oct 1950, Prague; d of the late Paul Laube and of Ina Laubeova; m Paul Dolansky 1980; one s one d. *Education:* Charles Univ. *Career:* Work experience with newspapers including Mladá Fronta 1969; Czech Corresp for German magazine Aktuell; Asst Prof Charles Univ 1976–. *Publications:* Portrait of F. X. Shalda, Literature and Journalism. *Leisure interests:* culture, theatre, skiing, water sports. *Address:* Navrátilova 9, 110 00 Prague 1, Czech Republic. *Telephone:* (2) 24216038.

DOLE, Elizabeth Hanford, MA, JD; American lawyer and government official; b 29 July 1936, Salisbury, NC; d of John Van Hanford and Mary E. Cathey; m Robert J. Dole 1975; one step-d. *Education:* Duke and Harvard Univs and Univ of Oxford (UK). *Career:* Called to the Bar, DC 1966; Staff Asst to Asst Sec for Educ, Dept of Health, Educ and Welfare 1966–67; practising lawyer, Washington, DC 1967–68; Assoc Dir Legis Affairs, then Exec Dir Pres's Comm for Consumer Interests 1968–71; Deputy Dir Office of Consumer Affairs, The White House, Washington, DC 1971–73; Commr Fed Trade Comm 1973–79; Asst to Pres for Public Liaison 1981–83; Sec of Transport 1983–87; Sec of Labor 1989–90; Pres American Red Cross 1990–98; Trustee Duke Univ 1974;

mem Visiting Comm, John F. Kennedy School of Govt 1988, Harvard School of Public Health 1992–, Bd of Overseers Harvard Univ 1989–95; numerous awards. *Address:* POB 58247, 700 New Hampshire Avenue, NW, Washington, DC 20037, USA.

DOMIN, Hilde, PH D; German writer; b 27 July 1912, Cologne; m Erwin W. Palm 1936 (died 1988). *Education:* Univs of Heidelberg, Cologne, Berlin, Rome and Florence (Italy). *Career:* Language teacher, UK, Prof Univ of Santo Domingo 1948–53; Lecturer in Poetry Univ of Frankfurt 1987–88, Univ of Mainz 1988–89; has given readings and lectures throughout Germany since 1961, also in USA, Canada, throughout Europe and overseas; mem Deutsche Akad für Sprache und Dichtung, PEN-Club; several medals and prizes including Rilke Prize 1976, Nelly-Sachs Prize 1983, Stadt Heidelberg Prize 1993, Stadt Freinsheim Prize 1994, Konrad-Adenaur Stiftung Prize 1999. *Publications include:* Poetry: Nur eine Rose als Stütze 1959, Rückkehr der Schiffe 1962, Hier 1964, Ich will Dich 1970, Gesammelte Gedichte 1951–86 1987; Das zweite Paradies (novel) 1968 (original text 1986), Wozu Lyrik heute (essays) 1968, Von der Natur nicht vorgesehen (autobiog) 1974, Aber die Hoffnung: Autobiographie aus und über Deutschland 1982, Das Gedicht als Augenblick von Freiheit Frankfurter Poetik-Vorlesungen 1988, Gesammelte autobiographische Schriften, Gesammelte Essays. *Leisure interests:* literature, music, nature. *Address:* Graimbergweg 5, 6900 Heidelberg, Germany. *Telephone:* (6221) 12545.

DOMITIEN, Elisabeth; Central African Republic politician. *Career:* Fmr mem Mouvement d'évolution sociale de l'Afrique noire (MESAN), Vice-Pres 1975–79; Prime Minister of Central African Repub 1975–76; imprisoned Nov 1979, on trial Feb 1980.

DOMOTO, Akiko, BA; Japanese politician and business executive; b 31 July 1932, Oakland, CA, USA; d of Takayuki and Ryuo Domoto. *Education:* Tokyo Women's Christian Coll. *Career:* Producer, Dir and Newscaster Tokyo Broadcasting System 1959–89; mem House of Councillors (Parl, Upper House) 1989–, mem Foreign Affairs Cttee, Special Cttee on the Environment; Chair Biodiversity Working Group for Global Legislators for a Balanced Environment (GLOBE) Int, Vice-Pres GLOBE Japan 1990–; Founder Int Children's Network Japan 1991–; Co-Founder Japan Women's Global Environmental Network 1991–; Gov Chiba Prefecture March 2001–; Japanese Citizens' Broadcasting League Award 1981; Conf of Japanese Journalists' Award 1981; Special Award (Japanese Cultural Broadcasting Foundation) 1981; Bronze Medal (New York Film Festival, USA) 1985. *TV documentaries include:* The Baby Hotel Series 1980–81, Tibet's Phantom Guge Kingdom (series) 1983–84, Monitoring Japan's ODA (Official Devt Assistance) 1987, The Age of Child Slavery 1989; *Publications include:* Women's Human Rights and Gender 1984, Post-War History of Japanese Women 1984, Street Children 1986, The South Pole Challenge: Story of Scott and Amundsen 1988. *Leisure interests:* mountain-climbing, tennis. *Address:* House of Councillors, 1-7-1 Nagata-cho, Tokyo 100, Japan; 422 Sangiin Kaikan, 2-1-1, Nagata-cho, Chiyoda-ku, Tokyo 100, Japan. *Telephone:* (3) 3508-8422; *Fax:* (3) 3506-8085.

DONAGHY, Rita, OBE, BA; British public servant; b 9 Oct 1944; d of the late William Scott Willis and Brenda Bryan; m 1st James Donaghy 1968 (died 1986); m 2nd Edward Easen-Thomas 2000. *Education:* Leamington Coll for Girls and St Mary's Coll (Durham). *Career:* Founded clerical br of Nat and Local Govt Officers Asscn (NALGO) 1969, Br Sec, Chair and Vice Chair 1970–85, mem Nat Exec Council 1973–2000, Pres 1989–90, Chair merger working group (led to the formation of UNISON 1993); mem TUC Gen Council 1987–2000, Pres TUC 1999–2000; Chair TUC Women's Cttee 1998–2000; mem Low Pay Comm 1997–2000, Equal Pay Comm 1999–2000; mem Govt Advisory Cttee on Employment of People with Disabilities 1994–97; Chair Advisory, Conciliation and Arbitration Service (ACAS) 2000–; mem Cttee on Standards in Public Service 2001–; contrib to Times Higher Educational Supplement. *Leisure interests:* theatre, reading, watching cricket, gardening. *Address:* Brandon House, 180 Borough High St, London SE1 1LW, UK. *Telephone:* (20) 7210-3670; *Fax:* (20) 7210-3664; *E-mail:* r.donaghy@acas.org.uk; *Internet:* www.acas.org.uk.

DONALD, Athene Margaret, PH D, FRS; British professor of experimental physics; b 15 May 1953; d of Walter Griffith and Annette Marian Taylor; m Matthew J. Donald 1976; one s one d. *Education:* Girton Coll (Cambridge). *Career:* Postdoctoral researcher Cornell Univ 1977–81; Science and Eng Research Council Research Fellow Univ of Cambridge 1981–83, Royal Soc Research Fellow 1983–85, Lecturer 1985–95, Reader 1985–98, Prof of Experimental Physics 1998–; mem Governing Council, Inst of Food Research 1999–; Samuel Locker Award in Physics, Univ of Birmingham 1989, Charles Vernon Boys Prize, Inst of Physics 1989, Rosenhain Medal and Prize, Inst of Materials 1995. *Publications:* Liquid Crystalline Polymers (jtly) 1992, Starch: Structure and Function (ed jtly) 1997, and numerous articles in scientific journals. *Address:* Cavendish Laboratory, University of Cambridge, Madingley Rd, Cambridge, CB3 0HE, UK.

DONALDSON, Dame (Dorothy) Mary, GBE, JP, FCROG; British local government official; b 29 Aug 1921, Wickham, Hants; d of the late Reginald George Gale and Dorothy Alice Warwick; m John Francis Donaldson (Baron Donaldson of Lymington) 1945; two d one s. *Education:* Portsmouth High School for Girls, Wingfield Morris Orthopaedic Hosp and Middx Hosp (London). *Career:* Chair Women's Nat Cancer Control Campaign 1967–69; Vice-Pres British Cancer Council 1970; served on numerous other medical and community bds and cttees; mem Inner London Educ Authority 1968–71; Alderman City of London (Ward of Coleman St) 1975–91, Sheriff 1981–82, first woman Lord Mayor of London 1983–84; Chair Interim Licensing Authority for In-vitro Fertilisation and Human Embryology 1985–91, Council responsible for Ombudsman in Banking 1985–94; mem Press Complaints Comm 1991–94; JP Inner London 1960; Hon Fellow Girton Coll, Cambridge; Hon D SC (City) 1983; Order of Oman 1982; Order of Bahrain 1984; Grand Officier de l'Ordre Nat du Mérite 1984; Pres's Medal Inst of Public Relations 1984. *Leisure interests:* sailing, gardening, skiing. *Telephone:* (1590) 675292 (Home).

DONATH, Helen; American opera and concert singer; b 10 July 1940, Corpus Christi, TX; d of Jimmy Erwin and Helen Hamauei; m Klaus Donath 1965; one s. *Education:* Roy Miller High School and Del Mar Coll (Texas). *Career:* Studied with Paola Novikova, later with husband Klaus Donath (by whom all song-recitals are accompanied); debuts in Germany at Cologne Opera House 1962, Hanover Opera House 1963–68, Bayerische Staatsoper, Munich 1968–72; guest appearances in London (Royal Opera House, Covent Garden), Vienna, Milan, San Francisco, Lisbon, New York, etc; has given concerts in all major European and American cities; over 100 recordings 1962–; Pope Paul Medal; Salzburg 50 Year Anniversary Medal; Bratislava Festival Award; Deutscher Schallplattenpreis and Großes Lob for her first song recital recording; Lower Saxony Prize for Culture 1990. *Operas include:* Die Zauberflöte, Don Giovanni, Die Meistersinger, Der Rosenkavalier, Le Nozze di Figaro, The Rake's Progress, Idomeneo, Carmen. *Leisure interests:* family, gardening, cooking, swimming, filming. *Address:* Bergstrasse 5, 30900 Wedemark, Germany.

DONGO, Margaret; Zimbabwean politician; b 1963; m; three c. *Career:* Joined ZANU (Zimbabwe African Nat Union) early 1960s; guerrilla fighter; worked for ZANU-PF 1980–90; Co-Founder Nat Liberation War Veterans Asscn 1989; first elected as ZANU-PF MP 1990; ran as ind cand 1995; defeated but reinstated in office after winning court case against Govt; Rep Zimbabwe Movt for Ind Electoral Cands for S Harare Constituency. *Address:* Zimbabwe Union of Democrats, South Harare, Zimbabwe.

DÖNHOFF, Gräfin (Countess) **Marion,** DR RER POL; German journalist; b 2 Dec 1909, Friedrichstein, E Prussia; d of August Graf and Ria (née von Lepel) Dönhoff. *Education:* In Potsdam, Königsberg, Frankfurt/Main and Basel Univ (Switzerland). *Career:* Engaged in admin of various agricultural estates in E Prussia 1936–45; joined Die Zeit 1946, Political Ed 1955, Chief Ed 1968–72, Publr 1972–; Hon Trustee Aspen Inst for Humanistic Studies, USA; Dr hc (Smith Coll, Columbia Univ, New School for Social Research, New York); Joseph E. Drexel Prize 1964; Theodor Heuss Prize 1966; Peace Prize of German Book Trade 1971; Wolfgang-Döring Medal 1984; Louise-Weiss-Stiftung prize, Paris 1985; Heinrich-Heine prize 1988; Roosevelt-Freiheitspreis 1994, Reinhold-Maier-Medal 1996. *Publications:* Namen, die keiner mehr nennt 1962, Die Bundesrepublik in der Ära Adenauers

1963, Reise in ein fernes Land (jtly) 1964, Welt in Bewegung 1965, Deutsche Außenpolitik von Adenauer bis Brandt 1970, Menschen, die wissen, worum es geht 1976, Hart am Wind, The Political Career of Helmut Schmidt (ed) 1978, Von Gestern nach Übermorgen – zur Geschichte der Bundesrepublik Deutschland 1981, Amerikanische Wechselbäder 1983, Weit ist der Weg nach Osten 1985, Südafrikanischer Teufelkreis 1987, Preußen – Maß und Maßlosigkeit 1987, Kindheit in Ostpreußen 1988, Bilder, die langsam verblassen 1989, Gestalten Unserer Zeit: Politische Porträts 1990, Deutschland, deine Kanzler 1992, Im Wartesaal der Geschichte 1993, Um die Ehre willen, Erinnerungen an der Freunde von 20 Juli 1994. *Leisure interest:* art (painting and graphic art). *Address:* Die Zeit, Postfach 106820, 22587 Hamburg, Germany (Office).

DONLON, Patricia Anne, PH D; Irish librarian; b 28 Jan 1943, Dublin; d of Patrick and Marcella (née Garr) McCarthy; m Phelim Donlon 1965; two d. *Education:* Holy Faith Convent (Dublin), Univ Coll Dublin and Univ of Madrid. *Career:* Radio Researcher Radio Telefís Éireann (RTE) 1964–66; Asst Librarian Royal Irish Acad 1979–81; Lecturer in Children's Literature Univ Coll Dublin 1979–89; Curator W Collection, Chester Beatty Library and Gallery of Oriental Art, Dublin 1981–89; Dir Nat Library of Ireland (first woman dir of an Irish nat inst) 1989–98; Trustee Chester Beatty Library 1989; Patron and Trustee Irish Children's Book Trust 1989; Chair Irish Museum's Trust 1991; John J. Burns Visiting Scholar in Irish Studies, John J. Burns Library, Boston Coll 2001; mem Library Council of Ireland, Irish Manuscripts Comm; Salamanca Scholarship to Madrid, Nat Univ of Ireland 1963. *Publications:* The Lucky Bag: Classic Irish Stories (ed) 1984, Twentieth Century Children's Writers (adviser and contrib) 1989, Moon Cradle: Lullabies and Dandling Songs (ed) 1991, Sunny Spells: Stories (ed) 1992. *Leisure interests:* music, film, theatre, embroidery, walking the dog. *Address:* c/o John J. Burns Library, Boston College, Chestnut Hill, MA 02467-3801, USA. *E-mail:* patricia.donlon@bc.edu.

DONNELLY, Marian; Irish party executive; b 10 Aug 1938, Castledawson, Co Derry; d of Frank Devlin and Margaret Scullion; m Francis Donnelly 1973; two d one s. *Education:* St Mary's Convent (Magherafelt, Co Derry) and St Mary's Coll of Educ (Belfast). *Career:* Teacher 1960–78, later part-time teacher; mem Worker's Party, Pres (first woman) 1992; mem Northern Ireland Civil Rights Asscn 1968–. *Leisure interests:* amateur drama, reading, talking, GAA. *Address:* Workers' Party, 28 Gardiner Place, Dublin 1, Ireland. *Telephone:* (1) 874-0716 (Dublin); (1648) 42070; *Fax:* (1) 874-8702 (Dublin).

DONOHOE, Amanda; British actress; b 1962. *Education:* Francis Holland School for Girls, Cen School of Speech and Drama (London). *Career:* Fmr mem Royal Exchange Theatre in Manchester; debut on Broadway, New York 1995. *Films include:* Foreign Body 1986, Castaway, The Lair of the White Worm, The Rainbow, Tank Malling, Diamond Skulls (Dark Obsession), Paper Mask, The Madness of King George, Liar Liar, Writer's Block, I'm Losing You; *TV appearances include:* LA Law (series, Golden Globe Award), Married to Murder, Shame, It's Nothing Personal (also co-exec producer), The Substitute, Shame II: The Secret (also co-exec producer); *Plays include:* Uncle Vanya 1995, The Graduate 2001.

DOODY, Margaret Anne, D PHIL; Canadian professor of English; b 21 Sept 1939, St John, NB; d of Rev Hubert Doody and Anne Ruth Cornwall. *Education:* Centreville Regional High School, Dalhousie Univ (Halifax) and Lady Margaret Hall (Oxford, UK). *Career:* Instructor in English 1962–64; Asst Prof English Dept, Victoria Univ 1968–69; Lecturer Univ Coll of Swansea, Wales, UK 1969–77; Visiting Assoc Prof of English Univ of California at Berkeley, USA 1976–77, Assoc Prof 1977–80; Prof of English Princeton Univ, USA 1980–89; Andrew W. Mellon Prof of Humanities and Prof of English Vanderbilt Univ, Nashville, TN, USA 1989–; Dir of Comparative Literature Programme 1992–99; John and Barbara Glynn Family Prof of Literature, Univ of Notre Dame 2000–; Commonwealth Fellowship 1960–62; Canada Council Fellowship 1964–65; Imperial Oil Fellowship 1965–68; Guggenheim Foundation Fellowship 1978; Hon LL D (Dalhousie) 1985; Rose Mary Crawshay Prize 1986. *Publications:* A Natural Passion: A Study of the Novels of Samuel Richardson 1974, Aristotle Detective 1978, The Alchemists 1980, The Daring Muse 1985, Frances Burney: The Life in the Works 1988, Samuel Richardson: Tercentenary Essays

(co-ed) 1989, The True Story of the Novel 1996, Anne of Green Gables (co-ed) 1997; Play: Clarissa (jtly), New York 1984. *Leisure interests:* travel, ancient paintings and mosaics, reading detective fiction, swimming in the sea, music (Mozart, bluegrass). *Address:* English Department, University of Notre Dame, Notre Dame, IN 46556, USA (Office); 435 Edgewater Drive, Mishawaka, IN 46545, USA (Home). *Telephone:* (219) 631-9723 (Office); (219) 257-7927 (Home); *E-mail:* margaret.doody.1@nd.edu.

DORE, Bonny Ellen, MA; American film and television production executive; b 16 Aug 1947; d of Reber Hutson and Ellen Elizabeth Barnes; m Sandford Astor 1987. *Education:* Univ of Michigan. *Career:* Gen Man WSDP-FM Radio Station, MI 1970–72; Production Supervisor Public TV, New York State Dept of Educ 1972–74; Producer WXYZ-TV 1974–75; Man Children's Programmes ABC TV, Los Angeles, CA 1975, Dir Children's Programmes 1975–76, Dir Prime Time Variety Programmes 1976–77; Dir of Devt Hanna-Barbera, Los Angeles 1977; Vice-Pres of Devt and Production Krofft Entertainment, Los Angeles 1977–81, Centerpoint Productions 1981–82; Pres and Propr in asscn with Orion TV, The Greif-Dore Co, Los Angeles 1983–87, Bonny Dore Productions Inc, Los Angeles 1988–; mem Caucus of Writers, Producers and Dirs 1989–, Fundraising Cttee, Univ of Michigan 1990–; numerous awards include Outstanding Young Teacher of the Year (Cen States Speech Asscn) 1973, Action for Children's TV Award 1975, Certificate of Appreciation (Gov of Michigan) 1985, Council on Social Work Educ 1990, Gold Medal for Best TV Mini-series 1990, Best TV Actress Award 1990, Best Mini Series (Houston Film Festival) 1990. *TV productions include:* The Krofft Superstar Hour (Two Emmy Awards) 1979, The ½ Hour Comedy Hour 1983–84, Sins 1986, First Impressions 1987–88, Glory! Glory! (Two ACE Cable Awards) 1988–89, Reason for Living, The Jill Ireland Story 1990–91, Captive 1991, The Sinking of the Rainbow Warrior 1993. *Address:* Bonny Dore Productions Inc, 9454 Wilshire Blvd, Beverly Hills, CA 90212, USA.

DORÉ, Christiane, L ÈS L; French business executive; b 20 March 1942, Strasbourg; d of Jean-Pierre and Suzanne Zinglé; m Jean-Michel Doré 1968; two s. *Education:* Inst d'Etudes Politiques and Univ of Lyons. *Career:* Journalist 1965–68; Editorial Sec-Gen Consommateurs actualités magazine 1969–70, Ed-in-Chief 1970–71; Editorial Sec-Gen 50 Millions de Consommateurs magazine 1971–73, Ed-in-Chief 1973–78; TV adviser 1973–78; mem staff Information Service, Directorate of Construction and Planning, Ministry of Town Planning 1978–79; Technical Ed-in-Chief, Technical Dir Jeune Afrique review 1979–80; Rep to Minister of Consumer Affairs 1981–82; Admin-Gen Banque Sonfinco 1982, Pres, Dir-Gen 1982–86; Dir-Gen responsible for New Markets and Communication, Excofinances (La Mondiale group) 1986–87; Pres, Dir-Gen SCAS Voyages 1987–90; Pres, Dir-Gen Diners' Club de France 1987–90; Pres Société Nat de Télévision en Couleur—Antenne 2 (A2—second TV channel) and France Régions 3 1990–93; Pres, Dir-Gen Vitrine de France (Cible group) 1993–96; Insp Gen of Posts and Telecommunications 1998–2000; Vice-Pres Charles Riley Consultants Int 2000–; Commdr de l'Ordre Nat du Mérite. *Leisure interests:* tennis, skiing, wind-surfing, swimming. *Address:* Charles Riley Consultants International, 35 rue Fortuny, 75017 Paris, France. *E-mail:* christiane.dore@industrie.gouv.fr.

DORÉ, Katharine; British dance and theatre producer; one s. *Education:* Central School of Speech and Drama. *Career:* Admin, Adventures in Motion Pictures (AMP) (dance co) 1988–, Co-Dir and Producer of works, then Exec Dir; f Katharine Doré Man; co-f TreeHouse Trust (charitable school for children with autism and related communication disorders) 1997. *Productions include:* Swan Lake (Olivier Award, DramaLogue Award), A Midsummer Night's Dream (Albery Theatre) 2001. *Address:* Adventures in Motion Pictures, 3rd Floor Gloucester Mansions, 140A Shaftesbury Ave, London WC2, UK. *Internet:* www.amp.co.uk.

DORIN, Françoise Andrée Renée; French actress and writer; b 23 Jan 1928, Paris; d of the late René Dorin and of Yvonne Guilbert; m Jean Poiret (b Poiré) (divorced); one d. *Career:* At Théâtre des Deux-Ânes, then du Quartier Latin (Les Aveux les plus doux 1957), then La Bruyère (Le Chinois 1958); Presenter TV programme Paris-Club 1969; playwright and writer 1967–; Chevalier de la Légion d'Honneur; Officier de l'Ordre Nat du Mérite; Officier des Arts et des Lettres; Trophée Dussane 1973, Grand Prix du théâtre (for l'Etiquette) 1981. *Publications:* Novels: Virginie et Paul, La seconde dans Rome, Va voir Maman, Papa travaille 1976, Les lits à une place 1980, Les miroirs truqués 1982, Les jupes-culottes 1984, Les corbeaux et les renardes 1988, Nini patte-en-l'air 1990, Au nom du père et de la fille 1993, La Mouflette 1995, Les Vendanges tardives 1997; Plays: Comme au théâtre 1967, La facture 1968, Un sale égoiste, Les bonshommes 1970, Le tournant 1973, Le tube 1974, L'autre valse 1975, Si t'es beau, t'es con 1976, Le tout pour le tout 1978, L'intoxe 1980, Les cahiers tango 1987, L'étiquette 1990, Et s'il n'en restait qu'un 1992, Le retour en Touraine 1994, Monsieur de St Futile 1995; *Songs include:* Que c'est triste Venise, N'avoue jamais, Faisons l'humour ensemble, les miroirs truqués 1982; lyrics for Vos gueules les mouettes 1971, Monsieur Pompadour 1972, l'Etiquette 1983, Les jupes-culottes 1984, La valise en carton (musical comedy) 1986, L'âge en question 1986, La Retour en Toupaine 1993, Monsieur de Saint-Futile (Vaudeville) 1996. *Address:* c/o Artmedia, 10 avenue George-V, 75008 Paris, France (Office).

DORJIN, Nergui, B ECONS; Mongolian economist; b 8 Oct 1959, Ulan Bator; m Tserenjavin Oynbikeg 1981; one d one s. *Education:* State Financial Acad (Moscow), Inst of Man Devt (Ulan Bator) and IMF Inst (Washington, DC, USA). *Career:* Economist State Bank of the Mongolian People's Repub 1983–86, Head of Div 1986–89, Head Dept 1989–91, apptd Dir of Monetary Policy Dept 1991; has drafted several legal acts since 1984. *Leisure interests:* ping-pong, eco-tourism. *Address:* State Bank of the Mongolian People's Republic, Commerce St 6, Ulan Bator, Mongolia (Office); Sh/h 186, Ulan Bator 21, Mongolia (Home). *Telephone:* 22847 (Office).

DORMANN, Geneviève; French writer and journalist; b 24 Sept 1933, Paris; d of Maurice and Alice Dormann; m 1st Philippe Lejeune (divorced); three d; m 2nd Jean-Loup Dabadie (divorced); one d. *Education:* Lycée La Fontaine (Paris). *Career:* Writer, Journalist on Le Figaro newspaper; Grand Prix du Roman, Ville de Paris 1981. *Publications:* Novels: La Fanfaronne 1959, Le chemin des dames 1964, La passion selon saint Jules 1967, Je t'apporterai des orages (Prix des Quatre Jurys) 1971, Le bateau du courrier (Prix des Deux Magots 1975) 1974, Mickey, l'ange 1977, Fleur de péché 1980, Le roman de Sophie Trébuchet (Prix Kleber Haedens, Prix de la Ville de Nantes) 1982, Amoureuse Colette 1984, Le livre du point de croix 1986, Le bal du Dodo (Grand Prix du Roman, Acad Française) 1989, Paris une ville pleine de lions 1991, La petite main 1993, La gourmandise de Guillaume Apollinaire 1994, Adieu phénomène (Prix Genevois) 1999; Short stories: La première pierre 1957. *Leisure interests:* swimming, sailing. *Address:* 9 rue de Poitiers, 75007 Paris, France.

DORNER, Marie-Christine Françoise; French designer; b 21 Aug 1960, Strasbourg; d of Marc and Christiane (née Pascal) Dorner; m Thierry Brumter 1990; one s one d. *Education:* Gymnase Jean Sturm (Strasbourg) and Ecole Camondo (Paris). *Career:* Trainee Canal architects 1980–83; Designer Jean-Michel Wilmotte interior design agency 1984–85; collaborated with Teruo Kurosaki 1986; est interior design agency, Paris 1987; designed furniture for Japanese, Italian, Spanish, French and Dutch manufacturers 1986–; designed porcelain objects produced in France 1990; exhibitions in Europe, Japan and the USA; Grand Prix du Design 1995; teacher Royal Coll of Arts, London 1998–. *Projects include:* La Villa Hotel, Comédie Française restaurant, presidential stand for 14 July parade (Paris) 1990–96, urban furniture (Nîmes) 1993. *Leisure interest:* travel. *Address:* 23 Haldane Rd, London SW6 7ET, UK. *E-mail:* dorner.design@dial.pipex.com.

DORNONVILLE DE LA COUR, Dorthe, LL B; Danish civil servant; b 8 Jan 1961, Copenhagen; m Flemming Sejer Larsen 1985; one s. *Career:* Responsible for Equal Opportunities and Treatment in Labour Market, Danish Employers' Confed, apptd Head of Section 1989; mem Danish Equal Status Council; involved in legal affairs relating to employment; responsible for annotated edn Danish Sex Discrimination Act 1992. *Leisure interests:* reading, films, cooking. *Address:* Danish Employers' Confederation, 113 Vester Volgade, Copenhagen V, Denmark (Office); Caroline Amalie Vej 30, 2800 Lyngby, Denmark (Home). *Telephone:* 33-93-40-00 (Home); *Fax:* 33-12-29-76 (Home).

DORONINA, Tatyana Vasiliyevna; Russian actress; b 12 Sept 1933, Leningrad (now St Petersburg); d of Vasiliy Ivanovich Doronin and Anna Ivanovna Doronina; m Robert Dimitrievich Takhnenko. *Education:* Studio School of Moscow Arts Theatre. *Career:* Lenin Komsomol State Theatre, Leningrad 1956–59; Maxim Gorky State Bolshoi Drama Theatre, Leningrad 1959–66; Moscow Gorky Arts Theatre 1966–71, 1983–, Artistic Dir 1987–; Moscow Mayakovski Theatre 1971–83; works as actress and stage dir; People's Artist of the USSR 1981. *Plays include:* Factory Girl, In Search of Happiness, Wit Works Woe, My Elder Sister, The Barbarians, Virgin Soil Upturned, The Idiot, Irkutsk Story, Loss of the Squadron, Three Sisters, Brothers Karamazov, The Seagull; *Films:* Elder Sister, Again about Love, First Echelon, Horizon, Roll Call, Stepmother; also acted in TV films. *Address:* Moscow Gorky Arts Theatre, 22 Tverskoi Blvd, 119146 Moscow, Russian Federation (Office). *Telephone:* (095) 203-74-66.

DÖRRIE, Doris; German film director; b 1955, Hanover. *Films include:* Straight Through the Heart 1983, In the Belly of the Whale 1984, Männer 1985, Paradies 1986, Me and Him 1988, Geld 1990, Happy Birthday Türke! 1992. *Address:* c/o William Morris Agency, 151 South El Camino Drive, Beverly Hills, CA 90212, USA.

DOSTÁLOVÁ, Květoslava, MU DR, C SC; Czech medical practitioner and university teacher; b 7 May 1936, Seč; d of the late Josef and Helena Franc; m Josef Dostál 1960; one s one d. *Education:* Palacký Univ (Olomouc). *Career:* Asst Lecturer Dept of Pathophysiology, Palacký Univ 1960–63, Sr Lecturer 1963–89, Asst Prof of Pathophysiology 1990–, Vice-Dean Faculty of Medicine; author approx 100 articles on neurochem and psychopharmacology 1965–, co-author medical textbooks 1987, 1989; Hon mem J. E. Purkyně Czech Medical Soc 1990, Czech Soc of Pathological Physiology. *Leisure interests:* music, literature, gardening. *Address:* Palacký Univ, Dept of Pathological Physiology, Hněvotínská 3, 775 15 Olomouc, Czech Republic (Office); Tř Míru 19, 779 00 Olomouc, Czech Republic (Home). *Telephone:* (68) 23551; *Fax:* (68) 414541.

DOSUNMU, Sholabomi Abiola (Chief Adele Erelu of Lagos); Nigerian business executive; b 29 April 1935, Lagos; four c. *Education:* Ideal Girls' School (Yaba), Fed Women's Training Coll (Ilesia) and Barrett St Tech Coll (London). *Career:* Training Man Ikorodu Trading Co 1960–62; founded a training inst for young women, homecrafts and dressmaking 1963–77; running pvt business from 1981; mem Rent Tribunal, Head of the Appeal Section 1978–81; mem Lagos Council representing Lagos Island 1986–87, Lagos Mainland Local Govt Educ Authority (LGEA) 1989, Lagos Isale Eko Dist Cttee of LGEA 1989; mem Lagos State Better Life Programme 1989, Sec Sub-Cttee on Social, Cultural and Political Awareness 1990; has attended several workshops and mem numerous cttees and orgs 1984–. *Leisure interests:* interior decorating, design and dressmaking, reading, travel, national and local culture and tradition, gardening, farming. *Address:* c/o Lagos Mainland Local Government Education Authority (LGEA), Lagos, Nigeria.

DOTTO, Lydia Carol; Canadian science writer; b 29 May 1949, Cadomin, AB; d of August and Assunta Dotto. *Education:* Carleton Univ (ON). *Career:* Joined Edmonton Journal 1969, Toronto Star 1970, 1971; science writer Toronto Globe and Mail 1972–78; has covered space missions 1972–; freelance writer 1978–; Exec Ed Canadian Science News Service 1982–92; two dives under arctic ice, Resolute Bay, NWT 1974; participant zero-gravity training flight, Johnson Space Center, Houston, TX, USA 1983; Canadian Science Writers' Awards for newspaper and magazine articles 1974, 1981, 1984, 1994; Canadian Meteorological Soc Award 1975; Stanford Fleming Medal (Royal Canadian Inst) 1982–83. *Publications include:* The Ozone War (jtly) 1978, Thinking the Unthinkable: Civilization and Rapid Climate Change 1988, Canada in Space 1987, Planet Earth in Jeopardy: The Environmental Consequences of Nuclear War 1986, Asleep in the Fast Lane: The Impact of Sleep on Work 1990, Losing Sleep: How Your Sleeping Habits Affect Your Life 1990, Blue Planet 1991, Ethics and Climate Change 1993, The Astronauts: Canada's Voyageurs in space 1993, Storm Warning 1999. *Leisure interests:* computers, swimming, theatre. *Address:* 599 Gilmour St, Peterborough, ON K9H 2K3, Canada. *E-mail:* ldotto@sympatico.ca.

DOUGLAS, Margaret Elizabeth, OBE; British broadcasting executive and former political adviser; b 22 Aug 1934, London; d of Thomas and Dorothy Jones Douglas; m Terence Lancaster. *Education:* Parliament Hill Grammar School. *Career:* Sec BBC 1951, then Researcher, Dir and Producer Current Affairs TV, worked on Panorama, Gallery, 24 Hours, Ed Party Conf coverage 1972–83, Chief Asst to Dir-Gen 1983–87, Chief Political Adviser 1987–93; Supervisor of Parl Broadcasting 1993–99. *Leisure interests:* watching politics, football. *Address:* Flat 49, The Anchor Brewhouse, 50 Shad Thames, London SE1 2LY, UK (Home). *Telephone:* (20) 7403-3568 (Home); *Fax:* (20) 7403-3568 (Home).

DOUGLAS, Susan, OC; Canadian actress and broadcasting executive; b 13 March 1928, Vienna; m Jan Rubes 1950; three s. *Career:* Moved to Canada 1959; f Young People's Theatre 1965, also Dir; Head of Radio Drama, CBC Radio Dept 1979; Pres The Family Channel 1987–; mem Bd St Lawrence Center, Ontario Arts Council; Woman of the Year (B'nai Brith, Toronto, ON) 1979. *Stage appearances include:* He Who Gets Slapped (Donaldson Award 1946), Druid Circle, Heart Song, Taming of the Shrew, Private Affairs of Bel'Ami, Lost Boundaries, Five, Forbidden Journey; *TV appearances include:* Studio One, Kraft Playhouse, Montgomery Presents, Guiding Light; *Radio appearances include:* Theatre Guild on the Air, March of Time, Inner Sanctum Mystery, Helen Trent, Backstage Wife, Big Sister; *Plays produced include:* Dandy Lion, Popcorn Man, The Diary of Anne Frank, The Lost Fairy Tale. *Address:* 44 Charles St W, Suite 3503, Toronto, ON M4Y 1R8, Canada.

DOUKAS, Sarah; British business executive; b 1952, Malta; three c. *Career:* Fmrly fashion model; Head Booker Laraine Ashton Models 1981–87; f Storm Model Man 1987, represents numerous fashion models including Kate Moss (qv), Sophie Dahl (qv) and Liberty Ross. *Address:* Storm Model Management, 5 Jubilee Place, London SW3, UK. *Telephone:* (20) 7376-7764; *Internet:* www.stormmodels.com.

DOUTINÉ, Heike; German writer; b 3 Aug 1945, Zeulenroda, Thuringia. *Career:* Numerous novels, short stories and poems; books have been translated into French, Polish, Dutch, Spanish, Urdu, Hungarian, Serbo-Croat and English; Guest Prof Univ of Los Angeles and Ford Foundation, USA; Prize for Novel, Neue Literarische Gesellschaft; Villa Massimo Prize (Italy) 1973/74. *Publications include:* Novels: Wanke nicht, mein Vaterland, Berta, Wir Zwei, Die Meute, Der Hit, Im Lichte Venedigs (jtly) 1987, Blutiger Mund: die Tage des Mondes 1991; Poetry: In tiefem Trauer, Das Herz auf dem Lanze, Blumen begießen, bevor es anfängt zu regnen (also short stories) 1986, Kieder und Canones 1995; Deutscher Alltag: Meldungen über Menschen (short stories). *Address:* Ohnhorststr 26, 22609 Hamburg, Germany.

DOVE, Rita Francis, BA, MFA; American writer and professor of English; b 28 Aug 1952, Akron, OH; d of Ray Dove and Elvira Hord; m Fred Viebahn 1979; one d. *Education:* Miami and Ohio Univs, Univ of Tübingen (Germany) and Univ of Iowa. *Career:* Asst Prof Arizona State Univ 1981–84, Assoc Prof 1984–87, Prof 1987–89; Prof Univ of Virginia 1989–93, Commonwealth Prof of English 1993–; Poet Laureate of USA 1993–95; Writer-in-Residence Tuskegee Inst (AL) 1982; mem Literary Panel, Nat Endowment for Arts 1984–86; Judge Pulitzer Prize in Poetry 1991, Nat Book Award in Poetry 1991; mem numerous editorial bds; numerous hon degrees and awards. *Publications:* The Yellow House on the Corner (poetry) 1980, Museum 1983, Fifth Sunday (short stories) 1985, Thomas and Beulah (poetry) (Pulitzer Prize 1987) 1986, Grace Notes (poetry) 1989, Through the Ivory Gate (novel) 1992, Selected Poems 1993, Darker Face of the Earth 1994 (verse drama), Mother Love (poetry) 1995, The Poet's World (essays) 1995, Evening Primrose (poetry) 1998, On the Bus with Rosa Parks (poetry) 1999, Best American Poetry (ed) 2000. *Address:* Dept of English, University of Virginia, Charlottesville, VA 22903, USA. *Telephone:* (804) 924-6618 (Office).

DOW, Sheila Christine, PH D; British economist; b April 16 1949, Dumfries; d of Rev W. G. Anderson and E. Anderson; m Alexander Dow 1970; two d. *Education:* Univs of St Andrews, Manitoba (Canada), McMaster (Canada) and Glasgow. *Career:* Economist Bank of England 1970–72; Economist, then Sr Economist Dept of Finance, Govt of Manitoba 1973–77; Lecturer in Economics Univ of Stirling 1979–89,

Reader 1988–96, Prof 1996–. *Publications:* Money Matters (jtly) 1982, Macroeconomic Thought 1985, Financial Markets and Regional Economic Development 1990, Money and the Economic Process 1993, The Methodology of Macroeconomic Thought 1996. *Leisure interests:* sports, travel, music. *Address:* University of Stirling, Department of Economics, Stirling FK9 4LA, UK. *Telephone:* (1786) 467469; *Fax:* (1786) 467469; *E-mail:* s.c.dow@stir.ac.uk.

DOWDESWELL, Elizabeth; Canadian international organization executive. *Career:* Fmrly Minister of the Environment, Canada; Exec Dir UN Environment Programme 1993–98. *Address:* c/o United Nations Environment Programme, POB 30552, Nairobi, Kenya.

DOWRICK, Stephanie Barbara; New Zealand publishing executive and writer; b 2 June 1947; d of Harold and Mary (née Brisco) Dowrick; one s one d. *Education:* Sacred Heart Coll (Lower Hutt) and Univ of Wellington. *Career:* Co-Founder The Women's Press, London 1977, Man Dir 1977–82, Chair 1991; Fiction Publr Allen and Unwin, NSW; writer and psychotherapist. *Publications include:* Land of Zeus 1975, Why Children? (co-ed) 1982, Running Backwards Over Sand 1985, Intimacy and Solitude 1991, Speaking With the Sun (co-ed) 1991, After the Gulf War: For Peace in the Middle East 1991, The Intimacy and Solitude Workbook 1993. *Leisure interests:* music, art, religion. *Address:* Allen and Unwin, 9 Atchison St, St Leonards, NSW 2065, Australia (Office); 15 Alberto St, Lilyfield, NSW 2040, Australia (Home). *Telephone:* (2) 810-3277 (Home); *Fax:* (2) 818-3232 (Home).

DOYLE, Noreen, MBA; American banking executive; b 5 May 1949, New York. *Education:* Coll of Mount St Vincent and Dartmouth Coll. *Career:* Mem staff US Banking Dept, Bankers Trust Co, New York 1975–79, Man Credit Training Program 1979–80, Vice-Pres BT Southwest Inc, Houston, TX 1980–83, Div Man Energy Finance Group, New York 1983–86, Man Dir Structured Sales Group (New York) 1986–90, Man Dir European Structured Sales (London) 1990–92; Head Syndications, Merchant Banking, EBRD (London) 1992–1994, Deputy Vice-Pres Credit and Commercial Co-financing 1995–; mem Bd of Overseers The Amos Tuck School 1989–, Bd of Trustees Coll of Mount St Vincent 1979–90, Financial Women's Asscn of New York, American Asscn of the Sovereign Knights of Malta; John XXIII Award for Leadership (Coll of Mount St Vincent). *Publications:* Handbook of Corporate Finance 1990, Leveraged Buy-Outs. *Leisure interests:* theatre, running, reading, travel. *Address:* c/o EBRD, 122 Leadenhall St, London EC3V 4EB, UK.

DRABBLE, Jane, OBE, BA; British media executive; b 15 Jan 1947; d of Walter and Molly (née Boreham) Drabble. *Education:* Univ of Bristol. *Career:* Studio Man BBC 1968–72, Producer radio current affairs 1972–75, Asst Producer then Producer TV current affairs 1975–87, Ed Everyman series 1987–91, Asst Man Dir Network TV 1991–94, Head of Faculty Programmes 1993–94, Dir of Educ 1994–99. *Leisure interests:* music, theatre, walking, sailing. *Address:* c/o BBC, White City, 201 Wood Lane, London W12 7TS, UK.

DRABBLE, Margaret, CBE; British writer; b 5 June 1939, Sheffield; d of the late J. F. and Kathleen (née Bloor) Drabble; sister of A. S. Byatt (qv); m 1st Clive Swift 1960 (divorced 1975); two s one d; m 2nd Michael Holroyd 1982. *Education:* Newnham Coll (Cambridge). *Career:* Ed The Oxford Companion to English Literature 1979–85, 2000; Chair Nat Book League 1980–82; Vice-Patron Child Psychotherapy Trust 1987–; Hon Fellow Sheffield City Polytechnic 1989; Hon D LITT (Sheffield) 1976, (Bradford) 1988, (Hull) 1992; Hon D UNIV (York) 1995; E. M. Forster Award, American Acad of Arts and Letters 1973. *Publications:* A Summer Bird-Cage 1963, The Garrick Year 1964, The Millstone (John Llewelyn Rhys Memorial Prize 1966) 1965, Jerusalem the Golden 1967, The Waterfall 1969, The Needle's Eye 1972, Arnold Bennett: A Biography 1974, The Realms of Gold 1975, The Genius of Thomas Hardy (ed) 1976, The Ice Age 1977, For Queen and Country: Britain in the Victorian Age 1978, A Writer's Britain 1979, The Middle Ground 1980, The Radiant Way 1987, A Natural Curiosity 1989, Safe as Houses 1990, The Gates of Ivory 1991, Angus Wilson: A Biography 1995, The Witch of Exmoor 1996, The Peppered Moth 2001. *Leisure interest:* walking and talking. *Address:* c/o PFD, Drury House, 34–43 Russell St, London WC2B 5HA, UK (Office). *Telephone:* (20) 7344-1000 (Office).

DRAKULIĆ, Slavenka; Croatian journalist and writer; b 1949. *Career:* Contribs to newspapers and magazines including The New Republic, La Stampa, Dagens Nyheter, Frankfurter Rundechau and The Observer. *Publications include:* How We Survived Communism and Even Laughed, Balkan Express, Cafe Europa, Holograms of Fear, Marble Skin, The Taste of a Man 1997. *Address:* c/o The Women's Press, 34 Great Sutton St, London EC1V 0DX, UK.

DRBOHLAVOVÁ, Jana; Czech actress; b 22 Nov 1940, Prague; d of Karel Drbohlav and Marie Švejdová; m Ladislav Županič 1971; one s. *Education:* DAMU Acad of Theatre (Prague). *Career:* Actress Na Fidlovačce musical theatre 1962–63; actress Komorní, Komedie and ABC theatres, Prague 1963–; TV and radio performances, recordings. *Plays include:* Irma la Douce, Amore-mio, Rinaldo Dragonera 1962–63, Hlava 22, Sliby-chyby, Zkrocení zlé ženy; *Films:* Arabela, Dívka na košťěti. *Address:* Národní tř 25, 110 00 Prague 1, Czech Republic. *Telephone:* (2) 262067.

DREIFUSS, Ruth; Swiss politician and trade union executive; b 9 Jan 1940, St Gall. *Education:* Ecole d'Etudes Sociales (Geneva) and Univ of Geneva. *Career:* Ed Coopération, Swiss Union of Co-operatives, Basle 1961–64; Asst Sociologist Centre Psycho-social Universitaire, Geneva 1965–68; Asst in Nat Accounting, Faculty of Econ and Social Sciences, Univ of Geneva 1970–72; mem staff Swiss Devt Corpn, Fed Ministry of Foreign Affairs 1972–81; Sec Swiss Fed of Trade Unions 1981–93; mem Swiss Fed Council 1993, Head Fed Dept of Home Affairs 1993–; Pres of Swiss Confed 1998–99; mem Social Democratic Party; Dr hc (Haifa) 1999, (Jerusalem) 2000. *Address:* Federal Dept of Home Affairs, Bundeshaus, Inselgasse, 3003 Berne, Switzerland (Office). *Telephone:* (31) 3228033 (Office); *Fax:* (31) 3221015 (Office); *E-mail:* info@gs-edi .admin.ch (Office); *Internet:* www.edi.admin.ch (Office).

DRESSELHAUS, Mildred Spiewak, PH D; American professor of physics and engineering; b 11 Nov 1930, New York; d of Meyer and Ethel Spiewak; m Gene F. Dresselhaus 1958; three s one d. *Education:* Hunter Coll (NY) and Univ of Chicago (IL). *Career:* Mem staff Lincoln Lab MIT, Lexington 1960–67, Prof of Electrical Eng MIT, Cambridge 1967–, Assoc Head Dept of Electrical Eng 1972–74, Abby Rockefeller Mauzé Chair 1973–85, Dir Center for Materials Science and Eng 1977–83, Prof of Physics 1983–, Inst Prof 1985–; Visiting Prof Dept of Physics, Univ of Campinas, Brazil 1971, Technion—Israel Inst of Tech 1972, 1990, Nihon and Aoyama Gakuin Univs, Japan 1973, IVIC, Caracas, Venezuela 1977; Graffin Lecturer American Carbon Soc 1982; mem Energy Research Advisory Bd 1984–90; mem Bd of Dirs The Alliance Fund, Rogers Corpn, Quantum Chem Corpn; mem Governing Bd Nat Research Council 1984–87, 1989–90, 1992–; mem Hall of Fame, Hunter Coll 1972; Alumnae Medal (Radcliffe Coll, MA) 1973; Killian Faculty Achievement Award 1986–87; Nat Medal of Science 1990. *Publications include:* Physical Properties of Fullerenes; numerous contribs to professional journals. *Address:* MIT, Rm 13-3005, Cambridge, MA 02139, USA.

DREW, Joanna Maria, CBE, MA; British art gallery director; b 28 Sept 1929, Naini Tal, India; d of Brig Francis Greville Drew and Sannie Frances Sands. *Education:* Dartington Hall, Edinburgh Univ and Edinburgh Coll of Art. *Career:* With Arts Council of GB 1952–88, Asst Dir of Exhibitions 1970, Dir of Exhibitions 1975, Dir of Art 1978—86; Dir Hayward Gallery, South Bank Centre, London 1987–92; organized exhibitions of Millet, Courbet, Renoir, etc; mem Council RCA 1979–82; Officier des Arts et des Lettres 1988; Officier de l'Ordre Nat du Mérite 1994. *Address:* c/o Hayward Gallery, South Bank Centre, Belvedere Rd, London SE1 8XZ, UK.

DREYER, Inge; German poet; b 12 June 1933, Berlin; d of Curt and Katharina Ganswindt. *Education:* Univ of Berlin Coll of Educ. *Career:* Teacher Fritz-Karsen-Schule, Berlin 1956–68; Headmistress Walt-Disney-Schule, Berlin 1968–78; retd from teaching 1978; professional writer 1978–; Hon Prof of Literature Paris 1992–; Hon D LITT (London) 1992, (Paris) 1992; Golden Crown World Poets' Award 1990; Int Cultural Diploma of Honour 1995. *Publications:* Achtung Stolperstelle 1982, Schule mit Dachschaden 1985, Tönende Stille 1985, Die Streuner von Pangkor 1987; contribs to several anthologies and literary journals. *Leisure interests:* dance, painting, illustration, dress design, various sports. *Address:* Winkler Str 4A, 14193 Berlin, Germany. *Telephone:* (30) 8915783.

DREYFUS, Françoise, D EN D; French lawyer; b 11 May 1942, Nice; d of Roger and Marie-Madeleine Dreyfus; m 1st Roland Beauroy (divorced); m 2nd Jean Jacques Glassner 1994. *Education:* Univ of Paris. *Career:* Asst Univ of Paris I (Panthéon-Sorbonne) 1969–74, Sr Asst in Public Law 1974, Dir Public Admin and Law Educ and Research Centre 1979–80, Vice-Pres of Univ 1989–91, Prof Law Faculty 1990; Sr Lecturer Centre Universitaire Antille-Guyane, Guyana 1975–77; Tech Adviser to Minister of Health 1981–83; Legal Adviser to Minister for New Caledonia 1985; Sr Lecturer Inst d'Etudes Politiques de Paris 1985–87; Prof of Law Univ d'Evry Val d'Essonne 1990, Univ Paris I Panthéon-Sorbonne 1997–. *Publications:* La liberté du commerce et de l'industrie, L'interventionisme économique, Les institutions politiques et administratives de la France 1985, L'invention de la bureaucratie, servir l'Etat de France, en Grande-Bretagne et aux Etats-Unis (XVIIIe – Xxe siècle) 2000; contribs to law journals. *Address:* Université Paris I, Département de science politique, 14 rue Cujas, 75231 Paris, France.

DRIVER, Minnie (Amelia); British actress; b 31 Jan 1970, London; d of Charles Driver and Gaynor Churchward (née Millington). *Education:* Bedales School (Hants). *Career:* Best Newcomer, London Circle of Film Critics 1997, Best Actress, London Circle of Film Critics 1998. *Films include:* Circle of Friends, Goldeneye, Baggage, Big Night, Sleepers, Grosse Point Blank, Good Will Hunting, The Governess, Hard Rain, An Ideal Husband, Slow Burn, Tarzan (voice), South Park: Bigger, Longer and Uncut, High Heels and Lowlifes; *Drama includes:* Chatsky; *TV includes:* God on the Rocks, Mr Wroe's Virgins, The Politician's Wife, The Chris Isaak Show. *Address:* c/o Lou Coulson, 1st Floor, 37 Berwick St, London W1V 3LF, UK. *Telephone:* (20) 7734-9633.

DROBYSHEVSKAYA, Inessa; Belarus medical practitioner and politician; b 23 Aug 1947; d of Mikhail Kliouchinski and Maria Kliouchinskaya; m Anatoki Drobyshevski 1970; one d. *Education:* Vitebsk State Univ. *Career:* Obstetrician and Gynaecologist Spartak Plant Gomel 1972–73; Radiologist and Gynaecologist, Oncology Dispensary Gomel 1973–94; Head of Oncology Dispensary and Chief Oncologist Gomel 1986–94; Minister of Health 1994; Excellent Medical Doctor award; Supreme Soviet Award; 10 scientific publications 1986–93. *Leisure interest:* growing flowers. *Address:* 220048 Minsk, vul Miasnikov 39, Belarus. *Telephone:* (172) 226095; *Fax:* (172) 226297.

DROZDOVA, Margarita Sergeyevna; Russian ballet dancer; b 7 May 1948, Moscow. *Education:* Moscow Choreographic School and State Inst of Theatre Art (GITIS). *Career:* Danced with Stanislavsky Musical Theatre Ballet Co, Moscow 1967–91, Coach 1991–; mem CPSU 1980–91; Anna Pavlova Award, Paris 1968; RSFSR State Prize 1980; People's Artist of USSR 1986. *Ballets include:* Swan Lake, Gayané, Optimistic Tragedy, Corsaire, Coppélia, Cinderella. *Address:* Stanislavsky and Nemirovich Danchenko Musical Theatre, Moscow, Pushkinskaya str 17, Russian Federation (Office). *Telephone:* (095) 299-31-36 (Home).

DRUBICH, Tatyana Lusienovna; Russian actress; b 7 June 1960, Moscow; m Sergey Soloviev (divorced); one d. *Education:* Third Moscow Medical Inst. *Career:* Worked as a nurse then as a physician; actress 1972–; Head of Russian Rep of German chemical factory Dr Weigert 1992–. *Films:* 15th Spring (debut) 1972, 100 Days after Childhood 1975, Disarray 1978, Particularly Dangerous 1978, The Rescuer 1979, The Direct Heiress 1982, Selected 1983, Tester 1984, Black Monk 1986, Keep Me, My Talisman 1986, Assa 1987, Black Rose – an Emblem of Sorrow, White Rose – an Emblem of Love 1989, Hey, Fools 1996, Moscow 2000. *Address:* Seleznevskaya str 30, korp 3, Apt 77, 103473 Moscow, Russian Federation. *Telephone:* (095) 281-60-82.

DRUZHININA, Svetlana Sergeyevna; Russian film director and actress; b 16 Jan 1936, Moscow; m Anatoly Mukasey; one s. *Education:* Higher School of Choreography of the Bolshoi Theatre and All-Union Inst of Cinematography. *Films include:* Actress: Behind the Shop Window 1956, It Happened in Penkovo 1958, Girls 1962, Loneliness 1965, Green Light 1965, Beloved 1970; Dir: Fulfilment of Wishes 1974,

Sun 1977, Marriage of the Hussar 1979, Dulcinea of Toboss 1981, Princess of the Circus 1982, Guardemarines, Forward Ahead, Vivat, Guardemarines, Guardemarines-3 1986–91; *TV:* Secrets of Court Coups (series) 2001–. *Address:* Chernyakhovskogo str 2, apt 11, 125319 Moscow, Russian Federation. *Telephone:* (095) 155-80-71.

DU GRANRUT, Claude; French civil servant and judge; b 16 Nov 1929, Versaille; d of Count and Countess de Renty; m Bernard du Granrut 1950; five c. *Education:* Lycée Molière (Paris), Inst des Etudes Politiques (Paris), Wellesley Coll and Mount Holyoke Coll (USA). *Career:* Journalist 1950–56; Civil Servant, Ministry of Agric 1968–72, Professional Training Nat Agency, Dept of Labour 1972–78; Gen Sec Council on Women's Work 1978–87; mem Nat Econ Council 1979–81; Deputy Mayor of Senlis 1977–; Vice-Pres Picardy Regional Council 1986–; High Court Judge 1988–; mem EU Cttee of Regions 1994–; Hon LHD (Mount Vernon) 1979; Officier de la Légion d'Honneur 1979; Officier de l'Ordre Nat du Mérite 1995. *Leisure interests:* horse riding, gardening. *Address:* 3 rue Louis David, 75116 Paris, France.

DUBOIS, Maria Hélène Henriette; French diplomatist; b 15 May 1933, Belgrade, Yugoslavia; d of Albert and Nadejda (née Kovatchevich) Dubois; m Guilherme Kramert (divorced); one s one d. *Education:* Paris, Brazil, and Univ of Paris, Ecole Nat des Langues Orientales Vivantes. *Career:* Deputy Dir Industrias Reunidas, Recife, Brazil 1955–63; Econ Expansion Dept at Embassy of France, Yugoslavia 1963–66; Vice-Consul, Archivist, Casablanca, Morocco 1966–68; worked at Cen Admin, Personnel, then Europe 1969–75, UN and int orgs 1975–83; First Counsellor, Ghana 1983–87; Consul-Gen to Florence (Italy) and San Marino 1987–91; Amb to Costa Rica 1991–93, to St Lucia 1996–98, to St Christopher and Nevis 1996–98; Amb and Permanent Rep to CSCE Minsk Group 1993–95; Hon mem Coll of Engineers (Tuscany, Italy); Chevalier de l'Ordre Nat du Mérite; Chevalier de la Croix du Sud (Brazil); Chevalier de l'Infant Don Enrique (Portugal). *Publication:* Nous, tous les trois, les chiens et moi 1992. *Leisure interests:* piano, golf, horse-riding, swimming, collecting icons and carpets. *Address:* 40 rue de la Source, 75016 Paris, France (Home).

DUBOIS, Marie (pseudonym of Claudine Rousseau); French actress; b 12 Jan 1937, Paris; d of Pierre and Cécile Huzé; m Serge Rousseau 1961; one c. *Education:* Conservatoire Nat d'Art Dramatique (Paris). *Career:* Numerous appearances on stage, in films and on TV; Prix Suzanne Bianchetti 1963. *Plays include:* La contessa 1962, Le monstre Turquin 1965, Bleus, blancs, rouges ou Les libertins 1967, Zirélia 1981, L'amour tue! 1983, Le rêve de d'Alembert 1984, Thomas More, Le fils 1987, Le gardien des odeurs 1988; *Films include:* Tirez sur le pianiste 1959, Jules et Jim 1961, La ronde 1964, La grande vadrouille 1966, Le cascadeur 1969, Antoine et Sébastien 1973, Les arpenteurs (Best Actress Prize) 1973, La menace (César for Best Supporting Actress) 1977, Il y a longtemps que je t'aime 1979, La femme en fuite 1981, L'ami de Vincent 1983, Descente aux enfers 1986, Grand Guignol 1986, Un jeu d'enfant 1990, Les enfants du vent 1990, La dernière saison 1992; *TV appearances include:* Marie Curie 1964, Ma femme 1970, La belle au bois dormant 1973, François le champi 1976, La propriété 1980, Un manteau de chinchilla 1982, Bel-ami 1983, Lames de fond 1985, Maria Vandamne, Faux-frères 1989, La mémoire 1990, Maigret: l'homme du banc 1993. *Address:* c/o Artmédia, 10 ave George V, 75008 Paris, France.

DUBRAVČIĆ-ŠIMUNJAK, Sanda, MD, M SC; Croatian medical practitioner and former ice skater; b 24 Aug 1964, Zagreb; d of Dragutin and Zora (née Lipošćak) Dubravčić; m Boris Šimunjak 1991; one d. *Education:* Univ of Zagreb. *Career:* Nat Champion Figure Skater 1976–84; participated in nine European, seven World and two Olympic Championships; awarded Silver Medal 1981; European Champion 1984; runner with Olympic Torch, Sarajevo 1984; Head Croatian Del to Winter Olympics, Albertville, France 1992, Lillehammer, Norway 1994; currently medical practitioner specializing in physical medicine and rehabilitation, SV DUH Gen Hospital, Zagreb; Int Skating Union Medical Adviser Dec 1999–; papers and articles in medical journals; Best Athlete in Yugoslavia 1981; H. A. Samaranch Award for Research (Int Olympic Cttee Congress, Barcelona, Spain) 1991. *Publications:* Stress Fractures in Figure Skating 1989, Standards for Isokinetic Testing of Lower Extremities – Hip, Knee, Ankle 2001. *Leisure interests:* films, music, concerts, friends. *Address:* General Hospital SV DUH,

Department of Physical Medicine and Rehabilitation, 10000 Zagreb, Sveti Duh 64, Croatia (Office); 10000 Zagreb, Crnatkova 14A, Croatia (Home). *Telephone:* (1) 4712285 (Office); (1) 4843373 (Home); *Fax:* (1) 3745527 (Office); *E-mail:* sanda-dubravcic.simunjak@zg.hinet.hr.

DUCKWORTH, Marylin, OBE; New Zealand writer; b (Marylin Rose Adcock) 10 Nov 1935, Auckland; d of Cyril John Adcock and Irene Robinson; sister of Fleur Adcock (qv); m 1st Harry Duckworth 1955 (divorced 1964); m 2nd Ian MacFarlane 1964 (divorced 1972); m 3rd Daniel Donovan 1974 (died 1978); m 4th John Batstone 1985; four d. *Education:* Queen Margaret Coll and Victoria Univ (Wellington). *Career:* 10 writers' fellowships 1961–96 including Katherine Mansfield Fellowship, Menton 1980, Fulbright Visiting Writer's Fellowship, USA 1987, Victoria Univ Writing Fellowship, Hawthornden Writing Fellowship, Scotland 1994, Sargeson Writing Fellowship, Auckland 1995, Auckland Univ Literary Fellowship 1996; NZ Literary Fund Award for Achievement 1963, NZ Book Award for Fiction 1985. *Plays:* Home to Mother, Feet First; *Publications including:* novels: A Gap in the Spectrum 1959, A Barbarous Tongue 1963, Disorderly Conduct 1984, Married Alive 1985, Pulling Faces 1987, A Message from Harpo 1989, Unlawful Entry 1992, Seeing Red 1993, Leather Wings 1995, Studmuffin 1997; short stories: Explosions on the Sun 1989; poems: Other Lovers' Children; memoir: Camping on the Faultline. *Leisure interest:* playing the violin. *Address:* 41 Queen St, Mt Victoria, Wellington, 6001, New Zealand. *Telephone:* (4) 384 9990; *Fax:* (4) 384 9990.

DUCZMAL, Jaroszewska Agnieszka; Polish conductor; b 7 Jan 1946, Krotoszyn; m; three c. *Education:* Acad of Music (Poznán). *Career:* Creator and Dir Radio Amadeus Chamber Orchestra 1968–; asst conductor Poznán Nat Philharmonic 1971–72, conductor of Poznán Opera 1972–81; performs in Europe, N and S America and Asia; over 20 recordings including live concerts for TV and performances for radio; won award at first Nat Competition for Conductors, Katowice 1970, Silver Medal of Herbert von Karajan at the Meeting of Young Orchestras, West Berlin 1976; La Donna del Mondo Award of St Vincent Int Culture Centre, Rome 1982. *Leisure interests:* dogs, mountains, literary classics, gardening, mountaineering. *Address:* Polish Radio Amadeus Chamber Orchestra, al Marcinkowskiego 3, 61-745 Poznán, Poland. *Telephone:* (61) 8516686; *Fax:* (61) 8516687.

DUDEN, Anne; German writer; b 1 Jan 1942, Oldenburg. *Education:* West Berlin. *Career:* Co-Founder Rotbuch Verlag (publrs), Berlin 1973, mem staff 1973–78; freelance writer, London from 1978; works translated into several languages; several literary awards, including Krahichsteiner Literaturpreis 1986. *Publications include:* Übergang 1982, Das Judasschaf 1985.

DUDINSKAYA, Nathalia Mikhailovna; Russian ballet dancer and choreographer; b 21 Aug 1912, Kharkov; d of Mikhail Dudinskiy and Natalya Grippenberg; m Konstantin Sergeyev 1947 (deceased). *Education:* Leningrad (now St Petersburg) School of Choreography. *Career:* Debut Kharkov 1919; Prima Ballerina Kirov Academic Opera and Ballet Theatre, Leningrad until 1961; teacher of classical dance for soloists Kirov Theatre 1951–71; Prin Teacher of classical dance Vaganova Ballet Acad, Leningrad (now St Petersburg) 1964–, Prof and Head Faculty of Classical Dance 1997–; guest artist in many countries; People's Artist of USSR 1957; Order of Esteem 1939; Order Red Banner of Labour 1940, 1972, 1983, 1988; State Prizewinner 1941, 1947, 1949, 1951; Medal for Defence of Leningrad; Order Friendship of Peoples 1982. *Ballets include:* all ballets by Tchaikovsky, Raimonda, Giselle, Les Sylphides, Don Quixote, La Bayadère, Laurencia, Gayane, Cinderella, The Bronze Horseman, Shuralé, The Polish Maiden in Taras Bulba, The Path of Thunder, The Masquerade, A Midsummer Night's Dream, The Sleeping Beauty, The Spanish Suite, Miniature, Pacquita; *Films include:* The Sleeping Beauty, Raimonda; *Choreography includes:* With K. Sergeyev: Hamlet 1970, Le Corsaire 1973, The Left-Hander 1976, Beethoven Apassionata 1977, Class-Concert 1981, Swan Lake (Boston Ballet, USA) 1989, The Fairy Doll 1990, Cinderella (Osaka, Japan) 1991, Giselle (Osaka, Japan) 1992, Le Corsaire (Bolshoi, Moscow) 1992, (Boston Ballet, USA) 1997; as sole choreographer: Sleeping Beauty (Boston Ballet) 1993, Symphony of St Petersburg (Osaka) 1994. *Leisure interests:* swimming, diving. *Address:* 2 Gogol St, Apt 13, St Petersburg 191184, Russian Federation. *Telephone:* (812) 314-71-72; *Fax:* (812) 315-53-90.

DUFF, Ann MacIntosh, RCA; Canadian artist; b Toronto, ON; d of John MacIntosh and Constance Hamilton Duff. *Education:* Cen Tech School (Toronto, ON) and Queen's Univ. *Career:* One-woman exhibitions include Picture Loan Soc 1959, 1961, 1963, 1964, Gallery Ustel 1968, Merton Gallery 1970–74, Sisler Gallery 1975, Prince Arthur Galleries 1980–82, Gadatsy Gallery 1984, 1985, 1988, Lake Galleries 1990, 1991, 1993, 1998, 2000, D & E Lake Ltd 1996; group exhibitions include Canada Nat Exhibition 1951, 1954, 1956, Eighth Burnaby Biennial 1975, Graphex 1, 2 and 3 1973, 1974, 1975, Fifty Years of Watercolour Painting, Art Gallery of Ontario 1975, Watercolours Japan-Canada, Tokyo, Montréal 1976–78; represented in perm collections including Nat Gallery of Canada, City of Toronto Archives, Art Gallery of Ontario, Univ of Toronto Art Centre, Huron Coll, Agnes Etherington Gallery, Sarnia Art Gallery, London Art Gallery, Toronto Dominion Bank, Princess Margaret Hosp, Esso Resources, Citibank, Kitchener-Waterloo Art Gallery, John Labatt Ltd, Oregon State Univ (USA), The Royal Coll of Drawings and Watercolours, Windsor Castle (UK); mem Canadian Soc of Painters in Water Colour (Hon Award 1984); Queen's Jubilee Medal 1977. *Address:* 133 Imperial St, Toronto, ON M5P 1C7, Canada.

DUFFIELD, Dame Vivien Louise, DBE, MA; British organization executive; b 26 March 1946; d of Sir Charles and Francine (née Halphen) Clore; m John Duffield 1969 (divorced 1976); one s one d. *Education:* Cours Victor Hugo (Paris, France), Lycée Français de Londres (London) and Lady Margaret Hall (Oxford). *Career:* Est own foundation 1967, currently administers five foundations; f Clore Gallery, Tate Gallery, London, Eureka! (interactive children's museum), Halifax, W Yorks 1992; mem Nat Soc for Prevention of Cruelty to Children (NSPCC) Centenary Appeal Cttee 1983, Financial Devt Cttee 1985, Bd Royal Ballet 1990–; Dir Royal Opera House Trust 1985–2001 (Chair 1988), Royal Opera House 1990–2001; Vice-Chair Great Ormond Street Hosp Wishing Well Appeal 1987, Royal Marsden Hosp Cancer Appeal 1990; Trustee Dulwich Picture Gallery 1993–; Hon mem Royal Coll of Music 1987; Hon D PHIL (Weizmann Inst) 1985; Hon D LITT (Buckinghamshire) 1990; Benefactor of the Year, Nat Art Collections Fund 1988. *Leisure interests:* skiing, opera, ballet, shooting. *Address:* Clore Foundation, Unit 3, Chelsea Manor Studios, Flood St, London SW3 5SR, UK (Office). *Telephone:* (20) 7351-6061 (Office).

DUFFY, Carol Ann, OBE, BA, FRSL; British poet; b 23 Dec 1955, Glasgow; d of Frank Duffy and May Black; one d. *Education:* St Joseph's Convent (Stafford) and Univ of Liverpool. *Career:* Poetry Ed of AMBIT 1983–; Lecturer in Creative Writing, Manchester Metropolitan Univ 1996–; Cholmondeley Award 1992; Lannan Award (USA) 1995; Signal Poetry Award 1997. *Publications include:* plays: Take My Husband 1984, Cavern Dreams 1986; poetry: Fleshweathercock 1973, Standing Female Nude (Scottish Arts Council Award) 1985, Selling Manhattan (Somerset Maugham Award) 1987, Home and Away 1988, The Other Country (Dylan Thomas Award) 1990, Mean Time (Whitbread Poetry Award, Forward Poetry Prize, Scottish Arts Council Book Award) 1993, Selected Poems 1994, The Pamphlet 1998, The World's Wife 1999, Time's Tidings. *Leisure interest:* holidays. *Address:* c/o Anvil Press, 69 King George St, London SE10 8PX, UK. *Telephone:* (20) 8858-2946.

DUFFY, Maureen Patricia, BA, FRSL; British writer; b 1933; d of Grace Rose Wright. *Education:* Trowbridge High School for Girls, Sarah Bonnell High School for Girls and King's Coll (Univ of London). *Career:* Co-Founder Writers' Action Group 1972–79; Chair Greater London Arts Literature Panel 1979–81, Authors' Lending and Copyright Soc 1982–95, British Copyright Council 1989–99 (Vice Pres 1999–), Copyright Licensing Agency 1996–99; Vice-Pres Beauty without Cruelty 1975–, European Writers' Congress 1991–, British Copyright Council 1998– (Vice-Chair 1981–86, Chair 1989–98); Pres Writers' Guild of GB 1985–88 (Jt Chair 1977–78). *Publications:* That's How It Was 1962, The Single Eye 1964, The Microcosm 1966, The Paradox Players 1967, Lyrics for the Dog Hour 1968, Wounds 1969, Rites 1969, Love Child 1971, The Venus Touch 1971, The Erotic World of Faery 1972, I Want to Go to Moscow 1973, A Nightingale in Bloomsbury Square 1974, Capital 1975, Evesong 1975, The Passionate Shepherdess 1977, Housespy 1978, Memorials of the Quick and Dead 1979, Inherit the Earth 1980, Gorsaga 1981, Londoners: an elegy 1983, Men and Beasts 1984, Collected Poems 1949–84 1985, Change 1987,

A Thousand Capricious Chances: Methuen 1889–1989 1989, Illuminations 1991, Ocean's Razor 1993, Henry Purcell 1994, Restitution 1998, England: the Making of a Myth from Stonehenge to Albert Square 2001. *Address:* 18 Fabian Rd, London SW6 7TZ, UK. *Telephone:* (20) 7385-3598.

DUFOIX, Georgina, D ÈS SC ECON; French politician; b 16 Feb 1943, Paris; d of Alain Negre and Antoinette Pallier; m Antoine Dufoix 1963; two s two d. *Education:* Lycée de Nîmes and Univs of Montpellier and Sorbonne (Paris). *Career:* Mem Man Cttee PS 1979; Sec of State for Family Affairs 1981–83, for Family Affairs, Population and Immigrant Workers 1983–84; Conseiller Gén for Gard 1982, Socialist Deputy 1986–88; Minister for Social Affairs and Nat Solidarity 1984–86; Sec of State for Family Affairs, for Women's Rights, and for Repatriates May–June 1988; Chargée de Mission to Pres of France 1988–92; Pres Admin Council French Red Cross 1989–92; Del Fight against Drugs 1989–93; mem Bd UNRISD, Bd Govs War-Torn Soc Project (WSP), Geneva; Communications Co Vera. *Leisure interest:* her vineyard. *Address:* 35 rue des Blancs-Manteaux, 75004 Paris, France (Home).

DUKAKIS, Olympia, MFA; American actress; b 20 June 1931, Lowell, MA; d of Constantine S. and Alexandra (née Christos) Dukakis; m Louis Zorich; two s one d. *Education:* Univ of Boston. *Career:* Founding mem Charles Street Playhouse, Boston, MA 1957–60; drama teacher Univ of New York 1967–70, 1974–83, Yale Univ 1976; founding mem and Artistic Dir Whole Theatre, Montclair, NJ 1976–; appeared in more than 100 regional theatre productions and off-Broadway shows. *Plays include:* La Ronde, The Breaking Wall, The Trojan Women, The Cherry Orchard, Peer Gynt, A Man's a Man (OBIE Award), The Marriage of Bette and Boo (OBIE Award), The Aspern Papers, Social Security, The Night of the Iguana; *Plays directed include:* One Flew Over the Cuckoo's Nest, Arms and the Man, Uncle Vanya, Talley's Folly 1984; *Films include:* Twice a Man 1964, Lilith 1964, John and Mary 1969, Made for Each Other 1971, Rich Kids 1979, The Wanderers 1979, The Idolmaker 1980, King of America, Flanagan 1985, Moonstruck (Acad Award for Best Supporting Actress) 1988, Golden Globe Award, NY Film Critics Award, LA Film Critics Award) 1987, In the Spirit 1988, Steel Magnolias 1988, Daddy's Home 1988, Dad 1989, Look Who's Talking 1989, Look Who's Talking Too! 1990, Over the Hill 1991, Look Who's Talking Now, Naked Gun 33 1/3, The Cemetery Club, Digger, Jeffrey, Mighty Aphrodite, Mr Holland's Opus, Picture Perfect; *TV films include:* Lucky Day 1991, The Last Act is a Solo 1991, Tales of the City (series) 1994, A Century of Women 1994. *Address:* William Morris Agency, 151 S El Camino Drive, Beverly Hills, CA 90212, USA (Office); 222 Upper Mountain Ave, Montclair, NJ 07043, USA (Home).

DUKE, Patty; American actress; b 14 Dec 1946, New York; d of John P. and Frances Duke; m 1st John Astin 1973 (divorced 1985); m 2nd Michael Pierce 1986; one s. *Education:* Quintano's School for Young Professionals. *Career:* Pres Screen Actors' Guild 1985–88; Lecturer American Film Inst 1988; Emmy Awards 1964, 1969, 1976, 1979. *Plays include:* The Miracle Worker 1959–61, Isle of Children 1962; *Films include:* The Miracle Worker (Acad Award for Best Supporting Actress) 1962, Valley of the Dolls 1967, Me, Natalie (Best Actress Golden Globe Award 1970) 1969, My Sweet Charlie 1970, Captains and the Kings 1976, Something Special 1987, Prelude to a Kiss 1992; *TV appearances include:* Armstrong Circle Theatre 1955, The Prince and the Pauper 1957, Wuthering Heights 1958, Swiss Family Robinson 1958, US Steel Hour, Meet Me in St Louis 1959, The Power and the Glory 1961, Patty Duke Show (series) 1964–66, Before and After 1979, Women in White, The Baby Sitter, The Women's Room, All's Fair 1981–82, Something So Right, Best Kept Secrets, September Gun, It Takes Two (series) 1983, A Time to Triumph (film), George Washington: The Forging of a Nation 1984, Fight for Life 1987, Perry Mason: The Case of the Avenging Angel, Fatal Judgement 1988, Everybody's Baby: The Rescue of Jessica McClure, Amityville: The Evil Escapes, To Face Her Past 1996, A Christmas Memory 1997. *Address:* c/o William Morris Agency, 151 El Camino, Beverly Hills, CA 90212, USA.

DUKE, Robin Chandler; American diplomatist; m Angier Biddle Duke (deceased). *Career:* Writer NY Journal American 1940s; fmr mem Bd Dirs American Home Products, Rockwell Int, Int Flavors and Fragrances; Dir US–Japan Foundation, Lucile and David Packard

Foundation, UN Assen of USA until 2000; fmr Vice-Chair and mem Advisory Bd Inst of Int Educ; Chair Del to 21st Session of UNESCO 1980, Amb 1980, to Norway 2000–; mem Council on Foreign Relations; Fellow Acad of Arts and Social Sciences. *Address:* American Embassy, Drammensvien 18, 0244 Oslo, Norway. *Telephone:* 22-44-85-50; *Fax:* 22-43-07-77; *E-mail:* olso@usis.no; *Internet:* www.usembassy.no.

DULMAA, Ajuriin, D SC; Mongolian scientist; b 18 Sept 1936, Ulan Bator; m L. Sanjaa 1956; one d one s. *Education:* Mongolian State Univ. *Career:* Teacher State Pedagogical Univ 1956–61; Ichthyologist and Hydrobiologist Inst of Biology, Mongolian Acad of Science from 1964, Chief of Hydrobiology and Animal Study Sector; discovered five species of acquatic organisms and bred three new fish in Mongolian lakes; Corresp mem Acad of Science 1986, Prof 1989, Academician 1991; mem New York Acad of Sciences 1999; American Biographical Inst (ABI) Woman of the Year 1996, 1997; Merited Scientist of Mongolia 2000; Bharat Mata Award (India). *Publications:* has published over 200 scientific works. *Leisure interests:* reading, fishing. *Address:* Mongolian Academy of Science, Inst of Biology, Dept of Hydrobiology, Ulan Bator, Mongolia. *Telephone:* 51781 (Office); 27617 (Home); *E-mail:* enkhtuul-mas@magicnet.mn; *Internet:* www.mas.ac.mn.

DUMAS, Rhetaugh Etheldra Graves, MS, PH D, RN, FAAN; American health and higher education administrator, nurse and psychologist; b 26 Nov 1928, Natchez, MS; d of Rhetaugh Graves and Josephine (Clemmons) Graves Bell; m A. W. Dumas, Jr 1950; one d. *Education:* Dillard Univ (New Orleans, LA), Yale Univ School of Nursing and Union Grad School (Yellow Springs, OH). *Career:* Dir Student Health Center, Dillard Univ, New Orleans 1957–59, Instructor in Psychiatric Nursing 1961; Yale-New Haven Hosp 1960; Research Asst and Instructor Yale Univ School of Nursing 1962–65, Asst Prof 1965–66, Assoc Prof 1966–72; Dir of Nursing Connecticut Medical Health Center, Yale-New Haven Medical Center 1966–72; Chief Psychiatric Nursing Educ Branch, Div of Manpower and Training 1972–75; Deputy Dir Div of Manpower and Training Programs, Nat Inst of Mental Health 1976–79, Deputy Dir Alcohol, Drug Abuse and Mental Health Admin, US Public Health Service 1979–81; Dean and Prof Univ of Michigan School of Nursing, Ann Arbor, MI 1981, Vice-Provost for Health Affairs, Univ of Michigan 1994–97, Cole Prof, School of Nursing 1994–, Vice-Provost Emer 1997–, Dean Emer 1997–; Pres American Acad of Nursing 1987–89; Pres Nat League of Nursing 1997–99; mem NAS Inst of Medicine; Hon D HUM LITT (Yale) 1989 and several other hon degrees and awards. *Leisure interests:* reading, music, singing. *Address:* The University of Michigan, 400 N Ingalls St, Room 4320, Ann Arbor, MI 48109, USA (Office); 6 Eastbury Court, Ann Arbor, MI 48105, USA (Home). *Telephone:* (734) 936-6213 (Office); (734) 668-6103 (Home); *Fax:* (734) 764-4546 (Office); (734) 761-6195 (Home); *E-mail:* rhetaugh@umich.edu (Office).

DUMASY, Lise, D ÈS L; French professor of literature; b 18 June 1954, Taza, Morocco. *Education:* Ecole Normale Supérieure (Sèvres). *Career:* Schoolteacher 1978–80; research engineer Centre Nat de Recherches Scientifiques (CNRS) 1980, seconded to Inst de France 1984; teacher Mannheim Univ 1987–88; Sr Lecturer Univ Stendhal (Grenoble-III) then Prof 1992, Head Dept of French Language, Literature and Civilization 1992–95, mem Scientific Council 1997, Prin March 1999–. *Address:* Bureau de la Présidente, Université Stendhal (Grenoble-III), BP 25, 38040 Grenoble, Cedex 9, France.

DUNANT, Sarah, BA; British broadcaster and writer; b 8 Aug 1950, London; d of David and Estelle (née Joseph) Dunant; two d. *Education:* Godolphin and Latymer School and Newnham Coll (Cambridge). *Career:* Actress 1972–73; teacher (Japan) 1973–74; travelling (Asia) 1973–74, (S and Cen America) 1976–77; Producer BBC Radio 1974–76; freelance journalist, novelist, scriptwriter, radio and TV presenter 1977–; sometime Presenter Woman's Hour, BBC Radio Four 1986–, The Late Show BBC2 TV 1989–95, Night Waves BBC Radio 3 1997–. *Publications:* Exterminating Angels (jtly) 1983, Intensive Care (jtly) 1986, Snow Storm in a Hot Climate 1988, Birth Marks 1991, Drowning in Punch, Fatlands (Silver Dagger Award) 1993, The War of the Words (ed) 1994, Under My Skin 1995, Transgressions 1997, The Age of Anxiety (ed) 1998, Mapping the Edge 1999, The Birth of Venus 2002. *Leisure interests:* travelling, gardening. *Address:* c/o Clare

Alexander, Aitken Associates, 29 Fernshaw Rd, London SW10 0TG, UK; 1A Highwood Rd, London N19 4PN, UK (Home). *Telephone:* (20) 7281-1555 (Home); *Fax:* (20) 7272-4147 (Home).

DUNAWAY, (Dorothy) Faye; American actress; b 14 Jan 1941, Bascom, FL; d of John and Grace Dunaway; m 1st Peter Wolf 1974; m 2nd Terry O'Neill 1981; one s. *Education:* Univs of Florida and Boston. *Career:* Spent three years with Lincoln Center Repertory Co in New York, appearing in A Man For All Seasons, After the Fall and Tartuffe; Off-Broadway in Hogan's Goat 1965; appeared at the Mark Taper Forum, Los Angeles in Old Times, as Blanche du Bois in A Streetcar Named Desire 1973, The Curse of an Aching Heart 1982. *Films include:* Hurry Sundown 1967, The Happening 1967, Bonnie and Clyde 1967, The Thomas Crown Affair 1968, A Place For Lovers 1969, The Arrangement 1969, Little Big Man 1970, Doc 1971, The Getaway 1972, Oklahoma Crude 1973, The Three Musketeers 1973, Chinatown 1974, Three Days of the Condor 1975, The Towering Inferno 1976, Voyage of the Damned 1976, Network (Acad Award for Best Actress) 1976, The Eyes of Laura Mars 1978, The Champ 1979, The First Deadly Sin 1981, Mommie Dearest 1981, The Wicked Lady 1982, Supergirl 1984, Barfly 1987, Burning Secret 1988, The Handmaid's Tale 1989, On a Moonlit Night 1989, Up to Date 1989, Scorchers 1991, Faithful 1991, Three Weeks in Jerusalem, The Arrowtooth Waltz, The Temp 1992, Don Juan DeMarco, Drunks, Dunston Checks In, Albino Alligatorr, The Chamber, Fanny Hill 1998, Love Lies Bleeding 1999, The Yards 1999, Joan of Arc 1999, The Thomas Crown Affair 1999; *TV appearances include:* After the Fall 1974, The Disappearance of Aimee 1976, Hogan's Goat, Evita! – First Lady 1981, 13 at Dinner 1985, Beverly Hills Madame 1986, The Country Girl, Casanova, The Raspberry Ripple, Cold Sassy Tree, Silhouette, Rebecca; *Publication:* Looking for Gatsby (autobiog, jtly) 1995. *Address:* c/o ICM, 8942 Wilshire Blvd, Beverly Hills, CA 90211, USA (Office).

DUNBAR, Bonnie J., PH D; American engineer and astronaut; b 3 March 1949, Sunnyside, WA; d of Robert Dunbar; m Ronald M. Sega. *Education:* Univs of Washington and Houston (TX). *Career:* Mem staff Boeing Computer Services 1971–73; Sr Research Engineer Space Div Rockwell Int; Visiting Scientist Harwell Labs, Oxford, UK 1975; Adjunct Asst Prof of Mechanical Eng, Univ of Houston; joined NASA 1978, Astronaut 1981, mission specialist flight STS 61-8 1985, STS 32 1990; mem AAAS, American Ceramic Soc, Soc of Biomedical Eng, Materials Research Soc. *Address:* NASA, Johnson Space Centre Astronaut Office, Houston, TX 77058, USA.

DUNMORE, Helen; British writer; b 1952, Yorks; m; one s one d one step-s. *Publications:* Poetry: The Sea Skater (Poety Soc's Alice Hunt Bartlett Award), The Raw Garden (Poetry Book Soc Choice), Secrets (Signal Poetry Award 1995); Novels: Zennor in Darkness (McKitterick Prize 1994), Burning Bright, A Spell of Winter (Orange Prize for women writers 1996), Talking to the Dead 1996, Your Blue-Eyed Boy 1998, With Your Crooked Heart 1999; Short stories: Love of Fat Men 1998, Ice Cream 2000; also children's novels. *Address:* c/o Caradoc King, A. P. Watt Ltd, 20 John St, London WC1N 2DR, UK. *Telephone:* (20) 7405-6774 (Office); *Fax:* (20) 7831-2154 (Office).

DUNN, Baroness (Life Peer), cr 1990, of Hong Kong Island in Hong Kong and of Knightsbridge in the Royal Borough of Kensington and Chelsea, **Lydia Selina Dunn,** DBE, JP, BS; Hong Kong business executive; b 29 Feb 1940, Hong Kong; d of the late Yenchuen Yeh and Chen Yin Chu Dunn; m Michael David Thomas 1988. *Education:* St Paul's Convent School (Hong Kong), Coll of Holy Names (Oakland, CA) and Univ of California at Berkeley (USA). *Career:* Exec Trainee Swire & Maclaine 1963, Dir 1973, Man Dir 1976, Exec Dir 1982–; Dir John Swire & Sons (Hong Kong) Ltd 1978–, Exec Dir 1996–; Exec Dir Swire Pacific Ltd 1982–; Chair Swire Loxley Ltd 1982–, Swire Marketing Ltd 1986–, Camberley Enterprises Ltd 1986–, Swire Source America, Inc 1988–, Asian American Man Inc 1988–, The Eagle's Eye Int Ltd 1988–, Christie's Swire (Hong Kong) Ltd 1989–, Swire Resources Ltd 1990–, Encomium Ltd; Dir Cathay Pacific Airways Ltd 1985–97 (Adviser to Bd 1997–), Hong Kong and Shanghai Banking Corpn Ltd 1981–96 (Deputy Chair 1992–96), Hong Kong and Shanghai Banking Corpn Holdings Plc 1990–, Volvo 1991–93 (mem Int Advisory Bd 1985–91), Christie's Int PLC 1996–98, Christie's Fine Art 1998–2000, Marconi PLC (fmrly GEC) 1997–, Christie's Swire

(Holding) Ltd 1989–, Hong Kong Seibu Enterprise Co Ltd 1989–; Pres Carroll Reed Int Ltd (USA) 1990–; mem HK Legis Council 1976–88, Sr mem 1985–88; mem Exec Council 1982–95, Sr mem 1988–95; Chair Hong Kong Trade Devt Council 1983–91, Hong Kong/Japan Business Co-operation Cttee 1988–95 (mem 1983–95); mem Council Chinese Univ of Hong Kong 1978–90, Hong Kong/US Econ Co-operation Cttee 1984–93, Hong Kong Br, Hong Kong Asscn 1983–, Int Council of Asia Soc 1986–, Inst of Dirs, Royal Soc for the Encouragement of Arts, Mfrs and Commerce; Chair Lord Wilson Heritage Trust 1993–95; Hon Fellow London Business School 2000; Hon LL D (Chinese Univ of Hong Kong) 1984, (Hong Kong) 1991, (BC, Canada) 1991, (Leeds) 1994; Hon D SC (Buckingham) 1995; Trade Award, Prime Minister of Japan 1987; To Peace and Commerce Award, USA Sec of Commerce 1988. *Publications:* In the Kingdom of the Blind 1983. *Leisure interest:* collecting antiques. *Address:* John Swire & Sons Ltd, Swire House, 59 Buckingham Gate, London SW1E 6AJ, UK.

DUNN, Susan, BA; American opera singer; b 23 July 1954, Malvern, AR. *Education:* Hendrix Coll and Indiana Univ. *Career:* Debut at Peoria (IL) Opera Co 1982; since then appearances at La Scala (Milan, Italy), Carnegie Hall, Lyric Opera (Chicago, IL), Vienna State Opera, Australian Opera, Washington Opera, San Diego Opera (CA); has performed with leading orchestras including New York Philharmonic, Chicago Symphony, Boston Symphony, Orchestre de Paris, Concert-gebouw Orchestra (Netherlands); Council Award (Nat Metropolitan Opera) 1981; winner Philadelphia Opera Co/Pavarotti Int Vocal Competition 1981, WGN-III Opera Competition 1983; G. B. Dealey Prize (Dallas Morning News-Dallas Opera) 1983; Richard Tucker Award 1983. *Operas include:* Aida, La Forza del Destino, Un Ballo in Maschera, Otello, Il Trovatore. *Address:* c/o Herbert H. Brelin Inc, 119 W 57th St, New York, NY 10019, USA.

DUNSMORE, Rosemary, BFA; Canadian actress; b 13 July 1952, Edmonton, AB; d of Robert James and Florence Ruth Dunsmore; m Peter Dvorsky 1981. *Education:* York Univ. *Career:* Actress 1974–; performed at Stratford Festival 1983, 1984, Edinburgh Festival; teacher of acting Centre for Actors' Study, Toronto, ON and Equity Showcase; Guest Teacher Langara Coll, Vancouver, BC; held workshop for professional actors, Vancouver; awards include Kari Award (Canadian Telecom) 1982. *Plays include:* Ten Lost Years, Buried Child, Getting Out, Single, Straight Ahead/Blind Dancers (Theatre Alliance Dora Award); *Film and TV appearances include:* Anne of Green Gables: The Sequel, Blind Faith (Best Actress Actra Nellie Award 1982), Skate, Dancing in the Dark, The Campbells, Mom P. I., MacGyver, LA Laq, My Two Dads, Twins, Total Recall. *Leisure interests:* tennis, cooking. *Address:* c/o Pam Friendly, Premiere Artists, 232C Gerrard St E, Toronto, ON M5A 2E6, Canada.

DUONG THU HUONG; Vietnamese writer and screenwriter; b 3 Jan 1947, Thai Binh province; m 1968 (divorced 1981); one s one d. *Education:* Ecole de Théorie Professionnelle (Ministry of Culture) and Ecole de Formation Littéraire Nguyen Du. *Career:* Volunteer Cultural Activities, Binh Tri Thien 1968–77; film studio work N Vietnam from 1977; mem Exec Cttee Asscn des Cinéastes 1989; First prize Concours de récit 1979; Gold Medal, two Silver Medals Vietnamese Film Festivals for feature films scripted. *Publications:* Thien Duong Mu (Paradise of the Blind); four scripts, one children's novel, three novels, ten collections of stories. *Leisure interests:* music, sport, literature. *Address:* Association des Cinéastes Vietnamiens, 51 rue de Tran hung Dao, Hanoi, Vietnam; c/o Editions Des Femmes, 6 rue de Mézières, 75006 Paris, France.

DUPEREY, Anny (pseudonym of Anny Legras); French actress; b 28 June 1947, Rouen; d of Lucien and Ginette Legras; fmr partner Bernard Giraudeau; one s one d. *Education:* Conservatoire d'Art Dramatique (Rouen and Paris). *Career:* Numerous appearances on stage, in films and on TV; Prix Dussane 1984; Chevalier de la Légion d'honneur. *Plays include:* La guerre de Troie n'aura pas lieu (Prix Gérard Philipe, Best Foreign Theatre Actress, Canada) 1975–78, Attention fragile (co-adaptor) 1978–80, Duo pour une soliste 1984, Le secret 1987, Le plaisir de rompre, Le pain de ménage 1990, Quand elle dansait 1994, Un mari idéal 1995; *Films include:* Stavisky 1973, Un éléphant ça trompe énormément 1976, Psy 1981, Le grand pardon 1982, Mille milliards de dollars 1982, Meurtres à domicile 1982, Les compères 1983, La triche 1984; *TV appearances include:* Un château au soleil (Sept d'or for Best

Actress) 1988, La face de l'ogre (also dir) 1988, Une famille formidable (Sept d'or for Best Actress) 1992, Charlemagne 1994, La vocation d'Adrienne 1997, Chère Marianne 1999; *Publications:* L'admiroir (Prix Alice Barthou, Acad Française) 1978, Le nez de Mazarin 1986, Le voile noir 1992, Je vous écris... 1993, Les chats de hasard 1999. *Leisure interests:* sewing, crafts. *Address:* Cinéart, 36 rue de Ponthieu, 75008 Paris, France.

DUPUY, Anne-Marie; French politician; b 18 Sept 1920, Pithiviers, Loiret; d of Pol and Louise (née Lacroix) Didier; two d one s. *Education:* Lycée Camille-Sée and Univ of Paris. *Career:* Personnel Officer Messieurs de Rothschild Frères 1952–63; Asst Sec to Prime Minister Georges Pompidou 1963–66, Prin Pvt Sec 1966–69; Prin Pvt Sec Secr-Gen of Presidency of the French Repub 1969–73; Prin Pvt Sec to Pres Georges Pompidou 1973–74; mem Council of State 1974–87, on secondment 1984; Regional Councillor, Alpes-Maritimes 1982–94; MEP (RPR) 1984–89; Mayor of Cannes 1983–89; Head of Dept Comm for Refugees 1990–98; mem Conseil d'Etat; Chair Cannes Professional Football Club 1987–89; Officier de la Légion d'Honneur; Officier de l'Ordre Nat du Mérite; Croix du Combattant Volontaire 1939–45. *Publication:* Le Destin et la Volonté (memoirs) 1996. *Leisure interests:* reading, classical music. *Address:* Conseil d'Etat, Palais Royal, 75100 Paris, France.

DUQUE, Sarah Amaro, MA, MFA; American artist and writer; b 30 May 1929, Los Angeles, CA; d of the late Victor Anthony and Sarah (née Millholland) Duque. *Education:* Stanford Univ, Dominican Univ of Calif, Villa Schifanoia (Florence, Italy) and Univ of Edinburgh (UK). *Career:* Teacher N Ranchito School Dist, CA 1951–53, Los Angeles City Schools, CA 1953–64; Prof of Art N Orange Co Coll Dist 1964–85; artist and writer 1985–; one-woman exhibitions at Serra Gallery (San Francisco, CA) 1963, Loyola-Marymount Univ Gallery (Los Angeles, CA) 1964, Galleria Mazzucchelli (San Domenico, Italy) 1971, Galleria Del Parione (Florence, Italy) 1973, Fullerton Coll Gallery (Fullerton, CA) 1974, Galleria San Marco (Florence) 1981, Brea Civic Center (CA) 1983, Woollahra Gallery (Sydney, Australia) 1984, Civic Gallery (Orvieto, Italy) 1988; group exhibitions include Nat Serigraph Soc (New York) 1953, Butler Inst of American Art (Youngstown, OH) 1963, Miracle Mile Art Show (Los Angeles, CA) 1965, Nat Tapestry Exhibition (Detroit, MI) 1968, Galleria Torra (Piccilli, Italy) 1982, Galleria Della Verna (Tuscany, Italy) 1982, Russian Tea Room and St Thomas More Foyer (New York) 1987; represented in numerous public and pvt collections including Modern Museum of Art (Manila), Vatican Museum of Modern Art, Galleria Mazzucchelli (San Domenico, Italy), Auschwitz Art Museum (Poland), Vallourec Inc (Houston, TX), Offices of Radio Free Europe (Paris), Monastario Benedistino Cuenavaca (Mexico) Mount Angel Abbey (St Benedict, Oregon) and at Franciscan Peace Centre (Assisi, Italy); Nat Endowment of Humanities 1977; Daniel Murphy Foundation 1988; Irvine Foundation of California 1996. *Publications include:* Accade una Volta Firenze 1984, Accade una Volta Venezia 1986, Accade una Volta Milano 1986, Sally and Father Serra 1987. *Leisure interests:* music, travel. *Address:* 2384 Carrotwood Drive, Brea, CA 92821, USA; Via Eaccia 24, Orvieto, Italy. *Telephone:* (714) 250-1886 (USA); (763) 66148 (Italy).

DURANT, Isabelle; Belgian politician; b 4 Sept 1954, Brussels. *Education:* Univ Coll London. *Career:* Registered nurse; teacher 1981–89; mem of Ecologist Party (AGALEV) 1989–, Attaché of Ecologist Parl Group at Regional Council of Brussels 1992–94; Fed Sec and Spokeswoman for ECOLO-AGALEV 1994–99; mem Fed Office of ECOLO-AGALEV 1995–99; Co-ordinator of Etats généraux de l'Ecologie politique (EGEP) 1996–; Deputy Prime Minister and Minister for Mobility and Transport July 1999–. *Address:* Ministry of Transport, Wetstraat 63–65, rue de la Loi, 1040 Brussels, Belgium. *Telephone:* (2) 237-67-11; *Fax:* (2) 237-67-11.

DURANTE, Viviana Paola; Italian ballet dancer; b 8 May 1967, Rome. *Career:* Joined Royal Ballet Co, London 1984, became Soloist 1987, Prin 1989, Guest Artist 1997, 1999; Premio Positano Award (Italy) 1991, Evening Standard Award, Time Out Award. *Ballets include:* Ondine, Romeo and Juliet, La Bayadère, Swan Lake, Sleeping Beauty, Cinderella, Prince of the Pagodas, My Brother and My Sisters, Requiem, Don Quixote, Manon, Nutcracker, Rhapsody, Capriccio, Anna Karenina, Carmen, Symphonic Variations; *Films (video) include:*

Mayerling, Sleeping Beauty. *Leisure interests:* yoga, swimming, travelling, reading, life. *Address:* c/o Royal Ballet Company, Royal Opera House, Covent Garden, London WC2E 9DD, UK (Office).

DURBEN, Maria-Magdalena; German writer; b 8 July 1935; d of Bernhard and Eva (née Klein) Block; m 2nd Wolfgang Durben 1967. *Education:* In Erfurt and Berlin. *Career:* Writes in collaboration with Wolfgang Durben; Dr hc (Gdańsk, Poland) 1977, (New York); Hon D LITT (Karachi) 1978, (World Acad of Languages and Literature, São Paulo, Brazil) 1978, (World Acad of Arts and Culture, Taipei) 1979; numerous awards. *Publications:* Ein Stückchen von Gott, Gruß an Taiwan, Wenn der Schnee fällt, Da schrie der Schatten fürchterlich, Schaukle am blauen Stern, Unterm Glasnadelzelt, Roter Rausch und weiße Haut, Wenn das Feuer fällt, Wenn die Asche fällt, Lichtrunne, Zwischen Knoblauch und Chrysanthemen, Haiku mit Stäbchen. *Address:* Schulstr 8-10, 66701 Beckingen, Germany.

DURHAM, Christine Meaders, JD; American judge; b 3 Aug 1945, Los Angeles, CA; d of William Anderson and Louise Meaders; m George Homer Durham 1966; three d two s. *Education:* Wellesley Coll (MA) and Duke Univ (NC). *Career:* Called to Bar, NC 1971, UT 1974; pvt practice Durham, NC 1971–73; Instructor of Legal Medicine, Duke Univ 1971–73; Adjunct Prof of Law, Brigham Young Univ, UT 1973–78; Partner Johnson, Durham and Moxley 1974–78; Judge Utah Dist Court 1978–82; Assoc Justice Utah Supreme Court 1982–; Pres Women Judges' Fund for Justice 1987–88; Fellow American Bar Foundation; mem ABA, American Judicature Soc. *Address:* Utah Supreme Court, POB 140210, Salt Lake City, UT 84114-1202, USA.

DURKEE, Sarah Bruce; American lyricist and writer; b 14 Feb 1955, Salem, MA; d of Allen Bruce and Patricia Durkee; m Paul Ross Jacobs 1988. *Education:* Pingree School (S Hamilton, MA). *Career:* Actress and teacher Celebration Mime Theatre, various cities 1973–76; comedienne and writer Nat Lampoon Shows, various cities 1977–79; Lyricist Andy's Summer Playhouse (Wilton, NH) 1980, Meat Loaf (New York) 1983–84, Sesame St 1987, Square One 1987, Children's TV Workshop 1987; Gold Award (Houston Int Film Festival) 1987; Emmy Award (for music direction and composition, Sesame St) 1987–90. *Address:* Children's TV Workshop, New York, NY, USA.

DURRANI, Tehmina; Pakistani writer; m Ghulam Mustafa Khar (divorced); two d. *Career:* Controversial writer; wrote autobiography after split with notorious fmr fuedal landlord Ghulam Mustafa Khar. *Publications:* My Feudal Lord (autobiog), Mirror to the Blind 1996, Blasphemy 1998. *Address:* c/o Viking Penguin, 27 Wright's Lane, London W8, UK.

DURRANT, Jennifer Ann; British artist; b 17 June 1942, Brighton; d of Caleb John Durrant and Winifred May Wright; m 1st William A. H. Henderson 1964 (divorced 1976); m 2nd Richard Alban Howard Oxby 2000. *Education:* Varndean Grammar School for Girls (Brighton), Brighton Coll of Art and Crafts, Slade School of Fine Art and Univ Coll (London). *Career:* Part-time Lecturer in Painting St Martin's School of Art, London 1974–87, RCA 1979–, Chelsea School of Art 1987–, Royal Acad Schools 1991–; Exhibition Selector Northern Young Contemporaries, Whitworth Gallery, Manchester, TV SW Arts; mem Painting Faculty The British School at Rome 1979–83; Newham Hosp Comm (in asscn with Greater London Arts Asscn and King Edward's Hosp Fund); Towner Art Gallery, Eastbourne; Artist-in-Residence Somerville Coll, Oxford 1979–80; solo exhibitions at Univ of Surrey (Guildford) 1975, Arnolfini Gallery (Bristol) 1979, Museum of Modern Art (Oxford) 1980, Nicola Jacobs Gallery (London) 1982, 1985, Arcade Gallery, Harrogate 1983, Northern Centre for Contemporary Art (Sunderland) 1986, Serpentine Gallery (London) 1987, Newlyn-Orion (Penzance) 1988, Lynne Stern Assocs (London) 1989; Group exhibitions include: Liverpool, Reykjavik, Boston (USA), Edmonton (Canada), New York, Aachen (Germany), Pittsburg (USA), Birmingham, Stoke On Trent, Sheffield 1988, Newcastle 1989, London, Lincoln 1990; works in collections of Arts Council of GB, British Council, Contemporary Art Soc, Tate Gallery, London Museum of Fine Arts, Boston (USA), Neue Gallerie (Aachen, Germany), etc and in pvt collections; Abbey Minor Travelling Scholarship 1964; Arts Council Award 1976; Arts Council Major Award 1978; Greater London Arts Asscn Award 1980; Athena Art Award 1988. *Leisure interests:* classical

music, including opera, archaeology, visiting museums, looking at paintings and sculpture. *Address:* 9–10 Holly Grove, London SE15 5DF, UK. *Telephone:* (20) 7639-6424.

DURRANT, Mignonette Patricia, BA; Jamaican diplomatist; b 30 May 1943. *Education:* Univ of West Indies. *Career:* Admin Officer, Ministry of Agric 1964–70; First Sec Ministry of Foreign Affairs 1971–72, Prin Asst Sec 1972–74; Minister-Counsellor, Mission to OAS, Washington, DC 1974–77; Asst Dir Political Div, Ministry of Foreign Affairs 1977–81, Deputy Dir 1981–83; Deputy Perm Rep to UN 1983–87, Perm Rep 1995–; Amb to Fed Repub of Germany 1987–92; Dir-Gen Ministry of Foreign Affairs and Foreign Trade 1992–95. *Address:* Permanent Mission of Jamaica to the UN, 767 Third Ave, 9th Floor, New York, NY 10017, USA. *Telephone:* (212) 935-7509; *Fax:* (212) 935-7607; *E-mail:* jamun@undp.org.

DURY, Raymonde; Belgian sociologist and politician; b 22 July 1947, Haine-St-Paul. *Career:* Press Attaché Socialist Group, EP 1976–82; MEP (PS) 1982–98, mem Cttee on Institutional Affairs, Del for Relations with Transcaucasus, Leader Belgian Del 1989, Vice-Chair Group of the Party of European Socialists; Gov of Brussels 1998–. *Address:* Rue Uyttenhove, bte 45, 1090 Brussels, Belgium.

DUSSERRE, Liliane Denise France, L ÈS SC, MD; French professor of medicine; b 6 March 1932, Dijon; d of Francis and Henriette (née Renaudin) Charignon; m Pierre Dusserre 1954; two s one d. *Education:* Lycée Marcel-Pardé (Dijon), Faculties of Science and of Medicine (Dijon) and Faculty of Medicine (Paris). *Career:* Intern 1957–61, Asst Lecturer in Biology Dijon hosps 1963–76, Biochem Tutor 1966–69, Tutor of Math, Statistics and Medical Computing 1969–76, Sr Lecturer, Hosp Biologist 1976–; Head of Medical Computing Dept, Centre Hospitalier Universitaire, Dijon; first woman mem Conseil Nat de l'Ordre des Médecins 1982; mem Conseil Nat des Universités 1987, Conseil Supérieur des Hôpitaux 1988, Asscn des Femmes Médecins, Asscn des Epidémiologistes de Langue Française, Soc Française de Biométrie; Chevalier de la Légion d'Honneur; Chevalier des Palmes Académiques; Officier de l'Ordre Nat du Mérite. *Publication:* L'information medicale, l'ordinateur et la loi 1999. *Leisure interests:* skiing, reading. *Address:* 2 bis ave de la 1r Armée Française, 21000 Dijon, France. *Telephone:* (3) 80-30-76-47; *Fax:* (3) 80-30-76-47.

DUVALL, Shelley; American actress and producer; b 7 July 1949, Houston, TX. *Career:* Founder TV production co Think Entertainment. *Films:* Brewster McCloud, McCabe and Mrs Miller, Thieves Like Us, Nashville, Buffalo Bill and the Indians, Three Women (Cannes Festival Prize 1977), Annie Hall, The Shining, Popeye, Time Bandits, Roxanne, Suburban Commando, The Underneath, Portrait of a Lady, Changing Habits, Alone, Home Fries, Space Cadet; *TV:* Bernice Bobs Her Hair, Lily, Twilight Zone, Mother Goose Rock 'n' Rhyme, Faerie Tale Theatre (Rumpelstiltskin, Rupunzel), Tall Tales and Legends (Darlin' Clementine); *Producer:* Faerie Tale Theatre, Tall Tales and Legends, Nightmare Classics, Dinner at Eight (film), Mother Goose Rock 'n' Rhyme, Stories from Growing Up, Backfield in Motion (film), Bedtime Stories, Mrs Piggle-Wiggle.

DVOŘÁKOVÁ, Vladimíra, PH D; Czech political scientist; b 11 Feb 1957; m Petr Dvořák 1977; one s one d. *Education:* Charles Univ (Prague) and Czech Acad of Sciences. *Career:* Assoc Prof Univ of Econs 1994–, Sec Centre of European Studies and Co-ordinator E European Constitutionalism; Man Ed Politologiscka reuve 1994–; Ed-in-Chief Současná Europa a Ceská republike 1996–; mem Exec Cttee Czech Political Sciences Asscn 1994–. *Publication include:* Nicaragua 1980, Transitions to Democracy (in Czech) 1994, Democracy and Constitutionalism (in Czech) 1996. *Leisure interest:* reading. *Address:* Pivovarnichá 9, 180 00 Prague 8, Czech Republic. *Telephone:* (2) 6846177; *Fax:* (2) 24220657; *E-mail:* dvorakv@nb.use.cz.

DWORKIN, Andrea, BA; American feminist and writer; b 26 Sept 1946, Camden, NJ; d of Harry and Sylvia Spiegel. *Education:* Bennington Coll. *Career:* Has worked as a waitress, receptionist and factory worker; Visiting Prof of Women's Studies and Law, Univ of Minnesota 1983, has taught classes sponsored by the Depts of Law and Women's Studies and the Faculty of Liberal Arts; delivered lectures in Ireland, UK, Norway, Sweden and Canada; organized seminars and workshops, and delivered lectures at numerous univs throughout the USA; formulated (jtly) legislation recognizing pornography as a violation of women's civil rights, revised version of civil rights bill for city of Indianapolis (IN); mem Authors' Guild, PEN, Southern Poverty Law Center (Klanwatch), Nat Abortion Rights Action League (NARAL), Planned Parenthood, Nat Women's Political Caucus, Amnesty Int, Nat Org for Women; Fellow Women's Inst for Freedom of the Press; several appearances on TV programmes in USA and UK. *Publications:* Woman Hating 1974, Our Blood: Prophecies and Discourses on Sexual Politics (essays) 1976, The New Woman's Broken Heart 1980, Pornography: Men Possessing Women 1981, Right-wing Women 1983, Ice and Fire (novel) 1986, Letters from a War Zone 1976–1987, 1989, Mercy 1991 (novel), Life and Death 1997, Scapegoat 2000; numerous contribs to anthologies and journals; books and articles translated into several languages.

DYACHENKO, Tatyana Borisovna; Russian politician; b 17 Jan 1960, Sverdlovsk; d of fmr Pres Boris and Naina Yeltsin; m Velery Mikhailovich Okulov; two s. *Education:* Moscow State Univ. *Career:* Engineer Construction Bureau Salut 1982–94, Construction Bureau Zarya Urala, Moscow 1994–95; mem Boris Yeltsin Election Campaign 1996; counsellor to Pres Yeltsin 1997–99. *Leisure interest:* tourism.

DYADKOVA, Larissa; Russian singer; b 9 March 1952, Zelenodolsk; m Alexandre Kogan 1985; one d. *Education:* Leningrad Conservatory class of J. Levando. *Career:* Soloist Mariinsky Theatre 1978–; toured with Mariinsky Theatre in European countries, guest soloist Metropolitan-Opera, La Scala, Communale Theatre, Florence, Deutsche Oper Berlin, Arena de Verona, San Francisco Opera, New Israeli Opera. *Music:* concert appearances: performs Verdi's Requiem in concerts, vocal series by Mussorgsky and Mahler, cantatas by Prokofiev; works with conductors Levine, Rostropovich, Mehta, Abbado, Temirkanov, Gergiev. *Address:* Mariinsky Theatre, Teatralnaya pl. 1, St Petersburg, Russian Federation. *Telephone:* (812) 114-3039; *Fax:* (812) 114-3039.

DYBKJÆR, Lone, M CHEM ENG; Danish politician; b (Lone Vincents) 23 May 1940, Copenhagen; d of Kristian and Else V. F. (née Jensen) Vincents; m 1st Ib Dybkjær; two d; m 2nd Poul Nyrup Rasmussen (Prime Minister of Denmark) 1994. *Education:* Rungsted Statsskole and Tech Univ of Denmark. *Career:* Sec Danish Acad of Tech Sciences 1964–66, Consultant 1977; Sec Biomedical Eng Cttee 1966–70; Head Information Secr Tech Univ of Denmark 1970–74; Consultant to Geotechnical Inst 1978–80; mem Folketing (Parl, Det Radikale Venstre/Danish Social-Liberal Party) 1973–77, re-elected 1979, Spokesperson on Energy, Labour Market and Environmental Questions 1979–87, 1990–94, on Foreign Affairs 1987–88; mem Danish Del to Nordic Council 1982–84, Chair Energy Cttee 1984–87, Tech Cttee 1987–88, Govt Rep on Nordic Council 1988–90; Minister of the Environment 1988–90; Govt Rep on Bd Citycorp Aktieselskab, Copenhagen 1986–88, Chair Arbejdmiljøinstitut 1998–, mem Bd Københavns Bank 1991–; mem Environmental Tech Expert Panel of Almindelig Brand Invest 1999–; Co-Chair Gender Task Force, Stability Pact for SE Europe, Working Table on Democratization and Human Rights 1999–; MEP (Danish Social-Liberal Party, Group of the European Liberal, Democrat and Reformist Group (ELDR)) 1994–, First Vice-Pres Cttee on Devt and Co-operation (responsible for human rights) 1999–, mem Cttee for Rules and Procedures, ELDR 1994–, mem Cttee on Women's Rights and Equal Opportunities 1999–, Temporary Cttee on Human Genetics and Other New Technologies in Modern Medicine 2000, substitute mem Cttee on Foreign Affairs, Human Rights, Common Security and Defence Policy 1999–2001, substitute mem Temporary Cttee on Echelon 1999–, substitute mem Cttee on Constitutional Affairs 2001; First Vice-Chair ACP–EU Ass; Chair Osteoporosis Asscn 1994–; Cyclist of the Year 1989; European Gold Medal for Conservation of Buildings 1991; Europa Preis für Denkmalpflege 1991; Bird Life Prize 1993. *Publications:* Tête à tête with a Modern Politician 1998, Strange Parliament 1999, Digital Denmark 1999. *Leisure interests:* tennis, reading. *Address:* European Parliament, ASP 10G 116, rue Wiertz, 1047 Brussels, Belgium (Office); c/o Det radikale Venstre, Christiansborg, 1240 Copenhagen K Denmark (Office); Allégade 6A, 2000 Frederiksberg, Denmark (Home). *Telephone:* (2) 284-7391 (Office); 33-37-47-56 (Home); *Fax:* (2) 284-9391 (Office); 33-37-72-51 (Home); *E-mail:* ldybkjaer@europarl.eu.int (Office); rvlody@ft.dk (Office); *Internet:* www.lone-dybkjaer.dk (Office).

DYKE, Beverley Janis, BA; Australian business executive; b 9 May 1951; d of Arthur and Jean Dyke. *Education:* Univ of New South Wales and Macquarie Univ. *Career:* Mem staff Tjuringa Ipec Group 1969–74; Nat Liaison Officer Nat Exec Australia Party 1974–75; Producer current affairs programme 2GB 1976; Accounts Exec Forcefield Promotions 1977–80; Marketing Consultant The Consultancy 1980–82; Consultant Polymex Consultants 1982; Dir and Shareholder Fox Communications 1982–85, Proprietor 1992–; Man Dir Issues Australia (fmrly Mojo Corpn) 1986–93, Chair 1993–; Fed Dir Advertising Fed of Australia 1993–97; Trade In Services Group 1987–90; Assoc Fellow Australian Marketing Inst; mem Australian Inst of Political Science, Women Chiefs of Enterprise, Bd Australia/Indonesia Inst 1989–94. *Leisure interests:* bush walking, swimming, cycling, weight training, reading, music. *Address:* 35 Grandview St, Pymble, NSW 2073, Australia.

DYSON, Esther, B ECON; American business executive; b 1952, Switzerland. *Education:* Harvard Univ. *Career:* Fmr Securities Analyst New Court Securities, Oppenheimer & Co; fmr reporter Forbes Magazine; Chair EDventure Holdings (fmrly Rosen Research) 1993–; sponsor of Annual PC (Platforms for Communication) Forum; Non-Exec Chair wpp.com; Publr Release 1.0 (monthly newsletter); fmr Chair ICANN (Internet Corpn for Assigned Names and Numbers); mem Govt Export Council Subcttee on Encryption; mem Bd Electronic Frontier Foundation, Santa Fe Inst, Global Business Network, Inst for East/West Studies; Founder-mem Russian Software Market Asscn; Partner Mayfield Software Fund; mem Software Pubrs Asscn. *Publication:* Release 2.0: A design for living in the digital age 1997. *Leisure interest:* swimming. *Address:* 104 5th Ave, 20th Floor, New York, NY 10011, USA.

E

EAGLE, Angela, BA; British politician; b 17 Feb 1961; d of André and the late Shirley Eagle. *Education:* Formby High School and St John's Coll (Oxford). *Career:* Mem Econ Directorate CBI 1984; Researcher Confed of Health Service Employees 1984, Press Officer 1986, Parl Officer 1992; MP (Lab) for Wallasey 1992–; Parl Under Sec of State, Dept of Social Security 1998–; mem Lab Party Nat Women's Cttee 1989–; mem BFI. *Leisure interests:* cricket, cinema, chess. *Address:* House of Commons, London SW1A 0AA, UK. *Telephone:* (20) 7219-4074.

EARLE, Sylvia Alice, MA, PH D; American biologist and oceanographer; b 30 Aug 1935, Gibbstown, NJ; d of Lewis and Alice Freas Reade. *Education:* Florida State and Duke Univs (NC). *Career:* Resident Dir Cape Haze Marine Lab, Sarasota, FL 1966–67; Research Scholar Radcliffe Inst 1967–69; Research Fellow Farlow Herbarium, Harvard Univ 1967–75, Researcher 1975; Research Assoc Univ of California at Berkeley 1969–75; Research Assoc (Botany) Natural History Museum, Los Angeles Co 1970–75, Fellow in Botany 1989–; Research Biologist and Curator California Acad of Sciences, San Francisco appt 1976; Founder, Pres, CEO Bd of Dirs Deep Ocean Tech Inc, Oakland, CA 1981–90; Founder, Pres, CEO Deep Ocean Eng, Oakland, CA 1982–90, mem Bd Dirs 1992–; mem Council World Wide Fund for Nature; Trustee Charles A. Lindbergh Fund (Pres 1990–), Center for Marine Conservation 1992–, Perry Foundation (Chair 1993–); Hon PH D (Monterey Inst of Int Studies) 1990, (Ball State) 1991, (George Washington) 1992, (Duke) 1993; Hon D SC (Duke) 1993, (Ripon Coll, Connecticut) 1994; numerous awards including Conservation Service Award (US Dept of the Interior) 1970, Conservation Service Award (California Acad of Sciences) 1979, Order of Golden Ark Prince (Netherlands) 1980, David B. Stone Medal (New England Aquarium) 1989, Gold Medal (Soc of Women Geographers) 1990, Medal (Radcliffe Coll) 1990, Pacon Int Award 1992. *Publications:* Scientific Results of the Tektite II Project (ed) 1972–75, Exploring the Deep Frontier 1980; numerous contribs to professional journals. *Address:* Deep Ocean Engineering, 1431 Doolittle Drive, San Leandro, CA 94577-2225, USA (Office); 12812 Skyline Blvd, Oakland, CA 94619, USA (Home).

EASTON, Michelle, BA, JD; American lawyer and civil servant; b 12 Aug 1950, Philadelphia, PA; d of Glenn and Jeanne (née Mulhall) Easton; m Ron Robinson 1974; three s. *Education:* Briarcliff Coll and American Univ (Washington, DC). *Career:* Called to the Bar, VA 1981; Asst to Exec Dir Young Americans for Freedom 1973–78; Asst to Public Relations Dir Nat Right to Work Comm 1978, Legal Asst Nat Right to Work Legal Defense Foundation 1979; mem staff Office of the Pres-Elect, Equal Employment Opportunity Comm, Washington, DC 1980–81; lawyer Dept of Justice, Washington, DC 1981, Dir Missing Children's Program, Office of Juvenile Justice and Delinquency Prevention 1985–87; Special Asst Dept of Educ, Washington, DC 1981–83, Dir of Intergovt Affairs 1987–88, Deputy Under-Sec for Intergovt and Interagency Affairs 1988–91, Exec Asst to Sec for Pvt Educ 1991–94; mem VA State Bd of Educ, Richmond 1994–98; Pres Clare Boothe Luce Policy Inst 1993; Liaison Officer Agency for Int Devt, Africa Bureau 1984; mem Bd Dirs The Family Foundation, Richmond 1998–.

EASTON, Sheena; British singer; b 27 April 1959, Bellshill; m Tim Delarm 1997; two c. *Education:* Royal Scottish Acad of Music and Drama. *Career:* First hit single followed appearance on TV show The Big Time; has collaborated with Prince; currently living in USA; Grammy Award for Best New Artist 1981. *Singles include:* 9 to 5, Modern Girl, For Your Eyes Only (theme to Bond film), Sugar Walls, U Got the Look (with Prince); *Albums include:* Take My Time 1981, You Could Have

Been with Me 1981, Madness, Money and Music 1982, Best Kept Secret 1983, A Private Heaven 1984, The Lover in Me 1988, Greatest Hits (jtly) 1989, Me gustas tal como eres (Grammy Award for Mexican-American Performance) 1984; *TV appearances:* Miami Vice (series), Body Bags, The Highlander, The Adventure of Brisco County Jr, Outer Limits 1995, Chicken Soup for the Soul 1999; *Musical:* Man of La Mancha. *Address:* c/o Harriet Wasserman Management, 18136 Califa St, Tarzana, CA 91356, USA (Office).

EASTWICK-FIELD, Elizabeth, FRIBA; British architect (retd); b (Elizabeth Gee) 21 Nov 1919, London; d of Philip Gee and Georgia Urban Smith; m John Eastwick-Field 1942; three s one d. *Education:* Privately (London), Schule der Angewandte Kunst (Munich, Germany), Cen School of Arts and Crafts (London), Bartlett School of Architecture (Univ Coll London). *Career:* Lecturer in sciography Bartlett School of Architecture 1940–41; freelance architectural design and draughting 1947–54; Partner Stillman and Eastwick-Field architects 1954–86, Consultant 1986– (projects included Camden School for Girls, London and Chase Farm Hospital, Enfield); illustrator of various architectural books and papers; Firm has received several architectural awards including from Ministry of Housing and Local Govt, Civic Trust and RIBA. *Leisure interests:* landscape gardening, horticulture, video film-making, computer graphics. *Address:* Low Farm, Low Rd, Denham, Eye, Suffolk IP21 5ET, UK. *Telephone:* (1379) 870219; *Fax:* (1379) 870219 (Home).

EBADI, Shirin; Iranian lawyer; b 1947. *Career:* Apptd Judge (first and only woman) Tehran 1974, forced to step down from the bench after 1979 revolution, retd 1984; currently runs own law practice, specializing in human rights; arrested on charges of 'disturbing public opinion' 2000, received suspended sentence Sept 2000; mem Cttee for the Defense of Rights of the Victims of Serial Murders; has written numerous books and articles; Human Rights Watch Award 1996.

EBERLEY, Helen-Kay, M MUS; American opera singer, record company executive and publisher; b 3 Aug 1947, Sterling, IL; d of William Elliott and P. Eberley. *Education:* Northwestern Univ. *Career:* Debut in Der Rosenkavalier with Lyric Opera, Chicago, IL 1973; has performed jazz with Duke Ellington and Dave Brubeck; numerous solo concerts including Continental Bank Concerts 1981–89; Chair, Pres, Artistic Co-ordinator Eberley-Skowronski Inc, Evanston, IL 1973–92; Founder EB-SKO Productions 1976; Exec Dir, performance consultant E-S Management 1985; Founder HKE Enterprises 1993–; singing coach; Guest Lecturer at colls and univs; numerous appearances on TV and radio; F. K. Weyerhauser Scholar, Metropolitan Opera 1967; volunteer Art Inst of Chicago 1995–; Milton J. Cross Award, Metropolitan Opera Guild 1968; numerous poetry awards including Poets and Patrons, Inc (Chicago). *Operas include:* Così fan Tutte, Le Nozze di Figaro, Dido and Aeneas, Tosca, La Traviata, Don Giovanni, Brigadoon; Producer, Annotator: Gentleman Gypsy 1978; Exec Producer: Separate But Equal 1976, All Brahms 1977, Opera Lady 1978, Eberley Sings Strauss 1980, Helen-Kay Eberley: American Girl 1983, Helen-Kay Eberley: Opera Lady II 1984; *Publications:* Angel's Song 1993, The Magdalena Poems 1994, Chapel Heart 1995, Desert Dancing 1998, Canyon Ridge 2000. *Leisure interest:* animal rights. *Address:* HKE Enterprises, 1726 Sherman Ave, Evanston, IL 60201, USA.

EBTEKAR, Massoumeh, D SC, PH D; Iranian politician; b 1961, Tehran; m; two s. *Education:* Martyr Beheshti Univ and Tarbiat Modarres Univ. *Career:* Univ Prof; fmr mem Ed Bd Keyhan Int newspaper; acting head of NGO Bureau of Women's Affairs; Vice-Pres in charge of Iran's Environment Protection Org Aug 1997– (first woman Vice Pres). *Publications:* numerous contribs to int journals. *Address:* c/o Office of the President, Tehran, Iran. *Internet:* www.president.ir.

ECLEO, Hon Glenda B., D ED; Philippine politician and business executive; b 10 May 1937, Iligan City; d of the late Roberto Buray and Rudina Oliveros; m Ruben E. Ecleo 1955 (deceased); four s four d. *Education:* Misamis Oriental High School, Univ of the Visayas and Cebu State Coll. *Career:* Mem House of Reps 1987–92, Chair House Cttee on Educ, Culture and Sports, Co-Chair Sub-Cttee on Public Educ, mem Cttees on Local Govt, Natural Resources, Health, Social Services, Family Relations and Population, and Rural Devt, mem Sub-Cttee on Educ Oversight; Propr Twin Dragon Printing Enterprises, Ecleo Caltex, RGE Stitchmark; Pres and Founder Don José Ecleo Memorial Educational Foundation; numerous awards include Outstanding Public Official (Philippine Youth Devt) 1984, Leadership Excellence Achievement Award (Asian Int Inst of Professional Devt) 1986, Plaque of Recognition (Philippine Media Practitioners Asscn) 1987, Maharlika Award (Asian Experimental Fellowships of the Philippines) 1987, Outstanding Business Exec and Civil Leader (Media Award) 1989, Outstanding Lady Solon (Public Eye Magazine) 1992. *Leisure interests:* outdoor games, sports, business. *Address:* 106 Swallow Drive, Corner Flicker Sts, Green Meadows Subdivision, Quezon City 1100, Philippines. *Telephone:* (73) 721-88-85.

EDELMAN, Judith, B ARCH, AIA; American architect; b 16 Sept 1923, Brooklyn, NY; d of Abraham and Frances Hochberg; m Harold Edelman 1947; two s. *Education:* Connecticut Coll, New York Univ and Columbia Univ (NY). *Career:* Schermerhorn Travelling Fellow 1950; Architect, pvt practice 1958–60; Partner Edelman and Salzman, New York 1960–79, Edelman Partnership, New York 1979–; Adjunct Prof of Architecture City Univ of New York 1972–76; numerous Visiting Lectureships including Washington Univ, St Louis (MO) 1974, Univ of Oregon 1974, MIT 1975, City Univ of New York 1975, 1977, Columbia Univ (NY) 1979, Univ of California at Berkeley, Univ of Southern California 1982; mem American Inst of Architects; major works include the restoration of St Mark's Church, New York 1970–82, Two Bridges Urban Renewal Area Housing 1970–96, Goddard Riverside Elderly Housing and Community Centre, New York 1983, Chung Pak Bldg, New York 1992; awards include Bard Award of Merit 1975, 1982, First Prize, Nat Trust for Historic Preservation 1983, Public Service Award, Settlement Housing Fund 1983, Woman of Vision Award, Nat Org for Women 1989, Pioneer in Architecture Award, American Inst of Architects (New York) 1990. *Address:* Edelman Partnership, 100 Lafayette St, Suite 602, New York, NY 10013, USA (Office); 37 W 12th St, New York, NY 10011, USA (Home). *Telephone:* (212) 431-4901 (Office); *Fax:* (212) 226-5958 (Office); *E-mail:* jedelman@teparchitects.com.

EDELMAN, Marian Wright, BA, LL B; American lawyer; b 6 June 1939, Bennettsville, SC; d of Arthur J. and Maggie Wright; m Peter B. Edelman 1968; three s. *Education:* Univs of Paris and Geneva (Switzerland), Spelman Coll and Yale Univ. *Career:* Called to the Bar, DC, MS, MA; Lawyer Nat Asscn for the Advancement of Colored People (NAACP) Legal Defense and Educ Fund Inc, New York 1963–64, Dir Legal Defense and Educ Fund, Jackson, MS 1964–68; Partner Washington Research Project, S Center for Public Policy 1968–73; Dir Center for Law and Educ, Harvard Univ, MA 1971–73; Pres Children's Defense Fund 1973–; mem Exec Cttee Student Non-Violent Co-ordinating Cttee 1961–63, Advisory Council Martin Luther King, Jr Memorial Library, Presidential Comm on Missing in Action 1977, Presidential Comm on Int Year of the Child 1979, Presidential Comm on the Agenda for the 1980s, Bd of Dirs NAACP Legal Defense and Educ Fund; numerous hon degrees including Hon LL D (Smith Coll) 1969, (Columbia, Pennsylvania, Yale, etc), Hon DHL (Trinity Coll, Washington) 1978, (Syracuse) 1979, (State Univ of New York) 1981, (Yale) 1985, (New School of Social Research) 1989, (DePaul) 1990, (Clark, Harvard, Union Coll) 1991, (Tuskegee, Washington, St Louis, Mercy Coll) 1992, (Sciences) 1979; Order of Golden Ark Prince (Netherlands) 1980, David B. Stone Medal (New England Aquarium) 1989, Gold Medal (Soc of Women Geographers) 1990, Medal (Radcliffe Coll) 1990, Pacon Int Award 1992. *Address:* Children's Defense Fund, 25 E St, NW, Washington, DC 20001, USA.

EDELSON, Mary Beth, MA; American artist; b 6 Feb 1933, E Chicago; d of Albert Melvin amd Mary Lou (née Young) Johnson; one s one d. *Education:* Depauw (IN) and New York Univs. *Career:* Instructor Corcoran School of Art, Washington, DC 1970–75; Artist-in-Residence Univ of Illinois 1982, 1988, Univ of Tennessee 1983, Columbia Univ (NY) 1984, Maryland Inst of Art 1985, Kansas City Art Inst 1986, Gilford Coll 1992, Univ of Colorado 1993, Clemson Univ (SC) 1994, Univ of S Florida 1995; exhibitions include Stichting de Appel (Amsterdam), Berlinische Gallerie (Berlin), Walker Art Gallery, Corcoran Gallery (Washington), Museum of Modern Art (New York), Guggenheim Museum of Art (New York), Everson Museum, Museu de Arte Contemporânea (São Paulo, Brazil), A/C Project Room (New York), Nicole Klagsbrun (New York), Creative Time (New York), Mercer Union (Toronto, Canada), The Agency (London), Nicolai Wallner (Copenhagen); lectures in field; Founder-mem Conf of Women in Visual Arts. *Publications:* Seven Cycles: Public Rituals 1981, To Dance: Painting with Performance in Mind 1985, Seven Sites 1987, Shape Shifter: Seven Mediums 1990, Firsthand: Photographs 1973–93, Shooter (series) 1993. *Leisure interests:* cooking, travel. *Address:* 110 Mercer St, New York, NY 10012, USA. *Telephone:* (212) 226-0832; *Fax:* (212) 226-0832.

EDENIUS, Ann-Kari, BA; Swedish magazine editor and civil servant; b 11 Sept 1962, Munkfors; d of Allan and Sonya Petersson; m Mats Edenius 1988. *Education:* Stockholm. *Career:* Information Asst 1984; Project Leader Rikstörbundet mot Astma-Allergi 1985–86; Ed Affärs Ekonomi Management business magazine 1986–87, Medborgaren political magazine 1987–91; apptd Deputy Press Sec to Prime Minister 1991. *Address:* c/o Prime Minister's Office, Rosenbad 4, 103 33 Stockholm, Sweden.

EDGAR, Patricia May, B ED, MA, PH D; Australian foundation executive and television producer; b 11 March 1937, Mildura, Vic; d of R. and E. Etherington; m Donald Ernest Edgar 1960; two d. *Education:* Mildura High School and Univs of Melbourne, Stanford (USA) and La Trobe. *Career:* Secondary school teacher, Vic 1959–62; Lecturer Council of Adult Educ, Vic 1965–66; Sec Victorian Asscn for the Teaching of English 1966; Professional Intern KQED TV, San Francisco, USA 1968; Acting Dir of Research Ford Foundation Project, Univ of Chicago, IL, USA 1969; Sr Lecturer Centre for the Study of Educational Communication and Media, School of Educ, La Trobe Univ 1970–81; Visiting Prof Dept of Communication and Dramatic Arts, Univ of Iowa, USA 1980; Task Force Dir Australian Children's Television Foundation 1981, Dir 1982–, Exec in charge of production (children's TV programmes) 1983–; Corresp mem Acad Argentina de Artes y Ciencias de la Comunicacion 1996; Hon D LITT (W Australia); Archbishop of Sydney Citation Award, World Communications Day 1992; Australian Coll of Educ Medal 1998. *Productions include:* Documentaries: Mexico '75 1975, Winners 1985, Kaboodle (I) 1986, (II) 1988–89, Touch the Sun 1987–88, Round the Twist (I) 1988–89, (II) 1992, (III) 1999, (IV) 2000, Songs of Innocence (documentary) 1992, Lift Off II 1994, First Day 1995, The Genie from Down Under 1995; Series: Winners 1985, More Winners 1990, Kaboodle 1986, Kaboodle II 1989, Touch the Sun 1987–88, Round the Twist (I) 1988–89, (II) 1992, (III) 1999, (IV) 2000, The Greatest Time on Earth 1990, Lift Off 1991–92, Sky Trackers 1993, The Genie from Down Under (I) 1995, (II) 1997, L'il Elvis Jones and the Truckstoppers 1996, The Crash Zone (I)1998, (II) 2000, Yolungu Boy (feature film) 1999; TV Film: Sky Trackers 1990; *Publications include:* Australia and Her Northern Neighbours (jtly) 1974, Media She (jtly) 1974, Children and Screen Violence 1977, The Politics of the Press 1979, The News in Focus 1980, Janet Holmes á Court 1999. *Leisure interests:* films, reading, walking. *Address:* Australian Children's Television Foundation, 145 Smith St, 3rd Floor, Fitzroy, Vic 3065, Australia (Office); 8 Mount St, Eaglemont, Vic 3084, Australia (Home). *Telephone:* (3) 9419-8800 (Office); (3) 9457-1441 (Home); *Fax:* (3) 9419-0660 (Office); (3) 9457-4696 (Home); *E-mail:* patricia.edgar@actf.com.au (Office); pdedgar@ozemail.com.au (Home).

EDISON, Hali Jean, BA, MS, PH D; American economist; b 28 May 1953, Santa Monica, CA; d of Jack and Suzanne Edison; m James H. Berry 1988; two s. *Education:* Univ of California at Santa Barbara and LSE (UK). *Career:* Economist Amex Bank, London 1978; Visiting Lecturer Univ of Bergen, Norway 1981–82; Economist Fed Reserve Bd,

Washington, DC 1982–90, Sr Economist 1990–95; Special Advisor to Deputy Sec, Dept of Treasury 1995–96; Consultant to Norwegian Cen Bank 1987; Lecturer Univ of Maryland at College Park 1988. *Publications:* The ECU Market (contrib) 1987, Economic Modelling in OECD (contrib) 1988, The Effectiveness of Central Bank Intervention, A Survey of the Literature after 1982 1993. *Address:* Board of Governors, Federal Reserve Board, Washington, DC 20551, USA. *Fax:* (202) 452-6424; *E-mail:* edisonh@frb.gov.

EDMISTEN, Jane Moretz, MA, JD; American lawyer; b 25 Oct 1938, Boone, NC; d of the late Ralph Dace and of Lola (née Thompson) Moretz; one d. *Education:* Univ of North Carolina and George Washington Univ. *Career:* Research Analyst Georgetown Univ 1962–63, Herner & Co, Washington, DC 1964; Military Assistance Analyst USAF, Washington, DC 1964–66; Head Legis Reference Section NASA 1966–69; called to Bar, NC 1967, DC 1967, US Supreme Court 1972; Trial Attorney Appellate Section, Tax Div, Dept of Justice 1970–74, 1976–77; Counsel Govt Nat Mortgage Asscn, Dept of Housing and Urban Devt 1977–79; Deputy Gen Counsel US Merit Systems Protection Bd 1979–81; mem Moore & Foster, Washington, DC 1981–82; Partner Prokop & Edmisten, Washington, DC 1983–84; pvt practice 1984–; Adjunct law schools of George Washington and Georgetown Univs; mem ABA; Justice Tom C. Clark Award 1980; University Wide Adjunct Teaching Award, American Univ (DC) 1984, Law School Adjunct Teaching Award 1986. *Publication:* BNA Portfolio (jtly) 1980. *Leisure interests:* reading, travel. *Address:* 4530 Wisconsin Ave, Suite 210, Washington, DC 20016, USA. *Telephone:* (202) 364-4220; *Fax:* (202) 966-6988.

EDSTRÖM, Ingrid Maria; Swedish media executive; b 25 March 1931, Stockholm; d of Axel and Karin Edström; one s. *Education:* Communal Girls' School (Västerås) and Axel Witzansky Theatre Studio. *Career:* Worked in experimental theatre 1952–57; TV Producer Sveriges Radio AB 1957–66, Staff Trainer 1966–68, Head of Children's TV, TV2 1968–78, Regional Man, Malmö 1978–82, Co-Dir of Programmes, TV2 1982–87; Theatrical Dir Swedish Nat Theatre Centre 1987–89; Man Dir Swedish Film Inst 1989–94; teacher Nat Film School 1994–98; mem Swedish Broadcasting Comm 1994; Chair EBU Working Party for Children and Youth 1985–87; Vice-Chair Eurimages 1990–95. *Leisure interest:* sailing. *Address:* Klyvarevägen 7, Nacka, 131 42 Stockholm, Sweden. *Telephone:* (8) 718 10 70; *Fax:* (8) 718 10 70.

EDWARDS, Meredith Ann, AM, B COM, PH D; Australian economist and civil servant; b 10 May 1941; d of John Wear Burton and Cecily Parker; m 1963 (divorced); one s one d. *Education:* Canberra High School, Univ of Melbourne and ANU. *Career:* Lecturer, then Sr Lecturer Coll of Advanced Educ 1972–83; joined Office of the Status of Women, Commonwealth Public Service 1983; Special Adviser on Youth Allowance, Dept of Educ, later Dept of Prime Minister and Cabinet 1984–85; staff mem ANU 1985; Consultant to Minister for Social Security 1986; Prin Adviser, later First Asst Sec, Social Policy Div, Dept of Social Security 1986–90; Dir Nat Housing Strategy, Dept of Health, Housing and Community Services, Canberra 1990–92; First Asst Sec Econ Div, Dept of Employment, Educ and Training 1983; Head Taskforce on Employment Opportunities, Dept of Prime Minister and Cabinet 1993, Deputy Sec, Dept of Prime Minister and Cabinet 1993–97; articles on finance and taxation; mem Council, Univ of Canberra, Australia Statistical Advisory Council. *Leisure interests:* jogging, swimming, tennis, reading, music, photography. *Address:* 1 Lomandra St, O'Connor, ACT 2602, Australia. *Telephone:* (6) 271 5204.

EDWARDS, Sian; British conductor; b 27 Aug 1959; partner Ian Kemp; one s. *Education:* Royal Northern Coll of Music (Manchester), Leningrad Conservatoire with Prof I. A. Musin (now St Petersburg, Russian Fed); studied with Sir Charles Groves, Norman del Mar, Neeme Järvi. *Career:* Won first Leeds Conductors' Competition 1984; has worked with many leading British orchestras including London Philharmonic, Royal Liverpool Philharmonic, Royal Scottish Orchestra, City of Birmingham Symphony, Halle, BBC Philharmonic, English Chamber orchestras, London Sinfonietta; other orchestras worked with include Los Angeles Philharmonic, St Paul Chamber Orchestra, Orchestre de Paris; operatic debut Mahagonny (Scottish Opera) 1986;

Music Dir English Nat Opera 1993–95. *Operatic productions include:* La Traviata, L'Heure Espagnole (Glyndebourne) 1987–88, Kat'a Kabanova, New Year (Glyndebourne Touring Opera) 1988–90, The Knot Garden, Rigoletto, Il Trovatore (Royal Opera House, Covent Garden, London) 1988–91, Greek (world première, Munich Biennale, Germany, Edinburgh Festival, UK) 1988, The Gambler (English Nat Opera (ENO)) 1990, Khovanschina (ENO) 1994, Mahagonny 1995, La Clemenza di Tito 1998, Eugene Onegin 2000; *Recordings include:* Tchaikovsky orchestral music (Royal Liverpool Philharmonic), Peter and the Wolf, Young Person's Guide to the Orchestra, Tchaikovsky's 5th symphony (London Philharmonic Orchestra). *Address:* 70 Twisden Rd, London NW5 1DN, UK.

EDWARDS, Tracy Karen, MBE; British yachtswoman; b 5 Sept 1962, Reading; d of the late Anthony H. and of Patricia Edwards. *Education:* Arts Educational School (Tring, Herts) and Gowerton Comprehensive School (Swansea). *Career:* Travelled 1978–1980; worked on charter boats throughout world 1980–1985; took part in Whitbread race on Atlantic Privateer 1985; began Maiden project 1986, Capt of Maiden (first all-female crew) in Whitbread round-the-world race 1989–90; set world fastest ocean record 1997; Man Dir Tracy Edwards Assocs Ltd 1990–. *Publications:* Maiden (also video) 1990, Living Every Second (autobiog) 2000. *Leisure interests:* riding, sailing, sport. *Address:* c/o 14 Vernon St, London W14 0RJ, UK.

EGERSZEGI, Krisztina; Hungarian swimmer; b 1974. *Career:* Gold Medallist 200m Backstroke, Olympic Games, Seoul, Republic of Korea 1988 (youngest Olympic swimming champion), Barcelona, Spain 1992; Gold Medallist 200m Backstroke, Bronze Medallist 400m Individual Medley Olympic Games, Atlanta, GA, USA 1996. *Address:* Budapest Spartacus, 1103 Budapest, Kőér u 1/a, Hungary.

EHLE, Jennifer; British actress. *Education:* Cen School of Speech and Drama (London). *Films:* This Year's Love, Bedrooms and Hallways, Wilde, Paradise Road, Backbeat, Sunshine; *Plays:* Summerfolk (Royal Nat Theatre), The Relapse (RSC), The Painter of Dishonour (RSC), Richard III (RSC) 1996, Tartuffe (Playhouse), The Real Thing (Albery) 1999, (Broadway) 2000; *TV:* Melissa, Pride and Prejudice (BAFTA Best Actress Award), Beyond Reason, Pleasure, Self Catering, The Maitlands, Micky Love, The Camomile Lawn. *Address:* c/o ICM, 76 Oxford St, London W1N 0AX, UK. *Telephone:* (20) 7636-6565.

EHRLICH, Sister Emilia; nun/Church official. *Career:* Mem Ursuline order; Special Sec Synod of Bishops (first woman) Oct 1994. *Address:* c/o Holy See Press Office, Via della Conciliazione 54, 00193 Rome, Vatican City.

EICHHORN, Lisa; American actress; b 2 April 1952, Glen Falls, NY. *Education:* Queen's Univ Ontario (Canada), St Peter's Coll (Oxford, UK) and Royal Acad of Dramatic Art (UK). *Films:* Yanks 1979, The Europeans 1979, Why Would I Lie? 1980, Cutter and Bone (Cutter's Way) 1981, The Weather in the Streets 1983, Wildrose 1984, Opposing Force (Hell Camp) 1987, Grim Prairie Tales, Moon 44 1989, King of the Hill 1993, The Vanishing 1993, Mr 247 1994, A Modern Affair, Judas Kiss; *Plays include:* roles in British Shakespearean productions, A Doll's House, A Golden Boy, The Speed of Darkness, The Summer Winds, The Common Pursuit, The Hasty Heart, Pass/Fair, Arms and the Man, Misfits 1996.

EISENBERG, Sonja Miriam, BA; American artist; b 10 June 1926, Berlin; d of Adolf and Meta Cecilie (née Bettauer) Weinberger; m Jack Eisenberg 1946; two d one s. *Education:* Queen's Coll, Middlebury Coll, New York Univ and Nat Acad School of Fine Arts (NY). *Career:* Arrived USA 1938, became US citizen 1947; solo exhibitions include Bodley Gallery, New York 1970, 1973, 1975, 1980, Galerie Art du Monde, Paris 1973, Buyways Gallery, Sarasota, FL 1973–1975, 1978, Galerie de Sfinx, Amsterdam 1974, Palm Springs Desert Museum, CA 1975, Cathedral of St John the Divine, New York 1983, 1985, The Millbrook Gallery, NY 1989; group exhibitions include Galerie Frédéric Gollong, St Paul de Vence, France 1978, Tokyo Metropolitan Art Museum 14th Int Art Friendship Exhibition 1989, Park Ave Armory, New York 1996, AKIM-USA, Mask's, New York 1996; Artist-in-Residence Cathedral of St John the Divine 1984–, Regent 1990–; Gold Medal Accademia Italia delle Arti e del Lavoro 1981; Gold Medal for Artistic Merit (Int Parl for

Safety and Peace) 1983; Palma D'Oro Europe 1986. *Leisure interests:* music, dance and relaxation, tennis, gardening, woodwork. *Address:* 1020 Park Ave, New York, NY 10028, USA. *Telephone:* (212) 249-7733.

EL ROUMI, Magida; Lebanese singer; b 13 Dec 1956, Kfarchima; d of Halim El Roumi and Marie Loutfi; m Antoine Dfouni 1977; two d. *Education:* Lebanese Univ. *Career:* Appearances include the Carthage Festival, Tunisia 1980, Syria and Kuwait 1987, United Arab Emirates 1987, 1991, Qatar and Bahrain 1991, the Jarash Festival, Jordan 1986, Beirut, Syria and Bahrain 1988, USA Convention Center (Los Angeles, CA) 1989, 1990, Palais des Congrès, Paris 1991, 1996; has won several int awards. *Songs include:* O les oiseaux, Panam Panam; one record for children; *Film:* Return of the Prodigal 1975 (Egyptian Critics' Prize). *Leisure interests:* reading, nature. *Address:* POB 1050, Jounieh, Lebanon. *Telephone:* (9) 916543; (9) 915629; *Fax:* (9) 915774.

EL SAADAWI, Nawal, MD; Egyptian medical practitioner and writer; b 27 Oct 1931; m Sherif Hetata 1964; one d one s. *Education:* Univ of Cairo. *Career:* Novelist and writer on women's problems in the Arab world 1956–; has produced 28 novels, plays, essays and collections of short stories in Arabic, of which 15 have been translated into several other languages; Dir-Gen Ministry of Health 1965–72; psychiatrist 1974–; imprisoned for three months and books banned in Egypt 1981; moved to USA 1992; has taught at Univ of Washington, WA, USA; Visiting Prof Duke Univ Center for Int Studies and Programme in Asian and African Languages and Literature 1993–94; Writer-in-Residence Asian and African Languages Dept, Duke Univ 1993–96; Pres Arab Women's Solidarity Asscn (shut down by Govt 1991); worked for the UN in Beirut (Lebanon) and Ethiopia; Hon D UNIV (York) 1994; Short Story Award (Cairo) 1974; Franco-Arab Literary Award (Paris) 1982. *Publications include:* Women and Sex 1971, The Hidden Face of Eve: Women in the Arab World, Woman at Point Zero, God Dies by the Nile, The Circling Song, The Fall of the Imam 1987, My Travels Around the World, The Innocence of the Devil 1994. *Leisure interests:* walking, swimming. *Address:* c/o Dept of Asian and African Languages, Duke University, Durham, NC 27708, USA; 25 Myrad St, 12211 Giza, Egypt (Home).

ELDERS, Jocelyn, MS; American surgeon-general; b 13 Aug 1933, Schaal, AR; d of Haller Jones; m Oliver Elders 1960; two s. *Education:* Philander Smith Coll and Univ of Arkansas. *Career:* Resident Univ of Arkansas Medical Center 1963–64, Chief Pediatric Resident 1964–67, Pediatric Research Fellow 1967–71, Assoc Prof of Pediatrics 1971–76, Prof 1976–87, 1994–; Dir AK Dept of Health 1987–93; Surgeon-Gen of USA 1993–94; Host Morning Talk Show, KSYG AK 1995; numerous articles in professional journals. *Publication:* M. Jocelyn Elders, MD (autobiog) 1998. *Address:* c/o University of Arkansas College of Medicine, Fayetteville, AR 72701, USA. *Internet:* www.uark .edu.

ELFYN, Menna, BA; British poet; b 1951, S Wales; d of Rev T Elfyn Jones and Rachel Maria Jones; m Wynfford James 1974; two c. *Education:* Univs of Swansea and Aberystwyth. *Career:* Lecturer St David's Coll (Lampeter) 1979–86; Lecturer in Educ Univ of Swansea 1989–92; Co-Dir of Creative Writing Trinity Coll (Carmarthen) 1997–; columnist Western Mail 1996–; Artist-in-Residence at various schools, colls and hosps (UK and USA); Writing Fellow (Univ of Wales) 1984; mem Gorsedd of Bards 1993; Best Vol of Eisteddfod 1977. *Publications include:* Aderyn Bach Mewn Llaw (Welsh Arts Council Prize) 1990, Eucalyptus 1995, Cell Angel 1996, Cusan Dyn Dall (Blind Man's Kiss) 2001; 7 vols of poetry; various works for music, produced as librettist for 4 US composers; works have been translated into 12 languages. *Leisure interests:* music, travel. *Address:* Cysgod y Craig, Stryd y Gwynt, Llandysul, Ceredigion, Wales; 113 Bedford St, Roalt, Cardiff, Wales, UK. *Telephone:* (1559) 362122; *E-mail:* menna.elfyn@talk21.com; *Internet:* www.menna.elfyn.co.uk.

ELIZABETH ANGELA MARGUERITE, HM Queen Elizabeth the Queen Mother, Lady of the Order of the Garter, Lady of the Order of the Thistle, CI, GCVO, GBE, Lord Warden of the Cinque Ports; British royal; b 4 Aug 1900; d of the 14th Earl of Strathmore and Kinghorne; m HRH The Duke of York, later HM King George VI 1923 (died 1952).

Career: Reigned as Queen 1936–52. *Address:* Clarence House, London SW1 1AA, UK; Royal Lodge, Windsor Great Park, Berks, UK; Castle of Mey, Caithness, Scotland, UK.

ELIZABETH II, (Elizabeth Alexandra Mary); Queen of Great Britain and Northern Ireland and of Her other Realms and Territories; b 21 April 1926, London; d of HRH Prince Albert, Duke of York (later HM King George VI), and Duchess of York (now HM Queen Elizabeth The Queen Mother, qv); m HRH The Prince Philip, Duke of Edinburgh 20 Nov 1947; four c: Prince Charles Philip Arthur George, Prince of Wales (heir apparent), b 14 Nov 1948; Princess Anne Elizabeth Alice Louise, The Princess Royal (qv), b 15 Aug 1950; Prince Andrew Albert Christian Edward, Duke of York, b 19 Feb 1960; Prince Edward Antony Richard Louis, b 10 March 1964. *Career:* Succeeded to The Throne following Her father's death, 6 Feb 1952. *Address:* Buckingham Palace, London SW1A 1AA, UK; Windsor Castle, Berkshire SL4 1NJ; Palace of Holyroodhouse, Edinburgh EH8 8DX, UK; Balmoral Castle, Aberdeenshire AB35 5TB, UK; Sandringham House, Norfolk PE35 6EN, UK.

ELKINS, Margreta Ann Enid, AM, MUS D; Australian opera singer and teacher; b 16 Oct 1930, Brisbane; d of George Geater and Elizabeth Smith Henderson; m Henry James 1950; one d. *Education:* Morningside State School, Commercial High School and Sacred Heart Convent (Qld). *Career:* On tour with Nat Opera of Australia, Australia and New Zealand 1954–55; resident mezzo-soprano Royal Opera House, Covent Garden, London 1957–67; voice coach Queensland Conservatorium 1982–; Head of Vocal Studies Hong Kong Acad for Performing Arts 1990–; numerous performances with Lyric Opera (Qld), Victoria State Opera, English Nat Opera, etc. *Leisure interests:* horses, walking, gardening. *Address:* c/o Jennifer Eddy Artists Management, The Cliveden, Suite 11, 596 St Kilda Rd, Melbourne, Vic 3004, Australia.

ELLES, Baroness (Life Peer), cr 1972, of the City of Westminster, **Diana Louie Elles,** BA; British politician; b 19 July 1921, Bedford; d of Col S. F. Newcombe, DSO; m Neil Elles 1945; one s one d. *Education:* Privately (London, Paris and Florence, Italy) and Univ of London. *Career:* Served Women's Auxiliary Air Force 1941–45; voluntary social work 1956–72; Del to UN Gen Ass 1972; mem House of Lords 1972–; Chair Int Office Cons Party 1973–79; Int Chair European Union of Women 1973–79; mem British Del to EP 1973–75, MEP 1979–89, Vice-Pres EP 1982–87, Chair Legal Affairs Cttee 1987–89; Gov Univ of Reading 1986–96, British Inst, Florence 1986–; Trustee Caldecott Community 1990–97. *Publication:* Human Rights of Aliens (UN Special Report) 1980. *Address:* 75 Ashley Gardens, London SW1P 1HG, UK. *Telephone:* (20) 7828-0175; *Fax:* (20) 7931-0046.

ELLIOT, Virginia Helen Antoinette, MBE; British sportswoman; b 1 Feb 1955; d of the late Ronald Morris and of Heather Holgate; m 1st Hamish Julian Peter Leng 1985 (divorced 1989); m 2nd Michael Eliot 1993. *Education:* Bedgebury Park (Goudhurst, Kent). *Career:* Three Day Eventer, Champion Jr European Championship 1973, Mini Olympics 1975, Burghley 1983–86, 1989, Badminton 1985, 1989, 1993, European Championship 1985, 1987, 1989, World Championship 1986; Team Silver Olympic Medal, Los Angeles, USA 1984, Seoul 1988; Bronze Individual Olympic Medals Los Angeles, USA 1984, Seoul 1988; currently trainer of Nat Hunt jockeys and horses. *Publications include:* Jtly: Ginny 1986, Priceless 1987, Ginny and Her Horses 1987, Training the Event Horse 1990; (novels) Winning 1995, Race Against Time 1996. *Leisure interests:* skiing, cooking, art, theatre. *Address:* Holliers, Middle Barton, Oxon OX5 3QH, UK.

ELLIOTT, Marianne, D PHIL, FRHISTS; Irish historian; b 25 May 1948, N Ireland; d of Terence J. and Sheila (née O'Neill) Burns; m Trevor Elliott 1975; one s. *Education:* Dominican Convent (Fort William, Belfast), Queen's Univ, Belfast and Lady Margaret Hall (Oxford). *Career:* French Govt research scholar, Paris 1972–73; other research in Ireland, UK, France, Netherlands and USA; Lecturer in History W London Inst of Higher Educ 1975–77; Research Fellow Univ Coll, Swansea 1977–82; Visiting Prof Iowa State Univ 1983, Univ of S Carolina 1984; Research Fellow Univ of Liverpool 1984–91; Simon Fellow Univ of Manchester 1988–89; Lecturer in History Birkbeck Coll, London 1991–93; John Rankin and Andrew Geddes Prof of Modern History and Dir Inst of Irish Studies, Univ of Liverpool 1993–; mem

Opsahl Comm on N Ireland 1993; James Donnelly Sr Award for History (American Conf for Irish Studies) 1991. *Publications:* Partners in Revolution: the United Irishmen and France (American History Asscn Leo Gershoy Award 1983) 1982, Watchmen in Sion: the Protestant Idea of Liberty 1985, The People's Armies (trans) 1987, Wolfe Tone: Prophet of Irish Independence (Sunday Independent/Irish Life Award for Biography 1990) 1989, A Citizens' Inquiry: The Opsahl Report on Northern Ireland (jtly) 1993, A History of the Catholics in Ulster 1998. *Leisure interests:* family, French culture, running, swimming, reading, music. *Address:* Dept of History, University of Liverpool, POB 147, Liverpool L69 3BX, UK (Office). *Telephone:* (151) 7943831; *Fax:* (151) 7943836; *E-mail:* sscl57@liv.ac.uk.

ELLIS, Alice Thomas (see Haycraft, Anna Margaret).

ELLIS, Fiona, BA; British arts administrator; b N Ireland. *Education:* Univs of Oxford and York. *Career:* Fmr Stage Man New End Theatre (Hampstead); fmr Programming Man Warminster Arts Centre; fmr Theatre Officer Regional Arts Asscn; fmr Asst Dir Calouste Gulbenkian Foundation; freelance grants assessor; now Dir Northern Rock Foundation. *Address:* c/o Helen Brass, 21 Lansdowne Terrace, Gosforth, Newcastle NE3 1HP, UK. *Telephone:* (191) 2848412; *Fax:* (191) 2848413; *Internet:* www.nr-foundation.org.uk.

ELLMANN, Lucy; American writer and critic; b IL; d of the late Richard Ellmann; one d. *Education:* Univ of Essex (UK) and Courtauld Inst (London). *Career:* Has lived in Oxford since the age of 13; regular contribs to various periodicals and newspapers including the Times Literary Supplement, The Guardian, Sunday Telegraph and the Observer; mem judging panel Irish Times–Aer Lingus Int Fiction Prize 1992. *Publications:* Novels: Just Desserts (Guardian Fiction Prize 1988), Varying Degrees of Hopelessness 1991, Man or Mango 1998. *Address:* c/o Hamish Hamilton Ltd, 27 Wrights Lane, London W8 5TZ, UK.

ELMALAN, Mireille; French politician; b 1949. *Career:* Clerk; Deputy Mayor Pierre-Benite (Rhône-Alpes); mem Cen Cttee PCF; MEP (GUE/Nordic Green Left, PCF) 1989–, mem Cttee on Social Affairs and Employment, mem Cttee on Women's Rights, Del for relations with Maghreb countries and Arab Maghreb Union. *Address:* European Parliament, rue Wiertz, 1040 Brussels, Belgium. *Telephone:* (2) 234-21-11; *Fax:* (2) 230-69-33.

ELMS, Lauris Margaret, OBE, AM; Australian opera singer; b 20 Oct 1931, Melbourne; d of Harry Britton and Jean Elms; m Graeme Ernest de Graaff 1958; one d. *Career:* London debut as Ulrica in Ballo in Maschera, Royal Opera House, Covent Garden 1957; perfomances with Victoria Philharmonic, Sutherland-Williamson Opera Co, Elizabethan Opera Co, Australian Opera Co, Musica Viva, Chamber Music Fed, London Philharmonic, Royal Philharmonic, Israel Philharmonic; Hon D MUS (Sydney) 1988; Queen's Jubilee Medal 1977. *Operas include:* Peter Grimes (also recording), Orfeo, Julius Caesar, Lucretia Borgia, Il Trovatore, Trojans, Bluebeard's Castle, Carmen; numerous recordings for Decca. *Leisure interests:* reading, sailing, bargello, needlework. *Address:* 10A Strathmore Parade, Chatswood, NSW 2067, Australia. *Telephone:* (2) 411 6727.

ELSON, Karen; British model; b 1979. *Career:* Started modelling career at age 15, signed up with Boss Agency, Manchester; appeared in Italian Vogue Jan 1997; joined agencies Ford Models, New York and Models 1, London; appearances in American Vogue, Harper's Bazaar; signed contract with Chanel cosmetics; Best Female Model of the Year Award 2000. *Address:* c/o Models 1, Omega House, 471–473 Kings Rd, London SW10 0LU, UK. *Telephone:* (20) 7376-5821.

ELVIN, Violetta; British ballet dancer; b (Violetta Prokhorova) 3 Nov 1925, Moscow; d of Vassili Prokhorov and Irena T. Grimusinskaya; m 1st Harold Elvin 1944 (divorced 1952); m 2nd Siegbert J. Weinberger 1953; m 3rd Fernando Savarese 1959; one s. *Education:* Bolshoi Theatre School (Moscow). *Career:* Mem Bolshoi Theatre Ballet 1942, evacuated to Tashkent 1943; Ballerina Tashkent State Theatre; rejoined Bolshoi Theatre as Soloist 1944; joined Sadler's Wells Ballet, Royal Opera House, Covent Garden, London (now the Royal Ballet) as Guest Soloist 1946, and later as regular mem, Prima Ballerina 1951–56 (concluded

her stage career 1956); Guest Artist Stanislavsky Theatre, Moscow 1944, Sadler's Wells Theatre 1947; Guest Prima Ballerina, La Scala, Milan, Italy 1952–53; Guest Artist Cannes (France) 1954, Copenhagen 1954, Teatro Municipal, Rio de Janeiro (Brazil) 1955, Festival Hall (London) 1955; Guest Prima Ballerina Royal Opera House, Stockholm 1956; Royal Opera House, Covent Garden 1956 (concluded her stage career); Dir Ballet Co San Carla Opera, Naples 1985–87. *Film appearances:* The Queen of Spades, Twice Upon a Time, Melba. *Leisure interests:* reading, walking, swimming. *Address:* Marina di Equa, 80066 Seiano, Bay of Naples, Italy. *Telephone:* (81) 8798520.

EMANUEL, Elizabeth Florence, MA, RCA, FCSD; British fashion designer; b 5 July 1953, London; d of Samuel Charles and Brahna Betty Weiner; m David Leslie Emanuel 1975 (separated 1990); one s one d. *Education:* City of London School for Girls and Harrow Coll of Art. *Career:* Opened London salon 1978; designed wedding gown for HRH Princess of Wales 1981; designed costumes for Andrew Lloyd Webber's Song and Dance 1982, sets and costumes for ballet Frankenstein, The Modern Prometheus, Royal Opera House, London, La Scala, Milan, Italy 1985, costumes for Stoll Moss production of Cinderella 1985, costumes for film Diamond Skulls 1990, uniforms for Virgin Atlantic Airways 1990, Britannia Airways 1995; launched int fashion label Elizabeth Emanuel 1991, Dir Elizabeth Emanuel PLC; launched Bridal Collection for Berkertex Brides UK Ltd 1994; launched bridal collection in Japan 1994. *Publication:* Style for All Seasons (with David Emanuel) 1982. *Leisure interests:* ballet, cinema, environmental and conservation issues. *Address:* 49 Dorset St, London W1H 3FH, UK. *Telephone:* (20) 7266-1055.

EMBDEN, Carole Joy, MA; Jamaican broadcasting executive; b 8 Sept 1956, St Catherine; d of Percival G. and Dorian Powell; m Donovan Wayne Embden 1977; three s. *Education:* St Hugh's High School for Girls, Univ of the W Indies (Kingston) and Univ of Windsor (ON, Canada). *Career:* Information Officer Jamaica Information Service 1980–81; Communications Media Officer Bureau of Health Educ 1981–82; Public Educ Officer Bureau of Women's Affairs 1982–84; apptd Producer Jamaica Broadcasting Corpn (JBC) 1984, Asst Dir and News Ed 1990; part-time Dir of Marketing and Public Relations Inst of Management Science; Part-time Lecturer in Communications Univ of W Indies and Creative Production and Training Centre; Rotary journalism scholarship 1987. *Publication:* The ABC of Health and Hygiene 1982. *Leisure interests:* drama, swimming, choral singing. *Address:* Jamaica Broadcasting Corpn (JBC), 5 S Odeon Ave, POB 100, Kingston 10, Jamaica (Office); 163 Border Ave, Kingston 19, Jamaica (Home). *Telephone:* 925-6032.

EMEAGWALI, Dale Brown, PH D; American scientist. *Education:* Coppin State Coll (Baltimore, MD) and Georgetown Univ (Washington, DC). *Career:* Teacher and Research Asst, Dept of Microbiology Georgetown Univ, Washington, DC 1977–80; Fellow Nat Inst of Allergy and Infectious Diseases, NIH, Bethesda, MD 1981–84, Dept of Pathology 1985–86; Est Molecular Biology Lab, Dept of Zoology and Physiology, Univ of Wyoming 1986–87; Asst Research Scientist, Dept of Pediatrics, Univ of Michigan 1987–92; Researcher and teacher of cell biology, Univ of Minnesota 1992–94, conducting research on protein kinase C 1994; mem AAAS, American Soc of Microbiology, Nat Tech Asscn; numerous contribs to professional journals; Nat Tech Asscn Scientist of the Year 1996. *Address:* 1180 Cushing Circle, Suite 113, Saint Paul, MN 55108-5015, USA.

EMECHETA, Buchi, B SC; British writer and lecturer; b 21 July 1944; d of Jeremy and Alice Emecheta; m Sylvester Onwordi 1960; three d two s. *Education:* Methodist Girls' High School (Lagos) and Univ of London. *Career:* Fmr librarian and community worker; Sr Research Fellow, Visiting Prof of English Univ of Calabar 1980–81; Lecturer Yale Univ, USA 1982, Univ of London 1982; numerous Visiting Professorships at univs in USA; Propr Ogwugwn Afo Publishing Co; mem Home Sec's Advisory Council on Race 1979, Arts Council 1982–83; listed in Best of Young British 1983. *Publications include:* In the Ditch 1972, The Bride Price 1976, The Slave Girl 1977, The Joys of Motherhood 1979, Naira Power 1982, Double Yoke 1982, The Rape of Shavi 1983, Head Above Water (autobiog) 1984, Gwendolen 1989, Kehinde 1994;

Children's books: Titch the Cat 1979, Nowhere to Play 1980, The Moonlight Bride 1981, The Wrestling Match 1981; contribs to newspapers. *Leisure interests:* gardening, music, theatre, reading.

EMERY, Lin; American sculptor; b 20 May 1958, New York City; d of Cornell Emery and Jean Weill; m S. B. Braselman 1962; one s. *Education:* Univs of Chicago and Sorbonne (Paris, France). *Career:* Worked in studio of Ossip Zadkine, Paris 1950; 46 solo exhibitions in US museums and galleries 1957–98; int exhibitions in Tokyo, Hong Kong, Manila, Sofia, Paris, London, Berlin, Brisbane, Kyoto and Frankfurt 1961–98; public sculpture erected in Civic Center New Orleans 1966–70, Fidelity Center Oklahoma City 1972, Humanities Center Columbia (SC) 1974, Marina Centre Singapore 1986, City of Oxnard (California) 1988, Fed Plaza Houma (LA) 1997, Osaka Dome Japan 1997; Visiting Prof Tulane School of Architecture (New Orleans) 1969–70, Newcomb School of Art (New Orleans) 1980; Visiting Artist and Lecturer Art Acad of Cincinnati, LA State Univ, Univ of New Orleans, Univ of Texas at Austin, Univ of Maine 1985–88; Chair 9th Int Sculpture Conf 1976, Co-Chair Mayor's Steering Cttees (New Orleans) 1979–80; Studio Chair Coll Art Assn 1979; mem Bd Contemporary Arts Center (New Orleans) 1997–; mem Loyola Univ Visiting Cttee 1996–99; advisor Artists Guild (New Orleans) 1997–99; mentor Center for Creative Arts (New Orleans) 1998; Mayor's Award for Achievement in the Arts (LA) 1980, Lazlo Aranyi Award for Public Art (VA) 1990, Delgado Award for Artistic Excellence (LA) 1997, Grand Prix for Public Sculpture (Japan) 1997. *Address:* 7520 Dominican St, New Orleans, LA 70118, USA. *Telephone:* (504) 866-7775; *Fax:* (504) 866-0144.

EMIN, Tracey; British artist; b 1964, Margate. *Education:* John Cass School of Art (London), Maidstone Coll of Art and Royal Coll of Art (London). *Career:* Exhibitions include White Cube Gallery (London) 1992, Minky Manky 1995; read a series of autobiographical short stories at Royal Festival Hall 1996; Founder Tracey Emin Museum, London 1996, solo exhibitions: My Major Retrospective, Part of What Made Me What I Am; made Why I Never Became a Dancer (short film). *Leisure interests:* writing poetry, watching sunsets. *Address:* The Tracey Emin Museum, 221 Waterloo Rd, London SE1, UK. *Telephone:* (20) 7261-1116.

ENACHE, Smaranda; Romanian journalist and human rights activist; b 31 March 1950, Tîrgu Mureş; d of Ioan and Marioara Enache; m 1st Paul-Vasile Szobotka 1972; one s; m 2nd Elek-Adalbert-Viktor Szokoly 1990. *Education:* Lycée d'études humanistes (Reghin) and Univ of Bucharest. *Career:* Teacher of French literature 1974–81; Man Tîrgu Mureş Youth Theatre 1981–91; Ed weekly Gazeta de Mureş, Tîrgu Mureş 1991–, quarterly Altera 1995–; Founder and Jt Chair Ligue Pro Europa, Tîrgu Mureş 1989–; Founder Civic Alliance of Romania, Directory Council of Civil Alliance Party; mem Groupe pour le Dialogue Social, Bucharest 1990–, Romanian Helsinki Cttee, Helsinki Citizens Ass Int Council; Prix Maecenas pour l'attitude civique exemplaire, Budapest 1990; Pro Amicitia prize for Interethnic Solidarity 1994. *Play:* Fables? Fables! (political allegory, banned by bd of censors) 1989. *Leisure interests:* theatre, travel, gardening, swimming. *Address:* 4300 Tîrgu Mureş, Pta Trandafirlior nr 5A, POB 1-154, Romania. *Telephone:* (65) 217584; *Fax:* (65) 168594.

ENDERS, Gisela, MD; German virologist and epidemiologist; b 25 May 1924, Stuttgart; d of Erwin and Olga Ruckle; m Gerhard Enders; two s. *Education:* Univs of Munich and Tübingen. *Career:* Worked at Univ Clinic, Tübingen then Inst für Virusforschung, Heidelberg; Fulbright Fellow, USA 1953–56; at Inst of Hygiene, Univ of Marburg 1957–63, Hon Prof 1975–; Dir Virus Dept, Medical Research Office, Stuttgart 1963–79; f own lab 1979; Hon Prof Univ of Hohenheim 1982–; f Inst für Virologie 1985; Del to WHO cttee on training of lab personnel; Adviser to Deutsche Stiftung für Entwicklungsländer (foundation for developing countries); numerous publs on virology, and many contribs to professional journals; Bundesverdienstkreuz; Gold Medal for work on prenatal diagnoses, Haackert-Stiftung 1990. *Leisure interests:* painting, music, architecture, tennis, skiing. *Address:* Laboratorium und Institut für Virologie, Infektiologie und Epidemiologie eV, Rosenbergstr 85, 70193 Stuttgart, Germany.

ENDOH, Keiko, MA; Japanese professor of sociology; b 28 Jan 1944, Sendai; d of Kazuo and Aiko Endoh; m 1970 (divorced 1973); one d. *Education:* Tohoku Univ. *Career:* Ed Igaku-Shoin Co (publrs) 1967–69; Lecturer Sendai Shirayur Jr Coll 1975–81; Lecturer Tohoku-Gakuin Univ 1981–83, Assoc Prof 83–90, apptd Prof Dept of Liberal Arts 1990; mem Social-Educational Council (Sendai) 1988; Head of Women's Council (Sendai) 1991. *Publications include:* Sociology – Theory and Application 1984, Watching Modern Times from a Sociological Viewpoint 1991, Sociology 1992, Family Sociology 1992. *Leisure interests:* travel, horse-riding. *Address:* Taihaku-ku Yagiyama Kasumicho 14-3, 982 Sendai, Japan. *Telephone:* (22) 229-0679.

ENGEL, Walburga (see Von Raffler-Engel, Walburga).

ENGELEN-KEFER, Ursula, DR RER POL; German trade unionist; b 20 June 1943, Prague, Czech Republic; m Klaus Engelen 1967; two s. *Education:* In Cologne. *Career:* Journalist based in New York for Die Zeit and Handelsblatt 1967–70; Adviser on Econ and Social Econ to Deutscher Gewerkschaftsbund (DGB—trade union conf) inst for labour market analysis and politics 1970, fmr Adviser to Fed Chair DGB on int social policy, currently Vice-Pres DGB; Vice-Pres Bundesanstalt für Arbeit 1984–90; numerous advisory and cttee positions in nat and int orgs, including EC, EC Econ and Social Cttee, ILO, etc. *Publications include:* Beschäftigungspolitik 1976, Arbeitslosigkeit 1978; contribs to books and journals. *Address:* Henriette-Herz-Platz 2, 10178 Berlin, Germany. *Telephone:* (30) 24060259; *Internet:* www.dgb.de.

ENGERER, Brigitte Marie; French pianist; b 27 Oct 1952, Tunis; d of Edgard and Marie-Rose Engerer; m Yann Queffelec 1982; one d one s. *Education:* Coll Notre-Dame de Sion (Tunis) and Conservatoire Nat Supérieur de Musique (Paris). *Career:* Studied under Lucette Descaves 1958–69, and Stanislav Neuhaus at Conservatory of Moscow (USSR, now Russian Fed) 1970–80; has given concerts in Europe and USA, with Berlin Philharmonic (with Herbert von Karajan) 1980–81 and Zubin Mehta, London Symphony Orchestra, New York Philharmonic Orchestra, and other major orchestras world-wide, including Canada, Czech Repub, Switzerland, Austria, Germany, Italy, Hungary, Netherlands, etc; gave recital at Théâtre des Champs-Elysées 1993; Chevalier des Arts et des Lettres; Prix Int Marguerite Long; Prix Int Tchaikovsky; Prix Int de la Reine Elisabeth de Belgique; Prix du Royaume de la Musique; numerous other awards. *Recordings include:* Les saisons (Tchaikovsky) 1982, Mélodie hongroise, Schubert's Klavierstücke D946 and Impromptus Opus 90 1983, Schumann's Carnaval and Carnaval de Vienne (Grand Prix, Acad du Disque Français) 1983, Chopin's Sonata No 3 and posthumous works, Piano romantique 1985, Tableaux d'une exposition and Une nuit sur le Mont-Chauve (Mussorgsky) 1988; *Video:* Richard Strauss' Burlesque 1988. *Leisure interests:* chess, mah-jong, reading, sailing. *Address:* Concerts de Valmalète, 7 rue Hoche, 92300 Levallois-Perret, France.

ENYA; Irish singer and composer; b (Eithne Ní Bhraonáin) 17 May 1961, Gweedore, Co Donegal; d of Leo and Maire Braonán. *Career:* Keyboard player with Clannad 1980–82; solo career 1982–; commissioned by David Puttnam to write music for film The Frog Prince, by BBC to write music for TV series The Celts; signed to Warner Music UK 1987; has collaborated with Christy Moore and Sinéad O'Connor (qv); two Grammy awards. *Recordings include:* Singles: Orinoco Flow 1988, Storms in Africa 1989, Oíche Chiún (Silent Night) 1989, Exile 1991, Caribbean Blue 1991, Book of Days 1992, Anywhere Is 1995, On My Way Home 1996; Albums: Enya 1987, Watermark 1988, Shepherd Moons 1991, The Celts 1992, The Memory of Trees 1995, Paint the Sky with Stars 1997, Day Without Rain 2000; With Clannad: Crann Ull 1980, Fuaim 1982; Video: Moonshadows 1991. *Address:* Ayesha Castle, Killiney, Co Dublin, Ireland.

EPHRON, Delia; American author and scriptwriter; b 1945, Beverly Hills, CA; d of the late Henry and of Phoebe (née Wollkind) Ephron; m Jerome Kass. *Career:* Began career as journalist, New York Magazine and New York Times; co-writer of screenplays with sister Nora Ephron (qv). *Publications include:* How to Eat Like A Child, Teenage Romance or How to Die of Embarrassment, Big City Eyes 2000; numerous children's books; *Screenplays include:* This is My Life 1992, Sleepless in

Seattle (exec producer) 1993, Mixed Nuts, Michael 1996, You've Got Mail 1998, Hanging Up 2000. *Address:* c/o Sam Cohn International Creative Management, 40 West 57th St, New York, NY 10019, USA.

EPHRON, Nora, BA; American writer and scriptwriter; b 19 May 1941, New York; d of the late Henry and of Phoebe (née Wollkind) Ephron; m 1st Dan Greenburg (divorced); m 2nd Carl Bernstein (divorced); two s; m 3rd Nicholas Pileggi. *Education:* Wellesley Coll. *Career:* Reporter New York Post 1963–68; freelance writer 1968–; Contributing Ed and columnist Esquire Magazine 1972–73; Sr Ed 1974–78; Contributing Ed New York Magazine 1973–74; co-writer of screenplays with sister Delia Ephron (qv); mem American Writers' Guild, Authors' Guild, PEN, Acad of Motion Picture Arts and Sciences. *Publications:* Wallflower at the Orgy 1970, Crazy Salad 1975, Scribble, Scribble 1978, Heartburn 1983, Nora Ephron Collected 1991, Big City Eyes 2000; *Screenplays:* Silkwood (with Alice Arlen) 1983, Heartburn 1986, When Harry Met Sally... 1989, Cookie 1989 (co-exec producer, co-screenwriter), My Blue Heaven 1990, This is My Life (Dir, co-writer) 1992, Sleepless in Seattle (also Dir) 1993, Mixed Nuts (also Dir), Michael (also Dir) 1996, You've Got Mail (also Dir) 1998, Red Tails in Love: a Wildlife Drama in Central Park (also Producer and Dir) 2000, Hanging Up (also Producer) 2000; *Film appearances:* Crimes and Misdemeanors, Husbands and Wives. *Address:* c/o Sam Cohn, International Creative Management, 40 W 57th St, New York, NY 10019, USA.

EPPS, Roselyn Elizabeth Payne, MA, MD; American paediatrician; b 11 Dec 1930, Little Rock, AR; d of William Kenneth and Mattie Elizabeth Payne; m Charles Harry Epps, Jr 1955; three s one d. *Education:* Howard Univ, Johns Hopkins Univ and American Univ. *Career:* Instructor, Researcher Howard Univ Coll of Medicine, Washington 1960–61, Prof Dept of Pediatrics and Child Health 1980–98, Head Div of Child Devt, Dir Child Devt Center 1985–89; Pediatrics Medical Officer Dist of Columbia Dept of Public Health, Washington 1961–75; Head Clinical Services Bureau, Dist of Columbia Dept of Human Services, Washington 1975–80; Acting Commr of Public Health 1980; Research Assoc, Visiting Scientist Smoking Tobacco and Cancer Program, Nat Cancer Inst, NIH, Washington, DC 1989–91, Expert Public Health Applications Research Br, Bethesda, MD 1991; Consultant on sickle cell desease to NIH 1984–88, Govt of Liberia and IBRD 1984, UN Fund for Population Activities 1984; Pres Bd of Dirs Hosp for Sick Children, Washington, DC 1986–90, mem 1984–94; columnist on various newspapers; has written over 140 scientific articles; numerous awards. *Address:* 1775 N Portal Drive, NW, Washington, DC 20012, USA.

EPSTEIN, Selma; American pianist and musicologist; b 14 Aug 1927, Brooklyn, NY; d of the late Samuel and Tillie (née Schneider) Schechtman; m Joseph Epstein 1950; two s two d. *Education:* Juilliard School and privately. *Career:* Debut as concert pianist Carnegie Hall, New York 1942; many concert tours in USA and world-wide, including People's Repub of China 1992–93; many concert tours with US Information Agency in Europe, the Far East and Australasia promoting music by 20th century, black and women composers 1964–; teacher Newcastle Conservatory of Music, NSW, Australia 1972–75; Dir of Publications Chromattica USA 1981–; art exhibitions in USA and Canada 1991–92; author eight group piano-teaching books 1975–, guide to researching music by women 1991, ed two historical anthologies of duets 1992. *Recordings include:* Selma Epstein plays Percy Grainger 1981. *Leisure interests:* reading, gardening, travel. *Address:* Chez Quatre Minous, 2443 Pickwick Rd, Dickeyville, MD 21207, USA. *Telephone:* (410) 448-3334; *Fax:* (410) 448-1433.

ERDENETOGTOKH, Altangerel; Mongolian economist, journalist and politician; b 11 March 1945, Ulan Bator; m Khatanbaatar 1967; two d one s. *Education:* Mongolian State Univ and Acad of Nat Economy (Moscow). *Career:* State Economic Planning Comm 1967–76; Political Commentator on TV 1980–87; mem People's Great Hural (Parl) 1990–92; fmrly Ed-in-Chief Government News, Parl Corresp 1992. *Leisure interests:* reading, theatre, cinema, friends. *Address:* People's Great Hural, Ulan Bator 12, Mongolia. *Telephone:* (1) 312220 (Office); (1) 320696 (Home); *Fax:* (1) 328602.

ERDRICH, (Karen) Louise, MA; American writer and poet; b 7 June 1954, Little Falls, MN; d of Ralph Louis and Rita Joanne (née Gourneau) Erdrich; m Michael Anthony Dorris 1981 (died 1997); five d one s (deceased). *Education:* Wahpeton High School (ND), Dartmouth Coll (NH), Johns Hopkins Univ (MD) and Univ Coll London. *Career:* Visiting Poetry Teacher N Dakota State Arts Council 1977–78; Teacher of Writing Johns Hopkins Univ, Baltimore 1978–79; Communications Dir and Ed Circle-Boston Indian Council 1979–80; Textbook Writer Charles Merrill Co 1980; mem PEN, mem Exec Bd 1985–; Guggenheim Fellow 1985–86; Nelson Algren Award 1982; Pushcart Prize 1983; Nat Magazine Fiction Award 1983, 1987; First Prize O. Henry Awards 1987. *Publications:* Imagination (textbook) 1981, Jacklight (poems) 1984, The Bluejay's Dance (non-fiction) 1995; Novels: Love Medicine (trans into more than 18 languages, Nat Book Critics' Circle Award for Best Work of Fiction 1984, LA Times Book Award) 1984, The Beet Queen (Nat Book Critics' Circle Nomination) 1986, Tracks 1988, Baptism of Desire 1989, Crown of Columbus (with Michael Dorris) 1991, The Bingo Palace 1994, Tales of Burning Love 1996, The Antelope Wife 1998, The Birchbark House 2000; short stories, children's stories, essays and poems publ in magazines. *Leisure interest:* family. *Address:* c/o Andrew Wylie Agency, 250 W 57th St, Suite 2114, New York, NY 10107, USA. *E-mail:* mail@wylieagency.com (Office).

ERENUS, Bilgesu, BA; Turkish playwright; b 13 Aug 1943, Bilecik; d of Avni and Aliye Duru; m M. Erenus 1967 (divorced 1990); one s. *Education:* Kadiköy High School for Girls (Istanbul), Istanbul Conservatory of Music and Univ of Istanbul. *Career:* Scriptwriter Türkiye Radyo Televizyon Kurumu (TRT—Turkish Radio-Television Corpn) 1965–73; playwright 1973–, 13 plays performed in Turkey, six published, several translated into French and German, one performed in Paris; social activist under mil regime 1980–83, prosecuted by martial courts and held in solitary confinement; First Prize World Children's Year Play Competition 1976; named Best Playwright in Turkey 1978. *Publications include:* L'Invité 1984, İkili Oyun (film script) 1989, Devlerin Ölümü (film script) 1990. *Leisure interest:* social activism. *Address:* Ayazpaşa Cami Sok, Saray Apt 10/12, Taksim, Istanbul, Turkey. *Telephone:* (1) 1432112.

ERIKSSON, Marianne; Swedish politician; b 17 March 1952, Brännkyrka. *Career:* Local Br Sec Nordic Green Left 1987–94; Int Affairs Sec 1995–; MEP (Bureau of GUE, Vänsterpartiet), mem Del for Relations with the Maghreb countries and the Arab Mahgreb Union, Del to the EU-Bulgaria Jt Parl Cttee; mem Budgetary Control Cttee; Vice Chair Cttee on Women's Rights and Equal Opportunities. *Address:* Gotlandsgaten 69, 11638 Stockholm, Sweden; European Parliament, rue Wiertz, 1047 Brussels, Belgium. *Telephone:* (2) 284-21-11 (Belgium); *Fax:* (2) 230-69-43 (Belgium).

ERLENDSDÓTTIR, Guðrún; Icelandic judge; b 3 May 1936, Reykjavík; d of the late Erlendur Ólafsson and Jóhanna V. Sæmundsdóttir; m Örn Clausen 1961; two d one s. *Education:* Univ of Iceland (Reykjavík). *Career:* Practiced law with husband 1961–70; teacher of Law Univ of Iceland 1970–86; first woman Judge of Supreme Court 1986–, Chief Justice 1991–92; Chair Equality Council 1973–80; books and articles on family law, law of succession and sexual equality. *Address:* Hæstiréttur Islands (Supreme Court), Reykjavík, Iceland (Office); Blikanes 3, 210 Garðabær, Iceland (Home). *Telephone:* 5540464; *Fax:* 5623995.

ERMAN, Verda; Turkish concert pianist; b 19 Dec 1944, Istanbul; d of Ilhami and Gilda Erman; m René Zapata 1974; one d. *Education:* Privately and Conservatoire Nat Supérieur de Musique de Paris (France). *Career:* Studied with Marguerite Long, Peter Feuchtwanger and Lazare Levy; Soloist Presidential Symphony Orchestra, Ankara 1971; has performed at concerts in over 44 countries; State Artist of Turkey 1972; Laureate of various int piano competitions including Montréal (Canada), Marguerite Long and Levintritt. *Recordings include:* Brahms, Schubert, Erkin, Bartók (for Pianissime collection). *Leisure interests:* opera, ballet, cooking. *Address:* 21 rue Georges Sand, 75016 Paris, France. *Telephone:* (1) 42-88-57-31.

ERNAUX, Annie; French writer; b 1 Sept 1940, Lillebonne; d of the late Alphonse Duchesne and Blanche Dumenil; m Philippe Ernaux 1964 (divorced 1985); two s. *Education:* Lycée Jeanne-d'Arc (Rouen) and Univs of Rouen, Bordeaux and Grenoble. *Career:* Teacher of literature 1966–2000; writer 1974–; Prix Renaudot 1984. *Publications:* Les Armoires Vides 1974, La femme gelée 1981, La place 1984, Une femme 1988, Passion simple 1992, La honte 1997, Je ne suis pas sortie de ma nuit 1997, L'événement 2000, Se perdre 2001. *Address:* 23 rue des Lozères, 95000 Cergy, France. *Fax:* (1) 30-31-27-74; *E-mail:* a .ernaux@infonie.fr (Home).

ERNST DE LA GRAETE, Brigitte Ulrique J. M. J. G., L EN D; Belgian politician; b 23 April 1957, Liège; two s. *Education:* Univ of Liège and Univ Catholique de Louvain. *Career:* Asst Dept of European Econ Law, Univ of Liège 1980–82; Municipal Councillor in charge of Recreation, Youth and Sports, Liège 1983–88; MEP 1989–94, mem Green group, mem Cttees on Econ and Monetary Affairs and Industrial Policy, Women's Rights and Devt and Co-operation; Dir Amnesty Int EU Asscn 1995–99; currently Fed Sec ECOLO (Ecologistes Confédérés pour l'Org de Luttes Originales). *Publication:* La commune, outil du développement économique local 1991. *Address:* 49 Thier de la Fontaine, 4000 Liège, Belgium (Home). *Telephone:* (4) 223-71-73 (Home); *Fax:* (4) 223-40-73 (Home); *E-mail:* brigitte.ernst@ecolo.be (Office); *Internet:* www.liege.be.

ERR, Lydie Clementine Nicole; Luxembourg politician; b 23 April 1949, Petange. *Education:* Univ of Strasbourg and Inst of Advanced European Studies (France). *Career:* Barrister 1976–, solicitor 1979–; mem Parti Ouvrier Socialiste Luxembourgeois (Socialist Party) 1983–, Nat Chair Socialist Women 1983–94, mem Supervision Cttee; Mem Chamber of Deputies (Parl) 1984–, Chair European and Foreign Affairs Cttee 1989; mem Ass of Council of Europe 1991, Vice-Pres 1996, Chair Cttee of Human Rights 1996, Cttee on Equal Opportunities for Women and Men; mem Ass of WEU 1991–98. *Address:* Chambre des Députés, 34 rue du Marché-aux-Herbes, Luxembourg.

ERRA, Mercedes, MBA; French advertising executive; b 23 Sept 1954, Barcelona, Spain; d of Valentin and Roser (née Alfaro) Erra; m Jean-Paul Valz; five s. *Education:* Lycées Bergson, Lamartine and Fénelon (Paris), Ecole des Hautes Etudes Commerciales (Jouy-en-Josas) and Univ of Paris IV (Paris-Sorbonne). *Career:* Asst, Head of Publicity Saatchi & Saatchi Advertising, France 1981–83, Group Head 1983–84, Client Man 1984–86, Assoc Man 1986–88, Asst Dir-Gen 1988–90, Dir-Gen 1990–95; Pres BETC EURO RSCG 1995–. *Address:* BETC EURO RSCG, 85–87 rue du Faubourg Saint Martin, 75010 Paris, France (Office); 7 ave André Guillaume, 92380 Garches, France (Home). *Telephone:* (1) 56-41-35-95 (Office); *Fax:* (1) 56-41-37-07 (Office); *E-mail:* mercedes.erra@betc.eurorscg.fr (Office).

ERZEN, Jale Nejdet, MFA, PH D; Turkish art historian and artist; b 12 Jan 1943, Ankara; d of Necdet and Selma Erzen. *Education:* Art Center Coll of Design (LA, USA) and Istanbul Tech Univ. *Career:* Taught part-time at various univs in Turkey; lectured widely in USA, Italy and France; mem staff Faculty of Architecture Middle East Tech Univ 1974–, Prof of History of Art and Aesthetics 1992–; Founder and Ed Boyut Fine Arts Journal 1980–85; Founder Pres SANART Asscn of Aesthetics and Visual Culture; advisor Int Asscn for Applied Aesthetics 1998–2001; works in pvt and state collections in Turkey and Europe; Consultant Istanbul Biennale 1992, Istanbul Contemporary Museum 1992–93, Ankara Contemporary Museum 2000–2001; also consultant for various architectural journals; Chevalier des Arts et des Lettres 1991; Best Critic Award, Istanbul Art Fair 2000. *Art Exhibitions:* solo and group exhibitions LA Arts Asscn and in France and Italy; exhibits regularly in Ankara and Istanbul; work in collections in Europe, USA and in nat and pvt collections in Turkey; *Films:* video exhibition of Suleiman the Magnificent, Grand Palais, Paris (with Stephane Yerasimos) 1989; *Publications:* books on Ottoman architects Sinan, Sabri Berkel, Erol Akyavas, Mehmet Aksoy; various articles on aesthetics, modern art, Ottoman architecture. *Leisure interests:* gardening, horse-riding, poetry. *Address:* Faculty of Architecture, Middle East Technical University, Inonu blv, 06531 Ankara, Turkey (Office); Sanart, Kenedi Cad 42, Kavaklidere, 06660 Ankara, Turkey (Home). *Telephone:* (312) 2102215 (Office); (312) 4464761 (Home); *Fax:* (312) 2101249 (Office); *E-mail:* erzen@arch.metu.edu.tr; *Internet:* www.metu.edu.tr.

ESCOBAR, Marisol; Venezuelan sculptor; b 22 May 1930, Paris; d of Gustavo and Josefina Hernandez Escobar. *Education:* Ecole des Beaux Arts (Paris), New School for Social Research (New York) and Hans Hoffman School of Art (New York). *Career:* Solo exhibitions include New York 1962–64, Museum of Modern Art, New York 1964, Sidney Janis Gallery 1966, 1967, 1973, 1975, 1978, 1981, 1986, London 1967, Netherlands 1968, Venice Biennale, Italy 1968, Japan 1987, Nat Portrait Gallery, Washington, DC 1991; rep perm collections including Museum of Modern Art, New York, Whitney Museum of Modern Art, Metropolitan Museum, New York, Albright-Knox Gallery, Buffalo, NY, Hakone Museum, Tokyo, Museum of Contemporary Arts, Caracas; has designed sets for Martha Graham Dance Co; mem American Acad of Arts and Letters 1975–; Dr hc (Rhode Island School of Design, State Univ of New York at Buffalo) 1992. *Address:* 421 Washington St, New York, NY 10013, USA. *Telephone:* (212) 966-2589.

ESCOBEDO, Helen (Elena), ARCA; Mexican sculptor; b 28 July 1934, Mexico City; d of Manuel G. and Elsie Fulda Escobedo; m 1st Fredrik Kirsebom (divorced 1982); one s one d; m 2nd Hans-Jürgen Rabe 1995. *Education:* Univ of Motolinia and RCA. *Career:* Dir of Fine Arts Nat Univ of Mexico 1961–74, Dir of Museums and Galleries 1974–78; Tech Dir Nat Museum of Art, Mexico 1981–82; Dir Museum of Modern Art, Mexico 1982–84; mem Espacio Escultórico design team 1978–79; Guggenheim Fellowship; Assoc mem Acad Royale de Belgique; Tlatilco Prize for Sculpture, Int Water Sculpture Competition Prize, New Orleans World Fair 1983, Order of the Lion (Finland). *Art Exhibitions:* Museo de Arte Moderno, Mexico City 1975, Nat Art Museum, Helsinki 1991, Museo Kufino Tamayo 1992; *Designs include:* Gateway to the Wind, Olympic Highway 68, Mexico City, 1968, Signals, Auckland Harbour 1971, The Great Cone, Jerusalem 1986; *Publications:* Mexican Monuments, Strange Encounters 1989. *Leisure interests:* reading, writing. *Address:* Mühlenberger Weg 16, 22587 Hamburg, Germany (March–Sept); 1A Cerrada de San Jerónimo 19, Mexico 10200 DF, Mexico (Oct–Feb). *Fax:* (40) 86-64-56-93 (Hamburg); (5) 683-4699 (Mexico).

ESCOFFERY, Gloria Blanche, BA, DIP ED; Jamaican artist, poet and journalist; b 22 Dec 1923, Jamaica; d of William I. and Sylvia Escoffery; one s (adopted). *Education:* McGill Univ (Montréal, Canada), Slade School of Fine Art (London) and Univ of the West Indies. *Career:* Many nat and int exhibitions of paintings; Columnist on the Daily Gleaner newspaper 1980–82; Art Critic for Jamaica Journal 1981–89; Jamaica Scholar 1943; Inst of Jamaica Centenary Medal 1979; Officer of the Order of Distinction (Jamaica) 1977; Silver Musgrave Medal, Inst of Jamaica 1985. *Publications:* Loggerhead (poetry) 1988, Mother Jackson Murders the Moon (poetry) 1998; poems published in anthologies. *Address:* 4 St Christopher Crescent, POB 14, Brown's Town, Jamaica. *Telephone:* 975-2268.

ESPERT ROMERO, Nuria; Spanish actress and director; b 11 June 1935, Hospitalet, Barcelona; m Armando Moreno 1955; two d. *Education:* Barcelona. *Career:* Began acting in professional productions aged 12 1947; played title role in Médée 1954; formed own co 1959; performed throughout world 1969–; has appeared in works by Shakespeare, O'Neill, Lope de Vega, Sartre, Genet, Lorca, Calderón de la Barca, etc; performed at Odeon Teatre d'Europe (Paris) 1996; began directing 1986; Dir The House of Bernarda Alba (London Evening Standard Drama Award) 1986; Dir of operas for Royal Opera House (Covent Garden, London) and La Monnaie theatre (Brussels), Olympic Games (Barcelona 1992), and in Tokyo (Japan); Artistic Dir Turandot, Liceo Theater, Barcelona 1999; author numerous int theatre publs; over 100 Spanish honours and awards; 17 int awards. *Operas directed include:* Madam Butterfly, Elektra, Rigoletto, La Traviata, Carmen, Medea, Elizabeth; *Plays:* The Seagle 1997, Master Class 1998, Who's Afraid of Virginia Woolf 1999, 2000. *Leisure interests:* resting, thinking, reading. *Address:* Pavía 2, 28013 Madrid, Spain. *Telephone:* (91) 7154958; *Fax:* (91) 3511177.

ESTEFAN, Gloria, BA; American singer and songwriter; b 1 Sept 1957, Havana, Cuba; d of José and Gloria Fajardo; m Emilio Estefan, Jr; one s one d. *Education:* Univ of Miami (FL). *Career:* Career took off following hit single Conga; Lead singer Gloria Estefan and Miami Sound Machine; has had 17 Top Ten hits, albums have sold over 20 million copies; several int tours and performances world-wide; performances at World Series Baseball, St Louis, MO (USA) 1987, Olympic Games, Seoul (Repub of Korea) 1988, Pan American Games 1988, Superbowl, Minneapolis, MN (USA) 1992; numerous awards include American Music Award 1987, Songwriter of the Year (British Music Industry), Grammy nomination. *Albums include:* Primitive Love 1986, Let it Loose 1987, Cuts Both Ways 1990, Coming Out of the Dark 1991, Greatest Hits 1992, Mi Terra 1993, Hold Me, Thrill Me, Kiss Me 1994, Destiny 1996, Gloria! 1998, Santo Santo 1999, Alma Caribend: Carribean Soul 2000; *Singles include:* Anything for You 1987, Live for Loving You 1991, Can't Forget You 1991, Coming Out of the Dark 1991, Always Tomorrow 1992, Go Away 1993. *Address:* Estefan Enterprises Inc, 6205 Bird Rd, Miami, FL 33155, USA (Office).

ESTERER-WANDSCHNEIDER, Ingeborg Charlotte Martha Katharina, PH D; German journalist; b 18 Feb 1926, Mainz; d of Jakob-Ernst and Charlotte Günther; m 1st Rainer Esterer 1951; m 2nd Hajo Wandschneider 1972; one s one d. *Education:* High schools (Mainz and Berlin) and Univs of Berlin and Hamburg. *Career:* Freelance journalist 1948–51, 1990–; Sec Inst Français Hambourg 1951–53; Ed Kristall (entertainment and science magazine) 1954–60; freelance radio journalist and trans of French and English books 1960–70; Public Relations Officer Amnesty Int (German Section) 1968–70; Leading Ed Vital (health and fitness magazine) 1970–83, Für Sie (women's magazine) 1983–90; First Prize (Medical Journalism—Ophthalmology) 1989. *Leisure interests:* literature, music, philosophy, art. *Address:* Cranachstr 39, 2000 Hamburg 52, Germany. *Telephone:* (40) 893154.

ESTEVAN BOLEA, Maria Teresa; Spanish politician; b 26 Oct 1936, Huesca. *Career:* MEP (EPP, PP), mem Cttee on Research, Technological Devt and Energy, Del to the EU-Hungary Jt Parl Cttee. *Address:* European Parliament, rue Wiertz, 1047 Brussels, Belgium. *Telephone:* (2) 284-21-11; *Fax:* (2) 230-69-43.

ESTEVE-COLL, Dame Elizabeth, DBE, BA, FRSA; British former university vice-chancellor and museum director; b 1938; d of P. W. and Nora Kingdon; m José Alexander Timothy Esteve-Coll 1960 (died 1980). *Education:* Birkbeck Coll (Univ of London). *Career:* Librarian, London Borough of Merton, Kingston Coll of Art, Kingston Polytechnic 1968–77; Head Dept of Learning Resources, Kingston Polytechnic 1977–82; Univ Librarian Univ of Surrey, Chair Arts Cttee 1982–85; Chief Librarian Nat Art Library, Victoria and Albert Museum 1985–87, Dir Victoria and Albert Museum 1988–95; Vice-Chancellor Univ of E Anglia 1995–97; Assoc Library Asscn; Hon LITT D (E Anglia) 1997. *Publication:* The Victoria and Albert Museum (jtly) 1992. *Address:* 27 Ursula St, London SW11 3DW, UK. *Telephone:* (20) 7652-3744.

ETCHELLS, (Dorothea) Ruth, MA, DD; British former college principal; b 17 April 1931; d of the late Rev Walter and Ada Etchells. *Education:* Merchant Taylor's School for Girls (Crosby, Liverpool), Univs of Liverpool and London. *Career:* Head of English Dept Aigburth Vale High School, Liverpool 1959–63; Lecturer in English Chester Coll of Educ 1963–65, Sr Lecturer in English and Resident Tutor 1965–1968; Part-time Lecturer in English and Resident Tutor Trevelyan Coll, Durham 1968–72, Vice-Prin 1972, Sr Lecturer 1973–79; Prin (first woman, first lay Prin) St John's Coll (Univ of Durham) with Cranmer Hall (ordination training) 1979–88, mem Council Univ of Durham 1985–88, Hon Fellow St John's Coll 1991–; Bishop's Council and Standing Cttee Durham Diocesan Synod 1975–97, Chair House of Laity, Durham Diocese 1988–96; Examining Chaplain to Bishop of Bath and Wells 1984–88; mem Gen Synod Church of England 1985–96, mem Doctrine Comm 1986–89, Crown Appointments Comm 1987–96; Vice-Chair Durham Family Health Services Authority Bd 1990–96, Chair Medical Services Cttee 1990–96; mem Governing Council Durham High School 1995–2002, Ridley Coll, Cambridge 1998–; Trustee Hosp of God at Greatham 1995–2000. *Publications include:* Unafraid to Be 1969, The Man with the Trumpet 1970, A Model of Making 1983, Poets and Prophets (ed, four vols) 1987, 1988, Praying with the English Poets 1990, Just As I Am: Personal Prayers for Every Day 1994, Set My People Free 1995, A Reading of the Parables of Jesus 1998. *Leisure interests:* friends, country walks, pets, working in stained glass, painting, sketching. *Address:* 12 Dunelm Court, South St, Durham DH1 4QX, UK. *Telephone:* (191) 3841497.

ETOMA, Lagi; Tuvaluan broadcasting executive; b 6 April 1943; d of Ienisei and Simolo Etoma; five s three d. *Education:* Elaine Bernacchi, Bikenibeu Tarawa (Kiribati). *Career:* Shopkeeper 1962–63; nurse 1963–65; broadcaster Radio Tuvalu 1968, radio programme producer, acting Broadcasting and Information Officer (Head Radio Tuvalu) 1990; mem Nat Council of Tuvalu women. *Leisure interests:* sport, reading, picnics. *Address:* POB 92, Funafuti, Tuvalu. *Telephone:* 732; *Fax:* 732.

EUVRARD, Catherine Andrée Pénélope; French business executive; b 5 June 1941, Boulogne-Billancourt; d of Michel and Suzanne (née Achillas-Achillopulo) Bernard; m Jean-Pierre Euvrard 1971; two s one d. *Education:* Lycée Molière and Ecole Notre-Dame de l'Assomption (Paris), W London Coll (UK) and Management Center Europe (Brussels). *Career:* Asst Commercial Section Kodak-Pathé (France) Co 1960–69; Publicity Dir Vichy (L'Oréal) lab 1969–73; Head Product Group Lachartre (Procter & Gamble) lab 1973–82; Dir Actuel magazine 1982–84; Dir-Gen Hebdo magazine 1984–86; Dir Courtaud group 1986–89; Vice-Pres Ores Search (Bossard group) co 1989–90; Founder, Pres Catherine Euvrard Consultants (Bossard group) 1990–; Admin Emmanuelle Khanh Int. *Leisure interests:* ballet dancing, roller-skating, jazz, collecting hats and glassware, tennis, golf, skiing. *Address:* Catherine Euvrard Consultants, 5 rue du Bois de Boulogne, 75116 Paris, France (Office); 5 bis blvd Richard Wallace, 92200 Neuilly-sur-Seine, France (Home). *Telephone:* (1) 45-55-17-94 (Office); *Fax:* (1) 45-00-29-98 (Office).

EVANGELISTA, Linda; Canadian fashion model; b St Catherine, Toronto, ON; m Gerald Marie (divorced 1993). *Career:* Top fashion model; endorses Diet Coke (on French TV); face of Yardley Cosmetics; models for all leading fashion houses and at major fashion shows. *Film:* Unzipped 1996. *Address:* c/o Elite Model Management, 40 Parker St, London WC2B 5PH, UK; Elite Model Management Corporation, 111 E 22nd St, Floor 2, New York, NY 10010, USA (Office). *Telephone:* (20) 7333-0888 (Office) (London).

EVANS, Janet; American swimmer; b 28 Aug 1971. *Career:* Gold Medallist 400m Freestyle and 800m Individual Medley, Olympic Games, Seoul, Repub of Korea 1988, 800m Freestyle, Olympic Games, Barcelona, Spain 1992; Silver Medallist 400m Freestyle, Olympic Games Barcelona, Spain 1992; winner 400m Freestyle Philips 66 Nat Swimming Championships, IN 1994; competitor, Olympic Games, Atlanta, GA, USA 1996; named US Swimmer of the Year 1987. *Address:* US Olympic Cttee, 1750 Boulder St, Colorado Springs, CO 80909, USA.

EVANS, Joni; American publishing executive. *Career:* Publr Linden Press, Simon & Schuster 1979–85, Pres Simon & Schuster Trade Div 1985–87; Publr Random House imprint 1987–90, Pres, Publr own imprint, apptd Exec Vice-Pres Random House Inc 1990; named one of the 101 Most Powerful People in Entertainment, Entertainment Weekly 1990. *Address:* c/o Random House Inc, 201 E 50th St, New York, NY 10022, USA.

EVANS, Lois Logan, BA; American banking executive and government official; b 1 Dec 1937, Boston, MA; d of Harlan deBaun and Barbara Logan; m Thomas W. Evans 1956; two d one s. *Education:* Vassar and Barnard Colls. *Career:* Alt Chief Del to UN Comm on the Status of Women, New York 1972–74; mem Bd of Dirs US Comm to UNESCO, Washington, DC 1974–78; Pres Acquisition Specialists Inc, New York 1975–, Chair Bd of Dirs; Exec Vice-Pres Campbell Shea Inc, New York 1988–89; Asst Chief of Protocol, State Dept, New York 1981–83; Chair of Bd Fed Home Bank, New York 1986–88; mem Bd US Export-Import Bank 1984–90; Co-Chair Reagan–Bush Campaign, New York 1984; mem S Pacific Comm 1990–92, Man Decision Lab, New York Univ, NY 1992. *Address:* Acquisition Specialists Inc, 919 3rd Ave, Suite 21, New York, NY 10022, USA.

EVATT, Hon Elizabeth Andreas, AC, LL M; Australian lawyer and former university chancellor; b 11 Nov 1933, Sydney, NSW; d of Clive Raleigh and Marjorie Hannah (née Andreas) Evatt; m Robert Southan 1960; one d. *Education:* PLC Pymble (Sydney), Univ of Sydney and Harvard Univ (MA, USA). *Career:* Called to the Bar, NSW 1955; Chair

Royal Comm on Human Relationships 1974–77; Chief Judge Family Court of Australia 1976–88; Pres Law Reform Comm 1988–; Chancellor Univ of Newcastle, NSW 1988–94; Deputy Pres Conciliation and Arbitration Comm 1973–89, Australian Industrial Relations Comm 1989–94; Vice-Pres Industrial Relations Comm 1973–94, H. V. Evatt Memorial Foundation 1982–87; Chair Arts Law 1985–88; Pres Australian Law Reform Comm 1988–93, mem 1993–94; mem UN Cttee on Elimination of Discrimination against Women 1984–92 (Chair 1989–91), Advisory Cttee Peace Research Centre ANU, Bd Pearl Watson Foundation 1985, Bd Australian Inst of Family Studies 1989, Macquarie Univ Council 1979–85; reviewed Aboriginal and Torres Strait Islander Heritage Protection Act 1984; Hearing Commr (part-time), Human Rights and Equal Opportunity Comm 1995–98; mem UN Human Rights Cttee 1993, World Bank Admin Tribunal 1998; Hon LL D (Sydney) 1985; Australian Human Rights Medal 1995. *Publication:* A Guide to Family Law (ed) 1986. *Leisure interests:* reading, walking, music. *Address:* Unit 2003, 184 Forbes St, Darlinghurst, NSW 2010, Australia. *E-mail:* eevatt@bigpond.net.au (Office).

EVER, Ita; Estonian actress; b 1 April 1931, Paide; m (divorced); one s. *Education:* Secondary School No 4 (Tallinn) and Theatre Inst (Moscow). *Career:* Actress Estonian Dramatic Theatre and film studios in Moscow, St Petersburg and Tallinn 1953–; has appeared in over 100 plays and 20 films and has had one record produced. *Address:* Sütiste tee 46–20, Tallinn 0034, Estonia. *Telephone:* (2) 521800.

EVERS-WILLIAMS, Myrlie, BA; American organization executive; b 17 March 1933, Vicksburg, MS; m Medgar Evers (died 1963); three c. *Education:* Alcorn State Univ (MS) and Pomona Coll (CA). *Career:* Dir Planning Clarmont Colls (CA) 1968–70; Vice-Pres Seligman & Latz, New York, NY; Dir of Consumer Affairs Atlantic Richfield Co; Commr Public Works Bd, Los Angeles, CA 1987–95; Chair Nat Asscn for the Advancement of Colored People (NAACP) 1995–98; Founder-mem Nat Women's Political Caucus; Lecturer on Civil Rights; Althea T. L. Simmons Social Action Award 1998; NAACP Spingarn Award 1998. *Publications include:* For Us the Living 1967. *Address:* MEW Associates Inc, 15 SW Colorado Ave, Suite 310, Bend, OR 97702-1149, USA.

EVERT, Chris(tine) Marie; American tennis player (retd); b 21 Dec 1954, Fort Lauderdale, FL; d of James and Colette Evert; m 1st John Lloyd 1979 (divorced 1987); m 2nd Andy Mill 1988; three s. *Education:* St Thomas Aquinas High School (Fort Lauderdale, FL). *Career:* Amateur player 1970–72, professional since 1972; S African Champion 1973; Wimbledon (UK) Singles Champion 1974, 1976, 1981; French Champion 1974, 1975, 1979, 1980, 1982, 1985, 1986; Italian Champion 1974, 1975, 1980; US Open Champion 1975, 1976, 1977, 1978, 1980, 1982, record 100 victories; Colgate Series Champion 1977, 1978; World Champion 1979; played Wightman Cup for USA 1971–73, 1975–82; played Fed Cup for USA 1977–82; won 1000th singles victory Australian Open Dec 1984; Pres Women's Tennis Asscn 1975–76, 1983–91; Founder Chris Evert Charities for needy and drug-abusive mothers and their children 1989; involved in Chris Evert/Ellesse Pro-Celebrity Tennis Classic for charity 1989–; owner Evert Enterprises/IMG, Boca Raton (FL) 1989–; Dir Pres's Council on Physical Fitness and Sports 1991–. *Publication:* Lloyd on Lloyd (with John Lloyd) 1985. *Address:* Evert Enterprises/IMG, 7200 W Camino Real, #310, Boca Raton, FL 33433, USA.

EVORA, Cesaria; Cape Verde musician; b 27 Aug 1941, Mindelo, San Vicente. *Career:* Singer specializing in 'morna' (traditional Cape Verdean songs), since 1959; recording artist for Mélodie 1990–; has performed at the New Morning Jazz Club and Olympia (Paris), in Japan, USA and throughout Europe. *Albums include:* La Diva aux pieds nus 1988, Distino di Belita 1990, Mar Azul 1991, Miss Perfumado 1992, Sodade les plus belles mornas de Cesaria 1994, Cesaria 1995, Cabo Verde 1997, Best of Cesaria Evora 1998, Café Atlantico 1999.

EVYATAR, Hena; Israeli artist, sculptor and ceramic artist; b (Hena Kohn) 1929, Łódź, Poland; m Azriel Evyatar 1949. *Career:* Works included in numerous group exhibitions; solo exhibitions include Buenos Aires 1955, New York (USA) 1964, 1977, 1985, Tel-Aviv 1971, 1976, 1982, 1983; created murals for Dan Carmel Hotel, Faculty Club, Technion and Deshanim Chemical Plant, Haifa; First Prize Cen Ceramic and Sculpture Exhibition, Chicago, USA 1960; Sculpture Prize Nat Sea Exhibition, Haifa 1975. *Publications:* Artists about themselves 1974, Moulding of Perspex 1975. *Address:* 18 Hagilboa St, Tel-Aviv 65223, Israel.

EWBANK, Inga-Stina, PH D; Swedish professor of English; b 13 June 1932; d of Gustav and Ingeborg Ekeblad; m Roger Ewbank 1959; two d one s. *Education:* Högre Allänna Läroverket för Flickor (Gothenburg), Univs of Carleton (ON, Canada), Gothenburg and Sheffield and Liverpool (UK). *Career:* William Noble Fellow Univ of Liverpool, UK 1955–57, Asst Lecturer 1960–63, Lecturer, then Sr Lecturer 1963–72; Research Fellow Shakespeare Inst, Univ of Birmingham, UK 1957–60; Reader in English Literature Bedford Coll, Univ of London 1972–74, Hildred Carlile Prof 1974–84; Prof of English Literature Univ of Leeds 1985–97; Visiting Lecturer Univ of Munich, Germany 1959–60; Visiting Assoc Prof Northwestern Univ, IL, USA 1966; Visiting Prof Harvard Univ 1974, Univ of Maryland 1981, Georgetown Univ (DC) 1982, Columbia Univ (New York) 1984; Dr hc (Oslo) 1999, (Lingnan, Hong Kong) 1999. *Publications:* Their Proper Sphere: A Study of the Brontë Sisters as Early-Victorian Female Novelists 1966, Shakespeare, Ibsen and the Unspeakable (lecture) 1975, Ibsen's John Gabriel Borkman: An English Version (jtly) 1975, Shakespeare's Styles (co-ed) 1980, Strindberg and the Intimate Theatre 1987, Three Chamber Plays by August Strindberg 1997, Anglo-Scandinavian Cross Currents 1999; numerous contribs to books including The Cambridge Companion to Shakespeare Studies 1986. *Leisure interests:* reading, theatre, children. *Address:* 19 Woodfield Rd, Ealing, London W5, UK.

EWING, Margaret Anne, MA; British politician; b 1 Sept 1945, Lanark; d of John and Peggie (née Lamb) McAdam; m Fergus Stewart Ewing 1983. *Education:* Univs of Glasgow and Strathclyde and Jordanhill Coll. *Career:* Asst teacher St Modan's High School (Stirling) 1970–73, Prin Remedial Educ 1973–74; joined SNP 1966, mem Nat Exec Cttee, Sr Vice-Chair 1984–87, Vice-Pres and Parl Leader 1987–; MP for E Dunbartonshire 1974–79, for Moray 1987–2001; mem Scottish Parl 1999–; Convenor Scottish Nat Party Group, Holyrood. *Leisure interests:* gardening, films, reading, folk music. *Address:* Scottish Parliament, Edinburgh, EH99 1SP, UK (Office); Burns Cottage, Tulloch's Brae, Lossiemouth, Morayshire IV31 6QY, UK (Home). *Telephone:* (131) 3485704 (Office); (1343) 551111 (Home); *Fax:* (1343) 813649 (Home).

EWING, Maria Louise; American opera singer (soprano); b 27 March 1950, Detroit, MI; d of Norman I. and Hermina M. (née Veraar) Ewing; m Sir Peter Hall 1982 (divorced 1989); one d. *Education:* Cleveland Inst of Music (OH). *Career:* Debut at New York Metropolitan Opera 1976; appearances with major orchestras including New York Philharmonic, Orchestre de Paris, London Philharmonic Orchestra, Royal Philharmonic Orchestra (UK), London Symphony Orchestra, City of Birmingham Symphony Orchestra (UK), at La Scala (Milan, Italy), Glyndebourne Festival (UK), Chicago Lyric Opera, Royal Opera House, Covent Garden, Earl's Court and Promenade Concerts (London), Salzburg Opera (Austria), Geneva Opera (Switzerland), Paris Opera, Metropolitan Opera (New York); also appears as concert and recital singer. *Operas include:* The Marriage of Figaro, The Barber of Seville, L'Incoronazione di Poppea, Carmen, Pelléas et Mélisande, The Dialogues of the Carmelites, Così fan Tutte, La Perichole, La Cenerentola, Salome, The Merry Widow, Tosca, Madam Butterfly, The Trojans; *Recordings include:* La Demoiselle Elue 1986, Mozart's Requiem (with Leonard Bernstein) 1988, Scheherezade 1990, Jazz Album 1990, Pelléas et Mélisande 1991, Lady Macbeth of Mtzensk 1994. *Leisure interest:* home and family. *Address:* c/o David Godfrey, Mitchell-Godfrey Management, 48 Gray's Inn Rd, London WC1X 8LT, UK (Office); c/o Marc Wilkins, Herbert H Breslin Inc, 119 W 57th St, New York, NY 10019, USA. *Telephone:* (20) 7831-3027 (Office); *Fax:* (20) 7831-5277 (Office); *E-mail:* davidgodfrey@mariaewing.com (Office).

EWING, Winifred Margaret, MA, LL B, FRSA; British politician and lawyer; b (Winifred Margaret Woodburn) 10 July 1929, Glasgow; d of George Woodburn and Christina B. Anderson; m Stewart Martin Ewing 1956; two s one d. *Education:* Queen's Park School, Univ of Glasgow and Peace Palace (The Hague). *Career:* Practising solicitor 1956–; MP for Hamilton 1967–70, for Moray and Nairn 1974–79; MEP 1975–, for the Highlands and Islands of Scotland 1979–99, mem for Highlands and

Islands, Scottish Parl 1999–, Chair Cttee on Youth, Culture, Educ, Information and Sport 1984–87, mem Cttee on Devt and Co-operation 1987–, ACP–EEC Jt Ass; Pres Scottish Nat Party, European Free Alliance 1991–; Vice-Pres European Democratic Alliance 1984–, Animal Welfare Intergroup (European Parl) 1989–99; Sec Glasgow Bar Asscn 1961–67, Pres 1970–71; mem Exec Cttee Scottish Co for Devt and Industry 1972–; Dr hc (Open Univ) 1993; Hon LL D (Glasgow) 1995; Freeman of Avignon. *Leisure interests:* hill-walking, collecting paintings, singing. *Address:* Goodwill, Milton Duff, Elgin, Moray IV30 3TL, UK (Home). *Telephone:* (1343) 541144; *Fax:* (1343) 540011.

EYAMBA-IDEM, Dorothy Nsa, LL B, BL; Nigerian high court judge; b 5 Oct 1947, Calabar; d of Chief Okon E. Okon and Agnes Edem; m 1st Archibong Omon 1975 (divorced 1980); m 2nd Eyamba-Idem 1980; five d one s. *Education:* Hope Waddell Training Inst (Calabar), Univ of Nigeria (Nsukka), Nigerian Law School and Nigerian Inst of Advanced Legal Studies (Lagos). *Career:* Mem Nat Youth Service Corpn, Ibadan 1974–75; Magistrate, later Chief Magistrate (Grade I), Cross River State 1975–85; Chair Rent Tribunal, Calabar Zone 1984–85; apptd Judge High Court of Justice, Cross River State 1985; Chair Comm on Inquiry into Nigeria Oil Palm Estates Privatization and Commercialization Review, Cross River State 1990. *Leisure interests:* reading, gardening, listening to gentle music. *Address:* High Court of Justice, Akamkpa, Cross River State, Nigeria (Office); 7 Okon Inok Estate, Ediba-Calabar, Cross River State, Nigeria (Home); POB 190, Housing Estate, Calabar, Nigeria (Postal Address). *Telephone:* (87) 224708.

EZRATTY-BADER, Myriam, L ÈS L; French judge; b 7 Dec 1929, Nice; m José Ezratty 1956. *Education:* Univ of Aix-en-Provence. *Career:* Head of Office Dept of Supervised Educ, then Dept of Civil and Legal Affairs, Ministry of Justice 1958–74; Tech Adviser to Minister of Health 1974–79; Pres of Chamber at Court of Appeal, Paris 1979–81, First Pres 1988–96, First Hon Pres of Court of Appeal, Paris; Dir of Supervised Educ 1981–83, of Prisons Admin 1983–86. *Address:* CIPC, 507 place d'Armes, Montréal, Québec, Canada.

F

FABÉNYI, Júlia, PH D; Hungarian art historian and archaeologist; b 27 Sept 1953, Budapest; d of Ede Fabényi and Ilona Tokay; m; one s. *Education:* Univ of Leipzig. *Career:* Asst Prof Univ of Social Sciences, Faculty of Art History of Leipzig 1977–82; curator Budapest Art Gallery 1990–94, Head of Exhibition Dept 1994–95, Man Dir 2000–; Dir Picture Gallery of Szombathely 1996–2000; Fine Arts Curator Int Book Fair, Frankfurt 1999–. *Address:* Mücsarnok, 1146 , Dózsa György út 37, Budapest (Office); 1023 Budapest, Zsigmond tér 8, Hungary (Home). *Telephone:* (343) 4145; *Fax:* (343) 5205; *E-mail:* lbeke@computronic .hu.

FABER, Sandra Moore, BA, PH D, D SC; American astronomer; b 28 Dec 1944, Boston; d of Donald Erwin and Elizabeth Mackenzie Moore; m Andrew L. Faber 1967; one s one d. *Education:* Swarthmore Coll and Harvard Univ. *Career:* Astronomer Lick Observatory, Santa Cruz, CA, Asst Prof 1972–77, Assoc Prof 1977–79, apptd Prof 1979; Nat Science Foundation Fellow 1966–71; Woodrow Wilson Fellow 1966–71; Alfred P. Sloan Fellow 1977–81; Tetelman Fellow Yale Univ 1987; Visiting Prof Princeton Univ 1978, Univ of Hawaii 1983, AZ State Univ 1985; Carnegie Lecturer Carnegie Inst, Washington, DC 1988; Feshbach Lecturer MIT 1990; Assoc Ed Astrophysics Journal Letters 1982–87; mem NAS, American Acad of Arts and Sciences, American Philosophical Soc 2000–; Bart J. Bok Prize, Harvard Univ 1978; Dir's Distinguished Lecturer Award Livermore Nat Lab 1986. *Address:* University of California, Lick Observatory, Santa Cruz, CA 95060, USA.

FABIANI, Simonetta (see Simonetta).

FAGIN, Claire Mintzer, PH D; American professor of nursing; b 25 Nov 1926, New York; d of Harry Fagin and Mae (Slatin) Mintzer; m Samuel Fagin 1952; two s. *Education:* Wagner Coll, Teachers' Coll, Columbia and New York Univs. *Career:* Staff Nurse Sea View Hosp, Staten Island, New York 1947, Clinical Instructor 1947–48; Bellevue Hosp, New York 1948–50; Psychiatric Mental Health Nursing Consultant, Nat League for Nursing 1951–52; Asst Chief Psychiatric Nursing Service Clinical Center, NIH 1953–54, Supt 1955; Research Project Co-ordinator Children's Hosp, Dept of Psychiatry, Washington, DC 1956; Instructor in Psychiatric-Mental Health Nursing, New York Univ 1956–58, Asst Prof 1964–67, Dir Grad Programs in Psychiatric-Mental Health Nursing 1965–69, Assoc Prof 1967–69; Prof and Chair Nursing Dept, Herbert H. Lehman Coll 1969–77; Dir Health Professions Inst, Montefiore Hosp and Medical Center 1975–77; Dean School of Nursing, Univ of Pennsylvania, PA 1977–92, Prof 1992–96, Pres (interim) 1993–94, Dean Emer, Prof Emer 1996–; Dir Salomon Inc 1994–97; Pres American Orthopsychiatric Asscn 1985; Pres (Elect) Nat League for Nursing; Consultant to many foundations, public and pvt univs, health care agencies; mem Inst of Medicine, NAS (Governing Council 1981–83), American Acad of Nursing (Governing Council 1976–78), Expert Advisory Panel on Nursing, WHO 1974–, Nat Advisory Mental Health Council, Nat Inst of Mental Health 1983–87, Bd of Health Promotion and Disease Prevention 1990–94, Comm on Human Rights 1991–; Pres Nat League for Nursing 1991–93; consultant to many foundations, public and pvt univs, health care agencies; speaker on radio and TV; Fellow Coll of Physicians of Philadelphia 1986; Hon D SC (Lycoming Coll, Cedar Crest Coll, Univ of Rochester, Medical Coll of Pennsylvania, Univ of Maryland, Loyola Univ, Wagner Coll); Hon LL D (Pennsylvania); Hon D HUM LITT (Hunter Coll, Rush Univ); numerous awards and distinctions. *Publications:* Nursing Leadership: Global Strategies (ed) 1990; more than 75 articles on nursing and health policy. *Address:* Nursing Education

Building, University of Pennsylvania, 354 NEB, Philadelphia, PA 19104, USA (Office); 200 Central Park South, Apt 12E, New York, NY 10019, USA (Home).

FAIRBAIRN, Hon Joyce, BA; Canadian journalist and politician; b 6 Nov 1939, Lethbridge, AB; d of the late Judge Lynden Eldon and Mary Elizabeth Fairbairn; m Michael Gillan 1967. *Education:* Univ of Alberta and Carleton Univ. *Career:* News Reporter Ottawa Journal 1961–62; Political Reporter and Columnist Parl Press Gallery Bureau, United Press Int 1962–64; Political Corresp F. P. Publications for Winnipeg Free Press, Calgary Albertan, Lethbridge Herald, Vancouver Sun, Victoria Times, Ottawa Journal 1964–70; Legis Asst to Rt Hon Pierre Trudeau 1970–84, Communications Co-ordinator Prime Minister's Office 1981–83; Senator for Lethbridge, Prov of Alberta 1984–97, mem Standing Senate Cttees on Legal and Constitutional Affairs, Agriculture and Forestry (Vice-Pres), Foreign Affairs, Aboriginal Peoples, Special Senate Cttees on Youth 1984–86, Terrorism and Public Safety 1986–87, Senate Leader, Minister with special responsibility for Literacy 1993–97; Vice-Chair N and W Liberal Caucus; mem Senate Univ of Lethbridge. *Address:* Centre Block, 571-S, Senate, Ottawa, ON K1A 0A4, Canada (Office); 34 Harmer Ave N, Ottawa, ON K1Y 0T4, Canada (Home).

FAIRCLOUGH, Rt Hon Ellen Louks, PC, OC, FCA; Canadian politician; b 28 Jan 1905, Hamilton, ON; d of the late Norman Ellsworth Cook and Nellie Bell Louks; m David Henry Gordon Fairclough 1931; one s (deceased). *Education:* Hamilton Public and Secondary Schools. *Career:* Public Accountant 1935–57; Alderman Hamilton City Council 1946–49, Controller, Deputy Mayor 1950; MP (Progressive Cons) 1950–63, Sec of State 1957, Minister of Citizenship and Immigration 1958, Postmaster-Gen 1962; mem Canadian Del to UN 1950; Del Conf of Parliamentarians from NATO Countries 1955; Dir Canada Permanent until 1980; Patron The Huguenot Soc of Canada 1969, United Empire Loyalists Asscn, Hamilton Br 1980; Hon mem Zonta Int 1990–; numerous contribs to newspapers and magazines; Hon LL D (McMaster Univ) 1975, (Brock) 1996; awards include Woman of the Year (Canadian Business and Professional Women) 1963, Eleanor Roosevelt Humanitarian Award (Israel) 1984, elected to Hamilton Gallery of Distinction 1985, Persons Award (Ottawa) 1989. *Publications:* Saturday's Child (autobiog), numerous short stories and articles. *Leisure interests:* reading, photography, crossword puzzles, solitaire. *Address:* 25 Stanley Ave, Hamilton, ON L8P 2K9, Canada. *Telephone:* (416) 522-5248.

FAIRSTEIN, Linda; American lawyer and writer; b 1947; m Justin N. Feldman 1986. *Career:* Lawyer Office of the District Attorney, Manhattan, New York 1972, Head Sex Crimes Unit 1974; provides training for police, prosecution and medical staff, and rape counsellors. *Publication:* Final Jeopardy 1996. *Address:* c/o Little Brown & Co, Inc, 34 Beacon St, Boston, MA 02108, USA. *Internet:* members.aol.com/ feldfair.

FAISAL, Taujan; Israeli politician; b 1949; m. *Career:* TV presenter until 1989; parl candidate 1989; mem Knesset (Parl—first woman) 1993; delivered lecture at SOAS, London, UK 1994. *Address:* Knesset, Kiryat Ben-Gurion, Hakirya, Jerusalem 91950, Israel. *Telephone:* (2) 661211.

FALCUCCI, Franca; Italian politician; b 22 March 1926, Rome. *Career:* Mem Christian Democrat Party (DC) 1944–, Deputy Political Sec 1975–76, Chair European Union of Christian Democrat Women 1978; Senator for Rome VII, then for Cerreto Sannita (Campania)

1968; fmr Under-Sec of State, Ministry of Educ; Minister of Educ 1986–87. *Address:* Camera dei Deputati, piazza Montecitorio, 00186 Rome, Italy.

FALK, Elizabeth Moxley; American opera and theatre producer; b 21 Sept 1942, Memphis, TN; d of the late Warren Luke and of Elizabeth (née Beshears) Moxley; m Lee Harrison Falk 1976. *Education:* Blytheville High School. *Career:* Actress and singer 1961; Marketing Exec BBDO Advertising 1970–86; Theatre Producer New York Town Hall; Stage Man, later Producer New York Vineyard Opera and Co Man New Artists' Coalition 1986–88; Founder, Producer and Artistic Dir Pala Opera Asscn from 1989; Fellow Accademia Rossiniana, Pesaro. *Productions include:* The Tempest, The Soldier's Tale, Il Viaggio a Reims, La Gazza Ladra 1990, The Quicksilver Celebration 1991, Othello Meets Otello 1991, La Donna del Lago 1992, Hail Macbeth! 1992, Rigoletto, The Fool 1992; *Publications include:* White Tie and Veils, Goldsmith's Last Rites. *Leisure interests:* theatre, opera, scuba-diving. *Address:* 7 W 81st St, Suite 12C, New York, NY 10024, USA. *Telephone:* (212) 269-8760; *Fax:* (212) 769-8760.

FALK, Gathie; Canadian artist; b 31 Jan 1928, Alexander, MB; d of Cornelius and Agatha Falk; m Dwight Swanson 1974 (divorced). *Education:* Univ of British Columbia. *Career:* Painter, sculptor, performance artist; solo exhibitions include Canadian Cultural Centre, Paris 1974, Nat Gallery tour 1976–77, 49th Parallel, NY 1987, Vancouver Art Gallery Retrospective 1968–2000 2000; group exhibitions include Australian Nat Library, Museum of Modern Art, Toyama, Japan; comms include mural for Canadian Embassy, Washington, DC, USA 1988; Canadian Council short term grant 1967, Arts Bursary 1968, 1969, 1971; Sr Grant 1980; Sun Award 1968. *Address:* Equinox Gallery, 2321 Granville St, Vancouver, BC V6H 3G3, Canada.

FALKENDER, Baroness (Life Peer), cr 1974, of West Haddon, Northants, **Marcia Matilda Falkender,** CBE, BA; British politician; b 10 March 1932, Longbuckby, Northants; d of Harry Field; m George E. C. Williams 1955 (divorced 1961). *Education:* Northampton High School for Girls and Queen Mary Coll (Univ of London). *Career:* Pvt Sec to Sec-Gen, Lab Party 1954–56; Pvt and Political Sec to Harold Wilson 1956–83; mem House of Lords 1974–; Political Columnist Mail on Sunday 1982–88; Dir Peckham Bldg Soc 1986–91, S London Investment and Mortgage Corpn 1986–90, Milford Dock Co 1986–87; Pres UK Cttee UN Devt Fund for Women 1990–95; Chair Canvasback Productions 1989–91; mem British Screen Advisory Council 1985–; Trustee National Silver Trust 1988–; Gov Queen Mary and Westfield Coll, London Univ 1987–93, mem External Relations Cttee 1987–97. *Publications:* Inside Number 10 1972, Downing Street in Perspective 1983. *Leisure interests:* film industry, reading. *Address:* House of Lords, London SW1A 0PW, UK (Office); 3 Wyndham Mews, Upper Montagu St, London W1H 1RS, UK (Home). *Telephone:* (20) 7402-8570 (Office); *Fax:* (20) 7402-3407 (Office).

FALLACI, Oriana; Italian writer and journalist; b 29 June 1930, Florence; d of Edoardo and Tosca (née Cantini) Fallaci. *Education:* Liceo Classico 'Galileo Galilei' (Florence), and medical school. *Career:* Entered journalism 1946, Special Corresp 1950, War Corresp since 1967 (Vietnam, Indo-Pakistan war, Middle East, insurrections in S America); Hon D LITT (Columbia Coll, Chicago); St Vincent Prize for Journalism (twice); Bancarella Prize for Best Seller 1991; Hemingway Prize for Literature; numerous other prizes. *Publications:* The Useless Sex 1960, The Egotists 1965, If the Sun Dies 1968, Interview with History 1974; Novels: Penelope at War 1963, Nothing and So Be It 1969, Letter to a Child Never Born 1975, A Man (Premio Viareggio) 1979, Insiallah 1990; numerous articles in Life, Look, New York Times Magazine, Washington Post, New Republic, etc, and in Europe, Asia and S America. *Address:* c/o Rizzoli Corpn, 31 W 57th St, 14th Floor, New York, NY 10019, USA. *Telephone:* (212) 308-2000.

FALUDI, Susan C.; American journalist and writer; b 1960, Yorktown Heights, NY. *Education:* Harvard Univ. *Career:* Contrib Harvard Univ student newspaper; mem staff New York Times; Reporter Miami Herald, Atlanta Constitution, San José Mercury News; Reporter Wall Street Journal, San Francisco bureau 1990–; contribs to Ms and Mother Jones magazines; Pulitzer Prize 1991. *Publication:* Backlash: The

Undeclared War Against American Women 1991. *Address:* Sandra Dijkstra Literary Agency, 1155 Camino del Mar, Suite 515, Del Mar, CA 92014, USA.

FAN HSU, Hon Rita Lai-Tai, OBE, JP, M SC, M SOC SC; Hong Kong politician; b 20 Sept 1945, Shanghai, People's Repub of China; m Stephen Fan Sheung-tak; two c. *Education:* Univ of Hong Kong. *Career:* Chair Bd of Educ; mem Legis Council; mem Council Family Planning Asscn of Hong Kong; Assoc Dir Academic Services and Continuing Educ, Hong Kong Polytechnic; Hon Adviser Hong Kong Subsidized Secondary Schools Council; mem Hong Kong Psychological Soc, British Psychological Soc. *Address:* Legislative Council, Legislative Council Bldg, 8 Jackson Rd, Central, Hong Kong Special Administrative Region, People's Republic of China. *Telephone:* 8440868; *Fax:* 8101691.

FANTHORPE, Ursula Askham, CBE, MA, FRSA, FRSL; British poet and writer; b 22 July 1929; d of the late Richard Fanthorpe and the late Winifrid Elsie Askham Redmore. *Education:* St Catherine's School, Bramley, St Anne's Coll (Oxford), London Inst of Educ, Univ of Swansea. *Career:* Asst Mistress Cheltenham Ladies' Coll 1954–62, Head of English 1962–70; English teacher Howells School, Llandaff 1972–73; temp clerical work Bristol 1973–74; clerk/receptionist Burden Neurological Hosp Bristol 1974–89; Arts Council Writer-in-Residence, St Martin's Coll Lancaster 1983–85; freelance writer 1989–; contrib to radio and television programmes, various workshops and collaborations with artists and musicians; mem Nat Trust, Wildlife and Wetlands Trust, CPRE, Compassion in World Farming, Medical Foundation, Religious Soc of Friends, PEN 1980, Soc of Authors 1995; Hon Fellow Cheltenham & Glos Coll of Higher Ed 1995; Hon D LITT (West of England) 1995; Dr hc 2000; Soc of Authors' Travelling Fellowship 1986, Hawthornden Fellowship 1987, 1997, Arts Council Writers' Award 1994, Soc of Authors' Cholmondeley Award 1995. *Publications include:* Side Effects 1978, Standing To 1982, Voices Off 1984, A Watching Brief 1987, Neck-Verse 1992, Safe as Houses 1995, Consequences 2000; anthologies: Selected Poems 1986, Penguin Modern Poets 6 1996, Double Act (audiobook, jtly) 1997, Poetry Quartets 5 1999. *Address:* Culverhay House; Wotton-under-Edge, Glos GL12 7LS, UK. *Telephone:* (1453) 843105; *Fax:* (1453) 843105.

FAQIR MUHOMMAD, Roshan Kumari; Indian dancer and choreographer; b 24 Dec, Ambala, Haryana; d of the late Chowdhry Faqir Muhommad and Zohra Begam. *Education:* Privately. *Career:* Founder and teacher Nritya Kala Kendra Dance Acad, Bandra, Bombay (now Mumbai); specializes in Kathak dance style; has performed for Jawaharlal Nehru, Indira Gandhi, Nikita Khrushchev, King Hussein of Jordan, the King of Nepal, Dr Milton Obote, etc; choreographed and appeared in film Jalsaghar; choreographed and composed for films Lekin and Samporan Krishnain; awarded nat title Padmashri; Gaurav Puraskar, Govt of Maharastra; Nritya Vilash; Nritya Shromani; Nritya Parangat; Sangeet Natak Akademi President's Award 1976; Maharashtra Gauray Puruskar 1990. *Leisure interests:* music, cooking, gardening. *Address:* 3/9 Kashi Kung, Water Field Rd, Bandra, Mumbai 400 050, India. *Telephone:* (22) 6427552.

FARAGÓ, Katinka; Swedish film producer; b 16 Dec 1936, Vienna, Austria; d of Alexander Faragó; m 1st Raymond Lundberg 1963; m 2nd Måns Reuterswürd 1984; two d. *Career:* Script-girl 1953; worked with Ingmar Bergman 1954–84; Head of Production Sandrew Film and Theatre, Stockholm from 1989. *Films include:*, Fanny and Alexander, Sacrifice, Good Evening Mr Wallenberg, Autumn Sonata 1978 (Golden Bug, Best Film in Sweden 1991), The White Lioness 1996. *Leisure interests:* film, family. *Address:* Sandrews, POB 5612, 114 86 Stockholm, Sweden (Office); Roddargatan 5, 185 32 Varholm, Sweden (Home). *Telephone:* (8) 234 700 (Office); *Fax:* (8) 103 850 (Office).

FAREMO, Grete, LL B; Norwegian politician; b 16 June 1955, Byglandsfjord, Setesdal; d of Osmund and Tora Faremo; partner Magne Lindholm; one c. *Career:* Fmr mem staff Ministry of Finance and Directorate for Devt Co-operation (NORAD); Head of Div Ministry of Devt Co-operation 1984, Minister of Devt Co-operation 1991–93; Chief Negotiating Officer Aker Eiendom 1986; Dir (of Cultural Affairs) Aker Brygge (business and leisure complex), Norsk Arbeiderpresse; Minister of Justice and Peace 1994–97; mem Arbeiderparti (Labour

Party), mem Bd Arbeiderparti Forum for Art and Culture. *Address:* c/o Norwegian Labour Party, Youngstorget 2, POB 8743, Oslo, Norway (Office); Theresesgt 7B, 0358 Oslo, Norway (Home).

FARHI, Nicole; French fashion designer; b 25 July 1946, Nice; d of Ephraim and Marcelle (née Babani) Farhi; fmr partner Stephen Marks; one d; m David Hare 1992. *Education:* Lycée Calmette (Nice) and Cours Berçot Art School (Paris). *Career:* Designer with Pierre D'Alby, Paris 1968; f French Connection, London with Stephen Marks 1973; fmr designer Stephen Marks; Founder and Designer Nicole Farhi 1983, Nicole Farhi For Men 1989, Nicole's Restaurant 1994; British Fashion Award for Best Contemporary Designer 1995, 1996, 1997. *Leisure interest:* sculpture. *Address:* 16 Foubert's Place, London W1V 1HH, UK. *Telephone:* (20) 7287-8787.

FARLEY, Carole, MUS B; American opera singer (soprano); b 29 Nov 1946, Le Mars, IA; d of Melvin and Irene (née Reid) Farley; m Jose Serebrier 1969; one d. *Education:* Indiana Univ and Hochschule für Musik (Munich, Germany). *Career:* US operatic debut in title role of La Belle Hélène, New York City Opera 1969; Paris debut Nat Orchestra 1975, London debut Royal Philharmonic Soc 1975, S American debut Teatro Colón (Buenos Aires) 1975, Metropolitan Opera as Lulu 1977; now appears regularly in leading opera houses of the world and in concert performances with major orchestras in the USA, S America, South Africa, Australia and Europe; Metropolitan Opera première of Shostakovich's Lady Macbeth of Mztensk (Katerina Ismailova); Wozzeck (Marie), Toulouse Opera; mem American Guild of Musical Artists; several awards and prizes including Grand Prix du Disque 1995, 1997. *Operas include:* Manon, Idomeneo, La Traviata, Tales of Hoffmann, Salome, Eugene Onegin, Wozzeck, Lady Macbeth of Mztensk, Mahagonny, Elektra; *Recordings include:* Le Pré aux Clercs, Behold the Sun, French Songs by Chausson, Duparc, Satie, Fauré (German Music Critics Award 1989), Prokofiev Songs, Poulenc's The Human Voice, Menotti's The Telephone (with Scottish Chamber Orchestra), Britten's Les Illuminations, Prokofiev's The Ugly Duckling, Kurt Weill songs, Milhaud songs (with John Constable), Tchaikovsky Opera Arias, Guntram, Strauss Final Scenes from Daphne and Capriccio, Beethoven's Symphony No 9, Delius songs with orchestra; *Film videos include:* Poulenc's La Voix Humaine, Menotti's The Telephone, Strauss's Four Last Songs and Songs with orchestra. *Leisure interests:* skiing, jogging, swimming, dancing, cooking, entertaining, reading. *Address:* 20 Queen's Gate Gardens, London SW7 5LZ, UK. *Telephone:* (20) 7584-7626; *Fax:* (20) 7584-7626; *E-mail:* michael@ rlombardo.com (Office); caspi123@aol.com (Home); *Internet:* www .phoenixartists.co.uk (Office).

FARLEY, Peggy, MA; American banking executive; b 12 March 1947; d of Harry E. and Ruth F. Farley. *Education:* Barnard Coll and Columbia Univ (NY). *Career:* Admissions Officer Barnard Coll, NY 1973–76; Admin Citibank NA, Athens, Greece 1976–77; Consultant Org Resources Counselors, New York, NY 1977–78; Sr Assoc Morgan Stanley and Co Inc, New York, NY 1978–84; Man Dir, CEO AMAS Securities Inc, New York, NY 1984–98, mem Bd Dirs AMAS Group, London; Pres, CEO, Bd Dirs Ascent/Meredith Asset Man Inc, New York 1999–. *Publication:* The Place of the Yankee and Euro Bond Markets in a Financing Program for The People's Republic of China 1982. *Address:* Ascent/Meredith Asset Management Inc, 712 Fifth Ave, New York, NY 10019, USA.

FARMER, Beverley Anne, BA; Australian writer; b 1941, Melbourne; one s. *Education:* Univ of Melbourne. *Publications:* Alone, Milk (NSW Premier's Prize for Fiction) 1984, Home Time, A Body of Water, The Seal Woman, The House in the Light, Place of Birth, Collected Stories. *Address:* c/o University of Queensland Press, POB 42, St Lucia, Queensland 4067, Australia.

FARRELL, Eileen; American opera singer; b 1920, Williamantic, CT; d of Michael Farrell and Catherine Kennedy; m Robert V. Reagan 1946; one s one d. *Career:* Debut with Columbia Broadcasting Co 1941, own programme until 1947; opera debut with San Francisco Opera, CA; has toured extensively in USA and world-wide; several hon degrees; Grammy Award. *Operas include:* Il Trovatore; *Albums include:* Handel: Messiah 1985, I Gotta Right to Sing the Blues 1991, Theresien Mass

1992, Greatest Hits: Opera 1994, Eileen Farrell Sings Verdi 1997, As You Like It 2000. *Address:* c/o International Creative Management Artists Ltd, 40 W 57th St, New York, NY 10019, USA.

FARRELL, Suzanne; American ballet dancer; b 16 Aug 1945, Cincinnati; d of Robert Ficker and Donna Holly; m Paul Mejia 1969 (divorced 1997). *Education:* Cincinnati Conservatory of Music and School of American Ballet. *Career:* New York City Ballet 1961–69, 1975–89, featured dancer since 1962, Prin Dancer 1965–89; also danced with Béjart Ballet, Brussels; appeared in numerous Balanchine ballets choreographed for her including Mozartiana, Chaconne, Meditation, Vienna Waltzes; staged seven Balanchine ballets at John F. Kennedy Center for Performing Arts, Washington, DC 1995 and many other stagings of Balanchine's works; repetiteur for Balanchine Trust, including Kirov Ballet, Royal Danish Ballet and Paris Opéra Ballet; mem Advisory Panel Princess Grace Foundation, Sr Advisory Bd of Arthritis Foundation; trains ballet dancers in camp The Adirondacks; Mademoiselle magazine Merit Award 1965; Dance magazine award 1976; New York City Award of Honor for Arts and Culture 1979; A. Einstein Coll of Medicine Spirit Achievement Award 1980; Emmy Award 1985; American Acad of Achievement Golden Plate Award 1987; New York State Gov's Arts Award 1988. *Ballets include:* Ah, Vous Dirais-je, Maman?, Romeo and Juliet, Nijinsky, Clown of God 1971, Bolero, The Rite of Spring, I Trionfi; *Film:* Midsummer Night's Dream; *TV programmes include:* Balanchine Dance in America; *Publication:* Holding on to the Air (autobiog) 1990. *Address:* Kennedy Center for the Performing Arts, Washington, DC 20566, USA.

FARRINGTON OF RIBBLETON, Baroness (Life Peer), cr 1994, of Fulwood in the County of Lancashire, **Josephine Farrington;** British organization executive; b 29 June 1940; m Michael James Farrington 1960; three s. *Career:* Chair Educ Cttee, Lancashire Co Council 1981–91, Chair 1992; Leader Lab Group, Asscn of Co Councils 1987–94, Vice-Chair 1990–94, Chair 1994–96, Chair Policy Cttee 1993–94; mem Consultative Council for Local Govt Finance 1987–; Pres Cttee for Culture, Educ and the Media, Council of Europe 1989–94; UK Rep Cttee of the Regions 1994–, Chair Educ and Training Cttee 1994–; UK Woman of Europe 1994. *Address:* 114 Victoria Rd, Fulwood, Preston PR2 4NN, UK. *Telephone:* (20) 7201-1500 (London); (1772) 718836 (Preston).

FARRIS, Vera King, PH D; American college president and zoologist; b 18 July 1940, Atlantic City, NJ; d of Henry King and Ida E. Norton; one s. *Education:* Tuskegee Inst and Univ of Massachusetts. *Career:* Fmrly Academic Vice-Pres Kean Coll (NJ), Vice-Provost Academic Affairs, State Univ of New York at Brockport, Dean State Univ of New York at Stony Brook; apptd Pres Stockton State Coll (NJ) 1983; Vice-Pres Middle States Asscn of Colls and Schools; mem Asscn of New Jersey Governing Bds, Acad of the Governor's Pride of New Jersey, Nominating Cttee of the American Asscn of State Colls and Univs; numerous contribs to professional journals; Hon D HUM LITT (St Peter's Coll, Marymount Manhattan Coll, Sojourner-Douglass); Hon D IUR (Monmouth Coll); Hon D SC (Johnson, Wales); awards include Hon Citizen of Atlanta (GA) 1984, Certification of Appreciation B'nai B'rith 1986, Award of Nat Asscn of Black Women in Higher Educ 1986, People of the Year Award (Galloway Township Educ Foundation) 1988. *Leisure interests:* knitting, plants, films, walking. *Address:* Stockton State College, Office of the President, Pomona, NJ 08240, USA (Office); 300 Shore Rd, Linwood, NJ 08221, USA (Home). *Telephone:* (602) 652-4521; *Fax:* (602) 652-4945.

FARROW, Maureen A., B SC; British economist and business executive; b 20 July 1943, Molesey; d of George Arthur and Winnifred Ivy (née Gregory) Pickett; m John E. L. Farrow 1969; one s. *Education:* Hull Univ and York Univ (ON, Canada). *Career:* Market Research Man Ultra Electronics 1966–69; Vice-Pres Singer Assocs, Canada 1972–82; Pres C. D. Howe Inst, Canada 1987–89; Partner, Chief Economist Coopers and Lybrand (now PricewaterhouseCoopers) Consulting Group 1982–92, Chief Economist Coopers and Lybrand Canada 1992; Pres Economap Canada 1992–; Economist Loewen, Ondaatje, McCutcheon Ltd 1994–99; Dir Canadian Chamber of Commerce 1990–96, Nat Ballet School 1991–95, Equitable Life Insurance Co; Pres Canadian Asscn of Business Economists 1983–85; mem Bd Social Sciences and Humanities Research Council of Canada 1985–91,

Ontario Round Table on the Environment and Econ (Mining and Energy Task Force) 1991, Nat Trustco Inc 1992–97; Trustee Imperial Oil Pension and Savings Fund 1993–97; Fellow Inst of Management Consultants of Ontario; numerous publs on the econ, competition and the environment. *Leisure interests:* current affairs, ballet, gardening, travel. *Address:* 30A Hazelton Ave, Toronto, ON M5R 2E2, Canada (Office); 15 Douglas Drive, Toronto, ON M4W 2B2, Canada (Home). *Telephone:* (416) 964-4486 (Office); *Fax:* (416) 964-4490 (Office).

FARROW, Mia Villiers; American actress; b 9 Feb 1945, CA; d of John Villiers Farrow and Maureen O'Sullivan; m 1st Frank Sinatra 1966 (divorced 1968); m 2nd André Previn 1970 (divorced 1979); partner Woody Allen, until 1992; fourteen c. *Career:* Stage debut 1963; French Acad Award for best actress 1969; David Donatello Award (Italy) 1969; Rio de Janeiro Film Festival Award 1969; San Sebastian Award. *Plays include:* The Importance of Being Earnest 1963, Mary Rose, The Three Sisters, House of Bernarda Alba 1972–73, The Marrying of Ann Leete 1975, The Zykovs 1976, Ivanov 1976, Romantic Comedy 1979; *Films include:* Guns at Batasi 1964, Rosemary's Baby 1968, Secret Ceremony 1969, John and Mary 1969, See No Evil 1970, The Great Gatsby 1973, Full Circle 1978, A Wedding 1978, Death on the Nile 1978, The Hurricane 1979, A Midsummer Night's Sex Comedy 1982, Zelig 1983, Broadway Danny Rose 1984, Purple Rose of Cairo 1985, Hannah and her Sisters 1986, Radio Days 1987, September 1988, Another Woman 1988, Oedipus Wrecks 1989, Crimes and Misdemeanours, Alice 1990, Husbands and Wives 1992, Widow's Peak 1994, Miami Rhapsody 1995, Private Parts 1997, Reckless, Coming Soon; *TV appearances include:* Peyton Place 1964–66, Johnny Belinda 1965, Peter Pan 1975, Goodbye Raggedy Ann (TV film), Miracle at Midnight; *Publication:* What Falls Away (autobiog) 1996. *Leisure interests:* reading, mind wandering, listening to music and certain people. *Address:* c/o Sam Cohn, International Creative Management, 40 W 57th St, New York, NY 10019, USA.

FASSBAENDER, Brigitte; German opera singer (mezzo-soprano); b 3 July 1939, Berlin; d of the late Willi Domgraf-Fassbaender and Sabine Peters. *Education:* Nuremberg Conservatoire and studied with father. *Career:* Debut Bavarian State Opera, Munich 1961; teacher of Solo Vocal Music Musikhochschule, Munich; appearances at La Scala (Milan, Italy), Vienna State Opera and Salzburg (Austria), Royal Opera House (Covent Garden, London), Metropolitan Opera (New York) and San Francisco (CA, USA); Teacher of Solo Vocal Music Musikhochschule, Munich; soloist, Dir of Opera, Braunschweig; Fellow Royal Northern Coll of Music (UK) 1991–; awards include Bundesverdienstkreuz am Bande, Bayerischer Verdienstorden; Dr hc. *Recording:* Hyperion Schubert Edn (vol 11) 1992. *Address:* c/o American Theatre, 38100 Braunschweig, Germany.

FASSIE, Brenda; South African singer; m Nhlanhla Mbambo 1989 (separated); one s. *Career:* Performed at Viva South Africa music festival, London, UK 1994. *Songs include:* Don't Follow Me I'm Married; *Album:* I'm Not a Bad Girl 1992.

FATHIMA BEEVI, M.S., B SC, LL B; Indian politician and judge; b 30 April 1927, Pathananthitta, Kerala; d of Meera Sahib. *Career:* Enrolled as advocate 1950; practised in civil, criminal, and revenue fields at Quilon and Ernakulam; Subordinate Judge 1968; Dist and Sessions Judge 1974; Judicial mem Income Tax Appellate Tribunal 1980; Judge, Kerala High Court 1983–89, Supreme Court of India 1989–92; Gov of Tamil Nadu 1997–; mem Nat Human Rights Comm 1993; Mahila Shiromani Award 1990. *Address:* Office of the Governor, Raj Bhavan, Chennai, Tamil Nadu, India; Anna Veedu, Petta, Pathananthitta, Kerala, India (Home). *Telephone:* (44) 5360099 (Office); (44) 2351313 (Home).

FATIN, Hon Wendy Francis, B SC; Australian politician; b 10 April 1941, Harvey, WA; one s one d. *Education:* W Australia Inst of Tech. *Career:* Registered Nurse; Adviser to Minister for Repatriation and Compensation and Minister for Social Security 1974–75; Political Research Asst 1975–77, 1981–83; mem House of Reps (Australian Lab Party) for Canning, WA 1983, for Brand, WA 1984–96, mem Govt Econ Cttee 1983–87, House of Reps Standing Cttee on Community Affairs 1987–96, on Employment, Educ and Training 1987–96; Minister for Local Govt, Minister assisting Prime Minister for Status of

Women 1990–93, Minister for Arts and Territories 1991–93; Foundermem Women's Electoral Lobby; Fellow Coll of Nursing of Australia. *Address:* Lot 46, Soldiers Rd, Roleystone, WA 6111, Australia.

FAULSTICH-WIELAND, Hannelore Hilde, PH D; German professor of educational science; b 10 Dec 1948, Hann Münden; d of Karl Heinz and Edith Wieland; m Peter Faulstich 1967; two s. *Education:* High School (Simi Valley, CA, USA), Hann Münden and Tech Univ of Berlin. *Career:* Asst Prof Tech Univ of Berlin 1973–77; Researcher in Educ, Göttingen, Kassel, Dortmund; Deputy Head Women's Research Center, Hanover 1982–84; Prof Fachhochschule, Frankfurt/Main 1984–92; Prof of Women's Studies Univ of Münster 1992–96; Prof of Educational Science Univ of Hamburg 1997–. *Publications:* Berufsorientierende Beratung von Mädchen 1982, Der Weg zur modernen Bürokommunikation 1987, Computer-Cultur 1988, Weibliche Identität 1989, Koedukation—enttäuschte Hoffnungen 1991, Entdramatisierung der Differenzen 1995, Trennt uns bitte, bitte nicht 1995, Geschlecht und Erziehung 1995, Individuum und Gesellschaft 2000. *Leisure interests:* swimming, science fiction. *Address:* University of Hamburg, Department of Education, 20146 Hamburg, Edmund-Siemers-Allee 1. *Telephone:* (5541) 912950; *Fax:* (5541) 912952; *E-mail:* faulstich-wieland@erzwiss.uni-hamburg.de; *Internet:* www.erzwiss .uni-hamburg.de.

FAWCETT, Farrah; American actress; b 2 Feb 1947, Corpus Christi, TX; d of James William and Pauline Alice Fawcett; m Lee Majors 1973 (divorced); partner Ryan O'Neal; one s. *Education:* Univ of Texas. *Career:* Signed by Screen Gems. *TV appearances include:* Series: Charlie's Angels, Good Sports, The Six Million Dollar Man, The Rockford Files; TV Films: Three's a Crowd, The Feminist and the Fuzz, The Girl Who Came Gift-Wrapped, Murder on Flight 502, Nazi Hunter: The Beate Klarsfeld Story, Poor Little Rich Girl: The Barbara Hutton Story, Margaret Bourke-White, Small Sacrifices, Criminal Behavior, The Substitute Wife, Children of the Dust; *Play:* Extremities 1983; *Films include:* Love is a Funny Thing, Myra Breckinridge, Logan's Run 1976, Somebody Killed Her Husband 1978, Sunburn 1979, Saturn 3, Cannonball Run 1980, Extremities 1986, See You in the Morning, Man of the House, The Apostle 1999, The Love Master 2000, Dr T and the Women 2000.

FAWSETT, Patricia C., MA, JD; American judge; b 1943. *Education:* Univ of Florida. *Career:* Pvt law practice Akerman, Senterfitt & Edison, Orlando, FL 1973–86; Commr 9th Circuit Judicial Nominating Comm 1973–75; Greater Orlando Crime Prevention Asscn 1983–86; Judge US Dist Court, Orlando 1986–; Commr Orlando Housing Authority 1976–80; mem ABA, American Judicature Soc, Asscn of Trial Lawyers of America. *Address:* US District Court, Federal Bldg, 80 N Hughey Ave, Orlando, FL 32801, USA.

FAYE, Safi, PH D; Senegalese film director; b 1943, Dakar. *Career:* Acting debut in Petit à petit, then feature film dir; first African woman to direct a feature film 1975. *Films directed:* La Passante (short) 1972, Kaddu Beykatt (Letter From a Peasant, special mention at Pan-African Film Festival, Ouagadougou, Burkina Faso) 1975, Fad'gal 1979, Goob Na Nu (The Harvest is Over, short) 1979, Man sa yay (I, Your Mother) 1980, Les âmes au soleil (short) 1981, Selbé parmi tant d'autres (short) 1981, Selbe: One Among Many 1983, Mosane 1996. *Address:* c/o Synergy Gender and Development, BP 3370, Dakar, Senegal.

FEDDEN, (Adye) Mary, OBE, RA; British artist; b 14 Aug 1915, Bristol; d of H. V. Fedden and I. M. Prichard; m Julian Trevelyan 1951 (died 1988). *Education:* Badminton School (Bristol) and Slade School of Art (London). *Career:* Taught painting Royal Coll of Art 1956–64, Yehudi Menuhin School 1964–74; exhibitions Redfern, Beaux Arts, Christopher Hull and New Grafton Galleries, London and various provincial galleries 1948–; works purchased by HM The Queen, Tate Gallery, Crown Prince of Jordan; Pres Royal W of England Acad 1984–88; Hon D LITT (Bath). *Leisure interests:* cycling, reading.

FEDORUK, Sylvia O., OC, MA, D SC; Canadian professor of physics and politician; b 5 May 1927, Canora, SK; d of Theodore and Annie Fedoruk. *Education:* Univs of Saskatchewan, Windsor and W Ontario. *Career:* Asst Physicist Saskatoon Cancer Clinic 1951, Sr Physicist 1957; Asst Prof Univ of Saskatchewan 1956, Prof of Physics 1973–86,

Chancellor 1986–89, now Prof Emer; Nuclear Medicine Consultant IAEA, Vienna 1966, 1968, 1969; mem Atomic Energy Control Bd of Canada 1973–88; Lieut-Gov Prov of Saskatchewan 1988–94; fmr Dir Sports Fed of Canada; Queen's Jubilee Medal 1977; YWCA Woman of the Year 1986. *Leisure interests:* curling, fishing, golf. *Address:* Government House, 4607 Dewdney Ave, Regina, SK S4P 3V7, Canada (Office); 49 Simpson Crescent, Saskatoon SK S7H 3C5, Canada (Home).

FEDULOVA, Alevtina Vasilevna; Russian party official; b 14 April 1940, Elektrostal, Moscow Region; m Gennadij Fedulov; one s. *Education:* Moscow Region Pedagogical Inst, Acad of Social Science. *Career:* Mem CPSU 1963–91; Sec then First Sec City Komsomol Cttee 1957–67, Sec Moscow Region Komsomol 1967–71, Sec Cen Komsomol Cttee 1977–84; Chair Cen Bd All-Union Pioneers' Org 1971–77; mem Cen Revision Comm, CPSU Cen Cttee 1981–86; Exec Sec Soviet Peace Cttee 1984–87; First Deputy Chair Cttee of Soviet Women 1987–91, Chair 1991–92; Chair Russian Union of Women 1991; mem State Duma (Parl) 1994–96, Deputy Chair 1994–96; numerous articles in newspapers and magazines; Leader Women of Russia Party; Order of Honour 1976; Order of Labour 1981; Order of Service to the Country 1985; Friendship of People's Order 1986. *Leisure interests:* crafts, flowers. *Address:* State Duma, 103009 Moscow, Okhotny Ryad 1, Russian Federation; 103832 Moscow, Glinishevskij per 6, Russian Federation. *Telephone:* (095) 292-08-52; (095) 229-32-32; *Fax:* (095) 200-02-74.

FEIJI, Vivi Mint; Mauritanian business executive. *Career:* Began career as Personnel Officer State Carpet Co, mid 1960s; Founder and Dir Matis Rugs 1990–. *Address:* c/o Union Mauritanienne des Femmes, Entreprenantes et Commercantes, BP 2858 Nouakchott, Mauritania.

FEILER, Jo Alison, MFA; American fine art photographer; b 16 April 1951, Los Angeles, CA. *Education:* Univ of California, Art Center Coll of Design and California Inst of the Arts. *Career:* Art Dir Log/An Inc 1975–85; Photography Ed, Coast Environment Magazine 1970–72; Asst Dir Frank Perls Gallery, Beverly Hills, CA 1969–70; numerous group and solo exhibitions including Susan Harder Gallery (New York) 1984, California Inst of the Arts 1975, Inst of Contemporary Art (London) 1975, Museum of Fine Arts (Houston, TX) 1983, Santa Fe Center for Photography (NM) 1983, Canon Photo Gallery (Amsterdam) 1980; represented in public and pvt collections including J. Paul Getty Museum (CA), Museum of Modern Art (New York), Metropolitan Museum of Art (New York), Smithsonian Inst (Washington, DC), Royal Photographic Soc of Great Britain, Victoria and Albert Museum (London), Bibliothèque Nat (Paris), Fondation Vincent Van Gogh (Arles, France); numerous comms for magazines; Certificate of Art Excellence, Los Angeles Co Musuem of Art 1968; Scholarship Grant Inst of the Arts, CA 1974; Cash Award, All California Photography Show 1976. *Leisure interests:* collecting art, books, cross-country skiing, music, cooking. *Telephone:* (212) 772-7187; *Fax:* (212) 772-0553.

FEINSTEIN, Dianne; American politician; b 22 June 1933, San Francisco, CA; d of Leon and Betty (née Rosenburg) Goldman; m 1st Bertram Feinstein 1962 (deceased); one d; m 2nd Richard C. Blum 1980. *Education:* Stanford Univ (CA). *Career:* Intern in Public Affairs Coro Foundation, San Francisco 1955–56; Asst to California Industrial Welfare Comm, Los Angeles and San Francisco 1956–57; Vice-Chair California Women's Bd Terms and Parole 1962–66; Chair San Francisco City and Co Advisory Comm for Adult Detention 1967–69; Superintendant City and Co of San Francisco 1970–78, Mayor 1978–88; Democrat Cand Governorship of California 1990; Senator from California 1993–; mem Bd of Govs Bay Area Council 1972–, Democratic Nat Cttee and numerous other public bodies; numerous hon degrees. *Address:* US Senate, 331 Senate Hart Office Bldg, Washington, DC 20510, USA.

FELLINGER, Imogen, PH D; German musicologist; b Munich; d of Wolfgang and Lola Margarete Fellinger. *Education:* Gymnasium (Munich), Univs of Munich and Tübingen. *Career:* Research Collaborator Int Inventory of Musical Sources (RISM) for W Germany and W Berlin 1957–62; Chair Research Dept for Music Bibliography (19th Century), Inst of Musicology, Univ of Cologne 1963–70; Chair 19th

Century Music Archive, State Inst for Music Research, Prussian Culture Collection, Berlin 1970–93, Sr Lecturer 1983–93; Chair Working Group on Music Periodicals, Int Asscn of Music Libraries, Archives and Documentation Centres (IAML) 1979–, Rep to Répertoire Int de la Presse Musicale 1992–; Founder-mem Johannes Brahms Gesamtausgabe 1983–; mem Kuratorium Österreichische Johannes Brahms Gesellschaft 1991–. *Publications:* Über die Dynamik in der Musik von J. Brahms 1961, Verzeichnis der Musikzeitschriften des 19. Jahrhunderts 1968, Klavierstücke, Opus 118 und 119 von J. Brahms (ed) 1974, Periodica Musicalia 1789–1830 1986, R. Fellinger, Klänge um Brahms 1997; numerous contribs to music periodicals, dictionaries, congress reports and collections. *Address:* St Anna-Platz 10, 80538 Munich, Germany. *Telephone:* (89) 225287.

FENG LANRUI; Chinese economist; b 17 Sept 1920, Guiyang, Guizhou Prov; d of Feng Shaotang and Xie Guangyu; m Li Chang 1946; two s two d. *Education:* Senior Party School of the CCP Central Cttee. *Career:* Ed and Reporter Jin-Cha-Ji Daily 1945–46; Ed-in-Chief Harbin Daily 1949–54; Dir Teaching and Research Section of Political Econ, Polytechnic Inst of Harbin 1956–59; Deputy Dir Heilongjiang Inst of Econs, Heilongjiang Provincial Bureau of Statistics 1959–64; Deputy Dir Policy Research Section, State Comm for Cultural Relations with Foreign Countries 1965–75; mem State Council Political Research Dept 1975–80; Sr Research Fellow, Prof Inst of Marxism-Leninism and Mao Zedong Thought, Chinese Acad of Social Sciences 1980–86, Deputy Dir 1980–82, Adviser 1983–86, Deputy Chair 1986–89, mem Academic Council 1990–; mem Editorial Cttee Encyclopedia of People's Repub of China (vol Scientific Socialism) 1980–, A Comprehensive Dictionary of Economics (vol Population, Labour and Consumption) 1983–; Sec-Gen China Council of Econ Asscns 1981–91; mem Standing Cttee Chinese People's Friendship Asscn 1986–94; Sun Yefang Prize 1984; Xinhya Digests Prize for Most Impressive Article of the Year 1998. *Publications include:* Labour: Payment and Employment (collected articles) 1982, On the Relationship between Employment and Economic Growth (jtly) 1983, On Letting Some People Get Rich Ahead of Others 1984, Overcome Egalitarianism and Let Some People Get Rich Ahead of Others 1985, More on Letting Some People Get Rich Ahead of Others 1986, Distribution According to Work, Wage and Employment 1988, On the Ageing of the Chinese Population 1989, The Labour Market of China 1991, Social Security Must be Unified 1994, Actively Foster the Labour Market 1995, Can Inflation be Reduced under 10% for the Current Year?, Unemployment in China: 21% by the year 2000? 1996, The Restructuring of China's Social Security System 1997, A Collection of Selected Economic Articles (2 vols) 1999, and numerous articles on the market economy. *Leisure interests:* art, literature. *Address:* 34 Dongzongbu Hutong, 100005 Beijing, People's Republic of China. *Telephone:* 6512 4654 (Home).

FENG YING; Chinese ballet dancer; b 28 Feb 1963, Harbin; m James Y. Ho 1989; one d. *Education:* Beijing Dance Acad. *Career:* Paris Opera Ballet School 1982–83; Prin Dancer Cen Ballet of China 1980–; leading role in many classical and Chinese ballets; guest artist, 2nd Paris Int Ballet Competition 1986; toured USA, UK, Russia, Japan, Singapore, Hong Kong, Taiwan; mem Chinese Dancers' Asscn 1982, China Ballet Art Soc 1992; First Prize Pas de Deux, Nat Ballet Competition 1987; award at 5th Japan World Ballet Competition 1987; First Class Dancer of the State 1987. *Address:* Central Ballet of China, 3 Taiping St, Beijing, 100050, People's Republic of China.

FENGER MØLLER, Grethe, BL; Danish politician; b 6 Nov 1941, Frederiksberg; d of Torben Fenger Møller. *Education:* Univ of Copenhagen. *Career:* Sec in Ministries of Labour and Social Affairs; Pres Dansk Kvindesamfund (Soc of Danish Women); mem Folketinget (Parl, Konservative Folkeparti—Cons People's Party) since 1977; Minister of Labour 1982–86; Dept of Social Affairs. *Address:* Ministry of Social Affairs, Holmens Kanal 22, 1060 Copenhagen K, Denmark. *Telephone:* 33-37-50-00; *Fax:* 33-32-85-36; *E-mail:* dpgfm@sm.dk.

FENNER, Dame Peggy Edith, DBE, DL; British politician; b 12 Nov 1922, London; m Bernard Sidney Fenner 1940; one d. *Career:* Local govt 1957–71; MP (Cons) 1970–97; Jr Minister of Agric, Fisheries and Food 1972–74, 1981–86; UK Rep to Council of Europe and WEU 1987–97. *Address:* House of Commons, London SW1A 0AA, UK. *Telephone:* (20) 7219-3000; *Fax:* (20) 7219-4956.

FENNING, Lisa Hill, BA, JD; American mediator and former federal judge; b 22 Feb 1952, Chicago, IL; d of Ivan Byron and Joan Hill; m Alan Mark Fenning 1977; four c. *Education:* Wellesley Coll and Yale Univ. *Career:* Legal clerk US Court of Appeals (7th circuit), Chicago 1974–75; called to Bar, IL 1975, CA 1979; Assoc Jenner & Block, Chicago 1975–77, O'Melveny & Myers, Los Angeles 1977–85; Judge US Bankruptcy Court, Los Angeles 1985–2000; Mediator JAMS, Orange, CA 2000–; Guest Lecturer Southwestern School of Law and School of Business, Univ of Southern California; Vice-Pres Nat Conf on Women's Bar Asscns, Baltimore 1985–86, Pres elect 1986–87, Pres 1987–88; mem Bd of Govs Nat Conf of Bankruptcy Judges 1989–92, mem Bd Trustees Endowment for Education 1992–, Chair 1994–95, Benchmarks Ed 'NCBJ Newsletter' 1991–; mem Bd Dirs American Bankruptcy Inst 1994–, Bd Advisors Nat Judicial Educ Program to Promote Equality for Women and Men in the Courts 1994–, Nat Asscn of Women Judges; Fellow ABA 1992, American Coll of Bankruptcy 1994. *Address:* JAMS, Suite 600, 500 N State College Blvd, Orange, CA 92868, USA.

FERAUD, Aura, PH D; Panamanian lawyer. *Education:* Colegio San Vincent, Instituto Pan-Americano, Univ Santa Maria La Antigua and Univ Complutense de Madrid (Spain). *Career:* Attorney Arias, Fabrega and Fabrega 1975–76, Mendoza and Assocs 1976–77; est her own law firm 1978; Gen Attorney Office of Gen Counsel of Panama Canal Comm (part-time) 1979–91; mem Christian Democratic Party 1986, Asst to the Presidency for Int Affairs 1987–89; Attorney-Gen for Admin 1990–91; Chair Nat Ethics Council 1995–; Consultant Fundación para la Promoción de la Mujer, Junta Comunal de Bella Vista; has given numerous lectures in Panama; mem Instituto Iberoamericano de Derecho Aeronautico y del Espacio y de la Aviación Comercial 1973–, Panama Bar Asscn 1975–, Inter-American Bar Asscn 1984–; awards include Andres S. Flemming Award (for outstanding services to US Fed Govt) 1983; Gold Medal Public Service Award, Panama Canal Comm 1985; Outstanding Woman of the Year, Asscn of Women from the Univ of Panama 1990; Distinguished Woman of the Community, Soroptomist International 1991. *Address:* Calle 42 no 9, y avda Cuba, CP 6899, Panamá, Panama. *Telephone:* 227-0627; *Fax:* 225-2211.

FERGE, Zsuzsa, PH D; Hungarian sociologist; b 25 April 1931, Budapest; d of George and Ágota (née Keller) Kecskeméti; m Sándor Ferge 1953 (died 1993); one d one s. *Education:* Univ of Econ Sciences and Hungarian Acad of Sciences. *Career:* Statistician Cen Statistical Office 1953–68; Sociologist Inst of Sociology, Hungarian Acad of Sciences 1968–89; Prof and Head Dept of Social Policy, Lóránd Eötvös Univ, Budapest 1989–2001; mem European Acad 1993–, Hungarian Acad of Sciences 1998–; has received state decorations, Széchenyi Prize 1995; hon degree (Edinburgh) 1997. *Publications include:* In English: A Society in the Making: Hungarian Social and Societal Policy 1945–1975 (1979), Dynamics of Deprivation (co-ed) 1987, Social Policy in a Changing Europe (co-ed) 1992; In Hungarian: Social Stratification 1969, Social Reproduction and Societal Policy 1982, Politics of Poverty in Hungary 1986, Is There a Fourth Road? 1989, Selected Essays on Societal Policy 1991, Inequalities Broke Loose 2001; over 200 papers in professional journals. *Address:* c/o Ministry of Foreign Affairs, Economic Development Division, POB 174, Belmopan, Belize. *Telephone:* (361) 372-2994; *E-mail:* fergesp@ludens.elte.hu.

FERGUSON, Marnie H., BA; Canadian business executive; b 10 April 1949, Linday (ON); d of Noble William Eberts and Gladys Eileen (née Smith-Emsley) Eberts; m Garry S. Ferguson 1969; three s. *Education:* Ryerson Polytechnic Inst, Waterloo Lutheran Univ and Univ of Waterloo. *Career:* Various human resources man posts in consumer packaged-goods industries; Dir Human Resources Monsanto Canada Inc 1989–91, Vice-Pres, People, Quality and EH&S 1991–95, People-Canada and Transformation and Change Monsanto Worldwide 1995–, Gen Man Monsanto Incite Consulting Div 1991–94, Dir Continuous Improvement Monsanto Canada, Sr Consultant Incite Div of Monsanto; Chair Council on Total Quality Man Conf Bd of Canada; mem Personnel Asscn of Ontario, American Man Asscn. *Leisure interests:* gardening, music, travel. *Address:* Monsanto Canada Inc, 2330 Argentia Rd, POB 787, Streetsville, Mississauga, ON L5M 2G4, Canada. *Telephone:* (905) 826-9222; *Fax:* (905) 826-8961.

FERGUSON, Stephney Winsome Lorraine, JP, BA, MLS; Jamaican librarian; b 20 Oct 1938; d of the late Doris and Jasper Ferguson; one d (adopted). *Education:* Univ of the West Indies and Indiana Univ (USA). *Career:* Sr Librarian Jamaica Library Asscn 1964–70; Librarian Coll of Arts, Science and Tech 1970–80; Dir Nat Library of Jamaica 1980–1990; Pres Commonwealth Library Asscn 1986–1990; Vice-Chair Conf of Dirs of Nat Libraries 1990–1992; Pres Cand Int Fed of Library Asscn 1991; Sr Lecturer Dept of Library Studies, Univ of the West Indies, Campus Librarian 1997–, Univ Librarian 1998–; Pres Asscn of Caribbean Univ, Research & Institutional Libraries 1999–2000; JP 1991; mem Editorial Cttee Alexandria, Interlending and Document Supply, Standing Cttee Int Fed of Library Asscns (IFLA) 1997–; Officer Section on Educ and Training (SET) 2000–2001; Inst of Jamaica Centenary Medal; Mutual Security Bank Award for Outstanding Achievement 1988; Officer of the Order of Distinction 1990. *Leisure interests:* reading, fishing, walking. *Address:* The Library, University of the West Indies, Mona, Kingston 7, Jamaica; 8 Wellington Place, Kingston 6, Jamaica (Home). *Telephone:* 927-2123; *Fax:* 927-1926; *E-mail:* sfergusn@uwimona.edu.jm.

FERNANDEZ, Gigi; American tennis player; b 22 Feb 1964, San Juan, Puerto Rico. *Career:* Mem US Fed Cup Team 1988, 1990–92, 1994–95; winner Doubles (with Robin White) US Open 1988, (with Martina Navratilova, qv) 1990, (with Natasha Zvereva, qv) 1992, 1995; winner Doubles (with Natasha Zvereva) French Open 1991, 1992, 1993, 1994, 1995; winner Doubles (with Natasha Zvereva) Wimbledon 1992, 1993, 1994; Gold Medallist in Doubles (with Mary Joe Fernandez, qv) Olympic Games, Barcelona, Spain 1992; winner Doubles (with Natasha Zvereva) Australian Open 1993, 1994; Singles Semi-finalist Wimbledon 1994; Finalist Doubles Australian Open, Wimbledon (UK) 1995; Finalist Mixed Doubles Australian Open, Wimbledon (UK), US Open 1995; winner Doubles (with Natasha Zvereva) Pan Pacific 1996; Founder Gigi Fernandez Charitable Foundation 1992; named Puerto Rican Female Athlete of the Year 1988; Corel WTA Tour Doubles Team of the Year Award (with Jana Novotná, qv) 1991, (with Natasha Zvereva) 1993–95. *Leisure interests:* golf, boating, skiing, hiking, biking, reading, beach volleyball, computers. *Address:* c/o Women's Tennis Association, 2665 S Bayshore Drive, Suite 1002, Miami, FL 33133, USA.

FERNANDEZ, Mary Joe; American tennis player; b 19 Aug 1971, Dominican Repub; d of José and Sylvia Fernandez. *Career:* Ranked No 1 in USA 1984; turned professional tennis player 1986; Quarter-finalist French Open 1986, Geneva 1987, Australian Open 1993; Semi-finalist Eastbourne (UK) 1988, French Open 1989, Wimbledon (UK) 1991, Australian Open 1991, Italian Open 1991, 1993, US Open 1992; Finalist in Singles and Doubles competitions Australian Open 1990, Singles competition 1992; Bronze Medallist in Singles, Gold Medallist in Doubles, Olympic Games, Barcelona 1992 (with Gigi Fernandez, qv); winner Singles competition Strasbourg 1994, winner (with Lindsay Davenport) French Open Doubles 1996; winner Doubles Hilton Head, Carolina 1997, Madrid 1997, won Singles title German Open 1997; mem US Fed Cup Team (Atlantic City, NJ) 1996.

FERNÁNDEZ SANZ, Matilde; Spanish politician and psychologist; b 24 Jan 1950. *Career:* Consultant Industrial Psychologist and mem personnel dept several firms; mem PSOE 1973–, Exec Sec and Sec for Women's Affairs 1984; Minister for Social Affairs 1989–93; Mem Congreso de los Deputados (Parl) for Cantabria 1989; Vice-Pres Women's Socialist Int; Gen Sec Chemistry and Energy Fed UGT Union; mem Council Regional Soc for Promotion of Principality of Asturias; mem Gov Body Coll of Mining Engineers, Inst of Women's Affairs. *Address:* c/o Ministry of Social Affairs, Calle de José Abasral, Madrid, Spain.

FERNÁNDEZ-ZAVALA, Margarita, MA; American (Puerto Rican) artist and college chancellor; b 7 Nov 1949; m Dennis A. Simonpietri 1974; two s one d. *Education:* Univ of Puerto Rico and New York Univ. *Career:* Artist, one-woman exhibitions 1981, 1983, 1984; apptd Lecturer of Puerto Rican Contemporary Art and Women's Art 1980; Art Critic since 1980; apptd Chancellor Escuela de Artes Plasticas 1988. *Film:* Puerto Rico: Arte e Identidad (jtly) 1991. *Leisure interests:* reading Latin-American literature, travel. *Address:* c/o Escuela de Artes Plasticas,

Apdo 4184, San Juan, PR, USA (Office); Regina Medina 16A, Santa Paula, Guaynabo, PR 00956, USA (Home). *Telephone:* 725-1522 (Office); 790-4898 (Home); *Fax:* 725-8111 (Office).

FERRARI, Beatriz; Uruguayan church official. *Career:* Pres of Evangelical Methodist Church, Uruguay until 2000; currently studying in Costa Rica. *Address:* c/o Iglesia Evangélica Metodista en el Uruguay, (Evangelical Methodist Church in Uruguay), San José 1457, CP 11200, Montevido, Uruguay. *E-mail:* mortimerarias@hotmail.com.

FERRARO, Geraldine Anne, JD; American lawyer, politician and journalist; b 26 Aug 1935, Newburgh, NY; d of the late Dominick and Antonetta L. (née Corrieri) Ferraro; m John Zaccaro 1960; two d one s. *Education:* Marymount Manhattan Coll, Fordham and New York Univs. *Career:* Called to the New York Bar 1961, US Supreme Court 1978; practised law in New York 1961–74, Asst Dist Attorney Queens Co, New York 1974–78; Chief Special Victims Bureau 1977–78; mem House of Reps 1979–84; first woman Democrat cand for US Vice-Pres (with Walter Mondale) 1984; Chair Democratic Platform Cttee 1984; Man Partner Keck Mahin Cate and Koether, New York 1993–94; US Amb to UN Human Rights Comm 1994, 1995, World Conf, Vienna 1993, 4th World Conf on Women 1995; Prof Georgetown Univ School of Public Policy; Pres Int Inst of Women Political Leaders; Dir Nat Democratic Inst for Int Affairs; mem several Congressional Cttees, Queens Co Women's Bar Asscn, Int Inst Women's Political Leadership; currently political analyst for FOX News; Fellow Harvard Inst of Politics 1988; several hon degrees including Dr hc (New York) 1984, (Hunter Coll) 1985, (Virginia State) 1989, (Briarcliff Coll for Business) 1990, (Potsdam Coll) 1991. *Publications include:*Ferraro, My Story (jtly) 1985, Changing History: Women, Power and Politics 1993, Framing a Life 1998; *TV appearances include:* co-host Crossfire, CNN 1996–98. *Leisure interests:* swimming, tennis, golf. *Address:* 218 Lafayette St, New York, NY 10012, USA (Office). *Telephone:* (212) 226-2965; *Fax:* (212) 925-7401.

FERRÉOL, Andréa Louise; French actress; b 6 Jan 1947, Aix-en-Provence; d of Paul and Aurélie (née Darbon) Ferréol. *Education:* Lycée Paul Cézanne and Ecole des Beaux-Arts (Aix-en-Provence) and Cours d'Art Dramatique J. L. Cochet (Paris). *Career:* Triomphe du Cinéma 1973; Officier des Arts et des Lettres 1989. *Plays include:* Les fraises musclées 1970, Turandot ou le congrès des blanchisseurs 1971, Crime et châtiment 1972, Roméo et Juliette 1973, Les gens déraisonnables sont en voie de disparition 1978, La valse du hasard 1986; *Films include:* La grande bouffe 1973, Despair 1977, Le dernier métro 1980, Les trois frères 1980, La nuit de Varennes 1981, Zoo 1985, Douce France 1985, Francesco 1988, Street of No Return 1988, Rouge Venise 1989, The Phantom of the Opera 1989, Il maestro 1992, Hors saison 1993, Le roi nu 1993, Domenica 1993; *TV appearances include:* Les louves 1985, Le fantôme de l'opéra 1990, Maria des eaux vives 1992. *Leisure interest:* swimming. *Address:* Artmédia, 10 ave George V, 75008 Paris, France.

FERRER I CASALS, Concepció; Spanish professor of literature and politician; b 27 Jan 1938, Ripoll (Girona). *Education:* Univs of Barcelona and Strasbourg. *Career:* Mem municipal council of Figueres 1979–80; mem Unió Democràtica de Catalunya (UDC) Exec 1978–84, 1987–, Chair UDC 1984–86; Deputy in Catalan Regional Parl 1980–87, First Vice-Pres 1980–84; Vice-Pres European Union of Christian Democrats EUCD 1983–86; Pres Union of Christian Democratic Women (UCDW) 1987–89; Vice-Pres Christian Democratic Int 1998–; MEP (Bureau of EPP) 1987–, mem Cttee Industry, External Trade, Research and Energy, Jt Parl Ass of ACP–EU; mem Social and Academic Council of the Int Univ of Catalonia 1995–; Grand Cross of the Order of Bernardo O'Higgins (Chile); Commdr of the Order of May (Argentina). *Address:* European Parliament, rue Wiertz, 1047 Brussels, Belgium. *Telephone:* (2) 284-21-11; *Fax:* (2) 230-69-43.

FERRES, Veronica Maria; German actress; b 10 June, Cologne. *Education:* Luwig-Maximilian-Univ (Munich). *Career:* Awards include Golden Camera Award, Germany 1998. *Films include:* The Mask of Desire, Bambi (Best Actress Award) 1992, Lateshow, The Ladies Room, Schtonk 1992, Superwoman 1996, Rossini 1997, Honeymoon, The Second Homeland, The Bride (Best Actress Award, 9th Int Film Festival, Pescara) 1999; *Plays:* The Casket 2000, The Geierwally, Talking With, The Bernauerin, Ghostride; *TV:* Bobby, Sans Famille,

The Manns, Jack's Baby, The Chaos Queen 1997, The Naughty Woman 1998, Dr Knock, Catherine the Great, Fatal Motherlove, Les Misérables 2000. *Leisure interests:* horse-riding, skiing, fencing, golf, scuba-diving, dancing. *Address:* Ferres Management, Kurfürstenstr 18, 80801 Munich, Germany. *Telephone:* (089) 1223510 (Office); (089) 399733 (Home); *Fax:* (089) 12001818 (Office); (089) 399744 (Home).

FERRETTI, Alberta; Italian designer and retailer; b 1951; m; two s. *Career:* Opened first boutique The Jolly Shop, Cattolica 1968; launched first collection under the name Alberta Ferretti 1974; launched new range under name Philosophy 1984; operates 17 Alberta Ferretti boutiques including London, Tokyo and New York brs; Vice-Pres Aeffe fashion workshop. *Leisure interests:* swimming, reading, sailing. *Address:* Via delle Querce 51, 47842 San Giovanni in Marignano (RN), Italy. *Internet:* www.albertaferretti.com.

FERRETTI, Janine, BA; Canadian environmentalist. *Education:* Univ of CA at Santa Cruz and York Univ (Toronto). *Career:* Research Asst IUCN (Int Union for the Conservation of Nature and Natural Resources, now World Conservation Union) 1977–78; Research Assoc ELCI (Environment Liaison Centre Int) Nairobi (Kenya) 1980–81; Co-ordinator Int Programs, Pollution Probe Foundation 1984–89, Exec Dir 1989–94; Dir N American Comm for Environmental Cooperation Feb 1998–. *Leisure interest:* sports. *Address:* 393 St Jacques St W, Suite 200, Montréal, PQ H2Y 1N9, Canada. *Telephone:* (514) 350-4303; *Fax:* (514) 350-4303; *E-mail:* jferretti@ccemte.org.

FERRIER-CAVERIVIÈRE, Nicole Marie Gabrielle, D ÈS L; French university rector and academic; b 14 Aug 1945, Limoges; d of Jean and Hélène (née Joyet-Lavergne) Caverivière; m Michel Ferrier 1968; one d one s. *Education:* Lycée de Limoges and Univ of Poitiers. *Career:* Asst Prof Univ of Limoges 1968–81; Prof Univ of Paris XII (Paris-Val-de-Marne) 1981–86; Auditor Inst des Hautes Etudes de Défense Nat 1985–86; Rector Acad de Dijon, Chancellor Univ of Dijon 1986–89; Prof Univ of Paris IV (Paris-Sorbonne) 1989–; Tech Advisor to Cabinet of the Prime Minister 1993–95; Dir Cabinet of Sec of State for Higher Educ, then Deputy Dir Cabinet of Minister for Nat Educ, Higher Educ and Research 1995–96; Rector Acad d'Orléans-Tours 1996–2000; Insp-Gen of Educ 2000–; Pres Soc des amis de Colette 1989, Soc d'études du XVIIème siècle 1990; Chevalier de l'Ordre Nat du Mérite 1987. *Publications:* L'image de Louis XIV dans la littérature française de 1660 à 1715 1981, Le grand roi à l'aube des lumières 1715–1751 1985, Colette et la mode 1991. *Leisure interests:* horse-riding, tennis. *Address:* 24 rue Emile Dubois, 75014 Paris, France.

FERRIOT, Dominique Renée, L EN D; French museum director and professor; b 9 Jan 1950, Algiers, Algeria; d of Paul and Renée Bernasconi; m Bertrand Ferriot 1972; one d. *Education:* Univ of Paris and Inst d'Etudes Politiques de Paris. *Career:* Journalist, art critic 1971–76; Deputy Dir Ecomusée du Creusot 1976–80; Head Partnership Dept Musée de la Villette 1980–84; Tech Adviser in Cabinet of the Minister of Research and Tech, then Dir of Del on Information, Communication and Scientific and Tech Culture 1984–87; Dir Musée Nat des Techniques, Conservatoire Nat des Arts et Métiers 1988–2000; Prof, Conservatoire Nat des Arts et Métiers 2001–; organizer int conf on industrial heritage 1981; Chevalier de l'Ordre Nat du Mérite 1990, Chevalier de la Légion d'Honneur 2000. *Publication:* Patrimoine industriel et technique 1981. *Leisure interest:* science popularisation. *Address:* CNAM, 292 rue Saint-Martin, 75003 Paris, France. *Telephone:* (1) 53-01-82-93; *Fax:* (1) 53-01-82-35; *E-mail:* ferriot@cnam.fr.

FETZ, Anita, L PH; Swiss women's organization official; b 19 March 1957. *Education:* In Basel and Berlin (Germany). *Career:* Teacher 1983–84; Asst Teachers' Seminar, Basel 1984–85; Founder, apptd Dir FEMMEDIA, Büro für Frauenförderung (org for the promotion of women) 1986; mem Nationalrat/Conseil Nat (Parl) 1985–90; apptd Man Adviser Alternative Bank Schweiz (ABS) 1990, Adviser to Swiss Greenpeace 1992. *Publications include:* Gene, Frauen und Missionen (jtly) 1988, Strukturwandel der Gesellschaft und Veränderung der Frauenrolle (jtly) 1988, Mut zur Karriere: Laufbahnplanung für Frauen 1992, Rahmenkonzept für die Aus- und Wieterbildung in öffentlichen Verwaltungen (jtly) 1992. *Address:* Oberer Rheinweg 37, 4058 Basel, Switzerland. *Telephone:* (61) 6810972.

FICHTEL-MAURITZ, Anja; German sportswoman; b 17 Aug 1968, Tauberischofsheim; m 1992; one s. *Career:* Fencer; Gold Medallist single and team foil competitions, Olympic Games, Seoul, Repub of Korea 1988; competitor team foil competition, Olympic Games, Barcelona, Spain 1992; Bronze Medallist women's team foil competition, Olympic Games, Atlanta, GA, USA 1996.

FIELD, Helen; British opera singer; b 14 May 1951, Wrexham, Clwyd. *Education:* Royal Northern Coll of Music (Manchester), Royal Coll of Music (London) and Germany. *Career:* Winner triennial Young Welsh Singers' Competition 1976; appearances with English Nat Opera, Welsh Nat Opera, Opera North, Metropolitan Opera (New York), Scottish Opera, Royal Opera (London) and with opera cos of Netherlands, Cologne (Germany) and Brussels; concert performances with several leading orchestras, regular radio and TV appearances. *Operas include:* Rigoletto, La Bohème, Eugene Onegin, Fidelio, Jenůfa, Othello, Khovanschina; *Recordings include:* Rigoletto, A Village Romeo and Juliet, Osud. *Address:* c/o Lies Askonas Ltd, 186 Drury Lane, London WC2B 5RY, UK.

FIELD, Sally; American actress; b 6 Nov 1946, Pasadena, CA; m Alan Greisman 1984; three c. *Education:* Actor's Studio. *Films include:* The Way West 1967, Stay Hungry 1976, Smokey and the Bandit 1977, Hooper 1978, Norma Rai (Cannes Film Festival Best Actress Award 1979, Acad Award 1980) 1979, Beyond the Poseidon Adventure 1979, Smokey and the Bandit II 1980, Absence of Malice 1981, Places in the Heart (Acad Award 1984) 1984, Murphy's Romance (also exec producer) 1985, Punchline 1987, Steel Magnolias 1989, Not Without My Daughter 1991, Soapdish 1991, Dying Young (co-producer) 1991, Homeward Bound: The Incredible Journey (voice only) 1993, Mrs Doubtfire 1993, Forrest Gump 1994, Eye for an Eye 1996, Where the Heart Is 2000, Time of Our Lives 2000, Say It Isn't So 2001; *TV appearances include:* Series: Gidget 1965, The Flying Nun 1967–69, The Girl With Something Extra 1973; Films: Maybe I'll Come Home In the Spring 1971, Marriage: Year One 1971, Home for the Holidays 1972, Bridges 1976, Sybil (Emmy Award 1977) 1976, A Woman of Independent Means, From the Earth to the Moon 1998, A Cooler Climate 1999, David Copperfield 2000, The Court 2001.

FIELDING, Fenella Marion; British actress; b 17 Nov 1934, London. *Education:* North London Collegiate School. *Career:* Acting career began 1954; many appearances in UK and USA; first appearance in New York 1970. *Plays include:* Cockles and Champagne 1954, Pay the Piper 1954, Jubilee Girl 1956, Valmouth 1958, 1959, 1982, Pieces of Eight 1959, Five Plus One 1961, Twists (Variety Best Revue Performance of the Year) 1962, Doctors of Philosophy 1962, Luv 1963, So Much to Remember – The Life Story of a Great Lady 1963, Let's Get a Divorce 1966, The Beaux Stratagem and the Italian Straw Hat 1967, The High Bid 1967, Façade 1970, Colette 1970, Fish out of Water 1971, The Old Man's Comforts 1972, The Provok'd Wife 1973, Absurd Person Singular 1974, 1975, Fielding Convertible 1976, Jubilee Jeunesse 1977, Look After Lulu 1978, A Personal Choice 1978, Fenella on Broadway 1979, Wizard of Oz 1983, The Jungle Book 1984, The Country Wife 1990, Mermaid 1990, A Dangerous Woman 1998, Blithe Spirit 1999; *Films include:* Drop Dead Darling, Lock Up Your Daughters, Carry On Screaming, Carry On Regardless, Doctor in Clover, Doctor in Distress, Doctor in Trouble, No Love for Johnnie, Robin Hood; *TV Series:* That Was The Week That Was, A Touch of Venus, Ooh La La, Stories from Saki, Dean Martin and the Gold-Diggers, Comedy Tonight, Rhyme and Reason. *Leisure interest:* reading. *Address:* CCA Management, 4 Court Lodge, 48 Sloane Square, London SW1W 8AT, UK.

FIELDING, Helen; British author and journalist. *Education:* Univ of Oxford. *Career:* Began career working for BBC; fmr columnist The Independent. *Publications include:* Cause Celeb, Bridget Jones's Diary, Bridget Jones: The Edge of Reason. *Address:* c/o Viking Books (author mail), Penguin Books, 27 Wrights Lane, London W8 5TZ, UK.

FIEUX, Michèle Marie, D SC; French oceanographer; b 25 Oct 1940, Neuilly-sur-Seine; d of Joseph and Paule (née Brunot) Fieux. *Education:* Lycée Hélène Boucher (Paris) and Faculty of Sciences (Paris). *Career:* Research Engineer Centre Nat pour l'Exploitation des Océans (CNEXO) 1968–77, CNRS 1978–; Research Assoc MIT, Woods Hole

Oceanographic Inst, USA 1973–75; Prof of Regional Oceanography, Ecole Nat Supérieure des Techniques Avancées (ENSTA) 1979–; Pres Indian Ocean working group of Cttee on Climatic Changes and the Ocean (CCCO) 1982–89; mem Comité Nat Français de Géodésie et de Géophysique (CNFGG) 1972–, Comité Nat Français de Recherches Océaniques (CNFRO) 1987–, Oceanography Soc 1991–, American Geophysical Union 1992–, Comité de Perfectionnement Institut Oceanographique 1996–; elected Corresp mem Acad de Marine 2001; numerous articles in int scientific journals on the hydrology and dynamics of the Indian Ocean and the Pacific–Indian oceans through-flow; French Oceanographic Soc Medal 1985; Albatross Award, American Miscellaneous Soc 1991; Tchihatchef Prize, Science Acad 1992; Chevalier de la Légion d'Honneur 2000. *Leisure interests:* flying, skiing, tennis, sailing. *Address:* University of Paris VI (Pierre et Marie Curie), Lab d'Océanographie Dynamique et de Climatologie, 4 place Jussieu, 75005 Paris, France (Office); 17 rue Tournefort, 75005 Paris, France (Home). *Telephone:* (1) 44-27-38-07 (Office); *Fax:* (1) 44-27-38-05 (Office); *E-mail:* fieux@lodyc.jussieu.fr.

FIGALA, Karin, DR RER NAT; German professor of the history of science; b 7 Aug 1938, Vienna; d of Norbert and Luzy (née Steude) Figala. *Education:* Univs of Berne, Bonn and Munich, in Hamburg and Tech Univ of Munich. *Career:* Worked in pharmaceutical industry, Ludwigshafen 1963–65; Asst Prof Zentralinst für Geschichte der Technik, Tech Univ of Munich 1978, Prof 1980–; mem Comité Int pour la Métrologie Historique 1975; Corresp mem Acad Int d'Histoire des Sciences 1978; mem Gesellschaft für Wissenschaftsgeschichte 1990; numerous contribs on history of science to professional journals; Prix de l'Acad d'Alsace 1974. *Leisure interests:* literature, fine art. *Address:* Zentralinstitut für Geschichte der Technik der Technische Universität München, Museuminsel 1, 80306 Munich, Germany (Office); Baader-str 23, 80469 Munich, Germany (Home). *Telephone:* (89) 2179401 (Office); *Fax:* (89) 2179324 (Office).

FIGES, Eva, BA; British writer; b 15 April 1932, Berlin; d of Emil and Irma Unger; m John Figes; one s one d. *Education:* Kingsbury Co School and Queen Mary Coll (London). *Career:* Awarded Guardian Fiction Prize. *Publications:* Patriarchal Attitudes 1970, Waking 1981, Light 1983, The Knot 1996. *Leisure interests:* music, films, theatre, visual arts. *Address:* c/o Rogers, Coleridge & White Ltd, 20 Powis Mews, London W11 1JN, UK.

FIGINI, Michela; Swiss skier; b 7 April 1966. *Career:* Gold Medal Winter Olympics, Sarajevo (fmrly Yugoslavia) 1984; Gold Medal World Championships 1985, two Silver Medals 1987; Silver Medal Winter Olympics, Calgary (Canada) 1988; winner 26 races in world championships. *Address:* c/o Swiss Ski Federation, Worbstr 52, 3074 Muri, Switzerland; 6773 Prato, Switzerland (Home). *Telephone:* (94) 301187 (Home).

FIGUERAU, Micheline Gabrielle Josette; French civil servant; b 23 Aug 1942, Villiers-St-Frédéric; d of Gabriel Figuereau and Renée Le Cam; one d. *Education:* Lycées (Niort and Le Mans). *Career:* At the Treasury 1963–75; trade unionist, Deputy Sec-Gen Syndicat Nat du Trésor Force Ouvrière (FO), Confed Asst FO 1975–85; Interministerial Del to Economie Sociale; Insp-Gen of Tourism 1989–98, Chief Insp-Gen 1998–; Gen Reporter of European Year of Tourism 1989; Del-Gen Fondation Jean Jaurès 1992–93; Chevalier de l'Ordre Nat du Mérite 1988. *Leisure interests:* cooking, reading, cinema, music. *Address:* Inspection Générale du Tourisme, 2 rue Linois, 75740 Paris Cedex 15, France. *Telephone:* (1) 45-75-62-16.

FILARDO, Leonor, MS; Venezuelan banking executive and finance official; b 1944; d of Jesus and Carmen Vargas de Filado; m (divorced); three d. *Education:* Caracas Catholic Univ and Univ of Surrey (UK). *Career:* Worked for Cen Bank of Venezuela 1970–75, Sr Vice-Pres Int Operations 1979–84; Sr Vice-Pres of Int Finance, Venezuelan Investment Fund 1975–79; Exec Dir World Bank Exec Bd 1984–86; Alt Exec Dir IMF 1986–88, Exec Dir 1988–90; Rep Office, Washington DC 1990; Vice-Pres Cen Bank of Venezuela 1993–94; Minister Counsellor Embassy USA 1994; fmr Adviser to Cen American and Venezuelan govts on stabilization and structural adjustment programmes, participant in negotiations with IMF for External Fund Facility for Venezuela; Francisco de Miranda Medal, (1st Class) Venezuela 1990. *Leisure interests:* art, music, opera, travel, workout.

FILATOVA, Ludmila Pavlovna; Russian opera singer (mezzo-soprano); b 6 Oct 1935, Orenburg; d of Pavel Filatov and Valentina Semoylova; m Rudakov Igor 1971. *Education:* Leningrad (now St Petersburg) State Univ. *Career:* Mem CPSU 1969–91; mem Kirov Opera Choir 1958–60; Soloist with Kirov (now Mariinsky) Opera 1962–; teacher of singing Leningrad Conservatoire 1973–; performs music of Shostakovich, Tchaikovsky, Rachmaninov, Glinka; Glinka Prize 1960; People's Artist of USSR 1983. *Opera roles include:* Lyubasha in A Bride for the Tsar, Marfa in Khovanshchina, Carmen, Marta-Ekaterina in Petrov's Peter I, Countess in The Queen of Spades. *Address:* Mariinsky Theatre, St Petersburg, Teatralnaya Pl 1, Russian Federation.

FILIMON, Valeria; Romanian journalist; b 29 May 1949, Butimanu; d of Ion and Maria Dumitrescu; m Vasile Filimon 1984. *Education:* Univ of Bucharest. *Career:* Freelance journalist for various Romanian dailies and literary magazines 1967–90; Assoc Prof 1970–90; journalist 1990–93; Ed-in-Chief, The Modern Woman (magazine) 1993–98, Regala 1998–, Olimp 1999–; Project Co-ordinator in Romania, Int Fed of Journalists 1996–; Vice-Pres Journalists' Soc of Romania; Romanian Writers' Union Prize. *Publications:* co-author of critical edition of Romanian novelist Liviu Rebreanu 1968–75; Lyceum (collection of literary criticism in two vols) 1974. *Address:* Bd Pache Protopopescu No 11, Sector 2, 70311 Bucharest, Romania. *Telephone:* (1) 3152482; *Fax:* (1) 3130675.

FILIPPINI, Rosa; Italian politician and organization executive; b 3 Nov 1954, Naples. *Career:* Radical activist 1971–79; mem Federazione Nazionale per le Liste Verdi (Green Party); Co-Founder Italian div Friends of the Earth, Pres 1983–87; apptd Councillor, Rome 1985; mem Congress of Deputies (Parl) for Genova-Imperia-La Spezia-Rimini 1987, Vice-Pres Green parl group, co-promoter nat referendum against hunting, mem Cttee for Justice, Regulatory Body; Pres Friends of the Earth, Italy 1999–. *Address:* Amici della Terra, Via di Torre Argentina 18, 00186 Rome, Italy.

FILKIN, Elizabeth, B SC S; British civil servant; b 24 Nov 1940; d of John Tompkins and Frances Trollope; m 1st David Geoffrey Nigel Filkin 1974 (divorced 1994); three d; m 2nd Michael John Honey 1996. *Education:* Clifton High School, Bristol (UK) and Univ of Birmingham (UK). *Career:* Organizer, Sparkbrook Asscn 1961–64 Whyndham Deedes Fellowship, Israel 1964; Research Asst, Research Assoc, Lecturer, Univ of Birmingham 1964–68; Lecturer and Community Worker, Nat Inst for Social Work 1968–71; Community Work Services Officer, London Borough of Brent 1971–75; Lecturer in Social Studies, Univ of Liverpool 1975–83; Chief Exec Nat Asscn of Citizens' Advice Bureaux 1983–88; Dir of Community Services, London Docklands Devt Corpn 1988–90, Asst Chief Exec 1990–92; Revenue Adjudicator 1993–95; The Adjudicator, Inland Revenue, Customs and Excise, and Contribs Agency 1995–99; Parl Commr for Standards 1999–; Non-Exec Dir Britannia Bldg Soc 1992–98, Hay Management Consultants 1992–98, Logica 1995–98, Weatherall, Green & Smith 1997–99; Chair Lord Chancellor's Advisory Cttee on Legal Aid 1991–94; mem Council Univ of East London 1997–; Hon Fellowship Queen Mary Coll, Univ of London. *Publications:* The New Villagers 1968, What a Community Worker Needs to Know 1974, Community Work and Caring for Children 1979, Caring for Children 1979, Women and Children First (ed) 1984. *Leisure interests:* walking, swimming. *Address:* House of Commons, London SW1A 0AA, UK. *Telephone:* (20) 7219-0320 (Office); *Fax:* (20) 7219-0490 (Office); *E-mail:* filkine@parliament.uk.

FINE, Rana Arnold, PH D; American oceanographer; b 17 April 1944, New York; d of Joseph and Etta (née Kreisman) Arnold; m 1st Shalle Fine 1965 (divorced 1980); m 2nd James Mattson 1983. *Education:* New York Univ and Univ of Miami. *Career:* Postdoctoral Research Assoc Rosenstiel School of Marine and Atmospheric Science, Univ of Miami 1976–77, Asst Prof 1977–80, Research Assoc Prof 1980–84, Assoc Prof 1984–90, Prof and Chair of Marine and Atmospheric Chem 1990–; mem Div Polar Programs Advisory Cttee NSF, Washington, DC 1987–90, Geophysics Study Cttee NAS 1989–92, Ocean Studies Bd

NAS 1992–; mem American Geophysicists Union, Fellow, Sec 1986–88, Pres-elect Ocean Science Section 1994–96, Pres 1996–; mem AAAS, American Meteorologists Soc, The Oceanography Soc; research grants from NSF 1977–, Office of Naval Research 1983–88, Nat Oceanography and Atmospheric Admin 1986–, NASA 1990–. numerous contribs to professional journals. *Leisure interests:* sailing, scuba diving, fishing, tennis, reading. *Address:* University of Miami, Rosenstiel School of Marine and Atmospheric Science, 4600 Rickenbacker Causeway, Miami, FL 33149, USA. *Telephone:* (305) 361-4722; *Fax:* (305) 361-4689.

FINLAY, Mary Louise, BA; Canadian journalist, broadcaster and writer; b 29 March 1947, Ottawa, ON; d of John Francis and Helen B. Finlay; one s. *Education:* Univ of Ottawa and Harvard Univ (USA). *Career:* Historical Researcher, Trans Canadian War Museum 1967–70; Current Affairs Interviewer, Producer 1970–75; Presenter Take 30 1975–77; Presenter, writer Finlay and Company 1976; contrib As It Happens (radio) 1977–78, 90 Minutes Live 1977–78; Presenter, Producer Live It Up 1978–81; Co-Presenter The National Driving Test 1980; Co-Presenter, Producer The Journal 1981–88; Presenter Sunday Morning 1988–94; Presenter Now The Details 1994–; Nieman Fellow Harvard Univ 1986; mem Canadian Civil Liberties Union. *TV documentaries scripted:* The Railroad Show 1974, The Mackenzie Valley Pipeline Inquiry 1976, All is Calm 1983, Timothy Findley's War 1983, Taking a Chance on Faro 1984, The Right to Die 1984, The Death of Clarence Warren 1985, Congress and the Contras 1985. *Leisure interests:* reading, skiing, tennis. *Address:* Box 500, Station A, Toronto, ON M5W 1E6, Canada (Office); 100 Edith Drive, Toronto, ON M4R 1Z2, Canada (Home).

FINNBOGADOTTIR, Vigdís; Icelandic former Head of State and teacher; b 15 April 1930, Reykjavík; d of Finnbogi Rutur Thorvaldsson and Sigridur Eiriksdóttir; m (divorced); one d (adopted). *Education:* Menntaskólinn i Reykjavík, Univs of Grenoble and Paris (Sorbonne) and Iceland. *Career:* Teacher of French Menntaskólinn i Reykjavík, Menntaskólinn vid Hamrahlid; Head Guide Training, Iceland Tourist Bureau; Dir Reykjavík Theatre Co 1972–80; teacher of French drama Univ of Iceland; mem staff Icelandic State TV; Pres of Iceland 1980–96; mem Advisory Cttee on Cultural Affairs in Nordic Countries 1976–80, Chair 1978–80; fmr Chair Alliance Française; Dr hc (Grenoble) 1985, (Bordeaux) 1987, (Smith Coll) 1988, (Luther Coll) 1989, (Manitoba) 1989; Hon LL D (Nottingham) 1990; Hon GCMG 1982. *Leisure interest:* theatre. *Address:* c/o Office of the President, Stornarráðshúsið, v/Lækjargötu, 150 Reykjavík, Iceland.

FINNEY, Joan Marie McInroy, BA; American politician; b 12 Feb 1925, Topeka, KS; d of Leonard McInroy and Mary M. Sands; m Spencer W. Finney 1957; two d one s. *Education:* Washburn Univ. *Career:* Mem staff of Senator Frank Carlson 1953–69; Commr of Elections Shawnee Co (KS) 1970–72; Admin Asst to Mayor of Topeka 1973–74; Treas State of KS 1971–91, Gov 1991–95; mem Bd Dirs Hayden High School, St Francis Hosp, Fed Democrat Women's Club; mem Democratic Nat Cttee. *Address:* c/o Governor's Mansion, State Capitol, Topeka, KS 67730, USA.

FINNIE, Linda Agnes; British opera and concert singer; b 9 May 1952, Paisley, Scotland; d of William and Agnes Finnie. *Education:* John Neilson Institution (Paisley), Carrick Acad (Maybole) and Royal Scottish Acad of Music and Drama. *Career:* Concert performances in Europe, Australasia, Far East and USA, regular radio broadcasts; has sung with all the major British orchestras and with Chicago, Boston, Pittsburgh and San Francisco Symphony orchestras (USA), Hong Kong Philharmonic, Orchestre de Paris and Orchestre Philharmonique de Radio France (France), RAI Orchestra (Italy), Danish Radio Orchestra, under many leading conductors including Abbado, Maazel, Barenboim, Previn, Tilson-Thomas, Tate, Pritchard, Davis, Rattle, Salonen, Jarvi and Hickox; has also sung at Geneva (Switzerland), Nice (France), Bayreuth and Frankfurt (Germany) festivals; Kathleen Ferrier Memorial Award; Kathleen Ferrier Prize; 'S-Hertogenbosch Concours; John Noble Bursary; Countess of Munster Scholarship. *Operas include:* Un Ballo in Maschera, Tristan und Isolde, Don Carlos; *Recordings include:* Alexander Nevsky, Elijah, Beethoven's 9th Symphony, Songs of the

British Isles, Armide, La Rondine and l'Enfant et les Sortilèges. *Leisure interests:* reading, driving, sewing, going to concerts and opera. *Address:* 16 Golf Course, Girvan, Ayrshire KA26 9HW, UK.

FINNIGAN, (Helen) Joan, BA; Canadian poet, playwright and oral historian; b 23 Nov 1925, Ottawa; d of Frank and Maye (née Horner) Finnigan; m Charles Grant MacKenzie (died 1965); two s one d. *Education:* Lisgar Collegiate (Ottawa), Carleton and Queen's Univs. *Career:* Gen Reporter Ottawa Journal; freelance journalist 1949–67; research, scriptwriting, idea production, interviewing Canadian Nat Film Bd 1969–1976; scriptwriter CBC Radio 1976–84; four photography exhibitions, guest lectures, radio and TV appearances; mem Writers' Union of Canada, League of Canadian Poets; Pres's Medal for Poetry, Univ of Western Ontario 1969; Philemon Wright Award 1983. *Publications include:* A Dream of Lilies (poetry) 1965, It Was Warm and Sunny When We Set Out (poetry) 1970, Living Together (poetry) 1976, Some of the Stories I Told You Were True (oral history) 1981, Legacies, Legends and Lies (Ottawa-Carleton Literary Award) 1985, Tell Me Another Story (oral history) 1988, The Dog Who Wouldn't Be Left Behind (children's) 1989, Wintering Over (poetry) 1992, Old Scores: New Goals 1992, The Watershed Collection (poetry) 1992, Witches, Ghosts and Loups-Garous 1994, Dancing at the Crossroads 1995, Down the Unmarked Roads (fiction) 1997, Second Wind, Second Sight (poetry) 1998, Tallying the Tales of the Old-Timers (oral/social history) 1999; Plays: The Best Damn Fiddler from Calabogie to Kaladar (screenplay, nine Genie Awards, Best Screenplay Canadian Film Awards) 1969, A Prince of Good Fellows 1976, Up the Vallee! 1978, Songs from Both Sides of the River 1987; Edited: A History of Lisgar Collegiate, 1843–1993 1993. *Leisure interests:* seven grandchildren, gardening, travelling to Ireland, begetting new ideas, storytelling, photography. *Address:* Moore Farm, Hartington, ON K0H 1W0, Canada. *Telephone:* (613) 374-3145.

FIORENTINO, Linda; American actress; b 9 March 1958, Philadelphia. *Education:* Rosemont Coll and Circle in the Square Theater School. *Career:* Mem Circle in the Square Performing Workshops. *Films:* Vision Quest 1985, Gotcha! 1985, After Hours 1985, The Moderns 1988, Queens Logic 1991, Shout 1991, Wildfire 1992, Chain of Desire 1993, The Desperate Trail 1994, The Last Seduction 1994, Bodily Harm 1995, Jade 1995, Unforgettable 1997, The Split 1997, Men in Black 1997, Kicked in the Head 1997, Dogma 1998, Ordinary Decent Criminal 1999, Where the Money Is 1999, What Planet Are You From? 2000; *TV films:* The Neon Empire 1989, The Last Game 1992, Acting on Impulse 1993, Beyond the Law 1994, The Desperate Trail. *Address:* c/o United Talent Agency, 9560 Wilshire Blvd, Floor 5, Beverly Hills, CA 90212, USA.

FIRSOVA, Elena Olegovna; Russian composer; b 21 March 1950, Leningrad (now St Petersburg); d of Oleg Borisovich Firsov and Victoria Evgenievna Firsova; m Dmitri Smirnov 1972; one s one d. *Education:* Moscow Conservatory. *Career:* Mem Composers' Union, Russia since 1976; moved to UK 1991; freelance composer since 1991. *Compositions include:* Misterioso (Quartet No 3) 1982, Three Poems by Mandelstam 1981, Earthly Life 1989, Forest Walks 1993. *Leisure interest:* reading. *Address:* c/o Boosey & Hawkes, 295 Regent St, London W1B 2JH, UK. *Telephone:* (20) 7580-2060; *Fax:* (20) 7436-5675.

FIRTH, Tazeena Mary; British stage and costume designer; b 1 Nov 1935, Southampton; d of Denis Gordon and Irene (née Morris) Firth. *Education:* St Mary's School (Wantage) and Châtelard School (Switzerland). *Career:* Stage Design with Timothy O'Brien 1961–80; ind stage designer 1980–; has designed for numerous plays and operas in Europe, USA, Australia, etc for cos including RSC, Nat Theatre and English Nat Opera; Gold Medal for Set Design (jtly), Prague Quadriennale 1975. *Stage designs include:* The Bartered Bride 1962, The Girl of the Golden West 1962, Tango 1966, All's Well that Ends Well 1967, The Merry Wives of Windsor 1968, The Latent Heterosexual 1968, Women Beware Women 1969, As You Like It 1973, Next of Kin 1975, The Marrying of Ann Leete 1976, The Force of Habit 1977, Evita 1979, The Rape of Lucretia 1982, Turandot 1983, La Traviata 1986, Rigoletto 1987, Romeo and Juliet 1988, Dido and Aeneas 1989, 1995, From the House of Dead 1990, Macbeth 1990, La Bohème 1991, Don Giovanni 1991, Rigoletto 1992, Carmen 1993, Magic Flute 1993, Peter Grimes 1993, Don Giovanni 1995, Oh Come ye Sons of Art, Bluebeards

Castle, Jenůfa, Copenhagen 1995, Peter Grimes, Göteborg and Finnish Nat Opera, and Jenůfa, Copenhagen 1998. *Leisure interests:* sailing, walking. *Address:* 33 Lansdowne Gardens, London SW8 2EQ, UK. *Telephone:* (20) 7622-5384.

FISCHER, Andrea; German politician; b 14 Jan 1960, Arnsberg. *Education:* Freie Univ Berlin 1985–90. *Career:* Trained as offset printer 1978–81; printer and corrector in Hamburg and Berlin 1981–85, also mem Print and Paper TU, German TU Fed; joined Greens Party 1985; worked as journalist 1985–90; research asst for labour market and social affairs European Parl 1990–91; researcher Berlin Science Centre 1991–94; mem Bundestag 1994–; spokesperson of Alliance 90/Greens Parl Group 1994–; Fed Minister of Health 1998–. *Address:* Ministry of Health, Am Proptshof 78A, 53121 Bonn, Germany. *Telephone:* (228) 9410; *Fax:* (228) 9414900; *E-mail:* www.bngesundheit.de.

FISCHER, Leni; German politician; b 18 July 1935, Haltern, Recklinghausen; m; three c. *Education:* Westfälische Wilhelms Univ, Münster. *Career:* Numerous teaching and acad posts 1969–76; mem Municipal Council, Neuenkirchen until 1980, Planning Team Inst for Int Solidarity, Konrad-Adenauer Foundation; mem CDU 1968–, apptd Chair Women's Asscn, Westphalia-Lippe 1975–87, N-Rhine-Westphalia 1987, elected Fed Vice-Chair Women's Asscn, mem N-Rhine-Westphalia Steering Cttee, Fed Steering Cttee 1989; mem Bundestag (Parl) 1976–, Chair Bundestag Cttee on Econ Co-operation, mem Cttee on Defence, substitute mem Cttee on Youth, Family, Women and Health, mem Sub-Cttee on Human Rights and Humanitarian Aid; Vice-Pres CDU/CSU Women's Asscn 1980; CDU/CSU Parl Group Deputy Spokesperson for Devt Policy 1982, Del to German Cttee for UNICEF; mem German Cttee for UN, Vice-Pres 1981–89; Substitute Council of Europe (CDU) 1985. *Address:* Emdettenerstr 12, 48485 Neuenkirchen, Germany.

FISCHER-JØRGENSEN, Eli; Danish professor of phonetics; b 11 Feb 1911, Nakskov; d of Kai and Emmy Daisy Smyth (née Hansen) Fischer-Jørgensen. *Education:* Univ of Copenhagen and in Germany, France, UK, Netherlands and USA. *Career:* Asst Lecturer in German, Univ of Copenhagen 1939–43, Lecturer in Phonetics 1943–66, Prof 1966–81, Prof Emer 1981–, mem Senate of Univ 1970–72; mem Research Council for the Humanities 1968–72, Int Council for the Congresses of the Phonetic Sciences 1960–91, (Vice-Pres 1983); Pres Linguistic Circle of Copenhagen 1968–72, Ninth Int Congress of Phonetic Sciences (Copenhagen) 1979; mem Editorial Bd Acta Linguistica 1947–56, 1964–79, Phonetica 1957, Journal of Phonetics 1972–89; mem Danish Royal Acad of Sciences and Letters 1968–, British Acad 1995–; Hon mem Linguistic Soc of America 1963, Phonetic Soc of Japan 1991, Linguistic Circle of Copenhagen 1992; Hon D PHIL (Aarhus) 1978, (Lund, Sweden) 1978, (Copenhagen) 1993, (Bayreuth) 2001; awards include Golden Medal, Univ of Copenhagen 1935. *Publications include:* The Importance of Dialect Geography for the Conception of Sound Laws 1935, General Phonetics 1948, Trends in Phonological Theory 1975, A Phonetic Study of the Stød in Standard Danish 1989, Stress in Earlier Danish 2001. *Leisure interests:* kayak paddling, sketching. *Address:* Kongestien 45, 2830 Virum, Denmark. *Telephone:* 45-85-35-13.

FISCHER-LICHTE, Erika, D PHIL; German professor of drama; b 25 June 1943, Hamburg; d of Walter and Erika (née Hanssen) Lichte; m B. Fischer 1967; one s. *Education:* Freie Univ (Berlin) and Univ of Hamburg. *Career:* Professor of Contemporary German Literature, Frankfurt 1973–86, Dir Inst of German Language and Literature 1978–79; Prof of Gen and Comparative Literature Univ of Bayreuth 1986–; Prof of Drama Johannes Gutenberg Univ (Mainz) 1990–; Prof and Man Dir Drama Institute, Freie Univ (Berlin) 1996; Guest Prof Univ of Indiana (Bloomington, USA) 1985, 1992, Univ of Washington (Seattle), Theatre Acad, St Petersburg; Founder-mem, Dir Inst für Weltliteraturlichen Studien, Univ of Bayreuth 1987; Pres German Asscn for Drama 1991–96, Int Fed of Theatre Research 1995; mem Bd German Asscn for Semiotics 1982–84 (Chair 1983), Advisory Bd Int Asscn of Semiotics of Performing Arts, Senate of German Research Asscn 1993, Standing Cttee of the Humanities of European Science Foundation 1994. *Publications include:* Bedeutung: Probleme einer semiotischen Hermeneutik und Ästhetik 1979, Schillers Don Carlos 1987, Geschichte des Dramas (2 vols) 1990, Kleists Michael Kohlhaas 1990, Kurze Geschichte des deutschen Theaters 1993, Semiotik des

Theaters (3rd edn) 1994, The Discovery of the Spectator: Paradigm Change on the Theatre of the 20th Century 1997, The Show and the Gauze of Theatre: A European Perspective 1997; The Own and the Other Theatre 1999, Transformations. Theatre of the nineties (with Doris Kolesch and Christel Weiler) 1999. *Leisure interests:* literature, theatre, film. *Address:* c/o Freie Universität Berlin, Institut für Theaterwissenschaft, Grunewald Str 35, 12165 Berlin, Germany; Freie Universität Berlin, Kaiserwerther Str 16–18, 14195 Berlin. *Telephone:* (30) 82041040.

FISCHEROVÁ, Sylva; Czech poet; b 5 Nov 1963, Prague; d of Josef Ludvík and Jarmila Fischerová. *Education:* Olomouc Grammar School and Charles Univ. *Career:* Poet; teaching asst Dept of Classical Studies, Charles Univ, Prague. *Publications:* Zvláštní znamení (anthology) 1985, Chvění závodních koní 1986, Velká zrcadla 1990, The Tremor of the Racehorses 1990. *Address:* 772 00 Olomouc, Dukelská 19, Czech Republic. *Telephone:* (68) 259454.

FISHER, Carrie; American actress and writer; b 21 Oct 1956, Beverly Hills, CA; d of Eddie Fisher and Debbie Reynolds (qv); m Paul Simon 1983 (divorced 1984); one d. *Education:* Beverly Hills High School and Cen School of Speech and Drama (London). *Career:* Appeared with her mother in nightclub act aged 13; appeared in chorus of Broadway production of Irene, starring Debbie Reynolds, aged 15; Broadway stage appearances in Censored Scenes from King Kong, Agnes of God; several TV credits. *Films include:* Shampoo (Photoplay Award as Best Newcomer of the Year) 1975, Star Wars 1977, The Empire Strikes Back 1980, The Blues Brothers 1980, Return of the Jedi 1983, The Man with One Red Shoe 1985, Hannah and Her Sisters 1986, Amazon Women on the Moon 1987, Appointment with Death 1988, The 'Burbs 1989, Loverboy 1989, She's Back 1989, When Harry Met Sally 1989, The Time Guardian, Sibling Rivalry 1990, Drop Dead Fred 1991, Soapdish 1991, This is My Life 1992, Austin Powers: International Man of Mystery, Scream 3 2000, Famous 2000; *TV appearances include:* Come Back Little Sheba, Classic Creatures, Return of the Jedi, Thumbalina, Paul Reiser, Out on a Whim, Two Daddies?, Trying Times, Laverne and Shirley, George Burns' Comedy Week; TV Films: Leave Yesterday Behind, Sunday Drive, Sweet Revenge; *Publications:* Postcards From the Edge (also screenplay) (PEN award) 1987, Surrender the Pink 1990, Delusions of Grandma 1994; short stories. *Address:* Creative Artists Agency, 9830 Wilshire Blvd, Beverly Hills, CA 90212.

FISHER, Elisabeth Neill, MA; British circuit judge; b 24 Nov 1944, Northampton; d of Kenneth Neill and Lorna Charlotte Honor Fisher. *Education:* Oxford High School for Girls (GPDST) and Univ of Cambridge. *Career:* Called to the Bar, Inner Temple 1968; Circuit Judge (Midland and Oxford Circuit) since 1989; mem Senate and Bar Council 1983–86, Criminal Justice Consultative Council 1992–99; Chair Birmingham Family Mediation Service 1996–, Home Sec's Advisory Bd on Restricted Patents 1998–; D UNIV (Cen England) 1997. *Address:* Queen Elizabeth II Law Courts, 2 Newton St, Birmingham B4 7NA, UK. *Telephone:* (121) 681-3300.

FISHER, Jimmie Lou; American state official; b 31 Dec 1941, Delight, AR. *Education:* Arkansas State Univ, John F. Kennedy School of Govt, Harvard Univ. *Career:* Treas Greene Co, AR 1971–78; Auditor, Little Rock, AR 1979, State Treas 1981–; Sec Arkansas State Bd of Finance; mem Arkansas Bd of Election Commrs; fmr Vice-Chair Democrat State Cttee; fmr mem Democrat Nat Cttee; Del Democrat Nat Convention 1988; Pres Nat Asscn of State Treasurers. *Address:* Treasury Dept, 220 State Capitol Bldg, Little Rock, AR 72201, USA.

FISHER, Valerie Claire, AO, OBE; Australian organization official; b 15 May 1927, Melbourne; d of Clyde and Nita Olholm; m Harold Robert Fisher 1950. *Education:* Royal Melbourne Inst of Tech. *Career:* Foundation mem Country Women's Asscn (Barnawartha Br) 1952, State Pres (Vic) 1973–75, Nat Pres 1975–77; Pres S Pacific Area Associated Country Women of the World 1973–83, Deputy Pres 1983–89, World Pres 1989–95; mem Women's Advisory Council to Prime Minister 1978–1981, Advisory Council to Vic Premier 1982–1984, Nat Breast Cancer Council 1996–; Queen's Silver Jubilee Medal 1978; Anzac of the Year Peace Award 1992; Nat Outstanding

Achiever of the Year 1992. *Leisure interests:* reading, gardening, church welfare work, swimming. *Address:* Avonlea, Barnawartha, Vic 3688, Australia. *Telephone:* (60) 26 7256; *Fax:* (60) 26 7256.

FITZGERALD, Frances; American writer; b 1940; d of Desmond Fitzgerald and Marietta Peabody Fitzgerald Tree. *Education:* Radcliffe Coll. *Career:* Writer of a series of profiles, Vietnam 1966 and of a series of profiles for Herald Tribune newspaper; Overseas Press Club Award 1967; Nat Inst of Arts and Letters Award 1973; Pulitzer Prize 1973; Nat Book Award 1973; Sydney Hillman Award 1973; George Polk Award 1973; Bancroft Award for History 1973. *Publications include:* Fire in the Lake: The Vietnamese and the Americans in Vietnam 1972, America Revised 1979. *Address:* c/o Simon and Schuster Inc, 1230 Ave of the Americas, New York, NY 10020, USA.

FITZGERALD, Judith Ariana, MA, PH D; Canadian poet, columnist and professor of English; b 11 Nov 1952, Toronto. *Education:* York Univ (ON) and Univ of Toronto. *Career:* Asst Prof Laurentian Univ (ON) 1981–83; Poetry Ed Black Moss Press 1981–87; critic The Toronto Star 1984–88, columnist 1987, 1992–93, 1997–1999; Ed Countrywave 1995–1996; creator and Sr Writer Today's Country 1992–1998; regular contrib to The Glode and Mail and The Globe Review; numerous writer-in-residenceships; juror Gov-Gen's Poetry Award 1998; Canada Council Arts Grant A 1988, 1990, 1991, 1993, Professional Writers' Grant 2000; Fiona Mee Award 1983; Silver Medal, New York Int Radio Festival 1995, 1996, 1997, Gold 1998. *Publications include:* Victory 1975, Lacerating Heartwood 1977, Easy Over 1981, Un Dozen: thirteen Canadian Poets (ed) 1982, Split/Level 1983, Beneath the Skin of Paradise: The Piaf Poems 1984, My Orange Gorange 1985, Given Names (Writers' Choice Award 1986) 1985, Whale Waddleby 1986, SP/ELLES: Poetry by Canadian Women/Poésie de femmes canadiennes (ed) 1986, Diary of Desire 1987, First Person Plural (ed) 1987, Rapturous Chronicles 1991, Ultimate Midnight 1992, Habit of Blues: Rapturous Chronicles II 1993, Walkin' Wounded 1993, River 1995, Building a Mystery: the Story of Sarah McLachlan and Lilith Fair 1997, Twenty-Six Ways Out of This World 1999, Sarah McLachlan: Building a Mystery 2000, Adagios 2000, Marshall McLuhan: Wise Guy 2001; numerous criticism and poetry in anthologies, journals and newspapers. *Leisure interests:* baseball, music, ornithology. *Address:* POB 876, Sundridge, ON P0A 1Z0, Canada. *Internet:* www.onlink.net/judithfitzgerald.

FITZGERALD, Sylvia Mary Denise, BA, FLS; British librarian; b 1939, London; d of Audeen Aengus and Doris Winifred (née Dickinson) Fitzgerald. *Education:* Convent of Our Lady of Sion (Worthing, Sussex) and Open Univ. *Career:* Librarian Science Museum 1956–57, British Museum 1957–63, Patent Office 1963–65, Ministry of Agric, Fisheries and Food 1965–79; Chief Librarian and Archivist Royal Botanic Gardens, Kew 1979–99; Assoc Library Asscn 1962–. *Leisure interests:* friends, music, teaching. *Address:* 139 London Rd, Ewell, Epsom, Surrey KT17 2BT, UK.

FITZGERALD, Tara; British actress; b 18 Sept 1969; d of the late Michael Callaby and of Sarah Geraldine Fitzgerald. *Career:* Stage debut in Our Song, London. *Plays include:* Our Song, Hamlet 1995, Antigone 1999; *Films include:* Hear My Song 1990, Sirens 1994, The Englishman Who Went Up a Hill But Came Down a Mountain 1995, Brassed Off 1996, Childhood 1997, Conquest 1998, New World Disorder 1998, The Cherry Orchard 1999, Rancid Aluminium 1999; *TV appearances include:* The Black Candle, The Camomile Lawn, Anglo-Saxon Attitudes, Six Characters in Search of an Author, Fall from Grace, The Tenant of Wildfell Hall, The Student Prince, The Woman in White, Frenchman's Creek, In the Name of Love. *Address:* c/o Caroline Dawson Associates, 19 Sydney Mews, London SW3 6HL. *Telephone:* (20) 7581-8111; *Fax:* (20) 7589-4800.

FIVE, Karin Cecilie (Kaci) Kullmann, MA; Norwegian business executive and former politician; b 13 April 1951, Oslo; d of Kjell and Anne-Lise (née Heiberg) Kullmann; m Carsten O. Five 1972; one s one d. *Education:* Univ of Oslo. *Career:* Deputy mem Storting 1977–81, mem 1981–; Deputy Chair Conservative Party 1982–88; Vice-Chair Conservative Party Parly Group 1985–89; mem Baerum Municipal Council 1975–81; Deputy mem Nat Council on Youth Affairs 1979–81; Exec Officer, Norwegian Employers' Fed 1980–81; Minister of Trade and

Shipping 1989–90; Leader Conservative Party 1991–94; Conservative Party Spokesperson for Foreign Affairs and EU 1994; Sr Adviser European Public Policy Advisers (EPPA) 1997–98; Sr Vice-Pres Aker RGI 1998–. *Address:* c/o Aker RGI AS, Fjordalléen 16, POB 1423 Vika, N-0115 Oslo, Norway. *Telephone:* 2413 0000; *Fax:* 2413 0101; *E-mail:* kaci@aker-rgi.com; *Internet:* www.aker-rgi.com/eng/1_html/l_five.html.

FLAHERTY, Mary Diana, BA; Irish politician; b 17 May 1953; d of Tom and Lucy (née McManamon) Flaherty; m Alexis Fitzgerald 1982; four s. *Education:* Holy Faith Convent (Dublin) and Univ Coll Dublin. *Career:* School teacher 1974–81; elected to Dublin City Council 1979, 1985, 1991; TD 1981–; Minister of State for Health and Social Welfare Jan–Nov 1981; Opposition Jr Spokesperson for Health 1987, for Devt Co-operation 1988; Front Bench Spokesperson for Health and Social Welfare 1989–91, for Energy 1991–93; Govt Convenor Social Affairs Cttee 1994. *Leisure interests:* gardening, walking, cooking, cycling. *Address:* Dáil Éireann, Leinster House, Kildare St, Dublin 2, Ireland (Office); 2 Richmond Place, Dublin 6, Ireland (Home). *Telephone:* (1) 614403 (Office); (1) 976620 (Home).

FLEMING, Jacky, BFA; British cartoonist and illustrator; b 19 Jan 1955, London; d of Gerald Fleming and Lore Erwine Librowicz. *Education:* N London Collegiate School, Chelsea School of Art and Univ of Leeds. *Career:* Fmrly teacher of Art, now freelance cartoonist and illustrator; first cartoon published 1978; contribs to the BBC, The Women's Press, Oxford Univ Press, Open Univ, The Independent on Sunday, The Guardian, New Statesman and Society, New Internationalist, etc. *Publications include:* Be a Bloody Train Driver 1991, Never Give Up 1992, Falling in Love 1993, Dear Katie 1994, Hello Boys 1996. *Leisure interests:* piano, painting. *E-mail:* jackyfleming1@hotmail.com; *Internet:* www.jackyfleming.co.uk.

FLEMING, Renée, M MUS; American opera singer (soprano); b 14 Feb 1959, Indiana; d of Edwin Davis Fleming and Patricia (Seymour) Alexander; m Richard Lee Ross 1989 (divorced 2000); two d. *Education:* Potsdam State Univ, Eastman School of Music (Univ of Rochester) and Juilliard School American Opera Center. *Career:* Fulbright Scholar to Germany 1984–85; intly renowned for her performances of vocal music by Mozart and Richard Strauss; George London Prize 1988, Richard Tucker Award 1990, Solti Prize, Acad du Disque Lyrique 1996, Vocalist of the Year (Musical America) 1977, Prize Acad du Disque Lyrique 1998, Grammy Award 1999. *Music:* debuts Houston Grand Opera (Marriage of Figaro) 1988, Spoleto Festival, Charleston and Italy 1986–90, New York City Opera (La Bohème) 1989, San Francisco Opera, Metropolitan Opera, Paris Opera at Bastille, Teatro Colon, Buenos Aires (all Marriage of Figaro) 1991, Glyndebourne (Così fan tutte) 1992, La Scala Milan (Don Giovanni) 1993, Vienna State Opera (Marriage of Figaro) 1993, Lyric Opera of Chicago (Susannah) 1993, San Diego Opera (Eugene Onegin) 1994, Paris Opera 1996. *Address:* c/o M. L. Falcone Public Relations, 155 W 68th St, Apt 1114, New York, NY 10023, USA. *Telephone:* (212) 580-4302; *Fax:* (212) 787-9638.

FLEMMING, Marilies, LL D; Austrian politician; b 1933, Wiener Neustadt; two c. *Education:* Univ of Cambridge (UK). *Career:* Works for Austrian Academic Asscn; mem Österreichische Volkspartei (ÖVP, Austrian People's Party); Sec-Gen Austrian Women's Movt (attached to ÖVP) 1977–84, elected Head 1984; mem Viennese Prov Council, Cttee for Social Affairs and Health, Cultural Cttee since 1978; fmr Minister for the Environment, Youth Affairs and Family; Chair Austrian Div European Women's Union, Christian Democrat Women's Union, Austrian Women's Asscn. *Address:* Ministry of the Environment, Youth and Family, Radetzkystr 2, 1031 Vienna, Austria.

FLESCH, Colette; Luxembourg politician and European Communities official; b 6 April 1937. *Education:* Wellesley Coll and Fletcher School of Law and Diplomacy (MA, USA). *Career:* Admin Gen Secr EC Council, Brussels 1964–69; nominated MEP 1969–79, elected 1979–80, 1984–85, 1989–90, Vice-Chair Cttee on Budgets and LDR group 1989–90, mem (fmr Chair) Cttee on Devt and Co-operation; mem Luxembourg Chamber of Deputies 1969–80, 1984–89; fmr Minister of Foreign Affairs, of Trade and Co-operation, of Justice; Mayor, Luxembourg 1970–80; Dir-Gen Directorate-Gen X (Informa-

tion, Communication and Culture), EU Comm. *Address:* c/o Directorate-General X, Commission of the EU, 200 rue de la Loi, 1049 Brussels, Belgium. *Telephone:* (2) 235-11-11; *Fax:* (2) 235-01-22.

FLETCHER, Betty Binns, BA, LL B; American federal judge; b 29 March 1923, Tacoma, WA; d of John Howard and Carrie (née Hammond) Binns; m Robert L. Fletcher 1942; two s two d. *Education:* Stanford Univ and Univ of Washington. *Career:* Fmr Dir Seattle Trust and Savings Bank; called to the Bar, WA 1956; Partner Preston, Thorgrimson, Ellis, Holman and Fletcher 1956–79; US Circuit Judge, 9th Circuit Court of Appeals 1979–; Pres Fed Judges' Asscn; mem American Law Inst, ABA, American Judicature Soc; Outstanding Judge Award, Seattle-King Co Bar Asscn 1990; ABA Margaret Brent Women Lawyers of Achievement Award 1992. *Address:* US Court of Appeals, 9th Circuit, 1000 US Courthouse, 1010 5th Ave, Seattle, WA 98104, USA. *Telephone:* (206) 553-2670; *Fax:* (206) 553-4788.

FLETCHER, Louise, BA; American actress; b 1936, Birmingham, AL; d of Robert Capers Fletcher. *Education:* Univ of N Carolina. *Career:* Mem Bd of Dirs Deafness Research Foundation; Hon LHD (Gallaudet Univ) 1982, (W Maryland Coll) 1986. *Films include:* Thieves Like Us 1973, Russian Roulette 1974, One Flew Over the Cuckoo's Nest (Acad Award for Best Actress) 1975, Exorcist II: The Heretic 1976, The Cheap Detective 1977, The Magician 1978, Natural Enemies 1979, The Lucky Star 1979, The Lady in Red 1979, Strange Behavior 1980, Brainstorm 1981, Strange Invaders 1982, Once Upon a Time in America 1982, Firestarter 1983, Overnight Sensation 1983, Invaders from Mars 1985, The Boy Who Could Fly 1985, Nobody's Fool 1986, Flowers in the Attic 1987, Two Moon Junction 1988, Blue Steel 1988, Best of the Best 1989, Shadowzone 1989, Blind Vision 1990, The Player 1991, Return to Two Moon Junction 1993, Tollbooth 1993; *TV appearances include:* Maverick, Wagon Train, The Law-Man, Playhouse 90, The Millionaire, Alfred Hitchcock, Thou Shalt Not Commit Adultery 1978, A Summer to Remember 1984, Island 1984, Second Serve 1985, Hoover 1986, The Karen Carpenter Story 1988, Final Notice 1989, The Hitchhiker 1990, Tales from the Crypt 1991, In a Child's Name 1991, Boys of Twilight 1991, The Fire Next Time 1992, Civil Wars 1993, Deep Space Nine 1994, 1995, The Haunting of Cliff House, Dream On 1994, Someone Else's Child 1995, VR5 1994, 1995, Twisted Path 1997, Brimstone 1998, Devil's Arithmetic 1999.

FLETT, Kathryn Alexandra; British journalist; b 1 April 1964, Herts; d of Douglas J. Flett and Patricia Jenkins. *Education:* Notting Hill and Ealing High School and Hammersmith and West London Coll. *Career:* Staff writer I-D magazine 1985–87; Fashion Ed then Features Ed The Face 1987–89; freelance contrib to numerous publications including The Times, The Sunday Times, The Observer, The Guardian, The Face, Arena, Elle, Harpers Bazaar, etc 1989–92; contributing Ed Arena 1991–92, Ed 1992–; Ed Arena Homme Plus 1992–; columnist The Observer 1994–. *Address:* Arena Magazine, Exmouth House, 3rd Floor Block A, Pine St, London EC1, UK. *Telephone:* (20) 7837-7270; *Fax:* (20) 7837-3906.

FLOCKHART, Calista; American actress; b 11 Nov 1964, Freeport, IL; d of Ronald and Kay Flockhart; one adopted s. *Films include:* Quiz Show 1994, Naked in New York 1994, Getting In 1994, The Birdcage 1996, Pictures of Baby Jane Doe 1996, Drunks 1997, Telling Lies in America 1997, Milk and Money 1997, A Midsummer Night's Dream 1999, Like a Hole in the Head 1999, Jane Doe 1999; *Plays on Broadway include:* The Glass Menagerie, The Three Sisters; *TV:* The Guiding Light 1978, Darrow 1991, An American Story 1991, Life Stories: Families in Crisis 1992, Ally McBeal (Best Actress Award Golden Globe 1998) 1997–. *Address:* c/o David E. Kelly Productions, Twentieth Century Fox, 10201 W Pico Blvd, Building 80, Los Angeles, CA 90064, USA.

FLODIN, May Valborg; Finnish boat constructor, nurse and politician; b 5 May 1934, Helsinki; d of Hjalmar and Astrid (née Lindholm) Rehnberg; m Nilstorsten Flodin 1959; one s one d. *Education:* Helsingfors Svenska Sjukvårdsinstitut, Univ of Helsinki, Åbo Akademi Univ and Nordic School of Public Health (Sweden). *Career:* Dist Nurse 1956–72; Nursing Educator and School Nurse 1973–76; Dir of Nursing 1976–; mem Landskapsstyrelsen (Åland Islands Govt) 1980–81, Deputy Chair 1984–91; mem Landsting (Åland Islands Parl) 1984–;

mem Nordic Council 1984–; Cross of Merit Order of the Lion of Finland 1984. *Leisure interests:* literature, art, organization work, theatre. *Address:* Ålands Landsting, PB 69, 22100 Mariehamn, Åland Islands, Finland. *Telephone:* (28) 25000; *Fax:* (28) 19155.

FLON, Suzanne; French actress; b 28 Jan 1918, Kremlin-Bicêtre. *Career:* Sec to singer Edith Piaf; numerous appearances in films, on stage and on TV; Chevalier des Arts et des Lettres; Grand Prix Nat des Arts et des Lettres (for Theatre) 1980; several other awards. *Plays include:* Le survivant 1943, La maison de Bernarda Alba, La mégère apprivoisée 1957, Long voyage vers la nuit 1973, De si tendres liens 1984–85, Gigi 1985, Léopold le bien-aimé (Molière Award for Best Actress) 1987, Fièvre romaine 1988, Une absence 1988, L'antichambre 1991, La chambre d'amis (Molière Award for Best Actress) 1995; *Films include:* Moulin Rouge, Tu ne tueras point (Coupe Volpi for Best Actress, Venice Festival) 1961, Amours célèbres, Tante Zita 1967, Teresa (Best Actress Award, Taormina Festival) 1970, Un amour de pluie 1974, Docteur Françoise Gailland, Quartet 1981, L'été meurtrier (César for Best Supporting Actress) 1983, En toute innocence 1988, Journal d'un vieux fou 1988, La vouivre (César for Best Supporting Actress) 1989, Gaspard et Robinson 1990, Voyage à Rome 1992, Les enfants du marais 1999, Je suis né d'une cigogne 1999; *TV appearances include:* Un voyage en province 1975, Dialogues de carmélites, Mademoiselle Clarisse 1984, Le dernier civil 1985. *Address:* c/o Nora Stern, 4 bis rue de la Grande Chaumière, 75006 Paris, France.

FLOOD, Josephine Mary, PH D; Australian archaeologist; b 25 July 1936, Yorks, UK; d of Philip Lowther and the late Mary Scarr; m 1st Philip Flood 1964 (divorced); m 2nd Nigel Peacock 1991; two s one d. *Education:* Lowther Coll (Abergele) and Girton Coll (Cambridge, UK). *Career:* Leader of Women's Himalayan expedition 1961; Lecturer in Classical Archaeology, ANU 1963–64; Dir Aboriginal Heritage Section, Australian Heritage Comm 1978–91, Asst Dir Australian Heritage Comm 1978–91; Prin Investigator Earthwatch (archaeology and rock art project in Northern Territory) 1988–92; researcher and writer 1991–; Fellow Royal Geographical Soc 1962, Australian Acad of the Humanities 1991. *Publications:* Four Miles High 1966, The Moth Hunters 1980, Archaeology of the Dreamtime 1983, The Riches of Ancient Australia 1990. *Leisure interests:* mountaineering, skiing, photography, rock art research. *Address:* 19 Chauvel Crescent, Tuross Head, NSW 2537, Australia.

FLOUZAT, Denise, D ÈS ECON; French economist; b 4 Dec 1928, Paris; d of Joseph and Juliette Chandelier; m 1st Maurice Flouzat (deceased); one s one d; m 2nd Juvénal Osmont d'Amilly 1992. *Education:* Univ of Paris and Inst d'Etudes Politiques de Paris. *Career:* Prof Univ of Toulon 1974–76, Univ of Paris X 1976–78; Prof Univ of Paris I (Panthéon-Sorbonne) 1978–86, Prof of Man 1988; Rector Acad of Orléans-Tours 1986–88; Dir CRERAP (Centre for Teaching and Research on the Econs of the Asia–Pacific Region) 1988; Vice-Pres Acad of Accountancy 1994–96, Pres 1996–; mem Council for Monetary Politics Banque de France, also mem Gen Council 1994–99; Auditor Inst of Higher Educ of Nat Defence 1980–81; Prin Attaché Gen Army Inspection 1986; Chevalier de la Légion d'Honneur; Chevalier de l'Ordre Nat du Mérite; Officier des Palmes Académiques. *Publications include:* Analyse économique-comptabilité nationale (5th edn) 1993, Economie contemporaine: (vol I) Les fonctions économiques (16th edn) 1994, (vol II) Les phénomènes monétaires nationaux et internationaux (13th edn) 1995, (vol III) Croissance, crise et stratégies économique (6th edn) 1991, L'Euro: les essentiels 1998, La nouvelle émergence de l'Asie 1999; articles on the economies of Japan, Repub of Korea and Indonesia. *Address:* 21 ave Marceau, 75016 Paris, France.

FLOWERS, Angela Mary; British gallery owner; b 19 Dec 1932, Croydon; d of Geoffrey and Olive Holland; m Adrian Flowers 1952 (divorced); three s one d; partner Robert Heller; one d. *Education:* Westonbirt School (Kent), Wychwood School (Oxford) and Webber-Douglas Acad of Dramatic Art (London). *Career:* Opened Angela Flowers Gallery, Soho, London 1970, Flowers East, Hackney 1988, Flowers West, Bergamot Station, Santa Monica, CA 1998; also summer exhibitions at Angela Flowers (Ireland) Inc, Downeen, Co Cork. *Address:* Flowers East Gallery, 199–205 Richmond Rd, Hackney, London E8 3NJ, UK. *Telephone:* (20) 8985-3333; *Fax:* (20) 8985-0067; *E-mail:* gallery@flowerseast.com; *Internet:* www.flowereast.co.uk.

FOALE, Marion Ann; British fashion designer; b 13 March 1939, London; d of Stuart and Gertrude (née Rayner) Foale; m Christopher Jones 1971; one s one d. *Education:* Ilford Co High School (London) and Royal Coll of Art. *Career:* Fashion designer 1962–; designed Queen's mantle for OBE dedication ceremony 1960; founding partner (with Sally Tuffin) Foale and Tuffin Ltd 1961–72; signed with Puritan Fashion Corps, NY 1965–70; designed clothes for films: Susannah York (qv) in Kaleidoscope 1966, Audrey Hepburn in Two for the Road 1966; f own label Marion Foale–Knitwear Designer 1982. *Publication:* Marion Foale's Classic Knitwear Book 1987. *Leisure interests:* swimming, cats, studying fine art. *Address:* Foale Ltd, 133A Long St, Atherstone, Warwicks CV9 1AD, UK (Office); Church Farm, Orton-on-the-Hill, Nr Atherstone, Warwicks CV9 3NG, UK. *Telephone:* (1827) 720333; *Fax:* (1827) 720444; *E-mail:* foale@talk21.com (Office).

FOCH, Nina; American actress and producer; b 20 April 1924, Leyden, Netherlands; d of Dirk and Consuelo (née Flowerton) Foch; m 1st James Lipton 1954; m 2nd Dennis de Brito 1959; m 3rd Michael Dewell 1967; one s. *Education:* Lincoln School and Univ of Southern California. *Career:* Founder, Actress Los Angeles Theater Group 1960–65, Nina Foch Studio 1973–; Adjunct Prof of Drama Univ of Southern California 1966–68, 1978–80; Adjunct Prof of Film Directing 1987–; Artist-in-Residence Univ of N Carolina 1966, Ohio State Univ 1967, California Inst of Tech 1969–70; Sr Faculty mem American Film Inst 1974–77; mem Bd Dirs Nat Repertory Theater 1967–75; creative consultant to numerous dirs, writers and producers. *Plays include:* John Loves Mary 1947, Twelfth Night 1949, Tonight at 8.30 1966–67 (dir), A Phoenix Too Frequent 1950, King Lear 1950, Second String 1960; *Films include:* Nine Girls 1944, My Name is Julia Ross 1945, I Love a Mystery 1945, The Guilt of Janet Ames 1947, The Dark Past 1948, An American in Paris 1951, Sombrero 1953, Executive Suite (Acad Award nomination) 1954, The Ten Commandments 1956, Spartacus 1960, Salty 1973, Rich and Famous 1981, Skin Deep 1988, Sliver 1994, Morning Glory 1994, It's my Party 1995, 'Til there was you 1996, Kilronan 1996; *TV appearances include:* Lou Grant (Emmy Award nomination 1980), War and Remembrance 1988, The Today Show, The Tonight Show, LA Law 1991. *Leisure interests:* cooking, swimming. *Address:* POB 1884, Beverly Hills, CA 90213, USA.

FOCKE, Katharina, D PHIL; German politician (retd) and journalist (retd); b 8 Oct 1922, Bonn; d of Ernest and Franziska (née Schulz) Friedlaender; m Ernst Günter Focke 1954 (died 1961). *Education:* Univ of Hamburg. *Career:* Journalist 1946–54; joined SPD 1964; mem N Rhine-Westphalia Lantag (regional Parl) 1966; mem Bundestag (Parl) 1969–80, mem Cttee for Devt 1976–79; Parl State Sec of Fed Chancellor 1969–72; Fed Minister for Youth, Family Affairs and Health 1972–76; MEP 1979–89, mem Cttee for Devt and Co-operation 1979. *Publications include:* Europa über den Nationen 1962, Europäer in Frankreich 1965. *Leisure interests:* cooking, gardening, music, travelling. *Address:* Drost-Hülshoffstr 21, 50968 Cologne 51, Germany. *Telephone:* (221) 385236; *Fax:* (221) 3779822.

FOGGO, Dianne Blair; Australian trade union executive; b 16 Nov 1947, Bairnsdale, Vic; d of Geoffrey Gordon and Neila Blair Foggo; m Paul Byrne 1989. *Education:* Darwin Community Coll, Victoria Coll of Educ and Univ of Melbourne. *Career:* School teacher 1969–82; Gen-Sec N Territory Teachers' Fed 1982–84; Industrial/Womens' Officer Australian Teachers' Union 1984–87, Industrial Officer 1986–88, Pres 1988–92; Exec mem Australian Council of Trade Unions 1988–92, Vice-Pres 1991–92; mem Bd Australian Broadcasting Comm 1990–92; inaugural mem Schools Council, Nat Bd of Employment Educ and Training 1988–90; Commr Australian Industrial Relations Comm 1992–. *Address:* Level 35, Nauru House, 80 Collins St, Melbourne, Vic 2000, Australia.

FOLEY, Carmel; Irish women's organization executive. *Career:* Chief Exec Council for the Status of Women; mem Comm for the Status of Women; Dir of Consumer Affairs Nov 1998–. *Address:* Office of the Director of Consumer Affairs, 4 Harcourt Rd, Dublin, 2, Ireland. *Telephone:* (1) 4025555; *Fax:* (1) 4025501; *Internet:* www.odca.ie.

FOLEY, Joan Eleanor, BA, PH D; Canadian professor emeritus of psychology and former university administrator; b 31 May 1936, Sydney; d of Alfred Joseph and Bessie Ridgway Mason; two s. *Education:*

Univ of Sydney. *Career:* Lives and works in Canada; Scientific Officer Defence Research Medical Labs, Downsview, ON 1960–62; Special Lecturer in Psychology Univ of Toronto 1963, Asst Prof 1963–65, Assoc Prof 1965–75, acting Chair Dept of Psychology 1969–70, Assoc Dean Faculty of Arts and Science 1971–74, Prof of Psychology 1975–2001, Prof Emer 2001–, Chair Dept of Psychology 1985, Univ Vice-Pres, Provost 1985–93; Chair Div of Life Science, Scarborough Coll 1975–77, Prin 1976–84, 1999–2000; Dir Donwood Inst 1973–88, Chair of Bd 1986–88; Dir Ontario Psychological Foundation 1987–92; Dir Int Devt Research Centre 1989–97, Vice-Chair 1992–95; has written numerous articles for academic journals on learning, perception, spatial orientation; Fellow Canadian Psychological Asscn. *Leisure interests:* gardening, tennis. *Address:* Div of Life Sciences, Scarborough College, University of Toronto, 1265 Military Trail, Scarborough ON M1C 1A4, Canada (Office); 168 Madison Ave, Toronto, ON M5R 2S5, Canada (Home). *Telephone:* (416) 287-7568; *Fax:* (416) 287-7569; *E-mail:* foley@utsc.utoronto.ca.

FOLEY, Johanna Mary (Jo), BA; British magazine editor; b 8 Dec 1945, Co Kerry, Ireland; d of the late John and Mary Foley; m Desmond Francis Conor Quigley 1973. *Education:* St Joseph's Convent (Kenilworth) and Manchester Univ. *Career:* Reporter Birmingham Post 1970; Beauty Ed Woman's Own 1972–73, Sr Asst Ed 1978; Launch Ed Successful Slimming 1976; Woman's Ed The Sun 1980; Ed Woman 1982, Observer Magazine 1986, Options 1988–91; Exec Ed The Times 1984–85; freelance journalist and media consultant 1991–; Magazine Ed of the Year 1983. *Leisure interests:* eating, reading, cinema, opera. *Address:* The Reform Club, Pall Mall, London SW1, UK.

FOLLETT, Barbara, B SC; British academic and organization executive; b 25 Dec 1942, Kingston, Jamaica; m 1st Richard Turner; m 2nd Gerald Stonestreet; m 3rd Leslie Broer; m 4th Ken Follett; two d one s one step-s one step-d. *Education:* LSE and Open Univ. *Career:* Teacher Berlitz School of Language, Paris 1963–64; Man (jt) of fruit farm, Stellenbosch, S Africa 1966–77; Regional Sec (acting) S African Inst of Race Relations, Cape Town 1970; Regional Man (Cape and Namibia) Kupugani 1971–74, Dir (with special responsibility for health educ projects) 1975–78; Asst Course Organizer and Lecturer Centre for Int Briefing, Farnham, Surrey 1980–84; freelance lecturer and consultant 1984–92; Founder-mem and Dir EMILY's List UK 1992–; Visiting Fellow Inst of Public Policy Research 1993–; Labour Party Parl Cand 1984, 1986–87; MP for Stevenage 1997; Founder mem Women's Movt for Peace, S Africa, Labour Party Women's Network (mem Steering Cttee 1988–); mem The Black Sash, Fawcett Soc, Nat Alliance of Women's Orgs, Nat Women's Network, Womankind. *Leisure interests:* film, theatre, reading, photography, Scrabble, Star Trek. *Address:* 4 Popple Way, Stevenage SG1 3TG, UK. *Telephone:* (1438) 817910 (Home); *Fax:* (1438) 810444 (Home); *E-mail:* barbara@barbara-follett .org.uk; *Internet:* www.barbara-follett.org.uk.

FOLLETT, Rosemary, BA; Australian politician; b 27 March 1948; d of Aubrey and Judith Follett. *Education:* Merici Coll (Canberra) and Univ of Canberra. *Career:* Fmr public servant; elected Lab Party mem Old House of Ass (Legis Ass) for Fraser 1985; Chief Minister Australian Capital Territory (first woman Head of State Govt in Australia) May–Dec 1989, 1991–95; Leader of Opposition 1989–91; ACT Discrimination Commr 1996–; Pres Australian Capital Territory br Lab Party 1987–89. *Leisure interests:* reading, music, sport. *Address:* ACT Human Rights Office, POB 158, Canberra, ACT 2601, Australia. *Telephone:* (6) 205 0000; *Fax:* (6) 205 0535; *E-mail:* follett@dpa.act.gov .au.

FOLLIOT, Yolande Isoline; French actress; b 12 Dec 1952, Le Mans; d of Gaston and Janine (née Blot) Folliot; m Guy Lerminier 1992; two c (adopted). *Education:* Conservatoire Supérieur d'Art Dramatique de Paris. *Career:* Actress; Bourse de la Vocation 1971; Kangouron d'Or; 7 d'Or 1981. *Plays include:* Le Jeu de l'Amour & du Hasard 1973, Melite 1976, Tartuffe 1979, Snap 1980, Le Mysanthrope 1981, Le Mariage de Figaro 1982, Six Personnages en Quête d'Auteurs 1983, L'Amuse Gueule, La Double Inconstance 1988, Reviens Dormir à l'Élysée 1990, La Paix Chez Soi 1991, Desire 1992, Le Canard a l'Orange 1993, Une Folie 1994, Archibald 1995; *TV includes:* Les Jeunes Filles 1977, Le Petit Paradis 1981, In Grand Avocat 1982, Claire 1985, Arsene Lupin 1988,

Le Temps Mort 1989, Mascarade 1991, Honorin & l'Enfant Prodigue 1993, Nestor Burma 1993, Engaged to the Empire. *Address:* 79 rue Truffaut, 75017 Paris, France (Home).

FONDA, Bridget; American actress; b 27 Jan 1964, Los Angeles, CA; d of Peter and Susan Fonda. *Education:* New York Univ Theater Programme, Lee Strasberg Inst and with Harold Guskin. *Films include:* Aria 1987, You Can't Hurry Love 1988, Scandal 1989, Shag 1989, Strapless 1990, Frankenstein Unbound, The Godfather Part III 1990, Leather Jackets, Out of the Rain, Iron Maze, Doc Hollywood 1991, Singles 1992, Single White Female 1992, Point of No Return 1993, Little Buddha 1994, It Could Happen To You 1994, Camilla 1994, The Road to Wellville 1994, Rough Magic 1995, Balto (voice) 1995, Grace of My Heart 1996, City Hall 1996, Drop Dead Fred, Light Years (voice), Iron Maze, Army of Darkness, Touch, Jackie Brown, Finding Graceland, The Break Up, South of Heaven West of Hell, Monkey Bone, Lake Placid, Delivering Milo; *TV appearances include:* Series: 21 Jump Street, Jacob Have I Loved, WonderWorks (episode) 1989, The Edge (The Professional Man); Film: Leather Jackets 1991, In the Gloaming 1997. *Address:* c/o IFA, 8730 W Sunset Blvd, Suite 490, Los Angeles, CA 90069, USA.

FONDA, Jane; American actress; b 21 Dec 1937; d of the late Henry and Frances (née Seymour) Fonda; m 1st Roger Vadim 1967 (divorced 1973, died 2000); one d; m 2nd Tom Hayden 1973 (divorced 1989); one s; m 3rd Ted Turner 1991 (separated). *Education:* Vassar Coll. *Career:* Has appeared in numerous films and TV programmes; has made several fitness and aerobics videos; Acad Award for Best Actress 1972, 1979; Golden Globe Award 1978. *Films include:* Tall Story 1960, A Walk on the Wild Side 1962, Period of Adjustment 1962, Sunday in New York 1963, The Love Cage 1963, La Ronde 1964, Histoires extraordinaires 1967, Barbarella 1968, They Shoot Horses Don't They? 1969, Klute 1970, Steelyard Blues 1972, Tout va bien 1972, A Doll's House 1973, The Blue Bird 1975, Fun with Dick and Jane 1976, Julia 1977, Coming Home 1978, California Suite 1978, The Electric Horseman 1979, The China Syndrome 1979, Nine to Five 1980, On Golden Pond 1981, Roll-Over 1981, Agnes of God 1985, The Morning After 1986, The Old Gringo, Stanley and Iris 1990, Lakota Woman (producer) 1994; *Plays include:* There Was a Little Girl, Invitation to a March, The Fun Couple, Strange Interlude; *TV appearances include:* The Dollmaker 1984 (Emmy Award); *Publications include:* Jane Fonda's Workout Book 1982, Women Coming of Age 1984, Jane Fonda's New Workout and Weight Loss Program 1986, Jane Fonda's New Pregnancy Workout and Total Birth Program 1989, Jane Fonda Workout Video, Jane Fonda Cooking for Healthy Living 1996. *Address:* c/o CAA, 9830 Wilshire Blvd, Beverly Hills, CA 90212, USA (Office).

FONG WONG KUT MAN, Nellie; Chinese politician and accountant; b 7 Feb 1949, Hong Kong; m Eddy C. Fong; one c. *Career:* Practises as chartered accountant; mem Hong Kong Urban Council 1983–89, Legis Council 1988–91, People's Repub of China Hong Kong Special Admin Region Preliminary and Preparatory Cttees 1993–97 (Leader Econ Sub-Group), Exec Council of Hong Kong Special Admin Region July 1997–; Chair Exec Cttee The Better Hong Kong Foundation 1995, China Operations, Arthur Andersen; mem Standing Comm on Civil Service Salaries and Conditions of Service 1989–93, Hong Kong Baptist Univ Council 1990–92, numerous other cttees and bds; Gold Bauhenia Star 1999. *Address:* Executive Council Secretariat, 1st Floor, Main Wing, Central Government Offices, Hong Kong Special Administrative Region, People's Republic of China. *Telephone:* 28520294; *Fax:* 28504092; *E-mail:* nellie.k.fong@hk.arthurandersen.com.

FONTAINE, Nicole, D EN D; French politician; b 16 Jan 1942, Normandy; d of Jean and Geneviève (née Lambert) Garnier; m Jean-René Fontaine 1964; one d. *Education:* Univ of Paris and Inst d'Etudes Politiques (Paris). *Career:* Deputy Sec-Gen Catholic Educ Secr (France) 1972–81, Chief Rep 1981–84; mem Nat Educ Council (France) 1975–81, Econ and Soc Council (France) 1980–84; MEP 1984–, Vice-Pres EP 1994–99, Pres 1999–; perm mem Conciliation Cttee 1994–; Chair EP del to COSAC (Conf of Bodies Specialising in Community Affairs); mem Governing Council, Exec Cttee and Political Bureau Nouvelle UDF Party, Chair cttee responsible for relations with the European insts. *Publications:* L'enseignement privé associé à l'Etat par contrat, L'école libre et l'Etat, Les Deputés Européens: Qui sont-ils?

Que font-ils? 1994, L'Europe de vos initiatives 1997, Le traité d'Amsterdam, à l'attention de ceux qui aimeraient s'intéresser à l'Europe si elle était moins obscure 1998. *Address:* European Parliament, rue Wiertz, 1047 Brussels, Belgium. *Telephone:* (2) 284-55-62; *Fax:* (2) 284-95-62.

FOOKES, Baroness (Life Peer), cr 1997, of Plymouth in the County of Devon, **Janet Evelyn Fookes,** DBE, BA; British politician; b 21 Feb 1936, London; d of the late Lewis Aylmer and Evelyn Margery Fookes. *Education:* Royal Holloway Coll (London). *Career:* Teacher 1958–70; MP (Cons) for Merton and Morden 1970–74, Plymouth, Drake 1974–97, Chair Educ, Arts and Home Affairs Sub-Cttee of Expenditure Cttee 1975–79, Parl Group for Animal Welfare 1985–92, mem Speaker's Panel of Chairs 1976–97, mem Select Cttee on Home Affairs 1984–92, Deputy Speaker, Second Deputy Chair Ways and Means Cttee 1992–97; mem Council Royal Soc for the Prevention of Cruelty to Animals (RSPCA) 1975–92, Chair 1979–81; mem Commonwealth War Graves Comm 1987–97; mem House of Lords 1997–; Hon D LITT (Plymouth). *Leisure interests:* gardening, gymnasium exercises, yoga, swimming, theatre. *Address:* House of Lords, London SW1A 0PW, UK. *Telephone:* (20) 7219-5353; *Fax:* (20) 7219-5979.

FOOT, Philippa Ruth, MA, FBA; British professor of philosophy; b 3 Oct 1920, Owston Ferry, Lincs; d of W. S. B. and Esther Cleveland Bosanquet; m M. R. D. Foot 1945 (divorced 1960). *Education:* Somerville Coll (Oxford). *Career:* Lecturer in Philosophy Somerville Coll, Oxford 1947–50, Fellow and Tutor 1950–69, Vice-Prin 1967–69, Sr Research Fellow 1970–88, Hon Fellow 1988–; Prof of Philosophy Univ of California at Los Angeles (USA) 1974–91, Griffin Prof 1988–91, Prof Emer 1991–; fmr Visiting Prof Cornell Univ, MIT, Univ of California at Berkeley, Princeton Univ and City Univ of New York (USA); Pres Pacific Div American Philosophical Asscn 1983–84; mem American Acad of Arts and Sciences; Dr hc (Sofia, Bulgaria) 2000. *Publications include:* Theories of Ethics (ed) 1967, Virtues and Vices 1978; articles and reviews in professional journals. *Leisure interests:* reading, walking, gardening. *Address:* 15 Walton St, Oxford OX1 2HG, UK. *Telephone:* (1865) 557130.

FORBES, Leonie Evadne; Jamaican actress, broadcaster and playwright; b 14 June 1937, Kingston; d of Jonathan and Gladys Forbes; m 1st Ludlow Galloway (divorced 1963); one s; m 2nd Keith Amil 1963 (divorced 1975); two d one s; m 3rd Paul Harvey 1978 (divorced 1987). *Education:* Kingston Sr School, Excelsior High School, Durham Coll and Royal Acad of Dramatic Arts (London). *Career:* Sec Extra Mural Dept, Univ of West Indies 1955–60; studies and work in UK 1961–66; Announcer Jamaica Broadcasting Corpn 1960–61, Producer, Presenter Radio and TV 1966–68, Producer, Presenter TV 1970–72, Head FM Radio 2 1972–75, Dir of Broadcasting 1976–77, Head Dept of Theatre 1978–79; Librarian Radio and TV, Australian Broadcasting Corpn 1968–70; Officer of the Order of Distinction 1980; Bronze Musgrave Medal 1974, Silver 1987; Award of Excellence (Caribbean Acad of Arts and Culture) 1991; Centenary Medal (Inst of Jamaica) 1991. *Plays and films include:* Miss Unusual, Sea Mama, The Rope and The Cross, Old Story Time, Champagne and Sky Juice – Children of Babylon, I Marcus Garvey, Milk and Honey, Passion and Paradise, Whiplash; *TV appearances include:* I Is a Long Memoried Woman, Orchid House, Songs of Praise, South of the Border, Dixon of Dock Green, Hugh and I, Martin; *Publications include:* Moments by Myself 1988, Re-entry into Sound, Part IV (jtly) 1989; Plays: Let's Say Grace, What's Good for the Goose, The Baby Born. *Leisure interests:* crochet, writing poetry and plays. *Address:* 6 Barbican Close, Kingston 6, Jamaica. *Telephone:* 927-3584.

FORD, Anna, BA; British broadcaster; b 2 Oct 1943; d of John Ford and Jean Beattie Winstanley; m 1st Alan Holland Bittles (divorced 1976); m 2nd Charles Mark Edward Boxer (died 1988); two d. *Education:* Minehead Grammar School, White House Grammar School (Brampton) and Univ of Manchester. *Career:* Work for students' interests, Univ of Manchester 1966–69; Lecturer Rupert Stanley Coll of Further Educ, Belfast 1970–72; staff tutor, Social Sciences, N Ireland Region, Open Univ 1972–74; presenter and reporter Granada TV 1974–76, Man Alive BBC 1976–77, Tomorrow's World BBC 1977–78; newscaster ITN 1978–80; with TV am 1980–82; freelance broadcasting and writing 1982–86; BBC news and current affairs 1989–; Trustee

Royal Botanic Gardens, Kew 1995–; Hon LL D (Manchester) 1998. *Publication:* Men: A Documentary 1985. *Leisure interests:* talking, writing, drawing. *Address:* BBC Television Centre, Wood Lane, London W12 7RJ, UK. *Telephone:* (20) 7624-9991.

FORD, Betty Bloomer; American organization executive; b 8 April 1918, Chicago, IL; d of William Stephenson and Hortence (née Neahr) Bloomer; m Gerald R. Ford (fmr Pres of USA) 1948; three s one d. *Education:* Bennington Coll. *Career:* Dance Instructor, MI 1932–48; Dancer Martha Graham Concert, New York 1939–41; Model John Powers Agency, New York 1939–41; Fashion Dir Herpolscheimer's Dept Store, MI 1943–48; First Lady of USA 1974–76; currently Pres Bd Dirs The Betty Ford Center, CA; trustee numerous orgs; Hon LL D (Michigan) 1976; Presidential Medal of Freedom 1991. *Publications:* The Times of My Life (autobiog) 1979, Betty: A Glad Awakening 1987. *Address:* POB 927, Rancho Mirage, CA 92270, USA.

FORD, Eileen, BS; American business executive; b 25 March 1922, New York; d of Nathaniel and Loretta Marie Otte; m Gerard William Ford 1944; two d one s. *Education:* Barnard Coll (NY). *Career:* Stylist Elliot Clarke Studio, New York, NY 1943–44, William Becker Studio 1945; Copywriter Arnold Constable, New York 1945–46; Reporter Tobe Coburn 1946; Co-Founder Ford Model Agency 1946, currently Chair; mem Bd Dirs London Philharmonic Orchestra 1948–; Harpers Bazaar Award; Woman of the Year in Advertising award 1983. *Publications:* Eileen Ford's Model Beauty, Secrets of the Model's World, A More Beautiful You in 21 Days, Beauty Now and Forever 1977. *Address:* Ford Modelling Agency, 142 Greene St, New York, NY 10012, USA.

FORDE, (Mary Marguerite) Leneen, LL B, AC, D UNIV; Australian university chancellor; b 12 May 1935; d of John Alfred and Evelyn Philomena (née Bujold) Kavanagh; m 1st Francis Gerard Forde 1955 (divorced 1966); three s two d; m 2nd Angus McDonald 1983 (divorced 1999). *Education:* Lisgar Collegiate (Ottawa) and Univ of Queensland. *Career:* Medical Lab Technician 1953–54; mem staff Haematology Dept, Royal Brisbane Hosp 1954–56; Law Clerk Alexander McGillivray 1969–70; Solicitor Cannan & Peterson 1971–74; Partner Sly, Weigall, Cannan & Peterson 1974–92; Gov of Qld 1992–97; Chancellor Griffith Univ 2000–; Chair Royal Comm of Inquiry into Abuse of Children in Qld Insts 1998–99; mem Bd St Leo's Coll 1998–2000, Brisbane Coll of Theology 1999–2001, Brisbane City Council Arts and Environment Trust 1999–2000, Qld Ballet 2000–, Qld Govt Forde Foundation 2000–; Founder Qld Women Lawyers' Asscn 1976; mem Qld Law Soc 1971–, Women Chiefs of Enterprise Int 1989–; Pres Zonta Int 1990–92, Scout Asscn of Australia 1997–; Patron Nat Pioneer Women's Hall of Fame 1999–; Paul Harris Fellow, Rotary Club of Brisbane 1990; Woman of Substance Award, Qld Girl Guides' Asscn 1990; Qldr of the Year 1991; Dame of the Order of St John of Jerusalem 1992; Hon D LITT (Qld) 1996; Hon D UNIV (Australian Catholic Univ) 2000. *Publication:* Queensland Annual Law Review 1991, 1992. *Leisure interests:* theatre, music, art, surfing, ballet. *Address:* 11 Eighth Ave, St Lucia, Qld 4067, Australia. *Telephone:* (7) 369 7744; *Fax:* (7) 369 9419.

FOREMAN, Amanda, BA, PH D; British historian and writer; b 1968, London; d of Carl Foreman. *Education:* Sarah Lawrence Coll (Bronxville, NY) Columbia Univ (NY) and Lady Margaret Hall (Oxford). *Career:* Henrietta Jex Blake Sr Scholarship, Univ of Oxford 1998; TV and radio presenter 1998–; freelance contrib to newspapers in UK and USA. *Publications include:* Georgiana: Duchess of Devonshire (Whitbread Biography of the Year Award) 1998, Mme de Pompadour (introduction) 2001. *Address:* c/o Random House, 20 Vauxhall Bridge Rd, London SW1V 2SA.

FORERO DE SAADE, María Teresa, D MED; Colombian politician and medical practitioner; b 28 Feb 1939, Vergara, Cundinamarca; m Rafael Saade Abdala; three s. *Education:* Instituto Pedagógico Nacional, Colegio Departamental de la Merced (Bogotá) and Pontificia Univ Javeriana. *Career:* Qualified as doctor 1966; Prof of Paediatrics Univ of Rosario 1968–69, Faculty of Nursing, Nat Red Cross 1971–72; Dir-Gen Colsubsidio Clinic for Children 1974–82; Deputy Senator 1978–82; Vice-Minister of Health 1982, Minister at Ministry of Health 1982; Minister of Labour and Social Security 1989–90; Minister of Health 1996–98. *Address:* FEPAFEM, calle 123, No 8–20, Bogotá, Colombia. *Telephone:* (571) 620-3630 (Office); *Fax:* (571) 213-6809 (Office).

FORESTIER, Sylvie; French curator; b 1 April 1935, Algiers, Algeria; d of Armand and Georgette Laurent; m 2nd Hubert Forestier; one s five step-c. *Education:* Univs of Algiers and Paris (Sorbonne), Inst d'Art et d'Archéologie (Paris) and Centre d'Etudes Supérieures de la Renaissance (Tours). *Career:* Philosophy teacher 1957–61; educational TV and radio Producer 1961–69; Curator Musée Nat du Palais de Compiègne 1969–73, Musée Nat des Arts et Traditions Populaires 1973–83; Curator, Dir Musée Nat le Message Biblique Marc Chagall 1983; Dir Nat 20th Century Collections, Provence-Alpes-Côtes d'Azur region 1993–; Prof Ecole du Louvre 1977–; Curator-Gen of Nat Heritage 1995. *Publications include:* Disputationes adversus astrologiam divinatricem de Pic de la Mirandole 1956, 1850–1900: Le réalisme et la démocratie 1969, Marc Chagall: L'œuvre monumentale, les vitraux 1986, Marc Chagall: L'œuvre gravée 1987, Les Chagall de Chagall 1988, Les céramiques de Chagall 1990, Voyage au cœur d'un chef d'œuvre: résistance, résurrection, libération de Marc Chagall 1990, Pablo Picasso: La guerra e la pace 1991. *Address:* 37 rue Rochambeau, 33000 Bordeaux, France.

FORGAN, Elizabeth Anne Lucy, BA, FRSA; British broadcasting executive; b 31 Aug 1944; d of Thomas Moinet and Jean Margaret Muriel Forgan. *Education:* Benenden School and St Hugh's Coll (Oxford). *Career:* Journalist Teheran Journal 1967–68, Hampstead and Highgate Express 1969–74, Evening Standard 1974–78, The Guardian 1978–81; Sr Commissioning Ed Channel Four TV 1981–86, Deputy Dir of Programmes 1987, Dir 1988–93; Man Dir Network Radio BBC 1993–96; Chair Heritage Lottery Fund April 2001–; Dir Most Media 1998–; mem Scott Trust 1988–93, Bd of Govs BFI 1989–91, Visiting Cttee RCA 1990–93, Human Fertilization and Embryology Authority 1990–; Fellow Royal Television Soc; Hon D LITT (Keele) 1994; Chevalier des Arts et des Lettres 1990. *Leisure interests:* church music, cheap novels, Scottish Islands. *Address:* 112 Regent's Park Rd, London NW1 8UG, UK.

FORGET, Nicolle, B COMM, L EN D; Canadian business executive; b 14 May 1941, Saint-Liguori, PQ; d of Léonard and Noella Forget. *Education:* Coll des Hautes Etudes Commerciales (Montréal) and Univ of Montréal. *Career:* Mem Admin Council Hydro-Québec 1978–85, Hydro-Québec Int 1978–82, Soc d'Energie de la Baie James 1978–84; Chair Admin Council Nouveler Inc 1981–85; mem Canadian Econ Council 1978–81; mem Admin Council Ecole Polytechnique de Montréal 1988; mem Nat Transport Office 1988–93; mem Admin Council Groupe Jean Coutu 1993; Founder-mem, Sec Fédération des Femmes du Québec 1967–68. *Address:* 1170 Maple, Longueuil, PQ J4J 4N6, Canada.

FORNALCZYK, Anna, PH D; Polish economist; b 7 Jan 1947, Łódź; d of Tomasz and Kazimiera Rybak; m Jerzy Fornalczyk 1966; two s. *Education:* Univ of Łódź. *Career:* Asst Prof Univ of Łódź 1968–90; Chair Solidarity Br at Faculty of Econ, Univ of Łódź 1980–89; Adviser to Solidarity, Łódź 1980–86, to Parl Office, Łódź 1989–90; Chief Senator Election Cttee, Łódź 1989; apptd Pres Anti-Monopoly Office 1990, Pres Founders' Council, Int Women Foundation 1992; Awards from Ministry of Educ 1976, 1981, 1987, Polish Economists' Asscn 1984. *Publications:* Integration of Enterprises in Yugoslav Economy 1977, Yugoslav Economic System 1979, Organizational Aspects of the Centrally Planned Economy 1987. *Leisure interests:* mountain-climbing, swimming, journals. *Address:* Anti-Monopoly Office, Plac Powstańców Warszawy 1, 00-950 Warsaw, Poland (Office); Pomorska 66/68 m 11, 91-409 Łódź, Poland (Home). *Telephone:* (22) 263414 (Office); (42) 784616 (Home); *Fax:* (22) 265076 (Office).

FORNER, Jane, B MUS; Canadian arts administrator; b 9 Jan 1939, St Stephen, NB; d of Aubrey and Ethel (née Williamson) Akerley. *Education:* Saint John High School (NB), Mount Allison Univ and Acad of Music and Dramatic Art (Vienna). *Career:* Asst Ed Opera Canada 1969–71; Publicist CBC 1971–72, Producer Music 1971–78, Exec Producer Music 1978–82; Dir of Music CentreStage Music 1982–87; Artistic Dir BACH 300, Toronto 1985; Dir Music Toronto 1987–89; freelance writer 1989–; Man Boris Brott Summer Music Festival 1991–; Dir Richmond Virginia Opera 1992; Dir of Marketing, Vancouver Symphony Orchestra 1995–. *Leisure interest:* sailing. *Address:* 601 Smithe St, Vancouver, BC V6B 5G1, Canada.

FORRAI, Katalin; Hungarian educationalist; b 25 Sept 1926, Debrecen; m Lázló Vikár; two s one d. *Career:* Prof Kindergarten Teachers' Coll 1950–60; children's broadcaster 1952–87; Supervisor Music Educ and Postgrad Courses, Hungarian Pedagogical Inst 1960–68; researcher into early childhood; Bd mem Int Soc for Music Educ 1976–86, Pres Elect 1986, Pres 1988–, Founding Chair Early Childhood Comm; Vice-Pres Int Kodály Soc 1979–83; Music Dir Kodaly Pedagogical Legacy videocassette series 1984; Pres Hungarian Music Council 1990–94; mem Hungarian Union of Composers, Franz Liszt Soc, Hungarian Pedagogical Soc. *Publications:* Children's Games Collection (2nd edn) 1956, Children's Songs of the Neighbouring Peoples 1965, European Children's Songs 1966, Music Methodology and Song Material for Kindergarten (3rd edn) 1974, Music Education in Pre-school (12th edn) 1995. *Address:* 1054 Budapest, Bajcsy 60, Hungary. *Telephone:* (1) 111-7088; *Fax:* (1) 246-8499.

FORRESTER, Helen; British writer; b 6 June 1919, Hoylake, Cheshire. *Education:* Privately. *Career:* Resident in Canada 1953–; Writer-in-Residence Lethbridge Community Coll 1980, Edmonton Public Library 1990; mem Writers' Union of Canada, Soc of Authors (London), Canadian Asscn of Children's Authors, The Authors' Lending and Copyrights Soc Ltd (London); Patron Chester Library Festival; Hon D LITT (Liverpool) 1988, LITT D (Alberta) 1993; Govt of Alberta Achievement Award for Literature 1979; YMCA Woman of the Arts 1987. *Publications include:* Thursday's Child (fmrly Alien There is None 1959), Twopence to Cross the Mersey (autobiog) 1981, Minerva's Stepchild (autobiog) 1979, Liverpool Daisy (Hudson's Bay Beaver Award) 1979, By the Waters of Liverpool (autobiog) 1981, Lime Street at Two (autobiog, Alberta Culture's Literary Award 1986) 1985, The Moneylenders of Shahpur (Hudson's Bay Beaver Award for best unpublished manuscript 1970) 1987, Yes, Mama (Writers' Guild Fiction Award 1989) 1987, The Lemon Tree 1991, The Liverpool Basque 1993, Mourning Doves 1996; numerous short stories, book reviews and contribs to journals. *Leisure interests:* reading, travel. *Address:* c/o Writers' Union of Canada, 24 Ryerson Ave, Toronto, ON M5T 9Z9, Canada.

FORRESTER, Maureen, CC, D MUS; Canadian musician and administrator; b 25 July 1930, Montréal, PQ; d of Thomas and Mary Domican Forrester; m Eugene Kash 1957 (separated); four d one s. *Education:* Dawson School (Montréal), privately and Univ of W Ontario. *Career:* Contralto; Trustee Nat Arts Centre Corpn 1973; Gov Thomson Hall 1982; Chair Canada Council 1984–1989; Fellow Strong Coll, York Univ; numerous honorary degrees; Nat Award in Music (Banff School of Fine Arts) 1967; Harriet Cohen Int Music Award 1968; Molson Prize 1971; Yale school of Music Samuel Simons Sanford Award 1983; Toronto Arts Award 1989. *Address:* Canada Council, POB 1047, 99 Metcalfe St, Ottawa, ON K1P 5V8, Canada.

FORRESTER, Viviane; French writer and critic; b 29 Sept 1925, Paris; d of Edgar and Yvonne (née Hirsch) Dreyfus; m 1st Simon Stollof (divorced); two s; m 2nd; m 3rd John Forrester 1967. *Career:* Literary critic La Quinzaine Littéraire 1974, 1994–, Nouvel Observateur 1975; mem Jury Prix Femina; Chevalier de la Légion d'Honneur; Chevalier de l'Ordre Nat du Mérite; Commdr des Arts et des Lettres. *Publications include:* Le grand festin 1971, Le corps entier de Marigda 1975, Violence du calme 1980, Les allées cavalières 1982, Van Gogh ou l'enterrement dans les blés (Prix Femina-Vacaresco) 1983, L'œil de la nuit 1987, Ce soir, après la guerre (Prix de l'Académie Française) 1992, L'Horreur économique (Prix Médicis essai) 1996, Une étrange dictature 2000, Au Louvre avec Viviane Forrester: Leonardo da Vinci 2001. *Leisure interests:* reading, reading, reading. *Address:* 40 rue du Bac, 75007 Paris, France (Home). *Telephone:* (1) 42-22-65-36.

FORST, Judith Doris, OC, B MUS; Canadian opera singer; b 7 Nov 1943, New Westminster, BC; d of Gordon Stanley and Euna Jessie Lumb; m Graham N. Forst 1964; one s one d. *Education:* Univ of British Columbia. *Career:* Has appeared in USA with New York Metropolitan Opera, New York City Opera, Seattle Opera, San Francisco Opera, New Orleans Opera, Fort Worth Opera, Santa Fe Opera, Washington, DC Opera, Miami Opera, Baltimore Opera and San Diego Opera Soc, in Canada with Canadian Opera Co (Toronto), Vancouver Opera, Calgary Opera, Montréal Symphony Orchestra, Vancouver Symphony Orchestra and Hamilton Symphony Orchestra, and in Europe with

Munich State Opera (Germany), Symphony Orchestra of Barcelona (Spain) and Orchestre de Radio France (Paris); Guest Lecturer Univ of British Columbia, Univ of Montréal; mem Asscn of Canadian TV and Radio, American Guild of Musical Artists; Hon LL D (Univ of British Columbia) 1992; won Metropolitan Opera auditions 1968, CBC Cross-Canada Talent Contest 1968; Canadian Woman of the Year 1978; Greater Miami Opera Asscn Performer of the Year 1980; Univ of British Columbia Distinguished Alumnus of the Year 1986; Freeman City of Port Moody 1992. *Address:* 428 Princeton Ave, Port Moody, BC V3H 3L3, Canada.

FORSTER, Margaret, BA; British writer; b 25 May 1938, Carlisle; d of Arthur Gordon and Lilian (née Hind) Forster; m Edward Hunter Davies 1960; two d one s. *Education:* Carlisle Co High School and Somerville Coll (Oxford). *Career:* School teacher 1961–63; novelist and biographer 1964–; Chief Non-fiction Reviewer London Evening Standard 1977–80; mem BBC Advisory Cttee on Social Effects of TV 1975–77, Arts Council Literary Panel 1977–81; Royal Soc of Literature Award for Biography 1989. *Publications include:* Non-fiction: The Rash Adventurer: the rise and fall of Charles Edward Stuart 1973, William Makepeace Thackeray: memoirs of a Victorian gentleman 1978, Significant Sisters: History of Active Feminism 1839–1940 1984, Elizabeth Barrett Browning: A Life 1988, Elizabeth Barrett Browning: selected poems (ed) 1988, Daphne du Maurier: The Authorised Biography 1993, Hidden Lives: A Family Memoir 1995, Rich Desserts and the Captain is Thin: A Family and Their Times 1831–1931 1997, Precious Lives 1998; Novels: Fenella Phizackerley 1970, Mr Bone's Retreat 1971, The Seduction of Mrs Pendlebury 1974, Mother, can you hear me? 1979, The Bride of Lowther Fell 1980, Marital Rites 1990, The Battle for Christabel 1991. *Leisure interests:* fell-walking, reading contemporary fiction. *Address:* 11 Boscastle Rd, London NW5 1EE, UK; Grasmoor House, Loweswater, near Cockermouth, Cumbria CA13 0RU, UK. *Telephone:* (20) 7485-3785 (London); (1900) 85303 (Cumbria).

FORT, Dame Maeve Geraldine, DCMG, MA; British diplomatist; b 19 Nov 1940; d of the late F. L. Fort. *Education:* Trinity Coll Dublin (Ireland) and Univ of Paris IV (Paris-Sorbonne). *Career:* Joined Foreign Service 1963; served in UK Mission, New York 1964–65, Commonwealth Relations Office 1965, FRG 1968, Nigeria 1971, mem Contact Group on Namibia 1978–82; seconded to SEATO, Bangkok 1966–68; Second then First Sec FCO 1973–78, Counsellor with special responsibility for Namibia 1982–83; Royal Coll of Defence Studies 1983; Counsellor, Head of Chancery and Consul-Gen, Chile 1984–86; Head W African Dept, FCO 1986–89; Amb to Chad (non-resident) 1987–89, to Mozambique 1989–92, to Lebanon 1992–96; High Commr to S Africa 1996–2000. *Leisure interests:* family, friends, dog, gardening, cinema, theatre. *Address:* Foreign and Commonwealth Office, King Charles St, London SW1A 2AH, UK (Office); Greystoke, 255 Hill Street, Pretoria 0083, South Africa.

FORTIER, Kimberly, BA; American publisher/editor; b 15 Oct 1960; d of M. R. Soloman and L Sanders; m 1st Michael Fortier 1988 (divorced); m 2nd Stephen Quinn 2000. *Education:* Vassar Coll (Poughkeepsie, NY, USA). *Career:* Marketing Dir Condé Nast 1989–98; publisher and CEO The Spectator 1998–2001; writes for The Wall Street Journal, The Telegraph, The Times, The Erotic Review. *Leisure interest:* 2nd tier Victorian novels. *Address:* The Spectator, 56 Doughty St, London WC1, UK. *Telephone:* (20) 7430-0186; *Fax:* (20) 7831-2111; *E-mail:* kimberly@spectator.co.uk.

FORTNEY, Judith A., PH D; American epidemiologist; b 28 Jan 1938, Cheshire, UK; d of Cyril and Jacqueline (née Faulkner) Cooper; m Lloyd R. Fortney 1961 (divorced 1986); one s one d. *Education:* Univ of London, Univ of Wisconsin and Duke Univ. *Career:* Various positions Family Health Int, NC 1974–87, Dir Scientific Affairs 1992–; Adjunct Prof Dept of Epidemiology, Univ of North Carolina 1986; Consultant NIH 1985–, WHO 1985–; Fellow American Coll of Epidemiology; mem American Public Health Asscn, Soc for Epidemiologic Research, Int Epidemiology Asscn; contribs to professional journals. *Address:* Family Health International, Box 13950, Research Triangle Park, NC 27709, USA.

FORWARD, Nancy Grace Augusta (Wake); British journalist, diplomatist and resistance worker; b 30 Aug 1912, Wellington, New Zealand; d of Charles Augustus and Ella Wake; m 1st Henri Fiocca 1939 (died 1943); m 2nd John Forward 1957. *Education:* N Sydney Girls' High School (Australia) and Queen's Coll for Ladies (London). *Career:* Freelance journalist 1936–39; Founder-mem Pat O'Leary Escape Route in Occupied France 1940–43; mem Specials Operations Exec (SOE), parachuted into France, Capt FANY (First Aid Nursing Yeomanry) 1943–45; Exec Officer Foreign Office, attached to Embassies in Paris and Prague 1952–58; Officer WRAF (Women's Royal Air Force) Air Ministry, London 1952–58; Patron Council of Ex-Servicewomen's Asscns; Dr hc (Griffith) 1995; George Medal; USA Medal of Freedom with Bronze Palm; Croix de Guerre with Palm and Bar; Croix de Guerre with Star; Médaille de la Résistance; Officier de la Légion d'Honneur 1985; Dr hc (Univ Griffith) 1995. *Publication:* The White Mouse 1985. *Leisure interests:* reading, writing, cooking, travel. *Address:* 5/82 William St, Port Macquarie, NSW 2444, Australia; POB 338, Port Macquarie, NSW 2444, Australia. *Telephone:* (65) 83 5886.

FOSSEY, Brigitte Florence; French actress; b 15 June 1947, Tourcoing; d of Roger and Marcelle (née Feuillade) Fossey; m 1st Jean-François Adam (divorced); one d; m 2nd Yves Samama 1988. *Education:* Marymount Int School, Cours Clouiet d'Orval, Coll Sévigné and Lycée Janson-de-Sailly (Paris). *Career:* Film career began at the age of five in Jeux interdits 1952. *Films include:* Le Grand Meaulnes 1967, Adieu l'ami 1968; M comme Mathieu 1970, L'homme qui aimait les femmes, Quintette 1977, Un mauvais fils 1980, La Boum 1980, Croque la vie 1981, La Boum II 1982, Enigma, Chanel solitaire 1983, Au nom de tous les miens 1983, Les fausses confidences, Un amour interdit 1984, Cinema Paradiso, 36-15 code Père Noël 1990, Le cri du papillon 1991, Les enfants du naufrageur 1992; *Plays include:* L'été 1967, Ivanov 1970, La mouette 1974, Reviens, James Dean, reviens! 1986, Paroles 1988, A croquer... ou l'ivre de cuisine 1991, Tempête sur le pays d'Egypte 1993; *TV appearances include:* Crime et châtiment 1969, Alice au pays des merveilles 1973, Salvator et les Mohicans de Paris 1975, Christophe Colomb 1976, L'été Indien 1980, L'affaire Caillaux 1986, Le château des oliviers 1993 (7 d'Or for Best Actress), Pour l'amour de Thomas 1994. *Address:* c/o Anne Alvarès Corréa, 18 rue Troyon, 75017 Paris, France.

FOSTER, Joanna Katharine; British organization executive; b 5 May 1939, Canterbury, Kent; d of the late Michael and Lesley Mead; m Jerome Foster 1961; one d one s. *Education:* Benenden School (Kent) and Univ of Grenoble (France). *Career:* Sec, Editorial Asst Vogue magazine (London and New York); journalist San Francisco Chronicle (CA, USA) 1957–61; Head Press Office, Cons Cen Office 1961–66; Management Adviser Industrial Soc 1967–71, Head Pepperell Unit 1981–88; Press Attachée and Ed INSEAD Business School, Fontainebleau, France 1971–79; Dir of Corp Educ Univ of Pittsburgh, PA, USA 1979–81; Chair Equal Opportunities Comm 1988–93; Deputy Chair Trustee Savings Bank Foundation for England and Wales 1991; Pres EC Comm Advisory Cttee on Equal Opportunities Jan–Dec 1992, Vice-Pres Jan–April 1993; Pres Relate Marriage Guidance 1993–96; Dir The BT Forum 1995–97, (Chair 1997–); Chair Lloyds TSB Foundation for England and Wales 1998–; mem advisory group on women's issues to Sec of State for Employment 1992, Industrial Soc, European Women's Foundation; Chair Nat Work-Life Forum 1998–; mem Govt Advisory Group on Work-Life Balance 2000–; Hon Fellow St Hilda's Coll, Oxford 1988; Hon D LITT (Kingston) 1993, (Salford) 1994; Hon LL D (Oxford Brooks) 1993, (Univ of West of England) 1993, (Strathclyde) 1994, (Bristol) 1996. *Leisure interests:* family, food, friends. *Address:* Confessor's Gate, Islip, Oxford OX5 2SN, UK.

FOSTER, Jodie (Alicia Christian), BA; American actress, film director and producer; b 19 Nov 1962, Los Angeles, CA; d of Lucius and Eileen 'Brandy' (née Almond) Foster; one s. *Education:* Yale Univ. *Career:* Acting debut in TV programme Mayberry 1969; Founder and Chief Exec Egg Pictures (production co) 1992; Hon DFA (Yale) 1997. *Films include:* Napoleon and Samantha 1972, Kansas City Bomber 1972, Menace of the Mountain, One Little Indian 1973, Tom Sawyer 1973, Alice Doesn't Live Here Any More 1975, Taxi Driver 1976, Echoes of a Summer 1976, Bugsy Malone 1976, Freaky Friday 1976, The Little Girl Who Lives Down the Lane 1977, Candleshoe 1977, Foxes 1980, Carny 1980, Hotel New Hampshire 1984, The Blood of Others 1984,

Siesta 1986, Five Corners 1986, The Accused (Acad Award for Best Actress 1989) 1988, Stealing Home 1988, Catchfire 1990, The Silence of the Lambs (Acad Award for Best Actress 1992) 1990, Little Man Tate (also dir) 1991, Shadows and Fog 1992, Sommersby 1993, Maverick 1994, Nell 1994, Home for the Holidays (dir and co-producer) 1996, Game, Contact 1997, The Baby Dance (exec producer only) 1997, Waking the Dead (exec producer only) 1998, Anna and the King 1999. *Address:* Egg Pictures Production Co, Jerry Lewis Annex, 5555 Melrose Ave, Los Angeles, CA 90038, USA (Office).

FOUQUE, Antoinette, DR RER POL; French psychoanalyst, feminist and publisher; b 1 Oct 1936, Marseilles; d of Alexis and Vincente Grugnardi; m René Fouque; one d. *Education:* Univ of Aix-Marseille and Ecole des Hautes Etudes (Paris). *Career:* Literary Critic and Trans 1964–68; Co-Founder Mouvement de Libération des Femmes (MLF) 1968; Organizer Politique et Psychanalyse group 1968; Founder, Dir Editions Des Femmes publrs 1973, Founder three Des Femmes bookshops in Paris, Lyons and Marseilles 1974; Dir Le Quotidien des Femmes magazine 1974, Des Femmes en Mouvements magazine 1978–82; Founder Inst de Recherche en Sciences des Femmes, Coll de Féminiologie 1978; Founder talking book co (books on cassette) 1980; Dir La Psychanalyste books 1983; Founder, Pres Alliance des Femmes pour la Démocratisation 1989; Rep for the creation of a women's art museum to Sec of State for the Rights of Women 1990; Ed at Passages 1991; Pres Alliance Française, San Diego (USA) 1986–88; Int Pres Women Int Center, San Diego 1987–88; Founder, Hon Pres Parité 2000 club 1992; Founder-mem Women of Europe cttee 1993; MEP (Energie Radicale list) 1994–99, Vice-Pres Comm on the Rights of Women 1994, mem official del to UN Int Conf on Women, Beijing; teacher Univ of Paris I (Panthéon-Sorbonne) 1990, Paris VIII (St Denis) 1992 (Dir of Research 1994); Dip Modern Literature; Officier de la Légion d'Honneur; Chevalier des Arts et des Lettres; awards include Living Legacy, San Diego (USA) 1986, Leading Women in Europe Award, Milan (Italy) 1989, Susan B. Antony Award (USA) 1990. *Publications:* Women in Movements, Yesterday, Today, Tomorrow 1992, Il y a deux sexes 1995. *Leisure interest:* swimming. *Address:* Editions Des Femmes, 6 rue de Mézières, 75006 Paris, France.

FOURCADE, Anne Marie; French architect; b 9 June 1950, Toulouse; d of Marc and Yvonne Fourcade; one d. *Education:* School of Architecture. *Career:* Founder Parcade Co 1993; multimedia Adviser to Int Youth Audiovisual Multimedia Festival. *Works include:* Renovation of Salle Pleyel 1983–84, Mirapolis, Cergy-Pontoise 1985–87, Mercier visitors' centre, Epernay 1987–88, Cusenier visitors' centre, Thuir 1987–88, Puy du Fou cultural area, Vendée 1988–89, bldg at La Villette 1990–91, hotel renovation, Nice 1992, hotel construction, Ramatuelle 1992, Espace Eugène Mercier 1994–95, renovation for Moët et Chandon 1994–95, reconstruction and renovation of SA Foncière ADP bldgs 1996, 1997, 1999, construction of a London bakery for Poilâne 1999. *Leisure interests:* music, festivals, exhibitions, cycling. *Address:* Agence Fourcade, 22 rue Poussin, 75016 Paris, France.

FOWLER, Rebecca, B SC; British newspaper editor; b 1958; m Niall Ferguson; one s one d. *Education:* Univ of Southampton. *Career:* Freelance journalist; Medical Corresp Mail on Sunday, then Features Ed; journalist Daily Mail; Assoc Ed Sunday Times 1991, then Deputy Ed; fmr Ed Sunday Express. *Address:* c/o Sunday Express, Ludgate House, 245 Blackfriars Rd, London SE1 9UX, UK.

FOX, Hazel Mary (Lady Fox), MA; British editor and lawyer; b 22 Oct 1928; d of J. M. B. Stuart; m Sir Michael Fox 1954; three s one d. *Education:* Roedean School and Somerville Coll (Oxford). *Career:* Called to the Bar, Lincoln's Inn 1950; Bar practice 1950–54; Lecturer in Jurisprudence, Somerville Coll, Oxford 1951–58, Fellow 1976–81, Hon Fellow 1988; Lecturer Council of Legal Educ 1962–76; Visiting Lecturer in Law, Univ of Oxford 1992–; Dir British Inst of Int and Comparative Law 1982–89, Ed Int and Comparative Law Quarterly 1987–98; Chair Tower Hamlets Juvenile Court 1968–76, London Rent Assessment Panel 1977, London Leasehold Valuation Tribunal 1981; mem Departmental Cttee on Jury Service, Home Office 1963–65; JP London 1959–77; Hon QC 1993. *Publications:* International Arbitraion (jtly) 1959, International Economic Law and Developing States (ed) Vol I 1988, Vol II 1992, Joint Development of Offshore Oil and Gas (ed) Vol I 1989, Vol II 1990, Armed Conflict and the New Law (co-ed) Vol II:

Effecting Compliance 1993. *Address:* c/o British Inst of International and Comparative Law, 17 Russell Square, London WC1B 5DR, UK. *Telephone:* (20) 7636-5802.

FOX, Kerry; New Zealand actress; m Jaime Robertson. *Education:* New Zealand Dama School. *Career:* Fmrly lighting designer; several TV and film appearances. *Films include:* Country Life, An Angel at my Table (Elvira Notary Best Performance award), The Last Days of Chez Nous, Friends, Shallow Grave; *TV includes:* Mr Wroe's Virgins, A Village Affair, Saigon Baby, The Affair.

FOX, Renée Claire, PH D; American professor of sociology; b 15 Feb 1928, New York; d of Paul Fox and Henrietta Gold. *Education:* Smith Coll (Northampton, MA), Radcliffe Coll and Harvard Univ. *Career:* Research Asst and Assoc, Bureau of Applied Social Research, Columbia Univ, New York 1953–58, Lecturer, Asst and Assoc Prof, Barnard Coll 1955–66; Lecturer in Sociology Harvard Univ 1967–69, Research Assoc Program on Tech and Soc 1968–71; Prof Dept of Sociology, Univ of Pennsylvania 1969, Chair 1972–78, Prof of Psychiatry, School of Medicine 1969, Prof of Sociology in Medicine 1972, Prof of Sociology, School of Nursing 1978, Annenberg Prof of Social Sciences 1978–98, Prof Emer 1998–; George Eastman Visiting Prof Balliol Coll, Oxford 1996–97; Assoc Ed Journal of Health and Social Behaviour 1985–87; mem Editorial Bd Bibliography of Bioethics 1979, Culture, Medicine and Psychiatry 1980–86, Journal of American Medical Asscn 1981; Chevalier Order of Leopold II 1995; eight books and numerous essays and articles published; numerous prizes, awards and honours. *Address:* University of Pennsylvania, Dept of Sociology, 507 McNeil Bldg, 3718 Locust Walk, Philadelphia, PA 19104, USA (Office); The Wellington, 135 S 19th St, Philadelphia, PA 19103, USA (Home). *Telephone:* (215) 898-7933 (Office); (215) 563-4912 (Home).

FOY, Hjordis Elsa Mannbeck, MD, PH D; American epidemiologist and physician; b 28 June 1926; d of Lewi and Elsa (née Lindbom) Mannbeck; m Robert E. Foy 1956; three d. *Education:* Karolinska Inst (Sweden) and Univ of Washington. *Career:* Researcher of acute respiratory diseases 1963–92; Prof of Epidemiology School of Public Health, Univ of Washington, Seattle 1968–, Dir of Preventive Medicine Training 1983–89; Consultant Ministry of Public Health, Thailand 1987; Fellow Infectious Disease Soc of America 1968, American Acad of Preventive Medicine 1968; has written over one hundred research papers. *Leisure interests:* hiking, travel. *Address:* University of Washington, Dept of Epidemiology, Box 357236, School of Public Health and Community Medicine, Seattle, WA 98195, USA (Office); 11016 NE 47th Pl, Kirkland, WA 98033, USA (Home). *Telephone:* (206) 685-1751 (Office); *Fax:* (206) 543-8525 (Office); *E-mail:* hfoy@u .washington.edu.

FRAGA ESTÉVEZ, Carmen; Spanish politician; b 19 Oct 1948, Léon. *Career:* MEP (EPP, PP), mem Cttee on Fisheries, mem Del for relations with the Maghreb countries and Arab Maghreb Union; Vice-Chair EPP 1999–. *Address:* European Parliament, rue Wiertz, ASP 11E206, 1047 Brussels, Belgium; Partido Popular, Grupo Popular – Parlamento Europeo, C/Génova, 13, 28004 Madrid, Spain. *Telephone:* (2) 284-21-11 (Belgium); *Fax:* (2) 230-69-43 (Belgium).

FRAHM, Sheila, BS; American politician; b 22 March 1945, Colby, Kan; m Kenneth Frahm; three d. *Education:* Fort Hays State Univ. *Career:* Mem Kan Senate, Topeka 1988–94, Senate Majority Leader 1993–94, Lieut-Gov Kan 1995–96; Republican Senator from Kansas 1996–; mem Shakespeare Fed, Kan Corn Growers, Kan Livestock Asscn. *Address:* Suite 401, 700 South West Jackson, Topeka, KS 66603, USA; 410 N Grant, Colby, KS 67701, USA (Home).

FRAIKIN, Hélène Solange; French business administrator; b 17 July 1935, Vizille-Isère; m Gerard Fraikin 1962; one d. *Education:* Univ of Grenoble. *Career:* Finance Dir Air Liquide 1957–62; Sec-Gen Societé Transports Fraikin, Chair Fraikin Ltd 1991, Vice-Pres, Dir-Gen Fraikin SA until 1992, mem Bd Dirs, Dir Gen Fraikin 1993; CEO Capex Investment Jan 2000–; Chevalier de l'Ordre Nat du Mérite. *Leisure interests:* skiing, sailing, tennis. *Address:* Capex Investment, 182 ave Charles de Gaulle, 92200 Neuilly-sur-Seine, France. *Telephone:* (1) 40-88-98-43; *Fax:* (1) 46-35-68-71.

FRAIN, Irène Marie Anne; French writer and journalist; b 22 May 1950, Lorient; d of Jean and Simone (née Martelot) Le Pohon; m François Frain 1969; one d. *Education:* High schools in Lorient and Rennes and Univ of Paris IV (Paris-Sorbonne). *Career:* Teacher secondary schools, then Univ of Paris III (Sorbonne-Nouvelle) 1971–86; first book published 1979; journalist on Paris Match magazine 1984–; Chevalier des Arts et des Lettres 1989; Chevalier de la Légion d'Honneur 1998. *Publications:* Quand les Bretons peuplaient les mers 1979, Contes du cheval bleu les jours de grand vent 1980, Le Nabab (Prix des Maisons de la Presse) 1982, Modern Style 1984, Désirs (Prix des Ecrivains de l'Ouest) 1986, Secret de Famille (Prix Radio-Télé Luxembourg—RTL Grand Public) 1989, Histoire de Lou 1989, La guirlande de Julie 1991, Devi 1993, Quai des Indes 1993, Vive la mariée 1993, La vallée des hommes perdus 1994, L'homme fatal 1995, L'inimitable 1998, A jamais 1999, La maison de la source 2000. *Leisure interests:* skiing, cycling, yachting, cooking. *Address:* c/o Editions Fayard, 75 rue des Saints-Pères, 75006 Paris, France. *Telephone:* (1) 43-06-06-71; *Fax:* (1) 43-06-06-81; *E-mail:* irene.frain@france-loisirs.com; *Internet:* www.irenefrain.com.

FRAME, Janet, CBE; New Zealand writer; b 1924, Dunedin. *Education:* Oamaru North School, Waitaki Girls' High School, Dunedin Training Coll and Otago Univ. *Career:* Subject of feature film An Angel At My Table 1991; Hubert Church Award for New Zealand Prose; New Zealand Scholarship in Letters 1964; Burns Fellow, Otago Univ (Dunedin). *Publications:* Lagoon 1951, Owls do Cry 1957, Faces in the Water 1961, The Edge of the Alphabet 1962, Scented Gardens for the Blind 1963, The Reservoir (short stories), Snowman, Snowman (fables), The Adaptable Man 1965, A State of Siege 1967, The Pocket Mirror (poetry), Yellow Flowers in the Antipodean Room 1968, Mona Minim and the Smell of the Sun (children's book) 1969, Intensive Care (novel) 1971, Daughter Buffalo (novel) 1972, Living in the Maniototo (novel) 1979, The Carpathians 1988, An Autobiography 1990.

FRANCA, Celia; British ballet dancer, director and choreographer; b 25 June 1921, London; m James William Morton 1960. *Education:* Guildhall School of Music and Royal Acad of Dance (London). *Career:* Ballet debut Mercury Theatre, London 1936; Dancer with numerous ballet cos 1936–; Guest Artist and Choreographer Sadler's Wells Theatre Ballet, London 1946–47; Ballet Mistress and Leading Dancer Metropolitan Ballet, London 1947–49; Guest Artist Ballet Rambert, London 1950; Founder Nat Ballet of Canada 1951, Prin Dancer 1951–59, Artistic Dir 1951–74; Co-Founder Nat Ballet School, Toronto 1959; mem Bd Canada Council 1982–89, York Univ 1985–88, School of Dance, Ottawa; mem Arts Advisory Bd, Canada-Israel Cultural Foundation; Patron Osteoporosis Soc of Canada; Hon LL D (Assumption) 1959, (Mount Allison) 1966, (Toronto) 1974, (Dalhousie, York) 1976, (Trent) 1977, (McGill) 1986; Hon D LITT (Guelph) 1976; Hon DCL (Bishop's Univ) 1967; numerous awards including Gold Key (City of Washington, DC USA) 1955, Hadassah Award of Merit 1967, Molson Award 1974, Admin Award (Int Soc of Performing Arts) 1979, Canada Dance Award 1984, Woman of the Year Award (St George's Soc of Toronto) 1987; Gov Gen Award for Performing Arts 1994. *Ballets include:* Danced in: Le Jardin aux Lilas, The Planets, Bar aux Folies-Bergère, The Rake's Progress, Gala Performance, Le Spectre de la Rose, The Sleeping Beauty, Mephisto Valse, The Mermaid, Giselle, Job, The Dances of Galanta, Coppélia, La Sylphide, Romeo and Juliet, Swan Lake, The Lovers' Gallery, Peter and the Wolf, Paris Soir, Suite of Airs; Choreographed: Dance of Salome, The Eve of St Agnes, Cinderella (Emmy Award 1970), Hansel and Gretel, Coppélia, Giselle, One in Five, Pineapple Poll, Romeo and Juliet (Prix René Barthelmy, Monte Carlo Int TV Festival 1966), Swan Lake (Emmy nomination 1968), The Sleeping Beauty (Emmy Award 1973); *Publication:* The National Ballet of Canada: A Celebration (jtly) 1978. *Address:* 203–350 Queen Elizabeth Drive, Ottawa, ON K1S 3N1, Canada.

FRANCESCHI DE AGUILERA, Mirtza Angelica, BA; Panamanian lawyer; b 16 Dec 1936, David, Chiriqui; m Manuel José Aguilera Rojas 1963; four s. *Education:* Nuestra Señora de Los Angeles High School (David, Chiriqui), French Coll (Mexico) and Nat Autonomous Univ of Mexico (UNAM). *Career:* Municipal judge, David, Chiriqui 1962–69; Legal Counselor to Nat Bank of Panama 1969–70; pvt practice 1970–89; Magistrate Pres of the Superior Court of Justice, David,

Chiriqui 1990–91; Magistrate of the Supreme Court of Justice 1992–99, Magistrate Pres 2000–2001; Honorific Mention UNAM 1959; Values of the Community, Rotary Club, David 1991–92; Distinguished Lawyer of the Americas, FIA 2000; Distinguished Woman of the Year 2000, Int Soroptimist Club, David. *Publications:* Corporates in Civil Law 1959; Lectures: Women's Rights in Panamanian Legal System 1987, Justice Administration in Panama 1992, Human Rights Administrative Contentious Proceeding in Panama 1994, Judiciary Ethics in Panama 1997. *Leisure interests:* reading, theatre. *Address:* Corte Suprema de Justicia, Edif 236, Ancon, Calle Culebra, Apdo 1770, Panama City, Panama (Office); Apdo 1866, Balboa, Ancon, Panama City, Panama (Home). *Telephone:* 262-1413, 262-1469 (Office); 232-5051 (Home); *Fax:* 212-0574 (Office); 232-5051; *E-mail:* pcsjrp@cwp.net.pa (Office); aguilera@sinfo.net (Home).

FRANCIS, Clare Mary, MBE, B SC; British writer and former yachtswoman; b 17 April 1946; d of Owen Francis; m Jacques Robert Redon 1977 (divorced 1985); one s. *Education:* Royal Ballet School and Univ Coll London. *Career:* Crossed Atlantic singlehanded in 37 days, Falmouth (UK) to Newport (USA) 1973; competed in Round Britain Race 1974, Azores Race 1975, L'Aurore Race 1975, 1976; women's record Observer Transatlantic Singlehanded Race (29 days) 1976; first woman skipper Whitbread Round the World Race 1977–78; Fellow Univ Coll London 1979; Hon Fellow UMIST 1981. *TV Series:* The Commanding Sea (co-writer and presenter) 1981; *Publications:* Nonfiction: Come Hell or High Water 1977, Come Wind or Weather 1978, The Commanding Sea 1981; Novels: Night Sky 1983, Red Crystal 1985, Wolf Winter 1987, Requiem 1991, Deceit 1993 (televised 2000), Betrayal 1995, A Dark Devotion 1997, Keep Me Close 1999. *Leisure interests:* music, opera. *Address:* c/o John Johnson Agency, 45–47 Clerkenwell Green, London EC1R 0HT, UK.

FRANCIS, Diana, BA; British international organization official; b 21 Nov 1944, Southport; d of Harold and Irene Ford; m Nicholas Francis 1967; two d one s. *Education:* St Hilda's Coll (Oxford). *Career:* Fmr school teacher; peace campaigner, non-violence trainer and mediator; apptd Pres Int Fellowship of Reconciliation 1984. *Leisure interests:* printmaking, sculpture. *Address:* 113 Dovers Park, Bathford, Bath BA1 7UE, UK. *Telephone:* (1225) 858294; *Fax:* (1225) 235113.

FRANCIS, Dorothy Delores; Canadian painter; b 1 Jan 1923, Dinsmore, SK; d of Remi Horace and Eva (née Emard) Leonard; m Harold Reid Francis 1942; three s (one deceased) two d. *Education:* Nutana Collegiate (Saskatoon) and Vancouver School of Art. *Career:* Professional artist 1953–; primarily portrays Inuit and Canadian native Indian people; numerous solo exhibitions; represented in numerous pvt and corp collections in Canada and abroad; work on perm display at Smithsonian Museum (USA), Pacific Northwest Indian Centre, Gonzaga Univ (USA). *Leisure interests:* interior decorating, photography. *Address:* 885 Berwick Park, Qualicum Beach, BC V9K 1N7, Canada. *Telephone:* (604) 752-3665.

FRANCK, Martine; French photographer; b Antwerp, Belgium; m Henri Cartier-Bresson 1971; one d. *Education:* Univ of Madrid and École du Louvre (Paris). *Career:* Photography apprenticeship under Eliot Elisofon and Gjon Mili at Time-Life (Paris); freelance photographer for Time-Life, The New York Times, French Vogue; Founder Viva (photographic agency) 1972; Assoc mem Magnum Photos (photographic agency) 1980, mem 1983–. *Exhibitions:* over 40 exhibitions around the world including Tibetan Tulkus: Images of Continuity, Rossi & Rossi Gallery, London 2000; *TV documentaries include:* What has happened to the American Indians?, Music at Aspen. *Address:* 5 passage Piver, 75011 Paris, France.

FRANKENHAEUSER, Marianne, PH D; Swedish professor of psychology; b (Marianne von Wright) 30 Sept 1925, Helsinki; d of Tor von Wright and Ragni Alfthan; m Bernhard Frankenhaeuser 1946 (died 1994); one d. *Education:* Oxford Univ (UK), Univs of Helsinki, Stockholm and Uppsala. *Career:* Asst Prof of Psychology Univ of Stockholm 1960–63; Research Fellow Swedish Council for Social Science Research 1963–65; Assoc Prof of Experimental Psychology Swedish Medical Research Council 1965–69, Prof 1969–80; Prof of Psychology Karolinska Inst 1980–92, Chair Dept of Psychology 1980–82, Head Psychology Div, Dept of Psychiatry and Psychology

1980–92; Resident Scholar Rockefeller Foundation Study and Conf Centre, Como, Italy 1980; Gildersleeve Prof Barnard Coll, Columbia Univ (USA) 1981; Prin Investigator, John D. and Catherine T. MacArthur Foundation Mental Health Network on Health and Behavior 1983–89; Research Fellow Swedish Inst for Research on Management and Work 1990–95; Chair Scientific Council of Swedish Psychological Asscn 1970–73; Pres European Brain and Behaviour Soc 1974–76; Deputy Gov American Biographical Inst Research Asscn (ABIRA) 1995–; Foreign Assoc NAS (USA) 1989, Foreign mem Finnish Soc of Sciences and Letters 1994; Corresp mem Acad Int de Philosophie des Sciences 1983; mem Academia Europaea 1989, New York Acad of Sciences 1992, Distinguished Bd of Advisors Int Encyclopedia of the Social and Behavioral Sciences 1998–, Hon Cttee XXVII Int Congress of Psychology, Stockholm 2000; Fellow Center for Advanced Study in the Behavioral Sciences, Stanford Univ (CA) 1995–96; Visiting Scholar Inst for Research on Women and Gender, Stanford Univ 1997–98; Hon mem Swedish Forum for Psychological Worklife Issues 1988; Hon DR RER POL (Turku, Finland) 1990; awards include The King of Sweden's Medal 1985, Swedish Nat Award for Zealous and Devoted Service 1986, Women of Achievement Award, Int Women's Forum 1989, Int Soc of Behavioral Medicine Award 1990. *Publications:* Estimation of Time 1959, Stress (jtly) 1987, Women, Work and Health (jtly) 1991, Stress and Gender 1993, and articles on psychology in scientific journals. *Leisure interests:* reading, writing, outdoor life in clean nature. *Address:* Dept of Psychology, University of Stockholm, 106 91 Stockholm, Sweden (Office); Skeppargatan 32, 114 52 Stockholm, Sweden (Home). *Telephone:* (8) 16 36 84 (Office); (8) 663-94-68 (Home); *Fax:* (8) 15 35 87 (Office); (8) 667-02-61 (Home); *E-mail:* mf@psychology.su.se.

FRANKENTHALER, Helen, BA; American artist; b 1928, New York; m Robert Motherwell 1958 (divorced 1971); m Stephen M. DuBrul, Jr 1994. *Education:* Bennington Coll (VT). *Career:* One-woman exhibitions throughout USA and Europe including André Emmerich Gallery 1959–91, Whitney Museum of American Art, Metropolitan Museum of Art 1973, Guggenheim Museum (New York) 1975–85, Corcoran Gallery (Washington, DC) 1975, John Berggman Gallery (San Francisco, CA and New York) 1972, 1976, 1979, 1982, 1986, 1987, Janie C. Lee Gallery (Houston, TX) 1973, (Dallas, TX) 1975, 1976, 1978, 1980, Knoedler Gallery (London) 1978, 1981, 1983, 1985, Sterling & Francine Clark Art Inst (Williamstown, MA) 1980, Knoedler & Co (New York) 1992–; travelling retrospective exhibitions 1985, 1986, 1989, 1993; mem American Acad 1990–, Chair 1991; mem Inst of Arts and Letters 1974, Nat Educ Asscn Council on the Arts 1985–90, Corpn of Yaddo 1973–78; Trustee Bennington Coll 1967–82; Fellow Calhoun Coll, Yale Univ 1968–; numerous hon degrees including Hon D HUM LITT (Skidmore Coll) 1969, Hon DFA (Smith Coll) 1973, (Moore Coll of Art) 1974, (Bard Coll) 1976, (Harvard) 1980, (Yale) 1981, (Brandeis) 1982, (Hartford) 1983, (Syracuse) 1985, (Marymount Manhattan Coll, Adelphi, Washington) 1989, Dr hc (George Washington) 1992, (Darthmouth Coll) 1994, (City Univ of New York) 1995, (Rhode Island School of Design, Pennsylvania) 1996; First Prize Paris Biennale 1959; Joseph E. Temple Gold Medal Award (Pennsylvania Acad of Fine Arts) 1968; Spirit of Achievement Award (Albert Einstein Coll of Medicine) 1970; Gold Medal of the Commune of Catania (Florence, Italy) 1972; Garrett Award (Art Inst of Chicago) 1972; Creative Arts Award (American Jewish Congress) 1974; Art and Humanities Award (Yale Women's Forum) 1976; Extraordinary Woman of Achievement Award (Nat Conf of Christians and Jews) 1978; Mayor's Award of Honor for Art and Culture (New York City) 1986; Connecticut Arts Award 1989; Distinguished Artist Award for Lifetime Achievement (Coll Art Asscn) 1994; Lotus Medal of Merit (The Lotus Club) 1994; Artist of the Year Award (ART—Art Resources in Teaching) 1995. *Address:* c/o M. Knoedler and Co Inc, 19 E 70th St, New York, NY 10021, USA.

FRANKLIN, Aretha; American singer; b 25 March 1942, Memphis, TN; d of Rev C. L. Franklin; m 1st Ted White (divorced); m 2nd Glynn Turman 1978. *Career:* Made first recordings at father's Baptist church (Detroit); toured as gospel singer; signed contract with Columbia Records (New York) 1960, with Atlantic 1966, with Arista 1980; numerous Grammy Awards 1967–87, American Music Award 1984, John F. Kennedy Center Award 1994, Rock and Roll Hall of Fame 1987. *Recordings include:* Aretha 1961, The Electrifying Aretha Franklin 1962, Laughing on the Outside, The Tender, the Moving, the Swinging Aretha Franklin 1963, Running out of Fools, The Gospel Sound of Aretha Franklin 1964, Soul Sister 1966, I Never Loved a Man the Way I Love You 1967, Lady Soul, Aretha Now, Aretha in Paris 1968, Aretha's Gold 1969, This Girl's in Love with You, Spirit in the Dark 1970, Live at Fillmore West 1971, Young, Gifted and Black, Amazing Grace 1972, Hey Now Hey, The Best of Aretha Franklin, The First Twelve Sides 1973, Let Me in Your Life, With Everything I Feel in Me 1974, You 1975, Sparkle, Ten Years of Gold 1976, Sweet Passion 1977, Almighty Fire 1978, La Diva 1979, Aretha 1980, Love All the Hurt Away 1981, Jump to It 1982, Get It Right 1983, One Lord, One Faith 1988, Through the Storm 1989, What You See Is What You Sweat 1991, Jazz to Soul 1992, Aretha After Hours, Chain of Fools 1993, Unforgettable: A Tribute to Dinah Washington 1995, Love Songs 1997, The Delta Meets Detroit 1998, A Rose is Still a Rose 1998, Amazing Grace 1999; *Film:* The Blues Brothers 1981; *Publication:* Aretha: From these Roots (with David Rib). *Address:* Arista Records, c/o Gwen Quinn, 6 West 57th St, New York, NY 10019, USA (Office); 8450 Linwood St, Detroit, MI 48206, USA.

FRANKLIN, Barbara Hackman, BA, MBA; American business executive and former government official; b 19 March 1940, Lancaster, PA; d of Arthur A. and Mayme M. (née Haller) Hackman; m 2nd Wallace Barnes 1986. *Education:* Pennsylvania State Univ and Harvard Business School. *Career:* With Singer Co, New York 1964–68; Asst Vice-Pres Citibank, New York 1969–71; Women's Recruitment Officer The White House, Washington, DC 1971–73, Co-Chair Finance Cttee 1988; mem Consumer Products Safety Comm 1973–79; Sr Fellow and Dir Govt and Business Program, Wharton School, Univ of Pennsylvania 1979–88; Pres and CEO Franklin Assocs 1984–92, Barbara Franklin Enterprises 1995–; Alt Rep and Public Del UN 1989, mem Advisory Cttee for Trade Policy and Negotiation 1982–86, 1989–92; Advisor to Comptroller-Gen 1984–92, 1995–98; US Sec of Commerce, Washington, DC 1992–93; Financial Chair CT Reps 1994–; Chair Heritage Foundation Advisory Council on Int Trade 1994–; Chair task force on tax reform 1985–86; mem Services Policy Advisory Cttee of US Trade Reps 1986–89; Alt Rep and Public Del to 44th Session of UN Gen Ass 1989–90; mem Bd of Dirs Aetna Inc 1979–92, 1993–, Dow Chemical Co 1980–92, 1993–, AMP Inc 1993–99, NASDAQ Stock Market 1995–98, MedImmune Inc 1995–, Milacron 1996–, Guest Services Inc 1998–, Watson, Wyatt & Co 2000–; fmr Dir Black & Decker Corpn, Nordstrom, Westinghouse Electric Corpn and other cos; mem Council on Foreign Relations 1991–, Bd Dirs Atlantic Council 1995–, Bretton Woods Cttee, US–China Business Council; Fellow Nat Asscn of Corp Dirs; Founder-mem Int Women's Forum; Distinguished Visting Fellow, Heritage Foundation, Nat Cttee for US–China Relations; mem and Dir Exec Cttee Bd of Trustees Econ Club of New York; several hon degrees and numerous awards for business and social achievement, including the John J. McCloy Award and the 2000 NACD Dir of the Year Award. *TV appearances include:* monthly commentator, 'Nightly Business Report', Public Broadcasting Service 1997–. *Leisure interests:* exercise, skiing, sailing, reading. *Address:* 2600 Virginia Ave, NW, Suite 506, Washington, DC 20037, USA (Office); 2700 Virginia Ave, NW, Apt 110, Washington, DC 20037 (Home); 1875 Perkins St, Bristol, CT 06010, USA. *Telephone:* (202) 337-9100 (Washington); (860) 582-2500 (Bristol); *Fax:* (202) 337-9104 (Office); *E-mail:* bh.franklin@aol.com (Office).

FRANKS, Lynne; British public relations executive; b 16 April 1948; d of Leslie Samuel and Angela (née Herman) Franks; m Paul Howie 1972 (separated 1992); one s one d. *Education:* Minchenden Grammar School (London). *Career:* Sec Petticoat Magazine 1965–67; Asst Ed Freemans Mail Order Staff Newspaper 1967–69; est Lynne Franks Ltd public relations consultants 1971, now Chair; clients have included Katharine Hamnett (qv), Ruby Wax (qv), Lenny Henry, Gerald Ratner, Jasper Conran, Neil Kinnock, Brylcreem, Swatch, Harvey Nichols, Next, Littlewoods, Comic Relief, Greenpeace, Amnesty Int. *Publication:* Absolutely Now!: A Futurist's Journey to Her Inner Truth 1997. *Leisure interests:* New Age spirituality, healing, the environment. *Address:* 327–329 Harrow Rd, London W9 3RB, UK. *Telephone:* (20) 7724-6777; *Fax:* (20) 7724-8484.

FRANSSEN, Margot A. C., BA; Canadian business executive; b 21 March 1952, Netherlands; d of Guilliame G. and Rose J. Franssen; m Hall A. Tingley 1983; one s. *Education:* York Univ. *Career:* Clerk, McLeod Young Weir & Co 1970–72; Sec United Funds Management 1972–73; Exec Sec Alfred Bunting & Co 1973–75; Pres The Body Shop, Canada 1979–; mem Canadian Retail Council, The Fashion Group; mem Bd Salvation Army, Toronto; mem Advisory Bd Imagine, Retail Directions Magazine; Fellow Ryerson Polytech Inst, Toronto; Retail Council Marketing and Communications Award 1987; Women Who Make a Difference Award 1989; Woman Of Distinction Business Award 1994; Henry Singer Award for Exceptional Leadership in Retailing and Services (Univ of Alberta). *Address:* 33 Kern Rd Don Mills, ON M3B 1S9, Canada (Office); 52 Warren Rd, Toronto, ON, Canada (Home).

FRASER, Lady Antonia, CBE, MA, FRSL; British writer; b 27 August 1932, London; d of the Earl and Countess of Longford (qv); m 1st Hugh Fraser 1956 (divorced 1977, died 1984); three s three d; m 2nd Harold Pinter 1980. *Education:* Dragon School (Oxford), St Mary's Convent (Ascot) and Lady Margaret Hall (Oxford). *Career:* Mem Cttee English PEN 1979–88, Pres 1988–89, Vice-Pres 1990–, Crimewriters Asscn 1980–86; Hon D LITT (Hull) 1986, (Sussex) 1990, (St Andrews) 1994; Norten Medlicott Medal, Historical Asscn 2000. *Publications include:* King Arthur 1954, Robin Hood 1955, Dolls 1963, History of Toys 1966, Mary, Queen of Scots (James Tait Black Memorial Prize) 1969, Cromwell: Our Chief of Men 1973, King James VI and I 1974, Scottish Love Poems, A Personal Anthology 1974, Kings and Queens of England (ed) 1975, Love Letters (anthology) 1976, Quiet as a Nun 1977 (adapted for TV 1978), The Wild Island 1978, King Charles II 1979, Heroes and Heroines (ed) 1980, A Splash of Red 1981, Cool Repentance 1982, Oxford In Verse (ed) 1982, Jemima Shore Investigates (adapted for TV 1983), The Weaker Vessel (Wolfson History Prize) 1984, Oxford Blood 1985, Your Royal Hostage 1987, Boadicea's Chariot: The Warrior Queens 1988, The Cavalier Case 1990, Jemima Shore at the Sunny Grove 1991, The Pleasure of Reading (ed) 1992, The Wives of Henry VIII 1992, Charles II: His Life and Times 1993, Political Death: A Jemima Shore Mystery 1994, The Gunpowder Plot (St Louis Literary Award 1996, CWA Non Fiction Gold Dagger 1996) 1996, The Lives of the Kings and Queens of England 1998, Marie Antoinette: the Journey 2001; *TV includes:* adaptations: Quiet as a Nun 1978, Jemima Shore Investigates 1983; plays: Charades 1977, Mister Clay 1985. *Leisure interests:* cats, grandchildren. *Address:* c/o Curtis Brown, Haymarket House, 28/29 Haymarket, London SW1Y 4SP, UK.

FRASER, Dawn, MBE, AO, JP; Australian swimmer and writer; b 4 Sept 1937; d of Rose Christina (née Miranda) and Kenneth George A. Fraser; m Gary Ware 1965 (deceased); one d. *Education:* Leichhardt High School (Sydney). *Career:* Competed in Olympic Games (Melbourne) 1956, (Rome) 1960 and (Tokyo) 1964, won four Gold and four Silver Medals; won six Gold and two Silver Medals in Commonwealth Games; first woman to swim 100m in under one minute; holder 100m freestyle record 1956–72, held 39 world records; mem House of Reps (Parl) for Balmain 1988–91; Chair Beachwatch; Vice-Pres Australia Day Council; Dir W Tigers Football Club; f mem World Sports Acad; Patron World Masters Swimming, Leichhardt Cttee of Red Cross, New S Wales Div, Lyndon Community; mem Int Sporting Events Advisory Cttee, Sydney 2000 Olympic Bid Cttee, Australians Abroad Council, Advertising Standards Council; Sponsor Nat Community Awareness Campaign on Aid and Devt (ACFOA); numerous awards include Australian Athlete of the Year, Helms Award 1961, ABC (Australian Broadcasting Corpn) Sportsman of the Year 1962, Australian of the Year 1964, Int Swimming Hall of Fame (Fort Lauderdale, FL, USA) 1965, Australia's Best Sportsperson for the last 25 years (ABC) 1975, Hall of Fame (American Women's Sports Foundation) 1985, Australia's Sports Hall of Fame 1985, Australian Female Athlete of the Century 1999, World's Greatest Living Female Water Sports Champion (Int Olympic Cttee, Vienna) 1999; Paul Harris Fellowship Medal Rotary Club 2000. *Publications:* Dawn Fraser 1979, Our Dawn (jtly) 1991, Dawn One Hell of a Life 2001. *Leisure interest:* sport, as spectator and participant. *Address:* POB 118, Balmain, Sydney, NSW 2041, Australia.

FRASER, Helen Jean Sutherland, MA; British publishing executive; b 8 June 1949, London; d of the late G. S. and of Paddy Fraser; m Grant James McIntyre 1982; two d. *Education:* Univ of Oxford. *Career:* Ed

Methuen Ltd 1972–74, Open Books Ltd 1974–76; Ed then Editorial Dir William Collins 1977–87; Publr William Heinemann 1987–91, William Heinemann and Mandarin Paperbacks 1991–93; Publishing Dir Reed Trade Books 1993–96, Man Dir 1996; currently Man Dir Penguin Gen Div. *Leisure interests:* opera, music, gardening. *Address:* c/o Penguin Books, 27 Wrights Lane, London W8 5TZ, UK. *Telephone:* (20) 7010-3240; *E-mail:* helen.fraser@penguin.co.uk.

FRASER, Honor; British model; b 18 Dec 1974, Beaufort Castle, Inverness; d of the late Hon Simon Augustine Fraser, Master of Lovat and Virginia (née Grose) Fraser; (granddaughter of the late 17th Lord Lovat). *Career:* First catwalk appearance in Milan at 19; with Storm Model Man, then with Select Model Man 1997–; campaign for Givenchy 1997; appeared in campaigns for Ungaro and Nina Ricci; columnist Scotland on Sunday 1998–. *Film:* The Cookie Thief. *Address:* Select Model Management, Thomas Archer House, 43 King St, London WC2E 8RJ, UK. *Telephone:* (20) 7470-5200; *Fax:* (20) 7470-5233.

FRASER, Sylvia Lois, BA; Canadian writer; b 8 March 1935, Hamilton, ON; d of the late George and Gladys Meyers; m Russell James Fraser 1959 (divorced 1978). *Education:* Univ of Western Ontario. *Career:* Feature writer The Toronto Star Weekly 1952–68; writer 1968–; Guest Lecturer Banff Centre 1973–79, 1985, 1987, 1988; Writer-in-Residence Univ of Western Ontario 1980; Women's Press Club Medal 1967, 1968; Pres's Medal for Canadian Journalism 1968; Nat Magazine Gold Medal 1994, Silver Medal 1996. *Publications:* Pandora 1972, A Candy Factory 1975, A Casual Affair 1978, The Emperor's Virgin 1980, Berlin Solstice 1984, My Father's House (Canadian Authors' Asscn Non-Fiction Book Award) 1987, The Book of Strange (also published as The Quest for The Fourth Monkey—American Library Asscn Booklist Medal) 1992, The Ancestral Suitcase 1996, The Rope in the Water: a Pilgrimage to India 2001. *Address:* 701 King St W No 302, Toronto, ON M5V 2W7, Canada. *Telephone:* (416) 703-7030; *Fax:* (416) 703-3824; *E-mail:* slfraser@interlog.com.

FRASER-MOLEKETI, Geraldine J.; South African politician; b 24 Aug 1960, Cape Town; m Jubulani Moleketi; three c. *Career:* Fmrly worked in Admin and Communications, World Lutheran Fed; fmr Personal Asst to Gen Sec of SA CP; fmr Office Manager and Nat Admin Union of Democratic Univ Staff; exiled from SA 1980–90; fmr mem Man Cttee and Convention for a Democratic SA; Nat Deputy Elections Coordinator, ANC 1993–94; MP 1994; Deputy Minister of Welfare and Population Devt 1995–96, Minister 1996–99, of Agric and Land Affairs 1999; fmr mem Patriotic Health Forum, Nat Health Forum; Co-Founder and fmr Trustee Jabulile Ndlovu Educare Trust; observer of nat elections, Pakistan 1993; mem Nelson Mandela Children's Fund. *Address:* c/o Ministry of Agriculture and Land Affairs, 184 Jacob Mare Building, corner Jacob Mare and Paul Kruger Streets, Pretoria, 0001, South Africa.

FRATINI, Georgina Carolin; British fashion designer; b 22 Sept 1931, Kobe, Japan; d of The Hon and Mrs Somerset Butler; m 2nd Renato Fratini 1961; m 3rd Jimmy Logan 1967 (divorced 1985). *Education:* Canada, India, Burma (now Myanmar), Hathrop Castle (Glos) and Royal Coll of Art. *Career:* Asst costume and set designer, Katherine Dunham Dance Group 1951–53; freelance designer 1953–63; Founder Designer and Dir Gina Fratini Ltd 1964–. *Leisure interests:* gardening, horse-racing.

FRÉCHETTE, Louise, BA; Canadian diplomatist; b 16 July 1946, Montréal; d of Léo and Gilberte (née Verville) Fréchette. *Education:* Coll Basile Moreau, Univ of Montréal and Coll d'Europe (Brussels). *Career:* Mem W European Div, Dept of External Affairs 1971, 1975–77, Deputy Dir W European Div 1982, Trade and Policy Div 1982–83, Dir European Summit Countries Div 1983–85; Second Sec, Athens 1973–75; First Sec UN Mission, Geneva 1979–82; attended CSCE, Madrid 1980–81; Amb to Argentina and Uruguay 1985–88; Asst Deputy Minister, Latin American and Caribbean Br, External Affairs and Int Trade Canada 1988–90, Asst Deputy Minister Econ Policy and Trade Competitiveness Br 1990–92; Amb and Perm Rep to UN (New York, USA) 1992–94, Assoc Deputy Minister Dept of Finance

1994–95, Dept of Defence 1995–98; Deputy Sec-Gen UN Jan 1998–. *Address:* Office of the Deputy Secretary-General, S-3862A, United Nations, New York, NY 10017, USA. *Telephone:* (212) 963-8010.

FREEDMAN, Amelia, MBE, FRAM; British music teacher and director; b 21 Nov 1940; d of Henry and Miriam (née Claret) Freedman; m Michael Miller 1970; two s one d. *Education:* St George's School (Harpenden), Henrietta Barnet School (London), RAM and Royal Coll of Music. *Career:* Teacher of Music King's School, and Perse School for Girls, Cambridge, Chorleywood Coll for the Blind, Sir Philip Magnus School, London 1961–65; Founder and Artistic Dir Nash Ensemble 1964–; Artistic Dir Bath Int Festival 1984–93, Bath Mozartfest 1995–; Musical Advisor Israel Festival 1989–; Programme Advisor Philharmonia Orchestra 1992–95; Head of Classical Music, South Bank Centre 1995–; chamber music consultant for numerous projects at the Barbican and South Bank Centre, London; Hon D MUS (Bath) 1993; Chevalier des Arts et des Lettres 1984; Chevalier de l'Ordre Nat du Mérite; Czech Govt Medal for Services to Czech Music in UK 1986. *Leisure interests:* ballet, cinema, children, opera, sport, stamp-collecting, theatre. *Address:* 14 Cedars Close, Hendon, London NW4 1TR, UK. *Telephone:* (20) 8203-3025; *Fax:* (20) 8203-9540.

FREEDMAN, Dawn Angela, LL B; British circuit judge; b 9 Dec 1942, London; d of Julius and Celia Freedman; m Neil John Shestopal 1970. *Education:* Westcliffe High School for Girls and Univ Coll London. *Career:* Called to the Bar, Gray's Inn 1966; Stipendiary Magistrate 1980–91; Crown Court Recorder 1989–90; Circuit Judge 1991–; mem Parole Bd 1992–96. *Leisure interests:* theatre, TV, cooking. *Address:* Harrow Crown Court, Hailsham Drive, Harrow, London HA1 4TU, UK. *Telephone:* (20) 8424-2294; *Fax:* (20) 8424-2209.

FREEDMAN, Rita B., BS, MA; American political organization official; b 26 Dec 1946, New York; d of Sidney and Betty Siegel; m Joel Freedman 1967; two s one d. *Education:* Cornell and Columbia Univs and Univ of Pennsylvania. *Career:* Asst Dir Youth Inst for Peace in the Middle East 1977–80; teacher of Labour, Foreign Policy and Latin American courses, Univ of Pennsylvania 1972–73, Seton Hall Univ 1975, Rutgers Univ 1975–76; Exec Dir Social Democrats USA 1980–, Rep at Socialist Int; mem Bd League for Industrial Democracy, Bayard Rustin Fund, Jewish Labor Cttee. *Address:* Social Democrats USA, 815 15th St, NW, Suite 511, Washington, DC 20005, USA. *Telephone:* (202) 638-1515; *Fax:* (202) 347-5585.

FREEDMAN, Sandra Warshaw, BA; American former mayor; b 21 Sept 1943, Newark, NJ; d of Joseph and Ruthe Warshaw; m Michael J. Freedman; two s one d. *Education:* Univ of Miami. *Career:* Mem Tampa City Council 1974–, Chair (first woman) 1983–86, Mayor City of Tampa (first woman) 1986–95; mem Arts Council of Tampa, Nat Council of Jewish Women, Florida Women's Network, US Conf of Mayors Task Force on City/State Relations; Vice-Pres Florida Gulf Coast Symphony 1979–80; mem Bd of Fellows Univ of Tampa; numerous honours and awards including City of Tampa Human Rights Award 1980, Woman of Achievement Award, Business and Professional Women 1986, First Ladies of Tampa Award, Tampa Women's Club 1990, Outstanding Representation Award, Distinguished Citizen Award, Univ of S Florida 1995. *Address:* 3435 Bayshore Blvd, Tampa, FL 33629, USA.

FREEMAN, Cathy; Australian athlete; b 16 Feb 1973, Mackay; d of Norman Freeman and Cecilia Barber. *Career:* Works as public relations adviser; winner Australian 200m 1990–91, 1994, 1996, Australian 100m 1996, Amateur Athletics Fed 400m 1992, 200m 1993; Gold Medallist 4x100m Commonwealth Games 1990; Gold Medallist 200m, 400m, Silver Medallist 4x100m Commonwealth Games 1994; Silver Medallist 400m, Olympic Games, Atlanta 1996; winner World Championships 400m, Athens 1997 (first Aboriginal winner at World Championships); Gold Medallist 400m, Olympic Games, Sydney 2000; set 2 Australian 200m records, 5 Australian 400m records 1994–96; Media and Communications Officer, Australia Post; numerous nat awards including Australian of the Year 1998. *Leisure interests:* family, pets, children, movies. *Address:* c/o Melbourne International Track Club, 43 Fletcher St, Essendon, Victoria 3040, Australia.

FREILICHER, Jane, MA; American artist; b 29 Nov 1924, New York; d of Martin and Bertha Freilicher; m Joseph Hazan 1957; one d. *Education:* Brooklyn Coll, Hans Hoffman School of Fine Arts and Columbia Univ (New York). *Career:* Solo exhibitions include Tibor de Nagy Gallery 1952–68, John Bernard Myers Gallery 1971, Fischbach Gallery 1975, 1977, 1979–80, 1983, 1985, 1988, 1990, 1992, 1995, Utah Museum of Fine Arts 1979, Lafayette Coll 1981, Kansas City Art Inst 1983, David Heath Gallery, Atlanta, GA 1990; group exhibitions include Metropolitan Museum of Art 1979–80, Denver Art Museum 1979, American Acad and Inst of Arts and Letters 1981, 1984–85, Brooklyn Museum 1984, Yale Univ 1986, Tibor de Nagy Gallery 1992, Whitney Museum 1995; represented in perm collections including Metropolitan Museum of Art, Hirschorn Museum, Rose Art Museum, Whitney Museum; mem American Acad and Inst of Arts and Letters; Nat Endowment of the Arts grantee 1976; Eloise Spaeth Award, Guild Hall Museum, Hampton, NY 1991.

FREIVALDS, Laila, LL B; Swedish politician and lawyer; b 22 June 1942, Rīga, Latvia; m Johan Hedström; one d. *Education:* Uppsala Univ. *Career:* Service in dist court 1970–72, Svea Court of Appeal 1973–74; Reporting Clerk Court of Appeal 1974; Counsel Västerås rent tribunal 1974–75; served in Riksdag (Parl) Information Office 1975–76; Sr Admin Officer, Head of Div Nat Bd for Consumer Policies 1976–79, Dir-Gen and Consumer Ombudsman 1983–88; Minister for Justice 1988–91, 1994–; Legal consultant, Baltic states 1991–94. *Address:* c/o Ministry of Justice, Rosenbad 4, 10333 Stockholm, Sweden; Riksdagen, 10012 Stockholm, Sweden.

FRENCH, Anne, MA; New Zealand writer and publishing executive; b 5 March 1956, Wellington; d of Derek Lawrence and M. Olive French; one s. *Education:* Wellington Girls' Coll, Victoria Univ of Wellington and Auckland Teachers' Coll. *Career:* Ed Oxford Univ Press (NZ br) 1979, then Literary Ed, apptd Publr 1982; Sec NZ PEN 1980, 1981; Councillor Book Publishers' Asscn of NZ 1984; mem Council Local Publishers' Forum 1991; Queen Elizabeth II Arts Council Writers' Bursary 1990; PEN Young Writers' Award 1973, 1974; NZ Book Award for Poetry 1988; PEN Best First Book Award 1988. *Publications include:* Poetry: All Cretans are Liars 1987, The Male as Trader 1988, Cabin Fever 1990. *Leisure interests:* singing, sailing, fishing, reviewing, running. *Address:* 53 Ngatiawa St, One Tree Hill, Auckland 5, New Zealand. *Telephone:* (9) 636-8910; *Fax:* (9) 524-6723.

FRENCH, Dawn; British actress and comedienne; b 11 Oct 1957; m Lenny Henry; one d (adopted). *Education:* Manchester Univ. *Career:* French and Saunders stage shows and TV series with Jennifer Saunders (qv); own show on BBC TV Murder Most Horrid; radio debut in play Birthdays 1992; opened shop 16–34 with Jennifer Saunders. *TV appearances include:* The Comic Strip (Strike, Consuela, Five Go Mad in Dorset, Supergrass, Ken, The Yob, Suzy), French and Saunders, The Vicar of Dibley; *Plays:* Silly Cow, When We Are Married 1996, A Midsummer Night's Dream 2001. *Address:* c/o BBC, Broadcasting House, London W1A 1AA, UK.

FRENCH, Marilyn, PH D; American writer and critic; b 21 Nov 1929, New York; d of E. C. and Isabel (née Hazz) Edwards; m Robert M. French, Jr 1950 (divorced 1967); one s one d. *Education:* Hofstra Coll and Harvard Univ. *Career:* Secretarial and clerical work 1946–53; Lecturer Hofstra Coll 1964–68; Asst Prof Holy Cross Coll, Worcester, MA 1972–76; Mellon Fellow Harvard Univ 1976–77. *Publications:* The Book as World – James Joyce's Ulysses 1976, The Women's Room (novel) 1977, The Bleeding Heart (novel) 1981, Shakespeare's Division of Experience 1981, Beyond Power: On Women, Men and Morals 1985, Her Mother's Daughter 1987, The War Against Women 1992, Our Father (novel) 1994, My Summer with George (novel) 1996, A Season in Hell (memoir) 1998. *Address:* c/o Charlotte Sheedy Literary Agency, 65 Bleecker St, New York, NY 10012, USA (Office).

FRENI, Mirella; Italian opera singer; b 27 Feb 1935, Modena; d of Ennio and Gianna (née Arcelli) Freni; m Leone Magiera 1955; one d. *Career:* Debut 1955; appearances include La Scala (Milan, Italy) 1962, Glyndebourne Festival 1961 and Royal Opera House (London) 1961, Metropolitan Opera (New York, USA) 1965, Vienna State Opera, Salzburg Festival (Austria) and other leading opera houses throughout the world. *Operas include:* Falstaff, La Bohème, Don Giovanni, Marriage of Figaro, L'elisir d'amore, La Traviata, Otello. *Address:* c/o John Coast Opera Management, 31 Sinclair Rd, London W14 0NS, UK (Office).

FRETWELL, Elizabeth, OBE; Australian opera singer and vocal coach; b Melbourne; m Robert Simmons; one s one d. *Education:* Privately. *Career:* Joined Nat Theatre, Melbourne 1950; joined Sadler's Wells, London 1956; mem Elizabethan Opera Co, Australia 1963; toured W Germany 1963, Canada, UK, USA 1964, Europe 1965; Guest Soprano Durban and Cape Town Opera Cos, S Africa 1970; mem Australian Opera 1970–87; appeared opening season Sydney Opera House 1973; professional adjudicator; mem music bd Opera Foundation, Australia 1982–. *Operas include:* La Traviata, Fidelio, Ariadne auf Naxos, The Flying Dutchman, The Girl of the Golden West, Il Trovatore, Aida, Peter Grimes, Forza del Destino, Falstaff, Masked Ball, Il Tabarro. *Address:* 47 Kananook Ave, Bayview, NSW 2104, Australia.

FRETWELL, Lady Mary, OBE; British organization executive; b 17 Oct 1939, Falmouth; d of Frederick and Isobel Dubois; m John Fretwell 1959; one s one d. *Education:* St Anne's Convent (Sanderstead) and Densons Secretarial Coll (London). *Career:* Founder Passports for Pets Lobby Group to reform UK quarantine system 1994. *Leisure interests:* riding, skiing, gardening. *Address:* Passports for Pets, 20 Seymour Rd, London SW18 5JA, UK; Le Presbytere, La Haye de Calleville, 27800 Eure, France. *Telephone:* (20) 8874-3708 (UK); *Fax:* (20) 8870-9223 (UK); *E-mail:* passports.forpets@virgin.net; *Internet:* www.homepage .virgin.net/passports.forpets.

FREUD, Bella Lucia; British fashion designer; b 17 April 1961, London; d of Lucian and Bernardine (née Coverley) Freud; two d. *Education:* Michael Hall School (E Sussex), Accademia di Costuma e di Moda (Rome) and Instituto Mariotti (Rome). *Career:* Asst to Vivienne Westwood (qv) 1986–89; Designer and Dir Bella Freud 1989–; exhibited at London Designer Show 1991, London Fashion Week 1993; Innovative Design – New Generation Award, British Fashion Council 1991. *Leisure interests:* eating, reading, looking at paintings, watching ice-skating. *Address:* 21 St Charles Square, London W10 6EF, UK. *Telephone:* (20) 8968-7579; *Fax:* (20) 8969-3602.

FREYH, Brigitte (née Mayer); German foundation curator; b 25 April 1924, Ahrensdorf; one s. *Career:* Manager Walter-Kolb-Stiftung, Frankfurt 1959–62; mem Bundestag (Parl) 1961–72; Parl State Sec at Ministry of Econ Co-operation 1969–72; Curator Deutsche Stiftung für Int Entwicklung (German foundation for int devt); mem German UNESCO Comm 1966. *Address:* Im Wingert 12A, 61440 Oberursel, Germany.

FREYNDLIKH, Alisa Brunovna; Russian actress; b 8 Dec 1934; d of Bruno Arturovich Freyndlikh. *Education:* Leningrad (now St Petersburg) Theatre Inst. *Career:* Worked with Komissarzhevskaya Theatre, Leningrad 1957–61, Lensoviet Theatre, Leningrad 1961–83, Gorky Theatre (Moscow) 1983–; worked in films 1958–; RSFSR State Prize 1976; USSR People's Artist 1981, State Prize 1995. *Films include:* Family Happiness 1970, My Life 1973, The Princess and the Pea 1977, An Everyday Novel 1977, Always With Me 1977, An Unofficial Romance 1978, Stalker 1980, An Old-Fashioned Comedy 1980, Agony 1981, The Canary Cage 1984, Success 1985, The Nights near Moscow, The Hunt; *Plays include:* Perfidy and Love 1990, Autumn Violins 1997, and many others. *Address:* 191002 St Petersburg, Rubinstein ul, dom 11, kv 7, Russian Federation. *Telephone:* (812) 314-88-40.

FRICHOT, Sylvette; Seychelles politician. *Career:* Minister of Local Govt, Youth and Sports. *Address:* Ministry of Local Government and Sports, Oceangate House, Victoria, Seychelles. *Telephone:* 24161; *Fax:* 21006.

FRICKER, Brenda; Irish actress; b 17 Feb 1945, Dublin. *Career:* Appearances with RSC, Royal Court Theatre and Nat Theatre, London, UK; numerous appearances in films and in TV series. *Films include:* My Left Foot (Acad Award for Best Supporting Actress) 1989, The Field 1991, So I Married An Axe Murderer 1992, Angels in the Outfield 1994, A Man of No Importance 1994, Deadly Advice 1994; *TV appearances include:* Casualty (series) 1986–90, The Ballroom Romance,

Licking Hitler, The House of Bernarda Alba, Brides Of Christ (mini-series) 1991, The Sound and the Silence. *Address:* United Talent Agency Inc, 9560 Wilshire Blvd, 5th Floor, Beverly Hills, CA 90212, USA.

FRIDAY, Nancy; American feminist and writer. *Publications include:* My Secret Garden: Women's Sexual Fantasies, My Mother, My Self, Jealousy, Forbidden Flowers, Men in Love, Women on Top, The Power of Beauty 1996, To Be Seen 1996, Self Exploration and Insatiable Lust 1991, The Power of Beauty 1996, The Mirrored Self 1997.

FRIDH-HANESON, Britt, PH D; Swedish academic; b 9 May 1925, Lund; d of Valdemar Haneson and Sonja Sandblad; m 1st Bengt E. Thomasson 1951; m 2nd Åke Fridh 1975; three s. *Education:* Univs of Lund and Göteborg and Swedish School of Classical Studies (Rome). *Career:* Asst Classics Dept, Univ of Lund 1951–61; Lecturer Classics Inst (Rome, Italy) 1961–64; Sr Asst Master 1969–90; Lecturer and Asst Prof Dept of Classical Studies, Univ of Göteborg 1968–90; Leader of expeditions to sites of archaeological interest 1971–; Adviser on Classical Archaeology, lecturer and speaker 1990–; Pres Swedish Assn of Univ Women 1987. *Leisure interests:* gardening, gym, theatre, theology, teaching young people about classical heritage. *Address:* c/o Utlandagatan 8c, 412 61 Göteborg, Sweden.

FRIEBE, Ingeborg; German politician; b 20 April 1931. *Career:* Mem SPD; mem N Rhine-Westphalia Landtag (regional Parl) 1975–, Pres Landtag 1990–95; Mayor of Monheim; Chair Verbandsversammklung des Rheinischen Sparkassen- und Giroverbandes (savings bank asscn of the Rhine). *Address:* Kirchfeldstr 60, 40217 Düsseldorf, Germany.

FRIEDAN, Betty; American feminist leader; b 4 Feb 1921, Peoria, IL; d of Harry and Miriam (née Horwitz) Goldstein; m Carl Friedan 1947 (divorced 1969); two s one d. *Education:* Smith Coll. *Career:* Founder Nat Org for Women 1966, first Pres 1966–70, Chair 1970–72; Organizer Nat Women's Political Caucus 1971, Int Feminist Congress 1973, First Women's Bank & Trust Co 1973; Visiting Prof of Sociology Temple Univ 1972, Yale Univ 1974, Queen's Coll 1975; Contributing Ed McCalls Magazine 1971–74; Jt Chair Nat Comm for Women's Equality; numerous lectures in USA and Europe; Distinguished Visiting Prof George Mason Univ 1995, Mount Vernon Coll 1996; mem PEN; Dr hc (Columbia) 1994; American Humanist Award 1975. *Publications:* The Feminine Mystique 1963, It Changed My Life: Writings on the Women's Movement 1976, The Second Stage 1982, The Fountain of Age 1993, Through the Prison of Gender 1998, Life So Far: A Memoir 2000; articles in McCall's, Harper's, etc. *Address:* 2022 Columbia Rd, NW, Washington, DC 20009, USA.

FRIEDMAN, Jane; American publishing executive. *Career:* Joined Random House 1968; fmr Pres Random House Audio; fmr Exec Vice-Pres Knopf Publishing Group, Random House Inc; fmr Publr Vintage Books; fmr mem Random House Exec Cttee; Pres, CEO HarperCollins 1997–. *Address:* c/o HarperCollins, 10 East 53rd St, New York, NY 10022, USA. *Telephone:* (212) 207-7000; *Fax:* (212) 207-7759; *E-mail:* www.harpercollins.com.

FRIEL, Anna; British actress; b 12 July 1976, Rochdale, Lancs; d of Desmond and Julie Friel. *Career:* Joined Oldham Theatre Workshop 1989; Best Actress, Nat Television Awards 1995; Best Supporting Actress, Drama Desk Awards (New York) 1999. *TV programmes include:* Coronation Street, Emmerdale, GBH 1990, Cadfael, Brookside 1993–95; *Films include:* Land Girls 1997, Rogue Trader 1998, A Midsummer Night's Dream 1998, Mad Cows 1999, Everlasting Peace 2000, War Bride Without You; *Theatre includes:* Closer (Broadway) 1999, Lulu (Almeida, London) 2000. *Address:* c/o Conway van Gelder Ltd, 3rd Floor, 18/21 Jermyn St, London SW1Y 6HP, UK. *Internet:* www.netshopuk.co.uk/annafriel.

FRIGGEBO, Birgit; Swedish politician; b 25 Dec 1941, Falköping; m 1st Lennart Rydberg 1968; one s; m 2nd Bo Södersten 1997. *Career:* Mem Folkpartiet (Liberal Party) 1957–, Sec 1983–85; accountant in estate agency 1960; chief negotiator Swedish Asscn of Municipal Housing Cos (SABO) 1969–76, rep at Rents and Tenancies Court of Appeal 1975–76; Chair Liberal Youth Stockholm 1963–64, mem Exec Cttee Liberal Party Nat Youth League 1964–69; mem Nat Bd Liberal

Party 1972–93, First Vice-Chair and mem Exec Cttee 1983–93, Sec 1983–85, Leader Parl Liberal Party Group Council 1990–91; mem Stockholm Social Welfare Bd 1967–70, Comm on Housing for Young Persons 1968–70, Stockholm County Council 1971–76; MP 1979–82, 1985–97; Minister of Housing and Physical Planning 1976–82, of Cultural Affairs and Immigration 1991–94; mem Parl Standing Cttee on the Constitution 1985–91, 1994–97 (Chair 1994–97), mem Bd Parl's Cen Services Office 1986–91, Cttee on Child Pornography 1995–97, Cttee on Local Pvt Radio 1996–97; mem Nat Debt Office, Data and Access to Information Comm, Cttee on Swedish Security 1985–88; Co-Gov Jönköping 1998–; mem Bd Nat Agency for Govt Employers 1999–, Nat Courts Admin 2000–; mem Bd Salusansvar Sakförsäkringar AB, Salus Bank AB 1998–. *Address:* County Administrative Board, 551 86 Jönköping, Sweden (Office); Skolgatan 5, 55316 Jönköping, Sweden (Home). *Telephone:* (36) 157001 (Office); *Fax:* (36) 150164 (Office); *E-mail:* birigit.friggebo@f.lst.se (Office).

FRITCHIE, Dame Rennie, DBE; British public servant; b 29 April 1942; d of Charles Fredrick Fennell and Eva Tordoff; m Don Jamie Fritchie 1960; one s (and one d deceased). *Education:* Ribston Hall Grammar School for Girls. *Career:* Admin Officer Endsleigh Insurance Brokers 1970–73; Sales Training Officer Trident Insurance Ltd 1973–76; Head of Training Confs and Specialist Training Advisor on Women's Devt, Food and Drink, ITB 1976–80; consultant Social Ecology Assocs 1980–81; Dir Transform Ltd 1981–85, Rennie Fritchie Consultancy 1985–89; Man Dir Working Choices Ltd 1989–91, Mainstream Devt Consultancy 1991–; mem Bd Stroud and Swindon Building Soc 1995–; Chair Gloucester Health Authority 1988–92, SW Regional Health Authority 1992–94, Nat Health Service (NHS) Exec S and W Region 1994–97; mem NHS Policy Bd 1994–97, Gen Medical Council 1996–99; Civil Service Commr for Public Appointments 1999–; mem Bd British Quality Foundation 1994–99; mem Selection Panel, Glos Police Authority 1994–99; Chair Pennell Initiative for Women's Health in Later Life 1997–99, Pres 1999–; Visiting Assoc Prof Univ of York 1996–; Pro-Chancellor Univ of Southampton 1998–; Fellow Cheltenham & Gloucester Coll of Higher Educ; Patron Headway 1989–, Healing Arts 1995–, Meningitis Trust 1998–, Effective Intelligence 2000–, SPACE 2000–, Swindon Arts Foundation, Lord Mayor's Appeal 2000–2001, Barts Cancer Centre 2000–; Companion of the Inst of Management 2000–; Hon PH D (Southampton) 1996; Hon D UNIV (York) 1998. *Publications include:* Working Choices 1988, The Business of Assertiveness 1991, Resolving Conflicts in Organisations 1998. *Leisure interests:* reading, swimming, theatre. *Address:* Commissioner for Public Appointments, 172 South Block, County Hall, 1B Belvedere Rd, London SE1 7GE, UK. *Telephone:* (20) 7207-2264.

FRITSCH, Elizabeth, CBE; British potter; b 1940, Shropshire; one s one d. *Education:* RAM and RCA (London). *Career:* Est Workshop, E London 1985; exhibitions include Crafts Council 1974, Leeds City Art Galleries 1978, Victoria and Albert Museum (London) 1980, RCA 1984, Künstler Haus (Vienna) 1986, Amsterdam 1988, Kyoto Nat Museum of Modern Art (Japan) 1988, Tokyo Nat Museum of Modern Art 1988, Besson Galleries (London) 1989, Royal Museum of Scotland 1990, Hetjens Museum (Düsseldorf) 1990 and Stuttgart (Germany) 1991, Oriel Gallery (Cardiff) 1991; numerous works in public collections; mem Crafts Council; Judge Fletcher Challenge Int Ceramics Competition, New Zealand 1990; Sr Fellow RCA 1995; Silver Medallist, RCA 1970; Royal Copenhagen Jubilee Competition 1970; Herbert Read Memorial Prize 1970; Gold Medal, Int Ceramics Competition, Poland 1976; Crafts Council Bursary 1980. *Leisure interests:* music, mountains, theatre.

FRITSCHE, Claudia; Liechtenstein diplomatist; b 26 July 1952; m Manfred Fritsche 1980. *Education:* Business and Language Schools (Schaan and St Gall). *Career:* Personal Sec to Head of Govt 1970–74; joined Office for Foreign Affairs 1978; Diplomatic Collaborator 1980–87; Sec to Liechtenstein Parl Del to Council of Europe and EFTA; First Sec Embassy of Liechtenstein in Germany 1987–90, in Vienna 1989–90; Perm Rep of Liechtenstein to UN, New York 1990–. *Address:* Permanent Mission of Liechtenstein to the UN, 633 Third Ave, 27th Floor, New York, NY 10017, USA (Office). *Telephone:* (212) 599-0220 (Office); *Fax:* (212) 599-0064 (Office); *E-mail:* liechtenstein@un.int; *Internet:* www.un.int/liechtenstein.

FROMAN, Ann; American sculptor; b 7 April 1942, Brooklyn, NY; d of Harry and Eleanor Froman; m Irvin Schwartz 1974; one d. *Education:* Palace of Fontainebleau School of Fine Arts (France), Fashion Inst of Technology (New York) and Nat Acad School of Fine Art (New York). *Career:* Solo exhibitions include Nat Arts and Antiques Festival, NY 1969, 1973, Hebrew Coll, Boston 1977, 1982, Bodley Gallery, NY 1978, Bennington Museum, VT 1981, Int Art Expo, NY, Dyansen Gallery, CA 1988; group exhibitions include Aleph Gallery, México, Int Arts Club, NY, Ella Lerner Gallery, MA, Nelson Rockefeller Collection, NY, US Customs Museum, NY, Images Int, Bethesda; collections and comms include Slater Museum, CT 1974, Hosp for Special Surgery, NY 1975, Metropolitan Museum of Art, NY 1976, Judaica Museum of Greater Phoenix, AZ 1978, St Raphael's Church, NJ 1979, Butler Museum of Art, OH 1979, Museum of Fine Art, MA 1979, Culinary Inst of America, NY 1982, Brooklyn Coll, NY 1990, Time Warner Inc, NY 1991, March of Dimes, NY 1992, Radcliffe Coll, MA 1992; represented in perm collections including Springrield Museum of the Fine Arts, MA, Temple Emanu-El, New York, St Raphael's Church, Livingston, NJ, Jewish Museum of Greater Phoenix, AZ, New York Hosp of Special Surgery; works featured in books and magazines; awards include Shoe Design Award 1968, Brooklyn Museum Sculpture Award 1970, Mortimer C. Ritter Award 1971, American Soc for Contemporary Artists Award 1980. *Leisure interests:* theatre, gardening, snorkelling, fund-raising. *Address:* S Anson Rd, Stanfordville, NY 12581-0367, USA. *Telephone:* (914) 868-1992.

FRONTIERE, Georgia; American football executive; m 1st Carroll Rosenbloom 1966 (deceased). *Career:* Pres and propr LA Rams football team 1979–, currently Man Partner St Louis Rams; mem numerous orgs; mem Bd American Air Museum in Britain, LA Boys and Girls Club; Trustee St Louis Univ; Dr hc (Pepperdine). *Address:* St Louis Rams, One Rams Way, Earth City, MO 63045, USA.

FROSTENSON, Katarina; Swedish writer; b 1953. *Career:* Novelist, playwright; elected to Swedish Acad 1992, mem adjudication panel Nobel Prize for Literature. *Address:* Swedish Academy, POB 2118, 103 13 Stockholm, Sweden.

FRUTOS GAMA, Manuela; Spanish politician; b 18 May 1956, Valverde de Merida. *Career:* MEP (PSE), mem Cttee on Regional Policy, Del to the EU-Bulgaria Jt Parl Cttee. *Address:* c/o European Parliament, rue Wiertz, 1047 Brussels, Belgium.

FRY, Hedy; Canadian politician and medical practitioner; b 1941 Trinidad; three s. *Education:* Coll of Physicians and Surgeons (Dublin). *Career:* Medical practitioner Vancouver, BC; Liberal Mem House of Commons (Parl) for Vancouver Centre 1993; Parl Sec to Minister of Health 1993; Sec of State for Multiculturalism and Status of Women 1996–; fmrly Pres BC Medical Asscn. *Leisure interests:* drama, racquetball. *Address:* House of Commons, Parliament Bldgs, Wellington St, Ottawa, ON K1A 0A6, Canada.

FRY, Marion Golda, B LITT, MA; Canadian university president (retd); b 16 April 1932, Halifax, NS; d of George and Marion Fry. *Education:* Univ of King's Coll, Dalhousie Univ and Oxford Univ (UK). *Career:* Asst Prof of Philosophy and Asst Dean of Women, Bishop's Univ, Lennoxville, PQ 1958–64; Prin Catharine Parr Traill Coll, Trent Univ 1964–69, Assoc Prof of Philosophy Trent Univ 1964–86, Vice-Pres 1975–79; Adjunct Prof Dept of Philosophy, Dalhousie Univ 1988–93; Pres and Vice-Chancellor Univ of King's Coll 1987–93; Hon DCL (King's) 1985; Hon D LITT (Trent) 1989. *Leisure interests:* travel, classical music, walking. *Address:* 652 Walkerfield Ave, Peterborough, ON K9J 4W2, Canada.

FRYE, Helen Jackson, MA, JD; American federal judge; b 10 Dec 1930, Klamath Falls, OR; d of Earl and Elizabeth Jackson; m 1st William Frye 1952; two d one s; m 2nd Perry Holloman 1980. *Education:* Univ of Oregon. *Career:* Teacher, OR 1956–63; called to Bar, OR 1966; pvt practice, Eugene, OR 1966–71; circuit court Judge, OR 1971–80; US Dist Judge, Portland, OR 1980–95, Sr Judge 1995–. *Address:* 1107 US Courthouse, 1000 SW 3rd Ave, Portland, OR 97204, USA.

FU MINGXIA; Chinese diver; b 1978, Hubei. *Education:* Special diving school (Beijing). *Career:* Began diving training at the age of seven; Gold Medallist Goodwill Games 1990, World Diving Championships 1991, 1994; Gold Medallist Olympic Games, Barcelona, Spain 1992, (then second-youngest Gold Medallist in Olympic history), Olympic Games, Atlanta, GA, USA 1996 (Women's Platform and Women's Springboard).

FU QIFENG; Chinese acrobat and historian; b 15 March 1941, Chengdu, Sichuan; d of Fu Tianzheng and Ceng Qingpu; m Xu Zhuang 1961; one s one d. *Education:* Peace Middle School (Shanghai) and Beijing Library. *Career:* Performer acrobatics troupe, Shanghai 1950–60; performer, teacher and archivist China Acrobatic Troupe, Beijing 1960–79; Founder and Ed Acrobatics and Magic (journal) 1980–91, Deputy Chief Ed 1991; mem Research Dept Asscn of Chinese Acrobats 1987–, Council Beijing br 1981, Council mem 1991–; mem Editorial Cttee Acrobatics, Contemporary China series 1991–; mem China Magic Cttee 1993–. *Publications:* Acrobatics in China (jtly) 1983, Chinese Acrobatics Through the Ages 1986, The Art of Chinese Acrobatics 1988, History of Chinese Acrobatics 1989, History of Chinese Artistic Skill (in Japanese) 1993, Literature and Art vol of China Concise Encyclopedia (jtly) 1994, Secret of Spiritualist Activities 1995, Illusions and Superstitions 1997. *Leisure interests:* dress designing, doll making. *Address:* 5-2-501 Hongmiao Beili, Jintai Rd, 100025 Beijing, People's Republic of China. *Telephone:* 65002547.

FUCHS, Anke, LL M; German politician and lawyer; b 5 July 1937, Hamburg; d of Paul Nevermann; m; two c. *Education:* Univs of Hamburg and Innsbruck (Austria) and School of Public Admin (Speyer). *Career:* Mem SPD 1956–, Party Council 1970–, Presidium 1986, Fed Man 1987–91, Chair Party Council 1993–; trade union activist 1964–76; Area Sec IG Metall (Metal Workers' Union) 1968, Man Dir, Frankfurt 1971; State Sec in Fed Ministry for Labour and Social Affairs 1977; mem Bd Bundesanstalt für Arbeit 1978; mem Bundestag (Parl) for Cologne-South 1980–; Parl State Sec Fed Ministry for Labour and Social Affairs 1980–82, Fed Minister for Youth, Family and Health Affairs April–Oct 1982; Vice-Chair Bundestag 1998–; Pres Deutscher Mieterbund (tenants' asscn) 1995–; Vice-Chair Friedrich Ebert-Stiftung; Dr hc 2000. *Address:* Deutscher Bundestag, Platz der Republik, 11011 Berlin, Germany (Office). *Telephone:* (30) 22772577 (Office); *Fax:* (30) 22776175 (Office).

FUKUDA, Haruko; Japanese international organization executive. *Career:* Fmr Partner, James Capel (stockbroker); fmr mem Nikko Research Centre; Sr Advisor to Lazard Bros (merchant bank); CEO World Gold Council May 1999–. *Address:* King's House, 10 Haymarket, London SW1Y 4BP, UK.

FULLER, Kathryn, MS, JD; American international organization executive; b 8 July 1946, New York, NY; d of Delbert Orison and Carol Scott Gilbert Fuller; m Stephen Paul Doyle 1977; two s one d. *Education:* Brown Univ (Providence, RI), Univ of Maryland and Univ of Texas. *Career:* Law clerk New York, Houston and Austin (TX) 1974–76, to Chief Justice John V. Singleton, Jr, US Dist Court, Southern Dist of TX 1976–77; Attorney and Advisor Office of Legal Counsel, Dept of Justice (Washington, DC) 1977–79, Attorney Wildlife and Marine Resources Section 1979–80, Chief Wildlife and Marine Resources Section 1981–82; Exec Vice-Pres, Dir TRAFFIC USA 1982–89; Pres and CEO World Wildlife Fund (WWF) 1989–; called to the Bar, DC and TX; mem council on Foreign Relations, International Council of Environmental Law, Overseas Devt Council; numerous articles in journals; Hon D SC (Wheaton Coll) 1990; Hon LL D (Knox Coll) 1992; Hon D HUM LITT (Brown) 1992; William Rogers Outstanding Graduate Award, Brown Univ 1990; UNEP Global 500 award 1990. *Leisure interests:* squash, trekking, scuba diving, gardening, fishing. *Address:* World Wildlife Fund (WWF), 1250 24th St, NW, Washington, DC 20037, USA. *Telephone:* (202) 293-4800.

FULLERTON, Fiona; British actress; b 10 Oct 1956, Kaduna, Nigeria; d of Brig B. V. H. and Pamela Fullerton; m 1st 1976 (divorced 1982); m 2nd Neil Shackell; one s one d. *Education:* Elmhurst Ballet School (Camberley, Surrey). *Career:* Has appeared in numerous plays, films and TV programmes. *Plays include:* The Royal Baccarat Scandal, Camelot, The Boyfriend, Gypsy, The Beggar's Opera, I Am A Camera, Caught

Napping, Something's Afoot, Cinderella, Revenge, Henry VIII, Valentine's Day, The Constant Wife, Pygmalion, Death and the Maiden; *Films include:* Run Wild Run Free, Nicholas and Alexandra, Alice's Adventures in Wonderland, The Human Factor, A View to a Kill, A Girl Named Harry; *TV appearances include:* The Charmer, A Taste for Death, Angels, Lev Tolstoy, A Question of Faith, Gaugin the Savage, Dick Barton Special Agent, A Friend Indeed, Shaka Zulu, Hold the Dream, The Life of Hemingway, A Hazard of Hearts, A Ghost in Monte Carlo, The Secret Life of Ian Fleming, To Be the Best, The Bogie-Man. *Leisure interests:* walking, reading, collecting antiques and paintings. *Address:* c/o Jean Diamond, London Management, 2–4 Noel St, London W1, UK. *Telephone:* (20) 7287-9000.

FUNCKE, Liselotte; German politician; b 20 July 1918, Hagen; d of Oscar and Bertha (née Osthaus) Funcke. *Education:* Commercial studies (Berlin). *Career:* Fmrly worked in industry and commerce (Hagen and Wuppertal); mem Landtag (regional Parl) of Nordrhein-Westfalen (N Rhine-Westphalia) 1950–61; mem Bundestag (Parl) 1961–79, Vice-Pres 1969–79, Chair Finance Cttee 1972–79; mem Presidium FDP 1968–82, Deputy Chair FDP 1977–82; Minister of Economy and Transport, N Rhine-Westphalia 1979–80; Fed Govt Rep responsible for integration of overseas workers and their families 1981–91; Hon mem governing bodies of evangelical church and social orgs; Dr hc (Bursa and Hagen); nat and int awards include Bundesverdienstkreuz mit Stern und Schulterband 1973; Dr hc; Bundesverdienstkreuz 1973 and other medals. *Publication:* Streets Tail History 1999. *Address:* Ruhr-Str 15, 58097 Hagen, Germany (Home). *Telephone:* (2331) 182034.

FUNDAFUNDA, Irene Bwalya, BA; Zambian civil servant; b 7 July 1947, Lusaka; d of Elija Fundafunda and Elizabeth Mwila; two d one s. *Education:* Univ of Zambia, Lusaka. *Career:* Asst District Sec 1973–79; Admin Officer Ministry of Foreign Affairs 1979–89, Dir of Int Org 1989; Del to UN Gen Ass New York 1984–92, UN Comm on the Status of Women, Vienna 1983, 1984, UN World Conf on Women Nairobi 1985, Comm on Human Rights 1991. *Leisure interests:* reading, gardening, music, cooking. *Address:* Ministry of Foreign Affairs, Directorate of International Organizations, POB RW, 50069 Lusaka, Zambia.

FURET, Marie Françoise Thérèse, D EN D; French professor of international law; b 9 March 1928, Montpellier; d of Jules and Juliette (née Pierron) Coste-Floret; m Robert Furet 1954; three d one s. *Education:* Inst Ste Odile, Univ of Montpellier, Inst d'Etudes Politiques (Paris) and Univ of Paris. *Career:* Barrister Court of Appeal, Montpellier 1952–57; Asst Faculty of Law, Univ of Paris 1966–69; Prof Faculty of Law, Univ of Poitiers 1969–70; Prof Faculty of Law, Univ of Montpellier I 1970–98 (Prof Emer 1998–); Chevalier de la Légion d'Honneur; Officier de l'Ordre Nat du Mérite 1980. *Publications:* Le désarmement nucléaire 1973, La guerre et le droit 1979, Le droit international et les armes (jtly) 1983, Commentaire de la Charte des Nations Unies (jtly) 1991, Paul et Alfred Coste-Floret: deux jumeaux et trois républiques 2001; numerous publs in professional journals. *Leisure interest:* piano. *Address:* 16 rue du Cardinal de Cabrières, 34000 Montpellier, France. *Fax:* (4) 67-60-65-21.

FURMANOVSKY, Jill, BA; British photographer; b 1953 Bulawayo, Rhodesia; d of Jack and Eva Furmanovsky; one d. *Education:* Central School of Art and Design. *Career:* Founder rockarchive.com 1998; Diamond Music Photographer of the Year 1987; Observer Portrait Award 1992; Kodak European Gold Award 1994; Woman of the Year (Music and Related Industries) 1998. *Publications:* The Moment – 25 Years of Music Photography 1995, Was There Then – 3 Years with Oasis 1997. *Leisure interests:* photography, music, travel. *Address:* 8 Fitzroy Rd, London NW1 8TX, UK. *Telephone:* (20) 7722-4716; *Fax:* (20) 7916-4930; *E-mail:* jill@rockarchive.com; *Internet:* www.rockarchive.com.

FURSE, Clara Hedwig Frances, B SC; British investment banker; b 16 Sept 1957; m Richard Furse 1981; two s one d. *Education:* St James's School (W Malvern) and LSE. *Career:* Man Dir UBS 1983–98; Deputy Chair London Int Financial Futures and Options (LIFFE) 1997–99; Group CEO Crédit Lyonnais Rouse 1998–2000; CEO The London Stock Exchange PLC 2001–. *Address:* The London Stock Exchange PLC, Old Broad St, London EC2N 1HP, UK. *Telephone:* (20) 7797-1000; *Fax:* (20) 7334-8916; *Internet:* www.londonstockexchange.com.

FUSZARA, Małgorzata, PH D; Polish sociologist; b 9 Dec 1951, Warsaw; d of Stanisław and Jadwiga Fuszara. *Education:* Univ of Warsaw. *Career:* Teaching Asst Warsaw Univ 1974–83, apptd Adjunct Prof 1983; research on conflict resolution and food rationing 1983; est Centre for Socio-Legal Studies on the Position of Women 1991, Dir 1991; apptd Pres Sociology of Law Br, Polish Sociological Asscn 1987; contribs to professional journals. *Leisure interests:* music, sightseeing. *Address:* University of Warsaw, Inst of Applied Social Sciences, Podchorążych 20, 00-721 Warsaw, Poland. *Telephone:* (22) 414811; *Fax:* (22) 414811.

FUTRELL, Mary Alice Hatwood, ED D; American organization executive; b 24 May 1940, Alta Vista, VA; d of Josephine Austin; m Donald Lee Futrell. *Education:* Virginia State Univ, George Washington Univ (DC), Univ of Maryland, Univ of Virginia and Virginia Polytechnic Inst. *Career:* Teacher of Business Educ, Parker-Gray High School, Alexandria, Virginia 1963–65, George Washington High School 1965–80; Pres Nat Educ Asscn (NEA) 1983–89, Educ Int, Washington, DC 1992; Sr Fellow, Assoc Dir Center for the Study of Educ and Nat Devt 1989–92; Dir Inst for Curriculum Studies, Washington, DC 1992; mem numerous asscns and orgs; Hon DHL (Virginia State, George Washington) 1984, (Spellman Coll) 1986, (Cen State) 1987; Hon ED D (Eastern Michigan) 1987, (George Washington) 1992; Hon PH D (Lowell, Adrian); Fitz Turner Human Rights Award 1976; Creative Leadership in Women's Rights Award 1982; Outstanding Black Business and Professional Person, Ebony magazine 1984; One of 100 Top Women in America, Ladies Home Journal magazine 1984; One of 12 Women of the Year, Ms magazine 1985; One of Top 100 Blacks in America, Ebony magazine 1985–89. *Address:* George Washington Univ, 2134 G St, NW, Washington, DC, USA.

FUTTER, Ellen Victoria, AB, JD; American museum administrator; b 21 Sept 1949; d of Victor and Joan Babette Futter; m John A. Shutkin 1974; two d. *Education:* Univ of Wisconsin, Barnard Coll and Columbia Univ (New York). *Career:* Called to the Bar, NY 1975; Assoc Milbank, Tweed, Hadley & McCloy, New York 1974–80; acting Pres Barnard Coll, New York 1980–81, Pres, Trustee 1981–93; Pres American Museum of Natural History, New York 1993–; mem Bd Dirs Fed Reserve Bank of New York, Deputy Chair; mem Bd Dirs Mutual Benefit Life, American Ass Consortium on Financing of Higher Educ; mem New York City Comm on Status of Women Partners; mem ABA, Council on Foreign Relations; Spirit of Achievement Award, A. Einstein Coll of Medicine; Abram L. Sachar Award, Brandeis Univ; YWCA Elizabeth Cutter Morrow award. *Address:* American Museum of Natural History, Cen Park W at 79th St, New York, NY 10024, USA.

FYFIELD, Frances (see Hegarty, Frances).

G

GABARASHVILI, Tamar; Georgian musician and music teacher; b 22 July 1937, Tbilisi; d of Boris and Buda Gabarashvili; m Irakli Khomeriki 1980. *Education:* Tbilisi Cen Musical School and Moscow Tchaikovsky Conservatoire. *Career:* Cellist; soloist with Mosconcert 1966–90, then with Tbilisi Symphonic Orchestra; teacher, Chair in Tbilisi Conservatoire; Gold Medal, Int Cello Competition, Helsinki 1962; Third Prize, Int Pablo Casals Competition, Budapest 1963; Laureate, Third Int Tchaikovsky Competition, Moscow 1966. *Film:* Pastoral (cellist) 1978; numerous recordings of solo concerts 1962–. *Leisure interests:* knitting, cooking. *Address:* 380079 Tbilisi, Larsi Str 2–6, Georgia. *Telephone:* (32) 226420; *Fax:* (32) 987187; *E-mail:* buniaga@fable7.ge.

GABOR, Zsa Zsa; American actress; b (Sari Gabor) 6 Feb 1918, Hungary; d of Vilmos and Jolie Gabor; m 1st Burhan Belge 1937 (divorced 1941); m 2nd Conrad Hilton 1942 (divorced 1947); one d; m 3rd George Sanders 1949 (divorced 1954); m 4th Herbert Hutner 1964 (divorced 1966); m 5th Joshua Cosden, Jr 1966 (divorced 1967); m 6th Jack Ryan 1975 (divorced 1976); m 7th Michael O'Hara 1977 (divorced 1982); m 8th Prince Frederick von Anhalt, Duke of Saxony 1986. *Education:* Budapest, Lausanne (Switzerland) and Acad of Music and Dramatic Arts (Vienna). *Career:* Has lived in USA since 1941; numerous TV appearances on talk shows. *Films include:* Lovely to Look At 1952, We're Not Married 1952, Moulin Rouge 1952, The Story of Three Loves 1953, Lili 1953, Three Ring Circus 1954, Death of a Scoundrel 1956, Girl in the Kremlin 1957, For the First Time 1959, Boys' Night Out 1962, Picture Mommy Dead 1966, Arrivederci, Baby! 1966, Jack of Diamonds 1967, Won Ton Ton, the Dog Who Saved Hollywood, Queen of Outer Space, Frankenstein's Great Aunt Tilly, A Nightmare on Elm Street 3, Naked Gun 2½: The Smell of Fear, Happily Ever After (voice); *Publication:* How to Get a Man, How to Keep a Man and How to Get Rid of a Man 1971.

GABORIAU, Simone Raymonde Andrée Jeanne, L EN D; French judge; b 8 May 1945, Bordeaux; d of Paul and Marie-Paulette (née Dumonteil) Monthioux; m Patrick Daniel Gaboriau 1965; one d one s. *Education:* Lycée Théodore Gardère (Bordeaux) and d'Etat (Talence) and Univ of Bordeaux. *Career:* Deputy Public Prosecutor, Chaumont 1971–73; Examining Magistrate, Tribunal de Grande Instance, Bordeaux 1973–79, First Examining Magistrate 1979–82, Vice-Pres 1982–85; Counsellor Court of Appeal, Bordeaux 1985–89; Pres Tribunal de Grande Instance, Limoges 1989–; Pres Syndicat de la Magistrature (trade union) 1982–86, Cercle Condorcet de Bordeaux 1988–89 (currently Hon Pres). *Leisure interests:* reading, cinema, travel. *Address:* Tribunal de Grande Instance de Limoges, Palais de Justice, place d'Aine, 87000 Limoges, France. *Telephone:* (5) 55-11-81-01; *Fax:* (5) 55-32-21-01; *E-mail:* p.tgi-limoges@justice.fr.

GABRENAITE, Egle; Lithuanian actress; b 24 Sept 1950, Moscow; d of Antanas Gabrenas and Genovaite Tolkute; m (divorced); one s. *Education:* Lithuanian Music Acad. *Career:* Actress 1972–. *Plays include:* Hamlet, King Lear, The Cherry Orchard, Antigone; *Films include:* Travel to Paradise 1978, The Black Birch 1979, Travel to the Country 1986. *Leisure interests:* jazz theatre, cats. *Address:* Vilnius 2038, Vysniu 2-29, Lithuania. *Telephone:* (2) 265476; *Fax:* (2) 616800.

GAD EL MAWLA, Nazli, BM, B CH, MD; Egyptian professor of medical oncology; b 16 June 1929, Cairo; d of the late M. A. Gad El Mawla and Sania Sultan; m M. W. Mattar 1958; two d. *Education:* Univ of Cairo. *Career:* Intern Cairo Univ Hosp 1953–54, Resident Intern in charge of Medicine 1955–67; Tutor Faculty of Medicine, Univ of Cairo 1968–70, Nat Cancer Inst 1970–74, Asst Prof 1974–75, apptd Prof 1975, Prof of Oncology from 1977; numerous articles and papers on oncology in

professional journals; awards for internal medicine and surgery 1952. *Leisure interest:* music. *Address:* National Cancer Institute (NCI), Cairo University, Fom-El-Khalig, Cairo, Egypt. *Telephone:* (2) 3416819; *Fax:* (2) 844720.

GADATSCH, Hannelore; German journalist and broadcaster; b 1 May 1941, Berlin; d of Friedrich and Lydia Rosentreter; m Claus Jürgen Gadatsch 1965; two s. *Education:* Heinrich von Kleist Schule (Berlin) and Freie Univ Berlin. *Career:* TV Journalist and Presenter on various German channels 1963–, currently with Südwestfunk, Baden Baden, in charge of programmes for European Culture Channel (Arte) and other programmes; programmes include documentaries for Report series 1977–88, Tagesthemen (Presenter) 1984, 1985, Eins Plus (Presenter, cable and satellite TV); also Ed political, social and cultural talk shows; received awards for programmes BAG 1974, Drought and Famine in Ethiopia 1984, Settlement by Force in Ethiopia 1987, and for programme on torture victims 1994. *Address:* Südwestfunk, Hans-Bredow-Str 6, 76530 Baden Baden, Germany. *Telephone:* (7221) 922819; *Fax:* (7221) 922026.

GADHOKE, Sneh, MD; Indian cardiologist; b 25 May 1933, Lyallpur; m Ved Gadhoke 1957; two s. *Education:* Lady Hardinge Medical Coll and All-India Inst of Medical Sciences (Delhi). *Career:* Medical career began in 1951; specialized in cardiology from 1961; carried out basic research into high altitude effects on the cardio-respiratory system, coronary artery disease and rheumatic heart disease; Asst Prof of Biometeorology All-India Inst of Medical Sciences 1969–72; Sr Consultant Cardiologist Ganga Ram Hosp 1973–75, Moolchand K. R. Hosp, New Delhi from 1973, Batra Hosp, G. M. Modi Hosp and Escorts Heart Inst and Research Centre, New Delhi; currently Hon Consultant Cardiologist and Head of Intensive Cardiac Care Moolchand K. R. Hosp; Fellow Nuffield Foundation; mem Nat Council of Women in India; numerous publs in Indian and int journals. *Leisure interests:* gardening, arts, Indian mythology, reading. *Address:* S 21 Panchshila Park, New Delhi 110 017, India. *Telephone:* (11) 6441311; *Fax:* (11) 4623117.

GADJIEVA, Leila-Shovket, D MED; Azerbaijani politician; b 1951, Baku. *Education:* Azerbaijan Medical Inst. *Career:* Researcher, Head of Div then Head Researcher Sklifosovsky Inst of Emergency Medicine, Moscow 1978–89; Head Dept Research Centre, Ministry of Public Health, Russian Fed and Head of group working on the devt of legislation in the field of public health, Supreme Soviet, Russian Fed 1990–93; Chair Int Movt for Democratic Reforms in Azerbaijan 1990; f Liberal Democratic Party 1993; State Sec Azerbaijan 1993–94; Amb to UN 1994; has written more than 100 articles on medicine, philosophy and politics. *Address:* Parliament House, Baku, Azerbaijan.

GAFFNEY, Maureen, MA; Irish psychologist and organization executive; b 18 May 1947, Cork; d of Vincent P. Gaffney and Margaret Barry; m Dr John W. Harris 1976; one d one s. *Education:* Nat Univ of Ireland (Univ Coll Cork) and Univ of Chicago (IL, USA). *Career:* Clinical psychologist; broadcaster and columnist with Irish Times on women's, equality and power issues; Law Reform Commr 1987; Sr Lecturer in Psychology, Trinity Coll Dublin 1992–; Chair Nat Econ and Social Forum 1993–. *Publications:* Parenting 1991, Glass Slippers and Tough Bargains: Women, Men and Power 1993, The Way We Live Now 1996; academic articles and reviews. *Leisure interests:* reading, cooking, running. *Address:* National Economic and Social Forum, Centre Block, Government Bldgs, Upper Merrion St, Dublin 2, Ireland. *Telephone:* (1) 678-5577; *Fax:* (1) 662-1095.

GAGE, Elizabeth (pseudonym of Susan Libertson), BA; American writer; b 28 Dec 1947, Chicago, IL; d of Kenneth H. and Alices Falces Rusch; m Joseph Libertson 1969; one d. *Education:* West Sr High (Madison, WI) and Northwestern Univ (Evanston, IL). *Publications:* A Glimpse of Stocking 1988, Pandora's Box 1990, The Master Stroke 1991, Taboo 1992, The Ghosts of War 1993, Intimate 1995, Confession 1998, Against All Odds 1998, The Hourglass 1999. *Address:* 145 N Kihei Rd, Kihei, Maui, HI 96753, USA.

GAGE, Frances Marie, RCA; Canadian sculptor; b 22 Aug 1924, Windsor, ON; d of Russel and Jean Mildred (née Collver) Gage. *Education:* Ontario Coll of Art, Art Students League (NY, USA) and Ecole des Beaux Arts (Paris). *Career:* Sculptor in wood and stone; tutor in field; exhibitions in Canada, Italy 1984, USA 1987, Finland 1990, Hungary 1994, Netherlands 1998 and UK; comms for Fanshaw Coll, London, ON 1962, Univ of Western Ontario 1963, Univ of Guelph 1966, Dr Andrew Smith Univ 1967, Mount Allison Univ 1968, Women's Coll Hosp, Toronto 1969, Univ of Toronto 1969, Royal Soc of Canada 1973, Standards Council of Canada, Roy Thompson Hall 1990, Donald Forster Sculpture Park 1990; mem Council Royal Canadian Acad of Art; Rothman Purchase Award 1965. *Leisure interests:* conservation, music. *Address:* 138 Ball's Lane, Cobourg, ON K9A 2L5, Canada.

GAGNON-TREMBLAY, Monique, BA, BL; Canadian politician; b 26 May 1940, Plessisville, PQ; d of Joseph and Antoinette Gagnon; m Jacques Tremblay 1970. *Education:* Quirion Business School, Univ of Laval (PQ) and Univ of Sherbrooke (PQ). *Career:* Exec Sec notary's office 1958–69; est notary office, Ascot Corner, PQ 1973; apptd Teaching Asst in Notarial Law Univ of Sherbrooke, PQ 1973; fmr Vice-Pres Shefford Inc chemical products, Granby, PQ; mem Québec Nat Ass for St-François 1985–; Minister responsible for the Status of Women, PQ 1985–89; Minister for Immigration and Cultural Communities, Vice-Pres Québec Treasury Bd PQ 1989–94; Deputy Premier, Pres Treasury Bd, Minister responsible for Admin and the Public Service 1994; currently Pres Official Opposition (Caucus), Nat Ass, PQ. *Address:* Hôtel du Parlement, Bureau 2.53, Québec, G1A 1A4, Canada; 27, 10E Ave Nord, Sherbrooke, Québec J1G 5G6, Canada. *Telephone:* (418) 644-2817 (Sherbrook); (819) 565-3667 (Parlement); *Fax:* (418) 643-6640 (Sherbrook); (819) 565-8779 (Parlement); *E-mail:* mgagnontremblay@assnat.qc.ca; *Internet:* www.assnat.qc.ca/eng/membres/gagm1.html.

GAIDA, Natalia V.; Belarus opera singer; b 1 May 1939, Sverdlovsk; m Youri Bastrikov 1965; one d. *Education:* Law Inst (Sverdlovsk) and Conservatoire (Sverdlovsk). *Career:* Debut, Sverdlovsk Opera 1965; Singer Belarus Musical Comedy 1970–; Prof Minsk Acad of Arts 1994–; mem Cen Cttee Cultural Workers' Union 1978–82, Presidium Union of Theatrical Players 1982–; People's Artist of the Repub of Belarus 1980; Order of the Insignia of Honour 1986; Kryštalnaja Paŭlinka Prize 1995. *Operas and shows include:* La Bohème, Don Juan, Fille de Neige, Silver, Maretza and the Princess of the Circus, My Fair Lady, Hello Dolly; over 60 operettas and 15 operas; *Film:* La soirée de gala avec les italiens 1970. *Leisure interest:* travel. *Address:* 220004 Minsk, vul Ramanaŭskaya Slabada 9-76, Belarus. *Telephone:* (172) 202153.

GAINSBOURG, Charlotte; French actress and singer; b 22 July 1971; d of the late Serge Gainsbourg and of Jane Birkin (qv). *Film appearances include:* An Impudent Girl (César Award), Paroles et Musique, Charlotte Forever, Merci la Vie 1991, The Cement Garden, Jane Eyre, Anna Oz; *Recordings include:* Lemon Incest, Charlotte Forever, Elastique.

GAJ, Bozena, MA; Polish politician; b 23 Dec 1951, Cracow; divorced; one s. *Education:* Jagiellonian Univ (Cracow). *Career:* Joined Solidarity 1980, Head of Cttee on Educ, Cracow 1989–91; joined Confederacy of Ind Poland 1989; elected to Sejm (Parl) 1991; f Alliance of Women Against Difficulties of Life 1992. *Leisure interests:* swimming, yoga. *Address:* Sejm PRI, ul Wiejski 4/6/8, 00-489 Warsaw, Poland; Os Dywizjonu 303, 39-38, Cracow, Poland. *Telephone:* (12) 486759 (Cracow).

GALABERT, Micheline, D ECON; French civil servant; b 29 Sept 1929, Paris; d of Bernard Jean and Germaine (née Jamet) Augé; m Jean Michel Galabert 1959; two s. *Education:* Inst d'Etudes Politiques de Paris, Univ of Paris, Inst Supérieur des Techniques d'Organisation and Deutsche Hochschule für Politik (Germany). *Career:* Mem staff Ecole Nationale d'Administration 1952–55; Insp-Gen of Social Security 1955–67; Social Counsellor Embassy of France, Morocco 1967–70; Tech Counsellor Ministry of Finance 1970–73; Dir Centre d'Etudes de l'Emploi 1973–80; Head of French Office, Bureau Int du Travail 1980–89; Insp-Gen of Social Affairs 1989–94; Vice-Pres Comité Int de Liaison des Asscns Féminines 1995; Pres Asscn des Femmes de l'Europe Méridionale 1966–; Officier de la Légion d'Honneur 1995. *Leisure interest:* hill-walking. *Address:* 48 rue Vaugirard, 75006 Paris, France. *Telephone:* (1) 43-25-80-95.

GALÁS, Diamanda; American singer and poet; b San Diego, CA. *Education:* Univ of CA. *Career:* First live performance, Festival d'Avignon (France) 1979; performed lead in opera Un Jour Comme un Autre (Avignon) 1980; performed at Theatre Gerard Philippe Saint-Denis; solo tour at European festivals including Donaueschingen, Inventionen, Biennale de Paris, Musica Oggi, Festivale de la Voce; performed at Int AIDS Conf (San Francisco) 1990, Olympic Festival (Barcelona, Spain) 1990, Helsinki Festival, Festival delle Colline (Italy), Serious Fun Festival (Lincoln Center, USA) 1993, Royal Festival Hall (London, UK) 1996. *Recordings include:* The Litanies of Satan 1982, Panoptikon, The Masque of the Red Death (triptych) 1989, Plague Mass (trilogy), Wild Women with Steak Knives, Tragouthia apo to Aima Exon Fonos (Song from the Blood of those Murdered), Vena Cava 1992, The Divine Punishment, Saint of the Pit, There are No More Tickets to the Funeral, The Singer, Insekta 1993, The Sporting Life 1994, Schrei X Live/Schrei 27 1996; *Publications:* The Shit of God 1996. *Address:* c/o Asphodel Records, 763 Brennan St, San Francisco, CA 94103, USA. *E-mail:* garth@diamandagalas.com; *Internet:* www.diamandagalas.com.

GALDIKAS, Birute M. F., PH D; Canadian primatologist; b 1947; m 1st Rod Brindamour (divorced 1979); one s; m 2nd Pak Bohap; one s one d. *Education:* Univ of California at Los Angeles. *Career:* Moved to Indonesia with Rod Brindamour to study Orangutans and record their behaviour in the wild 1971–; est Camp Leakey, nr Kaliman, Borneo, also rescued captive orangutans, rehabilitated and returned them to the forest until 1992; worked with Louis Leakey; Lecturer Simon Fraser Univ, Vancouver, BC, Canada. *Publication:* Reflections of Eden—My life With The Orangutans of Borneo 1995. *Address:* Camp Leakey, Sekonver River, Pangkalabun, Nr Kaliman, Borneo, Indonesia.

GALE, (Gwendoline) Fay, AO, PH D, D UNIV; Australian university vice-chancellor and geographer; b (Gwendoline Fay Gilding) 13 June 1932, Balakava, SA; d of Rev George Jasper and Kathleen Gertrude (née Pengelley) Gilding; one s one d. *Education:* Methodist Ladies' Coll and Univ of Adelaide. *Career:* Lecturer in Geography, then Sr Lecturer, Univ of Adelaide 1966–74, Reader 1974–78, Prof of Geography 1978–89, Pro-Vice-Chancellor 1988–89, Prof Emer 1989–; Australian Heritage Commr 1989–95; Vice-Chancellor Univ of Western Australia 1990–97; Visiting Prof Univ of Washington, USA 1978, Univ Coll London 1985; Pres Inst of Australian Geographers 1989–90, Australian Vice-Chancellors Cttee 1996–97; Pres Acad of Social Sciences in Australia 1998–; Chair Social Justice Advisory Cttee 1989, Festival of Perth, WA 1992–, W Australia Symphony Orchestra 1996–; mem Humanities and Social Science Panel, Australian Research Council 1987–89, Chair 1989; Exec mem Acad of the Social Sciences in Australia 1980–82, 1988–89; mem Council Co-operative Research Centre 1996–, Prime Minister's Science Council 1996–; Hon Fellow St Hugh's Coll, Oxford, UK 1972; Hon Life Fellow Australian Inst of Geographers 1994; Elin Wagner Fellowship 1971; Catherine Helen Spence Fellowship 1972; Fellow Acad of Social Sciences of Australia 1978, Australian Inst of Man 1995, mem Nat Comm of UNESCO, Australia 1999–, Australian Research Council 2000–; Hon D LITT (W Australia); British Council Award 1972; John Lewis Gold Medal 2000; Griffith Taylor Medal 2001. *Publications:* Women's Role in Aboriginal Society (ed) 1970, Urban Aborigines 1972, Race Relations in Australia: the Aboriginal situation (jtly) 1975, Poverty Among Aboriginal Families in Adelaide (jtly) 1975, We are Bosses Ourselves: the Status and Role of Aboriginal Women Today (ed) 1983, Tourists and the National Estate: Procedures to

Protect Australia's Heritage (jtly) 1987, Aboriginal Youth and the Criminal Justice System: the Injustice of Justice (jtly) 1990, Inventing Places: Studies in Cultural Geography (co-ed) 1991, Changing Australia 1991, Boyer Lectures 1991, Juvenile Justice: Debating the Issues 1993, Tourism and the Protection of Aboriginal Sites 1994, Cultural Geographies 1999, Making Space: Women and Education at St Aloysius College Adelaide 1880–2000 2000. *Leisure interests:* bush walking, camping, music, theatre, rock art. *Address:* c/o Office of the Vice-Chancellor, The University of Adelaide, Adelaide, S Australia 5005, Australia (Office). *Telephone:* (8) 8379-7476 (Office); *Fax:* (8) 8379-7378 (Office).

GALE, Kathy, BA; British publishing executive; b 13 Aug 1960, Cheltenham; d of George and Celia Margot Gale. *Education:* John Smeaton High School and Goldsmiths Coll (London). *Career:* Bookseller; worked for British Books in Print; Copy Ed Pan Books Ltd; Sr Ed Hodder and Stoughton; Editorial Dir of specialist fiction Pan Macmillan; Publishing Dir The Women's Press 1991–; activist in women's and peace orgs. *Address:* The Women's Press, 34 Great Sutton St, London EC1V 0PX, UK. *Telephone:* (20) 7251-3007; *Fax:* (20) 7608-1938.

GALEY, Geneviève; French journalist and television executive; b 13 April 1944, Paris; d of Louis-Emile and Marcelle Galey. *Education:* Lycées Victor Duruy and Sophie Germain and Inst Catholique (Paris). *Career:* Admin Sec Paris Match magazine 1966–69, journalist Political Section 1969–72; journalist on Le Point 1972–82; Corresp for TV programme Les visiteurs du jour; Deputy Head Télévision Française 1 (TF1) Political Service 1983, Head 1984–85, Deputy Chief Ed TF1 1986, Ed-in-Chief 1988–. *Leisure interests:* skiing, tennis. *Address:* TF1, 15 quai du Pont du Jour, 92656 Boulogne Cedex, France. *E-mail:* ggaley@tf1.fr.

GALICA, Divina; British sportswoman; b 1944. *Education:* Chatelard School (Switzerland). *Career:* Skier and racing driver; competitor downhill and giant slalom ski events Winter Olympic Games, Innsbruck, Austria 1964, Grenoble, France 1968, Sapporo, Japan 1972; twice took 3rd place downhill World Cup; won over 50 non-Formula One car races 1972–; British Women's Speed Record holder since 1994; instructor Skip Barber Racing School, Lakeville, CT, USA; competitor speed-skiing demonstration event Winter Olympic Games, Albertville, France 1992. *Address:* Skip Barber Racing School, 29 Brook St, Lakeville, CT 06039, USA (Office); Divina Galica Ltd, 51 Hasker St, London SW3 2LE, UK (Office); 1226 Nancesowee Ave, Sebring, FL 33870, USA (Home). *Telephone:* (860) 435-1300 (Office, USA); (941) 471-2027 (Home); *Fax:* (860) 435-1321 (Office, USA); (941) 471-2027 (Home).

GALINDO, Rosario Arias de; Panamanian publishing executive; b 4 Jan 1920, Panamá; d of Harmodio Arias (Pres of Panama 1932–36) and Rosario Guardia de Arias; m Gabriel Galindo V. 1940; two d one s. *Education:* Sacred Heart Convent (Santiago, Chile), schools in Brussels and Paris and Univ studies in Geneva, Paris and Panamá. *Career:* Mem Bd of Dirs Nat Red Cross 1952–62, Cttee for Human Rights 1980–89, Nat Ind Union for Democratic Action 1981–89, Inter-American Press 1991; apptd Pres Editora Panamá América, SA 1962; Publr El Panamá América and Crítica Libre daily newspapers; mem Bd of Trustees Isthmian Foundation for Econ and Social Studies 1991, Foundation for the Advancement of Women 1991; mem Latin American Inst for Advanced Studies, Panamanian Art Inst, Nat Concert Asscn; articles on Human Rights, freedom of the press and democracy in Panamanian and American newspapers including Freedom House (New York) and La Prensa (Panamá); Manuel Amador Guerrero decoration 1991; Keys to the City of Panamá 1991. *Leisure interests:* grandchildren and great-grandchildren, music, theatre, needlework. *Address:* POB B-4, Vía Fernández de Córdoba (Vista Hermosa), Panamá 9A, Panama. *Telephone:* 61-2300; *Fax:* 61-3152.

GALLAIRE, Fatima; Algerian playwright; b (Fatima Bourega), El Harrouch; m; two c. *Education:* Univs of Algiers and Paris VIII (Vincennes à St-Denis) and Cinémathèque (Algiers). *Career:* Visting Author Dept of French, Grinnell Coll, USA 2000; Arletty Prize for Drama in French 1990; AMIC Prize, Acad Française 1994. *Plays include:* Princesses (Soc des Auteurs Award) 1987, Les co-épouses 1990,

La fête virile 1992, Molly des sables 1994, Au cœur, la brûlure 1994, Les richesses de l'hiver 1996, Le secret des vieilles 1996. *Address:* c/o Department of French, Grinnell College, Grinnell, IA 50112, USA.

GALLANT, Mavis, CC, FRSL; Canadian writer and literary critic; b 1922, Montréal, PQ. *Career:* Employee Nat Film Bd of Canada and Montréal Standard; emigrated to France 1950; short stories published The New Yorker 1951–; has written reviews and essays for New York Review of Books, The New York Times Book Review; Writer-in-Residence Univ of Toronto 1983–84; Hon mem American Acad and Inst of Arts and Letters 1989; Hon LLD (Queen's) 1991; Tributee Int Authors Festival, Harbourfront, Toronto 1993; Canada Council Molson Prize for the Arts 1997. *Publications:* Short stories: The Other Paris 1956, My Heart is Broken 1964, The Pegnitz Junction 1973, The End of the World 1974, From the Fifteenth District 1978, Home Truths (Gov-Gen Award) 1981, Overhead in a Balloon 1985, In Transit 1988, Across the Bridge 1993, Paris Notebooks 1997; Novels: Green Water, Green Sky 1969, A Fairly Good Time 1970; Play: What is to Be Done? 1984; Non-fiction: Paris Journals: Selected Reviews and Essays 1986. *Address:* c/o McLelland & Stewart, Suite 900, 481 University Ave, Toronto, ON M5G 2E9, Canada.

GALLEY, Carol, BA; British business executive. *Education:* Gosforth Grammar School (Newcastle) and Univ of Leicester. *Career:* Joined Mercury Asset Man (now Merrill Lynch Investment Man 2000) 1971, Dir 1982, Vice-Chair 1995–2001, mem Exec Man Cttee; mem Nat Advisory Council for Educ and Training Targets. *Address:* c/o Merrill Lynch Investment Management PLC, 33 King William St, London EC4R 9AS, UK (Office). *Telephone:* (20) 7280-2800; *Fax:* (20) 7280-2453.

GALUN, Rachel, M SC, PH D; Israeli entomologist; b 3 April 1926; d of Yehuda and Dina Rabinowich; m Arjeh Galun 1948; one s one d. *Education:* Hebrew Univ and Univ of Illinois (USA). *Career:* Head Dept of Entomology Israeli Inst of Biological Research, Ness Ziona 1956–78; Prof of Entomology Univ of Tel Aviv 1968–78; Head Dept of Zoology Hebrew Univ 1980–84, Head Inst of Microbiology, Hadassah Medical School 1988–94; Visiting Scientist NIH, Bethesda, USA 1984, IAEA, Vienna 1987; mem Bd of Dirs Int Centre for Insect Physiology, Kenya 1978–88; consultant to various orgs; over 150 books and articles on entomology. *Leisure interests:* travel, bridge. *Address:* Hebrew University, Hadassah Medical School, POB 1172, Jerusalem 91010, Israel (Office); 29 Ben Zvi Blvd, Ramat Gan, Israel (Home). *Telephone:* (2) 7428095 (Office); (3) 6744297 (Home); *Fax:* (2) 784010 (Office).

GAMBLE, Christine Elizabeth, PH D; British cultural administrator; b 1 March 1950, Rotherham; d of late Albert Edward Gamble and Kathleen Laura Wallis; m Edward Barry Antony Craxton. *Education:* Royal Holloway Coll (Univ of London). *Career:* Worked in Anglo-French cultural org 1974–75; Office of the Cultural Attaché, British Embassy, Moscow 1975–76; joined British Council, New Delhi 1977; returned to UK (Stratford-upon-Avon) 1979, posted to Harare 1980–82, Regional Officer for the Soviet Union and Mongolia 1982–85, Deputy Dir Athens 1985–87, with Corp Planning Dept 1988–90, Head Project Pursuit Dept and Dir Chancellor's Financial Sector Scheme 1990–92, Dir Visitor's Dept 1992–93, Gen Man Country Services Group and Head European Services 1993–96; Cultural Councillor British Embassy, Paris and Dir British Council 1996–98; Dir Royal Inst of Int Affairs, London 1998–; Order of Rio Branco (Brazil) 2000. *Leisure interests:* literature, art, music, theatre. *Address:* Royal Institute of International Affairs, Chatham House, 10 St James's Square, London SW1Y 4LE, UK. *Telephone:* (20) 7957-5700; *Fax:* (20) 7957-5710.

GANDHI, Maneka Anand; Indian politician and environmentalist; b 26 Aug 1956, New Delhi; d of the late T. S. and of Amteshwar Anand; m Sanjay Gandhi 1974 (died 1980); one s. *Education:* Lawrence High School (Sanawar) and Jawaharlal Nehru Univ (New Delhi). *Career:* Fmr beauty queen; fmr adviser to Sanjay Gandhi; Ed Surya (Sun) newspaper 1975–80; attended Lucknow Convention 1982; Founder and Leader of Sanjay Vichar Manch (Sanjay Ideas Org) 1982, of political party Rashtriya Sanjay Manch (merged with Janata Party 1988) 1983; Minister of State for the Environment and Forests 1989–91, mem Rajya Sabha (Parl) 1996–; Minister for Social Justice and Empowerment 1999–; political and environmental columnist 1984–95; Managing

Trustee, then Pres Ruth Cowell Trust 1980–; Sr Advisor VOICE (consumer action forum) 1988; f Greenline 1992; Founder and Chair People for Animals Trust 1994; Chair Cttee on Control and Supervision of Experiments on Animals, Rugmark Foundation 1994, Delhi Soc for Prevention of Cruely to Animals (SPCA) 1995; Pres Sanjay Gandhi Animal Care Centre; Lord Erskine Award, Royal Soc for Prevention of Cruelty to Animals (RSPCA) 1992; Vegetarian of the Year 1995; Environmentalist of the Year 1995; Prani Mitra Award (Nat Animal Welfare Bd) 1997; Marchig Prize (Marchig Animal Welfare Trust, GB) 1997; Venu Menon Lifetime Achievement Award 1999; Bhagwan Mahavir Award 1999; Diwaliben Award 1999. *TV includes:* New Horizons, Heads and Tails, Maneka's Ark; *Publications:* Sanjay Gandhi 1980, Mythology of Indian Plants, Animal Quiz 1988, Brahma's Hair 1990, Penguin Book of Hindu Names 1992, The Complete Book of Muslim and Parsi Names 1994, Heads & Tails I 1994, First Aid for Animals, Animal Laws of India 1996, Rainbow and Other Stories, Natural Health for Your Dog, Heads & Tails II 1996. *Leisure interests:* wildlife, books, painting, animal hospitals, social service. *Address:* 202, C-Wing, Shastri Bhavan, New Delhi 110001, India (Office); A-4 Maharani Bagh, New Delhi 110065, India (Home). *Telephone:* (11) 3381001 (Office); (11) 6840402 (Home); *Fax:* (11) 3381902 (Office); (11) 6823144 (Home).

GANDHI, Sonia; Indian (b Italian) politician; b 9 Dec 1946, Italy; d of Stefano and Paola Maino; m Rajiv Gandhi 1968 (died 1991); one s one d. *Education:* Univ of Cambridge and Nat Gallery of Modern Art (Delhi). *Career:* Pres Congress (I) Party, India 1991, now mem; Chair Jawaharlal Memorial Fund, Indira Gandhi Memorial Fund 1991; Pres Rajiv Gandhi Foundation; mem All India Congress Cttee (I), leader 1998–; Leader of Opposition in Parl (Lok Sabha). *Publications:* Rajiv 1992, Rajiv's World 1994. *Leisure interests:* Indian art, restoring paintings. *Address:* Rajiv Gandhi Foundation, Jawahar Bhawan, Dr Rajendra Prasad Rd, New Delhi 110 011, India (Office); All India Congress Committee (I), 24 Akbar Rd, New Delhi 110011, India (Office); 10 Janpath, New Delhi 110011, India (Home). *Telephone:* (11) 3017470 (Office); (11) 3014161 (Home).

GANDHI VADRA, Priyanka; Indian politician; b 1972; d of Rajiv and Sonia Gandhi; m Robert Varda 1996; one s. *Career:* Descendent of the Nehru-Gandhi political dynasty; worked in orphanage and as school-teacher; canvassed for Congress party on behalf of her mother, Amethi Constituency 1999; mem All India Congress Cttee. *Address:* c/o All India Congress Committee, 24 Akbar Rd, New Delhi, 110 011, India.

GANNON, Lucy; British writer; b 1948; m (husband deceased); one d. *Career:* Fmrly nurse, residential social worker and military policewoman; has devised and written numerous TV series and dramas; Writer-in-Residence Royal Shakespeare Co 1987. *TV includes:* Keeping Tom Nice (Richard Burton Award 1987, John Whiting Award 1990), Wicked Old Nellie 1989, A Small Dance (Prix Europa 1991), Testimony of a Child, A Small Dance, Trip Trap, Soldier, Soldier, Peak Practice, Bramwell. *Address:* Cruck Barn, Ashbourne Rd, Church Broughton, Derby DE65 5AT, UK.

GAPRINDASHVILI, Nona; Georgian chess player; b 3 May 1941, Zugdidi; d of the late Terenti Gaprindashvili and of Vera Grigolia; m Anzor Chichinadze 1969; one s. *Education:* Tbilisi State Univ. *Career:* Teacher; Chess Champion of Georgia 1956; World Chess Champion five times 1962–78; Olympic Champion 11 times 1963–92, Gold Medals bearer; Int Grand Master (women's title) 1974; twice won European Cup of Champions; Laureate of first Chess Oscar 1982; Pres Georgian Nat Olympic Cttee 1985–96; Medal for Distinguished Service 1963; Order of Lenin 1966; USSR Order of Honour 1978; Order of Merit, Georgia 1994. *Publications:* Sense of My Life 1976, I Prefer Risk 1977; articles on chess in various magazines. *Leisure interests:* art (theatre, music, ballet), sport (snooker, billiards, table tennis, football). *Address:* Georgian Chess Federation, Tbilisi, Georgia (Office).

GARAS, Klára, PH D; Hungarian art historian; b 19 June 1919, Rákosszentmihály; d of Pál Garas and Irén Strasser. *Education:* Budapest Univ of Sciences. *Career:* Joined staff Budapest Museum of Fine Arts 1945, subsequent posts to Gen Dir 1964–84; Corresp mem Hungarian Acad of Sciences 1972, mem 1985–; Labour Order of Merit (golden degree) 1974, 1979. *Publications:* Magyarországi festészet a XVII

században (Hungarian Painting in the 17th century) 1953, Magyarországi festészet a XVIII században (Hungarian Painting in the 18th century) 1955, Olasz reneszánsz portrék a Szépmüvészeti Muzeumban (Italian Renaissance Portraits in the Museum of Fine Arts) 1965, 1973, Carlo Innocenzo Carloni (jtly) 1966, A velencei settecento festészete (Venetian Paintings of the 18th Century) 1977, Franz Anton Maulbertsch, Leben und Werk (his Life and Work) 1974, A 17 század német és osztrák rajzmüvészete (Deutsche und österreichische Zeichnungen des 18 Jahrhunderts) 1980; several publs on the Budapest Museum of Fine Arts. *Leisure interest:* 15th to 18th century European and Hungarian painting. *Address:* 1126 Budapest, Kiss János altábornagy u 48/c, Hungary. *Telephone:* (1) 156-3809.

GARAUD, Marie-Françoise; French civil servant and administrator; b 6 March 1934, Poitiers; d of Marcel and Yvonne (née Brion) Quintard; m Louis Garaud 1959; two s. *Education:* Inst de la Providence and Univ of Poitiers. *Career:* Barrister, Poitiers Bar 1954; Legal Asst Ministry of the Sea 1957–60; Parl Attachée to Cabinet of the Minister of Co-operation 1961–62; Rep to Cabinet of the Minister of Justice and Keeper of the Seals 1962–67; Rep to Cabinet of the Prime Minister 1967–68; Tech Adviser to Secr-Gen of the Presidency 1969–74; Public Auditor Cour des Comptes, Paris 1974–98, Head 1998–; MEP 1999–; Pres Inst Int de Géopolitique 1982–. *Publications:* De l'Europe en général et de la France en particulier (jtly) 1992, Maastricht, pourquoi non? 1992. *Leisure interests:* horse-riding, hunting. *Address:* 31 quai Anatole France, 75007 Paris, France (Office); 27 quai Anatole France, 75007 Paris, France. *Telephone:* (1) 47-05-60-35 (Office); *Fax:* (1) 45-51-77-77 (Office); *E-mail:* instit.geopol@wanadoo.fr.

GARCÍA, Marta; Cuban ballet dancer; b 1949, Havana. *Education:* Alicia Alonso's Ballet Acad and Prov School of Ballet (Havana). *Career:* Professional debut 1965, Soloist 1967, Prima Ballerina 1974, Prin Dancer Ballet Nacional de Cuba; performances in Europe, USA and Asia; Guest Dancer Bellas Artes Ballet, Mexico, Budapest Opera and Ballet Theatre, Choreographic Gala, Monte Carlo, Int Ballet Festival, Peru, Opera House, Rome; dancer of traditional and contemporary roles; Dr hc (Moscow) 1969; numerous awards and prizes including Gold Star, Paris 1970, Laureate's Medal, Tokyo 1978, Medal of Friendship, Vietnam 1978, Cuban Medal, Distinction for Nat Culture, Ministry of Cuba. *Address:* Calzada 510 esq D y E Vedado, 10400 Havana, Cuba. *Telephone:* 32-7151; *Fax:* 32-6343.

GARCÍA ARÍAS, Ludivina; Spanish politician; b 13 Dec 1945, Morelia, Mexico. *Career:* Teacher; elected MEP (PSE, PSOE) 1986; mem Cttee on Econ and Monetary Affairs and Industrial Policy, Cttee on Women's Rights, Del for Relations with the mem states of ASEAN, SE Asia and the Repub of Korea, Del to the EU-Slovak Repub Jt Parl Cttee. *Address:* c/o European Parliament, rue Wiertz, 1047 Brussels, Belgium.

GARCÍA MORENO, Amalia; Mexican politician; b Zacatecas; d of Francisco García and Conceptión Medina; one d. *Education:* Universidad Autónoma de Puebla. *Career:* Fed Deputy 1988–91; mem Rep Ass for Fed Dist 1991–94; Senator 1997–; Nat Pres Partido de la Revolución Democrática; mem Consultative Council of Women, Human Rights Comm. *Leisure interests:* reading, films. *Address:* Office of the President, Partido de la Revolución Democrática, Monterrey 50, Col Roma, CP, 06700 Mexico, DF, Mexico. *Telephone:* 207 1212; *Internet:* www.cen-prd.org.mx.

GARCIN, Sylviane Simone, L ÈS SC; French business executive; b 17 Sept 1946, Grenoble; d of Paul and Simone Cathiard; m Gaston Garcin 1973; two d one s. *Education:* Univ of Grenoble. *Career:* Admin Asst Genty-Cathiard 1970–72, Legal Adviser 1972–75, Dir-Gen 1975–90; Dir-Gen Go Sport 1975–90; Pres Château Haut Bergey 1991–. *Address:* Château Haut Bergey, 33850 Léognan, France.

GARDAM, Jane Mary, BA, FRSL; British writer; b 11 July 1928, Coatham, N Yorks; d of William and Kathleen (née Helm) Pearson; m David Hill Gardam 1954; two s one d. *Education:* Saltburn High School for Girls and Bedford Coll for Women. *Career:* Co-ordinator UK Hosp Libraries British Red Cross 1951–53. *Publications:* Novels: A Long Way From Verona 1971, The Summer After the Funeral 1973, Bilgewater 1977, God on the Rocks (Prix Baudelaire 1979) 1978, The Hollow Land

(Whitbread Award 1981) 1980, Bridget and William 1981, Horse 1982, Kit 1983, Crusoe's Daughter 1985, Kit in Boots 1986, Swan 1987, Through the Doll's House Door 1987, The Queen of the Tambourine (Whitbread Novel Award 1992) 1991, Earth Fox 1995, Tufty Bear 1996, The Green Man 1998, The Flight of the Maidens 2000; Short stories: A Few Fair Days 1971, Black Faces, White Faces (Winifred Holtby Award, David Highams Award) 1975, The Sidmouth Letters 1980, The Pangs of Love (Katherine Mansfield Award 1984) 1983, Showing the Flag 1989, Going into the Dark House 1994, Missing the Midnight 1997; Non-fiction: The Iron Coast 1994. *Leisure interests:* agriculture, gardening, travel, hospitality. *Address:* Haven House, Sandwich, Kent CT13 9ES, UK; Throstlenest Farm, Crackpot, N Yorks, UK; 34 Denmark Rd, London SW19, UK.

GARDNER OF PARKES, Baroness (Life Peer), cr 1981, of Southgate, Greater London, and of Parkes, NSW (Australia), **Rachel Trixie Anne Gardner,** BDS; Australian business executive, politician and dental surgeon; b 17 July 1927, Parkes; d of the late Hon J. J. Gregory and Rachel McGirr; m Kevin Anthony Gardner 1956; three d. *Education:* Monte Sant Angelo Coll (Sydney), E Sydney Tech Coll, Univ of Sydney and Cordon Bleu de Paris. *Career:* Came to UK 1955; dental surgeon; mem Westminster City Council 1968–78, Lady Mayoress 1987–88; mem GLC for Havering 1970–73, Enfield-Southgate 1977–86; Parl cand (Cons) for Blackburn 1970, N Cornwall 1974; JP (N Westminster) 1971; mem House of Lords 1981–, a Deputy Speaker and Deputy Chair of Cttees 1999–; mem London Electricity Bd 1984–90; Dir Gateway Building Soc 1987–88, Woolwich Building Soc 1988–93; British Chair European Union of Women 1978–82; mem Dept of Employment Advisory Cttee on Women's Employment 1980–88; British Rep UN Status of Women Comm 1982–88; Chair PLAN Int (UK) 1989–, Royal Free Hampstead Nat Health Service Trust 1994–97; Vice-Chair NE Thames Regional Health Authority 1990–94; Chair Suzy Lamplugh Trust 1993–97. *Leisure interests:* travel, family, needlework. *Address:* House of Lords, London SW1A 0PW, UK. *Telephone:* (20) 7219-6611; *Fax:* (20) 7219-5979; *E-mail:* gardnert@parliament.uk.

GAREWAL, Simi; Indian actress, producer, director and broadcaster; b 17 Oct 1947, Lahore, Pakistan; d of Jalawar Singh and Darshi Garewal. *Education:* Convent of Jesus and Mary (New Delhi) and Newland House School (London). *Career:* Film debut 1962; mem Int Jury Teheran Film Festival 1975; writer, producer and owner Siga Arts Int from 1982; Filmfare, Screen and Critic Awards; Paters Award for TV commercial (Australia) 1988; Balraj Sahni Award for Contrib to Indian Cinema 1991; Meena Kumari Award; Best TV anchor 1999; Filmgoers Award 2000. *Films include:* Tarzan Goes to India 1962, Days and Nights in a Forest, Padatik, Two Drops of Water, Do Badan (Filmfare Award) 1964, Saathi (Filmfare Award) 1967, Mera Naam Joker (All-India Film Critics Award) 1970, Siddhartha (India Cinegoers' Asscn Award 1974) 1972, Karz (All-India Film Critics Award) 1981, Rukhsat (writer and dir) 1989; *TV as writer, producer and dir includes:* It's A Woman's World (presenter), Maharajas (BBC) 1987, Living Legend Raj Kapoor (Channel Four) 1987, India's Rajiv (Channel Four) 1989–91, Rendezvous with Simi Garewal (Star Plus) 1997–. *Leisure interests:* snooker, backgammon, chess, puzzles, ice-skating, swimming, poetry, computer games. *Address:* Pavlova, 6th Floor, Little Gibbs Rd, Malabar Hill, Mumbai 400 006, India. *Telephone:* (22) 3641841; *Fax:* (22) 3644856.

GARG, Mridula, MA; Indian writer; b 25 Oct 1938, Calcutta (now Kolkata); d of Birendra Prasad and Ravi Kanta Jain; m Anand Garg 1963; two c. *Education:* Delhi School of Econs. *Career:* Lecturer in Econs 1960–63; writer of short stories, novels and plays in Hindi, later English. *Publications:* Novels: Uske Hisse Ki Dhoop (M. P. Sahitya Acad Award) 1975, Chittcobra 1979, Anitya 1980, Main Aur Main 1984, A Touch of Sun 1977, Daffodils on Fire (short stories) 1990; Plays include: Ek Aur Ajnabi (All India Radio Award) 1978. *Leisure interests:* reading, acting, flower-arranging. *Address:* E 118 Masjid Moth, GK 3, New Delhi 110 048, India. *Telephone:* (11) 6452140.

GARIBALDI, Marie Louise, BA, LL M; American judge; b 26 Nov 1934, Jersey City, NJ; d of Louis J. and Marie Garibaldi. *Education:* Connecticut Coll, Columbia and New York Univs. *Career:* Attorney Office of Regional Counsel, Internal Revenue Service, NY 1960–66; Assoc McCarter & English, Newark, NJ 1966–69; Partner Riker, Danzig, Scherer & Hyland, Newark, NJ 1969–82; Assoc Justice New Jersey Supreme Court, Newark, NJ 1982–2000; Co-Chair Thomas Keane's campaign for governorship of New Jersey 1981; mem Gov Byrne's Comm on Dept of Commerce 1981; mem New Jersey Bar Asscn, Pres 1982; mem Bd Dirs Columbia Univ School of Law Alumni Asscn; Trustee St Peter's Coll, Jersey City; Fellow American Bar Foundation; New York Univ Law Alumni of New Jersey and Columbia Univ Distinguished Alumni Awards 1982. *Address:* 34 Kingswood Rd, Weehawken, NJ 07087, USA; 583 Newark Ave, Jersey City, NJ 07306, USA.

GARNER, Kate; British fashion photographer; b 9 July 1954, Wigan; m W. Morrison 1989. *Education:* Notre Dame High School (Wigan) and Blackpool Coll of Art. *Career:* Freelance Photographic Asst 1977–80; formed Haysi Fantayzee (pop group, two Top 20 Hits) 1981–84; freelance Photographer working mainly on fashion, music and portraits 1988–; work has appeared in The Face, Vogue, Harpers and Queen, Sky, Arena, Daily Telegraph, The Guardian; work also used by all major recording cos. *Recordings include:* John Wayne is Big Leggy, Shiney Shiney, Battle Hymns for Children Singing 1981–84. *Address:* c/o David Parfitt Studio, 3 Lever St, London EC1, UK. *Telephone:* (20) 7253-5047; *Fax:* (20) 7608-0628; *Internet:* www.kategarner.com.

GARNIER-LANÇON, Monique; French international consultant; d of André Lançon and Yvonne Fargier; five c. *Career:* Technical Adviser to Minister of Cultural Affairs in charge of Press and Public Relations 1969–71; fmr journalist, Regional Councillor, Deputy Mayor of Paris, Paris Councillor, Co-Pres Western European Defence Asscn; Special Adviser for Europe, American Foreign Policy Council, Washington, DC, USA 1985, Dir 1987–1995; Vice-Pres Inst Européen de Sécurité, Luxembourg 1984–87, Pres 1986–95; Founder-mem Co-ordination Cttee of Asscn Euro-Atlantique pour la Coopération, in charge of relations with the USA and int orgs (including UN, NATO, EU, etc) 1992–95; Consultant to Int Policy Forum, Heritage Foundation, Council for Nat Policy, American Security Council, Hoover Inst (all USA); Del for Europe Center for Int Relations, Washington, DC, USA; Pres Asscn Culturelle Franco-Allemande pour la Jeunesse 1980–99; mem Council Promospace 1981; mem Council Fed des Asscns Franco-Allemandes (Franco-German Asscns) 1982–91, Pres 1991–; Chevalier de la Légion d'Honneur; Chevalier de l'Ordre des Palmes Académiques; Cross Ordre des Anciens Combattants d'Europe; Bronze Medal, Famille Française. *Address:* c/o 32 rue Rossini, 06000 Nice, France.

GAROUSTE, Elizabeth Catherine; French furniture designer; b 17 July 1946, Paris; d of Salomon and Blima Rochline; m Gérard Garouste 1970; two s. *Education:* Ecoles Alsacienne and Commando and Atelier Charpentier (Paris). *Career:* Solo exhibitions of furniture and objects in Paris, New York, Musée des Arts Décoratifs de Bordeaux, David Gill Gallery (London), Wunderhauss (Munich, Germany), Rome, Tokyo, etc; collaborates on furniture design with Christian Lacroix, Nina Ricci and other designers; creates glassware for Ricard and wallpaper for Aubusson; Prix Int des Créateurs de l'Année 1991. *Leisure interests:* reading, gardening. *Address:* la Mésangère, 27810 Marcilly-sur-Eure, France.

GARR, Teri; American actress; b 1952, Lakewood, OH; m John O'Neill 1993; one d (adopted). *Career:* Regular appearances on The Sonny and Cher Comedy Review 1974; also appeared in Law and Order 1976, and in Fresno. *Films include:* The Conversation 1974, Young Frankenstein 1974, Won Ton Ton, the Dog Who Saved Hollywood 1976, Oh God! 1977, Close Encounters of the Third Kind 1977, Mr Mike's Mondo Video 1979, The Black Stallion 1979, Tootsie 1982, One From the Heart 1982, The Sting II 1983, The Black Stallion Returns 1983, Mr Mom 1983, Firstborn 1984, After Hours 1985, Miracles 1986, Out Cold 1989, Let it Ride 1989, Short Time 1990, Waiting for the Light 1990, Mom and Dad Save the World 1992, Dumb and Dumber 1995; *TV films include:* Doctor Franken 1980, Prime Suspect 1982, The Winter of our Discontent 1983, To Catch a King 1984, Intimate Strangers 1986, Pack of Lies 1987, Flapjack Floozie 1988, Mother Goose Rock 'n Rhyme, Stranger in the Family 1991, Deliver Them From Evil: The Taking of Alta View 1992, Fugitive Nights: Danger in the Desert 1993. *Address:* c/o Brillstein/Grey, 91150 Wilshire Blvd, Suite 350, Beverly Hills, CA 90212, USA.

GARRARD, Rose, DIP AD; British sculptor and mixed media artist; b 21 Sept 1946, Bewdley, Worcs; d of W. V. and Germaine Garrard; m (divorced). *Education:* Stourbridge, Birmingham and Chelsea Colls of Art and Acad des Beaux Arts (Paris). *Career:* Freelance designer, model and prop-maker to magazines, theatres, advertisers and TV 1969–83; arts consultant to architects advising on public works projects including Liverpool Shopping Precinct and Elephant & Castle Shopping Centre, London 1971–74; Artist-in-Residence, Cen Foundation School for Girls, London 1982, Birmingham City Art Gallery 1983; part-time Sr Lecturer in Art and Social Context, Dartington Coll of Arts; solo exhibitions include Worcester 1967, London 1977, 1983, Cambridge 1983, Birmingham, Liverpool, Bristol, Nottingham and Rochdale 1984, Inst of Contemporary Art (ICA) London 1984; numerous group exhibitions in UK, Europe, USA, Canada, and Australia 1967–; works in perm collections including Victoria and Albert Museum, Contemporary Art Soc and Arts Council of GB; mem numerous selection panels; Int Multiples Prize Award by Paolozzi 1969; Prix d'Honneur de Paris for Sculpture 1971; Arts Council of GB Purchase Award 1979; Greater London Arts Asscn Major Award 1980. *Address:* Studio 21, 105 Carpenters Rd, London E18, UK. *Telephone:* (20) 8519-6321.

GARRATT, Sheryl, BA; British journalist and editor; b 29 March 1961, Birmingham; d of Frank and June (née Fray) Garratt; m Mark McGuire 1994; one s. *Education:* Barr Beacon Comprehensive School (Birmingham) and Univ Coll London. *Career:* Freelancer, mem staff and contrib to numerous publs including New Musical Express, Honey, Looks, News on Sunday, The Observer, The Sunday Telegraph; Music Ed City Limits; mem staff The Face magazine 1988–, Ed 1990–95; freelance journalist 1995–98; Ed The Observer Magazine 1998–. *Publications:* Signed, Sealed and Delivered 1984, Adventures in Wonderland – a Decade of Club Culture 1998. *Leisure interests:* clubbing, drinking, sitting up all night talking afterwards. *Address:* The Observer, 119 Farringdon Rd, London EC1R 3ER, UK (Office); 52 Milton Grove, London N16 8QY, UK (Home); 56C St Thomas's Rd, London N4 2QW, UK. *Telephone:* (20) 7713-4175 (Office); *Fax:* (20) 7503-6748 (Home); *E-mail:* sheryl.garratt@observer.co.uk (Office).

GARRETT, Lesley, FRAM; British opera singer; b 10 April 1955, Thorne, Yorks; d of Derek and Margaret (née Wall) Garrett; m 1991; one s one d. *Education:* Thorne Grammar School, Royal Acad of Music and Nat Opera Studio. *Career:* Studied under Henry Cummings and Joy Mammen; winner of Kathleen Ferrier Memorial Competition 1979; operatic debut Wexford Festival (Ireland) 1980; fmr singer with Opera North; joined English Nat Opera (Prin Soprano) 1984; appearances at The Last Night of the Proms, Welsh Nat Opera, Opera North, Wexford (Ireland) and Buxton festivals and at Glyndebourne; tours to Switzerland and the fmr USSR; Hon D Arts (Plymouth) 1995, Best Selling Classical Artist, Gramophone Award 1996. *Operas include:* Orlando, The Marriage of Figaro, Xerxes, A Midsummer Marriage, The Mikado, The Bartered Bride, A Masked Ball, The Magic Flute, The Merry Widow, Die Fledermaus 1991, The Cunning Little Vixen 1991, La Bohème 1991, Princes Ida 1992, Cosi fan Tutte, The Rise and Fall of the City of Mahaggony, Don Giovanni, Ariodante, Street Scene, Orpheus and Eurydice, La Belle Vivette; *Recordings include:* The Mikado, Diva! A Soprano at the Movies 1991, Wuthering Heights 1991, The Flower Duet from Lakme (single) 1992, Soprano in Hollywood 1996; *TV appearances include:* Street Scene (BBC) 1992, Motormouth (Children's TV), Lesley Garrett... Tonight (BBC TV series). *Leisure interest:* watching cricket. *Address:* The Music Partnership Ltd, 41 Aldebert Terrace, London SW8 1BH UK (Office). *Telephone:* (20) 7787-0361; *Fax:* (20) 7787-0364.

GARRISON-JACKSON, Zina; American tennis player (retd); b 16 Nov 1963, Houston, TX; m Willard Jackson, Jr 1989. *Career:* Winner WTA Championships 1985; Singles semi-finalist, Wimbledon (UK) 1985, finalist 1990 (lost to Martina Navratilova, qv); semi-finalist US Open 1988, 1989; Gold Medallist Ladies Doubles (with Pam Shriver), Olympic Games, Seoul 1988; winner Mixed Doubles (with S. Stewart), Australian Open 1987, Wimbledon (UK) 1988, 1990; winner Ladies Doubles (with Mary Joe Fernandez, qv), US Open 1993. *Address:* c/o USTA, 70 W Red Oak Lane, White Plains, NY 10604, USA (Office); c/o Advantage International, 1751 Pinnacle Drive, Suite 1500, McLean, VA 22102, USA.

GARTZ, Linda Louise, BA, M ED; American television producer, writer and executive; b 23 March 1949, Chicago, IL; d of Fred Samuel and Lillian Louise Gartz. *Education:* Northwestern Univ (Evanston, IL). *Career:* Teacher, Chicago 1971–72; teacher and TV lecturer, Winnetka, IL 1972–80; producer and writer Catholic TV Network, Chicago 1980–81; freelance Documentary Producer WLS-TV, Chicago 1981–82, News Researcher, Asst Producer 1982–83; Assoc Producer, Documentary Writer WBBM-TV, Chicago 1983–85; Pres Linda Gartz Productions, Chicago 1983; mem Nat Acad of TV Arts and Sciences (NATAS); Chicago Int Film Festival Certificate of Merit 1981, 1988; Associated Press Sports Award 1983; winner documentary category Columbus Int Film Festival 1988; San Francisco State Univ Broadcast Media Award 1988. *TV documentaries include:* Writer and Assoc Producer: Children and Divorce (Emmy Award 1985) 1984, The Class of '84 (Silver Award, New York Film Festival 1985), The Red Jacket (Emmy Award 1986) 1985, No Place Like Home (Illinois Broadcasters' Asscn, San Francisco Int Film Festival awards) 1985; Writer, Producer and Dir: Changing Habits (Emmy Award) 1986, Hispanic Mosaic (Emmy Award 1988) 1987.

GARZARELLI, Elaine Marie, B SC, MBA; American economist and business executive; b 13 Oct 1951, Philadelphia, PA; d of Ralph J. and Ida M. Garzarelli. *Education:* Drexel Univ (Philadelphia, PA) and NY Univ. *Career:* Lecturer in Economics; worked A. G. Becker, NY 1973–75, Vice-Pres, Economist 1975–84, Man Dir 1984; Exec Vice-Pres Shearson Lehman Bros 1984–94; Prin Garzarelli Int Inc 1994–; developed Sector Analysis, model used to predict profits and stock price changes; predicted stock market crash 1987; mem Nat Asscn of Business Economists, Women's Financial Asscn, American Statistical Asscn, Women's Bond Asscn; Businesswoman of the Year, Fortune magazine 1987. *Address:* Garzarelli Int Inc, 16661 Echo Hollow, Boca Raton, FL 33434, USA.

GASKELL, Christine Ann, BA; British business executive; b 16 April 1959; m Michael Paul Taylor 1987. *Education:* Univ of York. *Career:* Graduate Trainee British Leyland 1980, Personnel Man Leyland DAF 1980–92; Personnel Man Fisons Pharmaceuticals 1992–95; Personnel Dir Rolls Royce and Bentley Motor Cars Ltd 1995–. *Leisure interests:* skiing, golf, aerobics, reading, theatre. *Address:* 3 Westmorland Close, Bowdon, Altrincham, Cheshire WA14 3QR, UK. *Telephone:* (1270) 535434.

GASKIN, Catherine Majella Sinclair; Irish writer; b 2 April 1929, Co Louth; d of James and Mary (née Harrington) Gaskin; m Sol Cornberg 1955 (died 1999). *Education:* Holy Cross Coll (Sydney) and Sydney Conservatorium of Music (Australia). *Career:* Published first novel at age 17; many titles translated into several European languages. *Publications include:* This Other Eden 1946, With Every Year 1947, Dust in Sunlight 1950, All Else is Folly 1951, Daughter of the House 1952, Sara Dane (serialized for TV) 1955, Blake's Reach 1958, Corporation Wife 1960, I Know My Love 1962, The Tilsit Inheritance 1963, The File on Devlin (adapted as TV film) 1965, Edge of Glass 1967, Fiona 1970, A Falcon for a Queen 1972, The Property of a Gentleman 1974, The Lynmara Legacy 1975, The Summer of the Spanish Woman 1977, Family Affairs 1980, Promises 1982, The Ambassador's Women 1985, The Charmed Circle 1988. *Leisure interests:* reading, music. *Address:* Villa 139, The Manors, 15 Hale Rd, Mosman, NSW 2088, Australia. *Telephone:* (2) 9908-8089.

GASTAUT, Thérèse; United Nations official. *Career:* Dir UN Information Centre for Belgium, Luxembourg, Netherlands and Liaison Office with the European communities 1975–83, Dir UN Information Service, Geneva 1983–90, 1993–99; Manager Information Programme WHO 1990–92; Spokeswoman for the UN Sec-Gen 1993–96; Dir Public Affairs Div, Dept of Public Information 1999–. *Address:* UN, Palais des Nations, 1211 Geneva 10, Switzerland. *Telephone:* (22) 9172300; *Fax:* (22) 9170030.

GATZ, Christiane; German professor of plant genetics; b 1958. *Education:* Technical Univ (Darmstadt). *Career:* Prof of Plant Molecular Genetics, Bielefeld Univ 1993–95; mem Bd EFB Section Agri-Biotechnology; Postdoctoral fellow at the University of Wisconsin (Madison, USA); Alfried Krupp von Bohlen und Halbach-Prize for young univ lecturers 1994. *Address:* Albrecht-von-Haller Institute for

Plant Sciences, Dept of General and Developmental Plant Physiology, Untere Karspuele 2, 37073 Goettingen, Germany. *Telephone:* (1970) 828255; *Fax:* (1970) 828357; *E-mail:* cgatz@gwdg.de.

GAUCI, Miriam; Maltese opera singer; b 3 April 1957, Malta; d of Carmel Cutajar and Rosette Tabone; m Michael Laus 1987. *Education:* Conservatorio G. Verdi and Centro di Perfezionamento Artisti Lirici (Milan, Italy). *Career:* Debut at La Scala, Milan, Italy in La Sonnambula, L'Orfeo, Die Frau ohne Schatten; debut in USA in Madame Butterfly; appeared in La Bohème with Placido Domingo, Los Angeles, USA, Hamburg, Germany; appeared in La Traviata, Geneva, Switzerland, Dresden, Germany; 1st prize in various int competitions including Treviso, Bologna, Milan, Italy 1979. *Video:* Carmen 1989; *Recordings include:* Madame Butterfly 1992, Manon Lescaut, La Bohème, Deutscher Requiem, Verdi's Requiem, Egmont, Operatic Arias. *Leisure interests:* long walks, swimming. *Address:* Villa No 5, Salini St, Marsascala, Malta. *Telephone:* 820033; *Fax:* 690477.

GAUDRON, Mary Genevieve; Australian judge; b 1943; m John Fogarty. *Career:* Deputy Pres Australian Conciliation and Arbitration Comm 1974–79; Solicitor-Gen, NSW 1981–87; Judge High Court of Australia 1987–; mem Council Macquarie Univ 1981–86. *Address:* High Court of Australia, POB E435, Canberra, ACT 2604, Australia.

GAUGUSCH-DJAMBAZIAN, Christine; Austrian ballet dancer; b 4 March 1951, Vienna; d of Friedrich and Maria Gaugusch; m Eduard Djambazian 1980. *Education:* Ballet School of the Vienna State Opera. *Career:* Mem Vienna State Opera Ballet 1966–, Soloist 1982–. *Ballets include:* Romeo and Julia, Giselle, Sylvia, Sleeping Beauty, Daphnis and Chloë, Nutcracker, Midsummer Night's Dream, Don Quixote, Don Juan; *Film:* Peter und der Wolf 1969. *Address:* Himmelpfortgasse 7/32, 1010 Vienna, Austria.

GAUNT, Bobbie; Canadian business executive (retd); b Washington, PA. *Career:* Joined Ford 1972, Pres and Chief Exec, Ford Canada Ltd 1997–2001, Vice Pres Ford Motor Co 1999–2001; Co-Chair Int Women's Forum, Toronto; Founder-mem Canadian Chapter of Women's Automotive Asscn Int; mem Advisory Bd Richard Ivey School of Business, Bd of Visitors Katz School of Business (Univ of Pittsburg); Co-Chair Juvenile Diabetes Foundation Annual Dinner 1999, YMCA-Oakville's Capital Campaign; Hon Co-Chair fundraising gala for the Canadian Foundation for the Physically Disabled 1999, 2000; one of 100 Leading Women in the N American Auto Industry, Automotive News 2000; Women of Distinction Award 2000; Dr hc (Niagara) 2000, (Ryerson Univ) 2000, (Toronto) 2000, (Sheridan Coll, ON) 2000. *Address:* Canadian Rd, POB 2000, Oakville, ON, Canada.

GAVRON, Nicky; British public servant. *Career:* Councillor (Lab) for Haringey (Archway Ward, London) 1986–; Lab Leader London Planning Advisory Cttee (LPAC) 1991–, Chair 1994–; mem GLA, Deputy Mayor of Greater London 2000–; Vice-Chair Planning Cttee Local Govt Asscn (LGA); mem Govt Comm for Integrated Transport; Adviser to Govt's Urban Task Force. *Address:* Romney House, 43 Marsham St, London SW1P 3PY. *Telephone:* (20) 7983-4000; *Internet:* www.london.gov.uk/gla.

GAY, Marie-Louise; Canadian designer, writer and illustrator; b 17 June 1952, Québec City, PQ; d of Bernard Roland and Colette Gay; m David Toby Homel; two s. *Education:* Inst des Arts Graphiques de Montréal, Montréal Museum of Fine Arts School, Acad of Art Coll (San Francisco, CA, USA). *Career:* Graphic Designer Perspectives and Décormag magazines 1974–76; Art Dir La Courte Echelle publrs 1980; Lecturer in Illustration Univ of Québec, Montréal 1981–, Ahuntsic Coll 1984–85; Writer and Designer Bonne Fête Willy 1989, Qui a peur de LouLou? 1993, Le jardin de Babel (children's puppet plays) 1999; Set Designer La Boîte, Nat Film Bd of Canada animated film 1989; mem Canadian Children's Book Centre, Ibby Canada; numerous awards include two Canadian Council prizes 1985, Gov-Gen's Award 1988, 2000, Mr Christie's Book Award 1997–2000, CBA's Libris Award 2000, Ruth Schwartz Award 2000. *Publications:* Illustrator: Hou Ilva 1976, Dou Ilvien 1978, Hébert Luée 1980, Lizzy's Lion 1984, The Last Piece of Sky 1993, The Three Little Pigs 1994, When Vegetables Go Bad! 1994, The Fabulous Song 1996, Rumplestiltskin 1997, Dreams are More Real than Bathtubs 1998, The Christmas Orange 1998, How

to Take Your Grandmother to the Museum 1998, Yuck, A Love Story 2000; Writer and Illustrator: De Zéro à Minuit 1981, La Sœur de Robert 1983, La Drôle d'Ecole 1984, Moonbeam on a Cat's Ear 1986, Rainy Day Magic 1987, Angel and the Polar Bear 1988, Fat Charlie's Circus 1989, Willy Nilly 1990, Mademoiselle Moon 1992, Rabbit Blue 1993, Midnight Mimi 1994, Princess Pistache 1998, Stella, Star of the Sea 1999, Sur mon île 1999, Stella, Queen of the Snow 2000. *Leisure interests:* canoeing, cycling, reading, hiking, travelling. *Address:* 773 Davaar, Montréal, PQ H2V 3B3, Canada. *Telephone:* (514) 273-0368; *Fax:* (514) 273-5488.

GAYER, Yevdokiya Alexandra; Russian/Nanai ethnographer and politician; b 8 March 1934, Podali, Khabarovsk Territory; m (husband deceased); two s. *Education:* Vladivostok. *Career:* Researcher Inst of History, Archaeology and Ethnography USSR Acad of Sciences (Far E Br) 1969–89; People's Deputy of USSR, mem Soviet of Nationalities, Comm on Problems of Int Relations and Nat Policy 1989–92; Advisor to the Pres 1992–; Deputy Chair State Cttee on Social-Econ Devt of Russia 1993–; mem Council of Fed of Russia 1993–96; Deputy Chair Comm of the North and Indigenous Peoples 1996–; Sec-Gen Int League of Small Nations and Ethnic Groups 1996–; Chief Advisor State Cttee on Problems of Devt of North Territories 1997–98; Prof Int Acad of Marketing and Man (Mamarmen); mem Russian Acad of Natural Sciences, Acad of Information Science, Acad of Polar Medicine. *Address:* Rublyovskoye Sh 3, korp 2, Apt 388, 121609 Moscow, Russian Federation (Office). *Telephone:* (095) 413-76-95.

GAZARO, Wéré Régine; Togolese government official; b (Wéré Régine Palouki) 6 Oct 1958, Kara; m Abdel-Aziz Gazaro 1983; one d one s. *Education:* Kara, Univ 'Dunarea de Jos' din Galaţi (Romania), postgrad studies in Switzerland. *Career:* Responsible for Food Quality Control Dept of Nutrition and Food Tech 1985–91; Sec-Gen World Campaign to Fight against Hunger 1991; Prefect, Kozah 1991; Minister of Social Welfare and Nat Solidarity, Lomé 1991; Dir Organisation Africaine Propriété Intellectuelle (OAPI) 1995–. *Leisure interests:* reading, cinema, theatre. *Address:* c/o Organisation Africaine Propriété Intellectuelle, BP 887, Yaoundé, Cameroon.

GEBHARDT, Evelyne; German politician; b 19 Jan 1954, Montreuil-sous-Bois, France. *Education:* Lycée Lamartine (Paris) and Sorbonne (Paris). *Career:* Freelance translator 1977–; fmr lecturer; MEP (PSE, SPD), mem Cttee on Legal Affairs and the Internal market, Vice Chair Del for Relations with The People's Repub of China; mem Baden-Württemberg SPD Land Exec Cttee 1989–; Fed Vice-Chair Working Party of Social-Democratic Women 1992–; mem Exec of European Women's Org Grain de Sel (Paris) 1993–, Akademie für Ethik in der Medizin 1997–, Bd Asscn of Young People's Art Colls 1999–, Marie Schlei Asscn, Gegen Vergessen – Für Demokratie. *Address:* Europa-Büro, Lahmgrubengasse 1, 74653 Künzelsau, Germany; European Parliament, rue Wiertz, 1047 Brussels, Belgium. *Telephone:* (2) 284-21-11 (Belgium); *Fax:* (2) 230-69-43 (Belgium); *E-mail:* egebhardt@europarl.eu.int; egebhardt.mdep@t-online.de.

GEE, Maggie, PH D, B LITT, FRSL; British writer, journalist and lecturer; b 2 Nov 1948, Poole; d of V. V. and Aileen (née Church) Gee; m Nicholas Rankin 1983; one d. *Education:* Horsham High School and Somerville Coll (Oxford). *Career:* Writing Fellow Univ of E Anglia 1982; Visiting Fellow Sussex Univ 1986–, Teaching Fellow 1996–; Writer-in-Residence Northern Arts 1996; regular reviews in Daily Telegraph, Times Literary Supplement, Sunday Times; judge Booker Prize 1989; mem Man Cttee Soc of Authors 1991–94, mem Council 1999–; Hawthornden Fellow 1989; Best of Young British Novelists 1982. *Publications:* Dying in Other Words 1981, The Burning Book 1983, Light Years 1985, Grace 1988, Where are the Snows 1991, Lost Children 1994, The Ice People 1998. *Leisure interests:* visual arts, swimming, walking, film, theatre. *Address:* c/o David Godwin Associates, 55 Monmouth St, London WC2H 9DG. *Telephone:* (20) 7240-9992; *Fax:* (20) 7395-6110.

GEHLHOFF-CLAES, Astrid Veronica; German writer; b 6 Jan 1928, Leverkusen; d of Heinrich and Wilma Claes; m Joachim Gehlhoff 1957; two d. *Education:* Univ of Cologne. *Career:* Writer 1956–; Founder-Chair org for writers working with prisoners 1975–88; Deutsche Literaturfonds Scholarship 1985; Guest Villa Massimo 1991, 1992;

Bundesverdienstkreuz (First Class) 1986; other awards include För-derungspreis zum Gerhart-Hauptmann-Preis (Freie Volksbühne Berlin) 1962, Förderungspries zum Immermann-Preis (Düsseldorf) 1965, Verdienstorden des Landes Nordrhein-Westfalen 1990. *Publications include:* Poetry: Der Mannequin 1956, Meine Stimme mein Schiff 1962, Gegen Abend ein Orangenbaum 1983, Nachruf auf einen Papagei 1989; Play: Didos Tod 1964; Short stories: Erdbeereis 1980; Novel: Abschied von der Macht 1987; Publisher: Else Lasker-Schüler: Briefe an Karl Kraus 1959, 1960, Bis die Tür aufbricht: Literatur hinter Gittern (anthology) 1982, Einen Baum umarmen: Briefwechsel mit Felix Kamphausen 1976–91; trans to German of books by Henry James. *Address:* Rheinallee 133, 40545 Düsseldorf, Germany. *Telephone:* (211) 555925.

GEHRING, Gillian Anne, MA, D PHIL, FINSTP; British professor of physics; b 19 May 1941, Nottingham; d of H. L. (Max) and F. Joan Murray; m Karl A. Gehring 1968; two d. *Education:* Univs of Manchester and Oxford. *Career:* Leverhulme Postdoctoral Research Fellowship St Hugh's Coll, Oxford 1965–67, Fellow, Tutor in Physics 1968–70; NATO Fellowship Univ of California at Berkeley 1967–68; Common Univ Fund (CUF) Lecturer in Theoretical Physics, Univ of Oxford 1970–89; Prof of Solid State Physics Univ of Sheffield 1989–; author of research papers on theoretical condensed matter physics. *Leisure interest:* family activities. *Address:* Dept of Physics, University of Sheffield, Sheffield S10 2TN, UK (Office); 27 Lawson Rd, Broomhill, Sheffield S10 5BU, UK (Home). *Telephone:* (114) 276 8555 (Office); (114) 268 2238 (Home).

GEIGER, Erika L.; Swiss United Nations official; b 30 July 1942, Geneva. *Education:* Geneva Univ. *Career:* Legal Documentation Asst, WIPO 1975–77, Asst Legal Officer 1977–83, apptd Legal Officer Industrial Property Law Information Section 1983, Chief Advisor. *Address:* WIPO, 34 chemin des Colombettes, 1211 Geneva 20, Switzerland. *Telephone:* (22) 7309111; *Fax:* (22) 335428.

GEIGER, Michaela; German politician; b 29 Sept 1943, Ober-ammergau; m; one s. *Career:* TV picture technician Bayerisches Fernsehen, Munich-Freimann 1964–67; mem supervisory Bd Volks-bank, Garmisch-Partenkirchen 1975; Deputy Dist Chair CSU, Upper Bavaria 1977; Municipal Councillor, Garmisch-Partenkirchen 1978–81; mem Bundestag (Parl), Speaker of CDU/CSU parl group; Parl Sec of State for Econ Co-operation 1991–93, in Ministry of Defence 1993. *Address:* Bundestag, 11011 Berlin, Germany.

GEISER, Barbara; Swiss politician; b 20 April 1948, Langenthal. *Education:* Ecole normale (Langenthal) and Univs of Fribourg, Berne and Paris IV (Paris-Sorbonne). *Career:* Schoolteacher 1974–84, teacher of Educ 1985–89; mem Berne Council 1989, Pres 1996; mem Grand Council, Berne May–Dec 1998; Sec Femmes socialistes suisses 1989; Cen Sec Parti socialiste suisse/Sozialdemokratische Partei der Schweiz. *Leisure interests:* arts, political argument, travel. *Address:* Postgasse 28, 3011 Berne, Switzerland; Parti socialiste suisse/Sozialdemokratische Partei der Schweiz, Spitalgasse 34, 3001 Berne, Switzerland (Office). *Telephone:* (31) 3118932; *Fax:* (31) 3118932.

GELBER, Sylva M., OC; Canadian government official; b 4 Dec 1910, Toronto, ON; d of Louis and Sara (née Morris) Gelber. *Education:* Havergal Coll, Univ of Toronto and Columbia Univ. *Career:* Mem staff Social Work Bureau (Jerusalem, Israel) 1932–37, Hadassah Medical Org, Jerusalem 1937–42, Dept of Labour, Palestine 1942–48; Health Insurance Consultant, Dept of National Health and Welfare, Canada 1950–68; Dir Women's Bureau, Dept of Labour 1968–75; Special Advisor, Deputy Minister of Labour 1975–78; Del UN Gen Ass 1976, 1978, ILO Conf 1969, 1971, 1975, 1976; Rep UN Comm on the Status of Women 1970–74; Chair OECD Working Party 1973–78; Dir Sylva Gelber Music Foundation; mem Canadian Inst of International Affairs, UN Assoc of Canada; Hon mem Bd of Govs Trent Univ; Hon LL D (Queens) 1976, (Memorial) 1976, (Guelph) 1977; Hon D HUM LITT (Mount St Vincent) 1976. *Publications:* No Balm in Gilead: A Personal Retrospective of Mandate Days in Palestine 1989; numerous papers, reports and articles. *Leisure interest:* music. *Address:* 77 Placel Rd, Rockcliffe Park, Ottawa, ON K1L 5B9, Canada.

GELENCSÉR, Éva, PH D; Hungarian scientist; b 27 Feb 1950, Vésztő; d of Mihály and András Ilona Gelencsér; m Ferenc Pándi 1981; one s. *Education:* Budapesti Műszaki Egyetem. *Career:* Asst Dept of Chemistry, Coll for Food Industry 1973–79, Sr Scientist Product Devt Dept, Central Food Research Inst (KÉKI) 1979–84, apptd Head Dept of Biology 1984; contrib Acta Alimentaria, Journal of Food Agric since 1979; specializes in nutritional evaluation of plant and animal proteins during food processing and interchemistry of food proteins and food protein allergens; mem Hungarian Soc of Nutrition, Hungarian Biochemical Soc, Hungarian Food Dietetic Cttee, Hungarian Acad of Sciences Complex Food Cttee, Food Science Labour Section of Food Chemistry. *Address:* Központi Élelmiszeriapri Kutató Intézet, Central Food Research Institute, Biology Dept, 111 Budapest XI, Budafoki út 59, Hungary. *Telephone:* (1) 161-2404; *Fax:* (1) 155-8991.

GELHORN, Carolyn, B ED; Canadian business executive and inventor; b 3 March 1944, Winnipeg (MB); d of the late George John and of Elsie Bertha (née Kreger) Gelhorn; m Ralph Rampersad 1990; one s one d. *Education:* Univ of Manitoba. *Career:* Teacher 1970–79; Hotel Man, UK 1981; Marketing Rep Pitney Bowes 1980, 1981–82, Sales Man 1982–86, Marketing Advisory Bd 1983; Pres Carshaw Inc 1986–; Sec/Treas Quantum Enterprises, Ralcar Inc; mem Women Inventors Project. *Publications:* Individual Instruction in Music Through Learning Centres (ed) 1977, Street Smarts. *Leisure interests:* travel, reading. *Address:* 10–66 Edmonton St, Winnipeg, R3C 1P7, Canada. *E-mail:* cgelhorn@sprint.ca.

GELLER, Margaret, PH D; American astrophysicist; b Dec 8 1947, Ithaca, NY; d of Seymour and Sarah Geller. *Education:* Univ of California at Berkeley and Princeton Univ. *Career:* NSF Pre-doctoral Fellow 1970–73; Center Post-doctoral Fellow, Center for Astrophysics (Cambridge, MA) 1974–76; Lecturer Harvard Univ 1977–80; Sr Visiting Fellow Cambridge Univ 1978–80; Asst Prof Harvard Univ 1980–83; Sr Scientist Smithsonian Astrophysical Observatory 1983–; mem AAAS 1990, NAS 1992 (Council 2000–(03)); Fellow MacArthur Foundation 1990–95; Goodspeed-Richards Lecture, Univ of Pennsylvania 1992, Helen Sawyer Hogg Lecture, Royal Astronomical Soc of Canada 1993, Brickwedde Distinguished Lecturer, Johns Hopkins Univ 1993, Bethe Lecturer, Cornell Univ 1996, Hilldale Lecturer 1999, then Smithsonian Distinguished Lecturer, Univ of Wisconsin 2000; Hon DS (Connecticut Coll) 1995, (Gustavus Adolphus Coll) 1997, (Massachusetts) 2000; numerous awards including AAAS-Newcomb Cleveland Prize 1991, Klopsteg Award, American Asscn of Physics Teachers 1996. *Film:* Where the Galaxies Are (video) 1991, So Many Galaxies... So Little Time 1993. *Leisure interests:* film-making, reading, conversation, writing, travel, gardening. *Address:* Smithsonian Astrophysical Observatory, 60 Garden St, Cambridge, MA 02138, USA. *Telephone:* (617) 495-7409; *Fax:* (617) 495-7467.

GEMS, Iris Pamela (Pam); British playwright; b Bransgore, Dorset; d of the late Jim Price and Elsie Mabel Annetts; m Keith Leopold Gems 1949; two s two d. *Education:* Brockenhurst Grammar School and Univ of Manchester. *Career:* Playwright c1970–; f women's theatre season, Almost Free Theatre, London 1975; plays have been staged at the Royal Shakespeare Co's Other Place and on Broadway (New York); mem Dramatists' Guild (USA), Writers' Guild. *Plays include:* Betty's Wonderful Christmas 1974, Dusa, Fish, Stas and Vi 1976, Queen Christina 1977, Piaf 1978, Franz into April 1978, The Treat 1979, Pasionaria 1981, Aunt Mary 1983, Camille 1985, The Danton Affair 1986, Blude Angel 1991, Deborah's Daughter 1994, Stanley (Best Play, Evening Standard Awards 1996, Best Play, Olivier Awards 1997) 1995, Marlene 1996, The Snow Palace 1998; Adaptations: Uncle Vanya 1981, A Doll's House 1983, The Cherry Orchard 1984, Ghosts 1992, The Seagull 1994; *Novels include:* Bon Voyage, Mrs Frampton 1990. *Leisure interest:* gardening. *Address:* c/o Jenny Casarotto, National House, 60–66 Wardour St, London W1V 4ND, UK (Office). *Telephone:* (20) 7287-4450; *Fax:* (20) 7287-9128.

GENDREAU-MASSALOUX, Michèle; French public servant and former university rector; b 28 July 1944, Limoges; d of François Massaloux and Marie-Adrienne Delalais; m Pascal Gendreau 1970. *Education:* Ecole Normale Supérieure de Jeunes Filles (Sèvres) and Inst d'Etudes Politiques (Paris). *Career:* Univ Tutor Univ of Paris IV (Paris-Sorbonne), Villetaneuse (Univ of Paris XIII—Paris-Nord) and Univ of

Limoges; Rector Acad d'Orléans, Tours 1981–84, Acad de Paris 1989–98; Conseiller d'Etat 1998; Tech Adviser to Sec-Gen for Nat Educ and Univs, Presidency of the Repub, then to Sec-Gen for Admin Reform and Improvement of Relations between Public Services and their Users, Deputy Sec-Gen 1985–88, Spokesperson for the Presidency 1986–88, Head of Mission May 1988; Vice-Pres Conseil supérieur de l'educ nat 1989; mem Conseil supérieur de la langue française 1989, Comm Nat de la Communication et des Libertés 1988–89, French Comm for UNESCO 1991, Conseil orientation Ecole du Louvre 1991, Council Coll Univ Français de Moscou 1991, Council Coll Univ Français de Saint-Petersburg 1992, Scientific Cttee Bibliothèque de France 1992, Conseil Scientifique de la Cinquième 1996; Pres Assoc de préfiguration de la Cité de la musique 1990; mem Comm de contrôle des sondages 1999–; Dir Gen Agence Universitaire de la francophonie (AUF) 1999–; Chevalier de la Légion d'Honneur, Chevalier de l'Ordre Nat du Mérite, Ordre des Palmes Académiques. *Publication:* Recherche sur l'Humanisme de Francisco de Quevedo 1977, works and translations concerning the Spanish Golden Age. *Leisure interest:* music. *Address:* Conseil d'Etat, 75100 Paris 01 SP, France (Office); 38 ave Charles Floquet, 75007 Paris, France (Home). *Telephone:* (1) 40-46-20-02; *Fax:* (1) 40-46-24-77.

GENET, Jacqueline Hélène Juliette Valentine, D ÈS L; French professor of English; b 24 Feb 1932, Evreux; d of Jean and Hélène (née Delarue) Veyssié; m Jean Genet 1961; two s. *Education:* Ecole Normale Supérieure de Sèvres, Univ of Oxford (UK) and Univ of Paris (Sorbonne). *Career:* Secondary school teacher 1957–66; Lecturer, later Sr Lecturer Univ of Limoges 1966–74; Sr Lecturer Univ of Caen 1974–77, Prof 1977–92 (Prof Emer 1992–), Pres of Univ 1983–88; Pres Soc des Anglicistes de l'Enseignement Supérieur 1990–92; fmr Vice-Pres Int Asscn for the Study of Anglo-Irish Literature; Dr hc (Ireland) 1990, (Würzburg) 1995; Chevalier de l'Ordre Nat du Mérite; Commdr des Palmes Académiques. *Publications:* W. B. Yeats: les fondements et l'évolution de la création poétique: Essai de psychologie littéraire 1976, La poétique de W. B. Yeats 1990, Le Théâtre de W. B. Yeats 1995; numerous works of criticism, articles and translations. *Address:* University of Caen, Esplanade de la Paix, 14032 Caen Cedex, France (Office); 13 rue de Bretteville, 14000 Caen, France (Home). *Telephone:* (2) 31-85-21-78 (Home); *E-mail:* jacqueline.genet2@wanadoo.fr.

GENIYEVA, Yekaterina Yuryevna; Russian librarian; b 1 April 1946, Moscow; one d. *Education:* Moscow State Univ. *Career:* Nurse Moscow Hosp 1962–63; Sr Ed, Deputy Dir All-Union State Library of Foreign Literature 1971–93, Dir-Gen 1993–; Chair Exec Bd Inst Open Soc (Soros Foundation) 1995; mem Council on Culture, Russian Presidency 1996–; Vice-Pres Russian Library Asscn 1997–, Int Fed of Libraries; mem Russian Comm on Problems of UNESCO 1997–; mem Ed Bds journals Biblioteka, Libri, Inostrannaya Literatura, Znamya, Detskaya Literatura, Mir Bibliotek. *Publications:* monographs, trans of English authors, numerous articles. *Leisure interests:* books, travelling. *Address:* VGBIL, Nikoloyamskaya str. 1, 109189 Moscow, Russia. *Telephone:* (095) 915 3636; *Fax:* (095) 915 3637.

GENZKEN, Isa; German sculptor; b 27 Nov 1948, Bad Oldeslohe. *Education:* Hochschule für Bildende Künste (Hamburg and Berlin) and Staatliche Kunstakademie (Düsseldorf). *Career:* Teacher of sculpture Staatliche Kunstakademie, Düsseldorf 1977–78; teacher of structure Fachhochschule Niederrhein, Krefeld 1978–79; Guest Prof of Sculpture, Berlin 1990, Städelschule Frankfurt/Main 1992; exhibitions held in Munich 1988, Chicago (IL, USA), Frankfurt, Brussels 1992, New York 1997–98; Karl-Schmidt-Rottluff Scholarship 1978–80; Kunstpreis Berlin 1980. *Publications:* Exhibition Catalogues 1988, 1992. *Address:* c/o Jack Shainman Gallery, 513 West 20th St, New York, NY 10011, USA.

GEOGHEGAN-QUINN, Máire; Irish former business consultant and former politician; b 5 Sept 1950, Carna, Co Galway; d of the late John and of Barbara (née Folan) Geoghegan; m John Quinn 1973; two s. *Education:* Coláiste Muire and Carysfort Teacher Training Coll (Dublin). *Career:* Teacher, Dublin 1970–73, Galway 1973–75; TD (Fianna Fáil) for Galway W 1975; Parl Sec to Minister for Industry, Commerce and Energy 1977–78, Minister 1978–79; Minister for the Gaeltacht 1979–81 (first woman cabinet minister); Front Bench spokesperson on the Gaeltacht 1981–82; Minister for Youth and Sport,

Dept of Educ 1982; Front Bench spokesperson on Women's Rights 1982–87; Minister with responsibility for Co-ordination of Govt Policy and EC Affairs 1987–91; Minister for Tourism, Transport and Communications 1992–94, for Justice 1994; columnist Irish Times 1997–2000; mem European Court of Auditors 2000–; consultant to several cos; fmr Chair The Saffron Initiative; fmr Chair Fianna Fáil; fmr Non-Exec Dir The Ryan Hotel Group, Aer Lingus; fmr TV broadcaster; elected to Galway Borough Council 1985. *Publication:* The Green Diamond (novel) 1996. *Leisure interests:* reading, writing and travel. *Address:* European Court of Auditors, 12 rue Alcide de Gasperi, 1615 Luxembourg, Luxembourg (Office). *Telephone:* 4398-45370 (Office); *Fax:* 4398-46493 (Office); *E-mail:* www.eca.eu.int (Office).

GEORGE, Jennie, BA; Australian trade union official; b 20 Aug 1947, Italy. *Education:* Sydney Univ. *Career:* Gen Sec NSW Teachers Fed 1980–82, Pres 1986–89; mem Exec Australian Council of Trade Unions (ACTU) 1983, Vice-Pres 1987, Asst Sec 1991–95, Pres 1996–; Asst Nat Dir Trade Union Training Authority 1989–91. *Address:* CTU, North Wing, Trades Hall, 54 Victoria St, Carlton South, Vic 3053, Australia (Office).

GEORGE, Susan; British actress; b 26 July 1950; d of Norman Alfred George and Eileen Percival; m Simon MacCorkindale 1984. *Career:* Began acting career 1954; Partner Amy Int Productions, London; recorded album 2001. *Films include:* Cup Fever, Davey Jones' Locker, Billion Dollar Brain, Twinky 1969, Eyewitness 1970, Straw Dogs 1971, Dirty Mary and Crazy Larry 1974, Mandingo 1975, Out of Season 1975, A Small Town in Texas 1977, Tomorrow Never Comes 1978, Venom 1980, A Texas Legend 1981, The House Where Evil Dwells 1982, The Jigsaw Man 1984, Czechmate 1985, Lightning, The White Stallion 1986, Stealing Heaven (producer) 1987, White Roses (producer, Asquith Award for Best New Composer, BFI Awards 1990) 1988, The House That Mary Bought (also producer) 1994; *TV appearances include:* Swallows and Amazons, Human Jungle, The Right Attitude 1968, Dr Jekyll and Mr Hyde 1973, Lamb to the Slaughter 1979, Royal Jelly 1979, The Bob Hope Special 1979, Pajama Tops 1982, Masquerade 1983, Hotel 1985, Blacke's Magic 1986, Jack the Ripper 1987, Castle of Adventure 1990, Cluedo, Stay Lucky 1992, The House that Mary Bought 1995, EastEnders 2001; *Theatre includes:* The Sound of Music 1962, The Country Girl 1984, Rough Crossing 1987; *Publications:* illustrated book of poetry 1987, record album 2001. *Leisure interests:* Arab horse breeding, singing. *Address:* c/o Jean Diamond, 2–4 Noel St, London W1F 8GB, UK.

GEORGE, Susan Elizabeth, MS; American writer; b 26 Feb 1949, Warren, OH; d of Robert and Anne George; m Ira Toibin 1971 (divorced 1995). *Education:* Univ of California and California State Univ. *Career:* Teacher El Toro High School (El Toro, CA) 1975–87, Coastline Community Coll (Fountainvalley, CA) 1988–; has lectured at Irvine Valley Coll (Irvine, CA) 1989, Univ of California Extension 1990, Edinboro Univ Summer School at Exeter Coll, Oxford (UK) 1993, Univ of British Columbia (Canada) 1993, Univ of Oklahoma 1995; numerous honours and awards including the establishment of The Elizabeth George Collection at Boston Univ 1989, One of Forty Graduates Who Have Made a Difference, Univ of California, Riverside 1994, Visions and Visionaries, Honoring Six Graduates from California State Univ, Fullerton. *Publications:* A Great Deliverance (Anthony Award, Bouchercon XXI 1989, Agatha Award, Malice Domestic 1989, Le Grand Prix de Literature Policiere, Mystery Writers of France 1990) 1988, Payment in Blood 1989, Well-Schooled in Murder (MIMI Award 1991) 1990, Sisters in Crime, Vol II—The Evidence Exposed 1990, A Suitable Vengeance 1991, For the Sake of Elena 1992, Missing Joseph 1993, A Novel by Any Other Name 1994, Playing for the Ashes 1994, In the Presence of the Enemy 1996, Women on the Case (ed) 1996, Deception on His Mind 1998, In Pursuit of the Proper Sinner 1999, A Traitor to Memory 2001. *Leisure interests:* photography, skiing, theatre, film. *Address:* 4111 Shorebreak Drive, Huntington Beach, CA 92649, USA. *Internet:* ElizabethGeorgeOnline.com.

GERGELY, Judit, PH D; Hungarian economist and investment banking executive; b 5 Nov 1953, Budapest; d of István and Edith (née Poós) Gergely. *Education:* Univ of Econs (Budapest) and Inst of Devt Studies and Univs of Oxford and Cambridge (UK). *Career:* Scholar Central Planning Bureau, Budapest 1977; Economist Inst for World Economics

1978–83; Asst to Dir of Foreign Affairs Hungarian Econ Asscn 1979–81; Economist IBRD, Washington, DC, USA 1983–88; Man Dir InvestCenter, Hungary 1988–90; Vice-Pres First Hungary Fund 1990–91; apptd CEO Barclays de Zoete Wedd Ltd, Budapest 1991; speaker in field; 28 articles and papers in int journals 1978–88; British Acad of Sciences Scholarship 1980; Hungarian Econ Asscn Award 1981. *Leisure interests:* dance, rowing, music, travel, cycling, reading. *Address:* Budapest 1021, Hüvösvölgy út 1771/A, Hungary (Home).

GERHARDT, Renata; German publisher and translator; b 14 April 1926, Berlin; m Rainer M. Gerhardt 1948 (died 1954); two s. *Education:* Univs of Freiburg and Heidelberg. *Career:* Co-Founder, Publ Verlag der Fragmente, Freiburg and Breisgau until 1954; Co-Ed Fragmente Int Revue für Moderne Dichtung until 1954; Founder Gerhardt Verlag, Berlin 1962, publr of Surrealist art books and literature; trans to German of modern and Avant-Garde writers including Ezra Pound, Gertrude Stein, Henry Miller, Alfred Jarry, Antonin Artaud, Vladimir Nabokov, etc. *Leisure interests:* fine arts, literature. *Address:* c/o Jenaer Str 7, 10717 Berlin, Germany.

GERMANOVA, Yevdokiya Alekseyevna; Russian actress; b 8 Nov 1959, Moscow. *Education:* State Inst of Theatre Art. *Career:* With Oleg Tabakov Theatre Studio 1983–; roles in productions including Mystery by J. B. Priestley (production in Austria), Trust, Love, Hope by O. Horvat (dir M. Schell); numerous prizes for best women's roles at int and nat festivals in Kiev, Karlovy Vary, Nizhny Novgorod, Ange, Moscow. *Films include:* Moslem (dir V. Khotinenko), Close Circle (A. Konchalovsky), Kix (S. Livnev), Crazy (S. Garazov), Here is Freedom (A. Waida), Niagara (A. Vizir), We Cannot Guess (O. Narutskaya). *Address:* Chaplygina Str, 1A, Oleg Tabakov Theatre Studio, Moscow, Russian Federation. *Telephone:* (095) 916 2121.

GEROVA, Darina Dimitrova; Bulgarian writer and journalist; b 2 June 1934, Sofia; d of Dimitar Guerov and Nevena Guerova; m Vladimir Grancharov 1962 (died 1989); two s. *Education:* Univ of Sofia. *Career:* Ed and journalist Trud, Zhenata dnes (Women Today), Mladeg, Narodna Cultura, Septemvri, etc; numerous articles, reviews, essays and short stories on educ, youth, nat culture and status of women; awarded Saints Cyril and Methody Medal First Class 1983. *Publications include:* Novels: Noon Rain 1967, Dusty Sun 1969, Hut on the Top 1972, Hello Sun! 1976, Post Festum 1981, Eve From the Third Floor 1982 (film adaptation 1987), We Are Sinners, O Lord! 1987, Icons For Non-Believers 1990, The Pain of Woman 1995. *Leisure interests:* art, music, theatre, cinema. *Address:* 1618 Sofia, Buxton bl 19 vh E, Bulgaria. *Telephone:* (2) 56-18-69; *E-mail:* dardimger@abv.bg.

GERSOVITZ, Sarah Valerie, MA, RCA; Canadian artist and playwright; b Montréal, PQ; d of Solomon and Eva Gamer; m Benjamin Gersovitz 1944; two s one d. *Education:* Macdonald Coll School for Teachers (Québec, PQ) and Concordia Univ (Montréal, PQ). *Career:* Fmr teacher of Art and Art History; Art Critic Arts-Atlantic 1984–; solo exhibitions include Univ of Kaiserslautern, Germany, and Instituto Culturel Peruano, Lima; 70 int biennials in Canada, USA, Venezuela, Colombia, Brazil, Peru, UK, Norway, Germany, Switzerland, France, Spain, Italy, Yugoslavia, Czech Repub, Hungary, Bulgaria, Hong Kong, Repub of China (Taiwan), Australia, Repub of Korea, Poland, Chile; work represented in perm collections including Library of Congress, Washington, DC and New York Public Library (USA), Nat Gallery of S Australia, The Israel Museum, Jerusalem, Instituto Culturel Peruano, Lima, Montréal Museum of Fine Arts, The House of Humour and Satire, Gabrovo, Bulgaria; fmr mem Council RCA; mem Dramatists Guild; numerous awards include Nat Gallery of S Australia Purchase Award, First prize Nat Playwriting Competition, Ottawa, ON 1982, First prize Int Jury 9th Int Biennale, Gabrovo, Bulgaria 1989, First prize Concours Graphique, l'Université de Sherbrooke, First prize and Gold Medal (Seagram Fine Arts Exhibition), Graphic Art Prize (Winnipeg Show Biennial), Anaconda Award (twice, Canadian Painter-Etchers and Engravers); Finalist CBC Radio Drama Competition 1989. *Plays include:* A Portrait of Portia, The Picasso Affair (First prize Nat Playwriting Competition 1982), The Artist and Food for Thought, The Studio, Eh, Harry? (First prize, Jacksonville Univ 1988), The Winding Staircase (First prize Country Playhouse Playwriting Competition, Houston, TX 1985), Person-to-Person, Nighty-Night, The Panel, Survey Show, Desjardin's Garden, The Black Ceiling, Patchwork Quilt,

Box Camera, Ceremony, Reservation for Dinner, Lullaby, The Classical Hour, The Fine Art of Dealing Fine Art. *Leisure interest:* gardening. *Address:* 4360 Montrose Ave, Westmount, PQ H3Y 2B1, Canada. *Telephone:* (514) 933-5048; *Fax:* (514) 933-5048; *E-mail:* b.sv .gersovitz@sympatico.ca.

GESSENDORF, Mechthild; German opera singer (soprano); m Ernö Weil. *Career:* Performances with Bayerische Staatsoper (Munich), Hamburgische Staatsoper, Deutsche Oper (Berlin), Wiener Staatsoper (Vienna), Royal Opera House (Covent Garden, London), Grand Opéra (Paris), La Scala (Milan), Metropolitan Opera (New York), Monte Carlo Opera, etc; numerous appearances at int festivals including Salzburg (Austria), Aix-en-Provence (France) and Edinburgh (UK). *Operas include:* Der Rosenkavalier, Ariadne auf Naxos, Lohengrin, Die Walküre, Der fliegende Holländer, Jenufa, Die Frau ohne Schatten, Tannhäuser. *Address:* Nibelungen Str 23, 75179 Pforzheim, Germany.

GETTY, Estelle; American actress; b 25 July 1923, New York; m Arthur Gettleman 1947; two s. *Education:* New School for Social Research (New York) and at Herbert Berghof Studios. *Career:* Actress and comedienne in plays, films and on TV; Founder Fresh Meadows Community Theatre. *Plays include:* The Divorce of Judy and Jane 1971, Widows and Children First, Light Up the Sky, Torch Song Trilogy (Helen Hayes Best Supporting Performer in a Touring Show Award) 1981–83; *Films include:* The Chosen 1982, Tootsie 1982, Protocol 1984, Mask 1984, Mannequin 1987, Stop Or My Mom Will Shoot 1992, Fortune Hunters 1999, Stuart Little (voice) 1999; *TV appearances include:* The Golden Girls (series, Golden Globe Award, Emmy Award), The Golden Palace, Empty Nest, No Man's Land, Victims for Victims: The Teresa Saldana Story, Copacabana; *Publication:* If I Knew What I Know Now... So What? 1988. *Address:* Innovative Artists Talent and Literary Agency, 1999 Ave of the Stars, Suite 2850, Los Angeles, CA 90067, USA.

GEYER, Georgie Anne, B SC; American journalist; b 2 April 1935, Chicago, IL; d of Robert George and Georgie Hazel Geyer. *Education:* Northwestern Univ (IL) and Univ of Vienna. *Career:* Reporter Southtown Economist, Chicago 1958; Society Reporter Chicago Daily News 1959–60, Gen Assignment Reporter 1960–64, Latin America Corresp 1964–67, roving Foreign Corresp, columnist 1967–75; Syndicated Columnist Los Angeles Times Syndicate 1975–80; columnist Universal Press Syndicate 1980–; Lyle M. Spencer Prof of Journalism, Syracuse Univ, NY 1976; int lecture tours on American journalism sponsored by Int Communication Agency, Nigeria, Somalia, Tanzania, Zambia 1979, Indonesia, Philippines 1981, Belgium, Iceland, Norway, Portugal 1982; regular TV and radio appearances; Sr Fellow Annenberg, Washington 1992–; Fellow Soc of Professional Journalists 1992–; has interviewed many world political figures; several hon degrees (LITT D); numerous awards include American Newspaper Guild First prize 1962, Overseas Press Club award for best writing on Latin America 1966, Alumni Award (Northwestern Univ) 1991. *Publications:* The New Latins 1970, The New 100 Years War 1972, The Young Russians 1976, Buying the Night Flight (autobiog) 1983, Guerilla Prince: the Untold Story of Fidel Castro 1991. *Address:* The Plaza, 800 25th St, NW, Washington, DC 20037, USA.

GHEORGHIU, Angela; Romanian opera singer (soprano); b 1965, Adjud; m 1st Andrei Gheorghiu 1988; m 2nd Roberto Alagna. *Education:* Bucharest Acad. *Career:* Debut Nat Opera, Cluj 1990; has performed with Royal Opera, London, New York Metropolitan Opera, NY, Vienna State Opera and in Montréal, Canada and Tokyo, Japan; Belvedere Prize, Vienna, Schatzgraber-Preis, Hamburg State Opera, Gulbenkian Prize. *Operas include:* Don Giovanni, La Traviata, La Bohème, Turandot, Carmen, Cherubin, La Traviata, L'Elisir d'Amore, Falstaff, Roméo et Juliette; *Recordings include:* La Traviata (as Violetta) 1995, selection of arias. *Address:* c/o Royal Opera House, Covent Garden, London WC2, UK (Office); c/o M. Levon Sayan, 76–78 ave des Champs-Elysées, 75008 Paris, France.

GHEORGHIU, Virginia Míhaela, MA; Romanian political adviser and journalist; b 20 Jan 1965, Alba-Iulia; d of Vasile and Maria Gheorghiu; m Alin Adrian Nemecz 1984. *Education:* Cluj High School and Univ of Cluj. *Career:* NATO Scholar 1990–91; radio and TV Ed 1990–91; Spokesperson and Expert Council for Reform, Govt of Romania 1991,

Govt Spokesperson 1992, State Sec and Head Public Transportation Dept 1993; Public Affairs Dir Romanian American Enterprise Fund 1995–; TV presenter 1995–; fmrly Public Relations Dir Centre for Strategic Studies and Comparative Analysis and Exec Dir Young Politicians' Club of Romania; Fellow Chatham House, London 1993, Hubert Humphrey Fellow, American Univ, Washington, DC, USA 1994; numerous articles in Romanian press on politics, semiotics and philosophy; numerous appearances on TV and radio. *Leisure interests:* reading, music, walking. *Address:* Bucharest 1, Romanian American Enterprise Fund, 4 Vasile Conta, Romania (Office); Cluj 3400, 2 Horea St, Apt 18, Romania (Home). *Telephone:* (1) 2100701 (Office); (51) 132050 (Home); *Fax:* (1) 2100713.

GHEZALI, Salima; Algerian newspaper editor; m (divorced); two c. *Career:* Fmrly schoolteacher, Mitidja hills; Ed-in-Chief La Nation weekly newspaper 1994–; has received three int press awards including Int Press Club Award 1996. *Address:* c/o La Nation, Algiers, Algeria.

GHILARDOTTI, Fiorella; Italian politician; b 25 June 1946, Castelverde; m Sergio Graziosi; two s. *Education:* Univ of Milan. *Career:* Teacher; trade unionist, Dir Confed Italiana Sindacati Lavoratori (CISL) 1981–90; Pres Lombardy region 1992–94, Vice-Pres Cttee of Regions 1993–94; MEP (Bureau of PSE, Democratici di Sinistra) 1994–, mem Cttee on Employment and Social Affairs, on Women's Rights and Equal Oppertunities, mem Jt Parl Ass ACP-EU; Chair PSE Standing Cttee on Women 1997–. *Leisure interest:* reading. *Address:* European Parliament, rue Wiertz, 1047 Brussels, Belgium; Centro Dentro l'Europa, 7 Via Mercadante, 20124 Milan, Italy. *Telephone:* (2) 284-21-11 (Brussels); (2) 6906433 (Milan); *Fax:* (2) 6706433 (Milan); *E-mail:* fiorells.ghilardotti@stcom.com.

GHULOMOVA, Dilbar M.; Uzbekistan politician. *Career:* Deputy Prime Minister and Chair Women's Cttee. *Address:* Office of the Cabinet of Ministers, 700008 Tashkent, Government House, Uzbekistan. *Telephone:* (3712) 39-82-95; *Fax:* (3712) 39-86-01.

GHURAYIB, Rose, MA; Lebanese writer. *Education:* American Univ of Beirut. *Career:* Teacher of Arabic and History; fmr Ed Al-Raida, quarterly newsletter of Inst for Women's Studies in the Arab World, later Consultant; writer of books, poems and plays for children; researcher into the condition and liberation of women in the Arab world. *Publications include:* The Harem Window: Sisterhood is Global (ed) 1984, Adwa' Ala al-Haraka al-Nissaiya al-Mua'asirah (Highlights on the Contemporary Women's Movement) 1985. *Address:* c/o Institute for Women's Studies in the Arab World, Beirut University College, rue Mme Curie, POB 13-5053, Beirut, Lebanon.

GIBAULT, Claire; French conductor; b 31 Oct 1945, Le Mans; d of Louis and Suzanne Gibault. *Education:* Conservatoire du Mans and Conservatoire Nat Supérieur de Paris. *Career:* At Opéra de Lyon 1971–74, Conductor 1990–; fmr Dir Office de Radiodiffusion-Télévision Française (ORTF) Orchestra, Orchestre du Conservatoire de Paris, and Toulouse, Angers, Nantes and Mulhouse orchestras; Dir Opéra de Chambéry; conductor at concerts in France and abroad, and with orchestras including Orchestre de la Suisse Romande, Monte-Carlo, Nice-Provence-Côte-d'Azur, Turin, Rome, Lausanne, Brussels, Québec and San Francisco orchestras, at Royal Opera House, Covent Garden, London, etc; Chevalier de l'Ordre Nat du Mérite; Prix de la Fondation de la Vocation 1969 and numerous prizes from Conservatoire du Mans and Conservatoire Nat Supérieur de Paris. *Works conducted include:* The Magic Flute 1974, 1994, L'enlèvement au sérail 1987, Pelléas et Mélisande 1993, La station thermale (world première) 1995; numerous contemporary works; *Recordings:* Les mariés de la Tour Eiffel 1990, Les Brigands d'Offenbach (laser video). *Leisure interests:* walking, cycling, tennis. *Address:* Opéra de Lyon, 1 place de la Comédie, 69001 Lyons, France.

GIBBONS, Julia Smith; American judge; b 23 Dec 1950, Pulaski, TN; d of John Floyd and Julia (née Abernathy) Smith; m William Lockhart Gibbons 1973; one s one d. *Education:* Vanderbilt Univ (Nashville, TN) and Univ of Virginia. *Career:* Called to the Bar, TN 1975; Law Clerk to US Circuit Judge, 6th Circuit Court of Appeals 1975–76; Attorney Farris, Hancock, Gilman, Branan and Lanier 1976–79; Legal Advisor to Gov of Tennessee 1979–81; Circuit Court Judge (TN) 1981–83, US Dist Judge 1983–94, Chief Judge 1994–; Fellow American Bar Foundation, Tennessee Bar Foundation, Memphis and Shelby Co Bar Foundation; named Outstanding Judge of the Year 1985. *Address:* US District Court, 167 N Main St, 1157 Federal Bldg, Memphis, TN 38103, USA. *Telephone:* (901) 495-1265; *Fax:* (901) 495-1270.

GIBSON, Eleanor Jack, MA, PH D; American psychologist (retd); b 7 Dec 1910, Peoria, IL; d of William and Isabel Grier Jack; m James Gibson 1932; one s one d. *Education:* Smith Coll and Yale Univ. *Career:* Instructor Smith Coll, Northampton, MA 1933–40, Asst Prof 1940–49; Research Assoc in Psychology, later Prof of Psychology, Cornell Univ 1949–65; Visiting Prof MIT 1973, Univ of Pennsylvania 1984, Univ of S Carolina 1987, Emory Univ 1988–90, Univ of Connecticut 1988; Montgomery Fellow, Dartmouth Coll 1985; Pres Eastern Psychology Asscn 1968, Experimental Div, American Psychological Asscn 1977; Chair Div J, AAAS 1982–83; mem NAS, American Acad of Arts and Sciences; Guggenheim Fellow 1972–73; Hon D SC (Smith Coll) 1972, (Rutgers) 1973, (Trinity Coll) 1982, (Bates Coll) 1985, (S Carolina) 1987, (Emory Univ) 1990, (Middlebury Coll, VT) 1993; Hon D HUM LITT (Albany) 1984, (Miami) 1989, (Oxford, Ohio) 1989, (Yale) 1993; Hon Dr of Social Sciences (Yale) 1996; numerous awards include Distinguished Scientist Award (American Psychological Asscn) 1968, G. Stanley Hall Medal 1971, Wilbur Cross Medal (Yale) 1973, Howard Crosby Warren Medal 1977, Distinguished Scientific Contribution Award (SRCD) 1981, Medal for Distinguished Service (Columbia Univ) 1983, Gold Medal (American Psychological Foundation) 1986, Nat Medal of Science 1993. *Publications:* Principles of Perceptual Learning and Development 1969, Psychology of Reading (jtly) 1975, An Odyssey in Language and Perception 1991, An Ecological Approach to Perceptual Learning and Development (jtly) 2000; numerous articles in psychological journals. *Address:* 266 Washington St Ext Middlebury, VT 05753, USA (Home). *Telephone:* (802) 388-6340 (Home).

GIBSON, Elspeth; British designer; b 29 Nov 1963, Nottingham; d of Wendy and Roy Gibson; m Dominic George Lawlor; one d. *Education:* Tuxford Comprehensive School (Notts) and Mansfield and Notts Coll of Art and Design. *Career:* Opened first Elspeth Gibson boutique, London 1998; introduced range of bath products Oct 1999; New Generation Designer of the Year Award 1999; Elle Style Award 1999. *Leisure interests:* horse riding, painting, gardening, walking. *Address:* c/o Brower Lewis, 74 Gloucester Place, London, W1H 3HN, UK (Office); 22 Cheverton Rd, London N19 3AY, UK (Home). *Telephone:* (20) 7263-1878 (Office); *Fax:* (20) 7226-5644 (Office); *E-mail:* fashion@ elspethgibson.com (Office); *Internet:* www.elspethgibson.com.

GIBSON, Yvonne Francis; Saint Vincent and the Grenadines politician. *Career:* fmrly Minister of State for Educ, Youth and Women's Affairs and fmr Minister of Health and the Environment; Minister of State in the Prime Minister's Office 2000. *Address:* c/o Office of the Prime Minister, Government Bldgs, Kingstown, Saint Vincent and the Grenadines. *Telephone:* 456-1703; *Fax:* 457-2152.

GIELGUD, Maina Julia Gordon; British ballet dancer and artistic director; b 14 Jan 1945, London; d of Lewis Gielgud and Elisabeth Grussner. *Career:* Mem Ballet du Marquis de Cuevas 1962–63, Ballet Classique de France 1965–67, Ballet du XXème Siècle, Maurice Béjart 1967–72, London Festival Ballet 1972–77, Royal Ballet 1977–78; freelance dancer 1978–82; Rehearsal Dir London City Ballet 1981–82; Artistic Dir Australian Ballet 1983–96; Ballet Dir Royal Danish Ballet 1997–2000, The Boston Ballet 2000–; Hon AO 1991. *Ballets produced:* (for The Australian Ballet) The Sleeping Beauty 1985, Giselle 1987. *Address:* 1/9 Stirling Court, 3 Marshall St, London W1V 1LQ, UK (Home). *Telephone:* (20) 7734-6612 (Home); *E-mail:* gielgud@ibm.net (Home).

GILCHRIST, Ellen Louise, BA; American writer; b 20 Feb 1935, Vicksburg, MS; d of William Garth and Aurora Gilchrist; three s. *Education:* Millsaps Coll (MS) and Univ of Arkansas. *Career:* Freelance writer and journalist; Commentator Nat Public Radio news, Washington 1984–85; mem Authors' Guild; Nat Educ Asscn Grant 1979; Poetry Award Mississippi Arts Festival 1968; Univ of Arkansas Poetry Award 1976; New York Quarterly Craft in Poetry Award 1978; The Prairie Schooner Fiction Award 1981; Mississippi Acad of Arts and Science Fiction Award 1982, 1985; Saxifrage Award 1983; Univ of

Arkansas J. William Fulbright Prize 1985; Mississippi Inst of Arts and Letters Literary Award 1985. *Publications:* The Land Surveyor's Daughter 1979, In the Land of Dreamy Dreams 1981, The Annunciation 1983, Victory Over Japan (American Book Award) 1984, Drunk With Love 1986, Falling Through Space 1987, The Anna Papers 1988, Light Can Be Both Wave and Particle 1989, Riding Out the Tropical Depression (poetry), I Cannot Get You Close Enough 1991, Net of Jewels 1992, Starcarbon (Mississippi Acad of Arts and Science Fiction Award 1992) 1992, Anabasis 1994, The Age of Miracles 1994, The Courts of Love.

GILLESE, Eileen Elizabeth, BCL, BA; Canadian professor of law; b 8 July 1954, Edmonton, AB; d of John and Thelma Gillese; m Robert Donald Badun 1982; three d one s. *Education:* Univs of Oxford and Alberta. *Career:* Part-time Lecturer in Law Univ of Alberta 1980–83; called to the Bar Alberta 1981, Ontario 1988; with law practice Reynolds, Mirth and Cote 1980–83; Prof Faculty of Law, Univ of W Ontario 1983–99, Assoc Dean Student Affairs 1989–90, Assoc Dean Admin 1992–95, Dean 1996–99; mem Pension Comm of Ontario 1987–96, Vice-Chair 1989–94, Chair 1994–96; Justice Superior Court of Canada 1999–; mem Ontario Rhodes Scholar Selection Cttee 1986–, Sec 1989–95; 3M Fellow for Excellence in Teaching 1986; named Oustanding Woman, Fed Govt 1978; Inaugural Award for Faculty Excellence, Legal Soc 1986, 1992; Edward J. Pleva Award for Teaching Excellence 1993. *Publications:* Trusts (jtly, 3rd edn) 1987, Property Law (jtly, 2nd edn) 1990; numerous articles on business law, inheritance, trusts, etc. *Leisure interests:* public speaking, community work, reading, travel, squash, cycling. *Address:* Court House, 12th Floor, Unit K, 80 Dundas St, London ON N6A 2P3, Canada (Office); 77 Green Acres Drive, London ON N6G 2S4, Canada (Home).

GILLESPIE, Rhondda Marie, B MUS; Australian concert pianist; b 3 Aug 1941, Sydney; d of David and Marie Gillespie; m Denby Richards 1972. *Education:* Sydney Conservatorium of Music with Alexander Sverjensky and privately with Louis Kentner and Denis Matthews (London). *Career:* Debut on Australian radio aged eight 1949; first public recital 1953; winner ABC Concerto Competition, Sydney 1959; European debut in London with Tchaikovsky's 2nd Piano Concerto 1960; has played with major orchestras and conductors throughout the world and made many TV and festival appearances; formed Gillespie–Weatherburn Duo 1986, performed at many major venues including Sydney Opera House and Barbican Centre, London; has recorded for Philips, Decca Argo, EMI and Chandos; awarded Harriet Cohen Commonwealth Medal 1964. *Recordings:* Bliss and Lambert Sonatas, Charles Camilleri recital, Usko Meriläinen Piano Concertos Nos 1 and 2, Liszt Ballades and Sonata. *Leisure interests:* golf, languages, exotic cooking. *Address:* 2 Princes Rd, St Leonards-on-Sea, E Sussex TN37 6EL, UK. *Telephone:* (1424) 715167; *Fax:* (1424) 712214.

GILLETT, Margaret, MA, ED D; Canadian professor of education and writer; b 1 Feb 1930, Wingham, Australia; d of Frank Leslie and Janet Adele (née Vickers) Gillett. *Education:* Univ of Sydney, Russell Sage Coll and Columbia Univ (USA). *Career:* English teacher, Australia 1951–53; Educ Officer, Australia 1954–57; Asst Prof of Educ Dalhousie Univ, NS, Canada 1961–62; Registrar Univ of Addis Ababa, Ethiopia 1962–64; Prof of Educ McGill Univ, Montréal, Canada 1964, Macdonald Prof of Educ 1982–94, William C. Macdonald Emer Prof of Educ 1996–; Hon Life mem Grad Soc McGill Univ, Comparative Educ Soc of Canada, Canadian Soc for the Study of Educ 1995, James McGill Soc 1993; Hon LL D (Saskatchewan) 1988; Russell Sage Medal 1991; Woman of Distinction Award 1994. *Publications:* The Laurel and the Poppy: Francis Thompson 1966, We Walked Very Warily: A History of Women at McGill 1981, Dear Grace: A Romance of History 1986, Our Own Agendas 1995, A Fair Shake Revisited 1996. *Leisure interests:* tennis, gardening, music. *Address:* McGill University, Faculty of Education, 3724 McTavish St, Montréal, PQ H3A 1Y2, Canada; 150 Berloiz, Verdun, PQ H3E IK3, Canada (Home). *Telephone:* (514) 398-6746 (Office); (514) 766-9619 (Home).

GILMORE, Gail Varina, M MUS; American opera singer; b 21 Sept 1951, Washington, DC. *Education:* In New Orleans (LA) and Univ of Indiana at Bloomington. *Career:* Appearances at Oper am Rhein (Düsseldorf, Germany), Teatro la Fenice (Venice, Italy), Arena di Verona (Italy), Opernhaus Frankfurt (Germany), Houston Opera (TX),

Metropolitan Opera (New York), Bolshoi Theatre (Moscow); performances with José Carreras; numerous concert appearances. *Operas include:* Les Troyens, Carmen, Orfeo ed Euridice, Cavalleria Rusticana, Ariadne auf Naxos, Der Rosenkavalier, Aida, Macbeth, Il Trovatore, Don Carlos, Tannhäuser, Parsifal, Lohengrin. *Address:* Apollolaan 123, NL 1077 Amsterdam, Netherlands.

GILMORE, Rosalind Edith Jean, CB, MA, FRSA; British civil servant and business executive; b (Rosalind Fraser) 23 March 1937, London; d of Sir Robert and Lady (Betty) Fraser; m Brian Terence Gilmore 1962. *Education:* King Alfred School (London), Univ Coll London and Newnham Coll (Cambridge). *Career:* Entered HM Treasury 1960, Asst Prin 1960–62, Asst Pvt Sec to Chancellor of Exchequer 1962–65, Prin Pvt Sec to Paymaster-Gen 1973, Asst Sec 1975, Head Financial Insts Div 1977–80, Press Sec to Chancellor of the Exchequer 1980–82; Exec Asst to Econs Dir IBRD 1966–67; Cabinet Office 1974; Prin Pvt Sec to Chancellor of the Duchy of Lancaster; Gen Man Corp Planning Dunlop Ltd 1982–83; Dir of Marketing Nat Girobank 1983–86; Directing Fellow St George's House, Windsor Castle 1986–89; Dir Mercantile Group PLC, Mercantile Credit Co Ltd, London and Manchester Group PLC 1986–89, Regulatory Services, Lloyds 1994–95; Marketing Consultant FI Group PLC (Software) 1986–89; Deputy Chair and Commr Bldg Socs Comm 1989–91, Exec Chair 1991–94; Chief Registrar of Friendly Socs and Industrial Insurance Commr 1991–94; Chair Homeowners Friendly Soc Ltd 1996–98, Arrow Broadcasting 1996–98; Dir Moorfields Eye Hosp Trust 1994–, BAT Industries PLC 1996–98, Zurich Financial Services AG (Switzerland) 1998–, Allied Zurich PLC 1998, TU Fund Mans 1999–; mem Financial Services Act Tribunal 1986–89, Securities and Investment Bd 1993–96; Vice-Pres for Leadership, Int Women's Forum 1997–; Dir Leadership Foundation 1997–, Court Cranfield Univ 1992–, Bd Opera North 1993–96, Lloyd's Regulatory Bd 1994–98, Council RCM 1996–; Assoc Fellow Newnham Coll, Cambridge 1986–93, Hon Fellow 1993; Fellow Univ Coll London 1988; Fellow Chartered Inst of Marketing. *Publication:* Mutuality for the Twenty-first Century 1998. *Leisure interests:* music, reading, house in Greece, swimming. *Address:* c/o Zurich Financial Services, 22 Arlington St, London SW1A 1RW, UK (Office); 3 Clarendon Mews, London W2 2NR, UK (Home). *Telephone:* (20) 7317-3957 (Office); (20) 7402-8554 (Home); *Fax:* (20) 7317-3926 (Office); (20) 7402-8554 (Home); *E-mail:* rosalind.gilmore@alliedzurich.co.uk (Office).

GILMOUR, Mavis Gwendolyn, MD, FRCS; Jamaican politician; b 13 April 1926, St Elizabeth; d of Isaac and Adelaide Holness. *Education:* Howard Univ (Washington, DC, USA), and Univ of Edinburgh (UK). *Career:* Medical officer Kingston Public Hosp 1951, consultant surgeon 1960–72; mem House of Reps (Lab) for W Rural St Andrew 1976–; Minister of Educ 1980–86, of Social Security and Consumer Affairs 1986–89. *Leisure interests:* sewing, horticulture, reading. *Address:* House of Representatives, Gordon House, Duke St, Kingston, Jamaica.

GILOT, Françoise; French artist; b 26 Nov 1921, Neuilly-sur-Seine; d of Emile and Madeleine Gilot; partner Pablo Picasso (died 1973); two c (see Paloma Picasso); m 1st Luc-Rémi Simon 1955 (divorced 1961); one d; m 2nd Jonas Salk. *Education:* Univ of Paris. *Career:* One-woman exhibitions include La Hune Gallery (Paris) 1951, Alex Vomel Gallery (Düsseldorf, Germany) 1954, Coard Gallery (Paris) 1959, 1961, 1962, 1963, 1966, 1968, 1988, Mayor Gallery (London) 1960, 1962, David Findlay Gallery (New York) 1965, Gallery 32 (Milan, Italy) 1965, Chapman Kelley Gallery (Dallas, TX, USA) 1966, 1970, Georges Lavrove Gallery (Paris) 1984, Musée du Palais des Papes (Avignon) 1987, Musée Picasso (Antibes) 1987, Riggs Galleries (La Jolla, CA, USA) 1987, 1989, Robertson Gallery (Beverly Hills, CA, USA) 1988, El Paso Museum of Art (TX, USA) 1988, Atrium Gallery (Stockholm) 1988, Mia Joosten Gallery K318 (Amsterdam) 1989, Gallery Berggruen (Paris) 1990; paintings in collections of Musée d'Art Moderne de Paris; creator scenery and costumes for Héraclès ballet 1953; illustrator of poetry; Chevalier de la Légion d'Honneur; Commdr des Arts et des Lettres. *Publications:* Vivre avec Picasso 1965, Le regard et son masque 1975, Matisse et Picasso 1991. *Leisure interests:* horse-riding, swimming. *Address:* 36 ave Junot, 75018 Paris, France.

GINSBURG, Ruth Bader, LL B; American judge; b 15 March 1933, Brooklyn, New York; d of Nathan Bader and Celia Amster; m Martin Ginsburg 1954; one s one d. *Education:* Cornell (NY), Harvard (MA)

and Columbia (NY) Univs. *Career:* Called to the Bar, NY 1959, US Supreme Court 1967, DC 1975; Law Sec to judge, US Dist Court (Southern Dist), New York 1959–61; Research Assoc Columbia Univ Law School (NY) 1961–62, Assoc Dir project on int procedure 1962–63, Prof 1972–80; Asst Prof Rutgers Univ Law School (NJ) 1963–66, Assoc Prof 1966–69, Prof 1969–72; Circuit Judge, US Court of Appeals, DC Circuit (Washington, DC) 1980–93; Judge US Supreme Court 1993–; Fellow Center for Advanced Study in Behavioral Sciences, Stanford (CT) 1977–78; mem American Bar Asscn, AAAS, American Law Inst, Council on Foreign Relations; several hon degrees. *Publications include:* Civil Procedure in Sweden (jtly) 1965, Swedish Code of Judicial Procedure 1968, Sex-Based Discrimination (jtly). *Address:* United States Supreme Court, Supreme Court Bldg, 1 First St, NE, Washington, DC 20543, USA.

GINWALA, Frene Noshir, D PHIL; South African politician. *Education:* Univs of London and Oxford (UK). *Career:* In exile, in Tanzania, Zambia, Mozambique and UK until 1991, worked as freelance journalist The Guardian, Man Dir Standard and Sunday News 1969, Spokesperson for African Nat Congress (ANC), London; Chief Researcher for Nelson Mandela 1991; currently Speaker S African Nat Ass (first woman). *Address:* National Assembly, Cape Town, South Africa.

GIOVANNI, Nikki, BA; American poet; b 7 June 1943, Knoxville, TN; d of Jones Giovanni and Yolande Watson; one s. *Education:* Fisk Univ and Univ of Pennsylvania. *Career:* Asst Prof of Black Studies, City Coll of New York 1968; Assoc Prof of English, Rutgers Univ (NJ) 1968–72; Prof of Creative Writing, Coll Mt St Joseph on the Ohio 1985; Prof Virginia Polytechnic Inst and State Univ (Blacksburg, VA) 1987–; Visiting Prof Ohio State Univ 1984; f Nixtom Ltd 1970; numerous awards and hon degrees. *Publications include:* Black Feeling, Black Talk 1968, Black Judgement 1968, Re: Creation 1970, Poem of Angela Yvonne Davis 1970, Spin A Soft Black Song 1971, Gemini 1971, My House 1972, A Dialogue: James Baldwin and Nikki Giovanni 1973, Ego Tripping and Other Poems for Young Readers 1973, A Poetic Equation: Conversations Between Nikki Giovanni and Margaret Walker 1974, The Women and the Men 1975, Cotton Candy on a Rainy Day 1978, Vacationtime 1980, Those Who Ride the Night Winds 1983, Sacred Cows... and other Edibles 1988, Conservations with Nikki Giovanni 1992, Racism 101 1994, Grand Mothers 1994. *Address:* Virginia Polytechnic Institute and State University, Department of English, POB 0112, Blacksburg, VA 24063, USA.

GIROUD, Françoise; French journalist, writer and politician; b 21 Sept 1916, Geneva, Switzerland; d of Salih Gourdji and Elda Faragi; one s (deceased) one d. *Education:* Lycée Molière and Coll de Groslay. *Career:* Began in cinema as Continuity Girl 1932, Asst Dir 1937, adapted and wrote various film scripts; Ed Elle 1945–53; Co-Founder L'Express 1953, Ed 1953–71, Dir 1971–74; Chair Express-Union publrs 1970–74; mem Bd of Govs Express Group 1971–74; Chief Columnist Le Nouvel Observateur 1983–; Sec of State for Women's Affairs 1974–76, for Culture 1976–77; Vice-Pres Parti Radical 1975–76, Union pour la démocratie française 1978–; Pres Action Int contre la Faim 1984–88, Hon Pres 1988–, Pres Comm to improve cinema ticket sales 1989–91; literary critic Le Journal du Dimanche 1990–94, Le Figaro 1994–; mem Prix Femina Jury 1992–; Dr hc (Michigan) 1976, (Goucher Coll, USA) 1977; Chevalier de la Légion d'Honneur 1983. *Publications:* Le Tout-Paris 1952, Nouveaux portraits 1953, La nouvelle vague: portrait de la jeunesse 1958, Si je mens 1972, Une poignée d'eau 1973, La comédie du pouvoir 1977, Ce que je crois 1978, Une femme honorable (Acad Int Médicis de Florence award 1984) 1981, Alma Mahler ou l'art d'être aimée (Grand prix littéraire de la Femme) 1988, Leçons particulières 1990, Jenny Marx ou la femme du diable 1992, Les hommes et les femmes (jtly) 1993, Journal d'une parisienne 1993, Mon très cher amour 1994, Cœur de tigre 1995, Chienne d'année 1996, Cosima la sublime 1996, Gais-Z et contents 1997, Arthur ou le bonheur de vivre 1997, Deux et deux font trois 1998, Histoires (presque) vraies 2000, C'est arrivé hier (journal 1999) 2000; *Films scripted include:* Antoine et Antoinette 1947, La belle que voilà 1950, L'amour, madame 1951, Julietta 1953, Le bon plaisir (jtly) 1984, Le quatrième pouvoir 1985, Marie Curie (TV film, Nymphe d'Or Award Monte Carlo Int TV

Festival) 1991. *Address:* Editions Fayard, 75 rue des Saints Pères, 75006 Paris, France. *Telephone:* (1) 45-55-65-80; *E-mail:* francoise.giroud@ wanadoo.fr (Office).

GIRVAN, Marilyn Ann, BA; Canadian national organization executive; b 12 Dec 1939, Toronto, ON; d of Archibald Middleton and Beatrice Ann Girvan; divorced; two s. *Education:* Toronto Teachers' Coll and Carleton Univ (Ottawa, ON). *Career:* Teacher Toronto Bd of Educ 1959–65, (volunteer) Butimba Teachers' Coll, Tanzania 1965–67, Dar es Salaam Int School, Tanzania 1967–69, Remedial Reading Programme, Kingston, Jamaica 1971–75; Dir of Programme Funding CUSO, Ottawa, ON 1975–78; Exec Dir Match Int Centre 1978–81, Canadian Advisory Council on the Status of Women 1981–84, Canadian Bureau for Int Educ 1985–88; Dir Women in Devt and Gender Equity, Policy Br, Canadian Int Devt Agency (CIDA) 1988–96; mem bd Advisory Council for the Co-operative Programme in Int Devt Studies, Univ of Toronto. *Leisure interests:* travel, cinema. *Address:* 615 Burn St, Ottawa, ON K1K 1B4, Canada (Home).

GIVENS, Robin; American actress; b 27 Nov 1964, New York; m Mike Tyson 1988 (divorced 1989). *Education:* Sarah Lawrence Coll (Bronxville, NY) and Harvard Univ Grad School of Arts and Sciences (MA). *Career:* Fmr model. *Films include:* A Rage in Harlem 1991, Boomerang, Foreign Student, Blankman; *TV appearances include:* Head of the Class, Angel Street, Courthouse, Beverly Hills Madam, The Women of Brewster Place, The Penthouse, Dangerous Intentions, Everything's Jake. *Address:* 106 Central Park S, Apt 11F, New York, NY 10019, USA.

GJELLERUP, Pia, LL M; Danish politician; b 22 Aug 1959, Copenhagen. *Education:* Univ of Copenhagen. *Career:* Mem Town Council of Frederiksberg 1982–87; mem Folketing (Parl) 1987–, Sec Social Democratic Parl Group 1990–93, Leader 1994–98, mem Cttee of Social Democratic Group; Minister of Justice 1993, for Trade and Industry 1998–2000, for Finance 2000–; fmr Chair Parl Cttee on Tax and Duties; called to the Bar, Copenhagen 1990. *Address:* Folketing, Christiansborg, 1240 Copenhagen K, Denmark. *Telephone:* 33-37-55-00; *E-mail:* pia_gjellerup@socialdemokratiet.dk.

GJERGJI, Andromaqi, D SC; Albanian ethnologist; b 20 May 1928, Korçe; d of Llambi and Persefoni Jorgji. *Education:* Univ of Tirana. *Career:* Scientific Researcher Dept of Ethnography, Inst of History, Acad of Sciences, Tirana 1950–78; apptd Ethnologist Inst of Popular Culture 1978–; Asst Lecturer Acad of Fine Arts, Tirana; has conducted fieldwork throughout Albania; has collaborated on ethnographic exhibitions in Albania, Finland, Sweden, Rome, Paris, Bucharest; Contrib to Albanian Encyclopaedic Dictionary 1985; mem Editorial Bd Albanian Ethnographic Atlas and Kultura Popullore journal; Order of Naim Frashëri 1976. *Publications:* Bibliografi e Etnografisë Shqiptare 1944–79 1980, Veshje Shqiptare në Shekuj 1987, Veshjet Popullore Shqiptare (textbook) 1989, Histori e Artit Shqiptare (jtly) 1990; approx 100 contribs to scientific journals. *Leisure interest:* music. *Address:* Instituti i Kulturës Popullore, Rruge Kont Urani 3, Tirana, Albania. *Telephone:* (42) 223-23.

GJESTEBY, Kari; Norwegian politician; b 16 May 1947, Oslo; d of Omar A. and Ingrid E. (née Thoresen) Gjesteby; m Mikael Klingberg; two d. *Education:* Norwegian School of Econs and Business Admin (Bergen-Sandviken). *Career:* Exec Officer Ministry of Local Govt and Labour 1972–74; Political Sec Ministry of Consumer Affairs 1974–76; State Sec Ministry of Church and Educ 1976–86, Ministry of Finance 1979–81; Minister of Trade and Shipping 1981; First Deputy Gen Sec Nordic Council of Ministers Secr, Oslo 1983–86; State Sec Ministry of Foreign Affairs 1986–88; Business Consultant 1988–90; Dir Norges Bank 1989–; Minister of Justice 1990–92; fmr mem Nat Wages Arbitration Bd, Exec Dir 1992–. *Address:* c/o Norges Bank, Bankplassen 2, POB 1179, Sentrum, 0107 Oslo, Norway (Office); Lachmannsvei 30, 0495 Oslo 4, Norway (Home).

GJEVANG, Anne; Norwegian opera singer (contralto); b 24 Oct 1948, Oslo. *Education:* Conservatorio Santa Cecilia (Rome) and Hochschule für Musik und Darstellende Kunst (Vienna). *Career:* Operatic debuts in Austria and Germany, Bayreuth Festival 1983, Metropolitan Opera, New York 1987, Victoria Music Festival, London 1991; mem Zurich Opera House 1987–91; guest performer Berlin and London Philharmonics, Chicago Symphony Orchestra, USA, Orchestre de Paris; performed with famous conductors including Solti, Barenboim, von Karajan, Giulini, Abbado, Chailly, Albrecht, Perick, Haitink and Pappano; renowned for appearances as Erda in Wagner's Ring des Nibelungen; awarded Norsk Kritikerpris 1986. *Recordings include:* Anne Gjevang in Recital, Mahler's 3rd Symphony, Schumann's Das Paradies und die Peri, Handel: Messiah 1985, (Arias and Choruses) 1990, (Highlights) 1998. *Address:* Leinv 3, 1453 Bjørnemyr, Norway. *Telephone:* (9) 96-09-35; *Fax:* (9) 91-07-66.

GLASE, Anne-Karin; German politician; b 24 July 1954, Neuruppin. *Career:* MEP (EPP, CDU), mem Cttee on Social Affairs and Employment, Jt Parl Ass ACP-EU; mem Brandenburg CDU Land Exec, Women's Union, Brandenburg Rural Women's Asscn; Vice-Chair CDU Fed Cttee on Devt Policy; Chair Competence Centre for Conversion and Weapons Clearance; mem Bd European Centre for Worker's Questions. *Address:* European Parliament, rue Wiertz, 1047 Brussels, Belgium; H-Rau-Straße 31, 16816 Neuruppin, Germany. *Telephone:* (2) 284-21-11 (Belgium); *Fax:* (2) 230-69-43 (Belgium); *E-mail:* aglase@europarl.eu.int; *Internet:* www.cdu-csu-ep.de.

GLASPIE, April Catherine, MA; American diplomatist; b 26 April 1942, Vancouver, BC, Canada. *Education:* Johns Hopkins Univ (MD). *Career:* Joined State Dept 1966; Political Officer US Embassy, Egypt 1973–77, UK 1978–80; Asst to Asst Sec for Near E and SE Asian Affairs 1977–78, Dir Office of Jordan, Lebanon and Syrian Affairs 1985–87; UN Mission 1980–81, Dir Language Inst, US Embassy, Tunisia 1981–83; Deputy Chief of Mission, Syria 1983–85; Amb to Iraq 1987–90; Ambassador-in-Residence Univ of California, San Diego 1991–92; Dir Office of African Affairs 1993. *Address:* Department of State, Office of Southern African Affairs, 2201 C St, Rm 4238, Washington, DC 20016-2646, USA.

GLASSMAN, Caroline Duby, LL B; American judge; b 13 Sept 1922, Baker, OR; d of Charles Ferdinand and Caroline Marie Duby; m Harry Paul Glassman 1953; one s. *Education:* Willamette Univ (OR). *Career:* Called to Bar, OR 1944, CA 1952, ME 1969; Attorney Title Insurance and Trust Co, Salem, OR 1944–46; Assoc Belli, Ashe, Pinney & Melvin, San Francisco, CA 1952–58; Lecturer Univ of Maine School of Law 1967–68, 1980; Partner Glassman & Potter, Portland, ME 1973–78, Glassman, Beagle & Ridge, Portland 1978–83; Judge Maine Supreme Judicial Court, Portland 1983–97; mem American Law Inst, Maine Trial Law Asscn, Oregon, California and Maine Bar Asscns. *Publication:* The Legal Status of Homemakers in the State of Maine 1977. *Address:* 56 Thomas St, Portland, ME 04102, USA (Home).

GLAUERT, Audrey Marion, SC D; British research scientist; b 21 Dec 1925, Farnborough, Hants; d of Hermann and Muriel (née Barker) Glauert; m David Franks 1959 (divorced 1979). *Education:* Perse School for Girls (Cambridge) and Bedford Coll (Univ of London). *Career:* Asst Lecturer in Physics Royal Holloway Coll 1947–50; Sir Halley Stewart Research Fellow Strangeways Lab, Cambridge 1950–89; Fellow Clare Hall, Cambridge 1966–; JP, Cambridge 1975–88; Hon mem French Soc for Electron Microscopy 1967; Pres Royal Microscopical Soc 1970–72; Hon Fellow 1973; Hon mem Electron Microscopy Soc of America 1990 (now Microscopy Soc of America), received Distinguished Scientist Award 1990; Hon Fellow Royal Microscopical Soc. *Publication:* Practical Methods in Electron Microscopy 1972–1999. *Leisure interests:* sailing, gardening, working for prison reform. *Address:* 29 Cow Lane, Fulbourn, Cambridge CB1 5HB, UK. *Telephone:* (1223) 880463; *E-mail:* amg44@cam.ac.uk.

GLENDINNING, Hon Victoria, CBE, MA, FRSL; British writer and journalist; b 23 April 1937, Sheffield; d of Baron and Lady (née Hurst) Seebohm of Hertford ; m 1st O. N. V. Glendinning 1959 (divorced 1981); four s; m 2nd Terence de Vere White 1982 (died 1994); m 3rd Kevin Patrick O'Sullivan 1996. *Education:* St Mary's School (Wantage), Millfield School, Somerville Coll (Oxford) and Univ of Southampton. *Career:* Part-time teacher 1960–69; part-time psychiatric social worker 1970–73; Editorial Asst Times Literary Supplement 1974–78; Pres English Centre of PEN 2001–; Hon D LITT (Southampton) 1994, (Dublin) 1995; Dr hc (Ulster) 1995; Hon D UNIV (York) 2000. *Publications:* A Suppressed Cry 1969, Elizabeth Bowen: portrait of a writer 1977, Edith Sitwell: a unicorn among lions 1981, Vita: a

biography of V. Sackville-West 1983, Rebecca West: a life 1987, The Grown-Ups (novel) 1989, Hertfordshire 1989, Trollope 1992, Electricity (novel) 1995, Sons and Mothers (co-ed) 1996, Jonathan Swift 1998, Flight (novel) 2002; articles in newspapers and journals. *Address:* c/o David Higham Associates, 5–8 Lower John St, Golden Square, London W1R 4HA, UK.

GLENNIE, Evelyn Elizabeth Ann, OBE, FRSA, FRAM, FRCM; British musician; b 19 July 1965, Aberdeen; d of Herbert Arthur and Isobel Glennie; m Gregorio Malcangi 1993. *Education:* Ellon Acad (Aberdeenshire), Royal Acad of Music (London) and Japan (with Keiko Abe). *Career:* Toured UK and Scandinavia with Nat Youth Orchestra of Scotland; debut as percussionist Wigmore Hall 1986; concerto, chamber and solo percussion performances world-wide; tours in UK, Europe, USA, Canada, Australia, New Zealand, Far East, Middle East and South America; numerous TV appearances, including three documentaries on her life; composer of music for TV and radio; performs works written for her by Muldowney, McLeod, Bennett, Musgrave, Bourgeois, Bates, Heath and McMillan; first soloist percussionist to feature at the Proms, London 1989; f Evelyn Glennie Percussion Composition Award, Evelyn Glennie Nat Music Scholarship; Hon Pres Beethoven Fund for Deaf Children; Hon Fellow Welsh Coll of Music and Drama; Hon D MUS (Aberdeen) 1991, (Bristol) 1995, (Portsmouth) 1995, (Leicester, Surrey) 1997, (Queen's Coll, Belfast) 1998, (Exeter, Southampton) 2000; Hon D LITT (Warwick) 1993, (Loughborough) 1995, (Salford) 1999; Hon LL D (Dundee) 1996; Hon D UNIV (Essex, Durham) 1998; numerous prizes including Shell/LSO Music Gold Medal 1984, Queen's Commendation Prize at RAM 1985, Munster Trust Scholarship 1986, Grammy Award 1988, Scotswoman of the Decade 1990, Charles Heidsieck Soloist of the Year, Royal Philharmonic Soc 1991, Personality of the Year, Int Classical Music Awards 1993, Young Deaf Achievers Special Award 1993, Best studio percussionist, Rhythm Magazine 1998, 2000. *Recordings include:* Rebounds, Light in Darkness, Dancin', Rhythm Song, Veni, Veni, Emmanuel, Wind in the Bamboo Grove, Drumming, Her Greatest Hits, The Music of Joseph Schwantner, Sonata for Two Pianos and Percussion–Bela Bartok, Last Night of the Proms – 100th Season, Street Songs, Reflected in Brass, Shadow Behind the Iron Sun, African Sunrise – Manhattan Rave; *Publication:* Good Vibrations (autobiog) 1990, Great Journeys of the World, Beat It! *Leisure interests:* reading, walking, cycling, martial arts, antiques, collecting musical instruments. *Address:* POB 6, Sawtry, Huntingdon, Cambs PE17 5WE, UK (Office). *Telephone:* (1480) 891772; *Fax:* (1480) 893910 (Office); *E-mail:* chris@evelyn.co.uk (Office); *Internet:* www.evelyn.co.uk.

GLESS, Sharon; American actress; b 31 May 1943, Los Angeles, CA; m Barney Rosenzweig. *Education:* Gonzaga Univ. *Career:* Numerous appearances and starring roles in TV series and films; seven Emmy nominations, seven Golden Globe nominations; Hollywood Women in Radio and TV Genii Award; Ms Magazine Woman of the Year Award; Gideon Media Award 1992; Distinguished Artist Award 1992. *TV appearances include:* Faraday and Company 1973, Switch! 1975–78, The Immigrants 1978, The Last Convertible 1979, Turnabout 1979, House Calls 1981–82, Cagney and Lacey (Golden Globe Award 1985, Emmy Awards for Outstanding Lead Actress in a Drama Series 1986, 1987) 1982–88, The Trials of Rosie O'Neill (Golden Globe Award 1990) 1990–92; *TV films include:* All My Daughters 1972, My Darling Daughters' Anniversary 1973, Richie Brockelman: The Missing 24th Hour 1976, The Islander 1978, Crash 1978, Hardhat and Legs 1980, The Miracle of Kathy Miller 1981, Letting Go 1985, The Outside Woman 1989, Honor Thy Mother 1992, Separated by Murder 1994, Cagney and Lacey: The Return 1994; *Film:* The Star Chamber 1983; *Play:* Watch on the Rhine 1989. *Address:* William Morris Agency, 151 El Camino Drive, Beverly Hills, CA 90212, USA.

GLOAG, Ann Heron; British business executive; b 10 Dec 1942; d of Iain and Catherine Souter; m 1st Robin Gloag 1965; one s (deceased) one d; m 2nd David McCleary 1990. *Education:* Perth High School. *Career:* Trainee Nurse Bridge of Earn Hosp, Perth 1960–65; Ward Sister Devonshire Royal Hosp, Buxton 1965–69, Theatre Sister 1969–80; Co-Founder Stagecoach Ltd (fmrly Stagecoach Express Services) 1980–83, Co-Dir 1983–86, Exec Dir Stagecoach Holdings PLC 1986–2000 (Man Dir 1986–94), operater South-West Trains, holdings in New Zealand, Portugal, Africa and Sweden; Scottish Marketing Woman of the Year,

Scottish Univs 1989; Veuve Clicquot and Inst of Dirs Businesswoman of the Year 1989–90. *Leisure interests:* family, travel, supporting charities. *Address:* Stagecoach Holdings PLC, 10 Dunkeld Rd, Perth PH1 5TW, UK. *Telephone:* (1738) 442111.

GLOSTER, Elizabeth, BA, QC; British judge; b 5 June 1949; d of Peter and Betty (née Read) Gloster; m Stanley Eric Brodie 1973; one s one d. *Education:* Roedean School (Brighton) and Girton Coll (Cambridge). *Career:* Called to the Bar, Inner Temple (London) 1971, QC 1989, Bencher 1992; Judge Courts of Appeal (Jersey and Guernsey) 1993–, Recorder 1995–; mem Panel of Council who appear for Dept of Trade and Industry; mem Bd (non-exec) Civil Aviation Authority 1992–93. *Address:* 1 Essex Court, Temple, London EC4Y 9AR, UK. *Telephone:* (20) 7583-2000; *Fax:* (20) 7583-0118.

GLOVER, Jane Alison, MA, D PHIL, FRCM; British conductor; b 13 May 1949; d of Robert Finlay Glover and the late Jean Muir. *Education:* Monmouth School for Girls and St Hugh's Coll (Oxford). *Career:* Jr Research Fellow St Hugh's Coll, Oxford 1973–75, Lecturer in Music 1976–84, Sr Research Fellow 1982–84; Lecturer St Anne's Coll, Oxford 1976–80, Pembroke Coll 1979–84; mem Oxford Univ Faculty of Music 1979–; conducting debut Wexford Festival (Ireland) 1975; operas and concerts for BBC, Glyndebourne, Royal Opera House, Covent Garden, English Nat Opera, London Symphony Orchestra, London and Royal Philharmonic Orchestras, Philharmonia, Royal Scottish Orchestra, English Chamber Orchestra, BBC Welsh Symphony Orchestra, Bournemouth Sinfonietta; Prin Conductor London Choral Soc 1983–2000, Huddersfield Choral Soc 1989–96; Artistic Dir London Mozart Players 1984–91, Conductor until 1992; Gov RAM 1985–90, BBC 1990–95; mem BBC Cen Music Advisory Cttee 1981–85, Music Advisory Cttee Arts Council 1986–88; Hon D MUS (Exeter) 1986, (CNAA) 1991, (London) 1992, (City) 1995, (Glasgow) 1996; Hon D LITT (Loughborough) 1988, (Bradford) 1992; Dr hc (Open Univ) 1988, (Brunel) 1997. *TV appearances include:* Orchestra 1983, Mozart 1985; *Radio work includes:* Opera House 1995, Musical Dynasties 2000; *Publications:* Cavalli 1978; contribs to The New Monteverdi Companion 1986, Monteverdi 'Orfeo' Handbook 1986; articles in numerous journals. *Leisure interest:* The Times crossword puzzle and theatre. *Address:* c/o Askonas Holt Ltd, Lonsdale Chambers, 27 Chancery Lane, London WC2A 1PF, UK (Office). *Telephone:* (20) 7400-1700.

GLUBE, Hon Constance R., BA, LL B; Canadian judge; b 23 Nov 1931, Ottawa, ON; d of Samuel and Pearl Lepofsky; m Richard H. Glube 1952; three s one d. *Education:* Glebe Coll Inst (Ottawa), McGill Univ (Montréal, PQ) and Dalhousie Univ (Halifax, NS). *Career:* Called to Bar, NS 1956; Solicitor Kitz & Matheson, Halifax, NS 1964–66; Partner Fitzgerald & Glube 1966–68; Solicitor Legal Dept, City of Halifax 1969–74; mem Court House Comm 1972–74; QC 1974–; City Man, Halifax 1974–77; Metro Centre Bd 1975–77; Judge Trial Div Supreme Court of Nova Scotia 1977, Chief Justice 1982–98; Chief Justice Court of Appeal and Chief Justice of Nova Scotia 1998–; mem Bd of Dirs Canadian Judges' Conf 1979, 2nd Vice-Chair 1980–82; mem Exec and Bd Assn of Municipal Admins 1975–77, Bd of Dirs Canadian Inst for the Admin of Justice 1979–83, Bd Canadian Judicial Council 1982–, Exec 1985–88; mem Int City Mans' Assn, Canadian Bar Assn; Hon LL D (Dalhousie) 1983, (St Mary's Univ, Halifax) 1999; Hon D HUM LITT (Mount St Vincent Univ, Halifax) 1998; City of Halifax Award of Merit 1977; Frances Fish Women Lawyers Award 1997. *Leisure interests:* gardening, swimming. *Address:* Law Courts, 1815 Upper Water St, Halifax, NS B3J 3C8, Canada (Office); 5920 Inglewood Drive, Halifax, NS B3H 1B1, Canada (Home).

GLÜCK, Louise Elisabeth; American poet; b 22 April 1943, New York; d of Daniel and Beatrice (née Grosby) Glück; m 1st Charles Hertz (divorced); one s; m 2nd John Dranow 1977. *Education:* Sarah Lawrence Coll (Bronxville, NY) and Columbia Univ (NY). *Career:* Visiting Poet Goddard Coll, VT, Univs of N Carolina, Virginia and Iowa; Elliston Prof Univ of Cincinnati, OH 1978; Holloway Lecturer Univ of California at Berkeley 1982; Visiting Prof Univ of California at Davis 1983; Scott Prof of Poetry Williams Coll, MA 1983; Regents Prof of Poetry Univ of California at Los Angeles 1985–88; Baccalaureate Speaker Williams Coll 1993; Poet Laureate of Vermont 1994; visiting mem facutly Harvard Univ, MA 1995; Rockefeller Foundation Grant, Nat Educ Asscn 1969–70, 1979–80, 1988–89; Guggenheim Founda-

tion Grant 1975–76, 1987–88; American Acad and Inst of Arts and Letters Literary Award 1981; Nat Book Critics' Circle Award for poetry 1985; Poetry Soc of America Melville Cane Award 1986; Wellesley Coll Sara Teasdale Memorial Prize; Bobbitt Natil Prize, Library of Congress 1992; William Carlos Williams Award 1993. *Publications:* Firstborn 1968, The House on Marshland 1975, Descending Figure 1980, The Triumph of Achilles 1985, Ararat 1990, The Wild Iris (Pulitzer Prize for Poetry) 1993, Proofs and Theories (collected essays) 1994.

GLUCKMAN, Eliane; French haematologist; b 25 Feb 1940, Paris; m 1963; one s. *Education:* Univ of Paris. *Career:* Head of Bone Marrow Transplant Unit, Hôpital Saint-Louis, Paris 1973–, Prof of Medicine 1975–; Chevalier de la Légion d'Honneur; Officier de l'Ordre Nat du Mérite; approx 400 contribs to int scientific journals. *Address:* Hôpital Saint-Louis, 1 ave Claude Vellefaux, 75475 Paris, France (Office); 70 blvd du Port Royal, 75005 Paris, France (Home). *Telephone:* (1) 42-49-96-44; *Fax:* (1) 42-49-96-34.

GLUSHENKO, Yevgeniya Konstatinovna; Russian actress; b 4 Sept 1952; m Aleksandr Kalyagin. *Education:* Shchepkin Theatre School. *Career:* Worked with Maly Theatre 1974–. *Films include:* Unfinished Play for Mechanical Piano 1977, Profile and Front-View 1979, Oblomov 1980, First-Time Married 1980, In Love of One's Own Accord (Moscow and West Berlin Film Festival Prizes 1983) 1982, Zina Zinulya 1985; *Plays include:* Misfortune from Sense 1975, King Lear 1979, The Savage 1990, Infanticide 1991, The Hot Heart 1992, A Criminal Mother or the Second Tartuffe 1993, The Feast of Victors 1995, Queen Margo 1996. *Address:* 1905 Goda str 3, Apt 91, 123100 Moscow, Russian Federation. *Telephone:* (095) 205-26-54.

GODDARD, Mel, BA; British insurance consultant; b 10 Feb 1958, Bonn; d of Sir John and Lady Barnes; m Christopher Goddard 1989; one s one d. *Education:* Wycombe Abbey School (Bucks) and Univ of Manchester. *Career:* At H. Clarkson Insurance Brokers Ltd 1978–82, Fenchurch Group Ltd 1982–86, Sterling Underwriting Agency Ltd, Lloyd's of London 1986–92, QBE Int Insurance Ltd 1993–96; Active Underwriter Syndicate 1223, Lloyd's of London 1997–2000; Dir QBE Underwriting Agency Ltd; Assoc Chartered Insurance Inst (ACII); Ind Insurance Consultant and Expert Witness 2000–; mem Panel of Arbitrators ARIAS 2000–. *Leisure interests:* Arabian horses, piano, racing. *Address:* Hunters Farm, Blind Lane, Newick, E Sussex, UK. *Telephone:* (1825) 724325; *Fax:* (1825) 724325; *E-mail:* goddardmel@ aol.com.

GODDARD, Trisha; British broadcaster; b 1958, Hackney, London; m 1st (husband deceased); m 2nd; two c; m 3rd Peter Gianfrancesco. *Career:* Fmr air hostess and travel journalist; Sr Current Affairs Broadcaster, ABC (Australia) until 1999; Presenter, early morning TV show Trisha (Anglia TV) 1999–. *Address:* c/o Anglia TV, Anglia House, Norwich, NR1 3JG, UK.

GODIN, Raymonde Louise, BFA; French (b Canadian) painter; b 23 Dec 1930, Montréal, PQ; d of Erigène and Madeleine (née Paradis) Godin; m Paul Kallos 1957; one s. *Education:* Villa Maria and Concordia Univ (Montréal). *Career:* Art studies in Montréal, New York and Paris 1952–56; one-woman exhibitions include London 1963, Paris 1968–92, Brussels 1980, Montréal 1982–90, Washington, DC 1988, Québec 1989, Avignon 1992, Triennale des Amériques (Maubeuge) 1993, Joigny 1994, Pont de l'Arche 1995; numerous group exhibitions in France, USA, Italy, Spain, Sweden, Canada, etc; works feature in pvt and public collections in France, USA and Canada, including Art Gallery of Toronto, Galerie Nat du Canada (Ottawa), Musée d'Art Contemporain (Montréal), Musée d'Art Moderne de la Ville de Paris, Bibliothèque Nat de Paris; murals commissioned by the state for Hôpital Bichat, Paris 1989; Chevalier des Arts et des Lettres 1989. *Leisure interest:* music. *Address:* 22 rue de Saintonge, 75003 Paris, France.

GODLEY, Georgina, MA; British fashion designer; b 11 April 1955, London; d of Michael and Heather Godley; m Sebastian Conran 1988; two s. *Education:* Putney High School, Thames Valley Grammar School (London), Wimbledon School of Art, Brighton Polytechnic and Chelsea School of Art. *Career:* Designer Browns, London and Paris 1979–80; Partner and Designer Crolla, London 1980–85; Dir and sole Designer Georgina Godley Ltd (own label collections) 1986–; Designer/Co-ordinator Tabletop Habitat 1999, Head of Design Home Accessories, Habitat 2000; mem British Fashion Council Designer Cttee; Visiting Lecturer at various fashion and art colls in UK; work included perm exhibition at Victoria and Albert Museum, London and Bath Costume Museum; ICA Young Contemporaries award 1978. *Address:* 42 Bassett Rd, London W10 6UL, UK (Home). *Telephone:* (20) 7255-2545 (Office); *Fax:* (20) 7460-0299.

GODWIN, Fay S.; British photographer; b 17 Feb 1931, Berlin, Germany; d of Sidney Simmonds and Stella MacLean; m Tony Godwin; two s one step-d. *Education:* many schools all over the world. *Career:* No photographic training; started photography 1966; tour relating to publ of The Oldest Road 1975; commissioned by Nat Trust to photograph properties and sites, Wessex 1982; British Council's overseas tour of Godwin's Photographs 1984; landscape exhibition Serpentine Gallery, London 1985; Land exhibition Yale Center for British Art, USA; Our Forbidden Land exhibition Royal Photographic Soc Gallery and nat tour; retrospective, Barbican, London 2001; joined Network Photographers Picture Agency 1991; teaches at photographic schools and workshops; Pres Ramblers' Asscn 1987–90, Life Vice-Pres 1990–; Bradford Fellowship 1986–87; Fellow Nat Museum of Photography, Bradford 1987; Hon Fellow Royal Photographic Soc 1991, Royal Inst of Scottish Architects 1992; major award from Arts Council of GB 1978. *Publications:* The Oldest Road: An Exploration of the Ridgeway (jtly) 1975, The Oil Rush (jtly) 1976, The Drovers' Roads of Wales (jtly) 1977, Islands (jtly) 1978, Remains of Elmet: A Pennine Sequence (with poems by Ted Hughes) 1979, Romney Marsh and the Royal Military Canal (jtly) 1980, Tess: The Story of a Guide Dog (jtly) 1981, The Whisky Roads of Scotland (jtly) 1982, Bison at Chalk Farm 1982, The Saxon Shore Way from Gravesend to Rye (jtly) 1983, The National Trust Book of Wessex 1985, Land (jtly) 1985, The Secret Forest of Dean 1986, Our Forbidden Land 1990, The Edge of the Land 1995, Glassworks and Secret Lives 1999. *Leisure interests:* walking, photography, reading, painting. *Address:* c/o Faye Godwin Network, 3–4 Kirby St, London E4N 8TS, UK. *Telephone:* (20) 7831-3633.

GODWIN, Gail Kathleen, PH D; American writer; b 18 June 1937, Birmingham, AL; d of Mose Godwin and Kathleen Krahenbuhl; m 1st Douglas Kennedy 1960 (divorced 1961); m 2nd Ian Marshall 1965 (divorced 1966). *Education:* Peace Jr Coll (Raleigh, NC) and Univs of N Carolina and Iowa. *Career:* News reporter Miami Herald 1959–60; reporter, consultant US Travel Service, London 1961–65; Editorial Asst Saturday Evening Post 1966; Fellow Center for Advanced Study, Univ of Illinois, Urbana 1971–72; Lecturer Iowa Writers' Workshop 1972–73, Vassar Coll, NY 1977, Columbia Univ Writing Program 1978, 1981; American specialist US Information Service (USIS) 1976; mem PEN, Authors' Guild, Authors' League, Nat Book Critics' Circle; Guggenheim Fellow 1975–76; various awards and distinctions, including American Acad and Inst of Arts and Letters Literary Award 1981. *Publications include:* Novels: The Perfectionists 1970, Glass People 1972, The Odd Woman 1974, Violet Clay 1978, A Mother and Two Daughters 1982, The Finishing School 1985, A Southern Family 1987, Father Melancholy's Daughter 1991, The Good Husband 1994, Evensong 1998; short stories and librettos. *Address:* POB 946, Woodstock, NY 12498, USA.

GOEVA, Nusha (Tatyana) Vladimirova; Bulgarian artist; b 11 May 1959, Sofia; d of Vladimir Ivanov Goev and Elsa Borisova Goeva. *Education:* Acad of Fine Arts (Sofia). *Career:* Solo exhibitions in Old Town Plovdiv 1989, Dobrich 1990, Sapporo, Japan 1991, Krefeld, Germany 1992, Art Clasic Gallery, Plovdiv 1992, Arena Gallery, Sofia 1993, 1996, GEA, Bochum, Germany 1994, Seasons Gallery, Sofia 1995; group exhibitions in Moscow 1985, Paris 1985, Athens 1987, Kuwait 1988, Krefeld, Germany 1991, Sofia 1992, Bulgaria 1996; works in perm collections including Nat Art Gallery, Sofia, Germany, Greece and Netherlands; Hon Consul, Hamburg, Germany; won prizes at VIIIth Nat Exhibition of Young Artists, Sofia 1989, Int Biennial for Humour and Satire, Gabrovo 1991. *Leisure interests:* reading, cinema, old photographs and letters. *Address:* 1113 Sofia, Elemag Str 15, Bl 307, Apt 80, Bulgaria. *Telephone:* (2) 65-98-26.

GOGOBERIDZE, Lana Levanovna, D LITT; Georgian film director and politician; b 13 Oct 1928, Tbilisi; d of Levan and Ninio Gogoberidze; m Lado Aleksi-Meskhishvili 1958 (died 1978); two d.

Education: Tbilisi State Univ and State Univ of Cinematography (VGIK) (Moscow). *Career:* Mem CPSU 1965–89; Head of a Dir's Studio at Rustaveli Theatre School, Tbilisi 1975–; Dir Kartuli Filmi (Georgian Film) 1988–; Chair Liberal Democratic Faction 1992–95; mem Georgian Parl 1994–, Leader of Majority 1995–, Head, Georgia–France Friendship Group 1997–; mem Citizens' Union party 1997–; Head, Perm Nat Del to Council of Europe 1997–; Pres Int Asscn of Women Film-Makers; mem Bd of Union of Georgian Film-Makers; People's Artist of Georgian SSR 1979; Venice Film Festival Prize 1979, USSR State Prize 1980, Tokyo Film Festival Prize (Best Dir) 1986, Venice Film Festival Prize 1992, Berlin Film Festival Prize 1993; Culture Diploma of Honor, American Biographical Inst 1995; Chevalier de l'Ordre Nat du Mérite (France) 1997. *Films include:* Under the Same Sky 1961, I See the Sun 1965, Boundaries 1970, When the Almond Blossomed 1973, Interviews on Personal Problems 1979, A Day Longer than Night 1985, Turnover 1986, Waltz on the Pechora River 1986 (five prizes); Documentaries: Gelathi 1957, Tbilisi—1500 1958, Letters to the Children 1981; *Publications:* Walt Whitman 1955, Walt Whitman: Leaves of Grass (trans) 1956, Rabindranath Tagore (trans) 1957, Foreign Poetry in Georgian (trans) 1995. *Leisure interests:* tennis, skiing, painting. *Address:* Parliament of Georgia, Rustaveli Ave 8, Tbilisi, Georgia (Office); Kazbegi Str 17, Apt 26, Tbilisi, Georgia (Home). *Telephone:* (32) 93-19-92 (Office); (32) 22-76-79 (Home); *Fax:* (32) 99-58-53 (Office).

GOLANI, Rivka; Canadian (b Israeli) viola player and painter; b 22 March 1946, Tel Aviv, Israel; d of Jacob Golani and Lisa Gulnik; m Jeremy Fox 1993; one s. *Education:* Univ of Tel Aviv. *Career:* Studied with Oedon Partos; Prof of Viola Univ of Toronto (ON, Canada) 1974–; has performed with major orchestras including Boston Symphony (USA), Royal Concertbouw Orchestra, Israel Philharmonic, ORF Radio Orchestra (Vienna), Tokyo Metropolitan Orchestra (Japan), Royal Philharmonic Orchestra, BBC Symphony and Philharmonic, Hallé and other British orchestras, Bern Symphony and Radio Symphony Orchestra (Berlin, Germany); has had more than 200 works written for her by composers including Holloway, Hummel, Fontajn, Colgras, Vagn Holmboe, Yuasa, Turner and Holliger; has presented multi-media performances for viola and orchestra; exhibitions of paintings in Germany, Israel, USA and UK; Grand Prix du Disque 1985. *Recordings include:* Elgar Cello Concerto (arranged by Lionel Tertis), Phantasy for viola and orchestra, Rhapsody Concerto, Bartok Concerto, T. Serly Viola Concerto, T. Serly Rhapsody, Malcolm Arnold Concerto, Brahms Viola Sonatas op 120, Edmund Rubbra Viola Concerto, Colgrass Chaconne, Viola Nouveau, Prouesse; *Publication:* Birds of Another Feather (book of drawings). *Leisure interest:* painting. *Address:* c/o Margaret Barkman, 46 Yarrow Rd, Toronto, ON M6M 4E3, Canada (Office); 54 Crofton Rd, London SE5 8NB, UK; POB 22044, Tel Aviv 61220, Israel. *E-mail:* foxjones@inforamp.net.

GOLDBERG, Whoopi; American actress; b (Caryn Johnson) 13 Nov 1955; d of Robert Johnson and Emma Harris; one d; m 2nd Dave Claessen 1986 (divorced 1988); one d; m 3rd Lyle Trachtenberg 1994 (divorced 1995). *Career:* First stage appearance aged eight Hudson Guild Theater, New York; worked with Helena Rubinstein Children's Theater; Co-Founder San Diego Repertory Theater, appeared in Mother Courage, Getting Out; mem Blake St Hawkeyes Theater, San Francisco, CA; toured USA in The Spook Show; co-writer and star Moms (solo show); Broadway debut Lyceum Theater 1984; presented own TV show 1992–93; Grammy Award for Best Comedy Album 1985; acting award, Nat Asscn for the Advancement of Colored People (NAACP) 1993; Hans Christian Andersen Award for Outstanding Achievement by a Dyslexic; Mark Twain Prize for Humor, Kennedy Center of Arts 2001. *Films:* The Color Purple (Acad Award Nomination for Best Actress, NAACP Image Award, Golden Globe Award, Hollywood Foreign Press Asscn Award), Jumpin' Jack Flash, Burglar, The Telephone, Fatal Beauty, Ghost 1990, Sarafina 1992, Sister Act 1992, Soap Dish, Made in America 1992, Alice 1993, Sister Act II 1993, Corrina Corrina 1993, Boys on the Side 1994, Star Trek Generation 5, Moonlight and Valentino, Bogus 1996, Eddie, The Celluloid Closet, The Associate 1996, The Ghost of Mississippi 1996, How Stella Got Her Groove Back 1998, Deep End of the Ocean 1999, Jackie's Back! 1999, Girl Interrupted 1999; *TV appearances include:* Moonlighting (Guest Appearances, Emmy nomination 1985), Baghdad Café.

GOLDING, Baroness (Life Peer), cr 2001, of Newcastle-under-Lyme in the County of Staffordshire, **Llinos (Llin) Golding;** British politician; b 21 March 1933; d of Ness and Elina Victoria Edwards; m 1st John Roland Lewis 1957; two d one s; m 2nd John Golding 1980. *Education:* Caerphilly Girls' Grammar School and Cardiff Royal Infirmary School of Radiography. *Career:* Radiographer; Asst to John Golding, MP 1972–86; MP (Lab) for Newcastle under Lyme 1986, Opposition Whip for W Midlands, Women's Affairs, Energy and Tourism 1987–92, Spokesperson on Social Security 1992–95, on Children and Family 1993–95, on Agric, Fisheries and Food 1995–97, Chair All-Party Parl Group on Children, Jt Chair All Party Parl Group on the Homeless 1989–99, mem All-Party Parl Group on Drugs Misuse until 1998, Treas All-Party Parl Group on Racing and Bloodstock; Match Sec Lords and Commons Fly Fishing Club; Sec Newcastle Trades Council 1976–87; mem BBC Advisory Council, N Staffs District Health Authority 1983–87; mem Soc of Radiographers. *Address:* House of Lords, London SW1A 0PW, UK (Office); 6 Lancaster Ave, Newcastle-under-Lyme, Staffs ST5 1DR, UK (Home). *Telephone:* (20) 7219-3000 (Office); (1782) 636200.

GOLDRING, Mary, OBE, BA; British economist and broadcaster. *Education:* Our Lady's Priory (Sussex) and Lady Margaret Hall (Oxford). *Career:* Air and Science Correspondent, The Economist 1949–74, Business Ed 1966–74; economist and broadcaster 1974–; mem selection cttee Harkness Fellowships 1980–86; Trustee Science Museum 1987–97; delivered Fawley Foundation Lecture 1992; Hon D LITT (Univ of W of England) 1994; Blue Circle Award for Industrial Journalism 1979; Outstanding Personal Contrib to Radio, Broadcasting Press Guild 1986; Harold Wincott Award for Broadcasting 1991; Industrial Journalist of the Year, Industrial Soc and BP 1991. *TV and radio programmes includes:* Analysis (BBC—Sony Radio Award for Best Current Affairs Programme 1985) 1977–87, Answering Back (interviews, Channel 4) 1989–91, Goldring Audit (Channel 4) 1992, 1993, 1994, 1995; *Publication:* Economics of Atomic Energy 1957. *Leisure interest:* landscaping. *Address:* 37 Sloane Ave, London SW3 3JB, UK.

GOLEMI (KAZANXHI), Rushen, MD; Albanian surgeon and politician; b 16 July 1935, Durrës; d of Mahmud Golemi and Meleg Xejlani; m Alfred Kazanxhi 1959; two d one s. *Education:* Inst of Medical Studies (Tirana). *Career:* First female surgeon in Albania 1957; Surgeon, Tirana 1957–91, Peshkopi Dist 1959; nominated as univ teacher but appointment vetoed by govt 1974; Chief Surgeon, Gen Surgery Ward, Tirana Univ 1975–91; has performed over 10,000 operations, often using new operative methods; Deputy to People's Ass (Democratic Party of Albania – DPA) 1991–; author over 30 scientific surveys and medical textbooks; Good Service to the People Award 1981; 1st Class Professional Award 1990. *Publications include:* Medical textbook: Desimurgia; *Educational films:* Surgical Treatment of Mithral Sthenosis by the Close Method, Surgical Treatment of the Thyroid Gland. *Leisure interests:* Albanian and foreign literature, family. *Address:* Rruga Zhan D'Arc, Pallatet e Lanës, Shkalla 4, Apt 24, Tirana, Albania. *Telephone:* (42) 24226; (42) 27158.

GOLLANCZ, Livia Ruth, ARCM; British musician and publishing executive; b 25 May 1920; d of Victor Gollancz and Ruth Lowy. *Education:* St Paul's Girls' School and Royal Coll of Music (London). *Career:* French horn player London Symphony Orchestra 1940–43, Hallé Orchestra 1943–45, Scottish Orchestra 1945–46, BBC Scottish Orchestra 1946–47, Royal Opera House, Covent Garden, London 1947, Sadler's Wells, London 1950–53; Editorial Asst, Typographer Victor Gollancz Ltd, Publrs, London 1953, Dir 1954–90, Governing Dir, Jt Man Dir 1965–85, Chair 1983–89, Consultant 1990–93. *Publication:* Victor Gollancz, Reminiscences of Affection (ed) 1968. *Leisure interests:* gardening, hill-walking, classical music. *Address:* 26 Cholmeley Crescent, London N6 5HA, UK.

GOMBOS, Katalin; Hungarian actress; b 12 Feb 1929, Hódmezővásárhely; d of Pál and Etelka (née Voska) Gombos; m Imre Sinkovits 1951; one s one d. *Education:* Hungarian Acad of Dramatic and Cinematic Art. *Career:* Acting debut at age 16; mem Madách Theatre Co 1958–; tours to USA, Canada, Switzerland, Germany, Austria, Czech Republic, fmr USSR and Yugoslavia; Film Festivals of Mar del Plata, Warsaw, Moscow, Frunze; Medal of Merited Artist of Hungarian Repub 1985. *Plays include:* The Fellow of the Devil, The Marriage of

John Tanner, Georges Dandin, The Marriage of Figaro, As You Like It, A Midsummer Night's Dream, Comedy of Errors, Lorenzaccio; *TV and Film appearances include:* At Midnight 1957, Repulsion 1965, The Night of Secrets 1966, The Widow and The Captain 1967, Kira Georgievna 1969, Alfa, Romeo and Julia 1968, Me, Ferenc Prenn (series) 1969, The Teacher of the Underworld 1969, Men Recount 1972, The Ballad of the Fire 1972, Böszi and The Others, Answer (series) 1974, Galilei 1977, The Sipsirica (series) 1979, Pygmalion 1982, Caviar and Lentil 1984, János Apaczai Csere 1986, Bunker 1987, Actors Pair 1988. *Leisure interest:* dubbing films. *Address:* 1052 Budapest V, Petőfi tér 3, Vlem 16, Hungary. *Telephone:* (1) 118-3940.

GOMEZ, Geneviève Hélène; French business executive; b 13 April 1943, Paris; d of Francis and Simone Gomez; m Philippe Lagayette (divorced). *Education:* Lycée Stéphane Gsell (Oran, Algeria), Inst d'Etudes Politiques de Paris and Inst de la Construction et de l'Urbanisme. *Career:* Rep Banque Indosuez 1978–80, Sub-Dir 1980–82, Sec-Gen 1983–86, Dir 1987–90, Adviser on real estate 1990–; Pres, Dir-Gen SATIS real estate co 1987–; Pres, Dir-Gen Foncière des Champs-Elysées land promotion co 1991–93; Exec Dir Elf Aquitaine 1993–96; Pres SOFIPA and CPIH (subsidiaries of Elf-Gabon) 1993; Admin, Dir-Gen SOGERAP 1993–95, Pres, Dir-Gen 1995; Dir Soc Marseillaise de Crédit (SMC) 1997–. *Leisure interests:* golf, hunting. *Address:* SMC, 75 rue Paradis, 13006 Marseille, France; 139 blvd Malesherbes, 7507 Paris, France (Home).

GOMEZ, Jill, FRAM; British opera and concert singer; b 21 Sept 1942, New Amsterdam, British Guiana (now Guyana). *Education:* Royal Acad of Music and Guildhall School of Music. *Career:* Operatic debut Glyndebourne Festival Opera 1969; performed with The Royal Opera, Kent Opera and English, Scottish and Welsh Nat Operas; appearances include Covent Garden (London), Aldeburgh (UK), Wexford (Ireland), Bordeaux (France), Geneva (Switzerland), Frankfurt (Germany); recitals in France, Austria, Belgium, Germany, Netherlands, Scandinavia, Switzerland, Italy, Spain, USA; Festival appearances include Aix-en-Provence, Spoleto, Bergen, Versailles, Flanders, Netherlands, Prague, Edinburgh, Ludwigsburg, Zurich, Lyon and BBC Promenade concerts; masterclasses at Pears-Britten School, Aldeburgh, Trinity Coll of Music, London, Dartington Summer Festival, Meridian TV. *Operas and other performances include:* The Rake's Progress, The Marriage of Figaro, Elegy for Young Lovers, Gianni Schicchi, The Knot Garden, Voice of Ariadne 1974, Thaïs 1974, The Midsummer Marriage 1976, Miss Julie (radio) 1977, Eugene Onegin 1977, Don Giovanni 1978, 1985, 1988, Rigoletto 1979, Maddalena 1979, Così fan tutte 1979, Eighth Book of Madrigals 1979, La Traviata 1979, Lucio Silla 1981, Giulio Cesare 1981, The Turn of the Screw 1981, 1984, Benvenuto Cellini 1982, Les Pêcheurs de Perles 1982–83, Goyescas 1988, Midsummer Night's Dream 1990, Powder Her Face 1995; *Recordings include:* Vespro della Beata Vergine 1610 (Monteverdi), Acis and Galatea (Handel), The Knot Garden (Tippett), three recital discs of French, Spanish and Mozart songs, Quatre Chansons Françaises (Britten), Trois Poèmes de Mallarmé (Ravel), Chants d'Auvergne (Canteloube), Les Illuminations (Britten), Bachianas Brasileiras No 5 (Villa Lobos), Cabaret Classics with John Constable, Knoxville-Summer of 1915 (Barber), South of the Border (Down Mexico Way...), Britten's Blues (Britten and Cole Porter), Cantiga–The Song of Inês de Castro (David Matthews), Seven Early Songs (Mahler), A Spanish Songbook (jtly), Powder Her Face, Miss Julie. *Address:* 16 Milton Park, London N6 5QA, UK. *Telephone:* (20) 8348-4193.

GOMEZ DE ENTERRIA, Carmen, D EN D; Spanish European Union official; b 25 April 1939, Viana do Bolo; m Denis Rodriguez Sagaria 1978. *Education:* Univ of Toulouse (France) and Univ Autònoma de Barcelona. *Career:* Temp Assoc Prof of Public Int Law Univ Autònoma de Barcelona 1971–79; Legal Adviser Ministry for Relations with the EC, Madrid 1979–87; Dir-Gen Trans and Gen Services, Directorate-Gen VII, Secr-Gen of EP 1987; Encomienda de Isabel la Católica Reina de España 1985. *Address:* c/o European Parliament, Centre Européen, Plateau du Kirchberg, BP 1601, L-2929, Luxembourg; 10 rue d'Amsterdam, L-1126, Luxembourg.

GONG LI; Chinese actress; m Ooi Hoe-Seong 1996. *Films include:* Red Sorghum 1987, Raise the Red Lantern, Farewell My Concubine, To Live, Shanghai Triad, Temptress Moon.

GONG PUSHENG, MA; Chinese party official and diplomatist (retd); b 6 Sept 1913, Shanghai; m Chang Hanfu (deceased); two d. *Education:* Yenching Univ and Columbia Univ (USA). *Career:* Del CPPCC 1st Nat Congress 1949; mem 1st–4th Exec Cttees, All China Women's Fed 1949–84; Deputy Dir Dept of Int Orgs and Confs, Ministry of Foreign Affairs 1949–58, Dir 1963–67; Vice-Pres Red Cross Soc of China 1979–85, China UN Asscn 1985–; Amb to Ireland 1980–83; mem Nat Cttee CPPCC 1983–93, mem Foreign Affairs Cttee 1988–93; mem Exec Cttee Council of Chinese People's Inst of Foreign Affairs 1985–; Prof Coll of Foreign Affairs 1985–; Hon Pres Beijing Soc for Comparative Int Studies 1991–; Adviser China Soc for People's Friendship Studies 1994; Vice-Chair Bd Yenching Grad Inst 1995–. *Address:* c/o Ministry of Foreign Affairs, Chaoyangmennei St, Dongsi, Beijing, People's Republic of China. *Telephone:* (1) 65120585; *Fax:* (1) 65131831.

GONZÁLEZ ÁLVAREZ, Laura; Spanish politician; b 9 July 1941, Avilés, Asturias. *Career:* Mem Avilés City Council 1979; mem Regional Govt of Austurias 1979; mem IU Regional Exec in Asturias, IU Nat Exec; Pres Parl Austurias 1991; MEP (GUE, IU), mem Cttee on Petitions, on the Environment, Public Health and Consumer Policy, Del for Relations with the Countries of Cen America and Mexico; Vice-Chair GUE/Nordic Green Left Group 1994; mem Worker's Comms in Healthcare, numerous NGO's in the fields of women's rights, solidarity, help for drug addicts. *Address:* European Parliament, rue Wiertz, 1047 Brussels, Belgium. *Telephone:* (2) 284-21-11; *Fax:* (2) 230-69-43.

GONZÁLEZ DE LA ROCHA, Mercedes, PH D; Mexican sociologist; b 19 Oct 1954, México; d of Alberto González Salas and Gisella de la Rocha y de la Rocha; m Agustín Escobar Latapí 1978; one s one d. *Education:* Univ Iberoamericana (México) and Univ of Manchester (UK). *Career:* Visiting Scholar Univ of Texas, Austin; Researcher Centro de Investigaciones y Estudios Superiores en Antropología Social, Mexico; Visiting Tinker Prof Inst of Latin American and Iberian Studies, School of Int and Public Affairs, Columbia Univ (NY) 1998; numerous papers and articles on sociology in professional books and journals. *Leisure interests:* swimming, walking, reading. *Address:* c/o SIPA, Columbia University, Morningside Heights, New York, NY 10027, USA; Ciésas Occidente, Amado Nervo 201, Col Ladrón de Guevara, Guadalajara, Jalisco, Mexico. *Telephone:* (36) 16-54-08 (Mexico).

GONZÁLEZ MARTÍNEZ, Elda Evangelina, D HIST; Spanish historical researcher; b 2 July 1949, Buenos Aires, Argentina; d of Daniel González and Evangelina Martínez; m Fernando Giobellina 1985; one d. *Education:* Univ of Buenos Aires, Univ of Uppsala (Sweden) and Univ Complutense de Madrid. *Career:* Researcher Consejo Superior de Investigaciones Científicas (CSIC), Madrid 1990–. *Publications:* Spirits from the Margin 1990, Brasil: café e inmigración, Los españoles en São Paulo 1990, A marginália sagrada 1991. *Address:* CSIC, Centro de Estudios Históricos, Departamento de Historia de América, Duque de Medinacelli 6, 28014 Madrid, Spain (Office); Calle Prado 22, 2 interior, 28004 Madrid, Spain (Home). *Telephone:* (1) 5856029; *Fax:* (1) 5856197.

GONZALEZ QUEVEDO, Ofelia Maria, MA; Cuban ballet dancer; b 15 Feb 1953, Camaguey; d of Oscar Gonzalez Garcia and Ofelia Quevedo Estrada; m Pablo Moret Arechavaleta 1974; one s. *Education:* Nat School of Arts (Havana) and Higher Inst of Arts (Havana). *Career:* Debut with Nat Ballet of Cuba 1968, Soloist 1972, First Soloist 1976, Prin Dancer 1978, Prima Ballerina 1986–; tours of Europe, Asia, and N, Cen and S America with Nat Ballet of Cuba 1968–; Guest Artist Bellas Artes Ballet, Mexico, AMADE Gala, Spain, ATER, Italy, Colombian Inst of Classical Ballet; Special Mention, Fifth Int Ballet Competition, Varna, Bulgaria 1970; participant Second Int Ballet Competition, Moscow 1978; Medallist, Int Gala Performance, Teatro La Zarzuela, Madrid 1974. *Films:* Un retablo para Romeo y Julieta 1970, Edipo Rey 1971. *Address:* Santa Catalina 661, Apt 12, e/ Goss y La Sola, Havana, Cuba. *Telephone:* (7) 408030.

GOOD, Mary Lowe, MS, PH D; American chemist, business executive and civil servant; b 29 June 1931, Grapevine, TX; d of John Willace and Winnie Mercer Lowe; m Bill Jewel Good 1952; two s. *Education:* Arkansas State Teachers' Coll, Univ of Central Arkansas (Conway) and Univ of Arkansas (Fayetteville). *Career:* Lecturer Louisiana State Univ, Baton Rouge 1954–56, Asst Prof 1956–58, Boyd Prof of Materials Science, Div of Eng Research 1979–80, Assoc Prof Louisiana State Univ, New Orleans 1958–63, Prof 1963–80; Vice-Pres, Dir of Research UOP Inc, Des Plaines, IL 1980–84; Pres, Dir of Research Signal Research Center Inc, Des Plaines 1985–86; Pres Engineered Materials Research Div, Allied Signal Inc, Des Plaines 1986–88; Sr Vice-Pres Tech Allied Signal Inc, Morristown, NJ 1988–93; Under-Sec of Commerce for Tech, Dept of Commerce, Washington, DC 1993–97; Managing mem Venture Capital Investors LLC 1997–; mem Nat Science Bd 1980–91, Vice-Chair 1984, Chair 1988–90; mem American Chemical Soc, Pres 1987; numerous hon doctorates including Dr hc (Arkansas) 1979, (Duke) 1987, (Northeastern, IL) 1989, (Manhattan Coll, Coll of William and Mary, Polytech Univ) 1992; Agnes Faye Morgan Research Award 1969; Scientist of the Year Award, Industrial Research and Devt magazine 1982; Delmer S. Fahrney Medal, Franklin Inst 1988; Medallist Award, Industrial Research Inst 1991; AAAS Award 1992; Distinguished Public Service Award, Nat Science Foundation 1992; Albert Fox Demers Medal, Rensselaer Polytech Inst 1992; Roe Award, American Soc of Mechanical Engineers 1993. *Publications:* Biotechnology and Materials Science: Chemistry for the Future, Integrated Laboratory Sequence (Vol 3); approx 100 articles for tech journals. *Leisure interests:* Scottish history, holidays with grandchildren. *Address:* Venture Capital Investors LLC, 400 W Capitol Ave, Ste 1845, Little Rock, AR 72212, USA (Office); 13824 Rivercrest Drive, Little Rock, AR 72201, USA (Home).

GOODALL, Jane, CBE, PH D; British primatologist and environmentalist; b 3 April 1934, London; d of Mortimer Herbert and Vanne Morris-Goodall (née Joseph); m Hugo van Lawick 1964 (divorced 1974); one s; m 2nd M. Derek Bryceson 1975 (died 1980). *Education:* Uplands School and Univ of Cambridge. *Career:* Asst Ed Documentary Film Studio; Asst Sec to Louis Leakey, worked in Olduvai Gorge, Gombe Stream Game Reserve (now Gombe Nat Park), camp became Gombe Stream Research Centre 1964; Scientific Dir Gombe Wildlife Research Inst 1967–; Founder Cttee for Conservation and Care of Chimpanzees 1986; Hon Visiting Prof in Zoology, Dar es Salaam Univ 1973–; A. D. White Prof-at-Large Cornell Univ 1996–; Visiting Lecturer numerous univs including Yale Univ (USA); speaker on conservation issues, appeared on numerous TV programmes including 20/20, Nightline, Good Morning America; contrib to New York Times; Hon Foreign mem AAAS; Conservation Award, New York Zoological Soc; Franklin Burr Award (twice), Nat Geographic Soc; Nat Geographic Soc Centennial Award; Hubbard Medal 1995; Medal of Mt Kilimanjaro 1996; Public Service Award, Nat Scientific Bd 1998; John Hay Award, Orion Soc 1998; Int Peace Award, Reorganized Church of the Latter Day Saints. *Publications include:* In the Shadow of Man 1971, The Chimpanzees of Gombe 1986, The Chimpanzee Family Book 1989, Through a Window: My Thirty Years with the Chimpanzees of Gombe 1990, The Chimpanzee: The Living Link Between 'Man' and 'Beast' 1992, Visions of Caliban 1993, Jane Goodall: with love 1994, Dr White 1999, 40 Years at Gombe 1999, Brutal Kinship 1999, Reason for Hope 1999, Africa in My Blood: An Autobiography in Letters 2000. *Address:* c/o Jane Goodall Inst for Wildlife Research, Education and Conservation, POB 14890, Silver Spring, MD 20911, USA (Office). *Telephone:* (301) 565-0086; *Fax:* (301) 565-3188.

GOODMAN, Elinor Mary; British broadcaster and journalist; b 11 Oct 1946; d of Edward Weston Goodman and Pamela Longbottom; m Derek Scott 1985. *Education:* pvt schools and secretarial coll. *Career:* Consumer Affairs Corresp Financial Times newspaper 1971–78, Political Corresp 1978–82; Political Corresp Channel Four News (TV) 1982–88, Political Ed 1988–. *Leisure interests:* riding, walking. *Address:* Martinscote, Oare, Marlborough SN8 4JA, UK.

GOODY, Joan Edelman, MA, M ARCH, FAIA; American architect; b 1 Dec 1935, New York; d of Beril and Sylvia (née Feldman) Edelman; m 1st Marvin E. Goody 1960 (died 1980); m 2nd Peter H. Davison 1984. *Education:* Cornell Univ and Harvard Univ Grad School of Design. *Career:* Principal Goody, Clancy & Assocs Inc, Boston, MA 1961–; Design Critic and Asst Prof Harvard Univ Grad School of Design 1973–80, Eliot Noyes Visiting Critic 1985; Faculty for Mayors Inst for City Design 1989–; Chair Boston Civic Design Comm 1992–; Dir Historic Boston, WGBH-TV; received Henry Adams Award 1960, AIA

Citation for Excellence in Architecture 1980, in Urban Design 1988. *Projects include:* Heaton Court Housing 1979, 265 Franklin St 1984, 99 Summer St 1987, Harbor Point Housing 1988, Salomon Center (Brown Univ, RI) 1990. *Address:* Goody, Clancy & Assocs Inc, 334 Boylston St, Boston, MA 02116, USA. *Telephone:* (617) 262-2760; *Fax:* (617) 262-9512.

GOOLAGONG, Evonne Fay (see Cawley, Evonne).

GOONERATNE, Malini Yasmine, AO, PH D, D LITT; Australian professor of English, writer and poet; b 22 Dec 1935, Colombo, Sri Lanka; d of S. J. F. Dias and Esther Mary (née Ramkeesoon) Bandaranaike; m Brendon Gooneratne 1962; one s one d. *Education:* Bishop's Coll (Colombo), Univs of Ceylon and Cambridge (UK). *Career:* Lecturer in English Ceylon Univ 1965–72; Sr Lecturer in English Macquarie Univ, NSW, Australia 1972, Assoc Prof 1979, Dir Postcolonial Literature and Language Research Centre 1988–93, Chair of English Literature 1991–99, Prof Emer 1999–; Nat Co-ordinator Commonwealth Visiting Fellowship 1989; Resident Fellow Literary Criterion Centre, India 1990; Visiting Prof Edith Cowan Univ, WA 1991, Univ of Michigan, USA 1991; Patron Jane Austen Soc of Australia 1990; Vice-Pres FILLM 1990–; mem Australian Fed of Univ Women, Australian Soc of Authors; Marjorie Bainaid Literary Award for Fiction 1992; Raja Rao Award 2001. *Publications include:* English Literature in Ceylon 1815–1878 1968, Jane Austen 1970, Word, Bird, Motif (poems) 1971, The Lizard's Cry and Other Poems 1972, Alexander Pope 1976, Diverse Inheritance: a Personal Perspective on Commonwealth Literature 1980, 6,000 Feet Death Dive: Poems 1981, Relative Merits: the Bandaranaike Family of Sri Lanka 1986, A Change of Skies 1991, Celebrations and Departures: Poems 1991, The Pleasures of Conquest 1995, This Inscrutable Englishman: Sir John D'Oyly, Baronet (1774–1824) (with B. Gooneratne) 1999. *Leisure interests:* travel, theatre, embroidery, swimming. *Address:* Macquarie University, Dept of English, College of Humanities, N Ryde, NSW 2109, Australia. *Telephone:* (2) 9876-2111; *Fax:* (2) 9876-8698; *E-mail:* yasmine@humanities.mq.edu.au; *Internet:* www.nla.gov.au/ms/findaids/9094.html.

GORCHAKOVA, Galina Vladimirovna; Russian opera singer (soprano); b 1962, Novokuznetsk, Western Siberia; m Nikolai Petrovich Mikhalsky (divorced); one s. *Education:* Novosibirsk State Conservatory. *Career:* Soloist Sverdlovsk (now Yekaterinburg) Theatre of Opera and Ballet 1987–91; with Kirov Opera 1991–96; performances include Royal Opera House, London, Promenade Concerts (Proms), Royal Albert Hall, London 1991, Metropolitan Opera, New York 1992, La Scala, Milan, Italy 1994, Edinburgh Festival, UK 1992, Opera Bastille, also in Tokyo and Birmingham; recording artist for Philips; Merited Artist of Russia. *Operas include:* Madam Butterfly, The Fiery Angel, The Oprichnik, The Queen of Spades, Prince Igor, Eugene Onegin, Iolanta, The Force of Destiny, The Invisible City of Kitezh, Ruslan and Ludmila, Aida, Don Carlos, Tosca, Cavalleria Rusticana; *Recordings include:* Mazeppa, Prince Igor. *Leisure interest:* travelling by car. *Address:* c/o Askonas Holt, Lonsdale Chambers, 27 Chancery Lane, London WC2A 1PF, UK (Office). *Telephone:* (20) 7400-1700.

GORDIMER, Nadine, FRSL; South African writer; b 20 Nov 1923; d of Isidore Gordimer and Nan Myers; m 2nd Reinhold Cassirer 1954; one s one d. *Education:* Convent school. *Career:* Co-Ed South African Writing Today 1967; mem ANC 1990–; Patron and Founder-mem Congress of S African Writers; Charles Eliot Norton Lecturer in Literature, Harvard Univ 1994; Hon mem American Acad and Inst of Arts and Letters, American Acad of Arts and Sciences; Vice-Pres Int PEN; Hon D LITT (Yale, York, Harvard, Leuven, Cambridge, Oxford and others); awards include W. H. Smith Literary Award 1961, Thomas Pringle Award (English Acad of SA) 1969, James Tait Black Memorial Prize 1971, Grand Aigle d'Or Prize (France) 1975, CNA Literary Award (S Africa) 1974, 1979, 1981, 1991, Neil M. Gunn Fellowship (Scottish Arts Council) 1981, Modern Language Asscn Award (USA) 1981, Premio Malaparte (Italy) 1985, Nelly Sachs Prize (Germany) 1985, Bennett Award (USA) 1987, Benson Medal (RSL) 1990, Nobel Prize for Literature 1991; Commdr des Arts et des Lettres 1986. *Publications:* Novels: The Lying Days 1953, A World of Strangers 1958, Occasion for Loving 1963, The Late Bourgeois World 1966, A Guest of Honour 1970, The Conservationist (Booker Prize, jtly) 1974, Burger's

Daughter 1979, July's People 1981, Something Out There (novella) 1984, A Sport of Nature 1987, My Son's Story 1990, None to Accompany Me 1994, The House Gun 1997, The Pickup 2001; Short Stories: Face to Face 1949, The Soft Voice of the Serpent 1952, Six Feet of the Country 1956, 1986, Friday's Footprint 1960, Not For Publication 1965, Livingstone's Companions 1972, Selected Stories 1975, Some Monday for Sure 1976, A Soldier's Embrace 1980, Jump 1991, Crimes of Conscience 1991; Non-fiction: The Black Interpreters (literary criticism) 1973, The Essential Gesture (essays) 1988, Writing and Being (lectures) 1995, Living in Hope and History: Notes on our Century (essays) 1999. *Address:* c/o A. P. Watt, 20 John St, London WC1N 2DR, South Africa.

GORDON, Dame Elmira Minita, GCMG, GCVO, M ED, PH D; Belizean former governor-general; b 30 Dec 1930, Belize City. *Education:* Govt Training Coll (Belize), Univs of Nottingham, Birmingham (UK), Calgary and Toronto (Canada). *Career:* Teacher and missionary 1946–58; Lecturer Training Coll 1959–69; Govt Educ Officer 1969–81; JP 1974, Sr JP 1987; Dist Commr for Belize Dist 1970–77; Deputy Chair Domestic Wages Council until 1981; first Belizean Gov-Gen 1981–93; Leather Carver, winner of numerous prizes, solo exhibitions in Belize and Canada; Patron Belize Girl Guides Asscn, Boy Scouts Asscn; Hon mem Salvation Army Advisory Bd; mem Red Cross Belize 1951, Royal Commonwealth Soc 1986; Hon LL D (Victoria, BC) 1984, (Birmingham) 1986; Dame Minita Gordon Scholarship cr by Univ of Victoria, BC 1987. *Publication:* Brush Teeth Night and Morning (for Jr Red Cross) 1976. *Address:* c/o Office of the Governor-General, Belmopan, Belize.

GORDON, Hannah Cambell Grant, FRSAMD; British actress; b 9 April 1941; d of William Munro and Hannah Grant Gordon; m Norman Warwick 1970; one s. *Education:* Univ of Glasgow and Royal Scottish Acad of Music and Dramatic Art (Glasgow). *Career:* Awarded Royal Coll of Music and Dramatic Art James Bridie Gold Medal 1962; Fellow Royal Coll of Music and Dramatic Art; Hon D LITT (Glasgow). *Stage appearances include:* Can You Hear Me at the Back? 1979, The Killing Game 1980, The Jeweller's Shop 1982, The Country Girl 1983, Light Up the Sky 1985, Mary Stuart 1987, Shirley Valentine 1989, Hidden Laughter 1991, An Ideal Husband 1992, The Aspern Papers; *TV appearances include:* Johnson Over Jordan 1965; Series: Great Expectations 1969, Middlemarch 1969, My Wife Next Door 1972, Upstairs, Downstairs 1976, Telford's Change 1979, Goodbye Mr Kent 1983, Gardener's Calendar 1986, My Family and Other Animals 1987, Joint Account 1989, Midsomer Murders 1999, Watercolour Challenge presenter 1998; *Films include:* Spring and Port Wine 1970, The Elephant Man 1979; numerous radio performances. *Leisure interests:* cooking, gardening, tennis, walking. *Address:* c/o Conway Van Gelder Ltd, 18-21 Jermyn St, London SW1Y 6HP, UK.

GORDON, Lorraine; American jazz entrepreneur; m 1st Alfred Lyons; m 2nd Max Gordon (died 1990). *Career:* Owner and Manager The Village Vanguard jazz club, New York 1990–. *Address:* The Village Vanguard, 178 Seventh Ave South, New York, NY, USA.

GORDON, Mary Catherine; American writer. *Publications include:* Final Payments 1978, The Company of Women 1980, Men and Angels 1985, Temporary Shelter (short stories) 1987, The Other Side 1989, The Rest of Life: Three Novellas 1993, The Shadow Man: A Daughter's Search for Her Father (memoir) 1996, Seeing Through Places 2000, Joan of Arc 2000; Essays: Good Boys and Dead Girls 1991. *Address:* 15 Claremont Ave, New York, NY 10027, USA.

GORDON, Mildred; British politician; b 24 Aug 1923; d of Judah and Dora Fellerman; m 1st Sam Gordon 1948 (died 1982); one s; m 2nd Nils Kaare Dahl 1985. *Education:* Raines Foundation School (Stepney) and Forest Teachers' Training Coll (Walthamstow). *Career:* Teacher of English and History, London 1945–47, 1952–59, 1964–85, Visiting Teacher Holloway Prison 1960–62; mem London Lab Party Exec 1983–86, Chair London Lab Party Policy Cttee 1985–86; Adviser to GLC Women's Cttee; MP for Bow and Poplar 1987–97, Vice-Chair Parl Lab Party Social Service Cttee, Educ Cttee, Select Cttee on Educ, Science and Arts, Chair Parl All-Party Child Support Act Monitoring

Cttee 1995–97. *Leisure interest:* reading. *Address:* 28 Cumbrian Gardens, London NW2 1EF, UK. *Telephone:* (20) 7219-4125; *Fax:* (20) 7219-2495.

GORDON, Pamela, MBA; Bermudan politician; b 4 Sept 1955; d of E. F. Gordon. *Education:* Queen's Univ. *Career:* Fmr Minister of the Environment; Leader United Bermuda Party; Prime Minister of Bermuda 1997–98; Hon LL D (New Brunswick). *Address:* c/o United Bermuda Party, Central Office, 87 John F. Burrows Building, Chancery Lane, POB HM 715, Hamilton, HM CX, Bermuda. *Telephone:* 295-0729; *E-mail:* www.bermuda.bm/ubp.

GORMAN, Teresa Ellen, B SC; British politician; b 30 Sept 1931; m James Daniel Gorman; one c. *Education:* Univ of London. *Career:* Teacher and business exec; Founder and Chair Alliance of Small Firms and Self-Employed People Ltd 1974; Founder Amarant Trust 1986–; ind Parl Cand Streatham (London) 1974; Councillor Westminster City Council, London 1982–86; mem Cons Women's Nat Cttee 1983–2001; MP (Cons) for Billericay, Essex 1987–2001. *Publications include:* The Case for Private Enterprise 1976, Minimum Wage Laws and Small Firms 1979, Worried to Death 1983, The Bastards 1983, Business Still Burdened 1984, Quangos Just Grow 1985, The Enterprise Culture 1986, The Amarant Book of HRT 1989, Chichesgate (jtly) 1990; reports for Adam Smith Inst and Centre for Policy Studies, London. *Leisure interests:* travel, gardening. *Address:* c/o House of Commons, London SW1A 0AA, UK. *Telephone:* (20) 7219-3000.

GORZYNSKA, Barbara, MA; Polish violinist; b 4 Dec 1953, Cmielow; d of Zygmunt and Janina (née Nowak) Gorzynski; m Ryszard Rasinski 1982; one s. *Education:* Acad of Music (Łódź). *Career:* Performances as soloist with London Philharmonic Orchestra, Royal Philharmonic Orchestra (UK), Staatskapelle Dresden (Germany), Warsaw Philharmonic Orchestra, English Chamber Orchestra (UK), Halle Orchestra (Germany) 1981–; London debut Royal Festival Hall 1981; Visiting Prof Hochschule für Musik und Darstellende Kunst, Graz, Austria; recordings with Le Chant du Monde, WIFON, Polskie Nagrania; winner Zagreb Int Violin Competition 1977, Carl Flesch Int Violin Competition 1980. *Recordings include:* Chopin's Trio in G Minor 1986, Wieniawski's Pieces for Violin and Piano 1988, Mozart's Violin Concerto in D 1991. *Leisure interests:* film, theatre. *Address:* c/o Christopher Tennant Artists' Management, Unit 2, 39 Tadema Rd, London SW10 0PY, UK. *Telephone:* (20) 7376-3758; *Fax:* (20) 7351-0679.

GOSDEN, Christine Margaret, B SC, PH D; British scientist; b 25 April 1945, Newark; d of George G. H. and Helena Ford; m John R. Gosden 1971. *Education:* Loughton School and Univs of Edinburgh and London. *Career:* Research Fellow Univ of Edinburgh 1971–73; mem Sr Scientific Staff MRC Genetics Unit, Western Gen Hosp, Edinburgh 1973; Sr Lecturer in Human Genetics, King's Coll Hosp, London 1983–88, Visiting Prof Dept of Obstetrics and Gynaecology 1988; Insp Human Fertilization and Embryology Authority 1991–; Prof of Medical Genetics, Dept of Obstetrics and Gynaecology, Univ of Liverpool 1993–. *Publications include:* Is my baby alright?; over 100 articles and papers on mental illness and handicap, genetic diseases, prenatal diagnosis and therapy, and foetal medicine. *Leisure interests:* whales, conservation of endangered animals, birds and plants, books, harpsichord, wine. *Address:* University of Liverpool, Department of Obstetrics and Gynaecology, Liverpool Women's Hospital, Crown St, Liverpool L8 7SS, UK. *Telephone:* (151) 702-5100; *Fax:* (151) 702-4024; *E-mail:* cgosden@liverpool.ac.uk.

GÖTTE, Rose, D PHIL; German politician; b 21 March 1938; m Klaus Götte 1961; three c. *Education:* Bonn. *Career:* Scientific Researcher, Educational Theory of Pre-School Educ; mem Landtag (state parl), Rheinland-Pfalz 1979–87; mem Bundestag (Parl, SPD) 1987–91, mem Parl SPD Bd; State Minister for Educ and Culture, Rheinland-Pfalz 1991–94, for Culture, Youth, Family and Women 1994. *Publications:* Alzheimer – was tun? 1991, Sprache und Spiel im Kindergarten (9th edn) 1994.

GOULANDRIS, Niki; Greek ecologist and women's organization executive. *Career:* Co-Founder Goulandris Nat History Museum, Athens 1964, later Vice-Pres; Dir Centre Nat d'Information des

Femmes; Founder-mem Assn Européenne pour le Développement de l'Information des Femmes; Woman of Europe award 1990. *Address:* 71 ave de Cortenberg, 1040 Brussels, Belgium.

GOVIER, Katherine Mary, MA; Canadian writer; b 4 July 1948, Edmonton, AB; d of George Wheeler and Doris Eda Govier; m John Allen Honderich 1981; one s one d. *Education:* Univ of Alberta and York Univ (ON). *Career:* Writing first published 1972; fiction and non-fiction published by major British and Canadian magazines 1973–81; Lecturer in English Ryerson Polytech Inst, Toronto, ON 1973–74; Contrib, Ed Toronto Life magazine 1975–77; Visiting Lecturer Creative Writing Programme, York Univ 1982–86; Research Fellow Univ of Leeds, UK 1986; Chair Writers' Devt Trust 1990–91; mem PEN Canada (Vice-Pres 1996–97), Writers' Union of Canada; Nat Magazine Award 1979; Foundation for the Advancement of Canadian Letters Authors' Award 1979. *Publications:* Going Through the Motions 1981, Random Descent (3rd edn) 1987; Short stories: Fables of Brunswick Avenue 1985, Before and After (2nd edn) 1990; Novels: Between Men 1987, Hearts of Flame 1991, The Immaculate Conception Photography Gallery 1994, Angel Walk 1996; Short stories included in Oxford Book of Canadian Short Stories, Canadian Short Stories (ed R. Weaver) 1985, More Stories by Canadian Women (ed R. Sullivan) 1987, Oxford Book of Canadian Short Stories (ed M. Atwood and R. Weaver) 1995. *Leisure interests:* travel, skiing. *Address:* c/o Elaine Markson Agency, 44 Greenwich Ave, New York, NY 10011, USA (Agent); 54 Farnham Ave, Toronto, ON M4V 1H4, Canada (Home).

GOW, Lyn, PH D; Australian university pro vice-chancellor; b 24 Dec 1949, Sydney; d of Ernest W. Gow and Noelene B. Dutch; m John Robert Uhrin 1976; two d one s. *Education:* Alexander Mackie Teachers' Coll (NSW) and Macquarie Univ. *Career:* Held various teaching and lecturing posts; Sr Lecturer in Educ Univ of Wollongong 1985–91; Reader in Rehabilitation Sciences Hong Kong Polytechnic 1989–91; Dean (acting) Faculty of Educ, Univ of W Sydney 1991–92, Admin Dir Univ of W Sydney and Dir ESCLADE Research Centre 1991–93; apptd Pro Vice-Chancellor and Dean La Trobe Univ, Bendigo, Vic 1994; Ed and reviewer five professional journals; several awards. *Publications include:* Integration of People with Handicaps in Hong Kong (jtly) 1990, Mastering the Research Maze (jtly, 2nd edn) 1992, Including Us 1994, Annotated Bibliography on Integration 1994; over 200 papers, articles, book chapters, etc. *Leisure interests:* running, swimming, cycling, biathlons, triathlons, marathons. *Address:* La Trobe University, Bendigo Campus, POB 199, Bendigo, Vic 3550, Australia.

GRACHEVA, Nadezhda Aleksandrovna; Russian ballet dancer; b 21 Dec 1969, Semipalatinsk; d of Aleksander Aleksandrovich and Vera Petrovna Gracheva; m 1st Aleksei Yuryevich Seregin (divorced); m 2nd Yevgeny Kern. *Education:* Moscow School of Choreography. *Career:* With Bolshoi Theatre 1987–; leading parts in Bayadera, Swan Lake, Nutcracker, Sleeping Beauty, Les Sylphides, Stone Flower, Romeo and Juliet and others; toured in many European and American countries, Japan, Israel, New Zealand; Benoît Prize 1991; prizes at int competitions Varna 1984, 1986, Moscow 1987, Osaka 1995; State Prize of Russia 1996; People's Artist of Russia 1996. *Leisure interest:* cooking. *Address:* Bolshoi Theatre, Teatralnaya pl 1, 103009 Moscow, Russian Federation (Office); 1st Truzhennikov per 17, Apt 49, 119121 Moscow, Russia (Home). *Telephone:* (095) 248 2753 (Home).

GRADIN, Anita Ingegerd; Swedish politician; b 12 Aug 1933, Hörnefors, Västerbotten Co; d of Ossian and Alfhild (née Englund) Gradin; m Bertil Kersfelt; one d. *Education:* Coll of Social Work and Public Admin (Stockholm) and in USA. *Career:* Journalist 1950–63; mem staff Social Welfare Planning Cttee, Stockholm 1963–67; First Sec Cabinet Office 1967–82; mem Stockholm City Council 1966–68; mem Social Democratic Lab Party (SDP) Exec Cttee of Stockholm 1968–82; mem Riksdag (Parl, SDP) 1968–82; Del Council of Europe 1973–82, Chair Cttee on Migration, Refugees and Demographic Questions 1978–82; Minister with responsibility for Immigrant and Equality Affairs, Ministry of Labour 1982–86, Minister with responsibility for Foreign Trade, Ministry of Foreign Affairs 1986–92; Amb to Austria, Slovenia and to UN insts including IAEA, UNIDO and UNRWA 1992–94; EC Comm for Immigration, Home and Judicial Affairs 1995–99; Chair District Br, Fed of Social Democratic Women, Stockholm 1968–82; Chair Swedish Union of Social Workers and

Public Admin 1970–81; Chair Nat Bd for Intercountry Adoptions 1973–80; Chair of Stockholm Conf on Vietnam 1974–76, of Swedish Cttee for Vietnam, Laos and Cambodia 1977–82; mem Exec Cttee Nat Fed of Social Democratic Women in Sweden 1964–93, Vice-Chair 1975–93; mem Exec Cttee of RFSU (Nat Asscn for Sexual Enlightenment) and Otterfonden 1969–92; Vice-Chair Socialist Int Women's Council 1983–86; Pres Socialist Int Women 1986–92; Vice-Pres Socialist Int 1986–92; mem EFTA Del 1991–92; Pro Merito Medal, Council of Europe 1982; Wizo Woman of the year 1986; Cavalieri di Gran Croce (Italy) 1991; Das Grossen Goldene Ehrenzeichen am Bande (Austria) 1994; Marisa Bellizario European Prize (Italy) 1998. *Leisure interests:* fishing, philately, music. *Address:* Svartviksslingan 27, 16738 Bromma, Sweden (Home). *Telephone:* (8) 269872; *Fax:* (8) 269872; *E-mail:* gradin.kersfelt@telia.com.

GRADWELL, Mavis; British business executive; b 21 Jan 1948, Burnley; d of Philip and Anne Hall; m Mr Gradwell 1966; two s. *Education:* St Hilda's School for Girls (Burnley, Lancs). *Career:* Sec to Chair Simon Jersey Ltd 1974, then worked in accounts dept, production and sales, later Man Dir. *Leisure interests:* reading, dancing, socialising. *Address:* Syke Side Drive, Altham, Accrington, Lancs BB5 5YE, UK; 18 Pine Crescent, Oswaldtwistle, Accrington, Lancs BB5 3TF, UK. *Telephone:* (1254) 395382.

GRAENITZ, Ilona; Austrian politician; b 15 March 1943, Vienna. *Career:* Fmr mem Nationalrat (Parl); fmr MEP (PSE, Sozialdemokratische Partei Österreichs), mem Cttee on the Environment, Public Health and Consumer Protection, Cttee on Petitions, Del for Relations with the USA; currently Dir Global Legislators for a Balanced Environment (GLOBE) Europe. *Address:* 50 rue du Taciturne, 1040 Brussels, Belgium. *Telephone:* (2) 230-65-89; *Fax:* (2) 230-95-30; *E-mail:* globe .europe@village.uunet.be.

GRAF, Steffi; German tennis player; b 14 June 1969, Brühl; d of Peter Graf; partner Andre Agassi. *Education:* Coached by father, trained by Pavel Slozil. *Career:* Won Orange Bowl 12s 1981, European 14-and-under and European Circuit Masters 1982, Olympic demonstration event, Los Angeles, CA, USA 1984; winner German Open 1986, 1989, French Open 1987, 1988, 1993, 1995, 1996, 1999, Australian Open 1988, 1989, 1990, 1994, Wimbledon (UK), 1988, 1989, 1991, 1992, 1993, 1995, 1996, US Open 1988, 1989, 1993, 1995, 1996, ATP Tour World Championship 1996, German Open 1989, numerous Women's Doubles Championships with Gabriela Sabatini (qv), Fed Cup 1992; Olympic Champion Seoul, Repub of Korea 1988, Silver Medallist Barcelona, Spain 1992; ranked No 1 Aug 1987; named Official World Champion 1988; Grand Slam winner 1988, 1989; youngest player to win 500 Singles victories as a professional Oct 1991; 100 tournament wins, 21 Grand Slam titles (July 1996); announced retirement Aug 1999. *Address:* 6831 Brühl bei Mannheim, Germany.

GRAHAM, K. M. (Kathleen Margaret), BA, RCA; Canadian painter; b 13 Sept 1913, Hamilton, ON; d of Charles and G. Blanche (née Leitch) Howitt; m Wallace Graham 1938 (died 1962); one s one d. *Education:* Oakwood Coll (Toronto) and Trinity Coll (Univ of Toronto). *Career:* Wrote articles for various periodicals 1945–62; began painting 1962; solo and group exhibitions in N America and Europe 1967–; solo exhibitions include Pollock Gallery (Toronto, ON) 1971–75, David Mirvish Gallery (Toronto) 1976, Klonaridis Inc (Toronto) 1979–1991, Watson Willour (Houston, TX, USA) 1980, Lillian Heidenberg (NY, USA) Macdonald Stewart Art Centre (Guelph, ON) 1984, Glenbow Museum (Calgary, AB) 1984, Concordia Art Gallery (Montréal, PQ) 1985, Art Gallery (Newfoundland and Labrador) 1994, Costin and Klintworth (Toronto) 1995–96, Moore Gallery (Toronto) 2000, 2001; group exhibitions include Festival of Canada (Binghamton, NY, USA) 1971, 14 Canadians: A Critic's Choice (Hirschorn Museum, Washington, DC, USA) 1977, Four Toronto Painters (Dianne Brown Gallery, Washington, DC, USA) 1977, Works on Paper (Galerie Wentzel, Hamburg, Germany) 1977, Certain Traditions (toured major galleries in UK) 1979–80, Bolduc, Fournier, Graham: Recent Paintings (London, Paris, Brussels, Liverpool) 1982–83, Ontario House (Brussels) 1983, Associated American Artists (New York) 1986–89, Los Angeles Art Fair (CA, USA) 1986; work featured in numerous public and pvt collections in Canada and USA; work has appeared on numerous book covers, prints, posters and on TV and radio; designed

liturgical vestments for St Michael and All Saints Parish Church (Toronto) 1977; Hon Fellow Trinity Coll (Toronto) 1988. *Publications include:* numerous contribs to journals including Brick – A Literary Journal 1988, 1990, 1998, 2000, 2001; book and magazine covers including Views From the North: An Anthology of Travel Writing (ed Karen Mulhallen) 1984. *Leisure interests:* the Canadian Arctic, literature, gardening. *Address:* 26 Boswell Ave, Toronto, ON M5R 1M4, Canada. *Telephone:* (416) 921-3890.

GRAHAM, Patricia Albjerg, PH D; American professor of education; b 9 Feb 1935, Lafayette, IN; d of Victor L. and Marguerite Hall Albjerg; m Loren R. Graham 1955; one d. *Education:* Purdue and Columbia Univs. *Career:* Teacher Deep Creek and Maury High Schools, Norfolk, VA 1955–58; Chair History Dept, St Hilda's and St Hugh's School, New York 1958–60, Part-time Coll Advisor 1961–63, 1965–67; Lecturer Indiana Univ, School of Educ, Bloomington 1964–65; Asst Prof Barnard Coll and Columbia Teachers' Coll, New York 1965–68, Assoc Prof 1968–72; Prof 1972–74; Prof Harvard Univ Grad School of Educ, Cambridge, MA 1974–79, Warren Prof 1979–, Dean Grad School of Educ 1982–91; Dean Radcliffe Inst and Vice-Pres for Institutional Planning, Radcliffe Coll, Cambridge, MA 1974–76, Dean and Vice-Pres 1976–77; Dir Nat Inst of Educ 1977–79; Vice-Pres for Teaching, American Historical Asscn 1985–89; Pres Nat Acad of Educ 1985–89; Dir Spencer Foundation 1983–2000, Pres Chicago Br 1991–2000; Dir Johnson Foundation 1983–; mem AAAS (mem Council 1993–96, Vice-Pres 1998–); several hon degrees. *Publications:* Progressive Education: From Arcady to Academe, A History of the Progressive Education Association 1967, Community and Class in American Education, 1865–1918 1974, Women in Higher Education (co-ed) 1974, S.O.S. Sustain Our Schools 1992. *Address:* Harvard University Graduate School of Education, Longfellow Hall, Appian Way, Cambridge, MA 02135, USA; The Spencer Foundation, 900 N Michigan Ave, Suite 2800, Chicago, IL 60611, USA.

GRAMM, Wendy Lee, PH D; American organization executive; d of Joshua and Angeline Lee; m Senator William Philip Gramm 1970; two s. *Education:* Wellesley Coll (MA) and Northwestern Univ (Evanston, IL). *Career:* Mem staff Dept of Quantitive Methods, Univ of Illinois 1969; Asst Prof Texas A & M Univ 1970–74, Assoc Prof Dept of Econs 1975–79; mem research staff Inst of Defense Analyses 1979–82; Asst Dir Fed Trade Comm Bureau of Econs 1982–83, Dir 1983–85; Admin Office of Information and Regulatory Affairs, OMB 1985–87; Exec Dir Presidential Task Force on Regulatory Relief; Chair Commodity Futures Trading Comm 1988–93; currently Dir Regulatory Studies Program and Dist Sr Fellow Mercatus Center, George Mason Univ; contribs to professional journals. *Address:* Mercatus Center, George Mason University, 3301 N Fairfax Drive, Ste 450, Arlington, VA 22201, USA. *Telephone:* (703) 993-4930; *E-mail:* wgramm@gmu.edu.

GRANN, Phyllis, BA; American publishing executive; b 2 Sept 1937, London; d of Solomon and Louisa (née Bois-Smith) Eitingon; m Victor Grann 1962; two s one d. *Education:* Barnard Coll. *Career:* Sec Doubleday Publrs, New York 1958–60; Ed William Morrow Inc, New York 1960–62, David McKay Co, New York 1962–70, Simon & Schuster Inc, New York 1970, Vice-Pres 1976; Pres, Publr G. P. Putnam's & Sons, New York 1976–86, Putnam Publishing Group Inc (now Penguin Putnam Inc), New York 1986–96, CEO 1987–96, Chair 1997–. *Address:* Penguin Putnam Inc, 375 Hudson St, New York, NY 10014, USA (Office).

GRANT, Allison Jean, B MUS; Canadian actress and singer; b 23 Nov 1958, Vancouver, BC; d of Ian Van Felson and Antoinette Suzanne Grant. *Education:* Banff School of Fine Arts (AB), Univ of W Ontario, Morley Coll and The Dance Centre (UK). *Career:* Fmr teacher of Children's Drama, Alma Coll, MI, USA; performed Stratford Festival, ON 1982–85; co-writer musical featuring Gilbert and Sullivan compositions; Tyrone Guthrie Awards, Stratford, ON 1982, 1983. *Stage appearances include:* Cats, The Drunkard, Desert Song, The Magic Flute, Heat, Brigadoon, Not Available in the Stores (première), Guys and Dolls, They're Playing Our Song, The Secret Garden (world première, Dora Mavor Moore Award for best actress in a musical) 1986, Carousel 1991, The House of Martin Guerre (world première) 1993. *Leisure interest:* travel.

GRAPIN, Jacqueline G., L EN D; French international organization executive; b 15 Dec 1942, Paris; d of Jean and Raymonde (née Ledru) Grapin; m Michel Le Goc 1971; one d one s. *Education:* Inst d'Etudes Politiques de Paris, Univ of Paris (I) and Ecole des Hautes Etudes Commercials. *Career:* Auditor Inst des Hautes Etudes de Défense Nat, Paris 1980; writer for Le Monde newspaper 1967–81, Ed-in-Chief Europa (supplement) 1977–81, Econ Corresp, Washington, DC 1985–86; Prof Inst d'Etudes Politiques de Paris 1974–77; Assoc Ed World Paper, Boston, MA, USA 1980–93; Dir-Gen Interevia Publishing Group, Geneva, Switzerland 1982–86; Pres The European Inst, Washington, DC 1986–; Econ Corresp for Le Figaro newspaper, Washington, DC 1987–; Admin Int Women's Media Foundation 1991; mem Int Inst for Strategic Studies, London; Prix Vauban, Inst des Hautes Etudes 1977; Officier de la Légion d'Honneur. *Publications:* La guerre civile mondiale 1977, Radioscopie des Etats-Unis 1980, Fortress America 1984, Pacific America 1987. *Address:* The European Institute, 5225 Wisconsin Ave NW, Suite 200, Washington, DC 20015, USA. *Telephone:* (202) 966-5071; *Fax:* (202) 362-1088; *E-mail:* jgrapin@europeaninstitute.org.

GRATTAN, Michelle, BA; Australian journalist; b 30 June 1944, Melbourne. *Education:* Melbourne Univ. *Career:* Chief Political Corresp The Age 1976–93, Political Ed 1995–96; Ed Canberra Times 1993–95; Sr writer and columnist Australian Financial Review 1996–98; Chief Political Corresp Sydney Morning Herald 1999–. *Publications include:* Australian Prime Ministers 2000, Reconciliation 2000. *Address:* Press Gallery, Parliament House, Canberra, ACT 2600, Australia (Office); 147 Mugga Way, Red Hill, Canberra, Australia (Home). *Telephone:* 62737687 (Office); 62956554 (Home); *Fax:* 62404022 (Office).

GRAUER, Sherrard G. S. Meredith, BFA, RCA; Canadian artist; b 20 Feb 1939, Toronto; d of Dal and Shirley (née Woodward) Grauer; m John William Keith-King 1971; three s. *Education:* York House School (Vancouver), Brillantmont (Lausanne, Switzerland), Ecole du Louvre (Paris), Wellesley Coll (MA, USA) and San Francisco Art Inst (CA, USA). *Career:* Sculptor and painter; solo exhibitions include Mary Frazee Gallery, W Vancouver 1964, Bau-Xi Gallery 1965, 1967–68, 1970, 1975–76, 1978, 1980, 1985, 1987, 1989, 1992, Véhicule Art Inc, Montréal 1973, Nat Gallery of Canada 1975, Surrey Art Gallery, BC 1980; group exhibitions include Montréal Museum of Fine Arts 1967, Canadian Expo '67, Hamilton Art Gallery 1973, Vancouver Art Gallery 1983, 1986, Charles H. Scott Gallery, Vancouver 1985, Artropolis 1993; numerous touring exhibitions; works in perm collections including Nat Gallery of Canada, Vancouver Art Gallery, Musée de l'art contemporain, Montréal; comms include murals and stage settings; mem Bd and Hon Sec Vancouver Art Gallery 1975; Founder-mem Vancouver Arts, Sciences and Tech Centre 1980–84; Dir Women in Focus Arts and Media Centre 1991; mem Royal Canadian Acad of Arts 1979. *Leisure interests:* gardening, reading, watching. *Address:* 106-8828 Heather St, Vancouver, BC V6P 3S8, Canada. *Telephone:* (604) 321-3960; *Fax:* (604) 321-3967.

GRAY, Ann Maynard, BA, MBA; American broadcasting executive; b 22 Aug 1945, Boston, MA; d of Paul Maynard and Pauline Elizabeth MacFayden; one s one d. *Education:* Univ of Michigan and New York Univ. *Career:* Employee Chase Manhattan Bank, New York 1967–68, Chemical Bank, New York 1968–71, Asst Sec 1971–73; Dir Carteret Savings Bank, Morristown, NJ 1984–88; Asst to Treas, then Asst Treas American Broadcasting Co (ABC) Inc 1974–76, Treas 1976–81, Vice-Pres of Corp Planning 1979–86, Vice-Pres Capital Cities/ABC Inc 1986, Sr Vice-Pres of Finance ABC TV Network Group 1988–91; Pres Diversified Publishing Group 1991; Dir American Business Press 1991–95, Cyprus Amax Minerals Co Inc, Pan Energy Corpn; Trustee Martha Graham Center of Contemporary Dance, New York 1989, Cancer Care, NY 1990. *Address:* Capital Cities/ABC Inc, 77 W 66th St, New York, NY 10023, USA.

GRAY, Dulcie Winifred Catherine, CBE, FRSA, FLS; British actress, playwright, author; b (Dulcie Savage-Bailey) 20 Nov 1920, Kuala Lumpur, Federated Malaysian States (now Malaysia); d of the late Arnold Savage-Bailey and Kate Edith Clulow Gray; m Michael Denison 1939 (deceased). *Education:* England and Malaya. *Career:* Has worked in theatre since 1939; repertoire includes Aberdeen, Edinburgh, Glasgow, Harrogate; debut as Sorrel in Hay Fever 1939; Queen's Silver Jubilee Medal 1977. *Films:* They Were Sisters 1944, Wanted for Murder 1945, A Man about the House 1946, Mine Own Executioner 1947, The Glass Mountain 1948, There Was a Young Lady 1953, A Man Could Get Killed 1965, The Black Crow 1994; *Plays inculde:* The Little Foxes, Midsummer Night's Dream 1942, Brighton Rock, Landslide 1943, Lady from Edinburgh 1945, Dear Ruth, Wind is 90 1946, Queen Elizabeth Slept Here 1949, Sweet Peril 1952, We Must Kill Toni, The Diary of a Nobody 1954, Love Affair (also writer) 1956, Double Cross 1958, Let Them Eat Cake 1959, Candida 1960, Heartbreak House 1961, Where Angels Fear to Tread 1963, An Ideal Husband 1965, Happy Family 1967, Number 10 1967, Out of the Question 1968, Three 1970, The Wild Duck 1970, Ghosts 1972, At the End of the Day 1973, Time and the Conways (tour) 1977, A Murder is Announced 1977, Lloyd George Knew my Father (tour) 1980, A Coat of Varnish 1982, School for Scandal (British Council 50th Anniversary European Tour) 1983, The Living Room 1987, The Best of Friends (tour) 1990, 1991, The Importance of Being Earnest (tour) 1991, Tartuffe 1991–92, Two of a Kind (tour) 1995, The Ladykillers (tour) 1999, Les Liaisons Dangereuses (tour) 2000, The Lady Vanishes (tour) 2001; *TV:* Howards' Way (series) 1985–90, several plays; *Radio:* Front Line Family (BBC serial) 1941; numerous plays; *Publications:* Murder on the Stairs, Murder in Melbourne, Baby Face, Epitaph for a Dead Actor, Murder on a Saturday, Murder in Mind, The Devil Wore Scarlet, No Quarter for a Star, The Murder of Love, Died in the Red, The Actor and His World (with Michael Denison), Death in Denims, Butterflies on my Mind (Times Educational Supplement Sr Information Book Prize 1978), Dark Calypso, The Glanville Women, Anna Starr, Mirror Image, Looking Forward, Looking Back (autobiog), J. B. Priestly (biog). *Leisure interests:* swimming, butterflies. *Address:* Shardeloes, Missenden Rd, Amersham HP7 0RL, UK. *Telephone:* (1494) 725555.

GRAY, Hanna Holborn, PH D; American university professor; b 25 Oct 1930; d of Hajo and Annemarie Holborn; m Charles Montgomery Gray 1954. *Education:* Bryn Mawr Coll (PA), Univ of Oxford (UK) and Harvard Univ (MA). *Career:* Instructor Bryn Mawr Coll 1953–54; Teaching Fellow Harvard Univ 1955–57, Instructor 1957–59, Asst Prof 1959–60, Visiting Lecturer 1963–64; Asst Prof Univ of Chicago 1961–64, Assoc Prof 1964–72, Prof 1978–, Pres 1978–93, Harry Pratt Judson Distinguished Service Prof 1994–; Dean and Prof Northwestern Univ, IL 1972–74; Provost and Prof of History Yale Univ 1974–78, Acting Pres 1977–78; Visiting Prof Univ of California, Berkeley 1970–71; Co-Ed Journal of Modern History 1965–70; mem Bd Dirs Cummins Engine Co, Chair Bd; mem Harvard Corp, Andrew W. Mellon Foundation; mem Bd Regents Smithsonian Institution; Trustee Yale Corpn 1971–74, Comm on Econ Devt, Bryn Mawr Coll, Howard Hughes Medical Inst, Marlboro School of Music; Fellow Center for Advanced Study in Behavioral Sciences 1966–67, Visiting Scholar 1970–71; Fellow Newberry Library 1960–61, American Acad of Arts and Sciences; Hon Fellow St Anne's Coll, Oxford (UK) 1978–; numerous hon degrees; awards include Yale Medal 1978, Medal of Liberty award 1986, Medal of Freedom 1991, Sara Lee Frontrunner Award 1991, Charles Frankel Prize 1993, Centennial Medal (Harvard Univ) 1994, Distinguished Service Award in Educ (Inst of Int Educ) 1994, M. Carey Thomas Award, Bryn Mawr Coll 1997, Medal of Distinction, Barnard Coll 2000. *Address:* University of Chicago, Dept of History, 1126 E 59th St, Chicago, IL 60637, USA. *Telephone:* (713) 702-7799; *Fax:* (713) 702-4600; *E-mail:* h-gray@uchicago.edu.

GRAY, Linda Esther; British opera singer; b 29 May 1948; d of James and Esther Gray; m Peter McCrorie 1971; one d. *Education:* Greenock Acad and Royal Scottish Acad of Music and Drama. *Career:* London Opera Centre 1969–71, Glyndebourne Festival Opera 1972–75, Scottish Opera 1974–79, English Nat Opera 1979, Welsh Opera 1980; debut American performance 1981; appeared Royal Opera House, London 1982, 1983; Cinzano Scholarship 1969; Goldsmith Scholarship 1970; James Caird Scholarship 1971; Christie Award 1972; Kathleen Ferrier Award 1972. *Operas include:* Tristan und Isolde, die Walküre, Tosca, Parsifal, Fidelio; *Recordings:* Tristan und Isolde 1981, Die Feen 1983. *Leisure interests:* cooking, swimming. *Address:* 35 Green Lane, New Malden, Surrey KT3 5BX, UK.

GRÉCO, Juliette; French actress and singer; b 7 Feb 1927, Montpellier; d of Louis Gérard and Juliette Gréco; m 1st Philippe Lemair; one d; m 2nd Michel Piccoli; m 3rd Gérard Jouannest 1988. *Education:* Acting with Solange Sicard, Pierre Dux and Béatrice Dussane. *Career:* At Tabou cabaret (with Raymond Quesneau, Roger Vadim, Boris Vian, Jean-Paul Sartre, etc) 1946; numerous cabaret performances in France and abroad; concerts include shows at Olympia (Paris) 1954, 1957, 1966, 1991, Théâtre Nat de Paris (with Georges Brassens) 1966 and at the Odéon-Théâtre de l'Europe 1999; Chevalier des Arts et des Lettres; Grand Prix Nat de la Chanson 1990. *Songs include:* Si tu t'imagines... L'éternel féminin, Les feuilles mortes, Romance (Grand Prix du Disque) 1952, La valse brune, Si l'amour est un péché, Rêveuse et fragile, Toi que j'aime, Les pingouines, J'en tremble, Ta jalousie; *Films include:* Orphée 1950, Quand tu liras cette lettre 1953, Elena et les hommes 1955, Les racines du ciel 1958, Drame dans un miroir 1960, Maléfices 1962, Le désordre à 20 ans 1967; *TV appearances include:* Belphégor (series) 1965; numerous variety shows including Top à Juliette Gréco; *Publications include:* Jujube 1982, Un jour d'été et quelques nuits 1998. *Leisure interest:* tapestry. *Address:* c/o Maurice Marouani, 37 rue Marbeuf, 75008 Paris, France.

GREDLER, Martina, MP; Austrian medical practitioner and politician; b 29 Dec 1958, Vienna. *Education:* Athenee Royal (Rösrath, Germany). *Career:* Mem Nationalrat (Parl) 1994–95; elected MEP (LDR) 1995, mem Cttee on Budgets, Del for relations with Slovenia, Del for relations with the People's Repub of China; mem Bd of Liberales Forum 1993; Treas Liberal Int 1996. *Leisure interests:* diving, travelling. *Address:* c/o European Parliament, rue Wiertz, 1047 Brussels, Belgium.

GREEN, Joyce Hens, BA, JD; American federal judge; b 13 Nov 1928, New York; d of James S. and Hedy Hens; m Samuel Green 1965 (deceased); two s one d. *Education:* Univ of Maryland and George Washington Univ (DC). *Career:* Called to the Bar, DC 1951, VA 1956, US Supreme Court 1956; law practice, Washington 1951–68, Arlington, VA 1956–68; Partner Green & Green 1966–68; Judge Superior Court, DC 1968–79, US Dist Court, DC 1979–, Judge (Presiding) US Foreign Intelligence Surveillance Court 1988–95; Chair Task Force on Gender, Race and Ethnic Bias, DC Circuit Court; Chair (elect) ABA Nat Conf of Fed Trial Judges; mem Women's Bar Asscn, DC, Pres 1960–62; mem Exec Women in Govt, Chair 1977; mem Women's Forum of Washington, DC, Nat Asscn of Women Judges, Bd Dirs Fed Judges' Asscn; Fellow American Bar Foundation; Woman Lawyer of the Year 1979; Judicial Honoree of the Year, Bar Asscn of DC, 1994; Edmund J. Randolph Award, US Dept of Justice 1995. *Publications:* Marriage and Family Law Agreements (contrib to supplements) 1985–89, Dissolution of Marriage (jtly) 1986. *Address:* US District Court, US Courthouse, 333 Constitution Ave, NW, Washington, DC 20001, USA.

GREEN, Lucinda Jane, MBE; British former horsewoman; b 7 Nov 1953, Low Dow; d of the late George Errol and Lady Doreen Hersey Winifred Prior-Palmer; m David Green 1981 (separated); one s one d. *Education:* St Mary's School (Wantage) and Idbury Manor (Kingham, Oxon). *Career:* Mem Jr European Team 1971; winner Badminton Horse Trials 1973, 1976, 1977, 1979, 1983, 1984; winner Burghley Horse Trials 1977, 1981; European Champion 1975, 1977; World Champion 1982; mem Olympic team Montréal, Canada 1976, Los Angeles, CA, USA 1984; team Silver Medal and individual Gold Medal European Championships, Germany, 1975, team Gold Medal 1977, 1985, 1987; Co-Presenter Horses (Channel Four TV) 1987; fmr Consulting Ed Eventing magazine; currently columnist Daily Telegraph; runs cross-country riding clinics in the UK and abroad. *Publications:* Up, Up and Away 1977, Four Square 1980, Regal Realm 1985, Cross-Country Riding (2nd edn) 1995. *Leisure interests:* driving, skiing, diving, travel. *Address:* The Tree House, Appleshaw, Andover, Hants SP11 9BS, UK. *Telephone:* (1264) 771133.

GREEN, Pauline, BA, M SC; British politician; b 8 Dec 1948, Gzira, Malta; d of the late B. W. Wiltshire and of Lucy (née Vella) Wiltshire; m Paul A. Green 1971; one s one d. *Education:* John Kelly Secondary Modern School for Girls (Brent, London), Kilburn Polytechnic, Open Univ and LSE. *Career:* Fmr policewoman with Metropolitan Police; Lecturer Barnet Coll of Further Educ 1980–82; Sec Chipping Barnet Labour Party 1981, Chair 1983; Asst teacher Special Educ Unit 1982–85; Parl adviser on European Affairs to Co-operative Union 1985–89; MEP (Lab) for London N 1989–99, mem Cttee on the Environment, Public Health and Consumer Protection 1989; Leader,

EP Lab Party 1993–94, PSE 1994–99; mem Nat Exec Cttee Lab Party 1993–99; Vice-Pres Socialist Int Women 1994–99; Chief Exec Co-operative Union Ltd 2000–; Hon D UNIV (Middlesex) 1988, (N London); Medal of Honour, Greece 1994, Grand Golden Cross with Star, Austria 1995, Grand Commdr Order of Merit, Cyprus. *Leisure interests:* music, swimming, walking. *Address:* The Co-operative Union Ltd, Holyoake House, Hanover St, Manchester M60 0AS, UK (Office); 55 Slaithwaite Rd, Meltham, Holmfirth, West Yorks HD9 5PG, UK (Home); 8 Normandy Ave, Barnet, Herts EN5 2JA, UK (Home). *Telephone:* (161) 246-2900 (Office); *E-mail:* pgreen.coopunion@co-op .co.uk (Office).

GREEN, Rose Basile, FRSA, MA, PH D; American poet and writer; b 19 Dec 1914, New Rochelle, NY; d of Salvatore and Caroline Basile; m Raymond S. Green 1942; one d one s. *Education:* Coll of New Rochelle, Columbia Univ (NY) and Univ of Pennsylvania. *Career:* Teacher Torrington High School, CT 1936–42; Writer, Researcher Cavalcade of America, NBC 1940–42; Assoc Prof of English, Registrar Univ of Tampa, FL 1942–43; Special Lecturer in English Temple Univ, PA 1953–57; Prof of English Cabrini Coll, PA 1957–70; Exec Dir American Inst of Italian Studies; Vice-Pres, Dir Nat Italian-American Foundation; Chair Nat Advisory Council for Ethnic Heritage Studies; mem American Acad of Political and Social Sciences, Acad of American Poets, American Studies Asscn, Ethnic Studies Asscn, American Asscn of Univ Women; Hon LHD (Gwynedd-Mercy Coll) 1979, (Cabrini Coll) 1982; Cavalier of the Repub of Italy; Daughters of the American Revolution Nat Bicentennial Award for Poetry 1976; Nat Amita Award for Literature 1976. *Publications:* Cabrinian Philosophy of Education 1967, Lauding the American Dream 1980, The Life of Mother Frances Cabrini 1984, The Pennsylvania People 1984, Challenger Countdown 1988, Five Hundred Years of America 1492–1992 1992; Poetry: To Reason Why 1971, Primo Vino 1974, 76 for Philadelphia 1975, Woman, The Second Coming 1977, Century Four 1981, Songs of Ourselves 1982; Criticism: The Latin-American Novel 1974. *Address:* 308 Manor Rd, Lafayette Hill, PA 19444-1741, USA.

GREENBERG, Gloria, BFA; American artist; b 4 March 1932; d of Benjamin and Sara Greenberg; m Martin Bressler 1953; two c. *Education:* Music and Art High School, Cooper Union School of Art, Brooklyn Museum School of Art (New York) and Yale Univ School of Art. *Career:* Served in US Army 1957–58; Designer Harper and Row Publrs 1966–79; founding mem 55 Mercer Gallery, New York 1970; teacher of Art 1981–; MacDowell Colony Fellowship 1965, 1973. *Publication:* Chimes of Change and Hours: Views of Older Women in Twentieth Century America (contrib) 1983. *Leisure interest:* writing poetry and travel. *Address:* 118 E 17th St, New York, NY 10003, USA. *Telephone:* (212) 533-7625.

GREENE, Enid; American politician and lawyer; b 5 Oct 1958; d of Mr and Mrs D. Forrest Green; m (divorced); one d. *Education:* Univ of Utah and Brigham Young Univ (UT). *Career:* Commercial Litigator Ray, Quinnery and Nebeker 1983–90; Deputy Chief of Staff Gov Norm Bangerter 1990–92; Corp Counsel Novell Inc 1993–94; mem House of Reps 1995–96, mem House Rules Cttee 1995–96; mem Utah Econ Devt Corpn 1995–96; attorney Smith & Glauser, Salt Lake City 1998–. *Leisure interests:* reading, horseback riding, hiking, needlework, church and community work. *Address:* Smith & Glauser, 2180 S 1300 E, Salt Lake City, UT 84106, USA.

GREENE, Sally; British theatre executive; b 1957; m. *Career:* Fmr Man Richmond Theatre (London); restored and refurbished Richmond and Criterion Theatres (London); CEO Old Vic Productions; Dir Royal Exchange Theatre (Manchester); Gov Royal Shakespeare Co; Trustee Old Vic Theatre Trust 2000, Richmond Theatre Trust Ltd. *Address:* Park House, 26 North End Rd, London NW11 7PT, UK.

GREENE-MERCIER, Marie-Zoe, BA; American sculptor; b 31 March 1911, Madison, WI; d of Louis and Zoé (née Lassagne) Mercier; m Wesley Hammond Greene 1937; three s. *Education:* Harvard Univ and New Bauhaus (Chicago). *Career:* Solo exhibitions include Galerie Duncan (Paris) 1953, Art Inst (Chicago) 1955, Galleria d'arte Arno (Florence) 1965, Numero (Milan) 1966 and Artivisive (Rome) 1972, Amerika House (Stuttgart) 1979 and Skulpturenpark Museum (Bad Nauheim, Germany) 1986, Galerie Loehr (Frankfurt) 1991; group exhibitions include London Royal Inst Galleries 1954, Pagani Foundation 1966, 1969–72, Museum of Contemporary Art (Chicago) 1968, Salon de Mai (France) 1973–78, 1986, UNESCO (Paris) 1979, Kurhausgarten (Bad Homburg, Germany) 1979–81, Grand Palais (Paris) 1990, Kunstmesse, (Frankfurt) 1991; work in perm collections including Roosevelt Univ, Bauhaus Archiv Museum (Berlin), Museum of Modern Art (Venice, Italy), Int Film Bureau, Univ of Chicago, Oberhessisches Museum, Giessen, Germany 1995–; awards include: Gold Medal Cannes 1969, Hors Concours, Nice 1970, Mérite Belgo-Hispanique Palmes d'Or 1975, Mary Mildred Sullivan Award 1985; contribs to journals and catalogues. *Address:* 1232 E 57th St, Chicago, IL 60637-1613, USA. *Telephone:* (312) 324-2232.

GREENFIELD, Baroness (Life Peer), cr 2001, **Susan Adele,** CBE, D PHIL; British pharmacologist; b 1 Oct 1950; d of Reginald Myer and Doris Margaret Winifred Greenfield; m Peter William Atkins 1991. *Education:* Godolphin and Latymer School for Girls and St Hilda's Coll (Oxford). *Career:* MRC Training Fellow Univ Lab of Physiology, Oxford 1977–81; fmrly with Coll de France (Paris); MRC-INSERM French Exchange Fellow 1979–80; Jr Research Fellow Green Coll (Oxford) 1981–84, Lecturer in Synaptic Pharmacology 1985–96, Prof in Synaptic Pharmacology 1996–, Gresham Prof of Physics (Gresham Coll) 1995–; Dir Royal Inst 1998–; Visiting Fellow Inst of Neuroscience La Jolla, USA 1995; Sr Research Fellow Lincoln Coll (Oxford); Hon Fellow St Hilda's Coll (Oxford), Royal Coll of Physicians 2000; Visiting Distinguished Scholar Queen's Univ, Belfast 1996; Trustee Science Museum; awarded 18 Hon D SC degrees 1997–2001; Woman of Distinction, Jewish Care 1998, Michael Faraday Medal, Royal Soc 1998. *TV appearances include:* Dimbleby Lecture 1999, author and presenter of Brain Story ('Landmark' series of programmes on the brain) 2000; *Radio includes:* Start the Week, Any Questions and other discussion programmes; presenter of Turn On, Turn Off series on drugs and the brain; *Publications:* numerous articles in learned journals; Mindwaves (ed with C. B. Blakemore) 1987, Journey to the Centres of the Brain (with G. Ferry) 1994, Journey to the Centres of the Mind 1995, The Human Mind Explained (ed) 1996, The Human Brain: A Guided Tour 1997; Brainpower (ed) 2000, Brain Story 2000, Private Life of the Brain 2000. *Leisure interests:* aerobics, travel. *Address:* Department of Pharmacology, Mansfield Rd, Oxford OX1 3QT, UK (Office). *Telephone:* (1865) 271628 (Office); *Fax:* (1865) 271853 (Office); *E-mail:* susan.greenfield@pharm.ox.ac.uk.

GREENGROSS, Baroness (Life Peer), cr 2000, of Notting Hill in the Royal Borough of Kensington and Chelsea, **Sally Greengross,** OBE, FRSA; British member of the House of Lords; b 29 June 1935; m Sir Alan Greengross 1959; three d one s. *Education:* Brighton and Hove School and LSE. *Career:* Fmr lecturer, researcher, linguist and industrial exec; fmr Magistrate at Inner London Juvenile Court; mem UK Forum; Asst Dir Age Concern 1977–82, Deputy Dir 1982–87, Dir then Dir Gen 1987–2000; Exec Chair, The Experience Corps 2001–, Chair Int Longevity Centre, UK 2000–, Advisory Cttee to English Longitudinal Study on Ageing at Int Centre for Health and Society at Univ Coll London; Founder and Sec-Gen Eurolink Age 1981–2001; Jt Chair Bd, Age Concern Inst of Gerontology, King's Coll, London 1987–; Hon mem Bd Dirs Int Fed on Ageing 1982–83, Vice-Pres 1987–; mem UN Network on Ageing 1983–, WHO Network on Ageing 1983–, Standing Advisory Cttee on Transport for Disabled and Elderly People 1986–88, Advisory Panel Centre for Voluntary Orgs LSE 1991–, Advisory Group to Sec of State Dept of Health, on Health of the Nation 1991–, Advisory Cttee Carnegie Inquiry into Third Age 1992–93, European Year of Older People 1992–93, Advisory Council of European Movt 1992–, Advisory Cttee to Sec of State Dept of Employment, on Older Workers 1993–, Bd World Org for Care in Home and Hospice 1993–, Man Bd Hanover Housing Group, Advisory Cttee to Health Educ Authority on policy for older people, BT Forum Devt Advisory Group 1994–, HelpAge Int; Vice-Pres EXTEND 1996–; Pres Action on Elder Abuse 1994–, Patron 1999–; Patron Home Concern 1993–, James Powell UK Trust 1999–, Groundwork Foundation 1999–, ESRC Connect 1999–, Pennell Initiative 1999–; Consultant Journal of Educational Gerontology 1987–; Ed Adviser Home Care 1993–; Hon Pres Women for Europe 1999–; Hon D LITT (Ulster) 1994; Hon D UNIV (Kingston), (Exeter); named UK Woman of Europe 1990. *Publications:* Ageing, An Adventure in Living (ed) 1986, The Law and Vulnerable Elderly People (ed) 1991, Living, Loving and Ageing (jtly) 1991; numerous articles and

broadcasts on ageing. *Leisure interests:* theatre, music, the countryside. *Address:* House of Lords, Westminster, London SW1A 0PW, UK; 9 Dawson Place, London W2 4TD (Home). *Telephone:* (20) 7229-1939; *Fax:* (20) 7792-9238; *E-mail:* greengross@parliament.uk.

GREER, Germaine, PH D; Australian feminist and writer; b 29 Jan 1939, Melbourne; d of Eric Reginald and Margaret May (née Lafrank) Greer. *Education:* Star of the Sea Convent (Gardenvale, Vic), Univs of Melbourne, Sydney and Cambridge (UK). *Career:* Sr Tutor in English Univ of Sydney 1963–64; Asst Lecturer then Lecturer in English, Univ of Warwick, UK 1967–72, Prof of English and Comparative Studies, 1998–; lecturer throughout USA and Canada with American Program Bureau 1973–78; Visiting Prof Grad Faculty of Modern Letters, Univ of Tulsa, USA 1979, Prof of Modern Letters 1980–83; Founder Dir Tulsa Centre for the Study of Women's Literature, Founder Ed Tulsa Studies in Women's Literature 1981; Dir Stump Cross Books 1988–; Special Lecturer and Unofficial Fellow Newnham Coll, Cambridge (UK) 1989–98; broadcaster/journalist 1972–, numerous TV appearances and public talks including discussion with Norman Mailer in The Theatre of Ideas, New York; Jr Govt Scholarship 1952; Diocesan Scholarship 1956; Sr Govt Scholarship 1956; Teachers' Coll Studentship 1956; Commonwealth Scholarship 1964; Dr hc (Griffith, Australia) 1996, (York, Toronto) 1999, (UMIST) 2000. *Publications:* The Female Eunuch 1969, The Obstacle Race: The Fortunes of Women Painters and Their Work 1979, Sex and Destiny: The Politics of Human Fertility 1984, Shakespeare 1986, The Madwoman's Underclothes 1986, Kissing the Rod: An Anthology of 17th Century Verse (co-ed) 1989, Daddy, We Hardly Knew You (J. R. Ackerly Prize and Premio Internazionale Mondello) 1989, The Uncollected Verse of Aphra Behn (ed) 1989, The Change: Women, Ageing and the Menopause 1991, The Collected Works of Katherine Philips (ed), the Matchless Orinda, Vol III: The Translations (co-ed) 1993, Slipshod Sibyls: Recognition, Rejection and the Woman Poet 1995, The Surviving Works of Anne Wharton (co-ed) 1997, The Whole Woman 1999, John Wilmot, Earl of Rochester, Writers and Their Work 1999; articles for the Listener, Spectator, Esquire, Harper's Magazine, Playboy, Private Eye and other periodicals. *Leisure interest:* gardening. *Address:* c/o Gillon Aitken Associates, 29 Fernshaw Rd, London SW10 0TG, UK (Office).

GREEVY, Bernadette; Irish concert singer (mezzo-soprano); b 1940, Dublin; d of Patrick J. Greevy and Josephine F. Miller; m Peter A. Tattan 1965 (died 1983); one s. *Education:* Convent of the Holy Faith (Clontarf, Dublin). *Career:* London debut Wigmore Hall 1964; has since performed in Europe, USA, Canada and Far East; recordings of works by Brahms, Handel, Haydn, Bach, Berlioz, Britten, Elgar and Mahler; mem Bd Nat Concert Hall 1981–86, 1991–; Hon D MUS (Univ Coll, Dublin, Trinity Coll, Dublin); Harriet Cohen Int Music Award; Order of Merit (Order of Malta), Dame of the Holy Sepulchre, Pro Ecclesia et Pontifice (Vatican). *Leisure interests:* gardening, cooking, painting. *Address:* Melrose, 672 Howth Rd, Dublin 5, Ireland.

GREGER, Janet L., MS, PH D; American professor of nutritional sciences; b 18 Feb 1948, IL; d of Harold and Marjorie Greger. *Education:* Univ of Illinois and Cornell Univ (NY). *Career:* Asst Prof Purdue Univ, IN 1973–78; Asst Prof, Assoc Prof Univ of Wisconsin, Madison 1978–83, Prof of Nutritional Sciences 1983–, Assoc Dean Grad School 1990–96, Assoc Dean Medical School 1996–98; mem Bd of Man Council on Governmental Relations 1993–1999, NIH Regulatory Burden Working Group 2000–; AAAS Congressional Sciences Eng Fellow 1984–85. *Publication:* Nutrition for Living 1994; over 160 papers in scientific journals. *Leisure interests:* travel, reading. *Address:* University of Wisconsin, Dept of Nutritional Sciences, 1415 Linden Drive, Madison, WI 53706, USA. *Telephone:* (608) 262-9972 (Office); (608) 238-1550 (Home); *Fax:* (608) 262-5860; *E-mail:* jlgregor@ facstaff.wisc.edu (Office).

GRÉGOIRE, Marie (Ménie); French journalist and writer; b 15 Aug 1919, Cholet; d of Maurice and Marie (née Jactel) Laurentin; m Roger Grégoire 1943 (deceased); three d. *Education:* Univ de Paris (Sorbonne), Ecole des Hautes Etudes and Inst d'Art et d'Archéologie (Paris). *Career:* Psychoanalyst; speaker for the Alliance française in Finland, Italy, Sweden, USA 1950–; journalist with various newspapers and periodicals including Le Monde and Esprit; Editorial Writer Marie-Claire; presented two daily women's radio programmes on Radio-Télé

Luxembourg (RTL) 1967–81, Ed 1980–86; presented Avec le temps (TV) 1984; columnist France-Soir 1986–99; mem Conseil supérieur de l'information sexuelle, de la régulation des naissances et de l'éducation familiale 1974–, various nat comms; Officier de la Légion d'Honneur 1990. *Publications:* Le métier de femme 1964, Femmes (two vols) 1966, La belle Arsène, Passeport du couple 1967, Les cris de la vie 1971, Ménie Grégoire raconte... 1972, Telle que je suis 1976, Des passions et des rêves 1981, Tournelune 1983, Sagesse et folie des Français 1986, Nous aurons le temps de vivre 1987, La France et ses immigrés 1988, La Dame du Puy du Fou 1990, Le petit roi du Poitou 1992, La magicienne 1993, Le Bien aime 1996, Les dames de la Loire 2001. *Leisure interests:* sculpture, hunting and golf. *Address:* 3 rue Chapon, 75003 Paris, France. *Telephone:* (1) 42-77-53-81; *Fax:* (1) 40-27-08-95.

GREGORY, Cynthia Kathleen; American ballet dancer; b 8 July 1946, Los Angeles, CA; d of Konstantin and Marcelle Gregory; m 1st Terrence S. Orr 1966 (divorced); m 2nd John Hemminger 1976 (died 1984); m 3rd Hilary B. Miller. *Career:* Ford Foundation Scholar San Francisco Ballet 1961, Soloist 1962–65; Prin Dancer San Francisco Opera 1964–65; mem American Ballet Theatre, New York 1965, Soloist 1966, apptd Prin Dancer 1967; apptd Perm Guest Artist Cleveland San José Ballet 1986; has performed lead female roles in classical ballets and created roles for modern works; has appeared with Berlin State Opera Ballet, Nat Ballet of Cuba, New York City Opera, Ballet West, Zurich State Opera Ballet (Switzerland); Dance magazine Award 1975; Harkness Ballet Foundation 1st Annual Dance Award 1978; Cyril Magnin Award for Outstanding Achievement in the Arts (San Francisco Chamber of Commerce) 1986. *Publication:* Ballet is the Best Exercise. *Address:* American Ballet Theatre, 890 Broadway, New York, NY 10003, USA; Cleveland San José Ballet, 1 Playhouse Square, Suite 330, Cleveland, OH 44115, USA.

GREGORY, Mary Barbara, D PHIL; British economist; b 1 March 1941, Larkhall; d of Rev J. A. MacDonald and of Mrs J. MacDonald; m Norman L. Gregory 1968; three s. *Education:* Hamilton Acad, Univs of Glasgow and Oxford and Brown Univ (RI, USA). *Career:* Research Officer Nat Inst of Econ and Social Research, London 1969–71; Lecturer Dept of Political Economy, Univ of Glasgow 1972–82; Fellow, Tutor in Econs and Univ Lecturer, St Hilda's Coll, Oxford 1982–; mem Council Royal Econ Soc 1988–93; Ed Oxford Economic Papers 1988–95. *Publications:* Income Distribution Growth and Basic Needs in India 1982, Macroeconomic Theory and Stabilisation Policy 1988, A Portrait of Pay 1990. *Address:* University of Oxford, St Hilda's College, Cowley Place, Oxford OX1 2JD, UK. *Telephone:* (1865) 276810; *Fax:* (1865) 276816; *E-mail:* mary.gregory@economics.oxford.ac.uk.

GREKOVA, Irina Nikolaevna (pseudonym of Elena Sergeevna Venttsel); Russian writer; b 21 March 1907, Reval (now Tallinn), Estonia. *Education:* Leningrad (now St Petersburg) Univ. *Career:* Prof of Cybernetics Moscow Univ; published first story 1957. *Publications include:* Beyond the Entryway 1962, The Lady's Hairdresser 1963, Under the Streetlight 1966, During the Tests 1967, Little Garnsov 1970, The Landlady 1976, Life at the Department: Tales 1981, The Rapids (novel) 1984, A Legendary Figure 1987, The Break 1987, Soviet Women Writing (ed) 1991, Through Fresh Is Its Renown (novel) 1995. *Address:* 125167 Moscow, Leningradsky Prosp 44, kv 29, Russian Federation. *Telephone:* (095) 212-32-69.

GRENDELMEIER, Verena; Swiss politician and documentary film writer and director; b 16 Feb 1939, Zurich; d of Alois Grendelmeier. *Education:* Zurich, Basel, Paris and Vienna. *Career:* Stage Dir 1963–67; TV Dir 1967–73; mem Zurich Canton 1973–79; Vice-Pres Social Liberal Party of Independents 1980–96; mem Nationalrat/Conseil Nat (Parl) 1983–; Conseillère Nationale, mem Council of Europe, Pres Comm on the Media and Dir of documentaries Swiss TV, Zurich; mem Amnesty Int, Charity Council for Maltreated Women and Children. *TV Documentaries:* Im selben Boot – der psychisch Kranke und wir 1975, Gehirn und Verhalten (on neuro-psychology) 1976, Das gläserne Gefängnis (on autism) 1980, Das verordnete Glück (on Austria) 1982. *Leisure interests:* music, cooking, theatre, hiking, mountaineering. *Address:* Nationalrat/Conseil National, Parlamentsgebäude, 3003 Berne, Switzerland (Office); Witikonerstr 468, 8053 Zurich, Switzerland (Home). *Telephone:* (1) 4224718 (Home).

GRENVILLE, Kate, MA; Australian author; b 14 Oct 1950, Sydney; d of Kenneth Grenville Gee and Nance Russell; m Bruce Petty 1986; one s one d. *Education:* Univ of Sydney and Univ of Colorado at Boulder (USA). *Career:* Ed of documentary films, Film Australia 1971–76; freelance journalist, London and Paris 1977–80; Sub-Ed Subtitling Unit, Multicultural TV (Sydney) 1982–85; reviewer; journalist; Writer-in-Residence at univs and Nat Film School (Sydney) 1986–; Sr Fellowship, Australia Council Bicentennial Comm; Vogel/Australian Award 1985; Victorian Premier's Literary Award 1995. *Publications:* Bearded Ladies 1984, Lilian's Story 1985, Dreamhouse 1986, Joan Makes History 1988, The Writing Book 1990, Making Stories 1992, Dark Places 1995, The Idea of Perfection (Orange Prize 2001) 1999, From Start to Finish 2001. *Leisure interest:* learning cello. *Address:* c/o Barbara Mobbs Agency, POB 126, Edgecliff, NSW 2027, Australia. *E-mail:* kgrenville@bigpond.com; *Internet:* www.users.bigpond.com/kgreville.

GREY, Dame Beryl Elizabeth, DBE; British arts administrator and former ballet dancer; b 11 June 1927, London; d of Arthur Ernest and Annie Elizabeth (née Marshall) Groom; m Dr Sven Gustav Svenson 1950; one s. *Education:* Dame Alice Owens School (London), Madeline Sharp School, Royal Ballet School and de Vos School of Dance. *Career:* Debut Sadler's Wells Co 1941; first full-length ballet Swan Lake on 15th birthday; Prima Ballerina with Royal Ballet until 1957; freelance int Prima Ballerina 1957–; Royal Ballet tours of USA, Europe, Africa and Far East 1945–; guest artist Opera Houses in Norway, Finland, Sweden, Denmark, Belgium, Romania, Germany, Italy, S and Cen America, Middle East, SA, Rhodesia (now Zimbabwe), Australasia; first foreign guest artist to dance with Bolshoi Ballet (Moscow, Leningrad–now St Petersburg, Kiev, Tiflis) 1957–58, with Beijing and Shanghai Ballets 1964; Dir-Gen Arts Educational Trust (London) 1966–68; Artistic Dir London Festival Ballet 1968–79; produced and staged Swan Lake (London Festival Ballet, London) 1971, Giselle (Perth, Australia) 1984, 1986, Sleeping Beauty (Royal Swedish Ballet, Stockholm) 1985; Pres Dance Council for Wales 1982–; Vice-Pres Royal Acad of Dancing 1980–; Chair Imperial Soc of Teachers of Dancing 1982–91, Pres 1991–2001; Trustee Royal Ballet Benevolent Fund 1985–, Vice Chair 1987–92, Chair 1992–; Trustee London City Ballet; Dir Royal Opera House, Covent Garden 1999–; Vice-Pres Music Therapy Charity 1980–, Fed of Music Festivals 1987–, Keep-fit Soc; Gov Royal Ballet 1993–, Vice-Chair of Govs 1995–; Patron Dancers Resettlement Trust, Benesh Inst, Friends of Sadler's Wells Theatre 1991–, Osteopathic Centre for Children 1994, Amber Trust 1995; Fellow Imperial Soc of Teachers of Dancing 1966–; Hon D MUS (Leicester) 1970, (London) 1996; Hon D LITT (City Univ) 1974, (Buckingham) 1993; Hon DIP ED (CNAA) 1989; Queen Elizabeth II Coronation Award (Royal Acad of Dancing) 1996. *Ballets include:* Giselle, Sleeping Beauty, Sylvia, Nutcracker, Les Sylphides, Checkmate, Donald of the Burthens, Dante Sonata, Three Cornered Hat, Ballet Imperial, Lady and the Fool, Les Rendezvous; *Publications:* Red Curtain Up 1958, Through the Bamboo Curtain 1965; My Favourite Ballet Stories (ed) 1981. *Leisure interests:* piano playing, painting, swimming, opera. *Address:* Fernhill, Priory Rd, Forest Row, E Sussex RH18 5JE, UK. *Telephone:* (1342) 822539 (Home); *Fax:* (1342) 822539 (Home).

GREY, Deborah, BA, B EDUC; Canadian politician; b 1 July 1952, Vancouver, BC; d of Mansell and Joyce Grey; m Lewis Larson 1993. *Education:* Univ of Alta. *Career:* MP for Beaver River, Alta 1989–97, for Edmonton N, Alta 1997–; Chair Opposition Caucus, Canadian Alliance 1993–2001; Deputy Parl Leader 1995–; Canada 125 Medal 1992. *Leisure interests:* motorcycle riding, swimming. *Address:* House of Commons, Parliament Bldgs, Ottawa, ON K1A 0A6, Canada. *Telephone:* (613) 996-9778; *Fax:* (613) 996-0785; *E-mail:* greyd@parl.gc.ca.

GREY, Marina (pseudonym of Marina Chiappe); French writer and historian; b 5 March 1919, Ekaterinodar, Russia; d of Gen Anton Denikine; m 1st Jean Boudet 1941; one s; m 2nd Jacques Lassaigne 1948; m 3rd Jean-François Chiappe 1961. *Education:* Schools in Malakoff, Chartres and Sèvres. *Career:* Emigrated from Russia to France 1926; Journalist working on French radio and TV 1944–65; writer of novels and historical books 1965–; literary prizes from Société des Gens de Lettres 1973, Acad Française 1979, 1983, Ville de Paris 1984. *Publications include:* Les armées blanches 1968, La saga de l'exil (three novels) 1979, 1980, 1984, Hébert, le père Duchesne agent royaliste (Prix Eugène Colas, Acad de Paris 1983) 1983, Mon père, le général Denikine 1985, Enquête sur la mort de Louis XVII 1989, Les Romanov 1991, Le Baron de Batz, le d'Artagnan de la révolution 1991, Qui a tué Raspoutine. *Leisure interest:* travel. *Address:* 10 rue de Fontenay, 78000 Versailles, France. *Telephone:* (1) 39-50-55-45.

GREYLING, Brenda J.; South African financial executive; b 13 Nov 1949; (divorced). *Career:* Owner US co importing SA goods 1977–79; Vice-Pres South African Futures Industry Asscn (SAFIA) 1979–87, Man Dir 1987; Consultant Rand Merchant Bank 1987–88; Man Dir Brenda Greyling and Assocs (pty) Ltd, Chair Integrated Man SA and Sec-Gen Inst of Financial Markets; cr first Futures Expo (computer and tech trade show); articles in finance magazines; mem American Soc of Asscn Execs, Exec Women's Club of SA. *Address:* POB 561, Lonehill, Sandton 2062, South Africa. *Telephone:* (11) 8345963 (Office); (11) 7053333 (Home); *Fax:* (11) 8384400.

GRIER, Pam; American actress, writer and singer; b 1949, Winston-Salem, NC; d of Clarence Ransome Grier and Gwendolyn (Sylvia) Samuels. *Career:* Mem Acad of Motion Picture Arts and Sciences. *Films:* The Big Doll House 1971, Women in Cages 1971, Big Bird Cage 1972, Black Mama, White Mama 1972, Cool Breeze 1972, Hit Man 1972, Twilight People 1972, Coffy 1973, Scream, Blacula, Scream! 1973, The Arena 1973, Foxy Brown 1974, Bucktown 1975, Friday Foster 1975, Sheba Baby 1975, Drum 1976, Greased Lightning 1977, Fort Apache: The Bronx 1981, Something Wicked This Way Comes 1983, Stand Alone 1985, The Vindicator 1986, On the Edge 1986, The Allnighter 1987, Above The Law 1988, The Package 1989, Class of 1999 1991, Bill and Ted's Bogus Journey 1991, Tough Enough, Posse 1993, Serial Killer 1995, Original Gangstas 1996, Escape from LA 1996, Mars Attacks! 1996, Strip Search 1997, Fakin' Da Funk 1997, Jackie Brown 1997, Holy Smoke 1999, In Too Deep, Fortress 2; *Plays:* Fool for Love (NAACP Image Award 1986), Frankie and Johnnie, In the Claire De Lune; *TV:* (mini-series) Roots: The Next Generations 1979; (films) Badge of the Assassin 1985, A Mother's Right: The Elizabeth Morgan Story 1992, Family Blessings. *Leisure interests:* skiing, scuba diving, western and English horseback riding, tennis.

GRIFFIN, Jane Flanigen, PH D; American research chemist; b 26 March, 1933; d of Charles F. and Edith M. (née O'Connor) Flanigen; m Richard F. Griffin 1954; three s (one deceased) two d. *Education:* Holy Angels Acad, D'Youville Coll and State Univ of New York. *Career:* Industrial Lab Technician Linde Corpn 1952–53, Jr Research Scientist 1954–55; Danforth Fellow State Univ of New York, Buffalo 1967–72, Teaching Asst 1971–73; Research Fellow Molecular Biophysics Dept, Hauptman-Woodward Medical Research Inst (fmrly Medical Foundation of Buffalo, Inc) 1974–77, Research Scientist (I) 1977–80, Research Scientist (II) 1980–85, Sr Research Scientist (I) 1985–88, Head of Dept 1988, Asst Research Dir 1994; Scholar-in-Residence Dept of Chemistry, Queen's Univ, ON, Canada 1984; Bd of Dirs W New York Tech Devt Center 1987; Bd of Trustees D'Youville Coll 1989; Chair American Crystallographic Asscn 1980; named one of Outstanding Young Women of America 1963. *Publications:* Molecular Structure and Biological Activity (co-ed) 1982, Atlas of Steroid Structure (co-ed) 1984, The Hydrogen Bond: New Insights on an Old Story (ed) 1987. *Leisure interests:* reading, architectural history, tennis. *Address:* Hauptman-Woodward Medical Research Institute, 73 High St, Buffalo, NY 14203-1196, USA. *Telephone:* (716) 856-9600; *Fax:* (716) 852-6086; *E-mail:* griffin@hwi.buffalo.edu; *Internet:* www.hwi.buffalo.edu.

GRIFFITH, Melanie; American actress; b 9 Aug 1957, New York; d of Peter Griffith and Tippi Hedren; m 1st Don Johnson (divorced 1976); m 2nd Steven Bauer 1983 (divorced 1985); one s; m 3rd (for 2nd time) Don Johnson 1989 (divorced 1993); one d; m 4th Antonio Banderas 1996; one d. *Education:* Hollywood Professional School and acting with Stella Adler. *Career:* First TV commercial at the age of nine months; moved to LA aged four. *Films include:* The Garden 1975, Night Moves 1975, The Drowning Pool 1975, Smile 1975, One on One, Roar, Joyride, Body Double 1984, Fear City 1985, Something Wild 1986, Cherry 2000 1988, The Milagro Beanfield War 1988, Stormy Monday 1988, Working Girl (Golden Globe Award, Acad Award nomination) 1988, In the Spirit 1990, Pacific Heights 1990, The Bonfire of the Vanities, Shining Through, Paradise 1991, A Stranger Amongst Us

1992, Close to Eden 1993, Born Yesterday 1993, Milk Money 1994, Nobody's Fool 1994, Two Much, Mulholland Falls, Now and Then 1996, Lolita 1996, Celebrity, Crazy in Alabama, Cecil B. Demented 2000; *TV appearances include:* Once an Eagle (mini-series), Carter Country (series), Coast to Coast, Steel Cowboy, Golden Gate, She's in the Army Now, Starmaker. *Address:* c/o Creative Artists Agency, 9830 Wilshire Blvd, Beverly Hills, CA 90212, USA (Office).

GRIFFITH, Nanci; American singer and songwriter; b 6 July 1953, Seguin, TX; d of Griff and Ruelene Griffith. *Career:* Fmrly schoolteacher; appeared in Nanci Griffith on Broadway 1994. *Albums include:* There's A Light Beyond These Woods 1977, Once In A Very Blue Moon 1984, The Last Of The True Believers 1985, Poet In My Window 1986, Lone Star State of Mind 1987, Little Love Affairs 1988, One Fair Summer Evening 1988, Storms 1989, Late Night Grand Hotel 1991, The MCA Years – A Retrospective 1993, Other Voices, Other Rooms 1993 (Grammy Award for Best Folk Album), Flyer 1994; *Publications include:* Two Of A Kind Heart 1988, Love Wore A Halo Back Before The War.

GRIFFITHS, Rachel; Australian actress; b 1968, Melbourne. *Education:* Univ of Melbourne. *Film and TV appearances include:* Secrets 1993, Muriel's Wedding 1994, To Have and to Hold 1996, Jude 1996, Cosi 1996, Children of the Revolution 1996, Welcome to Woop-Woop, My Best Friend's Wedding, Since You've been Gone, My Son the Fanatic 1997, Among Giants, Divorcing Jack, Amy, Hilary and Jackie, Tulip, Me Myself I, Very Annie Mary 2000, Never Better 2000, Blow 2001, Six Feet Under 2001. *Address:* c/o Markham and Froggatt Ltd, 4 Windmill St, London W1P 1HF, UK.

GRIFFON-FOUCO, Martine Monique Suzanne, L ÈS SC; French nuclear engineer; b 11 Nov 1951, Béthines; d of Albert and Marie-Madeleine (née Brunet) Griffon; m Jean-Luc Fouco 1980; two s. *Education:* Conservatoire Nat des Arts et Métiers, Univ de Paris IV (Paris-Sorbonne), Inst Nat des Langues et Civilisations Orientales and Ecole Nat Supérieure de Mécanique et d'Aérotechnique (Poitiers). *Career:* Engineer Agence Nat pour l'Amélioration des Conditions de Travail 1977, Commissariat à l'Energie Atomique (CEA) 1978–82; Head Human Factors Group, Thermic Production Dept, Electricité de France (EDF) 1982–88; Head Safety and Quality Section Centre de Production Nucléaire du Blayais 1988–90, Head of Plant 1990–93, Deputy Dir 1993–94, Dir 1994–; has written articles on the incidence of human error in nuclear plants; Chevalier de l'Ordre Nat du Mérite. *Leisure interests:* motorcycling, jogging, gliding. *Address:* Centre de Production Nucléaire du Blayais, Braud et Saint-Louis, BP 27, 33820 Saint-Ciers-sur-Gironde, France.

GRIMMER, Margot; American ballet dancer, choreographer and director; b 4 May 1944, Chicago, IL; d of Vernon and Ann (née Radziwill) Grimmer; m Weymouth S. Kirkland, Jr 1987; one d. *Education:* New Trier High School (IL), Lake Forest Coll (IL) and Northwestern Univ (Evanston, IL). *Career:* Dancer New York City Ballet 1956–57, Kansas City Starlight Theatre 1958, St Louis Municipal Theatre 1959, Chicago Trust House Music Theatre 1960–61, Lyric Opera Ballet 1961, 1963–66, 1968, Ballet Russe de Monte Carlo 1962, Ruth Page Int Ballet 1965–70, Choreographer and Dir American Dance Co 1972–; Dancer and Choreographer Ravinia Concert 1973; performances with Chicago Symphony Orchestra 1974, Bob Hope 1975, at Washington DC Bicentennial 1976, Sebastopol Center for Arts 1990; teacher and dir American Dance School 1971–87; teacher Oakland Dance Collective 1989–; critic New Voice Publications 1980–82; TV Presenter Spotlight 1984–85; numerous grants from Illinois Arts Council and Nat Endowment for the Arts. *Performances include:* In-a-Godda-Da-Vida 1972, The Wasteland 1973, Rachmaninov: Theme of Variations 1973, Le baiser de la fée and Sonata 1974, Four Quartets 1974, American Expert 1975, Earth, Wind and Fire 1976, Blood, Sand and Empire 1977, Disco Fever 1978, Pax Romana and Xanadu 1979, Ishmael 1980, Vertigo 1982, Eye In The Sky 1984, Frankie Goes to Hollywood 1986, Power House Africano 1987, After Dark 1990, Cole Porter Tribute 1994; *Film:* Statics (Int Film Award) 1967. *Leisure interests:* photography, making videos, writing. *Address:* 970 Vernon Ave, Glencoe, IL 60022, USA. *Telephone:* (708) 835-2556.

GRINDENKO, Tatyana Tikhonovna; Russian violinist; b 29 March 1946, Kharkov, Ukraine; m 1st Gidon Kremer; m 2nd Vladimir Martynov. *Education:* Moscow State Conservatory. *Career:* Prize, World Int Youth Competition in Bulgaria 1968, Wieniawski Competition in Poland 1972; repertoire includes baroque, avant-garde, jazz, rock, experimental music; Co-Founder (with A. Lyubimov) and Artistic Dir Moscow Acad of Ancient Music. *Leisure interest:* driving sports cars. *Address:* Moscow State Philharmonia, Tverskaya str 31, 103050 Moscow, Russian Federation. *Telephone:* (095) 253 7425 (Home).

GROENEWOLD, Sabine, D PHIL; German publishing executive; b 18 Oct 1940, Hamburg; m Kurt Groenewold. *Education:* Univs of Hamburg, Tübingen and Salamanca (Spain). *Career:* Asst Prof, later Assoc Prof Univs of New York, Hamburg, Kassel and Berlin 1969–88; Publr and Ed Europäische Verlagsanstalt, Rotbuch Verlag, Hamburg 1989–; numerous articles on Spanish and Latin-American literature 1972–. *Address:* Europäische Verlagsanstalt GmbH, Parkallee 22000, Hamburg 20, Germany. *Telephone:* (40) 4501940; *Fax:* (40) 45019450.

GROL-OVERLING, Anne Catherine, MA; Netherlands educational psychologist and politician; b 20 March 1931, Doetinchem; d of A. J. Overling and M. A. C. van der Klugt; m Wenceslaus J. F. Grol 1961; one d one s. *Education:* Catholic Univ Nijmegen. *Career:* Lecturer in Psychology and Pedagogy 1952–65; Research Fellow, Tanzania 1963–69; Head Dept School of Social Work, Hengelo 1969–84; Lecturer in Group Dynamics Conservatory of Music, Enschede 1984–94; mem Town Council, Hengelo 1970–76; mem Provincial States Overÿssel 1978–82; mem First Chamber (Senate) of States-Gen 1982–. *Publication:* Primary Education in Sukumaland, Tanzania 1970. *Leisure interests:* reading, languages, music, theatre. *Address:* Eerste Kamer der Staten Generaal, Binnenhof 22, Postbus 20017, The Hague, Netherlands (Office); Stationsplein 22, 7511 70 Enschede, Netherlands (Home). *Telephone:* (53) 432-13-18 (Home).

GRØNDAHL, Kirsti Kolle; Norwegian politician; b 1 Sept 1943, Røyken; m Svein Erik Grøndahl 1967; two d. *Education:* Univ of Oslo. *Career:* Mem Røyken Municipal Council and Exec Bd 1972–77; Chair Røyken Labour Party 1980–82, Spikkestad Labour Party 1990–, mem Labour Party's Cttee for Environment 1983–; mem Storting 1977–; mem Standing Cttee on Church and Educ 1977–85, on Foreign and Constitutional Affairs 1989–, Minister of Church and Educ 1986–88, of Devt Co-operation 1988–89, Vice-Pres Storting 1990–93, Pres 1993–; mem Norwegian Del to Parl Ass of Council of Europe 1989–90; Leader Del to CSCE Parl Ass 1991–; mem Nordic Council and of Council's Presidium 1990–93, Leader Norwegian Del to Nordic Council 1992–93. *Address:* Stortinget, Karl Johansgt 22, 0026 Oslo 1, Norway (office). *Telephone:* 22-31-30-50 (Office); *Fax:* 22-31-38-50 (Office); *E-mail:* stortinget.postmottak@st.dep.telemax.no (Office); *Internet:* www.stortinget.no (Office).

GRÖNER, Lissy (Lieselotte); German politician; b 31 May 1954, Langenfeld; m Gerhard Gröner; one s one d. *Career:* Mem SPD 1971–; MEP (PSE) 1989–, Co-ordinator Cttee for Women's Rights, mem Cttee on Culture, Youth, Educ, the Media and Sport, Cttee on Women's Rights and Equal Opportunities, Jt Parl Ass ACP-EU; Vice-Pres Socialist Int, SIW (Socialist Int Women); Vice-Chair Children's Alliance; mem Bd of the Asscn of Social-Democratic Women; mem Workers' Welfare Association (AWO), BUND (Association for Nature and Environmental Protection), Information, Documentation and Action Centre against Xenophobia – for a Multicultural Future, DPG (German Postal Workers' Union), Europa-Union; mem IFFF (Women's Int League for Peace and Freedom), Friends of Nature Tourism Asscn, Berlin Women's Computer Centre Advisory Cttee. *Address:* European Parliament, rue Wiertz, 1047 Brussels, Belgium (Office); Parkstr 15, 91413 BRX Neustadt/Aisch, Germany (Home). *Telephone:* (2) 284-54-12 (Office); (9161) 1076 (Home); *Fax:* (2) 284-94-12 (Office); (9161) 1068 (Home); *E-mail:* lgroener@europarl.eu.int.

GRONKIEWICZ-WALTZ, Hanna Beata, LL D; Polish banking executive and lawyer; b 4 Nov 1952, Warsaw; d of Wojciech and Maria Gronkiewicz; m Andrzej Waltz 1973; one d. *Education:* Univ of Warsaw. *Career:* Academic researcher Div of Admin Comparative Law and State Econ Man Inst of Legal Admin Sciences 1975–; expert on Econ and Banking Law to Sejm PRI (Parl) 1989; mem Codifying Comm of Banking Law 1991; mem Faculty of Canon Law, Acad of Catholic Theology 1992; Pres Narodowy Bank Polski (Nat Bank of Poland) 1992–; charter mem Solidarity 1980; Chair faculty Solidarity branch 1989–92; ind cand in presidential election 1995; scholarship to Univ of Paris I (Panthéon-Sorbonne) 1983; 2nd best manager of a cen bank, Global Finance magazine, USA 1994; European Award 1995, 1998; Zycie Gospodarne Award 1995; The Warsaw Voice Award 1995. *Publications:* The Role of the Ministry of Industry in the Management of the Economy 1985, Central Bank: From Planned Economy to Market Economy: Legal Aspects 1993, Economic Law (jtly) 1996; over 40 works and articles in econ and financial journals. *Leisure interests:* American literature, classical music. *Address:* Narodowy Bank Polski, ul Świętokrzyska 21, 00-919 Warsaw, Poland (Office). *Telephone:* 653 10 00; *Fax:* (22) 263751.

GROSSETETE, Françoise D.; French politician; b 17 May 1946, Lyon. *Education:* Univ de Droit (Lyon). *Career:* Lecturer in law 1969–74; mem, then Fed Sec Republican Party 1984–94; Mayor of St Etienne 1983–92, Deputy Mayor 1992–; Regional Counsellor of Rhone-Alpes 1992–; MEP (EPP) 1994–, mem Cttee on the Environment, Public Health and Consumer Protection, Del for relations with the Maghreb countries and the Arab Maghreb Union, Del for relations with Russia, Pres Comm for Man of Country Parks and Forests 1998–; Treas Fed Nat des Parcs de France 1996–; mem Political Cttee Démocratie Libérale 1998–, Nat Sec for Equal Opportunities 1997–; Admin Inst Français de l'Environnement 1995–98. *Leisure interests:* walking, tennis, music, reading. *Address:* rue Wiertz, 1047 Brussels, Belgium; Hôtel de Ville, 42007 St Etienne, France. *Telephone:* (4) 77-42-87-39 (France); *Fax:* (4) 77-42-88-89 (France).

GROSSMAN, Nancy, BFA; American artist; b New York; d of Murray and Josephine Grossman. *Education:* Pratt Inst (New York). *Career:* Solo exhibitions include Krasner Gallery, New York 1964, 1965, 1967, Cordier and Ekstrom, New York 1968, 1969, 1971, 1973, 1975–76, Barbara Gladstone Gallery, New York 1980, 1982, Heath Gallery, Atlanta 1981, 1986, Exit Art, New York 1991, Hillwood Art Museum, Brookville, New York 1991, Sculpture Center, New York 1991, Binghamton Univ, Binghamton, NY 1992, Hooks-Epstein Galleries, Houston, TX 1993, 1995, Weatherspoon Art Gallery, Univ of N Carolina, Greensboro 1994, LedisFlam, New York 1994; group exhibitions include Whitney Museum of American Art, New York 1968–69, 1973, 1980–81, 1995–96, Fogg Art Museum, Cambridge, MA 1972, American Acad of Arts and Letters, New York 1974, 1987, tour of Hungary, Czechoslovakia, Poland 1978, Betté Stoler 1983, Exit Art, NY 1991, Michael Rosenfeld Gallery 1995, 1996, Andre Zarre 1996, Luise Ross Gallery 1996; works in perm collections including Whitney Museum of American Art, Smithsonian Inst, Dallas Museum of Fine Arts, Boymans Van Beuningen Museum, Rotterdam, Netherlands, Univ of California, Princeton Univ, Contemporary Arts Museum, Houston, Metropolitan Museum of Art, New York, Weatherspoon Art Gallery, Greensboro, NC; mem Sculptors' Guild; Guggenheim Fellow 1965; Fellow New York Foundation for the Arts 1991; Acad of Arts and Letters–Nat Inst of Arts and Letters Award 1974, Hassam, Speicher, Betts and Symons Purchase Award 1989; Nat Endowment for Arts Award 1984. *Address:* 105 Eldridge St, New York, NY 10002, USA.

GROULT, Benoîte Marie Rose, L ÈS L; French writer and journalist; b 31 Jan 1920, Paris; d of André and Nicole (née Poiret) Groult; m 1st Pierre Heuyer 1944 (died 1945); m 2nd Georges de Caunes 1946; two d; m 3rd Paul Guimard 1951; one d. *Education:* Univ of Paris (Sorbonne). *Career:* Fmr teacher of Latin; Journalist on Elle and Marie-Claire magazines; currently writer and freelance journalist; Pres Comm pour la Féminisation des noms de métiers 1985–; mem Jury Prix Fémina 1979–; Prix Bretagne 1975; Officier de la Légion d'Honneur 1995; Commdr de l'Ordre Nat du Mérite. *Publications include:* La part des choses (Prix de l'Acad de Bretagne) 1972, Ainsi soit-elle 1975, Le féminisme au masculin 1977, Les vaisseaux du cœur (English title Salt on our Skin 1992, trans also to German) 1989, Olympe de Gouges (biog), Pauline Roland (biog), Histoire D'une evasion (autobiog) 1998; With sister (Flora Groult): Journal à quatre mains (English title Double-handed diary) 1958, Le féminin pluriel (English title Feminine Plural) 1961, Il était deux fois. *Leisure interests:* sea, fishing. *Address:* 54 rue de Bourgogne, 75007 Paris, France; 3 rue de la Croix, 83400 Hyères, France. *Telephone:* (1) 47-05-33-30; *Fax:* (4) 94-65-81-95.

GROWE, Joan Anderson, B SC; American former state official; b 28 Sept 1935, Minneapolis, MN; d of Arthur F. and Lucille M. Anderson; three s one d. *Education:* St Cloud State Univ, Univ of Minnesota and Harvard Univ. *Career:* Elementary school teacher, MN 1956–58, 1964–66; mem Minnesota House of Reps (Democratic-Farmer-Labor Party) 1973–74, Sec of State, State of Minnesota, St Paul 1975–98; Cand US Senate 1984; mem Exec Council Minnesota State Bd of Investment; mem Bd of Dirs Women Execs in State Govt; mem Nat Asscn of Secs of State, Pres 1979–80; Minnesota School Bell award 1977; YMCA Outstanding Achievement award 1978; Distinguished Alumni Award, St Cloud State Univ 1979; The Woman Who Makes A Difference Award, Int Women's Forum 1991; Esther V. Crosby Leadership Award, Greater Minneapolis Girl Scout Council 1992. *Address:* 180 State St, St Paul, MN 55155-0001, USA.

GRUNBERG-MANAGO, Marianne, PH D; French biochemist; b 6 Jan 1921, Leningrad, USSR (now St Petersburg, Russian Fed); d of Vladimir Grunberg and Catherine Riasanoff; m Armand Manago 1948 (deceased); one s one d. *Education:* Univ of Paris. *Career:* Research Asst, subsequently Researcher then Sr Researcher, CNRS 1946–61, Head Dept of Biochem, Inst of Physico-Chemical Biology 1959, Dir of Research CNRS 1961, Head Biochem Div 1967–; Assoc Prof Univ of Paris VII 1972–; Ed-in-Chief Biochimie; Pres-elect Int Union of Biochemistry 1983, Pres 1985–88; Vice-Pres Comm for Sciences and Tech, UNESCO 1985; mem Acad des Sciences, Institut de France 1982–, Vice-Pres 1994, Pres 1995–; mem Soc de Chimie Biologique, American Soc of Biological Chemists, Int Council of Scientific Unions Gen Cttee; Foreign mem American Acad of Arts and Sciences, New York Acad of Sciences, Acad of Sciences of Russia (Ukraine), American Philosophical Soc; Foreign Hon mem NAS (USA); Fogarty Fellow 1977–82; Charles-Léopold Mayer Prize 1955, 1966; Chevalier de la Légion d'Honneur; Commdr de l'Ordre Nat du Mérite. *Publications:* Biosynthèse des acides nucléiques (jtly) 1974, Escherichia coli and Salmonella typhimurium 1987; more than 300 publications in scientific journals. *Leisure interest:* paintings. *Address:* Institut de Biologie Physico-chimique, 13 rue Pierre-et-Marie Curie, 75005 Paris, France; 80 blvd Pasteur, 75015 Paris, France. *Telephone:* (1) 43-25-26-09.

GRUNENBERG, Nina; German journalist; b 7 Oct 1936, Dresden; d of Valentin and Dorothea Grunenberg; m Reimar Lüst. *Career:* Corresp Die Zeit newspaper; awards include Theodor-Wolff-Preis 1973, Quandt-Medienpreis 1990. *Publications:* Journalisten, Reportagen-Sammlung 1967, Schweden-Report (jtly) 1973, Japan-Report (jtly) 1981, Reise ins andere Deutschland (jtly) 1986, Die Chefs 1990. *Address:* Bellevue 49, 2000 Hamburg 60, Germany.

GRYAZNOVA, Alla Georgiyevna, D ECON; Russian professor of economics; b 27 Nov 1937, Moscow; m; one c. *Education:* Moscow Inst of Finance. *Career:* Asst Lecturer, Lecturer, Sr Lecturer, Docent, Prof, Moscow Inst of Finance (now Acad of Finance of Russian Govt) 1964–74, Pro-rector on int relations and research 1976–85, Rector 1985–; organizer various int symposia and confs on banking problems; Ed-in-Chief Banking System in Russia; Merited Worker of Science of Russian Fed; mem New Way Movt 1995; First Vice-Pres, Guild of Financiers; Vice-Pres, Acad of Man and Market; mem Acad of Econ Sciences, Int Acad of Informatics, Int Acad of Eurasia; Pres Moscow Int School of Finance and Banking. *Publications:* over 200 articles on econ problems. *Leisure interests:* tennis, ballet, volleyball, poetry. *Address:* Academy of Finance, Leningradsky prosp 49, 125468 Moscow, Russian Federation. *Telephone:* (095) 943 9855 (Office).

GRZESKOWIAK, Alicja, PH D; Polish politician; b 10 June 1941, Swirz, Lvov Prov, Ukraine; m (husband deceased); one d. *Education:* Nicolaus Copernicus Univ (Torun). *Career:* Research worker Faculty of Law and Admin Nicolaus Copernicus Univ (Torun) 1966–96, Prof 1990; Catholic Univ of Lublin (KUL) 1990, Prof 1991, mem Scientific Council of John Paul II Inst; Lecturer in Religious Law Higher Ecclesiastic Seminary (Torun) 1994; mem Solidarity Trade Union 1980; Senator 1989–, Vice-Marshal of Senate 1991–93, Marshal 1997–; Del Parl Ass of the Council of Europe 1989–97, mem 1991–97; Chair Group of Christian Democrats 1992–97; mem Social Movt of Solidarity Election Action (RSAWS) 1998–; mem Admin Council of John Paul II Foundation, Vatican 1992; consulter of Pontifical Council for the Family 1993; f Foundation of Assistance to Single Mothers (Torun);

Dame of the Holy Sepulchre Friars of Jerusalem; Hon mem Ass of Catholic Families; Dr hc (Acad of Catholic Theology, Warsaw) 1995, (Holy Family Coll, Philadelphia) 1998, (Int Ind Univ of Moldova) 1999; Pro Ecclesia et Pontifice Medal 1991; Medal of 13th Jan of Lithuanian Rep; Great Cross, Order of Crown (Belgium) 1999. *Publications:* numerous scientific publs on penal law, human rights and family rights. *Leisure interests:* reading, listening to music. *Address:* Kancelaria Senatu RP, ul Wiejska 6, 00-902 Warsaw, Poland. *Telephone:* (22) 694 14 39; *Fax:* (22) 694 27 01.

GU XIULIAN; Chinese politician and party official; b 1935, Nantong City, Jiangsu Prov. *Education:* Metallurgical Machinery Coll (Shenyang). *Career:* Cadre State Council 1970–73; Vice-Minister State Planning Comm, State Council 1973–83; alt mem, Cen Cttee, CCP 1977; Vice-Chair Cen Patriotic Sanitation Campaign Cttee, Cen Cttee 1981–89; mem 12th Cen Cttee, CCP 1982–87; mem 13th Cen Cttee CCP 1987–92; mem 14th Cen Cttee CCP 1992–97; Deputy Sec CCP Prov Cttee, Jiangsu 1982–89; Gov of Jiangsu 1983–89; Minister of Chemical Industry 1989–93, 1993–98 (also Party Cttee Sec at the Ministry); mem 15th Cen Cttee CCP 1997–; fmr Standing mem Nat Fed of Women. *Address:* c/o Ministry of Chemical Industry, Hepingli St, Anding Menwai, Beijing 100723, People's Republic of China.

GUADALUPE MARTÍNEZ, Ana; Salvadorean political guerrilla and group leader and political negotiator. *Career:* Leader Ligas Populares del 28 de Febrero (LP-28), a prin group within the opposition org Frente Democrático Revolucionario-Frente Farabundo Martí para la Liberación Nacional (FDR-FMLN), El Salvador; mem team negotiating peace settlement with Pres Alfredo Cristiani 1990–91.

GUARDIA DE ALFARO, Gloria, MA; Panamanian writer and journalist; b 12 March 1940, San Cristóbal, Venezuela; d of Carlos A. Guardia-Jaén and Olga Zeledón de Guardia; m Ricardo A. Alfaro-Arosemena 1968; one d. *Education:* Colegio de las Esclavas del Sagrado Corazón (Panamá), Roycemore School for Girls (Evanston, IL), Vassar Coll (NY), Columbia Univ (NY, USA) and Univ Complutense de Madrid (Spain). *Career:* Began writing 1961; journalist Agencia Latinoamericana 1975–90; Columnist on La Prensa, Panamá 1980–83, El Panamá-América 1990; mem Panamanian Acad of Letters 1985, Librarian and mem Bd of Dirs 1990; apptd mem Editorial Bd Panorama Católico 1988, Editora Mariano Arosemena 1990; Hon mem Real Academia Española 1989; Hon Scholarship Vassar Coll 1958–1963; numerous awards including Honor al Mérito (Soc of Spanish and Latin-American Writers) 1961, Premio Nacional Ricardo Miró 1966, Cen American Book Award 1976. *Publications include:* Novels: El último juego 1977; Short stories; Otra vez Bach 1983, Cartas Apocrifas 1990, Hora Santa 1996; Essays: Estudios sobre el pensamiento poético de Pablo Antonio Cuadra 1971, La búsqueda del rostro 1983; Editor: Palabras preliminares, Obras completas de María Olimpia de Obaldía 1976; numerous monographs. *Leisure interests:* music, opera, ballet. *Address:* CP 101830, Zona 10, Santa Fe de Bogotá, Colombia; Calle 87, 11a–84, Santa Fe de Bogotá, Colombia (Home). *Telephone:* (1) 256-1540 (Home); *Fax:* (1) 218-4236.

GUBAIDULLINA, Sofia Asgatovna; Russian (b Tatar) avant-garde composer and conductor; b 24 Oct 1931, Chistopol; d of Asgat Gubaidulin and Fedossia Gubaidulina; m Peter Meschaninov; one d. *Education:* Kazan and Moscow Conservatories and under Nikolai Peiko, Vissarion Shebalin (composition) and Grigori Kogan (piano). *Career:* Gained int recognition Paris 1979; British debut 1987 (Symphony in 12 Movts); works commissioned for Helsinki Summer Festival 1991. *Compositions include:* Orchestral pieces: The Steps 1971, The Hour of Soul 1976, Offertorium 1980, Stimmen... verstummen (symphony) 1986, Seven Words, Zeitgestalten (symphony) 1994; Cantatas: The Night in Memphis 1968, Rubaiyat 1969, Perception 1983, Dedication to Marina Tsvefayeva 1984, Now Always Now 1993, Johannes Passion 2000; 2nd Cello concerto 1994, Viola concerto 1998; concertos for solo instruments with chamber orchestra; instrumental music for non-traditional groups. *Address:* 107061 Moscow, 2d Pugatchevskaya ul 8/5, kv 130, Russian Federation; Ziegeleiweg 12, 25482 Appen, Germany. *Telephone:* (095) 161-80-61 (Moscow).

GUEDDANA, Nabiha, MD; Tunisian politician and professor of medicine; b 26 Jan 1949, Tunis; d of Ben Aissa Abderrahmane; m Bechir Gueddana; two s one d. *Education:* Paris. *Career:* Sec of State for Social Advancement 1989–92, for Women's Affairs and the Family 1992–93; Prof of Preventive and Social Paediatrics, Faculty of Medicine, Univ des Sciences, des Techniques et de Médecine de Tunis (Tunis II) 1993–94; Pres, Dir-Gen Nat Office of the Family and Population, Ministry of Public Health 1994–; Prix du Centre Int de l'Enfance 1987; Prix du President de la Republique des Societies Maghrebines de Médecine 1990; Medaille de la Sante Publique 1993. *Publications:* L'Adolescent Tunisien: Sante et Environnement 1987, Un Enfant et Deux Tunisies 1989. *Leisure interest:* painting. *Address:* 42 ave de Madrid, 1002 Tunis, Tunisia. *Telephone:* (1) 341-088; *Fax:* (1) 340-335.

GUEILER TEJADA, Lidia; Bolivian politician and diplomatist; b 1926, Cochabamba. *Career:* Active role in revolution of 1952; Pvt Sec to Pres Paz Estenssoro 1952; left Movimiento Nacional Revolucionario and joined Partido Revolucionario de la Izquierda Nacional (PRIN) 1964; Founder PRIN-Gueiler (part of Alianza Democrática de la Revolución Nacional) 1979; mem Chamber of Deputies 1956, Pres 1979, Pres Congress 1979; interim Pres of Bolivia 1979–80 (overthrown in coup); in exile in Paris 1980–82; Amb to Colombia 1983–86, to Venezuela 1992–. *Address:* Embassy of Bolivia, Avda Luis Roche Con 6A Transversal, Attamira, Caracas, Venezuela; Ministry of Foreign Affairs, Cancellería de la República de Bolivia, Plaza Murillo esq Ingarí, La Paz, Bolivia. *Telephone:* (2) 261-4563 (Venezuela) (Office); *Fax:* (2) 261-3386 (Venezuela) (Office).

GUÉRIN, Isabelle; French ballet dancer; b 6 May 1961, Rosny-sous-Bois; d of Jean Claude Guérin and Christine Martre; m Jean-Pierre Frohlich 2000; one d. *Education:* Lycée de Rambouillet and Lycée Racine Aparis. *Career:* Danseuse Etoile Opera de Paris 1985–, has performed in ballets by Noureev, Balanchine, Forsythe, Neumeier, Robbins, Tharp, Kylian, Petit, Béjart, Prejlocay, Lifar and Lander; performances in the USA, Italy (La Scala, Milan), Russia (Bolshoi, Moscow) and Japan; Guest Artist NY Ballet; Prix de Conservatoire 1977; Prix Pavlova 1988; Prix Benois en Danse 1993; Chevalier des Arts et des Lettres; Chevalier de la Légion d'Honneur 2001. *Videos include:* Ceudrillon, La bayadère, Notre dame de Paris; *Films include:* Le Parc, L'Arlesienne. *Leisure interests:* gardening, travelling, theatre, cinema. *Address:* Opéra de Paris, 8 rue Scribe, 75009 Paris, France; 32 rue de Levis, Paris, France. *Telephone:* (1) 47-66-46-39; *Fax:* (1) 47-66-46-39.

GUERRA DE VILLALAZ, Aura E., LL D; Panamanian magistrate; b Bugaba, Chiriquí; m; four c. *Education:* Univ of Panamá and Univ Autónoma de México. *Career:* Exec Dir Second Judiciary Room, Supreme Court 1963–66; Judge 7th District, Penal Branch 1966–1969, Civil Branch 1969; part-time researcher Center for Judiciary Research, Univ of Panamá 1955–87, Dir 1969–72 (acting), 1978–87; part-time Prof of Penal Law Univ Sta María La Antigua 1969–76, 1981–84, 1987–90; Dir Nat Archives 1972–73; Prof of Penal Law Univ of Panamá 1974–91, Head Dept of Penal Law and Criminology, Faculty of Law 1985–89; apptd Magistrate Supreme Court 1990; Del for Latin America, Cttee for Crime Prevention and Criminal Justice, UN 1979–89; numerous articles in professional books and journals; attended numerous confs on crime prevention; Founder-mem Panamanian Asscn for Promoting Science 1985; mem Mexican Acad of Criminology 1975, Panamanian Asscn of Women Lawyers 1975, Panamanian Acad of Law 1980, Pres 1988; hon mem World Peace Through Law Center 1963. *Address:* Supreme Court, Apdo 1770, Panamá 1, Panama.

GUICHENEY, Geneviève Jeanne, L ÈS L; French journalist and broadcaster; b 13 May 1947, Draguignan; d of Pierre and Mady (née Pierrugues) Guicheney. *Education:* Univs of Rennes and Paris I (Panthéon-Sorbonne). *Career:* Teacher in Rennes 1968–69, in Saint-Denis 1972–73; worked at Union de Transports Aériens (UTA) 1970–72; interpreter Gen Dept of Cultural, Scientific and Tech Relations, Ministry of Foreign Affairs 1973–77; Producer series of interviews on France-Culture radio 1976; Journalist on Télévision Française 1 (TF1) 1977–78; Journalist and Presenter Soir 3 news programme on Société Nationale de Programmes—France Régions 3 (France 3) 1978–87; Ed-in-Chief Radio-Télé Luxembourg (RTL) 1987–89; mem Conseil Supérieur de l'Audiovisuel (supervisory org)

1989–97; Presenter France Télévision 1998–. *Address:* France Télévision, 7 esplanade Henri de France, 75907 Paris Cedex 15, France. *E-mail:* g.guicheney@france2.fr.

GUIGNABODET, Liliane, L ÈS L; French writer; b 26 March 1939, Paris; d of Moïse and Luba (née Néchéva) Graciani; m Jean Guignabodet 1961; two d one s. *Education:* Lycée Jules Ferry (Paris), Univs of Paris (Sorbonne) and London (UK). *Career:* Prof of French San José State Univ, USA 1961–62; Prof of Arts and Culture, Ecole Technique d'IBM France 1966–69; writer 1977–; mem PEN-Club Français, Asscn des Ecrivains Croyants, Soc des Gens de Lettres, Acad Européenne des Sciences, des Arts et des Lettres, Acad Valentin, Jury du Prix de Journalisme de l' Asscn Franco-Bulgare; Grand prix du Roman, Ville de Cannes 1991. *Publications:* L'écume du silence (Prix George Sand) 1977, Le bracelet indien 1980, Natalia (Grand Prix du Roman, Acad Française) 1983, Le livre du vent 1984, Dessislava 1986, Car les hommes sont meilleurs que leur vie 1991. *Leisure interests:* piano, travel, decorating, skiing. *Address:* 55 rue Caulaincourt, 75018 Paris, France; 16 chemin du Clos d'Agasse, 06650 Le Rouret, France.

GUIGOU, Elisabeth Alexandrine Marie, L ÈS L; French politician; b 6 Aug 1946, Marrakesh, Morocco; d of Georges Vallier and Jeanne Flecchia; m Jean-Louis Guigou 1966; one s. *Education:* Lycée Victor Hugo (Marrakesh), Lycée Descartes (Rabat), Facultés des Lettres (Rabat and Montpellier), Faculté des Sciences Economiques (Montpellier) and Ecole Nat d'Admin. *Career:* Civil servant Ministry of Finance 1974, Office of the Treasury 1974–75, Office of Banks 1976–78, Office of Financial Markets 1978–79; Deputy Chair Finance Cttee VIIth Plan 1975–78; Sr Lecturer Inst d'Etudes Politiques, Paris 1976; Financial Attaché Embassy, London 1979–81; Head Office for Europe, America and Asia, Treasury 1981; Tech Counsellor Office of Minister of Economy and Finance 1982–88, Deputy Dir 1985; Sec-Gen Interministerial Cttee on European Econ Co-operation 1985–90; Head Office of Pres of Repub 1988–90; Minister of European Affairs 1990–93; mem Regional Council of Provence Alpes Côte-d'Azur 1992–; MEP (PSE) 1994–97, mem Cttee on Institutional Affairs, Del for relations with the Maghreb countries and the Arab Maghreb Union; elected Deputy to Nat Ass for Vaucluse (Socialist Party) 1997; Minister of Justice 1997–2000, of Employment and Solidarity 2000–. *Publications:* Pour les européens 1994, Etre femme en politique 1997. *Address:* Ministry of Employment and Solidarity, 127 rue de Grenelle, 75700 Paris Cedex 01, France (Office); Conseil Régional de Provence Alpes Côte-d'Azur, 27 place Jules Guesde, 13481 Marseille Cedex, France (Office); 168 blvd de Montparnasse, 75014 Paris, France (Home). *Telephone:* (1) 40-56-60-00 (Office); *Fax:* (1) 40-56-67-60 (Office).

GUILFOYLE, Dame Margaret Georgina Constance, DBE, LL B; Australian former politician and organization executive; b 15 May 1926, Belfast, UK; d of the late William and Elizabeth Jane (née Ellis) McCartney; m Stanley Martin Leslie Guilfoyle 1952; two d one s. *Education:* ANU. *Career:* Chartered sec and accountant 1947–; Liberal mem Senate for Victoria 1971–87; Minister for Educ 1975, for Social Security 1975–80, for Finance 1980–83; Dir Mental Health Research Inst 1989–2001, Australian Children's TV Foundation 1990–, Jack Brockhoff Foundation 1990–; Deputy Chair Infertility Treatment Authority 1995–; Chair Judicial Remuneration Tribunal 1995–, Ministerial Advisory Cttee on Women's Health 1996–99, Australian Political Exchange Council 1996–; mem Bd Australian Inst of Family Studies 1993–2000; mem Nat Inquiry Concerning Human Rights of People with Mental Illness 1990–93, Review of the Australian Blood Banking and Plasma Product Sector 1999, Lyceum Club, Melbourne Beefsteak Club; Fellow Australian Certified Practising Accountants; Fellow Chartered Inst of Secs and Administrators. *Leisure interests:* reading, gardening, opera. *Address:* 21 Howard St, Kew 3101, Vic, Australia (Home). *Telephone:* (3) 9853-8516; *Fax:* (3) 9861-6027.

GUILLAUME, Angela Rae, CBE, BA; British politician; b 7 May 1938, Newcastle upon Tyne; d of the late Norman and Gladys Moffett; m 2nd John Guillaume 1976; three s. *Education:* Univ of Durham and Depauw Univ (IN, USA). *Career:* British Chair European Union of Women 1986–90, Int Chair 1993–; Vice-Chair Cons Women's Nat Cttee; mem Econ and Social Cttee of the EC 1990; carries out political and voluntary work, including fund-raising for hospices; mem Registered Insps Appeal

Tribunal 1994–; Trustee Dir Lymington Hospice. *Leisure interests:* family, sailing, skiing. *Address:* Economic and Social Committee (ECOSOC), 2 rue Ravenstein, 1000 Brussels, Belgium; Camelot, Ramley Rd, Lymington, Hants SO41 8LH, UK (Home). *Telephone:* (1590) 678466 (Home); *Fax:* (1590) 676782 (Home).

GUILLAUMONT, Sylviane Lucie Marie Jeanneney, D ÈS SC; French economist; b 6 April 1938, Grenoble; d of Jean Marcel and Marie Laure (née Monod) Jeanneney; m Patrick Guillaumont 1961; two s two d. *Education:* Faculty of Law and Econs (Paris). *Career:* Asst Faculty of Law and Econs, Paris 1962–64; Prof Univ of Dakar, Senegal 1965–68; Prof Univ of Clermont-Ferrand 1968–, Vice-Pres 1977–80; Dir Centre d'Etudes et de Recherches sur le Développement Int (CERDI-CNRS) 1991–; mem Supervisory Council of Caisse Français de Développement 1978–; Pres Stratégies de Développement 1988–, French Asscn of Econs 1991–, Ajustement et Développement 1994–. *Publications:* Pour la politique monétaire: défense d'une mal aimée (jtly) 1982, Zone Franc et développement africain 1984. *Address:* CERDI, 65 blvd de François Mitterand, 63009 Clermont-Ferrand Cedex, France. *Telephone:* (4) 73-43-12-05; *Fax:* (4) 73-42-12-28.

GUILLEM, Sylvie; French ballet dancer; b 23 Feb 1965, Le Blanc Mesnil. *Career:* Joined Ecole de Danse, Paris Opera 1976; joined Ballet de l'Opéra as Dancer 1981, apptd Leading Dancer 1982, Soloist 1983, Prin Dancer, later Prima Ballerina 1984; joined Royal Ballet, London as Prin Guest Artist 1989; Chevalier de la Légion d'Honneur; Commdr des Arts et des Lettres 1988; Prize for Excellence and Gold Medal, Varna Int Dance Competition 1983; Prix Carpeau 1984; Hans Christian Andersen Award 1988; Arpège Prize, Lanvin perfumes 1989. *Ballets include:* Romeo and Juliet, Don Quixote, Raymonda, Swan Lake, Giselle, Notre Dame de Paris, Cendrillon (cr), In the Middle, somewhat elevated (cr), Magnificat (cr), Le Martyre de Saint-Sébastien (cr), Manon; *TV includes:* Evidentia (cr and producer) 1995. *Address:* c/o Royal Ballet, Royal Opera House, London WC2E 9DD, UK (Office).

GUINCHARD-KUNSTLER, Paulette; French politician; b 1950. *Career:* Began career as psychiatric nurse; later Dir Regional Centre for Women's Rights, Franche-Comté; Municipal Councillor Besançon 1983–, Del 1997–; Reg Councillor 1986–97; mem Parti Socialiste (PS) 1986–; elected to Assemblée Nat as MP for 2nd Doubs Constituency June 1997; Sec of State for Elderly People March 2001–. *Publication:* Vieillir en France 1999. *Address:* Ministre de l'Emploi et de Solidarité, 127 rue de Grenelle, 75007 Paris, France; 8 ave de Ségur, 75007 Paris, France. *Telephone:* (1) 40-56-52-30; *Fax:* (1) 40-56-65-80.

GUINEBERTIERE, Armelle; French politician; b 27 July 1944, Carquefou. *Career:* Local Councillor, Cerizay 1983–; Gen Councillor Deux-Sèvres 1985–, then 2nd Vice-Pres; Regional Councillor Poitou-Charentes 1986–; MEP (Group Union for Europe, RPR); mem Cttee on Culture, Youth, Educ and the Media, Del for Relations with Slovenia, Del for Relations with Japan 1994–99. *Address:* Conseil Générale, 25 ave du Général Marigny, 79140 Cerizay, France. *Telephone:* (5) 49-80-02-34; *Fax:* (5) 49-80-05-96; *E-mail:* a .guinebertiere@cg79.fr.

GUISEWITE, Cathy Lee, BA; American cartoonist; b 5 Sept 1950, Dayton, OH; d of William Lee and Anne Guisewite. *Education:* Univ of Michigan. *Career:* Created Cathy comic strip syndicated in around 500 newspapers 1976–; TV specials featuring cartoon characters (Emmy Award 1987); numerous awards including Outstanding Communicator of the Year Award (Los Angeles Advertising Women) 1982; named one of America's Twenty-Five Most Influential Women 1984, 1986; Reuben Award, Nat Cartoonists Soc 1992. *Publications include:* The Cathy Chronicles 1978 (republished as What's a Nice Single Girl Doing with a Double Bed?! and I Think I'm Having a Relationship with a Blueberry Pie! 1981), Motherly Advice from Cathy's Mom 1987, A Hand to Hold, an Opinion to Reject 1987, My Granddaughter Has Fleas 1989, $14 in the Bank and a $200 Face in My Purse 1990, Reflections (A Fifteenth Anniversary Collection) 1991, Only Love Can Break a Heart, but a Shoe Sale Can Come Close 1992, Revelations from a 45-Pound Purse 1993; collections of daily cartoon strips. *Leisure interests:* tennis, skiing, shopping, films. *Address:* c/o Universal Press Syndicate, 4520 Main St, Suite 700, Kansas City, MO 64111-7701, USA.

GULEGINA, Maria (née Muradyan); Belarus/Armenian soprano; b 1959, Odessa; m Mark Gulegin. *Education:* Odessa Conservatory, with A. Dzhamagorzyan and Yevgeni Ivanov. *Career:* Soloist Minsk Opera Theatre 1983–90; teacher Minsk Conservatory 1986–90; regular appearances at major theatres in Europe; solo recitals in Germany, Italy, Switzerland, Austria, France and Hungary; First Prize All-Union Glinka Competition 1984. *Operas include:* Tosca, Manon Lescaut, Due Foscari, Il Trovatore, Un Ballo in Maschera, Ernani, Aida, Otello, Nabucco, La Gioconda, Cavalleria Rusticana, Andrea Chenier, Fedora, Yolanta, Eugene Onegin, Queen of Spades; *Concert performaces:* Verdi's Requiem, Janáček's Glagolitic Mass. *Address:* c/o Askonas Holt, Lonsdale Chambers, 27 Chancery Lane, London WC2A 1PF. *Telephone:* (20) 7400-1700; *Fax:* (20) 7400-1799.

GUNDAREVA, Natalya Georgiyevna; Russian actress and politician; b 28 Aug 1948, Moscow; m Mikhail Filippov. *Education:* B. Shchukin Theatre School. *Career:* Actress with Mayakovsky Theatre 1971–; cinema debut 1973; mem State Duma (Parl, Women of Russia party) 1993–96; USSR People's Actress; State Prize of Russia 1981; USSR State Prize 1984. *Films include:* Hello and Goodbye 1973, Autumn 1975, Sweet Woman 1977, Autumn Marathon 1979, Once Twenty Years Later 1981, The Term of Prescription 1983, Dogs' Feast 1990, The Promised Heaven 1991, Chicken 1991, The Petersburg Secrets 1997, and many others. *Address:* Mayakovsky Theatre, Moscow, Bolshaya Nikitskaya str 19, Russian Federation (Office); 125047 Moscow, Tverskaya 42, kv 14, Russian Federation (Home). *Telephone:* (095) 250-43-55 (Home).

GUNDERMANN, Iselin, D PHIL; German historian; b 28 May 1935, Magdeburg; d of Hans and Lieselotte (née Mewes) Gundermann. *Education:* Schools in Magdeburg and Halle and Univs of Berlin, Bonn, Innsbruck (Austria) and Cologne. *Career:* History Dept Univ of Bonn 1964–83; Librarian 1973–; Librarian Prussian State Archive, Berlin 1983–, Academic Dir and Head Public Relations Dept; retd 2000; participant in activities for ecclesiastical and scientific insts; Freiherr-vom-Stein-Preis (Alfred-Toepfer-Foundation, Hamburg) 1990. *Publications include:* Herzogin Dorothea von Preußen 1965, Untersuchungen zum Gebetbüchlein der Herzogin Dorothea von Preußen 1966, Berlin als Kongreßstadt 1978, Kaiser Friedrich III (catalogue) 1988, Alte Hauptstadt Berlin 1993, Allgemeines Landrecht für den Preußischen Staaten 1994, Via Regia – Preußens Weg zur Krone 1998. *Leisure interests:* music (opera), 19th Century paintings and sculptures. *Address:* Ilmenauer Str 7A, 14193 Berlin, Germany (Home). *Telephone:* (30) 8257609 (Home).

GUNNARS, Kristjana, MA; Icelandic writer, poet, translator and professor of English; b 19 March 1948, Reykjavík; d of Gunnar and Tove Bodvarsson; one c. *Education:* Oregon State Univ (USA) and Univ of Regina (SK). *Career:* Asst Ed Iceland Review, Iceland 1980–81; freelance writer, translator and ed 1981–; Writer-in-Residence Regina Public Library, Canada 1988–89, Univ of Alberta, Edmonton, Canada 1989–90, Assoc Prof of English 1991, Prof 1991–; Lecturer Okanagan Coll, BC, Canada 1990–91; mem PEN, Writers' Union of Canada, League of Canadian Poets, Composers', Authors' and Publishers' Asscn of Canada, Alliance of Canadian Cinema, TV and Radio Artists. *Publications:* Settlement Poems I and II 1980, 1981, One-Eyed Moon Maps 1981, Wake-Pick Poems 1982, Stephan G. Stephansson, In Retrospect (trans) 1982, The Axe's Edge 1983, The Night Workers of Ragnarök 1985, The Papers of Dorothy Livesay (jtly) 1985, Crossing the River: Essays in Honor of Margaret Laurence (ed) 1988, Stephan G. Stephansson, Selected Prose and Poetry (trans) 1988, The Prowler 1989, Carnival of Longing 1989, Zero Hour 1991, Unexpected Fictions, New Icelandic Canadian Writing (ed) 1992, The Guest House and Other Stories 1992, The Substance of Forgetting 1992, The Rose Garden 1993, Exiles Among You 1996, Night Train to Nyköbing 1996, When Chestnut Trees Blossom 2002. *Address:* University of Alberta, Dept of English, Edmonton, AB T6G 2E2, Canada.

GUNNARSDÓTTIR, Elfa-Björk, BA; Icelandic broadcasting executive; b 29 Sept 1943; d of Gunnar Þórit Halldórsson and Sigríður Halldórsdóttir. *Education:* In Reykjavík and Univ of Stockholm. *Career:* Work for the disabled and the blind 1974–75; Chief Librarian Reykjavík Public Library 1975–85; Dir of Radio and Chair Prog Bd, Ríkisútvarpið (Icelandic Nat Broadcasting Service) 1985; Chief of Health-circle 1989.

Leisure interests: health-care, yoga, music, reading. *Address:* c/o Ríkisútvarpið, Broadcasting Centre, Efstaleiti 1, 150 Reykjavík, Iceland (Office); Miðleiti 4, 103 Reykjavík, Iceland (Home). *Telephone:* (1) 679017 (Home).

GUNNELL, Sally, OBE; British athlete (retd) and broadcaster; b 29 July 1966, Chigwell, Essex; m Jon Bigg 1992; two c. *Career:* Coached by Bruce Longdon; competed 400m hurdles Olympic Games, Repub of Korea, Seoul 1988, Gold Medallist, Olympic Games, Barcelona, Spain 1992; Winner 100m hurdles Commonwealth Games 1986, 400m hurdles 1990; Silver Medallist 400m hurdles World Championship, Tokyo 1991; Bronze Medallist 400m relay Olympic Games, Barcelona, Spain 1992; women's team captain, Olympic Games, Barcelona 1992; Gold Medallist, 400m hurdles, World Championships, Stuttgart 1993, European Championships, Gothenberg 1994, Commonwealth Games, Victoria 1994; competitor Olympic Games, Atlanta, GA, USA 1996; retd from Athletics 1997; now works as TV presenter; fmr mem Essex Ladies Athletic Club; Head Commit to Get Fit Campaign 1993–98; Red Cross Amb to Angola 1996; Amb for Millennium Youth Games (Sports Council) 1998–; fitness consultant Crown Sports 2001–; Sunday Times Lifetime Achievement Award 1997. *TV Presenting includes:* Bodyheat 1994–96, World Championships (BBC) 1995, 1999, Channel 4 Athletics 1998–, Peak Performance 1999, GMTV 2000, Sydney Olympics (BBC) 2000, Live Talk 2001; *Publications:* Running Tall (biog, jtly) 1996, Be Your Best (fitness book) 2001. *Address:* MTC, 10 Kendall Place, London W1H 3AH, UK (Office); c/o MTC (UK) Ltd, 20 York St, London W1, UK (Office).

GUNSON, Ameral Blanche Tregurtha; British classical singer; b 25 Oct 1948, London; d of Charles and Auriol (née Lewis) Gunson; m 1st Maurice Powell 1969 (divorced 1974); m 2nd Philip Kay 1979; two s. *Education:* Convent of Jesus and Mary (London) and Guildhall School of Music and Drama. *Career:* Freelance singing career 1972–74, with BBC Singers 1976–80; solo singing career in UK, Europe and Far East; Proms Seasons 1979, 1985, 1988–90; Assoc Guildhall School of Music and Drama; Lubslith Asscn (Finland) Award for vocal teaching 1997. *Recordings include:* Angelica (Puccini), Gloria (Walton), In The Beginning (Copland), Peter Grimes (Gramophone Award) 1997. *Leisure interests:* gardening, reading, walking, Russian music, relaxation. *Address:* 40 Brooklands Way, Redhill, Surrey RH1 2BW, UK. *Telephone:* (1737) 762726.

GÜNTHER, Maren; German politician; b 18 June 1931, Dreilützow/Mecklenburg. *Career:* fmr MEP (EPP, CSU), mem Cttee on Devt and Co-operation, Subcttee on Security and Disarmament, Del to the EU-Malta Jt Parl Cttee. *Address:* c/o European Parliament, rue Wiertz, 1047 Brussels, Belgium.

GUO LANYING; Chinese opera and folk singer; b 31 Dec 1930, Ping Tao Co, Shanxi Prov; d of Guo Yingjie and Liu Furong; m Wan Mingyuan 1962; two d one s. *Education:* People's Univ (Beijing). *Career:* Mem Chinese Opera 1946–49, leading actress 1949–78; Pres Chinese Art Cttee and mem Council of China and Foreign Countries' Friendship Asscn 1949–78; Deputy 1st to 6th NPC; mem Cttee Chinese Literature and Art Asscn 1955–88; Prof China's Music Coll 1980–82; mem Council Chinese Music Asscn, Drama Asscn 1980–82; Dir Guo Lanying Art Troupe; Dir China's Nat Opera; Pres Chinese Nat Folk Art Coll of Guangzhou 1986; Stalin Prize 1954. *Films include:* Xiao Erhei's Marriage 1952, The East is Red 1964, Embroidering Silk Banner With Words of Gold 1965; *Recordings include:* The White-haired Girl, The Unjust Verdict of Widow Du E, The Best of Guo Lanying 1990; *Publication:* Selected Songs of Guo Lanying 1980. *Leisure interests:* literature, painting, Chinese Wushu. *Address:* Chinese National Folk Art College of Guangzhou, Fei E Ling, Shatou, Panyu Co, Guangzhou, 511490 Guangdong, People's Republic of China. *Telephone:* (20) 4870408 (Office); (20) 4878200 (Home).

GUO LIWEN; Chinese politician; b 1920, Weixian, Hebei. *Career:* Joined CCP 1938; counsellor Chinese Embassies in Hungary, Guinea, Italy, France 1964–80; Sec Chinese Women's Fed 1980–82, First Sec 1982–; mem 12th CCP Cen Cttee 1982–87; Deputy Hubei Prov, mem Law Cttee, Credentials Cttee, Standing Cttee 7th NPC 1988–, Adviser Law Cttee; Advisor All-China Fed of Women Lawyers 1993–. *Address:* Chinese Women's Federation, Beijing, People's Republic of China.

GURCHENKO, Ludmila Markovna; Russian actress; b 12 Nov 1935, Kharkov. *Education:* Moscow All-Union Inst of Cinema. *Career:* Worked in films 1956–; concert appearances as a singer; People's Artist of USSR 1983. *Films include:* Carnival Night, Night of Revelry, Baltic Sky, Old Walls (RSFSR State Prize 1976), Mother, Five Evenings, Mechanic Gavrilov's Favourite Woman (Best Actress Award, Manila Film Festival), Station for Two (Best Actress Award, 16th All-Union Cinema Festival, Leningrad 1983), Ideal Husband, Love and Loves, Dreams and Waking Flights, Secret of Her Youth, Applause, Applause, Forgive Us, Stepmother Russia, White Clothes, The Sex Tale, The Pretender, The Burn, Listen, Fellini; *Publication:* My Grown-up Childhood 1980, Applause, Applause. *Address:* 103001 Moscow, Trekhpruday per 5/15, kv 22, Russian Federation. *Telephone:* (095) 209-68-37.

GURLEY BROWN, Helen; American writer and editor; b 18 Feb 1922, Green Forest, AR; d of Ira M. and Cleo (née Sisco) Gurley; m David Brown 1959. *Education:* Texas State Coll for Women and Woodbury Coll. *Career:* Exec Sec Music Corpn of America 1942–45, William Morris Agency 1945–47; Copy-writer Foote, Cone & Belding advertising agency, Los Angeles 1948–58; advertisement writer and account exec Kenyon & Eckhard, Hollywood 1958–62; Ed-in-Chief Cosmopolitan magazine 1965–97, Editorial Dir Cosmopolitan Int Edns, Ed-in-Chief 1997–; mem Authors' League of America, American Soc of Magazine Eds, AFTRA; establishment of Helen Gurley Brown Research Professorship at Northwestern Univ 1985; Hon LL D (Woodbury) 1987; Hon D LITT (Long Island) 1993; Francis Holm Achievement Award 1956–59, Univ of Southern California School of Journalism 1971; Special Award for Editorial Leadership of American Newspaper Woman's Club 1972; Distinguished Achievement Award in Journalism, Stanford Univ 1977; New York Women in Communications Inc Award 1985; Publrs' Hall of Fame 1988; Henry Johnson Fisher Award, Magazine Publrs of America 1995. *Publications:* Sex and the Single Girl 1962, Sex and the Office 1965, Outrageous Opinions 1966, Helen Gurley Brown's Single Girl's Cook Book 1969, Sex and the New Single Girl 1971, Having It All 1982, The Late Show: A Semiwild but Practical Guide for Women over 50 1993, The Writer's Rules: The Power of Positive Prose 1998, I'm Wild Again: Snippets from My Life and a Few Brazen Thoughts 2000. *Address:* Cosmopolitan, 959 Eighth Ave, New York, USA (Office); 1 W 81st St, New York, NY 10024, USA (Home). *Telephone:* (212) 649-2222 (Office); *Fax:* (212) 245-4518 (Office).

GUTMAN, Natalia Grigorievna; Russian cellist; b 14 Nov 1942; m Oleg Kagan (deceased); three c. *Education:* Under R. Saposhnikov at Gnessin Music School (Moscow) and under Prof Kozolupova and Mstislav Rostropovich at Moscow Cen Conservatory. *Career:* Tours to Europe, USA and Japan; performances with Berlin Philharmonic Orchestra, Vienna Philharmonic Orchestra, London Symphony Orchestra, Orchestre Nat de France, Orchestre de Paris, Royal Philharmonic Orchestra (under Yuri Temirkanov), Concertgebouw, London Philharmonic, Munich Philharmonic, the LA Philharmonic (under André Previn), Chicago Symphony (under Claudio Abbado) 1988–89; Chamber Music tour of fmr USSR and Europe with Eliso Virsaladze and Oleg Kagan 1982; played sonatas, trios and quartets with Sviatoslav Richter; sonata and concerto written for her by Alfred Schnittke; Solo tours include the USA with Soviet State Symphony Orchestra (under Yevgeny Svetlanov), Italy with BBC Symphony (under Yuri Temirkanov), fmr USSR with Sir John Pritchard; has performed with Royal Philharmonic Orchestra (UK, under Yuri Temirkanov), the Concertgebouw, London Philharmonic, Orchestre Nat de France, LA Philharmonic (CA, USA, under André Previn), Chicago Philharmonic (IL, USA, under Claudio Abbado), teacher Moscow Conservatory 1967–77; Prof Stuttgart Conservatory 1997–; f Oleg Kagan Memorial Festival, Krems, Moscow; prizes at Vienna Student Festival Competition, Tchaikovsky Competition, Munich Chamber Music Competition and Dvořák Competition, Prague. *Address:* c/o Askonas Holt, Lonsdale Chambers, 27 Chancery Lane, London WC2A 1PF, UK (Office). *Telephone:* (20) 7400-1700 (London); (095) 203 3391 (Moscow).

GUTTMAN, Helene Nathan, PH D; American research scientist; b 21 July 1930, New York; d of Arthur and Mollie (née Bergovoy) Nathan. *Education:* Brooklyn Coll, Harvard and Columbia Univs. *Career:*

Research technician Public Health Research Inst, New York 1951–52; bacteriologist Burroughs-Wellcome, Inc 1952–53; Research Asst Haskins Labs 1953–56, Research Assoc 1956–60, microbiologist 1960–64; Lecturer Dept of Biology, Queens Coll, New York 1956–57; Research Assoc Dept of Biological Sciences, Goucher Coll, Towson, MD 1960–62; Asst then Assoc Research Prof, Dept of Biology, Univ of New York 1962–67; Assoc Prof Dept of Biological Sciences, Univ of Illinois 1967–75, Prof 1969–75, Dept of Microbiology, Medical School 1974–75, Assoc Dir of Research, Urban Systems Lab 1975; expert Nat Heart, Lung and Blood Inst, Bethesda, MD 1975–77, co-ordinator office of Program Planning and Evaluation 1977–79; Dept Dir Scientific Advisory Bd, Admin Office, Environmental Protection Agency 1979–80; co-ordinator food safety and human nutrition, Admin Office, US Dept of Agric 1980–83, nat animal care co-ordinator 1989–95; Assoc Dir Beltsville Human Nutrition Research Center, Agric Research Service 1983–89; Pres HNG Assocs 1983–; mem Bd of Advisors Monroe Inst 1993–; mem Editorial Bd Protozoology 1972–75, Journal of American Women's Asscn 1978–81, Methods in Cell Science 1994–; Fellow AAAS, American Inst of Chemists, American Acad of Microbiology; mem numerous professional orgs. *Publications:* Science and Animals: Addressing Contemporary Issues (sr ed) 1989, Guidelines for the Well-being of Rodents in Research (ed) 1990, Rodents and Rabbits: Current Research Issues (ed) 1994, Rodents and Rabbits: Addressing Current Issues (co-ed) 1994. *Address:* 5607 McLean Drive, Bethesda, MD 20814, USA (Home).

GUTTOWA, Alicja Barbara, PH D; Polish scientist; b 12 Jan 1924, Luck, fmr USSR; d of Bolesław and Bronisława Chmielewski; m Jan Gutt 1949; one s. *Education:* Univ of Warsaw. *Career:* Asst Researcher Univ of Warsaw 1947–50, Agric High School 1950–51; Asst Prof Inst of Parasitology, Polish Acad of Sciences 1970–79, Prof 1980–84, Dir 1984–90, apptd Head of Parasite Physiology Lab 1990; Gold Service Cross 1973; Polonia Restituta Cross 1983; 25th Anniversary Medal, Polish Acad of Sciences 1984. *Publications:* Diphyllobothriasis in the Baltic Sea Area 1970, Some Aspects of Physiological Adaptations in Helminths 1981; 85 papers on human and animal parasites. *Leisure interests:* theatre, gardening, reading. *Address:* Polish Academy of Sciences, Inst of Parasitology, Pasteura 3, 00-973 Warsaw, Poland. *Telephone:* (22) 222562.

GUYATT, Doris Elsie, CD, PH D; Canadian civil servant; b 29 April 1929, New Glasgow, NS; d of Joseph and Margaret Shield Woolcott; m Richard Glenn Guyatt 1950; three s one d. *Education:* Guelph Coll Vocational Inst, Univs of W Ontario and Toronto. *Career:* Lecturer Ryerson Polytech Inst, Toronto 1968–69; Researcher Vanier Inst of the Family 1970–71; Teaching Asst Faculty of Social Work, Univ of Toronto 1971–74; Programme Developer, Project Co-ordinator, Sr Programme Analyst, Sr Policy Analyst, then Sr Policy Adviser Ontario Ministry of Community and Social Services 1973–90, Acting Man 1990–91; Dir Royal Canadian Military Inst 1985–86; Acting Man Ontario Ministry of Health 1990–94, Chair United Way Campaign 1993; Aide de Camp to Lieutenant-Gov of Ontario 1975–95; First Vice-Pres Canadian Fed of Business and Professional Women's Clubs 1988–90, Pres 1990–92; First Vice-Pres Canadian Intelligence and Security Asscn 1994–96 (Dir 1988–94, 1998–); consultant D. E. Guyatt Devt Services 1995–; Queen's Silver Jubilee Medal 1977. *Publication:* The One-Parent Family in Canada 1972. *Leisure interests:* music, theatre. *Address:* 60 Inverlochy Blvd, Apartment 908, Thornhill, ON L3T 4T7, Canada.

GUZY, Carole; American photojournalist; m Jonathan Utz. *Education:* Northampton Co Area Community Coll and Art Inst of Fort Lauderdale. *Career:* Staff photographer Miami Herald 1980–88, The Washington Post 1988–; notable assignments include coverage of volcanic eruption in Colombia, famine in Ethiopia, civil war in Somalia and daily life in Haiti; Pulitzer Prize 1986, 1995, Photographer of the Year (Nat Press Photographers Asscn) 1990, 1993, 1997, Robert F. Kennedy Memorial Prize 1997 and numerous other awards. *Address:* c/o Washington Post, 1150 15th St NW, Washington, DC 20071, USA.

H

HAARMANN, Pirkko-Liisa, D JUR; Finnish judge; b 3 Feb 1938, Helsinki; d of Johannes and Bertta Autio; m Harald Haarmann 1987. *Education:* Univ of Helsinki. *Career:* Pvt law practice, Helsinki 1963, Asst Prof Univ of Helsinki 1973, Prof of Commercial Law 1978; Judge Supreme Court 1983–2001; Commdr Order of the White Rose of Finland 1988, 2000; Ståhlberg Award 1993. *Publications:* On Foundations (in Finland) 1971, Copyright (in Finland) 1992, 1999, Intellectual Property Rights 1994, 2001. *Leisure interests:* reading, films, music, walking in forests. *Address:* Unionkatu 6A1, 00130 Helsinki, Finland; Länsikaari 7, 54530 Lulimäki, Finland. *Telephone:* (358) 9-628085; *Fax:* (358) 5-4573310; *E-mail:* pirkko-liisa.haarmann@pp.inet.fi.

HAAS, Sandra Ingrid; German singer and songwriter; b 25 May 1951, Volkmarsen, Kassel. *Education:* Cologne. *Career:* Official German Rep as singer and songwriter Agustin-Lara World Song Festival, México, 6th Song Olympiad, Athens, World Song Festival, Seoul, Int Song Festival, Viña del Mar, Chile; numerous recordings (three albums, 11 singles), and TV and radio appearances; First Prize Talent Schuppen TV show, Germany. *Leisure interests:* photography, shooting, pets. *Address:* c/o Song Team Music, Utrechter Str 2, 5024 Pulheim-Stommeln, Germany.

HAAS-BERGER, Regina Maria, LL M; Netherlands politician and organization executive; b 22 Feb 1935, Abcoude; d of J. A. Berger and M. R. Berger-Reyne; m Adolf Haas 1956; one d. *Education:* Univ of Leiden. *Career:* Mem Leek Municipal Council; Pres Leek PvdA region, mem regional PvdA Bd; mem Second Chamber of States-Gen (Parl) 1971–91, Pres Standing Cttee on Health Care 1980–91; mem Council of Europe until 1991; Pres Nat Cttee for the Chronically Ill 1991–. *Address:* Nationale Commissie Chronisch Zieken, Plein van de Verenigde Naties 21, 2719 EG Zoetermeer, Netherlands (Office); Courbetstr 6, 1077 ZT Amsterdam, Netherlands (Home). *Telephone:* (79) 368-73-89 (Office); (20) 675-89-53 (Home); *Fax:* (79) 361-98-54 (Office); (20) 675-89-53 (Home).

HABBEMA, Cox; Netherlands actress and theatre director; b 21 March 1944, Amsterdam; m Eberhard Esche 1969. *Education:* Univ of Amsterdam. *Career:* Mem Centrum Theatre Group 1967–69, Deutsches Theater, Berlin; stage, film and TV appearances in Germany, Netherlands, France, Belgium; Man Dir Stadsschouwburg Theatre, Amsterdam 1986–; Dir Vondelpark Open Air Theatre, Amsterdam and Theatre Engelenbak, Frascati 1986–. *Films include:* Heart Beat Fresco 1966, To Grab the Ring 1968, Wie heiratet man einen König 1969, 11:50 from Zürich 1969, Leben mit Uwe 1973, Rufus 1975, De komst van Joachim Stiller 1976, De stilte rond Christine M. 1982; numerous TV appearances. *Leisure interests:* reading, opera, theatre. *Address:* Stadsschouwburg Amsterdam, Leidseplein 26, 1017 PT Amsterdam, Netherlands (Office); Berh Zweerskade 12, 1077 TX Amsterdam, Netherlands (Home). *Telephone:* (20) 52-37-70-0 (Theatre); (20) 66-26-55-5 (Home); *Fax:* (20) 62-38-68-5 (Theatre).

HABIB, Randa, MA; Jordanian/French journalist; b 16 Jan 1952, Beirut, Lebanon; d of Farid Habib; m Adnan Gharaybeh 1973; one s one d. *Education:* French Lycée, Rio de Janeiro and Univ of Beirut. *Career:* Corresp Agence France Presse (AFP) 1980, Dir and Head AFP Office, Amman 1987–; corresp Radio Monte Carlo 1988–, also for several int publs and TV including Politique Internationale; Médaille du Travail (France). *Leisure interests:* reading, swimming, painting. *Address:* Agence France Presse, Jebel Amman, 2nd Circle, POB 3340, Amman, Jordan. *Telephone:* (6) 4642976; *Fax:* (6) 4654680; *E-mail:* randa@afp.index .com.jo.

HÁBOVÁ, Dana; Czech translator; b 4 April 1951, Prague; m Věroslav Hába 1977; one s one d. *Education:* Inst of Translation and Interpreting (Prague). *Career:* Freelance translator 1973–; Robert Payne Award Columbia Univ, USA 1986. *Translations include:* Works of Miroslav Holub, W. Allen, P. Shaffer, S. Shepard, F. Weldon, J. Martin, P. Gems, S. Daniels. *Leisure interest:* gardening. *Address:* Klimentská 36, 11000 Prague, Czech Republic (Home). *Telephone:* (2) 2312963 (Home).

HADID, Zaha; Iraqi architect; b 31 Oct 1950, Baghdad. *Education:* American Univ (Beirut, Lebanon) and Architectural Asscn (London). *Career:* Winner design competition for The Peak leisure complex, Hong Kong 1982 (project cancelled); designed Sapporo restaurant interior 1991 (1st completed work); fire station for Vitra Furniture Co (Germany) 1991, block of flats (Berlin); Cardiff Bay Opera House Sept 1994 (project rejected by Millenium Comm Dec 1994), habitable bridge across the Thames, London (jt winner) 1996; commissioned to design Contemporary Art Center, Cincinnati (OH, USA) 1998, Mind Zone in Millennium Dome (London) 1999; garden exhibition centre, Weil am Rhein, Germany 1999; winner int competition, Rome 1999; Kenzo Tange Prof (Columbia Univ) 1994; Sullivan Prof (Univ of Illinois) 1997; guest Prof Hochschüle für Bildende Kunst (Hamburg) 1997; numerous exhibitions world-wide. *Address:* Studio 9, 10 Bowling Green Lane, London EC1R 0BD, UK. *Telephone:* (20) 7253-5147; *Fax:* (20) 7251-8322.

HADZI VASILEVA-MARKOVSKA, Verica, M SC; Macedonian organization executive; b 8 July 1956, Berovo; d of Ljubomir Hadzi Vasilev and Nada Hadzi Vasileva; m Mihajlo Markovski 1980; two d. *Education:* Univ of Skopje and Swinburne Univ of Tech (Melbourne, Australia). *Career:* Research Asst 1979–91; Asst Dir Devt Fund of Macedonia 1991–93; Deputy Dir Macedonian Agency for the Transformation of Enterprises with Social Capital 1993–95, apptd Dir 1995; has participated in numerous int and nat confs and workshops. *Publications include:* Prices Policy of Macedonian Enterprises 1987, Terminology of the Contemporary Market Economy (jtly) 1993, Entrepreneurial Management (jtly) 1994. *Leisure interests:* listening to music, swimming, reading, spending time with family. *Address:* 91000 Skopje, Dame Gruev 4, POB 410, Macedonia (Office); 91000 Skopje, bul Jane Sandanski 51/1, Macedonia (Home). *Telephone:* (91) 229275 (Office); (91) 417239 (Home); *Fax:* (91) 233633 (Office); *E-mail:* verica%mpa@itl.mk.

HAEBLER, Ingrid; Austrian pianist; b 20 June 1926, Vienna. *Education:* Vienna, Salzburg and Geneva. *Career:* Specializes in Haydn, Mozart, Schubert and Schumann; mem Faculty, Salzburg Mozarteum 1969–; First Prize, Int Competition, Munich, Germany 1954; Mozart Medal, Vienna 1971.

HAENDEL, Ida, CBE; British (b Polish) violinist; b 15 Dec 1928, Chelm, Poland. *Education:* Warsaw Conservatoire, pvt tuition in Paris and London. *Career:* Began playing violin at five years, won first medal at seven years, first prize at 15 years; studied with Carl Flesch and Georges Enesco; UK debut Queen's Hall, London 1938; performances in Los Angeles, Baltimore and New York (USA), Montréal (Canada), Berlin (Germany), Birmingham, London; performances with famous conductors including Beecham, Rattle, Barenboim, Pritchard; tours with BBC Symphony, English Chamber Orchestra and London Philharmonic Orchestra to Hong Kong, People's Repub of China, the fmr USSR, Australia and S America; participated in centenary anniversary Festival of Bronislav Huberman, Tel-Aviv 1982; celebrated 50th anniversary of debut at Promenade Concerts, London 1987; mem numerous int juries; numerous recordings with EMI; Hon mem RAM

1982–; Sibelius Medal (Finland) 1982. *Publication:* Woman with Violin (autobiog) 1970. *Leisure interests:* drawing, reading. *Address:* c/o Askonas Holt Ltd, 27 Chancery Lane, London WC2A 1PF, UK (Office). *Telephone:* (20) 7400-1751; *Fax:* (20) 7400-1799; *E-mail:* melanie .evans@askonasholt.co.uk (Office).

HAFNER, Ursula, D PHIL; Swiss former politician; b 10 June 1943, Schaffhausen; m Dieter Hafner 1968. *Education:* Kantonsschule Schaffhausen, Univs of Zurich, Caen (France) and Aberdeen (UK). *Career:* Teacher of French; became mem Schaffhausen cantonal council 1981; mem Nationalrat/Conseil National (Parl) for Schaffhausen (Sozialdemokratische Volkspartei der Schweiz—Social-Democratic Party) 1987–1999; apptd Pres Swiss Youth Bd 1990. *Address:* Saentisstr 45, 8200 Schaffhausen, Switzerland (Home). *Telephone:* (52) 6256475 (Home).

HAFTENDORN, Helga, D PHIL; German professor of political science; b 9 Sept 1933, Erfurt. *Education:* Univ of Frankfurt/Main. *Career:* Prof of Political Science Hochschule der Bundeswehr, Hamburg and Freie Univ of Berlin 1973–; Konrad Adenauer Chair Georgetown Univ, Washington, DC, USA 1978–79; Visiting Prof Stanford Univ, USA 1982–83; Visiting Fellow Harvard Univ, MA, USA 1988; Jean Monnet Chair European Univ Inst, Florence, Italy 1989; mem Berlin-Brandenburg Acad of Science 1993–; Research Award Max Planck Soc 1995. *Publications include:* Security and Detente: Conflicting Priorities in German Foreign Policy 1985, Sicherheit und Entspannung Zur Außenpolitik der Bundesrepublik Deutschland 1955–82 (2nd edn) 1986, Sicherheit und Stabilität Außenbezihungen der Bundesrepublik zwischen Ölkrise und NATO-Doppelbeschluß 1986, The Reagan Administration: Toward a Reconstruction of American Strength 1988, America and Europe in an Era of Change 1993, NATO and the Nuclear Revolution 1996. *Address:* Freie Universität Berlin, Department of Political Science, Ihnestr 21, 14195 Berlin, Germany.

HAGEN, Uta Thyra; American actress; b 12 June 1919, Göttingen, Germany; d of Oskar F. L. Hagen and Thyra Leisner; m 1st José V. Ferrer 1938; m 2nd Herbert Berghof 1957 (died 1990); one d. *Education:* Wisconsin High School, Royal Acad of Dramatic Art (London) and Univ of Wisconsin. *Career:* Debut as Ophelia in Hamlet, Dennis, MA 1937; teacher and Co-Founder Herbert Berghof Studio, School of Acting 1947–; Hon DFA (Smith Coll) 1978; Dr hc (De Paul Univ, Chicago) 1980; Hon D HUM LITT (Worcester Coll) 1982; Critics Award 1951, 1963; Tony Award 1951, 1963; Donaldion Award 1951; London Critics Award 1964; Mayors Liberty Award 1988; Lortel Award 1995, 1996; Drama League Lifetime Achievement Award 1996; OBIE Lifetime Achievement Award 1996; Antoinette Perry Lifetime Achievement Award 1999. *Plays include:* The Seagull, Arms and the Man, The Latitude of Love, The Happiest Days, Othello, The Master Builder, Angel Street, A Streetcar Named Desire, The Country Girl, Saint Joan, Tovarich, In Any Language, The Lady's Not For Burning, The Deep Blue Sea, Cyprienne, A Month in the Country, The Good Woman of Setzuan, The Affairs of Anatol, The Queen and the Rebels, Who's Afraid of Virginia Woolf?, The Cherry Orchard, Charlotte 1980, Mrs Warren's Profession 1985, You Never Can Tell 1987, Circle in the Square 1986, Mrs Klein 1995–96, (nat tour) 1996–97, Collected Stories 1998–2000; *Films:* The Other 1972, The Boys from Brazil 1978, Reversal of Fortune 1990; *Publications:* Respect for Acting 1973, Love for Cooking 1976, Sources (memoirs) 1983, A Challenge to the Actor 1990. *Leisure interests:* gardening, cooking, needlework. *Address:* Herbert Berghof Studio, 120 Bank St, New York, NY 10014, USA.

HAGON, Anne-Marie, L ÈS L; Belgian politician; b 24 June 1947, Gosselies; m Willy Corbisier. *Education:* Univ Catholique de Louvain. *Career:* Teacher 1970–76; Local Councillor, Montigny-le-Tilleul 1976–82, Deputy Mayor 1982–88; Prov Councillor 1985–87; became mem Chamber of Deputies (Parl) for Charleroi 1988, mem Comms and Council of French Community, apptd Pres of Ass 1992. *Address:* Chamber of Deputies, Palais de la Nation, Place de la Nation 2, 1000 Brussels, Belgium (Office); rue des Ronces 9, 6110 Montigny-le-Tilleul, Belgium (Home).

HAHN, Ulla, D PHIL; German writer; b 30 April 1946, Brachthausen. *Education:* Univs of Cologne and Hamburg. *Career:* Lecturer Univs of Hamburg, Bremen, Oldenburg 1975–80; Radio Ed, Bremen 1979–91;

freelance writer 1992–; Leonce und Lena Award 1981; Hölderlin Award 1985; Roswitha von Sandersheim Medal 1986; Medal of Fed Repub of Germany. *Publications include:* Poetry collections: Herz über Kopf 1981, Spielende 1983, Freudenfeuer 1985, Unerhörte Nähe 1988; Novel: Ein Mann im Haus 1991. *Leisure interests:* walking, reading, music, theatre. *Address:* DVA, Neckarstr 121, Postfach 106012, 7000 Stuttgart 1, Germany (Publr); Breitenfelderstr 86, 2000 Hamburg 20, Germany (Home). *Telephone:* (40) 485495 (Home).

HAILES, Julia P., MBE; British author and environmental consultant; b 23 Sept 1961, Templecombe, Somerset; m Edward de Courcy Bryant 1991; three s. *Education:* Knighton House (Dorset)and St Mary's School (Calne). *Career:* Dir SustainAbility Ltd 1987–95, Creative Consumer Cooperative Ltd (Out of This World) 1994–2000, Six Fox Ltd 1995–99, Jupiter Global Green Investment Trust 2001–; UN Global 500 Award for Outstanding Environmental Achievement. *Publications:* Green Pages: The Business of Saving the World 1987, The Green Consumer Guide 1988, The Green Consumer's Supermarket Shopping Guide 1989, The Young Green Consumer Guide 1990, The Green Business Guide 1991, Holidays That Don't Cost the Earth 1992, The LCA Sourcebook 1993, Who Needs It? 1995, MANUAL 2000: Life Choices for the Future You Want 1998, The New Foods Guide: What's Here, What's Coming, What it Means for Us 1999. *Leisure interests:* bridge, walking, tennis. *Address:* Tintinhull House, Tintinhull, Somerset BA22 8PZ, UK. *Telephone:* (1935) 823972; *Fax:* (1935) 826176; *E-mail:* hailes@tintinhull.demon.co.uk; *Internet:* www.juliahailes.com.

HALE, Rt Hon Dame Brenda Marjorie, DBE, PC, MA; British lawyer and judge; b 31 Jan 1945, Leeds; d of Cecil Frederick and Marjorie (née Godfrey) Hale; m 1st Anthony John Christopher Hoggett 1968 (divorced 1992); one d; m 2nd Julian Thomas Farrand 1992. *Education:* Richmond High School for Girls (Yorks), Girton Coll (Cambridge) and Gray's Inn (London). *Career:* Asst Lecturer Dept of Law, Univ of Manchester 1966–68, Lecturer 1968–76, Sr Lecturer 1976–81, Reader 1981–86, Prof 1986–89; Prof King's Coll, London 1990–99; Visiting Fellow, Nuffield Coll, Oxford 1997–; Practice Manchester Bar 1969–72; Law Commr 1984–93; Recorder 1989–94; Judge High Court, Family Div 1994–99; Lord Chief Justice of Appeal 1999–; Ed Journal of Social Welfare Law 1978–84; mem Mental Health Review Tribunal for the North-West 1979–80, Council on Tribunals 1980–84; Chair Nat Family Conciliation Council 1989–93; mem Judicial Studies Bd Civil and Family Cttee 1990–94, Human Fertilization and Embryology Authority 1990–93; Gov Centre for Policy on Ageing 1990–93; Pres Nat Family Mediation 1994–; Man Trustee Nuffield Foundation 1987–; Hon LL D (Sheffield) 1989, (London Guildhall) 1996, (Manchester) 1997. *Publications:* Women and the Law (jtly) 1984, Parents and Children (4th edn) 1993, The Family Law and Society: Cases and Materials (jtly, 4th edn) 1996, Mental Health Law (4th edn) 1996, From the Test Tube to the Coffin: Choice and Regulation in Private Life 1996. *Leisure interests:* bridge, theatre, home. *Address:* Royal Courts of Justice, Strand, London WC2A 2LL, UK.

HALIMI, Gisèle Zeïza Elise, L EN D, L PH; French lawyer, writer and politician; b 27 July 1927, La Goulette, Tunisia; d of Edouard Taieb and Fortunée Metoudi; m 1st Paul Halimi; m 2nd Claude Faux 1961; three s. *Education:* Lycée de jeunes filles (Tunis), Univ of Paris (Sorbonne), Inst d'Etudes Politiques (Paris). *Career:* Barrister Court of Appeal, Tunis 1949–56, Paris 1956–; represented FLN during war for Algerian independence 1954–62; represented writers, artists and the women's movt; int judicial observer in Spain, Morocco, Greece 1962–74; Chair Comm of Inquiry into War Crimes in Vietnam 1966; Founder and Pres CHOISIR feminist movt 1971–; mem French Nat Ass (Parl) for Isère 1981–84; Official Rep of Prime Minister 1984–85; Perm Rep of France to UNESCO 1985–86, mem UNESCO Exec Council 1985–87; political and feminist writer; gives lectures in France and abroad; Personality of the Year Award (Paris) 1983; Minerva int award (Rome) 1985; Grand Officier de l'Ordre de la République de Tunisie 1992; Chevalier de la Légion d'Honneur; Medal of Achievement of the Greek People. *Publications:* Djamila Boupacha 1962, Resistance Against Tyranny 1966, Le procès de Burgos 1971, Procès de Bobigny (jtly) 1973, La cause des femmes 1974, Procès d'Aix-en-Provence (jtly) 1978, Programme commun des femmes (jtly) 1978, Choisir de donner la vie (jtly) 1979, Quel président pour les femmes? (jtly) 1981, Fini le féminisme? (jtly) 1984, Le lait de l'oranger 1990, Djamila Boupacha

1991, La cause des femmes 1992, Femmes: moitié de la terre, moitié du pouvoir 1994, Une embellie perdue 1996, La nouvelle cause des femmes 1997, Fritna 1999. *Leisure interests:* classical music, poetry, history of art. *Address:* 102 rue Saint-Dominique, 75007 Paris, France. *Telephone:* (1) 47-05-21-48; *Fax:* (1) 45-51-56-10.

HALL, Dinny; British jewellery designer; b 1959; m; one d. *Education:* Cen School of Art. *Career:* Est own business 1982, opened first shop, London 1992, second shop 1995; designs fashion jewellery for Rifat Ozbek collections 1985–, and Isaac Mizrahi, New York; collection includes silver, semi-precious and fine jewellery; Accessory Designer of the Year 1989; Marie Claire Jeweller of the Year 1995. *Address:* 200 Westbourne Grove, London W11, UK.

HALL, Jerry; American model and actress; b 2 July 1956, Texas; m Mick Jagger 1990 (divorced 1999); two s two d. *Career:* Began modelling career in Paris in 1970s; numerous TV appearances including David Letterman Show, USA; stage debut in Bus Stop, Lyric Theatre, London 1990; Contributing Ed Tatler 1999–. *Films include:* Batman 1989, Princess Caraboo 1994, Diana and Me 1996, RPM 1996; *Plays include:* The Graduate 2000. *Address:* c/o ICM Ltd, Oxford House, 76 Oxford St, London W1N 0AX, UK.

HALL, Judith Myfanwy Sarah; British magazine editor; b 23 July 1947; d of Norman and Vera Hall; m Andrew Becker 1984; one s. *Education:* Eltham Hill Grammar School for Girls (London) and Univ of Warwick. *Career:* Book publishing 1968–71; Asst Fiction Ed Woman's Weekly 1971–74, later Ed 1987–92; Fiction Ed Woman's Journal 1974–76, Features Ed 1976–80; Deputy Ed Woman's World 1980–82; Deputy Ed Woman's Realm 1982–84, Ed 1984–87; freelance journalist and television script ed 1992–94; Ed BBC Homes & Antiques magazine 1994–. *Leisure interests:* theatre, cinema, reading, home crafts, family. *Address:* BBC Worldwide, 80 Wood Lane, London W12 0TT, UK. *Telephone:* (20) 8433-3483.

HALL, Kathleen Mary Veronica, MBE, MA; British international organization official; b 23 July 1925, Stranraer. *Education:* Univ of Glasgow and Lamorbey Park Coll (Sidcup, Kent). *Career:* Asst Psychotherapist, Sutton, Surrey 1946–47; Asst Teacher Sidcup Girls' Tech School 1947–50; Sr Careers Officer, Lanarkshire 1951–61; Deputy Dir Northern Ireland Youth Employment Service 1962–74; Sr Careers Adviser Northern Ireland Civil Service 1975–86; Sec-Gen Int Asscn for Educational and Vocational Guidance, Belfast 1985–91, Vice-Pres 1992–95, Sec-Gen (acting) and Consultant 1996; author of various articles for professional journals; Fellow Inst of Careers Guidance 1973–. *Leisure interests:* gardening, golf, bridge, reading, travel, arts. *Address:* International Asscn for Educational and Vocational Guidance, Dept of Economic Devt, Gloucester House, Chichester St, Belfast BT1 4RA, UK (Office); 66 Wellington Park, Belfast BT9 4DP, UK (Home). *Telephone:* (28) 90252299 (Office); (28) 90667160 (Home); *Fax:* (28) 90252266 (Office).

HALL, Margaret Dorothy, OBE; British designer; b 22 Jan 1936; d of Thomas Robson and Millicent Hall. *Education:* Bromley and Royal Colls of Art. *Career:* Design Asst Casson, Condor and Partners 1960–61, Westwood Piet and Partners 1961–63, Dennis Lennon and Partners 1963–64; Head of Design British Museum 1964–2001, exhibitions designed include Masterpieces of Glass 1968, Museum of Mankind 1970, Treasures of Tutankhamun 1972, Nomad and City 1976, Captain Cook in the South Seas 1979; Designer Manuscripts and Men, Nat Portrait Gallery 1969; mem Council RSA 1984–89; Chair Group of Designers/Interpreters in Museums 1978–81; Gov Ravensbourne Coll of Art 1973–78; Fellow Museums Asscn; Royal Designer for Industry (RSA) 1974. *Publication:* On Display: A Design Grammar for Museum Exhibitions 1987. *Address:* 13 Ferry Path, Cambridge CB4 1HB, UK.

HALL-ALLEYNE, Beverley Clare, MA; Jamaican linguist; b 25 April 1946, Kingston; d of the late Lloyd C. and of Sybil Hall; m 1980; two d one s. *Education:* Queen's School (St Andrew) and Univs of the West Indies and California (USA). *Career:* Asst to Head and Spanish Instructor Language Lab, Research Asst Univ of the West Indies 1968–70; Asst Lecturer in Spanish 1972–74; Research Fellow African-Caribbean Inst (ACIJ), Inst of Jamaica (IOJ) 1975–85, Dir ACIJ 1978–85, apptd Exec Dir IOJ 1985; Part-time Lecturer Intensive

Language Inst, State Univ of New York 1978–79; articles to local journals; mem UNESCO Cttee on Culture and Communication, Soc for Caribbean Linguistics, Int Org of Folk Art; Dir Nat Gallery of Jamaica; IOJ Day Medal for long and dedicated service 1989. *Leisure interests:* music, dance, gardening. *Address:* Institute of Jamaica, 12–16 E St, Kingston, Jamaica (Office); Kai-Nou, Aguilar Rd, Stony Hill, Jamaica (Home). *Telephone:* 922-0620; *Fax:* 922-1147.

HALLAHAN, Hon Elsie Kay, B SC S; Australian politician; b 4 Nov 1941, Perth, WA. *Education:* Western Australian Inst of Tech. *Career:* Mem Legis Council (Australian Lab Party) for E Metropolitan W Australia 1983–93, Minister for Community Services, Youth, Aged, Multicultural and Ethnic Affairs 1986, Minister Assisting Minister for Women's Interests 1986–90, for Local Govt, Lands, Family, Aged 1989, for Community Services, Family, Youth, Aged 1989–90, for Planning, Lands, Heritage, the Arts 1990, for Planning, Lands, Heritage 1990, for Educ Employment and Training, the Arts 1991–93, Deputy Leader of Govt, Legis Council 1987–93; mem Legis Ass (Australian Lab Party) for the Armadale W Australia 1993–96; Minister of Educ and Training, Arts, Media 1993–94; W Australia Deputy Leader of Opposition 1994; Shadow Minister for Fed Affairs 1994, for Racing and Gambling 1994; W Australia Shadow Minister for Tourism 1994, for Transport 1994; mem numerous house cttees. *Address:* Capita Centre, 20th Floor, 197 St George's Terrace, Perth, WA 6000, Australia. *Telephone:* (9) 222 9691; *Fax:* (9) 481 0223.

HALLANAN, Elizabeth V., JD; American federal judge; b 10 Jan 1925, Charlestown, WV; d of Walter Simms and Imogene Hallanan. *Education:* Univs of Charlestown (WV), West Virginia and Michigan. *Career:* Lawyer Crichton & Hallanan, Charleston, WV 1952–59, Lopinsky, Bland, Hallanan, Dodson, Deutsch & Hallanan, Charleston 1975–84; mem WV State Bd of Educ 1955–57, House of Dels, WV Legis, Charlestown 1957–58; Asst Commr of Public Insts, Charleston 1958–59; mem then Chair WV Public Service Comm 1969–75; Judge US Dist Court, WV 1983–; Woman of Achievement, YWCA 1997–. *Address:* US District Court, POB 2546, Charleston, WV 25329, USA.

HALLETT, Carol Boyd; American diplomatist and civil servant; b 16 Oct 1937, Oakland, CA. *Education:* Univ of Oregon. *Career:* Field Office Rep to mem of California State Ass and State Senator 1966, Staff Asst to mem House of Reps 1967–76; mem California State Ass 1976–82, Minority Floor Leader 1979–82, Dir of Parks and Recreation 1982–83; Asst to US Sec of the Interior 1984–85; Amb to Bahamas 1986–89; apptd US Commr of Customs, US Customs Service, Washington, DC 1989–93; Sr Govt Relations Advisor Collier, Shannon, Rill & Scott, Washington 1993–95, Pres, CEO Air Transport Asscn of America 1995; Consultant and Dir Foundation for Individual and Econ Freedom 1982–83; Western Regional Dir Citizens For America 1983–84, Nat Field Dir 1985–86. *Address:* Air Transport Association of America, Suite 1100, 1301 Pennsylvania Ave, NW, Washington, DC 20004, USA.

HALLIWELL, Geri; British singer. *Career:* Mem (with Victoria Adams (qv), Melanie Brown, Emma Bunton and Melanie Chisholm) The Spice Girls 1993–98; UN Goodwill Amb 1998–; Best Single (for Wannabe) Brit Awards 1997, Best Video for Say You'll Be There 1997; two Ivor Novello songwriting awards 1997; Best British Band Smash Hits Show 1997; three American Music Awards 1998; Special Award for Int Sales Brit Awards 1998. *Film:* Spiceworld the Movie 1997; *Music:* albums include: Spice Girls 1996, Spiceworld 1997, Schizophonic (solo), Scream If You Want to Go Faster 2001; Singles include: Wannabe 1996, Say You'll Be There 1996, 2 Become 1 1996, Mama/Who Do You Think You Are 1997, Spice Up Your Life 1997, Too Much 1997, Stop 1998, Viva Forever 1998, (solo) Look at Me 1999, Mi chico Latino 1999, Lift Me Up 1999, Bag it Up 2000, It's Raining Men 2001; *Publications:* If Only (autobiog) 1999. *Address:* c/o Chrysalis Records, 43 Brook Green, London W6 7EF, UK. *Telephone:* (20) 7605-5000.

HALLMAN, Viola; German business executive; b 8 Dec 1944, Hagen, North Rhine-Westphalia; d of Werner and Helga Flachmeier; m Olof J. Hallman 1971; one d. *Education:* Univs of Hamburg, Marburg and Padua (Italy). *Career:* Chief Exec Theis Group, Chief Exec Friedrich Gustav Theis Kaltwalzwerke GmbH 1972, Friedrich Gustav Theis GmbH & Co Flachdraht- und Profilwerk Hagen-Hohenlimburg 1972, Theis Verpackungssysteme GmbH, Packbandwerk Gelsenkirchen

1975, Alte & Schröder GmbH & Co, Stahl- und NE-Veredlungswerke Halver und Hagen-Halden 1979; Chair and CEO Theis Precision Steel Corpn, Bristol, CT, USA 1986–; Chair of Bd and Pres Theis of America, Inc, Wilmington, DE, USA 1986–, Theis Ibérica SA urbi-Basaurí, Vizcaya, Spain 1990–; mem Fed Cttee of Business Econs (BBW) of the RKW, Eschborn, VvU Asscn of Women Entrepreneurs, Cologne, ASU Working Asscn of Independent Business Entrepreneurs, Bonn; Manager of the Year 1979. *Publication:* Entrepreneur – Profession Without Future?. *Leisure interests:* riding, swimming, literature, history. *Address:* Bandstahlstr 14 – 18, 58093 Hagen-Halden, Germany. *Telephone:* (2331) 6930.

HALLOCK MULLER, Pamela, PH D; American oceanographer and bio-geologist; b 2 June 1948, Pierre, SD; d of Graydon B. and Marjorie L. (née Millard) Hallock; m Robert Glenn Muller 1969. *Education:* Univs of Montana and Hawaii. *Career:* Postdoctoral research Inst for Historical Geology and Paleontology, Univ of Copenhagen 1978, Inst of Gen Microbiology, Univ of Kiel, Germany 1979; Asst Prof Faculty of Earth Sciences, Univ of Texas of the Permian Basin 1978–83; Assoc Prof Dept of Marine Science, Univ of S Florida 1983–88, Prof 1988–; Assoc Ed Journal of Foraminiferal Research 1985–; mem Editorial Bd Marine Micropaleontology Journal 1990–, Geology Journal 1996–; mem Bd of Dirs Cushman Foundation for Foraminiferal Research 1989–95, Pres 1995–96, Fellow; Fellow Geological Soc of America; mem Paleontology Soc, Asscn of Women Geoscientists, Soc of Sedimentary Geology, American Littoral Soc; approx 40 articles published in scientific journals and symposia 1974–; NSF research grant 1981, 1985, 1987, 1989, 1992; NASA Summer Faculty Fellowship 1987; NOAA-NURC research contracts 1991–93, 1995–96; NURC Aquarius Aquanaut 1994. *Leisure interests:* scuba-diving, canoeing, natural history. *Address:* University of South Florida, Dept of Marine Science, 140 Seventh Ave S, St Petersburg, FL 33701, USA. *Telephone:* (813) 893-9567; *Fax:* (813) 893-9189.

HALLSTEIN, Ingeborg; German opera singer (coloratura soprano); b 23 May 1939, Munich; one d. *Career:* Mem Bayerische Staatsoper 1961–; numerous guest appearances in Germany and abroad, including Teatro Colón (Buenos Aires), Wiener Staatsoper (Vienna), Royal Opera House (Covent Garden, London), Royal Opera House (Stockholm), Concertgebouw (Amsterdam); has performed at many festivals in Austria, Germany, the Netherlands and Ireland; has performed operas, operettas and oratorios for radio and TV broadcasts; Prof Hochschule für Musik, Würzburg 1979; title Bayerische Kammersängerin conferred; Bundesverdienstkreuz 1976. *Operas include:* Die Schweigsame Frau, Die Zauberflöte, Der Rosenkavalier, Ariadne auf Naxos, Idomeneo; *Film:* Wälsungenblut. *Leisure interests:* music, poetry, drawing, cooking, walking, animals. *Address:* Tengstr 35, 80796 Munich 40, Germany.

HALONEN, Tarja Kaarina; Finnish Head of State; b 24 Dec 1943, Helsinki; m Pentti Arajair 2000; one d from a previous marriage. *Education:* Univ of Helsinki. *Career:* Lawyer Lainvalvonta Oy 1967–68; social welfare officer, organizing Sec Nat Union of Finnish Students 1969–70; lawyer Cen Org of Finnish Trade Unions 1970–; Parl Sec to Prime Minister Sorsa 1974–75; mem Helsinki City Council 1977–96; mem Eduskunta (Parl, Social Democratic Party) 1979–2000, Chair Parl Social Affairs Cttee 1984–87; Second Minister, Ministry of Social Affairs and Health 1987–90, for Nordic Co-operation 1989–91, Minister of Justice 1990–91, of Foreign Affairs 1995–2000; Pres of Finland 2000–. *Leisure interests:* swimming, sculpture, painting, gardening. *Address:* Office of the President of the Republic, Mariankatu 2, 00170 Helsinki, Finland (Office).

HALSEMA-KUBES, Wilhelmina, MA; Netherlands curator; b 12 June 1937, Groningen; m J. J. Halsema 1962. *Education:* Univ of Amsterdam. *Career:* Apptd Curator of sculpture Rijksmuseum, Amsterdam 1968; Buchelius Prize 1987. *Publications:* Beeldhouwkunst in het Rijksmuseum: Catalogus (jtly) 1973, Adriaen van Wesel, een Utrechtse beeldhouwer uit de late middeleeuwen (jtly) 1980. *Leisure interests:* gardening, classical music, opera. *Address:* Rijksmuseum Amsterdam, Hobbemastraat 21, 1071 XZ Amsterdam, Netherlands (Office); Lage Laarderweg 104, 1272 JD Huizen, Netherlands (Home). *Telephone:* (2152) 54-38-1 (Home).

HÄMÄLÄINEN, Sirkka Aune-Marjatta, D ECON; Finnish banking executive; b 8 May 1939, Riihimäki; d of Martti and Aune Hinkkala; m Arvo Hämäläinen 1961; one s one d. *Education:* Helsinki School of Econs and Business Admin. *Career:* Economist Bank of Finland 1961–1979, Acting Head Econs Dept 1979–1981, Dir Bank of Finland 1982–1991, mem Bd Bank of Finland 1991–1992, Gov and Chair 1992–1998; Chair Bd Financial Supervision Authority 1996–1997; mem Exec Bd European Central Bank 1998–; Dir Econs Dept Finnish Ministry of Finance 1981–1982; Prof Helsinki School of Economics and Business Administration 1991–; mem Econ Council of Finland 1992–1998, Nat Bd of Econ Defence 1992–1998, CEPS Int Advisory Council 1993–1998, Trilateral Comm (Europe) 1995–, Cen Bank Governance Steering Cttee Bank for Int Settlements 1996–, Devt Programme of Nat Strategy 1996–1998, Finnish Public R&D Financing Evaluation Group 1998; mem Delegation of Åbo Akademi University 1995–, Bd Foundation for Economic Education 1996–; mem Bd Finnish National Theatre 1992–1998, Bd of Trustees, Savonlinna Opera Festival Patrons' Asscn 1993–, Supervisory Bd of Finnish Cultural Foundation 1996–; Dr hc Univ of Turku (Finland) 1995; 1st Class Commander, Order of the White Rose of Finland; 1st Class Merit Medal, Order of the White Star (Estonia). *Address:* European Central Bank, 60066 Frankfurt am Main, Kaiserstr 29, Postfach 160319, Germany. *Telephone:* (69) 13440; *Fax:* (69) 13446000; *Internet:* www .ecb.int.

HÄMÄLÄINEN, Tuulikki Katriina Pia, B ECONS; Finnish politician; b 25 Nov 1940, Helsinki; d of Jaakko Kustaa and Alma Anna Liisa Ojala; one c. *Career:* Sec State Computer Centre 1963–65; broadcaster Oy Yleisradio Ab (Finnish Broadcasting Co) 1965–83; mem Hyvinkää Town Council (Suomen Sosialidemokraattinen Puolue—Social Democratic Party) 1976, Chair 1985, Chair City Admin Bd 1981–84; mem Pres Electorate 1982; mem Eduskunta (Parl) 1983–; Second Minister of Social Affairs and Health 1990–1992; Vice-Chair Admin Council of State Fuel Centre 1984; mem Finnish Workers' Savings Bank Man 1984. *Address:* c/o Ministry of Social Affairs and Health, Snellmaninkatu 4–6, POB 267, 00171 Helsinki, Finland.

HAMARI, Julia; Hungarian opera and concert singer (mezzo-soprano); b 21 Nov 1942, Budapest; d of Sándor Hamari and Erzsébet Dokupil; m Lajos Petö. *Education:* Franz Liszt Music Acad of Budapest. *Career:* Performed at Edinburgh and Glyndebourne (UK), Florence Maggio Musicale (Italy) festivals; specializes in Rossini, Mozart, Bellini; Lieder recitalist and oratorio performer; Prof Staatliche Hochschule für Musik, Stuttgart, Germany 1989–; Kodály Prize 1987. *Address:* Max Brodweg 14, Stuttgart 40, Germany.

HAMBLING, Maggi, OBE; British artist; b 23 Oct 1945, Sudbury, Suffolk; d of Harry Leonard and Marjorie Rose Hambling. *Education:* Hadleigh Hall School and Amberfield School (Suffolk), Ipswich School of Art, Camberwell School of Art (London) and Slade School of Fine Art (London). *Career:* Studied painting with Lett Haines and Cedric Morris 1960–; first solo exhibition at Hadleigh Gallery, Suffolk 1967; solo exhibitions London 1973, 1977, Nat Gallery 1981, Nat Portrait Gallery 1983, 1997, Serpentine Gallery 1987, Richard Demarco Gallery, Edinburgh 1988, Arnolfini Gallery, Bristol 1988, Bernard Jacobson Gallery 1990, Yale Center for British Art, USA 1991, Northern Centre for Contemporary Art 1993, Marlborough Fine Art 1996, 2001, Hugh Lane Gallery (Dublin) 1997, Gainsborough's House (Suffolk) 2000, Lady Margaret Hall 2001, Morley Coll (London) 2001; public collections include Arts Council, British Council, British Museum, Contemporary Art Soc, European Parl Collection, Imperial War Museum, Nat Gallery, Nat Portrait Gallery, Royal Army Medical Coll, Southampton Art Gallery, Tate Gallery, William Morris School, Birmingham City Art Gallery, Morley Coll, Clare Coll (Cambridge), Gulbenkian Foundation, HTV Bristol, Scottish Nat Gallery of Modern Art, Scottish Nat Portrait Gallery, St Thomas' Hosp, London, Univ Coll London, Wakefield Art Gallery, Art Gallery, All Souls Coll (Oxford), Ashmolean (Oxford), Victoria and Albert Museum, Nat Gallery of Australia and Yale Center for British Art; Monument to Oscar Wilde (Adelaide St, London) 1998; tutor Morley Coll; Hon LITT D 2000; Boise Travel Award 1969; Arts Council Award 1977; First Artist-in-Residence, Nat Gallery, London 1980–81; Jerwood Painting Prize

1995. *Publication:* Maggi and Henrietta 2001. *Leisure interest:* tennis. *Address:* Marlborough Fine Art, 6 Albemarle St, London W1X 4BY, UK; Morley College, Westminster Bridge Rd, London SE1 7HT, UK.

HAMBRAEUS, (Sigrid) Birgitta, BA; Swedish politician; b 11 April 1930, Västerås; d of Erik David Lindblom and Janesie Edström-Lindblom; m Olof Hambraeus 1959; two s. *Education:* Sigtuna Foundation Arts Grammar School, Vassar Coll (NY, USA) and Univ of Stockholm. *Career:* Youth leader 1954–71; school social worker 1964–66; teacher 1965–71; mem Orsa Town Council 1965–88; elected to Riksdag (Parl, Centerpartiet–CP/Centre Party) 1971, mem Parl Auditors 1988; mem Right Livelihood Awards Foundation. *Address:* Hamregården POB 25, 794 00 Orsa, Sweden (Home).

HAMBURG, Beatrix Ann, BA, MD; American psychiatrist; b 19 Oct 1923, Jacksonville, FL; d of Francis Minor and Beatrix (née Downs) McCleary; m 1951; one s one d. *Education:* Vassar Coll and Yale Univ. *Career:* Research Assoc Medical School, Stanford Univ, CA 1961–71, Assoc Dir Lab of Stress and Conflict 1974–76, Assoc Prof of Psychiatry 1976–80; Sr Research Psychiatrist, Nat Inst of Mental Health, Bethesda, MD 1978–80; Assoc Prof Harvard Medical School, Boston 1980–83, mem Div of Health Policy Research 1980– (Exec Dir 1981–83); Prof of Psychiatry and Pediatrics, Mt Sinai Medical School, New York 1983, Dir Child and Adolescent Psychiatry Div 1988–92; Pres W. T. Grant Foundation, New York 1992–; Dir Studies Pres's Comm on Mental Health 1977–78; mem Comm on Behavior and Soc, Nat Acad of Sciences 1983; mem Bd Dirs New World Foundation 1978–83, Bush Foundation, Revson Foundation, Greenwall Foundation 1986–; mem Bd of Trustees, New York Acad of Medicine 1992, Judge Baker Children's Center, Harvard Univ 1999–; Fellow American Acad of Child Psychiatry; mem AAAS, Soc of Professors of Child Psychiatry, Soc for the Study of Social Biology, Acad of Research in Behavioral Medicine; Outstanding Achievement Award, Alcohol, Drug Abuse and Mental Health Admin 1980. *Publications:* Behavioral and Psychosocial Issues in Diabetes 1980, School Age Pregnancy and Parenthood 1986; numerous articles in professional journals. *Address:* W. T. Grant Foundation, 515 Madison Ave, New York, NY 10022, USA. *Telephone:* (212) 752-0071.

HAMESSE, Jacqueline; Belgian historian and international organization executive; b 7 Dec 1942, Etterbeek; m Paul Tombeur 1975. *Education:* Catholic Univ of Louvain. *Career:* Treas Int Soc for the Study of Medieval Philosophy 1982–87, apptd Sec 1988; apptd Pres Inst of Medieval Studies, Catholic Univ of Louvain 1984, Pres Répertoire Int des Incipits de Manuscrits Médiévaux 1986; Sec Int Fed of Insts for Medieval Studies (FIDEM) 1988, Dir Leonard E. Boyle Foundation for Medieval Studies 1999. *Publication:* Auctoritates Aristotelis 1974. *Address:* ISP, Université Catholique de Louvain, 14 Place du Cardinal Mercier, 1348 Louvain-La-Neuve, Belgium. *Telephone:* 10-47-47-98; *Fax:* 10-47-48-07; *E-mail:* hamesse@risp.ucl.ac.be; *Internet:* www.isp .ucl.ac.be/isp/fidem.

HAMILTON, Linda; American actress; b 26 Sept 1956, Salisbury, MD; m 1st Bruce Abbott (divorced); one s; m 2nd James Cameron 1996; one d. *Career:* Actress on TV and in films. *Stage appearances include:* Looice 1975, Richard III 1977; *Films include:* T.A.G: The Assassination Game 1982, Children of the Corn 1984, The Stone Boy 1984, The Terminator 1984, Black Moon Rising 1986, King Kong Lives! 1987, Mr Destiny 1990, Terminator 2: Judgment Day 1991, Silent Fall 1994, The Shadow Conspiracy 1997, Dante's Peak 1997; *TV appearances include:* Series: The Secrets of Midland Heights 1980–81, King's Crossing 1982, Beauty and the Beast 1987–90; Films: Reunion 1980, Rape and Marriage – The Rideout Case 1980, Country Gold 1982, Secrets of a Mother and Daughter 1983, Secret Weapons 1985, Club Med 1986, Go Toward the Light 1988, On the Line 1998, Point Last Seen 1998, The Color of Courage 1999, The Secret Life of Girls 1999. *Address:* United Talent Agency, 5th Floor, 9560 Wilshire Blvd, Beverly Hills, CA 90212, USA (Office).

HAMMARSTRÖM, Stina Margareta, MA; Swedish publishing executive; b 21 Feb 1945, Stockholm; d of Sven and Karin Hammarström; m Gösta Åberg 1979; one d. *Career:* Ed Bokförlaget Prisma AB (publrs), Stockholm 1970–79; Publr Hammarström & Åberg Bokförlag AB

1979–90; apptd Ed AB Rabén & Sjögren Bokförlag, Stockholm 1990. *Address:* c/o Hammarström & Åberg Bokförlag AB, Föreningsvägen 33, 121 63 Johanneshov, Sweden.

HAMNETT, Katharine; British fashion designer; b 16 Aug 1948; d of James Appleton; two s. *Education:* Cheltenham Ladies' Coll and St Martin's School of Art. *Career:* Tuttabankem 1969–74; designed freelance in New York, Paris, Rome and London 1974–76; Founder Katharine Hamnett Ltd 1979; launched Choose Life T-Shirt collection 1983; involved in Fashion Aid 1985; opening of first Katharine Hamnett shop, London 1986, followed by two more shops in 1988; production moved to Italy 1989; Visiting Prof London Inst 1997–; numerous publs in major fashion magazines and newspapers; Int Inst of Cotton Designer of the Year 1982; British Fashion Industry Designer of the Year 1984; Bath Costume Museum Menswear Designer of the Year Award 1984; British Knitting and Clothing Export Council Award for Export 1988. *Address:* Katharine Hamnett Ltd, 202 New North Rd, London N1 7BJ, UK (Office). *Telephone:* (20) 7354-4400 (Office); *Fax:* (20) 7354-5246 (Office).

HAMPARTZOUMIAN, Yvette Achkar; Lebanese artist; b 1928, São Paulo, Brazil; m 1st John Sargologo (divorced); m 2nd Zavan Hampartzoumian; two c. *Education:* Lebanese Acad of Fine Art. *Career:* Participated in group exhibitions in Italy, Belgium and fmr Yugoslavia, biennales in Paris, Alexandria (Egypt) and São Paulo (Brazil).

HAMPSHIRE, Susan, OBE; British actress; b 12 May 1942; d of George Kenneth and June Hampshire; m 1st Pierre Granier-Deferre 1967 (divorced 1974); one s (one d deceased); m 2nd Eddie Kulukundis 1981. *Education:* Hampshire School (Knightsbridge). *Career:* Work to increase public awareness of dyslexia; Hon D LITT (City Univ, London) 1984, (St Andrews) 1986; Hon ED D (Kingston) 1993; Dr hc (Pine Manor Coll, Boston) 1994. *Plays include:* Expresso Bongo 1958, Follow that Girl 1960, Fairy Tales of New York 1961, Ginger Man 1963, She Stoops to Conquer 1966, On Approval 1966, The Sleeping Prince 1968, A Doll's House 1972, The Taming of the Shrew 1974, Peter Pan 1974, Romeo and Jeannette 1975, As You Like It 1975, Miss Julie 1975, The Circle 1976, Man and Superman 1977, Tribades 1978, An Audience Called Edouard 1978, The Crucifer of Blood 1979, Night and Day 1979, The Revolt 1980, House Guest 1981, Blithe Spirit 1986, Married Love, A Little Night Music 1989, The King and I 1990, Noel and Gertie 1991, Relative Values 1992, Susanna Andler 1996, Black Chiffon 1996, Relatively Speaking 2000–2001; *TV appearances include:* Andromeda, The Forsyte Saga (Emmy Award for Best Actress 1970), Vanity Fair (Emmy Award for Best Actress 1973), The First Churchills (Emmy Award for Best Actress 1971), The Pallisers, Dick Turpin 1980, The Barchester Chronicles 1982, Leaving 1984, Leaving II 1985, Going to Pot 1985, Don't Tell Father, The Grand 1996–98, Coming Home 1998–99, Nancherrow, Monarch of the Glen 1999–2001; *Films include:* During One Night 1961, The Three Lives of Thomasina 1963, Night Must Fall 1964, Wonderful Life 1964, Paris in August, The Fighting Prince of Donegal 1966, Monte Carlo or Bust 1969, Rogan, David Copperfield, Living Free 1972, A Time for Loving 1972, Malpertius (E. Poe Prizes du Film Fantastique, Best Actress) 1972, Neither the Sea Nor the Sand, Roses and Green Peppers, Bang; *Publications:* Susan's Story (autobiog) 1981, The Maternal Instinct, Lucy Jane at the Ballet 1985, Lucy Jane on Television 1989, Trouble Free Gardening 1989, Every Letter Counts 1990, Lucy Jane and the Dancing Competition, Lucy Jane and the Russian Ballet 1992, Rosie's First Ballet Lesson 1996. *Leisure interests:* gardening, music, studying antique furniture. *Address:* c/o Chatto & Linnit Ltd, 123A King's Rd, London SW3 4PL, UK. *Telephone:* (20) 7352-7722.

HAMPSON, Judith Elizabeth, B SC, PH D; British environmental scientist; b 16 March 1951, Bolton, Lancs; d of Richard and Anne Hampson. *Education:* Leigh Girls' Grammar School and Univ of Leicester. *Career:* Head Animal Experimentation Research Dept, Royal Soc for the Prevention of Cruelty to Animals (RSPCA) 1980–86; Rapporteur on animal experiments to Eurogroup for Animal Welfare and EC Econ and Soc Cttee 1980–90; mem Home Office Advisory Cttee on Animal Experiments 1980–90; became Ind Consultant on Animal Welfare to Australian Senate Select Enquiry for Australian and NZ Fed of Animal Socs 1986, Environmental Consultant on indigenous peoples' issues, the impact of business on the environment, the preservation of wilderness and wildlife and animal welfare 1991; journalist and broadcaster in field; Winston Churchill Travelling Fellow, USA 1981. *Leisure interests:* water sports, skiing, horses, nature, music, singing. *Telephone:* (1367) 52172 (Home); (1367) 53454 (c/o ERIBA).

HAMWEE, Baroness (Life Peer), cr 1991, of Richmond upon Thames, **Sally Rachel Hamwee,** MA; British lawyer and politician; b 12 Jan 1947, Manchester; d of Alec and Dorothy (née Saunders) Hamwee. *Education:* Manchester High School for Girls and Girton Coll (Cambridge). *Career:* Partner Clintons Solicitors 1979–; Lib Dem Spokesperson on the environment, local govt, planning and housing, House of Lords 1991–; Councillor London Borough of Richmond upon Thames 1978–; Chair London Planning Advisory Cttee 1986–94; Deputy Chair London Ass, GLA 2000–; mem Advisory Council London First 1996–, Dir 1993–96; mem Council Family Policies Study Centre 1994–. *Address:* House of Lords, Westminster, London SW1A 0PW, UK; 101A Mortlake High St, London SW14 8HQ, UK.

HAN SUYIN, MB, BS, LRCP, MRCS; British (b Chinese) writer and medical practitioner; b (Elizabeth Kuanghu Chow) 12 Sept 1917, Xinyang, China; d of Y. T. Chow (Zhou) and M. Denis; m 1st P. H. Tang 1938 (died 1947); one d; m 2nd L. F. Comber 1952 (divorced 1968); m 3rd Vincent Ruthnaswamy 1971; two adopted d. *Education:* Yenching Univ (Beijing), Univ of Brussels and Royal Free Hospital, Univ of London. *Career:* Employed Queen Mary Hosp, Hong Kong 1948–52, Johore Bahru Hosp, Malaya 1952–55; pvt medical practice 1955–64; Lecturer in Contemporary Asian Literature, Nanyang Univ, Singapore 1958–60, on China, USA 1965; has lectured in Europe, USA, Australia, Canada, Asia and Africa; Hon Prof Univ of Alberta (Canada) and several Chinese univs; Founder Han Suyin Fund for Scientific Exchange between China and the West, Han Suyin–Vincent Ruthnaswamy Fund for Cultural Relations Between India and China, Rainbow Prize for Translation, DUNHUANG (to facilitate exchanges between students from People's Republic of China and Kazakstan, Tajikistan and Uzbekistan) 1995; Hon Pres Bingxin Foundation; Pres Espace Enfant Fund (Switzerland); Amb of Friendship, People's Republic of China 1996; numerous awards. *Publications include:* Destination Chungking 1942, A Many-Splendoured Thing 1952, …And the Rain My Drink 1956, The Mountain is Young 1958, Cast But One Shadow 1962, Winter Love 1962, The Four Faces 1963, The Crippled Tree (autobiog) 1965, A Mortal Flower (autobiog) 1966, China in the Year 2001 1967, Birdless Summer (autobiog) 1968, Morning Deluge – Mao Tse-tung and the Chinese Revolution 1972, Wind in the Tower 1976, Lhasa, the Open City 1977, My House has Two Doors 1980, Phoenix Harvest 1980, Till Morning Comes 1982, The Enchantress (novel) 1985, A Share of Loving (autobiog) 1987, Tigers and Butterflies 1990, Fleur de soleil, Les yeux de demain, La peinture chinoise, Chine insolite, Wind in my Sleeve (autobiog) 1992, Eldest Son: Zhou Enlai and the Making of Modern China (1898–1976) 1994; three photography books. *Leisure interests:* economics, travel, lecturing. *Address:* 37 Montoie, Lausanne 1007, Switzerland.

HANCOCK, Beryl Lynette (Lyn), B ED, MA, LRAM; Canadian (b Australian) lecturer, writer, photographer and film producer; b 5 Jan 1938, E Fremantle, WA; d of Ted and Doris Taylor; m 1st David Hancock 1963 (divorced 1972); m 2nd Frank Schober 1991 (divorced 1998). *Education:* Perth Modern School, Graylands Teacher Training Coll, W Australia Univ and Simon Fraser Univ. *Career:* Prin Acad of Speech and Drama, W Australia 1954–59; teacher W Australia, London, Montréal, Vancouver, Victoria 1957–69; Sec, animal caretaker, writer and film maker, Wildlife Conservation Centre, Saanichton, BC 1964–73; freelance writer, photographer and lecturer 1964–; numerous appearances on TV and radio; Licentiate of Trinity Coll of Music, London; awards include American Express Travel Writing Award 1981, 1983. *Films include:* Co-Producer: Coast Safari, Pacific Wilderness, and TV documentary series; *Publications include:* Writer: There's A Seal in My Sleeping Bag (Pacific NW Booksellers' Award 1973) 1972, The Mighty Mackenzie 1974, There's A Raccoon in My Parka (Kortright Conservation Award 1978) 1977, Love Affair With A Cougar 1978, An Ape Came Out of My Hatbox 1980, Gypsy in the Classroom 1980, Tell Me, Grandmother 1985, Northwest Territories: Canada's Last Frontier 1986, Looking For The Wild (Kortright Conservation Award 1987) 1986, Alaska Highway: Road to Adventure 1988, Northwest Territories – Discover Canada 1993, Nunavut 1995,

Yukon 1996, Winging it in the North 1996, Great Canadian Fishing Stories (contrib) 1996, 2001, Vancouver Port City 1998, Western Canada Travel Smart 1998, 2001; Photographer: Coastal Canada 1985, Wilderness Canada 1986, The Last Wilderness: Images of the Canadian Wild 1990; contribs to magazines including Up Here, Canadian Geographic, BC Outdoors, Above and Beyond, Readers' Digest; over 1,000 articles published internationally. *Leisure interests:* hiking, kayaking, gardening, photography. *Address:* 8270 Sabre Rd, Lantzville, BC V0R 2H0, Canada. *Telephone:* (250) 390-9075; *Fax:* (250) 390-9074; *E-mail:* lynhancock@home.com; *Internet:* www.islandnet.com/pwacvic/hancoc00.html.

HANCOCK, Ellen, MA; American business executive. *Career:* Vice-Pres IBM computers 1985, Sr Vice-Pres 1992; Exec Vice-Pres and CEO Nat Semiconductor 1995; Exec Vice-Pres of Research and Devt and Chief Technology Officer Apple Computer 1996; currently Chair and CEO Exodus Communications Inc (CA); mem Council on Foreign Relations; mem Bd dirs Colgate-Palmolive, Aetna, American Electronics Association, Silicon Valley Manufacturing Group; mem Bd Trustees Marist Coll, Santa Clara Univ; mem Council on Foreign Relations, Cttee of 200 (women execs group), US Advisory Board of NTT DoCoMo Inc; Hon D HUM LITT (Univ of W Connecticut). *Address:* c/o Exodus Communications, 2831 Mission College Blvd, Santa Clara, CA 95054, USA. *Telephone:* (408) 346-2200; *E-mail:* inquiry@exodus.net.

HANCOCK, Sheila, OBE; British actress and director; d of the late Enrico and Ivy (née Woodward) Hancock; m 1st Alexander Ross (died 1971); one d; m 2nd John Thaw 1973; one d. *Education:* Dartford County Grammar School and Royal Acad of Dramatic Art. *Career:* Repertory Stratford East; Dir The Actors Centre 1978–; Assoc Dir Cambridge Theatre Co 1980–82; Artistic Dir RSC Regional Tour 1983–84; actress and Dir Nat Theatre 1985–86; Variety Club, London Critics and Whitbread Trophy Best Actress on Broadway Awards. *Plays include:* Rattle of a Simple Man 1962, The Anniversary 1966, A Delicate Balance 1969, So What About Love? 1969, Absurd Person Singular 1973, Déjà Revue 1974, The Bed Before Yesterday 1976, Annie 1978, Sweeney Todd 1980, The Winter's Tale 1981, 1982, Peter Pan 1982–83, The Cherry Orchard, The Duchess of Malfi 1985–86, Greenland 1988, Prin 1989, 1990, Entertaining Mr Sloane, A Judgement in Stone, The Way of the World 1992, Then Again 1997, Vassa 1999; Dir: The Soldier's Fortune 1981, A Midsummer Night's Dream 1983, The Critic 1986; *Films include:* The Love Child 1987, Making Waves 1987, Hawks 1988, Buster 1988, Three Men and a Little Lady 1990, Hold Back the Night 1999; numerous TV shows and appearances; *Publication:* Ramblings of an Actress (autobiog) 1987. *Leisure interests:* music, reading. *Address:* c/o ICM, 76 Oxford St, London W1N 0AX, UK.

HANES, Ursula Ann, RCA; Canadian sculptor; b 18 Jan 1932, Toronto; d of Prof Charles Samuel and Theodora Burleigh (née Auret) Hanes; m 1st David John Fry 1956 (divorced 1968); m 2nd Daniel P. Guthrie 1976 (divorced 1981); two d two s. *Education:* Perse School for Girls (Cambridge, UK), Cambridge School of Art, Art Students' League, Columbia Univ (NY, USA) and Univ of Toronto Inst of Child Study. *Career:* Audio-visual Consultant, Mali 1971–72; Co-Founder Les Ateliers Fourwinds art centre 1994; exhibitions include Columbia Univ, NY 1953, New England Soc of Artists 1953, Ontario Soc of Artists 1954–62, Stratford Festival, ON 1955, RCA 1955, 1957, 1959–62, Canadian Nat Exhibition 1956, 1959–60, Young Canadian Contemporaries 1957, Lanzarote, Canary Islands 1969–75, Saxe Gallery, Toronto 1980, Geneva, Switzerland 1986, Tréguier and La Rochelle, France (group exhibitions) 1988, Musée du Nouveau Monde, La Rochelle, France (one woman show) 1990, Arles, France 1991, Aix-en-Provence, France 1992, Avignon, France 1994, Ateliers Fourwinds, Aureille, France 1994, 1995, 1996, La Galerie Beaucaire (one woman) 2000, Hotel Mirande, Avignon (one woman) 2001; comms include busts, murals, fountains, painted wooden panels of 21 California mission saints for San Juan Bautista, CA 1983, Encounter Series (five bronze maquettes) 1984, six abstract figures in bronze, then marble 1986, Bathers (bronze bas-relief) 1987, Dragon in Arch (cast stone bas-relief) 1987, Abstractions on Mountain Forms (bronze maquettes, then marble) 1988, bust of Van Gogh for Nat Bank of Paris, Arles 1991, Women/Landscapes (bronze dolphin fountain), La Dame des Alpilles (limestone), Spinner Dolphin (bronze garden sculpture) 2001; mem

Ontario Soc of Artists, Sculptors' Soc of Canada (Pres 1964–65). *Leisure interests:* dance, reading, theatre. *Address:* La Julière, 13930 Aureille, France. *Telephone:* (4) 90-59-93-87 (Home); (4) 90-59-93-42 (Office); *Fax:* (4) 90-59-93-42; *E-mail:* redwinds4@aol.com.

HANFT, Ruth, PHD; American health policy consultant; b 12 July 1929; d of Max Samuels and Ethel Schechter; m Herbert Hanft 1951; one s one d. *Education:* School of Industrial and Labor Relations, Cornell Univ and Hunter Coll. *Career:* Social Science Analyst, Social Security Admin 1964–66; Prog Analyst Office of Econ Opportunity 1966–68, Dept of Health, Educ and Welfare 1968–72; Sr Research Assoc, Inst of Medicine, NAS 1972–76; Deputy Asst Sec, US Dept of Health and Human Services 1977–81; Health Policy Consultant 1981–88; Visiting Prof, Dartmouth Medical School 1976–; Consultant and Research Prof, Dept of Health Services and Admin, George Washington Univ 1988–91, Prof 1991–95, Consultant 1995–; mem Inst of Medicine, NAS; Fellow Hastings Inst; Walter Patenge Medal of Public Service. *Publications:* Hospital Cost Containment (jtly) 1978, Human in Vitro Fertilization; Political, Legal and Ethical Issues, in Gynecology and Obstetrics Vol 5, Chapter 98 1984, Improving Health Care Management in the Workplace (jtly) 1985, Physicians and Hospitals: Changing Dynamics, in The Health Policy Agenda (contrib) 1985; articles on medical ethics in professional journals. *Leisure interests:* gardening, needlepoint, travel. *Address:* 3340 Brookside Drive, Charlottesville, VA 22901, USA (Home).

HANNAH, Daryl; American actress; b 1960, Chicago, IL. *Education:* Univ of California at Los Angeles. *Career:* Studied with Stella Adler; studied ballet with Marjorie Tallchief; appeared on TV in Paper Dolls. *Films include:* The Fury 1978, The Final Terror, Hard Country 1981, Blade Runner 1982, Summer Lovers 1982, The Final Terror 1983, Splash 1984, The Pope of Greenwich Village 1984, Reckless 1984, Legal Eagles 1986, Roxanne 1987, Wall Street 1987, High Spirits 1988, Clan of the Cave Bear 1988, Steel Magnolias 1989, Crazy People 1990, At Play in the Fields of the Lord, Memoirs of an Invisible Man 1992, Grumpy Old Men, Attack of the 50 ft Woman, The Tie That Binds, The Last Supper (dir) 1994, A Hundred and One Nights (dir) 1995, Grumpier Old Men 1995, Two Much 1996, The Last Days of Frankie the Fly 1996, Wild Flowers 1999, My Favorite Martian 1999, Dancing in the Blue Iquand 2000, Cord 2000; *Plays include:* The Seven Year Itch 2000.

HANQUET, Huberte, D SC S; Belgian politician and administrator; b 29 Aug 1926, Liège. *Education:* Catholic Univ of Louvain. *Career:* Teacher Centre de Formation Sociale, Liège 1954–70, Dir 1970–74; Admin Comm d'Assistance Publique, Liège 1959–63, 1970–76; Occasional Lecturer Catholic Univ of Louvain 1976–85; Adviser Centre Public d'Aide Sociale, Liège 1977–85; Senator 1974–85, Co-opted Senator 1988–91, Hon Senator 1991–, Chair Comm on Foreign Affairs; mem Chamber of Reps (Parl, PSC) 1985–88; Chair Conseil Nat des Femmes Belges 1984–90; Pres Caritas Catholica en Communauté Française 1993, Vice-Pres Caritas Europe 1996; Médaille Civique de Première Classe 1981; Officier de l'Ordre de Léopold 1987. *Publications include:* Le travail professionnel des femmes et mutations sociales 1972. *Address:* quai Churchill 6B, bte 102, 4020 Liège, Belgium. *Telephone:* (41) 43-24-93.

HANSEN, Barbara Caleen, PH D; American scientist and university administrator; b 24 Nov 1941, Boston, MA; d of Reynold and Dorothy (née Richardson) Caleen; m Kenneth D. Hansen 1976; one s. *Education:* Univs of California at Los Angeles, Pennsylvania (PA) and Washington (Seattle). *Career:* Research Fellow Univ of Pennsylvania Inst of Neurosciences 1966–68; Asst and Assoc Prof Univ of Washington 1971–76; Prof and Assoc Dean Univ of Michigan, Ann Arbor 1977–83; Assoc Vice-Pres of Academic Affairs and Research and Dean of Grad School, Southern Illinois Univ, Carbondale 1983–85; Vice-Pres for Grad Studies and Research, Univ of Maryland, Baltimore 1986–90, Prof of Physiology and Psychology 1990–; Pres Int Asscn for Study of Obesity 1987–91; mem N American Asscn for the Study of Obesity (Pres 1985), American Physiological Soc, American Soc for Clinical Nutrition (Pres 1995–96), Int Asscn for Study of Obesity, NAS Inst of Medicine; Fellow Univ of Pennsylvania Inst of Neurosis 1966–68. *Publications:* Controversies in Obesity (ed) 1983, The Commonsense Guide to Weight Loss for People with Diabetes 1998, The Metabolic Syndrome X 1999;

book chapters and articles in learned journals. *Leisure interests:* sailing, scuba-diving, golf, reading. *Address:* Obesity and Diabetes Research Center, University of Maryland School of Medicine, MSTF6-00, 10 S Pine St, Baltimore, MD 21201, USA (Office); 6501 Bright Mountain Rd, McLean, VA 22101, USA (Home). *Telephone:* (301) 328-3904 (Office); (410) 706-3168 (Home); *Fax:* (301) 328-7540 (Office); (410) 706-7540 (Home).

HANSEN, Litten, B SC S; Danish business executive; b 24 Dec 1944; d of H. K. and G Hansen; m Knud Hauge 1992 (died 2000); one d. *Education:* Drama school and Univ of Copenhagen. *Career:* Actor and Theatre Dir 1974–81; mem Folketing (Parl) 1975–77; Pres COPY-DAN 1985–91, Gen Man 1994–; Head of Drama Nat Royal Theatre 1991–94; Pres Danish Actors' Asscn 1982–91; Chair Nat Theatre Council 1995–99; Ridder of Dannebrog. *Address:* Copy-Dan, Østerfælled Torv 10, 2100 Copenhagen 6, Denmark (Office); Holbergsgade 10, 1057 Copenhagen K, Denmark (Home). *Telephone:* 35-44-14-00 (Office); 33-14-15-45 (Home); *Fax:* 35-44-14-14 (Office); 33-32-15-47 (Home); *E-mail:* lha@copydan.dk (Office); litten@hansen.mail.dk (Home); *Internet:* www.copydan.dk (Office).

HAO JIANXIU; Chinese politician; b 1935, Qingdao. *Career:* Worker State Operated Cotton Factory No 6, Qingdao, Deputy Dir 1964, mem Standing Cttee Factory Revolutionary Cttee 1968; originated Hao Jianxiu Work Method; mem Exec Council, Women's Fed 1953; mem Cen Cttee, Communist Democratic Youth League 1953; joined CCP 1954; mem Cen Cttee Communist Youth League from 1964 until Cultural Revolution; mem Qingdao Municipality Revolutionary Cttee 1967, Vice-Chair 1971, Trade Union, Shandong 1975; Chair Women's Fed, Shandong 1975; mem Standing Cttee, Shandong Prov CCP Cttee 1977; mem 11th CCP Cen Cttee 1977–82, 12th Cen Cttee 1982–87, Financial and Econ Leading Group 1986, 13th Cen Cttee 1987–92, 14th Cen Cttee 1992–97, mem 15th Cen Cttee CCP 1997–; Vice-Minister of Textile Industry 1978–81, Minister 1981–83; Alt Sec Secr 1982, Sec 1985; Vice-Minister State Planning Cttee 1988–; mem Politburo 13th Cen Cttee CCP 1985; Deputy Dir Leading Group for the Placement of Demobilized Army Officers 1993–; Vice-Chair Cttee for Women and Children's Work 1987–; Nat Model Worker in Industry 1951; Hon Pres Factory Dirs' Study Soc, Acad of Social Sciences 1985–. *Address:* Zhonggong Zhongyang, A8, Taipingjie St, Beijing 100050, People's Republic of China.

HARAJDA, Helena Anna, MA, D SC; Polish acoustician and physicist; b 29 June 1921, Lublin; d of Jan M. and Kamilla Jasielski; m Ryszard J. Harajda 1942; four c. *Education:* S. S. Ursulae Secondary School (Stanisławów) and Adam Mickiewicz Univ in Poznań. *Career:* Asst Lecturer Adam Mickiewicz Univ 1950–53; Sr Lecturer Inst of Physics, Acad of Agriculture 1954–75; Asst Prof and Head of Dept of Music Educ, Pedagogical Univ, Zielona Góra 1975–77, Head of Dept of Acoustics, Zielona Góra 1977–91; Prof of Physics 1989; founding mem Polish Acoustical Soc 1962; mem Acoustics Cttee, Acoustics of Music Section, Polish Acad of Sciences 1965–80; over 100 papers contributed to scientific journals; Golden Cross of Merit 1975; Polonia Restituta Cross 1981; Distinction for Outstanding Services to Educ in Poland 1983. *Leisure interests:* travel, climbing, nature conservation. *Address:* Institute of Physics, Pedagogical University, Plac Słowiański 6, 65-069 Zielona Góra, Poland; ul Sucharskiego 30 m 6, 65-562 Zielona Góra, Poland. *Telephone:* (68) 261543.

HARDSTAFF, Veronica Mary; British politician; b 23 Oct 1941, Wellington, Salop. *Career:* MEP (PSE) 1994–99, mem Cttee on Agric and Rural Devt, Vice-Chair EU-Poland Jt Parl Cttee 1995–99. *Address:* 64 Linaker Rd, Sheffield S6 5DT, UK. *Telephone:* (114) 233-5414.

HARDWICK, Elizabeth, MA; American writer; b 27 July 1916, Lexington, KY; d of Eugene Allen and Mary (née Ramsey) Hardwick; m Robert Lowell 1949 (divorced 1972); one d. *Education:* Kentucky and Columbia Univs. *Career:* Assoc Prof Barnard Coll; Founder, Advisory Ed New York Review of Books; mem American Acad, Inst of Arts and Letters (Gold Medal for Criticism 1993), American Acad of Arts and Sciences; Guggenheim Fellow 1947; Dr hc (Smith Coll, Kenyon Coll, Skidmore Coll, Bard Coll); George Jean Nathan Award 1966. *Publications:* Novels: The Ghostly Lover 1945, The Simple Truth 1955, Sleepless Nights 1979; Essays: A View of My Own 1962, Seduction and

Betrayal 1974, Bartleby in Manhattan 1983, Sight Readings 1998; Other: The Selected Letters of William James (ed) 1960, Herman Melville, A Life 2000; contribs to New Yorker. *Address:* 15 W 67th St, New York, NY 10023, USA.

HARDWICK, Mollie, FRSA; British writer; b Manchester; d of Joseph Greenhalgh and Anne Frances Atkinson; m Michael John Drinkrow Hardwick 1961 (died 1991); one s. *Education:* Manchester High School for Girls. *Career:* Announcer BBC Radio, N Region 1940–45, Drama Dept 1946–62; freelance writer 1963–. *Publications include:* Stories from Dickens 1968, Emma, Lady Hamilton 1969, Mrs Dizzy 1972, Upstairs Downstairs: Sarah's Story 1973, The Years of Change 1974, The War to End Wars 1975, Mrs Bridges' Story 1975, Alice in Wonderland (play) 1975, The World of Upstairs Downstairs 1976, Beauty's Daughter (Elizabeth Goudge Award) 1976, The Duchess of Duke Street: The Way Up 1976, The Golden Years 1976, The World Keeps Turning 1977, Charlie is my Darling 1977, The Atkinson Heritage 1978, Thomas and Sarah 1978, Thomas and Sarah: Two for a Spin 1979, Lovers Meeting 1980, Juliet Bravo 2 1980, Monday's Child 1981, Calling Juliet Bravo: New Arrivals 1981, I Remember Love 1982, The Shakespeare Girl 1983, By the Sword Divided 1983, The Merrymaid 1984, Girl with a Crystal Dove 1985, Malice Domestic 1986, Parson's Pleasure 1987, Uneaseful Death 1988, Blood Royal 1988, The Bandersnatch 1989, Perish in July 1989, The Dreaming Damozel 1990, Come Away Death 1997; numerous publications with Michael Hardwick, plays and scripts for radio and TV and contribs to journals.

HARDY, Françoise Madeleine; French singer, writer and astrologer; b 17 Jan 1944, Paris; m Jacques Dutronc 1981; one s. *Education:* Univ of Paris. *Career:* Singer and songwriter 1960–; has given numerous concerts including performances at Olympia (Paris); has toured France and abroad; numerous TV appearances; now writes lyrics for musicians including Diane Tell, Julien Clerc, Khalil Chahine, Guesch Patti and composer-arranger Alain Lubrano; Presenter daily Horoscope radio programme on Radio-Télé Luxembourg (RTL); writer on astrology; Victoire de la Musique Best Song Award 1991. *Songs include:* Tous les garçons et les filles 1962, Ce petit cœur, Mon amie la rose, L'amitié, La maison où j'ai grandi, Rendez-vous d'automne, Comment te dire Adieu, Etonnez-moi, Benoît, Message personnel, Ce soir, Gin Tonic 1980, VIP 1986, Décalages 1988; *Album:* Le danger 1996; *Films include:* Château en Suède 1963, Une balle au cœur 1965, Grand prix 1966; *Publications include:* Le grand livre de la Vierge (jtly), Entre les lignes entre les signes (jtly) 1986, Notes secrètes (jtly) 1991; contribs to Françoise Hardy présente l'Astrologie Universelle 1986. *Leisure interests:* reading, especially books dealing with spirituality. *Address:* 13 rue Hallé, 75014 Paris, France.

HARKIN, Ruth R., BA, JD; American lawyer and business executive; b 27 Aug 1944, Vesta MN; d of Walter Herman and Virgina Coull Raduenz; m Tom Harkin 1968; two d. *Education:* Univ of Minnesota and Catholic Univ (Washington, DC). *Career:* Mem staff Dept of Army, Repub of Korea 1966–67; mem staff Polk Co Social Services, Des Moines, IA 1968; Clerk Lawyers Comm on Civil Rights under Law; Co Attorney Story Co, IA 1972–76; Special Prosecutor Polk Co 1977–78; Dep Gen Counsel Akin, Gump, Strauss, Hauer & Feld, LLP, Washington, DC 1983–93; Pres and CEO Overseas Pvt Investment Corpn 1993; Sr Vice-Pres for Int Affairs, United Technologies. *Address:* c/o Overseas Private Investment Corpn, 1100 New York Ave, Washington, DC 20527, USA.

HARLÉ, Laurence Marcelle; French cartoonist; b 15 April 1949, Paris; d of Alfred and Huguette Ferreux; m Nicolas Harlé 1969; two d one s. *Education:* Lycée Honoré de Balzac (Paris). *Career:* Trainee journalist 1965–68; designer 1968–77; cartoonist 1973–; collaborator on Pilote magazine 1978–84, on France Culture 1987–. *Cartoon publications:* Cartland 1975, Dernier convoi pour l'Orégon 1976, Le trésor de la femme-araignée 1978, La rivière du vent 1979, Les doigts du chaos 1982, Silver Canyon (Prize for Best Script 1985) 1983, La cavalerie américaine 1985, Les survivants de l'ombre (Prize for Best Cartoon Book, Angoulême 1988) 1987, L'enfant lumière 1989. *Leisure interests:* cinema, theatre, puzzles, gardening. *Address:* Editions Dargaud, 6 rue Gager Gabillot, 75015 Paris, France.

HARLECH, Lady Pamela, BA; British journalist and arts administrator; b 18 Dec 1934; d of Ralph Frederick Colin and Georgia Talmey; m Baron Harlech 1969 (died 1985); one d. *Education:* Smith and Finch Colls (MA, USA). *Career:* London Ed American Vogue 1964–69; Food Ed British Vogue 1971–82; freelance journalist 1972–; production work for special events 1986–87; Commissioning Ed Thames and Hudson Publrs 1987–89; Chair Women's Playhouse Trust 1984–94, Victoria & Albert Enterprises 1987–94, English Nat Ballet 1990–2000; mem Council British American Arts Assen 1990–92, Welsh Arts Council 1981–85, Arts Council of GB 1986–90, S Bank Bd 1986–94, Council Assen of Business Sponsorship for the Arts 1988–94, Man Bd Crusaid 1987–96; Trustee Victoria and Albert Museum 1986–94. *Publications include:* Feast Without Fuss 1976, Pamela Harlech's Complete Guide to Cooking, Entertainment and Household Management 1981, Vogue Book of Menus 1985. *Leisure interests:* music, cooking, laughing. *Address:* English National Ballet, 39 Jay Mews, London SW7, UK.

HARLOW, Carol Rhian, PH D, FBA; British barrister and professor of law; b 28 Aug 1935, London; d of Harold and Clare Williams; m 1958; one s one d. *Education:* Queen's Coll (London). *Career:* Lecturer Kingston Polytechnic 1972–75, LSE 1976–88, Prof of Public Law 1989–, Jean Monnet Prof, European Univ Inst 1995, 1996; mem Social Security Appeals Tribunal 1978–85; Chair Legal Action Group 1986–89; Hon QC. *Publications:* Compensation and Government Torts 1982, Law and Administration (jtly) 1984, Politics and Public Law 1986, Pressure Through Law (jtly) 1992, Introducing Tort Law 1994. *Leisure interests:* theatre, arts, gardening. *Address:* LSE, Dept of Law, Houghton St, London WC2A 2AE, UK (Office); 58 Mount Ararat Rd, Richmond TW10 6PJ, UK (Home). *Telephone:* (20) 7955-7248.

HARMAN, Rt Hon Harriet, PC; British politician and lawyer; b 30 July 1950; d of the late John Bishop Harman and of Anna Charlotte Harman; m Jack Dromey 1982; two s one d. *Education:* St Paul's Girls' School and Univ of York. *Career:* Mem staff Brent Community Law Centre 1975–78; Legal Officer Nat Council for Civil Liberties (NCCL) 1978–82; MP (Lab) for Peckham 1982–97, for Camberwell and Peckham 1997–, Opposition Chief Sec to the Treasury 1992–94, Opposition Spokesperson on Employment 1994–95, on Health 1995–96, on Social Security 1996–97; Sec of State for Social Security 1997–98; Solicitor Gen 2001–. *Publications include:* Sex Discrimination in Schools 1977, Justice Deserted: the Subversion of the Jury 1979, The Century Gap 1993. *Address:* House of Commons, London SW1A 0AA, UK. *Telephone:* (20) 7219-0650; *Fax:* (20) 7219-4877; *E-mail:* harmanh@parliament.uk; *Internet:* www.harriet.harman.labour.co.uk.

HARMS, Inger Birgitte; Danish politician; b 10 Aug 1942, Esbjerg; d of Vagn Harry and Ida (née Nielsen) Lund; m 1962 (divorced 1976); one s one d. *Education:* Esbjerg, Prairie High School (IA, USA), Åbenrå. *Career:* Chair Åbenrå branch Socialistisk Folkeparti (Socialist People's Party) 1981–; mem Folketing (Parl) 1981–90, Chair Cttee for Naturalization 1981; mem Nordic Council 1981; Del to UN Gen Ass 1986; mem Danish Del to Council of Europe 1987, Pres Communists and Allies group in Council of Europe 1987 (known as Unified European Left 1989–); mem Cttee for the Danish Minority in Germany 1990; author several articles on the EC, animal ethics, E-W relations; European Pro Merito Prize 1990. *Leisure interests:* politics, shooting. *Address:* c/o Frueløkke 328, 6200 Aabenraa, Denmark.

HARNEY, Mary, BA; Irish politician; b 1953, Ballinasloe, Co Galway. *Education:* Presentation Convent (Clondalkin, Co Dublin) and Trinity Coll (Dublin). *Career:* Mem Seanad Éireann (youngest ever Senator) 1977–81; TD 1981–, Co-Founder Progressive Democrats 1985, Minister for Environmental Protection 1989–92, Deputy Leader Progressive Democrats 1993, then Leader and Spokesperson on Justice, Equality and Law Reform; Minister for Enterprise and Employment 1997; currently Tánaiste (Deputy Prime Minister) and Minister for Enterprise, Trade and Employment; mem Dublin Co Council 1979–91. *Address:* Department of Enterprise, Trade and Employment, Kildare St, Dublin, 2, Ireland; 11 Serpentine Terrace, Ballsbridge, Dublin 4, Ireland. *Telephone:* (1) 631-2121; *Fax:* (1) 361-2827; *E-mail:* webmaster@entemp.ie; *Internet:* www.entemp.ie.

HARNOY, Ofra, CM; Canadian (b Israeli) cellist; b 31 Jan 1965, Israel; d of Jacob and Carmela Harnoy; m Robert S. Cash. *Education:* Studied with father in Israel, with William Pleeth in London, Vladimir Orloff in Toronto and in master classes with M. Rostropovich, Pierre Fournier and Jacqueline du Pré. *Career:* Professional debut aged 10, with Boyd Neel Orchestra, Toronto; solo appearances with orchestras in the USA, Canada, Japan, Europe, Israel and Venezuela; TV appearances in Canada, UK and other European countries, Japan and Australia; played world première performance Offenbach cello concerto, N American première Bliss cello concerto, world première recording of several Vivaldi cello concertos; numerous solo recordings; prizes and awards include JUNO Award for Best Classical Soloist (Canada) 1987/88, 1988/89, 1991, 1992, 1993, First Prize Montréal symphony competition 1978, Canadian Music Competition 1979, Concert Artists Guild (New York) 1982, Young Musician of the Year (Musical America magazine), USA 1983, Grand Prix du Disque, Critics' Choice, Best Records of the Year (The Gramophone) UK 1986, 1988, 1990. *Address:* 437 Spadina Rd, POB 23046, Toronto, ON M5P 2W0, Canada. *Telephone:* (416) 863-1060; *Fax:* (416) 861-0191.

HARPER, Heather, CBE, FRCM; British opera singer (soprano); b 8 May 1930, Belfast; d of Hugh and Mary Eliza Harper; m 2nd Eduardo J. Benarroch 1973. *Education:* Trinity Coll of Music (London). *Career:* Created soprano role in Britten's War Requiem, Coventry Cathedral 1962; toured USA with BBC Symphony Orchestra 1965, fmr USSR 1967; soloist the Maltings, Snape 1967, Queen Elizabeth Hall 1967; annual concert and opera tours USA 1967–91; Prin Soloist BBC Symphony Orchestra tour of Hong Kong and Australia 1982, Royal Opera House US tour 1984; concerts in Europe, Asia, Middle East, Australia, S America; prin roles at Covent Garden, Bayreuth Festival, La Scala (Milan, Italy), Teatro Colón (Buenos Aires), Edinburgh Festival, Glyndebourne, Sadler's Wells, Metropolitan Opera House (New York) and San Francisco (USA), Frankfurt (Germany), Deutsche Oper (Berlin), Japan, Netherlands Opera House, New York City Opera; renowned performances of works of Richard Strauss; TV roles in Peter Grimes, Owen Wingrave, Idomeneo, Don Giovanni, La Traviata, La Bohème, etc; 25 consecutive years as Prin Soloist at the Proms; Dir Singing Studies at the Britten–Pears School for Advanced Musical Studies, Aldeburgh, Suffolk 1986–; Prof of Singing and Consultant Royal Coll of Music, London 1986–; Visiting Lecturer-in-Residence, Royal Scottish Acad of Music 1987–; retd from operatic stage 1986; mem BBC Music Panel 1989–, Royal Soc of Arts 1989–; Hon Fellow Trinity Coll of Music; Hon mem RAM; Hon D MUS (Queen's Univ); Edison Award 1971; Grammy Award 1979, 1984, 1991. *Recordings include:* Les Illuminations (Britten), Symphony No 8 (Mahler), Don Giovanni, Requiem (Verdi) and Missa Solemnis (Beethoven), Seven Early Songs (Berg), The Marriage of Figaro, Peter Grimes, Four Last Songs (Strauss), 14 Songs with Orchestra. *Leisure interests:* gardening, painting, cooking, swimming, tennis.

HARPER, Jenny Gwynnydd, MA, M PHIL; New Zealand/British university professor; b 27 April 1950, Geraldine, NZ; d of George Cuthbert Lyon and Joan Gwynnydd (née Fulton) Harper; m 1982 (divorced 1994); one d. *Education:* Villa Maria Coll (Christchurch), Univ of Canterbury (Christchurch), Christchurch Teachers' Coll, Courtauld Inst of Art (Univ of London) and Univ of Sydney. *Career:* Trainee gen nurse Christchurch Hosp 1968–69; Tutor of Religious Studies Univ of Canterbury 1974–77; Teacher Naenae Coll (Lower Hutt) 1978–80; Asst Curator Australian Nat Gallery (Canberra) 1983; European Art Curator Queensland Art Gallery (Brisbane, Australia) 1983–86; Sr Int Art Curator Nat Art Gallery (Wellington) 1986–88, Dir 1990–93; mem Planning Team Museum of New Zealand Te Papa Tongarewa (Wellington) 1988–90, Dir Museum Projects 1994–; Prof, Head of Art History Victoria Univ of Wellington 1995–2001, Head of School of Art History, Classics and Religious Studies 2001–; Sir William Hartley Fellowship 1981–82; NZ Commemoration Medal 1990. *Publications:* Bridget Riley: An Australian Context 1985, Barbara Kruger (exhibition catalogue) 1988, Imants Tillers 19301 (exhibition catalogue) 1989, Boyd Webb 1997. *Leisure interests:* reading, visiting art museums, opera. *Address:* POB 9075, Marion Square, Wellington, New Zealand; Victoria Univ of Wellington, POB 600, Wellington, New Zealand. *Telephone:* (4) 463-5801; *Fax:* (4) 463-5024; *E-mail:* jenny .harper@vuw.ac.nz.

HARRELL-BOND, Barbara, M LITT, D PHIL; American anthropologist; b 7 Nov 1932, SD; d of Elmer and Irene Moir; two s one d. *Education:* Univ of Oxford (UK). *Career:* Research Fellow Univ of Edinburgh, UK 1967–69; Visiting Prof Dept of Anthropology, Univ of Illinois 1970; Sr Research Fellow Afrika-Studiecentrum, Leiden, Netherlands 1971–76, Univ of Warwick, UK 1976–79; Assoc for Africa, Univs Field Staff Int 1979–81; Sr Research Fellow Queen Elizabeth House, Univ of Oxford 1982; Dir Refugee Studies Programme, Univ of Oxford 1982–96; Visiting Prof Makewe Univ 1997–2000; Distinguished Adjunct Prof, American Univ in Cairo 2001–02. *Publications:* Modern Marriage in Sierra Leone 1975, The Imposition of Law (jtly) 1979, Imposing Aid 1986, Directory of Current Research on Refugees 1987, 1988. *Leisure interest:* horse-riding. *Address:* c/o University of Oxford, Refugee Studies Programme, 21 St Giles, Oxford OX1 3LA, UK.

HARRIS, Barbara Clementine; American church official; b 1930, Philadelphia, PA; d of Beatrice Harris; m 1962 (divorced). *Education:* Charles Morris Price School of Advertising and Journalism (Philadelphia, PA), Metropolitan Collegiate Center, Villanova Univ (PA) and Episcopal Divinity School. *Career:* Joined Joseph V. Baker Assocs, Pres 1958–68; joined Sun Oil Co 1968, Man Community Relations Dept 1973–1980; ordained Priest 1980, assigned to St Augustin of Hippo Parish, Norristown (PA), Chaplain to Philadelphia Co Prison System then Rector (interim) to Church of the Advocate 1988; Bishop Suffragan Episcopal Diocese of Massachusetts 1989 (first female bishop in history of Anglican communion); apptd Exec Dir Episcopal Church Publishing Co 1984; Hon D THEOL (Hobart) 1981. *Address:* Episcopal Diocese of Massachusetts, 138 Tremont St, Boston, MA 02111, USA.

HARRIS, Elizabeth; British public relations consultant; b 1 May 1942; d of Lord and Lady Ogmore; m 1st Richard Harris; m 2nd Rex Harrison; three s. *Education:* In Wales, England, Switzerland and at Royal Acad of Dramatic Art (London). *Career:* Fmrly actress, columnist on Western Mail and writer; worked in public relations 1984–, Founder Elizabeth Harris Assocs Ltd 1989, currently Man Dir; mem Inst of Public Relations. *Publication:* Love, Honour and Dismay (autobiog). *Leisure interests:* theatre, travel. *Address:* 7 Grove Court, Drayton Gardens, London SW10 9QY, UK. *Telephone:* (20) 7373-5800; *Fax:* (20) 7244-8302; *Internet:* elizabethhr@aol.com.

HARRIS, Emmylou; American singer; b 2 April 1947, Birmingham, AL; m 1st Brian Ahern; m 2nd Paul Kennerley 1985; two c. *Education:* Univ of N Carolina. *Career:* Singer 1967–, toured with Fallen Angels Band in USA and Europe; Pres Country Music Foundation 1983–; Grammy Awards 1976, 1977, 1980, 1981, 1984, 1987, 1992, 1996; Female Vocalist of the Year (Country Music Asscn) 1980; Acad of Country Music Album of the Year (with Dolly Parton and Linda Ronstadt, qv) 1987. *Recordings include:* Albums: Gliding Bird 1969, Pieces of the Sky 1975, Elite Hotel, Luxury Liner, Quarter Moon in a Ten-Cent Town, Blue Kentucky Girl 1979, Light of the Stable 1979, Evangeline 1981, Last Date 1982, White Shoes 1983, Thirteen, Trio (with Dolly Parton and Linda Ronstadt) 1987, Angel Band 1987, Bluebird 1989, Duets 1990, Cowgirl's Prayer 1993, Songs of the West 1994, Wrecking Ball 1995, Singin with Emmylou Harris, Vol I 2000. *Address:* c/o Vector Management, 1500 17th Ave S, Nashville, TN 37212, USA.

HARRIS, Julie; American actress; b 2 Dec 1925, Michigan; d of William Picket and Elsie (née Smith) Harris; m 1st Jay I. Julien 1946 (divorced 1954); m 2nd Manning Gurian 1954 (divorced 1967); one s; m 3rd Walter Erwin Carroll 1977 (divorced 1982). *Education:* Yale Drama School. *Career:* Numerous awards. *Plays include:* Sundown Beach 1948, The Young and Fair 1948, Magnolia Alley 1949, Montserrat 1949, The Member of the Wedding 1950, I am a Camera (New York Drama Critics' Award) 1951, The Lark 1956, Little Moon of Alban (Emmy Award) 1960, A Shot in the Dark 1961, Victoria Regina (Emmy Award) 1962, Marathon 33 1964, Ready When You Are, C. B. 1964, And Miss Reardon Drinks a Little 1971, Voices 1972, The Last of Mrs Lincoln 1973, In Praise of Love 1974, The Belle of Amherst (New York) 1976, (London) 1977, Break a Leg 1979, Mixed Couples 1980, Driving Miss Daisy 1988, Lucifer's Child 1991, Lettice and Lovage, The Fiery Furnace 1993, The Glass Menagerie 1996, The Gin Game 1997, Ellen Foster 1997, Love is Strange 1999; *Films include:* East of Eden (Antoinette Perry Award) 1955, I Am a Camera 1956, Poacher's

Daughter 1960, The Haunting, The Moving Target, Voyage of the Damned 1976, The Bell Jar 1979, Gorillas in the Mist 1988, The Dark Half, Housesitter, Carried Away, Bad Manners 1997, The First of May 1998; *TV includes:* Little Moon of Alban 1960, Knots Landing 1982, Scarlett, The Christmas Tree 1996, Ellen Foster 1997. *Address:* c/o Gail Naehlis, William Morris Agency, 151 S El Camino Drive, Beverly Hills, CA 90212-2775, USA.

HARRIS, Margaret, MS; American pianist, conductor and composer; b 1943, Chicago, IL; d of William and Clara Harris. *Education:* Juilliard School of Music. *Career:* Debut at three years, with Chicago Symphony Orchestra (IL) 1953; Conductor and Pianist Black New World, toured Europe as Dir of Black New World and Negro Ensemble Co; debut as Symphonic Conductor with Grant Park and Chicago Symphonic Orchestras 1971; Conductor St Louis (MN), San Diego (CA), Detroit (MI) and Winston-Salem (NC) Symphonies, Los Angeles Philharmonic, Opera Ebony (NY), Dayton Philharmonic 1991; Guest Conductor Brooklyn Philharmonic, New York 1994; tour of Europe as pianist 1994; American culture specialist US Information Agency, Porgy & Bess (in Russian) 1995; Pres Margaret R. Harris Enterprises; Artist-in-Residence Hillsborough Coll (FL) 1984; Visiting Distinguished Prof Univ of W Florida 1989–; Perm Artistic and Music Dir Olympus Music Soc, New York 1994; conductor and music dir numerous Broadway and TV shows; Dame Knights of Malta. *Compositions include:* David, Cycle of Psalms, Spiritual Suite, Stabat Mater, Mass in A, the Lord's Prayer, We are D.C.'s Future, Christ is Alive Here 1994.

HARRISON, Fiona, B SC; British business executive; b 1950, Hertfordshire; m. *Education:* Ware Grammar School (Herts) and Univ of Leicester. *Career:* Began career as Man Trainee, Metal Box; fmr Buyer Boots the Chemist, now Non-Exec Dir; worked in Product Devt Dept, Clairol 1977–80; Retail Dir Coats Viyella 1980–98; Career Consultant Stork & May 1998; CEO Liberty PLC 1998–. *Address:* Liberty, Regent St, London W1, UK.

HARRISON, Pauline, CBE, BA, D PHIL; British professor of biochemistry; b 24 Aug 1926, Henbury; d of Dr John MacQueen Cowan and Adeline May Cowan; m Royden John Harrison 1954; two d. *Education:* St Trinnean's School (Edinburgh), Univ of Edinburgh and Somerville Coll (Oxford). *Career:* Began career as Research Asst to Dorothy Hodgkin, Univ of Oxford 1946–52; Nuffield Fellow King's Coll (London) 1952–55; Research Assoc Univ of Wisconsin, USA 1964; Grantholder Ministry of Fuel and Power, Sheffield Univ 1956–58, MRC and Ind Research Worker 1958–64; Lecturer, later Sr Lecturer, Reader and Prof Univ of Sheffield 1965–91, now Prof Emer of Biochem; mem Cttee and Chair British Biophysical Soc; mem and Editorial Advisor Biochemical Soc; mem Cttee Inorganic Biochem Discussion Group, Int Soc of Biology and Inorganic Chem; Co-Founder Int Conf on Proteins of Iron Metabolism 1972–; Hon D SC (Sheffield) 1998; has published numerous specialist articles in scientific journals. painting, reading, walking, theatre and the arts, grandchildren. *Address:* Dept of Molecular Biology and Biotechnology, Faculty of Pure Science, University of Sheffield, Sheffield S10 2TN, UK (Office); 4 Wilton Place, Sheffield S10 2BT, UK (Home). *Telephone:* (114) 266-2003; *Fax:* (114) 272-8697; *E-mail:* p.harrison@sheffield.ac.uk (Office).

HARRY, Deborah Ann; American singer, songwriter and actress; b 11 July 1945, Miami, FL; d of Richard Smith and Catherine (née Peters) Harry; fmr partner Chris Stein. *Education:* Centenary Coll. *Career:* Fmr singer with Wind in the Willows; singer and songwriter with Blondie 1975–83; currently solo singer and songwriter; film actress; awarded Gold, Silver and Platinum discs. *Recordings include:* Albums: Blondie, Blondie: The Hunter, Plastic Letters, Parallel Lines, Eat to the Beat, The Complete Picture (compilation), Ku Ku (solo album), Autoamerican, Rockbird, Def, Dumb and Blond 1989, Blonde and Beyond 1993, Rapture 1994, Virtuosity 1995, Rockbird 1996, Der Einziger Weg 1999; Singles with Blondie: Rip Her to Shreds, Denis, I'm Always Touched By Your Presence Dear, Picture This, Heart of Glass, Sunday Girl, Call Me, Atomic, Union City Blue, The Tide is High, Rapture; Solo singles: I Want That Man, French Kissing in the USA, Well Did You Evah? (with Iggy Pop, for Red Hot and Blue compilation); *Films:* Union City Blue, Videodrome, Hairspray, Tales from the Darkside: The Movie 1990, Joe's Day 1999, 200 1999, Six Ways to Sunday 1999, Ghost Light 2000, Dueces Wild 2000, Red Lipstick 2000; *TV appearances:* Saturday Night Live, The Muppet Show, Tales from the Darkside, Wiseguys; *Plays include:* Teaneck Tanzi, The Venus Flytrap. *Address:* c/o Innovative Artists, Suite 2850, 1999 Ave of the Stars, Los Angeles, CA 90067, USA (Office).

HART, Josephine; Irish writer; b Mullingar, Co Westmeath; m Maurice Saatchi. *Career:* Founder Gallery Poets, London; Producer various plays in West End (London); Presenter Books by My Bedside (Thames TV); mem judging panel Irish Times–Aer Lingus Int Fiction Prize 1992. *Publications:* Novels include: Damage 1991, Stillest Day 1998. *Address:* c/o Random House, 20 Vauxhall Bridge Rd, London SW1V 2SA, UK.

HART, Romaine Jennifer, OBE; British film executive; b 14 June 1933, London; d of Goldie and Alexander Bloom; m 1958; two d. *Education:* Westcombe School and St Mary's Hall (Brighton). *Career:* Man Dir Mainline Pictures; opened first Screen cinema Screen on the Green, Islington 1970, Screen on the Hill, Hampstead 1977, Screen at Baker St 1984, Screen at Reigate 1988, Screen at Walton, Walton on Thames 1992, Screen at Winchester 1996; mem Bd British Screen Advisory Council, Friday Productions, Common Purpose, International Human Rights Watch Film Festival 1996; BFI Award for excellence in cinema exhibition. *Leisure interests:* theatre, swimming, tennis. *Address:* Mainline Pictures, 37 Museum St, London WC1, UK. *Telephone:* (20) 7242-5523; *Fax:* (20) 7430-0170.

HARTIGAN, Grace; American artist; b 28 March 1922, Newark, NJ; d of Matthew A. and Grace Hartigan; m 1st Robert L. Jachens 1941 (divorced 1948); one s; m 2nd Robert Keene 1959 (divorced 1960); m 3rd Winston H. Price 1960 (died 1980). *Education:* Pvt art classes. *Career:* Dir Graduate School of Painting, Maryland Inst 1965–; solo exhibitions include Tibor de Nagy Gallery, New York 1951–55, 1957–59, Vassar Coll Art Gallery 1954, Martha Jackson Gallery, New York, NY 1962, 1964, 1967, 1970, Gertrude Kasle Gallery, Detroit, MI 1968, 1970, 1972, 1974, Gres Gallery, Washington 1960, Univ of Minnesota 1963, William Zierler Gallery, New York 1975–, C. Grimaldis Gallery, Baltimore, MD 1979, 1981, 1982, 1984, 1986, 1987, 1989, 1990, 1993, Hamilton Gallery, New York 1989, ACA Gallery, New York 1991, 1992, 1994; numerous group exhibitions including Modern Art in US 1955–56, 4th Int Art Exhibition, Japan 1957, New American Painting Show 1958–59, World Fair, Brussels, Moca in Moca, Chicago, IL, Whitney Museum of Modern Art, New York 1992–93; represented in perm collections; Merit Award for Art, Mademoiselle Magazine 1957; Purchase Award, Nat Inst of Arts and Letters 1974. *Address:* 1701 1/2 Eastern Ave, Baltimore, MD 21231-2420, USA.

HARTLEY, Catharine; British Arctic/Antarctic explorer; b 14 Sept 1965, Manchester; d of Jim and Mary Hartley. *Education:* Chichester Coll of Tech and Guilford School of Acting. *Career:* Fmr Stage and Location Man; works for Blue Peter children's programme, BBC TV; extensive travel in SE Asia, Australasia etc; first British woman (with Fiona Thornewill, qv) to walk across the Antarctic to the Geographic S Pole 2000, also first British woman (with Fiona Thornewill) to walk to Geographic N Pole 2001, becoming first ever woman to manhaul own sledge to both N and S Poles; Pride of Britain Award 2000; People of the Year Award 2001. *Leisure interests:* rock climbing, watersports, travel. *Address:* c/o Blue Peter, BBC Broadcasting House, Portland Place, London W1A 1AA, UK. *Telephone:* (20) 7720-7760 (Office); (7714) 242359 (Mobile); *E-mail:* cath@sark.freeserve.co.uk.

HARUTUNIAN, Ludmila, PH D; Armenian sociologist; b 13 Jan 1941, Yerevan; d of Hakop Harutunian and Varsik Vartanian; m Albert Maksudian 1964; one s one d. *Education:* Yerevan State Univ, Inst of Continuing Educ (Moscow) and Univ of Paris (Sorbonne). *Career:* UNESCO expert on discrimination against women 1976; apptd Head Dept of Sociology, Yerevan State Univ 1986; People's Deputy of USSR, mem Supreme council of USSR 1989, mem Comm on Inter-ethnic Relations 1989, Chair Sub-Cttee of Ethnic Conflict 1990; Rep to European Org on Conflict Resolution 1992; Vice-Chair Women's Cttee of Armenia 1986; mem CIS Sociological Asscn 1978; Winner All-Union Competition for Sociologists 1973. *Publications include:* Mode of Life: Methodological Problems of Sociology Studies 1985, Destruction of Myths 1990, For Which Purpose am I again at Microphone 1991, Brightness and Poverty of President 1991, We Have to Free Ourselves of Love and Hatred 1992. *Address:* 375056 Yerevan, N-Nork III Microraion 30, kv 19, Armenia. *Telephone:* (8852) 646-774; *Fax:* (8852) 550-385.

HARVEY, Barbara Fitzgerald, CBE, MA, B LITT, FRHISTS, FSA, FBA; British academic; b 21 Jan 1928, Teignmouth, Devon; d of Richard Henry and Anne Fitzgerald (née Julian) Harvey. *Education:* Teignmouth Grammar School, Bishop Blackall School (Exeter) and Somerville Coll (Oxford). *Career:* Asst Univ of Edinburgh 1951–52; Lecturer Queen Mary Coll (Univ of London) 1952–55; Tutor Somerville Coll (Oxford) 1955–93, Fellow 1956–93, Emer Fellow 1993–, Vice-Prin 1976–79, 1981–83, Ford's Lecturer Univ of Oxford 1989, Reader in Medieval History 1990–93; Vice-Pres Royal Historical Soc 1986–90; Gen Ed Oxford Medieval Texts 1987–99; mem Royal Comm on Historical Manuscripts 1991–98. *Publications:* Westminster Abbey and its Estates in the Middle Ages 1977, The Westminster Chronicle, 1381–94 (co-ed) 1982, Living and Dying in England 1100–1540: The Monastic Experience (Wolfson Foundation History Prize – jtly 1993) 1993, The Short Oxford History of the British Isles: The Twelfth and Thirteenth Centuries (ed) 2001; articles in learned journals. *Address:* 66 Cranham St, Oxford OX2 6DD, UK. *Telephone:* (1865) 554766.

HARVEY, Cynthia Theresa; American ballet dancer and teacher; b 17 May 1957, San Rafael, CA; d of Gordon and Clara (née De Ojeda) Harvey; m Christopher D. Murphy 1990. *Education:* High School of Professional Children's School (New York). *Career:* Joined American Ballet Theater 1974, Prin Dancer 1982–86, 1988–; with Royal Ballet, London 1986–88; numerous guest appearances with Mikhail Baryshnikov, Rudolf Nureyev and Alexander Godunov and with Stuttgart Ballet, Germany, Birmingham Royal Ballet and Northern Ballet Theatre, UK; teacher at leading ballet schools in USA. *Publication:* The Physics of Dance and the Pas de Deux (jtly) 1994; *Film:* The Turning Pointe. *Leisure interests:* motor racing, music, theatre, football, design. *Address:* c/o American Ballet Theater, 890 Broadway, 3rd Floor, New York, NY 10003, USA. *Telephone:* (212) 477-3030.

HARVEY, Polly Jean (P. J.); British singer; b 1970, Dorset. *Career:* Folk singer, then rock singer with band P. J. Harvey; now solo singer; nominated for Mercury Awards. *Recordings include:* Albums: Dry, To Bring You My Love, Dance Hall at House Point; Singles: Dress, Sheela-Na-Gig, Down By The Water, C'mon Billy, Send His Love to Me, Is That All There Is? 1996, That Was My Veil 1996, Broken Homes 1998, A Perfect Day Elise 1998, The Wind 1998.

HARVOR, Erica Elisabeth Arendt, MA; Canadian writer; b 26 June 1936, Saint John, NB; d of Kjeld Deichmann and Erica Matthiesen; m Stig Harvor 1957 (divorced 1977); two s. *Education:* Saint John High School and Concordia Univ. *Career:* Tutor Concordia Univ 1986–87, currently Writer-in-Residence; Course Dir and Part-time Lecturer in Creative Writing, Div of the Humanities, York Univ (Toronto) 1987–93; mem Canadian juries; reader and tutor in field; First Prize CBC's New Canadian Writing Series 1965, Ottawa Short Story Competition 1970, The League of Canadian Poets' Nat Poetry Prize 1989, 1991; The Malahat Long Poem Prize 1990; Confed Poets' Prize 1991, 1992. *Publications:* Women and Children 1973 (re-issued as Our Lady of All The Distances 1991), If Only We Could Drive Like This Forever 1988, Fortress of Chairs (poems) 1992, Let Me Be The One 1996; works featured in journals, magazines and anthologies. *Address:* c/o The Writers' Union of Canada, 24 Ryerson Ave, Toronto, ON M5T 2P3, Canada.

HARWOOD, Vanessa Clare, OC; Canadian ballet dancer, teacher and choreographer; b 14 June 1947, Cheltenham, UK; d of Peter Griffiths and Hazel Marian Harwood; m Hugh E. Scully 1980; two step-d one d. *Education:* Nat Ballet School (Toronto, ON). *Career:* Teacher Studio Dance Theatre, Toronto; joined Corps de Ballet, Nat Ballet of Canada 1965, Soloist 1967, Prin Dancer 1970–87; Guest Dancer Australian Ballet 1977, Detroit Symphony (MI, USA) 1977, Chicago Ballet (IL, USA) 1978, Norfolk (VA, USA) 1978, Jacobs Pillow 50th Anniversary 1981, Dutch Nat Ballet 1979, Munich Opera Ballet (Germany) 1981, Godunov and Stars Tour (USA) 1982, Universal Ballet (Seoul) 1985; Dancer and Actress Canadian Pavilion Expo '86; stylist and coach Canadian Olympic Ice Dancers 1988; Artistic Dir Balletto Classico, debut with Kitchener Symphony 1989; Vice-Pres Actors Fund of

Canada 1991–; mem Canadian Actors' Equity Asscn, World Dance Alliance Council 1995–, Advisory Bd Dancer Transition Resource Centre 1997–; awarded Commemorative Medal for 125th Anniversary of Canadian Confed 1992;. *Ballets include:* Swan Lake, Pas de Deux, La Fille Mal Gardée, Giselle, Sleeping Beauty, Romeo and Juliet, Coppelia, Allure, Locatelli Sonata; *Play:* The Mousetrap; *Opera:* Merry Widow (also staged) 1989. *Address:* 328 Glengarry Ave, Toronto, ON M5M 1E6, Canada.

HASHEMI BAHREMANI (RAFSANJANI), Faezeh, MA; Iranian politician and sportswoman; b 1963, Qum; d of Ali Akbar Hashemi Bahremani (Pres Rafsanjani) and Effat Marashi Ali-abadi; m Hamid Lahouti Oshkevari 1980; one d one s. *Education:* Al-Zahra Univ and Islamic Azad Univ (Teheran). *Career:* Mem Majlis-e-Shura e Islami (Parl) 1996–; Vice-Pres Nat Olympic Cttee 1990–; Founder and Pres Islamic Countries Women Sports Solidarity Council (ICWSSC) 1991–; mem Cen Council of the Communications Network of Women's NGOs 1995–. *Publication:* The First Meeting 1993. *Leisure interests:* study, sport, cinema, music. *Address:* 10 Simin Alley, Asef St, Vali Asr Ave Zaferanieh, Tehran 19879, Iran. *Telephone:* (21) 8019934; *Fax:* (21) 8019906.

HASHMI, Mahmooda, PH D; Pakistani broadcasting executive; b 12 April 1946, Lahore; d of the late Mohammad Shah; m S. A. Shakoor 1986. *Education:* Punjabi Univ (India). *Career:* Joined Pakistan Broadcasting Corpn (fmrly Radio Pakistan) 1973, later Deputy Controller; Sec-Gen Pakistan Nat Rose Soc 1996–97, Ed Pakistan Rose Annual (magazine, in English). *Publications include:* Munis-ul-Ushaq; numerous articles. *Leisure interest:* gardening. *Address:* House 38, St no 5, F-8/3, Islamabad, Pakistan. *Telephone:* (42) 250971.

HASINA WAJED, Sheikh, BA; Bangladeshi politician; b 28 Sept 1947, Tungipara, Gopalganj Dist; d of the late Bangabandu Sheikh Mujibur Rahman and Sheikh Fajilatunessa Mujib; m Dr M. A. Wazed Mia 1969; one s one d. *Education:* Eden Girls' Coll (Dhaka) and Univ of Dhaka. *Career:* Pres Awami League (AL) 1981–; organized mass movt for democracy and civil rights 1981–91; leader eight-party opposition alliance 1983; formed Movt for Restoration of Democracy (MRD) with seven-party opposition group led by Begum Khalida Zia (qv) 1983; Leader of Opposition, Parl 1986–1991, 1991–96; Prime Minister 1996–, also Minister of the Armed Forces Div, of the Cabinet Div, of Special Affairs, of Defence, of Power, Energy and Mineral Resources, and of the Establishment; author of several books and numerous articles; Houphouet-Boigny Peace Prize (jtly) 1999. *Publication:* Ora Tokai Keno? 1989. *Leisure interests:* reading, writing, music. *Address:* Office of the Prime Minister, Old Sangsad Bhaban, Tejgaon, Dhaka, Bangladesh, Bangladesh (Office). *Telephone:* (2) 814100 (Office); *Fax:* (2) 813244 (Office); *E-mail:* pm@pmo.bdonline.com (Office).

HAŠKOVÁ, Věra, D SC; Czech scientist; b 4 April 1927, Pardubice; d of Josef Hočalek and Anna Marešova; m 1st Milan Hašek 1950 (divorced 1970); m 2nd Čestmír Hašek; two d one s. *Education:* State Gymnasium (Pardubice) and Charles Univ (Prague). *Career:* Researcher Dept of Experimental Biology and Genetics, Czech Acad of Sciences 1953–66, Inst of Clinical Experimental Surgery 1967–70, Inst of Clinical and Experimental Medicine 1970–93, Head Dept of Immunology until 1993; Lecturer in Transplant Immunology and Immunogenetics Charles Univ 1987–93; mem Czechoslovak Acad of Sciences; Hon mem Czech Biological Soc, Czech Immunological Soc; State Prize (jtly) 1961; G. Mendel Medal 1977; J. E. Purkyne Gold Medal, Czechoslovak Acad of Sciences 1987; more than 200 papers published in scientific journals. *Address:* Bohácova 862, 149 00 Prague 4, Czech Republic. *Telephone:* (2) 7950492; *Fax:* (2) 3123463.

HASLEGRAVE, Marianne Huggard; British international organization executive; b 2 Nov 1942, London; m 1st David B. Huggard 1968; m 2nd James Edward Haslegrave 1982; one s. *Education:* Durham Univ, Queen's Coll (New York) and City Univ of New York. *Career:* Co-ordinator Forum World Conf, UN Decade for Women 1979–80; Liaison Officer UN Conf on New and Renewable Sources of Energy 1981; Consultant Int Women's Issues 1984–88; Gen Sec Int Fed of Business and Professional Women 1988–92; Dir Commonwealth Medical Asscn 1992–. *Publication:* Forward From Nairobi 1985.

Address: Commonwealth Medical Association, BMA House, Tavistock Square, London WC1H 9JP, UK. *Telephone:* (20) 7383-6095; *Fax:* (20) 7383-6195.

HASSELFELDT, Gerda; German politician; b 7 July 1950, Straubing, Lower Bavaria; m Volker Hasselfeldt 1974; one s one d. *Career:* Worked at Fed Inst of Labour, Nuremberg 1975–77; Head Section for Training Placement, Munich Job Centre 1977–78; Careers Adviser to Abiturienten and Undergrads, Deggendorf Job Centre 1978–85, Head Careers Advice Dept 1985–87; joined Junge Union 1968; Chair Haibach Asscn 1968–74, mem various exec cttees 1968–85; Dist Chair Women's Union 1975; mem Regen Dist Council (Kreistag) 1978; CSU Dist Chair Regen 1987; mem Bundestag (Parl) 1987; Fed Minister for Regional Planning, Bldg and Urban Devt 1989–91, for Health 1991–92 (resigned); Chair of the Finances Working Group of the CDU/CSU Bundestag faction. *Address:* Workstation of the Republic, German Bundestag, Wilhelmstr 60, 11011 Berlin, Germany. *Telephone:* (30) 2277-2497; *Fax:* (30) 2277-6221; *E-mail:* gerda.hasselfeldt@bundestag .de; *Internet:* www.hasselfeldt.de.

HASSENBOHLER, Mireille; American ballet dancer; b New Orleans. *Education:* San Francisco Ballet School and Houston Ballet Acad. *Career:* Joined Houston Ballet as apprentice 1992, Corps de Ballet 1993, Prin Dancer 2000–. *Repertoire:* The Nutcracker, Sleeping Beauty, Swan Lake, Études, Les Patineurs, Theme and Variations, La Valse, Early's Dream, In the Middle, Somewhat Elevated, Sinfonietta, Manon, Elite Syncopations, Bound, Second before the Ground, Skeleton Clock, Firebird, Simple Gifts, The Rite of Spring, Cinderella, Peer Gynt, The Snow Maiden, Four Last Songs. *Address:* 1916 West Gray, Houston, TX 77019, USA.

HASTEDT, Annegret Heide; German business executive; b 7 Nov 1940, Bremen; d of Hermann and Marianne Buschmann; m Klaus Hastedt 1962; two s. *Education:* Kippenberg-Gymnasium (Bremen) and American Inst of Banking/American Bankers' Asscn (Cincinnati, OH, USA). *Career:* Southern Ohio Nat Bank, Cincinnati 1960–61; Norddeutsche Kreditbank AG (Nordkredit), Bremen 1961–62; Galerie-Moden, Bremen 1973–76; Mode-Kabinett, Bremen 1976, apptd Man Dir and Partner Mode-Kabinett A. Hastedt GmbH 1978; apptd Vice-Pres Fed of Business and Professional Women, Germany 1983; mem Bd Regional Women's Council, Bremen 1988; mem council Radio Bremen 1988; mem Bd Fed of Textiles Retail Business, Bremen 1990; mem responsible for Europe, Int Fed of Business and Professional Women–UN Status of Women Cttee 1991. *Leisure interests:* literature, classical music, tennis. *Address:* Emmastr 285, 2800 Bremen 1, Germany. *Telephone:* (421) 211119; *Fax:* (421) 215184.

HASTINGS, Deborah; American bass guitarist; b 11 May 1959, Evansville, IN; d of Mortimer Winthrop Hastings and Margaret Hastings Zimmerman. *Education:* Univ of Wisconsin. *Career:* Plays MIDI, five-string, fretless acoustic and fretted acoustic bass guitars; featured in live weekly country music radio programme 1975–; freelance photographer, Madison, WI 1976–81; played in numerous musical productions Madison Theater Guild 1978–85; mem American Jazz Express Big Band 1978–85; band leader Bo Diddley 1992–; numerous TV appearances 1985–; tours of Australia, Europe, Japan 1989; played at inauguration of Pres George Bush 1989; has played with Chuck Berry, James Brown, Ray Charles, Joe Cocker, Albert Collins, Robert Cray, Bo Diddley, Fats Domino, Mick Fleetwood, Marvin Hamlish, John Lee Hooker, B. B. King, Ben E. King, Huey Lewis, Jerry Lee Lewis, Little Richard, Wilson Pickett, Billy Preston, Ron Wood; mem Musicians' Union. *Publication:* Photographer's Market 1981. *Leisure interests:* videography, photography, computer music. *Address:* c/o Talent Consultants International, 1560 Broadway, Suite 1308, New York, NY 10036, USA. *Telephone:* (212) 582-9661.

HATCH, Heather Ann, BA; Canadian curator and arts administrator; b 5 Jan 1955, Hamilton, ON; d of William McLaren and Diane Franklin Hatch. *Education:* Univ of Guelph (ON). *Career:* Asst Curator Univ of Guelph Art Gallery 1976–78; Admin Asst to Dir The Winnipeg Art Gallery 1978, Devt Officer 1979, Asst to Chief Curator 1981; Curator/Arts Administrator City of Toronto (ON) 1982–90, Curator Market Gallery, City of Toronto Archives 1982–87, Admin Officer Toronto/Amsterdam Artists Exchange Programme 1984–90, staff liaison Public Art Comm City of Toronto 1985–90; Co-ordinator Olympic Arts Advisory Cttee, Toronto Olympic Council 1989; Chair Toronto Outdoor Art Exhibition 1986–89; Dir Toronto Arts Awards Foundation 1988–90; Pres The Haley Group 1991–; mem Asscn of Cultural Execs, Art Gallery of Ontario, The Corp Art Collectors' Group; has written several exhibition catalogues. *Leisure interests:* tennis, sailing, cycling. *Address:* City of Toronto Archives, City Hall, Toronto, ON M5H 2N2, Canada.

HAUG, Frigga, D PHIL; German sociologist and publisher; b 28 Nov 1937, Mülheim/Ruhr; d of Heinz and Melanie Langenberger; m 1st Mr Laudan 1959 (divorced 1965); one d; m 2nd Wolfgang Fritz Haug 1965. *Education:* Mädchengymnasium Mülheim/Ruhr and Free Univ of Berlin. *Career:* Nurse; social worker 1957–58; interviewer; interpreter; Ed and Publr Das Argument (social sciences journal) 1968–; Lecturer Univs of Copenhagen, Berlin, Marburg (Germany) 1971–; Prof Univs of Sydney (Australia) 1985, Innsbruck (Austria) 1988, Klagenfurt 1992, Toronto 1992, Durham (NC) 1997, Mexico 2001; Prof Hochschule für Wirtschaft und Politik, Univ of Hamburg 1978–2001; Ed Ariadne women's crime series 1988–1997; research into women's studies and labour; has published 20 books and approx 100 articles in ten languages; mem women's editorial bd 1981–. *Publications include:* Kritik der Rollentheorie 1974, Gesellschaftliche Produktion und Erziehung 1977, Development of Work 1978, Education for Femininity 1980, Subjekt Frau 1985, Contradictions in Automated Labour 1987, Sexualisierung des Körpers 1988, (English 1987, 2000), Kitchen and State 1988, Erinnerungsarbeit 1990, Die andere Angst 1991, Beyond Female Masochism 1992, Hat die Leistung ein Geschlecht? 1993, Sündiger enuß?, Filmerfahrungen von Frauen 1995, Frauen-Politiken 1996, Lustmolche und Köderfrauen 1997, Vorlesungen zur Einführung in die Erinnerungsarbeit 1999 (English 2002). *Leisure interests:* travel, walking, reading, women's politics, swimming, wine, writing, cooking, lecturing. *Address:* Wittumhalde 5, 73732 Esslingen/N, Germany; Isestr 76, 20149 Hamburg, Germany. *Telephone:* (711) 882-48-58 (Berlin); *Fax:* (711) 88-48-63 (Berlin); *E-mail:* FriggaHaug@aol.com.

HAUG, Jutta D.; German politician; b 8 Oct 1951, Castrop-Rauxel. *Career:* Fmr Town Councillor, Herten; MEP (PSE, SPD); mem Cttee on Budgets (Gen Rapporteur 2000), Del for relations with the mem States of ASEAN, SE Asia and the Repub of Korea; Chair W Westphalia dist Social Democratic Women's Asscn. *Address:* European Parliament, rue Wiertz, ASP 11G246, 1047 Brussels, Belgium. *Telephone:* (2) 284-21-11; *Fax:* (2) 230-69-43.

HAUSER, Rita Eleonore Abrams, LL B; American lawyer; b 12 July 1934, New York, NY; d of Nathan and Frieda Abrams; m Gustave M. Hauser 1956; two c. *Education:* Hunter Coll, Univs of Strasbourg and Paris (France), Harvard Univ (MA) and New York Univ. *Career:* Called to the Bar, DC 1959, NY 1961; Attorney US Dept of Justice 1959–61; in practice New York 1961–67; Partner Moldover, Hauser, Strauss & Volin 1968–72; Sr Partner Stroock & Stroock & Lavan, New York 1972–92, of counsel 1992–; Pres The Hauser Foundation 1990–; US Chair Int Center for Peace in the Middle East 1984–92; mem Bd Dirs Int Peace Acad 1990–, Chair 1993–; mem Visiting Cttee John F. Kennedy School of Govt, Harvard Univ 1992–; mem numerous orgs and advisory panels, Lecturer on Law at several colls and univs; Hon LL D (Seton Hall Univ, Finch Coll) 1969, (Univ of Miami) 1971. *Address:* The Hauser Foundation, 712 Fifth Ave, New York, NY 10019, USA.

HAUTALA, Heidi Anneli, M SC; Finnish politician; b 14 Nov 1955, Oulu; one s. *Education:* Univ of Helsinki. *Career:* Journalist; Chair Finnish Green Party 1987–91; mem Helsinki City Council 1985–94; mem Eduskunta (Parl) 1991–95; MEP (Group of the Greens, Vihreät) 1995–, mem Cttee on Legal Affairs and the Internal Market, Cttee On Women's Rights and Equal Oppertunities, Del for Relations with Switzerland, Iceland and Norway; currently Leader Green Party/European Free Alliance; mem Secretariat of the European Fed of Green Parties 1989–93; Vice Chair Verts/ALE Exec Cttee 1997–99, Second Chair 1999–. *Leisure interests:* environment, security, women, trade, hiking, knitting, debating. *Address:* Euoopan Parlamentti, Pohjoisesplanadi 31, 00100 Helsinki, Finland; European Parliament, rue Wiertz, 1047 Brussels, Belgium. *Telephone:* (2) 284-54-46 (Belgium); *Fax:* (2) 284-94-46 (Belgium); *E-mail:* hhautala@europarl.eu.int; hautala@ vihrealiitto.fi; *Internet:* www.vihrealiitto.fi/hautala.

HAUWEL, Adèle, D MED; Belgian international organization official; b 20 March 1920, Brussels; d of Florimond and Irma (née Verspecht) Hauwel. *Education:* Free Univ of Brussels. *Career:* Medical practitioner; Sec Belgian Open Door Group (for the Economic Emancipation of the Woman Worker) 1960–; Hon Sec Open Door Int; Prix Avon for women's liberation 1983. *Publications:* Ephémérides du féminisme 1975, La porte ouverte 1980–. *Leisure interest:* reading. *Address:* Open Door International, rue Américaine 16, 1060 Bussels, Belgium. *Telephone:* (2) 537-67-61.

HAWKINS, Paula; American politician; b Salt Lake City, UT; d of Paul B. and Leone (née Staley) Fickes; m Walter Eugene Hawkins 1947; two d one s. *Education:* Utah State Univ. *Career:* Del Republican Nat Convention 1968, 1972, 1976, 1980, 1984, Co-Chair Platform Comm 1984, mem Bd Dirs Florida Fed of Republican Women 1968–, Republican Nat Ctteewoman 1968–87; mem Florida Public Service Comm, Tallahassee 1972–79, Chair 1977–79; Republican Senator, FL 1981–87, mem numerous Comms, Chair Drug Enforcement Caucus 1981–87; mem Maitland Civic Cen 1965–76; Charter mem Bd of Dirs Florida Americans Constitutional Action Cttee of 100 1966–68, Sec-Treas 1966–68; mem Gov of Florida Comm on Status of Women 1968–71; mem OAS Perm Sub-Cttee on Narcotics Control and Terrorism 1981–; US Del to UN Narcotics Convention, Vienna 1987, to UN Convention, New York, NY 1994; mem Bd Dirs Freedom Foundation 1981; Chair Nat Comm on Responsibilities for Financing Postsecondary Educ 1988–92; Chair Paula Hawkins & Assocs, Inc 1988; fmr Chair Legis Comm Orange Co Drug Abuse Council, fmr Co-Chair Orange Co March of Dimes; fmr mem Cen Florida Museum Speakers Bureau; Hon HHD (Utah) 1982; Dr hc (Nova Univ, St Thomas Villa Nova, Rollins Coll); Citation for Service, Florida Republican Party; Above and Beyond Award, Outstanding Woman in Florida Politics; Tree of Life Award, Jewish Nat Foundation 1985; Albert Einstein Good Govt Award 1986. *Publication:* Children at Risk 1986. *Address:* 1214 Park Ave N, Winter Park, FL 32789, USA; POB 193, Winter Park, FL 32790-0193, USA. *Telephone:* (407) 677-3020; *Fax:* (407) 677-3055.

HAWLICEK, Hilde; Austrian politician; b 14 April 1942, Vienna. *Career:* Fmr Minister of Educ and the Arts; MEP (Vice-Pres PSE); mem Cttee on Culture, Youth, Educ and the Media, Del for relations with the Maghreb Countries and the Arab Maghreb Union. *Address:* European Parliament, rue Wiertz, 1047 Brussels, Belgium. *Telephone:* (2) 284-21-11; *Fax:* (2) 230-69-43.

HAWN, Goldie; American actress; b 21 Nov 1945, Washington, DC; d of Edward Rutledge and Laura Hawn; m 1st Gus Trikonis 1969 (divorced); m 2nd Bill Hudson (divorced); partner Kurt Russell; two s one d. *Education:* American Univ (Washington, DC). *Career:* Began career as chorus-line dancer, World's Fair, New York 1964; regular appearances in TV series Laugh In; f Cherry Alley Productions 1981; Partner Hawn/Sylbert Movie Co (with Anthea Sylbert, qv). *Stage appearances include:* Romeo and Juliet, Kiss Me Kate, Guys and Dolls; *Films include:* Cactus Flower (Acad Award) 1969, There's a Girl in my Soup 1970, Dollars 1971, Butterflies are Free 1972, The Sugarland Express 1974, The Girl from Petrovka 1974, Shampoo 1975, The Duchess and the Dirtwater Fox 1976, Foul Play 1978, Seems Like Old Times 1980, Private Benjamin (also producer) 1980, Lovers and Liars, Best Friends 1982, Protocol (also exec producer) 1984, Swing Shift 1984, Wildcats 1986, Overboard 1987, Bird On A Wire 1990, My Blue Heaven (co-exec producer) 1990, Deceived, Alone Together (also co-producer), Housesitter, Death Becomes Her, Something to Talk About (exec produced), The First Wives Club 1996, Everyone Says I Love You, The Out Of Towners 1999, Town and Country 1999; *TV series include:* Good Morning, World, Rowan and Martin's Laugh-In, Goldie and Kids—Listen to Us. *Address:* c/o Ed Limato, ICM, 8942 Wilshire Blvd, Beverly Hills, CA 90211, USA (Office).

HAY, Barbara, CMG, MBE, FRSA; British diplomatist; b 20 Jan 1953; d of the late Alfred and of Isa Hay. *Education:* Boroughmuir Sr Secondary School (Edinburgh). *Career:* Joined Diplomatic Service 1971, served in Moscow and Johannesburg, Asst Pvt Sec to Perm Under-Sec and Head of Diplomatic Service 1981–83, First Sec Moscow 1988–91, Consul Gen St Petersburg (Russian Fed) 1991–92, Jt Assistance Unit (Cen Europe), FCO 1992–94, Amb to Uzbekistan and Non-Resident Amb to

Tajikistan 1995–99; Counsellor, FCO 1999–2000. *Leisure interests:* Scottish country dancing, theatre, travel, music, keeping in touch with friends. *Address:* Foreign and Commonwealth Office, London SW1A 2AH, UK.

HAY, Elizabeth Dexter, AB, MD; American professor of embryology; b 2 April 1927, St Augustine, FL; d of Isaac Morris and Lucille Elizabeth Hay. *Education:* Public High School (Melbourne, FL, and Hayes, KS), Smith College (MA) and Johns Hopkins Univ School of Medicine (MD). *Career:* Intern in internal medicine Johns Hopkins Hosp, Baltimore, MD 1952–53; Instructor in Anatomy Johns Hopkins Univ School of Medicine 1953–56, Asst Prof 1956–57; Asst Prof Cornell Univ Medical Coll, NY 1957–60; Asst Prof Harvard Medical School, Boston, MA 1960–64, Louise Foote Pfeiffer Assoc Prof 1964–69, Louise Foote Pfeiffer Prof of Embryology 1969–, Chair Dept of Anatomy and Cellular Biology 1975–93, Prof of Cell Biology 1993–; contribs to professional journals 1952–; Hon SC D (Smith Coll) 1973, (Trinity Coll) 1989, (Johns Hopkins Univ) 1990; E. B. Wilson Award, American Soc of Cell Biology 1988; Excellence in Science Award, Fed of American Socs of Experimental Biology 1990. *Publications:* Regeneration 1966, Fine Structure of the Developing Avian Cornea (jtly) 1969, Development Biology Journal (Ed-in-Chief) 1971–75, Cell Biology of the Extracellular Matrix (ed, 2nd edn) 1991. *Leisure interests:* mycology, feline breeding. *Address:* Harvard Medical School, Dept of Cell Biology, 220 Longwood Ave, B-1-342, Boston, MA 02115, USA. *Telephone:* (617) 432-0407; *Fax:* (617) 277-2732.

HAY, Julie, M PHIL; British consultant and writer; b 15 July 1942, Edgware; two s. *Education:* Harrow Weald Grammar School and Henley Man Coll. *Career:* Consultant with experience in industry, govt and public sector; Civil Servant 1956–61; mem staff Kodak 1961–64, Dexion 1964–67, Amoco 1967, Glacier Metal 1967–71, London Borough of Harrow 1971–74, British Airways 1974–86; Chief Exec A. D. Int 1986–; Diploma in Management Studies. *Publications:* Working it Out at Work – Understanding Attitudes and Building Relationships 1993, Analyse Transactionnelle et Formation 1994, Donkey Bridges for Developmental TA: Making Transactional Analysis Memorable and Accessible 1995, Getting the Best out of Development Centres 1996, Transactional Analysis for Trainers 1996, The Gower Assessment and Development Centre 1997, Action Mentoring: Creating Your Own Developmental Alliance 1997, Dealing with Difficult People 1998, Transformational Mentoring: Creating Developmental Alliances for Changing Organizational Cultures 1999, Transactional Analysis Introductory Course 2001, Neuro Linguistic Programming Practitioner Course 2001. *Leisure interests:* travel, grandchildren, riding. *Address:* AD International, Sherwood House, 7 Oxhey Rd, Watford WD19 4QF, UK. *Telephone:* (1923) 224737; *Fax:* (1923) 210648; *E-mail:* julie@adinternational.com; *Internet:* www.adinternational.com.

HAYASE, Yasuko, B SC; Japanese demographer; b 17 Jan 1944, Mie-ken; d of Shiro and Toku Fujita; m Koichi Hayase 1968; one s one d. *Education:* Tsuda Univ (Tokyo). *Career:* Jr Officer then Chief of Statistical Planning and Analysis Div, then Sr Officer Inst of Developing Econs 1966, then Chief Japanese Editorial Div, Information and Publications Dept; Visiting Research Fellow Jilin Univ, People's Repub of China 1986–88; Academic Visitor Centre for Population Studies, London School of Hygiene and Tropical Medicine, UK 1994–95; Sr Research Assoc Institute of Devt Studies, Univ of Zimbabwe 1995–96; mem Council on the Health and Welfare Statistics, Ministry of Health and Welfare 1990–93; mem International Union for the Scientific Study of Population, Population Asscn of Japan, Japan Statistical Soc, Sociology Soc of Japan. *Publications:* Change in Mortality and Its Cause Structure Among Developing Countries 1986, Population Policy and Vital Statistics in China 1991, Population Change in China 1992; numerous contribs to journals. *Leisure interests:* tennis, travel. *Address:* Institute of Developing Economies (IDE), Information and Publications Department, 42 Ichigaya Honmura-cho, Shinjuku-ku, Tokyo 162, Japan. *Telephone:* (3) 3353-4231; *Fax:* (3) 3226-8475.

HAYASHI, Toshiko; Japanese politician; b 27 Feb 1940. *Education:* Gunma Univ. *Career:* Mem Japanese Communist Party (JCP), JCP Cen Cttee 1990; mem House of Councillors, mem Cttee on Agric, Forestry and Fisheries and Special Cttee on Disasters 1990. *Address:* House of Councillors, 1-7-1 Nagata-cho, Tokyo 100, Japan.

HAYCRAFT, Anna Margaret (pseudonym Alice Thomas Ellis), FRSL; British writer and journalist; b 9 Sept 1932, Liverpool; d of John and Alexandra Lindholm; m Colin Haycraft 1956 (died 1995); four s one d (also one s one d deceased). *Education:* Bangor Co Grammar School for Girls and Liverpool School of Art. *Career:* Columnist Spectator 1985–89, The Universe 1989–91, The Catholic 1990–96, The Oldie 1996–98, Catholic Herald 1998–2001; journalist all tabloids and broadsheets; Fellow Royal Horticultural Soc 1998; Welsh Arts Council Award 1977, Yorkshire Post Novel of the Year 1983, Writers Guild Award for Best Fiction 1991. *Works include:* The Summerhouse (screenplay) 1993, The Cats Whiskers (radio play) 1990, Unexplained Laughter (TV adaptation) 1987; *Publications include:* (as Alice Thomas Ellis) The Sin Eater (Welsh Arts Council Award) 1977, The Birds of the Air 1980, The Twenty-Seventh Kingdom 1982, The Other Side of the Fire 1983, Unexplained Laughter (Yorkshire Post Novel of the Year) 1985, Secrets of Strangers (jtly) 1986, Home Life 1986, More Home Life 1987, The Clothes in the Wardrobe 1987, The Skeleton in the Cupboard 1988, Home Life Three 1988, The Loss of the Good Authority (jtly) 1989, Wales: an anthology (ed) 1989, Home Life Four 1989, The Fly in the Ointment 1989, A Welsh Childhood 1990, The Inn at the Edge of the World (Writers' Guild Award for Best Fiction) 1990, Pillars of Gold 1992, Serpent on the Rock 1994, The Evening of Adam (short stories) 1994, Cat Among the Pigeons 1994, Fairy Tale 1996, Valentine's Day 2000; (as Anna Haycraft) Natural Baby Food 1977, Darling, You Shouldn't Have Gone to So Much Trouble (jtly) 1980. *Address:* c/o Robert Kirby, PFD, Drury House, 34–43 Russell St, London WC2B 5HA, UK. *Telephone:* (20) 7344-1000.

HAYDÉE PEREIRA DA SILVA, Marcia; Brazilian ballet dancer and choreographer; b 18 April 1937, Niterói; d of Alcides Pereira da Silva and Margarita Haydée Salaverry Pereira da Silva; m Günther Schöberl 1996. *Education:* Royal Ballet School (London) and with Olga Preobrajendska and Lubov Egorova (Paris). *Career:* Mem Grand Ballet du Marquise de Cuevas 1951–61; Prin Dancer Stuttgart Ballet (Germany) 1961, Artistic Dir 1976–96; Artistic Dir Ballet de Santiago de Chile 1992–96; has created numerous roles in ballets by John Cranko, John Neumeier and Maurice Béjart. *Address:* Stuttgart Ballet, Direktion, Oberer Schlossgarten 6, 70173 Stuttgart, Germany. *Telephone:* (711) 2032235; *Fax:* (711) 2032491.

HAYES, Cheryl Davis, MBA, MA; American researcher and administrator; b 27 Oct 1950, IA; d of James G. and Gloria Westerberg Davis; m John C. Hayes, Jr 1972; two s one d. *Education:* Skidmore Coll, Georgetown Univ and The Wharton School, Univ of Pennsylvania. *Career:* Research Fellow, Smithsonian Inst, Washington, DC 1972–74; Study Dir Study Project on Children's Service, NAS/NRC (Nat Research Council) 1978–80, Panels on Study of Policy Formation Process 1978–80, on Work, Family and Community, and on Adolescent Pregnancy and Childbearing 1984; Exec Officer Cttee on Child Devt Research and Public Policy 1980; Exec Dir Nat Comm on Children; mem Bd of Trustees, Nat Child Research Center; mem Bd Beauvoir School; several books on aspects of social policy research. *Address:* 4347 Forest Lane, NW, Washington, DC 20007, USA. *Telephone:* (202) 364-0742.

HAYHURST, Christine Ann, BA, MBA; British business executive; b 18 Feb 1951, Ashton-under-Lyme, Lancs; d of Leonard Peatfield and May Stafford; m William Henry Hayhurst 1975. *Education:* Liverpool Polytechnic and Polytechnic of Cen London. *Career:* Deputy Gen Sec Gen Ass of Unitarian and Free Christian Churches 1979–90; Chief Exec Inst of Administrative Man 1990–93; Inst Sec Inst of Man 1993, Dir of Int Activities 1996; Pres Int Asscn of Liberal Religious Women 1993; Vice-Pres Int Asscn for Religous Freedom 1996. *Leisure interests:* walking, swimming, Unitarianism, theatre, interfaith activities, women's issues. *Address:* 2 Savoy Court, Strand, London WC2R 0EZ, UK. *Telephone:* (20) 7497-0468; *Fax:* (20) 7497-0463; *E-mail:* savoy@inst-mgt.org.uk.

HAYTER, Dianne, BA; British political party executive; b 7 Sept 1949, Hanover, Germany; d of the late Alec Bristow and Nancy Hayter. *Education:* Trevelyan Coll (Durham). *Career:* Research Asst European Trade Union Confed (ETUC), Brussels 1973; Research Officer Trade Union Advisory Cttee to OECD, Paris 1973–74; Asst Gen Sec Fabian Soc 1974–76, Gen Sec 1976–81, mem Exec Cttee 1986–95; mem Exec Cttee London Lab Party 1977–83; Nat Constitution Cttee Labour Party 1987–98, NEC 1998–; Chief Exec European Parl Lab Party 1990–96; Chief Exec Pelican Centre 1999–; JP (Inner London) 1976–90; journalist on A Week in Politics (Channel 4 TV) 1981–83; Dir Alcohol Concern 1983–90; mem Royal Comm on Criminal Procedure 1978–80; Chair Fabian Soc 1992–93. *Publications:* The Labour Party: Crisis and Prospects 1977, Labour in the Eighties (contrib) 1980. *Leisure interests:* reading, politics. *Address:* Pelican Centre, North Hampshire Hospital, Aldermaston Rd, Basingstoke RG24 9NA, UK. *Telephone:* (1256) 314746; *Fax:* (20) 7428-7526; *E-mail:* d.hayter@btinternet.com.

HAZAN, Adeline, LL M; French lawyer and politician; b 21 Jan 1956, Paris; d of Edouard and Nicole (née Lanfranchi) Hazan; m Christophe Blandin 1997. *Education:* Univ of Paris (Pantheon-Sorbonne). *Career:* Judge Châlons-sur-Marne 1980–83, Juvenile Tribunal, Nanterre 1983–90; Head of Dept Gen Secr for Integration 1990–91, with responsibity for Crime Prevention, Interministerial Del 1991–95; Judge Juvenile Tribunal (Paris) 1995–97; Councillor Office of Ministry of Employment and Solidarity 1997–99; Regional Councillor for Champagne-Ardenne 1998–; MEP June 1999–; mem Nat Bureau Parti Socialiste (PS). *Address:* 31 rue Claude Bernard, 75005 Paris, France; European Parliament, rue Wiertz, 1047 Brussels, Belgium.

HAZZARD, Shirley, FRSL; American (b Australian) writer; b 30 Jan 1931, Sydney, Australia; d of Reginald and Catherine Hazzard; m Francis Steegmuller 1963 (died 1994). *Education:* Queenwood School (Sydney). *Career:* Combined Services Intelligence, Hong Kong 1947–48; UK High Commr's Office, Wellington, NZ 1949–50; UN (Gen Service Category), New York 1952–62; novelist, writer of short stories and contrib to The New Yorker 1961–; Boyer Lecturer, Australia 1984, 1988; mem Nat Inst of Arts and Letters; Guggenheim Fellow 1974; US Nat Inst of Arts and Letters Award in Literature 1966; First Prize O. Henry Short Story Awards 1976; Nat Critics' Circle Award for Fiction 1981; Hon Citizen of Capri 2000. *Publications:* Short stories: Cliffs of Fall 1963; Novels: The Evening of the Holiday 1966, People in Glass Houses 1967, The Bay of Noon 1970, The Transit of Venus 1980; History: Defeat of an Ideal: A Study of the Self-destruction of the United Nations 1973, Countenance of Truth: The United Nations and the Waldheim Case 1990, Greene on Capri (memoir) 2000. *Leisure interest:* Parthenophile. *Address:* Apt C-1705, 200 E 66th St, New York, NY 10021, USA.

HE LULI; Chinese paediatrician and administrator; b 7 June 1934, Shandong Prov; d of the late He Siyuan and He Yiwen; m Rong Guohuang 1958; two s. *Education:* Beijing Coll of Medicine. *Career:* Paediatrician Beijing Children's Hosp 1957–; Vice-Mayor Beijing Municipality 1988–96; mem, Vice-Chair CPPCC 8th Nat Cttee 1993–98; Vice-Chair Standing Cttee of 9th NPC 1998–; Vice-Pres Women and Youth Cttee, Revolutionary Cttee of Chinese Kuomintang 1988–96 (Chair 1997–), All China Women's Fed 1993–; Pres Cen Acad of Socialism 1999–. *Address:* Central Academy of Socialism, Beijing 100081, People's Republic of China.

HEAL, Barbara Jane, PH D, FBA; British professor of philosophy; b 21 Oct 1946, Oxford; d of William Calvert and Martha (née Hurst) Kneale; m John Gauntlett Benedict Heal 1968 (divorced 1987); one s one d. *Education:* Oxford High School for Girls and New Hall (Cambridge). *Career:* Research Fellow Newnham Coll, Cambridge 1971–74; Harkness Fellow of the Commonwealth Fund, Visiting Fellow Princeton and Berkeley, USA 1974–76; Lecturer in Philosophy, Univ of Newcastle upon Tyne 1976–86, Univ of Cambridge 1986–96, Reader in Philosophy 1996–99, Prof 1999–. *Publication:* Fact and Meaning 1989. *Address:* St John's College, Cambridge CB2 1TP, UK (Office). *Telephone:* (1223) 338668 (Office); (1223) 314317 (Home); *E-mail:* bjh1000@cam.ac.uk.

HEALY, Bernadine P., MD; American cardiologist; b 2 Aug 1944, New York; d of Michael J. and Violet Healy; m Floyd Loop 1985; two c. *Education:* Vassar Coll (NY) and Harvard Univ (CT). *Career:* Staff Fellow Pathology Section, Nat Heart and Lung Inst, NIH, Bethesda, MD 1972–74; Fellow Cardiovascular Div, Dept of Medicine, Johns Hopkins Univ, Baltimore, MD 1974–76, Fellow Dept of Pathology 1975–76, Asst Prof of Medicine and Pathology 1976–81, Assoc Prof of Medicine 1977–82, Asst Dean for Postdoctoral Programs and Faculty

Devt 1979–84, Assoc Prof of Pathology 1981–84, Prof of Medicine 1982–84; Dir Cardiac Care Unit, Johns Hopkins Hosp 1977–84; Dean Coll of Medicine and Public Health Johns Hopkins Univ School of Medicine, Prof Internal Medicine, Physiology 1995– (also active medicine and pathology, Johns Hopkins Hosp); Dean Medical School Ohio State Univ 1995–97; apptd Deputy Dir Office of Science and Tech Policy, Exec Office of the Pres, White House, Washington, DC 1990; Advisory Cttee to Dir NIH 1986, mem White House Science Council 1988, Special Medical Advisory Group, Dept of Veterans' Affairs 1990; Chair Research Inst, Cleveland Clinic Foundation, OH 1985–91, Advisory Panel for Basic Research for the 1990s, Office of Tech Assessment 1990; Trustee Edison BioTech Centre, Cleveland, OH 1990; Consultant Nat Heart and Lung Inst, NIH since 1976; mem numerous cttees, orgs and asscns; Award of American Heart Asscn 1983–84, 1990; Annual Award for Medicine (Medical Coll of Philadelphia) 1983. *Address:* American Red Cross, 430 17th St, NW, Washington, DC 20006, USA.

HEATON, Frances Anne, BA, LL B; British finance executive; b 11 Aug 1944, Winchester, Hants; d of John Ferris Whidborne and Marjorie Annie Maltby; m Martin Heaton 1969; two s. *Education:* Trinity Coll (Dublin), Civil Service Coll and London Business School. *Career:* Mem staff Treasury Dept 1967–80; joined Corp Finance Dept, Lazard Bros & Co Ltd 1980, Dir 1987–; Dir-Gen Takeover Panel 1992–94; Non-exec Dir W. S. Atkins 1990–, Non-exec Deputy Chair 1996–; Non-exec Dir Bank of England 1993–2001, Commerical Union 1994–, Harrisons and Crosfield 1994–, BUPA 1998–2001, World Pay Group PLC 2000–, Fountain GB 2001–; mem Cttee on Standards in Public Life 1997–. *Leisure interests:* bridge, gardening, riding. *Address:* c/o WS Atkins, Woodcote Grove, Ashley Rd, Epsom, Surrey KT18 5BW, UK.

HECHE, Anne; American actress; b 25 May 1969, Aurora, Ohio; d of Donald Heche. *Films:* An Ambush of Ghosts 1993, The Adventures of Huck Finn 1993, A Simple Twist of Fate 1994, Milk Money 1994, I'll Do Anything 1994, The Wild Side 1995, Pie in the Sky 1995, The Juror 1996, Walking and Talking 1996, Donnie Brasco 1997, Volcano 1997, Subway Stories, Wag the Dog 1997, Six Days Seven Nights 1998, A Cool Dry Place 1998, Psycho 1998, The Third Miracle 1999; *TV:* series: Another World; films: O Pioneers! 1992, Against the Wall 1994, Girls in Prison 1994, Kingfish: A Story of Huey P. Long 1995, If These Walls Could Talk 1996.

HECKERLING, Amy; American film director; b 7 May 1954, New York; m Neal Israel. *Education:* New York Univ and American Film Inst. *Career:* Dir of short and feature films. *Films:* Shorts: Modern Times, High Finance, Getting It Over With; Features: Fast Times at Ridgemont High 1982, Johnny Dangerously 1984, Into the Night (actress), National Lampoon's European Vacation 1985, Look Who's Talking (also writer) 1989, Look Who's Talking Too 1991, Look Who's Talking Now (co-exec producer, dir) 1993, Cheerless 1996; *TV includes:* Twilight Zone 1986, Fast Times at Ridgemont High (series), George Burns Comedy Hour, Fast Times, They Came From Queens; *Publication:* The No-Sex Handbook (jtly) 1990. *Address:* Creative Artists Agency, 9830 Wilshire Blvd, Los Angeles, CA 90028, USA.

HEDERMAN, Carmencita, MA; Irish politician; b 23 Oct 1939; d of George and Ita Cruess-Callaghan; m William P. Hederman 1962; three d two s. *Education:* Sacred Heart Convents (Dublin and Surrey), Trinity Coll Dublin, Univ of Paris (Sorbonne) and Istituto Palladio (Vicenza, Italy). *Career:* Elected Alderman Dublin City Council 1974; Lord Mayor of Dublin 1987–88; elected to Seanad Éireann (Senate) on Trinity Coll Panel 1989; Dir First Nat Building Soc, People in Need Trust, Bd of Dublin City Food Bank; mem Dublin Corpn Cttees on planning, youth and community, traffic, environment, protocol and selection; Patron War on Want, The AIDS Trust, The Alzheimer Soc of Ireland, Irish Nat Council for Soviet Jewry; mem Council Nat Collections of Ireland; Dr hc (Trinity Coll and Nat Univ of Ireland) 1988; People of the Year Award 1988; Spirit of Dublin Award 1988. *Leisure interests:* riding, gardening, patchwork. *Address:* Seanad Éireann, Leinster House, Kildare St, Dublin 2, Ireland (Office); 92 Upper Leeson St, Dublin 4, Ireland (Home). *Telephone:* (1) 680889 (Home); *Fax:* (1) 605913 (Home).

HEDSTRÖM, Lotta Nilsson; Swedish politician; b 13 Sept 1955, Stockholm; m Staffan Nilsson; two s. *Career:* Fmr teacher, farmer and devt worker in Nepal and Tanzania; Chief Municipal Admin; Co-Leader Miljopartiet de Grona; female spokesperson for the Swedish Green Party. *Leisure interests:* outdoor life, dancing, choir singing. *Address:* POB 2136, 103 14 Stockholm, Sweden; POB 16069, 10322 Stockholm, Sweden (Office). *Telephone:* (70) 340 6367; *E-mail:* lotta .nilsson.hedstrom@mp.se.

HEFNER, Christie Ann, BA; American business executive; b 8 Nov 1952, Chicago, IL; d of Hugh Marston and Mildred Hefner; m William A. Marovitz 1995. *Education:* Brandeis Univ (MA). *Career:* Freelance journalist 1974–75; Special Asst to Chair Playboy Enterprises Inc, Chicago, IL 1975–78, Vice-Pres 1978–82, mem Bd Dirs 1979–, Vice Chair 1986–88, Pres 1982–88, COO 1984–88, Chair and CEO 1988–, mem Bd Dirs Playboy Foundation-Playboy Enterprises Inc; mem Bd Magazine Publishers Asscn; mem Advisory Bd ACLU (IL), Nat Council on Crime and Delinquency; mem advisory Bd Canyon Ranch, Nat Cable TV Asscn Diversity Cttee, Aaron Diamon AIDS Research Center, CORE Foundation, Business Cttee for the Arts, Creative Coalition, Bd of Dirs Rush-Pres (St Luke's Medical Center, Chicago); numerous awards include Founders Award (Midwest Women's Center) 1986, Human Rights Award (American Jewish Cttee) 1987, Harry Kalven Freedom of Expression Award (American Civil Liberties Union) 1987, Spirit of Life Award (City of Hope) 1988, Champion of Freedom Award (Anti-Defamation League) 2000, Bettie B. Port Humanitarian Award (Mt Sinai) 2001; elected to Hall of Fame Women's Business Devt Center 1991. *Address:* Playboy Enterprises Inc, 680 N Lake Shore Drive, Chicago, IL 60611, USA. *Telephone:* (312) 751-8000; *Fax:* (312) 337-0271.

HEGARTY, Frances; British writer and lawyer; b 1949. *Career:* Part-time lawyer 1987–2000; novelist 1987–. *Publications include:* (as Frances Fyfield) A Question of Guilt 1988, Deep Sleep (Silver Dagger Award) 1991, A Clear Conscience 1994 (Grand Prix de Littérature Policière 1998), Without Consent 1996, Blind Date 1998 (televised 2000), Staring at the Light 1999, Undercurrents 2000; (as Frances Hegarty) The Playroom 1991, Half Light 1992, Let's Dance 1995. *Address:* c/o Rogers Coleridge White, 20 Powis Mews, London W11 1JN, UK.

HEGGESSEY, Lorraine Sylvia, BA; British television executive; b 16 Nov 1956; d of Sam and Doris Heggessey; m Ronald de Jong 1985; two d. *Education:* Uvyners School (Ickenham, Middx) and Univ of Durham. *Career:* Journalist Westminster Press Group; News Trainee and Sub Ed BBC 1979–83; worked on current affairs and factual programmes for BBC, ITV and Channel 4; Producer Panorama 1983–86; Ed Biteback 1991–92; Series Producer The Underworld 1992–94; Exec Producer BBC Science (QED 1995, Animal Hospital, The Human Body, Minders) 1994–97; Head of Children's Programmes BBC 1997–2000; Jt Dir of Factual and Learning Programmes BBC 2000; Dir of Programmes and Deputy Chief Exec BBC April 2000–; Controller of BBC1 Sept 2000–. *Leisure interests:* family, skiing, tennis, gym. *Address:* BBC Television Centre, Wood Lane, London W12 7RJ, UK. *Telephone:* (20) 8576-1622; *Fax:* (20) 8576-8248; *E-mail:* lorraine.heggessey@bbc .co.uk; *Internet:* www.bbc.co.uk.

HEIBERG, Astrid Nøklebye, DR MED; Norwegian politician and professor of psychiatry; b 14 April 1936, Oslo; d of Andreas and Else (née Holt) Nøklebye; m Arvid Heiberg 1963; two d. *Education:* Univ of Oslo Medical School. *Career:* Prof of Psychiatry Univ of Oslo 1981–; Jr Minister Dept of Health and Social Affairs 1981–85; mem of Storting (Parl, Høyre, Cons) 1985–89; leader Cons Women's Nat Fed 1985–89; Minister Dept of Consumer Affairs and Governmental Admin 1986; Deputy Chair Cons Party 1990–91; cand as Mayor of Oslo 1991; mem Oslo City Council 1991; Pres Norwegian Red Cross 1993. *Leisure interest:* homemaking. *Address:* Drammensveien 82D, 0271 Oslo 2, Norway. *Telephone:* (2) 14-55-90; (2) 55-18-29; *Fax:* (2) 49-58-61.

HEIDSIECK, Antoinette (Tania); French pianist; b 15 Sept 1939, St-Aubin-le-Cauf; d of Jean Bourgain and Marie Thérèse Génu de Lattre; m Eric Heidsieck 1960; three c. *Education:* Conservatoire de Musique de Versailles and Conservatoire Nat Supérieur de Musique de Paris. *Career:* Founded piano duo with husband Eric Heidsieck 1961–73, performances in Europe, Japan, USA, South America, the countries of the former USSR and on TV and radio; solo pianist 1973–; numerous recordings; 1er Prix de Piano et Prix d'Honneur, Conservatoire Nat Supérieur de Versailles; 1er Prix de Piano et de Musique de chambre, Conservatoire Nat Supérieur de Musique de Paris. *Works include:* La Cadence pour le Concerto en ré majeur K 537 de Mozart. *Leisure interests:* tapestry, writing, painting, ceramics. *Address:* 6 rue Papillon, 75009 Paris, France. *Telephone:* (1) 42-46-89-91; *Fax:* (1) 47-70-83-46.

HEILBRUN, Carolyn Gold (pseudonym Amanda Cross), PH D; American writer and professor of English literature; b 13 Jan 1926, East Orange, NJ; d of Archibald and Estelle (née Roemer) Gold; m James Heilbrun 1945; two d one s. *Education:* Wellesley Coll (MA) and Columbia Univ (New York). *Career:* Instructor Brooklyn Coll 1959–60; Instructor Columbia Univ, New York 1960–62, Asst Prof 1962–67, Assoc Prof 1967–72, Prof of English Literature 1972–, Avalon Foundation Prof of Humanities 1986–93; mem Mystery Writers of America, Exec Bd 1982–84; Guggenheim Fellow 1966; Rockefeller Fellow 1976; Hon DHL (Pace) 1996, (Brown) 1997; Nero Wolfe Award 1981; Life Achievement Award, Modern Language Asscn 1999. *Publications:* The Garnett Family 1961, Christopher Isherwood 1970, Towards Androgyny 1973, Reinventing Womanhood 1979, Writing A Woman's Life 1988, Hamlet's Mother and Other Women 1990, The Education of a Woman: The Life and Times of Gloria Steinem 1995, The Last Gift of Time 1997, Collected Stories 1997; (as Amanda Cross) eleven novels. *Address:* c/o Eilen Levine Literary Agency, Suite 1801, 15 E 26th St, New York 10010, USA.

HEINISCH, Renate Charlotte; German politician; b 15 Dec 1937, Boxberg. *Career:* MEP (EPP), mem Cttee on Culture, Youth, Educ and the Media, Del for relations with the countries of S America 1994–99. *Address:* c/o European Parliament, rue Wiertz, 1047 Brussels, Belgium.

HELGADÓTTIR, Guðrun; Icelandic politician and writer; b 7 Sept 1935; d of Helgi Guðlangsson and Ingigerður Eyjólfsdóttir; two s two d. *Education:* Reykjavík Grammar School and Univ. *Career:* Sec Reykjavík Grammar School 1957–67; Head of Dept, Nat Social Security Inst 1973–80; mem Reykjavík City Council 1978–82; elected mem Althingi (Parl, People's Alliance) 1979, Speaker 1988–91; Pres United Alliance 1988; writer of 16 books; numerous awards including The Nordic Prize for Children's Books 1992. *Leisure interests:* arts, gardening. *Address:* Althingi, v/Austurvöll, 101 Reykjavík, Iceland (Office); Túngata 43, 101 Reykjavík, Iceland (Home). *Telephone:* (1) 23124 (Home).

HELLSVIK, Gun, LL M; Swedish politician; b 27 Sept 1942, Ängelholm; m Per Hellsvik 1966; one s. *Education:* Lund Univ. *Career:* Lecturer in Commercial Law, Lund Univ 1972–82; Bd mem Inst of Tech, Lund 1984–91, Bd mem IDEON research park, Lund 1984–91; Municipal Commr and Chair Municipal Exec Bd, Lund 1982–91; leader municipal opposition group 1988; Minister of Justice 1991–94; MP 1994–2001, Chair Standing Cttee of Legal Affairs 1994–2001; Dir-Gen Swedish Patent and Registration Office 2001–; mem Nat Bd Moderate Party 1985–. *Leisure interest:* cooking. *Address:* Swedish Patent and Registration Office, Box 5055, 10242 Stockholm, Sweden. *Telephone:* (8) 782-25-00 (Office); *E-mail:* gun.hellsvik@prv.se (Office).

HELPER, Hon Bonnie Merilyn, LL B; Canadian judge; b 20 Aug 1943; d of Samuel L. and Pauline Zinman; m Michael Helper 1966; two s one d. *Education:* Univ of Manitoba. *Career:* Lecturer Manitoba Law School 1966–67; pvt practice 1967–78; Judge (part-time) Prov Judges Court, Family Div 1978–80, (full-time) 1980–83, Court of Queen's Bench, Family Div (MB) 1983–89, Court of Appeal (MB) 1989–. *Address:* Law Courts Bldg, Broadway and Kennedy, Winnipeg, MB R3C 0P9, Canada.

HEMINGWAY, Geraldine; British designer and consultant; b 7 Dec 1961, Burnley Lancs; m Wayne Hemingway; two s two d. *Education:* St Augustine's (Billington). *Career:* Together with husband started in business with market stall in Camden, London; cr footwear, clothing and accessory label Red or Dead 1992; collection retailed through eight Red or Dead shops in UK and three Red or Dead shops in Japan, and wholesaled to int network of retailers; left Red or Dead 1999; cr Hemingway design label 1999; designed annexe for Inst of Dirs 2001; Street Designers of the Year, British Fashion Awards 1995, 1996, 1997. *Publication:* Red or Dead: The Good, the Bad and the Ugly (with Wayne

Hemingway) 1998. *Address:* 15 Wembley Park Drive, Wembley, Middx, HA9 8HD, UK. *Telephone:* (20) 8903-1074 (Office); *Fax:* (20) 8903-1074 (Office); *E-mail:* gerardine@hemingwaydesign.co.uk.

HENDERSON, Yvonne Daphne, BA, DIP ED; Australian politician; b 16 May 1948, UK; d of Patrick W. and Daphne Finn; m Jeremy Henderson 1971; two s two d. *Education:* John Curtin High School and Univ of Western Australia. *Career:* Vice-Pres W Australia br Australian Labour Party 1981; elected to W Australia Parl for Gosnells 1983; Deputy Speaker W Australia Parl 1983; Minister for the Arts and Lands 1988, for Works Services and Consumer Affairs 1989, for Housing and Consumer Affairs 1990, for Productivity and Labour Relations and Consumer Affairs 1991; W Australian Shadow Minister for Productivity and Labour Relations 1993–94, for Public Sector Man 1993, for Environment 1994, for Heritage 1994, for Consumer Affairs 1994. *Leisure interests:* music, reading, walking. *Address:* Parliament House, 2 Havelock St, West Perth, WA 6005, Australia.

HENDRICKS, Barbara, B SC, B MUS; American opera singer (soprano); b 20 Nov 1948, Stephens, AR; d of M. L. and Della Hendricks; m Martin Engström 1978; one s one d. *Education:* Univ of Nebraska and under Jennie Tourel at Juilliard School of Music (New York). *Career:* Operatic debut, San Francisco Opera in L'Incoronazione di Poppea 1976; appeared with opera companies of Boston, Santa Fe, Glyndebourne (UK), Hamburg (Germany), La Scala (Milan, Italy), Berlin, Paris, Los Angeles, Florence (Italy), Royal Opera, Covent Garden (London) and Vienna; recitals in Europe and America; extensive tours of fmr USSR and Japan; concert performances with leading orchestras; appeared at numerous music festivals including Edinburgh (UK), Osaka (Japan), Montreux (Switzerland), Salzburg (Austria), Dresden (Germany), Prague (Czech Repub), Aix-en-Provence and Orange (France) and Vienna (Austria); nearly 50 recordings; nominated Goodwill Amb for Refugees at UN 1987; Hon mem Inst of Humanitarian Law, San Remo, Italy 1990; Hon D MUS (Nebraska Wesleyan Univ) 1988; Dr hc (Louvain) 1990, (Juilliard, NY) 2000; Chevalier de la Légion d'Honneur; Commdr des Arts et des Lettres. *Film appearance:* La Bohème 1988. *Leisure interest:* reading. *Address:* c/o Opéra et Concert, 1 rue Volney, 75002 Paris, France; c/o Société fiduciaire, 1 av de Florimont, 1820 Montreux, Switzerland.

HENDRY, Diana Lois, M LITT; British writer; b 2 Oct 1941, Meols, Wirral; d of Leslie and Amelia McLonomy; m George Hendry (divorced 1981); one s one d. *Education:* W Kirby Grammar School for Girls (Wirral) and Univ of Bristol. *Career:* Reporter, Feature Writer Western Mail, Cardiff 1960–65; freelance journalist 1965–80; teacher (part-time) Clifton Coll 1987–90; Tutor (part-time) in Literature Open Univ 1987–92, Bristol Polytechnic 1987–93; tutor in Creative Writing Univ of Bristol 1995–; fmr Writer-in-Residence Fairfield Grammar School, Writer-in-Residence Dumfries & Galloway Royal Infirmary; Third Prize Peterloo Poetry Competition 1991, Second Prize 1993; First Prize Honsman Soc Poetry Competition 1996. *Publications include:* Fiona Finds Her Tongue 1985, Double Vision 1990, Harvey Angell (Whitbread Literary Award, Children's Novel Section) 1991, Making Blue 1995, Strange Goings-on 1995, The Awesome Bird 1995, Harvey Angell and the Ghost Child (Scottish Arts Council Award) 1997, Fiona Says 1998; poems published in literary magazines and anthologies. *Leisure interests:* yoga, playing the piano, hats, talking, reading. *Address:* c/o 52 York Rd, Montpelier, Bristol BS6 5QF, Avon, UK.

HENLEY, Elizabeth Becker, BFA, PH D; American playwright and actress; b 8 May 1952, Jackson, MS; d of Charles and Lydy Henley. *Education:* Univ of Illinois. *Career:* Pulitzer Prize for Drama 1981; New York Drama Critics Circle Best Play Award 1981; George Oppenheimer/Newsday Playwriting Award 1980–81. *Publications:* Crimes of the Heart 1981, The Wake of Jamey Foster 1982, Am I Blue 1982, The Miss Firecracker Contest, The Debutante Ball 1985, The Lucky Spot 1987, Abundance 1989, The Debutante Ball 1991, Beth Henley: Monologues for Women 1992; Screenplays: Nobody's Fool 1986, Crimes of the Heart 1986, Miss Firecracker 1989, Signatures (also play) 1990, Control Freaks (play) 1993, Revelers (also play) 1994. *Address:* William Morris Agency, 151 S El Camino Drive, Beverly Hills, CA 90212, USA.

HENRY, Gloria, BA; Trinidad and Tobago politician and organization executive; b 20 April 1946, Port of Spain; d of Ralph and Norma Springer; m Ralph M. Henry 1968 (divorced 1987); two s one d. *Education:* St Joseph's Convent, Mausica Teachers' Training Coll, Univ of the W Indies (St Augustine). *Career:* Teacher; insurance and property salesperson; entered politics 1976; mem House of Reps (Parl, Nat Alliance for Reconstruction—NAR) for Arouca S 1986–91; Parl Sec Ministry of External Affairs and Int Trade 1986, Ministry of Industry, Enterprise and Tourism 1987; Minister of Social Devt and Family Services 1988–90, Minister of Educ 1990–91; mem Exec Bd Inter-American Comm of Women 1989–90, Bd of Dirs Inter-American Parl Group on Population and Devt; mem Nat Defence Council; apptd Chair of Bd Youth for Christ 1992, Chair of Bd and CEO Nat Youth Foundation of Trinidad and Tobago 1992; Leader Del to 26th UNESCO Gen Conf, Paris 1991; mem New World political group until 1968, Tapia House Movt. *Address:* National Youth Foundation of Trinidad and Tobago, 72 Picton St, Newtown, Port of Spain, Trinidad and Tobago (Office); 12A Leotaud Lands, O'Meara Rd, Arima, Trinidad and Tobago (Home). *Telephone:* 622-7126 (Office); *Fax:* 628-7816 (Office).

HENRY, Martha, OC; Canadian actress and director; b 17 Feb 1938, Detroit, MI, USA; d of Lloyd H. and Kathleen Buhs; one d. *Education:* Carnegie Mellon Univ (PA, USA). *Career:* Appearances in theatres throughout Canada and in UK, also on TV and radio and in films; Artistic Dir Grand Theatre 1988–95; mem Advisory Cttee Theatre Section, Canada Council 1985–87, Bd of Canada Council 1988–90; Hon DFA (Lawrence, York); Hon LL D (Toronto) 1986; Theatre World Award (NY, USA) 1970; Toronto Drama Bench Award for Outstanding Contribution to Canadian Theatre 1989. *Plays include:* You Can't Take It With You, The Seagull, Macbeth, A Midsummer Night's Dream, King Lear, Twelfth Night, Much Ado About Nothing, Comedy of Errors, Othello, A Winter's Tale, The Country Wife, Uncle Vanya, The Cherry Orchard, Three Sisters, Mother Courage, Three-penny Opera, Hamlet, Playboy of the Western World, Pal Joey, Warm Wind in China, The Cocktail Hour, The Stillborn Lover, Dancing at Lughnasa; *Films include:* The Wars (Genie Award Best Performance Film 1983), Dancing in the Dark (Genie Award Best Performance Film 1986), White Light; *TV includes:* Venus Observed, Orpheus and Eurydice, Lord Arthur Saville's Crime, Talking to a Stranger, The Master Builder, Ladies in Retirement, Waiting for the Parade, The Newcomers (Genie Award Best Performance TV 1979), Empire Inc, Mount Royal (Gemini Award Best Performance TV 1988), Glory Enough for All (Gemini Award Best Performance TV 1989). *Address:* 90 Mornington St, Stratford, ON N5A 5E8, Canada.

HENRY-MARTIN, Jacinth Lorna; Saint Christopher and Nevis politician; b 28 July 1961, Sandy Point; d of Samuel and Venetta Henry; m Michael McDonald Martin; three s. *Career:* Jr Minister, Ministry of Tourism, Culture and Environment with special responsibility for Culture Jan 2000; Minister of Youth, Sports and Culture (first female minister of Saint Christopher and Nevis Lab Party Govt) March 2000–. *Leisure interests:* writing short stories, poetry. *Address:* Ministry of Youth, Sports and Culture, Church St, POB 878, Basseterre, Saint Christopher and Nevis. *Telephone:* 465-2521 Ext 1400; *Fax:* 466-7628; *E-mail:* cultyouthsports@caribsurf.com.

HENRY-WILSON, Maxine-Antoinette, M SC; Jamaican politician; b 27 Feb 1951, Manchester, UK; d of Vincent G. and Olive Henry; m Gladstone Wilson 1986; one d. *Education:* St Andrew High School, Univ of the West Indies and Rutgers Univ (NJ, USA). *Career:* Lecturer Univ of West Indies 1986–92; Minister of State in the Office of the Prime Minister 1992–93, Minister without portfolio 1994, then Minister of Information; Gen Sec People's Nat Party (PNP) 1994–. *Leisure interests:* jazz, ceramics. *Address:* Office of the Prime Minister, 1 Devon Rd, Kingston 6, Jamaica; 4 Kings Mews, Kingston 10, Jamaica. *Telephone:* 927-9607; *Fax:* 968-6723.

HENSCHEL, Jane Elizabeth, BA; American opera singer; b 2 March 1957, Appleton, Wisconsin; d of Lester and Betty (née Lau) Haentzschel. *Education:* Univ of Southern California. *Career:* Ensemble mem in opera houses in Aachen, Wuppertal, Dortmund and Düsseldorf (Germany) 1981–92; began int career as Amme in Die Frau ohne Schatten, Royal Opera House (London); frequent guest at major European Opera Houses including: La Scala (Milan), Deutsche Oper (Berlin), Amsterdam Opera, Paris Opera, Bayerische Staatsoper (Munich), Staatsoper (Berlin); has performed with the following conductors: Seiji Ozawa, Sir Colin Davis, Daniel Barenboim, Bernard Haitink, Riccardo Muti, Christian Thielemann, Sir Andrew Davis, Lorin Maazel. *Recordings include:* Mahler's 8th Symphony, The Rake's Progress, Die Verlobung im Traum, Die Drei Groschen Oper. *Leisure interests:* reading, concerts.

HENSON, Lisa; American film company executive; b 1961; d of the late Jim and of Jane Henson. *Education:* Harvard Univ (MA). *Career:* Exec Asst to Head of Production, Warner Brothers 1983, Dir of Creative Affairs 1985, Exec Vice-Pres of Production 1992; Pres in charge of Production Columbia Pictures 1993, Studio Pres 1994–; mem Bd Jim Henson Productions. *Address:* Columbia Pictures, 3400 Riverside Drive, Burbank, CA 91505, USA.

HEPBURN, Katharine; American actress; b 12 May 1907, Hartford, CT; d of the late Dr Thomas N. Hepburn and Katharine Houghton; m Ludlow Ogden Smith (divorced). *Education:* Bryn Mawr Coll (PA). *Career:* Professional stage actress 1928–; film actress 1932–; also appears on TV; Dr hc (Columbia) 1992; Gold Medal for Best Film Actress, Venice 1934; Whistler Soc Award 1957; Lifetime Achievement Award (Annual American Comedy Awards) 1989. *Plays include:* The Lake, The Philadelphia Story, Without Love 1942, As You Like It 1950, The Millionairess 1952, The Taming of the Shrew 1955, The Merchant of Venice 1955, Much Ado About Nothing 1955, Coco (musical) 1970 (on tour 1971), A Matter of Gravity 1976 (on tour 1977), The West Side Waltz 1981; *Films include:* A Bill of Divorcement 1932, Morning Glory (Acad Award 1934) 1933, Little Women 1933, Alice Adams 1935, Sylvia Scarlett 1935, Mary of Scotland 1936, Quality Street 1937, Stage Doors 1937, Holiday 1938, The Philadelphia Story (New York Critics' Award) 1940, Woman of the Year 1942, Keeper of the Flame 1942, Sea of Grass 1947, State of the Union 1948, Adam's Rib 1949, The African Queen 1951, Pat and Mike 1952, The Rainmaker 1956, Suddenly Last Summer 1959, Long Day's Journey Into Night 1962, Guess Who's Coming to Dinner? (Acad Award 1968) 1967, The Lion in Winter (Acad Award 1969) 1968, The Madwoman of Chaillot 1969, The Trojan Women 1971, The Glass Menagerie (TV) 1973, Love Among the Ruins (TV) 1975, Rooster Cogburn 1975, Olly Olly Oxen Free 1976, The Corn is Green (TV) 1979, Christopher Strong 1980, On Golden Pond (Acad Award 1982) 1981, The Ultimate Solution of Grace Quigley 1984, Mrs Delafield Wants to Marry (TV) 1986, Laura Lansing Slept Here (TV) 1988, The Man Upstairs (TV) 1992, Love Affair 1993, This Can't Be Love (TV) 1994, One Christmas 1994; *Publications:* The Making of The African Queen 1987, Me (autobiog) 1991. *Address:* James D. Miller Ltd, 350 Fifth Ave, Suite 5019, New York, NY 10118, USA.

HEPPLEWHITE, Rosalind Mary Joy (Ros), BA; British charity administrator and civil servant; b 20 Dec 1952, Stoke-on-Trent; d of Anthony Gordon and Anne Phillips; m Julian Hepplewhite 1971; one s one d. *Education:* Portsmouth N Grammar School for Girls, Univ Coll (London) and Somerville Coll (Oxford). *Career:* Asst House Gov Bethlem Royal and Maudsley Hosps 1980–83, Hosp Sec 1983–84; Unit Admin (Mental Health) Hammersmith and Fulham Health Authority 1984–85; Unit Gen Man (Mental Health and Mental Handicap) Brighton Health Authority 1985–88, Dir of Corp Devt 1988–89; Nat Dir MIND (Nat Asscn for Mental Health) 1989–91; Chief Exec Child Support Agency 1992–94; Chief Exec and Registrar Gen Dental Council 1996–. *Leisure interests:* home, family, music. *Address:* General Dental Council, 37 Wimpole St, London W1M 8DQ, UK.

HEPTULLA, Najma, PH D; Indian politician and scientific researcher; b 13 April 1940, Bhopal; d of Yousuf Ali; m Akbar Heptulla; three d. *Career:* Mem Rajya Sabha (Parl), apptd Deputy Chair 1985, Gen Sec Bombay Pradesh Congress Cttee 1986–87, Sec Parl Science Forum; Deputy Chair Rajya Sabha 1985–86, 1988–; All-India Haj Advisory Bd; Pres Indo-Arab Soc; Jt Research Fellow Council of Scientific and Industrial Research, later Sr Fellow. *Address:* 4 Akbar Rd, New Delhi 110 011, India; Heptulla Park, 2nd Hasanabad Rd, Santa Cruz (West), Mumbai 400 054, India.

HERBERT, Jocelyn; British theatre designer; b 22 Feb 1917; d of Sir Alan Patrick and Gwendolen Herbert; m Anthony Lousada 1937 (divorced 1960); three d one s. *Education:* St Paul's Girls' School, London Theatre Studio and Paris and Vienna. *Career:* With Michel St Denis and George Devine, London Theatre Studio 1936–37; joined English Stage Co, Royal Court Theatre 1956; freelance designer 1958–; designer opera sets for Paris Opera, Metropolitan Opera (New York, USA), English Nat Opera. *Plays designed include:* The Chairs, The Lesson, Exit the King, Purgatory, Sport of My Mad Mother, Krapp's Last Tape, Happy Days, Not I, Footfalls, That Time, Roots, The Kitchen, I'm Talking about Jerusalem, Chips with Everything, The Merchant, Serjeant Musgrave's Dance, Trials by Logue, Antigone, The Trial of Cob and Leach, The Changeling, Richard III, Midsummer Night's Dream, Julius Caesar, Luther, A Patriot for Me, Inadmissible Evidence, Skyvers, The Lion and the Jewel, Life Price, Three Months Gone, Home, The Changing Room, Cromwell, Life Class, Early Days, Savages, The Portage to San Cristobal of A. H., What the Butler Saw, Teeth 'n' Smiles, Rum and Coca Cola, Mother Courage, Life of Galileo, A Woman Killed with Kindness, Tyger, The Oresteia, The Seagull, Joan of the Stockyard, The Trackers of Oxyrhynchus, Round House, Hamlet, Pygmalion, Saratoga, The Merchant, Heartbreak House, The Devil and the Good Lord, Gigi, Square Rounds 1992, Stages 1992, The Kaisers of Carnuntum! 1995, The Labourers of Herakles! 1995; *Films designed include:* Jim Jones 1961, Isadora 1968, Hamlet 1969, Ned Kelly 1970, O'Lucky Man 1972, Hotel New Hampshire 1983, Whales of August 1987. *Leisure interests:* painting, the country. *Address:* 45 Pottery Lane, London W11, UK. *Telephone:* (20) 7727-1104.

HERCUS, Luise Anna, AM, PH D; Australian linguist; b 16 Jan 1926, Munich, Germany; d of Alfred and Theodora Schwarzschild; m Graham Robertson Hercus 1955 (died 1974); one s. *Education:* Univ of Oxford (UK) and ANU (Canberra). *Career:* Tutor and Lecturer St Anne's Coll, Oxford 1948–54; Research Fellow Univ of Adelaide 1965–68; Sr Lecturer in Asian Studies Australian Nat Univ 1969–71, Reader in Sanskrit 1972–91, currently Visiting Fellow; much work on recording nearly extinct Aboriginal languages 1963–. *Publications include:* The Languages of Victoria: A Late Survey 1969, The Bagandji Language 1982, This is What Happened, Historical Narratives by Aborigines (co-ed) 1986, Nukunu Dictionary 1992, Wembawemba Dictionary 1992, Paakanyi Dictionary 1993, A Grammar of the Arabana–Wangkangurru Language, Lake Eyre Basin, South Australia 1994, A Grammar of the Wirangu Language from the West Coast of South Australia 1999; articles on Middle Indo-Aryan and on oral traditions of S Australian Aborigines. *Leisure interest:* raising orphaned marsupials. *Address:* Kintala, via Gundaroo, Dick's Creek Rd, NSW 2620, Australia. *Telephone:* (62) 36 8145; *Fax:* (62) 49 3252.

HERCUS, Hon Dame Margaret Ann, DCMG, BA, LL B; New Zealand politician, diplomatist and international consultant; b 24 Feb 1942, Hamilton; d of Horace and Mary (née Ryan) Sayers; m John Hercus; two s. *Education:* Victoria, Auckland and Canterbury Univs. *Career:* Lawyer and Staff Training Officer, Beath & Co, Christchurch 1969–70; mem Price Tribunal and Trade Practices Comm 1973–75; Deputy Chair Commerce Comm 1975–78; Chair Consumer Rights Campaign 1975; mem House of Reps (Lab) for Lyttelton 1978–87; Opposition Spokesperson on Social Welfare, Consumer Affairs and Women's Affairs 1978–84; Minister of Social Welfare, Police and Women's Affairs 1984–87; Perm Rep of NZ to the UN 1989–90; int consultant 1991–98; Chief of Mission, UN Force in Cyprus 1998–99. *Leisure interests:* collecting original NZ prints, theatre, reading. *Address:* 82A Park Terrace, Christchurch 8001, New Zealand.

HÉRIARD DUBREUIL, Dominique; French business executive; b 6 July 1946, Paris; d of André and Anne-Marie (née Renaud) Hériard Dubreuil; m Alain-Pierre Jacquet 1975; one d. *Education:* Univ of Paris II (Panthéon-Assas) and Inst des Relations Publiques. *Career:* Press Attaché Havas Conseil 1969–72; est public relations dept Ogilvy & Mather 1972; Programme Head Hill & Knowlton 1973–75; est public relations dept McCann-Erickson France 1975–77; Founder, Chair and Man Dir Agence Infoplan 1978–87; Man Dir E. Rémy Martin & Cie SA 1988–, Chair 1990–; Pres Fed of Wine and Spirit Exporters of France 1992–94; Pres Comite Colbert 1994–98, Vinexpo 1998; CEO Rémy Cointreau 1998–2000, Pres Bd Dirs 2001–; Chevalier de la Légion d'Honneur; Officier de l'Ordre Nat du Mérite. *Leisure interest:* visual arts. *Address:* 152 Ave des Champs-Elysées, 75008 Paris, France (Office). *Telephone:* (1) 44-95-11-58; *Fax:* (1) 46-53-51-11; *E-mail:* dominique.heriard.dubreuil@remy-cointreau.com.

HERMANGE, Marie-Thérèse; French politician; b 17 Sept 1947, Algiers, Algeria. *Education:* Inst of Political Studies. *Career:* Deputy Mayor Paris 1989–; RPR Nat Sec Responsible for Children, Training and Social Cohesion; MEP (EPP, RPR), Vice-Chair Cttee on Social Affairs and Employment; mem Del for Relations with Switzerland, Iceland and Norway; Vice-Pres Nat Council of French Women. *Address:* European Parliament, rue Wiertz, ASP13E216, 1047 Brussels, Belgium; Hôtel de Ville de Paris 75004 Paris, France. *Telephone:* (2) 284-21-11; *Fax:* (2) 230-69-43; *E-mail:* mhermange@europarl.eu.int; mhermange@easynet.fr; *Internet:* webperso.easynet.fr/mhermange.

HERMARY-VIEILLE, Catherine; French writer; b 8 Oct 1943, Paris; d of Jacques and Jacqueline (née Dubois) Hermary; m Jean Vieille 1962; one s one d. *Education:* Coll Ste Marie de Passy (Paris and Noisy), Ecole Nat des Langues Orientales (Paris), Univ de Paris VIII—Vincennes à St-Denis, Manhattanville Coll (NY, USA). *Career:* Asst Embassy of Cyprus, Paris 1968–69; began career as writer 1981; Reporter for various newspapers; mem PEN-Club, Islam-Occident, Asscn des Ecrivains de Langue Française; Prix Georges Dufau de l'Acad Française; Chevalier des Arts et des Lettres. *Publications:* Le grand vizir de la nuit (Prix Fémina) 1981, L'épiphanie des dieux (Prix Ulysse) 1982, La marquise des ombres 1984, L'infidèle (Prix Radio-Télé Luxembourg—RTL) 1986, Romy 1988, Le rivage des adieux 1989, Le jardin des Henderson 1990, Un amour fou (Prix des Maisons de la Presse) 1991, La piste des turquoises 1992, La pointe aux tortues 1994, Lola 1994, L'Initié 1996, L'Ange Noir 1998 (Prix Littéraire du Quartier Latin), Les Dames de Brières 1999, L'Etang du Diable 2000. *Leisure interests:* reading, golf, travel. *Address:* Shelton Mill, 371 Shelton Mill Rd, Charlottesville, VA 22903, USA.

HERMINE, Muriel Maryvonne Monique; French artist; b 3 Sept 1963, Le Mans; d of Remy and Monique (née Fabre) Hermine; m Yannick Quennehen 1991. *Education:* In Tours. *Career:* French synchronized swimming Champion ten times 1983–88; Third, World Championships 1986; European Champion 1983–87; Fourth, Olympic Games, Seoul, Repub of Korea 1988; Pres, Man Dir Muriel Hermine Productions (aquatic show) 1986–; Creator and Dir aquatic shows including Sirella 1991, Sirella et les trois royaumes 1992, Crescend'O 1997, 1998 (Disneyland, Paris 1999, 2000, 2001), Freedom Opera Gospel 2002; Chevalier des Arts et des Lettres 1992; Médaille d'Argent de la Ville de Paris 1988. *Publications:* Sirella, les pieds dans l'eau, la tête dans les étoiles 1992. *Address:* 6 rue de la Justice, 75020 Paris, France. *Telephone:* (1) 40-31-50-00; *Fax:* (1) 40-31-54-84; *E-mail:* ondinepnod@wanadoo.fr; *Internet:* www.murielhermine.com.

HÉROUX, Justine; Canadian film producer and executive; b 25 May 1942, Montréal; d of Philémon Bouchard and Cécile Hamelin; m Denis Héroux 1972; one s. *Education:* Maisonneuve Hosp. *Career:* First Asst Dir and Production Man of many films 1969–79; Producer 1979–; Pres Cinévidéo Plus and Cinéroux Films Inc 1990–. *Films include:* Atlantic City (assoc producer, Grand Prix Venice Film Festival) 1979, Les Plouffe (Int Press Award and several Génie Awards 1982) 1980, Little Gloria... Happy at Last 1982, Le crime d'Ovide Plouffe 1983, L'adolescente sucre d'amour 1984, Le matou 1985, Les fous de Bassan (exec producer) 1986, Flag (exec producer) 1987, Dames galantes (co-producer) 1990, A Star for Two, Sous le signe du poisson, Miss Moscou 1991, L'homme de ma vie 1992, La fenêtre 1992, Connections 1992, Flight from Justice 1993, Meurtre en Musique 1993, Crosswinds 1993, Tales of the Wild (series) 1994, The Adventures of Smoke Belliou (series) 1995. *Leisure interests:* films, theatre, classical music. *Address:* Cinévidéo Plus, 2100 rue Ste-Catherine Ouest, Suite 710, Montréal, PQ H3H 2T3, Canada (Office); 28 Roskilde, Outremont, PQ H2V 2N5, Canada (Home). *Telephone:* (514) 937-7986 (Office); (514) 937-7986 (Home); *Fax:* (514) 937-8332 (Office); (514) 937-8332 (Home); *E-mail:* 103601.1036@compuserve.com.

HERRERA, Carolina; Venezuelan fashion designer; b 1940, Caracas; m 1st Guillermo Behrens Tello (divorced 1965); two d; m 2nd Reinaldo Herrera 1968; four d. *Education:* privately. *Career:* Fashion Designer 1981–; Founder Carolina Herrera Inc, launched Carolina Herrera perfume 1988, Herrera for Men 1991, Flore perfume 1994, Aquaflore 1996, accessories 1997, 212 perfume 1997, 212 Men 1999, CH (diffusion collection) 2001; opened flagship store (Madison Ave) 2000; Patron The Children's Hosp of Washington, DC, Aids Project Los Angeles, CA and NY Women's Foundation; numerous wards include Hispanic Designer Fashion Award 1987, Bride Magazine Award 1989, American Perfume Asscn Award 1993, Int Fashion Center (NY) Special Distinction for a Career in the World of Design 1995, Spirit of Achievement Award (Albert Einstein Coll of Medicine, Yeshiva Univ) 1996, Woman with Heart Award (American Heart Asscn) 2001; appeared on Int Best Dressed List 1971–80, Harpers Bazaar Best Dressed List 2001, mem Best Design Hall of Fame 1980–. *Address:* 501 Seventh Ave, 17th Floor, New York, NY 10018, USA. *Telephone:* (212) 944-5757; *Fax:* (212) 944-7996.

HERRERA, Paloma; Argentine ballet dancer; b 21 Dec 1975, Buenos Aires; d of Alberto and Marisa Herrera. *Education:* Teatro Colón, Buenos Aires, Minsk Ballet School and School of American Ballet. *Career:* Joined American Ballet Theater (ABT) corps de ballet; roles in Sleeping Beauty, Don Quixote and La Bayadère; soloist, ABT 1992, prin dancer 1995; leading role in How Near Heaven (created for her by Twyla Tharp, qv) 1994; other notable roles include Clara in The Nutcracker, Medora in Le Corsaire, Kitri in Don Quixote, Juliet in Romeo and Juliet. *Address:* American Ballet Theatre, 890 Broadway, New York, NY 10003, USA.

HERRERA ARAUZ, Balbina, PH D; Panamanian politician. *Education:* University of Pananma. *Career:* Mayor of San Miguelito dist 1984–89; mem Legis Ass (Parl) for 8–6 Circuit; mem Perm Comms for Public Health 1989–90, for Foreign Relations 1989–90, for Public Works 1990–91, for Children's Rights 1992–93; Vice-Pres Comm for Foreign Affairs, for Children's Rights 1993–94; Pres of the Legis Ass 1994 (first Panamanian woman); Pres of Mayoral Asscn; has participated in many seminars on devt and human rights in Latin America. *Address:* c/o Asamblea Legislativa, Panamá 1, Panama.

HERSHEY, Barbara; American actress; b 5 Feb 1948, Hollywood, CA; d of William H. Herzstein; m Stephen Douglas 1992 (divorced 1995); one s. *Education:* Hollywood High School. *Career:* Debut in TV series The Monroes. *Film appearances include:* With Six You Get Eggroll, The Last Summer, The Baby Maker 1970, Boxcar Bertha 1972, The Stunt Man 1980, The Entity 1983, The Right Stuff 1983, The Liberation of Lord Byron Jones 1970, Love Comes Quietly, The Pursuit of Happiness 1971, Passion Flower, The Natural 1984, Hannah and Her Sisters 1986, Tin Men 1987, Shy People (Best Actress, Cannes Film Festival) 1987, The Last Temptation of Christ 1988, A World Apart (Best Actress, Cannes Film Festival) 1988, Beaches 1989, Defenceless 1989, Aunt Julia and the Scriptwriter 1990, Paris Trout 1990, A Killing in a Small Town (Best Actress Emmy and Golden Globe Awards) 1990, The Public Eye 1991, Defenseless 1991, Swing Kids 1993, Splitting Heirs, Falling Down 1993, The Bible (TV) 1993, A Dangerous Woman 1994, Last of the Dogmen, Portrait of a Lady 1996, A Soldier's Daughter Never Cries 1998, Frogs for Snakes 1998, The Staircase 1998, Breakfast of Champions 1999, Passion 1999. *Address:* CAA, 9830 Wilshire Blvd, Beverly Hills, CA 90212, USA (Office).

HERSOM, Naomi Louisa, M ED, PH D; Canadian former university president and professor of education; b 4 Feb 1927, Winnipeg, MB; d of Frederick and Anna Hersom. *Education:* Univs of Manitoba and Alberta. *Career:* Teacher and Prin, Winnipeg 1954–67; Prof of Curriculum Studies, Univ of Alberta 1969–75; Dir of Undergrad Progs and Assoc Dean (Academic), Univ of British Columbia 1975–79, Prof of Educational Admin 1979–81; Prof and Dean Coll of Educ, Univ of Saskatchewan 1981–86; Pres Mount St Vincent Univ 1986–91; Visiting Scholar Univ of Ottawa 1991–92; Dir and Vice-Pres Social Science Fed of Canada 1979–82; first woman Pres Canadian Educ Asscn 1989–90; mem numerous comms and task forces; Hon LL D (McGill, York) 1988, (Manitoba) 1989, (Ottawa) 1990, (St Mary's, Victoria) 1991; Dr hc (Alberta) 1992, (Providence Coll) 1998; George Croskery Memorial Award, Canadian Coll of Teachers 1985; Grand Dame of Merit, Kts of Malta 1988. *Publications:* Co-author: Curriculum Development for Classroom Teachers 1971, Locally Initiated School Evaluation 1973, Developing Evaluation Systems in Schools: Organizational Strategies 1975, A Study of Open Area Schools in the Edmonton Public School

System 1978, Women and the Canadian Labour Force 1982, contrib to Educational Leadership 1992. *Leisure interest:* bird-watching. *Address:* 405 Québec St, #301, Victoria, BC V8V 4Z2, Canada (Office). *Telephone:* (250) 360-1892; *Fax:* (250) 360-1892; *E-mail:* nhersom@islandnet.com (Home).

HERZIGOVA, Eva; Czech fashion model; b 10 March 1973, Litvinov; m Tico Torres. *Career:* Modelled for Guess advertisements 1992, model for Gossard Wonderbra; has appeared on the cover of several fashion magazines. *Film:* Inferno.

HERZOG, Pnina, PH D; Israeli civil servant. *Education:* Univs of Manchester (UK) and Ottawa (Canada) and George Washington Univ (DC, USA). *Career:* Joined Ministry of Health 1964, Pharmacist in charge of Registration of New Drugs, Pharmaceutical Div 1964–72, Deputy Head Dept of Clinical Pharmacology, Drug Monitoring Centre 1972–83, Acting Head 1983–84, Dir Int Relations 1985–95, Dir-Gen 1990–95, Sr Adviser 1995; mem Israeli Peace Talks Del 1994–95; Co-ordinator Advisory Cttee for Registration of New Drugs 1965–72, Cttee for Approval of Clinical Trials 1972–81; mem Advisory Cttee for Registration of New Drugs 1965–84; mem Advisory Group to WHO, Int Collaborating Scheme on Adverse Drug Reactions 1983–84; Chair Nat Cttee, World Health Day and World Non-Smoking Day 1985–95; mem WHO Exec Bd 1993–96, First Vice-Chair 1994–95, Exec Bd Rep at 49th WHO Ass 1996; Vice-Pres Int Council of Women 1988–94; Hon Pres Israel Asscn of Univ Women 1990; Chair Int Bd of Govs, Hebrew Univ of Jerusalem 1990–, Leon Bernard Foundation Prize Cttee 1995; mem Royal Pharmaceutical Soc of GB 1949–, Sasakawa Health Prize Cttee 1995; Bnot Brit Award 1975; Open Door Award 1986; Ramot Shapira Distinguished Service Award 1995; articles on the effects of drug therapy in professional journals. *Leisure interests:* piano, painting.

HESPEL, Véronique Thérèse, MA; French civil servant; b 23 May 1951, Paris; d of Bernard and Marie Beau; m 2nd Alain Hespel 1988; two d one s. *Education:* Univ of Paris VII, Inst d'Etudes Politiques de Paris and Ecole Nat d'Admin. *Career:* Tax Insp Insp-Gen of Finance 1978–82; Rep to Budget Directorate 1982–83, to Cabinet of Jacques Delors, then Minister of Econ, Finance and Budget 1983–84; Head Bureau of Social Questions 1984–85, Urban and Housing Bureau 1986–87; responsible for Third Dub-Directorate, Budget Directorate 1988–89; Financial Dir CEA (atomic energy comm) 1989–91; Rep to Directorate-Gen Union des Assurances de Paris insurance co 1992–; Insp-Gen of Finance 1994–98; Commissaire Adjoint au Plan 1998–. *Address:* Commission général du Plan, 18 rue de Martignac, 75007 Paris, France.

HESSE-HONEGGER, Cornelia; scientist and artist. *Career:* Fmrly scientific illustrator, Dept of Zoology, Univ of Zurich; began studying insects after the Chernobyl (Ukraine) nuclear explosion 1988; specialises in painting the mutations suffered by fruit flies exposed to radiation in lab experiments and specimens of bugs found in the vicinity of nuclear power plants in Europe and USA; made a study of insects around three nuclear power plants and one research plant in Aargua (Switzerland); exhibitions throughout Europe; contribs to newspapers and magazines; lectures in field. *Address:* c/o Locus +, Wards Bldg, 3rd Floor, Rm 17, 31–39 High Bridge, Newcastle upon Tyne NE1 1EW, UK.

HEWITT, Heather Agnes, BA, DIP ED; Australian college principal; b 14 July 1934; d of G. Fleming; m John Hewitt 1958; two s one d. *Education:* Univs of Melbourne (Vic) and New England (NSW) and La Trobe Univ (Vic). *Career:* Psychologist Royal Children's Hosp 1960–63; Sr Lecturer Lincoln Inst for Health Sciences 1964–70, Burwood State Coll of Advanced Educ 1979–80; Lecturer Inst of Early Childhood Devt 1979–80; Prin Univ Coll, Univ of Melbourne 1979–99; Chair Victoria Ascertainment Cttee for Pre-School Sensory Impaired Children and Deaf/Blind Children 1970–79, Ministerial Cttee on Early Identification and Assessment of Handicapped Persons 1973, Prems Cttee on Mental Retardation, Sub-Cttee Educ of Deaf, Blind and Deaf/Blind Children 1976, Int Asscn of Educ of Deaf/Blind, Int Council of Visually Impaired; mem Australian Group for Scientific Study of Mental Deficiency; Int Counsultant Christoffel Blindenmission (Germany), Helen Keller Int. *Publications include:* A Sensory Motor Program for Language Delayed Children two and a half to four and a half years (co-ed) 1980, Persons

Handicapped by Rubella: Victors and Victims (jtly) 1991; numerous contribs to professional journals. *Leisure interests:* reading, gardening. *Address:* 2 Kiata Drive, Mildura, Vic 3500, Australia. *Telephone:* (3) 344 4000; *Fax:* (3) 344 5104.

HEWITT, Rt Hon Patricia Hope, PC, MA, FRSA; British/Australian politician; b 12 Dec 1948, Canberra; d of Sir Lenox and Alison Hope Hewitt; m 1st Julian Gibson-Watt 1970 (divorced 1978); m 2nd William Birtles 1981; one d one s. *Education:* Girls' Grammar School (Canberra), Coll Cevenol (Chambon-sur-Lignon, France), ANU, Newnham Coll (Cambridge). *Career:* Public Relations Officer Age Concern 1971–73; Women's Rights Officer Nat Council for Civil Liberties (NCCL), London 1973–74, Gen Sec 1974–83; Parl Cand (Lab) for Leicester E constituency 1983; Press Sec to Leader of Opposition (Lab Party) 1983–87, Policy Co-ordinator 1987–89; Deputy Dir Inst for Public Policy Research 1989–94; Head of Research Andersen Consulting 1994–97; MP (Lab) Leicester W 1997–; mem Social Security Select Cttee 1997–98; Economic Sec to the Treasury 1998–99; Minister for Small Business and e-Commerce, Dept of Trade and Industry 1999–2001; Sec of State for Trade and Industry 2001–; mem Sec of State's Advisory Cttee on Employment of Women 1977–84, Nat Lab Women's Cttee 1979–83, Lab Party Enquiry into Security Services 1980–81; Co-Chair Human Rights Network 1979–81; mem Advisory Bd New Socialist 1980–90; mem Council Campaign for Freedom of Information 1983–89; mem Bd Int League for Human Rights 1984–; mem Exec Cttee Fabian Soc 1988–93; Deputy Chair Comm on Social Justice 1993–; Vice-Chair Healthcare 2000 1995–; Assoc Newnham Coll, Cambridge 1984–94;. *Publications include:* The Abuse of Power 1981, Your Second Baby (jtly) 1990, About Time: the revolution in work and family life 1993. *Leisure interests:* gardening, cooking, music, theatre, family. *Address:* House of Commons, London SW1A 0AA, UK; DTI, 1 Victoria St, London SW1H 0ET, UK. *Telephone:* (20) 7215-5621.

HEYHOE FLINT, Rachael, MBE, DL; British sportswoman, writer and broadcaster; b 11 June 1939, Wolverhampton; d of Geoffrey and Roma (née Crocker) Heyhoe; m Derrick Flint 1971; one s. *Education:* Wolverhampton Girls' High School and Dartford Coll of Physical Educ. *Career:* Head of Physical Educ Wolverhampton Municipal Grammar School 1960–62, Northicote School 1962–64; mem England Women's Cricket Team 1960–84, Capt 1966–77; mem England Hockey Team 1964; County Squash Player 1964–68; County Golfer 1982–84; Journalist Wolverhampton Express and Star 1965–72; Sports Writer Daily Telegraph 1967–84; Sports Ed Wolverhampton Chronicle 1969–71; First woman Sports Reporter, ITV 1972; freelance Public Relations and Sports Marketing Consultant to La Manga Club (Spain), Wolverhampton Wanderers Football Club 1980– (mem Bd 1997–); mem Bd Family Assurance Friendly Soc 1992–; mem Advisory Panel Faldo Jr Series 1998–; Chair MG Rover Dealership Trust 2000–; Best After-Dinner Speaker Award, Guild of Professional Toastmasters 1972; Hon Fellow Business Man (Univ of Wolverhampton). *Publications include:* Just for Kicks 1966, Women's Hockey 1975, Fair Play (jtly) 1976, Heyhoe (autobiog) 1977. *Leisure interests:* golf, cricket, watching all sports. *Address:* Danescroft, Wergs Rd, Tettenhall, Wolverhampton WV6 9BN, UK. *Telephone:* (1902) 752103; *Fax:* (1902) 765111.

HEYLIN, Angela Christine, OBE; British public relations consultant; b 17 Sept 1943; d of the late Bernard and of Ruth Victoria Heylin; m Maurice Minzly 1971; one s. *Education:* Apsley Grammar School and Watford Coll. *Career:* CEO Charles Barker Lyons 1984, Charles Barker Watney & Powell 1986–, Charles Barker Traverse-Healy 1987–; Dir Charles Barker Group 1986–89, Chair and CEO 1988, Charles Barker City 1989, Charles Barker Advertising 1989; CEO Chair Charles Barker PLC 1992–96, Chair 1996–99; UK Pres BSMG Worldwide 1999–; Dir Corp Communications 1989, The Young Vic 1992–, Mothercare PLC 1999–, Provident Financial PLC 1999–; Chair Public Relations Consultants' Asscn 1990–92, House of St Barnabas-in-Soho; mem Citizen's Charter Advisory Panel 1993–97; Trustee Historic Royal Palaces 1999–; Award for Outstanding Contrib to the Industry 1988. *Publication:* Putting it Across: The Art of Communicating, Presenting and Persuading 1991. *Leisure interests:* theatre, piano, entertaining. *Address:* BSMG Worldwide, 110 St Martin's Lane, London WC2N 4DY (Office), UK (Office); 46 St Augustine's Rd, London NW1 9RN,

UK (Home). *Telephone:* (20) 7841-5459 (Office); (20) 7485-4815 (Home); *Fax:* (20) 7841-5777 (Office); *E-mail:* acheylin@cbarker.bsmg .com (Office); home@minzly.fsnet.co.uk (Home).

HIBBIN, Sally, BA; British film producer; b 3 July 1953, London; d of Eric and Nina Hibbin. *Education:* Keele Univ and Univ Coll (London). *Career:* Researcher, sub-editor The Movie 1978–81; freelance journalist (film reviews, film books, sports sub-editor) 1981–93; documentary producer 1982–87; drama producer 1988–; Founder-mem and Dir Parallax Pictures Ltd; Jt Business Award, Women in TV and Film 1994. *Documentaries:* Live a Life 1982, The Road to Gdansk, Great Britain United; *TV and Film Productions:* A Very British Coup (BAFTA and EMMY Award) 1987, Riff Raff (FELIX European Film Award) 1991, Raining Stones 1993, Bad Behaviour (Exec Producer) 1993, Ladybird, Ladybird 1994, I.D. 1995, Land and Freedom (Exec Producer) 1995, The Englishman Who Went Up a Hill But Came Down a Mountain (Exec Producer) 1995, Carla's Song 1996, Stand and Deliver 1998, Dockers (drama) 1999, Hold Back the Night 1999, Liam (Exec Producer) 2000; *Publications:* Politics, Ideology and the State (ed) 1978, The Making of Licence to Kill 1989, The Making of Back to the Future III 1990, The Official History of the James Bond Films 1987, 1989, The Official History of the Carry On Films 1988; has contributed to various film journals, magazines and collections. *Leisure interests:* walking, cooking, Tottenham Hotspur Football Club. *Address:* Parallax Pictures Ltd, 7 Denmark St, London WC2, UK. *Telephone:* (20) 7836-1478; *Fax:* (20) 7497-8062; *E-mail:* sally@parallaxpictures.freeserve.co.uk (Office); *Internet:* parallaxpictures.co.uk (Office).

HICKS, Maureen Patricia; British organization executive and politician; b 23 Feb 1948, Barton-on-Sea, Hants; d of Ronald and Norah Cutler; m Keith Henwood Hicks 1973; one s one d. *Education:* Ashley Secondary School, Brokenhurst Grammar School, Furzedown Coll of Educ (London). *Career:* Teacher of English and Drama 1969–70; Man Marks & Spencer 1970–74; Asst Area Educ Officer, NW Surrey 1974–76; Dir Stratford-upon-Avon Motor Museum 1976–82; mem Stratford Dist Council 1978–83; MP (Cons) for Wolverhampton NE 1987–92, mem Select Cttee on Educ, Science and the Arts 1987–90, Sec Cons Backbench Tourism Cttee 1987–92; Parl Pvt Sec to Minister of State and to Parl Under-Sec of State, Foreign and Commonwealth Office 1991–92; Part-time Lecturer in Tourism and Retail Man; Non-Exec Dir David Clarke Associates 1992–96, S Warwicks Combined Care (fmrly Mental Health Services) NHS Trust 1994–; Dir of Fundraising and Marketing, Myton Hamlet Hospice, Warwick 1997–; mem Exec Heart of England Tourist Bd; Exec mem Man Bd Citizens' Advice Bureau; mem Women in Man Asscn; Hon Fellow Wolverhampton Univ 1992. *Leisure interests:* theatre, travel, music, golf. *Address:* UK.

HICKSON, Jill Lesley Norton, MBA; Australian literary agent and business executive; b 28 Sept 1948; d of Staveley Fredrick Norton Hickson and Jean Halse Rogers; m Neville K. Wran 1976; one d. *Education:* Univ of Sydney and Australian Graduate School of Management. *Career:* Programmer/Announcer 2MBS FM 1975–76; Int Relations Man Quantas Airways 1976–81; Literary Agent and Man Dir Hickson Assocs Pty Ltd 1983–99; consultant Curtis Brown Australia Pty Ltd 1999–; mem Bd Dirs Ansett NZ, NSW Conservatorium of Music 1984–89, Sydney Opera House Trust 1985–89, Sydney Symphony Orchestra 1986; mem Australian Inst of Int Affairs, Australian Soc of Authors, Australian Writers' Guild, Grad Man Asscn; Patron Fellowship of Australian Writers, United Music Teachers' Asscn of NSW, 2MBS FM Music Foundation, Domestic Animal Birth Control Soc; mem Cttee State Library NSW Foundation, Art Gallery NSW Foundation; Cecil Hall Prize, Australian Inst of Man 1972; Schroder Darling Finance Prize; Inst of Dirs Prize. *Leisure interests:* piano, books, nature conservation, animal welfare. *Address:* POB 271, Woollahra, NSW 2025, Australia.

HIGGINS, Julia Stretton, CBE, D PHIL, FRS; British polymer scientist; b 1 July 1942, London; d of George and Sheilah Stretton Downes. *Education:* Ursuline Convent School (Wimbledon) and Somerville Coll (Oxford). *Career:* Physics teacher Mexborough Grammar School 1966–68; Research Assoc Manchester Univ 1968–72, Centre de Recherche sur les Macromolécules (Strasbourg, France) 1972–73; physicist, ILL (Grenoble, France) 1973–76; mem academic staff

Imperial Coll (London) 1976–, Prof of Polymer Science 1989–; Foreign mem Nat Acad of Eng, USA; over 200 articles in scientific journals. theatre, opera, travel. *Address:* Department of Chemical Engineering, Imperial College, London SW7 2BY, UK. *Telephone:* (20) 7594-5565; *Fax:* (20) 7594-5638; *E-mail:* j.higgins@ic.ac.uk.

HIGGINS, Dame Rosalyn, DBE, JSD, QC, FBA; British judge and professor of international law; b 2 June 1937; d of the late Lewis Cohen and Fay Inberg; m Terence L. Higgins 1961; one s one d. *Education:* Burlington Grammar School (London), Girton Coll (Cambridge) and Yale Univ (USA). *Career:* UK Intern Office of Legal Affairs, UN 1958; Commonwealth Fund Fellow 1959; Visiting Fellow Brookings Inst Washington, DC, USA 1960; Jr Fellow in Int Studies, LSE 1961–63, Visiting Fellow 1974–78, Prof of Int Law 1981–95; staff specialist in int law Royal Inst of Int Affairs 1963–74; Prof of Int Law Univ of Kent at Canterbury 1978–81; Judge Int Court of Justice 1995–; mem UN Cttee on Human Rights 1985–; Visiting Prof Stanford Univ (USA) 1975, Yale Univ (USA) 1977; Vice-Pres American Soc of Int Law 1972–74; Dr hc (Paris XI); Hon DCL (Dundee) 1994, (Durham, LSE) 1995, (Cambridge, Sussex, Kent, City Univ, Greenwich, Essex) 1996, (Birmingham, Leicester, Glasgow) 1997, (Nottingham) 1999; Ordre des Palmes Académiques, Yale Law School Medal of Merit 1997, Manley Hudson Medal (ASIC) 1998. *Publications include:* The Development of International Law through the Political Organs of the United Nations 1963, Conflict of Interests 1965, The Administration of the United Kingdom Foreign Policy through the United Nations 1966, Law in Movement – essays in memory of John McMahon (co-ed) 1974, UN Peacekeeping: documents and commentary (four vols) 1969–81, Problems and Process: International Law and How We Use It 1995; numerous articles in professional journals. *Leisure interests:* sport, cooking, eating. *Address:* International Court of Justice, Peace Palace, 2517 KJ The Hague, Netherlands. *Telephone:* (70) 302-24-15; *Fax:* (70) 302-24-09; *E-mail:* mail@icj-cij.org (Office); *Internet:* www.icj-cij.org (Office).

HIGHTOWER, Rosella; American/French dance teacher, choreographer and artistic director; b 30 Jan 1920, Ardmore, USA; d of Charles Hightower and of Ula Fanning; m Jean Robier 1955; one d. *Career:* Worked with Léonide Massine at Ballets Russes de Monte-Carlo 1938–41; danced with American Ballet Theater, leading dancer with Marquise de Cuevas' Ballet 1947–61; created roles in Balanchine's Apollo, Tudor's Pillar of Fire, etc; Founded Centre de Dance Int, ballet school 1961; Artistic Dir Ecole Supérieure de Dance de Cannes Rosalind Hightower 1991–; Dir Ballet Marseilles Opera, Grand Théâtre de Nancy, Paris Opéra, La Scala (Milan, Italy); Officier de la Légion d'Honneur; Commdr de l'Ordre Nat du Mérite; Prix Porselli 1993; Lys d'Or 1994; Oklahoma Treasures 1997 and numerous other awards. *Address:* Centre de Danse International Rosella Hightower, Le Gallia, 27 blvd Montfleury, 06400 Cannes, France; Villa Piège de Lumière, Parc Fiorentina, ave de Vallauris, 06400 Cannes, France (Home). *Telephone:* (4) 93-06-79-79 (Office); *Fax:* (4) 93-06-79-78 (Office); *E-mail:* contact@cannesdance.com (Office).

HILDEBRANDT, Regine; German politician; b 26 April 1941; three c. *Career:* Biologist; mem staff Zentralstelle für Diabetes und Stoffwechselkrankheiten, Berlin; Minister of Labour, Social Affairs, Health and Women, Fed State of Brandenburg 1990; Woman of the Year 1991; Hoegur-Preis 1992. *Leisure interests:* plants, ornithology, geology, art history, photography, singing in a choir. *Address:* Ministry of Labour, Social Affairs, Health and Women, Rosa-Luxemburg-Str 3, 1020 Berlin, German.

HILGERTOVÁ, Štěpánka; Czech sportswoman; b 10 April 1968, Prague; d of Stanislav and Zdeňka Proškovi; m Luboš Hilgert 1986; one s. *Education:* Prague. *Career:* Became mem Nat Slalom Canoe Team 1986, Nat Olympic Slalom Canoe Team 1992; Nat Champion 1988, 1989, 1990; 3rd place World Championship Team 1989, 2nd place 1991; 2nd place European Championship 1996, 1998, 1st place 2000; 2nd place World Championship 1997, 1st place 1999; 2nd place World Cup 1989, 1999, 1st place 1992, 1998; 1st place Olympic Games Atlanta 1996, Sydney 2000; 2nd place Czech Athlete 2000; currently sports instructor; Czech Canoeist of the Century 2000. *Leisure interests:*

family, reading. *Address:* Kva, 148 00 Prague 4, Czech Republic. *Telephone:* (2) 7952161; *Fax:* (2) 71913262; *E-mail:* hilgertova@ladymail.cz.

HILL, Debra; American film director, producer and scriptwriter; b Philadelphia, PA. *Career:* Script supervisor, later Asst Dir and Second Unit Dir on various films; currently producer and scriptwriter. *Films include:* Halloween (also co-writer) 1978, The Fog 1980, Escape from New York 1981, Halloween II 1981, Halloween III: Season of the Witch 1982, The Dead Zone 1983, Head Office 1986, Adventures in Babysitting 1987, Big Top Pee-Wee 1988, Heartbreak Hotel 1988, Gross Anatomy 1989, The Fisher King 1991, Escape from LA, Replacement Killers, Crazy in Alabama; *TV work includes:* Adventures in Babysitting, El Diablo, Monsters, Dream On, Girls in Prison.

HILL, Pamela, BA; American broadcasting executive; b 18 Aug 1938, Winchester, IN; d of Paul and Mary Frances (née Hollis) Abel; m Tom Wicker 1974; one s. *Education:* Univ of Glasgow (UK), Bennington Coll (VT), Univ Autónoma del Estado de México (Toluca). *Career:* Foreign Affairs Analyst Nelson A. Rockefeller Presidential Campaign 1961–64; Researcher, Assoc Producer, Dir, Producer NBC News 1965–73; Dir White Paper series 1969–72; Producer Edwin Newman's Comment 1972; Producer Closeup documentary series ABC News, NY 1973–78, Exec Producer 1978; Vice-Pres ABC News 1979–89; Sr Vice-Pres, Sr Exec Producer Cable News Network (CNN) 1989–98; numerous personal awards and awards for Closeup series. *Publications:* United States Foreign Policy 1945–65 1968, Catching up with America (photographic contrib) 1969. *Leisure interests:* photography, horse-riding. *Address:* c/o Cable News Network (CNN), 5 Penn Plaza, 24th Floor, New York, NY 10001, USA.

HILL, Polly, PH D; British social anthropologist; b 10 June 1914, Cambridge; d of A. V. and Margaret N. (née Keynes) Hill; m 1953 (divorced 1961, died 1985); one d. *Education:* Newnham Coll (Cambridge). *Career:* Mem editorial staff Economic Journal, Cambridge 1936–38; Research Asst Fabian Soc, London 1938–39; civil servant Treasury, later Bd of Trade and Colonial Office 1940–51; mem editorial staff West Africa, London 1951–53; mem academic staff Univ of Ghana, Legon 1954–65; field work in N Nigeria, writing in Cambridge 1966–72; Smuts Reader in Commonwealth Studies Univ of Cambridge 1973–79, Emer Reader 1979–; field work in India 1977–78; Leverhulme Emer Fellow 1981–82; Fellow Clare Hall, Cambridge 1966–81, Emer Fellow 1981–; Hon Fellow SOAS 1998. *Publications include:* The Unemployment Services 1940, The Gold Coast Farmer 1956, The Migrant Cocoa Farmers of Southern Ghana 1963, Studies in Rural Capitalism in West Africa 1970, Rural Hausa: A Village and a Setting 1972, Population, Prosperity and Poverty: Rural Kano, 1900 and 1970 1977, Dry Grain Farming Families: Hausaland (Nigeria) and Karnataka (India) compared 1982, Development Economics on Trial: the Anthropological Case for a Prosecution 1986, Lydia and Maynard: The Letters of L. Lopokova and J. M. Keynes (co-ed) 1989, Who Were the Fen People? 1993 and many other publs. *Leisure interest:* embroidery. *Address:* 4 Earl St, Cambridge CB1 1JR, UK. *Telephone:* (1223) 315151.

HILL, Susan Elizabeth, BA, FRSL; British writer and playwright; b 5 Feb 1942; d of the late R. H. and Doris Hill; m Stanley W. Wells 1975; two d (and one d deceased). *Education:* Grammar schools (Scarborough and Coventry) and King's Coll (London). *Career:* Literary critic various journals 1963–; numerous plays for BBC 1970–; Fellow King's Coll, London 1978; presenter Bookshelf, BBC Radio 4 1986–87; Founder and Publr Long Barn Books 1996–. *Publications include:* The Enclosure 1961, Do Me a Favour 1963, Gentleman and Ladies 1969, A Change for the Better 1969, I'm the King of the Castle 1970, The Albatross 1971, Strange Meeting 1971, The Bird of the Night 1972, A Bit of Singing and Dancing 1973, In the Springtime of the Year 1974, The Cold Country and Other Plays for Radio 1975, The Ramshackle Company (play) 1981, The Magic Apple Tree 1982, The Woman in Black 1983 (stage version 1989), Through the Kitchen Window 1984, Through the Garden Gate 1986, The Lighting of the Lamps 1987, Lanterns Across the Snow 1987, Shakespeare Country 1987, The Spirit of the Cotswolds 1988, Family (autobiog) 1989, The Glass Angels 1991, Beware! Beware! 1993, King of Kings 1993, Reflections from a Garden (jtly) 1995, Contemporary Women's Short Stories (co-ed) 1995, Listening to the Orchestra (short stories) 1996, The Second

Penguin Book of Women's Short Stories 1997, The Service of Clouds 1998; For Children: One Night at a Time 1984, Mother's Magic 1986, Can it be True? 1988, Susie's Shoes 1989, Stories from Codling Village 1990, I Won't Go There Again 1990, I've Forgotten Edward 1990, Pirate Poll 1991. *Leisure interests:* walking in the English countryside, friends, reading, broadcasting. *Address:* Longmoor Farmhouse, Ebrington, Chipping Campden, Glos GL55 6NW, UK. *Telephone:* (1386) 593352; *Fax:* (1386) 593443.

HILL SMITH, Marilyn; British opera singer (soprano); b 9 Feb 1952, Carshalton, Surrey; d of George and Irene Smith; m Thomas Peter Kemp 1974. *Education:* Nonsuch High School for Girls (Cheam, Surrey) and Guildhall School of Music and Drama (London). *Career:* Pantomine, cabaret and concerts in UK, Australia, NZ and USA 1969–80; radio debut with BBC 1975; TV debut 1983; Prin mem English Nat Opera 1978–84; debut Royal Opera 1981, New Sadler's Wells Opera 1981, Canadian Opera 1984, Welsh Nat Opera 1987, Scottish Nat Opera 1988, New D'Oyly Carte Opera 1990, Lyric Opera, Singapore 1992; has appeared at several major European music festivals including Versailles, Granada, Aldeburgh, London Promenade Concerts and on television and radio; Adjudicator for Fed of Music Festivals 2001; Assoc Guildhall School of Music; Young Musician of the Year 1975 and other prizes. *Recordings include:* Vienna Première (Music Retailers Award for Excellence) 1984, Treasures of Operetta (Music Retailers Award for Excellence) 1985, Pirates of Penzance (Music Retailers Award for Excellence) 1991. *Leisure interests:* cooking, gardening, sleeping. *Address:* c/o Music International, 13 Ardilaun Rd, Highbury, London N5 2QR, UK. *Telephone:* (20) 7359-5183; *Fax:* (20) 7226-9792.

HILLER, Susan, MA; American/British artist; b 7 March 1942; d of Paul Hiller and Florence Ehrich; m David Coxhead 1962; one s. *Education:* Smith Coll and Tulane Univ. *Career:* Solo exhibitions at galleries in UK, USA, Europe and Australia 1973–; numerous group exhibitions in UK and abroad; Lecturer Slade School of Art, London 1982–90; Prof of Fine Art Univ of Ulster 1990–96; Artist-in-Residence, Univ of Sussex, UK 1973; Distinguished Visiting Prof Califonia State Univ, USA 1991; Visiting Art Council Chair Univ of California, USA 1992; Baehr Chair in Contemporary Art, Univ of Newcastle 2000–; Gulbenkian Foundation Fellow 1976, 1977; Hon Fellow Dartington Coll of Arts 1998; Guggenheim Fellowship 1998–99. *Publications:* Dreams: Visions of the Night (jtly) 1989, The Myth of Primitivism (ed) 1991, After the Freud Museum 1995, Thinking about Art: Conversations with Susan Hiller 1996. *Address:* 83 Loudoun Rd, London NW8 0DL, UK. *Telephone:* (20) 7372-0438 (Office); *Fax:* (20) 7229-5259 (Office).

HILLER, Dame Wendy, DBE; British actress; b Stockport; d of Frank Hiller and Marie Stone; m Ronald Gow 1937 (died 1993); one s one d. *Education:* Winceby House (Bexhill). *Career:* Trained at Manchester Repertory Theatre; Hon LL D (Manchester) 1984. *Plays include:* Love on the Dole 1935, The First Gentleman 1945, Tess of the d'Urbervilles, The Heiress 1947, Ann Veronica 1949, The Night of the Ball 1955, Waters of the Moon 1955, Moon for the Misbegotten 1957, Flowering Cherry 1958, Toys in the Attic 1960, The Aspern Papers 1962, 1984, The Wings of the Dove 1963, The Sacred Flame 1966, When We Dead Awaken 1968, The Battle of Shrivings 1970, Crown Matrimonial 1972, John Gabriel Borkman 1975, Lies 1976, The Importance of Being Earnest 1987, Driving Miss Daisy 1988; *Films include:* Pygmalion 1938, Major Barbara 1940, I Know Where I'm Going 1945, Separate Tables (Acad Award for Best Actress 1959) 1958, Sons and Lovers 1960, A Man for All Seasons 1966, David Copperfield 1969, Murder on the Orient Express 1975, Voyage of the Damned 1976, The Cat and the Canary 1977, The Elephant Man 1979, Making Love 1981, The Kingfisher 1982, The Lonely Passion of Miss Judith Hearne 1987; *TV includes:* The Importance of Being Earnest 1986, All Passion Spent 1987, A Taste for Death 1988, Ending Up 1989, The Best of Friends 1991, The Countess Alice 1991. *Leisure interest:* gardening. *Address:* c/o Chatto & Linnit, 123A King's Rd, London SW3 4PL, UK.

HILLS, Carla Anderson, AB, LL D; American lawyer and government official; b 3 Jan 1934, Los Angeles, CA; d of Carl and Edith (née Hume) Anderson; m Roderick Maltman Hills 1958; three d one s. *Education:* Stanford Univ (CA), St Hilda's Coll, Oxford (UK), Yale Law School. *Career:* Asst US Attorney Civil Div, Los Angeles, CA 1958–61; Partner

Munger, Tolles, Hills & Rickershauser law firm 1962–74; Adjunct Prof School of Law, Univ of California, Los Angeles 1972; Asst Attorney Gen Civil Div, US Dept of Justice 1974–75; Sec of Housing and Urban Devt 1975–77; Partner Latham, Watkins & Hills law firm 1978–86, Weil, Gotshal and Manges, Washington, DC 1986–88, Mudge, Rose, Gutherie, Alexander & Ferdon 1994–; US Trade Rep Exec Office of the Pres 1989–93; Chair and CEO Hills & Co 1993–; Co-Chair Alliance to Save Energy 1977–; Vice-Chair Bar of Supreme Court of the US, California State and Dist of Columbia Bars, Council Section of Anti-trust Law, American Bar Asscn 1974, American Law Inst 1974–, Fed Bar Asscn (Los Angeles Chapter, Pres 1963), Women Lawyers Asscn (Pres 1964), Los Angeles Co Bar Asscn, Chair of various cttees including Standing Cttee on Discipline, CA 1970–74; mem Bd of Dirs Int Business Machines (IBM), The Signal Co Inc, Standard Oil Co of California, American Airlines Inc, Int Exec Service Corpns, Time-Warner Inc 1993–, Chevron Corpn 1993–; mem Carnegie Comm on the Future of Public Broadcasting 1977–78, Sloan Comm on Govt and Higher Educ 1977–79, Advisory Cttee Woodrow Wilson School of Public and Int Affairs 1977–80, Yale Univ Council 1977–80, Fed Accounting Standards Advisory Council 1978–80, Trilateral Comm 1977–82, 1993–, American Cttee on East–West Accord 1977–79, Int Foundation for Cultural Co-operation and Devt 1977, Editorial Bd National Law Journal 1978, CA Gov's Council of Econ Policy Advisers 1993–, Council on Foreign Relations 1993–; Co-Chair Int Advisory Bd Center for Strategic and Int Studies; Vice-Chair Nat Cttee on US–China Relations 1993–; mem Bd Dirs US–China Business Council, Vice-Chair 1995–; Vice-Chair Interamerican Dialogue 1997–; Contributing Ed Legal Times 1978–88; Fellow American Bar Foundation 1975–; Trustee Pomona Coll 1974–79, Norton Simon Museum of Art 1976–80, Brookings Inst 1977, Univ of S California 1977–, Asia Soc, Inst for Int Econs, Americas Soc; Adviser Annenberg School of Communications, Univ of S California 1977–78; Chair Urban Inst 1983; Dr hc (Pepperdine Univ, CA) 1975, (Washington Univ, MO) 1977, (Mills Coll, CA) 1977, (Lake Forest Coll) 1978, (Williams Coll), (Notre Dame Univ), (Wabash Coll). *Publications:* Federal Civil Practice (jtly) 1961, Antitrust Adviser (ed and co-author) 1971. *Leisure interest:* tennis. *Address:* Hills & Company, 1200 19th St, NW, Suite 201, Washington, DC 20036, USA (Office); 3125 Chain Bridge Rd, NW, Washington, DC 20016, USA (Home).

HILTON, Janet Lesley; British clarinettist; b 1 Jan 1945, Liverpool; d of Howard and Eve Hilton; m David Vivian Richardson 1968; two s (one deceased) one d. *Education:* Belvedere School (Liverpool), Royal Manchester Coll of Music, Vienna Konservatorium. *Career:* BBC concerto debut 1963; clarinet soloist with major British orchestras including Royal Liverpool Philharmonic, Scottish Chamber, Bournemouth Symphony, Bournemouth Sinfonietta, City of London Sinfonia, BBC Scottish and Welsh Symphony, BBC Philharmonic; guest at Edinburgh, Aldeburgh, Bath, Cheltenham, City of London Festivals, Henry Wood Promenade concerts; appearances throughout Europe and N America; Prin Clarinet Welsh Nat Opera 1970–73, Scottish Chamber Orchestra 1975–80, Kent Opera 1984–88, Manchester Camerata; teacher Royal Scottish Acad of Music and Drama 1974–80, Royal Northern Coll of Music 1983–87; Visiting Tutor Birmingham Conservatoire 1989, Prof of Clarinet 1990, Head of Woodwind 1992–; Prof, Univ of Cen England 1993; Head of Woodwind, Royal Coll of Music, London 1998–; Dir Camerata Wind Soloists; dedicatee of works by Iain Hamilton, John McCabe, Edward Harper, Elizabeth Maconchy, Alun Hoddinott, Malcolm Arnold; Musicians' Union Scholarship to Royal Northern Coll of Music 1961, Assoc Royal Northern Coll of Music; Hiles Gold Medal 1964, Nat Fed of Music Socs Prize and Boise Foundation Scholarship 1965. *Recordings include:* all of Weber's music for clarinet with City of Birmingham Symphony Orchestra, Lindsay Quartet and Keith Swallow (Chandos); Neilsen and Copland Concertos with Scottish Nat Orchestra, Stanford Clarinet Concerto with Ulster Orchestra, Mozart Clarinet Quintet with the Lindsay Quartet 1998; recordings of McCabe, Harper, Maconchy and Hoddinott concertos with BBC Scottish Symphony Orchestra on Clarinet Classics 2001. *Leisure interests:* cookery, reading, family. *Address:* Flat D, 1 Primrose Gardens, London NW3 4UJ, UK. *Telephone:* (20) 7586-7374; *E-mail:* jhilton@rcm.ac.uk (Office).

HILTON, Tessa; British newspaper editor; b 18 Feb 1951; d of Michael and Phyllis Hilton; m Graham Ball 1976; two s one d. *Education:* St Mary's School (Gerrards Cross). *Career:* Journalist Sunday Mirror 1970–78, Ed 1994–; freelance writer 1978–85; Ed Mother magazine 1985–87; Exec Today 1987–91; Ed Femail, Daily Mail 1991–94; Asst Ed Sun 1994; Deputy Ed Express then Ed Express on Sunday magazine 1996–99. *Publication:* Great Ormond Street Book of Child Health 1990. *Leisure interest:* family. *Address:* c/o Express Newspapers, 245 Blackfriars Rd, London SE1, UK.

HILTON OF EGGARDON, Baroness (Life Peer), cr 1991, of Eggardon in the County of Dorset, **Jennifer Hilton,** MA; British police executive and member of the House of Lords; b 12 Jan 1936, Nicosia, Cyprus; d of John Robert and Margaret Frances Hilton. *Education:* Univs of Manchester and London. *Career:* Mem Metropolitan Police Force, London 1956–; mem staff Nat Police Coll 1973–74; Metropolitan Police Man Services Dept 1975–76; Supt Heathrow Airport, then Battersea 1977–81, Chief Supt Chiswick 1981–84; Commdr various posts including New Scotland Yard 1984–87; Head Metropolitan Police Training, Hendon 1988–90; mem House of Lords 1991–, Spokesperson on the Police and the Environment; mem EC Sub-Cttee on Environment 1991–95 (Chair 1995–98); Chair Advisory Panel on Works of Art 1998–; Sybil Hill Trophy 1964; First prize Police Gold Medal Essay Competition 1975; QPM 1989. *Publications:* The Gentle Arm of the Law (2nd edn) 1973, Individual Development and Social Experience (jtly, 2nd edn) 1981. *Leisure interests:* gardening, art history, travel. *Address:* House of Lords, Westminster, London SW1A 0PW, UK. *Telephone:* (20) 7219-3182.

HILTUNEN, Eila Vilhelmina; Finnish sculptor; b 22 Nov 1922, Sortavala (now in Russian Fed); d of Usko and Ester (née Nousiainen) Hiltunen; m Otso Pietinen 1944; two c. *Education:* Acad of Fine Arts (Helsinki). *Career:* Contribs to numerous int exhibitions; works in perm collections including Agnelli, Museum of Modern Art, Stockholm, UNESCO, Paris, UN, New York; City of Paris Silver Medal 1960; Pro Finlandia Award 1965; Fiorino Gold Medal 1971; Commendatore al Merito della Repubblica Italiana 1981. *Works include:* Sibelius Monument, Helsinki 1961–67, Lilienthal, Huntsville Space Center, AL, USA 1968, Palm Grow, Teheran (now Tehran) 1975, Sunflower Field, Jeddah, Saudi Arabia 1984. *Leisure interests:* history of art, languages, literature. *Address:* Nouttapolku 8, 00330 Helsinki, Finland; Il Cassero, 53020 Monticchiello, Siena, Italy. *Telephone:* (0) 483292 (Finland); (578) 755092 (Italy).

HIMMELFARB, Gertrude, PH D, FBA; American professor of history and writer; b 8 Aug 1922; d of Max and Bertha (née Lerner) Himmelfarb; m Irving Kristol 1942; one s one d. *Education:* Brooklyn Coll and Univ of Chicago. *Career:* Distinguished Prof of History Graduate School, City Univ New York 1965–88, Prof Emer 1988–; Fellow American Philosophical Soc, American Acad of Arts and Sciences, Royal Historical Soc, etc; many public and professional appointments; Guggenheim Fellow 1955–56, 1957–58, Nat Endowment for the Humanities Fellowship 1968–69, American Council of Learned Socs Fellowship 1972–73, Woodrow Wilson Int Center Fellowship 1976–77, Humanities Fellowship 1980–81; Hon LHD (Rhode Island Coll) 1976, (Kenyon Coll) 1985; Hon LITT D (Smith Coll) 1977, (Lafayette Coll) 1978; Hon D HUM LITT (Boston) 1987, (Yale) 1990; Rockefeller Foundation Award 1962–63. *Publications:* Lord Acton: A Study in Conscience and Politics 1952, Darwin and the Darwinian Revolution 1959, Victorian Minds 1968, On Liberty and Liberalism: The Case of John Stuart Mill 1975, The Idea of Poverty 1984, Marriage and Morals Among the Victorians 1986, The New History and the Old 1987, Poverty and Compassion: The Moral Imagination of the Late Victorians 1991, On Looking into the Abyss: Untimely Thoughts on Culture and Society 1994, The De-Moralization of Society from Victorian Virtues to Modern Values 1995. *Address:* 2510 Virginia Ave NW, Washington, DC 20637, USA.

HINDMARCH, Anya; British fashion designer; b 1968. *Career:* Launched career with handbag design for Harpers & Queen 1987; opened first Anya Hindmarch shop 1993; produces new collection of around 45 handbags each season. *Address:* First Floor, 91 Walton St, London SW3 2HP, UK. *Internet:* www.anyahindmarch.com.

HINGIS, Martina; Swiss tennis player; b 30 Sept 1980, Kosice, Czechoslovakia; d of Mélanie Hingis. *Career:* Competed in first tennis tournament 1985; family moved to Switzerland at age seven; winner French Open Jr championship 1993, Wimbledon Jr Championship 1994; has competed in the Italian Open, US Open, Chase Championship (NY) and Wimbledon; won first professional tournament Filderstadt (Germany) 1996; winner Australian Open 1997 (youngest winner of a Grand Slam title in Twentieth Century), 1998, 1999 (Singles and Doubles), US Open 1997, Kremlin Cup 2000; Wimbledon Singles Champion 1997. *Leisure interests:* horse-riding, roller-blading. *Address:* c/o AM Seidenbaum 17, 9377 Truebbach, Switzerland.

HINTON, Susan Eloise; American writer; b 1948, Tulsa, OK; m David Inhofe 1970; one s. *Career:* Writer of teenage fiction and films; Golden Archer Award 1983; Author Award American Library Asscn Young Adult Services Div/School Library Journal 1988. *Publications:* The Outsiders 1967 (Chicago Tribune Book, World Spring Festival Honour Book 1967, Media and Methods Maxi Award 1975, Massachusetts Children's Book Award 1979), That Was Then, This is Now 1971 (Chicago Tribune Book, World Spring Festival Honour Book 1971, Massachusetts Children's Book Award 1978), Rumble Fish 1975 (Land of Enchantment Award New Mexico Library Asscn 1982), Tex 1979 (Sue Hefly Award 1983), Taming the Star Runner 1988, Big David, Little David 1994; screenplay: Rumble Fish (jtly); *Film appearances:* Tex 1982, The Outsiders 1983. *Address:* Press Relations, Delacorte Press, 1540 Broadway Suite Bd, New York, NY 10036, USA.

HIRD, Dame Thora, DBE, D UNIV; British actress; b 28 May 1911; d of James Henry Hird and Mary Jane Mayor; m James Scott 1937 (died 1994); one d. *Education:* The Misses Nelson's Prep School (Morecambe, Lancs) and Lancs Royalty Theatre Repertory Co. *Career:* First appeared in West End of London 1940–42; Film contract Ealing Studios 1940; Pye Female Comedy Star Award 1984; Hon D LITT (Lancaster) 1989. *Films include:* Blacksheep of Whitehall, They Came in Khaki, A Kind of Loving, Once a Jolly Swagman, Maytime in Mayfair; *TV appearances include:* Meet the Wife, The First Lady, In Loving Memory, Hallelujah!, Last of the Summer Wine, Praise Be!, Thora on the Straight and Narrow, Cream Cracker under the Settee (BAFTA Award for Best TV Actress 1988), Waiting for the Telegram (BAFTA Award for Best TV Actress 1999), Lost for Words (BAFTA Award for Best TV Actress 2000); *Publications include:* Scene and Hird (autobiog) 1976, Praise Be Notebook 1991, Praise Be Yearbook 1991, Praise Be Christmas Book 1991, Praise Be Book of Prayers 1992, Praise Be I Believe 1993, Is It Thora? 1996, Not in the Diary 2000. *Leisure interests:* reading, travelling. *Address:* c/o Felix de Wolfe, Garden Offices, 51 Maida Vale, London W9 1SD, UK. *Telephone:* (20) 7723-5561.

HIRONAKA, Wakako, MA; Japanese politician and writer; b 11 May 1934, Tokyo; m Heisuke Hironaka; one s one d. *Education:* Ochanomizu Women's Univ and Brandeis Univ (MA, USA). *Career:* Mem House of Councillors (Parl, Komeito Party) 1986–, Dir-Gen Environment Agency and Minister of State 1993–94; Dir Communications Cttee, Special Cttee on Relocation of the Nat Diet and Related Orgs, mem Special Cttee on the Environment; mem World Comm on Forests and Sustainable Devt 1995, organizing cttee Microcredit Summit 1995; Hon PH D (Brandeis) 1987. *Publications include:* Between Two Cultures, Woman, Her Work and Family 1981, What Values Should We Leave for the Future Generations? 1982, What America Wants from Japan, Voices from the American Congress 1987, Politics is Unexpectedly Interesting 1989; has translated numerous works 1975–87. *Address:* House of Councillors, 1-7-1 Nagata-cho, Suite 403, Chiyoda ku, Tokyo 100, Japan. *Telephone:* (3) 5308-8403; *Fax:* (3) 3502-8817; *E-mail:* hironaka@st.rim.or.jp.

HITE, Shere D., MA, PH D; American feminist and writer; b St Joseph, MO; m Friedrich Hoericke 1985. *Education:* Univ of Florida and Columbia Univ (New York). *Career:* Dir feminist sexuality project Nat Org for Women (NOW), New York 1972–78; Dir Hite Research Int, New York 1978–; Instructor in female sexuality, New York Univ 1977–; Lecturer Harvard Univ, McGill Univ, Columbia Univ, also numerous women's groups, int lecturer 1977–2002; Visiting Prof Nihon Univ, Japan 1998–2002; mem Advisory Bd Foundation of Gender and Genital Medicine, Johns Hopkins Univ; Consultant Ed Journal of Sex Educ and Therapy, Journal of Sexuality and Disability; mem Nat Org for Women

(NOW), American Historical Asscn, American Sociological Asscn, AAAS, Acad of Political Science, Women's History Asscn, Society for Scientific Study of Sex, Women's Health Network; f Nike Prize for Women's Non-Fiction Writing, Frankfurt 1997; Distinguished Service Award, American Asscn of Sex Educators, Counselors and Therapists; Hon Award of Merit, Nihon Univ (Japan); Nike Award, Univ of Messina (Italy) and other awards. *Publications:* Sexual Honesty: By Women For Women 1974, The Hite Report: A Nationwide Study of Female Sexuality 1976, The Hite Report on Male Sexuality 1981, Hite Report on Women and Love 1987, Good Guys, Bad Guys (jtly) 1989, Women as Revolutionary Agents of Change: The Hite Reports and Beyond 1993, The Hite Report on the Family: Growing Up Under Patriarchy 1994, The Divine Comedy of Ariadne and Jupiter 1994, The Hite Report on Hite: A Sexual and Political Autobiography 1996, 2000, Women's View of Other Women 1996, How Women See Other Women 1998, Sexual Business: Ethics at Work 2000. *Address:* c/o Arcadia Books, 15 Nassau St, London W1N 7RE, UK (Office).

HJELM-WALLÉN, Lena, MA; Swedish politician; b 14 Jan 1943, Sala; d of Gustaf Hjelm and Elly Hjelm-Wallén; m Ingvar Wallén; one d. *Education:* Univ of Uppsala. *Career:* Teacher, Sala 1966–69; active in Social Democratic Youth League; elected to Riksdag (Parl) 1968; mem Exec Cttee Västmanland branch of Socialdemokratiska Arbetarepartiet (Social Democratic Labour Party—SDLP) 1968, mem SDLP Parl Exec 1976–82, SDLP spokeswoman on Educ 1991–94, mem Bd SDLP 1978–87; Minister without Portfolio, with responsibility for schools 1974–76; Minister of Educ and Cultural Affairs 1982–85, of Int Devt Co-operation 1985–91, for Foreign Affairs 1994–98; Deputy Prime Minister 1998–. *Leisure interests:* nature, books, gardening, family. *Address:* c/o Cabinet Office, Rosenbad 4, 103 33 Stockholm, Sweden. *Telephone:* (8) 405-10-00; *Fax:* (8) 723-11-71.

HLAVAC, Elisabeth, DR IUR; Austrian politician; b 25 Feb 1952; d of Herbert and Edith Hlavac. *Education:* Univ of Vienna. *Career:* Mem Socialist Party 1971–, mem Women's Cttee, Vienna 1986, Chair Women's Cttee 1988, Prov Exec Cttee 1988, Fed Exec Cttee 1989–; mem 19th District Council, Vienna 1978–88; mem Bundesrat (Parl, Second Chamber) 1988–89, Nationalrat (First Chamber) 1989–, Social Democrat Spokesman for Justice 1991–94; elected MEP (PSE) 1995, mem Cttee on Legal Affairs and Citizens' Rights, Del for relations with Estonia, Lithuania and Latvia. *Leisure interests:* reading, arts. *Address:* European Parliament, rue Wiertz, 1047 Brussels, Belgium. *Telephone:* (2) 284-21-11; *Fax:* (2) 230-69-43.

HLEDÍKOVÁ, Zdenka, PH D; Czech academic; b 23 Oct 1938, Prague. *Education:* Charles Univ (Prague). *Career:* Mem staff State Archives (Pilsen) 1960–62, Archives of the Cen Directory of Czechoslovak Film 1962–65; Asst Dept of Auxiliary Historical Sciences and Archive Sciences, Faculty of Arts, Charles Univ (Prague) 1969–96, Prof of Auxiliary Historical Sciences 1996; Dir Czech Historical Inst (Rome) 1994. *Publications:* The Post of General Vicars of the Prague Archbishop in the Pre-Hussite Period 1971, Protocollum visitationis archidiaconatus Pragensis annis 1379–1382 per Paulum de Janowicz, archidiaconum Pragensem, factae (jtly) 1973, Raccolta Praghese di scritti di Luca fieschi 1985, The History of Administration in Bohemian Lands till 1945 (jtly) 1989, The Prague Bishop Jan IV of Dražice 1301–1343 1991, Life of Arnestus of Pardubice according to Valentin Krautwald (jtly) 1997. *Leisure interests:* civilized culture, nature. *Address:* Faculty of Arts, Charles University, Nám Jana Palacha 2, 110 00 Prague 2, Czech Republic; Czech Historical Institute in Rome, Via Concordia 1, 00183 Rome, Italy. *Telephone:* (4202) 21619312; *E-mail:* zdenka.hledikova@ff .cuni.cz; chur@libero.it.

HOARE, Sara-Jane, BA; British fashion director; b 27 June 1955, London. *Education:* Putney High School (London) and Univ of Warwick (Coventry). *Career:* Fashion Ed The Observer 1985–87; Fashion Dir (British) Vogue magazine 1989–92; mem staff American Vogue; Fashion Dir Harpers Bazaar, New York 1992–. *Leisure interests:* piano, opera, ballet, classical music, scuba-diving. *Address:* Harpers Baazar, New York, USA. *Telephone:* (212) 903-5000; *Fax:* (212) 262-7101; *E-mail:* carole@waggingtail.com; *Internet:* www.studionet.com.

HOCQ, Nathalie; French business executive; b 7 Aug 1951, Neuilly (Hauts-de-Seine); d of Robert Hocq and Christiane Arnoult; m Patrick Choay. *Education:* Ecole Mary Mount (Neuilly), Cours Victor-Hugo (Paris) and Univ of Paris IX (Paris-Dauphine). *Career:* Publicity Asst Havas-conseil 1970; in charge of duty-free network Briquet Cartier 1970; Exec Cartier SA 1974, Gen Man 1977, Man Dir Devt 1979–81; Chair Cartier Int 1981; Chair Poiray Joailliers 1986–, Pres, Dir-Gen 1988–, René Boivin Joailliers 2000–. *Leisure interests:* riding, tennis, skiing, swimming. *Address:* Poiray Joailliers, 1 rue de la Paix, 75002 Paris, France (Office); 8 rue du Colonel Combes, 75007 Paris, France (Home).

HODAČOVÁ, Helena, PH D; Czech writer; b 16 Sept 1916, Jičín; d of O. Homoláč; m François Svoboda 1939; one s (and one d deceased). *Education:* Charles Univ (Prague) and Univ of Paris (Sorbonne). *Career:* Writer of poetry since age of 15; Publicist Lidové Noviny; first books part of Czechoslovak Avant-Garde movt, later publs deal with problems of everyday life. *Publications:* L'harpe éolienne 1943, Ciel blanc – terre noire 1964, La vie du peintre O. Homoláč, Demi-temps vertigineux, Les oiseaux s'envolent: biographie d'une librettiste du compositeur Smetana, The Chinese 1996. *Leisure interest:* travel. *Address:* Pod lipkami 4, 150 00 Prague 5, Czech Republic. *Telephone:* (2) 523436.

HODGE, Margaret Eve, MBE, B SC; British politician; b 8 Sept 1944, Alexandria, Egypt; d of the late Hans and Lisbeth Oppenheimer; m 1st Andrew Watson 1968 (divorced); m 2nd Henry Hodge 1978; three d one s. *Education:* LSE. *Career:* Leader Islington Council 1982–92; mem Lab Party Local Govt Cttee 1983–94; Sr Consultant Price Waterhouse 1992–94; MP (Lab) for Barking 1994–, Chair Task Force on under 5s policy, London Group of Lab MPs 1996–98; mem Educ Select Cttee 1997–98; Chair Asscn of London Authorities 1984–92, Circle 33 Housing Trust 1993–96; Gov LSE 1990–. *Publications:* Quality, Equality and Democracy 1991, Beyond the Town Hall 1994; numerous contribs to newspapers and journals. *Leisure interests:* family, opera, piano, travel, cooking. *Address:* House of Commons, London SW1A 0AA, UK; 10 Richmond Crescent, London N1 0LZ, UK (Home). *Telephone:* (20) 7219-6666 (Office); (20) 7607-8806 (Home); *Fax:* (20) 7219-3640 (Office); (20) 7700-1157 (Home).

HODGE, Patricia; British actress; b Grimsby; m Peter Owen; two s. *Education:* London Acad of Music and Dramatic Art. *Career:* Eveline Evans Award for Best Actress; Hon D LITT (Hull, Brunel) 1996. *Plays include:* No-one Was Saved, All My Sons, Say Who You Are, The Birthday Party, The Anniversary, Popkiss, Two Gentlemen of Verona, Pippin, Maudie, Hair, The Beggar's Opera, Pal Joey, Look Back in Anger, Dick Whittington, Happy Yellow, The Brian Cant Children's Show, Then and Now, The Mitford Girls, As You Like It, Benefactors, Noel and Gertie, A Little Night Music 1995–96; Royal National Theatre: Money (Olivier Award 2000) 1999, Summerfolk, Noises Off (also tour) 2000–01; *Films:* The Disappearance, Rose Dixon – Night Nurse, The Waterloo Bridge Handicap, The Elephant Man, Heavy Metal, Betrayal, Sunset, Just Ask for Diamond, The Secret Life of Ian Fleming, The Leading Man 1996, Prague Duet 1996, Jilting Joe 1997, The Memory of Water 2001; *TV appearances include:* Valentine, The Girls of Slender Means, Night of the Father, Great Big Groovy Horse, The Naked Civil Servant, Softly, Softly, Jackanory Playhouse, Act of Rape, Crimewriters, Target, Rumpole of the Bailey, The One and Only Mrs Phyllis Dixey, Edward and Mrs Simpson, Disraeli, The Professionals, Holding the Fort, The Other 'Arf, Jemima Shore Investigates, Hayfever, The Death of the Heart, Robin of Sherwood, O.S.S., Sherlock Holmes, Time for Murder, Hotel Du Lac, The Life and Loves of a She Devil, Rich Tea and Sympathy 1991, The Cloning of Joanna May 1991, The Legacy of Reginald Perrin 1996, The Moonstone 1996. *Address:* c/o ICM, Oxford House, 76 Oxford St, London W1R 1RB, UK.

HODGSON, Marjorie Jane; Canadian painter; b 30 March 1932, Hamilton, ON; d of George Henry and Florence (née Tweddall) Botting; m Joshua Hodgson 1950; three s. *Education:* Hamilton Tech, Artists' Workshop (Toronto), Ontario Coll of Art, Doon School of Fine Art (ON) and under Hortense Gordon and John Sloan. *Career:* Painter and instructor in watercolour; exhibitions include Ontario Soc of Artists, Canadian Soc of Painters in Water Colours 1967, 1972–84, Tokyo Nat Art Gallery 1975–76, Montréal Museum of Fine Arts 1975–76, Nancy Poole's Studio 1975, Visual Arts, Ontario 1976, Acadia Univ, O'Keefe

Centre 1978, 1981, 1985, 1990, Ontario House, London (UK) 1986, 1988, Kingsmount Art Gallery, Toronto 1991; represented in perm collections including Union Gas, Molson's Breweries, Henderson Hosp, Canada Perm, Ellerslie Investments, Windsor Castle; mem Canadian Soc of Painters in Water Colour 1974–, Life mem 1996–, Ontario Soc of Artists 1977–; Molson Purchase Award 1976. *Leisure interest:* gardening. *Address:* 1 East Haven Drive, Scarborough, ON M1N 1L8, Canada. *Telephone:* (416) 267-6749.

HODGSON, Patricia Anne, CBE, DU, MA; British broadcasting official; b 19 Jan 1947; d of Harold and Pat (née Smith) Hodgson; m George Donaldson 1979; one s. *Education:* Brentwood High School and Newnham Coll (Cambridge). *Career:* Freelance journalist and broadcaster UK and USA 1968–79; Educ Producer BBC and occasional Producer Today and Tonight current affairs programmes 1970–82, mem BBC Secretariat 1982–83, Deputy Sec 1983–85, Sec 1985–87, Head of Policy and Planning 1987–92, Dir of Policy and Planning 1993–2000; Chief Exec Ind TV Comm (ITC) 2000–; mem Haringey Borough Council (Cons) 1974–77; Chair Bow Group 1975–76; Ed Crossbow 1976–80; Dir Broadcasters' Audience Research Bd 1987–; mem London Electricity Consultative Council 1981–83, London Arts Bd 1991–, Monopolies and Mergers Comm 1993–99, Advisory Bd Judge Inst (Cambridge); Trustee Prince's Youth Business Trust 1992–95; Assoc Fellow Newnham Coll, Cambridge 1994–97. *TV productions include:* English Urban History 1978, Conflict in Modern Europe 1980, Rome in the Age of Augustus 1981. *Address:* ITC, 33 Foley St, London W1W 7TL, UK. *Telephone:* (20) 7306-7825; *Fax:* (20) 7306-7800; *E-mail:* Patricia.Hodgson@itc.org.uk.

HODROVÁ, Daniela, MA; Czech writer and literary theorist; b 5 July 1946, Prague; d of Zdeněek Hodr; m Karel Milota 1985. *Education:* Charles Univ (Prague). *Career:* Head Literary Theory Dept Inst of Czech and World Literature, Prague 1974–. *Publications include:* Hledání románu 1989, Visite Privée—Prague 1991, Trýznivé měesto (The Suffering City, trilogy of novels) 1991–92, Perůnuv den 1994. *Address:* Lucemburská 1, 130 00 Prague 3, Czech Republic.

HOEY, Rt Hon Catharine (Kate) Letitia, PC, B SC ECONS; British politician; b 21 June 1946; d of Thomas Henry and Letitia Jane Hoey. *Education:* Belfast Royal Acad, Ulster Coll of Physical Educ and City of London Coll. *Career:* Lecturer Southwark Coll 1972–76; Sr Lecturer Kingsway Coll 1976–85; Councillor London Borough of Hackney 1978–82, of Southwark 1988; Educ Advisor London Football Clubs 1985–89; MP (Lab) for Vauxhall 1989–; Opposition Spokeswoman Citizens' Charter and Women 1992–93; Parl Pvt Sec to Minister of State (Minister for Welfare Reform), Dept of Social Security 1997; Parl Under-Sec of State, Home Office 1998–99, Dept of Culture, Media and Sport 1999–2001, Minister for Sport 1999–2001. *Leisure interests:* keeping fit, watching football. *Address:* House of Commons, London SW1A 0AA, UK. *Telephone:* (20) 7219-3000; *E-mail:* hcinfo@ parliament.co.uk (Office).

HOFF, Magdalene; German politician; b 29 Dec 1940, Hagen. *Career:* Municipal Councillor, Hagen 1975–79; MEP (PSE, SPD), mem Cttee on Foreign Affairs, Human Rights, Common Security and Defence Policy, Security and Defence Policy. *Address:* Riegestraße 8–10, 58091 Hagen, Germany; European Parliament, rue Wiertz, 1047 Brussels, Belgium. *Telephone:* (2) 284-21-11 (Belgium); *Fax:* (2) 230-69-43 (Belgium).

HOFF, Ursula, AO, OBE, PH D; Australian lecturer in fine arts and writer; b 26 Dec 1909; d of H. L. Hoff. *Education:* Univs of Hamburg and Munich (Germany) and London. *Career:* Lecturer in Fine Arts, Univ of Melbourne 1950–, Sr Assoc 1985–; Asst Keeper Nat Gallery of Victoria 1943–49, Curator of Prints and Drawings 1956, Asst Dir 1968–73, Ed Bulletin 1973; Hon LL D (Melbourne); Hon LITT D (Monash, La Trobe); Britannica Award 1966. *Publications include:* Charles I, Patron of the Arts 1941, Charles Conder, His Australian Years 1960, Charles Conder, Lansdowne Australian Art Library 1972, European Painting and Sculpture before 1800 1973, The Art of Arthur Boyd 1986, European Paintings Before 1800 1995. *Leisure interests:* literature, music. *Address:* 678 Canning St, N Carlton, Vic 3054, Australia.

HOFFMAN, Grace; American opera singer (mezzo-soprano); b 14 Jan 1925, Cleveland, OH; d of Dave and Hermina Hoffman. *Education:* Western Reserve Univ and Manhattan School of Music (New York). *Career:* Completed musical studies in Italy (Fulbright Scholarship); appeared at Maggio Musicale, Florence; guest performance as Azucena (Il Trovatore), Zurich Opera, Switzerland and subsequently mem of co for two years; debut at La Scala, Milan, Italy as Fricka (Die Walküre); with Stuttgart Opera, Germany 1955–; has appeared at Edinburgh (UK) and Bayreuth (Germany) festivals; numerous guest appearances in leading roles at Teatro Colón, Buenos Aires, San Francisco Opera, Chicago Lyric Opera, Covent Garden, London, Metropolitan Opera, New York, the Vienna Opera, in Berlin, Brussels, etc; numerous oratorio and concert appearances in major European music centres; Prof of Voice Hochschule für Musik, Stuttgart 1978–; titles conferred Württembergische Kammersängerin 1960, Austrian Kammersängerin 1980; Vercelli Prize; Baden-Württemberg Medal of State 1978. *Leisure interest:* her house and furnishing it. *Address:* Bergstr 19, 72666 Neckartailfingen, Germany.

HOFFMANN, Adriana; Chilean environmentalist. *Career:* Leading environmentalist in various pressure groups such as Lahuen, Defenders of the Native Forests and Protege; plays leading role in the Chilean Science Soc, Biology Soc of Chile, Earth Foundation, Asscn of Chilean Female Leaders, UICN (Int Union for Conservation); Head Nat Environmental Comm (CONAMA) 2000–. *Publications include:* Flora silvestre de Chile 1983, El árbol urbano en Chile 1989, Cactáceas en la flora silvestre de Chile 1990, De cómo Margarita Flores puede cuidar su salud y ayudar a salvar el planeta (with Marcelo Mendoza) 1992. *Address:* Obispo Donoso 6, Castilla 520 via Correo 21, Providencia, Santiago, Chile. *Telephone:* 240-5600; *Fax:* 244-1262; *E-mail:* informaciones@conama.cl.

HOFFMANN, Eva Wydra, MA, PH D; Polish/American author and academic; b 1 July 1945, Cracow; d of Boris and Maria Wydr; m Barry Hoffman 1971 (divorced 1976). *Education:* Rice Univ (Texas) and Yale School of Music. *Career:* Journalist New York Times 1980–90; Visiting Prof Mass Inst of Technology (MIT); Visiting Fellow Townsend Center (Berkeley) 2000, Clare Hall (Cambridge) 2001; Amnesty Lecturer (Oxford) 2001; Guggenheim Fellowship. *Publications include:* Lost in Translation 1989, Exit into History 1993, Shtetl 1997. *Leisure interest:* playing the piano. *Address:* Clare Hall, Cambridge, UK.

HOGAN, Linda; American university professor and writer. *Career:* Currently Assoc Prof Univ of Colorado; has written poetry, novels and essays. *Publications include:* Mean Spirit, Savings, Red Clay (poems and stories), Solar Storms, Dwellings: A Spiritual History, Of The Living World, Stories We Hold Secret, The Book of Medicines (poetry), From Women's Experience to Feminist Theology. *Leisure interests:* native American rights, environmental issues. *Address:* University of Colorado, Central Office, Boulder, CO 80309, USA.

HOGG, Anne; British potter; b Nov 1939, Singapore. *Education:* Falmouth School of Art and Slade School of Fine Art (London). *Career:* Designs and produces bone china pots; exhibitions include Mid-Cornwall Galleries, Salt House Gallery, Boar's Hill (Oxford, jtly), York St Gallery (Bath), West Side Gallery (Richmond), Riverside Mill, Queen's Gallery, Buckingham Palace 1990; mem Cornwall Crafts Asscn, Devon Guild of Craftsmen. *Leisure interests:* making porcelain dolls, spinning, creative knitting, oil painting.

HOGG, Hon Caroline Jennifer; Australian politician; b 18 April 1942; d of G. Kluht; m Robert Hogg 1967; one s one d. *Education:* Univ of Adelaide. *Career:* Mem Legis Council (Australian Lab Party) for Melbourne N Victoria 1982–, Minister for Community Services 1985–87, for Educ 1987–88, for Post-Secondary Educ, Ethnic Affairs and the Aged 1988–89, for Health 1989–91, for Ethnic, Municipal and Community Affairs 1991–92; Deputy Leader Opposition Legis Council 1990–96; Shadow Minister for Agric, Rural Affairs, the Arts 1992–93, for Higher Educ and Training (and assisting with the Arts) 1993–96. *Leisure interests:* reading, cinema, swimming, cycling, politics. *Address:* 36A North St, Glenroy, Vic 3046, Australia.

HOGG, Baroness (Life Peer), cr 1995, of Kettlethorpe in the County of Lincolnshire, **Sarah Elizabeth Mary Hogg**, MA; British journalist and economist; b 14 May 1946; d of Lord Boyd-Carpenter; m Douglas M. Hogg 1968; one s one d. *Education:* St Mary's Convent (Ascot) and Lady Margaret Hall (Oxford). *Career:* Staff writer The Economist 1967, Literary Ed 1970, Econs Ed 1977; Econs Ed Sunday Times 1981; Econs Ed and Deputy Finance and Industry Exec Ed The Times 1984–86; Asst Ed and Business and City Ed The Independent 1986–89; Econs Ed The Daily Telegraph 1989–90; Presenter Channel 4 TV News 1982–83; Head Policy Unit Office of the Prime Minister, 10 Downing St (with rank of Second Perm Sec) 1990–95; Chair London Econs 1997–99 (Dir 1995–97), Frontier Econs 1999–; mem Int Advisory Bd Nat Westminster Bank 1995–97, Advisory Bd Bankinter 1995–98, House of Lords Select Cttee on Science and Tech 1995–98, House of Lords Select Cttee on Monetary Policy 2000–, Council Royal Econ Soc 1996–, Council Hansard Soc 1996–; Dir London Broadcasting Co 1982–90, Royal Nat Theatre 1988–91, Foreign & Colonial Smaller Cos Investment Trust 1995– (Chair 1997–), Nat Provident Inst 1996–99, GKN 1996–, 3 i 1997– (Deputy Chair 2000), P&O 1999–2000, P&O Princess Cruises 2000–, Martin Currie Portfolio Investment Trust 1999–; Gov BBC 2000–; Fellow Eton Coll 1996–; Hon Fellow Lady Margaret Hall, Oxford 1994; Hon MA (Open Univ) 1987; Hon D LITT (Loughborough) 1992; Wincott Foundation Financial Journalist of the Year 1985. *Publication:* Too Close to Call (jtly) 1995. *Address:* House of Lords, London SW1A 0AA, UK.

HOGGETT, Dame Brenda Marjorie (see Hale, Rt Hon Dame Brenda Marjorie).

HOHLER, Erla Bergendahl, PH D, FSA; Norwegian archaeologist and art historian; b 20 Nov 1937, Oslo; m Christopher Hohler 1961; three c. *Education:* Univ of Oslo and Courtauld Inst (London). *Career:* Asst Prof Inst of Art History, Univ of Oslo 1975; Keeper Medieval Dept, Univ Museum of Nat Antiquities (Oslo) 1987; Prof Inst of Archaeology, Art History and Numismatics, Univ of Oslo 1993–; Prof of Art History Univ of Tromsø 1994; mem Det Norske Videnskapsakademi 1994. *Publications:* The Capitals of Urnes Church 1975, Stavkirkene 1981, Stilentwicklung in der Holzkirchen Architektur 1981, Norwegian Stave Church Carving 1989, Norwegian Stave Church Sculpture I-II 1999, Catalogue Raisonné 1999. *Address:* Universitetets Kulturhistoriske Museer, Frederiks Gt 3, 0164 Oslo, Norway (Office); Lyder Sagens Gt 23, 0358 Oslo, Norway (Home). *Telephone:* 22 85 95 36 (Office); 22 85 18 52 (Home).

HÖHN, Charlotte, D PHIL; German demographer; b 19 Sept 1945, Wiesbaden; d of Rudolf and Ursula Junghans; m Günter-Jürgen Höhn 1968 (divorced 1982); one d. *Education:* Elly-Heuss-Schule (Wiesbaden) and Johann Wolfgang Goethe Univ (Frankfurt am Main). *Career:* Research Asst Goethe Univ Statistical Inst, Frankfurt am Main 1970–73; Population Statistician Fed Statistics Office, Wiesbaden 1973–80; Sr Researcher Fed Inst for Population Research, Wiesbaden 1980–88, Dir and Prof 1988–; Lecturer in Demography Justus-Liebig Univ, Giessen 1982–94; author three books, approx 100 articles, Ed four books on population; mem Council Int Union for the Scientific Study of Population (IUSSP) 1985–93; Pres European Asscn for Population Studies (EAPS) 1991–95, then Hon Pres. *Leisure interests:* tennis, skiing, opera. *Address:* Federal Institute for Population Research, Postfach 5528, 65180 Wiesbaden, Germany (Office); Walkmühlstr 66, 65195 Wiesbaden, Germany (Home). *Telephone:* (611) 752235; *Fax:* (611) 753960; *E-mail:* bib@statistik-bund.de.

HOLBROOK, Elizabeth Mary Bradford, RCA; Canadian sculptor; b 7 Nov 1913, Hamilton, ON; d of William Ashford and Alma Victoria (née Carpenter) Bradford; m John Grant Holbrook 1936; two s one d. *Education:* Hamilton Tech Inst (ON), Ontario Coll of Art (Toronto), Royal Coll of Art (London). *Career:* Self-employed professional sculptor; instructor Burlington Cultural Centre, ON 1989–90; works in perm collections including Nat Gallery of Canada, Ottawa 1958–, Nat Portrait Gallery, Washington, DC 1975–, Art Gallery of Ontario, Toronto 1979–, Sir Winston Churchill Collection, St John's, NF 1985–; solo retrospective exhibition at McMaster Univ, Hamilton 1989; mem Sculptors' Soc of Canada, Ontario Soc of Artists; Lieut-Gov's Silver Medal, Ontario Coll of Art 1935; Sculpture Soc of New York Gold Medal for Portrait Sculpture 1969; elected to Hamilton Hall of Distinction 1994. *Publication:* Face to Face – A Life in Three Dimensions (autobiog) 1992. *Leisure interests:* equestrian sports, pony breeding. *Address:* Brookford, RR 3, 1177 Mineral Springs Rd, Dundas, ON L9H 5E3, Canada. *Telephone:* (416) 648-3003.

HOLDEN, Anne Jacqueline, QSO, JP, MA, LL B; New Zealand writer and lawyer; b 11 May 1928, Whakatane; d of Harold A. and Mildred Dare; m Henry Curran Holden 1954; two s two d. *Education:* Auckland Girls' Grammar School, Hamilton High School, Univ of Auckland, Victoria Univ of Wellington, Auckland Coll of Educ. *Career:* Teacher of English and Art History 1951–86; Barrister and Solicitor 1989–; Case-worker Wellington Community Law Centre 1990–; Part-time Lecturer in Law Wellington Polytechnic 1990; mem Indecent Publications Tribunal 1991. *Publications:* Novels: Rata 1965, The Empty Hills 1967, Death After School 1968, The Witnesses 1971, The Girl on the Beach 1973, No Trains at the Bay 1976; Play: Going Up, Mr Martin? 1965; Film: The Bedroom Window 1987. *Leisure interests:* art, theatre, politics, travel, gardening. *Address:* 72 Amritsar St, Khandallah, Wellington 4, New Zealand. *Telephone:* (4) 479-2621.

HOLLÁN, R. Susan, MD, D SC; Hungarian professor of haematology; b 26 Oct 1920, Budapest; d of Dr Henrik Hollán and Dr Malvin Hornik; m Dr György Révész; one s one d. *Education:* Univs of Pécs and Budapest. *Career:* Intern Rokus Hosp, Budapest 1945–50; Lecturer Univ Medical School, Budapest 1950–54; Research Fellow and Consultant Inst for Experimental Medical Research 1954–; Dir Nat Inst of Haematology and Blood Transfusion 1959–85, Dir-Gen 1985–90; Prof of Haematology Postgrad Medical School 1970–90; Corresp mem Hungarian Acad of Sciences 1973, mem Presidium 1976–84, mem 1982–; mem WHO Global AIDS Research Steering Cttee; Hon mem Polish Soc of Haematology, German Soc of Haematology, Purkinje Soc (Czech Repub), Turkish Soc of Haematology, All-Union Scientific Soc of Haematology and Blood Transfusion (fmr USSR); Foreign Corresp mem Soc de Biologie, Collège de France, Paris; Pres Int Soc of Haematology 1980–84; Vice-Pres Hungarian Soc of Haematology, Nobel Prize Award, Int Physicians Prevention of Nuclear War 1983–89; Hon mem of six nat societies of Haematology; Hon Pres Hungarian Soc of Human Genetics; mem WHO Expert Cttee on Biological Standardization in Haematology, Clinical and Immunological Work Cttee of Hungarian Acad of Sciences, Bd of Special Cttee for Clinical Sciences; Exec mem Hungarian Medical Research Council; mem Academia Europea; Ed-in-Chief Hungarian Medical Encyclopaedia and Haematologia (quarterly); mem HSWP Cen Cttee 1975–89; Hungarian Academic Award 1970; State Prize 1974; Socialist Hungary Medal. *Publications:* Basic Problems of Transfusion 1965, Haemoglobins and Haemoglobinopathies 1972, Genetics, Structure and Function of Blood Cells 1980, Management of Blood Transfusion Services 1990; over 300 papers in Hungarian and int medical journals. *Leisure interests:* fine arts, sport. *Address:* National Institute of Haematology and Blood Transfusion, 1113 Budapest, Daróczi ut 24, Hungary (Office); 1025 Budapest, Palánta u 10-12, Hungary (Home). *Telephone:* 372-4210 (Office); (1) 3260-619 (Home); *Fax:* (1) 372-4352; *E-mail:* hollan@ella.hu (Office).

HOLLAND, Agnieszka; Polish film and television director and screenwriter; b 28 Nov 1948, Warsaw; m Laco Adamik; one d. *Education:* FAMU film school (Prague). *Career:* Asst to Kryzstof Zanussi during filming of Illumination 1973; mem production group 'X', Warsaw 1972–81; Dir first TV film 1973; worked in theatre, Cracow; co-scripted Rough Treatment 1978; wrote screenplay for Yurke Bocayevicz's Anna; has made numerous TV documentaries. *Films worked on:* With Andrzej Wajda: A Love in Germany, Man of Marble, Man of Iron, The Orchestra Conductor, Korczak, Danton; *Films directed include:* Screen Test (jtly) 1977, Provincial Actors (Critics' Award, Cannes) 1979, The Fever 1980, The Lonely Woman 1981, Angry Harvest 1985, To Kill A Priest 1988, Europa, Europa (Best Foreign Movie of the Year, New York and Boston, MA, Film Critics and Nat Bd of Review, USA) 1992, Oliver, Oliver 1993, The Secret Garden 1993, Total Eclipse 1995, Washington Square 1997, The Third Miracle 1999. *Address:* Agence Nicole Cann, 1 rue Alfred de Vigny, 75008 Paris, France. *Telephone:* (1) 44-15-14-21.

HOLLAND, Dulcie Sybil, AM; Australian composer; b 5 Jan 1913, Sydney; d of William Berry and Gertrude Holland; m Alan R. Bellhouse 1940; one d one s. *Education:* Shirey Coll (NSW), Sydney Conservatorium of Music, Royal Coll of Music (London). *Career:* Pianist, accompanist, musicologist, teacher, conductor, choir dir, writer, freelance broadcaster; compositions include 40 scores for documentary films 1946–66; Music Examiner 1967–84; Hon Sec Fellowship of Australian Composers 1970–79; Eisteddfod judge, organist, Musical Dir St Luke's Church of England, NSW 1976–87; mem Business and Professional Women's Club (NSW); Fellow Trinity Coll of Music, London; Assoc of Music, Australia; Royal Coll of Music Blumenthal Scholarship 1938; Australian Broadcasting Corpn–APRA Composers' Competition Prizes 1933, 1944, 1953; Cobbett Prize for Chamber Music Composition 1938; Rotary Award 1989. *Publications include:* Musicianship (seven vols) 1974, More Picture Pieces 1979, Practice in Musicianship 1980, Five Story Pieces 1981, Harmony Step by Step 1981, Australian Poems Set to Music 1984, Master Your Theory (eight vols) 1984–88, Two-Part Writing 1987, Cello Pictures 1988, Learn the Piano with Dulcie Holland (three vols) 1989, Sight-Reading Step by Step 1989, Aural Training 1990, Extra Practice in Harmony 1991, Tunes for New Trumpeters 1994, Sax-Happy 1996. *Address:* 67 Kameruka Rd, Northbridge, NSW 2063, Australia. *Telephone:* (2) 9958 7629.

HOLLINGWORTH, Clare, OBE; British journalist; b 10 Oct 1911; d of John Albert and Daisy Gertrude Hollingworth; m 1st Vyvyan Derring Vandeleur Robinson 1936 (divorced 1951); m 2nd Geoffrey Spence Hoare 1952 (died 1966). *Education:* Girls' Collegiate School (Leicester), Grammar School (Ashby-de-la-Zouch), School of Slavonic Studies, London. *Career:* Mem staff League of Nations Union 1935–38; worked in Poland for Lord Mayor's Fund for Refugees from Czechoslovakia 1939; journalist Daily Telegraph Poland, Turkey, Egypt (covered desert campaigns, troubles in Persia and Iraq, Civil War in Greece and events in Palestine) 1941–50, foreign 'trouble-shooter' (covered war in Vietnam) 1967–73; Corresp Manchester Guardian (covered Algerian War and troubles in Egypt, Aden and Vietnam), based in Paris 1950–63, Defence Corresp 1963–67; Far East Corresp Sunday Telegraph, Hong Kong 1981–; Research Assoc Centre for Asian Studies, Univ of Hong Kong 1981–; Hon D LITT (Leicester) 1993; Journalist of the Year Award 1963; Hannan Swaffer Award 1963; James Cameron Award for Journalism 1994. *Publications include:* Poland's Three Weeks War 1940, There's a German Just Behind Me 1945, The Arabs and the West 1951, Mao and the Men Against Him 1984, Front Line 1990. *Leisure interests:* visiting second-hand furniture and bookshops, collecting modern pictures and Chinese porcelain, music. *Address:* 19 Dorset Square, London NW1 6QB, UK; 302 Ridley House, 2 Upper Albert Rd, Hong Kong Special Administrative Region, People's Republic of China. *Telephone:* (20) 7262-6923 (London); 2868-1838 (Hong Kong).

HOLLIS OF HEIGHAM, Baroness (Life Peer), cr 1990, of Heigham in the City of Norwich, **Patricia Lesley Hollis,** PC, D PHIL, FRHISTS; British lecturer in modern history and member of the House of Lords; b 24 May 1941; d of Lesley and Queenie Rosalyn Wells; m James Martin Hollis 1965; two s. *Education:* Univ of Cambridge, Univ of California (USA) and Columbia Univ (NY). *Career:* Harkness Fellow 1962–64; Nuffield Scholar 1964–67; Sr Lecturer in Modern History Univ of East Anglia 1967–, Dean School of English and American Studies 1988–90; mem House of Lords 1990–, Opposition Whip 1990–97, opposition frontbench spokesperson on social security, disability, local govt and housing; Parl Under-Sec of State, Dept of Social Security 1997; Vice-Pres Asscn of Metropolitan Authorities 1990–97, Environmental Health Officers 1992, Nat Fed of Housing Asscns 1993; mem Norwich City Council 1968–91 (Leader 1983–88), Norfolk Co Council 1981–85, Regional Econ Planning Council 1975–79, BBC Regional Advisory Cttee 1979–83, Press Council 1989–90; Sr Fellow in Modern History, Univ of East Anglia; Hon LL D (Norfolk) 1994; Hon D LITT (Anglia Polytechnic Univ). *Publications include:* The Pauper Press 1970, Class and Conflict 1815–50 1973, Pressure from Without 1974, Women in Public 1850–1900 1979, Robert Lowery, Radical and Chartist (jtly) 1979, Ladies Elect: Women in English Local Government 1865–1914 1987, Jennie Lee: A Life 1997. *Leisure interests:* boating, singing, domesticity. *Address:* House of Lords, London SW1A 0PW, UK. *Telephone:* (20) 7219-3000.

HOLMES À COURT, Janet, AO, B SC, D UNIV; Australian business executive; b 1943, Perth, WA; m Robert Holmes à Court (died 1990); three s one d. *Education:* Perth Modern School and Univ of Western Australia. *Career:* Fmrly science teacher; Exec Chair Heytesbury Holdings Pty Ltd (family-owned co which includes Heytesbury Pastoral Group, John Holland Group, Stoll Moss Theatres and Key Transport); Chair John Holland Group, Australian Children's Television Foundation, Black Swan Theatre Co, W Australian Symphony Orchestra; Dir Goodman Fielder Ltd 1998–; fmr Pro-Chancellor, Univ of W Australia; mem Bd Reserve Bank of Australia, Bd Man Festival of Perth. *Leisure interest:* the arts. *Address:* Heytesbury Pty Ltd, 27/140 St George's Terrace, Perth, WA 6000, Australia.

HOLT, Hon Mary, LL B; British circuit judge; d of Henry James and Sarah Holt. *Education:* Girton Coll, Cambridge. *Career:* Called to the Bar, Gray's Inn 1949; Circuit Judge Northern Circuit 1977–95; mem Cons Nat Exec Council 1969–72, Woman's Nat Advisory Cttee 1969–70, Rep Cen Council 1969–71; MP (Cons) for Preston N 1970–74; Freedom of Cities of Dallas and Denton (TX, USA) 1987; Badge of Honour British Red Cross Soc. *Publication:* Benas and Essenhigh's Precedents of Pleading (2nd edn) 1956. *Leisure interest:* walking. *Address:* c/o The Session House, Preston, Lancashire, UK.

HOLT, Nancy Louise, BS; American artist; b 5 April 1938, Worcester, MA; d of Ernest Milton and E. Louise (née Jellicoe) Holt; m Robert I. Smithson 1963 (died 1973). *Education:* Tufts Univ (Medford, MA). *Career:* Visiting artist Univ of Rhode Island, Univ of Montana; Lecturer Princeton Univ, NJ; solo exhibitions include Univ of Montana Art Gallery 1972, Univ of Rhode Island Art Center, Kingston 1972, LoGiudice Gallery, New York 1973, Bykert Gallery, New York 1974, Walter Kelly Gallery, Chicago, IL 1974, Franklin Furnace, New York 1977, Whitney Museum Young American Film-makers Series, New York 1977, John Weber Gallery, New York 1979, 1982, 1984, 1986, Flow Ace Gallery, Los Angeles 1985; sculpture comms include Wild Spot (Wellesley Coll, MA) 1979–80, Star-Crossed (Miami Univ, OH) 1979–81, Dark Star Park (Arlington, VA) 1979–84, Inside Out (Washington, DC) 1980, Annual Ring (Saginaw, MI) 1981, Time Span (Laguna Gloria Art Museum, Austin, TX) 1981, Catch Basin (Toronto, ON, Canada) 1982, Sole Source (Dublin) 1983, Waterwork (Gallaudet Coll, Washington, DC) 1984, End of the Line/West Rock (S Connecticut State Univ, New Haven) 1985, Pipeline and Starfire (Anchorage, AK) 1986, Astral Grating (New York) 1987, Spinwinder (SE Massachusetts Univ) 1991; Nat Endowment for the Arts grants 1975, 1978, 1983, 1986, 1988, Beard's Fund Inc grant 1977; Guggenheim Fellow 1978. *Publications:* Ransacked 1980, Time Outs 1985; *Films include:* Swamp 1971, Pine Barrens 1975, Sun Tunnels 1978; *Videos include:* Underscan 1974, Revolve 1977, Art in the Public Eye 1988. *Telephone:* (212) 929-1947; *Fax:* (212) 929-1533.

HOLT, Thelma, CBE; British theatrical producer; b 4 Jan 1932, Barton-on-Orwell; d of David Holt and Ellen Finagh Doyle; m 1st Patrick Graucob (divorced 1968); m 2nd David Pressman 1969 (divorced 1970). *Education:* St Ann's School (Lytham, St Anne's) and Royal Acad of Dramatic Art (London). *Career:* Began career as actress 1953; Co-Founder (with Charles Marowitz) Open Space Theatre 1968; Dir Round House Theatre 1968; Exec Producer Theatre of Comedy 1983; Head of Touring and Commercial Exploitation, Royal Nat Theatre 1985 (Laurence Olivier Award for Outstanding Achievement 1987); Exec Producer Peter Hall Co 1989; f Thelma Holt Ltd 1990; Dir Theatre Investment Fund Ltd; Vice-Pres Citizen's Theatre (Glasgow); Cameron Mackintosh Prof of Contemporary Theatre and Fellow St Catherine's Coll (Oxford) 1998; Patron Oxford Univ Dramatic Soc 2001; Dir Nat Youth Music Theatre 2001; mem Arts Council of England 1993–98, Chair Drama Advisory Panel 1994–98, Council Royal Acad of Dramatic Art; Dr hc (Middx), Hon MA (Open Univ). *Productions:* Three Sisters, Tango at the End of Winter, Electra, Hamlet, Les Atrides, Le Baruffe Chiozzotte, Six Characters in Search of an Author, The Tempest, Medea, Much Ado about Nothing, Peer Gynt, The Clandestine Marriage, The Seagull, A Midsummer Night's Dream, Antony and Cleopatra, The Glass Menagerie, Observe the Sons of Ulster Marching Towards the Somme, A Doll's House, The Maids, Les Fausses Confidences, Oh Les Beaux Jours, Shintoku-Maru, The Relapse, Macbeth, King Lear, Miss Julie, Semi-Monde, Sotoba

Komachi, Yoroboshi. *Leisure interest:* bargain-hunting at antique fairs. *Address:* 11 Aldwych, London WC2B 4DG, UK. *Telephone:* (20) 7379-0438; *Fax:* (20) 7836-9832; *E-mail:* thelma@dircon.co.uk.

HOLZER, Jenny, MFA; American artist; b 29 July 1950, Gallipolis, OH; d of Richard Vornholt and Virginia Beasley Holzer; m Michael Andrew Glier 1984; one d. *Education:* Ohio Univ, Rhode Island School of Design and Whitney Museum of American Art Ind Study Program. *Career:* Became working artist, New York 1977; special projects and comms 1978– include 'Green Table', Univ of Calif, San Diego 1993, 'Lustmord', Süddeutsche Zeitung Magazin, no 46, Germany, 'Black Garden', Nordhorn, Germany 1994, 'Allentown Benches', Allentown, PA 1995, 'Erlauf Peace Monument', Erlauf, Austria 1995, installation at Schiphol Airport, Amsterdam, Netherlands 1995, Biennale di Firenze, Florence, Italy 1996, installation for Hamburger Kunsthalle, Hamburg, Germany 1996, perm installation at Guggenheim Museum, Bilbao, Literaturhaus Munich, Germany, Oskar Maria Graf Memorial 1997, Kunsthalle Zürich, Switzerland; Gallery Artist, Barbara Gladstone Gallery 1983–; Fellow American Acad, Berlin 2000; Dr hc (Ohio) 1994; Blair Prize, Art Inst of Chicago; Leone d'Oro, 44th Venice Biennale 1990; Gold Medals for Title and Design, Art Directors of Germany 1993; Silver Medal for Title and Editorial Design, Art Directors' Club of Europe 1993; Skowhegan Medal for Installation 1994, Crystal Award for outstanding contrib to cross-cultural understanding, World Econ Forum, Switzerland 1996. *Art Exhibitions:* Solo exhibitions include: Rüdiger Schöttle Gallery, Munich, Germany 1980, Barbara Gladstone Gallery, New York 1983, Dallas Museum of Art, Texas 1984, Des Moines Art Center, Iowa 1986, Am Hof, Vienna, Austria 1986, Rhona Hoffman Gallery, Chicago 1987, Contemporary Arts Museum, Houston 1987, Brooklyn Museum, New York 1988, American Pavilion, 44th Venice Biennale, Italy 1990, Art Tower Mito, Japan 1994, Bergen Museum of Art, Norway 1994, Williams Coll Museum of Art, Williamstown, MA 1995, Kunstmuseum Kartause Ittingen, Warth, Switzerland 1996, Index Gallery, Osaka, Japan 1997, Yvon Lambert Gallery, Paris 1998, Inst Cultural Itau, São Paulo 1998, Centro Cultural Bancodo Brasil, Rio de Janeiro 1999; Group exhibitions include: Museum of Modern Art, New York 1988, 1990, 1996, Guggenheim Museum, New York 1996, Centre Pompidou, Paris, France 1996, Nat Gallery Australia, Canberra 1998, Rhona Hofman Gallery, USA 1998, Oslo Museum of Contemporary Art 2000; *Publications:* A Little Knowledge 1979, Black Book 1980, Eating Through Living 1981, Truisms and Essays 1983. *Leisure interests:* reading, riding. *Address:* 80 Hewitts Rd, Hoosick Falls, NY 12090, USA. *Telephone:* (518) 686-9323 (Office); *Fax:* (518) 686-9019 (Office).

HOME, Anna Margaret, OBE, MA; British broadcasting executive; b 13 Jan 1938; d of James Douglas and Janet Mary (née Wheeler) Home. *Education:* Convent of Our Lady (St Leonards-on-Sea, Sussex) and St Anne's Coll (Oxford). *Career:* Radio Studio Man BBC 1960–64, Research Asst, Dir and Producer Children's TV 1966–70, Exec Producer Children's Drama Unit 1970–81; Controller of Programmes TVS (Southern regional BBC station), then Deputy Dir of Programmes 1981–86; Head of Children's Programmes BBC TV 1986–98; Chair Second World Summit on TV for Children, London 1998; Chief Exec Children's Film and TV Foundation 1998–; Fellow of Royal Television Soc 1987; Pye TV Award for Distinguished Services to Children's TV 1985; Eleanor Farjeon Award for Services to Children's Literature 1989; Lifetime Achievement Award, Women in Film and TV 1996; BAFTA Special Award for Lifetime Achievement in Childrens Programmes 1997. *TV series include:* Lizzie Dripping, Bagthorpe Saga, Moon Stallion, Grange Hill; *Publication:* Into the Box of Delights: A History of Children's Television 1993. *Leisure interests:* theatre, gardening, literature, travel. *Address:* 3 Liberia Rd, London N5 1JP, UK.

HOMES, Amy M.; American writer; b 1962, Chevy Chase, MD. *Career:* Judge Nat Book Award, Fiction 2000, NY Public Library Award 2001; mem Bd of Dirs Yaddo; numerous awards including Fellowships from The Center for Scholars and Writers, NY Public Library, Guggenheim Foundation, Nat Endowment for the Arts and NY Foundation for the Arts; Benjamin Franklin Award 2000. *Publications:* Jack (Deutscher Jugendliteraturpreis) 1989, The Safety of Objects 1990, In a Country of Mothers 1993, The End of Alice 1995, Appendix A 1995, Music for Torching 1999. *Address:* c/o Anchor Books, Transworld Publishers, 61 Uxbridge Rd, London W5, UK.

HONECKER, Margot; German politician; b (Margot Feist) 17 April 1927, Halle; m Erich Honecker 1953 (deceased); one d. *Career:* Co-Founder Anti-Fascist Youth Cttee, Halle 1945; mem CP 1945–89; Sec Freie Deutsche Jugend (FDJ) Cttee, Sachsen-Anhalt; Chair Young Pioneers and Sec Cen Council FDJ 1949–53; mem Volkskammer 1949–54, 1967–89; mem Cen Cttee Socialist Unity Party (SED) 1963–89; univ training in USSR 1953–54; Head Teacher Training Dept, Ministry of Educ 1955–58, Deputy Minister of Educ 1958–63, Minister of Educ 1963–89; with husband in Moscow 1991, sought asylum in Chilean Embassy, Moscow Dec 1991; left Embassy for Chile July 1992; mem Acad of Pedagogical Sciences; Dr hc; Karl-Marx-Orden, Vaterländischer Verdienstorden in Gold, Held der Arbeit, and other decorations. *Publication:* On Educational Policy and Pedagogics in the German Democratic Republic 1986. *Address:* c/o Rheinisch-Westfälische Akademie der Wissenschaften, Philosophical Section, Palmenstr 16, 4000 Düsseldorf, Germany.

HONEYMAN, Janice Lynne; South African actress, director and writer; b 14 Jan 1949, Cape Town; d of Frank Gordon and Marie Evelyn Honeyman; m Robin Hornibrook 1977. *Education:* Univ of Cape Town. *Career:* Dir and actress Market Theatre Co and Performing Arts Council of Transvaal 1970–; Dir Dogge's Troupe-Interaction, London 1977–78; Founder-mem Market Theatre Co, Resident Dir 1984–85; freelance Dir RSC 1988–89; Deputy Exec Dir (Artistic) Johannesburg Civic Theatre 1993–, Artistic Dir 2000–; Assoc Artist PACT; Trustee Market Theatre Foundation 1985–, Foundation for Equality 1993–2000; Ernest Oppenheimer Award for Resident Dir, Market Theatre; SA Young Artists Award; Breytenbach Epathalon, A. A. Vita Award for directing; Gallo Award for Best Performance, Johnnie Walker Black Label Achievers. *Publications:* This is for Keeps (jtly) 1984, Knickerbocker Knockabout 1988. *Leisure interests:* reading, opera, swimming, snorkelling, travelling. *Address:* 8A Seymour St, Westdene, Johannesburg 2092, South Africa. *Telephone:* (11) 403 3408 (Office); (11) 477 7626 (Home); *Fax:* (11) 403 3412.

HOOG, Simone; French curator; b 21 Feb 1934, Paris; d of René and Elise Virault; m Michel Hoog 1961; one s two d. *Education:* Univ of Paris (Sorbonne) and Ecole du Louvre. *Career:* Curator Musée Nat des Châteaux de Versailles et du Trianon 1960–86, Curator-in-Chief 1986–; Curator-Gen of Nat Heritage 1993; Chevalier de l'Ordre Nat du Mérite; Chevalier des Arts et des Lettres; Chevalier de l'Ordre Souverain (Malta). *Publications:* La manière de montrer les jardins de Versailles 1982, L'iconographie des Bourbon 1985, Le Bernin, Louis XIV, une statue déplacée 1989, Catalogue des sculptures du Château de Versailles 1993. *Leisure interests:* puzzles, cinema, swimming. *Address:* Musée National du Château de Versailles, 78000 Versailles, France.

HOOJA, Usha Rani, MA; Indian sculptor; b 18 May 1923, Delhi; d of Samuel and Grace Joseph; m Bhupender Hooja 1950; one s one d. *Education:* St Stephen's Coll (Delhi) and Polytechnic of Central London (fmrly Regent St Polytechnic). *Career:* Freelance sculptor specializing in monumental outdoor compositions 1955–, welded scrap metal 1975–, cast bronze miniatures 1985–; works situated in Bombay, Delhi, Jaipur, Jodhpur, Kota, Udaipur and abroad in Cambridge, Bath and Derby (UK), Fiji, Mauritius, Sweden and Washington (DC, USA); works include Power and Industry 1955, police memorial 1963, three compositions for hospitals 1972, 1975, 1979, three labour monuments 1973, 1978, 1981, atomic power monument 1979; Fellow Rajasthan Lalit Kala Akademi (Nat Acad of Art) 1991; Rajasthan Shree 1983; Ma Harana Mewar Award 1985; Veteran Arists (AIFACS) 1988; Nat Award for Sculpture (FIE Foundation) 1993. *Publication:* Songs and Sculpture (poems) 1975. *Leisure interests:* music, reading, poetry, needlework, gardening, cookery, travel. *Address:* 11 Uniara Garden, Jaipur 302 004, India. *Telephone:* (141) 622005.

HOOKER, Morna Dorothy, DD, PH D; British professor of divinity; b 19 May 1931, Beddington, Surrey; d of Percy Francis and Lily (née Riley) Hooker; m Rev Dr W. David Stacey 1978 (died 1993); two step-d one step-s. *Education:* Univs of Bristol and Manchester. *Career:* Research Fellow Univ of Durham 1959–61; Lecturer in New Testament Studies King's Coll, London 1961–70; Visiting Prof McGill Univ, Montréal, Canada 1968; Lecturer in Theology Univ of Oxford 1970–76, Keble Coll, Oxford 1972–76; Visiting Fellow Clare Hall, Cambridge 1974; Lady Margaret's Prof of Divinity, Univ of Cambridge

1976–, Fellow Robinson Coll, Cambridge 1977–; Visiting Prof Duke Univ, NC, USA 1987, 1989; Co-Ed Journal of Theological Studies 1985–; Fellow King's Coll, London 1979; Fellow Linacre Coll, Oxford 1970–76, Hon Fellow 1980; Fellow Westminster Coll, Oxford 1996–; Pres Studiorum Novi Testamenti Societas (SNTS) 1988–89; Hon D LITT (Bristol) 1994; Hon DD (Edinburgh) 1997. *Publications:* Jesus and the Servant 1959, The Son of Man in Mark 1967, What About the New Testament? (co-ed) 1975, Pauline Pieces 1979, Studying the New Testament 1979, Paul and Paulinism (co-ed) 1982, The Message of Mark 1983, Continuity and Discontinuity 1986, From Adam to Christ 1990, A Commentary on Mark 1991, Not Ashamed of the Gospel 1994, The Signs of a Prophet 1997, Beginnings: Keys that Open the Gospels 1997. *Leisure interests:* molinology, walking, music. *Address:* Robinson College, Cambridge CB3 9AN, UK. *Telephone:* (1223) 339149; *Fax:* (1223) 351794.

HOON, Premila, B SC, MBA; British banking executive; b 21 Oct 1953, Bombay (now Mumbai), India; m (divorced); one s. *Education:* St Joseph's Coll (Bangalore, India) and Xavier Inst (Jamshedpur, India). *Career:* Fmrly mem staff Chemco Financial Services Ltd, Head of Credit Manufacturer's Hanover Finance Ltd; Joined Guiness Mahon, Dir and Head Media and Entertainment Finance Activities 1986–98; Head of Media Project and Sectoral Finance Group, Société Générale 1998–; has financed or arranged finance for numerous films including Howard's End, Scandal, My Left Foot, Green Card, The Crying Game, Richard III, Surviving Picasso; mem Advisory Cttee on Film and Finance, Dept of Nat Heritage, Gov BFI 1990–96; Women in Film Business Award, Carlton TV 1995. *Leisure interests:* travel, reading. *Address:* c/o Société Générale, 41 Tower Hill, London EC3N 4HA, UK; 1 Ailsa Rd, St Margarets, Twickenham TW1 1QJ, UK. *Telephone:* (20) 7676-6000; (20) 7865-1030 (Direct Line); *Fax:* (20) 7667-2489; *Internet:* www .socgen.com.

HOOPER, Baroness (Life Peer), cr 1985, of Liverpool and of St James's in the City of Westminster, **Gloria Dorothy Hooper,** LL B; British politician; b 25 May 1939, Southampton; d of the late Frederick and Frances (née Maloney) Hooper. *Education:* Univ of Southampton and Univ Central (Quito, Ecuador). *Career:* Solicitor of Supreme Court 1973–; Partner Taylor Garrett 1974–84; MEP for Liverpool 1979–84, Vice-Chair Cttee on Environment, Public Health and Consumer Protection, Deputy Whip European Democrat Group; mem House of Lords 1985–, Govt Whip 1985–87; Parl Under-Sec of State, Dept of Educ and Science 1987–88, Dept of Energy 1988–89, Dept of Health 1989–92; Deputy Speaker House of Lords 1993–; mem Parl Del to Council of Europe, Western European Union 1992–97; Gov Centre for Global Energy Studies, Royal Ballet, English Speaking Union; Fellow Royal Geographical Soc, Industry and Parl Trust, Royal Soc of Arts; Pres Canning House 1997–. *Publications:* Cases on Company Law 1967, Law of International Trade 1968. *Leisure interests:* theatre, travel, walking. *Address:* House of Lords, Westminster, London SW1A 0PW, UK. *Telephone:* (20) 7219-3000.

HOPE, Emma; British fashion designer; b 1962, Southwick, Hants. *Education:* Cordwainers Coll (London). *Career:* Launched first shoe collection 1985; opened first shop in Islington (London) 1986; three London shops by 2001; has designed shoe collections for several well-known designers; launched first handbag collection 1997; five Design Council Awards; Martini Style Award 1988. *Address:* 53 Sloane Square, London SW1, UK.

HOPE-CROSBY, Polly, FRSA; British artist, designer, writer and photographer; b 21 June 1933, Colchester; d of Gen Hugh and Lady Stockwell; m 1st John Hope 1953; one s; m 2nd Theo Crosby 1990. *Education:* Heatherley, Chelsea and Slade Schools of Art. *Career:* Trained as a classical ballet dancer; has completed various commissions including pointillist mural for Barbican Centre, London, four life-size terracotta figures for Shakespeare's Globe Theatre; collaborated on bldg Shakespeare's Globe Theatre, vestments for Wakefield Cathedral 1999–2000 and many other public works; works with several composers writing librettos; has composed Greek song cycles; has written film scripts, made videos, films and animated films. *Art exhibitions include:* Spaces and Places, London, Italy, Cyprus 1998, Dhaka, Bangladesh 2000, South Bank Art Centre, London, Los Angeles, California and many other shows; *Animated film:* Memories, Memories 1995; *Plays:*

Freedom and Death 1992, General Anghie 1993; *Music:* Productions include: Il Giardino degli Uccelli (1 act opera, music by Quentin Thomas) 1999, Death of Lord Byron (1 act opera, music by Quentin Thomas) 2000, Bran's Singing Head (music by Geoffrey Alvarez) 1996; *Publications:* Here Away From it All 1969, Us Lot 1970, The Immaculate Misconception 1972, A Baker's Dozen of Greek Folk Songs 1994, Songs My Parrot Taught Me 1994, Egyptian Love Songs and Songs for Aphrodite 1998, Il Giardino degli Uccelli 1999. *Leisure interests:* music, sitting in the sun and sleeping. *Address:* 5A & B Heneage St, Spitalfields, London EI 5LU, UK. *Telephone:* (20) 7247-3450; *Fax:* (20) 7247-3450; *E-mail:* polly@doxy.demon.co.uk; *Internet:* www .hopeart.com.

HOPKIRK, Joyce, FRSA; British journalist and editor; b 2 March, Newcastle upon Tyne; d of Walter and Veronica (née Keelan) Nicholson; m 1st Peter Hopkirk 1962; one d; m 2nd William James Lear 1974; one s. *Education:* La Sagesse Convent and Middle St Secondary School (Newcastle upon Tyne). *Career:* Reporter Gateshead Post 1955; Founder Ed Majorcan News 1959; Reporter Daily Sketch 1960; Royal Reporter Daily Express 1961; Ed Fashion magazine 1967; Women's Ed Sun newspaper 1967; Launch Ed Cosmopolitan magazine 1971–72; Asst Ed Daily Mirror 1973–78, Asst Ed Sunday Mirror 1985; Women's Ed Sunday Times 1982; Editorial Dir Elle magazine 1984; Ed-in-Chief She magazine 1986–89; currently freelance journalist; Dir Editors Unlimited 1990–; Ed of the Year 1972; Women's Magazines Ed of the Year 1988. *Publications:* Successful Slimming 1976, Successful Slimming Cookbook 1978, Splash (jtly) 1995, Best of Enemies 1996; *Video cassette:* Successful Slimming 1978. *Leisure interests:* conversation, gardening, hockey, skiing, boating. *Address:* Gadespring, 109 Piccotts End, Hemel Hempstead, Herts HP1 3AT, UK. *Telephone:* (1442) 245608; *Fax:* (1442) 64868.

HOPPEN, Kelly; British interior designer, author and retailer; b 28 July 1959, Johannesburg; d of Stephanie Hoppen; m Ed Miller; two step-d. *Career:* Interior design in the field of interior accessories, rugs, woven floor coverings, paints and blinds; launched first fabric collection 1998; launched paint collection for Fired Earth 1998; Andrew Martin Interior Designer of the Year Award 1996. *Projects include:* First Class Cabins for British Airways, 112 Hotel, London and corp office space and pvt homes; *Publications:* Table Chic 1997, East Meets West 1997, In Touch 1999, Close Up 2001. *Leisure interests:* travel, music, art. *Address:* 2 Munden St, London W14, UK. *Telephone:* (20) 7471-3364; *Fax:* (20) 7471-3351; *E-mail:* kelly@kellyhoppen.com; *Internet:* www .kellyhoppen.com.

HORLICK, Nicola Karina Christina, BA; British banking executive; b 12 Dec 1960, Nottingham; d of Michael Robert Dudley Gayford and Suzanna Christina Victoria Czyzewska; m Timothy Piers Horlick 1984; three d one s. *Education:* Cheltenham Ladies' Coll, Birkenhead High School, Phillips Exeter Acad (USA) and Balliol Coll (Oxford). *Career:* Mem staff Mercury Asset Man 1983–91; joined Morgan Grenfell Asset Man 1991, Man Dir Morgan Grenfell Investment Man 1992, Dir Morgan Grenfell Asset Man 1992, Dir Morgan Grenfell Property Asset Man 1996; Fund Man SG Asset Man. *Publication:* Can You Have it All? 1998. *Leisure interests:* opera, theatre, literature, skiing. *Address:* SG Asset Management, 100 Ludgate Hill, London EC4M 7NL, UK. *Internet:* www.sgam.co.uk.

HORNE, Marilyn; American opera singer (mezzo-soprano); b 16 Jan 1934, Bradford, PA; d of Bentz and Berneice Horne; m Henry Lewis (divorced); one d; m 2nd Nicola Zaccaria. *Education:* Univ of Southern California (under William Vennard). *Career:* Performed with several German opera cos in Europe 1956; debut San Francisco Opera 1960; has since appeared at Covent Garden, London, Chicago Lyric Opera, La Scala, Milan, Italy, Metropolitan Opera, New York; performed at inauguration of US President Clinton 1993; many recordings; numerous hon doctorates; Nat Medal of Arts 1992, Kennedy Center Honor 1995, Musical American Musician of the Year 1995. *Operas include:* Don Carlo, Wozzeck, Norma, Anna Bolena, Aida, Carmen, Barbiere di Siviglia, Le Prophète, Mignon, L'Italiana in Algeri, I Capuletti ed i Montecchi, Tancredi, Orlando Furioso. *Leisure interests:* needlepoint, swimming, reading, sightseeing. *Address:* c/o Colombia Artists Management Inc, 165 W 57th St, New York, NY 10019, USA.

HORNER, Matina Souretis, PH D; American psychologist, former college president and business executive; b 28 July 1939, Boston, MA; d of Demetre John and Christine Souretis; m Joseph L. Horner 1961; two s one d. *Education:* Bryn Mawr Coll (PA) and Univ of Michigan. *Career:* Teaching Fellow Univ of Michigan, Ann Arbor 1962–66, Lecturer in Motivation Personality 1968–69; Lecturer on Social Relations Harvard Univ, MA 1969–70, Asst Prof of Clinical Psychology 1970–72, Consultant Univ Health Services 1971–89, Assoc Prof of Psychology 1972–89; Pres Radcliffe Coll, MA 1972–89, Pres Emer 1989–; Exec Vice-Pres TIAA-CREF, NY 1989–; mem Advisory Council Nat Science Foundation 1977–87, Chair 1980–86; mem Bd Dirs Women's Research and Educ Inst 1979– (Chair Research Comm 1982–), Council for Financial Aid to Educ 1985–89, Revson Foundation 1986–92 (Chair 1992–97), Beth Israel Hosp 1989–95; Trustee Massachusetts Gen Hosp, Inst of Health Professions 1988–; mem Advisory Cttee Women's Leadership Conf on Nat Security 1982–; mem Council on Foreign Relations 1984–; Roger Baldwin Award Massachusetts Civil Liberties Union Foundation 1982; Citation of Merit, Nat Conf of Christians and Jews, Northeast Region 1982; Career Contribution Award, Massachusetts Psychology Asscn 1987; Distinguished Bostonian Award 1990; Ellis Island Medal 1990.

HORROCKS, Jane; British actress; b 18 Jan 1964, Lancs; d of John and Barbara Horrocks; partner Nick Vivian; one s one d. *Education:* Royal Acad of Dramatic Art. *Films:* The Dressmaker 1989, Life is Sweet 1991 (Best Supporting Actress, LA Critics Award 1992), Little Voice 1998, Born Romantic 2001; *Plays include:* The Rise and Fall of Little Voice; TV: (film) Hunting Venus; (series) Red Dwarf, Absolutely Fabulous 1992–94, The Flint Street Nativity 1999. *Address:* c/o PFD, Drury House, 34–43 Russell St, London WC2B 5HA, UK. *Telephone:* (20) 7344-1010.

HOSPITAL, Janette Turner, MA; Australian writer; b 12 Nov 1942, Melbourne; d of Adrian C. and Elsie (née Morgan) Turner; m Clifford G. Hospital 1965; one s one d. *Education:* Univ of Queensland (Australia) and Queen's Univ (Kingston, ON, Canada). *Career:* Full-time writer of novels and short stories, resident in Australia, Canada and USA 1982–; teacher Queensland 1963–66; Librarian Harvard Univ, MA, USA 1967–71; Lecturer in English St Lawrence Coll, ON, Canada 1971–82, and in Fed men's prisons; Writer-in-Residence and Lecturer MIT, USA 1985–86, 1987, 1989; Writer-in-Residence Univ of Ottawa, Canada 1987, Univ of Sydney 1989, La Trobe Univ, Melbourne 1990–93, Queen's Univ at Herstmonceux Castle, UK 1994; Visiting Prof of Writing Univ of Boston, MA, USA 1991; Adjunct Prof in English Univ of Ottawa 1990–; Visiting Fellow and Writer-in-Residence Univ of E Anglia 1996; O'Connor Chair in Literature, Colgate Univ, Hamilton, NY 1999–; Dr hc Griffith Univ (Queensland) 1995; Atlantic First Award, USA 1978; Foundation for the Advancement of Canadian Letters First Prize for magazine fiction 1982; named among Canada's Best Ten Younger Writers 1986; Nat Magazine Awards Gold Medal for travel writing, Canada 1991. *Publications include:* Novels: The Ivory Swing (Seal First Novel Award) 1982, The Tiger in the Tiger Pit 1983, Borderline 1985, Charades 1988, A Very Proper Death (as Alex Juniper) 1991, The Last Magician 1992, Oyster 1996; Short story collections: Dislocations (Fellowship of Australian Writers Fiction Award and Canadian Asscn for the Blind Torgi Award 1988) 1986, Isobars 1990, Collected Stories 1995; numerous articles. *Leisure interests:* hiking, mountain climbing, music. *Address:* c/o Jill Hickson, POB 271, Woollahra, Sydney, NSW 2025, Australia; c/o Mic Cheetham, 11–12 Dover St, London W1X 3PH, UK; c/o Elaine Markson, 44 Greenwich Ave, New York, NY 10011, USA.

HOSSACK, Rebecca, BA, BLL; Australian gallery owner; b 15 Oct 1955, Melbourne; d of Joan John and Donald Hossack; m Matthew Henry Sturgis 1991. *Education:* Geelong Grammar School (Corio), ANU and Melbourne Univ. *Career:* Arrived London, UK 1980; opened Rebecca Hossack Gallery 1988, Charlotte St Gallery 2000; Cultural Attaché, Australian High Comm in London 1994–97; contrib to many journals and newspapers on subject of aboriginal and Australian art including The Independent, The Telegraph, The Express, Art Review and Oxford Dictionary of Art; Business Sponsorship of the Arts 1984. *Leisure interest:* aboriginal art. *Address:* Rebecca Hossack Gallery, 35 Windmill St, London W1T 2JS, UK. *Telephone:* (20) 7436-4899; *Fax:* (20) 7323-3182; *E-mail:* rebecca@r-h-g.co.uk; *Internet:* www.r-h-g.co.uk.

HOSSAIN, Hameeda, PH D; Bangladeshi women's organization official and historian; b 28 Dec 1936, Hyderabad, Sind; d of the late Abdulla Akhund and of Marian Shaikh; m Kamal Hossain 1964; two d. *Education:* Wellesley Coll (MA, USA) and St Anthony's Coll (Oxford, UK). *Career:* Research Asst Inst of Int Affairs, Karachi (Pakistan) 1958–61; Ed at Oxford Univ Press, Karachi and Dhaka 1962–64, 1972–74; involved in devt of women's employment and craft devt 1967–75, 1981–84; Ed Forum (political weekly), Dhaka 1969–71, banned by the military 1971; Founder Karika (craft co-operative) 1974; Vice-Pres Nat Crafts Council 1992; Founder-mem Ain O Salish Kendra (legal aid org) 1986; researched the history of women's involvement in political movts; Del to UN Decade for Women confs, Mexico 1975, Nairobi (Kenya) 1985; mem Steering Cttee DAWN (third world women's network) 1985–. *Publications:* Company Weavers of Bengal 1988, No Better Options? Industrial Women Workers of Bangladesh (jtly) 1990, From Crisis to Development, Coping with Disasters in Bangladesh (co-ed) 1992; contribs to historical journals. *Leisure interests:* reading, gardening, photography. *Address:* 7C New Bailey Rd, Dhaka 1000, Bangladesh. *Telephone:* (2) 407086; *Fax:* (2) 863883.

HÖTTGER, Ursula; German painter. *Career:* Solo exhibitions in Germany, Switzerland, Italy, USA and UK; specializes in portraits, landscapes and drawings; works acquired by collections including Royal Palace (Sweden) 1982, Victoria and Albert Museum (London) 1988, Guildhall (Windsor, UK) 1988, Univ of Liverpool Art Collection (UK) 1990, Guildhall (Winchester, UK) 1995; portraits include Hermann Hesse 1961, 1978, Marcel Marceau 1980, Karl Carstens 1984, Queen Elizabeth the Queen Mother 1988, Alfred Brendel 1989, Queen Elizabeth 1992, Yehudi Menuhin 1995. *Address:* Im Rottfeld 5, 40239 Düsseldorf, Germany.

HOUBEN, Francine M. J., M SC; Netherlands architect; b 2 July 1955, Sittard; m; two d one s. *Education:* Technical Univ Delft (Netherlands). *Career:* Graduated in Architecture 1984; Founder Mecanoo Architecten bv, Delft; Visiting Prof in Germany, Philadelphia Univ (USA), Univ of Calgary (Canada) and the Berlage Inst, Amsterdam; currently Prof of Aesthetics of Mobility, Faculty of Architecture, Delft Univ of Tech and at the Università della Svizzera Italiana, Accademia di Architettura, Mendrisio (Switzerland); numerous awards include Rotterdam-Maaskant Prize for Young Architects 1987, Nieuwe Maas Prize for Housing Hillekop, Rotterdam 1990, Berlagevlag Award for Offices for Gravura Lithographers, The Hague 1993, Jhr Victor de Stuerspenning for Herdenkingsplein, Maastricht 1994, Scholenbouwprijs 1996, Nationale Staalprijs for the Library of the Tech Univ of Delft 1998, 4° Bienal Internacional de Arquitectura Award, São Paolo, Brazil 2000, Corus Construction Award for the Millennium for the Library of the Tech Univ of Delft 2000, Bouwkwaliteitsprijs, Rotterdam 2000, TECU Architecture Award for the National Museum of Heritage, Arnhem 2001. *Publications include:* Maliebaan, een huis om in te werken 2000, Composition, Contrast, Complexity 2001. *Address:* Mecanoo Architecten bv, Oude Delft 203, 2611 HD Delft, Netherlands. *Telephone:* (15) 2798100; *Fax:* (15) 2798111; *E-mail:* info@mecanoo.nl; *Internet:* www.mecanoo.nl.

HOURS-MIEDAN, Magdeleine; French curator and historian; b 5 Aug 1913, Paris; d of Lucien and Suzanne (née Ricard) Miedan; m Jacques Hours 1935; three s. *Education:* Cours Désir (Paris), Ecole du Louvre (Paris), Ecole des Hautes Etudes (Paris), Univ of Paris (Sorbonne). *Career:* Attaché Oriental Antiquities Louvre museum, Paris 1936–46, Head of Lab 1946–85, Curator 1960–68, Head Curator 1968; three archaeological excavations, Carthage 1945–47; Producer TV programmes on history of art and conservation Office de Radiodiffusion-Télévision Française (ORTF) 1958–; Head of Research CNRS 1960; Insp-Gen of French Museums 1980; Officier de la Légion d'Honneur 1972; Commdr de l'Ordre Nat du Mérite; Commdr des Arts et des Lettres 1978. *Publications:* Les représentations figurées sur les stèles de Carthage (2nd edn) 1980, A la découverte de la peinture par les méthodes physiques 1958, Les secrets des chefs-d'œuvre 1964, Corot 1968, L'analyse scientifique des peintures, Une vie au Louvre (Prix Alice Louis-Barthou de l'Acad Française) 1987; *TV productions include:* Les secrets des chefs-d'œuvre 1958–64, Le musée imaginaire 1963, Trésors dans la ville 1964–65, Sur les chemins de l'invisible 1965.

Leisure interest: writing. *Address:* 10 bis rue du Pré-aux-Clercs, 75007 Paris, France; Le grand village à Courcoury, 17100, France. *Telephone:* (1) 45-48-75-35.

HOUSE, Karen Elliott; American financial executive and journalist; b 7 Dec 1947, Matador, TX; d of Ted and Bailey Elliott; m 1st Arthur House 1975 (divorced 1983); m 2nd Peter Xann 1984; one d one s. *Education:* Univ of Texas and Harvard Univ. *Career:* Educ Reporter Dallas Morning News 1970–71, with Washington bureau 1971–74; Regulatory Corresp Wall Street Journal 1974–75, Energy and Agric Corresp 1975–78, Diplomatic Corresp 1978–84, Foreign Ed 1984–89; Vice-Pres Dow Jones Int Group 1989–95, Pres 1995–; Dir German-American Council 1988–; Trustee Boston Univ (MA); Edward Weintal Award (Georgetown Univ) 1980–81; Fellow Nat Acad of Arts and Science, Harvard Univ 1982; Edwin Hood Award (Nat Press Club) 1982; Distinguished Achievement Award (Univ of S California) 1984; Pulitzer Prize 1984; Bob Considine Award (Overseas Press Club) 1984, 1988. *Address:* Dow Jones & Co, 200 Liberty St, New York, NY 10281, USA.

HOUSE, Lynda Mary; Australian film producer; b 30 April 1949, Tasmania; d of Graeme and Patricia House; m Tony Mahood 1993. *Career:* Mem Bd Film Vic 1993–96, Australian Film Finance Corpn 1997–. *Films:* Proof (Australian Film Inst Best Film 1991), Muriel's Wedding (Australian Film Inst Best Film 1994). *Leisure interests:* watching films, reading, gardening. *Address:* 117 Rouse St, Port Melbourne, Vic 3121, Australia. *Telephone:* (3) 9646-4025; *Fax:* (3) 9646-6336.

HOUSHIARY, Shirazeh, BA; Iranian artist; b 15 Jan 1955, Iran. *Education:* Teheran Univ, Chelsea School of Art (London) and Cardiff Coll of Art. *Career:* Sculptor Lisson Gallery, London; solo exhibitions include: Chapter Arts Centre 1980, Galleria Massimo Minini, Milan, Italy 1983, Valentina Moncada, Rome 1992, Camden Arts Centre, London, Fine Arts Center, Univ of Massachusetts, USA 1993–94; group exhibitions include: The Sculpture Show (Arts Council of GB, Hayward Gallery, Serpentine Gallery), New Art (Tate Gallery, London) 1983, Bruges La Morte Gallery, Belgium 1992, Sculptors' Drawings, The Body of Drawing (Univ of Warwick, Coventry and The Mead Gallery) 1993, Christmas Tree (Tate Gallery, London) 1993. *Address:* c/o Lehmann Maupin Gallery, 39 Greene St, New York, NY 10013, UK.

HOUSTON, Whitney; American singer and actress; b 9 Aug 1963, East Orange, NJ; d of John and Cissy Houston; m Bobby Brown 1992; one d. *Education:* Trained under direction of mother. *Career:* Mem New Hope Baptist Jr Choir 1974; backing vocalist Chaka Khan (qv), Lou Rawls, Cissy Houston 1978; appeared in Cissy Houston night-club act; debut record Hold Me (duet with Teddy Pendergrass) 1984; Hon DH (Grambling State Univ, LA); Grammy Award for Best Female Pop Performance 1985, 1987, for Best R & B Vocal Performance 2000; winner seven American Music Awards and other awards. *Albums include:* Whitney Houston 1985, Whitney 1986, I'm Your Baby Tonight 1990, The Bodyguard (film soundtrack, jtly), Waiting to Exhale (film soundtrack, jtly), The Preacher's Wife (film soundtrack, jtly), My Love is Your Love 1999; *Songs include:* Greatest Love of All, Saving All My Love For You, How Will I Know, Didn't We Almost Have It All, You're Still My Man, I'm Your Baby Tonight, Friends Can be Lovers (with Dionne Warwick, qv) 1993, I Will Always Love You, I'm Every Woman, I Have Nothing, Queen of the Night, Exhale; *Films include:* The Bodyguard 1992, Waiting to Exhale 1996, The Preacher's Wife 1996, Scratch the Surface 1997, Anything for You 2000. *Address:* c/o John Houston Nippi Inc, 2160 N Central Rd, Fort Lee, NJ 07024, USA.

HOWARD, Ann; British opera singer (mezzo-soprano); b 22 July 1936, Norwood, London; d of William A. and Gladys W. Swadling; m Keith Giles 1954; one d. *Education:* With Topliss Green and Rodolfa Lhombino (London) and Dominic Modesti (Paris) and at Royal Opera House (London). *Career:* Performed in world premières of Mines of Sulphur (Bennett) 1970, Rebecca (Josephs) 1982, The Tempest (Eaton, USA) 1985, The Plumber's Gift (Blake) 1989, The Doctor of Myddfai (Maxwell Davies) 1996 and in UK première of Le Grand Macabre 1981; series of Gilbert and Sullivan operas Performing Arts Center, NY State Univ 1993–98; has appeared in UK, France, Canada,

USA, Mexico, Chile and Italy and on BBC radio and TV; teaches privately. *Operas include:* Carmen, Samson et Dalila, Don Quichote, La Belle Hélène, Don Carlos, Il Trovatore, Aida, Italiana in Algeri, Orfeo, Lohengrin, Tristan und Isolde, The Rake's Progress, The Mikado, The Marriage of Figaro, The Gipsy Baron, Kiss Me, Kate, Electra, La Grande Duchesse de Gerolstein, Into the Woods, Die Fledermaus, Candide, Peter Grimes, Boris Goudonov, Rusalka, Street Scene, The Rise and Fall of the City of Mahagonny; *Recordings:* Candide (Bernstein), Into the Woods (Sondheim), The Valkyrie (Wagner); *Video recordings:* Rusalka (Dvořák), Ruddigore (Sullivan). *Leisure interests:* gardening, cooking. *Address:* c/o Stafford Law Associates, 6 Barham Close, Weybridge, Surrey KT13 9PR, UK. *Telephone:* (1932) 854489; *Fax:* (1932) 858521.

HOWARD, Elizabeth Jane, CBE, FRSL; British writer; b 26 March 1923; d of David Liddon and Katharine Margaret Howard; m 1st Peter M. Scott 1942; one d; m 2nd James Douglas-Henry 1959; m 3rd Kingsley Amis 1965 (divorced 1983, died 1995). *Education:* At home and London Mask Theatre School. *Career:* BBC TV modelling 1939–46; Sec Inland Waterways Asscn 1947; professional writer including plays for TV; Hon Artistic Dir Cheltenham Literary Festival 1962; Artistic Co-Dir Salisbury Festival of Arts 1973; John Llewellyn Rhys Memorial Prize 1950. *Publications:* Novels: The Beautiful Visit 1950, The Long View 1956, The Sea Change 1960, After Julius 1966, Something in Disguise 1970 (TV series 1982), Odd Girl Out 1972, Getting it Right (Yorkshire Post Prize) 1982, The Light Years (1st vol of The Cazalet Chronicle) 1990, Marking Time (2nd vol of The Cazalet Chronicle) 1991, Confusion (3rd vol of The Cazalet Chronicle) 1993, Casting Off (4th vol of The Cazalet Chronicle) 1995, Falling 1999; Short story collection: Mr Wrong 1976; Non-fiction: A Companion for Lovers (ed) 1978, Howard and Maschler on Food: Cooking for Occasions (jtly) 1987, Green Shades (gardening anthology) 1991; *Screenplays:* The Very Edge 1963, The Attachment 1986, Getting it Right 1985, The Attachment 1986. *Leisure interests:* music, gardening, the arts, travel, natural history, cooking, reading. *Address:* c/o Jonathan Clowes, Iron Bridge House, Bridge Approach, London NW1 8BD, UK.

HOWARD, Helen Barbara, RCA; Canadian painter and illustrator; b 10 March 1926, Long Branch, ON; d of Thomas Edmund and Helen Margaret Howard; m Richard Daley Outram 1957. *Education:* Chatham Coll Inst and W Tech and Commercial School (Toronto, ON). *Career:* Co-Founder and Propr (with Richard Daley Outram) The Gauntlet Press 1960–; one-woman exhibitions include Picture Loan Soc (Toronto) 1957, 1958, 1960, 1965, Towne Cinema, Int Cinema (Toronto) 1962, Wells Gallery 1966, 1984, Fleet Gallery (Winnipeg, MB) 1966, Victoria Coll (Toronto) 1966, Sisler Gallery (Toronto) 1974, 1976, Prince Arthur galleries (Toronto) 1980, Massey Coll (Toronto) 1984, Latcham Gallery (Stouffville) 1985, O'Keefe Centre (Toronto) 1986, Nat Library of Canada 1986, Univ Coll Toronto 1987, Georgetown Cultural Centre 1988; E. J. Pratt Library Univ of Toronto 1995; group exhibitions include Art Gallery of Ontario 1958, 1960, 1961, 1976, Nat Gallery of Canada 1966; represented in public and pvt collections including Nat Gallery of Canada, Art Gallery of Ontario, Nat Library of Canada, British Museum (London), Bodleian Library, Univ of Oxford (UK), Library of Congress (Washington, DC, USA). *Book designs and illustrations include:* Creatures 1972, Seer 1973, Thresholds 1973, Locus 1974, Turns and other Poems 1975, Arbor 1976, The Bass Saxophone 1977, Whale Sound 1977, The Promise of Light 1980, Selected Poems 1984, Man in Love 1985, Hiram and Jenny 1988, The Music is the Sadness 1988. *Leisure interests:* music, gardening, bookbinding.

HOWARTH, Judith; British opera singer (soprano); b 11 Sept 1962, Ipswich; m Gordon Wilson 1986. *Education:* Royal Scottish Acad of Music and studies with Patricia Macmahon. *Career:* Prin Soprano Royal Opera House, Covent Garden, London appt 1986; American debut 1986; appearances at Salzburg, Austria and Aix-en-Provence, France Festivals 1991; now freelance; numerous concert and recital engagements in UK, USA, Far East, Australia and NZ; debut at Salzburg Festival in Mozart's Der Schauspieldirektor 1991; has also appeared with Florida Grand Opera, Drottningholm Festival, Opera North and Glyndebourne Touring Opera; debut with Deutsche Staatsoper, Berlin in Cavalli's La Didone 1996. *Operas include:* Der Freischütz, Les Huguenots, Alcina, Don Giovanni, The Marriage of Figaro; *Recording:*

Mozart's Requiem 1991; *Films and videos:* Puccini 1984, Carmen, The Marriage of Figaro, Die Fledermaus, Der Schauspieldirektor. *Leisure interests:* cooking, walking, travel. *Address:* c/o Askonas Holt, Lonsdale Chambers, 27 Chancery Lane, London WC2A 1PF, UK. *Telephone:* (20) 7379-7700; *Fax:* (20) 7242-1831.

HOWATCH, Susan Elizabeth, LL B; British writer; b 14 July 1940, Leatherhead, Surrey; d of George and Anne Sturt; m Joseph Howatch 1964; one d. *Education:* Sutton High School and King's Coll (London). *Career:* Emigrated to USA 1964, lived in Ireland 1976–80, returned to UK 1980; first book published 1965; Lecturer in Theology and Natural Science (Cambridge) 1992; Fellow King's Coll London; Hon Fellow Univ of Wales at Lampeter, Sarum Coll Salisbury. *Publications:* Novels: Penmarric 1971 (adapted for TV 1978), Cashelmara 1974, The Rich are Different 1977, Sins of the Fathers 1980, The Wheel of Fortune 1984, Glittering Images 1987, Glamorous Powers 1988, Ultimate Prizes 1989, Scandalous Risks 1991, Mystical Paths 1992, Absolute Truths 1994, A Question of Integrity 1997, The High Flyer 1999. *Leisure interest:* theology. *Address:* c/o Gillon Aitkin Associates, 29 Fernshaw Rd, London SW10 0TG, UK. *Telephone:* (20) 7351-7561; *Fax:* (20) 7376-3594; *E-mail:* reception@aitkenassoc.demon.co.uk (Office).

HOWE, Tina, BA; American playwright; b 1937, New York; d of Quincy and Mary (née Post) Howe; m Norman Levy 1961; one s one d. *Education:* Sarah Lawrence Coll (Bronxville, NY) and Columbia and Chicago Teacher Training Colls. *Career:* Visiting Prof Hunter Coll 1983–90; Adjunct Prof Univ of New York 1983–; plays have been performed at Los Angeles Actors Theatre, New York Shakespeare Festival, The Kennedy Center, The Second Stage; mem Council Dramatists' Guild; Guggenheim Fellow 1990; Dr hc (Bowdoin Coll) 1988; Obie for Distinguished Playwriting 1983; Outer Critics Circle Award 1983; Tony nomination for Best Play 1987; American Acad of Arts and Letters Award in Literature 1993. *Plays include:* The Nest 1969, Birth and After Birth 1973, Museum 1976, The Art of Dining 1979, Appearances (unpublished) 1982, Painting Churches 1983, Coastal Disturbances, Approaching Zanzibar, One Show Off 1993. *Address:* c/o Flora Roberts Inc, 157 W 57th St, New York, NY 10019, USA. *Telephone:* (212) 355-4165.

HOWE OF ABERAVON, Lady Elspeth; British organization executive; m Lord Howe of Aberavon (Geoffrey Howe); three c. *Career:* Chair Opportunity 2000, Business in the Community (BITC) 1990–99, BOC Foundation for the Environment 1990–, Broadcasting Standards Council 1993–97, Broadcasting Standards Comm 1997–99; Non-Exec Dir Kingfisher 1986–, Legal and Gen 1986–97; mem Working Group on Women's Issues, Dept of Employment; Pres UK Cttee for UNICEF; Gov LSE; People's Peer 2001. *Address:* Broadcasting Standards Commission, 5 The Sanctuary, London SW1, UK. *Telephone:* (20) 7233-0544; *Fax:* (20) 7233-0397.

HOWELL, Margaret, DIP AD; British fashion designer; b 5 Sept 1946, Tadworth; d of E. H. Howell; m Paul Renshaw 1974 (divorced 1987); one s one d. *Education:* Deburgh Co-Educational and Goldsmith's Coll (London). *Career:* First Margaret Howell Collection 1972; opened Margaret Howell Ltd, London 1977; three shops in London; stocked by shops in Paris and Japan; opened Margaret Howell (France) 1996; over 50 retail outlets worldwide by end of 1996; Co-Dir Margaret Howell Ltd 1985–; Designer of the Year. *Leisure interests:* films, art exhibitions, visiting country houses and gardens, walking, the countryside. *Address:* Margaret Howell Ltd, 5 Garden House, 8 Battersea Park Rd, London SW8 4BG, UK. *Telephone:* (20) 7627-5587.

HOWELLS, Anne Elizabeth; British opera and concert singer; b 12 Jan 1941, Southport, Lancs; d of Trevor and Mona Howells; m 1st Ryland Davies 1966 (divorced 1981); m 2nd Stafford Dean 1981 (divorced 1998); one s one d. *Education:* Sale Co Grammar School and Royal Manchester Coll of Music. *Career:* Three seasons in Chorus with Glyndebourne Festival Opera 1964–66, took leading role at short notice in L'Ormindo (Cavalli) 1967, subsequent roles include Dorabella in Così fan tutte, Cathleen in world première Rising of the Moon (Nicholas Maw), Composer in Ariadne, Diana in Calisto; with Royal Opera House, Covent Garden 1969–71, appearing as Lena in world premiere of Victory (Richard Rodney Bennett), in The Barber of Seville and in The Marriage of Figaro; Guest Artist with Royal Opera House 1973–;

has also appeared with Welsh Nat Opera, Scottish Opera, English Nat Opera, Chicago Opera (USA), Geneva Opera (Switzerland), Metropolitan Opera, New York (USA), Lyons Opera, Marseilles Opera and Nantes Opera (France), Netherlands Opera; performed at La Scala, Milan (Italy), at Salzburg Festival (Austria) 1976, 1980 (Tales of Hoffmann and film version of Clemenza di Tito) and in Naples (Italy), San Francisco (USA), Belgium, Hamburg and Berlin (Germany); Prof Royal Acad of Music 1997–; Fellow Royal Manchester Coll of Music. *Leisure interests:* cinema, reading. *Address:* c/o IMG Artists, Media House, 3 Burlington Lane, London W4 2TH, UK.

HRADSKÁ, Viktoria, PH D; Czech politician; b 12 Feb 1944, Budapest, Hungary; d of Ladislav Hradský and Jiřina Kabíčková; m 1st Pavol Hokynek 1966 (divorced 1973), remarried 1977 (divorced 1981); m 2nd Alex Koenigsmark 1981; one s. *Education:* Charles Univ (Prague). *Career:* Researcher History of Czech Philosophy Czechoslovak (now Czech) Acad of Sciences 1969–89; apptd Deputy Minister of Foreign Relations, Vice-Pres Czech Foreign Relations Cttee 1990; first woman political party Chair (Liberal Democratic Party); Pres RDP Group; several awards for radio and stage plays 1988, 1989. *Publications:* Czech Vanguard and Philosophy 1987; several trans from Hungarian into Czech. *Leisure interests:* theatre, dogs, reading. *Address:* c/o RDP GROUP, Karmelitska 17, 118 00 Praha 1, Czech Republic. *Telephone:* (2) 57105120; *Fax:* (2) 57105124.

HU DAOFEN; Chinese scientist; b 10 Aug 1933, Shanghai; m Zheng Yibo 1958; one s one d. *Education:* Moscow Agricultural Coll. *Career:* Mem staff Zhejiang Agricultural Univ 1959–61, Chinese Acad of Agricultural Sciences, Beijing from 1961, apptd Dir Beijing Plant Cell Bio-engineering Lab 1986; Prof of Genetic Breeding; Beijing Special Class Award for Sciences and Tech 1984. *Leisure interest:* music. *Address:* Beijing Plant Cell Bio-engineering Laboratory, POB 2449, 100081 Beijing, People's Republic of China. *Telephone:* (1) 8418851.

HU QIHENG; Chinese scientist and administrator; b 15 June 1934, Beijing; d of the late Hu Shu Wei and Fan Wen Yi; m Lian Yuan Jian 1959; one s one d. *Education:* Inst of Chemical Machinery (Moscow). *Career:* Visiting Research Prof Case Western Reserve Univ, Cleveland, OH, USA 1980–82; Dir Inst of Automation, Chinese Acad of Sciences 1983–87, Sec-Gen Chinese Acad of Sciences 1987–88, Vice-Pres 1988–96; Pres Chinese Asscn of Automation 1984–93, Chinese Computer Fed 1985–96; mem CPPCC 1993–; Vice-Pres China Asscn for Science and Tech 1996; contribs to scientific publs; Important Tech Achievement Award (Nat First Congress of Sciences) 1978; Advanced Woman of the Country Award 1985. *Leisure interests:* reading novels, growing flowers, pets (kittens and guinea-pigs), bicycling, computer drawing. *Address:* Chinese Academy of Sciences, 52 San Li He Rd, 100864 Beijing, People's Republic of China. *Telephone:* (10) 62553590; *Fax:* (10) 62624476; 68512458.

HUBBARD, M. Ruth, BA, MS; Canadian civil servant; b 27 June 1942, Toronto; d of John S. and Winifred (née Moreton) Willis; m Martin Hubbard 1973; one s. *Education:* Queen's Univ at Kingston (ON) and Ohio State Univ (USA). *Career:* Mem staff Statistics Canada 1967–77; Dir Program Br, Treasury Bd Secr 1977–84, Asst Sec 1983–84; Assoc Commr FIRA 1984–85; Exec Vice-Pres Investment Canada 1985–88; Deputy Minister Revenue Canada (Customs and Excise) 1988–92, Employment and Immigration Canada (also Chair) 1992–93, Supply and Services Canada 1993; Master of the Royal Canadian Mint 1993–94; Pres Public Service Comm of Canada 1994–99; Sr Advisor to Privy Council Office 1999–. *Address:* Room 404G, Langevin Bldg, 80 Wellington St, Ottawa, ON K1A 0A3, Canada (Office); 44 Emerson Ave, Apt 503, Ottawa, ON K1Y 2L8, Canada (Home). *E-mail:* rhubbard@pco-bcp.gc.ca.

HUBER-HERING, Vita, D PHIL; Austrian opera director; b 27 Sept 1938, Salzburg. *Education:* Univ of Vienna. *Career:* Asst Landestheater Darmstadt, Germany 1963–71; Producer Staatstheater Wiesbaden, Germany 1972–75, Staatstheater Darmstadt 1976–81; Chief Producer Städtische Bühnen Augsburg, Germany 1981–82, Staatstheater Darmstadt 1982–84, Staatsoper Hamburg, Germany 1984–86, Deutsche Oper am Rhein, Düsseldorf-Duisburg, Germany 1986–. *Publications:* Ein großer Herr, Fürst Pückler (jtly) 1968, Flirt und Flitter,

Lebensbilder aus der Bühnenwelt 1970, Applaus für den Souffleur, Teather-Anekdoten 1973; trans of operas and plays. *Address:* Deutsche Oper am Rhein, Heinrich-Heine-Allee 16A, 4000 Düsseldorf, Germany.

HUBERT, Ana Maria Manuela (Annie), PH D; French anthropologist and scientific researcher; b 5 April 1941, Montevideo, Uruguay; d of René and Denise (née Rouchon) Hubert; m 1st Clark Cunningham 1958 (divorced 1967); two d one s; m 2nd Jean François Baré 1981. *Education:* Coll Français de Buenos Aires (Argentina), Ecole des Hautes Etudes en Sciences Sociales (Paris), Univ of Paris X (Paris-Nanterre). *Career:* First French anthropologist successfully to complete research into dietary factors in cancer and to collaborate with biologists and epidemiologists; anthropological research, Thailand 1959–66, 1968–71, Laos 1966–67; field-work on nasopharyngeal cancer China, Greenland, Tunisia; part-time Researcher Centre de Documentation et de Recherches sur le Monde Insulindien (CEDRASEMI), CNRS 1967–81, Inst Gustave Roussy 1981–83; Research Asst Inst Pasteur, Lyons 1983–84, Sr Researcher 1984–87; fmrly Research Asst Unité d'Epidémiologie des Virus Oncogènes of Inst Pasteur, Paris; part-time Researcher CNRS 1988–, now Research Dir Sociétés Santé Développement; Sec-Gen Int Comm for the Anthropology of Food. *Publications include:* Le pain et l'olive: aspects de l'alimentation en Tunisie 1984, L'alimentation dans un village yao de Thaïlande du Nord 1985, Modes de vie et cancers 1989, Le manger juste 1991, The Heritage of French Cooking 1991, Pourquoi les Eskimo vont pas de cholesterol 1995; has published around 250 scientific works. *Leisure interests:* cookery, music, walking. *Address:* Université de Bordeaux II, 3 place de la Victoire, 33000 Bordeaux, France (Office); 239 rue Mandron, 33000 Bordeaux, France (Home). *Telephone:* (5) 56-69-91-11; *Fax:* (5) 56-69-91-11; *E-mail:* ahubert@worldnet.fr; *Internet:* www.icafood.org.

HUBERT, Elisabeth Michèle Adélaïde Marie, D EN MED; French politician; b 26 May 1956, Le Lude; d of Auguste and Germaine Hubert. *Education:* Univ of Nantes. *Career:* Medical practitioner, Nantes 1982–94; Municipal Councillor, Nantes 1983–; mem Nat Ass (Parl, RPR) from Loire-Atlantique 1986, reelected 1988, 1993; Minister for Public Health and Health Insurance 1995; fmr mem Social and Cultural Affairs Comm; fmr mem RPR Political Bureau; fmr Vice-Pres RPR Parl Group; Chargée de Mission, Office of the Pres 1996–97; Dir-Gen Fournier et Débat (France) 1997–. *Address:* c/o Laboratoires Fournier et Débat, 153 rue de Buzenval, 92380 Garches, France.

HÜBSCHER, Angelika; German writer; b 4 April 1912, Busbach, nr Bayreuth; d of Ferdinand Maria Knote and Margarete Bernewitz; m Arthur Hübscher 1950; two step-d one s (died 1982). *Education:* Privately, Humanistisches Gymnasium (Bayreuth) and Univ of Heidelberg. *Career:* Sacked from Ministry of Foreign Affairs, Berlin by Gestapo 1940; interpreter for Heidelberg Police Dept after 1945; reader for Stahberg Verlag (publrs); Hon mem Bd of Dirs Schopenhauer Gesellschaft until 1992; Pres Int Women's Club 1986–87; f Cultura '87 1987; f Schopenhauer Foundation 1988; Chevalier des Palmes Académiques 1967; Bundesverdienstkreuz 1977; Ehrenbrief des Landes Hessen 1976. *Publications:* Ed: Casanova: Histoire de ma vie, Schopenhauer (Zurich edn); Schopenhauer und Frankfurt (catalogue and exhibition) 1994; writer, ed many books on Schopenhauer. *Leisure interests:* lyrics, eco-trophology. *Address:* Beethovenstr 48, 60325 Frankfurt/Main 1, Germany. *Telephone:* (69) 745219.

HÜBSCHLE, Michaela M. E. K. H., BA; Namibian politician; b 21 Sept 1950, Otjiwarongo. *Education:* University of Pretoria, South Africa. *Career:* Translator and Research officer German Embassy, Pretoria 1974–76; Environmentalist community pressure group, Tübingen, Germany 1976–83; Personnel Relations Officer Katutura community-based projects 1984–89; mem Constituent Ass (SW Africa People's Org—SWAPO) 1989; MP (Nat Ass) 1990; Deputy Whip SW Africa People's Org 1990–1995; Deputy Minister Ministry of Prisons and Correctional Services 1995; Chair Environment Cttee, SW Africa People's Org, mem Cen Cttee Women's Council; Deputy Finance and Project Officer of Namibian Nat Women Org; mem Commonwealth Parl Asscn, Parliamentarians for Global Action; Trustee CSPD Child Survival Protection and Devt Foundation. *Leisure interests:* music, theatre, fine arts, swimming. *Address:* Ministry of Prisons and Correctional Services, Goethe St, PMB 13323, Namibia.

HUDSON, Anne Mary, D PHIL; British academic; b 28 Aug 1938; d of the late R. L. and K. M. Hudson. *Education:* Dartford Grammar School for Girls and St Hugh's Coll (Oxford). *Career:* Lecturer in Medieval English, Lady Margaret Hall, Oxford 1961–63, Tutor 1963–91, Fellow 1963–, Prof 1989–; Common Univ Fund (CUF) Lecturer Oxford Univ 1963–81, Special Lecturer 1981–83; Sir Israel Gollancz Prize, British Acad 1985, 1991. *Publications:* Selections from English Wycliffite Writings (ed) 1978, English Wycliffite Sermons I (ed) 1983, II (ed) 1990, Lollards and their Books 1985, From Ockham to Wycliffe (co-ed) 1987, The Premature Reformation 1988, Two Wycliffe Texts (ed) 1993. *Address:* Lady Margaret Hall, Oxford OX2 6QA, UK.

HUDSON, Katherine M.; American business executive; b 1947. *Education:* Univ of Indiana. *Career:* Joined Eastman Kodak Co 1970, mem staff finance, community and investor relations depts, Gen Man Instant-Photography Unit 1984, later Dir Corp Information Systems and Dir of Information Systems and Processes, Corp Vice-Pres 1988–93, Vice-Pres and Gen Man Professional, Printing and Publishing Imaging Division 1992–1993; Pres and CEO W. H. Brady Co 1994–, Brady Corp 1999–; mem Bd Dirs CNH Global N. V. *Address:* Brady Corp, 6555 Good Hope Rd, POB 571, Milwaukee, WI 53201-0571, USA.

HUFSTEDLER, Shirley Mount, LL B; American lawyer and former judge; b 24 Aug 1925, Denver, CO; d of Earl Stanley and Eva E. (née von Behren) Mount; m Seth M. Hufstedler 1949; one s. *Education:* Univ of New Mexico (Albuquerque) and Stanford Univ (CA). *Career:* Staff mem Stanford Law Review 1947–49, book reviews Ed 1948–49; called to Bar, CA 1950; mem Beardsley, Hufstedler & Kemble pvt law practice 1951–61; Judge Los Angeles Co Superior Court 1961–66; Assoc Justice California Court of Appeal 1966–68; Circuit Judge 9th Circuit, US Court of Appeals 1968–79; US Sec of Educ 1979–81; Partner Hufstedler, Kaus & Ettinger pvt law practice 1981–; currently Sr Counsel Morrison and Forester; Dir Hewlett Packard Co, US West Inc, Harman Industries Int; mem Bd John T. and Catherine MacArthur Foundation 1983–; Trustee California Inst of Tech, Occidental Coll (Los Angeles, CA) 1972–89, Aspen Inst, Colonial Williamsburg Foundation (VA) 1976–95, Constitutional Rights Foundation 1978–80, Nat Resources Defense Council 1983–85, Carnegie Endowment for Int Peace 1983–96; mem ABA, American Law Inst, Council mem 1974–84, American Bar Foundation, Women Lawyers Asscn, Pres 1957–58, American Judicature Soc, Council on Foreign Relations; 20 hon doctorates 1967–81; Fellow American Acad of Arts and Sciences; Univ of California, Los Angeles (UCLA) Medal 1981; ABA Medal 1996. *Leisure interests:* gardening, mountaineering, music, books, art. *Address:* Morrison and Forester, 555 W 5th St, Suite 3500, Los Angeles, CA 90013, USA. *Telephone:* (213) 892-5804.

HUGGAN, Jean Isabel, BA; Canadian writer; b 21 Sept 1943, Kitchener, ON; d of Cecil Ronald and Catherine Innes Howey; m Bob Huggan 1970; one d. *Education:* Univ of Western Ontario. *Career:* Editorial Asst Macmillan Publishing Co 1965–66; teacher 1968–72; reporter, photographer and columnist The Belleville Intelligencer 1973–76; teacher of Creative Writing Univ of Ottawa 1985–87; First Prize for film script Nat Film Bd contest for women writers 1977; Joe Savago Award—New Voice of 1987 (Quality Paperback Book Club) 1987; Alan Swallow Literary Award 1987. *Publications include:* First Impressions 1980, Best Canadian Stories (contrib) 1983, The Elizabeth Stories 1984, 1987, Stories by Canadian Women (Vol II) 1987, New American Short Stories 1988, Soho Square 1990, The Time of Your Life (contrib) 1992, You Never Know 1993, Unbecoming Daughters of the Empire 1993, Gates of Paradise II (contrib) 1994, Serpent à Plumes 1994, The Seasons of Women 1996, When We Were Young 1997, Altre Terre 1997, Penguin Anthology of Stories by Canadian Women 1999, Dropped Threads 2000. *Leisure interests:* walking, reading, music.

HUGHES, Catherine Eva, CMG, MA; British former diplomatist and college principal; b (Catherine Eva Pestell) 24 Sept 1933, London; d of Edmund and Isabella (née Sangster) Pestell; m J. Trevor Hughes 1991. *Education:* Leeds Girls' High School and St Hilda's Coll (Oxford). *Career:* Joined Foreign Service 1955; served The Hague, Bangkok, Vientiane, OECD Del, Paris 1955–75; Counsellor E Berlin 1975, seconded to Cabinet Office 1978; Insp HM Diplomatic Service 1981–83; Minister (Econ), Bonn 1983–87; Asst Under-Sec FCO

1987–89; Prin Somerville Coll, Oxford 1989–96. *Address:* 2 Bishop Kirk Place, Oxford OX2 7HJ, UK. *Telephone:* (1865) 316669; *Fax:* (1865) 516021 (Home).

HUGHES, Helen, AO, MA, PH D; Australian professor emeritus; b 1 Oct 1928, Prague, Czechoslovakia (now Czech Repub); m Graeme Dorrance 1972; two s one d. *Education:* MacRobertson Girls' High School (Melbourne), Univ of Melbourne and LSE. *Career:* Business economist, Melbourne 1955–58; Lecturer in Econs Univ of NSW 1959–60; Sr Lecturer in Econs Univ of Queensland 1961–62; Research Fellow Dept of Econs, Research School of Pacific Studies, ANU (Canberra) 1963–68, Prof of Econs and Exec Dir Nat Centre for Devt Studies 1983–93; Dir Full Employment Project Univ of Melbourne 1994–95, Sr Fellow Centre for Ind Studies 1996–; various positions IBRD (Washington, DC) 1969–76, Dir Econ Analysis Dept 1976–83; Dir Nat Mutual Life Asscn of Australia 1987–95, AUSSAT Pty ltd 1983–91; mem UN Cttee for Devt Planning 1987–93; Fellow Acad of Social Sciences of Australia 1985; Hon D LITT. *Publications:* The Australian Iron and Steel Industry 1964, Australia in a Developing World 1985, Achieving Industrialization in East Asia (ed) 1988. *Leisure interests:* reading, music, art. *Address:* 12 Spring St, Double Bay, Sydney, NSW 2028, Australia. *Telephone:* (2) 324 4442; *Fax:* (2) 363 9989.

HUGHES, Linda Jean, BA; Canadian newspaper publisher; b 27 Sept 1950; d of Edward Rees and Madge Preston; m George Ward 1978; one s one d. *Education:* Univs of Victoria and Toronto. *Career:* Reporter on Victoria Times 1972–73, Head Legislature Bureau 1974–76; City Hall Reporter, Copy Ed on The Edmonton Journal 1976–77, Editorial Writer 1978–80, Head Legislature Bureau, Asst City Ed 1980, City Ed 1981–84, Asst Man Ed 1984–87, Ed 1987–91, Publr 1992–; Southam News Services, Ottawa 1979; Southam Fellow Univ of Toronto 1977–78; Hon D LITT (Athabasca) 1997. *Leisure interests:* reading, cycling, skiing. *Address:* The Edmonton Journal, POB 2421, Edmonton, AB T5J 2S6, Canada. *Telephone:* (403) 429-5129; *Fax:* (403) 429-5536.

HUGHES, Margaret Eileen, BA, LL M, M SW; Canadian lawyer; b 22 Jan 1943, Saskatoon, SK; d of E. Duncan and Eileen Farmer; m James Roscoe Hughes 1966; two d. *Education:* Univ of Saskatchewan (Canada) and Univ of Michigan (USA). *Career:* Mem Faculty of Law Univ of Windsor (ON) 1968–75; Exec Interchange Programme, Dept of Justice 1975–77; Prof of Law Univ of Saskatchewan 1978–84; Dean of Law Univ of Calgary 1984–89, now Prof; mem Faculty Sr Univ Administrators' Course (Banff) 1990–; Chair Council of Canadian Law Deans 1987–88; mem Exec Cttee and Bd Dirs Industrial Relations Research Group 1990–2000; mem Canadian Inst of Resources Law 1984–89, Research Inst for Law and the Family 1984–89, 1997–2001; mem Alberta, Saskatchewan, Ontario Law Socs; has written several book chapters. *Leisure interests:* swimming, hiking. *Address:* University of Calgary, Calgary, AB T2N 1N4, Canada. *Telephone:* (403) 220-5110; *Fax:* (430) 282-7298; *E-mail:* hughesm@ucalgary.ca.

HUGHES, Mary-Lorraine, PH D, MBA; British business executive; b 29 April 1951, Pwllheli. *Education:* Aldershop Co High School for Girls, Univ of Surrey and Manchester Business School. *Career:* Propr, Man retail business 1976–83; CEO numerous clothing manufacturing businesses, including Courtaulds Textiles 1983–94; CEO Portmeirion Potteries (Holdings) plc 1994–; Swann Scholarship 1973–76, Pilkington Scholarship, Manchester Business School 1980–82. *Leisure interests:* animal welfare, natural history, travel. *Address:* Portmeirion Potteries, London Rd, Stoke-on-Trent ST4 7QQ, UK (Office); 12 Dingle Lane, Sandbach, Cheshire CW11 1FY, UK (Home). *Telephone:* (1782) 744721; *Fax:* (1782) 744061.

HUGHES, Monica Mary; Canadian writer; b 3 Nov 1925, Liverpool, UK; d of Edward Lindsay and Phyllis (née Fry) Ince; m Glen Hughes 1957; two s two d. *Education:* Privately in UK. *Career:* Served WRNS 1943–46; Lab technician NRC, Ottawa 1952–57; writer of children's books 1971–; Canadian Council Prize for Children's Literature 1981, 1982; Writers' Guild of Alberta Award 1983, 1984, 1987; Silver Feather (Germany) 1988; Phoenix 2000 Award; Alberta Women of Vision Award 2000. *Publications include:* Novels: Gold-Fever Trail 1974, Earthdark 1977, The Tomorrow City 1978, Ghost Dance Caper 1978, The Keeper of Isis Light 1980, The Guardian of Isis 1981, The Isis Pedlar 1982, Hunter in the Dark 1982, Ring-Rise, Ring-Set 1982, Space

Trap 1983, My Name is Paula Popowich! 1983, Devil on my Back 1984, Sandwriter 1985, The Dream Catcher 1986, Log Jam 1987, The Promise 1989, The Refuge 1989, Little Fingerling 1989, Invitation to the Game 1990, The Crystal Drop 1992, The Golden Aquarians 1994, Castle Tourmandyne 1995, Where have you been, Billy Boy? 1995, The Seven Magpies 1996, The Faces of Fear 1997, The Story Box 1998, What if … ? (ed) 1998, The Other Place 1999, Storm Warning 2000; Short stories: Out of Time 1984, Dragons and Dreams (contrib) 1985, Window of Dreams (contrib) 1986, Take Your Knee Off My Heart (contrib) 1990, The Unseen 1994. *Leisure interests:* swimming, walking, travel, reading. *Address:* 13816 110A Ave, Edmonton, AB T5M 2M9, Canada. *Telephone:* (403) 455-5602; *Internet:* www.ecn.ab.ca/mhughes.

HUGHES, Penny; British business executive; b 1960. *Career:* Pres Coca-Cola, Great Britain and Ireland until Jan 1996; Non-Exec Dir Berisford, Body Shop Int. *Address:* Body Shop, Watersmead, Littlehampton, UK.

HUGHES, Shirley; British writer and illustrator; b 16 July 1927; d of Thomas James and Kathleen (née Dowling) Hughes; m John Sebastian Papendrek Vulliamy 1952; two s one d. *Education:* West Kirby High School for Girls, Liverpool Art School and Ruskin School of Art (Oxford). *Career:* Freelance writer and illustrator; lecturer in field; mem Man Cttee Soc of Authors 1983–86, Advisory Cttee Public Lending Rights Registrar 1984–88, Library and Information Services Council 1989–92; Children's Rights Award 1976; Kate Greenaway Medal 1978; Silver Pencil Award, Netherlands 1980; Eleanor Farjeon Award 1984. *Publications include:* Sally's Secret (3rd edn) 1976, Helpers (2nd edn) 1978, Lucy and Tom's Day (2nd edn) 1979, Dogger (4th edn) 1980, The Trouble With Jack (2nd edn) 1981, Moving Molly (3rd edn) 1981, Lucy and Tom's Christmas 1981, It's Too Frightening for Me (4th edn) 1982, Lucy and Tom at the Seaside (3rd edn) 1982, Alfie Gets in First (2nd edn) 1982, Lucy and Tom Go To School (4th edn) 1983, Up and Up (3rd edn) 1983, Charlie Moon and the Big Bonanza Bust-up (2nd edn) 1983, Alfie Gives a Hand 1983, Here Comes Charlie Moon (3rd edn) 1984, Alfie's Fee (2nd edn) 1984, An Evening at Alfie's 1984, Lucy and Tom's abc 1984, A Nursery Collection (six vols) 1985–86, Chips and Jessie 1985, Another Helping of Chips 1986, Lucy and Tom's 123 1987, Out and About 1988, The Big Alfie and Annie Rose Story Book 1988, Angel Mae 1989, The Big Concrete Lorry 1989, The Snow Lady 1990, Wheels 1991, The Big Alfie Out of Doors Story Book 1992, Stories by Firelight 1993, Giving, Bouncing, Chatting, Hiding 1994, Rhymes for Annie Rose 1995, Enchantment in the Garden 1996, Alfie and the Birthday Surprise 1997, The Lion and the Unicorn 1998, Mother and Child Treasury (ed) 1998, Abel's Moon 1999, Alfie's Numbers 1999, The Shirley Collection 2000. *Leisure interests:* needlework, paintings, illustrated diaries, writing. *Address:* 63 Lansdowne Rd, London W11 2LG, UK. *Telephone:* (20) 7229-0087.

HUI, Ann; Chinese film-maker; b 23 May 1947, Anshan, Liaoning Prov. *Education:* Univ of Hong Kong and London Film School. *Career:* Fmr asst to Hu Jingquan; began career making TV documentaries and features; joined RTHK 1978, directed three segments of Beneath the Lion Rock (series). *Films include:* The Secret, The Spooky Bunch, The Story of Woo Viet, Boat People, Love in a Fallen City, Summer Show (Silver Bear Award, Berlin Film Festival), Ordinary Heroes; *Publications:* The Secret 1979, Boat People 1982, Romance of Book and Sword 1987, Yakuza Chase 1991, Summer Snow 1995.

HULL, Andrea Douglas, BA, DIP ED; Australian arts administrator; b 13 March 1949, Sydney; d of W. G. and M. S. (née Gaynor) Hull; m Graham Pitts 1987; one d. *Education:* Abbotsleigh Girls' School and Univ of Sydney. *Career:* Journalist and teacher 1971–74; Sr Project Officer Community Arts Bd, Australian Council for the Arts 1974–79, Dir 1979–82, Dir Policy and Planning Div 1982–86, Dir of Strategic Devt 1986–88; Exec Dir W Australia Dept for the Arts 1988–94; Dir Victorian Coll of the Arts 1995–; mem Sidney Myer Performing Arts Award Cttee 1984–92, UNESCO Advisory Cttee on Cultural Heritage Conventions and Recommendations 1986–89, Australian Abroad Council 1990–95, Australia–Japan Foundation 1992–95, Premier's Cultural Consultative Cttee 1996–; mem Bd Australia–Korea Foundation 1992–, Nat Acad of Music 1995–98, Melbourne Theatre Co 1996–; Chair Arts Industry Tourism Council 1995–99; Trustee Victorian Arts Centre Trust 1995–98; articles on the arts, culture, the environment and youth to professional journals; W Australia Sr Exec Service Fellowship 1990. *Leisure interests:* yoga, swimming, tennis, reading, theatre. *Address:* 234 St Kilda Rd, Melbourne, Vic 3004, Australia (Office). *Telephone:* (3) 9685-9315; *Fax:* (3) 9682-1841.

HULL, Jane Dee, M SC; American lawyer and politician; b 8 Aug 1935, Kansas City; d of Justin D Bowersock and Mildred Swenson; m Terrance Ward Hull 1954; two s two d. *Education:* Univ of Kansas and Univ of Arizona. *Career:* Republican; House major whip, Arizona House of Reps 1987–88, Speaker of House 1989–93; Chair Ethics Cttee, Econ Devt Cttee 1993; mem Legis Council, Gov's Int Trade and Tourism Advancement Bd, Gov's Strategic Partnership for Econ Devt, Employment Implementation Task Force 1993; fmr Sec of State of Arizona, Gov 1997–; mem Bd Dirs Morrison Inst for Public Policy, Arizona Town Hall, Arizona Econ Council; mem Nat Org of Women Legislators, Nat Repub Legislators Asscn; Nat Legislator of the Year Award 1989; Econ Devt Award of Arizona Innovation Network 1993. *Address:* Office of the Governor, State Capitol, West Wing, 1700 West Washington St, Phoenix, AZ 85007, USA.

HULME, Keri; New Zealand writer; b 9 March 1947, Christchurch; d of John W. and Mary (née Miller) Hulme. *Education:* Univ of Canterbury (NZ). *Career:* Worked as tobacco picker, fish and chip cook, TV dir and woollen-mill worker; became full-time writer 1972, self-employed 1983–; Writer-in-Residence Otago Univ 1978, Univ of Canterbury, Christchurch 1985; New Zealand Book of the Year 1984; Mobil Pegasus Prize for Maori Literature 1984; Booker McConnell Prize for Fiction, UK 1985. *Publications include:* The Silences Between (Moderaki Conversations) 1982, The Bone People 1984, Te Kaihau: The Windeater (short stories) 1986, Bait 1992, Strands (poetry) 1992. *Leisure interests:* fishing, painting, reading, music, Maoritaka, family, eating, drinking. *Address:* c/o Hodder and Stoughton Ltd, 338 Euston Rd, London NW1 3BH, UK.

HULTHÉN, Anneli; Swedish politician; b 27 July 1960, Gothenburg. *Education:* Univ of Gothenburg. *Career:* Care Assistant 1976–85; mem Housing Corpn, Gothenburg 1985–, Housing Advisor 1987–92; mem Gothenburg City Council 1985–94, 1999–; Gothenburg City CEO 1992–; Ombudsman, Social Democratic Party Youth (SSU) 1985–87, Chair Gothenburg dist SSU 1984–87, Exec Cttee 1987–93; mem Exec Social Democratic Party Gothenburg; Deputy mem party Exec; MP 1987–91, 1994–95, Deputy mem Cabinet 1987–91, Deputy mem Cttee on Transport and Communications 1987–91, Cttee on Foreign Affairs 1988–91, 1994–95, Cttee on the Constitution 1994–95; Chair Govt del for housing for young people 1988–; MEP (PSE, Socialdemokratiska arbetarepartiet), mem Cttee on Environment, Public Health and Consumer Policy, Del for relations with Estonia, Lithuania and Latvia; mem State Youth Council 1989–, Nat Housing Bd 1988–92, Museum of Architecture 1990–92, Gothenburg police authority 1991, Swedish Radio 1993–94, Swedish TV 1994–95; Chair Narcotics Comm, Foundation for Strategic Environmental Research (MISTRA). *Address:* European Parliament, rue Wiertz, 1047 Brussels, Belgium. *Telephone:* (2) 284-21-11; *Fax:* (2) 230-69-43.

HUME, Valerie Elizabeth, DIP ED, PH D; Canadian civil servant; b 24 April 1934, Auckland, New Zealand; d of Frank Seddon and Edna (née Russell) Hume. *Education:* Epsom Girls' Grammar School (Auckland), Auckland Univ, Edinburgh Univ (UK), Auckland Teachers' Coll and Canadian Nat Defence Coll (Kingston). *Career:* Teacher, NZ 1954–60, Canada 1960–61, UK 1961–62, Switzerland 1962–66; Asst Prof York Univ, Toronto 1969–76; policy and planning specialist Dept of Indian Affairs and Northern Devt 1976–87, Head Land Programmes 1987–88, Policy Co-ordinator in Sustainable Devt 1989–; Adjunct Prof Carleton Univ, Ottawa 1978–79; Dir Physical and Mathematical Sciences, Natural Sciences and Engineering Research Council 1988–89; Founder and Pres Canadian Cttee for UNIFEM 1993–95; mem Canadian Inst of Int Affairs, American Asscn of Geographers, Canadian Red Cross, Canadian Asscn of Geographers, Zonta Int. *Leisure interests:* flute, outdoor activities. *Address:* 655 Richmond Rd, Unit 14, Ottawa, ON K2A 3Y3, Canada. *Telephone:* (613) 728-8617; *Fax:* (819) 953-2590; *E-mail:* vhume@home.com.

HUNAIDI, Rima Khalaf, MA, PH D; Jordanian politician and organization executive. *Education:* American Univ of Beirut (Lebanon) and Portland State Univ (Ohio). *Career:* Fmr Minister of Industry and Trade, of Planning; fmr Deputy Prime Minister; Senator Jordanian Upper House; mem Jordanian Econ Consultative Council; Asst Sec-Gen and Dir UNDP Regional Bureau for the Arab States (RBAS) June 2000–; speaker at numerous int confs. *Address:* UNDP, Regional Bureau for Arab States, One United Nations Plaza, DC1 – 22nd Floor, New York, NY 10017, USA. *Telephone:* (212) 906-5324; *Fax:* (212) 906-5364.

HUNEBELLE, Danielle; French journalist, writer and television producer; b 10 May 1922, Paris; d of Andrée and Germaine (née Cordon) Weill; two d. *Education:* Lycées Racine and Molière (Paris) and Univ of Paris (Sorbonne). *Career:* Actress 1945–48; Journalist 1948–; War Corresp in Greece 1948; worked in army information office in Indochina 1951; Special Envoy for Le Monde newspaper 1951; Sr Reporter for Réalités magazine 1952–72; TV Producer, made documentaries about Ho Chi Minh and Henry Kissinger and produced Jeux de Société series and docu-dramas; Founder Société des Publications Danielle Hunebelle 1973, Publr in French and English of La Lettre Int de Danielle Hunebelle; now retd; Chevalier de la Légion d'Honneur; Chevalier des Arts et des Lettres. *Publications:* Philippine, Les plumes du paon, Rien que les hommes, Dear Henry. *Leisure interests:* travel, music, reading, gardening, swimming, bridge. *Address:* Elia, 06190 Cap Martin, France. *Telephone:* (4) 93-57-77-47; *E-mail:* junior.anais@wanadoo.fr.

HUNLEY, Hon (Wilma) Helen, OC; Canadian former politician and Lieutenant-Governor; b 6 Sept 1920, Acme, AB; d of James Edgar and Esta May (née Hundley) Hunley. *Education:* Rocky Mountain House High School. *Career:* Telephone operator; attained rank of Lieut Canadian Women's Army Corps 1941–46; Int Harvester franchise 1948–68; owner and Man Helen Hunley Agencies Ltd 1968–71; mem Legis Ass 1971–79; Minister without Portfolio 1971; Solicitor-Gen 1973; Minister of Social Services and Community Health 1975–79; Lieut-Gov of Alberta 1985–91; Hon LL D (Alberta) 1985; Hon Lieut Col RCA 1990. *Leisure interests:* golf, bird-watching, reading. *Address:* 5315 53rd St, Rocky Mountain House, AB T0M 1T3, Canada. *Telephone:* (403) 845-3164.

HUNT, Caroline Rose, PH D; American business executive; b 8 Jan 1923, El Dorado; d of H. L. Hunt and Lyda Bunker; divorced; four s one d. *Education:* Mary Baldwin Coll, Univs of Texas and Charleston. *Career:* Beneficiary of Caroline Hunt Trust Estate which includes Corpn, Rosewood Properties, Rosewood Resources with interests in oil and gas properties, luxury hotels, office devts in maj cities; owner Lady Primrose's Shopping English Countryside; Hon Chair and Chair numerous socs and cttees; Pres Appointee J. F. Kennedy Center for Performing Arts; Dallas Historic Soc Award for Excellence in Community Service in the Field of Business 1984; Les Femmes du Monde Award 1988; Grande Dame d'Escoffier 1989; Nat Fragrance Council Award 1994, British American Commerce Award 1994. *Publication:* The Compleat Pumpkin Eater. *Leisure interests:* antiques, writing. *Address:* 100 Crescent Court, Suite 1700, Dallas, TX 75201, USA.

HUNT, Hon Justice Constance Darlene, LL M; Canadian judge; b 11 Jan 1950; d of Howard S. Hunt and Linda Fromm. *Education:* Univ of Saskatchewan and Harvard Law School (USA). *Career:* Legal Adviser Inuit Taririsat of Canada 1973–75; Assoc Prof Faculty of Law, Univ of Calgary 1976–80, Assoc Dean 1979–81, Prof 1980–81; Corp Counsel Mobil Oil of Canada Ltd, Calgary and London (UK) 1981–83; Exec Dir Canadian Inst of Resources Law and Prof Faculty of Law, Univ of Calgary 1983–89, Dean and Prof of Law, Univ of Calgary 1989–91; Justice Alberta Court of Queen's Bench 1991–95, Alberta Court of Appeal 1995–. *Publications:* Oil & Gas Law in Canada (jtly) 1990. *Leisure interests:* music, sport. *Address:* Court of Appeal, 530 7 Ave SW, Calgary, AB T2P 0Y3, Canada. *Telephone:* (403) 297-6698.

HUNT, Helen; American actress; b 15 June 1963, LA; d of Gordon and Jane Hunt. *Films:* Rollercoaster, Girls Just Want to Have Fun, Peggy Sue Got Married, Project X, Miles From Home, Trancers, Stealing Home, Next of Kin, The Waterdance, Only You, Bob Roberts, Mr Saturday Night, Kiss of Death, Twister, As Good As It Gets (Acad Award for Best

Actress 1998), Twelfth Night, Pay It Forward 2000, Dr T and the Women 2000; *Plays include:* Been Taken, Our Town, The Taming of the Shrew, Methusalem; *TV:* Swiss Family Robinson, Mad About You (Emmy Award 1996, 1997, Golden Globe Award 1997). *Address:* c/o Connie Tavel, 9171 Wilshire Blvd, Suite 436, Beverley Hills, CA 90210, USA.

HUNT, Linda; American actress; b 2 April 1945, Morristown, NJ. *Education:* Interlochen Arts Acad (MI) and Goodman Theater and School of Drama (Chicago, IL). *Career:* Has appeared on Broadway and in films 1975–. *Plays include:* Down by the River 1975, A Metamorphosis in Miniature (Obie Award) 1982, Top Girls (Obie Award) 1983, Little Victories 1983, Aunt Dan and Lemon 1985, Cherry Orchard 1988; Broadway appearances: Ah, Wilderness! 1975, End of the World 1984; *Films include:* Dune 1984, The Year of Living Dangerously (Acad Award for Best Supporting Actress) 1983, The Bostonians 1984, Eleni 1985, Silverado 1985, Popeye 1980, Waiting for the Moon 1987, She-Devil 1989, Kindergarten Cop 1990, If Looks Could Kill 1991, Rain Without Thunder 1993, Twenty Bucks 1993, Younger and Younger 1993, Prêt-a-Porter 1994, Pocahontas 1995 (voice), Eat Your Heart Out 1997, Amazon (voice) 1997, The Relic 1997, Out of the Past 1998, Pocahontas II: Journey to a New World (voice) 1998, The Century 1999 (narrator). *Address:* William Morris Agency, 151 S El Camino Drive, Beverly Hills, CA 90212, USA.

HUNTER, Angela Margaret Jane (Anji); British political advisor; b 1956, Malaysia; m Nick Cornwall 1980; one s one d. *Education:* St Leonard's, St Clare's (Oxford) and Brighton Polytechnic. *Career:* Asst to Prime Minister Tony Blair May 1997–; Dir of Govt Relations 2001–. *Address:* c/o 10 Downing St, London SW1, UK.

HUNTER, Holly, BFA; American actress; b 20 March 1958, Atlanta, GA; d of Charles Edwin and Opal Marguerite Hunter; m Janusz Kaminski 1995. *Education:* Carnegie Mellon Univ. *Career:* Actress in plays before film debut in The Burning 1981; Co-Founder the Met theatre co, Los Angeles, CA and has produced two plays; Dir California Abortion Rights Action League. *Stage appearances include:* Crimes of the Heart, The Wake of Jamey Foster, The Miss Firecracker Contest, A Weekend Near Madison, The Person I Once Was, Battery, A Lie of the Mind; *Films:* The Burning 1981, Swing Shift, Raising Arizona 1987, Broadcast News (Best Actress, New York Film Critics Circle, Best Actress, Berlin Film Festival) 1988, The End of the Line, Animal Behavior, Miss Firecracker 1989, Always 1989, Once Around 1990, The Firm 1993, The Piano (Acad Award 1994) 1993, Copycat 1995, Home for the Holidays 1995, Crash 1996, A Life Less Ordinary, Living Out Loud 1998, Time Code 2000; *TV films include:* Svengali, An Uncommon Love, With Intent to Kill, A Gathering of Old Men, Roe vs Wade (Emmy Award for Best Actress) 1989, Positively True Adventures of the Alleged Texas Cheerleader-Murdering Mom (Emmy Award for Best Actress).

HUNTER, Rita, CBE, RAM; British opera singer; b 15 Aug 1933; d of Charles Newton and Lucy Hunter; m John Darnley-Thomas 1960 (died 1994); one d. *Education:* Wallasey. *Career:* Joined Carl Rosa 1950; debut Berlin 1970, Royal Opera House, London 1972, Metropolitan Opera, New York 1972, Munich, Germany 1973, Australia 1978; performed at Seattle Wagner Festival (USA) 1980; conducts worldwide master classes; Founder (with John Darnley-Thomas) Maduo School of Singing, Australia 1986–; organized John Darnley Thomas Memorial Scholarship; Hon D LITT (Warwick) 1978; Hon D MUS (Liverpool) 1983. *Operas include:* Aida, Il Trovatore, Un Ballo in Maschera, Cavalleria Rusticana, Lohengrin, The Flying Dutchman, Idomeneo, Don Carlos, Turandot, Nabucco, Macbeth, Tristan und Isolde, Electra; *Publication:* Wait till the Sun Shines Nellie (autobiog) 1986. *Leisure interests:* swimming, caravanning, oil painting, reading, gardening, sewing. *Address:* 305 Bobbin Head Rd, N Turramurra, NSW 2074, Australia; c/o Mark Bonello, 52 Dean St, London W1V 5HJ, UK. *Telephone:* (2) 9944 5062 (Australia); (20) 7437-8564 (UK); *Fax:* (2) 9488 7526; *E-mail:* grane@arrakis.com.au.

HUNTINGFORD, Felicity Ann, PH D; British zoologist; b 17 June 1948, Wiltshire; d of Thomas and Jill Morgan; m Timothy Huntingford 1969; two d. *Education:* Univ of Glasgow and St Hilda's Coll (Oxford). *Career:* Reader Dept of Zoology, Univ of Glasgow 1974–, later Titular Prof Div of Environmental and Evolutionary Biology, Inst of Biomedical and Life Sciences; ed Animal Behaviour 1986–91. *Publications:* The Study of Animal Behaviour 1984, Animal Conflict 1986. *Address:* University of Glasgow, Institute of Biomedical and Life Sciences, Glasgow G12 8QQ, UK (Office); 14 Banavie Rd, Glasgow G11 5AN, UK (Home). *Telephone:* (141) 330-5975 (Office); (141) 357-2867 (Home).

HUO DA; Chinese writer; b 1945, Beijing. *Education:* Beijing Constructional Eng Coll. *Career:* Translator Beijing Bureau of Cultural Relics; screenplay writer Beijing TV Station and Beijing TV Art Centre; Vice-Chair Chinese Soc of Writers of Ethnic Minorities. *Publications include:* The Burial Ceremony of Muslims (Mao Dun Prize for Literature), Red Dust (4th Nat Prize), The Worry and Joy of Thousands of Households (4th Nat Prize), Dragon Foal (Best Film Screenplay Award), Magpie Bridge (Flying Apsaras Award), Collected Works of Huo Da (6 vols). *Address:* Beijing Television Station, Beijing, 100089, People's Republic of China.

HUPPERT, Isabelle Anne; French actress; b 16 March 1953, Paris; d of Raymond Huppert and Annick Beau; two s one d. *Education:* Lycée de Saint-Cloud, Ecole Nat des Langues Orientales Vivantes. *Career:* Pres Comm d'avances sur recettes 1994–; Prix Susanne Blanchetti 1976; Prix Bistingo 1976; Prix César 1978; Gold Palm, Cannes 1978; Prix d'interprétation, Cannes 1978; Chevalier de la Légion d'Honneur. *Films include:* Le bar de la Fourche, César et Rosalie, Les valseuses, Aloïse, Dupont la joie, Rosebud, Docteur Françoise Gailland, Le juge et l'assassin, Le petit Marcel 1976, Les indiens sont encore loin 1977, La dentellière, Violette Nozière 1978, Les sœurs Brontë 1978, Loulou 1980, Sauve qui peut (la vie), Les héritières 1980, Heaven's Gate 1980, Coup de torchon 1981, Dame aux camélias 1981, Les ailes de la colombe 1981, Eaux profondes 1981, Passion, travail et amour, La truite 1982, Entre nous 1984, My Best Friend's Girl 1984, La garce 1984, Sac de nœuds 1985, Cactus 1986, Sincerely Charlotte 1986, The Bedroom Window 1986, Une affaire de femmes (Story of Women) 1988, The Possessed 1988, Milan Noir 1990, Madame Bovary 1991, Milana 1991, Après l'amour 1992, La Séparation 1994, Amateur 1994, L'Inondation 1994, La Cérémonie (César Award for Best Actress 1996) 1995, Les Affinités électives 1996, Rien ne va plus 1997, Les Palmes de M. Schutz 1997, L'Ecole de la chair 1998, Pas de scandale 1999, Merci pour le chocolat 2000, Les Destineées Sentimentales 2000, la Fausse suivante et Saint-Cyr 2000, The Pianist 2001; *Plays include:* Mary Stuart 1996. *Address:* c/o VMA, 40 ave George V, 75008 Paris, France.

HUQ, Shireen Pervin, BA; Bangladeshi feminist; b 4 Sept 1953, Comilla; d of Mohammad Rafiqul Huq and Jaheda Khanum; m Zafrullah Chowdury 1992; one s. *Education:* Holy Cross Coll (Dhaka), Univ of Dhaka, Evergreen State Coll (Washington, DC, USA) and Univ of Sussex (UK). *Career:* Organizer Naripokkho (Pro-Women) women's activist group 1983–; freelance Women in Devt (WID) Consultant and Gender Analysis Trainer; Adviser on women's devt Royal Danish Embassy, Dhaka 1987–; has made documentary films. *Address:* House 51, Rd 9A, Dhanmandi, Dhaka 1209, Bangladesh. *Telephone:* (2) 811495; *Fax:* (2) 811431; *E-mail:* shireen@naripkho.pradeshta.net.

HURLEY, Elizabeth Jane; British actress, producer and model; b 10 June 1965; d of the late Roy Leonard Hurley and of Angela Mary Hurley. *Career:* Producer for Simian Films and producer of Extreme Measures 1996; Spokeswoman and model for Estée Lauder. *Films include:* Aria 1987, Rowing with the Wind 1987, The Skipper 1989, El Largo Invierno 1990, The Orchid House 1990, Passenger '57 1992, Mad Dogs and Englishmen 1994, Dangerous Ground 1995, Samson and Delilah 1996, Austen Powers: International Man of Mystery (ShoWest Award for Best Supporting Actress 1997) 1996, Permanent Midnight 1997, My Favourite Martian 1999, Ed TV 1999, Austin Powers: The Spy Who Shagged Me 1999, Mickey Blue Eyes (producer only) 1999, The Weight of Water 2000, Bedazzled 2000; *TV appearances include:* Christabel (series) 1988), The Orchid House, Act of Will, The Resurrector, Rumpole, Inspector Morse, The Good Guys, The Young Indiana Jones Chronicles, Sharpe's Enemy, Cry of the City; *Plays include:* The Cherry Orchard – A Jubilee (Russian and Soviet Arts Festival), The Man Most Likely To (Middle East tour). *Leisure* *interest:* gardening. *Address:* c/o Simian Films, 3 Cromwell Place, London SW7 2SE, UK. *Telephone:* (20) 7589-6822; *Fax:* (20) 7589-9405.

HURLEY, Dame Rosalinde, DBE, LL B, MD, FRCPATH, FRCOG; British professor of microbiology and barrister; b 29 Dec 1929, London; d of the late William and Rose (née Clancey) Hurley; m Peter Gortvai 1963. *Education:* Acad of the Assumption (Wellesley Hills, MA, USA), Queen's Coll (London), Univ of London and Inns of Court. *Career:* Called to the Bar, Inner Temple 1958; House Surgeon Wembley Hosp 1955; House Physician W London Hosp 1956; Sr House Officer Charing Cross Hosp and Medical School 1956–57, Registrar 1957–58, Lecturer and Asst Clinical Pathologist 1958–62; Consultant Microbiologist 1962–75; Prof of Microbiology, Royal Postgraduate Medical School's Inst of Obstetrics and Gynaecology 1975–95, Prof Emer 1995–; Consultant Microbiologist Queen Charlotte's and Chelsea Hosp, London 1963–95, Hon Consultant 1995–; Prof of Microbiology Royal Postgraduate Medical School Inst of Obstetrics and Gynaecology 1975–95, Prof Emer 1995–; Vice-Chair Cttee on Dental and Surgical Materials 1975–78, Chair 1979–81; Chair Medicines Comm 1982–94; mem Public Health Lab Service Bd 1982–90; Pres Asscn of Clinical Pathologists 1984–; Chair Asscn of Profs of Medical Microbiology 1987–94; European Parl Rep; mem Bd Man European Medicines Evaluation Agency 1994–; mem Advisory Bd, Sheffield Inst of Biotech Law and Ethics 1995; Hon D UNIV (Surrey) 1984; Hon Fellow Faculty of Pharmaceutical Medicine 1990, Royal Soc of Medicine 1995; Hon FRSM 1996; Hon FIBIOL 1999; Baron C. ver Heyden de Lancey Prize 1991; Medal of Royal Coll of Pathologists 1999. *Publications:* Candida Albicans (jtly) 1964, Symposium on Candida Infections (jtly) 1966, Neonatal and Perinatal Infections (jtly) 1979; numerous papers on candidosis and infections in pregnant women and the newborn. *Leisure interests:* reading, gardening. *Address:* 2 Temple Gardens, Temple, London EC4Y 9AY, UK.

HURTADO, Maria Elena, MA; Chilean journalist and development executive; b 5 July 1945, Santiago; d of Rene and Adriana (née Merino) Hurtado; m Rolando Gaete 1972; two s. *Education:* Catholic Univ of Santiago, Univ of London and Middlesex Polytechnic (UK). *Career:* Journalist Ercilla news magazine 1968–70; Head Publications Dept, Editora Quimanti 1970–73; Research and Information Officer, World Devt Movt 1978–80, Dir 1991–93, Council mem; Science and Tech Officer South magazine 1980–90, Asst Ed 1990–91; Ed Panoscope, The Panos Inst 1990–91; Dir of Global Policy and Campaigns, Consumers Int 1994–; articles in int journals. *Leisure interests:* reading, bridge, travel. *Address:* Consumers International, 24 Highbury Crescent, London N5 1RX, UK (Office); 32 Poets Rd, London N5 2SE, UK (Home). *Telephone:* (20) 7226-6663 (Office); *Fax:* (20) 7354-0607 (Office).

HUSAINI, Naazish, M PHIL; Indian broadcasting executive; b 3 June 1951; d of Ali Abbas Husaini; m Shri Khalid Sultan 1983; one d. *Education:* Aligarh Muslim Univ. *Career:* Mem staff ERTS Project, UNICEF 1974; Producer Doordarshan India (Television India) 1975, Asst Dir 1985, apptd Deputy Controller of Programmes, responsible for Science and Rural Audience Programmes 1989; Jt Dir of Software Univ Grants Comm 1986; Consultant Islam in India, Wisconsin Univ Project 1987, Race to Save the Planet WBGH Project 1987; contribs to professional journals; Doordarshan Award, Best Children's Programmes 1984, Best Edited Programmes 1985. *Leisure interests:* music, film, bird-watching, environment issues. *Address:* Doordarshan, Doordarshan Bhawan, New Delhi 110 001, India (Office). *Telephone:* (11) 387786.

HUSSEY, Gemma, BA; Irish writer and former politician; b 1938, Bray, Co Wicklow; m Dermot R. Hussey; two d one s. *Education:* Loreto Convent (Bray), Convent of the Sacred Heart (Mount Anville, Dublin) and Univ Coll Dublin. *Career:* Chair Women's Political Asscn 1973–75, Vice-Chair 1975–77; mem Council for the Status of Women 1973–75; mem Seanad Éireann (Senate, Fine Gael) 1977–82, Govt Leader of Seanad 1981–82; became mem Dáil Éireann (House of Reps) 1982; Minister for Educ 1982–86, for Social Welfare 1986–87; Dir European Women's Fed; mem Jury Reading the Future literary award, Radio Telefís Éireann (RTÉ). *Publications:* Cutting Edge 1991, Ireland Today 1994. *Address:* c/o RTE, Donnybrook, Dublin, 4, Ireland.

HUSTON, Anjelica; American actress and director; b 8 July 1951, Los Angeles, CA; d of the late John and Enrica (née Soma) Huston; fmr partner Jack Nicholson; m Robert Graham 1992. *Education:* In Ireland. *Films:* Sinful Davey, A Walk with Love and Death, The Last Tycoon 1976, The Postman Always Rings Twice 1981, Swashbuckler, This is Spinal Tap 1984, The Ice Pirates 1984, Prizzi's Honor (Acad Award for Best Supporting Actress, New York and Los Angeles Film Critics' Awards 1985), Gardens of Stone, Captain Eo, The Dead, Mr North, A Handful of Dust, The Witches, Enemies, A Love Story, Crimes and Misdemeanors 1989, The Grifters, The Addams Family 1991, Addams Family Values 1993, The Player, Manhattan Murder Mystery 1993, The Crossing Guard 1996, The Perez Family 1996, Bastard Out Of Carolina (dir) 1996, Phoenix 1997, Agnes Browne 2000; *TV appearances include:* The Cowboy and the Ballerina 1984, Faerie Tale Theatre, A Rose for Miss Emily, Lonesome Dove; *Stage appearances include:* Tamara, Los Angeles 1985. *Address:* c/o International Creative Management, 8942 Wilshire Blvd, Beverly Hills, CA 90211, USA.

HUTCHISON, Kay Bailey, LL B; American politician; b 22 July 1943, Galveston, TX; d of Allan and Kathryn Bailey; m Ray Hutchinson. *Education:* Univ of Texas. *Career:* TV news reporter Houston, TX 1969–71; pvt law practice 1969–74; Press Sec to Anne Armstrong (qv) 1971; Vice-Chair Nat Transport Safety Bd 1976–78; Asst Prof Univ of Texas, Dallas 1978–79; Sr Vice-Pres, Gen Counsel Repub of Texas Corpn, Dallas 1979–81; Counsel Hutchison, Boyle, Brooks & Fisher, Dallas 1981–91; mem House of Reps, TX 1972–76, Treas of Texas 1990, Senator from Texas 1993–; Fellow American Bar Foundation, Texas Bar Foundation; mem ABA, State Bar of Texas. *Address:* c/o US Senate, 370 Russell Senate Bldg, Washington, DC 20510, USA.

HUXLEY BARKHAM, Selma de Lotbinière, OC; British historical geographer and writer; b 8 March 1927, London, UK; d of Michael and Ottilie (née de Lotbinière Mills) Huxley; m John Brian Barkham 1954 (died 1964); two s two d. *Career:* Asst, Cttee on Geographic Names, Royal Geographic Soc, UK 1949; Librarian, Arctic Inst of N America, Montréal 1951–54; Founder African Students Asscn 1960s; prepared and presented brief to Royal Comm on Bilingualism and Biculturalism which was deemed instrumental in bringing French immersion to Canadian public school system; Founding Mem, French Section, Citizens' Cttee on Children; helped start first French Canadian theatre group for children in the Outaouais, 'La compagnie des Trouvères' 1960s; researcher for historic sites (including Louisbourg) 1964–68; teacher Instituto Anglo-Mexicano, Guadalajara, Mexico until moving to Spain 1969–72; identified earliest ports used by Basques and other Europeans and found earliest civil documents written in Canada 1972–87; Royal Canadian Geographic Soc grant to lead first expedition to identify 16th century Basque whaling sites in Labrador including what is now the Red Bay Nat Historic Site 1977; led teams of underwater and land archaeologists to these sites; worked for Public Archives of Canada in Spain 1973–85; Social Sciences and Humanities Research Council of Canada grant for publ of documents relating to Basques in NF and Labrador 1984–86; mem Historical Cttee, Museo Naval de San Sebastian 1992–, Advisory Cttee For Red Bay, Labrador, Nat Historic Site 1996–; advocates Basque Nat Trust for the Preservation of Basque Architecture 1993–; Co-Founder, Northern Peninsula Heritage Soc 1997–; fluent in several European languages; Hon Consul of Bilbao, Bizkaia Chamber of Commerce (first woman nominee) 1992; elected mem Réal Sociedad Bascongada de Amigos del Païs 1981; Dr hc (Memorial Univ of Newfoundland) 1993, (Windsor, ON) 1985; Gold Medal of Royal Canadian Geographical Soc (first woman) 1980; numerous publs, lectures and confs; Award for Culture, Fundacion Sabino Arana, Bilbao 1999. *Publications include:* Los Vascos en el Marco Atlantico Norte Siglos XVI y XVII, Itsasoa (Vol 3) 1987. *Leisure interest:* languages. *Address:* 7 Chapel St, Chichester, West Sussex PO19 1BU, UK; 23 Des Estacades, Cantley, PQ J8V 3J3, Canada. *E-mail:* alv-bar@cyberus.ca.

HUXTABLE, Ada Louise, AB; American writer and critic; b New York; d of Michael Louis and Leah (née Rosenthal) Landman; m L. Garth Huxtable 1942. *Education:* Hunter Coll and Inst of Fine Arts, New York Univ. *Career:* Asst Curator of architecture and design Museum of Modern Art, New York 1946–50; Fulbright Scholarship to study contemporary Italian architecture and design 1950, 1952; contributing Ed Progressive Architecture, Art in America, freelance writer on architecture and design 1952–63; New York Times architecture critic 1963–82; mem Times Editorial Bd 1973–82; independent architectural consultant and critic 1982–96; Architecture Critic, The Wall Street Journal 1996–; mem Corpn Visiting Cttees on Architecture, Harvard Univ and MIT, Rockefeller Univ Council, Smithsonian Council, Advisory Bd of the Buell Centre for the Study of American Architecture, Columbia Univ; mem Soc of Architectural Historians, American Acad and Inst of Arts and Letters, American Philosophical Soc; Hon mem American Inst of Architects; Hon Fellow Royal Inst of British Architects; Fellow American Acad of Arts and Sciences, New York Inst for the Humanities; Guggenheim Fellowship for Studies in American Architecture 1958; numerous hon degrees; awards include Frank Jewett Mather Award for art criticism (Coll Art Asscn) 1967, Pulitzer Prize for Distinguished Criticism 1970, Architectural Criticism Medal (American Inst of Architects) 1969, Special Award of Nat Trust for Historic Preservation 1970, Nat Arts Club Medal for Literature 1971, Diamond Jubilee Medallion of the City of New York 1973, US Sec of Interiors' Conservation Award 1976, Thomas Jefferson Medal for Architecture 1977, Jean Tschumi Prize for Architectural Criticism, Int Union of Architects 1987, Medal for Architectural Criticism, Acad d'Architecture Française 1988, MacArthur Prize Fellowship 1981–86, Henry Allen Moe Prize in the Humanities, American Philosophical Soc 1992. *Publications:* Pier Luigi Nervi 1960, Classical New York 1964, Will They Ever Finish Bruckner Boulevard? 1970, Kicked a Building Lately? 1976, The Tall Building Artistically Reconsidered: The Search for a Skyscraper Style 1985, Architecture, Anyone? 1986, Goodbye History, Hello Hamburger 1986, The Unreal America: Architecture and Illusion 1997. *Address:* 969 Park Ave, New York, NY 10028, USA.

HYLAND, Frances, OC; Canadian actress; b Regina, SK; m George McCowan (divorced); one s. *Education:* Royal Acad of Dramatic Art. *Career:* Debut in London; appearances at Stratford festival 1954, toured with The Canadian Players; helped to est regional theatres in Canada; Dir Canadian Theatre, Shaw Festival Theatre; mem Canada Council 1974; Hon LL D (British Columbia, Saskatchewan, Windsor); Drainie Award 1981; Gov Gen's Award for Performing Arts 1994. *Plays include:* A Streetcar Named Desire, The Winter's Tale, Crime and Punishment, The Idiot, A Woman of No Importance, Measure for Measure, Hamlet, Look Homeward Angel, A Time to Laugh. *Address:* c/o Canadian Actors' Equity Asscn, 260 Richmond St E, 2nd Floor, Toronto, ON M5A 1P4, Canada.

HYNDE, Chrissie; American singer, songwriter and musician; b 7 Sept 1951, Akron, OH; one d with Ray Davies; m 1st Jim Kerr (divorced); one d; m 2nd Lucho Brieva 1999. *Career:* Fmrly music journalist on publs including NME; lead singer with The Pretenders, first hit single Stop Your Sobbing 1979, singer, songwriter and guitarist new band formed 1983; tours in the UK, Europe and USA; sang with UB40 group on singles I Got You Babe and Breakfast in Bed; gold and platinum discs in the USA. *Recordings include:* Albums: Pretenders, Pretenders II, Packed, Extended Play, Learn to Crawl, Get Close, The Singles; Singles: Kid 1979, Brass in Pocket 1979, The Talk of the Town 1980, Message of Love, I Go to Sleep, Back on the Chain Gang, Middle of the Road, Thin Line Between Love and Hate, 2,000 Miles, Don't Get Me Wrong, Hymn to Her.

HYNES, Garry, BA; Irish artistic director; b 10 June 1953, Ballaghaderreen, Co Roscommon; d of Oliver and Carmel Hynes. *Education:* Dominican Convent (Galway) and Univ Coll (Galway). *Career:* Founder Druid Theatre Co 1975, Artistic Dir 1994–; tours to Sydney, London and New York; Dir RSC Stratford and London 1988, 1989; Artistic Dir Abbey Theatre, Dublin 1991–94; Hon LL D (Nat Council for Educ Awards) 1987, (Nat Univ of Ireland) 1998; Fringe First, Edinburgh 1980, Dir of the Year 1983, 1985; Harveys Award for Best Dir 1983; Time Out (London) Award for Direction 1988; People of the Year Award 1989. *Productions include:* Playboy of the Western World 1982, Conversations on a Homecoming 1985, Baile gan Gáire (jtly) 1985, The Leenane Trilogy, A Whistle in the Dark 1986, The Plough and the Stars 1991, The Power of Darkness, Famine, The Beauty Queen of Leenane 1996 (New York 1998, Tony Award for Direction 1998). *Leisure interests:* books, poker, food. *Address:* c/o Druid Theatre Co, Chapel Lane, Galway, Ireland. *Telephone:* (91) 568617.

I

IBRAHIM, Fatima; Sudanese feminist and organization executive; b 1934, Khartoum. *Education:* Studied journalism. *Career:* Worked as teacher; Pres Sudanese Women's Union and Ed-in-Chief Sawt Al-mara'ah (Women's Voice); first woman mem Parl in Sudan 1965; spent time under house arrest and in detention following coup d'état in 1969; released 1983; elected Pres Women's Int Democratic Fed 1991; mem Cen Cttee Sudanese Communist Party.

IBRAIMOVA, Elmira; Kyrgyzstan diplomatist and economist; b 13 April 1962, Frunze. *Education:* Moscow State Univ (Russian Fed). *Career:* Perm Rep to UN 1999–. *Address:* Permanent Mission of Kyrgyzstan to the United Nations, 866 United Nations Plaza, Suite 477, New York, NY 10017, USA. *Telephone:* (212) 486-4214; *E-mail:* kyrgyzstan@un.int.

ICAZA, Teresa; Panamanian artist; b 12 Oct 1940; d of Ricardo and Lilia Icaza; m 1st A. Gonzalez (divorced 1966); m 2nd J. R. Villalaz; two d. *Education:* Self-taught. *Career:* Dir Habitante Galerie 1981–82; Asst Dir Museum of Contemporary Art, Panamá 1982–85; solo exhibitions include Art Inst of Panama 1973, Nova Galerie, Panamá 1974, Galerie El Buho, Bogotá, Colombia 1977, The Seller of Panarte, Panamá 1980, Galerie Etcetera, Panamá 1983, Galerie Kandinsky, San José, Costa Rica 1990, Galerie Metropolitana, Quito 1992, The Americas Collection, Coral Gables, FL, USA 1993, 1995, Galería Arteconsult, Panamá 1993, 1995, Plástica Contemporánea, Guatemala 1994, 1996, Arawak Galería de Arte, Santo Domingo, Dominican Repub 1994, 1995, Freites-Revilla Gallery, Boca Raton, FL, USA 1996; group exhibitions include Cultural Festival, Colombia 1973, Women Int Center, New York 1976, Caracas, Venezuela 1983, Havana Biennial, Cuba 1984, Castagnino Museum, Argentina 1986, Espacio Gallery, San Salvador 1986, Miami Biennial, FL, USA 1986, São Paulo Biennial, Brazil 1987, Valparaíso Biennial, Chile 1990, The Auction Gallery, New York 1990, Cuenca Biennial, Ecuador 1991, Lisbon 1991, México Biennial, Mexico 1992, Art Miami '92, '93, '95 Miami, FL, USA, TRIO'S Galería de Arte, Tegucigalpa, Honduras 1993, Galería Filanbanco, Quito 1994, Galería Espacio, San Salvador 1994, Magnat Gallery, London 1994, The Americas Collection, Coral Gables, FL, USA 1994, 1995, Galería 1-2-3, San Salvador 1995, Santander Gallery, Banco Santander Int, Miami, FL, USA 1995; represented in numerous perm collections; awards include First Prize Nat Inst of Culture Painting Competition 1985, Ladies of Int Organisms Competition 1985, Second Prize Nat Painting Competition 1987. *Leisure interests:* etching, ceramics, silk-screen. *Address:* Calle 49 No 11, Bella Vista, POB 6321, Panamá 5, Panama. *Telephone:* 69-1897; *Fax:* 69-3537.

ICHINO, Yoko; American ballet dancer and teacher; b Los Angeles, CA; m David Nixon 1985. *Education:* RAD and under Mia Slavenska. *Career:* Dancer Joffrey Ballet 1973–75, Stuttgart Ballet, Germany 1975–76; Soloist American Ballet Theatre 1977–81; Prin Nat Ballet of Canada 1982–90; Dir of Professional Training Program Ballet Met, Columbus, OH Sept 1995–; freelance dancer and teacher; Guest Dancer with numerous cos including Australian Ballet, Ballet de Monte Carlo, Ballet Nat de Marseille (France), Birmingham Royal Ballet (UK), Deutsche Oper Ballet, Royal New Zealand Ballet, Tokyo Ballet; guest appearances include World Ballet Festival, Japan 1979, 1985, Ruth Page's production of Nutcracker 1981, 1986, 1987, 1990, 1991; teaching workshops in USA and Japan 1977–87; Guest teacher USA, Australia, Monaco, Germany, Canada, Japan, UK; first American winner Third Int Ballet Competition, Moscow 1977. *Ballets include:* Theme and Variations, Undertow, The River, Sleeping Beauty, Giselle, Swan Lake, Don Quixote, The Dream, La Fille Mal Gardée, Etudes, La Bayadère, Components, L'Ille Inconnue, Nutcracker, Coppelia, Chat

Botté, Romeo and Juliet, Les Sylphides, The Merry Widow, Flames of Paris, Swan Lake, Cinderella. *Address:* Ballet Met, 322 Mount Vernon Ave, Columbus, OH 43215, USA. *Fax:* (30) 3134395 (Germany).

IDRAC, Anne-Marie André, L EN D; French politician and civil servant; b 27 July 1951, Saint-Brieuc; d of André and Marguerite Colin; m Francis Idrac 1974; four d. *Education:* Univ of Paris II, Inst d'Etudes Politiques de Paris and Ecole Nat d'Admin. *Career:* Civil Servant Ministry of Equipment, Housing and Transport 1974–77, Technical Adviser to Sec of State for Housing, then to Minister of Environment 1979–81, Sub-Dir for Housing Improvement 1981–83, for Finance and Judicial Affairs 1983–87, Head Dept, Deputy Dir Construction Directorate 1987–90, Dir Ground Transport 1993–95, Sec of State for Transport 1995–97; Deputy to Nat Ass (UDF) for Yvelines 1997–; Sec Gen Force Démocrate, mem Conseil régional d'Ile de France 1998–; Vice-Pres UDF, Pres Mouvement Européen France 1999–; Rep to Prefect, Midi-Pyrénées region 1977–79; Auditor Inst des Hautes Etudes de Défense Nat 1986–87; Dir-Gen Etablissement Public d'Aménagement, Cergy-Pontoise (new town man co) 1990–93; Laureate, Fondation Nat des Entreprises Publiques 1977; Chevalier de l'Ordre Nat du Mérite. *Address:* Assemblée Nationale, 75355 Paris, France.

IHEKWEAZU, Edith, PH D; Nigerian educator; b 23 Aug 1941, Erlangen, Germany; m U. A. Ihekweazu 1969; two s one d. *Education:* Univ of Hamburg (Germany). *Career:* Lecturer Univ of Hamburg 1967–74; Lecturer, later Sr Lecturer Univ of Nigeria 1974–83, Head Dept of Languages 1986–88, Dean Faculty of Arts 1988–90; mem Int Fed of Univ Women, Int Asscn of German Studies, W African Languages Asscn. *Publications include:* Goethes West Östlicher Divan, Untersuchungen zur Struktur des lyrischen Zyklus 1971, Verzerrte Utopie, Bedeutung und Funktion des Wahnsinns in expressionistischer Prosa 1982, Peter Ruhmkorf: Bibliografie Essy zur Poetik 1984, Readings in African Humanities: Traditional and Modern African Culture (ed) 1985, Experience Abroad: African Travellers Discover the Western World 1986; numerous contribs to professional journals. *Address:* University of Nigeria, Dept of Languages, Nsukka, Anambra State, Nigeria; 1 King Jaja St, University of Nigeria, Nsukka Campus, Anambra State, Nigeria (Home). *Telephone:* (095) 771911 (Office); (095) 770417 (Home).

IHROMI-SIMATUPANG, Tapi Omas, MA, LL D; Indonesian anthropologist; b 2 April 1930, Pematang Siantar; m Prof Ihromi 1959; two d. *Education:* Univ of Indonesia, Cornell Univ (NY, USA) and Univ of Leiden (Netherlands). *Career:* Apptd Lecturer Faculty of Law, Univ of Indonesia 1955, Prof 1979; Chair Inst for Social Services 1986; Chair Srikandi Foundation for the Advancement of the Status of Women 1983; Educational Rep to Parl and People's Ass 1968–71; named Best Social Sciences Researcher, Univ of Indonesia 1990. *Publications:* The Status of Women and Family Planning in Indonesia 1973, Mothers with Single Rôles and with Double Rôles 1990. *Leisure interest:* reading. *Address:* Jalan Dempo 14, Jakarta Pusat 10320, Indonesia. *Telephone:* (21) 3904127.

IIVULA-ITHANA, Pendukeni; Namibian politician; b 11 Oct 1952, Ongandjera; d of E. Iivula; m Joseph M. Ithana 1987; two s one d. *Education:* High School Oshigambo, UN Inst for Namibia and Univ of London. *Career:* Leader SW Africa People's Org of Namibia (SWAPO) Women's Council and mem Cen Cttee SWAPO; Deputy Minister, later Minister of Youth and Sport 1991, now Minister of Justice and Attorney-Gen. *Leisure interests:* swimming, cooking, music, dance, reading. *Address:* Ministry of Justice, Justitia Bldg, Independence Ave, PMB 13248, Namibia. *Telephone:* (61) 2805111; *Fax:* (61) 221615.

ILLNEROVA, Helena, B SC; Czech medical scientist; b 28 Dec 1937, Prague; d of the late Karel Lagus and Libuše Lagusová-Baxová; m Michal Illner 1963; one s one d. *Education:* Charles Univ and Acad of Sciences. *Career:* Research Assoc Inst of Physiology, Acad of Sciences 1966–85, Head Dept of Neurohumoral Regulations 1990–; Research Assoc Inst for Cancer Research, Columbia Univ (USA) 1969–70; Sr Fellow in Neurosciences, Fogarty International Center, NIH, Univ of Massachusetts 1992, 1993, 1994; Vice-Pres Acad of Sciences 1993–; mem Advisory Bd Soc for Biological Rhythms Research 1987; mem Czech Learned Soc 1994; Award of Czech Physiology Soc 1981; Award of Czech Medical Soc J. E. Purkyně 1987; numerous contribs to books and journals. *Leisure interests:* grandchildren, literature, tourism, skiing. *Address:* Institute of Physiology, Vídeňská 1083, 142 20 Prague 4, Czech Republic. *Telephone:* (2) 24240527; *Fax:* (2) 4719117.

IMAI, Nobuko; Japanese viola player; b 18 March 1943, Tokyo; m Aart von Bochove 1981; one s one d. *Education:* Toho School of Music (Tokyo), Juilliard School of Music and Yale Univ (USA). *Career:* Mem Vermeer Quartet 1974–79; soloist with London Symphony Orchestra, Royal Philharmonic (UK), Chicago Symphony (USA), Concertgebouw (Netherlands), Montréal Symphony (Canada), Boston Symphony (USA), Vienna Symphony, Orchestre de Paris, Stockholm Philharmonic; festival performances include Marlborough, Casals, South Bank (London), Bath, Cheltenham and Aldeburgh (UK), London Proms, Int Viola Congress (Houston, TX, USA), Lockenhaus, Hindemith Festivals (Tokyo, New York and London) 1995–96; Prof High School of Music, Detmold, Germany 1985–; performed world première of Takemitsu Viola Concerto entitled A String Around Autumn 1989; First Prize Munich Int Viola Competition; Second Prize Geneva Int Viola Competition; Avon Arts Award 1993; Japanese Educ Minister's Art Prize for Music 1994; Mobil Prize (Japan) 1995; Suntory Hall Prize 1996. *Recordings include:* Tippett Triple Concerto, Berlioz: Harold in Italy, Takemitsu, Walter and Schnittke concertos. *Leisure interests:* cooking, golf. *Address:* c/o Kajimoto Concert Management Co Ltd, Tokyo, Japan. *Telephone:* (3) 3574-0969; *Fax:* (3) 3574-0980; *E-mail:* kajimoto@music.co.jp; *Internet:* www.music.co.jp/~kajimoto.

IMAN, (Iman Abdul Majid); Somali fashion model; b 25 July 1956; m 1st Spencer Haywood (divorced 1987); one d; m 2nd David Bowie 1992. *Education:* Univ of Nairobi. *Career:* Fashion model 1976–90, has modelled for Claude Montana and Thierry Mugler; signed Revlon Polish Ambers contract (first black model to be signed by int cosmetics co) 1979; launched own cosmetics co I-Iman; has made numerous TV appearances and has appeared on Michael Jackson video. *Films include:* Out of Africa, Star Trek VI: The Undiscovered Country, Houseparty II, Exit to Eden. *Internet:* www.i-iman.com.

INDJOVA, Reneta, PH D; Bulgarian economist and politician; b 6 July 1953, Nova Zgora; m Boyan Slavenkov 1977 (divorced 1977); one d. *Education:* Sofia Univ of Nat and World Economy. *Career:* Univ Asst Prof of Political Economy and Econs 1975–89; Co-Founder Union of Democratic Forces (UDF), co-author UDF's platform 1990; Econ Counsellor to Great Nat Ass 1990–91; expert govt's Agency for Econ Devt 1991–93; Head of Privatization Agency 1993, Exec Dir 1994; Prime Minister of Bulgaria 1994–95; Founder and Nat Chair political party 'For Real Reforms' 1997; Fellow Eisenhower Exchange Program, Philadelphia 1995; Trustee American Univ of Blagoevgrad 1996–; Distinguished Speaker Atlantic Club of Bulgaria 1995. *Leisure interests:* literature, music, tailoring. *Address:* 'Hadji Dimitar' bl 142, A, ap 4, Sofia, 1510, Bulgaria.

INDRANI, (pseudonym of Indrani Bajpai Rahman); Indian dancer; b 19 Sept 1930, Madras (now Chennai); d of Ramlal and Ragini (née Devi) Bajpai; m Habib Rahman 1946; two c. *Education:* Studied under Ragini Devi (mother), Tanjore Kittappa, Deva Prasad Das-Orissa, Chinammu Amma-Kerala and Pandanallur Chokkalingham Pillai. *Career:* Career as Indian classical dancer started at five years; world tours with mother and later with own dance co; dance tour Asia Soc of New York; acted as India's Cultural Ambassador, performances for Pres J. F. Kennedy, HM Queen Elizabeth II, Krushchev and Mao Zedong; Prof of Dance The Juilliard School, Lincoln Center, New York and Univ of New York; teacher of classical Indian dance styles including Orissi and Kuchipudi; numerous articles on dance; Padma Shree, Govt of India 1965, Sangeet Natak Akad Award 1982; Sahitya Kala Parishad, Delhi Admin 1972;

Key to City of New York 1973; Asscn of Indians in America Award 1984; Dr Taraknath Das Award, Columbia Univ, NY 1992. *Leisure interests:* reading, politics, theatre, friends. *Address:* 29A Oberoi Apts, 2 Alipur Rd, Delhi 54, India; 85 Fourth Ave, Apt 2H, New York, NY 10003, USA. *Telephone:* (11) 2528500 (India); (212) 228-0885 (USA); *Fax:* (212) 227-5719 (USA).

INDZHOVA, Reneta; Bulgarian former civil servant and politician; b 1953. *Career:* Fmr Head of Privatization Agency; Prime Minister (first woman) Oct–Dec 1994; mem Union of Democratic Forces (UDF). *Address:* Union of Democratic Forces, Blvd Rakovski 134, 1000 Sofia, Bulgaria. *Telephone:* (2) 88-25-01.

INGOLD, Catherine White, PH D; American university president; b 15 March 1949, Columbia, SC; d of Hiram Hutchison and Annelle White; m Wesley Thomas Ingold 1970; one c. *Education:* Univ of Paris (Sorbonne). *Career:* Assoc Prof of Romance Languages, Gallaudet Univ 1973–88, Dir Honours Programme 1980–85, Dean of Arts and Sciences 1985–86, Provost and Vice-Pres of Acad Affairs 1986–88; Pres American Univ of Paris, France 1988–92, Curry Coll, Milton, MA 1992–96; Deputy Dir Nat Foreign Language Center, Johns Hopkins Univ 1996–; Dr hc (Francis Marion) 1992; Prix Morot-Sir de Langue et Littérature Française. *Address:* National Foreign Language Center, 1617 Massachusetts Ave, NW, Washington, DC 20036, USA (Office); 1 rue de Belgrade, 75007 Paris, France (Home).

INNES, Sheila Miriam, MA, FRSA, FITD; British broadcaster and media educator; b 25 Jan 1931; d of James and Nora Innes. *Education:* Talbot Heath School (Bournemouth) and Lady Margaret Hall (Oxford). *Career:* Joined BBC 1955, Radio Producer World Service 1955–61, TV Producer family progs 1961–65, Further Educ progs 1965–73, Exec Producer Further Educ 1973–77, Head Continuing Educ 1977–84, Controller Educational Broadcasting 1984–87, Dir BBC Enterprises Ltd 1986–87; Chief Exec The Open Coll 1987–89, Deputy Chair 1989–92; Media and Educ Consultant 1991–; Chair cross-section Cttee for Devt and Review Business and Technician Educ Council (BTEC) 1986–87, for Product Devt 1989–92; Non-Exec Dir Brighton Health Care NHS Trust 1992–95; mem Adjudication Panel British Gas Training Awards 1988–92; mem Gen Bd Alcoholics Anonymous 1980–, Bd of Govs Centre for Information on Language Teaching and Research 1981–84, Council Open Univ 1984–87, Council for Educational Tech 1984–87, Educational Working Party, European Broadcasting Union 1984–87; Patron One World Broadcasting Trust 1988–; mem Educ Cttee RSA 1990–96, Age Concern Training Validation Cttee 1992–95, BIM Man Devt Project 1992–95; Vice-Pres Educ Section BAAS 1990; articles on language, training and broadcasting to professional journals; Companion, British Inst of Man 1988; Hon D LITT (South Bank) 1992. *Leisure interests:* music, languages, literature, countryside, swimming, photography, travel. *Address:* Wychwood, Barcombe, Lewes, E Sussex BN8 5TP, UK; Rowan Hill, Crook, Cumbria LA8 9HR, UK (Home). *Telephone:* (1273) 400268.

INOUE, Yuko; Japanese viola player; b Hamamatsu. *Education:* Royal Northern Coll of Music (Manchester, UK). *Career:* Frm prin viola of Netherlands Chamber Orchestra; now soloist and chamber musician; Prof at RAM (London); performed as soloist with Hungarian State Philharmonic Orchestra, Halle Orchestra, Netherlands Chamber Orchestra; performed as prin with Philharmonia Orchestra, London Sinfonietta; has appeared at Lockenhaus, Kuhmo, Cheltenham, Bath and Aldeburgh Festivals; winner of 17th Budapest Int Viola Competition.

INUI, Harumi, BA; Japanese politician; b 18 Oct 1934, Tokushima; m 1961; two d. *Education:* Univ of Tokushima. *Career:* Teacher of Health and Physical Educ 1957; staff mem Physical Educ and Health Div, Tokushima Bd of Educ 1973, Social Educ Div 1979; Asst Dir Youth and Women's Bureau, Tokushima Dept of Planning and Co-ordination 1982; elected to House of Councillors (Parl) for Tokushima 1989, mem Budget Cttee 1989; Parl Vice-Minister for Science and Tech 1993. *Leisure interests:* sports, reading, theatre, cinema. *Address:* 3-24-3 Kamiyoshino-cho, Tokushima-shi, Tokushima-ken 770, Japan. *Telephone:* (88) 654-1735; *Fax:* (88) 654-1735.

INUKAI, Tomoko, BA; Japanese journalist and writer; b 18 April 1931, Tokyo; d of Mototake and Katsuko Hatano; m Yasuhiko Inukai 1953 (divorced 1978); one s one d. *Education:* Univs of Gakushin and Illinois (USA). *Career:* Journalist Far E Bureau, Chicago Daily News 1957–60; published first book 1968; mem Cttee Social Policy Council, Econ Planning Agency 1988, Cttee Tokyo Metropolitan Marine Park 1990; solo art exhibition Tokyo 1992; Del to Jt Japan Inst for Social and Econ Affairs and Swiss Inst of Int Studies Japan Symposium, Zurich, Switzerland 1979. *Publications include:* How to Avoid Housekeeping: to be free from the house 1968, Men and Women: new relationships 1982, Suspicious Circuit 1986, Japan Rediscovering Kabuki 1989. *Leisure interests:* photography, art, driving. *Address:* 25-19 Kamiyama-cho, Shibuya-ku, Tokyo 150, Japan. *Telephone:* (3) 469-4691; *Fax:* (3) 460-3040.

INYUMBA, Aloysia; Rwandan politician. *Career:* Minister of Women's Affairs and the Family; mem Front patriotique rwandais (Inkotanyi). *Address:* Ministry of Women's Affairs and the Family, BP 790, Kigali, Rwanda. *Telephone:* 73481.

IOANNIDOU-ADAMIDOU, Irena; Cypriot writer and translator; b 5 Feb 1939, Famagusta; d of the late Cleanthis and of Anastasia (née Galanou) Ioannides; m Panos Adamides 1961; two d. *Education:* Brillantmont International Coll, Acad of Music (Lausanne, Switzerland) and Univ of Vienna. *Career:* Writer since the age of 16; collaboration with Cyprus Broadcasting Corpn and numerous other TV and radio stations and theatres 1962–; mem Public Relations Cttee Cyprus PEN 1980–86; mem Nat Soc of Greek Writers, Society of Greek Playwrights, Soc of Greek Literary Translators; numerous awards and prizes. *Publications include:* Novels: Hommes, chemins et destin 1959, Maria Cristina 1960, Symphonie Héroïque 1961, Dans les bras de la mer 1962, Mme Rime 1963, Mattinata 1964, Nous vivrons 1981, Un ciel comme le nôtre 1981; Plays: Le parfum 1968, Le suicide 1970, La vengeance 1975, Visite 1977, Conflit 1978, Le cerf-volant 1980, Le champ 1982, Délit prémédité 1983, Post mortem 1986, Lutte secrète 1987, Syméos 1989, Le conseil conjugal (First Prize, Cyprus Radio) 1990, The Suspects (winner VII Third World International Playwright Competition 1994), The Robbery; Short stories: Syméos (Pan-Hellenic Prize, Athens) 1986, La Fille de Théodore 1991; has translated works from French, English, Spanish, etc by writers including Alfred de Musset, Molière, Boris Vian, Romain Rolland, Diego Fabbri, Strindberg, Natalia Ginzburg, Arthur Miller. *Address:* 92 Makenios III Ave, Nicosia, Cyprus. *Telephone:* (2) 376899.

IRELAND, Patricia; American organization executive; b 19 Oct 1945, Oak Park, IL; d of James Ireland and Joan Filipek; m James Humble 1968. *Education:* Univ of Miami (FL). *Career:* Flight attendant Pan Am World Airlines 1967–75; Partner Stears, Weaver, Miller, Weissler, Alhadeff and Sitterson, Miami, FL; legal counsel Dade Co; legal counsel Florida Br, Nat Org for Women (NOW); Dir Project Stand Up for Women (NOW), Rep to EP, Nat Congress of Brazilian Women, German–American Women's Confs, Cuban Women's Fed, European Women's Solidarity Conf and Nat Abortion Campaign (UK), Exec Vice-Pres NOW 1987–91, Pres 1991–. *Address:* c/o National Organization for Women (NOW), 2nd Floor, 733 15th St, NW, Washington, DC 20005, USA.

IRUKWU, Enoh Maria Etuk, M SC; Nigerian broadcasting executive; b 16 Oct 1934, Etinan, Akwa Ibom State; m Joe Irukwu 1963; three d two s. *Education:* Boston Univ (MA, USA). *Career:* Joined Fed Radio Corpn of Nigeria (fmrly Nigerian Broadcasting Corpn), Dir External Service Programmes; mem Nat Electoral Comm (NEC) from 1987; Pres Media Women Asscn of Nigeria; Nat Pres Lagos Soroptimist; mem Nat Centre for Women Devt, Devt Policy Centre. *Leisure interests:* reading, cooking, travelling, music. *Address:* POB 30733, Ojetunji Aboyade House, DPC Rd/ Oba Akinyele St, Secretariat Ibadan, Agodi, Nigeria. *Internet:* www.dpcnig.org.

IRVING, Amy; American actress; b 10 Sept 1953, Palo Alto, CA; m Steven Spielberg 1985 (divorced); one s; one s with Bruno Barreto. *Education:* American Conservatory Theater and London Acad of Dramatic Art. *Career:* Frequent TV appearances. *Films include:* Carrie, The Fury, Voices, Honeysuckle Road, The Competition, Yentl, Mickey and Maude, Rumpelstiltskin, Who Framed Roger Rabbit? (voice), Crossing Delancey, Show of Force, An American Tail: Fievel Goes West (voice), Benefit of the Doubt, Kleptomania, Acts of Love (also co-exec producer), I'm Not Rappaport, Carried Away, Deconstructing Harry, One Tough Cop, Blue Ridge Fall, The Confession, The Rage: Carrie 2; *Stage appearances include:* Romeo and Juliet, Amadeus 1981–82, Heartbreak House 1983–84, The Road to Mecca 1988.

IRVING, Janet Turnbull, MA; Canadian literary agent; b 16 April 1954, Toronto; d of Donald Gibson and Joan Heloise Turnbull; m John Irving 1987. *Education:* Univ of Toronto. *Career:* Ed Authors' Marketing Services Ltd 1979; Ed Doubleday Canada Ltd 1980, Man Ed 1981; Vice-Pres, Publr and Dir Seal Books 1984–87; Pres The Turnbull Agency 1987–, Curtis Brown Canada Ltd 1989–99; Ed Bantam Canada Inc; Founding Pres The Canadian Business Task Force on Literacy. *Address:* POB 1048, Manchester Centre, VT 05255, Canada.

IRWIN, Flavia (Lady de Grey), RA; British artist; b 15 Dec 1916, London; d of Clinton and Everilda Irwin; m Sir Roger de Grey 1942; two s one d. *Education:* Hawnes School (Ampthill, Beds) and Chelsea School of Art. *Career:* Taught gen design at Medway Coll of Art 1970–75; Sr tutor Decorative Arts Course, City & Guilds of London Art School 1975–; solo exhibition Ansdell Gallery; several group exhibitions including Royal Acad of Arts Summer Exhibition, Gallery 10, Grosvenor St; work in collections including Westminster Conf Centre (London), Midland Montague Morgan Grenfell, Carlisle City Art Gallery, Dept of the Environment, Govt Art Collection; Hon Academician Royal West of England Acad (Bristol). *Leisure interests:* swimming, reading. *Address:* 5 Camer St, Meopham, Kent DA13 0XR, UK. *Telephone:* (1474) 812327.

ISAAC-SIBILLE, Bernadette, L ÈS L; French politician; b 30 March 1930, Lyons; d of Albert and Lucile (née Martin-Monchovet) Sibille; m Alain Isaac 1956; three s one d. *Education:* Belmont School, Inst of Ladies of Nazareth, Catholic Univ (Lyons) and Univ of Lyons. *Career:* Teacher 1959–65; Town Councillor, then Deputy Mayor, Lyons 1977–83, Municipal Councillor and sometime Mayor 1983–; Rhône District Councillor 1985–, Vice-Pres Gen Council; mem Nat Ass (Parl, UDF) for Rhône 1988–; Vice-Pres Rhône Gen Council; Chevalier de l'Ordre Nat du Mérite 1980; Médaille de la Famille Française 1982. *Leisure interests:* piano, music, reading. *Address:* Assemblée Nationale, 75355 Paris, France (Office); 25 rue François Genin, 69005 Lyons, France (Home). *Telephone:* (4) 78-36-61-19 (Home); *Fax:* (4) 72-32-16-60 (Home).

ISAKSEN, Eva; Norwegian film director; b 1956. *Career:* Asst Dir, Producer then Dir; first feature film 1985; Dir for Norsk Film A/S. *Films include:* You Are Not Alone, Burning Flowers 1985, Death at Oslo Central 1990.

ISHIOKA, Eiko; Japanese costume designer; b Tokyo. *Education:* Tokyo Nat Univ of Fine Arts and Music. *Career:* Worked as commercial graphic artist, art dir posters, record covers and books Japan 1961–80; moved to New York 1980; production designer Mishima (special award, Cannes Film Festival, France 1984); costume designer M Butterfly (nominated for Tony award 1988), Bram Stoker's Dracula (Best Costume Design Oscar 1993); elected to Hall of Fame, New York Art Dirs' Club 1992.

ISOHOOKANA-ASUNMAA, Tytti Maria, D SC S; Finnish politician and lecturer in history and social sciences; b 24 Sept 1947, Haukipudas; d of Kaarlo and Helvi (née Hekkala) Isohookana; m Martti T. Asunmaa 1974; one s. *Education:* Univ of Oulu. *Career:* Mem Haukipudas Municipal Council from 1972, First Vice-Chair 1989; elected to Eduskunta (Parl, Centre Party) for Haukipudas 1983; apptd Minister for Cultural Affairs 1992; Lecturer in History and Social Sciences, Dept of Teacher Educ, Univ of Oulu from 1973; Chair Council for Adult Educ 1985–87, Finnish Youth Asscn; mem Bd of Dirs, Finnish Film Foundation 1987. *Publications:* Teacher Training in Oulu 1953–73 1974, Birth and Development of the Agrarian Party in Northern Finland up to Independence 1976, The Agrarian Party, Development Between 1906–1939 1980, The Agrarian Party into the Majority Party in Kainuu 1985, Peace Education in Teachers' Awareness 1986. *Leisure interests:* reading, gardening. *Address:* c/o Eduskunta, Mannerheimintie 30, 00102 Helsinki, Finland (Office); Kellontie, 90820 Kello, Finland (Home). *Telephone:* (0) 13417585 (Office); (81) 402271 (Home).

ISOM, Harriet Winsar, BA, LL M; American former diplomatist; b 4 Nov 1936, Oregon; d of Blaine Eugene and Evelyn (née Struve) Isom. *Education:* Mills Coll (Oakland, CA) and Fletcher School of Law and Diplomacy (Medford, MA). *Career:* Foreign Affairs Analyst USAF 1960–61; entered diplomatic service 1961; postings in Asia and Africa including Deputy Chief of Mission to Burundi 1974–77; Consul Medan, Indonesia 1977–78, Political Counsellor, Jakarta 1978–81; Dir of Korean Affairs, US Dept of State 1984–86; Chargée d'Affaires, Laos 1986–89; Amb to Benin 1989–92, to Cameroon 1993–96; Pres's Award 1989. *Leisure interests:* reading, photography, amateur dramatics. *Address:* Isom Ranch, 74661 Yoakum Rd, Echo, OR 97826, USA.

ITZIK, Dalia, BA; Israeli politician and teacher; b 1952, Jerusalem; m; three c. *Education:* Herzliya Interdisciplinary Centre (Hebrew Univ). *Career:* Fmr Deputy Mayor of Jerusalem in charge of Educ; fmr Chair Legis Panel of Labour Party; fmr mem Labour Party Cen Cttee, Bd of Govs of Israel Broadcasting Authority, Bd of Jerusalem Theatre, Gerard Behar Centre; mem Knesset 1992–; served in Finance Cttee 1992–96, Educ and Culture Cttee 1992–99 (Chair 1995–96), Cttee on Status of Women 1992–99; Chair Special Cttee for Research and Scientific Technological Devt 1997–99; Minister of the Environment 1999–2001, of Industry and Trade 2001–. *Address:* Ministry of Industry and Trade, POB 299, 30 Rehov Agron, Jerusalem, 94190, Israel. *Telephone:* (2) 6220661; *Fax:* (2) 6222412; *E-mail:* dover@moit.gov.il; *Internet:* www .tamas.gov.il.

IVANOVA, Ludmila Nikolayevna, MD; Russian geneticist; b 19 Feb 1929, Novosibirsk. *Education:* Novosibirsk Inst of Med. *Career:* Head of Lab Inst of Cytology and Genetics Siberian Br, Russian Acad of Sciences 1971–; Corresp mem Russian Acad of Sciences 1991, mem 1997–; main research in cellular and molecular mechanisms of regulation of permeability of biological membranes; L. A. Orbeli Award, Russian Acad of Sciences. *Leisure interests:* music, cookery. *Address:* Institute of Cytology and Genetics, Akademika Lavretyeva prosp 10, Novosibirsk, Russian Federation. *Telephone:* (3832) 35-54-74; *Fax:* (3832) 33-12-78; *E-mail:* ludiv.bionet.nse.ru.

IVANOVA, Natal'ya Borisovna; Russian journalist. *Education:* Moscow State Univ. *Career:* Journalist Znamya 1972–86, Deputy Ed-in-Chief 1991–; journalist Druzhba narodov; mem Exec Cttee European Forum, Moscow; mem Aprel'lit movt, Moscow Asscn, Russian Fed Writers' Union, PEN Centre, Commonwealth of Writers' Unions 1992–, European Cultural Centre, Geneva, Switzerland. *Address:* Znamya, Moscow 103863, ul Nikolskaya 8/1, Russian Federation. *Telephone:* (095) 921-24-30.

IVERSON, Ann; American business executive; b 1944; d of John Earl Van Eenenaam and Dorothy Ann Knight; m 4th (divorced); one d one s. *Education:* Arizona State Univ. *Career:* Mem staff Bullock's Dept Store (Los Angeles, CA), Harzfield's (Kansas City, KS), T. H. Mandy (VA); Operating Vice-Pres Bloomingdales 1984, then Sr Vice-Pres of Stores; joined Storehouse, UK 1989, Stores Dir British Home Stores (BHS), Chief Exec Mothercare; Chief Exec Kay-Bee Toys, Laura Ashley 1995–97.

IVEY, Beryl Marcia; Canadian business executive and administrator; b 28 Dec 1924, Chatham, ON; d of Col W. I. and Beatrice Alice Nurse; m Richard M. Ivey 1949; three d one s. *Education:* Univ of Western Ontario and Ontario Coll of Educ. *Career:* Teacher of Physical Educ and English 1948–49; Vice-Pres and Dir Richard Ivey Foundation 1972–; Pres Beehive Investments Ltd 1973–; Dir Theatre London 1965–67, Shaw Festival Theatre 1969–75, Nat Theatre School, Montréal, PQ 1971–72, Ivest Corpn 1974–, Eskimo Arts Council 1975–78, World Wildlife Fund (Canada, now World Wide Fund for Nature) 1975–98, Nat Ballet School 1975–80, 1983–84, Univ Hosp, London 1982–92, Trillium Foundation of Ontario 1982–88, Canada Trustco Mortgage Co 1982–89, Galatea Art Int Corpn 1985–, CT Financial Services Inc 1987–89; Pres Arboretum Advisory Council, Univ of Guelph 1987–93. *Address:* 630 Richmond St, London, ON N6A 3G6, Canada (Office); 960 Wellington St, London, ON N6A 3T2, Canada (Home).

IVINS, Marsha S., BS; American aerospace engineer and astronaut; b 15 April 1951, Baltimore, MD; d of Joseph L. Ivins. *Education:* Univ of Colorado. *Career:* Pilot and Engineer NASA Lyndon B. Johnson Space Center from 1974, Station Design Br 1974–80, Astronaut 1985, mission specialist shuttle flight STS-32 1990, specialist shuttle Atlantis flight 1992; mem Experimental Aircraft Asscn 99's, Int Aerobatic Club. *Address:* NASA, Johnson Space Center, Astronaut Office, 201 Nasa Rd, Houston, TX 77058, USA.

IZQUIERDO ROJO, María, D PHIL; Spanish university professor and politician; b 13 Sept 1946, Oviedo. *Career:* Mem Congress of Deputies (Parl) 1977, 1986, mem Bureau 1979, Sec of State for the Regions 1982–87; MEP (Socialists Group), mem Cttees on Agric and Rural Devt, Regional Policy and Regional Planning, Interparl Del for Relations with Maghreb Countries, Del to EU-Malta Jt Parl Cttee, fmr Pres Del for Relations between Maghreb Countries and the Arab Maghreb Union; Chair EP Intergroup on the Mediterranean 1990–99, Women for Peace; Medal of Constitutional Merit. *Address:* European Parliament, rue Wiertz, 1047 Brussels, Belgium. *Telephone:* (2) 284-21-11; *Fax:* (2) 230-69-43; *E-mail:* mizquierdo@europarl.eu.int.

J

JAARSMA, Ria (Maria) F., D ED; Netherlands politician; b 19 June 1942, Amsterdam; m Piet Jaarsma 1966 (deceased). *Education:* Graphic School and Univ of Amsterdam. *Career:* Fmr publr and freelance consultant; Pres PvdA Group on Town Council 1974–75; mem Prov State N Holland 1975–87; mem Eerste Kamer (First Chamber) of States-Gen 1987; Chair Regional Employment Bd 1991; mem Council of Nat Inst for Educational Research, Foundation for Educational Research, Univ for Amsterdam, Exec Cttee Inst for Higher Educ; has written over 50 books, papers and studies on educ, equal opportunities, and the relation between educ and the labour market. *Address:* Eerste Kamer der Staten-Generaal, Binnenhof 22, Postbus 20017, The Hague, Netherlands (Office); Vreelandsweg 56, 1394 BN Nederhorst den Berg, Netherlands (Home). *Telephone:* (70) 62-45-71 (Office); (294) 25-15-91 (Home); *Fax:* (294) 25-49-56 (Home).

JÄÄTTEENMÄKI, Anneli Tuulikki, LL M; Finnish politician; b 11 Feb 1955, Lapua; d of Oiva Jaakoppi and Anna Irja (née Latvala) Jäätteenmäki. *Education:* Univ of Helsinki. *Career:* Political Sec Dept of Foreign Affairs, Municipal Lab Market Org 1982, Council of State Secr 1984; Legis Sec KP Parl Group 1986; Mem Eduskunta (Parl) 1987–, Minister of Justice 1994–95; mem Parl Council Bank of Finland 1992–94, 1995, Council of Europe 1996; Chair Advisory Cttee on Correctional Treatment of Prisoners, on Equal Rights; mem Advisory Cttee Asscn of Local Broadcasting, Admin Bd Asscn of Human Rights and Civil Liberties, Cen Council Vassa Dist Planning Asscn, Int Advisory Cttee on Human Rights. *Leisure interests:* reading, sport. *Address:* Eduskunta, 00102 Helsinki, Finland. *Telephone:* (0) 4321 (Office); (64) 4387038 (Home); *Fax:* (0) 4322274 (Office).

JACKSON, Betty, MBE, DIP AD; British fashion designer; b 24 June 1949, Bacup, Lancs; d of Arthur and Phyllis Gertrude Jackson; m David Cohen 1985; one s one d. *Education:* Bacup and Rawtenstall Grammar School and Birmingham Coll of Art and Design. *Career:* Chief Designer Quorum 1975–81; Founder and Dir Betty Jackson Ltd 1981–; opened Betty Jackson retail shop 1991; Fellow Birmingham Polytechic 1989, Univ of Cen Lancashire 1993; Hon Fellow RCA 1989, part-time tutor 1982, Visiting Prof 1999; Cotton Designer of the Year, Cotton Inst 1983; British Designer of the Year 1985; Fil d'Or, Int Linen Council 1985, 1989; Royal Designer for Industry (Royal Soc of Arts) 1988, 1989; Contemporary Designer of the Year 1999. *Leisure interests:* reading, listening to music. *Address:* Betty Jackson Ltd, 1 Netherwood Place, Netherwood Rd, London W14 0BW, UK. *Telephone:* (20) 7602-6023; *Fax:* (20) 7602-3050; *E-mail:* info@bettyjackson.com (Office).

JACKSON, Caroline Frances, MA, D PHIL; British politician; b 5 Nov 1946, Penzance; m Robert Jackson 1975; (one s deceased). *Education:* St Hugh's and Nuffield Colls (Oxford). *Career:* Oxford City Councillor 1970–74; mem Nat Consumer Council 1982–84; MEP (Cons) for Wilts 1984–99, for S W England 1999–, Chair Environment, Consumer Protection and Public Health Cttee 1999–. *Publications:* Young Person's Guide to Europe 1997, 2001, Playing by the Green Rules 2000. *Leisure interest:* gardening. *Address:* European Parliament, rue Wiertz, 1047 Brussels, Belgium (Office). *Telephone:* (2) 284-52-55; *Fax:* (2) 284-92-55; *E-mail:* cjackson@europarleu.int; *Internet:* www.carolinejacksonmep.org.uk.

JACKSON, Glenda, CBE; British actress and politician; b 9 May 1936, Birkenhead, Cheshire; d of Harry and Joan Jackson; m Roy Hodges 1958 (divorced 1976); one s. *Education:* Royal Acad of Dramatic Art (London). *Career:* Fmr mem Royal Shakespeare Co where roles included Ophelia in Hamlet and Charlotte Corday in Marat/Sade (London and New York); played Queen Elizabeth I in TV series Elizabeth R; selected as Lab Parl Cand for Hampstead and Highgate 1990, MP 1992–; Parl Under-Sec of State, Dept for the Environment and Transport 1997–99; Adviser on Homelessness, GLA 2000–; Pres Play Matters (fmrly Toy Libraries Asscn) 1976–; Dir United British Artists 1983–; Hon D LITT (Liverpool) 1978; Hon LL M (Nottingham) 1992; Hon Fellow Liverpool Polytechnic 1987. *Plays include:* Marat/Sade 1965, The Investigation 1965, Hamlet 1965, US 1966, Three Sisters 1967, Collaborators 1973, The Maids 1974, Hedda Gabler 1975, The White Devil 1976, Antony and Cleopatra 1978, Rose 1980, Strange Interlude 1984, 1986, Phaedra 1984, 1985, Across from the Garden of Allah 1986, The House of Bernarda Alba 1986, Macbeth 1988, Scenes from an Execution 1990, Mermaid 1990, Mother Courage 1990, Mourning Becomes Electra 1991; *Films include:* Marat/Sade 1966, Negatives 1968, Women in Love (Acad Award 1971) 1969, The Music Lovers 1970, Sunday, Bloody Sunday 1971, The Boy Friend 1971, Mary, Queen of Scots 1971, The Triple Echo 1972, Bequest to the Nation 1972, A Touch of Class (Acad Award 1974) 1973, The Romantic Englishwoman 1975, The Tempter 1975, The Incredible Sarah 1976, The Abbess of Crewe 1976, Stevie 1977, Hedda 1977, House Calls 1978, The Class of Miss McMichael 1978, Lost and Found 1979, Hopscotch 1980, The Return of the Soldier 1982, Giro City 1982, Summit Conference 1982, Great and Small 1983, And Nothing But the Truth 1984, Turtle Diary 1985, Beyond Therapy 1985, Business as Usual 1986, Salome's Last Dance 1988, The Rainbow 1989, The Secret Life of Sir Arnold Bax 1992; *TV appearances include:* Sakharov 1984. *Leisure interests:* gardening, reading, listening to music. *Address:* House of Commons, London SW1A 0AA, UK (Office); c/o Crouch Associates, 59 Frith St, London W1V 5TA, UK (Agent). *Telephone:* (20) 7734-2167 (Agent); (20) 7219-3000 (Office).

JACKSON, Janet Damita; American singer and choreographer; b 16 June 1966, Gary, IN; d of Joseph and Katherine Jackson; m James DeBarge 1984 (annulled 1985); partner Rene Elizondo. *Education:* Valley Professional School. *Career:* Singing debut at age seven; has toured internationally including All For You Tour 2001–02; three Grammy nominations; nine American Music Award nominations; American Music Award for Best Dance Artist, Best Female Pop Rock Artist and Best Female Soul R & B Artist 1991; MTV Video Vanguard Award 1990; Starlight Foundation Humanitarian of the Year Award 1991. *Albums:* Janet Jackson 1982, Dream Street 1984, Control (video choreographed by Paula Abdul, qv) 1986, Janet Jackson's Rhythm Nation 1814 1989, Rhythm Nation Compilation 1990, The Velvet Rope 1997; *Singles include:* Nasty (American Music Award, Best Female Soul Singer) 1987, What Have You Done For Me Lately? (also video, American Music Award, Best Female Soul Video) 1987, When I Think of You (also video, American Music Award, Best Pop Video) 1988, Alright 1990, Black Cat 1990, Come Back to Me 1990, Escape 1990, Love Will Never Do Without You 1990, If (also video, Best Female Video, MTV), That's the Way Love Goes (Grammy Award for Best R & B Song, jtly) 1994, All For You 2001; *Film:* Poetic Justice 1993; *TV includes:* Good Times 1977–79, A New Kind of Family, Diff'rent Strokes, Fame. *Address:* Creative Artists Agency, 9830 Wilshire Blvd, Beverly Hills, CA 90212, USA.

JACKSON, Margaret Anne, B ECONS, MBA, FCA; Australian business executive; b 17 March 1953, Vic; d of Wallace James and Dorothy Jean Jackson; m Roger Donazzan 1977; one s one d. *Education:* Monash Univ and Univ of Melbourne. *Career:* Accountant Price Waterhouse Co 1973–77; Accountant Nelson Parkhill BDO 1977–, Partner 1983–90; Partner KPMG Peat Marwick 1990–92; Chair Transport Accident Comm (Vic) 1993–; Chair Qantas Airways Ltd 2000–; Dir Telecom Australia 1983–90, Australian Wool Corp 1986–89, Int Wool Secr

1986–89, Qantas 1992–, Pacific Dunlop 1992–2000, Broken Hill Pty Co Ltd 1993–2000, New Zealand Banking Group Ltd 1994–; mem Vic State Council Inst of Chartered Accountants, 1985–93, Chair 1989–90, mem Nat Council 1988–91; mem Australian Science and Tech Council 1990–93, Nat Health and Medical Research Council 1991, Convocation Cttee Univ of Melbourne 1988–91; Distinguished Service Award, Inst of Chartered Accountants. *Leisure interests:* travel, bushwalking, skiing, reading, photography, gardening. *Address:* Qantas Airways Ltd, Qantas Centre, 203 Coward St, Mascot, NSW 2020, Australia.

JACKSON, Shirley Crite, MA, ED D; American civil servant; b 4 June 1940, Memphis, TN; d of Golden and Lucinda (née Berry) Crite; m Allen Jackson 1969; one s. *Education:* Northeastern Univ, Univ of Chicago, George Washington Univ and Catholic Univ of America. *Career:* Teacher 1961–72; Consultant in Communication Skills and Maths, Program Co-ordinator, DC Heath Publ Co, Lexington, MA 1972–75; Prof Univ of Maine 1975–77; Tech Asst Right to Read Program, US Office of Educ 1975, Devt Branch Chief 1975–77, Deputy Dir 1977, Dir 1977–78, Dir Nat Basic Skills Improvement Program 1978–81, basic educ programs 1979–81, Deputy Asst Sec educational support programs 1981–82, Dir local and State educational programs 1982; Assoc Dir Teaching and Learning Research Program, Nat Inst of Educ 1982–89; Assoc Commr Nat Center for Educ Statistics 1989–95; Dir of Analysis and Data Collection, Office of Civil Rights, Office of Educ Research and Improvement, Washington, DC; Dir Jacksons Enterprises 1995–; articles in professional journals and books; mem numerous cttees and panels on educ; mem Int Reading Asscn, Asscn of Supervision and Curriculum Devt, American Educational Research Asscn, Nat Council of Negro Women; US Dept of Educ certificates 1976, 1978, 1980, 1981. *Address:* 2120 Keating St, Temple Hills, MD 20748, USA.

JACKSON SMALL, Grace Rosemarie, BA, M SC; Jamaican athlete; b 14 June 1961, Priory, St Ann; d of the late Omri and of Edna Jackson; m Ronald Small 1990. *Education:* Alabama Univ and Queen's Coll (New York). *Career:* Bronze Medallist in 200m, World Univ Games 1983, Gold Medallist 1985, Bronze Medallist in 100m 1985; Silver Medallist in 100m and 200m, World Athletic Cup 1985; Silver Medal in 200m, Olympic Games, Seoul 1988; TAC Gold Medallist in 200m 1990; mem Int Amateur Athletics Fed comm 1989–; Jamaican Sportswoman of the Year 1986, 1988; Jamaican Order of Distinction 1988. *Leisure interests:* travel, music, sewing. *Address:* 34 Durie Drive, Kingston 8, Jamaica. *Telephone:* 925-7176; *Fax:* 925-4482.

JACOBSEN, Mette; Danish swimmer; b 20 March 1973, Nakskov; d of Per and Bente Jacobsen. *Education:* Tåstrup. *Career:* Gold Medallist European Championships 1991, (Vienna) 1995; Bronze Medallist World Championships (Perth, Australia) 1991, Gold Medallist (Rio de Janeiro, Brazil) 1995; mem Danish Olympic swimming team 1988, 1992, 1996, 2000; Sportswoman of the Year 1991, 1995. *Leisure interests:* boyfriend, books. *Address:* Klovtofteparken 38, 2630 Tåstrup, Denmark. *Telephone:* 43-99-71-66; *Fax:* 42-62-87-55.

JACOBY, Hildegard (Hilla); German writer and photographer; b 20 April 1922, Berlin; d of Heinrich and Else (née Klein) Gerberding; m Max-Moshe Jacoby. *Education:* Oberlyzeum Weissesee (Berlin). *Career:* Actress, Dir children's theatre and artistic producer 1945–; writer, photographer for illustrated books (with Max-Moshe Jacoby); exhibitions of photographs in Berlin and London 1990; two Kodak Photo Book Prizes (with Max-Moshe Jacoby). *Publications include:* Shalom 1978, The Land of Israel 1978, Sweden 1978, Hallelujah Jerusalem 1980, New York 1981, The Last Hours with Jesus 1982, The Jews, God's Chosen People 1983, I Am With You 1985, Who Saves Tina? (for children) 1985, Do Not Fear 1985, The Ten Commandments – That we may live 1987, Israel, the Miracle 1988, Walking With Jesus in the Holy Land 1989, Mit Jesus unterwegs 1990, Nächstes Jahr in Jerusalem 1995, The Land of the Bible 1997; also children's books. *Address:* Spessartstr 15, 14197 Berlin, Germany. *Telephone:* (30) 8211815.

JACOBY, Ruth, B PHIL; Swedish banking executive and diplomatist; b 13 Jan 1949, New York, USA; d of Erich H. and Charlotte F. Jacoby; m Björn Meidal 1976; two s. *Education:* Univ of Uppsala. *Career:* First Sec Ministry of Foreign Affairs, Stockholm 1972, Deputy Asst Under-

Sec 1984–88, Asst Under-Sec and Head Dept 1990–94; Asst Under-Sec Ministry of Finance 1989–90; Exec Dir Bd of IBRD (World Bank) representing Sweden, Norway, Finland, Denmark, Iceland, Estonia, Latvia and Lithuania 1994–97; Amb 1997–; mem Swedish del to OECD 1980–84. *Address:* Malmgardsvagen 6, 11638 Stockholm, Sweden; Malmogardsvagen 6, 11638 Stockholm, Sweden. *Telephone:* (8) 6412787; *Fax:* (8) 6412787; *E-mail:* meidal@swipnet.se (Home).

JACQUELINE-MARS; French sculptor; b Paris; d of Comte Yves de Constantin; m 1st Paul Collet 1974 (deceased); m 2nd Jean-Max Riboul de Pescay 1980 (deceased); two d. *Education:* Couvent de la Providence (Saint-Marc-sur-Mer) and self-taught. *Career:* Red Cross Diploma 1939; sculptures have been acquired by the State, museums, libraries, churches, town halls, public places, etc; Head arts section of a literary journal 1972–; Vice-Pres Jury (Fine Art), Acad Int de Lutèce, Paris 1982–; Vice-Pres Int Hight Cttee for World Culture, Rome 1985–; Chevalier des Arts et des Lettres 1967; Chevalier de l'Ordre de la Courtoisie Française; Chevalier de l'Ordre de Santa Maria de Bethléem 1980; Chevalier de l'Etoile de la Paix 1982; Médaille d'Or d'Arts-Sciences-Lettres, Paris 1985; Médaille d'Or de la Vallée des Rois, Château de Tours 1989. *Works include:* Sculptures of hands: Julien Benda, Jean Cocteau, Isabelle Durou, Marceau Constantin; Sculptures: Wilfrid Lucas, Bruno Saint-Hill, Frédéric Schneider; Monuments: A la gloire des parachutistes (Pau) 1960, Les compagnons de la paix (Monuments aux morts, Coullons) 1975, Plaque au Général de Gaulle (L'appel du 18 juin 1940, Coullons) 1990, Medallions for Europe '93 1992. *Leisure interests:* travel, yoga. *Address:* les Petits Marnaïr, 45720 Coullons-en-Sologne, France (Studio and gallery); 2 square du Vivarais, 75017 Paris, France (Home). *Telephone:* (2) 38-36-10-79 (Studio and Gallery); (1) 45-72-24-23 (Home).

JACQUEMARD, Simonne; French writer; b 6 May 1924, Paris; d of André and Andrée (née Raimondi) Jacquemard; m Jacques Brosse 1955. *Education:* Inst Saint-Pierre and Univ of Paris. *Career:* Teacher of Music, Latin and French; collaborator Laffont-Bompiani Dictionaries; contrib to Figaro littéraire, La table ronde; travelled in USSR, Egypt, Greece, Italy, N Africa and Spain; Chevalier de la Légion d'Honneur 1999, Officier des Arts et des Lettres; Grand Prix Thyde-Monnier 1984. *Publications:* Les fascinés 1951, Sable 1952, La leçon des ténèbres 1954, Judith Albarès 1957, Planant sur les airs 1960, Compagnons insolites 1961, Le veilleur de nuit (Prix Renaudot) 1962, L'oiseau 1963, L'orangerie 1963, Les derniers rapaces 1965, Dérive au zénith 1965, Exploration d'un corps 1965, Navigation vers les îles 1967, A l'état sauvage 1967, L'éruption du Krakatoa 1969, La Thessalienne 1973, Des roses pour mes chevreuils 1974, Le mariage berbère 1975, Danse de l'orée 1979, Le funambule 1981, Lalla Zahra 1983, La fête en éclats 1985, Les belles échappées 1987, L'huître dans la perle 1993, Le jardin d'Hérodote 1994, l'Ephèbe couronné de lierre 1995, La gloire d'Ishiwara 1996, Vers l'estuaire ébloui 1996, Trois mystiques grecs 1997, Orphée ou l'initiation mystique (jtly) 1998, l'Oiseau 1998 (Prix Jacques Lacroix, l'Académie Française 1999); studies on music (jtly) and on bird life and observation of wild animals. *Address:* 12 bis ave des Gobelins, 75005 Paris, France.

JACQUES, Paula; French writer and broadcaster; b 9 May 1949, Cairo; d of Jacques Abadi and Esther Sasson; m (divorced 1970). *Career:* Worked as comedienne in Africa; joined Radio France Internationale as reporter, worked on Après-midi de France-Culture, L'Oreille en coin 1975–90; presenter Nuits-noires France-Inter radio 1997–, Cosmopolitaine 2000–; sometime writer F Magazine; mem Prix Femina jury 1996–. *Play:* Zanouba; *Publications:* Lumière de l'oeil 1980, Un baiser froid comme la lune 1983, L'héritage de Tante Carlotta 1987, Deborah et les anges dissipés (Prix Femina 1991), La déscente au paradis 1995, Les femmes avec leur amour 1997. *Address:* France-Inter, 116 ave du Président Kennedy, 75220 Paris, Cedex 16, France.

JAFFREY, Madhur; Indian actress and cookery writer; b 13 Aug 1937, Delhi; m 1st Saeed Jaffrey (divorced 1965); three c; m 2nd Sanford Allen 1969. *Education:* Univ of Delhi and Royal Acad of Dramatic Art (London). *Career:* Has appeared in numerous radio and TV plays and acted on Broadway (New York) and in several films; writes on Indian cookery for the New York Times and other journals; currently living in the UK. *Films include:* Shakespeare Wallah (Best Actress Award, Berlin Film Festival, Germany), Guru, Autobiography of a Princess, Heat and

Dust, Assam Garden; *Play:* Medea; *TV appearances include:* Madhur Jaffrey's Indian Cookery (series), Firm Friends 1992; *Publications:* Invitation to Indian Cooking (latest edn) 1987, Madhur Jaffrey's Cook Book: Food for Family and Friends 1989, Far Eastern Cookery 1989, Days of the Banyan Tree 1990, Eastern Vegetarian Cooking (latest edn) 1990, A Taste of India (latest edn) 1991, Illustrated Indian Cooking. *Address:* c/o Jeremy Conway, Eagle House, 109 Jermyn St, London SW7 6HB, UK.

JAGAN, Janet; Guyanese politician, journalist and writer; b 20 Oct 1920, Chicago, IL, USA; d of Charles and Kathryn Rosenberg; m Cheddi Jagan (Pres of Guyana) 1943 (died 1997); one s one d. *Education:* Univ of Detroit, Wayne Univ (Detroit) and Michigan State Coll. *Career:* Gen Sec People's Progressive Party (PPP) 1950–70, Int Sec 1970–84, Exec Sec 1984–92; Ed Thunder 1950–56; Deputy Speaker House of Ass (Parl) 1953; six months' political imprisonment 1954; Minister of Labour, Health and Housing 1957–61, of Home Affairs 1963–64; mem Elections Comm 1967–68; Ed Mirror 1969–72, 1973–97; mem Nat Ass 1976–97; 1st woman Prime Minister of the Repub of Guyana 1997, President 1997–99; Amb to UN 1993; Pres Women's Progressive Org, Union of Guyanese Journalists; Chair Comm on the Rights of the Child, Cttee Nat Art Collection; Trustee and Chair Cheddi Jagan Research Centre; mem World Council of Women Leaders; Outstanding Woman Award, Univ of Guyana 1989, Order of Excellence 1993, Order of Liberator (Venezuela) 1998, UNESCO Mahatma Gandhi Gold Medal for Women's Rights 1998. *Publications:* History of the People's Progressive Party 1971, Army Intervention in the 1973 Elections in Guyana 1973, An Examination of National Service 1976; Children's stories: When Grandpa Cheddi Was a Boy and other stories 1993, Patricia the Baby Manatee and other stories 1995, Children's Stories of Guyana's Freedom Struggles 1995, Anastasia, the Ant Eater and other stories 1997, The Dog Who Loved Flowers 2000. *Leisure interest:* swimming. *Address:* Freedom House, 41 Robb St, Georgetown, Guyana. *Telephone:* 72095 (Office); *Fax:* 72096 (Office); *E-mail:* ppp@guyana.net.gy (Office).

JAGGER, (Alexis) Harriett; British fashion editor; b 30 Oct 1959; d of P. C. and E. L. Jagger; m Simon Gaul 1984. *Education:* King's High School for Girls (Warwick), Marlborough Coll and London Coll of Fashion. *Career:* Fashion Asst The Observer 1981–85; Fashion Ed Elle 1985–88; Sr Fashion Ed Vogue (UK) 1988–92; Fashion Ed-at-Large Tatler 1994–. *Leisure interests:* skiing, cricket, horse-racing, tennis, theatre, gardening. *Address:* Tatler, Vogue House, Hanover Square, London W1R OAD, UK. *Telephone:* (20) 7499-9080.

JAGGER, Bianca, MA; British (Nicaraguan) artist, film director and human rights activist; b 2 May 1950, Managua, Nicaragua; d of Carlos Perez-Mora and Dora Macias Somassiba; m Michael P. Jagger 1971 (divorced 1979); one d. *Education:* Inst of Political Sciences (Paris) and New York Univ. *Career:* Lecturer on Cen America at several colls and univs; Co-Founder Iris House, New York; has campaigned for human rights in Cen America, mem several US Congressional dels and dels from int human rights orgs; visited the fmr Yugoslavia to document alleged human rights violations and testified before the Helsinki Comm on Human Rights and the US Congressional Human Rights Caucus; has helped to evacuate children from Bosnia 1993–; works to protect rain forests in Honduras, Nicaragua and Brazil and indigenous peoples in Brazil; contribs to New York Times; mem Exec Dir's Leadership Council, Amnesty Int USA, Advisory Cttee Human Rights Watch America, Bd Dirs Action Council for Peace in the Balkans, Bd Hispanic Fed, New York; Special Advisor Indigenous Devt Int, Cambridge (UK); Hon DH (Stone Hill Coll, MA) 1983; UN Earth Day Int Award 1994; Humanitarian Award, Hispanic Fed of New York City 1996; 1996 Woman of the Year, Boys Town, Italy; Abolitionist of the Year Award, Nat Coalition to Abolish the Death Penalty 1996. *Films include:* Flesh Color, Success, Cannonball Run, Chud II; *TV includes:* Hotel, Miami Vice, The Colby's, The Rattles. *Leisure interests:* horse-riding, water-skiing. *Address:* 530 Park Ave, 18D, New York, NY 10021, USA. *Telephone:* (212) 512-5328; *Fax:* (212) 512-7474.

JAHANARA, Begum, M SC; Bangladeshi educationalist and politician; b 11 Feb 1942, Dhaka; d of Shajahan and Noor Jahan Begum; m Ahmed Murtafa 1962 (deceased); two s one d. *Education:* Dhaka Univ. *Career:* Apptd Prof Habidullah Bahar Coll 1976; mem Dhaka Univ Senate

1980; Jt Sec-Gen Bangladesh Nationalist Party (BNP) 1988; mem Parl from 1991; apptd Minister of State for Cultural Affairs 1991; Chair Asscn for Women's Rights Implementation in Bangladesh 1980; Gen Sec Bangladesh Home Econs Asscn 1978–90, Vice-Pres 1990; articles on child behaviour, nutrition and other topics in local newspapers. *Leisure interests:* reading, social work, cooking, spending time with children, making dolls. *Address:* Ministry of State for Cultural Affairs, Govt of Bangladesh, Bldg 6, Rm 1020, Bangladesh Secr, Dhaka, Bangladesh (Office); 149, Malibag Bazar Rd, Dhaka 1217, Bangladesh (Home). *Telephone:* (2) 402025 (Office); (2) 833745 (Home).

JAHR-STILCKEN, Angelika; German publishing executive; b 26 Oct 1941; m Rudolf Stilcken 1977; one s one d. *Career:* Publr and Ed-in-Chief Gruner und Jahr. *Address:* Schöner Wohnen, Gruner und Jahr AG & Co, Am Baumwall 11, Postfach 110011, 20459 Hamburg, Germany. *Telephone:* (40) 37032225; *Fax:* (40) 37035676.

JAKOBSEN, Mimi; Danish politician; b 19 Nov 1948, Copenhagen; d of Erhard Jakobsen. *Career:* Lecturer in German Philology and Phonetics, Univ of Copenhagen; mem Folketinget (Parl) 1977–; Minister for Cultural Affairs 1982–86, for Social Affairs 1986–88, of Business Affairs 1993–, of Industry 1994–; Chair Centrum-Demokraterne (Centre Democrat Party) 1989–; Chair Europaeiske Centrum-Demokraterne. *Address:* Centrum-Demokraterne, Folketinget, Christiansborg, 1240 Copenhagen K, Denmark. *Telephone:* 33-37-55-00; *Fax:* 33-32-85-36.

JÁMBOR, Ági, M MUS; American pianist; b 4 Feb 1909, Budapest, Hungary; d of Vilmos and Olga (née Riesz) Jámbor; m 1st Imre Patai 1933 (died 1949); m 2nd Claude Raines 1959 (divorced 1960); one s. *Education:* Budapest Acad of Music under Kodály and Weiner, and Musikhochschule (Berlin). *Career:* Debut at age 12; regular concert tours throughout USA and Europe; Full Prof Dept of Music and Anthropology/Ethno-Musicology, Bryn Mawr Coll, PA 1957–74, Prof Emer 1974–; Curator of Music Instruments Univ Museum, PA; numerous recordings of Bach, Chopin, Mozart, etc; Deutsche Akad Brahms Prize (Berlin) 1928; Int Chopin Prize (Warsaw) 1937. *Leisure interest:* reading. *Address:* Bryn Mawr College, Bryn Mawr, PA 19010, USA (Office); Beethoven Apartments No 104N, 1518 Park Ave, Baltimore, MD 21217, USA (Home). *Telephone:* (301) 383-0531 (Home).

JAMES, Geraldine; British actress; b 6 July 1950, Maidenhead, Berks; d of Gerald Trevor and Annabella (née Doogan) Thomas; m Joseph Sebastian Blatchley 1986; one d. *Education:* Downe House (Newbury) and Drama Centre London Ltd. *Career:* Stage and screen actress 1972–; repertory Chester 1972–74, Exeter 1974–75, Coventry 1975; Best Actress Awards from TV Critics 1977, Venice Film Festival, Italy 1989, Drama Desk (New York) for Best Actress 1990. *Plays include:* Passion of Dracula 1978, The White Devil 1981, Turning Over 1984, When I Was a Girl I Used to Scream and Shout 1987, Cymbeline 1988, The Merchant of Venice 1989, Death and the Maiden 1992, Lysistrata 1993, Hedda Gabler 1994, Give Me Your Answer Do 1998; *Films:* Sweet William 1978, Night Cruiser 1978, Gandhi 1981, The Storm 1985, Wolves of Willoughby Chase 1988, The Tall Guy 1989, If Looks Could Kill 1990, The Bridge 1990, Losing Track 1991, Prince of Shadows 1991, Teen Agent 1991, Beltenebros, No Worries, Words on the Window Pane 1993, Moll Flanders 1994, The Man Who Knew Too Little 1996, Testimony of Taliesin Jones 1999, First Love 1999, The Luzhin Defence 2000; *TV appearances include:* Series: The History Man 1980, Jewel in the Crown 1984, Blott on the Landscape 1985, Echoes 1988, Stanley and the Women 1991, Kavanagh QC 1994, 1995, Band of Gold 1994, 1995, Over Here 1995, Band of Gold 1996, Drovers' Gold 1996, Gold 1997, Kavanagh QC 1997, The Sins 2000; Films and guest appearances: Dummy 1977, She's Been Away 1989, Inspector Morse 1990, The Doll's House 1991, Ex 1991, Losing Track 1992, The Healer 1994, Doggin Around 1994, Rebecca 1996, See Saw 1997. *Leisure interests:* music, cinema. *Address:* c/o Julian Belfrage Associates, 46 Albermarle St, London W1, UK. *Telephone:* (20) 7491-4400; *Fax:* (20) 7493-5460.

JAMES, Dame Naomi Christine, DBE, MA, PH D; New Zealand academic and former yachtswoman; b 2 March 1949; d of Charles and Joan Power; m 1st Robert James 1976 (died 1983); one d; m 2nd Eric

Haythorne 1990 (divorced 1994). *Education:* Rotorua Girls' School. *Career:* Teacher 1972–74, 1997–99; mem Yacht Charter Crew 1975–77; solo world voyage 1977–78; first woman to sail solo around Cape Horn 1977–78; Ladies Prize, Observer Transatlantic Race 1980; winner (with husband) Round Britain Race 1982; Trustee Nat Maritime Museum 1986; mem Council Winston Churchill Memorial Trust; named New Zealand Yachtsman of the Year 1978; Chichester Trophy; Best Book of the Sea Award. *TV:* documentary: The Polynesian Triangle 1989; *Publications:* Woman Alone 1978, At One With the Sea 1979, At Sea on Land 1981, Courage at Sea 1987, Great Journeys 1989. *Leisure interests:* literature, philosophy, travel. *Address:* Shore Cottage, Currabinny, Carrigaline, Co Cork, Ireland. *Telephone:* (21) 437-8825; *Fax:* (21) 437-8825; *E-mail:* naomij@eircom.net.

JAMES OF HOLLAND PARK, Baroness (Life Peer), cr 1991, of Southwold in the County of Suffolk, **Phyllis Dorothy James,** OBE, JP, FRSL, FRSA; British writer; b 3 Aug 1920, Oxford; d of Sidney Victor and Dorothy Amelia (née Hone) James; m Connor Bantry White 1941 (died 1964); two d. *Education:* Cambridge Girls' High School. *Career:* Admin Nat Health Service 1949–68; Prin Home Office 1968; Police Dept 1968–72; Criminal Policy Dept 1972–79; JP Willesden 1979–82, Inner London 1984; Chair Soc of Authors 1984–86, Pres 1997–; Gov BBC 1988–93, Arts Council 1988–92; Chair Booker Prize Panel of Judges 1987, Arts Council Literary Advisory Panel 1988; mem Detection Club, Bd of British Council 1988–93, Church of England Liturgical Comm 1991–; Fellow Royal Soc of Arts; Assoc Fellow Downing Coll (Cambridge) 1986, Hon Fellow 2000; Hon Fellow St Hilda'a Coll (Oxford) 1996, Girton Coll (Cambridge) 2000; Hon D LITT (Buckingham) 1992, (Hertfordshire) 1994, (Glasgow) 1995, (Durham) 1998, (Portsmouth) 1999; Hon LITT D (London) 1993; Dr hc (Essex) 1996; 'Grand Master' Award of the Mystery Writers of America 1999. *Publications:* as P. D. James: Cover Her Face 1962, A Mind to Murder 1963, Unnatural Causes 1967, Shroud for a Nightingale 1971, The Maul and the Pear Tree (with T. A. Critchley) 1971, An Unsuitable Job for a Woman 1972, The Black Tower 1975, Death of an Expert Witness 1977, Innocent Blood 1980, The Skull Beneath the Skin 1982, A Taste for Death 1986, Devices and Desires 1989, The Children of Men 1992, Original Sin 1994, A Certain Justice 1997, Time to be in Earnest 1999, Death in Holy Orders 2001. *Leisure interests:* exploring churches, walking by the sea, reading. *Address:* c/o Greene and Heaton Ltd, 37A Goldhawk Rd, London W12 8QQ, UK.

JAMET, Marie-Claire Thérèse Odile; French harpist; b 27 Nov 1933, Reims; d of the late Pierre and Renée (née Hanson) Jamet; m Christian Lardé 1955; two s. *Education:* Conservatoire Nat Supérieur de Musique (Paris). *Career:* Has given over 2,000 concerts worldwide as soloist and with Christian Lardé; specializes in contemporary music; Soloist Ensemble Inter Contemporain 1976–; Prof Conservatoire Nat Supérieur de Musique, Paris 1984–95; Chevalier de l'Ordre Nat du Mérite 1983; Chevalier des Arts et des Lettres 1992; Chevalier de la Légion d'Honneur 1995; First Prize for Harp, Conservatoire Nat Supérieur de Musique 1948, First Prize for Chamber Music 1951; several prizes from Acad Charles Cros; numerous int prizes for recordings. *Recordings include:* Concerto pour flûte et harpe (Mozart), Les danses et sonate (Debussy), Introduction et allegro (Ravel), Musique du XVIIIème siècle 1978, La harpe au XXème siècle 1980, Harpe en élégance (jtly), Récital flute et harpe. *Leisure interests:* reading, swimming, yoga. *Address:* Bureau de Concerts Maurice Werner, 7 rue Richepance, 75008 Paris, France (Agent); 'Lou Bastidoun', chemin de Valbelette, 83780 Flayosc, France (Home). *Telephone:* (4) 94-70-41-36 (Home); *Fax:* (4) 94-84-60-25 (Home).

JAMIESON, Right Rev Penelope Ann Bansall, BD, PH D; New Zealand ecclesiastic; b 21 June 1942, Chalfont St Peter, Bucks; m Ian William Andrew Jamieson 1964; three d. *Education:* High School (High Wycombe, UK), Univ of Edinburgh (UK), Victoria Univ (Wellington) and Otago Univ (Dunedin). *Career:* Deacon 1982; Priest 1983; Asst Curate St James', Lower Hutt 1982–85; Vicar Karori W with Makara, Diocese of Wellington 1985–90; Bishop of Dunedin 1990–. *Publication:* Living at the Edge: Sacrament and Solidarity in Leadership 1997. *Address:* Diocese of Dunedin, POB 5445, Dunedin, New Zealand. *E-mail:* pennydn@dn.ang.org.nz.

JAMIN, Sylvie; French former sportswoman; b 19 Sept 1949, Paris; d of Jean Emile and Monique (née Boyer) Maurial; m Jean Michel Jamin 1974; two d one s. *Education:* Ecole Saint Pie X (Saint Cloud). *Career:* Jr French Water-Skiing Champion 1963, 1964, 1965; Jr European Champion 1965, 1966, 1967; European and World Vice-Champion (slalom) 1969, Champion 1973; European Champion 1970; French Champion 1968–1973; Silver and Bronze Medals European Championships 1971, Silver Medal 1972, Gold and Bronze Medals 1973; holds various records; Chevalier de l'Ordre Nat du Mérite 1973; Award from Union Mondiale de Ski Nautique 1971, 1973; Prix Féminin, Acad des Sports 1973. *Publication:* Le ski nautique en trois jours 1974. *Address:* Route de d'Olean, 33680 Lacanau, France. *Telephone:* (5) 56-03-09-01; *Fax:* (5) 56-26-22-48.

JAN, Simin Amin, BM, M SC; Pakistani medical practitioner; b 28 May 1958, Lahore; d of Mahmud and Surraya Mahmud Jan; m Amin Jan 1989; one s. *Education:* Univ of London (UK). *Career:* Asst Prof of Haematology, Khyber Medical Centre 1981–88, Consultant Haematologist 1989–; Nat Adviser on Health, All-Pakistan Women's Asscn 1981–; first Pakistani to perform bone-marrow transplant in UK 1983; WHO Fellow 1984–86; est Haematology Clinic and Lab, Peshawar 1989; Chief Exec Mohammad Medical Complex and Blood Transfusion Centre, Peshawar 1996; CEO Jan Trading Corpn Pvt Ltd 1995; mem Provincial Comm for Child Welfare and Devt, Govt of North-West Frontier Prov 1991; Pres Pakistan Blood Transfusion Services 1991, Save The Children (Pakistan) 1991; Gen-Sec Pakistan Fed of Business and Professional Women 1983; mem Govt Cttees for Women, Children, Local Govt and Rural Devt; Outstanding Young Persons of the World Award for Humanitarian and Voluntary Service, Jaycees Int 1988; elected to Int Professional and Business Women's Hall of Fame 1995. *Publications:* The Importance of Antenatal Care 1983, Developing the Potential of Women in the Field of Health 1983, The Kathore Village Rural Health and Welfare Scheme 1987, Voice Against Child Labour 1991, Field Trip to Hazardous Work-Sites involving Child Labour 1995, International Thalassaemia Day 1996. *Leisure interests:* family, music, walking. *Address:* 27 Shami Rd, Peshawar Cautt, Pakistan. *Telephone:* (521) 276462; *Fax:* (521) 276462.

JAN, Sylvie; French organization executive; b 26 Oct 1952; two s. *Education:* Centre Professionnel du Journalisme (Paris). *Career:* Pres Union des Femmes Françaises (UFF) 1992, Fed Democratique Int des Femmes (FDIF) 1994; Founder Clara feminist magazine 1987. *Leisure interests:* photography, art exhibitions, high mountains, meeting friends. *Address:* 25 rue du Charolais, 75012 Paris, France (Office); 3 rue Henri Ribière, 75019 Paris, France (Home). *Telephone:* (1) 40-01-90-90; *Fax:* (1) 40-01-90-81.

JANDA, Krystyna; Polish actress and director; b 18 Dec 1952, Starachowice; m; two s one d. *Education:* State Higher School of Drama (Warsaw). *Career:* Actress Atheneum Theatre (Warsaw) 1976–88, Powszechny Theatre (Warsaw) 1988–; acting in TV and cabarets; numerous awards in Poland and abroad; above 30 leading roles in classic and contemporary plays; Best Actress 40th Int Film Festival, San Sebastián. *Films:* Man of Marble 1976, Without Anaesthetic 1978, The Border 1978, The Conductor 1979, Die Grüne Vogel 1979, Golem 1979, Mephisto 1980, War Between Worlds 1980, Man of Iron 1981, Espion lève Toi 1981, Interrogation 1982, Ce fut un Bel Eté 1982, Bella Donna 1983, Gluth 1983, Der Bulle und das Mädchen 1984, Vertige 1985, My Mother's Lovers 1985, Laputa 1986, Short Film About Killing 1987, II Decalogue, V Decalogue 1988, Ownership 1989, Polish Kitchen 1991, Relieved of the Life 1992, Pestka (actress and dir) 1995, As 1995, Mother's Mother 1996, Unwritten Principles 1997, Last Chapter 1997, David Weissen 1999; *Plays include:* Bal manekinów 1974, Edukacja Rity 1984, Z zycia glist 1984, Biala bluzka 1987, Medea 1988, Shirley Valentine 1990, Kobieta zawieckiona 1996, Kotka na goracym blaszanym dachu 1997, Maria Callas Lelicja spiewa 1997, Harry i ja 1998; *TV:* Mierzejewska 1989, From Time to Time 1999. *Address:* Teatr Powszechny, ul Zamoyskiego 20, Warsaw, Poland.

JANEWAY, Elizabeth Hall, AB; American writer; b 7 Oct 1913, Brooklyn, New York; d of Charles H. and Jeannette F. (née Searle) Hall; m Eliot Janeway 1938 (died 1993); two s. *Education:* Barnard Coll. *Career:* Mem Council Authors Guild, Council Authors League America, PEN; Chair New York State Council for the Humanities; Assoc Fellow

Yale Univ; Hon PH D (Simpson Coll, Cedarcrest Coll, Villa Maria Coll); Hon DHL (Russell Sage Coll, Florida Int Univ, Simmons Coll) 1989; Fellow AAAS; Medal of Distinction, Barnard Coll 1981. *Publications:* The Walsh Girls 1943, Daisy Kenyon 1945, The Question of Gregory 1949, The Vikings 1951, Leaving Home 1953, Early Days of the Automobile 1956, The Third Choice 1959, Angry Kate 1963, Accident 1964, Ivanov Seven 1967, Man's World, Women's Place 1971, Between Myth and Morning: Women Awakening 1974, Harvard Guide to Contemporary American Writing 1979, Powers of the Weak 1980, Comprehensive Textbook of Psychology (contrib) 1974, 1980, Cross Sections from a Decade of Change 1982, Improper Behaviour 1987. *Address:* 350 E 79th St, New York, NY 10021, USA.

JANGARACHEVA, Mira, PH D; Krygyzstan politician; b 30 March 1952 Frunz (now Bishkek); d of Kamil Jangaraohev and of Fatima Baignldieva; m Kylychbek Berdybekov 1974; one d. *Education:* Kyrgyz State Univ and Moscow State Univ. *Career:* Lecturer Faculty of Social Sciences, Kyrgyz State Univ 1976–78, Technical Univ of Frunze (now Bishkek) 1981–88; Research Scholar Moscow State Univ 1989–92; Deputy Mayor of Bishkek 1992–95; mem Khogorku Kenesh (Parl) 1995–96; fmr Deputy Prime Minister. *Leisure interests:* literature, family. *Address:* 720003 Bishkek, Government House, Kyrgyzstan. *Telephone:* (3312) 231-652; *Fax:* (3312) 218-726.

JANIN, Christine Jacqueline Marie, MD; French medical practitioner and mountaineer; b 14 March 1957, Rome, Italy; d of Michel and Maryvonne (née Ollivier Henry) Janin; m Antoine Barthélémy. *Career:* Ascent of Gasherbrum II (Pakistan, first French woman to climb higher than 8,000m) 1981, Hidden Peak (Pakistan, first woman to reach summit) 1986, Mt Everest (Nepal, first French woman) 1990; mem expeditions to Kumbhakarna (Nepal, Makalu II and Baruntse mountains) 1983, medical expedition to Annapurna IV (Nepal) 1985, mountain bike expedition Katmandu–Lhassa (Tibet) 1986, Baffin kayaking expedition (Canada) 1988, scientific expedition Everest Turbo 1989; mem Top 7 Project (round the world via the highest peaks in each continent) 1992; Dir A Chacun son Everest asscn; Chevalier de la Légion d'Honneur 1993; Medal from Dept of Haute-Savoie 1990; Médaille de l'Acad des Sports 1991; Médaille du Sénat 1991. *Films:* Baffin 1988, Désir d'Everest 1991, Au Fil des Cimes 1993; *Publication:* Christine Janin: Première Française à l'Everest 1990, Le Tour du Monde par les Cimes 1993. *Address:* 113 route de Thônes, 74940 Annecy-le-Vieux, France. *Telephone:* (4) 50-64-01-20; *Fax:* (4) 50-64-00-64.

JANKOWSKA, Danuta Jadwiga, PH D; Polish scientist; b 15 March 1927, Żelechów; d of Stanisław Zieliński and Maria Zielińska; m Zygmunt Jankowski 1951; one d. *Education:* Medical Acad (Łódź). *Career:* Assoc Prof Inst of Paediatrics, Łódź 1974–87, apptd Head Clinic of Paediatric Surgery 1974, Deputy Dir of Inst 1976, Prof 1987; numerous scientific awards. *Publications:* Paediatry (jtly) 1984, Vade-mecum of Paediatry (jtly) 1990; 85 papers, articles and works on paediatry; four films. *Leisure interests:* reading, poetry. *Address:* Akademia Medyczna w Łódźi, Inst of Paediatrics, Al Koscinski 4, 909-419 Łódź, Poland (Office); Gdańska 116, m 2, 90-520 Łodź, Poland (Home). *Telephone:* (42) 367458 (Home).

JANKOWSKA-CIEŚLAK, Jadwiga, MA; Polish actress; b 15 Feb 1951, Gdańsk; d of Kazimierz Jankowski and Helena Jankowska; m Piotr Cieslak 1971; two s one d. *Education:* A. Zelwerowicz State Theatre Acad (Warsaw). *Career:* Actress Dramatozny Theatre Co 1973–81, later Nat Theatre Co and Polski Theatre Co, currently with Powszechny Theatre Co; apptd Prof of Acting A. Zelwerowicz State Theatre Acad 1990; 28 Cybulski Award 1972; Polish Film Festival Awards 1973, 1977; Polskie Radio i Telewizja (Polish TV and Radio) Award 1978; Cannes Film Festival Award 1982. *Films include:* This Love is Nonsense 1972, Nacht Dienst 1975, Exit 7 1978, Another Look 1982. *Leisure interests:* knitting, gardening and fishing. *Address:* Film Polski, ul Mazewiecka 6/8, 00-950 Warsaw, Poland.

JANOWITZ, Gundula; Austrian opera singer; b 2 Aug 1937, Berlin, Germany; d of Theodor and Else (née Neumann) Janowitz; m; one d. *Education:* Acad of Music and Performing Arts (Graz). *Career:* Debut with Vienna State Opera; has sung with Deutsche Oper, Berlin 1966, Metropolitan Opera, New York 1967, Teatro Colón, Buenos Aires 1970, Munich State Opera 1971, Grand Opéra, Paris 1973, Royal Opera House, Covent Garden, London 1976, La Scala, Milan, Italy 1978; concerts in major cities throughout the world, appearances at festivals, Bayreuth and Munich (Germany), Aix-en-Provence (France), Glyndebourne (UK), Spoleto (Italy), Salzburg; mem Vienna State Opera, Deutsche Oper, Berlin; recordings with Deutsche Grammophon, EMI, Decca. *Leisure interest:* modern literature. *Address:* 3072 Kasten 75, Austria, Austria.

JANOWITZ, Tama, MA; American writer; b 12 April 1957, San Francisco, CA; d of Frederick and Phyllis (née Winer) Janowitz. *Education:* Lexington High School, Barnard Coll, Hollins Coll (Roanoke) and Yale School of Drama. *Career:* Fmr model; Asst Art Dir Kenyon and Eckhardt advertising agency 1977; Alfred Hodder Fellow Princeton Univ 1988–89; Hon MFA (Columbia) 1985. *Publications:* Short Stories: Slaves of New York 1986 (writer of screenplay and actress in film version 1989); Novels: American Dad 1981, A Cannibal in Manhattan 1987. *Address:* 92 Horatio St, Suite 5E, New York, NY 10014, USA (Home).

JARAMILLO DE MAINCOURT, Carmenza, LL D; Colombian diplomatist; b 14 April 1958, Riosucio, Caldas; m Christophe Maincourt 1992; one d. *Education:* Univ de Paris II (France), LSE, Colegio Mayor de Nuestra Señora Rosario. *Career:* Joined Ministry of Foreign Affairs 1982–, Chargé d'Affaires Embassy Paris, France, then Counsellor, Consul-Gen Embassy Hong Kong, Amb to India 1993; mem del to UNESCO, Paris, France. *Leisure interests:* horse-riding, tennis, reading, music. *Address:* Embassy of Colombia, 82D Malcha Marg, Chanakyapuri, New Delhi 110 021, India. *Telephone:* (11) 3012771; *Fax:* (11) 3792485.

JARAY, Tess, DFA; British artist; b 31 Dec 1937, Vienna, Austria; d of Francis F. and Pauline Jaray; m 1960 (divorced 1983); two d. *Education:* Alice Ottley School (Worcester), St Martin's School of Art and Slade School of Fine Art (London). *Career:* Teacher Hornsey Coll of Art 1964–88, Slade School of Art 1968; commissioned to paint mural for British Pavilion, Expo '67, Montréal, Canada, terrazzo floor Victoria Station, London 1985, Centenary Square, Birmingham 1988, Wakefield Cathedral Precinct 1989, Terrace of Arts Council Headquarters, London 1991, Forecourt of Embassy of the UK, Moscow 1995, Hosp Square, Leeds 1998, Forecourt new British Embassy, Moscow 1999; solo exhibitions Grabowski Gallery, London 1963, Hamilton Galleries, London 1965, 1967, Axiom Gallery, London 1969, Whitechapel Gallery, London 1973, Adelaide Festival Centre, Australia 1980, Whitworth Art Gallery, Manchester 1984, Ashmolean Museum, Oxford 1984, Serpentine Gallery, London 1988; numerous group exhibitions in Rome, Liverpool, London, Bern etc; Hon FRIBA 1995; French Govt Scholarship 1961. *Address:* 29 Camden Square, London NW1, UK. *Telephone:* (20) 7485-5057.

JÄRV, Elo-Reet; Estonian leatherworks artist; b 6 Aug 1939, Tallinn; d of the late Eduard Järv. *Education:* State Art Inst. *Career:* Artist 1975–; solo exhibitions include Tallinn, Tartu, Moscow 1985, 1986, Tallinn, Parnu, Viljandi 1994, Kuressaare 1996, Tallinn 1998; has participated in numerous group exhibitions including Tallinn, Rīga (Latvia), Stockholm (Sweden) and Finland 1970–93, Erfurt Art and Crafts Quadrennial (Germany) 1982, Les Ulis, Paris 1989, Kassel (Germany) 1991, Expo-92 Seville (Spain) 1992, Södertälje (Sweden) 1993; Kristjan Raud Art Award 1983; Grand Prix, Baltic Art and Crafts Triennial (Tallinn) 1985, 1991; Estonian Leatherwork Artists Union Award 1999. *Works include:* The Beetles 1981, The Guards 1983, Trophies from the Border Zone 1984, To the Temples 1989–91, The Dragon 1992, Self Portrait as a Fossil Dragon 1995, Päkkamm 1999. *Leisure interests:* hiking, oriental philosophy. *Address:* J Koorti 16–56, Tallinn, 13623, Estonia. *Telephone:* (2) 632-3056 (Studio).

JAWAD, Haifaa-A, PH D; Iraqi university lecturer in Middle Eastern and Islamic studies; b 1952, Baghdad. *Education:* Univ of Baghdad, Univs of Exeter and Northbrook (UK). *Career:* Asst Lecturer in Politics, Al-Mustansriey Univ, Baghdad 1980–82; part-time Asst Lecturer in Middle Eastern Politics, Univ of Exeter, UK 1986; teacher of Arabic as a foreign language, Islamic Centre of the South West 1987; Asst Prof of Middle Eastern Politics, New England Coll, Arundel, UK; Sr Lecturer in Middle East and Islamic Studies, Westhill Coll, Birmingham, UK;

lectures in field; mem British Soc for Middle Eastern Studies. *Publications:* The Euro-Arab Dialogue 1980, Euro-Arab Relations: A Study in Collective Diplomacy 1992; The Middle East in the New World Order (ed, 2nd edn) 1996; articles in Islamic journals. *Leisure interests:* travel, research. *Address:* Westhill Coll, Weoley Park Rd, Selly Oak, Birmingham B29 6LL, UK. *Telephone:* (121) 472-7245.

JAWORSKA, Tamara, MFA, RCA; Canadian painter and fibre artist; b 20 July 1928, Archangielsk, fmr USSR (now Russian Fed); m Tad Jaworski 1959; one d. *Education:* State Acad of Fine Arts (Poland). *Career:* Freelance artist in fibre art 1952–; Art Dir and Chief Designer for numerous corpns, Poland 1954–63; Lecturer State Acad of Fine Arts, Poland 1952–68; part-time tutor Ontario Coll of Arts, Toronto 1980–90, conducts seminars for post-graduate students; solo exhibitions include State Gallery of Fine Arts, Warsaw 1965, Pushkin Nat Museum, Moscow 1966, Scottish Woollen Gallery, Galashields, UK 1968, Merton Gallery, Toronto 1970, London Art Gallery, ON 1971, Spain 1980–81, Canadian Cultural Centre Art Gallery, Paris 1981, Munich Art Gallery, Germany 1982, Galerie Inard, Toulouse, France 1982, 1991, John B. Aird Gallery, Toronto 1991, Iparmuveszeti Muzeum of Decorative Art, Budapest 1995, Dresden Design Centre, World Centre, Dresden, Germany 1996, Chateau de Tremblay Gallery, Fontenoy, France 1996, Retrospective Exhibition, Toronto 1997; group exhibitions include Galeria Lampertz Contempora, Cologne, Germany 1966, Rotterdam Art Gallery, the Netherlands 1967, Kunsthaus Gallery, Vienna 1967, The Hermitage, Leningrad (now St Petersburg, Russian Fed) 1968, Museum of Modern Art, México 1969, Montréal 1971, Vevey, Switzerland 1977, Royal Canadian Acad of Arts 1980, Art Gallery of Dallas, TX, USA 1983, Galerie Inard, Andorra 1985, Luxembourg 1985, Toulouse 1985, Salon des Arts de l'Air et de l'Espace, Toulouse, France 1989; collections include Gallery of European Art, Moscow, Nat Museum of Fine Arts, Warsaw, Canadian Embassy, Saudi Arabia, Nat Museum of the History of Weaving Art, Łódź, and collections in USA, Sweden, Switzerland, France and UK; mem Order of Canada, RCA, Accademia Italia delle Arti e del Lavoro, Ontario Soc of Artists; Gold Medal Triennale di Milano 1957; Medaglio d'Oro, Accademia Italia delle Arti 1980; Golden Centaur 1982; Gold Medal Int Art Competition, NY 1985; Gov Gen of Canada Commemoration Medal 1993. *Address:* 49 Don River Blvd, Willowdale, Toronto, ON M2N 2M8, Canada. *Telephone:* (416) 222-8491; *Fax:* (416) 222-8491; *E-mail:* tamtad@ica.net.

JAY, Baroness (Life Peer), cr 1992, of Paddington in the City of Westminster, **Margaret Ann Jay,** PC, BA; British politician, charity director and broadcaster; b 18 Nov 1939; d of Lord and Lady Callaghan of Cardiff; m Peter Jay 1961 (divorced 1986); two d one s; m 2nd M. W. Adler 1994. *Education:* Blackheath High School (London) and Somerville Coll (Oxford). *Career:* Broadcaster and journalist for BBC and ITV; programmes include Panorama and This Week; mem Parkside Health Authority 1985; Founder, Dir Nat AIDS Trust 1988–92; mem House of Lords 1992–, Prin Opposition Spokesperson on Health 1995–97, Deputy Leader 1997–98, Leader 1998–2001; Minister of State, Dept of Health 1997–98, Minister for Women 1998–2001; Non-Exec Dir Carlton TV 1996–97, Scottish Power 1996–97; mem Kensington, Chelsea and Westminster Health Authority 1992–97; Chair Nat Asscn Leagues of Hosp Friends 1994. *Publications:* How Rich Can We Get 1974, Battered, The Story of Child Abuse (jtly) 1987. *Address:* House of Lords, London SW1A 0PW, UK; 44 Blomfield Rd, London W9 2PF, UK.

JAYALALITHA JAYARAM, C.; Indian politician, former actress and singer; b 24 Feb 1948, Mysore City; d of the late R. Jayaram. *Education:* Stella Maris Coll. *Career:* Appeared in over 100 films; joined All-India Anna Dravida Munnetra Kazhagam 1982, Propaganda Sec 1983, Deputy Leader, Leader; mem Rajya Sabha (Council of States) 1984; Chief Minister Tamil Nadu 1991–96; Kalaimamani Award 1971–72. *Publications:* Manathai Thotta Malargal, Ennangal, Uravin Kaithigal, Ovuthike Sontham, Nenjile Oru Kanal, Nee Insi Naan Illai. *Leisure interests:* reading, music, swimming, cricket, horse-riding. *Address:* All-India Anna Dravida Munnetra Kazhagam (AIADMK), Lloyd's Rd, Chennai 600 004, India (Office); Vedo Nilayam 36, Poes Garden, Chennai 600 086, India (Home).

JEANMAIRE, Renée Marcelle (Zizi); French actress, dancer and singer; b 29 April 1924; d of Marcel Jeanmaire; m Roland Petit 1954; one d. *Education:* Paris Opera Ballet. *Career:* Dancer Paris Opera Ballet 1940–44, Ballets de Monte-Carlo, Ballets Col de Basil, Ballets Roland Petit; Dir (with Roland Petit) Casino de Paris 1969–; several music hall appearances; Chevalier de la Légion d'Honneur; Chevalier des Arts et des Lettres; Officier de l'Ordre Nat du Mérite. *Ballets include:* Aubade, Piccoli, Carmen, La croqueuse de diamants, Rose des vents, Cyrano de Bergerac, La dame dans la lune, La symphonie fantastique 1975, Le loup, La chauve-souris 1979, Hollywood Paradise Show 1985, Java for Ever 1988, Marcel et la belle excentrique 1992; *Films:* Hans Christian Andersen, Anything Goes, Folies Bergères, Charmants garçons, Black Tights, La revue, Zizi je t'aime; *Musical:* The Girl in Pink Tights. *Address:* c/o Ballets Roland Petit, 20 blvd Gabès, 13008 Marseille, France.

JEFFERSON, Kristin Marie, MFA; American film producer and museum director; b 15 Jan 1947; d of E. Harold and Helen C. Jefferson. *Education:* Bard and Hunter Colls (NY) and Tisch School of the Arts (Univ of New York). *Career:* Artist, writer and film maker; Prof of Art City (Univ of New York) 1971–79, Guest Lecturer in Art of Non-Western World and Comparative Aesthetics 1979–89; Art Dealer in Non-Western Art and Jewellery 1979–; freelance Curator in Comparative Aesthetics 1982–; Founder, Pres and Dir Museum of World Art (NY) 1989–; f Shared Visions film production co 2001–; Dr hc (New York) 1997. *Films:* Consciousness in the Arts 1973, The Choreography of Memory (video); produced: Free to Dance: American Masters Documentary 2001, Documentary of Hattie McDaniel 2001; *Publications:* She – Images of Women in African Art 1983, Magic in the Mind's Eye – The Alchemy of Collecting 1987. *Leisure interests:* reading, theatre, music, travel. *Address:* 330 W 56th St, Suite 5M, New York, NY 10019, USA. *Telephone:* (212) 245-1138; *E-mail:* sharedvisions@ mindspring.com.

JEFFORD, Barbara Mary, OBE; British actress; b 26 July 1930, Plymstock; d of the late Percival Francis and Elizabeth Mary Ellen (née Laity) Jefford; m 1st Terence Longdon 1953 (divorced 1961); m 2nd John Turner 1967. *Education:* Weirfield School (Taunton), Eileen Hartly-Hodder Studio (Bristol) and Royal Acad of Dramatic Art. *Career:* Acting debut 1949; acted in plays and films and on TV and radio; numerous and extensive tours; mem RSC 1950–54, 1992–, Old Vic Co 1956–62, Prospect 1977–79, Nat Theatre 1976–87; Queen's Jubilee Medal 1977; Pragnell Shakespeare Award 1994. *Plays include:* Measure for Measure, Henry VIII, Much Ado About Nothing, Henry IV, Othello, As You Like It, A Midsummer Night's Dream, The Taming of the Shrew, Tiger at the Gates, Coriolanus, Cymbeline, The Merchant of Venice, King Lear, Twelfth Night, Hamlet, St Joan, Macbeth, The Importance of Being Earnest, Mourning Becomes Electra, All For Love, Six Characters in Search of an Author, The Government Inspector, Tamburlaine The Great, Fathers and Sons, Ting Tang Mine (Clarence Derwent Award 1988), Ride A Cock Horse, Little Murders, Barbarians, Hedda Gabler, Medea, All's Well that Ends Well, A Collier's Friday Night, Night Must Fall, Misha's Party, Phèdre 1998, Britannicus 1998, Richard II 2000, Coriolanus 2000; *Films include:* Ulysses 1967, The Shoes of the Fisherman 1968, To Love a Vampire 1970, Hitler: the last ten days 1973, And the Ship Sails On 1983, When the Whales Came 1988, Reunion 1988, Where Angels Fear to Tread 1991, The Ninth Gate 2000. *Leisure interests:* the seaside, swimming, music, gardening. *Address:* c/o PFD, Drury House, 34–43 Russell St, London WC2B 5HA, UK. *Telephone:* (20) 7344-1010; *Fax:* (20) 7836-9523.

JELLICOE, Patricia Ann, OBE; British playwright and director; b 15 July 1927; d of John Jellicoe and Frances Jackson Henderson; m 1st C. Knight-Clarke 1950 (divorced 1961); m 2nd Roger Mayne 1962; one s one d. *Education:* Polam Hall (Darlington), Queen Margaret's (York) and Cen School of Speech and Drama (London). *Career:* Founder and Dir Cockpit Theatre 1952–54; Teacher Cen School of Speech and Drama 1954–56; Literary Man Royal Court Theatre 1973–75; Founder and Dir Colway Theatre Trust 1979–85, Pres 1986. *Publications include:* Plays: The Sport of My Mad Mother 1958, The Knack 1961, Shelley 1965, The Rising Generation 1967, The Giveaway 1969, You'll Never Guess! 1973, Clever Elsie, Smiling John, Silent Peter 1974, A Good Thing or a Bad Thing 1974, Flora and the Bandits 1976, The Reckoning 1978, The Bargain 1979, The Tide 1980, The Western Women 1984,

Mark og Mønt 1988, Under the God 1989, Changing Places; Translations: Rosmersholm 1960, The Lady From the Sea 1961, The Seagull (jtly) 1963, Der Freischütz 1964; Non-fiction: Some Unconscious Influences in the Theatre 1967, Shell Guide to Devon (jtly) 1975. *Address:* Colway Manor, Lyme Regis, Dorset DT7 3HD, UK.

JELVED, Marianne, M ED; Danish politician; b 5 Sept 1943, Charlottenlund; m. *Career:* School teacher 1967–89; teacher Royal Danish School of Educational Studies 1979–87; mem Gundsø Council (Social Liberal Party) 1982–89, Deputy Mayor 1982–85; mem Folketinget (Parl) 1987–, Minister of Economic Affairs and of Nordic Co-operation 1994; Leader Social Liberal Party 1988–; Minister for Econ Affairs 1993, for Nordic Co-operation 1994; Deputy Prime Minister of Denmark. *Publication:* BRUD: Radikale vaerdier i en forandret tid (jtly) 1994. *Address:* Ministry of Economic Affairs, Ved Stranden 8, 1061 Copenhagen K, Denmark. *Telephone:* 33-92-41-74; *Fax:* 33-93-60-20; *E-mail:* oem@oem.dk (Office); *Internet:* www.oem .dk (Office).

JENKINS, Elizabeth, OBE; British writer; b 31 Oct 1905. *Education:* Newnham Coll (Cambridge). *Publications:* The Winters 1931, Lady Caroline Lamb: a Biography 1932, Portrait of an Actor 1933, Harriet (Femina Vie Heureuse Prize) 1934, The Phoenix Nest 1936, Jane Austen – a Biography 1938, Robert and Helen 1944, Young Enthusiasts 1946, Henry Fielding, English Novelists Series 1947, Six Criminal Women 1949, The Tortoise and the Hare 1954, Ten Fascinating Women 1955, Elizabeth the Great 1958, Elizabeth and Leicester 1961, Brightness 1963, Honey 1968, Dr Gully 1972, The Mystery of King Arthur 1975, The Princes in the Tower 1978, The Shadow and the Light: A Life of Daniel Dunglass Home 1983, A Silent Joy (novel) 1992. *Address:* 121 Greenhill, London NW3 5TY, UK. *Telephone:* (20) 7435-4642.

JENKINS, Dame (Mary) Jennifer, (Lady Jenkins of Hillhead), DBE; British administrator; b 18 Jan 1921; d of the late Sir Parker Morris; m Roy Jenkins (Baron Jenkins of Hillhead) 1945; two s one d. *Education:* St Mary's School (Calne) and Girton Coll (Cambridge). *Career:* With Hoover Ltd 1942–43, Ministry of Lab 1943–46, Political and Econ Planning (PEP) 1946–48; part-time extra-mural Lecturer 1949–61; part-time teacher Kingsway Day Coll 1961–67; Chair Consumers Asscn 1965–76; mem Exec Bd British Standards Inst 1970–73, Design Council 1971–74, Cttee of Man Courtauld Inst 1981–84, Ancient Monuments Bd 1982–84, Exec Cttee Nat Trust 1984– (Chair 1986–90), Historic Bldgs and Monuments Comm 1984–85; Sec Ancient Monuments Soc 1972–75, Pres 1985–; Chair N Kensington Amenity Trust 1974–77; Historic Bldgs Council for England 1975–84, Royal Parks Review Group 1991–96, Architectural Heritage Fund 1994–97, Expert Panel Heritage Lottery Fund 1995–99; Trustee Wallace Collection 1977–83; Dir J. Sainsbury Ltd 1981–86, Abbey Nat PLC 1984–91; JP London Juvenile Courts 1964–74; Hon mem Royal Town Planning Inst 1988; Hon Fellow Landscape Inst 1995; Hon FRICS 1980, FRIBA 1982; Hon LL D (London) 1988, (Bristol) 1990; Hon D UNIV (York) 1990, (Strathclyde) 1993; Hon D CL (Newcastle) 1992; Hon D ARCH (Oxford Brookes) 1993; Hon D LITT (Greenwich) 1998. *Publications:* From Acorn to Oak Tree: The Growth of the National Trust 1994. *Address:* St Amand's House, East Hendred, OX12 8LA, UK; 2 Kensington Park Gardens, London W11 3HB, UK.

JENNER, Ann Maureen; Australian (b British) ballet dancer and teacher; b 8 March 1944, Ewell, Surrey; d of Kenneth George and Margaret Rosetta (née Wilson) Jenner; m Dale Robert Baker 1980; one s. *Education:* Royal Ballet School. *Career:* Dancer Royal Ballet Co 1961–78, Soloist 1964, Prin 1970; Principal Australian Ballet Co 1978–80; currently Full-Time Teacher The Australian Ballet School; Guest Teacher Nat Theatre Ballet School 1980, Assoc Dir 1987, Dir 1988; Guest Teacher Victorian Coll of the Arts, Melbourne, Australian Ballet and Queensland Ballet 1980–, San Francisco Ballet Co and School, USA 1985; freelance ballet teacher and choreographer and mem staff Dance World 301 (Melbourne, Vic). *Ballets include:* La fille mal gardée 1966, Coppelia 1968, Cinderella 1969, Sleeping Beauty 1972, Giselle 1973, Deux Pigeons 1974, Romeo and Juliet 1977, Mayerling 1978, Spartacus 1979, Don Quixote 1979, Anna Karenina 1980,

Pineapple Poll 1980. *Leisure interests:* swimming, music. *Address:* c/o The Australian Ballet School, 2 Kavanagh St, South Bank, Vic 3006, Australia. *Telephone:* (3) 9669-2700.

JENNINGS, Elizabeth, CBE, MA; British poet and critic; b 18 July 1926, Boston, Lincs; d of H. C. Jennings. *Education:* Oxford High School and St Anne's Coll (Oxford). *Career:* Asst Oxford City Library 1950–58; Reader Chatto & Windus Ltd 1958–60; freelance writer 1960–; Arts Council Prize for Poems 1953; Arts Council Award 1981; Paul Hamlyn Foundation Award 1997. *Publications:* Poetry: Poems 1953, A Way of Looking (Somerset Maugham Award 1956) 1955, A Sense of the World 1958, Michelangelo's Sonnets (trans) 1961, Song for a Birth or Death 1961, Recoveries 1963, The Mind has Mountains (Richard Hillary Prize) 1966, The Secret Brother (for children) 1966, Collected Poems 1967, The Animals' Arrival 1969, Lucidities 1971, Relationships 1972, Growing Points 1975, Consequently I Rejoice 1977, After the Ark (for children) 1978, Moments of Grace 1979, Celebrations and Elegies 1982, Extending the Territory 1985, Collected Poems 1953–86 (W. H. Smith Award 1987) 1986, Tributes 1989, Times and Seasons 1992, Familiar Spirits 1994, A Spell of Words 1997, Praises 1998, Timely Issues 2001; Criticism: Every Changing Shape 1961, Seven Men of Vision 1976; Batsford Book of Religious Verse (ed) 1982, In Praise of Our Lady 1982, Extending the Territory 1985; contribs to The New Yorker, Southern Review, Poetry (Chicago), Botteghe Oscure, Daily Telegraph, Encounter, New Statesman, Observer, Scotsman, Country Life, Listener and others. *Leisure interests:* theatre, music, looking at pictures, conversation. *Address:* c/o David Higham Assocs Ltd, 5–8 Lower John St, London W1R 4HA, UK.

JENSEN, Kirsten Maria; Danish journalist and politician; b 11 March 1961, Esbønderup. *Career:* Journalist; fmr MEP (Socialdemokratiet) 1989, Vice-Chair Cttee on Environment, Public Health and Consumer Protection, mem Del for relations with Cen Asia and Mongolia. *Address:* c/o European Parliament, rue Wiertz, 1047 Brussels, Belgium.

JENSEN, Lis; Danish politician; b 6 July 1952, Jetsmark. *Career:* MEP (Europe of Nations Group), mem Cttee on Social Affairs and Employment, Del to the EU–Bulgaria Jt Parl Cttee. *Address:* European Parliament, rue Wiertz, 1047 Brussels, Belgium. *Telephone:* (2) 284-21-11; *Fax:* (2) 230-69-43.

JENSEN, Marianne; Danish (Greenlandic) politician. *Career:* Fmrly Minister of Culture, Education and Research; Minister of Health, Environment and Research 1995; mem Siumut (Forward) party. *Address:* c/o Ministry of Health, Environment and Research, 3900 Nuuk, Greenland.

JEREN, Tatjana, MD, PH D; Croat medical practitioner; b 18 March 1941, Zagreb; d of Ivan and Andja (née Papić) Jeren; m Ivan Beus 1968. *Education:* Univ of Zagreb. *Career:* Mem staff Univ Hosp for Infectious Diseases, Zagreb 1966, Specialist on Infectology 1970, Head Dept of Cytology and Haematology 1976–; Asst Prof Medical Faculty, Univ of Zagreb 1981–88, Prof 1988–; mem Croatian Acad of Medical Sciences 1989; numerous papers in medical journals 1970–. *Leisure interests:* reading, paintings. *Address:* Sveučilište u Zagrebu, University Hospital for Infectious Diseases, 4100 Zagreb, Mirogojska 8, Croatia (Office); Zagreb, Šestinski kraljevec 100, Croatia (Home). *Telephone:* (1) 420880 (Home).

JÉRÔME-FORGET, Monique, PH D; Canadian organization executive; b 8 Aug 1940, Montréal, PQ; d of Frederick and Cécile (née Labelle) Jérome; m Claude Forget 1960; one s one d. *Education:* Coll Basile-Moreau and McGill Univ. *Career:* First Vice-Pres Canadian Advisory Council on Status of Women; Asst Deputy Ministry of Health and Welfare of Canada; Vice-Rector Concordia Univ 1982–86; Pres and CEO Québec Comm on Health and Safety at Work 1986–90; Pres and CEO Inst for Research on Public Policy 1991–; mem Nat Ass of Québec 1998–; Chair OECD Task Force on Social Policy; Chair Int Union of Family Orgs, Family Health Cttee; mem Bd of Dirs Canadian Council for Social Devt, Québec Fed of Women; Founder and Assoc mem Kellogg Center 1977–. *Publications:* The Family as Part of a Larger System (jtly), Working with the Family in Primary Care (jtly) 1984.

Leisure interests: travel, skiing, sailing. *Address:* Hôtel du Parlement, Bureau 3.135, Québec, G1A 1A4, Canada (Office); 82, 1227 rue Sherbrooke Ouest, Montréal, PQ H3G 1G1, Canada (Home).

JEVRIĆ, Olga; Yugoslav sculptor; b 29 Sept 1922, Belgrade; d of Srbislav Jevrić and Anna Radivojević-Vačić. *Career:* Solo exhibitions include Galerija ULUS, Belgrade 1957, Galeria Nofizie, Turin, Italy 1959, Drian Galleries, London, UK 1962, Galerija Suvremene Umjetnosti, Zagreb 1964, Salon Musée d'Art Moderne, Belgrade 1965, 1981; group exhibitions include 23rd Biennale Internationale, Venice, Italy 1958, Concorso Internationale del Bronrelto, Padua, Italy 1959–70, Biennale Internazionale, Carrara, Italy 1962, 1967, Salon de la jeune sculpture, Paris, France 1965, Pittsburgh International, PA, USA 1967, Kleinplastiken aus der Sammlung der Nationalgalerie, Berlin, Germany 1990; apptd Ed-in-Chief Dictionnaire des Arts Plástiques de SANU (ASAS) 1980; became mem Acad Serbe des Sciences et des Arts 1974; Prix Politika 1960; Prix Juillet 1979. *Works include:* Formes Complementaires, Formes Eccentriques, Composition Astatique, Composition Horizöntale. *Leisure interests:* music, photography, reading. *Address:* 11000 Belgrade, Braničevska 8, Yugoslavia. *Telephone:* (11) 439013.

JHABVALA, Ruth Prawer, CBE, MA; British/American writer; b 7 May 1927, Cologne, Germany; d of Marcus Prawer and Eleonora Cohn; m C. S. H. Jhabvala 1951; three d. *Education:* Hendon Co School and Univ of London. *Career:* Refugee to UK 1939; lived India 1951–75, USA 1975–; Neill Gunn Int Fellowship 1979; MacArthur Foundation Award 1984; Hon D LITT. *Publications:* Novels: To Whom She Will 1955, Nature of Passion 1956, Esmond in India 1958, The Householder 1960, Get Ready for Battle 1962, A Backward Place 1962, A New Dominion 1971, Heat and Dust (Booker Prize) 1975 (screenplay 1983), In Search of Love and Beauty 1983, The Nature of Passion 1986, Three Continents 1987, Poet and Dancer 1993, Shards of Memory 1995; Short story collections: A Stronger Climate 1968, An Experience of India 1970, How I Became a Holy Mother 1976, Out of India: Selected Stories 1986, East into Upper East 1998; Film Scripts (for Ismail Merchant and James Ivory): Shakespeare Wallah 1965, The Guru 1969, Bombay Talkie 1971, Autobiography of a Princess 1975, Roseland 1977, Hullabaloo over Georgie and Bonnie's Pictures 1978, Jane Austen in Manhattan 1980, Quartet 1981, A Room with a View (Acad Award 1987) 1986, Madame Sousatzka 1988, Mr and Mrs Bridge 1989, Howards End (Acad Award) 1992, The Remains of the Day 1993, Jefferson in Paris 1995, Surviving Picasso 1996, The Golden Bowl 2000. *Address:* 400 E 52nd St, New York, NY 10022, USA.

JIAGGE, Annie Ruth, LL D; Ghanaian former judge and voluntary worker; b 7 Oct 1918, Lomé, Togo; d of the late Rev Robert Domingo and Henrietta L. Baëta; m Fred K. A. Jiagge 1953. *Education:* Achimota Training Coll (Accra), LSE and Lincoln's Inn (UK). *Career:* Head-teacher Keta Presbyterian Sr Girls' School; called to the Bar, Ghana 1950, practised law 1950–55; Dist Magistrate 1955–57, Sr Magistrate 1957–59; Judge Circuit Court 1959–61, High Court 1961–69, Court of Appeal 1969–83, Pres 1980–83; Ghanaian Rep UN Comm on the Status of Women 1962–72, Chair 1968; Chair Comm on Investigation of Assets 1966, Ghana Council on Women and Devt 1975–82; mem Presidium WCC 1975–, Pres WCC 1975–83, Moderator Programme to Combat Racism 1984–91; Pres Cttee of Churches' Participation in Devt 1985–93; mem Cttee of experts to formulate draft constitution 1991–92, Pres's Transitional Cttee 1993, Council of State 1993; Vice-Pres World YWCA 1949; mem Court, Univ of Ghana, Legon 1968–, Int Advisory Bd Noel Foundation 1990–; Hon LL D (Ghana, Legon) 1974; Gimbles' Int Award for Humanitarian Work 1969; Ghana Grand Medal 1969. *Publication:* UN Declaration on Elimination of Discrimination against Women (basic draft) 1967. *Leisure interests:* music, gardening, crafts. *Address:* 8 Onyasia Crescent, Roman Ridge, POB 5511, Accra N, Ghana. *Telephone:* (21) 772046.

JIANG LIJIN, PH D; Chinese organic chemist; b 15 April 1919, Beijing; d of Jiong-Shang Jiang and Shu-Duan Li; m Guo-Zhi Xu 1954; two s. *Education:* Furen Univ and Univ of Minnesota (USA). *Career:* Assoc Prof Inst of Chem, Acad Sinica, Beijing 1956–74, Inst of Photographic Chem 1974–77, Prof and Sr Research Fellow 1978–, mem Standing Cttee, Chem Div 1981–93, Academician 1994–; mem Standing Cttee 6th CPPCC 1983–87, 7th CPPCC 1988–92, 8th CPPCC 1992–97;

Red Banner Pacesetter Award 1979–83. *Publications:* The Chemistry and Phototherapeutic Mechanism of Hypocrellins (Academia Sinica Natural Science Award Second Prize 1990), The Relationship between the Structures of the Phycobiliproteins and the Evolution of the Algal Species, The Study of the Mechanism of Energy Transfer (Academia Sinica Natural Science Award Second Prize 1993), The Photochemical, Photophysical and Photodynamical Actions of the Naturally Occurring Perylenohydroxylquinones (Second Prize, Natural Science Award, Acad Sinica 1996); numerous publs on hypocrellins and phycobiliproteins. *Leisure interests:* tennis, travel. *Address:* Inst of Photographic Chemistry, Academia Sinica, De Wai, Bei Sha Tan, Beijing 100101, People's Republic of China (Office); Apt 804, Bldg 812, Huang Zhuang, Haidian Qu, Beijing 100080, People's Republic of China (Home). *Telephone:* (10) 64888068 (Office); (10) 62569291 (Home); *Fax:* (10) 62029375.

JIRICNA, Eva Magdalena, CBE, RIBA, RA; British architect; b 3 March 1939, Ziln, Czechoslovakia. *Education:* Univ of Prague and Prague Acad of Fine Arts. *Career:* Worked with the GLC's School Div 1968; Louis de Soissons Partnership 1969–78, Project Architect; lectured at South Bank Polytechnic 1974–76; went into practice with David Hodges 1978; team leader at Richard Rogers Partnership 1982–84; formed her own practice 1984, reformed as Eva Jiricna Architects 1986–; External Examiner for RCA and the Schools of Architecture at Leicester, Sheffield, Oxford, Bath, Humberside and Plymouth Univs and for RIBA; Hon Fellow Royal Coll of Art 1990; Royal Designer for Industry 1991; Design Prize RA 1994; Hon Fellow Royal Inc of Architects in Scotland 1996; mem American Hall of Fame 1998, RIBA Council; D Tech (hc) Southampton, Brno (Czech Repub) 2000. *Major commissions include:* the Gehry Bldg, Prague, the New Orangery, Prague, Canada Water Bus Station, London, Faith Zone, Millennium Dome 1999; *TV:* Tales from Prague, BBC2, Architecture of the Imagination: Staircases, BBC2 1990, The Late Show – Czech Modernism 1994, Wideworld, Anglia TV 1997, The Dome: Trouble at the Big Top, BBC2 1999; *Publications:* Eva Jiricna: Design in Exile, The Joseph Shops: Eva Jiricna. *Address:* Eva Jiricna Architects, Third Floor, 38 Warren St, London, W1T 6AE, UK. *Telephone:* (20) 7554-2400; *Fax:* (20) 7388-8022; *E-mail:* mail@ejal.com.

JIROVA, Jitka, PH D; Czech scientist; b 12 March 1944, Vsetín; d of Prof Otto Engelberth; m 1967; one s one d. *Education:* Czech Tech Univ and Czech Acad of Sciences. *Career:* Researcher Inst of Theoretical and Applied Mechanics 1967–, biomechanics of artificial replacement of human joints and computational modelling, experimental methods and biomaterials 1979–, Chief Research Fellow 1987–, Head of Lab of Experimental Biomechanics 1989–; Scientific Sec Czech Soc of Biomechanics 1994–; numerous contribs to scientific journals; Award of Pres of State Cttee for Scientific and Tech Devt 1985. *Leisure interests:* photography, gardening, art. *Address:* Institute of Theoretical and Applied Mechanics, Prosecká 76, 190 00 Prague 9, Czech Republic (Office); Lužická 38, 120 00 Prague 2, Czech Republic (Home). *Telephone:* (2) 882121; *Fax:* (2) 884634; *E-mail:* jirova@itam.cas.cz.

JOENPELTO, Eeva Elisabeth; Finnish writer and artist; b 17 June 1921, Sammatti; m Jarl Helemann 1945 (until 1975); two s. *Education:* Lohja. *Career:* Writer of 26 novels 1951–94; several State Prizes 1955–, including Finlandia prize 1994. *Leisure interests:* history, shooting. *Address:* Werlanderintie 231, 09220 Sammatti, Finland. *Telephone:* (912) 356433.

JOHANASSON, Ylva; Swedish politician; b 13 Feb 1964, Huddinge; m Bo Hammar; two c. *Education:* Univ of Lund and Stockholm Inst of Educ. *Career:* Teacher 1988, 1992–94; Mem Riksdag (Parl, Left Party) 1988–91, mem Parl Reference Group for the Evaluation of Vocational Training in Sr Secondary Schools 1989–91, for the Curriculum Cttee 1991–92, Cttee on Young People 1989–91, on Grades and Marketing 1990–92; fmr Minister for Schools and Adult Educ at Ministry of Educ. *Address:* Ministry for Schools and Adult Education, Drottninggt 16, 103 33 Stockholm, Sweden. *Telephone:* (8) 405-10-00; *Fax:* (8) 723-11-92.

JOHANSEN, Hanna; Swiss (b German) writer; b 17 June 1939, Bremen, Germany; m Adolf Muschg 1967 (until 1990); two s. *Education:* Univs of Marburg and Göttingen and Ithaca Univ (NY, USA). *Career:* Writer of novels and children's stories since 1978; Marie-

Louise Kaschnitz Prize 1986; Conrad Ferdinand Meyer Prize 1987; Swiss Jugend Book Prize 1990. *Publications:* Novels: Die Stehende Uhr 1978, Trocadero 1980, Die Analphabetin 1982, Zurück nach Orambi 1986, Ein Mann vor der Tür 1988; Short stories: Über den Wunsch, sich Wohlzufühlen 1985, Die Schöne am Unteren Bild Rand 1990; five children's books 1983–89. *Address:* c/o Hanser Verlag, Kolbergerstr 22, Postfach 860420, 800 Munich 800, Germany (Office); Vorbühlstr 7, 8802 Kilchberg, Switzerland (Home). *Telephone:* (1) 7153029 (Home).

JOHNES, Jill, PH D; British economist; b 14 Dec 1962, Lytham, Lancs; d of Jim J. and Sheila Gregson; m Geraint Johnes 1987; three c. *Education:* Queen Mary School (Lytham) and Univ of Lancaster. *Career:* British Aerospace 1985–88; Lecturer in Regional Econs Univ of Lancaster 1988–91, part-time Lecturer 1991–; Consultant Govt of Isle of Man 1989–90; Deputy Ed Regional Studies 1989–1992; Review Ed Education Econs 1992–; Pilkington Award for Pedagogy 1991. *Publications:* Performance Indicators in Higher Education 1990; numerous articles in professional journals. *Leisure interests:* reading, needlework, sport, walking, watercolours. *Address:* University of Lancaster, Management School, Dept of Economics, Lancaster, Lancs LA1 4YW, UK (Office); 55 Moorside Rd, Brookhouse, Lancaster, Lancs LA2 9AJ, UK (Home). *Telephone:* (1524) 65201 (Office); (1524) 770767 (Home); *Fax:* (1524) 843087 (Office); *E-mail:* j.johnes@lancaster.ac.uk.

JOHNNY, Sonia M, BA, JP; Saint Lucia diplomatist and attorney. *Education:* Univ of the W Indies, Johns Hopkins School of Advanced Int Studies and Georgetown Law Center. *Career:* Attorney; Amb of St Lucia to USA. *Leisure interests:* reading, theatre, watching sports. *Address:* 3216 New Mexico Ave, NW, Washington, DC 20016, USA. *Telephone:* (202) 364 6792; *Fax:* (202) 364 6723; *E-mail:* eofsaintlu@aol.com.

JOHNOVÁ, Adriena; Czech artist; b 6 Aug 1926, Prague; d of the late Václav and Milena Simota; m Jiri John 1923 (died 1972); one s. *Education:* Univ of Industrial Arts. *Career:* Solo exhibitions include: Prague 1960, Uppsala, Sweden 1978, Baumgartner, W. Berlin 1983, Riverside Studios, London 1983, Galerie de France, Paris 1991, Gallery Gema, Prague, Berlin 1997; group exhibitions include: New York 1980, Osaka and Kyoto 1981, Munich 1983, Washington 1988, Repub of Korea 1988, Denmark 1984, Prague Castle 1996; Grand Prix for Graphics, (Ljubljana) 1979; Grand Prix Int for Drawings (Wroclaw), Gottfried von Herder Prize (Vienna); Medal of Merit (Prague) 1997. *Leisure interests:* human relations, literature, music, nature. *Address:* Nad Královskou oborou 15, 170 00 Prague 7, Czech Republic (Office); Na Podkovce 14, 140 00 Prague 4, Czech Republic (Home). *Telephone:* (2) 61213879.

JOHNSON, Betsey Lee, BA; American fashion designer; b 10 Aug 1942, Hartford, Conneticut; d of John Herman and Lena Virginia Johnson; m 1st John Cale 1966; one d; m 2nd Jeffrey Olivier 1981. *Education:* Pratt Inst (New York) and Syracuse Univ. *Career:* Editorial Asst Mademoiselle magazine 1964–65; Partner and Co-Owner Betsey, Bunky & Nini, New York 1969–; shops in NY, LA, San Francisco, Coconut Grove, Florida, Venice, California, Boston, Chicago, Seattle; Prin Designer for Paraphernalia 1965–69; designer Alvin Duskin Co, San Francisco 1970; Head Designer Alley Cat by Betsey Johnson (div of LeDamor Inc) 1970–74; freelance designer for Jr Womens' Div, Butterick Pattern Co 1971, Betsey Johnson's Kids Children's Wear (div of Shutterbug Inc) 1974–77, Betsey Johnson for Jeanette Maternities, Inc 1974–75; designer for Gant Shirtmakers Inc (women's clothing) 1974–75, Tric-Trac by Betsey Johnson (women's knitwear) 1974–76, Butterick's Home Sewing Catalog 1975– (children's wear); Head Designer jr sportswear co; designed for Star Ferry by Betsey Johnson and Michael Miles (children's wear) 1975–77; owner and Head Designer B. J. Inc designer wholesale co 1978; Pres and Treas B. J. Vines New York; opened Betsey Johnson store (New York) 1979; mem Council of Fashion Designers, American Women's Forum; Merit Award, Mademoiselle magazine 1970, Coty Award 1971, two Tommy Print Awards 1971. *Address:* 110 East 9th St, Suite A889, Los Angeles, CA 90079, USA.

JOHNSON, Gwenavere Anelisa, MA; American artist; b 16 Oct 1909, Newark, SD; d of Arthur and Susie (née King) Nelson; m John Johnson 1937; one s. *Education:* Univ of Minnesota and San Jose State Univ (CA). *Career:* Art Teacher, MN 1937–38, CA 1947–75; propr Tree Tops Studio 1975–; exhibitions include Treeside Gallery (Los Gatos), Los Gatos Art Museum, Rosicrucian Museum, Garden Art Show 1981–95, Centre d'Art Contemporain (Paris) 1983, Triton Art Museum 1983–95; mem San Jose Art League, Los Gatos Art Asscn, Santa Clara Art Asscn, Soc of Western Artists, Nat League of American Penwomen; numerous show awards; Golden Centaur Award, Accad Italia 1982; Golden Flame Award 1986. *Address:* 106 Fairview Ave, Capitola, CA 95010, USA.

JOHNSON, Louise Napier, PH D, FRS; British university professor; b 26 Sept 1940, Worcester; d of George Edmund and Elizabeth (née King) Johnson; m (huband deceased); one s one d. *Education:* Wimbledon High School, Univ Coll London and Royal Inst (London). *Career:* Research Asst Yale Univ 1996; demonstrator Zoology Dept, Univ of Oxford 1967–73, Lecturer in Molecular Biophysics 1973–90, David Phillips Prof of Molecular Biophysics 1990–, Additional Fellow Somerville Coll 1973–90, Hon Fellow 1991–, Professorial Fellow Corpus Christi Coll 1990–; mem EMBO 1991–; Assoc Fellow Third World Acad of Sciences 2000–; mem Council, Royal Soc 1998–2001, Scientific Advisory Council, European Molecular Biology Lab 1994–2000, Council for the Central Lab of the Research Councils 1998–2001; Trustee Cambridge Crystallographic Data Centre; Gov Westminster School; Hon D SC (St Andrews) 1992; Linderström-Lang Prize 1989, Charmian Medal, Royal Soc of Chem 1997, Datta Medal, Fed of European Biochemical Soc 1998. *Publications include:* Protein Crystallography (with T. L. Bluncell) 1976, Glycogen Phosphorylase (jtly) 1991; more than 150 scientific papers on lysozyme, phosphorylase protein kinases, allosteric mechanisms, cell cycle proteins, protein crystallography. *Leisure interests:* family, horses. *Address:* Laboratory of Molecular Biophysics, Department of Biochemistry, University of Oxford, Oxford OX1 3QU, UK. *Telephone:* (1865) 275365; *Fax:* (1865) 510454; *E-mail:* louise@biop.ox.ac.uk; *Internet:* www.biop.ox.ac.uk.

JOHNSON, Marlene, BA; American organization executive and politician; b 11 Jan 1946, Braham, MN; d of Beauford and Helen (née Nelson) Johnson; m Peter Frankel. *Education:* Macalester Coll. *Career:* Mem staff Face to Face Health and Counselling Clinic 1977–78, Working Opportunities for Women 1977–82; Lieut-Gov State of Minnesota, St Paul 1983–91; Assoc Admin for Admin at Gen Services Admin Washington, DC 1994–95; Sr Fellow Family Support Project Center for Policy Alternative 1991–93; Chair Minnesota Women's Political Caucus 1973–76, Child Care Task Force 1987, Nat Conf of Lieut-Govs 1987, Children's 2000 Comm; Co-Founder Women's Campaign Fund 1982; Vice-Pres for People and Strategy Rowe Furniture Corpn, Va 1995–97; CEO Asscn Int Educators 1998–; f Nat Leadership Conf of Women Execs in State Govt; mem Bd of Dirs Nat Child Care Action Campaign; mem Nat Asscn of Women Business Owners; named one of Ten Outstanding Young Minnesotans 1980; Children's Champion Award, Children's Defense Fund 1989.

JOHNSON, Nancy Lee, BA; American politician; b 5 Jan 1935, Chicago, IL; d of Noble Wishard and Gertrude (née Smith) Lee; m Theodore Johnson 1958; three d. *Education:* Radcliffe Coll and Univ of London (UK). *Career:* Lecturer in American Art, New Britain Museum of American Art 1968–71; Vice-Chair Charter Comm, CT 1976–77; mem Connecticut Senate for 6th Dist 1977–82; mem House of Reps (Parl) for Connecticut 6th Dist, Washington, DC 1983–. *Address:* 141 S Mountain St, New Britain, CT 06052, USA.

JOHNSON, Norma Holloway, BS, JD; American federal judge; b Lake Charles, LA. *Education:* Dist of Columbia Teachers' Coll and Georgetown Univ. *Career:* Called to the Bar, DC 1962, US Supreme Court 1967; pvt law practice Washington, DC 1963; Attorney Dept of Justice 1963–67; Asst Corp Counsel 1967–70; Judge Dist of Columbia Superior Court 1970–80, US Dist Court 1980–97, Chief Judge 1997–; mem Bd of Dirs Nat Children's Center, Washington, DC, Nat Street Law Inst; mem ABA, Nat Bar Asscn, Asscn of Women Judges. *Address:* US District Court, US Courthouse, 333 Constitution Ave, NW, Washington, DC 20001, USA.

JOHNSON, Susan Ruth; Australian writer; b 30 Dec 1956, Brisbane; d of John Joseph and Barbara Ruth (née Bell) Johnson; m 1st John Patrick Burdett 1989 (divorced 1991); m 2nd Leslie William Webb

1994; one s. *Education:* Clayfield Coll (Brisbane) and Univ of Queensland. *Career:* Journalist The Sydney Morning Herald and The Nat Times 1975–84; full-time writer 1984–; resident Keesing Studio, Cité Int des Arts, Paris (awarded by Literature Bd, Australia Council) until 1992; several fellowships awarded by Australia Council 1986–92. *Publications:* Latitudes: New Writing From the North (co-ed) 1986, Message From Chaos 1987, Flying Lessons 1990, A Big Life 1993, Hungry Ghosts 1996. *Leisure interests:* reading, travel, films, food, surfing. *Address:* c/o Margaret Connolly and Assocs, POB 48, Paddington, NSW 2021, Australia. *Telephone:* (2) 360 3935.

JOHNSON-SIRLEAF, Ellen; Liberian politician and civil servant. *Education:* Harvard Univ (MA, USA). *Career:* Asst Minister of Finance 1964–69, Deputy Minister of Finance 1977–80; Sr Loan Officer IBRD, Washington, DC 1973–77, 1980–81; fmr Pres Liberian Bank for Devt Investment; Vice-Pres Citibank Regional Office for Africa, Nairobi 1981–85; Vice-Pres and mem Bd of Dirs Equator Holders, Equator Bank Ltd, Washington, DC until 1992; Asst Admin UNDP and Dir Regional Bureau for Africa 1992–. *Address:* c/o UN Development Programme, 1 United Nations Plaza, New York, NY 10017, USA.

JOHNSTON, Alexandra Ferguson, PH D; American college principal and professor of English; b 19 July 1939, Indianapolis, IN; d of Geoffrey and Alexandra (née Sherwood) Johnston. *Education:* Brantford Coll Inst and Vocational School and Univ of Toronto (ON, Canada). *Career:* Asst Prof of English Queen's Univ 1964–67; Asst Prof Univ of Toronto 1967–70, Assoc Prof 1970–78, Prof of English 1978–, Prin Victoria Coll 1981–91; Dir Records of Early English Drama 1976–; Sec Int Soc for Medieval Theatre 1980–89, Pres 1989–92; Pres Medieval and Renaissance Drama Soc, Modern Language Asscn of America 1989–91; Pres Canadian Council of Churches 1994–; Hon LL D (Queen's) 1984; DD (Presbyterian Coll) 1990. *Publication:* The York Records, Records of Early English Drama (2 vols) 1979. *Address:* 150 Charles St W, Toronto ON M5S 1K9, Canada (Office); 39 Elgin Ave, Toronto, ON M5R 1G5, Canada (Home).

JOHNSTON, Hon Rita Margaret; Canadian former politician; b 22 April 1935, Melville, SK; d of John and Annie (née Chyzzy) Leichert; m George Johnston 1951; two d one s. *Career:* Alderman Dist of Surrey 1970–83; became mem Legis Ass (British Columbia Social Credit Party) 1983; Minister of Municipal Affairs, Recreation and Culture, Govt of British Columbia 1986–89, Minister of Transportation and Highways 1989–91, Deputy Premier 1990–91, Premier 1991 (first woman); Leader British Columbia Social Credit Party 1992; Man Bell Finance Ltd; Stenographer Household Finance and Bank of Montréal; mem Surrey Chamber of Commerce. *Address:* 3190 Gladwin Rd, Suite 1601, Abbotsford, BC V2A 6W8, Canada (Home).

JOHNSTONE, Diane Katrina, B ECONS; Australian diplomatist; b 23 Nov 1950, Sydney; d of the late C. H. S. and of Sheila Johnstone; m Gregory Luz 1988. *Education:* Queenwood School for Girls (NSW) and Univ of Sydney. *Career:* Mem staff Dept of Foreign Affairs and Trade, Canberra 1973, 1976–79, 1982–83, 1984–86, Head of Graduate Recruitment 1990–91, Dir of Defence Policy 1991–92, Indian Ocean Task Force 1995; mem staff Embassy, SA 1974–76, Liaison Officer, Zimbabwe (fmrly Rhodesia) 1979–80; at High Comm, Kenya 1980–82, Australian Mission to UN, New York, USA 1982; Olympic Liaison Officer Consulate-Gen, Los Angeles, CA, USA 1984; Amb to Nepal 1986–89; Dir Stategic Policy Section, Dept of Defence 1993–95; mem Bd Interchange Program Esso Australia Ltd 1983–84; contribs to professional journals and publs. *Leisure interests:* tennis, horse-riding, skiing, trekking, theatre, music. *Address:* Department of Foreign Affairs and Trade, Canberra, ACT 2600, Australia (Office); 81 Wybalena Grove, Cook, ACT 2614, Australia (Home). *Telephone:* (6) 153 1775 (Home).

JOHNSTONE, Rose M., PH D; Canadian professor of biochemistry; b 14 May 1928, Łódź, Poland; d of Jacob Mamelak and Esther Rotholc; m Douglas Johnstone 1953; two s. *Education:* McGill Univ (Montréal). *Career:* Asst Prof of Biochem, McGill Univ 1960–67, Assoc Prof 1967–77, Prof 1980–, Chair of Biochem 1980–90, Gilman Cheney Chair 1985; Treas Staff Asscn 1969–72, 1995–; numerous papers in scientific journals; Fellow Nat Cancer Inst of Canada; mem Canadian Biochemical Soc (Pres 1985–86), American Soc of Biological Chemists,

Int Org of Women Biochemists; Fellow Royal Soc of Canada 1987, Treas 1991–94; Moyse Travelling Fellowship 1954; Queen's Silver Jubilee Medal 1978; J. Manery Fisher Award 1991. *Leisure interests:* dance, tennis. *Address:* McGill University, Dept of Biochemistry, McIntyre Bldg, Suite 810, 3655 Drummond St, Montréal, PQ H3G 1Y6, Canada (Office); 4064 Oxford Ave, Notre Dame de Grace, PQ H4A 2Y4, Canada (Home). *Telephone:* (514) 398-7264 (Office); *Fax:* (514) 398-7384 (Office); *E-mail:* rmjohns@med.mcgill.ca.

JÓKAI, Anna, BA; Hungarian writer; b 24 Nov 1932, Budapest; d of Gyula and Anna (née Lukács) Jókai; m 3rd Sándor Kapocsi 1983; one s one d. *Education:* Univ Eötvös Loránd (Budapest). *Career:* Accountant 1951–61; teacher 1961–76; freelance writer 1976–; Pres Hungarian Writers' Asscn 1990–92; József Attila Prize 1971; Int Pietrczak Pax Literary Prize, Poland 1980; Kossuth Prize 1994; Hungarian Heredity Prize 1998, The Book of the Year Prize 1999; Council for Educational Tech Prize 1999; Hungarian Art Prize 2000. Publications: 19 novels including Have No Fear 1998, numerous short stories and essays and 3 plays 1968–. *Address:* 1074 Budapest, Dohány u 82, Hungary. *Telephone:* (1) 1423041; *Fax:* (1) 1423041.

JOKIPII, Liisa, MD; Finnish medical practitioner and university teacher; b 26 March 1943, Helsinki; m Anssi Jokipii 1968; two s two d. *Education:* Univ of Helsinki. *Career:* Asst Dept of Serology and Bacteriology, Univ of Helsinki 1973, Dozent in Clinical Microbiology and Immunology 1977–; Prof of Clinical Microbiology and Immunology, Univ of Oulu 1977; Prof of Bacteriology and Serology, Univ of Turku 1978; scientific articles on cell-mediated immunity, bacteriology and parasitology; contribs to textbooks on parasitology. *Leisure interests:* classical music (opera), old Finnish handicrafts and design. *Address:* Vanhaväylä 37, 00830 Helsinki, Finland (Home). *Telephone:* (0) 783827 (Home).

JOLAS, Betsy; French composer; b 5 Aug 1926, Paris; d of Eugène and Maria Jolas; m Gabriel Illouz 1949; two s one d. *Education:* Bennington Coll (USA) and Conservatoire Nat Supérieur de Musique (Paris). *Career:* Pianist, organist and chorister Dessoff Choirs, USA; Prof Conservatoire Nat Supérieur de Musique, Paris 1971–; has taught at Univs of Yale, Berkeley and Southern California, USA; Darius Milhaud Chair, Mills Coll, CA, USA; compositions have been performed by Boston Symphony Chamber Players, London Sinfonietta, Lincoln Center Chamber Music Soc, Ensemble Inter Comtemporain, Groupe Vocal de France, etc; mem American Acad of Arts and Letters 1983, American Acad of Arts and Sciences 1995; Chevalier de l'Ordre Nat du Mérite; Commdr des Arts et des Lettres; other awards include Laureate Int Orchestra Conducting Competition (Besançon) 1953, Copley Foundation Prize (Chicago, IL, USA) 1954, American Acad of Arts Prize 1973, Fondation Koussevitsky Prize 1974, Grand Prix Nat de la Musique 1974, Grand Prix de la Ville de Paris 1981. *Recordings of compositions:* D'un opéra de voyage, Episode quatrième, JDE, Points d'Aube, Quatuor II, Quatuor III, Sonate A 12, Stances, Episode huitième, Musique de jour, EA (petite suite variée); *Operas:* Le Pavillon au bord de la Riviere 1976, Le Cyclope 1986, Schliemann; numerous compositions for choirs, solo voices, orchestra, piano, etc. *Address:* c/o Conservatoire National Supérieur de Musique, 209 ave Jean Jaurès, 75019 Paris, France.

JOLIE, Angelina; American actress; b 1975; d of Jon Voight and Marcheline Bertrand; m 1st Jonny Lee Miller 1996 (divorced); m 2nd Billy Bob Thornton 2000. *Education:* Lee Strasberg Inst and New York Univ. *Films include:* Lookin' to Get Out 1982, Cyborg II: Glass Shadow 1995, Hackers 1995, Foxfire 1996, Mojave Moon 1996, Love is All There is 1996, True Women 1997, George Wallace (Golden Globe) 1997, Playing God 1997, Hell's Kitchen 1998, Gia (Golden Globe, Screen Actors Guild Award) 1999, Playing by Heart 1999, The Bone Collector 2000, Lara Croft Tomb Raider 2001.

JOLLEY, (Monica) Elizabeth, AO; British/Australian writer and lecturer; b 4 June 1923, Birmingham; d of Charles and Margarethe Knight; m Leonard Jolley 1945; two d one s. *Education:* Privately and Quaker Boarding School (Sibford, Oxon). *Career:* Trained as nurse St Thomas' Hosp, London and Queen Elizabeth Hosp, Birmingham 1940–46; moved to W Australia with family 1959; lectures and workshops throughout Australia including Maximum Security Prison, Fremantle, and Bandyup Women's Prison 1976–; part-time Lecturer

School of Communication and Cultural Studies, Curtin Univ 1986–, Prof of Creative Writing 1998–; Hon D TECH (Curtin) 1986; Hon D LITT (Macquarie) 1995, (Queensland) 1997; named Citizen of the Year in Arts, Culture and Entertainment 1987; ASAL Gold Medal for contrib to Australian Literature. *Publications include:* Plays: Night Report (Sound Stage Radio Drama Special Prize) 1975, The Performance 1976, The Shepherd on the Roof 1977, The Well-bred Thief 1977, Woman in a Lampshade 1979, Two Men Running (Australian Writers' Guild Award 1982) 1981, Paper Children 1988, Little Lewis Has Had a Lovely Sleep 1990, The Well 1992; Short stories: Hedge of Rosemary (Victoria State Short Story Award) 1966, Running on the Spot (Moomba Award) 1980, Palomino 1980, The Newspaper of Claremont Street 1981, The Libation (Moomba Award) 1981, Mr Scobie's Riddle (W Australia Week Award, Age Book of the Year Award) 1983, Woman in a Lampshade 1983, Five Acre Virgin 1984, The Travelling Entertainer 1984, Foxybaby 1984; Novels: Miss Peabody's Inheritance 1984, Milk and Honey (Premier's Prize for Fiction, NSW 1985) 1984, The Well (Booker Prize nomination 1986, Miles Franklin Award 1987, film 1997) 1986, The Sugar Mother (France-Australia Literary Translation Award) 1988, My Father's Moon (Age Book of the Year) 1989, Cabin Fever (Literature Award Australian Natives Asscn, Gold Medal Australian Literary Soc 1991) 1990, Central Mischief 1992, The Georges' Wife 1993, The Orchard Thieves 1995, Lovesong 1997, An Accommodating Spouse 1999; Essays: Central Mischief (Premier of WA Prize); one vol of poetry, one vol of radio plays. *Leisure interests:* orchardist and goose farmer, reading, walking. *Address:* Curtin University of Technology, School of English, POB U1987, Perth, WA 6001, Australia (Office); 28 Agett Rd, Claremont, WA 6010, Australia (Home). *Telephone:* (8) 9384 7879 (Home).

JONÁŠOVÁ, Jana; Czech concert and opera singer; b 28 April 1943, Plzeň; d of Václav Růžek and Anna Růužková; m Petr Jonáš 1964; one d. *Education:* Acad of Performing Arts (Prague). *Career:* Soloist Prague Nat Theatre 1970–; currently also tutor Acad of Performing Arts, Prague; has performed at opera houses throughout Europe and at numerous int festivals including Prague Spring Festival, Edinburgh Festival (UK), and in Madrid, Moscow, Strasbourg (France) and Paris, Hamburg (Germany), Salzburg (Austria); numerous recitals; UNESCO Prize 1970; Wiener Flotenuhr Prize 1974; Artist of Merit 1981; Czech Nat Artist 1985. *Operas include:* Hoffmann's Tales, Don Pasquale, Fidelio, Orpheus, Jenufa, Excursions of Mr Brouček, From the House of the Dead, Così fan tutte, The Magic Flute, Titus, Don Giovanni, Boris Godunov, Beautiful Helene, The Lady's Maid, The Kiss, Orlando, Lancelot, The Barber of Seville, Rigoletto, La Bohème, Ariadne auf Naxos, Two Widows, Little Cunning Vixen, La Traviata; *Recordings:* Mozart Arias for Soprano 1970, Bach Kantate 1978, Italian opera arias 1986, concert coloraturas 1990, Love Songs 1994. *Leisure interests:* gardening, swimming. *Address:* Ve Smečkách 2, 110 00 Prague 1, Czech Republic. *Telephone:* (2) 2360199.

JONATHAN, Lydia Thikhoi, PH D; Lesotho scientist and former university pro-vice-chancellor; b 6 March 1951, Leribe; d of the late Leabua and of Mantahli Jonathan. *Education:* Chelsea Coll (London) and Aston Univ (Birmingham, UK). *Career:* Sr Lecturer in Organic and Natural Products Chem, Nat Univ of Lesotho, Pro-Vice-Chancellor 1991–95; ex-officio mem Council and Senate; assoc mem Int Union of Pure and Applied Chem, Int Visitors' Programme on Higher Educ in the USA 1992; mem Natural Products Research Network for E and Cen Africa, American Soc of Pharmacologists, Lesotho Science and Tech Assocn; articles in scientific journals; Fulbright Fellow 1987–88; UNESCO Grant for study of chem of medicinal plants of Lesotho 1987–89. *Leisure interests:* reading, music. *Telephone:* 340601; *Fax:* 340000.

JONES, A. Elizabeth; American diplomatist; b 6 May 1948, Germany; d of William C. Jones and Sara Ferris; m Thomas A. Homan 1977; one d one s. *Education:* Swarthmore Coll (PA) and Boston Univ (MA). *Career:* Deputy Dir Lebanon, Jordan, Syria and Iraq, State Dept 1982–85; Econ Adviser to US Mission, Berlin, Germany 1985–88, Deputy Chief of Mission Islamabad 1988–92, Bonn 1992–93; Exec Asst to Sec of State 1993–94, Amb to Kazakhstan 1995. *Leisure interests:* skiing, hiking, softball, camping, snow-shoeing. *Address:* Embassy of the United States of America, Almaty, Furmanova 99, Kazakhstan. *Telephone:* (3272) 507626; *Fax:* (3272) 633883.

JONES, Catherine Zeta; British actress; b 25 Sept 1969, Swansea, Wales; d of David James Jones; m Michael Douglas 2000; one s. *Films:* Scheherazade, Coup de Foudre, Splitting Heirs 1993, Blue Juice 1995, The Phantom 1996, The Mask of Zorro 1997, Entrapment 1998, The Haunting 1999, Traffic 2000, America's Sweethearts 2001; *Plays include:* The Pyjama Game, Annie, Bugsy Malone, 42nd Street, Street Scene; *TV includes:* The Darling Buds of May, Out of the Blue, Cinder Path 1994, Return of the Native 1995, Titanic 1996. *Address:* c/o ICM Ltd, Oxford House, 76 Oxford St, London W1N 0AX. *Telephone:* (20) 7636-6565; *Fax:* (20) 7323-0101.

JONES, Dorothy V., PH D; American historian; b 14 Dec 1927, Washington, DC; d of Guy and Margaret Vincent; m Robert R. Jones 1947; two s. *Education:* Washburn Univ and Univs of Missouri and Chicago. *Career:* Exhibition curator Joseph Regenstein Library, Univ of Chicago, IL 1982–85; Visiting Scholar Dept of History 1986–91; Research Assoc Newberry Library, Chicago 1986–91, Scholar-in-Residence 1986–; Assoc History Dept, Northwestern Univ, Evanston 1991–; SSRC–MacArthur Fellow in Int Peace and Security 1986–88; Lionel Gelber Prize 1991. *Publications:* License For Empire: Colonialism by Treaty in Early America 1982, Splendid Encounters: The Thought and Conduct of Diplomacy 1984, Code of Peace: Ethics and Security in World of Warlord States (Lionel Gelber Prize for Best Book in Int Relations) 1991. *Leisure interests:* gardening, reading. *Address:* 1213 Main St, Evanston, IL 60202, USA.

JONES, Edith Hollan, BA, JD; American judge; b 7 April 1949, Philadelphia, PA; d of O. Roger and Edith (née Lingle) Hollan; m Sherwood Jones 1973; two s. *Education:* Cornell Univ and Univ of Texas. *Career:* Called to the Bar, TX 1974, US Supreme Court 1979, US Court of Appeals, US Dist Court of Texas; Assoc Andrews and Hurth 1974–82, Partner 1982–85; Judge US Court of Appeals (fifth circuit) 1985–; Gen Counsel Republican Party of Texas 1981–83; mem ABA, State Bar of Texas. *Address:* US Court of Appeals Bob Casey, US Courthouse, 515 Rusk Ave, Houston, TX 77002, USA.

JONES, Eurfron Gwynne, PH D; British broadcasting executive; b 24 Sept 1934, Aberdare, Glamorgan; d of William Gwynne and Annie (née Harries) Jones; m Michael John Coyle 1968; one s. *Education:* Aberdare Girls' Grammar School and Univ of Wales. *Career:* Teaching Asst in Zoology, Mt Holyoke Coll, MA, USA 1955–56; mem staff BBC 1959–83, 1984–94, Gen Trainee 1959, Producer School Radio and TV, and Continuing Educ 1959–75, Asst Head of School Radio 1983–84, Head of School TV 1984–87, Controller Educational Broadcasting 1987–92, Dir of Educ 1992–94; freelance Consultant Int Children's Centre 1975–1983; Visiting Prof Inst of Educ, Univ of London 1994; mem Wyatt Cttee on Violence 1986, Cttee on the Public Understanding of Science 1992–; mem Council Open Univ 1987–94, Royal Inst 1989–92, 1994–97, COPUS 1992–94; mem Educ Advisory Cttee Nat Museums and Galleries of Wales 1995–, Resident Panel Inst of Welsh Affairs 1996–; Chair Digital Coll for Wales 1997–; Fellow Royal Television Soc 1994; Hon LL D (Exeter) 1990. *Publications:* Children Growing Up 1973, The First Five Years 1975, How Did I Grow? 1977, Television Magic 1978, Lifetime I, Lifetime II 1982; numerous articles on educ and children. *Leisure interests:* photography, family, swimming.

JONES, Grace; American (b Jamaican) singer, model and actress; b 19 May 1952, Spanishtown, Jamaica; d of Robert and Marjorie P. Jones; m Atila Altaunbay 1996; one s. *Education:* Syracuse Univ (NY). *Career:* Moved to New York at age 12; fashion model in New York, then Paris; debut as singer New York 1977; recorded first album for Island Records 1977; opened La Vie en Rose restaurant, New York 1987. *Films include:* Conan the Destroyer 1984, A View to a Kill 1985, Vamp 1986, Boomerang 1991; *Recordings include:* Albums: Portfolio 1977, Fame, Muse, Amado Mio 1990, Island Life 1992; Singles: La Vie en Rose, Pull up to the Bumper, Warm Leatherette, Private Life, Slave to the Rhythm. *Address:* Island Pictures Inc, 8920 Sunset Blvd, 2nd Floor, Los Angeles, CA 90069, USA.

JONES, Dame Gwyneth, DBE, FRCM; British opera singer (soprano); b 7 Nov 1936, Pontnewynydd, Mon; d of the late Edward George and Violet (née Webster) Jones; m Till Haberfeld 1969; one d. *Education:* Royal Coll of Music (London), Accad Chigiana (Siena, Italy) and Zurich Int Opera Centre (Switzerland). *Career:* Mem Zurich Opera

House, Switzerland 1962–63, Royal Opera House, Covent Garden, London 1963–, Vienna State Opera House, 1966–, Deutsche Oper Berlin, Germany 1966–, Bavarian State Opera, Germany 1967–; guest performances include La Scala Milan and Rome Opera (Italy), Berlin State Opera, Munich State Opera and Hamburg (Germany), Paris, Metropolitan Opera (New York), San Francisco, Dallas, Chicago and Los Angeles, (USA), Zurich and Geneva (Switzerland), Teatro Colón (Buenos Aires), Tokyo, Bayreuth Festival (Germany), Salzburg Festival (Austria), Arena di Verona, Edinburgh Festival and Welsh Nat Opera; Hon mem Vienna State Opera 1989; recordings for Decca, DGG, EMI, CBS; Hon mem Vienna State Opera 1989; Hon D MUS (Wales); Kammersängerin title conferred in Austria and Bavaria; Shakespeare Prize (Hamburg) 1987; Bundesverdienstkreuz (Germany) 1988; Commdr des Arts et des Lettres 1993. *Operas include:* Il Trovatore, Otello, Aida, Fidelio, The Flying Dutchman, Medea, Die Walküre, Macbeth, Don Carlos, Madame Butterfly, Tosca, Don Giovanni, Salome, Parsifal, Tristan und Isolde, Aegyptische Helena, Die Frau ohne Schatten, Elektra, Tannhäuser, Der Rosenkavalier, Der Ring des Nibelungen, Lohengrin, La Fanciulla del West, Erwartung, La voix humaine; *TV films:* Fidelio, Aida, The Flying Dutchman, Beethoven 9th Symphony, Tannhäuser, L'Incoronazione di Poppea, Der Rosen-kavalier, Die Walküre, Siegfried, Götterdämmerung, Die Lustige Witwe. *Address:* POB 556, 8037 Zurich, Switzerland.

JONES, Marion; American athlete; b 12 Oct 1975, LA; m C. J. Hunter 1998. *Education:* Rio Mesa High School (Oxnard, CA). *Career:* Track and field athlete; Gold Medallist 100m, World Championships 1997, 1999; winner Gold Medals 100m, 200m, 4x400m relay, Bronze Medal Long Jump, 4x100m relay Olympic Games, Sydney 2000 (most medals won by a woman in a single Olympics); Gold Medallist 200m World Championships, Edmonton 2001; ranked number 1 in the world in 100m, 200m and Long Jump by Track and Field Magazine 1998 (also Women's Athlete of the Year 1997, 1998); Jesse Owens Award 1999. *Address:* c/o USA Track and Field, 1 Rca Dome, Suite 140, Indianapolis, IN 46225-1023, USA.

JONES, Merri Louise; Canadian banking executive; b 2 Dec 1950, Toronto, ON; d of the late William and of Betty Louise (née Smith) Poole; m Alan Jones 1974; two d. *Education:* Univ of Western Ontario. *Career:* Mem staff Royal Bank of Canada 1972–77, Chemical Bank, 1977–83, First Interstate Bank of Canada 1984–91, CIBE 1991–96; Vice-Chair and COO T.A.L. Pvt Man Ltd. *Address:* 93 Dinnick Crescent, Toronto, ON M4N 1L9, Canada.

JONES-BARBER, Angela, M ED; Jamaican management consultant; b 30 April 1950, St Andrew; d of Stanley and Pauline (née McCartney) Silvera; one s one d. *Education:* Univ of Miami (FL, USA) and St Benedict's Coll. *Career:* Counselling and Guidance Co-ordinator Ministry of Educ, Bahamas 1977–83; Lecturer St Benedict's Coll, St John's Univ, MN, USA, Continuing Educ Extension Prog, Nassau, Bahamas 1980–83; apptd Man Consultant and Pres Source Ltd 1983; Rapporteur Drugs and Alcohol Conf, World Fed for Mental Health, Nassau 1974; trans for int confs, Bahamas 1978, 1979; Chair Women Int Trade Fairs, Kingston 1984, 1985, 1986; Dizabras Gold Medal of Brazil; Nat Award for contribs to care of under-privileged children 1981. *Publications:* National Guidlines for Guidance and Counselling (jtly); contribs to numerous information booklets. *Leisure interests:* meditation, yoga, walking, reading.

JONES-SMITH, Jacqueline, LL B, MA; American civil servant; b 5 Nov 1952, New York; m Joshua Smith; one step-s. *Education:* American and Syracuse Univs. *Career:* Fmr assoc MAXIMA Corpn 1979–85; Asst Co Attorney, Motgomery Co 1985–87; Attorney Fed Election Comm; Chair Consumer Product Safety Comm 1989–94, Commr 1994; mem ABA, Nat Bar Asscn. *Address:* US Consumer Product Safety Commission, 4430 E W Highway, Suite 725 Bethesda, MD 20814, USA.

JONG, Erica Mann, MA; American writer and poet; b 26 March 1942, New York; d of Seymour and Eda (née Mirsky) Mann; m 1st Michael Worthman; m 2nd Allan Jong (divorced 1975); m 3rd Jonathan Fast 1977 (divorced 1983); one d; m 4th Kenneth David Burrows 1989. *Education:* Barnard Coll and Columbia Univ (New York). *Career:* Mem Faculty English Dept, City Univ of New York 1964–65, 1969–70, Overseas Div Univ of Maryland 1967–69; mem Literature Panel New

York State Council on Arts 1972–74; mem Faculty Salzburg Seminar, Salzburg, Austria 1993; Pres Authors' Guild 1991–93, mem Advisory Bd; Hon Fellow (Welsh Coll of Music and Drama) 1994; Nat Endowment of the Arts grantee 1973; Bess Hokin Prize, Poetry magazine 1971; Alice Faye di Castagnola Award, Poetry Soc of America 1972; Prix Litéraire, Deauville Film Festival 1997. *Publications:* Poems: Fruits & Vegetables 1971, Half-Lives 1973, At the Edge of the Body 1979, Ordinary Miracles 1983, Becoming Light 1991; Novels: Fear of Flying 1973, How to Save Your Own Life 1977, Fanny 1980, Parachutes and Kisses 1984, Serenissima: a Novel of Venice 1987, Any Woman's Blues 1990; Poetry and Non-fiction: Loveroot 1975, Witches 1981, Megan's Book of Divorce (for children, 2nd edn) 1996, Megan's Two Houses, The Devil at Large 1993, Fear of Fifty 1994, What Do Women Want? 1998; Composer: Zipless: Songs of Abandon from the Erotic Poetry of Erica Jong 1995. *Leisure interests:* sailing, flying. *Address:* Erica Jong Productions, c/o K. D. Burrows, 425 Park Ave, New York, NY 10019, USA. *Telephone:* (212) 980-6922; *Fax:* (212) 421-5279.

JÖNS, Karin, BA; German politician and journalist; b 29 April 1953, Kiel. *Education:* Univ of Mannheim. *Career:* Research Asst Univ of Mannheim 1975–77; Journalist working on daily newspapers 1976–78, Public Services Trade Union (ÖTV) 1978–80; mem SPD 1973–; Spokesperson Ministry for Fed Affairs, Bremen/Bonn 1980–82; Chef de Cabinet Ministry for Cultural Relations between France and Germany 1983–86; Officer in charge of Int and European Affairs, State Dept, Nord Rhein-Westfalen 1986–87; Perm Rep of Bremen to EU 1987–94; MEP (Socialists Group) 1994–, mem Cttees on Social Affairs and Employment, Del to ACP-EU Jt Parl Ass, fmrly Del for relations with Transcaucasus; mem Bremen SPD Land Exec 1998–. *Address:* European Parliament, rue Wiertz, 1047 Brussels, Belgium; SPD–Europa-büro, Findorffstrasse 106108, 28215 Bremen, Germany. *Telephone:* (2) 284-21-11 (Belgium); (421) 3501817 (Germany); *Fax:* (2) 230-69-43 (Belgium); (412) 353121 (Germany).

JONUSAUSKIENE, Milda; Lithuanian artist; b 13 April 1940, Seduva; m Aloyzas Jonusauskas 1968; two s. *Education:* Vilnius Art Acad. *Career:* Numerous exhibitions in Lithuania, Poland, France and Russian Fed; Third Prize World Poster Competition Against Nuclear War 1984. *Leisure interests:* painting, theatre, home. *Address:* Vokieciu 10-3, Vilnius, Lithuania. *Telephone:* (2) 615-749.

JOOF-COLE, Ami; Gambian broadcasting executive; b 9 Jan 1952, Bakau; d of Kebba Balla Modi Joof and Suntu Kamara; m 1980; three d two s. *Education:* St Joseph High School and Gambia High School (Banjul) and Univ of Ghana. *Career:* Head of Rural Broadcasting and Adult Educ, Radio Gambia 1983–, Co-ordinater and Producer radio drama series 'Pa Kube Jarra' 1989–94; Chair Nat Women's Council 1993–; Pres Gambian Cttee on Traditional Practices 1991–, Gambia Family Planning Asscn (first woman) 1996–; Dir African Women's Media Centre, Dakar 2001–; mem Bd WAMNET (West Africa Media Network for Gender) 1994–95, Nat Think Tank, Nat Consultative Cttee to Review AFPRC Timetable and Programming, African Asscn for Literacy and Adult Educ, Int Asscn of Women in Radio and TV, Nat Pop Comm, Nat AIDS Cttee; several awards including Special Prize for Radio 1981, Commonwealth Foundation Fellowship Award 1994. *Publications include:* Role of Radio Farm Forums in Rural Development in Ghana 1978, Making Broadcasting Work in Africa – Mass Media in the Gambia 1985, Partial Commercialisation of Radio Gambia 1990, Traditional Practices in the Gambia 1992, Radio Listening and Learning Groups in the Gambia 1992, An Experience of Rural Broadcasting in the Gambia 1971–96 1996. *Leisure interests:* dancing, listening to music, reading, cooking, walking. *Address:* Radio Gambia, Banjul, Gambia. *Telephone:* 497339; *Fax:* 495923.

JOPLING, Jane, MA; British United Nations official; b 23 April 1932, Amersham; d of Lindsay Millais and Joan Jopling. *Education:* Univ of Cambridge. *Career:* Journalist, UK and USA 1955–61; apptd UN Official with special interest in Econ, Social and Environmental issues, and in Policy Co-ordination in the UN System 1961, Dir Exec Office of the Sec-Gen of the UN 1988. *Leisure interests:* music, travel, tennis. *Address:* Executive Office of the Sec-Gen, United Nations, Rm S-384OD, New York, NY 10017, USA (Office); 305 E 40th St, New York, NY 10016, USA (Home). *Telephone:* (212) 599-8468 (Home); *Fax:* (212) 963-2155 (Home).

JORDAN, Deirdre Frances, AC, MBE, PH D; Australian university chancellor; b 18 Sept 1926, Loxton; d of Clement John and Helena Frances Jordan. *Education:* St Aloysius' Coll (Adelaide) and Univs of Adelaide and London. *Career:* Headmistress St Aloysius' Coll 1954–68; Sr Lecturer Educ Dept, Univ of Adelaide 1968–88, Deputy Chair 1973–82, Chair 1982–84; Chair Centre for Aboriginal Studies in Music 1974–77; Commr Tertiary Educ Authority of S Australia 1979–80; Pro-Chancellor Flinders Univ of S Australia 1980–88, Chancellor 1988; Chair Bd Govs Mercedes Coll 1994; Fellow Australian Coll of Educ 1987; mem Bd Trustees St Francis Xavier Seminary 1992–; Hon D LITT (Flinders) 1986. *Publications:* Transition from School to Univ 1968, Support Systems for Aboriginal Students in Higher Education 1984. *Leisure interests:* reading, opera, camping, bush walking. *Address:* Flinders University of S Australia, Sturt Rd, Bedford Park, S Australia (Office); 23 Victoria St, Prospect, SA 5082, Australia (Home). *Telephone:* (8) 201 2721 (Office); *Fax:* (8) 276 2271 (Office).

JOSHI, Damayanti, BA; Indian classical dancer; b 5 Dec 1932, Bombay (now Mumbai); d of Ramchandra and Vatsala Joshi. *Education:* Numerous schools of classical dancing. *Career:* Leading exponent of Kathak Dance; has held dance seminars throughout India and in Asia, Africa and Europe; Examiner in music and dance for numerous Indian univs; holds several public service posts connected with dance; Visiting Prof IndiraKala Sangeet Vishwavidyalaya, Khairagarh, conducts teachers' workshops; has performed before Heads of State of Nepal, Afghanistan, fmr USSR, Laos, Yugoslavia, Indonesia, Philippines and Mexico; choreographer of numerous productions, numerous TV appearances and contribs to journals; Chair Dancers' Guild, Bombay; Sangeet Nathak Award 1968. *Film:* Damayanti Joshi on Kathak Dance; *Publication:* Madame Menaka (monograph), articles for art magazines and newspapers. *Leisure interests:* reading, writing, sitar. *Address:* D-1, Jeshtharam Baug, Tram Terminus, Dadar, Mumbai 400 013, India. *Telephone:* (22) 4141589.

JOSHI, Heather Evelyn, FBA, MA; British demographer; b 21 April 1946, Plymouth; d of G. M. and M. F. Spooner; m 1st Mr Joshi 1969; m 2nd G. H. Martin 1982; one s one d. *Education:* Tavistock School, St Hilda's and St Antony's Colls (Oxford). *Career:* Lecturer St Hilda's Coll, Oxford 1969–73; Econ Adviser to UK Govt 1973–79; Research Fellow London School of Hygiene and Tropical Medicine 1979–83, Sr Research Fellow 1983–88, Sr Lecturer in Econ Demography 1990–93; Sr Research Fellow Birkbeck Coll, London 1988–90; Prof of Econ Demography City Univ, London 1993–98; Prof of Econ and Developmental Demography in Educ Inst of Educ, London Univ 1998–. *Publications:* Surplus Labour and The City (jtly) 1976, The Changing Population of Britain (ed) 1989. *Leisure interests:* family, music. *Address:* Centre for Longitudinal Studies, Institute of Education, 20 Bedford Way, London WC1H 0AL, UK (Office); 20 Rochester Terrace, London NW1 9JN, UK (Home). *Telephone:* (20) 7612-6874 (Office); (20) 7483-6627 (Home).

JOSHI, Sudha Vijay, BA; Indian politician and organization executive; b 10 June 1940, Bombay (now Mumbai); d of Vishwanath Rangrao Chitnis; m Vijay Chintaman Joshi 1964; one s one d. *Education:* Univ of Bombay. *Career:* Apptd Convenor Bombay Pradesh Mahila Congress 1978; Gen Sec Lokmanya Seva Sangh Vile Parle 1981–83; apptd Sec All India Mahila Congress 1984; mem Rajya Sabha (Council of States) 1984; Dir Nat Fed of Lab Co-operatives (NFLC), Chair Women's Section; Dir Maharashtra Tourism Devt Corpn 1982–85. *Leisure interest:* reading. *Address:* Rajya Sabha, Parl House, New Delhi 110 011, India (Office); 1/5 Shivanand Playground Crossroads, Vile Parle E, Mumbai 400 057, India (Home). *Telephone:* (11) 389977 (Office).

JOUDRY, Patricia; Canadian writer; b 18 Oct 1921, Spirit River, AB; m 1st Delmar Dinsdale (divorced 1952); two d; m 2nd John Steele (divorced 1975); three d. *Career:* Writer and theatre producer. *Publications include:* Plays: Teach Me How to Cry (Dominion Drama Award 1956), Henry Aldrich Show (radio), Penny's Diary (radio), The Sand Castle, Three Rings for Michele, The Song of Louise in the Morning, Stranger in My House, Walk Alone Together (Stratford-Globe Prize and London W End Prize 1959), Semi-Detached 1960, Valerie, God Goes Heathen, Think Again 1969, Now 1970, I Ching 1971, A Very Modest Orgy 1981; Novels: The Dweller on the Threshold 1973, The Selena Tree 1980; Non-fiction: And the Children Played

1975, Spirit River to Angels' Roost 1977, Sound-Therapy for the Walk Man 1984, Twin Souls (jtly) 1993. *Address:* POB 105, Lund, BC V0N 2G0, Canada.

JOVIČIĆ, Natasa, MA; Croatian politician and art historian; b 1 Dec 1962; one s (adopted). *Education:* Columbia Coll (Chicago, USA). *Career:* Est Multimedia Women's Center (one of first non-govt orgs in Croatia) 1993; organized and led 40 exhibitions in Croatia and the USA; teacher of women's issues and multicultural educ Depaul Univ, USA 1998–2000; Asst Minister of Educ and Sports 2000–; Columbia Coll Scholarship; Soroptimist Int Award for Human Rights. *Publications:* Fifth Quadrant 1995; author of articles and essays on art history and educ 1989–2001. *Leisure interests:* human rights, women's rights. *Address:* Ministry of Education and Sport, 4100 Zagrab, trg Hrvatskiy Velikana 6, Croatia (Office); 10000 Zagreb, Ljevakovićeva 30, Croatia (Home). *Telephone:* (1) 4569005 (Office); *Fax:* (1) 4610478 (Office); *E-mail:* natasa.jovicic@zg.tel.hr.

JOWELL, Tessa Jane Helen Douglas, MA; British politician; b 17 Sept 1947; d of Kenneth and Rosemary Palmer; m 1st Roger Jowell 1970 (divorced 1976); m 2nd David Mills 1979; one s one d. *Education:* St Margaret's School (Aberdeen), Univs of Aberdeen and Edinburgh. *Career:* Child Care Officer, Lambeth Council, London 1969–71; Psychiatric Social Worker Maudsley Hosp, London 1972–74; Ass Dir Mind 1974–86; Dir Community Care Special Action Project, Birmingham 1986–90, Community Care Programme Joseph Rowntree Foundation 1990–92; MP (Lab) for Dulwich 1992–97, for Dulwich and W Norwood 1997–; Opposition Whip 1994–97; Minister of State Dept of Public Health 1997–99, Dept for Educ and Employment 1999–2001; Minister for Women 1998–; Sec of State for Culture, Media and Sport June 2001–; Councillor Camden, London 1971–86; Chair Social Services Cttee, Asscn Metropolitan Authorities 1984–86; mem Mental Health Act Comm 1985–90; Sr Visiting Fellow Policy Studies Inst 1986–90, King's Fund Inst 1990–92; numerous contribs to professional journals. *Leisure interests:* gardening, reading, music, Italy. *Address:* House of Commons, London SW1A 0AA, UK.

JOYNER-KERSEE, Jacqueline (Jackie), BA; American athlete; b 3 March 1962, E St Louis, IL; 1962; d of Alfred and Mary Joyner; m Bobby Kersee 1986. *Education:* Univ of California at Los Angeles (UCLA). *Career:* Champion Long-Jump, World Championships 1987, 1991; Silver Medallist in Heptathlon, Olympic Games, Los Angeles 1984, Gold Medallist (set World record), Seoul 1988, Barcelona 1992; Gold Medallist Long-Jump (set Olympic record), Olympic Games, Seoul, Repub of Korea 1988, Bronze Medallist Barcelona, Spain 1992, Atlanta, GA, USA 1996; with Richmond Rage in American Basketball League; winner IAAF Mobil Grand Prix 1994; currently Asst Basketball Coach, Univ of California at Los Angeles (UCLA); Chair St Louis Sports Comm 1996–; Jim Thorpe Award 1993; Jackie Robinson Robie Award 1994, Jesse Owens Humanitarian Award 1999; Hon DHL (Spellman Coll) 1998, (Howard Univ) 1999, (George Washington Univ) 1999. *Publication:* A Kind of Grace (autobiog) 1997. *Address:* c/o Elite International Sports Marketing Inc, 1034 S Brentwood Blvd, Suite 1530, St Louis, MO 63117, USA.

JUDA, Annely, CBE; German art dealer; b 23 Sept 1914, Kassel; d of Kurt and Margarete Brauer; m Paul A. Juda 1939 (divorced 1955); two d one s. *Education:* State school (Kassel) and Reimann School for Art and Design (London). *Career:* Came to London 1937; Opened Molton Gallery, London 1960; Founder Hamilton Gallery 1963; Co-Founder, Dir and Consultant Annely Juda Fine Art 1967; publr numerous art catalogues; Cologne Prize 1993. *Leisure interests:* theatre, music, the arts. *Address:* Annely Juda Fine Art, 23 Dering St, London W1R 9AA, UK (Office); 74 Windermere Ave, London N3 3RA, UK (Home). *Telephone:* (20) 7629-7578 (Office); (20) 8346-0743 (Home); *Fax:* (20) 7491-2139 (Office); *E-mail:* ajfa@annelyjudafineart.co.uk; *Internet:* www.annelyjudafineart.co.uk.

JUDD, Ashley; American actress; b 19 April 1968, Granada Hills, CA. *Films include:* Ruby in Paradise 1993, Smoke 1995, Heat 1995, A Time to Kill 1996, Kiss the Girls 1997, Simon Birch 1998, Eye of the Beholder 1999, Double Jeopardy 1999, Dexterity 2000, Where the Heart Is 2000; *TV film:* Norma Jean and Marilyn 1996. *Address:* William Morris Agency, 151 S El Camino Drive, Beverly Hills, CA 90212, USA.

JUDD, Wynonna; American singer and musician; b 1964; d of Naomi Judd; one s. *Career:* Fmrly mem The Judds, country and western group; now soloist; Grammy Award 1985, 1986, 1987, 1989; Duet Award (with Naomi Judd); Acad of Country Music Award 1985–91, 1994; Vocal Duo Award (with Naomi Judd); Country Music Asscn Award 1984–91; nominated for two Grammy Awards 1994. *Recordings include:* Albums: The Judds, Why Not Me?, Rockin' with the Rhythm, Christmas Time with the Judds, Heartland, River of Time 1989, Love Can Build a Bridge 1990, Wynonna 1992, Tell me Wy 1993, Greatest Hits Vol I, Vol II, In Concert 1995, Revelations 1996, The Other Side 1997, The Judds Reunion: Live 2000, Number One Hits 2000; Singles: Had a Dream 1983, Mama He's Crazy 1984, Why Not Me 1984, Love is Alive 1985, Grandpa 1986; *Publication:* Love Can Build a Bridge (jtly) 1993. *Address:* Mercury Nashville, 66 Music Square W, Nashville, TN 37203.

JULIAN, Rae Scott, BA, DIP ED; New Zealand organization executive; b 17 March 1941, Marton; d of Robert A. and P. Joan Honeyman; m Robin Denis Julian 1963 (divorced 1986); one s one d. *Education:* Marton Dist High School, Rangitikei Coll (Marton), Canterbury Univ (Christchurch), Christchurch Teacher Training Coll and Massey Univ (Palmerston N). *Career:* Teacher Parl Labour Research Unit 1963–66, Research Officer 1976–83, Dir 1983–86; Human Rights Commr with special responsibility for Women's Rights 1987–92; Sec Council for Equal Pay and Opportunity 1976–79; Nat Pres Soc for Research on Women 1977–80; Civic Educ and Training Specialist, UN Volunteers, Cambodia 1992; J. R. McKenzie Fellow, New Zealand Council for Educational Research 1974–75. *Publications:* Brought to Mind 1977; Wilderness Women (contrib) 1989, New Zealand Politics (contrib, 3rd edn) 1992. *Leisure interests:* walking, reading, drama, music. *Address:* c/o Govt Research Unit, Parl Bldgs, Wellington, New Zealand (Office); 16 Orari St, Ngaio, Wellington, New Zealand (Home). *Telephone:* (4) 479-7925 (Home).

JULIANA, Louise Emma Marie Wilhelmina, HRH; former Queen of the Netherlands; b 30 April 1909; d of Queen Wilhelmina and Prince Henry of Mecklenburg-Schwerin; m Prince Bernhard of Lippe-Biesterfeld 1937; four d: Princess Beatrix Wilhelmina Armgard (now Queen Beatrix, qv), Princess Irene Emma Elisabeth, Princess Margriet Francisca, Princess Maria Christina. *Career:* Princess of the Netherlands, Princess of Orange-Nassau, Duchess of Mecklenburg, Princess of Lippe-Biesterfeld; went to Canada after German occupation 1940, in UK 1944, returned to Netherlands 1945; Princess Regent Oct–Dec 1947, May–Aug 1948; Queen of Netherlands 1948–80, abdicated 30 April 1980. *Address:* Palace of Soestdijk, Amsterdamsestraatweg 1, 3744 AA Baarn, Netherlands.

JULIUS, DeAnne, PH D; American economist; b 14 April 1949; d of Marvin Julius; m Ian A. Harvey 1976; one s one d. *Education:* Iowa State Univ and Univ of California at Davis. *Career:* Econ Adviser for Energy, IBRD 1975–82; Man Dir Logan Assocs Inc 1983–86; Dir of Econs Royal Inst of Int Affairs, London 1986–89; Chief Economist Shell Int Petroleum Co, London 1989–93, British Airways 1993–97; mem Monetary Policy Cttee, Bank of England 1997–2001; Chair British Airways Pension Investment Man Ltd 1995–97. *Publications:* Global Companies and Public Policy: The Growing Challenge of Foreign Direct Investment 1990, The Economics of Natural Gas 1990, Is Manufacturing Still Special in the New World Order? (jtly) (Amex Bank Prize) 1993 and articles on int economics. *Leisure interests:* skiing, windsurfing, bonsai. *Address:* c/o Bank of England, Threadneedle St, London EC2R 8AH, UK. *Telephone:* (20) 7601-4444.

JUNG, Claudia Cornelia; German ballet dancer; b 9 April 1961, Munich; d of Adolf and Christel-Karin Jung; m Wojchiech Hankiewicz 1984. *Education:* Musikhochschule (Munich). *Career:* Ballet studies in cities including Paris, Lisbon, New York, Moscow, Rome, Vienna and San Francisco; Soloist Städtische Bühnen Augsburg 1979–81, Deutsche Oper am Rhein, Düsseldorf/Duisburg 1981–85, Deutsche Oper Berlin 1985–; numerous guest appearances in Germany and abroad; Bronze Medal Int Ballet Competition, Varna (Bulgaria) 1980; Bronze Medal Int Ballet Competition Bolshoi Theatre, Moscow 1981; Förderpries Bayern 1983. *Address:* Parsbergstr 53, 82110 Germering, Germany. *Telephone:* (89) 843495.

JUNG, Doris; American opera singer and teacher; b 5 Jan 1924, Centralia, IL; d of John and May (née Middleton) Crittenden; m Felix Popper 1951; one s. *Education:* Univ of Illinois, Mannes Coll of Music, Vienna Acad of Performing Arts (Austria) and under Julius Cohen, Emma Zador, Luise Helletsgruber and Winifred Cecil. *Career:* Professional debut as Vitellia in Clemenza di Tito, Zurich Opera, Switzerland 1955; appearances with Hamburg State Opera and Munich State Opera (Germany), Vienna State Opera, Copenhagen Royal Opera, Stockholm Royal Opera, New York City Opera and Metropolitan Opera (New York), opera cos in Marseille and Strasbourg (France), Naples and Catania (Italy) and with Syracuse Symphony 1981; teacher New York 1970–. *Address:* 40 W 84th St, New York, NY 10024, USA. *Telephone:* (212) 873-3147; *Fax:* (212) 873-3147.

JUNKER, Karin; German politician and journalist; b 24 Dec 1940, Düsseldorf. *Career:* Journalist and publr; mem SPD 1964–, SPD Bureau, SPD Exec, Fed Chair Arbeitsgemeinschaft sozialdemokratischer Frauen 1992–, Deputy Chair SPD Media Comm; officer in Town Hall, Gelsenkirchen 1980–89; Consultant, Gelsenkirchen 1985–89; MEP (Socialists Group) 1989–, Vice-Pres ACP–EU Jt Ass, mem Media Comm 1985, Cttee on Devt and Co-operation, Vice-Chair Programme Cttee of WDR Broadcasting Authority 1986–; mem Programme Advisory Cttee of Supervisory Cttee, European Culture TV Channel (EKK) 1992. *Address:* European Parliament, rue Wiertz, 1047 Brussels, Belgium. *Telephone:* (2) 284-5429; *Fax:* (2) 284-9429; *E-mail:* kjunker@europarl.eu.int.

JUNZ, Helen B., MA; American economist and consultant; d of Samson and Dobra Bachner. *Education:* Univ of Amsterdam and New School for Social Research (New York). *Career:* Acting Chief Consumer Price Section, Nat Industrial Conf Bd, New York 1953–58; Research Officer Nat Inst of Social and Econ Research, London 1958–60; Economist Bureau of Econ Analysis, Dept of Commerce, Washington, DC 1960–62; Adviser Div of Int Finance, Bd of Govs, Fed Reserve System 1962–77, OECD, Paris 1967–69; Sr Int Economist Council of Econ Advisers, The White House, Washington, DC 1975–77; Deputy Asst Sec Office of Asst Sec for Int Affairs, Dept of the Treasury, Washington, DC 1977–79; Vice-Pres and Sr Adviser First Nat Bank of Chicago 1979–80; Vice-Pres Townsend Greenspan and Co Inc, New York 1980–82; Sr Adviser European Dept, IMF, Washington, DC 1982–87, Deputy Dir Exchange and Trade Relations Dept 1987–89, Special Trade Rep and Dir Geneva Office, Switzerland 1989–94; Dir Gold Econ Services, World Gold Council, Geneva, Switzerland 1994–96; Pres HBJ Int, London 1996–; numerous contribs to professional journals. *Address:* HBJ International, 23 Warwick Sq, London SW1V 2AB, UK. *Telephone:* (20) 7630-9727; *Fax:* (20) 7630-9727.

JURINAC, Sena; Austrian (b Yugoslav) singer; b 24 Oct 1921; m Josef Lederle. *Education:* Studied under Milka Kostrencíc. *Career:* First appearance as Mimi, Zagreb 1942; mem Vienna State Opera Co 1944–82; now works as voice teacher; has performed at Salzburg and Glyndebourne (UK) Festivals and Royal Opera House, Covent Garden (London); numerous tours and recordings; title Austrian State Kammersängerin conferred 1951, Ehrenkreuz für Wissenschaft und Kunst 1961, Grosses Ehrenzeichen für Verdienste um die Republik Österreich 1967; Ehrenring der Wiener Staatsoper 1968, Ehrenmitgleid der Wiener Staatsoper 1971. *Operas include:* Der Rosenkavalier 1966, 1971, Tosca 1968, Iphigénie en Tauride 1973. *Address:* c/o Vienna State Opera, 1010 Vienna, Austria.

JUST, Annette; Danish politician; b 27 June 1947, Gentofte, Copenhagen; two d. *Education:* Switzerland and UK. *Career:* Mem Jelling Town Council (Fremskridtspartiet, Progress Party) 1978–89; Chair Asscn of Councils for Progress Party 1978–84, Nat Pres Progress Party 1985–87; became mem Folketing (Parl) for Vejle Co 1987, mem Cttees on EC, Foreign Policy, Foreign Affairs, Nat Security, Defence, Trade and Industry; mem Women's Air Corp, Home Guard 1965–84; mem Bd Chr Islef & Co A/S 1981–91. *Address:* Fremskridtspartiet, Folketinget, Christiansborg Slot, 1240 Copenhagen K, Denmark (Office); Landsvalevej 10, 2970 Hørsholm, Denmark (Home). *Telephone:* 33-37-55-00 (Office); *Fax:* 33-32-85-36 (Office).

JUTTERSTRÖM, Christina, MA; Swedish journalist and professor of journalism; b (Christina Lewell) 27 March 1940, Stockholm; d of Siri and Gösta Lewell; m 1st Stig Jutterström; m 2nd Ingemar Odlander 1978; two d. *Education:* Uppsala Univ. *Career:* Political reporter Sveriges Radio AB (Swedish Broadcasting Corpn) 1966–69, political reporter 1969–73, Man Ed political news 1973–75, Man Ed Dagens Eko 1977–81; Foreign Corresp in Africa for Svenska Dagbladet newspaper 1975–77; Asst Man Ed Dagens Nyheter newspaper 1981–82, Ed-in-Chief 1982–95; Ed-in-Chief Expressen newspaper 1995–96; Prof of Journalism, Univ of Gothenburg 1997–; mem Bd IPI. *Address:* Bjursattersgard, 64032 Malmköping, Sweden. *Telephone:* (157) 44222; *Fax:* (157) 44201; *E-mail:* christina.jutterstrom@jmg.gu.se (Office).

JUUL, Kristine, M SC; Danish research fellow; b 13 Aug 1958, Copenhagen; d of Kjeld and Nina Juul; m Henrik Julius Nielsen 1989; one s. *Education:* Int School (Geneva, Switzerland), St Georges English School (Rome, Italy) Tranegårdskolen and Gentofte Statsskole (Gentofte) and Roskilde Univ Center (Roskilde). *Career:* Project co-ordinator school-building project Nicaragua 1983–84; Asst DANIDA (Danish Devt Agency) Tanzania 1987, Denmark 1987–88; Assoc Expert in Socio-Econ, Centre de Suivi Ecologique Dakar, Senegal 1988–92; Consultant COWI-Consult 1992; apptd Research Fellow Int Devt Studies, Univ of Roskilde 1992, Asst Prof 1996–; has written several essays and papers, contribs to journals. *Address:* c/o University of Roskilde, Dept of Geography and International Development Studies, Building 21.1, POB 260, 4000 Roskilde, Denmark. *Telephone:* (45) 46-74-21-49; *Fax:* (45) 46-74-30-31; *E-mail:* kristine@ruc.dk.

K

KAAL, Anu; Estonian opera singer; b 4 Nov 1940, Tallinn; m Hillar-Kalev Kaal 1961; one d. *Education:* Music Coll and Music Conservatory (Tallinn) and Scuola di Canto all Scala (Milan, Italy). *Career:* Opera singer Tallinn Opera House 1963–96; Prof Tallinn Music Acad 1984–; Folk Artist of Estonia 1977; Folk Artist of USSR 1981. *Operas include:* The Magic Flute, Porgy and Bess, Rigoletto, The Mighty Magician, The Warriors, Der Rosenkavalier, Don Carlos, The Telephone, Die Fledermaus, La Traviata, Don Giovanni, Cyrano de Bergerac, La Bohème, La Serva Padrona, The Bartered Bride, Un Ballo in Maschera, Boris Godunov, Mefistofele, Manon. *Leisure interests:* nature, travel. *Address:* Tallinn 0001, UUS-Tatari 16–33, Estonia. *Telephone:* (2) 682065.

KAAS, Patricia; French singer; b Stiring Wendel, nr Forbach. *Career:* Dancer at tea-dances and night-clubs aged 13 years; first recording aged 17 years; produces records through Note de Blues (her own co); toured Viet Nam and Cambodia 1994; has made four world tours and sold 14 million albums. *Recordings include:* Singles: Jalousie, Mademoiselle chante le Blues; Album: Je te dis vous, Rendez-vous, Le mot de passe. *Address:* c/o Talent sorcier, 3 rue des Petites Ecuries, 75010 Paris, France (Office). *Telephone:* (1) 44-59-99-00 (Office); *Fax:* (1) 44-59-99-01 (Office).

KABAIVANSKA, Raina; Bulgarian opera singer; b 15 Dec 1934, Burgas; d of Joachin and Staika Kabaivanska; m Franco Guandalini 1972; one d. *Education:* pvt singing tuition and Conservatorium of Sofia. *Career:* Debut in Puccini's Tabarro 1959; sang with Joan Sutherland and under direction of Maria Callas; has since performed with all major directors including Von Karajan in theatres world-wide; Premico Puccini; Premio Viotti; Verdi d'Oro. *Films:* Tosca, I Pagliacci, Falstaff, Il Trovatore, Madame Butterfly; *Records:* Tosca, Madame Butterfly, Adriana Lecouvreur, Francesca da Rimini; numerous videos. *Leisure interests:* literature, art collection, antiques. *Address:* viale Fabrizio 81, Modena, Italy. *Telephone:* (59) 211170.

KABI, Mamoshebi, BA, M ED; Lesotho politician; b 7 March 1936, Maseru; d of the late Rev and Mrs Elijah E. Phakisi; m Motete Kabi 1958; two s two d. *Education:* Nat Univ of Lesotho, Tennessee State Univ (USA) and St Francis Xavier Univ (Canada). *Career:* Extension Educator Inst of Extra Mural Studies, Nat Univ of Lesotho 1978–92; mem Basutoland Congress Party 1960–, fmr Sec-Gen Women's League, Nat Treas, Br Sec, Constituency Sec; detained and tortured for political convictions on numerous occasions during state of emergency 1970–81; Mem Nat Ass (Parl) 1993–, mem Business Cttee; Minister of Transport, Post and Telecommunications 1996; Co-Founder and mem Thamae Women's Devt Project, Moho Museum of Art and History, Moho Devt Foundation, Lesotho Literacy Network; mem OAU Observer Team, South African elections 1994, African Asscn for Literacy and Adult Educ; numerous articles. *Leisure interests:* reading, watching TV soap operas, knitting, sewing. *Address:* c/o Ministry of Transport, Post and Telecommunications, POB 413, Maseru, Lesotho (Office); Lower Thamae, POB 1320, Maseru 100, Lesotho (Home).

KADAR, Rabia; Chinese business executive; b 1948, Aletai, N Xinjiang; m Stick Aji; eleven c. *Career:* Founder March 8th Store 1987, leather-processing factory, Xinjiang, Rabia Store (Kazakstan), garment factory and knitting mill 1994; Chair Akdar Industrial and Trade Co 1992; Vice-Chair Xinjiang All Fed of Industries and Commerce, Xinjiang Women Entrepreneurs Asscn; mem nat and regional cttees of CPPCC.

KAEL, Pauline; American writer and film critic; b 19 June 1919, Two Rock, CA; d of Isaac and Judith (née Friedman) Kael; one d. *Education:* Univ of California at Berkeley. *Career:* Film critic The New Yorker 1968–91; contribs to numerous magazines including Partisan Review, Vogue, The New Republic, McCall's, The Atlantic, Harpers; Exec Consultant Paramount Pictures 1979; Guggenheim Fellow 1964; Hon D LL (Georgetown) 1972; Hon D ARTS and LIT (Columbia Coll) 1972; Hon D LIT (Smith Coll) 1973, (Alleghery Coll) 1979; Hon D HUM LITT (Kalamazoo Coll) 1973, (Reed Coll and Haverford Coll) 1975; Hon DFA (New York School of Visual Arts) 1980; George Polk Memorial Award for Criticism 1970; Best Magazine Column Award 1974; Distinguished Journalism Award 1983. *Publications:* I Lost it at the Movies 1965, Kiss Kiss Bang Bang 1968, Going Steady 1970, Deeper into Movies (Nat Book Award Arts and Letters 1974) 1973, Reeling 1976, When the Lights Go Down 1980, 5001 Nights at the Movies 1982 (expanded 1991), Taking It All In 1984, State of the Art 1985, Hooked 1989, Movie Love 1991, For Keeps 1994, Raising Kane and other essays 1996. *Address:* c/o The New Yorker, 4 Times Square, New York, NY 10036, USA.

KAHN, Paula, BA, FRSA; British publishing executive; b 15 Nov 1940; d of Cyril Maurice and Stella (née Roscoe) Kahn. *Education:* Chiswick Co High School and Univs of Bristol and London. *Career:* With Longman Group 1966–94, Ed, Publr, Publishing Dir, Div Man Dir 1966–79, English Language Teaching, Dictionaries, Trade and Reference Divs 1980–85, Int Sector 1986–88, Publishing Chief Exec 1988–89, Chair, Chief Exec 1990–94; Project Dir World Learning Network 1995–96; Man Dir Phaidon Press 1996–97; Chair Equality Works 2000–; Non-Exec Dir English Language Services Int Ltd 1998–, New Ways to Work (also Vice-Chair) 1998–, Stonewall 2000–; mem British Council English Teaching Advisory Comm 1989–, Council Publrs' Asscn 1990– (Vice-Pres 1994–95, Pres 1995–), Forum UK 1991, Educ and Training Sector Group, Dept of Trade and Industry 1993–, Bd Inst of Int Visual Arts 1994–, Islington Community Health Council (also Vice-Chair) 1998–; Founder-mem Bentick Group 1994–; mem Governing Body SOAS 1993–95; Gov Elizabeth Garrett Anderson School, Islington 1997–2000, Cripplegate Foundation 2000–; Companion of the Inst of Man. *Leisure interests:* cinema, theatre, France, books. *Address:* 4 Mica House, Barnsbury Square, London N1 1RN, UK. *Telephone:* (20) 7609-6964; *Fax:* (20) 7609-6965; *E-mail:* paulakahn@micahouse.co.uk.

KAILIS, Patricia Verne, AM, OBE, MB; Australian medical practitioner and business executive; b 19 Aug 1933, Castlemaine; d of George Alexander Hurse and Verne Amanda Daley; m Michael George Kailis 1960. *Education:* Chatham State School (Vic) and Presbyterian Ladies Coll (Melbourne, Vic). *Career:* Gen Practitioner (WA) 1960–69; Genetic Counsellor and Neurogeneticist Royal Perth Hosp (WA) 1970–95; Dir M. G. Kailis Group 1960; mem Bd Rocky Bay Inc 1980, Pres 1990; mem Council Presbyterian Ladies Coll (Perth, WA) 1990–96; Gov Univ Notre Dame 1995. *Leisure interests:* classical music, opera. *Address:* M. G. Kailis Group, 50 Mews Rd, Fremantle, WA 6160, Australia; Kastello, 5 Minim Close, Mosman Park, WA 6012, Australia. *Telephone:* (9) 385 5725; *Fax:* (9) 385 5715.

KAIN, Karen, CC; Canadian ballet dancer; b 28 March 1951, Hamilton, ON; d of Charles A. Kain and Winifred Mary Kelly; m Ross Petty 1983. *Education:* Nat Ballet School. *Career:* Joined Nat Ballet of Canada 1969, Prin Dancer 1970; has danced most of major roles in repertoire; appeared as Giselle with Bolshoi Ballet on tour of fmr USSR, in the Sleeping Beauty with London Festival Ballet in UK and Australia, in Swan Lake with Vienna State Opera Ballet; toured Japan and Repub of Korea with Ballet Nat de Marseille 1981; created roles of Chosen

Maiden in The Rite of Spring for Nat Ballet of Canada 1979, Giulietta in Tales of Hoffman for Ballet Nat de Marseille 1982, the Bride in The Seven Daggers/Los Siete Puñales, Alice 1986, La Ronde 1987, Daphnis and Chlöe 1988, Tagore 1989, Song of the Earth 1991; Pres The Dancer's Transition Centre; Hon Patron Kidney Foundation of Canada; Artistic Assoc, Nat Ballet of Canada 1999–2000; Hon LL D (York, McMaster, Trent); Silver Medal, 2nd Int Ballet Competition, Moscow 1973; Int Emmy Award for Karen Kain: Dancing in the Moment. *TV productions include:* Giselle, La fille mal gardée, The Merry Widow, Alice, La Ronde; *Publication:* Movement Never Lies 1994. *Leisure interests:* reading, swimming, theatre, music. *Address:* The Walter Carsen Centre for The National Ballet of Canada, 470 Queens Quay, Toronto, ON M5V 3K4, Canada.

KAL-YAM, Nonna, MA; Israeli painter and graphic designer; b 22 Aug 1959, Minsk, fmr USSR (now Belarus); m 1980; one d. *Education:* Acad of Arts (Belarus). *Career:* Graphic Designer Cultural Foundation of Belarus; Freelance painter; exhibitions in Minsk, Tel-Aviv and Jerusalem (Israel); mem Nat Asscn of Painters and Sculptors, Int Asscn of Painters and Sculptors; Painter of the Year, Belarus 1987; First Prize Painting Contest 1989. *Leisure interests:* travel, sports, literature. *Address:* POB 11117, Tel Aviv 61110, Israel. *Telephone:* (3) 6136275; *Fax:* (3) 5014450.

KALAPESI, Roshan Minocher, B SC; Indian business executive, writer and designer; b 21 May 1925, Bombay (now Mumbai); d of the late Khanbahadur Minocher dinsha Kalapesi and Khorshed Minocher (née Tata) Kalapesi. *Education:* Convent of Jesus and Mary (Bombay), Royal Inst of Science (Bombay) and Elphinstone Coll (Bombay). *Career:* Man Dir Shannon Chemical Works 1965–; Dir Artiste's Creative Theatre, Mumbai 1972–; fmr Art Dir and costume designer; Pres Crafts Council of India 1975–79; Chair Crafts Council of W India; has exhibited at Australia Museum, Sydney, Smithsonian Inst, USA, Nat History Museum, UK, Prince of Wales Museum, and several other museums in Europe, Canada and USA, also at Festival of India, UK; designed wardrobe for Reita Faria (Miss India and Miss World); Patron 'Paramparik Karigar', Asscn of Master Craftsmen; Dip of Art, J. J. School of Art; First Nat Award for Best Costumes for film 'Pestonjee' 1988. *TV includes:* The Raj Through Indian Eyes (Channel 4, UK); *Publications include:* Plays: The Splendoured One (Life of Zarathushtra), Cyrus the Great. *Leisure interests:* reading, theatre, sports. *Address:* 59 L Jagmohandas Marg, Mumbai 400 006, India. *Telephone:* (22) 3696927 (Office); (22) 3637336 (Home); *Fax:* (22) 3684719; *E-mail:* banyan@vsnl.com.

KALBASSI, Iran, PH D; Iranian associate professor; b 1 Dec 1939, Isfahan; m 1975; one s. *Education:* Univs of Teheran and Shiraz. *Career:* School teacher 1958–74; Assoc Prof and researcher 1974–96; has published six books and 30 articles. *Leisure interests:* reading, walking, writing. *Address:* 23 Hormoz Sttari St, Vali-i Asr Ave, 19689 Tehran, Iran. *Telephone:* (21) 8788191.

KALE, Oladele Olusiji, BA, MB, B CH; Nigerian medical practitioner and professor of medicine; b 19 Nov 1938, Ijebu-Ode, Ogun State; m Aderonke Oderinde 1969; five s. *Education:* Trinity Coll Dublin (Ireland), Univs of Liverpool and Bristol (UK). *Career:* House Physician and Surgeon Teaching Hosp, Univ of Lagos 1963–64; Registrar New Cross Hosp, London 1967; Sr Registrar Univ Coll Hosp, Ibadan 1971–73, Lecturer and Consultant 1973–76, Sr Lecturer and Consultant 1976–78; Reader in Preventive and Social Medicine Univ of Ibadan 1978–82, Prof 1982, Head of Dept 1983–87; apptd Dir Ibarapa Community and Primary Health Program 1983; Fellow Nigerian Medical Coll of Public Health 1971, W African Coll of Physicians 1971; mem Int Epidemiological Asscn, WHO Expert Advisory Panel on Parasitic Diseases, Steering Cttee, WHO Tropical Disease Scientific Working Group, Asscn for Study of Medical Educ; Chair Nat Cttee on Health Corpns; numerous contribs to medical books. *Leisure interests:* reading, word puzzles, writing, chess, darts. *Address:* University of Ibadan, Dept of Preventive and Social Medicine, College of Medicine, Oyo State, Nigeria (Office); 20 Paul Hendrickse Rd, New Bodija, Ibadan, Oyo State, Nigeria (Home). *Telephone:* (22) 400010 (Office); (22) 410017 (Home).

KALOYANOVA-SIMEONOVA, Fina Petrova, MD, PH D; Bulgarian medical practitioner; b 30 Dec 1926; d of Peter and Maria Kaloyanov; m Jordan Simeonov 1950; two s. *Education:* Higher Medical Inst (Sofia). *Career:* Scientific Researcher 1951–56; Sr Researcher 1956–69; mem WHO expert panel 1969–72; Dir Inst of Hygiene and Occupational Health 1972–84, apptd Head Dept of Toxicology 1984; has received many nat awards and decorations. *Publications:* Les Pesticides et l'Homme 1971, Human Toxicology of Pesticides 1991. *Leisure interest:* growing flowers. *Address:* Institute of Hygiene and Occupational Health, Medical Academy, 1431 Sofia, Bul Dimitar Nestorov 15, Bulgaria. *Telephone:* (2) 58-12-59-0; *Fax:* (2) 59-60-71.

KAMALI, Norma; American fashion designer; b 27 June 1945, New York; d of Sam Arraez and Estelle Galib; m M. H. Kamali (divorced). *Career:* Ind fashion designer, New York 1965–; opened first shop E 53rd St 1968, moving to Madison Ave 1974; retitled business OMO (On My Own) and moved to 56th St 1978; second boutique opened Spring St, New York 1986; OMO Home 1988–; collaboration with Bloomingdale's 1988–; OMO Tokyo 1990–; awards include Coty American Fashion Critics' Winnie Award 1981, 1982, Outstanding Women's Fashion Designer of the Year Award 1982, Council of Fashion Designers of America, American Success Award 1989, Pencil Award 1999, Fashion Outreach Style Award 1999. *Address:* 11 W 56th St, New York, NY 10019, USA.

KAMALKHANI, Zahra (Shahnaz), PH D; Iranian anthropologist; b 7 March 1954, Shiraz; d of Habib Kamalkhani and Nezhat Jahanmiri; m Hoshang Lahooti 1977; one d one s. *Education:* Univs of Teheran (Iran) and Bergen (Norway) and SOAS (London). *Career:* Asst Lecturer Inst for Middle East Language and Culture, Univ of Bergen (Norway) 1986–87, Dept of Social Anthropology, 1992, 1993, 1995; Nordic Visiting Fellow, Nordic Inst of Asian Studies (Copenhagen, Denmark) 1994. *Publications:* Iranian Immigrants and Refugees in Norway 1988, Women's Everyday Religious Discourse in Iran 1993, Family and Household Economic Management in the Context of Change 1993, Women's Islam: Religious Practice Among Women in Today's Iran 1996. *Leisure interests:* reading, swimming, mountain walking, tennis. *Address:* University of Bergen, Department of Social Anthropology, Fosswinckelsgatan 6, 5006 Bergen, Norway. *Telephone:* 55-58-92 (Office); 55-90-10-48 (Home); *Fax:* 55-58-92-60 (Office); *E-mail:* zahra.kamalkhani@sosantr.uib.no.

KAMEI, Shizuka; Japanese politician. *Career:* Mem House of Reps (Parl) for Hiroshima; Parl Vice-Minister of Transport, Minister 1994–95; Chair LDP Nat Org Cttee and Chair (acting) LDP Policy Research Council. *Address:* c/o Ministry of Transport, 2-1-3 Kasumigaseki Chiyoda-ku, Tokyo, Japan.

KAMESWARAN, Lalitha, BS, MB, PH D, F MED SCI; Indian medical practitioner and university vice-chancellor; b 27 July 1930, Madurai; d of S. and Vasumathi Bharati; m Shanmugam Kameswaran 1952; one s one d. *Education:* Univs of London and Madras. *Career:* Tutor in Pharmacology Madurai Medical Coll 1955–60, Asst Prof 1960–62, Reader 1962–64, Prof 1964–80; Dir Inst of Pharmacology, Madras Medical Coll 1980–82, first woman Dean 1982–83; concurrently Dean Govt Gen Hosp; first woman Dir of Medical Educ, Tamil Nadu 1983–88; Vice-Chancellor Tamil Nadu Dr M. G. R. Medical Univ, Madras 1988–93; First Vice-Chancellor Sri Ramachandra Deemed Medical Univ 1994; mem Exec Cttee Medical Council of India; fmr Pres Indian Pharmacological Soc; Fellow Coll of Allergy and Applied Immunology; numerous articles in scientific journals; numerous awards including Dr B. C. Roy Nat Award 1983, Shiromani Nat Award 1990. *Leisure interests:* travel, reading. *Address:* 5 Third Ave, Indira Nagar, Chennai 600 020, India. *Telephone:* (44) 4912575.

KAMP, Margreet M. H., PH D; Netherlands politician; b 22 June 1942, Borne. *Education:* Higher Professional School and Univ of Groningen. *Career:* Mem Volkspartij voor Vrijheid en Democratie (People's Party for Freedom and Democracy), Pres Nat Overall Cttee for Health and Welfare, Cttee for Social Devt; mem Tweede Kamer (Second Chamber) of States-Gen 1982, mem Cttees for Welfare and Culture, Public Health, Social Affairs and Agric. *Publications:* Cherchez la femme 1990; various articles on women and corp man. *Leisure interests:* walking, tennis. *Address:* Tweede Kamer der Staaten-Generaal, Binnenhof 1A, Postbus 20018, The Hague, Netherlands. *Telephone:* (70) 318-22-93; *Fax:* (70) 318-29-24.

KAN, Diana Artemis Mann Shu, FRSA; American artist; b 3 March 1926, Hong Kong; d of Kam Shek and Sing-Ying (née Hong) Kan; m Paul Schwartz 1952; one s. *Education:* Art Students League, Ecole des Beaux Arts (Paris) and Grande Chaumière (Paris). *Career:* Art Reviewer Villager 1960–69; Foreign Corresp and City Ed Cosmorama Pictorial Magazine, Hong Kong 1968; art lecturer Birmingham Southern Univ, Univ of New York, Mills Coll and Philadelphia Museum; solo exhibitions include Shanghai 1935, 1937, 1939 and Nanking (China, now People's Repub of China) 1936, 1938, Hong Kong 1937, 1939, 1941, 1947–48, 1952, London 1949, 1963–64, Paris 1949, San Francisco, (CA, USA) 1950, 1967, New York 1950, 1954, 1959, 1967, 1971–72, 1974, 1978, Naples (Italy) 1971, Taipei Nat History Museum (Repub of China—Taiwan) 1971; group exhibitions include Royal Acad of Fine Arts (London) 1963–64, Nat Acad (New York) 1967, 1969–70, 1974–76, Columbia Museum of Art 1969; works in perm collections including Metropolitan Museum of Art, Nelson Gallery, Dalhousie Univ (Canada), Taipei Nat History Museum; mem Pen and Brush Club, Nat Acad of Design, American Watercolour Soc, Nat League of Pen Women, Audubon Artists, Allied Artists of America; numerous prizes and awards. *Publications:* White Cloud 1938, The How and Why of Chinese Painting 1974. *Address:* 15 Grammercy Park S, New York, NY 10003, USA.

KAN, Lai-Bing, PH D; Hong Kong librarian; b Hong Kong. *Education:* Univ of Hong Kong and Univ of California (USA). *Career:* Asst Librarian Univ of Hong Kong Libraries 1959–70, Deputy Librarian 1970–72, Univ Librarian 1983–; Univ Librarian and Dir of Library System, Chinese Univ of Hong Kong 1972–83; Library Consultant, Univ of E Asia, Macau 1980–88; Dir of Studies, Programmes in Library and Information Science, School of Professional and Continuing Educ, Univ of Hong Kong 1961–; Certificate Course for Library Assts, Dept of Extra Mural Studies, Chinese Univ of Hong Kong 1973–; Chair, Vice-Chair Hong Kong Library Asscn, mem various cttees 1959–; Pres Int Asscn of Oriental Librarians 1990–93; Honorary Fellow Charles Sturt Univ, Australia 1990–93. *Publications include:* An Annotated Guide to Hong Kong Government Serials 1979, Newspapers of Hong Kong 1981, Serials of Hong Kong 1981, Libraries and Information Services in Hong Kong 1988; many articles in int, regional and local journals. *Leisure interests:* travelling, reading. *Address:* University of Hong Kong Library, Pokfulam Rd, Hong Kong. *Telephone:* 8592200; *Fax:* 8589420.

KANE, Carol; American actress; b 18 June 1952, Cleveland, OH. *Education:* Professional Children's School (New York). *Career:* Acting career began at the age of 14. *Plays include:* The Prime of Miss Jean Brodie 1966, The Tempest 1974, The Effect of Gamma Rays on Man-in-the-Moon Marigolds 1978, Arturo Ui, Macbeth 1980, Frankie and Johnny in the Claire de Lune 1988; *Films include:* Carnal Knowledge 1971, Dog Day Afternoon 1975, Hester Street (Acad Award nomination) 1975, Annie Hall 1977, The World's Greatest Lover 1977, The Muppet Movie 1979, Racing with the Moon 1984, Jumpin' Jack Flash 1986, Ishtar 1987, License to Drive 1988, Scrooged 1988, The Princess Bride 1989, Flashback, Joe vs the Volcano 1990, My Blue Heaven, The Lemon Sisters 1990, Ted and Venus 1991, In the Soup 1992, Addams Family Values 1993, When A Stranger Calls Back 1993, Even Cowgirls Get The Blues 1993, Baby on Board 1993, The Crazysitter 1995, Trees Lounge 1996, Office Killer 1997, The Tic Code 1998, Jawbreaker 1999, Man on the Moon 1999; *TV appearances include:* Taxi (series, Emmy Award) 1981–83, Noah's Ark 1999, several TV films. *Address:* c/o Krost/Chapin Management, 9465 Wilshire Blvd, Suite 430, Los Angeles, CA 90212, USA.

KANE, Margaret Brassler; American sculptor; b 25 May 1909, East Orange, NJ; d of Hans and Mathilde (née Trumpler) Brassler; m Arthur Kane 1930; two s. *Education:* Syracuse Univ, Art Students League, New York Coll of Music and John Hovannes Studio. *Career:* Freelance artist in fibre art 1952–; Art Dir and Chief Designer for numerous corpns, Poland 1954–63; Lecturer State Acad of Fine Arts, Poland 1952–68; part-time tutor Ontario Coll of Arts, Toronto 1980–90, conducts seminars for post-graduate students; solo exhibitions include State

Gallery of Fine Arts, Warsaw 1965, Pushkin Nat Museum, Moscow 1966, Scottish Woollen Gallery, Galashields, UK 1968, Merton Gallery, Toronto 1970, London Art Gallery, ON 1971, Spain 1980–81, Canadian Cultural Centre Art Gallery, Paris 1981, Munich Art Gallery, Germany 1982, Galerie Inard, Toulouse, France 1982, 1991, John B. Aird Gallery, Toronto 1991, Iparmuveszeti Muzeum of Decorative Art, Budapest 1995, Dresden Design Centre, World Centre, Dresden, Germany 1996, Chateau de Tremblay Gallery, Fontenoy, France 1996; group exhibitions include Galeria Lampertz Contempora, Cologne, Germany 1966, Rotterdam Art Gallery, the Netherlands 1967, Kunsthaus Gallery, Vienna 1967, The Hermitage, Leningrad (now St Petersburg, Russian Fed) 1968, Museum of Modern Art, México 1969, Montréal 1971, Vevey, Switzerland 1977, Royal Canadian Acad of Arts 1980, Art Gallery of Dallas, TX, USA 1983, Galerie Inard, Andorra 1985, Luxembourg 1985, Toulouse 1985, Salon des Arts de l'Air et de l'Espace, Toulouse, France 1989; collections include Gallery of European Art, Moscow, Nat Museum of Fine Arts, Warsaw, Canadian Embassy, Saudi Arabia, Nat Museum of the History of Weaving Art, Łódź, and collections in USA, Sweden, Switzerland, France and UK; mem Order of Canada, RCA, Accademia Italia delle Arti e del Lavoro, Ontario Soc of Artists; Gold Medal Triennale di Milano 1957; Medaglio d'Oro, Accademia Italia delle Arti 1980; Golden Centaur 1982; Gold Medal Int Art Competition, NY 1985; Gov Gen of Canada Commemoration Medal 1993. *Address:* 30 Strickland Rd, Cos Cob, CT 06807, USA.

KANETAKA, Rose Kaoru; Japanese journalist and broadcaster; b 28 Feb 1928. *Education:* Los Angeles City Coll (CA, USA). *Career:* Narrator, Dir and Producer current affairs programmes Tokyo Broadcasting System Network; numerous tours to film travel documentaries including The World Around Us 1959–90; Adviser Hyogo prefecture; Deputy-Chair Japan Travel Writers' Org, Yokohama Tourist Org; Commendation, Ministry of Foreign Affairs 1985; Cavalieri (Italy) 1987; Medal with Purple Ribbon, Ministry of Gen Affairs 1991. *Address:* 202 Ambassador Arms Bldg, 3-15-10 Roppongi, Minato-ku, Tokyo 106, Japan. *Telephone:* (3) 3582-9733; *Fax:* (3) 3582-9735.

KANOUN, Houda, MA; Tunisian politician; b 1 Jan 1940, Sfax. *Education:* Univ des Lettres, des Arts et des Sciences Humaines (Tunis I). *Career:* Teacher Sfax 1974–89; Deputy Mayor of Sfax 1975–1980; Gen Sec Feminine Youth 1974–1981; mem Cen Cttee Constitutional Democratic Rally 1988–; Mem Assemblée Nationale (Nat Ass—Parl) 1989–; has written several essays. *Leisure interests:* reading, swimming. *Address:* Immeuble Taparura, rue Habib Maazoun, Sfax 3000, Tunisia. *Telephone:* (4) 296369; *Fax:* (4) 227426.

KANTAROFF, Maryon, BA; Canadian sculptor, lecturer and writer; b 20 Nov 1933, Toronto, ON; d of Christopher and Irene (née Somlev) Kantaroff. *Education:* Royal Conservatory of Music (Toronto), Univ of Toronto, British Museum, Berkshire Coll of Art, Sir John Cass Coll of Art, Chelsea Coll of Art and Univ of London (UK). *Career:* Asst Curator Art Gallery of Toronto 1957–58; Art teacher 1958–59, 1962; Art Critic BBC E Europe Broadcasting 1959–62; freelance sculptor 1959–, first professional exhibition 1962; first Resident Sculptor Seneca Coll 1970; Organizer New Feminists in Toronto 1969; Art Lecturer and Feminist 1970–; Founder Art Foundry Inc 1974–78; first retrospective exhibition 1987; sculpture for Canadian Embassy Tokyo (installation) 1991; creations include environmental sculptures, limited jewellery edns; numerous solo and group exhibitions; mem Sculpture Soc of Canada, Canadian Art Asscn, Toronto Professional and Businesswomen's Asscn; Zonta Adventure Award 1975; YWCA Woman of Distinction 1982; Pres's Award for best sculpture, Sculpture Soc of Canada 1992. *Leisure interests:* reading, music, swimming. *Address:* 148 Lyndhurst Ave, Toronto, ON M5R 2Z9, Canada.

KANTCHEFF, Slava; German pianist and television presenter; b 15 July 1959, Wiesbaden; d of Kantcho and Mathilde Kantcheff; m Peter Horton 1986. *Education:* Conservatoire Nat Supérieur de Musique et de Danse (Paris). *Career:* First TV appearance aged seven; performed Beethoven and Mozart piano concertos with orchestra aged ten; recorded first album aged 23; Co-Presenter own TV series with Peter Horton 1989–91; has performed at more than 1,500 concerts. *Recordings:* four solo albums (Beethoven, Brahms, Schumann and

Chopin), five albums with Peter Horton. *Address:* Martin-Luther-Str 24/DT, 81539 Munich, Germany. *Telephone:* (89) 695689; *Fax:* (89) 6259189.

KANTER, Rosabeth Moss, MA, PH D; American professor of management, consultant and writer; b 15 March 1943, Cleveland, OH; d of Nelson Nathan and Helen (née Smolen) Moss; m 1st Stuart Alan Kanter 1963 (died 1969); m 2nd Barry Alan Stein 1972; one s. *Education:* Bryn Mawr Coll, Univ of Michigan and Harvard Univ Law School. *Career:* Assoc, Asst Prof Brandeis Univ 1967–77; Prof Yale Univ 1977–86; Class of 1960 Prof of Man Harvard Univ Business School 1986–; Visiting Prof MIT 1973–74, Harvard 1979–80; Chair Bd Goodmeasure Inc, Cambridge, MA 1980–; Consultant to BellSouth, Apple Computer, Proctor and Gamble, IBM, Int Harvester Co, Honeywell Corpn and numerous other cos; mem Bd Nat Org of Women Legal Defense and Educ Fund 1979–86, American Sociological Asscn (Exec Council 1982–85), Eastern Sociological Soc (Exec Council 1975–78, Gellman Award 1978), Acad of Man Cttee of 200 (also F), Bd NOW (Nat Org of Women) Legal Defence and Educ Fund, New York 1979–86, 1993–, American Production and Quality Center 1989–, Econ Policy Inst 1993–, Malcolm Baldridge Nat Quality Award 1994–, Gov's Council for Econ Growth, MA 1994–; Co-Chair int trade task force 1995–; Incorporator Babson Coll 1984–87, Boston Children's Museum 1984–; Trustee Coll Retirement Equities Fund 1985–89; Guggenheim Fellow; numerous hon degrees; Woman of the Year, New England Women's Business Owners 1981; Int Asscn Personnel Women 1981, MS Magazine 1985; Working Woman AT & T Hall of Fame 1986; Athena Award, Intercollegiate Asscn of Women Students 1980; McFeely Award, YMCA 1995, and other awards. *Publications include:* Work and Family in the US 1977, Men and Women of the Corporation (C. Wright Mills Award) 1977, The Change Masters 1983, Creating the Future: The Massachusetts Comeback and Its Promise for America (jtly) 1988, When Giants Learn to Dance (Johnson Smith, Knicely Award) 1989, The Challenge of Organization Change (jtly) 1992, World Class: Thriving Locally in the Global Economy 1995, Rosabeth Moss Kanter on the Frontiers of Management 1997, Evolve!: Succeeding in the Digital Culture of Tomorrow 2001, and six other books; has written more than 200 articles for professional journals, magazines, books etc. *Leisure interests:* tennis, swimming. *Address:* Harvard University Graduate School of Business Administration, Soldiers Field, Boston, MA 02163, USA. *Telephone:* (617) 495-6053; *Fax:* (617) 496-7167.

KANTŮRKOVÁ, Eva; Czech writer; b 11 May 1930, Prague; d of Jiří Síla and Dobromila Sílová; m 1st Mr Šternov 1949; m 2nd Mr Kantůrkov; two s. *Education:* Charles Univ (Prague). *Career:* Writer 1964–, unable to publish works in Czechoslovakia 1970–89; imprisoned by Czechoslovak authorities because of book which was printed abroad 1981–82; mem Czech Parl 1990–92; mem Czech Centrum PEN Club, Asscn of Czech Writers; numerous novels, short stories, essays, plays and screenplays; wrote screenplay for film Funeral Ceremony (2nd prize Film Festival, Montréal, Canada) 1990, TV film My Friends in the Black House (1st and 2nd prizes Cannes Film Festival); Tom Stoppard Prize 1985; Jan Palach Prize 1989. *Leisure interest:* cultivating blossoms. *Address:* Xaveriova 13, 150 00 Prague 5, Czech Republic; c/o Swedish PEN Club, Pennklubben, Bonniers, Box 3159, 103 63 Stockholm, Sweden. *Telephone:* (2) 546949 (Prague).

KAPLAN, Flora Edouwaye S., PH D; American anthropologist; b New York City, NY; m (divorced 1993); one d one s. *Education:* Hunter Coll and Graduate Center, City Univ of New York and Columbia Univ (New York). *Career:* Fmr Asst then Curator Dept of Primitive Art and New World Cultures, Brooklyn Museum of City of New York; Adjunct Lecturer Herbert H. Lehman Coll, City Univ of New York 1970–73, Lecturer 1973–74, Graduate Fellow 1974–76; Adjunct Asst Prof Dept of Anthropology, New York Univ 1976–77, Asst Prof 1977–84, Assoc Prof 1984–90, Dir Certificate Program in Museum Studies, Graduate School of Arts and Science 1977–, Prof of Anthropology and Museum Studies and Dir Program in Museum Studies 1990–99; Fulbright Prof Univ of Benin (Nigeria) and Centre for Social, Cultural and Environmental Research 1983–85; photographs chosen for American Anthropologist Appointment Calendar 1978, UNICEF calendars 1986, 1991, 1993; Assoc Center of Latin American, Caribbean Studies, New York Univ 1978–; mem Advisory Bd Inst for African-American Affairs 1981–; Consultant Dahesh Museum, New York 1993–; mem Ed Bd New York Univ Electronic Journal of Sciences and Arts, Ed Advisory Bd Encyclopedia of Cultural Anthropology, Yale Univ; Co-Ed book series 'Museum Meanings' (Routledge, London) 1997–; mem Exhibitions Cttee 1998–, Comprehensive Interpretive Plan (CIP) for Statue of Liberty Nat Monument and Ellis Island Immigration Museum, Nat Park Service, US Dept of Interior 2001–; elected US Bd American Asscn of Museums/Int Council of Museums (AAM/ICOM) 1981–83, 1983–86, 1998–2001; has organized numerous museum exhibitions and symposia; numerous fellowships, awards and grants 1968–; Benin Woman of Honour 1990. *Publications:* Women: Public and Private Places (jtly) 1980, Una Tradición Alfarera: Conocimento y Estilo 1980, Images of Power: Art of the Royal Court of Benin 1981, A Mexican Folk Pottery Tradition: Cognition and Style in Material Culture in the Valley of Puebla 1994, Museums and The Making of 'Ourselves': The Role of Objects in National Identity (ed) 1994–98, Queens, Queen Mothers, Priestesses and Power: Case Studies in African Gender and Power (ed) 1997–98, In Splendor and Seclusion: Royal Women at the Court of Benin, Nigeria 2002; 55 chapters and articles in learned journals, publications and books. *Leisure interests:* film, photography. swimming, music. *Address:* 140 Nassau St, New York, NY 10038, USA. *Telephone:* (212) 998-8084; *Fax:* (212) 608-5196.

KAPLAN, Nelly; French film director and writer; b 11 April 1936, Buenos Aires; d of Julio and Sima (née Efron) Kaplan. *Education:* Univ of Buenos Aires. *Career:* Asst Dir to Abel Gance 1954–64; has written and directed numerous short films on art 1961–, and several feature films and documentaries 1967–; Officier de l'Ordre Nat du Mérite; Chevalier de la Légion d'Honneur; Officier des Arts et des Lettres; Lion d'Or du Festival de Venise 1967, Médaille d'Or 1969. *Films include:* Gustave Moreau 1961, Rodolphe Bresdin 1962, Abel Gance, hier et demain 1963, Dessins et merveilles 1964, A la source, la femme aimée 1965, Le regard Picasso 1967, La fiancée du pirate 1969, Papa les petits bateaux 1971, Néa 1976, Charles et Lucie 1979, Abel Gance et son Napoléon 1983, Le regard dans le miroir 1985, Pattes de velours 1986, Crépuscule des loups 1987, Les Mouettes 1990, Plaisir d'amour 1991; *Publications:* Manifeste d'un art nouveau: la Polyvision 1956, Le sunlight d'Austerlitz 1960, Le réservoir des sens 1965, Le collier de Ptyx 1971, Mémoires d'une liseuse de draps 1974, Napoléon d'Abel Gance, Aux orchidées sauvages 1998, Un manteau de fou rire 1998, La petite fille en costume marin 1999. *Leisure interest:* swimming. *Address:* Cythère Films, 34 ave des Champs Elysées, 75008 Paris, France.

KAPUR, Promilla, PH D, D LITT; Indian social scientist; b 1 Oct 1928, Indore; d of Harkishanlal and Kaushalya Devi Dhawan; m Brig Teg Bahadur Kapur 1947; two s. *Education:* Agra and St John's Colls, Inst of Social Sciences (Agra), Inst of Public Admin (New Delhi) and Caron Foundation (USA). *Career:* Researcher and teacher 1960–75; Marriage and Family Counsellor and Therapist 1970–; Consultant Sociologist 1980; Drug Counsellor 1984; Sex, Human Rights and Human Values Counsellor 1990; Dir Integrated Human Devt Services Foundation 1984; numerous awards include Woman of the Year 1994, Special Media India Award 1994, Talented Ladies Award (Bharat Nirman) 1995, Commemorative Research Fellow Coin (American Biographical Inst) 1996, Plaque for Distinguished Social Services (Swatantra Lekhak Manch). *Publications:* Marriage and the Working Woman in India 1972, Love, Marriage and Sex 1973, The Changing Status of the Working Woman in India 1975, Love, Marriage, Sex and the Indian Women 1977, The Life and World of Call Girls in India 1978, The Indian Call Girls 1979, Conflict Between Adolescent Girls and Their Parents 1982, Family Violence Against Females – A Report 1988, Girl Child and Family Violence (ed) 1993, Girl Child in India (ed) 1995. *Leisure interests:* reading, travelling, watching TV. *Address:* Integrated Human Development Services Foundation, K/37A Green Park, New Delhi, India. *Telephone:* (11) 654409.

KARAMÜRSEL, Arin, MA; Turkish pianist; b 19 Oct 1936, Istanbul; d of Abdülkadir and Azade Karamürsel. *Education:* Conservatory (Istanbul), Acad Marguerita Long (Paris) and Tchaikovsky Conservatory (Moscow). *Career:* Began playing the piano aged eight 1944; First performance Istanbul 1948; has performed in many countries including Turkey, France, UK, Luxembourg, Switzerland, Finland, Poland, Mexico, Cuba, Japan, People's Republic of China, Kuwait, Bahrain, Qatar, UAE; has played with orchestras including Orchestre Lamoureux 1966; soloist State Symphony Orchestra, Istanbul since

1988; First Prize Tchaikovsky Conservatory 1980; Bright Interpretation Award, Cervantino Festival, Mexico 1983. *Leisure interests:* travel, reading, concerts, cinema, music, friends. *Address:* Ihlamur Yolu, Güney Apt 83/7, Tešvikiye, Istanbul, Turkey. *Telephone:* (1) 2300532.

KARAN, Donna, BFA; American fashion designer; b 2 Oct 1948, Forest Hills, NY; m 1st Mark Karan (divorced 1978); one d; m 2nd Stephan Weiss 1983. *Education:* Parsons School of Design (New York). *Career:* With Addenda Co until 1968; with Anne Klein 1968–71, Assoc Designer 1971–74, Jt Dir of Design 1974–84; Propr, Designer Donna Karan Co, New York 1984–96, Chair, Head Designer Donna Karan Int (public co) 1996–2001; Chief Designer Louis Vuitton Moët Hennessy (LVMH) 2001–; mem Fashion Designers of America; Coty Award 1977, 1981, 1984, Fashion Designers of America Women's Wear Award 1996. *Address:* Donna Karan International, 15th Floor, 550 Seventh Ave, New York, NY 10018, USA.

KARI, Hilda Thugea; Solomon Islands politician; b 29 April 1949, Pau Pau Village, Guadalcanal Island; d of Ishmael and Elizabeth (née Votaia) Avui; m Solomon Kari 1973; three s one d. *Education:* St Catherine's School (Sydney). *Career:* Joined the Colonial Secr 1971; Govt Admin, Personal Man 1978–89; MP (People's Alliance Party) for NE Guadalcanal 1990. *Leisure interests:* conservation, Christian activities. *Address:* POB 845, Honiara, Solomon Islands. *Telephone:* 23747.

KARIEVA, Bernara Rakhimovna; Uzbekistan ballet dancer; b 28 Jan 1936, Tashkent; d of Rakhim Kariev; m Kulakhmat Rizaev; two d. *Education:* Tashkent Choreography School (under N. A. Dovgelli and L. A. Zass) and Moscow School of Choreography (under M. A. Kozhukhova). *Career:* Prin Ballet Dancer Navoi Theatre, Tashkent 1955–86, Bolshoi Ballet 1957; mem CPSU 1967–91; has danced frequently with the Bolshoi and given many performances internationally; Prof of Dance Tashkent School of Choreography; Dir Bolshoi Opera and Ballet Theatre 1994; Dir-Gen Theatre East–West Int Festival 1993; mem UNESCO Nat Comm on Culture (Uzbekistan), Asscn of Actors of Uzbekistan 1984–98; Pres Bd Uzbek Union of Theatre Workers; elected USSR People's Deputy 1989–91; awards include Uzbek State Prize 1970, People's Artist of the USSR 1973, USSR State Prize 1982, Uzbek Order of Dustlike, 200th Anniversary of Pushkin Medal. *Ballets include:* Swan Lake, Francesca da Rimini, Young Lady and Hooligan, Anna Karenina, Don Juan, Love and the Sword, Cinderella, Ballet Princess, Dea, Madame Bovary, Spartacus, Maskarad, Neznakomka, Othello, Hamlet; *Film appearances include:* I'm a Ballerina, Born Miniatures, Variations. *Leisure interests:* piano music, visually discovering the world. *Address:* Navoi Opera Theatre, Tashkent, Uzbekistan; 28 Mustafo Kamol Otaturk St, Tashkent 700029, Uzbekistan (Home). *Telephone:* (371) 133-35-28 (Office); (371) 132-10-20 (Home); *Fax:* (371) 133-33-44 (Office); *E-mail:* gabt_uz@albatros.uz (Office); gabt_uz@operamail.com (Home); *Internet:* gabt-uz.narod.ru (Home).

KARINA, Anna (Hanne Karin Bayer); French (b Danish) actress; b 22 Sept 1940, Frederiksberg, Denmark; d of Carl Johann Bayer and Elva Helvig Frederiksen; m 1st Jean-Luc Godard (divorced); m 2nd Pierre-Antoine Fabre 1968 (divorced); m 3rd Daniel Georges Duval 1978. *Career:* Has appeared on TV and in theatre; Prix Orange. *Films include:* She'll Have To Go 1961, Une femme est une femme 1961, Vivre sa vie 1962, Le petit soldat 1963, Bande à part 1964, Alphaville 1965, Made in the USA 1966, La religieuse 1968, The Magus 1968, Before Winter Comes 1968, Laughter in the Dark 1969, Justine 1969, The Salzburg Connection 1972, Living Together 1974, L'assassin musicien 1975, Les œufs brouillés 1976, Boulette chinoise 1977, L'ami de Vincent 1983, Ave Maria 1984, Dernier été à Tanger 1987, Cayenne Palace 1987, L'Oeuvre au noir 1988, Last Song 1989, L'Homme qui voulait être coupable 1990; *Radio:* Une histoire d'amour 2000; *Publications:* Golden City 1983, On n'achète pas le soleil (novel) 1988. *Address:* Orban éditions, 76 rue Bonaparte, 75006 Paris, France.

KARL, Elfriede; Austrian politician; b 14 Sept 1933, Salzburg. *Education:* Acad for Social Studies. *Career:* Completed commercial apprenticeship 1950; saleswoman 1950–53; shorthand typist Building and Timber Workers Union, Salzburg 1953–60; Salzburg Chamber of Labour 1961–, Sec to Econs Dept 1968; Sec State for Family Affairs Policy, Kreisky Govt 1971–79, Sec State Fed Ministry of Finance 1979–83; Fed Minister for Family Affairs 1983–84; mem Austrian Socialist Party (SPÖ, now Social-Democratic Party of Austria). *Address:* c/o Social-Democratic Party of Austria, Löwelstr 18, 1014 Vienna, Austria.

KARLE, Isabella, PH D; American chemist; b 2 Dec 1921, Detroit, MI; d of Zygmunt A. and Elizabeth (née Graczyk) Lugoski; m Jerome Karle 1942; three d. *Education:* Univ of Michigan. *Career:* Assoc Chemist Univ of Chicago 1944; Instructor in Chem Univ of Michigan 1944–46; Physicist Naval Research Lab, Washington, DC 1946–; mem NAS, American Crystallographic Asscn, American Chemical Soc, American Physical Soc, American Biophysical Soc, American Peptide Soc, American Philosophical Soc, American Acad of Arts and Sciences; has written more than 320 scientific articles, chapters and reviews; Hon D SC (Michigan) 1976, (Wayne State) 1979, (Maryland) 1986, (Athens) 1997, (Pennsylvania) 1999; Hon D HUM LITT (Georgetown) 1984; Lifetime Achievement Award, Women in Science and Engineering 1986, Gregori Aminoff Prize, Swedish Royal Acad of Sciences 1988, Bijvoet Medal, Univ of Utrecht, Netherlands 1990, Bower Award, Franklin Inst 1993, Chemical Sciences Award (NAS) 1995, Medal of Science, awarded by Pres of USA 1995, and other awards and honours. *Leisure interests:* swimming, ice-skating, needlework. *Address:* Naval Research Laboratory, Code 6030, Washington, DC 20375, USA (Office); 6304 Lakeview Drive, Falls Church, VA 22041, USA (Home). *Telephone:* (202) 767-2624 (Office); *Fax:* (202) 767-6874 (Office).

KARMI, Ghada, PH D, MRCP; British medical practitioner; b 19 Nov 1939, Palestine; d of Hasan and Amina Karmi; m 1st Geoffrey Withers 1965; m 2nd Abdul-Rahman Ayyoub 1980; one d. *Education:* Henrietta Barnett School (London), Univs of Bristol and London and St Antony's Coll (Oxford). *Career:* Medical Practitioner various hosps 1964–72; became active in Palestinian politics 1970, Founder Palestine Action 1972–78, Palestine Medical Aid 1972–82, acts as Spokesperson on radio and TV on Palestinian and Middle East politics; Research Asst Univ of London 1972–80; Gen Medical Practitioner 1981–83; Public Health Specialist 1984–, specializing in the study of effects of migration on health (est unit within Nat Health Service); Consultant Physician in Public Health NW and NE Thames Regional Health Authorities 1989–95; Research Assoc SOAS, Univ of London 1990–, Research Fellow in History of Medicine, Wellcome Inst; Trustee Medical Aid for Palestinians. *Publications:* An Early Arabic Medical Dictionary (ed) 1991; various articles on the history of Arabic medicine and on the Arab–Israeli conflict. *Leisure interests:* theatre, opera, walking, history of medicine. *Address:* University of Durham, Centre for Middle Eastern and Islamic Studies, South Rd, Durham DH1 3TG, UK (Office); 51 Hodford Rd, London NW11 8NL, UK (Home).

KARPAN, Kathleen Marie, BS, MA, JD; American state official, lawyer and journalist; b 1 Sept 1942, Rock Springs, WY; d of Thomas and Pauline (née Taucher) Karpan. *Education:* Univs of Wyoming and Oregon. *Career:* Asst News Ed Cody Enterprise, WY 1964; press asst to Teno Roncalio, House of Reps, Washington, DC 1965–67, 1971–72, Admin Asst 1973–74; Asst News Ed, Wyoming Eagle, Cheyenne 1967; freelance writer 1968; teaching asst Dept of History, Univ of Wyoming 1969–70; Desk Ed Canberra Times, Australia 1970; Deputy Dir Office of Congressional Relations, Econ Devt Admin, Dept of Commerce, Washington, DC 1979–80; Attorney Adviser Office of Chief Counsel, Econ Devt Admin 1980–81; Campaign Man Rodger McDaniel 1981–82; Asst Attorney-Gen State of WY, Cheyenne 1983–84, Dir Dept of Health and Social Services 1984–86, Sec of State 1987–95; Dir Surface Mining Reclamation, Dept of the Interior 1997–2000, Deputy Asst Sec of the Interior for Lands and Minerals Man 2000–; mem Washington Bar Asscn, Nat Asscn of Secs of State. *Address:* Department of the Interior, 1951 Constitution Ave, NW, Washington, DC 20240, USA.

KARSIM, Marynur; Chinese party official; b 15 August 1929, Ili, Xinjiang; d of the late Ababakry and Guly; m Ahmatjan Karsim 1945 (died 1949); one s one d. *Education:* Cen Coll of the Communist Party of China. *Career:* Mem Cttee 2nd Nat People's Political Consultative of China, 1st, 2nd, 5th Nat People's Political Consultative of Uygur Autonomous Region of Xinjiang; Deputy 2nd, 3rd CCP Congress, 1st, 2nd, 3rd, 5th, 6th, 7th Uygur Autonomous Region NPC, 2nd, 3rd, 6th, 7th NPC; Clerk Nat Lead Org; Vice-Chair Nat Women's Asscn of

China, NPC of Uygur Autonomous Region; named Excellent Nat Worker, Cttee of Women and Children's Work Adjustment 1991. *Leisure interest:* sociological research. *Address:* National People's Congress of Xinjiang Uygur Autonomous Region, 10 Dongfeng Rd, Yurumqi, Xinjiang, People's Republic of China. *Telephone:* (991) 228645.

KARTOMI, Margaret Joy, AM, D PHIL, FAHA; Australian musicologist; b 24 Nov 1940, Adelaide; d of George and Edna Hutchesson; m Hidris Kartomi 1960; one d. *Education:* Univ of Adelaide and Humboldt Univ. *Career:* Chair, Lecturer in Music Monash Univ 1969–70, Sr Lecturer 1971–73, Reader 1974–88, Prof of Music, Head of Dept 1988–, Dir Inst of Contemporary Asian Studies 1989–91; Visiting Prof Univ of California at Berkeley 1986–87; Dir Monash-ANZ Centre for Int Briefing 1988, Monash Asia Inst 1988, Symposium of Int Musicological Soc, Melbourne 1988; Dir-at-Large Int Musicology Soc 1993–; Fellow Acad of Humanities 1982–; Alexander Clarke Prize for Pianoforte Performance 1960; Dr Ruby Davy Prize for Musical Composition 1961; German Record Critics' Prize 1983, 1999. *Publications include:* On Concepts and Classifications of Musical Instruments 1990; has written or edited eight other books and 100 articles and 300 articles in the New Grove Dictionary of Musical Instruments 1989. *Leisure interests:* tennis, badminton, concerts, theatre. *Address:* Monash University, Dept of Music, Wellington Rd, Clayton, Vic 3168, Australia (Office); 83 Grand View Rd, Wheelers Hill, Vic 3150, Australia (Home). *Telephone:* (3) 9565 3238 (Office); (3) 9560 3966 (Home); *Fax:* (3) 9905 3241; *E-mail:* margaretkartomi@arts.monash.edu.au.

KASATKINA, Natalya Dmitriyevna; Russian ballet dancer and choreographer; b 7 June 1934, Moscow; d of Dmitry A. Kasatkin and Anna A. (née Kardashova) Kasatkina; m Vladimir Vasilyov 1956; one s. *Education:* Bolshoi Theatre Ballet School (Moscow). *Career:* Dancer Bolshoi Theatre Ballet Company 1954–76; Chief Choreographer Moscow State Ballet Theatre 1977–; choreographed many ballets including Vanini Vanini 1962, Geologist 1964, Rites of the Sacred Spring 1965, Tristan and Isolde 1967, Preludes and Fugues 1968, Our Yard 1970, The Creation of the World 1971, Romeo and Juliet 1972, Prozrienie 1974, Gayane 1977, Mayakovsky (opera) 1981, Adam and Eve (film) 1982, The Magic Frock Cloak 1982, The Mischiefs of Terpsichore 1984, Blue Roses for a Ballerina 1985, Pushkin 1986, The Faces of Love 1987, Petersburg's Twilights 1987, Swan Lake 1988, The Fairy's Kiss 1989, Don Quixote (film ballet) 1990, Cinderella (also produced) 1993, Nutcracker (also produced) 1994, The Lady with Camelias (also libretto and production) 1995, Wonderful Mandarin (also libretto and production) 1996, Firebird (also libretto and production) 2000, Spartacus (also original libretto and production) 2002; Jt Head Moscow Classical Ballet 1977–; co-wrote libretto and co-produced opera Peter I 1975, Così fan Tutte 1978; Laureate of the Int Ballet Dancers and Choreographers Competitions; State Prize of USSR 1976; Order 'Red Banner of Labour' 1976; People's Actress of RSFSR 1984; People's Friendship Award 1994. *Ballets danced include:* Spartacus, Carmen, Rites of the Sacred Spring and others *Films include:* Choreographic Novels (TV), Blue Roses for a Ballerina, Romeo and Juliet, Nutcracker, Rites of the Sacred Spring, The Fairy's Kiss. *Leisure interests:* drawing, cooking. *Address:* Classical Ballet Theatre, 103012 Moscow, Pushechnaya 2/6, Russian Federation; 103006 Moscow, Karetny Riad ul 5/10, kv 37, Russian Federation (Home). *Telephone:* (095) 924-55-24 (Office); (095) 299-95-24 (Home); *Fax:* (095) 251-26-91 (Office); (095) 921-31-27 (Home); *Internet:* www.classicalballet.ru.

KASRASHVILI, Makvala; Georgian opera singer (soprano); b 13 March 1948, Kutaisi; d of Filimon Kasrashvili and Nina Nanikashvili; m (divorced). *Education:* Tbilisi Conservatory. *Career:* Soloist with Bolshoi Theatre, Moscow 1968; has performed internationally, including Royal Opera House, Covent Garden, London; Georgian State Prize 1983; People's Artist of USSR 1986; Grand Prix, Montréal Vocal Competition (PQ, Canada). *Operas include:* La Traviata, Eugene Onegin, Iolanthe, Tosca, Turandot, Aida, The Gambler. *Leisure interest:* driving cars. *Address:* Bolshoi Theatre, Moscow, Teatralnaya pl 1, Moscow, Russian Federation. *Telephone:* (095) 200-58-00.

KASSAYE, Elizabeth; Ethiopian organization executive; b 19 March 1960, Addis Ababa; d of Tekle Kassaye and Dechassa Ayelech. *Education:* Empress Menen Secondary School (Addis Ababa), Lakeview High School (IL, USA) and Univ of Addis Ababa. *Career:* Trans Embassy of the USA 1976–79; Producer Voice of Ethiopia radio programmes 1979–81; Information Officer Christian Relief and Devt Asscn 1981–82; Mass Media Consultant UN ECA/FAO Jt Agric Div 1982; Int Relations Officer Ethiopian Peace, Solidarity and Friendship Cttee 1984–85; apptd Head Press and Information Dept Ethiopian Red Cross Soc 1985–86, Int Relations Bureau 1986–90, Public Relations and Dissemination Dept 1990. *Publication:* From Disaster Relief to Development 1988. *Leisure interests:* tennis, swimming, reading. *Address:* Ethiopian Red Cross Society, Public Relations and Dissemination Dept, POB 195, Addis Ababa, Ethiopia (Office); POB 40178, Addis Ababa, Ethiopia (Home). *Telephone:* (1) 153139 (Office); (1) 167487 (Home); *Fax:* (1) 512643 (Office).

KASSEBAUM, Nancy Landon, MA; American politician; b 29 July 1932, Topeka; d of Alfred M. Kassebaum and Theo Landon; three s one d; m 2nd Howard Baker 1996. *Education:* Univs of Kansas and Michigan. *Career:* Mem Washington staff of Senator James B. Pearson of Kansas 1975–76; Senator (Republican) from Kansas 1979–97, mem several senate cttees; mem Bd Trustees Robert Wood Johnson Foundation 1997–. *Address:* c/o Robert Wood Johnson Foundation, College Rd E, POB 2316, Princeton, NJ 08543, USA.

KASURINEN, Anna-Liisa; Finnish politician; b 8 May 1940, Kivijärvi; d of Otto and Ida (née Autio) Oksanen; m Lauri Kasurinen 1989; three c. *Career:* Psychiatric nurse Pitkäniemi Hosp 1964–66; mem Kotka Town Council 1972, Chair 1981; mem Council SDP 1978; mem Presidential Electorate 1978, 1982; became mem Eduskunta (Parl) 1979; Minister of Educ 1987–92; mem Cen Admin Bd, Asscn of Nursing 1976–79. *Address:* c/o Ministry of Education, Meritullinkatu 10, POB 293, 00171 Helsinki, Finland.

KATZ, Hilda; American poet and artist; b 2 June 1909; d of Max and Lina (née Schwartz) Katz. *Education:* Nat Acad of Design. *Career:* Solo exhibitions include Bowdoin Coll Art Museum 1951, California State Library 1953, Jewish Museum 1956, Ball State Teachers' Coll 1957, Miami Beach Art Center, Richmond Art Asscn 1959, State Museum of Albany 1989, Jewish Theological Seminary of America 1989; special collections include US Nat Museum 1965, Univ of Maine 1965, Library of Congress 1965–71, Metropolitan Museum of Art 1965–66, 1980, Nat Gallery of Art 1966, Nat Collection of Fine Arts 1966–71, Nat Air and Space Museum 1970, New York Public Library 1971, 1978, US Museum of History and Tech 1972, Naval Museum 1972, Smithsonian Inst 1979, Israel Nat Museum (Jerusalem) 1980–81, Jewish Heritage (New York) 1989, Jewish Nat and Univ Library (Israel) 1990; works in perm collections including Fogg Museum, Colorado Springs Fine Arts Center, Newark Public Library, Addison Gallery of American Art, Safed Museum (Israel), Musée Nat d'Art Contemporain (Paris, France), Yad Vashem Memorial Archives (Israel); commemorative poetry at New York State Museum of Art. *Publications include:* (as Hilda Weber) Anthologies: The Bloom 1984–85, 1987, Perfume and Fragrance 1988, 1989, Lightning and Rainbows 1989, 1990. *Address:* 915 W End Ave, Apt 5D, New York, NY 10025, USA.

KAUGER, Yvonne, BS, JD; American judge; b 3 Aug 1937, Cordell, OK; d of John and Alice (née Bottom) Kauger; m Ned Bastow 1982; one d. *Education:* Southwestern State Univ, St Anthony's Hosp and Oklahoma City Univ. *Career:* Assoc Rogers, Travis and Jordan 1970–72; Judicial Asst Oklahoma Supreme Court 1972–84, Judge 1984–94, Vice-Chief Judge 1994–96, Chief Judge 1997–98, Judge 1998–; mem Appellate Div Court on Judiciary; mem State Capitol Preservation Comm 1983–84; mem Dean's Advisory Comm Faculty of Law, Oklahoma City Univ; Founder Gallery of Plains Indian 1987; mem Bd of Dirs Lyric Theatre Inc 1966–, Pres 1981; mem ABA; Oklahoma Business and Professional Women's Woman of the Year 1984; Oklahoma Trial Lawyers' Appellate Judge of the Year 1987; Down Towner Award, Red Earth 1990; Woman of the Year Award, Red Lands County Girl Scouts 1990; apptd to Washita Co Hall of Fame 1992; adopted by Cheyenne-Arapaho tribes 1985.

KAUR, Bibi Jagir; Indian religious leader; m (husband deceased); two d. *Career:* Fmr maths teacher; fmr Minister in Punjab State Govt; fmr Pres Shiromani Gurudwara Prabandhak Cttee (Sikh body). *Address:* Bhulath, Dist Kapurthala, Punjab, India. *Telephone:* (1822) 48051 (Home); *Fax:* (172) 687652.

KAUR, Prabhjot (see Prabhjot, Kaur).

KAUR, Surrinder, MD; Indian medical practitioner; b 7 March 1933; d of the late G. S. Talib and Lal Kaur; m Amarjit Singh 1960; two d one s. *Education:* Postgrad Inst of Medical Educ and Research (Chandigarh). *Career:* Registrar Postgrad Inst of Medical Educ and Research 1962–65, Lecturer 1965–72, Asst Prof 1972–79, Assoc Prof 1979–84, Prof and Head of Dermatology 1984–; Examiner and Expert for numerous univs and selection bds; Kshanika Oration Award 1981; Hari Om Ashram Alembic Research Award 1983; Glaxo Oration award 1991; over 200 publications on dermatology. *Leisure interests:* reading, music. *Address:* Postgraduate Institute of Medical Education and Research, Dept of Dermatology, Chandigarh 160 012, India (Office); 58 Sector 24-A Chandigarh 160 023, India (Home). *Telephone:* (172) 541032 (Office).

KAWAKUBO, Rei; Japanese fashion designer; b 1943, Toyko; m Adrian Joffe 1992. *Education:* Keio Univ (Tokyo). *Career:* Joined Asahikasei 1964; freelance designer 1966; launched Comme des Garçons Label 1969; Founder and Pres Comme des Garçons 1973; Japan Comme des Garçons Collection presented twice a year, Tokyo; 395 outlets in Japan, 5 Comme des Garçons shops and 550 outlets outside Japan; currently has 11 lines of clothing, 1 line of furniture, and a perfume; opened 1st overseas Comme des Garçons Boutique in Paris 1982; joined Fed Française de la Couture 1982; Founder Six magazine 1988; created costumes and stage design for Merce Cunningham's Scenario 1997; Dr hc (RCA, London) 1997; Mainichi Newspaper Fashion Award 1983, 1988; Chevalier des Arts et des Lettres. *Address:* c/o Comme des Garçons Co Ltd, 5-11-5 Minamiaoyama, Minatoku, Tokyo, Japan.

KAWECKA, Antonina; Polish opera singer; b 16 Jan 1923, Warsaw; d of Mieczysław and Janina Piekarska; m Antoni Bochniak 1948; one d. *Education:* The Conservatory (Warsaw). *Career:* Made operatic debut in Cavalleria Rusticana 1945; appeared in over 40 operas, Poland 1947–79; numerous guest performances and concerts in various countries including USA, People's Repub of China, fmr Czechslovakia, fmr USSR, Hungary, Yugoslavia, Bulgaria, Germany; tutor Acad of Music, Poznań since 1970; Kt's Cross Polonia Restituta 1953, Officer's Cross 1959, Commdr's Cross 1976; Polish Ministry of Culture Award 1982; Polish Asscn of Vocal Tutors Award 1992. *Operas include:* Carmen, Aida, Otello, Tannhäuser, Il Trovatore, Halka, Hrabina, Eugene Onegin, Un Ballo in Maschera; *Recordings include:* numerous operatic arias and duets, Polish songs of Chopin, Szymanowski and Moniuszko 1961. *Leisure interest:* monographic books. *Address:* Promienista str 164 a/12, 60-159 Poznań, Poland. *Telephone:* (61) 325143.

KAY, Jackie, PH D; British author; b 1961, Edinburgh; d of John and Helen Kay; partner Carol Ann Duffy; one s. *Education:* Stirling Univ (Scotland). *Career:* Worked at Arts Council 1991–93. *Publications:* The Adoption Papers (Eric Gregory Award, Saltire and Forward Prizes) 1991, Other Lovers (Somerset Maugham Award), Bessie 1997, Off Colour 1998, Trumpet (Guardian Fiction Prize) 1998; also several TV documentaries. *Leisure interests:* jazz, theatre, shopping, film. *Address:* c/o Picador Books, Macmillan Publishers, 25 Eccleston Place, London SW1W 9NF, UK.

KAYE, Mary Margaret, FRSL; British writer and illustrator; d of the late Sir Cecil and Lady Kaye; m G. Hamilton (died 1985); two d. *Career:* Writer of historical and detective novels and of books for children; illustrator. *Publications include:* Historical Novels: The Far Pavilions 1978 (TV adaptation 1984), Shadow of the Moon (2nd edn) 1979, Trade Wind (2nd edn) 1981; Detective Novels: Six Bars at Seven 1940, Death Walks in Kashmir (published as Death in Kashmir 1984) 1956, Later Than You Think (published as Death in Kenya 1983) 1958, House of Shade (published as Death in Zanzibar 1983) 1959, Night on the Island (published as Death in the Andamans 1985) 1960, Death in Berlin 1985; Children's Books: The Potter Pinner Books 1937–41, The Ordinary Princess 1980, Thistledown 1981; Autobiography Share of Summer: The Sun in the Morning (Vol 1) 1990, Golden Afternoon (Vol II) 1997, Enchanted Evening (Vol III) 1997; Illustrator: The Story of St Francis, Children of Galilee, Adventures in a Caravan. *Leisure interest:* painting.

KAZANKINA, Tatyana; Russian athlete; b 17 Dec 1951, Petrovsk, Saratov; d of Vasily Kazanking and Maria Kazankina; m Alexandre Kovalenko 1974; one d. *Career:* Int athlete since 1972; European Indoor Silver Medallist 1975; Olympic Gold Medallist 800m and 1500m, Montréal, Canada 1976, Gold Medallist 1500m Moscow 1980; held World records at 800m and 1500m (three times), 2000m, 3000m, 4×800 m; World Championships Bronze Medal 1983; suspended for life by Int Amateur Athletics Fed (IAAF) 1984, reinstated 1985; economist, St Petersburg; Asst Prof St Petersburg Acad of Physical Culture; Pres St Petersburg Union of Athletes; Hon PH D 1992; Hon Master of Sport 1976. *Leisure interests:* travel, human contacts. *Address:* c/o Light Athletic Federation, St Petersburg, Millonnaia ul 22, Russian Federation (Office); St Petersburg, Hoshimina ul 11-1-211, Russian Federation (Home). *Telephone:* (812) 114-69-31 (Office); (812) 595-09-40 (Home); *Fax:* (812) 315-97-95.

KAZARNOVSKAYA, Ljuba; Russian opera singer (soprano); b 18 July 1956, Moscow; m Robert Roszyk 1989. *Education:* Moscow Gnessin School of Music and Moscow Conservatory. *Career:* Professional debut as Tatyana in Eugene Onegin at Stanislawsky Opera Theatre, Moscow 1981; singer Stanislawsky Theatre 1981–89, Bolshoi Theatre 1986–89, Kirov Ballet, St Petersburg (fmrly Leningrad) 1989, Salzburg 1990, Royal Opera House, Covent Garden (London) 1991, Metropolitan Opera (New York) 1991, Vienna 1992; moved to Vienna 1989, has performed in maj opera houses of the world, in opera productions with Herbert von Karajan, Carlos Kleiber, Claudio Abbado, Riccardo Muti, Daniel Barenboim, James Conlon, Mrowinsky, Haitink, Svetlanov, Steinberg, Jansons and Temirkanov; also performs in concerts, including Requiem (Verdi), La voix humaine by Poulenc, and at festivals in Salzburg, Bregenz, Edinburgh and others; prize winner All-Union competition of singers 1981, Glinka competition 1981, UNESCO competition 1984, Int competition in Bratislava 1984. *Operas include:* Eugene Onegin, Iolanthe, La Bohème, Pagliacci, Faust, The Marriage of Figaro, Falstaff, The Force of Destiny, Boris Godunov, La Traviata, Salome; *Recordings include:* Don Giovanni (also film), Shostakovich's 14th Symphony; numerous TV appearances. *Leisure interests:* singing, swimming, jewellery, shoes. *Address:* c/o Hohenbergstr 50, 1120 Vienna, Austria.

KAZEM, Fatima M., PH D; Egyptian professor of rural sociology; b 25 Aug 1935, Alexandria; d of the late Mohamed Kazem Layer and Khadiaga Abe-Hadid; m M. Gamal Eldin Rashed 1961; two s one d. *Education:* Univs of Wisconsin (USA) and Assiut. *Career:* Journalist Akhbar Elyem, Cairo 1958–64; Researcher NMRU 3 1968–69; Research Supervisor Arab Inst for Devt, Tripoli, Libya 1975–76; Asst Prof Coll of Arts, King Saud Univ, Riyadh, Saudi Arabia 1986–90; apptd Assoc Prof Faculty of Agric, Univ of Assiut 1990; became mem Integrated Social Services Soc, Assiut 1991, mem Faculty Bd 1992. *Leisure interest:* rural community development. *Address:* University of Assiut, Faculty of Agric, Dept of Rural Sociology and Agricultural Extension, Assiut, Egypt (Office); Assiut Univ Housing, Bldg B, Apt 9, Assiut, Egypt (Home). *Telephone:* (88) 333722 (Office); *Fax:* (88) 332875 (Office).

KAZEMIPOUR, Shahla, M SC S; Iranian demographics researcher; b 28 Feb 1946; m 1969; one s one d. *Education:* Univ of Tehran. *Career:* Lecturer on demography Univ of Tehran 1968–, co-operates with Inst for Social Studies and Research. *Publications:* Social Indicator of Iran 1978, Demographic Analyses 1991; over 50 research papers. *Leisure interests:* reading, researching into social problems. *Address:* Demographic Centre, Institute for Social Studies and Reserach, University of Teheran, Tehran, Iran. *Telephone:* (21) 4883473.

KAZRAGYTE, Doloresa; Lithuanian actress; b 29 Sept 1942, Jaroslavl, Russia; m Viktoras Šinkariukas. *Education:* State Conservatoire (Vilnius). *Career:* Actress Vilnius Academic Theatre and Kalinas Academic Theatre 1968–96; All-Union Theatre Prize 1978; Lithuanian State Theatre Award 1976; Ministry of Culture Award for Best Woman's Part of the Season 1984. *Plays include:* A Streetcar Named Desire 1976, The

Last Ones 1981, Six Personages in Search of the Author 1982, Freken Julia 1984, Outcry 1984, The Creditors, By a Hairbreath from Destruction 1995; *Publications include:* The Railless Bridge (essays) 1986, Life Before the Life (essays) 1995, Pirelli (play) 1985, Rock 'n' Roll for Tomorrow (radio play, Lithuanian State Radio award 1996). *Leisure interest:* the countryside. *Address:* J Basanavičiaus al 51–19, Kaunas, Lithuania. *Telephone:* (7) 793-467.

KBIR-ARIGUIB, Najia, D ÈS SC; Tunisian scientist; b 26 Sept 1937, Tunis; m Abdelmagid Ariguib 1961; three s. *Education:* Univ of Paris. *Career:* Apptd Prof of Inorganic Chem Coll of Science, King Saud Univ, Riyadh, Saudi Arabia 1978, School of Higher Educ Univ of Sciences, Techniques and Medicine (Tunis II); Dir Nat Inst for Scientific and Tech Research 1983–87; Head Research Team carrying out studies in the field of phosphates, briny water and clays; mem Admin Council Research Center for Medical Studies and Sciences, Section for Women Students Center, Planning Cttee for setting up new scientific bldgs; Pres Advisory Comm for Recruiting Univ Profs of Chem; Vice-Pres Nat Comm of Mastership and Promotion of Industrial Tech; mem Nat Comm of Extra-Atmospheric Space, Nat Comm of Environment; has written more than 35 scientific publications; Fellow African Acad of Sciences, Third World Acad of Science 1985; Commandant de l'Ordre de L'Indépendance 1983. *Leisure interest:* reading. *Address:* King Saud University, College of Science, POB 22452, Riyadh 11495, Saudi Arabia (Office); 4 rue de la Jeunesse, 2033 Mégrine, Tunis, Tunisia (Home). *Telephone:* (1) 4785468 (Office); (1) 295273 (Home); *Fax:* (1) 430917 (Home).

KEARSE, Amalya Lyle, BA, JD; American federal judge and bridge player; b 11 June 1937, Vauxhall, NJ; d of Robert and Myra (née Smith) Kearse. *Education:* Wellesley Coll and Univ of Michigan. *Career:* Called to the Bar, NY 1963, US Supreme Court 1967; Assoc Hughes, Hubbard and Reed 1962–69, Partner 1969–79; Judge US Court of Appeals (2nd circuit) 1979–; Lecturer in Evidence Law Faculty, Univ of New York 1968–69; mem Bd of Dirs Nat Assocn for the Advancement of Colored People (NAACP) Legal Defence and Educational Fund 1977–79, Nat Urban League 1978–79; mem Editorial Bd Charles Goren 1974–; mem American Contract Bridge League Nat Laws Comm 1975–; Nat Women's Pairs Bridge Champion 1971, 1972, World Women's Pairs Champion 1986; Nat Teams Bridge Champion 1987, 1990, 1991; mem ABA, American Law Inst, Lawyers Comm for Civil Rights Under Law. *Publications:* Bridge Convention Complete 1975, Official Encyclopedia of Bridge (ed) 1976, Bridge Analysis (ed and trans) 1979, Bridge at Your Fingertips 1980. *Address:* US Court of Appeals, US Courthouse, Foley Square, New York, NY 10007, USA.

KEATON, Diane; American actress; b 5 Jan 1946, Santa Clara, CA. *Education:* Santa Clara Coll and Neighborhood Playhouse (New York). *Career:* Acting debut in Hair (New York) 1968; Directorial debut What Does Dorrie Want? 1982; has written several books on photography. *Plays include:* Play It Again Sam 1971, The Primary English Class 1976; *Films include:* Lovers and Other Strangers 1970, Play It Again Sam 1972, The Godfather 1972, Sleeper 1973, The Godfather Part II 1974, Love and Death 1975, I Will... I Will... For Now 1975, Harry and Walter Go To New York 1976, Annie Hall (Acad Award for Best Actress and other awards) 1977, Looking for Mr Goodbar 1977, Interiors 1978, Manhattan 1979, Reds 1981, Shoot the Moon 1982, Mrs Soffel 1985, Crimes of the Heart 1986, Trial and Error 1986, Radio Days 1987, Heaven (dir) 1987, Baby Boom 1988, The Good Mother 1988, The Lemon Sisters (producer) 1989, Running Mates 1989, The Godfather III, Secret Society (dir), Father of the Bride 1991, Twin Peaks (TV, dir), Manhattan Murder Mystery 1993, Unsung Heroes (dir) 1995, Father of the Bride II 1995, Marvin's Room, The First Wives Club 1996, The Only Thrill 1997, Hanging Up (also Dir) 1999, The Other Sister 1999, Town and Country 1999; *Publications:* Reservations (co-ed), Still Life (ed). *Address:* c/o John Burnham, William Morris Agency, 151 S El Camino Drive, Beverly Hills, CA 90212, USA.

KEDZIEZARWSKA, Dorota; Polish film director; b 1957, Łódź. *Education:* Cinema School Łódź, pupil of Wojciech Has. *Career:* Directs short and feature length films. *Films include:* Les diables, les diables (presented at Cannes Film Festival) 1991, Les Corneilles 1996.

KEHUSMAA-PEKONEN, Saara Tellervo, M SC, MBA; Finnish business executive; b 25 Nov 1941, Rovaniemi; d of Ali Armas and Senja Maria Kehusmaa (née Ronkainen); m Kari Pekonen 1969. *Education:* Helsinki. *Career:* Teacher at commercial coll (Espoo) 1967–71; Research Asst, IMF (Washington, DC, USA) 1973–75; Planner and Co-ordinator Helsinki School of Econ 1975–80, Sr Lecturer 1983–; Sr Training Adviser, Training Man PRODEC (Programme for Devt Co-operation), Helsinki School of Econs and Business Admin 1980–84, apptd Exec Dir 1985; Team Leader TACIS Tech Office (Minsk, Belarus) 1996–97; Order of the Lion of Finland 1993. *Address:* PRODEC, Töölönkatu 11A, 00100 Helsinki, Finland. *Telephone:* (0) 43138261; *Fax:* (0) 409880.

KEITH, Penelope Anne Constance, OBE; British actress; b 2 April 1940, Sutton, Surrey; d of Frederick Hatfield and Constance Mary Keith; m Rodney Timson 1978. *Education:* Annecy Convent (Seaford, Sussex), Convent Bayeux (France) and Webber Douglas School (London). *Career:* Made professional debut Civic Theatre, Chesterfield 1959; appeared in repertory Lincoln, Salisbury, Manchester 1960–63, Cheltenham 1967; mem RSC Stratford 1963, Aldwych 1965; Pres Actors' Benevolent Fund 1990–; Gov Queen Elizabeth's Foundation for the Disabled 1989–, Guildford School of Acting 1991–; Trustee Yvonne Arnaud Theatre 1992–; Best Light Entertainment Performance, British Acad of Film and TV Arts 1976, Best Actress 1977; Show Business Personality, Variety Club of GB 1976; BBC TV Personality 1979, Comedy Performance of the Year, Soc of West End Theatres (SWET) 1976, Female TV Personality, TV Times Awards 1976–78, BBC TV Personality of the Year 1978–79, TV Female Personality, Daily Express 1979–82. *Plays include:* Suddenly at Home 1971, The Norman Conquests 1974, Donkey's Years 1976, The Apple Cart 1977, The Millionairess 1978, Moving 1980, Hobson's Choice, Captain Brassbound's Conversion 1982, Hay Fever 1983, The Dragon's Tail 1985, Miranda 1987, The Deep Blue Sea 1988, Dear Charles 1990, The Merry Wives of Windsor 1990, The Importance of Being Earnest 1991, On Approval 1992, Relatively Speaking 1992, Glyn and It 1994, Monsieur Amilcar 1995, Mrs Warren's Profession 1997, Good Grief 1998; *Films include:* Rentadick, Take a Girl Like You, Every Home Should Have One, Sherlock Holmes, The Priest of Love; *TV appearances include:* The Good Life (Good Neighbors in USA) 1974–77, Private Lives 1976, The Norman Conquests 1977, To the Manor Born 1979–81, On Approval 1980, Spider's Web, Sweet Sixteen, Waters of the Moon, Hay Fever, Moving, Executive Stress, What's my Line? 1988, Growing Places, No Job for a Lady 1990, Law and Disorder 1994, Next of Kin, Coming Home 1999. *Leisure interest:* gardening. *Address:* London Management, 2 Noel St, London W1V 3RB, UK. *Telephone:* (20) 7287-9000.

KELLER, Evelyn Fox, PH D; American biophysicist; b 20 March 1936, New York; m Joseph B. Keller 1964 (divorced); one son one d. *Education:* Radcliffe Coll, Brandeis and Harvard Univs. *Career:* Asst Research Scientist, New York Univ 1963–66, Assoc Prof 1970–72; Assoc Prof State Univ of New York, Purchase 1972–82; Prof of Maths and Humanities, Northwestern Univ 1982–88; Prof Univ of Calif at Berkeley 1988–92; Prof of History and Philosophy of Science MIT 1992–; mem Inst of Advanced Studies, Princeton 1987–88; Visiting Fellow, later Scholar, MIT 1979–84, Visiting Prof 1985–86. *Publications include:* A Feeling for the Organism 1983, Reflections on Gender and Science 1985, Secrets of Life, Secrets of Death 1992, Keywords in Evolutionary Biology (Ed) 1994, Refiguring Life 1995, Feminism and Science (co-author) 1996, The Century of the Gene 2000. *Address:* Massachusetts Institute of Technology, E51-263B, 77 Massachusetts Ave, Cambridge, MA 02139, USA. *Telephone:* (617) 253-1000; *Fax:* (617) 253-8000; *Internet:* web.mit.edu.

KELLETT-BOWMAN, Dame Mary Elaine, DBE, MA; British politician; b 8 July 1924; d of the late Walter Kay; m 1st Charles Norman Kellett 1945 (deceased); three s one d; m 2nd Edward Thomas Kellett-Bowman 1971. *Education:* Queen Mary School (Lytham), The Mount School (York), St Anne's Coll and Barnett House (Oxford). *Career:* Called to Bar of England and Wales 1964; Lay mem Press Council 1964–68; Alderman Camden Borough Council 1968–74, Vice-Chair Housing Cttee 1968, Chair Welfare Cttee 1969; MP (Cons) for Lancaster 1970–97; MEP for Cumbria and N Lancs 1975–84; mem Social Affairs and Regional Policy Cttees 1975–84; mem Union of

European Women 1956; Del to Luxembourg 1958; Pres Bowland Village Trust 1990–96; Pres Nat Asscn of Widows 1999–; No 1 Country Housewife 1960; Christal MacMillan Law Prize 1963. *Leisure interests:* gardening, collecting and repairing antiques. *Address:* Endymion, Ampfield, Romsey, Hants SO51 9BD, UK; Redman House, 8 King's Arcade, Lancaster, UK (Home).

KELLEY, Kitty; American writer; b 1943; m Michael Edgley (divorced). *Career:* Fmr Press Asst; Researcher Washington Post; freelance journalist and writer of biographies 1971–; has written articles for magazines and newspapers including New York Times, Newsweek, McCall's, Los Angeles Times, Chicago Tribune; currently developing TV show The Kitty Kelley Show; awards include Outstanding Author Award (American Soc of Journalists and Authors) 1987, Philip M. Stern Award, named one of the most influential people in Washington, DC (Regardie's magazine), named one of 1991's Power Brokers (M.Inc magazine), Media Decade Hall of Fame (Vanity Fair). *Publications:* Jackie Oh! 1979, Elizabeth Taylor: The Last Star, His Way: The Unauthorized Biography of Frank Sinatra 1986, Nancy Reagan: The Unauthorized Biography 1991, The Royals 2001.

KELLY, Cathy; Irish writer; b Belfast. *Career:* Fmr Journalist, Dublin. *Publications include:* Woman to Woman, She's the One, Never Too Late, Someone Like You (Parker Romantic Novel of the Year) 2001. *Leisure interest:* reading. *Address:* c/o HarperCollins (author mail), Ophelia House, Fulham Palace Rd, London W6, UK. *Internet:* www.cathy-kelly .com.

KELLY, Judith Pamela (Jude), OBE, BA; British theatre director; b 24 March 1954, Liverpool; d of John and Ida Kelly; m Michael Bird 1983; one d one s. *Education:* Calder High School (Liverpool) and Univ of Birmingham. *Career:* Freelance folk and jazz singer 1970–75; Actress Leicester Phoenix Theatre 1975–76; Founder Solent People's Theatre Dir 1976–80; Artistic Dir Battersea Arts Centre (BAC) 1980–85; Dir of Plays Nat Theatre of Brent 1982–85; freelance dir 1985–88; Festival Dir York Festival and Mystery Plays 1988; Artistic Dir West Yorkshire Playhouse 1988–, Chief Exec 1993–; Chair Qualifications and Curriculum Authority Advisory Group on the Arts 2001–; mem Ind TV Comm 2000–; Hon Fellow Dartington Coll of Arts; Hon D LITT (Leeds Metropolitan) 1995, (Bradford) 1996, (Leeds) 2000, (York) 2001, (Open Univ) 2001. *Productions include:* The Seagull, The Tempest, The Elixir of Love (for English Nat Opera), Singin' in the Rain (2001 Olivier Award for Outstanding Musical Production), Half A Sixpence, Johnson Over Jordan. *Leisure interest:* windsurfing. *Address:* West Yorkshire Playhouse, Playhouse Square, Quarry Hill, Leeds LS2 7UP, UK. *Telephone:* (113) 2137800; *Fax:* (113) 2137250; *Internet:* www.wyp.co .uk.

KELLY, Ros, BA, DIP ED; Australian politician; b 25 Jan 1948, Sydney; d of M. and P. Raw; m David Morgan; one s one d. *Education:* Univ of Sydney. *Career:* High School teacher, NSW and ACT 1969–74; consultant and mem ACT Consumer Affairs Council 1974–79; mem ACT Legal Aid Comm 1976–79, House of Reps (Parl) 1980–95; fmr mem ACT Legis Ass; Sec Fed Lab Party Parl Caucus 1981–87; Minister for Defence Science and Personnel 1987–89, for Telecommunications and Aviation Support 1989–90, for the Arts 1990–93, for Sport, the Environment, Tourism and Territories 1990–94, Assisting the Prime Minister for the Status of Women 1993–94; mem Int Advisory Council, Normandy Ltd 1995–; Group Exec Dames and Moore, Australia and Asia 1995–; Dir Environmental Resources Man, Thiess Pty, Ltd, Greenfleet; Trustee World Wildlife Fund. *Leisure interests:* tennis, reading, films, aerobics. *Address:* c/o Dames and Moore, 1/41 McLaren St, N Sydney, NSW 2060, Australia; Building C, 33 Saunders St, Pyrmont, NSW 2009, Australia. *Telephone:* (2) 9955-7772; *Fax:* (2) 9955-7324.

KELLY, Sharon Pratt, BA, JD; American lawyer and politician (mayor); b 30 Jan 1944, Washington, DC; d of Carlisle and Mildred (née Petticord) Pratt; m 1st Arrington L. Dixon 1966 (divorced 1982); two d; m 2nd James R. Kelly, III 1991; one step-d. *Education:* Howard Univ (Washington, DC). *Career:* Called to the Bar, US Dist Court, US Court of Appeals, DC, US Tax Court 1970; Assoc Pratt and Queen PC 1971–76; lawyer, Prof Antioch School of Law, Washington, DC 1972–76; Assoc Gen Counsel Potomac Electric and Power Co 1976–79,

Dir Consumer Affairs 1979–83, Vice-Pres Consumer Affairs 1983–86, Vice-Pres Public Policy 1986–89; elected Mayor Washington, DC 1991–95; Chair Eastern Regional Caucus Nat Democratic Cttee 1976–85, Treas 1985–; Nat Ctteeperson Dist of Columbia State Cttee 1977; mem Bd Dirs Women's Research and Educational Inst 1986–88, Dist of Columbia Unified Bar, Dist of Columbia Bar Asscn; Hon D IUR (Howard, George Washington and Georgetown Univs and St Mary's Coll); Presidential Award 1983; Distinguished Service Award, Fed of Women's Clubs 1986, Nat Asscn of Black Women Attorneys 1987, 1988; Ebony Magazine Achievement Award 1991; Mary McCleod Bethune–W. E. B. DuBois Award 1991. *Address:* 1525 Iris St, NW, Washington, DC 20012, USA. *Telephone:* (202) 727-5011.

KELMENDI, Aferdita; Yugoslav (Serbian/Kosovan) broadcaster; b 1956; m. *Career:* Broadcaster with state-controlled radio station until 1989; Founder Radio 21 (Kosovo's first pvtly-run radio station) 1999. *Address:* Radio 21, Pristina, Kosovo, Serbia, Yugoslavia.

KELTOŠOVÁ, Ol'ga, B SC; Slovak politician; b 27 Feb 1943, Pezinok; m (divorced); one d one s. *Education:* Comenius Univ (Bratislava). *Career:* Worked on student magazines Echo of Bratislava Students and The Student, both proscribed in 1968; Translator Faculty of Natural History, Comenius Univ 1970–71; Press Sec Democratic Party 1989, expelled from Party 1991; mem Slovak Nat Council (Parl) 1990, Deputy Chair 1990–92; mem Movt for a Democratic Slovakia (HZDS) 1992–; Minister of Labour, Social Affairs and Family 1992–94; Chair Co-ordinating Cttee on Matters of Handicapped Citizens 1995, Co-ordinating Body for Problems of Women 1996–; mem Parl of Slovak Repub 1998–. *Address:* Political Party for Democratic Slovakia (HZDS), Tomásikova 32/A, Bratislava 1, Slovakia. *Telephone:* (7) 433-301-44.

KEMPSTON DARKES, V. Maureen, BA, LL B; Canadian business executive; b 31 July 1948, Toronto, ON; m Lawrence J. Darkes. *Education:* Univ of Toronto. *Career:* Mem Legal Staff Gen Motors of Canada Ltd 1975–79, Asst Counsel 1979, Head Tax Staff 1980–84, Gen Dir Public Affairs 1987, Vice-Pres of Corp Affairs and mem Bd Dirs 1991, Gen Counsel and Sec 1992, Pres and Gen Man 1994–; mem Legal Staff Gen Motors Corpn (Detroit, MI, USA) 1979–80, mem staff Treasurer's Office (New York, NY) 1985–87, Vice-Pres 1994–; mem Bd Dirs Hughes Aircraft of Canada, CAMI Automotive, CN Rail, Brascan Ltd, Thomson Corpn, Nat Quality Inst, Nat Research Council; mem Arts and Science Advisory Bd Univ of Toronto, Bd of Govs Univ of Waterloo, Business School Advisory Cttee Univ of Western Ontario, Bd Dirs Women's Coll Hosp Foundation, Bd New Directions; Hon D COMM (St Mary's) 1995; Hon LL D (Victoria, Toronto) 1996. *Address:* General Motors of Canada Ltd, 1908 Colonel Sam Drive, Oshawa, ON L1H 8P7, Canada.

KENDAL, Felicity, CBE; British actress; b 25 Sept 1946; d of Geoffrey and Laura Kendal; m 1st (divorced); one s; m 2nd Michael Rudman 1983 (divorced 1991); one s. *Education:* Six convents in India. *Career:* Made debut 1947, aged nine months in A Midsummer Night's Dream; grew up touring India and Far East with parents' theatre co; returned to UK 1965; London debut as Carla in Minor Murder, Savoy Theatre 1967; Variety Club Most Promising Newcomer 1974; Best Actress 1979; Clarence Derwent Award 1980; Rear of the Year Award; Evening Standard Best Actress Award 1989, Variety Club Best Actress Award 2000. *Plays include:* Henry V, The Promise 1968, Back to Methuselah, A Midsummer Night's Dream, Much Ado About Nothing 1970, 1989, Kean 1970, 1971, Romeo and Juliet, 'Tis Pity She's a Whore 1972, The Three Arrows 1972, The Norman Conquests 1974, Once Upon a Time 1976, Arms and The Man 1978, Clouds 1978, Amadeus, Othello, On the Razzle 1981, The Second Mrs Tanqueray, The Real Thing 1982, Jumpers 1985, Made in Bangkok 1986, Hapgood 1988, Ivanov 1989, Hidden Laughter 1990, Tartuffe 1991, Heartbreak House 1992, Arcadia 1992, An Absolute Turkey 1994, Indian Ink 1995, Mind Millie for Me 1996, The Seagull 1997, Waste 1997, Alarms and Excursions 1998, Fallen Angels 2000; *TV appearances include:* The Good Life (Good Neighbors in USA) 1974–77, Solo, The Mistress, The Woodlanders, Edward VII, Viola in Twelfth Night 1979, The Camomile Lawn 1992, The Mayfly and the Frog, Boy meets Girl, The Tenant of Wildfell Hall, Crimes of Passion, The Dolly Dialogues, Now is Too late, Deadly Earnest, The Marriage Counsellor, Home and Beauty, Favourite Things, How Proust Can Change Your Life 2000;

Films: Shakespeare Wallah 1965, Valentino 1976, Parting Shots; *Publication:* White Cargo (memoirs) 1998. *Leisure interest:* golf. *Address:* c/o Chatto and Linnit, 123A King's Rd, London SW3 4PL, UK. *Telephone:* (20) 7352-7722; *Fax:* (20) 7352-3450.

KENNARD, Olga, (Lady Burgen), OBE, SC D, FRS; British research scientist; b 23 March 1924, Budapest, Hungary; d of Joir and Catherine Weisz; m 1st David Kennard 1948 (divorced 1961); two d; m 2nd Sir Anthony Burgen 1993; two d. *Education:* Schools in Hungary, Prince Henry VIII Grammar School (Evesham) and Newnham Coll (Cambridge). *Career:* Research Asst Cavendish Lab, Cambridge 1944–48; mem MRC Scientific Staff London 1948–61, External Scientific Staff Univ of Cambridge 1961–89; Dir Cambridge Crystallographic Data Centre 1965–97; Head Crystallographic Chem, Univ Chem Lab, Cambridge; MRC Special Appt 1969–89; Visiting Prof Univ of London 1988–90; mem Academia Europaea, Council, Royal Soc 1995–97; has written 20 reference books and more than 200 articles for scientific journals and books on X-ray crystallography, molecular biology, information tech; Royal Soc Chem Prize for Structural Chem 1980. *Leisure interests:* swimming, music, modern architecture and design. *Address:* Keelson, 8A Hills Ave, Cambridge CB1 7XA, UK. *Telephone:* (1223) 415381.

KENNEDY, Angela; Australian swimmer; b 28 Feb 1976, Nambour, Qld; d of Bob and Helen Kennedy. *Education:* Queanbeyan High School. *Career:* Holder of World Record, 50m short course butterfly Feb 1995, Australian Record 50m short course backstroke and 50m butterfly Dec 1995; Gold Medallist Medley Relay, World Short Course Championship, Bronze Medallist 100m butterfly; mem Australian team 1996 Olympics Atlanta, GA, USA 1996; fmr Holder World Record 100m butterfly. *Leisure interests:* surf life-saving, reading, watching videos. *Address:* 19 Silky Oak, Carseldine Grove, Brisbane, Qld 4034, Australia. *Telephone:* (7) 3263-9815; *Fax:* (7) 3263-9815.

KENNEDY, Cornelia Groefsema, BA, JD; American federal judge; b 4 Aug 1923, Detroit, MI; d of Elmer and Mary (née Gibbons) Groefsema; m Charles Kennedy, Jr (deceased); one s. *Education:* Univ of Michigan. *Career:* Called to the Bar, MI 1947; Law Clerk US Court of Appeals, Washington, DC 1947–48; Assoc Elmer H. Groefsema, Detroit 1948–52; Partner Markle and Markle 1952–66; Judge Third Judicial Circuit, MI 1967–70, US Dist Court 1970–79, Chief Judge 1977–79; Circuit Judge US Court of Appeals (6th circuit) 1979–; Fellow American Bar Foundation; mem ABA, Fed Bar Asscn, American Judicature Soc, Nat Asscn of Women Lawyers, American Trial Lawyers Asscn, Nat Conf of Fed Trial Judges; Hon LL D (Northern Michigan, Eastern Michigan) 1971, (Western Michigan) 1973, (Detroit Coll) 1980, (Detroit) 1987. *Address:* US Court of Appeals 744, US Courthouse, 231 W Lafayette Blvd, Detroit, MI 48226, USA.

KENNEDY, Kathleen; American film producer; b 1954; m Frank Marshall. *Education:* San Diego State Univ. *Career:* Fmr camera operator, video ed, floor dir, production co-ordinator for TV; Production Asst on Steven Spielberg's 1941; Founder and Pres Amblin Entertainment 1992; Founder (with Frank Marshall) Kennedy/Marshall Co. *Films include:* Assoc Producer: Raiders of the Lost Ark 1981, Poltergeist 1982, E.T.: The Extra-Terrestrial (producer) 1982, Twilight Zone: The Movie 1983, Indiana Jones and the Temple of Doom 1984; Co-Exec Producer: Gremlins 1984, Goonies 1985, Back to the Future 1985, The Color Purple 1985, Young Sherlock Holmes 1985, An American Tail 1986, Innerspace 1987, Empire of the Sun 1987, Batteries Not Included 1987, Who Framed Roger Rabbit? 1988, The Land Before Time 1988, Indiana Jones and the Last Crusade 1989, Dad 1989, Always 1989, Joe versus the Volcano 1990, Gremlins II: The New Batch 1990, Hook 1991, Noises Off, Alive, A Far Off Place, Jurassic Park 1993, Milk Money, The Bridges of Madison County, Congo, The Indian in the Cupboard, Twister; Exec Producer: Schindler's List, A Dangerous Woman, The Flintstones; *TV includes:* Steven Spielberg's Amazing Stories, You're On, Roger Rabbit and the Secrets of Toontown.

KENNEDY, Pagan, MA; American writer and teacher; b 7 Sept 1962, Washington, DC. *Education:* Wesleyan (CT) and Johns Hopkins Univs (MD). *Career:* Publr Pagan's Head magazine 1988–93; columnist Village Voice 1990–93; Adjunct Instructor Boston Coll 1995–; contribs

to The Nation, Spin, Seventeen, Interview, etc; Nat Endowment for the Arts Award 1993. *Publications:* Stripping and Other Stories 1994, Platforms: A Microwaved Cultural Chronicle of the 1970s 1994, 'Zine 1995, Spinsters 1996. *Address:* High Risk Books, 180 Varick St, New York, NY 10014, USA. *E-mail:* pagan@user1.channel1.com.

KENNEDY OF THE SHAWS, Baroness (Life Peer), cr 1997, of Cathcart in the City of Glasgow, **Helena Ann Kennedy,** QC, FRSA; British lawyer; b 12 May 1950; d of Joshua Kennedy and Mary Jones; partner (Roger) Iain Mitchell 1978–84; one s; m Iain L. Hutchison 1986; one s one d. *Education:* Holyrood Secondary School (Glasgow) and Council of Legal Educ. *Career:* Called to the Bar, Gray's Inn 1972; mem Bar Council 1990–93, CIBA Comm into Child Sexual Abuse 1981–83, Council Howard League for Penal Reform 1989–; Visiting Lecturer British Postgraduate Medical Fed 1991–; Commr BAFTA inquiry into the future of the BBC 1990, Hamlyn Nat Comm on Educ 1991–; Visiting Lecturer, British Postgrad Medical Fed 1991–; Adviser, Mannheim Inst on Criminology, LSE 1992–; Leader of inquiry into health, environmental and safety aspects of Atomic Weapons Establishment, Aldermaston 1993; Chair British Council 1998–, Human Genetics Comm 2000–; author of official report (Learning Works) for Further Educ Funding Council on widening participation in further educ 1997; mem Advisory Bd, Int Centre for Prison Studies 1998; Chair London Int Festival of Theatre, Standing Cttee for Youth Justice; fmr Chair Charter 88 (resgnd); Pres London Marriage Guidance Council, Birth Control Campaign, Nat Children's Bureau, Hillcroft Coll; Vice-Pres Haldane Soc, Nat Ass of Women; mem British Council's Law Advisory Cttee Advisory Bd for Study of Women and Gender, Warwick Univ; mem Bd City Limits magazine 1982–84, New Statesman 1990–96, Counsel magazine 1990–; Chancellor Oxford Brookes Univ 1994–; presenter of various programmes on radio and TV and creator of BBC drama series Blind Justice 1988; Patron, Liberty; Hon Fellow Inst of Advanced Legal Studies, Univ of London 1997; Hon LL D (Strathclyde), (Wolverhampton) 1997, (Leicester) 1998 and 9 other hon degrees; Hon mem Council, Nat Soc for Prevention of Cruelty to Children; Women's Network Award 1992, UK Woman of Europe Award 1995, Campaigning and Influencing Award, Nat Fed of Women's Insts 1996, Times Newspaper Lifetime Achievement Award in the Law (jtly) 1997. *Publications include:* The Bar on Trial (jtly) 1978, Child Abuse Within the Family (jtly) 1984, Balancing Acts (jtly) 1989, Eve was Framed 1992; numerous articles on women, civil liberties and legal matters. *Leisure interests:* theatre, spending time with family and friends. *Address:* House of Lords, London SW1A 0PW, UK. *Telephone:* (1708) 379482; *Fax:* (1708) 379482.

KENNY, Yvonne Denise, AM, B SC; Australian opera singer; b 25 Nov 1950, Australia; d of the late Arthur Raymond and of Doris Jean Kenny. *Education:* Sydney Univ (Australia). *Career:* Debut Queen Elizabeth Hall, London 1975; Prin soprano Royal Opera House, London 1976–; appearances with Berlin Staatsoper, Vienna State Opera, Australian Opera and at La Scala (Milan, Italy), La Fenice (Venice, Italy), Paris, Hamburg (Germany) and Zurich (Switzerland); numerous recordings. *Operas include:* Die Zauberflöte, Idomeneo, Fidelio, Le Nozze di Figaro, L'Elisir d'Amore, Turandot, Mitridate, Alcina, Semele, Giulio Cesare, Don Giovanni, The Fairy Queen, Capriccio, Der Rosenkavalier; Falstaff. *Leisure interests:* swimming, walking, gardening. *Address:* c/o Askonas Holt Ltd, Lonsdale Chambers, 27 Chancery Lane, London WC2A 1PF, UK.

KENSIT, Patricia Jude (Patsy); British actress; b 4 March 1968, London; m 1st Dan Donovan; m 2nd Jim Kerr 1992 (divorced 1996); one s; m 3rd Liam Gallagher (divorced 2000) 1997; one s. *Career:* Film debut aged four in The Great Gatsby 1974; appeared in numerous commercials; made successful pop album Fearless with brother James Kensit's band Eighth Wonder. *Films include:* The Foundation, The Bluebird 1976, Absolute Beginners 1986, Alfie Darling, Hanover Street, Chorus of Disapproval 1989, The Skipper, Chicago Joe and the Showgirl 1990, Lethal Weapon II 1989, Twenty-One, Prince of Shadows, Does This Mean We're Married?, Blame It On The Bellboy, The Turn Of The Screw, Beltenebros, Bitter Harvest, Prince of Shadows, Angels and Insects, Grace of My Heart, Dream Man, Human Bomb, Janice Beard, Pavillions, Best, Things Behind the Sun, Bad Karma ; *TV includes:* Great Expectations, Frost in May, Quiet as a Nun, Silas Marner, Tycoon: The Story of a Woman, Adam Bede, The

Corsican Brothers, Aladdin. *Address:* 14 Lambton Place, London W11 2SH, UK. *Telephone:* (20) 7792-1040 (Office); *Fax:* (20) 7221-7625; *E-mail:* daggerents@aol.com (Office).

KENT, Jill Elspeth, BA, LL M, JD; American business executive, art dealer and lawyer; b 1 June 1948, Detroit, MI; d of the late Seymour and Grace (née Edelman) Kent; m Mark E. Solomons 1978. *Education:* Univ of Michigan and George Washington Univ. *Career:* Called to the Bar, DC 1975; Man Internship US Dept of Transport, Washington, DC 1971–73; Staff Analyst, Office Man and Budget Exec, Office of the Pres 1974–76, Sr Budget Examiner 1980–84; mem Legis Counsel US Treasury Dept 1976–78, Deputy Asst Sec for Departmental Finance, Planning and Man 1985–88; Dir Legis Reference Div, Health Care Financing Admin 1978–80; Chief Treasury Gen Services 1984–85; Asst Sec of the Treasury 1988–89; Chief Finance Officer US Dept of State 1989–93, Acting Under-Sec for Man 1991; Chief Finance Officer George Washington Univ Medical Center, Washington 1993–97; Vice-Pres IPAC 1997–98, The Columbus Group; Pres and CEO Atlantic Threadworks Inc; Gen Man The Frogeye Co 1995–; mem Bd Dirs China Foundation 1997–; Sr Counsellor Atlantic Council 1997–; Prin Council of Excellence in Govt 1993–; Asst Prof Corcoran Gallery of Art 1984–86; Adjunct Prof of Public Policy, Univ of Maryland 1993–; mem ABA, DC Bar, Bd Dirs Mobile Medical Care Inc 1987–91, Bd Trustees Newport Schools 1988–92, Advisory Bd Virginia Female Execs Asscn 1990–, Pres's Council on Man Improvement 1988–, Bd of the Foreign Service 1990–, Bd Trustees Washington Civic Symphony 1994–; Treas Exec. *Leisure interests:* classical music, art, antiques, travel. *Address:* 2101 Wilson Blvd, Arlington, VA 22201, USA (Office); 2419 California St, NW, Washington, DC 20008, USA (Home).

KENWORTHY, Joan Margaret, MA; British former college principal; b 10 Dec 1933, Oldham; d of the late Albert and Amy (née Cobbold) Kenworthy. *Education:* Girls' Grammar School (Barrow-in-Furness) and St Hilda's Coll (Oxford). *Career:* Leverhulme Overseas Research Scholar, Makerere Coll, Uganda 1956–58; Acting Tutor St Hugh's Coll, Oxford 1958–59; Tutorial Research Fellow Bedford Coll, London 1959–60; Asst Lecturer in Geography Univ of Liverpool 1960–63, Lecturer 1963–73, Sr Lecturer 1973–77, Warden Salisbury Hall 1966–77, Morton Hall 1974–77; Prin St Mary's Coll, Durham 1977–99; Visiting Lecturer Univ of Sierra Leone 1975, Univ of Fort Hare, Ciskei 1983; mem Council African Studies Asscn of UK 1969–71, 1994–97, Council Inst of British Geographers 1976–78, Cttee Merseyside Conf for Overseas Students Ltd 1976–77, Council Royal Meterological Soc 1980–83; Treas Asscn of British Climatologists 1976–79; N Chair Durham Univ Soc 1979–82; has contributed to and ed numerous geographical books and has written various articles on African climatology. *Address:* 3 Satley Plough, Satley, Bishop Auckland, Co Durham DL13 4JX, UK. *Telephone:* (1388) 730848.

KEOGH, Lainey; Irish designer; b 20 Sept 1957; d of Peter Keogh and Patricia Byrne. *Career:* Worked in medical sciences until 1983; began to work with yarn in 1983; recognized for work by Int Wool 1987; mem Secr Int Festival du Lin 1989, British Fashion Council 1994; Man Dir Lainey Keogh 1986–; developed fabrics for Dior couture studio 1998; Prix De Coeur (France) 1987; Cable Ace Award for Costume Design for film Two Nudes Bathing 1995; People of the Year Award (Ireland) 1997; Prix de Coeur (France) 1997. *Leisure interests:* sky, walking, looking. *Address:* 42 Dawson St, Dublin 2, Ireland. *Telephone:* (1) 6793299; *Fax:* (1) 6794975.

KEOHANE, Nannerl O., PH D; American academic and university president; b 18 Sept 1940, Blytheville, AR; d of James Arthur and Grace (née McSpadden) Overholser; m 1st Patrick Henry, III 1962 (divorced 1969); m 2nd Robert O. Keohane 1970; three s one d. *Education:* Wellesley Coll, St Anne's Coll (Oxford) and Yale Univ. *Career:* Mem Faculty Swarthmore Coll 1967–73, Stanford Univ 1973–81; Fellow Center for Advanced Study in the Behavioral Sciences, Stanford Univ 1978–79, 1987–88; Pres and Prof of Political Sciences Wellesley Coll 1981–93, Duke Univ 1993–; mem Bd of Dirs IBM 1986–, Bd Trustees The Colonial Williamsburg Foundation 1988–, Center for the Advanced Study of the Behavioral Sciences 1991–, The Nat Humanities Center 1993–; mem MIT Corpn 1992–; Fellow American Acad of Arts and Sciences, American Philosophical Soc; Marshall Scholar 1961–63; Elected to Nat Women's Hall of Fame 1995. *Leisure interests:* travel,

jogging, theatre, music. *Address:* Office of the President, Duke University, 207 Allen Bldg, Box 90001, Durham, NC 27708-0001, USA. *Telephone:* (919) 684-2424; *Fax:* (919) 684-3050; *E-mail:* president@duke.edu.

KEPNER, Rita Marie, BA, MA; American sculptor; b 15 Nov 1944, Binghamton, NY; d of Peter and Helena (née Piotrowski) Kramnicz; m John Matthiesen; one s. *Education:* State Univ of New York, Oklahoma Univ and City Univ (WA). *Career:* Solo exhibitions include Penryn Gallery (Seattle) 1970, 1973, 1976, Zoliborz Gallery (Warsaw) 1981, Yorkshire 501 (Norman, OK) 1988; group exhibitions include State Univ of New York 1966, Manawata Art Gallery, Portland Art Museum 1976, Die Roemer Gallery (Wiesbaden, Germany) 1988, Blue Heron Gallery (Port Hadlock, WA) 1991–92, Quimper Arts, Bruskin Gallery (Port Townsend, WA) 1993, 1994, Port Townsend Women's Center 1995, Ichikawa, Japan 1997, Scott Milo Gallery 2000; informal Cultural Amb to Poland 1976–81; Fed Women's Project Man, Schweinfurt, Germany 1986–87, Wiesbaden 1988; Artist-in-Residence City of Seattle 1975, 1977–78; Public Affairs Officer, Wiesbaden 1987–88; Instructor in writing and editing for Managers, Dept of Navy, Bremerton, WA 1991–93; apptd Public Information Officer, Fed Emergency Man Agency (Exxon Valdez oil spill), Mid-West 1993, S CA 1990, Northridge, CA 1994–, GA, OR, WA, AK 1994, North California floods 1995, Oklahoma City bombing 1995, WA floods 1996, NY floods and snowstorms 1996, CA storms and floods 1997, El Niño earthslides and floods 1998, Tropical Storm Floyd floods, NY 1999, Flight 990 Egyptian Airline crash 1999, Los Alamos fire, NM 2000, MN fires 2000, AR ice storm 2001, OK ice storm, windstorms, tornadoes and floods 2001, and other disasters 1997–2001; Commdr Corps of Engineers, US Army 1995; mem Bd of Dirs Aradia Medical Clinic, Seattle 1972–74, 1988–89; Founder Chimacum School of Distinguished Learning Boosters 1989; First Aid Trainer, Seattle; Co-Chair Marrowstone Island Groundwater Comm, Dept of Ecology; mem Int Artists Asscn of UNESCO, Int Artists' Co-operation; disaster reservist; numerous awards and honours. *Leisure interests:* sailing, gardening, reading. *Address:* 8643 Flagler Rd, Nordland, WA 98358-9600, USA. *Telephone:* (360) 385-5971.

KEPPELHOFF-WIECHERT, Hedwig; German politician; b 31 May 1939, Sudlohn. *Career:* Mem CDU Dist Exec 1981–, CDU Land Exec 1989–96; mem COPA Rural Women's Cttee, Brussels 1976–91, Vice-Chair 1986–89; MEP (EPP) 1989–, mem Cttee on Agric and Rural Devt, ACP-EU Jt Parl Ass, fmrly Del for relations with the mem States of Asean, SE Asia and the Rep of Korea; Chair German Fed of Women Farmers; Vice-Chair Women Farmers' Cttee, Cttee of Professional Agric Orgs. *Address:* European Parliament, rue Wiertz, 1047 Brussels, Belgium. *Telephone:* (2) 284-21-11; *Fax:* (2) 230-69-43; *E-mail:* h .keppelhoff@t-online.de.

KERJAN, Liliane Jeanine, L EN D, D ÈS L; French professor of American studies; b 13 Feb 1940, Lorient; d of Jean and Suzanne (née le Gouallec) Nicol; m Daniel Kerjan 1960; one s one d. *Education:* Univ of Rennes. *Career:* Dir of Studies Univ of Nantes 1965–67; Lecturer Univ of Rennes II (Univ of Haute Bretagne) 1967–77, Prof 1977–, Vice-Pres 1979–82, 1986–93, 1994–98; Admin Asscn des univs partiellement ou entièrement de langue française 1989–99; Rector Acad de Limoges 2000–; Fellow Salzburg Seminar of American Studies 1969, 1972, 1985; Drama Critic O'Neill Theater Center, USA 1973; Fulbright Prof Univ of San Diego, USA 1982; Learned Scholar Yale Law School 1987; worked at Nat Univ of Côte d'Ivoire 1989; mem UREF (French Univ Network) Bd 1986, EAIE (European Asscn for Int Educ) 1991; Officier des Palmes Académiques 1987. *Publications include:* Edward Albee 1971, The Theatre of Edward Albee 1978, L'Egalité aux Etats-Unis: mythes et réalités 1991; various articles on theatre, law and society. *Leisure interest:* gardening. *Address:* Rectorat de l'Académie de Limoges, 13 rue François Chénieux, 87031 Limoges, France (Office). *Telephone:* (2) 99-33-51-73 (Office); *Fax:* (2) 99-33-51-75 (Office); (2) 99-60-00-09 (Home).

KERNOT, Cheryl, BA, DIP ED; Australian politician; b 1948; one c. *Education:* Univ of Newcastle. *Career:* Fmr teacher; Senator for Queensland 1990–97, Spokesperson on Treasury and Finance, Commonwealth and State Relations, Aboriginal Affairs and Reconciliation, Women, Prime Minister and Cabinet; Leader Australian Democratic

Party 1993–97; Shadow Minister for Regional Devt, Infrastructure, Transport and Regional Services 1998–99, for Employment and Training 1999–. *Address:* Shop 3, 199 Gympie Rd, Strathpine, Qld 4500, Australia.

KERR, Deborah Jane, CBE; British actress; b 30 Sept 1921, Helensburgh, Dumbarton, Scotland; d of Arthur Kerr Trimmer and Colleen Smale; m 1st Anthony Bartley 1945 (divorced 1960); two d; m 2nd Peter Viertel 1960; one step-d. *Education:* Rossholme Prep (Weston-super-Mare) and Northumberland House (Bristol). *Career:* Made debut Open Air Theatre Regents Park 1939; film debut Contraband; first major role as Jenny Hill in Major Barbara; went to Hollywood 1946; film awards include four New York Critics' Awards 1947 (two), 1957, 1960, Hollywood Foreign Press Asscn Award 1956, 1958, Variety Club of GB Award 1961, six Acad Award nominations, BAFTA Special Award 1991, Hon Acad Award 1994. *Films include:* Love on the Dole 1940, Penn of Pennsylvania 1940, Hatter's Castle 1941, The Day Will Dawn 1941, The Life and Death of Colonel Blimp 1942, Perfect Strangers 1944, Black Narcissus 1945, I See a Dark Stranger 1945, The Hucksters 1946, If Winter Comes 1947, Edward My Son 1948, The Prisoner of Zenda 1948, Young Bess 1949, King Solomon's Mines 1950, Quo Vadis 1950, Rage of the Vulture 1951, Dream Wife 1952, From Here To Eternity 1953, The End of the Affair 1954, The Proud and the Profane 1955, The King and I (Hollywood Foreign Press Asscn Award) 1956, Heaven Knows Mr Allison 1957, An Affair To Remember 1957, Separate Tables 1957–58, The Journey 1958, The Blessing 1958, Beloved Infidel 1960, The Sundowners 1960, The Innocents 1961, The Chalk Garden 1963, The Night of the Iguana 1963, Marriage on the Rocks 1965, Gypsy Moths 1968, The Arrangement 1968–69, The Assam Garden 1984, Reunion at Fairborough 1984; *Plays include:* Heartbreak House 1943, Tea and Sympathy (Donaldson and Sarah Siddons Awards) 1953 (US tour 1954/55), The Day After the Fair (US tour 1973/74), Seascape 1974/75, Souvenir 1975, Long Day's Journey Into Night (US) 1977, Candida (London) 1977, The Last of Mrs Cheyney (US tour 1978), The Day After the Fair (Australian tour 1979), Overheard (London and UK tour 1981), The Corn is Green (London) 1985; *TV appearances:* A Song at Twilight 1981, Witness for the Prosecution (TV film) 1982, Ann & Debbie 1984, A Woman of Substance 1984, Hold the Dream 1986. *Leisure interests:* painting, gardening. *Address:* Wyhergut, 7250 Klosters, Grisons, Switzerland.

KERR, Jean; American writer; b July 1923, Scranton, PA; d of Thomas J. Collins and Kitty O'Neill; m Walter Kerr 1943; five s one d. *Education:* Catholic Univ of America (Washington, DC). *Career:* Mem Nat Inst of Arts and Sciences; Hon LHD (Northwestern Univ) 1962, (Fordham Univ) 1965; Campion Award 1971; Laetare Medal 1971. *Publications:* King of Hearts (jtly) 1954, Please Don't Eat the Daisies 1957, The Snake Has All the Lines 1960, Penny Candy 1970, How I Got to Be Perfect 1978; Plays: Jenny Kissed Me 1949, Touch and Go 1950, Mary, Mary 1962, Poor Richard 1963, Finishing Touches 1973, Lunch Hour (play) 1980. *Address:* 1 Beach Ave, Larchmont, Manor, New York, NY 10538, USA.

KERR, Rose, BA; British museum curator; b 23 Feb 1953; d of William Antony and Elizabeth (née Rendell) Kerr; m Stephen Lord 1990. *Education:* SOAS (Univ of London) and Languages Inst (Beijing). *Career:* Fellow Percival David Foundation of Chinese Art 1976–78; Research Asst Victoria and Albert Museum, London 1978–87, Chief Curator Far Eastern Collection 1987–; Pres Oriental Ceramic Soc 2000–; mem GB–China Educ Trust 1997–, Council of the Percival David Foundation of Chinese Art 2000–. *Publications:* Kiln Sites of Ancient China (jtly) 1980, Guanyin: A Masterpiece Revealed (jtly) 1985, Chinese Ceramics: Porcelain of the Qing Dynasty 1644–1911 1986, Later Chinese Bronzes 1990, Chinese Art and Design: The T. T. Tsui Gallery of Chinese Art (ed) 1991, Ceramic Evolution in the Middle Ming Period (jtly) 1994. *Leisure interest:* gardening. *Address:* Victoria and Albert Museum, Far Eastern Collection, Exhibition Rd, London SW7 2RL, UK. *Telephone:* (20) 7942-2243; *Fax:* (20) 7942-2252; *E-mail:* r.kerr@vam.ac.uk.

KERVIN, Alison Christine, M SC; British magazine editor; b 18 Feb 1967, Birmingham; d of Peter Kervin and of Cristine Kervin. *Education:* Chelsea Coll (Sussex). *Career:* Journalist Hastings Observer 1988;

Deputy Sports Ed Slough Observer 1989; Youth Devt Officer and Public Relations Officer England Rugby Team 1991; TV Presenter Rugby Special (first woman); Rugby correspondent on national newspaper (first woman); Features Ed Rugby World magazine, then Ed 1995; Cosmopolitan Woman of the Year 1993; IPC Writer of the Year Award 1995; Highly Commended British Sports Journalism Awards 1995. *Publications include:* Sports Writing Guide. *Leisure interests:* opera, sports, literature, music. *Address:* Rugby World, IPC Magazines Ltd, King's Reach Tower, Stamford St, London SE1 9LS, UK (Office); Flat 1, Poulett Lodge, Cross Deep, Twickenham TW1 4QJ, UK (Home). *Telephone:* (20) 7261-6770; *Fax:* (20) 7261-5419.

KERWIN, Claire; Canadian (b Belgian) artist; b Châtelet, Belgium; d of Emile and Elisabeth (née Fremersdorf) Roland; m George Kerwin 1947; one s one d. *Career:* Living in Canada 1947–; one-woman exhibitions include Merton, Pascal and Art Dialogue Galleries (Toronto), Alice Peck Gallery (Burlington), St Jean-de-Luz (France); group exhibitions include Canadian Embassy (Paris), Ontario House (London), Royal Canadian Acad of Art, Univ of Waterloo, Soc of Canadian Artists, John B. Aird Gallery, Shaw-Rimmington Gallery; commissioned to design set for Toronto Dance Theatre 1991; mem Council Royal Canadian Acad, John B. Aird Gallery, Print and Drawing Council of Canada; Medal of Merit, City of Toronto. *Leisure interests:* tennis, squash, farming. *Address:* 20 Monteith St, Toronto, ON M4Y 1K7, Canada. *Telephone:* (416) 923-5105.

KESTELMAN, Sara; British actress; d of the late Morris Kestelman and of Dorothy Mary Creagh. *Education:* Cen School of Speech and Drama (London). *Career:* Joined Liverpool Playhouse then Library Theatre, Manchester, RSC 1969. *Plays include:* The Crucible, The Importance of Being Earnest, Measure for Measure, The Silver Tassie, Much Ado about Nothing, Troilus and Cressida, Subject to Fits, A Midsummer Night's Dream, Gorky's Enemies, I Claudius, The Homecoming, Macbeth, Plunder, Uncle Vanya, Nine 1996, Hamlet 2000; *TV appearances include:* Tom Jones 1997, Kavanagh QC 1997, Anna Karenina 2000; *Film:* Zardoz; *Publication:* A Two Hander (poems, with Susan Penhaligon) 1996. *Leisure interests:* drawing, photography, writing.

KESWICK, Annabel Thérèse (Tessa); British organization executive and former civil servant; b 15 Oct 1942, Beauly, Scotland; d of Baron Lovat and Rosamund Delves-Broughton; m 1st Lord Reay 1964 (divorced 1978); two s one d; m 2nd Henry Neville Lindley Keswick 1985. *Education:* Convent of the Sacred Heart (Woldingham, Surrey). *Career:* Fmr mem staff J. Walter Thompson, the Spectator; Ed Business and Energy International 1975–78; Councillor (Cons) Royal Borough of Kensington and Chelsea (Queensgate Ward—London) 1982–86, mem Housing Cttee, Social Services Cttee; Conservative Cand for Inverness 1987; Special Adviser to Rt Hon Kenneth Clarke at Dept of Health 1989, Dept of Educ, Home Office, Treasury 1989–95; Exec Dir Cluff Investments 1980–96; Dir Centre for Policy Studies 1995–. *Leisure interests:* art, music, travelling, breeding horses. *Address:* Centre for Policy Studies, 57 Tufton St, London SW1P 3QL, UK. *Telephone:* (20) 7222-4488; *Fax:* (20) 7222-4388.

KEY, Mary Ritchie, PH D; American professor of linguistics; b 19 March 1924, San Diego, CA; d of George Lawrence and Iris Lyons Ritchie; m Audley E. Patton; two s (one s deceased) one d. *Education:* Univ of Texas. *Career:* Chair Program in Linguistics, Univ of California at Irvine 1969–71, 1975–77, 1987, Faculty Research Fellow 1984–85, then Prof of Linguistics; numerous guest lectureships; consultant to State of California, Modern Language Asscn, American Dialect Soc, etc; involved in linguistic research in languages including American Indian languages, Spanish in Mexico and S America, English dialects in Nova Scotia (Canada), Hawaii, Scotland, England and the USA; mem Editorial Bd several professional journals; mem Linguistic Soc of America, American Dialect Soc; Regent's Grant (Univ of California) 1974; Fulbright–Hays Award 1975; Book Award, Friends of the Library 1976; Rolex Award 1990. *Publications include:* Comparative Tacanan Phonology 1968, Male/Female Language 1975, The Grouping of South American Indian Languages 1979, Catherine the Great's Linguistic Contribution 1980, Polynesian and American Linguistic Connections 1984; numerous monographs and contribs to journals on linguistics.

Leisure interests: music, embroidery, gardening. *Address:* c/o University of California at Irvine, Dept of Linguistics, Irvine, CA 92717, USA. *Telephone:* (714) 731-8556.

KHAKAMADA, Irina Mutzuovna, CAND ECON; Russian politician; b 13 April 1955, Moscow; m 3rd Vladimir Sirotinsky; three c. *Education:* Russian Peoples' Friendship Univ (Moscow). *Career:* Mem staff Research Inst, State Planning Cttee 1981–85; teacher Tech Inst of Automobile Factory 1985–89; Sr Expert Russian Stock Exchange of Raw Materials 1990; mem Party of Econ Freedom 1992, Sec-Gen and Co-Chair 1992–94; Pres Liberal Women's Foundation 1994; mem State Duma (Parl) 1993–97, 1999–; Head Right Forces faction (Deputy Chair 2000–); Leader pre-election union Obshcheye Delo 1995; Chair State Cttee for Support of Small Enterprises 1997–98; Founder and Co-Leader pre-election union Pravoye Delo. *Publications include:* The Maiden Name. *Address:* State Duma, Okhotny Ryad 1, 103265 Moscow, Russian Federation. *Telephone:* (095) 292-80-41 (Office); *Fax:* (095) 292-80-44 (Office).

KHAKETLA, Masechele; Lesotho teacher and writer. *Education:* Morija Training Coll and Univ of Fort Hare. *Career:* Co-Founder and propr Iketsetseng Primary School; teacher Basutholand High School; High Court Assessor; Hon D LITT (Nat Univ) 1983. *Publications include:* Mosali eo o'nehileng Eena, Mahlopha a senya, Ka u Lotha, Khotosoaneng, Selibelo sa Nkhono, Pelo ea monna, Ho isa Lefung, Mosiuoa Masilo, Mantsopa, Molamu oa kotjana. *Leisure interest:* reading. *Address:* POB 65, Maseru 100, Lesotho. *Telephone:* 313877.

KHAL, Helen; Lebanese writer; b 1923, Allentown, PA, USA; m (divorced); two c. *Education:* Lebanese Acad of Fine Art and Art Students' League (New York). *Career:* Teacher of Art American Univ of Beirut; artist 1946–; exhibitions 1960–; Founder Gallery One 1963.

KHALIL, Sameeha Salameh; Palestinian organization executive; b 20 April 1923, Anapta; d of Yusif Mustafa al-Qubbaj and Helmeieh Hafeth Tuqan; m Salameh Khalil Salameh 1940; four s one d. *Education:* Friends Girls' School (El-Bireh) and Beirut Arab Univ. *Career:* Founder Arab Union Soc, El-Bireh 1952; Sec-Gen Union of Palestinian Women in Jerusalem 1965; Founder and Pres Soc of In'ash El-Usra, El-Bireh 1965; Head of Palestine Del to UN Conf on the Status of Women (Beijing) 1995; mem Nat Guidance Cttee of Palestine 1970–79, Exec Cttee Union of Charitable Socs in Jerusalem, Exec Bd Palestinian Union of Charitable Socs; Treas Higher Cttee of Adult Educ in Palestine; Pres Union of Voluntary Women's Socs; has received awards from various insts. *Publications:* From the Intifada to the State 1988; several magazine and newspaper articles and collections of Arabic poetry. *Leisure interests:* reading, writing popular Arabic poetry, making speeches. *Address:* Society of In'ash El-Usra, El-Bireh POB 3549, W Bank, via Israel. *Telephone:* (2) 9956876; *Fax:* (2) 9956544.

KHAN, Chaka (pseudonym of Yvette Marie Stevens); American singer; b 23 March 1953, Chicago; one c. *Career:* Singer with Rufus Musical Group 1972–76, Warner Brothers Records 1978–; Grammy Awards for Group Vocal and Vocal Arrangements 1983, for Best Rhythm and Blues Female Vocalist 1983, 1984. *Recordings include:* Rags to Rufus 1974, Rufus Featuring Chaka Khan 1975, Chaka 1979, Naughty 1980, Whatcha' Gonna Do For Me 1981, Chaka Khan 1982, I Feel For You 1984, Destiny 1986, CK 1989, I'm Every Woman 1989, It's My Party 1989, Life Is a Dance 1989, Love You All My Lifetime 1992, The Best of Chaka Khan 1996, Missing You (single jtly) 1996, Never Miss The Water (single) 1996, Come 2 My House 1998. *Address:* c/o Warner Bros Records, 75 Rockefeller Plaza, 20th Floor, New York, NY 10019, USA.

KHAN, Haseena Moin, MA; Pakistani screenwriter; b 20 Nov 1938, Kanpur, India; d of the late Moinuddin Khan. *Education:* Univ of Karachi. *Career:* Began writing stories and plays in coll; playwright Pakistan TV Corpn 1971–; Headmistress of a girls' high school; has written numerous plays and TV serials; awards include TV Writer Award, Awami Award, Civil Award, Governor Award, Pride of Performance Nat Award 1988, Nigar Award, Johns Hopkins Univ Award 1992. *TV serials:* Shahzori 1972, Kiran Kahani 1973, Zer Zabar Pesh 1974, Uncle Urfi 1975, Roomi 1976, Parchaiyan 1977, Dhund 1978, Ankahi 1979, Tanhaiyan 1981, Dhoop Kinaray 1983, Aahat 1987, Tansen 1991, Pal Do Pal; *TV plays include:* Sangsar, Gurya Ralta,

Paani Pe Likha tha, Chup Darya. *Leisure interests:* painting, sculpture, music, reading. *Address:* A 190, Block I, N Nazimabad, Karachi, Pakistan. *Telephone:* (21) 6630168 (Home).

KHANH, Emanuelle (pseudonym of Renée Nguyen); French fashion designer; b 12 Sept 1937; m Manh Khanh Nguyen 1957; one s one d. *Career:* Fmr fashion model for various fashion houses including Balenciaga and Givenchy; Designer of jr sportswear for Cacharel, Paris 1962–67; est own co launching Missoni knitwear, Paris 1970–; f own label specializing in embroidered clothes, accessories 1971–. *Address:* Emmanuelle Khanh International, 45 ave Victor Hugo, 75116 Paris, France. *Telephone:* (1) 44-17-31-00.

KHATAMI, Mahin, PH D; Iranian molecular biologist; b 9 May 1943, Teheran (now Tehran); d of Kazim and Badri Khatami. *Education:* Teacher Training Coll (Teheran), Teheran Univ, State Univ of New York at Buffalo and Univ of Pennsylvania (USA). *Career:* Teacher of Chem and Physics, Teheran (now Tehran) 1964–69; Medical Technologist 1970–72, 1977–80; Research Specialist Univ of Pennsylvania 1974–75; Biochem Instructor Philadelphia Coll of Pediatric Medicine, Chem Instructor Philadelphia Community Coll 1974–75; Research Specialist Hosp of the Univ of Pennsylvania 1976–77; Research Assoc Univ of Virginia School of Medicine 1980–81; apptd Research Asst Prof Univ of Pennsylvania School of Medicine 1985, Consultant Univs of Tabriz and Teheran, Burroughs Wellcome Co 1988, The Upjohn Co 1989; reviewer for various scientific periodicals 1986–; mem various academic cttees 1987–, Bd Coronary Heart Disease Research 1987–89; Chair Univ of Pennsylvania Symposium on Diabetic Complications 1989–91; has written numerous papers and articles; has spoken at more than 63 Nat and Int Symposia 1980–; Research Service Award, Nat Inst of Health 1982–85. *Leisure interest:* poetry. *Address:* Scheie Eye Institute, 51 N 39th St, Philadelphia, PA 19104, USA (Office); 1019 Radnor House, Rosemont, PA 19010, USA (Home). *Telephone:* (215) 662-8037 (Office); (215) 525-4757 (Home).

KHATOON, Akram, MA; Pakistani banking executive; b 26 Sept 1937, Ajmair, India; d of the late M. and of Hasina Shafi. *Education:* Punjab Univ (Lahore) and Inst of Bankers (Pakistan). *Career:* Trainee Officer State Bank of Pakistan; Man Muslim Commercial Bank All Women Branch 1961, then Regional Man, Deputy Head Personnel Div until 1981, Chief of Training Women's Banking Div 1981–89, Pres First Women Bank 1989; mem Bd Dirs Inst of Public Admin, Council Inst of Bankers in Pakistan; Woman of the Year Award 1990; has written numerous articles on banking and finance for nat newspapers and magazines. *Leisure interests:* reading, travel. *Address:* First Women Bank Ltd, 7th Floor, Mehdi Towers, SMCH Society, Shahrah-e-Faisal, Karachi, Pakistan. *Telephone:* (21) 4556093; *Fax:* (21) 4556983.

KHAW, Kay-Tee, MA, MB, M SC, MRCP; British professor of clinical gerontology; b 14 Oct 1950; d of Khaw Kai Boh and Tan Chwee Geok; m James Fawcett 1980; one s one d. *Education:* Girton Coll (Cambridge), St Mary's Hosp Medical School (London) and London School of Hygiene and Tropical Medicine. *Career:* Wellcome Trust Research Fellow, London School of Hygiene and Tropical Medicine, St Mary's Hosp and Univ of California at San Diego, USA 1979–84; Asst Adjunct Prof School of Medicine, Univ of California at San Diego 1985; Sr Registrar in Community Medicine School of Clinical Medicine, Univ of Cambridge 1986–89, Prof of Clinical Gerontology 1989–; numerous contribs to scientific journals; Daland Fellow American Philosophical Soc 1984. *Address:* Clinical Gerontology Unit, University of Cambridge School of Clinical Medicine, Addenbrooke's Hospital, Cambridge CB2 2QQ, UK.

KHOALI-MCCARTHY, Lisebo; Lesotho organization executive; b 15 Sept 1953; d of J. B. C. and Teresa E. Khoali; m Bryan McCarthy 1973 (divorced 1988); one d. *Education:* Nat Univ of Lesotho. *Career:* Devt Activist 1986–; Founder, Pres Lesotho Council of NGOs 1987; Country Programme Dir Unitarian Service Cttee. *Leisure interests:* music, travel, theatre, art-viewing, historic buildings, reading. *Address:* Unitarian Service Committee, Private Bag A11, Maseru 100, Lesotho. *Telephone:* (266) 315202; *Fax:* (266) 310237.

KHOURI, Carrie; American screenwriter. *Screenplay:* Thelma and Louise (Acad Award 1992) 1990. *Address:* c/o International Creative Management, 8899 Beverly Hills Blvd, Los Angeles, CA 90048, USA.

KHRISTOVA, Tsvetanka Mintcheva; Bulgarian sportswoman; b 14 March 1962, Kazanlŭk. *Education:* Nat Acad of Sports (Sofia). *Career:* European Champion in Discus, Athens 1982, Silver European Medallist, Stuttgart (Germany) 1986; Bronze Medallist World Championships, Rome 1987, Olympic Games, Seoul 1988; World Champion, Tokyo 1991; Silver Medallist Olympic Games, Barcelona 1992; Hon Master of Sports; World Athletic Gala Prize, Monte Carlo 1986, 1991. *Leisure interests:* mountain climbing, reading, music. *Address:* Kazanlŭk, Otets Paisiy Str 22, Apt 25, Bulgaria. *Telephone:* (431) 4-02-16.

KI-ZERBO, Jacqueline; Malian United Nations official; b 23 Sept 1933; d of the late Lazarre Coulibaly and Gertrude Traore; m Joseph Ki-Zerbo 1956; three s two d. *Education:* Collège des Jeunes Filles (Bamako), Ecole Normale de Rufisque (Senegal) and Univ of Paris (Sorbonne). *Career:* Teacher of English, Dakar 1958–59; Headmistress, Guinea 1959–60, Burkina Faso 1961–74; UNESCO Regional Educational Adviser on Population, Dakar 1975–76; Co-ordinator Sahel Improved Housing Programme (Perm Inter-State Cttee on Drought Control in the Sahel—CICSS) 1981–83, UNIFEM Devt Fund for Women (Cen and W Africa) 1987; has written various articles on educ and women's econ devt; Paul G. Hoffman Prize for Services to Nat and Int Devt (UN) 1984. *Leisure interests:* reading, visiting friends and family, letter-writing. *Address:* UNIFEM, BP 154, Dakar, Senegal. *Telephone:* 23-32-44; *Fax:* 23-55-00.

KIBRICK, Anne, BS, MA, ED D; American professor of nursing; b 1 June 1919, Palmer, MA; d of the late Martin and Christine Grigas Karlon; m Sidney Kibrick 1949; one s one d. *Education:* Boston, Columbia and Harvard Univs. *Career:* Head Nurse Worcs Hahnemann Hosp 1941–43; Staff Nurse Children's Hosp Medical Center, Boston 1943–45; Educ Dir Charles V. Chapin Hosp, Providence, RI 1945–47; Asst Educ Dir Veterans Admin Hosp 1948–49; Asst Prof of Nursing, Simmons Coll, Boston 1949–55; Dir Grad Programs in Nursing, Boston Univ 1958–63, Prof and Dean 1963–70; Dir Grad Programs in Nursing, Boston Coll 1970–74; Chair School of Nursing, Boston State Coll 1974–82; Dean School of Nursing, Univ of Massachusetts, Boston 1982–88, Prof 1988–93, Prof Emer 1993–; Consultant Nat Student Nurses' Asscn 1985–88, Cumberland Coll of Health Sciences (NSW, Australia), Menoufia Univ (Shebeen El-Koam, Egypt); mem Inst of Medicine, Nat Acad of Sciences 1970–, Bd of Dirs Post-Grad Medical Inst, Massachusetts Medical Soc 1983–96, Exec Cttee 1988–96, Brookline Town Meeting 1995–2000; Dir Landy-Kaplan Nurses Council 1992– (Treasurer 1994–); Charter mem Nat Acads of Practice 1985–; Fellow American Acad of Nursing 1973; Hon DHL (St Joseph's Coll); Mary Adelaide Nutting Award, Distinguished Service Award, Isabel Stewart Award, Nat League for Nursing, Service Award, Nat Hadassah Org, Chancellor's Medal, Univ of Massachusetts, Boston 1992, Hall of Fame, Nursing, Teacher's Coll, Univ of Columbia 1999, Massachusetts Nurses Asscn 2000. *Publications:* Explorations in Nursing Research (jtly) 1979; numerous articles in professional journals. *Leisure interests:* reading, knitting, travel. *Address:* 130 Seminary Ave, #221, Auburndale, MA 02466, USA (Home). *Telephone:* (617) 969-3225 (Home).

KIDD, Jodie; British fashion model; b 1979, Surrey; d of Johnny and Wendy Kidd. *Education:* St Michael's School (W Sussex). *Career:* Spent much of childhood in Barbados; fashion model 1995–; has modelled for numerous fashion magazines; also top int catwalk model for designers including Gucci, Prada, Karl Lagerfeld, Yves Saint Laurent, Chanel, John Galliano, Calvin Klein and Yohji Yamamoto; appeared on the Front cover of Tatler March 1996; make-up model for Chanel 1999 season; fmr Nat Jr Athletics Champion; holder of Under-15s High Jump record for Sussex; many awards as a jr show jumper. *Leisure interests:* riding, polo. *Address:* c/o IMG Models, Bentinck House, 3–8 Bolsover St, London W1P 7HG, UK. *Telephone:* (20) 7580-5885.

KIDJO, Angélique; Benin singer and songwriter; b 14 July 1960, Cotonou; d of Frank and Yvonne Kidjo; m Jean Hebrail 1987. *Education:* In Cotonou. *Career:* Began performing in her mother's theatre co aged six; joined Kidjo Brothers Band, Alafia, Pili Pili and later Parakou; recording debut 1980; appearance at Montreux Festival 1986; African Musician of the Year 1991. *Recordings include:* Pretty 1980, Ninive, Ewa Kadjo 1985, Parakou 1989, Logozo 1991, Fifa 1996; several albums (jtly). *Address:* c/o Island Records, 334 King St, London W6 0RA, UK.

KIDMAN, Dame Fiona Judith, DBE; New Zealand writer; b 26 March 1940, Hawera; d of Eric and Flora Cameron (née Small) Eakin; m Ian Kidman 1960; one s one d. *Education:* small rural schools in the north of NZ. *Career:* Founding Sec/Organiser NZ Book Council 1972–75; Sec NZ Centre, PEN 1972–76, Pres 1981–83; Pres NZ Book Council 1992–95, Pres of Honour 1997–; f Writers in Schools, Words on Wheels (touring writing co), Writers Visiting Prisons; mem Arts Bd, Creative NZ; teaches creative writing; many literary prizes including NZ Book Awards (fiction category), Queen Elizabeth II Arts Council Award for Achievement, Victoria Univ Writers' Fellow; NZ Scholarship in Letters; Dame Companion New Zealand Order of Merit. *Publications:* A Breed of Women 1979, Mandarin Summer 1981, Mrs Dixon and Friend (short stories) 1982, Paddy's Puzzle 1983, The Book of Secrets 1986, Unsuitable Friends (short stories) 1988, True Stars 1990, Wakeful Nights (poems selected and new) 1991, The Foreign Woman (short stories) 1994, Palm Prints (autobiog essays) 1995, Ricochet Baby 1996, The House Within 1997, The Best of Fiona Kidman's Short Stories 1998, NZ Love Stories; An Oxford Anthology (ed) 1999. *Leisure interests:* theatre, film, gardening. *Address:* POB 14-401, Kilbirnie, Wellington, New Zealand. *Fax:* (4) 386-1895; *E-mail:* fionakidman@compuserve.com.

KIDMAN, Nicole; American/Australian actress; b 20 June 1967, Hawaii, USA; d of Anthony Kidman and Janelle Glenny; m Tom Cruise 1990 (divorced 2001); one adopted d one adopted s. *Education:* N Sydney Girls' High School, St Martin's Youth Theatre, Melbourne, Australian Theatre for Young People (Sydney) and Sydney and Philip Street Theatre. *Career:* Acting debut in Australian film 1982; currently Goodwill Amb for UNICEF Australia and Amb for Australian Theater for Young People. *Films include:* , Vietnam (Best Actress Logie Award), The Emerald City, The Year My Voice Broke, Flirting, Dead Calm, Days of Thunder, Billy Bathgate, Far and Away, Malice, My Life, To Die For (Best Actress Golden Globe Award, Boston Film Critics' Award, Seattle Film Festival Award, Broadcast Film Critics' Award, London Film Critics' Award), Batman Forever, Portrait of a Lady, The Peacemaker, Eyes Wide Shut 1999, Practical Magic 1999, Moulin Rouge 2000, The Others 2000; *Plays include:* The Blue Room 1998–99; *TV appearances include:* Bangkok Hilton (mini-series) (Australian Film Inst Best Actress Award). *Leisure interests:* scuba-diving, sky-diving, tennis, kick-boxing, hiking, skiing, jogging, reading. *Address:* c/o Ann Churchill-Brown, Shanahan's Management, POB 478, King's Cross, NSW 2011, Australia. *Telephone:* (612) 358-4677.

KIDRON, Beeban; British film and television director; b 1961, London. *Education:* Camden School for Girls and Nat Film School (Beaconsfield). *Career:* Asst to photographer Eve Arnold 1976–77. *Film and TV work includes:* Carry Greenham Home, Oranges Are Not The Only Fruit 1990, Antonia and Jane, Used People 1992, Great Moments in Aviation 1992. *Address:* c/o BBC TV Centre, Wood Lane, London W12, UK.

KIDWAI, Mohsina; Indian politician; b 1 Jan 1932, Banda Dist, UP; d of the late Qutubuddin Ahmed; m Khalilur Rahman Kidwai 1953; three d. *Education:* Women's Coll (Aligarh). *Career:* Mem UP Legis Council 1960–74, Legis Ass 1974–77, Lok Sabha (Parl) 1978–79, 1980–84; Minister of State for Food and Civil Supplies, Govt of UP 1973–74, for Harijan and Social Welfare 1974–75, for Small-Scale Industries 1975–77; Union Minister of State for Labour and Rehabilitation 1982–83, for Health and Family Welfare 1983–84, Rural Devt Aug–Oct, Nov–Dec 1984; Minister of Health and Family Welfare 1984–88, of Urban Devt 1988–90; Pres UP Congress Cttee (I) 1976–80, 1982, Pres UP Congress Exec (I); Gen-Sec All-India Congress Cttee 1999–; mem Nat Comm of Population 2000–; Founder, Patron Nat Girls' Higher Secondary School, Bara Banki and other insts helping women, children and destitutes, including Harijans and Dalits. *Leisure interests:* reading biographies and other literary works, music, sports. *Address:* Civil Lines, Bara Banki, Uttar Pradesh, India; c/o All India Congress Committee, 24 Akbar Rd, New Delhi 110011, India.

KIEHL, Marina; German skier; b 12 Jan 1965. *Career:* Jr World Champion in skiing 1983; German Champion (alpine skiing) seven times; World Champion 1985, 1986; Olympic Champion, Calgary (Canada) 1988; Goldener Ehrenring der Landeshauptstadt München 1988. *Leisure interests:* sports, graphic design. *Address:* Hermine-Bland-Str 11, 8000 Munich, Germany.

KIELAN-JAWOROWSKA, Zofia, PH D; Polish palaeontologist; b 25 April 1925, Sokolow; d of Franciszek and Maria (née Osinska) Kielan; m Zbigniew Jaworowski 1958; one s. *Education:* Univ of Warsaw and Polish Acad of Sciences Inst of Paleobiology. *Career:* Asst Dept of Palaeontology, Univ of Warsaw 1948–52; Sr Scientist Polish Acad of Sciences Inst of Palaeobiology 1952–60, Prof, Dir of Inst 1961–82; Visiting Prof Musée Nat d'Histoire Naturelle, Inst de Paléontologie, Paris 1982–84; Head Vertebrate Palaeontology Lab, Inst of Palae- ontology, Polish Acad of Sciences 1984–87, Head Scientific Council 1996–; Prof of Palaeontology, Museum of Palaeontology, Univ of Oslo 1987–95; mem Polish Acad of Sciences 1967, Norwegian Acad of Sciences 1989; Hon mem Polish Copernicus Soc of Naturalists, Linnean Soc (London), Soc of Vertebrate Palaeontology (USA); Dr hc (Camerino, Italy) 1989; Polish State Prize 1974; Prize of Alfred Jurzykowski Foundation (USA) 1994; Romer-Simpson Medal, Soc of Vertebrate Paleontology (USA) 1996. *Publications:* Hunting For Dinosaurs 1969, Mesozoic Mammals: The First Two-Thirds of Mammalian History (jtly) 1979; over 180 papers and monographs in scientific journals. *Leisure interest:* downhill skiing. *Address:* Instytut Paleobiologii PAN, ul Twarda 51/55, 08-818 Warsaw, Poland; ul Sadowa 9, 05-520 Konstancin, Poland (Home). *Telephone:* (22) 7544434; *Fax:* (22) 7544435; *E-mail:* zkielan@twarda.pan.pl.

KIERAN, Sheila Harriet; Canadian writer and consultant; b 4 May 1930, Toronto, ON; d of Seymour and Ida (née Schulman) Ginzler; m 1951 (divorced 1968); four s two d (and one d deceased). *Education:* Columbia Univ (USA) and Univ of Toronto. *Career:* Dir Public Participation, Royal Comm on Violence in the Communications Industry 1975–77; Sr Policy Adviser Ministry of the Environment 1985–87; Speech-writer to several govt ministers 1987–90; writer of govt reports; Sr Editorial Adviser to Gov-Gen of Canada; Ed Royal Comm on the Future of the Toronto Waterfront and other govt reports and documents; numerous articles for TV, radio and journals. *Publications include:* The Non-Deductible Woman: A Handbook for Working Wives and Mothers 1970, The Chatelaine Guide to Marriage (contrib) 1974, The Family Matters: Two Centuries of Family Law and Life in Ontario 1986. *Address:* 66 Badgerow Ave, Toronto, ON M4M 1V4, Canada.

KILVET, Krista, BA; Estonian politician and diplomatist; b 31 May 1946, Tallinn; m (divorced); three d. *Education:* Univ of Tartu (Estonia). *Career:* Librarian Library of Acad of Sciences 1965–67; journalist Estonian radio 1967–90; Deputy Minister of State 1990–92; mem Riigikogu (Parl, Estonian Party of Devt) 1992–95, mem Foreign Affairs Cttee, Cttee on Culture and Educ; fmr Pres Estonian Women's Union, Estonian Group of Inter-Parl Union; currently Pres Int Zonta Club (Tallinn); Diplomat Ministry of Foreign Affairs; has translated plays for Estonian theatre and contrib political articles to newspapers and journals. *Leisure interests:* folklore, theatre, music, foreign relations. *Address:* Islandi Väljak 1, 15049 Tallinn, Estonia; Lükati Tee 6-7, 12012 Tallinn, Estonia (Home). *Telephone:* 631-7164 (Office); *Fax:* 631-7199; *E-mail:* krista.kilvet@mfa.ee.

KIM MYUNG-JA, PH D; South Korean politician; b 13 July 1944, Seoul; three c. *Education:* Seoul Nat Univ and Univ of Virginia (USA). *Career:* Visiting Researcher Univ of Tokyo (Japan) 1989; Prof of Chemistry and Dean Coll of Science Sookmyung Women's Univ 1974–; mem Advisory Council on Democratic and Peaceful Unification 1991–99; Commen- tator on Science and Tech Korean Broadcasting System (KBS) 1995–99; Policy Advisor Environment Forum of Nat Ass 1996–99; Advisor Presidential Council for Science and Tech 1997–99; mem Korean Cttee of UNESCO 1997–99, Environment Cttee of Korean Nat Council of Women 1997–99, Environmental Conservation Steering Cttee, Ministry of the Environment 1997–99, Metropolitan Environ- ment Council, Korean Organizing Cttee 1998–99; mem Bd Dirs Citizen's Justice Movt 1996–99, Korea Research Council of Funda- mental Science and Tech 1999; Minister of the Environment 1999–; Vice Pres Korean Science Writer's Asscn 1988; mem Korean Acad of

Science History 1990, Korean Acad of Science and Tech 1994–; Presidential Prize for Enhancement of Science and Tech. *Publications:* Structure of Scientific Revolution 1991, Scientific Tradition of Orient and Occident – Environment Movement 1991, Modern Society and Science 1992, Realm of Science and Technology 1998. *Address:* Ministry of the Environment, 1 Jungang-dong, Gwachon City, Kyonggi Prov, Republic of Korea (Office); 602 Hyochang Green Villat, 3–5 Hyochang-dong, Yongsan-ku, Seoul, Republic of Korea. *Telephone:* (2) 504-9211; (2) 504-9214; *Fax:* (2) 504-9200; *E-mail:* mjkim@me.go.kr; *Internet:* www.me.go.kr.

KIM SUNG-JOO; South Korean business executive; b 1956. *Education:* Amherst Coll, Harvard Business School (USA). *Career:* Pres Sung Joo Int (retail company) 1988–. *Publications:* I Want to be a Beautiful Outcast. *Address:* c/o International Small Business Consortium, 3334 Main St, #433, Norman, OK 73072, USA.

KIMANE, Itumeleng, PH D; Lesotho lecturer in sociology; b 5 July 1955, Welkom; d of Samuel Sellor and Elizabeth Matlale (née Pulc) Kimane; m Napo Mohale 1989; one d three step-d one step-s. *Education:* Nat Univ of Lesotho, Univ Coll (Cardiff) and Edinburgh Univ (UK). *Career:* Asst Teacher Nat Univ of Lesotho 1979, Lecturer 1982, Sr Lecturer 1991, Head Sociology Dept 1983–85, 1990, Deputy Dean Faculty of Social Sciences 1983–85; Dean Faculty of Postgraduate Studies 1996; mem univ cttees; winner Gender Issues Research Competition, Org of Social Science Research in E and Southern Africa. *Publications:* The Diagnosis and Management of Acute Respiratory Infections by Caretakers of Children Under the Age of Five in Lesotho: an anthropological study 1991, The Gender Planning System: enhancing the participation and performance of civil servants in Lesotho 1991. *Leisure interests:* music, films, cooking, reading. *Address:* National University of Lesotho, Dept of Social Anthropology and Social Studies, PO Roma 180, Maseru, Lesotho. *Telephone:* 340601; *Fax:* 340000.

KINCAID, Jamaica; Antigua and Barbuda writer; b (Elaine Potter Richardson) 25 May 1949, St John's; d of Annie Richardson; m Allen Shawn 1979; one s one d. *Career:* Staff writer The New Yorker 1976; writer 1978–; numerous hon degrees. *Publications:* At the Bottom of the River (short stories; American Acad and Inst of Arts and Letters Morton Dauwen Zabel Award) 1983, Annie John (novel; Ritz Paris Hemingway Award nomination) 1985, A Small Place (non-fiction) 1988, Lucy (novel) 1990, An Autobiography of My Mother 1996, My Brother 1997, My Favorite Plant 1998, My Garden (non-fiction). *Address:* c/o Farrar Straus & Giroux, 19 Union Square W, New York, NY 10003, USA.

KINCSES, Veronica; Hungarian opera and concert singer (soprano); d of György Kincses and Etelka Angyal; m József Vajda; one s. *Education:* Liszt Ferenc Music Acad (Budapest) and Accademia Santa Cecilia (Rome). *Career:* Soloist State Opera Budapest; Lieder and aria recitalist, also sings oratorio; guest performances USA, Argentina, Venezuela, Hong Kong, Singapore etc 1997–98; First Prize Int UNESCO Song Competition, Bratislava; Liszt Prize; Kossuth Prize; Merited Artist Award; Grand Prix du Disque, Paris. *Operas include:* Madam Butterfly, La Bohème, Manon Lescaut, Turandot, Le Villi, Le nozze di Figaro, Così fan Tutte, La Clemenza di Tito, Don Giovanni, Simone Boccanegra, La Forza del Destino, Carmen, Faust, Fiamma, Die Meistersinger von Nürnberg, Adriana Lecouvreur, Tosca, Bluebeard's Castle. *Leisure interest:* teaching singers. *Address:* International Manage- ment of the Hungarian State Opera, 1061 Budapest, Andrássy ut 22, Hungary; Robert Lombardo Associates, 61 W 62nd St, New York, NY 10023, USA. *Telephone:* (1) 332-7372 (Hungary); (212) 586-4453 (New York).

KING, Annette Faye, BA; New Zealand politician; b 13 Sept 1947, Murchison; one c. *Education:* Naimea Coll and Waikato Univ. *Career:* Branch Sec and Chair Lab Party; mem House of Reps (Parl) for Horowhenna 1984–87, 1987–91, Chair Parl Select Cttee on Social Services, mem House Select Cttee, Caucus Cttee on Women, Social Services and Community Affairs; Minister of Employment, of Immigra- tion and of Youth Affairs 1989–90; Under-Sec for Social Welfare, Employment and Youth Affairs; currently Minister of Health and Minister for Racing; Dental nurse 1965–70, 1973–82; tutor in dentistry 1982–84; Vice-Pres State Dental Nurses' Inst 1981–84; mem Tourism

2000 Task Force Cttee. *Address:* c/o House of Representatives, POB 18041, Wellington, New Zealand. *Telephone:* (4) 719199; *Fax:* (4) 990704.

KING, Billie Jean; American tennis player; b 22 Nov 1943, Long Beach, CA; d of Willard J. Moffitt; m Larry King 1965. *Education:* Los Angeles State Univ. *Career:* Amateur player 1958–67, Professional 1967–; Wimbledon Champion (UK) 1966, 1967, 1968, 1972, 1973, 1975; S African Champion 1966, 1967, 1969; US Champion 1967, 1971, 1972, 1974; Australian Champion 1968; Italian Champion 1970; German Champion 1971; French Champion 1972; has won record 20 Wimbledon titles (six singles, ten doubles, four mixed) and played more than 100 matches; had won 1,046 singles victories by 1984; f Women's Tennis Asscn 1973; Publr Women Sports 1974–; Sports Commentator ABC TV 1975–78; Commr US Tennis Team 1981–; CEO Domino's Pizza TeamTennis 1985–; Capt US Fed Cup Team 1995–96; Women's Olympic Tennis Coach 1996; Consultant Virginia Slims Championship Series; Top Woman Athlete of the Year 1973; named to Int Tennis Hall of Fame 1987, Nat Women's Hall of Fame 1990; Lifetime Achievement Award, March of Dimes 1994. *Publications:* Tennis To Win 1970, Billie Jean (jtly) 1974, We Have Come A Long Way: The Story of Women's Tennis 1988. *Address:* c/o World TeamTennis, 445 N Wells, Suite 404, Chicago, IL 60610, USA.

KING, Carolyn Dineen, BA, LL B; American federal judge; b 30 Jan 1938, Syracuse, NY; d of Robert and Carolyn (née Bareham) Dineen; m 2nd John King 1988; three s (by previous marriage). *Education:* Smith Coll and Yale Univ. *Career:* Called to the Bar, Washington, DC 1962, TX 1963; law practice Houston 1962–79; Judge US Court of Appeals (5th Circuit), Houston 1979–, Chief Judge 1999–; Trustee and mem Exec Comm Univ of St Thomas 1988–; Trustee, Sec, Treas, Chair of Audit Cttee, Finance Cttee and mem Man Cttee United Way Texas Gulf Coast 1979–85; mem Council American Law Inst 1991–; mem ABA, Fed Bar Asscn. *Address:* US Court of Appeals 11020, US Courthouse, 515 Rusk St, Houston, TX 77002-2694, USA.

KING, Coretta Scott, AB, MUS B; American singer and civil rights campaigner; b 27 April 1927, Marion, AL; d of Obidiah Scott and Bernice McMurray; m Martin Luther King, Jr 1953 (assassinated 1968); two s two d. *Education:* Antioch Coll, New England Conservatory of Music. *Career:* Concert debut as singer, Springfield, OH 1948; numerous concerts throughout USA, India 1959; Voice Instructor, Morris Brown Coll, Atlanta, GA 1962; Del to White House Conf on Children and Youth 1960; Sponsor Cttee for Sane Nuclear Policy, Cttee on Responsibility, Mobilization to End War in Vietnam 1966–67; mem Southern Rural Action Project, Inc; Pres Martin Luther King Jr Foundation; Chair Comm on Econ Justice for Women; mem Exec Cttee, Nat Cttee of Inquiry; Co-Chair Clergy and Laymen Concerned about Vietnam, Nat Comm for Full Employment 1974; Pres Martin Luther King Jr Center for Social Change; Co-Chair Nat Cttee for Full Employment; mem Exec Bd Nat Health Insurance Cttee, Bd S Christian Leadership Conf, Martin Luther King Jr Foundation, UK; Trustee Robert F. Kennedy Memorial Foundation, Ebenezer Baptist Church; Sponsor Margaret Sanger Memorial Foundation; Commentator Cable News Network (CNN), Atlanta 1980–; lecturer and writer; Hon LHD (Boston, Marymount-Manhattan Coll, NY) 1969, (Morehouse Coll, Atlanta) 1970; Hon HHD (Brandeis, MA) 1969, (Wilberforce, OH, Bethune-Cookman Coll, FL, Princeton) 1970; Hon LL D (Bates Coll, ME) 1971; Hon MUS D (New England Conservatory of Music, Boston) 1971; numerous awards including Universal Love Award (Premio San Valentine) 1968, Wateler Peace Prize 1968, Dag Hammarskjöld Award 1969, Pacem in Terris Award (Int Overseas Service Foundation) 1969, Leadership for Freedom Award (Roosevelt Univ) 1971, Martin Luther King Memorial Medal 1971, Int Viareggio Award 1971. *Publication:* My Life With Martin Luther King Jr 1969; articles in magazines. *Address:* Martin Luther King Jr Center for Nonviolent Social Change, 449 Auburn Ave, NE, Atlanta, GA 30312, USA; 671 Beckwith St, SW, Atlanta, GA 30314, USA.

KING, Lynn, LL B, MA; Canadian judge; b 19 April 1944, Ont; d of Harry and Madelin (née Tarshis) Waisberg; m M. T. Kelly 1981; two s. *Education:* Univ of Toronto and Fletcher School of Law and Diplomacy. *Career:* Lawyer 1973–85; Partner Copeland, King 1973–75; Lecturer Osgoode Hall Law School 1975–76; Partner King and Sachs 1976–86;

Instructor Bar Admission Course 1979–85; Judge Ontario Court of Justice 1985–. *Publications:*Law, Law, Law 1975, What Every Woman Should Know About Marriage, Separation and Divorce 1980, Women Against Censorship (jtly) 1986. *Leisure interests:* cycling, reading, wilderness canoeing, skiing, swimming. *Address:* 311 Jarvis St, Toronto, ON M5B 2C4, Canada. *Telephone:* (416) 327-6891.

KING, Marcia Gygli, BA, MFA; American artist; b 4 June 1931, Cleveland, OH; d of Robert and Ruth (née Farr) Gygli; m Rollin White King 1956 (divorced 1974); two s. *Education:* Smith Coll (Northampton, MA) and Univ of Texas at San Antonio (USA). *Career:* Art Critic Express News, San Antonio, TX 1976–77; Artist New York 1979–; Lecturer Nat Gallery of Art (Washington, DC) 1956–60, Univ of Texas 1976, Southern Methodist Univ (Dallas, TX) 1984, McNay Art Museum (San Antonio) 1984, Washington Project for the Arts 1985, Monserrat Coll of Art (Beverly, MA) 1987, Whitney Museum (New York) 1988, Lehman Coll (City Univ of New York) 1988; solo exhibitions include MacNamara O'Connor Museum, McNay Art Museum (San Antonio) 1984, Parker Smalley Gallery (New York) 1988, 1990, Haines Gallery (San Francisco, CA) 1988, Katzen Brown Gallery (New York) 1988–90, Wallace Wentworth (Washington, DC) 1989, Cleveland Center for Contemporary Art 1989–90, Hal Katzen Gallery (New York) 1992–94, Guild Hall Museum (East Hampton, NY) 1995, Brooklyn Botanic Garden (Brooklyn, NY) 2001; collections include Brooklyn Museum, Guggenheim Museum, Johnson Museum, Nat Museum of Women in the Arts, Cleveland Museum of Art (OH), Guild Hall Museum (East Hampton, NY), Newark Museum (NJ), Arkansas Arts Center; MTA Grant for Creative Stations Project (New York) 1995; Hon MFA (Texas) 1981; numerous awards and prizes including Artist of the Year, San Antonio Art League 2000. *Address:* 477 Broome St 63, New York, NY 10013, USA; 626 Evans Ave, San Antonio, TX 78209, USA. *Telephone:* (212) 925-5160; *Fax:* (212) 925-5160; *E-mail:* marciagk@aol.com.

KING, Mary Elizabeth; British equestrian; b 8 June 1961, Newark; d of Lieut-Commdr M.D.H. Thomson; m David King 1995; one s one d. *Education:* Manor House School (Honiton), King's Grammar School and Evendine Court (Cordon Bleu). *Career:* Team gold medals 1991, 1994, 1995, 1997; rep GB at Barcelona, Atlanta and Sydney Olympics; British Open Champion 1991, 1992, 1996; winner Badminton Horse Trials 1992, 2000, Burghley Horse Trials 1996; Watch Leader 'Sir Winston Churchill'. *Publications:* Mary Thomson's Eventing Year 1993, All the King's Horses 1997, William and Mary 1998. *Leisure interests:* tennis, snow and water-skiing. *Address:* School House, Salcombe Regis, Sidmouth EX10 0JQ, UK (Home); Matford Park Farm, Exminster, Exeter, Devon EX6 8AT, UK (Home). *Telephone:* (1395) 514882 (Office); *Fax:* (1392) 432531 (Office); *E-mail:* eluk@co.uk; *Internet:* www.eluk.co.uk/maryking.

KING, Poppy; Australian business executive; b 24 May 1972, Melbourne; d of the late Graham Nathan and Rachelle King. *Education:* Wesley Coll (Melbourne). *Career:* Founder Poppy Industries cosmetics co aged 18, CEO 1992–; Young Australian of the Year 1995. *Address:* Poppy Industries Pty Ltd, POB 4354, Melbourne, Vic 3000, Australia. *E-mail:* poppyk@poppy.com.au.

KING, Dame Thea, DBE, FRCM, ARCM, FGSM; British clarinettist; b 26 Dec 1925, Hitchin, Herts; d of Henry and Dorothea King; m Frederick J. Thurston 1953 (died 1953). *Education:* Bedford High School and Royal Coll of Music (London). *Career:* Sadler's Wells Orchestra 1950–52; Portia Wind Ensemble 1955–68; London Mozart Players 1956–84; Prof Royal Coll of Music 1961–87, Guildhall School of Music 1988–; mem English Chamber Orchestra, Melos Ensemble of London, Robles Ensemble; frequent soloist, broadcaster and recitalist; recordings include works by Mozart, Brahms, Spohr, Mendelssohn, Bruch, Finzi and Stanford, and 20th Century British music. *Publications:* Clarinet Solos (Chester Woodwind Series) 1977, Arrangement of J. S. Bach: Duets for Two Clarinets 1979, Clarinet Duets (Chester Woodwind Series) 1979, Schumann for the Clarinet (jtly) 1991, Mendelssohn for the Clarinet 1993, The Romantic Clarinet: A Mendelssohn Collection 1994, Tchaikovsky 1995. *Leisure interests:* cows, lace-making, skiing. *Address:* 16 Milverton Rd, London NW6 7AS, UK. *Telephone:* (20) 8459-3453.

KING-WYNTER, Sheila Dorothy, BS, MB, MD; Jamaican micro-biologist; b 28 Nov 1932, Barbados; d of Alfred and Henrietta (née Stuart) King; m Hugh Wynter 1959; two s one d. *Education:* Queen's Coll (Barbados), Univ Coll of the W Indies and Univ of London (UK). *Career:* Intern and resident Univ Hosp of the W Indies 1959–61, Asst Lecturer in Microbiology 1961–72, Head Dept of Microbiology 1972–84, Prof of Microbiology 1981; concurrently Dir WHO Influenza Surveillance Centre; numerous papers in scientific journals; Medal of Appreciation in Field of Medicine from Prime Minister 1983. *Leisure interest:* art. *Address:* University Hospital of the West Indies, Dept of Microbiology, Mona, Kingston 7, Jamaica (Office); 1 Millsborough Close, Kingston 6, Jamaica (Home). *Telephone:* 927-1660 (Office).

KINGSOLVER, Barbara, MS; American writer; b 8 April 1955, Annapolis, Maryland; m; two d. *Education:* DePauw Univ (Indiana). *Career:* Scientific writer, Office of Arid Land Studies, Univ of Arizona 1981–85; freelance journalist 1985–87; Bellwether Prize for Fiction 1997. *Publications:* The Bean Trees 1988, Holding the Line 1989, Homeland and Other Stories 1989, Animal Dreams 1990, Another America 1992, Pigs in Heaven 1993, High Tide in Tucson 1995, The Poisonwood Bible 1998, Prodigal Summer 2000.

KINGSTON, Maxine Hong, AB; American writer; b 27 Oct 1940, Stockton, CA; d of Tom and Ying Lan (née Chew) Hong; m Earll Kingston 1962; one s. *Education:* Univ of California at Berkeley. *Career:* Teacher of English, Sunset High School, Hayward, CA 1965–66, Kahuku High School, HI 1967, Kahaluu Drop-In School 1968, Kailua High School 1969, Honolulu Business Coll 1969, Mid-Pacific Inst, Honolulu 1970–77; Prof of English, Visiting Writer Univ of Hawaii 1977; Thelma McCandless Distinguished Prof Eastern Michigan Univ 1986; Chancellor's Distinguished Prof Univ of California at Berkeley 1990–; NEA Writing Fellow 1980; Guggenheim Fellow 1981; Mademoiselle Magazine Award 1977; Anisfield-Wolf Book Award 1978; Stockton Arts Comm Award 1981; Hawaii Award for Literature 1982; named Living Treasure of Hawaii 1980; American Acad and Inst Award in Literature 1990; award from American Acad of Arts and Sciences 1992; Nat Humanities Medal 1998; Fred Cody Lifetime Achievement Award 1998; Ka Palapola Po'okela Award 1999. *Publications:* The Woman Warrior: Memoirs of a Girlhood Among Ghosts (Nat Book Critics Circle Award for Non-fiction) 1976, China Men (Nat Book Award) 1981, Hawaii One Summer 1987, Through The Black Curtain 1988, Tripmaster Monkey: His Fake Books (PEN USA W Fiction Award) 1989; numerous short stories, articles and poems. *Address:* Department of English, University of California, 322 Wheeler Hall, Berkeley, CA 94720, USA.

KINIGI, Sylvie; Burundian politician. *Career:* Fmr Exec Officer Structural Adjustment Programme; Prime Minister of Burundi 1993–94; fmr mem Union pour le Progres Nat (UPRONA). *Address:* c/o Office of the Prime Minister, Bujumbura, Burundi.

KINNOCK, Glenys Elizabeth, BA, DIP ED, FRSA; British politician and organization executive; b 7 July 1944, Northampton; d of Cyril and Elizabeth (née Pritchard) Parry; m Neil Gordon Kinnock 1967; one s one d. *Education:* Holyhead Comprehensive School and Univ of Wales (Cardiff). *Career:* Teacher 1966–93; MEP (Lab) for S Wales E 1994–99, re-elected 1999–, mem EP Devt and Co-operation Cttee, and of Foreign Affairs, Human Rights, Common Security and Defence Policy Cttee; Vice-Pres EU/African, Caribbean and Pacific (ACP) Joint Ass; Rapporteur on the EU–S Africa Trade and Devt Agreement, and for Working Group on the Future of the EU/ACP relations; Labour Party Spokesperson for Int Devt in EP; EU Special Rep at elections in Cambodia 1998; Vice-Pres Univ of Wales, Cardiff 1988–95; Pres Coleg Harlech 1998–; Chair Forum on Early Warning and Early Response (FEWER); mem Council Voluntary Service Overseas; Pres Steel Action, One World Action; Patron Saferworld; Hon Fellow Univ of Wales Coll, Newport 1998; Hon LL D (Thames Valley) 1994; Dr hc (Brunel) 1997, (Kingston); has compiled and presented programmes on social and family issues for BBC Radio 4. *Publications:* Voices for One World (ed) 1988, Eritrea Images of War and Peace 1988, Namibia – Birth of a Nation 1990, By Faith and Daring 1993. *Leisure interests:* reading, theatre, cinema. *Address:* 1 Bridge View, Cwmfelinfach, Ynysddu, Newport, Gwent NP1 7HG, UK; North Wales Labour European Office, 47 Kirnel St, Rhyl LU8 1AG, UK. *Telephone:* (29) 2061-8337; *Fax:* (29) 2061-8226; *E-mail:* gkinnock@europe-wales.new.labour.org .uk.

KINSHOFER-GÜTHLEIN, Christa; German skier; b 24 Jan 1961, Munich; m Reinhard Güthlein 1985. *Career:* World Champion 1979, Vice-Champion 1980; Silver Medal Olympic Games, Lake Placid (USA) 1980; Silver and Bronze Medals Olympic Games, Calgary (Canada) 1988; numerous other medals; owner children's sport shops in Rosenheim and Munich; mem Olympic Asscn; Sportswoman of the Year 1980; Ski Sportswoman of the Year 1980, 1981. *Leisure interests:* reading, conversation, shopping, flea markets, decorating. *Address:* Münchner Str 44, 83022 Rosenheim, Germany.

KINSKI, Nastassja; American (b German) actress; b (Nastassja Nakszynski) 24 Jan 1961, W Berlin; d of the late Klaus Kinski and of Ruth Brigitte Kinski; m Ibrahim Moussa 1984; one s one d; one s with Quincy Jones. *Career:* Made film debut in Falsche Bewegung 1975; Bundespreis 1983. *Films include:* Stay As You Are 1978, Tess 1978, One From The Heart 1982, Cat People 1982, Moon In The Gutter 1983, Spring Symphony 1983, Unfaithfully Yours 1984, The Hotel New Hampshire 1984, Maria's Lovers 1984, Paris, Texas 1984, Harem, Revolution 1985, Torrents of Spring 1989, On a Moonlit Night 1989, Magdalene 1989, The King's Future 1989, Night Sun 1991, Faraway, So Close!, Terminal Velocity 1994, One Night Stand 1997, Little Boy Blue 1997, Father's Day 1997, Somebody is Waiting 1997, Sunshine 1998, Your Friends and Neighbors 1999, The Magic of Marciano 1999, The Intruder 1999, Town and Country 1999, The Lost 1999, The Claim 2000. *Address:* c/o William Morris Agency, 151 S El Camino Drive, Beverly Hills, CA 90212, USA.

KIRANOVA, Evgenia, LL B; Bulgarian journalist and magazine editor; b 23 Jan 1929, Sofia; m 1st Dencho Denchev 1948 (until 1967); one s one d; m 2nd Ivan Delchev 1973. *Education:* Univ of Sofia. *Career:* Sec World Democratic Fed of Women 1954–57; Deputy Ed Bulgarian-Soviet Friendship 1957–66; Head Foreign Dept Bulgarian Writers' Union 1966–67; Ed Pogled (Review) 1968–72; Foreign Commentator Bulgarian Radio and TV 1972–73; World Peace Council Sec, Helsinki 1973–82; Sec-Gen, Vice-Pres Int Cttee of Solidarity with Cyprus 1975; Political Observer Sofia Press Agency 1985–90; Ed-in-Chief Nie Jhenite women's magazine 1990; Founder, Pres Women's Union for Dignity and Equality; Vice-Pres Bulgarian section Int Women's Fed of Business and Professional Women. *Publications:* Well Known and Beloved 1960, Legal Defence of Motherhood 1965, Cyprus Drama, Women in the Contemporary World, Fight for Peace, Suomi. *Leisure interests:* tourism, swimming, cooking. *Address:* 1712 Sofia, J. K. Mladost 3, bl 316, vh A, Bulgaria. *Telephone:* (2) 74-40-22.

KIRBY, Pamela Josephine, B SC, PH D; British business executive; b 23 Sept 1953, Bristol; d of Patrick and Anne (née Ceridwen) Kirby. *Education:* King's Coll (London) and Cardiothoracic Inst (London). *Career:* Joined pharmaceutical industry as Medical Rep 1979; held variety of positions in clinical trials, sales and marketing 1979–88; Man Dir Astra Pharmaceuticals Ltd 1988–94, Vice-Pres of Corp Strategy and Regional Dir Astra AB 1995; mem Council Swedish Chamber of Commerce 1990–94, Bd of Welsh Devt Agency 1991–94. *Leisure interests:* classical music, piano, squash. *Address:* Astra Pharmaceuticals Ltd, Charles House, 6th Floor, 5–11 Lower Regent St, London SW1Y 4LR, UK.

KIRKBY, Emma, OBE, MA, FGSM; British singer; b 26 Feb 1949, Camberley, Surrey; d of the late Geoffrey Kirkby and of Beatrice Daphne Kirkby; one s by Anthony Rooley. *Education:* Sherborne School for Girls, Somerville Coll (Oxford) and pvt singing lessons with Jessica Cash. *Career:* Specialist singer of renaissance, baroque and classical repertoire; began full-time professional singing 1975; involved in revival of performances with period instruments and the attempt to recreate the sounds the composers would have heard 1975–; Henry Wood Promenade Concerts 1977–; freelance singer, particularly with Consort of Musicke, Taverner Players, Acad of Ancient Music; Hon D LITT (Salford) 1985; Hon D MUS (Bath) 1994, (Sheffield) 2000. *Recordings include:* Complete Songs of John Dowland 1976–77, Messiah (Handel) 1979, 1989, Madrigals by Monteverdi, Wert, Scarlatti and other Italians, Schütz, Grabbe, Wilbye, Ward and other English composers,

Handel's Athalia, Joshua, Judas Maccabaeus, Sequences by Hildegarde of Bingen (Hyperion), Vespers (Monteverdi) 1983, Exsultate Jubilate (Mozart) 1984, Mass in B minor (Bach) 1984, Italian Arias (Handel) 1985, Monteverdi duets (jtly), Mozart Concert Arias 1986, Songs by John Blow (jtly) 1987, Monteverdi Madrigals 1989, Dowland Songs 1989, Arias by Arne and Handel 1993, Vivaldi Opera Arias 1995, Handel Opera Arias, Songs and Cantatas of Maurice Greene 1995, Handel Opera Arias 1996, Stabat Mater (Pergolesi), Haydn's Creation, Mozart Motets, Mozart Concert Arias, Christmas Music with Westminster Abbey Choir. *Address:* c/o Consort of Musicke, 54A Leamington Rd Villas, London W11 1HT, UK. *Telephone:* (20) 7229-5142; *Fax:* (20) 7221-1282.

KIRKLAND, Gelsey; American ballet dancer; b 1953, Bethlehem, PA; m Greg Lawrence. *Education:* School of American Ballet. *Career:* Youngest mem New York Ballet at 15 in 1968, Soloist 1969–72, Prin Dancer 1972–74; American Ballet Theater 1974–81, 1982–84; Teacher and Coach American Ballet Theater 1992–; Guest Dancer Royal Ballet, London 1980, 1986, Stuttgart Ballet, Germany 1980. *Performances include:* Firebird, The Goldberg Variations, Scherzo Fantastique, An Evening's Waltzes, The Leaves Are Fading, Hamlet, The Tiller in the Field, Four Bagatelles, Stravinsky Symphony in C, Song of the Nightingale Connotations, Romeo and Juliet; *TV appearance:* The Nutcracker 1977; *Publications:* Dancing on My Grave (autobiog) 1987, The Shape of Love (jtly) 1990, The Little Ballerina and Her Dancing Horse 1993. *Address:* c/o Dubé Zakin Management Inc, 67 Riverside Drive, Apt 3B, New York, NY 10024, USA.

KIRKLAND-STROVER, Marie Claire, CM, QC, LL D, BA; Canadian former judge; b Palmer, MA, USA; d of the late Charles and of Rose (née Demers) Kirkland; m 1st P. Casgrain (divorced); m 2nd Wyndham Strover; two s one d. *Education:* McGill Univ. *Career:* With Cerini and Jamieson 1952; first woman elected to Québec Legis Ass 1961, re-elected 1970; first woman Cabinet Minister as Minister of Transport and Communications 1964, Minister of Tourism, Fish and Game 1970, of Cultural Affairs 1972–73; Judge Prov Court of Québec 1973–90; Founder, Pres Canadian section Int Alliance of Women; Hon LL D (Moncton) 1965, (York) 1975; mem Order of Canada; Chevalier de l'Ordre Souverain du Québec; Grande Dame de l'Ordre Souverain Militaire de St-Jean de Jérusalem; Persons Award, Gov-Gen 1993. *Leisure interests:* travel, fishing, golf. *Address:* 2865 Rothesay Rd, T/H 14, Rothesay, NB E2E 5X9, Canada.

KIRKPATRICK, Jeane Duane Jordan, MA, PH D; American diplomatist and professor of political science; b 19 Nov 1926, Duncan, OK; d of Welcher F. and Leona (née Kile) Jordan; m Evron M. Kirkpatrick 1955; three s. *Education:* Stephens Coll (Columbia, MO), Barnard Coll, Columbia Univ (NY) and Univ of Paris. *Career:* Research Analyst Dept of State 1951–53; Research Assoc George Washington Univ, Washington, DC 1954–56, Fund for the Republic 1956–58; Asst Prof of Political Science Trinity Coll, Washington, DC 1962–67; Assoc Prof of Govt, Georgetown Univ, Washington, DC 1967–73, Prof 1978–, Leavey Prof in Foundations of American Freedom 1978–; Sr Fellow American Enterprise Inst for Public Policy Research 1977–; Perm Rep to UN 1981–85; fmr Democrat, joined Republican Party 1985; fmr mem Democratic Nat Comm; Vice-Chair Comm on Vice-Presidential Selection 1972–74; mem Nat Comm on Party Structure and Presidential Nomination 1975, Int Research Council Center for Strategic and Int Studies, Georgetown Univ; Earhart Fellow 1956–57; numerous hon degrees, including Hon LHD (Georgetown and St Anselm's Univs, Univs of Pittsburgh and W Florida, Charleston and Mt Vernon Colls) 1978, Dr hc (Hebrew Univ of Jerusalem and Tel-Aviv Univ, Israel); Prix Politique; Award of the Commonwealth Fund; Gold Medal Veterans of Foreign Wars; Hubert H. Humphrey Award, American Political Science Asscn; Gold Medal, Nicholas Soc; Christian A. Herter Award, Boston World Affairs Asscn; Defender of Jerusalem Award; Distinguished Public Service Medal; Distinguished Alumna Award, Stephens Coll 1978; Distinguished Alumna Medal, Barnard Coll 1983; B'nai B'rith Award 1982; Pres Medal of Freedom 1985, Hubert Humphry Award (American Political Science Asscn) 1988. *Publications:* Foreign Students in the United States: A National Survey 1966, Mass Behavior in Battle and Captivity 1968, Leader and Vanguard in Mass Society: The Peronist Movement in Argentina 1972, Political Woman 1974, The New Presidential Elite 1976, Dismantling the Parties: Reflections on

Party Reform and Party Decomposition 1978, Dictatorships and Double Standards 1982, The Reagan Phenomenon 1983, Legitimacy and Force (2 vols) 1988, Foreign Affairs: America and the World 1989–90, The Withering Away of the Totalitarian State 1990; also articles in political journals. *Leisure interests:* contemporary fiction, Bach, gourmet cooking. *Address:* American Enterprise Institute, 1150 17th St, NW, Washington, DC 20036, USA. *Telephone:* (202) 862-5814.

KIRNER, Joan Elizabeth, AO, AM; Australian politician; b 20 June 1938, Essendon, Vic; d of John and Beryl Hood; m Ron Kirner 1960; two s one d. *Education:* Penleigh Ladies' Coll, Univ High School and Univ of Melbourne. *Career:* Teacher 1959–60; has held various voluntary posts in educ; mem Australian Schools Comm 1973–78, UNESCO Educ Cttee 1973–78; joined Australian Lab Party 1979, Pres Vic Br 1994–95; mem Victoria Parl for Melbourne W 1982–85; Minister of Conservation, Forests and Lands 1985–88, of Educ 1988–90, of Ethnic Affairs 1990–92; Deputy Premier of Victoria 1989–90, Premier 1990–92; Chair Employment Services Regulatory Authory 1994; Nat Chair Centenary of Fed Advisory Cttee 1994–95, mem 2000–; Vice-Pres Evatt Foundation 1994; Co-Convenor Emily's List Australia; f Nat Landcare Program; contrib to educational magazines; Fellow Australian Coll of Educ. *Leisure interests:* bush walking, reading, music. *Address:* Old Treasury Bldg, Cnr Spring and Collins St, Melbourne, Vic 3000, Australia.

KIRSCHSTEIN, Ruth Lillian, AB, MD; American medical practitioner and administrator; b 12 Oct 1926, Brooklyn, NY; d of Julius and Elizabeth (née Berm) Kirschstein; m Alan S. Rabson 1950; one s. *Education:* Long Island Univ (New York) and Tulane Univ School of Medicine (New Orleans, LA). *Career:* Instructor in Pathology Tulane Univ 1954–55; Medical Officer, Resident in Pathology Lab of Viral Products, NIH 1956–60, Head Section of Pathology, Lab of Viral Immunology 1960–62, Asst Chief of Lab 1962–64, Acting Chief Lab of Pathology 1964–65, Chief 1965–72, Asst Dir Div of Biologics Standards 1971–72, Dir Nat Inst of Gen Medical Sciences 1974–93, Acting Assoc Dir for Research on Women's Health 1990–91, Acting Dir NIH 1993, Deputy Dir 1993–; Acting Deputy Dir Bureau of Biologics, Food and Drug Admin 1972–73, Deputy Assoc Commr for Science 1973–74; mem Inst of Medicine NAS; elected to American Acad of Arts and Sciences 1992; Hon LL D (Atlanta) 1985; Hon D SC (Mount Sinai School of Medicine) 1984, (Medical Coll of Ohio) 1986; Hon D HUM LITT (Long Island) 1991; Dr hc (School of Medicine, Tulane Univ) 1997; Presidential Meritorious Exec Rank Award 1980; Presidential Distinguished Exec Rank Award 1985, 1995; Distinguished Exec Service Award, Sr Exec Asscn 1985; Dr Nathan Davis Award, American Medical Asscn 1990; Public Service Award, Fed of American Societies for Experimental Biology 1993; Nat Public Service Award, American Soc of Public Admin/Nat Acad of Public Admin 1994; Roger W. Jones Award, American Univ 1994; Georgeanna Seegar Jones Women's Health Lifetime Achievement Award 1995. *Publications:* The National Institute of General Medical Sciences Probes Cellular and Molecular Bases of Life 1983, The Virus and Poliomyelitis Vaccine 1984, Women's Health Report of the Public Health Service Task Force on Women's Health Issues 1985. *Leisure interests:* music, art. *Address:* National Institute Health Bldg 1, Rm 126, 1 Center Drive, MSC 0148, Bethesda, MD 20892-0148, USA; 6 West Drive, Bethesda, MD 20814, USA (Home). *Telephone:* (301) 496-2433 (Office); *Fax:* (301) 402-2700; *E-mail:* execsec1@od.nih.gov (Office); *Internet:* www.nih.gov (Office).

KIRSZENSTEIN-SZEWIŃSKA, Irena, M ECON; Polish athlete; b 24 May 1946, Leningrad (now St Petersburg), USSR (now Russian Fed); m; two s. *Education:* Warsaw Univ. *Career:* Silver Medallist for long jump and 200m, Olympic Games, Tokyo 1964, Gold Medal 4 x 100m relay, Bronze Medallist 100m and Gold Medallist 200m, Mexico 1968, Bronze Medallist 200m, Munich, Germany 1972, Gold Medal for 400m, Montréal, Canada 1976; seven times world record holder for 200m and 400m; mem Provisional Nat Council of Patriotic Movt for Nat Rebirth (PRON) 1982–83, Nat Council PRON 1983–89, All-Poland Peace Coalition 1989–, Vice-Chair 1989–; Pres Polish Women's Sport Asscn 1994–, Polish Athletic Asscn 1997–; Vice-Pres Polish Olympic Cttee 1988–, Polish Athletics Union 1989–, Polish Olympians Asscn 1993–, World Olympians Asscn 1995–; mem Council European Athletic Asscn 1995–, Women's Cttee, Int Amateur Athletic Fed, Int Olympic Cttee (IOC) 1998–, IOC Co-ordination Cttee 1998–; Pres

Irena Szewinska Foundation—Vita-Aktiva 1998–; Gold Cross of Merit 1964; Officer's Cross, Order of Polonia Restituta 1968, Commdr's Cross, Order of Polonia Restituta 1972, with Star 1999, Order of Banner of Labour (2nd Class) 1976. *Leisure interests:* jogging, books, theatre. *Address:* Polish Athletic Association, ul Ceglowska 68/70, 01-809 Warsaw, Poland. *Telephone:* (22) 6397015; *Fax:* (22) 6397016.

KIRTCHEVA, Elena Petkova, D JUR; Bulgarian diplomatist, politician and lawyer; b 18 Sept 1949, Lom; d of Petko Dimitrov Kirtchev and Maria Alexandrova (née Kadieva) Kirtcheva; m 1980; one s. *Education:* Univ of Sofia. *Career:* Legal Adviser industrial plant 1973–76; Lecturer in Nat and World Econ 1976–90; Legal Expert Nat Round Table 1990; Opposition Mem Grand Nat Ass 1990, Vice-Chair New Constitution Comm 1990, mem Bd of Dirs Parl Agrarian Party 1990, mem Bulgarian Parl Del to Ass of Council of Europe 1990; mem Bulgarian Del to Conf on Security and Co-operation in Europe (CSCE) 1990–91; Amb to Switzerland 1991; various scientific articles and studies and manuals and handbooks for univ students. *Leisure interest:* politics. *Address:* Embassy of Bulgaria, Berna Str 2–4, 3005 Berne, Switzerland (Office); Belpstrasse 45, 3007 Berne, Switzerland (Home); Sofia, Nishava St 128, Apt 49, Bulgaria (Home). *Telephone:* (31) 431455 (Office); (31) 3817743 (Switzerland, Home); (2) 59-00-23 (Bulgaria, Home); *Fax:* (31) 430064 (Office); (31) 3817743 (Switzerland, Home).

KISTLER, Darci; American ballet dancer; b 4 June 1964, Riverside, CA; d of Jack B. and Alicia (née Kinner) Kistler; m Peter Martins 1992. *Education:* Studied with Irina Kosmovska (Los Angeles) and School of American Ballet. *Career:* Prin Dancer in corps de ballet New York City Ballet under Balanchine 1980; injured 1982–85; teacher School of American Ballet 1994–; new roles created for her in Suite from Histoire du Soldat to Stravinsky score, neo-classical Tchaikovsky Symphony no 1 1980; New York Women's Award, Golden Plate Award, Dance Magazine Award. *Performances include:* Haydn Concerto 1979, Swan Lake 1979, Brahms–Schönberg Quartet, Divertimento No 15, Symphony in C, Raymonda Variations, Walpurgisnacht Ballet, Valse fantaisie, Tchaikovsky Suite No 3, The Nutcracker Suite, Who Cares?, Balanchine's Chaconne, Jacques d'Amboise's Irish Fantasy and Pastorale 1982, Robbin's Afternoon of a Faun, The Magic Flute 1981–82, Piano Rag-Music 1982, Prélude à l'après-midi d'un faune 1985, A Midsummer Night's Dream, Prodigal Son, Slaughter on Tenth Avenue, Variations pour une porte et un soupir, La sonnambula 1986, Serenade, Ivesiana, Danses concertantes, Mozartiana Jewels 1988–89, The Four Seasons 1989, Allegro brillante, The Goldberg Variations, Other Dances, Dances at a Gathering, In G Major 1989–90, La valse 1991, The Sleeping Beauty, The Nutcracker (film) 1993, Balanchine Celebration 1993, Symphonic Dances 1994, Apollo 1994; *Publication:* Ballerina: My Story 1993. *Address:* c/o New York City Ballet Inc, New York State Theater, 20 Lincoln Center, New York, NY 10023, USA.

KITSON, Linda Frances, MA; British artist and teacher; b 17 Feb 1945, London. *Education:* West Preston Manor School (Rustington), Tortington Park (Arundel), Ecole des Beaux Arts (Lyons, France), St Martin's School of Art and Royal Coll of Art (London). *Career:* Visiting Tutor Royal Coll of Art, St Martin's School of Art 1972–78, Chelsea School of Art, Camberwell School of Art and Crafts, City and Guilds of London Art School 1972–82; Lecturer Royal Coll of Art 1979–82, Visiting Tutor 1984; Official War Artist Falkland Islands Task Force 1982; has staged several one-woman exhibitions and contributed to Royal Acad Summer Exhibition 1971–; Pres Army Arts and Crafts Soc 1983; South Atlantic Medal (with rosette) 1983. *Publication:* The Falklands War: A Visual Diary 1982, The Plague 1985, Sun, Wind, Sand and Stars 1989. *Leisure interests:* rock-dancing, music. *Address:* 1 Argyll Mansions, Kings Rd, London SW3 5ER, UK. *Telephone:* (20) 7584-5020.

KITT, Eartha Mae; American singer and actress; b 26 Jan 1928, North, SC; d of John and Anna Kitt; m William McDonald 1960 (divorced); one d. *Career:* Soloist Katherine Graham Dance Group 1948; night club singer 1949–; numerous TV appearances; records for RCA; Woman of the Year, Nat Asscn of Negro Musicians 1968. *Films include:* New Faces 1953, St Louis Blues 1957, Anna Lucasta 1958, Mark of the Hawk (also known as Accused) 1958, Saint of Devil's Island 1961, Synanon 1965, Up the Chastity Belt 1971, Dragonard, All By Myself (documentary) 1982, Erik the Viking, Boomerang 1991, Fatal Instinct 1993; *Stage*

appearances include: Dr Faustus 1951, New Faces of 1952, Mrs Patterson 1954, Shinbone Alley 1957, Timbuktu 1978, Blues in the Night 1985, The Wizard of Oz 1998, The Wild Party 2000; *TV appearances include:* Batman (guest, as Catwoman); *Recordings include:* I'm Still Here 1989, Live on Broadway 1990, Primitive Man 1990, Where Is My Man 1990, Live in London 1991; *Publications:* Thursday's Child 1956, A Tart Is Not A Sweet, Alone with Me 1976, I'm Still Here 1990, Confessions of a Sex Kitten 1991, Down to Earth (jtly) 2000, How to Rejuvenate: It's Not Too Late (jtly) 2000. *Address:* c/o Eartha Kitt Productions, Flat 37, 888 Seventh Ave, New York, NY 10106, USA.

KITZINGER, Sheila Helena Elizabeth, MBE, M LITT; British writer, social anthropologist and birth educator; b 29 March 1929, Taunton, Somerset; d of Alex and Clare (née Bond) Webster; m Uwe Kitzinger 1952; five d. *Education:* Bishop Fox's Girls' School (Taunton), Ruskin and St Hugh's Colls (Oxford). *Career:* Research Asst Dept of Anthropology, Univ of Edinburgh 1952–53; Course Team Chair Open Univ 1981–83; Man Cttee Midwives' Information and Resource Service 1985–87, Ed Cttee 1987–; Chair Steering Cttee Int Homebirth Movt; Hon Prof Thames Valley Univ 1993; mem Bd Int Caesarean Awareness Network; Consultant Int Childbirth Educ Asscn; Adviser Baby Milk Coalition, Maternity Alliance; Patron Seattle School of Midwifery; Joost de Blank Award for Research 1971. *Publications:* Giving Birth 1971, Education and Counselling for Childbirth 1977, Women as Mothers 1978, The Place of Birth (co-ed) 1978, Birth at Home 1979, The Good Birth Guide 1979, Pregnancy and Childbirth 1980, Sheila Kitzinger's Birth Book 1981, Some Women's Experiences of Episiotomy (jtly) 1981, Episiotomy: physical and emotional aspects 1981, Birth Over Thirty 1982, The New Good Birth Guide 1983, Woman's Experience of Sex 1983, Episiotomy and the Second Stage of Labour (co-ed) 1984, Being Born 1986, The Experience of Childbirth (6th edn) 1987, The Experience of Breastfeeding (2nd edn) 1987, Celebration of Birth 1987, Freedom and Choice in Childbirth 1987, Some Women's Experiences of Epidurals 1987, Giving Birth: How It Really Feels 1987, The Midwife Challenge (ed) 1988, The Crying Baby 1989, The New Pregnancy and Childbirth 1989, Breastfeeding Your Baby 1989, Pregnancy Day by Day (jtly) 1990, Homebirth 1991, Tough Questions (jtly), Ourselves as Mothers, The Year after Childbirth 1995, The Complete Book of Pregnancy and Childbirth 1996, Becoming a Grandmother 1997, Breastfeeding 1999, Rediscovering Birth 2000, Midwifery Guidelines on Water Birth (jtly) 2000, Birth Your Way 2001. *Leisure interest:* painting. *Address:* The Manor, Standlake, Oxon OX27 7RH, UK. *Telephone:* (1865) 300266; *Fax:* (1865) 300438; *E-mail:* info@sheilakitzinger.com; *Internet:* www.info@sheilakitzinger.com.

KIZER, Carolyn Ashley, BA; American writer; b 10 Dec 1925, Spokane, WA; d of Benjamin and M. (née Ashley) Kizer; m 1st Stimson Bullitt 1948 (divorced); two d one s; m 2nd John Woodbridge 1975. *Education:* Sarah Lawrence Coll (Bronxville, NY), Columbia Univ (NY) and Univ of Washington. *Career:* Writer-in-Residence Univ of Ohio 1974, Center Coll (KY) 1979, E Washington Univ 1980, Bucknell Univ (PA) 1982, State Univ of New York 1982; Prof of Poetry Univ of Maryland 1976–77, Univ of Cincinatti 1981, Univ of Louisville (KY) 1982, Columbia Univ 1982, Stanford Univ 1986; Sr Fellow Princeton Univ 1986; Visiting Prof Univ of Arizona 1990, Univ of California, Davis 1991; Cole Royalty Chair, Univ of Alabama 1995; numerous festivals on poetry; mem PEN, Poetry Soc of America, Acad of American Poets, Amnesty Int; Hon D LITT (Whitman Coll) 1986, (St Andrew's) 1989, (Mills) 1990; American Acad and Inst of Arts and Letters Award 1985; Gov's Award, State of Washington 1965, 1985, 1995, 1998. *Publications include:* The Ungrateful Garden 1961, Knock Upon Silence 1965, Midnight Was My Cry 1971, Mermaids in the Basement: Poems for Women 1984, Yin: New Poems (Pulitzer Prize 1985) 1984, The Nearness of You (Theodore Roethke Prize 1988) 1987, The Essential Clare (ed) 1993, On Poems and Poets 1994, Picking and Choosing: Prose on Prose 1995, 100 Great Poems by Women (ed) 1995. *Address:* 19772 8th St E, Sonoma, CA 95476, USA.

KJÆRSGAARD, Pia Merete; Danish politician; b 23 Feb 1947, Copenhagen; d of Poul Kjærsgaard and Inge Munch Jensen; m Henrik Thorup 1967; one s one d. *Education:* Gentofte School and Copenhagen School of Commerce. *Career:* Office asst for insurance and advertising co 1963–67; Home help 1978–84; mem Folketinget (Parl, Dansk

Folkeparti – Danish People's Party) for Copenhagen Country Dist 1984–87, 1998–, for Fyen Country Dist 1987–98, mem Ministry of Justice's Rd Safety Comm 1986–87, Chair Parl Health Cttee 1988–91; mem, Deputy Chair Liberal Group, Nordic Council 1990–94, 1998–; mem Defence Cttee 1997; Deputy Chair Council of Foreign Affairs; mem Bd Danish Nat Bank 1989–96, Foreign Policy Bd 1993–, Bd for Political Foreign Affairs and OSCE, Intelligence Service Cttee, Political–Econ Bd, The Justice Comm, Bd Danish–Taiwan Asscn; Leader Fremskridtspartiet (Progress Party) 1985–94; Co-Founder, Chair Dansk Folkeparti 1995–; Knight of the Danish Flag; Kosan Prize 1986; Politician of the Year, Danish Nat Asscn of Business Interests 1989; Golden Post Horn, Danish Mail Order Asscn 1992; Medal of Honour, Friends of Overseas Chinese Asscn 1999. *Publication:* Men udsigten er god... (But The View Is Excellent...) (biog) 1998. *Leisure interests:* media, music, literature, gardening and physical fitness. *Address:* Dansk Folkeparti, Folketinget, Christiansborg, 1240 Copenhagen K, Denmark (Office); Kærmindevej 31, 2820 Gentofte, Denmark (Home). *Telephone:* 33-37-51-07; *Fax:* 33-37-51-93; *E-mail:* df@ft.dk; *Internet:* www.danskfolkeparti.dk.

KJER, Bodil; Danish actress; b 2 Sept 1917. *Career:* Has appeared at Royal Theatre of Denmark in more than 100 roles; numerous awards including four awards from Danish film critics (Bodil award named after her); Commdr Order of Dannebrog. *Films:* Elly Petersen, The Invisible Army, Jenny and the Soldier, Meet Me on Cassiopeia, The Missing Clerk, Copper, Mirror, Mirror, Tradition, Up Yours!, Babette's Feast (Acad Award), Sunset Boys. *Address:* Vestre Pavilion, Frydenlund, Frydenlunds Allé 19, 2950 Vedbaek, Denmark.

KJER HANSEN, Eva; Danish politician; b 22 Aug 1964, Åbenrå. *Career:* Fmr MEP (Group of the European Liberal, Democrat and Reform Party), mem Cttee on Budgetary Control, Del for relations with Russia. *Address:* c/o European Parliament, rue Wiertz, 1047 Brussels, Belgium.

KLAPISCH-ZUBER, Christiane Michèle Jeanne, PH D; French historian; b 30 Nov 1936, Mulhouse; d of the late Alfred Claude Zuber and Denise Sancery; m Robert Klapish 1964 (divorced); one d. *Education:* Lycée Lamartine, Ecole Normale Supérieure des Jeunes Filles, Ecole Pratique des Hautes Etudes (EPHE) VI Section (Paris). *Career:* Mem staff EPHE VI Section (subsequently Ecole des Hautes Etudes en Sciences Sociales—EHESS) 1962–, Dir of Studies 1981–, Deputy Dir, then Co-Dir Centre de Recherches Historiques 1978–85; Visiting Prof Villa I Tatti (Harvard Univ, MA, USA), Florence, Italy 1985–86; Visiting Scholar Getty Center for the History of Art, Los Angeles, CA, USA 1988–89; mem Inst for Advanced Study, Princeton Univ, NJ, USA 1995–96; Médaille de Bronze (CNRS) 1979; Prix Mgr Marcel, Acad Française 1991; Ultimo Novecento Prize, Pisa (Italy) 1991. *Publications:* Les maîtres du marbre, Carrare 1300–1600 1969, Les Toscans et leurs familles (jtly) 1978, Women, Family and Ritual in Renaissance Italy 1985, La maison et le nom: Stratégies et rituels dans l'Italie de la Renaissance 1990, Histoire des Femmes II: Le Moyen Age (ed) 1991. *Leisure interests:* reading, walking. *Address:* Centre de Recherches Historiques, 54 blvd Raspail, 75006 Paris, France (Office); 37 rue Pétion, 75011 Paris, France (Home). *Telephone:* (1) 49-54-24-40 (Office); (1) 45-35-00-92 (Home); *Fax:* (1) 49-54-23-99 (Office).

KLARSFELD, Beate Auguste; French (b German) war crimes investigator and writer; b 13 Feb 1939, Berlin, Germany; d of Kurt and Hélène (née Scholz) Künzel; m Serge Klarsfeld 1963; one s one d. *Education:* Berlin. *Career:* War crimes investigator 1967–; has been involved in numerous campaigns to expose Nazi criminals and bring them to trial, including the forced return to France of Klaus Barbie 1983; human rights activist and campaigner against anti-Semitism; has been arrested numerous times during her campaigns, including in Bolivia, Argentina, Uruguay, Chile, Paraguay, Poland, Czechoslovakia (now Czech Repub), Austria, Italy, Jordan, Turkey; has campaigned for the release of Israeli hostages in Beirut, and for peace between Israel and the Arab states; Co-Founder Beate Klarsfeld Foundation 1978; life made into film, Nazi Hunter: The Beate Klarsfeld Story 1986; Chevalier de la Légion d'Honneur 1984; Prix de la Fondation du Judaïsme Français 1984 (jtly); Hias Liberty Award (jtly) 1984; Jabotinsky Award (jtly) 1984; Golda Meir Prize 1987; Wallenberg Prize 1989. *Publications:* Wherever They May Be (autobiog) 1975; several documents on

the Holocaust (with Serge Klarsfeld). *Leisure interests:* dogs, cats, travels to Venice and Florence. *Address:* 32 rue de la Boétie, 75008 Paris, France. *Telephone:* (1) 45-61-18-78; *Fax:* (1) 45-63-95-58.

KLAß, Christa; German politician; b 7 Nov 1951, Osann. *Career:* Jt Man Ind Wine-Grower 1972–; mem Bernkastel-Wittlich Dist Council 1990–; Vice-Chair CDU Dist Asscn 1993–; mem Fed Exec Women's Union 1997–; MEP (EPP), mem Cttee on Women's Rights and Equal Opportunities, Environment, Public Health and Consumer Policy, fmrly Regional Policy, Del for relations with China, fmrly Del for relations with Switzerland, Iceland and Norway. *Address:* European Parliament, rue Wiertz, 1047 Brussels, Belgium. *Telephone:* (2) 284-21-11; *Fax:* (2) 230-69-43.

KLEE, Marie-Elisabeth; German United Nations official; b 13 Jan 1922, Worms; d of Freiherr von Heyl; m Eugen Klee 1945 (died 1956). *Career:* Asst Archivist Ministry of Foreign Affairs 1945; mem Bundestag (Parl), Parl Council, European Council, Vice-Pres WEU 1961–72; Foreign Affairs Officer Ministry of Culture, State of Rheinland-Pfalz 1973–79; Chair German Cttee for UNICEF 1985–93; Bundesverdienstkreuz (First Class) 1972; Orden del mérito civil 1972; Chevalier de l'Ordre Nat du Mérite 1972; Hon Medal of the European Council. *Publications:* La situation des églises en l'Europe orientale (Council of Europe) 1968. *Leisure interests:* music, art, hiking. *Address:* German Committee for UNICEF, Höninger Weg 104, 50969 Cologne 51, Germany (Office); Deutschherrenstr 137, 53179 Bonn, Germany (Home). *Telephone:* (221) 936500 (Office); *Fax:* (221) 93650279 (Office).

KLEIN, Naomi; Canadian journalist and author; b 1970; d of Bonnie Klein; m Avi Lewis. *Career:* Journalist intern Toronto Globe and Mail; fmr Ed The Magazine (alternative political magazine); unofficial spokesperson for anti-globalization movt. *Publications:* No Logo 2000. *Address:* Ophelia House, Fulham Palace Rd, London W6, UK.

KLEIN, Robin; Australian writer; b 28 Feb 1936, Kempsey, NSW; d of Lesley Macquarie and Mary (née Cleaver) McMaugh; m Karl Klein 1956 (divorced 1980); two s two d. *Education:* Newcastle Girls' High School (NSW). *Career:* Has written numerous children's books. *Publications include:* The Giraffe in Pepperell Street 1978, Honoured Guest 1979, Thing (Jr Book of the Year, Children's Book Council of Australia 1983) 1982, Sprung! 1982, Junk Castle 1983, Penny Pollard's Diary 1983, Oodoolay 1983, Hating Alison Ashley (Special Award, W Australian Young Readers' Book Award, Winner Sr Category, KOALA Awards 1987) 1984, Thalia the Failure 1984, Thingnapped 1984, Brock and the Dragon 1984, Penny Pollard's Letters 1984, Ratbags and Rascals 1984, Battlers 1985, Halfway Across the Country and Turn Left 1985, The Enemies 1985, Annabel's Ghost 1985, Snakes and Ladders 1985, Boss of the Pool 1986, The Princess Who Hated It 1986, Games 1986, Penny Pollard in Print 1986, The Lonely Hearts Club 1987, Robin Klein's Crookbook 1987, Get Lost 1987, The Last Pirate 1987, Christmas 1987, I Shot an Arrow 1987, Birk the Berserker 1987, Stanley's Smile 1988, Annabel's Party 1988, Irritating Irma 1988, The Kidnapping of Clarissa Montgomery 1988, Jane's Mansion 1988, Laurie Loved Me Best 1988, Penny Pollard's Passport 1988, Dear Robin 1988, Against the Odds 1989, The Ghost in Abigail Terrace 1989, Came Back to Show You I Could Fly 1989, Penny Pollard's Guide to Modern Manners 1989, Tearaways 1990, Boris And Borsch (Honour Book, Australian Children's Book Council Awards 1991) 1990, All in the Blue Unclouded Weather 1991, Dresses of Red and Gold 1992, Seeing Things 1993, Turn Right for Zyrgow 1994, The Sky in Silver Lace 1995. *Leisure interests:* gardening, embroidery, tapestry, house renovations. *Address:* c/o Curtis Brown Australia, POB 19, Paddington, NSW 2021, Australia.

KLEIST, Baroness Sabine von, D ÈS SC, DR MED; German professor of medicine; b 2 Dec 1933, Berlin; m Baron von Kleist 1959; two d. *Education:* Univs of Frankfurt/Main and Paris (Sorbonne). *Career:* Prof, Chair of Immune Biology, Faculty of Medicine, Univ of Freiburg 1978; discovered tumour associated antigens; Deputy Chair Deutsche Krebshilfe (German cancer asscn) 1986; Bundesverdienstkreuz (First Class) 1989; awards include Prix Essec 1974, Hartmann-Thieding

Medal 1989, Abbott Award 1990, Paracelsus Medal 1993. *Publication:* Das Carzinfötale Antigen 1981. *Address:* Stefan-Meier-Str 8, 7800 Freiburg, Germany.

KLEVELAND, Åse; Norwegian politician; b 18 March 1949, Stockholm; partner Oddvar Tuhus. *Career:* Fmr singer, contestant Eurovision Song Contest; fmr TV presenter; Man Tusenfryd Amusement Park; Sec, later Leader Norwegian Musicians' Union 1979–83, 1983–87; Minister of Cultural Affairs 1990; currently Man Dir Swedish Film Inst. *Address:* c/o Ministry of Culture and Scientific Affairs, Akersgt 42, POB 8030 Dep, 0032 Oslo, Norway.

KLIMENTOVA, Daria; Czech ballet dancer; b 23 June 1971, Prague; m Ian Comer 1999; one d. *Career:* Prin Ballet Dancer, English Nat Ballet. *Leisure interest:* digital photography. *Address:* English National Ballet, 39 Jay Mews, London SW7, UK. *E-mail:* daria@cwcom.net.

KŁOSKOWSKA, Antonina, PH D; Polish sociologist (retd); b 7 Nov 1919, Piotrków Trybunalski; d of Wincenty Kłoskowski and Cecylia Kłoskowska. *Education:* Lódz Univ. *Career:* Doctor 1950–54, Asst Prof 1954–66, Assoc Prof 1966–73, Prof 1973–; Expert UNESCO 1967–; Head Sociology of Culture Dept, Sociology Inst, Univ of Warsaw 1977–90; Head Research Unit on Culture and Politics, Inst of Political Sciences, Polish Acad of Sciences (PAN) 1991–2000; Ed-in-Chief Kultura i Spoleczenstwo 1981–; Chair Cttee of Sociological Sciences, PAN 1973–81; Corresp mem PAN 1974–, Ordinary mem 1983–, mem of Bd 1989–; mem Nat Cttee of Int Sociological Asscn attached to Social Sciences Dept of Polish Acad of Sciences 1984; Chair Scientific Council of Inst of Culture, Warsaw 1978–86; Chair Scientific Council of Inst of Political Studies, Polish Acad of Sciences 1990–96; Pres Polish Sociological Asscn 1989–94; mem Bd Cttee of Communication, Culture and Science, Int Sociological Asscn; Commdr's Cross, Order of Polonia Restituta; Scientific Prize, City of Lódz; Meritorious Teacher of People's Poland 1978. *Publications:* Kultura masowa, Krytyka i obrona 1964, Z historii i socjologii kultury 1969, Spoleczne ramy kultury 1973, Machiavelli jako humanista na tle wloskiego Odrodzenia 1954, Education in a Changing Society (co-ed) 1977, Socjologia kultury (Sociology of Culture) 1981, Oblicza polskosci (Images of Polishness) (ed 1990); Encyclopaedia of Polish Culture in the 20th Century, vol I: Concepts and Problems (ed) 1991, The Neighbourhood of Cultures (co-ed) 1994, Kultury narodowe u korzeni (National Cultures at Grass-Roots Level) 1996. *Leisure interests:* reading, television, holidaying in the country. *Address:* Dzika 6 m 270, 00-172 Warsaw, Poland (Home). *Telephone:* (22) 6255221.

KNEF, Hildegard; British (b German) actress, singer and writer; b 28 Dec 1925, Ulm, Germany; d of Hans Theodor and Frieda Auguste (née Groehn) Knef; m 2nd David Cameron; one d; m 3rd Paul Rudolph Schell 1977. *Education:* Art studio (Ufa Babelsberg). *Career:* Actress Schloßparktheater, Berlin 1945, 1960, Imperial Theater, New York 1955–56, Berliner Schaubühne 1961, 1964–65; Edison Prize 1972; Bundesverdienstkreuz (First Class) 1975; award for best female role, Karlsbad Film Festival 1976; Bundesfilmpreis 1959, 1977; Golden Tulip, Amsterdam 1981, Deutscher Video-Preis 1999 and many other film awards. *Films include:* Die Mörder sind unter uns 1946, Film ohne Titel 1948, Die Sünderin 1950, Entscheidung vor Morgengrauen 1951, Schnee am Kilimandscharo 1952, Alraune 1952, Illusion in Moll 1952, The Man Between 1953, Svengali 1954, La Fille de Hambourg 1958, Der Mann der sich verkaufte 1958, Lulu 1962, Landru 1962, Dreigroschenoper 1962, Das Große Liebesspiel 1963, Wartezimmer zum Jenseits 1964, The Lost Continent 1967, Jeder stirbt für sich allein 1975, Fedora 1977; numerous recordings and TV appearances; *Publications:* Der Geschenkte Gaul 1970, Ich brauche Tapetenwechsel 1972, Das Urteil (Mark Twain Prize 1980) 1975, Heimwehblues 1978, Nicht als Neugier 1978, So nicht 1982, Romy 1983. *Leisure interests:* music, painting. *Address:* c/o Agentur Jovanovic, Holbeinstr 4, 81679 Munich, Germany.

KNIGHT, Angela Ann, B SC; British business executive and former politician; b 31 Oct 1950; d of Andrew McTurk and Barbara Jean (née Gale) Cook; m David George Knight 1981 (divorced); two s. *Education:* Penrhos Coll (N Wales) and Univ of Bristol. *Career:* Man Air Products Ltd 1972–77; Man Dir and Chair Cook & Knight (Metallurgical Processors) Ltd 1977–84, Chair Cook & Knight (Process Plant)

1984–91; MP for Erewash 1992–97; Parl Pvt Sec to Minister for Industry 1993–94, to Chancellor of the Exchequer 1994–95; Econ Sec to HM Treasury 1995–97; Chief Exec Asscn of Pvt Client Investment Mans and Stockbrokers 1997–; Non-Exec Dir PEP and ISA Mans Asscn 1997–99, Scottish Widows 1997–, Saur Water Services and S E Water PLC 1997–, Mott MacDonald 1998–, Logica 1999–. *Leisure interests:* Walking, skiing, reading, music. *Address:* 112 Middlesex St, London E1 7HY, UK.

KNIGHT, Gladys (Maria); American singer; b 28 May 1944, Atlanta, GA; d of Merald and Elizabeth (née Woods) Knight; m 2nd Barry Hankerson 1974 (divorced 1979); one s and two c (from previous marriage). *Career:* Tours with Morris Brown Choir 1950–53; singer Gladys Knight and the Pips 1953–; singer Lloyd Terry Jazz Ltd 1959–61; tours in UK 1967, 1972, 1973, 1976, Australia, Japan, Hong Kong, The Philippines 1976; recordings with Brunswick 1957–61, Fury 1961–62, Everlast 1963, Maxx and Bell 1964–66, Motown 1966–73, Buddah, Capitol, Columbia and MCA 1988; TV and film appearances; four Grammy Awards; American Music Award 1984, 1988; Rock and Roll Hall of Fame 1996. *Recordings include:* Best of Gladys Knight and the Pips 1990, Best Thing That Ever Happened to Me 1990, Heart and Soul of Gladys Knight 1990, Midnight Train to Georgia 1990, Taste of Bitter Love 1990, Golden Hour of Gladys Knight and the Pips 1991, Good Woman (solo album) 1991, The Way We Were 1991, Imagination 1992, Claudine 1992, Missing You (single jtly) 1996, Blue Lights in the Basement 1996, Imagination 1996, The Lost Live Albums 1996. *Address:* c/o Shakeji Inc, 3221 LaMirada Ave, Las Vegas, NV 89120, USA.

KNIGHT, Gloria Delores, BA, M SC, LL D; Jamaican business executive; b Kingston; d of the late F. A. and of Inez (née Stothart) Samms; m Everett Knight 1960; four d one s. *Education:* Univ of the W Indies, Univ of Oxford (UK) and McGill Univ (Canada). *Career:* Various posts in Jamaican Civil Service, Ministries of Labour, Housing and Social Welfare, Devt, Finance and Planning 1953–66; Admin Sec Kingston Waterfront Redevt Co 1966–68; Gen Man Urban Devt Corpn 1968–89; Pres Mutual Life Assurance Soc 1989; concurrently Dir Urban Devt Corpn, Airprojam Ltd, Mutual Security Bank; Order of Jamaica; Commdr of the Order of Distinction 1977; Certificate of Honour for Distinguished Service 1980; Award for Distinguished Service 1985; Award for outstanding contribution to the insurance industry, Insurance Inst of Jamaica 1994; American Friends of Jamaica Int Achievement Awards 1994; Award for outstanding manager, Jamaica Inst of Management 1995. *Publications:* The State of Urban Planning in Jamaica 1976, Urban Settlements in the Caribbean and Central America 1976, Public Enterprises: Their Management and Some Problems. *Leisure interests:* badminton, reading. *Address:* 2 Oxford Rd, Kingston 5, Jamaica. *Telephone:* 926-9025.

KNIGHT, Baroness (Life Peer), cr 1997, of Collingtree, **Jill (Joan Christabel) Knight;** British politician; b 9 July 1927; d of Arthur and Alma Christie; m James Montague Knight 1947 (died 1986); two s. *Education:* Fairfield School (Bristol) and King Edward VI Grammar School (Birmingham). *Career:* Mem Northampton County Borough Council 1956–66; MP (Cons) for Edgbaston 1966–97, mem Party Select Cttee on Race Relations and Immigration 1969–72, Select Cttee for Home Affairs 1980–83, Chair Lords and Commons All-Party Child and Family Protection Group 1978–, Cons Back Bench Health and Social Services Cttee 1982–, mem Exec 1922 Cttee 1979–, Sec 1983–87, Vice-Chair 1987–88; mem Council of Europe 1977–78, 1999–, WEU 1977–78, 1999– (Chair Cttee for Parl and Public Relations, Presidential Cttee of WEU 1984–88); Chair British Inter-Parl Union 1994–97; Pres W Midlands Cons Political Centre 1980–83; Vice-Pres Townswomen's Guilds 1986–94; Co-Dir Computeach Int Ltd; Kentucky Col, USA 1973, Heckett MultiServ 1999–; Hon D SC (Aston). *Publications:* About the House 1995. *Leisure interests:* theatre, reading, needlework, antiques, singing. *Address:* House of Lords, London SW1A 0PW, UK. *Telephone:* (20) 7219-3000.

KNOWLES, Alison, BA; American artist; b 1933, New York; m Dick Higgins; two d. *Education:* Scarsdale High School, Middlebury Coll and Pratt Inst (New York). *Career:* Worked for Something Else Press; Asst Prof of Art California Inst of Arts; Resident Artist Banff Centre, Canada 1990; creative performances include The Importance of Caravaggio and

Loose Pages (New York), North Water Song (PA), Un Coup de Dés (with John Cage) 1989; radio performances include North Water Song 1988, Sounds from the True Crow 1989, Setsbun (jtly) 1990; video performances include A Book of Bean is its Reading 1983, Food Frames with un Coup de Dés 1987, Loose Pages 1989; solo exhibitions include A Finger Book and Palimpsest Prints, Emily Harvey Gallery (New York) 1988, A Finger Book and Assorted Cloth and Paper Works, Performance of North Water Song, Neuberger Gallery (New York) 1988, One-Woman Exhibition, Galerie Schöppenhauer (Cologne, Germany) 1992; group exhibitions include Editions of Franz Conz, Emily Harvey Gallery (New York), Le Vertu del Minestrone 1989, Breath Drawings: Leone Doro—Shoe Parts and Prints (Paris) 1989, Lines of Vision: Drawings by Contemporary Women, Long Island Univ (New York) 1989. *Publications:* Seven Days Running 1978, Natural Assemblages and the True Crow 1980, A Bean Concordance 1983. *Address:* 122 Spring St, New York, NY 10012, USA.

KNOX, Lesley, MA; British merchant banking executive; b 1953; d of the late Eric and of Vera Samuel; m Brian Knox; one d. *Education:* St Denis School (Edinburgh), Cheltenham Ladies' Coll and Univ of Cambridge. *Career:* Qualified with Slaughter & May, London 1979; with Shearman & Sterling, New York; Corp Finance Exec Kleinwort Benson 1981, Dir 1986–; Head Institutional Asset Man, Kleinwort Benson Investment 1991–96; Deputy Gov British Linen Bank 1997, Gov 1999–; Founder-Dir British Linen Advisers 2000–; Non-exec Dir British Bank of Scotland (first woman), Glenmorangie, Dawson Int, MFI Group, Cedar Group, Fulcrum, Alliance Trust, Thames Water, Strong & Fisher PLC, Scottish Provident. *Leisure interests:* family, contemporary art, fly fishing. *Address:* Bank of Scotland, The Mound, Edinburgh EH1 1YZ, UK; British Linen Advisers, 8 Frederick's Place, London EC2R 8HY, UK. *Telephone:* (20) 7710-8820 (London); *Fax:* (20) 7710-8813 (London); *E-mail:* lesley.knox@britishlinen.co.uk.

KNUDSEN, Lillian; Danish trade union official; b 27 July 1945, Aalborg; d of Lauritz Scorensen and Anna Krog; m Harald Borsting 1985; one d one s. *Career:* Employee Spokesperson Bates Sakkefabrik 1966–71; Shop Steward Kastrup Airport 1972–75; Sr Shop Steward 1975–77; Chair Kastrup br Kvindeligt Arbejderforbund (Women Workers' Union) 1977, mem Exec Bd 1978–85, Pres 1985; mem numerous Danish and int labour cttees. *Address:* Norholm Alle 17, 2770 Kastrup, Denmark. *Telephone:* 31-39-31-15; *Fax:* 31-39-05-40.

KNUDSEN, Lisbeth; Danish newspaper editor and executive manager; b 7 June 1953, Copenhagen. *Career:* Political Ed 'Berlingske Tidende' 1075–84, Business Ed 1984–88, Sunday Ed 1988–89, Ed 1989–90; Ed-in-Chief and Exec Man 'Apressen/Det Friaktuelt' 1990. *Address:* Soeager 20, 2820 Gentofte, Denmark. *Telephone:* 39-68-34-40; *Fax:* 39-68-34-40; *E-mail:* lisbeth.knudsen@aktuelt.dk.

KOBAN, Rita; Hungarian sportswoman. *Career:* Silver Medallist in 500 Kayak singles, canoe-kayak event, Bronze Medallist in doubles, Olympic Games, Barcelona, Spain 1992; Gold Medallist in 500 Kayak singles, canoe-kayak event, Olympic Games, Atlanta, GA, USA 1996.

KOBERDOWA, Irena, PH D; Polish historian; b 17 Sept 1916; d of Ludwik and Lydia Halwic; m 1st Joseph Sado 1939 (divorced 1948); m 2nd Wieslaw Koberda (divorced 1955); two s. *Education:* Univs of Poznań and Warsaw. *Career:* Teacher 1938–39, 1945–52; deported from German territory and interned in Nazi concentration camp 1939–45; worked for Acad of Social Sciences and Workers' Movt Inst 1952–66, 1973–82; Dir-Gen Warsaw Archives 1956–72; Polish Archivist and Researcher in various countries including fmr USSR, Netherlands and France 1964–83; retd 1983; Croix d'Or de Mérite 1970; Order of Polonia Restituta 1974; Médaille de la Comm de l'Educ Nat 1976; Méritée des Archives 1978. *Publications include:* Le grand duc Konstantin à Varsovie 1965, Dépêches politiques des consuls généraux de France à Varsovie 1860–64 1965, Le parti social-révolutionnaire Prolétariat 1981, La première internationale 1860–64 1987; almost 200 articles in various languages. *Leisure interest:* modern literature. *Address:* Ul Wiktorska 95-97 m 25, 02-582 Warsaw, Poland. *Telephone:* (22) 448357.

KODYMOVÁ, Jarmila, PH D; Czech scientist; b 15 Jan 1945, Libice; m 1978; one s one d. *Education:* Tech Univ of Prague and Acad of Sciences. *Career:* Scientific Research in physics of plasma and plasmachem, Inst of Physics, Acad of Sciences 1968–, research in photodissociation iodine laser system 1980–82, in chemical oxygen–iodine laser system 1985–, Sr Scientist and Head of Group of Chemical Lasers, Dept of Gas Lasers; has lectured at international confs and insts in Japan, People's Repub of China and USA 1990, 1992, 1994, 1996; has written more than 40 scientific papers, 12 research reports and projects and three patents 1970–96; Award of Acad of Sciences 1978. *Leisure interests:* classical music, reading, gardening, cycling, children. *Address:* Czech Academy of Sciences, Institute of Physics, Department of Gas Lasers, Na Slovance 2, 180 40 Prague 8, Czech Republic. *Telephone:* (2) 66052699; *Fax:* (2) 821227; *E-mail:* kodym@fzu.cz.

KOGARKO, Liya Nikolaevna, PH D; Russian geologist; b 17 May 1936, Moscow; m Igor H. Ryabchikov; one s. *Education:* Moscow State Univ. *Career:* Head Geochem, Alkaline Rocks Lab, Vernadsky Inst of Geochem and Analytical Chem, Russian Acad of Sciences; new mineral, kogarkoite, named after her 1973; has written numerous articles and contribs to books on minerals; Vernadsky Prize 1990. *Leisure interest:* reading historical novels. *Address:* Moscow, Dm Ulyanov ul 4-2-208, Russian Federation. *Telephone:* (095) 938-20-54; *Fax:* (095) 938-20-54.

KOGAWA, Joy Nozomi, CM; Canadian writer; b 6 June 1935, Vancouver, BC; d of the late Gordon Goichi and Lois Masui (née Yao) Nakayama; one s one d. *Education:* R. I. Baker School (Alberta) and Univ of Alberta. *Career:* Writer Prime Minister's Office 1974–76; Writer-in-Residence Univ of Ottawa 1978–; Dir Canadian Civil Liberties Asscn; mem Writers' Union of Canada, PEN Int; Fellow of Ryerson Polytechnical Inst 1991; Hon LL D (Lethbridge) 1991, (Guelph) 1992, (Simon Fraser) 1993; Hon DD (Knox Coll, Toronto) 1999; mem of the Order of Canada 1986. *Publications:* Poetry: The Splintered Moon 1967, A Choice of Dreams 1974, Jericho Road 1977, Woman in the Woods 1985; Novels: Obasan (Books in Canada First Novel Award 1981, Canadian Authors' Asscn Book of the Year Award 1982, Notable Book, American Library Asscn 1982, American Book Award, Before Columbus Foundation 1983, Periodical Distributors of Canada and Foundation for the Advancement of Canadian Letters Award for Paperback Fiction 1983) 1981, Naomi's Road 1986, Itsuka 1992, The Rain Ascends 1995. *Address:* 25 The Esplanade, Suite 2604, Toronto, ON M5E 1W5, Canada. *Telephone:* (416) 214-9547.

KÖHN, Rosemarie; Norwegian ecclesiastic; b 1940, Germany. *Career:* Family emigrated from Germany 1947; Priest (Lutheran) 1969–; Rector of Practical Theology Faculty, Oslo Univ 1989; Bishop of Hamar (first woman bishop in Norwegian church, third in the world) 1993–. *Address:* Council of Norwegian Bishoprics, POB 1937, Grønland, 0135 Oslo, Norway.

KÖKSAL, Fatma Zeynep, M SC, PH D; Turkish electronics engineer; b 5 Jan 1951, Ankara; d of Hamit and Süeda Tulga; m İlal Köksal 1973; one d. *Education:* Science Lycée and Middle East Tech Univ (Ankara). *Career:* Mem staff Ankara Nuclear Research and Training Centre since 1972, Head Nuclear Electronics Div; apptd Consultant to IAEA 1989; contribs to professional journals. *Leisure interests:* films, sports, music. *Address:* Ankara Nükleer Arastirma ve Eğitim Merkezi, Nuclear Electronics Div, Belsevler, Ankara, Turkey (Office); Güven Sokak No 20/8, A Ayranci, 06540 Ankara, Turkey (Home). *Telephone:* (4) 4673667 (Home); *Fax:* (4) 4368657 (Office).

KOLPAKOVA, Irina Aleksandrovna; Russian ballet dancer; b 22 May 1933, Leningrad (now St Petersburg); m Vladlen G. Semeonov 1955; one d. *Education:* Acad of Vaganova, Leningrad Choreographic School and Leningrad Conservatoire. *Career:* Debut 1951; Prima Ballerina, Kirov Theatre of Opera and Ballet, Leningrad (now Mariinsky Theatre, St Petersburg) 1951–91, Ballet Mistress 1987–91; teacher of ballet, American Ballet Theater, New York 1991–, Indianapolis Ballet School 1995–; Prof Acad of Russian Ballet 1995–; People's Artist of the USSR 1965; Grand Prix de Ballet, Paris 1966; USSR State Prize 1980; Hero of Socialist Labour 1983; Order of the Red Banner; Order of Lenin 1983. *Ballets include:* Sleeping Beauty, Romeo and Juliet, Othello, The Red Poppy, Fountain of Bakchisarai, Giselle, Zolushka, Raymonda, La Sylphide, Les Sylphides, Don Quixote, Pushkin, Creation of the World,

The Stone Flower, Legends of Love; *Films:* Sleeping Beauty, Raymonda, Les Sylphides. *Leisure interest:* ballet. *Address:* c/o American Ballet Theater, 890 Broadway, New York, NY 10003, USA.

KOMLEVA, Gabriela Trofimovna; Russian professor of ballet; b 27 Dec 1938, Leningrad (now St Petersburg); d of Trofim Ivanovich Komlev and Lucia Petrovna (née Kouljavik) Komleva; m Arkady Andreevich Sokolov-Kaminsky 1970. *Education:* Leningrad Ballet School (under Kostrovitskaya) and Leningrad Conservatoire. *Career:* Ballet Dancer with Kirov (now Mariinsky) Ballet 1957–88, teacher and Ballet Mistress 1978–, choreographer 1984–; teacher Leningrad Conservatoire 1987, Prof of Rehearsal Mastership 1994–; staged ballets in USSR and abroad; regular masterclasses in Europe and USA 1994–; Presenter Terpsichore's Finest Points, Leningrad TV 1985–89; awards include First Prize, USSR Competition of New Choreography 1967, Honoured Artist of the Daghestan ASSR 1968, of the RSFSR 1970, Russian Fed State Prize Winner 1970, People's Artist of USSR 1983. *Ballets include:* Swan Lake, Sleeping Beauty, La Bayadère, Raimonda, Giselle, Don Quixote, Cinderella, Les Sylphides, Moor's Pavana, The Firebird, Paquita, Pas de Quatre, Leningrad Symphony, Furious Isadora; *Films:* Don Quixote 1971, Dance Images 1975, The Firebird 1977, La Bayadère (Best Music Film of Year, BBC) 1979, The Sleeping Beauty 1979, Gabriela Komleva Dances 1981, Paquita 1982, Leningrad Symphony 1982, Pas de Quatre, Cinderella 1985, Moor's Pavana, Furious Isadora 1988; *Publication:* Dance – Happiness and Pain 2000. *Leisure interests:* painting, music. *Address:* 198005 St Petersburg, Fontanka Reka 116, kv 34, Russian Federation. *Telephone:* (812) 316-30-77; *Fax:* (812) 316-30-77.

KONDRAT'YEVA, Marina Viktorovna; Russian ballet dancer; b 1 Feb 1934. *Education:* Bolshoi Theatre Ballet School. *Career:* Mem Bolshoi Ballet Co 1953–80, Ballet Mistress 1980–; People's Artist of RSFSR 1976. *Ballets include:* Cinderella, Fountain of Bakhchisarai, Sleeping Beauty, Romeo and Juliet, The Stone Flower, Giselle, Gayane, Swan Lake, Legend of Love. *Address:* Bolshoi Theatre, Moscow, Tetralnaya Pl 1, Russian Federation. *Telephone:* (095) 291-27-97.

KONRAD, Helga; Austrian politician. *Career:* Fed Minister for Women's Affairs in the Fed Chancellery 1995; mem Socialdemokratische Partei Österreichs (SPÖ—Social-Democratic Party of Austria). *Address:* Office of the Federal Chancellor, 1014 Vienna, Ballhausplatz 2, Austria.

KONSTANTINOVA, Elka Georgieva, PH D; Bulgarian politician and professor of Bulgarian literature; b 25 May 1932, Sofia; d of Georgi K. and Vassilka M. (née Chakyrova) Gogov; one s. *Education:* Univ of Sofia. *Career:* Asst Prof, later Prof of Bulgarian Literature, Sofia Inst of Literature, Shoumen Higher Pedagogical Inst, Sofia Higher Inst of Theatre and Drama 1956–91; Minister of Culture 1991–92; currently Prof of Literature Inst of Literature, Bulgarian Acad of Sciences; mem Union of Bulgarian Writers 1978–83; Chair Radical Democratic Party (Union of Democratic Forces—UDF) 1978–83; Guest Lecturer Jagiellonian Univ (Poland); mem Exec Ctte All Bulgaria Gathering 2000; numerous books, studies and monographs. *Leisure interests:* science fiction, feminism. *Address:* Sofia, Blvd V. Levsky 47B, Bulgaria. *Telephone:* (2) 86-11-1; *Fax:* (2) 87-73-39.

KONVICKOVA, Svatava, PH D; Czech academic; b 2 April 1943, Český Brod; d of Stanislav Křížek; m Tomáš Konvička; one d one s. *Education:* Czech Tech Univ. *Career:* Researcher Sigma Research Inst 1967–83; Assoc Prof Czech Tech Univ 1983–95, Prof and Head Lab of Biomechanics of Man 1995–; Ministry of Educ Prize 1987; has written 110 research papers and articles in int journals and presented papers at int symposia 1970–95. *Leisure interests:* literature, theatre, travel. *Address:* Machovcova 19, 14700 Prague 4, Czech Republic. *Telephone:* (2) 496471; *Fax:* (2) 329386; *E-mail:* konickoc@fsid.cvut.cz.

KOPLOVITZ, Kay, BS, MA; American broadcasting executive; b 11 April 1945, Milwaukee, WI; d of William E. and Jane T. Smith; m William C. Koplovitz, Jr 1971. *Education:* Univ of Wisconsin and Michigan State Univ. *Career:* Dir WTMJ-TV, Milwaukee 1967; Ed Communications Satellite Corpn, Washington 1968–72; Dir of Community Services UA Columbia Cablevision, Oakland, NJ 1973–75; Vice-Pres and Exec Dir UA Columbia Satellite Services Inc, Oakland

1977–80; Founder, Pres and CEO USA Networks and Sci-Fi Channel, New York 1972–98; CEO Koplovitz & Co 1998–; mem Bd Dirs Nat Jr Achievement 1986–, Nat Cable TV Asscn 1984–, Int Council, Nat Acad TV Arts and Sciences 1984–93 (Chair 1994–95), Women in Cable (Pres 1982–83); numerous awards including Muse Award (New York Women in Film and TV) 1992, Ellis Island Medal of Honour 1993, Crystal Award (Women in Film) 1993, Broadcasting Magazine's Hall of Fame 1992. *Address:* Koplovitz & Co, Room 515-W, 237 Park Ave, Suite 2100, New York, NY 10017, USA (Office).

KOPP, Elisabeth, L EN D; Swiss politician; b 16 Dec 1936, Zurich; d of Max Jkle-Heberlein; m Hans W. Kopp 1960; one d. *Education:* Univ of Zurich. *Career:* Mem City Council Zumikon 1970–74, Mayor 1974–84; mem Council of Educ 1972–80; mem Nat Council (Parl) 1979–84; Minister of Justice 1984–89; currently Lawyer Kopp and Assocs, Zurich. *Publication:* Briefe 1991. *Leisure interests:* cooking, skiing, travel. *Address:* Drei Eichen, 8126 Zumikon, Switzerland. *Telephone:* (1) 9180311; *Fax:* (1) 9180593; *E-mail:* elisabeth.kopp@bluewin.ch.

KOPPE, Janna G, PH D; Netherlands professor; b 18 March 1935, Deventer. *Education:* Univ of Amsterdam and Univs of Maryland, Pittsburg, Cleveland and Nashville, Boston (USA). *Career:* Mem staff Dept of Neonatology, Univ of Amsterdam 1967–77, Vice-Chair 1977–87, Prof 1986, apptd Chair 1987; Chair Perinatology section Dutch Soc of Pediatricians 1984–87; Pres Dutch Soc of Perinatal Medicine 1989, Dutch Soc of Surfactant Medicine 1990, European Asscn of Perinatal Medicine 1990–92 (mem Exec Bd 1992–94); Pres XIIth European Congress of Perinatal Medicine in Amsterdam 1992 (mem scientific cttee, XVI European Congress 1992–94); mem several Cttes and Bds of Perinatal Medicine; has participated in numerous nat and int meetings and written over 150 articles in nat and int journals. *Leisure interests:* sports medicine, running, swimming, cross-country skiing. *Address:* Roosmarijnhof 29, 1115 DW Duivendrecht, Netherlands. *Telephone:* (20) 699-32-13.

KOŘÍNKOVÁ, Květoslava, DIP ENG, PH D; Czech politician; b 10 July 1940, Český Brod, Kolín Dist; d of Ladislav Kořínek and Marie Kořínková; m Antonín Peltrám 1975. *Education:* Inst of Transport (Žilina, Slovakia). *Career:* Worked on the railways, Deputy Head Goods Depot, Station of Český Brod 1957–64; technician, researcher Research Inst of Transport, Prague 1964–71; specialist working on transportation and container systems, Ministry for Technological Devt and Investment 1971–72; mem Presidium, Czech Council of the Czechoslovak Scientific-Technological Soc 1972–87, Chair Women's Comm 1970–89, Women's Club 1989–; Minister-Chair Fed People's Control and Auditing Cttee 1989–90; Fed Govt Minister of Control and Auditing 1990–92; teacher Pardubice Univ of Transport 1993–; mem Dels to UN on the rights of women and children 1980; mem Presidium EUROSAI (European Org of Supreme Audit Insts) 1990–92, Govt Comm for Equal Rights for Women 1990–; mem Municipal Metropolitan Council of Prague 1994–, Czech Social Democratic Party 1994–, Deputy Chair 1995–; mem Parl (Social Democratic Party) 1996–98, Vice-Pres Foreign Cttee of Parl 1996–, mem Standing Comm of Parl for banking until 1998, Standing Del for co-operation with EP until 1998; Insp-Gen of Railways 1998–2000; has written numerous articles and school text books on transport. *Leisure interests:* reading, music, the arts. *Address:* Vysoká škola dopravní, Pardubice, Czech Republic.

KOROI, Jokapeci Tagi Elizabeth; Fijian party official and former nurse; b 29 September 1931, Ono-i-Lau; d of Netani Edward and Veitinia Cavu; m Michael Aisea Koroi 1958; three d two s. *Education:* Lelean Memorial School (Nausori) and nursing training at Auckland Public Hosp. *Career:* Mem Nursing Educ Bd 1960–77, Council Fiji Nurses' Asscn 1970–87, Fiji Nat Council of Women 1979–87, Council of Reps of Int Council of Nurses 1979–87, Fiji Electricity Asscn Bd 1982–84; Pres Fiji Nurses' Asscn 1972–77; Vice-Pres Commonwealth Fed of Nurses 1986–87; Vice-Pres Fiji Lab Party 1985–91, Pres 1991–; has several nursing and teaching diplomas. *Leisure interests:* charity work, gardening, travel. *Address:* Fiji Labour Party, POB 2162, Suva, Fiji (Office); Lot 1 Deovji St, Tamavua, POB 14950, Suva, Fiji (Home). *Telephone:* 305811 (Office); 321036 (Home); *Fax:* 305808 (Office).

KOSTENKO, Lina Vasilievna; Ukrainian poet; b 12 March 1930, Rzhischevo, Kiev Region. *Education:* Maxim Gorky Inst of Literature (Moscow). *Career:* Ukrainian SSR State Prize 1987. *Publications:* Lights of the Earth 1957, The Winds 1958, Particles of the Heart 1961, Bank of the Eternal River 1977, Inimitablility 1980, Marusya Churay 1979–82, Scythian Woman 1981, Garden of Unmelting Snow 1987, Selected Poetry 1990; numerous publs in literary magazines. *Address:* 252054 Kiev, Chkalova str 52, kv 8, Ukraine (Home). *Telephone:* (44) 224-70-38 (Home).

KOTOVA, Elena, PH D; American economist; b 21 Nov 1956, Moscow; d of Victor Kotov and Natalia Kotova; m Nick Zimin 1985; one s. *Education:* Moscow State Univ. *Career:* Jr then Sr Researcher Inst of Oriental Studies, Moscow 1980–89; Chair Econ Policy Cttee, Moscow City Council 1989–90; Minister of Privatization Moscow City Govt, CEO Moscow State Property Cttee 1990–92; Visiting Lecturer Harvard Univ, Cambridge (MA, USA) 1991, Wharton School of Econ, Univ of Pennsylvania (PA, USA) 1993; Sr Asst to Exec Dir Russia IMF 1993; Man Enterprise Restructuring and Pvt Sector Devt Specialist IBRD 1993; Visiting Researcher Univ of New Delhi (India) 1989; mem Club of Rome 1991, Forum on Econ Transition in Russia (Bologna, Italy) 1991. *Publications:* External Debt and Economic Development of Asian Countries 1982, Elusive Privatization or What is the Primitive Capital Accumulation in Russia 1992, Processes of Monopolization in Oriental Economies 1990, Privatization in Russia: Institutional Challenges 1993, numerous contribs to newspapers and journals. *Leisure interests:* skiing, swimming, dance. *Address:* International Bank for Reconstruction and Development (World Bank), 1818 H St, NW, Washington, DC 20433, USA (Office); 2724 Stephenson Lane, NW, Washington, DC 20015, USA (Home). *Telephone:* (202) 473-5042 (Office); (202) 244-6247 (Home); *Fax:* (202) 522-1164; *E-mail:* ekotova@worldbank.org.

KOUBKOVÁ, Jana; Czech jazz singer and composer; b 31 Oct 1944, Prague; d of Jaroslav Koubek and Hana Koubková; m Jan Kunst 1967 (divorced 1969). *Education:* People's Conservatory (Prague). *Career:* Began singing with Czechoslovak Radio Children's Choir aged six 1950–57; Semafor Theatre 1975–76; Ludek Hulan Jazz Sanatorium 1975–79; Hot Tety and Hot Aunts Vocal Groups 1976–82; Co-Founder Vokalíza (annual jazz, blues and rock festival) 1981; singer with various big bands since 1982; Teacher of Music, State Conservatory; has written numerous articles on singing for Tvorba magazine, and writes rhythmical poetry; regular TV and radio appearances; Best Vocal Performance Award, Prague Jazz Festival 1977; Melody Magazine Award for Artistic and Organizational Work 1985. *Recordings include:* Horký dech 1982, Bosa 1985, Jazzperanto (jtly) 1988, Panta rhei 1989. *Leisure interests:* writing, reading, jogging, hiking, travel, learning. *Address:* Karmelitská 23, 118 00 Prague 1, Czech Republic. *Telephone:* (2) 539272.

KOUDIL, Hafsa Zinai; Algerian writer and film maker; b 1951. *Career:* Currently living in Tunisia; has written four novels; campaigns for the rights of women and against the Islamicization of Algeria; participant at Amiens Film Festival 1994, Int Women's Film Festival, Créteil, France 1995. *Publications include:* La fin d'un rêve (autobiog) 1984, Le passé décomposé 1993, Le mariage de jouissance (screenplay); *Film:* Le démon au féminin 1993.

KOUMI, Margaret (Maggie); British magazine editor; b 15 July 1942; d of the late Yiasoumis Koumi and of Melexidia Paraskeva; m Ramon Sola. *Education:* Buckingham Gate (London). *Career:* Sec Thomas Cook 1957–60; sub-ed, feature and fiction writer Visual Features Ltd 1960–66; sub-ed TV World 1966–67; Production Ed 19 Magazine 1967–69, Ed 1969–86, concurrently Ed Hair Magazine; Man Ed Practical Parenting, Practical Health, Practical Hair and Beauty 1986–87; Jt Ed Hello! 1988–93, Ed 1993–2001; Eds of the Year Award 1991. *Publication:* Beauty Care 1981. *Leisure interests:* work, reading. *Address:* c/o Hello! Ltd, Wellington House, 69–71 Upper Ground, London SE1 9PQ, UK.

KOURNIKOVA, Anna; Russian/American tennis player; b 7 June 1981, Moscow; d of Sergei and Alla Kournikov. *Career:* Began playing tennis at age of 5; mem Russian Fed Cup Team 1996–97, Russian Olympic Team 1996; Wimbledon Semifinalist 1997; Won first Sanex WTA Tour pro title (Doubles with Monica Seleš, qv) Princess Cup, Tokyo 1998;

Doubles Winner (with Barbara Schett) Sydney 2001; Sanex WTA Tour Most Impressive Newcomer Award 1996; Sanex WTA Tour Doubles Team of the Year Award (with Martina Hingis, qv) 1999; highest world ranking no 9, 2000. *Leisure interests:* dancing, music. *Address:* c/o Bank Lane, Roehampton, London SW15 5XZ, UK.

KOVACHEVICH, Elizabeth Anne, B COM, JD; American federal judge; b 14 Dec 1936, Canton, IL; d of Dan and Emilie (née Kuchan) Kovachevich. *Education:* Univ of Miami and Stetson Univ. *Career:* Called to the Bar, FL 1961, US Dist Court 1961, US Supreme Court 1968; Assoc DiVito and Speer, FL 1961–62; Counsel Rieck and Fleece Guilders Supplies Inc 1962; law practice 1962–73; Judge 6th Circuit, FL 1973–82, US Dist Court, Tampa, FL 1982–; Chief Judge, US Dist Court, Middle Dist, FL 1996–(2003); mem Florida Gov's Comm on the Status of Women 1968–71; mem Defense Advisory Cttee on Women in Service, Dept of Defense 1973–76; mem ABA, Asscn of Trial Lawyers of America, American Judicature Soc; Hon mem Bd of Overseers, Law Faculty, Stetson Univ 1986; awards include St Petersburg Panhellenic Appreciation Award 1964, Distinguished Alumni Award, Stetson Univ 1970, Beta Sigma Phi Woman of the Year Award 1970, US Navy Recruiting Command Appreciation Award 1975, Florida Fed of Business and Professional Women, Woman of the Year 1981, Ben C. Willard Memorial Award, Stetson Lawyer's Asscn 1983, Mrs Charles Ulrick Bay Award, Associated Women Students Woman of the Year Award, St Petersburg Rotary Award, St Petersburg Jr Coll Alumni of the Year Award 1994, Catholic Law Person of the Year 1998, FL Council on Crime and Delinquency Award for Distinguished Service in Judicial 1999, J-Ben Watkins Award, Stetson Univ Coll of Law 1999, Delta Delta Delta Woman of Achievement Award 2000, William Reece Smith Jr Award of Public Service 2001, Hillsborough Co Outstanding Jurist Award 2000–01. *Address:* US District Court, 801 N Florida Ave, Tampa, FL 33602, USA.

KOZENÁ, Magdalena; Czech opera singer; b 26 May 1973, Brno. *Education:* Brno Conservatoire and Acad of Music and Dramatic Art (Bratislava). *Career:* Guest of Janácek's Opera, Brno 1991–; soloist Volksoper, Vienna 1996–97; has toured in Europe, USA, Japan, Venezuela, Taiwan, Hong Kong, S Korea, Canada; First Place in Int Mozart Competition, Salzburg 1995; G. Solti Prize (France); Echo Preis (Germany) 2000; Golden CD for Bach's Airs 2000. *Opera roles include:* Dorabella in Così fan Tutte, Isabella in The Italian Girl in Algiers, Mercedes in Carmen, Annius in La Clemenza di Tito, lead in Orfo ed Eurydice (Gluck) 1999, Poppea in L'Incoronazione di Poppea (Monteverdi) 2000. *Leisure interests:* philosophy, music, swimming, cycling. *Address:* c/o Agency Symfonieta, Beethovenova 4, 602 00 Brno, Czech Republic (Office); Národní divadlo, Dvoráková 11, 600 00 Brno, Czech Republic (Home). *Telephone:* (5) 219780, (5) 219787 (Office); (5) 213099, (5) 321285 (Home).

KOZIOŁ-PRZYBYLAK, Urszula, BA; Polish writer; b 20 June 1931, Rakówka; d of Hipolit and Czestawa (née Kargol) Kozioł; m Felikes Prybylak 1960. *Education:* Univ of Wrocław. *Career:* High School teacher 1954–71; Literary Ed Poglądy (Opinions) 1956, Odra 1971–; awards include Literary Prize, Autumnal Encounters Festival of Gdańsk 1963, Władysław Broniewski Prize, Polish Students' Asscn 1964, Literary Prize of Wrocław 1965, Kościelski Foundation of Geneva Prize 1969, Polish Ministry of Culture Literary Prize 1971, Kommandeur-Kreuz zum Orden der Wiedergelurf Polens 1997, Kultur Preis Schlesien, Hanover 1998, PEN-Club Award 1998. *Publications include:* Poetry: Gumowe klocki (Rubber Blocks) 1957, W rytmie korzeni (In the Rhythm of the Roots) 1963, Smuga i promień (A Trace and a Ray) 1965, Lista obecności (Attendance Record) 1967, W rytmie słońca (In the Rhythm of the Sun) 1974, Wybór wierszy (Select Poetry) 1976, Poezje wybrane (2nd edn) 1986, W ptynnym słernie 1998, Słany nieocsynisłości 1999; (in English) Poems (trans from Polish) 1998; (in German) Im Zeichen des Feuers 1997, Voll Geheimnis Ganz wie die Welt 1998; Prose: Osobnepo sny i pnypomiści 1997; Novels: Postoje pamięci (Stations of Memory, 3rd edn) 1977, Ptaki dla myśli (Birds for Thought, 2nd edn) 1983; Short stories: Z poczekalni (From the Waiting Room) 1978, Osobnego sny i prypowieści (The Dreams and Parables of the Separate One) 1978, Noli me tangere 1984; Plays: Król malowany (The Painted King) 1978, Trzy Światy (Three Worlds) 1981, Podwórkowcy (Yard Kids) 1982, Sportolino 1982, Psujony (Spoilers) 1982, Zbieg z Babony (Escapee from Babona) 1983, Dziwna podróż

Bączka do Gryslandii (Strange Voyage of Bug to Grysland) 1984, Magiczne imię (A Magic Name) 1985, O stołku (About a Chair) 1987, Żalmik (Laments) 1989, Zgaga 1990, Postoje siowa (Stations of Words) 1995, Wielda Pawza (A Great Pause) 1996. *Leisure interest:* travel. *Address:* Komandorska 37/6, 53-342 Wrocław, Poland. *Telephone:* (71) 3673853; *Fax:* (71) 3435516.

KRABBE, Katrin; German athlete; b 1970; m Michael Zimmerman 1994; one s. *Career:* Mem Neubrandenburg team; winner of three gold medals in European Track and Field Championships 1990; 100m and 200m World Championships, Tokyo 1991; banned for taking pro-scribed drugs 1992–96, ban reduced by one year to March 1993, ban reversed by Regional Court, Munich May 1995; co-owner Sport and Fashion GmbH.

KRALL, Hanna; Polish journalist and writer; b 20 May 1937, Warsaw; m Jerry Szperkowicz; one d. *Education:* Univ of Warsaw. *Career:* Reporter Zycie Warszawy 1955–66, Polityka 1966–, corresp in Moscow 1966–69; corresp Tygodnik Powszechny, Gazeta Wyborcza; Prize of Minister of Culture and Art 1989, J. Shocken Literary Prize (Germany), Solidarity Cultural Prize 1995, Kulture Foundation Award 1999, Leipzig Book Fair Award 2000. *Publications:* Na wschód od Arbatu (To the East of Arbat) 1972, Zdazyc przed Panem Bogiem (To Outwit God) 1976, Szesc odcieni bieli (Six Shades of White) 1978, Sublokatorka (The Sub-tenant) 1983, Trudnosci ze wstawaniem (Difficulties Getting Up) 1988, Hipnoza (Hypnosis) 1989, Taniec na cudzym weselu (Dance at a Stranger's Wedding) 1993, Co sie stalo z nasza bajka (What's Happened to our Fairy Tale) 1994, Dowody na istnienie (Proofs of Existence) 1995, Tam jnz nie ma zadnej rzeki (There is No River Anymore) 1998 (translated into over 10 languages). *Address:* Stowarzyszenie Pisarzy Polskich, ul Krakowskie Przedmiescie 87/89, 00-079 Warsaw, Poland.

KRAM, Shirley Wohl, LL B; American federal judge; b 1922, New York. *Education:* Hunter Coll, City Univ of New York and Brooklyn Coll. *Career:* Attorney Legal Aid Soc 1951–53, 1962–71; Assoc Simons and Hardy 1954–55; law practice 1955–60; Judge Family Court, New York 1971–83, US Dist Court 1983–93, Sr Judge 1993–. *Publications:* The Law of Child Custody (jtly), Development of the Substantive Law. *Address:* US District Court, US Courthouse, 40 Foley Square, Rm 2101, New York, NY 10007, USA.

KRAMER, Dame Leonie (Judith), AC, DBE, D PHIL, FAHA, FACE; Australian professor emeritus of literature; b 1 Oct 1924; d of the late A. L. and G. Gibson; m Harold Kramer 1952 (deceased); two d. *Education:* Presbyterian Ladies Coll (Melbourne), Univs of Melbourne and Oxford (UK). *Career:* Tutor St Hugh's Coll, Oxford 1949–52; Assoc Prof Univ of New S Wales 1963–68; Prof of Australian Literature Univ of Sydney 1968–89, Prof Emer 1989–, Deputy Chancellor 1988–91, Chancellor 1991–; Vice-Pres Australian Asscn for Teaching of English 1967–70, Australian Soc of Authors 1969–71; Pres, then Vice-Pres Australian Council for Educ Standards 1973–; mem Univs Comm 1974–86; Commr Australian Broadcasting Comm (ABC) 1977–81, Chair 1982–83; Dir Australia and NZ Banking Group 1983–94, W Mining Corpn 1984–96, Quadrant Magazine Co Ltd 1987–99, (Chair 1988–99); mem Council Nat Roads and Motorists' Asscn 1984–95, Council Foundation for Young Australians 1989–, Asia Soc 1991–2000; Nat Pres Australia–British Soc 1984–93 Order of Australia Asscn 2001–; Chair Bd of Dirs Nat Inst of Dramatic Art (NIDA) 1987–92; Sr Fellow Inst of Public Affairs (IPA) 1988–; mem Univs Council 1974–85, Nat Literature Bd of Review 1970–73, Council Nat Library of Australia 1975–81, Council Australian Nat Univ 1984–87, Bd of Studies, NSW Dept of Educ 1990–, World Book Encyclopaedia Advisory Bd 1989–99, Int Advisory Cttee Encyclopaedia Britannica 1991–99, NSW Council of Australian Inst of Co Dirs 1992–; Chair Bd of Dirs Nat Inst of Dramatic Art (NIDA) 1987–91, Deputy Chair 1991–95; Sr Fellow Inst of Public Affairs (IPA) 1988–96; Commr Electricity Comm (NSW) 1988–95; Chair Operation Rainbow Australia Ltd 1996–; Hon Fellow St Hugh's Coll Oxford 1994; Hon D LITT (Tasmania) 1977, (Queensland) 1991, (NSW) 1992; Hon LL D (Melbourne) 1983, (ANU) 1984; Hon MA (Sydney) 1989; Britannica Award 1986. *Publications include:* (as L. J. Gibson): Henry Handel Richardson and Some of Her Sources 1954; (as Leonie Kramer): Australian Poetry (ed) 1961, Companion to Australia Felix 1962, Myself When Laura 1966, A. D. Hope 1979, The Oxford

History of Australian Literature (ed) 1981, The Oxford Anthology of Australian Literature (co-ed) 1985, My Country: Australian Poetry and Short Stories – Two Hundred Years (2 vols) 1985, James McAuley: Poetry, Essays, etc (ed) 1988, David Campbell: Collected Poems (ed) 1989, Collected Poems of James McAuley 1995. *Leisure interests:* gardening, music. *Address:* 12 Vaucluse Rd, Vaucluse, NSW 2030, Australia. *Telephone:* 93514164.

KRANTZ, Judith, BA; American writer; b 9 Jan 1928, New York City; d of Jack David Tarcher and Mary Brager; m Stephen Krantz 1954; two s. *Education:* Wellesley Coll. *Career:* Contrib to Good Housekeeping 1948–54, McCalls 1954–59, Ladies Home Journal 1959–71; contributing Ed Cosmopolitan 1971–79. *Publications:* Scruples 1978, Princess Daisy 1980, Mistral's Daughter 1982, I'll Take Manhattan 1986, Till We Meet Again 1988, Dazzle 1990, Scrulples II 1992, Lovers 1994, Spring Collection 1996, The Jewels of Teresa Kant 1998, Sex & Shopping: Confessions of a Nice Jewish Girl 2000; all works have been made into TV mini-series.

KRASNOHORSKÁ, Mária, PH D; Slovak diplomatist; b 15 Aug 1949, Topolčany; m Juraj Krasnohorský 1974; one d one s. *Education:* Comenius Univ (Bratislava). *Career:* Researcher Acad of Dramatic Arts, Bratislava, Head Language Dept and teacher of Modern French Drama 1972–91; mem staff Ministry of Foreign Affairs 1991–93; Counsellor Perm Mission to UNO (Geneva, Switzerland) 1993–94, Amb, Perm Rep 1994; has translated several plays from French and Russian 1970–91. *Leisure interests:* literature, theatre. *Address:* Permanent Mission of the Slovak Republic to the UNO, Ancienne route 9, 1218 Grand Saconnex, Geneva, Switzerland. *Telephone:* (22) 7986272; *Fax:* (22) 7880919.

KRATOCHVÍLOVÁ, Jarmila; Czech athlete; b 26 Jan 1951, Golčův Jeníkov. *Education:* Gymnasium (Čáslav). *Career:* Accountant Triola, Golčův Jeníkov 1970–71; mem Centre of Top-level Performance Sports, Vysoké školy, Prague 1971–87, now retd; currently sports coach; coach Czech Olympic team, Sydney 2000; world records include 400m track event, Helsinki 1983, 800m track event, Munich 1983; Gold Medal 400m track event, World Cup, Rome 1981, 400m, 800m track events, World Championships, Helsinki 1983; Silver Medal, Olympic Games, Moscow, USSR 1980, 400m track event, European Championships, Athens 1982; Order of Labour 1983; UNESCO Fair Play Prize 1988. *Publication:* Waiting (jtly). *Address:* TJ Slavoj Cáslav, TSM-Voaranty, 286 01 Cáslav, Czech Republic (Office); Pod Vyšehradem 207, 58282, Golčův Jeníkov Czech Republic (Home).

KRAVAEVA, Vessa, DIP AD; Bulgarian artist; b 17 Jan 1928; d of the late Doncho Kravaev and Velichka Kravaeva; m Ivan Ivanov 1950; one s one d. *Education:* Nat Acad of Fine Arts (Sofia). *Career:* Mem Bd of Govs Union of Bulgarian Artists 1971; Prof Acad of Arts, Tarnovo 1973–78; numerous exhibitions include Bulgaria, Germany, Sweden, The Mall Galleries (London) 1980–; represented in perm collections in Nat Gallery of Bulgaria, Sofia City Gallery, Bulgarian Ministry of Defence and at collections in France and UK; Cyril and Methodius Medal for contrib to nat culture (twice); Exceptional Contrib in the Cultural Life of Bulgaria 1970, 1990; The Masterpiece in Art award 1963–73; numerous prizes and awards at competition level 1980–. *Leisure interests:* reading, music. *Address:* 1126 Sofia, 16A Vishneva St, Bulgaria. *Telephone:* (2) 66-77-53.

KRAVITCH, Phyllis A., BA, LL B; American federal judge; b 23 Aug 1920, Savannah, GA; d of Aaron and Ella (née Wiseman) Kravitch. *Education:* Goucher Coll and Univ of Pennsylvania. *Career:* Admitted to the Bar, GA 1943, US Dist Court 1944, US Supreme Court 1948, US Circuit Court of Appeals 1962; law practice Savannah 1944–76; Judge Superior Court, Eastern Judicial Circuit Court of GA 1977–79, US Court of Appeals, Atlanta 1979–; Trustee Georgian Inst of Continuing Legal Educ 1979–82; mem Council Law Faculty, Emory Univ, Atlanta 1991–, Visiting Cttee Law Faculty, Univ of Chicago 1989–92; Fellow American Bar Foundation; mem ABA, American Judicature Soc, American Law Inst; Visiting Cttee Georgia State Univ Law School 1994–; Hon LL D (Goucher Coll) 1981, (Emory Univ) 1998; Savannah's Most Influential Woman 1978; Hannah G. Solomon Award, Nat Council of Jewish Women 1978; James Wilson Award, Univ of Pennsylvania Law Alumni Soc 1992; ABA Margaret Brent Women

Lawyers Achievement Award 1991; Arabella Babb Mansfield Award, Nat Asscn of Women's Lawyers 1999; Trailblazer Award, Greater Atlanta Hadassah Attorney's Council 2000; Kathleen Kessler Award, Georgia Asscn of Women Lawyers 2001. *Publication:* Jewish Women in America: An Historical Encyclopedia 1999. *Address:* US Court of Appeals, 56 Forsyth St NW, Suite 202, Atlanta, GA 30303, USA. *Telephone:* (404) 335-6300.

KREHL, Constanze Angela; German politician; b 14 Oct 1956, Stuttgart. *Career:* Vice-Chair SPD Group Volkskammer 1990, mem Bundestag (SPD) 1990, SPD Bureau, Vice-Chair SPD Land of Saxony 1996, Chair 1999–, mem SPD Exec 1999–; Observer EP 1991–94; MEP (PSE); mem Cttee on Budgets; Chair Del to EU–Russia Parl Cooperation Cttee, mem Conf of Del Chairs; fmr Deputy mem Cttee on Regional Policy, Transport and Tourism. *Address:* European Parliament, rue Wiertz, 1047 Brussels, Belgium. *Telephone:* (2) 284-51-34; *Fax:* (2) 284-51-34; *E-mail:* ckrehl@europarl.eu.int.

KREITUSE, Ilga, PH D; Latvian politician; b 5 July 1952, Tērvete, Dobele Dist; m Aivars Kreituss; one s one d. *Education:* Univ of Latvia and State Univ of Moscow. *Career:* Mem Faculty of History and Philosophy, Univ of Latvia, Party History Inst and Inst of History, Acad of Sciences; fmrly teacher Riga Secondary School No 1; fmrly Deputy Saeima (Parl), Chair (speaker) 1995; Pres candidate 1996; mem Democratic Party Saimnieks 1995–; has written three books (jtly) and more than 30 research papers. *Address:* Saeima, Jēkaba iela 11, Rīga 1811, Latvia.

KREMENTZ, Jill; American photographer and writer; b 19 Feb 1940, New York; d of Walter and Virginia (née Hyde) Krementz; m Kurt Vonnegut, Jr 1979; one d. *Education:* Drew Univ and Art Students League. *Career:* Staff mem Harper's Bazaar 1959–60, Glamour magazine 1960–61; Reporter Show magazine 1962–64; Staff Photographer Herald Tribune, New York 1964–65, Vietnam 1965–66; Assoc Ed Status-Diplomat magazine 1966–67; Contributing Ed NY magazine 1967–68; Corresp Time-Life Inc 1969–70; Contributing Photographer People magazine 1974–; works appeared in numerous magazines worldwide; solo exhibitions include Madison Art Center 1973, Univ of Massachusetts 1974, Nikon Gallery (New York) 1974, Delaware Art Museum 1975; collections in Museum of Modern Art and Library of Congress; mem PEN; Washington Post/Children's Book Guild Non-Fiction Award 1984; ACCH Joan Fassler Memorial Book Award 1990. *Publications include:* Photographer: The Face of South Vietnam 1968, Words and Their Masters 1974; Photographer and writer: Sweet Pea: A Black Girl Growing Up in the Rural South 1969, A Very Young Dancer 1976, A Very Young Rider 1977, A Very Young Gymnast 1978, A Very Young Circus Flyer 1979, The Writer's Image 1980, How It Feels When a Parent Dies 1981, How It Feels to be Adopted 1982, How It Feels When Parents Divorce 1984, The Fun of Cooking 1985, Jack Goes to the Beach 1986, Jamie Goes on an Airplane 1986, Taryn Goes to the Dentist 1986, A Visit to Washington, DC 1987, How It Feels to Fight for Your Life 1989, A Very Young Musician 1990, A Very Young Gardener 1990, A Very Young Actress 1991, How it Feels to Live with a Physical Disability 1992. *Address:* c/o Alfred A. Knopf Inc, 201 E 50th St, New York, NY 10022, USA.

KREPS, Juanita Morris, MA, PH D; American economist, business executive and government official; b 11 Jan 1921, Lynch, KY; d of the late Elmer and Cenia Blair Morris; m Clifton H. Kreps, Jr 1944 (deceased); one s two d. *Education:* Berea Coll (KY) and Duke Univ (Durham, NC). *Career:* Instructor in Econs Denison Univ, OH 1945–46, Asst Prof 1947–50; Lecturer Hofstra Univ, NY, 1952–54, Queens Coll, NY 1954–55; Visiting Asst Prof Duke Univ, NC, Asst Prof 1958–61, Assoc Prof 1962–67, Prof 1967–77, Dean of Women's Coll, Asst Provost 1969–72, James B. Duke Prof 1972–77, Vice-Pres 1973–77; US Sec of Commerce 1977–79; Ford Faculty Research Fellow 1964–65; Dir New York Stock Exchange 1972–77, J. C. Penney Co 1972–77, 1979–91, Eastman Kodak Co 1975–77, 1979–91, RJR Nabisco 1975–77, 1979–89, Citicorp 1979–89, UAL Inc 1979–92, AT&T 1980–91, Armco Inc 1980–91, Zurn Industries Inc 1982–, Deere & Co 1982–92, Chrysler Corpn 1983–91; mem Comm on Future of Worker-Management Relations to advise Secs of Commerce and Labor 1993–95; currently mem Council on Foreign Relations, Miller Center Comm on Separation of Powers; Fellow American Acad of Arts

and Sciences 1988; Trustee Berea Coll 1972–78, 1980–98, Coll Retirement Equities Fund 1972–77, Kenan Inst of Pvt Enterprise, Univ of N Carolina, Chapel Hill 1995–, Duke Endowment, Univ of N Carolina at Wilmington; Chair Bd of Trustees, Educational Testing Service 1975–76; Pres-Elect American Asscn for Higher Educ 1975–76; Overseer Teachers' Insurance and Annuity Asscn, Pres Bd of Overseers 1992–96; Chair Coll Retirement Equities Fund Bd of Overseers; has received 20 hon degrees; N Carolina Public Service Award 1976, Haskins Award 1984, Corp Governance Award, Nat Asscn of Corp Dirs (first recipient) 1987, Duke Univ Medal for Distinguished Meritorious Service and many other awards. *Publications:* Employment, Income and Retirement Problems of the Aged (ed) 1963, Technology, Manpower and Retirement Policy (ed) 1966, Lifetime Allocation of Work and Income (ed) 1971, Sex in the Marketplace: American Women at Work (ed) 1971, Principles of Economics (jtly, 2nd edn) 1965, Contemporary Labor Economics (jtly) 1974, Sex, Age and Work (jtly) 1975, Women and the American Economy, A Look to the 1980s (jtly) 1976; over 60 papers on ageing, retirement and econs. *Leisure interests:* music, art. *Address:* 115 E Duke Bldg, Box 90768, Duke University, Durham, NC 27708, USA; 29 Forest at Duke Drive, Durham, NC 27705, USA. *Telephone:* (919) 684-2616 (Office); *Fax:* (919) 684-8351.

KRESADLOVA-FORMANOVA, Vera; Czech actress and artist; b 28 Feb 1944, Prague; d of Bohuslav Kresadlo and Jirina Kresadlova; m Milos Forman 1964; three s. *Education:* School of Design Art. *Career:* Mem Semafor Theatre Co 1964–; has acted in more than 15 films and TV series 1964–90; singer with Swing Prague Band 1980–, tours of Germany, Netherlands; made recording 1986; glass designer 1990–. *Leisure interest:* art and design. *Address:* České Družiny 31, 160 00 Prague 6, Czech Republic. *Telephone:* (2) 3121636.

KRIEGER, Margarethe; German graphic artist and art critic; b 27 April 1936, Mannheim; d of Carl and Ingeborg Krieger; m Jürgen Schütz 1968. *Education:* Univ of Heidelberg and Kunstakademie Karlsruhe. *Career:* Art critic on Mannheimer Morgen 1961–; graphic artist, illustrator and portrait painter; exhibitions in Germany and abroad; graphic artist for films; Graphic Art Prize, Salon des Femmes Peintres (Musée d'Art Moderne, Paris) 1968; Prize for Foreign Painter (Musée d'Art Moderne, Paris) 1973; Gold Medal, Italian Acad of Arts 1978; Prize from Acad Salsomaggiore (Parma, Italy) 1981; Willibald-Kramm-Kunstpreis, Heidelberg 1992. *Leisure interest:* short films. *Address:* Mühltalstr 93, 69121 Heidelberg, Germany.

KRIKHELI, Eteri Anzorovna; Russian/Georgian cosmetologist; b 13 May 1965, Tbilisi; m Krikheli David Gavrilovich; two d. *Education:* Moscow Inst of Stomatology and Moscow Inst of Foreign Languages. *Career:* With Moscow Inst of Stomatology 1992–94; f Klazko co (Clinics of Laser Surgery) 1997; participated in confs in Barcelona, Paris, Monte Carlo, Dusseldorf, London, seminars on cosmetic surgery; numerous articles in magazines and journals. *Leisure interests:* jazz, soul, classical music. *Address:* Klazko, Serafimovicha str 2, 109072 Moscow. *Telephone:* (095) 959-30-69 (Office).

KRISTEVA, Julia, D ÈS L; French psychoanalyst and writer; b 24 June 1941, Bulgaria; m Philippe Sollers 1967; one s. *Education:* Univ of Sofia and Ecole des Hautes Etudes en Sciences Sociales (Paris). *Career:* Prof Univ of Paris VII; psychoanalyst and writer. *Publications include:* Le texte du roman, approche sémiologique d'une structure discursive transformationnelle 1970, La révolution du langage poétique: l'avant-garde à la fin du XIXème siècle, Lautréamont et Mallarmé 1974, Des chinoises 1974, Polylogue 1977, Pouvoirs de l'horreur: Essai sur l'abjection 1980, Le langage, cet inconnu 1981, Histoires d'amour 1985, Soleil noir, dépression et mélancolie 1987, Etrangers à nous-mêmes (Prix Henri Hertz 1989) 1988, Les Samouraïs 1990, Lettre ouverte à Harlem Désir 1990, Le vieil homme et les loups 1991, Les nouvelles maladies de l'âme 1993, Le temps sensible: Proust et l'expérience littéraire (essay) 1994, Possession 1996, Sens et non-sens de la révolte 1996, La révolte intime 1997, Le génie féminin, Vol 1: Hannah Arendt 1999, Vol 2: Melanie Klein 2000. *Address:* Université de Paris VII, 2 place Jussieu, 75005 Paris, France.

KRISTIANSEN, Ingrid; Norwegian athlete; b 1956. *Career:* Fmrly cross-country skier; began running marathons 1977; winner London Marathon 1985, Boston Marathon, USA 1986, 1989, New York

Marathon, USA 1989; World Record Holder at 5,000m 1986, 10,000m 1986 and marathon 1985; World Champion in 10,000m event, Rome 1987; only woman to win world titles in track, road and cross-country events.

KRISTOF, Agota; Swiss (b Hungarian) writer; b 30 Oct 1935, Csikvánd; d of Kristof Kálmán and Antonia Turchányi; m 1st Jean Béri 1954; m 2nd Jean-Pierre Baillod 1963; two d one s. *Education:* Szombathely (Hungary). *Career:* Writer since age of 14; left Hungary 1956; began writing plays in French 1970; factory worker 1983–88; first book published 1986; full-time writer 1988–; Prix Européen ADELF 1986; Prix France-Inter 1992. *Publications:* Un rat qui passe, La fille de l'arpenteur, l'Expiation, Le grand cahier 1986, La preuve 1988, Le troisième mensonge 1991. *Leisure interest:* reading. *Address:* c/o 13 rue de Vieux-Châtel, 2000 Neuchâtel, Switzerland.

KROLL, Rev Una Margaret Patricia, MA, MB; British deacon, writer and broadcaster; b 15 Dec 1925; d of George and Hilda Hill; m Leopold Kroll 1957 (died 1987); three d one s. *Education:* Girton Coll (Cambridge) and The London Hosp. *Career:* Medical practitioner in Africa 1953–60; Gen practice 1960–81; Clinical Medical Officer Hastings Health Dist 1981–85, Sr Clinical Medical Officer 1985–88; writer, broadcaster and active feminist 1970–89; worker Deacon 1970–88, Deacon Church in Wales 1988, Priest 1997–; Novice Sister Soc of the Sacred Cross 1990–94, currently a solitary in life vows; fmr mem Prov Validating Bd, Church of Wales, Royal Coll of Gen Practitioners. *Publications:* Cervical Cytology (contrib) 1969, Transcendental Meditation: a signpost to the world 1974, Flesh of my Flesh: a Christian view on sexism 1975, Lament for a Lost Enemy: study of reconciliation 1976, Sexual Counselling 1980, The Spiritual Exercise Book 1985, Growing Older 1988, In Touch with Healing 1991, Vocation to Resistance 1995, Trees of Life 1997, Forgive and Live 2000. *Leisure interests:* reading, gardening. *Address:* St Mary's Lodge, Priory St, Monmouth, Gwent NP5 3BR, UK. *Telephone:* (1600) 860244.

KRONE, Julieann (Julie) Louise; American jockey; b 24 July 1963, Benton Harbor, MI; d of Don and Judi Krone; m Matthew A. Muzikar 1996. *Career:* First win 1979 on Lord Farckle; winner Cornhusker Handicap on Gaily Gaily 1988; winner Budweiser Maryland Classic on Master Speaker 1989; winner Belmont Stakes on Colonial Affair 1993; winner Canadian Molson Millions on Peaks and Valleys 1995; woman jockey with most wins ever (c 3,400 races) 1986–; numerous TV appearances. *Leisure interests:* reading, show jumping, roller-blading. *Address:* Jockeys Guild Inc, POB 250, Lexington, KY 40588, USA.

KRONICK, Doreen, MA; Canadian psychologist; b 9 Nov 1931, Winnipeg, MB; d of Leon and Elsie A. Pape; m Joseph Kronick 1950; two s one d. *Education:* Skidmore Coll (NY) and York Univ. *Career:* Founder Ontario Asscn for Children with Learning Disabilities 1964, Canadian Asscn for Children with Learning Disabilities 1967; lecturer to univs, psychiatric insts, govt bodies, professional asscns; Lecturer in Social Work Univ of Toronto 1977–79, in Special Educ 1977–81; Asst Prof York Univ 1981–83, Assoc Prof 1983–87; Consultant Ontario Ministry of Educ 1978–95; Woman of the Year, Pioneer Women 1974; Lowen, Ondattje, McCutcheon Award 1980; first recipient Thérèse Casgrain Award, Canadian Govt 1983; Commemorative Medal Canada 125 1994. *Publications include:* Social Development of Learning Disabled Persons 1981, New Approaches to Learning Disabilities: Cognitive, Metacognitive and Holistic 1988, Teaching Children with Exceptionalities 1992; nine other books, contribs to ten books and numerous articles and papers in professional journals. *Leisure interests:* reading, travel, cooking, music. *Address:* 221 Broadway Ave, Toronto, ON M4P 1W1, Canada. *Telephone:* (416) 489-7858.

KRUEGER, Anne O., PH D; American economist and international organization official; b 12 Feb 1934, Endicott, NY; d of Leslie A. and Dora W. Osborn; m James M. Henderson 1981; one d. *Education:* Oberlin Coll and Univ of Wisconsin. *Career:* Asst Prof of Econs Univ of Minnesota 1959–63, Assoc Prof 1963–66, Prof 1966–82; Research Assoc Nat Bureau of Econ Research 1969–82, 1986–; Vice-Pres Econs and Research, IBRD 1982–86; Arts and Sciences Prof of Econs Duke Univ, Durham, NC 1987–92; Sr Fellow (non-resident) Brookings Inst 1988–94; Sr Research Fellow Inst for Policy Reform 1990–; Rep Int Econ Asscn 1991–; Commr Int Baltic Econ Comm 1991–; Herald L.

and Caroline L. Ritch Prof in Humanities and Sciences, Stanford Univ 1993–, Dir Center for Research on Econ Devt and Policy Reform 1996–; Deputy Dir-Gen IMF June 2001–; mem Advisory Council Korea Econ Inst of America 1991–; visiting prof at univs in USA, Denmark, Germany, France, Australia and Sweden; mem editorial Bds of several int econ journals; mem NAS; Pres American Econ Asscn 1996–97; Fellow American Acad of Arts and Sciences, Econometric Soc; Hon D HUM LITT (Georgetown) 1993; Hon D ECON (Monash Univ, Australia) 1996; Dr hc (Hacettepe, Ankara) 1990; Robertson Prize, Nat Acad of Science 1984; Bernhard-Harms Prize Kiel Inst of World Econs 1990; Kenan Enterprise Award 1990; Frank E. Seidman Distinguished Award in Political Economy 1993. *Publications:* Foreign Trade Regimes and Economic Development: Turkey 1974, The Benefits and Costs of Import Substitution in India: A Microeconomic Study 1975, Trade and Development in Korea (co-ed) 1975, Growth, Distortions and Patterns of Trade Among Many Countries 1977, Liberalization Attempts and Consequences 1977, The Development Role of the Foreign Sector and Aid: Korea 1979, Trade and Employment in Developing Countries (co-ed) 1981, Exchange Rate Determination 1983, Development With Trade: LDCs and International Economy (co-ed) 1988, The Political Economy of International Trade 1989, Aid and Development (jtly) 1989, Perspectives on Trade and Development 1990, The Political Economy of Agricultural Pricing Policy (co-ed) 1991, Political Economy of Policy Reform in Developing Countries 1993, American Trade Policy 1995, The WTO as an International Institution (ed) 1998. *Address:* Dept of Economics, Stanford University, Stanford, CA 94035-6072, USA; 41 Linaria Way, Portola Valley, CA 94028, USA (Home). *Telephone:* (650) 723-0188 (Office); *Fax:* (650) 723-8611 (Office); *E-mail:* akrueger@leland.stanford.edu (Office).

KRUGER, Barbara; American artist and writer. *Education:* Syracuse Univ, Parsons School of Design and School of Visual Art (NY). *Career:* Began career as graphic designer, art director and picture ed on various magazines; held teaching post California Inst of Art, School of Art Inst (Chicago) and Univ of California at Berkeley; Creative Artists Service Program Grant 1976–77; Nat Endowment for the Arts Grant 1983–84. *Exhibitions include:* Contemporary Arts Museum, Houston, TX 1985, LA County Museum of Art 1985, Rhona Hoffman Gallery, Chicago 1986, 1990, Mary Boone Gallery, NY 1987, 1989, 1991, 1994, Nat Art Gallery, Wellington, NZ 1988, Galerie Bebert, Rotterdam 1989, Kölnische Kunstverein, Cologne, Germany 1990, Magasin, Centre Nat d'Art Contemporain, Grenoble, France 1992, Museum of Contemporary Art, LA 1999; also various group exhibitions. *Address:* c/o South London Gallery, Peckham Rd, London SE5, UK.

KUBANOVA, Anna Alekseyevna; Russian dermatologist; b 21 Sept 1948, Sochi; d of Radyanov Aleksey Panteleyevich and Radyanova Vera Leonidovna; one s. *Education:* Second Moscow Inst of Medicine. *Career:* Therapist Research Inst of Automatic Apparatus, USSR Ministry of Radio Industry 1972–74; Jr Researcher 2nd Moscow Inst of Medicine 1974–88; Prof, Chair, Deputy Dir, then Dir Cen Research Inst of Dermatological and Venerological Studies 1988–; Chief Dermatologist Russian Ministry of Public Health; Pres Soc of Dermatologists and Venerologists; Deputy Ed-in-Chief Vestnik Demakologii i Venerologii journal; Corresp mem Russian Acad of Medical Sciences; mem Presidium, Pharmacological Soc of Ministry of Public Health. *Publications:* over 300 scientific papers, including 11 monographs. *Address:* Central Research Institute of Dermatological and Venerological Studies, Korolenko st 4, korp 4, Moscow, Russian Federation. *Telephone:* (095) 964-26-20; *Fax:* (095) 964-48-22; *E-mail:* kubanova@cnikvi.ru; *Internet:* www.cnikvi.ru.

KUBIŠOVÁ, Marta; Czech singer; b 1 Nov 1942, České Budĕvovice; d of Jan Kubič and Marta Geierovoá; m 1st Jan Nĕmec 1969; m 2nd Jan Moravec 1974; one d. *Education:* Podĕbrady Grammar School and Oriental Inst (Prague). *Career:* Singer with Stop Theatre, Paroubice 1962–63, Alfa Theatre, Pilsen 1963–64, Lokoko Theatre, Prague 1964–68, Golden Kids Group 1968–70; banned from singing until after the 'Velvet Revolution' 1990; construction work, Prague 1971–74, 1982–89; Spokesperson Charter 77 1978–79; several music awards. *Recordings include:* Songs and Ballads (Platinum Record 1990) 1969; songs on films and TV programmes. *Leisure interests:* animals, nature, music, films. *Address:* Zahradničkova 1122, 150 00 Prague 5, Czech Republic. *Telephone:* (2) 558410.

KUÇURADI, Ioanna, PH D; Turkish professor of philosophy; b 4 Oct 1936, Istanbul; d of Georgios and Ephemia Kuçuradi. *Education:* Zappeion Greek Lycée for Girls (Istanbul) and Istanbul Univ. *Career:* Asst Prof Dept of Philosophy, Istanbul Univ 1959–61; Asst Prof Dept of Humanities, Atatürk Univ, Erzurum 1965–68; Lecturer Dept of Educ, Hacettepe Univ, Ankara 1968–69, Founder, Chair Dept of Philosophy 1969; mem Steering Cttee Int Fed of Philosophical Socs 1983, Sec-Gen 1988; apptd Pres Philosophical Soc of Turkey 1980; mem Cttee for Social Sciences and Humanities, Turkish Nat Comm for UNESCO. *Publications include:* In Turkish: Behind the Curtains (poetry) 1962, The Tragic in Max Scheler and Nietzsche 1965, Nietzsche's Conception of Man 1967, Ethics 1977, 1988, Art from a Philosophical Point of View 1980, Among the Events of our Time 1981, Uludag Papers 1988; numerous articles and papers. *Address:* International Federation of Philosophical Societies, c/o E. Agazzi, Séminaire de Philosophie, Université, 1700 Fribourg, Switzerland (Office); Ahmet Rasim sok 8/4, Çankaya, 06550 Ankara, Turkey (Home). *Telephone:* (4) 4366157 (Home); *Fax:* (4) 4410297 (Home).

KUDELINA, Lubov' Kondratyevna; Russian politician; b 4 April 1955, Vladivostok. *Education:* Moscow Inst of Finance. *Career:* Mem staff Ministry of Finance 1977–; Head Dept of Financing of Mil Complex and Law-Enforcing Orgs (Ministry of Finance) 1996–99; Deputy-Minister of Finance July 1999–; mem Fed Anti-terrorist Comm, Govt Comm on Mil-Industrial Problems 1999–2001; Head Financial-Econ Dept 2001–; Deputy Minister of Defence on Financial-Econ Problems 2001–. *Address:* Ministry of Defence, 103160 Moscow, K0160, Russian Federation. *Telephone:* (095) 296-75-78.

KUHLMANN, Kathleen Mary; American opera singer (mezzo-soprano); b 7 Dec 1950, San Francisco, CA; d of Hugo S. and Elvira L. Kuhlmann; m Haydn John Rawstron 1983 (divorced 1998). *Education:* Mercy High School (San Francisco), Univ of San Francisco and Chicago Lyric Opera School. *Career:* Resident Mezzo-Soprano Cologne Opera, Germany 1980–82; freelance singer 1982–; int debuts incude La Scala, Milan, Italy 1980, San Francisco Opera 1982, Royal Opera House, Covent Garden, London 1982, Teatro Regio Parma, Italy 1983, Glyndebourne Festival Opera, UK 1983, Wiener Staatsoper 1983, Teatro Communale Pisa, Italy 1983, Chicago Lyric Opera 1984, Salzburger Festspiele, Austria 1985, Stuttgart Opera, Germany 1985, Hamburg State Opera, Germany 1985, Lausanne/Geneva, Switzerland 1986, Naples, Italy 1987, Tel-Aviv, Israel 1988, Metropolitan Opera House, New York 1989, Paris 1990, Semperoper, Dresden, Germany 1992, Munich State Opera, Germany 1994, Staatsoper Unter den Linden, Berlin 1995, Deutsche Oper, Berlin 1995, Aix-en-Provence 1996, Opéra de Paris 1997, Opera di Roma 1998, Opéra de Bordeaux 1998; renowned for her interpretation of Rossini, Händel and Monteverdi Mezzo repertoire. *Address:* c/o IMG Paris (Vocal Division), 54 ave Marceau, 75008 Paris, France.

KUHN, Annemarie; German politician; b 9 May 1937, Ludwigs-hafen/Rhein. *Education:* Banking studies. *Career:* Fmr bank clerk; mem SPD 1964–, Chair Mainz SPD 1972, mem Dist Bd Rheinhessen 1988; Local Councillor, Mainz 1974–91; trade unionist in Industriegewerkschaft Chemie-Papier-Keramik, Rheinland-Pfalz/Saarland Dist, Sec 1977; MEP 1991–99, fmr mem Cttees on the Environment, Public Health and Consumer Protection, Petitions, Social Affairs, Employment and the Working Environment (Substitute mem), ACP–EEC Jt Ass; Ehrenring der Stadt Mainz 1991. *Address:* Eichendorffstr 59, 55122 Mainz, Germany (Home). *Telephone:* (6131) 238159 (Home); *Fax:* (6131) 287825 (Home).

KULENTY, Hanna, B MUS; Polish composer; b 18 March 1961, Białystok; one d. *Education:* Acad of Music (Warsaw) and Conservatory (The Hague). *Career:* Studied under Włodzimierz, Kotoński and Louis Andriessen; Guest Performer Deutscher Akademischer Austauschdienst in Berliner Künstler Programm 1990–91; performances of works by many orchestras in countries including the Netherlands, Latvia, UK, Demark, Germany; Stanisław Wyspiański Award 1987; First Prize Composers' Competition, Polish Composers' Union 1986, 1987; has won other awards in music competitions. *Works include:* Ad Unum 1985, Symphony No 1 1986, Perpetuus 1989, Concerto (for Piano and Chamber Orchestra) 1990; works for solo instruments and Chamber Orchestras; *Recordings include:* 12½ Musis Sacrum, Chronicles from Warsaw Autumn Festivals, Hanna Kulenty: Ad Unum, Sesto, Arci. *Address:* c/o Jana Pawła II 69/52, 00-170 Warsaw, Poland.

KULLMANN FIVE, Karin Cecilie (Kaci) (see Five, Karin Cecilie (Kaci) Kullmann).

KUMARATUNGA, Chandrika Bandaranaike, PH D; Sri Lankan Head of State; b 29 June 1945, Colombo; d of the late S. W. R. D. Bandaranaike (fmr Prime Minister, assassinated 1959) and of Sirimavo R. D. Bandaranaike (qv, Prime Minister, first woman, died 2000); m Vijaya Kumaratunga 1978 (assassinated 1988); one s one d. *Education:* St Bridget's Convent (Colombo) and Univ of Paris. *Career:* Mem Exec Cttee Women's League, Sri Lanka Freedom Party (SLFP) 1974, 1980, Working Cttee 1980, Cen Cttee 1992, Deputy Leader 1992; Chair and Man Dir Dinakara Sinhala newspaper 1977–85; Vice-Pres Sri Lanka Mahajana Party (SLMP—Sri Lanka People's Party) 1984, Pres 1986, Leader SLMP and People's Alliance; Chief Minister, Minister of Law and Order, of Finance and Planning, Educ, Employment and Cultural Affairs, W Prov Council 1993–94; Prime Minister Aug–Nov 1994, Minister of Finance and Planning, Ethnic Affairs and Nat Integration July 1994–, of Defence, of Buddha Sasana Nov 1994–; Pres of Sri Lanka Nov 1994–; Additional Prin Dir Land Reform Comm 1972–75; Chair Janawasa Comm 1975–77; Expert Consultant FAO 1977–80; Research Fellow Univ of London 1988–91; Guest Lecturer Univ of Bradford (UK) 1989, Jawaharlal Nehru Univ (India) 1991; has written several research papers on land reform and food policies. *Leisure interests:* playing piano and guitar, tennis, swimming, Kandyan (national dance), reading, art, sculpture, drama, cinema, music. *Address:* Presidential Secretariat, Republic Square, Colombo 1, Sri Lanka. *Telephone:* (1) 324801; *Fax:* (1) 333702.

KUMIN, Maxine Winokur, AM; American writer and poet; b 6 June 1925, Philadelphia, PA; d of Peter and Doll (née Simon) Winokur; m Victor M. Kumin 1946; two d one s. *Education:* Radcliffe Coll. *Career:* Visiting Prof Washington and Columbia Univs 1975, Brandeis Univ 1978, MIT 1984, Univ of Miami 1995, Pitzer Coll 1996; Visiting Lecturer Princeton Univ 1978–79, 1981–82; McGee Prof of Writing Davidson Coll 1997; Writer-in-Residence Florida Int Univ 1998; Consultant in Poetry, Library of Congress 1981–82; Elector Poets' Corner Cathedral Church of St John the Divine 1990–; mem Poetry Soc of America, PEN America, Authors' Guild, Writers' Union; Woodrow Wilson Visiting Fellow 1991–92; American Acad and Inst of Arts and Letters Award 1980; Fellow Acad of American Poets 1985, Chancellor 1995–; Levinson Award, Poetry Magazine 1987; The Poets' Prize 1994, Aiken Taylor Poetry Prize 1995, Harvard Grad School of Arts and Sciences Centennial Award 1996, Levinson Award, Poetry magazine 1987, American Acad and Inst of Arts Award 1989, Centennial Award, Harvard Grad School of Arts & Sciences 1996. *Publications include:* Poetry: Halfway 1961, The Privilege 1965, The Nightmare Factory 1970, Up Country (Pulitzer Prize for Poetry 1973) 1972, House, Bridge, Fountain, Gate 1975, The Retrieval System 1978, Our Ground Time Here Will Be Brief 1982, The Long Approach 1985, Nurture 1989, Looking For Luck 1992, Connecting the Dots 1996, Selected Poems 1960–1990 1997; Novels: Through Dooms of Love 1965, The Passions of Uxport 1968, The Abduction 1971, The Designated Heir 1974; Essays: In Deep 1987, Women, Animals and Vegetables: Essays and Stories 1994; numerous children's books, essays and short stories. *Leisure interest:* breeding horses. *Address:* c/o Scott Waxman Agency Inc, 1650 Broadway, Suite 1011, New York, NY 10019, USA.

KUNIN, Madeleine May, MA, MS; American politician and diplomatist; b 28 Sept 1933, Zurich, Switzerland; d of Ferdinand May and Renée Bloch; m Arthur S. Kunin 1959 (divorced 1995); three s one d. *Education:* Univs of Massachusetts and Vermont, and Columbia Univ (NY). *Career:* Reporter Burlington Free Press, VT 1957–58; Asst Producer WCAX-TV, Burlington 1960–61; freelance writer and instructor in English Trinity Coll, Burlington 1969–70; mem (Democrat) Vermont House of Reps 1973–78; Lieut-Gov of Vermont 1979–82, Gov 1985–91; Deputy Sec of Educ 1993–96; Amb to Switzerland 1996–99; Lecturer Middlebury Coll, St Michael's Coll 1984, now Scholar-in-Residence, Middlebury Coll; Fellow Inst of Politics, Kennedy School of Govt, Harvard Univ 1983–93; Bunting Fellow Radcliffe Coll, Cambridge, MA 1991–92; has written various articles for newspapers and magazines; has received several hon degrees and other distinctions. *Publication:* The Big Green Book (jtly) 1976, Living a Politicial Life 1994; numerous articles in professional journals, magazines and newspapers. *Address:* Geonomics House, Middlebury College, Middlebury, VT 05753, USA (Office). *E-mail:* mkunin@middlebury.edu (Office).

KUO, Shirley W. Y., BA, D ECON, PH D; Taiwanese politician and economist; b 25 Jan 1930; m Nieh Wenya; three d. *Education:* Nat Taiwan Univ, Kobe Univ (Japan) and MIT (USA). *Career:* Lecturer and Assoc Prof Nat Taiwan Univ, Prof 1966–89; Deputy Gov Cen Bank of China 1979–88; Minister of Finance 1988–90; Minister of State 1990, later Minister without Portfolio; Vice-Chair Council for Econ Planning and Devt 1973–79, Chair 1990. *Publications:* The Taiwan Economy in Transition, Growth with Equity: The Taiwan Case, The Taiwan Success Story: Rapid Growth with Improved Distribution in the Republic of China 1952–79, Macroeconomics, Microeconomics. *Address:* Office of the Executive Yuan, Chunghsiao E Rd, Section 1, No 1, Taipei 105, Taiwan; 11th Floor-1, 289 Tunhua S Rd, Section 1, Taipei, Taiwan.

KUPFER, Monica E., PH D; Panamanian art historian and curator; b 29 May 1957; m John F. Kirton. *Education:* Tulane Univ (New Orleans, LA) and Univ of Texas at Austin (USA). *Career:* Slide Curator, Tulane Univ 1978–79; Curatorial Asst, Italy 1980; Asst Prof in Art History, Tulane Univ 1981, Univ of Texas 1984–85; Art Consultant 1982–84; Guest Curator Museo de Arte Contemporáneo, Panama 1983, Curator 1985–88, apptd Adjunct Curator 1988; licensed trans in Spanish, English, German; mem Int Cttee for Museums of Modern Art, ICOM, Panamanian Nat Cttee of Museums, Coll Art Asscn of America; mem of numerous art panels and exhibition juries; has written various articles and essays on Latin American art. *Exhibitions organized include:* Diálogo y Pintura 1978, Concurso Panarte 1978, Grabados y Litografías 1979, Arte Erótico 1981, Encuentro de la Plástica Nal 1982, Retrospectiva de la Obra de Juan Manuel Cedeno 1983–84, Manuel Chong Neto: Vision Retrospectiva 1986, Encuentro de Escultural 1987. *Address:* Apdo 8082, Panamá 7, Panama. *Telephone:* (507) 26-2456; *Fax:* (507) 23-6614.

KÜR, Pinar, D ÈS L; Turkish writer and lecturer; b 15 April 1943, Bursa; d of Behram and Halide Ismet (née Zerluhan) Kür; m Can Kolukisaoğlu 1964 (divorced 1979); one s. *Education:* Forest Hills High School and Queens Coll (New York), and Univs of the Bosphorus (Istanbul) and Paris (Sorbonne). *Career:* Writer State Theatre of Ankara 1971–73; apptd Lecturer in English, Istanbul Univ 1979; Lecturer in Literature, Istanbul Bilgi Universifesi 1996; Sait Faik Award 1984. *Publications include:* Novels: Yarin, Yarin (Tomorrow, Tomorrow) 1976, Küçük Oyuncu (Petty Player) 1977, Asılacak Kadan (A Woman to Hang) 1979, Bitmeyen Aşk (Unending Love) 1986, Bir Cinayet Romanı (A Crime Novel) 1989, Sonuncu Sonbahar (The Last Fall); Short stories: Bir Deli Ağaç (A Tormented Tree) 1981, Akışı Olmayan Sular (Still Waters, Sait Faik Award 1984) 1983; numerous magazine and newspaper articles and translations into Turkish. *Leisure interests:* reading, classical music, summer sports. *Address:* Turna Sokak 7/3, Elmadăg, 80230 Istanbul, Turkey. *Telephone:* (1) 2415148; *E-mail:* kurpinar@hotmail.com.

KURIHARA, Harumi; Japanese business executive, cook, writer and broadcaster; b Shimoda; m; two s. *Career:* Celebrity cook and homemaker; Head of publishing, design and retail business; author of several multi-million selling cookbooks; designer of tableware, gardening tools and bedlinen; launched Harumi K range of luxury brands; owns Yutori no Kuukan restaurant, Tokyo; numerous appearances on TV talk shows. *Address:* c/o Yutori no Kuukan, Sendagaya 3-16-5, Tokyo, Japan. *Telephone:* 5410-8845.

KŮROVÁ, Jana; Czech ballet dancer; b Prague; d of Miroslav Kůra and Jarmila (née Manšingrová) Kůrová. *Education:* State Conservatory (Prague) and the Bolshoi Academic Choreographic School of Ballet (Moscow). *Career:* Prin Dancer Nat Theatre of Prague 1977–; made US debut All Star Gala, New York 1979; Founder Czech Ballet Theatre and Czech Ballet Theatre Foundation Inc, Prague 1991–; has performed numerous leading roles in romantic and classical ballets; has appeared in several films in Czech Repub (fmrly Czechoslovakia), Germany and the USA; has performed for Queen Sophia of Spain in Gran Gala de las Estrellas de la Dansa, Madrid 1980; Guest Artist Nat Ballet of Canada

1981; has performed in The World Ballet Festival, Tokyo 1982, Int Ballet Festival, Cuba 1986; has toured Italy 1983 and USA 1989, 1990, 1991, 1992; Prix de Lausanne, Médaille d'Or 1976; First Prize Prague Ballet Competition 1976; Second Prize The World Ballet Concours, Tokyo 1978; Second Prize Int Ballet Competition, USA 1979; First Prize Classical Pas de deux 1979. *Performances include:* Giselle, Swan Lake, The Sleeping Beauty, The Nutcracker, La Fille Mal Gardée, Don Quixote, La Bayadère, Paquita, Le Pas de Quatre, Sylvia, Cinderella, Romeo and Juliet, The Tales of Hoffman, Spartacus, Satanella, La Péri, Le Corsaire, La Esmérelda, The Birds, The Ur; *Films:* Cinderella 1977, Pas de Deux 1981, Giselle 1991. *Address:* Lodecká 3, Nové Město, 110 00 Prague 1, Czech Republic. *Telephone:* (2) 2310402; *Fax:* (2) 2310402.

KUROYANAGI, Tetsuko, BA; Japanese actress and writer; b 9 Aug 1933, Tokyo; d of Moritsuna and Cho Kuronyanagi. *Education:* Tokyo Coll of Music and at Bungakuza Theatre (Tokyo) and Mary Tarcai Studio (New York). *Career:* TV debut with Japanese Broadcasting Corpn (NHK) 1954; Host Tetsuko's Room (chat show), Asahi Nat Broadcasting Co 1976–94; regular guest Discover Wonders of the World (quiz show), Tokyo Broadcasting System 1987–; numerous stage appearances throughout Japan; Founder and Pres Totto Foundation (for training deaf actors) 1981–; Dir Chihiro Iwasaki Art Museum of Picture Books 1995–; Trustee World Wide Fund for Nature, Japan 1977–; UNICEF Goodwill Amb 1984–; Minister of Foreign Affairs Award. *Publications:* From New York with Love 1972, Totto-chan: The Little Girl at the Window 1981, Animal Theatre (photographic essay) 1983, Totto-channel 1984, My Friends 1986, Totto-chan's children: A Goodwill Journey to the Children of the World. *Leisure interests:* travel, calligraphy, study of giant pandas. *Address:* Yoshida Naomi Office, No 2 Tanizawa Bldg, 4th Floor, 3-2-11 Nishi-Azabu, Minato-ku, Tokyo 106-0031, Japan. *Telephone:* (3) 3403-9296; *Fax:* (3) 3403-5322.

KURTI, Tinka; Albanian actress; b 17 Dec 1932, Sarajevo, Bosnia; m Paloke Kurti 1951; one s. *Education:* Artistic school. *Career:* Actress Shkodër Theatre since 1949, banned from working nine times; now retd; Honoured Artist 1951; Artist of the People 1979; numerous awards for acting. *Films include:* Tana 1958; 31 film roles; *Plays include:* Othello, Macbeth; 158 roles in plays by Ibsen, Molière, Dürrenmatt, Shakespeare, etc. *Address:* Mihal Gramene, P 11 8, H I, Apt 8, Tirana, Albania. *Telephone:* (42) 26342.

KURYS, Diane; French film director; b 3 Dec 1948, Lyons. *Career:* Actress with Jean-Louis Barrault's theatre group; film scriptwriter, producer and dir. *Films:* Diabolo Menthe (Peppermint Soda, writer, dir, co-producer, Prix Louis Deluc for Best Picture) 1977, Coup de Sirocco (co-producer), Le grand pardon (co-producer), Cocktail Molotov (dir), Coup de Foudre (Acad Award nomination) 1984, Entre Nous (dir), A Man in Love (dir), La Baule-les-Pins, C'est la vie.

KUSAMA, Yayoi; Japanese sculptor, painter and writer; b 22 March 1929, Nagano Prefecture. *Education:* Kyoto Arts and Crafts School and The Art Students' League (New York). *Career:* Started painting around age 10; went to USA 1957 and showed large paintings and environmental sculptures; in late 1960s staged many body-painting festivals, fashion shows and anti-war demonstrations; has organized numerous group and solo exhibitions; has written several novels and contributed to magazines and newspapers; invented the infinity mirror room; apptd Pres Japan Educ Ltd 1977; produced open-air pieces for the Fukuoka Kenko Center, the Fukuoka Municipal Museum of Art, the Bunka-mura on Benesse Island, Naoshima, the Kirishima Open-Air Museum, and a mural for Lisbon subway station; solo exhibitions include Aggregation One Thousand Boats (New York) 1963, Driving Image Show (New York) 1964, Sex Food Obsession Show (The Hague, Netherlands) 1965, Phallus Garden Environment (Europe, USA, Japan) 1965–66, Endless Love Show 1966, Driving Image Show (Milan, Italy) 1966, Sex Food Obsession Compulsion Furniture Repetitive Vision (Essen, Germany) 1966, Fillmore East Theatre Happening 1968, Garden Nude Orgy Happening (Museum of Modern Art, New York) 1969, Airplane Happening in Air Over Holland 1969, Fashion Show Nude Happening (Venice, Italy) 1970, Cage/Painting/Women (The Hague) 1970–72, Ginza (Tokyo) 1975–76, 1980, (Italy) 1983, (Paris) 1986, (Calais, France) 1987, (New York) 1989, (Oxford, UK) 1989, (Venice Biennale) 1993, (New York) 1996, Los Angeles 1998, Tokyo

(1999), France 2000; has collaborated with photographer Nobuyoshi Araki, musician Peter Gabriel and fashion designer Issey Miyake; awards and prizes include Tenth Literary Award for New Writers, Yasei Jidai magazine 1983, Int Asscn of Art Critics Best Art Gallery Show (New York) 1996, Educ Minister's Art Encouragement Prize 2000, Foreign Minister's Commendations 2000, Asahi Prize 2001. *Publications include:* Novels: Manhattan Suicide Addict 1978, Christopher Gay Brothel 1984, The Burning of St Mark's Church 1985, Between Heaven and Earth 1988, Wood Stock Phallus Cutter 1988, Arching Chandelier 1989, Distress Like This 1990, Angels in Cape Cod 1990, Digitalis at Central Park 1991, Lost in Swapland 1992, The New York Story 1993, The Mental Hospital of Ants 1993, Violet Obsession 1998, New York '69 1998; Anthologies: Feeling Melancholy 1989; *Film:* Kusama's Self-Obliteration (also produced) (prizes at 4th Int Experimental Film Competition (Belgium) 1968, Ann Arbor Film Festival 1968) 1968, Topaz. *Address:* 1008 Ushisome Heim, Shinjuku-ku 30-2-chome, Haramachi, Tokyo, Japan; Benten Bldg, 111-7 Benten-cho, Shinjuku-ku, Tokyo 162-0851, Japan. *Telephone:* (3) 3202-1217; *Fax:* (3) 3202-1217; *E-mail:* yayoi@super.win.ne.jp.

KUSHNER, Eva M., OC, MA, PH D, FRSC; Canadian former university president and professor of French and comparative literature; b 18 June 1929, Prague, Czechoslovakia (now Czech Repub); d of the late Josef Dubsky and Anna (née Kakfa) Dubsky-Cahill; m Donn Jean Kushner 1949; three s. *Education:* Coll classique de jeunes filles (Cognac, France), Coll Marie de France and McGill Univ (Montréal). *Career:* Sessional Lecturer in Philosophy Sir George Williams Univ 1952–53; Sessional Lecturer in French McGill Univ 1952–55; Lecturer in French and Comparative Literature Univ Coll, London 1958–59, Carleton Univ (Ottawa) 1961–63, Asst Prof 1963–65, Assoc Prof 1965–69, Prof 1969–76, Chair Comparative Literature 1965–69, 1970–72, 1975–76, Hon Adjunct Prof of Comparative Literature 1976–79; Prof of French and Comparative Literature McGill Univ 1976–87; Pres Victoria Coll, Univ of Toronto 1987–94; Dir Comparative Literature, Univ of Toronto 1994–95; Visiting Prof Princeton Univ 2000; mem Acad Européenne des lettres, des sciences et des arts 1980, Royal Soc of Canada 1971–, Vice-Pres 1980–82; Pres Acad des lettres et sciences humaines 1980–82; mem Exec Cttee Canada Council 1975–81; mem Social Sciences and Humanities Research Council of Canada 1983–86, Vice-Pres 1984–86; mem Advisory Bd Nat Library of Canada 1977–81, Research Council Canadian Inst for Advanced Research 1983–87, Canadian Cttee for Women in Engineering 1989–91, Int Comparative Literature Asscn, Pres 1979–82; Vice-Pres Int Fed for Modern Languages and Literatures 1987–93, Pres 1996–; Hon D LITT (Acadia) 1988; Hon DD (United Theological Coll) 1992; Hon D LITT (Univ of St Michael's Coll) 1993, (Western Ontario) 1996; Dr hc (Szeged) 1997. *Publications include:* Patrice de la Tour du Pin 1961, Le Mythe d'Orphée dans la littérature française contemporaine 1961, Chants de Bohême 1963, Rina Lasnier 1967, 1969, Saint-Denys Garneau 1967, François Mauriac 1972, L'avènement de l'esprit nouveau 1400–1480 (co-ed) 1988, Théorie de la littérature: problèmes et perspectives (co-ed) 1989, La problématique du sujet chez montaigne (ed) 1995, Histoire des poétiques 1997. *Leisure interests:* reading, writing, swimming, travel. *Address:* Victoria University, 73 Queen's Park, Toronto, ON M5S 1K7, Canada (Office); 63 Albany Ave, Toronto, ON M5R 3C2, Canada (Home). *Telephone:* (416) 585-4592 (Office); (416) 538-0173 (Home); *Fax:* (416) 585-4592 (Office); (416) 585-4591 (Home); *E-mail:* eva.kushner@utoronto.ca.

KÚTVÖLGYI, Erzsébet; Hungarian actress; b 1950, Budapest; d of István Kútvölgyi and Erzsébet Nagy; m 1st Antal Örkény; m 2nd Zsolt Zákányi; two s. *Education:* In Budapest. *Career:* Actress in films and on stage and TV; worked with Vígszínház theatre co; Awards 1974, 1990. *Plays include:* La Mancha Lovagja, Romeo and Juliet, Crime and Punishment, Three Sisters; *Recordings include:* Popeesztival 1972, Bors Néni 1974, 30 Eves Vagyok 1975, Edith Piaf 1985. *Address:* 1054 Budapest, Szabadság tér 11-I-1, Hungary.

KUUSKOSKI, Eeva Maija Kaarina, LIC MED; Finnish politician and paediatrician; b 4 Oct 1946, Aura; d of Timo Mauri and Kirsti Mirjam (née Haapanen) Kuuskoski; m 1st Juha Ville Vikatmaa 1973 (deceased); one d (deceased); m 2nd Pentti Manninen 1991; one d. *Career:* Medical Officer Turku Health Centre 1973–79; Asst Turku Univ Public Health Studies Inst 1973; mem Turku City Council 1973–80; Admin Bd Student Health Care Foundation 1975–81; Asst Physician Helsinki Univ Hosp 1976–80; mem Eduskunta (Parl, Finnish Centre Party) 1979–95, Minister for Social Affairs and Health 1983–87, 1991–92; Program Dir Mannerheim League for Child Welfare 1995–; Commdr of the Order of the Lion of Finland. *Publication:* With People 1991. *Leisure interests:* opera, handcrafts. *Address:* Mannerheim League for Child Welfare, POB 141, 00531 Helsinki, Finland. *Telephone:* (0) 34811550; *Fax:* (0) 34811565; *E-mail:* eeva.kuuskoski@mll.fi; *Internet:* www.mll.fi.

KVARATSKELIA, Gucha Shalvovna, D SC; Georgian academic; b 1940. *Career:* Sr Researcher Inst of Language Study; Prof Tbilisi State Pedagogical Inst; People's Deputy of the USSR; mem Cttee on Science, Nat Educ, Culture and Educ, Supreme Soviet 1989–91. *Address:* Tbilisi State Pedagogical Institute of Foreign Languages, 380062 Tbilisi, Pr Chavchavadze 45, Georgia.

KWAN-KISAICHI, Shirley, BA, MS; American writer and producer; b 2 Oct 1958, Madrid, Spain; d of Hon Cheun and Kazuko (née Yoshioka) Kwan; m Kazuhiro Kisaichi 1988. *Education:* Washington State Univ and Columbia Univ. *Career:* Acting Educational Ed WNET-TV, New York 1980, Consultant 1980–81; News Writer Satellite News Channel, Stamford 1982–83, Newsday, Melville, New York 1983–84; Copyreader Dow Jones and Co, New York 1984–85; freelance writer and producer 1985–; Corresp Cross and Talk, Tokyo 1986–89; Consultant and Assoc Producer WETA-TV, Washington, DC 1986–87; Consultant ALC Press Inc, Tokyo 1986–88; numerous contribs to films, videos and journals; mem Asian American Journalist Asscn, Asian Cine-Vision, Asian American Int Film Festival Cttee. *Productions include:* Who Killed Vincent Chin? (reporter and production man, Acad Award nomination) 1986, Soho Murder (producer) 1988, Time of Your Life, Bourgeois Blues, Mail Order Matchup. *Address:* 244 Dean St, Brooklyn, NY 11217, USA.

KYO, Machiko; Japanese actress; b 1924. *Career:* Dancer Shochiku Girls' Opera Co, Osaka; film debut in Saigo ni Warau Otoko (Last Laughter) 1949; has appeared in over 80 films; Jussie (Finland) Award 1957. *Films include:* Rashomon (Best Actress Award) 1950, Ugetsu Monogatari 1953, Gate of Hell 1954, Story of Shunkin 1955, Akasen Chitai (Street of Shame), Teahouse of the August Moon 1956, Yoru no Cho (Night Butterflies) 1957, Odd Obsession 1959, Floating Weeds 1959, A Woman's Testament 1960, Ugetsu.

L

LA PLANTE, Lynda; British actress and writer; b 1946, Formby, Liverpool; m Richard La Plante 1976. *Education:* Streatham House School for Ladies (Crosby) and Royal Acad of Dramatic Art. *Career:* Actress 1972–, toured with Brian Rix; appearances include Liverpool Playhouse, Sheffield Crucible Theatre 1974; numerous TV appearances; currently TV script writer and novelist. *TV appearances include:* Fox, Minder, The Sweeney, The Gentle Touch; *Plays include:* Calamity Jane 1974; *TV scripts include:* Widows 1982, Prime Suspect (BAFTA Award 1992) 1991, 1993, 1995, Civvies 1992, Framed, Seekers, White Slaves (film), Comics 1993, Cold Shoulder 2 1996, Cold Blood, Bella Mafia 1997, Trial and Retribution 1997–, Killer Net 1998, Mind Games 2000; *Publications include:* The Legacy, The Talisman, Bella Mafia, Entwined, Cold Shoulder, The Governor, She's Out, Cold Heart 1998, Sleeping Cruelty 2000. *Address:* La Plante Productions Ltd, Paramount House, 162–170 Wardour St, London W1V 3AT, UK (Office).

LA ROCHE, Marie-Elaine A., BS, MBA; American banking executive; b 17 August 1949, New York, NY; d of Anre and Madeleine La Roche; three c. *Education:* Georgetown Univ (Washington, DC) and American Univ. *Career:* Mem Equity Sales Dept Morgan Stanley Investment Banking Co, New York 1978–81, Vice-Pres Investment Banking 1981–84, Principal Marketing Dir Fixed Income Div 1985–86, Man Dir Fixed Income Div 1986–, Man Dir and Dir World-wide Fixed Income Marketing 1986–89, Man Dir and Dir Public Finance Dept 1989–94; Vice-Pres Morgan Stanley Investment Banking Co, London 1984–85; Nat Co-Chair Women's Campaign Fund; mem Forum for Women Dirs, Cttee of 200 1991; f WISH List; named to YWCA Acad of Women Achievers 1983. *Address:* Morgan Stanley & Co Inc, 1251 Ave of the Americas, 4th Floor, New York, NY 10020, USA.

LA YACONA, Maria; American photographer; b 18 Nov 1926, Cleveland, OH; d of the late Mario and Anna La Yacona. *Education:* Winona School of Photography (IN, USA). *Career:* Photographer 1945–, mem staff Time Inc 1950–55, assigned to Life magazine, Time magazine and Sports Illustrated; freelance photographer 1956–; photographer Nat Dance Theatre Co of Jamaica 1964–91; mem Bd Nat Gallery of Jamaica; one-woman exhibition Brooks, San Francisco, CA, USA 1951, Jamaica: Portraits 1955–93; has participated in group exhibitions in Nat Gallery of Jamaica 1988–91; Silver Musgrave Medal for Photography 1972; Centenary Medal, Inst of Jamaica 1979; Third Place BBC 150 Years of Photography Competition 1988. *Publications:* Roots and Rhythms 1972, Dance Jamaica (2nd edn) 1985, Rum Cook Book 1972, Edna Manley—Sculptor 1990, Jamaica Portraits 1955–1998. *Leisure interests:* collecting and refurbishing antique furniture, gardening, playing cards. *Address:* 2A Bamboo Ave, Bamboo Court #10, Kingston 6, Jamaica. *Telephone:* (876) 927-1452; *Fax:* (876) 977-2642.

LABELLE, Huguette, OC, PH D; Canadian former civil servant; b 15 April 1939, Rockland, ON; d of Alderic and Aurore (née Chretien) Rochon. *Education:* Univ of Ottawa. *Career:* Consultant Govts of Haiti and Cuba 1974–76; Dir-Gen of Policy, Research and Evaluation Indian and Inuit Affairs Programme 1976–78; Asst Deputy Minister of Corp Policy, Dept of Indian and Northern Affairs 1979–80; Under-Sec of State for Canada 1980–85; Assoc Sec to the Cabinet and Deputy Clerk to the Privy Council 1985; Deputy Minister of Transport 1990–93; Pres Int Devt Agency 1993–; currently Chancellor Univ of Ottawa; Chair Bd Algonquin Coll, Ottawa-Carleton United Way, Ottawa Health Sciences Centre Inc; Pres Man Consulting Inst, Canadian Nurses' Asscn; Vice-Pres Canadian Safety Council; mem Bd of Govs Carleton Univ, Canadian Comprehensive Auditing Foundation, Council of Govs Canadian Centre for Occupational Health and Safety, Bd of Dirs Collaboration Santé Int, Exec Cttee Inst of Public Admin of Canada, Advisory Council Master of Public Man, Faculty of Business, Univ of Alberta, Advisory Bd School of Public Admin, Dalhousie Univ, Bd of Dirs Public Policy Forum, Advisory Bd Faculty of Admin, Univ of Ottawa; Chair Bd of Trustees Ottawa Gen Hosp; Pres Transportation Asscn of Canada; Hon LL D (Brock) 1982, (Saskatchewan) 1984, (Carleton, Ottawa) 1986, (York, Windsor) 1990, (Mt Saint Vincent), (Manitoba), (St Paul Univ), (St Francis Xavier Univ); numerous awards including Vanier Medal, Inst Public Admin of Canada, l'Ordre de la Pléiade. *Address:* 5 Robin Crescent, Ottawa, ON K1J 6J3, Canada. *Telephone:* (613) 746-2522; *Fax:* (613) 842-5341; *E-mail:* huguette .labelle@home.com.

LABÈQUE, Katia; French pianist; b Bayonne; fmr partner John McLaughlin. *Education:* Paris. *Career:* Performs world-wide with sister Marielle Labèque (qv); performs works by Mozart, Gershwin, Bernstein, Berio, Boulez, Miles Davis, Chick Corea, Schubert, etc. *Recordings include:* Visions de l'Amen (jtly), Little Girl Blue. *Leisure interest:* jazz. *Address:* TransArt (UK) Ltd, 8 Bristol Gardens, London W9 2JG, UK.

LABÈQUE, Marielle; French pianist; b Bayonne; partner Semyon Bychkov. *Education:* Paris. *Career:* Performs world-wide with sister Katia Labèque (qv); performs works by Mozart, Gershwin, Bernstein, Berio, Boulez, Miles Davis, Chick Corea, Schubert, etc. *Recordings include:* Visions de l'Amen (jtly). *Leisure interests:* camellias, ancient roses and Christmas roses, walking. *Address:* TransArt (UK) Ltd, 8 Bristol Gardens, London W9 2JG, UK.

LABIN, Suzanne, L ÈS SC; French writer and journalist; b 6 May 1913, Paris; m Edouard Labin 1935. *Education:* Univ of Paris (Sorbonne). *Career:* Articles published world-wide; conf and lecture tours world-wide; human rights activist; Pres Freedom League; Sec Société des Gens de Lettres; Dr hc (London); Prix de la Liberté; Grand Officier de l'Ordre du Mérite Européen; Prix Henri Malherbe, Asscn des Ecrivains Combattants. *Publications include:* Stalin the Terrible 1950, The Anthill 1959, Techniques of Soviet Propaganda 1960, Fifty Years USSR/USA 1962, Sellout in Vietnam 1964, Promise and Reality 1967, Hippies, Drugs, Promiscuity 1970, Le monde des drogués 1975, La violence politique 1978, Israël: le crime de vivre 1981, Les colombes rouges 1985, Les états térroristes, La guerre des lâches 1987, Vivre en dollars et votez en roubles 1988, Les pièges de Gorbatchev 1990, Des menteurs masochistes vous trompent: Voulez vous savoir pourquoi? 1992, Les Indignations selectives de la gauche: Anti-colonialistes, anti racistes, anti sexistes selectifs 1993, L'Etonnante Suzanne Labin: son coeur, sa lutte, son message 1995. *Leisure interests:* horses, skiing. *Address:* 3 rue Thiers, 75116 Paris, France. *Telephone:* (1) 45-53-74-09.

LABROUSSE, Jeanne, BA; French business executive; b 21 Nov 1935, Paris; m Christian Labrousse 1966; one s one d. *Education:* Univ of Paris (Sorbonne), Inst des Etudes Politiques (Paris), Centre de Recherches d'Urbanisme (Paris), Centre de Sociologies Européennes (Paris)and Inst for Study of Nat Defence (Paris). *Career:* Sr Lecturer Inst des Etudes Politiques 1964–80; Researcher CNRS; Head of Studies, later Dir French Inst of Public Opinion (IFOP) 1964–80; Head of Communications Pechiney-Ugine-Kuhlmann 1980–83; Dir French Publicity Admin 1983–86; Dir Eurotunnel (France) 1987–95, Pres Eurotunnel Services GIE and Admin Eurotunnel Devt SA 1989–95; Dir Altedia Conseil 1996, Adviser Altedia Communication 1996–; Consultant Jeanne Labrousse Conseil 1996–; Adviser Médiamétrie 1996–; Official Expert to Argentina–Paraguay Binat Comm for the construction of the Buenos-Aires/Colonia bridge and Brazil–Argentina highway

1994–99. *Leisure interests:* Greek and Roman ruins, gardening. *Address:* 55 blvd des Batignolles, 75008 Paris, France. *E-mail:* jlabrousse@altedia .r.

LACAMBRA MONTERO, Carmen; Spanish librarian; b 3 Feb 1947, Madrid. *Education:* Univ Complutense (Madrid). *Career:* Has held various posts at Gen Directorate of Books and Libraries, Ministry of Culture; Dir Int Standard Book Nos (ISBN), Spanish Agency 1987; Dir Centro del Libro y de la Lectura 1988–91; Dir-Gen Organismo Autónomo Biblioteca Nacional 1991. *Address:* Biblioteca Nacional, Paseo de Recoletos 20, 28071 Madrid, Spain.

LACHANCE, Janice Rachel, BA, DR IUR; American lawyer and trade union official; b 17 June 1953, Biddeford, MN; d of Ralph L. and Rachel A. Lachance. *Education:* Tulane Univ (LA) and Manhattanville Coll (NY). *Career:* Dir of Personnel US House Small Business Subcttee on Antitrust 1982–83; Admin Asst to Congresswoman 1983–84; Asst Press Sec Mondale Presidential Campaign 1984; Press Sec to Congressman 1985; Partner Lachance and Assocs 1985–87; Dir of Communications and Political Action, American Fed of Govt Employees 1987–93; Dir of Policy and Communications, US Office of Personnel Man 1993–96, Chief of Staff 1996–97, Deputy Dir 1997, Dir 1997–. *Leisure interest:* antiques. *Address:* US Office of Personnel Management, 1900 E St, NW, Suite 5F12, Washington, DC 20415, USA.

LACOSTE, Catherine; French sportswoman; b 27 June 1945, Paris; d of René and Simone (née Thion de la Chaume) Lacoste; m 1st Jaime de Prado y Colón de Carvajal 1970 (divorced); three d one s; m 2nd Angel G. Piñero 2001. *Education:* Cours Lacascade et Victor Hugo, Lycée Janson-de-Sailly (Paris) and Ecole Supérieure d'Interprètes et de Traducteurs. *Career:* Golfer 1953–; mem nat women's team 1964–, winners World Cup 1964, Spanish, British, American, French Championships 1969; has participated in numerous nat and int tournaments; Pres Golf de Chantaco; French Jr Champion 1964, 1966; US Open Champion 1967; Winner Carven Cup 1965, 1966, 1967, Gaveau Cup 1968; Champion of France 1967, 1968, 1972; Winner Colorado Springs Tournament, USA 1968; British Open Champion 1969; Winner USA Amateur Tournament 1969; Chevalier de l'Ordre Nat du Mérite; Chevalier de la Légion d'Honneur; Médaille d'Argent de la Ville de Paris 1966; Médaille d'Argent de la Ville de Saint-Jean-de-Luz; Prix Virginie-Hériot, Acad of Sports 1964, 1967. *Leisure interests:* guitar, painting, computer. *Address:* Calle Begonia 6, 4 Drcha, El Soto de la Moraleja, 28190 Alcobendas, Madrid, Spain. *Telephone:* (1) 6500865 (Spain); *Fax:* (1) 6507720 (Spain).

LADD, Diane, MA; American actress; b 19 Nov 1944, Meridian, MI; d of Mary and Preston Ladnier; m 1st Bruce Dern 1965; one d (Laura Dern, qv); m 2nd William Sharpe 1977. *Education:* Seventh Day Inst. *Career:* Dancer Copa Girls, New York; Film debut in Wild Angels 1966; Spokesperson PATH; lecturer in health and nutrition; Eleanor Duse Award. *Plays include:* Texas Trilogy, One Night Stands of a Noisy Passenger, Love Letters; *Films include:* Chinatown 1974, Alice Doesn't Live Here Anymore (British Acad Award, Acad Award nomination, Golden Globe Award) 1976, All Night Long 1981, Black Widow 1987, National Lampoon's Christmas Vacation 1989, A Kiss Before Dying 1990, Wild at Heart (Palme d'Or, Acad Award and Golden Globe nominations) 1991, Rambling Rose (Spirit Award, Acad Award and Golden Globe nominations, Chicago Critics Award) 1992, Hollywoodland... Forever 1992, Hold Me Thrill Me Kiss Me 1992, Carnosaur 1993, Fatherhood 1993, Spirit Realm 1993, Obsession 1994, Mrs Munck (also dir) 1994; *TV appearances include:* Alice (series, Golden Globe Award), The Lookalike, Crime of Innocence, Dr Quinn Medicine Woman, City of Angels, The Secret Storm (series), Alice (series, Golden Glove Award). *Leisure interests:* health, nutrition. *Address:* c/o Diane Ladd Productions Inc, POB 17111 Beverly Hills, CA 90209-3111, USA.

LAFFAN, Brigid, PH D; Irish professor of European politics; b 6 Jan 1955; d of Con and Aileen Burns; m Michael Laffan 1979; two d one s. *Education:* Univ of Limerick, Coll of Europe (Bruges, Belgium) and Trinity Coll, Univ of Dublin. *Career:* Researcher European Cultural Foundation 1977–78; Lecturer Coll of Humanities, Univ of Limerick 1979–86, Inst of Public Admin (IPA) 1986–89; Newman Scholar Univ Coll Dublin 1989–90, Lecturer Dept of Politics 1990–91, Jean Monnet

Prof of European Politics 1991–; Visiting Prof Coll of Europe 1992–. *Publications:* Ireland and South Africa 1988, Integration and Co-operation in Europe 1992, Constitution Building in the European Union (ed) 1996, The Finances of the European Union 1997, Europe's Experimental Union: Re-thinking Integration (jtly) 1999; numerous articles on Irish foreign policy, EC budgetary policy, insts, governance and political union. *Leisure interests:* theatre, reading, swimming. *Address:* Dept of Politics, University College, Belfield, Dublin 4, Ireland (Office); 4 Willowbank, The Slopes, Monkstown, Co Dublin, Ireland (Home). *Telephone:* (1) 706 8344 (Office); (1) 286 2617 (Home); 86 8195793 (Mobile); *Fax:* (1) 706 1171 (Office); (1) 284 5331 (Home); *E-mail:* brigid.laffan@ucd.ie (Office).

LAFONT, Bernadette; French actress; b 28 Oct 1938, Nîmes; d of Roger Lafont and Simone Illaire; m György Medveczky (divorced); one s two d (one deceased). *Education:* Lycée de Nîmes. *Career:* Pres Assoc Acas 1990–; Triomphe du cinéma 1973, Swann du coup de foudre de l'année, Festival of Romantic Film 1998; Chevalier de la Légion d'Honneur, Commdr des Arts et des Lettres. *Films:* Les Mistons 1957, L'Eau à la bouche 1959, Les Bonnes femmes 1959, Compartiment tueurs 1965, Le Voleur 1966, La Fiancée du pirate 1969, Out One 1971, La Maman et la putain 1972, Zig-Zag 1974, Retour en force 1979, La Bête noire 1983, Le Pactole 1984, L'Effrontée 1985, Masques 1987, Prisonnières 1988, L'Air de rien 1990, Ville à vendre 1992, Personne ne m'aime 1994, Pourquoi partir? 1996, Rien sur Robert 1999, Recto! Verso 1999; *Plays include:* Bathory la Comtesse sanglante 1978, La Tour de la défense 1981, Désiré 1984, Barrio Chino 1987, Pattes de velours 1987, Le Baladin du monde occidental 1988, Les Joyeuses et horrifiques farces du père Lalande 1989, La Frousse 1993, La Traversée 1996, L'Arlésienne 1997, Une table pour six 1998; *Publications:* La Fiancée du cinéma 1978, Mes Enfants de la balle 1988, Le Roman de ma vie 1997 (autobiog). *Address:* c/o Intertalent, 5 rue Clément Marot, 75008 Paris, France.

LAGUILLER, Arlette Yvonne; French political party leader; b 18 March 1940, Paris; d of Louis and Suzanne (née Janin) Laguiller. *Education:* Coll d'Enseignement Général (Lilas). *Career:* Mem militant Trotskyist party La Voix Ouvrière 1960–68; Nat Co-ordinator Lutte Ouvrière, spokesperson, cand presidential elections 1974, 1981, 1988, 1995; has worked at Crédit Lyonnais 1956–99; Municipal Councillor for Lilas (Seine-Saint-Denis) 1995, Regional Councillor for Ile-de-France 1998; MEP (Lutte Ouvrière et Ligue Communiste Révolution-naire) 1999–. *Publications:* Moi, une militante 1973, Une travailleuse révolutionnaire dans la campagne présidentielle 1974, Il faut changer le monde 1998, C'est toute ma vie 1996, Paroles de Prolétaires 1999. *Leisure interest:* music. *Address:* European Parliament, rue Wiertz, 1047 Brussels, Belgium; Lutte Ouvrière, BP 233, 75865 Paris Cedex 18, France. *Telephone:* (1) 48-04-72-00.

LAGUNA, Frederica de, PH D; American anthropologist and writer; b 3 Oct 1906, Ann Arbor, MI; d of Theodore and Grace Andrus de Laguna. *Education:* Phoebe Anna Thorne School (Bryn Mawr, PA), Bryn Mawr Coll and Columbia Univ. *Career:* Mem staff Univ of Pennsylvania Museum 1931–34; US Soil Conservation Service 1935–36; Lecturer Bryn Mawr Coll 1938–41, Asst Prof 1941–42, 1946–49, Assoc Prof 1949–55, Prof of Anthropology 1955–75, Chair Dept of Sociology and Anthropology, 1950–66, Dept of Anthropology 1967–72, R. Kenan Jr Prof 1974–75, Prof Emer 1975–; USNR 1942–45; Bryn Mawr Coll European Fellow 1927; Rockefeller Post-War Fellow 1945–46; Fellow Columbia Univ 1930–31, Nat Research Council 1936–37, Viking Fund 1949, Social Science Research Council Faculty 1962–63, AAAS, American Anthropological Asscn (Pres 1966–67); Hon Fellow Rochester Museum of Arts and Sciences, NY 1941; Fellow, Hon Life mem Arctic Inst of N America; mem NAS, Soc for American Archaeology; Hon Life mem Alaska Anthropological Asscn; Hon Pres Asscn for N Studies 1991–; Hon D HUM LITT (Alaska); Lindback Award for Distinguished Teaching 1975; Distinguished Service Award, American Anthropological Asscn 1986, Fiftieth Anniversary Award, Soc for American Archaeology 1988, Alaska Anthropology Asscn Award for Lifetime Contribs 1993, American Book Award, Before Columbus Foundation 1995. *Publications:* The Archaeology of Cook Inlet, Alaska 1934, The Eyak Indians of the Copper River Delta, Alaska (jtly) 1938, Chugach Prehistory: The Archaeology of Prince William Sound, Alaska 1956, Under Mount Saint

Elias: The History and Culture of the Yakitat Tlingit 1972, Voyage to Greenland: A Personal Initiation into Anthropology 1977, The Tlingit Indians (ed) 1991, Tales from the Dena 1995; Novels: The Thousand March: Adventures of an American Boy with Garibaldi 1930, The Arrow Points to Murder 1937, Fog on the Mountain 1938; contribs to learned journals. *Address:* The Quadrangle, Apt 1310, 3300 Darby Rd, Haverford, PA 19041-1067, USA. *Telephone:* (610) 658-2298.

LAINE, Dame Cleo (Clementina Dinah), DBE; British singer and actress; b 28 Oct 1927, Southall, Middx; m 1st George Langridge 1947 (divorced 1957); one s; m 2nd John Philip William Dankworth 1958; one s one d. *Career:* Joined Dankworth Orchestra 1953; est Dankworth Performing Arts Centre, Wavendon Stables 1969; performed at Edinburgh Festival 1966, 1967; numerous tours and appearances with symphony orchestras and on TV; Hon MA (Open Univ) 1975; Hon D MUS (Berklee Coll of Music, Boston, USA) 1982; Hon D MUS (York) 1993; Dr hc (Luton) 1994; Melody Maker, New Musical Express Top Girl Singer Awards 1957; Winner Int Critics' Poll American Jazz magazine Downbeat 1965; Woman of the Year, 9th Annual Golden Feather Awards 1973; Edison Award 1974; Variety Club of GB Show Business Personality Award (jtly) 1977; TV Times Viewers' Award, Most Exciting Female Singer 1978; Grammy Award Best Female Jazz Vocalist 1985; Presidential Lifetime Achievement Award, Nat Asscn of Record Merchandisers 1990; Vocalist of the Year, British Jazz Awards 1990; Lifetime Achievement Award (USA) 1991, Distinguished Artist Award, Int Society for the Performing Arts 1999; awarded several Gold and Platinum discs. *Performances include:* Flesh To a Tiger (Moscow Arts Theatre Award) 1958, Façade, Show Boat 1971, Colette 1980, A Little Night Music 1983, Hedda Gabler, Valmouth, A Time to Laugh, The Women of Troy, The Mystery of Edwin Drood (Best Actress in a Musical Award, Tony Award, Theatre World Award) 1986, Into the Woods 1989, Noyes Fludde 1990; *Recordings include:* Feel the Warm, I'm a Song, Live at Melbourne, Best Friends, Sometimes When We Touch; *Film:* Last of the Blonde Bombshells 2000; *Publications:* Cleo: An Autobiography 1994, You Can Sing if You Want To 1997. *Leisure interest:* painting. *Address:* The Old Rectory, Wavendon, Milton Keynes, MK17 8LT, UK. *Telephone:* (1908) 584414.

LAING, Jennifer Charlina Ellsworth; British advertising executive; b 1947, Southampton; d of the late James Ellsworth Laing and of Mary (née Taylor) McKane; m (divorced). *Education:* Bournemouth Municipal Coll and NW London Polytechnic. *Career:* Joined Garland Compton 1969, firm subsequently taken over by Saatchi & Saatchi, Dir Saatchi & Saatchi Garland Compton 1977; Dir Leo Burnett 1978–80; rejoined Saatchi & Saatchi, Deputy Chair 1981–87, Jt Chair 1987–88, Chair Saatchi & Saatchi Advertising 1995–96, Chief Exec N American Operations, NY 1996–2000, mem Exec Bd Saatchi & Saatchi Advertising Worldwide 1996–2000; Chair CEO Aspect Hill Holliday 1988; formed Laing Henry Ltd 1990, merged with Saatchi & Saatchi 1995; Dir Remploy Ltd; Non-Exec Dir Great Ormond Street Hosp for Children NHS Trust; Fellow Marketing Soc, Inst of Practitioners in Advertising. *Leisure interests:* racing, ballet, opera. *Address:* c/o Saatchi & Saatchi, 375 Hudson St, New York, NY 10014, USA.

LAIT, Jacqueline; British politician; b 16 Dec 1947; d of Graham Harkness Lait and Margaret Stewart; m Peter Jones 1974. *Education:* Paisley Grammar School and Univ of Strathclyde. *Career:* Mem staff Govt Information Service, Scottish Office, Privy Council then Dept of Employment 1974–80; Parl Adviser Chemical Industries Asscn 1980–84; Parl Consultancy 1984–92; MP (Cons) for Hastings and Rye 1992–97, for Beckenham 1997–; Jr Whip (first Cons woman) 1996–97, 1999–2000, Front Bench Spokesperson on Pensions and Social Security 2000–; Chair City and E London Family Health Services Authority 1988–91, British Section European Union of Women 1990–92; Vice Chair Cons Women's Nat Cttee 1990–92. *Leisure interests:* walking, theatre, food, wine. *Address:* House of Commons, London SW1A 0AA, UK. *Telephone:* (20) 7219-3000.

LAKE, Ricki; American television presenter; b 21 Sept 1968, New York; m Rob Sussman 1995; one s. *Career:* Presenter of Ricki Lake and Adult Ricki 1993–97; has appeared in several feature and TV films and written a children's book. *Film appearances include:* Hairspray 1988, Cry Baby

1990, Serial Mom 1994, Mrs Winterbourne 1996. *Leisure interests:* fitness, animals, shopping. *Address:* William Morris Agency, 151 S El Camino Drive, Beverly Hills, CA 90212-2704, USA.

LAKHDAR, Zohra Ben, PH D; Tunisian professor of molecular spectroscopy. *Education:* Univ of Paris VI and Univ of Tunis. *Career:* Fmr Head Spectroscopy Lab, Supervisor postgrad students for Tunisian DEA Diploma, Co-Chair Molecular Spectroscopy Group for Master's Degree and PH D courses; Prof of Physics, Univ of Tunis 1992–; Founder-mem Tunisian Physics Soc, Tunisian Astronomy Soc; Fellow Islamic Acad of Sciences. *Address:* Université des Sciences, des Techniques et de Médecine de Tunis, Manar II, 2092 Tunis, Tunisia. *Telephone:* 873-366; *Fax:* 872-055.

LAKHIA, Kumudini; Indian dancer, teacher and choreographer; b 17 May 1930, Bombay (now Mumbai); d of Dinkar and Leela Jayakar; m Rajnikant Lakhia 1953; one s one d. *Education:* Univ of Allahabad. *Career:* F-Dir Kadamb Centre for Dance; teacher of Kathak traditional dance; has choreographed several films; Exec mem Sangeet Natak Akademi, New Delhi, Chair Gujarat State; Highest Artistic Merit Award, Cuba 1973; Sangeet Natak Akademi Award, Gujarat State 1978, New Delhi 1982; Padma Shri Award, Indian Govt 1987. *Address:* Kadamb Centre for Dance and Music, Paromal Garden, CG Rd, Ahmedabad 380 006, India (Office); 8 NBK Society, Ahmedabad 380 006, India (Home). *Telephone:* (272) 462560 (Office); (272) 79572 (Home).

LAKHOVA, Yekaterina Filippovna; Russian politician; b 26 May 1948; m; one d. *Education:* Sverdlovsk State Medical Inst. *Career:* Pediatrician, Deputy Head of Div, Sverdlovsk (now Yekaterinburg) City Dept of Public Health, Deputy Head, Main Dept of Public Health, Sverdlovsk Regional Exec Cttee 1972–90; RSFSR Peoples' Deputy, mem Council of Repub RSFSR Supreme Soviet, Chair Cttee on Problems of Women, Motherhood and Childhood 1990–93; State Adviser on Problems of Family, Protection of Motherhood and Childhood 1992–; adviser to Russian Pres on Problems of Family, Protection of Motherhood and Childhood 1992–94; Chair Cttee on Problems of Women, Family and Demography of Russian Presidency 1992–; Founder and Chair political movt Women of Russia 1993; mem State Duma 1993–; mem Socialist Party of Russia 1996, Otechestvo (Homeland) political movt 1998. *Address:* State Duma, Okhotny Ryad 1, 103265 Moscow, Russian Federation. *Telephone:* (095) 292 1900 (Office).

LAKO, Natasha; Albanian politician and writer; b 13 May 1948, Korça; m Sjevlan Shanaj 1970; one s one d. *Education:* Univ of Tirana. *Career:* Teacher 1966–68; journalist 1968–71; scriptwriter 1976–88; freelance writer 1989–91; Mem Parl (Kuvendi Popullor—Democratic Party) 1991; Film Festival Prize for Screenplays 1980. *Publications include:* March in US 1971, Worl's First Word 1976, Stardom of Words (poetry, Migjeni Prize 1986), White Sheets 1990; poems translated into German and Dutch. *Leisure interests:* swimming, walking. *Telephone:* (42) 23502; *Fax:* (42) 22540.

LALIQUE, Marie-Claude; French business executive and designer; b 19 April 1935, Paris; d of Marc and Suzanne Lalique. *Education:* Inst Merici and Ecole Nat Supérieure des Arts Décoratifs. *Career:* Designer Lalique glassware co 1957–75, Dir of Design 1975–, Pres, Dir-Gen 1977–94; jewellery collections shown at Cartier, New York 1967, Lalique, Paris 1968; exhibition of sculptures Galerie d'Art, Paris 1974; creator Lalique perfume and line of leather goods 1994. *Address:* Lalique, 11 rue Royale, 75008 Paris, France.

LALLA AICHA, HRH Princess; Moroccan diplomatist; eldest d of the late King Mohammed V. *Career:* Amb to UK 1965–69, to Italy 1969–73 (also accred to Greece); Pres Moroccan Red Crescent; Grand Cordon of Order of the Throne. *Address:* c/o Ministry of Foreign Affairs, ave Franklin Roosevelt, Rabat, Morocco.

LALUMIÈRE, Catherine, D EN D; French politician; b 3 Aug 1935, Rennes; m Pierre Lalumière 1960 (deceased); one c. *Career:* Asst Lecturer Inst of Political Studies, Univ of Bordeaux I 1960–71; Lecturer Univ of Paris I (Panthéon-Sorbonne) 1971–81; mem PS 1973–, Nat

Officer for Civil Service 1975, mem Steering Cttee 1979; mem Nat Ass (Parl) for Gironde 1981–89; Sec of State for Civil Service and Admin Reforms 1981; Minister for Consumer Affairs 1981–83; Sec of State for Civil Service 1983–84; Adviser to Pres on Civil Service, Sec of State for European Affairs 1984–86; mem Council of Europe Parl Ass 1987–89, Vice-Pres Foreign Affairs Cttee, Vice-Pres Del to EC, Sec-Gen Council of Europe 1989–94; Vice-Pres European Parl 1999– ; Urban Community Councillor Bordeaux 1989– ; Municipal Councillor Talence 1989– ; MEP 1994–, mem Cttee on Foreign Affairs, Security and Defence Policy, Del for relations with Ukraine, Belarus and Moldova; Deputy Pres Radical France 1996 (now Radical Socialist Party); Hon DCL (Durham) 1995. *Leisure interests:* walking, reading. *Address:* European Parliament, rue Wiertz 60, 1047 Brussels, Belgium. *Telephone:* (2) 284-20-05; *Fax:* (2) 230-75-55; *E-mail:* epbrussels@europarl .eu.int; *Internet:* www.europarl.eu.int/brussels.

LAMB, Christina, MA; British journalist; b 15 May 1965, London; d of Kenneth Ernest Edward and Anne Doreen Lamb. *Education:* Nonsuch High School (Surrey) and Univ Coll (Oxford). *Career:* News Reporter Cen TV 1987–88; Financial Times Corresp in Afghanistan and Pakistan 1988–89, in Brazil 1990; Young Journalist of the Year 1988. *Publication:* Waiting for Allah 1991. *Leisure interests:* opera, jazz, poetry, tennis. *Telephone:* (21) 263-8845; *Fax:* (21) 263-8845.

LAMBERT, Eva Fleg; British (b German) artist; b 2 July 1935, Dresden, Germany; d of Gustave Gerson and Anne (née Dahlmann) Fleg; m 1st Stephen MacDonald 1957 (divorced 1970); two d one s; m 2nd Anthony Lambert 1970; one s. *Education:* Boston Univ (MA, USA) and Univ of Edinburgh. *Career:* Weaver, painter 1961– ; Dir An Tuireann Arts Centre, Isle of Skye 1990– ; numerous solo and group exhibitions including New Arts Fed, Royal Soc of Women Pastelists, Royal Soc of Portrait Painters, Crafts Edinburgh 1974, Crafts Biennale (Edinburgh) 1974, Kes Mosaics (Edinburgh) 1980, Royal Inc Architects (Glasgow) 1984, Netherbow Arts Centre (Edinburgh) 1985, Highland Open 1989; commissioned by German Speaking Union to weave pulpit drop for Bicentenary of St Andrew's and St George's Church, Edinburgh 1984; has written various articles on craft and tourism 1985– ; mem Skye Connection Arts Touring Group 1991– , Scottish Craft Centre; grantee Highland Craftpoint. *Publications:* Garden Grows Cookery Book 1978; articles on crafts and tourism. *Leisure interests:* Islamic art, tourism and its effects on local people, sheep husbandry. *Address:* 10 Carnach, Waternish, Isle of Skye IV55 8GL, UK. *Telephone:* (1470) 083297; *Fax:* (1470) 083306.

LAMBERT, Jean Denise, BA; British politician; b 1 June 1950, Orsett, Essex; d of Frederick and Margaret (née Archer) John; m Stephen Lambert 1977; one s one d. *Education:* Palmers Grammar School for Girls (Grays, Essex), Univ Coll (Cardiff) and St Paul's Coll (Cheltenham). *Career:* Secondary school teacher, Waltham Forest 1972–82; Examiner GCE/CSE Spoken English and English Language 1982–85; mem Green Party 1977– , London Area Co-ordinator 1977–81, Co-Chair Council 1982–85, 1986–87, Rep European Green Parties 1985–86, 1988–89, Speaker 1988– , Rep EP 1989–94, Jt Prin Speaker 1992–93, Chair Exec 1993–94; MEP (Green) for London Region 1999– ; f Ecology Bldg Soc 1981, mem Bd 1981–84, Chair 1982–83, Patron 1984– ; mem Council Charter 88 1990– , Hansard Soc Comm on Electoral Guidelines, 300 Group, Waltham Forest Council for Racial Equality; mem Cttee Voting Reform Group 1995– ; contrib numerous articles to journals. *Leisure interests:* reading detective fiction, cooking, dance. *Address:* Unit 56-59, Hop Exchange, 24 Southwark St, London, SE1 1TY, UK. *Telephone:* (20) 7407-6269 (Office); (20) 8520-0676 (Home); *E-mail:* jeanlambert@greenmeps.org.uk.

LAMBERT, Mary Ann, BA, MBA; American banking executive; b 10 Dec 1946, Atlanta, GA; d of John J. and Mary (née Kelleher) Lambert; m Michael F. Robinson 1984 (divorced 1991). *Education:* Univs de los Andes (Colombia) and Dijon (France), Trinity Coll (Washington, DC) and Georgia State Univ. *Career:* Researcher Inst Centroamericano de Admin de Empresas, Managua, Nicaragua 1972–74; Bank Strategy and Lending, Bankers Trust Co, New York 1974–79; Vice-Pres Multinat Lending Dept, ABN Bank 1979–85, Eurobond Underwriting Rep 1985–86, Sr Vice-Pres and Chief Operating Officer Capital Markets 1987–91, apptd Man Dir and Chief Investment Officer ABN AMRO Asset Man (USA) 1992; Fulbright Travelling Fellow and Latin

American Teaching Fellow 1972; several articles in banking journals. *Leisure interests:* gardening, tennis, travel, cross-country skiing, reading, history. *Address:* ABN Capital Markets Corporation, 335 Madison Ave, 14th Floor, New York, NY 10017, USA (Office); 505 E 79th St, New York, NY 10021, USA (Home); 696 E Rd, Clarksburg, MA 01247, USA (Home). *Telephone:* (212) 808-5315 (Office); (212) 988-1005 (Home, NY); (413) 664-8472 (Home, MA).

LAMBERT, Phyllis B., OC, M ARCH, RCA, FRAIC, FRSC; Canadian architect; b 24 Jan 1927, Montréal; d of Samuel and Saidye (née Rosner) Bronfman. *Education:* The Study (Montréal), Vassar Coll (NY, USA) and Illinois Inst of Tech (Chicago, USA). *Career:* Architect, Consultant and Dir of Planning Seagram Bldg, NY (American Inst of Architects 25 Year Award of Excellence 1984, New York Landmarks Conservancy Award 1989) 1954–58, Toronto Dominion Centre 1962, Saidye Bronfman Center (Montréal Massey Medal, Royal Architecture Inst of Canada 1970) 1963–68, Jane Tate House renovation 1974–76, Biltmore Hotel renovation, LA 1976, Ben Ezra Synagogue Restoration Project, Cairo (Egypt) 1981–94, Canadian Centre for Architecture 1984–89; mem planning studies staff Douglas Community Org 1968–69, Fogg Museum Space Study 1972; Founder, Dir Curator's Office Joseph E. Seagram and Sons Inc, NY 1972, Centre Canadien d'Architecture 1979 (Dir and Chair Bd of Trustees 1979–99, Consulting Architect 1984–89); Pres Soc d'Amélioration Milton Parc 1979–85; Chair, Prin Ridgeway Ltd Architects/Developers 1972–84; Dir Groupe de recherche sur les bâtiments en pierre grise de Montréal 1973, Seagram Bicentennial Project 1974–79; Architect/Developer Biltmore Hotel 1976; Project Dir renovation of Ben Ezra Synagogue, Cairo 1987–93; Adjunct Prof School of Architecture, McGill Univ 1986– ; Assoc Prof School of Architecture, Univ of Montréal 1989– ; Founder, mem Bd Int Confed of Architectural Museums (Pres 1985–89); Chair Temple Hoyne Buell Centre 1984–89; created Fonds d'investissement de Montréal, pvt fund for revitalization of Montréal neighbourhoods 1997; est IFCCA Prize for Design of Cities 1999; mem Bd Trustees Inst Fine Arts, New York Univ, Visiting Cttee Princeton Univ, NJ, Visiting Cttee GSD Harvard Univ, MA; mem Bd of Overseers, Coll of Architecture, IL Inst of Tech; Founder-mem Bd Int Confed of Architectural Museums; mem numerous cttees and orgs; exhibitions include McCord Museum 1975, 1980, 4th Floor Gallery, Seagram Bldg, NY, 1977, Kunsthaus Lempertz, Cologne, Germany 1982, Art Inst of Chicago 1983, Cooper Hewitt Museum 1983, Montréal Museum of Fine Arts 1983, 1984, Centre Nat d'Art et de Culture Georges-Pompidou, Paris 1984, Nat Gallery of Canada 1984, Canadian Centre for Architecture/Centre Canadien d'Architecture 1990, 1993; Hon FRIBA; numerous hon degrees; awards include Award of Honor (American Inst of Architects, S California Chapter) 1978, Int Design Award (American Soc of Interior Designers) 1980, Nat Honor Award (American Inst of Architects) 1980, Nat Preservation Honor Award 1981, Médaille de l'Acad de l'Architecture (Paris) 1988, Gabrielle Léger Award (Heritage Canada Foundation) 1988, Cyclist of the Year 1989, Prix d'Excellence en Architecture (Ordre des Architectes du Québec) 1989, Grand Prix, Conseil des arts, Communauté urbaine de Montréal 1990, European Gold Medal for Conservation of Buildings 1991, Gold Medal of the Royal Architectural Inst of Canada 1991, AIA Award, 1992, Lescarbot Award (Govt of Canada) 1992, Prix Gérard-Morisset (Govt of Quebec) 1994, Ordre de la Pléiade (Assemblée int des parlementaires de langue français) 1995, Hadrian Award (World Monuments Fund) 1997, Int Montblanc Arts Patronage Award 2001; Chevalier de l'Ordre Nat du Québec 1985. *Publications include:* Court House: A Photographic Document 1978, Photography and Architecture 1839–1939 1983, Planned Assaults 1987, The First Five Years 1988, Opening the Gates of Eighteenth-Century Montreal (ed) 1992, Fortifactions and the Synagogue: The Fortress of Babylon and the Ben Ezra Synagogue, Cairo (ed) 1994, Viewing Olmsted: Photographs by Robert Burley, Lee Friedlander and Geoffrey James (ed) 1996, Mies in America (ed) 2001. *Address:* c/o Centre Canadien d'Architecture, 1920 rue Baile, Montréal, PQ H3H 2S6, Canada. *Telephone:* (514) 939-7000; *Fax:* (514) 939-7020; *Internet:* www.cca.qc.ca.

LAMBERT, Verity Ann; British film and television producer; b 27 Nov; d of Stanley Joseph Lambert and Ella Corona Goldburg. *Education:* Roedean and Univ of Paris (Sorbonne). *Career:* Producer BBC TV 1963, 1973; Producer London Weekend TV 1970; Controller of Drama Thames TV 1974, Dir of Drama 1981–82, Dir Thames TV 1982–85;

Chief Exec Euston Films 1979–82; Dir of Production Thorn EMI Films Ltd; Founder, Dir Cinema Verity Productions Ltd 1985–; Gov British Film Inst 1981–86, Nat Film and Television School 1984–; delivered McTaggart Lecture Edinburgh TV Festival 1990; Hon LL D (Strathclyde) 1988; Veuve-Clicquot Businesswoman of the Year 1982. *Films:* Link, Morons from Outer Space, Restless Natives, Dreamchild, Not for Publication, Clockwise, A Cry in the Dark; *TV productions include:* Dr Who, Adam Adamant Lives, Somerset Maugham Short Stories (BAFTA Award 1969), Budgie, Between the Wars 1974, Rock Follies, Rumpole of the Bailey, Edward and Mrs Simpson, The Naked Civil Servant, Minder, Quatermass, The Flame Trees of Thika, Reilly: Ace of Spies, The Sailor's Return, The Knowledge, May to December (series) 1989–, The Boys from the Bush, Sleepers, GBH 1991, Eldorado 1992, Comics 1993, Class Act 1994, Class Act II 1995, She's Out 1995. *Leisure interests:* reading, eating. *Address:* 11 Addison Ave, London, W11 4QS, UK.

LAMBRAKI, Irini; Greek politician; b 5 Jan 1949, Ioannina. *Career:* MEP (PSE) until 1999, fmr mem Cttee on Agric and Rural Devt, Cttee on the Rules of Procedure, the Verification of Credentials and Immunities, Del for relations with the US. *Address:* c/o European Parliament, rue Wiertz, 1047 Brussels, Belgium. *Telephone:* (2) 284-21-11; *Fax:* (2) 230-69-43.

LAMM, Vanda Éva, PH D; Hungarian professor of law; b 26 March 1945, Budapest; d of Robert I. and Hedvig (née Vandel) Lamm. *Education:* Univ of Budapest, Faculté int pour l'enseignement du droit comparé (Strasbourg, France), Hague Acad of Int Law (Netherlands) and Columbia Univ (USA). *Career:* Research Fellow Inst for Legal Studies, Hungarian Acad of Sciences, Dir 1991–; Prof of Int Law Univ of Miskolc 1998, Univ of Budapest-Győr; mem Perm Court of Arbitration 1999–; Deputy mem Court of Arbitration of OSCE; mem UN's CEDAW cttee monitoring implementation of 1979 Convention on Elimination of Discrimination against Women; Pres Int Nuclear Law Asscn 2000–; Sec-Gen Hungarian Br, Int Law Asscn; Vice-Chair Group of Governmental Experts on Third Party Liability, OECD-NEA; Ed-in-Chief Állam- és Jogtudomány; Ed Acta Juridica Hungarica. *Publications:* numerous publs on nuclear law and int law. *Address:* Institute for Legal Studies, Hungarian Academy of Sciences, POB 25, I. Országház u. 30, 1250 Budapest, Hungary. *Telephone:* 355 73 84; *Fax:* 375 78 58.

LAMOTTE, Carole Geneviève Marie, BA; French business executive; b 16 July 1947, Paris; d of the late Daniel and of Maïte Kiefe; m Pierre-Yves Lamotte 1972; two s one d. *Education:* Saint Cloud Girls' School and Univ of Paris. *Career:* Set up Press and Public Relations Office then Press Officer Kiefe & Cie 1970–78; Dir of Devt Cassegrain 1978–82, Gen Dir 1982–98; Gen Dir Hamon 1999–. *Leisure interests:* reading, cinema, travel, children. *Address:* Société Hamon, 5 rue d'Uzès, 75002 Paris, France.

LAMPERT, Catherine Emily, MFA; American art gallery director; b 15 Oct 1946, Washington, DC; d of Chester G. Lampert and Emily F. Schubach; m Robert Keith Mason 1971; one d. *Education:* Brown and Temple Univs (USA) and Univ of London. *Career:* Asst Curator Museum of Art, Rhode Island School of Design, USA 1968–69; Studio Int 1971–72; Sr Exhibition Organizer Hayward Gallery 1973–88; Dir Whitechapel Art Gallery 1988–2001. *Publications include:* Rodin: sculpture and drawings 1986, Lucian Freud 1993; numerous contribs to exhibition catalogues. *Address:* 92 Lenthall Rd, London E8 3JN, UK. *Telephone:* (20) 7249-7650.

LANCASTER, Carol J., PH D; American academic; b 23 Aug 1942, Washington, DC; m Curtis Farrar 1980; one s. *Education:* Georgetown Univ (DC) and LSE (UK). *Career:* Budget Examiner Office of Man and Budget 1972–76; mem Policy Planning Staff, Dept of State 1977–89, Deputy Asst Sec of State for Africa 1980–81; Dir of African Studies Georgetown Univ 1981–89, Asst Prof 1989–; Deputy Admin USAID 1993–96; Visiting Fellow Inst for Int Econs 1987–91, Overseas Devt Council 1992–93. *Publications include:* African Debt and Financing 1986, US Aid to Africa 1988, Economic Reform in Africa 1989. *Address:* 11 Dupont Circle, NW, Washington, DC 20036, USA. *Telephone:* (202) 328-9000; *Fax:* (202) 328-5432.

LANCIAUX, Concetta, MBA, PH D; Italian business executive; b 26 Feb 1942, Accetura; d of Giovanni Carestia and Rosina Deramo; m 1st James Greenfield (divorced); one s; m 2nd Didier Lanciaux 1978. *Education:* Catholic Univ (Milan), Univ of N Carolina (USA), Carnegie Mellon Univ (Pittsburgh, USA) and Institut d'Administration des Entreprises (Paris, France). *Career:* Assoc Prof Humanities and Social Sciences Faculty, Carnegie Mellon Univ, Pittsburgh, PA 1970–78, Dir School of Business Admin Training Center 1975–78; European Training Dir Texas Instruments Europe 1978–80; Vice-Pres of Human Resources Intel Europe 1980–85; Dir Corp Human Resources Groupe Financière Agache (Groupe Arnault) 1985–90; Exec Vice-Pres of Human Resources and Adviser to the Pres Moët Hennessy Louis Vuitton SA (LVMH) 1990–; Personnel Manager of the Year, L'Expansion 1989; ranked in Top 50 Human Resources Dirs, HR World Review 2000; honoured as one of the 30 most influential businesswomen in Europe, Wall Street Journal, USA 2001. *Publications:* Computer Aided Translation 1978, Humanist and Scholastic Poetics 1981, Stratégies de la Récompense 1990. *Address:* LVMH Moët Hennessy Louis Vuitton SA, 30 ave Hoche, 75008 Paris, France (Office); 26 rue Vineuse, 75016 Paris, France (Home). *Telephone:* (1) 44-13-21-35 (Office); *Fax:* (1) 44-13-21-90 (Office); *E-mail:* c .lanciaux@lvmh.fr (Office).

LANCTÔT, Micheline, BA; Canadian actress, writer and film producer; b 12 May 1947, Montréal, PQ; d of Bernard and Simone Lanctôt; m Hubert Yves 1981; two c. *Education:* Coll Jésus-Marie d'Outremont. *Career:* Instructor (part-time) Concordia Univ 1980–; Prin Stopfilm Inc 1981–; mem Bd Canadian Film Inst, Canadian Centre of Advanced Film Studies, Asscn de réalisateurs/réalisatrices de film du Québec, Union des artistes; Special Achievement Award, 1981 Canadian Film Awards. *Films include:* Actress: The True Nature of Bernadette 1972, The Apprenticeship of Duddy Kravitz 1974; Writer/ Director: L'homme à tout faire 1980 (5 Genie nominations, Silver Medal San Sebastian Film Festival) 1980, Sontaine (Silver Lion Venice Film Festival, awards in France and Portugal) 1984; *Publications:* Armand Dorion, homme à tout faire 1980, Garage Meo Mina 1982. *Address:* 350 rue Birch, St-Lambert, PQ J4P 2M6, Canada.

LANDOWSKI, Françoise-Louise; French pianist and artist; b 3 March 1917, Boulogne-Billancourt; d of Paul and Louise Amélie (née Cruppi) Landowski; m Gérard Caillet 1942; two d. *Education:* Lycée Français (Rome) and Conservatoire Nat de Musique de Paris. *Career:* Int concert pianist 1945–70; teacher of piano and painting 1968–88; creator, performer Musique et Peinture (art and music) show 1974–92; Presenter programmes on music and painting, history of music, music and prayer, etc on French radio 1985–92; currently gives pvt piano lessons; solo exhibitions in France, Belgium and Switzerland; mem Asscn des Chrétiens pour l'abolition de la torture; awards include First Prize in Piano, Conservatoire Nat de Musique de Paris, Médaille d'Argent des Arts et des Lettres, Acad du Var 1975, Prize for Contemporary Art, New York 1978. *Leisure interests:* gardening, reading, walking. *Address:* 3 rue Falconet, 92310 Sèvres, France; Les Lauves, 334 chemin de la Gardiole, Le Brusc, 83140 Six-Fours, France. *Telephone:* (5) 45-07-29-80.

LANDRIEU, Mary, BA; American state government official; b 23 Nov 1955; m E. Frank Snellings. *Education:* Louisiana State Univ. *Career:* Louisiana State Rep, Dist 90 1979–89, State Treas 1987–95; Del Democratic Nat Convention 1980; Senator from Louisiana 1997–; mem Women Execs in State Govt, Fed of Democratic Women. *Address:* 702 Hart Senate Office Bldg, Washington, DC 20510, USA.

LANDRY, Monique; Canadian consultant and former politician; b 25 Dec 1937, Montréal; d of Auguste and Antoinette (née Miquelon) Bourbeau; m Jean-Guy Landry 1958; three s one d. *Education:* Univ of Montréal. *Career:* Physiotherapist Montréal Children's Hosp 1957–58, pvt practice 1958–63; publicist 1963–80; propr, Vice-Pres Cordevin Int 1980–84; mem House of Commons for Blainvile-Deux-Montagnes 1984–; Parl Sec to the Sec of State 1984–85; Minister for Int Trade 1985–86, for External Relations and Int Devt 1986–92, Canadian Int Devt Agency 1986–92, Minister of State for Indian and Northern Affairs 1991–92, of Science and Sec of State Jan–Nov 1993; fmr mem Standing Cttee on Communications and Culture, Jt Cttee on Official Languages Policy and Programs and the Standing Cttee on Finance, Trade and

Econ Affairs, Canada–Europe Parl Asscn, Canada–France Inter-Parl Asscn, Canada–NATO Parl Asscn; Consultant Dessau Int 1994–96, Pres 1996–99, Pres Dessau-Soprin Int 1998–; Pres Québec Arthritis Soc Public Awareness Campaign 1988–; Woman of the Year 1988, Salon de la Femme de Montréal 1988. *Leisure interests:* golf, tennis. *Address:* Dessau-Soprin International Inc, 1200 St Martin Blvd, Suite 300, Laval, Quebéc, H7S 2E4, Canada.

LANE, Carla, OBE; British writer; b Liverpool; two s. *Career:* Won a poetry prize at the age of seven; has published several short stories and poems, and has written for radio and TV; contrib to Northern Drift series; cr and writer numerous comedy series and plays for BBC TV. *TV series and plays include:* The Liver Birds, Butterflies, Bread, Happy Christmas, I Love You, I Woke Up One Morning, The Last Song, The Last Supper, Leaving, Mistress, No Strings, Solo, Screaming. *Address:* c/o Jonathan Clowes Ltd, 10 Iron Bridge House, Bridge Approach, London NW1 8BD, UK. *Telephone:* (20) 7722-7674; *Fax:* (20) 7722-7677.

LANE, Nancy Jane, OBE, D PHIL, PH D, SC D, FIBIOL, FRSA; Canadian biologist; b NS; d of Temple Haviland and Frances Deforest (née Gilbert) Lane; m R. N. Perham 1969; one s one d. *Education:* Dalhousie Univ (NS), Lady Margaret Hall (Oxford, UK), Girton Coll (Cambridge, UK) and Trumbull Coll, Yale Univ (CT, USA). *Career:* Official Fellow and Lecturer in Cell Biology, Graduate Tutor, Girton Coll, Cambridge 1968–, Researcher, Sr Prin Scientific Officer Dept of Zoology, Univ of Cambridge 1968–90, Sr Wellcome Research Assoc 1990–; Visiting Prof Venezuela, Brazil, Italy, USA; Non-Exec Dir Smith and Nephew 1991–2000, Peptide Therapeutics 1995–98; Ed-in-Chief Cell Biology International; has written numerous articles for scientific journals; mem Advisory Panel Citizen's Charter 1991–94; Deputy Chair Athena Project (UK) 2000–; Hon LL D (Dalhousie) 1985; Hon D SC (Salford); Fellow Inst of Biology (Pres 2001–), Zoological Soc of London (Vice Pres and mem Council 1998–2001). *Leisure interests:* theatre, ballet, modern dance, 20th-century painting, opera. *Address:* Girton College, Cambridge CB3 0JG, UK; Zoology Department, Downing St, Cambridge CB2 3EJ, UK (Offices); 107 Barton Rd, Cambridge CB3 9LL, UK (Home). *Telephone:* (1223) 330116; (1223) 336600; *Fax:* (1223) 336676; (1223) 330116; *E-mail:* njl1@cam.ac.uk; *Internet:* www.zoo.cam.ac.uk.

LANE FOX, Martha, BA; British business executive; b 10 Feb 1973. *Education:* Oxford High School, Westminster School and Magdalen Coll (Oxford). *Career:* Business analyst Spectrum Strategy Consultants 1994–96, Assoc 1996–97; Business Devt Dir Carlton Communications 1997–98; Co-Founder (with Brent Hoberman) and COO lastminute.com 1998–. *Address:* 4 Buckingham Gate, London SW1E 6JP, UK (Office). *Telephone:* (20) 7802-4200 (Office); *Fax:* (20) 7802-9350 (Office); *Internet:* www.lastminute.com.

LANG, kd (Katherine Dawn—kd lang); Canadian singer and songwriter; b 1961, Consort, AB; d of Adam and Audrey L. Lang. *Career:* Fmrly performance artist Edmonton, AB; mem Texas swing fiddle band 1982, then The Reclines; performed with Bruce Springsteen, Sting, Peter Gabriel and Tracy Chapman on Amnesty Int Tour 1988; appeared on TV special with Roy Orbison, Tom Waits, Bruce Springsteen and Elvis Costello and on Tonight show; acting debut in film Salmonberries 1991; Entertainer of the Year, Canadian Country Music 1989; three Grammy awards. *Recordings include:* Singles: Friday Dance Promenade, So in Love, Crying (duet with Roy Orbison), Constant Craving, Just Keep Me Moving, If I Were You; Albums: A Truly Western Experience 1984, Angel with a Lariat 1986, Shadowland 1988, Absolute Torch and Twang 1990, Ingénue 1992, Even Cowgirls Get the Blues (film soundtrack) 1993, All You Can Eat 1995, Drag 1997, Australian Tour 1997; Films include: Salmonberries (Best Film, Montréal Film Festival) 1991, Teresa's Tattoo 1994, The Last Don 1997. *Address:* c/o WEA Records, The Warner Bldg, 28 Kensington Church St, London W8 4SP, UK; Sire Records, 75 Rockefeller Plaza, New York, NY 10019, USA. *Telephone:* (20) 7937-8844; *Fax:* (20) 7938-3563.

LANG-DILLENBURGER, Elmy; German writer and artist; b 13 Aug 1921, Pirmasens; d of Hermann and Else (née Haber) Lang; one s. *Education:* In Munich, Göttingen, Paris and Salzburg (Austria). *Career:*

Fmr foreign corresp; currently freelance writer and journalist; stories have appeared in newspapers, magazines and anthologies; mem Die Kogge (writers' asscn), European Authors Asscn, Asscn Européenne François Mauriac; Diploma di Merito dell'Univ delle Arti, Salsomaggiore (Italy) 1982; Landgrafenmedaille der Stadt Pirmasens 1986; Gran Premio d'Europa La Musa dell'Arte 1990; ELK-Feder 1991. *Publications include:* Novels: Frühstück auf französisch, Der Rabenwald 1985, ICH—Vincent van Goch 1990; Poetry: Ping-pong Pinguin (also English), Blick ins Paradies 1978, 1980, Das Wort 1980, Limericks 1984, Stufen zum Selbst 1986, Lebenszeichen 1988, Der Schäfer von Madrid, Verdammt geliebtes Leben, Vie maudite bien aimée 1993; Paradies mit Streifen (short stories) 1994; also children's books. *Address:* Strobelallee 62, 66953 Pirmasens, Germany. *Telephone:* (6331) 41425.

LANGE, Jessica; American actress; b 20 April 1949, Cloquet, MN; d of Al and Dorothy Lange; m Paco Grande 1970 (divorced 1982); one d (with Mikhail Baryshnikov); one s one d (with Sam Shepard). *Education:* Univ of Minnesota. *Career:* Student of mime with Etienne DeCroux, Paris; dancer Opéra Comique, Paris; model Wilhelmina Agency, New York; in Summer stock production Angel On My Shoulder, NC 1980. *Films include:* King Kong 1976, All That Jazz 1979, How to Beat the High Cost of Living 1980, The Postman Always Rings Twice 1981, Frances 1982, Tootsie (Acad Award for Best Supporting Actress) 1982, Country 1984, Sweet Dreams 1985, Crimes of the Heart 1986, Everybody's All American 1989, Far North 1989, Music Box 1989, Men Don't Leave 1989, Cape Fear 1991, Far North 1991, Night and the City 1993, Losing Isiah, Rob Roy 1994, Blue Sky (Golden Globe Best Actress Award, Acad Award for Best Actress 1995) 1994, A Streetcar Named Desire (Golden Globe Award) 1996, A Thousand Acres 1997, Hush 1998, Cousin Bette 1998, Titus 1999; *TV appearance:* Cat On A Hot Tin Roof 1984; *Plays include:* A Streetcar Named Desire (Theatre World Award) 1996, Long Day's Journey into Night 2000. *Address:* c/o Toni Howard, ICM, 8942 Wilshire Blvd, Beverly Hills, CA 90211, USA.

LANGE, Mechthild, MA; German journalist; b Hamburg. *Education:* In Hamburg, Berlin, Munich and Geneva (Switzerland). *Career:* Freelance journalist; Dramatic Adviser Deutsches Schauspielhaus, Hamburg 1986–89; mem editorial staff, producer NDR-Fernsehen TV 1972–; has written numerous theatre reviews for Frankfurter Rundschau nat newspaper; Adolf-Grimme Preis 1972. *Publication:* Regie im Theater (jtly) 1989. *Leisure interest:* travel. *Address:* NDR-Fernsehen, Red Kunst, Literatur Theater, Gazellenkamp, 2 Hamburg, Germany (Office); Isestr 134, 20149 Hamburg, Germany (Home). *Telephone:* (40) 415465225 (Office); (40) 4603738 (Home); *Fax:* (40) 41565470 (Office).

LANGENHAGEN, Brigitte; German politician; b 8 Dec 1939, Hamburg. *Career:* Fmr MEP (EPP), mem Cttee on Regional Policy, on Fisheries, Del for relations with the People's Repub of China. *Address:* c/o European Parliament, rue Wiertz, 1047 Brussels, Belgium.

LANGLEY, Gillian Rose, PH D; British scientist; b 10 Aug 1952, London; d of James and Rose Dymond; m Christopher Langley 1979. *Education:* Parkstone Grammar School (Poole) and Girton Coll (Cambridge). *Career:* Researcher in Neurochem Univ of Cambridge 1974–78; Research Assoc in Cell Culture Univ of Nottingham 1978–79; Scientific Adviser British Union for the Abolition of Vivisection 1979–81; Gen Sec Dr Hadwen Trust for Humane Research 1981–88, Scientific Adviser 1988; freelance scientific consultant to several orgs 1988–. *Publications:* Vegan Nutrition: A Survey of Research 1988, Animal Experimentation: The Consensus Changes 1989, Faith, Hope and Charity: An Enquiry into Charity-Funded Research 1990. *Leisure interests:* running, mountain walking, cross-country skiing, reading, photography, cycling. *Address:* Dr Hadwen Trust, 46 Kings Rd, Hitchin, Herts SG5 1RD, UK. *Telephone:* (1462) 455300.

LANGLOIS-GLANDIER, Janine, L EN D; French broadcasting executive; b 16 May 1939, Paris; d of Jean and Fernande Louise (née Ruellan) Glandier; m Philippe Langlois 1969; one d one s. *Education:* Lycée Victor Hugo, Ecole Nat de Commerce, Inst d'Etudes Politiques and Univ of Paris. *Career:* Began working for ORTF (Office de Radiodiffusion-Télévision Française) 1967, Radio France Finance Dept 1972–74, Treas 1974–75; Sec-Gen SFP (Société Française de Production) 1971–85, Man Dir 1981, CEO 1982–85; Chair and CEO Soc

Nat de Programmes—France Régions 3 (FR3) 1985–86; Head Supervisory Council La Sept 1986–87; Pres Inst Nat de l'Audiovisuel 1987–90; Chair and CEO Pathé TV and Pathé Interactive 1991–97, Dir Gen Pathé Cinéma 1996; mem Conseil Supérieur de l'Audiovisuel (CSA) 1997–; Admin Festival d'Automne et de la Cinémathèque française 1995–, Libération newspaper 1996–; Chevalier de la Légion d'Honneur; Chevalier de l'Ordre Nat du Mérite; Officier des Arts et des Lettres. *Leisure interests*: music, cinema, golf. *Address*: CSA, Tour Mirabeau, 39-43 quai André Citroën, France (Office); 4 square Alboni, 75016 Paris, France (Home); Darazac, 19220 Saint Privat, France (Home). *Telephone*: (1) 49-24-43-43 (Office); *Fax*: (1) 49-24-43-50 (Office).

LANGSLEY, Eileen, DIP ED; British photographer; b 6 Dec 1943, Sheffield; d of Leslie and Sally Jepson; m 1971. *Education*: High Storrs Grammar School for Girls (Sheffield) and Lady Mabel Coll of Physical Educ. *Career*: Head Physical Educ for Girls King Edward VII School 1965–76; first professional British woman sports photographer 1979; Founder Supersport Photographs 1979, Int Asscn of Women Sports Photographers 1988; Official Photographer Fed Int de Gymnastique 1984, Women's Sports Foundation 1986; Chair Professional Sports Photographer's Asscn 1990, 1991; contribs to many int publications; awards include Asscn Int de la Presse Sportive Photo Competition 1982, Sports Picture of the Year (jtly) 1986, British Sport Asscn for the Disabled Media Awards 1989. *Publications*: Gymnastics: The Art of Sport 1996, Gymnastics: In Perspective 2000. *Leisure interests*: tennis, music, contemporary dance. *Address*: Wayside, White Lodge Lane, Baslow, nr Bakewell, Derbyshire DE4 1RQ, UK. *Telephone*: (1246) 582376; *Fax*: (1246) 582227; *E-mail*: eileenlangsley@hotmail.com.

LANSBURY, Angela, CBE; British actress; b 16 Oct 1925, London; d of Edgar Lansbury and of the late Moyna Macgill; m 1st Richard Cromwell (divorced); m 2nd Peter Shaw; one s one d one step-s. *Education*: Webber Douglas School of Singing and Dramatic Art (London). *Career*: Made film debut in Gaslight 1944; numerous appearances on stage in London and New York, USA and on TV; Hon D HUM LITT (Boston) 1990; Silver Mask for Lifetime Achievement BAFTA 1991, Lifetime Achievement Award, Screen Actors' Guild 1997, several Tony awards for plays and numerous other awards. *Films include*: National Velvet, The Manchurian Candidate, In the Cool of the Day, Harlow, Moll Flanders, Bedknobs and Broomsticks, Death on the Nile, The Lady Vanishes, The Mirror Cracked, The Pirates of Penzance, Company of Wolves, Beauty and the Beast (voice); *TV appearances include*: Pantomime Quiz (series), Murder She Wrote (series) 1984–96, The Shell Seekers 1989, South by Southwest 1997, A Story to Die For 2000; *Publication*: Angela Lansbury's Positive Moves (jtly) 1990. *Address*: c/o Corymore Productions, Bldg 426, 100 Universal City Plaza, Universal City, CA 91608, USA; c/o William Morris, 31 Soho Square, London W1V 6HH, UK.

LANSING, Sherry Lee, BS; American actress, film producer and business executive; b 31 July 1944, Chicago, IL; d of Norton and Margot Lansing; m 2nd William Friedkin 1991; one step-s. *Education*: Northwestern Univ (Evanston, IL). *Career*: Teacher of maths, Public High Schools, Los Angeles, CA 1966–69; model, TV commercials, Max Factor and Alberto-Culver 1969–70; Exec Story Ed Ray Wagner Int 1970–73; Vice-Pres for Production Heyday Productions 1973–75; Exec Story Ed, Vice-Pres for Creative Affairs MGM Studios 1975–77; Vice-Pres, Sr Vice-Pres for Production Columbia Pictures 1977–80; Pres 20th Century-Fox Productions 1980–83; ind producer, Jaffe-Lansing Productions LA 1983–; Chair and CEO Paramount Motion Picture Group 1992–. *Films include*: Actress: Loving, Rio Lobo 1970; Producer: Racing with the Moon 1984, Firstborn 1984, Fatal Attraction 1987, The Accused 1989, Black Rain 1990, School Ties 1992, Indecent Proposal 1993. *Address*: Paramount Pictures Corp, 5555 Melrose Ave, Los Angeles, CA 90038-3197, USA. *Telephone*: (213) 956-5000.

LANYON, Ellen, MFA; American artist; b 21 Dec 1926, Chicago, IL; d of Howard Wesley and Ellen (née Aspinwall) Lanyon; m Roland Ginzel 1948; one s one d. *Education*: Art Inst of Chicago, Univ of Iowa and Courtauld Inst of Art (London). *Career*: Teacher of Art Art Inst of Chicago 1952–54, Rockford Coll, IL 1953, Summer School, MI 1961–62, 1967–70, 1971–72, 1978, Univ of Illinois 1970, Univ of Wisconsin 1971–72, Pennsylvania State Univ 1974, Univ of California

1974, Sacramento State Univ 1974, Stanford Univ 1974, Boston Univ 1975, Kansas State Univ 1976, Univ of Missouri 1976, Univ of Houston 1977; Adjunct Visiting Prof Southern Illinois Univ at Carbondale, Northern Illinois Univ, State Univ Coll at Purchase, NY 1978, Cooper Union, NY 1978–79, Parsons School of Design 1979; Distinguished Visiting Prof Univ of San Diego, Univ of California at Davis 1980, School of Visual Arts, NY 1980–83; Assoc Prof Cooper Union, NY 1980–94; Founder Chicago Graphic Workshop 1952–55; illustrator The Wandering Tattler 1975, Perishable Press 1976–, Red Ozier Press 1980–; solo exhibitions include Stewart Richart Gallery (San Antonio) 1962, 1965, Zabriskie Gallery (New York) 1962, 1964, 1969, 1972, Richard Gray Gallery (Chicago, IL) 1970, 1973, 1976, 1979, 1982, 1985, Odyssia Gallery (Rome) 1975, Harcus Krakow (Boston, MA) 1977–, Odyssia Gallery (New York) 1980, Printworks Ltd (Chicago, IL) 1989, Struve Gallery (Chicago, IL) 1990, 1993, Berland Hall Gallery (New York) 1992, Sioux City Art Center 1992; Museum of Art (Iowa) 1994, Andre Zarre Gallery (New York) 1994, TBA Exhibition Space (Chicago, IL) 1996 ; travelling exhibitions include American Fed of Arts 1946–69, Art Inst of Chicago 1946–73, Denver Art Museum 1950–52, Library of Congress 1950–52, Metropolitan Museum of Art 1953, Museum of Modern Art 1953, 1962, Birds and Beasts 1969–71, Chicago Imagists 1972, Bicentennial America 76, Downtown Whitney (New York) 1978–, Queens Museum 1978, Walkerk Art Center 1981, Art of the Quilt 1985, Made in America 1987, Art of the Screen 1986–, Lines of Vision: Drawings by Contemporary Women 1989, Symbolism 1989, Landscape As Stage 1992, Face To Face 1992, From America's Studio 1992; group exhibitions include Nat Museum of Women in the Arts (Washington, DC) 1994–95, Rutgers Univ 1996, Wadsworth Atheneum (Hartford, CT) 1996, Museum of Contemporary Art (Chicago, IL) 1996, Rockford Art Museum (IL), Museum de Jade Fidel Tristan (San José, Costa Rica) 1997; rep in many perm collections; mem Ed Bd Coll Art Journal 1982–; grantee Nat Endowment for Arts 1974, 1987, Herewood Lester Cook Foundation 1981; numerous awards. *Leisure interests*: reading, gardening. *Address*: 138 Prince St, New York, NY 10012, USA. *Telephone*: (212) 966-9758.

LAPOTAIRE, Jane; British actress; b 26 Dec 1944, Ipswich; d of Louise Elise Burgess-Lapotaire; m 1st Oliver Wood 1965 (divorced 1967); m 2nd Roland Joffé 1974 (divorced 1982); one s. *Education*: Northgate Grammar School (Ipswich) and Bristol Old Vic Theatre School. *Career*: Actress Bristol Old Vic Theatre Co 1965–67, Nat Theatre Co 1967–71, 1983–84, RSC 1974–75, 1978–81, 1986–87, Prospect Theatre Co 1975–76, Compass Theatre Co 1984, Fortune Theatre 1986, Royal Court 1988–89; has appeared in numerous films and TV serials; Pres Bristol Old Vic Theatre Club 1985–, Friends of Shakespeare's Globe 1985–; mem Cttee Marie Curie Memorial Foundation Appeals 1986–88; Visiting Fellow Univ of Sussex 1986–; Hon Assoc Artist RSC. *Plays include*: Measure for Measure, Flea in her Ear, Dance of Death, The Way of the World, The Merchant of Venice, Oedipus, The Taming of the Shrew, Twelfth Night, Uncle Vanya 1974–75, A Month in the Country, A Room With A View 1975–76, As You Like It 1977, Love's Labours Lost 1978–79, Piaf (Soc of W End Theatres—SWET Award 1979, London Critics Award, Variety Club Award 1980, Broadway Tony Award 1981) 1978–81, Eileen 1983, Kick For Touch 1983, Belvidera, Venice Preserved, Antigone 1984, St Joan 1985, Double, Double 1986, Misalliance 1986, Archbishop's Ceiling 1986, Greenland 1988, Shadowlands (Variety Club Best Actress Award) 1989, Hamlet 1992–93, Ghosts 1993–94, Henry VIII 1996–98 (Helen Hayes Award 1998), one-woman show Shakespeare As I Knew Her 1996; *Films*: Eureka 1983, Lady Jane 1986, Surviving Picasso 1996; *TV appearances includes*: Marie Curie 1977, Antony and Cleopatra 1981, Macbeth 1983, Seal Morning 1985, Napoleon and Josephine 1987, Blind Justice (Best Actress Award, British Press Guild) 1988, The Dark Angel 1989, Love Hurts 1991, Johnny and the Dead 1995, Ain't Misbehavin' 1996; *Publication*: Grace and Favour 1988. *Leisure interest*: walking. *Address*: Storm Artists Management, 47 Brewer St, London W1R 3FD, UK (Office). *Fax*: (20) 8870-4240 (Home).

LAPPE, Frances Moore, BA; American lecturer and development worker; b 10 Feb 1944, Pendleton, OR; d of John and Ina Moore; m 1st Marc Lappe 1967 (divorced 1977); m 2nd J. Baird Callicott 1985 (divorced 1991); one s one d; m 3rd Paul Martin DuBois 1991. *Education*: Earlham Coll (IN). *Career*: Co-Founder and mem staff Inst for Food and Devt Policy, San Francisco, CA 1975–90; Co-Founder and Co-Dir Centre for Living Democracy, Brattleboro, VT 1990; Hon PH D (St Mary's Coll) 1983, (Lewis and Clark Coll) 1983, (Macalester Coll) 1986, (Hamline Univ) 1987, (Earlham Coll, Kenyon Coll) 1989, (Michigan, Nazareth Coll) 1990, (Niagara Coll) 1993; named to Nutrition Hall of Fame, Center for Scientific and Public Interest 1981; Mademoiselle Magazine award 1977; World Hunger Media Award 1982; Right Livelihood Award 1987. *Publications include:* Diet for a Small Planet 1971, Now We Can Speak 1982, What To Do After You Turn Off the TV: Fresh Ideas for Enjoying Family Time 1985, What Can We Do? 1980, Aid as Obstacle 1980, Nicaragua: What Difference Could a Revolution Make?, Food and Farming in the New Nicaragua 1982, World Hunger: Ten Myths 1982, World Hunger: Twelve Myths (jtly) 1986, Mozambique and Tanzania: Asking the Big Questions (jtly) 1980, Casting New Molds: First Steps Toward Worker Control in a Mozambique Factory (jtly) 1980, Food First: Beyond the Myth of Scarcity (jtly) 1977, Betraying the National Interest (jtly) 1987, Rediscovering America's Values 1989, Taking Population Seriously (jtly) 1990, The Quickening of America: Rebuilding Our Nation, Remaking Our Lives 1994. *Address:* Center for Living Democracy, Black Fox Rd, Brattleboro, VT 05301-3085, USA.

LAPPING, Anne Shirley Lucas; British television producer; b 10 June 1941; d of the late Frederick and of Freda Lucas Stone; m Brian Michael Lapping 1963; three d. *Education:* LSE. *Career:* With London Weekend TV 1970–73; writer The Economist 1974–82; TV Producer and Dir Brook Lapping Productions 1982–; Dir Channel Four 1989–94, Scott Trust 1994–; Vice-Chair Brent, Kensington, Chelsea and Westminster NHS Trust 1999–; mem Social Science Research Council (now Econ and Social Research Council) 1977–79, Nat Gas Consumers' Council 1978–79; Gov LSE 1994–. *Leisure interests:* literature, housework. *Address:* 61 Eton Ave, London NW3 3ET, UK. *Telephone:* (20) 7586-1047.

LARIVE, Jessica; Netherlands politician; b 24 Nov 1945, Voorburg; m Jan-Julius Groenendaal 1976; one d. *Education:* Univ of Amsterdam and Leiden Univ. *Career:* Legal adviser Benelux economic union and Ed Benelux (periodical) 1974; Political Asst Liberal, Democratic and Reform Group, EP 1978; MEP (VVD) 1984–99, Chef de Cabinet for EC Commr Martin Bangemann 1984, mem Cttee on Econ and Monetary Affairs and Industrial Policy, Cttee on Women's Rights, Del for relations with the countries of Cen America and Mexico. *Address:* c/o European Parliament, rue Wiertz, 1047 Brussels, Belgium.

LARKEN, Commdt Anthea, CBE; British navy officer; b 23 Aug 1938; d of Frederick William and Nance Saville; m Rear Adm Edmund Shackleton Jeremy Larken. *Education:* Stafford Girls' High School. *Career:* Range Assessor WRNS 1956, Commdr 1960, Photographic Interpreter 1961, Secretarial Officer 1967, Staff Officer, Singapore 1964–66, in command of Officers' Training, Britannia Royal Naval Coll (BRNC), Dartmouth 1976–78, NATO Military Agency for Standardization, Brussels 1981–84, Chief Staff Officer to Flag Officer, Plymouth 1985–86, Royal Coll of Defence Studies 1987, ADC to Queen 1988–91, Dir WRNS 1988–91; Dir and Co Sec Operational Command Training Org Ltd 1991–96; Gov Royal Naval School, Haslemere 1988–91. *Leisure interests:* theatre, music, reading, home, family, friends.

LARMELA, Kaisa, MA; Finnish magazine editor; b 28 Nov 1943, Turku; d of Kaarlo and Sirkku Honka; m Harri Larmela 1965; one d one s. *Education:* Helsinki Univ. *Career:* Journalist 1964–, Ed 1976–; Ed-in-Chief et-lehti 1989; Julius-Journalist-Prize, Finnish Asscn of Magazine Eds-in-Chief 1993; numerous articles in magazines 1964–96. *Leisure interests:* literature, gardening, home, family. *Address:* et-lehti, Höy Läämötie 1, POB 100, 00040 Helsinki, Finland. *Telephone:* (0) 1205475; *Fax:* (0) 1205428; *E-mail:* kaisi.larmela@helsinkimedia.fi.

LARMORE, Jennifer May, B MUS; American opera singer; b 21 June 1958, Atlanta, GA; d of William C. and Eloise O. Larmore; m William Powers 1980. *Education:* Sprayberry High School (Marietta, GA) and Westminster Choir Coll (Princeton, NJ). *Career:* Operatic debut with L'Opéra de Nice, France 1985, debut with Metropolitan Opera, NY 1995, Salzburg Festival debut 1993, Tanglewood Festival debut 1998; specialises in music of the Bel Canto and Baroque Periods; Spokesperson and Fundraiser, US Fund for UNICEF 1998–; William M.

Sullivan Fellowship 1983; Maria Callas Vocal Competition, Barcelona 1984, McAllister Vocal Competition, Indianapolis 1986, Alumni Merit Award, Westminster Choir Coll 1991, Gramophone Award 1992 for Best Baroque Album, Richard Tucker Foundation Award, NY 1994, selected by the US Olympic Cttee to sing the Olympic Hymn for the closing of the Atlanta Olympic Summer Games 1996. *Music:* over 40 recordings of operatic and solo repertoire; operatic appearances with most of the world's leading cos; recital appearances include Carnegie Hall, NY, Wigmore Hall, London, Musik Verein, Vienna, Concertgebauw, Amsterdam, Palais Garnier, Paris, LG Arts Center, Seoul, Teatro Colón, Buenos Aires, Teatro Liceo, Barcelona, Teatro Monnaie, Brussels, Arts Center, Melbourne, etc; *TV:* appearances include Star Trek 30th Anniversary broadcast, live Christmas Eve service from St Patrick's Cathedral, numerous live broadcasts from the Metropolitan Opera. *Leisure interests:* playing with pet dog, relaxing pool-side, shopping. *Address:* c/o ICM Artists Ltd, 40 W 57th St, New York, 10019, USA. *Telephone:* (212) 556-5633; *Fax:* (212) 556-6851; *E-mail:* jenniferlarmore@aol.com.

LAROQUE, Michèle; French actress and film producer; b 15 June 1960, Nice; d of Claude Laroque and Doïna Trandabur; m Dominique Deschamps (divorced); one d. *Education:* Univ of Nice. *Career:* Founder own production co PBOF (Please Buy Our Films); Chevalier des Arts et des Lettres. *Films:* The Hairdresser's Husband, Pédale Douce, Le Plus Beau Métier du Monde, Ma Vie en Rose, Serial Lover, Doggy Bag, Epouse-moi, Le Placard; *Plays:* Silence en coulisses, Ils s'aiment, Ornifle, La Face cachée d'Orion, Une Folie. *Leisure interests:* tennis, skiing, riding, golf. *Address:* c/o Claire Blondel, Artmedia, 20 av Rapp, 75007 Paris, France.

LARROCHA, Alicia de; Spanish concert pianist; b 23 May 1923, Barcelona; d of Eduardo and Teresa (née de la Calle) de Larrocha; m Juan Torra 1950; one s one d. *Education:* Pvt school. *Career:* First public recital, Barcelona 1928; first orchestral concert with Madrid Symphony Orchestra under Fernandez Arbós, Madrid 1935; concert tours in Europe, S America, USA, Canada, Japan, SA, NZ, Australia; Dir Academia Marshall, Barcelona 1959; mem Bd Dirs Musica en Compostela 1968; Hon Pres Int Piano Archives, New York 1969; Corresp mem Hispanic Soc of America, New York 1972; Gold Medal, Academia Marshall 1943; Harriet Cohen Int Music Award 1956; Grand Prix du Disque, Acad Charles Cros, Paris 1960, 1974; Paderewski Memorial Medal 1961; Orders of Civil Merit 1962, of Isabel la Católica 1972; Edison Award, Amsterdam 1968, 1978; First Gold Medal, Mérito a la Vocación 1973; Grammy Award, USA 1974, 1975; Musician of the Year (Musical America Magazine) 1978; Gold Medal, Spanish Int (USA) 1980.

LATASI, Naama; Tuvaluan politician; b 19 Aug 1943, Niutao; d of Maheu Naniseni; m Kamuta Latasi 1966; two s two d. *Education:* Elaine Bernacchi Girls' School (Kiribati), S Devon Tech Coll (Torquay, UK), Tech Training Inst (Kiribati) and Training Inst (Sydney, Australia). *Career:* Commr for Tuvalu; Exec mem Nat Council of Youth, Tuvalu Asscn of NGOs; Vice-Pres and Pres Funafuti and Kiribati Women's Groups; Minister of Health and Human Resources Devt 1989–93; mem Parl Nanumea Island, responsible for Educ, Culture, Women's Affairs, Youth, Sport, Community Affairs, NGOs, Museums, Libraries and Archives. *Leisure interests:* gardening, needlework, youth activities, women's affairs.

LATOS-VALIER, Paula, M PHIL; American art gallery director; b 6 Feb 1946, Philadelphia, PA. *Education:* Univs of Dijon (France), New Hampshire and Yale and Ecole des Beaux Arts (Dijon, France). *Career:* Freelance Design and Public Art Projects 1973–77; Lecturer School of Art, Decordova Museum 1974–76; Asst Dir Boston Visual Artists Union Gallery 1974–76; Man Int Exhibitions, Australian Gallery Dirs Council (AGDC) 1979–81; Consultant to Dir of Arts and Entertainment, Australian Bicentennial Authority 1985–88; Asst Dir Sydney Biennale 1981–88, Exec Officer 1989–90; apptd Dir and CEO Art Gallery of WA 1990; mem Visual Arts Crafts Bd 1988–89, International Programme Man 1989–90; Chair Int Cttee for Visual Arts 1988–89; mem numerous asscns and cttees including Fulbright Selection Cttee for WA, Australian Nat Cttee ICOM (International Council of Museums), Regional Galleries Asscn of NSW, Nat Asscn of Visual Arts, The Coll Art Asscn (USA); as an artist and designer has participated in solo and group exhibitions including Inst of Contemporary Art, Boston, USA, National Print Exhibition, Silvermine, USA, MIT, USA, Library of Congress, USA, Smithsonian Inst, Washington, DC; comms include Art Gallery of NSW, Melbourne Univ Gallery, Commercial Galleries Asscn of Australia; has designed and created banners for several city centres and major bldg centres. *Publications:* Crafty Animals 1987, Alphabet Animals 1989. *Leisure interest:* traditional and tribal art. *Address:* 8A/70 Terrace Rd, E Perth, WA 6004, Australia. *Telephone:* (9) 328 7233; *Fax:* (9) 328 6353.

LATTY, Carmen, MA; Jamaican business executive; b 3 Jan 1943, Clarendon; d of Z. F. and K. Latty; one s. *Education:* Clarendon Coll, Mico Teachers' Coll, Kansas Univ (USA) and Univ of the West Indies. *Career:* Int trade consultant Embassy of USA, Kingston 1989–; Dir Mico Coll Foundation; several awards including Mico College 150th Anniversary Appreciation Medal for Outstanding Contribution to the Devt of Educ Publishing in the Caribbean Region 1987. *Leisure interests:* gardening, interior decorating, music, reading, teaching, collecting art. *Address:* 6 Purley Close, Kingston 8, Jamaica. *Telephone:* 925-7069; *Fax:* 929-4850.

LAU, Cheryl, PH D, JD; American politician; b 7 Dec, Hilo, HI; d of Ralph and Beatrice Lau; m Garth Dull 1987. *Education:* Indiana Univ, Smith Coll (Northampton, MA) and Univs of Oregon and San Francisco (CA). *Career:* Called to the Bar 1986; Deputy Attorney-Gen Nevada Motor Vehicles and Public Safety Dept, Attorney-Gen's Office; Sec of State of Nevada 1991–95; Gen Counsel House of Reps, Washington, DC 1995; Fellow John F. Kennedy School of Govt, Harvard Univ 1997–98; Indiana Univ Merit Scholarship 1965, 1966, Foundation Award 1966, Service Award 1966, Arthur B. Metz Scholar 1966; Smith Coll Grad Assistantship 1966–67; Univ of Oregon Research Fellowship 1970–71; Vice-Chair Legal Comm American Asscn of Motor Vehicle Admins; Mediator Bay Area Lawyers for the Arts. *Publications:* Talking About the Cheng and the Seh 1972, An Investigation of the Chinese Fiddle and Its Music 1972, Non-Western Music 1983; several articles in journals. *Leisure interests:* reading, skiing, hiking. *Address:* c/o John F. Kennedy School of Government, Harvard University, Cambridge, MA 02138, USA.

LAU, Evelyn Yee-Fun; Canadian writer; b 2 July 1971, Vancouver. *Career:* Published poems and short stories in magazines from the age of 12; Air Canada Award for Most Promising Writer Under 30; Vantage Women of Originality Award 1999. *Publications include:* Runaway: Diary of a Street Kid (autobiog, adapted for TV as The Diary of Evelyn Lau) 1989, You Are Not Who You Claim (Milton Acorn People's Poetry Award) 1990, Oedipal Dreams 1992, Fresh Girls & Other Stories 1993, Other Women 1995, Choose Me (short stories) 1999.

LAUDER, Estée; American business executive; b New York; m Joseph Lauder (deceased) ; two s. *Career:* Chair Bd Estée Lauder Inc 1946–; Hon LL D (Pennsylvania) 1986; Chevalier de la Légion d'Honneur; recipient of numerous awards including Neiman-Marcus Fashion Award 1962, Spirit of Achievement Award (Albert Einstein Coll of Medicine) 1968, Harper's Bazaar Top Ten Outstanding Women in Business 1970, Médaille de Vermeil de la Ville de Paris 1979, Athena Award 1985, Golda Meir 90th Anniversary Tribute Award 1988, Pres's Award (Cosmetic Exec Women) 1989. *Publication:* Estée: A Success Story 1985. *Address:* Estée Lauder Inc, 767 Fifth Ave, New York, NY 10153, USA.

LAUFER, Jacqueline, PH D; French professor of business studies; b 30 Sept 1944; d of Raymond and the late Annick (née Beau) Huppert; m Romain Laufer 1969; one d. *Education:* Univ of Paris X (Paris-Nanterre), Paris IV (Paris-Sorbonne), Ecole Pratique des Hautes Etudes (Paris) and Cornell Univ (USA). *Career:* Prof Groupe HEC (Hautes Etudes Commerciales, fmrly Centre d'Enseignement Supérieur des Affaires) 1972–, develops research and business teaching activities; Prix de la Fondation HEC 1986. *Publications:* Monsieur Personnel et le développement des hommes 1978, La féminité neutralisée? Les femmes dans l'entreprise 1982, L'entreprise et l'égalité des chances 1993. *Leisure interests:* walking, swimming, theatre. *Address:* Groupe HEC, Dept MRH, 1 rue de la Libération, 78351 Jouy-en-Josas Cedex, France (Office); 139 bis ave M Renaudin, 92140 Clamart, France (Home). *Telephone:* (1) 39-67-73-18 (Office); *Fax:* (1) 39-67-70-88 (Office).

LAUPER, Cyndi; American singer and songwriter; b 20 June 1952, New York; d of Fred Lauper and Catrine Dominique; m David Thornton 1991. *Career:* Mem Blue Angel 1980; toured with Doc West's Disco Band Flyer; signed with Portrait Records as a solo artist 1983; concert tours in UK, Australia, Japan and Hawaii; appeared on several TV shows; One of the Women of the Year 1984; Best Female Video Performer, MTV Video Music Awards 1984; Best Female Performer, American Video Awards 1985; received six Grammy and two American Video Awards 1985. *Albums include:* She's So Unusual 1983, A Night to Remember 1989; Twelve Deadly Cyns... And Then Some 1994; *Songs:* Girls Just Want to Have Fun, She Bop, Money Changes Everything, Time After Time, Goonies R Good Enough 1985, True Colors 1986, A Night to Remember 1989, I Drove All Night; *Films:* Vibes 1988, Off and Running 1992, Life with Mikey 1993, The Opportunists 1999. *Address:* Epic Records, c/o Sony Music Entertainment, 550 Madison Ave, New York, NY 10022, USA.

LAUREL-TRINIDAD, Lally (see Trinidad, Lally Laurel).

LAURIE, Piper; American actress; b 22 Jan 1932, Detroit, MI; m Joseph Morgenstern 1962; one c. *Career:* Has appeared on TV, on Broadway and in films; mem Acad of Motion Picture Arts and Sciences; Emmy Award, Acad of TV Arts and Sciences 1987, Golden Globe Award 1990. *Plays include:* The Glass Menagerie 1965, Rosemary and the Alligators 1961; *Films include:* The Milkman, Francis Goes to the Races, Prince Who Was a Thief, Son of Ali Baba, Has Anybody Seen My Gal, No Room for the Groom, Mississippi Gambler, Kelly and Me, Signal, Ain't Misbehavin', Until They Sail, The Hustler, Carrie, Tim, Return to Oz, Children of a Lesser God, Appointment with Death, Other People's Money 1990, Storyville 1992, Rich in Love 1992, Trauma 1993, Wrestling Ernest Hemingway 1993; *TV appearances include:* Days of Wine and Roses, Playhouse 90, The Deaf Heart, The Ninth Day, G. R. Theatre, Play of the Week, Hallmark Hall of Fame, Nova: Margaret Sanger, The Woman Rebel, In the Matter of Karen Ann Quinlan, Rainbow, Skag, The Thorn Birds, Twin Peaks; Films: The Bunker 1981, Love Mary 1985, Mae West 1985, Toughlove 1985, Promise 1986, Lies and Lullabies 1993, Shadows of Desire 1994, Fighting for My Daughter 1995, Inherit the Wind 1999. *Address:* c/o Jonathan Howard, William Morris Agency, 151 S El Camino Drive, Beverly Hills, CA 90067, USA.

LAURIEN, Hanna-Renate, PH D; German politician; b 15 April 1928, Danzig (now Gdańsk, Poland); d of Helmut and Charlotte Laurien. *Education:* In Berlin. *Career:* Teacher 1951–; School Prin 1965–; joined Rheinland-Pfalz Ministry of Culture, Mainz 1970, State Sec 1971–76, Minister of Culture 1976–81; Senator for Educ, Youth and Sport, Berlin 1981–85, for Educ, Vocational Training and Sport 1985–89, Chair Petitions Cttee 1989–91, Pres Berlin House of Reps 1991; Mayor of Berlin 1986; mem Fed Bd CDU 1976; Chair Women's Union of Berlin CDU, Educ Comm, Diocesan Council of Berlin Catholics; mem Exec Cttee, Cen Cttee of German Catholics, Bd Int Fed for Youth Social Work; Großes Bundesverdienstkreuz 1981; Theodor-Heuß-Medaille 1994; Dame Commdr of the British Empire. *Publications:* Not Yes and Not Amen: A Woman in Politics Invokes Christianity 1985, Thoughts 1988, What Moves the Laity 1989, Abgeschrieben? 1995; numerous essays and contribs on educ, status of women and religion. *Leisure interests:* reading, philosophy, theology, cooking. *Address:* Abgeordnetenhaus Berlin, 10111 Berlin-Mitte, Germany.

LAURILA, Ritva Tellervo; Finnish politician; b 13 April 1932, Helsinki. *Career:* MEP (EPP) until 1999, fmr mem Cttee on Foreign Affairs, Security and Defence Policy, Del for relations with Japan. *Address:* c/o European Parliament, rue Wiertz, 1047 Brussels, Belgium.

LAURISTIN, Marju; Estonian politician and sociologist; b 7 April 1940, Tallinn; d of Johannes Lauristin (fmr Prime Minister of Estonia) and Olga Lauristin; m Peeter Vihalemm 1978; two d. *Education:* Tartu Univ (Estonia). *Career:* Sociologist, Head Dept of Journalism Tartu Univ until 1989, Prof 1994–; mem CPSU until 1990; leading dissident in Estonia, Founder Popular Front of Estonia 1988, mem governing council 1988–; Chair Estonian Social Democratic Party 1990–94; People's Deputy 1989–90; Deputy Speaker Estonian Supreme Council (Parl) 1990–92; mem Riigikogu (Parl) 1992–95; Minister of Social Affairs 1992–94. *Publication:* Return to the Western World: Cultural and

Political Perspectives on the Estonian Post-Communist Transition (co-ed). *Leisure interest:* literature. *Address:* Tartu, Ropka 19–12, Estonia. *Telephone:* (7) 471532; *Fax:* (7) 375440.

LAUSTSEN, Agnete, LL D; Danish politician; b 25 Sept 1935, Copenhagen; d of Else and Otto Laustsen; m Ole Tjellesen 1996. *Education:* Univ of Copenhagen. *Career:* Chair Council of Students of Law 1958–60; mem City Council of Copenhagen (Cons) 1962–88; mem Folketing (Parl) 1979–, mem Ministry of Interior, Head of Office, Ombudsman for Consumer Affairs 1979–, Chair Parl Social Cttee 1983–87; Minister of Health 1987–88, of Housing and Bldg 1988–91; Pres Danish Section European Union of Women 1975–, Int Chair Pol Comm European Union of Women; Danish Del to UN Gen Ass 1991; Vice-Pres Danish Section Int Parl Union 1992–; mem Bd Copenhagen City Foundation of Culture 1970–87, Thorvaldsen Museum 1972–80, Ny Carlsberg Glyptoteket Museum 1986–87; has written several articles for Danish and foreign periodicals; Commdr of the Order of Dannebrog; Officier de l'Ordre Nat du Mérite. *Leisure interests:* travel, ballet, art. *Address:* c/o Frederiksholms Kanal 20, 1220 Copenhagen, Denmark.

LAUVERGEON, Anne Alice Marie, DIP ENG; French civil servant; b 2 Aug 1959, Dijon; d of Gérard and Solange (née Martellière) Lauvergeon; m Jean-Eric Molinard 1986. *Education:* Lycée Lakanal (Sceaux), Lycée Voltaire (Orléans), Ecole Normale Supérieure and Ecole Nat Supérieure des Mines (Paris). *Career:* Engineer, later Head of Econ Studies Usinor 1983–84; Engineer Nuclear Protection and Safety Inst, Centre for Atomic Energy; Head of Ground-level and Underground Div, Dept of Research and Industry 1985–88; Asst Head Gen Council of Mining; Head of Study School of Mining Eng, Paris 1988–90; Head of Mission on Int Econs and Foreign Trade 1990; Asst Sec-Gen to Presidency 1990–91, Deputy Chief of Staff 1991–; Man Dir Lazard Frères et Cie 1995–98; Pres Dir-Gen Compagnie générale des matières nucléaires 1999–; Deputy Dir-Gen Alcatel Alsthom 1997–; mem Bd Pechiney 1996–, Framatome 1998. *Publication:* Sur les traces des dirigeants ou la vie du chef dans les grandes entreprises (jtly) 1988. *Address:* Cogema, 2 rue Paul Dautier, BP 4, 78141 Vélizy-Villacoublay Cedex, France (Office); 12 rue César Franck, 75015 Paris, France (Home).

LAVANANT, Dominique; French actress; b 24 May 1944, Morlaix; d of Yves and Annick (née Thézé) Lavanant. *Education:* Lycées de Morlaix and Kérichen à Brest, Faculté de Brest, and Univ of Paris Inst Nat des Langues et Civilisations Orientales. *Career:* Dancer in Gene Robinson ballets 1972–73; actress 1970–. *Plays:* Jarry sur la butte 1970, L'assemblée des femmes 1971, Un pape à New York 1972, One Woman Show 1974, 1978–79, Frisson sur le secteur 1975–78, Commissaire Nicole Bouton 1978–79, 1980–82, Excès contraire 1987–88, Les rustres 1992–93, Ma sœur est un chic type 1993–94; *Films:* Les Galettes de Pont-Aven 1970, Calmos 1972, Cause toujours tu m'intéresses 1978, Diabolo Menthe 1978, Courage, fuyons 1978, Pourquoi pas nous 1979, Le Cheval d'Orgueil 1980, Inspecteur La Bavure 1980, Est-ce bien raisonnable? 1981, Les hommes préfèrent les grosses 1981, Hôtel des Amériques 1981, Y-a-t-il un Français dans la salle? 1982, Coup de foudre 1982, Papy fait de la résistance 1983, Debout les crabes, la mer monte 1983, Paroles et musique 1984, Les Nanas 1984, Sac de nœuds 1985, Rendez-vous 1985, Trois hommes et un couffin 1985, Billy Ze Kick 1985, Je hais les acteurs 1986, Mort un dimanche de pluie 1986, Soigne ta droite 1987, Agent trouble 1987, Les années sandwiches 1987, Quelques jours avec moi 1987, Un jeu d'enfant 1990, La Fracture du myocarde 1990, Ville à vendre 1991, Les amies de ma femme 1992, Secret de famille 1992, Grosse fatigue 1993, Le monstre 1994, Désiré 1995; *TV includes:* Imogène (series) 1990–91, Pepita 1993. *Leisure interests:* tennis, windsurfing, painting, piano. *Address:* VMA, 10 ave George V, 75008 Paris, France.

LAVERICK, Elizabeth, OBE, C ENG, PH D, FIEE, FINSTP, FRSA; British consultant engineer; b 25 Nov 1925, Amersham, Bucks; d of William and Alice Maria (née Garland) Rayner; m Charles Laverick 1946 (divorced 1960). *Education:* Dr Challoner's Grammar School (Amersham) and Univ of Durham. *Career:* Tech Asst Radio Research Station, Slough 1942–43; Microwave Engineer GEC 1950–54, Elliot Bros 1954–57; Head Radar Research Labs, Elliot-Automation Radar Systems Ltd 1958–68, Gen Man 1968–69; Tech Dir Marconi Avionics 1969–71; mem Electronics Div Bd IEE 1967–70, Council 1969–70,

Deputy Sec 1971–85, Electronics Project Dir 1982–85, Chair Eng Careers Co-ordinating Cttee 1983–85, Consultant in Advanced Manufacturing in Electronics 1985–88; Ed Woman Engineer journal 1984–90, Hon Sec 1990–95; mem Advisory Cttee on Women's Employment 1970–82, Inst of Physics Council 1970–73, Advisory Cttee for Electronic and Electrical Eng, Univ of Sheffield 1984–87, Nat Electronics Council 1986–90, Court City Univ 1991–95; Pres Women's Eng Soc 1967–69; Chair Women in Physics Cttee, Inst of Physics 1985–90, Int Conf of Women Engineers and Scientists Ninth Conf 1989–91; has written various articles for professional journals; Liveryman Worshipful Co of Engineers 1985; Hon Fellow UMIST 1969; Hon mem City and Guilds 1991. *Leisure interests:* tapestry, music, gardening. *Telephone:* (1494) 772465.

LAWRENCE, Carmen Mary, PH D; Australian politician and former psychologist; b 2 March 1948, WA; d of Ern and Mary Lawrence; m 1979; one s. *Education:* Santa Maria Coll (Perth). *Career:* Sr Tutor, Dept of Psychiatry and Behavioural Science, Univ of Western Australia (WA) 1979, Lecturer, and Course Controller in Behavioural Science applied to Medicine 1980–83; Research Psychologist in Research and Evaluation Unit, Psychiatric Services, Health Dept of WA 1983–86; mem House of Reps 1986–, apptd Minister for Educ 1988, fmr Minister for Educ and Aboriginal Affairs, Premier of WA 1990–93, also Treas, Minister for the Family and for Women's Interests; Leader of the Opposition, Shadow Treasurer, Shadow Minister for Employment, for Fed Affairs 1993–94; Fed Shadow Minister of Health 1994–96, on Status of Women and on Environment and the Arts 1996–97; mem Fed Parl for Fremantle 1994–; has written several academic papers on psychology; awards include Benjamin Rosenstamm Prize in Econs, British Psychological Soc Prize for Psychology, Australian Psychological Soc Prize for Psychology, H. I. Fowler Prize for Research in Psychology, J. A. Wood Memorial Prize. *Leisure interests:* reading, theatre, music. *Address:* Unit 7, Queensgate Mall, William St, Freemantle, WA 6160, Australia.

LAWRENCE, Joan Margaret, AM, MB, BS, FRCPSYCH; Australian psychiatrist; b 14 Dec 1933, Gordonvale; d of John R. and Thelma M. Lowrey; m Michael Lawrence 1967. *Education:* Gordonvale State School, Brisbane Girls' Grammar and Univ of Queensland. *Career:* Medical Officer, Dir Child Welfare and Guidance Clinics 1962–64; Consultant Psychiatrist Student Health Service, Univ of Queensland 1962–72; Psychiatry Supervisor, Lowson House, Royal Brisbane Hosp 1964–70, Visiting Psychiatrist in Charge, Day Therapy Centre 1972–83, Sr Consultant Psychiatrist 1988–; Medical Adviser Huntington's Disease Asscn 1978–; also runs pvt practice; Pres Australian Medical Asscn 1986–87, Royal Australian and New Zealand Coll of Psychiatrists 1987–89, Australian Fed of Medical Women 1988–91, Doctors' Health Advisory Service 1989–; Fed Councillor for Psychiatry Australian Medical Asscn 1988–91; Exec mem Alcohol and Drug Foundation 1987; Australian Medical Asscn, Royal Australia and New Zealand Coll of Psychiatrists, Royal Coll of Psychiatrists; Corresp Fellow American Psychiatric Asscn; contribs to professional journals 1988–. *Leisure interests:* breeding and exhibiting Afghan hounds and Löwchens, yachting. *Address:* Watkins Medical Centre, 225 Wickham Terrace, Brisbane, Qld 4000, Australia. *Telephone:* (7) 3831 6868; *Fax:* (7) 3832 1176.

LAWRENCE, Josie; British actress and comedienne. *Career:* Performed for nine years with The Rupert Pupkin Collective, the Comedy Store Players and The Kray Sisters, then appeared in Channel 4 TV shows Comedy Wavelength, Whose Line Is It Anyway? and Josie 1991; appearances include the Comedy Store, London and RSC. *Plays include:* The Taming of the Shrew; *Musical:* The King and I 2001; *Film:* Enchanted April 1991; *TV includes:* Outside Edge. *Address:* c/o ICM, 76 Oxford St, London W1N 0AX, UK.

LAWRIE, Mary Jane Murray, BA, LL B; Australian judge; b 14 Oct 1946, Murwillimbah, NSW; d of Charles Malcolm and Heather Murray Lawrie. *Education:* Ascham School and Univ of Sydney. *Career:* Solicitor Supreme Court of New S Wales 1972; called to the Bar, NSW 1975; Justice Family Court of Australia 1986–. *Address:* Family Court of Australia, POB 1991, Sydney, NSW 2001, Australia. *Telephone:* (2) 581-7110; *Fax:* (2) 223-8049.

LAWSON, Lesley (Twiggy); British model, singer and actress; b 19 Sept 1949, London; d of William and Helen (née Reeman) Hornby; m 1st Michael Whitney Armstrong 1977 (died 1983); one d; m 2nd Leigh Lawson 1988. *Education:* Brondesbury and Kilburn Grammar School. *Career:* Fashion model 1966–70; Dir Twiggy Enterprises Ltd 1966–; own British TV musical series 1975–76 and numerous TV dramas in UK and USA; has made several records; f Twiggy & Co 1998–; launched Twiggy skin care range 2001; two Golden Globe Awards 1970. *Films include:* The Boy Friend 1971, There Goes the Bride 1979, Blues Brothers 1981, The Doctor and the Devils 1986, Club Paradise 1986, Harem Hotel, Istanbul 1988, Madame Sousatzka 1989, Woundings 1998; *Plays:* Cinderella 1976, Captain Beaky 1982, My One and Only 1983, Blithe Spirit, Chichester 1997, Noel and Gertie 1998, If Love Were All 1999; *TV:* Young Charlie Chaplin 1989, Take Time With Twiggy 2001, Good Morning (presenter) 2001–; *Publications:* Twiggy: An Autobiography 1975, An Open Look 1985, Twiggy: In Black and White 1998. *Leisure interests:* daughter Carly, music, design. *Address:* c/o Maureen Vincent, PFD, Drury House, 34-43 Russell St, London, WC2B 5HA, UK. *Telephone:* (20) 7344-1010; *Fax:* (20) 7836-9544; *E-mail:* postmaster@pfd.co.uk (Office); *Internet:* www.twiggylawson.co.uk.

LAWSON, Sonia, MA, RA, RWS; British artist; b 2 June 1934, Darlington; d of the late Frederick and Muriel (née Metcalfe) Lawson; m Charles William Congo 1969; one d. *Education:* Leyburn, Southwick Girls' School, Doncaster School of Art and Royal Coll of Art (London). *Career:* Lecturer Harrow School of Art 1960–65; Visiting Tutor St Martin's School of Art, Royal Coll of Art, W Surrey Coll of Art, Byam Shaw London, Cheltenham School of Art 1965–70; Tutor Royal Acad Schools, London, Visiting Lecturer 1985–; solo exhibitions include Zwemmer, London 1960, New Arts Centre 1963, Leeds 1964, 2000, Trafford Gallery, London 1967, Billingham/Middlesbrough 1973, Harrogate 1979, Darlington Art Gallery 1979, City Art Gallery, Manchester 1987, Wakefield, Bradford 1988–89, Boundary Gallery, London 1989, 1995, Dean Clough Galleria, Halifax (retrospective) 1996, London 1998, 2000; group exhibitions include Fragments Against Ruin, The Subjective Eye, Tolly Cobbold Nat Exhibitions, Moira Kelly Fine Art 1981–83, Hayward Annual, New York 1983, Fruitmarket Gallery, Edinburgh, Royal Acad Annual, Royal Inst of Fine Art, Glasgow 1990, John Moores, Liverpool 1991–92, Britain Salutes, New York; retrospective travelling exhibition Shrines of Life 1982–83, Milton Keynes 1982, Sheffield 1982, Bradford 1982, 1989, Leicester and Hull 1983, 1987, Wakefield 1988, Birmingham 1994, Halifax (retrospective) 1996, Stafford 1999, Bristol 2000; featured artist RWS London 2001, Carlow Arts Festival, Ireland 2001; works held in perm collections including Imperial War Museum, Arts Council of GB, Harrogate Art Galleries, Sheffield, Bradford, Huddersfield, Bolton, Leeds, Oxford and Birmingham Univs, Open Univ, RCA Collection, RA Collection, Lambeth Palace and The Vatican 1989, Chatsworth Coll, Univ Centre Birmingham 1994, Barclays Capital, Paris 1998; Rowney Drawing Prize, Royal Acad 1984; Gainsborough House Drawing Prize, Eastern Arts 1984, 1989; Lorne Award, Slade School of Fine Art 1986; Eastern Arts Open Drawing Prize 1990. *Leisure interest:* denizen watching. *Address:* c/o Royal Academy of Arts, Burlington House, Piccadilly, London W1V 0DS, UK (Studio). *Telephone:* (20) 7300-5680 (Academicians' Affairs Office, Royal Acad); *Fax:* (20) 7300-5812; *E-mail:* art@sonialawson.co.uk (Home); *Internet:* www.sonialawson.co.uk (Home).

LAXTON, Sonja, M SC; South African sportswoman; b 6 Aug 1948, Ermelo; d of P. H. S. and H. van Zyl; m Thomas Ian Laxton 1974; one d. *Education:* Pearson High School (Port Elizabeth) and Univ of the Witwatersrand (Johannesburg). *Career:* Mem staff Chamber of Mines 1972–75; Lecturer Univ of Durban-Westville 1975–78, Rand Afrikaans Univ 1978–79; Head of Quality Control EPOL 1980–82; Athlete (middle and long distance) 1962–, rep South Africa 17 times in track, road and cross-country events, set many nat records, received numerous awards including Best Veteran (running). *Leisure interests:* cinema, theatre. *Address:* 10 Cestrum Ave, POB 220, Morningside 2057, Johannesburg, South Africa. *Telephone:* (11) 7831205; *Fax:* (11) 8839283.

LAYCOCK, Gloria, B SC, PH D, FRSA; British crime scientist and civil servant; b 29 June 1947, New Brighton; d of Frank Robinson and Eleanor Burnham; m David Laycock 1968 (divorced 1990); two s one d. *Education:* Holly Lodge High School (Liverpool) and Univ Coll, London. *Career:* Psychologist Home Office Prison Service 1968–78, Home Office Research Unit 1978–83; Research Dir Home Office Crime Prevention Unit 1983–92; Head of Police Research Group 1992–99; Int Visiting Fellow US Dept of Justice, Washington DC 1999–2000; Visiting Fellow and Consultant, Australian Inst of Criminology (Canberra) 2001; Prof Jill Dando Inst of Crime Science (Univ Coll London) May 2001–; Assoc British Psychological Soc. *Leisure interest:* gardening. *Address:* Jill Dando Institute of Crime Science, University College London, 29-30 Tavistock Square, London WC1H 9QU, UK. *Telephone:* (20) 7679-4990; *Fax:* (20) 7679-4969; *E-mail:* g.laycock@ucl.ac.uk; *Internet:* www.jdi.ucl.ac.uk.

LAZUTINA, Larissa; Russian cross-country skier; b 1966; m. *Career:* Eight world championship ski titles including Olympic relay gold medals 1992, 1994 and three titles in 1995; mem Russian Olympic ski team 1992, 1994, 1998; first Olympic individual gold medal for cross-country sprint, Hakuba, Nagano Winter Olympics (Japan) 1998. *Address:* c/o Int Ski Federation, Marc Hodler House, Blochstrasse, 3653 Oberhofen/Thunersee, Switzerland.

LE BON, Yasmin; British fashion model; b 1964; m Simon Le Bon; three d. *Career:* Models at top fashion shows in Paris, New York, USA etc; cover-girl on numerous magazines; mem Friends of the Earth. *Address:* Models One, 12 Macklin St, London, WC2, UK.

LE CAVELIER, Nada; Lebanese jewellery designer. *Career:* Exhibitions include Beirut 1982, La Porta Art Gallery, Florence, Italy 1983, Antiquarium Fine Ancient Art Gallery, New York 1984, Jadis Art Gallery, Bahrain 1985, Al Zaira Center Kuwait City 1987, Tanit Art Gallery, Munich, Germany 1987, Myriam Ancient Art Gallery, Washington, DC, USA 1988, New York Jewelry Fair, New York 1991, Basel Int Jewellery Fair, Switzerland 1991, Tokyo Fair 1991; represented in perm collection A. R. El Khalil Museum, Jeddah, Saudi Arabia 1985–, and in numerous pvt collections.

LE DOUARIN, Nicole Marthe, D ÈS SC; French scientist; b 20 Aug 1930, Lorient; d of Urbain and Marthe (née Le Quefellec) Chauvac; m Georges Le Douarin 1952; two d. *Career:* Teacher of Natural Sciences 1954–60; Researcher Coll de France 1958–60; staff mem, Head of Research CNRS 1960–64; Sr Lecturer Faculty of Sciences, Clermont-Ferrand 1965–66, Univ of Nantes 1966–71, Prof 1971–75; Dir of Research 1975–88, Inst of Cell and Molecular Embryology, CNRS, Coll de France 1975–, Titular Prof 1988–; Pres Admin Council Etablissement Français des Greffes (French transplant org) 1994–95; mem Scientific Council of CNRS, Inst Pasteur 1981–90, Comité de l'énergie atomique, Advisory Bd of Montréal Br Ludwig Inst, Basel Inst for Immunology, Inst of Biotechnology, Univ of Helsinki, French Acad of Sciences 1982, NAS (USA) 1989, Royal Socs of UK 1989, Belgium and Spain 1990; Dr hc (Columbia Univ, NY) 1989, (Univ Complutense de Madrid) 1990; Officier de la Légion d'Honneur 1991; Commdr de l'Ordre Nat du Mérite; Prix Kyoto 1986; Médaille d'Or CNRS; Prix Louis Jeautet de Médecine 1990. *Publications:* The Neural Crest 1982, Chimaeras in Developmental Biology 1984. *Address:* Institut d'Embryologie Cellulaire et Moléculaire du CNRS, 49 bis ave de la Belle Gabrielle, 94736 Nogent sur Marne Cedex, France; Collège de France, place Marcellin Barthelot, 75005 Paris, France. *Telephone:* (1) 48-73-60-90; *Fax:* (1) 48-73-43-77.

LE GUIN, Ursula Kroeber, MA; American writer; b 1929, Berkeley, CA; d of Alfred L. and Theodora K. Kroeber; m Charles A. Le Guin 1953; two d one s. *Education:* Radcliffe Coll (Cambridge, MA) and Columbia Univ (New York). *Career:* Teacher of French Mercer Univ, Univ of Idaho 1954–56; teacher, Resident Writer, Visiting Lecturer at numerous univs including Univ of Washington, Portland State Univ, Pacific Univ, Reading Univ, UK, Univ of California at San Diego, Indiana Writers' Conf, Kenyon Coll 1971–; Mellon Prof Tulane Univ 1986; mem Science Fiction Research Asscn, Authors' League, Writers' Guild W, PEN; Fellow Columbia Univ 1952; Fulbright Fellow 1953; Hon D LITT (Bucknell Univ, Lawrence Univ, Oregon, W Oregon State); Hon D HUM LITT (Lewis and Clark Coll, Occidental Coll,

Emory Univ, Kenyon, Portland State); numerous awards include Hubbub Annual Poetry Award 1995, Asimov's Reader's Award 1995, Nebula Award 1996, James Tiptree Jr Retrospective Award 1995, 1997, Locus Readers Award 1995, 1996, Distinguished Service Award, Univ of Oregon, Bumbershoot Arts Award, Seattle 1998, Robert Kirsch Lifetime Achievement Award, LA Times 2000, Lifetime Achievement Award, Pacific NW Booksellers Asscn 2001. *Publications include:* Novels: Rocannon's World 1966, Planet of Exiles 1966, City of Illusions 1966, A Wizard of Earthsea 1968, The Left Hand of Darkness (Nebula Award, Hugo Award) 1969, The Lathe of Heaven 1971, The Tombs of Atuan 1971, The Farthest Shore (Nat Book Award) 1972, The Dispossessed (Hugo Award) 1974, The Word for World is Forest 1976, Malafrena 1979, The Beginning Place 1980, The Eye of the Heron 1983, Always Coming Home (Kafka Award 1986) 1985, Dancing at the Edge of the World 1988, Tehanu 1990, Searoad 1991, A Fisherman of the Inland Sea 1994, Four Ways to Forgiveness 1995, Unlocking the Air 1996, The Twins, The Dream 1997, Lao Tzu: Tao Te Ching: A Book about The Way and the Power of The Way 1997, Jane on her Own 1998, Steering the Craft 1998, Tom Mouse and Ms Howe 1998, The Sixty Odd 1999, The Telling (Locus Readers Award 2001) 2000, The Other Wind 2001; Short stories: The Wind's Twelve Quarters 1975, Orsinian Tales 1975, The Compass Rose 1982, Buffalo Gals 1987, Searoad 1991, A Fisherman of the Inland Sea 1994, Four Ways to Forgiveness 1995, Unlocking the Air 1996, Tales from Earthsea 2001, The Birthday of the World (Locus Readers Award 2001) 2002; Poetry: Wild Angels 1974, Hard Words 1981, In the Red Zone (jtly) 1983, Wild Oats and Fireweed 1987, Blue Moon over Thurman Street (jtly) 1993, Going Out with Peacocks 1994, Sixty Odd 1999, The Twins, The Dream/*Las Gamelas, El Sueño* 1997, Lao Tzu: *Tai Te Ching:* A Book About the Way and the Power of the Way 1997; Criticism: The Language of the Night 1989, Dancing at the Edge of the World (revised edn) 1992, Steering the Craft, Eighth Mountain 1998; Jr fiction: A Visit from Dr Katz 1988, Catwings 1988, Solomon Leviathan 1988, Catwings Return 1989, Fire and Stone 1989, A Ride on the Red Mare's Back 1992, Fish Soup 1992, Wonderful Alexander and the Catwings 1994, Jane On Her Own 1999, Tom Mouse, Roaring Brook 2002; Screenplay: King Dog 1985; Edited: Nebula Award Stories XI 1977, Interfaces 1980, Edges 1980, The Norton Book of Science 1993. *Address:* c/o Virginia Kidd, Box 278, Milford, PA 18337, USA; c/o Matthew Bialer, William Morris Agency, 1350 Ave of the Americas, New York, NY 10019, USA. *Telephone:* (212) 903-1355 (New York).

LE PONCIN-LAFITTE, Monique Maria Jeanne, D ÈS SC; French research scientist and neuro-psychologist; b 1 Jan 1948, Crehen; d of Maurice and Janine Le Poncin; m Jean Claude Lafitte 1977; one s. *Education:* Univs of Rouen and Paris. *Career:* Pharmacological Asst Faculty of Medicine, Univ of Rouen 1974–79; Lecturer Faculty of Pharmacy, Dijon, later Paris, then in charge of training Faculty of Sciences, Univ of Paris VII 1981–82; staff Faculty of Pharmacy Châtenay-Malabry 1982; Founder, Pres INRPVC (nat inst for research into the prevention of cerebral ageing) 1984–; Dir Centre Monique Le Poncin (centre for optimization and rehabilitation of the memory and intelligence) 1995–; organizer numerous confs in France; has given papers at confs abroad; mem Int Cerebral Blood Flow and Metabolism Soc, Int Psychogeriatric Asscn. *Publications:* Gym cerveau 1987 (game) 1991, Croque cerveau 1989, Guide santé Larousse 1990; collaborations on numerous publs; over 230 publs. *Leisure interests:* reading, painting. *Address:* Centre Monique Le Poncin, 10 rue Royale, 75008 Paris, France.

LEA, Ruth, BA, M SC, FRSA, FRSS; British business executive; b 22 Sept 1947; d of Thomas and Jane (née Brown) Lea. *Education:* Lymm Grammar School, Univs of York and Bristol. *Career:* Asst Statistician then Sr Economist HM Treasury 1970–73; Lecturer in Econs Thames Polytechnic 1973–74; Statistician CS Coll 1974–77, HM Treasury 1977–78, Cen Statistical Office 1978–84; Dept of Trade and Industry 1984–87; Deputy Dir Invest in Britain Bureau, Dept of Trade and Industry 1987–88; Sr Economist Mitsubishi Bank 1988–90, Chief Economist 1990–93; Chief UK Economist Lehman Brothers 1993–94; Econs Ed Independent TV Network 1994–95; Head, Policy Unit Inst of Dirs 1995–; mem Retail Prices Advisory Cttee 1992–94, Nat Consumer Council 1993–96, Rowntree Foundation Income and Wealth Inquiry Group 1993–94, Nurses' Pay Review Body 1994–98; Econ and Social Research Council (ERSC) Research Centres Board 1996–97, Research

Priorities Bd 1996–97, Statistics Advisory Cttee, Office of Nat Statistics 1996–97; Trustee New Europe Research Trust 1999–; mem judging panel for many nat awards; has written numerous research papers and various publs for the Inst of Dirs on business and econ topics; Hon DBA (Greenwich) 1997. *Leisure interests:* singing, philately, cat worship. *Address:* Policy Unit, The Institute of Directors, 116 Pall Mall, London SW1Y 5ED, UK (Office); 25 Redbourne Ave, London N3 2BP, UK (Home). *Telephone:* (20) 7451-3291 (Office); (20) 8346-3482 (Home); *Fax:* (20) 7839-2337 (Office); (20) 8346-3482 (Home).

LEACH, Penelope, PH D; British psychologist and writer; b 19 Nov 1937; d of the late Nigel Marlin Balchin and Elisabeth Balchin; m Gerald Leach 1963; one s one d. *Education:* Newnham Coll (Cambridge) and LSE. *Career:* Mem staff Home Office 1960–61; Lecturer in Psychology LSE 1965–67; Research Officer and Research Fellow MRC 1967–76; Medical Ed Penguin Books 1970–78; Research Consultant Int Centre for Child Studies 1984–90; Founder and Dir Lifetime Productions (childcare videos) 1985–87; Founder and Parent Educ Co-ordinator End Physical Punishment for Children 1989–; Commr Comm on Social Justice 1993–95; Vice-Pres Pre-School Playgroups Asscn 1977, Health Visitors Asscn 1982–98; Pres Child Devt Soc 1992–93 (Chair 1993–95), Nat Childminding Asscn 2000–; Prin Investigator and Dir Families Children and Childcare Study; mem Voluntary Licensing Authority on In-vitro Fertilisation 1985–89, Advisory Council American Inst for Child, Adolescent and Family Studies 1993–; Hon Fellow British Psychological Soc 1988, Dept of Mental Health (Bristol) 1988; Hon Sr Research Fellow Royal Free and Univ Coll Medical School 1998–, Tavistock Centre 2000–; Hon D ED. *Publications include:* Babyhood 1974, Baby and Child 1977, 1989, Who Cares? 1979, The Parents' A-Z 1984; The First Six Months 1987, The Babypack 1990, Children First 1994, Your Baby and Child: New Version For a New Generation 1997. *Leisure interests:* cooking, family and friends, gardening, travel. *Address:* 3 Tanza Rd, London, NW3 2UA, UK. *Telephone:* (20) 7435-9025; *Fax:* (20) 7431-6147.

LEAHY, Anne Suzanne Lucette, MA; Canadian diplomatist; b 18 Nov 1952, Québec; d of Jean and Suzanne (née Pratte) Leahy. *Education:* Ursulines de Québec, Queen's Univ at Kingston and Univ of Toronto. *Career:* Joined diplomatic service 1974–, mem Mission to the EC 1974–76, mem staff Embassy, Moscow 1980–82, Rep to the Devt Assistance Cttee, Paris 1982–86, Dir of Personnel, External Affairs 1987–89, Amb to Cameroon, Chad and Cen African Repub 1989–92, Dir-Gen Policy and Planning Staff, External Affairs and Int Trade Canada 1992; Amb to Poland 1993–96, to Russian Fed (also to Uzbekistan, Armenia and Belarus) 1996–99; Diplomat-in-Residence York Univ, Toronto. *Leisure interests:* tennis, theatre. *Address:* Centre for International and Security Studies, York University, 4700 Keele St, Toronto, ON M3J 1P3, Canada. *E-mail:* aleahy@yorku.ca.

LEAR, Evelyn; American opera singer (soprano); b 8 Jan 1930, Brooklyn, New York; d of Nina Quartin; m 2nd Thomas Stewart 1955; one s one d by previous marriage. *Education:* New York Univ, Hunter Coll (NY), Juilliard School (NY) and Lincoln Teachers Coll. *Career:* Soprano London Symphony Orchestra 1957, Berlin Opera 1959, Deutsche Oper 1959, Vienna State Opera 1964, Frankfurt Opera, Germany 1965, Royal Opera House, Covent Garden, London 1965, Chicago Lyric Opera 1966, Metropolitan Opera, New York 1967, La Scala, Milan, Italy 1971; has performed regularly with leading opera cos in Europe and USA; soloist with numerous orchestras including New York Philharmonic, Chicago Symphony, Philadelphia Orchestra, Boston Symphony, San Francisco Symphony, Los Angeles Philharmonic; has given many recitals and operatic performances with Thomas Stewart; currently Master Class teacher and lecturer; mem Kansas City Performing Arts Foundation 1965; Fulbright Scholar 1957; Concert Artists' Guild Award 1955; Grammy Award for Best Operatic Performance 1965. *Performances include:* Reuben, Reuben, Four Last Songs (Strauss), Ariadne auf Naxos, Wozzeck, Der Rosenkavalier, The Marriage of Figaro, Cosìe fan tutte, Tosca, Manon, Otello, The Trojans, Don Giovanni, Boris Godunov, Eugene Onegin, Mourning Becomes Electra, Lulu; *Film:* Buffalo Bill 1976; *Recordings include:* Wozzeck, Lulu, The Flying Dutchman, The Magic Flute, Boris Godunov, Eugene Onegin, Bach's St John Passion, Pergolesi's Stabat Mater, Der Rosenkavalier. *Leisure interests:* golf, reading, teaching. *Address:* 414 Sailboat Circle, Fort Lauderdale, FL 33326, USA.

LEAR, Frances Loeb; American writer and business executive; b 14 July 1923, New York; d (adopted) of Herbert Adam and Aline Loeb; m Norman Lear 1956 (divorced); two d. *Education:* Sarah Lawrence Coll (Bronxville, NY). *Career:* Asst buyer Bloomingdales New York 1945–51; Buyer Lord and Taylor 1952–59; f A Woman's Place, Lear, Purvis, Walker & Co 1972; Chair Women's Lobby, Washington, DC 1975–80; Founder and Ed-in-Chief Lears magazine for women over 30 1988–94; Pres Lear Television 1994; Ed of the Year, Advertising Age 1989. *Publication:* The Second Seduction (autobiog) 1992; *Video appearance:* Take Control of Your Money 1995. *Address:* Lear Television, 110 E 59th St, New York, NY 10022-8043, USA.

LEARY, Patricia Lilian; Australian industrial relations executive; b 10 Feb 1940; d of C. P. Branagan. *Education:* Coburg High School (Vic). *Career:* Industrial Officer and Paymaster Port Jackson and Manly Steamship Co Ltd 1964–74; Asst Industrial Adviser, then Industrial Relations Man Brambles Industries Ltd 1975–84; currently Commr Australian Industrial Relations Comm. *Leisure interests:* reading, travel, sport. *Address:* Australian Industrial Relations Commission, 448 Elizabeth St, Hobart, Tasmania 7002, Australia.

LEBRANCHU, Marylise; French university lecturer and politician; b 25 April 1947, Loudéac (Côtes-d'Armor); d of Adolphe Perrault Lebranchu and Marie Epert; m Jean Lebranchu 1970; three c. *Career:* Responsible for research, Nord-Finistère Semi-public Co 1973–78; joined Parti Socialiste Unifié (PSU) 1972, Parti Socialiste (PS) 1977; Parl Asst to Marie Jacq 1978–93; municipal councillor, Morlaix (Finistère) 1983, Mayor 1995–97, regional councillor 1986–; Deputy in Nat Ass for Morlaix Constituency 1997–; Minister of State attached to Minister for the Economy, Finance and Industry, with responsibility for small and medium-sized enterprises, trade and artisan activities 1997–; Jr Lecturer in Econs applied to town and country planning, Univ of Brest 1990–. *Leisure interest:* music. *Address:* Secrétariat d'Etat aux Petites et Moyennes Entreprises, au Commerce et à l'Artisanat, 80 rue de Lille, 75700 Paris, France.

LEDEN, Judy, MBE; British hang-glider; b 23 Dec 1959, London; d of Tom and Nina Leden. *Education:* St Bernard's Convent (Slough, Berks), Windsor Coll of Further Educ and Welsh Nat School of Medicine (Cardiff). *Career:* Broke Women's World Distance Record 1983; Women's European Champion 1986, World Champion 1987, 1991; made the first flight from Cotopaxi volcano, Ecuador, the world's highest active volcano 1990; Royal Aeroclub Silver Medal 1989; Cosmopolitan/Clairol Sportswoman of the Year 1991. *Publication:* Flying with Condors (autobiog). *Leisure interests:* micro-light flying, paragliding, travel. *Address:* 8 Burnham Manor, Gibbet Lane, Camberley, Surrey GU15 3UP, UK. *Telephone:* (1276) 28649; *Fax:* (1276) 66599.

LEE, Hermione, MA, M PHIL, FRSL, FBA; British academic; b 29 Feb 1948, Winchester; d of Benjamin and Josephine Lee; m John Barnard 1991. *Education:* Univ of Oxford. *Career:* Instructor Coll of William and Mary, Williamsburg, VA, USA 1970–71; Lecturer Dept of English, Univ of Liverpool 1971–77; Lecturer Dept of English, Univ of York 1977–87, Sr Lecturer 1987–90, Reader 1990, Prof 1993–98; Goldsmith's Prof of English Literature and Fellow New College (Oxford) 1998–; Presenter Book Four, Channel Four TV 1982–86; reviewer and broadcaster; Hon Fellow St Hilda's Coll, Oxford 1998, St Cross Coll, Oxford 1998. *Publications:* The Novels of Virginia Woolf 1977, Elizabeth Bowen 1981, 1999, Philip Roth 1982, The Secret Self I 1985, II 1987 (revised 1995), The Mulberry Tree: Writings of Elizabeth Bowen 1986, Willa Cather: A Life Saved Up 1989, Virginia Woolf 1996. *Leisure interests:* reading, music, countryside. *Address:* New College, Hollywell St, Oxford, OX1 3BN, UK. *Telephone:* (1865) 279500; *Fax:* (1865) 279590; *E-mail:* hermione.lee@new.ox.ac.uk.

LEE, (Nelle) Harper; American author; b 28 April 1926, Monroeville, AL; d of Amasa Coleman and Frances Finch Cunningham Lee. *Education:* Huntingdon Coll, Univ of Alabama and Univ of Oxford. *Career:* Began career as airline reservation clerk, Eastern Airlines and BOAC (NY) during the 1950s; writing debut 1960; Alabama Library Asscn Award 1961; mem Nat Council of Arts 1966; several honorary doctorates including Hon D HUM LITT (Spring Coll, AL) 1997. *Publications:* To Kill A Mockingbird 1960 (Pulitzer Prize for Fiction

1961); numerous magazine articles and essays. *Leisure interest:* golf. *Address:* c/o HarperCollins Publishers (author mail), Ophelia House, Fulham Palace Rd, London, W6, UK.

LEE, Tanith; British writer; b 19 Sept 1947, London; d of Bernard and Hylda Lee; m John Kaiine 1992. *Education:* Prendergast Grammar School. *Career:* Full-time writer 1975–; has written two episodes of Blake's Seven (BBC TV), several radio plays and collections of short stories; World Fantasy Award. *Publications include:* Birthgrave 1975, Flat Earth Series 1978–87 including Death's Master (August Derleth Award) 1985, Women As Demons: The Male Perception of Women Through Space and Time 1989, Blood of Roses 1990, Black Unicorn 1995, The Book of the Mad 1998, The Book of the Dead 1998, The Castle of Dark 2001, East of Midnight 2001, Queen of the Wolves 2001. *Leisure interests:* classical music, theatre, cinema, reading, painting. *Address:* c/o Hodder Headline, 338 Euston Rd, London, NW1 3BH, UK.

LEEGWATER-VAN DER LINDEN, Marlies E., D SC; Netherlands civil servant; b 26 Jan 1948, Amsterdam; m A. N. J. Leegwater 1970; two d one s (fostered). *Education:* Univ of Amsterdam. *Career:* Teacher of animal husbandry and anatomy, Kenya 1971–74; Researcher in parasitology, nutrition and pest man and tsetse control 1976–83; Civil Servant Ministry of Educ, Culture and Science 1985–, Co-ordinator for Devt Co-operation and Int Educ; author of scientific publs on nutrition, parasitology and tsetse rearing. *Address:* Ministry of Education, Culture and Science, Postbus 25000, 2700 LZ Zoetermeer, Netherlands. *Telephone:* (79) 323-29-04; *Fax:* (79) 323-23-20.

LEET, Mildred Robbins, BA; American development consultant; b 9 Aug 1922, New York; d of Samuel Milton and Isabella Elowsky; m 1st Louis J. Robbins 1941 (died 1970); m 2nd Glen Leet 1974. *Education:* New York Univ. *Career:* Sec and Vice-Pres of Conf Groups, US Nat Orgs at UN 1961–64, 1976–78, Vice-Chair and Sec 1962–64, mem Exec Cttee 1961–65, 1975–; Vice-Chair Exec Cttee NGOs UN Office of Public Information 1976–78; Chair Cttee on water, desertification, habitat and environment, Conf of NGOs with consultative status with UN/ECOSOC 1976–; Partner Leet and Leet (devt consultants) 1978–; Co-Founder and Dir Trickle Up Program 1979–, Co-Pres 1991–; Vice-Pres Save the Children Fed 1986, US Cttee, UN Devt Fund for Women 1983–; Co-Chair Women in Devt Cttee, Interaction 1985–91; Rep Int Peace Acad at UN 1973–77, Int Soc for Community Devt 1977–; mem Task Force on Poverty 1977–, Overseas Devt Bd 1988–; mem Bd Dirs Int Devt Conf 1991–; numerous honours and awards include Crystal Award (Coll of Human Services) 1983, Woman of Conscience Award (Nat Council of Women) 1986, Temple Award (Inst of Noetic Sciences) 1987, Rose Award (World Media Inst jtly) 1987, Human Rights Award (UN Devt Fund for Women jtly) 1987, Leadership Award (US Peace Corps), Matrix Award (Women in Communications Inc), Spirit of Enterprise Award (Rolex Industries) 1990, Int Humanity Award (ARC Overseas Asscn) 1992, Excellence Award (US Cttee for UNIFEM) 1992, Champion of Enterprise Award (Avon) 1994. *Address:* 54 Riverside Drive, New York, NY 10024, USA.

LEFANU, Nicola Frances, D MUS, FRCM; British composer; b 28 April 1947, Essex; d of William Richard LeFanu and Elizabeth Violet Maconchy; m David Newton Lumsdaine 1979; one s. *Education:* St Mary's School (Calne), St Hilda's Coll (Oxford) and Royal Coll of Music. *Career:* Dir of Music St Paul's Girls' School 1975–77; Composer-in-Residence New S Wales Conservatorium of Music, Sydney, Australia 1979; Del to Moscow Int New Music Festival 1984; Prof of Music Univ of York 1994–; has composed over 50 works including opera, orchestral works, chamber music with and without voice, choral music and solo pieces; Mendelssohn Scholar 1972; Harkness Fellow for composition study Harvard Univ (MA, USA) 1973–74; Hon Fellow St Hilda's Coll (Oxford); Leverhulme Research Award 1989; Cobbett Prize for chamber music 1968; First Prize, BBC Composers Competition 1971. *Leisure interests:* natural history, conservation, peace movement, women's movement. *Address:* Department of Music, University of York, Heslington, York YO10 5DD, UK. *Telephone:* (1904) 432445; *Fax:* (1904) 432450.

LEHANE, Maureen; British opera singer (retd); b London; m Peter Wishart 1966. *Education:* Queen Elizabeth's Girls Grammar School (Barnet, London) and Guildhall School of Music and Drama (London). *Career:* Studied under Hermann Weissenborn and John and Aida Dickens; professional debut Glyndebourne 1967; has performed with Handel opera socs in UK, USA, Poland, Sweden, Germany and Holland and at numerous festivals including Stravinsky Festival (Cologne), City of London Festival, Aldeburgh, Cheltenham, Three Choirs Festival (Bath), Oxford Bach Festival, Göttingen Handel Festival (Germany), also appearances in Berlin, Lisbon and Rome; fmr instructor at Guildhall School of Music, Univ of Reading and Welsh Coll of Music and Drama, now teaches pvtly; mem jury Int Singing Competition (Netherlands) 1982, Llangollen Int Eisteddfod 1991–93; Founder and Artistic Dir Great Elm Music Festival 1987–98, Jackdaws Educational Trust 1993–; numerous TV appearances. *Operas include:* Ariodante, Clytemnestra 1974, Dido and Aeneas 1976, La Cenerentola, Adriano 1982, The Lady of the Inn 1983, The Falcon 1983, Faust; *Recordings include:* Bach, Haydn, Mozart, Handel, including the first complete recording of Handel's Belshazzar; *Publication:* Songs of Purcell (jt-ed). *Leisure interests:* gardening, cooking, reading. *Address:* Bridge House, Great Elm, Frome, Somerset BA11 3NY, UK. *Telephone:* (1373) 812383; *Fax:* (1373) 812083; *E-mail:* music@jackdaws.org.

LEHR, Ursula M., PH D; German politician and professor of gerontology; b 5 June 1930, Frankfurt am Main; d of Georg Josef and Gertrud (née Jandorff) Leipold; m Helmut F. Lehr 1950 (died 1994); two s; m 2nd Hans Thomae 1998. *Education:* Rheinische Friedrich-Wilhelms Univ (Bonn). *Career:* Research Asst, Univ of Bonn 1955–60, Research and Teaching Asst, Inst of Psychology 1960–68, mem perm staff 1968–69, Additional Prof and Head Dept of Developmental Psychology 1969–72, Chair Dept of Psychology and Dir Inst of Psychology 1976–86, Hon Prof 1987–; Chair of Pedagogics and Pedagogical Psychology, Albertus Magnus Univ, Cologne 1972; Dir Inst of Gerontology, Ruprecht Karls Univ, Heidelberg 1986–88, 1991–96; Head German Centre for Research on Ageing, Heidelberg 1996–; mem Parl 1990–94; Fed Minister of Youth, Families, Women and Health 1988–91; mem Families Advisory Bd, Fed Ministry of Youth, Families and Health 1972–80; mem Swiss Soc of Gerontology 1976, Mexican Soc of Gerontology and Geriatrics 1982, WHO Expert Advisory Panel on Health of Elderly Persons 1983–87, American Soc of Gerontology, Int Council of Psychologists, Int Soc for the Study of Behavioural Devt, Int Asscn of Applied Psychology 1987; Vice-Pres German Gerontological Soc 1973–78, 1980–84, Pres 1997–; Founder-mem Acad of Sciences, Berlin 1987–91; Corresp mem Acad of Sciences, Austria 1994–, Sächsische Akad der Wissenschaften 1998–; Hon PH D (Fribourg); Max-Bürger Award of Gerontology 1973; Egner Award, Univ of Zurich 1989; René Schubert Award, Louise Eylmann Donation 1991; Grosses Bundesverdienstkreuz 1996; Landesverdienstmedaille Baden-Württemberg 1999. *Publications include:* Die Frau im Beruf 1969, Die Bedeutung der Familie im Sozialisationsprozeß 1973, Interventionsgerontologie 1974, Psychologie des Alterns (5th edn) 1985, Formen seelischen Alterns 1987; over 700 contribs to professional journals. *Leisure interests:* art, history of art (paintings of the Middle Ages and the 16th and 17th centuries). *Address:* German Centre for Research on Ageing, University of Heidelberg, Bergheimerstr 20, 69115 Heidelberg, Germany (Office); Am Büchel 53B, 53173 Bonn, Germany (Home). *Telephone:* (6221) 548101 (Office); (228) 352849 (Home); *Fax:* (6221) 548100 (Office); (228) 352741 (Home); *E-mail:* lehr@dzfa .uni-heidelberg.de (Office); ursula.lehr@t-online.de.

LEI JIEQIONG, MA; Chinese politician and jurist; b 1905, Guangzhou, Guangdong Prov; d of Lei Zichang and Li Peizhi; m Yan Jingyao 1941. *Education:* USA. *Career:* Prof Yenching Univ, 1931–52; Vice-Dean Inst of Politics and Law 1953–73; mem Cttee for Implementation Campaign of Marriage Laws 1953; Deputy Dir Bureau of Foreign Experts Admin under State Council 1956–66; Prof Beijing Univ 1973–; Vice-Mayor of Beijing 1979–83; Chair China Asscn for Promoting Democracy 1987–97; Hon Pres China Asscn of Women Judges, Asscn for Int Understanding of China, Western Returned Students' Asscn, China Social Workers' Asscn; mem Standing Cttee 5th CPPCC 1978–83; mem Standing Cttee 6th NPC 1983–88, Vice-Chair 1986–88, Vice-Chair of Law Cttee 1983–88; Vice-Chair 7th NPC 1988–93; Vice-Chair

Standing Cttee 8th NPC 1994–98; numerous other appointments and hon positions. *Address:* c/o 19 Xi Jiaomen Xiang, Xicheng District, Beijing, People's Republic of China.

LEIBOVITZ, Annie; American photographer; b 2 Oct 1949, CT. *Education:* San Francisco Art Inst. *Career:* Photographer Rolling Stone magazine 1970–73, Chief Photographer 1973–83, Vanity Fair 1983–; photographer for advertisements 1987–; owner Annie Leibovitz Studio, New York; numerous exhibitions including retrospective exhibition Smithsonian Nat Portrait Gallery, Washington, DC 1991, Palais de Tokyo, Paris 1992; Innovation in Photography Award, American Soc of Magazine Photographers 1987. Celebrity portraits include: John Lennon, Mick Jagger, Mikhail Baryshnikov, Bette Midler, Louis Armstrong, Ella Fitzgerald, Jessye Norman, Arnold Schwarzenegger, Tom Wolfe; *Publications include:* Annie Leibovitz Photographs 1970–1990 1992, Women (jtly) 2000. *Address:* c/o Jim Moffat, Art and Commerce, 755 Washington St, New York, NY 10014, USA.

LEIGH, Irene May, FRCP, MBBS, MD, F MED SCI, D SC (MED); British professor of medicine; b 25 April 1947; m 1st P. Nigel Leigh 1969 (divorced 1999); three d one s; m 2nd John E. Kernhalter 2000. *Education:* Merchant Taylor Girls' School (Crosby) and London Hosp Medical Coll. *Career:* Prof of Dermatology Barts and the London School of Medicine and Dentistry, Queen Mary's Coll 1992–99, Asst Warden (Research) 1997–; Prof of Cellular and Molecular Medicine and Dir Imperial Cancer Research Foundation (ICRF) Skin Tumour Lab 1999–; Pres European Soc of Dermatological Research 1999–2000. *Publications:* numerous scientific publs in specialist journals. *Leisure interests:* music, art, theatre, opera. *Address:* ICF Skin Tumour Laboratory, Centre for Cutaneous Research, Barts and the London, Queen Mary's School of Medicine and Dentistry, 2 Newark St, London E1 2AT, UK. *Telephone:* (20) 7882-7170; *Fax:* (20) 7882-7171; *E-mail:* i.leigh@icrf.icnet.uk.

LEIGH, Jennifer Jason; American actress; b 5 Feb 1962, Los Angeles, CA; d of the late Vic Morrow and of Barbara Turner. *Education:* Palisades High School. *Career:* Film debut in Walt Disney TV movie The Young Runaways 1977. *Stage appearance:* Sunshine 1989; *Films include:* Eyes of a Stranger 1981, Fast Times at Ridgemont High 1982, Grandview USA 1984, Flesh and Blood 1985, The Hitcher 1986, The Men's Club 1986, Heart of Midnight 1989, The Big Picture 1989, Miami Blues 1990, Last Exit to Brooklyn 1990, Crooked Hearts 1991, Backdraft 1991, Rush 1992, Single White Female 1992, Short Cuts 1993, The Hudsucker Proxy 1994, Mrs Parker and the Vicious Circle 1994, Georgia 1995, Kansas City 1996, Washington Square 1997, eXistenZ 1999, The King is Alive 2000; *TV appearances include:* The Young Runaways 1977, The Killing of Randy Webster 1981, The Best Little Girl in the World 1981, King of the Hill (voice) 1997, Hercules (voice) 1997. *Address:* c/o Tracey Jacobs, ICM, 8942 Wilshire Blvd, Beverly Hills, CA 90068-2464, USA.

LEIRNER, Sheila; Brazilian art critic and curator; b 25 Sept 1948, São Paulo; d of Abraham L. and Giselda (née Leirner) Klinger; m 1st Décio Tozzi 1970 (divorced 1972); m 2nd Gustavo Halbreich 1974 (divorced 1988); two s. *Education:* Univ of Vincennes and Univ of Paris (Sorbonne). *Career:* Production Asst to Luis S. Person and film critic 1970; visual arts columnist on Ultima Hora, São Paulo 1971–74; art critic on O Estado de São Paulo 1975–90; ind curator and art critic; Exec Dir Latin American Asscn of Visual Arts, Buenos Aires 1984; corresp Colombia magazine and D'Ars, Milan, Italy 1984–90; mem Brazilian Asscn of Art Critics 1976, Cen Advisory Bd Fantastic Art in Latin America, Indianapolis Museum 1984, Arts and Culture Comm São Paulo Biennial Foundation 1982–87; Gen Curator 18th and 19th São Paulo Biennial 1984–88; Curator Painterly/Pictorico, Los Angeles Municipal Art Gallery, Museu de Arte de São Paulo 1989–90; has written selected works of art criticism. *Leisure interests:* literature, music, collecting dolls' houses.

LEITH, Prudence Margaret, OBE, FRSA; British cook and business executive; b 18 Feb 1940, Cape Town, S Africa; d of the late Sam Leith and of Margaret Inglis; m Rayne Kruger; one s one d. *Education:* Haywards Heath (Sussex), Univ of Cape Town (SA), St Mary's Univ (Johannesburg, SA), Sorbonne Univ (Paris) and Cordon Bleu (London). *Career:* Catering service from flat, London 1960–65; f Leith's

Ltd (fmrly Leith's Good Food) 1960, Chair 1994–; Propr (jt) and Dir Leith's Restaurant 1969–95; f Leith's School of Food and Wine 1975, Dir 1975–95; Cookery Corresp Daily Mail 1969–73, Sunday Express 1976–80, The Guardian 1980–85, The Mirror 1995–98; Non-Exec Dir British Railways 1980–85, Safeway PLC 1988–89, Argyll Group PLC 1989–96, Halifax PLC 1995–96, Whitbread PLC 1995–, Triven PLC 1999–; mem numerous cttees and councils including Food from Britain Council 1983–86, Nat Training Task Force 1989–91, Nat Council for Vocational Qualifications (NVQs) 1992–96, Nuffield Bio-ethics Cttee on Genetical Modification of Plants 1997–99; mem RSA 1984–, Council 1992, Exec Cttee 1994, Chair 1995–97, Deputy Chair 1997–2000; Chair Restaurateurs' Assoc of GB 1990–94, UK Cttee New Era Schools' Trust 1994–2000, The British Food Heritage Trust 1997–; Gov Ashridge Man Coll 1992–; Chair 3E's Enterprises 1998–, King's Coll 1998; Patron Prue Leith Coll of Food and Wine (SA) 1996–; Trustee Forum for the Future 1998–, Training for Life 1999–, Places for People 1999–; Freedom of the City of London 1994; Corning Food Journalist of the Year 1979; Glenfiddich Trade Journalist of the Year 1983; Veuve Clicquot Business Woman of the Year 1990; Deputy Lieut Greater London 1998; Hon Fellow Hotel Catering and Institutional Man Asscn 1986, Salford Univ 1992, City and Guilds of London Inst 1992–97; Hon DBA (Greenwich) 1996; Hon D SC (Manchester); Hon D LITT (Queen Margaret Coll, Edinburgh) 1997; Dr hc (Open Univ) 1997, (Oxford Brookes) 2000. *Publications include:* Leith's All-Party Cook Book 1969, Parkinson's Pie 1972, Cooking For Friends 1978, The Best of Prue Leith 1979, Leith's Cookery Course (jtly) 1979–80, The Cook's Handbook 1981, Prue Leith's Pocket Book of Dinner Parties 1983, Dinner Parties 1984, Leith's Cookery School (jtly) 1985, Entertaining with Style (jtly) 1986, Confident Cooking 1989–90, Leith's Cookery Bible 1991, Leith's Complete; Novels: Leaving Patrick 1999, Sisters 2001. *Leisure interests:* writing, walking, fishing, gardening, tennis, old cookbooks, kitchen antiques, Trollope. *Address:* The Office, Chastleton Glebe, Moreton-in-Marsh, Gloucestershire GL56 0SZ, UK. *Telephone:* (1608) 674865; *Fax:* (1608) 674083; *E-mail:* pmleith@dial.pipex.com.

LEJEUNE, Rita Marguerite Joséphine, D ÈS L; Belgian professor emeritus of medieval literature; b 22 Nov 1906, Herstal; d of Jean Lejeune and Adrienne Vercheval; m Fernand Dehousse (died 1976); one s one d. *Education:* Univ of Liège and Ecole Pratique des Hautes-Etudes, La Sorbonne (Paris). *Career:* Researcher in Romance Philology Fonds Nat de la Recherche Scientifique 1929–37; Prof of Romance Philology Univ of Liège 1954–77, Emer Prof 1977–; Co-Dir Le Moyen Âge review 1960–; Dr hc (Bordeaux) 1964; Prix Achille Fould, Inst de France 1968; Grand Officier de l'Ordre de la Couronne 1991. *Publications include:* L'œuvre de Jean Renart 1935, Recherches sur le thème: les chansons de geste et l'histoire 1948, La Légende de Roland dans l'art du moyen âge (2 vols, jtly) 1968, Littérature et société occitane au moyen âge 1979. *Leisure interests:* reading, listening to classical music. *Address:* 17 rue St-Pierre, 4000 Liège, Belgium. *Telephone:* (41) 22-13-26.

LEMPER, Ute; German singer, dancer and actress; b 4 July 1963, Münster; m David Tabatsky; one s one d. *Education:* Dance Acad, Cologne and Max Reinhardt Seminar on Dramatic Art (Vienna). *Career:* Leading role in Viennese production of Cats 1983; appeared in Peter Pan (Berlin), Cabaret (Düsseldorf and Paris (Molière Award 1987)), Der Blaue Engel (Berlin) 1992, Chicago (London, Laurence Olivier Award) 1997–98; performances at Barbican Centre, London and Edinburgh Festival, UK 1994; French Culture Prize 1993. *Albums include:* Ute Lemper Sings Kurt Weill 1988, (Vol 2) 1993, Threepenny Opera 1988, Mahagonny Songspiel 1989, Songbook 1989, Illusions 1992, Espace Indécent 1993, City of Strangers 1994, Berlin Cabaret Songs 1996, Nuit Étrange 1997, All that Jazz/The Best of Ute Lemper 1998; *Film appearances include:* L'Autrichienne 1989, Prospero's Books 1989, Jean Galmont—Adventurer, Moscou Parade 1992, Coupable d'Innocence 1993, Bogus 1995, Prêt à Porter 1995, Combat de Fauves 1996, A River Made to Drown In, Appetite; *TV apearances include:* L'Affaire Dreyfus, Tales from the Crypt, Illusions, The Look of Love; *Publication:* Unzensiert (autobiog) 1995. *Address:* c/o Oliver Gluzman, 40 rue de la Folie Régnault, 75011 Paris, France. *Telephone:* (1) 44-93-02-02; *Fax:* (1) 44-93-04-40; *E-mail:* info@visiteursdusoir.com (Office); *Internet:* www.visiteursdusoir.com (Office).

LENG, Victoria Helen Antoinette (see Elliot, Virginia Helen Antoinette.

LENNOX, Annie, ARAM; British singer and songwriter; b 25 Dec 1954, Aberdeen; d of the late Thomas A. Lennox and of Dorothy (née Ferguson) Lennox; m 1st Radha Raman 1984; m 2nd Uri Fruchtman; two d. *Education:* Aberdeen High School for Girls and Royal Acad of Music (London). *Career:* Partner of Dave Stewart in pop group The Tourists 1978–80, The Eurythmics 1982–90, tours UK, Europe, USA 1983, 1984, world tours 1986–87, 1989–90, recorded numerous albums; now solo artist, recorded first solo album 1992; f DnA Ltd (with Dave Stewart) 1981; awards include Best UK Video (for Love is a Stranger) 1982, Grammy Awards for Best Video Album and for Best Female Performance (for Sweet Dreams), Ivor Novello Award for Best Pop Song (Sweet Dreams), American Soc of Composers Award, BPI Award for Best Female Vocalist 1982/83, 1987/88, 1989/90, 1992/93, BPI for Best Album (for Diva) 1992/93, Ivor Novello Award for Best Song (for Why), Brit Award for Best Female Vocalist 1996, Grammy Award for Best Female Pop Vocals (for No More I Love You) 1996. *Recordings include:* With Eurythmics: The Garden 1981, Sweet Dreams Are Made of This 1983, Touch 1984, 1984, Be Yourself Tonight 1985, Revenge 1986, Savage 1987, Greatest Hits 1991; Solo Album: Diva 1992, Medusa (Best Female Pop Vocal Award, Grammy Awards, USA for No More I Love You's, single 1996) 1995; *Film:* Revolution 1985. *Address:* c/o Tara Goldsmid, 19 Management Ltd, Unit 32, Ransomes Dock, 35–37 Parkgate Rd, London SW11 4NP. *Telephone:* (20) 7801-1920.

LENTRODT, Ursula; German harpist; b Berlin; d of Wilhelm and Clara (née von Occolowitz) Lentrodt; one d. *Education:* Hochschule für Musik (Berlin) and in Paris. *Career:* Solo harpist with orchestras including Berliner Rundfunk and Bayerischer Rundfunkorchester 1953–74; numerous solo concerts in Germany and abroad; teacher Musikhochschule, Munich; contribs to professional journals; Bundesverdienstkreuz 1986; Bayerischer Verdienstorden 1991; Citoyen d'Honneur (France). *Address:* Wagnerstr 1A, 80802 Munich, Germany. *Telephone:* (89) 395826.

LENZ, Marlene; German politician; b 4 July 1932, Berlin. *Education:* Heidelberg Univ. *Career:* Trans and fmr Official Comm of EC; Gen Sec European Women's Union 1967–71, mem Exec 1975–77, Vice-Pres 1977–; Adviser External Relations Office, Nat Exec CDU 1972–75; Rapporteur Bundestag (Parl) Cttee of Enquiry on Women and Soc; MEP (CDU) 1979–99, Vice-Chair Enquiry into Situation of Women in Europe 1979–84, Chair Cttee on Women's Rights 1984–87, Cttee on Human Rights 1994–99. *Publication:* Der Weg der Frau in der Politik. *Address:* Burgatraße 102, 53177 Bonn, Germany. *Telephone:* (228) 31-8845; *Fax:* (228) 31-8236.

LEONG, Adeline Shuk Ken Pung, BA; Malaysian librarian; b 16 March 1949, Singapore; d of Pung Onn Fah and Rosie Chia Qui Tee; m K. C. Leong 1975; one d. *Education:* ANU (Canberra) and Royal Melbourne Inst of Tech (Australia). *Career:* Dir Sabah State Library 1973–; mem Bd Dirs Inst Devt Studies Sabah; Chair Sabah Rhino and Wildlife Public Relations Subcttee 1986–88, Visitors Bd Taman Seri Putri 1987–88, Sabah Women's Asscn (PEWASA) Research and Devt Bureau 1987–89, Intan Bldg Cttee of the Intan Jaycees 1987–89, Sabah Women's Advisory Council 1988–91, Round Table on Mobile Libraries, Int Fed of Libraries Asscn 1988–91, Jaycees Malaysia Senate Asscn 1991–92; Assoc Australian Library Asscn; mem Int Fed Libraries Asscn, Libraries Asscn of Malaysia, Sabah Women's Asscn 1985–, Cttee Sabah Rhino and Wildlife Conservation 1986–88, SOS Heart Fund Asscn; Exec Vice-Pres Jaycees Int 1987; Pres Kota Kinabalu Toastmaster Club 1994–95, Area Gov PAN-SEA Toastmasters Dist 1995–96, Div Gov Dist 5IP 1996–; has attended numerous int confs and has written papers and articles on library devt for professional journals; All Intan Jaycee Award, Intan Jaycees 1980; Ahli Darjah Kinabalu, State Govt 1982; Outstanding Exec Vice-Pres Award, Jaycees Int 1987; Ahli Setia Darjah Kinabalu, State Govt 1988; Outstanding Young Malaysian Award, Jaycees Malaysia 1988; Hennessy Certificate of Honour, Kota Kinabalu Lions Club 1989; Most Active Working Mother Award, Kota Kinabalu Women's Br 1989; Ahli Mangku Negara, Fed Govt 1989; PGKD, State Govt 1993. *Address:* Sabah State Library, 88572 Kota Kinabalu, Sabah, Malaysia (Office); 3 Lorong Mawas, Taman Foh

Sang, 88300 Kota Kinabalu, Malaysia (Home). *Telephone:* (88) 225865 (Office); (88) 249292 (Home); *Fax:* (88) 233167; *E-mail:* adeline@sbh .lib.edu.my.

LEONI, Tea; American actress; b 25 Feb 1966; m David Duchovny 1997. *Films:* Switch 1991, A League of Their Own 1992, Wyatt Earp 1994, Bad Boys 1995, Flirting with Disaster 1996, Deep Impact 1998, There's No Fish Food in Heaven 1999; *TV:* sitcoms: Naked Truth, Flying Blind 1995. *Address:* c/o ICM, 8942 Wilshire Blvd, Beverly Hills, CA 90211, USA.

LEPAGE, Corinne Dominique Marguerite; French politician and lawyer; b 11 May 1951, Boulogne-Bilancourt; d of Philippe Lepage and Jacqueline Schulmann; m 1st Christian Jessua; one d; m 2nd Christian Huglo; one s. *Education:* Lycée Molière, Univ of Paris II and Inst d'Etudes Politiques (Paris). *Career:* Worked at legal practice 1971–76; barrister, Paris 1978–; Dir of Studies Univ of Paris II 1974–77, Course Dir 1982–86, Univ of Paris XII 1984–; Dir of Educ Univ of Metz 1978–80; Maître de Conférences Inst d'Etudes Politiques, Paris 1979–87; mem Bar Council 1987–89; Vice-Pres, Pres Asscn of Admin Law Advocates 1989–95; Minister of the Environment 1995–97; Pres Asscn nationale des docteurs en droit 1998–; Vice-Pres Environnement sans frontières 1998–, Asscn européenne des Générations emploi mondialisation 1999–; Pres CRII-GEN, CAP 21. *Publications include:* Code annoté des procédures administratives contentieuses 1990, Les audits de l'environnement 1992 On ne peut rien faire, Madame le ministre 1998, Bien gérer l'environnement, une chance pour l'entreprise 1999, La Politique de précaution 2001; numerous articles in La gazette du Palais. *Leisure interests:* cinema, reading, tennis, skiing, swimming. *Address:* Villa 40, rue André Prempain, 75008 Paris, France (Office); Jérôme, 1 ave du Casino Ouest, 14390 Cabourg, France (Home).

LEPERRE-VERRIER, Odile; French politician; b 18 Oct 1950, Orléans. *Career:* MEP 1994–99 (Group of the European Radical Alliance, mem Cttee on Culture, Youth, Educ and the Media, Cttee on Petitions, Del for relations with the countries of S Asia and the S Asia Asscn for Regional Cooperation (SAARC), Del for relations with Canada; Vice-Pres Mouvement des Radicaux de Gauche in charge of Educ and Culture 1996–98, mem Political Bureau 1998–. *Address:* Parti radical de gauche, 13 rue Deroc, 75007 Paris, France.

LÉPINE, Michèle Marie Geneviève, L ÈS L; French magistrate; b 25 March 1945, Casablanca, Morocco; m Jean Luc Lépine 1978; two s. *Education:* Univ of Aix-en-Provence and Inst des Etudes Politiques (Paris). *Career:* Civil Servant Ministry of Foreign Affairs 1968–86; Asst to Pres of the Repub 1975–88; Magistrate Cour des Comptes (Revenue Courts) 1986–; Chevalier de l'Ordre Nat du Mérite 1985. *Leisure interests:* golf, tennis, skiing, reading. *Address:* Cour des Comptes, 13 rue Cambon, 75100 Paris RP, France (Office).

LEPOMME, Linda; Belgian actress, singer and artistic director; b 16 March 1955, Lokeren; d of Willy Lepomme and Irma Hereman. *Education:* Higher Inst of Dramatic Art (Antwerp). *Career:* Mem Teater Arena, Ghent until 1985; rep Belgium in Eurovision Song Contest 1985; Asst Artistic Dir of Musicals Royal Ballet of Flanders, Musical Div 1985–91, Dir 1989. *Appearances include:* Rocky Horror Picture Show, The Fantasticks, Chicago, Company, Grease, Side by Side by Sondheim, My Fair Lady, West Side Story, Dear Fox. *Leisure interests:* golf, travel. *Address:* Krogstraat 169, 1860 Meise, Belgium. *Telephone:* (3) 234-34-38; *Fax:* (3) 233-58-92.

LERKSAMRAN, Lalita, M ED, PH D; Thai politician; b 23 Feb 1949; m Mr Pantawee 1974; two d. *Education:* Srinakarintaraviroj and Chula-longkorn Univs (Bangkok). *Career:* Lecturer Ramkamhaene Univ 1972–86, Head Dept of Testing and Research 1976; mem House of Reps 1986, Sec-Gen Inter-Parl Union 1989–91, Sec Ministry of Univ Affairs 1990–91, apptd Sec Cttee of Educ 1992. *Publications:* Intro-duction to Educational Research 1980, Evaluation of Learning English 1981. *Leisure interests:* reading, badminton, aerobics. *Address:* House of Representatives, U-Thong Nai Rd, Bangkok 10300, Thailand (Office); 15/188 Soi Sunannivet, Sukapiban 1 Rd, Bangkapi, Bangkok, Thailand (Home). *Telephone:* (2) 2826181 (Office); (2) 3781128 (Home).

LESNEVSKAYA, Irena Stefanovna; Russian journalist and business-woman; b 30 May 1942, Urlyutyup, Kazakhstan; divorced; one s. *Education:* Moscow State Univ. *Career:* Mem State Cttee of TV and Radio Broadcasting 1966–, Asst Dir Broadcasting for Children 1966–78; author of TV programmes About Time and Ourselves, Portraits, Cinema Poster, Cinema Panorama; Founder and Dir REN-TV (pvt TV co) 1991, Pres TV channel REN-TV 1997; Pres Bd Dirs Joint Stock co, Asscn of Ind TV-Producers; mem Bd Dirs Russian Public TV 1995–; mem Acad of Russian TV 1996–. *Address:* REN-TV Company, Zubovsky blvd 17, 117847 Moscow, Russian Federation. *Telephone:* (095) 246-59-33.

LESSING, Doris May, CH; British writer; b 22 Oct 1919, Kermanshah, Persia (now Iran); d of Capt Alfred Cook Tayler and Emily Maude McVeagh; m 1st Frank Charles Wisdom 1939 (divorced 1943); m 2nd Gottfried Anton Nicolai Lessing 1944 (divorced 1949); two s (one deceased) one d. *Education:* Roman Catholic Convent and Girls' High School (Salisbury (now Harare), S Rhodesia (now Zimbabwe)). *Career:* Assoc mem American Acad of Arts and Letters 1974, Nat Inst of Arts and Letters (USA) 1974; mem Inst for Cultural Research; Pres Book Trust 1996–; Distinguished Fellow in Literature, Univ of E Anglia 1991; Hon Fellow MLA (USA); Dr hc (Bard Coll) 1994, (Harvard) 1995; Hon D LITT (Princeton) 1989, (Durham) 1990, (Warwick) 1994, (Bard Coll New York State) 1994, (Harvard) 1995, (Oxford) 1996; five Somerset Maugham Awards, Soc of Authors 1954; Austrian State Prize for European Literature 1981: Shakespeare Prize, FVS Foundation (Hamburg) 1982; Grinzane Cavour Award (Italy) 1989; Woman of the Year, Norway 1995; Premi Internacional Catalunya 1999; David Cohen Literary Prize 2001; Principe de Asturias 2001. *Publications include:* The Grass is Singing 1950, Martha Quest 1952, A Proper Marriage 1954, Going Home 1957, The Habit of Loving 1958, Each His Own Wilderness (play) 1958, A Ripple from the Storm 1958, In Pursuit of the English (reportage) 1960, The Golden Notebook (Prix Medici 1976) 1962, Play With a Tiger (play) 1962, A Man and Two Women 1963, Landlocked 1965, Particularly Cats 1967, The Four Gated City 1969, Briefing for a Descent into Hell 1971, The Story of a Non-Marrying Man (short stories) 1972, The Summer Before the Dark 1973, Collected Edn African Stories (2 vols) This Was the Old Chief's Country and The Sun Between Their Feet 1973, The Memoirs of a Survivor 1974, To Room Nineteen (collected stories, vol 1), The Temptation of Jack Orkney (collected stories, vol 2), Canopus in Argos: Archives: Re Colonised Planet Shikasta 1979, The Marriages Between Zones 3, 4 and 5 1980, The Sirian Experiments 1981, The Making of the Representative for Planet 8 1982, The Sentimental Agents in the Volyen Empire 1983, The Diary of a Good Neighbour, If the Old Could (under pseudonym Jane Somers, later as The Diaries of Jane Somers by Doris Lessing) 1984, The Good Terrorist (W. H. Smith Literary Award 1986, Palermo Prize, Premio Internazionale Mondello 1987) 1985, The Wind Blows Away our Words 1987, Prisons We Choose to Live Inside 1987, The Fifth Child 1988, The Libretto of the Making of the Representative for Planet 8 1988, Particularly Cats and More Cats 1989, The Real Thing 1991, London Observed 1992, African Laughter: Four Visits to Zimbabwe 1992, Under My Skin (Los Angeles Times Book Prize, James Tait Memorial Prize 1995) 1994, Playing the Game 1995, Love, Again 1996, Walking in the Shade 1997, Mara and Dann 1999, Ben, in the World 2000, The Sweetest Dream 2001. *Address:* c/o Jonathan Clowes Ltd, 10 Iron Bridge House, Bridge Approach, London NW1 8BD, UK.

LETOWSKA, Ewa Anna, LL D; Polish lawyer; b 22 March 1940, Warsaw; m (husband deceased). *Education:* Univ of Warsaw. *Career:* Asst Prof 1975, Extraordinary Prof 1985; scientific worker, Inst of State and Law, Polish Acad of Sciences (Warsaw) 1961–87, Head of Team for civil law 1975–87, Prof Inst of Legal Sciences 1992–; Lecturer Univ of Warsaw and Postgraduate Training Centre of Admin Personnel 1961–87; Civic Rights' Intercessor (Ombudsman) 1988–92; mem of Bd, Int Ombudsman Inst; numerous scientific awards; Kt's Cross Order of Polonia Restituta. *Publications:* Wzorce umowne—ogólne warunki, wzory, regulaminy 1975, Obywatel—przedsiebiorstwo Zagadnienia prawne swiadczen na rzecz konsumenta (ed and co-author) 1982, Tendencje rozwojowe prawa cywilnego 1983 (ed and co-author), Komentarz do ogólnych warunków umów konsumenckich (co-author)

1985, Przygoda z opera (with J. Letowski) 1991. *Leisure interests:* serious music, vocalism. *Address:* Instytut Nauk Prawnych PAN, ul Nowy Swiat 72, 00-330 Warsaw, Poland. *Telephone:* (22) 826 78 53.

LETTE, Kathy; Australian author; b 11 Nov 1958, Sydney; d of Mervyn and Val Lette; m Geoffrey Robertson 1990; one s one d. *Career:* Fmr Columnist, Sydney and NY; fmr satirical news writer and presenter Willasee Show, Channel 9; fmr TV Sitcom Writer, Columbia Pictures (LA); fmr guest presenter This Morning with Richard and Judy (ITV, UK). *Books include:* Puberty Blues 1979, Hit & Ms 1984, Girls' Night Out 1988, The Llama Parlour 1991, Foetal Attraction 1993, Mad Cows 1996, Altar Ego 1998, Nip 'n' Tuck 2001; *Plays include:* Grommits, Wet Dreams, Perfect Mismatch, I'm So Happy For You I Really Am. *Leisure interest:* girls' nights out. *Address:* c/o Pan Macmillan, 25 Eccleston Place, London SW1W 9NF, UK; c/o Ed Victor, 6 Bayley St, Bedford Square, London WC1B 3HB, UK. *Telephone:* (20) 7304-4100; *Fax:* (20) 7304-4111; *E-mail:* kathy.lette@virgin.net; *Internet:* www.kathylette.com.

LEUNG, Oi Sie (Elsie), LL M, JP; Chinese legal official; b 24 April 1939, Hong Kong. *Education:* Univ of Hong Kong. *Career:* Admitted as solicitor, Supreme Court of Hong Kong 1968, as overseas solicitor, UK Supreme Court 1976; Notary Public 1978; admitted as barrister and solicitor of Vic, Australia 1982; founding mem and Hon Sec Hong Kong Fed of Women Lawyers 1976; Country Vice-Pres Int Fed of Women Lawyers 1978, First Vice-Pres 1992, Pres 1994–; del 7th People's Congress, Guangdong, People's Repub of China 1989, 8th Nat People's Congress 1993; founding mem and mem Exec Cttee Hong Kong Fed of Women 1993; Sec for Justice of Hong Kong Special Admin Region 1997–; Fellow Int Acad of Matrimonial Lawyers 1994. *Address:* Department of Justice, Secretary for Justice's Office, 4th Floor, High Block, Queensway Government Offices, 66 Queensway, Hong Kong Special Administrative Region, People's Republic of China. *Telephone:* (852) 28692001; *Fax:* (852) 28773978; *E-mail:* elsie-os-leung@doj.gcn .gov.hk.

LEUTENEGGER, Gertrud; Swiss writer; b 7 Dec 1948, Schwyz; m M. von Wartburg 1989; one d. *Education:* Schauspielakademie (Zurich). *Career:* Prizes include Ingeborg Bachmann Critics Prize 1978, Droste-preis 1979. *Publications include:* Vorabend 1975, Ninive 1977, Lebewohl, Gute Reise 1980, Gouverneur 1981, Komm ins Schiff 1983, Kontinent 1985, Meduse 1988, Acheron 1994, Sphärenklang 1999. *Address:* Scheideggstrasse 85, 8038 Zurich, Switzerland.

LEUTHEUSSER-SCHNARRENBERGER, Sabine; German politician; b 26 July 1951, Minden, Westphalia; m E Schnarrenberger. *Education:* Univs of Göttingen and Bielefeld. *Career:* Mem staff Patent Office 1979–90; Head of Admin, Personnel and Budget Dept 1990; mem Bundeshau (Free Democratic Party (FDP)) 1990–; Minister of Justice 1992–96; Chair FDP Dist Asscn, Starnberg 1984–, mem Nat Exec 1991–96 and of numerous cttees. *Leisure interests:* mountaineering, skiing. *Address:* Bundeshaus, 53113 Bonn, Germany. *Telephone:* (228) 1685162; *Fax:* (228) 1686402.

LEVEL, Brigitte Marie Adélaïde, D ÈS L; French writer; b 31 Oct 1918, Paris; d of Maurice and Jacqueline (née Ancey de Curnieu) Level; m Christian Léon-Dufour 1941 (died 1983); four s (two deceased) four d (one deceased). *Education:* Cours du Colisée (Paris) and Univ of Paris (Sorbonne). *Career:* Prof Univ of Paris 1959–85; participant in numerous confs since retirement 1985; Producer Radio-Courtoisie 1988–; Pres Acad of Still Life Art 1994; Pres French Poets Soc 1985; Vice-Pres Défense de la langue française; Officier des Palmes Académiques 1971, Officier de Mérite Agricole 1981, Officier des Arts et des Lettres 1986; Chevalier de l'Ordre Nat du Mérite 1989; numerous other awards including Prix Acad française, Prix Acad des Jeux floraux (églantine), Grand Prix Pascal Bonetti 1988, Grand Prix des Poètes français 1996, Prix Daudet 1998 and Médaille de Vermeil de la Ville de Paris. *Publications include:* As Anne Acoluthe, Geneviève Minne, Zoé Zou: Poetry: La girafe dépeignée, L'oiseau bonheur, L'arche de Zoé, Le temps des guitars masques 1990, Le zoo de zoulou 1994; Prose: Le caveau 1729–1939, Correspondance Apollinaizre–André Level, Le poète et l'oiseau. *Leisure interest:* cats. *Address:* 22 rue Legendre, 75017 Paris, France. *Telephone:* (1) 46-22-71-25.

LEVETE, Amanda; British architect; b 17 Nov 1955, Bridgend; d of Michael and Gina (née Seagrim) Levete; m Jan Kaplicky 1997; one s. *Education:* St Paul's Girls' School, London, Hammersmith School of Art and Architectural Asscn, London. *Career:* Prin Future Systems 1979–; worked with Alsop & Lyall 1980–81, YRM Architects 1982–84, Powis & Levete 1983–86, Richard Rogers & Partners 1984–89; mem Bd ARB 1997–2000, Architecture Foundation 1997–, Artangel 2000–. *Work includes:* Stonehenge Visitor Centre (1st Prize AJ/Bovis Royal Acad Award 1993), Haver King House 1995 (1st Prize Aluminium Award 1995), Floating Bridge, W India Quay, London 1997 (RIBA Award 1998), Wild At Heart (RIBA Award 1998), Media Centre at Lord's Cricket Ground 1999 (Stirling Prize 1999, BCIA 1999), Future Systems, RIBA, London and Storefront, New York 1991, 1992, Inst of Contemporary Arts, London 1998. *Address:* Future Systems, The Warehouse, 20 Victoria Gardens, London, W11 3PE, UK. *Telephone:* (20) 7243-7670; *Fax:* (20) 7243-7690; *E-mail:* email@future-systems .com; *Internet:* www.future-systems.com.

LEVI-MONTALCINI, Rita; Italian research scientist; b 22 April 1909, Turin; d of Adamo Levi and Adele Montalcini. *Education:* Univ of Turin Medical School. *Career:* Neurological researcher in Turin and Brussels 1936–41, in a country cottage in Piedmont 1941–43; in hiding in Florence during German occupation 1943–44; medical practitioner working among war refugees in Florence 1944–45; resumed academic positions at Univ of Turin 1945; has worked in St Louis, USA with Prof Viktor Hamburger 1947–, Assoc Prof 1956, Prof 1958–77; Dir Inst of Cell Biology, Italian Nat Council of Research, Rome 1969–78, Guest Prof 1979–89, Guest Prof Inst of Neurobiology 1989–; Pres Inst della Enciclopedia Italiana Treccani; Nobel Prize for Medicine (jtly) 1986 for work on nerve growth factors which control growth and devt in humans and animals. *Publication:* In Praise of Imperfection: My Life and Work 1988. *Address:* Institute of Neurobiology, CNR, viale Carlo Marx 15, 00137, Rome, Italy. *Telephone:* (6) 86090510; *Fax:* (6) 86090269.

LEVICK, Barbara Mary, D PHIL; British historian and former university lecturer; b 21 June 1931, London; d of Frank Thomas and Mary (née Smart) Levick. *Education:* Brighton and Hove High School and St Hugh's Coll (Oxford). *Career:* Librarian St Hilda's Coll, Oxford 1956–91, Lecturer in Classics 1956–59, Fellow and Tutor in Literae Humaniores 1959–98. *Publications:* Tiberius the Politician 1976, The Government of the Roman Empire 1985, Claudius 1990, Vespasian 1999. *Leisure interests:* gardening, music. *Address:* St Hilda's College, Oxford OX4 1DY, UK (Office); 120 Morrell Ave, Oxford OX4 1NA, UK (Home). *Telephone:* (1865) 791889; *E-mail:* barbara.levick@ st-hildas.ox.ac.uk.

LEVINE, Ellen; American magazine editor; b 19 Feb 1943; d of Eugene Jack and Jean Jacobson; m Richard U. Levine 1964; two s. *Education:* Wellesley Coll. *Career:* Reporter The Record, Hackensack, NJ 1964–70; Ed Cosmopolitan, New York 1976–82; Ed-in-Chief Cosmopolitan Living 1980–81, Woman's Day 1982–91, Redbook 1991–94, Good Housekeeping 1994–; Dir N. J. Bell, Newark, NJ; Commr Attorney-Gen's Comm on Pornography 1985–86; mem Exec Cttee Sen Bill Bradley 1984–; awards include Matrix Award (New York Women in Communications Inc) 1989, Honor Award (Birmingham Southern Coll) 1991. *Publications:* Planning Your Wedding, Waiting for Baby, Rooms That Grow With Your Child. *Address:* Good Housekeeping, 959 Eighth Ave, New York, NY 10019, USA. *Internet:* www .goodhousekeeping.com.

LEVINE, Marilyn (Anne), M SC, MA, MFA; Canadian artist; b 22 Dec 1935, Medicine Hat, AB; d of Herman R. and Annie Louise Hayes; m Sidney Levine. *Education:* Univ of Alberta (Edmonton) and Univ of California at Berkeley (USA). *Career:* David P. Gardner Faculty Fellow Award, Univ of Utah 1975; Visual Artists Fellowship Grant, Nat Endowment for the Arts 1976, 1980; Sr Arts Grant Award, Canada Council 1976; solo exhibitions include Norman Mackenzie Art Gallery (Regina, SK) 1974, 1998, O. K. Harris Works of Art (New York) 1974, 1976, 1979, 1981, 1984, 1985, 1991, Hansen Fuller Gallery (San Francisco, CA, USA) 1971, 1975, 1980, 1983, Inst of Contemporary Art (Boston, MA, USA) 1981, Galerie Alain Blondel (Paris, France) 1981, Rena Bransten Gallery (San Francisco, CA, USA) 1990, Canadian Clay and Glass Gallery 1999; group exhibitions include Nat Museum of Modern Art (Kyoto, Japan) 1971, Sidney Janis Gallery

(New York) 1972, Musée d'Art de la Ville de Paris 1973, Whitney Museum of American Art (New York) 1974, Museum of Contemporary Crafts (New York) 1975, Australian Nat Gallery (Canberra) 1977, Everson Museum of Art (Syracuse, NY, USA) 1979, Pennsylvania Acad of Fine Arts (Philadelphia, PA, USA) 1981–83, Mackenzie Art Gallery, Univ of Saskatchewan (Canada) 1980, Abbaye Saint André (Meymac, Corrèze, France) 1983, American Craft Museum (New York) 1986–92, Philbrook Museum of Art (Tulsa, OK, USA) 1987–89, Scripps Coll (Claremont, CA, USA) 1994–96; rep in perm collections including Berkeley Univ Art Museum (CA, USA), Canada Council Art Bank, Australian Nat Gallery, Nelson-Atkins Museum of Art (Kansas City, MO, USA), Nat Museum of Modern Art (Kyoto, Japan), Montréal Museum of Fine Art (PQ). *Address:* 950 61st St, Oakland, CA 94608, USA. *Telephone:* (510) 658-1690; *Fax:* (510) 658-1690; *E-mail:* info@marilynlevine.com; *Internet:* www.marilynlevine.com.

LEVY, Andrea, BA; British writer; b 7 Mar 1956, London; d of Amy and Winston Levy; partner Bill Mayblin; two step-d. *Education:* Highbury Hill High School (London) and Middlesex Univ. *Career:* Arts Council Award 1998. *Publications:* Every Light in the House Burnin 1994, Never Far from Nowhere 1996, Fruit of the Lemon 1999. *Leisure interests:* reading, films, TV and swimming. *Address:* c/o Review Press, Hodder Headline, 338 Euston Rd, London, NW1, UK; c/o David Grossman Literary Agency, 118B Holland Park Ave, London W11 4VA, UK. *Telephone:* (20) 7221-2770; *Fax:* (20) 7221-1445.

LEVY, Julia G., PH D, FRSC; Canadian professor of microbiology; b 15 May 1935, Singapore; d of Guillaume Albert and Dorothy Frances Coppens; m Edwin Levy 1969; two s one d. *Education:* Univ Coll London (UK) and Univ of British Columbia. *Career:* Instructor Dept of Microbiology, Univ of British Columbia 1958, Asst Prof 1962, Assoc Prof 1967, Prof 1972–; Vice-Pres of Research and Devt, Quadralogic Technologies Inc 1986–; Consultant Monsanto Chemicals 1978–80, Allied Chemicals 1985–87, Triton Biosciences 1986–87; Dir Helix Biosciences 1988–93; Sr Vice-Pres Scientific Affairs and Chief Scientific Officer, Quadralogic 1968–98; Pres and CEO QLT Photo Therapeutics Inc 1995–; Chair Premier's Advisory Council on Science and Tech, BC 1992–; MRC Industrial Professorship 1987–90; Pres Canadian Soc of Immmunology 1980–82; numerous contribs to textbooks and professional journals; Killam Sr Travel Fellow 1982–83; Hon D UNIV (Ottawa) 1989; Hon D LITT (Mount St Vincent) 1990; Bieley Research Award 1980; Gold Medal for Medical Research 1982; Killam Sr Research Prize 1986. *Leisure interests:* tennis, camping, swimming. *Address:* 520 W Sixth Ave, Vancouver, BC V5Z 4H5, Canada.

LEWIN, Olive; Jamaican musician and civil servant; b 28 Sept 1927, Vere, Clarendon; d of the late Richard J. M. and Sylvia Elliott Lewin; one d. *Education:* Royal Acad of Music (London) and Queen's Univ of Belfast (UK). *Career:* Teacher of Music 1949–65; piano recitals in Jamaica and UK, and for BBC radio and TV London; mem OAS Inter-American Cttee on Culture 1985; apptd Dir of Art and Culture, Ministry of Youth, Culture and Community Devt (fmrly Ministry of Information and Culture) 1981; Officer of the Order of Distinction; Jamaica Certificate and Badge of Honour; Silver Musgrave Medal; Woman of the Year 1978. *Publications include:* Some Folk Songs 1970, Forty Folk Songs of Jamaica 1973, Brown Girl in De Ring 1974, Beeny Bud: Dandy Shandy 1975, Alle, Alle, Alle 1976. *Leisure interests:* music therapy, folklore, reading, youth club activities, nature study. *Address:* Grace Kennedy and Co Ltd, HRD Division, 4 Duke St, Kingston, Jamaica. *Telephone:* 922-1710.

LEWINER, Colette, D ÈS SC; French organization executive; b 19 Sept 1945, Cairo, Egypt; d of the late Maurice and of Judith (née Hakim) de Botton; m Jacques Lewiner 1968; two s one d. *Education:* Lycée Français d'Alexandrie (Egypt), Lycées Molière and Janson-de-Sailly (Paris), Ecole Normale Supérieure (Sèvres) and Univ of Paris VII. *Career:* Lecturer Univ of Paris VII 1974–79; Head Research and Studies Dept, Electricité de France (EDF) 1979–82, Attaché Dept of Hydrocarbons 1982–83, Head Uranium Section 1983–85, Asst Head Fuel Dept 1986–87, Head 1987–88, Asst Dir, Head Marketing Devt Service 1988–89, Dir Devt and Commercial Strategy 1989–92; Pres, Dir-Gen Société Générale pour les Techniques Nouvelles (SGN) 1992–97; Pres Eurisys, Pres, Dir-Gen Eurisys Consultants 1993–97; Dir Gen Global Market Utilities, Cap Gemini 1998–; Pres European Nuclear Soc

1992–93; mem American Nuclear Soc, Bd French Nuclear Energy Soc, French Lighting Asscn, Bd French Electricity Cttee, French Soc of Electricians and Electronics Engineers, Admin Council French Energy Inst, Parisian Urban Heating Co; Chevalier de la Légion d'Honneur; Chevalier de l'Ordre Nat du Mérite 1991. *Publication:* Les centrales nucléaires 1988. *Leisure interests:* alpine skiing, modern painting, theatre, cinema, opera. *Address:* Cap Gemini, 76 ave Kléber, 75016 Paris, France (Office); 7 ave de Suresnes, 92110 Saint Cloud, France (Home).

LEWIS, Denise, MBE; British athlete; b 27 Aug 1972, West Bromwich; d of Joan Lewis. *Career:* Heptathlete; Commonwealth Champion 1994; Bronze Medallist, Olympic Games, Atlanta, GA, USA 1996; British record holder; Silver Medallist, World Athletics Championships 1997; Gold Medal European Championships 1998; Gold Medal Commonwealth Championships 1998; Silver Medal World Championship 1999; New Commonwealth Record (6,831 points) 2000; Gold Medallist, Olympic Games, Sydney 2000; British Athletics Writers Female Athlete of the Year 1998, 2000; Sports Writers Asscn Sportswoman of the year 2000. *Address:* c/o MTC (UK) Ltd, 20 York St, London W1U 6PU, UK. *Telephone:* (20) 7935-8000; *Fax:* (20) 7935-8066; *E-mail:* info.mtc-uk.com (Office); *Internet:* www.mtc-uk.com (Office).

LEWIS, Donna; British singer-songwriter; b Cardiff. *Career:* Fmrly piano player in bars; now singer-songwriter; appeared on David Letterman and Jay Leno TV shows, USA. *Recordings include:* Album: Now In A Minute 1996; Single: I Love You Always Forever. *Address:* c/o Atlantic Records, 35 Portman Square, London W1, UK. *Telephone:* (20) 7467-2550; *Fax:* (20) 7629-4947.

LEWIS, Juliette; American actress; b 21 June 1973, Fernando Valley, CA; d of Geoffrey and Glenis Batley Lewis. *Films include:* My Stepmother is an Alien 1988, Meet the Hollowheads 1989, National Lampoons Christmas Vacation 1989, Cape Fear 1991, Crooked Hearts 1991, Husbands and Wives 1992, Kalifornia 1993, One Hot Summer, That Night 1993, What's Eating Gilbert Grape 1993, Romeo is Bleeding 1993, Natural Born Killers 1994, Evening Star 1996, From Dusk Till Dawn 1996, The Audition, Full Tilt Boogie 1997, The Other Sister 1999, The 4th Floor 1999, Way of the Gun 2000; *TV appearances include:* Homefires (mini-series), I Married Dora 1988, Too Young To Die (film) 1989, A Family For Joe 1990. *Address:* c/o William Morris Agency, 151 S El Camino Blvd, Beverly Hills, CA 90212, USA.

LEWIS, Sarah; British international organisation executive; b 29 Nov 1964; d of John and Pamela Littman (née Hart) Lewis; partner Jorne Kasine. *Education:* City of London School for Girls and Ecole de Ski Etude (Moutiers, France). *Career:* Trainee Kent Imports Ltd (Ski Equipment Importers) 1981–83; Marketing and Promotions Asst Kent Schuss Ltd 1983–88; f own co Consultanski (public relations consulting) 1989–91; Alpine Dir British Ski Fed 1990–94; Co-ordinator for Continental Cups, Int Ski Fed (FIS), Switzerland 1994–98, Dir FIS 1998–2000, Sec-Gen 2000; Sec Asscn of Int Winter Sports Feds 2000–; mem British Alpine Ski Team 1982–88, represented Britain at World Skiing Championships (Crans, Montana) 1987, Olympic Games (Calgary, Canada) 1988; British Slalom Champion 1983; Lowlanders Slalom Champion 1984, 1986, 1988. *Leisure interests:* Arsenal Football Club, all sports as spectator, communications/Internet. *Address:* Marc Hodler House, Blochstrasse 2, 3653 Oberhofen/Thunersee, Switzerland. *Telephone:* (33) 2446161; *Fax:* (33) 2446171; *E-mail:* lewis@fisski.ch.

L'HEUREUX-DUBÉ, Claire, BA, LL L; Canadian judge; b 7 Sept 1927, Québec City; m Arthur Dubé 1957 (died 1978); one s (died 1994) one d. *Education:* Monastère des Ursulines (Rimouski), Collège Notre-Dame de Bellevue and Laval Univ (Québec). *Career:* Called to the Bar, PQ 1952; Partner Bard, L'Heureux and Philippon 1952–69, Sr Partner L'Heureux, Philippon, Garneau, Tourigny, St-Arnaud and Assocs 1969–73; Counsellor 1968–70; QC 1969; Puisne Judge Superior Court of Québec 1973, Supreme Court of Canada 1987–; Judge Court of Appeals, Québec 1979; fmr Prof Dept of Mines and Metallurgy, Laval Univ, Québec; lecturer in field; Vice-Pres Int Bd, Int Comm of Jurists 1992–98, Pres 1998; mem Canadian Bar Asscn, Canadian Inst for the Admin of Justice, Int Fed of Women Lawyers, Québec Asscn of Univ Women, American Law Inst 1995; Hon mem American Coll of Trial Lawyers 1995; assoc mem Int Academia of Comparative Law 1992;

mem Nat Council, Canadian Human Rights Foundation 1980–84; mem Bd of Dirs, Int Soc on Family Law 1977, Vice-Pres 1982–88; mem American Law Inst 1995; contribs to professional journals; Hon LL D (Dalhousie) 1981, (Laval) 1984, (Ottawa) 1988; Dr hc (Montréal) 1983, (Québec) 1989, (Toronto) 1994, (Queen's Univ) 1995, (Gonzaga Univ) 1996, (Windsor) 2000, (York) 2001; Medal Int Year of the Family, Québec 1994; Prix de la Justice, Canadian Inst for the Admin of Justice 1997; Margaret Brent Women Lawyers of Achievement Award, ABA Comm on Women in the Profession 1998. *Address:* Supreme Court of Canada, Wellington St, Ottawa, ON K1A 0J1, Canada. *Telephone:* (613) 996-9218; *Fax:* (613) 952-1882.

LI KEYU; Chinese fashion and costume designer; b 15 May 1929, Shanghai; m Yuan Mao 1955. *Education:* Cen Acad of Fine Arts. *Career:* Chief Costume Designer of Cen Ballet; Deputy Dir Chinese Soc of Stage Design; mem Bd All-China Artists' Asscn, Chinese Dancers' Asscn; Deputy Dir China Export Garments Research Centre; Sr Consultant Beijing Inst of Fashion Tech; has designed costumes for many works including Swan Lake, Le Corsaire, The Maid of the Sea, The Fountain of Bakhchisaria, La Esmeralda, The Red Detachment of Women, The East is Red, The New Year Sacrifice (Ministry of Culture Costume Design Prize), Zigeunerweisen (Ministry of Culture Costume Design Prize), Othello (for Peking Opera, Beijing's Costume Design Prize), Tang Music and Dance, Zheng Ban Qiao, La Péri (for Houston Ballet, TX, USA); winner sole Costume Design Prize, 4th Japan World Ballet Competition, Osaka 1984; has published two vols of sketches. *Address:* 21 Gong-jian Hutong, Di An-Men, Beijing 100009, People's Republic of China. *Telephone:* (1) 4035474.

LI LI; Chinese television director and producer; b 5 Jan 1944, Beijing; d of Cao Yu and Li Yu Ru. *Education:* Cen Acad of Drama (Beijing). *Career:* Dir Shanghai TV; has directed numerous films and TV serials; Red Banner Award 1979. *Films include:* Qin Wen (Fei Tein Award), Family Air (Fei Tein Award, Gold Falcon Award); *TV serials include:* Family, Spring, Autumn (Gold Falcon Award), Yang Nai Wu and Xiao Bai Cai (Fei Tein Award). *Leisure interests:* opera, kun qu. *Address:* Shanghai Television Co (Dianshi Tai), Nanjing Xi Lu 651, Shanghai, People's Republic of China. *Telephone:* (21) 2565899; *Fax:* (21) 2587854.

LI LIN; Chinese physicist; b 31 Oct 1923, Beijing; d of J. S. Lee and Lin Hsu; m C. L. Tsou 1949; one d. *Education:* Univs of Birmingham and Cambridge (UK). *Career:* Returned to China 1951; researcher Mechanics Lab, Academia Sinica 1951–57, Research Fellow Physics Inst 1978–, mem Dept of Maths and Physics 1980–; Research Fellow Beijing Atomic Energy Inst 1958; mem Chinese Acad of Sciences; winner of several collective prizes. *Leisure interest:* music. *Address:* Institute of Physics, Chinese Acad of Sciences, POB 603, Beijing 100080, People's Republic of China. *Telephone:* (10) 82649175 (Office); (10) 68422342 (Home); *Fax:* (10) 82649531 (Office); *E-mail:* lilin@aphy.iphy.ac.cn (Office); annalee@yeah.com (Home).

LI LINGWEI; Chinese badminton player; b 1964. *Career:* Winner women's singles title, 3rd World Badminton Championships, Copenhagen 1982; Winner Women's Singles and Women's Doubles (with Wu Dixi) 5th ALBA World Cup, Jakarta 1985; Winner Women's Singles, World Badminton Grand Prix, Tokyo 1985, Dunhill China Open Badminton Championship, Nanjing 1987, Malaysian Badminton Open, Kuala Lumpur 1987, World Grand Prix, Hong Kong 1988, China Badminton Open 1988, Danish Badminton Open, Odense 1988, All-England Badminton Championships 1989, 6th World Badminton Championships, Jakarta; elected seventh in list of ten best Chinese athletes 1984. *Address:* China Sports Federation, Beijing, People's Republic of China.

LI SHIJI; Chinese opera singer; b May 1933, Suzhou Co, Jiangsu Prov. *Career:* Head First Troupe, Beijing Opera Theatre 1989–; mem 7th CPPCC 1987–92, 8th 1993–. *Address:* Beijing Opera Theatre, 11 Hufang Rd, Xuanwu District, Beijing 100052, People's Republic of China.

LI WEIKANG; Chinese opera singer; b Feb 1947, Beijing. *Education:* China Acad of Traditional Operas. *Career:* Dir Troupe No 2, China Peking Opera Co, performer Beijing Peking Opera Co 1987–; Plum

Blossom Award 1984; Gold Album Award, for Lead Role at Nat Theatrical Performance Ass; Gold Prize at Nat Mei Lanfang Grand Competition; Gold Eagle Award for Best Actress. *Address:* Beijing Opera Company, Beijing, People's Republic of China.

LI YIYI; Chinese metallurgist; b 20 Oct 1933, Suzhou, Jiangsu Prov. *Education:* Beijing Univ of Iron and Steel Tech. *Career:* China's first female workshop chief in charge of a blast furnace in 1950s; researcher Metal Research Inst, Chinese Acad of Sciences 1962–, Vice-Dir 1986, Dir 1990–98; mem 4th Presidium, Chinese Acad of Sciences 2000–; Fellow Chinese Acad of Sciences; Vice-Pres Chinese Soc for Metals and Chinese Materials Research Society; developed five series of hydrogen-resistant steels; Nat Science and Tech Advancement Award (twice); Chinese Acad of Sciences Award for Advancement in Science and Tech (three times). *Publications:* more than 150 research papers. *Address:* Metal Research Institute, Chinese Academy of Sciences, 72 Wenhua Rd, Shenyang, 110015, People's Republic of China. *Telephone:* (24) 3843531; *Fax:* (24) 3891320; *E-mail:* yyli@imr.ac.cn.

LI YUANCHAO; Chinese politician; b 1950, Lianshui Co, Jiangsu Prov. *Education:* Shanghai Fudan Univ. *Career:* Joined CCP 1978; Sec Communist Youth League 1983; Sec Shanghai Br of the Communist Youth League 1983; Dir Nat Cttee for Young Pioneers' work under the Communist Youth League 1984; Vice-Chair Youth Fed 1986–; Deputy Dir First Bureau, Information Office 1993–, Cen Office for Overseas Publicity 1994–; Vice-Minister of Information Office, State Council 1993–96, of Culture 1996–2000; Vice-Sec CCP Jiangsu Prov Cttee 2000–; Vice-Chair Women and Youth Cttee; mem CPPCC 7th Nat Cttee 1988–. *Address:* Chinese Communist Party, Jiangsu Provincial Committee, Nanjing, People's Republic of China.

LIBERAKI, Margarita; Greek writer; b 22 April 1919, Athens; d of Themistocle and Sapho (née Fexi) Liberaki; m Georges Karapanos 1941 (divorced); one d. *Education:* Univ of Athens. *Career:* Lives in Paris and Greece, writes in Greek and French; plays performed at Festival d'Avignon (France), Festival of Athens. *Publications include:* Fiction: The Trees 1947, The Straw Hats (televised 1995) 1950, Trois étés 1950, The Other Alexander 1952, The Mystery 1976; Plays: Kandaules' Wife 1955, The Danaids 1956, L'autre Alexandre 1957, Le saint prince 1959, La lune a faim 1961, Sparagmos 1965, Le bain de mer 1967, Erotica 1970, Zoe 1985; Film scripts: Magic City 1953, Phaedra 1961, Three Summers (TV series) 1996, Diaspora 1999. *Leisure interest:* painting. *Address:* 7 rue de L'Eperon, 75006 Paris, France; 2 Strat Sindesmou, Athens 10673, Greece. *Telephone:* (1) 46-33-05-92 (Paris); (1) 3624968 (Athens).

LIBERIA-PETERS, Maria Philomina; Netherlands Antilles politician; b 20 May 1941, Curaçao; d of the late James Louis Peters and of Mable Albertine Hassell; m Niels Francisco 1972; one s one d. *Education:* Univ of Netherlands Antilles. *Career:* Head Teacher 1962–67; Supervisor early childhood public schools 1967–72, Roman Catholic schools for early childhood 1972–75; Teacher Training Coll for Teachers, Curaçao 1972–75; Commr Exec Council Local Govt of Curaçao 1975–80, 1983–84; mem Legis Council 1975–80; Early Childhood Schools Insp, Ministry of Educ 1981–; Mem Staten (Parl) 1982–, Minister of Econ Affairs 1982–83, Prime Minister 1984–85, 1988–93; Leader Nat Volkspartij (Nat People's Party) 1982–94; Chair Bd Standing Regional Conf for the Integration of Women in the Devt of Latin America and the Caribbean, ECLAC 1991–94; Founder-mem Business and Professional Women's Club, Steering Cttee for Women's Orgs in the Netherlands Antilles; awards include Grootofficier in de Orde van Oranje Nassau (Netherlands), Gran-Cruz del Orden de Boyaca (Colombia), Gran Cordon en el Orden del Libertador (Venezuela), Sol de Carabobo Primera Clase (Venezuela). *Leisure interests:* watching sport, walking. *Address:* c/o Partido Nashonal di Pueblo, Willemstad, Curaçao, Netherlands Antilles. *Telephone:* (9) 613988; *Fax:* (9) 672473.

LICHTMAN, Judith L., BS, LL B; American lawyer and organization executive; b 23 July 1940; m Elliott Lichtman; two d. *Education:* Univ of Wisconsin. *Career:* Fmrly at the Urban Coalition and US Comm on Civil Rights; Legal Adviser to Puerto Rico; joined Women's Legal Defense Fund 1974, apptd Pres 1988; Founder-mem Alliance for Justice, mem Bd of Dirs; currently Pres Nat Partnership for Women &

Families; mem Dist of Columbia Judicial Nomination Comm, Bd of Dirs Int Women's Health Network; named one of 100 Most Powerful Women in Washington, Washingtonian magazine 1989; Sara Lee Corpn Frontrunner Award, Humanities 1989; Hannah G. Solomon Award, Nat Council of Jewish Women 1992. *Address:* National Partnership for Women & Families, 1875 Connecticut Ave, NW, Suite 710, Washington, DC 20009, USA. *Telephone:* (202) 986-2600; *Fax:* (202) 986-2539; *E-mail:* info@nationalpartnership.org; *Internet:* www.nationalpartnership.org.

LIDDELL, Rt Hon Helen, PC; British politician; b 6 Dec 1950; d of Hugh and of the late Bridget Lawrie Reilly; m Alistair Henderson Liddell 1972; one s one d. *Education:* St Patrick's High School, Coatbridge and Strathclyde Univ. *Career:* Head Econ Dept Scottish TUC 1971–75, Asst Sec 1975–76; Econ Corresp BBC Scotland 1976–77; Scottish Sec Labour Party 1977–88; Dir Personnel and Public Affairs, Scottish Daily Record and Sunday Mail Ltd 1988–92; Chief Exec Business Venture Programme 1993–94; MP for Monklands E 1994–97, for Airdrie and Shotts 1997–, Opposition spokeswoman on Scotland 1995–97; Econ Sec HM Treasury 1997–98, Minister of State Scottish Office 1998–99; Minister of Transport 1999–2001; Sec of State for Scotland 2001–. *Publications:* Elite 1990. *Leisure interests:* cooking, hill-walking, music, writing. *Address:* House of Commons, Westminster, London, SW1A 0AA, UK. *Telephone:* (20) 7219 3000.

LIDMAN, Sara; Swedish writer; b 30 Dec 1923; d of Andreas and Jenny (née Lundman) Lidman. *Education:* Uppsala Univ. *Career:* Has written several books dealing with life in sparsely populated areas including N Sweden, SA 1960, Kenya 1962–64 and N Viet Nam 1965. *Publications include:* Tjärdalen 1953, Hjortronlandet 1955, Aina 1956, Regnspiran 1958, Bära mistel 1960, Jag o min son 1961, Med fem diamanter 1964, Samtal i Hanoi 1966, Gruva 1968, Vänner o uvänner 1969, Marta, Marta 1970, Fåglarna i Nam Dinh 1973, Libretto till två baletter, Inga träd skall väcka dig 1974, Balansen 1975, Din tjänare hör 1977.

LIEBERKNECHT, Christine; German politician; b 7 May 1958, Weimar; m Martin Lieberknecht 1978; one s one d. *Education:* Friedrich-Schiller Univ (Jena). *Career:* Curate (Thuringia) 1982; Pastor (Weimar) 1984–90; mem Thuringia Landtag (Regional Ass) 1991–, Pres Oct 1999–; Regional Minister of Religion 1990–92, of Fed and European Affairs 1992–94; Minister for Fed Affairs, State Chancellor's Office 1994–99; mem Fed Cttee Christlich Demokratische Union (CDU) 1991–99, Vice Chair CDU/CSU Evangelical Working Group 1991–; mem Bd Konrad-Adenauer Foundation; mem Synod German Evangelical Church (EKD); Chair Soc of Thuringian Castles and Gardens; mem Cttee European Movt of Germany 1993–, German Soc for Foreign Affairs 1994–; Pres Thuringia Ramblers Asscn. *Leisure interests:* Painting, music, walking. *Address:* Arnstadter Str 51, 99096 Erfurt, Thüringen, Germany. *Telephone:* (361) 3772001; *Fax:* (361) 3772009; *E-mail:* liberknecht@landtag.thueringen.de; *Internet:* www.landtag.thueringen.du.

LIEBERMANN, Berta R.; Austrian poet; b 16 March 1921, Glashütten; m Albert Liebermann 1967. *Career:* Hon D LITT (Albert Einstein Acad, MO, USA); prizes include Salsomaggiore award 1982, Albert-Einstein-Medaille (USA) 1990. *Publications include:* Heimweh, Planet der Glücklichkeit, Traumnetz der silberner Spinne, Spätlicht, Verwehte Spuren, Rückruf der Vergangenheit, Roter Oleander, Urlaute der Schöpfung, Urwind der Frühe, Verstreute Blüten III, Gespräche mit einem Engel; contribs to newspapers on the arts. *Leisure interests:* palaeontology, genealogy, anti-vivisection. *Address:* Kieferbachstr 6, 83088 Kiefersfelden, Germany. *Telephone:* (8033) 8104.

LIEFLAND, Erika; German sculptor; b 4 Dec 1936; m Reinhard Liefland 1963; two s one d. *Education:* Engineering Coll (Mannheim). *Career:* Has exhibited work in over 50 European towns; Stipendium Inst Italiano di Cultura 1990; First Prize for Ceramics, German-American Soc. *Leisure interest:* trips around the world. *Address:* Talstr 11, 64367 Mühltal, Germany. *Telephone:* (6151) 57998.

LIENEMANN, Marie-Noëlle; French politician; b 12 July 1951, Belfort; d of Pierre and Françoise Lienemann; m Patrice Finel 1976; one s one d. *Education:* High School of Tech Educ and Univ of Paris IX (Paris-Sud). *Career:* Deputy Mayor of Massy (PS) 1972–89; mem PS

Man Cttee 1978, Exec Office 1981–89, Deputy Nat Sec 1983–85; mem Essonne Co Council 1979–89; MEP 1984–88, 1997–, Vice-Pres EP 1999–; mem Nat Ass (Parl) for Essonne 1988; Minister for Housing 1992–93, Sec of State for Housing March 2001–; Mayor of Athis-Mons 1989–; mem Econ and Social Council 1994; Vice-Pres Asscn of Mayors in France 1996–. *Publications include:* Pour réussir à gauche (jtly) 1983, La Fracture 1991, Coup de gueule contre la technocratie. Les cannibales de l'Etat 1994, Madame le maire 1997, 7 jours dans la vie d'Attika 2000. *Leisure interests:* knitting, cinema. *Address:* Mairie, place du Général de Gaulle, 91200 Athis-Mons, France; 24 avenue du Chateau de Chaiges, 91200 Athis-Mons, France (Home). *Telephone:* (1) 69-54-54-21; *Fax:* (1) 69-54-54-57; *E-mail:* mlienemann@mairie-athis-mons.fr.

LIEPA, Ilza; Russian/Latvian ballet dancer; b 22 Nov 1963; d of Maris Liepa and Margarita Zhigunova; m Vladislovas A. Paulius. *Education:* Moscow Choreographic School of Bolshoi Theatre. *Career:* Joined Bolshoi Ballet 1981–, then Soloist; debut in UK concert Stars of World Ballet, Covent Garden (Firebird); tours with Bolshoi Theatre in most countries of Europe and America, independently toured in Argentina, Greece, Taiwan, Japan; Artistic Dir Golden Age Asscn 1994–98; f Maris Liepa Foundation; awards include Prize of Russian Trade Unions; Chaika 2000; Crystal Turandote 2001; Distinguished Artist of Russia, Hon Artist of Russian Fed. *Ballets include:* Legend about Love, Romeo and Juliet, The Firebird, Don Quixote, Corsair, Raimonda, Prince Igor, Your Sister and Captive, Catherine II in The Empress's Dream; *Films include:* The Shining World 1983, Mikhailo Lomonossov 1984, Bambi's Childhood 1984, Lermontov 1986, Lomononov 1987, Vision of the Rose 1989, Return of the Firebird 1994, Empire Under Strike 2000; *Plays include:* Your Sister and Captive 1999, The Empress's Dream 2000; *Publication:* Circle of the Sun (play) 2000. *Leisure interest:* cats. *Address:* Bryusov per 17, kv 12, 103009 Moscow, Russian Federation; Bolshoi Theatre, Teatralnaya pl 5, Moscow, Russian Federation. *Telephone:* (095) 229-23-88; *Fax:* (095) 229-23-88; *E-mail:* vpaulius@stk.mmtel.ru.

LIÉVANO DE MÁRQUEZ, Mirna, MBA; Salvadorean economist; b 1 July 1954, San Salvador; d of Rodolfo Liévano and Norma de Morán; m Jose Márques; one d. *Education:* Universidad Centroamericana José Simeón Cañas (San Salvador) and Univ de Louvain (Belgium). *Career:* Pres Social Investment Fund (FIS); Minister of Planning and Co-ordination of Econ and Social Devt 1990; Gov EBRD and Inter-American Devt Bank; Deputy Dir then Dir Econ and Social Research Dept, FUSADES; Pres MARCABLE; Dir Escuela Superior de Economía y Negocios; Economist of the Year 1995. *Publication:* El Salvador un pais en transición. *Leisure interest:* dance. *Address:* Escuela Superior de Economía y Negocios, Urb La Cima II, final Av Principal Pasaje 7, Políg A, San Salvador, El Salvador. *Telephone:* 273-1031; *Fax:* 372-8843.

LIFSHITZ, Chava (Eva), PH D; Israeli professor of chemistry; b 26 March 1936, Vienna, Austria; d of Salomon and Sara (née Müller) Wolf; m Assa Lifshitz 1958; two d one s. *Education:* Hebrew Univ of Jerusalem. *Career:* Mem Israeli Army 1954, 1958–61; Research Assoc Cornell Univ, Ithaca, NY, USA 1961–63; Lecturer in Chem Studies Hebrew Univ of Jerusalem 1963–76, Chair 1972–76, Prof 1976–, apptd Chair Inst of Chem 1994; Visiting Scientist Aeronautical Research Lab, OH, USA 1969–70, Cornell Univ, USA 1969, Wright Patterson AF Base, OH 1969–70, 1972, Wright State Univ, OH 1976–77; mem Israeli Bd of Higher Educ 1986–91, American Soc for Mass Spectrometry, American Chem Soc, Asscn of Profs for Political and Econ Strength in Israel; has written over 180 articles for scientific journals; Koltoff Prize, Israeli Inst of Tech 1985; Sherman Chair in Physical Chem, The Archie Sherman Charitable Trust 1989; Max Planck Research Award 1991. *Leisure interests:* classical music, theatre. *Address:* Hebrew University of Jerusalem, Dept of Physical Chem, Givat Ram, Jerusalem 91904, Israel; 1 Granoth St, Jerusalem 93706, Israel (Home). *Telephone:* (2) 6585866; *Fax:* (2) 6522472.

LIFSHITZ, Lea, BFA; Israeli painter; d of Ga Nahom Lasky; m Herzel Lifshitz; two s. *Education:* Univ of Tel-Aviv. *Career:* Solo exhibitions include Chemerinsky Gallery, Tel-Aviv 1972, Union Int Club, Frankfurt, Germany 1973, Cornell Univ, Ithaca, NY, USA 1976, Int Gallery, New York 1976, Ltd Edns Gallery, Beverly Hills, CA, USA

1979, 1986, 1989, Glucksmann Gallery, Zurich, Switzerland 1982, 1986, Tipheret Gallery 1985; group exhibitions include House of Artists, Tel-Aviv 1969, 1972–73, 1984, Bezalel, Jerusalem 1974, Cultural Israeli-American Art, New York 1975, Zohar Gallery, Toronto, Canada 1982 and Jourdan Gallery, Montréal, Canada 1982; works held in perm collections including Coca Cola Bldg, Tel-Aviv, Cornell Univ, various Israeli politicians and in USA, Canada, Germany, Switzerland, UK and Israel; named Creative Woman of the Year 1976.

LIGON, Janie, MBA; American business executive. *Education:* Northwestern Univ (Evaston, IL). *Career:* Business Planning Man Del Monte; Man Consultant McKinsey, Chicago, IL; Joined Levi Strauss 1980, Merchandising Man for women's jeans world-wide, Dir of Operations 1986–91, Nat Sales Man (Womenswear), Levi Strauss N America, Gen Man Levi Strauss UK 1994. *Address:* Levi Strauss UK, Moulton, Northants, UK.

LIJADU, Olayinka; Nigerian business executive; b April 1934, Lagos; five c. *Education:* CMS Grammar School and King's Coll (Lagos). *Career:* Joined Royal Exchange Assurance Co 1954, Exec Asst Fire Dept 1963–70; Fire Man Nat Insurance Corpn of Nigeria (NICON) 1970, later Deputy Gen Man, Man Dir (acting) 1975–77, Man Dir 1977–89; Visiting Lecturer in Insurance, W African Insurance Inst, Monrovia, Liberia; Dir NAL Merchant Bank, Daily Times of Nigeria, Nigeria Insurance Co; Treas W Africa Insurance Cos Asscn; Assoc Chartered Insurance Inst, London; Assoc mem Inst of Arbitrators (UK), Nigerian Inst of Management; mem Exec Cttee African Insurance Org, Nairobi, Kenya, Insurance Inst of Nigeria since 1965, later Chair Editorial Cttee and Fellow. *Leisure interests:* music, table tennis, drama.

LIJN, Liliane; American artist; b 22 Dec 1939, New York; d of Herman and Helena (née Kustanowicz) Segall; m 1st Takis Vassilakis 1961; one s; m 2nd Stephen Weiss 1968; one s one d. *Education:* Univ of Paris (Sorbonne). *Career:* Artist, Paris until 1966, London 1966–; has been exhibiting internationally since 1963; exhibitions include Electra, Musée d'Art Moderne de la Ville de Paris 1983, 20th Century Drawings and Watercolours, Victoria and Albert Museum, London 1984, Heads, Galerie Peter Ludwig, Cologne, Germany 1985, Livres des Artistes, Centre Nat d'Art et de Culture Georges-Pompidou, Paris 1985, Technologia e Informatica, Venice Biennale, Italy 1986, Fischer Fine Art, London 1987, Images du Futur 88, Cité des Arts et des Nouvelles Technologies de Montréal, Licht und Transparenz, Museum Bellerive, Zurich, Switzerland, Artec 89 Int Biennale, Japan, Chagall to Kitaj: Jewish Experience in 20th Century Art, Barbican Art Gallery, London 1990, Le Livre Illustré, Bibliothèque Municipale, Besançon, France 1991, Les Artistes et La Lumière, Le Manège, Reims, France 1991; comms include Birchwood Science Park, Warrington Devt Corp 1981, Norwich Cen Library 1982, Nm Schroder, Poole 1988, Labs of the Govt Chemist, London 1988, St Mary's Hosp, Isle of Wight 1990, Inner Light, Prudential Insurance HQ, Reading 1993, Dragon's Dance, Marks & Spencer, Cardiff 1993, Earth Sea Light Koan, St Mary's Hosp, Isle of Wight 1997; works featured in perm collections include Tate Gallery and Victoria & Albert Museum, London, Arts Council of GB, Musée de la Ville de Paris, Museum of Modern Art, New York, Chicago Inst, Bibliothèque Nat, Paris, Museum of Fine Arts, Bern, Glasgow Museum, Museum of NSW, Australia, City Art Gallery, Manchester, Henry Moore Foundation, Leeds; LFPA Production Award for 'Look A Doll' (video). *Publications:* Six Throws of the Oracular Keys 1982, Crossing Map 1983, Her Mother's Voice 1996, First Words 2000. *Leisure interests:* cooking, walking, gardening, travelling, mythology, physics. *Address:* 99 Camden Mews, London NW1 9BU, UK. *Telephone:* (20) 7485-8524; *Fax:* (20) 7485-8524; *E-mail:* lijn@lineone .net; *Internet:* www.lijn.net.

LIM, Catherine, PH D; Singaporean writer; one s one d. *Education:* Regional English Language Centre. *Career:* Writer, first book published 1978. *Publications include:* Little Ironies: Stories of Singapore 1978, Or Else: The Lightning God and Other Stories 1980, The Serpent's Tooth 1982, The Shadow of a Dream: Love Stories of Singapore 1987, Love's Lonely Impulses 1992, Deadline for Love & Other Stories 1992, The Best of Catherine Lim 1993, The Woman's Book of Superlatives 1993, Meet Me on the Queen Elizabeth II 1993, The Bondmaid 1997, The Teardrop Story Woman 1998. *Address:* 5 Upper St Martin's Lane, London, WC2H 9EA, UK.

LIMBACH, Jutta; German judge. *Career:* Pres fed Constitutional Court 1994–. *Address:* Bundesverfassungsgericht (Federal Constitutional Court), 76131 Karlsruhe, Schlossbezirk 3, Postfach 1771, Germany. *Telephone:* (721) 91010; *Fax:* (721) 9101382.

LIMERICK, Countess of, **Sylvia Rosalind Pery,** CBE, MA; British organization executive; b 7 Dec 1935; d of Maurice Stanley Lush; m Viscount Glentworth (now 6th Earl of Limerick) 1961; two s one d. *Education:* St Swithun's (Winchester) and Lady Margaret Hall (Oxford). *Career:* Research Asst Foreign Office 1959–62; Nat HQ Staff British Red Cross Soc 1962–66, Pres Kensington and Chelsea Div 1966–72, Vice-Pres London Br 1972–85, Chair British Red Cross 1985–95 (Hon Vice-Pres 1999), a Vice-Pres Int Fed of Red Cross and Red Crescent Socs 1993–97; Vice-Chair Community Health Council, S Dist of Kensington, Chelsea, Westminster Area 1974–77, Foundation for the Study of Infant Deaths 1971–; Pres Community Practitioners' and Health Visitors' Asscn 1984–; Chair Expert Group to investigate Cot Death Theories 1994–, Eastman Dental Inst 1996–99; Non-Exec Dir Univ Coll Hosps NHS Trust 1996–; Vice-Pres UK Cttee for UN Children's Fund 1979–, Nat Asscn for Maternal and Child Welfare 1985–90; mem Bd Govs St Bartholomew's Hosp 1970–74, Kensington, Chelsea and Westminster Area Health Authority 1977–82, Cttee of Man, Inst of Child Health 1976–96, Council King Edward's Hosp Fund 1981–89, Civil Service Occupational Health Service Advisory Bd 1989–92, Bd Eastman Dental Hosp SHA 1990–96; Trustee Child Accident Prevention Trust 1979–87; Hon FRCP; Hon Fellow Coll of Paediatrics and Child Health, Inst of Child Health 1996; Fellow Royal Soc of Medicine; Hon D LITT (Council for Nat Acad Awards) 1990. *Publication:* Sudden Infant Death: Patterns, Puzzles and Problems (jtly) 1985. *Leisure interests:* music, mountain-climbing, skiing. *Address:* 30 Victoria Rd, London W8 5RG, UK; Chiddinglye, W Hoathly, E Grinstead, W Sussex RH19 4QT, UK. *Telephone:* (20) 7937-0573 (London); (1342) 810214 (Sussex).

LIN, Maya, PH D; American architect and sculptor; b 5 Oct 1959, Athens, OH; d of Henry H. and Julia (née Chang) Lin. *Education:* Yale Univ. *Career:* Architectural designer Pers Forbes & Assocs (New York) 1986–87; pvt practice (New York) 1987–; mem Batey & Mack (San Francisco) 1983, Fumihiko Maki Assoc (Tokyo) 1985; mem Bd Nat Resources Defense Council. *Major projects include:* Vietnam Veterans Memorial, Washington; Peace Chapel, Juniata Coll, Pennsylvania; Women's Table, Yale Univ; Langston Hughes Library, Clinton, Tennessee; Civil Rights Memorial, Montgomery, AL; The Wave Field, Univ of Michigan Coll of Eng; Federal Courthouse, Manhattan; *Publications:* Maya Lin: Public/Private 1994, Boundaries 2000. *Address:* Maya Lin Studio, New York, USA.

LIN CHING-HSIA, LL B; Taiwanese film actress; b 1955, Taiwan. *Career:* Lived in California, USA 1979–81; now lives mainly in Hong Kong; has appeared in 82 films. *Films include:* Outside the Window, Dream Lovers, Police Story, Starry, Starry Night. *Address:* c/o Taiwan Cinema and Drama Association, 10/F, 196 Chunghua Rd, Sec 1, Taipei, Republic of China (Taiwan).

LINARES, Olga F., PH D; American anthropologist; b 10 Nov 1936, David, Panama; m Martin H. Moynihan (died 1996). *Education:* Vassar Coll and Harvard Univ. *Career:* Instructor in Anthropology, Harvard Univ 1964; Lecturer in Anthropology, Univ of Pennsylvania 1966–71; Visiting Asst Prof in Anthropology, Swarthmore Coll, PA 1967; Researcher, Sr Scientist Smithsonian Tropical Research Inst 1973; Visiting Assoc Prof, Univ of Texas at Austin 1974; Fellow Center for Advanced Study in the Behavioral Sciences, Stanford Univ, CA 1979–80, Visiting Prof Dept of Anthropology 1982; Overseas Visiting Fellow St John's Coll, Cambridge, UK 1986–87; Consultant Inst Nat de Cultura; Rep Consultant Comm Univ of Panama; numerous field trips to Panama, Senegal, Colombia, India, Malaysia, The Gambia and Indonesia; mem American Anthropological Asscn, AAAS, Soc for American Archaeology, Latin American Studies Asscn, Royal Anthropological Inst, Acad Panameña de la Historia, Asociación Panameña para el Avance de la Ciencia, NAS; Pres Asociación Panameña de Antropología. *Publications:* Power, Prayer and Production: The Jola of Casamance 1992; numerous articles in journals and books on the anthropology and archaeology of Panama and Cen America. *Address:*

Smithsonian Tropical Research Institute, Unit 0948, Apo AA 34002-0948, USA. *Telephone:* (507) 212-8083; *Fax:* (507) 212-8148; *E-mail:* linareso@tivoli.si.edu.

LINCOLN, Abbey; American jazz singer, actress and songwriter; b (Anna Marie Woolfridge) 1930, Jackson, MI; m Max Roach 1960 (deceased). *Career:* Singer with rhythm-and-blues bands, Honolulu, HI 1952, at Moulin Rouge club, CA (as Gaby Lee) 1955; performed at Lincoln Center, New York in a tribute to Billie Holiday, in a retrospective of the music of Max Roach and at the fifth annual Classical Jazz series 1991. *Films include:* The Girl Can't Help It, Nothing but a Man, For the Love of Ivy, Mo' Better Blues; *Recordings include:* Straight Ahead, The World Is Coming Down, You Gotta Pay the Band, Devil's Got Your Tongue.

LINCOLN, Blanche Lambert, BA; American politician; b 30 Sept 1960, Helena, Arkansas. *Education:* Randolph-Macon Woman's Coll. *Career:* Fmr mem of US House of Reps from Arkansas; Senator from Arkansas Jan 1999–; Democrat. *Address:* 359 Dirksen Senate Building, Washington, DC 20510, USA. *Telephone:* (202) 224-4843.

LINDBERG, Gunilla; Swedish international organisation executive; b 6 May 1947; m; two c. *Career:* Head Swedish Olympic Cttee 1969; Admin Chief Olympic Games (Winter and Summer) 1972, 1976, 1980; mem Bd Swedish Bob and Luge Fed 1976–78; Asst Sec-Gen Swedish Olympic Cttee 1984, Sec-Gen 1989–; Asst Chef de Mission and Chief of Press (Winter and Summer Games) 1984, 1988, 1992, 1994, 1996; mem Asscn of Nat Olympic Cttees (ANOC) Comm for the Preparation of the Olympic Games 1989, mem ANOC Exec Bd 1995; mem Int Olympic Cttee (IOC) 1996–, IOC Working Group on Women and Sport 1996–, IOC Press Comm 1997–, IOC Working Group on the Olympic Programme (for 2000 and 2004) 1997–, Exec Cttee 2000–. *Address:* Château de Vidy, Case Postale 356, 1007 Lausanne, Switzerland; Swedish Olympic Committee, Idrottens Hus, 12387 Farsta, Sweden.

LINDBLOM, Gunnel; Swedish actress and director; b 1931, Gothenburg. *Career:* Has worked with Ingmar Bergman in plays and films since c 1955. *Films include:* The Seventh Seal, Wild Strawberries, The Virgin Spring, Winter Light, The Silent, My Love is a Rose, Rapture, Loving Couples, Hunger, Woman of Darkness, The Girls, The Father, Brother Carl, Scenes From A Marriage, Misfire, Bakom, Jalusin; *Films directed include:* Paradise Place, Sally and Freedom, Summer Nights On The Planet Earth.

LINDÉN, Suvi, M SC; Finnish politician; b 19 April 1962, Helsinki; d of Lasse and Eine Lindén; m Timo Mehtala. *Education:* Univ of Oulu. *Career:* Silver Medal Finnish Jr Championship diving 1978; Bronze Medal Finnish Championship springboard 1978; Bronze Medal Finnish Championship women's diving 1997; Councillor Oulu City Council 1985–; MP 1995–; Minister of Culture April 1999–. *Leisure interest:* golf. *Address:* c/o Meritullinkatu 10, POB 293, 00171 Helsinki, Finland; POB 293, Helsinki, Finland. *Telephone:* (9) 13417412; *Fax:* (9) 13416978; *E-mail:* suvi.linden@minedu.fi; *Internet:* www.kokoomus.fi/linden.

LINDEPERG, Michèle; French politician; b 20 Sept 1941, Lyon; m Gérard Lindeperg 20 March 1961; one s one d. *Career:* Municipal Councillor for Grigny, MEP (PSE) 1994–99, mem Cttee on Civil Liberties and Int Affairs, Del for relations with the mem States of ASEAN, SE Asia and the Repub of Korea; mem Econ and Social Council 1999–. *Address:* 20 rue du Midi, 42000 Saint-Etienne, France.

LINDGREN, Astrid; Swedish writer; b 1907, Smoland; m 1931; one d. *Career:* Moved to Stockholm 1926; fmrly mem staff Raben and Sjogron publrs. *Publications include:* Pippi Longstocking, Bill Bergson Master Detective, The Bix Bullerby Children, Karleson On The Roof, Emil (series), Mio, My Mio, The Brothers Lionheart, Ronia The Robber's Daughter. *Address:* c/o Puffin Books, (Penguin Books), 27 Wrights Lane, London W8, UK.

LINDH, (Ylva) Anna Maria, BL; Swedish politician and youth worker; b 19 June 1957, Stockholm; d of Staffan and Nancy (née Westman) Lindh; m Bo Holmberg 1991; two s. *Education:* Sanobro School

(Enkoping) and Uppsala Univ. *Career:* Pres of the Nat Council of Swedish Youth 1980–83; mem Riksdag (Parl), mem Standing Cttee on Taxation 1982–85; Pres Govt Council of Alcohol and Drug Policy 1986–91; Pres Social Democratic Youth League 1984–90; Vice-Pres Int Union of Socialist Youth 1987–89; mem Exec Cttee Social Democratic Party 1991–; Vice-Mayor Stockholm City Council 1991–94; Pres Culture Cttee and Leisure Cttee 1991–94; Pres Cttee for Home Affairs, Party of European Socialists 1992–94; Minister of the Environment 1994–98, for Foreign Affairs 1998–; Pres Stockholm City Theatre 1991–94. *Leisure interests:* theatre, music, literature. *Address:* Ministry for Foreign Affairs, Gustav Adolfstorg 1, POB 16121, 103 39 Stockholm, Sweden. *Telephone:* (8) 405-10-00; *Fax:* (8) 723-11-76.

LINE, Frances Mary, OBE, FRSA; British broadcaster; b 22 Feb 1940; d of Charles Edward and Leoni Lucy (née Hendriks) Line; m James Lloyd 1972. *Education:* James Allen's Girls' School (London). *Career:* Joined BBC as a clerk/typist 1957–63, Radio Production Asst 1963–65, TV Production Asst 1966–67, Radio Producer 1967–73, Sr Radio Producer 1973–79, Chief Asst Radio Two 1979–83, Radio Four 1983–85, Head Radio Two Music Dept 1986–90, Controller Radio Two 1991–96; mem Council The Radio Acad (Vice-Chair 1988–89), Arts Minister's Cttee for Nat Music Day, Living Image Appeal Cttee; Hon Fellow Radio Acad 1996. *Leisure interests:* theatre, Sussex, happy-snaps. *Address:* 13 Naomi Close, Eastbourne, BN20 7UU, UK.

LINET, Christiane; Belgian environmentalist; b 29 April 1934; m (husband deceased). *Education:* Univ of Brussels. *Career:* With World Wildlife Fund (WWF) 1966–, Pres WWF Belgium 1992–99, mem Bd; Order of the Golden Ark (Netherlands) 1975; WWF Int Mem of Honour 1998. *Leisure interests:* skiing, water colours, golf, choral singing. *Address:* World Wildlife Fund, 608 Chaussée de Waterloo, 1050 Brussels, Belgium; Rue du Doyenne 110, 1180 Brussels, Belgium. *Telephone:* (2) 343-02-72; *Fax:* (2) 340-09-33.

LING-VANNERUS, Kerstin Margareta; Swedish business executive; b 19 Dec 1935; d of Herbert and Greta Hallin; m Ulf Ling-Vannerus 1957; one s one d. *Education:* Örebro School for Girls, Örebro Coll for Business and Admin (Sweden) and American Univ (Washington, DC, USA). *Career:* News Reporter Swedish Broadcasting Corpn 1956–57, Ed 1966–67, Producer 1971–80; Programme Dir, Skövde 1967–68, Västergötlands Tourist Traffic Asscn 1969–71; Marketing Dir Karlstad 1982–85; f Projectea (public relations and consulting co) 1987; Chair Swedish Broadcasting Corpn Regional Org 1972–75, Business and Professional Women 1970–76, 1982–86; mem Bd Int Fed of Business and Professional Women, Chair THEME Cttee 1987–91, Fundraising Cttee 1991–94, Membership Cttee, Baltic Region 1994–. *Publication:* Stiletik 1991. *Leisure interests:* travel, tennis, bridge, skiing, family. *Address:* Ynglingag 19, 113 47 Stockholm, Sweden; Liden 1, 456 32 Kungshamn, Sweden. *Telephone:* (8) 34 05 34; (523) 705 77; *Fax:* (8) 34 05 34.

LINI, Hilda; Ni-Vanuatu politician; b Pentecost Island; d of Harper and Jean Lini; m Jean-Marie Vaaganu; two c. *Career:* Mem Vanua'aku Party (fmrly New Hebridean Cultural Asscn) 1962–; est S Pacific Comm Women's Bureau, Noumea 1971; Ed Vanua'aku Viewpoints 1976, MP (first woman) 1987; Leader Del to sixth Nuclear-Free and Ind Pacific Conf, New Zealand 1990; Ed Pacific Island Profile 1990–91. *Address:* c/o Vanua'aku Party, Port Vila, Vanuatu.

LINTROP, Renita; Estonian film director; b 11 Dec 1955, Tallinn; m 1982; one d. *Education:* Tartu Univ. *Career:* Ed Estonian TV-film studio 1974–85; Story Ed animated films Tallinnfilm studio 1986–88, Dir Documentaries 1989–90; Script-writer and Dir SEE (ind film studio) 1991–; mem jury Tampere Int Film Festival 1995. *Works include:* The Palace 1982, The Youth 1984, This Catcher... 1987, The Hero of Our Time 1988, Cogito, ergo sum (First Prize for Short Film, Aurillac '90, France, Best Documentary of the Year, Estonia 1990) 1989, The Master 1989, To Shura (Jury Award, Pärnu Int Film Festival, Estonia 1990, Best Documentary, Tampere Int Film Festival, Finland 1991, Bronze Dragon, Krakow Int Film Festival, Poland 1991, Special Commendation, Melbourne Int Film Festival, Australia 1991, Cultural Year Prize, Estonia 1991, Audience Award for Best Short Film, Créteil Int Film Festival, France 1991) 1990, The Punishment (Grand Prix, St-Flour Int Film Festival, France 1992) 1992, The Circle 1993, Estonians

Life 1994, Too Tired to Hate 1995, Illusion of Safety 1996. *Leisure interests:* walking, reading. *Address:* Kalmistu tee 4–13, Tallinn 0012, Estonia. *Telephone:* (2) 446644; *Fax:* (2) 446644.

LION, (Emma) Elizabeth, L ÈS L; French civil servant; b 12 July 1944, Tunis, Tunisia; d of Raymond and Dolly (née Yana) Lizan; m Bernard Lion 1965; one s one d. *Education:* Schools in Tunis and Marseilles, Faculty of Letters (Lyons) and Ecole Practique des Hautes Etudes (Paris). *Career:* Joined Agence Nat pour l'Emploi 1972–77; Head of Dept Ministry of Labour 1977–81, ministerial cabinet 1981–86, 1988, Ministry of Social Affairs 1986–88, 1989–92, Rep to Interministerial Mission on Employment Initiatives 1992–93; Tech Advisor to Dir of Social Security, Ministry of Social Affairs (now Ministry of Employment) 1994–; Pres Service Social des Jeunes 1989–; Chevalier de l'Ordre Nat du Mérite 1990. *Leisure interests:* travel, exhibitions, theatre. *Address:* 1 ave Bugeaud, 75116 Paris, France. *Telephone:* (1) 47-27-46-34.

LIONAES, Aase; Norwegian politician; b 10 April 1907, Oslo; d of Erling and Anna Lionaes; m Kurt Jonas 1938; one d. *Education:* Univ of Oslo and LSE (UK). *Career:* Labour Mem Storting (Parl) 1953; Vice-Pres of the Lagting (Upper House) 1965–69, the Odelsting (Lower House) 1969–77; mem Govt Del to UN 1946–65; mem Nobel Peace Prize Cttee 1948, Pres 1968–79; Hon LL D (Oxford Coll, OH, USA). *Address:* Pans Vei nr 8, Ulvøya, N Oslo, Norway. *Telephone:* (2) 28-24-08.

LIPMAN, Maureen Diane, CBE; British actress; b 10 May 1946; d of the late Maurice and of Zelma Lipman; m Jack Morris Rosenthal 1973; one d one s. *Education:* Newland High School for Girls (Hull) and London Acad of Music and Dramatic Art. *Career:* Made professional acting debut Watford 1969; performed at Stables Theatre, Manchester 1970, Nat Theatre (Old Vic) 1971–73, RSC 1973; magazine columnist Options 1983–88, Riva, She 1988–92, Good Housekeeping 1993–; has appeared in numerous plays, films and TV series; has made 55 British Telecom commercials (TV Times Awards 1988); Hon D LITT (Hull) 1994, Hon MA (Salford) 1995; Columnist of the Year, IPA 1991. *Plays include:* The Knack 1969, The Front Page, Long Day's Journey Into Night, The Good Natur'd Man 1970–73, As You Like It 1973, Candida 1976, Outside Edge 1978, Chapter Two 1981, Meg and Mog 1982, On Your Way 1983, Messiah 1983, See How They Run (Laurence Olivier Award, Variety Club of GB Award) 1984, Wonderful Town (Variety Club of GB Award) 1986, Re: Joyce 1988–91, The Cabinet Minister 1992, Lost in Yonkers (Variety Club of Great Britain Award) 1994, The Sisters Rosensweig 1994, Oklahoma!, Peggy For You 2000, The Vagina Monologues 2001; *Films include:* Up The Junction 1969, Educating Rita 1983, Water 1984, Carry On Columbus 1992, Solomon and Gaenor 1998, Captain Jack 1999, The Discovery of Heaven 2000, The Pianist 2001; *TV appearances include:* The Evacuees, Smiley's People, The Knowledge, Rolling Home, Outside Edge, Love's Labour's Lost, Absurd Person Singular, Shift Work, Absent Friends, Agony, All In At No 20 (TV Times Award 1989), About Face 1989, 1990, Re: Joyce, Agony Again 1995, Eskimo Day 1996, Cold Enough For Snow, Oklahoma! (video); *Publications:* How Was It For You? 1985, Something To Fall Back On 1987, You Got An 'Ology? 1988, Thank You For Having Me 1990, When's It Coming Out? 1992, You Can Read Me Like A Book 1995, Lip Reading 1999. *Leisure interests:* films, walking, lying down, eating, pretending to exercise, radio. *Address:* c/o Conway Van Gelder Ltd, 18-21 Jermyn St, London, SW1Y 6HP, UK.

LIPOVSEK, Marjana; Austrian (b Yugoslav) opera singer; b 3 Dec 1946, Ljubljana, Yugoslavia. *Education:* Music Acad (Graz, Austria). *Career:* Joined Vienna State Opera, then Hamburg State Opera; has performed at leading European opera houses including Berlin, Madrid, Frankfurt, Germany, La Scala, Milan, Italy, Vienna State Opera and Bavarian State Opera, Munich, Germany; made int debut as recitalist Salzburg Festival 1985; Prix Spécial du Jury Nouvelle Acad du Disque Français, Gustav Mahler Gold Medal (Bavaria) 1993, (Vienna) 1996. *Operas include:* Così fan Tutte, The Ring, Aïda, Un Ballo in Maschera, The Merry Wives of Windsor, Orfeo ed Euridice, Il Trovatore, Khovanshchina, Wozzeck, Der Rosenkavalier; *Recordings include:* the Bach Passions, Gluck's Orfeo, Handel's Messiah, Beethoven's Choral Symphony (No 9), Wagner's Das Rheingold, Johann Strauss' Die Fledermaus and Frank Martin's Cornet (Grand Prix du Disque); *TV includes:* Carmen, Samson and Delila, Der Ring des Nibelungen, Die

Frau ohne Schatten, Tristan und Isolde. *Address:* c/o Artists Management Zürich, Rütistr 52, 8044 Zürich-Gockhausen, Switzerland. *Telephone:* (1) 8218957 (Office); *Fax:* (1) 8210127 (Office); *E-mail:* schuetz@artistsman.com.

LIPOWICZ, Irena Ewa, DR IUR; Polish politician; b 9 June 1953; d of Edmund and Maria (née Opara) Lipowicz. *Education:* Silesian Univ (Katowice), Univs of Tübingen and Heidelberg (Germany). *Career:* Tutor Law Faculty, Silesian Univ 1976; mem Solidarity 1980; mem Sejm (Parl, Democratic Union Party) 1991; has written two books and over 20 articles. *Leisure interests:* history, theatre, literature. *Address:* Grabowa 5A/14, 40-178 Katowice, Poland. *Telephone:* (3) 583694.

LISNYANSKAYA, Inna Lvovna; Russian writer; b 24 June 1928, Baku; m Semen I. Lipkin. *Career:* First works published 1949; contribs to literary almanack Metropole 1979; resigned from Union of Writers 1980 (membership restored 1989). *Publications include:* This Happened to Me 1957, Faithfulness 1958, Not Simply Love 1963, The Light of Grape 1978, Verse 1970–83 1984, On the Edge of Sleep 1984, The Circle 1985, Airy Layer 1990, Poetry 1991, After All 1994, The Lonely Gift 1995, The Box with a Triple Bottom (study on Without the Hero, poem by Akhmatova) 1995, Selected Poetry 2000. *Address:* 125315 Moscow, Usievicha ul 8, kv 16, Russian Federation. *Telephone:* (095) 155-75-98.

LISSAKERS, Karin Margareta, MA; American international civil servant; b 16 Aug 1944; m two c. *Education:* Univ of Ohio and Johns Hopkins Univ. *Career:* Mem staff Cttee on Foreign Relations, US Senate, Washington, DC 1972–78; Deputy Dir Econ Policy Planning Staff, US Dept of State 1978–80; Sr Assoc Carnegie Endowment for Int Peace (New York) 1981–83; Lecturer in Int Banking, Dir Int Business and Banking Programme, School of Int Public Affairs, Columbia Univ (NY) 1985–93; US Exec Dir IMF 1993–. *Publications:* Banks, Borrowers and the Establishment 1991; articles in professional journals. *Address:* International Monetary Fund, 700 19th St, NW, Room 13-320, Washington, DC 20431, USA.

LISTER, Marquita, M MUS; American opera singer; b 24 April 1961, Washington, DC. *Education:* New England Conservatory of Music and Oklahoma City Univ. *Career:* Has performed with opera cos in London, Houston (TX), Mexico, Portland (OR), Baltimore (MD), Berlin, San Francisco (CA), Utah, Pittsburgh (PA), Japan, Milan (Italy), Paris; concerts with Plácido Domingo 1991, Sir Neville Marriner and the Acad of St Martin in the Fields 1994, Keith Lockhart and the Boston Pops 1995–96, Leipzig Radio Orchestra 1995–96; Enid-Phillips Symphony Young Artist Award 1984; Wichita Symphony-Naftzger Young Artist Voice Award 1985; Stewart Awards-Eleanor Steber Music Foundation Award 1988; MacAllister Award 1989; Female Artist of the Year, Pittsburgh Opera 1995–96. *Operas include:* Porgy and Bess 1989, 1993, Carmen 1990, La Clemenza di Tito 1991, 1993, Aïda 1991, 1992, 1993, Falstaff 1992, Turandot 1992, I Pagliacci 1993. *Leisure interests:* walking, reading, pets, teaching. *Address:* c/o Caroline Woodfield, International Creative Management, 40 W 57th St, New York, NY 10019, USA. *Telephone:* (212) 556-6883; *Fax:* (212) 556-5647.

LISZCZ, Teresa, PH D; Polish politician and professor of law; b 26 May 1945, Choiny; d of Leon and Janina Pezda; m Leszek Jan Liszcz 1970. *Education:* Marie Curie-Skłowska Univ (Lublin) and Univ of Łódź. *Career:* Asst to Prof Lab Law Dept, Marie-Curie Skłowska Univ 1968–70, Prof of Law 1987–; mem Sejm (Parl, Centre Alliance) 1989–, Sec-of-State at the Chancellery of the Pres 1991, Chair Parl Legis Cttee; mem Lublin Scientific Asscn; Gold Cross of Merit 1989; has written over 80 articles on employment law and nat insurance. *Leisure interests:* mountain-climbing, cats, literature. *Address:* Pana Balcera 1/201, 20-631 Lublin, Poland. *Telephone:* (81) 554308.

LITTLE, Tasmin E., ARCM; British violinist; b 13 May 1965, London; d of George and Gillian Little; m Michael Hatch 1993. *Education:* Yehudi Menuhin School and Guildhall School of Music. *Career:* Studied with Lorand Fenyves in Canada; has performed with major orchestras including Leipzig Gewandhaus, Berlin Symphony, London Symphony, Royal Philharmonic (London), Hallé, Royal Liverpool Philharmonic, European Community Chamber Orchestra, Royal Danish and Stavanger Symphony; has given concerto and recital performances in the

UK, Europe, Scandinavia, South America, Hong Kong, Oman, South Africa, Australia, New Zealand, USA and Zimbabwe and has appeared at music festivals throughout the UK including the Proms since 1990; several TV appearances including BBC Last Night of the Proms 1995; Hon D LITT (Bradford) 1996; Gold Medal, Guildhall School of Music 1986; Woman of Tomorrow in the Arts, Cosmopolitan magazine 1990. *Recordings include:* Fratres, Tabula Rasa, The Lark Ascending, Bruch Concertos, Dvorak Concertos, Delius Double, Brahms and Sibelius Concertos, Saxton Concerto, Rubbra Concerto, Delius Concerto, Walton Concerto, George Lloyd Violin Sonatas. *Leisure interests:* theatre, cinema, swimming, languages. *Address:* c/o Askonas Holt Ltd, 27 Chancery Lane, London WC2A 1PF, UK. *Telephone:* (20) 7400-1700; *Fax:* (20) 7400-1799.

LITTLEWOOD, Joan (Maud); British theatre director and artist; b 6 Oct 1914, London. *Career:* Dir Theatre of Action, street theatre co, Manchester 1931–37; Founder Theatre Union, Manchester, introducing the Individual Work System 1937–39; freelance writer, banned from BBC and Entertainments Nat Service Asscn for political opinions 1939–45; Co-Founder Theatre Workshop 1945, Artistic Dir 1945–75, tours in UK and Europe with original works 1945–53, Theatre Royal with classics 1953–75, invited to Theatre of the Nations, Paris 1955–, transfers to West End, London and Broadway, New York 1960–61, Centre Culturel, Hammamet, Tunisia 1965–67, Image India, Calcutta, India 1968; cr children's entertainments outside Theatre Royal Stratford 1968–75; working in France 1975–; Seminar, Relais Culturel, Aix-en-Provence 1976; mem French Acad of Writers 1964–; Dr hc (Open Univ) 1977, (Open Univ, Brussels) 1995; Commdr des Arts et des Lettres 1986; Gold Medal for production of Lysistrata, Berlin, German Democratic Repub 1958, Olympic Award, Taormina 1959; Best Production of the Year (three times), Theatre of the Nations, Paris; SWET Award 1983; Woman of Achievement in the Arts Award, Arts Council of GB 1993, The Vildrosen Award, Folkkulturcentrum, Stockholm 1995, Lifetime Achievement Award, Directors Guild of GB 1995. *Productions include:* The Quare Fellow 1956, A Taste of Honey, The Hostage 1958, Lysistrata (Gold Medal for Production, Berlin) 1958, Taormina (Olympic Award) 1959, Fings Ain't Wot They Used T'Be 1959, Oh, What a Lovely War! (jtly) 1963, Sparrers Can't Sing (film) 1962; *Publications:* Milady Vine: Biography of Philippe de Rothschild 1984, Joan's Book (autobiog) 1994. *Address:* c/o Theatre Royal Stratford East, Gerry Raffles Square, Newham E15 1BN, UK (Office). *Telephone:* (20) 8534-7374 (Office).

LITVINOVA, Renata Muratovna; Russian actress and scriptwriter; b 11 Jan 1968, Moscow; d of Murat Vergazov and Mikhailovna Litvinova; m Mikhail Dobrovsky. *Education:* All-Union State Inst of Cinematography. *Career:* Mem Union of Theatre Workers. *Films include:* Passions, Two Arrows, Three Stories, The Border – Taiga Romance; *Scriptwriter for films:* Leningrad, November, Non-Love, Tractorists 2, Men's Confessions, Principal and Compassionate Eye, Three Stories, There is No Death for Me (Dir); *Publications:* Prize of Film Festival Centaurs for Passions. *Leisure interests:* antiques, cats. *Address:* Menzhinskogo str 38 korp 1, Apt 104, Moscow, Russian Federation. *Telephone:* (095) 470 3552 (Home).

LIU LIYING; Chinese civil servant; b 1932, Dongping, Shandong Prov. *Education:* Harbin Public Security Bureau Cadre School. *Career:* Joined CCP 1949; fmrly Vice-Chief and then Chief Cadre Section, Dir Political Dept, Vice-Chief Constable of Shenyang Public Security Bureau; Vice-Dir Discipline Inspection Dept, Discipline Inspection Cttee of CCP Cen Cttee, mem Standing Cttee 1983–; Vice-Sec Discipline Inspection Cttee of CCP Cen Cttee 1997–; headed the investigation into several maj corruption cases. *Address:* Discipline Inspection Committee of Chinese Communist Party Central Committee, Beijing, People's Republic of China.

LIU XIAOQING; Chinese actress; b 30 Oct 1955, Chengdu City, Sichuan Prov; d of Ran Changru and Liu Huihua; m Chen Guojun (divorced 1991). *Education:* Sichuan Music School. *Films include:* Strong Defence On The South China Sea 1975, Thank You, Comrades, Song Of Spring 1978, Little Flower, Wedding, What A Family 1979, Mystic Buddha Statue, On The Savage Land, Xu Mao And His Daughters 1981, In The Deep Of The Heart, The Invisible Net 1982, The Burning of Yuanmingyuan 1983, Red Beans At The North 1984, Three Young

Men in Shenzhen 1985, Hibiscus Town 1986, Furong Zhen (Lotus Town, 10th Hundred Flowers Best Actress Award, 7th Golden Cock Best Actress Award) 1986, Yuanye (11th Hundred Flowers Best Actress Award) 1988, Chun Tao (12th Hundred Flowers Best Actress Award 1989), Dream Of The Red Chamber 1988; *Publication:* My Way, My Eight Years, From a Movie Star to Billionaire. *Address:* POB 38, Asia Sport Village, Beijing, People's Republic of China. *Telephone:* (10) 4915988; *Fax:* (10) 4915899.

LIVELY, Penelope Margaret, OBE, FRSL; British writer; b 17 March 1933, Cairo, Egypt; d of Roger Low and Vera Greer; m Jack Lively 1957 (died 1998); one s one d. *Education:* St Anne's Coll (Oxford). *Career:* Mem Soc of Authors, PEN; has written TV and radio scripts; fmr mem Bd British Library; fmr Chair Soc of Authors; mem Bd British Council 1998–; Hon D LITT (Tufts Univ) 1992, (Warwick) 1998. *Publications include:* Fiction: The Road to Lichfield 1977, Nothing Missing But the Samovar and other stories (Southern Arts Literature Prize) 1978, Treasures of Time (Nat Book Award) 1979, Judgement Day 1980, Next to Nature, Art 1982, Perfect Happiness 1983, Corruption 1984, According to Mark 1984, Pack of Cards (short stories) 1986, Moon Tiger (Booker Prize) 1987, Passing On 1989, Going Back 1991, City of the Mind 1991, Cleopatra's Sister 1993, Heat Wave 1996, Spiderweb 1998; Jr fiction: Astercote 1970, The Whispering Knights 1971, The Wild Hunt of Hagworthy 1971, The Driftway 1972, The Ghost of Thomas Kempe (Carnegie Medal) 1973, The House in Norham Gardens 1974, Going Back 1975, Boy Without A Name 1975, A Stitch in Time (Whitbread Award) 1976, The Stained Glass Window 1976, Fanny's Sister 1976, The Voyage of QV66, Fanny and the Monsters 1979, Fanny and the Battle of Potter's Place 1980, The Revenge of Samuel Stokes 1981, Uninvited Ghosts and other stories 1984, Dragon Trouble 1984, Debbie and the Little Devil 1987, A House Inside Out; Non-fiction: The Presence of the Past 1976, Oleander, Jacaranda (autobiog) 1994, Beyond the Blue Mountains 1997, A House Unlocked 2001. *Leisure interests:* gardening, landscape history, talking, listening. *Address:* c/o David Higham Associates, 5–8 Lower John St, Golden Square, London W1R 4HA, UK. *Telephone:* (20) 7437-7888; *Fax:* (20) 7437-1072; *Internet:* www.penelopelively.net.

LIVNE, Lea; Israeli artist and teacher; b 25 Jan 1935, Haifa; d of Eliezer and Yona Carmi; m Yigal Livne 1952; two s two d. *Education:* Teaching Seminary, Art classes in Haifa, Avni School of Art, trained with Jean Clarte of Heiter Art (Paris). *Career:* Numerous solo and group exhibitions in France, SA, Spain, Italy, Yugoslavia and USA; solo exhibitions include To The Sea, Kibbutz Gallery 1969, Yad Labanim, Haifa 1975, Johannesburg 1977, Tzavta, Tel Aviv 1988, Hôtel des Augustins, Aix en Provence, France, Jewish Community Centre, Strasbourg, France, Akad Gallery 1990, 1994; group exhibitions include Erotica, Haifa 1975, print exhibition Haifa 1979, Int Memory Collection, Tervum, Belgium 1991, Tribute to Miró in Art, Olympic Games, Barcelona, Spain 1992, Humour and Satire, Bulgaria, Under the Auspices of Myrtos, Japan 1992, Yokohama-Kanagawa, Japan 1992; mem Israeli Arts Asscn; Kibbutz Gallery and Ocean Gallery Scholarship; Pomrok Award; Maritime Museum Nat Prize; First Diploma Annual Int Graphic Art Exhibition, Art Addiction, Stockholm 1995. *Leisure interests:* sport, music. *Address:* Kibbutz Ma'agan Michael, Mobile Post Menashe 37805, Israel. *Telephone:* (6) 6394491; *Fax:* (6) 6394888.

LIZIN, Anne-Marie, B SC; Belgian politician; b 5 Jan 1949, Huy; m Michel Lizin 1971. *Education:* Univ of Liège. *Career:* Alderman Commune of Ben-Ahin 1970–76; mem Cabinet of the Minister for Econ Affairs 1972–73; EC Commr 1973–77; mem Women's Cttee Belgian Socialist Party, Vice-Chair 1985; Counsellor Huy 1976–80, Alderman 1980–83, Mayor 1983; Counsellor Cabinet of the Minister for Foreign Affairs 1977–79; MEP 1979–88, mem Energy, Econ and Monetary Cttee, Cttee for Women's Rights 1979; mem UN Int Cttee on Solidarity with the struggle of the Women of SA and Namibia 1980, Walloon Cttee for Union of Towns; apptd Sec of State for Europe 1992 1988; Woman of Europe 1986. *Publications:* La sécurité nucléaire 1982, Dix femmes qui ont marqué leur époque 1982, Femmes d'Europe et du Tiers Monde, quelle solidarité? 1983, La gauche face aux illusions néo-libérales 1987, Demain, la Social-Démocratie 1991. *Leisure interests:*

reading, music. *Address:* Chaussée d'Ardenne 6, 4500 Huy, Belgium; Hôtel de Ville, Grand-Place 1, 4500 Huy, Belgium. *Telephone:* (85) 23-08-64; *Fax:* (85) 127-75-03; *E-mail:* anne-marie.lizin@huy.be.

LLEWELLYN SMITH, Elizabeth Marion, CB, MA; British university administrator (retd); b 17 Aug 1934, Upshire, Essex; d of the late John Clare Llewellyn Smith and of Margaret Emily Frances (née Crawford) Llewellyn Smith. *Education:* Christ's Hosp (Hertford), Girton Coll (Cambridge) and Royal Coll of Defence Studies. *Career:* Fmr civil servant, Deputy Dir-Gen of Fair Trading 1982–87, Deputy Sec Dept of Trade and Industry 1987–90; Dir European Investment Bank 1987–90; Prin St Hilda's Coll, Oxford 1990–2001; mem Business Appointments Panel, DTI 1996–; Hon Fellow St Mary's Coll, Univ of Durham 1999. *Leisure interests:* travel, books, entertaining. *Address:* St Hilda's College, Oxford OX4 1DY, UK; Brook Cottage, Taston, Charlbury OX7 3JL, UK. *Telephone:* (1608) 811874.

LLOYD, Barbara Bloom, PH D; American social psychologist and psychotherapist; b 25 Feb 1933, NJ; d of the late Samuel A. and Lily Bloom; m 1st Robert A. Le Vine 1953 (divorced 1963); m 2nd Peter C. Lloyd 1964; one d one s. *Education:* Univ of Chicago and Boston and Northwestern Univs. *Career:* Research Fellow Univ of Ibadan, Nigeria 1961–64, Univ of Sussex, UK 1970–71; Lecturer in Psychology Univ of Birmingham, UK 1964–67; Lecturer in Social Psychology Univ of Sussex 1967–75, Reader 1975–; mem British Asscn of Psychotherapists 1985–; Fellow British Psychological Soc 1982. *Publications:* Sex and Gender (jtly) 1985, Social Representatives and the Development of Knowledge (jtly) 1990, Gender Identities and Education (jtly) 1992, Smoking in Adolescence: Images and Identities (jtly) 1998. *Leisure interests:* theatre, travel, walking. *Address:* University of Sussex, School of Social Sciences, Falmer, Brighton, Sussex BN1 9SN, UK (Office); 10 Withdean Rd, Brighton BN1 5BL, UK (Home). *Telephone:* (1273) 678035 (Office); (273) 501252 (Home); *Fax:* (1273) 673563; *E-mail:* b.lloyd@sussex.ac.uk.

LLOYD, Emily; British actress; b 1971, London; d of Richard Lloyd Pack. *Career:* Debut in Wish You Were Here at 15 years 1987. *Films:* Cookie 1989, In Country 1989, Chicago Joe and the Showgirl 1990, Scorchers 1992, A River Runs Through It, Under the Hula Moon, When Saturday Comes 1996, Sarajevo 1996; *Screenplay:* Max Klapper–A Life in Pictures 1996. *Address:* c/o Triad Artists, Los Angeles, CA 90067, USA.

LLOYD, Phyllida, BA; British director; b 17 June 1957, Bristol; d of Patrick and Margaret (née Douglas-Pennent) Lloyd. *Education:* Lawnside School (Great Malvern) and Univ of Birmingham. *Career:* Theatre, opera and film director; fmr Floor Asst BBC TV; Assoc Dir Manchester Royal Exchange. *Theatre includes:* Six Degrees of Separation 1992, Hysteria (Royal Court) 1993, Pericles 1993, The Threepenny Opera 1994, The Way of the World 1995, Dona Rosita (Almeida) 1997, The Prime of Miss Jean Brodie (Royal Nat Theatre) 1998, Mamma Mia! (London, Toronto, Melbourne, NY) 1999–2001, Boston Marriage (Donmar) 2001; *Opera includes:* Gloriana 1993, La Bohème 1993, Medea (Opera North) 1996, Carmen 1998, The Carmelites 1999, Macbeth (Paris Opera) 1999, Verdi Requiem (English Nat Opera) 2000, The Handmaid's Tale (Copenhagen) 2000; *Film:* Gloriana 1999. *Leisure interests:* running, photography. *Address:* c/o Annette Stone Associates, 2nd Floor, 22 Great Marlborough St, London, W1F 7HU, UK. *Telephone:* (20) 7734-0626; *Fax:* (20) 7734-2346.

LOBO, Suely Maria de Paula e Silva, MA; Brazilian professor of English; b Andrelândia, Minas Gerais; d of Ary Siffert and Ambrosina de Paula e Silva; m Achilles Masetti Lobo 1966; two c. *Education:* Catholic Pontifical Univ of Minas Gerais and Fed Univ of Minas Gerais. *Career:* Asst Prof Catholic Pontifical Univ of Minas Gerais 1964–70, Assoc Prof 1970–76, apptd Prof 1976, Co-ordinator of Literary Programmes 1980, Head Dept of English 1984–94; Visiting Prof Fed Univ of Minas Gerais 1980; Rep of S America at Seminar on Contemporary Literature, Univ of Cambridge, UK 1988; mem Charles Dickens Int Fellowship, Keats-Shelley Memorial Asscn; Santos Dumont Medal 1985; Literary Research Award, Govt of Brazil; Award of Fulbright Comm 1988; Inconfidência Medal 1989. *Address:*

Pontifícia Universidade Católica de Minas Gerais, Av Dom José Gaspar 500, CP 2686, 30550 Belo Horizonte, MG, Brazil. *Telephone:* (31) 319-1112.

LOCKE, Sondra; American actress and film director; b 28 May 1947, Shelbyville, TN. *Career:* Acting debut 1968; directing debut 1986. *Films include:* The Heart is a Lonely Hunter 1968, Cover Me Babe, Willard, A Reflection of Fear, The Second Coming of Suzanne, The Outlaw Josey Wales, Death Game, The Gauntlet, Every Which Way But Loose, Bronco Billy, Any Which Way You Can, Sudden Impact, Ratboy (also dir), Impulse (dir), Dirty Harry IV; *TV appearances include:* Friendships, Secrets and Lies, Rosie: The Rosemary Clooney Story, Amazing Stories. *Address:* c/o Bauer Bendeck, 9255 W Sunset Blvd, Suite 716, Los Angeles, CA 90069, USA.

LOCKWOOD, Baroness (Life Peer), cr 1978, of Dewsbury, W Yorks, **Betty Lockwood,** DL; British politician; b 22 Jan 1924, Dewsbury; d of Arthur and Edith Alice Lockwood; m Cedric Hall 1978 (died 1989). *Education:* Eastborough Girls' School (Dewsbury) and Ruskin Coll (Oxford). *Career:* Nat Women's Officer Lab Party 1967–75; Vice-Pres Int Council of Social Democratic Women 1969–75; Chair Mary Macarthur Educational Trust, Holiday Homes 1971–94, Equal Opportunities Comm 1975–83, EC Comm Advisory Cttee on Equal Opportunities for Men and Women 1982–83, 1984–91, House of Lords EC Subcttee on Social and Consumer Affairs; Ed Lab Woman 1967–71; a Deputy Speaker House of Lords 1989–; mem Dept of Employment Advice Cttee on Women's Employment 1969–83, Advice Council on Energy Conservation 1977–80, Council Advertising Standards Authority 1983–93, Leeds Urban Devt Corpn 1988–, Council Univs of Bradford 1983–, Leeds 1985– (Chair 1992–); Pres Hillcroft Coll 1987–95; Hon Fellow UMIST 1986, Birkbeck Coll 1987; Hon D LITT (Bradford) 1981; Hon LL D (Strathclyde) 1983. *Leisure interests:* music, country life. *Address:* House of Lords, Westminster, London SW1A 0PW, UK (Office); 6 Sycamore Drive, Addingham, Ilkley, W Yorks LS29 0NY, UK (Home). *Telephone:* (20) 7219-3107 (Office).

LODGE, Juliet, D LITT, PH D; British professor of European politics and integration; b London; three c. *Education:* Univs of Reading, Heidelberg (Germany) and Toulouse (France). *Career:* Lecturer in Politics Univ of Auckland, NZ; Visiting Fellow in Int Relations, LSE 1977; Lecturer, Sr Lecturer, Reader Univ of Hull 1978–91, Dir European Community Research Unit 1985–95, Prof of European Politics, Jean Monnet Prof of European Integration 1991–; Dir Centre for European Studies, Univ of Leeds 1996–; Prof of European Integration and Jean Monnet Prof of EU Policy and Politics 1996–; British Woman of Europe 1992, European Woman of the Year 1992. *Publications include:* The European Community and New Zealand 1981, European Union: The European Community in Search of a Future 1986, The Threat of Terrorism 1988, The European Community and the Challenge of the Future 1989, The 1989 Election of the European Parliament 1990, National Parliaments and the Euro 1998, The 1999 Elections to the European Parliament; over 130 articles on European and Int affairs in professional journals. *Leisure interests:* art, literature, satire. *Address:* University of Leeds, Centre for European Studies, Leeds LS2 9JT, UK. *Telephone:* (113) 233-4443; *Fax:* (113) 233-5056; *E-mail:* j.e.lodge@leeds.ac.uk.

LODHI, Maleeha, PH D; Pakistani diplomatist and journalist; m (divorced); one s. *Education:* LSE. *Career:* Lecturer in Politics and Sociology, LSE 1980–85; fmr Lecturer Dept of Public Admin Quaid-i-Azam Univ, Islamabad; Ed The Muslim; Ed and Co-Founder The News (daily newspaper) 1985–93, 1997–2000; Amb to USA 1993–97, (with rank of Minister of State) 2000–; Fellow Pakistan Inst of Devt Econs; award from All Pakistan Newspaper Soc 1994. *Publications:* Pakistan's Encounter with Democracy, The External Dimension 1994; numerous contribs to int journals. *Address:* Embassy of Pakistan, 2315 Massachusetts Ave, NW Washington, DC 20008, USA. *Telephone:* (202) 939-6200; *Fax:* (202) 387-0484; *E-mail:* info@pakistan_embassy .com; *Internet:* www.imran.com/pakistan.

LOLLOBRIGIDA, Gina; Italian actress; b 4 July 1927, Sibiaco; d of Giovanni and Giuseppina Mercuri; m Milko Skofic 1949; one s. *Education:* Liceo Artistico (Rome). *Career:* Film debut 1947, since then has appeared in numerous films. *Films include:* Pagliatta 1947, Campane a Martello 1948, Cuori senza Frontiere 1949, Achtung, banditi! 1951,

Enrico Caruso 1951, Fanfan la Tulipe 1951, Altri Tempi 1952, The Wayward Wife 1952, Belles de nuit 1952, Pane, amore e fantasia 1953, La Provinciale 1953, Pane, amore e gelosia, La Romana 1954, Il Grande Gioco 1954, La Donna più Bella del Mondo 1955, Trapeze 1956, Notre Dame de Paris 1956, Solomon and Sheba 1959, Never So Few 1960, Go Naked in the World 1961, She Got What She Asked For 1963, Woman of Straw 1964, Le Bambole 1965, Hotel Paradiso 1966, Buona Sera Mrs Campbell 1968, King, Queen, Knave 1972, The Bocce Showdown 1990, Plucked, Bad Man's River, The Lonely Woman, Bambole; *Publications:* Italia Mia (photography) 1974, The Philippines. *Leisure interest:* photography. *Address:* via Appia Antica 223, 00178 Rome, Italy.

LOLOVA, Tatyana; Bulgarian actress; b 10 Feb 1934, Sofia; d of Zhelyasko Lolov and Maria Gorbatenko; m 1st Evelin Monev (divorced 1962); m 2nd Svetoslav Svetoslavov 1963; one s. *Education:* High School and Theatrical Inst (Sofia). *Career:* Actress 1955–, with Rousse Nat Theatre 1956–78, Theatre Sofia 1978–89, Sofia Theatre of Satire 1989, has performed in many plays, several films and TV series and has made one recording 1986. *Leisure interest:* travel. *Address:* 1111 Sofia, Geo Milev Compl, Bl 266, Apt 28, Postoyanstvo St, Bulgaria. *Telephone:* (2) 70-03-76.

LOM, Helen, MA; American attorney and international organization official; b 21 May 1947, Czechoslovakia (now Czech Repub); two d. *Education:* Swarthmore Coll and Boston Univ. *Career:* Researcher and teacher Costa Rica Univ, Pontificia Univ Catolica de Rio de Janeiro and Inst of Municipal Admin, Rio de Janeiro, Brazil 1972–75; Assoc Curtis Mallet-Prevost, Colt and Masle, NY 1976–79; with WIPO 1980–, currently Dir of the Developing Countries Div (Madrid and The Hague Systems), Sector of Co-operation for Devt. *Address:* WIPO, 34 chemin des Colombettes, 1211 Geneva 20, Switzerland. *Telephone:* (22) 338-9124.

LOMAX, (Janis) Rachel, MA, M SC; British civil servant; b 15 July 1945, Swansea; d of William and Dilys Salmon; m Michael Lomax 1967 (divorced 1990); two s. *Education:* Cheltenham Ladies Coll, Girton Coll (Cambridge) and LSE. *Career:* Econ Asst HM Treasury 1968–72, Econ Adviser 1972–78, Sr Econ Adviser 1978–85, Prin Pvt Sec to Chancellor of the Exchequer 1985–86, Under Sec 1986–90, Deputy Chief Econ Adviser 1990–92, Deputy Sec (Financial Insts and Markets) 1992–94; Deputy Sec Cabinet Office 1994–95; Vice Pres and Chief of Staff IBRD (World Bank) 1995–96; Perm Sec Welsh Office 1996–99, Dept for Work and Pensions 1999–; Chair UK Selection Cttee Harkness Fellowships 1995; mem Council Royal Econ Soc 1989–94. *Leisure interests:* walking, theatre, jazz, reading. *Address:* Permanent Secretary, Department for Work and Pensions, Richmond House, 79 Whitehall, London, SW1A 2NS, UK.

LONG, Shelley; American actress; b 23 Aug 1949, Fort Wayne, IN; m Bruce Tyson; one d. *Education:* Northwestern Univ. *Career:* Actress in comedy films and on TV. *Films:* A Small Circle of Friends 1980, Caveman 1981, Night Shift 1982, Losin' It 1983, Irreconcilable Differences 1984, The Money Pit 1986, Outrageous Fortune 1987, Hello Again 1987, Troop Beverly Hills 1989, Don't Tell Her It's Me 1990, Frozen Assets 1992, The Brady Bunch 1995; *TV includes:* Series: Cheers (Emmy Award for Outstanding Actress in a Comedy Series 1983) 1982–87, Good Advice 1993–94; Films: The Cracker Factory 1979, The Princess and the Cabbie 1981, Promise of Love, Voices Within: The Lives of Truddi Chase 1990, Memory of a Murder 1992, A Message from Holly 1992, The Women of Spring Break 1995, Dr T and the Women 2000. *Address:* c/o Ron Meyer, Creative Artists Agency, 9830 Wilshire Blvd, Beverly Hills, CA 90212, USA.

LONG WENPEI, PH D; Chinese professor of English; b 10 Nov 1926, Changsha; d of Long Boxin and Xiang Yuzhen; m Xu Yaozhou 1980; five step-s. *Education:* Nanjing Univ. *Career:* Mem Dept of Foreign Languages and Literature, Fudan Univ 1952–90, Vice-Chair of Dept 1964–80, Head Western Literature Section 1980–84; Adviser Eugene O'Neill Research Centre, Cen Acad of Drama 1985–; mem Council China Asscn For the Study of American Literature 1979–91, Vice-Pres 1991; Adviser T. S. Eliot–E. Pound Soc in China 1995–; has written numerous articles on Eugene O'Neill for literary journals. *Publications:* Selected Readings in American Literature (ed, jtly) Vol I 1985, Vol II 1987, Vol III 1996, Eugene O'Neill: A Collection of Critical Essays (ed)

1988, On O'Neil's Late Plays (Excellent Essay, All China Asscn of Foreign Literature Teaching and Research in Insts of Higher Learning 1995). *Leisure interests:* reading Chinese classics, watching stage plays. *Address:* Fudan University, Dept of Foreign Languages and Literature, Shanghai 200433, People's Republic of China. *Telephone:* (21) 5492222; *Fax:* (21) 5491875; *E-mail:* english@ms.fudaneduc.sh.cn.

LONGFORD, Countess of, **Elizabeth Pakenham,** CBE, FRSL; British writer; b 30 Aug 1906, London; d of N. B. Harman and Katherine Chamberlain; m Francis A. Pakenham (later Earl of Longford) 1931 (died 2001); four s four d (one deceased). *Education:* Headington School (Oxford) and Lady Margaret Hall (Oxford). *Career:* Parl Candidate (Lab) Cheltenham 1935, Oxford 1950; Trustee Nat Portrait Gallery 1967–78; mem Advisory Bd Victoria and Albert Museum 1969–75, British Library 1976–80; Hon D LITT (Sussex) 1970. *Publications:* Jameson's Raid 1959, Victoria RI (James Tait Black Prize) 1964, Wellington: The Years of the Sword (Yorkshire Post Book of the Year) 1969, Wellington: Pillar of State 1972, Winston Churchill 1974, The Royal House of Windsor 1974, Byron's Greece (jtly) 1975, Byron 1976, Wilfrid Scawen Blunt 1978, Louisa, Lady in Waiting to Queen Victoria and Queen Alexandra 1980, The Queen Mother 1981, Eminent Victorian Women 1981, Elizabeth R 1983, The Pebbled Shore: The Memoirs of Elizabeth Longford 1986, The Oxford Book of Royal Anecdotes (ed) 1989, Darling Loosy, The Correspondents of Princess Louise 1856–1939 1991, Wellington (abridged) 1992, Poets' Corner: an anthology 1992, Royal Throne: The Future of the Monarchy 1993. *Leisure interests:* Victoriana, literature, social history including the woman's movement, gardening. *Address:* 18 Chesil Court, Chelsea Manor St, London SW3 5QP, UK, UK; Bernhurst, Hurst Green, East Sussex, TN19 7QN, UK. *Telephone:* (20) 7352-7794 (London); (1580) 86248.

LONGO, Jeannie Michèle Alice; French cyclist; b 31 Oct 1958, Annecy; d of Jean and Yvette Longo; m Patrice Ciprelli 1985. *Education:* Inst d'Etudes Commerciales (Grenoble) and Univ of Limoges. *Career:* French Cycling Champion 1979–86; World Champion (road) 1985, 1987; winner Tour of Colorado, USA 1986, 1987, Tour of Colombia 1987, 1988, Tour of Norway 1987, Tour de France 1987; Silver Medal World Track Race 1987, World Champion 1988, 1989; holder of several world records, including world record for 3km, covered track, Grenoble 1992; winner French Cycle Racing Championship 1992; Silver Medallist Olympic Games, Barcelona, Spain 1992; Gold Medallist road race, Olympic Games, Atlanta, GA, USA 1996; consultant France Télévision 1999–; Médaille d'Or, La Jeunesse et les Sports; Médaille d'Or, Acad des Sports. *Address:* Fédération Française de Cyclisme, 5 rue de Rome, 93561 Rosny-sous-Bois, France. *Internet:* www.jeannielong.com (Home).

LONSDALE, Anne M., MA; British university administrator; b 16 Feb 1941, Huddersfield, Yorks; d of A. C. G. and Molly Menzies; m 1st Geoffrey Griffin 1962 (died 1962); m 2nd Roger Lonsdale 1964 (divorced 1994); one s one d. *Education:* St Anne's Coll (Oxford). *Career:* Lecturer in Classical Chinese, St Anne's Coll, Oxford 1965–73; Univ Admin, Univ of Oxford 1973–86, Dir External Relations Office 1986–93; Sec-Gen Cen European Univ 1994–96; Pres New Hall, Cambridge 1996–, Pro-Vice-Chancellor Cambridge Univ 1998–; Council of Senate, Cambridge Univ 1997–; mem Commonwealth Scholarship Comm 1996–; mem Governing Body of the GB Assoc for Cen and Eastern Europe; Trustee Moscow School of Social and Econ Sciences, LEAD Int UK; has written reviews and translations of Chinese literature and reports on univ admin in People's Repub of China, India, etc; Cavaliere Ordine al Merito della Repubblica Italiana 1992. *Leisure interest:* travel. *Address:* New Hall, Cambridge CB3 0DF, UK. *Telephone:* (1223) 762201; *Fax:* (1223) 762217.

LOPATKINA, Ulyana Vyacheslavovna, D MED; Russian ballet dancer; b 23 Oct 1973, Kerch. *Education:* Vaganova Acad of Russian Ballet. *Career:* Soloist Mariinsky Theatre 1991–; leading roles in Giselle, Sleeping Beauty, Anna Karenina, Fountain of Bakhchisarai, Raimonda, Chekherezada, Swan Lake, Bayadera, Corsair, performs in Goya-Divertissement; tours with Mariinsky Theatre in Europe, N and S America; State Prize of Russian Fed 1998. *Address:* c/o Mariinsky Theatre, Teatralnaya pl 1, St Petersburg, Russian Federation. *Telephone:* (812) 315 5724.

LOPEZ, Jennifer; American actress singer and dancer; b 24 July 1970, Bronx, NY. *Career:* Golden Globe 1998; MTV Movie Award 1999. *Films:* My Little Girl, My Family – Mi Familia, Money Train 1995, Jack 1996, Blood and Wine 1996, Anaconda 1997, Selena 1997, U-Turn 1997, Out of Sight 1998, Thieves 1999, Pluto Nash 1999, The Cell 2000, The Wedding Planner 2000, Angel Eyes 2000; *TV includes:* Second Chances, Hotel Malibu, Nurses on the Line: The Crash of Flight 7; *Music:* albums: On the 6, J. Lo 2001. *Address:* United Talent Agency, 9560 Wilshire Blvd, 5th Floor, Beverly Hills, CA 90212, USA.

LOREN, Sophia; Italian actress; b 20 Sept 1934, Rome; d of Riccardo Scicolone and Romilda Villani; m Carlo Ponti 1957 (marriage annulled 1962; m 1966); two s. *Education:* Scuole Magistrali Superiori. *Career:* First screen appearance as an extra in Quo Vadis; has appeared in numerous films and TV programmes; Chair Nat Alliance for Prevention and Treatment of Child Abuse and Maltreatment; Goodwill Amb for Refugees 1992; Hon Acad Award 1991; Chevalier de la Légion d'Honneur; Hon Acad Award 1991. *Films include:* Quo Vadis, Africa sotto i Mari, E Arrivato l'Accordatore 1951, La Tratta delle Bianche, La Favorita 1952, Aida 1953, Il Paese dei Campanelli, Miseria e Nobiltà, Il Segno di Venere 1953, Tempi Nostri 1953, Carosello Napoletano 1953, L'Oro di Napoli 1954, Attila 1954, Peccato che sia una canaglia, La Bella Mugnaia, La Donna del Fiume 1955, Boccaccio 1970, Matrimonio All'Italiana, The Pride and the Passion 1955, Boy on a Dolphin, Legend of the Lost 1956, Desire Under the Elms 1957, That Kind of Woman 1958, Houseboat 1958, The Key 1958, The Black Orchid (Venice Festival Award) 1959, It Started in Naples, Heller in Pink Tights 1960, La Ciociara (Acad Award) 1960, The Millionairess 1961, Two Women (Cannes Film Festival Award) 1961, El Cid 1961, Madame Sans Gêne 1962, Yesterday, Today and Tomorrow 1963, The Fall of the Roman Empire 1964, Lady L 1965, Operation Crossbow 1965, Judith 1965, A Countess from Hong Kong 1965, Arabesque 1966, More Than a Miracle 1967, The Priest's Wife 1970, Sunflower 1970, Hot Autumn 1971, Man of La Mancha 1972, Brief Encounter (TV) 1974, The Verdict 1974, The Voyage 1974, The Cassandra Crossing 1977, A Special Day 1977, Firepower 1978, Brass Target 1979, Blood Feud 1981, Two Women 1989, Prêt à Porter 1995, Grumpier Old Men; *Publications:* Eat with Me 1972, Sophia Loren on Women and Beauty 1984. *Address:* Case Postale 430, 1211 Geneva 12, Switzerland.

LORIOD, Yvonne; French pianist; b 20 Jan 1924, Houilles; d of Gaston and Simone (née Bilhaut) Loriod; m Olivier Messiaen 1961 (died 1992). *Career:* Hon Prof of Piano Conservatoire Nat de Musique, Paris; specializes in interpretation of complete works including Bach's Well-Tempered Klavier, Beethoven sonatas, Mozart piano concertos, works of Chopin and Debussy and complete works of Olivier Messiaen; first performances in Paris of Bartók's 1st and 2nd concertos, Schoenberg concerto and works by Messiaen, Jolivet, Boulez and other contemporary composers; has toured Europe, Japan, S America, N America; Commdr de la Légion d'Honneur; Officier des Arts et des Lettres; Grand Officier de l'Ordre Nat du Mérite; Grand Prix du Disque (seven times); Prix Henry Dauberville; Grand Prix de la Sacem 1986. *Address:* c/o Bureau de Concerts Maurice Werner, 17 rue du 4 Septembre, 75002 Paris, France. *Telephone:* (1) 45-10-92-80.

LOROUPE, Tegla; Kenyan marathon runner; b 1971. *Career:* First int success with fourth place at 10,000 m final, World Championships (Stuttgart, Germany) 1993; winner NY Marathon 1994, 1995; new world record time, Rotterdam Marathon 1998; third place 10,000 m final, World Championships (Seville, Spain) 1999; winner London Marathon Women's Race 2000. *Address:* c/o London Marathon, 10 Theed St, London, SE1, UK.

LOSINSKA, Kathleen Mary, OBE; British former trade union official; b 5 Oct 1922, Croydon; d of James Henry Conway and Dorothy Marguerite Hill; m Stanislaw Losinski 1942; one s. *Education:* Selhurst Grammar School for Girls (Croydon). *Career:* Civil Service Trade Union Leader until 1988; mem Trade Union Nuclear Energy Review Comm (first woman from the West to visit Chernobyl one year after nuclear disaster); Commr Civil Service Appeals Bd; Vice-Chair Civil Service Retirement Fellowship; mem Man Cttee Civil Service Benevolent Fund, European Christian Trade Union; Queen's Jubilee Medal;

Order of Polonia Restituta (1990). *Leisure interests:* historical research, writing, music. *Address:* Loretto, Baggotstown West, Bruff, Co Limerick, Ireland.

LOTT, Dame Felicity Ann, DBE, BA, FRAM; British opera and concert singer (soprano); b 8 May 1947, Cheltenham; d of John A. and Whyla (née Williams) Lott; m 1st Robin Golding 1973 (divorced); m 2nd Gabriel Woolf 1984; one d. *Education:* Pate's Grammar School for Girls (Cheltenham), Royal Holloway Coll (London) and Royal Acad of Music. *Career:* Debut with English Nat Opera 1975, at Glyndebourne 1977; has performed at Royal Opera House, Covent Garden, Glyndebourne Festival, English Nat Opera, Metropolitan Opera, New York, Vienna, La Scala, Milan, Italy, Paris Opera, Brussels, Hamburg and Munich, Germany, Chicago, USA; wide recital repertoire; Founder mem Songmakers' Almanac; Hon Fellow Royal Holloway Coll; Dr hc (Sussex) 1990; D LITT (Loughborough) 1996, (Oxford) 2001; Hon D MUS (London) 1997, (Royal Scottish Acad of Music and Drama) 1998; Officier des Arts et des Lettres 2000. *Recordings include:* St Matthew Passion (Bach), Messiah (Handel), Sacred Music by Vivaldi, Complete Mélodies of Ravel, Louise (Charpentier), French songs, Le Nozze di Figaro, Strauss Orchestral Songs, Peter Grimes, The Turn of the Screw, Così fan Tutte, The Merry Widow; *Videos:* Intermezzo, The Rake's Progress, A Midsummer Night's Dream. *Leisure interests:* reading, gardening. *Address:* c/o Askonas Holt Ltd, Lonsdale Chambers, 27 Chancery Lane, London WC2A 1PF, UK. *Telephone:* (20) 7400-1700; *Fax:* (20) 7400-0799; *E-mail:* info.@askonasholt.co.uk (Office); *Internet:* www.askonasholt.co.uk (Office).

LOUIE, Alexina Diane, B MUS, MA; Canadian composer; b 30 July 1949, Vancouver, BC. *Education:* Univ of British Columbia and Univ of California at San Diego (USA). *Career:* Professional Solo Pianist, Vancouver, BC 1966–71; Music Copyist 1970–73; Instructor of Music Pasadena City Coll, CA, USA 1974–80; Composer-in-Residence Canadian Opera Co 1996–; Composition Grantee Canada Council for the Arts 1974, 1980, 1981; Composer of the Year, Canada Music Council 1986; Juno Award 1988. *Compositions include:* Molly 1972, O Magnum Mysterium: In Memoriam Glenn Gould 1982, Songs of Paradise, Music for a Thousand Autumns, Concerto for Piano and Orchestra, Love Songs for a Small Planet, The Eternal Earth, Winter Music, Music for Heaven and Earth. *Address:* 323 Sunnyside Ave, Toronto, ON M6R 2R5, Canada (Home).

LOUISY, Dame Calliopa Pearlette, GCMG, PH D; Saint Lucia politician and educator; b 8 June 1946, Laborie, St Lucia; d of Rity Louisy. *Education:* St Joseph's Convent Secondary School, Univ of the West Indies, Université Laval (Canada) and Univ of Bristol (UK). *Career:* Grad teacher St Joseph's Convent 1969–72, 1975–76; tutor Saint Lucia 'A' Level Coll 1976–1981, Prin 1981–86; Dean Sir Arthur Lewis Community Coll 1986–94, Vice-Prin 1994–95, Prin 1996–97; Gov-Gen of Saint Lucia 1997–; Commonwealth Scholar 1972; Hon LL D (Bristol) 1999; Int Woman of the Year 1998; Grand Cross Order of Saint Lucia 1997. *Publications:* A Guide to the Writing of Creole 1981, The Changing Role of the Small State in Higher Education 1994, Dilemmas of Insider Research in a Small Country Setting 1997. *Leisure interests:* the performing arts, culture, gardening. *Address:* Government House, Morne Fortune, Castries, Saint Lucia, West Indies. *Telephone:* (758) 452 2481 (Office); (758) 452 2481 (Home); *Fax:* (758) 453 2731; *E-mail:* govgenslu@candw.lc.

LOVE, Courtney; American singer and actress; b 9 July 1965, San Francisco, CA; m Kurt Cobain 1992 (died 1994); one s one d. *Career:* Lead singer Hole rock group (f in LA 1989), has toured Europe. *Recordings include:* Albums: Pretty on the Inside 1991, Live Through This 1994; Singles: Retard Girl 1990, Beautiful Son 1993, Dicknail, Teenage Whore; *Films include:* Feeling Minnesota, Sid and Nancy, Straight to Hell, The People vs Larry Flynt, Basquiat 1996, Life 1997, Man on the Moon 1999. *Address:* c/o David Geffen Co, 9130 W Sunset Blvd, Los Angeles, CA 90069, USA.

LØVEID, Cecilie Meyer; Norwegian writer; b 21 Aug 1951, Mysen; d of Erik Løveid and Ingrid Meyer; m Bjørn H. Ianke 1978; one s two d. *Education:* Bergen. *Career:* Mem editorial staff, Profil (magazine) 1969; Sec Norsk Forfattersentrum, Vestlandsardelingen 1974; teacher Writing Arts Centre, Bergen 1986; mem Literary Council, Den norske

Fordatterforening 1987; Prix Italia 1982; Aschehons Prize; Donblans Prize. *Publications:* Most (novel) 1972, Sug (novel) 1979, Måkespisere (radio play) 1982, Balansedame (play) 1986, Maria Q. (play) 1991, Rhindøtrene (play) 1996. *Leisure interests:* old wooden toys, walking in the mountains, swimming. *Address:* Huitfeldtsgt 36, 0253 Oslo, Norway. *Telephone:* 22 83 05 63; *Fax:* 22 83 43 73.

LOVELL, Patricia Anne, MBE, AO; Australian film producer; d of H. G. Parr; m Nigel Lovell 1956; one s one d. *Career:* Actress, TV presenter and reporter 1959–74; freelance film and TV producer 1971–. *Films include:* Break of Day 1976, Summerfield 1977, Picnic at Hanging Rock, Gallipoli (Australian Film Inst Award) 1980, Monkey Grip (Australian Film Inst Award) 1982, The Perfectionist 1985; *TV productions include:* The Perfectionist 1985. *Leisure interests:* theatre, gardening, walking dogs. *Address:* POB 71, Avalon Beach, NSW 2107, Australia.

LOWRY, Noreen Margaret (Nina), LL B; British judge; b 6 Sept 1925, London; d of the late John Edmund and Hilda Grace Sarah Collins; m 1st Edward Lucas Gardner 1950 (divorced 1962); one s one d: m 2nd Richard John Lowry 1963; one d. *Education:* Bedford High School and Univ of Birmingham. *Career:* Called to the Bar, Gray's Inn 1948, Barrister SE Circuit, Cen Criminal Court, Inner London Sessions 1948–67; Metropolitan Stipendiary Magistrate 1967–76; Circuit Judge 1976–95; mem Criminal Law Revision Cttee 1975–, Criminal Injuries Compensation Bd 1995–2000; Hon LL D (Birmingham) 1992. *Leisure interests:* theatre, travel. *Address:* c/o Central Criminal Court, Old Bailey, London EC4M 7EH, UK.

LOWTHER, Merlyn, M SC; British banking executive; b 3 March 1954; d of Norman Edward Douglas and Joan Margaret (née Hewitt) Humphrey; m David John Lowther 1975; one s one d. *Education:* Manchester High School for Girls, Univ of Manchester and London Business School. *Career:* With Bank of England 1975–, Sr Dealer Gilt-Edged Div 1985–87, Head of Banking Div and Deputy Chief Cashier 1991–96, Personnel Dir 1996–98, Deputy Dir and Chief Cashier 1999–; Hon LL D (Manchester) 1999. *Leisure interests:* theatre, singing, reading, family. *Address:* Bank of England, Threadneedle St, London EC2P 2EH, UK. *Telephone:* (20) 7601-4444; *Fax:* (20) 7601-4771; *E-mail:* merlyn.lowther@bankofengland.co.uk; *Internet:* www.bankofengland.co.uk.

LU, (Hsiu-Lien) Annette; Taiwanese politician; b 7 June 1944, Taoyuan. *Education:* Taiwan Prov Taipei First Girls' High School, Nat Taiwan Univ and Univ of Illinois. *Career:* Fmr Sr Specialist, Section Chief Exec Law and Regulations Cttee of Exec Yuan; participated in street demonstrations; sentenced to twelve years' imprisonment 1979, released after 5 years and 4 months on medical parole; f N American Taiwanese Women's Asscn, Clean Election Coalition 1985–90; organized and led Alliance for the Promotion of UN Membership for Taiwan 1991; Democratic Progressive Party (DPP) mem Legis Yuan for Taoyuan, mem Foreign Affairs Cttee 1992–95; Nat Policy Adviser to Pres 1996; Magistrate for Taoyuan Co 1996–99; Vice-Pres of Taiwan 2000–; Chair Third Global Summit of Women, Taiwan 1994; f Center for Women's and Children's Safety. *Publications:* (novels) These Three Women, Empathy; (non-fiction) New Feminism, I Love Taiwan, Viewing Taiwan from Abroad, Retrying the Formosa Case. *Address:* Office of the President, Chiehshou Hall, 122 Chungking South Rd, Sec 1, Taipei, 100, Taiwan. *Telephone:* (2) 23718889; *Fax:* (2) 23611604; *E-mail:* public@mail.oop.gov.tw; *Internet:* www.oop.gov.tw.

LU QI-HUI; Chinese sculptor; b 8 April 1936, Shanghai; d of Ren Jin; m Fang Zenxian 1960; one s one d. *Education:* Cen Art Acad, E China Br. *Career:* Sculptor China Sculpture Factory E China Br 1955–61; teacher Shanghai Art Coll 1961–65; professional sculptor Shanghai Oil Painting and Sculpture Inst 1965–, Prof 1988–; mem Chinese Artists' Asscn. *Works include:* Transplanting Rice Seedlings 1957, Statue of Child Labourers 1974, Sculpture for Chairman Mao Memorial Hall 1977, Statue of Lu Xun 1979, Angrily Seeking Verses Against Reign of Terror 1980, Plateau in the Morning Sun 1986, Bada, an Ancient Chinese Artist (exhibited New York, USA in Contemporary Oil Painting from the People's Republic of China) 1987, The Emotion at Plateau 1989, Zhang Zhong-Jingi a Beginner of Chinese Medical Science 1990, Song Jie-Cai Rang of a Tibetan 1990, Hawk-dancing 1991 (statue), Wang Ge-Ji memorial (bronze) 1992, Magic Painter Mar-Lang (bronze) 1993, work for Shanghai Memorial Hall 1994, work for Japanese Fukuoka 1995, Xia-Qiu-Son (bronze) 1995, Balzac Memorial (bronze), Garden of Famous People, Shanghai 1996, Wu Fu-Zhi memorial (bronze) 1998. *Leisure interests:* Chinese painting, sport. *Address:* 100-301, 398 Xin-Pei Rd, Xin-Zuan, Shanghai, People's Republic of China. *Telephone:* (21) 64987283.

LUBICH SILVIA, Chiara; Italian evangelist; b 22 Jan 1920; d of Luigi and Luigia Lubich. *Education:* Teachers' Training Inst, Catholic Univ of Milan and Univ of Venice. *Career:* Founder, Pres Focolare Movt, a worldwide spiritual movt currently active in 184 countries with approval of successive Popes 1943–; participated in extraordinary Synod of Bishops 1985, Synod on the Vocation and Mission of the Laity 1987; Consultant Pontifical Council for the Laity; Hon Pres World Conf on Religion and Peace; Cross of Order of St Augustine of Canterbury 1981; Byzantine Cross, Phanar, Istanbul 1984; Plaque of St Catherine of Siena 1987; Templeton Foundation Prize for Progress in Religion 1977; Festival of the Peace of Augsburg Prize 1988; First Int Prize, Franciscan Int Centre of Studies for Dialogue among Peoples 1993; Ardent Eagle of St Wenceslaus; Seal of City of Trent 1995, UNESCO Prize for Peace Educ 1996, Cross of the South (Brazil) 1997, Human Rights Prize, Council of Europe 1998; numerous hon doctorates and other decorations. *Publications:* four vols of Spiritual Writings, Diary 1964/65 1967, It's A Whole New Scene 1969, Conversations with the Gen 1974, To the Gen 3, I 1974, II 1976, Why Have You Forsaken Me, The Key to Unity 1984, Encounters with the Orient 1986, On the Holy Journey 1987, From Scripture to Life 1991, Into the Light 1996, Journey to Heaven 1997, And Christmas Comes Back 1997, Where Life Lights Up 1998, Love Wins 1998. *Address:* via di Frascati 306, 00040 Rocca di Papa, RM, Italy. *Telephone:* (6) 947989.

LUCAS, Sarah, BA; British artist; b 1962, London. *Education:* Working Men's Coll (London), London Coll of Printmaking and Goldsmiths Coll, London. *Career:* Works with variety of materials and media, including photographs, sculpture and installations. *Solo Art Exhibitions include:* Got a Salmon On (Prawn), Anthony d'Offay Gallery, London 1994, Supersensible, Barbara Gladstone Gallery, NY 1995, Is Suicide Genetic?, Contemporary Fine Arts, Berlin 1996, Sarah Lucas, Portikus, Frankfurt 1996, Car Park, Ludwig Museum, Cologne 1997, Odd-bod Photography, Sadie Coles HQ, London 1998, The Old in Out, Barbara Gladstone Gallery 1998, Beautiness, Contemporary Fine Arts, Berlin 1999, Sarah Lucas, Tomio Koyama, Tokyo 2000, Sarah Lucas – Beyond the Pleasure Principle, Freud Museum, London 2000, The Fag Show, Sadie Coles HQ 2000; *Group Exhibitions include:* Material Culture, Hayward Gallery, London 1997, Real Life: New British Art, Tochigi Prefectural Museum of Fine Arts (and tour to Fukuoka City Art Museum, Hiroshima City Museum of Contemporary Art, Tokyo Museum of Contemporary Art and Ashiya City Museum of Art and History) Japan 1998–99, Sensation: Young British Artists in the Saatchi Collection, Brooklyn Museum, NY 1999, Intelligence, New British Art 2000, Tate Britain, Millbank, London 2000, Century City, Tate Modern, London 2001, Public Offerings, Museum of Contemporary Art, LA 2001, Summer Exhibition, RA, London 2001; *Films include:* Sausage Film 1990, The Shop (film for Century City exhibition, Tate Modern, London) 2001. *Address:* c/o Sadie Coles HQ Ltd, 35 Heddon St, London, W1, UK. *Telephone:* (20) 7434-2227; *Fax:* (20) 7434-2228; *E-mail:* press@sadiecoles.com; *Internet:* www.sadiecoles.com.

LUCHKO, Klara Stepanovna; Russian actress; b 1 July 1925, Poltava, Ukraine; d of Stefan and Anna Luchko; m 1st Sergey Lukianov 1959 (died 1963); m 2nd Dmitriy Mamleev; one d. *Education:* VGIK. *Career:* Actress, Cinema Actors' Theatre-Studio 1948–; has appeared in numerous films 1948–; mem Nika Cinema Acad; People's Artist of USSR; Badge of Honour, Cinema Actors Guild's Prize for Outstanding Contrib to Profession 1999; Order For Services to Motherland 2000. *Films include:* Cossacks from the Kuban (USSR State Prize) 1955, Twelfth Night, Red Leaves, The Gipsies (TV), Another's Child 1982, We – The Undersigned (TV) 1982, Badulai's Return 1986, Play in Death 1991, Eyes 1993, Parable 1995, Legend 1997; *TV work includes:* narrator in weekly programme Films of our Memory 1993–96 and Movie Star 1997–2000; *Publication:* My Biography: Am I Guilty? (screenplay and book). *Leisure interests:* travelling, music, the arts, writing. *Address:* 109240 Moscow, Kotelnicheskaya Nab, 1/15 Korpus B, kv 308, Russian Federation. *Telephone:* (095) 915-43-67.

LUCID, Shannon W., PH D; American biochemist and astronaut; b 14 Jan 1943, Shanghai, People's Repub of China; d of Joseph O. Wells; m Michael F. Lucid; two d one s. *Education:* Univ of Oklahoma. *Career:* Sr Lab Technician Oklahoma Medical Research Foundation 1964–66, Research Assoc 1974–; Chemist Kerr-McGee 1966–68; Astronaut NASA Lyndon B. Johnson Space Center, Houston, TX 1979–, Mission Specialist flights STS-51G and STS-34; mission specialist Shuttle Atlantis flight 1991; on board Russian Fed space station Mir March–Sept 1996. *Address:* NASA, Johnson Space Center, CB-Astronaut Office, Houston, TX 77058, USA.

ŁUCZKOWSKA, Jolanta Barbara, MA; Polish business executive; b 16 April 1954, Warsaw; one s. *Education:* Warsaw Univ. *Career:* Journalist 1977–81; Sec Ingersoll Rand 1982–87; Commercial Asst ICI, Poland 1987–90; Sales Rep Johnson and Johnson 1990, apptd Sr Sales Rep 1991; Adviser Foundation for Polish Agric Devt; Vice-Pres Business and Professional Women's Club; fmr mem Solidarity. *Leisure interests:* theatre, American and Russian literature. *Address:* Johnson & Johnson, ul Korkowa 89, 04-519 Warsaw, Poland (Office); Sapieżyńska 7m 35, 00-215 Warsaw, Poland (Home). *Telephone:* (2) 39121408 (Office); (22) 313016 (Home).

LUCZYWO, Helena; Polish media executive; b 1946; m; one d. *Education:* Univ of Warsaw. *Career:* Began career as English translator; later Ed of underground newspapers Robotnik (The Worker) and Tygodnik Mazowsze (Mazovia Weekly); Ed Gazeta Wyborcza (Election Gazette) 1989–; Co-Founder and Editorial Dir Agora SA (media corpn). *Address:* Gazeta Wyborcza, Agora SA, ul Czerska 8/10, 00-732 Warsaw, Poland.

LUDWIG, Christa; Austrian opera singer (mezzo-soprano); b 16 March 1928, Berlin, Germany; d of Anton Ludwig and Eugenie Besalla-Ludwig; m 1st Walter Berry 1957 (divorced 1970); one s; m 2nd Paul-Emile Deiber 1972. *Career:* Opera debut aged 18; mem Vienna State Opera 1955–, Hon mem 1981–, Vienna Konzerthaus; appearances at Athens Festival, Epidauros 1965 and festivals in Salzburg and Bayreuth, Germany, Lucerne, Switzerland, Netherlands, Prague, Saratoga, USA, Stockholm; guest appearances in Vienna, New York and Chicago, USA, Buenos Aires, Milan, Italy, Berlin and Munich, Germany; numerous recitals and solo performances in concerts; winner Bach-Concours; title Kammersängerin conferred, Austrian Govt 1962; Silver Rose, Vienna Philharmonic 1980; Golden Ring, Staatsoper, Vienna 1980; Golden Gustav Mahler Medal 1980; Hugo Wolf Medal 1980; Goldenes Ehrenzeichen, Salzburg; Gold Medal, City of Vienna 1988; Commdr des Arts et des Lettres 1989; Chevalier de la Légion d'Honneur 1989, Grosses Ehrenreichen 1994; Commdr de l'Ordre pour le Mérite (France) 1997. *Recordings include:* Norma (with Maria Callas), Lohengrin, Così fan tutte, Der Rosenkavalier, Carmen, Götterdämmerung, Die Walküre, Herzog Blaubarts Burg, Don Giovanni, Die Zauberflöte, Le Nozze di Figaro, Capriccio, Fidelio, Venus in Tannhäuser (Prix des Affaires Culturelles) 1972; *Publication:* In My Own Voice (biog) 1994. *Leisure interests:* music, archaeology, reading, home movie making, cooking, sewing, fashion, shopping, weaving, rug knitting, travel. *Address:* 14 Rigistr, 6045 Meggen, Switzerland (Home).

LUKASHEVA, Yelena Andreyevna, DR JUR; Russian lawyer; b 28 July 1927, Kharkov, Ukraine. *Education:* Moscow State Univ. *Career:* Head of div journal Sovietskoye Gosudarstvo i Pravo 1953–61; Sr researcher Inst of State and Law, USSR Acad of Sciences 1961–; mem Scientific Council, Head Sector of Human Rights 1989–; mem Scientific Council, Centre of Theory and History of State Law; Dir Expert Group on Politology and Law (Russian Humanitarian Foundation) 1990–2000; Merited Jurist of Russian Fed. *Publications:* books and articles on problems of theory of law, human rights, legal and social state, including Law, Morality, Personality 1986, General Theory of Human Rights (ed) 1996, Human Rights as a Factor of Strategic Stability of Development (ed) 2000, Human Rights (text book) 2000. *Leisure interest:* Russian classical music and literature. *Address:* Institute of State and Law, Znamenka str 10, 119841 Moscow, Russian Federation. *Telephone:* (095) 291-34-90; (095) 291-87-56 (Office); (095) 917-00-62 (Home).

LULING HAUGHTON, Rosemary Elena Konradin; American/British writer, lecturer, philosopher and theologian; b 13 April 1927, London; d of Theodore Dunham and Sylvia Elizabeth (née Thompson) Luling; m Edward Algernon Haughton 1948; seven s three d. *Education:* Farnham Girls' Grammar School (Hants), Queen's Coll and Slade School of Art (London). *Career:* Began writing 1965; lectures in USA, Europe, Australia 1968–; mem Lothlorien experimental therapeutic rural community, Dumfriesshire 1974–81; mem Admin Team Wellspring House Inc, org for social justice especially for women and children, including shelter for homeless families, educ, affordable housing and small businesses, MA, USA 1981–; Dr hc (St Mary's Coll, IN) 1977, (Notre Dame, IN) 1978, (Rochester Coll) 1984, (Georgian Court Coll, NJ), (Nazareth Coll, NY); Avila Award; Elizabeth Seton Award. *Publications include:* On Trying to be Human 1965, The Transformation of Man 1966, The Drama of Salvation, Tales from Eternity 1967, Elizabeth's Greeting, Act of Love 1968, Love 1968, The Catholic Thing 1978, The Passionate God 1980, The Re-Creation of Eve 1986, Song in a Strange Land 1990, The Tower that Fell (illustrated), Images for Change 1998; 25 other books, numerous articles and essays. *Leisure interests:* wood-carving, embroidery, gardening, reading, country cottage. *Address:* Wellspring House, 302 Essex Ave, Gloucester, MA 01930, USA; 5 Draper Corner, Heptonstall, Hebden Bridge, W Yorkshire, HX7 7EY, UK. *Telephone:* (508) 281-3221 (USA).

LULLING, Astrid Anne; Luxembourg politician; b 11 June 1929, Schifflange; d of Nic and Catherine Lulling. *Career:* Mem Chamber of Deputies (Parl, PCS) 1965–89, Exec mem 1984–87; nominated mem EP 1965–74, MEP 1989–, mem Cttees on Econ and Monetary Affairs, Industrial Policy, Women's Rights 1989–; Mayor of Schifflange 1970–85; mem NATO Ass 1979–84, Benelux econ union Interparl Council 1979–84; Pres Lab Cttee 1980–, European Centre, Int Council of Women; Pres Nat Fed of Women. *Leisure interests:* travel, reading, swimming. *Address:* European Parliament, rue Wiertz, 1047 Brussels, Belgium (Office); 28 chemin Vert, 3878 Schifflange, Luxembourg (Home). *Telephone:* (2) 284-53-31 (Office); 54-82-56 (Home); *Fax:* (2) 284-93-31 (Office); 54-88-50 (Home).

LULU, (Marie Lawrie Frieda); British singer and actress; b 3 Nov 1948, Glasgow. *Career:* Appearances on stage include Royal Command Performance and concerts in Las Vegas, Hollywood and Miami (USA); own shows on radio and TV. *Songs and recordings include:* Man Who Sold the World 1974, The Man with the Golden Gun (theme to Bond film) 1975, I Could Never Miss You, If I Were You 1982; *Stage performances include:* Peter Pan 1975–76, 1987–88, Aladdin 1976–77, Song and Dance, Guys and Dolls, The Mystery of Edwin Drood; *Films:* Swinging UK, Gonks Go Beat 1966, To Sir with Love; *TV appearances include:* Lulu 1966–74, 1982–83, Let's Rock, Some You Win 1983–84, The Growing Pains of Adrian Mole 1987, Perfect Scoundrels 1989–90. *Address:* c/o Susan Angel Associates Ltd, 1st Floor, 12 d'Arblay St, London W1V 3FP, UK.

LUMLEY, Joanna Lamond, OBE; British actress; b 1 May 1946, Kashmir, then British India; d of James Rutherford and Thyra Beatrice Rose Lumley; m 1st Jeremy Lloyd (divorced); one s; m 2nd Stephen Barlow 1986. *Education:* Army School (Kuala Lumpur), Mickledene (Kent) and St Mary's (St Leonards on Sea). *Career:* Hon D LITT (Kent) 1994; Hon D UNIV (Oxford Brookes) 2000; BAFTA Award 1992, 1994, Special BAFTA 2000. *Plays include:* Blithe Spirit 1986, Vanilla 1990, Revengers Comedies 1991, The Letter 1995, Hedda Gabbler, The Cherry Orchard, Private Lives, An Ideal Husband; *Films include:* Some Girls Do, Tam Lin, The Breaking of Bumbo, Games That Lovers Play, Don't Just Lie There Say Something, On Her Majesty's Secret Service, Trail of the Pink Panther, Curse of the Pink Panther, Satanic Rites of Dracula 1978, That Was Tory, Mistral's Daughter, A Ghost in Monte Carlo, Shirley Valentine, Forces Sweetheart, Innocent Lies 1995, James and the Giant Peach 1996, Cold Comfort Farm 1996, Prince Valiant 1997, Parting Shots 1998, The Tale of Sweeney Todd 1998, Mad Cows 1999, Maybe Baby 1999, The Cat's Meow 2000; *TV appearances include:* Release, Mark II Wife, Comedy Playhouse, It's Awfully Bad for Your Eyes Darling, Satanic Rites of Dracula 1973, Coronation Street, The Protectors, General Hospital 1974–75, The New Avengers 1976–77, Steptoe and Son, Are You Being Served?, The Cuckoo Waltz, Up The Workers, Sapphire and Steel 1978, A Perfect Hero 1991, Absolutely Fabulous (series) 1992–94, Class Act 1994; Girl Friday (documentary) 1994, White Rajahs of Sarawak (documentary), Joanna Lumley in the Kingdom of the Thunder Dragon (documentary)

1997, Coming Home 1998, A Rather English Marriage 1998, Nancherrow, Dr Willoughby, MD; *Publications include:* Stare Back and Smile (memoirs) 1989, Forces' Sweethearts 1993, Girl Friday 1994, Joanna Lumley in the Kingdom of the Thunder Dragon 1997. *Leisure interests:* walking, gardening, collecting things, painting, music, travelling. *Address:* c/o Conway van Gelder, 3rd Floor, 18–21 Jermyn St, London SW1 6HP, UK.

LUMSDEN, Lynne Ann; American publishing executive; b 30 July 1947, Battle Creek, MI; d of Arthur Lumsden and Ruth Pandy; m Jon Harden 1986; one d. *Education:* Univ of Paris, Sarah Lawrence Coll (New York), City Grad Center and New York Univ. *Career:* Copy Ed Harcourt Brace, Jovanavich, New York 1970–71; Ed Appleton-Century Crofts, New York 1971–73, Coll Div, Prentice Hall 1974–78, Sr Ed Coll Div 1978–81; Asst Vice-Pres, Ed-in-Chief Spectrum Books 1981–82, Vice-Pres, Editorial Dir, Gen Publishing Div 1982–85; Exec Vice-Pres, Publisher, Co-Owner Dodd, Mead & Co Inc, New York 1985–89; Owner, Chair JBH Communications Inc, Hartford, CT 1989–; Business Man Hartford News and Southside Media 1989–. *Address:* 11 Hammer St, Hartford, CT 06114, USA (Office).

LUNDBY-WEDIN, Wanja; Swedish trade union executive. *Career:* Fmr local govt worker; Vice-Pres Swedish Trade Union Confed (LO), Chair (first woman) Dec 2000–. *Address:* Landsorganisationen i Sverige (Swedish Trade Union Confederation), Barnhusgt 18, 105 53 Stockholm, Sweden. *Telephone:* (8) 796-28-00; *Fax:* (8) 796-28-00.

LUNDHOLT, Anne Birgitte, M SC; Danish politician; b 11 June 1952, Fredericia; d of N. E. and A. A. Lundholt. *Education:* Aarhus Univ and Copenhagen Business School. *Career:* Negotiator Fed of Danish Business Employers 1977–80; Head of Dept, Fed of Danish Textile Industry 1980–86, Co-Dir 1986–88; Man Dir Fed of Danish Furniture Industry 1988–89; Minister of Industry 1989–90, of Industry and Energy 1990–92; Politician of the Year 1990; Commdr of Dannebrog 1990. *Leisure interest:* golf. *Address:* c/o Ministry of Industry, Slotsholmsgade 12, 1216 Copenhagen K, Denmark.

LUNGHI, Cherie; British actress. *Career:* Numerous appearances in films and on TV in the UK and USA. *Films include:* Excalibur, King David, The Mission, To Kill a Priest, Jack and Sarah 1995, Frankenstein 1995; *TV appearances include:* Films: Sign of Four, Praying Mantis; Series: Master of the Game, Tales of the Unexpected, Strangers and Brothers 1984, Harem 1987, The Monocled Mutineer 1987, The Manageress 1988–91; numerous TV plays. *Address:* c/o Elspeth Pearson, August Management, 38 Hart Grove, London, W5 3NB, UK.

LUNN, Janet Louise Swoboda; Canadian writer and editor; b 28 Dec 1928, Dallas, TX, USA; d of Herman A. and Margaret Swoboda; m Richard Lunn 1950; four s one d. *Education:* Queen's Univ (ON). *Career:* Literary Consultant Ginn and Co 1968–78; Children's Ed Clarke, Irwin and Co 1972–75; Conducted Writers' Workshops with Ontario Arts Council; Writer-in-Residence Regina Public Library 1982–83, Kitchener Public Library 1988; mem Bd Dirs The Canadian Children's Book Centre 1990–93, (Vice-Pres 1990), IBBY Canada 1989; Second Vice-Chair Writers' Union of Canada 1979–80, Vice-Chair 1983–84, Chair 1984–85; mem Canadian Soc of Children's Authors, Illustrators and Performers, PEN Int; Hon LL D (Queen's) 1992; Hon Dip (Loyalist Coll, Belville, ON) 1993; Order of Ontario 1996. *Publications include:* The County (jtly) 1967, Double Spell (first published as Twin Spell 1968), Larger than Life 1979, The Twelve Dancing Princesses (IODE Toronto Br Children's Book Award) 1979, The Root Cellar (Book of the Year, Canadian Library Asscn 1982, Booklist's Reviewers' Choice, Teachers' Choice, American Nat Council of Teachers of English 1983, Honour List Int Bd of Books for Young People 1984, chosen in Jr High Category, California Young Reader Medal programme 1988), Shadow in Hawthorn Bay (Children's Book Award, Canadian Library Asscn, Young Adult Book of the Year Award, Saskatchewan Library Asscn, Children's Book of the Year, IODE Nat Chapter, Honour List, Int Bd of Books for Young People 1984, one of 40 books of the year, Int Children's Library, Munich, Germany 1986), Amos's Sweater (Ruth Schwartz Award, Canadian Booksellers' Asscn 1989, Amelia Frances Howard Gibbon Award, Gov-Gen's Award) 1988, Duck Cakes for Sale 1989, One Hundred Shining Candles 1990, The Story of Canada for Children 1992, The Hollow Tree, Umbrella

Birthday, Mr and Mrs Hat, Come to the Fair 1997, Charlotte 1998. *Leisure interests:* gardening, cooking, reading. *Address:* 115–3260 Southgate Rd, Ottawa, ON K1V 8W9, Canada. *E-mail:* janetlunn@sympatico.ca; *Internet:* www.keith-n.com/jlunn.

LUPONE, Patti, BFA; American singer; b 21 April 1949, Northport, NY; d of Orlando Joseph and Angela Louise LuPone; m Matt Johnston; one s. *Education:* Juilliard School (New York). *Theatre performances include:* School for Scandal, Three Sisters, The Beggar's Opera, The Robber Bridegroom, Measure for Measure, Edward II, The Water Engine, The Baker's Wife, The Woods, Working, Catchpenny Twist, As You Like It, The Cradle Will Rock, Stars of Broadway, Edmond, Evita (Tony Award), Oliver!, Anything Goes, Les Misérables, Sunset Boulevard; *Films:* 1941, Fighting Back, Witness, Wise Guys, Driving Miss Daisy, Family Prayers; *TV includes:* Life Goes On (series) 1989–93, LBJ: The Early Years, The Water Engine, Frasier, Falcone 2000. *Address:* ICM, 40 W 57th St, 16th Floor, New York, NY 10019, USA.

LURIE, Alison, AB; American writer; b 3 Sept 1926, Chicago, IL; d of Harry Lawrence and Bernice Stewart Lurie; m 1st Jonathan Peale Bishop 1948 (divorced 1985); three s; m 2nd Edward Hower 1996. *Education:* Radcliffe Coll (Cambridge, MA). *Career:* Lecturer in English Cornell Univ 1969–73, Adjunct Assoc Prof 1973–76, Assoc Prof 1976–79, Prof 1979–, currently Frederic J. Whiton Prof of American Literature; Yaddo Foundation Fellow 1963, 1964, 1966, 1984; Guggenheim Fellow 1965; Rockefeller Foundation Fellow 1967; Literature Award, American Acad of Arts and Letters 1978; Pulitzer Prize in Fiction 1985. *Publications:* V. R. Lang: a Memoir 1959, Love and Friendship 1962, The Nowhere City 1965, Imaginary Friends 1967, Real People 1969, The War Between the Tates 1974, V. R. Lang: A Memoir 1975, Only Children 1979, Clever Gretchen and Other Forgotten Folktales 1980, The Heavenly Zoo 1980, The Language of Clothes 1981, Fabulous Beasts 1981, Foreign Affairs (Pulitzer Prize) 1985, The Truth About Lorin Jones (Prix Femina Etranger 1989) 1988, Don't Tell the Grown Ups: Subversive Children's Literature (essays) 1990, The Garland Library of Children's Classics (co-ed), Women and Ghosts 1994, The Last Resort 1998, Familiar Spirits 2001; stories and articles in journals. *Address:* Dept of English, Cornell University, Ithaca, New York, NY 14853, USA. *E-mail:* al28@cornell.edu (Office).

LUTHER, Usha Masson, PH D; Indian educator; b 26 July 1926, Ferozepore; d of D. R. and C. K. Masson; m M. M. Luther 1981. *Education:* Univ of Delhi. *Career:* Lecturer Miranda Coll, Univ of Delhi 1964; Fellow George Washington Univ, Washington DC 1965–67; Asst Prof, Assoc Prof State Univ Coll at New Paltz, NY, Chair Asian Studies Dept 1967–75, Project Research Assoc 1976; Sr Research Fellow Indian Council of Social Sciences Research 1978–81, Indian Council of Historical Research 1985–87; Project Dir Historical Atlas, Turkey 1981–84; Co-Dir Univ Grants Comm, Jawaharlal Nehru Univ, New Delhi 1987–90; Pres Inst of Creative Academic Packages on India, New Delhi 1988–; Dir Educ Research Services and Publications 1989–; practising neuropath, Gurgaon 1998–; has served on several nat and int cttees; contribs to Indian Studies journals; numerous awards including Woman of the Year, American Biographical Inst Research Asscn (ABIRA), USA 1990, Twentieth Century Achievment Award (ABIRA) 1997, voted as one of Five Hundred Leaders of Influence (ARIBA) 1997. *Publications:* Historical Route Network of Anatolia 1550–1850s 1989, Historical Routes of the NW Indian Subcontinent 1550s–1850s 1990, Urvadiyan (The Valleys of Heart) (Hindi poems) 1998. *Leisure interests:* performing arts, handicrafts, museums, music, poetry, palmistry, homeopathy. *Address:* 100 Silver Oaks Apts, DLF Qutub Enclave, Phase 1, Gurgaon 122 002, India; D,416 Defence Colony, New Delhi 110024, India. *Telephone:* (124) 363232; *E-mail:* mmluther@usne.com.

LUTZ, Julie Haynes, PH D; American professor of astronomy; b 17 Dec 1944, Mount Vernon, OH; d of Willard Dannon and Julia Awilda Haynes; m Thomas Edward Lutz 1967; two c. *Education:* San Diego State Univ (CA) and Univ of Illinois. *Career:* Asst Prof of Astronomy Washington State Univ 1972–78, Asst Dean of Science 1978–79, Assoc Prof 1978–84, Assoc Provost 1981–82, Prof 1984–, Chair of Mathematics and Astronomy 1992–96; Research Fellow Univ Coll London, UK 1976–77, 1982–83; Visiting Resident Astronomer Cerro Tololo Inter-American Observatory 1988–89; Dir Div of Astronomy, NSF 1990–91, Div of Astronomical Sciences 1990–92; Fellow Royal

Astronomy Soc; mem AAAS, American Astronomy Soc of the Pacific (Pres 1990–92), Int Astronomers Union, Astronomy Soc of the Pacific. *Address:* Washington State University, Program in Astronomy, Pullman, WA 99164-3113, USA (Office); NE1200 McGee Way, Pullman, WA 99163, USA (Home).

LUVSANDANZABGIIN, Ider, BA; Mongolian diplomatist; b 1 March 1937, Ulan Bator; d of Yondongiin and Kulista Botasheva Luvsandanzan; m Pureviin Zorigt 1960; one d one s. *Education:* Inst of Int Relations and Diplomatic Acad (Moscow). *Career:* Mem staff Ministry of Foreign Relations 1963–73, 1977–79, 1981–86, apptd Dir Dept of Treaty and Legal Affairs 1989; Second Sec to UK 1973–76; Chargé d'affaires to France and Perm Rep to UNESCO 1986–89; Rapporteur Third Cttee UN Gen Ass 1972, Chair Cttee on Elimination of Discrimination Against Women 1982–84, mem 1985–86, mem Cttee on Econ, Social and Cultural Rights 1991–94; Amb Extraordinary and Plenipotentiary 1991; articles on human rights and the status of women. *Leisure interests:* reading, walking. *Address:* c/o Ministry of Foreign Relations, Dept of Treaty and Legal Affairs, Ulan Bator, Mongolia (Office); Flat 59, House 2B, Mikrorayon 5, Horoo 3, Sukhebaataryn rayon, Ulan Bator, Mongolia (Home). *Telephone:* 21803 (Home).

LUZ, Virginia Erskine, RCA; Canadian artist; b 15 Oct 1911, Toronto, ON; d of G. John and Jessie Luz. *Education:* Cen Tech School (Toronto) and McLane Art Inst (New York). *Career:* Freelance artist, Toronto 1932–38; Instructor of Illustration Art Dept, Cen Tech School, Toronto 1940–47, Asst Dir of Art 1965–69, Dir 1969–74; exhibitions include Royal Canadian Acad 1952–88, Ontario Soc of Artists 1945–88, Expo '67, Canadian Group of Painters 1945–52, Canadian Women Artists Show, New York 1947, Canadian Tour 1948–49, Montréal Museum of Fine Arts 1948–53, Canadian Nat Exhibition Shows (solo) 1948, 1976, 1981, 1993, 1994, (jt) 1951, 1953, Sisler Gallery, Toronto Tribute to 10 Women 1975, Artists Choice Etobicoke Civic Centre 1981; rep in numerous pvt and public collections including Dept of External Affairs, Ottawa, J. S. McLean Coll, London, ON and Robert McLaughlin Gallery; mem Canadian Soc of Painters in Water Colour 1960, Ontario Soc of Artists 1953, mem Exec Council 1963–65, Royal Canadian Acad of Arts 1977. *Address:* 602 Melita Crescent, Apt 319, Toronto, ON M6G 3Z5, Canada.

LYMAN, Peggy; American dance educator and artistic director; b 28 June 1950; d of James Louis and Anne Earlene Morner; m 1st David Stanley Lyman 1970 (divorced 1979); m 2nd Timothy Scott Lynch 1982 (divorced 1997); one s. *Career:* Prin Dancer Martha Graham Dance Co, New York 1973–88, Rehearsal Dir 1989–90, mem faculty Martha Graham School 1975–, Artistic Dir Martha Graham Ensemble 1990–91, Site Dir 1992, 1993; Head of Dance Div, N Kentucky Univ 1977–78; Artistic Dir Peggy Lyman Dance Co 1978–89; Asst Prof of Dance and Guest Choreographer Florida State Univ, Tallahassee 1982–89; Teacher Hartford Ballet School 1992–, E Connecticut Concert Ballet 1992–; Chair Dance Dept Hartt School, Univ of Hartford, CT 1994–; Guest Choreographer Southern Methodist Univ, Dallas, TX 1986; guest artist (with Rudolph Nureyev) on Invitation to Dance, CBS-TV 1980, numerous other guest appearances. *Address:* Dance Connecticut, 224 Farmington Ave, Hartford, CT 06105-3597, USA. *E-mail:* dancectplyman@snet.net.

LYMPANY, Dame Moura, DBE, FRAM; British concert pianist; b 18 Aug 1916, Saltash, Cornwall; d of John Johnstone and Beatrice Lympany; m 1st Colin Defries 1944 (divorced 1950); m 2nd Bennet H. Korn 1951 (divorced 1961); one s (deceased). *Education:* In Belgium, Austria, UK. *Career:* Debut Harrogate 1929; has played in USA, Canada, S America, Australia, NZ, India and most European countries including the fmr USSR; performed at Festival de la Musique et du Vin (Rasiguères, France) 1981, Festival des Sept Chapelles (Brittany, France) 1986; Chevalier des Arts et des Lettres 1992, Commdr Order of the Crown, Belgium 1980, Medal of Cultural Merit, Portugal 1989, Charles Heidsieck Prize, Royal Philharmonic Soc 1989, Order of Prince Henry the Navigator (Portugal) 1996. *Publication:* Moura Lympany: her autobiography 1991. *Leisure interests:* gardening, reading, tapestry. *Address:* c/o Transart, 8 Bristol Gardens, London W9 2JG, UK.

LYNCH, Jennifer Ann; New Zealand magazine editor; b 23 Sept 1938; d of William Leslie and Phyllis Joy Lynch; m 1991. *Education:* Epsom Girls' Grammar School (Auckland), Moorhead Sr High (MN, USA) and Concordia Coll (Moorhead, MN). *Career:* Actress until 1963; journalist, graphic artist 1963–; has worked for New Zealand Weekly News, Sunday Herald, Thursday Magazine; joined New Zealand Woman's Weekly 1975, Ed 1987. *Leisure interests:* theatre, opera, reading, gardening, animal welfare. *Address:* 1/7 Orcades Place, Lynfield, Auckland, New Zealand.

LYNCH, Patricia Gates; American former ambassador and broadcasting executive; b 20 April 1926, Newark, NJ; d of William Charles and Mary Frances Lawrence; m 1st Mahlon Eugene Gates 1942 (divorced 1972); m 2nd William Dennis Lynch; one d one s. *Education:* Dartmouth Inst. *Career:* Broadcaster WFAX-Radio, VA 1958–68, NBC-Radio Europe, Iran and USSR 1960–61; TV Host WETA, Washington, DC 1967–68; Int Broadcaster and Producer Voice of America, Washington, DC 1962–69; staff asst to First Lady Mrs Nixon, White House 1969–70; Host Breakfast Show, Morning Show 1970–86; Amb to Madagascar and The Comoros 1986–89; Dir of Corp Affairs Radio Free Europe/Radio Liberty, Washington, DC 1989–94; lectured worldwide 1968–86; mem Council of American Ambs, American Women in Radio and TV, American News Women's Club; United States Information Agency Grantee 1983; Public Service Award, US Army 1960.

LYNN, Loretta Webb; American singer; b 14 April 1935, Butcher Hollow, KY; d of Ted and Clara Webb; m Oliver V. Lynn, Jr 1948; three d two s (one deceased). *Career:* Sec and Treas Loretta Lynn Enterprises; Vice-Pres United Talent Inc; Hon Chair Bd Loretta Lynn Western Stores; Hon Rep United Giver's Fund 1971; recording artist with MCA 1961–; first female country singer to record a certified Gold album; Female Vocalist of the Year, Country Music Assn 1967, 1972, 1973; Grammy Award 1971; Entertainer of the Year 1972; Top Duet 1972–75; American Music Award 1978; Entertainer of the Decade, Acad of Country Music 1980; mem Country Music Hall of Fame 1988. *Recordings include:* Just a Woman 1985, Making Believe (jtly) 1988, The Country Music Hall of Fame 1991, Greatest Hits Live 1992, Country's Favorite Daughter (reissue) 1993; *Publication:* Coal Miner's Daughter 1976. *Address:* c/o United Talent Inc, POB 23470, Nashville, TN 37202, USA.

LYNN, Dame Vera, DBE; British singer; b 20 March 1917; d of Bertram and Ann Welch; m Harry Lewis 1941; one d. *Education:* Brampton Road School (East Ham). *Career:* Joined singing troupe 1928; Owner, Man dancing school 1932; broadcast with Joe Loss, joined Charlie Kunz band 1935; singer with Ambrose Orchestra 1937–40; solo singer 1940–; voted most popular singer in Daily Express competition 1939; own radio show Sincerely Yours 1941–47; sang to troops abroad during Second World War, named 'Forces' Sweetheart'; appeared in Applesauce, London 1941; post-war radio and TV shows and numerous appearances abroad including Denmark, Canada, S Africa and Australia; most successful record Auf Wiederseh'n; Pres Printers' Charitable Corpn 1980; Hon Citizen Winnipeg 1974; Freedom of City of London 1978; Commdr Order of Orange-Nassau (Netherlands); Burma Star Medal; War Medal 1985; Variety Club Int Humanitarian Award; European Woman of Achievement Award 1994. *Publications:* Vocal Refrain (autobiog) 1975, We'll Meet Again (jtly) 1989, The Woman Who Won the War (jtly) 1990, Unsung Heroines 1990. *Leisure interests:* gardening, painting, sewing, swimming.

LYNNE, Gillian, CBE; British choreographer, dancer and actress; d of the late Leslie and Barbara (née Hart) Pyrke; m Peter Land 1980. *Education:* Baston School (Bromley, Kent) and Arts Educational School. *Career:* Leading Soloist Sadler's Wells ballet 1944–51; Star Dancer London Palladium 1951–53; numerous TV, film and theatre appearances; has choreographed, directed and staged numerous musicals, plays, TV shows and films in Europe and USA; role in film Master of Ballantrae 1952; lead in Can-Can, Coliseum, London 1954–55; numerous roles as dancer, actress and revue artist; conceived, directed, choreographed and starred in Collages, Edinburgh Festival 1963; choreography for numerous TV shows; Patron Ind Dancers' Resettlement Trust, Liverpool Inst for Performing Arts, British Asscn of Choreographers, Adventures in Motion Pictures Ltd. *Appearances* *include:* Vanity Fair 1956, Samson and Delilah 1957, Aïda, Tannhäuser 1957, A Midsummer Night's Dream 1958, Chelsea at Nine 1957, New Cranks, Wanda, Rose Marie, Cinderella, Out of My Mind; *Stage productions include:* England Our England (revue) 1961, A Comedy of Errors, Stratford 1976 (TV musical 1977), musical As You Like It, Stratford 1977; *Choreography includes:* The Owl and the Pussycat 1962, Wonderful Life 1963–64, Every Day's a Holiday, Three Hats for Lisa, The Flying Dutchman 1966, Half a Sixpence 1966–67, Midsummer Marriage 1968, The Trojans 1969, Phil the Fluter, Man of La Mancha 1972, The Way of the World 1978, My Fair Lady 1979, Parsifal 1979 (also Assoc Dir), The Card, Cats (Olivier Award 1981, Molière Award for Best Musical, Paris 1989) 1981), Cabaret 1986, My Fair Lady, The Phantom of the Opera 1986, Café Soir, A Simple Man (ballet) 1988, The Brontës (also Dir) 1995, The Secret Garden 2000; TV: Peter and the Wolf 1966, There was a Girl, The Fool on the Hill, Muppet Show (series) 1976–80, Alice in Wonderland; Director: Paris 1989, What the World Needs 1997–98; A Midsummer Night's Dream (co-dir), Stratford 1977, Jeeves Takes Charge 1980, La Ronde, RSC (additional dir) 1982, Cabaret 1986; *TV work includes:* The Simple Man 1987 (BAFTA Award for direction and choreography), The Look of Love 1989, That's What Friends Are For! 1996; *Publications:* Cats, The Book of the Musical (contrib), numerous contribs to journals and articles in Dancing Times. *Address:* Lean Two Productions Ltd, 18 Rutland St, London SW7 1EF, UK (Office).

LYON, Christina Margaret, LL B, FRSA; British professor of law; b 12 Nov 1952, Liverpool; d of Edward Arthur and Kathleen Joan Harison; m Adrian Pirrie Lyon 1976; one d one s. *Education:* Univ Coll London. *Career:* Tutor and Lecturer in Law, Univ Coll London 1974–75; Trainee and Asst Solicitor Bell and Joynson 1975–77; Tutor in Law (part-time) Liverpool Univ 1976–77, Lecturer 1977–80, Prof of Common Law, Head Dept of Law 1993–97, Dean Faculty of Law 1994–97, Dir Centre for the Study of the Child, the Family and the Law 1995–, Queen Victoria Prof of Law 1998–; Solicitor 1977; Lecturer in Law, and Law and Social Work, Manchester Univ 1980–86, Sub-Dean Faculty of Law 1986; Prof of Law, Head Dept and School of Law Keele Univ 1987–93; Asst Recorder 1998–2000, a Recorder 2000–; Jt Ed Journal of Social Welfare and Family Law (fmrly Journal of Social Welfare Law) 1984–; mem Research Grants Cttee, Econ and Social Research Council (ESRC) 1988–91, Child Policy Review Group, Nat Children's Bureau 1989–, Nat Exec Cttee and Fundraising Cttee Relate (frmly Marriage Guidance Council) 1990–; Trustee Ind Representation for Children in Need 1989–; Dr Barnardo's Research Fellow 1987–; Maxwell Law Prize, Univ Coll London 1974. *Publications include:* Matrimonial Jurisdiction of Magistrates' Courts 1981, Cohabitation without Marriage 1983, Butterworth's Family Law Service Encyclopaedia (ed) 1983–, Law of Residential Homes and Day Care Establishments 1984, Child Abuse 1990, The Law Relating to Children in Principles and Practice of Forensic Psychiatry 1990, Butterworth's Family Law Handbook 1991, Atkins Court Forms on Infants vol I, vol II 1992, The Law Relating to Children 1993, Child Abuse 1993, Legal Issues Arising from the Care and Control of Children with Learning Disabilities who also Present Severely Challenging Behaviour vol I, Policy Guidance vol II, A Guide for Parents and Carers 1994, Child Protection and the Civil Legal Framework in The Child Protection Handbook 1995, Children's Rights and The Children Act 1989 in Children's Rights 1995, Working Together: an analysis of collaborative inter-agency responses to the problem of domestic violence 1995, Law and Body Politics 1995, Effective Support Services for Children (jtly) 1998, A Trajectory of Hope (jtly) 2000, Loving Smack, Lawful Assaults: a contradiction in human rights and law 2000. *Leisure interests:* horse-riding, swimming, foreign travel, reading, opera, theatre. *Address:* Faculty of Law, University of Liverpool, Chatham St, Liverpool, L69 3BX, UK; 54 Cromptons Lane, Calderstones, Liverpool L18 3EX, UK (Home). *Telephone:* (151) 722-7360 (Home).

LYON, Mary Frances, PH D, SC D, FRS, FIBIOL; British geneticist; b 15 May 1925, Norwich; d of Clifford James and Louise Frances (née Kirby) Lyon. *Education:* Woking Grammar School and Girton Coll (Cambridge). *Career:* Mem MRC Scientific Staff, Inst of Animal Genetics, Edinburgh 1950–55, Radiobiology Unit, Harwell 1955–90, Head of Genetics Section 1962–87; Clothworkers Visiting Research Fellow, Girton Coll, Cambridge 1970–71; Foreign Assoc NAS 1979; numerous scientific papers on genetics in professional journals; Foreign Hon mem American Acad of Arts and Sciences 1980; Francis Amory Prize, American Acad of Arts and Sciences 1977; Royal Medal, Royal Soc 1984; San Remo Int Prize for Genetics 1985; Gairdner Int Award 1985; William Allan Award, American Soc of Human Genetics 1986; Wolf Prize in Medicine 1997. *Address:* MRC Mammalian Genetics Unit, Harwell, Didcot, Oxon OX11 0RD, UK. *Telephone:* (1235) 834393; *Fax:* (1235) 834776; *E-mail:* m.lyon@har.mrc.ac.uk (Office).

M

MA YUAN; Chinese judge; b 30 June 1930, Xinmin Co, Liaoning Prov; two s. *Education:* Chinese People's Univ, Beijing. *Career:* Ed Chinese People's Univ, Beijing; mem CCP 1953–; teacher Dept of Law, Beijing Univ 1955–62, and part-time lawyer 1955–62, part-time Prof 1990–; Judge Civil Court, Supreme People's Court 1981–82, Vice-Pres Civil Court 1982–85, Vice-Pres Supreme People's Court 1985–; mem Standing Cttee All China Women's Fed; Vice-Pres China Marriage and Family Research Inst 1983–; Pres Chinese Asscn of Women Judges 1994–; Asst Sec-Gen Civil and Econ Law Cttee, China Law Soc 1983–. *Address:* Supreme People's Court, 27 Dong Jiaomin Xiang, Beijing 100745, People's Republic of China.

MAATHAI, Wangari, PH D; Kenyan environmentalist and biologist; b 1 April 1940, Nyer; d of Muta Njugi and Wanjiru Kibichoi; m Mwangi Maathai 1969 (divorced 1980); two s one d. *Education:* Mt St Scholastica Coll (Atchison, KS, USA) and Univs of Pittsburgh (USA) and Nairobi. *Career:* Visiting Research Asst Univ of Munich, Germany 1967–69; Lecturer Univ of Nairobi 1969–71, Sr Lecturer 1973, Assoc Prof 1978, Head Dept of Veterinary Anatomy 1973–81; Dir Kenya Red Cross Society 1973–77; Founder, Co-ordinator The Green Belt Movt 1977–; mem, later Chair of Bd Environment Liaison Center Int 1974–84; mem Nat Council Women of Kenya 1977–87, Club of Rome 1987–, Forum for Restoration of Democracy, Comm on Global Governance 1992–95, Ind Working Group on the Future of the UN 1994–95, UN Advisory Bd on Disarmament; arrested 1992; public speaker on human rights, women's issues, devt and the environment; Hon LL D (Williams Coll, USA) 1990; Hon D HUM LITT 1992; Hon Dr of Veterinary Medicine (Giessen, Germany) 1992; has received numerous awards including Judge Sasakawa Environment Prize, Woman of the Year Award 1983, Right Livelihood Award 1984, Better World Soc Award 1986, Global 500 Roll of Hon (UNEP, first woman) 1987, Woman of the World Award 1989, Green Century Environmental Award for Courage 1990, Goldman Environment Prize 1991, Hunger Project Prize (jtly) 1991, Edinburgh Medal 1993, Order of the Golden Ark, Goldman Environment Prize 1994 and others. *Publications:* The Green Belt Movement 1985, The Green Belt Movement: Sharing the Approach and the Experience 1988, The Manual of the Green Belt Movement 1991; numerous scientific papers in journals. *Leisure interests:* walking, swimming, reading. *Address:* The Green Belt Movement, POB 67545, Nairobi, Kenya. *Telephone:* (2) 504264; *Fax:* (2) 504264.

MABHENA, Sinqobile; Zimbabwean tribal chief; b 1974; d of the late Chief Mabhena and of Nomalanga Mabhena. *Career:* Chief Ndebele tribe (first woman) 1995–; studied to become a teacher.

McALEESE, Mary Patricia, LL B, MA, FRSA; Irish Head of State; b 27 June 1951, Belfast, N Ireland; d of Patrick and Claire (née McManus) Leneghan; m Martin McAleese 1976; two d one s. *Education:* Queen's Univ (Belfast), Inn of Court (N Ireland), King's Inns (Dublin) and Trinity Coll (Dublin). *Career:* Reid Prof Trinity Coll, Univ of Dublin 1975–79, 1981–87; political journalist and TV Presenter RTE (Radio Telefis Éireann), Dublin 1979–81, part-time 1981–85; Dir Inst of Professional Legal Studies, Queen's Univ of Belfast 1987–97, Pro Vice-Chancellor 1994–97; Pres of Repub of Ireland 1997–; Non-Exec Dir N Ireland Electricity 1992–97, Channel 4 TV 1993–97; mem Catholic Church Episcopal Delegation to the New Ireland Forum 1984, and to the N Comm on Contentious Parades; fmr mem Belfast Women's Aid, Irish Comm for Prisoners Overseas, Campaign for Homosexual Law Reform (Dublin); mem European Bar Asscn, Int Bar Asscn (N Ireland Rapporteur), Inns of Court (N Ireland), King's Inn (Dublin), Royal Irish Acad; Hon Fellow Inst of Engineers of Ireland, Trinity Coll (Dublin), Royal Coll of Surgeons, Coll of Anaesthetists, Liverpool John Moore's, Royal Coll of Physicians and Surgeons (Glasgow); Hon Bencher King's Inns, Inns of Court (N Ireland); Hon D HUM LITT (Rochester Inst of Technology (NY)); Hon LL D (Nat Univ of Ireland, Nottingham 1998, Victoria Univ of Technology (Australia), St Mary's (Halifax), Queen's (Belfast), Loyola Law School (LA, USA), Aberdeen, Surrey, Trinity Coll (Dublin), Manchester Metropolitan; Dr hc (Surrey) 2000; Silver Jubilee Commemoration Medal, Charles Univ (Prague). *Publications include:* The Irish Martyrs 1995, Reconciled Beings 1997. *Leisure interests:* skiing, reading, hill-walking. *Address:* Áras an Uachtaráin, Phoenix Park, Dublin 8, Ireland (Office). *Telephone:* (1) 617-1000 (Office); *Fax:* (1) 617-1001 (Office); *E-mail:* webmaster@aras.irlgov.ie; *Internet:* www.irlgov.ie/aras.

McALISKEY, (Josephine) Bernadette (née Devlin); politician; b 23 April 1947; d of the late John James and Elizabeth Devlin; m Micheal McAliskey 1973; three c. *Education:* St Patrick's Girls' Acad (Dungannon) and Queen's Univ (Belfast). *Career:* Elected MP (Ind Unity party) for Mid-Ulster (youngest woman) 1969–74; Founder-mem, mem Exec Irish Republican Socialist Party 1975–76; contested seats (Ind) for EP 1979, Dáil Eireann (Irish Parl, People's Democracy) 1982; shot by Loyalist gunmen 1981. *Publication:* The Price of My Soul 1979. *Leisure interests:* walking, folk music, doing nothing, swimming.

MACAPAGAL ARROYO, Gloria, PH D; Philippine politician; b 4 May 1948, Lubago Pampanga; d of the late Diosdado and Evangelina Macaraeg Macapagal; two s one d. *Education:* Assumption Coll, Georgetown Univ, Ateneo de Manila Univ and Univ of the Philippines. *Career:* Under-Sec Dept of Trade and Industry 1986–92; Senator 1992–98; Sec Dept of Social Welfare and Devt, Vice-Pres of Repub 1998–2001; Pres of The Philippines Jan 2001–; Outstanding Senator, Asiaweek; Woman of the Year by Catholic Educ Asscn of Philippines. *Address:* Office of the President, New Executive Building, Malacañang Palace Compound, J.P. Laurel St, San Miguel, Metro Manila, Philippines. *Telephone:* (2) 7356047; *Fax:* (2) 7358006; *E-mail:* gma@easy.net.ph.

MacARTHUR, Ellen, MBE; British yachtswoman; b 1977, Whatstandwell, Derbyshire; d of Ken and Avril MacArthur. *Career:* Circumnavigated UK single-handed (youngest person to pass Yachtmaster Offshore Qualification) 1995; took part in Mini Transat race 1997; Class Winner Route du Rhum race 1999; Second place in Vendée Globe Race (94 days' solo sailing, youngest woman to circumnavigate the globe single-handedly) 2001; BT/YJA Yachtsman of the Year 1998, Sailing's Young Hope (France) 1998. *Address:* c/o Offshore Challenges Ltd, Cowes Yacht Haven, Cowes, Isle of Wight PO31 7AY, UK. *Internet:* www.ellenmacarthur.com.

MACAULEY, Margaret Oluwatosin, M SC; Nigerian scientist; b 30 Jan 1964. *Education:* Queen's School (Ibadan), Univs of Ibadan and Ife. *Career:* Teacher New Bussa Teacher Training Coll 1975–76; mem Schools Bd of Kawa 1976–77, of Oyo 1979–80; Researcher US Geological Survey, Reston, VA 1978; Lecturer in Geology, Dept of Environmental Sciences, Ibadan Polytech 1980–86; part-time Lecturer Univ of W Indies 1987; apptd Man Dir and Chief Consultant Geo-Man Consultants Ltd, Lagos 1989; mem Science Asscn of Nigeria, Nigerian Asscn of Petroleum Explorationists, Jamaican Soc for Scientists and Geologists; mem Council Nigerian Mining and Geosciences Soc, Water and Sanitation Soc. *Leisure interests:* singing, religion, environmental protection. *Address:* Geo-Man Consultants Ltd, 4 Turnbull Rd, Ikoyi, Lagos, Nigeria.

McCALLION, Kathryn Elizabeth, BA; Canadian diplomatist; b 19 June 1945, Toronto, ON; d of David John and Norah Jean McCallion. *Education:* St Mildred's Coll, Jarvis Coll Inst and Univ of Waterloo (ON). *Career:* Second Sec, Mexico 1973–75; Consul and Trade Commr, USA 1975–78; Exec Asst to Deputy Minister for Int Trade, Ottawa 1981–82, Dir Food Policy Div 1982–83; Counsellor Perm Del OECD, Paris 1983–87; High Commr to Jamaica, Bahamas and Belize 1987–90; Dir-Gen W Europe, External Affairs, Ottawa 1990–94, Asst Deputy Minister, Latin America and Caribbean Br, Foreign Affairs 1990–94; Chief Trade Commr 1996–99; Asst Deputy Minister for Int Business and Communications 1996–97, for Int Business, Passport and Consular Affairs 1998–99, for Corp Services, Passport and Consular Affairs 1999–; Pres Professional Asscn of Foreign Service Officers 1980–81; Vice-Pres CS CO-OP 1995–96, Pres 1997–98; mem Bd Dirs Canadian Commercial Corpn 1997–98; Head of Public Service Award; Univ of Waterloo Faculty of Arts Achievement Award. *Leisure interests:* sports, reading. *Address:* 125 Sussex Drive, Ottawa, ON K1A 0G2, Canada. *Telephone:* (613) 996-7065; *Fax:* (613) 996-4519; *E-mail:* kathryn.mccallion@dfait-maeci.gc.ca.

McCANN, Judith; New Zealand film production executive; b 1947, Christchurch. *Career:* Worked for Canadian Govt in film policy and certification 1978–80; Deputy Dir Telefilm Canada 1980–88; apptd Exec Dir New Zealand Film Comm 1989. *Address:* c/o New Zealand Film Commission, 36 Allen St, POB 11-546, Wellington, New Zealand.

McCARTHY, Arlene, BA; British politician; b 10 Oct 1960, Belfast; d of John and June McCarthy. *Education:* Polytechnic of S Bank (London), UMIST and Freie Univ (Berlin). *Career:* Researcher for Socialist Group, EP 1989–90; Researcher and Press Officer for leader of European Parliamentary Lab Party 1990–91; Lecturer in Politics Freie Univ, Berlin 1991–92; Prin European Liaison Officer 1992–94; MEP 1994–; mem European Parliamentary Lab Party, Party of European Socialists (Spokesperson on Regional Policy 1994–). *Publication:* Changing States (co-ed) 1996. *Leisure interests:* dance, swimming, anthropology. *Address:* 3–5 st John St, Manchester, M3 4DN, UK. *E-mail:* arlene.mccarthy@geoz.poptel.org.uk.

McCARTHY, Doris Jean, CM, OC, BA, RCA; Canadian artist; b 7 July 1910, Calgary, AB; d of George Arnold and Jeannie McCarthy. *Education:* Ontario Coll of Art, Cen School of Arts and Crafts (London) and Univ of Toronto. *Career:* Teacher of Art Cen Tech School, Toronto 1932–72; regular exhibitor 1933–; calligrapher, liturgical and landscape artist; has staged more than 40 solo exhibitions; designer City of Scarborough flag; rep in many public and pvt collections including Wynick Tuck Gallery, Toronto, Canadian Art Galleries, Calgary, Robert McLaughlin Gallery, Oshawa, the Library of Windsor Castle; retrospective exhibitions include A Feast of Incarnation (on tour) 1991–; subject of film Doris McCarthy, Heart of a Painter 1983; Pres Canadian Soc of Painters in Water Colour 1953–55, Ontario Soc of Artists 1963–66; Hon LL D (Calgary) 1995; Award of Merit of the City of Scarborough 1987; Woman Artist of the Year 1983; Fellow of the Ontario Coll of Art 1990. *Publications:* A Fool in Paradise 1990, The Good Wine 1991 (autobiog vols 1 and 2). *Leisure interest:* writing. *Address:* 1 Meadowcliff Drive, Scarborough, ON M1M 2X8, Canada. *Telephone:* (416) 261-7727.

McCARTNEY, Stella, BA; British fashion designer; b 1972; d of Paul and the late Linda McCartney. *Education:* Cen St Martin's Coll of Art and Design. *Career:* Work with Christian Lacroix at age 15 and later with Betty Jackson; work experience in Fashion Dept, Vogue magazine; after graduating set up own design co in London; Chief Designer for Chloe, Paris until 2001. *Address:* Chloe, Faubourg St, Honoré, Paris, France.

McCLANAHAN, Rue, BA; American actress; b Healdton, OK; d of William Edwin and Dreda Rheua-Neil McClanahan; m 1st Tom Bish 1958; m 2nd Norman Hartweg; m 3rd Peter DeMaio; m 4th Gus Fisher 1976; m 5th Tom Keel 1984 (divorced 1985). *Education:* Univ of Tulsa (OK). *Career:* Actress Erie Playhouse, PA 1957–58; appeared in numerous plays, films and TV programmes, Los Angeles, CA 1959–64, New York 1964–73; mem Actors' Studio, Actors' Equity Asscn, Screen Actors' Guild; Best Actress in a Comedy Emmy Award 1987; Woman of the Year, Pasadena Playhouse 1986. *Plays include:* Who's Happy Now (Leading off-Broadway role, Obie Award) 1970, Jimmy Shine 1968–69,

Sticks and Bones 1972, California Suite 1977; *Films include:* They Might Be Giants, The People Next Door, The Pursuit of Happiness, Modern Love; *TV appearances include:* Maude 1973–78, Apple Pie 1978, Mama's Family 1982–84, Golden Girls (Emmy Award 1987) 1985–92, The Golden Palace 1992–93; *TV films:* Having Babies III 1978, Topper 1979, The Great American Traffic Jam 1980, Word of Honor 1981, The Day the Bubble Burst 1982, The Little Match Girl 1987, Liberace 1988, To the Heroes 1989, After the Shock 1990, Children of the Bride 1990, To My Daughter 1990, The Dreamer of Oz 1990, Baby of the Bride 1991, Mother of the Bride 1993, Danielle Steele's Message from Nam 1993, Burning Passion: The Margaret Mitchell Story 1994. *Address:* c/o Agency for the Performing Arts, Suite 1200, 9000 Sunset Blvd, Los Angeles, CA 90069, USA.

McCLURG, Patricia A., BA, BD; American church official; b 14 March 1939; d of the late T. H. and Margaret (née Smith) McClurg. *Education:* Austin Coll (Sherman, TX), Presbyterian School of Christian Educ (Richmond, VA), Austin Presbyterian Theological Seminary (Austin, TX) and Southern Methodist Univ (Dallas, TX). *Career:* Dir of Christian Educ Second Presbyterian Church, Newport News, VA 1963–65; Asst Pastor Westminster Presbyterian Church, Beaumont, TX 1967–71; Assoc Pastor First Presbyterian Church, Pasadena, TX 1969–71; Assoc Exec Synod of Red River, Denton, TX 1972–75, Presbytery of Elizabeth, Plainfield, NJ 1986–91; Dir Gen Ass Mission Bd Presbyterian Church, Atlanta, GA 1975–86; Presbytery Exec, Newark, DE 1991–; Vice-Pres Nat Council Churches of Christ in the USA 1985–87, Pres 1988–89; Chair WCC Ass 1985; mem Churches' Special Comm on S Africa, New York 1985–; contribs to professional journals; Distinguished Alumni Award (Austin Coll) 1979; Hon DD (Austin Coll) 1978. *Leisure interests:* walking on the beach, collecting sea shells, reading. *Address:* New Castle Presbytery, E-62 Omega Drive, Newark, DE 19713-2061, USA. *Telephone:* (302) 366-0595.

McCOLGAN, Elizabeth (Liz), MBE; British athlete; b 24 May 1964, Dundee, Scotland; d of Martin Lynch and Elizabeth Fearn; m Peter McColgan 1987; one d. *Education:* Univ of Alabama. *Career:* Coached by Grete Waitz; Gold Medal Commonwealth Games 10,000m 1986, 1990; Silver Medal World Cross Country Championships 1987, Bronze Medal 1991; Silver Medal Olympic Games 10,000m 1988; Silver Medal World Indoor Championships 3,000m 1989; Bronze Medal Commonwealth Games 3,000m 1990; Gold Medal World Championships 10,000m 1991; Gold Medal World Half-Marathon Championships 1992; first in New York City Marathon 1991; first in Tokyo Marathon 1992, third in 1996; third in London Marathon 1993, fifth in 1995, first in 1996, second in 1997, 1998. *Leisure interests:* cooking, cinema, crosswords. *Address:* c/o Marquee UK, 6 George St, Nottingham NG1 3BE, UK. *Telephone:* (115) 948-3206; *Fax:* (115) 952-7203.

McCOY, Anna Brelsford, BA; American artist; b 26 Sept 1940, Wilmington, DE; d of John W. McCoy, II and Anne (née Wyeth) McCoy; m 1st George A. Weymouth 1961 (until 1977); one s; m 2nd Kenneth C. Lindsay 1986 (until 1988); m 3rd C. Patrick Mundy 1994. *Education:* Tower Hill School (Wilmington), Shipley School (Bryn Mawr, PA) and Bennett Coll (Millbrook, NY). *Career:* Studied under Caroline Wyeth, Charles Vinson and Rea Redifer; exhibitions include Gallery I, Rockland, ME 1988, 1991, Chadds Ford Gallery, PA 1989–90, Artworks, PA 1992, Somerville-Manning Gallery, DE 1993, Caldbeck Gallery, ME 1996; portrait painter, also painter in oils and watercolour; collector and dealer in antiques. *Leisure interest:* antique furniture.

McCOY, Elaine Jean, QC, BA, LL B; Canadian politician and barrister; b 7 March 1946, Brandon, MB; d of John Frederick and Jean Stewart (née Hope) McCoy; m Miles H. Patterson 1988. *Education:* Univs of Alberta and British Columbia. *Career:* Called to the Bar, AB 1970; Sr Legal Counsel Alberta Public Utilities Bd; Barrister, Solicitor Black and Co; Head of Course Admin Advocacy Bar Admission Programme, Alberta Law Soc; mem Alberta Legis Ass for Calgary W 1986–; Minister of Labour with responsibility for Consumer and Corp Affairs 1986–89, Women's Issues 1987–92, Human Rights and Personnel Admin 1989–92; Pres McCoy Group 1993–, Macleod Inst for Environmental Analysis 1995–; founding Trustee Angela Cheng Musical Foundation; mem Canadian Bar Asscn, Law Soc of Alberta, United Church, Progressive Cons Party. *Leisure interests:* golf, fly-fishing, reading, crossword puzzles. *Address:* ES 1040, 2500 University Drive NW, Calgary, Alberta T2N 1N4, Canada; 223, 20 Coachway Rd SW, Calgary, AB T3H 1E6, Canada (Home). *Telephone:* (403) 220-5271; *Fax:* (403) 282-1287; *E-mail:* macleod@macleodinstitute.com; *Internet:* www.macleodinstitute.com.

McCRACKEN, Kathleen Luanne, PH D; Canadian poet and literary critic; b 26 Oct 1960, Dundalk, ON; d of Robert Ivan and Shirley Marguerite McCracken. *Education:* York Univ and Univ of Toronto (ON). *Career:* Teaching Asst, Course Dir and Lecturer Univ of Toronto and Ryerson Polytechnic Inst 1985–89; Course Dir Dept of English, York Univ 1988–89; Postdoctoral Fellowship, Social Sciences and Humanities Research Council, Univ Coll Dublin, Ireland 1989–91; Lecturer in American Studies Univ of Ulster at Jordanstown, Belfast, NI 1992–; has presented papers at confs in Canada, Ireland and USA; Ontario Arts Council Writers' Grantee (four times); Univ of Toronto Open Fellowship; Ontario Grad Scholarships; mem League of Canadian Poets, Modern Language Asscn, Anglo-Irish Literature. *Publications include:* Reflections 1978, Into Celebration 1980, The Constancy of Objects 1980, Reflections: A Creative History of the One-Room Schoolhouse in Proton Township (jtly) 1978, A Geography of Souls 2002; poetry and literary criticism published in various Canadian, American, Irish and British journals. *Leisure interests:* swimming, sailing, photography. *Address:* Faculty of Humanities, University of Ulster at Jordanstown, Shore Rd, Newtownabbey, Co Antrim, Northern Ireland BT37 0QB, UK. *Telephone:* (2890) 366192; *Fax:* (2090) 852611; *E-mail:* kl.mccracken@ulst.ac.uk.

McCULLOUGH, Colleen; Australian writer; b 1 June 1937, Wellington, NSW; m Ric Robinson 1984. *Education:* Holy Cross Coll (Woollahra), Univ of Sydney and Univ of London Inst of Child Health (UK). *Career:* Neurophysiologist in Sydney and London, and at School of Int Medicine, Yale Univ, CT, USA 1967–76; living on Norfolk Island, S Pacific 1980–; several novels have been made into films or TV series; Hon D LITT (Macquarie) 1993. *Publications:* Novels: Tim 1974, The Thorn Birds 1977, An Indecent Obsession 1981, A Creed for the Third Millennium 1985, The Ladies of Missolonghi 1987, The First Man in Rome 1990, The Grass Crown 1991, Fortune's Favorites 1993, Caesar's Women 1996, Caesar 1997, The Song of Troy 1998, Morgan's Run 2000; Non-fiction: Cooking with Colleen McCullough and Jean Easthope 1982 Roden Cutler, VC (biog) 1998. *Address:* POB 333, Norfolk Island, Oceania, via Australia. *Telephone:* (6723) 22642; *Fax:* (6723) 23313.

McDERMOTT, Alice; American writer; b 1953, Long Island, NY; m David Armstrong; two c. *Education:* State Univ of New York and Univ of New Hampshire. *Career:* Mem staff Houghton Mifflin publrs; writer, short stories published in Ms, Redbook, Seventeen and Mademoiselle magazines; teacher writing workshops American Univ (DC). *Publications include:* A Bigamist's Daughter 1982, That Night 1987, At Weddings and Wakes. *Address:* c/o Farrar, Straus and Giroux, 19 Union Square W, New York, NY 10003, USA.

MACDONALD, Hon Flora Isabel, CC, PC; Canadian politician and consultant; b 3 June 1926, N Sydney, NS; d of George Frederick and Mary Isabel (née Royle) MacDonald. *Education:* N Sydney High School, Empire Business Coll and Nat Defence Coll (Kingston). *Career:* Exec Dir Progressive Cons HQ 1957–66, Nat Sec Progressive Cons Asscn 1966–69; Admin Officer, tutor Dept of Political Studies, Queen's Univ 1966–72; mem Parl for Kingston and the Islands, ON 1972–88; Opposition Spokesperson for Indian Affairs and N Devt, Fed–Prov Relations, External Affairs and the Status of Women 1972–79; Sec of State for External Affairs 1979–80; Minister for Employment and Immigration 1984–86, Minister of Communications 1986–88; Visiting Fellow, Centre for Canadian Studies (Univ of Edinburgh) 1989; Special Adviser Commonwealth of Learning (Vancouver) 1990–91; host North South TV series 1990–94; Chair Int Devt Research Centre 1992–97, Carnegie Comm Re Preventing Deadly Conflict 1994–99, Co-Chair Canada Co-ordinating Cttee UN Year of Older Persons 1999; mem UN Eminent Person's Group to study Trans-Nat Corpns in SA 1989; Chair Capital Fundraising Campaign Mount St Vincent Univ (Halifax) 1990–94, HelpAge Int (UK), Shastri Indo-China Advisory Council; mem Bd Canadian Council for Refugees, CARE Canada, Friends of the Nat Library, Future Generations (Franklin, WV), Nat Museum of

Scotland, Partnership Africa Canada, UNIFEM; Pres World Federalists of Canada; Hon Pres Asscn of Canadian Clubs 1999–; Patron Commonwealth Human Rights Initiative; Hon Patron for Canada of Nat Museums of Scotland; Dr hc (Maine, Queen's, McMaster, Mt St Vincent, Acadia, State Univ of New York, York, Royal Military Coll, Edinburgh, Carleton, St Andrews Presbyterian Coll, Brock St Catherine's); Order of Ontario 1995; Pearson Peace Medal 1999. *Leisure interests:* travel, reading, speed-skating. *Address:* 1103–350 Queen Elizabeth Driveway, Ottawa, ON K1S 3N1, Canada (Home). *Telephone:* (613) 238-1098; *Fax:* (613) 238-6330; *E-mail:* flora@intranet.ca (Home).

McDONALD, Gabrielle Kirk, LL B; American judge; b 12 April 1942, St Paul; d of James G. and Frances R. Kirk; m Mark T. McDonald. *Education:* Howard Univ. *Career:* Fmr law professor; Fed judge, Houston, Tex 1979–88; partner Matthews Branscomb, Austin, Tex 1988–; serving on UN int tribunal on war crimes in fmr Yugoslavia, the Hague 1993–, Pres Nov 1997–; mem ABA, Nat Bar Asscn. *Address:* United Nations International Criminal Tribunal for Former Yugoslavia, POB 15833, Churchillplein, The Hague, 2501 EU, Netherlands.

MACDONALD, Morag, CBE, LL B, FRSA; British civil servant and business executive; b 8 Feb 1947; d of Murdoch and Isobel Macdonald; m 1st Adam Somerville 1970; m 2nd Walter Simpson 1983; one d. *Education:* Bellahouston Acad (Glasgow) and Univ of Glasgow. *Career:* Called to the Bar, Inner Temple 1974; joined Post Office as grad trainee 1968, in Telecommunications and Corp HQ 1969–79, Personal Asst to Man Dir Girobank 1980, Deputy Sec of Post Office 1983–85, Sec 1985–94; mem Council St George's Hosp Medical School 1994–97. *Leisure interests:* walking, embroidery, very indifferent piano playing. *Address:* Ardshiel, Gwydyr Rd, Crieff, Perthshire PH7 4BS, UK.

McDONALD, Oonagh, CBE, PH D; British consultant and politician; b Stockton-on-Tees, Co Durham; d of H. D. McDonald. *Education:* Univ of London. *Career:* Teacher St Barnabas School 1959–62, Hornsey Grammar School and Boreham Wood School 1964–65; Lecturer in Sociology Toynbee Hall 1964–65, Univ of Bristol 1965–76; MP (Lab) for Thurrock 1976–87, Parl Pvt Sec to Chief Sec to Treasury 1977–79, Opposition front bench Spokesperson on Defence 1981–83, on Treasury and Econ Affairs 1983–87, on Civil Service 1983–87, mem Public Accounts Cttee 1977–78, Select Cttee on Employment 1981, Jobs and Industry Policy Cttee 1985–87; mem Industrial Policy Sub-Cttee, Lab Party Nat Exec Cttee 1976–83, Council Consumers' Asscn 1988–94, Union of Shop Distributive and Allied Workers (USDAW) 1990; Consultant Unity Trust Bank PLC 1987–88; Gov Birkbeck Coll 1987–95; Non-Exec Dir Investors' Compensation Scheme 1992–, SAGA Group 1995–98; Dir Financial Services Authority (fmrly Savings and Investment Bd) 1993–98, Chair Consumer Panel 1994–95, FSA Ombudsman Scheme 1999–;Trustee Research Inst for Consumer Affairs 1992–93; Gwilym Gibbon Research Fellow Nuffield Coll, Oxford 1988–89; Sr Research Fellow Univ of Warwick 1990; devised TV documentary A Woman's Life. *Publications include:* The Economics of Prosperity (jtly) 1980, Own Your Own: social ownership examined 1989, Parliament at Work 1989, The Future of Whitehall 1992; contribs to professional journals. *Address:* c/o Birkbeck College, Malet St, London WC1E 7HX, UK. *Telephone:* (20) 8940-5563.

MACDONALD, Sharman, MA; British writer; b 8 Feb 1951, Glasgow; d of Joseph Henry Hosgood and Janet Rewat (née Williams) Macdonald; m Will Knightly 1976; one s one d. *Education:* Hutchesons' Girls' Grammar School (Glasgow), George Watson's Ladies' Coll (Edinburgh) and Univ of Edinburgh. *Career:* Actress with 7:84 at Royal Court Theatre 1972–84; Thames TV Writer-in-Residence 1985; London Evening Standard Award for Most Promising Playwright 1984. *Publications:* Plays: When I Was A Girl I Used To Scream And Shout 1984, The Brave 1987, When We Were Women 1987, All Things Nice 1990; Novels: The Beast 1984, Night, Night 1987; Filmscript: Wild Flowers 1988, The Winter Guest 1995, Borders of Paradise 1995, After Juliet 1999; radio: Sea Urchins (adapted for stage 1998), Gladly My Cross-Eyed Bear 2000; opera libretto: Hey Persephone! 1998. *Leisure interest:* guitar. *Address:* c/o Patricia Macnaughton, MLR Ltd, Douglas House, 16-18 Douglas St, London SW1P 4PB, UK.

McDORMAND, Frances; American actress; b 23 June 1957, IL; m Joel Coen. *Education:* Yale Univ School of Drama. *Career:* Travelled 'Bible Belt' with family (father a Disciples of Christ preacher), lived in Pennsylvania from age of eight; appearances in films, plays and on TV; actress with O'Neill Playwrights Conf. *Films include:* Blood Simple 1984, Raising Arizona 1987, Mississippi Burning (Acad Award nomination) 1988, Chattahoochee 1990, Dark Man 1990, Miller's Crossing 1990, Hidden Agenda 1990, The Butcher's Wife 1991, Passed Away 1992, Short Cuts 1993, Beyond Rangoon 1995, Fargo (Acad Award for Best Actress) 1996, Lone Star, Primal Fear, Palookaville, Paradise Road 1997, Johnny Skidmarks 1997, Madeline 1998, Talk of Angels 1998, Wonder Boys 1999, Almost Famous 2000; *Plays include:* Twelfth Night, Mrs Warren's Profession, Awake and Sing 1984, Painting Churches 1984, The Three Sisters 1985, All My Sons 1986, On The Verge, A Streetcar Named Desire (Tony Award nomination) 1988, Moon for the Misbegotten 1992, The Sisters Rosenzweig 1993, The Swan 1993; *TV appearances include:* Leg Work (series), Crazy in Love (film), The Good Old Boys (film). *Address:* c/o William Morris Agency, 1325 Ave of the Americas, New York, NY 10019.

McDOUGALL, Hon Barbara Jean, OC, PC, BA; Canadian former politician and financial executive; b 12 Nov 1937, Toronto; m. *Education:* Univ of Toronto. *Career:* Economist Canadian Imperial Bank of Commerce, Toronto 1962–62; Market Research Analyst, Toronto Star 1962–63; Business Writer Vancouver Sun 1963–64; Investment Analyst Odlum Brown Ltd 1964–74; Portfolio Man North West Trust and Seaboard Life Assurance Co, also Business commentator TV news, Edmonton 1974–76; mem staff A. E. Ames & Co Ltd (later Dominion Securities Ames Ltd), later Man Options Dept, then Vice-Pres, Toronto 1976–82; Exec Dir Canadian Council of Financial Analysts 1982–84; financial columnist and commentator for publs and CBC TV, Toronto; elected to Parl for St Paul's, Toronto (Progressive Cons) 1984–93, Minister of State for Finance 1984–86, for Privatization 1986–88, Minister Responsible for Status of Women 1986–90, Minister for Regulatory Affairs 1986–88, of Employment and Immigration 1988–91, Sec of State for External Affairs 1991–93; Chair Cabinet Cttee on Foreign Affairs and Defence Policy 1991–93, mem Cabinet Cttees for Planning and Priorities, Canadian Unity and Constitutional Negotiations 1991–93; Pres and CEO Canadian Inst of Int Affairs 1999–; Chair Morguard Real Estate Investment Trust 1997–99, AT&T Canada Corpn 1996–99; Dir Int Crisis Group 1995–, Individual Order of Forresters 1998–, Corel Corpn 1998–, Bank of Nova Scotia 1999–, Stelco Inc 1999–, Sun Media Corpn 1999–; mem Int Advisory Bd Council on Foreign Relations (NY) 1995–; Gov York Univ 1995–; Hon LL D (St Lawrence, New York). *Address:* 1 Clarendon Ave, Apt 401, Toronto, ON M4V 1H8, Canada; Canadian Inst of Int Affairs, 2nd Floor Glendon Hall, Glendon Coll, 2275 Bayview Ave, Toronto, ON M4N 3M6, Canada. *Telephone:* (416) 487-6830; *Fax:* (416) 487-6737; *E-mail:* bmcdoug@ciia.org.

MacDOWELL, Andie (Rose Anderson); American actress and model; b 21 April 1958, SC; m Paul Qualley; three c. *Career:* Model for L'Oréal cosmetics. *Films:* Greystoke: The Legend of Tarzan Lord of the Apes 1984, St Elmo's Fire 1985, Sex, Lies and Videotape (Best Actress, Los Angeles Film Critics) 1989, Green Card, The Object of Beauty, Hudson Hawk, The Player 1992, Ruby 1992, Groundhog Day 1993, Short Cuts 1993, Bad Girls 1994, Four Weddings and a Funeral 1994, Unstrung Heroes 1995, Multiplicity 1996, Michael, The End of Violence 1997, Town and Country 1998, Shadrack 1998, The Scalper 1998, Just the Ticket 1998, Muppets From Space 1999, The Music 2000, Town and Country 2001; *TV appearances include:* Domestic Dilemma, Women and Men 2, In Love There Are No Rules 1991, Sahara's Secret. *Address:* c/o ICM, 8942 Wilshire Blvd, Beverly Hills, CA 90211, USA.

McDOWELL, Catherine Mary, BA; British banking executive; b 25 Aug 1957, Portadown, NI; m Roger A. Jenkins 1980; one d. *Education:* Reigate Grammar School for Girls (Surrey), and Univs of Leeds and Harvard (USA). *Career:* Man Trainee Barclays Bank Int 1978, apptd Man Int Cash Man 1982; seconded to BZW Equities, New York 1987; apptd Head of Investor Relations, Barclays PLC 1991; Dir Barclays Pvt Banking responsible for Offshore Islands 1993. *Leisure interests:* theatre, travel, reading, skiing. *Address:* Barclays Private Banking, 49 Grosvenor St, London W1X 9FH, UK. *Telephone:* (20) 7487-2079; *Fax:* (20) 7487-2044.

McELHONE, Natascha; British actress; b 1971, Brighton; step-d of Roy Greenslade; m 1998. *Education:* London Acad of Music and Dramatic Art. *Films include:* Surviving Picasso, The Truman Show, The Devil's Own, Ronin, Love's Labour's Lost. *Address:* c/o ICM, Oxford House, 76 Oxford St, London W1D 1BS, UK.

McENTIRE, Reba, B ED; American country music singer and actress; b 28 March 1955, McAlester, OK; d of Clark and Jacqueline McEntire; m Narvel Blackstock 1989; one s. *Education:* Southeastern Oklahoma State Univ (Durant, OK). *Career:* Co-Founder Starstruck Entertainment (with husband/manager) 1988. *Albums:* What Am I Gonna Do About You 1986, Greatest Hits 1987, The Last One to Know 1987, Reba 1988, Sweet Sixteen 1989, Reba Live! 1989, Rumor Has It 1990, For My Broken Heart 1991, It's Your Call 1992, Greatest Hits II 1993, Read My Mind 1994, Starting Over 1995, What If It's You 1996, If You See Him 1998, So Good Together 1999; *Films:* Tremors 1990, The Gambler Returns 1991, Is There Life Out There 1994, North 1994, Little Rascals 1994, Buffalo Girls 1995, Forever Love 1998, One Night at McCool's 2000; *Publications:* Reba: My Story 1994, Comfort from a Country Quilt 1999. *Leisure interests:* reading, spending time with family. *Address:* c/o Trisha McClanahan, Starstruck Entertainment, 40 Music Square W, Nashville, TN 37203, USA.

McEWAN, Geraldine; British actress; b 9 May 1932, Old Windsor, Berks; d of Donald and Norah McKeown; m Hugh Cruttwell 1953; one s one d. *Education:* Windsor County Girls' School. *Career:* First engagement Theatre Royal, Windsor 1949; Nat Theatre 1965–71; has appeared in numerous plays, films and on TV; has also directed several productions 1988–; Evening Standard Best Actress Award 1984, 1995. *Plays include:* Who Goes There? 1951, Sweet Madness, For Better For Worse 1953, Love's Labour's Lost 1956, A Member of the Wedding 1957, The Entertainer 1957–58, Twelfth Night, Pericles, Much Ado About Nothing 1958, 1961, Hamlet 1961, The School For Scandal 1962, Armstrong's Good Night, Love For Love, A Flea in Her Ear, Dance of Death, Edward II, Home and Beauty, Rites, Way of the World, The White Devil, Amphitryon 1965–71, Dear Love 1973, Chez Nous 1974, The Little Hut 1974, Oh! Coward 1975, On Approval 1975, Look After Lulu 1978, The Browning Version 1980, Harlequinade 1980, The Provoked Wife 1980–81, The Rivals (Evening Standard Drama Award), You Can't Take It With You 1983–84, A Lie Of The Mind 1987, Lettice and Lovage 1988–89, Hamlet 1992, The Bird Sanctuary 1994, The Way of the World (Evening Standard Drama Award) 1995, The Chairs 1997–8, Hay Fever 1999; *Plays directed:* As You Like It 1988, Treats 1989, Waiting For Sir Larry 1990, Four Door Saloon 1991, Keyboard Skills 1993; *TV appearances include:* The Prime of Miss Jean Brodie (TV Critics Best Actress Award 1978) 1977, L'Elegance 1982, The Barchester Chronicles 1982, Come Into The Garden, Maude 1982, Mapp and Lucia 1984–85, Oranges Are Not The Only Fruit (BAFTA Best Actress Award 1991) 1990, Mulberry 1992, The Red Dwarf 1999, Thin Ice 2000, Victoria Wood's Christmas Special 2000; *Films include:* The Adventures of Tom Jones 1975, Escape from the Dark 1978, The Dance Of Death, Foreign Body 1986, Henry V 1989, Robin Hood: Prince of Thieves 1991, Moses 1995, The Love Letter 1999, Love's Labour's Lost 1999, Titus 2000, The Contaminated Man 2001, Magdalene 2001. *Address:* c/o Marmont Management Ltd, 303-308 Regent St, London W1R 5AL, UK.

McFADDEN, Mary; American fashion designer; b 1 Oct 1938, New York; d of Alexander Bloomfield McFadden and Mary Josephine Cutting; m 1st Philip Harari 1964 (divorced); one d; m 2nd Frank McEwan 1968 (divorced); m 3rd Armin Schmidt (divorced); m 4th Kohle Yohannan 1989 (divorced 1992); m 5th Vasilios Calitsis 1996. *Education:* Ecole Lubec (Paris), Univ of Paris (Sorbonne), Traphagen School of Design, Columbia Univ (New York) and New School for Social Research (New York). *Career:* Dir of Public Relations, Christian Dior, New York 1962–64; merchandising Ed Vogue, SA 1964–65; political and travel columnist Rand Daily Mail, SA 1965–68; Founder Vukutu Sculpture Workshop, Rhodesia (now Zimbabwe) 1968; freelance Ed My Fair Lady, Cape Town and French Vogue 1968–70; Special Projects Ed American Vogue 1970–73; fashion and jewellery designer (noted for tunics made from African and Chinese silks), New York 1973–; Chair Mary McFadden Inc 1976–; Partner MMcF Collection by Mary McFadden 1991–; adviser Nat Endowment for Arts; contribs to Vogue and House & Garden; awards include Neiman

Marcus Award 1979, Best Dressed List Hall of Fame 1979, Coty American Fashion Critics' Hall of Fame Award 1979, Woman of the Year, Police Athletic League 1990, New York Landmarks Conservancy 1994, Designer of the Decade and Beyond, Fashion Group Int and Philadelphia Breast Health Inst 1997, Legends Award, Pratt School of Design 2000. *Films include:* Zaoni–The Last Chak Empress, Sufism in India; *TV includes:* QVC, Worldly Accessories. *Leisure interests:* tennis, squash, travelling the world. *Address:* Mary McFadden Bldg, 240 W 35th St, Floor 17, New York, NY 10001, USA; 525 E 72nd St, Apt 2A, New York, NY 10021, USA (Home). *Telephone:* (212) 736-4078 (Office); (212) 772-1125 (Home); *Fax:* (212) 239-7259 (Office); *E-mail:* mmcfcouture@aol.com (Office); *Internet:* www.marymcfadden .couture.com (Office).

MACFARLANE, Alison Jill, BA; British statistician; b 29 March 1942, Watford; d of Angus and Joan (née Perkins) Macfarlane. *Education:* Western Jr High School (Washington, DC, USA), Watford Girls' Grammar School, Univ of Oxford and Univ Coll (London). *Career:* Statistician Rothamsted Experimental Station 1966–67, Hertfordshire Co Council Planning Dept 1967–70, MRC Environmental Hazards Unit 1972–75, London School of Hygiene and Tropical Medicine 1973–78; Programmer Experimental Cartography Unit, Royal Coll of Art 1970–72; Medical Statistician Nat Perinatal Epidemiology Unit 1978–2001; Prof of Perinatal Health, City Univ, London 2001–. *Publications:* Birth Counts (jtly) 1984, (2nd edn) 2000 Three, Four and More: A Study of Triplet and Higher Order Births (jtly) 1990, Where to be Born? The Debate and the Evidence (jtly, 2nd edn) 1994. *Leisure interests:* playing traditional music, history, politics, hill-walking. *Address:* Department of Midwifery, City University, 20 Bartholomew Close, London EC1A 7QN, UK. *Telephone:* (20) 7040-5832; *Fax:* (20) 7040-5717; *E-mail:* A.J.Macfarlane@city.ac.uk.

McFARLANE-COKE, Daisy, MA; Jamaican actuary and international organization adviser; b 15 October 1937; d of Allan J. McFarlane and Murtella M. McPherson-McFarlane; m Astley H. R. Coke 1968; two s. *Education:* Univs of the West Indies, Toronto (ON, Canada) and Oxford (UK) and Inst of Actuaries (UK). *Career:* Asst Lecturer Dept of Mathematics, Univ of the West Indies 1959–60; civil servant Ministry of Finance and Planning 1962–70, Govt Actuary 1970–72; Resident Partner Bacon Woodrow and deSouza 1972–77; Vice-Pres Jamaica Mutual Life Assurance Soc 1977–79; Sr Partner Coke and Assocs 1978–; Deputy Chair Eagle Merchant Bank Ltd, Jamaica Broadcasting Corpn (also Dir); Chair Public Service Comm, Caribbean Actuarial Asscn; Dir Crown Eagle Life Insurance Co, First Equity Corpn of Florida, Eagle Permanent Bldg Soc, Trafalgar Devt Bank; mem Bd Nat Insurance Fund; mem Int Actuarial Asscn, Int Asscn of Consulting Actuaries; Fellow Inst of Man Consultants of Jamaica, Pvt Sector Org of Jamaica; Woman of Distinction Award, Finance 1985; Nat Honour Commdr of Distinction. *Leisure interests:* talking, music, sewing, reading. *Address:* Coke and Associates, 60 Lady Musgrave Rd, Kingston 10, Jamaica (Office); 13 Glenalmond Drive, Kingston 8, Jamaica (Home). *Telephone:* 927-4329 (Office); *Fax:* 927-8366 (Office).

McGIBBON, Pauline Mills, OC, BA; Canadian former university chancellor and business executive; b 20 Oct 1910, Sarnia, Ont; d of Alfred William and Ethel Selina (née French) Mills; m Donald Walker McGibbon 1935. *Education:* Univ of Toronto. *Career:* Chancellor Univ of Toronto (first woman) 1971–74, Univ of Guelph 1977–83; Gov Upper Canada Coll (first woman) 1971–74; Pres Canadian Conf of the Arts (first woman) 1972–73; Lieut-Gov of Ontario 1974–80; Hon Col 25 Toronto Service Battalion (first Canadian woman) 1975–83; Hon Life mem Royal Canadian Military Inst; Dir Donwoods Inst 1973–85, Mt Sinai Inst 1981–86; Dir IBM Canada (first woman) until 1974, Imasco Ltd (first woman) until 1974, George Weston Ltd 1981–; Dir Mercedes-Benz Canada Inc 1983–91; Chair Bd of Trustees, Nat Art Centre 1980–84; Dir Massey Hall-Roy Thompson Hall 1980–; Hon LL D (Alberta) 1967, (Western, Queen's) 1974, (Toronto) 1975, (McMaster, Carleton) 1981, (Windsor) 1988; Hon D UNIV (Ottawa) 1972, (Laval) 1976; Hon D HUM LITT (St Lawrence) 1977; Hon D LITT (Victoria) 1979; Hon D ADMIN (Northland Open) 1990; decorations include Dame, Order of St Lazarus of Jerusalem 1967, Dame Grand Cross 1982, Grand Prior 1982–85, Dame of Grace, Order of St John of Jerusalem 1974; Queen's Jubilee Medal 1977; Eleanor Roosevelt Humanities Award, State of Israel Bonds 1978; Pauline

McGibbon Hon Award in Theatre Arts named after her 1980; 125th Anniversary of the Confed of Canada Medal 1992. *Address:* c/o Apt 2004, 20 Avoca Ave, Toronto, ON M4T 2B8, Canada.

McGILLIS, Kelly; American actress; b 9 July 1957, Newport Beach, CA; m Fred Tillman 1988; three c. *Education:* Pacific School of Performing Arts and Juilliard School of Music (New York). *Career:* Film debut in Reuben, Reuben 1983. *Films include:* Witness 1985, Private Sessions, Top Gun 1986, Made in Heaven 1987, The Sweet Revenge (TV) 1987, The Accused 1988, House on Carroll Street 1988, Dreamers, Promised Land 1988, Winter People 1989, Lie Down With Lions, Cat Chaser, Before and After Death, Grand Isle, The Babe, North, Painted Angels, Ground Control, Morgan's Ferry, At First Sight; *Plays include:* The Merchant of Venice 1988, Measure for Measure, Much Ado About Nothing; several TV films.

MacGLASHAN, Maureen Elizabeth, CMG, LL M; British former academic and diplomatist; b 7 Jan 1938; d of Kenneth and Elisabeth MacGlashan. *Education:* Luton Girls' High School and Girton Coll (Cambridge). *Career:* Mem staff Foreign Office 1961–67, Second Sec Tel-Aviv 1964–67; FCO 1967–72, Head Western European Dept 1991–92; Head of Chancery, E Berlin 1973–75; UK Rep to EC 1975–77; seconded to Home Civil Service 1977–82; Counsellor, Bucharest 1982–86; Asst Dir Research Centre for Int Law, bye-Fellow Girton Coll, Cambridge 1986–90; Counsellor, Consul-Gen, Deputy Head of Mission, Belgrade 1990–91; Resident Chair Civil Service Selection Bd 1992–95; Amb to Vatican City 1995–98; Ed Iran–US Claims Tribunal Reports vols 8–22, Law Reports vols 78–104. *Address:* 16G Main St, Largs, Ayrshire KA30 8AB, UK.

McGOVERN, Elizabeth; American actress; b 18 July 1961, Evanston, IL; m Simon Curtis; one d. *Education:* American Conservatory Theatre (San Francisco) and Juilliard School of Dramatic Art (New York). *Career:* Film debut in Ordinary People 1980; numerous film and TV appearances, theatre appearances on Broadway, New York, Los Angeles and London; lives in London. *Films include:* Ordinary People 1980, Ragtime (Acad Award nomination), Lovesick, Racing with the Moon, Once Upon a Time in America, The Bedroom Window, She's Having a Baby, Johnny Handsome, The Handmaid's Tale, A Shock to the System, Tune in Tomorrow, King of the Hill, Me and Veronica, The Favor, Wings of Courage, The Scarlet Pimpernel 1998, The Scarlet Pimpernel meets Madame Guillotine 1999, The Scarlet Pimpernel and the Kidnapped King 1999; *Plays include:* To Be Young Gifted and Black 1981, My sister in This House (Theatre World and Obie Awards), Painting Churches, The Hitch-Hiker, A Map of the World, Aunt Dan and Lemon, Two Gentlemen of Verona, A Midsummer Night's Dream, Love Letters, Twelfth Night, Major Barbara, Ring Around the Moon, Maids of Honour, The Three Sisters, As You Like It, The Misanthrope 1996; *TV appearances include:* If Not for You (series), Women and Men: Stories of Seduction, Broken Trust, Tales From Hollywood 1992, The Changeling 1993. *Address:* Writers and Artists Agency, 11726 San Vicente Blvd, Suite 300, Los Angeles, CA 90049, USA.

McGOWAN, Margaret Mary, CBE, PH D, FBA; British professor of French; b 21 Dec 1931; d of George and Elizabeth McGowan; m Sydney Anglo 1964. *Education:* Stamford High School for Girls, Univs of Reading and Strasbourg (France). *Career:* Lecturer Univ of Glasgow 1957–64, Univ of Sussex 1964–74, Prof of French 1974–, Dean 1979–82, Pro-Vice-Chancellor (Arts and Social Studies) 1982–87, Sr Pro-Vice-Chancellor 1989–96; Freedom of the City of Tours, France 1982. *Publications:* L'Art du ballet de cour 1963, Montaigne's Deceits 1974, Louis XIII's Ballets 1986, Ideal Forms in the Age of Ronsard 1985, Moy qui me voy 1989, The Vision of Rome in Late Renaissance France 2000. *Leisure interests:* music, gardening, tennis. *Address:* 59 Green Ridge, Withdean, Brighton BN1 5LU, UK.

McGOWAN, Monica Maud; Jamaican dance educator and artistic director; b 22 May 1932, Kingston; d of Mr and Mrs Vernon McGowan. *Education:* Holy Childhood High School, Univ of the W Indies, and Michigan State Univ and Hope Coll (Holland, MI, USA). *Career:* Dancer with Ivy Baxter Creative Dance Group, Soohih School, Univ of the W Indies Dance Summer Schools; Founder-mem Nat Dance Theatre Co of Jamaica (NDTC) 1962, Prin Dancer, tours to UK, USA, Canada, Australia, Germany, Russia, Mexico, Venezuela, Panama,

Costa Rica and the Caribbean region; teacher of Physical Educ, Christian Living and Dance Holy Childhood Prep School; Founder and Artistic Dir Holy Childhood Ballet School 1968, Sr Teacher 1978, Lecturer 1988; Ballet Tutor Edna Manley Coll of the Visual and Performing Arts; Guest Tutor and Lecturer on Caribbean Folk Music and Dance; Rep Nat Bd Cecchetti Council of America in Jamaica and English Speaking W Indies; Inst of Jamaica Centenary Medal 1979; Nat Dance Theatre Co (NDTC) Award 1982, NDTC Lifetime Achievement Award 1997; Hall of Fame Award, Caribbean Devt for Arts and Culture Foundation 1996; Jamaica Teachers' Asscn/Alcan Golden Torch Award for Long and Distinguished Service 1996; Long Service Awards (Holy Childhood Preparatory School, Jamaica Ind Schools Asscn, RC Education Asscn) 1998. *Ballets include:* Ni—Woman of Destiny, The Rope and the Cross, Mountain Women, The Gospel According to..., Shadows, Lucifer Lucifer, Islands. *Leisure interests:* music, painting, sewing, cooking. *Address:* 3 Wickham Ave, Kingston 8, Jamaica. *Telephone:* 925-7791.

McGRATH, Judith, BA; American television executive; b 1952, Scranton. *Education:* Cedar Crest Coll (Allentown, PA). *Career:* Fmr Copy Chief, Glamour Magazine; fmr Sr Writer Mademoiselle Magazine; fmr copywriter, Nat Advertising (PA); fmr copywriter Warner Amex Satellite Entertainment Co (later MTV Networks) 1981, subsequently Editorial Dir MTV, Exec Vice-Pres, Creative Dir, then Co-Pres and Creative Dir; Pres Networks; mem Bd LIFEbeat, People for the American Way, New York City Ballet, Rock the Vote. *Address:* c/o MTV, 1515 Broadway, New York, NY 10036, USA.

MacGREGOR, Joanna Clare, BA, FRAM; British concert pianist; b 16 July 1959, London; d of Alfred and Angela MacGregor; m Richard Williams 1986; one d (deceased). *Education:* South Hampstead High School for Girls, New Hall Coll (Cambridge), and Royal Acad of Music. *Career:* Young Concert Artists Trust concerts and recitals, UK 1985–88; recitals and concerts UK and many other countries; has performed with all leading UK orchestras including London Symphony, Royal Philharmonic, Halle, City of Birmingham Symphony, Royal Scottish and Philharmonia and with Berlin, Oslo, Singapore, Sydney and Munich Symphony Orchestras; Artistic Dir Platform Contemporary Music Festival 1991–93, Sound Circus (Bridgewater Hall, Manchester) 1996–; numerous radio and TV appearances including Last Night of the Proms 1997; mem Arts Council of England 1998–; Fellow Trinity Coll of Music; European Encouragement Prize for Music 1995. *Publications:* Music Tuition Book, Joanna MacGregor's Piano Work (3 vols) 1999. *Leisure interests:* cinema, horse riding. *Address:* c/o Ingpen and Williams, 26 Wadham Rd, London SW1S 2LR, UK. *Telephone:* (20) 8874-3222.

MacGREGOR, Susan Katriona, (Sue), OBE; British broadcaster; b 30 Aug 1941, Oxford; d of James and Margaret MacGregor. *Education:* Herschel School (Cape Town, SA). *Career:* Announcer and Producer South African Broadcasting Corpn 1962–67; BBC Radio Reporter World at One, World This Weekend, PM 1967–72, Presenter Woman's Hour BBC Radio 4 1972–87, Today 1984–, (BBC TV) Around Westminster, Dateline London; Visiting Prof of Journalism Nottingham Trent Univ 1995–; mem Royal Coll of Physicians Cttee on Ethical Issues in Medicine 1985–2000; mem Bd Royal Nat Theatre 1998–; Hon D LITT (Nottingham); Hon MRCP 1995; Hon D LITT (Nottingham) 1996, (Nottingham Trent) 2000; Hon LL D (Dundee) 1997. *Leisure interests:* theatre, cinema, skiing. *Address:* c/o BBC News Centre, Stage 6, Wood Lane, London W12 7RJ, UK. *Telephone:* (20) 8624-9644.

McGUINNESS, Catherine, MA, SC; Irish judge; b 14 Nov 1934, Belfast; d of Rev Canon Robert C. and Sylvia (née Craig) Ellis; m Proinsias MacAonghusa; two s one d. *Education:* Alexandra Coll, Univ of Dublin Trinity Coll and King's Inns (Dublin). *Career:* Teacher and writer until 1977; called to the Bar, Dublin 1977; mem Seanad Éireann (Senate) 1979–87; mem Council of State (advisory bd to Pres) 1988–91; fmr Judge of the Circuit Court, apptd High Court Judge 1996, apptd Supreme Court Judge 2000; Chair Nat Coll of Art and Design 1987–93, Employment Equality Agency 1988–93, Forum for Peace and Reconciliation 1994–; mem Gen Synod of the Church of Ireland, numerous state bds; Fellow Int Acad of Matrimonial Lawyers 1986–; Hon D LITT (Ulster). *Leisure interests:* choral singing, gardening. *Address:* 4 New Park Rd, Blackrock, Co Dublin, Ireland; The Supreme Court, Four Courts, Dublin 7, Ireland. *Telephone:* (1) 289-5300; *Fax:* (1) 289-3775.

MACHÁČKOVÁ, Ivana, PH D; Czech plant physiologist; b 5 July 1946, Prague; d of the late Robert Nittel and Miluše Nittelová; m Karel Macháček 1969; two s. *Education:* Charles Univ (Prague). *Career:* Researcher in Plant Nutrition, Inst for Crop Production, Prague 1977–84; researcher in Hormonal Regulation of Morphogenesis, Inst of Experimental Botany, Prague 1984–96, apptd Head Dept of Developmental Physiology 1994; Research Prof De Montfort Univ, Leicester, UK 1995; has written two textbooks and 80 papers in scientific journals 1976–96; Award from Acad of Sciences of Czech Repub 1992. *Leisure interest:* classical music. *Address:* Berkovská 1/1265, 160 00 Prague 6, Czech Republic. *Telephone:* (2) 3115949.

MACHADO DE SOUSA, Maria Leonor, PH D; Portuguese national library director and professor; b 11 Nov 1932, Lisbon; m Rogério Luís Machado de Sousa 1958; two s two d. *Education:* Univ of Lisbon. *Career:* Lecturer New Univ of Lisbon 1974–79, apptd Prof 1979; Organizer Portuguese Open Univ 1980, Vice-Rector 1988–90; Dir Biblioteca Nacional 1990–; Premio Calouste Gulbenkian 1986. *Publications:* A Literatura de Terror em Portugal nos sécs XVIII e XIX 1978, Inês de Castro: Um Tema Português na Europa 1987; several further books written and edited, and numerous articles. *Leisure interests:* reading, cinema. *Address:* Biblioteca Nacional, Campo Grande 83, 1751 Lisbon Codex, Portugal (Office); Rua de Sao Joaquim 6, 3° Dto, 1200 Lisbon, Portugal (Home). *Telephone:* (1) 687568 (Office); (1) 764720 (Home); *Fax:* (1) 7933607.

MACHAVELA, Esperança Alfredo, BL; Mozambican diplomatist; b 1 Aug; d of Alfredo Samuel and Vitòria (née Batista) Machavela; m 1976; one s. *Education:* Escola Feminina da Munhava (Beira), Liceu Antònio Enes, Univ Eduardo Mondlane (Maputo). *Career:* Sec to the Minister of Foreign Affairs 1976–80; mem Exec Secr Asscn de l'Amitié avec les Peuples 1980–; Legal Adviser Dept of Consular Affairs 1983–86; Amb to Cuba 1986–90, to Portugal 1990; mem Cen Cttee Frente de Libertação de Moçambique (Frelimo) 1991. *Leisure interests:* reading historical novels, tennis. *Address:* Embassy of Mozambique, Av de Berna 7, 1000 Lisbon, Portugal. *Telephone:* (1) 761676; *Fax:* (1) 7932720.

McINTOSH, Anne Caroline Ballingall, LL B; British politician and lawyer; b 20 Sept 1954, Edinburgh; d of Dr A. B. and G. L. McIntosh. *Education:* Harrogate Coll and Univs of Edinburgh and Aarhus (Denmark). *Career:* Trainee Comm of the EC, Brussels 1978; lawyer with Didier and Assocs, Brussels 1979–81; Bar apprenticeship with Simpson and Marwick, Edinburgh 1981–82; admitted to Faculty of Advocates 1982; worked at EC Comm Law Office, Belmont, Brussels 1982–83; Adviser to European Democratic Group (EDG), EP, Brussels 1983–89; MEP (Cons) for NE Essex 1989–94, for Essex N and Suffolk 1994–99, British Cons Spokesperson on Transport, Tourism and EP Rules of Procedure, mem Interparl Del for Relations with Norway, jr whip EDG 1989–92, mem Transport and Legal Affairs cttees; MP for Vale of York 1997–; Pres Anglia Enterprise in Europe; contribs to professional journals. *Leisure interests:* swimming, reading, cinema, hill-walking. *Address:* House of Commons, London, SW1A 0AA, UK; The Old Armoury, 3 Museum St, Saffron Walden, Essex, UK (Home).

McINTOSH, Fiona; British magazine editor. *Career:* Fmrly worked for the Daily Mirror newspaper; Ed Company magazine 1995. *Address:* c/o Company, National Magazine House, 72 Broadwick St, London W1V 2BP, UK. *Telephone:* (20) 7439-5000; *Fax:* (20) 7437-6886.

McINTOSH OF HUDNALL, Baroness (Life Peer), cr 1999, of Hampstead in the London Borough of Camden, **Genista Mary (Jenny) McIntosh,** BA, FRSA; British theatre administrator; b 23 Sept 1946, London; d of the late Geoffrey and of Maire Tandy; m Neil Scott Wishart McIntosh 1971 (divorced 1990); one s one d. *Education:* Hemel Hempstead Grammar School and Univ of York. *Career:* Casting Dir RSC 1972–77, Planning Controller 1977–84, Sr Admin 1986–90, Assoc Producer 1990; Dir Marmont Man Ltd 1984–86; Exec Dir Royal Nat Theatre 1990–96, 1997–; Chief Exec Royal Opera House 1997–; Dr hc (York) 1998. *Leisure interests:* music, gardening, reading. *Address:* Royal National Theatre, Upper Ground, London SE1 9PX, UK. *Telephone:* (20) 7452-3333; *Fax:* (20) 7452-3350.

McINTYRE-PIKE, Marguerite Diana; Jamaican business executive; b 19 Sept 1951, Kingston, Jamaica; d of Mark H. Conway McIntyre and Ceceline Shaw-McIntyre; m Carey Pike 1981 (deceased); two s. *Education:* St Andrew High School, Bishop's High School, Cambridgeshire Coll of Arts and Technology and Carl Duisberg, Munich (Germany). *Career:* Guest Relations Dir Holiday Inn (Montego Bay) 1974; Public Relations/Entertainment Dir Runaway Bay Hotel 1974–75; Founder Dee Ltd and South Coast Marketing Ltd; Dir Caribbean Hotel Asscn; first Vice-Pres Manchester Parish Investment Cttee Ltd; Outstanding Citizens Award 1979; Heritage Award in Tourism 1984; UN Award (Decade for Women) for outstanding service in tourism 1985. *Leisure interests:* social work, journalism, driving, creative dancing. *Address:* The Astra Country Inn, 62 Ward Ave, Mandeville, Manchester, Jamaica.

MACIUCHOVÁ, Hana; Czech actress; d of Jarmila Maciuchová. *Education:* Olomouc Grammar School and Prague Acad of Performing Arts. *Career:* Actress 1964–; mem Theatre Behind the Gate, Prague 1968–71, then Theatre Vinohrady, Prague; Czechoslovak prizes for TV and Stage roles 1977, 1982, 1987. *Plays include:* Cyrano de Bergerac, Faust and Master, Othello, Crime and Punishment, Twelfth Night; *Films include:* Man Against The Destruction 1989; many TV appearances. *Leisure interests:* music, travel, arts, reading. *Address:* Londýnská 23, 120 00 Prague 2, Czech Republic. *Telephone:* (2) 254195 (Home).

McIVER, Susan Bertha, BA, M SC, PH D; American writer and biologist; b 6 Nov 1940, Hutchinson, KS; d of Ernest D. and Thelma Faye (née McCrory) McIver; m T. A. Hostetter 1989. *Education:* Univ of California at Riverside and Washington State Univ. *Career:* Research Scientist, Asst Prof of Parasitology Univ of Toronto, Canada 1967–72, Assoc Prof of Microbiology and Parasitology 1972–80, Prof of Zoology and of Microbiology 1980–84; Prof, Chair of Environmental Biology Univ of Guelph, ON, Canada 1984–90; Consultant in Entomology US Army 1975–79, 1986–89; Consultant Study Group on Tropical Medicine and Parasitology, NIH 1983–85; full-time writer 1990–; Coroner Province of British Columbia 1993–; Dir Women-in-Crisis 1980–87, Chair 1988–89; mem Entomological Soc, Biological Council of Canada, Entomological Soc of America, Canadian Soc of Zoology, American Soc of Parasitology, Canadian Microscopic Soc, Mosquito Control Asscn; has written more than 100 scientific research papers and articles 1964–90 and numerous short stories 1990–; Int Fellowship in Tropical Medicine 1973; C. Gordon Hewitt Award, Entomological Soc of Canada 1978; Medical Research Council Fellowship 1978; 125th Confed Anniversary Silver Medal for Contribs to Community, Compatriots and Canada. *Leisure interests:* travel, art, hiking. *Address:* POB 968, Penticton, BC V2A 7N7, Canada. *Telephone:* (604) 493-1579 (Office); (604) 490-9049 (Home); *E-mail:* smciver@vip.net.

McKAY, Heather Pamela, MBE, AM; Australian squash player and coach; b 31 July 1941, Queanbeyan, NSW; d of Francis Linton Leslie and Dulcie Blundell; m Brian H. McKay 1965. *Education:* Queanbeyan Intermediate High School. *Career:* Competed in 14 Australian Women's Squash Championships 1960–73, 16 British Women's Squash Championships 1962–77, two Women's World Squash Championships 1976, 1979; USA Amateur Racquetball Champion 1979; USA Professional Racquetball Champion 1980, 1981, 1984, Canadian Professional Racquetball Champion 1980, 1982, 1983, 1984, 1985; Sr Squash Coach Australian Inst of Sport 1985–98. *Publication:* Heather McKay's Complete Book of Squash. *Leisure interests:* tennis, reading. *Address:* 8 Premworth Place, Runcorn, Qld 4113, Australia. *Telephone:* (7) 3345 7906.

MACKAY, Shena; British writer; b 6 June 1944, Edinburgh; d of Benjamin Mackay; m Robin Brown 1964 (divorced 1982); three d. *Education:* Tonbridge Girls' Grammar School (Kent) and Kidbrooke Comprehensive (London). *Career:* Began career working in antique shop (Chancery Lane, London); Fawcett Prize 1987. *Publications:* Dust Falls on Eugene Schlumberger 1964, Toddler on the Run 1964, Music Upstairs 1965, Old Crow 1967, An Advent Calendar 1971, Babies in Rhinestones 1983, A Bowl of Cherries 1984, Redhill Rococo 1986, Dreams of Dead Women's Handbags 1987, Dunedin 1992, The Laughing Academy 1993, Such Devoted Sisters (ed) 1993, Collected Stories 1994, The Orchard on Fire 1996, Friendship (ed) 1997, The

Artist's Widow 1998, The World's Smallest Unicorn 1999. *Address:* c/o Vintage Books, Random House Group, 20 Vauxhall Bridge Rd, London SW1V 2SA, UK.

McKECHNIE, Dame Sheila Marshall, DBE, MA; British organization executive; b 3 May 1948, Falkirk, Scotland. *Education:* Falkirk High School and Univs of Edinburgh and Warwick. *Career:* Research Asst Univ of Oxford 1971–72; Asst Gen-Sec Staff Section, Wall Paper Workers' Union 1972–74; Tutor Workers' Educational Asscn 1974–76; Health and Safety Officer Asscn of Scientific, Technical and Managerial Staffs (ASTMS, now part of Union for Manufacturing, Science and Finance MSF) 1976–85; Dir Shelter, Nat Campaign for the Homeless 1985–1994; Head Consumers' Asscn 1995–; Non-Exec Dir Bank of England 1998–; Hon D UNIV (Open) 1994; Hon D SC (Edinburgh) 1994. *Address:* Consumers' Association, 2 Marylebone Rd, London NW1 4DF, UK (Office). *E-mail:* mckechnies@which.co.uk (Office).

McKEE, Margaret Jean, AB; American federal government official; b 20 June 1929, New Haven, CT; d of Waldo McCutcheon and Elizabeth Brooks (née Thayer) McKee. *Education:* Vassar Coll (NY) and Univ of S California. *Career:* Staff Asst New York Republican State Cttee 1953–55, Crusade for Freedom 1955–57; Researcher Stricker and Henning Research Assocs Inc, New York 1957–59; Exec Sec New Yorkers for Nixon 1959–60; Asst to Raymond Moley 1961; Asst Campaign Cttee Louis J. Lefkowitz for Mayor 1961; Research Programmer, Treas Consensus Inc 1962–67; Special Asst to Senator Jacob K. Javits 1967–73, Admin Asst 1973–75; Deputy Admin American Revolution Bicentennial Admin 1976, Acting Admin 1976–77; Chief of Staff Perry B. Duryea, New York State Ass 1978; Public Affairs Consultant 1979–80; Dir Govt Relations Gen Mills Restaurant Group 1980–83; Exec Dir Fed Mediation and Conciliation Service 1983–86; mem Fed Labor Relations Authority 1986–89, Chair 1989–94; Chair Advisory Bd Workplace Solutions 1996–; mem Nat Partnership Council 1993–94; Co-Dir New York Republican State Campaign Cttee 1964; Dir Interamerican Life Insurance Co 1979–86; Treas VNNC Inc 1992–97; mem US Advisory Comm on Public Diplomacy 1979–82, Exec Women in Govt, Annual Fund Advisory Cttee Vassar Coll 1992–. *Address:* 3001 Veazey Terrace, Apt 1225, Washington, DC 20008, USA; 532 S Brooksvale Rd, Cheshire, CT 06410, USA (Home).

McKENNA, Patricia; Irish politician; b 13 March 1957, Monaghan. *Career:* MEP (The Green Group in the European Parliament); mem Cttee on Environment, Public Health and Consumer Protection, on Fisheries, on Women's Rights, Del for relations with the countries of SE Asia and the S Asia Asscn for regional Co-operation. *Address:* European Parliament, 97–113 rue Belliard, 1047 Brussels, Belgium. *Telephone:* (2) 284-21-11; *Fax:* (2) 230-69-43.

McKENNA, Virginia; British actress and conservationist; b 7 June 1931, London; d of Terence Morrell and Anne (née Dennis) McKenna; m 1st Denholm Elliot (divorced); m 2nd Bill Travers 1957 (died 1994); three s one d. *Education:* Herons Ghyll (Horsham, Sussex), Herschel Coll (SA) and Cen School of Speech and Drama (London). *Career:* Made TV debut 1951; film debut in The Second Mrs Tanqueray; has appeared in numerous stage productions, TV plays and films; has performed in poetry, prose and music evenings; Co-Founder Zoo Check Charitable Trust 1984 (renamed The Born Free Foundation 1991); Patron Plan Int, Children of the Andes, Wildlife Rehabilitation Centre, Leatherhead, Elizabeth Fitzroy Homes, Earthkind. *Films include:* The Second Mrs Tanqueray, Father's Doing Fine, The Cruel Sea, Simba, The Ship that Died of Shame, A Town Like Alice (Best Actress British Acad Award), The Smallest Show on Earth, The Barretts of Wimpole Street, Carve Her Name with Pride (Belgian Prix Femina Award), The Passionate Summer, Wreck of the Mary Deare, Two Living, One Dead, Born Free (Variety Club Best Actress Award), Ring of Bright Water, An Elephant Called Slowly, Waterloo, Swallows and Amazons, The Disappearance, Holocaust-2000, Staggered 1993, Sliding Doors 1999; *Plays include:* Love's Labour's Lost 1955, As You Like It 1955, Richard II 1955, A Winter's Tale, The Devils, The Beggar's Opera, A Little Night Music, The King and I (SWET Best Actress Award) 1983, Hamlet 1985, Winnie 1988, Sons and Mothers, It's a Lovely Day Tomorrow, The Lily and the Tiger, Larry's Stable (tribute to Laurence Olivier), The River Line, Penny for a Song, I Capture the Castle, A Personal Affair, The Bad

Samaritan; *TV appearances include:* Romeo and Juliet (Guild of TV Producers and Dirs Best Actress Award) 1955, A Passage To India, The Deep Blue Sea, The Lion at World's End (documentary) 1971, Cheap in August, Julius Caesar, Duel of Hearts, Lovejoy 1990, The Camomile Lawn 1991, Ruth Rendell Mysteries 1992, September 1994 (miniseries), Puccini, Girls in Uniform, Peter Pan, Waters of the Moon, The Scold's Bridle 1998, The Whistle Blower 2001; *Radio work includes:* The Devils, The Flame Trees of Thika; *Publications:* On Playing with Lions (jtly) 1966, Some Of My Friends Have Tails 1970, Into the Blue 1992, Journey to Freedom 1997; Co-Ed and Contrib: Beyond the Bars, Headlines from the Jungle (verse) 1990, Back to the Blue 1997. *Leisure interests:* classical music, poetry, walking in the countryside. *Address:* The Born Free Foundation, 3 Grove House, Foundry Lane, Horsham, W Sussex RH13 5PL, UK. *Telephone:* (1403) 327838; *Fax:* (1403) 327838; *E-mail:* wildlife@bornfree.org.uk; *Internet:* www.bornfree.org.

McKENZIE, Julia Kathleen, FGSM; British actress, director and singer; b 17 Feb 1941, London; d of Albion and Kathleen (née Rowe) McKenzie; m Jerry Harte 1972. *Education:* Tottenham County School and Guildhall School of Music and Drama. *Career:* Actress on stage and TV, and in musicals; also director. *Plays and Musicals include:* Maggie May 1965, Follies, Company 1972, Side By Side By Sondheim 1977, Guys and Dolls 1982, Woman in Mind 1986, Into The Woods 1990, Sweeney Todd 1993–94, Communicating Doors 1995; *Films:* Shirley Valentine 1989, The Old Curiosity Shop 1996; *TV appearances include:* Fame is the Spur, Glory Glory Days, Hotel du Lac, Absent Friends, Maggie and Her, Fresh Fields (series), French Fields (series), Julia and Co, Blott on the Landscape (series), Adam Bede 1991, The Shadowy Third 1994, Jack and the Beanstalk: The Real Story 2001; *Plays and TV programmes directed:* Stepping Out 1984, Steel Magnolias 1989, Just So 1989, Putting it Together, The Mercury Workshop Musical Revue 1994, The Musical of the Year (for Danish TV) 1996, Honk! (Scarborough 1997, Royal Nat Theatre, London 1999, N Shore Theatre, Beverly, USA 2000 and UK tour 2001), A Little Night Music, Tokyo 1999; *Recordings:* Album of Show Songs 1992, Anyone Can Whistle 1997, The King and I 1997, Sondheim: A Celebration 1997. *Leisure interests:* cooking, reading, gardening. *Address:* c/o April Young, 11 Woodlands Rd, Barnes, London SW13 0JZ, UK. *Telephone:* (20) 8876-7030; *Fax:* (20) 8878-7017.

MACKENZIE, Ruth, OBE, MA, FRSA; British theatre director and adviser; b 24 July 1957; d of Kenneth Mackenzie and Myrna Blumberg. *Education:* S Hampstead High School (London), Univ of Paris (Sorbonne) and Newnham Coll (Cambridge). *Career:* Ed's Asst Time Out magazine 1980–81; Co-Founder, Dir and Writer for Moving Parts Theatre Co 1980–82; Fellow in Theatre, Dir of Theatre in the Mill, Univ of Bradford 1982–84; Drama Officer responsible for Theatre Writing, Arts Council of GB 1984–86; Head of Strategic Planning S Bank Centre 1986–90; Exec Dir Nottingham Playhouse 1990–97; Consultant Artistic Programmer Theatr Clwyd 1995–96; Consultant Theatre Programmer Barbican Centre 1995–96; Gen Dir Scottish Opera 1997–99; Special Adviser, Sec of State for Culture, Media and Sport 1999–; Chair Paines Plough Theatre Co 1990–97; Judge British Gas Working for Cities Awards 1993–, Prudential Arts Awards 1995; mem Gulbenkian Foundation Large Scale Projects Cttee 1989–90, Arts Council Touring Advisory Panel 1992–96, British Council Dance and Drama Panel 1992–97, Bd Dance 4 1992–97, Bd London Int Festival of Theatre 1993–97, Arts Council Nat Lottery Panel 1994–97; Hon Fellow Univ of Nottingham 1994; Hon D LITT (Nottingham Trent) 1994, (Nottingham) 1997. *Leisure interest:* work. *Address:* Nottingham Playhouse, Wellington Circus, Nottingham NG1 5AF, UK. *Telephone:* (115) 947-4361; *Fax:* (115) 979-9546.

McKERROW, Shirley Margaret; Australian business executive and former party official; b 18 Sept 1933, Melbourne; d of Dante and Margaret (née Kelly) Gardini; m John McKerrow 1955 (divorced 1995); two s two d. *Education:* Genazzano Convent (Kew, Vic), Invergowrie Home Crafts Hostel (Hawthorn), Univ of Melbourne and La Trobe Univ (Vic). *Career:* Cen Council Rep Gisbourne Electorate 1972; Jr Vice-Pres Nat Party of Australia 1975, Sr Vice-Pres, State Pres (Vic) 1976–80, Fed Pres (first woman) 1981–87; Chair Darwin Branch, NT Country Liberal Party 1995; Dir Mandary House Pty 1993–, Hard Drive Café Pty 1995–, Samarinda Services Pty Ltd 1988–; Chair Bd Dirs John McEwen House 1997–; Dir World Interchange Pty Ltd

1998–; mem Northern Territory Liquor Comm 1998–2000, Licensing Comm 2000–; Trustee Sir Earle Page Memorial Trust 1999–. *Leisure interests:* watching cricket, cryptic crosswords, learning Indonesian, tennis, yoga, reading. *Address:* Samarinda Services Pty, 153 Mitchell St, Larrakeyah, NT 0820, Australia.

McKINNEY, Cynthia, BA; American politician; b 17 March 1955; d of Billy and Leola McKinney; one s. *Education:* Univ of Southern California and Fletcher School of Law and Diplomacy, Tufts Univ (MA). *Career:* Diplomatic Fellow Spelman Coll, Atlanta, GA 1984; teacher of political science Clark Atlanta Univ and Agnes Scott Coll, GA; mem Georgia House of Reps 1988–92; mem House of Reps (Democrat) from Georgia's 4th Dist 1993–, mem House Cttee on Banking and Financial Services, Int Relations Cttee, Congressional Black Caucus, Progressive Caucus, Women's Caucus (Sec and Head Task Force on Children, Youth and Families), Democratic Caucus Whip for Region 8; mem Bd HIV Health Services Planning Council of Metro Atlanta, Nat Council of Negro Women, NAACP, Sierra Club. *Address:* House of Representatives, 124 Cannon Bldg, Washington, DC 20515-1011, USA; 124 Cannon Bldg, Washington, DC 20515, USA. *Telephone:* (202) 225-1605.

MACKRELL, Judith, BA; British journalist; b 26 Oct 1954, London; m Simon Henson 1977; two s. *Education:* Univs of York and Oxford. *Career:* Dance Critic The Independent 1986–95, The Guardian 1995–; Hon Fellow Laban Cen, London. *Publications:* Reading Dance 1995, Life in Dance (with Darcey Bussell, qv) 1998, Oxford Dictionary of Dance (jtly) 2000. *Leisure interests:* family, travel, music, food. *Address:* c/o The Guardian, 119 Farringdon Rd, London EC1, UK. *Telephone:* (20) 7249-5553; *E-mail:* judith.mackrell@guardian.co.uk.

McLACHLIN, Beverley M., MA; Canadian supreme court judge; b 7 Sept 1943, Pincher Creek, AB; m 1st Roderick McLachlin (deceased); one s; m 2nd Frank E. McArdle 1992. *Education:* Univs of Alberta and British Columbia. *Career:* Called to the Bar, AB 1969, BC 1971; Lawyer Wood, Moir, Hyde and Ross, Edmonton 1969–71, Thomas, Herdy, Mitchell and Co, Fort St John 1971–72, Bull, Housser and Tupper, Vancouver 1972–75; Lecturer, Assoc Prof, Prof with tenure Univ of British Columbia 1974–78; apptd to Co Court of Vancouver 1981, Supreme Court of British Columbia 1981–85, Court of Appeal of British Columbia 1985–88; Chief Justice Supreme Court of British Columbia 1988–89; Judge Supreme Court of Canada 1989–, Chief Justice 2000–; mem Editorial Advisory Bd Family Law Restatement Project 1987–88, Civil Jury Instructions 1988; numerous contribs to professional journals; Hon LL D (Toronto) 1995, (York) 1999, (Ottawa) 2000, (Calgary) 2000, (Brock Univ) 2000, (Simon Fraser Univ) 2000. *Address:* Supreme Court of Canada, Wellington St, Ottawa, ON K1A 0J1, Canada. *Telephone:* (613) 992-6940; *Fax:* (613) 952-3092.

MacLAINE, Shirley; American film actress, writer and film director; b (Shirley MacLean Beaty) 24 April 1934, Richmond, VA; d of Ira and Kathlyn (née MacLean) Beaty; m Steve Parker 1954; one d. *Education:* Washington and Lee High School (Arlington, VA). *Career:* Fmr chorus girl and dancer; acting debut aged 19 in The Pajama Game; has acted in over 39 films; has also produced several films and TV series; Star of the Year Award, Theater Owners of America 1967; Las Vegas Entertainment Award; Woman of Achievement, Anti-Defamation League; Best Actress, Nat Bd of Review; Master Artist, USA Film Festival; Lifetime Achievement Award, Berlin Film Festival 1999. *Plays include:* Me and Juliet 1953, The Pajama Game 1954, If They Could See Me Now 1974, Out There Tonight 1990; *Films include:* The Trouble With Harry, Artists and Models, Around The World in 80 Days, Hot Spell, Ask Any Girl (Berlin Film Festival Silver Bear Award), Can-Can, All In A Night's Work, The Apartment (Best Actress, Venice Film Festival, British Film Acad), My Geisha, Irma La Douce (David di Donatello Award), The Yellow Rolls-Royce, Woman Times Seven, The Bliss of Mrs Blossom, Sweet Charity, Two Mules For Sister Sara, Desperate Characters (Best Actress Award, Berlin Film Festival 1971), The Possession of Joel Delaney, Amelia 1975, The Turning Point 1977, Being There 1979, Loving Couples 1980, The Change of Seasons 1981, Slapstick 1981, Cannonball Run II, Terms of Endearment (Acad Award for Best Actress, David di Donatello Award) 1984, Out On A Limb 1987, Madame Sousatzka (Golden Globe Award for Best Actress) 1989,

Steel Magnolias 1989, Waiting for the Light 1990, Postcards from the Edge 1990, Used People 1993, Wrestling Ernest Hemingway 1993, Guarding Tess 1993, Mrs Westbourne 1996, The Celluloid Closet, Evening Star 1996, Looking for Lulu, Bet Bruce, Bruno (also dir); *TV shows include:* Shirley's World 1970–71, The Other Half of the Sky: A China Memoir 1973, Shirley MacLaine: If They Could See Me Now 1974, Gypsy In My Soul 1975–76, To London With Love 1976, Where Do We Go From Here? 1976–77, Shirley MacLaine At The Lido 1979, Shirley MacLaine... Every Little Movement 1980, The Shirley MacLaine Special (Golden Rose of Montreux Award), London 1982, Out There Tonight 1990; *TV appearances include:* The West Side Waltz 1993, Joan of Arc; *Video:* Shirley MacLaine's Inner Workout 1989; *Publications:* Don't Fall Off the Mountain 1970, McGovern: A Man and His Beliefs (ed) 1972, The New Celebrity Cookbook 1973, You Can Get There From Here 1975 (Vols 1 and 2 of autobiog), Out on a Limb (Vol 3) 1983, Dancing in the Light (Vol 4) 1985, It's All in the Playing (Vol 5) 1987, Going Within: A Guide for Inner Transformation (Vol 6) 1989, Dance While You Can (Vol 7) 1991, My Lucky Stars (Vol 8) 1995, The Camino 2000. *Address:* MacLaine Enterprises Inc, 25200 Malibu Rd, Suite 101, Santa Monica, CA 90265, USA.

McLAREN, Dame Anne Laura, DBE, MA, D PHIL, FRS, FRCOG; British biologist; b 26 April 1927; d of 2nd Baron Aberconway; m Donald Michie (divorced); one s two d. *Education:* Univ of Oxford. *Career:* Researcher Univ Coll London 1952–55, Royal Veterinary Coll, London 1955–59; mem staff ARC Unit of Animal Genetics, Univ of Edinburgh 1959–74; Dir MRC Mammalian Devt Unit 1974–92; Prin Research Assoc Wellcome/Cancer Research Campaign Inst, Cambridge 1992–; Research Fellow King's Coll, Cambridge 1992–96, Hon Fellow 1996–; Foreign Sec Royal Soc 1991–96, Vice-Pres 1992–96; Pres BAAS 1993–94; mem ARC 1978–83, Cttee of Mans, Royal Inst 1976–81, Royal Soc Council 1985–87, 1991–96; Chair Governing Body, Lister Inst of Preventative Medicine 1994–; Trustee Nat History Museum 1994–; has written numerous papers on reproductive biology, embryology, genetics and immunology; Hon Fellow Univ Coll London 1993; Scientific Medal, Zoological Soc 1967; Gold Medal, Royal Soc 1990. *Address:* Wellcome/CRC Institute, Tennis Court Rd, Cambridge CB2 1QR, UK (Office); 40 Ainger Rd, London NW3 3AT, UK (Home).

McLARTY, Velma Corrine, BA; Jamaican business executive; b 9 Nov 1930; d of the late Horace Ford and Ellen Jane Wilmot-Ford; m Horace George McLarty 1957; two d one s. *Education:* Univ of the West Indies. *Career:* Dir Personnel Devt, Ministry of Mining and Natural Resources; Under-Sec Ministry of Public Service; Man Dir Sugar Industry Housing 1974–77, Nat Housing Trust 1977–80, Jamaica Nat Investment Promotion 1981–88; Pres JAMPRO (Jamaican Promotions) Ltd 1988–89, Econ Devt Consultants Inc; Dir Workers' Savings and Loan Bank, Workers' Bank Trust, Merchant Bank; Trustee Kingston Public and Victoria Jubilee Hosps Trust; UN Int Decade for Women Award 1985. *Leisure interests:* reading, theatre, gardening. *Address:* 99 Dumbarton Ave, Kingston 10, Jamaica (Office); 3 Tavistock Heights, St Andrew, Jamaica (Home). *Telephone:* 929-1768 (Office).

McLAUGHLIN, Hon Audrey, PC, M SC S; Canadian politician; b 7 Nov 1936, Dutton, ON; d of William M. and Margaret Brown; m Don McLaughlin 1954; one s one d. *Education:* Univs of Western Ontario and Toronto. *Career:* Mink rancher until 1964; teacher, Adisadel Coll, Ghana 1964–67; Caseworker Metro Toronto Children's Aid Soc; Exec Dir Canadian Mental Health Asscn 1975; mem New Democratic Party (NDP) 1960–, Leader 1989–95, Man Roger Kimmerly's election campaigns 1981, 1985; mem House of Commons (Parl) for Yukon 1987–97, Chair Parl Caucus, then NDP Finance Spokesperson; Special Rep Govt of Yukon on Circumpolar Affairs 1997–; apptd to the Privy Council 1991. *Publication:* A Woman's Place; My Life and Politics 1992. *Leisure interests:* travel, cinema, spending time alone. *Address:* 410 Hoge St, Whitehorse, Yukon, Y1A 1W2, Canada (Home).

McLEAN, Sheila Ann Manson, LL B, M LITT, PH D; British academic; b 20 June 1951, Glasgow; d of William Black and Bethia Wilson Manson; m Alan Vincent McLean 1976 (divorced 1987). *Education:* Glasgow High School for Girls and Univ of Glasgow. *Career:* Area Reporter to the Children's Panel, Strathclyde Region 1972–75; Lecturer, later Sr Lecturer Univ of Glasgow 1975–90, Int Bar Asscn Chair, Prof of Law and Ethics in Medicine 1990–. *Publications:* Legal Issues in Medicine (ed) 1981, Human Rights: From Rhetoric to Reality (co-ed) 1986, The Legal Relevance of Gender (co-ed) 1988, A Patient's Right to Know 1989, Legal Issues in Human Reproduction (ed) 1990, The Case for Physician Assisted Suicide (co-author) 1997, Old Law, New Medicine 1999; several monographs on medicine and the law. *Leisure interests:* playing the guitar, wine, friends. *Address:* University of Glasgow, Inst of Law and Ethics in Medicine, Glasgow G12 8QQ, UK (Office); 1/2, 47 Novar Drive, Glasgow G12 9UB, UK (Home). *Telephone:* (141) 3305577 (Office); *Fax:* (141) 3304698; *E-mail:* s.a.m .mclean@law.gla.ac.uk.

McLELLAN, Rt Hon Anne, BA, LLB, PC; Canadian politician; b 31 Aug 1950, Hants County, NS; d of Howard Gilmore McLellan and Joan Mary Pullan. *Education:* Dalhousie Univ and King's Coll (London, UK). *Career:* Asst Prof of Law Univ of New Brunswick 1976–80; Acting Assoc Dean and Assoc Prof of Law Univ of Alberta 1980–89, Assoc Dean 1985–87, Prof 1989–93, Acting Dean 1991–92; MP for Edmonton W 1993–; Minister of Natural Resources and Fed Interlocutor for Métis and Non-Status Indians 1993–97; Minister of Justice and Attorney-Gen 1997–; Chair Social Union Cttee 1997–; Vice Chair Special Cttee of Council 1997–; mem Econ Union Cttee 1997–, Treasury Bd 1997–; fmr mem Bd Dirs Canadian Civil Liberties Asscn, Alberta Legal Aid; fmr Vice-Pres Univ of Alberta Faculty Asscn. *Address:* Dept of Justice Canada, E Memorial Building, 284 Wellington St, Ottawa, ON K1A 0H8, Canada. *Telephone:* (613) 992-4621; *Fax:* (613) 990-7255; *E-mail:* McLellan.A@parl.gc.ca; *Internet:* www.annemclellan .ca.

McLELLAN, Nora; Canadian actress and singer; b 29 Oct 1954, Vancouver, BC; d of Godfrey and Jeanne McClelland. *Education:* Univ of British Columbia and HB Studio (New York, USA). *Career:* Stage debut at the age of nine, Vancouver Opera Asscn; actress with Canadian Theatre 1972–87, with Shaw Festival Theatre, and at numerous Canadian Theatres; Co-Founder AIDS Relief Fundraising (ARF) for Actors' Fund of Canada 1987. *Performances include:* La Bohème, A Respectable Wedding, Overruled, The Magistrate, Saint Joan, See How They Run, The Singular Life of Albert Nobbs, Candida, The Simpleton of the Unexpected Isles, Skin of Our Teeth, The Women, Cavalcade, Arms and the Man, Back to Methuselah, Peter Pan, Anything Goes, Julius Caesar, Scrooge, A Doll's House, Godspell, Lovers, You're a Good Man Charlie Brown, Jacques Brel is Alive and Well and Living in Paris, A Bistro Car, Starting Here Starting Now, Uncle Vanya, Harry's Back in Town, Children, Pinocchio, Time and the Conways, Road (Jessie Award), Who's Afraid of Virginia Woolf (Jessie Award) 1997, Hello Dolly! 1998, Music for Contortionist 2000. *Leisure interests:* travel, reading. *Address:* POB 353, Niagara-on-the-Lake, ON L0S 1J0, Canada.

McLOUGHLIN, Merrill, BA; American journalist; b 6 Jan 1945, Skowhegan, ME; d of Comerford W. and Elizabeth M. McLoughlin; m Michael A. Ruby 1986. *Education:* Smith College (Northampton, MA). *Career:* Educ Ed Newsweek Magazine 1973–78; technology writer Newsweek 1978–1982, Nat Affairs Ed 1982–1986; Asst Man Ed US News & World Report 1986–89, Co-Ed 1989. *Leisure interests:* music, skiing, hiking. *Address:* US News & World Report, 2400 N St, NW, Washington, DC 20037-1196, USA. *Telephone:* (202) 955-2306; *Fax:* (202) 955-2056; *E-mail:* mmcloughlin@usnews.com.

MacMANUS, Susan Ann, MA, PH D; American professor of political science; b 22 Aug 1947, Tampa, FL; d of Harold Cameron and Elizabeth Riegler MacManus. *Education:* Florida State Univ and Univ of Michigan. *Career:* Instructor of Political Science, Valencia Community Coll, Orlando, FL 1969–73; Asst Prof of Political Science Univ of Houston, TX 1975–79, Assoc Prof 1979–84; Visiting Prof of Political Science Univ of Oklahoma 1981–; Prof of Urban Affairs and Political Science Cleveland State Univ 1984–87; Prof of Public Admin and Political Science, Univ of S Florida 1987–, Chair Dept of Govt and Int Affairs 1990–, mem Bd of Dirs USF Research Foundation Inc 1990–; mem Advisory Bd, James Madison Inst for Public Policy Studies 1987–, Center for the Study of States, Rockefeller Inst of Govt, State Univ of New York 1990–; adviser and consultant to numerous univ and govt bodies; mem numerous editorial bds including Policy Studies Journal 1981–, Journal of Politics 1982–, Int Journal of Public Admin 1989– (Chair 1990–94); Pres Urban Politics Section, American Political

Science Assn 1995–96; mem American Soc for Public Admin, Policy Studies Org, Int Political Science Assn; Pres-Elect American Soc for Public Admin; named one of Outstanding Young Women of America 1980; Theodore and Venette Askounes-Ashford Distinguished Scholar Award, Univ of S Florida 1991. *Publications include:* Revenue Patterns in US Cities and Suburbs: A Comparative Analysis 1978, Selected Bibliography of State Government 1973–78 1979, Reapportionment and Representation in Florida: A Historical Collection 1991, Doing Business with Government: Federal, State, Local and Foreign Government Purchasing Practices for Every Business and Public Institution 1992, Young v Old: Generational Combat in the 21st Century 1996; numerous articles, papers, lectures, contribs to books, reports and monographs, TV and radio appearances. *Address:* University of South Florida, College of Arts and Sciences, Dept of Govt and Int Affairs, 4202 E Fowler Ave, SOC 107, Tampa, FL 33620-8100, USA (Office); 2506 Collier Parkway, Land O'Lakes, FL 34639, USA (Home). *Telephone:* (813) 974-2384 (Office); (813) 949-0320 (Home); *Fax:* (813) 974-2668 (Office); (813) 949-6923 (Home).

MACMILLAN, Judy Ann; Jamaican artist; b 3 Dec 1945, St Andrew; d of Dudley G. Macmillan and Vida J. Fullerton-Macmillan; one s. *Education:* Wolmer's Girls' School. *Career:* Fourteen solo exhibitions 1966–96; several group exhibitions in Jamaica and abroad including Caribbean Focus Exhibition, Commonwealth Inst, London 1986; Man Dir Colony Realty Co, Cross Roads Devt Co. *Leisure interests:* travel, swimming, reading, films. *Address:* Macmillan Advertising, 29 Old Hope Rd, Kingston 5, Jamaica. *Telephone:* 926-1796.

McMILLAN, Terry, BA; American writer; b 1952, Port Huron, MI; one s. *Education:* Univ of California at Berkeley and Columbia Univ Film School. *Career:* Fmr sec; Guest Columnist 'Hers' column, New York times; book reviewer for New York Times Book Review, Atlanta Constitution, Philadelphia Inquirer; fmr Assoc Prof of English Univ of Arizona; fmr Visiting Prof in Creative Writing, Univ of Wyoming, Stanford Univ; Prof Univ of Arizona 1988–91; Fiction Judge Nat Book Awards 1990; Nat Endowment for the Arts Fellow 1988; Doubleday/Columbia Univ Literary Fellow; Fellow Yaddo Artist Colony, Macdowell Colony. *Publications:* Mama (Nat Book Award, Before Columbus Foundation) 1987, Disappearing Acts 1989, Breaking Ice (ed) 1990, Waiting To Exhale 1995 (co-writer screenplay), How Stella Got Her Groove Back 1996. *Address:* c/o Viking Studio Books, 375 Hudson St, New York, NY 10014- 3657, USA.

McNALLY, Eryl Margaret, BA; British politician; b 11 April 1942; m James McNally 1964; one s one d. *Education:* Newbridge Grammar School, Univ of Bristol and Univ of Wales, Swansea. *Career:* Language teacher in secondary schools and colls of further educ; OFSTED (Office for Standards in Educ) Insp; Adviser Buckinghamshire Co Council; mem (Lab) Three Rivers Dist Council; Deputy Leader Hertfordshire Co Council; MEP (PSE) for Bedfordshire and Milton Keynes 1994–, Vice-Chair Research, Technological Devt and Energy Cttee, mem Switzerland, Iceland and Norway Interparl Del. *Leisure interests:* languages, swimming, reading. *Address:* European Parliament, rue Wiertz, 1047 Brussels, Belgium; 146 Abbots Rd, Abbots Langley, Herts WD5 0BL, UK. *Telephone:* (2) 284-21-11 (Office); (1908) 314974 (Home); *Fax:* (2) 230-69-43 (Office); (1923) 270608 (Home); *E-mail:* 100443.1574@compuserve.com.uk.

McNISH, Althea Marjorie; British textile designer; b Trinidad; d of the late J. Claude and Margaret McNish; m John Weiss 1969. *Education:* London Coll of Printing and Cen School of Art and Crafts. *Career:* Freelance textile designer 1957–, comms from Ascher and Liberty's 1957; interior design for Govt of Trinidad and Tobago in New York and Washington, USA and London 1962; Cotton Bd Travelling Scholarship to report on export potential for British printed cotton goods in Europe 1963; designed collection of dress fabrics for ICI and Tootal Thomson 1966; designs etched silver dishes (with John Weiss) 1973–; interior design for Sec-Gen of Commonwealth 1975, improvements to London Office of High Commr for Trinidad and Tobago (jtly) 1981; designer bedlinen collection for Courtaulds 1978, textile hangings for British Railways Bd Offices, London 1979, banners for Design Centre 1981, fashion textiles for Slovene textile printers 1985–91, furnishing textile designs for Fede Cheti, Milan, Italy 1986–91; murals and hangings for Royal Caribbean Cruise Line, MS Nordic Empress 1990, MS Monarch

of the Seas 1991; has taken part in numerous exhibitions and rep in numerous perm collections; Visiting Lecturer Cen School of Art and Crafts 1960–, USA 1972–, Italy, Germany and Yugoslavia 1985–; Advisory Tutor in Furnishing and Surface Design, London Coll of Furniture 1972–90. *Publications include:* Did Britain Make It?, M. Schoeser, Fabrics and Wallpapers 1986; numerous contribs to professional journals. *Leisure interests:* skiing, travel, music, gardening. *Address:* 142 West Green Rd, London N15 5AD, UK. *Telephone:* (20) 8800-1686.

MACPHERSON, Elle; Australian fashion model and business executive; b 29 March 1963, Killara, Sydney; d of Peter Gow and Frances Macpherson; m Gilles Bensimon (divorced 1989); one s by Arpad Busson. *Career:* Chief Exec Elle Macpherson Inc; designs and promotes own lingerie for Brendon; promotes Elle Macpherson sportswear; co-owner Fashion Café, New York. *Films include:* Sirens 1994, Goldeneye 1995, Bookworm, Jane Eyre 1996, If Lucy Fell 1996, The Mirror Has Two Faces 1996, Batman and Robin, Beautopia 1998, With Friends Like These 1998; *Videos include:* Stretch and Strengthen, The Body Workout 1995. *Address:* Artist Management, Penn House, B414 East 52nd St, New York, NY 10022, USA.

MacPHERSON, Ishbel Jean Stewart, MA; British investment banking executive; b London; d of Sir Thomas and Lady MacPherson. *Education:* Fettes (Scotland) and Univ of Edinburgh. *Career:* At Barclays de Zoet and Webb 1983–94; Head of Smaller Cos, Hoare Govett 1994–99; Head of Emerging Companies Dresdner Kleinwort Wasserstein 1999–. *Leisure interests:* riding, friends, videos. *Address:* 37 Connaught Square, London W2 2HL, UK. *Telephone:* (20) 7475-7146; *Fax:* (20) 7283-4667.

McSHARRY, Deirdre Mary; Irish journalist; b 4 April 1932, London; d of the late John and of Mary (née O'Brien) McSharry; m 1st 1953 (until 1955); m 2nd 1970 (until 1980). *Education:* Dominican Convent (Co Wicklow) and Trinity Coll (Dublin). *Career:* Actress Gate Theatre, Dublin 1953–55; writer The Irish Times 1953; mem staff Evening Herald, Dublin 1955–56; worked for Book Dept, Metropolitan Museum of Art, New York, USA 1956; reporter Women's Wear Daily, New York 1957–59; mem staff Woman's Own 1959–62; Fashion Ed Evening News 1962, The Sun 1967–71, Cosmopolitan 1972, Ed 1973–85; Woman's Ed Daily Express 1963–67; Ed-in-Chief Country Living 1986–89; Ed Countryside, New York 1991–92; Consultant Nat Magazine Co and Magazine Div The Hearst Corpn 1990–92; Chair Bath Friends of The American Museum in Britain, Bath; mem Council of the American Museum; Ed of the Year, Periodical Publrs' Assn 1981, 1987, Mark Boxer Award: Editor's Ed 1991. *Publication:* Inspirations: The Textile Tradition Then and Now (American Museum Catalogue) 2001. *Leisure interests:* architecture, the arts, gardening, travel, Celts, textiles, decorative arts. *Address:* Southfield House, 16 High St, Rode BA3 6NZ, UK. *Telephone:* (1373) 831263 (Home); *Fax:* (1373) 831263 (Home).

McSWEENEY, Brenda Gael, PH D; American UN official; b 23 July 1943, Boston, MA. *Education:* Smith Coll (Northampton, MA), Fletcher School of Law and Diplomacy, Grad Inst of Int Studies and Inst of European Studies (Geneva, Switzerland) and Inst of Political Science (Paris). *Career:* Researcher, teacher Fletcher School, Tufts and Harvard Univs 1966–71; Economic Analyst 1971; Programme Officer UNDP, then Asst Resident Rep Burkina Faso 1972–78, Sr Policy Analysis Officer, New York 1979–82, UNDP Resident Rep and Co-ordinator UN systems operational activities for devt, Jamaica, Bahamas, Turks and Caicos Islands, Bermuda 1982–88; apptd Exec Co-ordinator UN Volunteers 1988–98; UN Resident Co-ordinator in India and UNDP Resident Rep 1998–; has written various articles on devt; Fulbright Scholar, Paris 1967–69. *Address:* United Nations Development Programme, 55 Lodi Estate, New Delhi, 110 003, India. *E-mail:* brenda.mcsweeney@undp.org.in; *Internet:* www.undp.org.in.

McTEER, Janet; British actress; b 5 Aug 1961; d of Alan and Jean McTeer. *Education:* Royal Acad of Dramatic Arts (London). *Career:* Olivier Award; Evening Standard Award; Tony Award; Bancroft Gold Medal 1983. *Plays include:* Much Ado About Nothing, Uncle Vanya, Simpatico, Vivat! Vivat Regina 1995, A Doll's House 1996–97; *Films:* Tangleweeds 1999, The King is Alive 2000; *TV includes:* The Governor,

A Masculine Ending, Don't Leave Me This Way, A Portrait of a Marriage, Precious Bane. *Leisure interests:* cooking, gardens. *Address:* c/o Michael Foster, ICM Ltd, Oxford House, 76 Oxford St, London W1N 0AX, UK. *E-mail:* (20) 7636-6565; *Internet:* (20) 7323-0101.

McWILLIAM, Candia Frances Juliet, BA; British writer; b 1 July 1955, Edinburgh; d of Colin and Margaret McWilliam; m 1st Quentin Gerard Carew Wallop (now Earl of Portsmouth) 1981; one s one d; m 2nd Fram Dinshaw; one s. *Education:* Sherborne School (Dorset) and Girton Coll (Cambridge). *Publications:* novels: A Cast of Knives 1988, A Little Stranger 1989, Debatable Land 1994; short stories: Wait Till I Tell You 1997. *Address:* 21 Beaumont Buildings, Oxford OX1 2LL, UK. *Telephone:* (1865) 511931.

MADARIAGA, Isabel de, BA, PH D, FBA, FRHISTS; British professor of Russian studies; b 27 Aug 1919, Glasgow; d of Salvador de Madariaga and Constance Archibald; m Leonard B. Schapiro 1943 (divorced 1976). *Education:* Ecole Int (Geneva, Switzerland), Headington School for Girls (Oxford, UK), Instituto Escuela (Madrid) and Univ of London. *Career:* BBC Monitoring Service 1940–43; Cen Office of Information, London 1943–47; Econ Information Unit, Treasury 1947–48; Editorial Asst Slavonic and E European Review 1951–64; Part-time Lecturer in History LSE 1953–66; Lecturer in History Univ of Sussex 1966–68; Sr Lecturer in Russian History Univ of Lancaster 1968–71; Reader in Russian Studies School of Slavonic and E European Studies, Univ of London 1971–81, Prof 1981–84, Emer Prof 1984–; corresp mem Royal Spanish Acad of History. *Publications:* Britain, Russia and the Armed Neutrality of 1780 1963, Opposition (jtly) 1965, Russia in the Age of Catherine the Great 1981, Catherine II: A Short History 1990, Politics and Culture in Eighteenth Century Russia 1998; many scholarly articles. *Leisure interest:* music. *Address:* 25 Southwood Lawn Rd, Highgate, London N6 5SD, UK. *Telephone:* (20) 8341-0862.

MADDOCK, Baroness (Life Peer), cr 1997, of Christchurch in the County of Dorset, **Diana Margaret Maddock;** British politician; b 19 May 1945; d of Reginald Derbyshire and Margaret Evans; m 1st Robert Frank Maddock 1966; two d; m 2nd Rt Hon Alan Beith 2001. *Education:* Brockenhurst Grammar School, Shenstone Training Coll and Portsmouth Polytechnic. *Career:* Teacher Weston Park Girls' School, Southampton 1966–69, Extra-Mural Dept Stockholm Univ 1969–72, Sholling Girls' School, Southampton 1972–73, Anglo-Continental School of English, Bournemouth 1973–76, Greylands School of English, Southampton 1990–91; Councillor (Liberal, now Lib Dem) Southampton City Council 1984–93; MP (Lib Dem) 1993–97; Lib Dem Spokesperson on Housing 1993–97, House of Commons 1997–, (House of Lords 1997–), Women's Issues 1995; mem House of Lords 1997–; Pres Lib Dem Party 1998–; Vice-Chair All-Party Parl Group on Homelessness and Housing Need, Electoral Reform, Building Socs. *Leisure interests:* theatre, music, reading, travel. *Address:* House of Lords, London SW1A 0PW, UK. *Telephone:* (20) 7219-1625; *E-mail:* maddockd@parliament.uk.

MADDY, Penelope Jo, BA, PH D; American professor of philosophy; b 4 July 1950, Tulsa, OK; d of Richard and Suzanne Parsons; m David Malamont. *Education:* Univ of California at Berkeley and Princeton Univ. *Career:* Lecturer, then Asst Prof of Philosophy Univ of Notre Dame 1978–83; Assoc Prof of Philosophy Univ of Illinois at Chicago 1983–87; Assoc Prof of Philosophy and Math Univ of California at Irvine 1987–89, Prof 1989–98, Prof of Logic and Philosophy of Science 1998–, Chair Dept of Philosophy 1991–95, Founding Chair Dept of Logic and Philosophy of Science 1998–2001; Westinghouse Science Scholarship 1968–72; Marshall Scholarship 1972–73; American Asscn of Univ Women Fellowship 1982–83; NSF Fellowships 1986, 1988–89, 1990–91, 1994–95; Fellow American Acad Arts and Sciences 1998–. *Publication:* Realism in Mathematics 1990, Naturalism in Mathematics 1997. *Address:* Dept of Logic and Philosophy of Science, School of Social Sciences, University of California at Irvine, Irvine, CA 92697-5100, USA. *Telephone:* (949) 824-4133.

MADKOUR, Nazli, MA; Egyptian artist; b 25 Feb 1949, Cairo; d of Mokhtar Madkour and Malak Salem; m Mohamed Salmawy 1970; one s one d. *Education:* Univ of Cairo and American Univ (Cairo). *Career:* Fmr econ expert for Industrial Devt Centre for Arab States; professional artist 1981–; numerous solo and collective exhibitions; represented in

public and pvt collections in Egypt and internationally. *Publication:* Egyptian Women and Artistic Creativity 1989. *Leisure interests:* travel, reading, music. *Address:* 9 St 216 Digla, Maadi, Cairo, 11435, Egypt. *Telephone:* (2) 5197047 (Office); (2) 5199752 (Home); *Fax:* (2) 5197047.

MADONNA, (Madonna Louise Veronica Ciccone); American singer and film actress; b 1958, Bay City, MI; d of Sylvio and Madonna Ciccone; m Sean Penn 1985 (divorced 1989); one d by Carlos Leon; m 2nd Guy Ritchie 2000; one s. *Education:* Alvin Ailey Dance School. *Career:* Multi-million record-selling performing artist worldwide; toured UK 1983, 1987, France 1987, Germany 1987; several world tours, including Blonde Ambition Tour 1990–91 and Drowned World Tour 2001; f Maverick entertainment co 1992; appeared in play Speed-the-Plow 1988; made commercial for Pepsi Cola 1989; Vice-Pres ICA, London; face of Max Factor. *Albums:* Madonna – the First Album, Like A Virgin, True Blue, You Can Dance, I'm Breathless 1990, The Immaculate Collection 1991, Erotica 1992, Bedtime Stories 1994, Something to Remember 1995, Ray of Light (3 Grammy Awards, including Best Pop Album 1999) 1998, Music 2000; *Singles include:* Everybody, Burning Up, Holiday, Borderline, Like a Virgin, Material Girl, Into the Groove, Dress You Up, Crazy for You, Papa Don't Preach, La Isla Bonita, Who's That Girl?, True Blue, Like a Prayer, Vogue, Justify My Love 1990, This Used To Be My Playground 1992, Erotica 1992, Bedtime Stories 1994, Frozen 1998, Beautiful Stranger 1999, American Pie 2000, Music 2000, Tell Me 2000; *Films include:* Desperately Seeking Susan, Shanghai Surprise, Who's That Girl?, Bloodhounds of Broadway, Dick Tracy 1989, Soapdish 1990, Shadows and Fog 1991, In Bed With Madonna (US title Truth or Dare) 1991, A League of Their Own, Murder She Wrote (TV film), Body of Evidence 1992, Snake Eyes 1994, Dangerous Game 1994, The Girlie Show 1994, Evita 1996, Four Rooms 1996, The Next Best Thing 2000; *Publication:* Sex 1992. *Address:* Maverick Recording Company, 9348 Civic Centre Drive, Suite 100, Beverly Hills, CA 90210, USA.

MADSEN, Mette; Danish writer and former politician; b 3 July 1924, Pandrup, N Jutland; d of Holger and Nina Fruensgaard; m Gunnar Madsen 1965. *Career:* Mem (Liberal) Folketing (Parl) 1971–87; mem of Presidium Folketing 1981–84; Minister for Ecclesiastical Affairs 1984–88; Chair Supervisory Cttee Danish Royal Theatre 1978–84, Cttee of Information and Culture, N Atlantic Council 1982–84; honours include Ravn-Joensens Mindelegat 1968, Fanfareprisen Chr IV Laug 1997, Commdr of the Order of Dannebrog, Iceland Falcon Kt (Second Class), French Nat Order of Culture. *Publications include:* Hen På Eftermiddagen, Sommerens Veje (poetry), Og Så Er Der Kaffe (political memoirs) 1992, I Anledning Af (songs and poetry) 1994, Husk Nu at Neje (childhood memoirs) 1997, Tiden der Fulgte: 20 Top-Chefers Farvel til Magten (Goodbye to Power) 1998; contribs to anthologies of poetry and has written satirical songs. *Address:* Blegdalsparken 53, 9000 Ålborg, Denmark.

MAES, Nelly Sidonie Leona; Belgian politician; b 25 Feb 1941, Sinaai; two d one s. *Education:* Inst Onze-Lieve-Vrouw Presentatie (Sint-Niklaas). *Career:* Teacher until 1970; Councillor Sint Niklaas 1970, Alderman 1988, Alderman for Culture, Educ, Youth, Agric Devt Co-operation, Emancipation 1989; mem Chamber of Reps (Parl – Volksanie, Flemish Nationalist Party) 1971–78, 1985–91; Senator 1981–85, 1991; Sec Office of Chamber of Reps 1988; mem Chamber of Reps Advisory Cttee on European Affairs, Flemish-Arabic Soc, Comm on Foreign Relations, Nat Women's Council, Flemish Council Comm on Educ; Chair Vlaams Int Centre. *Leisure interest:* art.

MAGNUSSEN-CELLA, Karen Diane, OC; Canadian figure-skater; b 4 April 1952, Vancouver, BC; d of Alf John and Gloria (née Johansson) Magnussen; m Anthony Robert Cella 1977; two s one d. *Education:* Delbrook High School, Carson Graham Secondary High School and Simon Fraser Univ (Vancouver). *Career:* Olympic Silver Medallist 1972; World Champion 1973; Star Skater Ice Capades 1973–77; Coach N Shore Winter Club, N Vancouver; Founder Karen Magnussen Foundation 1973, Champion's Way Skating Schools; Life mem N Shore Winter Club, Vancouver Parks and Recreations 1973; Hon Citizen Thunder Bay, ON 1973; Hon Life mem Pacific Nat Exhibition 1973; Hon Coach Special Olympic Games USA 1981; mem Bd of Dirs British Columbia Sports Hall of Fame; Awards include British

Columbia Jr Athlete of the Year 1967, Sr 1971, 1972, Canada's Female Amateur Athlete of the Year 1971, 1972, British Columbia Overall Athlete of the Year 1972, Vanier Outstanding Young Canadian Award 1972, Special Achievement Award, Sons of Norway of America 1972, Award of Merit, Canadian Figure Skating Asscn 1973; mem British Columbia and Canadian Sports Hall of Fame 1973, Canadian Figure Skating Hall of Fame 1997; Best Athlete of the Quarter Century, Sport BC 1991, Distinguished Citizen Award, District of N Vancouver 1991, First Freeman, District of N Vancouver,. *Leisure interests:* golf, swimming. *Address:* 2852 Thorncliffe Drive, N Vancouver, BC V7R 2S8, Canada. *Telephone:* (604) 988-9230.

MAHARRY, Sharon Scott, BA; American advertising executive; b 30 Sept 1949, Roanoke, VA; d of Conrad Young and Mildred Scott; m Robert H. Maharry 1986. *Education:* Roanoke Coll (VA). *Career:* Copywriter Creative Advertising 1971–72, Lawler-Ballard Advertising 1979–81; Prin Image Advertising 1972–79; Sr Writer Young and Rubicam/Zemp, St Petersburg, FL 1981–82, Sr Vice-Pres and Creative Dir 1982–84; Exec Vice-Pres and Creative Dir Johanesson, Kirk and Maharry, Clearwater, FL 1984–85, ICE Communications, Rochester, NY 1985–86; apptd Sr Vice-Pres and Creative Dir Hutchins/Young and Rubicam, Rochester, NY 1986; Pres and Creative Dir Paradigm Communications 1997–98; f (with husband) Mind Control Inc (strategic marketing and creative communications co) 1998; numerous awards include Clio Award 1978, 1982, 1984, 1985, 1987–89, IBA Award, Hollywood Radio and TV Awards 1981, 1987–89, Andy Award, Advertising Club of New York 1980–85, Addy Award, American Advertising Fed 1977, 1982, 1983, 1987–89, One Show Award, New York Art and Copy Club 1982, Creativity Award, Art Dirs Magazine 1982, 1983, 1976, 1988, 1989, Gold Medal, Int TV and Radio Festival 1985, 1987, 1988, Gold Medal Award, London Int Advertising 1987.

MAHLAB, Eve, AO, LL B; Australian business executive; b 30 May 1937, Vienna, Austria; d of Robert Dickins and Gertrud Albers; m Frank Mahlab 1959; two d one s. *Education:* Melbourne Univ. *Career:* CEO Mahlab and Assocs 1968–85, Exec Dir 1985; Founder and Chair Know Biz 1985–90; Founder and Man Dir Thought Partners 2000–; mem Co-ordinating Cttee Women's Electoral Lobby 1975–78, Council Monash Univ 1975–81, Victoria Cttee of Enquiry into Status of Women 1975, Australia Canned Fruit Bd 1984–89, Victoria State Training Bd 1988, Women Chiefs of Enterprise, Bd Walter and Elisa Hall Inst of Medical Research 1990–; Co-Founder Liberal Feminist Network 1980; Non-Exec Dir Westpac Banking Corpn 1992–; Deputy Chairperson Film AustraliaBusiness Woman of the Year 1982; Hon LL D (Monash). *Leisure interests:* business, status of women, human resources, film production, law, legal profession, direct mail. *Address:* Level 44, 55 Collins St, Melbourne, Vic 3000, Australia.

MAHY, Margaret Mary, BA; New Zealand writer; b 21 March 1936; d of Francis George Mahy and Helen May Penlington; two d. *Career:* Asst Librarian Petone Public Library 1959; Asst Children's Librarian Christchurch Public Library 1960, Children's Librarian 1977; Librarian in charge of school requests, School Library Service, Christchurch Br 1967; writer 1980–; Carnegie Medal 1982; Esther Glen Medal. *Publications include:* Picture books: The Dragon of an Ordinary Family 1969, Mrs Discombobulous 1969, Pillycock's Shop 1969, The Little Witch 1970, The Princes and the Clown 1971, The Boy with Two Shadows 1971, The Man Whose Mother Was a Pirate 1971, The Rare Spotted Birthday Party 1974, The Ultra-Violet Catastrophe 1975, The Wind Between the Stars 1976, The Boy Who was Followed Home 1977, Jam 1985, The Great White Maneating Shark 1989; Short stories: Nonstop Nonsense 1977, The Great Piratical Rumbustification, The Librarian and the Robbers 1978, The Chewing-Gum Rescue 1982, The Birthday Burglar and a Very Wicked Headmistress 1984, Wibble Wobble 1984, The Spider in the Shower 1984, The Downhill Crocodile Whizz 1986, The Three Wishes 1986, The Door in the Air 1988, Tick Tock Tales 1994; Jr fiction: The Bus Under the Leaves 1975, The Pirate Uncle 1977, Raging Robots and Unruly Uncles 1981, The Adventures of a Kite 1985, Sophie's Singing Mother 1985, A Very Happy Bathday 1985, Clever Hamburger 1985, The Man Who Enjoyed Grumbling 1986, The Pop Group 1986, The Terrible Topsy-Turvy Tissy-Tossy Tangle 1986, Mr Rumfitt 1986, My Wonderful Aunt 1986, The Blood and Thunder Adventure on Hurricane Peak 1989, The Cousins Quartet (4 books) 1994; School books: The Crocodile's Christmas Jandals 1982,

The Bubbling Crocodile 1983, Shopping with a Crocodile 1983, The Great Grumbler and the Wonder Tree 1984, Fantail Fantail 1984, The Crocodile's Christmas Thongs 1985, Horrakapotchin 1985; also books for older children and for children learning to read. *Leisure interests:* reading, gardening. *Address:* No 1 RD, Lyttleton, New Zealand. *Telephone:* (3) 299-703.

MAITLAND, Lady Olga; British politician and journalist; b 23 May 1944; d of Earl of Lauderdale; m Robin Hay 1969; two s one d. *Education:* School of St Mary and St Anne, Abbots Bromley and Lycée Français de Londres. *Career:* Reporter Fleet St News Agency, Blackheath, District Reporter 1965–67; journalist Sunday Express 1967–91; Inner London Educ Authority Cand, Holborn and St Pancras 1986; Cons parl cand Bethnal Green and Stepney 1987; MP (Cons) Sutton and Cheam 1992–97; mem Select Cttee on Educ, on Procedures; Sec Cons Backbench Defence Cttee; Founder and Chair Families for Defence 1983–; Pres Defence and Security Forum 1992–; Patron St Raphael's Hospice Appeal 1992–. *Publications:* Margaret Thatcher: The First Ten Years 1989, Faith in the Family 1997; Peace Studies in our Schools (jtly) 1984; Political Indoctrination in Schools (jtly) 1985. *Leisure interests:* family, gardening, the arts, travel. *Address:* 21 Cloudesley St, London N1 0HX, UK. *Telephone:* (20) 7837 9212.

MAITRA, Jayanti, PH D; Indian historian and writer; b 6 Aug 1946, Calcutta (now Kolkata); d of Robin and Purnima Mukherjee; m Rana Maitra 1975; one d. *Education:* Jadavpur Univ and Presidency Coll (Calcutta). *Career:* Lecturer of History Jadavpur Univ 1980–86; Researcher in the history and culture of the UAE, studying progress and devt of women in collaboration with the Documentaries and Studies Centre, Rás al Khaymah 1986–; has presented papers at int confs; Govt of W Bengal Scholarship 1963; Univ Grants Comm (India) Research Scholarship 1970–73, Book Publication Grant 1981; Awards for Outstanding Academic Merit and for Proficiency in Indian Classical Dancing. *Publications:* Muslim Politics in Bengal 1855–1906 1982; articles in professional journals in India and abroad and in newspapers in UAE. *Leisure interests:* Indian classical music and dancing, studying places of historical interest. *Address:* POB 4525, Abu Dhabi, United Arab Emirates. *Telephone:* (2) 666124.

MAJOR, Dame Malvina Lorraine, DBE; New Zealand opera singer (soprano); b 28 Jan 1943, Hamilton; d of Vincent and Eva Major; m Winston William Richard Fleming 1965 (died 1990); one s two d. *Education:* Hamilton Tech Coll and London Opera Centre. *Career:* Debut as Rosina in The Barber of Seville, Salzburg Festival 1968; performances in Europe, UK, USA, Australia, Japan, Jordan, Egypt and NZ; concerts, opera and recording with NZ Symphony Orchestra, Auckland Philharmonic and Southern Symphony Orchestra; f Dame Malvina Major Foundation (for excellence in the performing arts) 1991; Amb for the NZ Year of the Family 1994; Prof of Singing, Canterbury Univ; Hon life mem NZ Horticultural Soc; Patron Christchurch City Choir, Canterbury Opera, Nelson School of Music, Waikato Multiple Sclerosis; NZ winner Mobil Song Quest 1963; winner Kathleen Ferrier Competition 1966; Outstanding Achievements in Music Award 1988; NZ Medal 1990; Entertainer and Int Performer of the Year 1992; NZ Music Award – Classical Disc 1993, 1994; numerous other awards for services to music. *Leisure interests:* family, golf, sewing. *Address:* POB 11-175, Manners St, Wellington, New Zealand. *Telephone:* (4) 495 7483.

MAKARA, Mpho 'Mampeke, BA, MA; Lesotho writer, teacher and student guidance counsellor; b 28 Oct 1954, Quthing; d of the late Tefo Stephen and Malesia Maria (née Masilo) Moroeng; m Thabo Makara 1977; two d one s. *Education:* Morija Girls' Training Coll, Nat Univ of Lesotho and Univ of Bath (UK). *Career:* Primary school teacher 1974–77; Asst Teacher 1982–85, Deputy Head 1987, Teacher, Counsellor of the Lower School, Machabeng Coll 1987, Co-ordinator Middle Years Programme 2000–. *Publications:* Plays: Mali A Llelana 1986, Ke Fahliloe 1990, Sehaeso I 1991, II 1993, III 1994; Novel: Mohanusa 1996; Short stories: Sepettele, Materaseng 1997; Poetry: U Elsang Uena 2002; has also written language courses. *Leisure interests:* reading, singing in a choir, walking, drama coaching, writing, travel. *Address:* Machabeng College, International School of Lesotho, POB 1570, Maseru, Lesotho; POB 15291, Maseru 100, Lesotho. *Telephone:* 315480; *Fax:* 316109; *E-mail:* machabhm@lesoff.co.za; *Internet:* www .lesoff.co.za/machab.

MAKAROVA, Inna Vladimirovna; Russian actress; b 28 July 1926, Taiga, Kemerovo Dist; d of Vladimir Makarov and Anna German; m 1st S. Bondarchuk 1947; m 2nd M. Perelman; one d. *Education:* All-Union Film Inst. *Career:* USSR State Prize 1949; Order of the Red Banner of Labour; People's Artist of the USSR 1985; Order of Merit of the RSFSR 1967. *Appearances include:* Young Guard 1948, Vysota 1957, My Dear Man 1958, Girls 1962, Women 1966, The Rumyantsev Affair 1956, Balsaminov's Wedding 1965, Russian Field 1972, Poskechonsk Old Times 1977, The Meek Love 1980, Dead Souls 1983, Childhood and Youth of Bembi 1988, A Loan for Marriage 1990. *Leisure interest:* gardening. *Address:* 121059 Moscow, Ukrainsky bul 11, Apt 14, Russian Federation. *Telephone:* (095) 243-00-93.

MAKAROVA, Natalia Romanova; Russian ballet dancer; b 1940, Leningrad (now St Petersburg); m 3rd Edward Karkar 1976; one s. *Education:* Vagonova Ballet School (Leningrad). *Career:* Mem Kirov Ballet 1959–70; sought political asylum, London 1970; Prin Dancer American Ballet Theatre 1970–; appeared with Kirov Co in London 1988, USSR 1989; f Makarova and Co 1980; Guest Artist Royal Ballet 1972, London Festival Ballet 1984; acted in Tovarich, Chichester Festival Theatre 1991; best known for performance of Giselle; retd from dancing 1992; actress St Petersburg theatres 1991–; Honoured Artist of the RSFSR. *Publications:* A Dance Autobiography 1979, On Your Toes 1984. *Address:* c/o American Ballet Theatre, 888 Seventh Ave, New York, NY 10019, USA.

MAKEBA, Miriam (Zenzile); South African singer; b 4 March 1932, Prospect Township, Johannesburg; m 1st James Kubay 1950 (divorced 1952); one d (deceased 1985); m 2nd Sonny Pillay 1959; m 3rd Hugh Masekela 1964 (divorced 1966); m 4th Stokely Carmichael 1968 (divorced 1978); m 5th Bageot Bah 1980. *Education:* Methodist Training School, Pretoria. *Career:* Sang at concert in Highbury Fields, London 1994; Amb to FAO 1999–. *Albums include:* Miriam Makeba 1960, The World of Miriam Makeba 1962, The Click Song 1965, Sangoma 1988, Welela 1989, Eyes on Tomorrow 1991, Miriam Makeba and the Skylarks 1991, The Best of Miriam Makeba and the Skylarks 1998, Live from Paris and Conakry 1998, Homeland 2000; *Publications include:* Makeba: My Story 1988 (autobiog). *Address:* c/o Souo Disc, 85 rue Foudary, 75015 Paris, France.

MÄKELÄ, Tina Elise; Finnish politician; b 30 June 1955, Lahti; m Lasse Antti Mäkelä 1976; two c. *Career:* Nurse and Church Social Worker; Chair SMP (Finnish Rural Party) 1991–92; mem Eduskunta (Parl). *Address:* Vapaudenkatli 24в 45, 40100 Jyväskylä, Finland.

MAKHALINA, Yulia Victorovna; Russian ballet dancer; b 23 June 1968, St Petersburg. *Education:* Vaganova Acad of Russian Ballet. *Career:* Ballet dancer Mariinsky Theatre 1985–89, prima ballerina 1989–; Winner Int Ballet Competition in Paris 1990 (Gold Medal and Grand Prix), Merited Artist of Russia. *Roles include:* Aurora and Lilac Fairy (Sleeping Beauty), Giselle and Myrtha (Giselle), Kitri (Don Quixote), Medora (Le Corsaire), Odette/Odile (Swan Lake), Nikiya and Gamzatti (La Bayadère), Mekhmene and Banu (Legend of Love), Maria (Fountain of Bakhchisarai), Zobeide (Sheherazade), Fire Bird (Firebird), Maria Taglioni (Pas de Quatre), Anna (Anna Karenina), Cinderella (Cinderella), Carmen (Carmen), Countess Elba (Goya Divertissement);. *Address:* Mariinsky Theatre, Teatralnaya pl 1, St Petersburg, Russian Federation.

MAKHMALBAF, Samira; Iranian film director; b 1980, Tehran; d of Mohsen Makhmalbaf. *Films include:* The Apple (Jury Prize, Cannes Film Festival) 1998, Takhte Siah (Blackboards) 2000. *Address:* c/o Hojatoleslam Sayed Muhammad Khatami, Office of the President, Pastor Avenue, Tehran, Iran.

MAKINDA, Anna; Tanzanian politician; b 26 July 1949; d of Wilson Makinda and Tulakela Samnyuka; one d. *Education:* Masasi and Kilakala Girls' Schools and Inst of Devt Man (Mzumbe). *Career:* MP 1975–; mem Parl Public Accounts Cttee 1975–83; First Vice-Pres and Minister of State in the Office of the Prime Minister 1983–90; Minister for Community Devt, Women's Affairs and Children 1991; Chair Pan African News Agency 1986–88. *Address:* c/o Ministry for Community Development, Women's Affairs and Children, POB 3448, Dar es Salam, Tanzania.

MAKRAM-EBEID, Mona, PH D; Egyptian professor of political science and politician; b Cairo; m; one s. *Education:* Harvard Univ (MA, USA), Univ of Cairo and American Univ in Cairo. *Career:* Prof of Political Science and Political Sociology, American Univ in Cairo; mem People's Ass (Parl) 1990–95, mem Foreign Affairs and Educ Cttees; Pres Parliamentarians for Global Action 1990–95; Founder-mem Arab Org for Human Rights; Adviser to World Bank for the Middle East and North Africa Region 1992; Consultant to Search for Common Ground, Initiative for Peace and Co-operation in the Middle East, Washington, DC; Exec mem Ibn Khaldum Centre for Developmental Studies, Nat Centre for Middle Eastern Studies; mem Int Consultative Group for the Middle East Center for Strategic and Int Studies, Washington, DC 1991, UNICEF Women for Devt Cttee, Women for Foreign Policy Group, Washington, DC, The Arab Thought Forum, Amman; several articles on politics in journals and magazines published in English, Arabic and French; Fulbright Scholar 1981, 1983; Chevalier de la Légion d'Honneur 1994; Woman of the Year, Civil Soc Review 1994; Commdr de la Pléiade, AIPLF (Int Asscn for French-speaking Parliamentarians) 1995. *Leisure interests:* tennis, theatre, ballet, swimming. *Address:* Apt 16, 4th Floor, 14 Guezira St, Zamalek, Cairo, Egypt. *Telephone:* (2) 3407603; *Fax:* (2) 2608288.

MAKSAKOVA, Ludmila Vasilyevna; Russian actress; b 26 Sept 1941, Moscow; d of Maria Maksakova; m two c. *Education:* Moscow Shchukin Theatre School. *Career:* Leading actress Moscow Vakhtangov Theatre 1961–; numerous film roles; RSFSR Merited Artist 1971, RSFSR People's Artist 1980, State Prize of Russian Fed (for Guilty without Guilt) 1995, Order for Service to Motherland. *Plays include:* Princess Turandot in Adelma, Masha in Alive Corpse, Nicol in The Prodigious Snob, Nastasha Filipovna in Idiot, Anna Karenina, Duchess of Marlborough in Glass of Water, Korzinkina in Guilty without Guilt, the Countess in The Queen of Spades. *Address:* Bryusov per 7, Apt 70, 103009 Moscow, Russian Federation. *E-mail:* (95) 229-94-98.

MAKSIMOVA, Yekaterina Sergeyevna; Russian ballet dancer and dance teacher; b 1 Feb 1939, Moscow; d of Sergey Maksimov and Tatiana Maksimova; m Vladimir Vasiliyev. *Education:* Bolshoi Theatre Ballet School and State Inst of Theatrical Arts. *Career:* Mem Bolshoi Theatre Ballet Co 1958–88, coach 1998–; toured widely; coach, Kremlin Ballet 1995–; Gold Medal, Varna (int competition) 1964, Pavlova Prize, Paris Acad of Dance 1969, Marius Petipa Prize, Paris Acad of Dance 1972, People's Artist of USSR 1973, Prize for Best Female Role, Prague Int TV Film Festival 1979, Honoured Artist of the RSFSR, Order of Red Banner, USSR State Prize 1981, Jino Tagni Int Prize, Rome 1989, Russian State Order of Merit 1999. *Ballets include:* Nutcracker, Stone Flower, Seventh Waltz, Chopiniana, Fountain of Bakhchisarai, Giselle, Song of the Forest, Flames of Paris, Anyuta, Paganini, Thunder Road, Cinderella, Sleeping Beauty, Don Quixote, Spartacus, Hussars' Ballad, Romeo and Juliet, Natalie (or The Swiss Milkmaid), Blue Angel, Nijinsky, Gaieté Parisienne, Eugene Onegin, Swan Lake, Icarus, Petrushka, Creation of the World; *Films:* Galatea, The Old Tango, Anyuta, Fouette, Traviata, Adam and Eva, Dame of Class, Chapliniana, Crystal Shoe, These Charming Sounds, Fragments of One's Biography, Trapezium; *TV documentaries include:* Creation of Dance, Road to Big Ballet, World of Dance, Pages of Modern Dance, Katya and Volodya, Yekaterina Maksimova, Duet, ...And There Is Always Something Unsaid. *Leisure interests:* reading, sewing. *Address:* c/o State Academic Bolshoi Theatre, Moscow, Teatralnaya pl 1, Russian Federation; Smolenskaya Naberezhnaya 5/13-62, 121099 Moscow, Russian Federation (Home). *Telephone:* (095) 292-06-55 (Office); (095) 244-02-27 (Home); *Fax:* (095) 254-73-68 (Office); (095) 244-02-27 (Home); *E-mail:* panart@mail.com (Office); info@vasiliev.com (Home); *Internet:* www.bolshoi.ru (Office); www.maximova.bolshoi.ru (Home).

MALFITANO, Catherine; American opera singer (soprano); d of Joseph Malfitano and Maria Maslova; one d. *Career:* Has appeared at Lyric Opera (Chicago), Metropolitan Opera (NY), La Scala (Milan), Deutsche Oper (Berlin), Royal Opera House (Covent Garden, London), Salzburg Festival, Paris, Geneva, Vienna, Rome, Marseilles,

LA, Florence, Hamburg, Barcelona, Israel; received Emmy for Tosca. *Opera appearances include:* Madame Butterfly 1995, 1997, Il Trittico, Salome, Wozzeck, Eugene Onegin, Tosca, Don Giovanni, Fidelio, McTeague (world première), Antony and Cleopatra, The Makropulos Case.

MALKKI, Susanna; Finnish conductor and cellist; b 1970, Helsinki. *Education:* Sibelius Acad (Helsinki) and Royal Acad of Music (London). *Career:* Prin Gothenburg Symphony Orchestra (Sweden) 1995–98; Conductor Musica Nova Festival (Helsinki) 1999; Guest Conductor Birmingham Contemporary Music Group. *Address:* c/o CBSO Centre, Berkley St, Birmingham, B1 2LF, UK.

MALLALIEU, Baroness (Life Peer), cr 1991, of Studdridge in the County of Buckinghamshire, **Ann Mallalieu,** LL M; British barrister and member of the House of Lords; b 27 Nov 1945; d of Sir William and Lady Mallalieu; m Timothy Felix Harold Cassel 1979; two d. *Education:* Newnham Coll (Cambridge). *Career:* Pres (first woman) Cambridge Union Soc 1967; called to the Bar, Inner Temple 1970, Bencher 1992; Recorder 1985–93; mem House of Lords (Lab) 1991, Opposition Spokesman on home affairs and legal affairs 1992–97; mem Gen Council of the Bar 1973–75; Chair Suzy Lamplugh Trust 1997–; Pres Countryside Alliance 1998–; Hon Fellow Newnham Coll, Cambridge 1992;. *Leisure interests:* sheep, hunting, poetry, horse-racing. *Address:* House of Lords, London SW1A 0PW, UK. *Telephone:* (20) 7219-3000.

MALLORY, Penny; British journalist, broadcaster and former rally car driver; m David Mallory; two d. *Education:* Ashford School for Girls and Highworth Grammar School (Kent). *Career:* Fmr Nat Ladies Rally Champion; 1st woman to enter World Rally Championships; currently TV presenter. *Leisure interests:* rally driving, interior design and house renovation, horses, travel. *Address:* Cunningham Management Ltd, 271 King St, London W6 9LZ, UK. *Telephone:* (20) 8233-2824; *Fax:* (20) 8283-2825; *E-mail:* info@cunningham-management.co.uk; *Internet:* www.cunningham-management.co.uk.

MALLOY, Eileen Anne, BS; American diplomatist; b 9 July 1954, New Jersey; d of John J. and Mary Langan Malloy; m 1st Ilmar Paegle 1975 (divorced); m 2nd James G. McLachlan 1985; two d. *Education:* Georgetown Univ (Washington, DC). *Career:* Reporter and Div Man Dun and Bradstreet, New York 1975–78; joined Foreign Service 1978; worked at US Embassies in London, Moscow and Dublin, and Consulate-Gen in Calgary, Canada; worked at Dept of State as UK Desk Officer, Analyst in Consular Affairs, Head of Secr staff for Sec of State, Special Asst to Under-Sec for Political Affairs; Amb to Kyrgyzstan 1994. *Leisure interests:* reading, gardening, clay-pigeon shooting, photography, architecture. *Address:* USA.

MALONE, Bernie, BCL; Irish politician; b 26 March 1948, Dublin; m Frank Malone 1972. *Education:* Dominican Coll (Dublin, Bruges, Belgium) and Univ Coll Dublin. *Career:* Co Councillor, Dublin 1979–94, Chair Co Council 1985; MEP 1994–99, Vice-Chair Foreign Affairs Cttee, Vice-Chair Socialist Group 1994–99. *Leisure interests:* reading, TV. *Address:* 43 Molesworth St, Dublin, Ireland.

MALONE, Beverly, PH D, RN; American nurse and nursing administrator. *Education:* Univ of Cincinnati and Rutgers State Univ. *Career:* Nurse (NJ) early 1970s; f pvt practice (OH) 1975; Asst Admin for Nursing, Univ Hosp Cincinnati 1983–86; Pres American Nurses Asscn 1996–2000; Dean, Interim Vice Chancellor of Academic Affairs and Prof N Carolina A&T State Univ School of Nursing 1996–2001; Deputy Asst Sec for Health, US Office of Public Health Services 2000–2001; Sec Gen Royal College of Nursing (RCN), Cardiff, UK Jan 2001–; mem US Del to World Health Ass 1998; mem Pres Clinton's Advisory Comm on Consumer Protection and Quality in Health Care Industry 1996–98. *Address:* Copse Walk, Cardiff Gate Business Park, Cardiff CF23 8XG, UK. *Telephone:* (0845) 7726100; *Internet:* www.rcn.org.uk.

MALONEY, Nina Eslyn; Saint Vincent and the Grenadines broadcasting executive; b 30 June 1935, Calliaqua, St Vincent; d of Adolphus and Violet Maloney. *Education:* Kingstown Anglican School. *Career:* Primary school teacher 1950–56; telephone operator 1956–65; Sec to Postmaster-Gen, Postage Stamp Cttee 1965–76; Announcer Nat

Broadcasting Corpn (NBC) Radio 705, Operator 1976–87, Religious Broadcast Co-ordinator 1986–92, Programme Asst 1987–88, Deputy Gen Man Personnel and Admin 1988–90, Exec Dir 1990; Dist Commr Girl Guides 1959–69, Sec Dist Council 1963–71; Pres St Vincent Jaycettes 1972–74, Friends of Bishop's Coll 1974–92; Sec Duke of Edinburgh's Award Scheme, St Vincent and the Grenadines 1976–92; Public Relations Officer, World Food Day Cttee 1988–92, Regional Constituent Ass, Org of E Caribbean States (OECS) 1991, Carnival Devt Cttee (Deputy Chair 1989–91); Jaycette of the Year 1970; Certificate for Outstanding Services as Pres, Friends of Bishop's Coll 1990; Long Service Medal, Girl Guides Asscn 1991. *Leisure interests:* singing, travel, social work, visiting shut-ins. *Address:* NBC, POB 705, Kingstown, Saint Vincent and the Grenadines (Office); Upper Edinboro, St Vincent and the Grenadines (Home). *Telephone:* 71111 (Office); 71202 (Home); *Fax:* 62749 (Office).

MANCHET, Eliane; French opera singer (soprano); b 16 May 1935, Bamako, Mali; d of Georges Schaaf and Claire Cote; m 1st Lucien Manchet (deceased); m 2nd Pierre Médecin 1970; two s. *Education:* Lycée (Montbeliard), Faculty of Medicine (Besançon) and Conservatoire Nat de Musique (Strasbourg). *Career:* Operatic debut Lyons 1966; performances in Paris, Bordeaux, Toulouse, Strasbourg, Nice 1966–78, in La Scala (Milan, Italy), Staatsoper (Vienna), Brussels, Amsterdam (Netherlands), Munich, Frankfurt/Main, Cologne and Berlin (Germany), Venice and Florence (Italy), Geneva (Switzerland) 1978–; appeared at Festival in Spoleto (Italy); int tours in Budapest, Munich 1985–; Prof of Singing, Nice Conservatoire 1985–95, Parisian Conservatoires 1988–; Grand Prix Int Singing Competition, Toulouse 1965. *Recordings include:* Les Brigands (Acad Charles Cros Prize, also film) 1969, Pelléas et Mélisande 1988, Cocteau – Melodies 1990, Die Fledermaus 1991. *Leisure interests:* tapestry, swimming, gardening. *Address:* 42 rue de la Pompe, 75116 Paris, France. *Telephone:* (1) 45-03-12-33.

MANCINO, Nicola; Italian politician and lawyer; b 15 Oct 1931, Montefalcione, Avellino. *Career:* Fmr communal, prov and regional councillor, Chair Campania Regional Exec Council (twice), Christian Democrat (DC) Prov Sec, Avellino, Regional Sec Campania; elected Senator from Avellino 1976, 1979, 1983, 1987; Chair DC Parl Group 1984; Minister of Interior 1992–94, Pres of Senate May 1996–. *Address:* The Senate, Rome, Italy.

MANDEL, Ruth Blumenstock, PH D; American university professor; b 29 Aug 1938, Vienna, Austria; m 1st Barrett John Mandel; m 2nd Jeffrey Lucker 1991; one d. *Education:* Brooklyn Coll (NY) and Univ of Connecticut. *Career:* Lecturer Univ of Pittsburgh 1968–70; Asst Prof Rider Coll 1970–71; Asst Prof Rutgers Univ 1973, Assoc Prof 1978, apptd Prof 1985, Educational Co-ordinator, now Dir, Center for the American Woman and Politics (CAWP), Dir of Educational Programs and Admin 1971, 1973; writes and speaks widely about women and women's issues, frequent TV and radio appearances, lectures throughout USA; Co-Founder Public Leadership Educ Network; Co-Chair Advisory Cttee, Inst for Research on Women 1982, Research Council, Advisory Panels on Social Sciences 1982–85; mem Pres's Comm on the Arts, Humanities and Social Sciences in an Era of High Technology 1983–84, Provost's Cttee on Political Oppression 1985, Provost's Budget and Planning Cttee 1988–90, Faculty Council and Planning Cttee 1990, Univ Faculty Budget Cttee 1990, Presidential Search Cttee 1990. *Publications include:* In the Running: The New Woman Candidate 1981, The Political Woman in the American Woman 1988–89; numerous contribs to professional journals. *Address:* Center for the American Woman and Politics, Eagleton Institute of Politics, Rutgers University, New Brunswick, NJ 08901, USA.

MANDELA, (Nomzano) Winnie; South African politician; b 1934, Bizana, Pondoland, Transkei; m Nelson Mandela 1958 (divorced 1996); two d. *Career:* Active mem of African Nat Congress (ANC); campaigned constantly on behalf of her husband gaoled for political activities 1964–90; held in solitary confinement 1969–70; named a "banned person" by S African authorities 1976; Head ANC Social Welfare Operations 1990–92; suspended from ANC's Women's League 1992; sentenced to six years' imprisonment on four counts of kidnapping and of being an accessory to assault 1991, sentence upheld on appeal, except charge of being accessory to assault; prison term waived to suspended two-year term, fine imposed June 1993; suspended from ANC Women's League 1993, Head April 1997–; mem ANC Nat Exec Cttee 1994; Deputy Minister for Arts, Culture, Science and Tech, Govt of Nat Unity 1994–95; Third World Prize 1985. *Publication:* Part of My Soul Went With Him 1985. *Address:* Orlando West, Soweto, Transvaal, South Africa.

MANDRELL, Barbara Ann; American singer; b 25 Dec 1948; d of Irby Matthew and Mary Ellen Mandrell; m Kenneth Lee Dudney 1967; three c. *Career:* Country music singer and entertainer 1959–; mem Grand Ole Opry, Nashville, TN 1972–; has performed throughout USA and abroad; mem Musicians' Union, Screen Actors' Guild, Country Music Asscn, Order of Eastern Star; Miss Oceanside (CA) 1965; Most Promising Female Singer, Acad of Country and Western Music 1971; Female Vocalist of the Year 1978, 1979, 1980; Entertainer of the Year 1980; People's Choice Awards 1982–84. *Recordings include:* Midnight Oil, Treat Him Right, This Time I Almost Made It, This is Barbara Mandrell, Midnight Angel, Barbara Mandrell's Greatest Hits, Morning Sun, Standing Room Only, The Barbara Mandell Collection 1995, Folled by a Felling 1995; *TV appearances include:* Barbara Mandrell and the Mandrell Sisters 1980–82, Barbara Mandrell: Get To the Heart 1987, The Wrong Girl 1999, Stolen from the Heart 2000; *Publications include:* Get To the Heart: My Story (jtly) 1990. *Address:* c/o Creative Artists Agency, 3310 West End Ave Fl 5, Nashville, TN 37203-1028, USA.

MANEVA, Tsvetana Georgieva; Bulgarian actress; b 30 Jan 1944, Plovdiv; d of George Manev and Nadezhda Maneva; m Javor Miloushev; one d. *Education:* The Higher Inst of Dramatic Art (Sofia). *Career:* Actress Dramatic Theatre of Plovdiv 1966–; Vice-Pres Bulgarian Actors' Union 1982–86; mem Nat Ass (Parl) 1976–90; teacher of acting New Bulgarian Univ; has acted in over 42 cinema and 39 theatre productions; has received numerous nat awards for theatre and cinema work including People's Actress Award. *Films include:* Last Word, Difficult Love, Useless Interval, How Long I've Been Waiting For You; *Plays include:* Nora 1972, Romeo and Juliet 1974, Julia 1977, The Two Gentlemen of Verona 1976, Much Ado About Nothing 1979, Tears and Laughter 1979, Medea, Antigone 1985, Who's Afraid of Virginia Woolf? 1990. *Leisure interests:* flowers, self-analysis, interest in the origins of the universe. *Address:* 1407 Sofia, 52 Buntovnik Str, Apt 30, Bulgaria. *Telephone:* (2) 65-82-65.

MANGESHKAR, Lata; Indian singer and actress. *Career:* Has appeared in numerous films. *Films include:* Pahill Mangala Gaur, Apki Sewa Mein, Majboor; *Producer:* Wadal, Kanchanjanga; *Directed music:* Ram Ram Pahume, Sadhi Manse. *Address:* 'Prabhu Kunj', 101 Peddar Rd, 400026 Mumbai, India.

MANGOLD, Sylvia Plimack, BFA; American artist; b 18 Sept 1938, New York; d of Maurice and Ethel Plimack; m Robert Mangold 1961; two s. *Education:* Cooper Union (New York) and Yale Univ (New Haven, CT). *Career:* Solo exhibitions include Fishbach Gallery, New York 1974, 1975, Daniel Weinberg Gallery, San Francisco 1974, Droll/Kolbert Gallery, New York 1978, 1979, 1980, Annemarie Verna, Zurich, Switzerland 1978, Young Hoffman Gallery, Chicago 1980, Wadsworth Atheneum, Hartford 1981, 1992; perspective exhibitions include Contemporary Arts Museum, Houston 1981, Brooke Alexander 1982, Rhona Hoffman Gallery 1985, Texas Gallery, Houston 1986, Fuller Goldeen Gallery, San Francisco 1987, The Elm Tree 1991, Univ of Michigan Museum of Art 1992, Retrospective 1994–96 (Albright Knox Art Gallery 1994, Wadsworth Atheneum 1995, Sarah Campbell Blaffer Gallery, Univ of Houston 1995, Museum of Fine Art, Boston 1995, 1996); group exhibitions include Visual Arts Museum 1968, Weatherspoon Art Gallery, American Fed of Arts 1969, 1972, The Aldrich Museum of Contemporary Art 1971, California Inst of the Arts 1974, Indianapolis Museum of Art 1974, The New York Cultural Center 1974, Hawthorn Gallery 1975, Indianapolis Museum of Art 1976, 1980, Genesis Galleries Ltd 1976, Rosa Esman Gallery 1976, Kassel, Germany 1977, The Madison Art Center 1977, Albright-Knox Gallery 1978, Mitchell Museum 1979, Phoenix Art Museum 1979, Thorpe Intermedia Gallery 1980, Art Latitude Gallery 1980, Castle Gallery 1982, Thomas Segal Gallery 1983, Siegal Contemporary Art 1983, The Hudson River Museum 1984, Sardonia Art Gallery 1985, Stamford Museum and Nature Center 1985, Delaware Museum of Art

1986, Flanders Contemporary Art 1987, Weatherspoon Art Gallery 1987, Fay Gold Gallery 1988, New York State Museum 1989, Cincinnati Art Museum 1989, John Stoller and Co 1990, Davison Art Center 1991, American Acad and Inst of Arts and Letters 1992; works featured in public collections of numerous US modern art museums and galleries. *Address:* 71 Bull Rd, Washingtonville, NY 10992, USA.

MANIERI, Maria Rosaria, PH D; Italian politician; b 30 May 1943, Nardò, Lecce. *Career:* Prof of Moral Philosophy Univ of Lecce 1972–; Councillor Nardò 1975–, Deputy Mayor and Assessor for Public Instruction, Culture and Sport; mem Senate (PSI) for Gallipoli-Galatina 1987, mem Cttees on Public Instruction and Cultural Heritage, Sec to Presidency of Senate; mem Bd of Dirs PSI. *Publications:* Donna e Capitale 1977, Bisogni e Potere—Oltre Hegel e oltre Marx 1984. *Address:* Senato, Palazzo Madama, 00186 Rome, Italy. *Telephone:* (6) 6543746.

MANION, Margaret Mary, AO, PH D, FACE, FAHA; Australian professor of fine arts; b 7 March 1935; d of the late Harold J. and Mary Ella (née Gibbs) Manion. *Education:* Loreto Convent (Normanhurst, NSW), Bryn Mawr Coll (PA, USA) and Univ of Melbourne (Vic). *Career:* Prin Loreto Coll, Mary's Mount 1962–66; Lecturer Christ Coll, Melbourne 1967, tutor 1967–68; Lecturer St Mary's Coll 1972–73, Vice-Prin 1972–75, Sr Lecturer 1973–78; Herald Prof of Fine Arts Univ of Melbourne 1979–95, mem Council 1984–88, Pro-Vice Chancellor 1985–88, Chair Academic Bd 1987–88, Head of Dept 1989–95; mem Council of Trustees Nat Gallery of Victoria 1975–90, Bldg Cttee 1979–80, Victoria Arts Centre Trust 1980–90, Australia Council 1981–90, Bd Council of Adult Educ 1988–; Fellow Australian Acad of the Humanities 1990; Fellow Australian Coll of Educ 1990. *Publications:* The Wharncliffe Hours 1972, The Wharncliffe Hours Facsimile (ed) 1982, Illuminated Manuscripts in Australian Collections (jtly) 1984, Medieval and Renaissance Manuscripts in New Zealand Collections (jtly) 1989, Medieval Texts and Images (co-ed) 1991, The Art of the Book – Its place in Medieval Worship (co-ed) 1998. *Leisure interests:* music, reading, walking. *Address:* 180 Curtain St, Carlton, Vic 3054, Australia.

MANKILLER, Wilma Pearl, BA; American tribal chief; b 18 Nov 1945, Stilwell, OK; d of Charley and Clara Irene Mankiller; m Hector N. Olaya 1963 (divorced 1975); two d. *Education:* San Bruno Coll and San Francisco State Coll (CA), Union Coll (OK) and Univ of Arkansas. *Career:* Community Devt Dir Cherokee Nation, Tahlequah, OK 1977–83, Deputy Chief 1983–85, Prin Chief 1985–87; Pres Inter-Tribal Council, OK; Trustee Ford Foundation, Citizen's Trust; mem Oklahoma Women's Hall of Fame 1986, Nat Women's Hall of Fame, Oklahoma Hall of Fame; American Leadership Award, Harvard Univ 1986. *Publication:* Mankiller: A Chief and Her People (jtly) 1993. *Leisure interests:* reading, writing. *Address:* POB 308, Park Hill, OK 74451, USA.

MANLEY, Beverley Lois, M SC; Jamaican political scientist and lecturer; b 8 Nov 1941, Kingston; m Michael Manley 1972 (divorced 1990); one d one s. *Education:* St Hugh's High School (Kingston), Univ of the W Indies and Howard Univ (USA). *Career:* Freelance Consultant on Gender and Devt; apptd Consultant Dir Bureau of Women's Affairs, Kingston 1991. *Publication:* Gender and the State: A Caribbean Perspective 1991. *Leisure interests:* walking, reading. *Address:* 28 Hopefield Rd, Kingston 6, Jamaica. *Telephone:* 927-6840; *Fax:* 929-0549.

MANN, Erika; German politician; b 28 Jan 1946, Naumburg. *Career:* Fmr MEP (PSE), mem Cttee on External Econ Relations, Del for relations with Ukraine, Belarus and Moldova. *Address:* c/o European Parliament, rue Wiertz, 1047 Brussels, Belgium.

MANN, Jill (Gillian) Lesley, PH D, FBA; British professor of Medieval and Renaissance English; b 7 April 1943; d of the late Edward William and Kathleen (née Bellamy) Ditchburn; m Michael Mann 1964 (divorced 1976). *Education:* Bede Grammar School (Sunderland), St Anne's Coll (Oxford) and Clare Hall (Cambridge). *Career:* Research Fellow Clare Hall, Cambridge 1968–71; Lecturer Univ of Kent at Canterbury 1971–72; Official Fellow Girton Coll, Cambridge 1972–88, Asst Lecturer 1974–78, Lecturer 1978–88, Professorial Fellow 1988–98; Endowed Prof Dept of English, Univ of Notre Dame 1999–;

British Acad Research Reader 1985–87; Hon Fellow St Anne's Coll, Oxford 1990. *Publications:* Chaucer and Medieval Estates Satire 1973, Ysengrimus 1987, The Cambridge Chaucer Companion (co-ed) 1986, Geoffrey Chaucer 1991; numerous articles on Middle English and Medieval Latin. *Leisure interests:* riding, walking, travel. *Address:* Dept of English, University of Notre Dame, Notre Dame, IN 46556, USA; Girton College, Cambridge CB3 0JG, UK.

MANNING, Jane Marian, OBE, FRAM, FRCM, GRSM; British concert and opera singer (soprano); b 20 Sept 1938, Norwich; d of the late Gerald Manning and of Lily (née Thompson) Manning; m Anthony Edward Payne 1966. *Education:* Norwich High School for Girls, RAM (London) and Scuola di Canto (Cureglia, Switzerland). *Career:* London debut concert 1964; int freelance soprano soloist specializing in contemporary music 1964–; more than 350 BBC broadcasts; US debut 1981, Australia 1978; appearances at all leading European festivals and concert halls; more than 250 world premières including several operas; Founder, Artistic Dir Jane's Minstrels 1988; Visiting Prof Mills Coll, Oakland, CA 1981, 1982, 1983, 1986, Royal Coll of Music, London 1995–; Visiting Lecturer UK, USA, Australia, NZ, Scandinavia; Visiting Artist Univ of Manitoba, Canada 1992; Hon Prof Univ of Keele 1996–(2002); mem Exec Cttee Musicians' Benevolent Fund; Hon D UNIV (York) 1988; Special Award for Services to British Music, Composers' Guild of GB 1974. *Recordings include:* The Complete Vocal Works of Messiaen; *Publications:* New Vocal Repertory 1986, (Vol II) 1996, A Messiaen Companion 1995. *Leisure interests:* reading, cooking, ornithology, cinema, philosophy. *Address:* 2 Wilton Square, London N1, UK. *Telephone:* (20) 7359-1593; *Fax:* (20) 7226-4369; *E-mail:* jane@ wiltonsq.demon.co.uk; *Internet:* www.classical-artists.com/ janemanning.

MANNING, Jo (Joan Elizabeth); Canadian artist; b 11 Dec 1923, Sidney, BC; d of Frederick William and Elizabeth Manning; two s two d. *Education:* Gen Amherst Secondary School. *Career:* One-woman exhibitions include Pollock Gallery 1965, 1968, Gallery Pascal 1974, 1977, 1980, Univ of Waterloo 1968, Mira Godard Gallery, Montréal 1976, Calgary 1981, Gadatsy Gallery 1984, Bishop's Univ; group exhibitions include Nat Gallery of Canada, Montréal Museum of Fine Art, Canada Council Art Bank, Dept of External Affairs, Nat Library of Canada, and in USA, Europe, S America and Australia; First Prize, Fourth American Print Biennale (Santiago, Chile) 1970; Gold Medal, Second Print Biennale (Florence, Italy) 1970; Hon Mention, Norwegian Print Biennale 1976; Medal Sixth Int Grafix Biennale (Frechen, Germany) 1980. *Address:* 445 Montréal St, Victoria, BC V8V 4Z7, Canada. *E-mail:* jmanning@islandnet.com.

MANNION, Rosa; British opera singer (soprano); b 1962; one c. *Education:* Royal Scottish Acad of Music. *Career:* Fmr singer with Scottish Opera; Prin Soprano English Nat Opera, London 1989–92; appearances in Lisbon, Amsterdam (Netherlands), Berlin, Paris, Salzburg (Austria), Aix-en-Provence (France), Glyndebourne, Royal Opera House, Covent Garden (London). *Operas include:* L'Elisir d'amore, Rigoletto, Der Rosenkavalier, La Traviata, Manon, Show Book, Die Zauberflöte, Le Roi malgré lui, Werther, A Masked Ball, Xerxes, Figaro's Wedding. *Address:* c/o IMG Artists, 616 Chiswick High Rd, London W4 5RX, UK.

MANSON, Shirley; British singer; b 1966, Edinburgh. *Career:* Lead singer with various pop bands including August 1984, Wild Indians, Goodbye, Mr Mackenzie and Angelfish, before joining band Garbage. *Recordings include:* Garbage 1995, Version 2.0 1998, The World is Not Enough. *Address:* c/o UNI/ALMO, 2220 Colorado Ave, Santa Monica, CA 90404, USA.

MANTEL, Hilary Mary, B JUR, FRSL; British writer; b 6 July 1952, Hadfield, Derbyshire; d of Henry and Margaret Mary Thompson; m Gerald McEwen 1972. *Education:* Hanytown Convent (Cheshire), London School of Econs and Univ of Sheffield. *Career:* Assoc London Coll of Music. *Publications:* Every Day is Mother's Day 1985, Vacant Possession 1986, Eight Months on Ghazzah Street 1988, Fludd 1989 (Winifred Holtby Memorial Award, Southern Arts Literature Prize, Cheltenham Festival Prize), A Place of Greater Safety 1992 (Sunday Express Book of the Year Award 1993), A Change of Climate 1994, An

Experiment in Love 1995 (Hawthornden Prize 1996), The Giant, O'Brien 1998. *Leisure interest:* sleeping. *Address:* c/o A. M. Heath & Co, London, WC2N 4AA, UK.

MAOR, Galia, MBA; Israeli banker; m; three c. *Career:* Joined Bank of Israel, supervisor of banks 1982–89; with Bank Leumi 1991–, Man Dir and CEO 1995–; mem various cttees. *Address:* Bank Leumi le-Israel BM, POB 2, 24-32 Yehuda Halevi St, Tel Aviv, 65546, Israel (Office). *Telephone:* 3-5148111 (Office); *Fax:* 3-5661872 (Office); *E-mail:* www .bankleumi.co.il.

MAPISA-NQAKULA, Nosiviwe; South African political campaigner; m Charles Nqakula; one s. *Career:* Head African National Congress (ANC) Taskforce to relaunch Women's League 1990, Nat Organizer 1991; mem ANC Nat Exec Cttee; mem SA Communist Party (SACP); MP, Chair Intelligence Portfolio Cttee (Nat Ass); mem Judicial Services Comm 2001–. *Address:* ANC, Munich Re Centre, 3rd Floor, 54 Sauer St, Johannesburg 2000, South Africa.

MARADEN, Marti; Canadian actress and theatre director; b 22 June 1945, El Centro, CA, USA; d of Ole Woodrow and Mildred Genevieve Maraden. *Education:* Univ of Minnesota and Michigan State Univ. *Career:* Actress Stratford Festival Theatre 1974–79, BAM Theatre Co (off-Broadway) 1979–80, Hudson Guild Theatre 1981, 1983, Shaw Festival Theatre 1982, 1983, 1985; numerous TV and radio appearances in Canada 1971–82; Dir Shaw and Stratford Festival Theatres 1988–; Tyrone Guthrie Award 1990. *Plays include:* Romeo and Juliet, Hamlet, Three Sisters, Uncle Vanya, Winter's Tale, The Barbarians, Waiting for the Parade, Blood Relations, The Tempest, Number Our Days, Cyrano de Bergerac, The Dining Room; *Plays directed include:* Breaking the Silence, He Who Gets Slapped 1988, Getting Married 1989, Home, The Two Gentleman of Verona, The Illusion. *Address:* 101 Geoffrey St, Toronto, ON M6R 1P2, Canada.

MARAINI, Dacia; Italian writer; b 13 Nov 1936; d of Fosco Maraini and Alliata Topazia; partner Alberto Moravia (died 1990). *Education:* Collegio SS Annunziata Florence and Rome. *Career:* Has written numerous novels, plays and essays; Co-Founder Teatro Porcospino; f Teatro della Maddalena (women's theatre). *Plays include:* La famiglia normale 1967, Il ricatto a teatro 1968, I Sogni di Clitennestra (5 plays) 1981, Lezioni d'Amore (6 plays) 1982; *Novels include:* The Holiday, The Age of Discontent (Prix Formentor) 1963, A Memoria 1967, Donna in Guerra 1975, The Train, Lettere a Marina 1981, Isolina 1985 (trans into English 1993), The Silent Duchess (five awards, including Premio Campiello) 1992, Bagheria (trans into English) 1994; *Poetry includes:* Crudeltà all'Aria Aperta 1966, Mangiami Pure 1980, Dimenticato di Dimenticare 1983; *Other publications:* La Vacanza 1962, L'Età del Malessere (Prix Formentor) 1962, Memoirs of a Female Thief 1973, Devour me too (short stories) 1987, La Bionda, la bruna e l'asino (essays) 1987. *Address:* Via Beccaria 18, 00196 Rome, Italy. *Telephone:* (6) 3611795.

MARALDO, Pamela Jean, BS, PH D; American nurse and organization executive; b 27 Oct 1947, Wilmington, DE; d of Ernest and Helen (née Antonini) Maraldo. *Education:* Adelphi and New York Univs. *Career:* Nurse; Cardiovascular Nurse, New York Univ Medical Centre 1970–74; Research Assoc Nat Health Council, New York 1975–78; Dir of Public Policy Nat League for Nursing, New York 1978–83, Chief Exec 1983–92; Pres Planned Parenthood Fed of America, New York 1992; mem Health Care Faculty, American Express, New York 1982, New York City Bd of Health 1988; Fellow American Acad of Nursing; Hon LHD (Worcester State) 1989. *Address:* Planned Parenthood Federation of America, 810 Seventh Ave, New York, NY 10019, USA.

MARANGOU, Niki; Cypriot writer; b 23 May 1948, Limassol; d of George Marangos and Kaety Chasapis; m 1st Michael Attalides 1970 (divorced 1975); one d; m 2nd Constantin Candounas 1999. *Education:* In Nicosia and Free Univ (Berlin, Germany). *Career:* Dramaturgist Nicosia State Theatre 1975–85; Dir Kochlias Bookshop, Nicosia 1980–; regular newspaper columnist; seven exhibitions of painting, participated in Biennale of Graphic Arts, Ljubljana 1993, Alexandria 1996; State Prize for Poetry 1981, 1987, State Prize for Prose 1990, Cavafy Prize for Poetry in Alexandria 1998, Biannual State Prize for Prose 2000. *Publications:* Ta Apo Kipon 1981, Arhi Indiktou 1987, Mia Strosi

Ammou 1991, Paramythia tis Kyprou (Fairy Tales from Cyprus) 1994, Is the Panther Alive? 1998, Recipes for Katerina 2000, Selections from the Divan 2001. *Leisure interests:* wild plants, painting. *Address:* Ioanni Metaxa 14, Ayios Dometios, Nicosia, Cyprus. *Telephone:* (2) 761766; *Fax:* (2) 766258; *E-mail:* kochlias@spidernet.com.cy; *Internet:* www .marangou.com.

MARCEAU, Sophie; French actress; b (Sophie Danièle Sylvie Maupu) 17 Nov 1966, Paris; d of Benoît and Simone (née Morisset) Maupu; one s. *Career:* Film and theatre actress. *Films:* La boum 1981, La boum 2 (César award 1984) 1983, Fort Saganne 1984, Joyeuses Pâques 1985, L'amour braque (Best Actress award) 1985, Police 1985, Descente aux enfers 1986, Chouans! 1987, L'étudiante 1988, Mes nuits sont plus belles que vos jours 1989, Pacific palisades 1989, Pour Sacha 1991, La note bleue 1991, Fanfan 1993, La fille de D'Artagnan 1994, Braveheart 1995, Beyond the Clouds 1995, Anna Karenina 1996, Marquise 1997, The World is not Enough 1998, La Fidélité 1999; *Plays:* Eurydice (Molière for Best Theatre Newcomer) 1991, Pygmalion 1993; *Publication:* Menteuse 1996. *Leisure interests:* music, reading, countryside, travel. *Address:* c/o Artmédia, 10 ave Georges V, 75008 Paris, France. *Telephone:* (1) 44-31-22-00.

MARCHAK, Maureen Patricia, PH D, FRSC; Canadian professor of sociology; b 22 June 1936, Lethbridge, AB; d of Adrian Ebenezer and Wilhelmina Rankin (née Hamilton) Russell; m William Marchak 1956; two s. *Education:* Univ of British Columbia. *Career:* Lecturer in Anthropology and Sociology Univ of British Columbia 1965–72, Asst Prof 1972–75, Assoc Prof 1975–80, Prof 1980–, Head Dept of Anthropology and Sociology 1987–90, Dean of Faculty 1990–96; Visiting Prof Carleton Univ 1987; Pres Canadian Sociology and Anthropology Asscn 1979–80; Chair Adjudication Cttee, Social Sciences and Humanities Research Council of Canada 1985–87, British Columbia Bldgs Corpn 1992–95; Vice-Pres Humanities and Social Sciences Acad, Royal Soc of Canada 1993–95; Consultant Open Learning Inst of British Columbia 1979, 1981–82, Ontario Council for Grad Studies 1979, 1984, Environment Canada 1982, Canadian Forestry Services 1982, Memorial Univ, NF 1989, 1995; mem Cecil Rhodes Scholarship Trust Selection Cttee 1988, Academic Council British Columbia Open Univ 1988–90, Bd of Univ Hosp 1991, Bd Ecotrust 1992–, Selection Cttee Nat Networks Centers of Excellence (Phase II) 1993; External Assessor Centre for Resource and Environmental Studies, ANU (Canberra) 1995; Fellow Royal Soc of Canada 1987–; Outstanding Contribution of the Year, Canadian Sociology and Anthropology Asscn 1990. *Publications include:* Ideological Perspectives on Canada 1975 (revised edns 1987, 1991), The Working Sexes (ed) 1977, In Whose Interests 1979, Green Gold: The Forest Industry in British Columbia (John Porter Memorial Award 1986) 1983, Uncommon Property (co-ed) 1987, The Integrated Circus: The New Right and the Restructuring of Global Markets 1991, Logging the Globe 1995. *Leisure interests:* hiking, swimming, skiing, music. *Address:* University of British Columbia, Dept of Anthropology and Sociology, 6303 NW Marine Drive, Vancouver, BC V6T 1Z1, Canada (Office); 4455 W First St, Vancouver, BC V6R 4H9, Canada (Home). *Telephone:* (604) 822-2911 (Office); *Fax:* (604) 822-6096 (Office).

MARCOS, Imelda Romualdez; Philippine politician; b c 1930; m Ferdinand E. Marcos (died 1989); two d one s. *Career:* Gov of Metro Manila 1975–86; Roving Amb; visited Beijing 1976; took part in negotiations in Libya over self-govt for S provinces 1977; leader Kilusan Bagong Lipunan (New Society Movt) 1978–81; mem Batasang Pambansa (Interim Legis Ass) 1978–83; Minister of Human Settlements 1978–79, 1984–86, of Human Settlements and Ecology 1979–83; mem Cabinet Exec Cttee 1982–84; Chair S Philippines Devt Authority 1980–86; indicted for embezzlement 1988, acquitted 1990; returned to Philippines 1991; Presidential cand 1992; sentenced to 18–24 years' imprisonment for criminal graft Sept 1993; convicted of two charges of corruption, sentenced to 9–12 years on each Sept 1993; sentenced on appeal to Supreme Court; facing four charges of corruption Sept 1995; mem Senate 1995. *Recordings include:* Imelda Papin featuring songs with Mrs Imelda Romualdez Marcos 1989.

MARCUS, Gill, B COMM; South African banker; b 10 Aug 1949, Johannesburg; d of Nathan and Molly Marcus. *Education:* Univ of S Africa. *Career:* Mem Nat Exec Cttee, African Nat Congress (ANC) 1991–99; MP 1994–99, Chair Jt Standing Cttee on Finance 1994–96, Deputy Minister of Finance 1996–99; Deputy Gov S African Reserve Bank 1999–, Chair Financial Services Bd, Policy Bd and Others. *Leisure interests:* reading, debating. *Address:* POB 427, Pretoria, 0001, South Africa (Office); 370 Church St, Pretoria 0002, South Africa (Home). *Telephone:* (12) 313-3465 (Office); *Fax:* (12) 313-3616 (Office); *E-mail:* Gill.Marcus@resbank.co.za.

MARCUS, Ruth Barcan, PH D; American professor of philosophy; b 2 Aug 1921, New York; d of Samuel Barcan and Rose Post; m Jules A. Marcus 1942 (divorced 1976); two s two d. *Education:* New York and Yale Univs. *Career:* Research Assoc Inst for Human Relations, Yale Univ 1945–47; Assoc Prof Roosevelt Univ 1959–64; Prof, Chair Dept of Philosophy, Univ of Illinois 1964–70; Prof Northwestern Univ 1970–73; Reuben Post Halleck Prof of Philosophy, Yale Univ 1973–93, Sevrin Scholar 1994–; Visiting Distinguished Prof, Univ of California at Irvine 1994–99; Adviser Oxford Univ Press, New York 1980–; Guggenheim Fellow 1953–54; NSF Fellow 1963–64; Fellow Center for Advanced Studies, Stanford Univ 1979, Inst for Advanced Study in the Humanities, Univ of Edinburgh, UK 1983, Wolfson Coll, Oxford, UK 1985, 1986, Clare Hall, Cambridge, UK 1988, American Acad of Arts and Sciences; mem, Vice-Pres Inst Int de Philosophie, Paris, Pres 1989–92, Hon Pres 1993–; Chair Nat Bd of Officers, American Philosophical Asscn 1977–83; Pres Asscn for Symbolic Logic 1983–86, Pres Elizabethan Club 1988–90; mem Council on Philosophical Studies (Pres 1988–), Steering Cttee, Fed Int Soc de Philosophie 1985–99 (Pres 1990–93, Hon Pres 1994–), numerous editorial bds; Hon D HUM LITT (Illinois) 1995; Medal, Coll de France 1986; Wilbur Cross Medal, Yale Univ 2000. *Publications:* The Logical Enterprise (co-ed) 1975, Logic Methodology and Philosophy of Science (ed) 1986, Modalities 1993, 1995; numerous articles in professional journals. *Address:* Dept of Philosophy, Box 208306, Yale University, New Haven, CT 06520, USA (Office); 311 St Ronan St, New Haven, CT 06511, USA (Home). *Telephone:* (203) 432-1665 (Office); *Fax:* (203) 432-7950 (Office).

MARCUSE, Judith Rose; Canadian choreographer and dancer; b 13 March 1947, Montréal, PQ; d of Frank Howard and Phyllis Margolick; m Richard Frederick Marcuse 1972; one d. *Education:* Nat Ballet Summer School, Royal Ballet School (London), School of American Ballet and Banff School of Fine Arts. *Career:* Dancer with Les Grands Ballets Canadiens 1965–68, Ballet de Genève (Switzerland) 1969, Bat-Dor Dance Co (Israel) 1970–72, Ballet Rambert (London) 1974–76; Artistic Dir Judith Marcuse Dance Projects Soc 1980–, Judith Marcuse Dance Co 1984–; mem Canadian and British Actors' Equity Asscns, Dance in Canada Asscn, Bd of Dirs Vancouver Dance Centre 1993, apptd Vice-Chair 1994; Chalmers Award for Choreography 1976; Clifford E. Lee Award for Choreography 1979; Vancouver Award for Excellence in Theatre 1986; W Vancouver 75 Achiever Award 1987; Commemorative Medal for 125th Anniversary of Canadian Confed 1993; Silver Prize NY Dance Video and Film Festival 1993, 1994. *Choreography and Direction includes:* SpeakEasy 1978, Side by Side by Sondheim 1979, Mirrors, Masques and Transformations 1980, Spring Dances 1981, Cuts 1981, HMS Pinafore 1981, Playgrounds 1981, Transfer 1981, We Can Dance 1982, Romeo and Juliet 1982, Reflections on Crooked Walking 1982, 1983, 1987, In Concert 1983, Cole 1984, Blue Skies 1985, Traces 1985, The Home Return of the Flying Ferromanganese Players 1987, Moving Past Neutral (commissioned by the Calgary Winter Olympics Arts Festival) 1988, Bach and Blue 1989, Madrugada 1990, Crooked Hearts (film) 1990, Second Nature (film) 1993, At The Races (film) 1994. *Leisure interests:* cooking, literature, travel. *Address:* 1128A W 15th St, N Vancouver, BC V7P 1M9, Canada (Office); 6754 Dufferin Ave, W Vancouver, BC V7W 2K2, Canada (Home).

MARDİN, Betul; Turkish public relations executive; b 1 Dec 1927, Istanbul; d of Muhıddın Arıf and Fahıre Kocataş Mardin; m 1st Akgün Usta 1950 (divorced 1957); m 2nd Haldun Dormen 1959 (divorced 1967); one s one d. *Education:* American Coll for Girls (Istanbul) and BBC Course, London. *Career:* Journalist Tercüman and Yeni Sabah newspapers 1956–61; Producer Dormen Theatre 1959–66; Producer Turkish Radio-Television Corpn, Radio and TV Ankara 1964–68; Public Relations Consultant 1968; Lecturer in Radio and TV Programming, Univ of Istanbul 1969–71; Founder and Jt Partner A &

B Public Relations 1974–84; Co-Founder IMAGE Public Relations Consultancy Ltd, Istanbul 1984, Pres 1987; Jt Partner Strategy Public Relations, IMAJ Communications 1984; Lecturer in Public Relations, Bosphorus Univ 1990; Chair Public Relations Asscn of Istanbul (IPRA) 1977–84, currently mem; mem CERP; Public Relations in Action award, IPRA 1979; American Hotel and Motel Asscn Gold Key Award 1982; Sheraton Hotels EAME, in recognition of Public Relations work 1983, 1984. *Address:* Hacı Adil Sokak 4, Aralik 2, Levent, 80620 Istanbul, Turkey (Office); Teşvikiye Palas 107/1, Teşvikiye, Istanbul, Turkey (Home). *Telephone:* (1) 1789363 (Office); *Fax:* (1) 1785333 (Office).

MARGARET ROSE, HRH The Princess, Countess of Snowdon, CI, GCVO, GCSTJ; British royal; b 21 Aug 1930, Glamis Castle, Angus, Scotland; d of the late HRH Prince Albert, Duke of York (later HM King George VI) and Duchess of York (now HM Queen Elizabeth the Queen Mother, qv); sister of HM Queen Elizabeth II (qv); m Antony Armstrong-Jones (now 1st Earl of Snowdon) 1960 (divorced 1978); one s one d. *Career:* Pres English Folk Dance and Song Soc, Friends of the Elderly and Gentlefolk's Help, The Guide Asscn, Horder Centre for Arthritis, Nat Soc for the Prevention of Cruelty to Children, The Royal Ballet, Royal Scottish Soc for Prevention of Cruelty to Children, Birmingham Royal Ballet, Scottish Children's League, Victoria League for Commonwealth Friendship, Commonwealth Trust; Grand Pres St John Ambulance Asscn and Brigade; Jt Pres Lowland Brigade Club; Pres and Chair of Council Invalid Children's Aid Nationwide; Patron Architects' Benevolent Soc, Asscn of Anaesthetists of GB and Ireland, Barristers' Benevolent Asscn, Bristol Royal Soc for the Blind, Ladies' Guild of the British and Int Sailors' Soc, Combined Theatrical Charities Appeals Council, Friends of the Iveagh Bequest, Kenwood, Friends of St John's Smith Square, Friends of Southwark Cathedral, Friends of the London Hosp (Whitechapel), Hallé Concerts Soc, Heart Disease and Diabetes Research Trust, Light Infantry Club, London Lighthouse, Mary Hare Grammar School for the Deaf, Mathilda and Terence Kennedy Inst of Rheumatology, Migraine Trust, Mustique Educational Trust, Nat Pony Soc, Northern Ballet Theatre, Olave Baden-Powell Soc, Pottery and Glass Trades' Benevolent Inst, Queen Alexandra's Royal Army Nursing Corps Asscn, Royal Coll of Nursing and Nat Council of Nurses of the UK, St Margaret's Chapel Guild, Edinburgh Castle, St Pancras Housing Asscn in Camden, Services Sound and Vision Corpn, Suffolk Regimental Asscn, Tenovus and Tenovus Scotland, Union of Schools for Social Service, Youth Clubs Scotland, Zebra Trust, Clarence House Restoration Trust, Purine Research Laboratory; Hon Life Fellow Zoological Soc of London; Hon Life mem Century House Asscn (British Columbia); Hon mem Automobile Asscn, Order of the Road, Royal Automobile Club, Sealyham Terrier Breeders' Asscn; Patron and Hon mem Grand Antiquity Soc of Glasgow; Hon Patron Winnipeg Art Gallery; Life mem British Legion Women's Section; mem Court of Assistants, Worshipful Co of Haberdashers; Master of the Bench Hon Soc of Lincoln's Inn; Patron-in-Chief English Harbour Repair Fund; Hon Fellow Royal Inst of British Architects, Royal Coll of Obstetricians and Gynaecologists, Royal Coll of Surgeons of England, Royal Photographic Soc of GB, Royal Soc of Medicine; Hon Pres British Museum Devt Trust; Vice-Patron Royal Anglian Regt Asscn; Visitor King George VI and Queen Elizabeth Foundation of St Catherine's; Col-in-Chief The Bermuda Regt, Highland Fusiliers of Canada (Militia), Queen Alexandra's Royal Army Nursing Corps, Royal Highland Fusiliers (Princess Margaret's Own Glasgow and Ayrshire Regt), The Princess Louise Fusiliers (Royal Canadian Infantry Corps-Militia), The Light Dragoons; Deputy Col-in-Chief The Royal Anglian Regt; Hon Air Commodore RAF Coningsby; Freeman of the City of London; Hon Life mem RAF Club; Sponsor HMS Illustrious, HMS Norfolk; Hon D MUS (London); Hon LL D (Keele); Awarded the Royal Victorian Chain 1990. *Address:* 1A Kensington Palace, London W8 4PU, UK.

MARGARIDO, Maria Manuela; São Tomé and Príncipe diplomatist. *Career:* Perm Rep of São Tomé and Príncipe to European Communities. *Address:* 42 ave Brugmann, 1060 Brussels, Belgium. *Telephone:* (2) 347-53-75.

MARGRETHE II; Danish Queen of Denmark; b 16 April 1940; d of late King Frederik IX and of Queen Ingrid; m Count Henri de Laborde de Monpezat (now Prince Henrik of Denmark) 1967; two s: Prince Frederik André Henrik Christian (heir apparent) b 26 May 1968; Prince Joachim Holger Waldemar Christian b 7 June 1969. *Education:* Univs of Copenhagen, Aarhus, Cambridge, Paris (Sorbonne) and LSE. *Career:* Succeeded to the throne 14 Jan 1972; has undertaken many official visits abroad with her husband, travelling extensively in Europe, the Far East, N, S America; artist, illustrator, set and costume designer; designed scenery and costumes for TV Theatre's The Shepherdess and the Chimney Sweep 1987, A Folk Tale (ballet); exhibitions held at Køge Art Gallery 1988, Millesgården, Stockholm 1989, Blåfarveværket, Norway 1991, Gammel Holtegaard 1993, Reykjavik, Iceland 1998, Gallery J.M.S., Oslo, Norway 1999; Patron Royal Danish Ballet; Royal Fellow Soc of Antiques of London 1974; Hon KG 1979; Hon mem Swedish Royal Acad of Science, History and Antiques 1988; Hon Fellow LSE 1975, Lucy Cavendish Coll (Cambridge) 1989, Girton Coll (Cambridge) 1992; Hon Bencher of the Middle Temple 1992; Hon LL D (Cambridge) 1975, (London) 1980; Dr hc (Iceland) 1986; Hon D UNIV (Oxford) 1992, (Edinburgh) 2000; Medal of the Headmastership, Univ of Paris 1987; Hon Freedom of the City of London 2000. *Publications:* Simone de Beauvoir's All Men are Mortal (trans, jtly) 1981, The Valley (trans) 1988, The Fields (Trans) 1989, The Forest (trans) 1989, The Wind on the Moon (trans) 1991; illustrations: The Lord of the Rings 1977–78, Norse Legends as Told by Jorgen Stegelmann 1979, Bjarkemaal 1982, Poul Ørum's Komedie i Florens 1990, Cantabile (poems) 2000;. *Address:* Amalienborg Palace, 1257 Copenhagen K, Denmark. *Telephone:* (33) 40-10-10; *E-mail:* Hofmarskallatet@mail.dk; *Internet:* www.kongehuset.dk.

MARGULIS, Lynn Alexander, PH D; American biologist; b 5 March 1938, Chicago, IL; d of Morris and Leona Wise Alexander; m 1st Carl Sagan 1957; two s; m 2nd T. N. Margulis 1967; one s one d. *Education:* Univs of Chicago, Wisconsin and California at Berkeley. *Career:* Research Assoc Dept of Biology, Brandeis Univ 1963–64, Lecturer in Biology 1963–65, Biology Co-ordinator Peace Corps, Colombia Project 1965–66; Consultant The Elementary Science Study, Educational Services 1963–67; Adjunct Asst Prof Dept of Biology, Boston Univ 1966–67, Asst Prof 1967–71, Assoc Prof 1971–77, Prof 1977–88, Univ Prof 1986–88; Instructor Chatauqua Short Course NSF Program 1978, 1983; Visiting Prof Scripps Inst of Oceanography Dept of Marine Biology 1980, California Inst of Tech Div of Geology and Planetary Science 1980, NASA-Ames Planetary Biology Microbial Ecology Summer Research Course 1980, 1982, 1984, Univ Autónoma de Barcelona Dept of Microbiology (Spain) 1986, 1988; Visiting Scholar Marine Science Research Center, State Univ of New York 1986; Co-Admin Planetary Biology Internship 1981–92; Distinguished Univ Prof Dept of Biology, Univ of Massachusetts 1988–99; Assoc Ed Precambrian Research 1979–; has given many lectures internationally; Co-Founder Soc for Evolutionary Protistology; mem NAS, numerous cttees and editorial bds; Hon D SC (Southeastern Massachusetts), (Westfield State Coll, MA) 1989, (Plymouth State Coll, NH) 1991, (Washington Coll, MD) 1995, (Tulane, LA) 1996; Commdr de l'Ordre des Palmes Académiques 1989; Sherman Fairchild Distinguished Scholar, California Inst of Tech 1976–77; Fellow AAAS 1975; Guggenheim Foundation Fellow 1979; Fellow World Acad of Art and Science 1995; Boston Univ Faculty Publication Merit Award 1967; George Lamb Award, Univ of Nebraska 1971; Diamond Award 1975; NASA Public Service Award 1981; Univ of Chicago Citation for Professional Excellence 1985; Boston Univ MacDonald Award for Excellence in Research 1986; Miescher-Ishida Award, Int Soc for Endocytobiology 1986; Distinguished Service Award, Nat Asscn of Biology. *Publications include:* Origin of Eukaryotic Cells 1970, Origins of Life I and II (ed) 1970, 1971, Origins of Life: Planetary Astronomy (ed) 1973, Origins of Life: Chemistry and Radioastronomy (ed) 1973, Limits of Life (co-ed) 1980, Symbiosis in Cell Evolution 1981, Early Life 1982, Five Kingdoms: An Illustrated Guide to the Phyla of Life on Earth (jtly) 1982, Origins of Sex (jtly) 1986, Microcosmos: Four Billion Years of Evolution From Our Bacterial Ancestors (jtly, 2nd edn) 1991, Garden of Microbial Delights 1988, Biospheres From Earth to Space (jtly) 1988, Global Ecology (jtly) 1989, Handbook Protoctista (ed) 1990, Mystery Dance (jtly) 1991, Symbiosis as a Source of Evolutionary Innovation: Speciation and Morphogenesis (co-ed) 1991, Environmental Evolution: The Effect of the Origin and Evolution of Life on Planet Earth (co-ed) 1992, Concepts of Symbiogenesis: A Historical and Critical Study of the Research of Russian Botanists (co-ed, trans of book by L. N. Khakhina's), Diversity of Life: The Five Kingdoms 1992, Symbiosis in

Cell Evolution: Microbial Communities in the Archean and Proterozoic Eons 1993, Illustrated Glossary of the Protoctista (co-ed) 1993, The Illustrated Five Kingdoms: A Guide to the Diversity of Life on Earth (jtly) 1994, What Is Life? (jtly) 1995, Slanted Truths (jtly) 1997, What Is Sex? (jtly) 1998; numerous papers and contribs to professional journals; also videos and films. *Leisure interests:* fiction, ballet, Spain, pre-Columbian Mexican culture. *Address:* Dept of Geosciences, Morrill Science Center, University of Massachusetts, Amherst, MA 01003, USA (Office); 20 Triangle St, Amherst, MA 01002, USA (Home). *Telephone:* (413) 545-3244 (Office); (413) 256-8113 (Home); *Fax:* (413) 545-1200 (Office).

MARIĆ, Ljubica, MA; Yugoslav composer; b 18 March 1909, Kragujevac (Serbia); d of Katarina Djordjević Marić. *Education:* Belgrade School of Music and State Conservatory (Prague). *Career:* All compositions dedicated to her mother; compositions played at festivals in Amsterdam (Netherlands) and Strasbourg (France) 1933; Prof of Musical Theory Acad of Music, Belgrade 1945–67; wrote major compositions for symphony orchestra 1956–63, chamber music 1980–; mem Serbian Acad of Arts and Sciences 1963–; 7 July Award for Lifetime Achievement 1965; Charter of the Serbian Acad of Arts and Sciences 1987. *Compositions include:* Songs of Space (Cantata, October Award, City of Belgrade 1957) 1956, Passacaglia (for symphony orchestra) 1958, Byzantine concerto (for piano and orchestra) 1959, Ostinato Super Thema Octoicha (for piano, harp and strings) 1963, Chants from the Darkness (cantata) 1984, Asymptote (for violin and string orchestra) 1986, Archaia (for violin, viola and cello) 1992, Wonderful Milligram (for flute and soprano) 1992. *Address:* 11000 Belgrade, Džordža Vašingtona 36, Yugoslavia. *Telephone:* (11) 322-4992.

MARIN, Marguerite (Maguy); French choreographer; b 2 June 1951, Toulouse. *Education:* Conservatoire de Toulouse. *Career:* Joined Maurice Béjart's Ballet du XXème Siècle; joined Ballet Théâtre de l'Arche (subsequently Compagnie Maguy Marin) 1979; Grand Prix Nat de la Choréographie 1983; Chevalier des Arts et des Lettres. *Works choreographed include:* May B 1981, Babel Babel 1982, Jaléo 1983, Hymen 1984, Calambre 1985, Cinderella 1985, Eden 1986, Leçons de Ténèbres 1987, Coups d'états 1988, Groosland 1989, Cortex 1991, Made in France 1992, Ay Dios 1993, Waterzooï 1993. *Address:* Compagnie Maguy Marin, Maison des Arts et de la Culture, place Salvador Allende, 94000 Céteil, France.

MARIN, Marilena; Italian politician; b 24 July 1947, Conegliano Veneto. *Career:* MEP (Group Union for Europe) until 1999; mem Cttee on Culture, Youth Educ and the Media, Del to the EU-Romania Jt Parl Cttee until 1999. *Address:* c/o European Parliament, rue Wiertz, 1047 Brussels, Belgium.

MARININA, Lieut-Col Aleksandra Borisovna (pseudonym of Marina Anatolyevna Alekseyeva), PH D; Russian writer and former criminologist; b 19 June 1957, Lviv, Ukraine; m Col Sergey Zatochny. *Education:* Moscow State Univ. *Career:* Fmr mem of staff Acad of Internal Affairs; began writing detective stories 1991–; mem of staff Moscow Inst of Justice, Ministry of Internal Affairs 1994–97. *Publications include:* Death and Some Love, Ghost of Music, Stolen Dream, I Died Yesterday, Men's Game, Forced Murderer, Black List, Requiem, When Gods Laugh 2000. *Address:* COP Literary Agency, Zhukovskogo str 4, Apt 29, 101000 Moscow, Russian Federation (Office); Krasnoprudnaya str 13, Apt 107, 107140 Moscow, Russian Federation (Home). *Telephone:* (095) 928-84-56 (Office); (095) 975-46-72 (Home); *Fax:* (095) 928-84-56 (Office); (095) 975-46-72 (Home); *E-mail:* alexandra@marinina.ru; *Internet:* www.marinina.ru.

MARINUCCI, Elena; Italian politician; b 18 Aug 1928, L'Aquila. *Career:* MEP (Group of the Party of European Socialists) until 1999; mem Cttee on Environment, Public Health and Consumer Protection, Del for relations with the countries of Central America and Mexico until 1999. *Address:* c/o European Parliament, rue Wiertz, 1047 Brussels, Belgium.

MARK, Mary Ellen; American photographer; b Philadelphia 1940; m Martin Bell. *Career:* Has photographed prostitution in India, street children in USA, heroin addiction in London, African famines;

Photographer Magnum agency, Life magazine; many awards including First Prize, Robert F. Kennedy Journalism 1985, Philippe Halsman Award, American Soc of Magazine Photographers, Photojournalism Award, George W Polk 1988.

MARKOVA, Dame Alicia (Lilian Alicia Marks), DBE; British ballet dancer; b 1 Dec 1910, London; d of Arthur Tristman Marks and Eileen Barry. *Education:* Privately in UK and Europe. *Career:* Debut in Dick Whittington at the Kennington Theatre 1920; studied under Astafieva and appeared with Legat Ballet Group 1923; mem Diaghileff Russian Ballet 1924–29, studying under Enrico Cecchetti (Song of a Nightingale created for her); Prima Ballerina Rambert Club 1931–34; First Prima Ballerina of Vic-Wells (now the Royal Ballet) 1933–35; Founder, mem Markova-Dolin Ballet Co 1935–38, 1944–45, Ballet Russe de Monte Carlo 1938–41, American Ballet Theatre 1941–44, Festival Ballet 1950–52 (Co-Founder); numerous guest appearances 1946–47; concerts with Dolin in USA, Far East and S Africa 1947–49; 1950–52; Guest Artist Teatro Colón, Buenos Aires 1952, Sadler's Wells, Ballet Theatre, Marquis de Cuevas Ballet and Metropolitan Opera, New York 1953, Royal Winnipeg Ballet, Canada 1953; mem Cuevas Ballet, London 1954, Royal Danish Ballet 1955, Royal Ballet, Covent Garden 1957, 1960; British Prima Ballerina Assoluta; Dir Metropolitan Opera Ballet of New York 1963–69; Distinguished Lecturer on Ballet Cincinnati Univ 1970, Prof of Ballet and Performing Arts 1970–; producer Les Sylphides, Australian Ballet 1976, London Festival Ballet 1977, N Ballet Theatre 1978, Royal Ballet School 1978, Royal Winnipeg Ballet 1979; presenter 'Masterclass' BBC TV series 1980; Pres London Ballet Circle 1981–, All England Dance Competition 1983–, Arts Educational Trust Schools 1984–, London Festival Ballet 1986–, English Nat Ballet 1989–; Vice-Pres Royal Acad of Dancing 1958–; Guest Prof Royal Ballet School 1972–; Gov Royal Ballet 1973–; Prof Yorkshire Ballet Seminars 1973–; int consultant 1990–; London Studio Centre consultant 1990–; Guest Prof de Danse, Paris Opera Ballet 1975; Guest Prof Australian Ballet 1976; Pres Int Dance Competition, Paris 1986; Patron Abingdon Ballet Seminars 1990–; Hon MUS D (Leicester) 1966, (E Anglia) 1982. *Publications:* Giselle and I 1960, Markova Remembers 1986. *Leisure interest:* music. *Address:* c/o Royal Ballet School, Talgarth Rd, London W14 9DE, UK.

MARKOVIĆ, Mirjana; Yugoslav (Serbian) politician; m Slobodan Milosevic. *Career:* Fmr Leader Yugoslav Left (JUL), leftist bloc, allegedly within the Socialist Party of Serbia; columnist for magazine Duga. *Address:* c/o Socialist Party of Serbia (Socijalistička Partija Srbije), 11000 Belgrade, bul Lenjina 6, Federal Republic of Yugoslavia.

MARKS, Shula Eta, OBE, PH D, FBA; British historian; b 14 Nov 1936, Cape Town, SA; m Isaac Meyer Marks 1957; one s one d. *Education:* Cape Town Univ (SA) and Univ of London. *Career:* Lecturer in History of Africa, Inst of Commonwealth Studies and School of Oriental and African Studies (SOAS) until 1976, Reader in History of Southern Africa 1976–84, Dir Inst of Commonwealth Studies 1983–93, Prof of Commonwealth History, Univ of London 1984–93, Prof of History of Southern Africa, SOAS 1993–2001; Hon D LITT (Cape Town); Hon D SOC SCI (Natal). *Publications include:* Reluctant Rebellion: An Assessment of the 1906–08 Disturbances in Natal 1970, The Ambiguities of Dependence in Southern Africa, Class, Nationalism and the State in Twentieth Century Natal 1966, Not Either an Experimental Doll: The Separate Worlds of Three South African Women (ed) 1987, Divided Sisterhood: Race, class and gender in the South African nursing profession 1994, chapters in Cambridge History of Africa, Vols 3, 4 and 6. *Address:* School of Oriental and African Studies, Thornhaugh St, London WC1H 0XG, UK. *Telephone:* (20) 7637-2388; *Fax:* (20) 7323-6046.

MARLAND, Caroline; British business executive. *Career:* Mem Bd Guardian Newspapers (The Guardian and The Observer newspapers) 1984, later Deputy Man Dir and Advertisement Dir, Man Dir 1996); Non-Exec Dir Burton Group; mem Council Inst of Dirs; fmr Chair Marketing and Media Cttee Royal Marsden Hosp. *Address:* The Guardian, 119 Farringdon Rd, London EC1R 3ER, UK.

MÁROVÁ, Libuše; Czech opera singer; b 24 Dec 1943, Sušice; d of František and Libuše Mára; m 1st Norbert Snitil 1968 (divorced 1976); m 2nd Tomáš Šimerda 1980 (divorced 1986). *Education:* Music Acad

(Prague). *Career:* Soloist Plzeň Theatre 1965–66, Nat Theatre, Prague 1966–; has performed in Germany, Netherlands, Austria, Italy, Belgium, France, Spain, Yugoslavia, Norway, Turkey; has recorded recitals and oratorios, and made TV films of Czech and Slovak operas. *Address:* Francouzská 11, 120 00 Prague 2, Czech Republic. *Telephone:* (2) 258520.

MARRE, Béatrice Michèle Marie-Odile, L ÈS SC; French politician and civil servant; b 2 April 1952, Paris; d of Jean and Louise-Marie Marre. *Education:* Univ of Paris X (Paris-Nanterre) and Inst d'Etudes Politiques. *Career:* Man Société Générale 1976–77; Man Asst for econ interest asscn 1978; Rep to Cabinet of the Sec of State for Public Security 1983–84; Sub-Prefect and Dir of Cabinet of the Prefect of Gard Dept 1984–85; Sub-Prefect of Château-Chinon 1985–87; Rep to Cabinet of the Pres 1987, Head of Cabinet 1988–95; Prefect Sources d'Europe econ interest asscn 1995–; Deputy for Oise (Socialist Group) 1997. *Leisure interests:* music, astronomy, horse-riding. *Address:* Assemblée Nationale, 75355 Paris, France; 126 rue de l'Université, 75007 Paris, France. *Telephone:* (1) 41-25-12-12; *Fax:* (1) 41-25-12-13.

MARRINAN QUINN, Paulyn, BA, BL; Irish barrister and insurance ombudsman; b 29 Oct 1945, Belfast, N Ireland; d of Patrick and Carmel Grace Marrinan; m Brendan P. Quinn 1971; one d two s (one deceased). *Education:* St Augustine's Priory (London), Trinity Coll (Dublin) and the Hon Soc of Kings Inns (Dublin). *Career:* Called to the Bar, Ireland 1979, Middle Temple (UK) 1982, N Ireland 1992; Ombudsman for Ireland's insurance industry 1992–98; Columnist on social and current affairs on IT (Irish Tatler) Magazine 1979–83; Producer, Presenter series Generations for Channel 4 (UK) on leading Irish women 1986; story broadcast on BBC Radio 4's Morning Story; Rep for Ireland, OECD Working Party on the Role of Women in the Economy 1988; fmr Chair Women's Political Asscn; Chair Network (org for women in business) Annual Confs 1989, 1992; Non-Exec Dir Attic Press Publishing House 1989, Chair of Bd 1993–94; mem Fund-Raising Cttee Irish Youth Foundation, Sub-Cttee of British and Irish Ombudsman Asscn reporting on Standards of Best Practice for Ombudsmen 1994–95, Irish Man Inst; Fellow Chartered Inst of Arbitrators. *Leisure interests:* walking, tennis, swimming, theatre and art galleries, promotion of the arts. *Address:* 4 Cluain Mhuire, Upper Glenageary Rd, Co Dublin, Ireland.

MARSDEN, Lorna R., PH D; Canadian university president and former politician; b 6 March 1942, Sidney, BC; d of John E. and Grace (née Simister) Bosher; m Edward B. Harvey 1962. *Education:* Univ of Toronto and Princeton Univ (USA). *Career:* Asst Prof of Sociology Univ of Toronto 1972–76, Assoc Prof 1976–79, Chair Dept of Sociology 1977–79, Prof 1979–92, Assoc Dean School of Grad Studies 1979–82, Vice-Provost 1983–84; Senator for Toronto-Taddle-Creek 1984–92; Pres, Vice-Chancellor Wilfrid Laurier Univ, Waterloo, Ont 1992–97; Pres York Univ 1997–; Chair Editorial Bd Addiction Research Fund 1984–88; Chair Liberal Party of Canada 1975–84; Pres Nat Action Cttee on the Status of Women 1975–77; Dir Air Canada 1978–84; mem Ontario Cttee on the Status of Women 1971, Advisory Cttee Women and the Economy, Nat Econ Council of Canada 1983; Trustee Elsie Gregory McGill Memorial Foundation 1984; Fellow Princeton Univ (USA) 1968–69; Sr Fellow Massey Coll, Toronto 1982, Woodsworth Coll 1983; Hon D JUR (New Brunswick) 1990; Queen's Silver Jubilee Medal 1977. *Publications:* Population Probe (jtly) 1972, The Fragile Federation: Social Change in Canada (jtly) 1979, Lives of Their Own (jtly) 1990. *Leisure interests:* travel, gardening, politics. *Address:* Ross Bldg, South 949, 4700 Keele St, Toronto, ON M3J 1P3, Canada; 206 Roxborough Drive, Toronto, ON M4W IX8, Canada (Home).

MARSH, Jean Lyndsey Torren; British actress; b 1 July 1934; d of Henry Charles and Emmeline Susannah Marsh; m Jon Devon Roland Pertwee 1955 (divorced 1960). *Career:* Actress with Nottingham and Huddersfield repertory cos; Co-Creator Upstairs Downstairs and The House of Eliott TV series (with Eileen Atkins, qv); Artistic Dir Adelphi Univ Theatre, New York, USA 1981–83; Hon DH (Maryland Coll, NY) 1980. *Plays include:* Much Ado About Nothing 1959, Bird of Time 1961, Habeas Corpus, The Importance of Being Earnest, Too True to be Good, Twelfth Night, Blithe Spirit, Whose Life is it Anyway?, Uncle Vanya, On the Rocks, Pygmalion, Hamlet, The Chalk Garden; *Films include:* Return to Oz, Willow; *TV appearances include:* Upstairs

Downstairs (Emmy Awards 1972, 1974, 1975), Nine to Five, A Connecticut Yankee in King Arthur's Court; *Publications include:* The Illuminated Language of Flowers 1978, The House of Eliott 1993; articles for Sunday Times, Washington Post, Los Angeles Times and New York Times (USA). *Leisure interests:* cross-country skiing, walking, reading, cooking, eating. *Address:* Hamstead Farm Cottage, Drift Lane, Chidham, W Sussex PO18 8PP, UK.

MARSH, Jeanette Isabel, B ECONS; Australian organization executive; b 24 Feb 1948, Melbourne; d of Ronald Herbert and Myra Roslyn White; m Peter Ronald Marsh 1971; one d. *Education:* Methodist Ladies' Coll (Kew, Vic) and Monash Univ (Vic). *Career:* Australian Council of Trade Unions Research Officer 1970–79, Industrial Advocate 1979–87; Deputy Pres Australian Conciliations and Arbitration Comm 1988–89, Industrial Relations Comm 1989–; mem Nat Council of Women Cttee on Employment, Nat Women's Advisory Council 1978–81, Council La Trobe Univ 1975–78; Dir Australian Broadcasting Corpn 1983–85; Commr Victoria Tourism Comm 1983–87. *Leisure interests:* swimming, reading, yoga. *Address:* Australian Industrial Relations Commission, 80 William St, E Sydney, NSW 2011, Australia. *Telephone:* (2) 8374-6596.

MARSHALL, Consuelo Bland, LLB; American federal judge; b 28 Sept 1936, Knoxville, TN; d of Clyde Theodore and Annie (née Brown) Arnold; m George E. Marshall Jr 1959; one s one d. *Education:* Los Angeles City Coll and Howard Univ (Washington, DC). *Career:* Called to Bar, CA 1962; Deputy Attorney City of Los Angeles 1962–67; Assoc Cochran and Atkins 1967–70; Commr Los Angeles Superior Court 1970–76, Judge 1977–80, Inglewood Municipal Court 1976–77, US Dist of California Cen Court 1980–; mem Advisory Bd Richstone Child Abuse Center, California Women Lawyers' Asscn, California Asscn of Black Lawyers, California Judges' Asscn; Ernest Stahlhut Award 1986; Judicial Excellence Award Criminal Courts Bar Asscn 1992. *Leisure interests:* walking, skiing, hiking. *Address:* US District Court, 312 N Spring St, Los Angeles, CA 90012, USA. *Telephone:* (213) 894-6314; *Fax:* (213) 894-6960.

MARSHALL, Margaret Anne, OBE; British opera and concert singer; b 4 Jan 1949, Stirling; d of Robert and Margaret Marshall; m Graeme G. K. Davidson 1970; two d. *Education:* High School of Stirling and Royal Scottish Acad of Music and Drama. *Career:* Operatic debut in Orfeo ed Euridice, Florence, Italy 1977; has since sung at La Scala (Milan, Italy), Royal Opera House, Covent Garden (London), Glyndebourne and Scottish Opera (UK), Barcelona (Spain), Hamburg and Cologne (Germany), and Salzburg (Austria); concert performances in major European and US cities and festivals with major orchestras; numerous recordings; First Prize, Munich Int Competition 1974; James Gulliver Award for Performing Arts in Scotland. *Leisure interests:* squash, golf, cooking. *Address:* Woodside, Main St, Gargunnock, Stirling FK8 3BP, UK.

MARSHALL, Penelope Jane Clucas, BA; British journalist; b 7 Nov 1962, Addlestone; d of the late Alan and of Mary (née Hanlin) Marshall; m Tim Ewart 1991; three d. *Education:* LSE. *Career:* Foreign Corresp for ITN (Independent TV News), Moscow coverage 1990, Bosnia coverage 1992, Defence and Diplomatic Corresp 1994–, SA Corresp 1999–2001; BAFTA Award 1992; Royal TV Soc award; Gold, Silver and Bronze Medals (New York). *Leisure interests:* singing, swimming, history. *Address:* c/o ITN, 200 Grays Inn Rd, London WC1X 8X2, UK. *Telephone:* (20) 7430-4411; *Fax:* (20) 430-4687; *E-mail:* penny .marshall@itn.co.uk.

MARSHALL, Penny (C. Marshall); American actress and director; b 15 Oct 1943, New York; d of Anthony Marshall and Marjorie Ward; m 1st Michael Henry (divorced); one d; m 2nd Robert Reiner 1971 (divorced 1979). *Education:* Univ of New Mexico. *Career:* Has made numerous TV and film appearances. *TV appearances include:* The Odd Couple 1972–74, Friends and Lovers 1974, Let's Switch 1974, Chico and the Man 1975, Mary Tyler Moore 1975, Heaven Help Us 1975, Saturday Night Live 1975–77, Battle of Network Stars 1976, Barry Manilow Special 1976, The Tonight Show 1976–77, Mike Douglas Show 1975–77, Merv Griffin Show 1976–77, $20,000 Pyramid 1976–77, Laverne and Shirley 1976–83, More Than Friends (TV film) 1978, Love Thy Neighbour (TV film) 1984; *Film appearances:* How

Sweet It Is 1967, The Savage Seven 1968, The Grasshopper 1979, 1941 1979, Movers and Shakers 1985, She's Having a Baby 1988, The Hard Way 1991, Hocus Pocus 1993, Get Shorty 1995; *Films directed:* Jumpin' Jack Flash 1986, Big 1988, Awakenings 1991, A League of Their Own 1992, Renaissance Man 1994, The Preacher's Wife 1996, The Time Tunnel: The Movie 1999; *Films produced:* Calendar Girl (exec producer), Getting Away With Murder 1995, With Friends Like These 1998, Saving Grace 1998, Live from Baghdad. *Address:* Parkway Productions, 10202 Washington Blvd, Culver City, CA 90232, USA.

MARTIN, Agnes, BS, MFA; American artist; b 22 March 1912, Maklin, SK, Canada; d of Malcolm I. Martin and Margaret Kinnon. *Education:* Columbia Univ. *Career:* First showing in Betty Parsons Gallery, New York 1958; retrospective exhibitions ICA Philadelphia 1955, Pasadena 1956, Hayward Gallery, London 1977, Stedelijk Museum, Amsterdam, Netherlands 1977, 1990, Whitney Museum, New York 1991; represented in perm collections Museum of Modern Art, New York, Albright-Knox Gallery, Solomon R. Guggenheim Museum, Tate Gallery, London, and many others. *Address:* Pace Gallery, 32 E 57th St, New York, NY 10022, USA; 414 Placitas Rd, Taos, NM 87571, USA. *Telephone:* (212) 421-3292 (NY); (505) 758-9636 (NM).

MARTIN, Elaine Miriam Wilson, PH D; Australian lecturer in social administration; b 4 July 1937, Melbourne; two d one s. *Education:* Univ High School, Univ of Melbourne and LSE (UK). *Career:* Researcher, teacher in social work and social welfare Univ of Melbourne and various welfare agencies 1962–72; Lecturer in Social Admin Flinders Univ of S Australia 1974–79, Sr Lecturer 1979–, Dean School of Social Sciences 1985–87, Acting Pro Vice-Chancellor 1989, Head of Discipline of Social Admin 1990–92, mem Univ Council 1982–89; mem various S Australia Govt Advisory Cttees; Researcher, Consultant social welfare orgs; Flinders Univ Distinguished Service Award 1995. *Publications:* High Living (jtly); contribs on aspects of social work, human service orgs and women's orgs to books and scholarly journals. *Address:* The Flinders University of S Australia, Social Admin, School of Social Sciences, POB 2100, Adelaide, SA 5001, Australia; 11 Frances St, Clarence Park, SA 5034, Australia. *Telephone:* (8) 201 2677; *Fax:* (8) 201 2566.

MARTIN, Evelyn Fairfax, OBE, FRSA; British organization executive; b 12 Aug 1926, Liverpool; d of the late Kenneth Gordon and of Beatrice (née Munro) Robinson; m Dennis William Martin 1949; three d (one deceased). *Education:* Belvedere Girls' School, Huyton Coll for Girls (Liverpool) and Mrs Hoster's Secretarial Coll (London). *Career:* Remedial Teacher, Trinidad 1950–51; Head Nursery School, Lagos 1958–60; Foster Parent 1960–78; Chair Battered Wives' Hostel 1980–82, Well Woman Centre, Liverpool 1982–86; Pres Nat Council of Women 1986–88, Company Sec 1992–; Co-Chair Women's Nat Comm 1991–93. *Leisure interests:* gardening, foreign travel, animals. *Address:* 32 Clifton Rd, Halifax HX3 0BT, UK. *Telephone:* (1422) 360438; *Fax:* (1422) 360438; *E-mail:* evelyn.martin@btinternet.com.

MARTIN, Lynn; American politician; b 26 Dec 1939, Chicago, IL; d of Lawrence and Helen Morley; m Harry Leinenweber; two d five step-c. *Education:* Univ of Illinois. *Career:* Fmr teacher; mem Winnebago Co Bd 1972–76; mem Illinois House of Reps 1977–79, Senate 1979–81, US House of Reps 1981–91; Sec of Labor 1991–93; Vice-Chair House Republican Conf 1982–86; Co-Chair Bi-partisan Ethics Task Force; mem House Rules Cttee, House Budget Cttee, Cttee on Public Works and Transportation, Cttee on Dist of Columbia; Prof of Govt, Harvard Univ 1993–; John Marshall Law School Freedom Award 1992. *Leisure interests:* reading, horse-riding, decorating. *Address:* Dept of Government, Harvard University, Cambridge, MA 02138, USA.

MARTIN, Marilyn, BA, M ARCH; South African gallery director; b 16 Aug 1943, McGregor, Cape Province; d of Mattheus van Blommenstein and Catharina Magdalena (née Kramer) Human; m Norman Martin 1969 (divorced 1976); one s one d. *Education:* Heidelberg High School (Cape Province), Univ of S Africa and Univ of the Witwatersrand (Johannesburg). *Career:* Fashion model, journalist, sec 1960–68; Lecturer in History of Art Univ of Durban-Westville 1974–77; Admin Officer Univ of the Witwatersrand 1977–81, Lecturer, then Sr Lecturer in Architecture 1982–89; Dir S African Nat Gallery 1990; Nat Vice-Pres, then Pres S Africa Asscn of Arts 1984–89, Life-long Vice-Pres 1990; Hon Curator Nat Monuments Council 1985–89; Dir Foundation

for the Creative Arts 1989; has written numerous articles on art and architecture for professional journals. *Leisure interest:* transcendental meditation. *Address:* South African National Gallery, Govt Ave, POB 2420, Cape Town 8000, South Africa. *Telephone:* (21) 451628; *Fax:* (21) 451607.

MARTÍNEZ, Conchita; Spanish tennis player; b 16 April 1972, Monzón; d of Cecilio and Conchita Martínez. *Career:* Turned professional 1988; reached last 16 French Open 1988, quarter-finals French Open 1989, 1990, 1991, 1992, 1993, semi-finals Italian Open 1991, French Open 1994, Australian, French, and US Opens and Wimbledon 1995, French and US Opens 1996, quarter-finals Olympic Games 1992; won Olympic Doubles Silver Medal (with Arantxa Sánchez-Vicario, qv) 1992; won Italian Open 1993, Hilton Head (SC), Italian Open, Stratton (VT) 1994, Wimbledon Singles Championship 1994; reached semi-finals French Open 1996. *Leisure interests:* golf, horse riding, music, soccer.

MARTINEZ, Herminia S., M SC; American international organization official, banking executive and economist; b Havana, Cuba; d of Carlos and Amelia Martínez Sánchez. *Education:* American and Georgetown Univs (DC) and Nat Univ of Mexico. *Career:* Instructor George Mason Univ, VA 1967–68; Researcher IBRD 1967–69, Industrial Economist, Industrialization Div 1969–71, Loan Officer in charge of Cen America 1971–79, Loan Officer and Economist, Mexico 1973–74, Venezuela and Ecuador 1973–77, Sr Loan Officer, Panama and Dominican Repub 1977–81, Middle E and N Africa 1981–84, W Africa 1985–87, Sr Economist, Africa 1988–91; Principal Operations Officer, Africa region 1991–97; Mid-career Fellow Princeton Univ, NJ 1988–89; mem American Econ Soc, Int Devt, Brookings Inst, Latin America Study Group. *Address:* World Bank, 1818 H St, NW, Washington, DC 20433, USA; 5145 Yuma St, NW, Washington, DC 20016, USA (Home).

MARTÍNEZ DE PERÓN, María Estela (Isabelita); Argentine politician and former dancer; b 6 Feb 1931, La Rioja Prov; m Gen Juan Domingo Perón (Pres of Argentina 1946–55, 1973–74) 1961 (died 1974). *Career:* Joined troupe of travelling folk dancers; danced in cabaret in several S American countries; lived in Spain 1960–73; returned to Argentina with Juan Perón 1973; Vice-Pres of Argentina 1973–74, Pres 1974–76 (deposed by mil coup 1976); Chair Peronist Party 1974–85; detained 1976–81; settled in Madrid, Spain 1985.

MARTINSON, Ida Marie, PH D; American professor of nursing; b 8 Nov 1936, Mentor, MN; d of the late Oscar and Marvel Sather; m Paul V. Martinson 1962; one s one d. *Education:* St Luke's Hosp School of Nursing (Duluth, MN) and Univs of Minnesota and Illinois. *Career:* Instructor in Tuberculosis Nursing St Luke's Hosp 1957–58; Instructor in Nursing Thornton Jr Coll, Harvey, IL 1967–69; Asst Prof, Chair of Research Univ of Minnesota School of Nursing 1972–74, Assoc Prof 1974–77, Dir of Research 1974–82, Prof 1977–82; Prof Dept of Family Health Care Nursing, Univ of California at San Francisco 1982–, Chair 1982–89, leave of absence 1996–; Carl Walter and Margaret Davis Walter Visiting Prof Frances Poyne Botton School of Nursing, CWRU 1994–96; Chair, Prof of Nursing and Head of Health Sciences, Hong Kong Polytechnic Univ, Hong Kong 1996–2000; Co-Founder Children's Cancer Foundation Taiwan; Pres Children's Hospice Int 1986–88; mem Inst of Medicine, NAS 1981–, Governing Council 1984–86; f East Asia Forum of Nursing Schools (EAFONS); Fellow American Acad of Nursing; four American Journal Nursing Book of the Year Awards; Children's Hospice Award 1989; Sigma Theta Tau Int Soc of Nursing 1999. *Publications:* Home Care: A Manual for Implementation of Home Care for Children Dying of Cancer 1978, Home Care: A Manual for Parents (jtly) 1979, Family Nursing 1989, Home Care Health Nursing 1989; more than 100 articles in journals, 56 book chapters (1994) and one film; ed of several books on home and family nursing. *Leisure interests:* skiing, walking, reading. *Address:* 2 Koret Way, Room N411Y, Dept of Family Health Care Nursing, University of California, San Francisco, CA 94143-0606, USA. *Telephone:* (415) 476-4694 (Office); *Fax:* (415) 753-2161 (Office); *E-mail:* ida .martinson@nursing.ucsf.edu (Office).

MARTON, Eva Heinrich; German opera singer; b 18 June 1943, Budapest, Hungary; d of Bela and Ilona (née Krammer) Heinrich; m Zoltan Marton 1965; one s one d. *Education:* Franz Liszt Acad

(Budapest) and with Gerald Mortier and Laszlo Halasz. *Career:* Singer Budapest State Opera 1968–72, Frankfurt Opera 1972–77, Hamburg State Opera 1977–80, Maggio Musicale Fiorentino (Italy), Vienna State Opera, La Scala (Milan, Italy), Rome Opera (Italy), Metropolitan Opera (New York), Lyric Opera (Chicago), Grand Opera (Houston) and San Francisco Opera (USA), Bayreuth Festival, Teatro Liceo, Barcelona (Spain), Teatro Colón, Buenos Aires, (Argentina), Royal Opera House Covent Garden, London, (UK); mem Vienna State Opera 1988–; mem Hungarian Nat Volleyball team; has made many solo records; Gold Star, Repub of Hungary 1989; Bartók Award 1990. *Operas include:* Turandot, Die Meistersinger, Tannhäuser, Il Trovatore, Lohengrin, Salome, Ariadne, Fedora, Tosca, Andrea Chenier, Manon Lescaut, La Forza del Destino, Fidelio, Elektra, Die Frau ohne Schatten, Der Fliegende Holländer; *Films include:* Turandot, Il Trovatore, Lohengrin, Tannhäuser, Elektra, La Gioconda, Tosca; *Recordings include:* Turandot, Andrea Chenier, Fedora, Bluebeard's Castle, Violanta, Tiefland, Mefistofele, Die Walküre, La Wally. *Leisure interests:* reading, films, tennis, cycling. *Address:* c/o Organisation Internationale Opéra et Concert, 19 rue Vignon, 75008 Paris, France.

MARWAH, Kanta, PH D; Indian/Canadian economist. *Education:* Punjab Univ and Univ of Pennsylvania (USA). *Career:* Consultant to UN Conf on Trade and Devt, developed a world model for int trade that facilitated the forecasting of market shares and trade flows *c*1968–1973; currently Prof of Econs; researcher on Canadian foreign exchange markets. *Publications:* A History of Macroeconometric Model-Building (jtly – Book of the Year, American Library Asscn Journal, Choice); numerous papers on Canadian economy.

MARZIEH, (pseudonym of Ashrafolsadat-Khadijeh-Marzieh Mortezaii); Iranian singer; b 21 March 1924, Teheran (now Tehran); d of the late Hassan Mortezaii and Ehteram Kavesh; m 1st Hassan Amini 1950 (divorced); m 2nd H. Malek Afzali 1953; one s one d. *Education:* Coll of Esmatieh (Teheran), music studies under grand masters of classical traditional Persian music at Nat Music Asscn of Iran. *Career:* Debut in play Shirin and Farhad, Barbod Theatre Co 1942; singer of traditional and classical Iranian music; numerous radio performances; numerous concert performances in Iran before the revolution in 1979; refused to sing in Iran after 1979, came to Europe 1994; performances world-wide, including the Royal Albert Hall and Earls Court (London), Germany, Stockholm, Moscow, Los Angeles and other cities in the USA; distinguished for her innovation in and influence on Persian music; Hon mem Nat Council of Resistance of Iran 1994, Artistic and Cultural Affairs Adviser to its leader, Maryam Rajavi; numerous recordings of arias, operettas, classical-traditional, folk music, jazz, etc; awards include US Congressional Record 1995, Award from Mayor of City of Los Angeles 1995, awards from cultural and academic insts in Iran. *Leisure interests:* literature, tennis, butterfly collection, antiques, flowers. *Address:* Culture en Liberté, 3 rue St-Germain, 95240 Cormielles-en-Parisis, France. *Telephone:* (1) 39-31-23-00; *Fax:* (1) 39-97-04-31.

MASAKO, Princess; Japanese royal; b 9 Dec 1963; d of Hisashi and Yumiko Owada; m Crown Prince Naruhito 1993. *Education:* Univs of Harvard (MA, USA), Tokyo and Oxford (UK). *Career:* Joined Ministry of Foreign Affairs 1987, mem staff Second N America Div, N American Affairs Bureau, mem trade relations negotiating teams in talks with US Sec of State and Trade Reps, responsible for formulating policy on semiconductors, resigned 1993. *Leisure interests:* music, walking, skiing, tennis. *Address:* Imperial Household Agency, 1-1, Chiyoda, Chiyoda-ku, Tokyo 100, Japan.

MASDIT, Supatra, MA; Thai politician; b 9 Jan 1950, Nakhon Si Thammarat Prov; m Pathompong Kesornsook. *Education:* Chulalangkorn Univ and Univ of Hawaii (USA). *Career:* Lecturer Kasetsart Univ 1971–73, Thammasat Univ 1973–79; Sec Integrated Rural Devt; mem House of Reps (Parl) 1979; Democratic Party Spokesperson 1983–88, Democrat Party Spokesperson on Foreign Affairs Standing Cttee 1983–86, mem Cttee 1983–88, Chair House Affairs Standing Cttee 1983–88, Rep Thai Unit, Interparl Union 1983–86; Sec to Minister to Prime Minister's Office 1986–88; Minister responsible for Public Relations Dept 1988–90, for Nat Educ 1988–90; Vice-Pres Nat Comm on Women's Affairs 1989–90; Pres Nat Public Relations Planning Bd 1989–90, Nat Film Bd 1989–90, Creative Media Foundation 1989; Kt Grand Cordon of the Most Noble Order of the

Crown of Thailand 1989, of the Most Exalted Order of the White Elephant 1990. *Address:* House of Representatives, U-Thong Nai Rd, Bangkok 10300, Thailand.

MASEKELA, Barbara; South African political activist and diplomatist; b 1941. *Career:* In exile from SA for 27 years; has lived in Ghana, UK and USA; fmr mem staff African Nat Congress (ANC), Zambia; first S African Amb to France 1994. *Address:* c/o Ministry of Foreign Affairs, Union Bldgs, East Wing, Government Ave, Pretoria, 0002, South Africa.

MASHAM OF ILTON, Baroness (Life Peer), cr 1970, **Susan Lilian Primrose Cunliffe-Lister, (Countess of Swinton),** DL; British member of the House of Lords; b 14 April 1935, Lyth-Caithness; d of Ronald Sinclair and Reba Blair; m Lord Masham (Earl of Swinton) 1959; one s one d. *Education:* Heathfield School (Ascot) and London Polytechnic. *Career:* Mem House of Lords 1970–; voluntary social worker; mem Peterlee and Newton Aycliffe New Town Corpn 1973–85, Parl All-Party Disabled Cttee 1970–, Penal Affairs Cttee 1975–, Yorkshire Regional Health Authority 1982–90, N Yorks Family Health Services Authority 1990–, Children's Group; Vice-Chair All-Party Parl Drug Misuse Cttee 1984–, AIDS Cttee; Pres N Yorks Red Cross 1963–88, Patron 1989–; Pres Yorks Asscn for the Disabled 1963–, Chartered Soc of Physiotherapy 1975–82, Spinal Injuries Asscn 1982–, Papworth and Enham Village Settlements; Vice-Pres British Paraplegic Sports Soc, British Sports Asscn for the Disabled, Disabled Drivers' Asscn, Disabled Drivers' Motor Club, Asscn of Occupational Therapists, Action for Dysphasic Adults; Chair Phoenix House Bd of Dirs 1986–92 (currently Patron), Home Office Working Group on Young People and Alcohol 1987; mem Bd of Visitors Wetherby Young Offenders Inst 1963–94, Winston Churchill Memorial Trust 1980–; Trustee Spinal Research Trust; Patron Disablement Income Group, Yorks Faculty of Gen Practitioners; Gov Ditchley Foundation 1980–; Hon Fellow of the Royal Coll of Gen Practitioners 1981; Hon Fellow Bradford and Ilkley Community Coll 1988, Chartered Soc of Physiotherapists; Hon MA (Open Univ) 1981; Hon D UNIV (York) 1985; Hon LL D (Leeds) 1988 (Teesside); Hon D SC (Ulster) 1990, Hon D LITT (Keele); Freedom of the Borough of Harrogate 1989. *Publication:* The World Walks By 1986. *Leisure interests:* breeding highland ponies, gardening, charity work. *Address:* Dykes Hill House, Masham, Nr Ripon, N Yorks HG4 4NS, UK; 46 Westminster Gardens, Marsham St, London SW1P 4JG, UK. *Telephone:* (1765) 689241 (N Yorks); (20) 7834-0700 (London); *Fax:* (1765) 688184 (N Yorks); *E-mail:* baroness.marsham@breathemail.net.

MASON, Angela, OBE, BA, M SC; British organization executive; b 9 Aug 1944, High Wycombe; d of Nancy and Charles Weir; one d. *Education:* Bedford Coll and LSE. *Career:* Founder-mem Gay Liberation Front 1969, Rights of Women 1970; Solicitor Law Centres, Camden, London 1973–92; Exec Dir Stonewall Lobby Group 1992–; Mike Rhodes Award for promoting lesbian and gay rights during the Age of Consent campaign 1994; Liberty Human Rights Award 1997. *Publications include:* The Cohabitation Handbook 1971, The Case For Change 1993, Queer Bashing: A National Survey of Lesbian and Gay Hate Crime 1995. *Leisure interests:* poodles, reading, painting. *Address:* Stonewall Lobby Group, 46–48 Grosvenor Gardens, London SW1W 0EB, UK. *Telephone:* (20) 7881-9440; *Fax:* (20) 7881-9444; *E-mail:* angela@stonewall.org.uk; *Internet:* www.stonewall.co.uk.

MASON, Bobbie Ann, PH D; American writer; b 1 May 1940, Mayfield, KY; d of Wilburn Arnett and Christy Lee Mason; m Roger Rawlings 1969. *Education:* Univs of Kentucky and Connecticut and Binghamton Univ (NY). *Career:* Short stories have appeared in numerous journals including The New Yorker, Harper's, The North American Review, The Washington Post Magazine, The Atlantic, The Boston Globe Magazine, The Paris Review, Oxford American, DoubleTake; contrib to journals Esquire and Vanity Fair; Grantee Nat Endowment for the Arts 1983, Pennsylvania Arts Council 1983, 1989; Guggenheim Fellow 1984; several short story awards 1981–; Appalachian Medallion Award, Univ of Charleston 1991. *Publications include:* Shiloh and Other Stories (Ernest Hemingway Foundation Award 1982, Award of American Acad and Inst for Arts and Letters 1984) 1982, In Country (Award for Cultural Contrib to the Arts, Vietnam Veterans of America 1989, made into feature film 1989) 1985, Spence + Lila 1988, Love Life 1989,

Feather Crowns 1993, Midnight Magic 1998, Clear Springs (shortlisted for Pulitzer Prize) 1999, Zigzagging Down A Wild Trail 2001. *Address:* c/o Amanda Urban, International Creative Management, 40 W 57th St, New York, NY 10019, USA.

MASON, Marsha; American actress; b 3 April 1942, St Louis, MO; d of James and Jacqueline Mason; m 1st Gary Campbell 1965 (divorced); m 2nd Neil Simon 1973 (divorced). *Career:* Has appeared in numerous plays, films and TV programmes; f herbal farm Resting in the River 1996, launched first product range 2000; Dr hc (Webster). *Plays include:* Cactus Flower 1968, The Deer Park 1967, The Indian Wants the Bronx 1968, Happy Birthday, Wanda June 1970, Private Lives 1971, You Can't Take It With You 1972, A Doll's House 1972, The Crucible 1972, Cyrano de Bergerac 1972, The Good Doctor 1973, King Richard III 1974, The Heiress 1975, Mary Stuart 1982, The Big Love (one-woman show) 1988, With The Naked Angels 1994; *Films include:* Blume in Love 1973, Cinderella Liberty (Golden Globe Award 1974) 1973, Audrey Rose 1977, The Goodbye Girl (Golden Globe Award 1978) 1977, The Cheap Detective 1978, Promises in the Dark 1979, Chapter Two 1979, Only When I Laugh 1981, Max Dugan Returns 1982, Heartbreak Ridge 1986, Drop Dead Fred 1990, I Love Trouble 1994; *TV appearances include:* Cyrano de Bergerac 1974, The Good Doctor 1978, Lois Gibbs and the Love Canal 1981, Surviving 1985, Trapped in Silence 1986, The Clinic 1987, Dinner At Eight 1989, The Image 1990, Broken Trust 1994, Frasier 1997. *Address:* Resting in the River, 528 Don Gaspar, Santa Fe, NM 87501, USA. *Telephone:* (888) 465-0563.

MASON, Monica; British arts administrator and former dancer; b 6 Sept 1941; d of Richard Mason and E. Fabian; m Austin Bennet 1968. *Education:* Royal Ballet School (London). *Career:* Mem Corps de Ballet, Royal Ballet 1958–, Sr Prin until 1989, Asst to Prin Choreographer 1980–84, Prin Répétiteur 1984–, Asst Dir 1989–. *Ballets include:* Rite of Spring 1962, Diversions, Elite Syncopations, Electra, Manon, Romeo and Juliet, Rituals, Adieu, Isadora, The Four Seasons, The Ropes of Time. *Address:* Royal Opera House, Covent Garden, London WC2E 9DD, UK. *Telephone:* (20) 7240-1200.

MASSALITINOVA, Tatyana Nicolaevna; Bulgarian actress; b 2 Sept 1921, Prague, Czechoslovakia; d of Nicolas Massalitinov and Katrine (née Krasnopolska) Massalitinova; m 1st Leonid Essaoulenko 1945; one d; m 2nd Paul Richard Greenevitch 1975. *Education:* St Joseph Coll, Foreign Language School, Acad of Fine Arts and Drama School. *Career:* Actress, Nat Theatre, Sofia 1946–89, then with Mrs Barboukoff's pvt theatre, Sofia and on tour in Bulgaria; tours of Bulgaria, USA, Czechoslovakia, Austria, Netherlands, Russia, Poland, Germany; recently worked for three theatre cos in Sofia; articles in theatrical magazines; playwright and recording artist; awards include Prize of the Bulgarian Artists' Union; Nat Artist of the People 1971. *Address:* 1113 Sofia, bul Samokoff 80, Bl 306, Apt 58, Bulgaria. *Telephone:* (2) 65-99-78.

MASSEVITCH, Alla Genrikhovna, D SC; Russian astronomer; b 9 Oct 1918, Tbilisi; d of Genrik Massevitch and Natalie Zhgenti; m Joseph Friedlander 1942; one d. *Education:* Moscow Industrial Pedagogical Inst and Moscow Univ. *Career:* Asst Prof of Astrophysics Moscow Univ 1946–48, Prof 1948–; Vice-Pres Astronomical Council, Soviet (now Russian) Acad of Sciences 1952–88, Chief Scientific Researcher 1980–83, in charge of optical (visual, photographic and laser ranging) tracking of Soviet (now Russian) space vehicles 1958–89; mem Nat Cttee for the Int Space Year 1989–93; Chair Working Group I, Cttee for Space Research (COSPAR) 1961–66; Vice-Pres Comm 44 JAU (Extraterrestrial Astronomy) 1961–67; Pres Comm 35 JAU (Internal Structure of Stars) 1967–70; Deputy Sec-Gen UNISPACE 1957–89, Pres of Section Satellite Tracking for Geodesy, Inter-Cosmos Co-operation 1968–89; Vice-Pres Inst for Soviet-American Relations 1967; Vice-Pres Bd Soviet Peace Cttee 1967; Foreign mem Royal Astronomical Soc 1963, Indian Nat Acad of Sciences 1980, Austrian Acad of Sciences 1985; mem Int Acad of Astronautics 1964; has written three books on stellar evolution, one on satellite geodesy, several popular books on astronomy, 168 papers on internal structure of stars, stellar evolution and optical tracking of satellites, mainly in Astronomical Journal of the USSR, Publications of the Sternberg Astronomical Inst and Scientific Information of the Astronomical Council 1945–; Hon

mem Russian Acad of Cosmonautics 1997; Int Astronautics Prize (Galaber Prize) 1965; USSR State Prize 1975; Honoured Scientist of Russia 1980 and decorations from Russia, Bulgaria, Mongolia and Poland. *Leisure interest:* collecting coffee machines and cookery books. *Address:* Astronomical Institute of the Russian Acad of Sciences, 48 Pyatnitskaya St, 109017 Moscow, Russian Federation (Office); 6 Pushkurev per, Apt 4, Moscow 103045, Russian Federation (Home). *Telephone:* (095) 931-3980 (Office); (095) 208-9333 (Home); *Fax:* (095) 230-2081; *E-mail:* vmyakurin@inasan.zssi.ru (Office).

MASSEY, Anna (Raymond); British actress; b 11 Aug 1937, Sussex; d of the late Raymond Massey and of Adrianne Allen; m 1st Jeremy Huggins 1958 (divorced 1963); one s; m 2nd Uri Andres 1988. *Education:* UK, USA, France, Italy and Switzerland. *Career:* Many performances with Nat Theatre. *Plays include:* The Reluctant Debutante 1955, Dear Delinquent 1957, The Elder Statesman 1958, Double Yolk 1959, The Last Joke 1960, The Miracle Worker 1961, The School for Scandal 1962, The Doctor's Dilemma 1963, The Right Honourable Gentleman 1964, The Glass Menagerie 1965, The Prime of Miss Jean Brodie 1966, The Flip Side 1967, First Day of a New Season 1967, This Space is Mine 1969, Hamlet 1970, Spoiled 1971, Slag 1971, Jingo 1975, The Seagull 1981, Heartbreak House 1975, Close of Play 1979, The Importance of Being Earnest (Best Supporting Actress Award, Soc of West End Theatre 1983), Family Voices, Other Places 1982, A Kind of Alaska (Best Supporting Actress, British Theatre Asscn 1986), King Lear 1986, Broadway Bound 1991, Mary Stuart 1996; *Films include:* Gideon's Day 1957, Peeping Tom 1960, Bunny Lake is Missing 1965, The Looking Glass War 1969, David Copperfield 1969, De Sade 1971, Five Days One Summer 1982, Another Country 1984, The Chain 1985, La Couleur du Vent 1988, The Tall Guy 1989, A Tale of Two Cities, Haunted 1995, The Grotesque 1995, The Slab Boys 1997, Déjà Vu 1997, Captain Jack 1998, Mad Cows 1998, Room to Rent 2001, Possession 2001; *TV appearances include:* Rebecca, I Remember Nelson, The Cherry Orchard, Mansfield Park, Journey into the Shadows: Portrait of Owen John (Best Actress, Locarno Film Festival 1984) 1983, Sakharov, Sacred Hearts (Royal TV Soc Award 1986) 1985, Hotel du Lac (BAFTA Award for Best Actress 1987, Royal TV Soc Award 1986) 1986, The Christmas Tree 1987, Sunchild 1988, A Tale of Two Cities 1989, Man From the Pru 1990, Shalom, Joan Collins 1990, Broadway Bound 1991, A Respectable Trade (series) (BAFTA Award for Best Actress 1998), The Sleeper 2001; *Radio work includes:* many radio plays and narration of This Sceptred Isle BBC Radio 1999. *Address:* c/o Markham and Froggatt Ltd, 4 Windmill St, London W1P 1HF, UK.

MASSEY, Doreen Barbara, MA, FRSA; British professor of geography; b 3 Jan 1944, Manchester; d of Jack and Nancy Massey. *Education:* Manchester High School for Girls, St Hugh's Coll (Oxford) and Univ of Pennsylvania (USA). *Career:* Mem staff Centre for Environmental Studies 1968–79; Prof of Geography Open Univ 1982–; mem staff Inst Nicaragüense de Investigaciones Económicas y Sociales (INIES), Nicaragua 1985–86; fmr mem Bd GLC Greater London Enterprise Bd; Hon Fellow St Hugh's Coll (Oxford); Vic Medal, Royal Geographical Soc 1994; Vautrin Lud Int Prize for Geography 1998. *Publications:* Capital and Land, Spatial Divisions of Labour, Anatomy of Job Loss, Nicaragua: urban and regional issues, Geography Matters, Uneven Re-Development, Space, Place and Gender, Geographical Worlds, and a Place in the World? Places, Cultures and Globalisation; numerous articles. *Address:* Open University, Faculty of Social Sciences, Walton Hall, Milton Keynes MK7 6AA, UK. *Telephone:* (1908) 654475.

MASTERKOVA, Svetlana Aleksandrovna; Russian athlete; b 1 Jan 1968, Achinsk; m Asyat Saitov; one d. *Career:* Track and field athlete; works with coaches Yakov Yelyanov and Svetlana Styrkina; 1996 Atlanta Olympic Games Champion (800m and 1500m); winner Silver Medal World Winter Championship 1993; winner Bronze Medal European Winter Championship 1996; twice World Record holder; Order For Service to Motherland; lives in France, Italy, Russia; Best Woman Athlete of the Year, Monte Carlo 1996; Merited Master of Sports; Best Woman Athlete of Russia 1996, 1997. *Address:* All-Russian Athletic Federation, Luzhnetskaya nab 8, 119871 Moscow, Russian Federation. *Telephone:* (095) 201 0150.

MASTERSON, Mary Stuart; American actress; b 28 June 1966, Los Angeles, CA; d of Peter Masterson and Carlin Glynn. *Education:* Goddard Coll. *Career:* Film debut at the age of eight in The Stepford Wives 1975; mem Actor's Studio; numerous film, TV and theatre appearances. *Films include:* Heaven Help Us, At Close Range, My Little Girl, Some Kind of Wonderful, Gardens of Stone, Mr North, Chances Are, Immediate Family (Nat Bd of Review Award 1989), Funny About Love, Fried Green Tomatoes at the Whistlestop Cafe, Mad at the Moon, Married to It, Benny & Joon, Bad Girls, Radioland Murders, Heaven's Prisoners, Bed of Roses; *TV appearances include:* Love Lives On (film), Amazing Stories; dir and writer Showtime 2000; *Plays include:* Been Taken, Lily Dale, The Lucky Spot, Moonlight and Valentines, Three Sisters. *Address:* c/o Creative Artists Management, 9830 Wilshire Blvd, Beverly Hills, CA 90212, USA.

MASTERSON, Valerie, CBE, FRCM; British opera and concert singer; b Birkenhead; d of Edward and Rita (née McGrath) Masterson; m Andrew March 1965; one s one d. *Education:* Holt Hill Convent and with Edwardo Asquez. *Career:* Made debut Landestheater, Salzburg, Austria; has sung with D'Oyly Carte Opera, Glyndebourne, Royal Opera House, Covent Garden and English Nat Opera, and on TV and radio; also in major opera houses internationally including Paris, Aix-en-Provence and Toulouse (France), Munich (Germany), Geneva (Switzerland), San Francisco (USA), Barcelona (Spain), Milan (Italy), Santiago (Chile) and Chicago (USA); Prof of Voice, Royal Acad of Music, London 1992–; Vice Pres British Youth Opera until 2000; Hon Fellow RAM 1994; Hon D LITT (South Bank Univ) 2000; Award for Outstanding Individual Performance of the Year in a New Opera, Soc of West End Theatre 1983. *Operas include:* La Traviata, Manon, Le Nozze di Figaro, Faust, Alcina, Die Entführung aus dem Serail, Così fan Tutte, La Bohème, Semele (Soc of W End Theatres—SWET Award) 1983, Die Zauberflöte, Julius Caesar, Rigoletto, Romeo and Juliet, Carmen, Count Ory, Mireille, Louise, Idomeneo, Les Dialogues des Carmélites, The Merry Widow, Xerxes, Orlando, Der Rosenkavalier, The Pearl Fishers, Die Fledermaus, Lucia di Lammermoor; *Recordings include:* Julius Caesar, La Traviata, Elisabetta Regina d'Inghilterra, Bitter Sweet, The Ring Cycle, Scipione, various Gilbert and Sullivan works. *Leisure interests:* tennis, swimming. *Address:* c/o Music International, 13 Ardilaun Rd, London N5 2QR, UK.

MASTRANTONIO, Mary-Elizabeth; American actress; b 17 Nov 1958, Oak Park, IL. *Education:* Univ of Illinois. *Career:* Singer and dancer before stage debut in West Side Story, New York. *Plays include:* Copperfield 1981, Oh Brother, Amadeus, Sunday in the Park With George, The Human Comedy, Henry V, Figaro, Measure for Measure, The Knife, Twelfth Night; *Films:* Scarface 1983, The Color of Money (Acad Award nomination) 1986, Slam Dance 1987, The January Man 1989, The Abyss 1989, Fools of Fortune, Class Action, Robin Hood: Prince of Thieves 1991, White Sands, Consenting Adults, A Day to Remember, Three Wishes; *TV appearances include:* Mussolini: The Untold Story, Uncle Vanya. *Address:* c/o ICM, 8942 Wilshire Blvd, Beverly Hills, CA 90211, USA.

MATHAI, Rachel, MB, MRCP, FRCP; Indian medical practitioner; b 22 July 1929, Mavelikara, Kerala; d of the late Jacob and Mary Eapen; m K. V. Mathai 1956; one d one s. *Education:* Baker Memorial School for Girls, CMS Coll (Kottayam), Christian Medical Coll (Vellore), Madras Medical Coll and Royal Coll of Physicians and Surgeons of Glasgow (UK). *Career:* Mem staff Christian Medical Coll, Vellore 1956; Prof of Dermatology, Venereology and Leprosy 1976; Consultant Dermatologist Muthoot Medical Centre, Kozhencherry 1989; Ed Indian Journal of Dermatology, Venereology and Leprosy 1974–83; Fellow Royal Coll of Physicians and Surgeons of Glasgow 1978; has written numerous articles for professional journals. *Leisure interests:* gardening, embroidery, cooking. *Address:* Konnanilkunnathil, Kolabhagam PO, Thadiyoor 689 545, India.

MATHIEU, Mireille; French singer; b 22 July 1946, Avignon; d of Roger and Marcelle Mathieu. *Education:* In Avignon. *Career:* Singer 1962–; numerous concerts and concert tours in France and abroad, including concerts at Olympia (Paris) 1967, Palais des Congrès (Paris) 1986, 1990, New York 1986, and tours of People's Repub of China 1986 and fmr USSR 1987; Chevalier de l'Ordre Nat du Mérite; Chevalier des Arts et des Lettres. *Songs include:* Mon credo, Viens dans

ma rue, Un homme et une femme, La dernière valse, Noël blanc, La première étoile, La parade des chapeaux melons, Paris un tango, Adieu je t'aime, La paloma adieu, Un jour tu reviendras, Le silence, Mille colombes, Santa Maria de la mer, A blue Bayou, Tous les enfants chantent avec moi, Toi et moi, Le village oublié, Un enfant viendra, Love story, Une femme amoureuse, L'enfant que je n'ai jamais eu, Ce soir je t'ai perdu, La Marseillaise (Nat Anthem, with Garde Républicaine and French army choir, for the bicentenary of the French Revolution) 1989, Mireille Mathieu chante Piaf; *Publication:* Oui je crois 1988. *Address:* Abilene Disc, 122 ave Wagram, 75017 Paris, France.

MATHIS, Edith; Swiss opera singer (soprano); b 11 Feb 1938, Lucerne. *Education:* Lucerne Conservatoire. *Career:* Made debut Lucerne 1956; sang with Cologne Opera, Germany 1959–62; appeared Salzburg Festival, Austria 1960, Deutsche Oper, Berlin 1963; made debut Glyndebourne (UK) in Le Nozze di Figaro 1962, Royal Opera House, Covent Garden, London in Le Nozze di Figaro 1970, Metropolitan Opera House, New York, USA in The Magic Flute 1970; mem Hamburg State Opera, Germany 1960–75. *Address:* c/o Ingpen & Williams Ltd, 26 Wadham Rd, London, SW15 2LR, UK; c/o Bueker-Management, Postfach 1169, Hanover, Germany. *Telephone:* (20) 8874-3222 (London).

MATHIS-EDDY, Darlene Fern, PH D; American poet and professor of English; b 19 March 1937, Elkhart, IN; d of the late William Eugene and Fern Roose (née Paulmer) Mathis; m Spencer Livingston Eddy, Jr 1964 (died 1971). *Education:* Goshen Coll and Rutgers Univ (NJ). *Career:* Instructor in English Douglass Coll 1962–64, Rutgers Univ 1964, 1965, Rutgers Univ Coll (Adult Educ) 1967; Asst Prof of English Ball State Univ (BSU) 1967–70, Assoc Prof of English 1970–75, Prof of English 1975–, Poet-in-Residence 1989–93; Consulting Ed Blue Unicorn 1995–; Founding Ed The Hedge Row Press 1995–; Poetry Ed BSU Forum; has written numerous articles and poetry for literary reviews 1968–; mem Comm on Women Nat Council of Teachers of English 1976–79; Woodrow Wilson Nat Fellow 1959–62, Notable Woodrow Nat Fellow 1991; Rutgers Univ Grad Honors Fellow 1964–65, Dissertation Honors Fellow 1966–67; numerous creativity and research awards 1967. *Publications:* The Worlds of King Lear 1970, Leaf Threads 1986, Wind Rhymes 1986, Snowy Egret (contrib ed) 1988–90, Weathering 1991, Reflections: Studies in Light 1993. *Leisure interests:* gardening, music, antiques, reading, sketching, photography, bird watching, cooking. *Address:* Dept of English, Robert Bell Bldg, Office No 248, Ball State University, Muncie, IN 47306-0460, USA (Office); 1409 W Cardinal St, Muncie, IN 47306, USA (Home). *Telephone:* (317) 285-8580.

MATLIN, Marlee; American actress; b 24 Aug 1965, Morton Grove, IL. *Education:* John Hersey High School (Chicago) and William Rainey Harper Coll. *Career:* Performer with Children's Theatre of the Deaf, Des Plaines at age eight. *Films:* Children of a Lesser God (Acad Award, Golden Globe Award) 1986, Walker 1987, The Man in the Golden Mask, The Linguini Incident, Hear No Evil; *TV appearances include:* Reasonable Doubts (series), Bridge To Silence (film) 1989, Against Her Will: The Carrie Buck Story (film), Face the Hate, Meaning of Life, Free to Laugh, Creative Spirit, Picket Fences 1993, 1994–96, Seinfeld 1993, Spin City 1996, ER 1999, Judging Amy 1999, Where the Truth Lies 1999. *Address:* c/o ICM, 8942 Beverley Hills Blvd, Beverly Hills, CA 90211, USA.

MATOLA, Sharon, BA; Belizean (b American) environmentalist and zoo director; b 3 June 1954, MD; d of Edward and Janice Matola. *Education:* New Coll of the Univ of S Florida. *Career:* Founder, Dir Belize Zoo 1983, developed Zoo as Tropical Educ Centre. *Publication:* Hoodwink the Owl (children's story book on conservation). *Leisure interest:* scientific expedition work. *Address:* The Belize Zoo and Tropical Centre, POB 474, Belize City, Belize. *Telephone:* (2) 50145523; *Fax:* (2) 50178808.

MATSEPE-CASABURRI, Ivy F., PH D; South African politician and broadcasting executive; d of the late Dorrington Matsepe and of Violet Matsepe; divorced. *Education:* Rutgers Univ (NJ, USA) and Fort Hare Univ. *Career:* Academic Registrar and Sr Lecturer UN Inst for Namibia, Lusaka, Zambia 1985–90; Exec Dir Educ Devt Trust 1990–93; Chair S African Broadcasting Corpn (SABC) 1993–; Pres Asscn of African

Women for Research and Devt 1988–; Minister of Posts, Telecoms and Broadcasting 1999–. *Publications:* articles published in African Journal of Political Economy. *Leisure interests:* music, reading, sports. *Address:* Ministry of Posts, Telecommunications and Broadcasting, Iparioli Office Park, Nkululeko House, 339 Duncan St, Hatfield, Pretoria 0083, South Africa; POB 91123, Auckland Park 2006, South Africa. *Telephone:* (12) 4278111 (Office); (11) 714 3900; *Fax:* (12) 3626915 (Office); (11) 714 3569.

MATTHÄUS-MAIER, Ingrid; German politician; b 9 Sept 1945, Werlte, Aschendorf Co; d of Heinz-Günther and Helmtraud (née von Hagen) Matthäus; m Robert Maier 1974; one s one d. *Education:* Law studies in Giessen and Münster. *Career:* Academic Asst Higher Admin Court, later Judge Admin Court, Münster; mem Bundestag (Parl, FDP) 1976–82, (SPD) 1983–99, Chair Finance Cttee 1979–82, Deputy Chair, Financial Policy Spokesperson SPD Parl Group 1988–99; mem Bd Kreditanstalt für Wiederaufbau 1999–. *Address:* Palmengartenstr 5–9, 60325 Frankfurt am Main, Germany (Home). *Telephone:* Telephone: (69) 7431 4466 (Office); *Fax:* (69) 7431 4141 (Office).

MATTILA, Karita Marjatta; Finnish opera singer; b 5 Sept 1960, Somero; d of Erkki and Arja (née Somerikko) Mattila; m Tapio Kuneinen 1992. *Education:* Perniö High School, Sibelius Acad (Helsinki) and pvt study with Liisa Linko-Malmio and Vera Rozsa (London). *Career:* Made debut Finnish Nat Opera in The Marriage of Figaro 1983; int debut Brussels Opera 1984; Royal Opera House, Covent Garden, London 1986–89; appeared at Barenboim-Ponnelle Festival, Paris 1986, Tel-Aviv 1987, 1990; appearances at Washington Opera 1985, Chicago Lyric Opera 1988, 1991 and Houston Grand Opera (USA) 1988, 1991, Royal Opera House, Covent Garden, London 1986, 1989, 1992, 1996, 1997, Vienna State Opera 1989, 1990, San Francisco 1989, 1997, and Metropolitan Opera, New York (USA) 1990, 1993, 1996, 2000, Opéra de Paris 1996, 1997, 2001; has also appeared in Washington, Houston, Chicago and San Francisco; recitals throughout Europe; has worked under major conductors including Sir Colin Davis, Claudio Abbado, von Dohnanyi, Giulini, Sinopoli; recordings for Philips and Deutsche Grammophon; First Prize Finnish Nat Singing Competition 1981; First Prize BBC Singer of the World, Cardiff 1983; Evening Standard Award 1997; Acad du Disque Lyrique Award 1997; Grammy Award for Best Opera 1998. *Operas include:* The Marriage of Figaro 1983, 1984, Die Fledermaus 1984–85, Così fan Tutte 1986, The Magic Flute 1986, 1989, Der Freischütz 1989, Don Giovanni 1992, Die Meistersinger 1993, Don Carlos 1996, Lohengrin 1997; *Recordings:* Der Freischütz, Don Giovanni, Così fan Tutte, Fierrabras, Schubert's Mass, Mendelssohn's 2nd Symphony, Das Paradies und die Peri, Strauss Songs. *Leisure interests:* languages, sailing, sport, golf. *Address:* c/o IMG Artists Europe, Lovell House, 616 Chiswick High Rd, London W4 5RX, UK. *Telephone:* (20) 8233-5800.

MATULOVIC-DROPULIC, Marina; Croatian politician. *Career:* Mem Christian Democratic Union; Minister of Construction, Urban Planning and Housing 1995; Župan (mayor) of Zagreb and prefect of Zagreb county 1996. *Address:* Office of the Župan, 10000 Zagreb, Skupš-Županija Grad Zagreb, Croatia. *Telephone:* (1) 511141; *Fax:* (1) 511546.

MATUTE AUSEJO, Ana María; Spanish writer; b 26 July 1925, Barcelona; d of Facundo Matute and Mary Ausejo; m 1952 (divorced 1963); one s. *Education:* 'Damas Negras' French Nuns Coll. *Career:* Has collaborated on literary magazine Destino; Visiting Lecturer Indiana Univ 1965–66, Oklahoma Univ, USA 1969–; Writer-in-Residence Univ of Virginia, USA 1978–79; mem Hispanic Soc of America; 'Highly Commended Author', Hans Christian Andersen Jury, Lisbon 1972. *Publications:* Los Abel 1947, Fiesta Al Noroeste (Café Gijón Prize) 1952, Pequeño Teatro (Planeta Prize) 1954, Los Niños tontos 1956, Los Hijos muertos (Nat Literary Prize and Critics Prize) 1959, Primera Memoria (Nadal Prize) 1959, Tres y un sueño 1961, Historias de la Artamila 1961, El Río 1963, El Tiempo 1963, Los Soldados lloran de noche (Fastenrath Prize 1969) 1964, El Arrepentido y otras Narraciones 1967, Algunos Muchachos 1968, La Trampa 1969, La Torre Vigia 1971, Olvidado Rey Gudu 1974; Children's books: El Pais de la Pizarra 1956, Paulina 1961, El Sal Tamontes Verde 1961, Caballito Loco 1961, El Aprendiz 1961, Carnavalito 1961, El Polizón del 'Ulises' (Lazarillo Prize) 1965. *Leisure interests:* painting, drawing, cinema.

MATVEYEVA, Novella Nikolaevna; Russian poet and singer; b 7 Oct 1934, Pushkin, nr Leningrad (now St Petersburg); d of Nikolai Nikolaevitch Matveyev-Bodryi and Nadeyda Timofeevna (née Orleneva) Matveyeva; m Ivan Semyonovitch Kiuru 1963. *Publications:* Lirika 1961, Little Ship 1963, Selected Lyrics 1964, The Soul of Things 1966, Reflection of a Sunbeam 1966, School for Swallows 1973, River 1978, The Song's Law 1983, The Land of the Surf 1983, Rabbit's Village 1984, Selected Works 1986, Praising the Labour 1987, An Indissoluble Circle 1988, Poems 1988, The Foretelling of an Eagle (play, in Theatre magazine) 1988; *Recordings:* A Gipsy Girl 1966, What a Strong Wind! 1966, Poems and Songs 1973, A Princess on a Peascorn 1980, A Trail Is My Home 1982, The Music of Light (jtly) 1984, My Small Raven 1985, Ballads 1985, A Red-haired Girl 1986, The Inseparable Circle (jtly) 1991, The Poetic Dialogue (jtly) 1993, Hosanna to Skhodnya 1993, Sonnets to Dashkova 1994, Minuet 1994. *Leisure interests:* listening to the radio (plays, classical music), reading. *Address:* 103009 Moscow, Kammergerski per 2, Apt 42, Russian Federation. *Telephone:* (095) 292-33-61.

MATVIYENKO, Valentina Ivanova; Russian politician; b 7 April 1949, Sheptovka USSR (now Ukraine); m Vladimir Vasilyevich Matviyenko; one s. *Education:* Leningrad Inst of Chem and Pharmaceuticals and Acad of Social Sciences at CPSU Cen Cttee. *Career:* Comsomol work 1972–84; First Sec Krasnogvardeysk Dist CP Cttee, Leningrad 1984–86; Deputy Chair Exec Cttee Leningrad City Soviet on Problems of Culture and Educ 1988–89; USSR Peoples' Deputy, mem Supreme Soviet 1989–92; mem of Presidium, Chair Cttee on Problems of Family, Motherhood and Childhood Protection 1989–91; Russian Amb to Malta 1991–95, to Greece 1997–98; rank of Amb Extraordinary and Plenipotentiary; Dir Dept on Relations with Subjects of Russian Fed, Parl and Public Orgs Ministry of Foreign Affairs 1995–97, Deputy Prime Minister of Russian Fed Sept 1998–, Chair Comms on Int Humanitarian Aid and Religious Orgs. *Address:* House of Government, Krasnopresnenskaya nab 2, 103274 Moscow, Russian Federation. *Telephone:* (095) 205 5143; *Fax:* (095) 205-45-44.

MAURA, Carmen, BA; Spanish actress; b 15 Sept 1945, Madrid; d of Antonio Maura. *Career:* Worked as a cabaret singer and trans; has appeared in numerous films including many of Pedro Almódovar's productions; Premio Nacional de Cinematografía 1988. *Films include:* Pepi, Luci, Bom y otras chicas del montón (Pepi, Luci, Bom... And a Whole Lot of Other Girls) 1980, Hábitos oscuros (Dark Habits), Sal Gorda 1983, Sé infiel y no mires con quién 1985, ¿Qué he hecho yo para merecer esto? (What Have I Done to Deserve This?), Matador, Extramuros 1985, Tata mía 1986, Mujeres al borde de un ataque de nervios (Women on the Verge of a Nervous Breakdown, (Best Actress, European Film Awards) 1988, Ley del deseo (Law of Desire) 1989, ¡Ay Carmela! (Best Actress, European Film Awards 1991) 1990, Baton Rouge, Le Saut Périlleux, Between Heaven and Earth, In Heaven as on Earth, How to be a Woman and Not Die in the Attempt, The Anonymous Queen, Shadows in a Conflict, Louis the Child King, How to Be Miserable and Enjoy it, The Flower of My Secret, Una Pareja de Tres, El Palomo cojo, Happiness in the Field, Tortilla y cinema, Alliance cherche doigt, Elles.

MAXWELL, Claudette Angella, M SC; Jamaican accountant and financial executive; b 6 Feb 1957, Hanover; d of Gladstone and Myrtle Whitelocke; m Stanhope Maxwell 1980 (divorced 1991); one d. *Education:* St Andrew High School for Girls (Kingston), Univ of the W Indies and American Univ (DC, USA). *Career:* Public Accountant Touche Ross Thorburn 1981–84; Financial Man Consultant KPMG Peat Marwick McLintock 1984–88; apptd Dir of Finance and Investments Workers' Savings and Loan Bank 1988–1991, Gen Man Finance and Admin 1991; Vernon Tate Scholarship 1976. *Leisure interests:* reading, music, swimming, cycling. *Address:* Workers' Savings and Loan Bank, 134 Tower St, Kingston, Jamaica (Office); 12 Foresythe Drive, Kingston 6, Jamaica (Home). *Telephone:* (809) 922-6499.

MAY, Elaine; American actress, film director and entertainer; b 1932, Philadelphia; d of Jack Berlin; m 1st Marvin May (divorced); one d; m 2nd Sheldon Harnick 1962 (divorced 1963). *Career:* Appeared on radio and stage as a child; performed Playwright's Theatre, Chicago; appeared in student production Miss Julie, Univ of Chicago; mem improvisatory theatre group, The Compass (nightclub), Chicago until 1957; improvised nightclub double-act with Mike Nichols; appearances include New York Town Hall 1959, An Evening with Mike Nichols and Elaine May, Golden Theatre, New York 1960–61; numerous TV and radio appearances, weekly appearance NBC radio show Nightline. *Films:* Luv 1967, A New Leaf (also dir) 1972, The Heartbreak Kid (dir) 1973, Mikey and Nicky (dir) 1976 (writer, dir remake 1985), California Suite 1978, Heaven Can Wait (co-author screenplay) 1978, In The Spirit 1990, The Birdcage 1996 (co-author screenplay), Primary Colors (co-author screenplay); *Publications:* Better Part of Valour 1983, Hotline 1983, Mr Gogol and Mr Preen 1991, Death Defying Acts 1995. *Address:* c/o Julian Schlossberg, Castle Hill Productions, 1414 Ave of the Americas, New York, NY 10019, USA.

MAY-WEGGEN, Hanja Johanna R.; Netherlands politician; b 29 Dec 1943; m Peter May 1965; two d. *Education:* Univ of Amsterdam. *Career:* High school teacher 1965–77; mem Dutch UN Del 1977–79; MEP 1979–89, 1994–99, leader Dutch del in EPP group; Minister of Transport and Public Works and Water Man 1989–94; mem Christian Democratic Appeal; Richard Martin Award 1986; Schumann Médaille 1990. *Address:* Aquariuslaan 53 5632 BB Eindhoven, Netherlands (Home).

MAYHEW, Elza Lovitt, MFA, RCA; Canadian sculptor; b 19 Jan 1916, Victoria, BC; d of George and Alice (née Bordman) Lovitt; m Charles Alan Mayhew 1938 (died 1943); two s one d. *Education:* Univs of British Columbia (Canada) and Oregon (USA). *Career:* Studied with Jan Zach 1955–58; has staged numerous exhibitions 1960–; solo exhibitions include The Point Gallery, Victoria 1960, 1962, Art Gallery of Greater Victoria 1961, 1964, 1971, Fine Arts Gallery, Univ of British Columbia 1961, Lucien Campbell Plaza Univ of Oregon, USA 1963, Venice Biennale Canadian Pavilion 1964, Dorothy Cameron Gallery, Toronto 1965, EXPO '67, Montréal, The Backroom Gallery, Victoria 1978, Burnaby Art Gallery 1979, Equinox Gallery, Vancouver 1980, Albert White Gallery, Toronto 1980, Wallack Gallery, Ottawa 1981, EXPO '86, Vancouver, Port Angeles Fine Art Center 1988; rep in nat and int group exhibitions; rep in perm collections including Canada Nat Gallery, Nat Capital Comm; subject of film Time Makers: The Sculpture of Elza Mayhew 1985; Dir Int Sculpture Center, Kansas, USA 1968–79; Consultant British Columbia Cttee on Art 1974–76; mem Acquisitions Cttee, Art Gallery of Greater Victoria 1983–85; Sir Otto Beit Medal, Royal Soc of British Sculptors 1962; British Columbia Centennial Sculpture Exhibition Purchase Award 1967; Dr hc (Vic) 1989. *Address:* 698 Beaver Lake Rd, Victoria, BC V8Z 5N8, Canada. *Telephone:* (250) 744-1728; *Fax:* (250) 744-4058.

MAYHEW, Judith, LL M; New Zealand government official, lawyer and academic; b 18 Oct 1948; m 1976 (divorced 1986). *Education:* Otago Girls' High School and Univ of Otago, NZ. *Career:* Barrister and solicitor, NZ 1973, solicitor, England and Wales 1993; Lecturer in Law, Univ of Otago 1970–73; Lecturer in Law and Sub Dean, Univ of Southampton, UK 1973–76, King's Coll London 1976–89; Dir Anglo-French law degree, Sorbonne, Paris 1976–79; Dir of Training and Employment Law, Titmuss Sainer Dechert 1989–94; Dir of Educ and Training, Wilde Sapte 1994–; Chief City and Business Adviser to Mayor of Greater London 2000–; mem Corpn of City of London 1996, Chair Policy and Resources Cttee 1997–; Special Adviser to Chair of Clifford Chance; mem City Disputes Panel 1996–, London Devt Partnership 1998–; Dir Gresham Coll 1990–, English-Speaking Union 1993–, Geffrye Museum 1995–, British Invisibles 1996–; Trustee Natural History Museum 1998–; Gov London Guildhall Univ 1992– Birkbeck Coll London 1993–. *Leisure interests:* opera, theatre, old English roses, tennis. *Address:* Corporation of London, Guildhall, London, EC2P 2EJ, UK. *Telephone:* (20) 7606-3030.

MAYNTZ, Renate, PH D; German sociologist; b 28 April 1929, Berlin; d of Walter and Annemarie (née Günther) Pflaum; m 2nd Hann Trier. *Education:* Wellesley Coll (USA) and Freie Univ (Berlin). *Career:* Visiting Asst Prof, Columbia Univ, New York, USA 1959; Prof Freie Univ, Berlin 1965, School of Admin Science 1971, Univ of Cologne 1973; Founder, Dir Max-Planck Inst for Social Research, Cologne 1985; Hon Prof Univ of Cologne 1985; Dr hc (Uppsala) 1977, (Paris X) 1979; Arthur-Burkhardt Prize 1991; Schader-Stiftung Prize 1999. *Publications:* Parteigruppen in der Großstadt 1959, Soziologie der

Organisation 1963, Policy-making in the German Federal Bureaucracy (jtly) 1975, Soziologie der öffentlichen Verwaltung (3rd edn) 1985, Forschungsmanagement—Steuerungsversuche zwischen Scylla und Charybdis 1985. *Leisure interest:* gardening. *Address:* Max-Planck Inst für Gesellschaftsforschung, Lothringer Str 78, 50677 Cologne 1, Germany. *Telephone:* (221) 336050; *Fax:* (221) 3360555.

MAYRÖCKER, Friederike; Austrian writer; b 20 Dec 1924, Vienna; d of Franz and Friederike Mayröcker. *Education:* Secondary school and teacher training coll (Vienna). *Career:* English teacher 1946–68; first book published 1956; freelance writer 1969–; about 70 publications (prose, poetry, radio plays and children's books); awards include Österreichischer Würdigungspreis für Literatur 1975, Literature Prize (City of Vienna) 1977, Großes Österreichisches Staatspreis für Literatur, Roswitha-von-Gandersheim Preis, Austrian Insignia for Arts and Letters, Friedrich-Hölderlin-Preis 1993, Manuskripte-Preis 1994, Großer Literaturpreis der Bayerischen Akad der Schönen Künste 1996. *Publications include:* Lorifari 1956, Die Abschiede, Gute Nacht, guten Morgen, Magische Blätter (4 vols), Reise durch die Nacht, Das Herzzerreißende der Dinge, Winterglück, Mein Herz mein Zimmer mein Name, Gesammelte Prosa, Stilleben, Das besessere Alter, Ausgewählte Gedichte 1944–78, Lektion, Notizen auf einem Kamel (poems) 1996; Play: Nada—Nichts; *Recordings:* Sprech Klavier, Umarmungen. *Leisure interests:* fine art, hiking. *Address:* Zentagasse 16/40, 1050 Vienna, Austria. *Telephone:* (1) 54-57-80.

MAZIDAH BINTI HJ ZAKARIA; Malaysian politician. *Career:* Mem Dewan Negara (Senate) 1986; Chair Sungei Wang Plaza Sdn Bhd. *Address:* Dewan Negara, Parliament House, 50680 Kuala Lumpur, Malaysia.

MAZUR, Marilyn; Danish composer and percussionist; b 18 Jan 1955, New York, USA; one s. *Education:* Royal Danish Conservatory of Music (Copenhagen). *Career:* Living in Denmark 1961–; Dancer with Creative Dance Theatre 1971; formed Zirenes band 1973; percussionist, drummer and singer working with various groups 1975–; mem Miles Davis band 1985–89; has worked with groups including Six Winds, Primi Band and Mazur/Markussen Quartet; band leader, composer and percussionist with own group, Future Song 1989–; mem Jan Garbarek Group 1991–; tours with Miles Davis 1985, Gil Evans 1986, Wayne Shorter 1987; has composed numerous works for big band/orchestra, rhythmic ensembles, choirs, TV, etc; several grants from Danish Nat Art Foundation; Ben Webster Prize 1983; Jasa Prize. *Recordings include:* Six Winds 1982, Primi Band: Primi 1984, Mazur/Markussen Quartet: MM4 1984, Ocean Fables 1986, Marilyn Mazur's Future Song 1992, Ocean Fables: Havblik 1992, Marilyn Mazur and Pulse Unit: Circular Chant 1995, Miles Davis Live (recorded 1988) 1996; appearances on 25 albums 1982–95. *Leisure interests:* cooking, dance. *Address:* Storegade 7, 2650 Hvidovre, Denmark. *Telephone:* 36-78-36-08; *Fax:* 36-78-36-19.

MBA, Lucie, L ÈS L; Gabonese politician; b 27 Dec 1950; two d. *Education:* In France, Spain and UK. *Career:* Asst Univ of Gabon 1981; Pres's Adviser on Nat Comm of UNESCO 1986; mem Cen Cttee Parti démocratique gabonais (PDG) 1986; Minister of Foreign Affairs, Co-operation and Francophone Affairs 1990–91, of Public Health and Population 1991–92. *Leisure interests:* walking, reading. *Address:* Ministry of Public Health, BP 5955, Libreville, Gabon. *Telephone:* 730985.

MBENGUE, Aminata; Senegalese politician. *Career:* Mem Parti socialiste sénégalais; Fmr Minister of Women's, Children's and Family Affairs. *Address:* Ministry of Women's, Children's and Family Affairs, Dakar, Senegal.

MBOYA, Pamela Arwa, BA; Kenyan diplomatist/UN official. *Education:* Makerere Univ, Uganda and Western Coll for Women, OH, USA. *Career:* Perm Rep to Habitat 1980–; Leader and Deputy Leader of Kenya Del to Comm on Human Settlements 1980–; Dir of the preparations of the UN Decade for Women Conf 1984–86; bd mem Kenyatta Univ Council 1990–; mem of Kenya Del to UNCED Preparatory Meetings and Conf in Rio de Janeiro, Brazil 1992; mem Kenyan Del to the UN Gen Ass 1984, 1985, 1987, 1993, 1994, 1995, Task Force on Laws and Practices relating to women in Kenya 1993–, Exec and Co-ordinating Cttee, Beijing Conf 1995 1993, Del fourth

Women's Decade Conf, Beijing 1995; awarded Cert of Merit by Nat Council of Women for work in the field of Diplomatic Services and Human Settlements 1994. *Address:* POB 67830, Nairobi, Kenya.

MDEE, Lineo Khubelu, MA; Lesotho town and country planner; b (Lineo Khubelu Letsie) 27 Dec 1954, Maseru; m Franciscus Mdee 1983; one s two d. *Education:* Nat Univ of Lesotho and Univ of Nottingham (UK). *Career:* Physical Planner, Govt of Lesotho 1980, Sr Physical Planner 1985, Chief Physical Planner 1988, apptd Commr of Lands 1989; has presented many papers at int confs and seminars, including Int Conf on Planning Legislation in Africa, Maseru 1981. *Leisure interests:* cooking, studying languages, singing, reading. *Address:* c/o Dept of Lands, Surveys and Physical Planning, POB 876, Maseru, Lesotho.

MEADOWS, Pamela Catherine, BA, M SC; British organization executive; b 9 Jan 1949, Wallasey; d of Sidney James and Hilda Catherine Meadows; m Paul Ormerod 1975; one s. *Education:* Univ of Durham and Birkbeck Coll (Univ of London). *Career:* Research Officer Nat Inst of Econ and Social Research 1970–74; Sr Econ Asst and Econ Adviser Home Office 1974–78; various posts at Dept of Employment 1978–93, later Dir of Econs Research and Evaluation; Dir Policy Studies Inst 1993–98; Sr Fellow Nat Inst of Econ and Social Research 1998–; mem Better Regulation Task Force 1997–; mem Exec Cttee Public Man and Policy Asscn 1998–; Trustee Employment Policy Inst 1995–; Gov Birkbeck Coll 1997–. *Address:* 35 The Avenue, Kew, Richmond, Surrey TW9 2AL, UK.

MEDINA, Ann Hillyer, MA; American film producer and news correspondent; b 9 May 1943, New York; d of the late Harold Raymond, Jr and of Janet (née Williams) Medina; m John Welch 1989. *Education:* Wellesley Coll (MA), Harvard Univ (Cambridge, MA), Univ of Chicago (IL), Cleveland State Law School and Univ of Edinburgh (UK). *Career:* Grad Asst Prof of Philosophy Univ of Illinois 1967–69; Trainee Reporter WMAQ-TV, Chicago 1969–70; Reporter WKYC-TV, Cleveland 1970–73; Network Producer NBC News 1973; Network Corresp ABC News 1973–75, Documentary Producer 1974; Reporter, Producer Newsmagazine, CBC News 1975–80, Exec Producer 1980–81; Sr Journalist, Producer The Journal, CBC 1981–86, Beirut Bureau Chief 1983–84, Presenter Saturday Report 1986–87; Producer, Resident Fellow Canadian Centre for Advanced Film Studies 1988, Sr Resident Fellow 1989–90; ind producer 1990–; Vice-Chair Exec Bd Acad of Canadian Cinema and TV 1986, Chair 1992–97; mem Nat Exec Bd Alliance Canada of Cinema, TV and Radio Artists 1987–89, Bd Toronto Women in Film and Video 1989–90, Canadian Film and TV Production Asscn 1991–, Calmeadow Foundation 1987–97, Canfar for AIDS; Herschel Fellow, Univ of Chicago 1966; Emmy Award for Outstanding Individual Achievement 1972; Gold Medal, Columbus Int Film Festival 1973; Broadcast Award, San Francisco State Univ 1974; Golden Sheaf, Yorkton Short Film Festival 1985; Gold Hugo, Chicago Film Festival 1988; Chris Plaque Award, Columbus Int Film Festival 1986. *Leisure interests:* sailing, ornithology. *Address:* 112 Alcina Ave, Toronto, ON M6G 2E8, Canada. *Telephone:* (416) 656-8850; *Fax:* (416) 654-3209.

MEDZIHRADSKÁ, Lucia; Slovak skier; b 14 Nov 1968, Brezno; d of Robert M. and Emilia Medzihradská; m Mr Pacak 1996. *Education:* Comenius Univ of Bratislava. *Career:* Jr World Giant Slalom Champion 1986; mem Czechoslovak Olympic team 1988, 1992; Nat Champion 1986–92; participant at Jr World Championships (First in Giant Slalom, First in Combination, Second in Slalom) 1986; participant Ski World Championship 1987, 1989, 1993; mem Slovak Nat Ski Team 1992–95; mem Slovak Olympic Team 1994; participant Univ Ski World Championship 1995; Czechoslovak Sportswoman Honour 1988. *Leisure interests:* tennis, windsurfing, cycling, music, design, fine art, sport photography, reading. *Address:* POB 57, Goughs Bay, Vic 3723, Australia. *Telephone:* (57) 77 3757.

MEEHAN, Elizabeth Marian, D PHIL, FRSA; British professor of politics; b 23 March 1947, Edinburgh; d of David Charles Meehan and Marian Byas MacKenzie. *Education:* Peebles Burgh and County High School, Edinburgh Coll of Art, Univ of Sussex and Nuffield Coll (Oxford). *Career:* Mem Diplomatic Service London and Lagos 1966–73; Lecturer in Politics Univ of Bath 1979–90; Hallsworth Fellow

Univ of Manchester 1989–90; Prof of Politics Queen's Univ (Belfast, N Ireland) 1991–, Dean Faculty of Econ and Social Science 1995–97; Visiting Fellow Policy Inst, Trinity Coll (Dublin) 1998–99; mem Fawcett Soc and Liberty 1976–, Asscn of Univ Teachers 1979–, British Fed of Univ Women 1985–, Irish Research Council for the Humanities and Social Sciences 2000–; Trustee Political Studies Asscn UK 1979, Scarman Trust 1991–, Irish Political Studies Asscn 1991–; Chair Bryson House charity 1998–: Dir Democratic Dialogue 1996–; mem New York Acad of Sciences. *Publications:* Women's Rights at Work 1985, Equality, Politics and Gender (jtly) 1991, Citizenship and the European Community 1992, Citizenship and the European Community 1993, Free Movement Between Ireland and the UK 2000. *Leisure interests:* reading, classical music, travel. *Address:* Queen's University, Dept of Politics, Belfast BT7 1NN, UK. *Telephone:* (2890) 245133; *Fax:* (2890) 235373; *E-mail:* e.meehan@qub.ac.uk.

MEERAPFEL, Jeanine, PH D; German (b Argentine) film director, scriptwriter, producer and professor; b 14 June 1943, Buenos Aires. *Education:* Hochschule für Gestaltung (Ulm, Germany). *Career:* Journalist, Ed Buenos Aires 1961–64; living in Germany 1964–; teacher of film Adult Educ Centre, Ulm 1970–80; Prof Acad of Media Arts, Cologne 1990–; made first long feature 1980; Dir, Producer Malena Films GmbH, Berlin; freelance film critic; mem Acad of Arts, Berlin, European Film Academy; Film Artist Award, North-Rhine-Westphalia 2000. *Films:* Malou (winner FIPRESCI award, Cannes 1981, First Prize Young Filmmakers, San Sebastián, First Prize Collective, Chicago 1981) 1980, Im Land meiner Eltern (Golden Ducat, Mannheim Festival) 1981, Solange es Europa noch gibt—Fragen an den Frieden (with Peter Schäfer) 1983, Die Kümmeltürkin geht (Interfilms Award, Berlin, German Film Critics' Award) 1985, Die Verliebten 1986, Desembarcos—when memory speaks (City of Strasbourg Award) 1986–89, La Amiga (German Fed Award 1989, Peace Award, Berlin 1990) 1988, Amigomío (Wiliam Dieterle Award) 1990–1993, Anna's Summer 2000–01. *Address:* Kunsthochschule für Medien, Peter Welter Platz 2, 50676 Cologne, Germany (Office); Droysenstr 6, 10629 Berlin, Germany (Home). *Telephone:* (221) 201890 (Office); *Fax:* (221) 2018924 (Office); *E-mail:* meerapfel@khm.de; *Internet:* www.meerapfel .de.

MEERT, Marie-Paule; Belgian civil servant; b 1949, Brussels. *Education:* Free Univ of Brussels. *Career:* Freelance journalist, TV and radio dir until 1973; Spokesperson for PSC (Christian Social Party) Minister 1973, for various ministers 1973–79; Belgian Spokesperson UN Year of the Handicapped 1979; Press Sec to Minister 1980–84; joined Prime Minister's press office 1984, apptd Spokesperson for Prime Minister 1985; fmr Communication Dir Belgian Olympic Cttee; fmr Public Affairs Dir Burston-Marsteller, Brussels; currently Sr Consultant and mem Man Team European Communications Strategies (CS). *Leisure interests:* family, photography, arts, travel, sports. *Address:* CS, Chaussée de la Hulpe 189, 1170 Brussels, Belgium. *Telephone:* (2) 674-22-50; *Fax:* (2) 675-58-70; *E-mail:* mail@cs-brussels.com; *Internet:* www.cs-brussels.com.

MEGAWATI SUKARNOPUTRI; Indonesian Head of State; b 23 Jan 1947, Jogjakarta; d of the late Achmed Sukarno (Founding Pres of Indonesia) and Fatmawati; m 1st Surendro (deceased); m 2nd Hassan Gamal Ahmad Hassan; m 3rd Taufik Kiemas; three c. *Career:* Elected to House of Reps (Parl) 1987; Leader Partai Demokrasi Indonesia (Indonesian Democratic Party) 1993–96 (deposed); now Chair Partai Demokrasi Indonesia Perjuangan (PDI-P); Vice-Pres of Indonesia 1999–2001, Pres of Indonesia July 2001–. *Address:* Office of the President, Istana Merdeka, Jakarta, Indonesia; c/o Partai Demokrasi Indonesia, Jalan Diponegoro 58, Jakarta 10310, Indonesia. *Telephone:* (21) 3840946.

MEHL, Ulrike, DIP ENG; German politician; b 6 Aug 1956, Leibolz; m Ulrich Mehl 1980; two d. *Education:* Fachhochschule. *Career:* Mem staff Ministry of Agric and Forestry, State of Schleswig-Holstein 1978–80, State Office for the Environment, Schleswig-Holstein 1980–81; leader environmental campaign BUND 1982–83, State Chair then Deputy Fed Chair 1986–90; mem Bundestag (Parl, SPD) 1990, mem Cttee for Environment and Agric. *Publication:* Häuser im lebendigen Grün. *Leisure interests:* reading, nature, children. *Address:* Johannisstr 12, 24589 Nortorf, Germany.

MEI YI; Chinese government official and translator; b 1913, Shantou, Guangdong Prov. *Career:* Spokesman for CCP Del negotiating with CNP Govt and US Special Envoy Gen G. Marshall 1946–47; Deputy Ed-in-Chief Xinhua News Agency 1947–49; Dir State Broadcasting Admin Bureau 1952–66; Deputy, 1st NPC 1954–58, 2nd NPC 1958–64; Vice-Pres Journalists' Asscn 1954–66; Dir Planning Bureau of the Acad of Social Sciences 1979–; Vice-Pres Acad of Social Sciences 1980–86; Vice-Pres Overseas Chinese History Soc 1981–; mem Standing Cttee 6th NPC 1983–87; mem Cen Advisory Comm CCP Cen Cttee 1985–93; Ed-in-Chief Encyclopedia of China Publishing House; Pres Gerontological Soc of China 1986–. *Address:* Academy of Social Sciences, Jianguomenwai St, Beijing, People's Republic of China.

MEIDINGER-GEISE, Inge, D PHIL; German writer; b 16 March 1923, Berlin; d of the late Kurt and Irene (née Minsberg) Geise; m Konrad Meidinger 1946 (died 1979). *Education:* Univs of Berlin and Erlangen. *Career:* Has written over 50 books including essays, poems, radio plays and historical works 1954–; Chair Die Kogge (European Asscn of Writers) 1967–88, Hon Chair 1988–; mem PEN (Germany); awards include Kulturpreis Erlangen 1972, Literaturpreis Mölle (Sweden) 1979 and Wolfram-von-Eschenbach-Preis 1988. *Publications include:* Sündenbrand (plays) 1976, Alle Katzen sind nicht grau (short stories) 1982, Menuett in Schwarz (short stories) 1990, Bodenpreise (novel) 1993. *Leisure interest:* Baroque music. *Address:* Schobertweg 1A, 91056 Erlangen, Germany. *Telephone:* (9131) 41307.

MEIER MIRÓ-QUESADA, Martha Elvira; Peruvian journalist and photographer; b 12 Dec 1961, Lima; d of the late Konrad Dietrich Meier and of Marta Elvira Miró-Quesada de la Fuente. *Education:* Villa María School for Girls, and the Taller Armando Robles Godoy de Cinematografía (Lima). *Career:* Producer ADV-Peru, Full Sail Studios, FL, USA 1980–87; scientific and environmental journalist 1988–; Publr of scientific magazine for local newspaper 1988–89; Head Ecology Section El Comercio newspaper 1989; Consultant Peace, Women and the Environment Project and Communication and Culture for Women; Del Interamerican Conf on Women and the Environment 1991; mem Bd of Dirs Servicios Editoriales de Edición—SED, Establecimiento Gráfico AMAUTA; FAO Award 1990; City of Qusqo (Cuzco) Award 1991; Benjamin Roca Muelle Award, Nat Chamber of Tourism 1991; Kukuli Press Award, Nat Episcopate Council 1991. *Publications:* Woman and the Environment in Peru (OAS) 1991; various articles and essays for magazines and newspapers. *Leisure interests:* horse-riding, painting, medicinal herb gardening. *Address:* Diario El Comercio, Jirón Antonio Miró Quesada 300, Lima 1, Peru. *Telephone:* (14) 287660; *Fax:* (14) 310810.

MEIN, Joy, OBE; Australian political administrator; d of S. B. Newman; m Ian Pulteney 1941 (died 1979); one s one d. *Education:* St Margaret's School. *Career:* Chair Fed Strategy Cttee, Liberal Party of Australia 1975, mem Fed Exec Cttee 1976–90, Pres Victoria Br 1976–79, Fed Vice-Pres 1979–90; State Treas and Chair Women's Affairs Group PDU 1983–; Chair Int Women's Democrat Union 1990–; Chair Australia Britain Soc 1992–98. *Leisure interests:* golf, music. *Address:* Flat 6, 116 Anderson St, South Yarra, Vic 3141, Australia.

MEISAMI, Julie Scott, PH D; American lecturer in Persian; b 29 July 1937, Berkeley, CA; d of Victor Roland and Muriel Ann (née Drake) Anderson; m E. Meisami 1967 (divorced 1988); two d. *Education:* Berkeley High School and Univ of California at Berkeley. *Career:* Researcher American Univ in Cairo 1962–63; Lecturer Univ of Teheran 1971–80; Researcher, CA 1980–85; Lecturer in Persian, Faculty of Oriental Studies, Fellow Wolfson Coll, Univ of Oxford 1985–; Nat Endowment for the Humanities Grants 1984, 1985, 1989–91, 1995–97; Persian Heritage Foundation Award 1985; Fellow Wolfson Coll, Oxford 1985. *Publications:* Medieval Persian Court Poetry 1987, The Sea of Precious Virtue (trans) 1991, Nizami, the Haft Paykar (trans) 1995; numerous articles and reviews for literary journals. *Leisure interests:* reading, travel. *Address:* The Oriental Institute, Pusey Lane, Oxford OX1 2LE, UK. *Telephone:* (1865) 278200; *Fax:* (1865) 278190; *E-mail:* meisami@server.orient.ox.ac.uk.

MEJÍA, Cecilia, MBA; Colombian business executive and government official; b 27 March 1945, Bogotá; d of Jorge and Julia (née Hernández) Mejía. *Education:* Convent of the Sacred Heart (Greenwich, CT), Univ de los Andes (Bogotá) and Columbia Univ (NY, USA). *Career:* Publr, Propr Editorial Jeroglífico 1977–; Man Consultant 1977–; Researcher Fedesarrollo, econs research inst 1977–81; Dir Business Man Programs, Univ de los Andes 1981–84, Nat Bldg Fund, Ministry of Public Works 1987–90; Exec Resurgir Bogotá 1985–86; Exec Dir Fundación Horizontes 1993; Amb Columbia Univ Business Grads Abroad 1987–; mem Bd of Dirs Nat Landmarks Comm 1987–89, Nat Calamities Prevention Fund 1987–89, Paz de Río 1992. *Leisure interests:* horse-riding, photography, travel. *Address:* Carrera 9 No 75-50, Santa Fe de Bogotá, Colombia. *Telephone:* (1) 212-8962; *Fax:* (1) 212-7381.

MEJÍA, María Emma; Colombian politician. *Career:* Fmr Minister of Educ, Minister of Foreign Affairs 1996–98; Presl Cand 1998; apptd a govt rep to negotiations with FARC 1999. *Address:* Ministry of Foreign Affairs, Palacio de San Carlos, Calle 10A, No 5-51, Santa Fe de Bogotá, Colombia. *Telephone:* (1) 282-7811; *Fax:* (1) 341-6777.

MELANDRI, Giovanna, B ECONS; Italian politician; b 28 Jan 1962, New York, USA. *Career:* Co-ordinator Industrial and Tech Policy Unit, Montedison 1983–87; Head Int Office Legambiente (Environmental League) and Chair Scientific Cttee 1988–94; mem Italian Del to Conf on Sustainable Devt, Bergen 1990, to UN Conf on Environment and Devt, Rio de Janeiro 1992; mem Exec Cttee Legambiente 1982–89, Nat Secr 1989–; mem Nat Exec Cttee Partito Democratico Socialista (PDS) 1991–, Democratici di Sinistra 1998–; mem Exec with responsibility for Communications Policy 1996–; mem Camera dei Deputati 1994–; Minister of Culture 1998–2000; fmr mem Progressisti-Federativo Group, in charge of work on bioethics and assisted reproduction, External Cttee to Special Comm on Child Welfare, fmr Pres Cttee on Human Rights, fmr mem Comm on Culture; del to first UN World Forum on TV 1997; Pres Madre Provetta 1995–99; f Italian Emily's List 1998; ed Ambiente Italia (annual environmental report of Legambiente) 1989–94, Italian World Watch Magazine 1986–91, Digitalia, l'ultima rivoluzione 1998; mem editorial cttee Tomorrow and La Nuova Ecologia environmental periodicals 1986–91, Madre Provetta News 1997–. *Address:* c/o Ministero per i beni e le attività culturali, Via del Collegio Romano 27, 00186 Rome, Italy.

MELEAGROU, Evie (Ivi), BA; Cypriot writer; b 27 May 1928, Nicosia; d of Efstathios Hadjidemetriou and Euridice Akritas; m Ioannis Meleagros 1952; two d one s. *Education:* Pancyprian Gymnasium (Nicosia), Athenerum Inst (Athens), Ecole de St Joseph (Nicosia) and Univ of London (UK). *Career:* Secondary school teacher of English and French 1947–52; broadcaster 1952–55; Ed Cyprus Chronicles literary magazine 1960–72, George Seferis' works 1969–72; Pres Pancyprian Women's Asscn 1974–81; Official Rep World Writers' Conf 1965, Panhellenic Congress on the Status of Women 1975, TV discussion on Cyprus, Greece 1984; public speaker on Cyprus in many countries; numerous TV appearances in UK, USA, Norway, Lebanon, France, etc; First Prize Pancyprian Short Story Competition 1952, Pancyprian Novella Competition 1957, Cyprus Nat Novel Award 1970, 1981, Hellenic Nat Novel Award 1981. *Publications:* Solomos Family 1957, Anonymous City (short stories) 1963, Eastern Mediterranean 1969, Conversation With Che 1970, Penultimate Era 1980, Persona is the Unknown Cypriot Woman (essays and poetry) 1994, The Virgin Plunge in the Ocean Depths (short stories and novellas) 1996; short stories have been translated into English, German, Russian and Hungarian. *Leisure interests:* country walking, swimming, travel, philosophy. *Address:* 22 Mesolongi St, Nicosia 100, Cyprus. *Telephone:* (2) 463507.

MELLINK, Machteld Johanna, PH D; Netherlands archaeologist; b 26 Oct 1917, Amsterdam; d of Johan Kellink and Machteld Kruyff. *Education:* Univs of Amsterdam and Utrecht. *Career:* Field Asst Tarsus excavations 1947–49; Asst Prof of Classical Archeology Bryn Mawr Coll 1949–53, Assoc Prof, Chair Dept of Classical and Near Eastern Archeology 1953–62, Prof 1962–88, Prof Emer 1988–; mem staff Gordion excavations organized by Pennsylvania Univ Museum 1950, during which the putative tomb of King Midas was discovered 1957; Field Dir Excavations at Karataş-Semayük in Lycia 1963–; excavator archaic and Graeco-Persian painted tombs near Elmali 1969–; Adviser Troy excavations, Univs of Tübingen and Cincinnati 1988–; Pres Archaeological Inst of America 1981–84; Vice-Pres American Research Inst in Turkey 1980–, Pres 1988–92; Hon LL D (Pennsylvania) 1987; Hon D HIST (Eskişehir, Turkey) 1990; L. Wharton Drexel Medal

1994. *Publications:* Hyakinthos 1943, Archaeology in Anatolia (reports in American Journal of Archaeology) 1955–93, A Hittite Cemetery at Gordion 1956, Dark Ages and Nomads 1964 (ed), Frühe Stufen der Kunst (jtly) 1974, Troy and the Trojan War (ed) 1986, Elmali-Karataş (Vol I, ed) 1992, (Vol II, ed) 1994. *Address:* Dept of Classical and Near Eastern Archaeology, Bryn Mawr College, Bryn Mawr, PA 19010-2899, USA; 264 Montgomery Ave, Haverford, PA 19041, USA (Home). *Telephone:* (610) 526-5339 (Office); (610) 642-3896 (Home); *Fax:* (610) 526-7479 (Office).

MELLOR, Julie Thérèse, B SC, MA; British equal opportunities director; b 29 Jan 1957, Bedford; d of Edward Vernon and the late Patricia Mellor; m Nicholas Reed 1990; one s one d. *Education:* Winchester County High School for Girls, Brasenose Coll (Oxford) and Cornell Univ (Ithaca, NY, USA). *Career:* Teacher Educ Research on Women and Work 1979–81; Employee Relations Adviser, Shell 1981–83; Employment Devt Officer London Borough of Islington 1983–84; Deputy Head of Contract Compliance on Equal Opportunities, GLC 1984–86; Employment Policy Adviser Inner London Educ Authority 1986–89; Equal Opportunities Man TSB 1989–92; apptd Dir of Equal Opportunities and Human Resources Dir British Gas PLC 1992–96; owner and prin consultant Julie Mellor Assocs 1996–99; Chair Equal Opportunities Comm 1999–, launched Valuing Women (campaign for equal pay) 1999, Equal Pay Task Force 1999; Commr Comm for Racial Equality 1995–; mem Bd Employers' Forum on Disability; Trustee Youth at Risk; Eleanor Emerson Fellow in Labour Educ, Cornell Univ 1979–81. *Leisure interests:* theatre, travel, food, family. *Address:* Equal Opportunities Commission, 36 Broadway, London SW1H 0XH, UK; Overseas House, Quay St, Manchester M3 3HN, UK. *Telephone:* (20) 7222-1110; *Fax:* (20) 7222-2810; *E-mail:* julie.mellor@eoc.org.uk; *Internet:* www.eoc.org.uk.

MENA DE QUEVEDO, Margarita, DR IUR; Colombian politician; b Concordia, Antioquía; m José Ignacio Quevedo. *Education:* Univ of Medellín (Antioquia). *Career:* Specialist in commercial and econ law; Pvt Sec Ministry of Public Works; Head of Personnel Superintendence of Socys; Vice-Pres Council of Medellín; Sec of Educ for Antioquía; Vice-Minister Mines and Energy, then Minister of Mines and Energy 1989–90. *Address:* c/o Ministry of Mines and Energy, Centro Administrativo Nacional, Avda Eldorado, Bogotá, Colombia.

MENA RIVERA, Julia; Nicaraguan politician; b 1951. *Career:* Vice-Pres Nat Ass 1995; mem Ind Liberal Party. *Address:* c/o Office of the Vice-President, Casa de Gobierno, Apdo 2398, Managua, Nicaragua.

MENCHÚ TÚM, Rigoberta; Guatemalan human rights activist; b 9 Jan 1959, San Miguel Uspantán; d of the late Vicente and Juana Menchú; m Angel Canil 1995; two c. *Career:* Began campaigning for rights for Indians as a teenager; fled to Mexico after parents and brother murdered by security forces 1980; Founder Guatemalan Opposition in Exile (RUOG), Nat Cttee for Reconciliation 1987; co-ordinated American Continent's Five Hundred Years of Resistance Campaign against 500th anniversary of arrival of Columbus in Americas 1992; Int Goodwill Amb UNESCO 1996–; mem UN Int Indian Treaty Council; Nobel Peace Prize 1992. *Publication:* I, Rigoberta (trans into 12 languages) 1983. *Address:* c/o Vicente Menchú Foundation, POB 5274, Berkeley, CA 94705, USA.

MENDOZA, June Yvonne, AO, RP; Australian portrait painter; b Melbourne; d of John Morton and Dot Mendoza; m Keith Mackrell 1960; three d one s. *Education:* Lauriston School for Girls (Melbourne) and St Martin's School of Art (London). *Career:* Portraits include HM Queen Elizabeth II, HM Queen Elizabeth, the Queen Mother, HRH The Prince of Wales, HRH The Princess of Wales, Margaret Thatcher, Lee Kuan Yew, Vigdís Finnbogadóttir, Corazón Aquino and numerous other govt, academic, regimental, theatrical, sporting and industrial personalities, internationally known musicians, large boardroom and family groups; large canvas for the House of Commons (440 portraits) of the House in session, for Australian House of Reps (170 portraits) for Parl, Canberra; has made numerous TV appearances and lectures regularly in UK and overseas; mem Royal Inst of Oil Painters, Royal Soc of Portrait Painters; Hon mem Soc of Women Artists; Hon D LITT (Bath) 1986, (Loughborough); Freedom of City of London 1997. *Exhibitions include:* solo exhibition Mall Galleries, London 1999. *Leisure*

interests: classical and jazz music, theatre. *Address:* 34 Inner Park Rd, London SW19 6DD, UK. *Telephone:* (20) 8788-7826 (Home); *Fax:* (20) 8780-0728 (Home).

MENEGOZ, Margaret; French film producer; b 21 April 1941, Hungary. *Career:* Co-Dir Films du Losange; Producer of all Eric Rohmer's films, and of films by Andrzej Wajda, Volker Schlöndorff and Wim Wenders. *Films include:* La Marquise d'O 1975, L'ami americain 1977, Flocons d'or 1978, Le passe-montagne 1979, Aurelia Steiner Vancouver 1979, Petit Pierre 1980, Le pont du nord 1981, Comédies et proverbes 1 1981, 2 1982, 3 1982, 4 1984, 5 1985, 6 1986, Mauvaise conduite 1983, De bruit et de fureur 1987, Europa Europa 1989, Louis, enfant roi 1991, Lautrec 1997, Pan tadeusz 1998, La saison des hommes 1999, La vierge des tueurs 1999. *Address:* Films du Losange, 22 ave Pierre I de Serbie, 75116 Paris, France. *Telephone:* (1) 44-43-87-12; *Fax:* (1) 49-52-06-40; *E-mail:* p.fief@filmsdulosange.fr; *Internet:* www.filmsdulosange.fr.

MENKEN, Jane Ava, PH D; American professor of sociology and demography; b 29 Nov 1939; d of Isaac Nathan and Rose Ida (Sarvetnick) Golubitsky; m Matthew Menken 1960 (divorced 1985), m Richard Jessor; one s one d. *Education:* Univ of Pennsylvania, Harvard and Princeton Univs. *Career:* Mem research staff Office of Population Research, Princeton Univ (NJ) 1969–71, 1975–87, Asst Dir 1978–86, Assoc Dir 1986–87, Prof of sociology 1980–82, of sociology and public affairs 1982–87; Prof of sociology and demography Univ of Pennsylvania 1987–, Dir Population Studies Center 1989–; mem Bd Dirs Alan Guttmacher Inst 1981–90, 1993–, population advisory cttee Rockefeller Foundation 1981–93, cttee on population 1983–85, on nat statistics 1983–89, on AIDS research 1987–94; mem Child Health and Human Devt Council 1988–91, Comm on Behavioral and Social Sciences and Educ 1991–; Co-Chair panal data and research priorities for arresting AIDS in Sub-Saharan Africa 1994–; John Simon Guggenheim Foundation Fellow 1992–93; Center for Advanced Study in Behavioral Sciences Fellow 1995–. *Publications:* Mathematical Models of Conception and Birth (jtly) 1973, Natural Fertility (ed) 1979, Teenage Sexuality, Pregnancy and Childbearing 1981, World Population and US Policy: The Choices Ahead 1986; contributes to professional journals. *Address:* Population Studies Center, University of Pennsylvania, 3718 Locust Walk, Philadelphia, PA 19104-6298, USA.

MENKES, Suzy Peta, MA; British journalist and author; b 24 Dec 1943, Beaconsfield; d of Edouard and Betty Curtis (née Lightfoot) Menkes; m David Spanier (died 2000); three s one d. *Education:* Brighton and Hove High School and Newnham Coll (Cambridge). *Career:* Jr Reporter The Times 1966–69, Fashion Ed 1979–87; Fashion Ed The Evening Standard 1968–77; Women's Ed Daily Express 1977–79; Fashion Ed The Independent 1987–88, Int Herald Tribune 1988–; writes monthly column in the Tribune and The New York Times; British Press Awards Commendations 1983, 1984; Freedom, City of Milan 1986, City of London 1987; Eugenia Sheppard Award for Fashion Journalism, Council of Fashion Designers of America. *Publications include:* The Royal Jewels 1985, The Windsor Style 1987, Queen and Country 1992. *Leisure interests:* family life, royal history, Indian history, reading, opera. *Address:* c/o International Herald Tribune, 6 bis rue des Graviers, 92521 Neuilly, Cedex, France. *Telephone:* (1) 41-43-94-28; *Fax:* (1) 41-43-93-38; *E-mail:* smenkes@iht.com.

MENYHÁRD, Nora Anna, D SC; Hungarian physicist; b 26 March 1935, Budapest; d of I. Menyhárd; m Peter Szèpfalusy 1963; one s. *Education:* Loránd Eötvös Univ (Budapest). *Career:* Scientific Researcher into dynamic critical phenomena 1966–67; Scientist Univ des Saarlandes, Germany 1978–79, 1982–83; Head Solid State Physics Dept, Inst for Solid State Physics 1991–95; current research interest numerical simulations of non-equilibrium phase transitions; has written over 50 articles for int physics journals. *Leisure interests:* music, hiking, dogs. *Address:* Inst for Solid State Physics, 1525 Budapest, POB 49, Hungary. *Telephone:* (1) 165-4707; *Fax:* (1) 155-1193.

MERCIER, Eileen Ann, MA, MBA; Canadian financial executive; b 7 July 1947, Toronto; d of Thomas S. (Paddy) and Frances K. Falconer; m Ernest C. Mercier 1980; two step-s two step-d one s. *Education:* Waterloo Lutheran Univ (ON), Univ of Alberta, Inst of Canadian Bankers (Toronto) and York Univ. *Career:* Worked for Toronto-

Dominion Bank Corp Finance Div, Capital Group 1972–78; Dir US Communications Operations Canwest Capital Corpn 1978–81; Man Corp Finance, Strategy and Planning Gulf Canada Ltd 1981–86; Vice-Pres The Pagurian Corpn 1986–87; Vice-Pres Corp Devt Abitibi-Price Inc 1987–90, Sr Vice-Pres, Chief Financial Officer 1990–95; Pres Finvoy Man Inc 1995–; mem Bd of Dirs CGI Group Inc, Teekay Shipping Corpn, C. I. Covington Fund Inc, Quebecur World Inc, Winpak Ltd; Vice-Chair Workplace Safety Insurance Bd of On; mem Bd of Govs York Univ; Trustee Univ Health Network; Fellow of the Inst of Canadian Bankers; Business Leader of the Year Award, Wilfrid Laurier Univ 1991. *Leisure interests:* golf, travel, the arts. *Address:* 199 Cranbrooke Ave, ON M5M 1M6, Canada. *Telephone:* (416) 487-3106; *Fax:* (416) 487-6114; *E-mail:* eileen_mercier@wsib.on.ca.

MERCIER, Michèle Jocelyne Yvonne Renée; French actress; b 1 Jan 1939, Nice; d of René-Emile and Francia Mercier; m Claude Bourillot (divorced). *Career:* Dancer at Opéra de Nice 1947 and Théâtre des Champs-Elysées (Ballets de la Tour Eiffel) 1954; numerous film appearances in French, Italian, British and American films. *Films include:* Tirez sur le pianiste 1960, Fury at Smugglers Bay, A Global Affair, La Marquise des Anges, Merveilleuse Angélique 1964, Le tonnerre de Dieu 1965, La seconde vérité, Angélique et le Roi, Soleil noir 1966, Le plus vieux métier du monde 1966, Comment j'ai appris à aimer les femmes 1967, Indomptable Angélique, Une corde et un colt, Lady Hamilton, Angélique et le Sultan 1968, Une veuve en or 1969, Les baroudeurs 1970, Macédoine 1971, L'appel de la forêt 1972, Les femmes du monde 1977, Goetz de Berlichingen 1978, Jeans tonic 1984, La Rumbera 1998; *Publication:* Angélique à cœur perdu 1988, Angéliquement vôtre 1996. *Address:* c/o Cabinet d'Affaires ACR, BP 32, 91490 Milly-la-Fôret, France.

MERCURE, Monique, OC, B MUS; Canadian actress; b 14 Nov 1930, Montréal, PQ; d of Eugene and Yvonne Emond; m Pierre Mercure 1949; three c. *Education:* Ecole Supérieure de Musique d'Outrement, Ecole Jacques Le Coq (Paris, France) and Montréal Drama Studio. *Career:* Has performed at Théâtre de l'Egregore, Théâtre du Nouveau Monde, Comédie Canadienne, Prairie Theatre, Nat Arts Centre (Ottawa), Stratford Festival, Free Theatre (Toronto), Alliance Theatre (Atlanta, GA, USA), Théâtre de Quatre, Théâtre Nat de Strasbourg (France); Visiting Lecturer l'Ecole Nat de Théâtre 1978, 1980, 1983; Dir-Gen Nat Theatre School of Canada 1991–; Gov Gen Award for Performing Arts 1993; Québec's Denise-Pelletier Award for Performing Arts 1993; Gascon-Roux Award for Best Actor 1993. *Plays include:* Le pélican, Summer and Smoke, Une femme douce, Magie rouge, Les maxibules, La paix du dimanche, The Maids, Un simple soldat, Le soulier de satin, Man for Man, Orphée, The Trojan Women, Les belles sœurs, Quatre à quatre, Equus, Le père humilié, Le balcon, For Ever Yours Marie Lou, Le journal d'un four, Patriote, Le pays du dragon, Toi et tes nuages, Les richesses naturelles, The Saga of the Wet Hens, Night of the Iguana, Les Dialogues des Carmélites, Memoir; *Films include:* Felix Leclerc Troubadour, Ce n'est pas le temps des romans (Prix de la critique, Tours Festival), Mon oncle Antoine, J. A. Martin Photographe (Palme d'Or, Cannes Film Festival, Etrog Award, Canadian Film), The Third Walker, La chanson de Roland, Quintet, La quarantaine. *Address:* 1, 440 Bonsecours, Montréal, PQ H2Y 3C4, Canada.

MEREDITH, Gwenyth Valmai, OBE, BA; Australian former playwright; b 18 Nov 1907, NSW; d of George and Florence Meredith; m Ainsworth Harrison 1938. *Education:* Sydney Girls' High School and Univ of Sydney. *Career:* Freelance writer; scriptwriter Australian Broadcasting Comm 1942–76; cr radio serials The Lawsons and Blue Hills; Propr Chelsea Book Club, Sydney 1932–39. *Publications include:* Novels: The Lawsons, Blue Hills, Beyond Blue Hills, Into the Sun; Travel Book: Inns and Outs; Plays: Wives Have Their Uses, Great Inheritance. *Leisure interests:* painting, gardening, fishing, bridge. *Address:* Unit 45, Kenilworth Gardens, Kangaloon Rd, Bowral, NSW 2576, Australia.

MERHAUTOVÁ, Anežka, PH D, D SC; Czech art historian; b 29 Dec 1919, Hranice; d of the late Marie Křístková; m 1st Mr Livora 1943; one d one s; m 2nd Mr Merhaut 1951. *Education:* Secondary school in Hranice, school for social assistants and Charles Univ (Prague). *Career:* Asst Cardiological Soc, Prague 1941–45; worked at Nat Gallery and Inst for the Protection of Monuments 1949–52; at Inst of Art History and

Acad of Sciences, Prague 1952–79; now retd; State Prize; Odeon Prize; F. Palacký Medal 2000. *Publications:* Bazilika sv Jiří na Pražském hradě 1966, Einfache mitteleuropäische Rundkirchen 1970, Romanische Kunst in Polen, der Tschech… 1974, Románské umění v Čechách a na Moravě (jtly) 1984, Vznik a význam svatovàclavské přilly 2000, Europas Mitte um 1000 (articles) 2000. *Leisure interest:* Romanesque architecture. *Address:* Institute of Art History, Dvouletky 341, 100 00 Prague, Czech Republic. *Telephone:* (2) 7820953.

MERKEL, Angela, DR RER NAT; German politician; b 17 July 1954, Hamburg. *Education:* Univ of Leipzig. *Career:* Research Assoc Zentralinstitut für physikalische Chemie, Berlin 1978–90; joined Demokratischer Aufbruch (DA) 1989, Press Officer 1990; Deputy Spokesperson for GDR 1990; joined CDU 1990, Deputy Fed Chair 1991–98, Gen Sec 1998–2000, Chair 2000–; mem Bundestag 1990–; Minister for Women and Youth 1991–94, for Family, Women, Youth and Sr Citizens 1994, Minister of the Environment, Nature Conservation and Nuclear Safety 1994–98. *Address:* CDU, 53113 Bonn, Konrad-Adenauer-Haus, Friedrich-Ebert-Allee 73–75, Germany. *Telephone:* (228) 5440; *Fax:* (228) 544216; *E-mail:* organisation@cdu.de; *Internet:* www.cdu.de.

MERLE, Carole; French skier; b 24 Jan 1964, Barcelonnette; d of Jean-Claude and Geneviève (née Michel) Merle; m Philippe Pellet 1991. *Education:* Lycée de Barcelonnette. *Career:* Professional skier since 1979; French Champion Giant Slalom 1985, 1987, combination and downhill 1987; Silver Medal Giant Slalom World Championships, Vail, CO, USA 1989; Super Giant Slalom Champion since 1990; Silver Medal Super Giant Slalom, Saalbach, Austria 1991; World Cup Giant Slalom Champion 1992; Silver Medal Olympic Games, Albertville, France 1992; Gold Medal World Championships, Morioka, Japan 1993; Chevalier de la Légion d'Honneur; Chevalier de l'Ordre Nat du Mérite. *Leisure interests:* reading, music, cooking, horse riding, sailing. *Address:* Fédération Française de Ski, 50 rue des Marquisats, 74000 Annecy, France (Office); Hôtel le Pyjama, Super Sauzé, 04400 Barcelonnette, France (Home).

MERNISSI, Fátima, PH D; Moroccan sociologist and writer; b 1941, Fez. *Education:* Univ of Paris (Sorbonne) and in the USA. *Career:* Sociologist, feminist and expert in the Koran; Prof Univ Mohammed V, Rabat. *Publications include:* Fear of Modernity or The Political Harem, Dreams on the Threshold. *Address:* University Mohammed V, BP 554, 3 rue Michelifen, Agdal, Rabat, Morocco.

MERRIL, Judith; American writer, broadcaster and anthologist; b 21 Jan 1923, New York; d of Samuel Solomon and Ethel Grossman; two c. *Education:* City Coll of New York and Rochdale Coll (Toronto, ON, Canada). *Career:* Teacher Rochdale Coll, Univ of Toronto, SEED School, Wesleyan Univ and Trent Univ, Canada; Writer-in-Residence Centennial Coll, Toronto Public Libraries 1987, Brampton Public Libraries 1989; Univ of Toronto 1991–92; Founder and Resource Person Spaced-Out Library; has written numerous TV and radio documentaries and commentaries including 108 mini-documentaries for TV Ontario, Doctor Who and radio documentaries for CBC; Dir Stafford Beer Foundation, Hiroshima-Nagasaki Relived; mem Toronto Anti-Intervention Coalition, Writers' Union of Canada, PEN, Speculative Writers' Asscn of Canada; Fourth Annual Canadian Science Fiction and Fantasy Award 1983; Casper Award 1986; 1990 Milford Award for Lifetime Achievement in Science Fiction and Fantasy Editing. *Publications include:* Shadow on the Hearth 1950, Gunner Cade (jtly) 1952, Outpost Mars (jtly) 1952, The Tomorrow People 1960, Out of Bounds 1963, Daughters of Earth 1969, The Best of Judith Merril 1976, Survival Ship 1977, Daughters of Earth and other stories 1985; Edited: Science fiction: Shot in the Dark 1950, Beyond Human Ken 1952, Beyond the Barriers of Space and Time 1954, Human? 1954, Galaxy of Ghouls 1955, The Year's Greatest Science Fiction and Fantasy (vols 1–12) 1956–68; Science fiction: The Best of the Best 1967, England Swings SF 1968, Tesseracts 1985. *Leisure interests:* conversation, reading, music, dancing, water sports, grandchildren. *Address:* 40 St George St, Toronto, ON M5S 2E4, Canada.

MESLEM, Chafika; Algerian United Nations official; b 2 Oct 1934, Algiers; three d. *Education:* Univ of Algiers. *Career:* Minister Plenipotentiary, Deputy Chief Div of Int Orgs and Chief of Service for Multilateral Co-operation 1971–77; Deputy Perm Rep to UN in charge of

UNCTAD, Geneva, Switzerland 1977–81, Deputy Sec-Gen Third Women's World Conf, Nairobi, Kenya 1983–85, Dir Div for the Advancement of Women 1981–87; Dir Div for Economic Co-operation among Developing Countries and Special Programmes 1995; contribs to UN journals. *Address:* Buchleitengasse 3/2A/5, 1180 Vienna, Austria.

MESPLÉ, Magdeleine (Mady); French opera singer and teacher; b 7 March 1931, Toulouse; d of Pierre and Yvonne (née Sesquière) Mesplé; m 1st René Guedon 1957; one d; m 2nd Raymond Dawalibi 1983 (divorced). *Education:* Inst Sainte-Elisabeth and Conservatoire Nat de Musique (Toulouse). *Career:* Coloratura Soprano 1952–; made debut Liège, Belgium 1952; has appeared at major opera houses including Théâtre de la Monnaie, Brussels 1954, Opéra de Paris 1956–, Bolshoi Theatre, Moscow, USSR (now Russian Fed) 1972, Palais Royal 1972, Metropolitan Opera, New York, USA 1973, Aix en Provence festival; teacher Conservatoire Nat de Région de St-Maur-des-Fossés, Bordeaux, Lyon, Conservatoire Européen, Paris; has taught masterclasses in Toronto, Beijing, Shanghai, Taipei, Hong Kong, La Réunion etc; mem jury for numerous int competitions including Washington, Bucharest, Paris, Cologne, Bilbao, Toronto; has had works written for her by Betsy Jolas, Maurice Ohana, Charles Chaynes; Officier de la Légion d'Honneur; Commdr de l'Ordre Nat du Mérite; Commdr des Arts et des Lettres. *Performances include:* Lakmé 1952, Lucia di Lammermoor 1960, Il était une fois l'operette 1972, 1974, Les Dialogues des Carmélites, Guillaume Tell, Le Barbier de Séville, Rigoletto, Les contes d'Hoffman, Elégie pour jeunes amants, Cloches de Corneville, Vie Parisienne, Les Saltimbanques; *Recordings include:* Lakmé, Werther, Véronique, Valses de Vienne, Le maître de chapelle, Les Saltimbanques, Art de la coloratura (No 1 Airs français, No 2 Airs italiens); *TV includes:* Château des Carpathes. *Leisure interests:* travel, animals. *Address:* 9 bis rue Girardon, 75018 Paris, France. *Telephone:* (1) 42-23-67-49; *Fax:* (1) 42-23-67-49.

MESSAGER, Annette; French artist; b 30 Nov 1943, Berck-sur-Mer; d of André and Marie L. (née Chalessin) Messager. *Education:* Ecole Nat Supérieure des Arts Décoratifs. *Career:* Solo exhibitions include Munich, Germany 1973, Grenoble 1973, Musée d'Art Moderne, Paris 1974, 1984, 1995, Rheinisches Landesmuseum, Bonn 1976, 1978, Galerie Seriaal, Amsterdam, Netherlands 1977, Holly Solomon Gallery, New York 1978, Galérie Gillespie-Laage, Paris 1979, 1980, Fine Arts Gallery, Univ of California at Irvine, San Francisco Museum of Modern Art 1981 and PS 1 New York, Galerie Hans Mayer, Düsseldorf, Germany 1981, Artist's Space, New York 1982, Musée des Beaux-Arts, Calais, Galérie Gillespie-Laage-Salomon, Paris 1983, 1988, Vienna and Zurich, Switzerland 1984, Riverside Studio, London 1985, Galerie Gillespie-Laage-Salomon, Sydney, Australia 1985, Consortium Dijon 1988, Centre d'Art Contemporain, Castres 1988, Musée de Grenoble 1989, Musée de la Roche sur Yon, Musée de Rochechouart, Bonner Kunstverein and Düsseldorf Kunstverein, Germany, Galerie Crousel-Robelin, Paris 1990, Galerie Elisabette Kaufmann, Basel, Switzerland, Mercer Union, Cold City Gallery, Toronto, Canada 1991, Arnolfini, Bristol, UK 1992, LACMA, Los Angeles, USA 1995, Museum of Modern Art, New York 1995–96, Art Inst of Chicago, USA 1996, CAPC, Bordeaux 1996, Larry Gagosian Gallery, New York 1997, Musée des Arts d'Afrique et d'Océanie, Paris 1998, Museo Nacional Centro de Arte Reina Sofia, Madrid 1999, Galerie Marian Goodman, Paris 2000; Chevalier des Arts et des Lettres. *Address:* 146 blvd Camelinat, 92240 Malakoff, France. *Telephone:* (4) 42-53-45-77.

MÉSZÁROS, Marta; Hungarian film director; b 19 Sept 1931, Budapest; d of László Mészáros; m 2nd Jan Nowicki. *Education:* Moscow Film School (USSR, now Russian Fed). *Career:* Emigrated with family to USSR 1936; now lives in Hungary; Golden Bear Award OCIC 1975; Béla Balázs Prize 1977; Artist of Merit 1989. *Films include:* End of September 1973, Free Breath 1973, Adopted Child 1975, Nine Months 1976, The Two of Them 1977, En Route 1979, Heritage 1980, Diary for my Children 1982, Fata Morgana Land 1983, Diary for my Loves 1986, Diary III 1989. *Address:* c/o MAFILM Studio, 1149 Budapest, Lumumba ut 174, Hungary. *Telephone:* (1) 183-1750.

METCALF, Laurie; American actress; b 16 June 1955, Edwardsville, IL. *Education:* Illinois State Univ. *Career:* Original mem Steppenwolf Theatre Co; has acted in plays on Broadway, New York, Chicago and Los Angeles. *Films include:* Desperately Seeking Susan 1985, Making Mr

Right, Candy Mountain, Stars and Bars, Miles from Home, Uncle Buck, Internal Affairs, Pacific Heights, Frankie and Johnny, JFK, Mistress, A Dangerous Woman, Blink, Leaving Las Vegas, (voice) Toy Story, Hellcab, U-Turn, Scream, Bulworth, Toy Story 2, Runaway Bride 1999; *TV appearances include:* Roseanne (series, three Emmy Awards 1992–94), The Execution of Raymond Graham (film) 1985, Dharma & Greg 1997, King of the Hill 1997, The Norm Show (series) 1999, (voice) God, The Devil and Bob 2000. *Address:* c/o ICM, 8942 Wilshire Blvd, Beverly Hills, CA 90211, USA.

METGE, Dame (Alice) Joan, DBE, PH D; New Zealand anthropologist; b 21 Feb 1930, Auckland; d of the late Cedric Leslie and of Alice Mary (née Rigg) Metge. *Education:* Matamata Dist High School, Epsom Girls' Grammar School, Univ of Auckland and LSE (UK). *Career:* Jr Lecturer in Geography Univ of Auckland 1952; engaged in studies and fieldwork 1953–61; Lecturer Univ Extension, Univ of Auckland 1961–64; Sr Lecturer in Anthropology Victoria Univ of Wellington 1965–67, Assoc Prof 1968–88, Capt James Cook Research Fellow 1981–83, Hon Fellow of Anthropology 1988–94; Hutchinson Medal, LSE 1959; Elsdon Best Memorial Medal, Polynesian Soc 1987; NZ Commemoration Medal 1990; Te Rangi Hiroa Medal, Royal Soc of NZ 1997. *Publications:* A New Maori Migration 1964, The Maoris of New Zealand 1976, Talking Past Each Other (jtly) 1978, In and Out of Touch 1986, Te Kohao o Te Ngira 1990, New Growth from Old 1995, Korero Tahi (Talking Together) 2001. *Leisure interests:* drama, literature, gardening. *Address:* 3 Mariri Rd, Onehunga, Auckland 1006, New Zealand. *Telephone:* (9) 634-5757; *Fax:* (9) 634-4172.

METZLER-ARNOLD, Ruth, LIC IUR, LL M; Swiss accountant and politician; b 23 May 1964, Sursee; m Lukas Metzler-Arnold 1991. *Education:* Univ of Freiburg. *Career:* Began career as accountant with UBS Berne 1989–90; accountant PriceWaterhouseCoopers PLC (St Gallen) 1990–99; Dist Judge, Appenzell 1992–95, Cantonal Judge 1995–96; Govt Councillor and Dir of Finance, Canton of Appenzell 1996–99, mem Bd Dirs of Finance 1999–; elected Fed Councillor March 1999; Dir Ministry, Fed Dept of Justice and Police March 1999–. *Leisure interests:* skiing, hiking, scuba diving. *Address:* Bundeshaus-West, Bundesgasse, 3003 Bern, Switzerland. *Telephone:* (31) 3224002; *Fax:* (31) 3227832; *E-mail:* ruth.metzler-arnold@gs-ejpd.admin.ch; *Internet:* www.ejpd.admin.ch.

MEVES, Christa; German psychoanalyst; b Neumünster; d of Carl and Elsa Mittelstaedt; m Harald Meves; two d. *Education:* In Neumünster, Breslau, Kiel and Hamburg. *Career:* Psychotherapist specializing in children and young people, Uelzen 1960–; writer on psychological themes 1969–; has published 83 books; books have been translated into 12 languages; columnist on various German newspapers; Bundesverdienstkreuz (First Class) 1985; Wilhelm-Bölsche Medaille, Kosmos Verlag 1974; Prix Amade 1976; Konrad-Adenauer-Preis 1978; Niedersächsischer Verdienstorden 1979; Goldmedaille, Herder Verlag 1977; Medal of Merit 1985; prizes for publications. *Publications include:* Schulnöte, Mut zum Erziehen 1970, Wunschtraum und Wirklichkeit 1972, Aus Vorgeschichten lernen 1985, Eltern-ABC 1990, Wahrheit befreit 1993, Problemkinder brauchen Hilfe 1995, Unsere Kinder wachsen heran 1995, Liebe und Agression 1996, Erziehen lernen 1996. *Leisure interests:* writing, painting, grandchildren. *Address:* Albertstr 14, 29525 Uelzen, Germany.

MEYERS, Janis L., BA; American former politician; b 20 July 1928, Lincoln, NE; d of Howard and Lenore Crilly; m Louis Meyers 1956; one d one s. *Education:* William Woods Coll (MO) and Univ of Nebraska–Lincoln. *Career:* Mem Overland Park City Council, KS 1967–70, Pres 1970–72; mem Kansas Senate 1972–84, First Chair Mid-American Regional Council; Pres League of Kansas Municipalities; mem US House of Reps (3rd Dist, Kansas) 1985–96, mem Cttees for Foreign Affairs, Small Businesses and Ageing, House Vice-Chair Environment and Energy Study Conf, Co-Chair Republican 92 Group, mem-at-large Republican Policy Cttee; mem Johnson Co Community Coll Foundation, Bd Dirs Johnson Co Mental Health Asscn; Golden Bulldog Award, Watchdogs of the Treasury Inc 1985–90; Guardian of Small Business Award, Nat Fed of Ind Business 1986, 1988, 1990; Spirit of Enterprise Award, US Chamber of Commerce 1988, 1989; Taxpayer Hero, Citizens Against Govt Waste 1990, 1991; numerous other awards. *Address:* US House of Representatives, 2303 Rayburn House Office Bldg, Washington, DC 20515, USA. *Telephone:* (202) 225-2865; *Fax:* (202) 225-0554.

MHLOYI, Marvellous, PH D; Zimbabwean sociologist; b 15 Sept 1952; m Gilford Mhloyi 1971; one d. *Education:* W Chester Univ and Univ of Pennsylvania (USA). *Career:* Teacher Zimbabwe 1973–74, 1977, Botswana 1976; Data Processor Analyst Philadelphia History Project, USA 1980; Asst Computer Programmer Univ of Pennsylvania 1981–82; Founder, Co-ordinator, apptd Lecturer Population Studies Programme Univ of Zimbabwe 1984, Chair Sociology Dept 1988–90; has written numerous contribs on African health and devt to professional journals; mem Int Union for the Scientific Study of Population, Union for African Sciences, Research Council of Zimbabwe, Social Science Cttee, Cttee Zimbabwe AIDS Control Programme, Bd Post and Telecommunications 1988, Selection Cttee Rhodes Scholarship 1988, Advisory Bd Journal of Studies in Family Planning, The Population Council 1988–91, Editorial Bd Health Transition Review ANU 1991, various WHO task forces 1991–93; Rockefeller Scholar Univ of Pennsylvania 1980; Population Council Scholar 1983; Fulbright Professional Devt Award; McArthur Fellowship of the Harvard Center for Population and Devt Studies 1991; Distinguished Alumni Award, W Chester Univ 1992. *Leisure interests:* music, tennis, community education in family health. *Address:* University of Zimbabwe, Dept of Sociology, POB MP167, Mount Pleasant, Harare, Zimbabwe (Office); 40 Quorn Ave, Mount Pleasant, Harare, Zimbabwe (Home). *Telephone:* (4) 303211 (Office); (4) 308082 (Home); *Fax:* (4) 732828 (Office).

MICALLEF, Doris (Maria Dolores); Maltese artist and business executive; b 20 Feb 1938, Birkirkara; d of Emmanuel and Stella Calleja; m Maximilian Micallef 1960; two s two d. *Education:* Malta School of Arts and Malta Soc of Arts, Manufactures and Commerce. *Career:* Co-Founder, Dir, Man Dormax Press 1969–; artist 1980–; solo exhibitions include Auberge de Provence 1985, 1990, Dormax Press 1986, Medisle Village 1987; group exhibitions include Council of Women, Museum of Fine Arts 1984, Permartex '85, '86, Royal British Legion, Maltafest, Auberge de Provence 1986–90, Malta 25 Sena Indipendenza, Museum of Fine Arts 1989, Malta Int Trade Fair 1989; rep in pvt collections; Dame of the Knights of St Agatha 1977. *Leisure interests:* gardening, water sports, fencing. *Address:* 43 Dormax House, Wignagourt St, Birkirkara 08, Malta. *Telephone:* 445511; *Fax:* 441092; *E-mail:* dmicallef@malta.com; *Internet:* www.maltaart.com/dorismicallef.

MICELI, Pauline Carmen; Maltese broadcaster and writer; b 5 Oct 1949, Zabbar; d of Joseph and Andreana Camilleri; m Charles Miceli 1975; one d. *Education:* M'Assunta Secondary School, Teacher Training Coll and Univ of Malta. *Career:* Teacher of Integrated Science 1970–75; Producer, Presenter Women's Programme Nat Radio 1976–80; Scriptwriter, Producer of educational programmes for schools 1980–89; activist in feminist group Min-Naha tan-Nisa 1980–85; regular newspaper columnist on social and women's issues 1980–; mem nat and int confs on women's issues 1980–. *Publications:* L-Avventuri ta' Heliks 1991, Maria-Eva: Maltese Women Tell Their Stories (2nd edn) 1992. *Leisure interest:* gardening. *Address:* 5 Alley 2, Main St, Naxxar 04, Malta. *Telephone:* 412338.

MICHAEL, Phryne, B ECONS; Cypriot business executive; b Limassol; two d. *Education:* Univ of Vienna and Vienna Conservatorium (Austria). *Career:* Joined Cyprus Tourism Org (CTO) 1971, later Head of Planning Dept, apptd Chief Tourist Officer 1983, Dir-Gen 1990–; papers and articles on tourism. *Address:* Cyprus Tourism Organisation, POB 4535, Zena Bldg, 18 Th Theodotou St, Nicosia, Cyprus.

MICHAELS, Anne; Canadian poet and novelist; b 1958, Toronto. *Publications include:* The Weight of Oranges 1986 (Commonwealth Prize for the Americas), Miner's Pond 1991 (Canadian Authors Asscn Award), Fugitive Pieces (several awards including Trillium Prize, Beatrice and Martin Fischer Award, Orange Prize, Guardian Fiction Award) 1997. *Address:* c/o Bloomsbury Publishing, 38 Soho Square, London, W1, UK.

MICHAUX-CHEVRY, Lucette Adrien, L EN D; French (b Guadeloupe) politician; b 5 March 1929, Saint-Claude, Guadeloupe; d of Edouard and Florentine Chévry; m Emile Michaux (deceased); one s

one d. *Education:* Univ of Paris. *Career:* Lawyer Basse-Terre 1955–; Municipal Councillor, Sainte-Claude 1959–65; mem Departmental Council of Guadeloupe, Chair 1982–85; Founder Political Party for Guadeloupe (LPG) 1984; mem Regional Council 1984, Chair 1992–; Deputy to Nat Ass (Parl, France, RPR) for Guadeloupe 1986, 1988–; State Sec for French-speaking World, Govt of France 1986–88, Minister with special responsibility for Humanitarian Measures and Human Rights 1993–95; Senator from Guadeloupe (RPR) 1995–; mem Comm of Foreign Affairs and Nat Defence; Mayor of Gourbeyre 1987. *Address:* Conseil Régional de la Guadeloupe, place du Champ d'Arbaud, 97100 Basse-Terre, Guadeloupe.

MIDGLEY, Elizabeth, AB; American administrator; b 17 May 1929, Philadelphia, PA; m 1st Thomas Farmer 1951 (divorced 1970); m 2nd John Midgley 1970; two d one s. *Education:* Johannes Gutenberg-Univ of Mainz (Germany) and Radcliffe Coll (Harvard). *Career:* Foreign Affairs Analyst Dept of State 1951–54, Research Asst to Walter Lippmann 1961–67; Producer and Corresp Nat Educational TV 1967–70; Producer CBS News 1970–88; mem Bd Trustees Migration Dialogue. *Address:* 2715 36th Place, NW, Washington, DC 20007, USA. *Telephone:* (202) 337-2715.

MIDLER, Bette; American singer, entertainer and actress; b 1 Dec 1945, Honolulu, HI; m Martin von Haselberg 1984; one d. *Career:* Made acting debut in film Hawaii 1965; mem of cast in Fiddler on the Roof, New York 1966–69, Salvation, New York 1970, Tommy, Seattle Opera Co 1971; night-club concert performer 1972–; numerous TV appearances include Tonight Show; After Dark Ruby Award 1973; Grammy Award 1973; Special Tony Award 1973; Emmy Award 1978. *Recordings include:* The Divine Miss M 1973, Bette Midler 1973, Broken Blossom 1977, Live at Last 1977, Thighs and Whispers 1979, New Depression 1979, Divine Madness 1980, No Frills 1984, Some People's Lives 1990; *Films include:* The Rose 1979, Jinxed 1982, Down and Out in Beverly Hills 1986, Ruthless People 1986, Outrageous Fortune 1987, Big Business 1988, Beaches 1989, Stella 1990, Scenes from a Mall 1991, For The Boys 1991, Hocus Pocus 1993, First Wives Club 1996, That Old Feeling 1997, Get Bruce 1999, Isn't She Great? 1999; *TV includes:* The Tonight Show, Gypsy 1993, Seinfeld 1996, Diva Las Vegas 1997, Murphy Brown 1998; *Publications include:* A View from a Broad 1980, The Saga of Baby Divine 1983. *Address:* c/o Warner Bros Records, 3300 Warner Blvd, Burbank, CA 91505, USA.

MIDORI, (pseudonym of Midori Goto); Japanese violinist; b 25 Oct 1971, Osaka; d of Setsu Goto. *Education:* The Professional Children's School and Juilliard School of Music (New York, USA). *Career:* Began playing violin at the age of four; living in USA 1981–; American debut Aspen Music Festival, CO 1981; Canadian debut 1985; UK debut with London Symphony Orchestra 1987; performances with all major orchestras including European Youth Orchestra, Berlin Philharmonic, Boston Symphony, Montréal Symphony, Canada, Chicago Symphony, Orchestre de Paris, Vienna Symphony, Monte Carlo Philharmonic, New York Philharmonic; has performed with conductors including Zubin Mehta, Leonard Bernstein, Leonard Slatkin, Pinchas Zukerman, James Conlon, Charles Dutoit; Founder, Pres Midori Foundation 1992–; appearances include Tanglewood Music Festival, MA 1986; tours of USA, Asia, Japan, Canada, Europe; Best Artist of the Year Japanese Govt 1988; Dorothy B. Chandler Performing Arts Award 1990; New York State Asian-American Heritage Month Award 1991; Crystal Award (Japan), Suntory Award 1994. *Recordings include:* Bach and Vivaldi Double Concertos 1986, Paganini's First Violin Concerto 1988, Tchaikovsky's Sérénade mélancolique 1988, Dvořák's Violin Concerto 1989, Romance for Violin and Orchestra 1989, Bartók Concerti 1989–90, Paganini's Caprices (Grammy nomination 1990) 1989, Live at Carnegie Hall 1990. *Leisure interests:* music, reading, cooking, writing, karate. *Address:* c/o ICM Artists Ltd, Oxford House, 76 Oxford St, London W1N 0AX, UK; Sony Classical, Sony Music Entertainment Inc, 550 Madison Ave, New York, NY 10022, USA.

MIGENES, Julia; American opera singer; b 1948, New York; m 4th Peter Medak. *Education:* Juilliard School of Music (New York). *Career:* Opera debut at 3½ years; has appeared in operas, on Broadway, on TV and in films; performances include Royal Opera House, Covent Garden, London 1987, Earl's Court, London, UK 1991. *Operas include:* Madam

Butterfly, Manon Lescaut 1987, Tosca 1991; *Film:* Carmen; *TV series:* Magnum, The Twilight Zone; *Theatre includes:* West Side Story; *Recordings include:* Carmen, Kismet, Rags.

MIGGIANI, Anna Maria, B PHARM; Maltese artist and pharmacist; b 27 July 1954, Sliema; d of Frank and the late Eileen (née Engerer) Miggiani. *Education:* Maria Regina Secondary School and Univ of Malta. *Career:* Began painting 1980; has frequently exhibited internationally; group exhibitions include Gallery Montage 1981, Maltese Women Artists, Galleria Fenici 1982, Maltafest Contemporary Art Exhibitions 1983–90, Malta, Graphics, Paintings, Ceramics, Munich, Germany 1984, Malta Union of Teachers 1984, L-Ghajta Siekta, Il Piazzetta, Sliema 1984, Council of Women, Museum of Fine Arts 1984, Cathedral Museum, Mdina 1985, UNESCO HQ, Paris 1987, Lions Club Exhibition 1987, The Art of the Rising Generation, Chamber of Commerce 1988, 25th Anniversary Independence Celebrations, Museum of Fine Arts 1989, 50th Year Anniversary De La Salle Coll, Pharmacists in Art, Cathedral Museum, Mdina 1989, Din L-Art Helwa Exhibition, San Pawl Tat-Targa 1990, 1991, Melitensia Art Gallery 1991; solo exhibitions at Museum of Fine Arts, Valletta 1987, Cathedral Museum, Mdina 1991; Medical Rep SmithKline Beecham Pharmaceuticals. *Publication:* All Malta 1988. *Leisure interests:* painting, reading, sailing, films. *Address:* Wixy, Triq Il-Kartocc, Jal-Ibrag, Malta. *Telephone:* 370125; *Fax:* 230426.

MIGONGO-BAKE, Elizabeth Wangoi, M SC, PH D; Kenyan agronomist; b 18 June 1953, Nakuru; d of Livingstone and Kesiah Resiata Migongo; m Gernot Bake 1983; one d. *Education:* Univ of Nairobi and Colorado State Univ (USA). *Career:* Ecology Consultant 1977–80; research on ecology and animal physiology 1980–84; Agro-Forester OAU, N Cameroon 1986–89; Consultant Kenyan Wildlife Services 1990–; Forage Agronomist 1990–; numerous papers on animal physiology. *Leisure interests:* horse-riding, swimming. *Address:* ICRAF, POB 30677, Nairobi, Kenya. *Telephone:* (2) 521450; *Fax:* (2) 521001.

MIKHALCHENKO, Alla Anatolevna, MA; Russian ballet dancer; b 3 July 1957, Moscow; d of Anatoly A. Dmitriev and Irina A Mikhalchenko. *Education:* Moscow Choreographic School, Russian Acad of Theatrical Arts. *Career:* Soloist Bolshoi Ballet 1976–99; Dir own ballet co 1994–; Lecturer Russian Acad of Theatrical Arts 1999–; Co-Founder, Co-ordinator Bolshoi Ballet School in Brazil 1999–; First Prize All-Soviet Competition 1976, First Prize and Distinction Varna Ballet Competition 1976; First Prize, Gold Medal Moscow Int Ballet Competition 1977; People's Artist of the RSFSR 1986. *Ballets include:* Swan Lake, Don Quixote, The Seagull, Angara, Indian Poem, Golden Age, Giselle, Ivan the Terrible, Raymonda, La Bayadère, Legend of Love, Prodigal Son; *Videos:* Swan Lake, Legend of Love, These Enchanting Tunes 1981, I Want to Dance 1985, Fragments of One's Biography 1985, An Evening with the Bolshoi 1986. *Leisure interests:* learning yoga and Eastern philosophy. *Address:* 123242 Moscow, Malaya Gruzinskaya ul 12, kv 18, Russian Federation. *Telephone:* (095) 252-26-09; *Fax:* (095) 292-90-32.

MIKHAYLOVA, Lilyana; Bulgarian writer; b 11 May 1939, Plovdiv; m Mladen Denew 1968; one s. *Education:* Univ of Sofia. *Career:* Teacher 1962–68; journalist 1968–74; Chief Ed in a publishing house 1974–90; has written screenplays and scripts and over 20 books; First Prize Varna Int Film Festival 1974, 1984; Nat Award for Contemporary Literature 1984; Sofia Award for Literature 1986. *Leisure interest:* fishing. *Address:* Sofia 1126, Brest 11, Bulgaria. *Telephone:* (2) 66-32-32.

MIKULSKI, Barbara Ann, BA; American politician; b 20 July 1936, Baltimore, MD; d of William Mikulski and Christina Eleanor Kutz. *Education:* Mount St Agnes Coll and Maryland Univ. *Career:* Mem of staff Baltimore Dept Social Services 1961–63, 1966–70, York Family Agency 1964, VISTA Teaching Center 1965–70; teacher Mount St Agnes Coll 1969, Community Coll, Baltimore 1970–71; Democratic Nominee to US Senate 1974, to House of Reps 1976; mem 96th–99th Congresses from Third Maryland Dist; Senator from Maryland 1987–; mem Democratic Nat Strategy Council, Nat Bd of Dirs Urban Coalition, Nat Asscn of Social Workers; Hon LL D (Goucher Coll) 1973, (Hood Coll) 1978. *Address:* US Senate, 709 Hart Office Bldg, Washington, DC 20510, USA.

MILES, Sarah; British actress; b 31 Dec 1941; m Robert Bolt 1967 (divorced 1976), remarried 1988 (died 1995). *Education:* Royal Acad of Dramatic Art (London). *Career:* Made first film appearance in Term of Trial 1962; mem Nat Theatre Co 1964–65, Shakespeare stage season 1982–83. *Films include:* Those Magnificent Men in Their Flying Machines 1964, I Was Happy Here 1966, The Blow-Up 1966, Ryan's Daughter 1970, Lady Caroline Lamb 1972, The Hireling 1973, The Man Who Loved Cat Dancing 1973, Great Expectations 1975, Pepita Jiménez 1975, The Sailor Who Fell From Grace With the Sea 1976, The Big Sleep 1978, Venom 1981, Hope and Glory 1987, White Mischief 1988, The Silent Touch; *TV appearances include:* James Michener's Dynasty, Great Expectations, Harem, Queenie, A Ghost in Monte Carlo, Dandelion Dead, Ring Around the Moon, The Rehearsal; *Plays include:* Vivat! Vivat Regina!, Asylum 1988; *Publications:* Charlemagne (play) 1992, A Right Royal Bastard (memoirs) 1993, Serves me Right (memoirs) 1994, Bolt from the Blue (memoirs) 1996. *Telephone:* (20) 7734-9361.

MILJAKOVIĆ, Olivera; Yugoslav opera singer; b 26 April 1939, Belgrade; one d. *Education:* In Belgrade. *Career:* Opera singer at Belgrade Opera House 1960; Soloist Vienna State Opera 1962–; guest appearances in Europe, USA, Japan, S America, etc; has performed at numerous festivals in Germany, Austria and Yugoslavia; Kammersängerin 1984. *Leisure interests:* history of art, philosophy, sport. *Address:* Neulinggasse 37, 1030 Vienna, Austria.

MILKINA, Nina; British concert pianist; b 27 Jan 1919, Moscow, Russia (now Russian Fed); d of Jacques and Sophie Milkine; m Alastair R. M. Sedgwick 1943; one s one d. *Education:* Privately in UK and France and Paris Conservatoire. *Career:* Studied under Leon Conus and Profs Harold Craxton and Tobias Matthay, and composition with Glazunov and Sabaniev; made debut aged 11 with Lamourex Orchestra, Paris; chosen by BBC to broadcast all Mozart's piano sonatas; gave Mozart Bicentennial recital at Edinburgh Int Festival 1991; int adjudicator; Hon Fellow RAM. *Recordings include:* Mozart piano concertos and recitals, Chopin Mazurkas, Scarlatti Sonatas, Mozart and Haydn Sonatas, works by Rachmaninov, Prokofiev, Scriabin. *Leisure interests:* chess, reading, travel. *Address:* 17 Montagu Square, London W1H 1RD, UK. *Telephone:* (20) 7487-4588.

MILLER, Christine Odell Cook, BA, JD; American federal judge; b 26 Aug 1944, Oakland, CA; d of the late Leo Marshall and Carolyn Grant (née Odell) Cook; m 1st Paul Henry Nettesheim 1978; m 2nd Dennis F. Miller. *Education:* Stanford Univ and Univ of Utah. *Career:* Called to the Bar, UT 1969, WA 1972, CA 1982; Clerk to Chief Judge US Court of Appeals, UT 1969–70; Trial Attorney Foreign Litigation Unit and Court of Claims Section, Civil Div, US Dept of Justice 1970–72; team leader attorney Bureau of Consumer Protection Div, Fed Trade Comm, Washington, DC 1972–74; Specialist in Litigation Hogan and Hartson, Washington, DC 1974–76, Shack and Kimball PC 1980–83; Special Counsel Pension Benefit Guaranty Corpn, Washington, DC 1976–78; Deputy Gen Counsel, then Asst Gen Counsel US Railway Asscn 1978–80; Judge US Court of Fed Claims, Washington, DC 1983–; mem State Bar Asscn of California, Dist of Columbia Bar Asscn; certified as Professional Gemologist. *Leisure interests:* jogging, gemology. *Address:* US Court of Federal Claims, 717 Madison Place, NW, Washington, DC 20005, USA. *Telephone:* (202) 219-9546; *Fax:* (202) 219-9542.

MILLER, Heidi G., PH D; American business executive. *Education:* Princeton and Yale Univs. *Career:* Chief Financial Officer Citigroup; Sr Exec Vice-Pres, Strategic Planning and Admin Priceline.com 2000–. *Address:* Priceline.com Inc, 800 Connecticut Ave, Norwalk, CT 06854, USA.

MILLER, Shannon; American athlete; b 10 March 1977, Rollo, MO; m 1999. *Education:* Univ of Houston (TX). *Career:* Gymnast; Silver Medallist, all-round competition, uneven bars, Olympic Games, Barcelona, Spain 1992; Bronze Medallist floor exercises, balance beam and team bronze, Olympic Games 1992; Gold Medallist all-round competition, floor exercises and uneven bars, World Championships, Birmingham, UK 1993; Gold Medallist all-round competition and balance beam, World Championships, Brisbane, Australia 1994; Gold Medallist Team Competition, balance beam, Olympic Games, Atlanta, GA, USA 1996; awards include Up and Coming Award Women's

Sports Foundation 1991, Steve Reeves Fitness Award 1992, Comeback Award 1992, Dial Award 1994, Athlete of the Year, USA Gymnastics Congress 1994. *Publication:* Winning Every Day: Gold Medal Advice for a Happy, Healthy Life! 1998. *Leisure interests:* scuba diving, figure skating, golf, reading. *Address:* 2415 Newbridge Ct, Pearland, TX 77584, USA. *Telephone:* (713) 436-1236; *Fax:* (713) 436-3660; *E-mail:* franmil555@aol.com; *Internet:* www.shannonmiller.com.

MILLETT, Katherine Murray, PH D; American feminist campaigner and artist; b 14 Sept 1934, St Paul; m Fumio Yoshimura 1965. *Education:* Univ of Minnesota, St Hilda's Coll (Oxford, UK) and Columbia Univ (NY). *Career:* Sculptor, Tokyo 1961–63; teacher Barnard Coll 1964–68; Distinguished Visiting Prof Sacramento State Coll, CA 1973–; f Women's Art Colony Farm, Poughkeepsie, NY; exhibitions include Minami Gallery (Tokyo), Judson Gallery 1967, Soho Gallery (New York) 1976, 1978 1980, 1982, 1984, 1986, Women's Bldg (Los Angeles, CA) 1977, Andre Wanters Gallery (New York) 1977, Chuck Levitan Gallery (New York), deVille Galerie (New Orleans, LA), Emmy Gallery (Berlin) 1977; mem Congress of Racial Equality 1965–. *Publications include:* Sexual Politics 1970, The Prostitution Papers 1973, Flying 1974, Sita 1977, The Basement 1979, Going to Iran 1982, The Loony Bin Trip 1990, The Politics of Cruelty 1994. *Address:* c/o Georges Borchardt Inc, 136 E 57th St, New York, NY 10022, USA.

MILLINGTON, Caroline, BA; British broadcasting executive; b 4 Aug 1949, Chelmsford; d of Ernest Millington and Gwen Pickard. *Education:* Grey Coat Hospital School (Westminster, London) and Univ of York. *Career:* Producer BBC radio and TV news and current affairs programmes and factual documentaries 1970–86, Asst Head, then Head BBC radio Magazine Programme Dept 1987–93, Controller of Production BBC Network Radio 1993; Founder and first Chair UK Radio Acad 1983–1986; Fellow Radio Acad 1995. *Leisure interests:* sketching, walking, making music. *Address:* BBC, Broadcasting House, Portland Place, London W1A 1AA, UK.

MILLS, Dame Barbara Jean Lyon, DBE, MA, QC; British lawyer and civil servant; b 10 Aug 1940; d of John and Kitty Warnock; m John Angus Donald Mills 1962; four c. *Education:* St Helen's School (Northwood) and Lady Margaret Hall (Oxford). *Career:* Called to the Bar, Middle Temple 1963, Bencher 1990; Jr Prosecuting Counsel to Inland Revenue 1977, Sr Prosecuting Counsel 1979; Jr Treasury Counsel Cen Criminal Court 1981–86; Recorder Crown Court 1982–92; QC 1986, QC (NI) 1991; Dept of Trade and Industry Insp under Section 177 of Financial Services Art 1986 (re Jenkins–British Commonwealth) 1986; Legal Assessor to Gen Medical Council and Gen Dental Council 1988–90; Dir Serious Fraud Office 1990–92; Dir of Public Prosecutions, Head Crown Prosecution Service 1992–98; The Adjudicator 1999–; Chair Forum UK 1999–2001, Council of Management, Women's Library 2000–; Non-Exec Dir Royal Free Hampstead Nat Health Service Trust 2000–; Gov London Guildhall Univ 1999–; Trustee Victim Support 1999–; mem Criminal Injuries Compensation Bd 1988–90, Parole Bd 1990; mem Gen Advisory Council of BBC 1991–92; Hon Vice-Pres, Inst for Study and Treatment of Delinquency 1996; Hon Fellow Lady Margaret Hall 1991, Soc for Advanced Legal Studies 1997; Companion of Honour, Inst of Man 1993; Hon LL D (Hull, Nottingham Trent) 1993, (London Guildhall) 1994. *Leisure interest:* family. *Address:* 72 Albert St, London NW1 7NR, UK. *Telephone:* (20) 7388-9206; *Fax:* (20) 7388-3454.

MILLS, Hayley Cathrine Rose Vivien; British actress; b 18 April 1946, London; d of Sir John and Lady (née Mary Hayley Bell) Mills; m Roy Boulting 1971 (divorced 1977); two s. *Education:* Elmhurst Ballet School and Inst Alpine Vidamanette. *Career:* Made debut in Tiger Bay 1959; on contract to Walt Disney; first stage appearance as Peter Pan 1969; Silver Bear Award, Berlin Film Festival 1958; British Acad Award; Special Oscar (USA). *Films include:* Pollyanna 1960, The Parent Trap 1961, Whistle Down the Wind 1961, Summer Magic 1962, In Search of the Castaways 1963, The Chalk Garden 1964, The Moonspinners 1965, The Truth about Spring 1965, Sky West and Crooked 1966, The Trouble with Angels 1966, The Family Way 1966, Pretty Polly 1967, Twisted Nerve 1968, Take a Girl Like You 1970, Forbush and the Penguins 1971, Endless Night 1972, Deadly Strangers 1975, The Diamond Hunters 1975, What Changed Charley Farthing?

1975, The Kingfisher Caper 1975, Parent Trap II 1986, Appointment with Death 1987, Parent Trap III, IV 1989, After Midnight 1992; *Plays include:* The Wild Duck 1970, Trelawny 1972, The Three Sisters 1973, A Touch of Spring 1975, My Fat Friend 1978, Hush and Hide 1979, The Importance of Being Earnest, The Summer Party 1980, Talley's Folly 1982, The Secretary Bird 1983, Dial M for Murder 1984, Toys in the Attic 1986, The Kidnap Game 1991, The King and I 1991/92, Fallen Angels 1994, The Card 1995, Dead Guilty 1996, Brief Encounter 1997–98, The King and I (US tour) 1997–98, Suite in Two Keys (New York) 2000, Vagina Monologues (New York) 2000, Little Night Music 2001; *TV appearances include:* The Flame Trees of Thika 1981, Parent Trap II 1986, Good Morning Miss Bliss, Murder She Wrote, Back Home, Tales of the Unexpected, Walk of Life 1990, Parent Trap III, IV, Amazing Stories; *Publication:* My God (jtly) 1988. *Leisure interests:* riding, reading, children, cooking, scuba-diving. *Address:* 123A Kings Rd, London SW3, UK.

MILNE, Paula; British screenwriter; b 1947; m 1st; three c; m 2nd 1988; one s. *Career:* Began career as a professional writer 1979; script reader, script editor BBC TV; contributed to TV series including Coronation Street, Z cars, Crown Court. *TV series include:* Angels, Play for Today, The Politician's Wife, My Cousin Rachel, Die Kinder, The Fragile Heart; *Film:* Mad Love. *Address:* c/o Channel Four Television Corp, 124 Horseferry Rd, London SW1P 2TX, UK. *Telephone:* (20) 7396-4444.

MILNE, Rose Eleanor, D ITT, OC, CM, RCA; Canadian sculptor; b 14 May 1925, St John, Neb; d of William Harold and Irene Eleanor Mary Milne. *Education:* Montréal Museum School of Fine Art, McGill Lab of Anatomy, Cen Coll of Arts and Crafts (London, UK), Ecole des Beaux Arts (Montréal) and Syracuse Univ (NY, USA). *Career:* Official Sculptor of Canada 1961–93; Consultant, Arctic Coll, Iqualuit, Hamlet of Coral Bay, NWT, The Tomb of the Unknown Soldier, Dept of Public Works, Monumental Art; stained-glass window creator, wood engraver, painter in water colours, makes bronze castings, has designed and built statues in wood, bronze, and stone for indoor and outdoor use, low-relief panels in wood, stone and bronze; designed and carved History of Canada (high-relief frieze) in lobby of House of Commons, also 12 stained-glass windows and 12 stones for Chamber of House of Commons; designed and made carving and mosaic for First Speaker's chair for Yellowknife, NWT; designed First Speaker's table and carved bronze mace cradle for Whitehorse, YT; Visiting Lecturer Carleton Univ, Ottawa; represented in several perm and pvt collections in People's Repub of China, UK and Canada; mem and Adjudicator The Centennial Coins and Medallions Cttee; mem numerous orgs and cttees including Smithsonian Inst, Canadian Wildlife; Hon D LITT (Carleton); Hon D HUM (Windsor); Hon LL D (Queen's). *Leisure interests:* landscape gardening, modern history, restoration of carved wood detail and stone masonry of early 19th century houses. *Address:* 229 Powell Ave, Ottawa, ON K1S 2A4, Canada (Home). *E-mail:* arnoo@ottonline.net.

MILNER DAVIS, Jessica Ruth, PH D; Australian (b British) academic and consultant; b 7 July 1943, Rugby, UK; d of Christopher John and E. Joyce Milner; m Geoffrey Guy Ashcroft Davis 1971; one d. *Education:* Homefield School (Rugby), N Sydney Girls' High School, Univ of New S Wales and Univ of Bristol. *Career:* Writer 1972–; Visiting Scholar Bristol Univ 1965–66, Stanford Univ 1976–78; mem Governing Council Univ of NSW 1965–70, 1981–, Deputy Chancellor 1981–90, Pro Chancellor 1999–; Hon Visiting Fellow Faculty of Arts, Univ of NSW 1990–; Consultant on gifted and talented children 1989–; Sr Vice-Pres Nat Union Australian Univ Students 1965–66; Dir Nat Inst of Dramatic Art 1984–86; Pres Int Soc for Humour Studies 1995–96; mem Australian Cttee World Univ Service 1964–70, Univ of New S Wales Alumni Asscn Bd 1980–, New S Wales Police Educ Advisory Council 1985–89; Dir New Coll Bd Sydney 2001–. *Publications:* Farce 1978, Readings from International Conference on Humour (ed) 1997, Understanding Humour in Japan 2001; has written papers on psychology, comedy and educ. *Leisure interests:* theatre, opera, bush regeneration, committees. *Address:* 75 Coolawin Rd, Northbridge, NSW 2063, Australia. *Fax:* (9) 967-2041.

MIN HUIFEN; Chinese musician; b 23 Nov 1945, Yixing Co, Jiangsu Prov; one s. *Education:* Shanghai Music Inst. *Career:* Began playing the erhu (traditional Chinese instrument) at age eight; became an erhu soloist in China Art Ensemble 1969, then in Shanghai Philharmonic Orchestra and in Shanghai Art Ensemble; mem Shanghai Traditional Instruments Orchestra 1978–; has made 10 solo records; Prof Shanghai Music Inst 1993–; mem 5th Nat Cttee CPPCC 1978–82, 6th 1983–87, 7th 1988–92, 8th 1993–; Shanghai Art and Literature Award 1987; first Gold Disc Award by China Records Factory; Nat Outstanding Artist award 1988; Best Performance Prize in Spring of Shanghai 1991. *Address:* Room 1101, Bldg 151, Weihai Rd, Shanghai 200003, People's Republic of China.

MINDSZENTY, Andrea, PH D; Hungarian geologist; b 19 Aug 1946, Budapest; d of János and Olga (née Baló) Mindszenty. *Education:* Loránd Eötvös Univ and Hungarian Acad of Sciences (Budapest). *Career:* Worked at Eng and Research Centre of Hungalu, Budapest 1969–70, 1972–77, Bauxite Prospecting Co 1977–81; Research Asst Loránd Eötvös Univ Dept of Mineralogy 1970–72, scientist 1981–90, Assoc Prof of Applied Geology 1989–, apptd Head of Dept 1991; mem bauxite prospecting expeditions to Mongolia 1971, Nigeria 1973, N Vietnam 1974, 1975, expeditions to Pakistan 1976, Cuba 1979, India 1985–86; Visiting Scientist Univ of Naples, Italy 1987–88, 1990–91, Univs of N Carolina and Oregon, USA 1992; Visiting Prof of Bauxite Geology Univ of Vienna 1990; Co-Leader Project 287 'Tethyan Bauxites', Int Geological Correlation Programme, UNESCO 1989–92; Vice-Pres Hungarian Geological Soc 1991–93; has written several articles in scientific journals. *Leisure interests:* horse-riding, skiing, mountain-hiking, classical music. *Address:* 1121 Budapest XII, Fülemile u 12/18 4 ép fsz 2, Hungary. *Telephone:* (1) 175-1096; *Fax:* (1) 266-4992; *E-mail:* andrea@ludens.elte.hu.

MING, Maureen, B COM, CA; South African business executive; b 2 May 1949, Johannesburg; d of the late Yet Ming and of Heng (née Ah) Ming. *Education:* End St Convent (Johannesburg) and Univ of the Witwatersrand. *Career:* First woman Audit Partner Ernst and Young (fmrly Ernst and Whinney) and first woman Audit Partner in int SA firm of CAs 1981. *Leisure interests:* gardening, reading. *Address:* c/o Ernst and Young House, Chartered Accountants (SA), 4 Pritchard St, POB 2332, Johannesburg 2000, South Africa.

MINNELLI, Liza; American actress and singer; b 12 March 1946, Los Angeles, CA; d of the late Vincente Minnelli and Judy Garland; m 1st Peter Allen 1967 (divorced 1972); m 2nd Jack Haley, Jr 1974 (divorced 1979); m 3rd Mark Gero 1979 (divorced 1992). *Education:* In California, Switzerland and at Univ of Paris (Sorbonne). *Career:* Made film debut aged three with mother in Good Old Summertime 1949; left school to tour in The Diary of Anne Frank, The Fantasticks, Carnival, The Pajama Game; numerous int concert appearances, including AIDS/tribute to Freddie Mercury concert, London 1992; Female Star of the Year, Nat Asscn of Theatre Owners 1972; Las Vegas Entertainer of the Year Award; Star on Hollywood Walk of Fame 1991. *Theatre includes:* Best Foot Forward (Theatre World Award) 1963, Flora, The Red Menace (Tony Award) 1965, Liza at the Winter Garden (Special Tony Award) 1973, Chicago 1975, The Act (Tony Award) 1977–78, Liza at the Winter Garden 1973 (Special Tony Award), Are You Now or Have You Ever Been?, The Rink 1984, Liza Minnelli Stepping Out at Radio City 1992, Victor-Victoria 1997; *Films include:* Charlie Bubbles 1968, The Sterile Cuckoo (David di Donatello Best Foreign Actress Award) 1969, Tell Me That You Love Me, Junie Moon 1971, Cabaret (Acad Award for Best Actress, Hollywood Foreign Press Golden Globe Award, British Acad Best Actress Award, David di Donatello Best Foreign Actress Award) 1972, That's Entertainment 1974, Lucky Lady 1976, A Matter of Time 1976, Silent Movie 1976, New York, New York 1977, Arthur 1981, The Muppets Take Manhattan, That's Dancing, Rent-A-Cop 1988, Arthur 2: On the Rocks 1988, Sam Found Out 1988, Stepping Out 1991, Trust 1991, Parallel Lives 1994; *TV appearances include:* The Flame Trees of Thika 1981, Parent Trap II 1986, Good Morning Miss Bliss, Murder She Wrote, Back Home, Tales of the Unexpected, Walk of Life 1990; *TV Specials include:* Liza, Liza with a Z (Emmy Award) 1972, Goldie and Liza Together 1980, Baryshnikov on Broadway 1980 (Golden Globe Award), A Time to Live 1985 (Golden Globe Award), My Favourite Broadway: The Leading Ladies 1999; *Recordings include:* Liza with a Z, Liza Minnelli: The Singer, Liza Minnelli: Live at the Winter Garden, Tropical Nights, The Act, Liza Minnelli: Live at Carnegie Hall, The Rink, Liza Minnelli at Carnegie

Hall, Results 1989; *Publication:* My God (jtly) 1988. *Leisure interests:* riding, reading, children, cooking, scuba-diving. *Address:* Capital Records Inc, 1750 Vine St, Hollywood, CA 90028, USA.

MINOGUE, Kylie Ann; Australian singer and actress; b 28 May 1968, Melbourne; d of Ronald and Carol Minogue. *Education:* Camberwell High School. *Career:* Began acting aged 11 in Skyways, The Sullivans, then Neighbours 1986 (all TV series); first female vocalist to have her first (released) five singles obtain silver discs in UK; many hit singles in Europe, Australia, Japan etc; numerous awards include Most Popular Actress Silver Logie 1987, Most Popular Personality on TV Logie 1988, 'Most Fanciable Female', Best Female Singer (Smash Hits Magazine) 1988, 1989, Best Int Female Artist (Irish Record Industry Awards) 1989, Recording Artist of the Year (Australian Variety Club) 1989, Best Female Vocalist (Japan Radio Music Awards) 1989, Best Radio Artist in France 1989, Top Female Artist in Israel 1989, Woman of the Decade award 1989, Mo Award (Australian Variety Industry) 1990, Int Outstanding Achievement Award 1990, Diamond Award 1990, Best Selling Australian Artist (World Music Awards) 1991, 'Sexiest Person on the Planet' (DMC and Mix-Mag magazines) 1992, 'World's Coolest Female in Music' (Select magazine) 1993, Best Single and Best Female Solo Singer (Smash Hits Awards) 1994. *Recordings:* Singles: I Should Be So Lucky (Platinum Record, Record of the Year, Japanese Popular Discs Awards 1988) 1988, Got To Be Certain 1988, The Locomotion (Platinum Record 1987, Highest Selling Record Award 1987, Most Popular Music Video Logie 1987), Je Ne Sais Pas Pourquoi 1988, Especially For You (jtly) 1988, Turn It Into Love 1988, It's No Secret, Hand On Your Heart 1989, Wouldn't Change A Thing 1989, Never Too Late (Best Video Logie) 1989, Tears On My Pillow 1990, Better The Devil You Know 1990, Step Back In Time 1990, What Do I Have To Do? 1991, Shocked 1991, Word Is Out, If You Were With Me Now (jtly) 1991, Give Me Just a Little More Time 1992, Finer Feelings 1992, What Kind of Fool 1992, Celebration 1992, Confide in Me 1994, Put Yourself in My Place (Best Australian Video, Australian Record Industry Awards 1995) 1994, Where the Wild Roses Grow (jtly) 1995, Where is the Feeling 1996, Some Kind of Bliss 1997, Breathe 1998, Spinning Around 2000, On a Night Like This 2000, Kids (jtly) 2000, Please Stay 2000; Albums: Kylie (Platinum Record, Top Album 1989, Music Week, Ampex Golden Reel Award) 1988, Enjoy Yourself (Triple Platinum Record) 1989, Rhythm of Love (Platinum Record) 1990, Lets Get To It 1991, Greatest Hits 1992, Kylie Minogue 1994 Kylie Minogue (Impossible Princess) 1998, Light Years 2000; *Videos:* Kylie Minogue: The Videos 1988, Kylie Minogue: The Videos 2 1989, Kylie... on the Go, Live in Japan 1990, Kylie Live in Dublin 1991, Kylie Let's Get to... The Videos 1992, Kylie's Greatest Hits 1992; *TV series:* Skyways 1980, The Sullivans 1981, The Henderson Kids 1984–85, Neighbours 1986–88; *Films:* The Delinquents 1989, Streetfighter 1994, Hayride to Hell (short) 1995, Biodome 1996, Sample People 1999, Cut 1999, Moulin Rouge 2001; *Plays:* The Tempest 1999; *Publication:* Kylie 1999. *Address:* c/o Terry Blamey Management Pty Ltd, 329 Montague St, Albert Park, Vic 3206, Australia; c/o Terry Blamey Management, POB 13196, London SW6 4WF, UK. *Telephone:* (3) 9696 2544 (Australia); (20) 7371-7627 (London); *Fax:* (3) 9690 9663 (Australia); (20) 7731-7578 (London); *E-mail:* info@terryblamey.com (Office); *Internet:* Kylie.com (Office).

MINOVES TRIQUELL, Judi F., MA M PHIL; Andorran diplomatist; b 15 Aug 1969, Andorra la Vella. *Education:* Yale Univ (USA). *Career:* Counsellor first Perm Mission of Andorra to the UN 1993–94, Deputy Perm Rep and Chargé d'Affaires 1994–95, Perm Rep 1995–; Alt Head Andorran del to World Summit on Social Devt, Copenhagen, Special Plenipotentiary Rep of Andorran Govt in negotiations to est diplomatic relations with various govts 1994–95; contrib to Andorra 7 magazine; literary and journalism awards. *Publications:* a novel and a collection of short stories. *Address:* Permanent Mission of Andorra to the United Nations, 2 United Nations Plaza, 25th Floor, New York, NY 10017, USA (Office). *Telephone:* (212) 750-8064 (Office); *Fax:* (212) 750-6630 (Office).

MINTOFF BLAND, Yana, PH D; Maltese economist and teacher; b 21 Aug 1951; d of Dominic Mintoff and Moyra Devere Bentwick; m David Bland 1991; one d one s. *Education:* Girls' Jr Lyceum and Univ of Malta. *Career:* Researcher econs of health and devt 1983–90; apptd Lecturer, Researcher Univ of Malta 1990; Organizer Mediterranean and Arab

Women's Solidarity Asscn 1990–92; mem of various forums on women, ecology, Socialist Peace; has written articles for academic magazines and newspapers 1972–. *Leisure interests:* swimming, walking. *Address:* Zebbug Zghir, Gnien Joanne, Tarxien, Malta. *Telephone:* 816644.

MINTON, Yvonne Fay, CBE; Australian opera singer (mezzo-soprano); b 4 Dec 1938, Sydney; d of the late Robert T. and of Violet (née Dean) Minton; m William Barclay 1965; one s one d. *Education:* Sydney Conservatorium of Music and studied in London with H. Cummings and Joan Cross. *Career:* Debut Royal Opera House, Covent Garden, London 1965, Prin Mezzo-Soprano 1965–71; US debut, Lyric Opera, Chicago 1972; Guest Artist Cologne Opera, Germany 1969–, Australian Opera 1972–73, Metropolitan Opera, New York, USA (in Der Rosenkavalier) 1973; has also appeared with Hamburg State Opera, and at Bayreuth and Munich, Germany, Paris, Salzburg, Austria, Chicago, New York and San Francisco, USA; Hon Fellow RAM. *Recordings include:* Der Rosenkavalier, Le Nozze di Figaro, La Clemenza di Tito, Mozart's Requiem, Elgar's The Kingdom, The Knot Garden, Lulu, Pelléas et Mélisande, The Dream of Gerontius. *Leisure interests:* reading, gardening. *Address:* c/o Ingpen and Williams, 26 Wadham Rd, London SW15 2LR, UK. *Telephone:* (20) 8874-3222; *Fax:* (20) 8877-3113.

MIOU-MIOU, (pseudonym of Sylvette Héry); French actress; b 22 Feb 1950, Paris; one d by the late Patrick Dewaere; one d by Julien Clerc. *Career:* Worked as child in Les Halles wholesale market; apprenticed in upholstery workshop; with comedian Coluche helped create Montparnasse café-theatre 1968; stage appearance in Marguerite Duras' La Musica 1985. *Films include:* La cavale 1971, Les valseuses 1974, Quelques messieurs trop tranquilles, Les granges brûlées, La grande trouille, Lily aime-moi, F comme Fairbanks, Al piacere di rivederla, Dites-lui que je l'aime, Les routes du sud, L'ingorgo una storia imposibile, Au revoir...à lundi, La dérobade (César Award) 1979, La femme flic, Est-ce raisonnable?, La gueule du loup, Guy de Maupassant, Entre nous, Attention, une femme peut en cacher une autre!, Canicule, Blanche et Marie, Tenue de soirée, Les portes tournantes, La lectrice, Netchaiev est de retour, Milou in May, The Jackpot, Le bal des casse-pieds, Germinal; *Play:* La Musica 1985.

MIRABELLA, Grace, BA; American magazine publishing executive; b 10 June 1930, Maplewood, NJ; d of Anthony and Florence Mirabella; m William G. Cahan 1974. *Education:* Skidmore Coll (NY). *Career:* Mem Exec Training Programme Macy's, New York 1950–51, Fashion Dept Saks Fifth Ave, New York 1951–52; mem public relations staff Simonetta and Fabiani, Rome 1954–56; mem staff Vogue Magazine 1952–54, 1956–58, Assoc Ed 1965–71, Ed-in-Chief 1971–88; apptd Publishing Dir Mirabella 1988; Lecturer New School of Social Science; Outstanding Grad Achievement Award (Skidmore Coll) 1972; Cavalier Order of Merit, Repub of Italy, Officer 1987; Fashion Critics Award (Parsons School of Design) 1985; Woman of Distinction Award (Birmingham-Southern Coll) 1985; Girl Scouts American Leadership Award 1987; Excellence in Media Award (Susan G. Komen Foundation) 1987; Equal Opportunity Award (NOW) 1987; Mary Ann Magnin Award 1988; Achievement Award (American Asscn of Plastic and Reconstructive Surgery) 1988; Special Merit Award (Council of Fashion Designers of America) 1989. *Address:* c/o Mirabella Magazine, 1633 Broadway, New York, NY 10019, USA.

MIRANDA DE LAGE, Ana; Spanish politician; b 7 May 1946, San Sebastián. *Career:* Fmr Admin Officer PSOE; MEP (PSE) 1986–99, fmr mem Cttee on External Econ Relations, on Petitions, Del for relations with the countries of S America. *Address:* c/o European Parliament, rue Wiertz, 1040 Brussels, Belgium.

MIRHOSSEINI, Akramossadat, D EN D; Iranian organization executive; b 28 Oct 1940, Iran; d of Hossein and Touran Aliabadi; divorced; one s. *Education:* Univ of Teheran. *Career:* Mem staff Ministry of Water and Electricity 1962–65, Dir Dept of Org, Methods and Training 1965–68; Specialist State Org for Admin and Employment 1968–70, Deputy Dir Dept of Org and Methods 1970–73, Dir-Gen Dept of Salary and Remuneration and Tech Sec at Council of State for Salary and Remuneration 1973–79; Dir of Human Resources Aciéries d'Ahwaz steel co 1984–85; political refugee in France 1986–; Founder, Pres Ligue des Femmes Iraniennes pour la Démocratie (LFID—League of Iranian Women for Democracy, fmrly known as Org Mondiale de la Solidarité des Femmes Iraniennes), Paris 1989–; contribs to books and newspapers on Iran and women's affairs. *Address:* c/o LFID, 73 rue du Château, 92100 Boulogne Billancourt, France. *Telephone:* (1) 48-99-06-26; *Fax:* (1) 48-99-06-26.

MIRICIOIU, Nelly; Romanian opera singer; b 31 March 1952, Adjud; d of Voicu and Maria Miricioiu. *Education:* Conservatoire G. Enesco (Iaşi). *Career:* Made professional debut as Queen of the Night in The Magic Flute in Romania 1970; W European debut as Violetta in Scottish Opera production of La Traviata 1981; debut at Royal Opera House, Covent Garden, London as Nedda in Pagliacci 1982, at La Scala, Milan as Lucia in Lucia di Lammermoor 1983; has since appeared at numerous opera houses including Verona and Florence (Italy), San Francisco (USA), Vienna (Austria), Berlin, Hamburg (Germany), Madrid (Spain) and in recitals and concerts; performed at concert in aid of Romanian Children's Hosps and Community Projects, Barbican Centre, London 1991; made first recording, recital Wigmore Hall, London 1986; winner 10 int competitions. *Operas include:* La Bohème, I Capuleti e I Montecchi, Rigoletto, Mefistofele, Carmen, Faust, La Traviata, Manon Lescaut, Anna Bolena, Lucrezia Borgia, Norma, Tancredi. *Leisure interests:* literature, television, cooking, socializing. *Address:* 53 Midhurst Ave, Muswell Hill, London N10, UK. *Telephone:* (20) 8883-8596.

MIRMAN, Sophie; British business executive; b 28 Oct 1956; d of Simone and Serge Mirman; m Richard Philip Ross 1984; one s one d. *Education:* French Lycée (London). *Career:* Mem staff Marks and Spencer 1974–81; Man Dir Tie Rack 1981–83; Co-Founder Sock Shop Int 1983, Chair and Jt Man Dir Sock Shop Int PLC 1983–90; Jt Man Dir Trotters Childrenswear and Accessories 1990–. *Leisure interests:* family, sport. *Address:* 34 King's Rd, London SW3 4UD, UK. *Telephone:* (20) 7259-9622.

MIRREN, Helen Lydia; British actress; b 26 July 1945, London; m Taylor Hackford 1997. *Career:* Made debut Nat Youth Theatre Old Vic 1965; mem RSC 1967–83; toured Africa and USA with Peter Brook's Centre Int de Recherches Théâtrales 1972–73; Dr hc (St Andrews) 1999. *Plays include:* Antony and Cleopatra 1965, 1982–83, The Revenger's Tragedy 1967, All's Well That Ends Well 1967, Troilus and Cressida 1968, Much Ado About Nothing 1968, Bartholomew Fair 1969, Richard III, Hamlet, The Two Gentlemen of Verona 1970, Enemies 1971, Miss Julie, The Balcony 1971, Man of Mode 1972, Macbeth 1975, Teeth 'n' Smiles 1975, The Seagull, The Bed Before Yesterday 1975, Henry VI Parts 1, 2 and 3 1977–78, Measure For Measure 1979, The Duchess of Malfi 1980, 1981, Faith Healer 1981, The Roaring Girl 1983, Extremities (Evening Standard Award) 1984, Madame Bovary 1987, Two Way Mirror 1989, Sex Please, We're Italian 1991, The Writing Game 1993, The Gift of the Gorgon 1994, A Month in the Country 1994, Orpheus Descending 2001; *Films include:* Age of Consent 1969, Savage Messiah 1971, O Lucky Man! 1973, Caligula 1976, Hussy, The Long Good Friday 1979, Fu Man Chu 1980, Excalibur 1981, Cal (Best Actress Award, Cannes) 1983, 2010 1984, White Nights 1985, Heavenly Pursuits 1986, Mosquito Coast 1987, Pascali's Island 1988, When the Whales Came 1988, Bethune, Making of a Hero 1989, The Cook, the Thief, his Wife and her Lover 1989, The Comfort of Strangers 1989, Where Angels Fear to Tread 1990, The Gift 1991, The Hawk, The Price of Jutland 1991, The Madness of King George (Acad Award nomination, Cannes Film Festival Award) 1995, Losing Chase 1996, Some Mother's Son 1996, Killing Mrs Tingle 1998, The Pledge 2000, No Such Thing 2001; *TV appearances include:* Behind the Scenes, Cousin Bette 1971, Miss Julie 1972, Coffin for the Bride 1973, Jackanory, The Changeling 1974, The Philanthropist 1975, Mussolini and Claretta Petacci 1975, The Collection 1976, The Country Wife, As You Like It 1978, Blue Remembered Hills, The Serpent Son, A Midsummer Night's Dream 1981, Mrs Reinhart, After the Party, Cymbeline, Soft Targets 1982, Coming Through 1985, Cause Célèbre 1987, Red King, White Knight 1988, Prime Suspect (BAFTA Award) 1991, Prime Suspect II 1992, Prime Suspect III 1993, Prime Suspect: Scent of Darkness (Emmy Award for Best Actress 1996), Losing Chase (Golden Globe Award for Best Actress 1997), Painted Lady 1997, The Passion of Ayn Rand 1998. *Address:* c/o Ken McReddie Ltd, 91 Regent St, London W1R 7TB, UK.

MIRZOYEVA, Zukhra; Tajikistan medical practitioner and politician; b 24 Aug 1947; d of Amondullo Arbobov and Sharifmo Arbobova; m Sulton Khudoidodovich 1968; two s. *Education:* Dushanbe Medical School No 1 and Abualil ibn Sino Tajik State Medical Inst (Dushanbe). *Career:* Internship Tajik Maternity Hosp No 1 1973–74; graduate Inst of Special Genetics, Acad of Medical Sciences of the USSR 1974–78; Sr Research Asst Abuali ibn Sino State Medical Inst 1977–80; Sr Research Asst Inst for the Protection of Mothers and Children, Tajik Ministry of Health, USSR; Chair Cen Cttee of the Tajik Trade Union of Health Workers 1986–95; Deputy Minister of Health, Tajikistan 1995; has published 18 scientific articles and theses. *Leisure interests:* classical music, art of the Renaissance period. *Address:* c/o Ministry of Health, 734026 Dushanbe, I. Somoni 59, Tajikistan.

MISRA, Susheela, B MUS, MA; Indian musician and writer; b 15 Sept 1921, Kerala; d of Prof and Mrs P. Sankaran-Nambiyar; m Shiv Sharan Misra 1944 (deceased); one s. *Education:* Presidency Coll (Madras) and Bhatkhande Coll (Lucknow). *Career:* Producer of classical music All India Radio 1952–80; apptd Vice-Chair, Fellow Uttar Pradesh Sangeet Natak Acad 1990; Culture Critic The Times of India, The Hindu; has written more than 600 articles on dance and music; mem various cttees and orgs; Hon D MUS (Kanpur Univ); Sharangdey Fellow, Sur Singar Sansad (Bombay); Bhatkhande Centenary Award. *Publications:* Music Profiles 1955, Great Masters of Hindustani Music 1981, Music Makers of the Bhatkhande College 1985, Invitation to Indian Dances 1987, Some Immortals of Hindustani Music 1990, Musical Heritage of Lucknow 1991, Lucknow ki Sangeet Parampara, Some Dancers of India (2nd edn) 1992. *Leisure interests:* reading, writing, music, painting. *Address:* 1 Shahnajaf Rd, Lucknow 226 001, India. *Telephone:* (522) 242656.

MITAL, Christine Marie Michelle, L ÈS L, MA; French journalist; b 24 April 1946, Lyons; d of Antoine and Lucette Riboud; m Gérard Mital 1969; two s. *Education:* Univ of Lyons and Inst d'Etudes Politiques de Paris. *Career:* Ed on France Soir 1971–72, Informations 1973; Ed on Nouvel Economiste 1974–76, Head Social Section 1976–79; Ed on L'Expansion 1979–85, Sr Reporter 1985–87, Deputy Ed-in-Chief 1990, Ed-in-Chief then Deputy Editorial Dir 1991–99; Co-Dir Le Monde des Affaires (supplement to Le Monde) 1987–88; Ed-in-Chief Le Nouvel Observateur 2000–; Asst Ed-in-Chief Capital 1999–. *Leisure interest:* skiing. *Address:* Le Nouvel Observateur, 10–12 place de la Bourse, 75002 Paris, France.

MITCHAM, Constance Viola, LL B; Saint Christopher and Nevis politician; b 19 Nov 1947, Sandy Point; d of Rosina Augusta (née Benjamin) Mitcham. *Education:* Girls' High School (St Christopher), Kingston Coll (Surrey), Univ of London and The Inns of Court School of Law (London, UK). *Career:* Called to the Bar, England and Wales 1972; Election Supervisor British Virgin Islands 1973; Partner Mitcham and Benjamin Legal Firm; Chief Magistrate British Virgin Islands 1974–76; Minister of Women's Affairs 1984–89, of Health and Women's Affairs 1989, Acting Minister of Educ 1986–87, 1989, of Tourism and Labour 1987; Third Vice-Pres St Christopher's People's Action Movt, Ed People's Action Movt 25th Anniversary Historical Magazine 1990; Ed Int Business in St Christopher and Nevis Inner Temple Yearbook 1991; Int Woman of the Year, Business and Professional Women's Club 1975. *Leisure interests:* research and history of political parties, gardening, walking. *Address:* Franklands Estate, St Christopher, Saint Christopher and Nevis. *Telephone:* 465-2521; *Fax:* 465-6077.

MITCHELL, Joni (Roberta Joan Anderson), AB; Canadian singer and songwriter; b 7 Nov 1943, Fort Macleod, AB; d of William A. and Myrtle (née McKee) Anderson; m 1st Chuck Mitchell 1965 (divorced); m 2nd Larry Klein 1982; one d by Brad McGrath. *Education:* Alberta Coll. *Career:* Juno Award 1981, Century Award, Billboard Magazine 1996, Polar Music Prize (Sweden) 1996, Gov Gen's Performing Arts Award 1996, Nat Acad of Songwriters Lifetime Achievement Award 1996; inducted into Rock & Roll Hall of Fame 1997, into Nat Acad of Popular Music–Songwriters Hall of Fame 1997. *Recordings include:* Albums include: Songs to a Seagull, Clouds, Ladies of the Canyon, Blue, For the Roses, Court and Spark, Miles of Aisles, The Hissing of Summer Lawns, Hejira, Don Juan's Reckless Daughter, Mingus (Jazz Album of the Year, Rock-Blues Album of the Year, Downbeat Magazine

1979), Shadows and Light 1980, Dog Eat Dog 1986, Chalk Mark in a Rainstorm 1988, Night Ride Home 1991, Turbulent Indigo (Grammy Awards for Best Pop Album, Best Art Direction 1996) 1994, Hits 1996, Misses 1996; Singles include: Both Sides Now, Michael from Mountains, Urge for Going, Circle Game; *TV includes:* Joni Mitchell: Intimate and Interactive (Gemini Award 1996); *Publication:* Joni Mitchell: The Complete Poems and Lyrics. *Address:* c/o S. L. Feldman & Associates, 1505 W 2nd Ave, Suite 200, Vancouver, BC V6H 3Y4, Canada.

MITCHELL, Katie, BA; British theatre director; b 23 Sept 1964, Reading; d of Michael and Sally Mitchell. *Education:* Univ of Oxford. *Career:* Pres Univ of Oxford Dramatic Soc 1984; awarded a Winston Churchill Memorial Trust award to research E European theatre in Russia, Lithuania, Georgia, Poland and Germany 1989; Founder Classics on a Shoestring Theatre Co 1990; Assoc Dir RSC 1997–98; Assoc Dir Royal Court Theatre, London 2000; Assoc Dir Abbey Theatre 2000; dir of plays for Royal Court Theatre, RSC, Nat Theatre, Welsh Nat Opera, Abbey Theatre etc; Evening Standard Award for Best Dir 1996. *Plays directed include:* Arden of Faversham, Vassa Zheleznova, Women of Troy (Classics on a Shoestring), A Woman Killed with Kindness, The Dybbuk, Ghosts, Rutherford & Son, Henry VI, The Machine Wreckers, The Phoenician Women (Evening Standard Award for Best Director) 1996, The Mysteries 1997, The Beckett Shorts 1997, Uncle Vanya 1998, The Oresteia 1999, The Widowing of Mrs Holroyd 1995, Endgame 1996, Don Giovanni 1996, Jenufa 1998, Attempts on Her Life 1999, The Maids 1999, The Country 2000, Katya Kabanova 2001, The Last Ones, Iphigenia in Aulis 2001, Mountain Language Ashes to Ashes 2001; *TV work includes:* The Widowing of Mrs Holroyd 1995, The Stepdaughter 2000. *Leisure interests:* accordion, travel. *Address:* c/o Sebastian Born, The Agency, 24 Pottery Lane, London W11 4LZ, UK.

MITKOVA, Tatyana Vyacheslavovna; Russian broadcaster; b 13 Sept 1957, Moscow; m Solovyev V. Mitkova; one s. *Education:* Moscow State Univ. *Career:* TV appearances Leningrad (now St Petersburg) 1980–, ed, sr ed, reporter, special corresp until 1990; commentator Cen TV in Moscow 1990–93; during the putsch of 1991 refused to give official communications on air, was dismissed from work; Co-Founder, leading journalist NTV (ind channel) 1993, Head Information Broadcasting, NTV May 2001–; American Acad of Journalism Prize, Org for Defence of Journalism Prize 1991; winner Competition of Broadcasters of Information programmes 1991; Teffi (Russian TV Acad) Prize 1997. *TV Presenting includes:* 120 Minutes, Int Panorama, Segodnya (Today). *Leisure interest:* Music. *Address:* Nezavisimoe televidenie—NTV, Novy Arbat str, 36, 121205 Moscow, Russian Federation. *Telephone:* (095) 217 5624.

MITROVÁ-BELLOVÁ, Eva Judita, MD, PH D, D SC; Slovak medical practitioner and diplomatist; b 5 July 1937, Košice; d of Ignác Bella and Zofia Szekeráková; m 1st Alexander Mitro; one d; m 2nd Vlastimil Mayer. *Education:* Comenius Univ (Bratislava). *Career:* Lecturer, Asst Prof Medical Faculty, Comenius Univ 1962–78; Sr Research Worker, Research Inst for Preventive Medicine and Chief Lab of Slow Virus Neuroinfections 1978–92; Vice-Chair House of the People, Fed Ass (Parl) 1992; Amb of Czechoslovakia, later Slovakia to Council of Europe 1992–94, Amb of Slovakia to Hungary 1994; Pres Democratic Union of Women in Slovakia 1992; J. E. Purkinje Award, Ministry of Health Care 1987; Golden Medal for activities in women's NGO 1987. *Publications:* Viral Infections and their Mitigation (jtly) 1975, Focal Accumulation of CJD in Slovakia 1980, Some New Aspects of CJD Epidemiology in Slovakia 1991. *Leisure interests:* literature, history, archaeology, piano, gardening, painting, organization of fine art exhibitions. *Address:* Púpavova Str 4, 841 04 Bratislava, Slovakia (Home).

MITTWOCH, Ursula, PH D, D SC; British geneticist; b 21 March 1924; d of Prof Eugen and Dr Hermine (née Lipmann) Mittwoch; m Bernard Victor Springer; one d. *Education:* Henrietta Barnett School (London) and Univ of London. *Career:* Mem external staff MRC 1958–62; Reader Univ Coll London 1980–85, Prof of Genetics 1985–89 (Emer 1989–), Hon Research Fellow 1989–; Hon Visiting Prof London Hosp Medical Coll 1989–90; Visiting Prof Queen Mary and Westfield Coll, London 1990–96. *Publications include:* Sex Chromosomes 1967, Genetics of Sex

Differentiation 1973. *Address:* University College London, Dept of Biology, Wolfson House, 4 Stephenson Way, London, NW1 2HE, UK; 73 Leverton St, London NW5 2NX, UK. *Telephone:* (20) 7267-1560; *E-mail:* u.mittwoch@ucl.ac.uk.

MLÍKOVSKÁ, Jiřina; Czech choreographer; b 3 Feb 1925, Plzeň; d of Jindřich and Růužena Kovářik; m Čestmír Mlíkovský 1950 (divorced 1963); one d one s. *Education:* Lycée Classique (Plzeň) and Akademie Múzických Umění (Prague). *Career:* Dancer Plzeň Theatre 1943–45, Nat Theatre, Prague 1945–48; Choreographer of folk dances 1950–60; Ballet Choreographer Prague; External Prof of Choreography and Ballet Production Akademie Múzických Umění 1984–; has choreographed works in numerous theatres and for Czechoslovak TV; many publs on choreography; numerous awards. *Leisure interests:* grandchildren, writing a family history, photography, architecture. *Address:* Akademie Múzických Umění, MalostranskÉnAm 12, 11800 Prague 1, Czech Republic. *Telephone:* (2) 535041.

MNOUCHKINE, Ariane; French theatre director; b 1938, Boulogne-sur-Seine. *Education:* Oxford Univ (UK). *Career:* Founder Paris-based Théâtre du Soleil 1964; Grand Prix de la Société des auteurs et compositeurs dramatiques (SACD) 2000. *Productions include:* Gengis Khan 1961, Les Petits Bourgeois, The Kitchen 1967, Clowns 1968, 1789 1970, L'Age d'or 1975, Mephisto 1979 (UK 1986), L'Indiade, Les Atrides, The King of Cambodia 1983. *Address:* Le Théâtre du Soleil, Cartoucherie de Vincennes, Vincennes, Paris, France.

MODAHL, Diane; British athlete; b 1967; m Vicente Modahl; one d. *Education:* Univ of Manchester. *Career:* Participant Commonwealth Games 1994, suspended after positive drug test, banned from athletics for four years 1994, ban overturned 1995; mem winning team Nat Team Cross-Country Championship 1996; participant Olympic Games, Atlanta, GA, USA 1996; ranked UK number 1 800m 1987–90, 1992–94, 1998; now sports journalist and presenter. *Address:* Show-Sport Management Ltd, 3 The Old Mill, Church Lane, Sale, Cheshire M33 5QQ, UK.

MÖDL, Martha; German opera singer. *Education:* Munich and Nuremberg Conservatoires. *Career:* Has made numerous appearances at German and foreign opera houses, and at Bayreuth Festivals 1951–; mem Staatsoper Stuttgart 1953–. *Address:* Perlacherstr 19, 8082 Grünwald, Germany.

MOERPRATOMO, A. Sulasikin; Indonesian politician; b 18 April 1927, Jakarta. *Education:* Univ of Indonesia. *Career:* Sec then Vice-Chair PERIWAR Women's Org 1953–56, Sec to Cen Bd of Educ Standing Cttee 1962–67; Chair Prov Bd PERISCA POSTEL (Asscn of Women in Dept of Posts and Telecommunications) 1962–72; Programme Officer UNICEF 1958–83; Chair Public Information Standing Cttee, Fed of Kindergarten Teachers' Asscn 1965–67, Presidium Nat Comm on the Status of Women 1975–78; mem Dewan Perwakilan Rakyat (House of Reps, Parl) 1982–87; Minister of State for Women's Affairs 1988–93; mem Majelis Permusyawaraten Rakyat (People's Consultative Ass) 1983–92. *Address:* c/o Office of the Minister of State for Women's Affairs, Jalan Merdeka Barat 15, Jakarta Pusat 10110, Indonesia.

MOFE-DAMIJO, May Ellen Ezekiel (Mee), BA; Nigerian journalist and writer; b 19 Dec 1956, Takoradi, Ghana; d of the late Warri Owegberu and of Victoria Ezekiel; m 2nd Richard Mofe-Damijo 1989; one d two step-s. *Education:* Ghana Nat Coll, St Theresa's Grammar School, Nigerian Inst of Journalism (Lagos) and Univ of Wisconsin (USA). *Career:* Journalist Sunday Concord newspaper 1982–84; Asst Ed Newswatch 1985–86; Ed Quality magazine 1987–1989; Publr, CEO Classique Magazine 1989–; has set up scholarship fund in the area of educ; has received Inner Wheel, Rotary and Jaycees Awards for charity work. *Publications:* Novels: Dream-Maker 1988, Centrespread 1989, Pilgrim Souls (in preparation); Non-fiction: Windsongs 1991, Women Like Us: a study of 20 successful Nigerian women 1992; Children's book: Tales Papa Told (in preparation). *Leisure interests:* charity work, reading, watching people. *Address:* Classique Magazine, Panache Communications Ltd, 3 Allen Ave, Ikeja, Lagos State, Nigeria. *Telephone:* (1) 967368.

MOFFO, Anna; American opera singer (soprano); b Wayne, PA; d of Nicholas and Regina (née Cinti) Moffo; m Robert Sarnoff 1974. *Education:* Curtis Inst. *Career:* Has appeared in TV opera Madam Butterfly, Italy; singer opera houses including Paris, London, Salzburg (Austria), Vienna, Milan (Italy); American debut Lyric Opera Co, Chicago 1957, Metropolitan Opera Co, New York 1959; appeared in Voice of Firestone telecast 1957; has made numerous recordings; Order of Merit (Italy); Young Artists award, Philadelphia Orchestra; Fulbright Award for study in Europe; Liebe Augustin Award. *Operas include:* Norma, La Bohème, Mignon, Rigoletto, Falstaff, Madam Butterfly, The Barber of Seville, La Traviata, Thaïs, The Daughter of the Regiment, Stiffelio, Tosca, Hansel and Gretel, Faust, Don Pasquale, Romeo and Juliet, The Magic Flute, Turandot, La Juive, The Marriage of Figaro, Otello, Il Trovatore, Luisa Miller, La Belle Hélène, The Gypsy Princess.

MOGGACH, Deborah, BA FRSL; British writer; b 28 June 1948, London; d of Richard and Helen Charlotte Hough; m Anthony Moggach 1971 (divorced); one s one d. *Education:* Camden School for Girls and Univ of Bristol. *Career:* Chair Soc of Authors. *Play:* Double Take; *TV dramas:* To Have and To Hold 1986, Stolen 1990, Goggle-Eyes (adaptation) 1993 (Writers' Guild Award for Best Adapted TV Serial), Seesaw 1998, Close Relations 1998, Love in a Cold Climate (adaptation) 2001; *Publications:* novels: You Must Be Sisters 1978, Close to Home 1979, A Quiet Drink 1980, Hot Water Man 1982, Porky 1983, To Have and To Hold 1986, Driving in the Dark 1988, Stolen 1990, The Stand-in 1991, The Ex-Wives 1993, Seesaw 1996, Close Relations 1997, Tulip Fever 1999, Final Demand 2001; short stories: Smile 1987, Changing Babies 1995. *Leisure interests:* swimming in rivers, walking round cities. *Address:* c/o Curtis Brown, 28/29 Haymarket, London, SW1P 4SP, UK. *Telephone:* (20) 7396-6600; *Fax:* (20) 7396-0110.

MOGHADAM, Valentine M., PH D; American (b Iranian) specialist on women in the Middle East; b 17 Sept 1952, Teheran (now Tehran); d of Victor and Germaine Mirza-Moghadam. *Education:* Community High School (Teheran), Univ of Waterloo (ON, Canada) and The American Univ (Washington, DC, USA). *Career:* Reporter Kayhan Int 1970–72; teacher of English Iranian Air Force Language School 1972–74; Lecturer in Devt and Middle East Studies, New York and Rutgers Univs 1986–89; Researcher in Gender Brown Univ Pembroke Center, RI 1988–89; Researcher in Women and Devt, UNU-WIDER, Helsinki 1990–92, Sr Researcher, Co-ordinator Research Programme 1992–95; Dir of Women's Studies, Illinois State Univ 1996; Official Del to World Summit for Social Devt, Copenhagen 1995, Fourth World Conf on Women, Beijing 1995; ACLS Award Research Travel Grant 1988; Fulbright Award 1990; IREX Travel Grant 1993; CAORC Fellowship 1996. *Publications:* Modernizing Women: Gender and Social Change in the Middle East 1993, Identity Politics and Women: Cultural Reassertions and Feminisms in International Perspective 1994, Gender and Development in the Arab World (jtly) 1995, Patriarchy and Development: Women's Positions at the End of the Twentieth Century 1996. *Leisure interests:* theatre, cinema, fiction, walking, photography, swimming, music. *Address:* Women's Studies Program, Illinois State University, 604 S Main, Campus Box 4260, Normal, IL 61790-4260, USA. *Telephone:* (309) 438-2947.

MOGHAIZEL, Laure, L EN D; Lebanese lawyer and campaigner; b (Laure Nasr) 1929, Lebanon; m Joseph Moghaizel 1953; three d two s. *Education:* Sœurs de Besançon and Univ Saint Joseph (Beirut). *Career:* Promoter, mem Cttee of Political Rights of Lebanese Women 1949–53, Cttee for Equality in Inheritance 1955–59, Cttee for Amendment of the Penal Law 1970; Founder-mem Lebanese Asscn of Jurist Women, Lebanese Univ Grad Women Asscn, Nat Council of Lebanese Women, Lebanese Asscn for Human Rights, Non-Violence Movt; Vice-Pres Arab Women Fed; Counsellor Int Council of Women; has written and contributed to several books; mem UNESCO Nat Cttee, Governmental Del to the Regional Meeting of Human Rights 1986, Arab Council for Childhood and Devt, Advisory Cttee on Arab Women and Devt, Abolitionist Int Fed, Comm to the UN Int Women's Conf, Nairobi 1985, Int Fed of Women Jurists; participant at numerous int confs; Lebanese Merit Decoration. *Leisure interest:* reading. *Address:* The Lebanese Association for Human Rights, 145 Tabaris Square, SNA

Bldg, POB 16-6742, Beirut, Lebanon (Office); 831 Damascus St, Museum Place, Beirut, Lebanon (Home). *Telephone:* (1) 333753 (Office); (1) 384470 (Home); *Fax:* (1) 328607 (Office).

MOHAMED, Sittou Raghadat, PH D; Comoran politician; b 6 July 1952, Ouani, Anjouan; m 1975; two s two d. *Education:* Mutsamudu and Ecole Normale des Instituteurs (Moroni). *Career:* Teacher 1983–91; campaigner for human rights (especially for women and children) and for democracy; first woman Sec of State for Population and Women's Affairs 1991; High Commr responsible for Women's Affairs 1992; Minister of Social Affairs, Labour and Employment 1994. *Publication:* Mémoire sur la condition de la femme Comorienne 1983. *Leisure interests:* music, reading. *Address:* c/o Ministry of Social Affairs, Labour and Employment, BP 520, Moroni, Comoros.

MOHAPI, Sophia Malikotsi, B COMM, CA; Lesotho accountant; b 13 July 1942, Maseru; d of the late Meshack and Esther Taole; m George Albert Mohapi 1963 (died 1975); three s one d. *Education:* Univ of Manitoba (Canada) and Lesotho Inst of Accountants (Maseru). *Career:* Deputy Finance Controller, Lesotho Nat Devt Corpn 1982–84; Lecturer in Financial Accounting and Tax, Centre for Accounting Studies 1984–88, Deputy Dir 1988–89; Deputy Financial Controller Lesotho Highlands Devt Authority 1989–91, apptd Deputy Chief Exec of Finance and Admin 1991; mem Council and Chair Disciplinary Cttee, Lesotho Inst of Accountants 1990. *Leisure interests:* tennis, music, knitting. *Address:* Lesotho Highlands Development Authority, POB 76, Maseru, Lesotho. *Telephone:* 311280; *Fax:* 310060.

MOISEIWITSCH, Tanya, CBE; British stage and costume designer; b 3 Dec 1914; d of the late Benno Moiseiwitsch and Daisy Kennedy; m Felix Krish 1942 (deceased). *Education:* Privately and Cen School of Arts and Crafts (London). *Career:* Scene painting student Old Vic, London and Abbey Theatre, Dublin, Ireland 1935–39, Q Theatre 1940; first West End production Golden Cuckoo, Duchess 1940; weekly repertory Oxford Playhouse 1941–44; Designer for Old Vic Co 1944–, Playhouse, Liverpool 1944–45, Theatre Royal, Bristol 1945–46; Consultant Designer Crucible Theatre, Sheffield 1971–73; Assoc Dir Laureate, Stratford Festival, Canada; Designer for numerous theatre and opera cos in UK and abroad; Hon Fellow Ontario Coll of Art 1979; Diplôme d'Honneur, Canadian Conf of the Arts; Hon D LITT (Birmingham) 1964, (Waterloo, ON) 1977, (Minnesota) 1994; Hon LL D (Toronto) 1988. *Stage and Costume designs include:* Bless the Bride 1947, Peter Grimes 1947, Beggar's Opera 1948, Treasure Hunt 1949, Home at Seven 1950, The Holly and the Ivy 1950, Captain Carvallo 1950, Figure of Fun 1951; for Old Vic: Uncle Vanya, The Critic, Cyrano de Bergerac 1945–46, The Cherry Orchard 1948, 1955, 1966, A Month in the Country 1949, Midsummer Night's Dream 1951, Timon of Athens 1952, Henry VIII 1953 (also RSC 1950), The Two Gentlemen of Verona 1957; for RSC: The History Cycle 1951, Othello 1954, Measure for Measure 1956, Much Ado About Nothing (scenery) 1958, All's Well that Ends Well 1959, 1977, Cymbeline 1970, The Imaginary Invalid 1974, Mary Stuart (costumes) 1982, Tartuffe 1983, The Government Inspector 1985, The Matchmaker (Edinburgh Festival) 1954, (New York) 1955, Merchant of Venice 1959; for Tyrone Guthrie Theatre, Minneapolis (USA): Hamlet 1963, The Miser, Three Sisters 1964, Saint Joan 1965, Volpone 1965, The Way of the World 1966, As You Like It 1967, Skin of Our Teeth (jtly) 1967, The House of Atreus 1973; Metropolitan Opera New York: Peter Grimes 1967, Rigoletto 1977, La Traviata 1981; for National Theatre: Volpone 1968, The Misanthrope 1973, Phaedra Britannica 1975, The Double Dealer 1978; for Abbey Theatre, Dublin: Swift 1969, Red Roses for Me 1980; The Barber of Seville, Brighton Festival 1971, The Voyage of Edgar Allan Poe (world première) 1976, The Clandestine Marriage 1984, King Lear (for Granada TV) 1983. *Address:* 17B St Alban's Studio, St Alban's Grove, London, W8 5BT, UK.

MOLINA, Angela; Spanish actress; three c. *Career:* Trained as dancer; actress (discovered by Luis Buñuel) 1977–; has appeared in over 50 films. *Films include:* That Obscure Object of Desire, Las Cosas del Querer.

MOMEN, Wendi, PH D, B SC; British publisher and religious organization official; b 21 Oct 1950, Hollywood (CA, USA); d of Robert Wirtshafter and Carol Allen (née Morris); m Moojan Momen 1971; one

s one d. *Education:* LSE. *Career:* Ed George Ronald publishing co, Oxford 1979–; editorial services OneWorld Publications (Oxford) 1989–, Intellect Books (Oxford) 1991–; Chair Man Exec Bahá'í Publishing Trust (UK) 1989–94, Ed 1991–, Asst Ed The Bahá'í Encyclopedia, Bahá'í Publishing Trust (USA) 1991–94; mem Nat Spiritual Ass of the Bahá'ís of the UK 1982–, Treas 1984–90, 2001–, Chair 1990–2000, Asst Sec 2000–2001; Pres European Bahá'ís Business Forum 1991–, Pres 1993–; TV programmes for Broomsticks Productions (Tonga) 1994–96; JP Biggleswade (now Bedford) Petty Sessional Div 1982–, Court Chair 1994–; Non-Exec Dir Beds Family Health Services Authority 1990–94, 1999–2001; mem Int Steering Cttee Global Women sector of Global Forum 1994; Trustee One World Trust 1997–, BASED-UK 1997–, Multi-Faith Centre (Derby Univ) 2000–. *Publications:* Call Me Ridvan 1982, Family Worship 1989, A Basic Bahá'í Dictionary 1989, Jewels (series) 1994, Meditation 1996, I'm a Bahá'í, Basic Bahá'í Chronology (with Glenn Cameron) 1996, To Be a Mother 1999, Paradise Created (with Brenton Edwards) 2001, numerous conference papers. *Leisure interests:* theatre, travel, reading. *Address:* Wixamtree, Sand Lane, Northill, nr Biggleswade, Beds SG18 9AD, UK. *Telephone:* (1767) 627626; *Fax:* (1767) 627626; *E-mail:* wendi@northill.demon.co.uk.

MONGELLA, Gertrude; Tanzanian United Nations official; four c. *Education:* Univ of Dar Es Salaam. *Career:* Fmr teacher and politician; fmr Amb to India; mem staff UN, responsible for organization of Fourth UN Conf on the Status of Women, Beijing 1995. *Address:* c/o United Nations, UN Plaza, New York, NY 10017, USA.

MONK, Lorraine Althea Constance, OC, MA, LL D; Canadian writer and producer of photographic books; b Montréal, PQ; d of Edwin and Eileen Marion (née Nurse) Spurrell; m John McGaughan Monk; two s two d. *Education:* McGill Univ. *Career:* Exec Dir Canadian Museum of Photography; Exec Dir Still Photography Div, Nat Film Bd of Canada; Centennial Medal 1967; Excellence of Service Award, Fed int de l'art photographique; Gold Medal Nat Asscn of Photographic Art; Silver Medal Leipzig Book Fair 1975; First Prize Int Craftsman Guild 1983. *Publications include:* A Year of the Land 1967, Ces visages qui sont en pays 1967, Stones of History 1967, Call Them Canadians 1968, A Time To Dream – Reveries en couleurs 1971, The Female Eye 1975, Between Friends (Gold Medal Int Book Fair, Leipzig, Germany) 1977, Robert Bourdeau Monograph 1979, Image (series), Signature (series), Canada With Love 1982, Celebrate our City 1983, Ontario: A Loving Look 1984, Photographs That Changed the World 1989, Canada: Romancing the Land 1996, These Things We Hold Dear – An Album of Photographic Memories (producer) 1999. *Address:* 176 Balmoral Ave, Toronto, ON M4V 1J6, Canada. *Telephone:* (416) 929-9357.

MONK, Marilyn, M SC, PH D; Australian scientist; b 6 Sept 1938, Melbourne; d of Frederick E. and Edna I. J. Monk; m Julian D. Gross 1968 (divorced 1982); two s. *Education:* Upwey High School (Vic) and Univs of Melbourne and London. *Career:* Scientist MRC of GB 1968–; Researcher in molecular genetics of mammalian devt; developed techniques for molecular studies of early embryos and pioneer work on detection of genetic defects in single cells; has been awarded several scholarships. *Publications:* Mammalian Development 1987, Genomic Imprinting 1990. *Leisure interests:* arts, literature, music, walking, swimming, horses. *Address:* MRC Mammalian Development Unit, Wolfson House, 4 Stephenson Way, London NW1 2HE, UK. *Telephone:* (20) 7387-9521; *Fax:* (20) 7383-0964.

MONK, Meredith Jane; American composer, director and choreographer; b 20 Nov 1942; d of Theodore G. Monk and Audrey Lois (Zellman). *Education:* Sarah Lawrence Coll (Bronxville, NY). *Career:* Founder, Artistic Dir House Foundation for the Arts 1968–; formed Meredith Monk & Vocal Ensemble 1978; Dr hc (Bard Coll) 1988, (Univ of the Arts) 1989, (Juilliard School of Music) 1998, San Francisco Art Inst 1999; Golden Eagle Award 1981, Nat Music Theatre Award 1986, German Critics' Award for Best Recording of the Year 1981, 1986, Samuel Scripps Award 1996 and numerous other awards. *Works include:* Break 1964, 16 Millimeter Earrings 1966, Juice: a theatre cantata 1969, Key 1971, Vessel: an opera epic 1971, Paris 1972, Education of the Girlchild 1973, Quarry 1976, Songs from the Hill 1976, Dolmen Music 1979, Specimen Days: a civil war opera 1981, Ellis Island 1981, Turtle Dreams Cabaret 1983, The Games 1983, Acts from Under and Above

1986, Book of Days 1988, Facing North 1990, Atlas: an opera in three parts 1991, Three Heavens and Hells 1992, New York Requiem 1993, Volcano Songs 1994, American Archaeology 1994, The Politics of Quiet 1996, Magic Frequencies 1998. *Leisure interests:* gardening, horse-riding. *Address:* House Foundation for Arts, 131 Varick St, New York, NY 10013, USA.

MONOGAROVA, Tatyana Alexeyevna; Russian opera singer (soprano); b (Tatyana Alexeyevna Kapustina) 16 Feb 1967, Moscow; d of Alexey Alexeyevich Monogarov and Svetlana Pavlovna Monogarova; m two c. *Education:* Russian Acad of Arts. *Career:* Soloist Moscow Chamber Theatre Helicon Opera 1989–91; soloist Moscow Stanislavsky and Nemirovich-Danchenko Music Theatre 1991–; guest soloist in European countries including Opera houses of Bologna, Bern, Nantes, Venice, Vienna (Kammeroper) and Riga; has performed with many conductors including Vladimir Fedoseyev, Vladimir Spivakov and Peter Feranec. *Repertoire includes:* Micaela in Carmen, Lia in Prodigal Son, Violanta in La Finta Giardinera, Countess in The Marriage of Figaro, Pamina in Die Zauberflöte, Xenia in La Bohème, Manon in Manon Lescaut, Butterfly in Madame Butterfly, Liu in Turandot, Luisa in Luisa Miller, Violetta in La Traviata, Leonora in Il Trovatore, Elisabetta in Don Carlos, Desdemona in Othello, Amelia in Simon Boccanegra, Lida in La Batalia di Legnano, Tsaritsa in Immortal Kashchey, Swan Princess in The Tale of Tsar Saltan, Parasha in Mavra (Stravinsky), Tatyana in Eugene Onegin, Yolanta, Oksana in Cherevichki, Lisa in Pique Dame, Electra in Oresteya (Taneyev), Rosalinda in Die Fledermaus (Strauss); Solo parts in: Magnificat (Bach), An die Freunde Op 125 (Beethoven), Requiem (Verdi), Symphony No 4 (Mahler), Requiem (Mozart), Motet Exultate, Jubilate, Mess in G Major (Schubert). *Address:* Moscow Stanislavsky and Nemirovich-Danchenko Music Theatre, Bolshaya Dmitrovka, 17, Moscow, Russian Federation. *Telephone:* (095) 229-00-48 (Theatre); (095) 366-89-07 (Home).

MONSPART, Sarolta, M SC; Hungarian sportswoman; b 17 Nov 1944, Budapest; d of Elemér and Sarolta (née Nagy) Monspart; m Péter Feledy 1981; one s. *Education:* Physical Educ High School and Loránd Eötvös Univ (Budapest). *Career:* Teacher of Math and Physics; mem nat Orienteering, Marathon, Ski-Orienteering, Ski-Cross-country teams 1962–78; World Orienteering Champion 1972; ran Marathon in under three hours (first woman in Europe), Budapest 1972; Team Leader of Healthy Lifestyle Programme, Nat Inst for Health Promotion 1990–; Merited Sportsperson of Hungary 1973; Merit Prize of Youth 1977, 1978, 1982. *Publication:* The Marvellous World of Running (jtly) 1990. *Leisure interests:* running, health promotion, the forest. *Address:* 1062 Budapest, Andrássy út 82, Hungary (Office); 1125 Budapest, Szilágyi E fasor 2, Hungary (Home). *Telephone:* (1) 332-7380 (Office); (1) 155-5025 (Home); *Fax:* (1) 331-6112; *E-mail:* FB7072@mail.matav.hu.

MONTAGU, Jennifer Iris Rachel, PH D, FBA; British curator; b 20 March 1931; d of the late Ewen Edward Samuel Montagu. *Education:* Benenden School (Kent), Lady Margaret Hall (Oxford) and Warburg Inst (London). *Career:* Asst Regional Dir Arts Council of GB, NW Region 1953–54; Lecturer in History of Art, Univ of Reading 1958–64; Asst Curator of Photograph Collection, Warburg Inst 1964–71, Curator 1971–91, Hon Fellow 1991; Slade Prof Univ of Cambridge and Fellow Jesus Coll, Cambridge 1980–81; Andrew W. Mellon Lecturer Nat Gallery of Art, Washington, DC 1991; Invited Prof Coll de France 1994; mem Academic Awards Cttee, British Fed of Univ Women 1963–89, Exec Cttee Nat Art-Collections Fund 1973–, Consultative Cttee Burlington Magazine 1975–, Cttee of the Jewish Museum 1983–, Reviewing Cttee on the Export of Works of Art 1987–96; Trustee Wallace Collection 1989–, British Museum 1994–; Hon Academician Acad Clementina, Bologna (Italy) 1988; Serena Medal for Italian Studies, British Acad 1992; Officier des Arts et des Lettres 1991; Chevalier de la Légion d'Honneur 1999. *Publications include:* Bronzes 1963, Alessandro Algardi (special Mitchell Prize) 1985, Roman Baroque Sculpture: the industry of art 1989, The Expression of the Passions 1994, Gold, Silver and Bronze:metal sculpture of the Roman Baroque 1996; exhibition catalogues and contribs to professional journals. *Address:* Warburg Institute, Woburn Square, London WC1H 0AB, UK; 10 Roland Way, London SW7 3RE, UK.

MONTAGUE, Diana, ARCM; British opera and concert singer (mezzo-soprano); b 8 April 1953, Winchester; d of N. H. and Mrs Montague; m Philip Doghan 1978; one s. *Education:* Testwood School (Totton, Hants), Winchester School of Art and Royal Manchester Coll of Music. *Career:* Made professional debut at Glyndebourne 1977; Prin Mezzo-Soprano Royal Opera House, Covent Garden, London 1978; freelance artist 1984–; has toured throughout Europe and USA appearing at Metropolitan Opera, New York, USA and Bayreuth, Germany, Aix-en-Provence, France, Salzburg, Austria and Glyndebourne festivals. *Leisure interests:* horse-riding, country life in general. *Address:* 28, 91 St Martin's Lane, London WC2, UK; 17 Sheridan Gardens, Testbourne Farm, Hants, UK. *Telephone:* (20) 7836-3770 (London); (170386) 0457 (Hants).

MONTAGUE, Air Cdre Ruth Mary Bryceson, B SC, FRSA; British former air force officer; b 1 June 1939; d of the late Griffith John and Nancy Bryceson Griffiths; m Roland Arthur Montague 1966. *Education:* Bedford Coll (Univ of London). *Career:* Commissioned RAF 1962, served UK and Far East 1962–66, UK 1966–80, HQ Strike Command 1980–83, RAF Staff Coll 1983–86, Deputy Dir Women's RAF 1986–89, Dir 1989–94, ADC to the Queen 1989–94; Chair of Council Friends of St Clement Danes, Cen Church of the RAF 1995; mem Council RAF Benevolent Fund 1994–, Council Royal Holloway (Univ of London) 1994–. *Leisure interests:* cookery, tapestry, gardening, world travel, clay pigeon shooting, swimming. *Address:* c/o National Westminster Bank, Marlow Br, POB 873, 7 High St, Marlow, Bucks SL7 1BZ, UK.

MONTE, Marisa; Brazilian singer. *Education:* studied lyrical art in Italy. *Career:* has performed over 200 concerts in Brazil, Europe and USA. *Recordings include:* Ao Vivo 1989, Rose and Charcoal, Red Hot+Rio, Aguas de Março (jtly), A Great Noise 1996. *Address:* c/o Ministry of Culture, SBN, Quadra 2, Bloco F, Edif Central, 70.040 Brasília, DF, Brazil.

MONTEIL, Martine Marcelle; French police commissioner; b 1950; one d. *Career:* Apptd first woman police Commr 1979; worked in Paris Anti-Drug Squad, later Head Anti-Prostitution Div; Commr Brigade Criminelle (Paris police criminal investigation unit) 1996–2000; Sub Dir for Human Resources and Logistics, Paris Judiciary Police 2000–. *Address:* 36 quai des Orfèvres, 75001 Paris, France.

MONTERO M., Clara; Costa Rican diplomatist. *Career:* Amb to Venezuela 1996–. *Address:* Embassy of Costa Rica, Avda San Juan Bosco, entre 1° y 2° transversal, Edif For You PH, Altamira, Apdo 62239, Caracas, Venezuela. *Telephone:* (2) 267-1104; *Fax:* (2) 262-0038.

MOORE, Carole Irene, MS; Canadian librarian; b 15 Aug 1944, Berkeley, CA, USA. *Education:* Stanford and Columbia Univs (USA). *Career:* Reference Librarian Columbia Univ Libraries 1967–68, Univ of Toronto Library 1968–73; Asst Head Reference Dept, Univ of Toronto Library 1973–74, Head 1974–80, Head Bibliographic Processing Dept 1980–86, Assoc Librarian, Tech Services 1986–87, Chief Librarian 1986–; Research Libraries Group Dir 1994–96; Bd Dirs Univ of Toronto Press 1994–; Columbia Univ School of Library Service Centenary Distinguished Alumni Award 1987. *Publications:* Labour Relations and the Librarian (ed) 1974, Canadian Essays and Collections Index 1972–73 1976. *Leisure interest:* gardening. *Address:* Robarts Library, 130 St George St, Toronto, ON M5S 1A5, Canada (Office); 5 Albermarle Ave, Toronto, ON M4K 1H6, Canada (Home).

MOORE, Darla D.; American business executive; b 1955, Lake City, NC. *Career:* Joined Chemical Bank 1982, in charge of Debtor-in-Possession Financing Group 1984–1991; Man Dir in charge of Mfrs' Restructuring and Reorganization Group, Manufacturers Hanover Trust Co 1991.

MOORE, Debbie; British business executive; b 31 May 1946. *Career:* Fmrly fashion model; f Pineapple Dance Studio 1979; first woman chair in Stock Exchange when Pineapple went public 1982; Veuve Cliquot Businesswoman of the Year 1984. *Publications:* The Pineapple Dance Book 1983, When a Woman Means Business 1989 (trans into Chinese

2000). *Address:* Debbie Moore Studios Ltd, 7 Langley St, London WC2H 9JA, UK. *Telephone:* (20) 7379-8090; *Fax:* (20) 7240-4531; *E-mail:* mail@pineapple.uk.com; *Internet:* www.pineapple.uk.com.

MOORE, Demi; American actress; b (Demi Guynes) 11 Nov 1962, Roswell, NM; d of Danny and Virginia Guynes; m Bruce Willis (divorced 2000); three d. *Career:* Model 1978–, Cover-girl for Vanity Fair magazine 1992; made film debut 1981; numerous appearances in TV series and films; runs own film production co Moving Pictures; made magazine advertisement for Donna Karan with Bruce Willis 1996. *Films:* Choices 1981, Parasite, Young Doctors In Love, Blame It On Rio, No Small Affair, St Elmo's Fire, One Crazy Summer, About Last Night..., Wisdom, The Seventh Sign, We're No Angels, Ghost, Nothing But Trouble, Mortal Thoughts (also co-producer), The Butcher's Wife, A Few Good Men, Indecent Proposal, Disclosure, The Scarlet Letter, Striptease 1995, The Juror 1996, GI Jane 1996, The Hunchback of Notre Dame (voice) 1996, Now and Then (also co-producer), If These Walls Could Talk, Deconstructing Harry 1997, Austin Powers: International Man of Mystery (producer) 1997, Passion of Mind, Airframe; *TV includes:* Kaz, Vegas, General Hospital, Bedroom, Tales From the Crypt, Bedroom; *Play:* The Early Girl (Theatre World Award) 1987. *Address:* Creative Artists Agency Inc, 9830 Wilshire Blvd, Beverly Hills, CA 90212, USA.

MOORE, (Georgina) Mary, MA, LL D; British college principal and writer; b 8 April 1930, Oxford; d of the late Prof V. H. Galbraith and Georgina R. Cole-Baker; m Antony R. Moore 1963 (died 2000); one s. *Education:* The Mount School (York) and Lady Margaret Hall (Oxford). *Career:* Joined HM Foreign (later Diplomatic) Service 1951; served in Budapest 1954, UK Perm Del at UN, New York 1956; First Sec 1961; resgnd on marriage 1963; Prin St Hilda's Coll, Oxford 1980–90; Trustee British Museum 1982–92, Rhodes Trust 1984–96, Pilgrim Trust 1991– (Chair 1993–); mem Council for Industry and Higher Educ 1986–90. *Publications:* (as Helena Osborne) The Arcadian Affair 1969, Pay Day 1972, White Poppy 1977, The Joker 1979, various plays for TV and radio including Testimonies 1990. *Leisure interests:* theatre, travel. *Address:* Touchbridge, Boarstall, Aylesbury, Bucks HP18 9UJ, UK. *Telephone:* (1844) 238247.

MOORE, Gillian, MBE, B MUS (HONS), MA, FRCM; British musical director; b 20 Feb 1959, Glasgow; d of Charles Moore and Sara Queen; partner Bruce Nockles; one s. *Education:* Univ of Glasgow, Royal Scottish Acad of Music and Drama, Univ of York and Harvard Univ. *Career:* Educ Dir London Sinfonietta 1983–93, Artistic Dir 1998–; Head of Educ Royal Festival Hall 1993–96, Music Audience Devt Man 1996–; Artistic Dir ISCM World Music Days, Manchester 1997–98; Visiting Prof Royal Coll of Music 1996–; Gov Nat Youth Orchestra of GB; mem British Govt Nat Curriculum Working Group on Music; freelance work as broadcaster, lecturer and writer in music, consultant on music and educ; Hon mem Guildhall School of Music 1993; Sir Charles Grove Award for Outstanding Contrib to British Music 1992, Asscn of British Orchestras Award for Contrib of Most Benefit to Orchestral Life in the UK 1999. *Address:* London Sinfonietta, 4 Maguire St, London, SE1, UK (Office); 108 Waller Rd, London SE14 5LU, UK (Home). *Telephone:* (20) 7928-0828 (Office); (20) 7639-6680 (Home); *Fax:* (20) 7928-8557 (Office); (20) 7639-6675.

MOORE, Julianne, BA; American actress; b 1951. *Education:* Univ of Boston. *Career:* With the Guthrie Theatre 1988–89. *Plays include:* Serious Money 1987, Ice Cream with Hot Fudge 1990, Uncle Vanya, The Road to Nirvana, Hamlet, The Father; *TV includes:* As the World Turns (series), The Edge of Night (series), Money, Power Murder 1989, Lovecraft 1991, I'll Take Manhattan, The Last to Go, Cast a Deadly Spell; *Films include:* Tales from the Darkside 1990, The Hand That Rocks the Cradle 1992, The Gun in Betty Lou's Handbag 1992, Body of Evidence 1993, Benny & Joon 1993, The Fugitive 1993, Short Cuts 1993, Vanya on 42nd Street 1994, Roommates 1995, Safe 1995, Nine Months 1995, Assassins 1995, Surviving Picasso 1996, Jurassic Park: The Lost World 1997, The Myth of Fingerprints 1997, Hellcab 1997, Boogie Nights 1997, The Big Lebowski 1998, Eyes Wide Shut, The End of the Affair 1999, Map of the World 1999, Magnolia 1999, Cookie's Fortune 1999, An Ideal Husband 1999, Hannibal 2000. *Address:* c/o Creative Artists Agency, 9830 Wilshire Blvd, Beverly Hills, CA 90212, USA.

MOORE, Mary Tyler; American actress; b 29 Dec 1936, New York; d of George and Marjorie Moore; m 1st Richard Meeker; m 2nd Grant Tinker 1963 (divorced 1981); m 3rd Robert Levine 1983; one s (deceased). *Career:* Chair MTM Enterprises Inc, Studio City, CA; has appeared in numerous TV programmes, films and on Broadway; Emmy Awards 1964–65, 1973–74, 1976; Golden Globe Awards 1965, 1981; named to TV Hall of Fame 1985. *TV appearances include:* Series: Richard Diamond Private Eye 1957–59, Dick Van Dyke Show 1961–66, Mary Tyler Moore Show 1970–77, Mary 1978, 1985, Mary Tyler Moore Hour 1979, Lincoln 1988, How to Survive the Seventies 1978, How To Raise a Drug Free Child; Films: Love American Style 1969, Run a Crooked Mile 1969, First You Cry 1978, Heartsounds 1984, Finnegan Begin Again 1984, The Last Best Year 1990, Thanksgiving Day 1990, Stolen Babies 1993 (Emmy Award), New York News 1995, Mary and Rhoda 1998; *Films include:* X-15 1961, Thoroughly Modern Millie 1967, Don't Just Stand There 1968, What's So Bad About Feeling Good? 1968, Change of Habit 1969, Ordinary People 1980, Six Weeks 1982, Just Between Friends 1986, Keys to Tulsa 1996, Flirting with Disaster 1996, Reno Finds Her Mum 1997, Labour Pains 1999; *Broadway appearances include:* Whose Life Is It Anyway? 1980, Sweet Sue 1987. *Address:* c/o William Morris Agency, 151 S El Camino Drive, Beverly Hills, CA 90212, USA.

MOORHOUSE, Jocelyn; Australian film director; m Paul J. Hogan; one c. *Education:* Australian Film and TV School. *Films directed include:* Proof 1991, Rowena's Wedding (with Paul J. Hogan), Snake in the Grass (with Paul J. Hogan), Muriel's Wedding, How to Make an American Quilt 1996.

MORAES-RAMIREZ, Mónica, M SC, PH D; Bolivian botanist; b 4 May 1960, La Paz; d of Oscar Moraes and Graciela Ramírez; m Jaime Sarmiento 1989; one s. *Education:* German School, Univ Mayor de San Andrés (La Paz), Univ Autónoma de Madrid (Spain) and Aarhus Univ (Denmark). *Career:* Asst in Botany Nat Museum of Natural History 1983–90; apptd Prof Univ Mayor de San Andrés 1990; Botanic Researcher and Palms Curator Herbario Nacional de Bolivia 1989–; has written several articles for professional journals 1989–. *Leisure interests:* Bolivian flora, Amazonian vegetation, Bolivian palms, conservation and sustainable use. *Address:* Herbario Nacional de Bolivia, Casilla 10077, Correo Central, La Paz, Bolivia. *Telephone:* (2) 792582; *Fax:* (2) 797511; *E-mail:* monica@palma.bo.

MORATH, Ingeborg Hermine, BA; American photographer; b 27 May 1923, Graz, Austria; d of Prof Edgar and Mathilde Morath; m Arthur Miller 1962; one d. *Education:* Univ of Berlin. *Career:* Trans, Ed ISB Feature Section, Salzburg, Vienna; Ed Der Optimist (literary monthly) 1945–52; Austria Ed Heute Magazine; freelance writer for magazines and radio; joined Magnum Photos 1952, mem 1955–; teacher and lecturer various univs, including Univ of Miami, Univ of Michigan and Harvard Univ; Hon DFA (Hartford) 1984; Great Austrian State Prize for Photography 1992; City of Vienna Gold Medal 1999; Gold Medal Nat Arts Club, New York 1999; Gold Medal City of Graz 2001. *Publications include:* Fiesta in Pamplona 1956, Venice Observed 1956, From Persia to Iran 1961, Tunisia 1961, Le Masque 1967, In Russia 1969, East West Exercises 1973, Boris Pasternak: My Sister Life 1976, In the Country 1977, Chinese Encounters 1979, Images of Vienna 1982, Salesman in Beijing 1984, Portraits 1987, Russian Journal 1991, Inge-Morath: Photographs from 1952 to 1992 1992, Spain in the Fifties 1994, The Danube 1995, Inge Morath Pamplona 1997, Inge Morath Portaits El Camino de Santiago 1999, Saul Steinberg Masquerade 2000. *Leisure interests:* looking at paintings, travel, hiking. *Address:* Magnum Photos, 151 W 25th St, New York, NY 10001-7024, USA (Office); RRI Box, 232 Tophet Rd, Roxbury, CT 06783, USA (Home). *Telephone:* (212) 929-6000 (Office); *Fax:* (212) 929-9325 (Office).

MORATTI, Letizia Brichetto; Italian broadcasting executive and politician; b 1950. *Career:* Fmr Chair Italian Insurance Brokers' Asscn; ran own research and other cos; elected to Chamber of Deputies (Parl) 1994; fmr Chair RAI; Non-Exec Dir BSkyB May–Sept 1999; Chair News Corpn Europe 1998–99. *Address:* c/o BSkyB, 6 Centaurs Business Park, Grantway, Isleworth, Middx, TW7 5QD, UK (Office).

MORAVCOVÁ, Jana, PH D; Czech writer and translator; b 8 May 1937, Černčice; d of Jindřich and Anna Moravec; m Bohumil Neumann 1959; one d. *Education:* Charles Univ (Prague). *Career:* Writer and Trans from Russian and Spanish; publishing house Ed 1959–; Ed-in-Chief Int Asscn of Crime Writers' Czech Section; has written over 20 novels and collections of poetry; has won numerous awards for literature. *Publications include:* Club of Unmistakables 1973, Snow Circle 1974, Still Life With Citadel 1978, Silent Cormorant 1979, Second Glass 1990, Fear Has Long Legs 1992, Holidays With Monica 1994, Fixdictionary 1996, J. Petrovická (biog) 1999, Cases of a Kind Detective 2000, Thirteen Colours of Love 2000. *Leisure interests:* literature, travel. *Address:* Podolská 1487, 147 00 Prague 4, Czech Republic. *Telephone:* (2) 44460015.

MORAWIŃSKA, Agnieszka, PH D; Polish art historian, museum curator and diplomatist; b 29 June 1944, Warsaw; d of the late Jan Morawiński and of Maria Morawińska-Brzezicka; m Andrzej Wanat 1985 (divorced 1990). *Education:* Univ of Warsaw and Center for Studies in the History of Landscape Architecture (Washington, DC, USA). *Career:* Lecturer Theatre School of Warsaw 1972–91; Curator of Polish Art Nat Museum, Warsaw 1976–; Under-Sec of State Ministry of Culture and Arts 1991–92; Curator of Art Royal Castle, Warsaw 1992; curator int exhibitions including Symbolism in Polish Painting 1890–1914, Detroit Inst of Arts, USA 1984, 19th Century Polish Painting, Nat Acad of Design, New York, USA 1988, Voices of Freedom, Polish Women Artists and the Avant-Garde, Nat Museum of Women in the Arts, Washington, DC 1991–92; Amb to Australia 1993, New Zealand 1993, Papua New Guinea 1994; has written many articles on art and art history; mem UNESCO Polish Cttee, Cultural Heritage Cttee Council of Europe, Coll Art Asscn of America. *Leisure interest:* theatre. *Address:* Zamekkrólewski, Plac Zamkowy 4, 00-277 Warsaw, Poland (Office); Wernyhory 18, 02-727 Warsaw, Poland (Home). *Telephone:* (2) 6357399 (Office); (22) 430870 (Home); *Fax:* (2) 6350498 (Office).

MORAY, Sherry; American ballet dancer; b 20 Sept 1963, Highland, IL; d of Richard Dean and Mary Maxine Murray. *Career:* Dancer Stuttgart Ballet Co, Germany 1977–79; Dancer Chicago City Ballet, IL 1980–87, Prima Ballerina 1988; Guest Dancer with various ballet cos, has taken part in ballet festivals including Jacobs Pillow and Edinburgh Arts Festival, UK. *Ballets include:* Cinderella, Romeo and Juliet, Swan Lake, The Nutcracker, Apollo, Le Corsaire, Rubies, Agon, Four Temperaments, Allegro Brillante, Hamlet, Die Fledermaus, Don Quixote, Divertimento No 15, Concerto Barocco, Valse Fantaisie, Raymonda, Who Cares?, Sylvia Variations, Stars and Stripes, Love Songs, Brandenburg II, A Little Mozart, Unanswered Question, Ave Maria, Seven Poetic Waltzes, Glazunov's Violin Concerto, Tango Classico, Rodin, Ballo Imperiale, The Sirens, Capriccio Per Domani, River Suite. *Address:* 1939 Berry Lane, Des Plaines, IL 60018, USA.

MORCOS, Gamila, PH D; Canadian Emeritus professor of French; b 8 Jan 1928, Assiout, Egypt; d of Tawfik N. Roweis and Nozha Y. Boulis; m Fouad Morcos 1951 (died 1988); three s. *Education:* Univs of Cairo and Paris (Sorbonne) and Bryn Mawr Coll (PA, USA). *Career:* High school teacher 1950; Asst, then Assoc Prof Ain Shams Univ, Cairo 1957–67, Laurentian Univ of Sudbury 1967–80, Dean of Humanities 1975–80; Dean Univ of Alberta 1980–85, Prof of French Literature 1985–93; participant at int confs in Togo 1982, Portugal 1983, Côte d'Ivoire 1986, Brazil 1987, India 1990, etc; mem Int Order of Merit, Asscn francophone int de recherche scientifique en éducation, Asscn Int de Docteurs des Univs de France, Asscn Int des Critiques Littéraires, Int Comparative Literature Asscn, World Asscn for Educ Research, American Asscn of Teachers of French, Asscn Canadienne-Française pour l'Avancement des Sciences, Asscn des Profs de français des Univs et Colls du Canada; Officier de l'Ordre des Palmes Académiques 1984; Prix de la Faculté Saint-Jean 1990; Rutherford Award for Excellence in Undergrad Teaching, Univ of Alberta 1991. *Publications:* Bilinguisme et enseignement du français 1989, Introduction and Notations to Albertaines (Georges Bugnet) 1991, Dictionnaire des artistes et des auteurs francophones de l'Ouest canadien (jtly) 1998; numerous articles on European literature and educ for professional journals. *Leisure interests:* reading, travel, music, good food. *Address:* No 2503, 1480 Riverside Drive, Ottawa, ON K1G 5H2, Canada (Home); University of Alberta, Faculté Saint-Jean, 8406 91st St, Edmonton, AB T6C 4G9, Canada (Office). *Telephone:* (403) 465-8700 (Office); (613) 521-6572 (Home); *Fax:* (403) 465-8750 (Office); (613) 521-7982 (Home).

MORDKOVITCH, Lydia, PH D; British (b Soviet) violinist; b 30 April 1944, Saratov, USSR (now Russian Fed); d of Mendel and Golda Shtimerman; m 1st Leonid Mordkovitch 1962 (divorced); one d; m 2nd Malkia Chayoth 1977 (divorced 1983). *Education:* School for Talented Children (Kishinev), Stoliarski School (Odessa), Nezhdanovna Conservatoire (Odessa), Tchaikovsky Conservatoire (Moscow) and studied with David Oistrakh. *Career:* Went to Israel 1974; living in UK 1980–; Sr Lecturer Kishinev Inst of Art 1970–73, Rubin Acad of Music, Jerusalem 1974–80; Prof of Violin Royal Northern Coll of Music, Manchester, UK 1980–95, Royal Acad of Music 1995–; made UK debut Hallé Orchestra 1979, US debut Chicago Symphony Orchestra; has played with many int orchestras including Philadelphia Orchestra, Scottish Nat Orchestra, London Philharmonic, New London Orchestra, The Hague Residentie Orchestra; violin soloist in recitals, concerts, on radio and TV in fmr USSR, Europe, USA, S and Cen America 1974–; has made more than 45 recordings 1978–; Hon Fellow Royal Northern Coll of Music; Hon ARAM; Prizewinner Nat Young Musicians Competition 1967, Long Thibaud Int Competition, Paris 1969, three Diapason d'Or Awards, Woman of the Year Award, American Biog Inst 1996, 1997, 1998, 1999, 2000, Outstanding Woman of the 20th Century, Outstanding Woman of the 21st Century, American Biog Inst. *Recordings include:* Strauss, Fauré, Schumann, Brahms and Franck Sonatas, Ravel's Sonata Tzigane, Brahms Concerto, Bartók, Honneger and Prokofiev Sonatas for violin solo, Schubert's Fantasy, Tchaikovsky, Glazunov, Prokofiev and Rachmaninov Russian music for violin, Ysaye's Six Sonatas for solo violin, Bruch's Concerto No 1, Prokofiev's Two Concertos (Diapason d'Or Award, Spanish Compact Disc Review Award), Bach's Sonatas and Partitas for solo violin, Moeran Concerto, Stanford's Irish Rhapsody No 6, Nielsen's Two Sonatas, Khatchaturian and Kabalevsky Concertos for violin, Shostakovich's Two Concertos (with Royal Scottish Orchestra, Gramophone Award 1990, Diapason d'Or Award 1990), Szymanowsky's Sonata, Nocturne and Tarantella, Three Myths, Busoni's Violin Sonatas, Walton's Concerto, Respighi's Concerto Gregoriano and Poème Automnal, Respighi and Ravel Sonatas, Alwyn's Concerto, Dyson's Concerto, Bartók's 44 Duos, Scharwenka works for violin, piano and cello, Vaughan Williams works for violin and piano. *Leisure interests:* theatre, literature, art. *Address:* Royal Academy of Music, 11 Deansway, London N2 0NR, UK (Office); 25b Belsize Ave, London NW3 4BL, UK (Home). *Telephone:* (20) 7873-7373 (Office); (20) 8442-0801 (Home); *Fax:* (20) 8442-0801 (Home).

MORDYUKOVA, Nonna (Noyabrina) Victorovna; Russian actress; d of Victor Konstantinovitch Mordyukov and Irina Petrovna Mordyukova. *Education:* All-Union Inst of Cinematography (Moscow). *Career:* Made first film 1950; has made over 100 films usually playing peasant women; Chair Art Council Studies; mem Russian Prize Comm; USSR State Prize 1949, USSR People's Actress 1974; Order of People's Friendship; Order Znak Pochiota; prize-winner int and all-union festivals; has had a planet named after her. *Films include:* Molodaya Guardia 1950, Somebody Else's Kinsfolk, Ekaterina Voronina, Paternal House, The Simple Story 1967, The Commissar 1968, The Marriage of Balzaminov 1972, Small Crane, Russian Field, Quagmire, Diamond Hand, Railway Station for Two, Relatives 1982, Luna Park 1992; *Publications:* That's Our Life (novel); short stories. *Leisure interests:* writing, dogs. *Address:* 121609 Moscow, Rubliovskoye sh 34/2, kv 549, Russian Federation. *Telephone:* (095) 413-87-05.

MOREAU, Gisèle; French politician; b 30 June 1941, Paris. *Career:* Fmr MEP (Confed Group of the European United Left/Nordic Green Left); fmr mem Cttee on Transport and Tourism, Del for relations with the USA. *Address:* c/o European Parliament, rue Wiertz, 1047 Brussels, Belgium.

MOREAU, Jeanne; French actress; b 23 Jan 1928, Paris; d of Anatole-Désiré Moreau and Katherine Buckley; m 1st Jean-Louis Richard 1949 (divorced); one s; m 2nd William Friedkin 1977 (divorced). *Education:* Collège Edgar-Quinet and Conservatoire Nat d'Art Dramatique. *Career:* Stage actress with Comédie Française 1948–52, Théâtre Nat Populaire 1953; Pres Cannes Film Festival 1975, Paris Int Film Festival 1975, Acad des Arts et Techniques du Cinéma 1986–88; Pres Comm des Avances sur Recettes 1993–94; mem Acad des Beaux-Arts; Officier de la Légion d'Honneur; Officier de l'Ordre Nat du Mérite; Commdr des Arts et des Lettres; Fellow BAFTA, British Acad; Molière Award 1988; European Cinema Prize, Berlin 1997; Hon Acad 1998; Golden Bear, Int Film Festival, Berlin 2000. *Films include:* Touchez pas au grisbi, Le salaire du péché, Ascenseur pour l'échafaud, Les amants, Moderato Cantabile, Les liaisons dangereuses, Dialogue des Carmélites, Jules et Jim, Eve, The Victors, La baie des anges, Peau de banane, Le train, Le journal d'une femme de chambre, Mata Hari—H21, The Yellow Rolls-Royce 1964, Viva Maria 1965, Mademoiselle 1965, Chimes at Midnight 1966, L'amour à travers les âges 1967, The Sailor from Gibraltar 1967, La mariée était en noir (English title The Bride Wore Black) 1967, La Grande Catherine (English title The Great Catherine) 1968, Le corps de Diane 1970, Une histoire immortelle, Monte Walsh, L'humeur vagabonde, Comptes rebours 1971, Chère Louise 1972, Jeanne, la Française 1972, Nathalie Granger 1972, Je t'aime 1973, Les valseuses 1973, La race des seigneurs 1973, Pleurs 1974, Le jardin qui bascule 1974, Souvenirs d'en France 1974, Lumière (also dir) 1976, The Last Tycoon 1976, Mr Klein 1976, Le Petit Théâtre de Jean Renoir 1976, L'adolescente 1978, Madame Rosa 1978, L'intoxe 1980, Plein Sud 1981, Mille milliards de dollars 1982, Au-delà de cette limite votre billet n'est plus valable 1982, Querelles 1982, La truite 1982, Le paltoquet 1986, Sauve-toi Lola 1986, Till the End of the World, Alberto Express 1989, Nikita 1990, Anna Karamazoff 1989–90, La femme fardée 1990, The Suspended Step of the Stork 1991, La Vieille qui marchait dans la mer 1992, L'Amant (English title The Lover, narrator) 1992, Until The End of The World 1992, La nuit de l'océan 1992, A demain 1992, The Summer House 1994, Les cents et une nuits 1995, The Proprietor 1996, Un amour de sorcière 1997, A tout jamais (une histoire de Cendrillon) 1999; *Plays include:* L'heure éblouissante, La machine infernale, Pygmalion, La chatte sur un toit brûlant, La bonne soupe, La chevauchée sur le lac de Constance, Lulu, L'intoxe, Night of the Iguana, Le Récit de la Servante Zerline 1986, La Célestine 1989. *Leisure interest:* reading. *Address:* Spica Productions, 4 square du Roule, 75008 Paris, France.

MOREAU, Louise, L ÈS SC; French politician; b 29 Jan 1921, Grenoble; d of Pierre-François and Marie-Pierette Mont-Reynaud; m Pierre Moreau (deceased); one s. *Career:* Rep to USA for provisional govt, Del to San Francisco Conf 1945; Sec-Gen First Congress of Asscn Interparlementaires Europe-Afrique 1959; Mayor of Mandelieu-la-Napoule 1971–95; mem Nat Ass (Parl, UDF) for Alpes-Maritimes 1978–; MEP (Union pour la France en Europe) 1979–84; Vice-Pres Nat Ass 1984–85, Vice-Pres UDF group 1986–; fmr mem French Del to European Movt; Officier de la Légion d'Honneur; Croix de Guerre 1939–45; Rosette de la Résistance. *Leisure interests:* golf, horse-riding, sailing. *Address:* Assemblée Nationale, 75355 Paris, France.

MORGAN, Mair Eluned; British politician; b 16 Feb 1967; d of Rev Bob Morgan and Elaine Morgan; m Dr Rhys Jenkins 1996. *Education:* Atlantic Coll (S Wales) and Univ of Hull. *Career:* Researcher with BBC Wales 1991; researcher and reporter Agenda TV 1992, documentary researcher, BBC TV 1993; MEP (PSE) for Mid and W Wales 1994–99, (Lab) for Wales 1999–; mem Cttee on Culture, Youth, Educ and the Media, Del for relations with the People's Rep of China, Cttee on Budgetary Control 1997–, substitute mem Budgets Cttee 1997–; Spokesperson for Social Group on Budgetary Control 1999. *Leisure interests:* guitar, travel. *Address:* Labour European Office, 16 Sachville Ave, Cardiff CF14 3NY, UK. *Telephone:* (29) 2061 8337; *Fax:* (29) 2061 8226.

MORGAN, Michèle (pseudonym of Simone Roussel); French actress; b 29 Feb 1920; d of Louis Roussel; m 1st Bill Marshall; one s; m 2nd Henri Vidal (deceased). *Education:* Studied with R. Simon (Paris). *Career:* Actress 1936–; numerous TV apperances; French 'Victoire' for Best Actress 1946, 1948, 1950, 1952, 1955; Médaille de Vermeil, Paris 1967; Officier de la Légion d'Honneur; Officier de l'Ordre Nat du Mérite; Commdr des Arts et des Lettres. *Films include:* Quai des brumes, Symphonie pastorale (Cannes Festival Prize for Best Actress 1946), Fabiola, Les septs péchés capitaux, Les orgueilleux, Obsession, Les grandes manœuvres, Marguerite de la nuit, Marie Antoinette, Si Paris nous était conté, Le miroir à deux faces, Femmes d'un été, Pourquoi viens-tu si tard? Les scélérats, Fortunat, Le puits aux trois vérités, Les lions sont lâches, Rencontres, Le crime ne paie pas, Landru, Constance

aux Enfers, Les yeux cernés, Dis-moi qui tuer, Les centurions, Benjamin, Le chat et la souris 1975, Ils vont tous bien (English title Everybody's Fine) 1989; *Publications:* Mes yeux ont vu 1965, Avec ces yeux-là 1977, Le fil bleu 1993. *Address:* Agents Associés, 201 rue du Faubourg Saint-Honoré, 75008 Paris, France.

MORGAN, Robin Evonne; American magazine editor and feminist writer; b 29 Jan 1941, Lake Worth, FL; one c. *Education:* Columbia Univ (NY). *Career:* Freelance book ed 1961–69; Ed Grove Press 1967–70; Ed and Columnist World Ms Magazine, New York 1974–87, Ed-in-Chief 1990–93, Int Consulting Ed 1993–; Visiting Chair and Guest Prof New Coll, Sarasota, FL 1973; Distinguished Visiting Scholar and Lecturer Centre for Critical Analysis of Contemporary Culture, Rutgers Univ 1987; Special Consultant UN Cttee, UN Convention to End All Forms of Discrimination Against Women, Brazil 1987; Special Adviser to Gen Ass Conf on Gender, UN Int School 1985–86; guest speaker numerous confs; organized first feminist demonstration against Miss America Pageant 1968; Co-Founder and mem Bd Dirs Feminist Women's Health Network, Nat Battered Women's Refuge Network, Nat Network Rape Crisis Centers; Founder Sisterhood Is Global Inst (Int think-tank) 1984, Officer 1989–97, Chair Advisory Bd 1997–; Founding mem Nat Museum of Women in Arts; mem Bd Dirs Women's Foreign Policy Council; mem Feminist Writers' Guild, Media Women, Women's Action Alliance, N America Feminist Coalition, Pan Arab Feminist Solidarity Asscn; Grantee Writer-in-Residence Yaddo 1980, Nat Endowment for Arts 1979–80, Ford Foundation 1982, 1983, 1984; Hon DHL (Connecticut) 1992; Front Page Award; Wonder Woman Award 1982. *Publications include:* Sisterhood is Powerful: An Anthology of Writings from the Women's Liberation Movement (also compiler and ed) 1970, Monster 1972, Lady of the Beasts (poetry) 1976, Going Too Far: The Personal Chronicle of a Feminist 1978, The Anatomy of Freedom: Feminism, Physics and Global Politics 1982, Sisterhood is Global: The International Women's Movement Anthology (also compiler and ed) 1984, Dry Your Smile: A Novel 1987, The Demon Lover: On the Sexuality of Terrorism 1989, The Mer-Child: A New Legend (poetry) 1990, Saturday's Child: A Memoir 2000. *Address:* c/o Edite Kroll Literary Agency, 12 Grayhurst Park, Portland, ME 04102, USA.

MORGAN, Susan Margaret, MA; British journalist; b 7 Feb 1944, Exeter; d of Frederick and H. M. Morgan. *Education:* Redland High School for Girls, Univ Coll of Wales (Aberystwyth) and Univ of Essex. *Career:* Teacher Univ of Qusqo (Cuzco), Peru 1966–68; Simultaneous Interpreter, Geneva 1968–70; freelance journalist and writer, Cen America, N Africa, Middle East, UK 1970–. *Publication:* In Search of the Assassin (also film documentary 1988) 1991. *Leisure interests:* reading, travel, painting, walking. *Address:* Garden Flat, 22 Belsize Gardens, London NW3 4LH, UK. *Telephone:* (20) 7483-2817.

MORGAN OF HUYTON, Baroness (Life Peer), cr 2001, of Huyton in the County of Lancashire, **Sally Morgan,** MA EDUC; British politician; b 28 June 1959; d of Albert Edward and Margaret Morgan; m John Lyons 1984; two s. *Education:* Belvedere Girls' School (Liverpool) and Univ of Durham. *Career:* Secondary school teacher 1981–85; Student Organizer, Labour Party 1985–87; Sr Targeting Officer 1987–93, Dir Campaigns and Elections 1993–95; Head of Party Liaison for Leader of the Opposition 1996–97; Political Sec to the PM 1997–2001; Women's Minister, Cabinet Office 2001–; mem House of Lords 2001–. *Address:* House of Lords, London SW1A 0PW, UK.

MORI, Hanae; Japanese fashion designer; b 8 Jan 1926, Shimane; d of Tokuzo and Nobu (née Matsuura) Fujii; m Ken Mori 1947; two s. *Education:* Women's Christian Univ (Tokyo). *Career:* Founder Studio of Film Costume Creation, for Tokyo Films, Tokyo 1953; First New York collection 1965, Paris 1975; Founder, Pres, Designer Hanae Mori Co 1977–; currently has 67 Hanae Mori shops in Japan, a store in New York, three shops in Paris and one in Monaco; mem Chambre Syndicale de la Haute Couture, Paris (first Asian mem) 1977–; retrospective exhibition at The Space, Hanae Mori Bldg, Tokyo 1989; Chevalier des Arts et des Lettres 1984; Chevalier de la Légion d'Honneur 1989; Fashion Eds' Club Award, Japan 1960; Neiman Marcus Award 1973; Pioneer Award 1978; Médaille de la Ville de Paris 1978; The Woman of Quality Award 1983; Night of Stars Award 1987; Asahi Prize (Japan) 1988; Purple Ribbon Award (Japan) 1988. *Address:* Hanae Mori Haute

Couture, 17–19 ave Montaigne, 75008 Paris, France (Office); 3 rue du Cirque, 75008 Paris, France (Home); 361 Kita Aoyama, Minato-ku, Tokyo, Japan (Home). *Telephone:* (1) 47-42-76-68; *Fax:* (1) 42-66-91-74.

MORIN-POSTEL, Christine Jacqueline Michèle; French business executive; b 6 Oct 1946, Paris; d of Roger and Marie-Paule Postel; m Jean-Paul Morin (divorced); one s one d. *Education:* Inst d'Etudes Politiques de Paris and Inst de Contrôle de Gestion. *Career:* Mem staff then Head Admin and Econ Research Services, Chambre Régionale de Commerce et d'Industrie de Haute-Normandie 1968–73; Man Sofinnova-Sofinindex group 1976–79; Man Lyonnaise des Eaux, Deputy Dir-Gen responsible for Devt and Int Operations, then Exec Vice-Pres 1979–93; Pres, Dir-Gen Compagnie Générale de Chauffage à Distance 1984–86; Gen Partner Financière Indosuez 1993–96; Chair and CEO CREDISUEZ 1996–; CEO Suez Lyonnaise des Eaux; Non-Exec Dir NFC PLC, The Rank Org PLC (UK); Chevalier de l'Ordre Nat du Mérite 1992, Chevalier de la Légion d'Honneur 1996. *Address:* CREDISUEZ, 1 rue d'Astorg, 75008 Paris, France.

MORISSETTE, Alanis; Canadian singer and songwriter; b 1 June 1974, Ottawa. *Career:* Released first single and f own record label at the age of 10; TV appearances in You Can't Do That On Television and on The David Letterman Show; signed contract as songwriter with MCA Publishing aged 14, recorded two albums for MCA's recording div; moved to Toronto, later to LA, USA; Juno Award for Most Promising New Female; Brit Award for Best Int Newcomer 1996; four Grammy Awards including Album of the Year and Best Rock Album, Best Female Award, MTV European Music Awards 1996. *Recordings include:* Alanis 1991, Now is the Time 1992, Jagged Little Pill (co-written) 1995, Supposed Former Infatuation Junkie 1998; *Film:* Dogma 1999. *Address:* c/o Warner Bros Records, 3 East 54th St, New York, NY 10022, USA.

MORITS, Yunna Petrovna; Russian poet and writer; b 2 June 1937, Kiev, USSR (now Ukraine); m Yuri Grigoryevich Vasilyev; one s. *Education:* Gorky Literary Inst. *Career:* Began publishing poetry 1954; has taken part in int poetry festivals in London, Cambridge (UK), Toronto, etc; has made solo singing recordings; mem Russian PEN, Int Fed of Journalists, Russian Acad of Natural Sciences; Award of Merit 1987; Triumph Prize 2001. *Publications include:* Conversation on Happiness 1957, The Headland of Desire 1961, The Vine 1970, The Brown Thread 1974, By Light of Life 1977, The Third Eye 1980, The Blue Flame 1985, On This High Shore 1987, In the Den of Voice 1990; six books for children, incl The Great Secret for a Small Company 1987; poems appeared in journal Oktyabr 1993–97; short stories, essays, scripts for animated cartoons. *Leisure interest:* painting and drawing. *Address:* 129010 Moscow, Astrakhansky per 5, kv 76, Russian Federation. *Telephone:* (095) 280-08-16.

MORIYAMA, Mayumi; Japanese politician; b 7 Nov 1927. *Education:* Univ of Tokyo. *Career:* Fmr Parl Deputy Minister for Foreign Affairs; fmr Chief Cabinet Sec; fmr Minister of Educ, Science, Culture and Sports; mem House of Councillors (Parl, LDP) for Tochigi, Komoto 1990–, mem Cttee on Educ 1990–; Minister of Justice 2001–. *Address:* House of Councillors, 1-7-1 Nagata-cho, Tokyo 100, Japan. *Telephone:* (3) 5813111.

MORPURGO DAVIES, Anna Elbina, D LITT, MA, FBA; Italian professor of philology; b 21 June 1937, Milan; d of the late Augusto and Maria (née Castelnuovo) Morpurgo; m J. K. Davies 1962 (divorced 1978). *Education:* Liceo-Ginnasio Giulio Cesare (Rome) and Univ of Rome. *Career:* Asst Univ of Rome 1959–61; Jr Fellow Center for Hellenic Studies, Washington, DC 1961–62; Lecturer in Classical Philology Univ of Oxford 1964–71, Fellow St Hilda's Coll 1966–71, Hon Fellow 1971–, Somerville Coll 1971–, Univ Prof of Comparative Philology 1971–; Visiting Prof Univ of Pennsylvania 1971, Yale Univ, USA 1977; Collitz Prof, Linguistic Soc of America 1975; Sather Prof Univ of California at Berkeley 2000; Hon foreign mem American Acad of Arts and Sciences 1986; Corresp mem Österreichische Akademie der Wissenschaften 1988, Bayerische Akademie der Wissenschaften 1998; Corresp mem Inst de France (Acad des Inscriptions et Belles-Lettres) 1992; mem Academia Europaea 1989, American Philosophical Soc 1991; Hon mem Linguistic Soc of America 1993; Hon D LITT (St Andrews) 1981; Premio Linceo per la linguistica 1996; Hon DBE 2000.

Publications: Mycenaeae Graecitatis Lexicon 1963, Studies Greek, Italic, and Indo-European linguistics offered to Leonard R. Palmer (ed with W. Reid) 1976, Linear B: A 1984 Survey (ed with Y. Duhoux) 1985, La linguistica dell'ottocento 1996, Nineteenth Century Linguistics (ed with W. Reid) 1998; articles on comparative, Near Eastern and classical linguistics. *Address:* Somerville Coll, University of Oxford, Oxford OX2 6HD, UK. *Telephone:* (1865) 270600; *Fax:* (1865) 270620.

MORRIS, (Catharine) Jan, CBE, MA, FRSL; British writer; b 2 Oct 1926. *Career:* Mem editorial staff The Times 1951–56, The Guardian 1957–62; Commonwealth Fellowship, USA 1954; George Polk Memorial Award for Journalism (USA) 1961; mem Yr Academi Gymreig, Gorsedd of Bards, Welsh Nat Eisteddfod; Hon Fellow, Univ Coll Wales; Hon FRIBA; Hon D LITT (Univ of Wales, Univ of Glamorgan); Heinemann Award for Literature 1961. *Publications:* (as James Morris) Coast to Coast 1956, Sultan in Oman 1957, The Market of Seleukia 1957, Coronation Everest 1958, South African Winter 1958, The Hashemite Kings 1959, Venice 1960, The Upstairs Donkey (for children) 1962, The Road to Huddersfield 1963, Cities 1963, The Presence of Spain 1964, Oxford 1965, Pax Britannica 1968, The Great Port 1970, Places 1972, Heaven's Command 1973, Farewell the Trumpets 1978; (as Jan Morris) Conundrum 1974, Travels 1976, The Oxford Book of Oxford 1978, Spain 1979, Destinations, The Venetian Empire, My Favourite Stories of Wales 1980, The Small Oxford Book of Wales, Wales The First Place (jtly), A Venetian Bestiary, Spectacle of Empire 1982, Stones of Empire 1983, Journeys 1984, The Matter of Wales 1984, Among the Cities 1985, Last Letters from Hav 1985, Stones of Empire: The Buildings of the Raj 1986, Scotland, The Place of Visions (jtly) 1986, Manhattan '45 1987, Hong Kong: Xianggang 1988, Pleasures of a Tangled Life 1989, Ireland Your Only Place 1990, O Canada 1992, Sydney 1992, Locations 1992, Travels with Virginia Woolf (ed) 1993, A Machynlleth Triad 1994, Fisher's Face 1995, 50 Years of Europe 1997, Wales: Epic Views of a Small Country 1999, Lincoln: A Foreigner's Quest 1999, Our First Leader 2000, Trieste and the Meaning of Nowhere 2001. *Address:* Trefan Morys, Llanystumdwy, Cricieth, Gwynedd LL52 0LP, UK. *Telephone:* (1766) 522222; *Fax:* (1766) 522426; *E-mail:* janmorris1@msn.com (Home).

MORRIS, Estelle, B ED; British politician; b 17 June 1952; d of Charles Richard and Pauline Morris. *Education:* Whalley Range High School (Manchester), Coventry Coll of Education and Univ of Warwick. *Career:* Teacher 1974–92; Councillor Warwick District Council 1979–91, Lab Group Leader 1981–89; MP for Birmingham, Yardley 1992–; Opposition Whip 1994–95, Opposition Front Bench Spokesperson on Educ 1995–97; Parl Under-Sec of State and School Standards Minister, Dept for Educ and Employment (DFEE) 1997–98, Minister of State 1998–2000; Sec of State for Educ and Skills 2001–. *Address:* House of Commons, London SW1A 0AA, UK. *Telephone:* (20) 7219-3000.

MORRISON, Frances M. (Fran), MA, FRSA; British former broadcaster and business executive; b 27 Jan 1949, Glasgow; d of William and Hilary (née Wootton) Morrison; m Trevor C. Deaves 1984 (divorced 1987); two s. *Education:* Univ of St Andrews. *Career:* Reporter, writer, producer BBC Radio 1971–77, BBC TV News and Current Affairs 1977–86; Presenter Newsnight (TV) 1979–81, Nationwide, 60 Minutes, Watchdog (TV) 1981–86, Woman's Hour (Radio); freelance Media Consultant and Broadcaster 1986–91; Man Media Relations/Communications Shell UK Ltd 1991; mem Inst of Petroleum 1992. *Leisure interests:* visual arts, theatre, children. *Address:* Shell UK Ltd, Head Office, Shell-Mex House, Strand, London WC2R 0DX, UK.

MORRISON, Margaret, OBE, BEM; British trade unionist; b 20 March 1924; d of William and May Campbell; m Thomas Morrison 1943; one d. *Education:* Sandyford Secondary Modern (Newcastle). *Career:* Mem Nat Exec Cttee, Civil Service Union 1968–78, Vice-Pres 1978–79, Pres 1980–87; Deputy Pres Nat Union of Civil and Public Servants 1987–89; Co-Chair Women's Nat Comm 1989–91; Vice-Chair Northern Regional TUC 1980; mem TUC Women's Cttee 1979–89, European Women's TUC and Steering Cttee 1982; Dir Northern Devt Co 1984–89, Entrust 1984; mem Civil Service Appeal Bd 1991; TUC Gold Badge, Woman Trade Unionist of the Year 1973. *Leisure interests:* music, swimming, reading, conversation. *Address:* Women's National Commission, Govt Offices, Horse Guards Rd, London SW1P 3AL, UK. *Telephone:* (20) 7270-5903.

MORRISON, Toni (Chloe Anthony Morrison), MA; American writer; b (Chloe Wofford) 18 Feb 1931, Lorain, OH; d of George and Ella Ramah (Willis) Wofford; m Harold Morrison 1958 (divorced 1964); two c. *Education:* Howard and Cornell Univs. *Career:* Teacher of English and Humanities Texas Southern Univ 1955–57, Howard Univ 1957–64; Ed Random House, New York 1965–; Assoc Prof of English State Univ of New York 1971–72, Schweitzer Prof of the Humanities 1984–89; Robert F. Goheen Prof of the Humanities, Princeton Univ 1989–; mem Council Authors' Guild; Nobel Prize for Literature 1993; Commdr des Arts et des Lettres; Nat Medal of Arts 2000. *Publications:* The Bluest Eye 1970, Sula 1974, Song of Solomon 1977, Tar Baby 1983, Beloved (Pulitzer Prize and Robert F. Kennedy Book Award 1988) 1987, Jazz 1992, Playing in the Dark: Whiteness and the Literary Imagination 1992, Nobel Prize Speech 1994, Birth of a Nationhood: Gaze, Script and Spectacle in the O. J. Simpson Trial 1997. *Address:* Princeton University, 111 Dickinson Hall, Princeton, NJ 08544, USA; c/o Suzanne Gluck, International Creative Management, 40 57th St West, New York, NY 10019, USA.

MORSHCHAKOVA, Tamara Georgyevna, D JUR; Russian judge; b 28 March 1936, Moscow; d of G. F. Morshchakov and R. I. Yarovitskaya; m 1st V. A. Homyakov 1957 (divorced 1963); m 2nd I. L. Petrukhin 1971; one d. *Education:* Moscow State Univ. *Career:* Researcher Inst of State and Law, Moscow 1958–71; Sr Researcher Inst of Soviet Legislation 1971–91; mem Scientific-Consultative Council, Supreme Court of Russian Fed 1985–; Prof Moscow State Juridical Acad 1987–; Lecturer Moscow Law Inst 1989–, Prof 1990–; mem Constitutional Court of the Russian Fed 1991–95, Vice-Pres 1995–; mem Drafting Cttee of New Constitution 1993; Honoured Jurist of the Russian Fed, Honoured Scientist of the Russian Fed. *Publications:* Efficiency of Justice 1975, Criteria for Assessing the Quality of the Trial 1987, The Judicial Reform 1990. *Leisure interests:* theatre, literature, poetry. *Address:* Constitutional Court of Russian Federation, Ilyinka str 21, 103132 Moscow, Russian Federation. *Telephone:* (095) 206-16-29.

MORTIMER, Katharine Mary Hope, B PHIL, MA; British business executive and financial adviser; b 28 May 1946, Burford; d of the late Robert Cecil and Mary Hope (née Walker) Mortimer; m 1st John Noel Nicholson 1973 (divorced 1986); one s; m 2nd Robert Michael Dean 1990. *Education:* School of Sts Mary and Anne (Abbots Bromley) and Somerville Coll (Oxford). *Career:* Mem staff IBRD 1969–72, Cen Policy Review Staff 1972–78; N. M. Rothschild Asset Man Ltd 1978–84; Dir N. M. Rothschild and Sons Int Corp Finance 1984–88; seconded to Securities and Investment Bd as Dir of Policy 1985–87; Man Dir Walker Books Ltd 1988–89; Financial Adviser to UK Know How Fund for Eastern Europe 1989–99; mem Bd of Crown Agents Financial Services Ltd and Crown Agents Asset Man Ltd 1990–; Non-Exec Dir Nat Bus Co 1979–91, Inst of Devt Studies 1983–95, Mast Devt Co 1989–90, BNF (British Nuclear Fuels) PLC 1993–2000, Pennon Group PLC 2000–; mem Econ and Social Research Council 1983–86, Royal Comm for the Exhibition of 1851 1988–, Governing Body Centre for Econ Policy Research 1986–91, Imperial Coll, London 1987–89, Monopolies and Mergers Comm 1995–2001; Trustee Inst for Public Policy Research 1989–94. *Address:* Lower Corscombe, Okehampton, Devon EX20 1SD, UK. *Telephone:* (1837) 840431; *Fax:* (1837) 840467.

MOSALA, Euna 'Mathabiso; Lesotho politician; b 15 July 1931, Lesotho; m Mr Mosala 1952; three s three d. *Education:* Nat Univ of Lesotho. *Career:* Founder-mem Lesotho Nat Council of Women 1964; elected mem Senate 1993; Vice-Moderator Southern Africa Alliance of Reformed Churches 1994–; f Red Cross Jr Links 1975; Dir Nat Council of Women Vocational Centres; mem Bd of Dirs Basotho Enterprise Devt Co-operation 1978–95, Project Advisory Cttee Skillshare Africa 1992, Selection Cttee Africa 2000 1992, Bd of Govs SOS Lesotho 1994; Exec mem Lesotho Council of NGOs 1984–86; Trustee Lesotho Handspun Mohair 1986; has published reports of confs attended; mem Most Meritorious Order of Mohlomi 1992. *Leisure interests:* knitting, crocheting, reading, project proposal writing. *Address:* 172 Stadium Area, Box 1340, Maseru 100, Lesotho. *Telephone:* 322511; *Fax:* 312768.

MOSCOSO DE GRUBER, Mireya Elisa; Panamanian politician and Head of State; b 1 July 1946, Panama; d of Plinio Antonio and Elisa Rodríguez de Moscoso; m Arnulfo Arias (died 1988); one s. *Education:* Colegio Comercial María Inmaculada and Miami Dade Community Coll. *Career:* Fmr Exec Sec Social Security Agency; fmr Sales Man, Deputy Man and Gen Man Arkapal SA (coffee co); govt rep on numerous int missions; spent ten years in exile in USA; Pres Partido Arnulfista; Pres of Panana Sept 1999–; fmr Pres Arias Foundation, Madrid; mem Asscn of Boquete Coffee Growers, Asscn of Milk Producers, Nat Asscn of Ranchers. *Address:* Office of the President, Palacio Presidential, Valija 50, Panamá 1, Panama. *Telephone:* 227-4062; *Fax:* 227-0076; *E-mail:* ofasin@presidencia.gob.pa.

MOSELEY-BRAUN, Carol, BA, JD; American politician and lawyer; b 16 Aug 1947, Chicago, IL; d of Joseph J. and Edna A. (née Davie) Moseley; m Michael Braun 1973 (divorced 1986); one s. *Education:* Univ of Illinois at Chicago. *Career:* Asst US Attorney US Dist Court, IL 1973–77; mem (Democrat) Illinois House of Reps 1979–88; Recorder of Deeds Cook Co, IL 1988–92; Senator (for Illinois), Washington, DC 1993–99, mem Senate Judiciary Cttee, Finance Comm, Sub-comm on Social Security and Family Policy, on Medicare, Long-term Care and Health Insurance, on HUD Oversight and Structure, on Int Financial and Monetary POlicy, on Financial Insts and Regulatory Relief, Comm on Banking, Housing and Urban Affairs; Amb to NZ 1999–2001. *Address:* c/o American Embassy, 29 Fitzherbert Terrace, POB 1190, Wellington, New Zealand.

MOSER, Anastasia; Bulgarian politician. *Career:* Co-Chair Bulgarian Agrarian People's Union. *Address:* Bulgarian Agrarian People's Union, (Bulgarski Zemedelski Naroden Sayuz), 1000 Sofia Yanko Zabunov St 1, Bulgaria.

MOSER, Edda; German opera singer (soprano); b 27 Oct 1942, Berlin; d of the late Hans-Joachim and of Dorothea Moser. *Education:* Conservatory of Berlin. *Career:* Has performed with numerous opera cos, including Vienna, Munich, Hamburg, Cologne and Metropolitan Opera, New York, USA; specializes in Mozart operas; own show on TV; title of Kammersängerin Wien conferred 1982; awarded Grand Prix du Disque three times. *Film:* Don Giovanni; *Publication:* Mehr als Worte (contrib). *Address:* Oper der Stadt Bonn, Am Boeselagerhof 1, 5300 Bonn 1, Germany.

MOSIEK-URBAHN, Marlies; German politician; b 9 Aug 1946, Leipzig. *Career:* MEP (PPE); mem Cttee on Legal Affairs and Citizens' Rights, on Rules of Procedure, the Verification of Credentials and Immunities, Del for relations with the countries of S Asia and the S Asia Asscn for Regional Co-operation. *Address:* European Parliament, rue Wiertz, 1047 Brussels, Belgium. *Telephone:* (2) 284-21-11; *Fax:* (2) 230-69-43.

MOSKALEWICZ, Bozena Maria, MA; Polish sociologist; b 27 Nov 1944; d of Władysław and Helena Moskalewicz; m Ryszard Perschke 1967; two s. *Education:* Univ of Warsaw. *Career:* Lecturer in Sociology Medical Centre of Postgrad Educ, Warsaw 1971–83; Researcher Inst of Rheumatology 1983–, apptd Head of Org Dept 1991; Researcher Inst of Paediatry 1985–91; Pres Warsaw Business and Professional Women's Club 1990–. *Publications:* Health Sector Structures: The Case for Poland 1987, Exploited and Then Forgotten: Elderly People 1990; over 30 articles and papers contributed to professional journals. *Leisure interests:* music, tourism, photography. *Address:* Bacha 12/105, 02-743 Warsaw, Poland. *Telephone:* (22) 436563.

MOSKVINA, Tamara, PH D; Russian ice-skating coach; b 26 June 1941, Leningrad (now St Petersburg); d of the late Nikolay and Seraphima Bratous; m Igor Borisovich Moskvin 1964; two d. *Education:* P. F. Lesgaft State College of Physical Culture (Leningrad) and Rimsky-Korsakov Music School. *Career:* Figure-skating coach 1970–; Prof P. F. Lesgaft State Coll of Physical Culture 1971–87; coached Olympic Champions Valova–Vassiliev 1984, Mishkutionok–Dmitriev 1992, Kazakova–Dmitriev 1998, World Pair Skating Champions 1981, 1983, 1985, 1987, 1991, 1992, 1997, 1998, 1999; currently nat coach of Russian figure-skating team; has co-written two books on skating; Honoured Master of Sports of the USSR 1969; Honoured Coach of the

USSR 1981; State Order of the Red Banner 1984, of People Friendship 1988; Honoured Figure of the Arts of Russia 1994; State Order of Achievement Before the Motherland 1998. *Leisure interests:* ballet, music. *Address:* St Petersburg 191104, Rileeva 1, Apt 35, Russian Federation. *Telephone:* (812) 279-1211; *Fax:* (812) 279-1211; *E-mail:* moskvina@softhome.net.

MOSS, Kate; British model; b 16 Jan 1974, Addiscombe; d of Peter Edward and Linda Rosina Moss. *Education:* Croydon High School. *Career:* Has modelled for The Face, Harpers and Queen, Elle, Vogue, Dolce & Gabana, Katherine Hamnett, Versace, Yves Saint Laurent; exclusive contract world-wide with Calvin Klein 1992–99; Fashion Personality of the Year, Lloyds Bank Fashion Awards 1995; Female Model of The Year Award, VH1 1996. *Film:* Unzipped 1996; *Publication:* Kate 1994. *Address:* c/o Storm Model Management, 1st Floor, 5 Jubilee Place, London SW3 3TD, UK. *Telephone:* (20) 7376-7764.

MOTA, Rosa; Portuguese athlete; b 1958. *Career:* Marathon runner; European Champion 1982, 1986, 1990; World Champion 1987; Winner Boston Marathon (USA) 1987, 1988, 1990; Gold Medal, Marathon, Olympic Games, Seoul 1988.

MOTEANE, May Ada, M SC; Lesotho accountant; b 20 May 1949; d of Daniel and Catherine Agbaraji; m 1975; one s. *Education:* Ahmadu Bello Univ (Nigeria) and Univ of Illinois at Urbana-Champaign (USA). *Career:* First female chartered accountant in Lesotho to start own practice, M. A. Moteane & Co 1986–93; Man Partner Ernst & Young (incorporating M. A. Moteane & Co), Lesotho 1993; First Registrar Lesotho Inst of Accountants; Founder, First Pres Women In Business, Lesotho 1990–96; Lesotho Rep to int confs incl UN Conf, Beijing 1995; Country Co-ordinator Council for Econ Empowerment of Women in Africa 1994. *Publications:* Women Entrepreneurs: Role in a Small Economy 1993, Improving Micro-Credit Delivery to Women in Lesotho. *Leisure interests:* travel, health clubs, African music. *Address:* c/o Ernst & Young, Private Bag A169, Maseru 100, Lesotho.

MOTROSHILOVA, Nelly Vassilyevna, D PHIL; Russian professor of philosophy; b 21 Feb 1934, Khartov dist; m (husband deceased); one s. *Education:* Moscow State Univ and USSR Acad of Sciences. *Career:* Jr researcher, sr researcher, then Head of Dept Inst of Philosophy (Russian Acad of Sciences) 1959–; Prof Moscow State Univ, All-Union Inst of Cinematography, Semashko Acad of Medicine, State Humanitarian Science Univ; Ed int journals Deutsche Zeitschrift für Philosophie, Studia Spinzana, Voprosy Filosofii; Humboldt Prize 1994; Plekhanov Prize (Russian Acad of Sciences) 2001. *Publications:* over 300 scientific papers, 100 monographs including Principles and Contradictions of Phenomenological Philosophy, Cognition and Society, Creation and Development of Physolophical Ideas 1994, The Way of Gegel to the Science of Logic 1984. *Leisure interest:* gardening. *Address:* Institute of Philosophy, Russian Academy of Sciences, Volkhonka str 14, Moscow, Russian Federation. *Telephone:* (095) 232-32-11; (095) 203-91-09 (Office); (095) 203-91-98 (Home); *E-mail:* nvm@iph.ras.ru.

MOUNTBATTEN OF BURMA, Countess, cr 1947, **Patricia Edwina Victoria Knatchbull,** CBE, CD, DL, JP; British member of the House of Lords; b 14 Feb 1924, London; d of Earl and Countess (née Edwina Ashley) Mountbatten of Burma; m Lord Brabourne 1946; five s (one deceased) two d. *Education:* Malta, London and New York. *Career:* Served in WRNS 1943–46; JP 1971–76; Col-in-Chief Princess Patricia's Canadian Light Infantry 1974–; Vice Lord-Lieutenant of the Co of Kent 1984–95; Chair Sir Ernest Cassel Educational Trust; Pres SOS Children's Villages, Friends of Cassel Hosp, Friends of William Harvey Hosp, Shaftesbury Homes and Arethusa, Kent Br of the NSPCC, Save The Children Fund, Relate (fmrly Marriage Guidance Council); Vice-Pres British Red Cross Soc, Nat Soc for the Prevention of Cruelty to Children (NSPCC), Family Planning Asscn, Nat Childbirth Trust, Soldiers', Sailors' and Airmen's Families Asscn, Royal Lifesaving Soc, Shaftesbury Soc, Nat Soc for Cancer, Royal Nat Coll for the Blind, Kent Voluntary Service Council, The Aidis Trust, Royal Coll of Nursing; Hon Pres Soc for Nautical Research, British Maritime Charitable Foundation; Patron Commando Asscn, HMS Cavalier Trust, Legion of Frontiersmen of the Commonwealth, Foudroyant Trust, HMS Kelly Reunion Asscn, Nuclear Weapons Freeze, Voluntary Aid Detachments

(Royal Navy), Compassionate Friends, Nurses' Welfare Trust; Vice-Patron Burma Star Asscn; Hon DCL (Kent); Dame of Justice, Most Venerable Order of the Hospital of St John of Jerusalem. *Address:* Newhouse, Menthorn, Ashford, Kent TN25 6NQ, UK. *Telephone:* (1233) 503636; *Fax:* (1233) 502244.

MOUSKOURI, Joanna (Nana); Greek singer and politician; b 13 Oct 1934, Athens; d of Constantin and Alice Mouskouri; m George Petsilas; one s one d. *Education:* Athens Nat Conservatory. *Career:* Singer 1956–; living in Paris 1962–; has given concerts world-wide; numerous TV appearances including Numéro 1 1979 and Nana Mouskouri à Athènes 1984; UNICEF Amb 1993–94; MEP 1994–; has received 300 Gold and Platinum Discs world-wide; Greek Broadcasting Festival Award 1959, Barcelona Festival Award, No 1 French Female Singer 1979; No 1 Female Singer World-wide, Canada 1980 and numerous other awards and prizes. *Songs include:* Roses blanches de Corfou, L'enfant au tambour, Les parapluies de Cherbourg, C'est bon la vie, Tous les arbres sont en fleurs, Plaisir d'amour, Ave Maria, Voici le mois de mai, Toi qui t'en vas, L'amour en héritage, Only love; *Publication:* Chanter ma vie 1989. *Leisure interests:* collecting antique jewellery, antiques and paintings, swimming. *Address:* c/o Polygram, 20 rue des Fossés Saint-Jacques, 75005 Paris, Paris; Aharnon 289, GR112 53, Athens, Greece. *Telephone:* 1 856 19 02 (Greece); *Fax:* 1 960 05 55 (Greece).

MOUSSAVOU MISSAMBO, Paulette; Gabonese politician; b 20 Sept 1949, Lastoursville; d of Luc Poungul and Simone Binounou; m Alphouse Moussavou-Doukagh 1972; one d. *Education:* Omar Bongo Univ and Univ of Lille III. *Career:* Deputy Head Lycée d'Etat de Pont-Gentil 1981–82, Head 1982–87; Head Lycée National Léon UZBA 1987–90; Minister for Civil Service 1990–91; elected mem of Nat Ass 1991; Minister of National Educ 1991; Chevalier dans l'ordre de l'Education Nationale; Officier des Palmes Académiques Françaises; Officier dans l'ordre de l'Etoile Equatoriale. *Leisure interests:* reading, gardening. *Address:* c/o Ministry of National Education, BP 6 Libreville, Gabon.

MOUT, Marianne Elisabeth Henriette Nicolette, D LITT; Netherlands historian; b 31 May 1945, Wassenaar; d of Arie Mout and Maria Helena van Tooren; m 1st Robbert Salomon van Santen (divorced 1979); m 2nd Peter Felix Ganz 1987. *Education:* Rijnlands Lyceum (Wassenaar) and Univ of Amsterdam. *Career:* Research student, Czechoslovakia 1966, 1967; Asst Keeper Jewish Historical Museum, Amsterdam 1969; Ed Martinus Nijhoff publrs 1970; Lecturer in Modern History, Utrecht Univ 1975–76; Sr Lecturer in Dutch History, Leiden Univ 1976–, Prof of Cen European Studies 1990–, Prof of Modern History 1994–; Fellow Netherlands Inst for Advanced Studies, Wassenaar 1987–88, 1993–94; Man Ed Tijdschrift voor Geschiedenis 1981–86; Pres Conseil Int pour l'édition de oeuvres d'Erasme; mem Bd Inst of Netherlands History (Instituut voor Nederlandse Geschiedenis) 1989–; mem Royal Netherlands Acad of Arts and Sciences, Austrian Acad of Arts and Sciences. *Publications include:* Komenský v Amsterodamu (jtly) 1970, Bohemen en de Nederlanden in de zestiende eeuw 1975, Plakkaat van Verlatinge 1581 1979, Gerhard Oestrich, Antiker Geist und moderner Staat bei Justus Lipsius 1989 (ed), Die Kultur des Humanismus: Reden, Briefe, Traktate, Gespräche von Petrarca bis Kepler 1998; numerous articles, mainly on 16th–17th-century Dutch and Cen European history of ideas and cultural history; Ed and Co-Ed of several books, including Gerhard Oestreich, Antiker Geist und moderner Staat bei Justus Lipsius 1989, Erasmianism Idea and Reality 1997; numerous articles on 16th–17th century Dutch and Cen European history of ideas and cultural history. *Address:* Leiden University, Dept of History, POB 9515, 2300 RA Leiden, Netherlands (Office); Oranje Nassaulaan 27, 2361 LB Warmond, Netherlands (Home). *Telephone:* (71) 527-26-51 (Office); *Fax:* (71) 527-26-52; *E-mail:* M.E.H.N.mout@let.leidenuniv.nl; *Internet:* www.let.leidenuniv.nl/history/sub/ag/Mout.htm.

MOWLAM, Rt Hon Marjorie (Mo), PC, PH D; British politician; b 18 Sept 1949; d of Tina Mowlam; m Jon Norton 1995. *Education:* Coundon Court Comprehensive School (Coventry), Univ of Durham and Univ of Iowa (USA). *Career:* Research Asst to MP Tony Benn 1971–72, Alvin Toffler 1972–73; Lecturer Univ of Wisconsin 1976–77 and Florida State Univ, USA 1977–78, Univ of Newcastle upon Tyne 1979–83; Sr Admin N Coll, Barnsley 1984–87; MP (Lab) for Redcar

1987–2001; Opposition Spokesperson on N Ireland 1988–89, on City and Corp Affairs 1989–92, on Citizen's Charter and Women 1992–93, for Nat Heritage 1993–94, Shadow Sec of State for NI 1994–97; Sec of State for N Ireland 1997–99; Minister for the Cabinet Office and Chancellor of Duchy of Lancaster 1999–2000; mem Lab Party 1969–, mem Lab Party Nat Exec Cttee Sub-Cttee on Energy, has held various Party positions at constituency and dist levels; Hon LL D (Queen's, Belfast) 1999. *Publications include:* Debate on Disarmament (co-ed) 1982. *Leisure interests:* walking, jigsaws, swimming. *Address:* 14B Queen St, Redcar, Cleveland TS10 1AE, UK. *Telephone:* (1642) 490404; *Fax:* (1642) 489260.

MTHEMBI-MAHANYELE, Sankie, BA; South African politician; b 23 March 1951, Sophiatown; d of the late Mkhomazi and Emma Gabaza Mthembi; m Mohale Mahanyele; three d. *Education:* Sekano-Ntoane High School and Univ of the North. *Career:* Fmr punch card operator Standard Bank; became involved in ANC underground, left SA 1977 to work for ANC; with Radio Freedom 1977–81; Ed women's journal Voice of Women 1979–87; fmr sub-Ed Dawn; mem Nat Exec Cttee of Women 1980–87, 1987–89, Admin Sec mission in West Africa 1986–89, Admin Sec mission in Sweden 1983–84, Chief Rep mission for Germany and Austria 1989–93, mem Nat Exec 1993–, Deputy Head Dept of Int Affairs 1993–94; Deputy Minister of Welfare 1994–95; Minister of Housing 1995–99. *Publications:* Flames of Fury (poetry), One Never Knows (short stories). *Leisure interests:* music, reading. *Address:* c/o Ministry of Housing, 240 Walker St, Sunnyside, Pretoria 0002, South Africa.

MUDJIDELL, Bridget; Australian artist; b 1935, Yagga Yagga; d of Tampa Nampitjin; m 1952 (husband deceased, name taboo); four s two d. *Career:* Raised in a traditional nomadic way; Sr Custodian traditional Aboriginal Women's Law for the Ngarti People in the desert areas of W Australia; artist 1988–; has exhibited in Australia, UK, USA. *Leisure interests:* traditional cultural activities, hunting, collecting craft materials, ceremonial performances. *Address:* c/o Warlayirti Artists, Balgo Hills, via Halls Creek, WA 6770, Australia. *Telephone:* (91) 68 8960; *Fax:* (91) 68 8959.

MUIR, (Isabella) Helen (Mary), CBE, MA, D PHIL, D SC, FRS; British biochemist; b 20 Aug 1920, Naini Tal, Uttar Pradesh, India; d of the late Basil Fairlie and Gwladys Helen Muir. *Education:* Somerville Coll (Oxford). *Career:* Research Fellow Univ of Oxford 1947–48; Research Scientist Nat Inst for Medical Research 1948–54; worked at St Mary's Hosp 1954–66, Empire Rheumatism Council Fellow 1954–58, Pearl Research Fellow 1959–66; Head of Div Kennedy Inst of Rheumatology 1966–86, Dir 1977–90; Bunim Lecturer US Arthritis Asscn 1978; Visiting Prof of Biochem, Queen Elizabeth Coll 1981–85; Newcastle Univ 1995; Hon Prof of Biochem Charing Cross Hosp Medical School 1979–; Gov Strangeways Research Lab 1980–90; currently Hon Visiting Prof of Biochem School of Biological Sciences, Univ of Manchester; mem Arthritis and Rheumatism Council Research Sub-Cttee 1962–75, Editorial Bd Biochemical Journal 1964–70, Annals of Rheumatic Diseases 1971–77, Connective Tissue Research 1971–85, Journal of Orthopaedic Research 1983–; Scientific mem MRC Council 1973–77; Hon Fellow Somerville Coll, Oxford; Hon mem American Soc Biological Chemists; Foreign mem Royal Swedish Acad of Sciences; mem Council Royal Soc 1982–83, Council Chelsea Coll 1982–85; Wellcome Trustee 1982–90; has written more than 200 articles, mainly on biochem of connective tissues in relation to arthritis and inherited diseases and contributed to several specialist books; Hon D SC (Edinburgh) 1982, (Strathclyde) 1983, (Brunel) 1990; awards include Heberden Orator and Medallist 1976, Feldberg Prize 1977, Bunim Medal, American Arthritis Asscn 1978, Co-Winner Basic Science Section Volvo Prize 1980, Neil Hamilton Fairley Medal 1981, CIBA Medal, Biochemical Soc 1981, Steindler Award, Orthopaedic Research Soc, USA 1982, CIBA Int Award 1993. *Leisure interests:* gardening, music, horses, natural history, ballet. *Address:* Longlands House, Hornby, Bedale, North Yorks DL8 1NG, UK.

MUJAWAHA, Marcienne; Burundi politician. *Career:* Mem Front pour la démocratie au Burundi (FRODEBU); Fmr Minister of Human Rights, Social Affairs and Women's Affairs. *Address:* c/o Ministry of Human Rights, Social Affairs and Women's Affairs, Bujumbura, Burundi.

MUJURU, Joyce Teurai-Ropa; Zimbabwean politician; b 15 April 1955, Mt Darwin; m Tapfumanei Ruzambu Solomon Mujuru 1977; four d. *Career:* Minister of Youth, Sport and Recreation 1980–81, of Community Devt and Women's Affairs 1981–88, of Community and Co-operative Devt 1989–92, of Rural Resources and Water Devt 1996–; Gov and Resident Minister of Mashonaland Cen Prov 1993–96. *Leisure interests:* church and women's meetings, knitting, sewing, cooking, outdoor life. *Address:* Ministry of Rural Resources and Water Development, Makombe Complex, Private Bag 7701, Causeway, Harare, Zimbabwe. *Telephone:* (4) 706081.

MUKASA, Eva Nagawa, B COMM, MBA; Ugandan banking executive; b 29 Jan 1944, Kampala; d of Enricho Semugema and Edith Nakimbugwe; m Ntensibe Mukasa 1966; two s two d. *Education:* Gayaza High School for Girls, Univ Coll (Nairobi, Kenya), Makerere Univ (Kampala) and Harvard Inst for International Development (USA). *Career:* Income Tax Assessor E African Community 1971–73; Devt Banker E African Devt Bank 1973–93, Dir of Finance 1986; Gen Man Uganda Women's Finance Trust Ltd (micro-finance NGO); mem Bd Trustees Women's World Banking, New York, Bd Uganda Insurance Comm, Bd New Vision Printing & Publishing Corpn. *Leisure interests:* gardening, rotary club activities, serving poor women. *Address:* c/o East African Development Bank, POB 4575, Kampala, Uganda; c/o Uganda Women's Finance Trust, POB 6972, Kampala, Uganda. *Telephone:* (41) 251109; *Fax:* (41) 255144; *E-mail:* uwft@swiftuganda.com.

MUKERJEE, Rita; Indian broadcasting executive; b 3 June 1941, New Delhi; d of Sudhansu and Suhasini Mukerjee. *Education:* Lady Shri Ram Coll for Women (New Delhi), Univ of Delhi, Int Inst of Journalism (Berlin) and All India Radio Staff Training Inst. *Career:* Co-Founder, Producer Youth Service Radio 1969–77; Network Broadcaster 1977–81; worked for All India Radio 1981–86, Deputy Dir Gen Overseas Services, External Services Div 1986–89, Dir Commercial Services 1988–89, apptd Chief Producer Cen Features Unit 1989; Guest Lecturer Indian Inst of Mass Communication; has received awards for productions. *Leisure interests:* Indian and Western music, reading, travel, meeting people, homeopathy. *Address:* C-167, Greater Kailash 1, New Delhi 110 048, India (Home). *Telephone:* (11) 6461735 (Home); (11) 3710486 (Office).

MUKHERJEE, Bharati; American (b Indian) lecturer and writer; b 1950; m Clark Blaise; two s. *Education:* Univs of Calcutta, Baroda and Iowa. *Career:* Prof of English McGill Univ, Canada; Lecturer Skidmore Coll; Lecturer in Literature and Creative Writing, Queen's Coll, New York. *Publications include:* The Tiger's Daughter 1971, Wife 1975, Days and Night in Calcutta 1977, Darkness 1985, The Sorrow and the Terror (with Clark Blaise) 1987, The Middleman and Other Stories (Nat Book Critics Circle Award for Fiction) 1988, Jasmine 1989, The Holder of the World 1993, Leave it to Me 1996. *Address:* c/o Grove Weidenfeld, 841 Broadway, New York, NY 10003, USA.

MUKHERJEE, Meenakshi, PH D; Indian professor of literature; b 3 Aug 1937, Calcutta (now Kolkata); d of Basanta Kumar and Parul Banerjee; m Sujit Mukherjee 1959; two d. *Education:* Univs of Patna, Delhi and Pennsylvania (USA). *Career:* Teacher New York State Univ, Univs of Delhi and of Hyderabad; Visiting Prof Univs of Texas at Austin and of Chicago; Founder, Ed Vagartha 1973–79; apptd Prof of English Jawaharlal Nehru Univ, New Delhi 1986; Meyer Foundation Fellow in Australia 1983; Nat Lecturer 1991. *Publications:* The Twice Born Fiction 1971, Realism and Reality 1985, Considerations (ed) 1977, Another India (co-ed) 1990, Jane Austen 1991. *Leisure interests:* film, theatre. *Address:* 329 Hauz Khas Apts, New Delhi 110 016, India. *Telephone:* (11) 657610.

MULLARKEY, Mary J., BA, LL B; American judge; b 28 Sept 1943, New London, WI; d of John Clifford and Isabelle A. (née Steffes) Mullarkey; m Thomas E. Korson 1971; one s. *Education:* St Norbert Coll (DePere, WI) and Harvard Law School (Cambridge, MA). *Career:* Called to the Bar, WI 1968, CO 1974; Attorney-Adviser Dept of the Interior 1968–73; Asst Regional Attorney Equal Opportunities Comm 1973–75; First Asst Attorney-Gen, Colorado Dept of Law 1975–79, Solicitor-Gen 1979–82; Legal Adviser to Colorado Gov 1982–85; Partner Mullarkey and Seymour, Denver, CO 1985–87; Justice Colorado Supreme Court 1987–; Hon D JUR (St Norbert Coll) 1989;

St Norbert Coll Alumni Award 1980; Colorado Women's Bar Asscn's Recognition Award 1986; Alma Mater Award 1993. *Address:* Supreme Court, 435 Colorado Judicial Building, 2 E 14th Ave, Denver, CO 80203, USA. *Telephone:* (303) 861-1111.

MÜLLER, Edith; German politician; b 3 March 1949, Kaldenkirchen. *Career:* Fmr MEP (The Green Group in the European Parl); fmr mem Cttee on Budgets, on Budgetary Control, Del for relations with the countries of S America, Del to the EU–Romania Jt Parl Cttee. *Address:* c/o European Parliament, rue Wiertz, 1047 Brussels, Belgium.

MULLOVA, Viktoria; Austrian (b Russian) violinist; b 27 Nov 1959, Moscow, USSR (now Russian Fed); d of Juri Mullov and Raisa Mullova; one s one d. *Education:* Cen Music School (Moscow) and Moscow Conservatory. *Career:* Left USSR 1983; has appeared with Berlin Philharmonic, Israel Philharmonic, Orchestre de Paris, Royal Philharmonic, Royal Concertgebouw, The Youth Orchestra of a United Europe, Chamber Orchestra of Europe, London Philharmonic, London Symphony, Philharmonia, Boston, Chicago, Philadelphia, Cleveland, Washington and Los Angeles Symphony Orchestras, etc; has worked with Kurt Masur, Claudio Abbado, Michael Tilson Thomas, Vladimir Ashkenazy and André Previn; First Prize Sibelius Competition, Helsinki 1980; Gold Medal Tchaikovsky Competition, Moscow 1982; Edison Prize and Diapason d'Or for recordings. *Recordings include:* Tchaikovsky and Sibelius Violin Concertos with Boston Symphony under Seiji Ozawa (Grand Prix du Disque), Vivaldi's Four Seasons, Bartók, Bach and Paganini solo works, Shostakovich Concerto No 1, Prokofiev Concerto No 2, Paganini Concerto No 1, Vieuxtemps Concerto No 5, Mendelssohn Concertos with Acad of St Martin in the Fields under Sir Neville Marriner, Brahms Concerto with Berlin Philharmonic under Claudio Abbado, Brahms and Beethoven Trios with André Previn and Heinrich Schiff, Bach Concertos with Mullova Ensemble, Bach Partitas (solo violin), Janácek, Prokofiev and Debussy Sonatas, J S Bach Violin Concertos, Concerto for Violin and Oboe; Stravinsky Concerto; Bartok Concerto No 2, Through the Looking Glass (incl works by Miles Davis and Yousso N'Dour). *Leisure interests:* reading, cinema, skiing, tennis, mountain climbing. *Address:* c/o Askonas Holt, Lonsdale Chambers, 27 Chancery Lane, London WC2A 1PF, UK. *Telephone:* (20) 7400-1700; *Fax:* (20) 7400-1799.

MUNNELL, Alicia Haydock, PH D; American economist and banking executive; b 12 June 1942, New York; d of Walter Howe Haydock and Alicia Wildman Haydock Roux; m 1st Thomas Clark Munnell 1963 (divorced 1977); two s; m 2nd Henry Scanlon Healy 1980. *Education:* Harvard Univ, Boston Univ and Wellesley Coll. *Career:* Teaching Fellow Econs Dept, Boston Univ 1965–66, Harvard Univ 1971–73; Research Asst The Brookings Inst 1966–68; Asst Prof of Econs, Wellesley Coll 1974; Economist Fed Reserve Bank of Boston 1973–76, Asst Vice-Pres and Economist 1976–78, Vice-Pres and Economist 1979–84, Sr Vice-Pres and Dir of Research 1984–93; Asst Sec for Econ Policy Dept Treasury 1993–; mem Nat Acad of Public Admin 1985, Nat Acad of Social Insurance 1986, Inst of Medicine, NAS 1986, Research Advisory Bd, Econ Policy Inst 1988, Econs Visiting Cttee, MIT 1989. *Publications include:* The Impact of Social Security on Personal Saving 1974, Options for Fiscal Structure Reform in Massachusetts (jtly) 1975, The Future of Social Security 1977, Pensions for Public Employees 1979, The Economics of Private Pensions 1982, Lessons from the Income Maintenance Experiments (ed) 1987, Massachusetts in the 1990s: The Role of State Government (jtly) 1990, Retirement and Public Policy (ed) 1991, Is There A Shortfall in Public Capital Investment? (ed) 1991, Pensions and Economy: Sources, Uses and Limitations of Data (co-ed) 1992; numerous contribs to professional books and journals. *Leisure interests:* tennis, skiing, needlepoint. *Address:* US Treasury Dept Office of Econ Policy, 1500 Pennsylvania Ave, NW, Washington, DC 20220, USA (Office); 6 W Cedar St, Boston, MA 02108, USA (Home). *Telephone:* (617) 973-3385 (Office); (617) 720-4530 (Home); *Fax:* (617) 973–3957 (Office).

MUNRO, Alice; Canadian writer; b 10 July 1931, Wingham, ON; d of Robert Eric and Anne Clark (née Chamney) Laidlaw; m 1st James Armstrong Munro 1951 (divorced 1976); three d; m 2nd Gerald Fremlin 1976. *Education:* Wingham Public and High Schools and Univ of W Ontario. *Career:* Winner Gov-Gen's Award for Literature 1968, Canadian Booksellers' Award 1971, Canada-Australia Literary Prize,

Fiction Prize, Nat Book Critics Circle 1999. *Publications include:* Dance of the Happy Shades (Winner Gov-Gen Award for Literature) 1968, Lives of Girls and Women (Canadian Booksellers' Award) 1971, Something I've Been Meaning To Tell You 1974, Who Do You Think You Are? (The Beggar Maid in the USA and UK) 1978, The Moons of Jupiter 1982, The Progress of Love 1986, Friend of My Youth 1990, Open Secrets 1994, Selected Stories 1996, The Love of A Good Woman 1999. *Address:* The Writers Shop, 101 5th Ave, New York, NY 10003, USA (Office); POB 1133, Clinton, ON N0M 1L0, Canada (Home).

MURATOVA, Kira Georgievna; Russian/Ukrainian film director; b 5 Nov 1934, Soroki, Moldavia; m 1st Alexandre Muratov (divorced); m 2nd Yevgeni Golubenko. *Education:* All-Union Inst of Cinematography with Sergey Gerasimov. *Career:* Debut feature film with A. Muratov On Steep Bank; acted in several films; USSR State Prize 1989; Int Andrzey Wajda Prize 2000. *Films:* Our Harvest Bread 1965, Short Meetings 1968, Long Partings 1972 (Fipressi Prize, Locarno 1987), Cognizing the White World 1980, Among Grey Stones 1983, Change of Fate 1988, Asthenic Syndrome 1990 (Nika Prize 1990), The Sentimental Militiaman 1991, Animations 1994, Three Stories 1996. *Address:* Proletarsky blvd 14B, apt 15, 270015 Odessa, Ukraine. *Telephone:* 28 65 51 (Home).

MURDOCH, Anna Maria, MA; Australian media executive; b 30 June 1944, Scotland; d of J Torv; m Rupert Murdoch 1967 (divorced 1999); two s one d. *Education:* Univ of New York (USA). *Career:* Fmr Journalist Daily Telegraph, Daily Mirror, Sunday Mirror, Australia; fmr Dir, Vice-Pres News America Publishing Inc, fmr Dir, Vice-Pres News America Holdings; now Dir News Corpn Ltd; Chair Bd Regents Children's Hosp (LA); Pres Bd Children's Inst Int. *Publications:* In Her Own Image 1985, Family Business 1988, Coming to Terms 1991. *Address:* News Corporation Ltd, POB 4245, Sydney, NSW 2001, Australia.

MURDOCH, Elisabeth, BA; American (b Australian) broadcasting executive; b 22 Aug 1968, Sydney, Australia; d of Rupert and Anna Maria (née Torv) Murdoch; m Elkin Pianim 1993; two d. *Education:* Brearley School and Vassar Coll (NY, USA). *Career:* Presentation and Promotions Asst Nine Network Australia 1990–91, researcher and producer 1991–93, Programming and Promotion Man Fox TV Studios Jan–Sept 1992; Programme Dir KSTV–Fox 13 1992–93; Network Dir of Programme Acquisitions Fox Cable Network LA 1994–95; Pres and CEO EP Communications 1995–96 (Peabody Award for Broadcast Excellence 1995); Gen Man Broadcasting Dept, BSkyB Ltd 1996, Dir of Programming 1996–98, Man Dir Sky Networks 1998–2000; Dir Future Publishing 2000–. *Address:* British Sky Broadcasting Ltd, Grant Way, Isleworth, Middx TW7 5QD, UK. *Telephone:* (20) 7705-3998; *Fax:* (20) 7705-6990.

MURPHY, Caryle Marie, BA; American journalist; b 16 Nov 1946, Hartford, CT; d of Thomas Joseph and Muriel Kathryn (née McCarthy) Murphy. *Education:* Jeanne d'Arc Acad High School (Milton, MA), Trinity Coll (Washington, DC) and Johns Hopkins School for Advanced Int Studies. *Career:* Teacher of English and History, Nyeri, Kenya 1968–70; Staff Reporter Brockton Enterprise, Brockton, MA 1972–73; Freelance Foreign Corresp, Angola 1974–76; joined Washington Post 1976, Foreign Corresp for S Africa 1977–82, Staff Reporter Washington, DC 1982–89, Middle E Corresp 1989–94; awards for reporting from Kuwait following its invasion by Iraqi troops 1990 include Int Women's Media Foundation Award for Courage in Journalism 1990, George Polk Award for Foreign Reporting, Long Island Univ 1990, Pulitzer Prize for Int Reporting 1991, Edward Weintal Journalism Prize for Diplomatic Reporting 1991; Edward R Murrow Fellow Council on Foreign Relations, NY 1994–95. *Address:* The Washington Post, Foreign Desk, 1150 15th St, NW, Washington, DC 20071, USA. *Telephone:* (202) 334-7400; *Fax:* (202) 334-5547.

MURPHY, Dervla Mary; Irish writer and critic; b 28 Nov 1931, Cappoquin, Co Waterford; d of Fergus Murphy and Kathleen Rochfort-Dowling; one d. *Education:* Ursuline Convent (Waterford). *Career:* American–Irish Foundation Literary Award 1975; Ewart-Biggs Memorial Prize 1978; Irish–American Cultural Inst Literary Award 1985. *Publications:* Full Tilt 1965, Tibetan Foothold 1966, The Waiting Land 1967, In Ethiopia with a Mule 1968, On a Shoestring to Coorg 1976, Where the Indus is Young 1977, A Place Apart 1978, Wheels Within

Wheels 1979, Race to the Finish? 1981, Eight Feet in the Andes 1983, Muddling Through in Madagascar 1985, Ireland 1985, Tales from Two Cities 1987, Embassy to Constantinople, The Travels of Lady Mary Wortley Montague (ed) 1988, In Cameroon with Egbert 1989, Transylvania and Beyond 1992, The Ukimwi Road 1993, A Better World in Birth 1997, South from the Limpopo 1997, Visiting Rwanda 1998, One Foot in Laos 1999. *Leisure interests:* classical music, reading, swimming, cycling, walking. *Address:* The Old Market, Lismore, Co Waterford, Ireland.

MURPHY, Diane E., BA; American federal judge. *Education:* Univ of Minnesota and Johannes Gutenberg Univ (Mainz, Germany). *Career:* Teaching asst Dept of History, Univ of Minnesota 1955–58; Temporary Substitute for Exec Dir, Minneapolis Commn on Human Relations 1965; Minnesota State Trial judge 1976–1980; US District Judge District of Minnesota 1980–94; Judge US Court of Appeals (8th circuit) Minneapolis 1994–; Dir and immediate past Pres Fed Judges Asscn; Dir and immediate past Chair American Judicature Soc; American Bar Asscn Standing Cttee on Judicial Selection, Tenure and Compensation; elected mem American Law Inst; mem Minnesota State Bar Asscn, Nat Asscn of Women Judges, Minnesota Women Lawyers; Chair Bd Trustees Twin Cities Public Television; Dir Bush Foundation; Trustee and Vice-Chair of Bd Science Museum of Minnesota; fmr Chair Minneapolis Charter Commn, Pres Minneapolis League of Women Voters; has written numerous articles in law journals; Fulbright Scholarship 1954–55; YWCA Outstanding Achievement Award 1981; Univ of Minnesota Outstanding Achievement Award 1983; Distinguished Citizen Award Alpha Gamma Delta 1985. *Address:* 11 E US Courthouse, 300 S 4th St, Minneapolis, MN 55415, USA.

MURPHY, Jill; British writer; b 1949, Wimbledon, London; one s. *Education:* Chelsea Coll of Art. *Career:* Fmr nanny, now writer of jr fiction; numerous awards. *Publications include:* The Worst Witch (has been made into musical), Five Minutes' Peace, Peace At Last, Whatever Next!, A Piece of Cake. *Address:* c/o Puffin Books, 27 Wrights Lane, London W8, UK.

MURRAY, Dame (Alice) Rosemary, DBE, MA, D PHIL, DL, JP; British chemist and former university administrator; b 28 July 1913, Havant; d of the late A. J. L. Murray and Ellen Maxwell Spooner. *Education:* Downe House School (Newbury) and Lady Margaret Hall (Oxford). *Career:* Lecturer in Chem Royal Holloway Coll, London 1938–41, Univ of Sheffield 1941–42; WRNS 1942–46; Fellow and Tutor Girton Coll, Cambridge 1946–54; Pres New Hall, Cambridge 1954–81; Univ Demonstrator in Chem 1947–52, Vice-Chancellor Cambridge Univ 1975–77; City Magistrate, Cambridge 1953–83; Pres Nat Inst of Adult Educ 1977–80; Dir Midland Bank 1978–84, The Observer 1981–93; DL (Cambridgeshire) 1982; Chair, mem cttees and councils colls of educ, schools, Wages Councils, Armed Forces Pay Review Body, Girls' Public Day School Trust; Hon D SC (Ulster) 1972, (Leeds) 1975, (Pennsylvania) 1975, (Wellesley Coll, MA) 1976, (Southern Caliornia) 1976; Hon DCL (Oxford) 1976; Hon LL D (Sheffield) 1977, (Cambridge) 1988; Liveryman Goldsmiths Co 1976. *Leisure interests:* foreign travel, gardening, book-binding. *Address:* 3 Oxford Rd, Old Marston, Oxford OX3 0PQ, UK.

MURRAY, Ann; Irish opera singer (mezzo soprano); b 27 Aug 1949, Dublin, Ireland; m Philip Langridge 1981; one s. *Education:* Royal Northern Coll of Music (Manchester, UK). *Career:* Fmrly performed with English Nat Opera, Royal Opera; European recital tours 1990, 1993, 1994; has performed in festivals at Aldeburgh, Edinburgh, Munich, Salzburg. *Address:* c/o Askonas Holt Ltd, Lonsdale Chambers, 27 Chancery Lane, London WC2A 1PF, UK.

MURRAY, Anne, OC; Canadian singer; b 20 June 1945, Springhill, NS; d of Carson and Marion Murray. *Education:* Univ of New Brunswick. *Career:* Teacher 1966–67; musician 1967–; Top Canadian Female Vocalist 1970; Top Canadian Female Entertainer of the Year 1970; Best Female Newcomer of the Year (Record World Magazine, USA) 1970–71; Top Newcomer Female Vocalist of the Year (Cashbox Magazine, USA); Juno Award, Top Female Vocalist 1970–86; Best Female Vocalist Grammy Award 1974; Nashville's Country Music Hall of Fame, Walkway of Stars 1974; Vanier Award, Outstanding Young Canadian; Canadian Female Recording Artist of Decade; star placed in

Walkway of Stars 1980; Best Female Vocal Performance 1978, 1979, 1980, 1983. *Recordings include:* Anne Murray's Sounds of London, Anne Murray's Greatest Hits Volume II 1989; *TV Specials include:* Anne Murray's Christmas Special 1981, Anne Murray's Caribbean Cruise 1983, Anne Murray's Winter Carnival from Quebec 1984, Sounds of London 1985, Anne Murray's Family Christmas 1988, Anne Murray in DisneyWorld 1991, Anne Murray in Nova Scotia 1999, Croonin' 1993. *Leisure interest:* sports. *Address:* c/o Bruce Allen Talent, 406-68 Water, Vancouver, BC V6B 1A6, Canada.

MURRAY, Cherry Roberts, BFA; American artist; b 3 Jan 1921, Colfax, LA; d of John Bunyon and Mary Roberts; m John Lewis Murray 1942; two d two s (one deceased). *Education:* Univs of N Mexico and Texas. *Career:* Artist USA 1939–54, 1970–, Japan 1954–56, 1960–64, Pakistan 1965–68, Repub of Korea 1965–68, Indonesia 1968–70; Instructor in Fine Arts Pima Coll E, Tucson, AZ 1979–; exhibitions include Baluche Regiment (Cherat, Pakistan) 1965–68, American Embassy Residence (Seoul) 1965–68, Jakarta (Indonesia) 1968–70, Abba Gallery 1978–80, Kay Bonfoey Gallery 1980, Rentschler Gallery 1980, Casa Grande Art Gallery (Tucson) 1980; represented in numerous perm and pvt collections including Univ of Texas, Univ of N Mexico, Nagayama Studio (Tokyo), Ayub Kahn, Baluche Regiment (Pakistan), Mitha Collection (Lahore, Pakistan), Sir Ian McKenzie (UK), H. Allen Loomes (Australia), Amb Yehuda Horam (Israel), Chote Kholgvista (Thailand); numerous awards include Creative Artist of the Year Award 1976, Best of Show Award, Nat League of American PEN Women 1978. *Address:* Pima Community College, 8202 E Poinciana Drive, Tucson, AZ 85730, USA.

MURRAY, Florence Kerins, LL B; American judge; b 21 Oct 1916, Newport, RI; d of John X. and Florence (née MacDonald) Kerins; m Paul F. Murray 1943; one s. *Education:* Syracuse and Boston Univs, Rhode Island Coll of Educ, Brown Univ and Univ of Rhode Island. *Career:* In army 1942–45, Lieut Col 1945, currently Hon Reserve; called to the Bar, MA 1942, RI 1947; law practice 1947–56; admitted to US Dist Court 1948, Supreme Court 1948, Tax Court 1948; mem Rhode Island Senate 1948–56; Nat Coll and Practicing Law Inst 1960–77; Assoc Judge Rhode Island Superior Court 1956, Presiding Justice 1978, Assoc Justice Rhode Island Supreme Court 1979–; Adviser Nat Judicial Coll, Reno, NV 1971, mem Bd of Dirs 1975–87, Chair Emer 1990; mem Bd Dirs State Justice Inst 1994; Chair Family Court Study Cttee 1956–58; apptd by Sec of Defense to Nat Defense Advisory Cttee on Women in the Service 1952–58; mem Civil and Political Rights Cttee, Pres's Comm on the Status of Women 1960–63; Adviser Nat Coll of the State Trial Judges 1970, 1971, 1972; Sec Exec Cttee Nat Conf of Trial Judges 1977; mem Gov's Justice Comm 1978; Chair Special Supreme Court Cttee to Develop Uniform Rules of Evidence 1981; mem American Law Inst, ABA; Fellow American Bar Foundation 1977, Inst of Judicial Admin 1980; Hon D ED (Rhode Island Coll of Educ) 1956; Hon LL D (seven times) 1956–81; Hon DBA (Johnson and Wales Coll) 1977; numerous awards including army awards, Judge of the Year Award (Nat Asscn of Women Judges) 1984, Melvin A. Eggers Sr Alumni Award (Syracuse Univ) 1992, Merit Award Rhode Island Bar Asscn 1994. *Leisure interests:* swimming, reading. *Address:* c/o Rhode Island Supreme Court, 250 Benefit St, Providence, RI 02903, USA (Office); 2 Kay St, Newport, RI 02840, USA (Home). *Telephone:* (401) 222-3266 (Office); *Fax:* (401) 222-3599 (Office).

MURRAY, Jenni, OBE, BA, D UNIV; British broadcast journalist; b 12 May 1950, Barnsley; d of Alvin and Win (née Jones) Bailey; two s. *Education:* Barnsley High School for Girls and Univ of Hull. *Career:* Fmr columnist The Yorkshire Post; presenter BBC Radio Bristol 1973–78, BBC TV South 1978–83, Newsnight 1983–85, BBC Radio 4 Today 1985–87, BBC Radio 4 Woman's Hour 1987–, Points of View 1993, This Sunday 1993, 1994, Dilemmas 1994; Prof of London Inst 2000; Pres Fawcett Soc 2001; D LITT (Bradford) 1994; Broadcasting Press Guild Broadcaster of the Year 1996. *Publications:* The Woman's Hour Book of Humour 1993; The Story of Women in Britain 1946 1996; has written numerous articles for leading newspapers and periodicals; *TV documentaries include:* The Duchy of Cornwall 1985, Every Man: Stand By Your Man 1987, Breaking The Chain 1988, As We Forgive Them 1989, Women in Politics 1989, Here's Looking At You 1991, Is It Me Or Is It Hot In Here – A Modern Woman's Guide to the Menopause 2001. *Leisure interests:* reading, horses, theatre, watching sons play rugby. *Address:* Radio 4, BBC Broadcasting House, Portland Place, London W1A 1AA, UK. *Telephone:* (20) 7765-4314; *E-mail:* jenni .murray@bbc.co.uk.

MURRAY, Joan, MA; Canadian writer, artist and former curator; b 12 Aug 1943, New York, USA; d of Sidney Arnold and Lucia Grace (née de Castro) Charlat; m W. Ross Murray 1959; two d one s. *Education:* Univ of Toronto and Columbia Univ (NY, USA). *Career:* Curator of Canadian Art, Art Gallery of Ontario 1970–73, Acting Chief Curator 1973; Dir The Robert McLaughlin Gallery 1974–2001; Lecturer in Art York Univ 1970–71, 1973–75, Scarborough Coll 1975–76; Adviser Toronto Western Hosp Art Cttee 1973, Ontario Cancer Inst, Princess Margaret Hosp 1977–78; Consultant Ontario Arts Council 1972–75; Broadcaster Arts National, CBC 1976–79; Art Ed The Canadian Forum 1970–74; Contributing Ed Canadian Art 1984–86; contributor The Art Post 1984–87; has staged numerous one-person shows 1983–; mem Council Canadian Museums Asscn 1974–76, Exec Council Ontario Asscn of Art Galleries 1974–76, Advisory Bd Artmagazine 1974–78, Bd of Govs Canadian Confed of the Arts 1975–76, Canadian Art Museum Org 1975–, Bd of Dirs Ontario Heritage Foundation 1975–78, Advisory Cttee on Art, Dept of Public Works 1976–78, Advisory Council Bata Shoe Museums Foundation 1980–. *Publications:* Letters Home: 1855–1906, The Letters of William Blair Bruce 1982, The Beginning of Vision: The Drawings of Lawren S. Harris (jtly) 1982, Kurelek's Vision of Canada 1983, Frederick Arthur Verner: The Last Buffalo 1984, Daffodils in Winter: The Life and Letters of Pegi Nicol MacLeod 1984, The Best of the Group of Seven 1984, The Best of Tom Thomson 1986, The Best of Contemporary Canadian Art 1987, Northern Lights: Masterpieces of Tom Thomson and the Group of Seven 1994, Tom Thomson: The Last Spring 1994, Confessions of a Curator: Adventures in Canadian Art 1996, Tom Thomson: Design for a Canadian Hero 1996, Home Truths: A National Album from Paul Peel to Christopher Pratt 1997, Canadian Art in the Twentieth Century 2000, Tom Thomson: Trees 2000; more than 100 catalogues and 200 articles on Canadian art. *Leisure interests:* swimming, reading. *Address:* 400 Saint John St W, Whitby, ON L1N 1N7, Canada (Home). *Telephone:* (905) 668-1904 (Home).

MURRAY, Noreen Elizabeth, PH D, FRS, FRSE; British professor of molecular genetics; b 26 Feb 1935, Burnley, Lancs; d of John and Lilian G. Parker; m Kenneth Murray 1958. *Education:* Lancaster Girls' Grammar School, King's Coll (London) and Univ of Birmingham. *Career:* Research Assoc Dept of Biological Sciences, Stanford Univ, CA, USA 1960–64; Research Fellow Botany School, Cambridge Univ 1964–67; Lecturer Univ of Edinburgh Inst of Cell and Molecular Biology, Sr Lecturer 1974–80, Reader 1982–88, Prof of Molecular Genetics 1988–; mem MRC Molecular Genetics Unit 1968–74; Group Leader European Molecular Biology Lab, Heidelberg, Germany 1980–82; Pres Genetical Soc of GB 1987–90; Fred Griffith Lecturer of Soc of Gen Microbiology 2001; has written numerous articles in specialist publications and journals; Hon D SC (Birmingham) 1995, (UMIST) 1995, (Warwick) 2001; Gabor Medal of the Royal Soc 1989. *Leisure interest:* gardening. *Address:* University of Edinburgh, Inst of Cell and Molecular Biology, King's Bldgs, Mayfield Rd, Edinburgh EH9 3JR, UK; 4 Mortonhall Rd, London EH9 2HW, UK. *Telephone:* (131) 650-5374; *Fax:* (131) 668-3970; *E-mail:* Noreen.Murray@ed.ac.uk.

MURRAY, Patty, BA; American politician; b 11 Oct 1950, Bothell, WA; d of David L. Johns and Beverly A. (McLaughlin); m Robert R. Murray 1972; one s one d. *Education:* Washington State Univ. *Career:* Teacher Shoreline Community Coll, Seattle 1984–87; campaigned against proposed closure of Washington State parent educ prog 1980; fmr mem Washington State Senate; US Senator (Democrat) from Washington 1993–, Vice Chair Senate Democratic Policy Cttee, mem Budget Cttee, Appropriations Cttee etc. *Address:* US Senate, 111 Russell Senate Office Bldg, Washington, DC 20510, USA (Office); 528 NW 203rd Place, Seattle, WA 98177, USA (Home).

MUSCARDINI, Cristiana; Italian politician; b 6 Nov 1948, Cannolio. *Career:* Fmrly journalist; fmr mem Camera dei Deputati (Chamber of Deputies, Parl); mem Cen Cttee MSI-DN; MEP 1989–, mem Cttee on Foreign Affairs, Security and Defence Policy, Del for relations with Russia. *Address:* c/o European Parliament, rue Wiertz, 1040 Brussels, Belgium.

MUSGRAVE, Susan; Canadian writer; b 12 March 1951, Santa Cruz, CA, USA; d of Edward Lindsay and Judith Bradfield (née Stevens) Musgrave; m Stephen Douglas Reid 1982; two d. *Career:* Writer since the age of 16; Bi-weekly Columnist Toronto Star, Vancouver Sun; book reviewer CBC Journal; Writer-in-Residence Univ of Waterloo 1983–85, Univ of New Brunswick 1985, Univ of W Ontario 1992–93; teacher of English Arvon Foundation 1975, 1980, Univ of Waterloo 1983–84, Kootenay School of Writing 1986, Camosun Coll, Victoria 1988–91; frequent judge and jury mem of poetry competitions; Toronto Univ Presidential Writer-in-Residence Fellowship 1995; Nat Magazine Award (Silver) 1981; b. p. nichol Poetry Chapbook Award 1991; CBC/Tilden Award for Poetry 1996; Vicky Metcalf Short Story Editors Award 1996. *Publications include:* Poetry: Songs of the Sea-Witch 1970, Entrance of the Celebrant 1972, Grave-Dirt and Selected Strawberries 1973, Gullband 1974, The Impstone 1976, Kiskatinaw Songs 1977, Selected Strawberries and Other Poems 1977, Becky Swan's Book 1978, A Man to Marry, A Man to Bury 1979, Tarts and Muggers: Poems New and Selected 1982, Cocktails at the Mausoleum 1985, Kestrel and Leonardo 1990, In The Small Hours of the Rain 1991, The Embalmer's Art 1992, Forcing the Narcissus 1994; Novels: The Charcoal Burners 1980, Hag Head 1980, The Dancing Chicken 1987; Essays: Great Musgrave 1989; has written numerous articles and poems for periodicals and anthologies. *Address:* 10301 W Saanich Rd, POB 2421, Sidney, BC V8L 3Y3, Canada. *Telephone:* (604) 656-5037.

MUSGRAVE, Thea, MUS DOC; British composer; b 27 May 1928, Edinburgh; d of James and Joan (née Hacking) Musgrave; m Peter Mark 1971. *Education:* Edinburgh Univ and Paris Conservatoire (under Nadia Boulanger). *Career:* Lecturer Extra-Mural Dept, London Univ 1958–65; Visiting Prof Univ of California at Santa Barbara, USA 1970; Distinguished Prof Queen's Coll, City Univ of New York, USA 1987; Hon D MUS (Council for Nat Academic Awards, Smith Coll and Old Dominion Univ); Koussevitzky Award 1972; Guggenheim Fellow 1974–75, 1982–83; Hon D MUS (Council for Nat Academic Awards, Smith Coll and Old Dominion Univ). *Works include:* Chamber Concerto 1, 2 & 3 1966, Concerto for Orchestra 1967, Clarinet Concerto 1968, Beauty and the Beast (ballet) 1969, Night Music 1969, Horn Concerto 1971, The Voice of Ariadne (chamber opera) 1972–73, Viola Concerto 1973, Space Play 1974, Mary, Queen of Scots (opera) 1976–77, A Christmas Carol (opera) 1978–79, An Occurrence at Owl Creek Bridge (radio opera) 1981, Harriet, A Woman Called Moses 1980–84, Black Tambourine for women's chorus and piano 1985, Pierrot 1985, For the Time Being for chorus 1986, The Golden Echo 1987, Narcissus 1988, The Seasons (orchestral) 1988, Simón Bolívar (opera) 1989–92, Rainbow (orchestral) 1990, Autumn Sonata 1993, Journey through a Japanese Landscape (marimba concerto) 1993, On the Underground (vocal) 1994, Helios (oboe concerto) 1995, Phoenix Rising (orchestral) 1997; chamber music, songs, choral music, orchestral music. *Leisure interests:* cooking, cinema, reading. *Address:* c/o Novello and Co Ltd, 8–9 Frith St, London W1D 3JB, UK. *Telephone:* (20) 7434-0066; *Fax:* (20) 7287-6329; *E-mail:* promotion@musicalis.co.uk.

MUSSALLEM, Helen Kathleen, CC, MA, ED D; Canadian health consultant; b Prince Rupert, BC; d of Solomon and Annie (née Bassette) Mussallem. *Education:* Vancouver Gen Hosp School of Nursing, Univ of Washington (USA), McGill Univ (Montréal) and Columbia Univ (USA). *Career:* Lieut Royal Canadian Army Medical Corps 1943–46; Staff Nurse, later Head Nurse and Supervisor, Vancouver Gen Hosp School of Nursing 1947–57; Dir project assessing Canadian School of Nursing, Canadian Nurses Asscn 1957–60, Dir Special Studies 1960–63, Exec Dir 1963–81; Consultant to nat and int health orgs 1981–; Sec-Treas Canadian Nurses Foundation 1966–81; mem Bd of Dirs Int Council of Nurses 1981–85; mem numerous nat and int orgs including WHO, Econ Council of Canada, Commonwealth Foundation, Royal Soc of Health, Canadian Red Cross Soc, Canadian Public Health Asscn, Law Reform Comm of Canada; Life mem Canadian Coll of Health Service Exec 1982; Fellow Royal Coll of Nursing (UK); Hon D SC (Memorial); Hon LL D (New Brunswick), (Queens) 1983; Dr hc (McMaster, BC), (Ottawa); Dame of Grace, Most Venerable Order of St John of Jerusalem; Int Red Cross Florence Nightingale Medal 1981; Medal of Distinguished Service (Columbia Univ); Queen's Jubilee Medal 1977; Hon life mem seven provincial nurses' asscns, Aboriginal Nurses' Asscn of Canada, Canadian Nursing Students' Asscn, Canadian Public Health Asscn, Univ of British Columbia Alumni Asscn

1994. *Publications include:* Spotlight on Nursing Education 1960, Path to Quality 1964, Social Change and Nursing Education 1974, A Glimpse of Nursing in Cuba 1973, Nurses and Political Action 1977, Succeeding Together 1983, Continuing Education: An Essential to Nursing Strategy and Network in Primary Health Care 1983, Changing Role of Professional Organizations 1986, Training of Nurse Teachers and Managers in Primary Health Care 1986, Volunteerism: Unmeasured Productivity 1990; over 40 articles in professional journals. *Leisure interest:* gourmet cooking. *Address:* National and International Health Related Agencies, Suite 1706, 20 The Driveway, Ottawa, ON K2P 1C8, Canada (Office); # 602, 2580 Tolmie St, Vancouver, BC V6R 4R4, Canada (Home). *Telephone:* (613) 234-5408 (Office); (604) 234-5408 (Home); *Fax:* (613) 234-5408 (Office).

MUTAFCHIEVA, Vera, PH D; Bulgarian writer and historian; b 28 March 1929, Sofia; d of Petar and Nadia (née Tritonova) Mutafchiev; m 1st Jossif Krapchev 1950 (divorced 1956); m 2nd Atanas Slavov 1961 (divorced 1967); two d. *Education:* Univ of Sofia. *Career:* Sr Researcher in Ottoman History, Inst of History, Sofia 1958–63, Inst of Balkan Studies 1963–79; Prof Inst of Literature 1979–91, Inst of Demographic Studies, Acad of Sciences 1991, Univ of Sofia 1991; Dir Language and Ancient Civilization Centre 1979–80, Bulgarian Inst of Research, Austria 1980–82; Sec Union of Bulgarian Writers 1982–86; has written 12 novels, several plays, numerous essays, monographs and translations; has published 67 scientific studies 1952–92; Gottfried von Herder Preis, Hamburg, Vienna 1980; State Prize 1982. *Leisure interests:* exotic travel, gardening, cooking, sewing. *Address:* 1113 Sofia, Latinka st bl 77B, Bulgaria. *Telephone:* (2) 72-61-28.

MUTI, Ornella (pseudonym of Francesca Romana Rivelli); Italian actress; b 9 March 1955, Rome. *Career:* Numerous appearances in films in Italy, Europe and USA. *Films include:* Mogli piu Bella 1970, Leonor 1975, Nuori Mostri 1977, Flash Gordon 1980, Tales of Ordinary Madness 1983, Casanova 1987, Oscar 1991, Swann in Love.

MUTOLA, Maria Lurdes; Mozambican athlete; b 1972. *Career:* Attended school in Oregon, USA with help from Olympic Solidarity Fund; came fourth in 800m, Tokyo World Championships, fifth at Olympic Games, Barcelona, Spain 1992; winner Bronze Medal in 800m, Olympic Games, Atlanta, GA, USA 1996.

MUTSCH, Lydia; Luxembourg politician; b 17 Aug 1961, Dudelange; d of Antoine and Antoinette (née Baum) Mutsch. *Education:* Lycée Hubert Clement (Esch-sur-Alzette) and Georg-August Univ (Göttingen, Germany). *Career:* Freelance journalist 1985–87; consultant, head publicity and public relations agency 1987–90; Communal Counsellor Esch-sur-Alzette 1987–90; apptd mem Chamber of Reps (Parl) 1990, Spokesperson for Socialist Group, Chair Environment Cttee; Int Sec Young Luxembourg Socialists; Vice-Chair Cttee for Middle Classes and Tourism; mem Luxembourg Socialist Party (POSL), Foreign Affairs, Sport and Youth and Econ Cttees, Control Comm of Int Union of Socialist Youth. *Leisure interest:* environment. *Address:* 22 rue du Commerce, 4067, Esch-sur-Alzette, Luxembourg. *Telephone:* 46-68-60; *Fax:* 54-72-13.

MUTTER, Anne-Sophie; German violinist; b 29 June 1963, Rheinfelden/Baden; d of Karl-Wilhelm and Gerlinde (née Winter) Mutter; one d. *Education:* Konservatorium Winterthur (Switzerland) and with Aida Stucki. *Career:* Began playing piano and violin 1969; performed in Int Music Festival Lucerne, Switzerland 1976; debut with Berlin Philharmonic Orchestra, Pfingstfestspiele Salzburg, Austria 1977; Soloist with orchestras, mem string trios, quartets internationally 1977–; performances include world premières of Witold Lutosławski's Chain II (1986) and Wolfgang Rihm's Gesungene Zeit 1992; Int Chair Violin Studies Royal Acad of Music, London 1985; Hon Pres Mozart Soc, Oxford Univ 1983; awards include Jugend musiziert Prize for violin 1970, 1974, for piano 1970, Künstler des Jahres, Deutscher Schallplattenpreis 1979, Record Acad Prize, Tokyo 1982, Grand Prix Int du Disque 1989, Int Schallplattenpreis 1993, Bundesverdienstkreuz (First class), Order of Merit (of Germany, of Bavaria). *Recordings include:* Beethoven, Mendelssohn, Bruch and Brahms Violin Concertos (with Herbert von Karajan and Berlin Philharmonic Orchestra), Bartók Violin Concerto No 2 and Moret Concerto En Rêve (with Seiji Ozawa and Boston Symphony Orchestra), Lutosławski Paríta, Chain II and

Stravinsky Violin Concerto (with Lutosławski and BBC Symphony Orchestra), Beethoven String Trios (with Rostropovich and Givranna), Berg's Violin Concerto and Rihm's Time Chant (with James Levine and Chicago Symphony Orchestra). *Leisure interests:* collecting modern art, English silver antiques, mountain-climbing, graphic arts, sport. *Address:* Effnerstr 48, 81925 Munich, Germany.

MUWANGA, Ree; British business executive. *Education:* Univ Coll (London) and LSE. *Career:* Mem staff, later Dir BZW Investment Man 1986–96; Head Unitised and Specialist Funds, AMP Asset Man 1996. *Address:* AMP Asset Management, 55 Moorgate, London EC2R 6PA, UK. *Telephone:* (20) 7477-5555; *Fax:* (20) 7477-5888.

MWAKESI, Irene Wakio, B ED; Kenyan international organization executive; b (Irene Tuja) 22 Sept 1953, Taita; m Fred Kimori Mwakesi 1978; two s one d. *Education:* State House Girls' Secondary School (Nairobi) and Univ of Nairobi. *Career:* Producer Voice of Kenya 1976–88; worked on Anvil Magazine 1988–89; Controller of Programme Radio, Kenya Broadcasting Corpn 1989–93; Information Officer UNICEF ESARO 1993–94; Information Officer UN Information Centre, Nairobi 1994; mem African Asscn of Science Eds. *Leisure interests:* aerobics, reading, meeting people. *Address:* United Nations Information Centre, POB 30552, Nairobi, Kenya; c/o Fred Mwakesi, POB 30067, Nairobi, Kenya. *Telephone:* (2) 623677; *Fax:* (2) 623692.

MWENDA, Deborah Chihota; Tanzanian broadcasting executive; b 11 May 1940, Harare, Zimbabwe; d of the late Z. A. and of Anne Chihota; m John Baptist Mwenda 1962; two s two d. *Education:* Tabora School and broadcasting courses in Germany and Netherlands. *Career:* Joined Radio Tanzania 1962, Head Nat Service 1979–82, Commercial Service 1982, Educational Dept 1987–90, Regional Relations 1990, Regional and Int Relations Dept 1991; Project Man Jt Radio Tanzania/UNFPA Population Drama Serial Project 1992; Publr Property Digest magazine 1989; Pres YWCA 1981–82; Hon Sec Tanzania Businesswomen Asscn 1989. *Leisure interests:* reading, gardening, writing, voluntary work. *Address:* Radio Tanzania, POB 9191, Dar es Salaam, Tanzania (Office); POB 3748, Dar es Salaam, Tanzania (Home). *Telephone:* 38022 (Office); *Fax:* 29416 (Office).

MY-ANH; French (b Vietnamese) sculptor; b (My-Anh Ung) 1 Feb 1947, Cantho, Vietnam; d of Nguyên van Ung and Mung thi Luu; m 1st Nghiêm Do Quang 1970 (divorced); one s one d; m 2nd Serge Polivka 2000. *Education:* Univs of Saigon and Paris and Ecole Nat Supérieure des Beaux Arts (Paris). *Career:* First exhibition in Saigon; in Paris 1968–; sculptures in bronze, polychromes, paper, metal; in charge of Sculpture Workshop, Municipal Culture Office, Croissy-sur-Seine 1988–; Prix Bigel, Saint-Cloud 1983; Prix Charles Regnier, Taylor Foundation 1984; Prix Sculpture, Ville du Vésinet 1985. *Sculptures include:* Sculpture for La Route des Epices restaurant, Paris 1984, SOGEA co, Bordeaux 1987, sculpture for l'Après-midi Show (TV) 1989, sculpture La Rencontre for Technoparc, Croissy-sur-Seine 1992, trophy for Salon Multimédia World Show 1995, Sculpture La Rencontre for SNCF 2000, Sculpture for Strasbourg station 2001. *Address:* 49 Ave de Verdun, 78290 Croissy sur Seine, France. *Telephone:* (1) 39-76-24-18; *E-mail:* myanh@noos.fr.

MYERS, Brenda Joyce, B SC; Canadian international organization executive; b 12 Nov 1952, Halifax (NS, Canada). *Education:* Dalhousie Univ (Halifax, NS, Canada). *Career:* Physiotherapist 1973–84; admin Health Service 1986–87; Exec Dir Canadian Physiotherapy Asscn 1987–95; Sec-Gen World Confed for Physical Therapy 1995. *Address:* World Confederation for Physical Therapy, 4A Abbot's Place, London NW6 4NP, UK. *Telephone:* (20) 7328-5448; *Fax:* (20) 7624-7579.

MYERS, Jodi, FRSA; British arts administrator; b 25 May 1952, London. *Education:* Central School of Speech and Drama (London). *Career:* Stage Man 1972–74; Publicity Asst English Nat Opera 1974–76; Publicity Officer English Music Theatre 1976–77, Marketing/Touring 1977–85; Deputy Dir Touring Arts Council of GB 1985–90; Dir Warwick Arts Centre (Coventry) 1991–96; Dir Performing Arts Royal Festival Hall (London) 1996–; mem Council Theatrical Man Asscn 1992–2000; mem Bd Dirs New Shakespeare Co; Adviser WoodHouse Centre, Royal Coll Music (London); Fellow Royal Soc of Arts. *Address:*

Royal Festival Hall, South Bank Centre, London, SE1 8XX, UK. *Telephone:* (20) 7921-0916; *Fax:* (20) 7928-2049; *E-mail:* jmyers@rfh .org.uk; *Internet:* www.rfh.org.uk.

MYERS, Margaret Jane (Dee Dee), BS; American government official, broadcaster and magazine editor; b 1 Sept 1961, Quonset Point, RI; d of Stephen George Myers and Judith Ann Burleigh; one d. *Career:* Press Asst Mondale for Pres Campaign (LA) 1984, to deputy Senator Art Torres (LA) 1985; Deputy Press Sec to Maj Tom Bradley (LA) 1985–87, Tom Bradley for Gov Campaign 1986; California Press Sec Dukakis for Pres Campaign (LA) 1988; Press Sec Feinstein for Gov Campaign (LA and San Francisco) 1989–90; Campaign Dir Jordan for Mayor Campaign (San Francisco) 1991; Press Sec Clinton for Pres Campaign (Little Rock) 1991–92, (White House, Washington) 1993–94; co-host Equal Time, CNBC (Washington) 1995–97; Ed Vanity Fair magazine, Washington 1995–; mem Bd Trustees, California State Univ 1999–; Robert F. Kennedy Award, Emerson Coll, Boston 1993. *Leisure interests:* running, cycling, music, major league baseball. *Address:* c/o White House, 1600 Pennsylvania Ave, NW, Washington, DC 20500, USA.

MYLES, Lynda Robbie, MA; British film producer; b 2 May 1947; d of the late Alexander Watt Myles and Kathleen Kilgour Myles (née Polson); m Dr David John Will 1972 (divorced). *Education:* Edinburgh Univ. *Career:* Dir Edinburgh Film Festival 1973–80; film consultant Channel 4 TV 1982–83; Producer Enigma Films 1983–86; Sr Vice-Pres Creative Affairs Europe, Columbia Pictures 1986–88; Commissioning Ed for Drama BBC TV 1989–91; independent film producer 1991–; has produced films for Alan Parker and Stephen Frears; mem Film Policy Review Bd, Dept for Culture, Media and Sport 1997–; Gov BFI 1993–96; BFI Award 1981. *Films include:* Defence of the Realm, The Commitments, The Snapper, The Van, The Life of Stuff. *Address:* 20 Ossington St, London, W2 4LY, UK.

MYLLER, Ritta; Finnish politician; b 12 July 1956, Joensuu. *Career:* MEP (PSE); mem Cttee on Regional Policy, Del for relations with Estonia, Lithuania and Latvia. *Address:* c/o European Parliament, rue Wiertz, 1047 Brussels, Belgium.

MYLONA, Lia, MA; Cypriot former business executive and administrator; b 15 April 1931. *Education:* French School (Cyprus), American Acad (Cyprus) and Univ of Edinburgh (UK). *Career:* Welfare Officer Cyprus Welfare Services 1956–60; Sr Industrial Relations Officer, Cyprus Employers' Fed 1962–67; Personnel Man Coca Cola (Cyprus) 1967–70, Cyprus Petroleum Refinery Ltd 1970–81; Dir Industrial Training Authority 1981–91; trained to work with cancer and AIDS sufferers in UK; fmr Pres Pancyprian Asscn for Equal Rights and Opportunities; fmr mem Red Cross Council, Pancyprian Safety Council, Cyprus Mental Health Asscn. *Leisure interests:* reading, writing, painting, music, travel, film classics, engraving. *Address:* c/o Industrial Training Authority, Nicosia, Cyprus.

N

NAG, Dipali, MA; Indian musician and musicologist; b 22 Feb 1922, Darjeeling; d of J. C. and Tarulata Taluqdar; m B. D. Nagchaudhuri 1943; one s. *Education:* Agra Univ and Trinity Coll of Music (London). *Career:* Lecturer on Indian Music Royal Asiatic Soc, London, Anjumane Musiqui, Teheran, Univ of California at Berkeley, USA, East-West Center, Honolulu, HI, USA, Music Coll, Colombo, Sri Lanka and at insts in India 1950–91; nat and int concert performances on radio and TV 1948–90; Head Research Dept, Sangeet Research Acad, Calcutta; has made numerous recordings, including one for the Int School of Comparative Music, Venice, Italy 1955; has written books on Ragpradhan, on notation of Western music and about Ustad Fayaaz Khan; awards from Nat Cttee for Gandhi Centenary (New Delhi) 1970, Andhra Univ 1987, Sir C. V. Raman Award (Acoustical Soc of India) 1984. *Leisure interests:* teaching and composing music for choral groups, interior decoration, writing about musical subjects. *Address:* Sangeet Research Academy, Research Dept, 1 Netaji Subhas Chandra Bose Rd, Tollygunge, Kolkata 700 040, India. *Telephone:* (33) 463395; *Fax:* (33) 296523.

NAGEL, Mónica; Costa Rican politician, lawyer and international organization executive; b 5 May 1960, Chile; m (divorced); two d. *Education:* Univ Autónoma de Centro América (San José). *Career:* Law teacher; worked in law office 1984–90; Vice-Minister of Justice with special responsibility for the rights of children 1990; Rep of Costa Rica on Inter-American Comm on Drug Abuse Control (CICAD), OAS 1990–94, Vice-Chair 1992–93, Chair 1993–94; mem Exec Bd UNICEF 1995; Pres Chair Third Conf of Ministers of Justice or Attorney Gens of the Americas 1998–, Bd Dirs of the Justice Studies for the Americas 2000–; Minister of Justice and Grace 1998–(2002); articles on drugs and rights of children in newspapers and magazines 1990–. *Leisure interests:* politics, rights of women and children, penitentiary system, alternative dispute resolution. *Address:* Ministry of Justice, Apdo 5.658, 1000 San José, Costa Rica. *Telephone:* (506) 280-9054; *Fax:* (506) 234-7959; *E-mail:* mnagel@gobnet.go.cr.

NAGUCKA, Ruta Rafaela, MA, PH D; Polish professor of English linguistics; b 23 March 1930, Zebrzydowice; d of Adam and Emilia (née Pustówka) Sikora; m Anthony Nagucki 1966 (died 1993). *Education:* Jagiellonian Univ (Cracow). *Career:* Asst then Sr Asst Jagiellonian Univ, Cracow 1955–63, Adjunct 1963–68, Docent 1968–78, Assoc Prof 1978–84, Prof 1984; mem Ministry of Nat Educ Comm on Awards 1988, Cen Qualifying Comm for Academic Appointments 1988; Ford Foundation Scholar to Univ Coll, London 1958–59; US Dept of State Grant to carry out research at Indiana Univ, Bloomington, USA 1965–66; Ministry of Higher Educ Awards 1964, 1969, 1979, 1985, 1999; Golden Cross of Merit 1975; Medal of the Cttee of Nat Educ 1982; Officer's Cross Order of Polonia Restituta 1995. *Publications:* The Syntactic Component of Chaucer's 'Astrolabe' 1968, Negatively Phrased Utterances in English 1978, An Integrated Analysis of Syntax and Semantics of Obsolete English Constructions 1984, The Language-to-Cognition Interface: the Old English Prepositional Phrase and the Four-dimensional Continuum 1997; numerous articles and reviews in linguistic journals. *Leisure interests:* music, photography. *Address:* Jagiellonian University, Gołębia 24, 31-007 Cracow, Poland (Office); J Lea 30 m 5, 30-052 Cracow, Poland (Home). *Telephone:* (12) 4221033 (Office); (12) 6361494 (Home); *Fax:* (12) 4226793 (Office); *E-mail:* rutanag@vela.filg.uj.edu.pl.

NAGY, Phyllis; American playwright; b New York. *Career:* Debut at Royal Court Theatre, London, now Writer-in-Residence; playwrighting fellowships from Nat Endowment of the Arts, McKnight Foundation, New York Foundation for the Arts. *Plays include:* Butterfly Kiss, Entering Queens, Girl Bar, Plaza Delores, The Scarlet Letter, Trip's Crinch, Weldon Rising, The Strip, Disappeared. *Address:* c/o Mel Kenyan, Casarotto Ramsay Ltd, 60–66 Wardour St, London, W1V 3HP, UK; c/o Joyce Ketay, 1501 Broadway, Suite 1910, New York, NY 10036, USA. *Telephone:* (20) 7287-4450; *Fax:* (20) 7287-9128.

NAIR, Mira; Indian film director and producer; b 1957, Bhubaneswar, Orissa; m 1st Mitch Epstein; m 2nd Mahmood Mamdani; one s. *Education:* Irish Catholic boarding school (Simla), Univ of Delhi and Harvard Univ (USA). *Career:* Performed with experimental theatre co, Calcutta (now Kolkata); began career as documentary and feature film-maker at Harvard Univ. *Films include:* India Cabaret (American Film Festival Award for Best Documentary of 1985) 1985, Children of Desired Sex (documentary), Salaam Bombay! (Cannes Film Festival Camera d'Or Award for Best First Feature by a New Dir and Prix du Publique, Acad Award nomination) 1988, Mississippi Masala 1991, Buddha, The Perez Family 1996, Kama Sutra 1996.

NAISH, Bronwen, ARCM; British musician; b 19 Nov 1939, Burley, Hants; d of E. F. E. Naish and G. J. Grant; m Roger Best 1959 (divorced 1981); three d two s. *Education:* Holyhead Grammar School and Royal Northern Coll of Music (Manchester). *Career:* Began playing double bass 1966; teacher and performer N England; Sub-Prin Bass Northern Sinfonia 1967–73; recital debut King's Hall, Newcastle-upon-Tyne 1971, Purcell Room, London 1974; pursued solo career in N Wales 1976–; tours include Channel Islands 1980, 1988, Australia 1988; created Slap and Tickle with Maurice Horhut 1988; performed Edinburgh Fringe Festival 1989, 1990; player of musical saw 1990–; examiner, Assoc Bd of Royal Schools of Music. *Publication:* Another String to my Bow 1982. *Leisure interests:* beekeeping, do-it-yourself. *Address:* Moelfre, Cwm Pennant, Garndolbenmaen, Gwynedd LL5 9AX, UK. *Telephone:* (176) 675356.

NAJMIR NUR, Begum, MA, M PHIL; Bangladeshi university teacher; b 27 Nov 1944, Dhaka; d of T. U. Ahmed and N. Nahar; m Gholam Mohammad 1964; two s one d. *Education:* Rangpur Girls' School, Rajshahi Govt Coll, Dhaka Univ and Massey Univ (New Zealand). *Career:* Apptd Asst Prof Inst of Social Welfare and Research, Dhaka Univ 1973; apptd Research Officer NIPA 1989; has attended numerous int confs including Int Conf on Women's Health (Manila, Philippines) 1990, and Family: Builders of a New Society (Madras, India) 1991. *Publications include:* Pay or Purdah: Women and Income-earning in Rural Bangladesh 1987, Introduction to Social Research (3rd edn) 1990, seven research studies and 19 papers. *Leisure interests:* gardening, reading, travelling. *Address:* Dhaka University, Institute of Social Welfare and Research, Dhaka, Bangladesh (office). *Telephone:* (2) 413967; (2) 507242.

NAJŽAR-FLEGER, Dora, PH D; Croatian professor of dentistry; b 10 Oct 1931, Sv Petar Orehovec; d of Antun and Marija Najžar; m Branko Fleger 1958; one d one s. *Education:* Univ of Zagreb School of Dentistry. *Career:* Dentist 1957–60; Asst Dental Pathology Dept, Univ of Zagreb 1960–71, Asst Prof 1972–86, apptd Head Dept of Operative Dentistry and Endodontics Dental Clinic 1981, Head Dept of Dental Pathology 1982–91, Full Prof 1987; Pres Dental Pathology Section, Croatian Medical Asscn 1986–89; Post-doctoral Fellow Univ of British Columbia, Vancouver, Canada 1982–83. *Publications:* Accidents in Dental Practice (contrib) 1988, Lexicon of Dentistry (contrib) 1990, Preventive Programs in Dentistry (contrib) 1990, Operative Dentistry (contrib) 1992; contribs to professional journals. *Leisure interests:* literature, nature. *Address:* University of Zagreb, School of Dentistry,

41000 Zagreb, Gundulićeva 5, Croatia (Office); 41000 Zagreb, Novomarofska 37, Croatia (Home). *Telephone:* (41) 321780 (Office); *Fax:* (41) 276071 (Office).

NAKAMURA, Hiroko; Japanese pianist; b 25 July 1944, Tokyo; m Shoji Fukuda 1974. *Education:* Studied piano under Aiko Iguchi, Leonid Kochanski, Rosina Lhevinne, Zbigniev Dzriewiecki, Stefan Askenazy. *Career:* Began playing piano at the age of three; debut with Tokyo Philharmonic Orchestra; Soloist NHK Symphony; performed with Moscow Philharmonic, State Acad Symphony Orchestra of the USSR, Leningrad Philharmonic, USSR now Russian Fed; has performed at over 3,000 concerts during her career, including tours of USA, Canada, UK, Europe, fmr USSR, People's Repub of China and Repub of China (Taiwan); first Japanese to win scholarships from Rockefeller Foundation and Juilliard School of Music, USA 1962; youngest winner of All-Japan Jr Student Piano Competition 1954, All-Japan Sr Student Piano Competition 1956, Japan Music Concours 1959; winner Juilliard Concours, Aspen Music Festival Prize, USA; youngest winner Int Piano Competition, Warsaw; Int Juror 1982, 1986, 1990–. *Recordings include:* Rachmaninov's Second and Third Piano Concertos, Tchaikovsky's First Piano Concerto, Chopin's First Piano Concerto; numerous other pieces with Sony; *Publications:* The Tchaikovsky Concours (Ohya Non-Fiction Prize), Savages Called Pianists. *Leisure interest:* animals. *Address:* 1302 Park Mansion, 2-3-34 Mita, Minato-ku, Tokyo 108, Japan. *Telephone:* (3) 454-6659; *Fax:* (3) 454-9547.

NAMAZOVA, Adila Avaz Kyzy; Azerbaijani politician; b 1926, Agdam. *Education:* Azerbaijan Medical Inst. *Career:* Asst Dept of Children's Diseases, Azerbaijan Medical Inst 1958–65, Prof, Head of Chair 1966–, currently Faculty Chief Azerbaijan Medical Inst; fmr mem Council of Nationalities; CP mem fmr Supreme Soviet Cttees on Women's Affairs, Family Protection, Motherhood and Childhood; mem Acad of Medical Sciences, Acad of Sciences of Azerbaijan; Pres Children's Doctors Soc, Pediatrics Asscn of Turkish-Speaking Countries; Honoured Science Worker; winner State Prize. *Publications:* has written over 250 monographs, works and textbooks. *Address:* Azerbaijan Medical Institute, 370022 Baku, Ul Bakizkhanova 23, Azerbaijan.

NAMIR, Ora; Israeli politician; b 1930, Hadera. *Education:* Levinsky and Givat Hashlosha Teacher Seminaries and Hunter Coll (New York). *Career:* Officer Israel Defence Forces, War of Independence; Sec-Gen Na'amat (Working Women and Volunteers Org) 1967; mem Knesset (Parl—Lab) 1973–, Sec Mapai Knesset faction, Sec Coalition Exec, Chair Prime Minister's Cttee on the Status of Women 1975, Educ and Culture Cttee 1977–84, Labour and Social Welfare Cttee 1984–92; Minister of the Environment 1992–94. *Address:* Knesset, Hakirya, Jerusalem 91000, Israel.

NAMJOSHI, Suniti, PH D; Canadian/British writer; b 20 April 1941, Bombay (now Mumbai), India; d of Manohar and Sarojini Namjoshi. *Education:* Univ of Poona (India) and McGill Univ (Montréal). *Career:* Fmr academic in Canada; currently lives and writes in Devon. *Publications:* Feminist Fables 1981, 1994, Saint Suniti and the Dragon 1994, Building Babel 1996, Goja 2000. *Leisure interests:* computers, gardening. *Address:* Grindon Cottage, Combpyne Lane, Rousdon, nr Lyme Regis DT7 3XW, UK. *Telephone:* (1297) 443422; *Fax:* (1297) 443422; *E-mail:* suniti@freeuk.com.

NAOMI MATA'AFA, Fiame; Western Samoan politician; b 1956; d of Fiame Mata'afa Mulinu'u. *Career:* Apptd Minister of Educ and Labour 1991; fmr Minister of Educ, Youth, Sport and Culture, currently Minister of Educ. *Address:* Ministry of Education, POB 1869, Apia, Western Samoa. *Telephone:* 21911; *Fax:* 21917.

NAPSIAH BTE OMAR, M SC; Malaysian politician; b 21 April 1943, Kuala Pilah, Negeri Sembilan. *Education:* Tunku Khursiah and Tunku Mohamad Schools, Telopea Park High School (Canberra, Australia), ANU and Cornell Univ (NY, USA). *Career:* Admin Officer Dept of Settlers Devt, FELDA, Kuala Lumpur 1967–69; Lecturer Coll of Agriculture, Serdang 1972; Co-ordinator Home and Nutrition Tech Dept, Univ Pertanian Malaysia 1972–73, Acting Head 1973–76, Head of Devt Studies Dept 1978–80, Assoc Prof 1981–82, concurrently Head of Coll Accommodation 1974–82; first woman mem Dewan Rakyat (House of Reps) for Kuala Pilah 1982–86, 1986; Deputy Fed Minister

of Housing and Local Govt 1982–87, Minister of Public Enterprises 1988–90, Minister of Nat Unity and Community Devt 1991–94; mem Supreme Council United Malay Nat Org (UMNO) 1988, apptd Deputy Chief Wanita UMNO 1988, Chair Wanita UMNO Movt, Negeri Sembilan 1988, Chief of Kuala Pilah Div 1988; Founder and Vice-Pres Australian Overseas Student Asscn, Canberra 1963–65; mem Cttee Life, Family Planning, Nat Co-operative Devt; Commdr of the Order of Negeri Sembilan. *Address:* c/o Ministry of National Unity and Community Development, Wisma Shen, 6th–16th Floors, Jalan Masjid India, 50562 Kuala Lumpur, Malaysia (Office); Kementerian Perusahaan Awam, Tingkat 3 Wisma PKNS, Jalan Raja Laut, 50652 Kuala Lumpur, Malaysia (Home).

NARAYAN, Irene, L TH, MA; Fijian politician; b 23 Feb 1932, Lucknow, India; d of the late G. and Violet Hannah Hamilton; m Jai Narayan 1954; three s one d. *Education:* Isabella Thorburn Coll and Lucknow and Benares Hindu Univs. *Career:* Prin DAV Girls' Coll 1958–62; elected to Legis Council 1966–71; mem House of Reps (Parl) 1972–86, Opposition Whip 1977–79, Deputy Leader of Opposition 1979–85; Minister of Indian Affairs 1987–92; Fijian Rep Commonwealth Parl Asscn Confs, Australia 1969, Jamaica 1978. *Address:* 11 Mataritosuva St, Suva, Fiji. *Telephone:* 211370.

NARDI-RIDDLE, Clarine, BA, JD; American lawyer and state official; b 23 April 1949, Clinton, IN; d of Frank and Alice (née Mattioda) Nardi; m Mark Alan Riddle 1971; one s one d. *Education:* Univ of Indiana. *Career:* Called to the Bar, IN 1974, US Dist Court, IN 1974, CT 1979, Fed Dist Court, CT 1980, US Supreme Court 1980, US Court of Appeals (2nd circuit) 1986, (DC circuit) 1994; Staff Attorney Indiana Legis Services Agency, Indianapolis 1974–78, Legal Counsel 1978–79; Deputy Corp Counsel City of New Haven, CT 1980–83; Counsel to Attorney-Gen State of Connecticut 1983–86, Deputy Attorney-Gen 1986–89, Acting Attorney-Gen 1989, Attorney-Gen 1989–91; Judge Superior Court, CT 1991–93; Sr Vice-Pres for Governmental Affairs, Gen Counsel Nat Multi-Housing Council, Nat Apartment Asscn 1995–; Asst Counsel Connecticut Gen Ass 1979; Legal Research Asst Yale Univ 1979; Legal Counsel Indianapolis State Bar Asscn 1979; mem Chief Justice's Task Force on Gender Bias 1988–90, Indiana Section of Ethics and Values Comm 1989–90, Gov's Missing Children Comm, Hartford Child Support Guidelines Comm, Gov's Task Force on Justice for Abused Children 1988–90; mem ABA, Nat Asscn of Attorneys-Gen; Hon LL D (St Joseph's Coll) 1991; named Connecticut History Maker, US Dept of Labor Perm Comm on Status of Women 1989. *Address:* National Multi-Housing Council, 1850 M St, NW, Washington, DC 20036, USA.

NARUSOVA, Ludmila Borisovna; Russian politician and academic; b 2 May 1951, Bryansk; d of Boris Moiseyevich Narusov and Valentina Vladimirovna Narusova; m Anatoly Sobchak (deceased); one d. *Education:* Leningrad State Univ and USSR Acad of Sciences. *Career:* Docent Leningrad State Univ 1979–95; mem State Duma 1995–99; f Hospis movt 1989, Maryinsky Foundation 1991, Foundation of Anatoly Sobchak (also Pres) 2000; invited His Highness, the Great Count Vladimir Kiryllovich Romanov to visit St Petersburg, took part in organising his funeral in St Petersburg; initiated and took part in organising funerals of the Tsar's family in the St Paul and St Peter Cathedral (St Petersburg) 1998; has carried out scientific works on public movts and history of Russian liberalism; has given lectures in USA, Austria, Germany, France; Rep to Austrian and German Foundations paying compensation to former victims of fascism. *Address:* Nab Moyki 31, Apt 8, 191186 St Petersburg, Russian Federation. *Telephone:* (812) 315-54-71 (St Petersburg); (095) 136-62-44 (Moscow).

NASRALLAH, Emily, BA; Lebanese writer and feminist; b 6 July 1931, Kfeir; d of Daoud Abi Rashed and Lutfa Abou Nasr; m Philip Nasrallah 1957; two s two d. *Education:* Shoueifat Nat Coll, Beirut Univ Coll and American Univ of Beirut. *Career:* Mem writing staff Al-Sayyad magazine and Al-Anwar newspaper 1955–70; Cultural and Public Relations Consultant Beirut Univ Coll 1973–75; Feature Writer and Ed Fayruz Magazine 1981–87; ECWA Del to UN Women's Forum on Population and Devt, New York, USA 1974; writer and feminist, one of the Beirut Decentrist women writers; participated in Olympics Authors' Festival, Calgary, Canada 1988; panellist and guest reader PEN Int Congress,

Toronto and Montréal, Canada 1989; Fayruz Magazine Prize for Outstanding Literary Works 1983; Khalil Gibran Prize, Arab Heritage Union in Australia 1991. *Publications:* (in Arabic): Novels: Birds of September (translated into several languages, Laureate Best Novel, Said Akl Prize, Friends of the Book Prize) 1962, The Oleander Tree 1968, The Bondaged (translated into German 1996) 1974, The Resplendent Flower 1975, Those Memories 1980, Flight Against Time (translated into several languages) 1981, Sleeping Ember 1995; Short story collections: The Island of Illusions 1973, The Source 1978, The Woman in Seventeen Stories 1983, The Lost Mill 1984, Our Daily Bread 1990, A House Not Her Own 1992, Stations of Emigration 1996; Non-fiction: Pioneer Women, from East and West (two vols) 1986. *Leisure interests:* gardening, cooking. *Address:* Osman Bldg, Ain-el-Tineh, Verdun St, POB 11-6245, Beirut, Lebanon. *Telephone:* (1) 862483; *Fax:* (1) 862483.

NASREEN, Taslima; Bangladeshi feminist and writer; b 1962, Mymensingh; d of Dr Rojab Ali; m 3rd (divorced). *Education:* Mymensingh Medical Coll and Dhaka Univ. *Career:* Practiced as a gynaecologist; Columnist Ajker Kagoj 1989; books banned in Bangladesh, fatwa (death threat) pronounced against her for blasphemy 1993; left Bangladesh to live in Sweden 1994, returned 1998; has published 15 books; winner Ananda Bazar Patrika Literary Prize 1992, Sakharov Prize (EP) 1994. *Publications include:* Fera (Return), Nirbachito Column (Selected Columns), Laija (Shame) (novel) 1993.

NASSONOVA, Valentina Aleksandrovna, DR MED; Russian rheumatologist; b 4 July 1923 Dniepropetrovsk, Ukraine; m (husband deceased); one s. *Education:* Moscow Inst of Medicine. *Career:* Research Asst, Asst, then Therapy Chair 1st Moscow Inst of Med 1953–58; Sr Research Asst Inst of Rheumatology (Russian Acad of Medical Sciences) 1958–60, Head of Dept 1960–70, Dir 1970–; f Russian Rheumatic Service incorporating therapeutical and diagnostical centre in regional hosps; WHO expert on rheumatic diseases 1975–; Vice–Pres EULAR 1975, Pres-Elect 1977, Pres 1979–81; Pres European Congress of Rheumatologists 1983, Asscn of Rheumatologists of Russia 1993–97; mem Ed Bd journal Therapeutical Archives, Practical Rheumatology 2000–; Hon mem American Coll of Rheumatologists, British, Japanese, Finnish, Yugoslavian, Bulgarian, Polish, German, French, Romanian socs of rheumatologists, and Ukrainian Asscn of Rheumatologists; Corresp mem Russian Acad of Medical Sciences 1974, mem 1984; Dr hc (Kishinev Medical Univ). *Publications:* over 500 scientific works including 10 monographs on systematic rheumatic diseases, rheumatoid arthritis, pathogenesis of rheumatic fever, anti-inflammatory therapy and its tolerability; contribs to Pharmacology in Rheumatology (Moscow) 1976, Lupus Erythematosus Vasceralis (Berlin). *Address:* Institute of Rheumatology Russian Academy of Medical Sciences, Kashirskoye shosse 34A, Moscow, Russian Federation. *Telephone:* (095) 114-44-90; *Fax:* (095) 114-44-68.

NATARAJAN, Jayanthl, BA, BL; Indian politician; b 7 June 1954, Madras (now Chennai); d of C. R. Sundararajan; m V. K. Natarajan. *Career:* Mem Rajya Sabha (Council of States, Parl) 1986; mem Cttee on Privileges, Social Welfare Bd 1988; social worker All India Women's Conf; lawyer with interest in legal aid for the underprivileged; Minister of State for Civil Aviation and Parl Affairs 1997–98. *Address:* Ab-8, Pandara Rd, New Delhi 1, India (Office); 'Badri', 47 Warren Rd, Mylapore, Chennai 600 004, India (Home).

NATHAN, Sara; British broadcasting executive; b 1956; m Malcolm Singer; one s one d. *Education:* Wimbledon High School, Univ of Cambridge and Stanford Univ (USA). *Career:* News Trainee BBC TV, later worked on Newsnight, The Money Programme and Breakfast News; launched The Magazine on BBC Radio 5 Live 1993; Ed Channel 4 News 1995–97; freelance programme ed 1998–; media columnist The Scotsman 1999–; mem Human Fertilization and Embryology Authority 1998–, BAFTA, Radio Authority 1999–, Gambling Review Body 2000–. *Address:* c/o Channel 4 News, Channel 4, 124 Horseferry Rd, London SW1, UK. *E-mail:* snathan@talk21.com.

NATTRASS, E.M.B. (Sue), FAIM; Australian arts administrator and director; b 15 Sept 1941, Horsham, Vic; d of John Elliott Nattrass and Elizabeth Claven Saul. *Education:* Univ of Melbourne and Melbourne Business School. *Career:* Stage Man, Lighting Designer and Production

Dir 1963–79; Gen Man J. C. Williamson Productions Ltd 1980–83; Dir Playbox Theatre Co 1981–84; Theatre Operations Man, Victorian Arts Centre 1983–88, Deputy Gen Man 1988–89, Gen Man 1989–96; Artistic Dir Melbourne Int Festival of the Arts 1997–99; Exec Dir Producer Services Millmaine Entertainment 2000–; numerous public appts including mem Drama Advisory Panel, Vic Ministry for the Arts 1983–85, 1987–88, mem Bicentennial Arts and Entertainment Cttee 1987–88, Ministerial Advisory Cttee, Queen Vic Women's Centre 1993–94, Patron 1996–; Pres Australian Entertainment Industry Asscn 1994–; Deputy Pres Victorian Coll of Arts 1992–; Dir Leadership Vic 1996–, Theatre Royal Hobart 2000–, Fed Square Pty Ltd 2000–, Harold Mitchell Foundation 2000–; mem Melbourne and Olympics Parks Trust 2000–; Patron Victorian Theatres Trust and the Song Room Inc; Premier Award; AGE Performing Arts Awards; St Michael's Medal 1996; Vic Day Award for Community and Public Service 1999. *Leisure interests:* cooking, walking, staring at trees, the bush. *Address:* 7 Martin St, S Melbourne, Vic 3205, Australia (Office); 5 Havelock Street, St Kilda, Vic 3182 Australia (Home). *Telephone:* (3) 9534-6269; (3) 9690-9766 (Office); *Fax:* (3) 9525-4392; *E-mail:* suen@millmaine.com.au (Office); nattrass@smart.net.au (Home); *Internet:* www.millmaine.com.au.

NAUCLER, Charlotte Elisabeth Helene, LLB; Finnish (b Swedish) politician; b 7 March 1952, Eda, Sweden; d of Per Olof Axel and Karen Helene (née Narvestad) Naucler; m Ben Valdemar Listherby 1980; one s one d. *Education:* Uppsala Univ (Sweden) and Univ of Helsinki. *Career:* Sec Law-drafting Dept, Govt of Åland 1979–83; Deputy Sec to Åland Parl 1983–86, then Sec Finance Cttee; Sec-Gen Åland Del, Nordic Council; mem Bd Int Scientific Council for Island Devt (Insula) 1989; apptd Pres Cercle Franco-Ålandais 1992; Lega Navale Italiana di Agrigento Castor and Pollux Prize for Men of the Sea 1992. *Leisure interests:* reading, politics. *Address:* Government of Åland, Södragt 5, 22100 Mariehamn, Åland Islands. *Telephone:* (28) 25474; *Fax:* (28) 19771.

NAVAROVÁ, Zuzana; Czech singer and composer; b 18 June 1959, Hradec Králové; d of Radovan Navara and Olga (née Kvapilová) Navarová; m Luis Tejada Medina 1989. *Education:* Charles Univ, State Conservatory (Prague) and Univ of Havana (Cuba). *Career:* Singer and guitar player 1978–, mem Nerez (music group) 1982–, Tres (music group) 1995–; composer of musical scores for theatre, film and cartoons; Vokalíza Award 1982; Czech Music Fund Award 1990. *Recordings include:* Masopust 1986, Na Vařený nudli 1988, Ke zdi 1990, Co se nevešlo 1991, Caribe 1992, Staráláska Nerez a vy 1993, Morytáty a balady 1993, Nerez v Betlémě 1993, Tres 1995, Nerez antologie 1995; Scores: Národní divadlo, Křížovka 1990, Řeči, Řeči, Řeči, 1991, Milionáři Bídy 1992. *Leisure interests:* flowers, cats, cooking. *Address:* Českolipská 11/388, 190 00 Prague-Prosek 9, Czech Republic. *Telephone:* (2) 3429611; *Fax:* (2) 321882.

NAVARRO-TOLENTINO, Rora, B SC, LL B; Philippine diplomatist; b 6 April 1946, Cebu City; d of Constantino C. Navarro, Sr and Helene Herrera-Navarro; m Abelardo M. Tolentino, Jr 1972; two d one s. *Education:* Coll of the Holy Spirit (Manila) and Univ of the Philippines. *Career:* Prin Asst Office of Consular Affairs, Dept of Foreign Affairs 1972, Acting Div Dir Office of Policy Planning 1972–76, Asst Sec for Public Affairs 1986–88, Dir-Gen for Asian and Pacific Affairs 1988–89; Consul, San Francisco, CA, USA 1976–78; First Sec, Consul-Gen, Thailand 1978–81, Minister-Counsellor 1981–85, Deputy Chief of Mission 1985–86; Alt Perm Rep to ESCAP, Thailand 1982–86; Amb to Australia 1989–94, also accredited to Nauru 1991, to France 1994, also accredited to Portugal 1994; Permanent Rep to UNESCO, Paris 1994; Coll Scholar Univ of the Philippines 1967. *Address:* Embassy of the Philippines, 4 Hameau de Boulainvilliers, 75016 Paris, France. *Telephone:* (1) 44-14-57-00; *Fax:* (1) 46-47-56-00.

NAVRATILOVA, Martina; American (b Czechoslovakian) tennis player; b 18 Oct 1956, Prague; d of Miroslav Navratil and Jana Navratilova. *Career:* Defected to USA 1975; professional lawn tennis player since 1975, ranked No 1 1982–85; Wimbledon Singles Champion 1978, 1979, 1982, 1983, 1984, 1985, 1986, 1987, 1990, finalist 1988, 1989, Doubles Champion 1976, 1979, 1982, 1983, 1984, 1985; French Champion 1982, 1984; Australian Champion 1981, 1983, 1985; US Open Champion 1983, 1984, 1987; Avon Champion

1978, 1979, 1981; runner-up Wimbledon 1994; 54 Grand Slam Titles, 149 other singles titles; World No 1 for 332 weeks at retirement (Nov 1994); eight Wimbledon titles (1993); set professional women's record for consecutive victories 1984; won 100th tournament of career 1985; only player to win 100 matches at Wimbledon 1991; has beaten Chris Evert's (qv) record with 158 singles wins (1992); Pres Women's Tennis Asscn 1979–80, 1983–84, 1994–95; World Champion 1980; Played Fed Cup for Czechoslovakia 1973, 1974, 1975; 1,400 victories (Oct 1993); 167 singles titles (Nov 1994); designer own fashion-wear; Dr hc (George Washington) 1996. *Publication:* Being Myself (autobiog) 1985, The Total Zone (jtly) 1994, The Breaking Point (jtly) 1996, Killer Instinct (jtly) 1998. *Leisure interests:* golf, snowboarding, skiing, basketball. *Address:* IMG, 1360 E 9th St, Cleveland, OH 44114, USA; US Professional Tennis Association, 6701 Highway 58, Harrison, TN 37341, USA.

NAYAK, Nalini, M SC S; Indian development worker; b 31 Dec 1947. *Education:* Tata Inst of Social Sciences (Bombay). *Career:* Lived and worked in artisanal fishing village 1967–77; supporter of nat and int campaign for the rights of artisanal fish workers 1980–; involved in environmental regeneration of estuarine vegetation; Ashoka Foundation Fellow; Gold Medal Tata Inst of Social Sciences 1971. *Publications:* Religion and Culture in the Fishing Community 1986, The Impact of Motorisation on Small-Scale Fishing in India 1992. *Address:* Sadanand, Choola Lane, Anayara, Trivandrum 695 029, India. *Telephone:* (471) 60108.

NAZARENKO, Tatyana Georgievna; Russian painter; b 24 June 1944, Moscow; m. *Education:* Moscow Surikov State Fine Arts Inst. *Career:* Worked Studio of USSR Acad of Fine Arts 1969–72; mem USSR (now Russian) Union of Painters 1969; solo exhibitions France, USA, Spain, Russia, Germany 1987–; Acad of Arts Silver Medal 1987; Russian State Prize 1993. *Address:* Moscow Artists' Union, Starosadsky Per 5, 101000 Moscow, Russian Federation. *Telephone:* (095) 921-51-88.

NCUBE, Sister Bernard; South African politician; b 9 March 1935, Pietersburg, Transvaal; d of Benedict and Anne Ncube. *Education:* St Thomas' School (Heidelberg, Germany) and St Mary's Teacher Training Coll (Lesotho). *Career:* Teacher St Angela's 1955; Field Worker SA Catholic Bishops' Conf 1980–87; worker Inst of Contextual Theology 1987; Co-Founder Fed of Transvaal Women, then Pres 1984; has been arrested and detained on several occasions; United Democratic Front Del to USA 1989. *Address:* Federation of Transvaal Women, c/o African National Congress of South Africa (ANC), Munich Re Centre, 3rd Floor, 54 Sauer St, Johannesburg 2000, South Africa.

NDIAYE, Ndioro, MD, PH D; Senegalese politician; b 6 Nov 1946, Bignona; m; six c. *Education:* Univ Cheikh Anta Diop of Dakar and Univ of Paris VII. *Career:* Head Oral Health Section, Bopp Medical Centre 1976–78; Asst Inst of Odonto-Stomatology, Faculty of Medicine and Pharmacy, Univ Cheikh Anta Diop of Dakar 1976–77, Lecturer 1982, Head Preventive and Social Odontology Section 1983, Acting Head 1983, Prof, Head of Inst 1988–; Head of Specialized Nursing Training in Odontology 1976–77; Head of Studies Nat School of Advanced Technicians in Odontology 1977–79, Acting Dir 1979, Head 1980; Technical Adviser Ministry of Public Health 1982–88; Minister of Social Devt 1988, for Women and Children 1990; Chief SEN HMD 001, Int Oral Fed Project in co-operation with WHO 1983, apptd Rep 1985; WHO expert in Oral Health for Africa Region 1985; Gen Sec Nat Asscn of Oral Surgeons 1975–77; Gen Sec Secr of Oral Health for Africa; Pres Fifth Regional Conf of African Women 1995; Head Del from Senegal, Int Conf on Population, Cairo 1995; mem UN Advisory Bd in preparation for int summit, Copenhagen 1995; participant at numerous confs; has worked with a number of int NGOs; numerous papers and contribs to academic journals; Commdr dans l'Ordre des Palmes Académiques 1992. *Address:* University Cheikh Anta Diop of Dakar, Faculty of Medicine and Pharmacy, Dept of Odonto-Stomatology, Dakar, Senegal (Office); Villa 7, Cité Fayçal, Cambérène, Dakar, Senegal (Home). *Telephone:* 251944.

NDIKUMANA, Victoire; Burundi politician; b 18 July 1957, Menyi; d of Emile Ndikumana and Augusta Gahimbare; m Daniel Sejiji 1979; two s one d. *Education:* Univ of Burundi. *Career:* Man Ministry of Commerce and Industry 1982–87, Dir of Internal Trade 1987–88, of External Trade 1988–90, Chair Admin Bd Nat Trade Office 1988–89, Head Trade Promotion Dept APEE 1990–91; Minister of Women's Advancement and Social Protection 1991–93; mem Admin Bd Office du Thé du Burundi (OTB—Burundi Tea Agency) 1984–89; Vice-Chair Admin Bd Compagnie de Gérance du Coton (COGERCO—Cotton Man Co) 1984–90; mem Municipal Consultative Council, Bujumbura; Chair Admin Bd Textile Complex, Bujumbura 1989–91. *Leisure interests:* reading, gymnastics, walking. *Address:* 10 ave Ntwarante, Rohero, Bujumbura, Burundi. *Telephone:* (2) 223619.

NEAL, Patricia; American actress; b 20 Jan 1926, Packard, KY; d of William Burdette Neal and Eura Mildred Petrey; m Roald Dahl 1953 (divorced 1983, died 1990); four d (one deceased) one s. *Education:* Northwestern Univ (IL). *Career:* Debut on Broadway 1946, followed by numerous TV, film and stage appearances; public lectures in America and abroad. *Stage appearances include:* Voice of the Turtle 1946, Another Part of the Forest (Tony Award, Donaldson Award, Drama Critics Award) 1946, The Children's Hour 1953, A Roomful of Roses 1954, Suddenly Last Summer 1958, The Miracle Worker 1959; *Films include:* John Loves Mary 1949, The Hasty Heart 1949, The Breaking Point 1950, Three Secrets 1950, The Day the Earth Stood Still 1951, Diplomatic Courier 1952, Something for the Birds 1953, Face in the Crowd 1957, Breakfast at Tiffany's 1961, Hud (Academy Award) 1963, The Third Secret 1964, In Harm's Way 1965, The Subject was Roses 1968, The Road Builder 1970, The Night Digger 1970, The Boy 1972, Happy Mother's Day Love George 1973, Baxter 1973, Widow's Nest 1976, The Passage 1978, All Quiet on the Western Front 1979, Ghost Story 1981, An Unremarkable Life 1989; *Publication:* As I Am (autobiog, jtly) 1988. *Leisure interests:* needlepoint, gardening, cooking. *Address:* 45 E End Ave, New York, NY 10028, USA. *Telephone:* (212) 772-1268.

NEARY, Jennifer Catherine, BA, DIP ED; Australian organization executive; b 16 Aug 1947; d of M. L. and Z. Neary. *Education:* Gosford High School (NSW) and Univs of Newcastle (NSW) and Singapura (Singapore). *Career:* Teacher 1971–74; Sr Research and Educ Officer, Commonwealth Dept of Educ 1974–75; Exec Officer, Disadvantaged Schools Programme Schools Comm 1975–77; Sec Bruce Tech and Further Educ (TAFE) Coll, Guild, ACT 1978–80; Dir Working Women's Centre, SA 1980–81; Head Women's Co-ordination Unit, New S Wales Dept of TAFE 1981–83; Dir Women's Bureau, Commonwealth Dept of Employment and Industrial Relations 1983–86, Dir of Programmes 1986–87; Exec Dir and Deputy Chair, Victoria Dept of TAFE 1987; Gen Man Programmes Div, Victoria State Training Bd 1987–88, Portfolio Policy Co-ordination Div 1988–89; Deputy Chief Exec Worksafe Australia 1989–91; Chief Exec Comcare Australia 1991–94; Nat Gen Man, Risk Management and Insurances GIO Australia 1994–95; Gen Man, Workers' Compensation, FAI Insurances 1996–. *Leisure interests:* sailing, opera, skiing. *Address:* FAI Insurances Ltd, Level 5, 333 Kent St, Sydney, NSW 2999, Australia.

NEARY, Patricia Elinor; American ballet dancer and director; b Miami, FL; d of James Elliott and Elinor (née Mitsitz) Neary. *Career:* Dancer corps de ballet, Nat Ballet of Canada, Toronto 1957–60; Prin Dancer New York City Ballet 1960–68; Dancer Geneva Ballet, Switzerland 1968–70, Dir 1973–78; Guest Dancer Stuttgart Ballet, Germany 1968–71; Asst Dir and Dancer W Berlin Ballet 1970–73; Dir Zurich Ballet (Switzerland) 1978–86, La Scala, Milan Ballet Co, Italy 1986–88; apptd Artistic Dir Ballet of British Columbia, Vancouver, Canada 1989. *Address:* c/o Ballet of British Columbia, Vancouver, Canada.

NECHUTOVÁ, Jana, PH D; Czech professor of philology; b 28 Nov 1936, Olomouc (Moravia); d of Ludvík Nechuta and Otilie Nechutová; m Prof Radislav Hošek 1975; one s one d. *Education:* Masaryk Univ (Brno). *Career:* Univ accreditation, Masaryk Univ 1991, Prof of Classical Philology (specializing in medieval Latin) 1993–, Dean Faculty of Letters 1995–98; publs on medieval literature, trans of Roman writers including Lucan and Seneca; Commenius Prize, Czechoslovak Govt 1992. *Publications include:* Nicolas of Dresda in the Early Reformation Thought 1967, Mallhiae de Janov Regulae Veleris et Novi Testamenti (ed) 1993, Medieval Latin 1995, Latin Literature of Medieval Czech 2000. *Leisure interests:* dogs, nature, classical music. *Address:* Masaryk

University Brno, Faculty of Philosophy, Arne Nováka 1, 660 88 Brno, Czech Republic (Office); Tomáškova 6, 615 00 Brno, Czech Republic (Home). *Telephone:* (5) 41121381; *Fax:* (5) 41121380; *E-mail:* nechutov@phil.muni.cz.

NEDD, Priscilla Anne; American film editor; b 6 April 1955, Indianapolis; d of Jerome Hoard and Betty Anne (née Dorn) Nedd. *Education:* Pierce Jr Coll (CA). *Career:* Freelance Assoc Film Ed 1981–82, Film Ed 1982–; mem Motion Picture Editors' Guild, American Cinema Editors, Acad of Motion Picture Arts and Sciences. *Films:* An Officer and a Gentleman 1981–82, Eddie and the Cruisers 1982–83, The Flamingo Kid 1984, No Small Affair 1984, Century City 1985, Street Smart 1986, Tucker: The Man and His Dreams 1987–88, Dead Poets Society 1989, Pretty Woman 1989–90, Guilty By Suspicion 1990.

NEEDHAM, Nina Camille, BA; Jamaican/British tourist organization executive; b 16 Aug 1952, St Catherine; d of Oscar and Joyce Chin; m Frank Merrick Needham 1981; one s. *Education:* The Queen's and St Andrew High Schools (Kingston), Univ of the W Indies, Mona Campus and Royal Inst of Public Admin (London). *Career:* Training Officer, later Admin School Services Div, Ministry of Educ, Jamaica 1973–80; Asst Gen Man Jamaica Hotel and Tourist Asscn 1980–81, Gen Man 1983–95, Exec Dir 1995–; Asst to Man Dir Caribtours, London 1982–83; Chair Hospitality and Tourism Advisory Cttee, Univ of Technology of Jamaica; Dir Tourism Product Devt Co, Tourism Action Plan Ltd. *Leisure interests:* theatre, reading. *Address:* Jamaica Hotel and Tourist Association, 2 Ardenne Rd, Kingston 10, Jamaica. *Telephone:* 926-2796; *Fax:* 929-1054; *E-mail:* cneedham@jhta.org.

NEGUS, Norma; British judge; d of G. D. Shellabear and K. L. Calvert; m 1st Richard Negus 1956; m 2nd David Turner-Samuels 1976. *Education:* Malvern Girls' Coll. *Career:* Fashion promotion and advertising 1950–68; called to the Bar, Gray's Inn 1968, mem Middle Temple; Metropolitan Stipendiary Magistrate 1984–90, Recorder 1989–90, Circuit Judge 1990–97; mem Parole Bd 1991–94, Mental Health Review Tribunal 1996–98. *Leisure interests:* reading, travel. *Address:* c/o Cloisters, 1 Pump Court, Temple, London EC4Y 7AA, UK.

NEIERTZ, Véronique; French politician; b 6 Nov 1942, Paris; d of Michel and Hélène (née Querenet) Dillard; m Patrick Neiertz 1965; two s one d. *Education:* Centre Nat des Arts et Métiers and Ecole des Hautes Etudes Commerciales pour Jeunes Filles. *Career:* Lecturer Univ of Madagascar 1967–70; Head Political, Econ and Social Documentation Service, PS 1972–79, Nat Sec for Women's Rights 1979–81, mem Bd of Dirs and Exec Cttee 1979–, Head Int Relations 1981; contrib to l'Unité 1976–; mem Nat Ass (Parl) for Seine Saint-Denis (Bondy-Romainville) 1981–88, 1993–, Sec Comm for Foreign Affairs 1981–86, Vice-Pres Parl France-Québec Friendship Group 1981–, Parl France-USSR Friendship Group 1986–, Pres French Section France-Canada Interparl Asscn 1981–86, Nat Ass Apartheid Study Group 1988, Nat Noise Council 1982–86; Spokesperson Socialist Group 1983–86, Vice-Pres Socialist Group 1986; assigned to Ministry of Foreign Affairs 1982; Sec of State for Consumer Affairs, Ministry of the Economy, Finance and the Budget 1988–91, Sec of State for Women's Rights and Daily Life 1991–92, Sec of State for Women's Rights and Consumer Affairs (Ministry of Economy and Finance) 1992–93; Regional Councillor Ile de France 1981–86, 1992–93; Deputy Mayor of Bondy 1983–95; Gen Councillor Seine-Saint-Denis 1988–; Pres Conseil Supérieur de l'adoption 1998–. *Publication:* Véridique histoire d'un septennat peu ordinaire 1987. *Leisure interests:* tennis, mountain sports. *Address:* Assemblée Nationale, Palais Bourbon, 126 Ave de l'Université, 75355 Paris, France (Office); Hôtel de Ville, 93140 Bondy, France (Office).

NELLIGAN, Kate; Canadian actress; b 16 March 1951, London, ON; d of Patrick Joseph and Alice (née Dier) Nelligan. *Education:* St Martin's Catholic School (London, ON), York Univ (Toronto), and Cen School of Speech and Drama (London). *Career:* Debut Little Theatre, Bristol, UK 1972; actress Little Theatre and Theatre Royal for Bristol Old Vic 1972–73, Nat Theatre Co, RSC, Stratford, UK; Best Actress Award, London Evening Standard 1978. *Plays include:* Barefoot in the Park 1972, Knuckle 1974, Heartbreak House 1975, Plenty, Misalliance, A Streetcar Named Desire, The Playboy of the Western World, London

Assurance, Private Lives, Moon for the Misbegotten 1984, As You Like It, Serious Money 1988, Spoils of War 1988, Eleni; *Films include:* The Count of Monte Cristo, The Romantic Englishwoman, Dracula 1979, Patman, Eye of the Needle 1980, Agent 1980, Without a Trace 1983, Eleni 1986, White Room, Frankie and Johnny 1991, The Prince of Tides 1991, Shadows and Fog, Fatal Instinct, Wolf, How to Make an American Quilt, Up Close and Personal, US Marshals, Stolen Moments (voice), Boy Meets Girl, The Cider House Rules; *TV appearances include:* The Onedin Line, The Lady of the Camellias, Licking Hitler, Measure for Measure, Thérèse Raquin 1980, Forgive our Foolish Ways 1980, Count of Monte Cristo, Victims, Kojak, Love and Hate, Old Times, Love is Strange, Swing Vote. *Leisure interests:* reading, cooking. *Address:* c/o Innovative Artists, Suite 2850, 1999 Avenue of the Stars, Los Angeles, CA 90067, USA.

NELMES, Dianne; British broadcasting executive; m Ian McBride 1985. *Education:* The Holt Girls' Grammar School (Wokingham) and Univ of Newcastle upon Tyne. *Career:* Fmr Ed Courier, Univ of Newcastle student newspaper, fmr Pres Students' Union; graduate trainee Thomson Newspapers; Journalist Look North, BBC TV from 1978; Exec Producer of Entertainment, Granada TV Ltd until 1992, responsible for many new programmes including This Morning, You've Been Framed, Cluedo, Stars in their Eyes; fmrly Researcher World in Action, Exec Producer 1992. *Address:* c/o Granada TV Ltd, Granada TV Centre, Quay St, Manchester M60 9EA, UK.

NELSON, Dorothy Wright, JD; American federal judge; b 30 Sept 1928, San Pedro, CA; d of Harry Earl and Lorna Amy Wright; m James F. Nelson; one s one d. *Education:* Univ of California at Los Angeles and Univ of Southern California Law Center. *Career:* Faculty mem Univ of Southern California Law Center 1957–, Prof and Interim Dean 1967, Dean 1969–80, Adjunct Prof 1980–; Circuit Judge Court of Appeals (Ninth Circuit) 1979–95, Sr judge 1995–, mem Judicial Council 1985; sat with Supreme Courts of Federated States of Micronesia 1984 and Israel 1985, High Courts of Bombay and Calcutta, India 1986; Vice-Pres American Judicature Soc 1977–79, Chair Bd of Dirs 1979–81; Chair Bd of Dirs Western Justice Center Foundation, Inc 1986–; Co-Chair Sino-American Conf on Mediation and Arbitration, Beijing 1992, Dialogue on Transition to a Global Soc, Switzerland 1992; mem Bd of Dirs Fed Reserve Bank of San Francisco 1977–80, Pres's Comm on Pension Policy 1979, Bd of Trustees James Madison Memorial Fellowship Foundation 1988–90, Fed Judicial Center's Cttee on Appellate Educational Programs 1989–91, Advisory Bd World Law Inst 1997–; mem ABA; Fellow American Bar Foundation; Lustman Fellow, Yale Univ 1977, Fellow Davenport Coll 1977; Hazen Foundation Fellow, Aspen Inst Exec Seminar Program 1977; Hon LL D (Western State) 1980, (Southern California) 1983, (Georgetown) 1988, (Whittier) 1989, (Santa Clara) 1990; awards include Times Woman of the Year 1986, AWARE Int Award 1970, Univ of Judaism Humanitarian Award—Torah Award 1973, Award of the World Peace Through Law Center 1975, American Judicature Soc Justice Award 1985. *Publications:* Judicial Administration and the Administration of Justice 1975, Foreword to University of Southern California Law Review Symposium on Gender Bias in the Courts 1994, Rutter Group Practice Guide, Federal, 9th Circuit Civil Appellate Practice (jtly) 1994; numerous publs on law reform and women's issues. *Address:* US Court of Appeals Circuit, 125 S Grand Ave, Suite 303, Pasadena, CA 91105, USA.

NELSON, Eleanor Francis, LL B; Australian judge; b 7 May 1944; d of R. Nelson; m Earle Williams 1972; one s one d. *Education:* Adelaide Girls' High School and Univ of Adelaide. *Career:* Called to the Bar, Southern Australia 1967, NT 1980, WA 1995; Barrister and Solicitor 1967–75, Barrister 1975; QC 1982; mem Bd of Examiners, Supreme Court 1975–89; Chair Comm and Bd, Pvt Agents 1977–82; mem Legal Services Comm 1980–82; Chair Parole Bd of SA 1983–; Chair Casino Supervising Authority 1990–95; mem Council, Law Soc 1976–82. *Address:* Rose Park Chambers, 148 Fullerton Rd, Rose Park, SA 5067, Australia.

NELSON, Judith, BA; American concert and opera singer; b 10 Sept 1939; d of Virgil D. Nelson and Genevieve W. Manes; m Alan H. Nelson 1961; one s one d. *Education:* St Olaf Coll (Northfield, MN). *Career:* Alfred Hertz Memorial Fellowship Univ of California at Berkeley 1972–73; European debut 1972; specializes in baroque repertoire; has performed with most major baroque orchestras in US and Europe including Acad of Ancient Music, Tafelmusik, Toronto, Canada, Philharmonia, San Francisco and with San Francisco, St Louis, Baltimore and Washington Nat Symphony Orchestras and Los Angeles Philharmonic; has appeared in opera in Boston, Los Angeles, Brussels, Innsbruck, Austria, Venice, Turin and Rome, Italy and at Maryland Handel Festival; Master Classes at Univ of California at Los Angeles, Univ of Chicago, Bath Summer School, UK Bruges Festival, Belgium, Jerusalem Music Center, Israel; Hon DFA (St Olaf Coll) 1979. *Leisure interests:* languages, support of local arts orgs, local politics. *Address:* 2600 Buena Vista Way, Berkeley, CA 94708, USA. *Telephone:* (415) 848-1992.

NELSON, Karin Becker, MD; American neurologist; b 14 Aug 1933, Chicago, IL; d of George and Sylvia (née Demansly) Becker; m Phillip G. Nelson 1955; three d one s. *Education:* Univs of Minnesota and Chicago. *Career:* Asst Resident in Neurology Univ of Maryland School of Medicine 1958–59; Resident in Neurology George Washington Univ School of Medicine 1959–62; Consultant in Medical Neurology St Elizabeth's Hosp, Washington, DC 1960–62; Outpatients Registrar Nat Hosp, London 1963; Medical Officer Perinatal Research Br, Nat Inst of Neurological Disorders and Blindness, NIH 1964–67, Medical Officer 1972–; Medical Staff Children's Hosp of Dist of Columbia 1962–, Assoc Neurologist 1967–71, Attending Neurologist 1971–73, 1978–; Instructor in Neurology George Washington Univ 1967–70, Asst Prof of Neurology 1970–72, Assoc Clinical Prof of Neurology 1972–; Consultant Nat Inst of Child Health and Human Devt 1975–80, Food and Drug Admin 1983–86, Boston Collaborative Drug Surveillance Group 1985–86, American Acad of Pediatrics 1985, 1987, Birth Monitoring Group, California State Dept of Health 1986–, Birth Defects Monitoring Comm, Center for Disease Control 1987; ed numerous scientific journals; mem Advisory Bd Int School of Neurosciences, Venice, Italy, Revision Bd Nat Inst of Aging, Child Neurology Soc, Nat Inst of Neurology and Communicative Disorders and Blindness, American Acad for Cerebral Palsy and Devt Medicine, American Epilepsy Soc, American Neurological Asscn; Fellow American Acad of Neurology; US Public Health Service Special Recognition Award 1977; Special Achievement Award 1981; United Cerebral Palsy Weinstein-Goldenson Research Award 1990. *Address:* NIH, 7550 Wisconsin Ave, Rm 700, Bethesda, MD 20892, USA.

NELSON HACKETT, Karen; American business executive; b 1954. *Career:* Fmr employee ING Barings, Head of Brokerage until 2000; joined Susquehanna Int Group; has worked for nearly 30 years at NY Stock Exchange (NYSE), Gov (first woman) 1999–. *Address:* New York Stock Exchange, Inc, 11 Wall St, New York, NY 10005, USA. *Telephone:* (212) 656-3000; *Internet:* www.nyse.com.

NĚMCOVÁ, Miriam; Czech conductor; b 2 Aug 1961, Prague; d of Mudr Zvonimié Němec and Dagmar Němcová. *Education:* Prague Conservatory, Acad of Music (Prague) and Conservatoire Nat Supérieur de Musique (Paris). *Career:* Choir Mistress Rosa Chamber Chorus, Prague 1977–89, Charles Univ 1980–85, Prague Radio 1987–88; Conductor Prague Madrigalists 1987–88, Asst Choir Mistress 1988–89; Conductor Liberec Opera Theatre 1989–90, Karlsbad Symphony Orchestra 1990, Prague Chamber Opera 1990–91, Karlovy Vary Symphony Orchestra 1991; Founder Praga Sinfonietta 1990; Artistic Dir and Conductor F. X. Šalda Theatre, Liberec 1991. *Address:* Čs Armády 5, 160 00 Prague 6, Czech Republic. *Telephone:* (2) 320054; *Fax:* (2) 320054.

NERINA, Nadia; South African ballet dancer; b Oct 1927, Cape Town; m Charles Gordon 1955. *Career:* Joined Sadler's Wells School, then Theatre Ballet 1946; Dancer Sadler's Wells Ballet until 1951, Royal Opera House (now Royal Ballet) 1951–67, Soloist 1967–69; danced in Europe, SA, USA, Canada, fmr USSR, Bulgaria and Romania; guest appearances with Turkish Nat Ballet 1957, Bolshoi and Kirov Ballets 1960, Munich Ballet 1963, Nat Finnish Ballet, 1964, Royal Danish Ballet 1964, Stuttgart Ballet 1965, Chicago Opera House 1967 and at London Palladium 1969, 1971, 1972; Hon Ballet Consultant Univ of Ohio, USA 1967–69; British Jury mem third Int Ballet Competition, Moscow 1977; Fellow Cecchetti Soc 1959, Patron 1964; mem Council Royal Soc for the Prevention of Cruelty to Animals (RSPCA) 1969–74. *Ballets include:* The Sleeping Beauty, Swan Lake, Coppelia, Giselle,

Cinderella, Firebird, La boutique fantasque, Petrushka, Carnaval, Les Sylphides, Les rendezvous, Façade, Homage to the Queen, La fille mal gardée, Electra; *Publication:* Ballet and Modern Dance 1974. *Address:* c/o Royal Opera House, Covent Garden, London WC2, UK.

NESBITT, Lenore Carrero, BS, LL B; American federal judge; m Joseph Nesbitt; one s one d. *Education:* Northwestern Univ and Univs of Florida and Miami. *Career:* Pvt Practice Nesbitt and Nesbitt 1960–63; Special Asst Attorney-Gen 1961–63; Research Asst Dade Co Circuit Court 1963–65, Law Offices 1969–73; Counsel Florida State Bd of Medical Examiners 1970–71, Petersen, McGowan and Feder 1973–75; Judge Florida State Courts 1975–82, US Dist Court, Miami 1983–; mem American and Florida Bar Asscns, US Judicial Conf Comm on Criminal Law and Probation Admin. *Address:* US District Court, 301 N Miami Ave, Miami, FL 33128-7784, USA.

NESHAT, Shirin, MFA, MA; Iranian photographer and video artist; b 1957, Qazvin. *Education:* Univ of California at Berkeley (USA). *Career:* Artist-in-Residence Henry Street Settlement, New York 1991–92; several grants and fellowships including Sponsored Project Grant, New York State Council on the Arts 1989, Tiffany Foundation Grant 1996, New York Foundation for Arts Photography Fellowship 1996; Gold Lion, Venice Biennale 1999. *Works include:* series of photographs Women of Allah 1993–97; split-screen video installations: Turbulent 1998, Rapture 1999, Fervor 2000; solo exhibitions include: Franklin Furnace (New York) 1993, Annina Nosei Gallery (New York) 1995, 1997, Lucio Amelio Gallery (Naples) 1996, Marco Noire Contemporary Arts (Turin) 1996, Centre d'Art Contemporain (Fribourg) 1996, Lumen Travo (Amsterdam) 1997, Galleria d'Arte Moderna (Bologna) 1997, Moderna Galerija (Ljubljana, Slovenia) 1997, Kunsthalle Wien, Whitney Museum of American Art, Tate Gallery (London), Serpentine Gallery (London) 2000, Hamburger Kunsthalle 2001; group exhibitions include: Venice Biennale 1999, Malmö Konsthall 2000.

NESTEROVA, Natalya Vasilyevna; Russian academic; b 1952. *Education:* Moscow State Univ and Moscow Pedagogical Inst. *Career:* Worked in different higher educ insts of Moscow; Founder and Pres Moscow Centre of Educ 1990–; f Humanitarian Gymnasium of N Nesterova 1991–; Founder and Rector New Humanitarian Univ and Acad of Dance N Nesterova 1992–; f Acad of Painting 1994–. *Address:* New Humanitarian Centre of Education, Varshavskoye shosse 38, 115230 Moscow, Russian Federation. *Telephone:* (095) 113 5544.

NETANYAHU, Shoshana, LL B; Israeli judge; b 6 April 1923, Danzig (now Gdańsk, Poland); d of Bernard and Rebecca Shenburg; m Elisha Netanyahu 1949 (died 1986); two s. *Education:* Reali School (Haifa) and Jerusalem Law School. *Career:* Law practice 1947–48, 1949–1969; Deputy Judge, Advocate-Gen Israeli Air Force 1948–49; Judge Magistrate's Court, Haifa 1969–74, Dist Court, Haifa 1974–82, Justice Supreme Court 1982–93; part-time Lecturer Faculty of Law, Univ of Haifa 1993–97, Hebrew Univ of Jerusalem 1993–; Chair State Comm of Inquiry into the Health System of Israel 1988–90; apptd Deputy Chair Israel Council of Higher Educ 1992; contribs to legal publs; Dr hc (Haifa) 1997; Distinction Award, Council of Women's Orgs in Israel 1988; 'Woman of Distinction', Women's League for Conservative Judaism 1998; Honour of Distinction, Movt for Quality Government in Israel 2001. *Publications include:* The Direct Right of the Insured Against the Insurer in Liability Insurance 1998, The Insurer's Duty of Good Faith and the Foreseeability Test of Damages 2000. *Leisure interests:* music, swimming. *Address:* The Supreme Court, 15/29 Diskin St, Jerusalem 96440, Israel. *Telephone:* (2) 5664473; *Fax:* (2) 5664875.

NEUBERGER, Rabbi Julia Babette Sarah, MA; British rabbi and broadcaster; b 27 Feb 1950, London; d of the late Walter Schwab and of Alice Schwab; m Anthony John Neuberger 1973; one s one d. *Education:* S Hampstead High School for Girls, Newnham Coll (Cambridge) and Leo Baeck Coll (London). *Career:* Rabbi S London Liberal Synagogue 1977–89; Lecturer and Assoc Fellow Leo Baeck Coll 1979–97; Assoc Newnham Coll, Cambridge 1983–96; Chancellor Univ of Ulster 1994–2000; Chair Rabbinic Conf, Union of Liberal and Progressive Synagogues 1983–85, Camden and Islington Community Health Services NHS Trust 1993–97; presenter Choices programme, BBC TV 1986, 1987; Visiting Fellow King's Fund Inst 1989–91; Fellow King's Fund Man Coll; Harkness Fellow Harvard Univ, USA 1991–92;

Trustee Runnymede Trust 1990–97, Imperial War Museum 1999–; Gov British Inst of Human Rights 1989–95; Chair Patients Asscn 1988–91, Royal Coll of Nursing Comm on Health Service 1988; Sec and Chief Exec The King's Fund 1997–; mem Nat Cttee SDP 1982–88, Policy Planning Group Inst of Jewish Affairs 1986–90, Univ Coll London Council 1993–97, MRC 1995–2000, NHS Complaints Review 1993–94, Gen Medical Council 1993–, Bd of Visitors, Memorial Church, Harvard Univ 1994–, Save the Children Fund Council 1995–96, Forum UK Cttee, Funding Review of BBC 1999, numerous other cttees, and public and charitable appts; Harkness Fellow, Commonwealth Fund of New York; Visiting Fellow, Harvard Medical School 1991–92; Hon Fellow, City and Guilds Inst, Mansfield Coll (Oxford); Dr hc (Open Univ, City Univ, Humberside, Ulster, Stirling, Oxford Brookes, Teesside, Nottingham, Queen's Belfast). *Publications:* The Story of Judaism 1986, Caring for Dying Patients of Different Faiths 1986, Days of Decision (ed) 1987, Whatever's Happening to Women? 1991, A Necessary End (co-ed) 1991, Ethics and Healthcare: the Role of Research Ethics Committees in the UK 1992, The Things that Matter 1993, On Being Jewish 1995, Dying Well – A Health Professional's Guide to Enabling a Good Death 1999; contribs to various books on cultural, religious and ethical factors in nursing; contribs to Nursing Times; reviews in journals and newspapers. *Leisure interests:* riding, sailing, Irish life, opera, setting up the old girls' network, children. *Address:* The King's Fund, 11–13 Cavendish Square, London W1G 0AN, UK. *Telephone:* (20) 7307-2400; *Fax:* (20) 7307-2803.

NEUFELD, Elizabeth Fondal, PH D; American professor of biological chemistry; b 27 Sept 1928, Paris, France; m 1951. *Education:* Univ of California at Berkeley. *Career:* US Public Health Service Fellow Univ of California at Berkeley 1956–57, Asst Research Biochemist 1957–63; mem staff Nat Inst of Arthritis, Metabolism and Digestive Diseases, Bethesda 1963–84, Research Biochemist 1963–73, Head of Human Biochemistry and Genetics Dept 1973–79, Head of Genetics and Biochemistry Br 1979–84; Prof and Chair Dept of Bio-chemistry, School of Medicine, Univ of California at Los Angeles 1984–; Sr Laureate Passano Foundation 1982; Fellow AAAS; mem NAS, American Acad of Arts and Sciences, American Soc of Human Genetics, American Chemistry Soc, American Soc of Biological Chemists, American Soc of Cell Biology, American Soc of Clinical Investigation; Dr hc (Paris) 1978; Hon D SC (Troy) 1981, (Hahnemann) 1984; Dickson Prize, Pittsburgh 1974; Hillebrand Award 1975; Gardner Foundation Award 1981; Albert Lasker Clinical Medical Research Award 1982; William Allan Award 1982; Elliot Cresson Medal 1984; Wolf Foundation Prize 1988; Nat Medal of Science 1994. *Address:* University of California at Los Angeles, School of Medicine, Dept of Biological Chemistry, Los Angeles, CA 90095-1737, USA. *Telephone:* (213) 825-4321.

NEUGARTEN, Bernice Levin, PH D; American social scientist; b 11 Feb 1916, Norfolk, NE; d of David L. and Sadie (née Segall) Levin; m Fritz Neugarten 1940; one s one d. *Education:* Univ of Chicago. *Career:* Research Asst Dept of Educ, Univ of Chicago 1937–39, Research Assoc Comm on Human Devt 1948–50, Asst Prof 1951–60, Assoc Prof 1960–64, Prof 1964–80, Chair 1969–73, Rothschild Distinguished Scholar and Prof Emer 1988–93, Emer Prof 1993–; Prof of Educ and Sociology, Northwestern Univ 1980–88, mem various advisory bodies; Fellow American Council on Educ 1939–41, AAAS, American Psychological Asscn, American Sociology Asscn, American Acad of Arts and Sciences; mem Inst of Medicine, NAS, Int Asscn of Gerontology; Hon D SC (Southern California) 1980; Hon PH D (Nijmegen) 1988; awards include Kleemier Award 1972, Brookdale Award 1980, Sandoz Int Prize 1987, Ollie Randall Award 1993, Gold Medal Award, American Psychological Foundation 1994. *Publications:* Co-author or ed: American Indian and White Children: A Social-Psychological Investigation 1955, Society and Education 1957, Personality in Middle and Late Life 1964, Middle Age and Aging 1968, Adjustment to Retirement 1969, Social Status in the City 1971, Age or Need? Public Policies for Older People 1982; numerous articles in professional journals. *Address:* 5801 Dorchester Ave, Chicago, IL 60637, USA.

NEUHÄUSER, Mary Helen; American artist and playwright; b 17 Feb 1943, San Antonio, TX; d of Gotthelf Friedrich and Edna Earl (née Walling) Neuhäuser; m Federico Andrea Canuto 1972 (divorced 1981). *Education:* Bethesda-Chevy Chase High School, Catholic Univ, Car-

negie Mellon Univ and Studio Nera Simi (Florence, Italy). *Career:* Group and one-woman exhibitions include Potters House Gallery, Washington, DC, Martha Washington Library, Alexandria, VA, Nat Museum of Fine Arts, Washington, DC, Smithsonian Inst, Washington, DC, Corcoran Gallery of Art, Veerhoff Galleries, Washington, DC, Capricorn Galleries, Bethesda, MD, Lorenz Gallery, Bethesda, Art and Design Gallery, Chantilly, VA, Thirty-Year Retrospective, Friendship Gallery, Chevy Chase, MD 1989; official portrait comms include FBI Bldg, House of Reps Bldg, Trinity Coll, Sidwell Friends School, Washington, DC; contribs to newspapers including The Washington Post, The Evening Star, Capitol Hill Roll Call; poet and writer for Democratic Presidential Campaign 1988; First Place The Washington Post (Portraits) 1961, 1964; numerous awards for abstract paintings 1961–76. *Plays:* The Great Sin, Awkwright and Murgatroyd. *Leisure interests:* charity work, homeless aid, orphanages, political and health care issues, foreign languages (Italian, Spanish, French). *Address:* 2107 Belvedere Blvd, Apt 6, Silver Spring, MD 20902, USA. *Telephone:* (301) 754-6365.

NEUMAN, Maxine Darcy, M MUS; American cellist and professor of music; b 1 July 1948, Philadelphia, PA; d of Marvin and Helga (née Hennigson) Neuman; m Reinhard Humburg 1987; one d one s. *Education:* Manhattan School of Music (New York). *Career:* Cellist New Jersey Symphony Orchestra 1969–71, Mostly Mozart Festival Orchestra, American Ballet Theatre, American Composers Orchestra 1971–80, Walden Trio 1972–, Contemporary Trio 1975–80, Berkshire Chamber Players 1980–85, Crescent String Quartet 1979–, St Luke's Chamber Ensemble 1980–, Breve, Ensemble for Early Music 1985–, Claremont Duo, Germany 1998–; Prof of Music Bennington Coll, VT 1981–95, Chair Music Dept 1985–86, 1990; Prof of Music Williams Coll, MA 1994–95, 1998; Prof of Music Hawthorne Valley School 1996–; mem Faculty School for Strings, New York 1996–; annual solo tours to Europe, S America, Japan, USA; mem Bd of Dirs Bronx Opera Co 1972–85, Chamber Music Conf of the NE 1987–; mem American Fed of Musicians 1969–, Chamber Music America 1980–; Double Award of Merit, Nat Fed of Music Clubs 1976; Int Congress on Women in Music Award, UN 1990. *Recordings:* Nighthawks (film score); numerous recordings on int labels 1980–. *Leisure interests:* photography, travel, reading, cooking, hiking. *Address:* Box 42, Park St, N Bennington, VT 05257, USA (Office); 200 Claremont Ave, New York, NY 10027, USA (Home). *Telephone:* (802) 442-2349 (Office); (212) 222-7896 (Home).

NEUWIRTOVÁ, Radana, MD; Czech haematologist; b 10 Oct 1927, Prague; d of Záviš and Marta Renelt; m Jan Neuwirt 1952; two d. *Education:* Charles Univ (Prague). *Career:* Mem staff Second Medical Clinic, Charles Univ, Prague 1957, Gerontology Dept 1968–73, Outpatient Dept Third Medical Clinic and Haematology Consultant 1974–82, Asst Prof Dept of Clinical Haematology 1982; mem Cttee Chemotherapy Section, Medical Soc J. E. Purkynje, Int Gesellschaft für Chemo- und Immunotherapie, Vienna, European Org for Research and Therapy of Cancer; numerous contribs to nat and int textbooks, medical journals and confs. *Leisure interests:* creative arts, pictures, books, gardening, tennis, skiing, natural sciences. *Address:* Charles University, Dept of Clinical Haematology, Ovocný trh 5, 116 36 Prague 1, Czech Republic (Office); Holečkova 48, 150 00 Prague 5, Czech Republic (Home). *Telephone:* (2) 295388 (Office); (2) 5733483 (Home).

NEVILLE-JONES, Dame (Lilian) Pauline, DCMG, FRSA, MA; British business executive, former diplomatist and civil servant; b 2 Nov 1939, Birmingham; d of Roland Neville-Jones and Cecilia Emily M. Rath. *Education:* Leeds Girls' High School and Lady Margaret Hall (Oxford). *Career:* Harkness Fellow Commonwealth Fund, USA 1961–63; Foreign Service 1963, 1968–71, 1975–77, Head of Planning Staff 1983–87, Third Sec, Rhodesia (now Zimbabwe) 1964–65, Third, then Second Sec, Singapore 1965–68, First Sec, Washington, DC 1971–75; mem Cabinet, later Chef de Cabinet to Commr responsible for the Budget, Financial Control, Financial Insts and Taxation, Comm of the EC 1976–82; Visiting Fellow Royal Inst of Int Affairs and Inst français des relations internationales 1982–83; Econs Minister then Political Minister and Deputy Head of Mission, Germany 1987–91; Deputy Sec to Cabinet, Cabinet Office (Office of Minister for the Civil Service) 1991–94, Chair Jt Intelligence Cttee 1993–94; Political Dir and Deputy Under-Sec of State FCO 1994–96; Head UK Del to Dayton, OH, USA talks on Bosnian crisis 1996; Man Dir and Head of Global Business Strategy, NatWest Markets (investment banking section of NatWest Group) 1996–98; a Gov BBC 1998–; mem Advisory Bd Hawkpoint Partners Ltd 1998–, Chair 1998–2000; Hon D UNIV (Open Univ) 1998; Hon D SC (ECON) (London) 1999. *Leisure interests:* cooking, gardening, antiques. *Address:* c/o National Westminster Bank PLC, 41 Lothbury, London EC2P 2BP, UK. *Telephone:* (20) 7352 0610; *E-mail:* gdr57@dial.pipex.com.

NEVILLE-ROLFE, Lucy Jeanne, MA; British civil servant; b 2 Jan 1953; d of Edmund and Margaret (née Evans) Neville-Rolfe; m Richard John Packer; four s. *Education:* Somerville Coll (Oxford). *Career:* Joined Ministry of Agriculture, Fisheries and Food 1973, Pvt Sec to Minister 1977–79, responsible for EC Sheepmeat and Milk 1979–86, for Land Use 1986–88, for Food Safety Act 1988–90, Head of Personnel 1990–92; mem Prime Minister's Policy Unit 1992–94; Under-Sec 1994; Dir Deregulation Unit, DTI then Better Regulation Unit, Cabinet Office 1995–97; Dir of Corp Affairs, Tesco PLC 1997–; mem Bd of Man FCO 2000–; mem Econs and Europe Cttees CBI 1998–; Vice-Pres European Commerce Steering Cttee; mem UNICE Task Force on Enlargement, Bd of Man British Retail Consortium 1998–. *Address:* Tesco PLC, Tesco House, Delamare Rd, Cheshunt, Herts EN8 9SL UK. *Telephone:* (20) 7215-6637.

NEVILLE-ROLFE, Marianne Teresa, CB, BA; British civil servant; b 9 Oct 1944; d of Edmund and Margaret (née Evans) Neville-Rolfe; m David William John Blake 1972 (divorced 1992). *Education:* St Mary's Convent (Shaftesbury) and Lady Margaret Hall (Oxford). *Career:* Mem staff CBI 1965–73, Head of Brussels Office 1971–72; Prin Dept of Trade and Industry 1973, Asst Sec 1982, Under-Sec Internal European Policy Div 1987; Chief Exec and Prin Civil Service Coll 1990; Dir Top Man Programme, Office of the Minister for the Civil Service, later Office of Public Service and Science, Cabinet Office 1990–94; Regional Dir Govt Office for the NW 1994–99; Chief Exec N E Manchester Ltd 2000–. *Leisure interests:* travel, opera. *Address:* 17 Stilton Drive, Beswick Shopping Centre, Manchester M11 3SB, UK. *Telephone:* (161) 230-2109.

NEVO, Ruth, PH D; Israeli painter and former professor of humanities; b 1924, Johannesburg, SA; d of Benjamin and Henrietta (née Goldsmith) Weinbren; m Natan Nevo 1952; three s. *Education:* Univ of the Witwatersrand (Johannesburg) and Hebrew Univ of Jerusalem. *Career:* Tutor Dept of English, Hebrew Univ 1952–, Prof 1973–, Renee Lang Prof of Humanities 1982–87; full-time painter 1987–; solo exhibitions 1986, 1991, 1993, 1995, 1997, 1998, 2000; mem Israel Acad 1985–, Israel Asscn of Painters and Sculptors 1989–. *Publications:* The Dial of Virtue 1963, Tragic Form in Shakespeare 1972, Comic Transformations in Shakespeare 1980, Shakespeare's Other Language 1987; Trans: Selected Poems by Bialik 1981, Travels by Amichai 1986. *Address:* Hehalutz 22, Jerusalem, Israel; Dept of English, Hebrew University, Mount Scopus, Jerusalem, Israel. *Telephone:* (2) 6523752.

NEWBOLD, Yve; British business executive; b 1941. *Career:* Solicitor; fmr Legal Adviser to Walt Disney Productions, Xerox Corpn, Rank Xerox, IBM; joined Hanson PLC 1986, Co Sec 1986–95; Chief Exec PRO NED 1995–97; Partner Heidrick & Struggles 1998–2000; Chair Ethical Trading Initiative 2000–; Non-Exec Dir BT (fmrly British Telecom) 1991–97; Coutts & Co 1994–98; Gov London Business School 1990–; mem London First, Demos (political 'think-tank'), Royal Comm on Criminal Justice 1991–93, Sr Salaries Review Body 1994–97, Advisory Bd Inst of Global Ethics 1997–. *Address:* Ethical Trading Initiative, 78 Long Lane, London EC1A 9EX, UK.

NEWBY-FRASER, Paula; Zimbabwean sportswoman; b 2 June 1962. *Education:* Univ of Natal (Durban, SA). *Career:* Began competing in triathlon events 1985; eight time winner Women's Champion Ironman Triathlon World Championship (Hawaii), est women's record 1992.

NEWCOMBE, Hanna, PH D; Canadian (b Czechoslovakian) peace researcher and writer; b 5 Feb 1922, Prague; d of Arthur and Paula (née Seger) Hammerschlag; m Alan Newcombe 1946; two s one d. *Education:* Univ of Toronto and McMaster Univ. *Career:* Moved to Canada 1939; part-time Lecturer McMaster Univ, Hamilton, ON 1955–58; high school maths and science teacher, Ontario 1961; Ed Peace Research

Abstracts Journal 1962–, Peace Research Reviews Journal 1967–; Co-Founder Canadian Peace Research and Educ Foundation 1965; Search for World Peace Instructor (part-time) York Univ, Ont 1976–96; Dir Peace Research Inst, Dundas, ON; Pres World Law Foundation 1974–84, World Fed Authority Cttee 1980–; mem several UN cttees; Hon LL D (McMaster) 1982; World Fedists of Canada Peace Award 1972; Lentz Int Peace Research Award (jtly) 1974; Woman of the Year (jtly), Hamilton 1985. *Publications include:* Alternative Approaches to World Government 1974, World Unification Plans and Analyses 1980, Design for a Better World 1983, Survey of Peace Research 1983; numerous chapters, articles and conf papers. *Leisure interests:* writing essays and poetry, swimming. *Address:* 25 Dundana Ave, Dundas, ON L9H 4E5, Canada. *Telephone:* (416) 628-2356; *Fax:* (416) 628-1830.

NEWELL, Frances Mary, FRSA, FCSD; British design consultant; b 19 Jan 1947, Surrey; d of the late Alexander C. and Julie S. Newell; m John William Sorrell 1974; two s one d. *Career:* Founder and Chair Newell & Sorrell (identity & design consultants, merged with Interbrand 1997) 1976–97; Group Creative Dir Interbrand Newell and Sorrell 1997–; Chair City & Guilds Nat Advisory Cttee on Art, Craft and Design 1994–96, mem Colour Group 1996–, City & Guilds Sr Awards Cttee 1996–; mem Bd Dirs Royal Acad Enterprises 1996–99, Exec Cttee Mencap Blue Sky Appeal 1996–98, Advisory Bd of Nat Museum of Photography, Film and TV; awards include 11 DBA Design Effectiveness Awards, 5 Silver D&ADs, 5 Clios, 1 Grand Award for British Airways Corp Identity and 5 Gold Awards in New York Festivals, 2 Art Dirs' Club of Europe Awards. *Leisure interests:* art, travel, gardening. *Address:* Interbrand Newell and Sorrell, 4 Utopia Village, Chalcot Rd, London NW1 8LH, UK. *Telephone:* (20) 7722-1113; *Fax:* (20) 7722-0259.

NEWMAN, Jocelyn Margaret, LL B; Australian politician; b 8 July 1937, Melbourne, Vic; d of the late L. T. and M. E. Mullett; m K. E. Newman 1961; one s one d. *Education:* Univ of Melbourne. *Career:* Barrister and Solicitor 1962–; voluntary worker 1963–86; farmer 1974–81; retailer 1978–86; property developer 1982–86; mem Senate for Tasmania 1986, 1987–, mem Cttees for Scrutiny of Bills 1986–87, Estimates 1986–, Educ and the Arts 1986–87, Foreign Affairs, Defence and Trade 1987–90, Educ of Gifted and Talented Children 1987–88, fmr Shadow Minister for Defence Science and Personnel 1988–92, the Aged and Veterans' Affairs 1992–93, Assisting Leader on Status of Women 1989–93, Family Health, Assisting Leader on Family Matters, Chair Health, Welfare and Veterans' Affairs Group 1993–94, Shadow Minister for Defence 1994–96; Minister for Social Security and Minister Assisting Prime Minister on Status of Women 1996–98, for Family and Community Services and Minister Assisting Prime Minister on Status of Women 1998–; Founder-mem Women's Shelters, Hobart and Launceston. *Leisure interest:* gardening. *Address:* Parliament House, Canberra, ACT 2600, Australia (Office); 11 Elphin Rd, Launceston 7250, Tasmania, Australia (Home). *Telephone:* (6) 277-7560 (Office); *Fax:* (6) 273-4122 (Office).

NEWMAN, Nanette; British actress and writer; b Northampton; d of Sidney and Ruby Newman; m Bryan Forbes 1955; two d. *Education:* Sternhold Coll, London Italia Conti Stage School and Royal Acad of Dramatic Art. *Career:* Film and TV actress; author of children's books and cookery books; Presenter BBC Radio Two programme 1991–. *Films include:* The L-Shaped Room 1962, The Wrong Arm of the Law 1962, Seance on a Wet Afternoon 1963, The Whisperers 1966, The Madwoman of Chaillot 1968, Captain Nemo and the Underwater City 1970, The Raging Moon (Variety Club Best Actress Award 1972) 1971, The Stepford Wives 1974, International Velvet (Evening Standard Best Actress Award) 1978; *TV appearances include:* The Fun Food Factory, London Scene, Stay With Me Till Morning, Jessie, Let There Be Love, Late Expectations 1987, The Endless Game 1988, Newman Meets (series) 2000, Celebrations (series); *Publications include:* God Bless Love 1972, Lots of Love 1973, All Our Love 1978, Fun Food Factory 1976, The Root Children 1978, Amy Rainbow 1980, That Dog 1980, Reflections 1981, Dog Lovers Coffee Table Book 1982, Cat Lovers Coffee Table Book 1983, My Granny was a Frightful Bore 1983, Christmas Cookbook 1984, Cat and Mouse Love Story 1984, The Best of Love 1985, Pigalev 1985, Archie 1986, The Summer Cookbook 1986, Small Beginnings 1987, Bad Baby 1988, Entertaining with Nanette Newman 1988, Charlie the Noisy Caterpillar 1989, Sharing

1989, ABC 1990, 123 1991, Cooking For Friends 1991, Spider, The Horrible Cat 1992, There's a Bear in the Bath 1993, Take 3 Cooks 1996, There's a Bear in the Classroom 1996, Up to the Skies and Down Again 1999, Little Book of Kids Talk 1999, To You with Love 1999. *Leisure interests:* needlepoint, china painting. *Address:* Chatto & Linnit Ltd, 123A King's Rd, London SW3 4PL, UK. *Fax:* (1344) 845174.

NEWMAN, Pauline, PH D; American federal judge; b 20 June 1927, New York; d of Maxwell Henry and Rosella Newman. *Education:* Vassar Coll and Columbia, Yale and New York Univs. *Career:* Research Chemist American Cyanamid Co, NJ 1951–54; mem Patent Staff FMC Corpn, New York 1954–75, Philadelphia 1975–84, Dir Dept of Patent and Licensing 1969–84; Programme Specialist Dept of Natural Sciences, UNESCO, Paris 1961–62; Called to the Bar, NY 1958, US Supreme Court 1972, US Court of Customs and Patent Appeals 1978, US Court of Appeals 1981, US Fed Court of Appeals 1982; Judge US Court of Appeals (Fed Circuit) 1984–; mem State Dept Advisory Comm on Int Industrial Property 1974–84; Lecturer in field; Trustee Philadelphia Coll Pharmacy and Science 1983–84; mem ABA, Bd Dirs Midgard Foundation 1973–84, Medical Coll, PA 1975–84, Research Corpn 1982–84, US Trademark Asscn 1975–79 (Vice-Pres 1978–79), American Inst of Chemists 1960–66, 1970–76, American Chemical Soc 1972–81, American Patent Law Asscn 1981–84; Pres Pacific Industrial Property Asscn 1979–80; numerous contribs to professional journals. *Address:* US Court of Appeals, National Courts Bldg, 717 Madison Place, NW, Washington, DC 20439, USA.

NEWMAN, Rachel, BA; American magazine editor; b 1 May 1938, Walden, MA; d of Maurice and Eythe Brenda (née Techell) Newman; m Herbert Bleiweiss 1973. *Education:* Pennsylvania State Univ and New School of Interior Design. *Career:* Accessories Ed Women's Wear Daily, New York 1964–65; Designer and Publicist Grandoe Glove Corpn, New York 1965–67; Assoc Ed McCall's Sportswear and Dress Merchandiser magazine, New York 1967, Man Ed McCall's You-Do-It Home Decorating 1968–70; Man Ed Ladies Home Journal Needle and Craft magazine, New York 1970–72; Ed-in-Chief American Home Crafts, New York 1972–77; Fashion Dir Good Housekeeping, New York 1977–78, Dir of Home Bldg and Decorating 1978–82; Ed Country Living 1979–; Founding Ed Country Cooking 1985–90, Dream Homes 1989–, Country Kitchens 1990–93, Country Living Gardener 1993–; Healthy Living 1996–; mem American Soc of Magazine Editors; Fellow Pennsylvania State Univ Alumni 1986; Distinguished Alumni Pennsylvania State Univ 1988. *Publications:* Living with Folk Art, Country Look and How to Get It, Country Gardens, Country Quilts, Country Decorating, Country Kitchens, Country Christmas, New Country Kitchens. *Address:* Country Living, 224 W 57th St, New York, NY 10019-3203, USA (Office). *Telephone:* (212) 649-3511 (Office); *Fax:* (212) 956-3857 (Office).

NEWTON, Elaine Merle Lister, MA; Canadian professor of humanities; b 10 March 1935, Toronto; d of Lou and Faye (née Gorvoy) Lister; m Alan Wilder 1991; two d one s. *Education:* Univ of Toronto and York Univ. *Career:* Prof of Humanities York Univ, Ont 1968–, mem Senate; Visiting Prof Carleton Univ, Ottawa 1979, Univs of Cape Town (SA) 1983, 1984, Sydney (Australia), Victoria Univ of Wellington 1990–91, Univ of Pittsburgh (USA) 1992–93; Guest Lecturer in Canada, Indonesia, UK, Israel, NZ, Australia, SA, USA; several scholarships from Univ of Toronto; Gov-Gen's Award 1953, 1954; Province of Ontario Teaching Award 1973; City of Toronto Academic of the Year 1981. *Publications:* Mirror of a People (ed); publs in journals on psychology and literature, literary methodology, ethnic studies, contemporary fiction. *Leisure interests:* tennis, swimming, hiking, theatre, music, reading. *Address:* York University, Dept of Humanities, 4700 Keele St, N York, ON M3J 1P3, Canada (Office); 44 Duplex Ave, Toronto, ON M5P 2A3, Canada (Home). *Telephone:* (416) 736-2100 (Office); *Fax:* (416) 440-1343 (Office).

NEWTON, Thandie; British actress; b Nov 1972, London; m Oliver Parker 1998. *Education:* Downing Coll (Cambridge). *Films:* Flirting, Jefferson In Paris, Interview with a Vampire, Beloved, It Was an Accident.

NEWTON-JOHN, Olivia, OBE; British singer and actress; b 26 Sept 1948, Cambridge; d of Brin Newton-John and Irene Born; m Matt Lattanzi 1984; one d. *Career:* Has appeared in several films and TV shows; co-owner Koala Blue 1982–; UNEP Goodwill Amb 1989–; Humanitarian Award US Red Cross 1999 and numerous other awards. *Recordings include:* Let Me Be There, If You Love Me, Let Me Know, Clearly Love, Come On Over, Don't Stop Believin', Making a Good Thing Better, Totally Hot, Physical, Soul Kiss 1986, Early Olivia 1989, The Rumour 1989, Warm and Tender 1989, Gaia, Heathcliff, Back with a Heart, The Main Event; *Videos:* Physical 1984, 1991, Down Under 1989, Soul Kiss 1989; *Films include:* Grease 1978, Xanadu 1980, Two of a Kind 1983; *TV appearances include:* It's Cliff Richard (BBC series). *Leisure interests:* horse-riding, song-writing, cycling, astrology, animals, conservation. *Address:* MCA, 70 Universal City Plaza, N Hollywood, CA 91608, USA (Office); POB 2710, Malibu, CA 90265, USA (Home).

NEYELOVA, Marina Mstislavovna; Russian actress; b 8 Jan 1948; m Kyrill Gevorgyan; one d. *Education:* Leningrad Inst of Theatre, Music and Cinema. *Career:* Actress Moscow Theatre Studio of Film Actors 1968–71, Mossoviet Theatre 1971–74, Sovremennik 1974–; prin roles in classical and contemporary repertoire including Chekhov's plays; debut in cinema 1968; numerous roles in films including Old, Old Tale 1970, Monologue 1973, Autumn Marathon 1979 (State Prize of Russia), Prison Romance; People's Artist Russian Fed 1980; USSR State Prize 1990; Prize Nika 1994; Order Friendship of Peoples 1996. *Address:* Potapovsky per 12, Apt 24, 117333 Moscow, Russian Federation (Home).

NEYTS-UYTTERBROECK, Annemie, BA; Belgian politician; b 17 June 1944, Brussels; m Freddy Neyts 1971. *Education:* Free Univ of Brussels. *Career:* Teacher, Zaventen 1966–73; Press Attaché to Minister of Justice 1973–75; Jr Chief-of-Staff Vice Gov of Prov of Brabant 1975–81; Pres Partij vor Vrijheid en Vooruitgang (PVV—Liberal Party, Dutch Wing), Brussels 1977–85, mem Perm Exec 1980–81, Vice-Pres, later Pres PVV Women 1982, Pres PVV 1985–89; mem Chamber of Reps (Parl) for Brussels-Town 1981; Local Councillor for Brussels 1983, Regional Councillor 1989; mem Perm Cttee of European Liberals and Democrats 1983; Co-Pres 2nd Congress of Flemish Citizens in Brussels 1979–81. *Publications:* Tussen Halle en Vilvoorde 1985. *Leisure interests:* travel, reading. *Address:* Chambre des Représentants/Kamer van Volksvertegenwoordigers, Palais de la Nation, 2 place de la Nation, 1000 Brussels, Belgium (Office; Léon Lepagestraat 24, 1000 Brussels, Belgium (Home). *Telephone:* (2) 519-81-11 (Office); (2) 512-87-64 (Home); *Fax:* (2) 512-65-33 (Office).

NGIRIYE, Julie, L ÈS S; Burundi politician; b 5 Dec 1955, Busiga; d of Philippe and Angèle (née Nabundibundi) Ngiriye; m Vital Ntibushemeye 1986; two d. *Education:* Univ of Burundi. *Career:* Teacher 1975–77; Educ Counsellor Teaching Programme Office; Asst Tutor Univ of Burundi; Minister of Social Affairs 1988–91, of Labour and Social Security 1988–93; mem Interparl Cttee on Privatization 1991; Founder-mem Asscn for the Progress of Women and Children 1989; Foundation for the Children of Burundi 1990, Martin Luther King Foundation for Non-Violence 1990; mem Cen Cttee Union pour le Progrès Nat (UPRONA) Party 1992; articles on social and working conditions. *Leisure interests:* reading, volley-ball, art, cooking, needlework.

NGO DINH NHU, Madame; Vietnamese politician; m Ngo Dinh Nhu (deceased; brother and adviser to the late Pres Ngo Dinh Diem). *Career:* Arrested by Viet Minh, escaped 1946; organized first popular demonstration in support of Govt of Prime Minister Ngo Dinh Diem 1954; Official Hostess for Pres Ngo Dinh Diem 1955–63; fmr mem Quoc Hoi (Nat Ass), responsible for Family Bill; f programme of paramilitary service for women 1961; Founder-Pres Vietnamese Women's Solidarity Movt.

NGUYEN THI BINH, Madame; Vietnamese politician; b 1927. *Education:* Saigon. *Career:* Student political leader in Saigon; organized (with Nguyen Huu Tho) first anti-American demonstration 1950; imprisoned by French authorities 1951–54; Vice-Pres S Vietnamese Cttee for Solidarity with the American People; Vice-Pres Union of Women for the Liberation of S Vietnam; mem Cen Cttee Nat Liberation

Front (NLF), apptd spokesperson to four-party peace talks, Paris 1968; Minister for Foreign Affairs, Provisional Revolutionary Govt of S Vietnam 1969–76, in Saigon 1975–76; Minister of Educ, Socialist Repub of Vietnam 1976–87; Vice-Pres of Viet Nam 1992–93; Vice-Pres Vietnamese Women's Union, Hanoi 1976, OSPAA. *Address:* c/o Ministry of Education, 21 Le Thanh Tong, Hanoi, Viet Nam.

NHLABATSI, Lindiwe Audrey, BA; Swazi diplomatist; b 21 Aug 1945; m Bethuel V. Nhlabatsi 1967; one s two d. *Education:* Carleton Univ (Ottawa), American Univ (Washington, DC), Univ of Swaziland, Univ of Bradford (UK), Univ of Australia and ILO Univ (Turin, Italy). *Career:* Data processor 1967–71; Asst Tourist Officer 1971–73; Asst Sec, Foreign Affairs 1973–79; Economist 1983–89; Counsellor 1990–94; Deputy Head of Mission, Ottawa 1995; Chair SADC Counsellors Group, African Diplomatic Club; Rep to UN Gen Ass Cttees 1983–95, to Comm of the Status of Women, New York 1996; Exec mem Business Women's Asscn of Swaziland; Co-Founder, Vice-Pres African Sisters Abroad, USA 1993; Commonwealth Award for Int Relations, Canberra 1975; UN Award for Human Rights, Univ of Bradford 1976; Business Award, USA 1987. *Publications include:* The Problem of Refugees in Swaziland 1985, The Role of Swazi Women and Population 1986, The Integration of Women in Development for Eastern and Southern African States 1986, Women and Employment in the Kingdom of Swaziland 1988, The Integration of Women's Issues in the Swaziland National Development Plan 1989. *Leisure interests:* classical music, photography, reading, voluntary work, writing, dancing, travel, lecturing, gardening, walking. *Address:* c/o High Commission for the Kingdom of Swaziland, 130 Albert St, Suite 1204, Ottawa, ON K1P 5G4, Canada.

NHU, Madame (see Ngo Dinh Nhu, Madame).

NÍ CHUILLEANÁIN, Eiléan, B LITT, MA; Irish poet and lecturer; b 28 Nov 1942, Cork; d of Cormac Ó Cuilleanáin and Eilis Dillon; m Macdara Woods 1978; one s. *Education:* Univ Coll Cork, and Lady Margaret Hall (Oxford). *Career:* Lecturer Trinity Coll, Dublin 1966–, then Sr Lecturer in English; Co-Founder Cyphers literary magazine 1975–; Irish Times Poetry Prize 1966; Patrick Kavanagh Prize 1973; O'Shaughnessy Prize for Poetry 1992. *Publications include:* Irish Women: Image and Achievement 1985; Poems: The Second Voyage (2nd edn) 1986, The Magdalene Sermon 1989, The Brazen Serpent 1994. *Leisure interests:* travel, Italy, food. *Address:* University of Dublin Trinity College, Dept of English, Dublin 2, Ireland (Office); 3 Selskar Terrace, Dublin 6, Ireland (Home). *Telephone:* (1) 772941 (Office); (1) 4978866 (Home); *Fax:* (1) 772694 (Office).

NÍ DHOMHNAILL, Nuala, BA, DIP ED; Irish poet; b 16 Feb 1952, St Helens, Lancs, UK; d of Séamus Ó Domhnaill and Eibhlín Ní Fhiannachta; m Doğan Leflef 1973; three d one s. *Education:* Laurel Hill Convent FCJ (Limerick) and Univ Coll Cork. *Career:* Travel overseas 1973–80; Writer-in-Residence Univ Coll, Cork 1992–93; various Oireachtas awards 1982, 1984, 1990; Irish American O'Shaughnessy Award 1988; Ireland Fund Literary Prize 1991. *Publications:* An Dealg Droighinn 1981, Feár Suaithinseach 1984, Feis 1991. *Leisure interests:* swimming, mountain walks, reading. *Address:* 2 Little Meadow, Pottery Rd, Cabinteely, Co Dublin, Ireland. *Telephone:* (1) 2857465; *Fax:* (1) 2834327.

NIBLAEUS, Kerstin Sigrid Elida, PH D; Swedish chemist and international organization executive; b 17 Dec 1946, Ljusdal; d of Sigvard and Greta Niblaeus; m Ulf Dahlsten 1969; one s one d. *Education:* Royal Inst of Tech (Stockholm). *Career:* Under-Sec of State for Research 1982–85, Dir-Gen Nat Chemicals Inspectorate 1986–95; Dir-Gen Gen Secr, EU Council of Ministers 1995–; mem Royal Acad of Agriculture and Forestry 1987, Royal Acad of Engineering Sciences 1989, Royal Acad of Sciences 1991. *Leisure interests:* family, reading, skating, skiing, trekking. *Address:* General Secretariat, European Union Council of Ministers, 1048 Brussels, Belgium (Office); 44 Clos des Chênes, 1170 Brussels, Belgium (Home). *Telephone:* (2) 285-74-21 (Office); *Fax:* (2) 285-76-81 (Office); *E-mail:* kerstin.niblaeus@ consilium.eu.int.

NICHANIAN, Véronique Christine; French fashion designer; b 3 May 1954, Boulogne-Billancourt; d of Jean and Antoinette (née Godon) Nichanian. *Education:* Lycée Henri Bergson (Paris) and Ecole de la Chambre Syndicale de la Haute Couture de Paris. *Career:* Freelance designer 1976–78; Asst Designer Cerruti 1976–78, then designer Men's Collection; Dir Men's Collections Hermès 1988–; Prix Jeune Créateur de la Ville de Paris 1988. *Leisure interests:* art galleries, museums, skiing. *Address:* Hermès, 24 rue du Faubourg St-Honoré, 75008 Paris, France.

NICHOLAS, Cindy, CM, B SC, LL B; Canadian politician and swimmer; b 20 Aug 1957, Toronto, ON; d of James Paul and Victoria Mary (née Dube) Nicholas; m Raymond LeGrow 1987; one d. *Education:* Univs of Toronto and Windsor. *Career:* Called to the Bar, Ontario 1984; law practice Eagleson 1990–; Sr Programme Officer Donner Canadian and Max Bell Foundations 1984–87; elected mem Provincial Parl 1987; long-distance swimmer, crossed Lake Ontario 1974, the English Channel 1975–82—first woman to swim both ways in a single crossing 1977; Canadian Woman Athlete of the Year 1977; Queen of the English Channel (for making 19 crossings); Scarborough Award of Merit 1974; City of Toronto Award of Merit 1975; Canada Sports Hall of Fame. *Address:* 17 Annis Rd, Scarborough, ON M1M 2Y8, Canada.

NICHOLLS, Christine Stephanie, D PHIL; British editor and writer; b 23 Jan 1943, Bury, Lancs; d of Christopher James and Olive (née Kennedy) Metcalfe; m Anthony James Nicholls 1966; two d one s. *Education:* Kenya High School, Lady Margaret Hall and St Antony's Coll (Oxford). *Career:* Henry Charles Chapman Research Fellow Inst of Commonwealth Studies, Univ of London 1968–69; freelance writer for BBC 1970–74, Research Asst 1975–76; Jt Ed Dictionary of Nat Biography 1977–89, Ed 1989–95; Ed Sutton Pocket Biographies 1996–; Assoc Fellow St Antony's Coll, Oxford 1990–. *Publications:* The Swahili Coast 1971, Dictionary of National Biography 1961–70 (co-ed) 1981, 1971–80 (co-ed) 1986, 1981–85 (ed) 1990, Cataract (jtly) 1985, Power: a political history of the 20th Century 1990, Dictionary of National Biography Missing Persons 1986–90 (ed) 1993, 1996, Hutchinson Encyclopedia of Biography 1996, David Livingstone 1998, The History of St Antony's Coll, Oxford 1950–2000 2000. *Leisure interests:* playing the flute, reading novels. *Address:* 27 Davenant Rd, Oxford OX2 8BU, UK (Home). *Telephone:* (1865) 511320.

NICHOLS, Grace; Guyanese writer and poet; b 1949; d of the late Iris Nichols; partner John Agard; two d. *Career:* Came to UK 1976. *Publications:* i is a long memoried woman (Commonwealth Prize 1983), Fat Black Woman's Poems, Lazy Thoughts of a Lazy Woman, Can I Buy a Slice of Sky (ed), A Quartet of Poems, Give Yourself a Hook, Sunris, Asane and the Animals; has also written one autobiographical novel.

NICHOLSON, Baroness (Life Peer), cr 1997, of Winterbourne in the County of Berkshire, **Emma Harriet Nicholson,** LRAM, ARCM, FRSA; British politician; b 16 Oct 1941, Oxford; d of Sir Godfrey Nicholson and Lady Catherine Constance Lindsay; m Sir Michael Harris Caine 1987 (died 1999). *Education:* Portsdown Lodge School (Sussex), St Mary's School (Wantage, Berks) and RAM (London). *Career:* Computer Programmer, Engineer and Consultant ICL 1962–66, John Tyzack and Partners 1967–69, McLintock Mann and Whinney Murray 1969–73; Dir of Int Devt Save the Children Fund 1974–77, Dir of Fundraising 1977–85; Vice-Chair Cons Party with Special Responsibility for Women 1983–87; MP (Cons) for Devon W and Torridge 1987–95, Founder, Jt Chair All-Party Parl Group for Romanian Children, Founder, Chair All-Party European Information Market (EURIM) Group 1991, Chair Cons Back Bench Environment Cttee, mem Select Cttee on Employment, Steering Cttee on Cons Council on Eastern Europe, Parl Panel for Royal Coll of Nursing, Medical Research Council; Parl Pvt Sec to Minister of State, Home Office 1992–93, Ministry of Agric 1993–95, to Financial Sec to the Treasury 1995; MP (Lib-Dem) for W Devon and Torridge 1995–97, Lib-Dem Spokesperson for Human Rights and Overseas Devt 1996; mem House of Lords 1997–; MEP (Liberal, Democrat and Reform Group) 1999–, mem Cttees on Foreign Affairs, Human Rights, Common Security and Defence Policy, Vice-Chair Cttee on Devt and Cooperation, Del ACP-EU Jt Parl Ass; Founder-mem Comité d'Honneur Sauvez les Enfants, France 1983; Founder and mem Bd Stichting Redt de Kinderen, Netherlands 1982–88; Pres AMAR Int Charitable Foundation, Sir

Michael Caine Foundation for African Writing; Patron CRUSAID; Chair Access for Disabled People to Arts Premises Today (ADAPT); Dir Cities in Schools; Visiting Fellow St Antony's Coll, Oxford 1995–96, now Assoc mem; Dr hc (North London) 1998. *Publication:* Why Does the West Forget? 1993, Secret Society: Inside – and Outside – the Conservative Party 1996. *Leisure interests:* music, singing, horse-riding, walking. *Address:* House of Lords, London SWIA 0PW, UK (Office); Croft, Winkleigh, Devon EX19 8HR, UK (Home); 4 Maunsel St, London SW1P 2QL, UK (Home). *Telephone:* (20) 7828-4992 (Office); (18053) 209 (Devon); (20) 7834-2261 (London); *Fax:* (1837) 83873 (Devon).

NICKS, Stevie (Stephanie); American singer and songwriter; b 26 May 1948, CA. *Career:* Singer and songwriter with Lindsey Buckingham, then with the group Fleetwood Mac 1975. *Recordings include:* With Buckingham: Buckingham Nicks 1973; With Fleetwood Mac: Fleetwood Mac 1975, Rumours 1977, Tusk 1979, Fleetwood Mac Live 1980, Mirage 1982, Tango in the Night 1987, Behind the Mask 1990; Solo: Bella Donna 1981, The Wild Heart 1983, Rock a Little 1985, Time Space 1991, Street Angel 1994; Composer: Rhiannon, Landslide, Leather and Lace, Dreams, Sara, Edge of Seventeen, If Anyone Falls (jtly), Stand Back (jtly), I Can't Wait (jtly), The Other Side of the Mirror, Time Space, Street Angel, Seven Wonders (jtly). *Address:* WEA Corporation, 79 Madison Ave, Floor 7, New York, NY 10016, USA.

NICOL, Baroness (Life Peer), cr 1983, of Newnham in the County of Cambridgeshire, **Olive Mary Wendy Nicol,** FRGS, JP; British politician; b 21 March 1923; d of the late James and Harriet Rowe-Hunter; m Alexander Douglas Ian Nicol 1947; two s one d. *Education:* Cahir School (Ireland). *Career:* Mem Civil Service 1942–48, Inland Revenue 1942–44, Admiralty 1944–48; JP, Cambridge 1972–86; mem Cambridge City Council 1972–82, Deputy Mayor 1984; mem Supplementary Benefits Tribunal 1976–78, Chair Environment Cttee 1978–82, Careers Service Consultative Panel 1978–81; mem House of Lords (Lab) 1983, Opposition Whip 1983–87, Deputy Chief Whip 1987–89, Environment Team Spokesperson on Green Issues 1985–94, Front Bench Spokesperson on the Environment 1987–, Deputy Speaker 1995–; Dir Cambridge and District Co-operative Bd 1976–85, Pres 1981–85; Trustee United Charities 1967–86; mem Council Granta Housing Asscn 1975–; mem European Communities Cttee 1993–95, Sustainable Devt Select Cttee 1994–95; mem Bd Parliamentary Office of Science and Tech 1998–99. *Leisure interests:* reading, walking, conversation. *Address:* House of Lords, London SW1A 0PW, UK. *Telephone:* (20) 7219-6705.

NICOLESCU, Tatiana, DS; Romanian professor of Russian language and literature; b 9 July 1932, Chisinau; m G. C. Nicolescu 1953 (died 1967); two d. *Education:* Univ of Bucharest. *Career:* Visiting Prof Univs of Moscow 1972–78, Bergamo 1981 and Milan, Italy 1982–91; apptd Prof of Russian Language and Literature, Researcher and Literary Critic Univ of Bucharest 1972, currently Prof of English; Visiting Prof Univ Inst of Modern Languages, Milan 1988; articles for professional journals; Awards for translation and literary criticism Univs of Moscow 1970, and Bucharest 1975. *Leisure interest:* reading. *Address:* Bucharest, Str Dr Muscel 17, Romania; University Institute of Modern Languages, via Salutati 4, Milan, Italy. *Telephone:* (2) 48014480 (Milan).

NICOLET, Aurèle; Swiss flautist and music teacher; b 1926, Neuchâtel. *Education:* Univ of Zurich and Conservatory of Music (Paris). *Career:* Solo flautist with Winterthur City Orchestra and Berlin Philharmonic; teacher Musikhochschule, Berlin and Staatlische Hochschule für Musik, Freiburg, Germany; numerous concert appearances and recordings; Music Prize, Verband der Deutschen Kritiker 1964.

NICOLOPULOS, Thania; Brazilian poet and writer; b 12 Jan 1924, Pernambuco; d of Elias Nicolopulos Pablopulos and Georgina (née Joanides) Reissis; m Ricardo Farias Rosas 1942; one s one d. *Education:* La Prensa, Mexico. *Career:* Freelance writer 1960–; Founder and Ed Centro Editorial Mexicano Osiris 1974; Fellow Altrusas, Red Cross, Fed of Int Volunteers; mem Asscn Escritores Poetas Mexicanos, Soc Autores Compositores, Anthropology Museum of Mexico. *Publications:* Interpretación de los Sueños 1965, El Mágico Lenguaje de los Sueños 1967, Antologí del Pensamiento 1973, Tlaltelolco Presente 1974, El Despertar de los Sentidos 1975, Metáforas y Paradijas 1975, Un album

de poesie musicale 1979, Interpretación de las Manos 1980, Sebastiana la Medium 1981, El Verano de la Vida 1982, La Ofrenda 1983, Remonicencias 1983, Poesía Haiku en español 1990. *Address:* Sierra Ventana 545, 11000 México, DF, Mexico.

NIE LI (LILI), Maj-Gen; Chinese administrator; b 1930; d of the late Marshal Nie Rongzhen; m Ding Henggao. *Career:* Vice-Chair Scientific and Tech Cttee, Comm of Science, Tech and Industry for Nat Defence 1983–; promoted to Maj-Gen PLA 1988; Vice-Chair of Nat Examination Cttee for Science Award; mem 8th NPC 1994–; Vice-Chair All-China Women's Fed 1992–; mem Internal and Judicial Affairs Cttee. *Address:* National Examination Committee for Science Award, Sanlihe, Beijing, People's Republic of China.

NIEHUIS, Edith, D PHIL; German politician and educationalist; b 2 Aug 1950, Görliehenfeld; m Gerhard Niehuis; one s one d. *Education:* Univs of Oldenburg and Göttingen. *Career:* Worked in insts of adult educ 1973–87; mem Dist Exec Cttee SPD, Hanover 1987–; mem Bundestag (Parl, SPD) for Northeim-Osterode 1987–, Chair Cttee on women and Youth 1991–94, on Families, Senior Citizens, Women and Youth 1994–98; Parl State Sec for Family Affairs, Senior Citizens, Women and Youth 1998–. *Publications:* Analyse der Erwachsenenbildung in der BRD und DDR 1973, Dezentraler Kindergarten, Elternmitwirkung und Elternbildung 1976, Politische Erwachsenenbildung in Landgemeinden 1976, Das Landjahr 1984, Orientierungskurs für Frauen in der Lebensmitte 1986. *Leisure interest:* family. *Address:* Parlementarische Staatssekretärin bei der Bundesministerin für Familie, Senioren, Frauen und Jugend, Taubenstraße 42/43, 10117 Berlin, Germany. *Telephone:* (30) 206551100; *Fax:* (3) 206554110.

NIEMI, Irmeli, D PHIL; Finnish former civil servant and university professor; b 3 Feb 1931, Helsinki; d of Taneli Kuusisto and Kyllikki Valtonen; m Mikko Niemi 1953; one s two d. *Education:* Univ of Helsinki. *Career:* Freelance trans, literature and theatre critic, Ed 1950–68; Jr Research Fellow Acad of Finland 1968–69, Research Prof 1981–84; Sr Teacher Theatre Acad Helsinki 1964–96; Assoc Prof of Comparative Literature and Drama, Univ of Turku 1970–78, Prof 1978–81, 1984–90; Research Prof Acad of Finland 1981–84; Dir-Gen Dept of Culture, Ministry of Educ 1990–96; Chair Finnish Research Council for the Humanities 1986–88, Bd of Finnish Nat Opera 1996–, Finland Festivals 1998–; mem Science Policy Council of Finland 1986–90. *Publications include:* Maria Jotunin näytelmät 1964, Nykydraaman ihmiskuva 1969, Nykyteatterin juuret 1975, The Role of the Spectator 1984, Suomalainen alueteatteri 1978–82 1984. *Leisure interests:* modern music, forest walks, travel. *Address:* Osmalahdentie 437, 21570 Sauvo, Finland (Home). *Telephone:* (2) 4701833; *Fax:* (2) 4701893; *E-mail:* irniemi@saunalahti.fi (Home).

NIGOGHOSSIAN, Sonia; French opera singer; b 3 April 1944, Arnouville-lès-Gonesse; d of Nigoghos Nigoghossian and Hermine Keutahialian. *Education:* Conservatoire Nat Supérieur de Musique et de Danse (Paris). *Career:* Operatic debut Opéra de Nantes; numerous nat and int recitals; has taken part in Aix-en-Provence Festivals; First Prize for singing and lyric art, Conservatoire Nat Supérieur de Musique et de Danse, Paris. *Operas include:* Les Indes Galantes, Alceste, The Marriage of Figaro, Così fan tutte, La Clemenza di Tito, The Barber of Seville, Tancrède, L'occasion fait le larron; many oratorios and Armenian music; *Recordings include:* Les Indes Galantes, Hyppolite et Aricie, Alceste, Les leçons de ténèbres. *Leisure interests:* theatre, cinema, drawing and painting, collecting silver objects and books on miniatures, swimming, walking. *Address:* 121 ave Henri Barbusse, 95400 Arnouville-lès-Gonesse, France.

NIJENHUIS, Emmie te, PH D; Netherlands ethnomusicologist; b 11 Nov 1931, Bussum; d of Dirk te Nijenhuis and W. Margarete Küchenthal; m 1965–70; one s. *Education:* Utrecht Conservatory and Utrecht Univ. *Career:* Teacher of theory and history of Western Music, Zwolle Conservatory 1958–61; Reader Indian Musicology, Utrecht Univ 1964–88; Visiting Lecturer Univs of Oxford, UK and Basel, Switzerland 1978, 1984; mem Royal Netherlands Acad of Sciences 1978. *Publications:* Dattilam: Compendium of Ancient Indian Music 1970, Indian Music, History and Structure 1974, The Ragas of Somanatha (2 vols) 1976, Musicological Literature 1977, Sacred Songs of India: Muttusvami Diksitar's Cycle of Hymns to the Goddess Kamala

(2 vols) 1987, Saṅgítaśiromani, A Medieval Handbook of Indian Music 1992; various articles in the Journal of the Royal Asiatic Soc 1971, Journal of the Music Acad, Madras 1972, 1975, Festschrift Josef Kuckertz, Salzburg 1992 and Musik in Geschichte und Gegenwart (encyclopedia of music), Kassel 1995. *Address:* Verlengde Fortlaan 39, 1412 CW Naarden, Netherlands. *Telephone:* (35) 694-93-22.

NIKOI, Gloria, MA; Ghanaian diplomatist and banking executive; three c. *Education:* Achimota Secondary School, Univ of St Andrews (UK). *Career:* Research Fellow in Econs, Univ of Ghana; Officer, Ministry of Trade and Development and Finance; Sec, Econ Counsellor and Deputy Chief of Mission to UN 1969–74; Head Dept of Relations with the USA, Ministry of Foreign Affairs 1974, later Prin Sec; Comm (Minister) of Foreign Affairs 1979; Chair Bank for Housing and Construction until 1995. *Address:* c/o Bank for Housing and Construction (BHC), 24 Kwame Nkrumah Ave, POB M1, Adabraka, Accra, Ghana.

NIKOLAYEVA-TERESHKOVA, Valentina Vladimirovna; Russian former astronaut; b 6 March 1937, Maslennikovo; d of the late Vladimir Tereshkov and Elena Fyodorovna Tereshkova; m Andrei Nikolayev 1963; one d. *Career:* Fmr textile worker Krasny Perekop mill, Yaroslavl; Sec local Komsomol 1960; mem (fmr) CPSU from 1962, Cen Cttee 1971; People's Deputy 1966, mem Presidium 1970–90; Pres Soviet Women's Cttee 1968; joined Cosmonaut Training Unit 1962, first woman in space, made 48 orbital flights of the earth in spaceship Vostok VI 1963; mem Yaroslavl Air Sports Club 1959; Chair Russian Asscn of Int Co-operation 1992–; Hero of the Soviet Union; Order of Lenin; Gold Star Medal; Order of the October Revolution; Joliot–Curie Peace Medal; numerous awards and honours from countries world-wide. *Address:* Moscow, Zvezkny Gorodok, Russian Federation.

NILSSON, Birgit, (Fru Bertil Niklasson); Swedish opera singer (soprano); b 17 May 1918, Karup; m Bertil Niklasson 1948. *Education:* Stockholm Royal Acad of Music. *Career:* With Stockholm Opera 1947–51; performances include Glyndebourne, UK 1951, Bayreuth 1954, 1957–70 and Munich 1954–58, Germany, Hollywood Bowl, USA, Buenos Aires and Florence, Italy 1956, Royal Opera House, Covent Garden, London 1957, 1962, 1963, 1973, La Scala, Milan and Naples, Italy, Vienna, Chicago and San Francisco, USA 1958, Metropolitan Opera, New York, USA 1959, Moscow 1964; Royal Court singer 1954; retd 1985; Hon mem Vienna State Opera 1968, Royal Acad of Music, London 1970; Austrian and Bavarian Kammer-sängerin title conferred; Hon Prof Swedish Gov 1999, Royal Music School Stockholm 2000; Dr hc (Andover Music Univ, Manhattan School of Music, Michigan State Univ of Fine Arts); honours and awards include Medal Litteris et Artibus 1960, Medal for Promotion of Art of Music, Royal Acad of Music, Stockholm 1968, Swedish Gold Medal 1978, First Commdr Order of Vasa 1974, Commdr Order of St Olav First Class, Norway 1975, Swedish Gold Medal 1978, Commdr des Arts et des Letters 1991. *Operas include:* Der Freischütz, Idomeneo, Turandot, Elektra, Salome, Die Walküre, Siegfried, Götterdämmerung, Tristan und Isolde; particularly well known for her Wagner and Verdi roles; *Publications include:* My Memories in Pictures 1977, La Nilsson 1995. *Address:* Box 527, S-10130, Stockholm C, Sweden.

NISHIZAKI, Takako; Japanese violinist; d of Shiniji Nishizaki. *Education:* Toho School of Music and Juilliard School (New York, USA). *Career:* Studied with father, then became first student of Shinichi Suzuki, creator of Suzuki Method of violin teaching. *Recordings include:* complete Fritz Kreisler Edn (ten vols), many contemporary Chinese violin concertos, concertos by Spohr, Briot, Cui, Respighi, Rubinstein and Joachim; for Naxos: Vivaldi's Four Seasons, Mozart's Violin Concertos, sonatas by Mozart and Beethoven, the Bach, Mendelssohn, Tchaikovsky, Beethoven, Bruch and Brahms Concertos.

NIX, Beverly Ann, BA, JD; American broadcasting executive; b 1 April 1951, Hobbs, NM; d of Vance I. and Betty Lea (née Hunsinger) Nix. *Education:* Univ of California at Los Angeles and Southwestern Univ. *Career:* Staff Attorney Legal Dept, Warner Brothers TV, Burbank, CA 1979–80, Assoc Dir Legal and Admin Affairs 1980–82, Dir Business Affairs 1982–83, Vice-Pres 1983–90, apptd Sr Vice-Pres 1990; mem

Acad of TV Arts and Sciences, Advisory Council Nat Captioning Inst Corpn, California Arboreteum Foundation. *Address:* c/o Warner Bros TV, 4000 Warner Blvd, Burbank, CA 91522, USA.

NIZAMI, Ghazala, B SC, B ED; Pakistani educational administrator; b 4 Oct 1951, Karachi; d of Nooruddin and Maryam Faruqi; m Rumman Nizami 1982; one d. *Education:* Univ of Karachi, Univ of London and Univ of Toledo, Ohio, USA. *Career:* Teacher St Joseph's Convent School 1972–73; Teacher, Headmistress, Vice-Prin and Prin Happy Home Secondary School Karachi; Prin Happy Home Int Schools Karachi and Dubai, UAE. *Address:* Happy Home International School, Shaheed E. Millat Rd, Karachi, Pakistan (Office); Happy Home International School, POB 15284, Dubai, UAE (Office); 86 B-II, South Circular Ave, Defence Housing Authority, Phase II, Karachi, Pakistan (Home). *Telephone:* (21) 4557412 (Pakistan, Office); (4) 824179 (Dubai, Office); *Fax:* (21) 4559444 (Pakistan, Office); (4) 280110 (Dubai, Office).

N'JIE, Louise, DIP ED; Gambian politician; m; one s. *Education:* Methodist Girls' High School, Portsmouth Training Coll and Univ of Oxford (UK). *Career:* Worked as education officer, school teacher and headmistress; elected to House of Reps (Parl, People's Progressive Party) 1982; Parl Sec Ministry of Health, Labour and Social Welfare 1982–85; Minister of Education, Youth, Sports and Culture 1985–88, of Health, Labour, Social Welfare and Environment 1988–92; Pres Gambia Red Cross Society; mem Gambia Women's Fed. *Leisure interest:* gardening. *Telephone:* 27223; *Fax:* 27122.

NJIE-SAIDY, Isatou; Gambian politician and teacher; m; four c. *Career:* Started work as schoolteacher 1970; active in Nat Women's Council; Sec of State for Social Welfare and Women's Affairs, Vice-Pres of The Gambia. *Address:* Office of the Vice-President, State House, Banjul, The Gambia (Office). *Telephone:* 227881 (Office); *Fax:* 227034 (Office).

NJUKI, Proscovia Margaret, B SC; Ugandan broadcasting executive; b 25 June 1951; d of Rev and Mrs Benoni Lwanga-Kagwa; m Samwiri H. K. Njuki 1977; two d one s. *Education:* Gayaza High School and Univ of Nairobi. *Career:* First female engineer in Uganda 1974; Tele-communications Engineer Uganda TV (UTV) 1974, Head UTV Engineering Services 1994, Commr for UTV 1995; Founder-mem Asscn of Women Engineers, Technicians and Scientists in Uganda 1989; mem Institution of Professional Engineers, mem Exec Council 1990–93. *Leisure interests:* Christian fellowship, reading, cooking, sewing. *Address:* Uganda Television, POB 4260, Kampala, Uganda. *Telephone:* (41) 245376; *Fax:* (41) 256888.

NOAKES, Baroness (Life Peer), cr 2000, of Goudhurst in the County of Kent, **Sheila (Valerie) Masters,** DBE, LL B, FCA; British business executive; b 23 June 1949, London; d of Albert Frederick and Iris Sheila (née Ratcliffe) Masters; m (Colin) Barry Noakes 1985. *Education:* Eltham Hill Grammar School (London) and Univ of Bristol. *Career:* Joined Peat Marwick Mitchell & Co 1970; seconded to HM Treasury 1979–81; partner KPMG (fmrly Peat Marwick Mitchell & Co, then KPMG Peat Marwick) 1983–; seconded to Dept of Health as Dir of Finance, Nat Health Service Man Exec 1988–91; Dir Bank of England 1994 (Chair Cttee of Non-Exec Dirs 1998–); mem Council Inst of Chartered Accountants in England and Wales 1987– (Deputy Pres 1998–99), Inland Revenue Man Bd 1992–99, Chancellor of Ex-chequer's Pvt Finance Panel 1993–97, Court of Bank of England 1994–; Commr Public Works Loan Bd 1995–; Assoc Inst of Taxation; Trustee Reuters Founders Share Co 1998–; Hon LL D (Warwick) 2000, (Bristol) 2000. *Leisure interests:* early classical music, opera, horse-racing, skiing. *Address:* 8 Salisbury Square, London EC4Y 8BB, UK. *Telephone:* (20) 7311-1000.

NOCHLIN, Linda, MA; American art historian. *Education:* Vassar Coll, Columbia Univ and NY Univ Inst of Fine Arts. *Career:* Mary Conover Mellon Prof of Art History, Vassar Coll 1971–79; Dist Prof of Art History City Univ, NY 1980–90; Prof of Art History and Humanities Yale Univ 1989–92; now Lila Acheson Wallace Prof of Modern Art, NY Univ Inst of Fine Arts; Fellow American Acad of Arts and Sciences, NY Univ Inst for the Humanities; Guggenheim Fellowship 1984–85. *Publications:* Women as Sex Objects: Studies in Erotic Art 1730–1970 1972, Realism and Tradition in Art 1848–1900, Impressionism and

Post-Impressionism 1874–1904, The Politics of Vision: Essays on Nineteenth Century Art and Society. *Address:* Institute of Fine Arts, New York University, 1 East 78th St, New York, NY 10021, USA (Office).

NOELLE-NEUMANN, Elisabeth, D PHIL; German professor emeritus of communications research; b (Elisabeth Noelle) 19 Dec 1916, Berlin; d of Ernst and Eva (née Schaper) Noelle; m 1st Erich P. Neumann 1946 (died 1973); m 2nd Heinz Maier-Leibnitz 1979 (died 2000). *Education:* Univs of Königsberg and Munich, School of Journalism, Univ of Missouri and Univ of Berlin. *Career:* Journalist 1940–45; Founder and Dir Inst für Demoskopie Allensbach, first German survey research inst 1947–; Lecturer in Communications Research, Free Univ of Berlin 1961–64; Prof of Communications Research Univ of Mainz 1964–, Dir Inst für Publizistik 1966–1983, currently Emer Prof; Visiting Prof Dept of Political Science, Univ of Chicago 1978–91, Univ of Munich 1993–94; Hon Prof Moscow External Univ of the Humanities; Public Opinion Analyst, Frankfurter Allgemeine Zeitung 1978–; Co-Ed Int Journal of Public Opinion Research 1989–; f Allensbach Foundation for Public Opinion Research 1996; mem Council World Asscn for Public Opinion Research (WAPOR) 1972–88, Pres 1978–80; mem Bd Konrad-Adenauer Foundation 1984–, Ludwig Erhard Foundation, Academia Scientiarum et Artium Europaea 1991–; Hon Citizen of Allensbach 1977; Hon mem German Univ Asscn 2000; Dr hc (St Gallen); awards include Großes Bundesverdienstkreuz, Alexander Rüstow Medal 1978, Nürnberger Trichter Award 1985, Viktor Matajy Medal 1987, Order of Merit, Baden-Württemberg 1990, Helen Dinerman Award 1990, Boveri Award 1997, Schleyer Foundation Award 1999. *Publications:* Allensbacher Jahrbücher der Demoskopie (ed, 9 vols) 1947–92 (English trans The Germans: Public Opinion Polls—2 vols 1967, 1980), Öffentlichkeit als Bedrohung 1977, Die Schweigespirale: Öffentliche Meinung—unsere soziale Haut 1980 (trans into several other languages), Macht Arbeit krank? Macht Arbeit glücklich? (jtly) 1984, Die verletzte Nation (jtly) 1987, Demoskopische Gessichtsstunde 1991, Massenkommunikation (co-ed) 1994, Öffentliche Meinung: Die Entdeckung der Schweigespirale (new edn) 1996, Alle, nicht jeder: Einführung in die Methoden der Demoskopie (jtly, new edn) 1996, Kampa. Meinungsklima und Medienwirkung im Bundestagwahlkampf 1998, 1999. *Leisure interest:* painting. *Address:* Institut für Demoskopie Allensbach, Radolfzellerstr 8, 78472 Allensbach/Bodensee, Germany (Office). *Telephone:* (7533) 8050 (Office); *Fax:* (7533) 3048 (Office); *E-mail:* enoelle-neumann@ifd-allensbach.de (Office).

NOLTE, Claudia; German politician; b 7 Feb 1966, Rostock; m; one s. *Career:* Mem Bundestag (Parl, CDU); mem CDU local Cttee (Thuringia) for Family Affairs 1992–94; Minister for Family Affairs, Sr Citizens, Women and Youth 1994. *Leisure interests:* piano, walking, painting. *Address:* c/o Ministry of Family Affairs, Senior Citizens, Women and Youth, 53123 Bonn, Rochusstr 8–10, Germany.

NOONAN, Peggy, BA; American writer; b 7 Sept 1950, Brooklyn, NY; d of James J. and Mary Jane (née Byrne) Noonan; m Richard Rahn 1985 (divorced); one s. *Education:* Fairleigh Dickson Univ (Rutherford, NJ). *Career:* Adjuster Aetna Insurance Co, Newark, NJ until 1970; scriptwriter, producer and later Editorial Dir WEEI (CBS), Boston; Writer, Ed CBS 1977–81, writer radio commentaries 1981–84; Scriptwriter for Pres of USA 1984–89; Adviser Bush–Quayle 1992 Campaign; Columnist Mirabella Magazine, New York Times, Forbes Magazine, Newsweek 1990–92; Hon HLD 1990 (Fairleigh); Esquire Magazine Achievement Award 1984; Republican Nat Women's Club Award for Journalism 1992. *Publications:* I Am Often Booed Because of Who My Friends Are, What I Saw at the Revolution: A Political Life in the Reagan Era 1990, Life, Liberty and the Pursuit of Happiness 1994, When Character was King (autobiog) 2001. *Leisure interest:* considering walking. *Address:* c/o Random House Inc, 1540 Broadway, New York, NY 10036, USA.

NOOR AL-HUSSEIN, Queen of Jordan, BA; Jordanian royal; b (Lisa Najeeb Halaby) 23 Aug 1951; m King Hussein I of Jordan 1978 (died 1999); four c. *Education:* Princeton Univ (USA). *Career:* Architectural and urban planning projects in Australia, Iran and Jordan 1974–78; Founder in Jordan of Royal Endowment for Culture and Educ 1979, annual Arab Children's Congress 1980, annual int Jerash Festival for Culture and the Arts 1981, Jubilee School 1984, Noor Al-Hussein Foundation 1985, Nat Music Conservatory 1986; Chair Nat Task Force for Children, Advisory Cttee for UNU Int Leadership Acad Amman; Patron Gen Fed of Jordanian Women, Nat Fed of Business and Professional Women's Clubs, Int Union for Conservation of Nature and Natural Resources 1988, Landmine Survivors Network 1998, and various environmental, cultural, sports and nat devt orgs; Founder-mem Int Comm on Peace and Food 1992; Pres United World Colls 1995; Dir Hunger Project; Hon Pres Birdlife Int 1996–; Pres and Patron British Soc of St John Ophthalmic Hosp Jerusalem; mem Int Eye Foundation Hon Bd, Gen Ass SOS-Kinderdorf Int, Int Council Near East Foundation; Trustee Mentor Foundation; many other affiliations; numerous hon doctorates, int awards and decorations for promotion of environmental conservation and awareness, econ and social devt of women, children and communities, cross cultural exchange, int understanding and world peace. *Leisure interests:* skiing, horseback riding, tennis, gardening, reading, photography. *Address:* Royal Palace, Amman, Jordan.

NOOYI, Indra K.; Indian/American business executive; b 1955, India. *Career:* Fmr Pres and Dir of Corp Strategy and Planning, Motorola; Sr Vice-Pres of Strategic Planning and Strategic Markets, Asea Brown Boveri until 1994; Sr Vice-Pres PepsiCo Inc 1994–2001, Chief Financial Officer 2000–, Pres 2001–. *Address:* 700 Anderson Hill, Purchase, NY 10577, USA.

NORDBØ, Eldrid, B SC S; Norwegian politician; b 12 Aug 1942, Skien; m Bjorn Skogstad Aamo. *Career:* Exec Officer Ministry of Health and Social Affairs until 1970, Pvt Sec to Minister 1971, Sec-Gen 1993–96; Research Officer Research Bureau of the labour movt 1970–71; Municipal Councillor for Health and Social Affairs, Oslo 1972–79; Consultant Int League of the Red Cross, Geneva 1980–81; Dir-Gen Ministry of Municipal Affairs and Labour 1981–86; State Sec Office of the Prime Minister 1986–89; Special Adviser Ministry of the Environment 1990, 1992–93, apptd Dir-Gen 1996; Minister of Foreign Trade and Shipping 1990–91. *Address:* Ministry of the Environment, POB 8013 Dep, 0030 Oslo, Norway.

NORDMANN, Marielle Isabelle; French harpist; b 24 Jan 1941, Montpellier; d of Robert and Josette (née Trèves) Nordmann; m Patrice Fontanarosa 1968; two d one s. *Education:* With Lily Laskine and Conservatoire Nat Supérieur de Musique (Paris). *Career:* Founder-mem Trio Nordmann, Lily Laskine–Nordmann Duo; Soloist with the English Chamber Orchestra, Ensemble orchestral de Paris, I Solisti Veniti; int concerts and recitals in Europe, America, Israel, Japan; has made over 20 recordings, including solo harp, concerts, chamber music and duos; Chevalier de l'Ordre Nat du Mérite 1990; Chevalier des Arts et des Lettres 1992; Premier Prix Harpe; Premier Prix Musique de Chambre (Conservatoire Nat Supérieur de Musique). *Leisure interests:* reading, films, swimming, skiing. *Address:* c/o Bureau de Concerts Marcel de Valmalète, 11 ave Delcassé, 75008 Paris, France.

NORMAN, Marsha; American playwright; b 21 Sept 1947, Louisville, KY; d of Billie Williams and Bertha Conley; m 1st Michael Norman (divorced 1974); m 2nd Dann C. Byck, Jr (divorced); m 3rd Timothy Dykman; one s one d. *Education:* Agnes Scott Coll and Univ of Louisville. *Career:* Rockefeller Playwright-in-Residence grantee 1979–80; American Acad and Inst for Arts and Letters grantee; Pulitzer Prize for Drama 1983; Tony Award 1991; numerous other awards and prizes. *Publications include:* Plays: Getting Out 1977, Third and Oak 1978, Circus Valentine 1979, The Holdup 1980, 'Night, Mother 1982, Traveler in the Dark 1984, Sarah and Abraham 1987, Four Plays by Marsh Norman (collection) 1988, D. Boone 1992, Loving Daniel Boone 1992, Trudy Blue 1995; TV plays: It's the Willingness 1978, In Trouble at Fifteen 1980, The Laundromat 1985, Third and Oak: The Pool Hall 1989, Face of a Stranger 1991; Novel: The Fortune Teller 1987; Musical lyrics: The Secret Garden 1991, The Red Shoes 1992. *Address:* c/o Jack Tantleff, 375 Greenwich St, Suite 700, New York, NY 10013, USA.

NORRIS, Frances McMurtray, BS, MA; American business executive; b 27 March 1946, Jackson, MI; d of William and Helen Frances (née Dutton) McMurtray; m Stephen Leslie Norris 1981. *Education:* Univs of Mississippi, Kentucky and Tennessee. *Career:* Legal Asst US House of Reps 1974–78, Staff Asst Rules Comm 1979–80, Asst to Republican Whip 1981–82; Dir Legislation Liaison, Dept of Educ 1983, Deputy Asst Sec for Legislation 1984–85, Asst Sec 1986–88; Dir Congressional Relations Office of Nat Drug Control Policy 1988–90; Special Asst for Legis Affairs to Pres of USA 1990; Vice-Pres The Dutko Group 1995; Pres Mississippi Soc of Washington 1983–84; US Govt Fellow Univ of Kentucky, Lexington 1969–70. *Address:* 412 First St, SE, Washington, DC 20003, USA (Office); 8015 Greenwich Woods Drive, McLean, VA 22102, USA (Home).

NORTON, Eleanor Holmes, LL B, MA; American politician and lawyer; b 15 June 1937, Washington, DC; d of Coleman and Vela (née Lynch) Holmes; m Edward W. Norton 1965; one s one d. *Education:* Antioch Coll and Yale Univ. *Career:* Law Clerk Fed Dist Court 1964–65; called to the Bar, PA 1965, US Supreme Court 1968; Asst Legal Dir American Civil Liberties Union 1965–70, Chair Nat Advisory Council; Exec Asst to Mayor of New York 1971–74; Chair Comm on Humanities 1970–77, Chair Comm on Humanities, Equal Employment Oportunity Comm 1977–81; Sr Fellow Urban Inst 1981–82; Prof of Law Univ of Georgetown 1982–; Dist of Columbia Del to US Congress 1990–; Trustee Community Foundation, Rockefeller Foundation; mem Bd Dirs A. Philip Randolph Inst; mem Advisory Bd Nat Women's Political Caucus, Women's Law and Policy Fellowship, Workplace Health Fund; Chair Comm on the Future of Women in the Workplace; mem Center for Nat Policy, Martin Luther King, Jr Center for Social Change, Nat Black Leadership Roundtable, Nat Political Congress of Black Women, Nat Urban Coalition, Council on Minority Educ, Council for Foreign Relations, US Citizens' Comm to Monitor Helsinki Accords; mem Exec Ford Foundation, NAS, Comm on the Effects of Technological Change on Employment and the Working Environment; Harper Fellow Yale Law School 1976; Hon LL D (Cedar Crest) 1969, (Bard) 1971, (Princeton) 1973, (Marymount) 1974, (New York) 1975, (Wayne State) 1980, (Syracuse, Yeshiva) 1981, (Lawrence, Pennsylvania) 1983, (Tufts) 1984, (Bowdoin) 1985; Young Woman of the Year Award, Jr Chamber of Commerce 1965; One of 25 Most Influential Women in America, Newspaper Enterprise Asscn 1977. *Publications:* Sex Discrimination and the Law: causes and remedies (jtly) 1975; numerous articles in professional journals. *Address:* University of Georgetown Law Center, 600 Jersey Ave, NW, Washington, DC 20001, USA.

NORTON, Gale Ann, BA, JD; lawyer and politician; b 11 March 1954, Wichita, KS; d of Dale Bentsen and Anna Jacqueline (née Lansdowne) Norton; m John Goethe Hughes 1990. *Education:* Univ of Denver. *Career:* Judicial Clerk Colorado Court of Appeals 1978–79; called to the Bar, CO 1979, US Supreme Court 1981; Sr Attorney Mountain States Legal Foundation, Denver 1979–83; Nat Fellow Hoover Inst, Univ of California at Stanford 1983–84; Asst to Deputy Sec, US Dept of Agric 1984–85; Assoc Solicitor US Dept of Interior 1985–87; policy analyst, Presidential Council on Environmental Quality 1985–88; pvt law practice 1987–90; Attorney-Gen of Colorado 1991–99; attorney Brownstein, Hyatt & Farber PC, Sr Counsel 1999–2001; Sec of the Interior Jan 2001–; Dir Transportation Law Program, Univ of Denver 1978–79, Lecturer Law Faculty 1989; contribs to environmental and professional journals; Murdock Fellow Political Economy Research Centre (Bozeman) 1984; Sr Fellow Indiana Inst 1988–90; fmr Chair Nat Asscn of Attorneys Environmental Cttee; Co-Chair Nat Policy Forum Environmental Council; Chair Environmental Comm of Republican Nat Lawyers Asscn; Appointee Colorado Legislature's Vision Comm 1988; mem Policy Comm YWCA 1988–90; mem Federalists Soc, Colorado Bar Asscn, Colorado Women's Bar Asscn; Young Career Woman, Business and Professional Women 1981; Federalist Soc's Young Lawyer of the Year 1991; Order of St Ives. *Leisure interests:* skiing, travel. *Address:* Department of the Interior, 1849 C St, NW, Washington, DC 20240, USA (Office). *Telephone:* (202) 208-3171; *Fax:* (202) 208-5048.

NORWOOD, Janet Lippe, PH D; American economist and civil servant; b 11 Dec 1923, Newark, NJ; d of M. Turner and Thelma (née Levinson) Lippe; m Bernard Norwood 1943; two s. *Education:* Douglass Coll and Tufts Univ. *Career:* Instructor Wellesley Coll 1948–49; economist William L. Clayton Center, Tufts Univ 1953–58; economist Bureau of Labor Statistics, Dept of Labor 1963–75, Deputy Commr, later Acting Commr 1975–79, Commr 1979–91; Sr Fellow The Urban Inst 1992–99; has written numerous papers and reports in field; Dir Inst of

Global Ethics; mem American Econ Asscn, Industrial Relations Research Asscn, Women's Caucus in Statistics, Comm of Status of Women Economists Profession, Int Statistics Inst, Int Asscn of Official Statistics, Nat Acad of Public Admin, American Statistical Asscn; Fellow AAAS, American Statistical Asscn, Royal Statistical Soc, Nat Asscn of Business Economists; Hon LL D (Florida Int) 1979, (Carnegie Mellon) 1984; Dept of Labor Distinguished Achievement Award 1972, Special Commendation Award 1977; Philip Arnow Award 1979; Elmer Staats Award 1982; Public Service Award 1984; Presidential Distinguished Exec rank conferred 1988. *Publications:* Organizing to Count, Change in the Federal Statistical System 1995. *Address:* 5610 Wisconsin Ave, Apt 21D, Chevy Chase, MD 20815-4415, USA.

NORWOOD, Mandi; British magazine editor; b 9 Oct 1963, Oldham, Lancs; m Martin Kelly 1995; two d. *Education:* Lord Lawson Comprehensive School, Park View Grammar School, Darlington Coll of Tech and London Coll of Fashion. *Career:* Sub-Ed then Deputy Chief Sub Look Now magazine 1984–86; freelance journalist 1986–87; Features Ed Clothes Show magazine Aug–Oct 1987; Deputy Ed More! magazine 1987–89; Ed Looks magazine 1989–90, Company magazine 1990–95, Cosmopolitan 1995–2000; Ed-in-Chief Mademoiselle, New York 2000–; mem British Soc of Magazine Eds 1990, Periodical Publrs Asscn Editorial Cttee; Women's Magazine Ed of the Year Award, British Soc of Magazine Eds 1993, 1999. *Address:* Mademoiselle, 4 Times Square, New York, NY 10036, USA (Office); 312 E 69th St, New York, NY 10021, USA (Home).

NOTAT, Nicole; French trade union executive; b 26 July 1947, Châtrices. *Career:* Sec Syndicat Gen de l'Educ Nat (SGEN, educ trade union) and Confédération Française Démocratique du Travail (CFDT), Meuse 1970; mem Regional Exec Cttee SGEN, Lorraine 1978; mem Exec Cttee and Nat Sec for Educ 1982, for Professional Training 1985; Jt Sec-Gen for Gender Equality 1988–92; CFDT Sec Gen 1992–, Pres 1992–94, 1996–98; Sec Union Nat pour l'emploi dans l'industrie, le commerce et l'agric (Unedic) 1994–. *Address:* CFDT, 4 blvd de la Villette, 75955 Paris, Cedex 19, France. *Telephone:* (1) 42-03-80-10; *Fax:* (1) 42-03-81-44; *E-mail:* nnotat@cfdt.ft; *Internet:* www.cfdt.fr.

NOTHOMB, Amélie; Belgian author; b 1967, Kobe, Japan; d of Patrick Nothomb. *Education:* Université Libre de Bruxelles. *Publications include:* Hygiène de l'assassin 1992, Le sabotage amoureux 1993, Les combustibles 1994, Les Catallinaires 1995, Péplum 1996, Attentat 1997, Mercure 1998, Stupeur et tremblements (Grand Prix, Académie française) 1999, Métaphysique des tubes 2000. *Address:* c/o Editions Albin Michel, 22 rue Huyghens, 75014 Paris, France.

NOVAK, Kim; American actress; b (Marilyn Novak) 13 Feb 1933, Chicago, IL. *Education:* Wright Jr Coll and Los Angeles City Coll. *Career:* Began career as a model; film debut 1954; named World's Favourite Actress, Brussels World Fair. *Films include:* The French Line 1954, Five Against the House, Picnic, Pal Joey, Vertigo, Bell Book and Candle, Middle of the Night, Strangers When We Meet, Boys' Night Out, Of Human Bondage, The Amorous Adventures of Moll Flanders, The Great Bank Robbery, Tales That Witness Madness 1973, The White Buffalo, The Mirror Crack'd 1980, Just a Gigolo 1981, The Children, Liebestraum 1991; *TV appearances include:* Alfred Hitchcock Presents (guest) 1985, Falcon Crest (series); TV films: Third Girl From the Left, Satan's Triangle, Malibu. *Address:* William Morris Agency, 151 S El Camino Drive, Beverly Hills, CA 90212, USA.

NOVARO, María; Mexican film director; three s. *Education:* Film school. *Career:* Began filming documentaries while working as a sociologist; feature films shown at Berlin, New York and Havana film festivals and at La quinzaine des réalisateurs, France. *Films include:* Lola (Awards from Berlin, New York and Havana film festivals), Danzon. *Leisure interest:* dance halls.

NOVELLO, Antonia Coello, MD, M PH; American public health official and former surgeon-general; b 23 Aug 1944, Fajardo, PR; d of Antonio and Ana D. (née Flores) Coello; m Joseph R. Novello 1970. *Education:* Univ of Puerto Rico and Johns Hopkins School of Hygiene. *Career:* Intern, Mott Children's Hosp, Univ of Mich Ann Arbor 1970–71; Resident in Paediatrics Michigan Medical Center 1971–73, Instructor in Diagnosis 1973–74, Paediatric Nephrology Fellow 1973–74; Paediatric Nephrology Fellow Georgetown Univ Hosp, Washington, DC 1974–75, Consultant Renal Dialysis Center 1975–78, Clinical Prof of Paediatrics 1986, 1989; Paediatric Consultant Psychiatric Inst, Washington, DC 1979–83; Project Officer Nat Inst of Arthritis, Metabolism and Digestive Disorders, NIH, Bethesda, MD 1978–79, Staff Doctor 1979–80, Exec Sec of Gen Medicine, Research Grants Div 1981–86, Deputy Dir Nat Inst of Child Health and Human Devt 1986–90; Capt US Public Health Service 1984, Vice-Admiral 1990; Clinical Prof Univ of Health Sciences 1989; Consultant WHO, Geneva, Switzerland 1989; Chair Sec's Work Group on Paediatric HIV Infection and Disease, Dept of Health and Human Services, Washington, DC 1988, Surgeon-Gen 1990–93; UNICEF Special Rep for Health and Nutrition 1993–; mem Georgetown Medical Center Interdepartmental Research Group 1984; mem Comm on Research in Paediatric Nephrology 1981; mem American Medical Asscn, Int Soc of Nephrology, Soc for Paediatric Research, Asscn of US Military Surgeons, Pan-American Medical and Dental Soc; numerous articles in professional books and journals; Public Health Service Commendation Medal 1983, Citation Award 1984, Oustanding Medal 1988, Unit Commendation 1988, Surgeon-Gen's Exemplary Service Medal 1989, Outstanding Unit Citation 1989; NIH Certificate of Recognition 1985; Dept of Health and Human Services Certificate of Commendation 1989. *Address:* c/o UNICEF, 3 United Nations Plaza, Room 634, New York, NY 10017, USA.

NOVETZKE, Sally Johnson; American diplomatist; b 12 Jan 1932, Stillwater, MN; m Richard C. Novetzke 1953; two s two d. *Education:* Carleton Coll (Northfield, MN). *Career:* Chair Iowa Precinct Republican Comm 1976–88, Co-Chair Linn Co Republican Party 1979–80, Chair 1980–83, mem State Cen Cttee 1982–85, Co-Chair Iowa Republican Party 1985, State Chair 1985–87, mem Advisory Bd, Iowa Fed of Republican Women 1987–89, Vice-Chair of Campaigns, Nat Fed of Republican Women and mem Nat Women's Coalition 1987–89; involved in numerous political campaigns, including Reagan–Bush presidential campaigns 1980, 1984; Amb to Malta 1989–93; mem Exec Cttee Hoover Presidential Library 1982–, Vice-Pres Trustees; Hon HLD (Mount Mercy Coll) 1991. *Leisure interests:* skiing, tennis, sailing, walking, reading, gardening. *Address:* 4747 Mount Vernon Rd SE, Cedar Rapids, IA 52403, USA.

NOVODVORSKAYA, Valeria Ilyinichna; Russian politician; b 17 May 1950. *Education:* Krupskaya Moscow Region Pedagogical Inst. *Career:* In dissident movt from late 1960s, arrested as student on charge of organizing underground anti-Soviet group 1969; organized political action against invasion of Czechoslovakia Dec 1969; Trans Second Moscow Medicine Inst 1975–90; arrested, discharged 1972; initiator of and participant in anti-Soviet meetings; arrested 17 times 1985–91; imprisoned for anti-Soviet activities 1978, 1985, 1986, 1991; mem Co-ordination Council of Democratic Union, participated in political seminar Democracy and Humanism 1988; Leader Party of Democratic Union 1992; political reviewer Khozyain 1993–95, Stolitsa 1995–; has written articles in newspapers and magazines. *Leisure interests:* reading, mountain climbing, swimming. *Address:* Democratic Union, Onezhskaya str 4, Apt 113, Moscow, Russian Federation. *Telephone:* (095) 453-37-76.

NOVOTNÁ, Jana; Czech tennis player; b 2 Oct 1968, Brno (then Czechoslovakia); d of Frantisek Novotný and Libuse Novotná. *Career:* Won US Open Jr Doubles 1986; turned professional 1987; won her first title Adelaide, Australia 1988; Olympic Silver Medallist in Doubles with Sukova 1988; won Australian and US Open Mixed Doubles with Pugh 1988; won six women's Doubles titles 1989; with Sukova won Australian Open, French Open and Wimbledon Doubles 1990; reached quarter-finals French Open 1991; won seven Doubles titles with L. J. Savchnenko-Neiland 1992; runner-up Ladies Doubles, Wimbledon (with L. J. Savchenko-Neiland) 1992, 1993, (with A. Sánchez Vicario, qv) 1994, winner (with A. Sánchez Vicario) 1995; runner-up, Wimbledon 1993; won Singles titles Osaka, Japan and Brighton, UK 1993, Leipzig and Essen, Germany and Brighton 1994; reached semi-finals, Wimbledon 1996; Olympic Bronze Medal in singles, Silver Medal in doubles with Suková, Atlanta 1996; won Wimbledon singles 1998, Wimbledon women's doubles 1998; announced retirement 1999.

NOVOTNÁ, Klára, D PHIL; Slovak diplomatist; b 11 May 1961, Nove Zamky, Czechoslovakia (now Slovakia); d of Juraj Tobakos and Anna Tobakosova; m Lubomir Novotny 1983; one s. *Education:* Comenius Univ (Bratislava). *Career:* Civil servant 1985–91, at Ministry for Int Relations 1991–92; diplomatist Emb of Czechoslovakia in Germany 1992–94; Amb to Sweden 1994. *Leisure interests:* philosophy, history. *Address:* Oračska 1, 831 06 Bratislava, Slovakia.

NOVOTNÁ, Květa; Czech pianist; b 1 July 1950, Prague; d of Josef Novotný and of the late Květa Novotná; two d one s. *Education:* Acad of Music (Prague). *Career:* Prof Acad of Music, Prague; Third Prize Prague Spring Int Competition 1972; Fourth Prize Int Competition Bolzano, Italy 1973; Fourth Prize Int Competition Naples, Italy 1973; Finalist Zwickau, fmr GDR 1974. *Recordings include:* Schumann's Davidsbündlertänze, Papillons and Toccata 1989, Kinderszenen, Waldszenen and Faschingsschwank aus Wien 1991, Sonata and Novelleten 1992, Dvořák's Poetic Tone-Pictures 1992. *Address:* Kocanda 129, 252 42 Jesenice, Czech Republic. *Telephone:* (2) 6438343.

NOWOTNY, Helga, D JUR, PH D; Austrian professor of social sciences; b 9 Aug 1937, Vienna. *Education:* Realgymnasium (Vienna), Univ of Vienna and Columbia Univ (New York). *Career:* Research Fellow Inst for Advanced Studies, Vienna 1969–72; Visiting Researcher King's Coll Cambridge, UK 1972–73; Founder, Dir European Centre, Vienna 1974–87; Visiting Prof of Bielefeld Univ, Germany 1978–79; Fellow Wissenschaftskolleg, Berlin 1981–82; Dir of Studies Maison des Sciences de l'Homme, Paris 1987; apptd Prof of Sociology Inst for Theory and Social Studies of Science, Univ of Vienna 1987; Resident Fellow Rockefeller Study Centre, Bellagio, Italy 1988; Guest Prof Wissenschaftszentrum, Berlin 1988; Chair Standing Comm on Social Sciences, European Science Foundation, Strasbourg, France 1985; mem Acad Europae 1989– (mem Exec Council 1991). *Publications:* Kern Energie 1979, Wie Männlich ist die Wissenschaft? 1986, Eigen Zeit 1989, Science as a Self-Organizing System 1990; contribs to professional journals. *Address:* University of Vienna, Inst for Theory and Social Studies of Science, Sensengasse 8, 1090 Vienna, Austria. *Telephone:* (222) 402-76-01-14; *Fax:* (222) 408-88-38.

NTAKATSANA, Limakatso Rebecca, D ED; Lesotho politician; b 28 Feb 1940, Mohales Hoek Dist; d of the late John Hlakanesa and Rosina Malipuo Ntakatsane. *Education:* Univ of Hull (UK) and Nat Univ of Lesotho. *Career:* Fmr shepherdess; teacher; f eight schools in Lesotho (five pre-schools and three primary schools); mem staff Ministry of Agriculture, est more than 15 village co-operatives 1983; youth co-ordinator 1960–; Dir Lithoteng Pvt Cen; Leader Kopanang Basotho Party (Basotho Unite); mem numerous cttees and orgs nationally and internationally; rep for Lesotho at int confs 1974, 1979; mem Nat UNESCO Comm 1975; several publs on schooling and for teaching pre-schoolers; awards for youth work in UK 1972; Int Olympic Comm Award, Maseru 1986; Award for Outstanding Voluntary Service, Maseru 1988. *Leisure interests:* sports, agricultural productivity, women's issues, youth work. *Address:* Lithoteng Ha Seoli, Private Bag A133, Maseru 100, Lesotho. *Telephone:* 317715.

NTIMO-MAKARA, 'Matora, MA, M ED, PH D; Lesotho university administrator; b 1 Sept 1945, Maseru; divorced; two d. *Education:* Ball State Univ and Hall Univ. *Career:* Lecturer in Educ 1974–78; Sr Extension Educator, Inst of Extra-Mural Studes, Nat Univ of Lesotho 1978–85; Sr Lecturer in Educational Foundations, Nat Univ of Lesotho 1986–, Head Dept of Educational Foundations 1991–94, Chair House Allocations Cttee, Chair Faculty of Educ Research and Conf Cttee, mem Univ Council 1987–90, then Pro-Vice Chancellor; mem Lesotho Educational Research Asscn, Sec 1986–89, Vice-Sec 1989–92, Chair 1992; Consultant to World Bank 1995; mem Lesotho Asscn for Non-Formal Educ, Women's Research Collective, S African Comparative and History of Educ Soc; mem Ministry of Educ Task Force 1987, Lesotho Research Team for Women and Law Project in S Africa 1990; papers presented at numerous seminars and confs, contribs to journals. *Address:* National University of Lesotho, PO Roma 180, Lesotho. *Telephone:* 340601.

NUGA, Simba, MBA, MA; British media executive; b 11 May 1961, Nigeria; d of Prince Christopher O. and Esther O. Otubushin; m Julius Nuga 1997; one s. *Education:* Girls Grammar School (Lagos, Nigeria),

Hammersmith & W London Coll, Middx Univ, Kingston Univ and Inst of Chartered Secretaries and Administrators. *Career:* Accounts Asst Pacific Printers 1978–79; Admin Trainee Chartered Inst of Man Accountants 1983–84; Accounts and Fundraising Asst Nat Autistic Soc 1986–87; accountant Programmes Training Ltd 1987–89; accountant The Voice Group Ltd 1990–93, Co Sec 1991–94, Financial Dir 1993–94, Man Dir 1994–96, Gen Man 2001–; Lecturer in Business Strategy, Middx Univ 1996–97; E-Commerce Co-ordinator Spar UK Ltd 1997–2001; columnist Women 2 Women magazine (supplement in The Voice newspaper); mem British Inst of Man, Chartered Inst of Marketing, Inst of Dirs (Diploma in Co Direction). *Leisure interests:* music, reading, current affairs, theatre, painting, socializing. *Address:* The Voice Group Ltd, 8th & 9th Floor, Bluestar House, 234–244 Stockwell Rd, London SW9 9UG, UK; 3 Grange Court, Sudbury Ave, Sudbury, Middx HA0 3AJ, UK. *Telephone:* (20) 8795-4832; *Fax:* (20) 8795-4832; *E-mail:* simbo.nuga@the-voice.co.uk.

NUGENT, Nelle, BS; American theatre and television producer; b 24 May 1939, Jersey City; d of John Patrick and Evelyn Adelaide (née Stern) Nugent; m 1st Donald G. Baker 1960 (divorced 1962); m 2nd Benjamin Janney 1969 (divorced 1980); m 3rd Jolyon Fox Stern 1982; one d. *Education:* Skidmore Coll. *Career:* Stage Man 1960–64; Production Asst on Broadway 1964–65, Stage Man 1964–68, Production Supervisor, then Gen Man 1969–70; Assoc Man Nederlander Corpn 1970–76; Chair Bd McCann and Nugent Productions Inc, New York 1976–86; apptd Pres Foxboro Productions Inc, New York 1985; Exec Producer Dick Clark Productions 1988–90; Pres and CEO Foxboro Entertainment 1990–94, Pres The Foxboro Co, Inc; Co Prin Golden Fox Films, Inc. *Productions include:* Theatre: Dracula (Tony Award) 1977, The Elephant Man (Tony Award, Drama Critics Award) 1978, Morning's At Seven (Tony Award) 1980, Home (Tony nomination) 1980, Amadeus (Tony Award) 1981, The Life and Adventures of Nicholas Nickleby (Tony Award, Drama Critics Award) 1981, The Dresser (Tony nomination) 1981, Painting Churches (Obie Award) 1983, All's Well That Ends Well (Tony nomination) 1983, Much Ado About Nothing (Tony nomination) 1984, Cyrano de Bergerac (Tony nomination) 1984, Leader of the Pack (Tony nomination) 1985; TV: Morning's at Seven, Piaf, Pilobolus, A Fighting Choice 1986, A Conspiracy of Love 1987, Morning Maggie (exec producer) 1987, The Final Verdict 1990, In the Presence of Mine Enemies 1995–96 (Silver Star Award, Houston Festival), A Town Has Turned to Dust 1997 (Silver Medal, World Festival) 1998, After the Storm 2000; Films: Student Body 1993, Getting In 1994, Jane Doc 1996. *Address:* Foxboro Co Inc, 133 E 58th St, Suite 301, New York, NY 10022, USA.

NURMESNIEMI, Vuokko Eskolin; Finnish textile artist; b Helsinki. *Education:* Inst of Industrial Arts (Helsinki). *Career:* Designer of fabrics, clothes, ceramics, glass and rugs; designed fabrics for Marimekko and Printex 1953–60, fabrics and clothes for Vuokko 1964–88; Head Designer Marimekko 1953–60; designer of church fabrics for Kaleva Church, Tampere 1968; exhibitions include Hälsingborg, Sweden 1955, Triennale di Milano (Gold Medal for Glass 1957), Italy 1957, 1962, Galerie Artek, Helsinki 1957, Galerie Artek, Stockholm 1958, Victoria and Albert Museum, London 1958, 1982, Lunning Winners, Copenhagen 1964, Centre Nat d'Art et de Culture Georges-Pompidou, Paris 1978, Milan 1980, Design Centre, Helsinki 1985; represented in perm collections including Victoria and Albert Museum, Museum of Industrial Design, Copenhagen, Metropolitan Museum of Art, New York, Museum of Applied Arts, Helsinki, Musée de l'Impression sur Etoffes, Mulhouse, France; Hon Royal Designer for Industry, RSA, London 1988; awards include Grand Prix for Realization of the Finnish Section, Triennale di Milano (jtly) 1964, Danish-American Lunning Prize 1964, Pro-Finlandia Medal KT of the Finnish Lion 1968, Prince Eugen Medal, Sweden 1986, Japan Design Foundation Award 1991. *Address:* Hopeasalmentie 27, 00570 Helsinki, Finland.

NUSSBAUM, Martha Craven, MA, PH D; American professor of law and ethics; b 6 May 1947, New York; d of George and Betty (née Warren) Craven; m Alan J. Nussbaum 1969 (divorced 1987); one d. *Education:* Wellesley Coll, Washington Square Coll, Univ of New York and Harvard Univ. *Career:* Asst, later Assoc Prof of Philosophy and Classics, Harvard Univ 1975–83; Assoc Prof, later Prof of Philosophy, Classics and Comparative Literature, Brown Univ 1984–95, David

Benedict Prof 1987–89; Visiting Prof of Law, Univ of Chicago 1994, Prof of Law and Ethics 1995–96; Ernst Freund Prof 1996–99; Fellow American Acad of Arts and Science; mem American Philosophical Asscn (Chair Cttee on Status of Women 1994–97); Brandeis Creative Arts Award for Non-Fiction 1990; PEN Spielvogel-Diamondstein Award 1991. *Publications:* Aristotle's De Moto Animalium 1978, The Fragility of Goodness 1986, Love's Knowledge 1990, The Quality of Life (ed, jtly) 1993, Passions and Perceptions (jtly) 1993, The Therapy of Desire 1994, Women, Culture and Development (jtly) 1995, Poetic Justice 1996, For Love of Country 1996, Cultivating Humanity 1997, Sex and Social Justice 1998. *Leisure interests:* music, running, hiking. *Address:* University of Chicago, Law School, 111 E 60th St, Chicago, IL 60637, USA. *Telephone:* (410) 863-2718; *Fax:* (401) 863-2719.

NÜSSLEIN-VOLHARD, Christiane, PH D; German scientist; b 20 Oct 1942, Magdeburg; d of Rolf and Brigitte (née Haas) Volhard. *Education:* Goethe-Univ (Frankfurt/Main) and Univ of Tübingen. *Career:* Postdoctoral Fellow (EMBO Fellowship) Biozentrum Basel, Switzerland 1975–76, Univ of Freiburg 1977; Head Group European Molecular Biology Lab (EMBL), Heidelberg 1978–80; Lab Research Assoc Max-Planck-Inst für Virusforschung, Tübingen 1972–74, Group Leader Friedrich-Miescher-Laboratorium, Max-Planck-Gesellschaft, Tübingen 1981–85, mem scientific team Max-Planck-Gesellschaft and Dir Max-Planck-Institut für Entwicklungsbiologie 1985–90, Dir Dept of Genetics 1990–; mem EMBO, Acad Europaea, Nat Acad of Sciences (USA), Royal Soc (UK), Deutsche Akad Leopoldina, American Acad of Arts and Sciences, Berlin-Brandenburgische Akad der Wissenschaften; American Philosophical Soc; author of 55 scientific articles; Hon SC D (Yale); Dr hc (Yale) 1990, (Utrecht, Princeton) 1991, (Freiburg, Harvard) 1989; Hon Prof (Tübingen) 1989; Leibnizpreis der Deutschen Forschungsgemeinschaft 1986; Carus-Medaille der Deutschen Akad Leopoldina, Halle 1989; Rosenstiel Medal, Brandeis Univ 1990; Mattia Award, Roche Inst 1990; Albert Lasker Medical Research Award, New York 1991; Prix Louis Jeantet de Médecine, Genever 1992; Otto Bayer Preis, Bayer AG 1992; Alfred Sloan Prize, Gen Motors Co 1992; Gregor Mendel Medal, Genetical Soc, UK 1992; Louisa Gross Horwitz Prize, Columbia Univ, New York 1992; Otto Warburg Medal, Deutsche Gesellschaft für Biochemie 1992; Theodor Boveri Preis, Univ Würzburg 1993; Ernst Schering Preis, Berlin 1993; Bertner Award, Anderson Cancer Research Center, Houston 1993; Bundesverdienstkreuz (First Class) 1994; Nobel Prize for Medicine (jtly) 1995; Leibnizpreis der Deutschen Forschungsgemeinschaft; Franz-Vogt-Preis, Univ of Giessen; Rosenstiel Medal, Brandeis Univ. *Address:* Max-Planck-Institut für Entwicklungsbiologie, Spemannstr 35/III, 72076 Tübingen, Germany. *Telephone:* (7071) 601487.

NWOSU, Maria Obiageli, PH D; Nigerian plant taxonomist; b 20 Oct 1948, Jos; d of Isaac I. and Philomena Akuegboagu Nwosu. *Education:* Queen's Coll (Lagos) and Univ of Heidelberg (Germany). *Career:* Lecturer in Botany (Plant Taxonomy and Biosystematics) Coll of Educ, Awka 1981–83; apptd Sr Lecturer Univ of Nigeria, Nsukka 1983; took part in German Academic Exchange Programme (DAAD) 1989; mem Int Asscn for Plant Taxonomy 1989, Botanical Asscn of Nigeria, Asscn of Univ Women; Fellow Linnean Soc of London; contribs to professional journals and publs. *Leisure interests:* sewing, tennis, gardening, swimming, foreign languages. *Address:* University of Nigeria, Dept of Botany, Plant Taxonomy Lab, Nsukka, Enugu State, Nigeria. *Telephone:* (42) 771577; *Fax:* (42) 770644.

NYAMBO, Brigitte Theofil, M SC, PH D; Tanzanian entomologist; b 14 July 1948, Moshi. *Education:* Univ of Dar es Salaam and Imperial Coll, (London). *Career:* Head Cotton Entomology, W Tanzania 1975–87; Sr Scientist ICIPE 1989–92; Head of Plant Protection, Horticultural Research Inst Tengeru Arusha 1992–93; Sr Scientist, IPM Specialist Int Inst of Biological Control, Kenya Station 1994, Sr Scientific Officer 1996; over 15 contribs to int journals. *Leisure interests:* reading, walking, sewing. *Address:* CABI International Institute of Biological Control, POB 76520, Nairobi, Kenya. *Telephone:* (154) 32394; *Fax:* (154) 32090.

NYGAARD HAUG, Agnes, LL B; Norwegian judge; b 27 Aug 1933; d of Marius and Eva Nygaard; m Bjørn Haug 1956; one s one d. *Education:* Univs of Oslo and California at Berkeley (USA). *Career:* Asst Judge, Oslo 1958–59; Legal Adviser Ministry of Justice 1959–70, Head of

Section 1970–77; Judge Eidsivating Court of Appeals 1977–86, Presiding Judge 1986–89, First Presiding Judge 1989; Norwegian Del to Int Union of Judges 1986. *Address:* Eidsivating Court of Appeals, POB 8017 Dep, 0030 Oslo 1, Norway (Office); Dyrlandsvn 11, 0875 Oslo, Norway (Home). *Telephone:* (2) 33-46-50 (Office); *Fax:* (2) 41-33-25 (Office).

NYLAND, Margaret Jean, LL B; Australian judge; b 19 Nov 1942; d of J. J. Nyland. *Education:* Adelaide Girls' High School and Univ of Adelaide. *Career:* Solicitor and Barrister, pvt practice 1965–87; Judge S Australia Dist Court 1987–93, Supreme Court of S Australia 1993–; Chair Social Security Appeals Tribunal, SA 1975–87; Chair Family Law Section, S Australia Law Soc 1976–84, 1985–87, S Australia Sex Discrimination Bd 1985–87, Nat Legal Aid Advisory Cttee 1991–94, Law Foundation S Australia Inc 1995–, Meryl Tankard Australian Dance Theatre Ltd 1996–; Dir Australian Asscn of Women Judges 1994–2001; mem Appeals Cttee, S Australia Dog Racing Control Bd 1977–87, Legal Practitioners' Complaints Cttee 1982–87, working party on access in child abuse cases 1986–87, Bd Art Gallery of S Australia 1990–94, Council St Ann's Coll Inc 1995–; Convenor Social Security Appeals Tribunal 1986–87; Deputy Presiding Officer Equal Opportunity Tribunal 1986–87; Rep for S Australia, Fed Cross Vesting Monitoring Cttee 1994–95; Pres John Bray Law Chapter, Univ of Adelaide Alumni Asscn 1998–2000; Patron Flinders Law Soc 1999, Women in Insurance 1999–, Women Lawyers' Asscn, S Australia 2000–, Roma Mitchell Community Legal Centre 2000–. *Leisure interests:* travel, theatre, Australian Rules football. *Address:* Supreme Court of S Australia, 1 Gouger St, Adelaide, SA 5000, Australia. *Telephone:* (8) 8204 0394; *Fax:* (8) 8204 0244; *E-mail:* margaret.nyland@courts.sa .gov.au.

NYOKONG, Tebello, PH D; Lesotho lecturer in chemistry; b 20 Oct 1951; one s one d. *Education:* Univ of Lesotho and McMaster Univ and Univ of Western Ontario (Canada). *Career:* Teaching Asst Univ of Lesotho 1978–80, Lecturer in Inorganic Chemistry 1981–86, in Physical Chemistry 1986–91; apptd Lecturer in Chemistry Rhodes Univ, Grahamstown, SA 1992; has written several conf papers; Fulbright Scholar 1990. *Leisure interests:* gardening, knitting. *Address:* Rhodes University, Chemistry Dept, POB 94, Grahamstown 6140, South Africa. *Telephone:* (461) 26631.

O

OAKAR, Mary Rose, MFA; American politician; b 5 Mar 1940, Cleveland, OH; d of Joseph M. and Margaret Mary (née Ellison) Oakar. *Education:* Ursuline Coll, John Carroll Univ. *Career:* Instructor in English and Drama Lourdes Acad, Cleveland, OH 1963–70; Asst Prof of English, Speech and Drama Cuyahoga Community Coll, Cleveland 1968–75; mem Cleveland City Council 1973–76; mem Congress (Parl) for 20th Dist, OH 1977–92, mem Peeper Comm on Long Term Health Care and numerous other comms and cttees on the aged, policing, finance and the community; Founder, Volunteer, Dir Near West Side Civic Arts Center, Cleveland 1970; Ward Leader Cuyahoga Co Democratic Party 1972–76; mem Ohio 20th Dist Democratic Cen Comm 1974; Partner Mary Rose Oakar and Assocs; Sec Conf to Establish Nat Action Plan on Breast Cancer 1994; apptd to Bd Dirs Builders for Peace 1994, White House Conf on Aging; Trustee Fed of Community Planning, Health and Planning Comm, Community Information Service, Cleveland Soc for Crippled Children, Public Services Occupational Group Advisory Comm, Cuyahoga Community Coll, Cleveland Ballet, YWCA; Hon LHD (Ursuline Coll) 1962; Hon LL D (Ashland); KT of the Order of St Ladislaus of Hungary; Outstanding Service Awards Office of Economic Opportunity 1973–78; three Community Services Awards 1973, 1974, 1976; Cuyahoga County Democratic Woman of the Year 1977; Women's Political Caucus Woman of the Year 1983; numerous awards from American Lebanese League, Irish Nat Caucus, Spanish Christian Org, Fed of American-Syrian Lebanese Clubs. *Address:* 2621 Lorain Ave, Cleveland, OH 44113, USA.

OAKLEY, Ann, PH D; British sociologist and writer; b 17 Jan 1944; d of Richard Titmuss; m Robin Oakley (divorced); three c. *Education:* Chiswick Polytechnic (now W London Inst of Higher Educ) and Somerville Coll (Oxford). *Career:* Prof of Sociology; Head of Research Unit Inst of Educ, Univ of London 1991–. *Publications include:* Novels: The Men's Room (adapted as a BBC TV serial 1991), Matilda's Mistake, The Secret Lives of Eleanor Jenkinson 1992, Scenes Originating in the Garden of Eden 1994, A Proper Holiday 1996; Non-fiction: The Sociology of Housework, From Here to Maternity, The Captured Womb, Taking It Like a Woman (autobiog, 2nd edn) 1992, Social Support and Motherhood 1992, Essays on Women, Medicine and Health 1993, Man and Wife 1996, Experiments in Knowing 2000. *Address:* c/o Edinburgh University Press, 22 George St, Edinburgh EH8 9LF, UK.

OATES, Joyce Carol, MA; American writer; b 16 June 1938, Lockport, NY; d of Frederic J. Oates and Caroline Bush; m Raymond J. Smith 1961. *Education:* Syracuse Univ and Univ of Wisconsin. *Career:* Prof of English Univ of Detroit 1961–67, Univ of Windsor, ON, Canada 1967–87; Writer-in-Residence Princeton Univ 1978–81, Prof 1987–; mem American Acad, Inst of Arts and Letters; Guggenheim Fellow 1967–68; O. Henry Prize Story Award 1967, 1968; Rea Award for Short Story 1990; Elmer Holmes Bukst Award 1990. *Publications include:* Novels: With Shuddering Fall 1965, A Garden of Earthly Delights 1967, Wonderland 1971, Do With Me What You Will 1973, The Assassins 1975, Childwold 1976, The Triumph of the Spider Monkey 1977, Son of the Morning 1978, Unholy Loves 1979, Cybele 1979, Bellefleur 1980, A Sentimental Education 1981, Angel of Light 1981, A Bloodsmoor Romance 1982, Mysteries of Winterthurn 1984, Solstice 1985, Wild Nights 1985, The Lives of the Twins 1987, You Must Remember This 1988, American Appetites 1989, Because It Is Bitter, and Because It Is My Heart (Nat Book Award nomination) 1990, Nemesis 1990, I Lock the Door Upon Myself 1990, Snake Eyes 1991, Black Water 1992, Foxfire 1993, What I Lived For 1994, Man Crazy 1997, My Heart Laid Bare 1998, The Collector of Hearts 1999, Broke

Heart Blues 1999, Blonde: A Novel 2000; Short stories: Heat 1991, Where Is Here? 1992, The Oxford Book of American Short Stories (ed) 1992; several volumes of poems including Them (Nat Book Award 1970) 1969, Nemesis (under pseudonym of Rosamond Smith) 1990, I Lock the Door Upon Myself 1900; George Bellows: American Artist (biog) 1995; The Oxford Book of American Short Stories (ed) 1993; plays, stories, essays, fiction in nat magazines. *Address:* c/o John Hawkins, 71 W 23rd St, Suite 1600, New York, NY 10010, USA.

OBENG, Letitia Eva Takyibea, M SC, PH D, FRSA; Ghanaian hydro-biologist, parasitologist and environmental scientist; b 10 Jan 1925, Anum; d of the late Rev Emmanuel V. and Dora Asihene; m George A. Obeng 1953 (deceased); two s one d. *Education:* Achimota School (Ghana) and Univs of Birmingham and Liverpool (UK). *Career:* Lecturer Coll of Science and Tech, Kumasi 1952–59; Research Scientist Nat Research Council, Ghana 1960–63; Researcher Ghana Acad of Sciences 1963–65; First Ghanaian woman PH D 1964; Founder, Dir Inst of Aquatic Biology, Council for Scientific and Industrial Research (CSIR), Ghana 1965–74; Co-Man UNDP/Ghana Govt Volta Lake Research Project, Sr Programme Officer and Dir Regional Office for Africa, UNEP and Regional Rep 1974–85; Distinguished Int Visitor Radcliffe Coll, Cambridge, MA, USA 1992–93; est network of African Environment Officers; currently consultant on water, health, the environment; participated in Environment Confs, Stockholm 1972 and Rio de Janeiro, Brazil 1992; participated in women's confs Mexico and Copenhagen, Denmark; Trustee Bd of Int Rice Research Inst, Int Irrigation Man Inst, Human Ecology Foundation; Dir Bd Stockholm Environment Inst, PANOS; mem Exec Council Africa Leadership Forum 1992; Fellow Ghana Acad of Arts and Sciences 1964; mem Royal Soc of Arts, UK; Silver Medal Royal Soc of Arts, UK 1972, Commonwealth Council for Scientific and Industrial Research (CSIR) Award for Distinguished Service 1997, Nat Science and Tech Award 1998, CSIR Science Lab named the 'Letitia Obeng Block' 1999. *Publications:* Simuliidae of North Wales, Man-made Lakes (ed) 1969, Environment and the Responsibility of the Privileged, Environment and Population, The Right to Health in Tropical Agriculture, Parasites – the Sly and Sneaky Enemies Inside You; numerous contribs to scientific books and journals. *Leisure interests:* painting flowers, poetry, traditional cultural of Ghana. *Address:* POB C223, Accra, Ghana. *Telephone:* (21) 776248.

OBERLANDER, Cornelia Hahn, CM, BA, B ARCH; Canadian (b German) landscape architect; b 20 June 1921, Mülheim, Germany; d of Franz and Beate (née Jastrow) Hahn; m Peter Oberlander 1953; two d one s. *Education:* Smith Coll (Northampton, MA, USA) and Harvard Univ (USA). *Career:* Architect Kahn, Stonorov and Kiley until 1974; Landscape Architect Arthur Erickson Architects 1974, then Assoc Landscape Architect Moshe Safdie Architects 1983; projects include Philadelphia Int Airport (USA) 1952–54, EXPO '67, Robson Square, Vancouver 1974–82, Univ of British Columbia Museum of Anthro-pology 1976, World Trade Center, Vancouver 1984–86, Hong Kong Bank of Canada 1984–86, EXPO '86, Nat Gallery of Canada (American Soc of Landscape Architects Nat Award) 1988, Canadian Chancery, Washington, DC (Nat Landscape Award 1990) 1989, NW Territories Legis Ass Bldg, Yellowknife 1991, Simon Fraser Univ 1991 and numerous pvt residences in Canada and USA; Co-Founder and mem Advisory Bd, Children's Play Resource Center, Vancouver 1978; mem Nat Task Force on Children's Play, Canadian Council on Children and Youth 1973–77, Vancouver City Council Art in Public Places Subcttee 1986, Canadian Soc of Landscape Architects, (Fellow 1981, Pres 1986–87, Environmental Chair 1987–88), American Soc of Landscape Architects (Fellow) 1992; Hon LL D (British Columbia) 1991;

Presidential Award; winner Peace-Keeping Monument Competition, Ottawa (jtly) 1990. *Publications:* Trees in the City (jtly) 1977; numerous articles for professional journals. *Leisure interests:* skiing, hiking, swimming, gardening. *Address:* 1372 Acadia Rd, Vancouver, BC V6T 1P6, Canada. *Telephone:* (604) 224-3967; *Fax:* (604) 224-7347.

OBERMAIEROVÁ, Jaroslava; Czech actress; b 10 April 1946, Prague; d of the late Karel and Květa Obermaier; m Richard Čech 1979 (divorced 1981); one s. *Education:* Acad of Performing Arts (Prague). *Career:* Film debut in Virgin's Sign during drama studies 1964; actress Kladno Theatre 1967–71, E. F. Burian Theatre, Prague 1971–91; Czech Nat Council Award 1981. *Films:* Virgin's Sign 1964, Seven Killed 1966; *TV appearances include:* Major Zeman (series) 1970–75, Once Upon a Time There Was a House 1977; *Plays include:* Grandmother 1970, Everybody's Sky 1982; leading parts in Chekhov plays. *Leisure interests:* woodcraft, music, poetry, literature. *Address:* Blahoslavova ul 4, 130 00 Prague 3, Czech Republic. *Telephone:* (2) 7986133.

OBERMAN, Helena, PH D; Polish scientist; b 25 June 1925, Wilno; two d. *Education:* Univ of Łódź. *Career:* Docent in Tech Microbiology Inst of Fermentation Tech and Microbiology, Faculty of Food Chemistry, Łódź Tech Univ 1968, apptd Dir of Inst 1973, Asst Prof 1977, Prof 1987; Cross of Merit 1977; Polish Acad of Sciences Prize 1980; Ministry of Higher Educ Prize 1981; Comm of Nat Educ Medal 1982; Ministry of Industry Prize 1989; contribs to nat and int books and journals on physiology, improvement of lactic acid bacteria, inter-generic fusion of yeast protoplasts, food microbiology, etc. *Leisure interests:* travel, classical music. *Address:* Łódź Technical University, Inst of Fermentation Technology and Microbiology, Ul Wólczańska 175, Łódź, Poland (Office); Narutowicza 79A6, 90-138 Łódź, Poland (Home). *Telephone:* (42) 784140 (Office); *Fax:* (42) 363522 (Office).

OBOLENSKY, Ariane Sophie; French civil servant; b 13 Jan 1950, Cognac; d of Paul and Jacqueline (née Bonnet) Obolensky. *Education:* Cours Fremyot de Chantal, Lycée Claude Monnet (Paris), Univ of Paris, Inst d'Etudes Politiques and Ecole Nat d'Admin (Paris). *Career:* Admin Treasury Dept, Ministry of the Economy, Finance and the Budget 1974–78, Chief Clerk 1980–84, Cabinet Dir Office of the Treasury Dir 1984, Deputy Dir of Bilateral Affairs, Int Affairs Dept 1985–88, Head Monetary and Financial Affairs Dept 1988–92, Head Int Affairs 1992; Financial Attaché Perm Rep of France to the EC 1978–80; Tech Adviser Office of the Prime Minister 1988; Vice-Pres European Investment Bank 1994. *Leisure interests:* opera, concerts, golf, yoga. *Address:* c/o European Investment Bank, 100 blvd Konrad Adenauer, L-2950, Luxembourg (Office); 22 rue de l'Eau, L-1449 Luxembourg (Home).

OBRAZTSOVA, Yelena Vasiliyevna; Russian opera singer (mezzo-soprano); b 7 July 1939, Leningrad (now St Petersburg); d of Vasily Alekseevich Obraztsov and Nataliya Ivanovna (née Bychkova) Obraztsova; m 1st Vyacheslav Makarov (divorced 1983); m 2nd Algis Ziuraitis 1983 (died 1998). *Education:* Leningrad Conservatoire (under Prof Grigoriyeva). *Career:* Attached to Staff, Moscow Conservatoire; soloist at Bolshoi with debut as Marina in Mussorgsky's Boris Godunov 1964–; numerous int appearances including Sofia, Brno, Prague Nat and Smetana, Paris and Marseilles, Wiesbaden, Berlin Komische Oper and Staatsoper (Germany), Budapest, Rome Caracalla, Monte Carlo, Bucharest, Majorca and Barcelona, Kiev, Leningrad, Moscow Bolshoi and Stanislavsky and Tbilisi (fmr USSR), San Francisco and New York Metropolitan 1975, La Scala, Milan 1976 and London; Hon mem Pushkin Acad 1995; Glinka Prize 1963; prize-winner Tchaikovsky Int Competition, Moscow 1970, Francisco Viñas Int Competition, Barcelona 1970, Medal of Granados 1971, Gold Pen of Critics, Wiesbaden 1972, Gold Verdi, Italy 1978, Bartók Memorial Medal, Hungary 1982; State Prize of Russia 1974, Lenin Prize 1976; Gold Star-Hero of Labour; People's Artist of USSR and other decorations. *Operas include:* Il Trovatore, Carmen, La Favorite, Werther, Le Nozze di Figaro, Boris Godunov, Khovanshchina, War and Peace, Samson et Dalila, Oedipus Rex, Queen of Spades, Aida, Un Ballo in Maschera, Don Carlos, Prince Igor, The Tsar's Bride, A Midsummer Night's Dream; also song-cycles by Glinka, Tchaikovsky, Rachmaninov and Schumann, and oratorios by Bach and Handel; *Films include:* Carmen, A Masked Ball, Cavalleria Rusticana, Merry Widow. *Leisure interests:* dogs, horses, fishing,

mushrooms. *Address:* c/o Bolshoi Theatre, Teatralnaya pl 1, 103009 Moscow, Russian Federation. *Telephone:* (095) 292-31-08; *Fax:* (095) 292-90-32.

O'BRIEN, Edna; Irish writer; b 15 Dec 1936, Tuamgraney, Co Clare; d of Michael O'Brien and Lena Cleary; m Ernest Gébler 1954 (divorced 1964); two s. *Education:* Convents and Pharmaceutical Coll of Ireland. *Career:* Engaged in writing from an early age; Hon D LITT (Queen's) 1999; Yorkshire Post Novel Award 1971; Kingsley Amis Award, Writers' Guild of GB Award 1993; European Prize for Literature 1995. *Publications:* The Country Girls 1960 (film 1983), The Lonely Girl 1962, Girls in Their Married Bliss 1963, August is a Wicked Month 1964, Casualties of Peace 1966, The Love Object 1968, A Pagan Place 1970 (play 1971), Night 1972, Mother Ireland 1976, Johnny I Hardly Knew You 1977, Arabian Days 1977, Mrs Reinhardt (adapted for TV) 1981, A Christmas Treat 1982, Stories of Joan of Arc (film) 1984, Vanishing Ireland 1987, The High Road 1988, On the Bone (poetry) 1989, Time and Tide 1992, House of Splendid Isolation 1994, Down by the River 1996, Maud Gonne (screenplay) 1996, James Joyce 1999, Wild Decembers 1999; Plays: The Wicked Lady, Virginia 1979, The Hard Way 1980, Home Sweet Home 1984, Flesh and Blood 1987, Madame Bovary 1987, Song of Love 1996; Short stories: A Scandalous Woman 1974, Mrs Reinhardt and other stories 1978, Returning: A Collection of New Tales 1982, A Fanatic Heart 1985, Scandalous Woman and other stories 1990, Lantern Slides (ed) 1990; Children's stories: The Dazzle, Tales for the Telling 1987. *Leisure interests:* reading, walking, dreaming. *Address:* c/o David Godwin Associates, 55 Monmouth St, London WC2H 9DG, UK. *Telephone:* (20) 7240-9992.

OBST, Lynda; American film executive; b 14 April 1950, New York. *Education:* Pomona Coll and Columbia Univ. *Career:* Ed New York times Magazine 1976–79; Exec Polygram Pictures 1979–81, Geffen Films 1981–83; Co-Producer Paramount 1983–85; Producer Walt Disney 1986, later at Columbia. *Films include:* Assoc Producer: Flashdance; Producer: Adventures in Babysitting, Heartbreak Hotel, The Fisher King, This is My Life; Exec Producer: Sleepless in Seattle.

O'CATHAIN, Baroness (Life Peer), cr 1991, of The Barbican in the City of London, **Detta O'Cathain,** OBE, BA, FRSA; British business executive; b 3 Feb 1938, Cork, Ireland; d of Caiomhghin and Margaret (née Prior) O'Cathain; m William Ernest John Bishop 1968 (died 2001). *Education:* Laurel Hill School (Limerick, Ireland) and University Coll (Dublin). *Career:* Asst Economist Aer Lingus, Dublin 1961–66; Group Economist Tarmac Ltd 1966–69; Econ Adviser Rootes Motors 1969–72; Sr Economist Carrington Viyella 1972–73; Econ Adviser British Leyland 1973–74, Dir Market Planning Leyland Cars 1974–76; Corp Planning Exec Unigate 1976–81; Agricultural Marketing Adviser to Minister of Agriculture 1979–83; Head of Strategic Planning, Milk Marketing Bd 1981–83, Dir and Gen Man 1984, Man Dir Milk Marketing 1985–88; Man Dir Barbican Centre, London 1990–95; Non-Exec Dir Midland Bank 1984–93, Channel Four 1985–86, Tesco 1985–2000, Sears 1987–94, British Airways 1993–, BET 1994–96, BNP Paribas UK PLC 1995–, Thistle Hotels PLC 1996–, S E Water PLC 1997–, Allders PLC 2000–, Wm Baird PLC 2000–; Fellow Chartered Inst of Marketing 1987 (Pres 1998–2001). *Leisure interests:* music, reading, swimming, gardening, walking. *Address:* House of Lords, London SW1A 0PW, UK (Office); Eglantine, Tower House Gardens, Arundel, W Sussex BN18 9RU, UK (Home). *Telephone:* (20) 7219-0662 (Office); (1903) 883775 (Home); *Fax:* (1903) 883775 (Home); *E-mail:* ocathaind@parliament.uk.

OCKRENT, Christine; Belgian journalist and broadcasting executive; b 24 April 1944, Brussels; d of Roger and Greta (née Bastenie) Ockrent; m Bernard Kouchner; one s. *Education:* Collège Sevigné (Paris), Univ of Cambridge (UK) and Inst d'Etudes Politiques de Paris. *Career:* Journalist Information Office, EC 1965–66; Asst Producer NBC News, USA 1967–68; Producer, journalist CBS News, USA 1968–76, Corresp 1976–77; journalist, Producer Société Nat de Programmes—France Régions 3 (FR3) TV, France 1976–80, several posts as journalist, ed and presenter on news programmes 1980–82; Ed Europe 1 radio station 1980–81; Man Ed, Presenter evening news on Société Nat de Télévision en Couleur—Antenne 2 1981–85; Ed, commentator Radio-Télé Luxembourg (RTL) radio 1985–87; Deputy Dir-Gen Télévision Française 1 (TF1) 1987–88; Deputy News Controller Antenne 2

1988–89, Ed, Anchor and Producer news programmes until 1992, on France 3 1992–95; Producer, Presenter (for Antenne 2) Carnets de route, Qu'avez-vous fait de vos 20 ans? 1990–91, Direct 1992–, (for France Inter radio) Portraits 1992–; Ed-in-Chief and Dir L'Express 1995–96; Deputy Dir BFM 1996–2000; Ed-in-Chief Dimanche Soir programme France 3 1996–98; Ed-in-Chief and Presenter France Europe Express 1997–; Dir L'Européen 1998–99; Sept d'or for Best Presenter 1985; Sept d'or for Personality of the Year 1985. *Publications:* Dans le secret des Princes 1986, Duel 1988, The Evil Empire (with Count de Marenches) 1988, Qu'avez-vous fait de vos 20 ans? (two vols) 1990, Les Uns et Les Autres 1993, Portraits d'eci et d'ailleurs 1994, La Mémoire du cœur 1997, Les Grands patrons (jtly) 1998, L'Europe racontée à mon fils, de Jules César à l'euro 1999. *Leisure interests:* swimming, skiing, sailing, tennis. *Address:* France 3, esplanade Henri de France, 75907 Paris Cedex 15, France; L'Européen, 94 bis rue de Suffren, 75015 Paris, France. *Telephone:* (1) 40-54-31-43.

OCKRENT, Isabelle Cécile Sophie, L ÈS L; Belgian business executive and civil servant; b 23 Jan 1950, Uccle; d of Roger and Greta (née Bastenie) Ockrent; four c. *Education:* Collège Sévigné, Cours Victor Hugo (Paris), Univ of Nanterre, Ecole des Hautes Etudes en Sciences Sociales (Paris) and Inst d'Etudes Politiques de Paris. *Career:* Admin OECD 1972–84; Tech Communications Adviser Office of the Minister of Defence 1984–85; Communications Adviser Office of the Del-Gen for Armament 1985–86; Communications Dir Int Metal Service (IMS) 1986–87, Française de Brasserie-Heineken 1987–90, Soc Nat d'Exploitation Industrielle des Tabacs et des Allumettes (SEITA) 1990; mem Entreprise et Média. *Address:* SEITA, 53 quai d'Orsay, 75340 Paris Cedex 07, France (Office); 9 ave de Suffren, 75007 Paris, France (Home); 10 rue de la Pointe, 56790 Larmor-Baden, France (Home). *Telephone:* (1) 45-56-61-50 (Office); *Fax:* (1) 45-56-67-70 (Office).

O'CON-SOLORZANO, Thelma, MA; Nicaraguan United Nations official; b 24 Feb 1942. *Education:* Women's Univ (Mexico), Univs of Pittsburgh and New York (USA) and Inst of Political Science (France). *Career:* Third Sec to Perm Mission, UN 1966–67; Protocol Officer Exec Office of the Sec-Gen, UN 1968–74; Information Officer Non-Govt Section, External Relations Div, Dept of Public Information 1974; Dir UN Information Centre, Colombia 1974–76, El Salvador 1976–77, Argentina 1980; Political Affairs Officer, Office of the Under-Sec-Gen for Special Political Affairs, UN 1977–80; Dir and Rep UN and UNICEF 1987–88; Dir UN Information Office for Australia, Fiji, Kiribati, Nauru, New Zealand, Tonga, Tuvalu, Vanuatu and W Samoa 1988; UN Rep and Resident Co-ordinator of the UN in Armenia 1992–94; Dir UN Information Centre for Mexico, Cuba and the Dominican Repub, México 1994; mem American Soc of Int Law 1968. *Publications:* The Central American Union Research on the Exploration and Exploitation of the Seabed 1961, El Caso Nicaragua 1983. *Address:* UN Information Centre, Presidente Masaryk 29, 6th Floor, Chapultepec Morales, 11570 México, DF, Mexico. *Telephone:* (5) 203-9406; *Fax:* (5) 203-8638; *Internet:* serpiente.dgsca.unam.mx/cinu.

O'CONNOR, Charmian Jocelyn, CBE, JP, PH D, D SC, FRSNZ, C CHEM, FRSC; New Zealand professor of chemistry and university administrator; b 4 Aug 1937, Woodville; d of Cecil J. and Kathrene M. Bishop; m Peter S. O'Connor 1963 (divorced 1971); one s one d. *Education:* Univ of Auckland and Univ Coll London. *Career:* Post-doctoral Fellow Univ Coll London 1967, Univ of California at Santa Barbara, USA 1967–68; Lecturer Univ of Auckland 1958–66, Sr Lecturer 1967–71, Assoc Prof 1972–85, Prof of Chemistry 1986–, Asst Vice-Chancellor on Equal Employment Opportunities and Staff Devt 1989–97, Deputy Vice-Chancellor 1994; Visiting Prof Texas A & M Univ, USA 1972, Nagasaki Univ, Japan 1982, 1986, 1987, Tokushima Univ, Japan 1987, Nagoya Univ and Nagoya Inst of Tech 1994, 1996, 1998; Fellow NZIC; numerous awards and prizes has written 300 articles in int journals and several book chapters; numerous conf presentations. *Leisure interests:* walking, knitting, watching TV, gardening, swimming. *Address:* University of Auckland, Dept of Chemistry, Private Bag 92019, Auckland, New Zealand. *Telephone:* (9) 373-7599; *Fax:* (9) 373-7422; *E-mail:* cj .oconnor@auckland.ac.nz (Office).

O'CONNOR, Deirdre Frances, LL B; Australian federal judge; b 5 Feb 1941; d of Charles Anthony O'Connor and Daphne Anzac Buff; m Michael John Joseph 1974; five s. *Education:* Bethlehem Coll (Ashfield)

and Univs of Sydney and New England. *Career:* Lecturer in Law Univ of New S Wales 1974–75; part-time Lecturer in Media and Law, Australian Film, Television and Radio School, NSW 1975–80; Lecturer in Law Macquarie Univ, NSW 1975–78, Sr Lecturer 1978–80; called to the Bar, NSW 1980; Commr New S Wales Law Reform Comm 1983–85; Chair Australian Broadcasting Tribunal 1986–91; Pres Admin Appeals Tribunal 1990–94; Judge Fed Court of Australia 1990–; Pres Australian Industrial Relations Comm 1994; Australian Govt Rep to UNESCO 1978; mem Council Order of Australia 1990–96, Univ of Canberra 1992–95; Ethics Prize; Prize for Family Law Publ. *Leisure interests:* walking, antiques (especially silver). *Address:* Federal Court of Australia, Level 16, Law Courts Bldg, Queens Square, Sydney, NSW 2000, Australia (Office); 25 Glenview Crescent, Hunter's Hill, NSW 2110, Australia (Home). *Telephone:* (2) 332-0889 (Office).

O'CONNOR, Gillian Rose; British financial journalist; b 11 Aug 1941; d of Thomas McDougall and Kathleen Joan (née Parnell) O'Connor. *Education:* Sutton High School for Girls and St Hilda's Coll (Oxford). *Career:* Ed Investors Chronicle 1982–94; Personal Finance Ed Financial Times 1994–98, Mining Corresp 1999–. *Address:* Financial Times, 1 Southwark Bridge, London SE1 9HL, UK.

O'CONNOR, Sandra Day, BA, LL B; American judge; b (Sandra Day) 26 March 1930, El Paso, TX; d of Harry A. and Ada Mae (née Wilkey) Day; m John Jay O'Connor III 1952; three s. *Education:* Stanford Univ. *Career:* Legal practice, CA and Frankfurt, Germany 1952–57; pvt practice, Phoenix, AZ 1959–65; Asst Attorney-Gen, AZ 1965–69; Arizona State Senator 1969–74, Majority Leader 1973–74; elected Superior Court Judge, AZ 1975, Judge of Appeals 1979–81; Assoc Justice US Supreme Court Sept 1981–; Dir Nat Bank of Arizona, Phoenix 1971–74; Pres Heard Museum, Phoenix 1979–81; Trustee Stanford Univ (CA) 1976–80; Hon mem Gray's Inn Bench 1982; mem Nat Bd Smithsonian Assocs 1981–82; 25 hon degrees; recipient Distinguished Achievement Award, Arizona State Univ 1980, Fordham-Stein Prize, Fordham Univ 1992, Service to Democracy Award, American Ass 1982, Award of Merit, Stanford Law School 1990; elected to Nat Women's Hall of Fame, Seneca Falls, NY 1995. *Address:* Supreme Court Bldg, 1 First St, NE, Washington, DC 20543, USA. *Telephone:* (202) 479-3151.

O'CONNOR, Sinead; Irish singer, songwriter and actress; b 8 Dec 1966, Dublin; d of John and the late Marie O'Connor; m John Reynolds (divorced); one s one d. *Education:* Dublin Coll of Music. *Career:* Band mem Ton Ton Macoute 1985–87; refused to accept Grammy Award for Best Alternative Album 1991; ordained priest Sister Bernadette in Latin Tridentine Church (Roman Catholic splinter group) 1999. *Recordings include:* Albums: The Lion and the Cobra 1987, I Do Not Want What I Haven't Got (three Grammy nominations and Grammy Award for Best Alternative Album 1991, Rolling Stone Artist of the Year 1991) 1990, Am I Not Your Girl? 1992, Universal Mother 1994, Gospeloak 1997; Songs: Heroin 1986, Mandinka 1987, Jump in the River 1988, Nothing Compares 2 U 1990, Three Babies 1990, You Do Something To Me (for Red Hot and Blue compilation) 1990, Silent Night 1991, My Special Child 1991, Visions of You (with Jah Wobble's Invaders of the Heart) 1992, Emperor's New Clothes 1992, Secret Love 1992, Success Has Made a Failure of Our Home 1992; *Video films:* Value of Ignorance 1989, The Year of the Horse 1991; *TV Film:* Hush-a-Bye-Baby. *Telephone:* (20) 7336-8802 (UK).

O'DAY, Anita; American jazz singer; b 18 Oct 1919, Chicago, IL; d of James and Gladys (née Gill) Colton; m 1st Don Carter 1936 (divorced); m 2nd Carl Hoff 1943 (divorced 1955). *Career:* Singing debut 1939; Co-Founder Hi Note jazz club, Chicago 1949; performed Newport Jazz Festival 1958; toured Sweden, Germany 1959, Japan 1964, 1969, 1975, 1976; UK debut Beaulieu Jazz Festival 1961; f Emily Records (record co) 1970s; performances in Los Angeles, New York, London, Rome, Hong Kong, New York, Montréal 1985–2000; has toured worldwide; awards from Down Beat magazine include New Star of the Year 1941, one of Top Five Female Singers 1942, Best Band Singer 1945. *Albums include:* Anita, Pick Yourself Up, Anita Sings the Most, Anita O'Day Swings Cole Porter, Cool Heat, Waiter, Make Mine Blues, All the Sad Young Men, Time For Two, Travelin' Light, In a Mellow Tone (Grammy nomination) 1989, The Rules of The Road 1993, Jazz Masters, Skylark, Swingtime in Hawaii, Ultimate Anita O'Day, Legends of the Swing Era; *Songs include:* Let Me Off Uptown, Thanks For the Boogie Ride, That's What you Think, And Her Tears Flowed Like Wine, Boogie Blue, Opus One; *Films:* Gene Krupp Story 1959, Zigzag 1970, The Outfit 1974; *Publication:* High Times Hard Times (autobiog) 1981. *Address:* c/o Alan Eichler, 6064 Selma Ave, Los Angeles, CA 90028, USA.

ODDY, Christine, LL B, M SC, FRSA; British former politician, lecturer and consultant; b 20 Sept 1955, Coventry. *Education:* Univ Coll London, Birkbeck Coll (London) and Inst of European Studies (Brussels). *Career:* Articled Clerk 1980–82; Solicitor 1982–; Lecturer 1984–89; Gov City of London Polytechnic; MEP (Lab) for Midlands Cen 1989–94, for Coventry and N Warks 1994–99, mem Cttees on Legal Affairs and Citizen's Rights, Social Affairs, Women's Rights, Del on Cen America; Sec Anti-Racism Working Group 1989–99; Treas European Parliamentary Labour Party 1994–99; mem Haldane Soc of Socialist Lawyers, Royal Inst of Int Affairs; Br Sec Nat Asscn of Teachers in Further and Higher Educ 1985–89, Regional Exec Cttee 1987–88. *Address:* 33 Longfellow Rd, Coventry CV2 5HD, UK. *Telephone:* (24) 7645-6856.

O'DELL, June Patricia, OBE, FRSA; British business and organization executive; b 9 June 1929, Sliema, Malta; d of the late Leonard Frederick and Myra Sarah (née Soden) Vickery; m Ronald Desmond O'Dell 1951 (divorced 1963); two d one s. *Education:* Edgehill Girls' Coll and Plymouth Tech Coll. *Career:* Prin Chesney's Estate Agents 1965–88; Nat Pres UK Fed of Business and Professional Women 1983–85; Chair Employment Cttee, Int Fed of Business and Professional Women 1983–87; Deputy Chair Equal Opportunities Comm 1985–90, Chair Legal Comm 1985–90; Dir Eachdale Devts Ltd 1988–; Non-Exec Dir Aylesbury Vale Community Healthcare NHS Trust 1991–98; Trustee Women Returners Network 1994–; mem Women's Nat Comm 1983–85, Industry Matters Women's Working Group 1985–, European Advisory Cttee for Equal Treatment between Women and Men 1986–90, RSA Women's Advisory Group 1986–, Authorised Conveyancing Practitioners Bd 1991–95, Legal Aid Advisory Cttee 1993–94, Bd Probus Women's Housing Soc 1993– (Chair 1998–); Fellow Nat Asscn of Estate Agents 1986; mem Council Royal Soc of Arts 1992. *Leisure interests:* music, opera, writing, literature, countryside, horses. *Address:* Gable End, High St, Great Missenden, Berks HP16 9AA, UK. *Telephone:* (1296) 614030.

ODIE-ALI, Stella, B SC, MA; Guyanese politician; b 20 Oct 1942; d of the late Basil Simon and of Hilda Bakridan Odie. *Education:* Univ of Guyana, Univ of the West Indies (Jamaica) and Morgan State Univ (USA). *Career:* School teacher 1959–69; Social Worker 1969–78; Lecturer 1978–85; mem Nat Ass (Parl, People's Nat Congress—PNC), Minister of Home Affairs 1986–92. *Publication:* Women in Agriculture in Guyana 1983. *Leisure interests:* reading, music, walking. *Address:* 186 Wills St, Republic Park, E Bank, Demerara, Guyana (Home). *Telephone:* 65054 (Home); *Fax:* 60936 (Home).

ODINAMADU, Oyibo Ekwulo, MA; Nigerian business executive; b 3 March 1930; d of the late Jacob Ekemezie and Dinah Mgboye (née Nwolisakwe) Akwuba; m Benedict Obidinma Odinamadu 1957 (died 1979); two s two d. *Education:* Lincoln Univ High School and Lincoln Univ (Jefferson City, MO, USA) and Columbia Univ (NY). *Career:* Anglican CMS Mission pupil-teacher, Nigeria 1943–47; Asst Sec E Nigeria Devt Corpn 1954–57; Educ Officer Inspectorate of Educ, E Nigeria Civil Service 1957–71, Insp of Educ 1963; teacher Women's Training Coll, Enugu 1957–62, Coll Prin 1962; Head Examinations and Registration Br of Ministry of Educ 1965–70; Prin Queen's School, Enugu 1970–71; Chair, Man Dir Echo Enterprises PLC, Enugu 1971–; f League of Women Voters of Nigeria 1978; Nat Vice-Pres Unity Party of Nigeria (now proscribed) 1979–83 and cand for post of Deputy State Governor 1979; Chair Abatete Task Force Group on Devt 1985; Pres Nat Council of Women's Socs of Nigeria 1960–79, now Life mem; Sec Provincial Mothers' Union (Anglican Communion) 1989; mem Nat Advisory Council on Educ for Citizenship 1978; mem Order of the Niger 1963; mem of the Order of Biafra, Govt of the Repub of Biafra (now Nigeria) 1966; mem Order of the Knighthood of St Christopher of the Diocese on the Niger (Anglican Communion) 1978; Certificate of Merit, Nat Asscn of University Women 1980. *Publication:* Politics and the Igbo Elite 1980. *Leisure interests:* charitable and voluntary activities

and orgs, public speaking, radio and TV programmes, reading and writing, games, travel, gardening. *Address:* Echo Enterprises PLC, 171 Zik Ave, POB 8424, Enugu, Enugu State, Nigeria. *Telephone:* (42) 335769.

ODIO BENITO, Elizabeth, L EN D; Costa Rican lawyer and politician. *Career:* Prof of Law; Solicitor-Gen 1978; Minister of Justice 1978–82, 1990–94; Second Vice-Pres of Costa Rica. *Address:* c/o Office of the President, San José, Costa Rica.

ODJIG, Daphne, OC; Canadian artist; b 11 Sept 1919, Wikwemikong (Manitoulin Island), ON; d of Dominic and Joyce Emily (née Peachey) Odjig; m Chester Beavon 1963; two s two step-s one step-d. *Career:* Mem Odawa tribe; solo exhibitions include Bashford and Schwarz Gallery, Calgary 1966, Lakehead Art Centre, ON 1967, Int Peace Gardens 1970, Warehouse Gallery of Native Art, Winnipeg 1974, Lefebvre Gallery, Edmonton 1979, Griffin Galleries, Vancouver 1979, Children of the Raven Gallery, Vancouver 1981; group exhibitions include Minot State Univ 1970, L'Agence de Cooperation Culturelle et Technologique 1971, Gallery Anthropos, London 1973, Royal Ontario Museum, Toronto 1974, Dominion Gallery, Montréal 1975, Woodland Indian Cultural Educational Centre, Brantford 1975, São Paulo Museum of Art and Rio de Janeiro Museum of Modern Art, Brazil 1977, Oklahoma Museum of Art, USA 1978, Jt Indian Individualist Show 1982; rep in perm collections including Manitoba Indian Brotherhood, Canadian Council Art Bank, Govt of Israel, Petro Canada, Ameco Canada Petroleum Ltd; comms include Earthmother, Canadian Pavilion, Expo '70, From Mother Earth Flows the River of Life, Ministry of Indian and Northern Affairs 1974, El Al; Founder-mem Professional Native Indian Artists Inc 1973; book illustrator, has written and illustrated series of ten books, Nanbush Indian Legends for Children 1971; featured in TV documentaries; Researcher Soc of Canadian Artists of Native Ancestry 1983; mem RCA; Hon LL D (Laurentian) 1982, (Toronto) 1985; Dr hc (Nipissing) 1996; Canadian Silver Jubilee Medal 1977; presented with Eagle Feather by Chief Wakageshig 1978, Commemorative Medal, 125th Anniversary of Confed of Canada 1992; Aboriginal Award, Toronto 1998. *Address:* 102–102 Forest Brook Place, Pentirton, BC V2A 7N4, Canada. *Telephone:* (250) 493-7475.

ODONE, Cristina, MA; Italian journalist and writer; b 11 Nov 1960, Nairobi; d of Augusto and Ulla (née) Sjöström Odone. *Education:* Univ of Oxford (UK). *Career:* Vice-Pres Odone Assocs consultancy, Washington, DC; Ed The Catholic Herald, UK 1992–96; Diary Journalist The Times newspaper, UK 1991–; TV reviewer Daily Telegraph newspaper 1996–98; Deputy Ed New Statesman 1998–. *Publications:* The Shrine 1996, Renewal 1997, A Perfect Life 1998. *Leisure interests:* travel, walking, entertaining, swimming. *Address:* New Statesman, Victoria Station House, 7th Floor, 191 Victoria St, London SW1E 5NE, UK. *Telephone:* (20) 7828-1232; *Fax:* (20) 7828-1881; *E-mail:* info@newstatesman.co.uk.

O'DONOGHUE, Denise, OBE; British broadcasting executive; b 1955. *Education:* Convent school (Harrow) and Univ of York. *Career:* Fmr Man Consultant; fmr Dir Independent Programme Producers' Asscn; Co-Founder and Man Dir Hat Trick Productions 1995–; RTS, BAFTA, Emmy and Press Guild awards. *TV programmes produced include:* Whose Line Is It Anyway?, Harry Enfield Television Programme, Have I Got News for You?. *Leisure interests:* running, relaxing. *Address:* Hat Trick Productions, 10 Livonia St, London W1V 3PH, UK.

O'DONOGHUE, Lois, CBE, AM, AC; Australian Aboriginal organization executive; b 1 Aug 1932; d of L. Woodford; m Gordon Smart 1979 (died 1991). *Education:* Unley G Technical High School and Royal Adelaide Hosp. *Career:* Fmr nurse; Commr Aboriginal Devt Comm 1980–84, 1988–89, Chair 1989–90; Deputy Chair Aboriginal and Torres Strait Islander Comm 1989–90, Chair 1990–; mem Aboriginal Negotiating Team for Native Title Legislation 1993, Republican Advisory Cttee 1993; Dir Aboriginal Hostels Ltd 1976–82, 1990– (Chair 1982–90); Chair Co-op Research Centre for Aboriginal and Tropical Health 1997–; Chair Sydney Olympic Nat Indigenous Advisory Cttee 1998–, mem Sydney Olympic Volunteers 2000 Advisory Cttee 1998–; mem PM's Advisory Cttee on changing Australia to a repub 1993; Hon LL D (ANU); Hon D UNIV (Murdoch, Flinders, ANU, S Australia);

Advance Australia Award 1982; Australian of the Year 1984. *Leisure interest:* gardening. *Address:* Yunggorendi First Nations Centre for Higher Education and Research, Sturt Rd, Bedford Park, SA 5042, Australia.

O'DONOVAN, Kathleen Anne, B SC; British business executive; b 23 May 1957, Warwicks. *Education:* Univ Coll London. *Career:* Accountant; joined Ernst and Whinney (now Ernst and Young) auditing co 1975, Auditor for BTR Industries Ltd, Group Audit Partner 1989–1991; Finance Dir BTR Industries Ltd (now Invensys PLC) 1991–; Non-Exec Dir EMI Gp 1997–; mem Court Bank of England 1999–. *Address:* Invensys PLC, Carlisle Place, London SW1P 1BX, UK. *Telephone:* (20) 7834-3848.

OELZE, Christiane; German opera and concert singer (soprano); b 9 Oct 1963, Cologne; m Bodo Primus; one d. *Career:* Studied with Klesie Kelly-Moog and Erna Westenberger; won several Lieder competitions including Hugo-Wolf-Wettbewerb 1987, Hochschule Wettbewerb für Lied-Duo 1988; recital tours USA, S America, Japan; has worked with many maj int conductors and has appeared on all important European concert stages and at int festivals, including Salzburg Festival 1997; began singing in opera 1990; roles include: Despina (Ottawa), Pamina (Leipzig, Lyon, Munich), Konstanze (Salzburg, Zürich), Anne Trulove (Glyndebourne), Regina (in Mathis der Maler, Covent Garden), Zdenka (Covent Garden), Zerlina (Covent Garden), Ännchen (in Der Freischütz, Covent Garden), Mélisande (Glyndebourne), Servilia (in La Clemenza di Tito, Covent Garden). *Recordings include:* two solo recitals, concert arias, Mass in C minor (Mozart), Christmas Oratorio, St John and St Matthew Passions, Webern songs and cantatas, Le Nozze di Figaro and many others. *Address:* c/o Pieter G. Alferink Artists' Management, Apollolaan 181, 1077 AT Amsterdam, Netherlands. *Telephone:* (20) 6643151; *Fax:* (20) 6752426; *E-mail:* alferink@ worldonline.nl.

O'FAOLÁIN, Julia, MA; Irish writer; b 1932, London; d of Sean and Eileen (née Gould) O'Faoláin; m Lauro R. Martines 1957; one s. *Education:* Sacred Heart Convent (Monkstown, Co Dublin), Univs of Dublin, Paris (Sorbonne) and Rome. *Career:* Writer and translator 1968–. *Publications include:* We Might See Sights! and Other Stories 1968, Godded and Codded, Man in the Cellar, Women in the Wall, No Country for Young Men 1980, The Obedient Wife, The Irish Signorina, Daughters of Passion 1982, The Judas Cloth 1992, Not in God's Image (co-ed), Women in History from the Greeks to the Victorians (co-ed). *Leisure interests:* gardening, karate. *Address:* c/o Rogers, Coleridge and White Ltd, 20 Powis Mews, London W11 1JN, UK. *Telephone:* (20) 7221-3717.

OGATA, Sadako, MA, PH D; Japanese United Nations official; b 16 Sept 1927, Tokyo; m Shijuro Ogata; two c. *Education:* Georgetown Univ (Washington, DC) and Univ of California at Berkeley (USA). *Career:* Prof, Dir Inst of Int Relations, then Dean Faculty of Foreign Studies, Sophia Univ, Tokyo until 1990; Sr mem Japanese Del to UN 1976–79; fmr Chair Exec Bd UNICEF; Japanese Rep to UN Comm on Human Rights, Geneva (Switzerland) 1982–85, led human rights mission, Myanmar 1990; fmr Dir Inst of Int Relations, Sophia Univ Tokyo, Dean Faculty of Foreign Studies until 1990; UN High Commr for Refugees 1991; mem Trilateral Comm 1984; author numerous books on diplomacy and int relations; Dr hc (Harvard) 1994. *Address:* UN High Commission for Refugees, CP 2500, 1202 Geneva, Switzerland.

OGILVIE, Dame Bridget Margaret, DBE, PH D, SC D, FIBIOL, FRCPATH, F MED SCI; Australian scientist; b 24 March 1938, Glen Innes, NSW; d of the late John Mylne Ogilvie and Margaret Beryl McRae. *Education:* New England Girls' School (Armidale, NSW) and Univs of New England (NSW) and Cambridge (UK). *Career:* Wellcome Animal Health Trust Fellow 1963–66; mem Scientific Staff MRC 1966–81; mem of staff The Wellcome Trust 1979–, Dir 1991–98; fmr Visiting Prof Imperial Coll, London 1998–; Non-Exec Dir Lloyds Bank 1995–, Lloyds TSB Group PLC 1996–2000, Zeneca Group PLC 1997, AstraZeneca 1999–; mem UK Council for Science and Tech 1993–2000, Advisory Council for Chem, Univ of Oxford 1997–, Australian Health and Medical Research Strategic Review 1998; Trustee Nat Museum of Science and Industry 1992–, Royal Coll of Veterinary Surgeons Trust Fund 1998–, Nat Endowment for Science

and Tech and the Arts 1998–, Cancer Research Campaign 2000–; Chair Governing Body Inst for Animal Health 1997–, Cttee on the Public Understanding of Science 1998–, British Library Advisory Cttee for Science and Business 1999–; has written several papers, contribs to reviews and books on the immune response of man and animals to parasitic infections 1964–84; Hon mem British and American Socs of Parasitology, British Veterinary Asscn, Hon MRCP, Hon FRCP; Hon Assoc Royal Coll of Veterinary Surgeons; Hon Fellow Univ Coll London, Girton Coll Cambridge, St Edmunds Coll Cambridge, Royal Australian Coll of Physicians, Inst of Biology, Royal Soc of Medicine; Foundation Hon Fellow Royal Veterinary Coll; Commonwealth Scholarship; Ian McMaster Fellow; Hon MD (Newcastle); Hon D SC (Nottingham, Salford, Westminster, Bristol, Glasgow, ANU, Buckingham, Dublin, Nottingham Trent, Oxford Brookes, Greenwich, Auckland, Durham, Kent, Exeter, London, Leicester, Manchester); Hon LL D (Trinity Coll, Dundee); Dr hc (Edinburgh); Univ Medal (Univ of New England); Inaugural Distinguished Alumni Award (Univ of New England); Lloyd of Kilgerran Prize 1994; Wooldridge Memorial Medal 1998; Australian Soc of Medical Research Medal 2000. *Leisure interests:* friends, looking at landscapes, swimming, walking, music, gardening. *Address:* c/o Medical Administration, University College London, Gower St, London WC1E 6BT, UK. *Telephone:* (20) 7679-4538; *Fax:* (20) 7383-2462; *E-mail:* rachel.chapman@ucl.ac.uk (Office).

OGILVY, HRH Princess Alexandra (Helen Elizabeth Olga Cristabel), the Hon Lady, GCVO; British royal; b 25 Dec 1936; d of the late Duke of Kent (fourth s of King George V) and Princess Marina (d of the late Prince Nicholas of Greece); m Hon Angus James Bruce Ogilvy 1963; one s one d. *Education:* Heathfield School (Ascot). *Career:* Chancellor Univ of Lancaster; Col-in-Chief The King's Own Royal Border Regt, The Queen's Own Rifles of Canada and the Canadian Scottish Regt (Princess Mary's); Deputy Col-in-Chief The Light Infantry; Deputy Col-in-Chief Queen's Royal Lancers 1993–; Deputy Hon Col The Royal Yeomanry (Territorial Army Voluntary Reserves); Patron and Air Chief Commdt Princess Mary's Royal Air Force Nursing Service; Patron Queen Alexandra's Royal Naval Nursing Service; Pres or Patron of many charitable and social welfare orgs; rep HM Queen Elizabeth II at independence celebrations of Nigeria 1960 and St Lucia 1979, 150th anniversary celebrations, Singapore 1969; Hon Fellow Royal Coll of Physicians and Surgeons of Glasgow, Royal Coll of Physicians, Royal Coll of Anaesthetists, Royal Coll of Obstetricians and Gynaecologists; Hon Air Commodore RAF Cottesmore; Hon Liverywoman Worshipful Co of Clothworkers; Hon Freedom of the City of Lancaster, City of London; Dr hc (Queensland, Hong Kong, Mauritius, Liverpool); decorations from Mexico, Peru, Chile, Brazil, Japan, Finland, Canada, Luxembourg, Netherlands. *Leisure interests:* music, reading, tapestry, outdoor recreations including swimming, skiing, riding. *Address:* Buckingham Palace, London SW1A 1AA, UK.

OGLESBY, Katherine Leni, BA, MA, DIP ED, FRSA; British university pro-vice-chancellor; b 2 Oct 1943, Manchester; d of William Henry and Elizabeth Oglesby; m Alan Wellings 1974; one s one d. *Education:* Univs of Wales, Leicester and Manchester. *Career:* Lecturer in Further Educ, Liverpool 1966–68; Lecturer in Adult Educ, Univ of Leicester 1970–75; apptd Lecturer in Post-Compulsory Educ, Univ of Sheffield 1976; Head of Dept, Univ of Lancaster 1993–96; Head of School of Educational Studies, Univ of Surrey 1996–99; Pro-Vice-Chancellor and Dean, The Manchester Metropolitan Univ 1999–; Hon Officer Standing Conf on Univ Teaching and Research in the Educ of Adults 1979–82; Hon Officer for Women's Educ, European Bureau of Adult Educ, the Netherlands 1985–87, apptd Pres 1988; Policy Officer, Higher Educ Funding Council (England) 1991–93; Hon Officer Nat Inst of Adult Continuing Educ 1986; Chair Standing Conf on Studies in Educ 1997; Fellow Royal Soc of Arts. *Publications:* Vocational Education for Women in Western Europe: The Legal Position, Issues and Programs 1988, Adult Education and Women 1989, European Issues for Staff Development 1991, Adult Education in Europe: Future Issues 1992. *Leisure interest:* gardening. *Address:* European Bureau of Adult Education, 32 Hallam Gate Rd, Sheffield S10 5BS, UK. *Telephone:* (161) 247-2001; *Fax:* (161) 247-6327; *E-mail:* k.l.oglesby@mmu.ac.uk.

ÖGRÜK, S. Özden; Turkish cartoonist; b 7 Feb 1955, Istanbul; m Galip Takin 1981 (divorced). *Education:* Art Inst of Istanbul. *Career:* Currently caricaturist for weekly comic-strip magazine Girgir; played in first women's football team in Istanbul 1968–72; Successful Pencil Award for the Most Renowned Caricaturist 1989. *Publication:* Çilgin Bediş (comic-strip album) 1987. *Leisure interest:* travelling to exotic and seldom-visited places. *Address:* Ihlamurdere Cad 148, D7, Beşiktaş, Istanbul, Turkey. *Telephone:* (1) 1603756.

OH, May Buong Yo Lau; Singaporean business executive and lawyer; b 20 May 1940, Singapore; d of Hu Liu Lau Cung Liu Hu; m Siew Leong Oh 1965; two c. *Education:* Anglo Chinese Jr Coll. *Career:* Barrister-at-Law, Lincoln's Inn, London 1964; called to the Bar, UK 1965, Singapore 1967; Advocate and Solicitor Supreme Court of Singapore 1967; Specialist American and int corp law, transactions, accounting and taxation; Legal Asst Lee and Lee 1966–67; Legal Officer Housing and Devt Bd 1967; Asst Man Mobil Oil Malaysia 1967, Co Sec 1968; Legal Counsel Mobil East, New York 1970, Mobil Europe, London 1970; Gen Counsel Mobil Oil Singapore 1970, Exec Dir (first Asian) 1971, Head of Govt Affairs 1973, Dir Legal and Govt Affairs for Singapore, Malaysia and Thailand 1973–84; Dir Mobil Asia 1974–84; Partner May Oh and Co 1984; Sr Partner May Oh and Wee Advocates and Solicitors 1985; mem Advisory Bd Int Comparative Law Center, Dallas, TX, USA; Chair Int Energy Confs in Asia 1984–86, 1988; mem American Inst of Man, Council Fellow 1981; mem Singapore Law Soc, Singapore Econ Soc, Singapore American Business Council, Int Bar Asscn, Law Asscn for Asia and Western Pacific. *Address:* May Oh and Wee, 21 Collyer Quay No 14-02, Hong Kong Bank Bldg, Singapore 0104, Singapore (Office); 27 Ewart Park, Singapore 1027, Singapore (Home).

O'HARA, Maureen (pseudonym of Maureen FitzSimons); American actress; b 17 Aug 1921, Dublin; m Charles Blair (deceased). *Education:* Abbey School of Acting and London Coll of Music. *Career:* Film debut in USA in Jamaica Inn 1939. *Films include:* My Irish Molly 1938, Jamaica Inn 1939, The Hunchback of Notre Dame, How Green Was My Valley, Ten Gentlemen from West Point, The Black Swan, The Fallen Sparrow, Buffalo Bill, Sentimental Journey, Miracle on 34th Street, Sinbad the Sailor, Sitting Pretty, Forbidden Street, Bagdad, Rio Grande, Quiet Man, Redhead from Wyoming, Fire over Africa, Lady Godiva, Everything But the Truth, Wings of Eagles, Our Man in Havana, The Parent Trap, Mr Hobbs Takes a Vacation, McLintock, Spencer's Mountain, Big Jake 1971, Only the Lonely 1991; *TV appearances include:* The Red Pony (film), Mrs Miniver, Spellbound, High Button Shoes, Who's Afraid of Mother Goose. *Address:* c/o Charles FitzSimons, 11445 Berwick St, Los Angeles, CA 90049, USA.

OHM, Kirsten; Norwegian diplomatist; b 27 Sept 1930, Narvik; d of Karsten and Dagny Marie Ohm. *Education:* Univ of Oslo, LSE (UK), Bryn Mawr Coll (USA) and Diplomatic School, Ministry of Foreign Affairs (Oslo). *Career:* Sec, Paris 1961–64, Counsellor 1972–75; Norwegian Del to the UN 1964–67; Counsellor Ministry of Foreign Affairs 1967–72, Special Adviser on Human Rights 1982–87; Amb to the Council of Europe, Strasbourg, France 1975–82, to Ireland 1988–92; Chevalier de la Légion d'Honneur 1962; Commdr of the Order of St Olav 1989; has written articles on int orgs and European co-operation. *Leisure interests:* walking, bird-watching, literature, stamps. *Address:* c/o Ministry of Foreign Affairs, 7 juni pl 1, POB 8114 Dep, 0032 Oslo, Norway.

OHTA, Tomoko, PH D; Japanese geneticist; b 7 Sept 1933, Miyoshi; d of Mamoru and Hatsu Harada; m Yasuo Ohta 1960 (divorced 1972); one d. *Education:* Univ of Tokyo and N Carolina State Univ (USA). *Career:* Researcher Kihara Inst for Biological Research 1958–62; Research mem Nat Inst of Genetics, Mishima 1967–69, Researcher 1969–76, Assoc Prof 1976–84, Prof 1984–97, Prof Emer 1997–, Head Dept of Population Genetics 1988–97; Vice-Pres Soc for the Study of Evolution 1994; mem Editorial Bd scientific journals; Foreign Hon mem American Acad of Arts and Sciences, Fellow 2000; Saruhashi Prize for Bright Future Women Scientists 1981; Japan Acad Prize 1985; Weldon Memorial Prize Univ of Oxford, UK 1986. *Publication:* Evolution and Variation of Multigene Families, Lecture Notes in Biomathematics Vol 37 1980. *Leisure interest:* reading. *Address:* National Institute of Genetics, 1111 Yata, Mishima 411-8540, Japan (Office); 20-20 Hatsunedai, Mishima-shi, Shizuoka-ken, Mishima 411-0018, Japan (Home). *Telephone:* (559) 72-4638 (Home); *Fax:* (559) 72-4638 (Home); *E-mail:* tohta@lab.nig.ac.jp (Office).

OJUN, Eredenebatiin, PH D; Mongolian theatre producer and writer; b 27 Dec 1918, Ulan Bator; d of Erdenebat and Tsetseg; m Col Purev 1935 (died 1951); one s one d. *Education:* Mongolian State Univ. *Career:* Trans, Asst Theatre Producer 1934–52, Theatre Producer 1957–80; now retd, researching into the history of the theatre; State Prize Laureate 1946; title of People's Actress conferred 1959. *Publications:* Plays: I don't go there, The Love, My Beautiful Mother; has written more than ten plays and 30 short stories, and translated over 40 plays into Mongolian. *Leisure interest:* reading. *Address:* State Drama Theatre, Ulan Bator, Mongolia; Central Post Office, POB 265, Ulan Bator, Mongolia.

OKAMOTO, Ayako; Japanese golfer; b 2 April 1951, Hiroshima; d of Shoichi and Tsuzuko Okamoto. *Education:* Imbari Meitoku High School (Ehime Prefecture). *Career:* Mem Japan Ladies' Professional Golf Asscn (JLPGA) 1975–; joined United States Ladies' Professional Golf Asscn (USLPGA) Tour 1981; JLPGA Money Queen 1981; USLPGA Money Queen 1987; has won 35 tournaments in Japan, 17 in USA and one in Europe (1996); Japan Prime Minister's Award (for contribution to encouraging and developing sports in Japan) 1987. *Leisure interests:* reading, listening to music, fishing. *Address:* PG Planning USA, Inc, 23307 Adolph Ave, Torrance, CA 90505, USA. *Telephone:* (310) 373-7619; *Fax:* (310) 373-5507.

O'KANE, Maggie, BA; Irish journalist; b 8 June 1962, Ardglas, Co Down, NI; d of Peter O'Kane and Maura McNeil; m John Mullin 1995; one s. *Education:* Loreto Convent (Balbriggan, Co Dublin), Univ Coll Dublin, Coll de Journalistes en Europe (Paris) and Coll of Commerce (Dublin). *Career:* Reporter on Irish TV 1982–84, Sunday Tribune newspaper, Dublin 1984–87; Reporter, TV Producer and Presenter 1987–89; Foreign Corresp and Feature Writer, The Guardian newspaper 1989–, covered revolutions in Eastern Europe 1989–91, the Gulf War (one of 32 int journalists to remain in Baghdad in Jan 1991) and post-war refugee crisis in Kurdistan 1991–92, civil war in the fmr Yugoslavia 1992–94, Bosnia, the US occupation of Haiti and problems in Cuba 1994–96, Afghanistan, Cambodia, Kosovo, Yugoslavia 2000; writer and Presenter Channel 4 TV documentary for the fifth anniversary of the Gulf War, BBC TV documentary on Haiti post-Aristide 1995, Channel 4 Frontline documentary Bloody Bosnia (Documentary of the Year, Royal TV Soc) 1994, The Face of Debt (Channel 4) 1999, Kosovo and E Timor 2000, Burma and The Hague 2001; Journalist of the Year 1992; Foreign Corresp of the Year 1993; Reporter of the Year (commended) 1994; Amnesty Int Foreign Corresp of the Year 1994; James Cameron Award for Journalism 1996. *Publications:* A Woman's World: Beyond the Headlines 1996, Mozambique. *Leisure interests:* swimming, cooking, running, walking, reading. *Address:* The Guardian, 119 Farringdon Rd, London EC1R 3ER, UK. *Telephone:* (20) 7278-2332; *E-mail:* maggie.okane@guardian.co.uk.

OKOSHI, Sumiye; American artist; b 26 April 1921, Seattle, WA; d of Masanari and Riyoko (née Fukuda) Ushiyama; m George Mukai 1976. *Education:* Rikkyo Jogakuin Univ (Tokyo), Univ of Seattle and Henry Fry Museum of Modern Art (Seattle). *Career:* Abstract artist specializing in paper on canvas; solo exhibitions include Gallery Int, New York 1970, Miami Museum of Modern Art 1970, Westbeth Courtyard Gallery, New York 1972, Galerie Salson, Tokyo 1982, Living Room Gallery, New York 1987, Viridian Gallery, New York 1987, Port Washington Public Library 1989; group exhibitions include Metropolitan Museum of Art, New York 1977, World Trade Center, New York 1979, Tokyo Nat Museum 1979, Pace Univ Gallery, New York 1981, Joslyn Center for Arts, CA, Newark Museum 1983, Bergen Museum of Art and Sciences 1983, American Acad of Arts and Sciences 1984, Nassau Community Coll 1985–86, Ann Javits Fed Bldg 1986, São Paulo and New York Culture Exchange 1988, Hyndai Gallery, Korea 1988; rep in perm collections including Miami Museum of Modern Art, Lowe Gallery, Univ of Miami, Port Washington Public Library, Nat Women's Educ Center, Japan, Nat Acad of Science, Washington, DC; mem Japanese Artists' Asscn, New York, Nat Women Artists' Asscn; recipient Belle Crimer Award 1986, Ziutal and Joseph Akston Award 1989, Ralph

Mayor Memorial Award 1991. *Leisure interests:* drawing, music, travel. *Address:* 55 Bethune St, Studio G226, New York, NY 10014, USA. *Telephone:* (212) 924-1167.

OKSAAR, Els, D PHIL; German professor of linguistics; b 1 Oct 1926, Pernau (now Estonia); d of Juhan and Luise (née Anderson) Järv; m Arved Oksaar 1947; one s. *Career:* Mem staff Univ of Stockholm, then Univ of Hamburg 1965–, Prof of Gen and Comparative Linguistics 1967–; Guest Prof ANU, Canberra, ACT 1967; Fellow Wissenschaftskolleg, Berlin 1987–88; Guest Lecturer USA, Asia, Australia; Pres Int Asscn for the Study of Child Language; Vice-Pres Int Soc of Applied Socio-Linguistics 1982–85; mem Finnish Acad of Sciences 1979–, Soc Royale des Lettres de Lund (Sweden); Fellow Japanese Soc for the Promotion of Science 1979; Dr hc (Helsinki) 1986, (Linköping, Sweden) 1987 (Tartu, Estonia) 1996; Research Prize, Immigrant Inst, Sweden; Konrad Duden Prize (Mannheim); Essay Prize, Deutsche Akad für Sprache und Dichtung; Research Prize, Stiftelsen Språk och Kultur (Sweden). *Publications:* Semantische Studien im Sinnbereich der Schnelligkeit 1958, Mittelhochdeutsch 1965, Berufsbezeichnungen im heutigen Deutsch: soziosemantische Untersuchungen 1976, Spracherwerb im Vorschulalter (2nd edn, trans to English and Japanese) 1987, Fachsprachliche Dimensionen 1988, Kulturemtheorie, ein Beitrag zur Sprachverwendungsforschung (trans to Korean) 1988 Sprache und Gesellschaft 1992, Mehrsprachigkeit bei Kindern—eine Chance, kein Hindernis (4th edn) 1996; ed and jt ed of numerous books and journals. *Leisure interest:* music. *Address:* Parkberg 20, 2000 Hamburg, Germany. *Telephone:* (40) 6070803.

OLDENBOURG, Zoé; French (b Russian) writer; b 31 March 1916, Petrograd (now St Petersburg); d of Sergius Oldenbourg and Ada Starynkevitch; m Heinic Idalie 1948; one s one d. *Education:* Lycée Molière and Univ of Paris (Sorbonne). *Career:* Writer 1925–; mem Jury of Prix Fémina 1961–; Commdr de l'Ordre Nat du Mérite, Commdr des Arts et des Lettres 1980; Chevalier de la Légion d'Honneur 1986. *Publications:* Argile et cendres 1946, La pierre angulaire (Prix Fémina) 1953, Bûcher de Montségur 1956, Les brûlés 1957, Les cités charnelles 1961, Les Croisades 1960, Catherine de Russie 1961, Saint Bernard 1969, L'épopée des cathédrales 1973, La joie des pauvres 1975, Que vous a donc fait Israël? 1976, Visages d'un autoportrait 1977, La joie-souffrance 1980, Le procès du rêve 1982, L'évêque et la vieille dame 1983, Que nous est Hécube? 1984, Les amours égarées 1988, Déguisements 1989, Aliénor 1992. *Leisure interests:* painting, manual work. *Address:* 4 rue de Montmorency, 92100 Boulogne-Billancourt, France. *Telephone:* (1) 48-25-35-96.

O'LEARY, Hazel R., BA; American politician and lawyer; b 17 May 1937, Newport News, VA; d of Russell Ried and Hazel Palleman; m John F. O'Leary 1980 (deceased); one s. *Education:* Fisk Univ (Nashville, TN) and Rutgers State Univ (NJ). *Career:* Fmr prosecutor, then Asst Attorney-Gen, NJ; fmr Vice-Pres and Gen Counsel O'Leary Assocs (consultants on energy econs and planning) 1981–89, Pres O'Leary and Assocs 1997–2000; COO Blaylock & Partners, New York 2000–; fmr mem staff Dept of Energy and Fed Energy Admin; joined Northern States Power Co, MN 1989, subsequently Exec Vice-Pres; Sec of Energy 1993–97; Democrat. *Address:* Blaylock & Partners L P, 609 Fifth Ave, New York, NY 10017, USA.

OLESEN, Aase; Danish politician; b 24 Sept 1934, Horsens; d of Eigill and Erna (née Nielsen) Larsen; m Tormod Olesen 1954; one s one d. *Career:* Teacher 1956–58; housewife 1958–70; Co-owner architectural practice 1970–; mem Folketing (Parl) 1974–77, 1979–90; mem Exec Cttee and Gen Council Radical Liberal Party 1986, Sec to Parl Group 1980–90; Chair Parl Social Cttee 1987–88; Minister of Social Affairs 1988–90; Chair Bd Arbejdsmarkedets Feriefond, Kofoeds Skole, Videnscenter for Aeldreområdet and Raadet for Social-og sundkeds uddannelserne. *Address:* Ndr Strandvej 254B, 3140 Aalsgaarde, Denmark (Office). *Telephone:* 4970-7645 (Home); *Fax:* 4970-7651 (Home); *E-mail:* aao@email.dk (Home).

OLESEN, Dorte Marianne, PH D, D SC; Danish mathematician; b 8 Jan 1948, Hillerød; d of Knud H. and Irene M. (née Pedersen) Olesen; m Gert K. Pedersen 1971; two s one d. *Education:* Univ of Copenhagen. *Career:* Academic Sec Ministry of Educ 1974–76; Post-doctoral Fellow Univ of Copenhagen 1976–79, Lecturer in Maths 1980–88, Dean

Faculty of Natural Sciences 1986–88, apptd Dir Danish Computing Centre for Research and Educ 1989; mem Math Sciences Research Inc, Univ of California at Berkeley, USA 1984–85; Prof of Maths Roskilde Universitetscenter 1988–; mem Danish Council for Research Policy and Planning 1987–93; Gold Medal Univ of Copenhagen 1974; Tagea Brandt Award 1988; contribs to professional journals. *Leisure interests:* history, architecture. *Address:* Danish Computing Centre for Research and Educ, Vermundsgade 5, 2100 Copenhagen Ø, Denmark. *Telephone:* 35-87-88-89; *Fax:* 35-87-88-90.

OLIN, Lena Maria Jonna; Swedish actress; b 22 March 1955, Stockholm; d of Stig Olin and Britta Alice Holmberg; one c. *Career:* Mem Royal Dramatic Theatre, Stockholm; stage appearances include Miss Julie, New York; worked with film dir Ingmar Bergman. *Films include:* The Adventures of Picasso, Fanny and Alexander 1983, Grasanklingar, After the Rehearsal 1984, Friends, The Unbearable Lightness of Being 1988, Enemies, A Love Story (Acad Award nomination) 1989, Havana, Mr Jones, Romeo is Bleeding, The Night and the Moment, The Polish Wedding 1996, Night Falls on Manhattan 1997, The Ninth Gate 1999, Mystery Men 1999, Chocolat 2000; several TV appearances. *Address:* c/o ICM, 8942 Wilshire Blvd, Beverly Hills, CA 90211, USA.

OLIPHANT, Betty, CC; Canadian (b British) ballet dancer and teacher; b 5 Aug 1918, London, UK; d of Stuart and Yvonne (née Mansfield) Oliphant; two d. *Education:* Queen's Coll School (London), and studied ballet under Tamara Karsavina and Laurent Novikoff. *Career:* Moved to Canada 1947; est Betty Oliphant School of Ballet 1948–59; apptd Ballet Mistress Nat Ballet of Canada 1951, Assoc Artistic Dir 1969–75; Founder Nat Ballet School 1959, Dir and Prin 1959–89; reorganized Royal Swedish Opera Ballet School 1967, Royal Danish Ballet School 1978; fmr Guest Bolshoi and Kirov Ballet Schools, fmr USSR; Founder-mem Canadian Asscn of Professional Dance Orgs; Guest of Honour First Int Ballet Concours, Moscow 1969, mem Jury 1977, 1981; mem Jury Third US Int Ballet Competition, Jackson, MS 1986, Prix de Lausanne 1991; Fellow and Examiner Imperial Soc of Teachers of Dancing; Fellow Ontario Inst for Studies in Educ 1985; Hon LL D (Queen's and Brock) 1978, (Toronto) 1980; Hon D LITT (York); Hon Dip for Distinguished Service to the Arts in Canada, Canadian Conf of the Arts 1982; Molson Prize 1978; Nat Dance Award for Contrib to the Art of Dance in Canada, Canadian Dance Teachers Asscn 1981; Lifetime Achievement Award, Toronto Arts Awards Foundation 1989; Order of Napoleon, Maison Courvoisier, France 1990. *Publication:* Miss O: My Life In Dance (autobiog) 1996. *Leisure interests:* swimming, reading, music, film, theatre. *Address:* The National Ballet School, 105 Maitland St, Toronto, ON M4Y 1E4, Canada (Office); 137 Amelia St, Toronto, ON M4X 1E6, Canada (Home). *Telephone:* (416) 964-3780 (Office); *Fax:* (416) 964-3632 (Office).

OLIVOVÁ, Věra, PH D; Czech historian; b 13 Nov 1926, Prague; m Pavel Oliva 1949; one s one d. *Education:* Charles Univ (Prague). *Publications:* The Doomed Democracy 1972, Sports and Games in the Ancient World 1984. *Leisure interests:* literature, art. *Address:* Na Míč 18, 16000 Prague 6, Czech Republic. *Telephone:* (2) 3114715.

OLLERTON, Jacqueline, M SC; British information scientist/librarian; b 29 May 1945, Barnsley, Yorks; d of Jack and Kathleen Ollerton; m Owen Luder 1989. *Education:* Univ of Loughborough. *Career:* Librarian Farmer & Dark Architects/Engineers 1968–72; Sr Information Officer Polytechnic of Cen London 1972–73; Head of Information Services and Data Bank (ACCESS) GLC Dept of Architecture and Design 1974–79, Head of ACCESS 1979–80; Computing and New Tech Officer, Head of Technical Information, GLC Dir-Gen's Dept 1980–85; Information Man Institution of Mechanical Engineers 1985; articles in a variety of journals including Local Govt Chronicle, ASLIB Information, Eng News; Special Award, Library Asscn/FARRIES Public Relations and Publicity Award 1990; Assoc Library Asscn. *Leisure interests:* poetry, reading, art, swimming. *Address:* Institution of Mechanical Engineers, 1 Birdcage Walk, Westminster, London SW1H 9JJ, UK (Office); 2 Smith Square, Westminster, London SW1P 3HS, UK (Home). *Telephone:* (20) 7973-1260 (Office); *Fax:* (20) 7222-8762 (Office).

OLSZEWSKA, Maria Joanna, PH D; Polish professor of plant cytology and cyto-chemistry; b 21 April 1929, Dąbrówka Polska-Sanok; d of Tadeusz and Stefania (née Strzelbicka) Skwarczyński; m Wacław Olszewski 1948; one d. *Education:* School of Agronomy (Łódź) and Univ of Łódź. *Career:* Plant Physiology Asst School of Agronomy, Łódź 1949–50; Botany Asst Pedagogical Coll, Łódź 1950–53; mem staff Dept of Plant Cytology, Univ of Łódź 1953–, Asst Prof, Head Cyto-chemistry Lab 1961–69, Head Dept of Plant Cytology and Cyto-chemistry 1969–, Assoc Prof 1969–78, Prof 1978–; Head Dept of Plant Anatomy and Cytology, Marie Curie-Skłodowska Univ, Lublin 1961–65; elected to Polish Acad of Sciences (PAN) 1989; Polonia Restituta Cross (Third Class) 1972, (Second Class) 1990, (First Class) 1999; numerous scientific awards. *Publications:* Plant Cytology (in Polish) 1971, Topochemical Methods in Tissues (jtly) 1975, Methods of Chromosome Studies (jtly, co-ed) 1981, Fundamentals of Cell Biology (jtly, co-ed, 4th edn) 1992, Plant Cytogenetics 1999; numerous contribs to professional journals. *Leisure interests:* picking mushrooms, cats, reading. *Address:* Łódź University, Dept of Cytology and Cytochemistry, Banacha 12–16, 90-237 Łódź, Poland (Office); Wierzbowa 38, m 43, 90-245 Łódź, Poland (Home). *Telephone:* (42) 786493 (Home); *E-mail:* olszewsk@biol.uni.lodz.pl.

OMAN, Julia Trevelyan, CBE, FCSD, DES RCA; British designer; b 11 July 1930, London; d of Charles Chichele Oman and Joan Trevelyan; m Dr (now Sir) Roy Strong 1971. *Education:* Royal Coll of Art. *Career:* Designer BBC TV 1955–67, including TV film Alice in Wonderland 1966; theatre designs include Brief Lives, London and New York 1967, 1974, Forty Years On 1968, The Merchant of Venice 1970, Othello 1971, The Importance of Being Earnest, Burgtheater, Vienna 1976, The Wild Duck, Lyric, Hammersmith, London 1980, The Shoemaker's Holiday, Nat Theatre 1981, Separate Tables 1982, The Consul, Edinburgh and USA 1985, A Man for All Seasons, Chichester Festival and Savoy, London 1987; ballet designs include Enigma Variations, Royal Ballet, London 1968, Swan Lake, Boston Ballet, USA 1981, Nutcracker, Royal Ballet, London 1984; opera designs include Eugene Onegin, Royal Opera House, Covent Garden, London 1971, Un Ballo in Maschera, Hamburg, Germany 1973, La Bohème, Royal Opera House 1974, A Month in the Country, Royal Ballet, London 1976, Die Fledermaus, Royal Opera House 1977, Le Papillon, Pas-de-Deux 1977, Otello, Stockholm 1983, Arabella, Glyndebourne Opera 1984; film designs include The Charge of the Light Brigade (art dir) 1967, Laughter in the Dark (art dir) 1968, Julius Caesar (production designer) 1969; exhibitions include Samuel Pepys, Nat Portrait Gallery 1970, Hay Fever, Danish TV 1979; other designs include Mme Tussaud's Hall of Historical Tableaux, London 1979, The Bear's Quest for the Ragged Staff—A Spectacle, Warwick Castle 1981, Die Csárdasfürstin, Kassel, Germany 1982, The Best of Friends 1988; Dir Oman Productions Ltd; mem Dept Educ and Science Visiting Cttee, Royal Coll of Art 1980; Hon D LITT (Bristol) 1987; Silver Medal, Royal Coll of Art; Royal Scholar, Royal Coll of Art; elected Designer, Royal Coll of Art; Designer of the Year Award 1967; ACE Award for Best Art Dir, NCTA, USA 1983. *Publications:* Street Children (jtly) 1964, Elizabeth R (jtly) 1971, Mary Queen of Scots (jtly) 1972, The English Year (jtly) 1982, A Celebration of Gardens (jtly) 1991, A Country Life (jtly) 1994, Garden Party (jtly) 2000. *Address:* c/o Curtis Brown, 4th Floor, Haymarket House, London SW1Y 4SP, UK. *Telephone:* (20) 7396-6600; *Fax:* (20) 7396-0110.

OMAR, Dato Napsiah binti, M SC; Malaysian politician; b 21 April 1943; m (husband deceased). *Education:* ANU (Canberra) and Cornell Univ (New York). *Career:* Admin Officer Fed Land Devt Authority, Kuala Lumpur 1967–69; started Women's and Family Devt Programme 1967; Lecturer Agricultural Coll Malaya Serdang 1972; Co-ordinator Food Tech, Home and Food Tech Div, Agricultural Univ 1972–73, Deputy Head Dept of Home Tech 1973–76, Head Dept of Human Devt Studies 1978–80, Warden Fourth Residential Coll 1974–82; Assoc Prof Dept of Human Devt Studies 1981; Deputy Minister of Housing and Local Govt 1981–87; Minister of Public Enterprises 1988–90, of Nat Unity and Social Devt 1990–95; Sr mem Exec Council of Negri Sembilan State Govt; Chair Econ Bureau UMNO 1986–88, mem Exec Cttee UMNO Women Malaysia 1987–90, Deputy Leader 1995, Chair Unity Bureau, UMNO Malaysia 1987–90, mem Supreme Council UMNO; Chair Women's Inst of Man; Pres Malaysian Girl Guides.

Address: c/o Ministry of Public Enterprises, WISMA PKNS, 3rd Floor, Jalan Raja Lant, 50652 Kuala Lumpur, Malaysia. *E-mail:* admin@wim .p.o.my; *Internet:* www.jaring.my/wimnet/.

O'MARA WALSH, Eileen; Irish organization executive. *Career:* Co-Founder Irish Tourist Industry Confederation (ITIC) 1980s, Chair 1984–88, 1998; owns O'Mara Travel co; Chair Great Southern Hotels, Forbairt (govt-sponsored business and enterprise programme); Dir Aer Lingus PLC. *Address:* c/o Irish Tourist Industry Confederation, Alliance House, Adelaide St, Dún Laoghaire, Co Dublin, Ireland.

O'MEALLY-NELSON, Blossom, DIP ED, PH D; Jamaican foundation executive; b 6 Sept 1940, Retirement, St Elizabeth; d of Albert and Sybil Nelson; m Dudley Clifford Stokes (divorced); two s one d. *Education:* St Andrew High School and Univ of the West Indies Mona Campus. *Career:* Jamaica Library Services 1960–61; Missionary for Jamaica Baptist Union, Turks and Caicos Islands 1961–65; high school teacher 1968–78; Sr Lecturer, Dept Head Sam Sharpe Teachers' Coll 1978–84; Man Consultant Caribbean Applied Tech Centre 1984–87; Exec Dir Nat Devt Foundation of Jamaica 1987–94; Pres Virtual Corporations Ltd; Man Consultant Workforce Devt Consortium; Chair Jamaica Conservation and Devt Trust, Bd of Studies for Educ at Univ of the West Indies, Council Coll of Arts, Science and Tech; Pres Asscn of Devt Insts; Vice-Pres Nat Council on Small Business; mem Univ Council of Jamaica; Int Visitors' Fellowship, US Information Service 1990; has written numerous professional articles. *Leisure interests:* gardening, sewing, animal rights, social service activities. *Address:* Workforce Development Consortium, 39 Hope Rd, Kingston 5, Jamaica; Virtual Corporations Ltd, 62 Duke St, Kingston, Jamaica (Office); 12 Forest Glen, Forest Gardens, Kingston 19, Jamaica (Home). *Telephone:* 978-6797 (Workforce Devt Consortium); 922-6455/2271 (Virtual Corporations Ltd); 929-3812 (Home).

OMOROGBE, Oluyinka Osayame, LL M; Nigerian university lecturer and lawyer; b 21 Sept 1957, Ibadan; d of Samuel O. and Irene E. B. Ighodaro; m Allan Omorogbe 1984; one s one d. *Education:* Obafemi Awolowo Univ, Nigerian Law School (Lagos) and LSE (UK). *Career:* Nat Youth Service 1979–80; Pvt Legal Practitioner for Solomon Asemota and Co 1980–81; Lecturer Dept of Jurisprudence and Int Law, Univ of Benin 1983–90, Head of Dept 1988–89; Sr Lecturer Dept of Jurisprudence and Int Law, Univ of Lagos 1990–; Dir Centre for Petroleum, Environment and Devt Studies, Lagos 1996–; mem Exec Cttee Petroleum Energy and Mining Law Asscn of Nigeria 1986–, Int Bar Asscn, African Soc of Int and Comparative Law; Treas Nigerian Soc of Int Law 1994–97, Sec 1997–; has written numerous articles in int journals on petroleum and energy law, and on int econ law. *Leisure interests:* cooking, baking, handcrafts, doodling. *Address:* POB 9261, Ikeja, Lagos, Nigeria; POB 9261, Ikeja, Lagos, Nigeria. *Telephone:* (1) 822321 (Office).

ONAY, Gülsün; Turkish pianist; b 12 Sept 1954, Istanbul; d of Jochen and Gülen Reusch; m 1st Ersin Onay 1975 (divorced 1986); one s; m 2nd Norbert Schappacher 1987. *Education:* Conservatoire Nat Supérieure de Musique (Paris) and under Nadia Boulanger, Monique Haas, Pierre Sancan and Bernhard Ebert. *Career:* First concert at the age of six; appearances with Warsaw Philharmonic, Staatskapelle Dresden and Berlin Radio Symphony Orchestra, (Germany), Salzburg Mozarteum Orchestra (Austria), Tokyo Symphony, Japan Philharmonic and the Bavarian, Danish, Austrian and Finnish Radio Symphony Orchestras; winner numerous int competitions; Turkish State Artist since 1986; Dr hc (Bosphorus) 1988. *Recordings include:* Chopin—Debussy—Saygun 1990, Bartok—Saygun 1991. *Address:* c/o Schlossgasse 20, 7800 Freiburg, Germany.

O'NEAL, Tatum; American actress; b 5 Nov 1963, Los Angeles; d of Ryan O'Neal and Joanna Moore; m John McEnroe 1986 (separated); two s one d. *Career:* Debut in Paper Moon 1973. *Films include:* Paper Moon (Acad Award) 1973, The Bad News Bears 1976, Nickelodeon 1976, International Velvet 1978, Little Darlings 1980, Circle of Two 1980, Certain Fury 1985, Little Noises 1992, Basquiat 1996; TV appearances in 15, Getting Straight. *Address:* c/o Innovative Artists, 1999 Ave of the Stars, Suite 2850, Century City, CA 90067, USA.

O'NEILL OF BENGARVE, Baroness (Life Peer), cr 1999, of The Braid in the County of Antrim, **Onora Sylvia O'Neill,** CBE, PH D, FBA; British philosopher and college principal; b 23 Aug 1941, Aughafatten, NI; d of the late Sir Con O'Neill and of Lady Garvey (née Rosemary Pritchard); m Edward Nell 1963 (divorced 1976); two s. *Education:* St Paul's Girls' School (London), Somerville Coll (Oxford) and Harvard Univ (USA). *Career:* Asst Prof Barnard Coll, Columbia Univ, USA 1970–76, Assoc Prof 1976–77; Lecturer Univ of Essex 1977–78, Sr Lecturer 1978–82, Reader 1982–87, Prof 1987–92; Prin Newnham Coll, Cambridge 1992–; Chair Nuffield Foundation 1998–, Human Genetics Advisory Cttee 1997–99; Dr hc (E Anglia) 1995, (Essex) 1996, (Nottingham) 1999. *Publications:* Faces of Hunger: An Essay on Poverty, Development and Justice 1986, Constructions of Reason: Explorations of Kant's Practical Philosophy, Towards Justice and Virtue: A Contrastive Account of Practical Reasoning 1996. *Leisure interests:* walking, talking. *Address:* Newnham College, Cambridge CB3 9DF, UK. *Telephone:* (1223) 330469; *Fax:* (1223) 359155.

ONER, Gulsen, MD, PH D; Turkish professor of physiology; b 3 Jan 1944, Kemah, Erzincan. *Education:* Univ of Istanbul and Hacettepe Univ. *Career:* Asst Prof, Surgical Research Centre, Hacettepe Medical School 1972–76, Assoc Prof and Sr Researcher 1976–85; Asst Prof Medical Research Centre, Univ Coll Hosp (London) 1976; Assoc Prof and Sr Researcher Dept of Pharmacology, Univ of Calgary 1980, Dept of Endocrinology, Univ of Saskatchewan 1981–82; Prof of Physiology, Head Dept of Physiology and Biophysics and Dir Medical Research Centre, Antalya Medical School. *Publications:* over 50 scientific medical publs on endocrinology, serology and allergy diseases. *Address:* Antalya Medical School, Akdeniz University, Antalya, Turkey. *Telephone:* (242) 227-52-66; *Fax:* (242) 227-55-40; *E-mail:* webmaster@akdeniz.edu.tr; *Internet:* www.akdeniz.edu.tr.

ONGG, Judy, BA; Japanese actress, singer and woodcut artist; b 24 Jan 1950, Taipei, Taiwan; d of Pin Y. and Yun Ngo Ongg; m H. Suzuki 1991. *Education:* American School (Tokyo) and Sophia Univ Int Div (Tokyo). *Career:* Joined Himawari Theatre 1960; film and TV debuts 1961; has starred in Chinese and Japanese films, TV shows and plays, nat and int variety shows, and made 50 records; host World Popular Song Festival 1975–89; Amb of Friendship UNICEF Japan Aqua Aid Project 1987; Producer Judy Collection (fashion) and Pres Heemory Co and Judy Ongg Tennis Classic Tournament; Organizer Great Wall Peace Project for 1995; Order of Brightness Medal, People's Repub of China; other awards include Best Actress in a Leading Role Award (Golden Horse, Asian Film Festival) 1972, Special Performance Award (19th Annual Asia Film Festival) 1973, Best Actress in a TV Drama Series (Kyoto Film Festival) 1974, Golden Canary Award (Tokyo Music Festival) 1979, Best Vocalist of the Year (Japanese Recording Acad) 1979; 3 Feb designated Judy Ongg Day, NV, USA 1990. *Plays include:* Hobson's Choice 1983, The World of Suzie Wong 1984, Fiddler on the Roof 1985, Roots 1987; *TV appearances include:* Story of a Boy Called Santa 1961, Judy Ongg Talk Show 1967–70, Young 720 (talk show) 1967–71; That's Music 1983; *Films include:* The Big Wave 1961, Goodbye Mr Tears 1968, Forgive, Forgot, Forgotten 1974; *Recordings include:* Tasogare no Akai Tsuki (Red Moon at Dusk) 1967, Miserarete (Enchanted—single, Gold Disk of Nihon Record Award) 1979, Oshin (theme music, Golden Record Grand Prix, Hong Kong) 1988; *Woodcut prints include:* Fuyunohi (First Prize Japan Fine Art Acad) 1983, Abura-ya II (Second Prize Japan Fine Art Acad) 1984, Ageya (Third Prize Japan Fine Art Acad) 1985, Iris 1987; *Publications:* Enchanted (essays) 1981, Judy's Healthy Food 1988, My Grandfather (fiction) 1991. *Leisure interests:* tennis, horse-riding, Chi-Kong (Chinese Kung-Fu), woodcut printing, travel, books. *Telephone:* (3) 3265-7895; *Fax:* (3) 3265-7896.

ONKELINX, Laurette, LL B; Belgian politician; b 2 Oct 1958, Ougrée; d of Gaston and Germaine (née Ali Bakir) Onkelinx; m Abbés Guenned 1987. *Education:* Univ of Liège. *Career:* Barrister-at-Law, Liège 1981; teacher of Admin Science 1982–85; mem (Parti Socialiste (PS)) Chamber of Reps (Parl) 1987, apptd Vice-Pres PS Group 1989; mem Council of French Community 1989; Pres Interfed Comm of Socialist Women; Chair Interfed Comm of Socialist Women; Vice-Chair Socialist Group, House of Reps; Chair Justice Cttee, House of Reps; Vice-Pres House of Reps; Minister for Social Integration, Health and Environment 1992–93; Minister-Pres in Govt of Communauté fran-

çaise in charge of Civil Service, Childhood and Promotion of Health 1993–95, Minister-Pres in charge of Educ, Audio-visual, Youth Help and Promotion of Health 1995–99; Deputy Prime Minister and Minister for Employment July 1999–; special interest in justice, consumer rights and the environment; Pres Ougrée Medical Home, Medical Service Village for the Disabled. *Publications include:* Continuons le débat, Théâtre du jeune public. *Address:* Ministry of Employment and Labour, Belliardstraat 51–53, rue Belliard, 1040 Brussels, Belgium. *Telephone:* (2) 233-51-11; *Fax:* (2) 230-10-67.

ONO, Yoko; American conceptual artist and singer; b 18 Feb 1933, Tokyo, Japan; m 1st John Lennon 1969 (died 1980); two s; m 2nd Samuel Havadtoy. *Education:* Student Peers School, Gakushuin and Harvard Univs. *Career:* Solo exhibitions include Albert Hall, London 1967, Birmingham 1968 and Univ of Wales (UK) 1969, Everson Museum, Syracuse, NY 1971, Budapest 1992, Royal Festival Hall, London 1997; group exhibitions include School of Art, Falmouth (UK) 1972; opened art gallery in Budapest (jtly) 1992; scriptwriter; composer of film scores. *Recordings:* With John Lennon: Two Virgins 1968, Life With Lions 1969, Wedding Album 1970, Live Peace in Toronto 1970, Some Time in New York City 1972, Double Fantasy (Grammy Album of the Year 1981) 1980, Milk and Honey 1984; Solo recordings: Yoko Ono/Plastic Ono Band, Fly, Approximately Infinite Universe, Feeling the Space, Season of Glass, Starpeace 1985, Walking on Thin Ice (Grammy nomination 1981), Don't Be Sad, Rising; *Video film:* Then and Now 1990; *Publications include:* Grapefruit 1964, John Lennon: Summer of 1980 1984, Acorns 1996. *Address:* c/o John Hendricks, 488 Greenwich St, New York, NY 10013, USA.

ONO, Yuriko; Japanese politician; b 20 Jan 1942, Osaka; m 1971; one s one d. *Education:* Kyoto Univ. *Career:* Joined Ushio publishing co 1971; mem House of Reps (Parl, Komeito, Clean Govt Party) 1990, mem Party Subcttee on Consumers and Prices 1990, Party Health and Welfare Subcttee 1990; Dir Party Women's Bureau. *Leisure interests:* reading, swimming. *Address:* 27-32, Kamirenjyaku 5-chome, Mitaka-shi, Tokyo, 181, Japan (Home). *Fax:* (3) 3592-9062 (Home).

ONODI, Henrietta; Hungarian gymnast; b 22 May 1974, Békéscsaba. *Career:* Came fourth jr beam competition European Championship, Karlsruhe, Germany 1986; Came second jr bars European Championship, Avignon, France 1988; First bars European Championship, Brussels 1989; Third gen and floor European Championship, Athens 1990; First horse, Second floor World Cup, Brussels 1990; Second horse World Championship, Indianapolis, USA 1991; First horse, Second floor World Championship, Paris 1992; jt Gold Medallist vault, Silver Medallist floor Barcelona Olympic Games, Spain 1992; scholarship to Univ of Minnesota. *Address:* c/o 5600 Békéscsaba, Szerdahelyi út 7.II.7, Hungary.

OOMEN-RUIJTEN, Maria; Netherlands politician; b 6 Sept 1950, Echt. *Career:* Mem Second Chamber of the States-Gen (Parl, CDA) 1981–; elected MEP (PPE) 1989, mem Cttees on Social Affairs, Employment and the Working Environment 1989–99. *Address:* c/o European Parliament, rue Wiertz, 1047 Brussels, Belgium.

OPIE, Iona Margaret Balfour, CBE, FBA; British writer and folklorist; b 13 Oct 1923; d of the late Sir Robert Archibald and Olive Cant; m Peter Mason Opie 1943 (died 1982); two s one d. *Education:* Sandecotes School (Parkstone). *Career:* Served with meteorological section of Women's Auxiliary Air Force (WAAF) 1941–43; writer and folklorist 1947–; Hon mem Folklore Soc 1974; Hon MA (Oxon) 1962, (Open) 1987; Hon D LITT (Southampton) 1987, (Nottingham) 1991; jt recipient Coote-Lake Medal 1960. *Publications:* I Saw Esau (jtly) 1947, The Oxford Dictionary of Nursery Rhymes (jtly) 1951, The Oxford Nursery Rhyme Book (jtly) 1955, Christmas Party Games (jtly) 1957, The Lore and Language of Schoolchildren (jtly) 1959, Puffin Book of Nursery Rhymes (jtly, European Prize City of Caorle, Italy) 1963, Children's Games in Street and Playground (jtly, Chicago Folklore Prize) 1969, The Oxford Book of Children's Verse (jtly) 1973, The Classic Fairy Tales (jtly) 1974, A Nursery Companion (jtly) 1980, The Oxford Book of Narrative Verse 1983, The Singing Game (Katharine Briggs Folklore Award, Rose Mary Crawshay Prize, Children's Literature Asscn Book Award) 1985, Tail Feathers From Mother Goose 1988, The Treasures of Childhood (co-ed) 1989, A Dictionary of

Superstitions 1989, Babies: an unsentimental anthology (jtly) 1990, The People in the Playground 1993, My Very First Mother Goose 1996, Here Comes Mother Goose 1999. *Leisure interest:* opsimathy. *Address:* Mells House, Farnham Rd, W Liss, Hants GU33 6JQ, UK. *Telephone:* (1730) 893309.

OPIE, Lisa, MBE; British squash player; b 15 Aug 1963, Guernsey, Channel Islands; d of Rex and Robina (née Waller) Opie. *Education:* Blanchelande Convent Coll (St Martin's, Guernsey). *Career:* Began playing squash at the age of 11, turned professional at 17; has won four nat titles and played for England over 50 times; Capt England winning team World Championships 1989; winner British Open competition 1991; ranked no three in the world 1992; Squash Rackets Asscn Player of the Year 1991; Runner-Up Sports Writers' Awards 1992. *Leisure interests:* sport, cooking, art, listening to music. *Address:* Flat 1B, Newcastle Drive, The Park, Nottingham NG7 1AA, UK.

OPPENHEIM, Martha Kunkel, MUS M; American pianist; b 25 June 1935, Port Arthur, TX; d of Samuel Adam and Grace (née Moncure) Kunkel; m Russell Edward Oppenheim 1960; two d. *Education:* Univ of Texas, Juilliard School of Music (New York) and American Conservatory (Fontainebleau, France). *Career:* Piano soloist Amarillo Symphony, Austin Symphony, Univ of Texas Orchestra, San Antonio Symphony and Dallas Symphony TX and Heilbronner Kammer Orchestra, Germany; recitals in Texas, New York and France; mem Halcyon Trio 1974–77; Asst Teacher Univ of Texas 1957–59, 1968–69; pvt teacher 1962–; mem Music Teachers Nat Asscn, Texas Music Teachers Asscn, San Antonio Music Teachers Asscn; winner of numerous local, nat and int competitions. *Address:* 9118 E Valley View Lane, San Antonio, TX 78217, USA.

OPPENHEIM-BARNES, Baroness (Life Peer), cr 1989, of Gloucester in the County of Gloucestershire, **Sally Oppenheim-Barnes,** PC; British politician and executive; b 26 July 1930, Dublin, Ireland; d of Mark and Jeanette Viner; m 1st Henry M. Oppenheim (died 1980); two d one s; m 2nd John Barnes 1984. *Education:* Sheffield High School and Lowther Coll (N Wales). *Career:* Fmr Exec Dir Industrial & Investment Services Ltd; fmr Social Worker, School Care Dept Inner London Educ Authority; MP (Cons) for Gloucester 1970–87; Vice-Chair Cons Party Parl Prices and Consumer Protection Cttee 1971–73, Chair 1973–74; Opposition Spokesperson on Prices and Consumer Protection 1974–79; mem Shadow Cabinet 1975–79; Minister of State for Consumer Affairs, Dept of Trade 1979–82; Non-Exec Dir and mem Main Bd, Boots Co PLC 1982–93, HFC Bank PLC 1989–98, Fleming High Income Trust 1989–97; fmr Nat Vice-Pres Nat Union of Townswomen's Guilds 1973–79, 1989–90; Pres Glos Dist Br British Red Cross Soc 1973–; Chair Nat Consumer Council 1987–89, Man Council, Nat Waterways Museums Trust 1988–89. *Publication:* Oppenheim Report on pedestrian safety at level crossings 1986. *Leisure interests:* tennis, bridge, theatre. *Address:* House of Lords, London SW1A 0PW, UK (Office); Quietways, The Highlands, Painswick, Glos GL6 6SL, UK (Home). *Telephone:* (20) 7219-3000 (Office).

ORBACH, Susie, BA, PH D; British/American psychotherapist and writer; b 6 Nov 1946, London; d of Maurice Orbach and Ruth Huebsch; partner Joseph Schwartz; one d one s. *Education:* City Univ of New York, Stony Brook Univ (USA) and Univ Coll London (UK). *Career:* Psychotherapist 1972–; Co-Founder Women's Therapy Centre, London 1976; Co-Founder Women's Therapy Centre Inst, New York 1981; columnist The Guardian newspaper 1991–99; consultant World Bank; Co-Founder ANTIDOTE, Psychotherapists and Counsellors for Social Responsibilities; Master of Social Work. *Publications:* Fat is a Feminist Issue 1976, Fat is a Feminist Issue II 1982, Understanding Women (jtly) 1982, What Do Women Want (jtly) 1983, Bittersweet (jtly) 1986, Hungerstrike 1985, What's Really Going On Here 1994, The Impossibility of Sex 1999, Towards Emotional Literacy 1999, On Eating 2001. *Address:* 2 Lancaster Drive, London NW3 4HA, UK. *E-mail:* susieorbach@aol.com.

ORBETZOVA, Verbka Tzekova, D MED; Bulgarian politician and professor of chemical pathology; b 4 Dec 1938, Popitza, Vratsa; d of Tzeko Peev Dankov and Maria T. (née Ivanova) Dankova; m Mitko Angelov Orbetzov 1972; one s one d. *Education:* Medical Acad (Sofia). *Career:* Paediatrician Byala Slatina Dist Hosp 1962–66; Research Fellow

Bulgarian Acad of Sciences 1969–76; Assoc Prof Medical Acad, Sofia 1976–84, apptd Prof of Chemical Pathology 1984; apptd Chief Cen Clinical Lab Dept, Medical Faculty, Univ of Sofia 1984; mem Narodno Sobraniye (Nat Ass, Bulgarian Socialist Party—fmrly Bulgarian Communist Party) 1990, Pres Medical Educ Sub-Comm; mem Bulgarian Socialist Party Cen Cttee 1990–91, Scientific Council of Bulgaria; Excellent Physician Award, Ministry of Health 1985. *Publications:* NAD/NADH Redox System in the Conditions of Keto-acidosis 1969, Lipoprotein Metabolism and its Regulation in Atherogenic and Antiatherogenic Conditions of Resistent and Atherosclerosis-prone Animals 1979. *Leisure interests:* folk medicine, investigation of paranormal phenomena, charity work. *Address:* National Assembly, 1000 Sofia, pl Narodno Sobraniye 3, Bulgaria (Office); 1505 Sofia, bul Christo Kabaktchiev 41, b2, Bulgaria (Home). *Telephone:* (2) 85-01 (Office); (2) 43-00-65 (Home).

O'REGAN, Katherine Victoria, JP; New Zealand politician; b 24 May 1946, Te Mata; m Michael Cox 1992; one s one d. *Education:* Hamilton Girls' High School. *Career:* Fmr nurse and Pharmacy Asst; mem Waipa Co Council (first woman) 1977–84; elected mem House of Reps (Parl, NZ Nat Party) for Waipa 1984, fmr Opposition Spokesperson for Consumer Affairs, Statistics, Women's Affairs and Family Issues; Minister of Consumer Affairs, Assoc Minister of Health, Assoc Minister of Women's Affairs and Assoc Minister for Social Welfare, responsible for community funding 1990–; Rep of Nat Opposition to Commonwealth Parl Asscn, Australia 1985, China–NZ Del 1985; has taken part in speaking tours of Indonesia, Repub of Korea, Japan, Israel and Geneva (Inter-Parl Union Women's Symposium); mem Bd Nat Soc for Alcohol and Drug Addiction. *Leisure interests:* reading, art, music, tennis. *Address:* Parliament Bldgs, POB 1473, Wellington, New Zealand (Office); 1856 Rewi St, Te Awamutu, New Zealand (Home). *Telephone:* (4) 742-750 (Office); (7) 871-7397 (Home); *Fax:* (7) 871-7414 (Home).

O'REILLY, Sheila; British administrator. *Career:* Sec-Gen Commonwealth Countries League. *Address:* Commonwealth Countries League, 14 Thistleworth Close, Isleworth, Middlesex TW7 4QQ, UK. *Telephone:* (20) 8737-3572.

ORESHONKOVA, Anna Vladimirovna, PH D; Belarusian philologist; b 21 Nov 1928, Nesviz, Novogrudok region; d of Vladimir Vikentievich Kvyatkovsky and Adelia Frantsevna Kvyatkovska; m Pyotr Dmitrievich Oreshonkov 1951; one s one d. *Education:* Belarusian State Univ and Acad of Sciences of Belarus. *Career:* Jr Researcher Inst of Linguistics, Acad of Sciences of Belarus 1959–63, Sr Researcher since 1967; Reader, Russian Language Chair, Minsk Pedagogical Univ 1963–67; mem Int Cttee of Slavic Linguistic Atlas 1989; Laureate USSR State Prize 1971. *Publications:* Dialectological Atlas of the Belarusian Language (jtly) 1963, Linguistic Geography and Grouping Belarusian Dialects 1969, Belarusian Grammar (Part 1, jtly) 1985, Government in Belarusian and Russian Languages 1991, Lexical Atlas of the Belarusian National Dialects: Vegetable words and animal-breeding (Part 1, jtly) 1993, Brief Dictionary of the Belarusian Language: Spelling, Pronunciation, Accent, Inflexion, Word Usage (jtly) 1994, Theory and Practice of the Belarusian Terminology (jtly) 1999, Slavic Linguistic Atlas: Lexical and word-formational: Animal-breeding (Vol 2, jtly) 2000, Slavic Linguistic Atlas: The Series of Vocabulary and Word-formation: Vegetable words (Vol 3, jtly) 2000. *Leisure interests:* knitting, growing flowers, painting. *Address:* 22049 Minsk, Volgogradskaya str, 53a-18, Belarus; Surganova str, 1/2/1010, Institute of Linguistics, Academy of Sciences of Belarus, 220072 Minsk, Belarus. *Telephone:* (17) 2628674.

O'RIORDAN, Marie; British magazine editor; b 1961. *Career:* Fmr Ed More!; Ed Elle magazine 1996–99; Group Publishing Dir EMAP Elan 1999–. *Address:* EMAP Elan, Endeavour House, 189 Shaftesbury Ave, London WC2H 8JG, UK. *Telephone:* (20) 7957-8383; *Fax:* (20) 7930 0184.

ORLAN; French performance artist; b 1948. *Career:* Art consists of undergoing plastic surgery operations, as part of 10-year The Reincarnation of St Orlan project; has had seven operations, including face sculpting broadcast live by satellite to galleries world-wide 1993 and operation to have 'horns' implanted in forehead; plans operation to have largest nose possible grafted onto face; touring exhibition My Body, This is My Software in UK at Inst of Contemporary Arts, London and Zone Gallery, Newcastle upon Tyne 1996; subject of debate on Concepts of Beauty, 22nd Annual Conf of Asscn of Art Historians, Newcastle 1996.

ORMOND, Julia; British actress; b 1965; m Rory Edwards (divorced). *Education:* Guildford High School, Cranleigh School, Farnham Art School and Webber Douglas Acad. *Career:* Worked in repertory, Crucible Theatre, Sheffield, Everyman Theatre, Cheltenham and on tour with Royal Exchange Theatre, Manchester. *Plays include:* Faith, Hope and Charity (London Drama Critics Award) 1989, The Crucible, Wuthering Heights, Treats, The Rehearsal (West End début), My Zinc Bed 2000; *TV appearances include:* Traffik (series), Ruth Rendell Mysteries, Young Catherine 1990, Captives, Stalin; *Films include:* The Baby of Macon, Legends of the Fall, First Knight, Sabrina, Smilla's Sense of Snow 1997, The Barber of Siberia 1998. *Address:* c/o CAA, 9830 Wilshire Blvd, Beverly Hills, CA 90212, USA.

ORMOS, Mária, PH D, D SC; Hungarian historian; b 1 Dec 1930, Debrecen; d of János Ormos and Elza Förster; one s one d. *Education:* Kossuth Lajos Univ (Debrecen) and Loránd Eötvös Univ (Budapest). *Career:* Asst Lecturer Historic Science Inst 1963; Univ Prof 1983; Rector Janos Pannonius Univ, Pécs 1984–92; Ordinary mem and mem Presidium, Hungarian Acad of Sciences 1987; mem Nat Cttee of Historians; Vice-Pres Asscn d'histoire des relations internationales; Pres Italian-Hungarian Mixed Cttee of Historians; Széczhenyi Prize 1995; Szentgyörgyi Prize 1995; Leo Sziliard Prize 2000. *Publications:* Franciaország és a keleti biztonság 1931–36 (France and Eastern Security) 1969, Merénylet Marseilleben (Assassination in Marseilles) 1984, Mussolini: a political portrait 1987, Nazism and Fascism 1987, Never as Long as I Shall Live: the last crowned Habsburg's attempted coup in 1921 1989, Civitas fidelissima 1990, From Padova to Trianon 1991, Hitler 1993, Magyarország a világháborúk korában 1914–45 (Hungary in the Age of the World Wars 1914–45) 1997, Európa a nemzetközi Kuzdotéren. Felemelkedés és hanyatlás 1814–1945 (Europe in the International Arena. Rise and Decline) (jtly) 1998, Hitler – Sztálin (Hitler–Stalin) (jtly) 1999. *Leisure interests:* reading, theatre, music. *Address:* c/o Janus Pannonius University (PJPT), 7621 Pécs, Rákóczi út 30, Hungary. *Telephone:* (72) 1315-942.

O'ROURKE, Mary; Irish politician; b 31 May 1937, Athlone; d of P. J. Lenihan; m Enda O'Rourke; two s. *Education:* St Peter's Convent, Univ Coll Dublin and St Patrick's Coll (Maynooth, Co Kildare). *Career:* Fmr secondary school teacher; mem Westmeath Co Council 1979–; TD (Parl, Fianna Fail) 1982; Minister for Educ 1987–91, for Health 1991–92, for Lab Affairs 1993–94, for Public Enterprise 1997–; Deputy Leader Fianna Fáil. *Address:* Aisling, Arcadia, Athlone, Co Westmeath, Ireland. *Telephone:* (902) 75065; *Fax:* (902) 78218.

ORTIZ, Cristina; Brazilian concert pianist; b 17 April 1950, Bahia; d of Silverio M. and Moema Fabricio Ortiz; m Jasper W. Parrott 1974; two d. *Education:* Conservatório Brasileiro de Música (Rio de Janeiro), Acad Int de Piano (with Magda Tagliaferro, Paris) and Curtis Inst of Music (with Rudolph Serkin, Philadelphia, PA, USA). *Career:* Has appeared in concerts with the Vienna Philharmonic, the Concertgebouw (Netherlands), Chicago Symphony (USA), Berlin Philharmonic, New York Philharmonic (USA), Israeli Philharmonic, Los Angeles Philharmonic, all the leading British orchestras, etc, and has undertaken many tours of N and S America, the Far East, NZ and Japan; has made TV appearances in the UK, Sweden, Germany, etc; has recorded extensively for EMI, Decca, Pantheon, Collins Classics and Pickwick Records; has undertaken to promote works of obscure Brazilian composers such as Lorenzo Fernandez and Fructuoso Vianna; First Prize Concours Magda Tagliaferro, Paris 1968, First Prize Van Cliburn Int Competition, TX, USA 1969. *Leisure interests:* tennis, music, master-classes, private lessons, reading, sketching, painting. *Address:* c/o Harrison/Parrott Ltd, 12 Penzance Place, London W11 4PA, UK. *Telephone:* (20) 7313-3500; *Fax:* (20) 7221-5042.

ORTIZ, Oneida Rivera de, BA; American librarian; b 12 Oct 1930, Salina, Puerto Rico; d of the late Celso Rivera and Aurelia Arzola; m Felix Luis Ortiz 1950; one d. *Education:* Univs of Puerto Rico, Drexel (PA) and New York. *Career:* Acting Dir Mayaguez Campus 1968–69; Asst Dean of Students Puerto Rico Jr Coll 1969–70; Library Dir Bayamón Regional Coll 1970–81, Humacao Univ Coll 1981–83;

Library Dir Univ of Puerto Rico, Dir of Learning Resources Center, Head and Acting Dir of Periodicals, Dir of Public Services; Dir Inst for Public Libraries; apptd Exec Sec Asscn of Caribbean Univ, Research and Institutional Libraries and Library Consultant 1979; Pres Puerto Rico Library Asscn; Treas World Asscn of Women Journalists and Writers; articles for professional books and journals; named Distinguished Educator of 1981. *Publications:* Integración de los Recursos 1976, Ensayos Educativos (co-ed) 1986, ALA World Encyclopedia of Library and Information Services (2nd edn) 1986, Pre Conferencia de Casa Blanca (2nd edn, co-ed) 1992. *Leisure interests:* reading, acting, sewing, puzzles. *Address:* Association of Caribbean University, Research and Institutional Libraries, Box 23317, University Station, San Juan 00931, Puerto Rico (Office); 39 Humacao St, Villa Avila, Guaynabo 00696, Puerto Rico (Home). *Telephone:* (809) 790-8054 (Office); *Fax:* (809) 765-5385.

OSBORN, June Elaine, BA, MD; American professor of epidemiology, paediatrics and communicable diseases; b 28 May 1937, Endicott, NY; d of Leslie A. and Dora W. (née Wright) Osborn; two s two d. *Education:* Oberlin Coll and Western Reserve Univ. *Career:* Intern, then Resident in Paediatrics Harvard Univ Hosp 1961–64; Postdoctoral Fellow Johns Hopkins Hosp 1964–65, Univ of Pittsburgh Hosp 1965–66; Paediatrics Specialist Madison, WI 1966–84; Faculty mem Univ of Wisconsin Medical School 1966–84, Prof of Paediatrics and Microbiology 1975–84, Assoc Dean of Graduate School 1975–84; Prof of Epidemiology, Paediatrics and Communicable Diseases and Dean School of Public Health, Univ of Michigan 1984–96, Prof Emer 1996–; Pres Josiah Macey Jr Foundation 1997–; mem Bd of Dirs Stetler Research Fund for Women Physicians 1971–75; mem Revision Panel on Viral Vaccine Efficacy, Food and Drug Admin 1973–79, Vaccines and Related Biological Products Advisory Comm 1981–85; mem Experimental Virology Study Section, Div Research Grants, NIH 1975–79; mem Medical Affairs Comm Yale Univ Council 1981–86, Medical Research and Devt Advisory Comm, US Army 1983–85, AIDS Task Force Inst of Medicine 1986, Advisory Comm Health Services Program of Robert Wood Johnson Foundation 1986–91, Rockefeller Foundation Advisory Comm, WHO Global Comm on AIDS 1988–92; Chair Revision Panel Nat Research Council 1981–84, Working Group on AIDS and Nat Blood Supply, NHLBI 1984–89, WHO Planning Group on AIDS and Int Blood Supply 1985–86, Nat Comm on AIDS 1989–93; mem Council Inst of Medicine 1995–; Trustee Kaiser Foundation 1990–; Fellow American Acad of Pediatrics, American Acad of Microbiology, Infectious Diseases Soc; mem Soc of Pediatric Research, American Asscn of Immunologists. *Address:* Josiah Macey Jr Foundation, 44 E 64th St, New York, NY 10021, USA.

OSBORNE, Judith Anne, MA, LL M; Canadian academic; b 18 May 1955, Sheffield, UK; d of Charles and Agnes Murray Hogg (née Gray) Osborne. *Education:* Boroughmuir High School and Univs of Edinburgh (UK), Toronto and British Columbia. *Career:* Tutor and Researcher Centre of Criminology and Woodsworth Coll, Univ of Toronto 1978–81; Researcher and Consultant Commonwealth Section 1978–80; Asst Prof School of Criminology, Simon Fraser Univ 1981–, Assoc Dir School of Criminology 1986–; Treas LIFE Resource Centre 1986; numerous articles in professional journals. *Address:* Simon Fraser University, School of Criminology, Burnaby, BC V5A 1S6, Canada (Office); 302-9148 Saturna Drive, Burnaby, BC V3J 7K2 Canada (Home).

OSEI-BONSU, Margaret; Ghanaian business executive; b 16 April 1957, Accra; d of Ben Ofori Agyeman and Grace Owusu; m Daniel Addae Osei-Bonsu 1978; five d. *Education:* Inst of Adult Educ (Accra). *Career:* Sec Ghana Water and Sewerage Corpn 1977–78; apptd Deputy Dir Camco Shipping Co, Tema 1979, Dir Magbon Farms Ltd 1981, Nat Pres Ghana Fed of Business and Professional Women 1991. *Leisure interests:* tennis, reading, films. *Address:* Camco, POB 870, Community 7, Tema, Ghana. *Telephone:* (221) 2285.

O'SHANE, Patricia June (Pat), AM, LL M; Australian university chancellor and magistrate; b 19 June 1941, Mossman, Qld; d of P. J. O'Shane; m 1st Michael Miller 1962 (divorced 1975); two d; m 2nd Allan Coles. *Education:* Cairns State High School, Queensland Teachers' Coll, Univs of Queensland, New South Wales and Sydney. *Career:* Called to the Bar (first Aborigine) 1976; Permanent Head

Aboriginal Affairs Dept, NSW 1981–86; Commr Commonwealth Tertiary Educ Comm 1983–86; Magistrate New S Wales Local Court 1986–; Chancellor Univ of New England 1995–; Hon LL D (Sydney Univ of Tech, Wollongong). *Leisure interests:* cycling, swimming, golf, bodybuilding. *Address:* Chamber of Magistrates, Downing Centre, Level 5, Downing St, 143 Liverpool St, Sydney, NSW 2000, Australia.

ÖSTBERG, (Karin) Ullastina, BA; Swedish magazine editor; b 12 April 1951, Falköping; d of the late Walther and Iris (née Andersson) Östberg. *Education:* Göteborg and Stockholm Univs. *Career:* Ed Det Bästa of Reader's Digest 1974–82, Staff Writer 1982–85, Ed-in-Chief 1985; Nat Dir Safety and Training, Swedish Parachute Asscn 1984–86, Head Safety and Training Cttee 1990–94. *Leisure interests:* parachuting, aerobatics, motorcycling. *Address:* c/o Det Bästa of Reader's Digest, POB 25, 164 93 Kista, Sweden.

OSTEN, Suzanne (Carlota); Swedish playwright and theatre and film director; b 20 June 1944, Stockholm; d of Carl Otto and Gud Osten; m; one d. *Education:* Lund Univ. *Career:* Dir first production at the age of 19; formed freelance theatre group 1967; joined City Theatre of Stockholm 1971; formed Unga Klara Stadsteatern ind repertory co within Municipal Theatre 1975; has written and directed more than 30 plays; film career began 1980; Dir own co; Prof Dramatic Inst 1995–; Nat Theatre Critics Prize 1982; Paris-Creteil Prize 1993 and other nat and int prizes for films. *Films:* Mamma – Our Life is Now 1982, The Mozart Brothers (Guldbagge Award for Direction) 1986, Lethal Film 1988, Guardian Angel 1990, Speak Up It's So Dark 1992, Only You and Me 1994, Carmen's Revenge 1996. *Leisure interest:* dance and poetry. *Address:* Upplandsgt 19, 113 60 Stockholm, Sweden. *Telephone:* (8) 32 54 23.

OSTERIA, Trinidad S., D SC; Philippine social scientist; b 4 Feb 1944; d of Asisclo and Teodocia Osteria. *Education:* Johns Hopkins Univ (MD, USA) and Univ of the Philippines. *Career:* WHO Visiting Scientist, UK, Switzerland, USA 1977; Project Expert UN Econ and Social Comm for Asia and the Pacific (ESCAP), Bangkok 1978–81; UN Visiting Scientist, Int Nutrition Programme, Harvard Univ, USA 1981–82; UN Consultant Maternal and Child Health Programme, Vanuatu 1983–84; Dir Research Centre, De La Salle Univ 1984–85, apptd Assoc Prof Dept of Behavioural Studies 1992; Fellow and Regional Co-ordinator of Urban and Women's Projects, Inst of SE Asian Studies, Singapore 1986–92; articles in professional journals. *Leisure interests:* collecting antique porcelain, playing the piano. *Address:* Social Devt and Research Centre, De La Salle University, 2401 Taft Ave, Manila, Philippines. *Telephone:* (2) 59-51-77; *Fax:* (2) 521-90-94.

OSTROWER, Fayga Perla; Brazilian (b Polish) artist and writer; b 14 Sept 1920, Łódź, Poland; d of Froim and Frimeta Krakowski; m Heinz Ostrower 1941; one s one d. *Education:* Fundação Getúlio Vargas (Rio de Janeiro). *Career:* Lecturer in Theory of Composition and Analysis Museum of Modern Art, Rio de Janeiro 1954–70, Univ Fed de Minas Gerais 1966–70; John Hay Whitney Lecturer Spelman Coll, Atlanta, GA, USA 1964; Post-graduate Prof Univ of Rio de Janeiro 1982–; numerous solo exhibitions and works in collections in the Americas and Europe; Special Show Mexico Bienal 1981, Puerto Rico Bienal 1995; mem Jury for São Paulo Bienal, Nat Show of Fine Arts, Rio de Janeiro and Grabado Inter Americano Bienal, Puerto Rico 1995; Vice-Pres Brazilian Cttee, Int Asscn of Plastic Arts, Int Council of Int Centre for Integrative Studies (ICIS), New York; Vice-Pres Brazilian Cttee, Int Soc for Educ through Art (INSEA), UNESCO 1983, fmr Pres; mem Bd Cultural Council Museum of Modern Art, Rio de Janeiro, Escola de Artes Visuais Parque Lage, Rio de Janeiro; Counsellor Inst Cultural Brasil-Alemanha, Goethe Inst, Rio de Janeiro; elected mem State Council for Culture, Rio de Janeiro; Hon mem Accad delle Arti del Disegno, Florence, Italy; numerous prizes including awards at São Paulo Bienal 1955, 1957, 1961, 1963, Venice Biennale 1958, 1962, Venezuela Bienal 1967, Rio de Janeiro City Award 1969 and II Biennale Internazionale della Grafica (Florence, Italy) 1970; Grand Int Prize, Venice; Chevalier Order of Rio Branco 1972; Hon Citizenship of Rio de Janeiro 1985; Grand Nat Award for the Arts (Brazil) 1994; Gran Nat Prize of Art (Brazil) 1995; Grand Prize of Fine Arts, Brazilian Ministry of Culture 1998; Ordem do Mérito Cultural. *Publications:* Criatividade e Processos de Criaçaõ (Creativity and Creative Processes) 1977, Universos de Arte 1983, Acasos e Criaçaõ Artística (Chance and Artistic

Creation) 1990, Os Caprichos de Goya 1995, Goya, Life and Work 1996, Goya, Artista Revolucionário e Humanista 1997, A Sensibilidade do Intelecto 1998 (Jabuti Literary Prize, Câmara Brasileira do Livro 1999). *Leisure interest:* art. *Address:* Avda Rui Barbosa 532, Apdo 1001, 22250-020 Rio de Janeiro, RJ, Brazil. *Telephone:* (21) 551-3015; *Fax:* (21) 551-8916.

OSTRY, Sylvia, OC, PH D, FRSC; Canadian economist and university chancellor; b 3 June 1927, Winnipeg; d of Morris Jack and Betsy Deborah (née Stoller) Knelman; m Bernard Ostry 1956; two s. *Education:* McGill Univ and Univ of Cambridge (UK). *Career:* Teaching and research at Canadian univs and Univ of Oxford Inst of Statistics, UK; joined Fed Govt 1964; Chief Statistician Statistics Canada 1972–75; Deputy Minister of Consumer and Corp Affairs and Deputy Registrar-Gen 1975–78; Chair Econ Council of Canada 1978–79; Head Econ and Statistics Dept, OECD, Paris 1979–83; Deputy Minister (Int Trade) and Co-ordinator for Int Econ Relations, Dept of External Affairs 1984–85; Amb for Multilateral Trade Negotiations and Personal Rep of the Prime Minister, Econ Summit, Dept of External Affairs 1985; Sr Research Fellow, Univ of Toronto 1989–90, Chair Centre for Int Studies 1990–97, Distinguished Research Fellow 1997–; Chancellor Univ of Waterloo 1990–97; Western Co-Chair Blue Ribbon Comm for Hungary's Econ Devt 1990–94; Chair Council Canadian Inst for Int Affairs 1990–94; Sylvia Ostry Foundation annual lecture series launched 1992; Dir Power Financial Corpn; Chair Int Advisory Council, Bank of Montréal; Expert Adviser Comm on Transnat Corpns, UN; Founder-mem Pacific Council on Int Policy; mem Int Cttee of InterAmerican Devt Bank/Econ Comm for Latin America and the Caribbean project, Bd UNU/World Inst for Devt Econs Research (Helsinki), Int Advisory Council Centre for European Policy Studies (Brussels), Advisory Bd Inst of Int Econs (Washington, DC), Bd of Distinguished Advisers Center for the Study of Cen Banks; delivered Per Jacobsson Foundation Lecture, Washington 1987; Volvo Distinguished Visiting Fellow, Council on Foreign Relations, New York 1989; Chair Council Canadian Inst for Int Affairs 1990–92; mem several learned socs and professional orgs; Fellow Royal Soc of Canada 1991; 18 hon degrees; Outstanding Achievement Award, Govt of Canada 1987; Career Achievement Award, Canadian Policy Research 2000. *Publications:* Labour Economics in Canada, International Economic Policy Co-ordination (jtly) 1986, Governments and Corporations in a Shrinking World: The Search for Stability 1990, Technonationalism and Technoglobalism: Conflict and Co-operation (jtly) 1995, Rethinking Federalism: Citizens, Markets and Governments in a Changing World (jtly) 1995, The Halifax G7 Summit: Issues on the Table (jtly) 1995, Who's on First? The Post Coldwar Trading System 1997, The Future of the World Trading System 1999, Convergence and Sovereignty: Policy Scope for Compromise 2000, Business, Trade and the Environmental 2000, The Changing Scenario in International Governance 2000; articles on labour econs, demography, productivity, competition policy. *Leisure interests:* films, theatre, contemporary reading. *Address:* Munk Center for International Studies, 1 Devonshire Place, Room 361S, Toronto, ON M5S 3K7, Canada. *Telephone:* (416) 946-8958; *Fax:* (416) 946-8915; *E-mail:* sylvia.ostry@utoronto.ca; *Internet:* www.utoronto.ca/cis/ostry.html.

O'SULLIVAN, Sally Angela, BA; British magazine editor; b 26 July 1949; d of Lorraine and Joan Connell; m 1st Thaddeus O'Sullivan 1973 (divorced); m 2nd Charles Wilson 1980; one s one d. *Education:* Ancaster House School and Trinity Coll Dublin. *Career:* Deputy Ed Woman's World 1977–78; Women's Ed Daily Record 1980, Sunday Standard 1981; Ed Options 1982–88; Launch Ed Country Homes & Interiors 1986; Ed She 1989, Harpers & Queen 1989–91, Good Housekeeping 1991–95; Ed-in-Chief Ideal Home, Homes and Ideas, Women and Home, Homes and Gardens, Country Homes and Interiors, Beautiful Homes, Living, etc magazines 1996–98; Chief Exec Cabal Communications 1998–; Non-Exec Dir London Transport 1995–, Anglian Water 1996–; mem Broadcasting Standards Council 1994, Nuffield Council of Bioethics 1995–; Magazine Ed of the Year 1986, 1994. *Leisure interests:* family, horses. *Address:* Cabal Communications, 374 Euston Rd, London NW1 3BL, UK.

O'SULLIVAN, Sonia; Irish athlete; b 28 Nov 1969, Cóbh, Co Cork; d of John and Mary O'Sullivan. *Education:* Accountancy studies in Villanova, USA. *Career:* Gold Medallist in 1,500m, Silver Medallist in

3,000m, World Student Games 1991; holds seven nat records; set new World record (her first) in 2,000m TSB Challenge, Edinburgh 1994, new European record in 3,000m TSB Games, London 1994, Gold Medallist in 3,000m European Athletic Championships, Helsinki 1994; winner Grand Prix in 3,000m 1993 (second overall); Silver Medallist in 1,500m, World Championships, Stuttgart, Germany 1993; Gold Medallist in 5,000m World Championships, Gothenburg, Sweden 1995; Gold Medallist in 4km and 8km World Cross Country Championships 1998; Gold Medallist in 5,000m and 10,000m European Championships 1998; Female Athlete of the Year 1995. *Leisure interests:* mountain biking, reading, films. *Address:* c/o Kim McDonald, 201 High St, Hampton Hill, Middlesex TW12 1NL, UK. *Telephone:* (20) 8941-9732; *Fax:* (20) 8941-9734.

OSUNKIYESI, Julie Olufunmilayo (née Williams); Nigerian radiographer (retd); m S. C. Osunkiyesi; four c. *Education:* Fed School of Radiography (Gen Hosp, Lagos) and St Bartholomew's Hosp School of Radiography (London). *Career:* Part-time Lecturer Fed School of Radiography, Gen Hosp, Lagos 1958–61; Nat Chair YWCA Relief and Rehabilitation Cttee during Nigerian Civil War 1968–72; State Chief Radiographer, Lagos; Hon Sec-Gen Better Life for Rural Dwellers, Lagos State Chapter and voluntary social worker; f Zonta Int Org in Nigeria, Pres Zonta Int Club of Lagos 1983–85; Del from Zonta Int Org to UN End of Decade for Women Conf, Nairobi 1985; apptd Rep of Lagos State Govt to Radiographers' Registration Bd of Nigeria 1989; Commr State Comm for Women 1991; Fellow, Life mem Asscn of Radiographers of Nigeria, Nat Pres 1990; Life mem British Soc of Radiographers; numerous papers given at nat and int confs on radiography. *Address:* Better Life for Rural Dwellers, Secretariat (Lagos State Chapter), Military Governor's Office, Alausa, Ikeja, Nigeria (Office); 29 Akerele St, Surulere, Lagos, Nigeria (Home).

OTA, Fusae; Japanese politician; b 1952. *Career:* Fmr Official Ministry of Int Trade and Industry (MITI); Gov of Osaka (first woman) 2000–. *Address:* Osaka Prefectural Government, 1-22, Ohtemae 2-chome, Chou-Ku, 540 Osaka, Japan. *Telephone:* (6) 944-6625; *Fax:* (6) 944-6622; *E-mail:* koho@office.pref.osaka.jp; *Internet:* www.pref.osaka.jp.

OTCHIROVA, Alexandra, PH D; Russian politician and organization executive; b 5 July 1949, Razon region; m Otchirov 1993; one d. *Education:* Moscow State Univ. *Career:* Research Fellow Inst of Philosophy, USSR Acad of Science 1976–89; Consultant to mem USSR Presidential Council 1990–91; Vice-Pres Acad of Creation 1991–92; mem State Duma (Parl) for Ingushetia, Russian Fed 1993–95, Co-Chair Cttee on Int Affairs; Founder, Pres Int Women's Centre 'Woman's Future', one of first NGOs in Russia; Co-Chair Women's League; mem Int Acad of Creative Endeavours; several state prizes for science and culture. *Publications:* Pluralism: Sources and Essences (Lenin Prize for Science and Tech); monographies and articles on philosophical and political problems and on the devt of civil soc. *Leisure interest:* writing poetry. *Address:* Moscow, Dolgorukovskaya Str 40, Bldg 6, fl 156, Russian Federation. *Telephone:* (095) 257-1694; *Fax:* (095) 257-0436.

OTTEY, Merlene; Jamaican athlete; m Nathaniel Page 1984 (divorced 1987). *Education:* Ruseas High School, Vere Tech High School and Univ of Nebraska—Lincoln (USA). *Career:* Has participated in many int athletics competitions; Bronze Medallist individual track 200m sprint and Silver Medallist relay, Pan-American Games, San Juan, PR 1979, Bronze Medallist 200m, Olympic Games, Moscow, USSR (now Russian Fed) 1980, Gold Medallist 100m, Int Athletic Meeting, Helsinki 1981, Gold Medallist 200m, Silver Medallist 100m and Bronze Medallist relay, Commonwealth Games, Brisbane, Australia 1982, Silver medallist 200m and Bronze medallist relay, First World Athletic Championship, Helsinki 1983, Bronze Medallist 100m and 200m, Olympic Games, Los Angeles, USA 1984, Bronze Medallist 100m, World Athletics Championships, Tokyo 1991, Bronze Medallist 200m, Olympic Games, Barcelona, Spain 1992; set 100m and 200m records, Commonwealth Games 1985; world champion 200m 1993; Silver Medallist 100m, 200m Olympic Games, Atlanta, USA 1996; apptd Roving Amb for Jamaica 1993; Officer of the Order of Distinction, Jamaica; Sportswoman of the Year, Carreras Sports Foundation, Jamaica 1979–85. *Address:* c/o Mrs Joan Ottey, Great Valley PO, Hanover, Jamaica.

OTTO, Kristin; German journalist and former swimmer; b 7 Feb 1966, Leipzig. *Education:* Leipzig Univ. *Career:* Professional swimmer 1982–89; Gold Medallist (seven medals) World Championships 1982, 1986, Gold Medallist (nine medals) European Championships 1983, 1987, 1989, Gold Medallist Olympic Games, Seoul 1988; currently TV journalist; Paek-Sang Crown 1988; Fina Prize 1991. *Leisure interests:* sport, collecting china. *Address:* Zentralstr 4 7010 Leipzig, Germany.

OTTOLINA, Rhona; Venezuelan politician. *Career:* Pres Formula 1 political party (formed legislative coalition with Derecha Emergente de Venezuela—DEV party). *Address:* Esq de Pajaritos, Edif Administrativo, Congreso Nacional, Caracas, Venezuela. *Telephone:* (2) 483-2085.

OTUNBAYEVA, Rosa Isakovna, C PHIL SC; Kyrgyzstan politician and diplomatist; b 23 Aug 1950; m; one s one d. *Education:* Univ of Moscow. *Career:* Lecturer and Chair of Dialectical Materialism, State Univ of Kyrgyzstan, Frunze (now Bishkek) 1975–81; Second Sec Frunze Local CP Cttee 1981–83, Sec Frunze Municipal CP Cttee 1983–86; Deputy Chair and Minister of Foreign Affairs, Council of Ministers, Kyrgyzstan 1986–89; Exec Sec USSR Comm on UNESCO Problems 1989–90, Chair 1990–91; Amb of USSR to Malaysia 1991–92; Vice-Prime Minister and Minister of Foreign Affairs, Repub of Kyrgyzstan Feb–May 1992; Amb of Kyrgyzstan to USA 1992–94 (also accredited to Canada); Minister of Foreign Affairs 1994–97; Amb of Kyrgyzstan to UK 1997–. *Address:* Embassy of Kyrgyzstan, 119 Crawford St, London W1H 1AF, UK. *Telephone:* (20) 7935-1462; *Fax:* (20) 7935-7449.

OUEDRAOGO, Marie-Michelle, PH D; Burkinabè professor of geography; b 6 Nov 1946, Korhogo, Côte d'Ivoire; d of Sibiri Slambéré; m Philippe Ouedraogo; two s two d. *Education:* Univ of Abidjan (Côte d'Ivoire) and Univ of Bordeaux III (France). *Career:* Univ of Ouagadougou 1976–, Head Dept of Geography 1977–81, Dir of External Relations 1988–91; Perm Sec Nat Comm of Dip Equivalence 1983–88; Nat Dir Unité d'Enseignement et de Recherche en Démographie (UERD) 1991; Pres Scientific and Admin Council CERPOD 1991. *Publications:* Approvisionnements de Ouagadougou en produits vivriers, en eau et en bois 1974, Urbanisation, organisation de l'espace et développement au Burkina Faso 1988. *Leisure interests:* reading, cinema, travel. *Address:* University of Ouagadougou, Dept of Geography, BP 7021, Ouagadougou, Burkina Faso (Office); Unité d'Enseignement et de Recherche en Démographie (UERD), BP 7118, Ouagadougou, Burkina Faso (Office). *Telephone:* 36-21-15 (Univ); 30-01-007 (UERD); *Fax:* 36-21-38 (University); 30-72-42 (UERD).

OUSSET, Cécile; French pianist; b 23 Jan 1936, Tarbes. *Education:* Paris Conservatoire. *Career:* French debut with Orchestre de Paris; British debut Edinburgh Festival 1980; US debut with Los Angeles Philharmonic 1984; prizewinner, Van Cliburn, Queen Elisabeth of Belgium, Busoni and Marguerite Long-Jacques Thibaud competitions. *Recordings include:* Recording of Brahms 2nd Piano Concerto (Grand Prix du Disque), concertos by Rachmaninov, Liszt, Saint-Saëns, Ravel, Grieg, Mendelssohn, recitals of Chopin, Debussy, Liszt.

OUTRAM, Dorinda, MA, PH D; British historian; b 11 Dec 1949, Leicester; d of Earnest Albert Outram and Rosemary Elenor Collins; m James Antony Burns 1976 (divorced 1980); one s. *Education:* Univ of Cambridge. *Career:* Research Fellowship British Acad 1974, Univ of Reading 1975; Lectureship and Research Fellowships, Univ of London 1977–81; Asst Prof Univ of Montréal, Canada 1981–82; Research Fellowship, Girton Coll, Cambridge 1982–84; Lecturer in Modern History, Univ Coll, Cork, Ireland 1984–98; Clark Prof of History, Univ of Rochester, NY 1998–; Visiting Prof Griffith Univ, Australia 1990; Landon Clay Visiting Assoc Prof Harvard Univ, USA 1991–92; Editorial Dir Comité int pour l'édition de la correspondance de Georges Cuvier 1983–; mem Editorial panel Dictionary of Irish Biography 1984–; Ed Bulletin of Irish Asscn for Research in Women's History 1987–88; Trustee British Soc for History of Science; Hon Sec Irish Nat Cttee for Research in Women's History 1988–; Vellacott Historical Essay Prize, Cambridge 1971; Royal Soc of London Research Award 1982; CNRS Research Award, Paris 1982. *Publications:* Science, Vocation and Authority in Post-Revolutionary France, Georges Cuvier 1984, Uneasy Careers and Intimate Lives: Women in Science 1987, The Body and the French Revolution 1989, The Enlightenment 1994;

numerous articles. *Leisure interests:* walking, talking, language learning, visiting France, Italy and Germany. *Address:* Department of History, University of Rochester, Rochester, NY 14627, USA.

OWEN, Deborah; American/British literary agent; b 8 July 1942, NY; d of the late Kyrill Schabert and Mary Babcock Smith; m David Anthony Llewellyn Owen (now Lord Owen) 1968; two s one d. *Career:* Founder and Literary Agent Deborah Owen Ltd 1971; Vice-Pres Cttee Asscn of Authors' Agents 1991–94; mem Bd of Dirs Viva radio 1993, Advisory Bd London Symphony Orchestra, Fulbright Comm. *Address:* 78 Narrow St, Limehouse, London E14 8BP, UK. *Telephone:* (20) 7987-5119.

OWEN, Nora, B SC; Irish politician; b 22 June 1945; d of James O'Mahony and Katherine Collins; m Brian J. Owen 1968; three s. *Education:* Dominican Convent (Wicklow) and Univ Coll Dublin. *Career:* Industrial chemist in pharmaceutical industry 1965–72; elected to Dublin Co Council (Fine Gael) 1979–94; TD 1981–, Chair Jt Parl Cttee on Overseas Devt 1981–87, Opposition Spokesperson on Overseas Devt 1981–82, 1989–92, mem EC Secondary Legislation Parl Cttee, mem British/Irish Parl Body 1989–92; Minister for Justice 1994–96; Exec mem Asscn of W European Parliamentarians for Action for Africa (AWEPAA). *Leisure interests:* reading, theatre, bridge. *Address:* c/o Dept of Justice, 72–76 St Stephen's Green, Dublin 2, Ireland (Office); 17 Ard na Mara, Malahide, Co Dublin, Ireland (Home). *Telephone:* (1) 6789711 (Office); (1) 8451041 (Home); *Fax:* (1) 6767797 (Office).

OWEN, Rena; New Zealand actress. *Career:* Fmr nurse; spent eight months in prison for drugs offences, UK 1984; playwright and actress; plays performed at London fringe venues, prisons and rehabilitation centres. *Films:* Once Were Warriors, Rapa Nui, You're My Venus.

OWEN, Ursula Margaret, BA; British publishing executive; b 21 Jan 1937, Oxford; d of Werner and Emma Sachs; m Roger Owen 1960 (divorced 1977); one d; partner Frank Kermode. *Education:* Putney High School, St Hugh's Coll (Oxford) and Bedford Coll (Univ of London). *Career:* Social Worker and Researcher into social issues 1960–69; Ed Barrie and Jenkins Ltd publrs; Founder-mem Virago Press 1973, Editorial Dir and Jt Man Dir 1974–90, Non-Exec Dir 1990–95; Cultural Policy Adviser to Lab Party, Dir Hamlyn Fund 1990–92; joined Index on Censorship 1990, Ed and CEO 1993–; mem Bd New Statesman magazine 1985–90, Cttee Royal Literary Fund 1990–94; Chair Educ Extra 1992– ; Vice-Pres Hay on Wye Festival of Literature. *Publications:* Fathers: Reflections by Daughters (ed) 1984, Whose Cities? (co-ed) 1990. *Leisure interests:* playing and listening to music, walking, cinema, travel, reading. *Address:* Index, 33 Islington High St, London N1 9LH, UK (Office); 1c Spencer Rise, London NW5 1AR UK (Home). *Telephone:* (20) 7278-2313 (Office); (20) 7485-9060 (Home); *E-mail:* ursulaibook@freeuk.net.

OWEN-ALLEN, Alison, BA; British film producer; three c. *Career:* Head of Devt Limelight Film and TV; Producer of feature films. *Films:* Hear My Song 1991, The Young Americans 1992, Moonlight and Valentino 1994, Roseanna's Grave 1996. *Address:* Working Title Films, 76 Oxford St, London W1, UK.

OWERS, Anne Elizabeth, BA; British organization executive; b 23 June 1947; d of William and Anne Smailes (née Knox) Spark; m Rev Ian H. Owers 1968; two s one d. *Education:* Washington Grammar School (Tyne and Wear) and Girton Coll (Cambridge). *Career:* Teacher and Researcher, Zambia 1968–71; Researcher, UK 1971–74; Adviser to Chair race advice groups 1974–81; Research and Devt worker Jt Council for the Welfare of Immigrants 1981–86, Gen Sec 1986–92; Dir Justice 1992–; Chair Bd of Trustees Refugee Legal Centre 1994–98; mem Bd Centre for Research into Ethnic Relations, Univ of Warwick 1990–, Advisory Council NCVO (Nat Council of Voluntary Orgs) 1994–, Lord Chancellor's Advisory Cttee on Legal Educ and Conduct 1997–99, Home Office Task Force on Human Rights 1999–, Legal Services Consultative Panel 2000–. *Leisure interests:* theatre, music, reading, friends. *Address:* Justice, 59 Carter Lane, London EC4V 5AQ, UK.

OXNER, Sandra Ellen, BA, LL B; Canadian judge; b 3 Oct 1941; d of Garnet and Mabel (née MacCalder) Oxner; m Donald P. Keddy 1985. *Education:* Univ of King's Coll and Dalhousie Univ. *Career:* Called to the Bar, NS 1965; Legal Dept City of Halifax, NS 1965–71; Judge Provincial Court (Criminal), Halifax 1971–; Chair Atlantic Advisory Cttee to Solicitor-Gen on Maximum Security Penitentiaries 1974–75; Criminal Law Consultant to Law Reform Comm of Canada 1976–77; Lecturer School of Journalism, Univ of King's Coll, Halifax 1980–89, Assoc Fellow 1982–90; Gov Canadian Inst for Advanced Legal Studies 1978–83, Commonwealth Trust 1989–91; Pres Canadian Asscn of Prov Court Judges 1977, Canadian Inst for the Admin of Justice 1981; Hon Life Vice-Pres Commonwealth Judges' and Magistrates' Asscn; Hon Life Pres Royal Commonwealth Soc; mem Nat Advisory Cttees Nat Council Canadian Human Rights Asscn; Mohr/Cullis Lecture-Fellowship 1982; Commonwealth Foundation Fellow 1988; Freedom of the City of London 1988. *Publications:* Discipline and Removal from Office of Provincial Court Judges 1978, The Trial Process (ed) 1981, Criminal Justice 1982, Law in a Colonial Society 1982. *Leisure interests:* legal history, dog-breeding. *Address:* Provincial Court House, 5250 Spring Garden Rd, Halifax, NS B3J 1E7, Canada (Office); 1354 Robie St, Halifax, NS, Canada (Home). *Telephone:* (902) 477-6277 (Home); *Fax:* (902) 477-1086 (Home).

ØYANGEN, Gunhild, MA; Norwegian politician; b 31 Oct 1947, Levanger; d of Kåre Utnes and Hildur Bergljot Nilsen; m Egil Øyangen; three c. *Education:* Univ of Trondheim. *Career:* Chair Agdenes Labour Party, mem Co Council 1982–, mem Nat Bd of Lab Party, Agricultural Cttee 1985–; Minister of Agric 1986–89, 1990; mem Storting (Parl) and Deputy Leader Standing Cttee on Agric 1989–90; Leader Social Cttee in Parl 1996–. *Address:* Stortinget, 0026 Oslo, Norway.

OYUN, Sanjaasurengin, PH D; Mongolian politician; b 18 Jan 1964; d of Dorjpalam and Sanjaasuren Oyun. *Education:* Secondary School No 13 (Ulan Bator), Charles Univ (Prague) and Univ of Cambridge. *Career:* Mem State Great Hural (Parl); Pres Citizens Will Party; Head Zorig Foundation. *Leisure interests:* karate, chess, hiking. *Address:* State Great Hural, Government House 303, Ulan Bator 12, Mongolia. *Telephone:* (11) 323645; *Fax:* (11) 322866; *E-mail:* oyun@mail.parl.gov.mn.

OZAY; Turkish actress and singer; b 1954. *Career:* Moved to Berlin 1971; Sec US Air Force, Berlin 1971; co-writer No More, stage musical; moved to Paris 1991; German Fed Award for Best Actress 1987. *Films include:* Forty Square Meters of Germany (Locarno Festival Silver Leopard), The Fisherman From Halikirnas 1992.

OŽELYTE, Nijole; Lithuanian politician and actress; b 1954. *Education:* Lithuanian Conservatoire. *Career:* Actress in Films and TV 1974–; Deputy Supreme Council of Lithuania 1990–92. *Address:* Taikos 87–49, Vilnius 232017, Lithuania. *Telephone:* (2) 427-908.

OZICK, Cynthia, MA; American writer; b 17 April 1928, New York City; d of William and Celia (née Regelson) Ozick; m Bernard Hallote 1952; one d. *Education:* New York and Ohio State Univs. *Career:* Writer of novels, short stories, essays and literary criticism; contribs to numerous journals and anthologies; mem PEN, Authors' League, American Acad of Arts and Sciences, American Acad and Inst of Arts and Letters; Hon LHD (Yeshiva, Hebrew Union Coll) 1984, (Williams Coll) 1986, (Hunter Coll) 1987, (Jewish Theological Seminary) 1988, (Adelphi) 1988, (State Univ of New York) 1989, (Brandeis) 1990, (Bard Coll, Spertus Coll) 1991, (Skidmore Coll) 1992, (Seton Hall, Rutgers) 1999, (Univ of NC) 2000, (New York) 2001; Guggenheim Fellow 1982, Lucy Martin Donnelly Fellow, Bryn Mawr Coll 1992; mem PEN, Authors' League, American Acad of Arts and Sciences, Dramatists Guild, Phi Beta Kappa; Founder mem Academie Universelle des Cultures (Paris); awards include Mildred and Harold Strauss Living Award, American Acad of Arts and Letters 1983, Phi Beta Kappa orator, Univ of Harvard 1985, Rea Short Story Award 1986, PEN/Spiegel-Diamonstein Award for the Art of the Essay 1997, Harold Washington Literary Award, City of Chicago 1997, John Cheever Award 1999, Lotos Club Medal of Merit 2000, Lannan Foundation Award for Fiction 2000, Koret Foundation Award for Literary Studies 2001. *Publications include:* Trust 1966, The Pagan Rabbi and Other Stories 1971, Bloodshed and three novellas 1976, Levitation: Five

Fictions 1982, Art and Ardor (essays) 1983, The Cannibal Galaxy 1983, The Messiah of Stockholm 1987, Metaphor and Memory (essays) 1989, The Shawl 1989, Epodes: First Poems 1992, What Henry James Knew, Other Essays on Writers 1994, Blue Light (play) 1994, Portrait of the Artist as a Bad Character 1996, The Cynthia Ozick Reader 1996, Fame and Folly 1996, The Shawl (play) 1996, The Puttermesser Papers 1997, Best American Essays (guest ed) 1998, Quarrel and Quandry (essays, guest ed) 2000; also poetry, criticism, reviews, translations, essays and fiction in numerous periodicals and anthologies. *Address:* c/o Alfred A. Knopf Co, 201 E 50th St, New York, NY 10022-7703, USA (Office); 34 Soundview St, New Rochelle, NY 10805-3914, USA (Home). *Telephone:* (914) 636-1970 (Home); *Fax:* (941) 654-6583 (Home).

P

PACK, Doris; German politician; b 18 March 1942, Schiffweiler/Saar; m; two c. *Career:* Headteacher; mem CDU 1962–, Vice-Chair Women's Union and Fed Advisory Cttee on European Policy; mem Local Council, Bübingen 1969–74, City Council, Saarbrücken 1974–76; mem Bundestag (Parl) 1974–83, 1985–89; mem Council of Europe and WEU until 1989; elected MEP 1989, mem Cttee on Culture, Youth Educ and the Media, substitute mem Cttee on Foreign Affairs, Security and Defence Policy, Chair Del for Relations with South-East Europe; mem Bureau EPP Group; Chair Südosteuropa Inst, Frankfurt. *Address:* Bei der Weiss Eich 1, 66129 Saarbrücken, Germany (Home). *Telephone:* (6805) 1654 (Home); *Fax:* (6805) 21580 (Home).

PADILLA GIL, Dora Nancy, LIC EN BIOL, M SC; Colombian biologist and heteropterist; b 16 Jan 1966, Santa Fe de Bogotá; d of Miguel Padilla Sarmiento and Ana Delia Gil de Padilla; m Alvaro Rugeles 1997; one s. *Education:* Colegio Nuestra Señora de la Sabiduría, Univ Pedagógica Nacional and Univ Nacional de Colombia. *Career:* School teacher 1988–; Teacher of Biology, Dept of Biology, Univ de Nariño (Colombia) 1994–; collector of aquatic insects, butterflies and beetles. *Publication:* Three New Species of Corixidae from Colombia (jtly) 1992, Compendio de las Cerridae (Hemiptera) de Colombia con descripción de una nueva especie de *Tachygerris* 2002. *Address:* Condominio San Diego MD c9 Pasto, Apdo Aéreo 1574 Pasto, Nariño, Colombia. *Telephone:* (7) 297071; *Fax:* (7) 313106; *E-mail:* dnpadilla@udenar.edu .co.

PADMORE, Elaine Marguirite, B MUS, MA; British artistic director and broadcaster; b 3 Feb 1947, Haworth, Yorks; d of Alfred and Florence Padmore. *Education:* Newland High School (Hull), Arnold School (Blackpool), Univ of Birmingham and Guildhall School of Music. *Career:* Lecturer in Liberal Studies Coll of Art, Croydon and Kingston 1968–70; Books Ed Music Dept, Oxford Univ Press 1970–71; Producer Music Div, BBC 1971–76, Presenter Festival Comment 1973–81, Chief Producer Opera, BBC Radio 1976–83, Announcer Radio Three 1982–90, Programmes include Parade, Music of Tchaikovsky's Russia, England's Pleasant Land; opera singer; Lecturer in Opera RAM 1979–86; Artistic Dir Wexford Festival Opera 1982–94, Dublin Grand Opera Soc 1989–90; Artistic Dir Royal Danish Opera 1993–2000; Dir of Opera, Covent Garden; contrib to musical books and journals; Hon ARAM; recipient Hungarian Pro Musica Award for Summertime on Bredon 1973, Prix Musical de Radio Brno for The English Renaissance 1974, Sunday Independent Award for Services to Music in Ireland 1985. *Leisure interests:* gardening, travel, art exhibitions. *Address:* Royal Opera House, Covent Garden, London WC2E 9DD, UK; 11 Lancaster Ave, Hadley Wood, Barnet, Herts EN4 0EP, UK.

PAGE, Geneviève (pseudonym of Geneviève Bonjean); French actress; b 13 Dec 1927, Paris; d of Jacques and Germaine (née Lipmann) Bonjean; m Jean-Claude Bujard 1959; one s one d. *Education:* Lycée Racine (Paris), Couvent des sœurs de Ste-Catherine (Lectoure), Cours Sorbon (Paris), Ecole du Louvre and Conservatoire Nat d'Art Dramatique. *Career:* Prin actress in the Comédie Française and the Jean-Louis Barrault co and TNP Jean Vilar; has appeared in many famous classical and tragic stage roles; Chevalier du Mérite Sportif; *Plays include:* Les larmes amères de Petra von Kant (Critics' Prize for Best Actress 1980), La nuit des rois, L'aigle à deux têtes, Angelo, tyran de Padoue 1984, Perséphone 1988, Mère Courage 1988, Le balcon 1991, Paroles de poètes 1992, La peste 1992, La femme sur le lit (Colombe Prix, Plaisir du Théâtre Best Actress) 1994, Les Orandes Forêts 1997, Delicate Balance 1998; *Films include:* Ce siècle a cinquante ans, Pas de pitié pour les femmes, Fanfan la tulipe, Lettre ouverte, Plaisirs de Paris, Nuits andalouses, L'étrange désir de M Bard, Cherchez la femme,

L'homme sans passé, Foreign Intrigue, The Silken Affair, Michael Strogoff, Un amour de poche, Song Without End, Le bal des adieux, El Cid, Les égarements, Le jour et l'heure, L'honorable correspondence, Youngblood Hawke, Le majordome, L'or et le plomb, Trois chambres à Manhattan, Grand Prix, Belle de jour 1967, Mayerling 1968, A Talent for Loving, The Private Life of Sherlock Holmes 1970, Les Gémeaux, Décembre 1973, Buffet Froid 1979, Beyond Therapy 1987, Les bois noirs 1991, Lovers 1999; *TV appearances include:* La nuit des rois 1962, La chambre 1964, Les corsaires 1966, La chasse aux hommes 1976, Athalie 1980, Les gens ne sont pas forcément ignobles 1990. *Leisure interests:* antiques, skiing, diving. *Address:* 52 rue de Vaugirard, 75006 Paris, France.

PAGE, Jennifer Anne, CBE, BA; British civil servant and business executive; b 12 Nov 1944; d of Edward and Olive Page. *Education:* Barr's Hill Grammar School (Coventry) and Royal Holloway Coll (London). *Career:* Civil Service 1968–, Prin Dept of Educ 1974, Asst Sec Dept of Transport 1980, seconded to BNOC 1981; London Docklands Devt Corpn 1983–84; Sr Vice-Pres Pallas Investment SA 1984–89; Chief Exec Historic Bldgs and Monuments Comm for England (English Heritage) 1989–95; Chief Exec Millennium Comm 1995–97, New Millennium Experience Co Ltd 1997–2000; mem Bd Railtrack Group 1994–, Equitable Life Assurance Soc 1994–. *Address:* c/o Railtrack Group PLC, Railtrack House, Euston Square, London NW1 2EE, UK. *Telephone:* (20) 7340-2001; *Fax:* (20) 7340-2000.

PAGÉ, Lorraine, DIP ED; Canadian trade union executive; b 17 Dec 1947, Montréal; two d. *Education:* Univs of Montréal and Québec (Montréal). *Career:* Pres Alliance des Professeures et Professeurs de Montréal (Union of Masters and Women Teachers) 1985–88; first woman Pres Centrale de l'enseignement du Québec trade union 1988; papers on unions, educ and the status of women; Prix Chomedey-de-Maisonneuve, SSJB 1987; Ordre des francophones d'Amérique 1990. *Leisure interests:* reading, theatre, arts, travel. *Address:* Centrale de l'enseignement du Québec, 9405 rue Sherbrooke Est, Montréal, PQ H1L 6P3, Canada. *Telephone:* (514) 356-8888; *Fax:* (514) 356-9999.

PAGE, Patricia Kathleen, CC; Canadian writer and painter; b 23 Nov 1916, UK; d of the late Lionel F. and Rose Laura (née Whitehouse) Page; William Arthur Irwin 1950. *Education:* St Hilda's School for Girls (Calgary). *Career:* Solo exhibitions in Mexico and Canada, numerous group exhibitions; works featured in collections including Nat Gallery of Canada and The Art Gallery of Ontario; subject of film Still Waters 1991, of two-part sound feature The White Glass 1996; Hon D LITT (Victoria) 1985, (Guelph) 1990, (Toronto) 1998, (Winnipeg) 2000; Hon D IUR (Calgary) 1989, (Simon Fraser) 1990; recipient Oscar Blumenthal Award for Poetry 1954, Gov-Gen's Award for Poetry 1954, Nat Magazine Gold Award 1985, Canadian Authors' Asscn Literary Award for Poetry 1986, Banff Centre Nat Award 1989; Tribute at the Vancouver Writers' Festival 2000. *Publications:* The Sun and The Moon 1944, As Ten as Twenty 1946, The Metal and the Flower 1954, Cry Ararat! – Poems New and Selected 1967, The Sun and The Moon and Other Fictions 1973, Poems – Selected and New 1974, To Say the Least (ed) 1979, Evening Dance of the Grey Flies 1981, The Travelling Musicians (text) 1984, The Glass Air 1985, Brazilian Journal (Hubert Evens Prize, British Columbia Book Awards 1988) 1987, A Flask of Sea Water 1989, The Glass Air (poems) 1991, The Travelling Musicians (children's book) 1991, Unless the Eye Catch Fire 1994, The Goat that Flew 1994, Hologram – A Book of Glosas (poems) 1994, A Children's Hymn (with music by Harry Somers), The Malahat Review (special issue) 1996, The Hidden Room – Collected Poems 1997, Alphabetical (poem) 1998, Compass Rose (poems in Italian trans) 1998, A

Somewhat Irregular Renga (jtly) (for the CBC) 1999, An Invisible Reality (text (poems) for oratorio by Derek Holman) 2000, A Children's Millennium Song (with music by Oscar Peterson) 2000, And Once More Saw the Stars – Four Poems for Two Voices (letters and poems) 2001, A Kind of Fiction (short stories) 2001; numerous poems, short stories, essays, art criticism, drawings in various nat and int magazines and anthologies. *Address:* 3260 Exeter Rd, Victoria, BC V8R 6H6, Canada.

PAGELS, Elaine, PH D; American writer and professor of religion; m 1st Heinz Pagels (died 1988); three c (one s died 1987); m 2nd Kent Greenawalt. *Education:* Stanford Univ (CA), modern dance at the Martha Graham studio (New York) and Harvard Univ (CT). *Career:* Harrington Spear Paine Prof of Religion, Princeton Univ; MacArthur Fellowship 1981. *Publications:* Gnostic Gospels (Nat Book Award, Nat Book Critics Circle Award) 1979, Adam, Eve and the Serpent, The Origin of Satan 1995. *Address:* University of Princeton, Harrington Spear Paine Professor of Religion, Princeton, NJ 08544, USA.

PAGLIA, Camille, M PHIL, PH D; American writer and professor of humanities; b 2 April 1947, Endicott, NY; d of Pasquale J. and Lydia Colapietro Paglia. *Education:* Harpur Coll (State Univ of New York at Binghamton) and Yale Univ. *Career:* Teacher Bennington Coll, VT 1972–80; Visiting Lecturer Wesleyan and Yale Univs 1980–84; Asst Prof, Philadelphia Coll of Performing Arts (now Univ of the Arts) 1984–87, Assoc Prof 1987–91, Prof of Humanities 1991–2000, Univ Prof and Prof of Humanities and Media Studies 2000–; columnist Salon.com 1996–; many TV appearances; numerous lecture tours; numerous magazine and newspaper articles. *Publications:* Sexual Personae: Art and Decadence from Nefertiti to Emily Dickinson 1990, Sex, Art, and American Culture 1992, Vamps and Tramps: New Essays 1994, Alfred Hitchcock's The Birds 1998. *Address:* University of the Arts, 320 S Broad St, Philadelphia, PA 19102, USA. *Telephone:* (215) 717-6265; *Fax:* (212) 980-3671 (Agent).

PAGOWSKA, Teresa; Polish painter; b 12 June 1929, Warsaw; m Henryk Tomaszewski; one s. *Education:* High School of Plastic Arts (Poznan). *Career:* Prof Acad of Fine Arts, Warsaw 1988; Hon mem Asscn Réalités Nouvelles 1963, Nouvelle Ecole de Paris 1964; numerous solo and group exhibitions in Poland and abroad; works in numerous collections; City of Warsaw Prize 1989; Alfred Jurzykowski Foundation Award, New York 1990; Kt's Cross Order of Polonia Restituta; Golden Cross of Merit. *Address:* Ul Jazgarzewska 13, 00-730 Warsaw, Poland. *Telephone:* (22) 40 11 51.

PAHLAVI, Farah Diba; Iranian former Empress of Iran; b 14 Oct 1938; d of Sohrab and Farida Diba; m HIM Shah Mohammed Reza Pahlavi 1959 (died 1980); two s two d. *Education:* Jeanne d'Arc School, Razi School (Teheran) and Ecole Spéciale d'Architecture (Paris). *Career:* Foreign Assoc mem Fine Arts Acad, France 1974; fmr Patron Farah Pahlavi Asscn (admin of Social Educ Asscn), Iran Cultural Foundation, and 34 other educational, health and cultural orgs; left Iran Jan 1979; living in Egypt 1980.

PAIGE, Elaine, OBE; British actress and singer; b 5 March 1948, Barnet; d of Eric and Irene Bickerstaff. *Education:* Aida Foster Stage school. *Career:* Tours of UK, Ireland, Australia 1985, UK 1987; numerous TV appearances; 14 solo albums; four multi-platinum albums, eight consecutive gold albums; awards include Variety Club Award for Showbusiness Personality of the Year 1986, Recording Artist of the Year 1986, British Asscn of Songwriters, Composers and Authors Award 1993, Lifetime Achievement Award, Nat Operatic and Dramatic Asscn 1999. *Films include:* Oliver, What Ever Happened to What's His Name; *TV appearances include:* Love Story, The Ladykillers, Phyllis Dixey; *Stage appearances include:* Hair 1968, Jesus Christ Superstar 1973, Grease 1973, Billy 1974, Evita (Show Business Personality of the Year) 1978, Cats 1981, Abbacadabra 1983, Chess 1986, Anything Goes 1989, Piaf 1993–94, Sunset Boulevard 1995–96, The Misanthrope 1998, The King and I 2000; *Albums include:* Stages 1983, Cinema 1984, Chess, Love Hurts, Memories, The Queen Album, Heart Don't Change My Mind 1991, Love Can Do That 1991, Well Almost 1991; *Video:* Elaine Paige in Concert 1991. *Leisure interests:* antiques, gardening, skiing, tennis. *Address:* E. P. Records, 1st Floor, 754 Fulham Rd, London SW6 5SH, UK.

PAIK, Nam June; Korean/American kinetic artist; b 1932, Korea. *Education:* Univ of Tokyo (Japan). *Career:* Left Repub of Korea 1949, moved permanently to New York 1964; mem Fluxus (anarchic, neo-dadaist movt) 1961; major exhibitions at Galerie Parnassus, Wuppertal (Germany) 1963, Video Works 1963–68, Hayward Gallery, London 1988. *Major works include:* Urmusik 1961, Opera Sextronique 1967, The K-456 Robot.

PAILLER, Aline; French politician; b 27 July 1955, Casablanca, Morocco. *Career:* MEP (Confed Group of the European United Left/Nordic Green Left, PCF), mem Cttee on Civil Liberties and Internal Affairs, on budgetary control, Del for relations with the People's Rep of China, for relations with the mem states of ASEAN, SE Asia and the Repub of Korea until 1999; TV presenter Intime Conviction (France Culture) 1999–; Vice-Pres Conseil Economique et Social 1999–. *Address:* Conseil Economique et Social, 9 place d'Iéna, 75775 Paris, Cedex 16, France.

PAINTAL, Priti; British composer; b 1960; partner Robert Maycock. *Career:* Works in collaboration with Shiva Nova group (sitar, tabla, cello, flute and keyboards); uses Indian classical, African, Western, Caribbean and Central American and other ethnic musical traditions in compositions; fmr mem Bd Arts Council; campaigns on behalf of ethnic music through Main Music Agenda; works commissioned by Royal Opera House, Covent Garden, Barbican and S Bank Centre, London. *Works include:* Survival Song 1988, Biko 1992, Gulliver 1995, Polygamy, Improvisations; *Recording:* Polygamy, Improvisations. *Address:* Peregrine, Grange Rd, St Michaels, Tenterden, Kent TN30 6TJ, UK.

PAJKIC, Snezana; Yugoslav athlete; b 23 Sept 1970, Čuprija; d of Aleksandar and Verica Pajkic; m Milan Jolovic 1993; one d. *Education:* Univ of Novi Sad. *Career:* Came third in 1,500m race, World Jr Athletics Championship 1986, second 1988; first in 1,500m race, European Jr Athletics Championship 1987, 1989; second in 1,500m race, Mediterranean Games 1987; first in 1,500m race, European Sr Athletics Championship 1990; Sportsperson of the Year, Čuprija 1985–92; October Prize, Town of Čuprija 1990. *Leisure interests:* reading, films. *Address:* Kruševačka BB 4/13, 35230 Čuprija, Yugoslavia. *Telephone:* (35) 462322.

PAL, Bachendri, B ED, MA, FRGS; Indian mountaineer and business executive; b 24 May, Nakuri Uttarkashi, Uttar Pradesh; d of Kishan Singh and Hansa Devi Pal. *Education:* Garhwal Univ and Nehru Inst of Mountaineering. *Career:* Lecturer Rand Afrikaans Univ 1977–82, Sr Lecturer 1982–84, Chair Dept of Communication Science 1982–92, Prof 1984–94; Guest Lecturer Univ of California at Sacramento, USA 1986; Distinguished Visiting Radcliffe Prof, Baylor Univ, Texas, USA 1992; Consultant to various S African cos 1980–89; Ed Communicare (official journal for communication sciences in SA) 1984–92; apptd Exec Dir Asscn of Advertising Agencies 1995; invited by Council on Foreign Relations, New York to testify on the nature, effects and implications of the media restrictions then existing in SA 1988; Del Inst for a Democratic Alternative for S Africa, African Nat Congress (ANC), Harare, Zimbabwe 1989; Guest Speaker Advista Arabia IV Conf, Bahrain 1996; mem Council USA SA Leadership Exchange Prog 1990–94; mem South African Acad of Arts and Science; numerous contribs to professional books and journals—over 45 scientific publs and papers, nat and int; named in Women We Remember 1886–1986 by Johannesburg City Council 1986; Finalist Boss of the Year 1992. *Publication:* Everest – My Journey to the Top (autobiog) 1988. *Address:* Tata Iron and Steel Co Ltd, Jamshedpur 831 001, India. *Telephone:* (657) 428924 (Office); (657) 424923 (Home); *Fax:* (657) 431140.

PALACIO DEL VALLE-LERSUNDI, I. Loyola de, LIC EN DER; Spanish politician; b 16 Sept 1950, Madrid. *Education:* Liceo Frances de Madrid and Univ Complutense de Madrid. *Career:* Lawyer; First Gen Pres Nuevas Generaciones 1977–78; Tech Sec Gen Fed of Press Asscns 1979–82; Senator (Vice-Pres Grupo Popular) 1986–89; Deputy to Congress of Deputies for Segovia, mem Exec Cttee PP 1988–89, Vice-Pres PP Parl Group 1989–96; Minister of Agriculture, Fisheries and Food 1996–99; with European Comm, Alt Vice-Chair Cttees on Environment, Regional Planning and Local Authorities and Relations with European Non-mem Countries; Vice-Pres of European Comm and Commr for Relations with European Parl, Transport and Energy Sept

1999–; Rep to Council of Europe, mem Subcttee on Europe Prize, on CSCE. *Address:* European Commission, 200 rue de la Loi, 1049 Brussels, Belgium; Fernández Cancela 2, 28016 Madrid, Spain (Home). *Telephone:* (2) 299-11-11; *Fax:* (2) 295-01-38.

PALACIO VALLELERSUNDI, Ana; Spanish politician; b 22 Aug 1948, Madrid. *Career:* Lawyer; MEP (PPE, PP) 1994–; mem Cttee on Transport and Tourism, on the Rules of Procedure, the Verification of Credentials and Immunities, Del for relations with SE Europe; Pres Cttee on Legal Affairs and the Internal Market (EP) 1999–; Hon mem Bar of England and Wales. *Address:* European Parliament, rue Wiertz, 1047 Brussels, Belgium. *Telephone:* (2) 284-21-11; *Fax:* (2) 230-69-43; *E-mail:* apalacio@europarl.eu.int; *Internet:* www.anapalacio.com.

PALÁNKAY, Klára; Hungarian opera singer; b 3 June 1924, Budapest; m László Hódy 1957. *Education:* Franz Liszt Acad of Music (Budapest) and in Rome. *Career:* Mem Hungarian Opera House 1944–70; tours of Austria, UK, France, Netherlands, Belgium, fmr USSR, Germany and Poland; Distinguished Artist Award 1968; title of Kammersängerin conferred 1990. *Operas include:* Carmen, Peter Grimes, Samson and Delilah, Bluebeard's Castle; *Recordings include:* Don Carlos 1953, Bánk-Bán, Bluebeard's Castle 1956, Aida 1989. *Leisure interest:* gardening. *Address:* 1065 Budapest, Lázár u 10, IV 21, Hungary. *Telephone:* (1) 311808.

PALČINSKAITE, Violeta; Lithuanian writer; b 20 Nov 1943; divorced. *Education:* Univ of Vilnius. *Career:* First book of poetry published 1961; first children's play performed by Lithuanian State Youth Theatre 1966; twenty of her books have been published; awarded Gold Medal Int Children's Film Festival, Italy 1982, Int Bd on Books for Young People Honours List 1992. *Publications include:* Stairs (poetry) 1985, The Dolls of the Old City (children's poetry) 1987, I am Going After Summer (plays) 1988, A Spotted Snail of Dreamland 1997; *Film scripts include:* Andrius, Train to Bulziber, The Iron Princess. *Leisure interests:* travel, music. *Address:* Antakalnio 8-3, 2055 Vilnius, Lithuania. *Telephone:* (2) 625-628; *E-mail:* violpalc@takas.lt.

PALEČKOVÁ, Veronika; Czech artist; b 25 April 1962, Prague. *Education:* Industrial Arts Univ (Prague), Ecole Nat Supérieure des Beaux-Arts (Paris) and Acad of Fine Arts (Prague). *Career:* Painter, sculptor, engraver and book illustrator; solo exhibitions include The Golden Melon Gallery, Prague 1990, Československý spisovatel, Brno 1990; group exhibitions include Kobe, Japan 1986, Mánes, Czechoslovakia 1989, Salon de Mai, Paris 1990, Basle 1991, Burgwedel, Bremen, Germany 1991, Mexiko, Egypt 1991, Nuremburg, Germany 1991, Hollar Gallery, Prague 1992; mem Hollar Soc of Graphic Artists; Prize Int Biennale of Graphic Design, Brno 1988. *Address:* Nad Zámečnicí 15, 150 00 Prague 5, Czech Republic. *Telephone:* (2) 521830.

PALEY, Grace; American writer and academic; b 11 Dec 1922, The Bronx, NY; d of Isaac and Manya Ridnik Goodside; m 1st Jess Paley 1942 (divorced 1969); m 2nd Robert Nichols 1972; one s one d. *Education:* Hunter Coll and New York Univ. *Career:* Mem teaching staff Sarah Lawrence Coll 1966, Columbia Univ, New York 1984; mem Inst of American Writers; Guggenheim Fellow; Dr hc (Wesleyan, Colgate); Edith Wharton Award, NY; First New York State Author. *Publications:* The Little Disturbances of Man 1959, Enormous Changes at the Last Minute 1974, Later the Same Day 1984, Leaning Forward (poems) 1985, Long Walks and Intimate Talks 1991, New and Collected Poems 1992, The Collected Stories 1994, Just As I Thought 1998, Begin Again Poems 2000; poems and short stories. *Address:* POB 620, Thetford Hill, VT 05074, USA. *Telephone:* (802) 785-7608.

PALEY, Maureen, MA; American gallery owner and art dealer; b 1953, New York City; d of Alfred and Sylvia Paley. *Education:* Sarah Lawrence Coll (NY), Brown Univ (Providence, RI) and Royal Coll of Art (London). *Career:* Founder, Dir Maureen Paley Interim Art 1984–; has also curated a number of large-scale public exhibitions including Riverside Studios (London) 1986, Photographers' Gallery (London) 1986, PPOW Gallery (New York) 1986, Cornerhouse (Manchester) 1987, Museum für Gestältung (Zürich), Arts Council Touring Exhibition of Wall Drawings 1992–94, Camden Arts Centre (London) 1993, Henry Moore Studio Trust 1996; lectures at her gallery and at art colls in London and abroad including the Tate Gallery, Goldsmith's

Coll, The Slade, Chelsea Coll of Art & Design; contribs as a broadcaster on BBC Radio 4; Bursary Winner 1982, 1983; Minnie Helen Hicks Prize, Brown Univ (RI) 1975; Pentax Prize, RCA 1980. *Publications include:* Wall to Wall, The Cauldron, Technique Anglaise, Art London. *Address:* Interim Art, 21 Herald St, London E2 6JT, UK. *Telephone:* (20) 7729-4112; *Fax:* (20) 7729-4113.

PALLEY, Claire Dorothea Taylor, MA, LL B, PH D; British former college principal; b 17 Feb 1931; d of Arthur Aubrey Swait; m Ahrn Palley 1952 (divorced 1985); five s. *Education:* Durban Girls' Coll and Univs of Cape Town and London. *Career:* Called to the Bar, Middle Temple; Advocate S Africa and Rhodesia (now Zimbabwe); Queen's Univ of Belfast 1966–67, Prof of Public Law 1970–73, Dean Law Faculty 1971–73; Prof of Law Univ of Kent 1973–84, Master of Darwin Coll 1974–82; Prin St Anne's Coll, Oxford 1984–91; mem Council, Minority Rights Group 1975–94, UN Sub-Comm on Prevention of Discrimination and Protection of Minorities 1988; Constitutional Adviser African Nat Council, Constitutional talks on Rhodesia 1976, Govt of Repub of Cyprus 1980–; Hon LL D (Queen's, Belfast) 1991. *Publications:* The Constitutional History and Law of Southern Rhodesia 1966, The United Kingdom and Human Rights 1991; contribs to professional journals. *Address:* POB 3433, Nicosia, Cyprus.

PALLI-PETRALIA, Fanny, LL B; Greek politician; b 10 Aug 1943, Athens; d of Epaminondas Petralias; m Nicolas Pallis 1966; three d one s. *Education:* Arsakio Coll (Athens) and Univ of Athens. *Career:* Lawyer; mem Vouli (Parl, Nea Demokratia party) for Athens 1985–; Under-Sec of State for Sports and Youth 1990–91, for Social Welfare 1992–93; mem Bd Pres's Cttee of Advisers; Pres Women's Org, Nea Demokratia party 1985–88 (mem Political Bureau 1992), mem Cen and Exec Cttee Nea Demokratia 1986–89, Head Secr for Culture, Environment and Sports 1994, later responsible for Equality and Human Rights; Pres Exec Cttee 11th Mediterranean Games 1991; Founder, Pres Athens Women's Org 1982–88; Pres Foreign Affairs Cttee, European Union of Women 1984, mem Exec Cttee 1995; Vice-Pres Women's Section, European People's Party 1992; Prix de la Francophonie, French Sports Acad 1992. *Publications:* A Modern Woman With a Modern Family in a Modern Republic 1989, Europe, Sports, The Future 1991. *Leisure interests:* Greek folklore, poetry, sailing. *Address:* Akademias 28, 106 71 Athens, Greece (Office); Stravonos 26, 116 74 Glyfada, Athens, Greece (Home). *Telephone:* (1) 362 8782 (Office); (1) 894 0610 (Home); *Fax:* (1) 364 3909 (Office).

PALMA, Milagros, D ÈS L; French (b Nicaraguan) anthropologist, writer and publisher; b 26 March 1949, León, Nicaragua; d of Alicia Guzmán; m Claude Feuillet 1974; two s one d. *Education:* León, Paris and Univ of Paris X (Paris-Nanterre). *Career:* Ed Côte-Femmes publrs 1989–; Maison des Ecrivains grant for foreign writers 1987. *Publications:* Palabra mítica de la Gente del Agua 1983, El Cóndor, dimensión mítica del Ave Sagrada (2nd edn) 1984, Los viajeros de la Gran Anaconda, Le ventre de la grande femme de l'Amazonie 1986, La mujer es puro cuento 1987, Senderos Míticos de Nicaragua, Revolución tranquila de Santos, Diablos y Diablitos 1988, Nicaragua: Once mil vírgenes 1988, Bodas de cenizas (novel) 1990, Le ver et le fruit ou L'apprentissage de la féminité en Amérique latine 1991, Desencanto al amanecer (novel) 1995. *Leisure interests:* reading, walking in the forest. *Address:* Côte-Femmes, 4 rue de la Petite Pierre, 75011 Paris, France. *Telephone:* (1) 43-79-74-79; *Fax:* (1) 43-79-46-87.

PALMER, Felicity Joan, CBE, FGSM; British opera singer; b April 1944, Cheltenham; d of Sylvia and Marshall Palmer. *Education:* Erith Grammar School and Guildhall School of Music and Drama. *Career:* Soprano, then Mezzo-Soprano; has performed at all major int opera houses, including La Scala, Milan, Royal Opera House, Covent Garden, Opéra de Paris, Netherlands Opera and Glyndebourne; Assoc, then Fellow Guildhall School of Music; Kathleen Ferrier Memorial Prize 1970. *Operas include:* Elektra, Semele, Mahagonny, Pelléas et Mélisande, The Ring Cycle, Falstaff, Un Ballo in Maschera; *Recordings include:* Poèmes pour mi, Holst Choral Symphony, The Music Makers, Sea Pictures, Phaedra, songs by Poulenc, Ravel and Fauré, Victorian ballads. *Address:* 27 Fielding Rd, London W4 1HP, UK (Home); c/o Askonas Holt Ltd, Lonsdale Chambers, 27 Chancery Lane, London WC2A 1PF, UK (Office). *Telephone:* (20) 8995-8792; *Fax:* (20) 8742-0182 (Home).

PALOMINO, Gloria E.; Jamaican business executive; b 23 Oct 1936; d of the late William and Mary Lyn Ah Ping; one s two d. *Education:* Alpha Convent of Mercy High School and Commercial Coll. *Career:* Established Diesel Equipment and Service Company Ltd 1955, Company Dir, Man Dir 1974–; Dir Diesel Power Ltd, Lychee Gardens Restaurant Ltd, Eagle Commercial Bank Ltd; f Police Civic Cttee 1963, Pres St Andrew Cen, Vice-Chair St Andrew N; Chair The Jamaica Lawn Tennis Asscn; Founding mem Woman Inc; Badge of Honour for Meritorious Service. *Leisure interests:* tennis, golf, gardening. *Address:* 156 Spanish Town Rd, Kingston 11, Jamaica; Manor Courts Apartments, Manor Park, Kingston 8, Jamaica. *Telephone:* 923-7055 (Office).

PALTROW, Gwyneth; American actress; b 29 Sept 1973, Los Angeles; d of Bruce Paltrow and Blythe Danner. *Education:* Spence School (New York) and Univ of California at Santa Barbara. *Films include:* Shout 1991, Hook, Flesh and Bone 1994, Malice, Mrs Parker and the Vicious Circle, Jefferson in Paris 1995, Seven 1995, The Pallbearer 1996, Moonlight and Valentino 1996, Emma 1996, Sydney, Great Expectations, The Rise and Fall of Little Voice, Sliding Doors 1998, A Perfect Murder 1998, Shakespeare in Love (Acad Award for Best Actress) 1998, The Talented Mr Ripley 1999, Duets 1999, Bounce 2000, The Intern 2000, The Anniversary Party 2001; *TV appearances include:* Cruel Doubt (film); *Plays include:* Picnic, The Adventures of Huck Finn, Sweet Bye and Bye, The Seagull. *Address:* c/o Rick Kurtzman, CAA, 9830 Wilshire Blvd, Beverly Hills, CA 90212, USA; Screen Actors Guild, 5757 Wilshire Blvd, Los Angeles, CA 90036, USA.

PAMFILOVA, Ella Alexandrovna; Russian politician; b 12 Sept 1953, nr Tashkent, Uzbekistan; d of the late Alexandre and of Polina Lekomtsev; m 1st Nikita L. Pamfilov 1976 (divorced 1993); one d; m 2nd. *Education:* Moscow Inst of Power Eng. *Career:* Electronics Engineer 1976–89; fmr Chair Trade Union Cttee, Moscow Maintenance and Repair Plant; People's Deputy of USSR 1989–91; Sec Comm of Supreme Soviet on Privileges Jan–Nov 1991; Russian Fed Minister of Social Protection of the Population 1991–94; mem State Duma (Parl) 1993–, mem Cttee on Security 1995–98; Chair Council on Social Policy under Presidential Admin 1994; Founder and Head Healthy Russia Movt (later Movt for Civic Dignity) 1996; Pres Acad Revival. *Leisure interests:* gardening, recitation. *Address:* State Duma, 103009 Moscow, Okhotny Ryad 1, Russian Federation (Office); 103727 Moscow, Slavyanskaya pl 4, Russian Federation (Home). *Telephone:* (095) 292-83-01.

PAN, Marta; French (b Hungarian) sculptor; b 12 June 1923, Budapest; d of Zsigmond and Marie (née Piltzer) Pan; m André Wogenscky 1952. *Education:* Ecole Normale Supérieure des Beaux-Arts (Budapest and Paris). *Career:* One-woman exhibitions and numerous nat and int group shows in cities including Paris, San Francisco, New York and Los Angeles, USA, Amsterdam, Brussels, Basle, Switzerland, Budapest, Vienna, Tokyo, Osaka and Sapporo, Japan 1952–; works on show Musée d'Art Moderne, Paris, Museo de Arte Moderna, Rio de Janeiro, Brazil, Museum Boymans–Van Beuningen, Rotterdam, Netherlands, Hirshhorn Museum and Sculpture Garden, Washington, DC, Musée d'art contemporain de Montréal, Canada, Ministry of Nat Defence, Beirut, Lebanon, Yokohama Cultural Centre, Japan; created fountains for the Champs Elysées and Place des Fêtes, Paris; jt producer two ballets with mobile sculptures; currently working on monumental architectural sculptures; Officier des Arts et des Lettres 1986, Commdr 1994, Chevalier de la Légion d'Honneur 1997; Médaille des Arts Plastiques, Acad d'Architecture 1986; Praemium Imperial 2001. *Works include:* Charnières 1952, Le Teck 1956, Balance en deux 1957, floating sculptures 1961, 1969, 1971, 1973, 1978, Les Lacs (Brest, France) 1988, Jardin de la ligne blanche, Fragment de Paysage (Japan) 1991, Highway Signal (nr Lyons, France) 1994, numerous monuments in Japan (Tokyo, Gifu, Kagashima) 1994, Three Islands (floating sculpture) (Luxembourg) 1999, Atami (Japan) 2000, Sculpture en U (Kanazawa, Japan) 2001, Fragment of a Landscape (nr London) 2001. *Leisure interests:* swimming, ornithology, gardening, music. *Address:* 80 ave du Général Leclerc, 78470 Saint-Rémy-lès-Chevreuse, France. *Telephone:* (1) 30-52-00-47; *Fax:* (1) 30-52-73-20.

PAN HONG; Chinese actress; b 4 Nov 1954, Shanghai; m Mi Jingshan (divorced 1990). *Education:* Shanghai Drama Acad. *Career:* Actress Shanghai Film Studio, Shanghai 1977–80, Omei Film Studio, Chengdu

1980–; mem 5th Nat Cttee, Fed of Literary and Art Circles 1988–. *Films include:* The Last Aristocrat, A Slave's Daughter, Camel Bell in the Desert, A Bitter Smile, A Middle-aged Woman (3rd Golden Rooster Best Actress Award) 1983, Well (8th Golden Rooster Best Actress Award) 1988. *Address:* Omei Film Studio, Tonghui Menwai, Chengdu City, Sichuan Province, People's Republic of China. *Telephone:* (28) 22991.

PAN RONGWEN, MD; Chinese medical practitioner; b 1 July 1931, Jiangsu Prov; d of Pan Yu Qi and Pan Cao Shi; m Lu Shi Cai 1960; one s one d. *Career:* Alt mem 12th CCP Cen Cttee 1982; Physician-in-Charge, Changzheng Hosp 1982, Vice-Pres 1983–, Prof 1986–. *Address:* Changzheng Hospital, 428 Feng Yang Rd, Shanghai 200003, People's Republic of China. *Telephone:* (21) 3275997.

PAN XIA; Chinese director; b Aug 1937, Yidu, Shandong Prov. *Education:* Tongji Univ (Shanghai). *Career:* Ed and Dir Literature and Arts Dept, Chinese People's Cen Radio Station 1959–75; Dir TV Drama Troupe, Cen Broadcasting Art Co 1975–83; Dir China TV Drama Centre 1983–; Best TV Drama Award 1980; Flying Apsaras Award 1982, several Gold Eagle Awards; Nat Jinguo Pacesetter for Meritorious Service 1991 and Nat Sanba Standard-Bearer 1992. *TV:* The Sacred Mission, Multi-Prism, Walking into the Storm, Xiang Jingyu, The Pioneers' Footsteps, Madame Sun Yatsen and Her Sisters; *Publications:* over 20 research papers. *Address:* China TV Drama Centre, Beijing, People's Republic of China.

PANDEY, Manorama, LL B, MA; Indian politician; b 23 July 1932, Buxar; d of the late Rama Kant Pandey; m J. N. Pandey 1954; three s. *Education:* Banaras Hindu Univ. *Career:* Mem Legis Ass (Congress Party) for Bihar 1957–77, Parl Sec of Finance and Gen Admin 1961–66, Deputy Minister of Information and the Home 1972, State Minister 1972–74; mem Rajya Sabha (Council of State, Parl) 1980; Chair Bihar State Finance Corpn 1977–78; mem various Parl Cttees. *Leisure interests:* gardening, sport. *Address:* Rajya Sabha, Parliament House, New Delhi 100 011, India (Office); Nehru Nagar, Patna 800 013, India (Home).

PANG TAO, MA; Chinese artist; b 20 Aug 1934, Shanghai; d of Pang Xun Qin and Qiu Ti; m Lin Gang 1959; one d. *Education:* Cen Inst of Fine Arts (Beijing). *Career:* Art teacher Oil Painting Dept, Cen Inst of Fine Arts, Beijing 1955–89; Visiting Artist Ecole des Beaux-Arts, Paris 1984–85; lived and worked in USA 1989–90, Artist-in-Residence, Beijing; one-woman exhibitions include Guangzhou 1947, Yily Art Gallery, Shanghai 1948, Cen Inst of Fine Arts Museum 1986; group exhibitions in China, Asia and Europe, including Pang's Art Exhibition, Lung Men Art Gallery, Repub of China (Taiwan) 1990, 24th Festival Int de la Peinture, Cagnes-sur-Mer, France 1992; First Prize Beijing City Art Exhibition (for Tibetan Girl) 1981; Prize of Honour Beijing and Nat Art Shows (jtly, for Eventful Years) 1985. *Publications:* Paintings by Lin Gang and Pang Tao 1984, Modern Materials and Techniques of French Paintings (trans and ed, revised edn) 1992. *Leisure interests:* mural, furniture and fashion design, classical music, stamp-collecting. *Address:* 68 Xiao Wei Lane, No 242, Beijing 100005, People's Republic of China. *Telephone:* (1) 5130504 (People's Republic of China); (818) 307-0670 (USA).

PANIGRAHI, Sanjukta; Indian dancer and choreographer; b 24 Aug 1944, Berhampur; d of the late Abhiram and of Shakuntala Mishra; m Raghunath Panigrahi 1960; two s. *Career:* First performance aged four; has toured extensively in Europe giving lecture demonstrations and performances in Odyssi style; has appeared at int festivals of music, dance and drama in India, fmr USSR, Australia, Japan, Indonesia, UK etc; conducts regular workshops at cultural and educ insts abroad; Life Pres Kalinga Kala Kshetra and the Natyotkala; mem Gen Council Orissa Sangeet Natak Acad; mem Governing Bd Utkal Sangeet Mahavidyalaya, Bhubaneswar; numerous articles in journals in India and overseas; several awards including Cen Sangeet Natak Acad Award 1976, State Acad Award 1977, Padmashree (Govt of India) 1978, Tirupati Nat Award 1987, All-India Critics' Asscn Award 1989. *Address:* Plot No 4114/A, Ashok Nagar E, Unit II, Bhubaneswar 751 009, Orissa, India. *Telephone:* (674) 50638.

PANINA, Yelena Vladimirovna; Russian civil servant; b 29 April 1948, Smolensk Region; m Aleksandr Andreyevich Panin; one d. *Education:* Moscow Inst of Finance and Higher School of Econs. *Career:* On staff Control-Audit Dept Ministry of Finance, Russian Fed 1970–75; Head of Dept, Deputy Dir-Gen Production Union 1975–86; Sec Dist CP Cttee Moscow Region 1986–88; Head of Dept Moscow CP City Cttee 1988–91; Dir-Gen USSR Trade Chamber 1991–92; mem Exec Bd Russian Union of Businessmen 1992–; Chair Russian Zemsvto Movt 1993–; Deputy Head World Russian People's Sobor 1995–; Co-Chair, Co-ordinator Moscow Confed of Businessmen 1992–; Dir-Gen Centre of Business Projects (Interbusinessproekt) 1992–97; mem State Duma 1997–. *Address:* Interbisnesproekt, Novy Arbat 21, Moscow, Russian Federation. *Telephone:* (095) 291 9874.

PANNETT, Juliet Kathleen, MBE; British artist; d of Charles and May (née Brice) Somers; m M. R. D. Pannett 1938 (died 1980); one d one s. *Education:* Harvington School (Ealing), Wistons School (Brighton) and Brighton Coll of Art. *Career:* Special Artist to Illustrated London News 1957–64; Official Artist Quantas Inaugural Jet Flights 1959, 1964, Air Canada Inaugural Flight 1968; exhibitions include Royal Festival Hall, London 1957, 1958, New York 1960, Coventry Cathedral Festival 1962, Fine Art Gallery, London 1969, Wigmore Hall, London 1989, 1991, Royal Acad, Royal Soc of Portrait Painters, Scottish Nat Portrait Gallery of Edinburgh; works in perm collections including Nat Portrait Gallery, London (22 portraits), Bodleian Library, Oxford, Painter Stainers' Hall, London, Univ of Edinburgh; Freeman City of London 1960; Freeman Painter Stainers' Co 1960, Gold Medal 1960. *Paintings include:* D Day (for Devon and Dorset Regt) 1963, HRH Prince Andrew, HRH Prince Edward (for HM The Queen) 1974, Lord Baden-Powell, Group Capt Sir Douglas Bader, Lord Dacre, Lord Denning, C. S. Lewis, Lord Hailsham, Dr Quett Masire (Pres of Botswana), Lord Mountbatten of Burma, Rt Hon Margaret Thatcher, Sir Barnes Wallis, The Duke of Kent (for Devon and Dorset Regt) 1982, HRH Princess Alexandra 1984, HM The Queen 1989, Sir Wilfred Thesiger DSO 1996, Sir Laurens van der Post; drawings reproduced in The Times, The Daily Telegraph, Radio Times, The Lancet, The Artist, Law Guardian, etc. *Leisure interests:* the garden, talking books, music. *Address:* Pound House, Roundstone Lane, Angmering, Sussex BN16 4AL, UK. *Telephone:* (1903) 784446; *Fax:* (1903) 784446.

PANTOJA, Yvonne Magno; Brazilian diplomatist; b 9 Nov 1926, Belém, Pará; d of Raymundo Da Silva and Odalea (née Pantoja) Magno; m Diego De Aldecocea Pantoja 1948 (divorced 1985); one d. *Education:* Ministry of Foreign Affairs Diplomatic School (Rio de Janeiro), Northwestern Univ (USA) and Univs of Rio de Janeiro, Michigan, California (at Berkeley) and Houston (USA). *Career:* Vice-Consul, New York 1959–62; Second Sec and FAO Rep, Rome 1962–66; Asst Head of Culture, Ministry of Foreign Affairs, Rio de Janeiro 1966–67, Head of Documentation 1967–68; First Sec, Copenhagen 1969–72; Consul, Trieste, Italy 1972–74, Chicago, IL, USA 1974–76, Houston, TX, USA 1976–81, San Francisco, CA, USA 1981–84; apptd Chair Comm on History of Rio de Janeiro 1969; teacher Baptist Church Prog 1985; mem Houston Chamber of Commerce, Japan American Soc, Christian Women's Club; given title of Cavaliere (Italy), Dannebrog Commdr (Denmark); recipient Honour Cross (Copenhagen). *Publication:* The Women of Brazil (First Library Prize, Brazil) 1946. *Address:* c/o 1223 Post Oak Park Drive, Houston, TX 77027, USA.

PANTON, Verma Wevlyn, B ARCH; Jamaican architect; b 17 April 1936, St Elizabeth; d of the late Vernon George and of Laura Louise Panton. *Education:* Carvalho's and Ardenne High Schools and McGill Univ (Canada). *Career:* First female architect in Jamaica and the W Indies; Asst Land Surveyor's Dept 1956–58; Project Architect Ministry of Educ 1964–68; Assoc McMorris, Sibley, Robinson 1968–82; Partner Landmark Devt Co Ltd 1983–84; currently Prin Verma W. Panton Architect–Planner; Chair Organizing Cttee Pan-American Fed of Architects Conf 1974; Exec mem and Chair Jamaica Inst of Architects Public Relations Cttee; mem Technical Subcttee Nat Advisory Council on Energy Conservation, Kingston Restoration Co Ltd Grants Review Cttee, Housing Cttee for Devt of the Nat Policy Statement for Women; Jamaica Govt Scholarship in Architecture 1958; two awards from Jamaica Inst of Architects; Honourable Mention architectural design

competitions 1967, 1973. *Leisure interests:* reading, jogging, squash, swimming. *Address:* 4 Avesbury Ave, Kingston 6, Jamaica. *Telephone:* 927-7963.

PAPACHRISTIDIS, Niky; Canadian shipping executive; b 10 April 1941, Montréal, PQ; d of Phrixos Basil and Mariette (née Vachon) Papachristidis; m Pierre Bove 1964; two s. *Education:* Coll Marie de France and McGill Univ (Montréal). *Career:* Sec-Treas Papachristidis Maritime Inc 1975–80, Vice-Pres 1980–81; Sec-Treas Papachristidis Tankers Ltd 1975–80; Dir Papachristidis (UK) Ltd; Pres Papachristidis (Canada) Ltd 1981; Chair Probulk (Canada) Ltd 1987–89; Dir Saint-Laurent Soc of Econ Devt; Chair Ballets-Jazz of Montréal, Canadian Mediterranean Inst, McGill Chamber Orchestra, Young Virtuosi; mem Young Pres Org, Montréal Bd of Trade, Montréal Chamber of Commerce. *Address:* 3 Westmount Square, Westmount, PQ H3Z 2P9, Canada.

PAPANDREOU, Margaret Chant; Greek feminist; b 1926, America; m Andreas Papandreou (deceased). *Career:* Campaigner for Greek Women's Movt; f Women's Union; Leader Int Women for Mutual Security network; numerous speeches at Int confs. *Address:* c/o The Womens Union of Greece, Ainianos 8, Athens, Greece. *Telephone:* (1) 823-49-37.

PAPANDREOU, Vasiliki (Vasso), M SC, PH D; Greek politician and former European Communities official; b 9 Dec 1944, Valimitika. *Education:* Athens School of Econs and Business Science and Univs of London and Reading (UK). *Career:* Lecturer Univs of Exeter and Oxford, UK 1971–74, Univ of Athens 1981–85; Founder-mem Greek Socialist Party PASOK 1974, mem Cen Cttee 1974–, Exec Bureau 1984–88; Dir Hellenic Org of Small and Medium-sized Businesses, Athens 1981–85; mem Admin Council Greek Commercial Bank 1982–85; mem Vouli (Parl) 1985–89; Deputy Minister of Industry, Energy and Tech 1985–86, Alt Minister 1986–87, Alt Minister of Commerce 1988–89; Commr EC Comm responsible for Employment, Industrial Relations and Social Affairs, Human Resources, Educ, Vocational Training, Youth and Relations with the Econ and Soc Cttee 1989–93; Minister for Devt 1996–99; Minister of the Interior, Public Admin and Decentralization 1999–; Hon ED D (London) 1992; Dr hc (Sheffield) 1992, (Toulouse) 1993; Chevalier du Tastevin, France 1991; Special Hon Distinction, Univ of Athens 1991; Chevalier de la Légion d'Honneur, Grand-Croix, Belgium. *Publications:* Multinational Companies and Less Developed Countries: The Case of Greece 1981; numerous papers on politics and econs. *Address:* Ministry of the Interior, Public Administration and Decentralization, Odos Stadiou 27, 101 83 Athens, Greece. *Telephone:* (1) 3221915; *Fax:* (1) 3240631; *E-mail:* kominatos@ypes.gr; *Internet:* www.ypes.gr.

PAPARIGA, Alexandra, BA; Greek politician; b 1945, Athens. *Education:* Univ of Athens. *Career:* Gen Sec Cen Cttee, Communist Party of Greece (KKE) 1991–. *Address:* Communist Party of Greece (KKE), Leoforos Irakliou 145, 142 31 Athens, Greece.

PAPAS, Irene; Greek actress; b 3 Sept 1926. *Education:* Drama school. *Career:* Film debut in Lost Angels 1951, theatre debut 1958. *Plays include:* The Idiot, Journey's End, The Merchant of Venice, Inherit the Wind, That Summer, That Fall, Iphigenia in Aulis; *Films include:* The Unfaithful, Attila the Hun, Tribute to a Bad Man, The Guns of Navarone, Antigone (Salonika Film Festival Best Actress Award), Electra (Salonika Film Festival Best Actress Award), Zorba the Greek, The Brotherhood, Anne of the Thousand Days, A Ciascuno il Suo, The Odyssey, The Trojan Women, Moses, Mohammed: Messenger of God, Iphigenia, Bloodline, Lion of the Desert, Erendira, Into the Night, The Assisi Underground, Sweet Country, High Season, Drums of Fire, Banquet, Zoe, Up Down and Sideways, Party 1996.

PAPATHANASSIOU, Aspassia; Greek actress; b 1920, Amphissa; m Kostas Mayrommatis 1944. *Education:* Dramatic Art School of Nat Theatre of Greece. *Career:* Underground activities during the war; played a variety of leading roles with various Greek theatrical groups; Founder-mem Piraikon Theatre 1957, Intellectual and Artistic Asscn 1974, Inst for study of Greek tragedies 1990; performances include Mayakovsky Theatre, Moscow and Acad Ukrainian Theatre, Kiev, USSR (now Ukraine), Royal Opera House, London, Toho Theatre Co,

Tokyo; has toured extensively in Europe and N and S America; appearances at Int Festivals in Berlin, Paris, Florence and Vienna; over 450 performances of ancient tragedy; has appeared on TV in UK, fmr USSR, USA and several other countries; mem Patriotic Front (PAM); Gold Medal of City of Athens 1962; Kotopouli Prize 1963; Officier des Arts et des Lettres 1991; Nat Greek Acad Award for interpretation of roles in ancient Greek drama 1991. *Plays include:* Persians, Orestia, Electra (Int First Prize, Théâtre des Nations, Paris 1960, Best Actress of 1963, Int Theatrical Prizes of Palermo, Italy), Medea, Antigone, Andromache, Les Troyens, The Cherry Orchard; *Films include:* Electra. *Address:* Xenokratous 38, 106 76 Athens, Greece. *Telephone:* (1) 7242243; *Fax:* (1) 7214050.

PAPILIAN-TODORUTIU, Cornelia, MD; Romanian pathologist; b 4 Nov 1923, Babdiu, Cluj; d of Andrei and Amalia (née Bud) Todorutiu; m Victor V. Papilian 1958 (died 1982). *Education:* Secondary school (Sibiu) and Univ of Cluj-Napoca. *Career:* Dept of Gen Pathology and Experimental Medicine, Univ of Cluj-Napoca Faculty of Medicine 1948–49, Asst Prof Dept of Histology 1949–55, Sr Lecturer 1955–59; First Research Fellow, Head Dept of Experimental Pathology, Oncological Inst, Cluj-Napoca 1960–91, Research Fellow 1991; scientific publs in int journals. *Leisure interests:* history, languages, literature, classical music, painting, sculpture. *Address:* Institutul Oncologic Cluj-Napoca, Dept of Experimental Pathology, 3400 Cluj-Napoca, Str Republicii 34-36, Romania (Office); 3400 Cluj-Napoca, Str Pietroasa 20, sc 3, Apt 31, Romania (Home). *Telephone:* (51) 95154050 (Home); *Fax:* (51) 95118365 (Office).

PAPON, Christiane; French politician; b 3 Sept 1924, Vienna, Austria; d of Alexandre and Marie-Louise (née Garnier) Eraud; m Jean-Pierre Papon (divorced). *Education:* Lycée de Nantes, Insts Jeanne de Chantal and Chavagnes (Nantes), Univ of Paris and Inst d'Etudes Politiques de Paris. *Career:* Press attaché Ministry of Foreign Affairs 1953–54; journalist Radiodiffusion française 1956–58; Dir Social Affairs and Labour at the Fédération des industries électriques, électroniques et informatiques 1958–78, Dir Gen Services 1978–83; mem RPR Cen Cttee 1976–, Political Bd 1979–84, 1990–93; Municipal Councillor, Neuilly-sur-Seine 1977–89; mem Nat Ass (Parl) for Val-de-Marne 1986–93, Sec of Nat Ass 1988–93; MEP 1987–89; Vice-Pres Carrefour du gaullisme 1976–93; Pres Femme-Avenir asscn 1975–88, Hon Pres 1988–; Officier de la Légion d'Honneur. *Address:* 1 bis blvd de la Saussaye, 92200 Neuilly-sur-Seine, France.

PAQUET-SÉVIGNY, Thérèse, PH D; Canadian former United Nations official and academic; b 3 Feb 1934, Sherbrooke, PQ; d of René and Marie-Reine (née Cloutier) Paquet; m Robert Sévigny 1956; one s one d. *Education:* Univ of Paris (Sorbonne) and Univ of Montréal. *Career:* Journalist on La Tribune and L'Actualité and communications researcher Montréal and Laval Univs 1952–61; Man Dir of Consumer Research, Steinberg Ltd 1961–66; mem staff Communications Dept, Univ of Montréal, McGill Univ and Ecole des Hautes Etudes Commerciales, Montréal 1969–76; Vice-Pres of Research and Planning, BCP Advertising Ltd 1969–71, Vice-Pres and Man Dir 1974–81, Pres and Chief of Operations 1981–83; Vice-Pres RSGL Advertising Ltd 1971–74; Vice-Pres Communications, CBC 1983–87; Under-Sec-Gen of Public Information, UN 1987, Dir Dept of Information until 1992; Prof of Communications Québec Univ, Montréal 1993–; Dir UNESCO Chair in Communication and Int Devt 1993–; Int Consultant 1993–; Sec-Gen Orbicom (Int Network of UNESCO Chairs in Communications) 1993–98, Sr Advisor 1999–; contribs to books and journals; Dr hc (Sherbrooke) 1991, (Bishop's Univ) 1991. *Leisure interests:* reading, walking, friends, films. *Address:* POB 8888, Downtown Station, Montréal, PQ H3C 3P8, Canada; 1509 Sherbrooke St W, Apt 29, Montréal, PQ H3G 1M1, Canada (Home).

PAQUIN, Anna; New Zealand actress; b 1983; d of Mary Paquin. *Films:* The Piano (Acad Award for Best Supporting Actress), Jane Eyre 1995, Fly Away Home 1996, Amistad 1997, Over the Moon 1998, Hurly-Burly 1998, Begin the Beguine 1998, Sleepless Beauty 1998, A Walk on the Moon 1999, She's All That 1999, X-Men 2000. *Address:* c/o William Morris Agency, 151 E Camino Drive, Beverly Hills, CA 90212, USA; c/o Gail Cowen, Double Happy Talent, Wellington, New Zealand.

PARAMONOVA, Tatyana Vladimirovna; Russian banking executive; b 1950; m; one s. *Education:* Moscow Plekhanov Inst of Nat Econs. *Career:* Economist, later Head of Dept, USSR State Bank 1972–91; Vice-Pres Petrocommerz Bank 1992; Head of Dept, Deputy Chair Cen Bank of Russian Fed 1992–; Acting Chair 1994–95; First Deputy Chair Exec Bd Elbimbank 1997–; mem Bd of Dirs and Observation Bd Savings Bank of Russian Fed 1999–; Chair Cttee on Bank Inspection, Cen Bank of Russian Fed 1999–. *Address:* Central Bank of the Russian Federation, Neglinnaya str 12, 103016 Moscow, Russian Federation. *Telephone:* (095) 923 1641; *Fax:* (095) 924 6524; *E-mail:* webmaster@ cbr.ru; *Internet:* www.cbr.ru.

PARASKEVA, Janet, BA, JP; British law administrator; b 28 May 1946; d of Antonis and Doris (née Fowler) Paraskeva; m Alan Hunt 1967 (divorced 1983); two d two step s. *Education:* Open Univ (UK). *Career:* HM Insp of Schools Dept of Educ and Science (now Dept for Educ and Employment) 1983–88; Dir Nat Youth Bureau 1988–91; CEO Nat Youth Agency 1991–95; Dir Nat Lotteries Charities Bd, England 1995–2000; CEO Law Soc of England and Wales 2000–; mem Fosse Community Nat Health Service Trust, Council of Univ of Leicester. *Leisure interests:* golf, riding, gardening. *Address:* c/o The Law Society's Hall, 113 Chancery Lane, London WC2A 1PL, UK. *Telephone:* (20) 7242-1222; *Fax:* (20) 7831-0344; *E-mail:* www.lawsoc.org.uk.

PARENT, Marthe Louise Elizabeth, L ÈS L; French banking executive and civil servant; b 22 Sept 1938, Paris; d of Hermana and Louise (née Gerndt) Hadjadj; m Roland Parent 1962; two d. *Education:* Lycée de Jeunes Filles (Arras), Lycée Fénelon (Paris), Univ of Paris (Sorbonne) and Ecole Nat d'Admin (Paris). *Career:* History teacher, Pontoise 1963–68; civil servant Dept of External Econ Relations 1972–76; Official Cour des Comptes (admin tribunal) 1976–77; Tech Adviser on Int Financial Questions to Minister-Del of the Economy, Finance and the Budget 1977–78, to Minister of the Economy, Finance and the Budget 1978–79; Financial Attaché Embassy of France to the USA, temp Admin Officer for France at IBRD 1979–81; Chief Energy and Transport Dept, Treasury Dept, Ministry of the Economy, Finance and the Budget and Sec Fonds de développement économique et social (FDES) 1981–82; Head Financial Service Gen Industry Dept, Ministry of Industry and Research 1983–84; Rep to Banque Paribas 1984–86, Deputy Dir 1986, Dir for Operational Risk Man 1997; Dir Banque Worms 1982–, Banque d'Inodev 1983–, Paribas Asie Ltd; Chevalier de la Légion d'Honneur. *Leisure interests:* films, gardening, skiing, tennis. *Address:* Banque Paribas, 3 rue d'Antin, 75002 Paris, France (Office); 3 ave Fénelon, 78600 Maisons-Laffitte, France (Home). *Telephone:* (1) 42-98-12-34 (Office); *Fax:* (1) 42-98-13-31 (Office).

PARENTI, Tiziana; Italian politician. *Career:* Mem Chamber of Deputies (Parl) 1994–, Head parl comm investigating the Mafia. *Address:* c/o Camera dei Deputati, Palazzo di Montecitorio, 00816 Rome, Italy.

PARETSKY, Sara N., MBA, PH D; American writer; b 8 June 1947, Ames, IA; d of David Paretsky and Mary E. Edwards; m S. Courtenay Wright 1976; three c. *Education:* Univs of Kansas and Chicago. *Career:* Man Urban Research Center, Chicago 1971–74, CNA Insurance Co, Chicago 1977–85; writer of crime novels 1985–; Pres Sisters in Crime, Chicago 1986–88; Dir Nat Abortion Rights Action League, IL 1987–; mem Crime Writers' Asscn (Silver Dagger Award 1986); Ms Magazine Woman of the Year 1987. *Publications include:* Indemnity Only 1982, Deadlock (Friends of American Writers Prize 1985) 1984, Killing Orders 1986, Bitter Medicine 1987, Blood Shot 1988, Burn Marks 1990, Guardian Angel 1992, A Woman's Eye (ed) 1992, Tunnel Vision 1994; numerous short stories and articles. *Address:* c/o Sally McMartin Assocs, POB 432, Millerton, NY 12546, USA.

PAŘÍZKOVÁ, Jana, MD, PH D, D SC; Czech physiologist; b 9 May 1931, Prague; d of Jan B. Čapek and Vlasta Čapková; m Jiří Pařízek 1958. *Education:* Charles Univ and Czechoslovak Acad of Sciences (Prague). *Career:* Sr Research Officer Research Inst for Physical Educ 1956–92 (became Biomedical Centre FTVS, Charles Univ 1991); Assoc Prof, Sr Scientist Lab of Health Promotion, Medical School, Charles Univ 1992–; main topics of research are growth and devt, influence of nutrition and physical activity, body composition and physical fitness and health promotion; posts for WHO including Visiting Prof and

Consultant; mem European Acad of Nutritional Sciences, New York Acad of Sciences, Int Comm on Anthropology of Food (Int Union of Anthropological and Ethnological Sciences), European Asscn for the Study of Obesity, Czech Medical Asscn of J. E. Purkyně, Advisory Bd for Nutrition (Ministry of Health), Int Asscn for the Advancement of Kinanthropometry (mem Exec 1980–), American Asscn of Physical Educ 1985–, Panel of Experts on Energy and Protein Requirements (WHO, FAO, UNU) 1991; invited speaker at numerous int congresses and symposia; numerous publs, including 429 articles in nat and int scientific journals, monographs, etc; Fellow Laboratoire de Nutrition Humaine, Hôpital Bichat, Paris; Philip Noel Baker Prize, ICSPE by UNESCO 1977; Memorial Medal, Charles Univ 1978. *Leisure interests:* music, reading, walking in the woods, travel, skiing. *Address:* Laboratory of Health Promotion, 4th Dept Internal Medicine, U Nemocnice 2, 128 06 Prague 2, Czech Republic (Office); Myslíkova 32, 120 00 Prague 2, Czech Republic (Home). *Telephone:* (2) 24962106 (Office); (2) 299496 (Home); *Fax:* (2) 298694 (Office); (2) 299496 (Home); *E-mail:* parizek@mbox.cesnet.cz.

PARK, Dame Merle Florence, DBE; British ballet dancer; b 8 Oct 1937, Salisbury, Rhodesia (now Harare, Zimbabwe); m 1st James Monahan (divorced 1970, he died 1985); one s; m 2nd Sidney Bloch 1971; one s. *Education:* Elmhurst Ballet School and Royal Ballet School. *Career:* Joined Royal Ballet 1954, Soloist 1955–, later Prin; opened own ballet school 1977; Dir Royal Ballet School 1983–; awards include Adelaine Genée Medal, Queen Elizabeth Award, Royal Acad of Dancing 1982. *Ballets include:* Façade, Coppelia, Sleeping Beauty, La fille mal gardée, Giselle, Les Sylphides, The Dream, Romeo and Juliet, Triad, The Nutcracker, La Bayadère, Cinderella, Shadow Play, Anastasia, Pineapple Poll, Swan Lake, The Firebird, Walk to the Paradise Garden, Dances at a Gathering, Shadow, Don Quixote, Deux Pigeons, Serenade, Scène de Ballet, Wedding Bouquet, Les Rendez-vous, Mirror Walkers, Symphonic Variations, Daphnis and Chloë, Serenade, In the Night, Laurentia, Mamzelle Angot, Manon, Apollo, Flower Festival, Le Corsaire, The Moor's Pavane, Aureole, Elite Syncopations, Lulu, The Taming of the Shrew, Mayerling, Birthday Offering, La Fin du Jour, Adieu, Isadora, Raymonda. *Leisure interests:* travel, sunbathing, music. *Address:* Royal Ballet School, 144 Talgarth Rd, London W14, UK.

PARK OF MONMOUTH, Baroness (Life Peer), cr 1990, of Broadway in the County of Hereford and Worcester, **Daphne Margaret Sybil Désirée Park,** CMG, OBE; British former diplomatist and university administrator; b 1 Sept 1921. *Education:* Ross Bassett School and Somerville Coll (Oxford). *Career:* First Aid Nursing 1943–47, Allied Comm for Austria 1946–48; Joined FO 1948; mem UK Del to NATO 1952–54; Second Sec, Moscow 1954–56; FCO 1956–59, 1961–64, 1967–69, 1973–79; Consul and First Sec, Léopoldville (now Kinshasa, Zaire) 1959–61, Lusaka 1964–67; Consul-Gen, Hanoi 1969–70; Chargé d'affaires ia, Ulan Bator 1972–73; Hon Research Fellow Univ of Kent 1971–72; Prin Somerville Coll, Oxford 1980–89, Hon Fellow 1990, Pro-Vice-Chancellor Univ of Oxford 1985–89; Gov BBC 1982–87; Chair Legal Advisory Cttee to Lord Chancellor 1985–90; Chair Royal Comm on the Historical Monuments of England 1989–94; mem RSA, Council of Voluntary Service Overseas 1981–84, British Library Bd 1983–89, Bd Sheffield Devt Corp 1989–, Royal Inst of Int Affairs, Royal Asiatic Soc, Thatcher Foundation 1992–; Dir Zoo Devt Trust 1989–90; Trustee Royal Armouries Devt Trust, Jardine Educational Trust; Hon LL D (Bristol) 1988. *Leisure interests:* conversation, politics, foreign travel. *Address:* House of Lords, London SW1A 0PW, UK.

PARK YOUNG SOOK, BA; South Korean politician; b 1933. *Education:* Ewha Univ. *Career:* Deputy Leader Peace and Democracy Party (PPD); mem Nat Ass, mem Cttee on Health and Social Affairs; Man Dir and Vice-Pres Korean Women's Orgs Asscn; Chair Women's Cttee, Korean Nature Conservancy Council; Chair Cttee Boo Chun Police Station Campaign Against Sexual Torture; Pres Campaign Movt for Refusal to Pay TV Licence Fee; Man Korea YWCA; Chair Women's Cttee, Asian Christian Asscn. *Address:* 326-1, Soo Yoo Dong, Do Bong Ku, Seoul, Republic of Korea (Home). *Telephone:* (2) 784-0911 (Office).

PARKER, Sarah Jessica; American actress; b 25 March 1965, Nelsonville, Ohio; m Matthew Broderick 1997. *Films include:* Rich Kids 1979, Somewhere Tomorrow 1983, Firstborn 1984, Footloose 1984, Girls Just Want to Have Fun 1985, Flight of the Navigator 1986, LA Story 1991, Honeymoon in Vegas 1992, Hocus Pocus 1993, Striking Distance 1993, Ed Wood 1994, Miami Rhapsody 1995, If Lucy Fell 1996, Mars Attacks! 1996, The First Wives Club 1996, Extreme Measures 1996, 'Til There was You 1997, A Life Apart: Hasidism in America 1997, Isn't She Great 1999, Dudley Do-Right 1999; *Plays include:* The Innocents 1976, The Sound of Music 1977, Annie 1978, The War Brides 1981, The Death of a Miner 1982, To Gillian on Her 37th Birthday 1983–84, Terry Neal's Future 1986, The Heidi Chronicles 1989, How To Succeed in Business Without Really Trying 1996, Once Upon A Mattress 1996; *TV includes:* Equal Justice 1990–91, Sex and the City 1998–. *Address:* c/o Jane Berliner, Creative Artists Agency, 9830 Wilshire Blvd, Beverly Hills, CA 90212, USA.

PARKIN, Sara Lamb; British environmentalist; b 9 April 1946, Aberdeen; d of George Lamb McEwan and Mairie Munro Rankin; m Donald Maxwell Parkin 1969; two s. *Education:* Barr's Hill Grammar School (Coventry) and Edinburgh Royal Infirmary. *Career:* Ward Sister Edinburgh Royal Infirmary and Research Asst Nursing Research Unit, Univ of Edinburgh 1973–74; Family Planning Nurse Brook Clinic, Edinburgh and Leeds Area Health Authorities 1976–80; mem Ecology Party 1977–(became Green Party 1985), Int Liaison Sec 1983–90, Speaker 1990–91, Exec Chair 1991–92; Co-Sec European Green Co-ordination 1985–90; Programme Dir Forum for the Future 1994–; mem Population Concern 1995–; Trustee Friends of the Earth Trust 1995–, Groundwork Foundation 1998–99. *Publication:* Green Parties: an international guide 1989, Green Futures 1990, Green Light on Europe 1991, The Life and Death of Petra Kelly 1994. *Leisure interests:* reading, films, opera, theatre, walking, camping, gardening, squash. *Address:* 227A City Rd, London EC1V 1JT, UK; 18 blvd Pinel, 69003 Lyons, France. *Telephone:* (4) 72-33-65-97 (France).

PARKS, Suzan-Lori; American playwright. *Career:* Avant-garde playwright; plays have been performed off-Broadway. *Plays include:* The Venus Hottentot, The American Play.

PARLY, Florence Marie Jeanne; French politician; b 8 May 1963, Boulogne-Billancourt. *Education:* Institut d'Etudes Politiques (Paris) and Ecole Nationale d'Administration (Paris). *Career:* Admin Budget Dept, Ministry for Economy, Finance and the Budget 1987–91; Tech Adviser Office of Minister of State, Public Affairs and Admin Reform 1991, Office of Minister for Equipment, Housing, Transport and Space 1991–93; Head Bureau of Social Security and Social Services, Budget Office, Ministry of Economy and Finance 1993–94, Bureau of Equipment, Housing, Towns and Town Planning 1994–95, Bureau of Culture and Media 1995–97; Budget Adviser Office of the Prime Minister (Lionel Jospin) 1997–98; Sec of State for Budget 1999–. *Leisure interest:* skiing. *Address:* 139 rue de Bercy, 75572 Paris, Cedex 12, France.

PARLY, Jeanne-Marie; French civil servant; b 1 April 1935, Toulouse. *Career:* Sr Lecturer Univ de Clermont-Ferrand 1967–68; fmrly Sr Lecturer, Prof Univ de Paris IX, Prof 1985–89; with Ministry of Nat Educ 1984, 1993–, adviser 1997–98, Dir 1998–; Rector Acad of Caen 1989–. *Address:* c/o Ministry of National Education, 110 rue de Grenelle, 75700 Paris, France.

PARMINTER, Kate; British charity administrator; b 24 June 1964; d of James and June Parminter; m Neil Sherlock; one d. *Career:* Fmr grad trainee Nestlé; fmr mem Horsham Dist Council; fmr Head Press and Public Affairs RSPCA; Dir CPRE 1998–. *Address:* Council for the Protection of Rural England, Warwick House, 25 Buckingham Palace Rd, London SW1W 0PP, UK. *Telephone:* (20) 7976-6433; *Fax:* (20) 7976-6373; *E-mail:* katep@cpre.org.uk.

PARNES, Pauline (Penny) H., B SC, DSPA; Canadian speech pathologist; b 8 Feb 1947, Toronto, ON; d of the late Morris L. and of Anne (née Pomotov) Rosner; m Richard Parnes 1969; two d. *Education:* Univ of Toronto. *Career:* Speech and Language Pathologist in numerous Hosps 1969–75; Speech Pathologist, specializing in Augmentative

Communication 1972–; Dir Augmentative Communication Service, Hugh MacMillan Medical Centre 1980–90, Co-Dir Microcomputer Applications Programme 1982–90; Founder-mem and Bd mem Dirs Int Soc for Augmentative and Alternative Communications 1983–, Pres 1990–91; Student Research Adviser Univ of Toronto 1984–88, 1990–91, Asst Prof of Communication Disorders 1990–93; Consultant Ontario Ministry of Health 1985–86; Asst Prof of Applied Health Sciences Univ of Western Ontario; Vice-Pres Hugh MacMillan Rehabilitation Centre, Toronto 1990–96; mem Advisory Bd US Trace Centre 1984, 1985, Ontario March of Dimes; Ed Bd Rehabilitation Technology; lectures in field; mem Bd Int Centre for the Advancement of Community Based Rehabilitation 1991–; mem Ontario and Canadian Speech and Hearing Asscns, Rehabilitation Eng Soc of N America, Communication Awareness and Action Group; numerous articles in professional journals; recipient Editor's Award 1987, Prentke-Romich AAC Award. *Leisure interests:* hiking, sports, travel, family, reading. *Address:* 17 Croydon Rd, Toronto, ON M6C 1S6, Canada (Home).

PARR, Carolyn Miller, MA, JD; American federal judge; b 17 April 1937, Palatka, FL; d of Arthur Charles and Audrey Ellen (née Dunklin) Miller; m Jerry Studstill Parr 1959; three d. *Education:* Stetson, Vanderbilt and Georgetown Univs. *Career:* Called to the Bar, MD 1977, US Supreme and Tax Courts 1977, DC 1979; Sr Trial Attorney Internal Revenue Service 1972–82; Special Counsel to Asst Attorney-Gen, Dept of Justice Tax Div 1982–85; Fed Judge US Tax Court 1985–; mem Nat and Int Asscn of Women Judges 1985–, ABA, World Jurist Asscn 2000–, Asscn for Conflict Resolution 2000–; Co-Founder Servant Leadership School, Washington DC 1990, Joseph's House (AIDS hospice), Washington DC 1990; Hon LL D (Stetson) 1986; Distinguished Alumni Award, Stetson Univ 1992; Honouree, Nat Debate for Peace in El Salvador 1992, Women's Fund for Justice 1995. *Leisure interests:* church and charity work, world travel. *Address:* US Tax Court, Rm 422, 400 Second St, NW, Washington, DC 20217, USA. *Telephone:* (202) 376-2871; *Fax:* (202) 249-9106; *E-mail:* carolynparr@hotmail.com.

PARR-JOHNSTON, Elizabeth, PH D; Canadian economist and university president; b 15 Aug 1939, New York, USA; d of F. Van Siclen and Helene Elizabeth (née Ham) Parr; m Archibald F. Johnston 1982; two s two d (by previous marriage). *Education:* Wellesley Coll and Yale Univ (USA). *Career:* Visiting Scholar (Econs) Wesleyan Univ, CT, USA 1970–71; Academic Assoc Carleton Univ, ON 1971–72; worked for Statistics Canada 1972, Dir Econ Devt Analysis of Regional Econ Expansion 1973–75; Dir Govt Affairs Inc Ltd 1975–79; Sr Policy Adviser and Chief of Staff Dept of Employment and Immigration 1979–80; Man Shell Canada Ltd 1980–90; Pres Mount St Vincent Univ 1991–96; Pres and Vice-Chancellor Univ of New Brunswick 1996–; Chair Council of Nova Scotia Univ Presidents 1992–94, Atlantic Asscn of Univs 1994–96; Dir The Mutual Life Assurance Co of Canada 1991–94, Metro (Halifax) United Way 1991–94, Nova Scotia Power Inc 1991–; Bank of Nova Scotia 1994–, Empire Co Ltd 1995–, Fishery Products Ltd 1995; mem Ontario Econ Council 1980–84, Nat (Labour) Innovations Advisory Bd 1992–; writer several govt studies on regional devt; Yale Univ Woodrow Wilson Fellow. *Leisure interests:* skiing, golf, sailing. *Address:* 58 Waterloo Row, Fredericton, NB E3B 5A3, Canada. *Telephone:* (506) 455-1363; *Fax:* (506) 455-1463.

PARSLOE, Phyllida, BA, PH D; British university administrator; b 25 Dec 1930; d of the late Charles Guy and Mary Zirphie (née Munro) Parsloe. *Education:* Univs of Bristol and London. *Career:* Probation Officer Devon Co Council 1954–59; Psychiatric Social Worker St George's Hosp 1959–65; Lecturer LSE 1965–70; Assoc Prof Law Faculty, Univ of Indiana, USA 1970–73; Prof of Social Work Univ of Aberdeen 1973–78; Prof of Social Work Univ of Bristol 1978–96, Pro-Vice-Chancellor 1988–91, Warden of Wills Hall 1991–97, now Emer Prof and Sr Research Fellow; Chair N Bristol NHS Trust 1999–; mem Cen Council for Educ and Training in Social Work 1986–, Common-wealth Scholarships Comm. *Publications:* The Work of the Probation and After Care Officer 1967, Juvenile Justice in Britain and America 1978, Social Services Teams: the practitioner's view (jtly) 1978, Social Services Area Teams 1981, Data Protection in Health and Social Services (jtly) 1988, Aiming for Partnership 1990; contribs to professional journals. *Leisure interests:* hill-walking, crafts, gardening. *Address:* School for Policy Studies, 8 Woodland Rd, Bristol BS8 1TN, UK; Lion House, 9 Castle St, Thornbury, S Glos BS35 1HA, UK.

PARTON, Dolly Rebecca; American singer, songwriter and actress; b 19 Jan 1946, Locust Ridge, Sevier Co, TN; d of Robert Lee and Avie Lee (née Owens) Parton; m Carl Dean 1966. *Career:* Radio appearances include Grand Ole Opry, WSM Radio, Cass Walker Program; owner Dollywood theme park, est 1985; star TV series Dolly 1987, numerous other TV appearances; awards include Vocal Group of the Year 1968, Vocal Duo of the Year All Country Music Asscn 1970, 1971, Nashville Metronome Award 1979, Female Vocalist of the Year 1975, 1976, Country Star of the Year 1978, Female Vocalist of the Year Acad of Country Music 1980, People's Choice Award 1980, 1988, E Tennessee Hall of Fame 1988. *Albums and singles include:* Dumb Blonde, Something Fishy, I Couldn't Wait Forever, Daddy Was An Old Time Preacher Man, Joshua, Jolene, Coat of Many Colors, I Will Always Love You, Love is Like a Butterfly, The Bargain Store, The Seeker, We Used To, All I Can Do, Odd Jobs, Here You Come Again (Grammy Award 1978), Nine to Five (Grammy Award 1981, Acad Award and Golden Globe Award nominee), Real Love 1985, Just the Way I Am 1986, Heartbreaker, Great Balls of Fire, Trio (with Emmylou Harris qv, and Linda Ronstadt, qv, Grammy Award 1987), Rainbow 1988, White Limozeen 1989, The Love Album 1990, Home For Christmas 1990, Eagle When She Flies 1991, Country Girl 1991, Anthology – Dolly Parton 1991, Slow Dancing with the Moon 1993, Honky Tonk Angels 1994, The Essential Dolly Parton 1995, Just the Way I Am 1996, Super Hits 1996, I Will Always Love You and Other Greatest Hits 1996 (with others), Hungary Again 1998, Grass is Blue 1999, Best of the Best-Porter 2 Doll 1999; *Films include:* Nine to Five 1980, The Best Little Whorehouse in Texas 1982, Rhinestone 1984, Steel Magnolias 1989, Straight Talk 1992, The Beverly Hillbillies; *Radio:* Grand Ole Opry, WSM Radio, Cass Walker Program; *Publication:* Dolly: My Life and Other Unfinished Business 1994, Coat of Many Colours. *Address:* c/o RCA, 6 W 57th St, New York, NY 10019, USA.

PARTRIDGE, Frances Catherine, CBE, D LITT, FRSL; British writer; b 15 March 1900; d of William Cecil and Margaret Ann (née Lloyd) Marshall; m Ralph Partridge 1933 (died 1960); one s. *Education:* Bedales School and Newnham Coll (Cambridge). *Career:* Antiquarian bookseller, 1922–28; translator of numerous books from French and Spanish until 1965. *Publications include:* (ed with husband) The Greville Memoirs, 8 vols 1938, A Pacifist's War 1978, Memories 1981, Julia 1983, Everything To Lose 1986, Friends in Focus 1987, Hanging On 1990, Other People 1993, Good Company 1994, Life Regained 1998. *Leisure interests:* music, reading, botany. *Address:* 15 West Halkin St, London SW1XC 8JL, UK. *Telephone:* (20) 7235-6998.

PARTRIDGE, Linda, BA, D PHIL, FRS, FRSE; British biochemist; b 18 March 1950, Bath; d Goerge Albert and Ida (née Tucker) Partridge; m 1st Vernon French (divorced 1989); m 2nd Michael John Morgan 1996. *Education:* Convent of Sacred Heart (Tunbridge Wells) and Univ of Oxford. *Career:* Demonstrator, then Lecturer, Reader, Prof of Evolutionary Biology Univ of Edinburgh 1976–1993; Weldon Prof of Biometry Univ Coll London 1994–; Nat Environment Research Council (NERC) Research Prof 1997–. *Leisure interests:* sailing, gardening. *Address:* Department of Biology, University College London, Wolfson House, 4 Stephenson Way, London NW1 2HE, UK. *Telephone:* (20) 7679-7418; *Fax:* (20) 7383-2048.

PASCAL-TROUILLOT, Ertha; Haitian politician and attorney; b 13 Aug 1943, Pétionville; d of Thimocles Pascal and Louise Clara Dumornay; m Ernst Trouillot 1971 (died 1987); one d. *Education:* State Univ of Haiti. *Career:* Attorney-at-law; Judge, Civil Court 1979–86, Supreme Court 1986–90; Acting Pres of Haiti 1990–91, taken hostage and forced to announce resignation during unsuccessful coup attempt Jan 1991, arrested in connection with this incident April 1991, later released and went to USA; mem French Writers' Asscn 1973–; Lauréate du Concours de l'Alliance Française, Prix Littéraire 1965. *Publications:* Code de Lois Usuelles (Vols 1 and 2) 1978–98. *Leisure interests:* travelling, music, theatre (classical and modern), cinema, sports (wrestling). *Address:* POB 150, Port-au-Prince, Haiti (Office); Christ-Roi 21, Port-au-Prince, Haiti (Home). *Telephone:* 245-6760 (Office); *Fax:* 245-6760 (Office).

PASCOE, Eva, BA; Polish business executive; b 1965. *Education:* Univ of Warsaw and Univ Coll (London). *Career:* Set up software co in Poland; now lives in London; Co-Founder Cyberia Cafés, London (world's first 'cybercafé'), Manchester, Birmingham, Edinburgh, Dublin, Paris, Tokyo, Rotterdam, New York, Manila, Bangkok; cafés in other int locations planned; co-creator TransCyberia and SubCyberia venues, Cyberia accessories, on-line dating agency, Cyberia magazine, Channel Cyberia TV, Cyberia Records. *Address:* c/o Cyberia Cafe, 39 Whitfield St, London W1, UK.

PASKALEWA, Virginia Stefanova, D HIST; Bulgarian historian; b 1 June 1928, Sofia; m T. Zahariev 1956; one d. *Education:* Foreign language school (Sofia) and Univ of Sofia. *Career:* Painting classes 1949–50; taught special courses in history at Univ of Sofia, worked with Inst of History; Chief Ed Bulgarian Historical Revue; has written three monographs and 250 articles and other publs; Order of Zlatarski; Herder Prize (Vienna) 1990. *Leisure interest:* drawing. *Address:* 1116 Sofia, 14-20 Georgi Sofiiski Rd, A III, Bulgaria. *Telephone:* (2) 51-39-02.

PASTIZZI-FERENCIC, Dunja, PH D; Croatian economist and United Nations official; b 13 Oct 1936, Zagreb; m Dr Ante Ferencic 1961; two d. *Education:* Univs of Zagreb, Panama and Paris (Sorbonne). *Career:* Fmr Sr Researcher and Sr Programme Co-ordinator Inst of Developing Countries, and African Research Inst, Zagreb; fmr Int Consultant to Govts of Venezuela and Panama, and to UNDP for establishment of technical co-operation between developing countries; joined UN as first Dir Int Research and Training Inst for the Advancement of Women (INSTRAW), Santo Domingo 1981, Dir Div for Natural Resources and Energy, UN Dept of Technical Co-operation for Devt, New York 1990, Chair Editorial Bd Natural Resources Forum 1990–93, Dir of Science, Tech, Energy, Environment and Natural Resources Div, Dept of Econ and Social Devt, New York 1992; Deputy Exec Sec UN Econ Comm for Europe; fmr mem Editorial Bd Review of Economic Trends in Developing Countries; Del to int confs and multilateral meetings; numerous UN publs on natural resources, energy, women and devt 1964–93; several awards and recognitions from NGO and women's orgs. *Leisure interests:* classical music, swimming, outdoor activities. *Address:* UN Economic Commission for Europe, Palais des Nations, 1211 Geneva 10, Switzerland (Office); Zagreb, Radnicki Dol 38A, Croatia (Home). *Telephone:* (22) 917-26-94 (Office); (1) 413-613 (Home); *Fax:* (22) 917-00-36 (Office).

PATACHOU, (pseudonym of Henriette Eugénie Jeanne Ragon); French singer and actress; b 10 June 1918, Paris; d of Maurice and Marie-Célestine (née Vizet) Ragon; m 1st Jean Billon (divorced); one s; m 2nd Arthur Lesser 1963. *Education:* Ecole Communale de la rue Gambetta (Paris). *Career:* World-wide singing tours include tours of the UK and USA 1963–65, 1972, Japan and Sweden 1972; has performed in Paris at La tête de l'art cabaret 1966, Eiffel Tower restaurant 1969–71, Théâtre des Variétés 1972, Théâtre Fontaine 1973; appearances in films Napoléon, Le Piano des Pauvres, French–Cancan, Faubourg Saint-Martin 1986, La Rumba 1987, Pola X 1999, Drôle de Félix 2000; Chevalier de la Légion d'Honneur; Chevalier des Arts et des Lettres; Médaille de Vermeil de la Ville de Paris 1973. *Songs include:* Bal chez Temporel, Et si j'avais marié un grec, Le meilleur de ma vie, Le tapin tranquille, Toutes les femmes de mon mari, Je voyage, Vive les hommes, L'Amazone, Avec le soleil, Le piano du pauvre, La chose; *Plays include:* Impasse de la fidélité, Le sexe faible 1985, Poussières 1989, Des journées entières dans les arbres 1990; *Films include:* Napoléon, Le piano des pauvres, French-Cancan, Faubourg Saint-Martin 1986, La rumba 1987; *TV appearances include:* Fugue en femme majeure 1985, L'inconnu du 7 octobre, La lettre perdue 1987, Orages d'été 1989. *Address:* c/o Babette Pouget, 6 square Villaret de Joyeuse, 75017 Paris, France.

PATEL, Marilyn Hall, BA, JD; American federal judge; b 2 Sept 1938, Amsterdam, NY; d of Lloyd Manning and Nina J. (née Thorpe) Hall; m Magan C. Patel 1966; two s. *Education:* Wheaton Coll and Fordham Univ. *Career:* Man Attorney Benson and Morris, New York 1963–65; own practice, New York 1965–67, San Francisco 1971–76; Attorney Dept of Justice, San Francisco 1967–71; Judge Alameda Co Municipal Court, Oakland, CA 1976–80, US Dist Court, San Francisco 1980, Chief Judge 1998–; Adjunct Prof of Law Hastings Coll of Law, San Francisco 1974–76; mem ABA, American Civil Liberties Union, Nat Org for Women, American Law Inst, American Judicature Soc, California Conf of Judges; Co-Founder Nat Asscn of Women Judges

and Advisors for Women. *Publications:* Immigration and Nationality Law 1974; numerous articles. *Address:* US District Court, 450 Golden Gate Ave, POB 36060, San Francisco, CA 94102, USA.

PATHIAUX, Geneviève; French librarian; b 25 May 1941, Neuilly. *Education:* Syracuse and Antioch Univs (USA). *Career:* OECD Library, Paris 1965–80; Information Officer ICC, Paris 1990–. *Publication:* Key Words in International Trade 1989, 1996. *Address:* c/o ICC, 38 Cours Albert 1er, 75008 Paris, France.

PATIL, Pratibha Devisingh, LL B, MA; Indian politician; b 19 Dec 1934, Jalgaon, Mahar; d of Narayanrao and Gangaji Patil; m D. R. Shekhawat; one s one d. *Career:* Mem Mahar Ass 1962–85, Deputy Minister 1967–72, Cabinet Minister for Social Welfare 1972–74, for Public Health and Social Welfare 1974–75, for Prohibition, Rehabilitation and Cultural Affairs 1975–76, for Educ 1977–78, for Urban Devt and Housing 1982–83; Deputy Chair Rajya Sabha (Council of States, Parl); Vice-Chair Nat Fed for Co-op Urban Banks and Credit Soc; Chair Bhartiya Granin Mahila Sangh, Mahar; Organizer Women Home Guards, Jalgaon Dist 1962; mem Standing Cttee, All India Women's Council; Convener first Women's Conf, Delhi. *Address:* Rajya Sabha, Parliament House, New Delhi 100 011, India (Office); 84 Rajul-B Apts, 9 Harkness Rd, Malabar Hill, Mumbai 400 006, India (Home).

PATON WALSH, Jill, CBE, MA, DIP ED, FRSL; British writer; b 29 April 1937; d of John Llewelyn Bliss and Patricia Paula DuBern; m Anthony Paton Walsh 1961 (separated); two d one s. *Education:* St Michael's Coll (Finchley) and St Anne's Coll (Oxford). *Career:* Teacher 1959–62; Arts Council Creative Writing Fellow, Brighton Polytechnic 1976–78; Gertrude Clark Whitall Memorial Lecturer, Library of Congress, USA 1978; Visiting Faculty mem Center for Children's Literature, Simmons Coll, Boston, MA, USA; Judge Whitbread Literary Award 1984; Chair Cambridge Cttee, Children's Writers' and Illustrators' Group; Adjunct British Bd of Children's Literature, New England. *Publications include:* Gen fiction: Farewell, Great King 1972, Lapsing 1986, A School for Lovers 1989, The Wyndham Case 1993, Knowledge of Angels 1994, A Piece of Justice 1995; Children's books: Hengest's Tale 1966, The Dolphin Crossing 1967, Wordhoard (jtly) 1969, Fireweed (Book World Festival Award) 1970, Goldengrove 1972, Toolmaker 1973, The Dawnstone 1973, The Emperor's Winding Sheet (jtly, Whitbread Prize) 1974, The Butty Boy 1975, The Island Sunrise: pre-historic Britain (non-fiction) 1975, Unleaving (Boston Globe/Horn Book Award) 1976, Crossing to Salamis, The Walls of Athens, and Persian Gold 1977–78, A Chance Child 1978, The Green Book 1981, Babylon 1982, Lost and Found 1984, A Parcel of Patterns (Universe Prize) 1984, Gaffer Samson's Luck (Smarties Prize Grand Prix 1984) 1985, Five Tides 1986, Torch 1987, Birdy and the Ghosties 1989, Can I Play? (series of fourtitles) 1990, Grace 1992, When Grandma Came 1992, Little Pepi and the Secret Names 1994, Connie Came to Play 1995, Thomas and the Tinners 1995, When I Was Little Like You 1997. *Leisure interests:* photography, gardening, reading. *Address:* c/o David Higham Associates, 5–8 Lower John St, Golden Square, London W1R 4HA, UK.

PATRICK, Ruth Jo, MLS, PH D; Canadian university librarian; b 6 July 1939, Saskatoon, SK; d of Jim and Josephine (née Homey) Patrick; m John Aubry 1974; one s. *Education:* Univs of Saskatchewan and California at Berkeley (USA) and Ontario Coll of Educ. *Career:* Analyst Systems Devt Corpn, Santa Monica, CA, USA 1969–73; Co-ordinator of Continuing Educ and Visiting Lecturer, School of Information Studies, Univ of Syracuse, NY, USA 1974–76; Asst Dir of Library Operations, Wayne State Univ, MI, USA 1978–83; Dean of Library Services, Univ of Montana, USA 1983–90; Librarian Univ of British Columbia 1990; Doctoral Fellow Univ of California at Berkeley 1969; Higher Educ Asscn Fellowship 1970–72; Council on Library Resources Grant 1983–84. *Publications:* Guidelines for Library Co-operation 1971, The Public Library and Federal Policy (jtly) 1973, The Impact of Microcomputers in Academic Research Libraries 1984, Self-Directed, Contract Learning for the Reference Librarian 1990. *Leisure interests:* cooking, gardening, walking. *Address:* University of British Columbia, Main Library, 1956 Main Mall, Vancouver, BC V6T 1Y3, Canada. *Telephone:* (604) 822-2298; *Fax:* (604) 822-3893.

PATRICK, Sue Ford, MA; American diplomatist; b 9 Nov 1946, Union Springs, AL; d of Oscar and Mildred (née Hunter) Ford; m Henderson M. Patrick 1973; one d. *Education:* Notre Dame Coll (MD), Virginia State Univ, Univs of Boston and Virginia and Nat War Coll (Washington, DC). *Career:* Vice-Consul, Thailand 1973–74; Desk Officer Dept of State 1976–78, First Sec 1981–84, Special Asst Refugee Programmes 1984–85; Second Sec, Kenya 1978–81; First Sec for Political Affairs, Côte d'Ivoire 1985–88; Deputy Chief of Mission, Rwanda 1988–91; detailed to OSD/ISP/NATO Policy, Pentagon, Washington, DC 1992–93; Dir Office of Foreign, Civil and Military Affairs 1993–94; Congressional Affairs Advisor Office Regional Security Policy, Dept State, Washington, DC 1994; mem American Foreign Service Asscn; Dept of State Meritorious Honor Award, Superior Honor Award 1990. *Leisure interests:* jogging, jazz, reading. *Address:* Office Regional Security Policy EAP/RSP, Rm 5313 Dept State, Washington, DC 20520, USA (Office); 2715 Colt Run Rd, Oakton, VA 22124, USA (Home).

PATTAMMAL, D.K.; Indian musician and singer; b 28 March 1919, Kancheepuram; d of F. D. Krishnaswami Dikshithar and M. Rajammal; m H. R. Iswaran 1940; two s. *Education:* High School (Kancheepuram). *Career:* First public performance 1932; has given concerts in Germany, France, Switzerland, Canada, the USA, Sri Lanka and all Indian states; numerous recordings and film music; Fellow of the Sangitnatak Acad; numerous awards, including awards from Music Acad, Madras and Govt of India. *Leisure interests:* house-keeping, teaching music to deserving youngsters, reading. *Address:* No 50 Gandhi Mantap Rd, Kotturpuram, Chennai 600 085, India. *Telephone:* (44) 414129.

PATTERSON, Adeline Wynante, MB, BS, M PH; Jamaican medical practitioner and international organization executive; b 8 May 1932, Dominica; m Victor Ignatius Patterson 1958; two d one s. *Education:* Univ of London (UK) and Johns Hopkins Univ (USA). *Career:* Sr Registrar Victoria Jubilee Hosp; Medical Dir Nat Family Planning Bd 1971; Chief Medical Officer 1977–81; Health Adviser Pan-Caribbean Disaster Preparedness Project, Antigua 1981–83; Dir Caribbean Food and Nutrition Inst, Jamaica 1983–; Fellow American Coll of Obstetrics and Gynaecology 1974. *Publications:* Teenage Pregnancies – Their Implication for the Individual and Community 1964, Anaemia in the Turks and Caicos Islands 1987, Haemoglobin Levels in West Indian Antenatals 1987. *Address:* Caribbean Food and Nutrition Institute, Jamaica Centre, W Indies University Campus, POB 140, Kingston 7, Jamaica. *Telephone:* 927-1540; *Fax:* 927-2657.

PATTERSON, Kay Christine Lesley, BA, DIP ED, PH D; Australian politician; b 21 Nov 1944, Sydney. *Education:* Univ of Sydney and Monash Univ (Clayton, Vic). *Career:* Tutor Educ Dept, Univ of Sydney 1970; Sr Tutor Psychology Dept, Monash Univ 1974–76, Lecturer 1977–83, Sr Lecturer 1983–85, mem Univ Council 1978–; Prin Lecturer and Chair School of Behavioural Sciences, Lincoln Inst of Health Sciences 1986–87; Kellogg Fellow Inst of Gerontology, Univ of Michigan, USA; Visiting Scholar Gerontology Centre, Pennsylvania State Univ 1985; mem Liberal Party of Australia 1983–; elected to Senate for Victoria 1987–; Parl Sec to Chair Opposition Social Policy and Health Group 1990–93, Shadow Minister for Senior Citizens and Aged Care, Shadow Minister Assisting the Leader on Women's Affairs and the Arts 1993–94, Parl Sec to Shadow Minister for Community Services, Senior Citizens and Aged Care 1994–96, mem Senate Cttee 1996, Chair Senate Environment, Recreation, Communication and Arts Cttee 1996; Fed Parl Sec to Minister for Immigration and Multicultural Affairs 1998, to Minister for Foreign Affairs 2000–; mem Australian Psychological Soc, Victoria State Council of the Girl Guides Asscn 1974–. *Address:* Senate, Parliament House, Rm S113, Canberra, ACT 2600, Australia; 270 Clayton Rd, Clayton, Vic 3168, Australia. *Telephone:* (3) 954 47411.

PATUREAU, Nicole Germaine Antoinette; French archivist and palaeographer; b 24 Dec 1943, Vendôme; d of René and Anne-Marie (née Suard) Patureau. *Education:* Lycées Hélène-Boucher, Jules-Ferry and Henri IV (Paris) and Ecole Nat des Chartes. *Career:* Dir Indre Archive Services, Curator Indre Antiques and objets d'art 1967–92; Dir Departmental Archives, Loir-et-Cher 1992–; Chevalier de l'Ordre Nat du Mérite; Chevalier des Arts et des Lettres; Chevalier des Palmes Académiques. *Publications:* Visages du Bas-Berry (contrib) 1970,

Nohant (2nd edn) 1995. *Leisure interest:* music. *Address:* 2 rue Louis Bodin, 41000 Blois, France (Office); 10 rue de la Vallée, 41100 Selommes, France (Home).

PAULET, Marie-Odile; French trade union official. *Career:* Teacher 1969–81; Head of Regional Employment Training CFDT, Midi-Pyrénées 1981–87, Nat Sec 1987–91; Sec-Gen Union Confédérale des Cadres et Ingénieurs (UCC-CFDT) 1991–. *Address:* UCC-CFDT, 47/49 ave Simon Bolivar, 75950 Paris Cedex 19, France; 14 rue du Coustou, 31500 Toulouse, France. *Telephone:* (1) 42-02-44-43; *Fax:* (1) 42-02-48-58.

PAULO SAMPAIO DA COSTA MACEDO, Maria Teresa, M PHIL; Portuguese international organization official; b 19 Jan 1943, Anadia. *Education:* Univ of Lisbon. *Career:* Prof Univ Autónoma de Lisboa 'Luís de Camões'; mem Ass of the Repub, Sec of State for Family Affairs, Pres three Interministerial Comms on the Family; Perm mem Superior Council of Social Action; Pres Int Union of Family Orgs (IUFO, Paris); Dir Cttee Confed of Family Orgs in the EC (COFACE); Vice-Pres European Union of Women; Pres Nat Bd Nat Confed of Family Asscns, Instituto de Estudos e Acção Familiar, Centro de Investigação e Informação da Família, Cooperativa de Formação e Animação Cultural, Cooperativa de Apoio ao Desenvolvimento Cultural, Escola Politécnica de Lisboa – Cooperative de Ensino (CRL); Dir Portuguese–Arabian Inst of Co-operation; mem Ibero-American Cttee for the Family; has delivered guest lectures internationally organized by the UN, UNESCO and NATO; awards include Medal of Merit for Family Service (Luxembourg), City Medal (Saint-Germain, France) 1982, Woman of the Year (Brazil) 1982, City Gold Medal (Paris) 1987, Paul Harris Medal of Merit 1989. *Address:* International Union of Family Organisations, 28 place Saint-Georges, 75009 Paris, France. *Telephone:* (1) 48-78-07-59; *Fax:* (1) 42-82-95-24.

PAULSEN, Nancy; American publishing executive. *Career:* Fmr Ed-in-Chief Puffin Books, apptd Publr 1991; fmr Sr Ed Viking Children's Books. *Address:* Puffin Books, Penguin USA, 375 Hudson St, New York, NY 10014, USA.

PAVLÁSKOVÁ, Irena; Czech film director; b 28 Jan 1960; d of Alois Pavlásek and Nelly Pavlásková; m Jihří Chlumecký 1991. *Education:* Film and TV Faculty (FAMU, Prague). *Career:* Film Dir and Scriptwriter 1985–; Grand Prix, Digne, France; Critics' Award, Moscow; Award for most original film, Harare, Zimbabwe. *Films:* Time of the Servants (Hon Mention, Caméra d'Or, Cannes Film Festival, France 1990, main prize for début film, Montréal, Canada 1990) 1989, Corpus delicti 1991. *Leisure interests:* literature, music, theatre. *Address:* Americká 26, 120 00 Prague 2, Czech Republic. *Telephone:* (2) 258074.

PAVLYCHKO, Solomea, PH D; Ukrainian literary scholar, writer and translator; b 15 Dec 1958, Lviv (Lvov); d of Dmytro and Bohdana Pavlychko; m Myhailo Zahrebelnyj 1982 (divorced 1991); one d. *Education:* Kiev T. G. Shevchenko State Univ. *Career:* Apptd Research Assoc Inst of Literature, Ukrainian Acad of Sciences 1985; organizer of first academic seminar on feminism in the Ukraine; mem Rukh (People's Movt for Perestroika in the Ukraine), Founder-mem and writer of the statutes of the Rukh Women's Community. *Publications:* Transcendental Poetry of the American Romanticism 1988, Byron: His Life and Work 1989, Labyrinths of Thought: The Intellectual Novel in Great Britain 1992, Letters from Kiev 1992; trans into Ukrainian of books by D. H. Lawrence, William Golding, Lillian Hellman; contribs to books on British, American and Ukrainian literature. *Address:* Ukrainian Academy of Sciences, Inst of Literature, 252001 Kiev, Hrushevskoho ul 4, Ukraine (Office); 252023 Kiev, Kuibysheva ul 32, kv 13, Ukraine (Home). *Telephone:* (44) 224-84-88.

PAYE, Laurence Hélène Marianne, PH D; French civil servant and researcher; b 8 Jan 1944, Grenoble; d of Jean-Marcel and Marie-Laure (née Monod) Jeanneney; m Jean-Claude Paye 1963; two d two s. *Education:* Lycée de Jeunes Filles (Grenoble), Lycées Montaigne and Victor Duruy (Paris), Univ of Paris (Sorbonne) and Goethe Inst (Brussels). *Career:* Worked at Fondation nat des sciences politiques 1965–67; teacher Lycée Français, Brussels 1969–73; joined CNRS 1975, Head Office of Scientific Co-operation with Industrialized Countries 1975–78, Rep to Dir-Gen 1978–79, Head of Office of the

Pres and Dir-Gen 1979–82, Rep to Dir-Gen of Higher Educ and Research 1982–84, Dir Regional and Univ Affairs 1986–89; Deputy Dir-Gen of Higher Educ and Research, Ministry of Nat Educ 1984–86; Town Councillor, Rioz 1989–; Sec-Gen of Research Renault 1990–98; Prof Conservatoire Nat des Arts et Métiers 1998–; Pres OECD Asscn Rencontres 1984–96; mem Admin Bd CNRS 1999–; Chevalier de la Légion d'Honneur; Chevalier de l'Ordre Nat du Mérite; Chevalier des Palmes Académiques. *Publication:* Le chantier universitaire 1988. *Leisure interests:* tennis, swimming. *Address:* Conservatoire National des Arts et Métiers, 292 rue Saint-Martin, 75141 Paris Cedex 03, France (Office); 1 place Alphonse Deville, 75006 Paris, France (Home); 4 rue Charles de Gaulle, 70190 Rioz, France (Home).

PAYNE, Marie-Therese Augusta; Dominican banking executive; b 28 Aug 1928, Dominica; d of the late A. R. and Sybil (née Potter) Colls-Lartigue; m Horace W. Payne 1955 (deceased); three d one s. *Education:* St Joseph's Convent (Grenada). *Career:* Asst Dir Barclays Bank until 1977; Deputy Man Dir Nat Commercial Bank (NCB) 1978–88, Dir 1989–; Dir NCB Jamaica Ltd, NCB Trust and Merchant Bank Ltd, NCB (Investments) Ltd, W Indies Trust Co Ltd, Carp Corpn Ltd, R. Hanna and Sons Ltd, Gen Industries Ltd, Gleaner Co Ltd and Jamaica Banana Producers'Asscn Ltd; Chair Cope Ltd. *Leisure interests:* music, swimming, dance. *Address:* NCB of Jamaica Ltd, 32 Trafalgar Rd, Kingston 5, Jamaica (Office); 10 Millsborough Meadows, 1A Millsborough Ave, Kingston 6, Jamaica (Home). *Fax:* 968-1342 (Home).

PAZ, Miriam; Bolivian diplomatist. *Career:* Fmrly Amb to France, later Minister-Counsellor and Chargé d'Affaires, Embassy of Bolivia, Ottawa, Canada. *Address:* c/o Ministry of Foreign Affairs and Worship, Calle Ingavi, esq. Junin, La Paz, Bolivia.

PEACOCK, Elizabeth Joan, FRSA; British politician; b 4 April 1937; two s. *Education:* St Monica's Convent (Skipton). *Career:* JP 1975–79; Election Agent (Cons) 1979; Councillor N Yorks Co Council 1981–84; MP for Batley and Spen 1983–97, Parl Pvt Sec to Minister of State at the Home Office 1991–92, to Minister of State at Dept of Social Security 1992, mem Select Cttee on Employment 1983–87, Exec Cttee Cons Back Bench 1922 Cttee 1987–91, Select Cttee on House of Commons Services 1988–91, Exec Cttee UK Br Commonwealth Parl Asscn 1987–92, Vice-Chair All-Party Group for the Prevention of Solvent and Volatile Substance Abuse; mem BBC Gen Advisory Cttee 1988–93; Vice-Pres Yorks and Humberside Devt Asscn; Pres Yorks Area Conservative Trade Unionists 1991–98; Fellow Industry and Parl Trust; DL (W Yorks) 1998. *Address:* Spen House, 87 George Lane, Notton, Wakefield, W Yorks WF4 2NQ, UK (Office); 27A Northgate, Cleckheaton, W Yorks BD19 3HH, UK (Constituency Office). *Telephone:* (1274) 872-968.

PEARCE, (Ann) Phillipa, MA, FRSL; British writer; d of Ernest Alexander and Gertrude Alice (née Ramsden) Pearce; m Martin James Graham Christie (deceased); one d. *Education:* Perse Girls' School (Cambridge) and Girton Coll (Cambridge). *Career:* Civil servant 1942–45; Producer and Scriptwriter for BBC Radio School Programmes 1945–58; Ed Educ Dept Clarendon Press 1958–60; Children's Ed André Deutsch Ltd 1960–67; freelance writer 1967–; lectures in field; reviews for Times Literary Supplement and The Guardian newspapers. *Publications:* From Inside Scotland Yard (jtly) 1963, A Dog So Small (2nd edn) 1964, The Strange Sunflower 1966, The Elm Street Lot 1969, The Squirrel Wife 1971, Stories From Hans Christian Anderson (ed) 1972, Beauty and the Beast 1972, What the Neighbours Did and other stories (2nd edn) 1974, Minnow on the Say (3rd edn) 1974, Mrs Cockle's Cat (2nd edn) 1974, Tom's Midnight Garden (Carnegie Medal 1959, 3rd edn) 1976, The Shadow Cage and other stories of the supernatural 1977, The Battle of Bubble and Squeak (Whitbread Award) 1978, The Way to Sattin Shore 1983, Lion at School and other stories 1985, Who's Afraid? and other strange stories 1986, The Toothball 1987, Emily's Own Elephant 1987, Freddy 1988, The Children of Charlecote (jtly, 3rd edn) 1989, Old Belle's Summer Holiday 1989, Here Comes Tod 1992, Dread and Delight: A Century of Children's Ghost Stories (ed) 1995. *Address:* c/o Viking Kestrel Books, 27 Wright's Lane, London W8 5TZ, UK. *Telephone:* (20) 7938-2200.

PEARCE, Jessica; British diplomatist; b 1 Sept 1957. *Career:* Joined FCO 1985, Asst Desk Officer (Research and Analysis) 1985–86, Desk Officer (East European Dept) 1986–87, (African Dept) 1992–94, Second Sec Embassy Dakar 1987–90, First Sec 1990, Head of Unit, UN Dept (London) 1990–92, language training 1994–95, Amb to Belarus 1996–99; Deputy-Head Non-Proliferation Dept, Foreign and Commonwealth Office 1999–. *Address:* Foreign and Commonwealth Office, London SW1A 2AH, UK.

PEARL, Valerie Louise, D PHIL, FRHISTS, FSA; British historian and former college president; b 31 Dec 1926, Newport, Mon; d of Cyril R. and Florence (née Bowler) Bence; m Morris L. Pearl 1949; one d. *Education:* King Edward VI High School (Birmingham) and St Anne's Coll (Oxford). *Career:* Graham Research Fellow and Lecturer in History Somerville Coll, Oxford 1965–68; Reader in History of London, Univ Coll London 1968–76, Prof 1976–81; Ford Special Lecturer Univ of Oxford 1980; Pres New Hall, Cambridge 1981–95; McBride Visiting Prof Bryn Mawr Coll, PA, USA 1974; Woodward Lecturer Yale Univ, USA 1974; Lecturer Indian Council for Social Science, Calcutta 1977; convenor founding conf and Ed-in-Chief The London Journal 1973–77; Literary Dir Royal Historical Soc 1975–77; Gov Museum of London 1978–92; Syndic Cambridge Univ Library 1982, Cambridge Univ Press 1984; Commr Royal Comm on Historical Manuscripts 1983–92; Hon Fellow St Anne's Coll, Oxford 1993; Leverhulme Research Award 1962. *Publications:* London and the Outbreak of the Puritan Revolution 1625–43 1961, The Interregnum 1972, Puritans and Revolutionaries 1978, Change and Stability 1979, Social Policy in Early Modern London 1981; articles and contribs to books, encyclopedias and professional journals. *Leisure interests:* walking, gardening, swimming. *Address:* New Hall, Huntingdon Rd, Cambridge CB3 0DF, UK. *Telephone:* (1223) 351721; *Fax:* (1223) 352941.

PEARSE, Barbara Mary Frances, B SC, PH D, FRS; British scientist; b 24 March 1948, UK; d of Reginald W. B. and Enid Alice (née Mitchell) Pearse; m Mark Steven Bretscher 1978; one s one d. *Education:* Lady Eleanor Holles School and Univ Coll (London). *Career:* Postdoctoral Fellow MRC Lab of Molecular Biology 1972–81; staff scientist 1981–; Visiting Prof Stanford Medical Center, USA 1984–85; mem EMBO 1982; Fellow Univ Coll London 1996; Jack Drummond Prize 1968; K. M. Stott Prize 1979; EMBO Gold Medal 1987. *Publication:* European Molecular Biology Organization Review 1987. *Leisure interest:* garden and woodland. *Address:* Medical Research Council, Laboratory of Molecular Biology, Hills Rd, Cambridge CB2 2QH, UK (Office); Ram Cottage, 63 Commercial End, Swaffham Bulbeck, Cambridge CB5 0ND, UK (Home). *Telephone:* (1223) 248011 (Office); (1223) 811276 (Home); *Fax:* (1223) 412142 (Office); *Internet:* www2.mrc-lmb.cam.ac.uk (Office).

PECKOVÁ, Dagmar; Czech opera singer (mezzo soprano); b 4 April 1961, Chrudim; m 2nd Ales Kasprík 1997; one s; m 3rd Klaus Schiesser. *Education:* Prague Conservatory. *Career:* With Music Theatre, Prague 1982–85; soloist with numerous cos including Czech Philarmony 1985–, with Semper Opera, Dresden 1985–88, with State Opera Berlin 1989–91; concert tours Austria, Switzerland, Germany, UK, France, USA 1997–99; roles include: Leonora (Basel), Cherubino in The Marriage of Figaro (London), Rosina in The Barber of Seville (Berlin, Dresden), Carmen (Prague); First Prize Antonin Dvorák Competition 1982; European Foundation for Music prize 1993; Thalia Prize (for Carmen) 2000. *Recordings include:* Martinu — Nipponari 1991, Mozart — Che Bella 1994, Janácek — Moravian Folk Poetry in Song 1994, Mahler — Adagietto, Kindertotenlieder 1996, Songs of Mahler and Berio 1997, Janácek—Káta Kabanová 1997, Janácek—Diary of One Who Disappeared 1999, recital of music by Wagner, Schoenberg, Zemlinsky and Brahms 2000, Lieder by Strauss, Schoeck, Berg 2001, Lieder by Dvorák 2001. *Leisure interests:* reading, car driving. *Address:* Na Pankráci 101, 140 00 Prague 4, Czech Republic. *Telephone:* (2) 4140-6665; *Fax:* (2) 4140-7599; *E-mail:* bellamaya@iplus.cz.

PEDRETTI, Erica; Swiss writer and artist; b Feb 1930, Sternberg (Czechoslovakia, now Czech Repub); m Gian Pedretti 1952; five c. *Education:* Schule für Gestaltung (Zürich). *Career:* Lived in Switzerland 1945–50, USA 1950–74, Switzerland 1974–; Bachmann-Preis 1984; Großer Literatur-Preis des Kantons Bern 1990; Berliner-Preis, Bobrowski-Medaille 1994; M. L. Kaschnitz-Preis 1996. *Publications:*

Harmloses, bitte 1970, Heiliger Sebastian, Valerie oder das Unerzogene Auge 1986, Engste Heimat 1995, Zerhümmerung 1996. *Address:* 4 chemin de Beausite, 2520 La Neuveville, Switzerland. *Telephone:* (38) 513561.

PEDRO, Maria; business executive; b 1952; divorced. *Career:* Has established a multi-media company with Peter Gabriel; PR adviser to celebrities and pop stars including Jeremy Guscott, Tony Underwood, Jonathan Webb, Steve Ojomoh, Laurent Cabannes, Jason McAteer and Alan Stubbs.

PEI YANLING; Chinese actress; b Aug 1947, Shuning Co, Hebei Prov. *Career:* Vice-Chair Hebei Fed of Literary and Art Circles 1993–; mem 7th CPPCC 1987–92, 8th 1993–. *Performances include:* The Man and the Ghost, Lotus Lantern. *Address:* Hebei Federation of Literary and Art Circles, Shijiazhuang City, People's Republic of China.

PEIJS, Karla M. H.; Netherlands politician; b 1 Sept 1944, Tilburg; m I. Platschorre; one s one d. *Education:* Catholic Univ. *Career:* Lecturer Utrecht Univ 1985–88, Head Int Relations Faculty 1988–89; elected MEP (EPP) 1989, Chair Parliamentary Intergroup on Small and Medium Enterprises, Vice-Chair Subcttee on Monetary Affairs, Del for Relations with the USA, mem Cttee for Econ and Monetary Affairs and Industrial Policy, Cttee for Women's Rights, substitute mem Cttee on Regional Policy, Regional Planning and Relations with Regional and Local Authorities, Co-Pres Ind Business and Econ Asscn of the EPP. *Address:* c/o European Parliament, rue Wiertz, 1040 Brussels, Belgium.

PEINEMANN, Edith; German concert violinist; b 3 March 1939, Mainz; d of Robert and Hildegard (née Rohde) Peinemann. *Education:* Studied under her father and later with Heinz Stauske and Max Rostal, Guildhall School of Music (London). *Career:* First Prize, ARD competition, Munich 1956; since then has performed with leading orchestras and conductors worldwide; Prof of Music Hochschule für Musik und Darstellende Kunst, Frankfurt; numerous recordings 1965–; Plaquette Eugène Ysange, Liège, Belgium. *Leisure interests:* art, hiking, cooking, wine, cross-country skiing. *Address:* c/o Pro Musicis, Rütistr 38, 8032 Zurich, Switzerland; Hochschule für Musik und Darstellende Kunst, Frankfurt, Germany. *Telephone:* (1) 2516533 (Zurich).

PELAYO DUQUE, María Dolores, LIC EN DER; Spanish politician; b 21 Nov 1943, Santa Cruz, Tenerife; d of Juan Maria and Mónica Pelayo Duque; m Salvador Dorta Reyes 1970; one s one d. *Education:* Univ de la Laguna. *Career:* Senator for Santa Cruz 1977–79; mem Congress of Deputies (PSOE) for Santa Cruz 1979–92, First Vice-Pres Comms on Defence and Agriculture, Third Sec Comm of the Congress of Deputies; awarded Gran Cruz de San Raimundo de Peñafort, Gran Cruz del Mérito Agricola. *Address:* c/o Congreso de los Diputados, Secretaría Tercera, Carrera de San Jerónimo s/n, Madrid, Spain.

PELLETIER, Monique Denyse, L EN D; French barrister and politician; b 25 July 1926, Trouville-sur-Mer; d of Jean and Christiane Lair (née Dubreuil) Bédier; m Jean-Marc Pelletier 1948; four s three d. *Education:* Lycée Racine (Paris) and law studies. *Career:* Barrister and Assessing Judge Tribunal pour Enfants, Paris-Nanterre 1948–60; Dir Ecole des parents et des éducateurs 1972–77; Municipal Councillor (UDF), Neuilly 1971–77, Deputy Mayor 1977–83; mem Exec UDF 1977; mem Study Group on Problems of Drug Addiction 1977; Sec of State to Minister of Justice and Keeper of the Seals 1978; Minister for Women's Rights 1980–81; Barrister, Paris Bar 1981–; mem Conseil Constitutionnel 2000–; Officier de la Légion d'Honneur; Commdr de l'Ordre Nat du Mérite. *Publications:* Le droit dans ma vie 1975, Nous sommes toutes responsables 1981, La ligne brisée 1996. *Address:* 45 ave Montaigne, 75008 Paris, France (Office); 67 ave Kleber, 75116 Paris, France. *Telephone:* (1) 47-20-92-92; *Fax:* (1) 47-23-91-55; *E-mail:* m.pelletier@ngo-avocats.com.

PELOSI, Nancy; American politician; b 1941, Baltimore, MD; d of Thomas J. D'Alesandro, Jr; m Paul Pelosi; four d one s. *Education:* Trinity Coll. *Career:* Chair California State Democratic Cttee 1981; mem Cttee Democratic Nat Cttee 1976, 1980, 1984; elected to US Congress from 5th Dist of California 1987–92, from 8th Dist of California 1993–; Financial Chair Democratic Senatorial Campaign Cttee 1987. *Address:* US House of Representatives, 2457 Rayburn Bldg, Washington, DC 20515-0508, USA.

PELTOMÄKI, Lea; Finnish business executive; b 24 Jan 1931, Kauhajoki; d of Väinö and Elsa Yli-Havunen; m Antti Johannes 1958 (died 1986); one d. *Education:* School of Social Studies (Helsinki). *Career:* Tax Sec, later Auditor and Chief of Finance, City of Pori 1977–87; mem Pori City Council 1988–; apptd Chair RKL (Technical and Real Estate Cttee), City of Pori 1990; auditor for several public and pvt orgs; Pres Nat BPW 1986–90, UNIFEM Pori 1986– (mem Bd UNIFEM Finland 1989–94); Hon Counsellor of Social Welfare 1994; Merit Cross of Finland, Lion Order 1986; Benevolentia Medal, Social Security Cen Fed 1988; Merit Mark, Finland's Communal Fed 1990; Defence Medal, Defence Medal Cttee 1992. *Leisure interests:* fitness, women's issues. *Address:* Liisankatu 17A 17, 28100 Pori, Finland. *Telephone:* (2) 6335949.

PEMA, Jetsun; Tibetan (now Chinese) politician and development worker; b 7 July 1940, Lhasa; d of the late Choekyong and Dickey Tsering; m 1964; two d one s. *Education:* Schools in Darjeeling (India) and in Switzerland and UK. *Career:* Dir Tibetan Children's Villages school for Tibetan refugees (Dharamsala and several brs, India) 1964–; Head Dalai Lama's Del to report on the state of educ in Tibet 1980; elected Minister of Educ in Cabinet of Tibetan Govt-in-Exile 1990; elected first Vice-Pres Tibetan Youth Congress 1970, advisor Tibetan Women's Asscn 1984; mem Pres Council SOS-Kinderdorf Int, Vienna; numerous articles in newspapers and magazines; Hermann Gmeiner Medal 1991. *Leisure interests:* reading, gardening. *Address:* Retreat Cottage, Dharamsala Cantt-176 216, Himachal Pradesh, India. *Telephone:* (1892) 2507.

PENCHEVA, Stanka Mikhaylova; Bulgarian writer; b 9 July 1929, Sliven; d of Michael Penchev and Maria Pencheva; m 1st Kliment Tzachev 1951 (divorced 1965); m 2nd Georgy Bourmov 1984 (died 1991); one d. *Education:* Univ of Sofia. *Career:* Journalist and Literary Ed Bulgarsko Radio, Septemvri magazine 1959–75, Otechestvo magazine 1975–86; trans three books of poetry; writer of 19 anthologies of poetry and three books of essays, including one on the contemporary Bulgarian woman, 1952–89; participated in Bulgarian womens' movt; mem Union of Bulgarian Writers; Union of Bulgarian Writers award for poetry 1970. *Publications include:* A Baker's Dozen (ed, anthology of 13 Bulgarian women poets) 1990. *Leisure interests:* ancient history, literature, culture, science fiction. *Address:* 1113 Sofia, 20-3 Tintyava Str, Entr G, Bulgaria. *Telephone:* (2) 72-86-01.

PENG LIYUAN; Chinese singer; b Nov 1952, Yuncheng, Shandong Prov. *Education:* Shandong Acad of Arts and China Acad of Music. *Career:* Solo singer Qianwei Song and Dance Troupe of Ji'nan Mil Command 1980–84; solo singer Song and Dance Troupe, PLA Gen Political Dept 1984–. *Address:* Song and Dance Troupe, People's Liberation Army General Political Department, Beijing, People's Republic of China.

PENG PEIYUN; Chinese politician; b 1929, Liuyang Co, Hunan Prov; d of Peng Zhen. *Education:* Southwest Associated Univ and Qinghua Univ. *Career:* CP Party Sec, Qinghua Univ 1949–50; Deputy Sec Univ Comm 1964–66; Deputy Dir Beijing Chemical Eng Inst 1977–78; Dir Policy Research Office, Ministry of Educ 1979–82; Vice-Minister of Educ 1982–85, of State Econs Comm 1985–88; Minister of State Family Planning Comm 1988; State Councillor 1993–; Vice-Chair Standing Cttee, Nat People's Congress 1998–. *Address:* Quanguo Renmin Diabiao Dahui (National People's Congress), Beijing, People's Republic of China.

PENG XIAOLIAN, MFA; Chinese film director and writer; b 26 June 1953; d of Boshan Peng and Weiming Zhu. *Education:* Beijing Film Acad and New York Univ (USA). *Career:* Worked as a farmer during the 'Cultural Revolution' 1969–78; Commissioning Dir Shanghai Film Studio 1982–89, Contract Film Dir 1996–; Visiting Scholar New York Univ 1989–90; independent film-maker 1990–; film Random Thoughts (writer and Dir) cancelled half-way through production for political reasons 1989, script won Second Prize, Rotterdam Film Festival 1991; Best Screenplay Award, Shanghai Young People's Cultural Competition (for Come Back in the Summer) 1986. *Films directed:* Me and My Classmates (Best Film, Best Dir, Second Chinese Children's Film Festival 1987, Golden Rooster Award for Best Children's Film, People's Repub of China 1987, Special Prize, Chinese Cen Film Bureau 1988) 1986, Women's Story (People's Choice Best Feature Film, Hawaii Film Festival 1988, Special Jury Prize, Paris Women's Film Festival 1990) 1988. *Address:* 863 Ju Lu Rd, 2nd Floor, Shanghai 200040, People's Republic of China. *Telephone:* (21) 62473796; *Fax:* (21) 64395609; *E-mail:* xlpeng@ms.fudan.sh.cn.

PENNEFATHER, Joan, MA; Canadian film commissioner; b 7 May 1943, Montréal, PQ; d of John and Marjorie (née Smeaton-Murphy) Pennefather; one s one d. *Education:* Marianopolis Coll, McGill Univ, Concordia Univ and Univ of Oxford (UK). *Career:* TV Promotion CFCF-TV 1975–76; Producer Nat Film Board of Canada 1977–81, Vice Film Commr and Dir of Corp Affairs 1986–88, Chair 1989–94; Canadian Govt Film Commr 1988–89; Exec Dir Nat Arts Centre, Ottawa 1994–95; Vice-Pres Thornley Fallis Inc Communications Counsel 1996–98; Commr Canadian Radio, TV and Telecommunications Comm (CRTC) 1998–; Chair UNESCO Int Symposium Women and the Media 1995; mem Communications Canada Research Advisory Bd on Broadcast Tech; mem Bd Nat Arts Centre, Telefilm Canada; mem Canadian Fed of Univ Women; Employer of the Year Award NFB Canadian Women in Radio and TV, 1992; Astral Award, Toronto Women in Film and TV 1994. *Leisure interests:* skiing, swimming, canoeing, music. *Address:* 1 Promenade du Portage, Hull, PQ K1A 0N2, Canada (Office); 84 Belmont Ave, Ottawa, ON K1S 0V3, Canada (Home).

PENNEY, Jennifer Beverley; Canadian former ballet dancer; b 5 April 1946; d of the late James Beverley G. and of Gwendolyn F. (née McKie) Penney; m Philip Ian Porter 1983 (divorced 1984). *Education:* Kelowna High School (BC) and Royal Ballet School (UK). *Career:* Mem Royal Ballet Co 1963–68, Soloist 1966–68, Prin Dancer 1970–88, retd 1988; London Evening Standard Ballet Award 1980. *Ballets include:* The Dream, Petrushka, Anastasia, The Four Seasons, Elite Syncopations, The Sleeping Beauty, The Nutcracker, Swan Lake, Manon (also video film), Cinderella, La Bayadère, Mayerling, Mam'zelle Angot, Illuminations, Giselle, Romeo and Juliet. *Leisure interests:* pottery, water-colour painting, gardening, do-it-yourself. *Address:* 2–258 Lower Ganges Rd, Salt Spring Island, BC V8K 1S7, Canada. *Telephone:* (604) 537-2052.

PENNEY, Sherry Hood, PH D; American university professor; b 4 Sept 1937, Marlette, MI; d of Terrance and B. Jean (née Stoutenburg) Hood; m 1st Carl Murray Penney 1961 (divorced 1978); two s; m 2nd James Duane Livingston 1985. *Education:* Albion Coll, Univ of Michigan and State University of New York at Albany. *Career:* Visiting Asst Prof Union Coll, Schenectady, NY 1972–73; Assoc Higher Educ, New York Educ Dept 1973–76; Assoc Provost Yale Univ 1976–82; Vice-Chancellor Academic Programs, Policy and Planning State Univ of New York 1982–88; Chair Bd of Dirs Nat Higher Educ Man Systems 1985–87; Acting Pres State Univ Coll at Plattsburgh, NY 1986–87; Chancellor Univ of Massachusetts, Boston 1988–95, 1996–2000, Pres Univ of Massachusetts System (acting) 1995, Prof of Leadership 2001–; mem American Council of Educ Comm on Women 1979–81, Comm on Govt Relations 1990–, Bd of Dirs N Star, TERI (also Chair), NE Aquarium, Boston Municipal Research Bureau, Greater Boston Chamber of Commerce; Trustee John F. Kennedy Library Foundation; consultant Ed Change magazine, Journal of Higher Education Management; Hon LL D (Albion Coll) 1989, (Quincy Coll); NE Women's Leadership Award; Chamber of Commerce Award for Lifetime Achievement. *Publications:* Patrician in Politics 1974, Women in Management in Higher Education (ed) 1975; contribs to professional journals. *Address:* University of Massachusetts, College of Management, M432, 100 Morrissey Blvd, Boston, MA 02125-3393, USA. *Telephone:* (617) 287-3890; *Fax:* (617) 287-3894; *E-mail:* sherry.penney@umb.edu.

PENNINGTON, Sheila, BA, M ED, PH D; Canadian psychotherapist; b 8 April 1932, Toronto, ON; d of Charles Edward and Marion (née Haddow) Catto; m Ben Harrison 1975; three s one d. *Education:* Univ of Toronto, Toronto Teachers' Coll and Ontario Inst for Studies in Educ. *Career:* Dancer CBC and mem Canadettes CNE Grandstand 1949–55; New York Bd of Educ 1956–59; Research Dept Toronto Bd of Educ 1962–65; Psychotherapist Scarborough Gen Hosp 1970–71;

pvt practice in self-healing 1971–; Pres Centre for the Healing Arts Inc 1987–; TV and radio appearances; guest speaker in USA, Canada and Europe; mem Asscn of American Humanistic Psychologists, Canadian Centre for Arms Control and Disarmament, Canadian Peace Alliances, Amnesty Int, Greenpeace, Canadian Civil Liberties Asscn, Writers' Union of Canada; Clinical mem America and Ontario Asscns of Marriage and Family Therapists; recipient Ontario Psychologists Presidential Award for scientific excellence in a thesis 1981. *Publication:* Healing Yourself: Understanding How Your Mind Can Heal Your Body 1988, The Little Princess Who Rescued Herself 1995. *Leisure interests:* ballet, swimming, music, animals, knitting, nature, Tai Chi, walking, reading. *Address:* 14 Thurloe Ave, Toronto, ON M4S 2K2, Canada. *E-mail:* healer@on.aibn.com.

PEONIDOU, Elli; Cypriot writer; b 21 Nov 1940; m Panos Peonides 1963; one s one d. *Education:* Charokopios School (Athens). *Career:* Has written eight books of poetry, eight children's books and several other works; works published in Bulgaria, Czech Repub, France, Poland, Hungary, Russia, Yugoslavia, etc; two children's plays staged in Cyprus and abroad; Repub of Cyprus Awards 1978, 1980, 1984; Asscn of Children's Books Awards 1987, 1991, 1992; awards for books 1994, 1996, for plays 1994. *Leisure interests:* theatre, cinema, travel. *Address:* 14 M Parides St, 3091 Limassol, Cyprus. *Telephone:* (5) 354142.

PÉPIN, Lucie; Canadian politician and nurse; b 7 Sept 1936, St-Jean d'Iberville, PQ; d of Jean and Thérèse (née Bessette) Pépin; two d. *Education:* Univ of Montréal and McGill Univ. *Career:* Head Nurse Gynaecology Dept, Notre-Dame Hosp, Montréal 1960–61; Family Planning Clinic, Faculty of Medicine, Univ of Montréal 1966–70, Instructor in Contraception, Dept of Nursing 1972–77, Instructor in Contraception and Sexuality 1976–78; Canadian Rep WHO 1972–74; Nat Co-ordinator Canadian Cttee for Fertility Research 1972–79; Co-ordinator Fed Badgley Report (on Operation of the Abortion Law), Justice Canada 1975–77, mem Fed Badgley Report (on Violence Against Children and Youth), Health and Welfare Canada 1980–83; Co-ordinator Nat Symposium, Canadian Fertility Soc 1977–79, Int Symposium on Family Planning 1979; Vice-Pres Canadian Advisory Council on Status of Women 1979–81, Pres 1981–84; mem House of Commons for Outremont 1984–91, mem Parl Task Force on Child Care, Health and Welfare 1986–87; Commr Royal Comm on Electoral Reform and Party Financing 1989–92; mem Appeal Div, Nat Parole Bd of Canada 1993–97; Senator 1997–; Dir Canadian Hemophilia Soc 1992; mem Québec Chamber of Commerce, Asscn of Univ Women, Vanier Inst of the Family, Thérèse Casgram Foundation. *Leisure interests:* tennis, sailing, painting, horse-riding. *Address:* 213 East Block, The Senate of Canada, Ottawa, ON K1A 0A4, Canada.

PÉREC, Marie-José Juliana; French athlete; b 9 May 1968, Basse-Terre, Guadeloupe; d of José and Joëlle Pérec. *Education:* Inst Nat du Sport et de l'Educ Physique. *Career:* Indoor European Champion 1989; Bronze Medallist European Championships 1990; Gold Medallist 400m event World Championships, Tokyo 1991, Olympic Games, Barcelona, Spain 1992, European Championships, Helsinki 1994, World Athletics Championships, Gothenburg, Sweden 1995; Olympic Games, Atlanta, GA, USA 1996; Gold Medallist 200m event, Olympic Games, Atlanta, GA, USA 1996; also fashion model. *Leisure interest:* fashion. *Address:* c/o Ars Athletica, 20 rue d'Hauteville, 75010 Paris, France.

PEREIRA, Francisca; Guinea-Bissau politician; b 12 June 1942; d of Zeferino Lucas Pereira and Maria Teresa Gomes; three d one s. *Education:* In Bissau, Algeria and Ukraine. *Career:* Sec-Gen Org of Women 1982; Minister for Women's Affairs 1990–; Pres Comm Action for Children 1991; First Vice-Pres Nat People's Ass (Parl) 1994; mem Comité Int de suivi des Assises de l'Afrique 1996; numerous awards. *Leisure interests:* reading, cinema, tourism. *Address:* 62 rua Osvaldo Vieira, Bissau, Guinea-Bissau (Office); Apdo 560, 1038 Bissau Codex, Guinea-Bissau (Home). *Telephone:* 201992 (Office); 201161 (Home).

PERETTI, Elsa; Italian jewellery designer; b 1 May 1940, Florence. *Career:* School teacher, France and Italy; mem staff Dado Torrigiani (Architect), Milan; Model, Spain, France, UK and USA; jewellery designer Halston, Giorgio Sant'Angelo 1969–; designer of accessories and creator of perfume Tiffany and Co, New York 1974–; Coty Award

1971; Pres's Fellow Award, Rhode Island School of Design 1981; Fashion Group Night of the Stars Award 1986. *Address:* c/o Tiffany & Co, 725 Fifth Ave, New York, NY 10022, USA.

PEREZ, Mireya; Chilean army officer; b 1950. *Career:* Head of Directorate for Police Protection of Family, Santiago; apptd Chile's first female gen, Nov 1998. *Address:* Comandancia en Jefe, Zenteno 45, Piso 4, Santiago, Chile.

PERKINS, Alice, BA; British civil servant; b 24 May 1949; d of Derrick Leslie John and Elsa Rose Perkins; m John Whitaker (Jack) Straw 1978; one s one d. *Education:* North London Collegiate School for Girls and St Anne's Coll (Oxford). *Career:* Joined Civil Service, DHSS (now DSS) 1971, Principal 1976–84, Asst Sec 1984–88, Dir of Personnel 1988–93; Under-Sec Defence Policy and Material Group HM Treasury 1993–95, Deputy Dir Public Spending (Overseas and Agric) 1995–98; Dir Corp Man, Dept of Health 1998–2001; Head of Civil Service Corp Man, Cabinet Office Jan 2001–; Trustee Whitehall and Industry Group 1993–; Non-Exec Dir Littlewoods Org 1997–. *Leisure interests:* gardening, looking at paintings, riding. *Address:* Cabinet Office, 70 Whitehall, London SW1A 2AS, UK. *Telephone:* (20) 7276-1566; *Fax:* (20) 7276-1479; *E-mail:* aperkins@cabinet-office.x.gsi.gov.uk.

PERLMAN, Rhea; American actress; b 31 March, Brooklyn, NY; m Danny DeVito 1982; two d one s. *Education:* Hunter Coll. *Career:* Appeared in numerous Broadway plays; Co-Founder Colonades Theatre Lab, New York and New Streets production co (with Danny DeVito). *TV appearances include:* Series: Taxi 1978–82, Cheers (Emmy Award for Best Supporting Actress 1984, 1985, 1986, 1989), H-E Double Hockey Sticks 1999; Films: I Want to Keep My Baby! 1976, Stalk the Wild Child 1976, Intimate Strangers 1977, Having Babies II 1977, Mary Jane Harper Cried Last Night 1977, Like Normal People 1979, Drop Out Father 1982, The Ratings Game 1984, Dangerous Affection, A Family Again, Love Child, My Little Pony (voice), Enid is Sleeping, Radio Flyer, Houdini 1998, In the Doghouse 1999, A Tail of Two Bunnies 2000, Secret Cutting 2000. *Address:* c/o Creative Artists Agency, 9830 Wilshire Blvd, Beverly Hills, CA 90212, USA.

PERNOT, Anne-Marie, DR IUR; Belgian civil servant and organization executive; b 6 Jan 1948, Antwerp; m Renard 1970; two s one d. *Career:* Solicitor 1977–89; Researcher in Women's Studies Univ of Louvain 1980–89; apptd Conciliator Ministry of Labour 1989, Pres Equal Opportunity Comm 1990. *Leisure interests:* reading, tennis. *Address:* c/o Ministry of Labour, 51 rue Belliard, 1047 Brussels, Belgium.

PERÓN, María Estela (Isabelita) (see Martínez de Perón, María Estela (Isabelita)).

PERREIN, Michèle Marie-Claude; French writer; b 30 Oct 1929, La Réole; d of Roger Barbe and Anne-Blanche Perrein; m Jacques Laurent (divorced). *Education:* Univ of Bordeaux and Centre de Formation des Journalistes. *Career:* Literary Ed and contrib to periodicals Arts-Spectacles, La Parisienne, Marie-Claire, La Vie Judiciaire, Votre Beauté, Le Point, F Magazine and Les Nouvelles Littéraires. *Publications:* Novels: La sensitive 1956, Le soleil dans l'œil 1957, Barbastre 1960, La Flemme 1961, Le cercle 1962, Le petit Jules 1965, M'oiselle S, La Chineuse 1970, La partie de plaisir 1971, Le buveur de Garonne 1973, Le mâle aimant 1975, Gemma Lapidaire 1976, Entre chienne et louve 1978, Comme une fourmi cavalière 1980, Ave Caesar 1982, Les cotonniers de Bassalane 1984, La Margagne 1989; Plays: L'hôtel Racine 1966, a+b+c = La clinique d'anticipation 1971, L'alter-auto 1971; Film collaborator: La vérité 1959. *Leisure interests:* tapestry, swimming, skating. *Address:* c/o Grasset et Fasqualle, 61 rue des Saints-Pères, 75006 Paris, France.

PERRY, Ruth; Liberian politician; b Tewor Dist, Grand Cape Mount Co; m McDonald M. Perry (deceased); seven c. *Career:* Fmrly with Chase Manhattan Bank of Liberia; Senator from Cape Mount Co 1986–90; Chair Council of State (of Liberian Nat Transitional Govt) 1996–97; mem Women's Initiatives in Liberia. *Address:* c/o Office of the President, Monrovia, Liberia.

PERRY OF SOUTHWARK, Baroness (Life Peer), cr 1991, of Charlbury in the County of Oxfordshire, **Pauline Perry,** MA, LLD, DIP ED, FRSA; British university administrator; b 15 Oct 1931, Wolverhampton; d of John and Elizabeth Welch; m George W. Perry 1952; three s one d. *Education:* Girton Coll (Cambridge). *Career:* University Lecturer in philosophy, Univs of Manchester, Massachusetts, Exeter and Oxford 1956–70; joined HM's Inspectorate 1970, Staff Insp 1975, Chief Insp of Schools 1981–87; Vice-Chancellor S Bank Polytechnic (now S Bank Univ), London 1987–93; Pres Lucy Cavendish Coll, Cambridge 1994–2001; Pro-Chancellor Univ of Surrey 2001–; Chair Dept of Trade and Industry Export Group for Educ and Training Sector 1993–98; mem Prime Minister's Advisory Group on the Citizen's Charter 1993–97; mem House of Lords (Cons) 1991–, House of Lords Select Cttee on Science and Tech 1992–95, on Scrutiny of Delegated Powers 1995–98, on Cen and Local Govt Relations 1995–96; mem Jt Select Cttee on Human Rights 2001–, Bd of Patrons, Royal Soc Appeal 1995–; Vice-Pres City & Guilds of London Inst 1994–99; Chair Judges Panel on Citizen's Charter 1997–; Hon Fellow Coll of Preceptors (City and Guilds), Coll of Teachers, Swedish Acad of Science (Pedagogy), RSA, Girton Coll (Cambridge), Lucy Cavendish Coll (Cambridge), Cambridge Univ Foundation 1997–; Companion, Inst of Management; Hon LL D (Aberdeen, Bath); Hon D LITT (Sussex, South Bank, City Univ); Hon D UNIV (Surrey); Hon D ED (Wolverhampton); Liveryman Worshipful Co of Bakers; Freeman City of London. *Publications:* author of three books and numerous articles in nat press and educ journals, contrib chapters to ten books. *Leisure interests:* music, walking, gardening. *Address:* House of Lords, Westminster, London SW1A 0PW, UK; Lucy Cavendish College, Cambridge CB3 0BU, UK. *Telephone:* (20) 7219-5474 (London); (1223) 332192 (Cambridge); *Fax:* (20) 7738-2911 (London); (1223) 339056 (Cambridge); *E-mail:* pp204@supanet.com.

PERSCHY, Maria; Austrian actress; b 23 Sept 1938, Eisenstadt; m John Melson (deceased); one d. *Education:* Max-Reinhardt-Seminar (Vienna). *Career:* Film debut in Nasser Asphalt 1958; has appeared in over 80 int films; numerous TV appearances; Kunstförderungspreis, Vienna 1956; Best Female Actress Award, San Sebastián Festival 1959; Laurel Award for one of Top Ten Newcomers 1963. *Films include:* Freud, Squadron 633, Ride the High Wind, Murders in the Rue Morgue, The Desperate Ones, The Tall Woman, Witch Without a Broom; *TV appearances include:* General Hospital, Hawaii Five-O. *Leisure interests:* classical music, reading, skiing, tennis.

PÉRY, Nicole; French politician; b 15 May 1943, Bayonne; d of Jean and Marie-Rose (née Duhart) Duprat; m Albert Péry 1964; one d one s. *Education:* Secondary school in Bayonne, Ecole Normale (Pau) and Univ of Bordeaux. *Career:* Mem PS 1971–, Fed Sec 1974–81, mem Nat Cttee; Deputy Mayor Ciboure 1977–83; MEP 1981–, Vice-Pres of EP 1984–97, mem Cttee on Devt and Co-operation, ACP–EEC Jt Ass, Cttee on Fisheries; Town Councillor, Bayonne 1983–; Regional Councillor, Aquitaine 1986–95; Deputy to Nat Ass (Parl) for Pyrénées-Atlantiques 1997–98; Sec of State for Women's Rights and Professional Training 1998–. *Leisure interests:* music, mountain sports. *Address:* Secrétariat d'Etat aux Droits des femmes et à la Formation Professionnelle, 8 ave de Ségur, 75350 Paris, 07 SP, France (Office); Villa Xori-Kanta, rue Massy, Ciboure, 64500 Saint-Jean-de-Luz, France (Home).

PESCHEL-GUTZEIT, Lore Maria, D IUR; German judge; b 26 Oct 1932, Hamburg; d of Hans and Eva (née Brüggmann) Gutzeit; two d one s. *Education:* Univs of Freiburg and Hamburg. *Career:* Judge Hamburg High Court 1960–72, Hamburg Court of Appeal 1972–84, Presiding Judge 1984–91; Lecturer in Family Law, Hamburg Univ 1987–91; Senator for Justice, Hamburg 1991–93, Berlin 1994–; Deputy mem Bundesrat (Parl) 1991–93; mem Hamburg Parl 1993–94; Fed Chair German Union of Female Lawyers 1977–83; Chair State of Hamburg Women's Council 1990–92; chair various comms on women's rights, family law, children's rights and civil service employment statutes; mem Bd and Exec Bd SPD Hamburg 1991–93, Treas SPD Berlin 1996; mem Council Deutsche Liga für das Kind 1977–94, mem Bd 1994–. *Address:* Senatsverwaltung für Justiz, Salzburger Str 21–25, 10825 Berlin, Germany. *Telephone:* (30) 78763225; *Fax:* (30) 78763699.

PESCUCCI, Gabriella; Italian costume designer; b Castiglioncello, Tuscany. *Education:* Accademia di Belle Arti (Florence). *Career:* Worked as Asst to Piero Tosi on set of Luchino Visconti's films Death in Venice and Ludwig; solo debut designing costumes for Charlotte Rampling in Italian film adaptation of 'Tis Pity She's a Whore 1971; designed costumes for Maria Callas in Medea, for Sean Connery in The Name of the Rose, Montserrat Caballé in Norma at La Scala (Milan), and for City of Women, Once Upon a Time in America, The Adventures of Baron Munchausen, The Scarlet Letter, The Age of Innocence (Acad Award 1996); other prizes and awards include two Donatello Davids, Italian Acad of Cinema, and two BAFTA Awards.

PESIC, Vesna; Yugoslav (Serbian) politician, philosopher and sociologist; b 6 May 1940, Groska. *Education:* Belgrade Univ. *Career:* On staff Inst of Social Sciences 1964–72, Inst of Social Politics 1972–78; Sr Researcher Inst of Philosophy and Social Theory, teacher Higher School for Social Workers 1978–91; Co-Founder Union for Yugoslavian Democratic Initiative (IZDI) 1991–, Helsinki Cttee in Belgrade, Cen of Antimil Actions Daily Time; mem Cttee for Freedom of Speech and Self-Expression; Chair Civil Union of Serbia; Leader Civic Alliance Party; active participant opposition block Union of Reform Forces of Serbia; mem Skuptsina (Parl) of Serbia; participant mass demonstrations of protest against S Milosevic 1996–97; Award for Democracy, Nat Foundation of Democracy, Washington, 1993. *Publications include:* Social Traditions and Style of Life 1977, Ethnomethodology and Sociology 1985, Social Deviations: Criticism of Social Pathology (jtly) 1981, Brief Course of Equality 1988, Theory of Changes and Parsons Concept of Contemporary Society 1990, Yugoslavian Military Crisis and World Movement 1992, Nationalism, War and Disintegration of Communist Federation 1993, articles in scientific journals and periodicals. *Address:* Civic Alliance of Serbia, Belgrade, Federal Republic of Serbia.

PESOLA, Anja Helena, M SC S; Finnish organization executive and former politician; b 2 July 1947, Kuopio; d of Jussi and Eini Heinonen; m Tapio Pesola 1971. *Education:* Univ of Jyväskylä. *Career:* Public Relations and Information Chief, Chamber of Commerce of Cen Finland and Information Chief of the Jyväskylä Fair 1971–73; Acting Financial Man Social Welfare Office of the City of Jyväskylä 1978–79; MP (Nat Coalition Party) 1979–91; Minister of Social Affairs and Health 1987–89; Dir Social Insurance Inst 1990–. *Leisure interests:* cross-country skiing, gardening, visual arts. *Address:* The Social Insurance Institution, Nordenskiöldinkatu 12, 00250 Helsinki, Finland. *Telephone:* (20) 43411; *Fax:* (20) 4341784.

PESQUIÉ-NIKITINE, Isabelle Françoise Michèle; French business executive; b 31 May 1958, Petit-Quevilly; d of Jean and Denise (née Cambonie) Pesquié; m Boris Nikitine (divorced). *Education:* Inst Rey and Lycée Corneille (Rouen), Conservatoire Nat des Arts et Métiers (Paris) and Univ of Oxford (UK). *Career:* Engineer Research Dept, Soc Nat Elf Aquitaine 1980, Project Head Innovation Dept 1982–84; Prof of Computer Science Inst Nat Supérieur de l'Enseignement Technique, Côte d'Ivoire 1980–81; Project Head Sligos 1980–81; Business Engineer Sogeris-Prestor 1984–85; Co-Founder, Pres Dir-Gen PNB Co 1985. *Leisure interests:* music, Egyptology. *Address:* c/o PNB, 4 rue Jean Macé, 92150 Suresnes, France.

PESTELL, Catherine Eva (see Hughes, Catherine Eva).

PETERS, Ellen Ash, BA, LL B; American judge; b 21 March 1930, Berlin, Germany; d of Ernest Edward and Hildegard (née Simon) Ash; m Phillip I. Blumberg; two s one d. *Education:* Swarthmore Coll and Yale Univ. *Career:* Assoc in Law Univ of California at Berkeley 1955–56; Prof of Law Yale Univ 1956–78, Adjunct Prof of Law 1978–84; Law Clerk to Judge US Circuit Court 1954–55; called to the Bar, CT 1957; Assoc Justice Connecticut Supreme Court, Hartford 1978–84, Chief Justice 1984–96, Judge Trial Referee 2000–; mem Bd Dirs Conf of Chief Justices, Trustee 1984–, Pres 1994; mem Bd Mans Swarthmore Coll 1970–81; Trustee Yale New Haven Hosp 1981–85, Yale Corpn 1986–92; Hon Chair US Constitution Bicentennial Cttee 1986–; mem Perm Comm on Status of Women 1973–74, Connecticut Bd of Pardons 1978–80, Connecticut Law Revision Comm 1978–84, ABA, Connecticut Bar Asscn, American Law Inst; mem Bd Dirs National Center State Courts 1992–, Chair 1994; Hon MA (Yale) 1964; Hon LL D (Swarthmore) 1983, (Georgetown) 1984, (Yale, Connecticut Coll, New York) 1985, (Colgate) 1986, (Trinity, Bates, Wesleyan) 1987, (DePaul) 1988, (Univ of Connecticut) 1992, (Rochester) 1994; Hon HLD (Hartford) 1985, (Alberta Magnus) 1990; awards include Ella Grasso Award 1982, Judicial Award (Connecticut Trial Lawyers' Asscn) 1982, Pioneer Woman Award (Hartford Coll for Women) 1988. *Publications:* Commercial Transactions: cases, texts and problems 1971, Negotiable Instruments Primer 1974; numerous articles in professional journals. *Address:* Supreme Court, 95 Washington St, Hartford, CT 06106, USA.

PETERS, Mary Elizabeth, DBE; British former athlete and business executive; b 6 July 1939, Halewood, Liverpool; d of the late Arthur Henry and Hilda Mary (née Ellison) Peters. *Education:* Portadown Coll (Co Armagh, N Ireland). *Career:* Rep N Ireland at Commonwealth Games 1958–74, Silver Medallist in Shot 1966, Gold Medallist in Pentathlon and Shot 1970, Gold Medallist in Pentathlon 1974; rep Britain in int events until 1974; came fourth in Pentathlon, Tokyo Olympics 1964, Gold Medallist in Pentathlon (world record), Munich Olympics, Germany 1972; Team Man British Women's Athletics Team 1979–84; Man Dir Mary Peters Sports Ltd 1977–; Chair N Ireland Cttee on Sport for the Disabled 1984–90; Founder-mem Ulster Games Foundation 1984, Chair 1991–; Pres British Athletics Fed 1996–, Lady Taverner's (N Ireland), Action Cancer; Vice-Pres Asscn of Youth Clubs (GB), Youth Action, Riding for the Disabled, Driving for the Disabled, Nat Playbus Asscn; mem Sports Council 1974–80, 1987–, N Ireland Sports Council 1974–93, (Vice-Chair 1977–80), Sports Aid Foundation, BBC Broadcasting Council for N Ireland 1982–84, Int Amateur Athletic Fed (Women's Cttee) 1995–99, Radio Telefis Eireann Authority; Deputy Mem N Ireland Tourist Bd; Hon D SC (Ulster) 1974; Dr hc (Loughborough), (Queen's Univ Belfast); awards include Churchill Foundation Fellowship 1972, BBC Sports Personality Award 1972, Elizabeth Arden Visible Difference Award 1976, Living Action Award 1985, Evian Health Award 1985. *Publication:* Mary P., an autobiography 1974. *Leisure interests:* keeping fit, walking, patchwork, gardening. *Address:* Willowtree Cottage, River Rd, Dunmurry, Belfast, Northern Ireland BT1T 9DP, UK. *Telephone:* (2890) 618882.

PETERS, Roberta, D LITT, D MUS; American opera singer; b 4 May 1930, New York; d of Sol and Ruth (née Hirsch) Peters; m Bertram Fields 1955; two s. *Education:* Elmira and Ithaca Colls. *Career:* Debut in Don Giovanni, Metropolitan Opera, New York 1950; has performed at numerous opera houses and festivals including Royal Opera House, Covent Garden, London, Vienna State Opera, Munich Opera and West Berlin Opera, Germany, Vienna and Salzburg, Austria, and Munich festivals, Bolshoi Theatre and Kirov Opera, USSR, now Russian Fed; tours include USA, Russian Fed, Israel, People's Repub of China, Japan, Repub of China (Taiwan), S Korea and Scandinavia; Chair Nat Inst Music Theater 1991–; mem Nat Council of Arts 1992; Hon LHD (Westminster) 1974, (Leligh) 1977; Hon D MUS (Colby) 1980; Hon DFA (St John's) 1982; Hon D LITT (New Rochelle) 1989; first American recipient of Bolshoi Medal; named Woman of the Year by Fed of Women's Clubs 1964. *Publication:* Début at the Met. *Address:* ICM Artists Ltd, 40 W 57th St, New York, NY 10019, USA (Office); Scarsdale, New York, NY 10583, USA (Home).

PETERSEN, Marita; Danish (Faroese) politician. *Career:* Prime Minister with responsibility for Constitutional Affairs, Foreign Affairs, Admin and Judicial Affairs 1994; Speaker Løgting (Parl) 1995; Chair Javnaðarflokkurin (SDP). *Address:* Foroya Landsstyri, Tinganes, POB 64, 110 Tórshavn, Faroe Islands.

PETITPIERRE, Anne, DR JUR; Swiss international organization official. *Career:* barrister; Prof of Law Univ of Geneva; mem Exec Council, Int Cttee of the Red Cross, Vice-Pres 1987–. *Address:* International Committee of the Red Cross, 19 ave de la Paix, 1202 Geneva, Switzerland. *Telephone:* (22) 7346001; *Fax:* (22) 7332057.

PETKOWA, Wania, PH D; Bulgarian poet; b 10 July 1954, Sofia; one d one s. *Education:* Cuba and Bulgaria and Inst Gamal Abdel Nasser. *Career:* Fmrly journalist, now interpreter and poet; has had over 25 books of poetry published; has received numerous Bulgarian and int awards for her poetry. *Leisure interests:* art, children, grandsons. *Address:* 1612 Sofia, Georgi Avramov St, Block 134-5, Apt 75, Bulgaria. *Telephone:* (2) 59-37-82.

PETRÁŇOVÁ, Lydia, PH D; Czech historian and ethnographer; b 24 March 1941, Kolín; d of the late Ladislav Soukup and of Marie Urbánková; m Josef Petráň 1966; one s one d. *Education:* Charles Univ (Prague). *Career:* Participant in academic visits and confs, Bautzen, Germany (fmrly GDR) 1987, Warsaw 1988, Münster, Germany 1989, London 1991; mem Int Comm for Research into European Food History 1989; research worker 1991–. *Publication:* Domovní znamení staré Prahy (Old House Signs of Prague, 2nd edn) 1991. *Leisure interest:* gardening. *Address:* Novodvorská 415, 142 00 Prague 4, Czech Republic. *Telephone:* (2) 4719134.

PETRE, Zoe, PH D; Romanian historian; b 23 Aug 1940, Bucharest; d of E. Condurachi and Florica Moisil; m Aurelian Petre 1961 (died 1982); two s. *Education:* Classical High School (Bucharest) and Univ of Bucharest. *Career:* Specialist in ancient world history; Asst in Ancient Greek and Roman History Faculty of History, Univ of Bucharest 1961–78, Lecturer 1978–90, Prof, Dean of the Faculty of History, mem Univ Bd 1990–; Lecturer Strasbourg Univ 1968–69; Assoc Prof École des Hautes Études en Sciences Sociales, Centre de Recherches Comparées sur les Sociétés Anciennes, Paris 1982, 1991, 1993; Sr Adviser to Pres of Romania 1996–; archive studies in France, Italy, Switzerland, UK and Greece; mem Romanian socs of Classical Studies, Historical Sciences, and Anthropology, Asscn pour l'encouragement d'études grecques, France, East–West Inst, New York; Vice-Pres nat Cttee of South-East European Studies; Timotei Cipariu Prize, Romanian Acad 1981. *Publications:* Commentaire aux 'Sept Contre Thèbes' d'Eschyle (jtly) 1981, Istoria Greciei (1st vol) 1992; around 75 studies in Greek history 1965–92; articles in magazines specializing in ancient history, culture and philology. *Leisure interests:* literature, music, film. *Address:* University of Bucharest, 70609 Bucharest, Blvd M. Kogălniceanu 64, Romania (Office); 73106 Bucharest, 39 Kiritescu Str, Romania (Home). *Telephone:* (0) 143508 (Office); *Fax:* (0) 120419 (Office).

PETRI, Michala; Danish musician; b 7 July 1958, Copenhagen; d of Kanny Sambleben and Hanne Petri; m Lars Hannibal 1992; two d. *Education:* Staatliche Hochschule für Musik und Theater (Hanover). *Career:* Recorder player; first appearance in Danish Radi 1963; first concert as soloist in Tivoli 1969; extensive world tours 1975–, has given over 3,000 concerts throughout Europe, the USA, Israel, Far East and Australia; has played with Pinchas Zukerman, James Galway and Keith Jarrett; formed duo with Lars Hannibal 1992; ed of several works for Wilhelm Hansen, Verlag Moeck and Amazing Music World.com; has issued 35 compact discs for Philips and BMG; Order Knight of Dannebrog 1995; Deutscher Scallplattenpreis 1997; Wilhelm Hansen Music Prize 1998; H. C. Lumbye Prize 1998; Sonning Music Prize 2000. *Leisure interests:* children, reading, cooking, philosophy. *Address:* Nordskrænten 3, 2980 Kokkedal, Denmark; Karen McDonald, 4 Addison Bridge Place, London W14 8XP, UK (Agent). *Telephone:* 45-86-25-77; *Fax:* 45-86-56-77; *E-mail:* mail@michalapetri.com; *Internet:* www.michala.com.

PETROVA, Dimitrina Gueorguieva, PH D; Bulgarian politician and philosopher; b 11 Jan 1957, Burgas; d of Georgy and Trendaphila Petrovi; m 1st Todor Gueorguiev 1978 (divorced 1984); one d; m 2nd Krassimir Kanev 1984; one d. *Education:* Univ of Sofia. *Career:* Apptd Lecturer in Philosophy Univ of Sofia 1982; engaged in underground dissident activities 1985; Founder-mem Ecoglasnost dissident movt 1989 (wrote policy statement 1990), Int Network for Democratic Solidarity 1991; mem Grand Nat Ass 1990–91; apptd Consultant to Pres of Bulgaria on pardoning of prisoners 1990; Visiting Lecturer at univs in USA and Ireland 1990, 1991; Research Asst and Programme Co-ordinator Centre for the Study of Democracy 1991; apptd Dir Public Inst of Environmental and Social Research 1991; Nat Co-ordinator Helsinki Citizens' Ass 1991; mem Editorial Bd several magazines; numerous publs in professional journals, periodicals and newspapers; has written many conf papers; Hon Citizen Tucson, AZ, USA 1990. *Leisure interests:* sports, literature, children, dance. *Address:* University of Sofia, Dept of Philosophy, 1000 Sofia, K62, Blvd Ruski 15, Bulgaria (Office); Public Institute of Environmental and Social Research, 1000 Sofia, Narodno Sabranie Square, 12A, 4th Floor, Bulgaria (Office); 1231 Sofia, Zh K Nadezhda 6, Bl 636 Vhod B, Apt 85, Bulgaria (Home). *Telephone:* (2) 88-34-06 (Office); *Fax:* (2) 88-51-94 (Office).

PETRUSHEVSKAYA, Lyudmila Stefanovna; Russian writer and playwright; b 26 May 1938, Moscow; d.of Stefan Antonovitsh Petrushevskij and Valentina Nikolaevna Jakovleva; m 1st Evgenil Kharatian 1939; one s; m 2nd Boris Pavlov 1940; one s one d. *Education:* Moscow Univ. *Career:* Journalist 1957–73; started writing short stories 1968, plays 1971; stage productions and publication of works were forbidden for many years; first underground performance 1975, first official performance, Tallinn 1979; mem Bayerische Akad der Schönen Kunste 1997; Int A. Pushkin Prize 1991; prizes for the best short story of the year from 'Ogoniok' 1988, 1989, and 'Oktiabr' 1993, 1996; Moscow-Penne Prize (Russia/Italy) 1996. *Publications include:* Plays: Two Window 1971, Music Lessons 1973, Cinzano 1973, Love 1974, The Landing 1974, Andante 1975, The Execution, A Glass of Water, Smirnova's Birthday 1977–78, Three Girls in Blue 1980, Colombina's Flat 1981, Moscow Choir 1984, The Golden Goddess 1986, The Wedding Night 1990, The Men's Quarters 1992, The Time: Night (Grand Prize, Annual All-Russian Theatre Festival of Solo Theatre, Perm 1995); Screenplay: Tale of Tales (jtly, Prize for Best Animated Film of All Time, Los Angeles, USA 1980); Children's Books: Vasili's Treatment 1991, Once Upon a time There Was a Trrr! 1994, Real Fairy Tales 1997, The Alphabet's Tale 1997; Complete Works (5 vols) 1996, The Girl's House 1998, Find Me, My Dream 2000; Other Publications: Immortal Love 1988, Songs of the 20th Century 1988, On the Way to the God Eros 1993, The Mystery of the House 1993, Girl's House 1998. *Leisure interest:* watercolour painting. *Address:* 107113 Moscow, Staroslobodsky per 2A, kv 20, Russian Federation. *Telephone:* (095) 269-74-48; *Fax:* (095) 269-74-48.

PETTERSEN, Oddrunn, BA, B ED; Norwegian politician; b 5 March 1937, Hadsel, Finnmark; d of Omar and Kristine Hansen; m Birger Pettersen 1961. *Education:* Cambridge Univ and Tromsø Coll of Educ. *Career:* Fmr teacher; Mayor of Berlevåg 1976–77; mem Bd Asscn of Local Authorities; mem Storting (Parl) 1977, mem Standing Cttees on Local Govt, the Environment, Communications and Shipping and Fisheries; Minister of Labour and Govt Admin 1989, of Fisheries 1990–92; Del UN Gen Ass 1982. *Address:* c/o Ministry of Fisheries, Øvre Slottsgt 2, POB 8118 Dep, 0032 Oslo 1, Norway.

PETURSDOTTIR, Solveig; Icelandic politician; b 11 March 1952; d of Pétur Hannesson and Guðrún Margrét Árnadóttir; m Kristinn Björnsson; two s one d. *Education:* Reykjavík Junior Coll and Univ of Iceland. *Career:* Deputy Reykjavík Probate Court 1977–78; Deputy, law office of the Supreme Court Advocate, Reykjavík 1979–80; teacher Commercial Coll of Iceland 1983–86; lawyer Reykjavík Mothers' Assistance Soc; mem Reykjavík City Council for Ind Party (Cons) 1986–91, Reykjavík Social Affairs Council 1986–90, Reykjavík Health Clinics Bldg Cttee, Social Security Bd 1987– (Vice-Chair 1991–); Deputy mem Reykjavík Bd of Public Health 1986–90; First Deputy Mem of the Althing (Parl) for the Ind Party for Reykjavik 1987–91, Mem Feb 1991–; elected to the Althing (MP) April 1991–, Chair Gen Cttee 1991–; Minister of Justice and Ecclesiastical Affairs May 1999–; Rep, North Atlantic Parliamentarians Asscn 1991– (Chair 1993–); Deputy Chair Nat Affairs Club Vörður 1990–. *Address:* Arnarhvali, 150 Reykjavik, Iceland. *Telephone:* 560- 9015; *Fax:* 551-0477; *E-mail:* solveig.petursdottir@dkm.stjr.is; *Internet:* www.stjr.is.

PEYTON, Kathleen Wendy; British writer; b 2 Aug 1929; d of William Joseph and Ivy Kathleen Herald; m Michael Peyton 1950; two d. *Education:* Wimbledon High School and Manchester School of Art. *Career:* Art teacher, Northampton 1953–55; writer 1947–; Carnegie Medal 1969; Guardian Award 1970. *Publications include:* (as K. Herald): Sabre, the Horse from the Sea 1947, The Mandrake 1949, Crab the Roan 1953; (as K. M. Peyton): North to Adventure 1959, Stormcock Meets Trouble 1961, The Hard Way Home 1962, The Maplin Bird (New York Herald Tribune Award 1965) 1964, Thunder in the Sky 1966, Flambards Trilogy (Guardian Award 1970): Flambards 1967, The Edge of the Cloud (Carnegie Medal) 1969, Flambards in Summer 1969, Fly-by-Night 1968, Pennington's Seventeenth Summer 1970, The Beethoven Medal 1971, The Pattern of Roses 1972, Pennington's Heir 1973, The Right-Hand Man 1977, A Midsummer Night's Death 1978, Marion's Angels 1979, Flambards Divided 1981, Dear Fred 1981, Going Home 1983, Who Sir? Me Sir? 1983, The Last Ditch 1984, Froggett's Revenge 1985, The Sound of Distant Cheering 1986, Downhill All the Way 1988, Darkling 1989, Skylark 1989, No Roses

Round the Door 1990, Late Smile 1992, The Boy Who Wasn't There 1992, The Wild Boy and Queen Moon 1993, Snowfall 1994, The Swallow Tale 1995, Unquiet Spirits 1997, Firehead 1998, Blind Beauty 1999. *Leisure interests:* horse-riding, walking, gardening, sailing. *Address:* Rookery Cottage, N Fambridge, Chelmsford, Essex CM3 6LP, UK. *Telephone:* (1621) 828545; *Fax:* (1621) 828545.

PEYTON-JONES, Julia, MA; British arts administrator; b 18 Feb 1952. *Education:* Tudor Hall, Byam Shaw School of Art and Royal Coll of Art. *Career:* Various academic and admin posts in art galleries; fmr mem staff Arts Council; Dir Serpentine Gallery, London 1991–; mem Court of Govs London Inst 1989–. *Address:* 25 Sudeley St, London N1 8HW, UK.

PFAELZER, Mariana R., BA, LL B; American federal judge; b 1926. *Education:* Univ of California at Los Angeles. *Career:* Assoc Wyman, Bautzer, Rothman and Kuchel 1957–78, Partner 1969–78; called to the Bar 1958; Judge US Dist Court (Cen Dist) California; Pres Ninth Circuit Dist Judges Asscn; mem ABA. *Address:* US District Court, 312 N Spring St, Los Angeles, CA 90012, USA.

PFAFF, Judy; American artist; b 22 Sept 1946, London, UK. *Education:* Wayne State Univ (Detroit), S Illinois Univ, Univ of Washington and Yale Univ. *Career:* Numerous solo exhibitions including Webb & Parsons Gallery, New York 1974, Daniel Weinberg Gallery, Los Angeles 1984; numerous group exhibitions including Razor Gallery 1973 and Holly Solomon Gallery, New York 1984, Whitney Museum of American Art, Houston Contemporary Art Museum, Wacoal Art Center, Tokyo, Brooklyn Museum, Venice Biennale, Italy, Museum of Modern Art, New York; Guggenheim Fellowship for Sculpture.

PFARR, Heide Maria Anna, D JUR; German politician and professor of industrial law; b 12 Oct 1944. *Career:* Teacher Fachhochschule für Wirtschaft, Berlin 1974–76, Prof 1976–78; Prof of Industrial Law Univ of Hamburg 1978–; Senator for Fed Affairs, Rep of Berlin State to Fed Govt and Berlin Senate European Rep until 1990; Minister for Women, Labour and Social Affairs, Fed State of Hessen and mem Bundesrat (Parl, Upper House) 1991–93; Chief Man Hans Böckler Foundation 1995. *Publications:* Auslegungstheorie und -praxis im Zivil- und Arbeitsrecht der DDR 1972, Lohngleichheit 1981, Gleichbehandlungsgesetz 1985, Quoten und Grundgesetz 1988, Diskriminierung im Erwerbsleben 1989. *Address:* Hans-Böckler-Stiftung, Bertha-von-Suttner-Platz 3, 40227 Düsseldorf, Germany (Office); Sängelsrain 270, 34128 Kassel, Germany (Home). *Telephone:* (211) 7778187 (Office); (561) 66618 (Home); *Fax:* (211) 7778177 (Office); (561) 66628 (Home).

PFEIFFER, Michelle; American actress; b 29 April 1958, Santa Ana, CA; m 1st Peter Horton (divorced 1987); one adopted d; m 2nd David E. Kelly 1993; one s. *Education:* Fountain Valley High School and Golden West Coll. *Career:* Fmr Miss Orange Co; modelling assignments and several TV shows before film debut in Falling in Love Again; co-owner film production co. *Films include:* Hollywood Nights, Charlie Chan and The Curse of the Dragon Queen, Grease 2 1982, Scarface 1983, Into the Night 1985, Ladyhawke 1985, One Too Many (TV film) 1985, Sweet Liberty 1986, Amazon Women on the Moon 1987, The Witches of Eastwick 1987, Natica Jackson (TV film) 1987, Married to the Mob 1988, Tequila Sunrise 1988, Dangerous Liaisons (Acad Award nomination) 1988, The Fabulous Baker Boys (Best Actress Nat Soc of Film Critics, New York Film Critics Circle, Chicago Film Critics, Nat Bd of Review, Golden Globe Award, Acad Award nomination) 1989, The Russia House 1989, Love Field, Frankie and Johnny 1991, Batman Returns 1992, The Age of Innocence 1993, Wolf 1994, My Posse Don't Do Homework 1994, Dangerous Minds 1995, Up Close and Personal 1996, To Gillian On Her 37th Birthday, One Fine Day 1997, A Thousand Acres 1997, Privacy 1997, The Story of Us 1999, The Deep End of the Ocean 1999, A Midsummer Night's Dream 1999, Being John Malkovich 1999, What Lies Beneath 2000. *Address:* c/o ICM, 8492 Wilshire Blvd, Beverly Hills, CA 90211, USA.

PHANTOG; Chinese mountaineer; b Aug 1939, Xigaza, Tibet; d of Cirhen and Cijiu Phantog; m Jia-shang Deng 1963; two d one s. *Education:* Cen Coll of Nationalities. *Career:* First Chinese woman to climb Everest 1975; Deputy Dir Wuxi Sports and Physical Culture Comm 1981–. *Leisure interests:* table tennis, badminton. *Address:* Wuxi Sports and Physical Culture Commission, Jiangsu, People's Republic of China. *Telephone:* (25) 225810.

PHILLIPS, Julia; American film producer; b 7 April 1944, Brooklyn, NY; m Michael Phillips (divorced). *Education:* Mt Holyoke Coll. *Career:* Production Asst McCall's Magazine; copywriter Macmillan publs; Story Ed Paramount pictures; Creative Exec First Artists Productions; formed Bill/Phillips Productions (jtly) 1970. *Films include:* Steelyard Blues, The Sting (Acad Award for Best Film), Taxi Driver, The Big Bus, Close Encounters of the Third Kind, The Beat (co-producer); *Publication:* You'll Never Eat Lunch in This Town Again 1991.

PHILLIPS, Marisa, BA, D LITT; British barrister; b 14 April 1932, Milan, Italy; d of the late Dr J. and B. Fargion; m Philip H. Phillips 1956; one d one s. *Education:* Univs of Rome and Redlands (CA, USA). *Career:* Worked for US Information Service, Rome 1954–56; called to the Bar, Lincoln's Inn 1963; joined Office of Dir of Public Prosecutions (now Crown Prosecution Service) 1964, Asst Dir 1981–85, Prin Asst Dir 1985–86, Asst Head Legal Services 1986–87, Dir Legal Services 1987–89; Legal Adviser Police Complaints Bd 1977; Sr Legal Adviser to Banking Ombudsman 1990–; Pres Mental Health Review Tribunal 1990–; Commr Mental Health Act Comm 1991–95; Chair London Rent Assessment Panel 1992–; Fulbright Scholar, Fellow 1952. *Leisure interests:* music, travel, the arts. *Address:* Dane Court, 6 Kidderpore Ave, London NW3 7SP, UK. *Telephone:* (20) 7435-9293.

PHILLIPS, Sarah; American fashion designer; b 1956, Manhattan, New York. *Education:* Parsons School of Design (New York). *Career:* Worked for Ralph Lauren and Christian Dior; started own business 1991; designed ball-gown Hillary Clinton (US First Lady) wore on Inauguration Day 1993; shops selling her designs include Saks Fifth Ave and Neiman Marcus.

PHILLIPS, Siân, CBE, BA, FRSA; British actress; b Bettws, Wales; d of D. and Sally Phillips; m 1st D.H. Roy 1956 (divorced 1959); m 2nd Peter O'Toole 1959 (divorced 1979); two d; m 2nd Robin Sachs 1979 (divorced 1992). *Education:* Pontardawe Grammar School, Cardiff Coll (Univ of Wales) and Royal Acad of Dramatic Art (London). *Career:* Mem BBC repertory co 1953–55; toured for Welsh Arts Council with Nat Theatre Co 1953–55; Arts Council Bursary to study drama outside Wales 1955; Chichester Festival Season 1978; Royal TV Soc annual televised lecture 1992; Vice Pres Actors Benevolent Fund; mem Gorsedd of Bards (for services to drama in Wales) 1960; Fellow Cardiff Coll 1982, Polytechnic of Wales 1988, Welsh Coll of Music and Drama (also Vice-Pres) 1990, Swansea 1998, Trinity Coll Carmarthen 1998; Hon D LITT (Wales) 1984. *Plays include:* Hedda Gabler 1959, The Duchess of Malfi 1960–61 (RSC), The Lizard on the Rock 1961, Ride a Cock Horse 1965, The Burglar 1967, Epitaph for George Dillon 1972, A Nightingale in Bloomsbury Square 1973, Spinechiller 1978, You Never Can Tell 1979, Pal Joey 1980, 1981, Dear Liar 1982, Major Barbara 1982, Peg (musical) 1984, Love Affair 1984, Gigi 1986, Thursday's Ladies 1987, Brel (musical) 1987–88, Paris Match 1989, Vanilla 1990, The Manchurian Candidate 1991, Painting Churches 1992, Ghosts (Artist of the Year nomination) 1993, The Lion in Winter 1994, An Inspector Calls (Broadway) 1995, A Little Night Music 1995, Marlene 1996 (S Africa 1998, Paris 1998, NY 1999), Falling in Love Again 1999, Almost Like Being in Love 2001, Lettice and Lovage 2001, Divas 2001; *TV appearances include:* Shoulder to Shoulder 1974, How Green Was My Valley (BAFTA Award) 1975, I, Claudius (Royal Television Soc Award and BAFTA Award 1978) 1976, Boudicca, The Oresteia of Aeschylus 1978, Crime and Punishment 1979, Tinker, Tailor, Soldier, Spy 1979, Sean O'Casey 1980, Churchill: The Wilderness Years 1981, How Many Miles to Babylon 1982, Smiley's People 1982, A Painful Case, Beyond All Reason, The Shadow of the Noose 1988, Snow Spider 1988, Freddie & Max, Emlyn's Moon, Tonight at 8.30, Perfect Scoundrels 1990, Hands Across the Sea 1991, Ways and Means 1991, Huw Weldon TV Lecture 1993, Summer Silence (musical), The Vacillations of Poppy Crew, Mind to Kill 1995, Scolds Bridle 1997, The Aristocrats (series) 1998, Alice Through the Looking Glass (feature film) 1998, Nikita 1999, The Magician's House 1999, Ballykissangel 2000; *Films include:* Becket 1963, Goodbye Mr Chips (Critics' Circle Award, New York Critics' Award, Famous Seven Critics' Award) 1969, Murphy's War 1970, Under Milk Wood 1971,

The Clash of the Titans 1979, Dune 1983, Ewok II, The Two Mrs Grenvilles, Valmont 1988, Dark River 1990, Age of Innocence 1992, House of America 1996, Alice Through the Looking Glass 1999, Coming and Going 2000; *Radio series:* Phédre, Oedipus, Henry VIII, Anatomy and Cleopatra, Bequest to a Nation, The Maids, The Leopard in Autumn 2001; *Cabaret appearances:* Falling in Love Again, New York and UK; *Recordings include:* Bewitched, Bothered and Bewildered, Pal Joey, Peg, I Remember Mama, Gigi, A Little Night Music 1990, A Little Night Music (2) 1995, Marlene 1996; *Publication:* Siân Phillips' Needlepoint 1987, Private Faces (autobiography vol I) 1999, Public Places (vol II) 2001. *Leisure interests:* canvas embroidery, travelling, gardening, painting. *Address:* c/o Lindy King, PFD, Drury House, 34–43 Russell St, London WC2B 5HA, UK. *Telephone:* (20) 7344-1010; *Fax:* (20) 7370-4314; *E-mail:* sianp@dircon.co.uk.

PHILLIPS, Susan Meredith, M SC, PH D; American university dean and professor of finance; b 23 Dec 1944, Richmond, VA; d of William and Nancy Phillips. *Education:* Agnes Scott Coll and Louisiana State Univ. *Career:* Asst Prof Louisiana State Univ 1973–74; Asst Prof of Business Admin Univ of Iowa 1974, Brookings Econ Policy Fellow 1976–77, Assoc Prof 1978–79, Acting Vice-Pres for Finance and Univ Services 1979–80, Assoc Vice-Pres 1980, Vice-Pres and Prof of Finance, Coll of Business Admin 1987–91; Econ Fellow Securities and Exchange Comm (SEC) 1978–79; mem Commodity Futures Trading Comm (CFTC) 1981, Chair 1983, Commr and Chair 1985–87; Gov, mem Bd of Govs, Fed Reserve System 1991–98; Dean and Prof of Finance, School of Business and Public Man, The George Washington Univ 1998–; mem US Congress Office of Tech Assessment Advisory Panel 1988–90, CFTC Regulatory Co-ordination Advisory Cttee 1991; mem Bd of Trustees Agnes Scott Coll 1983–91, Bd of Dirs Johnson County Youth Services Foundation 1988–91, Chicago Mercantile Exchange 1988–91, Nat Asscn of Coll and Univ Business Officers 1989–91, State Street Research Funds 1998–, Cantor Exchange 1998–, State Farm Mutual Automobile Insurance Co 1988–91, 1999–, Chicago Bd Options Exchange 2000–, Nat Futures Asscn 2000–; Chicago Bd Options Exchange Pomerance Prize for Outstanding Research in Options. *Publications:* The SEC and Public Interest (jtly) 1981; numerous papers and articles on econs in professional journals. *Leisure interests:* travel, music, reading. *Address:* School of Business and Public Management, The George Washington University, 710 21st St NW, Suite 206, Washington, DC 20052, USA (Office); 1200 N Nash St, No 550, Arlington, VA 22209, USA (Home). *Telephone:* (202) 994-6380 (Office); (703) 528-8559 (Home); *Fax:* (202) 994-2286 (Office); *E-mail:* sbpmdean@gwu.edu.

PIBULSONGGRAM, Nitya, MA; Thai diplomatist; b 1941; m. *Education:* Dartmouth Coll and Brown Univ. *Career:* Joined Foreign Service; Third Sec Foreign News Div, Information Dept 1968, SEATO Div, Int Orgs Dept 1969–72, Office of Sec to Minister of Foreign Affairs 1973, Office of Under-Sec of State, Policy Planning Div 1974; Head SE Asia Div, Political Dept 1975; First Sec Perm Mission to UN 1976–79, Deputy Perm Rep 1979–80, Perm Rep 1988–; Deputy Dir-Gen Information Dept, Ministry of Foreign Affairs 1980, Political Dept 1981; Amb-at-Large 1982; Dir-Gen of Int Orgs 1983–88; Amb to USA 1996–. *Address:* Royal Thai Embassy, 1024 Wisconsin Avenue, NW, Washington, DC 20007, USA. *Telephone:* (202) 944-3600; *Fax:* (202) 944-3611.

PICADO, Sonia, LIC EN D; Costa Rican diplomatist, lawyer and international organization executive; b 20 Dec 1936, San José; d of Antonio and Odile (née Sotela) de Picado; m (divorced); one s one d. *Education:* Univ of Costa Rica. *Career:* Dean Law Faculty, Univ of Costa Rica (first Latin-American woman) 1980–84, Cathedratical Chair 1984–; Co-Chair Int Comm for Cen American Recovery and Devt 1987–89; mem Cttee of Jurists World Conf on Refugees, UNHCR, Geneva, Switzerland 1988–89; Exec Dir Inter-American Inst of Human Rights 1988–94; Vice-Pres Inter-American Court of Human Rights 1991–; Amb to USA 1994–99; Inter-American Women's Comm Award 1986; Max Planck/Humboldt Award, Germany 1991; Monseñor Leonidas Proaño Award, Ecuador 1991. *Publications:* Women and Human Rights 1986, Philosophic Fundamentals of Human Rights in Latin America 1987, Religion, Tolerance and Liberty: A Human Rights

Perspective 1989, Peace, Development and Human Rights 1989. *Address:* c/o Ministry of Foreign Relations, Apdo 10.027, 1000 San José, Costa Rica. *Telephone:* 340404; *Fax:* 340955.

PICARD, Ellen Irene, B ED, LL M; Canadian judge; b 2 Feb 1941, Blairmore, AB; d of Norman N. W. and Irene M. (née Wells) Picard; m; one s. *Education:* Univ of Alberta. *Career:* Barrister and Solicitor Matheson & Co 1967–72; Prof of Law Univ of Alberta 1972–86, Assoc Dean Faculty of Law 1974–75, 1980–81, McCalla Prof 1982–83; Founder and Dir of Health Law Inst, Univ of Alberta 1977–86; Visiting Prof Univ of Auckland 1985, Willis Cunningham Visiting Professor, Queens Univ 1986; Founder and Chair Law & Medicine Section Canadian Asscn of Law Teachers 1976–79; Co-Founder and Chair Health Law Section Canadian Bar Asscn; mem Bd Alberta Inst of Law Research & Reform 1975–79; Vice-Pres Law Reform Comm of Canada 1991–92; mem Bd bioethics cttees at various hosps 1979–86; apptd to the Court of Queen's Bench of Alberta 1986, to the Court of Appeal 1995; Dir Canadian Inst for the Admin of Justice 1993; Chair Nat Judicial Computer Cttee 1993, Nat Judicial Inst Appellate Judges' Seminars 1996–98, Nat Judicial Council & Einstein Inst for Health, Science and the Courts Seminars 2000–2001; Hon Prof of Law and of Medicine 1986–; Picard Lecture in Law 1991; Hon LL D (Alberta) 1992. *Publications:* Studies in Canadian tort Law 1977, Legal Liability of Doctors and Hospitals in Canada (3rd edn) 1996; chapters in various books on the law and contribs to professional journals. *Leisure interests:* skiing, antique cars. *Address:* Judges' Chambers, The Law Courts, Court of Appeal of Alberta, 1A Sir Winston Churchill Square, Edmonton, AB T5J 0R2, Canada. *Telephone:* (780) 422-2349; *Fax:* (780) 427-5507; *E-mail:* picarde@just.gov.ab.ca.

PICASSO, Paloma; French designer; b 19 April 1949, Paris; d of Pablo Picasso and Françoise Gilot (qv); m Rafael Lopez-Cambil (Lopez-Sanchez) 1978 (divorced 1998); m 2nd Eric Thevennet 1999. *Education:* Univ of Paris (Sorbonne). *Career:* Studied jewellery design and fabrication; Fashion Jewellery Designer for Yves St Laurent 1969; jewellery for Zolotas 1971; costumes and sets for Lopez-Cambil's Parisian productions, L'interprétation 1975, Succès 1978; with Lopez-Cambil created Paloma Picasso brand, creations designed by her include jewellery for Tiffany & Co 1980, fragrance (Paloma Picasso 1984, Minotaure 1992) and cosmetics for L'Oréal, women's accessories for Lopez-Cambil, Ltd 1987, hosiery, eyewear, bone china, crystal, silverware and tiles for Villeroy & Boch, home linens for KBC, fabrics and wall coverings for Motif; pieces in perm collections of Smithsonian Inst (Washington, DC), Musée des Arts Décoratifs (Paris) and Die Neue Zamlang (Munich); Paloma Picasso boutiques in Japan and Hong Kong; Council of Fashion Design of America (CFDA) Accessory Award 1989. *Film:* Immoral Tales 1974. *Address:* Paloma Picasso Parfums, 6 bis rue des Graviers, 92521 Neuilly Cedex, France; Quintana Roo Ltd, 291A Brompton Rd, London SW3 2DY, UK. *Telephone:* (20) 7589-9030 (London); *Fax:* (20) 7589-7712 (London).

PICK-HIERONIMI, Monica Maria Anna; German opera and concert singer; b 14 Dec, Olpe; d of Jacob Pick and Helene Schäfer; m Otto Hieronimi 1968; one s. *Education:* Rheinische Musikschule (Cologne). *Career:* Numerous nat and int opera and concert appearances including performances in Munich, Mannheim, Frankfurt, Stuttgart, Vienna Staatsoper, Hamburg, Barcelona Theatre del Liceu, Spain, Rome, Deutsche Staatsoper Berlin, Paris, Milan, Italy, Zurich, Switzerland, Brussels, Prague, Verona (first German Aida), Italy 1992, Carnegie Hall, New York 1992; has performed at many festivals, including Buxton, UK, Würzburg Mozartfest, Schleswig-Holstein, Karlsruhe Händelsfestspiele, Prague Spring Festival, Arena di Verona Int Festival, Vienna Festival Weeks, Festival di Caracalla, Rome 1991; Carpine d'Oro, Brescia 1990; Prof Staatliche Hochschule für Musik, Cologne 1992–. *Operas include:* Don Giovanni, Norma, Elektra, La Forza del Destino, Ariadne, La Clemenza di Tito, Otello, Il Trovatore, Un Ballo in Maschera, Aida; *Recordings:* Christ on the Mount of Olives 1987, Verdi's Requiem 1989, Don Giovanni 1991, Nabucco, under Guadaguo with Arena di Verona 1996. *Leisure interests:* flowers, gardening. *Address:* Steinackerweg 25, 64658 Fürth-Steinbach, Germany. *Telephone:* (6253) 3906; *Fax:* (6253) 4761.

PICKENS, Jo Ann; American opera singer (soprano); b 4 Aug 1950, Robstown, TX; d of Anne Belle Sanders. *Career:* Commenced career with Chicago Lyric Opera; recitals and concerts around the world; performed with the conductors Solti, Dorati, Rattle, Norrington, Pesek and Sanderling; performances include Berlioz's The Trojans 1987, Armide 1988; Int Competition for Singers Award, Paris 1980; Metropolitan Opera Regional Auditions 1981; Benson & Hedges Gold Award 1981. *Address:* c/o Norman McCann International Artists Ltd, The Coach House, 56 Lawrie Park Gardens, London SE26 6XJ, UK.

PICKFORD, Lillian Mary, D SC, MRCP, FRS, FRSE; British scientist and endocrinologist; b 14 Aug 1902, India; d of Herbert Arthur and Lillian Minnie Pickford. *Education:* Bedford Coll and Univ Coll Hospital (London). *Career:* Physiologist and endocrinologist; lectured in the USA, Canada and S America; carried out research in Australia, New Zealand, Malaysia, Russia, Austria and India; wrote papers in physiology, pharmacology and endocrinology, for the Lancet and the Royal Society of Edinburgh 1926–72; Beit Memorial Fellowship 1936–39; now retd; Hon mem Physiological, Pharmacological and Endocrinological Socs; Hon D SC (Heriot-Watt Univ) 1991. *Publication:* Central Role of Hormones 1969. *Leisure interests:* painting, walking, riding. *Address:* Winton House, Nether Wallop, Stockbridge, Hants SO20 8HE, UK. *Telephone:* (1264) 781014.

PIECHOTKA, Maria, M SC; Polish architect; b 12 July 1920; d of Kazimierz and Zofia Huber; m Kazimierz Piechotka 1944; two s. *Education:* Warsaw Univ of Tech. *Career:* Designer, then Chief Designer Govt Design Offices, Warsaw 1956–80; Researcher into Jewish Urban Spaces and the Architecture of Synagogues in Polish Towns from 12th–19th Centuries 1955–; works with Inst of Fine Arts, Polish Acad of Sciences (PAN); Town Planning and Architectural Cttee of Warsaw Prize 1957, 1960, 1969; Polish Nat Prize 1974. *Publications:* Wooden Synagogues 1957, 1959, Jewish Urban Spaces and Synagogues in Polish Towns From 12th–19th Centuries (jtly). *Address:* ul Kleczewska 1, 01-851 Warsaw, Poland. *Telephone:* (2) 342731.

PIERCE, Mary; Canadian tennis player; b 15 Jan 1975, Montréal; d of Jim and Yannick Pierce. *Career:* Coached by Sven Groeneveld and Nick Bollettieri; turned professional 1989; moved to France 1990; represented France in Fed Cup 1991; first career title, Palermo, Italy 1991; runner-up French Open 1994; winner Australian Open 1995, Tokyo Nichirei 1995; semi-finalist Italian Open, Canadian Open 1996; finalist Australian Open 1997; winner of Doubles (with Martina Hingis, qv) Pan Pacific. *Address:* c/o WTA, 133 First St NE, St Petersburg, FL 33701, USA.

PIERCY, Marge, MA; American writer; b 31 March 1936, Detroit, MI; d of Robert Douglas and Bert Bernice (née Bunnin) Piercy; m Ira Wood. *Education:* Univ of Michigan and Northwestern Univ. *Career:* Poet-in-Residence Univ of Kansas 1971; Distinguished Visiting Lecturer Thomas Jefferson Coll, Grand Valley State Colls 1975, 1976, 1978, 1980; Elliston Poetry Fellow Univ of Cincinnati 1986; DeRoy Distinguished Visiting Prof Michigan Univ 1992; mem Artistic Advisory Bd American Poetry Center; numerous awards including Literary Award, Gov of MA's Comm on Status of Women 1974, Nat Endowment of Arts Award 1978, Carolyn Kizer Poetry Prize 1986, 1990, Sheaffer-PEN New England Award for Literary Excellence 1989, Golden Rose Poetry Prize 1990, May Sarton Award, New England Poetry Club 1991, Notable Book Award 1997, Paterson Poetry Prize 2000. *Publications include:* The Last White Class (play, jtly) 1979, Parti-Colored Blocks for a Quilt (essays) 1982; Fiction: Breaking Camp 1968, Hard Loving 1969, Going Down Fast 1969, Dance the Eagle to Sleep 1970, Small Changes 1973, Woman on the Edge of Time 1976, Vida 1980, Braided Lives 1982, Gone to Soldiers 1987, Summer People 1989, He, She and It 1991, Body of Glass (Arthur C. Clarke Award 1993) 1992, The Longings of Women 1994, Eight Chambers of the Heart 1995, City of Darkness, City of Light 1996, What Are Big Girls Made Of? 1997, Storm Tide 1998, Early Girl 1999, The Art of Blessing the Day 1999, Three Women 1999; Poetry: Breaking Camp 1968, Hard Loving 1970, To Be of Use 1973, The Twelve-Spoked Wheel Flashing 1978, The Moon is Always Female 1980, Circles on the Water (Selected Poems) 1982, My Mother's Body 1985, Available Light 1988, Mars and Her Children 1992. *Address:* POB 1473, Wellfleet, MA 02667, USA. *Telephone:* (508) 349-3163.

PIETIKÄINEN, Sirpa Maria, M SC; Finnish politician; b 19 April 1959, Parikkala; d of Erkki Pietikäinen and Sylvi Susanna Hirvelä. *Education:* Helsinki School of Econs and Business Admin. *Career:* Mem Hämeenlinna City Council 1980; elected mem Eduskunta (Parl, Nat Coalition Party) 1983; Minister of the Environment 1991–95; Presidential Elector 1988; apptd Vice-Chair Nat Coalition Party 1989; mem Finnish Del to Nordic Council 1987–91; Chair European Union of Democrats Environmental Cttee 1990. *Leisure interest:* literature. *Address:* c/o Ministry of the Environment, Ratakatu 3, 00121 Helsinki, Finland.

PIGOTT, Jean; Canadian business executive and politician; b 20 May 1924, Ottawa, ON; d of George Cecil and Margaret Jane Kelly (née Cotter) Morrison; m Arthur Campbell Pigott 1955; one s one d. *Education:* Ottawa Ladies' Coll and Albert Coll. *Career:* Pres and CEO Morrison Lamothe Food 1967–76, Chair of Bd Morrison Lamothe Inc 1980–84; Chair Ottawa Regional Hosp Planning Council 1973–76; fmr Vice-Pres Local Council of Women; fmr Dir and mem Audit Cttee Ontario Hydro, Canadian Devt Corpn and Dir Council of Christians and Jews until 1976; elected to House of Commons 1976; Sr Adviser on Human Resource to PM 1979; mem Govt transitional team 1984–85; first woman Chair Nat Capital Comm 1985; Chair Ottawa Congress Centre 1993; mem Canadian Asscn of the Club of Rome; Bd of Dirs Canadian Tire Corpn and Ben's Bakery; Chair Ottawa Gen Hosp Foundation; Gov Carleton Univ; Dir Trillium Corpn; Hon D UNIV (Ottawa) 1988; recipient Centennial Medal 1967, Ottawa Bd of Trade Distinguished Service to the Business Community Award 1975, Asscn des Détaillants en Alimentation Award 1975, Queen's Jubilee Medal 1977, KT of the Golden Pencil Award 1978, B'Nai Brith Award of Merit 1987. *Publications:* Feeding the Nations of the World 1979, Special Interest Advocacy: a right, a necessity or a danger?. *Address:* 55 Colonel By Drive, Ottawa, ON K1N 9J2, Canada (Office); 29-255 Botanica Lane, Ottawa, ON K1Y 4P8, Canada (Home).

PIKE, Baroness (Life Peer), cr 1974, of Melton in the County of Leicestershire, **Irene Mervyn Parnicott Pike,** DBE, BA; British politician; b 16 Sept 1918; d of Samuel Pike. *Education:* Univ of Reading. *Career:* Women's Auxiliary Air Force (WAAF) 1941–46; Dir Watts, Blake and Bearne 1964–; Cons election cand Pontefract 1951, Leek 1955; MP for Melton 1956–74; Asst Postmaster-Gen 1959–63; Jt Parl Under-Sec of State, Home Office 1963–64; mem House of Lords 1974–; Nat Chair Women's Royal Voluntary Service 1974–81; Chair Broadcasting Complaints Comm 1981–85. *Leisure interests:* walking, reading, gardening. *Address:* House of Lords, Westminster, London SW1A 0PW, UK (Office); Hownam, Kelso, Roxburgh, UK (Home). *Telephone:* (20) 7219-3000 (Office).

PILAROVÁ, Eva; Czech singer and actress; b 9 Aug 1939, Brno; d of Ladislav Bojanovský and Fransiška Horčičková Bojanovská; m Van Kolomatuík 1952; one s. *Education:* Brno School of Econs and Acad of Music. *Career:* Actress and Singer Semafor Theatre 1960–62, 1964–65, 1992–, Pokoko Theatre 1962–64; Singer with her own group 1965–; Grand Prix du Disque 1967. *Films include:* Good Walking Trip 1966, Crime in Cabinet 1968; *Publications:* I Remember 1991. *Leisure interest:* cooking. *Address:* Pod Královkov 5, 169 00 Prague 6, Czech Republic. *Telephone:* (2) 357854.

PILCHER, Rosamunde; British writer. *Career:* Recipient of Deutscher Videopreis 1996, Bambi Award, Bunte magazine 1997, Goldene Kamera Award, Hörzu 1998. *Publications include:* September 1990, Carousel 1993, Coming Home 1995 (Romantic Novelist of the Year, RNA 1996) (adapted for TV 1998), World of Rosamunde Pilcher 1996, Winter Solstice 2000. *Address:* Penrowan, Longforgan, Dundee DD2 5ET, UK.

PILIPOVÁ, Lucie; Czech foundation executive; b 7 July 1968, Olomouc; m Ivan Pilip 1991. *Education:* Univ of Econs (Prague) and Universidad Complutense (Madrid). *Career:* Marketing and Project Co-ordinator Int Org of Students of Econ Sciences (AIESEC); Interpreter BVV Int Trade Fairs, Brno 1986–89, Filmlabsystems Int, London July–Aug 1989; Interpreter and Personal Asst to British Corresp, Daily Telegraph, Prague 1989–91; Cen Europe Corresp, Antena 3 de Radio, Madrid 1991–92; Home News Reporter, Czech TV, Prague May–Aug 1992; Spokesperson to the Minister of Foreign Affairs, Prague 1992–94;

Exec Dir Bohemiae Foundation 1994; mem Czech Comm for UNESCO, Women's Forum, Bd of Dirs Foundation for Int Studies, Editorial Bd Czech Panorama. *Leisure interests:* horse-riding, hunting, tennis. *Address:* Nad Kajetánkou 4, 169 00 Prague, 6, Czech Republic. *Telephone:* (2) 316-49-83 (Home).

PINÓS, Carmen; Spanish architect; b 23 June 1954, Barcelona. *Education:* Escuela Superior de Arquitectura de Barcelona, Int Lab of Architecture with Urban Design (ILAUD) (Urbino) and Columbia Univ (USA). *Career:* Partnership with Enric Miralles, Barcelona 1983–91, projects included Cemetery of Igualada, Barcelona (Barcelona City Prize), Barcelona Olympics Archery Grand (Biannual Prize for European Architecture); est own architectural practice 1991, projects include Footbridge, Petrer (Alicante), Hogar School of Morella (Nat Prize for Architecture 1995); fmr Visiting Prof Acad Van Boukunst, Amsterdam; Ecole Speciale d'Architecture, Paris; Plym Prof Univ of Ill at Urbana–Champaign 1994–95; fmr Prof Kunstakademie, Dusseldorf; currently Prof Columbia Univ NY; winner MOPU competition (1st Prize) 1982; Mies Van de Rohe Prize and numerous other awards. *Major works:* El Croquis 1986, Arte Cemento 1987, Baumeister 1989. *Address:* Ave Diagonal 490, 3o2C, 08026 Barcelona, Spain. *Telephone:* (3) 4160372; *Fax:* (3) 4153719; *E-mail:* estpinos@arquired.es.

PINSKER, Essie Levine, BA; American sculptor; b New York; d of Harris and Sophia (née Feldman) Levine; m Sidney Pinsker; one s one d. *Education:* Brooklyn Coll, Univs of Columbia, New York, Oxford and Cambridge (UK), New York Univ and Museum of Modern Art. *Career:* Buyer Ohrbach's, and Arkwright, New York; fashion model; Ed Women's Wear Daily; Press Dir American Symphony Orchestra; Pres Essie Pinsker Advertising Assocs Inc 1960–82; Fashion Ed Woman Golfer magazine; journalist New York Times; Lecturer Fashion Inst of Technology; solo exhibitions include Bodley Gallery, New York 1981, Vorpal Gallery, New York 1987; group exhibitions include Metropolitan Life 1969, Huntington Art League 1977, Knickerbocker Artists, New York 1982, Cadme Gallery, PA 1984, River Gallery, CT 1984, Clark Whitney, MA 1985, Images Gallery, CT 1987, Arco Int Art Fair, Madrid 1988, Konstmassan Int Art Fair, Stockholm 1988, Galleri Atrium, Stockholm 1988, Galerie Atrium, Marbella, Spain 1988, Feingarten Galleries, LA 1989, Nina Owen Ltd, Chicago 1989, The Art Collector, San Diego 1989, Galerie IlseLommel' Leverkusen, Germany 1989, Sandra Higgins Fine Art, London 1989, Hampton Square Gallery, NY 1990, Left Bank Gallery, Laguna Beach; works feature in perm collections including Nat Portrait Gallery, Washington, DC, Aldrich Museum of Contemporary Art, CT, Oklahoma Art Center, Minnesota Museum of Art, Daytona Beach, FL, Museum of Modern Art, Warsaw, War Memorial, Israel, Art Inst of S California, Laguna Beach, Museum of Arts and Sciences, Daytona Beach, Everson Museum, Syracuse, City of Brea, CA, Paramount Group, LA, Granard Communications Ltd, London; Exec Producer Pupae (Cine Eagle Award) 1973; mem Nat Museum of Women in the Arts, Int Sculpture Center, Artists' Equity, Fashion Group of New York, Advertising Women of New York, Fashion Coalition of New York; recipient Knickerbocker Artists' Sculpture Award, Metropolitan Life Sculpture Award. *Address:* 8 Peter Cooper Rd, New York, NY 10010, USA.

PINTASILGO, Maria de Lourdes; Portuguese politician, engineer and diplomatist; b 18 Jan 1930, Abrantes; d of Jaime de Matos and Amélia Ruivo da Silva Pintasilgo. *Education:* Inst Superior Técnico (Lisbon). *Career:* Mem Research and Devt Dept Companhia União Fabril (CUF) 1954–60; Pres Pax Romana 1956–58; Int Vice-Pres The Grail 1965–69; apptd mem women's ecumenical liaison group by Holy See 1966–70; Dept of Politics and Gen Admin, Corporative Chamber 1969–74; Chair Nat Comm on Status of Women 1970–74; mem Portuguese Mission to UN 1971–72; Minister of Social Affairs 1974–75; Sec of State for Social Security, First Provisional Govt 1975; Amb to UNESCO 1976–79, mem Exec Bd UNESCO 1976–80; Prime Minister 1979–80; Adviser to Pres of Repub 1981–85; Ind Candidate to Portuguese Presidency 1986; MEP 1987–89; Pres Independent Comm on Population and Quality of Life 1992–; Chair Working Group on Equality and Democracy, Council of Europe, Strasbourg 1993–94; mem Interaction Council of Fmr Heads of Govt 1983–94, Deputy Chair 1989–94; mem World Policy Inst 1989–, UN Univ Council 1983–89, Club of Rome 1989–, Bd World Order Models Project 1987–; UN Advisory Cttee on Science and Tech for Devt 1989–91, Nat Council of Ethics for Life-Sciences 1990–, Bd

WIDER-UNU (World Inst for Devt Econs Research) Council (also Chair) 1991–. *Publications:* Les nouveaux féminismes 1980, Dimensão da mudança 1985; over 100 articles on int affairs, devt and the status of women. *Leisure interests:* poetry, piano. *Address:* Alameda Santo António dos Capuchos 4–5°, 1100 Lisbon, Portugal. *Telephone:* (1) 354-31-68; *Fax:* (1) 314-25-14.

PINTER, Frances Mercedes Judith, PH D; American (b Venezuelan) publisher; b 13 June 1949, Venezuela; d of George and Vera Hirschenhauser Pinter; m David Percy 1985. *Career:* Research Officer Centre for Criminological Research, Univ of Oxford, UK 1976–79; Man Dir Pinter Publrs 1979–94, Cen European Univ Press 1994–96; Chair Ind Publrs Guild 1981–82, Publrs Asscn E European Task Force 1990–; Deputy Chair Book Devt Council 1985–89; Exec Dir Centre for Publishing Devt, Open Soc Inst 1996–99; Chair Bd of Trustees, Int House 2001; Visiting Fellow Centre for Civil Soc, LSE 2000–2002; mem Bd UK Publrs Asscn 1987–92, IBIS Information Services 1988–90, Libra Books 1991–. *Leisure interests:* reading, travel, hiking. *Address:* 25 Belsize Park, London NW3 4DU, UK. *E-mail:* frances@pinter.org.uk (Office).

PINTO CORREIA, Clara, PH D; Portuguese writer and scientist. *Education:* Portugal and USA. *Career:* Journalist; researcher on developmental biology. *Publications:* Agrião 1984, Adeus Princesa (Goodbye Princess) 1987, The Ovary of Eve, Secondary Messengers 1999; numerous other publications including short stories, children's books, histories of science and an opera libretto. *Address:* c/o University of Chicago Press, 1427 E 60th St, Chicago, IL 60637, USA.

PIONTEK, Danuta; Polish business executive and economist; b 24 May 1937, Warsaw; d of Czesław and Eugenia Gocławski; m Eugeniusz Piontek 1978; two s one d. *Education:* High School of Econs (Warsaw). *Career:* Founder pvt business enterprise 1956; Gen Man in Kano State, Nigeria 1971–76; ran boutique, Warsaw 1977–82; Rep Farmtex foreign trade enterprise 1983–; Founder, Pres Soroptimist Int, Warsaw 1990–, Asscn of Real Estate Pvt Owners 1991–; Pres Polish Business Asscn 1990, Business Convention of Industrial Manufacturers, Trade and Agricultural Producers 1991; Vice-Pres Econ Party for the Repub of Poland 1992; Pres Confed of Asscns of Entrepreneurs; numerous TV appearances; Nat Jr Rowing Champion 1952, 1953. *Publication:* Banking Systems 1991. *Leisure interests:* sports, film, theatre. *Address:* ul H Wieniawskiego 9a, 01-572 Warsaw, Poland. *Telephone:* (22) 393405.

PIPER, Christa, MA; German painter and writer. *Education:* Kunst Schüle Westerd (Frankfurt/Main). *Career:* Paintings and drawings exhibited in Germany, fmr GDR, Austria, Switzerland, Israel, People's Repub of China, Monaco, Norway; Producer lyric/sound/dance collage Wieviel Erde braucht das Mensch 1984; Study Prize Heussenstammschen Stiftung, Frankfurt 1984. *Publications include:* Illustrated poems: Alltag 1969, Der Übermensch (Persiflage auf die Menschen im Jahr 3000) 1970, Spiel zu zweit 1976; Novels: Trotzdem Christine 1984, Im Zeichen der Rose 1984, Nimm dir dein Leben 1986, Die Wolke und der Regenbogen 1991, Wenn Dr Wieder 'Anion' Sagst 1998; work featured in calendars and catalogues. *Address:* Koselstr 19, 60318 Frankfurt am Main, Germany. *Telephone:* (69) 557899.

PIPER-PYLARINOU, Eftychia; Greek banking executive. *Career:* Responsible for Lending, First New York Bank for Business 1988–91; apptd Gov Hellenic Industrial Devt Bank SA investment bank (first woman Gov of a Greek bank) 1991. *Address:* c/o Hellenic Industrial Development Bank SA, Odos Panepistiniou 18, 106 72 Athens, Greece.

PISAR, Judith, BA; American arts administrator; b 17 Feb 1938, New York; d of Sol and Beatrice (née Gottsegen) Frehm; one s; m Samuel Pisar 1971; one d. *Education:* Vassar Coll, New York Univ and Juilliard School of Music (New York). *Career:* Founder Composer Speaks Inc 1962, responsible for composers including Luciano Berio, John Cage, Lukas Foss, Karlheinz Stockhausen, Iannis Xenakis; Hon Dir of Artistic Org Museum of Modern Art, New York 1964–65; Exec Dir Merce Cunningham Dance Co 1964–69, mem Admin Bd Cunningham Dance Foundation; Dir of Music Brooklyn Acad of Music 1969–71; Chair Admin Bd American Center, Paris 1976–95, Hon Pres 1995–; Pres d'Arts France-USA 1997–; Pres George Gershwin Centenary 1998, Festival Africain Américain 2000; participated in org of Costakis

Collection, Guggenheim Museum 1980; mem Higher Council of Cultural Patronage 1987–, Higher Council of Dance 1995–; mem Weisman Foundation, LA, New World Music Foundation; mem Artistic Bd Centre Nat Art et Technologie, Maison de la Culture de Reims, France; mem Admin Bd Régine Chopinot dance co; author articles for Musical America, USA, and Passion Magazine, Paris; Chevalier de la Légion d'Honneur; Chevalier des Arts et des Lettres. *Leisure interests:* modern dance, contemporary music, politics, collecting contemporary objects d'art, water sports, tennis. *Address:* 23 square de l'ave Foch, 75016 Paris, France (Office and Home); 870 Fifth Ave, New York, USA.

PISIER, Evelyne Andrée Thérèse, D ÈS L; French professor of political science; b 18 Oct 1941, Hanoi, Vietnam; m 1st B. Kouchner 1970; m 2nd Olivier Duhamel; three s two d. *Education:* Lycées Louis-le-Grand and Henri IV (Paris) and Univ of Paris. *Career:* Asst Law Faculty, Univ of Paris 1965–72; Sr Lecturer Univ of Reims 1972–79; Prof of Political Science Univ of Paris I (Panthéon-Sorbonne) 1979–; Pres Centre Nat des Lettres 1989–93; fmr Dir Centre d'études des conceptions politiques classiques et modernes (CNRS, Univ of Paris I); teacher Inst d'Etudes Politiques de Paris 1989–93; Dir of Books and Culture, Ministry of Culture, Communications and Major Public Works 1989–93; fmr Co-Dir Recherches politiques collection, Presses Universitaires de France; Vice-Pres Comm for Planning and Culture 1992; Editorial Adviser to Editions Hermann 1993–95; mem Univs Consultative Cttee 1977–80, Fondation Saint-Simon 1987–, State Efficiency Comm 1988–89. *Publications:* Les Marxistes et la politique (jtly) 1975, Dictionnaire des œuvres politiques (jtly) 1982, Les conceptions politiques du XXème siècle (jtly) 1983, Histoire des idées politiques (jtly) 1983, Les interprétations du stalinisme 1983, Le paradoxe du fonctionnaire (jtly) 1988, La dernière fois (novel) 1994. *Address:* University of Paris I (Panthéon-Sorbonne), 17 rue de la Sorbonne, 75005 Paris, France.

PITANGUY, Jaqueline; Brazilian organization executive. *Career:* Fmr Cabinet mem as Pres Brazilian Nat Council for Women's Rights; Dir of Citizenship, Studies, Information and Action (CEPIA) (Rio de Janeiro, Brazil); Chair-elect Global Fund for Women; mem Bd Comm on Citizenship and Reproduction Allen Guttmacher Inst, Inter-American Dialogue; mem Bd UNESCO Inst for Educ; mem Int Rights Council of the Carter Center. *Address:* Global Fund For Women, 1375 Sutter St, Suite 400, San Francisco, CA 94109, USA; Rua do Russel, 694/ 201 Gloria, Rio de Janeiro, RJ 22210, Brazil. *E-mail:* gfw@ globalfundforwomen.org; *Internet:* www.globalfundforwomen.org.

PITMAN, Jennifer Susan, OBE; British consultant and former racehorse trainer; b 11 June 1946, Leicester; d of George and Mary Harvey; m Richard Pitman 1965 (annulled); two s; m 2nd David Stait 1997. *Education:* Sarson Secondary Girls' School. *Career:* Nat Hunt Trainer 1975–99; Dir Jenny Pitman Racing Ltd 1975–99; Racing and Media Consultant, DJS Racing 1999–; race winners include Watafella (Midlands Nat 1977), Bueche Giorod (Massey Ferguson Gold Cup 1980), Corbiere (Welsh Nat 1982, Grand Nat 1983), Burrough Hill Lad (Welsh Nat 1984, Cheltenham Gold Cup 1984, King George VI Gold Cup 1984, Hennessey Gold Cup 1984), Smith's Man (Whitbread Trophy 1985), Stearsby (Welsh Nat 1986), Gainsay (Ritz Club Nat Hunt Handicap 1987, Sporting Life Weekend Chase 1987), Crumpet Delite (Philip Cornes Saddle of Gold Final 1988), Garrison Savannah (Cheltenham Gold Cup 1991), Wonderman (Welsh Champion Hurdle 1991), Don Valentino (Welsh Champion Hurdle 1992), Royal Athlete (Grand Nat 1995), Willsford (Scottish Nat 1995); first woman to train Grand Nat winner 1983; numerous awards including Racing Personality of the Year, Golden Spurs 1983, Commonwealth Sports Award 1983, 1984, Piper Heidsieck Trainer of the Year 1983/84, 1989/90, Variety Club of GB Sportswoman of the Year 1984. *Publications include:* Glorious Uncertainty (autobiog) 1984, Jenny Pitman: The Autobiography 1999. *Address:* Jenny Pitman Racing Ltd, Weathercock House, Upper Lambourn, nr Newbury, Berks, UK; Owls Barn, Kintbury, Hungerford, Berks RG17 9XS, UK (Home). *Telephone:* (1488) 668774 (Office); (1488) 669191 (Home); *Fax:* (1488) 668999 (Office).

PITT, Ingrid; British actress and writer. *Education:* Goethe Schule (Berlin, Germany). *Career:* Acting career began with Berliner Ensemble; defected from fmr GDR to USA 1962; joined Spanish Nat Theatre 1966, toured USA; int film debut in Where Eagles Dare 1968; writer 1980–; formed Monaco Films Ltd 1987, Co-Dir; Mar del Plata Best Actress Award. *Films include:* The Vampire Lovers, The House That Dripped Blood, Wild Geese 2, Countess Dracula 1971, Nobody Ordered Love, The Omegans, The Wicker Man, El Lobo, Who Dares Wins 1983, Parker, Requiem, Underworld 1987, Innocent Heroes 1988; *Publications include:* Cuckoo Run 1980, Katarina 1985, The Perons (jtly), Eva's Spell (jtly) 1986, Pitt of Horror, Hisako San, Bertie the Bus, Dragonhunter, Bertie to the Rescue. *Leisure interests:* flying, golf.

PIVETTI, Irene; Italian politician; b 1965; d of Grazia Gabrielli; m Paolo Taranta 1988 (separated 1992). *Education:* Catholic Univ of the Sacred Heart (Milan). *Career:* Journalist; mem Chamber of Deputies (Parl) 1992–, Speaker 1995–96; fmr mem Northern League; Founder Unione Democratic per l'Europa (UDEUR) 1999, Pres. *Address:* Camera dei Deputati, Palazzo di Montecitorio, 00186 Rome, Italy. *Telephone:* (6) 6760.

PIYASHEVA, Larisa, D ECON; Russian economist; b 10 July 1947, Moscow; m Boris Pinsker (divorced); two d. *Education:* Plekhnov Inst of Nat Econ. *Career:* Researcher Inst if Int Wrokers' Movt, USSR Acad of Sciences 1969–91; Head, Chair of Econs, Prof Moscow State Open Univ 1991–93, Dean of Faculty 1996–; Head Finance-Economy Dept, Council of Fed Staff 1994–; Dir F. von Hayek Pvt Inst of Econs and Law 1995–; Dir-Gen Dept of Moscow Maj Office Feb–Sept 1992. *Publications:* Anti-Communist Manifesto (jtly); monographs and scientific articles on problems of Soviet economy. *Address:* 113191 Moscow, Serpukhovskoy Val 17/23, kv 9, Russian Federation. *E-mail:* (095) 292-12-83.

PIZZEY, Erin Patria Margaret; British writer and campaigner; b 19 Feb 1939, People's Repub of China; d of Cyril Edward Antony and Ruth Patricia (née Balfour-Last) Carney; m 1st John Leo Pizzey 1961 (divorced 1979); one s one d; m 2nd Jeffrey Scott Shapiro 1980; seven s (adopted). *Education:* Leweston Manor (Dorset). *Career:* Protests on behalf of women and children's rights led to several court appearances; Founder first Shelter for Battered Wives and their children 1971; toured USA to help set up shelters 1974, New Zealand 1978; now writer; works as trans to Japanese, Russian, Greek, Portuguese, Polish, Latvian, Hebrew, Italian; contribs to The New Statesman, The Sunday Times, Cosmopolitan and to other int magazines; resident expert on family violence on Phil Donahue Show, TV 1982; gave evidence to Attorney-Gen's Task Force on Family Violence, USA 1984; Guest of Honour at conf of Int Supreme Court Judges, Rome 1994; Lunch of Honour on Capitol Hill, Washington, DC, sponsored by Congresswomen; lecture tours, New Zealand 1978, USA 1979; numerous awards, including Diploma of Honour (Int Order of Volunteers for Peace Italy) 1981, Nancy Astor Award for Journalism 1983, Distinguished Leadership Award (World Congress of Victimology) 1987, St Valentino Palm d'Oro Int Award for Literature (Italy) 1994. *Publications:* Non-fiction: Scream Quietly or the Neighbours Will Hear (also film 1979) 1974, Infernal Child (autobiog) 1978, The Slut's Cookbook (jtly) 1981, Prone to Violence 1982, Erin Pizzey Collects 1983; Fiction: The Watershed 1983, In the Shadow 1984, The Pleasure Palace 1986, First Lady 1987, The Consul General's Daughter 1988, The Snow Leopard of Shanghai 1989, Other Lovers 1991, Swimming with Dolphins, For the Love of a Stranger, Kisses, The Wicked World of Women 1996, The Fame Game 1999; Short Stories: The Man in the Blue Van, The Frangipani Tree, Addictions, Dancing, Sand. *Leisure interests:* reading, writing, cooking, antiques, violin, gardening, wine, food, travel. *Address:* Flat 5, 29 Lebanon Park, Twickenham TW1 3DH, UK; Il Molino Di Trove, 23 San Giovanni D'Asso, 53020 Siena, Italy. *Telephone:* (577) 823170 (Italy); *Fax:* (577) 823170 (Italy); *E-mail:* pizzey@sienanet.it.

PLAKWICZ, Jolanta, BA; Polish translator and feminist campaigner; b 18 Nov 1948, Legnica; d of Sobiesław and Danuta Lenkiewicz; m Stanisław Plakwicz 1972 (divorced 1991). *Education:* Univ of Warsaw. *Career:* Freelance translator 1980–; Co-Founder Polskie Stowarzyszenie Feministyczne (Polish Feminist Asscn) 1989–95, Co-Founder Fed for Women and Family Planning 1991, PSF Women's Centre (feminist foundation) 1995; Polcul Foundation Award for "starting feminism in Poland" 1995. *Publications:* Translator: Surfacing (Margaret Atwood) 1987, Three Men on the Bummel (Jerome K. Jerome) 1992; Writer:

Between State and Church, Polish Women's Experience in Super-women and the Double Burden 1992. *Leisure interests:* books, travel, driving, dog, cat. *Address:* PSF Women's Centre, ul Mokotowska 55, 00-542 Warsaw, Poland. *Telephone:* (22) 6294847; *Fax:* (22) 6294847.

PŁANETA-MAŁECKA, Izabela, MD; Polish paediatrician; b 8 Dec 1930, Lvov; m Ignacy Małecki 1955; one d. *Education:* Medical Acad (Łódź). *Career:* Asst Pharmacology Research Centre 1953–55, Gen and Social Hygiene Research Centre 1955–58, Medical Acad, Łódź; Asst Paediatric Ward Władysław Biegański Isolation Hosp, Łódź 1955–60; Sr Asst and Lecturer Military Medical Acad, Łódź 1960–78, Asst Prof of Children's Diseases Dept 1978–83, organizer and Head II Children's Diseases Dept, organizer and Head II Children's Diseases Clinic of Paediatric Dept 1983, Extraordinary Prof 1985–; organizer first gastroenterological dispensary in Poland for children, Łódź 1968; Deputy Dir for paediatric matters, Health Centre of Mother-Pole, Łódź 1987–; Minister of Health and Social Welfare 1988–89; numerous articles, mainly on gastroenterology; mem Polish Paediatric Soc 1955–, Polish Gastroenterological Soc 1978–, Polish Women's League, Deputy Chair Łódź Bd 1982; mem Nat Council of Patriotic Movt for Nat Rebirth (PRON) 1983–89, fmr mem Exec Cttee; mem World Peace Council 1983–; decorations include KT's Cross of Polonia Restituta Order, Gold Cross of Merit, Nat Educ Comm Medal. *Leisure interests:* music, belles-lettres, contemporary literature. *Address:* ul Biegańskiego 25 m 1, 91-473 Łódź, Poland. *Telephone:* (42) 452064 (Office); (42) 576555 (Home).

PLATELL, Amanda, BA; Australian newspaper executive. *Career:* Fmr mem staff Perth Daily News; moved to London 1986; joined Today newspaper, later Features Production Ed, then Deputy Ed; fmr mem staff London Daily News; Group Man Dir Mirror Group Newspapers 1995–96, Head of Promotions for MGN Titles, mem subsidiary MGN Bd, Group Man Dir and Acting Ed Sunday Mirror 1996–97; Ed Sunday Express 1998–99; Head of Media, Cons Party 1999–2001. *Publication:* Scandal 1999. *Address:* c/o Conservative Central Office, 32 Smith Square, Westminster, London SW1P 3HH, UK.

PLATILOVÁ, Dagmar, MUS M; Czech harpist; b 15 Aug 1943, Slapy; d of Josef and Jarmila Platilovi; m Myron Yadzyn 1971 (divorced 1985). *Education:* Acad of Musical Arts (Prague), Hartt School of Music (Univ of Hartford, USA) and Juilliard School of Music (New York). *Career:* Mem Prague Duo (flute and harp) 1962–68, 1976–, New York Harp Ensemble 1972–75; Prin Harpist Czech Radio Orchestra 1976–; appearances include Cisac Int Festival of Contemporary Music, Prague 1966, Int Music Festival, Bergen, Norway 1967, 1974, Prague Spring Festival 1967, Icam Festival, Hartford, CT 1969; Corresp for World Harp Congress Review 1985–99; many TV appearances; numerous recordings. *Address:* Zvonická 21, 160 00 Prague 6, Czech Republic. *Telephone:* (2) 33336953.

PLATT OF WRITTLE, Baroness (Life Peer), cr 1981, of Writtle in the County of Essex, **Beryl Catherine Platt,** CBE, DL, F ENG, FRCS, FRSA; British engineer and member of the House of Lords; b 18 April 1923; d of Ernest and Dorothy Myatt; m Stewart Sydney Platt 1949; one s one d. *Education:* Westcliff High School and Girton Coll (Cambridge). *Career:* Tech Asst Hawker Aircraft 1943–46, British European Airways (BEA) 1946–49; mem Chelmsford Regional Dist Council 1958–74, Essex Co Council 1965–85, Vice-Chair 1980–83, Chair Educ Cttee 1971–80; mem House of Lords 1981–, mem Select Cttee for Science and Tech 1982–85, 1990–94, Select Cttee on Relations between Cen and Local Govt 1995–96; mem of Court Univ of Essex 1964–99, City Univ 1969–78, Brunel Univ 1985–92; Vice-Pres UMIST 1985–94; Chancellor Middx Univ 1993–2000; Chair Equal Opportunities Comm 1983–88; Dir British Gas 1988–94, Smallpiece Trust 1989–95; Pres Nat Soc for Clean Air and Environmental Protection 1991, Pipeline Industries Guild 1994–96; Hon Fellow Polytechnic of Wales 1985, Girton Coll, Cambridge 1988; Hon FITD 1984, FICE 1991; Hon Fellow Inst of Structural Engineers, Inst of Gas Engineers; Hon D SC (Salford, City) 1984, (Cranfield Inst of Tech) 1985; Hon D UNIV (Open Univ) 1985, (Middx, Loughborough); Hon D ENG (Bradford) 1985; Hon D TECH (Brunel) 1986; Hon LL D (Cambridge) 1988. *Leisure interests:* cooking, reading, swimming. *Address:* House of Lords, Westminster, London SW1A 0PW, UK. *Telephone:* (20) 7219-5242; *Fax:* (20) 7219-6396.

PLAVŠIĆ, Biljana, PH D; Bosnia and Herzegovina politician and biologist. *Career:* Mem 'Crisis Cttee' (military and civilian govt which ordered mass expulsion of Muslims and Croats from E and Cen Bosnia 1991–92); Vice-Pres, then Acting Pres, then Pres Serb Republic of Bosnia and Herzegovina 1996–98; Chair Serb Nat Alliance; surrendered herself to trial at the war crimes tribunal in The Hague 2001, charged with genocide and crimes against humanity. *Address:* c/o Srpski Narodni Savez (SNP), Banja Luka, Serb Republic of Bosnia and Herzegovina.

PLISETSKAYA, Maiya Mikhailovna; Russian ballet dancer; b 20 Nov 1925, Moscow; m Rodion Shchedrin. *Education:* Moscow Bolshoi Theatre Ballet School. *Career:* Soloist, then Prin Dancer Bolshoi Ballet 1943–90; Artistic Dir Ballet Roma Opera 1984–85, Nat Ballet of Spain 1987–89; f Maya Plisetskaya Int Ballet Competition, St Petersburg 1994; Pres Imperial Russian Ballet 1996–; Co-Producer Anna Karenina 1972; Hon Prof Moscow Univ 1993; Hon mem Portuguese Dance Centre; First Prize Budapest Int Competition 1949; honours include People's Artist of the RSFSR 1951, People's Artist of the USSR 1959, Anna Pavlova Prize 1962, Lenin Prize 1964, Hero of Socialist Labour 1985, Triumph Prize 2000; Chevalier de la Légion d'Honneur 1986, and other decorations. *Ballets include:* Swan Lake, Raimonda, The Fountain of Bakhchisarai, Don Quixote, Romeo and Juliet, Shuralye, Laurencia, Spartak, Carmen Suite, Anna Karenina 1972, The Seagull 1980, Lady with a Lap Dog 1983, La folle de Chaillot 1992, Karazuka 1995; *Publication:* I Am Maiya Plisetskaya. *Address:* Theresien Str 23, 80333 Munich, Germany (Home); 103050 Moscow, Tverskaya 25/9, kv 31, Russian Federation (Home). *Telephone:* (89) 285834 (Germany); (095) 299-72-39 (Russian Federation).

PLOIX, Hélène Marie Joseph, MA, MBA; French civil servant and business executive; b 25 Sept 1944, Anould; d of René and Antoinette (née Jobert) Ploix; m Alexandre Lumbroso 1988. *Education:* Univ of California (USA) and Inst des Etudes Politiques de Paris. *Career:* Man Consultant McKinsey and Co, Paris 1968–78; Special Asst to Cabinet of Sec of State for Consumer Affairs 1977–78; Dir Compagnie Européenne de Publication 1978–82; Pres, Man Dir Banque Industrielle et Mobilière Privée 1982–84; mem of Bd Comm des Opérations de Bourse 1983–84; Adviser for Econ and Financial Affairs Office of the Prime Minister 1984–86; Exec Dir representing France IMF and IBRD 1986–89; Deputy CEO Caisse des dépôts et consignations 1989–95; Chair Caisse autonome de refinancement 1990–95, CDC Participations 1992–95; Chair and CEO Pechel Industries 1997; Chevalier de l'Ordre Nat du Mérite; Chevalier de la Légion d'Honneur. *Leisure interest:* golf. *Address:* Pechel Industries, 9 ave Percier, 75008 Paris, France.

PLOOIJ-VAN GORSEL, Elly, PH D; Netherlands politician; b 20 March 1947, Tholen; m J. Plooij 1969 (deceased); one s one d. *Education:* Univ of Utrecht. *Career:* Assoc Prof Univ of Leiden 1973–87; employed in business sector in various sr man positions 1987–; MEP (liberal party) 1994–, Spokesperson on Research, Technological Devt and Information Tech, mem EU–US and EU–China Interparl Del; takes a special interest in biotech information and communication tech; Pres European Internet Foundation; mem Transatlantic Policy Network; author of several scientific and political publs. *Leisure interests:* tennis, golf. *Address:* European Parliament, Wiertzstraat ASP 10 G257, 1047 Brussels, Belgium. *Telephone:* (2) 284-56-08; *Fax:* (2) 230-96-08; *E-mail:* plooij@planet.nl; *Internet:* www.plooij.nl.

PLOWRIGHT, Joan Anne, CBE; British actress; b 28 Oct 1929, Brigg, Lancs; d of William and Daisy (née Burton) Plowright; m 1st Roger Gage 1953 (divorced); m 2nd Sir Laurence (later Lord) Olivier 1961 (died 1989); two d one s. *Education:* Scunthorpe Grammar School, Laban Art of Movement Studio and Old Vic Theatre School. *Career:* Mem Old Vic Co, toured South Africa 1952–53; first leading role in The Country Wife, London 1956; mem English Stage Co 1956; at Nat Theatre 1963–74; Vice-Pres Nat Youth Theatre; mem Council English Stage Co; 18th Crystal Award, Women in Films (USA) 1994. *Plays include:* The Chairs 1957, The Entertainer 1958 (film 1960), Major Barbara 1958, Roots 1959, A Taste of Honey (Tony Best Actress Award) 1960, Uncle Vanya 1962, 1963, 1964, 1988, St Joan (Evening Standard Best Actress Award 1964) 1963, Hobson's Choice 1964, The Master Builder 1965, Much Ado About Nothing 1967, Tartuffe 1967, Three Sisters 1967, 1969 (film 1969), The Advertisement 1968, 1969, Love's Labour's Lost 1968, 1969, The Merchant of Venice, 1970,

1971–72 (TV 1973), Rules of the Game, Woman Killed with Kindness 1971–72, The Taming of the Shrew, Doctor's Dilemma 1972, Rosmersholm 1973, Saturday Sunday Monday 1973, Eden's End 1974, The Sea Gull 1975, The Bed Before Yesterday (Variety Club Award 1976) 1975, Filumena (Best Actress, Soc of West End Theatre – SWET 1978) 1977, Enjoy 1980, Who's Afraid of Virginia Woolf? 1981, Cavell 1982, The Cherry Orchard 1983, The Way of the World 1984, Mrs Warren's Profession 1985, The House of Bernarda Alba 1986, Conquest of the South Pole 1989, Time and the Conways 1991, If We Are Women; *Films include:* Equus 1976, Richard Wagner 1982, Revolution 1985, Drowning by Numbers (Variety Club Film Actress of the Year Award) 1987, The Dressmaker 1988, I Love You to Death 1989, Avalon 1990, Enchanted April 1991, Stalin (Golden Globe Award, Acad Award nomination) 1992, Denis the Menace 1992, A Place for Annie 1993, Last Action Hero 1993, A Pin for the Butterfly 1993, Widow's Peak 1993, On Promised Land 1994, Hotel Sorrento 1994, A Pyromaniac's Love Story 1994, The Scarlett Letter 1994, Jane Eyre 1995, Mr Wrong 1995, Picasso 1995, 101 Dalmatians 1996, The Assistant 1996, Shut Up and Dance 1997, Tom's Midnight Garden 1997, Tea with Mussolini 1998, Return to the Secret Garden 1999, Frankie and Hazel 1999, Bailey's Mistake 2000, Global Heresy 2000; *TV appearances include:* Daphne Laureola 1977, Saturday Sunday Monday 1977, Brimstone and Treacle 1982, The Importance of Being Earnest 1988, And a Nightingale Sang 1989, Oranges Are Not the Only Fruit, The House of Bernarda Alba 1991, Clothes in the Wardrobe 1992, Return of the Native 1994. *Leisure interests:* reading, music, entertaining. *Address:* c/o The Malthouse, Horsham Rd, Ashurst, Steyning, W Sussex BN44 3AR, UK.

PLOWRIGHT, Rosalind Anne, LRAM; British opera singer (soprano); b 21 May 1949; d of Robert Arthur and Celia Adelaide Plowright; m James Anthony Kaye 1984; one s one d. *Education:* Notre Dame High School (Wigan) and Royal Northern Coll of Music (Manchester). *Career:* London Opera Centre 1973–75; Glyndebourne Chorus and Touring Co 1974–77; debut with English Nat Opera as Page in Salome 1975, at Royal Opera House, Covent Garden as Ortlinde in Die Walküre 1980, debuts in Philadelphia and San Diego (USA), Paris, Madrid and Hamburg (Germany) 1982; appearances with Berne Opera (Switzerland) 1980–81, Frankfurt and Munich Operas (Germany) 1981, at La Scala, Milan (Italy), Edinburgh Festival, San Francisco and Carnegie Hall, New York 1983, with Deutsche Oper, Berlin 1984, Houston and Pittsburgh (USA), Venice and Verona (Italy) 1985, Rome, Florence (Italy) and the Netherlands 1986, Tulsa (USA), Buenos Aires, Santiago, Israel and Bonn 1987, with New York Philharmonic and Paris Opera 1987, in Lausanne and Geneva (Switzerland), Oviedo and Bilbao (Spain) 1988, Zurich (Switzerland), Copenhagen and Lisbon 1989, Vienna State Opera 1990, in Nice (France) 1991, Wiesbaden (Germany) 1992, Leeds (UK) 1993; has given recitals and concerts in UK, Europe and USA; First Prize 7th Int Competition for Opera Singers, Sofia 1979; Prix Fondation Fanny Heldy, Acad Nat du Disque Lyrique 1985. *Operas include:* Turn of the Screw (SWET award) 1979, Ariadne, Alceste, Médée, Norma, Mary Stuart, Andrea Chénier, The Tales of Hoffman, Don Giovanni, La Clemenza di Tito, Madame Butterfly, Manon Lescaut, Suor Angelica, Il Tabarro, Aida, Nabucco, Otello, I Vespri Siciliani, Un Ballo in Maschera, La Forza del Destino, La Traviata, Don Carlos, Il Trovatore, Macbeth; has made numerous recordings. *Leisure interests:* wind-surfing, cliff-climbing, fell walking. *Address:* c/o Artists Management Ltd, 2 Fir Hill Villas, Hollywater Rd, Bordon, Hants GU35 0AG, UK; 83 St Mark's Ave, Salisbury, Wilts SP1 3DW, UK.

PODOLSKY, Ilana Mihaela, MFA; Israeli artist; b 25 June 1957, Bucharest; m Simon Podolsky 1985; one d. *Education:* Special High School of Fine Arts and Acad of Fine Arts (Bucharest). *Career:* Graphic Designer, Bucharest 1981–85; teacher of print techniques, Painters' and Sculptors' Asscn, Tel-Aviv 1987; group exhibitions include Bucharest 1981–86, Tulcea, Romania 1981–85, Painters' and Sculptors' Asscn Gallery, Israel 1987, Municipal Museum, Ramat-Gan 1991, Minority Gallery, Gratz, Germany 1991; int exhibitions in Moscow 1982, Tokyo 1985, Brussels 1986, New York 1986, Budapest 1986, Toronto, Canada 1988, Spain 1990; solo exhibition Gallery of The World Bank Art Soc, Washington, DC 1987; touring exhibitions to Austria 1982, France 1987, USA 1987; works feature in perm collections in Israel,

Austria, Romania, Yugoslavia, USA; mem Painters' and Sculptors' Asscn of Israel; Gold Medal New York Art Expo 1986; Josef Kozkowsky Prize 1987.

POGONOWSKA-JUCHA, Emilia-Janina, LL M; Polish judge; b 10 Feb 1939; d of Henryk and Marianna Laskowska; m Lesław Jucha 1965; two s. *Education:* Secondary school in Łuków and Marie Curie-Skłodowska Univ. *Career:* Served apprenticeship in Białystok Dist Court 1963–65; Judge Gizycko Dist Court 1965–67, Krosno Dist Court 1967–75, Krosno Voivodship Court 1975–90, Rzeszów Court of Appeal 1990; mem Sejm (Nat Ass) 1985–91; mem State Court of Justice, Warsaw from 1991; Gold Award, Polish Lawyers' Asscn 1979; Silver Cross of Merit 1980; Polonia Restituta Cross 1988. *Publications:* Polish Consular Treaties 1963, Consumer Law in Poland 1980, Member of Parliament Rights and Duties 1990. *Leisure interests:* theatre, music, travel, books. *Address:* Marii Konopnickiej 3, 38-400 Krosno, Poland. *Telephone:* (131) 21235.

POIANI, Eileen Louise, BA, MS, PH D; American professor of mathematics; b 17 Dec 1943, Newark; d of Hugo Francis and Eileen Louise (née Crecca) Poiani. *Education:* Douglass Coll (New Brunswick) and Rutgers Univ (NJ). *Career:* Teaching Asst Rutgers Univ 1966–67; Asst Counsellor Douglass Coll 1967, 1969–70; Maths Instructor St Peter's Coll, Jersey City 1967–70, Asst Prof 1970–74, Dir of Self-Study 1974–76, Assoc Prof 1974–80, Prof 1980–, Asst to Pres 1976–80, Asst to Pres for Planning 1980–; Chair US Comm on Mathematical Instruction, Nat Research Council of NAS, Washington, DC 1983–; Founder and Nat Dir Women and Math Lectureship Program 1975–81, mem Advisory Bd 1981–; Project Dir Consortium for the Advancement of Pvt Higher Educ 1986–88; mem New Jersey Supreme Court Ethics Comm, Trenton 1986–; US Rep Int Congress on Math Educ, Budapest 1988; mem US Del to Int Congress on Math Educ, Canada 1992; mem Planning Cttee Nat Conf of Christians and Jews 1988–; mem American Math Soc, American Asscn of Univ Profs, Nat Council of Math Teachers; Trustee St Peter's Preparatory School 1986–; numerous articles, contribs and papers; apptd Danforth Assoc, Danforth Foundation 1972–86; named Outstanding Educator of America 1973, 1974, Outstanding Young Woman of America 1974; recipient Douglass Soc Award 1982; C. C. MacDuffee Award for Distinguished Service to Maths 1995; Christopher Columbus Foundation Award for Outstanding Community Service 1994; Mathematical Asscn Award (NJ Section) for Distinguished Coll or Univ Teaching 1993; Certificate of Appreciation for Outstanding Contribs as Nat Dir of Women and Maths Prog, Mathematical Asscn of America 1993. *Leisure interests:* gourmet cooking, golf, travel. *Address:* St Peter's College, 2641 Kennedy Blvd, Jersey City, NJ 07306, USA (Office); 49 Carrie Court, Nutley, NJ 07110, USA (Home). *Telephone:* (201) 915-9018 (Office); (201) 667-5297 (Home).

POKKA, Hannele, LL M; Finnish politician; b 25 May 1952, Ruovesi. *Career:* Lawyer; mem Keskustapuolue (KP, Centre Party), Chair KP Women; mem of Eduskunta (Parl) 1979–; mem Presidential Electorate 1982; Minister of Justice 1992–94; Councillor Nat Pensions Inst 1983; mem Farm Producers' Cen Asscn 1976. *Address:* c/o Ministry of Justice, Eteläesplanadi 10, 00130 Helsinki, Finland.

POLAK, Julia Margaret, MD, PH D, D SC, FRCP, FRCPATH, F MED SCI; British professor and consultant in histopathology; b 26 June 1939, Buenos Aires; m Daniel Catovsky; two s one d. *Education:* Univs of Buenos Aires and London. *Career:* Medical posts in Buenos Aires 1961–67; Research Asst Dept of Histochemistry, Royal Postgrad Medical School, Hammersmith Hosp (London) 1968–69, Asst Lecturer 1970–73, Lecturer in Histochemistry 1973–79, Sr Lecturer 1979–82, Reader 1982–84, Hon Consultant in Histopathology, Dept of Histo-chemistry 1979–, Deputy Dir of Dept 1988–91, Prof and Chair of Dept 1992–; EC Apptd Project Leader 1994; Chair British Endocrine Pathologists Group 1988–; Chair Cognate Research Group, Imperial Coll School of Medicine 1997–; Pres Tissue and Cell Eng Soc 1998–; Dir Tissue Eng Centre 1998–; mem 34 editorial bds and scientific and medical socs; Dr hc (Univ Computense, Madrid, Spain) 1997; awards include Benito de Udaondo Cardiology Prize 1967, Soc for Endo-crinology Medal 1984, Sir Eric Sharpe Prize for Oncology (Cable and Wireless) 1986/87, Erasmus Wilson Distinguished Lecturer (Royal Coll of Surgeons) 1992, Swedish Soc of Medicine Medal for Valuable

Contrib to The Annual Gen Meedint, Stockholm 1998. *Publications include:* Introduction to Immunocytochemistry (ed) 1997, Modern Visualisation of the Endothelium. Endothelial Cell Research Series (ed), Nitric Oxide in Bone and Joint Disease (ed) 1998; over 700 articles, book chapters and case reports, etc. *Leisure interest:* walking. *Address:* Tissue Engineering Centre, Imperial College School of Medicine, 3rd Floor, Chelsea & Westminster Hospital, 369 Fulham Rd, London SW10 9NH, UK; 11 Thames Quay, Chelsea Harbour, London SW10 0UY, UK (Home). *Telephone:* (20) 8237-2670 (Office); (20) 7352-1400 (Home); *Fax:* (20) 8746-5619 (Office); *E-mail:* julia.polak@ic.ac.uk.

POLESE, Kim, BS; American computer executive. *Education:* Univ of California at Berkeley and Univ of Washington. *Career:* Product Man Sun Microsystems 1988–95; Co-Founder Marimba Inc 1996–, also Pres and CEO. *Address:* Marimba Inc, 440 Clyde Ave, Maintain View, CA 94043, USA.

POLFER, Lydie, LL D; Luxembourg politician; b 22 Nov 1952, Luxembourg; m Hubert Wurth 1981; one d. *Education:* Lycée Robert Schuman and Univ of Grenoble (France). *Career:* Called to the Bar, Luxembourg 1977; Researcher European Parl Liberal , Democratic and Reformist Group; mem Parti Démocratique; mem Chamber of Deputies (Parl) 1979–85, 1989, mem Comms on Foreign Affairs, Justice, Public Works, Constitutional Reform, Community Affairs, Housing and Urbanism; mem Luxembourg Dist Council 1981–87; Mayor of Luxembourg 1981–99; MEP 1985–89, 1990–94; Chair Democratic Party 1994–; Vice-Prime Minister, Minister of Foreign Affairs and External Trade, Minister of Civil Service and Admin Reform 1999–; mem Council of Europe, mem Comms on Law, Migration, Parl and Public Relations; mem Union de l'Europe Occidentale Comms on Gen Matters and Parl Relations. *Address:* Ministry of Foreign Affairs and Trade, 5 rue Notre Dame, 2240, Luxembourg. *Telephone:* 487 2301; *Fax:* 223 285; *E-mail:* cecile.peysen@mae.etat.lu.

POLGÁR, Judit; Hungarian chess player; b 23 July 1976, Budapest; d of László and Klara Polgár. *Education:* High School. *Career:* Began playing chess at the age of five; Women's Grand Master 1988; winner World Chess Championships 1988, 1990; won five Gold Medals, Chess Olympiad, Thessaloniki, Greece 1988, Novi Sad, Yugoslavia 1990; winner Hungarian Super-Championship; youngest chess Int Grand Master and number one in the Int Chess Rating List 1992; Oscar Prize 1988. *Publications:* Polgár Tactics: 77 Chess Combinations (jtly) 1991, Le phénomène Polgár (jtly) 1991. *Leisure interests:* table-tennis, karate, tennis, music, swimming, excursions. *Address:* 1052 Budapest, Semmelweis u 10, Apt 39, Hungary. *Telephone:* (1) 137-5675; *Fax:* (1) 137-5675.

POLGÁR, Zsófia; Hungarian chess player; b 2 Nov 1974; d of László and Klara Polgár. *Education:* High School. *Career:* Int Chess Master and Women's Grand Master; mem Hungarian Gold Medal winning team, Chess Olympiad, Thessaloniki, Greece 1988 and Novi Sad, Yugoslavia 1990; winner int chess competition with 8.5 out of a possible 9 points, Rome 1989. *Publications:* Polgár Tactics: 77 Chess Combinations (jtly) 1991, Le phénomène Polgár (jtly) 1991. *Leisure interests:* table-tennis, karate, tennis, music, swimming, excursions. *Address:* 1052 Budapest, Semmelweis u 10, Apt 39, Hungary. *Telephone:* (1) 137-5675; *Fax:* (1) 137-5675.

POLGÁR, Zsuzsa; Hungarian chess player; b 19 April 1969; d of László and Klara Polgár. *Career:* Int Chess Grand Master; first woman to receive men's Grand Master title; highest-rated female chess player in the world 1984–86; mem Hungarian Gold Medal winning team, Chess Olympiad, Thessaloniki, Greece 1988, Novi Sad, Yugoslavia 1990. *Publications:* Polgár Tactics: 77 Chess Combinations (jtly) 1991, Le phénomène Polgár (jtly) 1991. *Leisure interests:* table-tennis, karate, tennis, music, swimming, excursions. *Address:* 1052 Budapest, Semmelweis u 10, Apt 39, Hungary. *Telephone:* (1) 137-5675; *Fax:* (1) 137-5675.

POLI BORTONE, Adriana, B LITT; Italian politician; b 25 Aug 1943, Lecce; m; two c. *Career:* Assoc Prof of Latin Literature, Univ of Lecce; elected Councillor for Lecce 1967–; mem Chamber of Deputies (Parl) for Lecce, Brindisi and Taranto (Movimento Sociale Italiano) 1983–87,

1987–94, (Alleanza Nazionale) 1994–; Minister of Agric 1994–95. *Address:* c/o Ministero delle Politiche Agricole Alimentari e Forestali, Via XX Settembre, 00187 Rome, Italy.

POLISHCHUK, Lyubov Grigoryevna; Russian actress; b 21 May 1949, Omsk; m; one d. *Education:* Creative Workshop of Variety Arts (Russian Concert Agency) and Moscow Lunacharsky Inst of Theatre Art. *Career:* In variety shows 1965–76; actress Theatre Hermitage 1980–87; leading actress Theatre School of Contemporary Play 1989–; in cinema 1976–; Merited Artist of Russian Fed. *Films:* Zatsepin Family 1976, Twelve Chairs 1976, Love with Privileges, Play of Imagination, New Odeon, Golden Mine, Daphnis and Chloë. *Address:* Tsandera str 7, Apt 386, 129075 Moscow, Russian Federation (Office). *Telephone:* (095) 215-66-18 (Home).

POLL AHRENS, Sylvia Ursula; Costa Rican swimmer; b 24 Sept 1970, Managua, Nicaragua. *Education:* Humboldt Schule (San José) and Univ of Costa Rica. *Career:* More than 15 Gold Medals won in Cen American and Caribbean Swimming Championships 1983–87; awarded three Gold, three Silver and two Bronze Medals, Pan-American Games, Indianapolis, IN, USA 1987; Silver Medallist in 200m freestyle, Olympic Games, Seoul 1988; competitions also include World Swimming Championships, Madrid 1986, Perth, Australia 1991; Sports Man Cariari Swimming Asscn; named Best Athlete of Latin America, Prensa Latina 1987, 1988; World Trophy for S America, Amateur Athletic Foundation of Los Angeles, CA, USA 1987; voted Best Athlete of Costa Rica 1986, 1987, 1988, and Athlete of the Decade. *Leisure interests:* reading English, German and Latin American literature, photography. *Address:* CP 7368, San José, Costa Rica.

POLLACK, Anita Jean, M SC; Australian politician; b 3 June 1946, Lismore; d of John Samuel and Kathleen (née Emerson) Pollack; m Philip Bradbury 1986; one d. *Education:* City of London Polytechnic and Univ of London. *Career:* Advertising Copywriter 1967–70; book ed 1971–75; Political Researcher for MEP 1980–89; MEP (Lab) for London SW 1989–99, mem Cttees on Environment, Public Health, Consumer Protection and Women's Rights; Head of European Liaison English Heritage 2000–. *Leisure interest:* family. *Address:* English Heritage, 23 Savile Row, London SW1, UK.

POLLACK, Ilana, BA; Israeli librarian; b 13 Aug 1946, Tel-Aviv; d of Leon Pinsky and Mala First; m Joseph Pollack 1977 (died 1994); two s. *Education:* Re'alit High School, Rishon Le Zion, Tel-Aviv Univ and Hebrew Univ of Jerusalem. *Career:* Served in Israeli Army 1964–66; Librarian Weizmann Inst of Science, Rehovot 1966, Librarian-in-Charge, Physics Faculty Library 1975, Chief Librarian Weizmann Inst of Science 1983–; has written numerous articles in Israeli-published information and library science journals. *Address:* Wix Library, Weizmann Institute of Science, Rehovot 76100, Israel (Office); 22 Sheankin St, Rishon Le-Zion 75282, Israel (Home). *Telephone:* (8) 9343583 (Office); (3) 9692186 (Home); *Fax:* (8) 9344176 (Office); *E-mail:* ilana.pollack@weizmann.ac.il; *Internet:* www.weizmann.ac.il/wis-library.home.htm (Office).

POLLARD, Eve; British newspaper editor; b 25 Dec 1945; d of Ivor and Mimi Pollard; m 1st Barry L. D. Winkleman 1968 (divorced 1978); one d; m 2nd Sir Nicholas M. Lloyd 1978; one s. *Career:* Fashion Ed Honey 1967–68; Fashion Ed Daily Mirror Magazine 1968–69, top feature writer 1969–70, Women's Ed Sunday Mirror 1971–81, Ed (and responsible for launch of Sunday Mirror Magazine) 1988–91; Women's Ed Observer Magazine 1970–71; Asst Ed Sunday People 1981–83; Features Ed, Presenter TV-AM 1983–85; Ed Elle USA (and launched magazine, New York) 1985–86, Sunday magazine News of the World 1986, You magazine Mail on Sunday 1986–88, Sunday Express and Sunday Express Magazine 1991–94; f Wedding Magazine 1999; TV Presenter The Truth About Women; Founder and Chair Women in Journalism 1995–; mem English Tourism Council (fmrly English Tourist Bd) 1993–2000, Competition Comm 1999–; Ed of the Year, Focus Awards 1991. *Publication:* Jackie: Biography of Mrs J. K. Onassis 1971, Splash! 1995. *Address:* c/o Simpson–Fox Associates, 52 Shaftesbury Ave, London W1V 7DE, UK.

POLLARD, Magda; Guyanese home economist and international organization official; b 29 March 1931, Guyana; d of the late Fitzgerald Hilbertus and Muriel Loretta Pollard. *Education:* Glasgow and W of Scotland Coll of Domestic Science and Queen Elizabeth Coll (Univ of London). *Career:* Prin Carnegie School of Home Econs 1962–; Lecturer for Certificate in Educ (Home Econs), Univ of Guyana 1975–77; Women's Affairs Officer CARICOM Secr 1980–, Rep at regional and int confs on women 1980–91; public speaker and consultant on women's issues; Pres Guyana Girl Guides Asscn 1974; Chair Guyana Home Econs Asscn, Nat Preparatory Cttee for Fourth World Conf on Women (Beijing) 1995, Nat Comm on Women 1996–99; Dir Nat Bank of Industry and Commerce 1997; mem and Consultant Caribbean Home Econs Asscn; mem Nat Insurance Tribunal, Expert Cttee of Commonwealth Secr for the preparation of a Commonwealth Plan of Action for Women 1987, 1994–95; Fourth CARICOM Triennial Award for Contribution to the Caribbean Women's Movt 1993; Special Award, Caribbean Asscn of Home Economists 1995; Golden Arrow of Achievement Nat Award 1996; Cacique Crown of Honour Nat Award 1998. *Publications:* Teaching Home Economics in the Caribbean (jtly) 1983. *Leisure interest:* choral singing. *Address:* 241 Bourda St, Lacytown, Georgetown, Guyana. *Telephone:* (2) 66675.

POLLEN, Arabella Rosalind Hungerford; British fashion designer and business executive; b 22 June 1961, Oxford; d of Peregrine and Patricia Pollen; m Giacomo Dante Algranti 1985; two s. *Education:* Ecole Française (New York), Nightingale Bamford, Hatherop Castle School (Glos), St Swithun's (Winchester) and Queen's Coll (London). *Career:* Founder Arabella Pollen Ltd in jt venture with Namara Ltd 1981; bought out Namara Ltd and entered jt partnership with Peregrine Marcus Pollen 1983–; Designer for other labels 1983–. *Leisure interests:* music, piano, literature.

POLLOCK, Griselda Frances Sinclair, PH D; British/Canadian professor and art historian; b 11 March 1949, Bloemfontein, SA; d of the late Alan Winton Seton Pollock and Kathleen Alexandra Sinclair; m Antony Bryant 1981; one s one d. *Education:* Queen's Coll (London), Lady Margaret Hall (Oxford) and Courtauld Inst of Art (London). *Career:* Mem teaching staff Univs of Reading and Manchester 1972–77, Univ of Leeds 1977–90, currently Prof of Social and Critical Histories of Art (Leeds) 1990–; Dir Arts and Humanities Research Bd (AHRB) Centre for Cultural Analysis, Theory and History 2000–. *Films:* Deadly Tales 1996, Eurydice 1997; *TV:* J'accuse... Van Gogh 1990; *Publications:* Millet 1977, Cassatt 1979, Old Mistresses: Women, Art and Ideology (jtly) 1981, Framing Feminism: Art and the Women's Movement 1987, Vision and Difference 1988, Avant-Garde Gambits 1888–1893: Gender and the Colour of Art History 1992, Dealing with Degas 1992, Generations and Geographies 1996, Avant-Gardes and Partisans Reviewed 1996, Mary Cassatt 1998, Differencing the Canon 1999, Looking Back to the Future 2000, The Case against Van Gogh 2001. *Leisure interests:* running, tennis, opera. *Address:* University of Leeds, Dept of Fine Art, Leeds LS2 9JT, UK. *Telephone:* (113) 233-5267; *Fax:* (113) 245-1977; *E-mail:* g.f.s.pollock@leeds.ac.uk.

POLLYEVA, Djokhan Redzherpovna; Russian jurist and politician; b 1960, Ashkhabad; m; one s. *Career:* Researcher, Head of Div Inst of Youth Research Centre, Cen Comsomol Cttee and State Cttee of Labour 1986–90; consultant Moscow City Soviet of People's Deputies 1990–91; Head Div of Social-Econ Analysis and Prognosis, Service of State Counsellor on Legal Problems 1991–92; Admin consultant to Pres B. Yeltsin 1992–93; played active role in Pres B. Yeltsin election campaign; counsellor to Deputy-Prime Minister S. Shakhrai 1993–95, to Deputy-Prime Minister B. Nemtsov 1995–97; Sr Asst to Russian Pres, Head of speech-writing group 1997–98; counsellor, Dir-Gen Agency Interfax 1995–98; Head Secr of Prime Minister S. Kiriyenko May–Aug 1998; Deputy Head of Admin for Russian Pres 1999, Head of speech-writing group and Dept of Political Planning 1999. *Address:* Kremlin, korpus 14в, Moscow, Russian Federation. *Telephone:* (095) 206-07-34.

POLOZKOVA, Lidia Pavlovna; Russian speed-skater; b 8 March 1939, Zlatoust; d of Pavel I. Skobilikov and Klavdia N. Skobilikova; m Alexander G. Polozkov; one s. *Career:* Fmr World Champion Speed-skater 1963–64; winner of 40 Gold Medals (25 at world level, 15 in fmr USSR), including 6 Winter Olympic Gold Medals 1960, 1964; mem CPSU 1964–91; Head Dept of Physical Educ Moscow Higher School of All-Union TU Movt 1974–88; Sr Vice-Pres All-Union TUs Soc for Physical Culture and Sports 1988–92; Vice-Pres Russian Speed-Skating Fed 1992–95; Head, Fund for Support of Sports Veterans 1997–; numerous publications on sport and physical culture; honours include two orders and title of Honoured Master of Sport 1960. *Leisure interests:* reading, theatre, forest walking, sports, knitting. *Address:* c/o Russian Speed-Skating Federation, Moscow, Luzhnetskaya nab 8, Russian Federation. *Telephone:* (095) 201-10-40.

PÓŁTAWSKA, Wanda Wiktoria, MD; Polish neuropsychiatrist, professor and writer; b 2 Nov 1921, Lublin; m Andrzej Półtawski 1947; four d. *Education:* Ursuline Sisters' High School (Lublin) and Jagiellonian Univ. *Career:* Polish Resistance 1939–41; interned in Nazi concentration camps 1941–45; teaching asst Psychiatric Clinic, Medical Acad Cracow 1957–69; Consultant to Educ and Therapeutic Consulting Office of the Chair of Psychology, Jagiellonian Univ 1954–72; Prof of Pastoral Medicine Pontifical Inst Giovanni Paolo II, Univ Lateranense, Rome 1981–84; Prof of Pastoral Medicine Pontifical Theological Acad, Cracow 1955–, Dir Family Inst 1967–; expert Pontifical Council for Pastoral Care; mem Pontifical Council for the Family, Pontifical Acad of Life; Hon DD (Notre Dame Pontifical Catechetical Inst, Arlington, VA, USA) 1987; Gold Medal for Social Work for the City of Cracow 1964; Cross 'Pro Ecclesia et Pontifice' 1981; Medal of the Polish Senate 1999; Pontifical Commandery of the Order of St Gregory the Great 1999; Medal of St Hedwig (Pontifical Acad, Cracow). *Publications:* And I Am Afraid of My Dreams 1961, I boję się snów 1961, Stare rachunki (Old Settlements) 1969, Przygotowanie do Małżeństwa (Preparation for Marriage) 1993, Samo Życie (The Very Life) 1995, Na kanwie 'Listu do Rodzin' Ojca Świętego Jana Pawła II (On the Canvas of 'Letter to the Families of John Paul II') 1995; numerous articles in Polish, English, German and Italian. *Leisure interest:* mountain tourism. *Address:* Bracka 1/3, 31-005 Cracow, Poland. *Telephone:* (12) 226898.

PON, Nicolina; Netherlands fine art dealer; b 26 Jan 1933, Leiden, Netherlands; d of Bernardus Marinus and Cornelia Clasina (née Parlevliet) Pon; three d. *Education:* Netherlands and Switzerland. *Career:* Art Collector; f Galerie Nicolina Pon, Zurich, Switzerland 1972, Ponova Gallery Inc, Toronto 1981; pvt art dealing office specializing in Old Masters, Impressionists and selected works of modern art, Zug, Switzerland 1985; Specialist Adviser Real-Estate Projects, Blue Falcon Investments Ltd; mem Confed Int des Négociants en Oeuvres d'Art 1974–, Swiss Kunsthandelverband 1974–; Dir and Chief Trustee Conias Foundation. *Address:* Nicolina Pon Fine Art, 7157 Siat, Switzerland. *Telephone:* (81) 925-22-26.

PONOMAREVA, Ksenya Yuryevna; Russian journalist; b 19 Sept 1961, Moscow; one s one d. *Education:* Moscow State Univ. *Career:* Schoolteacher 1984–86, teacher of Slavic languages Diplomatic Acad 1986–88; on staff Kommersant Publrs 1988–95, Deputy Ed Kommersaut Daily 1992–93; Ed-in-Chief Revisor (magazine) 1993–95; First Deputy Dir Information and Political Broadcasting Russian Public TV 1995–96; concurrently gen producer information programmes 1996–97; mem Bd of Dirs Russian Public TV 1996–, Dir-Gen 1997–98. *Address:* Akademika Koroleva str 12, 127000 Moscow, Russian Federation. *Telephone:* (095) 217-98-38;(095) 215-18-95 (Office).

PONS-DELADRIÈRE, Geneviève Anne-Marie, L EN D; French European Union official; b 11 Feb 1956, Tunis; d of Roger Deladrière and Paule Marchika; m Jean-François Pons 1980; one d one s. *Education:* Lycée Edouard Herriot (Lyons), Univ of Paris I (Panthéon-Sorbonne) and Ecole Nat d'Admin. *Career:* Adviser Admin Tribunal 1984–89; Nat Expert to EC Legal Service 1989–91; mem Cabinet of EC Comm Pres Responsible for Questions of the Environment, of Law Infractions and of State Aid 1991. *Leisure interests:* reading, tennis, skiing, swimming. *Address:* 45 ave d'Auderghem, 1040 Brussels, Belgium. *Telephone:* (2) 235-64-60; *Fax:* (2) 236-31-15.

PONTOIS, Noëlla Chantal Georgette; French ballet dancer and teacher; b 24 Dec 1943, Vendôme; d of Jean and Josette (née Usal) Pontois; m Daini Kudo (divorced); one d. *Education:* Ecole de Danse de l'Opéra (Paris). *Career:* Ballet Dancer Théâtre Nat de l'Opéra 1953, mem Corps de Ballet 1960–65, Soloist 1965, Prin Dancer 1966–68,

Prima Ballerina 1968; Guest Prima Ballerina 1984; guest appearance with London Festival Ballet in the Sleeping Beauty 1967; teacher Opéra de Paris 1988–; has danced with Rudolf Nureyev and Mikhail Baryshnikov; Chevalier de la Légion d'Honneur, Chevalier des Arts et des Lettres; Officier de l'Ordre Nat du Mérite; Prix René Blum 1964, Prix Anna Pavlova 1969; Grand Prix Nat de la Danse 1981. *Ballets include:* Sleeping Beauty 1967, Swan Lake, Giselle 1968, 1975, Extase, The Nutcracker (also special performance 1993), Daphnis et Chloé, Coppelia, Notre-Dame-de-Paris, La Bayadère, Pas de deux, L'après-midi d'un faune, Les Sylphides, Spartacus, Romeo and Juliet, Ivan the Terrible, Petrouchka, Quatre saisons, Le Bourgeois Gentilhomme, La fille mal gardée 1981. *Address:* Théâtre National de l'Opéra, 8 rue Scribe, 75009 Paris, France (Office); 25 rue de Maubeuge, 75009 Paris, France (Home).

POOK, Jocelyn; British composer and viola player; b 14 Feb 1960, Birmingham; d of Wilfred Pook and Mary Cecil Williams. *Education:* King Edward VI (Bury St Edmunds) and Guildhall School of Music and Drama. *Career:* Has performed with pop acts The Communards (3 year tour) Massive Attack, Meat Loaf, P. J. Harvey etc; composer of numerous TV and Film scores; wrote Blow the Wind – Pie Jesu which appeared on Orange Mobile Phone Advert; Assoc Guildhall School of Music and Drama; American Soc of Authors, Composers and Publrs Prize 1999. *Musical scores include:* Films: Strange Fish (Prix Italia) 1994, Mothers and Daughters 1994, Eyes Wide Shut (Golden Globe nomination) 1999; TV: Half the People 1997, Saints and Sinners (documentary series) 1998, Just Enough Distance 1998, Trouble at the House 1998, The Establishment (documentary series) 1999, Butterfly Collectors 1999, In a Land of Plenty 2001; *Recordings include:* Deluge 1997, Flood 1999, Untold Things 2001. *Address:* c/o Chester Music Ltd, 8–9 Frith St, London W1D 3JB, UK. *Telephone:* (20) 7434-0066; *Fax:* (20) 7254-1363.

POOL, Léa; Canadian film director; b 8 Sept 1950, Geneva, Switzerland; d of Jacques and Sylvia (née Pool) Mohr. *Education:* Univ of Québec. *Career:* Produced videos and TV Programmes Univ of Québec at Montréal 1975–79, films 1979–, concurrently Tutor of Cinema and Video 1978–83; mem staff World Festival of Film Montréal; Producer radio programmes on cultural minorities for Radio-Québec 1980–83; writer documentary on America 1988. *Films:* Strass Café 1980, La femme de l'hôtel (seven prizes including Génie for Best Actress, Int Press Award) 1984, Anne Trister 1986, A Corps Perdu 1988, La Demoiselle Sauvage 1991.

POPE, Angela; British film director. *Career:* Fmr Dir TV documentaries. *Films include:* Yesterday's Men (TV documentary) 1970, The Best Years? (TV documentary) 1977, Shift Work, Sweet As You Are (Royal TV Soc Award for Best Film), Captives 1994, The Hollow Reed 1997.

POPHAM, Amanda, MA; British ceramic artist; b 6 Nov 1954, W London. *Education:* Bradford Coll of Art, Portsmouth Polytechnic and RCA (London). *Career:* Numerous solo and group exhibitions throughout the UK 1977–; group exhibitions include Best of the Summer Wine Exhibition (Brown Bros Fine Art Award) 1988; works sold at retail outlets including Liberty (London).

PORTEOUS, Emma; British costume designer; b 26 June 1936, Calcutta (now Kolkata), India; d of Arthur and Cynthia E. V. Baldwin; m Peter McKenzie Porteous 1963; two d. *Education:* St Margaret's Boarding School (Darjeeling, India) and Bedford High School for Girls. *Career:* Fashion sketcher for Frederick Starke 1955–64; costume designer ATV and Rediffusion TV 1965–68; costume designer for some 42 films. *Films include:* Performance 1968, Leo the Last 1969, Entertaining Mr Sloane 1969, Triple Echo 1972, Jekyll and Hyde (Emmy nomination) 1972, Clash of the Titans (Hollywood Award for Fantasy and Science Fiction) 1979, Five Days One Summer 1981, Octopussy 1982, A View to a Kill 1984, Aliens 1985, My Life So Far, High Spirits, Living Daylights 1986, Around the World in Eighty Days (Emmy nomination) 1988, The Gravy Train, Robin Hood, Judge Dredd. *Leisure interests:* tapestry, travel. *Address:* 1 Masons Court, High St, Ewell Village, Surrey KT17 1RJ, UK. *Telephone:* (20) 8786-7736.

PORTER, Anna Maria, OC, MA; Canadian (b Hungarian) publishing executive; b Budapest; d of Steven and Maria (née Racz) Szigethy; m Julian Porter 1971; two d. *Education:* Univ of Canterbury (Christchurch, NZ). *Career:* Mem staff Cassell and Co, UK, Collier Macmillan Ltd, London 1967–69, Toronto 1970; Pres and Publr McClelland-Bantam Ltd (Seal Books) until 1982, Pres 1987–92; Publr, CEO and Dir Key Porter Books 1982–; Chair Doubleday Canada 1986–91; Dir Key Publrs, Alliance Communications Ltd, Young Naturalists Foundation, Imperial Life Assurance Co, People's Jewelry Ltd, York Univ, Conf Bd of Canada, WWF—World Wide Fund for Nature, Canada; mem Asscn of Canadian Pubs, Asscn for Export of Canadian Books, UNICEF (advisory), Information Highway Council. *Address:* Key Porter Books, 70 The Esplanade, Toronto, ON M5E 1R2, Canada.

PORTER, Marguerite Ann; British ballet dancer; b 30 Nov 1948; d of William Albert and Mary Porter; m 2nd Nicky Henson 1986; one s. *Education:* In Doncaster and at Royal Ballet School. *Career:* Dancer Royal Ballet Co 1966–, Soloist 1972–76, Prin then Sr Prin Dancer 1976–85, Guest Artist 1986–. *Ballets include:* Romeo and Juliet, Manon, A Month in the Country, Swan Lake (New York) 1999; *Film:* Comrade Lady; *Publication:* Ballerina: a dancer's life 1989. *Leisure interest:* family and friends. *Address:* c/o Richard Stone Partnership, 2 Henrietta St, London WC2E 8PS, UK.

PORTUONDO, Omara; Cuban singer; b 30 Oct 1930; d of Bartolomes Portunondo and Esperanza Pelaez; one s. *Education:* Univ of Havana. *Career:* Professional debut at Caberet Tropicana 1945; mem Cuarteto Las D'Aida for 15 years; debut solo album 1959; mem Oquestra Aragón 1970s; recorded a track for film Buena Vista Social Club; participated in Buena Vista performances Amsterdam and New York; Guardia Nacional de Cuba (5 times); Federación de Mujeres Cubanas Hon Prize. *Albums:* Buena Vista Social Presents... (contrib) (Best World Music Album 2000, nominated for Grammy 2000, Latin Grammy 2001), Buena Vista Presents...Omara Portuondo. *Leisure interests:* family, swimming. *Address:* c/o World Circuit Records, 106 Cleveland St, London W1P 5DP, UK. *E-mail:* post@worldcircuit.co.uk.

POSADA CHAPADO, Rosa María, LL D; Spanish politician; b 1940, Madrid. *Education:* Univ Complutense de Madrid and Univs of Strasbourg (France) and Oxford (UK). *Career:* Lawyer; Senate cand for Madrid; Cabinet Political Sec 1981; Sec of State for Information; apptd Pres Legis Ass (Parl), Autonomous Region of Madrid 1987. *Address:* c/o Asamblea de Madrid, San Bernardo 49, 28015 Madrid, Spain.

POSKITT, Elizabeth Margaret Embree, OBE, MA, MB, B CHIR, FRCP; British paediatrician; b 1939, Bolton, Lancs; d of Frederick R. and Margaret (née Turner) Poskitt. *Education:* Cheltenham Ladies' Coll, Girton Coll (Cambridge) and St Thomas's Hosp Medical School. *Career:* Medical Officer MRC Child Nutrition Unit, Kampala, Uganda 1968–71; Sr Registrar in Paediatrics, Birmingham 1971–74; Research Fellow Inst of Child Health, Birmingham 1974–76; Sr Lecturer in Child Health Univ of Liverpool 1977–93; Hon Consultant Paediatrician, Liverpool Health Authority 1977–93; Head of Section, MRC Dunn Nutrition Group, Kenebe, The Gambia 1993–98; Hon Sr Lecturer Int Nutrition Group, London School of Hygiene and Tropical Medicine 1998–; First Vice-Pres Int Fed of Univ Women 1989–92, Pres 1995–98; Vice-Pres British Fed of Women Grads 2001–(2004); Fellow Royal Coll of Paediatrics and Child Health. *Publications:* Practical Paediatric Nutrition 1988, Child and Adolescent Obesity (co-ed); numerous other publs on malnutrition, obesity in children, congenital heart disease etc. *Leisure interests:* travel, walking, gardening, music, development issues. *Address:* International Nutrition Group, Public Health Nutrition Unit, London School of Hygiene and Tropical Medicine, 49–51 Bedford Square, London W1B 3DP, UK. *Telephone:* (20) 7636-8636; *Fax:* (20) 7299-4666; *E-mail:* elizabeth.poskitt@lshtm.ac.uk.

POSPÍŠILOVÁ, Vlasta; Czech animator and film maker; b 18 Feb 1935, Prague; d of Miloš and Růžena Jurajda; m Emil Pospíšil 1959; one s two d. *Education:* Acad of Applied Arts (Prague). *Career:* Graphic Artist Publicity Dept Čedok 1954–56; joined Jiří Trnka Puppet Film Studio as animator working on puppet films, animated cut-outs and experimental films 1956, animator and film Dir Krátký films, Studio Jiřího Trnky, Prague 1978–; has received awards from the Festival of Children's Films (Zlín, Jiří Trnka Prize) 1980, 1988, 1991, Int Festival of Children's

Films, Chicago, IL, USA 1984, Espinho Int Festival, Portugal 1991, Isfahan Int Festival, Iran 1991. *Films:* Maryshka and Wolf's Castle 1980, Lady Poverty 1984, Mean Barka 1988, After the Oak Shed its Leaves 1991, Fireflies (series) 1995, The Fulfilled Dream (30 vol series) 2000. *Leisure interests:* gardening, cross-country skiing, puppet theatre. *Address:* Novodvorská 1123, 142 00 Prague 4, Czech Republic. *Telephone:* (2) 4713578; *Fax:* (2) 24250535; *E-mail:* emilpos@volny.cz.

POTT, Elisabeth, DR MED; German medical administrator; b 10 Jan 1949, Bochum; m Hans-Michael Pott 1974. *Education:* Univs of Bonn and Kiel. *Career:* Surgeon until 1977; Del Akademie für öffentliche Gesundheitswirtschaft (Acad for Public Health Economy), Düsseldorf, Fed State Hosp, Osnabrück, Fed Health Office, Berlin; Consultant to Fed Ministry of Labour and Social Affairs 1978; Deputy Chief Consultant Ministry of Social Affairs, Fed State of Lower Saxony 1980, Chief Consultant 1981; Dir Bundeszentrale für gesundheitliche Aufklärung (Fed Centre for Health Educ) 1985–; teacher of Social Medicine Medizinische Hochschule, Hanover; Scientific Adviser Deutsche Gesellschaft für Sozialpädiatrie. *Address:* Ostmerheimer Str 200, 51109 Cologne, Germany.

POTTER, Judith Marjorie, LL B; New Zealand lawyer; b 23 Aug 1942, Auckland; d of Philip Ernest and Winifred Marjorie Potter. *Education:* Epsom Girls' Grammar School (Auckland) and Univ of Auckland. *Career:* Called to the Bar 1964; apptd Partner Kensington Swan barristers and solicitors 1972; elected to Auckland Dist Law Soc Council 1977, Pres 1988–89; mem New Zealand Securities Comm 1988; elected to New Zealand Law Soc Council (first woman) 1985, Vice-Pres 1989–90, apptd Pres 1991; contribs on securities and corp law to professional journals; Sesquicentennial Medal for Services to Women 1990. *Leisure interests:* golf, tennis, music, walking and trekking, theatre, opera, family. *Address:* 15 Domett Ave, Epsom, Auckland 3, New Zealand.

POTTER, Ronda May, PH D; Australian engineer and company executive; b 20 Nov 1944; m Leonard Furys 1982; two d. *Education:* Univ of Adelaide. *Career:* Dir Teletraffic Research Centre, Univ of Adelaide 1989–90; Dir of CPE Network Operability, Technical Man responsible for new telecommunications voice and data interface specification prototypes, technical auditing and application devt 1990–94; Dir Educ Technology, Bell Communications Research 1994–95; Vice-Pres Global ADSI (Analog Display Services Interface) Solutions Inc 1995; contribs to publs on telecommunications. *Leisure interests:* yoga, gardening, running, hiking, music, dancing. *Address:* 100 Campus Drive, Suite 103, Morganville, NJ 07751, USA. *Telephone:* (908) 972-5333; *Fax:* (908) 972-5335; *E-mail:* rmpotterl@aol.com.

POTTS, Nadia; Canadian ballet dancer and dance teacher; b 1949, UK. *Education:* Nat Ballet School (Toronto). *Career:* Dancer Nat Ballet Co 1966–68, Soloist 1968–69, Prin 1969; Dir of Dance Programme Ryerson Polytechnic Univ 1989–; partnered Baryshnikov 1975 and Nureyev 1976; recipient prize for best Pas de deux, and Bronze Medal for Solo Dance, Int Ballet Competition, Varna, Bulgaria 1970. *Ballets include:* Bayaderka 1966, The Nutcracker, Cinderella 1967, Giselle 1976. *Address:* Ryerson Polytechnic University, 350 Victoria St, Toronto, ON M5B 2K3, Canada.

POULSEN, Birte, LL M; Danish diplomatist; b 4 Dec 1941, Vedsted. *Education:* Stephens Coll (MO, USA), Univ of Copenhagen, Coll of Europe (Bruges, Belgium) and NATO Defence Coll (Rome). *Career:* Joined Danish Foreign Service 1973; First Sec Danish Del to NATO, Belgium 1977–75, Counsellor Danish Del to OECD, Paris 1985–88, Deputy Perm Rep to UNESCO, Paris 1986–88, Amb to Zimbabwe 1993. *Leisure interests:* music, literature, golf. *Address:* c/o Ministry of Foreign Affairs, Asiatisk Plads 2, 1448 Copenhagen K, Denmark.

POUR-EL, Marian Boykan, PH D; American professor of mathematics; b New York; d of Joseph and Mattie (née Caspe) Boykan; m Akiva Pour-El; one d. *Education:* Hunter Coll (New York) and Harvard Univ. *Career:* Asst Prof of Maths Pennsylvania State Univ 1958–62, Assoc Prof 1962–64; Assoc Prof of Maths Univ of Minnesota 1964–68, apptd Prof 1968; mem Inst of Advanced Study, Princeton, NJ 1962–64; lecturer at int congresses on logic and computer sciences, UK 1971, Hungary 1967, Czechoslovakia 1973, Germany 1983, Japan 1985, 1988,

People's Repub of China 1987; Visiting Lecturer Polish Acad of Sciences (PAN) 1974; additional lectures in Germany 1980, 1989, 1991, Sweden 1983, 1994, Japan 1985, 1987, 1990, 1993, People's Repub of China 1987, Finland 1991, Estonia 1991, Russia 1992, Netherlands 1992; mem Fulbright Comm on Maths 1986–89; Fellow Japan Soc for the Promotion of Science 1993; elected Fellow AAAS; elected to Hunter Hall of Fame. *Publications:* Computability in Analysis and Physics (monograph, jtly) 1989; numerous articles on mathematical logic and theoretical computer science. *Leisure interests:* ballet, art, biological and physical sciences. *Address:* University of Minnesota, School of Maths, Vincent Hall, Minneapolis, MN 55455, USA. *Telephone:* (612) 625-9347; *Fax:* (612) 626-2017.

POWELL, Janet Frances, BA, DIP ED; Australian politician; b 29 Sept 1942, Nhill, Vic; d of Colin G. and Frances M. (née Kilpatrick) McDonald; m 1st 1965 (divorced); two d two s; m 2nd Harold Fraser 1994. *Education:* Ballarat Grammar School, Nhill High School and Univ of Melbourne. *Career:* Deputy Nat Pres Australian Democratic Party 1984–86; Senator for Vic 1986–92, 1992–93; Deputy Nat Pres Australian Democratic Party 1984–86, Parl Leader 1990–91; Consultant 1993–; Pres Young Women's Christian Asscn (YWCA), Vic 1998–. *Leisure interests:* reading, travel. *Address:* 14 Lynne St, Donvale, Vic 3111, Australia (Office); 25/51 Foley St, Kew, Vic 3101, Australia (Home). *Telephone:* (62) 77 3750; *Fax:* (62) 277 5786.

POWELL, Sandy; British costume and set designer; b 7 April 1960. *Education:* Cen St Martin's Coll of Art and Design (London). *Career:* Costume designer for all shows by The Cholmondoleys and The Featherstonehaughs; Evening Standard Award for film of Edward II; Best Tech Achievement Award; Evening Standard Award for Orlando 1994; Acad Award for Shakespeare in Love 1998; BAFTA Award for Velvet Goldmine 1998. *Films include:* Costumes: Cobachan, The Last of England, Stormy Monday, The Pope Must Die, Edward II, Caravaggio, Venus Peter, The Miracle, The Crying Game, Orlando, Being Human, Interview with a Vampire, Rob Roy, Michael Collins, The Butcher Boy, The Wings of the Dove, Felicia's Journey, Shakespeare in Love, Velvet Goldmine, Hilary and Jackie, The End of the Affair, Miss Julie; *Plays include:* Sets: Edward II (RSC), Rigoletto (Netherlands Opera) and Dr Ox's Experiment (ENO). *Address:* c/o PFD, Drury House, 34–43 Russell St, London WC2B 5HA, UK. *Telephone:* (20) 7344-1000; *Fax:* (20) 7836-9543; *E-mail:* lmamy@pfd.co.uk.

POWERS-FREELING, Laurel Claire, BA, MS; American business executive; b 16 May 1957, MI; d of Lloyd Marion and Catharine Joyce (née Berry) Powers; m Anthony Nigel Stanley Freeling 1989; one s. *Education:* Columbia Univ (New York) and MIT (Cambridge, MA). *Career:* Sr Consultant Price Waterhouse, Boston and New York 1979–84; Man McKinsey & Co, Atlanta, GA, New York and London 1984–89; Head of Corp Finance Morgan Stanley Int, London 1989–91; Exec Prudential Corpn PLC, London 1991–94, Dir of Corp Strategy and Planning 1992–94; Finance Dir Lloyds Abbey Life 1994. *Leisure interests:* music, wines, design. *Address:* 38 Bath Rd, Bedford Park, London W4 1LH, UK.

PRABHJOT KAUR, BA; Indian poet and politician; b 6 July 1924, Langaryal; d of Nidhan Singh; m Brig Narenderpal Singh 1948; two d. *Education:* Khalsa Coll for Women (Lahore) and Punjab Univ. *Career:* First collected poems published 1943; has written a total of 62 books of poems, short stories, etc; Indian Rep at numerous int literary confs 1956–; mem Legis Council, Punjab 1966; Ed Vikendrit and Byword magazines; mem Sahitya Akademi (Nat Acad of Letters), Exec Bd 1978; mem Cen Comm of UNESCO, Nat Writers' Cttee of India; Fellow Emer, Govt of India; honours include Sahitya Shiromani 1964 and Padma Shree 1967; named Rajya Kavi (Poet Laureate) by Punjab Govt 1964, Woman of the Year, UPLI, Philippines 1975; awards include Sahitya Akademi Award 1965, Golden Laurel Leaves, United Poets Int, Philippines 1967, Grand Prix de la Rose de la France 1968, Most Distinguished Order of Poetry, World Poetry Soc Intercontinental, USA 1974, Sewa Sifti Award 1980, NIF Cultural Award 1982, Josh Kenya Award 1982, Delhi State Award 1983. *Publications include:* Poems: Supne Sadhran 1949, Do Rang 1951, Pankheru 1956, Lala (in Persian) 1958, Bankapasi 1958, Pabbi 1962, Khai 1967, Plateau (French) 1968, Wad-darshi Sheesha 1972, Madhiantar 1974, Chandra Yug 1978, Dreams Die Young 1979, Shadows and Light (Bulgarian) 1980, Him

Hans 1982, Samrup 1982, Ishq Shara Ki Nata 1983, Shadows (English and Danish) 1985; Short stories: Kinke 1952, Aman de Na 1956, Zindgi de Kujh Pal 1982, Main Amanat Naheen (Hindi), Kuntith, Casket (English); Autobiog: Jeena vi 9k Ada Hai. *Leisure interests:* reading, travel. *Address:* D-203, Defence Colony, New Delhi 110024, India. *Telephone:* (11) 4626045.

PRADA, Miuccia; Italian fashion designer; b 1950; d of Luisa Prada; m Patrizio Bertelli; c. *Career:* Head of Prada since 1979, launched collection of women's clothing 1988, Miu Miu collection 1992, men's collection 1994.

PRAEGER, Cheryl Elisabeth, AM, D PHIL, D SC, FAA; Australian professor of mathematics; b 7 Sept 1948, Toowoomba; d of the late Eric Noel and of Queenie Hannah Elisabeth Praeger; m John David Henstridge 1975; two s. *Education:* Nambour State High School, Brisbane Girls' Grammar School, and Univs of Queensland and Oxford (UK). *Career:* Research Fellow in Maths ANU 1973–75, Visiting Fellow 1989; Lecturer Univ of Western Australia 1976–81, Sr Lecturer 1982–83, Prof of Maths 1983–, Dean Postgrad Research Studies 1996–97; Visiting Prof Univs of Auckland 1988, Waterloo, Canada 1989; mem Curriculum Devt Council, Canberra 1984–87, PM's Science Council, Canberra 1989–92; Commonwealth Scholarship and Fellowship Plan Scholarship to Univ of Oxford, UK 1970–73; Visiting Fellow Commoner, Queens Coll, Oxford 1995, 1998, 2000; Hon D SC (Prince of Songkla Univ, Thailand) 1993; Certificate of Merit Royal Humane Soc of New S Wales 1976. *Leisure interests:* cycling, hiking, spinning, reading. *Address:* University of Western Australia, Dept of Mathematics and Statistics, 35 Stirling Highway, Crawley, WA 6009, Australia. *Telephone:* (8) 9380-3344; *Fax:* (8) 9380-1028.

PRASHAR, Baroness (Life Peer), cr 1999, of Runnymede in the County of Surrey, **Usha Kumari Prashar,** CBE, BA, FRSA; British organization executive; b 29 June 1948; d of Nauhria Lal and Durga Devi Prashar; m Vijay Kumar Sharma 1973. *Education:* Duchess of Gloucester School (Nairobi), Wakefield Girls' High School and Univs of Leeds and Glasgow. *Career:* Mem Race Relations Bd 1971–75; Asst Dir Runnymede Trust 1976–77, Dir 1977–84; Resident Fellow Policy Studies Inst 1984–86; Dir Nat Council for Voluntary Orgs 1986–91; Vice-Chair British Refugee Council 1987–89; part-time Civil Service Commr 1990–96; Non-Exec Dir Channel Four TV 1992–99; mem Arts Council of GB 1979–81, Study Comm on the Family 1980–83, Social Security Advisory Cttee 1980–83, Exec Cttee Child Poverty Action Group 1984–85, Greater London Arts Asscn 1984–86, London Food Comm 1984–90, BBC Educ Broadcasting Council 1987–89, Advisory Council Open Coll 1987–89, Solicitors' Complaints Bureau 1989–90, Lord Chancellor's Advisory Cttee on Legal Educ and Conduct 1991–97, Royal Comm on Criminal Justice 1991–93, Council Policy Studies Inst 1992–97, Bd Energy Saving Trust 1992–98, Arts Council of England 1994–97; Chair Parole Bd 1997–; Hon Vice-Pres Council for Overseas Student Affairs 1986–; Trustee Thames Help Trust 1984–86, Charities Aid Foundation 1986–91, Independent Broadcasting Telethon Trust 1987–92, Acad of Indian Dance 1987–91; Chair English Advisory Cttee Nat AIDS Trust 1988–89; Patron Sickle Cell Soc 1986–, Elfrida Rathbone Soc 1988–; Gov De Montfort Univ 1996, Chancellor 2000–; contributed to works on race relations, sickle cell anaemia and health care; Hon LL D (De Montfort, S Bank Univ) 1994, (Greenwich, Leeds Metropolitan) 1999, (Ulster, Oxford Brookes) 2000. *Leisure interests:* painting, reading, music, countryside, squash. *Address:* House of Lords, London SW1A 0PW, UK.

PRATHER, Lenore Loving, BS, JD; American judge; b 17 Sept 1931, West Point, MS; d of Byron Herald and Hattie Hearn (née Morris) Loving; m Robert Brooks Prather 1957; two d one s. *Education:* Mississippi State Coll for Women and Univ of Mississippi. *Career:* Called to the Bar, MS 1955; practice with B. H. Loving, West Point 1955–60, own practice 1960–62, 1965–71, assoc practice 1962–65; Municipal Judge for City of West Point 1965–71; first woman Chancery Court Judge for 14th Dist of State of Mississippi 1971–82; first woman Supreme Court Justice for State of Mississippi, Jackson 1982–92, Presiding Judge 1993–97, Chief Justice 1998–; mem Mississippi State Bar Asscn, Mississippi Conf of Judges, Daughters of the American Revolution. *Address:* Mississippi Supreme Court, POB 117, Jackson, MS 39205, USA.

PRATS, Michèle Hermine, L ÈS L; French civil servant; b 10 April 1939, Paris; d of Henri and Suzanne (née Dupont) Peube-Locou; m 2nd Yves Prats 1965; four c (two from first marriage). *Education:* Lycée de Jeunes Filles (Antananarivo, Madagascar), Lycée de Versailles, Inst Maintenon (Paris), Univ of Antananarivo, Inst Nat des Langues Orientales Vivantes and Ecole Nat d'Admin. *Career:* Ed at Consulate-Gen, Antananarivo 1960–64; Admin Asst Cen Admin (on leave) 1965–66; Rep to Dir of Entertainment, Music and the Arts, Ministry of Culture 1969–70; Deputy Regional Dir of Cultural Affairs, Loire region 1970–71, Rep to Préfet responsible for Amenities, Tourism and Environment 1971–73; Regional Commr for Public Bldgs and Historic Monuments, Provence-Alpes-Côte d'Azur region 1973–79, Regional Del for Architecture and the Environment 1979–82; Head Dept of Int Affairs, Ministry of Transport 1982–84; Under-Sec Ministry of Urban Affairs, Housing and Transport 1985; Regional Dir of Amenities, Haute-Normandie 1986–87; Dir External Relations Domaines Prats 1987–90; Under-Sec for Int Affairs, Ministry of Equipment, Housing, Transport and the Sea 1990; Technical Counsellor Cabinet of Minister of the Environment 1992–93, Under-Sec Ministry of the Environment 1993–95; Under-Sec and Rep to Gen Council for Highways 1995, Insp-Gen of Equipment 1995–; Sec-Gen Nat Cttee on City Access 1995–; with Ministry of Equipment 1998–, responsible for neology and terminology; Chevalier de l'Ordre Nat du Mérite. *Address:* Conseil Général des Ponts et Chaussées, Tour Pascal B, 92055 La Défense, Cedex, France; 85 rue Lamarck, 75108 Paris, France (Home).

PRATT, Jeanne, AO; Australian foundation executive; b 1 Feb 1936; d of S. Lasker; m Richard Pratt 1959; two d one s. *Education:* Sydney Girls' High School and Univ of Sydney. *Career:* Journalist Australian Jewish News 1957–, Australian Consolidated Press Ltd 1957–59, No Man's Land (TV current affairs programme) 1975–77; Dir Visy Bd Co Pty Ltd 1979–, Victoria State Opera 1983–97, Spoleto Melbourne Foundation 1984–93; Chair Victoria Opera Foundation 1980–99; Chair The Production Co (Australia) Pty Ltd 1998–, Arts 2000 1998–; Dir Emergency Services Foundation 1985–; Trustee Epworth Medical Foundation 1985–; mem Man Bd Melbourne Theatre Co 1985–94, Advisory Cttee Victorian Community Foundation 1988–, Inst of Dirs of Australia, Nat Council Metropolitan Opera, USA, Opera Australia 1995–; Exec Cttee Nat Centre for Women 1993–; mem Bd Govs Jewish Museum Australia 1994–; Patron Cat Protection Soc of Victoria 1988–, Museum Lilydale 1995–; Life Gov Opera Foundation Australia 1999; mem Ministerial Advisory Cttee on Educ of Gifted Students 1996–. *Leisure interests:* reading, writing, theatre, scrabble. *Address:* Pratt Group, Level 39, 55 Collins St, Melbourne, Vic 3000, Australia.

PRATT, Mary Frances, BFA; Canadian artist; b 15 March 1935, Fredericton, NB; d of the Hon William J. and Katherine E. (née McMurray) West; m Christopher Pratt 1957; two d two s. *Education:* High School (Fredericton) and Mt Allison Univ. *Career:* Major exhibitions include Some Canadian Women Artists, Nat Gallery of Canada 1975, solo nat touring shows 1979–81, Mira Godard Gallery, Toronto 1985–87, 1996, Equinox Gallery, Vancouver 1986, 1994, Douglas Udell Gallery, Edmonton 1993, Survivors in Search of a Voice: The Art of Courage, Royal Ontario Museum, Toronto (and nat touring exhibition) 1995, The Art of Mary Pratt: The Substance of Light, Beaverbrook Art Gallery, Fredericton (and nat touring exhibition) 1995–97; works in collections including Nat Gallery of Canada, Ottawa, Canada House, London, Art Gallery of Ontario, Toronto, Art Gallery of Nova Scotia, Halifax; mem Fed Cultural Policy Review Comm 1978–81, Bd of Regents Mt Allison Univ 1981–89, Canada Council 1987–93; Atlantic Rep Royal Canadian Acad of the Arts 1994–; featured in two TV documentaries; Hon LL D (Dalhousie) 1985, (Memorial Univ of Newfoundland) 1986, (St Thomas) 1989, (Toronto) 1990; Dr hc (Mt Allison) 1992; Hon DFA (Victoria) 1996; Ontario Coll of Art Fellowship Award 1990; Canadian Conf of the Arts Commemorative Medal for 125th Anniversary of Confed 1993; Newfoundland and Labrador Arts Council Hall of Honour 1994. *Publications:* Across the Table – a celebration of Canadian food (jtly) 1985, Mary Pratt (jtly) 1989, The Art of Mary Pratt: The Substance of Light (jtly) 1995. *Address:* 161½ Waterford Bridge Rd, St John's, NF A1E 1C7, Canada. *Telephone:* (709) 726-5355; *Fax:* (709) 726-4007.

PRESKA, Margaret Louise Robinson, BS, MA, PH D; American business executive and former university president; b 23 Jan 1938, Parma, NY; d of Ralph Craven and Ellen Elvira (née Niemi) Robinson; m Daniel C. Preska 1959; two s one d. *Education:* State Univs of New York and Pennsylvania and Claremont Grad School. *Career:* Instructor LaVerne Coll, CA 1968–75, Asst Prof, Assoc Prof and then Academic Dean 1972–75; Instructor Starr King School for Ministry, Berkeley, CA 1975; Vice-Pres of Acad Affairs and Equal Opportunities Officer Mankato State Univ, MN 1975–79, Pres 1979–92; Distinguished Service Prof, Minnesota State Univs; Dir Kaliningrad (Russia) Retraining Project 1992–; propr Build-A-Bike.com Inc 2000–; mem Bd of Dirs Northern States Power Co, Southeastern Minnesota Business Innovation Center, Elderhostel Int 1983–, Minnesota Agricultural Interpretive Center 1983–, American Asscn of State Colls and Univs, Moscow on the Mississippi – Minnesota meets the Soviet Union; Chair The Fielding Inst, Santa Barbara 1983–86, Gov's Council on Youth 1983–86, Minnesota Educ Forum 1984; Nat Pres Campfire Inc 1985–87; Commr Great Lakes Gov's Econ Devt Council 1986; mem Gov's Comm on Econ Future of Minnesota 1985–, Nat Coll Athletic Asscn Pres's Comm 1986–, American Asscn of Univ Women, League of Women Voters, American Council on Educ, American Asscn of Univ Administrators; YWCA Leader Award 1982; Exchange Club Book of Golden Deeds Award 1987; Wohelo Camp Fire Award 1989. *Address:* Build-A-Bike.com Inc, 10 Summer Hills, Mankato, MN 56001, USA (Office); 3573 Bailey Bridge Bay, Woodbury, MN 55125, USA (Home).

PRESLEY, Priscilla Beaulieu; American actress; b (Priscilla Ann Wagner) 24 May 1945, Brooklyn, NY; m Elvis Presley 1967 (divorced 1973, died 1977); one d one s. *Education:* Steven Peck Theatre Art School and studied acting with Milton Katselas. *Career:* Founder Bis and Beau co selling dress designs; formed Navarone Productions TV production co; has made several TV commercials; launched perfume 'Moments' 1990. *TV appearances include:* Those Amazing Animals (host) 1980–81, Dallas (series) 1983–1988; TV films: Love is Forever, Elvis and Me (producer) 1987, Elvis (co-exec producer) 1989; *Films include:* The Naked Gun: From the Files of Police Squad! 1988, The Adventures of Ford Fairlane, The Naked Gun 2½: The Smell of Fear 1991, Naked Gun 33 ⅓: The Final Insult; Exec Producer The Road to Graceland 1998; *Publication:* Elvis and Me (jtly) 1985. *Leisure interests:* karate, dancing, diving. *Address:* c/o Michelle Bega, Rogers & Cowan, 1888 Century Park E, Los Angeles, CA 90067, USA.

PRESS, Tamara Natanovna; Russian athlete and trade union official; b 10 May 1937, Kharkov. *Education:* Leningrad Construction Engineering Inst and Higher Party School of Cen Cttee of CPSU. *Career:* Women's Shot-put champion, Olympic Games 1960, 1964, Discus champion 1964; Women's European Discus Champion three times 1958, 1960, 1962; winner of Soviet Championship 1958–66; mem CPSU 1962–91; worked for All-Union Cen Council of Trade Unions (now Commonwealth of Ind States—CIS Labour Union Fed) 1967–; Vice-Pres Sports Soc of Russian Trade Unions and Pres Physical Culture and Health Charity Fund 1992–; Order of Lenin; Order of Badge of Honour; Honoured Master of Sports of USSR 1960. *Address:* Sports Society Rossiya, 109017 Moscow, Maly Tolmachevsky per 4, Russian Federation. *Telephone:* (095) 238-63-87; *Fax:* (095) 230-76-26.

PRESTON, Frances W.; American business executive; three s. *Education:* Lincoln Coll (IL). *Career:* Mem staff Broadcast Music Inc (BMI), Nashville 1958, Vice-Pres 1964–85, Sr Vice-Pres of Performing Rights New York 1985, Exec Vice-Pres and CEO 1986, apptd Pres and CEO 1986; mem Film, Entertainment and Music Comm Advisory Council, TN, John Work Memorial Foundation, Leadership Nashville, Admin Council Confed of Int Socs of Authors and Composers; Trustee Country Music Foundation Inc; Hon Trustee Nat Acad of Popular Music; fmr mem Comm on White House Record Library; mem Bd of Dirs Rock and Roll Hall of Fame, Peabody Awards; Vice-Pres Nat Music Council; Founder-mem Black Music Asscn; mem Country Music Asscn, Nat Acad of Recording Arts and Sciences, Gospel Music Asscn, American Women in Radio and TV, Nashville Songwriters' Asscn; Dr hc (Illinois); awards include Achievement Award (Women's Equity Action League), Citation Award (Nat Acad of TV Arts and Sciences), Golden Baton Award (Young Musicians' Foundation), Irving Waugh Award of Excellence (Country Music Asscn); named One

of America's Fifty Most Powerful Women by Ladies' Home Journal. *Address:* Broadcast Music Inc (BMI), 320 W 57th St, Floor 3, New York, NY 10019, USA.

PRETTY, Katharine Bridget (Kate), PH D, FSA; British archaeologist and college principal; b 18 Oct 1945, Cheshire; d of Maurice Walter and Bridget Elizabeth Whibley (née Marples) Hughes; m 1st Graeme Lloyd Pretty (divorced 1975); m 2nd Tjeerd Hendrik van Andel 1988. *Education:* King Edward VI High School for Girls (Birmingham) and New Hall (Cambridge). *Career:* Fellow and Lecturer New Hall, Cambridge 1972–91, Emer Fellow 1995–, Chair Faculty of Archaeology and Anthropology 1991–, Council of the School of Humanities and Social Sciences 1997–; Prin Homerton Coll, Cambridge 1991–; Chair RESCUE, British Archaeological Trust 1978–83; Vice-Pres RSA 1999; Medal, British Archaeological Awards 1998. *Publications:* The Excavations of Wroxeter Baths-Basilica 1997. *Leisure interests:* archaeology, botany and gardening. *Address:* Homerton Coll, Hills Rd, Cambridge CB2 2PH, UK. *Telephone:* (1223) 507131; *Fax:* (1223) 507130; *E-mail:* kp10002@cam.ac.uk.

PRÉVÔT-LUCAS, Liliane Ingrid, D ÈS SC; French geologist; b 17 Oct 1940, Strasbourg; d of Edgar Prévôt and Anne Schulé. *Education:* Lycée de Jeunes Filles and Univ of Strasbourg. *Career:* Editorial Sec Sciences Géologiques periodical 1961–73; Sec-Gen CNRS Research Centre 1966–80, Research Engineer 1972–; co-leader Project 325 for Int Geological Correlation Prog (IGCP)/UNESCO; organizer int scientific confs 1983, 1989, 1991, 1996; mem UN Scientific Comm; Co-Ed vols on Phosphorites 1979, 1985, 1989; Lucien Cayeux Prize, Acad des Sciences 1989. *Leisure interests:* music, reading, travel. *Address:* Centre de géochimie de la surface du CNRS, 1 rue Blessig, 67000 Strasbourg, France (Office); 3 rue Touchmolin, 67000 Strasbourg, France (Home). *Telephone:* (3) 88-35-85-40 (Office); *Fax:* (3) 88-36-72-35 (Office).

PRICE, Leontyne; American opera singer (soprano); b 10 Feb 1927, Laurel, MS; d of James Anthony and Kate (née Baker) Price; m William Warfield 1952 (divorced 1973). *Education:* Central State Coll (Wilberforce, OH) and Juilliard School of Music (New York). *Career:* Appeared as Bess in Porgy and Bess, Vienna, Berlin, Paris, London and New York 1952–54; soprano recitalist and soloist 1954–; soloist Hollywood Bowl 1955–59, 1966; singer with NBC-TV 1955–58, San Francisco Opera Co 1957–59, 1960–61, Vienna Staatsoper 1958, 1959–60, 1961; recording artist RCA-Victor 1958–; performed at Royal Opera House, Covent Garden, London 1958–59, 1970, Chicago 1959, 1960, 1965, La Scala, Milan, Italy 1960–61, 1963, 1967, Metropolitan Opera, New York 1961–62, 1963–70, 1972, 1985, Paris Opéra 1968; retd 1985; Master Class Instructor Juilliard School, New York; Hon Vice-Chair US Cttee UNESCO; Fellow American Acad of Arts and Sciences; Trustee Int House; Hon D MUS (Howard Univ, Cen State Coll, Ohio); Hon DHL (Dartmouth); Hon DH (Rust Coll, MS); Hon D HUM LITT (Fordham); Presidential Medal of Freedom; Order of Merit, Italy; Nat Medal of Arts 1985, over 20 Grammy Awards for classical recordings. *Publication:* Aïda as told by Leontyne Price (for children) 1990. *Address:* c/o Columbia Artists Management Inc, 165 W 57th St, New York, NY 10019, USA; Price Enterprises, Room 920, 1133 Broadway, New York, NY 10010, USA.

PRICE, Dame Margaret Berenice, DBE; British opera singer; b 13 April 1941, Tredegar, Wales; d of the late Thomas Glyn Price and of Lilian Myfanwy Richards. *Education:* Pontllanfraith Grammar School and Trinity Coll of Music (London). *Career:* Operatic debut with Welsh Nat Opera in The Marriage of Figaro; renowned for Mozart operatic roles; has sung in world's leading opera houses and at festivals, on radio and TV; numerous recordings of opera, oratorio, concert works and recitals; Fellow Coll of Wales 1991; Hon Fellow Trinity Coll of Music; Hon D MUS (Wales) 1983; Elisabeth Schumann Prize for Lieder; Ricordi Prize for Opera; Silver Medal of the Worshipful Co of Musicians. *Operas include:* The Marriage of Figaro, The Magic Flute, Così fan Tutte, Don Giovanni, Die Entführung aus dem Serial, Simone Boccanegra, Der Freischütz, Otello, Don Carlo, Aida, Norma, Un Ballo in Maschera. *Leisure interests:* cookery, reading, walking, swimming, driving. *Address:* c/o Stefan Hahn, Artist Management HRA, Sebastian-platz 3, 80331 Munich, Germany.

PRIEST, Mary Hartwell Wyse (see Wyse Priest, Mary Hartwell).

PRIESTMAN, Jane, OBE, FCSD; British design management consultant; b 7 April 1930; d of late Reuben Stanley and Mary Elizabeth (née Ramply) Herbert; m Arthur Martin Priestman 1954 (divorced 1986); two s. *Education:* Northwood Coll and Liverpool Coll of Art. *Career:* Design practice 1954–75; Design Man, Gen Man Architecture and Design British Airports Authority 1975–86; Dir Architecture and Design British Railways Bd 1986–91; Visiting Prof De Montfort Univ 1997–; mem London Regional Transport Design Panel 1985–88, Jaguar Styling Panel 1988–91, Percentage for Art Steering Group, Arts Council 1989–91; Council mem, Design Council 1996–2000; Gov Commonwealth Inst 1987–98, Kingston Univ 1988–96; Hon FRIBA, FRSA; Hon Dr of Design (De Montfort) 1994, (Sheffield Hallam) 1998. *Leisure interests:* textiles, city architecture, opera, travel. *Address:* 30 Duncan Terrace, London N1 8BS, UK. *Telephone:* (20) 7837-4525; *Fax:* (20) 7837-4525.

PRIMACHENKO, Mariia Oksent'evka; Ukrainian artist; b 13 Jan 1908, Bolotnia; d of Oksent Gregorivich and Proskovia Vasilivna Primachenko; one s. *Career:* Worked in workshop producing decorative paintings 1935–37; nat and int exhibitions 1937–; exhibitions include Kiev and Moscow on numerous occasions 1936–88, Leningrad (now St Petersburg) 1936, 1977, Paris 1937, 1957, Sofia 1958, Vienna 1959, Tallinn, Estonia and Vilnius, Lithuania 1961, Riga, Latvia 1961, 1974, Budapest 1965, Montréal (Canada) 1967, 1972, Tomsk, Russian Fed 1969, 1976, Prague 1968, USA 1970, Belgium 1976, Yerevan, Azerbaijan 1982, Austria 1983, Malmö (Sweden) 1984, Denmark 1984, Cracow (Poland) 1985, Portugal 1986, Omsk, Sverdlovsk (now Yekaterinburg) and Kamensk-Ural'sky, Russian Fed 1987, Tbilisi, Georgia 1988; mem Artists' Union 1958–; Nat Artist of Ukraine; Order of Poch'et 1962; T. Shchevchenko Laureate 1966. *Leisure interests:* painting, teaching children, great-grandchildren and others to draw. *Address:* 255300 Kiev, Ivankov Raion, Bolotnia, ul Bogdana Khmel'nitskovo 59, Ukraine. *Telephone:* (044) 521-75.

PRIMAROLO, Dawn, BA; British politician; b 2 May 1954, London; d of Roy Alfred and Joyce Clara Gasson; m 1st 1972 (divorced); m 2nd Thomas Ian Ducat 1990; one s. *Education:* Thomas Bennett Comprehensive School (Crawley, Sussex), Bristol Polytechnic and Univ of Bristol. *Career:* Legal Sec and advice worker; Sec Avon Co Council 1975–78; mem Lab Party 1973–; Co Councillor, Avon 1985–87, Vice-Chair Equal Opportunities Cttee; MP for Bristol S 1987–, mem Select Cttee on Mems' Interests, All-Party Group on Autism; Shadow Health Minister 1992–94, Shadow Financial Sec 1994–97; Financial Sec 1997–99, Paymaster Gen 1999–; Patron of Bristol Home Start, Bristol Family Mediation, Knowle West Against Drugs, Lifeskills Project, Terence Higgins Trust, S Bristol Construction Co. *Address:* House of Commons, London SW1A 0AA, UK; POB 1002, Bristol BS99 1WH, UK (Office). *Telephone:* (20) 7219-3608 (London); (117) 909-0063 (Bristol); *Fax:* (20) 7219-2276 (London); (117) 909-0064 (Bristol).

PRINCE, Alison; British writer (children's fiction). *Career:* Fmrly farmer, art teacher and TV scriptwriter; currently writer and illustrator of childrens' fiction; organizes creative writing workshops in schools in Scotland, sponsored by Scottish Arts Council; columnist The Arran Banner. *Publications include;* Having Been in the City 1994, Witching Tree 1996, Blue Moon Day 1996, The Sherwood Hero (Guardian Children's Fiction Award, jtly 1996) 1996. *Leisure interests:* cats, dogs, music, reading. *Address:* Macmillan General Books Ltd, 18–21 Cavaye Place, London SW10 9PG, UK.

PROCTER, Jane Hilary Elizabeth; British magazine editor; b London; d of Gordon H. and Florence Bibby Procter; m Thomas C. Goldstaub 1985; one s one d. *Education:* Queen's Coll (London). *Career:* Ed Tatler 1990–99; Editorial Dir PeopleNews Network 1999–. *Publication:* Dress Sense. *Leisure interests:* skiing, sailing. *Address:* c/o Tatler, Vogue House, 1 Hanover Square, London W1R 0AD, UK.

PROCTER, (Mary) Norma; British opera and concert singer (retd); b 15 Feb 1928, Cleethorpes, Lincs; d of John and Clarice Procter. *Education:* Wintringham Secondary School (Grimsby), vocal and music studies in London with Roy Henderson, Alec Redshaw, Hans Oppenheim and Paul Hamburger. *Career:* London debut Southwark Cathedral 1948; operatic debut Aldeburgh Festival in Rape of Lucretia 1959, 1960; first appearance at Royal Opera House, Covent Garden in Orpheus 1961; specialist in concert works, oratorios and recitals; has performed at festivals and with major orchestras in Germany, France, Netherlands, Belgium, Spain, Italy, Portugal, Norway, Denmark, Sweden, Finland, Austria, Luxembourg, Israel and S America; Hon RAM 1974. *Recordings include:* The Messiah, Elijah, Samson, Second, Third and Eighth Symphonies and Das Klagende Lied (Mahler), First Symphony (Hartmann), Scenes and Arias (Nicholas Maw), Le Laudi (Hermann Suter), The Rarities (Britten) 2001. *Leisure interests:* reading, tapestry, sketching, TV, painting. *Address:* 194 Clee Rd, Grimsby DN32 8NG, UK. *Telephone:* (1472) 691210.

PROCTOR, Diane Nyland; Canadian director and choreographer; b 20 Jan 1944, Kitchener, ON; d of Lloyd Gofton and Frieda Martha (née Tschoeltsch) Nyland; m Frank Proctor 1970; one s one d. *Education:* Elizabeth Ziegler Elementary School and Kitchener-Waterloo Coll Inst. *Career:* Dancer on stage, film and TV; Dancer Nat Ballet Co 1961–62, 1964–65, 1967–68; performances include Anne of Green Gables, Charlottetown Festival 1965–69, The Trouble With Tracy, CTV 1970–71; Dir and Choreographer of 50 productions including Nunsense (Dora Mavor Moore Award for Choreography) 1986–87, Rose is a Rose, Canadian Opera Co 1987; Artistic Dir Press Theatre 1982–85; Kawantha Summer Theatre 1994, 1995; mem Cabaret and Musical Theatre Alliance, Canadian Actors' Equity Asscn, Alliance Canadian Cinema, TV and Radio. *Leisure interest:* golf. *Address:* Talent House, 186 Dupont St, Toronto, ON M5R 2E8, Canada.

PROSSER, Margaret Theresa, OBE, MS; British trade union official; b 22 Aug 1937, London; d of Frederick and Lilian James; m Joseph Prosser 1957 (divorced 1978); two d one s. *Education:* St Philomena's Convent (Carshalton, Surrey) and Polytechnic of NE London. *Career:* Advice Centre organizer, London Borough of Southwark 1974–76, Community Law Centre Employment Rights Adviser 1976–83; S London trade union dist organizer 1983–84; Nat Women's Sec Transport and Gen Workers' Union 1984–93, Nat Organizer 1993–99; mem Gen Council TUC 1985–, Pres 1995–96; mem Equal Opportunities Comm 1987–93, Employment Appeal Tribunal 1995–, Cen Arbitration Cttee 2000–. *Leisure interests:* walking, cooking, reading, gardening. *Address:* 24 Shannon Way, Beckenham, Kent BR3 1WG, UK. *Telephone:* (20) 8771-5487.

PROULX, Edna Ann (E. Annie), MA; American writer; b 22 Aug 1935, Norwich, CT; d of George Napoleon and Lois Nelly (née Gill) Proulx; m James Hamilton Lang 1969 (divorced 1990); three s one d. *Education:* Colby Coll (ME), Univ of Vermont and Sir George Williams Univ (now Concordia Univ, Montréal). *Career:* Fmr journalist; f Vershire Behind the Times newspaper, Vershire, VT; short stories appeared in Blair & Ketchums Country Journal, Esquire etc; has contributed more than 50 articles to magazines and journals; active anti-illiteracy campaigner; Kress Fellow Harvard Univ 1974, Ucross Foundation Residency, WY 1990, 1992, Fellow VT Arts Council 1989, Nat Educ Asscn 1991, Guggenheim Foundation 1993; mem PEN; Hon D HUM LITT (Maine) 1994; Alumni Achievement Award, Univ of Vermont 1994; New York Public Library Literary Lion 1994; Dos Passos Prize for Literature 1996; American Acad of Achievement Award 1998; Book Award, The New Yorker 2000. *Publications include:* Heart Songs and Other Stories 1988, Postcards (PEN-Faulkner award) 1992, The Shipping News (Nat Book Award for fiction 1993, Chicago Tribune Heartland award 1993, Irish Times Int fiction award 1993, Pulitzer Prize for fiction 1994) 1993, Accordion Crimes 1996, Best American Short Stories of 1997 (ed), Brokeback Mountain 1998. *Leisure interests:* cross-country skiing, hunting, fishing, canoeing, playing the fiddle. *Address:* POB 230, Centennial, WY 82055, USA. *Telephone:* (307) 742-6159.

PROUST, Joëlle Renée Elise, D ÈS L; French philosopher; b 3 Feb 1947, Orléans; d of the late Guy and of Mauricette (née Chenard) Proust; m Reda Bensmaïa 1973 (divorced 1989); two s. *Education:* Univ of Provence (Aix-en-Provence). *Career:* Philosophy teacher 1969–72; Curator Museum of Antiquities, Algiers 1973–74; Asst Prof Univ of Algiers 1974–76; Researcher CNRS at Univ of Aix-Marseille I (Univ de Provence) and Centre de Recherche en Epistémologie Appliquée (CREA), Ecole Polytechnique, Paris 1976–2000; Dir of Research CNRS/CREA 1990–2000, Institut Jean-Nicod, Ecole des Hautes Etudes en Sciences Sociales (EHESS) 2001–; Alexander von Humboldt-Stiftung Research Grant 1972–73. *Publications:* Questions de forme: logique et proposition analytique de Kant à Carnap (Bronze Medal CNRS 1987, trans to English 1990) 1986, Comment l'Esprit vient aux bêtes 1997, Vocabulaire des sciences cognitives (jtly) 1998. *Leisure interests:* opera, piano, hiking in the wilderness. *Address:* Institut Jean-Nicod (EHESS), 1 bis ave de Lowendal, 75007 Paris, France (Office); 16 rue des Cornouillers, 60170 Tracy-le-Mont, France (Home). *Telephone:* (1) 53-59-32-87 (Office); (3) 44-75-38-13 (Home); *Fax:* (1) 53-59-32-99 (Office); *E-mail:* jproust@ehess.fr; *Internet:* www .institutnicod.org.

PRUNSKIENĖ, Kazimiera-Danutė, D ECON; Lithuanian economist and politician; b 26 Feb 1943, Vasiulishke; d of Pranas Stankevičius and Ona Stankevičienė; m 1st Povilas Prunskus 1961; one s two d; m 2nd Algimantas Tarvydas 1990 (divorced). *Education:* Vilnius State Univ. *Career:* Lecturer in Econs Vilnius Univ 1965–86; Deputy Dir Lithuanian Inst of Agricultural Econs 1986–88; Chancellor Inst of Man 1988–89; mem Council of Sąjūdis (Lithuanian Movt for Reconstruction) 1988; Deputy Lithuanian Parl 1989–92, Deputy Prime Minister 1989–90, Prime Minister Lithuanian Repub 1990–91; Pres Lithuanian-European Inst 1991–, K. Prunskiene-Consulting (pvt consulting co) 1993–; Founder, Pres Lithuanian Women's Asscn (now Party) 1992–, Chair 1995–; mem Cen for Econ Policy Studies Int Advisory Council 1992–, Int Cttee for Econ Reform and Co-operation 1994–, Council of Women World Leaders 1997–; Pres Baltic Women's Basketball League 1994–; Minerva Prize for Politics, Women's Club Il Delle Donne, Italy 1991. *Publications include:* Amber Lady's Confession 1991, Leben für Litauen 1992, Europa – ein Kontinent gewinnt Gestalt (jtly) 1991, Backstairs 1992, Challenge to Dragon 1992, Price of Liberation 1993, Markt Balticum 1994, Transformation, Co-operation and Conversion 1996, Science and Technology Policy of the Baltic States and International Co-operation 1997, Intellectual Property Rights in Central and Eastern Europe: the Creation of Favourable Legal and Market Preconditions 1998. *Leisure interests:* sports, music, literature, knitting, cookery, forests. *Address:* Lithuanian–European Institute, Vilniaus St 45-13, 2001 Vilnius, Lithuania (Office); Kriviu 53A-13, 2007 Vilnius, Lithuania (Home). *Telephone:* (2) 222-114 (Office); *Fax:* (2) 221-955.

PRZECŁAWSKA, Anna Maria, PH D; Polish professor of education; b 9 Aug 1929, Warsaw; d of Henryk Sadkowski and Halina Sadkowska; m Krzysztof Przecławski 1951; one s one d. *Education:* Univ of Warsaw. *Career:* Participated in the Warsaw Uprising 1944; Asst Univ of Warsaw 1957, Asst Prof 1969, apptd Prof 1978, Dir Inst of Educ 1979–81, Dean Faculty of Educ 1981–87, Vice-Dean 1988, Chair of Social Pedagogics 1981; Golden Cross of Merit 1978; Bachelor's Cross of the Order of Polonia Restituta 1981, Officer's Cross 1988. *Publications:* The Young Reader and the Contemporary Times 1966, Books, Youth and Cultural Changes 1967, The Cultural Differentiations of the Young and the Problems of Education 1976. *Leisure interests:* reading, tourism, international cuisine. *Address:* University of Warsaw, Faculty of Education, Krakowskie Przedmieście 26-28, 00-325 Warsaw, Poland; Wilcza 55/63, 37, 00-679 Warsaw, Poland. *Telephone:* (2) 6286424; *Fax:* (22) 470822.

PSOTA, Irén; Hungarian actress; b 28 March 1929; d of the late István Psota and Ilona Dávid; m 1st F. Sobok; m 2nd J. Molnar; m 3rd T. Unguari (divorced). *Education:* Nat Drama School (Budapest). *Career:* Mem Madách Theatre Co 1952–80, 1990; mem Hungarian Nat Theatre 1980–90; awards include Jászai Prize (twice), Kossuth Prize, Erdenes Kivalo Prize. *Plays include:* The Caucasian Chalk Circle 1960, Saint Joan 1967, Irma la Douce 1963, Hello Dolly 1968, Yerma 1965, Rose Tattoo 1970, Mother Courage 1973, Margarida 1981, Cabaret 1991; *Film and TV appearances include:* House Under the Rocks 1957, Elektra 1963, Lovers 1969, Tsardas Princess 1971. *Leisure interests:* walking, travel, animals. *Address:* 1027 Budapest, Bem RKP 30, Hungary. *Telephone:* (1) 201-8140.

PUGACHEVA, Alla Borisovna; Russian singer; b 5 April 1949, Moscow; m 2nd Filipp Kirkorov; one d. *Education:* M. Ippolitov-Ivanov Music High School and A. Lunacharsky State Inst of Theatre Art. *Career:* Debut as Soloist Lipetsk vocal-instrumental group 1970; O. Lundstrem Jazz Orchestra 1971; Soloist Veselye Rebyata Ensemble 1973–78; Founder Theatre of Songs 1988, All Co 1993, All Magazine 1993; repertoire includes numerous songs by popular Soviet composers

including R. Pauls, A. Muromtsev, A. Zatsepin and others, also songs of her own; acted in films; several concert programmmes; tours in USA, Germany, Switzerland, India, France, Italy, etc; numerous prizes and awards including Third Prize All-Union Contest, Moscow 1974, Grand Prix, Int Competition Golden Orpheus, Bulgaria 1975, Int Festival Sopot 1978, USSR People's Artist; Ovation Prize 1994; State Prize of Russia 1995. *Address:* Tverskaya-Yamskaya str, Apt 57, Moscow, Russian Federation. *Telephone:* (095) 250-95-78.

PUJARI, Porama; Indian politician; b 1 July 1954, Bodobharandi; d of the late Boli Pujari; m Simanchal Das 1980; one s. *Career:* Elected Sarapanch to Bodobharandi Gram-Panchayat 1974; mem Advisory Cttee All India Radio 1976, Programme Advisory Cttee 1991; elected mem Legis Ass for Orissa 1980–85; Deputy Minister Govt of Orissa 1986–90; Jt Sec Orissa Pradesh Congress Cttee 1985; Vice-Pres Korapul Dist Congress Cttee 1992. *Leisure interests:* reading, travel, horticulture. *Address:* Bodobharandi, via Dabugam, Koraput, Orissa, India.

PULEIO, Jacqueline; Panamanian concert pianist; b 31 March 1961, Panamá; d of Luis Puleio and Griselda Cervera; m Pierre Deschamps 1980; three d. *Education:* Coll Privado de Maria Inmaculada and Conservatoire Européen de Musique (Paris). *Career:* First piano recital at age ten; debut as Soloist with Nat Symphonic Orchestra at Nat Theatre, Panamá 1975; Paris debut as Soloist with UNESCO Philharmonic Orchestra 1977; has given recitals at the Festival de Musique de Sceaux, Paris, with the Paillard Chamber Orchestra; other concerts and recitals (with Pierre Deschamps) include appearances in Paris, Santiago, Viña del Mar, Chile, Panama, Quito, Lima, London; has recorded four compact discs with Pierre Deschamps; Dip of Excellence, Conservatoire Européen de Musique, Paris 1979; Hon Cultural Attaché Embassy of Panama, Paris 1990. *Address:* 35 rue Prosper Dufour, 78370 Plaisir les Gâtines, France. *Telephone:* (1) 30-54-06-97; *Fax:* (1) 34-81-23-57.

PULVER, Liselotte; Swiss actress; b 11 Oct 1929, Berne; d of Eugen and Germaine (née Bürki) Pulver; m Helmut Schmid 1961 (died 1992); one s one d (deceased). *Education:* Conservatory of Music and Theatre (Berne). *Career:* Worked at Berne and Zurich City Theatres; appearances at Salzburg Festival, Austria 1957, Berlin Festival 1959; Bundesverdienstkreuz (BVK) 1985; other awards include German Film Critics' Prize 1958, Bundesfilmpreis 1958, 1980, Filmband in Gold 1980. *Plays include:* Regenmacher 1968, Monsieur Chasse 1973, Dame von Maxim 1979, 1980, Lauf doch nicht immer weg 1984–87; *Films include:* Ich denke oft an Piroschka (Prix Femina Belge du Cinéma 1956), Arsène Lupin, Zeit zu leben – zeit zu sterben, Buddenbrooks, Die Nonne, Trèfle à cinq feuilles 1972, Die sechzehn-jährigen 1974, Brot und Steine 1978; *TV appearances include:* Regenmacher 1966, Calamity Jane 1969, Hoopers letzte Jagd 1972, Sesamstraße 1977–83, Jeden Mittwoch 1981, Drunter und Drüber 1980, Leib und Seele 1988; *Publications:* Lachstory – Oh diese Ferien 1973, Wenn man trotzdem lacht (journal) 1990. *Leisure interest:* horse-riding. *Address:* 1166 Perroy/Lake Geneva, Switzerland.

PUOLANNE, Ulla Kaija, B ECONS; Finnish politician; b 28 June 1931, Lahti; d of Eero Eemil and Maili Matilda (née Penttilä) Raivo; m (divorced). *Education:* Helsinki. *Career:* Corresp Asko Oy 1959–65, Head of Dept 1965–68; Financial Man Reijo Puolanne and Partners Ltd; mem Lahti Town Council 1969–84, Admin Bd 1972–75; elected Kansallinen Kokoumus (KoK, Nat Coalition Party) mem of Eduskunta (Parl) 1975–91, mem Pres Electorate 1978, 1982, Chair Cons Party Parl Group 1984–87, Second Minister of Finance 1987–91; Knight (1st Class) of the Order of the Lion of Finland. *Leisure interest:* swimming. *Address:* Rullakatu 6E30, 15900 Lahti, Finland. *Telephone:* (18) 513388.

PURCELL, Joan; Grenada politician. *Career:* Fmrly Minister of Tourism with Responsibility for Civil Aviation and Women's Affairs; Minister of Communications and Works, Information and Carriacou and Petit Martinique Affairs; Head of Mercy Comm; Deputy Leader Nat Democratic Congress. *Address:* National Democratic Congress, St George's, Grenada.

PURI, Premlata, B SC, M MUS; Indian musician; b 30 May 1939, Dehradun; d of Bihari Lal and Maya Devi Puri. *Education:* Univs of Lucknow and Delhi. *Career:* Lecturer on Indian culture in Europe, USA and Japan, Indian Del to UNESCO confs on educ, art, culture 1968–95; mem Exec Cttee India Int Centre, Kendriya Vidyalaya Sangatan, Steering Cttee of Working Group on Art and Culture (Dept of Educ), Cen Bd of Secondary Educ, Nat Council of Science Museums; Dir-Gen Centre for Cultural Resources and Training, New Delhi 1994–; has contributed articles and papers on Indian culture to books and journals; Govt of India Scholarship in Music 1964; Italian Scholarship for the Study of Italian Language and W Music 1967. *Leisure interests:* reading, writing, social services. *Address:* Centre for Cultural Resources and Training, Bahawalpur House, Bhagwandas Rd, New Delhi 110 001, India; Triveni Kala Sangam, Flat 4, 205 Tansen Marg, New Delhi, India (Home). *Telephone:* (11) 3382300 (Office); (11) 3714506 (Home); *Fax:* (11) 3382757 (Office).

PUROHIT, Sharayu Mhatre, PH D; Indian sociologist; b 2 March 1942, Bombay (now Mumbai); m Vinayak Purohit 1972. *Education:* Fergusson Coll (Pune) and Univ of Bombay. *Career:* Apptd Jt Dir Indian Inst of Soc Research 1983. *Publications:* Bank Credit to Women: A Study of Working Class Lunch Suppliers 1980, Professionalisation and Indian Banking 1980, Multiple Transitions for Tribal Women 1981, Material Basis for Women's Liberation (jtly) 1987. *Leisure interests:* films, Indian music. *Address:* Indian Institute of Social Research, No 3, 2nd Floor, 372a Cadell Rd, Dadar, Mumbai 400 028, India. *Telephone:* (22) 4309049.

PURVES, Elizabeth Mary (Libby), OBE, MA; British writer and broadcaster; b 2 Feb 1950, London; d of James Grant and Mary (née Tinsley) Purves; m Paul Heiney 1980; one s one d. *Education:* Convent of the Sacred Heart (Tunbridge Wells) and St Anne's Coll (Oxford). *Career:* BBC local radio, Oxford 1972–76; Reporter Today Programme BBC Radio 4 1976–79, Presenter 1979–81, currently Presenter on Radio 4 and BBC World Service; Presenter BBC TV Choices 1982, BBC Radio Midweek 1984–; Ed Tatler magazine 1983; Pres Council for Nat Parks 2000–; writer for newspapers and magazines including The Times and Good Housekeeping. *Publications include:* Sailing Weekend Book 1985, Where Did You Leave the Admiral 1987, The English and their Horses (jtly) 1988, How Not to be a Perfect Mother 1988, One Summer's Grace 1990, How Not to Raise a Perfect Child 1991, Casting Off (novel) 1995, A Long Walk in Wintertime (novel) 1996, Grumpers' Farm (with Paul Heiney) 1996, Home Leave (novel) 1997, Holy Smoke 1998, More Lives than One (novel) 1998, Regatta (novel) 1999, Nature's Masterpiece: A Family Survival Book 2000, Passing Go (novel) 2000. *Leisure interests:* sailing, writing, walking. *Address:* c/o Lisa Eveleigh, 26A Rochester Square, London NW1 9SA, UK.

PUTANOV, Paula, PH D; scientist; b 14 July 1925, Darda; d of Stevan Putanov and Ranka Lokić. *Education:* Univ of Belgrade. *Career:* Research scientist Serbian Acad of Sciences and Arts 1952–59, Pres Interacademic Bd for Catalysis 1986; Founder and Head Dept for Catalysis, ICTM Belgrade 1959–68; Prof of Physical Chemistry Univ of Novi Sad 1966–90, Vice-Rector 1975–77; has contributed to scientific publications on catalysis and physical chemistry; mem Vojvodina Acad of Sciences and Arts 1979, Serbian Acad of Sciences and Arts 1992; October Award (City of Novi Sad) 1981. *Leisure interest:* poetry. *Address:* 11000 Belgrade, Serbian Academy of Sciences and Arts, Knez Mihailova 35 (Office), Yugoslavia; Belgrade, Dž Vašingtona 38A, Yugoslavia (Home). *Telephone:* (11) 634055; *Fax:* (11) 182825.

PÜTZ, Ruth-Margret; German opera singer (coloratura and lyric soprano); b 26 Feb 1932, Krefeld; m 1966; two d. *Education:* Singing studies in Cologne and Hanover. *Career:* Mem Württemberg State Opera, Stuttgart 1959–, Vienna State Opera 1960–64, Hamburg Opera 1963–; guest appearances in Milan and Rome, Italy, London, Paris, Madrid, Lisbon, Moscow and Leningrad (now St Petersburg), USSR (now Russian Fed), Stockholm, Helsinki and Buenos Aires; has performed at many festivals including Bayreuth, Salzburg, Austria and Edinburgh, UK; numerous recordings for Columbus, Electrola, CBS and Decca; title of Kammersängerin conferred 1962; awarded Soviet Culture Prize. *Leisure interests:* music, painting, travel. *Address:* Herderstr 5, 71229 Leonberg, Germany.

PUYBASSET, Michèle Marie-Antoinette, L EN D; French civil servant; b 25 Aug 1933, Ajaccio, Corsica; d of Dominique and Pauline (née Clementi) Peretti; m Jean Puybasset (died 1983); three s one d. *Education:* Lycées d'Ajaccio and Fénelon (Paris), Univ of Paris (Sorbonne) and Ecole Nat d'Admin. *Career:* Official at the Council of State 1960–67, Maître des Requêtes (Counsel) 1967–84, Sec-Gen 1979–83, mem 1985–; Reporter Higher Bd of Social Security 1961–62, Deputy Sec-Gen 1963–66; Reporter Refugee Comm 1962–63; Legal Adviser Ministry of Nat Educ 1966–77; Sec-Gen Fonds d'intervention culturelle 1977–79; Dir Secr-Gen of Govt 1983–93; Dir-Gen Centre Int de l'Enfance 1993–96; Pres Bd Acad de France, Rome 1990–96; Pres Comm d'Accès aux Documents Administratifs 1999–, Office Nat de Diffusion Artistique 1999–; mem Conseil d'Etat; Officier de la Légion d'Honneur; Commdr des Palmes Académiques; Officier de l'Ordre Nat du Mérite; Officier des Arts et des Lettres; Médaille d'Or de la Jeunesse et des Sports. *Leisure interests:* theatre, travel, music, cooking, skiing, cycling. *Address:* Conseil d'Etat, 75100 Paris, France (Office); 10 rue des Marronniers, 75016 Paris, France (Home).

PYLKKÄNEN, Alison, MA; British magazine editor; b 1963, Maltby (S Yorks); d of Betty and Michael Green; m Jussi Pylkkänen 1986; one s one d. *Education:* Lady Margaret Hall (Oxford). *Career:* Fmr Sub-Ed, later Deputy Ed Good Housekeeping; Ed She magazine 1996–. *Leisure interests:* cinema, eating out, fishing, crosswords, music. *Address:* She Magazine, National Magazine House, 72 Broadwick St, London W1V 2BP, UK. *Telephone:* (20) 7439-5000; *Fax:* (20) 7439-5350.

PYNE, Natasha; British actress; b 9 July 1946, Crawley, Sussex; d of John and Iris Pyne; m Paul Copley 1972. *Education:* Hurlingham Comprehensive School (London). *Career:* Entered film industry 1961; mem Young Vic Theatre Co and Exchange Co, Manchester 1980–81; mem BBC Radio Drama Co 1985–87, 1994–95. *Plays include:* A Party for Bonzo (Soho Poly) 1985–87, Twelfth Night (Middle East and Africa Tour) 1989–90, Rafts and Dreams 1990, Alfie 1992–93; *Films include:* The Idol, Taming of the Shrew, Breaking of Bumbo, One of Our Dinosaurs is Missing, Madhouse; *TV appearances include:* Father Dear Father (series), Hamlet, Silas Marner, A Brush with Mr Porter on the Road to Eldorado 1981, Gems 1987–88, Van der Valk 1991–92, The Bill (series) 1991, 1993, 2001, Virtual Murder 1992, McLibel! (drama-documentary) 1997, Cadfael III (film series) 1997; *Radio work includes:* On May-Day 1986, The Snow Queen 1994, Tipperary Smith 1994, Galileo 1995, Ben Hur (serial) 1995, Westway (serial) 1997–98, Young PC (series) 1997, Westway (serial) 1998–2001. *Leisure interests:* cycling, reading, cooking, travel, photography. *Address:* c/o Kate Feast Management, 10 Primrose Hill Studios, Fitzroy Rd, London NW1 8TR, UK. *Telephone:* (20) 7586-5502; *Fax:* (20) 7586-9817.

Q

QASIMI, Shaikha Lubna al-; Dubai information technology expert; niece of Shaikh of Sharjah. *Education:* UAE and USA. *Career:* Head Dubai Port Authority's Information Tech Div 1993–2000, Dubai's e-govt initiative to oversee transition to e-business tech for the public sector 2000–, tejari.com (website to promote interaction between businessmen); speaker at numerous Information Tech confs.

QIAN YI, MS; Chinese environmental scientist; b 1936, Suzhou, Jiansu Prov; d of Qian Mu. *Education:* Tongji Univ (Shanghai) and Tsinghua Univ. *Career:* Teaching Asst, Lecturer, Assoc Prof then Prof Tsinghua Univ 1959–; Dir State Key Jt Lab of Environmental Simulation and Pollution Control; science consultant Environmental Protection Comm of State Council; Vice-Chair, Gen Cttee of ICSU; Vice-Chair Eng and Environment Cttee of the World Fed of Eng Orgs; mem Standing Cttee 8th and 9th NPC; Nat Science and Tech Advancement Award (2nd Class); State Educ Comm Science and Tech Advancement Award (1st Class) 1987. *Publications:* Modern Wastewater Treatment Technology; The Prevention and Control of Industrial Environmental Pollution; Water Pollution Volume of Environmental Engineering Handbook, and about 100 research papers. *Address:* Dept of Environmental Engineering, Tsinghua Univ, Beijing, 100084, People's Republic of China. *Telephone:* (10) 62585684; *Fax:* (10) 62595687; *E-mail:* denqy@ tsinghua.edu.cn.

QIN YI; Chinese actress; b 2 Feb 1922, Shanghai. *Career:* Mem 6th CPPCC 1983–87, 7th 1987–92, 8th 1993–; Outstanding Film Artist Prize 1992. *Films include:* Remote Love, Song of Youth, Fog is no Fog 1993. *Address:* Shanghai Film Studio, 595 Caoxi North Rd, Shanghai 200030, People's Republic of China.

QU XIXIAN, BA; Chinese composer; b 23 Sept 1919, Shanghai; d of the late Qu Baowen and Zhu Pingyü; two d. *Education:* St John's Univ (Shanghai) and Shanghai Conservatory of Music. *Career:* Teacher of Harmony and Music History Beijing Art Inst 1948; composer for Music Ensemble, Cen Conservatory of Music 1949–54; composer Cen Philharmonic Soc 1954–; mem music dels to Hungary 1960, Bulgaria 1962, Japan 1964, Korea 1985; Adviser Chinese Film Music Inst 1981–; apptd Vice-Chair Chinese Musicians' Asscn 1985; Hon Chair Chinese Children's Music Inst 1987–. *Compositions include:* Pastorale (Mongolian folk-song), The Wusuli Boat Song (Heze folk-song), Waiting for You till Dawn (Sinjiang folk-song), The Red Army Base Cantata 1958, Song of the Youth (film) 1959, Listening to Mamma Telling the Past (First Prize Children's Song Contest) 1980, The Rickshaw Boy (film) 1982, Call Me by my Pet Name (collection) 1985, We and You (First Prize Children's Song Contest) 1987, The Flying Petals (First Prize Teachers' Song Contest) 1988, Releasing Pigeons at the Great Wall (First Prize Children's Song Contest) 1992; *Recordings:* The Flying Petals (chorus collection, jtly). *Leisure interests:* reading, friends. *Address:* Central Philharmonic Society, He-ping-li, Beijing 100013, People's Republic of China. *Telephone:* (1) 64216157.

QUACHEY, Lucia Akosua; Ghanaian business executive; b 11 Oct 1942, Mamfe, Cameroon; d of Benno Dotse and Catherine Eno Afagbegge; m Felix Stephen Quachey 1970; three s three d. *Education:* Holy Child Secondary School (Calabar, Nigeria) and Singer Sewing School (Lagos, Nigeria). *Career:* Self-employed Man Lucia Fashion Spot 1969–71, Man Dir Lucia Manufacturing Industry Ltd 1971–80, Exec Dir 1981; Man Dir Micro Rural Enterprise Devt Co; Founder-mem Ghana Fed of Business and Professional Women 1976, Nat Pres 1989–91, mem Bd of Dirs 1991; Rep Women in Management Forum, Canada 1989; Project Cttee mem for Africa, Int Fed of Business and Professional Women 1989; Founder and Pres Asscn of Women in Devt

Experts 1990; Council mem and Chair Garment and Knitting Subcttee of Asscn of Ghana Industries; Pres Fed of African Women Entrepreneurs 1991; mem Asscn of Women in Devt, Virginia, USA 1991, Inter-Univ Consortium for Int Social Devt, USA 1991, Commonwealth Asscn for Local Action and Econ Devt 1991, Bd UNDP Entrepreneurial Devt and Training Project 1991–92, Pvt Sector Advisory Cttee, Ministry of Finance and Econ Planning 1991–92. *Leisure interests:* music, films, reading. *Address:* POB 7600, Accra-North, Ghana. *Telephone:* (21) 222459; *Fax:* (21) 228398.

QUAN ZHENGHUAN; Chinese mural artist, painter and university professor; b 16 June 1932, Beijing; d of Quan Liang-Su and Qin Xiao-Qing; m Li Huaji 1959; two d. *Education:* Cen Acad of Fine Arts (Beijing). *Career:* Asst Lecturer Cen Acad of Fine Arts 1955–56, Cen Acad of Applied Arts 1956–59, Lecturer 1959–78, Asst Prof 1978–87, Prof and mem Academic Cttee 1987–; mem Standing Cttee Artists' Asscn of China. *Works include:* Murals: The Story of the White Snake (Beijing Int Airport) 1979, Jin Wei Filled the Ocean (Beijing Yian Jing Hotel), Dances of China (Beijing Opera House) 1984; Other works: Cries of Harmony (Monte Carlo Art Festival) 1988. *Leisure interests:* opera, 1930s' and 1940s' films, football. *Address:* Central Academy of Applied Arts, Beijing, People's Republic of China (Office); 3-601, 6/F Hongmiao Beili, Beijing 100025, People's Republic of China (Home). *Telephone:* (1) 5963912 (Office); (1) 5015522 (Home).

QUANT, Mary, OBE, FSIAD; British fashion, cosmetic and textile designer; b 11 Feb 1934, London; d of Jack and Mildred (née Jones) Quant; m Alexander Plunket Greene 1957 (died 1990); one s. *Education:* Goldsmiths' Coll of Art (London). *Career:* Dir of Mary Quant Group of cos 1955–; mem Design Council 1971–74, UK-USA Bicentennial Liaison Cttee 1973–, Advisory Council Victoria and Albert Museum, London 1976–78; retrospective exhibition of 1960s fashion, London Museum 1974; Sr Fellow Royal Coll of Art 1991; Hon Fellow Goldsmiths Coll, Univ of London 1993; Hon FRSA 1995; Dr hc (Winchester Coll of Art) 2000; awards include Sunday Times Int Fashion Award, Rex Award (USA), Annual Design Medal, Soc of Industrial Artists and Designers, Piavolo d'Oro (Italy), Royal Designer for Industry, Hall of Fame Award, British Fashion Council Award for outstanding contrib to British fashion 1990. *Publications include:* Quant by Quant 1966, Colour by Quant 1984, Quant on Make-up 1986, Mary Quant Classic Make-up and Beauty Book 1996. *Address:* Mary Quant Ltd, 3 Ives St, London SW3 2NE, UK. *Telephone:* (20) 7584-8781; *Fax:* (20) 7589-9443.

QUATRO, Suzi; American rock singer; b 3 June 1950, Detroit, MI. *Albums include:* Baby You're a Star 1989, Rock Hard 1990, The Wild One 1990; *Singles include:* Devilgate Drive, Can the Can, Daytona Demon.

QUEFFÉLEC, Anne Bénédicte Marie; French concert pianist; b 17 Jan 1948, Paris; d of Henri Queffélec and Yvonne Pénau; m Luc Dehaene 1983; two s. *Education:* Conservatoire National (Paris). *Career:* Tours in Europe, Japan, Israel, Africa, Canada and USA 1968–; performances with BBC Symphony, London Symphony, Royal Philharmonic, Bournemouth Symphony, Hallé, Scottish Chamber, City of Birmingham Symphony, Miami Symphony, Tokyo Symphony orchestras, Nouvel Orchestre Philharmonique de Radio-France, Orchestre Nat de Radio-France, Orchestre de Strasbourg; has performed under conductors including Zinman, Groves, Leppard, Marriner, Boulez, Semkow, Skrowaczewski, Eschenbach, Gardiner, Pritchard, Atherton; appearances at numerous festivals including Strasbourg, Dijon, Besançon, Bordeaux and Paris (France), King's Lynn, Bath and

London Proms (UK); judge in several int piano competitions; masterclasses in France, England and Japan; many appearances on musical programmes for TV and radio but has also appeared on literary and religious programmes; Pres Asscn des Amis d'Henri Queffélec, Asscn Musicale 'Ballades'; Chevalier de la Legion d'Honneur 1998; First Prize Munich Int Piano Competition, Germany 1968; Prizewinner Leeds Int Piano Competition, UK 1969; Best Performer of the Year, Victoires de la Musique 1990. *Recordings include:* Satie, Scarlatti, Chopin, Schubert, Fauré, Ravel, Debussy, Liszt, Hummel, Beethoven, Mendelssohn and Bach with Erato-RCA and Virgin Classics, and complete piano works of Henri Dutilleux 1996. *Leisure interests:* literature, theatre, art exhibitions, friends, children, humour, cycling. *Address:* 15 ave Corneille, 78600 Maisons-Laffitte, France. *Telephone:* (1) 39-62-25-64; *Fax:* (1) 39-62-25-64.

QUELER, Eve; American conductor; b New York. *Education:* Mannes Coll of Music (New York), City Coll of New York, piano with Isabella Vengerov, conducting with Carl Bamberger, Joseph Rosstock, Walter Susskind and Igor Markevich. *Career:* Began as pianist, Asst Conductor New York City Opera 1958 and 1965–70; later became a Conductor; guest-conducted Philadelphia, Cleveland, Montréal Symphony, New Philharmonia, Australian Opera, Opéra de Nice, Opera de Barcelona, San Diego Opera, Edmonton Symphony, Nat Opera of Czechoslovakia (now Czech Repub), Hungarian State, Hungarian Operahaz and various other orchestras; Music Dir Opera Orchestra of New York 1968; has written articles for Musical America Magazine; Dr hc (Russell Sage Coll, Colby Coll); Musician of the Month, Musical American Magazine; Martha Baird Rockefeller Fund for Music Award. *Recordings include:* Puccini's Edgar, Verdi's Aroldo, Massenet's Le Cid, Boito's Nerone, Strauss' Guntram. *Leisure interest:* organic gardening. *Address:* c/o Alix Barthelmes, Manager Opera Orchestra, 239 W 72nd St, New York, NY 10023, USA.

QUÉRÉ, Maryse, D ÈS SC; French civil servant and professor of computer science; b 24 Jan 1944, Longwy; d of Marcel and Louise (née Nalli) Tommasini; m Alain Quéré 1968; two d one s. *Education:* Lycée de Longwy and Univ of Nancy. *Career:* Head Dept of Computer Science, Inst universitaire de tech (IUT), Nancy 1980–83; Dir Centre de formation à l'informatique et à ses applications pédagogiques (centre for computer educ), Acad de Nancy-Metz 1981–85, Dir Centre d'initiation à l'enseignement supérieur (CIES) 1989–91; Prof of Computer Science Univ of Nancy II; Dir of Information and Communication, Ministry of Nat Educ 1991–92, Adviser on new technology to Dir-Gen of Higher Educ 1993; Rector Acad de Caen 1997–. *Address:* Rectorat, Académie de Caen, 168 Rue Caponiere, BP 6184, 14034 Caen, Cedex, France.

QUESTIAUX, Nicole Françoise; French politician and civil servant; b 19 Dec 1930, Nantes; d of Pierre Valayer and Elisabeth Mills; m Paul Questiaux 1951; one s one d. *Education:* Lycée de Casablanca (Morocco) and Ecole Nat d'Admin. *Career:* Auditor Council of State 1955, mem Second sub-section, Disputes Section, Maître des Requêtes (Counsel) 1962, Govt Commr Assemblée du Contentieux (Litigation Ass) 1963–74; Pres Joint Cttee for Study of Problems Relating to the Elderly 1969; Surrogate Govt Commr Tribunal des Conflits 1973–74; Councillor of State 1980–81; Minister of State 1981, Minister of Nat Solidarity 1981–82; Pres Fourth sub-section Council of State 1983–; Pres Council Centre d'étude des revenus et des coûts 1984–, Public Works Section, Council of State 1988–95; Vice-Pres Comité consultatif nat d'ethique des sciences et de vie, Comm nat des comptes de l'environnement. *Publications:* Le contrôle de l'administration et la protection des citoyens (jtly) 1973, Traité du social; Situations, luttes politiques, institutions (jtly) 1976. *Address:* 13 ave de Bretteville, 92200 Neuilly-sur-Seine, France (Home).

QUIN, Rt Hon Joyce Gwendolen, PC, BA, M SC; British politician; b 26 Nov 1944, Tynemouth, Northumberland; d of Basil Godfrey and Ida (née Ritson) Quin. *Education:* Univ of Newcastle upon Tyne and LSE. *Career:* Political Researcher Lab Party Int Dept, London 1969–72; Lecturer in French Univ of Bath 1972–76; Resident Tutor St Mary's Coll and Lecturer in French and Politics Univ of Durham 1977–79; MEP for S Tyne and Wear 1979–89; MP (Lab) for Gateshead E 1987–97, for Gateshead E and Washington W 1997–, mem Select Cttee on Treasury and Civil Service 1987–89, Opposition Front Bench Spokesperson on Trade and Industry 1989–92, on Employment 1992–93, on European Affairs 1993–97; Minister of State, Home Office 1997–98, Foreign and Commonwealth Office (Minister for Europe) 1998–99; Minister of State and Deputy Minister, Ministry of Agric, Fisheries and Food 1999–2001; Hon Fellow Sunderland Polytechnic (now Univ of Sunderland) 1986, St Mary's Coll, Univ of Durham 1998. *Leisure interests:* history and folk music of NE England, walking, cycling, reading. *Address:* House of Commons, London SW1A 0AA, UK; Design Works, William St, Felling, Gateshead NE10 03P, UK. *Telephone:* (20) 7219-3000 (London); (191) 469-6006 (Gateshead); *Fax:* (20) 7219-6052 (London).

QUINN, Andrea; British conductor and music director. *Education:* Royal Acad of Music (London). *Career:* Music Dir London Philharmonic Youth Orchestra 1994–97, Royal Ballet 1998–2001; Music Dir (desig) New York City Ballet 2001–; has conducted London Symphony Orchestra, London Philharmonic, Philharmonia and other leading orchestras; operas and music theatre pieces conducted include Misper (Glyndebourne), Four Saints in Three Acts (English Nat Opera), Harrison Birtwistle's Pulse Shadows (UK tour). *Address:* New York City Ballet, New York State Theater, New York, NY, USA. *Telephone:* (212) 870-5570; *Internet:* www.nycballet.com/programs/print_pr061200.html.

QUINN, Catherine; Australian ballet dancer; b 8 April 1961, Townsville; d of Brian Edward and Margaret Elizabeth James. *Education:* Queensland Univ of Tech. *Career:* Dancer with Expressions Dance Co, Brisbane 1983–86, Dance North, Townsville 1987–88, Siobhan Davies Co, London 1988–89, Rambert Dance Co, London 1989; nominated for Dancer of the Year and Contemporary Dancer of the Year Awards 1991. *Film:* White Man Sleeps (by Siobhan Davies) 1989. *Leisure interests:* swimming, opera, backgammon. *Address:* Rambert Dance Co, 94 Chiswick High Rd, London W4, UK. *Telephone:* (20) 8995-4246.

QUIROGA, Elena; Spanish writer; b 1921, Santander. *Career:* Mem Royal Spanish Acad of Language. *Publications:* Viento del Norte (Nadal Prize) 1951, La Sangre 1952, La Otra Ciudad 1953, Algo Pasa en la Calle 1954, La Enferma 1954, La Careta 1955, Plácida la Joven 1956, La Última Corrida 1958, Tristura (Critics' Prize) 1960, Escribo tu Nombre (Spanish entry in Rómulo Gallegos literary competition) 1965, Grandes Soledades, Presencia y Ausencia de Alvaro Cunqueiro (essay) 1984. *Address:* c/o Agencia Balcells, Diagonal 580, 08021 Barcelona, Spain.

QUISTHOUDT-ROWOHL, Godelieve, PH D; German politician; b 18 June 1947, Etterbeek, Belgium; m Michael Rowohl 1973; three s one d. *Education:* Univ Catholique de Louvain (Belgium). *Career:* Max Planck Inst for Biophysical Chemistry 1972–73; Asst Prof Inst for Medicine, Hanover 1974–78, Inst for Applied Linguistics, Hildesheim Univ 1979–89; elected MEP (EPP, CDU) 1989, mem Cttee on Energy, Research and Tech 1989, Vice-Chair, Del for relations with Japan. *Publication:* Analysis of Technical Texts for Translation Students 1985. *Address:* European Parliament, rue Wiertz, 1047 Brussels, Belgium. *Telephone:* (2) 284-21-11; *Fax:* (2) 230-69-43.

R

RABL-STADLER, Helga, LL D; Austrian politician and business executive; b 2 June 1948, Salzburg; m Peter Rabl 1977; two s. *Education:* Univ of Salzburg. *Career:* Journalist Die Presse, Die Wochenpress, Kurier, Vienna 1970–78; lawyer Salzburg and Linz 1978–; Co-Propr Resmann fashion house, Salzburg 1983; apptd Vice-Pres Salzburg Chamber of Commerce 1985, Pres 1988; mem Nationalrat (Nat Council—Österreichische Volkspartei) for Salzburg 1983–90; elected Vice-Chair Österreichische Volkspartei 1991; mem Bd Inst for Econ Promotion 1980; Chair Salzburg Br, Austrian Employers' and Trade People's Fed 1980; Pres Woman in the Business World. *Publication:* Arbeitszeitverkürzung aus der Sicht eines Handelsbetriebes 1989. *Leisure interests:* reading, travel, opera. *Address:* Handelskammer Salzburg, Julius-Raab-Platz 1, 5027 Salzburg, Austria. *Telephone:* (662) 888-83-28; *Fax:* (662) 888-85-88.

RACELIS, Mary, PH D; American United Nations official; b 11 Jan 1932, Manila, Philippines; m Mr Hollsteiner 1954; four d one s. *Education:* Univ of The Philippines, De la Salle Univ (Philippines) and Cornell Univ (New York). *Career:* Sec UN 1954–55; teacher 1957–60; Research Assoc and Dir, Inst of Philippine Culture 1969–77; Prof Dept of Sociology and Anthropology, Ateneo de Manila Univ 1969–77; Sr Adviser and Policy Specialist, UNICEF 1979–83, apptd Regional Dir, Regional Offices for E and S Africa 1983; currently Dir Inst for Philippine Culture, Ateneo de Manila University, Philippines; Pres Community Organizers Multiversity of the Philippines. *Publications:* The Dynamics of Power in a Philippine Municipality 1963, Society, Culture and the Filipino: Readings in Sociology and Anthropology 1973, Metropolitan Growth: Poverty Eradication through Popular Participation; over 200 articles on sociological, anthropological, political and developmental issues. *Address:* Institute of Philippine Culture, Ateneo de Manila University, POB 154, Manila, Philippines.

RACINE, Yolande, BA, MFA; Canadian curator; b 29 Feb 1948, Montréal, PQ; d of Jacques and Simone (née Legault) Racine; one s one d. *Education:* Coll Jean-de-Brébeuf (Montréal) and Univ of Montréal. *Career:* Researcher Musée Ferme Saint-Gabriel, Montréal 1971, Pre-archivist of Art History Documentation, Cegep Vieux-Montréal 1972, Pedagogical Consultant Fine Arts Dept 1978; Head of Educ Animation and Communications Dept, Museum of Contemporary Art, Montréal 1973–74, Curator 1978–82; Curator of Contemporary Art, Montréal Museum of Fine Arts 1982–92; teacher Faculty of Fine Arts Concordia Univ, Montréal 1992–94; Curator, Museum of Contemporary Art, Montréal 1993, Head of Multi-Media Creations 1993; Dir La Pulperie de Chicoutimi 1997–; freelance researcher 1975–76, in Asia, Middle E and N Africa 1977; mem Jury Canadian Council of Ottawa, Québec Ministry of Cultural Affairs; mem Québec Museum Soc, Canadian Museum Asscn, Int Council of Museums; Award of Excellence, American Fed of Arts 1988. *Publications:* L'architecture traditionnelle (jtly) 1973, Le mobilier traditionnel (jtly) 1973, L'Orfèvrerie traditionnelle (jtly) 1973, Les instruments d'artisanat (jtly) 1973, Albert Dumouchel rétrospective de l'œuvre gravé (jtly) 1974, Tendances actuelles au Québec (jtly) 1980, Theatre of the Imagination 1984, Betty Goodwin: works from 1971–1987 1987, Le monde selon Graff (jtly) 1987. *Address:* 300 rue Dubuc, Chicoutimi, PQ G7J 4M1, Canada (Office); 51 rue Duvernay, Chicoutimi, PQ G7J 2C7, Canada (Home).

RADCLYFFE, Sarah; British film producer; b 14 Nov 1950, London. *Career:* Producer 1978–; Dir Channel 4 1995–99, Film Council 1999–; Gov British Film Inst 1996–99. *Films include:* My Beautiful Launderette 1986, Sammy and Rosie Get Laid 1987, Wish You Were Here 1987, A World Apart 1990, Fools of Fortune 1990, Robin Hood 1991, Sirens 1993, Second Best 1993, Bent 1996, Cousin Bette 1997, Les Miserables 1998, The War Zone 1999, There's Only One Jimmy Grimble 2000. *Address:* Sarah Radclyffe Productions, 83/84 Berwick St, London W1V 3PJ, UK. *Telephone:* (20) 7437-3128; *Fax:* (20) 7437-3129; *E-mail:* srpltd@globalnet.com.uk.

RADEVA, Radka Koleva, PH D; Bulgarian mathematician; b 21 Nov 1936, Gabrovo; d of the late Koljo Radev and of Nadezhda Vassileva Minchev; m Vergil Dimitrov Vassilev 1957; two s. *Education:* Aprilov High School (Gabrovo), Univ of Sofia and Leningrad (now St Petersburg) State Univ (USSR, now Russian Fed). *Career:* Asst Prof of Maths Higher Mechanical and Electrical Engineering Inst (HMEEI), Gabrovo 1964, Sr Asst Prof 1966, Lecturer 1968, Sr Lecturer 1970, Assoc Prof 1977, then Pres; Pres Gabrovo Br Maths, Physics and Chem Section, Union of Bulgarian Scientists 1980; numerous publs in the field of multi-dimensional singular integral equations; reviewer for mathematical publs; Order of Cyril and Methodius 1986; Golden Badge (HMEEI) 1986, Badge of Honour, Union of Bulgarian Scientists; Gold Award of Achievement, American Biographical Inst; Commemorative Medal, Int Biographical Centres, Cambridge, UK. *Leisure interest:* music. *Address:* 5300 Gabrovo, 21 Orlovska Str, Bulgaria. *Telephone:* (66) 2-49-90.

RADULOVIC, Veronika; German artist; b 1954, Delbrück. *Education:* Fachhochschule Bielefeld. *Career:* Exhibitions include Museum of Modern Art (Tarragona, Spain) 1981, Kunstbaustelle (Munich) 1983, Frauenmuseum (Bonn) 1985, Kunstpassage (Münster) 1986, Stadthalle (Detmold) 1986, Regionalmuseum (Xanten) 1987, Künstlerhaus (Bonn) 1987, Galerie am Abdinghof (Paderborn) 1988, Vajda-Lajos-Studio (Szentendre, Hungary) 1989, Produzentengalerie (Kassel) 1990, Kunsthalle Bielefeld 1990; works held in perm collections including Stadtgeschichtliche Museen (Nuremberg), Kunstsammlung Gemeinde Steinhagen, Kunsthalle Bielefeld; artist in Vietnam 1993–94; Guest Lecturer Dept of Fine Art, Acad of Fine Art, Hanoi 1994–95.

RADZYMIŃSKA, Józefa, BA; Polish writer; b Lesznowola; d of Julian Radzymiński and Helena Ładyńska; m Franciszek Płodowski 1945; one s. *Education:* Acad of Political Sciences (Warsaw). *Career:* Served in Polish underground army (Armia Krajowa) 1939–45, imprisoned by the Nazis 1941, 1944–45; took part in Warsaw Uprising 1944; lived in Italy, UK and Argentina 1945–62, returned to Poland 1962; mem PEN, Asscn of Polish Writers 1962; awarded Polonia Restituta Cross, Armia Krajowa Cross, Warsaw Rising Cross, numerous other medals 1973–83. *Publications:* Second Time Ashes, The White Eagle on Río de la Plata, Not Destroyed by Thunder, Independent for Ever; 25 vols of poetry, novels, memoirs and monographs. *Leisure interests:* painting, music. *Address:* Broniewskiego 14/29, 00-771 Warsaw, Poland. *Telephone:* (22) 39-90-40.

RAE, Barbara, CBE, RA, RSA; British artist and lecturer; b 10 Dec 1943, Scotland; d of James Rae and Mary Young; one s. *Education:* Edinburgh Coll of Art. *Career:* Lecturer Glasgow School of Art 1975–96; Trustee British School (Rome) 1997–, Hospitalfield House (Arbroath) 1997–99; mem Bd Royal Fine Art Comm 1995–; Invited Artist, Royal Acad (London) 1994, 1995, 1996, Royal Hibernian Acad (Dublin) 1995, 1996; numerous group exhibitions UK, USA, Germany, Netherlands, Spain; works held in public and pvt collections including Scottish Nat Gallery of Modern Art, Scottish Arts Council, Univs of Edinburgh, Glasgow and York, Royal Bank of Scotland, Bank of England, TSB Group PLC, HRH the Duke of Edinburgh, Lord Avonside; mem Royal Scottish Soc of Painters in Watercolours (RSW); several awards including Guthrie Award, RSA 1977, Sir William Gillies

Travel Award 1983, Calouste Gulbenkian Printmaking Award 1983. *Leisure interests:* interior decoration, gardening, antique collecting. *Address:* c/o Art First, 9 Cork St, London W1X 1PD, UK.

RAE, Fiona, BA; British artist; b 1963, Hong Kong. *Education:* Croydon Coll of Art and Goldsmiths' Coll (London). *Career:* Solo exhibitions include Waddington Galleries, London 1991, 1995, Kunsthalle Basel, Basle 1992, ICA, London 1993–94, John Good Gallery, New York 1994, Galerie Nathalie Obadia, Paris 1994, Contemporary Fine Arts, Berlin 1996. *Address:* c/o Waddington Galleries, 11 Cork St, London W1, UK.

RAFFERTY, Hon Dame Anne (Judith), (Dame Anne Barker), Hon Mrs Justice Rafferty, DBE, LL B, FRSA; British barrister; b 1950; m Brian John Barker 1977; four d (one deceased). *Education:* Univ of Sheffield. *Career:* Called to the Bar, Gray's Inn 1973, Inner Temple *ad eundem* 1996, Bencher 1998; QC 1990; Crown Court Recorder 1991–2000; Head of Chambers 1994–2000; Deputy High Court Judge 1996–2000; Judge High Court of Justice, Queen's Bench Div 2000–; mem Cttee Criminal Bar Asscn 1986–91, Sec 1989–91, Vice-Chair 1993–95, Chair 1995–97; Chair Bar Conf 1992; mem Royal Comm on Criminal Justice 1991–93; mem Pigot Cttee 1988–89, Circuit Cttee, SE Circuit 1991–94; mem Criminal Cttee Judicial Studies Bd 1998–. *Address:* Royal Courts of Justice, Strand, London WC2A 2LL, UK.

RAFIDAH AZIZ, Paduka; Malaysian politician. *Career:* Minister of Int Trade and Industry. *Address:* Ministry of International Trade and Industry, Block 10, Kompleks Pejabat Kerajaan, Jalan Duta, 50622 Kuala Lumpur, Malaysia. *Telephone:* (3) 6510033; *Fax:* (3) 6512306; *E-mail:* mitiweb@miti.gov.my; *Internet:* www.miti.gov.my.

RAFSANJANI, Faezeh (see Hashemi Bahreman (Rafsanjani), Faezeh).

RAGGI, Reena, JD; American federal judge; b 11 May 1951, Jersey City, NJ; d of Edward J. and Tina (née Navarchi) Raggi; m David W. Denton 1983; one s. *Education:* Wellesley Coll (MA) and Harvard Univ Law School (MA). *Career:* Called to the Bar, NY 1977; US Attorney Dept of Justice, Brooklyn, NY 1986, US Dist Judge 1987–; Partner Windels, Marx, Davies & Ives, New York 1987. *Address:* US Courthouse, 225 Cadman Plaza E, Brooklyn, NY 11201, USA.

RAGINSKY, Nina, OC, BA, RCA; Canadian photographer and painter; b 14 April 1941, Montréal, PQ; d of Bernard Boris and Helen Thérèsa Raginsky; one d. *Education:* Rutgers Univ (New Brunswick, NJ, USA). *Career:* Photographer 1964–; Instructor in Photography Vancouver School of Art 1972–81; solo exhibitions include Vancouver Art Gallery, Victoria Art Gallery, Edmonton Art Gallery, Art Gallery of Ontario, San Francisco Museum of Art, Acadia Univ, Nancy Hoffman Gallery (New York); photographs included in several Nat Film Bd publs including Call Them Canadians, Canada Year of the Land, Between Friends—Entre Amis, BANFF Purchase; work has appeared in numerous nat and int journals. *Leisure interests:* walking, birding, gardening. *Address:* 272 Beddis Rd, Salt Spring Island, BC V8K 2J1, Canada. *Telephone:* (604) 537-4515.

RAHMAN, Indrani (see Indrani).

RAHMAN, Sarwari; Bangladeshi politician. *Career:* Fmr Minister of State for Women's Affairs until 2000. *Address:* c/o Ministry of Social Welfare and Women's Affairs, Bangladesh Secretariat, Bhaban 6, New Bldg, Dhaka, Bangladesh.

RAINE, Kathleen Jessie, CBE, MA, FRSL; British poet; b 1908; d of the late George and of Jessie Raine; m 1st Hugh Sykes; m 2nd Charles Madge (divorced, died 1996); one s one d. *Education:* Girton Coll (Cambridge). *Career:* Fellow Girton Coll, Cambridge 1956–; Co-Ed Temenos (review) 1982–93; Founder Temenos Acad 1992–; Blake Scholar; Hon D LITT (Leicester) 1974, (Durham) 1979; Officier, Ordre des Arts et des Lettres; numerous British and American poetry prizes and awards including W. H. Smith Literary Award; named one of ten greatest living writers, Royal Soc of Literature 1991; Queen's Medal for Poetry 1992. *Publications:* Poems: Stone and Flower 1943, Living in Time 1946, The Pythoness 1949, The Year One 1952, Collected Poems

1956, The Hollow Hill 1965, William Blake, Selected Poems 1970, The Lost Country (W. H. Smith Literary Award) 1971, On a Deserted Shore 1972, The Oval Portrait 1977, The Oracle in the Heart 1979, Collected Poems 1981, The Presence 1988, Selected Poems 1988, Living with Mystery 1992, Collected Poems 2000; Novels and essays: Stone and Flower 1943, Living in Time 1946, The Pythoness 1949, The Year One 1952, Blake and Tradition (Andrew Mellon Lectures) 1969, Selected Writings of Thomas Taylor the Platonist (jtly) 1969, Faces of Day and Night (French edn 1989) 1973, The Human Face of God 1982, India Seen Afar 1990, Golgonooza, City of the Imagination 1991; Autobiography: Farewell Happy Fields 1973, The Land Unknown 1975, The Lion's Mouth 1977; Criticism: Defending Ancient Springs 1967, Yeats, the Tarot and the Golden Dawn 1973, Death in Life and Life in Death 1973, David Jones and the Actually Loved and Known 1978, From Blake to a Vision 1978, Blake and the New Age 1979, The Inner Journey of the Poet and other papers 1982, L'imagination créatrice de William Blake 1986, Yeats the Initiate 1986, Le Monde Vivant de l'Imagination 1998, W. B. Yeats and the Learning of the Imagination 1999. *Address:* 47 Paultons Square, London SW3 5DT, UK.

RAINER, Luise; Swiss/American actress and painter; b 12 Jan; d of Heinz Rainer; m 1st Clifford Odets 1937 (divorced 1940); m 2nd Robert Knittel 1945 (died 1989); one s. *Education:* In Germany and Switzerland. *Career:* First stage appearance at 16 years, later starred in films in Hollywood; solo exhibition Patrick Seale Gallery (London) 1978; Best Actress Award, Motion Picture Acad of Arts and Sciences 1936, 1937; George Eastman Award, George Eastman Inst (New York) 1982; Grand Cross First Class, Order of Merit (Germany) 1985. *Appearances include:* Films: Escapade, The Great Ziegfeld, The Good Earth, Emperor's Candlesticks, Big City, Toy Wife, The Great Waltz, Dramatic School, On Her Own; Dramatic recitation: Enoch Arden (US tour) 1981–82, 1983. *Leisure interests:* writing, walking, wandering, mountain-climbing. *Address:* 54 Eaton Square, London SW1W 9BE, UK.

RAITT, Bonnie Lynn; American singer and musician; b 8 Nov 1949, Burbank, CA; d of John and Marjorie (née Haydock) Raitt. *Education:* Univ High School (Hollywood), Poughkeepsie High School (NY) and Radcliffe Coll (Cambridge, MA). *Career:* Mem staff American Friends Service Cttee 1968; performer blues clubs, E Coast; concert tours UK 1976, 1977; Co-Founder Musicians United for Safe Energy 1978; mem Christic Inst, Sanctuary Movt, CoMadres. *Albums include:* Bonnie Raitt 1971, Give It Up 1972, Takin' My Time 1973, Streetlights 1974, Home Plate 1975, Sweet Forgiveness 1977, The Glow 1979, Green Light 1982, Nine Lives 1986, Nick of Time (Grammy Awards for Best Album, Best Female Rock Vocal, Best Female Pop Vocal, Best Traditional Blues 1990) 1989, I'm in the Mood (jtly, Grammy Award for Best Traditional Record) 1990, The Bonnie Raitt Collection 1990, Luck of the Draw 1991 (Grammy Award for Best Female Rock Vocal), Longing In Their Hearts 1994 (Grammy Award for Best Pop Album), Road Tested 1996, Fundamental 1998; *Songs include:* Something To Talk About 1992 (Grammy Award for Best Female Country Performance), Good Man, Good Woman (jtly, Grammy Award for Best Rock Duo Vocal) 1992. *Leisure interest:* political activism. *Address:* POB 626, Los Angeles, CA 90078, USA.

RAJAVI, Maryam, B SC; Iranian politician; b 3 Dec 1953, Tehran; m 1980; one d. *Education:* Sharif Univ of Tech (Tehran). *Career:* Leader anti-Shah student movt; joined People's Mojahedin of Iran (leading Iranian opposition group) 1970s, Parl cand for Tehran in 1st post-revolutionary parl elections 1979; official in social dept 1980–81, organized demonstrations against Khomeini Govt 1980–1981; left Iran for Paris 1982; elected jt-leader of Mojahedin 1985, Sec-Gen 1989–93; Deputy Commdr-in-Chief Nat Liberation Army of Iran (NLA) 1987–93, launched programme for introduction of women in front-line combat and combat pilots 1987, transformed NLA from infantry to armoured force 1989–93; Pres-elect of the Nat Council of Resistance of Iran (572-mem Parl in exile) 1993–; proposed platform for women's int alliance against fundamentalism 1993; prominent int campaigner for women's rights 1993–; Guest-speaker Parls of Norway and GB 1995–96; awards include Medal of Honour for contrib to emancipation of women, Nat Comm for Gender Equality (Italy) 1993, one of the The Times 100 Most Powerful Women (UK) 1996. *Publications:* Charter of Fundamental Freedoms in Post-dictatorship Iran 1995, Message to

Fourth International Women's Conference in Beijing 1995, A Message of Tolerance 1995, Women, Islam and Fundamentalism 1996, Women, Voice of the Oppressed 1996, United Front Against Fundamentalism 1996, Message to 'Women in Frontline' (conference) 1997, Price of Freedom 2001; numerous lectures, TV appearances, interviews in int media. *Leisure interest:* reading. *Address:* National Council of Resistance of Iran, 17 rue des Gords, 95430 Auvers-sur-Oise, France (Office). *Telephone:* (1) 34-48-07-28 (Office); (1) 34-48-07-28; *Fax:* (1) 34-48-04-33 (Office); (1) 34-48-01-34.

RAJENDRAN, Sulochana, PH D; Indian journalist and art critic; b 25 Oct 1934, Rangoon (now Yangon), Myanmar; d of V. V. Ramamoorthy and K. Kamala; m S. Rajendran 1965; two d. *Education:* Lady Willingdon High School (Madras), Madras Christian Coll and Heras' Inst of Indian History and Culture (Bombay). *Career:* Asst Lecturer Ismail Yusuf Coll, Bombay 1955–56; Karnatak music vocalist, has appeared on All India Radio (AIR) since 1958; Asst Ed Thought magazine, New Delhi 1959–64; Lecturer Sri Venkateswara Coll, New Delhi 1964–66; freelance art critic (music and dance) 1960–; mem Man Cttee Sri Shanmukhananda Fine Arts and Sangeetha Sabha, Bombay 1987–91; Ed Shanmukha journal 1989; Dir Shanmukhananda Sangeetha Vidyalaya, Bombay 1991. *Leisure interest:* comparative studies in Hindustani and Karnatak music. *Address:* No 1, BIT, 3 Rms, King's Circle, Mumbai 400 019, India. *Telephone:* (22) 481322.

RAMA RAU, Santha; Indian writer; b 24 Jan 1923, Madras (now Chennai), Tamil Nadu; d of the late Sir Benegal Rama Rau and Lady Rama Rau (Dhanvanthi Handoo); m 1st Faubion Bowers 1951 (divorced 1966, died 1999); one s; m 2nd Gurdon W. Wattles 1970 (died 1995); two step-s two step-d. *Education:* St Paul's Girls' School (London) and Wellesley Coll (MA, USA). *Career:* Travel to Europe, India, America, SE Asia, Japan and Russia; fmr teacher Hani Freedom School, Tokyo; English teacher Sarah Lawrence Coll, Bronxville, NY, USA 1971–73; Dr hc (Bates, Brandeis, Roosevelt and Russell Sage Colls); Achievement Awards Asia Soc, NY, The Secondary Educ Bd, NJ, The Asscn of Indians in America. *Publications:* Home to India 1945, East of Home 1950, This is India 1953, Remember the House 1955, View to the South-East 1957, My Russian Journey 1959, A Passage to India (dramatization of E. M. Forster novel) 1962, Gifts of Passage (autobiog) 1962, The Cooking of India 1969, The Adventuress 1971, A Princess Remembers 1976, An Inheritance 1979; numerous articles and short stories. *Leisure interests:* opera, reading, travel. *Address:* 508 Leedsville Rd, Amenia, NY 12501, USA; 16 Sutton Place, New York, NY 10022, USA. *Telephone:* (845) 373-9124 (Amenia); (212) 755-3684 (New York); *Fax:* (845) 373-7730.

RAMBO, Sylvia H., BA, JD; American federal judge; b 17 April 1936, Royersford, PA; d of Granville A. and Hilda E. (née Leonhardt) Rambo; m George F. Douglas, Jr 1970. *Education:* Dickinson Coll and Dickinson School of Law (PA). *Career:* Called to the Bar, PA 1962; Attorney Trust Dept, Bank of Delaware 1962–63; Attorney pvt practice (Carlisle) 1963–76; Public Defender, later Chief Public Defender, Cumberland Co 1976; Judge Court of Common Pleas, Cumberland Co 1976–78, US Dist Court of Harrisburg (Middle Dist, PA) 1979–99, Chief Judge 1992–99, Fed Judge 2000–; Asst Adjunct Prof of Law, Dickinson School of Law 1973, 1976, 1977; mem Nat Asscn of Women Judges; Hon LL D (Wilson Coll) 1980; Hon LL D (Dickinson Coll) 1995; Hon LL D (Shippensburg Univ of Pennsylvania) 1996. *Address:* US District Court, POB 868, Harrisburg, PA 17108, USA.

RAMDAS, Kavita N., MA; Indian organization executive; b 22 Sept 1962, New Delhi; d of Laxminarayan and Lalita Ramdas; m Zulfigar Ahmad 1990; one d. *Education:* Mount Holyoke Coll and Woodrow Wilson School of Public and Int Affairs, Univ of Princeton (USA). *Career:* Program officer worked on issues of US poverty and econ devt and int population issues, John D. and Catherine T. MacArthur Foundation, Chicago, IL; Pres and CEO Global Fund for Women 1996–; mem Advisory Council Woodrow Wilson School of Public and Int Affairs, Univ of Princeton, Bd Rural Devt Inst, Seattle (WA); fmr mem Cttee on Women and Devt, Advisory Bd UN Econ Comm for Africa; fmr Trustee Gen Service Foundation; founding mem Bd and fmr Chair Asian Americans and Pacific Islanders in Philanthropy (AAPIP); fmr mem Bd Women and Philanthropy (affinity groups of the Council on Foundations); Henry Crown Fellow Aspen Inst 1999; Women's

Funding Network Award 1999. *Address:* Global Fund for Women, 1375 Sutter St, Ste 400, San Francisco, CA 94109, USA. *Telephone:* (415) 202-7640; *Fax:* (415) 202-8604; *E-mail:* kavita@globalfundforwomen .org; *Internet:* www.globalfundforwomen.org.

RAMIA, Carmen; Venezuelan organization executive. *Career:* Dir Ateneo de Caracas (Cultural Asscn of Caracas). *Address:* Ateneo de Caracas, Plaza Morelos, Parque los Caobos, Caracas, Venezuela. *Telephone:* (2) 573-4622.

RAMOS, María Elena; Venezuelan museum director and writer. *Career:* Dir Museo de Bellas Artes. *Address:* c/o Museo de Bellas Artes, Plaza Morelos, Parque Los Caobos, Caracas, Venezuela.

RAMPHELE, Mamphela Aletta, MB, CH B, B COM, DPH, PH D; South African international organization executive and former university chancellor; b 28 Dec 1947, Pietersburg; d of Pitsi Eliphaz and Rangoato Rahab (née Mahlaela) Ramphele; Partner Steve Biko (killed 1977); two s (one s with Steve Biko). *Education:* Bethesda Normal Coll (Pietersburg), Setotolwane High and Univ of Natal. *Career:* Medical practitioner and social anthropologist; mem Black Consciousness Movt, SA 1970s; f Zanempilo Community Health Centre, E Cape 1975; Br Man, E Cape Black Community Progs (nat network of projects) 1976; imprisoned for four months 1976, placed under banning order 1977, sent to NE Transvaal where she set up health centre, banning order lifted 1984; Research Fellow Dept of Anthropology, Univ of Cape Town 1984, Sr Researcher 1986, Deputy Vice-Chancellor 1991–95, Vice-Chancellor (first black and first woman) 1996–2000; Man Dir IBRD 2000–; Dir Inst for Democracy, Public Information Centre 1995–; Researcher and Consultant to Western Cape Hostel Dwellers' Asscn 1986–92; Non-Exec Dir Anglo-American Corpn 1992–95, Old Mutual 1993–; Founder-mem Black Consciousness Movt 1969; gave Canon Collins Memorial Address for British Defence and Aid Fund for Southern Africa; Hon D HUM LITT (Hunter Coll, New York) 1984; Hon MD (Natal) 1989, (Sheffield) 1998; Hon D SC (Univ Coll, London) 1997; Hon LL D (Princeton) 1997, (Brown Univ) 1998, (MI) 1998; Hon D PHIL (Univ of Orange Free State); Dr hc (Tufts Univ, MA) 1991, (Inst of Social Studies, Netherlands) 1997; Barnard Medal of Distinction, Barnard Coll, New York 1991. *Publications:* Children on Frontline (UNICEF report) 1987, Uprooting Poverty: The South African Challenge (with David Philip) 1989 (Noma Award for publishing in Africa 1991), Bounds of Possibility: The Legacy of Steve Biko and Black Consciousness (jtly) 1991, A Bed Called Home: Life in the Migrant Labour Hostels of Cape Town (jtly) 1993, Mamphela Ramphele: A Life (jtly) 1995, Across Boundaries: The Journey of a South African Woman Leader 1996, Produce from Untilled Fields: Adolescents in New Crossroads, Stretching Across Boundaries: An Autobiographical Reflection. *Leisure interests:* reading, walking. *Address:* International Bank for Reconstruction and Development, 1818 H St, Washington, DC 20433, USA (office); 4515 - Foxhall Crescents, Washington, DC 20007, USA (Home). *Telephone:* (202) 473-2419 (Office); *Fax:* (202) 522 1638 (Office); *E-mail:* mramphele@worldbank.org (Office).

RAMPLING, Charlotte, OBE; British actress; b 5 Feb 1946, London; m 1st; one s; m 2nd Jean-Michel Jarre; one s one step-d. *Career:* Film debut 1963; Chevalier des Arts et des Lettres 1986. *Films include:* The Knack 1963, Rotten to the Core, Georgy Girl, The Long Duel, Kidnapping, Three, The Damned 1969, Skibum, Corky 1970, 'Tis Pity She's a Whore, Henry VIII and His Six Wives 1971, Asylum 1972, The Night Porter, Giordano Bruno, Zardoz, Caravan to Vaccares 1973, The Flesh of the Orchid, Yuppi Du 1974–75, Farewell My Lovely 1975, Foxtrot 1975, Sherlock Holmes in New York, The Purple Taxi 1976, Orca—The Killer Whale 1977, Stardust Memories 1980, The Verdict 1983, Viva la vie 1983, Beauty and Sadness 1984, He Died With His Eyes Open 1985, Max mon Amour 1985, Angel Heart 1987, Paris by Night 1988, Dead on Arrival 1989, The Riddle, Ocean Point, Helmut Newton, Frames From the EdgeHammers Over the Anvil 1991, Time is Money 1992, La marche de Radetzky (TV film) 1994, Asphalt Tango 1995, Wings of a Dove 1996, The Cherry Orchard 1998, Signs and Wonders, Aberdeen 1999, Fourth Angel, Under the Sand, Superstition 2000; numerous TV plays. *Address:* c/o Artmédia, 20 ave Rapp, 75007 Paris, France. *Telephone:* (1) 43-17-33-00.

RAN, Shulamit, PH D; American/Israeli composer; b 21 Oct 1949, Tel-Aviv, Israel; d of Zvi and Berta Ran; m Abraham N. Lotan 1986; one s. *Education:* Mannes Coll of Music (New York). *Career:* Moved to USA 1963; William H. Colvin Prof of Composition Univ of Chicago, IL 1973–; Visiting Prof Princeton Univ, NJ 1987; Composer-in-Residence Chicago Symphony Orchestra 1990–; Brena and Lee Freeman, Sr Composer-in-Residence Lyric Opera of Chicago 1994; Visiting Prof Princeton Univ 1987; works performed by New York Philharmonic Orchestra 1963, Israel Philharmonic Orchestra 1971, Chamber Music Soc (Lincoln Center, New York) 1987, Chicago Symphony Orchestra 1988, 1991, 1993, 1995, Philadelphia Orchestra 1990, Cleveland Orchestra 1991, 1993, Orchestre de la Suisse Romande, Amsterdam Philharmonic; piano performances in the USA, Europe and Israel; numerous comms; Fellow American Acad of Arts and Sciences; Dr hc (Mount Holyoke Coll) 1988, (Spertus Inst) 1994, (Beloit Coll) 1996; Guggenheim Foundation Awards 1977, 1990; American Acad and Inst of Arts and Letters Award 1989. *Works include:* O the Chimneys 1969, Concert Piece for Piano and Orchestra 1970, Hyperbolae 1977, Verticals 1983, Sonata-Waltzer 1983, String Quartet No 1 1984, Concerto da Camera I 1985, Concerto for Orchestra 1986, Concerto for Orchestra 1986, East Wind (for solo flute) 1987, Concerto da Camera II 1987, String Quartet No 2 (Vistas) 1988–89, Mirage for 5 Players 1990, Symphony (Pulitzer Prize in Music) 1991, Legends for Orchestra 1993, The Dybbuk (opera, in progress). *Leisure interests:* spending time with husband, sons, parents and special friends. *Address:* University of Chicago, Dept of Music, 5801 S Ellis Ave, Chicago, IL 60637, USA.

RANDALL, Joan Walwyn, BA; Canadian business executive and university administrator; b 27 Feb 1928, Toronto, ON; d of Arthur G. and Ruth (née Harris) Walwyn; m William O. Randall (deceased). *Education:* St Clement's School and Univ of Toronto. *Career:* Dir and mem Audit Cttees, The Halifax Insurance Co and N. N. Life Insurance Co of Canada 1977–; Trustee and mem Acquisition Cttee Nat Gallery of Canada; Gov Ridley Coll 1977–; mem Governing Council Univ of Toronto 1980–89, Vice-Chair 1985–88, Chair 1988–89, mem Exec Cttee 1983–89, Univ Hosp Bd 1985–89, Admissions Cttee Faculty of Medicine 1989–, Advisory Cttee Faculty of Man 1989–; Chair Bd of the Univ Coll/Univ of Toronto Art Gallery 1994–; Vice-Chair Univ Coll Cttee 1994–; mem Bd of Trustees Royal Ontario Museum 1972–77, 1988–89, Sunnybrook Hosp 1988–89, Nat Museums of Canada, Nat Museum of Natural Science, Nat Gallery of Canada; Trustee Banting Research Foundation 1981–84, mem Investment Cttee 1982–84; mem Celebration Cttee Toronto Int Festival 1982–84; mem Inst of Contemporary Culture 1993–; mem and Public Rep to Council, Inst of Chartered Accountants of Ontario 1995–; Founder, Pres Arthritis Soc (Rosedale); Founder-mem and Sec Canadian Fed Friends of Museums 1977–; mem Canadian Museum Asscn, American Asscn of Museums, Metropolitan Museum of Art (New York, USA), Art Gallery of Ontario; First Annual Outstanding Achievement Award for Volunteerism, Ministry of Citizenship and Culture 1986; Arbor Award, Univ of Toronto 1990. *Address:* 39 S Drive, Toronto, ON M4W 1R2, Canada.

RANDALL, Paulette; British theatre director; b 1963. *Education:* Dick Sheppard Secondary School (London) and Rose Bruford Coll. *Career:* Variety of jobs before training as Dir under Max Stafford-Clark at Royal Court theatre; Dir of plays for theatre, TV and radio. *Plays include:* Five Guys Named Mo, Loud! (tour by Lenny Henry, dir), The Piano Lesson, Pecong, Leave Taking, Two Trains Running (dir) 1996; *TV includes:* Desmond's (producer).

RANDHAWA, Ravinder, BA; British writer; b 25 Jan 1952, India; d of Pakhar Singh and Kartar Kaur Randhawa; two d. *Education:* Leamington Coll for Girls (Leamington Spa). *Career:* Came to UK aged seven years; worked for women's groups setting up refuges and resource centres for Asian women 1978–84; Founder Asian Women Writers' Collective 1984. *Publications:* A Wicked Old Woman 1987, Hari-jan 1992, The Coral Strand 2001. *Leisure interests:* music, films, theatre, swimming. *Address:* 59 Helix Rd, London SW2 2JR, UK.

RANDZIO-PLATH, Christa; German politician; b 29 Oct 1940, Ratibor; m Ronald Randzio 1975. *Education:* Rheinische Friedrich-Wilhelms-Univ Bonn, Christian-Albrechts Univ zu Kiel and Univs of Amsterdam (Netherlands), Strasbourg (France), Pescara (Italy) and Lausanne (Switzerland). *Career:* Journalist 1970–72; Lawyer 1972–74;

Finance Dir, Hamburg 1974–89; mem Hamburg Bürgerschaft (City Council) 1986–89; MEP 1989–, Pres Monetary Sub-Cttee, mem Cttee on External Econ Relations. *Publication:* Frauen im Süden 1995. *Leisure interests:* reading, writing, ballet. *Address:* European Parliament, rue Wiertz, 1047 Brussels, Belgium (Office); Alter Fischmarkt 11, 20457 Hamburg, Germany (Home). *Telephone:* (2) 284-21-11 (Office); (40) 249229 (Home); *Fax:* (2) 284-69-43 (Office); (40) 331744 (Home).

RANIA AL-ABDULLAH, Queen of Jordan, BBA; Jordanian royal; b Rania al-Yassin 31 Aug 1970, Kuwait; m Prince Abdallah of Jordan (now King Abdallah of Jordan) 1993; two d one s. *Education:* American Univ (Cairo). *Career:* Est support network for battered and abused children; f Jordan River Foundation (JRF) 1995; Pres Jordan Soc for Organ Donation; Head Jordan Blood Disease Society; Int Patron Osteoporosis Foundation; Dr hc (Exeter) 2001. *Leisure interests:* reading, water skiing, running, cycling, cooking. *Address:* Royal Palace, Amman, Jordan. *Internet:* www.kinghussein.gov.jo/queen_rania.

RANKAITIS, Susan, MFA; American artist and photographer; b 10 Sept 1949, Cambridge, MA; d of Alfred Edward and Isabel (née Shimkus) Rankaitis; m Robbert Flick 1976. *Education:* Univs of Illinois and Southern California. *Career:* Art instructor Orange Coast Coll, Costa Mesa, CA 1977–83; Chair Dept of Art Chapman Coll, Orange, CA 1983–90; Fletcher Jones Chair in Art Scripps Coll, Claremont, CA 1990; solo exhibitions include Los Angeles Co Museum of Art 1983, Int Museum of Photography—George Eastman House 1983, Meyers/Bloom Gallery (Santa Monica, CA) 1989, 1990, 1992, Gallery Min (Tokyo) 1988, Light Gallery (New York and Los Angeles), Schneider Museum 1990, Center for Creative Photography 1991, Museum of Contemporary Photography (Chicago, IL) 1994, Robert Mann Gallery (New York) 1994; works held in perm collections including Center for Creative Photography (Univ of California at Los Angeles), Los Angeles Co Museum of Art, San Francisco Museum of Modern Art, Museum of Modern Art (Łódź, Poland), Nat Museum of American Art (Washington, DC); Nat Endowment for the Arts Grantee 1980, 1988; US/France Fellowship 1989; Agnes Bourne Fellow, Djerassi Foundation 1989; Graves Award 1985. *Leisure interests:* gardening, politics. *Address:* Scripps College, Dept of Art, 1030 Columbia, Claremont, CA 91711, USA. *Telephone:* (909) 607-4439; *Fax:* (909) 626-7811.

RANKIN, Joanna Marie, PH D; American professor of astronomy; b 10 March 1942, Denver, CO; d of Robert McCordy Rankin and Julia Bernice Pelsor; partner Mary Fillmore. *Education:* Southern Methodist Univ, Tulane Univ of Louisiana and Univ of Iowa. *Career:* Research Assoc in Physics/Astronomy, Univ of Iowa 1970–74, in Earth/Planetary Sciences MIT 1973–74; mem Scientific Staff Arecibo Observatory, Puerto Rico 1970–78, Acting Head Computer Dept 1975; Asst Prof of Astronomy, Cornell Univ, NY 1974–78, Sr Research Assoc History Dept and Center for Radiophysics and Space Research 1978–80; Assoc Prof of Physics Univ of Vermont 1980–88, apptd Prof Physics Dept 1988; Visiting Scientist Raman Research Inst, Bangalore, India 1988, 1991,1994; organizer Int Astronomical Union Colloquium 128 on the Magnetospheric Structure and Emission Mechanism of Radio Pulsars, Lagow, Poland 1990; series of six papers entitled 'Toward an Empirical Theory of Pulsar Emission' published in the Astrophysical Journal 1983–92; NSF Grantee 1978, 1981, 1990–93, 1994; Van Allen–Link Fellow, Dept of Astronomy, Univ of Iowa 1968–70; Fulbright Fellow 1994; Finalist Kellogg Foundation Nat Fellowship 1982; Indo-US Fellow, CIES 1991. *Address:* University of Vermont, Physics Dept, A-405 Cook Bldg, Burlington, VT 05405, USA. *Telephone:* (802) 656-0051; *Fax:* (802) 656-0817.

RANKINE, Jean Morag, M PHIL; British museum executive; b 5 Sept 1941, Hinckley; d of the late Alan and of Margaret Mary S. (née Reid) Rankine; m N. A. Hall 1992. *Education:* Cen Newcastle High School, Univ Coll London and Univ of Copenhagen (Denmark). *Career:* Grad Asst Durham Univ Library 1966–67; Research Asst Dept of Printed Books, British Museum 1967–73, Asst Keeper Dir's Office 1973–78, Head of Public Services 1973–83, Deputy Dir 1983–97. *Leisure interests:* rowing, skiing, fell-walking, opera. *Address:* 49 Hartington Rd, London W4 3TS, UK. *Telephone:* (20) 8994-9854; *E-mail:* jean@rankine49.freeserve.co.uk.

RANNEY, Helen M., MD, SC D; American professor emeritus of medicine; b 12 April 1920, Summer Hill, New York; d of Arthur C. and Alesia (née Toolan) Ranney. *Education:* Barnard Coll and Columbia Univ. *Career:* Asst Prof of Clinical Medicine Columbia Univ 1958–60; Assoc Prof of Medicine Albert Einstein Coll of Medicine 1960–65, Prof 1965–70; Prof of Medicine State Univ of New York 1970–73; Prof of Medicine Dept of Medicine, Univ of California at San Diego 1973–90, Chair 1973–86, Prof Emer 1990–; Distinguished Physician, Dept of Veterans' Affairs Medical Center, San Diego, CA 1986–91; mem staff Alliance Pharmaceutical Corpn, San Diego 1991–; mem NAS, Asscn of American Physicians, American Acad of Arts and Sciences, American Soc for Clinical Investigation, Inst of Medicine; numerous papers on haemoglobin in medical journals; Asscn of American Physicians Kober Medal 1996. *Address:* c/o Alliance Pharmaceutical Corporation, 3040 Science Park Rd, San Diego, CA 92121, USA (Office); 6229 La Jolla Mesa Drive, La Jolla, CA 92037, USA (Home). *Telephone:* (858) 459-6768 (Home); *Fax:* (858) 459-6780 (Home); *E-mail:* hranney@ucsd .edu (Home).

RANTZEN, Esther Louise, OBE, MA; British TV presenter and producer; b 22 June 1940; d of Harry and Katherine Rantzen; m Desmond Wilcox 1977 (died 2000); two d one s. *Education:* N London Collegiate School and Somerville Coll (Oxford). *Career:* Studio Man (Sound Effects) BBC Radio 1963–65; joined BBC TV 1965, Researcher 1965, Dir 1967, Reporter Braden's Week 1968–72, Producer and Presenter That's Life 1973–94, Scriptwriter 1976–, Producer The Big Time 1976–78, Presenter Drugwatch 1985–86, Esther Interviews... 1988, Hearts of Gold 1988, Childwatch, Esther 1994–, The Rantzen Report 1996, Producer and Presenter The Lost Babies 1983–84, The Gift of Life 1988, Trouble in Mind 1989, Never Too Late 1995, reporter, producer and presenter of numerous documentaries and current affairs programmes; mem Nat Consumer Council 1981–90, Health Educ Authority 1989–95, Dept of Health Task Force to Review Services for Drug Misusers 1994–95; Chair Childline; Pres Asscn of Youth with ME 1996–; Pres Meet-a-Mum Asscn; Vice-Pres (jt) Asscn for Spina Bifida and Hydrocephalus, Health Visitors' Asscn, Nat Children's Soc, Rose Road Appeal; Patron Addenbrookes Kidney Patients' Asscn, Contact-a-Family, Downs Children's Asscn, DEMAND, Jewels for Children, Headway (Nat Head Injuries Asscn), Children's Head Injuries Trust, Hesley Foundation, South Wessex Addiction Centre, ADFAM (Nat Charity for Families and Friends of Drug Users), SIMR (Seriously Ill for Medical Research), John Grooms Asscn; Trustee Ben Hardwick Memorial Fund; Hon Pres ME Asscn Young People's Group; Hon mem NSPCC Council 1989; Fellow Royal TV Soc 1995; Hon D LITT (Southampton Inst for Further Educ) 1994; Royal TV Soc Personality of the Year 1974; BBC TV Personality of 1975, Variety Club of GB; Special Judges' Award for Journalism, Royal TV Soc 1986; Richard Dimbleby Award, BAFTA 1988; Snowdon Award for Services to Disabled People 1996; Royal TV Soc Hall of Fame Award 1998. *Publications:* Kill the Chocolate Biscuit (jtly) 1981, Baby Love 1985, Ben: The Story of Ben Hardwick (jtly) 1985, Once Upon a Christmas 1996, Esther: The Autobiography 2000. *Leisure interests:* family, countryside, pantomime, work and fantasy. *Address:* BBC TV White City, 201 Wood Lane, London W12 7RJ, UK; Billy Marsh Associates, 174–178 North Gower St, London NW1 2NB, UK. *Telephone:* (20) 8752-5252; (20) 7388-6858.

RAPACZYNSKI, Wanda, MA; Polish business executive; b 1948; m; one d. *Education:* Univ of New York and Yale Univ. *Career:* Researcher and Project Dir Yale Univ Family TV Research and Consultation Center until 1982; fmr Exec, Vice-Pres and Head of Project Devt Citibank (NY) until 1992; Pres and CEO Agora SA (media corpn) 1992–. *Address:* Gazeta Wyborcza, Agora SA, ul Czerska 8/10, 00-732 Warsaw, Poland.

RAPHAEL, Beverley, AM, BS, MD, FASSA, FRACP, FRCPSYCH; Australian psychiatrist; b 4 Oct 1934; d of G. Raphael; one d. *Education:* Casino High School and Univ of Sydney. *Career:* Resident Psychiatrist New S Wales Health Comm 1973–74; Assoc Prof Univ of Sydney Repatriation Gen Hosp, Concord 1975–78; Foundation Prof of Psychiatry Faculty of Medicine, Univ of Newcastle 1978–87; Consultant in Psychiatric Aspects of Disaster, Australia and New S Wales Govts 1979; WHO Consultant in Psychiatric Educ, People's Repub of China 1984; Chair Dept of Psychiatry, Univ of Queensland, Dir Div of Psychiatry, Royal Brisbane Hosp and Dir Nat Centre for HIV Social Research 1990–94; Dir Centre for Mental Health, NSW Health Dept 1996–; Adjunct Prof Dept of Psychological Medicine, Univ of Sydney 1996–; Chair Mental Health Care Cttee, Nat Health and Medical Research Council 1981–93; Hon Consultant Psychiatrist Royal Prince Alfred Hosp 1978; Assoc Fellow American Psychiatric Asscn; Pres Nat Asscn for Loss and Grief 1977–81, Royal Australia and New Zealand Coll of Psychiatrists 1983–85; mem Nat Mental Health Working Party for AHMAC, Exec Health Care Cttee, Accreditation Cttee, New York Acad of Sciences. *Publications:* Anatomy of Bereavement 1983, When Disaster Strikes 1986, International Handbook of Traumatic Stress Studies (co-ed) 1990, Handbook of Preventive Psychiatry 1994, Psychological Debriefing (co-ed) 2000. *Leisure interests:* swimming, walking, reading, films. *Address:* Centre for Mental Health, NSW Health Dept, Locked Mail Bag 961, N Sydney, NSW 2059, Australia.

RAS, Eva Marija Balassa Wagner Stević; Hungarian actress, writer and painter; b 1 Jan 1941, Subotica; m Radomir Stević Ras 1963 (died 1982); one d (died 1993). *Education:* Gimnazija 'Moša Pijade' (Subotica) and Faculty of Dramatic Arts (Belgrade). *Career:* Actress since 1960s; Co-Founder (with husband) of Nat Theatre Drama 1964–72; mem Ljubiša Ristić's Troupe; solo and group exhibitions of paintings in Yugoslavia, Hungary, Germany, Canada, Cyprus etc; Chair Serbian Naive Artists' Asscn. *Plays include:* Der Shut 1964, Der Schatz der Azteken, Man is Not a Bird, The Switchboard Operator 1967, It rains in my Village 1969, Beasts 1976, Beauty of Evil 1986, Father is Away on Business 1986, Gorilla is Bathing at Noon 1993; has acted in seven Hungarian films; *Publications:* Novels: Don't Crow After Me on the Stairs that I am the Nicest 1971, The Grey Lady, When my Mum buys me Money, A Yellow Quince; also poetry for children, plays, film and TV scripts. *Address:* Belgrade, Sindjelićeva 36, Yugoslavia. *Telephone:* (11) 432590; *Fax:* (11) 553070.

RASHID, Salma Ahmed; Libyan diplomatist. *Career:* Secretary of Women's Affairs 1994–95; Amb to the League of Arab States (Arab League, first woman) 1996. *Address:* c/o League of Arab States, Arab League Bldg, Tahrir Square, Cairo, Egypt. *Telephone:* (2) 5750511; *Fax:* (2) 5775626.

RASMUSON, Marianne T., PH D; Swedish geneticist; b 2 Oct 1921; d of Rütger Essén and Ingeborg Nordström; m Bertil Rasmuson 1945; four s two d. *Education:* Stockholm Univ. *Career:* Asst Prof of Genetics Uppsala Univ 1955–59; Asst Prof of Genetics Umeå Univ 1969–79, Prof 1979–87, Prof Emer 1987–; mem Royal Swedish Acad of Sciences 1980. *Publications:* Genetics at the Population Level 1961, Genetics from Darwin to DNA 1988, Evolution 1997, Född att tänka 2000, Från vaggan till graven 2000; numerous articles on biology. *Leisure interests:* outdoor life, reading fiction and scientific publications. *Address:* Umeå Universitet, Inst of Genetics, 901 87 Umeå, Sweden (Office); Nydalavägen 22b, 903 39 Umeå, Sweden (Home). *Telephone:* (90) 786 5554 (Office); *Fax:* (90) 167 665 (Office); *E-mail:* rasmuson@telia.com.

RASTOLL, Frédérique Marie-Claude; French organization executive; b 13 Jan 1953, Vialar, Algeria; d of Antoine and Renée (née Eck) Rastoll; one d. *Education:* Lycée Jean Perrin (Lyons). *Career:* Primary school teacher 1974; Admin, Treas Maison des jeunes et de la culture, Briey 1981; Pres Hautes-Alpes Union of Confédération Générale du Logement (CGL) 1983, Confed Sec 1983–, Nat Sec 1989–; fmr Nat Pres CGL; now Tech Adviser Sec of State for Housing. *Leisure interests:* films, reading, ju-jitsu. *Address:* Secrétariat d'Etat au Logement, 3 place de Fontenoy, 75700 Paris, France (Office); Bâtiment A2, 1 rue Pottier, 78150 Le Chesnay, France (Home).

RASUL, Santanina Tillah, BA, MPA; Philippine politician; b 4 Sept 1930, Siasi, Sulu; m Abraham Abubakar. *Education:* Sulu High School, Univ of the Philippines and Nat Defence Coll of the Philippines. *Career:* Elected Barrio Councillor 1960–61, 1962–63; Special Consultant Nat Econ Council 1966–67; mem Prov Bd of Sulu 1971–76; studied rural devt Saudi Arabia and Egypt 1973; Chair Cttee and Political Subcttee Mindanao Exec Devt Acad 1975; Head Dept of Political Science, Nat Defence Coll of the Philippines 1976–78; Head of Del Int Seminar on Muslim Women, Morocco 1977; Resource Person Review of Proposed Local Govt Code 1973, Nat Comm on role of Filipino Women 1978–85, World Bank Seminar on Women's Involvement, Washington,

DC 1983; Del UNESCO Regional Literacy Workshop, India 1979; Alt Del UN World Conf on Women 1980; Chair Nat Women's Congress 1981–85; Head of Del SE Asia and Pacific Regional Conf on Muslim Women in Devt 1983; mem Philippine Comm of UNESCO 1986; Dir project on adult literacy, Ministry of Educ, Culture and Sports 1986; apptd Senator 1987, Chair Cttees on Civil Service and Govt Reorganization, on Women and Family Relations, Subcttee on Peace; mem Del Int Conf on Worldwide Educ for Women, USA 1987, ILO Conf, Geneva, Switzerland 1988; Founder first family planning clinic, Jolo; Nat Pres Muslim Professional and Business Women Asscn of the Philippines; mem Bd of Dirs Philippine Foundation for Rehabilitation of the Disabled 1978–79, Film and TV Review Bd 1982–85; numerous articles for newspapers and journals; numerous awards including Most Useful Citizen Award, Women's Univ 1977, Tandano Sora Award for Govt and Community Service 1981, UNESCO Award of Merit 1983, Outstanding Muslim Women Leader, Mindanao Information Network 1985, UNESCO Nesim Habif Award, Family Unit and Individual Achievements Award, Civic Ass of Women of the Philippines 1988. *Address:* Congress of the Philippines - Senate, Batasang Pambansa Bldg, Quezon City, Manila, Philippines (Office); 155 Lopez Rizal St, Mandakiyong, Metro Manila, Philippines (Home).

RATEB M. SOAD, Aisha, PH D; Egyptian diplomatist and professor of law; b 22 Feb 1928, Cairo; d of Mohamed Soad Rateb; m 1953 (separated); two s. *Education:* Cairo and Paris (France). *Career:* Minister of Social Affairs and Social Insurance 1971–77; Amb to Denmark 1979, to Fed Repub of Germany 1981; Amb Ministry of Foreign Affairs; currently Prof of Int Law, Univ of Cairo; numerous awards and distinctions. *Publications:* Principles of International Law, International Organizations, Neutrality, International Arab Relations, Some Legal Aspects of the Arab-Israeli Conflict, Legal Studies, etc. *Address:* Faculty of Law, University of Cairo, POB 12611, Orman, Giza, Cairo, Egypt; 6 Ibn Malek Street, Giza, Cairo, Egypt.

RATTE, Evelyne Isabelle Alice; French civil servant and magistrate; b 15 March 1951, Lyons; d of Jacques and Simone (née Tinel) Chalaye; m Philippe Ratte 1977; three s one d. *Education:* Lycée Simone Weil (Le Puy), Lycées Victor Duruy and Fénelon (Paris), Univ of Paris I (Panthéon-Sorbonne), Inst d'Etudes Politiques de Paris and Ecole Nat d'Admin (Paris). *Career:* Civil Servant Ministry of the Economy, Finance and the Budget 1979–83; Financial Attaché Embassy of France to fmr FRG 1983–85; Office Chief Budget Dept, Ministry of the Economy, Finance and the Budget 1985–86; Cabinet Dir to Minister Del to the Prime Minister for the Civil Service and Planning 1986–88; Public Auditor Cour des Comptes 1988–93; Dir Cabinet of Minister of Housing 1993–95; Rep to Ministry of Foreign Affairs 1995–96; Finance Dir Assistance Publique–Hôpitaux de Paris 1996–; mem Comm for Consumer Protection 1991–. *Address:* 17 ave de Breteuil, 75007 Paris, France (Office).

RATUSHINSKAYA, Irina Borisovna; Russian poet and writer; b 4 March 1954; d of Boris Ratushinski and Irina Ratushinskaya; m Igor Gerashchenko 1979; two s. *Education:* Odessa Pedagogical Inst. *Career:* Physics teacher, Odessa and Kiev 1975–82; arrested for poetry-writing 1982, convicted of 'subverting the Soviet régime' and sentenced March 1983 to seven years' hard labour and five years' internal exile, in prison and labour camp 1982–86, released Oct 1986; settled in UK 1986–, stripped of Soviet citizenship 1987; Visiting Scholar Northwestern Univ, IL, USA 1987–88; formed Democracy and Independence Group 1989–; Poetry Int Rotterdam Award (Netherlands) 1986; Ross McWhirter Foundation Award (UK) 1987; Christopher Award (USA) 1988. *Publications include:* Poetry: Poems (trilingual text) 1984, No, I'm Not Afraid 1986, Off Limits (in Russian) 1986, I Shall Live to See It (in Russian) 1986, Beyond the Limit 1987, Aan Allen 1987, Pencil Letter 1988; Non-fiction: Grey Is the Colour of Hope 1988, In the Beginning 1990, The Odessans 1996, Fictions and Lies 1998; poetry appeared in samizdat publs, W European Russian language journals, translations in American and British press and in USSR 1989. *Leisure interests:* drawing, swimming, travel. *Address:* c/o Vargius Publishing House, Kazakova str 18, 107005 Moscow, Russian Federation. *Telephone:* (095) 785-09-62.

RAU, Santha Rama (see Rama Rau, Santha).

RAVITCH, Diane S., PH D; American historian and civil servant; b 1 July 1938, Houston, TX; d of Walter Cracker and Ann Celia (née Katz) Silvers; m Richard Ravitch 1960 (divorced 1986); three s (one s deceased). *Education:* Wellesley Coll (MA) and Columbia Univ (NY). *Career:* Asst Prof of History and Educ Teachers' Coll, Columbia Univ, NY 1975–78, Assoc Prof 1978–83, Adjunct Prof 1983–91; Counsellor to the Sec, US Dept of Educ; Dir Woodrow Wilson Nat Fellowship Foundation 1987–91; Chair Educational Excellence Network, Washington, DC 1988–91; Adviser to Teachers' Solidarity and Ministry of Educ, Poland 1989; Asst Sec Office of Research and Improvement Dept of Educ, Washington 1991–93, Counsellor to Sec of Educ 1991–93; Visiting Fellow Brookings Inst 1993–94; Sr Research Scholar New York Univ 1994–, Brown Chair in Educ Policy 1997–; Sr Research Scholar NY Univ 1994–98, Research Prof 1998–; Sr Fellow Progressive Policy Inst 1998–; Adjunct Fellow Manhattan Inst 1996–; Trustee New York Historical Soc 1995–98; New York Council on the Humanities 1996–; numerous lectures abroad; mem PEN Int, Nat Acad of Educ 1979, American Acad of Arts and Sciences 1985 and numerous public policy bodies; Guggenheim Fellow; Hon D HUM LITT (Williams Coll) 1984, (Reed Coll) 1985, (Amherst Coll) 1986, (State Univ of New York) 1988, (Ramopo Coll) 1990, (St Joseph's Coll, NY) 1991; Hon LHD (Middlebury Coll) 1997, (Union Coll) 1998; Hon Citizen of California; Henry Allen Moe Prize in the Humanities, American Philosophical Soc 1986; Medal of Distinction, Polish Govt 1991. *Publications:* The Great School Wars: New York City 1805–1973 1974, The Revisionists Revised 1978, The Troubled Crusade: American Education 1945–1980 1983, The Schools We Deserve 1985, What Do Our 17-Year-Olds Know? (jtly) 1987, The American Reader (ed) 1990, The Democracy Reader (ed, jtly) 1992, National Standards in American Education 1995, Debating the Future of American Education (ed) 1995, Learning from the Past (ed, jtly) 1995, New Schools for a New Century (co-ed) 1997, Left Back 2000, City Schools (ed) 2000; 300 articles and reviews. *Leisure interest:* gardening. *Address:* New York University, 26 Washington Place, New York, NY 10003, USA. *Telephone:* (212) 998-5146.

RAWSON, Jessica Mary, CBE, BA, FBA; British college warden, museum curator and writer; b 20 Jan 1943; d of Roger Nathaniel and Paula Quirk; m John Rawson 1968; one d. *Education:* New Hall (Cambridge) and Univ of London. *Career:* Asst Prin Ministry of Health 1965–67; Second Asst Keeper Dept of Oriental Antiquities, British Museum 1967–71, First Asst Keeper 1971–76, Deputy Keeper 1976–87, Keeper 1987–94; Warden Merton Coll, Oxford 1994–; Visiting Prof Kunsthistorisches Inst, Heidelberg, Germany 1989, Dept of Art, Univ of Chicago, IL, USA 1994; has given numerous lectures including Levintvitt Memorial Lecture, Harvard Univ, USA 1989, A. J. Pope Lecture, Smithsonian Inst, USA 1991, Harvey Buchanan Lecture, Cleveland Museum of Art, USA 1993; Chair Oriental Ceramic Soc 1993–96; Vice-Chair Exec Cttee, GB–China Centre 1985–87, Bd of Govs SOAS, Univ of London 1999–; mem British Library Bd 1999; Hon D SC (St Andrews) 1997; Hon D LITT (Cambridge) 1991, (Sussex) 1998, (Royal Holloway, London) 1998, (Newcastle) 1999. *Publications:* Chinese Jade Throughout the Ages (jtly) 1975, Animals in Art 1977, Ancient China, Art and Archaeology 1980, Chinese Ornament: the lotus and the dragon 1984, Chinese Bronzes: art and ritual 1987, The Bella and P. P. Chiu Collection of Ancient Chinese Bronzes 1988, Western Zhou Ritual Bronzes from the Arthur M. Sackler Collections 1990, Ancient Chinese and Ordos Bronzes (jtly) 1990, The British Museum Book of Chinese Art (ed) 1992, Chinese Jade from the Neolithic to the Qing 1995, The Mysteries of Ancient China (ed) 1996. *Leisure interest:* fell-walking. *Address:* Merton College, Oxford OX1 4JD, UK. *Telephone:* (1865) 276352; *Fax:* (1865) 276282; *E-mail:* wardensoffice@admin.merton.ox .ac.uk.

RAWSTHORN, Alice, MA; British museum director; b 15 Nov 1958, Manchester; d of Peter Rawsthorn and Joan Schofield. *Education:* Clare Coll (Cambridge). *Career:* Journalist Financial Times 1985–2001; Trustee Design Museum 1992–2001, Dir 2001–; Trustee Whitechapel Art Gallery 1996–; Judge Turner Prize for Contemporary Art 1999. *Publications:* Yves St Laurent: A Biography 1996, Marc Newson 2000. *Leisure interests:* art, architecture, design, film, music, books, fashion. *Address:* Design Museum, Shad Thames, London SE1 2YD, UK. *Telephone:* (20) 7940-8778; *Fax:* (20) 7378-6540; *E-mail:* director@ designmuseum.org.uk; *Internet:* www.designmuseum.org.uk.

RAYET, Jacqueline; French ballet dancer and teacher; b 26 June 1933, Paris; d of René and Yvonne (née Jager-Fougerouze) Rayet; m Pierre Heuline 1966. *Education:* Ecole de Danse de l'Opéra de Paris. *Career:* Began dancing career in Second Quadrille, Opéra de Paris 1946, Soloist 1951, Prin Dancer 1956, Danseuse Etoile 1960, debut as Prima Ballerina 1961, Ballet Mistress 1979–80, Visiting Prof 1985–; Founder and organizer Les Nuits de Ballets, Festival de Brantôme 1958–; f Les Cadets du Ballet de l'Opéra de Paris 1976; toured S America, USSR, USA, Belgium, Hungary, Japan, SA; ballet performances in Hamburg (Germany), Geneva (Switzerland), Granada (Spain), Rome and Florence (Italy); Ballet Mistress and teacher Ballet du XXème Siècle Maurice Béjart 1980–81; teacher and Prof La Scala, Milan, Italy 1985–86; teacher Conservatoire Nat Supérieur de Musique et de Danse, Paris 1986–99; Visiting Prof Bulgaria, Japan, etc; mem int juries in Paris, Moscow, Lausanne (Switzerland) and Tokyo; Chevalier des Arts et des Lettres 1967; Chevalier de la Légion d'Honneur 1973. *Ballets include:* Giselle 1961, Swan Lake, Le sacre du printemps, Formes, Nutcracker, La bourrée fantasque, Blanche-Neige, Symphonie inachevée, Romeo and Juliet, Pelléas et Mélisande, La nuit transfigurée, Boléro, Formes, Les sept péchés capitaux, Pas de deux, Delta T 1971, Solo 1972, Slow, Heavy and Blue, La plus que lente 1977, La Dame de Pique 1979. *Address:* Vallon Saint-Martin, 13520 Les Baux-de-Provence, France.

RAYNER, Claire Berenice, OBE; British writer and broadcaster; b 22 Jan 1931, London; m Desmond Rayner 1957; two s one d. *Education:* Royal Northern and Guy's Hosps (London). *Career:* Nurse and midwife until 1960; writer advice columns in Petticoat, The Sun, The Sunday Mirror 1980–88, Today newspaper, Woman's Own 1966–88, Woman magazine 1988–92; has made numerous radio broadcasts for BBC, LBC radio and Capital Radio (London); many TV appearances including Pebble Mill at One, Kitchen Garden (co-presenter), Claire Rayner's Casebook 1980, 1983, 1984, BBC Breakfast TV, TV-AM Advice Spot 1985, A Problem Shared (British Sky Broadcasting TV), The David Frost Programme; has produced In Company with Claire Rayner, women's health and family life videos; Pres Gingerbread, The Patient's Asscn, British Humanist Asscn 1999–; fmr mem Royal Coll of Nursing Cttee on Ethics; mem Video Appeals Cttee British Bd of Film Classification, Council Charter 88, Royal Comm on Funding of Care of the Elderly 1998–99; Assoc Non-Exec Dir Royal London Hosps Trust (Barts and the London); Patron the Terrence Higgins Trust; Hon Fellow Univ of N London; Freeman City of London 1981; Medical Journalist of the Year 1987; Best Specialist Columnist of the Year, Publisher Magazine 1988. *Publications include:* Fiction: The Hive 1967, The Meddlers 1970, A Time to Heal 1972, The Performers (12 vol saga) 1973–1986, Reprise 1980, Family Chorus 1984, The Virus Man 1985, Maddie 1988, The Poppy Chronicles (8 vols) 1987–, Omnibus of Three Hospital Novels (reprint, as Sheila Brandon) 1989, Postscripts 1991, Dangerous Things 1992, The Barnabus crime novels 1993, 1994, 1995, 1996; Non-Fiction: For Children 1967, Mothercraft (as Ann Lynton) 1967, Woman's Medical Dictionary 1971, Kitchen Garden (jtly) 1976, Related to Sex 1979, Claire Rayner's Lifeguide 1980, Baby and Young Child Care 1981, Growing Pains 1984, The Getting Better Book 1985, Safe Sex 1987, The Don't Spoil Your Body Book 1989; books published in many countries; contribs to Design magazine (journal of the Design Council), nat newspapers, professional medical journals. *Leisure interests:* talking, cooking, theatre, giving parties. *Address:* Holly Wood House, Roxborough Ave, Harrow-on-the-Hill, Middx HA1 3BU, UK. *Telephone:* (20) 8864-9898; *Fax:* (20) 8422-3710; *E-mail:* clairerayner@ harrowhill.demon.co.

RÁZLOVÁ, Regina; Czech actress, teacher and director; b 16 July 1947, Brno; d of Stanislav Rázl; divorced 1977; one s one d. *Education:* Film Coll (Čimelice), Drama and Film Schools of Acad of Arts (Prague). *Career:* Actress Theatre Kladno 1969–73; mem various theatres, Barrandov Film Studio, Prague 1973–80; teacher Acad of Arts, Prague 1973; mem Nat Theatre of Prague 1980; several awards for theatre and film work. *Films include:* Utrpení mladého Boháčka 1969, Tatínek na neděli 1971, Lucie a zázraky 1971. *Leisure interests:* arts, psychology, pedagogy, alternative medicine, sport. *Address:* Slunečná 25, 100 00 Prague 10, Czech Republic. *Telephone:* (2) 779588; *Fax:* (2) 779588.

READ, Imelda Mary (Mel), BA; British politician; b 8 Jan 1939, Hillingdon; d of the late Robert Alan and of Teresa Mary Hocking; m Michael Teague 1991; one s one d one step-s. *Education:* Bishops Halt School (Hillingdon) and Univ of Nottingham. *Career:* Lab technician, Plessey Telecommunications 1964–74; Researcher and teacher 1977–84; Employment Officer Nottingham Community Relations Council 1984–89; MEP (EPP, Lab) for Leicester 1989, for Nottingham and Leicestershire NW 1994–99, for E Midlands 1999–, mem Cttees on Trade, Industry and Research 1999–, sub-mem Cttee on Legal Affairs 1999–, Pres EU/US Del 1999–; Chair British Labour Group 1990–92; mem Women's Advisory Cttee, TUC. *Publication:* Against a Rising Tide 1990. *Leisure interests:* bee-keeping, gardening. *Address:* European Parliament, rue Wiertz, 1047 Brussels, Belgium (Office); The Marlene Reid Centre, 85 Belvoir Rd, Coalville, Leics, LE67 3PH, UK. *Telephone:* (2) 284-55-11 (Brussels); (1530) 830780 (UK); *Fax:* (2) 284-95-11 (Brussels); (1530) 830781 (UK); *E-mail:* readm@labmeps-emids.fsnet .co.uk; *Internet:* www.labmeps-emids.fsnet.co.uk.

REAGAN, Nancy Davis (Anne Francis Robbins), BA; American former First Lady; b 6 July 1923, New York; d of Kenneth and Edith (née Luckett) Robbins, step-d of Loyal Davis; m Ronald Reagan 1952; one s one d, one step-s one step-d. *Education:* Smith Coll (MA). *Career:* Actress Metro-Goldwyn-Mayer 1949–56; fmr author syndicated column on prisoners-of-war and soldiers missing in action; civic worker active on behalf of Vietnam War veterans, sr citizens, disabled children and drugs victims; mem Bd of Dirs Revlon Group Inc 1989–; Hon Nat Chair Aid to Adoption of Special Kids 1977; one of Ten Most Admired American Women, Good Housekeeping Magazine 1977; Woman of the Year, LA Times 1977; perm mem Hall of Fame of Ten Best Dressed Women in US; Lifetime Achievement Award, Council of Fashion Designers of USA 1988. *Films include:* The Next Voice You Hear 1950, Donovan's Brain 1953, Hellcats of the Navy 1957; *Publications:* Nancy 1980, To Love A Child (jtly), My Turn 1989. *Address:* 2121 Ave of the Stars, 34th Floor, Los Angeles, CA 90067, USA.

REARDON, Katherine (Kate) Genevieve; British fashion editor; b 20 Nov 1968, New York, USA; d of P. W. J. Reardon and J. H. A. Wood. *Education:* Cheltenham Ladies' Coll and Stowe School (Buckingham). *Career:* Worked at American Vogue, New York 1988–90; apptd Fashion Ed Tatler Magazine, London 1990, later Fashion Dir. *Leisure interests:* riding, music. *Address:* Tatler Magazine, Vogue House, 1 Hanover Square, London W1, UK. *Telephone:* (20) 7499-9080; *Fax:* (20) 7409-0451.

REBÉRIOUX, Madeleine, D ÈS L; French historian and human rights activist; b 8 Sept 1920, Chambéry; d of Pierre and Elise (née Thonon) Amoudruz; m Jean Rebérioux 1946; three s one d. *Education:* Lycées (Lyons and Clermont-Ferrand), Ecole Normale Supérieure de Sèvres and Univ of Paris (Sorbonne). *Career:* Teacher 1945–61; Asst then Sr Lecturer Sorbonne 1962–69; Sr Lecturer, then Prof Univ of Paris VIII–Vincennes à St-Denis 1969–88, Prof Emer 1988–; Sr Lecturer Ecole des Hautes Etudes en Sciences Sociales, Paris 1978–; Vice-Pres Musée d'Orsay 1981–87; Head CNRS research group (Greco 55) on work and workers in 19th- and 20th-century France; Dir Le mouvement social, journal 1971–82; Pres Soc d'études jaurésiennes 1981–, Asscn française pour les célébrations nationales 1982–86; mem Cen Cttee Ligue des Droits de l'Homme et du Citoyen 1962–, Pres 1991–95, Hon Pres 1995Ý; anti-war activist during Vietnam and Indo-China campaigns. *Publications:* Les idées de Proudhon en politique étrangère, La République radicale 1898–1914, La deuxième internationale et l'Orient, Jaurès et la classe ouvrière, Les ouvriers du livre et leur fédération, Ils ont pensé nos droits, L'extrême droite en questions 1991, Jaurès 1994, Parcours engagé dans la France contemporaine 1999. *Address:* 104 blvd Arago, 75014 Paris, France (Home).

REBEYROL, Yvonne Colette, L ÈS L; French journalist and geographer; b 29 June 1928, Rouen. *Education:* Univ of Paris and Clark Univ (MA, USA). *Career:* Cartographer Le Monde 1951, Scientific Ed specializing in earth and archaeological sciences 1956–93; Officier de l'Ordre Nat du Mérite 1979; Silver Medal for Protection of Nature 1964; Silver Medal Soc for Geography 1965; Prix de l'Information Scientifique, Acad of Sciences 1990. *Publications:* Lucy et les siens, chroniques préhistoriques 1988, La Terre toujours recommencée, ou Trente ans de progrès dans les sciences de la terre 1990, Tourbillons et turbulences, la machine des climats 1990. *Leisure interests:* travel, photography. *Address:* 31 rue Gazan, 75014 Paris, France. *Telephone:* (1) 45-88-55-04.

REBOUL, Jacquette Suzanne Danièle, PH D; French librarian and writer; b 5 Dec 1937, Valence; d of Paul and Camille (née Marchal) Reboul. *Education:* Lycée de Jeunes Filles (Valence), Univ of Paris (Sorbonne) and Ecole Nat Supérieure de Bibliothécaires. *Career:* Librarian Univ of Rennes Library 1966–70; Librarian Library of the Sorbonne 1970–85, Chief Librarian 1986–98; retd; Chevalier de la Légion d'Honneur; Officier des Palmes Académiques; Prix Louis Guillaume for poetry. *Publications:* Le lever de l'aurore 1969, Le vieux Roi 1972, A l'intérieur de la vue 1973, Du bon usage des bibliographies 1973, La nuit scintille 1975, L'apprentie sorcière (Prix Louis Guillaume) 1982, Les cathédrales du savoir ou les bibliothèques universitaires de recherche aux Etats-Unis 1982, La liberté pour l'ombre 1985, Face à face 1986, Critique universitaire et critique créatrice 1986, L'œil du monde 1990, Raison ardente 1992, Cristal 1996, Psyché 2001. *Leisure interests:* music, travel in Europe, Africa, America and the Far East. *Address:* c/o La Maison des Ecrivains, 53 rue de Vaneuil, 75007 Paris, France. *E-mail:* courrier@maison-des-ecrivains.asso.fr (Office); reboulj@noos.fr (Home).

REBUCK, Gail, CBE, BA, FRSA; British publishing executive; b 10 Feb 1952, London; d of Gordon and Mavis Rebuck; m Philip Gould 1985; two d. *Education:* Lycée Français (London) and Univ of Sussex. *Career:* Production Asst Grieswood and Dempsey 1975–76; Ed, then Publr Robert Nicholson Guide Books, Barrie and Jenkin 1976–78; Non-Fiction Publr Hamlyn 1978–82; Co-Founder and Dir Century Publishing 1982–85; Publr Century Hutchinson 1985–89; Chair Random House Div, Random Century 1989–91, Chair and Chief Exec The Random House Group Ltd 1991–; Co-Founder Women in Man in Publishing; mem Cttee on the Public Understanding of Science 1995–97; Creative Industries Task Force 1997–; Trustee Inst for Public Policy Research 1993–; finalist 1991 Veuve Clicquot Business Woman of the Year. *Leisure interests:* reading, travel. *Address:* The Random House Group, 20 Vauxhall Bridge Rd, London SW1V 2SA, UK. *Telephone:* (20) 7840-8888; *Fax:* (20) 7233-6120; *E-mail:* grebuck@randomhouse.co.uk.

REDDY, Katakam Radha; Indian classical dancer; b 15 Feb 1950, Kotalgaon, AP; d of Enugu Raja Reddy and Venkat Laxmi; m Raja Reddy 1964; two d. *Education:* Limba Khurd and Kala Kshetram Kuchipudi Dance Inst (Eluru). *Career:* Came to Delhi to learn choreography (Govt of Andhra Pradesh Scholarship) 1966; performances of Kuchipudi Indian classical dance world-wide in partnership with husband Raja Reddy; Dir Natya Tarangini Kuchipudi Dance Inst; first Indian dancer to participate in Int Dance Festival, Avignon (France) 1974; subject of Indian and German documentary films, along with Raja Reddy; State Govt Award for Excellence in Kuchipudi Dance 1982; Govt of India Padmashree Award 1984; Sangeet Nataka Acad Award 1992. *Films include:* Vishwamitra. *Leisure interests:* interior decoration, cooking. *Address:* DII/57, Kaka Nagar, New Delhi 110 003, India. *Telephone:* (11) 4636630; *Fax:* (11) 4636640.

REDEL, Donna; American finance executive; b 1953; d of Irving Redel. *Career:* Exec Vice-Pres Redel Trading co; mem Bd New York Commodity Exchange (Comex), apptd Chair 1992; fmr Chief Information and Tech Officer, Prudential Securities Int; Head Centre for Global Industries, World Econ Forum (WEF) 2000–, Man Dir WEF 2001–. *Address:* World Economic Forum, 91–93 route de la capitale, 1223 Cologny/Geneva, Switzerland. *Telephone:* (22) 8691212; *Fax:* (22) 7862744; *Internet:* www.weforum.org.

REDGRAVE, Lynn; British actress; b 8 March 1943, London; d of the late Sir Michael Redgrave and Rachel Kempson; sister of Vanessa Redgrave (qv); m John Clark 1967; two d one s. *Education:* Queensgate School (London) and Cen School of Speech and Drama (London). *Career:* Numerous appearances on TV, in films and plays in UK and USA; performed at American Shakespeare Festival; actress Nat Theatre 1963–66; Presenter Fighting Back TV Show. *Plays include:* Black Comedy, My Fat Friend 1974, Mrs Warren's Profession, Knock Knock, Misalliance, St Joan, Twelfth Night (American Shakespeare Festival), Sister Mary Ignatius Explains It All for You, Aren't We All?, Sweet Sue, Les Liaisons Dangereuses, Three Sisters 1990, Shakespeare for My Father (one-woman show) 1993, Moon over Buffalo 1996; *Films include:* Tom Jones, Girl With Green Eyes, Georgy Girl (New York Critics' Award, Golden Globe Award and IFIDA Award), The Deadly Affair,

Smashing Time, The Virgin Soldiers, The Last of the Mobile Hot-Shots, Viva La Muerta Tua, Every Little Crook and Nanny, Everything You Have Always Wanted to Know About Sex, Don't Turn the Other Cheek, The National Health, The Happy Hooker, The Big Bus, Sunday Lovers, Home Front, Morgan Stewart's Coming Home, Midnight, Getting It Right, Shine, Gods and Monsters, Strike, The Simian Line, Touched, The Annihilation of Fish; *TV appearances include:* Whatever Happened to Baby Jane 1990. *Leisure interests:* cooking, gardening, horse riding. *Address:* c/o John Clark, POB 1207, Topanga, CA 90290, USA. *Telephone:* (310) 455-1334; *Fax:* (310) 455-1032.

REDGRAVE, Vanessa, CBE; British actress; b 30 Jan 1937; d of the late Sir Michael Redgrave and Rachel Kempson; sister of Lynn Redgrave (qv); m Tony Richardson 1962 (divorced 1967, died 1991); two d (Natasha Richardson and Joely Richardson, qqv) one s by Franco Reio. *Education:* Queensgate School (London), Ballet Rambert School and Cen School of Speech and Drama (London). *Career:* Co-Founder Moving Theatre 1974; mem Workers' Revolutionary Party (Cand for Moss Side 1979); Fellow BFI 1988; Dr hc (MA) 1990; London Evening Standard Award for Best Actress 1961; Variety Club Award 1961; Laurence Olivier Award 1984; Commdr des Arts et des Lettres 2001. *Plays include:* A Midsummer Night's Dream 1959, The Taming of the Shrew 1961, As You Like It 1961, Cymbeline 1962, The Seagull 1964, 1985, The Prime of Miss Jean Brodie 1966, Cato Street 1971, Threepenny Opera 1972, Twelfth Night 1972, Antony and Cleopatra 1973, 1986, Design for Living 1973, Macbeth 1975, Lady from the Sea 1976, 1979, The Aspern Papers 1984, Ghosts 1986, The Taming of the Shrew 1986, A Man for all Seasons 1988, A Touch of the Poet 1988, Orpheus Descending 1988, A Madhouse in Goa 1989, Three Sisters 1990, Lettice and Lovage 1991, When She Danced (Evening Standard Award for Best Actress) 1991, Heartbreak Hotel 1992, Maybe 1993, The Flag 1994, Brecht in Hollywood 1994, Vita and Virginia 1994, The Liberation of Skopje 1995, Antony and Cleopatra 1995, 1996, Julius Caesar 1996, John Gabriel Borkman 1996, Song at Twilight 1999, The Tempest 2000; *Films include:* Morgan – A Suitable Case for Treatment (Award for Best Actress, Cannes Film Festival 1966) 1965, A Man for all Seasons 1966, Camelot 1967, Blow Up 1967, Charge of the Light Brigade 1968, Isadora Duncan (Award for Leading Actress, US Nat Soc of Film Critics and Best Actress Award, Film Critics' Guild) 1968, The Seagull 1968, A Quiet Place in the Country 1968, The Trojan Women 1970, The Devils 1970, Mary Queen of Scots 1971, Murder on the Orient Express 1974, Julia (Acad Award for Best Supporting Actress 1978) 1977, Agatha 1978, Yanks 1978, Bear Island 1979, Wagner 1982, The Bostonians 1983, Prick Up Your Ears 1987, Comrades 1987, Consuming Passions 1988, Diceria dell'intore 1989, Young Catherine (ACE Award for Best Supporting Actress 1992) 1990, The Ballad of the Sad Cafe 1991, Howards End (Acad Award nomination) 1991, Mother's Boys 1993, The House of the Spirits 1993, Crime and Punishment 1993, They 1993, A Month by the Lake 1994, Little Odessa 1994, Mission Impossible 1995, Wind in the Willows (voice), The Willows in Winter (voice), Smilla's Sense of Snow 1996, Mrs Dalloway 1998, Deep Impact 1998, Cradle Will Rock 2000; produced and narrated documentary film The Palestinians 1977; *TV appearances include:* Katherine Mansfield (BBC) 1973, Playing for Time (CBS, Best Actress Award 1981) 1979, My Body My Child (ABC) 1981, Whatever Happened to Baby Jane 1990, Great Moments in Aviation 1993, For the Love of Tyler 1996; *Publications:* Pussies and Tigers 1963, An Autobiography 1991. *Leisure interest:* changing the status quo. *Address:* c/o Gavin Barker Associates, 45 S Molton St, London W1Y 1HD, UK. *Telephone:* (20) 7434-3801; *Fax:* (20) 7494-1547.

RÉDING, Viviane, PH D; Luxembourg politician; b 27 April 1951, Esch-sur-Alzette, Luxembourg m Dimitris Zois 1981; three s. *Education:* Univ of Paris. *Career:* Journalist and Ed Luxemburger Wort 1978–99; mem Luxembourg Parl 1979–89, Pres Social Cttee, mem Office of Chamber of Deputies, Benelux Parl, N Atlantic Ass (Leader of Christian Democrat/Conservative Group) 1983–89; mem Council City of Esch 1981–99, Pres Cultural Affairs Cttee 1992–99; MEP 1989–99, Pres Petitions Committee 1989–92, Vice-Pres Social Cttee 1992–94, Civil Liberties and Internal Affairs Cttee 1997–99, Head of Luxembourg Del to EPP, mem of EPP group office 1995–99; EU Commr for Educ, Culture, Youth, Media and Sport 1999–; Pres Luxembourg Union of Journalists 1986–98, Nat Pres Christian-Social Women 1988–93; Vice-Pres Christian Social Party 1995–99. *Address:* Commission of the European Communities, 200 rue de la Loi, 1049 Brussels, Belgium. *Telephone:* (2) 298-16-00; *Fax:* (2) 299-92-01; *E-mail:* viviane.reding@cec.eu.int; *Internet:* europa.eu.int.

REDONDO JIMENEZ, Encarnación; Spanish politician; b 18 April 1944, Molinos de Razón. *Career:* MEP (EPP, PP), mem Cttee on Agric and Rural Devt, Del for relations with Israel, Del to the EU-Romanian Jt Parl Cttee. *Address:* European Parliament, rue Wiertz, 1047 Brussels, Belgium. *Telephone:* (2) 284-21-11; *Fax:* (2) 230-69-43.

REDPATH, Norma, OBE; Australian sculptor; b 20 Nov 1928; d of H. C. Redpath; m Antonio de Altamer 1974. *Education:* Strathcona Girls' Grammar School, Tech Colls, Swinburne and Melbourne and Univ of Perugia (Italy). *Career:* Creative Arts Fellow ANU 1972; exhibitions and comms include Nat Gallery of Victoria, Art Gallery of New S Wales, Western Australia Art Gallery, Nat Collection of Canberra, Newcastle City Art Gallery, Benalla City Art Gallery, McClelland Gallery, Univ of Melbourne 1958, BP Bldgs, Vic 1964, Victoria Arts Centre 1968, Reserve Bank of Australia (Brisbane) 1969–72, Victoria Coll of Pharmacy 1970–72, Canberra School of Music 1972–75, State Bank of Victoria 1980–85; rep in perm collections in Australia and overseas; works include columns, murals, fountains, sculptures and carvings; Transfield Prize for Sculpture 1966; Mildura Prize for Monumental Sculpture 1961, 1964. *Address:* 4 Painsdale Place, Carlton, Vic 3053, Australia.

REED, Barbara Joan, BA, LL M; Canadian federal judge (retd); b 25 March 1937, St Catharines, Ont; d of Joseph Cornwall and Marjorie (née Grainge) Savage; m Robert Barry Reed 1960; two s one d. *Education:* Univ of Toronto and Dalhousie Univ. *Career:* Called to the Bar, ON 1971; Asst Prof Common Law Section, Univ of Ottawa 1971–73; joined Dept of Justice, Ottawa 1973, Legal Officer Constitutional Law Section 1973–74, Constitutional Adviser to Privy Council Office and Fed-Prov Relations Office 1974–80, Dir Legal Services Fed-Prov Relations Office 1980–82, Legal Counsel Privy Council Office and Fed-Prov Relations Office 1982–83; QC 1982; Justice Trial Div, Fed Court of Canada 1983–2000; Chair Competition Tribunal 1986–. *Leisure interests:* cross-country skiing, volleyball, photography, drama, needlework. *Address:* 160 Clearview, Ottawa, ON K1Z 6S5, Canada (Home).

REED, Jane Barbara, CBE, FRSA; British publishing and newspaper executive; b 31 March 1940, Letchworth, Herts; d of the late William and Gwendoline Reed. *Education:* Royal Masonic School. *Career:* Mem staff Woman's Own magazine 1965–69, Ed 1969–79; Publr IPC Magazines Ltd Women's Monthly Magazines Group 1979–81; Ed-in-Chief Woman magazine 1981–83; Asst Man Dir IPC Specialist Educ and Leisure Group 1983; Man Dir IPC Holborn Publishing Group 1983–85; Man Ed Features Section Today newspaper 1985–86, Man Ed 1985–89; Dir of Corp Affairs, News Int PLC 1989–2000; fmr Pres Media Soc; mem Council Nat Literacy Trust; Non-Exec Dir Media Trust; Trustee St Katharine & Shadwell Trust. *Publications:* Girl About Town 1965, Kitchen Sink—or Swim? (jtly) 1981. *Leisure interests:* painting, music, people. *Address:* News International PLC, POB 495, 1 Virginia St, London EC1 9XY, UK (Office); 41 Chipstead St, London SW6 3SR, UK (Home). *Telephone:* (20) 7782-6090; *Fax:* (20) 7782-6097.

REES, Lesley Howard, MD, D SC, FRCP, FRCPATH; British professor of chemical endocrinology and former college dean; b 17 Nov 1942; d of the late Howard Leslie Davis and Charlotte Patricia Siegrid Young; m Gareth Mervyn Rees 1969. *Education:* Pates Girls' Grammar School (Cheltenham), Malvern Girls' Coll and Univ of London. *Career:* Prof of Chemical Endocrinology St Bartholomew's and Royal London School of Medicine and Dentistry, Queen Mary and Westfield Coll (fmrly St Bartholomew's Hosp Medical Coll) 1978–, Sub-Dean 1983–88, Dean 1989–95; Ed Clinical Endocrinology 1979–84; Public Orator Univ of London 1984–86; Dir Int Office Royal Coll of Physicians 1997–, Education Dept 1997–; Chair Soc for Endocrinology 1984–87; Sec-Gen Int Soc of Endocrinology 1984–; mem Press Complaints Comm 1991–94. *Leisure interests:* music, poetry, reading, skiing, administrative gardening. *Address:* 23 Church Row, Hampstead, London NW3 6UP, UK. *Telephone:* (20) 7794-4936.

REEVES, Marjorie Ethel, CBE, PH D, D LITT, FRHISTS, FBA; British former university lecturer and writer; b 17 July 1905, Bratton, Wilts; d of Robert John and Edith Saffery (née Whitaker) Reeves. *Education:* Trowbridge High School for Girls (Wilts), St Hugh's Coll (Oxford) and Westfield Coll (London). *Career:* History teacher Roan School for Girls, London 1927–29; Lecturer in History St Gabriel's Coll, London 1931–38; Tutor, later Fellow, St Anne's Coll, Oxford, Univ Lecturer 1938–72, Vice-Prin 1948–68; Hon D LITT (Bath) 1992, (Queen Mary and Westfield Coll, London) 1998; Medlicott Medal 1993, Hon Citizen of San Giovanni, Italy 1994. *Publications:* The Influence of Prophecy in the Later Middle Ages 1969, The Figurae of Joachim of Fiore 1972, Joachim of Fiore and the Prophetic Future 1976, Sheepbell and Ploughshare 1978, Joachim of Fiore and the Myth of the Eternal Evangel in the Nineteenth Century (jtly) 1987, Competence, Delight and the Common Good: reflections on the crisis in higher education 1988, The Diaries of Jeffrey Whitaker 1739–1741 (jtly) 1989, Prophetic Rome in the High Renaissance Period (ed) 1992 Pursuing the Muses: A Study of Culture and Education from Two Collections of Family Papers 1700–1900 1996, Christian Thinking and Social Order, 1930 to the Present Day (ed and contrib) 1999, The Prophetic Sense of History in Medieval and Renaissance Europe 1999, Favourite Hymns: 2000 Years of Magnificat 2001; numerous books in the Then and There Series. *Leisure interests:* gardening, music. *Address:* 38 Norham Rd, Oxford, OX2 6SQ, UK. *Telephone:* (1865) 557039.

REEVES, Saskia; British actress; b London; d of Peter Reeves. *Education:* Guildhall School of Music and Drama (London). *Career:* Toured S America, India and Europe with Cheek By Jowl theatre co appearing in A Midsummer Night's Dream and The Man of Mode; mem RSC 1991–. *Plays include:* Metamorphosis, Who's Afraid of Virginia Woolf?, Separation, Measure For Measure, Smelling A Rat, Ice Cream, Two Gentlemen of Verona, The Virtuoso, 'Tis Pity She's a Whore 1991, 1992, A Woman Killed With Kindness, The Darker Face of the Earth; *Films include:* December Bride, The Bridge 1991, Close My Eyes 1991, The Butterfly Kiss, Much Ado About Nothing 1998; *TV appearances include:* Children Crossing, Antonia and Jane, In My Defence (part of Talking Heads series).

REGAN, Lesley, MD, FRCOG; British obstetrician and gynaecologist; b 8 March 1956; m John Summerfield 1990; two d, four step-c. *Career:* Hon Consultant in obstetrics and gynaecology, St Mary's Hospital, London 1990–96; Prof and Head of Dept Imperial Coll School of Medicine at St Mary's Hospital, London 1996–; specializes in research into multiple miscarriages. *Publications:* Miscarriage: What Every Woman Needs to Know 1997, numerous chapters in reproductive medicine textbooks and contribs to professional journals. *Address:* Department of Obstetrics and Gynaecology, Imperial College School of Medicine at St Mary's Hospital, South Wharf, Paddington, London W2 1NY, UK.

REGÀS, Rosa; Spanish writer; b 1934, Barcelona; m; five c. *Education:* Barcelona Univ. *Career:* With publrs Seix Barral 1964–70, currently Edhasa; translator UN; Founder and Ed La Gaya Ciencia. *Publications include:* Novels: Memoria de Almator 1991, Azul (Premio Nadal 1994) 1993.

RÉGINE, (pseudonym of Régina Zylberberg); Belgian singer and cabaret artist; b 26 Dec 1929, Etterbeck; d of Joseph and Tauba (née Rodstein) Zylberberg; m 2nd Roger Choukroun 1969; one s (from previous marriage). *Education:* Privately in Aix-en-Provence, Lyons and Paris (France). *Career:* Cabaret compère at Chez Régine, Paris 1958–61, in Paris 1961–81, Deauville (France) 1965, Régine's Club, Paris 1971–, Monte-Carlo 1971–, Regine's, Rio de Janeiro and Bahia (Brazil), Regine's New York (USA), Le Palace, Paris 1992–; has performed in numerous nat and int concerts and tours, including concerts at L'Olympia 1968, 1990 and Bobino, Paris 1973, Bouffes-du-Nord 1993, tours of Belgium 1970, Canada and USA; Creator 'Régine's' perfumes 1989; Co-Founder Presse et Public public relations co 1990–; Pres SOS Drogue Int 1985–; Chevalier des Arts et des Lettres; Grand Prix Acad du Disque Français 1969; Ruban Rouge, Chanson Française. *Songs include:* J'ai la boule au plafond, La Grande Zoa, Rue des rosiers, Patchouli-Chinchilla, Mille fois par jour, Les balayeurs, La fille que je suis, Fais-moi danser, La bonne adresse pour chiens perdus, La guimauve; *Films:* Mazel Tov ou le mariage 1968, Sortie de secours 1970,

Le train 1973, Les Ripoux 1984; *Publications:* Appelle-moi par mon prénom (Prix Bruno Coquatrix) 1985, La drogue, parlons-en 1987. *Leisure interests:* cooking, collecting valuable boxes. *Address:* c/o Patrick Goavec, 10 ave Georges V, 75008 Paris, France.

REGO, Paula; British artist; b 26 Jan 1935, Lisbon, Portugal; d of José and Maria de San José Paiva Figueiroa Rego; m Victor Willing (died 1988); two d one s. *Education:* St Julian's School (Carcavelos, Portugal), Slade School of Fine Art and Univ Coll London. *Career:* Solo exhibitions in London, Lisbon, Amsterdam (Netherlands) and Bristol 1979–; Retrospective exhibitions include Gulbenkian Foundation, Lisbon 1989, Serpentine Gallery, London 1989, 1992, Tate Gallery, Liverpool 1997, Centro Cultural de Belém, Lisbon 1997, Dulwich Picture Gallery, London 1998; group exhibitions include Paris, Rome, São Paulo (Brazil), Tokyo, Madrid, Baden-Baden (Germany), New York (USA) and UK; works rep by Marlborough Fine Art; Assoc Artist Nat Gallery 1990–; Sr Fellow Royal Coll of Art 1989; Dr hc (St Andrews, E Anglia), (Rhode Island School of Design, USA) 2000. *Publications include:* Etchings: Peter Pan 1992, Nursery Rhymes 1994, Pendle Witches 1996, Children's Crusade 1999. *Address:* c/o Marlborough Fine Art, 6 Albemarle St, London W1X 4BY, UK. *Telephone:* (20) 7629-5161.

REHN, (Märta) Elisabeth, MA, MBA, D SC; Finnish international official and politician; b 6 April 1935, Helsinki; d of Andreas Petrus and Ruth Leonida (née Weurlander) Carlberg; m Ove Rehn 1955; three d one s. *Education:* School of Econs (Helsinki). *Career:* Office Man Oy Renecta AB 1960–79, Oy Rehn Trading AB 1978–79; Careers teacher 1973–77; mem Kauniainen City Council 1973–80, City Bd 1979–80; mem Eduskunta (Parl, Swedish People's Party) 1979–95, mem Advisory Bd of Econ Relations between Finland and Developing Countries, Comm on Archipelago Matters, Chair Swedish People's Party Parl Group 1987–90; Minister of Defence, Minister Responsible for Equality Affairs 1990–94; Presidential Elector 1982; Presidential Cand 1993–94; MEP 1995–96; UN Special Rapporteur for Human Rights in fmr Yugoslavia 1995–98; Special Rep of Sec-Gen of the UN in Bosnia and Herzegovina 1998–; mem Party Exec Swedish People's Party 1985–; mem Bd of Trustees Kirkkonummi Merchant Bank 1984–, (Chair 1988–), Merchant Banks Cen Sharebank 1987–; mem Admin Council World Wide Fund for Nature (fmrly World Wildlife Fund – WWF) 1982–89, 1992–; mem Admin Bd and Chair Finnish Cttee for UNICEF 1988–93, Chair Standing Group, Nat Cttees for UNICEF 1990–94; KT (First Class) of the White Rose of Finland 1989. *Leisure interests:* nature, sports, fine arts, politics. *Address:* UNMIBH, O/SRSG, Geodetski Zavod, Mese Selimovica 69, 71210 Ilidza, Sarajevo, Bosnia and Herzegovina.

REID, Barbara Jane; Canadian illustrator and writer; b 16 Nov 1957, Toronto, ON; d of Robert Johnstone and Dora Ann Reid; m Ian Robert Crysler 1981; two d. *Education:* Lawrence Park Coll Inst and Ontario Coll of Art. *Career:* Author and illustrator of children's books 1980–; mem Canadian Asscn of Photographers and Illustrators in Communications, Children's Book Centre; Illustration Award, Ind Order of Daughters of the Empire 1986; Canadian Council Prize 1986; Ruth Schwartz Award for Children's Literature 1986; Elizabeth Cleaver Award 1987, 1993; Ezra Jack Keats Award 1988; Mr Christie Book Award 1991; Amelia Francis Howard Gibbon Award 1995, 1997; Gov-Gen's Award 1997. *Illustrated works include:* The New Baby Calf 1984, Have You Seen Birds 1986, Sing a Song of Mother Goose 1987, Playing With Plasticene, The Zoe Series 1991, Two By Two 1992, Gifts 1994, The Party 1997, The Golden Goose 2000. *Address:* 37 Strathmore Blvd, Toronto, ON M4J 1P1, Canada.

REID, Elizabeth Anne, BA, B PHIL; Australian United Nations official; b 3 July 1942, Taree, NSW; d of James and Jean Reid; m 1st Ronald Weir 1967; one s; m 2nd William Pruitt 1981 (deceased); one s. *Education:* Somerville Coll (Oxford) and ANU. *Career:* F-Dir and Project Man UN Asian and Pacific Centre for Women and Devt, Teheran 1977–79; Consultant in Devt Assistance, USAID, Peace Corps and ESCAP 1981–83; Consultant on AIDS and Devt Australia, Zaire and the Pacific 1985–87; Sr Consultant on Nat HIV/AIDS Strategy, Dept of Community Services and Health, Canberra 1987–89; Adviser WHO Global Programmes on AIDS, Geneva, Switzerland 1987–89; freelance corp consultant on HIV personnel policies and staff training 1987–89; Consultant HIV Policy, Programme Devt and Delivery,

UNDP and other int orgs 1987–89, Programme Dir Div for Women in Devt and Policy Adviser to Admin on HIV/AIDS and Devt 1989–92, apptd Dir HIV and Devt Programme 1992; Visiting Fellow Nat Centre for Devt Studies, ANU 1979–81; Commonwealth Travelling Scholar, Univ of Oxford, UK 1966–69; Fellow Inst of Politics, Harvard Univ 1976; has written numerous articles on AIDS and Devt; Nat Undergrad Scholar and Tillyard Prize, ANU 1965. *Leisure interests:* surfing, swimming, music. *Address:* Division for Women in Development, UNDP, Rm FF-1094, 304 E 45th St, New York, NY 10017, USA (Office); 59 Fourth Ave, Apt 1A, New York, NY 10003, USA (Home). *Telephone:* (212) 906-6976 (Office); (212) 989-5308 (Home); *Fax:* (212) 906-6336 (Office).

REID, Lynne McArthur, MD, MRCP, FRCP, FRCPATH; British (b Australian) pathologist; b 11 Nov 1923, Melbourne, Vic; d of Robert Muir and Violet Annie (née McArthur) Reid. *Education:* Wimbledon Girls' School (London), Presbyterian Ladies' Coll (Melbourne), Univ of Melbourne, Royal Melbourne Hosp, Univ Coll Hosp (London) and Brompton Hosp and Cardio-Thoracic Inst (British Postgrad Medical Fed, Univ of London). *Career:* Research Asst Inst of Diseases of the Chest, Univ of London 1950–55, Lecturer, then Sr Lecturer in Pathology Univ of London 1955–65, Reader in Experimental Pathology 1964–67, Prof 1964–76, Dean of Cardio-Thoracic Inst 1973–76, Hon Prof Univ Coll London 1976–; Hon Consultant in Experimental Pathology Brompton Hosp, London 1963–76; Simeon Burt Wolbach Prof of Pathology Harvard Medical School, Boston, MA, USA 1976–; Pathologist-in-Chief Children's Hosp, Boston, MA 1976–89, Pathologist-in-Chief Emer 1990–; Guest Lecturer, Guest Prof at numerous insts including Univ of California Medical School at Los Angeles, USA 1965, Univ of Colorado and Stanford Univ, USA 1977, Royal Coll of Physicians (London) 1981, Albert Einstein Medical Center (Philadelphia, PA, USA) 1983 and Univ of Minneapolis 1985, Louisiana State Univ Medical School 1987, Indiana Univ 1988 and American Heart Asscn, USA 1990; speaker at numerous confs and symposia including Int Congress on Hypoxia and Pulmonary Pathophysiology, People's Repub of China 1990 (also Vice-Pres); mem Steering Cttee Primary Pulmonary Hypertension Registry, NIH Nat Heart, Lung and Blood Inst 1986–; Founder-mem Royal Coll of Pathologists 1964; mem Royal Australian Coll of Physicians 1950, Fellow 1964; Hon Fellow Royal Coll of Radiologists 1995; Sidney Farber Lecturer, Soc of Pediatric Pathology, Washington, DC 1996; Edward Livingston Trudeau Medal, American Thoracic Soc 1991. *Publications:* The Pathology of Emphysema 1967; numerous book chapters and scientific articles. *Leisure interests:* music, travel, reading. *Address:* Children's Hospital, Dept of Pathology, 300 Longwood Ave, Boston, MA 02115, USA (Office); 50 Longwood Ave, Brookline, MA 02446, USA (Home). *Telephone:* (617) 735-7440 (Office); (617) 731-4581 (Home); *Fax:* (617) 735-7429 (Office).

REID, Margaret Elizabeth, LL B; Australian politician; b 28 May 1935, Crystal Brook, SA. *Education:* Univ of Adelaide. *Career:* Barrister and solicitor; selected Australian Capital Territory Rep to Senate 1981, mem Senate 1983–, mem Estimates Cttee A 1981–83, C 1982–83, F 1983–87, 1987–, E 1987, Chair Jt Standing Cttee on Australian Capital Territory 1981–83, mem 1983–, mem Cttees for Educ and the Arts 1981–83, for New Parl House 1983, for Procedure 1987, Deputy Govt Whip in Senate 1982–83; Deputy Opposition Whip 1983–87, Opposition Whip 1987–95; Deputy Pres of the Senate and Chair of Cttees 1995–96, Pres 1996–; mem Advisory Council on Australian Archives 1985–; Queen's Jubilee Medal 1977; Order of Polonia Restituta 1987. *Leisure interests:* cooking, gardening. *Address:* Senate, Parliament House, Rm M13, Canberra, ACT 2600, Australia; Shopfront, 62 Northbourne Ave, Canberra, ACT 2601, Australia. *Telephone:* (62) 727 111.

REID, Marion Loretta; Canadian politician; b 4 Jan 1929, N Rustico, PEI; d of the late Michael Joseph and of Loretta Josephine (née Whelan) Doyle; m Lea P. Reid 1949; five d four s. *Education:* N Rustico and Stella Maris Elementary Schools and Univ of Prince Edward Island. *Career:* Prin St Ann's Elementary School; mem Bd of Govs and Sec Prince Edward Island Teachers' Fed 1970–77; mem Teacher Recruitment Team, Curriculum Comm, Negotiating Strategy Comm, Status of Women Comm; Founder-mem QEH Foundation; mem Prince Edward Island Legis Ass 1979, 1982, 1986, Deputy Speaker 1979, Speaker 1983, Leader of the Opposition 1986–89, mem Standing Cttees on

Educ, Health and Welfare, Agriculture, Tourism and Parks; Lieut-Gov Prince Edward Island 1990; Hon Patron Laubach Literacy of Canada; Dame of Grace Order of St John 1990. *Address:* Stanley Bridge, R R 1, Breadalbane, PEI C0A 1E0, Canada.

REID, Sue Titus, PH D, JD; American lawyer and sociologist; b 13 Nov 1939, Bryan, TX; d of Andrew Jackson, Jr and Loraine (née Wylie) Titus. *Education:* Texas Woman's Univ, Univs of Missouri and Iowa. *Career:* Instructor, then Assoc Prof of Sociology Cornell Coll, Mount Vernon 1963–72, Acting Chair Dept of Sociology 1965–66; Assoc Prof and Chair Dept of Sociology Coe Coll, Cedar Rapids 1972–74; Assoc Prof of Law Univ of Washington 1974–76; Dean and Prof of Law, School of Criminology, Florida State Univ 1988–90, Acting Chair Dept of Sociology, Coll of Social Sciences 1990; Visiting Assoc Prof Univ of Nebraska 1970; Visiting Distinguished Prof of Law and Sociology Univ of Tulsa 1977–78, Prof of Law 1978–88, Assoc Dean 1979–81; Visiting Prof of Law Univ of San Diego 1981–82; Exec Assoc American Sociological Asscn 1976–77; called to the Bar, IA 1972, US Court of Appeals (DC) 1978, US Supreme Court 1978; Consultant Evaluation Policy Research Inc, Milwaukee 1976–77, Idaho Dept of Corrections 1984, American Correctional Inst; George Beto Prof of Criminal Justice Sam Houston Univ, Huntsville 1984–85; mem People-to-People Crime Prevention Del to People's Repub of China 1982; mem American Correctional Asscn, American Soc of Criminology, Acad of Criminal Justice Sciences; one of Oklahoma's Young Leaders of 1980's, Oklahoma Monthly 1980. *Publications:* Population Crisis: An Inter-disciplinary Perspective (co-ed) 1972, The Correctional System: An Introduction (jtly) 1981, Criminal Law (3rd edn) 1989, Criminal Justice: Procedures and Issues (4th edn) 1996, Crime and Criminology (8th edn) 1997; numerous articles in professional journals. *Address:* Florida State University, School of Public Admin and Policy, 635 Bellamy Bldg, Tallahassee, FL 32306, USA.

REID BANKS, Lynne; British writer; b 31 July 1929, London; d of James and Pat Reid Banks; m Chaim Stephenson 1965; three s. *Education:* In Canada and Royal Acad of Dramatic Art (London). *Career:* Stage career 1949–54; freelance journalist 1954–55; News Reporter (first woman in UK) Independent TV News (ITN) 1955–62; taught English in Israel 1962–71; writer, playwright and journalist 1971–; awards for children's literature, Australia, Italy and USA; Smarties Prize. *Publications include:* The L-Shaped Room (film 1962) 1960, An End to Running 1962, Children at the Gate 1968, The Adventures of King Midas 1976, Dark Quartet: the story of the Brontës (Yorkshire Arts Literature Award 1977) 1976, Path to the Silent Country: Charlotte Brontë's years of fame 1977, My Darling Villain 1977, I, Houdini 1978, The Indian in the Cupboard (numerous children's book awards, USA, made into feature film, released 1995) 1980, Defy the Wilderness 1981, Maura's Angel 1984, The Warning Bell 1984, Casualties 1986, Melusine 1988, The Magic Hare 1991, Yoshi and the Tea-Kettle (children's play) 1991, The Mystery of the Cupboard 1993, Broken Bridge 1994, Harry the Poisonous Centipede 1997, Fair Exchange (for adults) 1999, Alice-by-Accident 2000, Harry the Poisonous Centipede's Big Adventure 2000, The Dungeon 2002; works translated into other languages; contribs to newspapers including The Times, The Guardian, Observer, Times Literary and Educational Supplements, The Independent, Saga Mag. *Leisure interests:* theatre, travel, teaching English abroad. *Address:* c/o Watson, Little Ltd, Capo di Monte, Windmill Hill, Hampstead, London NW3 6RJ, UK; 4 Bradley Gardens, W Ealing, London W13 8HF, UK. *Telephone:* (1308) 862679; *Fax:* (1308) 863926; *E-mail:* lynne.stephenson@ukgateway.net; *Internet:* www.lynnereidbanks.com.

REIDY, Carolyn Kroll, PH D; American publishing executive; b 2 May 1949, Washington, DC; d of Henry August and Mildred Josephine (née Mencke) Kroll; m Stephen Reidy 1974. *Education:* Middlebury Coll (VT) and Indiana Univ. *Career:* Various positions up to Man of Subsidiary Rights, Random House, New York 1975–83; Dir Subsidiary Rights William Morrow & Co, New York 1983–85; Vice-Pres and Assoc Publr, Vintage Books, New York 1985–87, Publr 1987–88; Publr Anchor Books, Doubleday & Co, New York 1988; Pres and Publr, Avon Books, New York 1988–92, Adult Publ Group, Simon and Schuster, New York 1992–; Dir NAMES Project 1994–98, New York Univ Center for Publishing 1997–, Literacy Partners, Inc 1999–. *Address:* Simon and Schuster, 1230 Ave of the Americas, New York, NY 10020, USA (Office); 345 W 13th St, New York, NY 10014, USA (Home). *Telephone:* (212) 698-7323 (Office); *Fax:* (212) 698-7035 (Office); *E-mail:* carolyn.reidy@simonandschuster.com (Office); *Internet:* www .simonsays.com (Office).

REIFF, Patricia Hofer, M SC, PH D; American space physicist; b 14 March 1950, Oklahoma City; d of William Henry and Maxine Ruth (née Hoffer) Reiff; m Thomas Westfall Hill 1976; two d one s. *Education:* Wellesley Coll, Oklahoma State Univ and Rice Univ (Houston, TX). *Career:* Research Assoc Space Physics and Astronomy Dept, Rice Univ, Houston 1975, Adjunct Asst Prof 1976–78, Asst Prof 1978–81, Asst Chair 1979–85, Assoc Research Scientist 1981–87, Adjunct Assoc Prof 1983, Sr Research Scientist 1987–90, Distinguished Faculty Fellow 1990–92, Prof 1992–, apptd Chair 1996; Resident Research Assoc Marshall Space Flight Center, Huntsville 1975–76; mem Science Team Atmosphere Explorer Mission, Dynamics Explorer Mission, Global Geospace Scientific Mission, Image Mission; Consultant Houston Museum of Natural Sciences 1986–; mem Air Quality Comm, Houston and Galveston Area Council 1980–83, Green Ribbon Comm 1981–83, Advisory Comm on Atmospheric Sciences, NSF, Washington, DC 1988–, Strategic Implementation Study Panel, NASA, Washington, DC 1989–90, Exec Comm George Observatory, Houston 1989–, Space Science Advisory Cttee, NASA 1993–96, Cosmos Club 1992–; Designer Sundial-Solar Telescope 1989; numerous contribs to scientific journals; Trustee Citizens' Environment Coalition, Houston 1978–, Pres 1980–85; mem American Geophysics Union, American Meteorological Soc, Int Union of Geophysics; Nat Acad of Sciences Research Fellow 1975, Research Fellow Outstanding Young Women of America 1977, 1980; Houston's Woman on the Move 1990. *Address:* Rice University, Dept of Space Physics and Astronomy, 6100 S Main St, Houston, TX 77257-1892, USA.

REINIG, Christa; German writer; b 6 Aug 1926, Berlin; d of Wilhelmine Reinig. *Education:* Humboldt-Univ of Berlin. *Career:* Curator Mär-kisches Museum, Kultur-historisches Museum der Stadt Berlin 1958–63; mem PEN-Zentrum, Bayerische Akad der Schönen Künste; Literature Grant, Munich 1980; Bundesverdienstkreuz 1976; other awards include Literature Prize (Bremen) 1964, Tukan-Preis (Munich) 1969, Verband der deutschen Kritiker Prize 1976, Literature Prize (Südwestfunk—SWF, Baden-Baden) 1984, Literature Prize (Stadt Gandersheim) 1993. *Publications include:* Poetry: Die Steine für Finisterre 1960, Schwabinger Marterln 1968, Schwalbe von Olevano 1969, Müßiggang ist aller Liebe Anfang 1979, Sämtliche Gedichte 1984; Fiction and prose: Der Traum meiner Verkommenheit 1961, Drei Schiffe 1965, Orion trat aus dem Haus: Neue Sternbilder 1968, Die himmlische und die irdische Geometrie 1975, Entmannung 1976, Der Wolf und die Witwen 1980, Die Frau im Brunnen 1984; Short stories: Die ewige Schule 1982, Gesammelte Erzählungen 1986, Nobody 1989, Glück und Glas 1991; Das Aquarium (radio play, Kriegsblinden Prize). *Address:* Bertholdstr 11, 80809 Munich, Germany. *Telephone:* (89) 3512505.

REINSHAGEN, Gerlind; German writer; b 4 May 1926, Königsberg; d of Ekkehard and Friedel Technau; m 1949. *Education:* Studies in pharmacy. *Career:* Freelance writer of novels, theatre and radio plays, screenplays, poetry, essays and criticism; plays performed in Frankfurt/Main, Darmstadt, Staatstheater Stuttgart, Düsseldorf, Bremen and Zurich, Switzerland; mem German PEN, Deutsche Akad der Darstellenden Künste; awards include Fördergabe Schillerpreis, Baden Württemberg 1974, Mühlheimer Dramatikerpreis 1977, Roswitha von Gandersheim Medaille 1984, Ludwig Mülheimes Preis 1993, Niedersächsischer Kunstpreis 1997, Niedersächsischer Staatspreis 1999. *Publications include:* Novels: Rovinato oder Die Seele des Geschäfts 1981, Die flüchtige Braut 1984, Gesammelte Stücke 1986, Zwölf Nächte 1989, Jäger am Rand der Nacht 1993, Am grossen Stern 1996, Göttergeschichte 2000; Plays: Doppelkopf 1968, Leben und Tod der Marilyn Monroe 1971, Himmel und Erde (TV film 1976) 1974, Sonntagskinder (Mülheimer Dramatikerpreis, TV film 1981) 1974, Das Frühlingsfest 1980, Eisenherz 1982, Die Clownin 1985, Die Feuer-blume 1987, Tanz, Marie! 1989, Die fremde Tochter 1992, Drei Wünsche frei 1992, Die grüne Tür 1999; 11 radio plays; Gesammelte Stücke (collected pieces) 1986; contribs to theatrical journals and yearbooks. *Address:* Rheingaustr 2, 12161 Berlin, Germany. *Telephone:* (30) 8217171.

REINSHAGEN, Maria; Swiss business executive; b 23 Jan 1936; one s one d. *Career:* Fmr primary school teacher, Zürich; fmr Dir Prints Dept Felix Landau Gallery (LA); joined Christie's 1978, mem Bd (Europe) 1985, (London) 1990, Head of Zürich office, Deputy Chair Switzerland, Vice-Chair Europe 1996; mem Bd Union Bank of Switzerland 1994–2001. *Address:* c/o Christie's (Int) AG, Steinwlesplatz, 8032 Zürich, Switzerland. *Telephone:* (1) 268-10-10; *Fax:* (1) 268-10-11.

REIS, Steffa Amalia; British/Israeli artist; b 1 July 1931, Berlin; d of Michael and Ilse Fabian-Tenennbaum; m Nicolas Daniel Reis 1954 (divorced 1979); three c. *Education:* Harrow School of Art (UK), Royal Acad of Art (London) and Art Inst Oranim (Israel). *Career:* Teacher of art; specializes in inter-disciplinary arts and interaction of music with painting; regular solo exhibitions 1976–, including New York, (USA) and 10-year Retrospective, Berlin; toured S America; rep in perm and pvt collections; numerous articles and exhibition catalogues; awarded studio by Tel-Aviv municipality. *Leisure interests:* travel, music, film, theatre, fine cuts. *Address:* 228 Ben Yehuda St, Tel-Aviv 63473, Israel; Artists Colony, Zefat, Israel. *Telephone:* (3) 5443399 (Tel-Aviv); (69) 22022 (Zefat); *Fax:* (3) 5443399 (Tel-Aviv).

REISFELD, Renata, PH D; Israeli professor of chemistry; b Chełmza, Poland; d of Zdzisław and Anna Sobel; m Eliezer Reisfeld; two s. *Education:* Hebrew Univ of Jerusalem. *Career:* Prof Hebrew Univ of Jerusalem 1978–; Guest Prof Univ of Geneva, Switzerland 1974–, Univ of Paris VI (Pierre et Marie Curie) 1989, Univ of Paris XI (Paris-Sud) 1990; inventor of the visible solid state glass laser; Dr hc (Lyons, France) 1993; Chemical Soc of Israel Prize 1965; Distinguished Lecturer Award 1985. *Publications:* Laser and Excited States of Rare Earth (jtly) 1977, Chemistry, Spectroscopy and Application of Sol-Gel Glasses (co-ed, vol 77) 1992, Optical and Electronic Phenomena in Sol-Gel Glasses and Modern Applications (co-ed) 1996; 390 pubs on solid state chem, lasers, non-linear optics and spectroscopy in glasses. *Leisure interests:* sports, music, literature, plastic arts. *Address:* Hebrew University of Jerusalem, Dept of Inorganic Chemistry, Jerusalem, Israel; Straus 10A, Jerusalem, Israel (Home). *Telephone:* (2) 585323; *Fax:* (2) 585319.

REISS, Elaine Serlin, BA, LL M; American advertising executive and lawyer; b 27 Oct 1940, New York; d of Morris and Dorothy (née Geyer) Serlin; m Joel A. Reiss 1963; one s one d. *Education:* Univs of New York and Columbia. *Career:* Called to the Bar, New York 1965; Man Legal Dept, Doyle Dane Bernbach Advertising 1965–68; Man Legal Clearance Dept, later Vice-Pres and Man Legal Dept Ogilvy and Mather, New York 1968–78, Sr Vice-Pres and Man 1978–82, apptd Gen Counsel US Bd of Dirs 1982, Exec Vice-Pres 1985; Gen Counsel Ogilvy Group Inc, New York 1988, Sec 1989; Industry Adviser Seminar Series on Children, Law Faculty Georgetown Univ 1978–79; part-time mem Tisch School of Arts, Univ of New York 1982; mem American Asscn of Advertising Agencies, ABA, New York City Bar Asscn, Legal Aid Soc; New York Women in Communications Matrix Award in Advertising 1987. *Address:* Ogilvy & Mather Advertising, Worldwide Plaza, 309 W 49th St, New York, NY 10019, USA.

REJCHRTOVÁ, Noemi, PH D; Czech professor of church history; b 1 Nov 1940, Prague. *Career:* Worked in hosp and factory before studying history externally; Scientific Asst to church historian Amedeo Molnár, Assoc Prof 1984; fmr Researcher Historical Inst, Czech Acad of Sciences, Prague; Head Dept of Church History, Evangelical Theological Faculty, Charles Univ, Prague 1993, Prof of Church History 1994; mem Bibliographia Patristica int comm, editorial bd Lutherjahrbuch; also lyric painter. *Publications include:* The Correspondence of Karel Senior of Žerotín 1982, Czech Evangelical Politician Václav Budovec of Budov 1984, Comenius on Himself 1987, Critical Edition of the 'Anti-Alkoran' by V. Budovec 1989, 'On the Mother-School' by Comenius 1992. *Address:* Charles University, Evangelical Theological Faculty, Ovocný trh 5, 116 36 Prague 1, Czech Republic.

REKAI, Catherine (Kati), CM; Canadian (b Hungarian) writer; b 20 Oct 1921, Budapest; d of Desider and Ilona (née Hajdu) Elek; m John Rekai 1941; two d. *Education:* Mariaterezia Gymnazium (Budapest, Hungary). *Career:* Writer; newspaper and radio reporter; Public Relations Consultant Cen Hosp, Toronto; Dir Canadian Scene, Performing Arts Magazine; Vice-Pres Canadian Ethnic; mem Multicultural Advisory Cttee, Toronto History Bd, Writers' Union of Canada, External Affairs Cttee, Asscn of Children's Writers and Illustrators, PEN Int, George R. Gardiner Museum, Stratford Festival, Nat Ballet of Canada, Canadian Opera Co, Ethnic Journalists and Writers Club, TMAC-Travel Media Asscn of Canada; Prix Saint-Exupéry Francophonie 1988; Certificate of Honour for Contribution to Canadian Unity; KT Order of St Laszlo of Hungary; Cross of the Order of Merit (Hungary) 1993; Ziniak Award for Excellence in Multilingual Media 1996. *Publications include:* Plays: The Great Totem Pole Caper (also video), The Boy Who Forgot, The Tale of Tutenkhamen; Children's Books: Children's travel book series: The Adventures of Mickey, Taggy, Puppo and Cica and How They Discover... [... Toronto, Ottawa, Montréal, Budapest, Vienna, The Netherlands, Switzerland, Kingston, The Thousand Islands, France, The George R. Gardiner Museum of Ceramic Art in Toronto, Canada, Italy, Greece]; books published in French, Polish, Romanian, Hungarian and braille; numerous contribs to newspapers and radio programmes. *Leisure interests:* swimming, walking, travel, opera, theatre, reading. *Address:* 21 Dale Ave, No 727, Toronto, ON M4W 1K3, Canada. *Telephone:* (416) 922-5841; *Fax:* (416) 921-8322.

REMBO, Sonja Marie Hillevi; Swedish politician; b 17 Jan 1933, Gothenburg; d of Alvar and Junis (née Gregorsson) Rembo. *Education:* Inst of Commerce (Gothenburg). *Career:* Sec Swedish Ball Bearings Co Ltd 1968–79; mem Bd Nat Insurance Inspection 1982; mem bd Swedish Del for Marine Resources 1985–90, Port of Gothenburg Ltd 1985; mem Bd Moderata Samlingsparteit (MS, Moderate Party), Gothenburg and Bohuslän 1973–83, First Vice-Chair 1978–83, mem Social Dist Bd, Gothenburg 1974–79, mem Bd, Gothenburg 1989; First Vice-Chair Cons Women's Fed 1976–81; elected mem Riksdag (Parl) 1979, mem Labour Market Cttee, Nat Insurance Cttee, Parl Salaries Del 1979–85, Parl Bd of Trustees, MS 1985; mem War Del 1988. *Address:* Sylvestergt 7, 411 32 Gothenburg, Sweden.

REMINGTON, Deborah Williams, BFA; American artist; b 25 June 1935, Haddonfield, NJ; d of the late Malcolm van Dyke Remington and Hazel Irwin Stewart. *Education:* San Francisco Art Inst and calligraphy and Japanese painting in Japan. *Career:* Adjunct Prof of Painting The Cooper Union for the Advancement of Science and Art 1973–96; solo exhibitions include Dilexi Gallery (San Francisco) 1962, 1963, 1965, San Francisco Museum of Art 1964, Bykert Gallery (New York) 1967, 1969, 1972, 1974, Galerie Darthea Speyer (Paris) 1968, 1971, 1973, 1992, Hamilton Gallery (New York) 1977, Portland Center for Visual Arts (OR) 1977, Ramon Osuna Gallery (Washington, DC) 1983, Newport Harbor Art Museum (Newport Beach, CA) 1983, Oakland Museum of Art (CA) 1984, Ianuzzi Gallery (Phoenix, AZ) 1985, Jack Shainman Gallery (New York) 1987, Shoshana Wayne Gallery (Los Angeles, CA) 1988, Mitchell Algus Gallery, New York 2001; numerous group exhibitions in USA, France, Switzerland, Portugal, etc; rep in numerous perm collections including Whitney Museum (New York), Centre Nat d'Art et de Culture Georges-Pompidou and Bibliothèque Nationale (Paris), Museum Boymans–Van Beuningen (Rotterdam, Netherlands), Art Inst of Chicago, San Francisco Museum of Art, Nat Collection of American Art (Washington, DC), Cleveland Museum of Art; Tamarind Fellow, Artist-in-Residence 1973; mem Nat Acad of Design, New York; Nat Endowment Fellow 1979–80; Guggenheim Fellow 1984–85; Pollock-Krasner Foundation Grant 1999; Hassam and Speicher Purchase Award, American Acad and Inst of Arts and Letters 1988. *Leisure interest:* gardening/horticulture. *Address:* 309 W Broadway, New York, NY 10013-2226, USA. *Telephone:* (212) 925-3037; *Fax:* (212) 925-3037.

RENAUD, Line (pseudonym of Jacqueline Gasté); French singer and actress; b 2 July 1928, Nieppe; d of Edmond and Simone (née Renard) Enté; m Louis Gasté 1950 (deceased). *Career:* Singing debut, Paris 1945; singer in cabaret shows including the Moulin Rouge, Paris 1950, 1954, 1957, Casino de Paris 1959–63, 1966–67, 1976–79, Las Vegas (USA) 1964–65, 1968–70, 1970–71; nat and int tours; numerous TV appearances, also Co-Producer of shows broadcast by Office de Radiodiffusion-Télévision Française (ORTF) 1972–73; Chevalier de la Légion d'Honneur; Officier des Arts et des Lettres; other awards include prizes for records, radio and TV appearances, Médaille de Vermeil, Ville de Paris, Silver Mask for Career (Italy) 1988. *Plays and cabaret shows include:* Désirs 1966–67, Flesh (producer) 1970–71, Parisline 1976–79, Folle Amanda (Archange for Best Actress of the Year) 1982, Pleins feux

1991; *Films include:* La route du bonheur, La Madelon (Prix du Prestige français) 1955, Mademoiselle et son gang 1956, Sur la piste du rock and roll 1959, Le mariage de Figaro 1989, Ripoux contre Ripoux 1990; *Publications:* Bonsoir mes souvenirs 1963, Les brumes d'où je viens 1989. *Leisure interest:* dancing. *Address:* 5 rue du Bois-de-Boulogne, 75116 Paris, France (Home); Les Cèdres bleus, La Jonchère, 92500 Rueil-Malmaison, France (Home).

RENDELL, Phylis; Falkland Islander government official. *Career:* Dir Dept of Education until 1996; Dir Dept of Oil 1996. *Address:* Dept of Oil, Stanley, Falkland Islands. *Telephone:* 27322.

RENDELL OF BABERGH, Baroness (Life Peer), cr 1997, of Aldeburgh in the County of Suffolk, **Ruth Barbara Rendell,** FRSL; British crime novelist; b 17 Feb 1930; d of Arthur Grasemann and Ebba Kruse; m Donald Rendell 1950 (divorced 1975, remarried 1977, died 1999); one s. *Education:* Loughton County High School. *Career:* Writer of crime novels; Dr hc (Essex) 1990; awards include Arts Council Nat Book Award for Genre Fiction 1981, Sunday Times Award for Literary Excellence 1990 and other awards. *Publications include:* Novels: From Doon with Death 1964, Wolf to the Slaughter 1967, One Across Two Down 1971, Some Lie and Some Die 1973, The Face of Trespass 1974, A Judgment in Stone 1976, The Lake of Darkness 1980, The Tree of Hands 1984, An Unkindness of Ravens 1985, Live Flesh 1986, Heartstones 1987, Talking to Strange Men 1987, The Veiled One 1988, A Warning to the Curious – The Ghost Stories of M. R. James (ed) 1988, The Bridesmaid 1989, Ruth Rendell's Suffolk 1989, The Third Wexford Omnibus 1989, Mysterious 1990, Going Wrong 1990, The Strawberry Tree 1990, Walking on Water 1991, Kissing the Gunner's Daughter 1992, The Ruth Rendell Omnibus 1992, The Crocodile Bird 1993, The Third Ruth Rendell Omnibus 1994, Simisola 1994, Blood Lines, Long and Short Stories 1995; (ed) The Reason Why: An Anthology of the Murderous Mind 1995, Harm Done 2000; (as Barbara Vine) A Dark-Adapted Eye 1986, A Fatal Inversion 1987, The House of Stairs 1988, Gallowglass 1990, King Solomon's Carpet 1991, Asta's Book 1993, The Children of Men 1994, No Night Is Too Long 1994, The Keys to the Street 1996, The Brimstone Wedding 1996, The Chimney Sweeper's Boy 1998, A Sight For Sore Eyes 1998, Grasshopper 2000, Piranha to Scurfy and Other Stories 2000; Short stories: The Fallen Curtain 1976, Means of Evil 1979, The Fever Tree 1982, The New Girl Friend 1985, Collected Short Stories 1987, The Copper Peacock 1991. *Leisure interests:* reading, walking, opera. *Address:* 26 Cornwall Terrace Mews, London NW1 5LL, UK; House of Lords, London SW1A 0PW, UK.

RENDER, Arleen; American diplomatist. *Career:* Joined Foreign Service, Dept of State 1970, worked in Côte d'Ivoire, Iran and Italy 1971–78, int relations officer 1979–81, Deputy Chief of Mission, The Congo 1981–84, Ghana 1986–89, Consul-Gen, Jamaica 1984–86, Amb to the Gambia 1990–93, Dir Office of Central African Affairs (Washington DC) 1993–; Amb to Zambia 1996–99; Dir for S African Affairs, Dept of State 1999–. *Address:* Dept of State, Directorate of S African Affairs, Washington, DC 20521, USA.

RENDL-MARCUS, Mildred, MBA, PH D; American economist and artist; b 30 May 1928, New York; d of Julius and Agnes (née Hokr) Rendl; m Edward Marcus 1956. *Education:* Univ of New York and Radcliffe Coll (MA). *Career:* Economist Gen Electric Co 1953–56, Bigelow-Sanford Carpet Co Inc 1956–58; Researcher 1958–59; Instructor in Econs Hunter Coll, New York 1959–60; Lecturer in Econs Columbia Univ 1960–61; Researcher in Econ Devt, Nigeria 1961–63; Sr Economist Int Div, Nat Industrial Conf Bd 1963–66; Asst Prof Grad School of Business Admin, Pace Coll 1964–66; Assoc Prof Manhattan Community Coll, City Univ of New York 1966–71, Prof 1972–85; Visiting Prof Florida Int Univ 1986; Prin MRM Assocs, Rendl Fine Art; consultant and appraiser of fine arts; participant numerous confs on economy; exhibitions include New Canaan Art Show 1982–85, Silvermine Galleries 1986, Stanford Art Asscn 1987, Phoenix Gallery (New York) 1988, Parkview Point Gallery (Miami Beach, FL) 1982–89, Art Complex (New Canaan) 1988–89, Lever House (New York) 1990, Lincoln Center (New York) 1990, Women's Caucus for Art (San Antonio, TX) 1990, Broom St Gallery (New York) 1991; mem Bd of Dirs New York City Council on Econ Educ 1970; Columnist on the econs of art, Women in Art; Research in industrialization, debtor nations

and buffer stock schemes; participant New York Univ Art and Personal Property Appraisal 1986–88; Founder-mem Int Schumpeter Econs Soc; mem American Econ Asscn, Metropolitan Econ Asscn, Industrial Relations Research Asscn, American Asscn of Univ Women, New York City Women in Arts, Audubon Artists and Nat Soc of Painters in Casein; Fellow Gerontological Asscn; Distinguished Service Award, City Univ of New York 1985. *Publications:* Investment and Development of Tropical Africa (jtly) 1959, International Trade and Finance 1965, Monetary and Banking Theory 1965, Economics 1969, Principles of Economics (jtly) 1969, Economic Progress and the Developing World 1970, Economics 1978; articles and papers in field. *Address:* Art Complex, POB 814, New Canaan, CT 06840, USA (Office); 7441 Wayne Ave, Miami Beach, FL 33141, USA (Home).

RENGER, Annemarie; German politician; b 7 Oct 1919, Leipzig; d of Fritz and Martha (née Scholz) Wildung; m 1st Emil Renger 1938 (deceased); one s; m 2nd Aleksandar Renger-Lončarević 1965 (died 1973). *Career:* Pvt Sec to Dr Kurt Schumacher 1945–52; mem SPD 1945–, mem Presidium 1961–73, Man Berlin offices 1946; mem Bundestag (Parl) 1953–, Pres 1972–76, Jt Vice-Pres 1976–90, Man SPD Parl Group 1969–72; fmr mem Advisory Ass of European Council and Ass of WEU; Vice-Pres Int Council of Social Democratic Women, Socialist Int 1972–76; Hon Fellow Hebrew Univ, Jerusalem; Hon D UNIV (Ben Gurion, Beersheba, Israel); Grosses Bundesverdienstkreuz. *Address:* c/o Deutscher Bundestag, Platz der Republik, 11011 Berlin, Germany.

RENO, Janet, BA, LL B; American lawyer and government official; b 21 July 1938, Miami, FL; d of Henry Reno and Jane Wood. *Education:* Cornell and Harvard Univs. *Career:* Called to the Bar, FL 1963; Assoc Brigham & Brigham 1963–67; Partner Lewis & Reno 1967–71; Staff Dir Judiciary Comm, Florida House of Reps, Tallahassee 1971–72; Admin Asst State Attorney 11th Judicial Circuit Florida, Miami 1973–76, State Attorney 1978–93; Partner Steel, Hector & Davis, Miami 1976–78; US Attorney-Gen 1993–2001; mem American Bar Asscn, American Law Inst, American Judicature Soc; Democrat. *Address:* c/o Dept of Justice, 10th St and Constitution Ave, NW, Washington, DC 20530-0001, USA.

RENOUARD, Isabelle Anne Marie, L EN D; French diplomatist; b 13 July 1940, Saintes; d of Michel and Suzanne (née Garnier) Herr; m François Renouard 1965; two d one s. *Education:* Lycée Jules Ferry (Paris), Univ of Paris, Inst d'Etudes Politiques and Ecole Nat d'Admin (Paris). *Career:* Assigned to Ministry of Foreign Affairs 1964–69; Second Sec, Canada 1969–72; First Sec, Algeria 1972–75; Second Counsellor French Del to N Atlantic Council, Brussels 1975–78; Deputy Dir Ministry of Foreign Affairs, Head Strategic Affairs and Disarmament, Deputy Dir Political Affairs 1978–85, Dir of French People Living Abroad and Foreigners Living in France (Consular Affairs) 1986–96; Sec-Gen de la Défense Nat 1996–98; mem Admin Bd Fondation Nat des Sciences Politiques 1996; Officier de l'Ordre Nat du Mérite; Officier de la Légion d'Honneur; Dame, Order of Isabel la Católica, Spain; Order of Merit, Greece. *Address:* 9 rue Barennes, 33000 Bordeaux, France.

RESNICK, Alice Robie, BA, JD; American judge; b 21 Aug 1939, Erie, PA; d of Adam Joseph and Alice Suzanne (née Spizarny) Robie; m Melvin L. Resnick 1970. *Education:* Siena Heights Coll (Adrian, MI) and Univ of Detroit. *Career:* Called to the Bar, OH 1964, MI 1965, US Supreme Court 1970; Asst Co Prosecutor Lucas Co, Toledo 1964–75, Trial Attorney 1965–75; Judge Toledo Municipal Court 1976–83, Ohio Sixth Dist Court of Appeals 1983–88, Ohio Supreme Court 1989–; Instructor Univ of Toledo 1968–69; organizer Crime Stopper Inc, Toledo 1981–; Trustee Siena Heights Coll 1982–; mem Mayor's Drug Council, ABA, Toledo Bar Asscn, Nat Asscn of Women Judges, American Judicature Soc, Toledo Women's Bar Asscn, Toledo Museum of Art, Int Inst of Toledo. *Address:* Supreme Court, Office, 30 E Broad St, Columbus, OH 43266, USA; 2407 Edgehill Rd, Toledo, OH 43615, USA (Home).

RESNIK, Regina; American opera singer (mezzo-soprano); b 30 Aug 1924; d of Samuel and Ruth Resnik; m 1st Harry W. Davis 1947; one s; m 2nd Arbit Blatas 1975. *Education:* Hunter Coll (New York). *Career:* Opera debut New Opera Co 1942; has performed in over 80 roles as soprano and mezzo-soprano; has appeared at major opera houses including México 1943, New York City Opera 1943–44, Metropolitan Opera, New York 1944–1983, Royal Opera House, Covent Garden, London, Vienna State Opera, Bayreuth (Germany), Salzburg (Austria), San Francisco, Chicago, La Scala, Milan (Italy), Paris, Buenos Aires, Berlin, Brussels; Stage Dir Hamburg and Wiesbaden (Germany), Venice (Italy), Sydney (Australia), Vancouver (Canada), Strasbourg (France), Warsaw, Lisbon, Madrid; appeared on Broadway in Cabaret 1987, in A Little Night Music 1990, New York City Opera, 50th anniversary celebrations Danny Kaye Playhouse; Master Classes at Metropolitan Opera House, Opéra Bastille (Paris); 50th anniversary of career celebrated in New York, Vienna and Venice (Italy); Trustee Hunter Foundation, Metropolitan Opera Guild Bd; Dr hc (Hunter) 1992; Lincoln Center and Vienna State Opera Awards; Pres's Medal; Commdr des Arts et des Lettres, France. *Address:* American Guild of Musical Artists, 1727 Broadway, USA.

RESTELLI, Augusta; Italian trade union executive; b 9 Jan 1938; d of Enrico and Maria Restelli. *Career:* Mem Internal Comm De Angeli FRUA co 1958–68; Union Rep for Castellanza/Saronno (Varese) 1969–74; Sec Responsible for Industry and the Co-ordination of Women, Varese Prov Confederazione Italiana dei Sindacati Lavoratori (CISL) trade union 1974–77; Nat Sec Responsible for Man and Structures, Federazione Italiana dei Lavoratori Tessili e Abbigliamento (FILTA-CISL) trade union 1977–85, Sec-Gen 1985. *Leisure interests:* reading, mountain-climbing. *Address:* FILTA-CISL, via Goito 39, 00185 Rome, Italy (Office); via Palmi 3, Rome, Italy (Home). *Telephone:* (6) 4270041 (Office); (6) 7021436; *Fax:* (6) 4462544 (Office).

REYES, Alicia Llamado, MBA, CPA; Philippine business executive and government official; b 14 Oct 1933, Pasay City; d of Crispin Aure, Sr and Graciana (née Pérez) Llamado; m Renato G. Reyes (died 1968); two d one s. *Education:* Univ of Santo Tomás, Univ of the East and Harvard Univ (USA). *Career:* Sec to Supervising Gov, Devt Bank of The Philippines, Makati 1961, Head of Research and Admin Services Div, Br and Agencies Dept 1965–66, Asst Man Securities Marketing Dept 1966–67, Investment Banking and Econ Research Dept 1967–69, Man 1969–73, Man Industrial Projects Dept 1974–75, Exec Officer 1975–80, Gov 1980–86; apptd Chair and CEO Philippine Amusement and Gaming Corpn, Manila 1986; Chair Lucky Textile Mills; mem Philippine Inst of CPAs, Philippines American Studies Asscn; Smith/Mundt/Fulbright Scholar 1959, Univ of the East Scholar; Certificate of Honor, Philippine Inst CPAs 1973, Outstanding Public Accountant in Govt 1983. *Address:* Philippine Amusement and Gaming Corpn, 1330 Roxas Blvd, Manila, Philippines.

REYES TOLEDO, Eugenia, M SC; Chilean biologist and naturalist; b 19 July 1939, Talca; d of José Reyes and Ana M. Toledo; m Emilio Ginouvés 1966; three s. *Education:* Licio de Niñas de Talca, Univ of Chile and Univ of Minnesota (USA). *Career:* Biologist Univ of Concepción, specializing in biological devt of mammals 1966–92, Assoc Prof 1992–; leader Programme for the Conservation of the Chilean deer *pudu puda (Mammalia, Cervidae)* 1983–; involved in Programme on Species of the World in Danger of Extinction 1983–90; Co-ordinator of Research Sociedad de Vida Silvestre de Chile (Chilean Wildlife Soc) 1990–; has produced videos and scientific publs on the biology and conservation of the species *pudu puda;* Prize for scientific videos 1989. *Address:* University of Concepción, Faculty of Biological Sciences and Natural Resources, Casilla 2407, Apdo 10, Concepción, Chile. *Telephone:* (41) 234985; *Fax:* (41) 240280.

REYNOLDS, Anna, FRAM; British opera and concert singer; b 5 June 1936, Canterbury; d of Paul Grey Reynolds and Vera Cicely Turner. *Education:* Benenden School and Royal Acad of Music. *Career:* Studied with Prof Debora Fambri, Rome; has performed at numerous int festivals including Spoleto (Italy), Edinburgh, Aix-en-Provence (France), Salzburg Easter Festival (Austria), Vienna, Bayreuth (Germany), Tanglewood (USA); appeared with leading orchestras including Chicago Symphony, New York Philharmonic, Berlin Philharmonic, London Symphony; performances include New York Metropolitan Opera, (USA), La Scala, Milan (Italy), Royal Opera House, Covent Garden (UK), Bayreuth, Rome, Chicago Lyric Opera, Teatro Colón, Buenos Aires, Teatro Fenice, Venice; recordings with Decca, EMI, Polydor, Philips. *Leisure interests:* reading, piano, travel, world-wide

correspondence. *Address:* Peesten 9, 8658 Kasendorf, Germany. *Telephone:* (9228) 1661; *Fax:* (9228) 8468; *E-mail:* jean.cox@t-online.de.

REYNOLDS, Barbara, PH D; British former professor of Italian; b 13 June 1914; d of the late Alfred Charles Reynolds; m 1st Lewis Thorpe 1939 (died 1977); one s one d; m 2nd Kenneth Imeson 1982 (died 1994). *Education:* St Paul's Girls' School and Univ Coll London. *Career:* Asst Lecturer in Italian LSE 1937–40; Asst Lecturer in Italian Univ of Cambridge 1940–45, Lecturer in Italian Literature and Language 1945–62, mem Senate Council 1961–62; Chief Exec and Gen Ed The Cambridge Italian Dictionary 1948–81; Warden Willoughby Hall, Univ of Nottingham 1963–69, Reader in Italian Studies 1966–78; Visiting Prof Univ of California at Berkeley, USA 1974–75, Wheaton Coll, IL, USA 1977–78, 1982, Trinity Coll Dublin 1980, 1981, Hope Coll, MI, USA 1982; Hon Reader in Italian, Univ of Warwick 1975–80; Man Ed Seven Anglo-American literary review 1980–89; Pres Dorothy L. Sayers Soc 1995–; Hon D LITT (Wheaton Coll) 1979, (Hope Coll, MI) 1982; Silver Medal, Italian Govt 1964; Edmund Garner Prize 1964; Silver Medal Prov Admin of Vicenza 1971; Cavaliere Ufficiale al Merito della Repubblica Italiana 1978. *Publications include:* Tredici Novelle Moderne (jtly) 1947, The Linguistic Writings of Alessandro Manzoni: a textual and chronological reconstruction 1950, The Cambridge Italian Dictionary (vol I) 1962, (vol II) 1981, Guido Farina, Painter of Verona (jtly) 1967, Concise Cambridge Italian Dictionary 1975, Cambridge-Signorelli Dizionario 1986, The Translator's Art (co-ed) 1987, The Passionate Intellect: Dorothy L. Sayers' encounter with Dante 1989, Dorothy L. Sayers: Her Life and Soul 1993, The Letters of Dorothy L. Sayers (vol I) 1995, (vol II) 1997, (vol III) 1998, (vol IV) 2000; several translations of Italian works including Orlando Furioso (vol I, Int Literary Prize 1976) 1975; numerous articles in professional journals. *Leisure interest:* friendship and family life. *Address:* 220 Milton Rd, Cambridge CB4 1LQ, UK. *Telephone:* (1223) 565380; *Fax:* (1223) 424894.

REYNOLDS, Carolyn; British television producer; b 26 Dec 1957, Bury; d of James Douglas Brooks and Elsie Heap; m Simon Nicholas Reynolds 1985; two s. *Education:* Harrogate Coll and Univ of Nancy (France). *Career:* TV Production Asst, later Producer 1979–, Creator Families drama series for ITV 1989; Producer Coronation Street (series) for Granada TV 1992, Head of Drama Serials 1994. *Leisure interests:* skiing, reading, walking. *Address:* Granada TV, Quay St, Manchester M60 9EA, UK. *Telephone:* (161) 832-7211.

REYNOLDS, Debbie; American actress; b 1 April 1932, El Paso, TX; one d (Carrie Fisher, qv). *Career:* Film debut in June Bride 1948; stage debut at Blis-Hayden Theater 1952; Prin Debbie Reynolds Hotel/Casino and Hollywood Motion Picture Museum, Las Vegas 1993–. *Films include:* The Daughter of Rosie O'Grady, Three Little Words, Two Weeks With Love, Singin' in the Rain, Give a Girl a Break, Susan Slept Here, Athena, Hit the Deck, Tender Trap, Tammy and the Bachelor, This Happy Feeling, The Mating Game, It Started with a Kiss, The Rat Race, Second Time Around, How the West Was Won, The Unsinkable Molly Brown, The Singing Nun, How Sweet It Is, That's Entertainment!, The Bodyguard, Heaven and Earth, That's Entertainment III; *TV includes:* The Debbie Reynolds Show, Aloha Paradise, Sadie and Son, Jack Paar is Alive and Well; *Publication:* Debbie: My Life 1988. *Address:* Debbie Reynolds Studios, 6514 Lankershim Blvd, N Hollywood, CA 91606, USA.

REYNOLDS, Fiona Claire, M PHIL; British organization executive; b 29 March 1958, Alston, Cumbria; d of Jeffrey Alan Reynolds and Margaret Mary Watson; m Robert W. T. Merrill 1981; three d. *Education:* Rugby High School for Girls and Newnham Coll (Cambridge). *Career:* Sec Council for Nat Parks 1980–87; Asst Dir (Policy) CPRE 1987–91, apptd Dir 1992; UNEP Global 500 Award 1990; Dir Women's Unit, Cabinet Office 1998–2000; Dir-Gen Nat Trust 2001–. *Leisure interests:* walking in the countryside, classical music, opera, literature. *Address:* National Trust, 36 Queen Anne's Gate, London SW1H 9AS, UK.

REYNOLDS, Joyce Maire, MA, FBA; British lecturer in Classics (retd); b 18 Dec 1918, London; d of William Howe and Nellie Farmer Reynolds. *Education:* Walthamstow Co High School for Girls, St Paul's

Girls' School (Hammersmith) and Somerville Coll (Oxford). *Career:* Temp Admin Officer, Bd of Trade 1941–46; Rome Scholar, British School at Rome 1946–48; Lecturer in Ancient History, King's Coll, Newcastle upon Tyne 1948–51; Fellow, Lecturer and Dir of Studies in Classics, Newnham Coll, Cambridge 1951–84, Asst Lecturer, then Lecturer in Classics, Univ of Cambridge 1952–83, Reader in the Epigraphy of the Roman Empire 1983–84, Hon Fellow Newnham Coll 1984–; Hon Fellow Somerville Coll, Oxford 1988; Visiting mem Inst of Advanced Studies, Princeton, NJ, USA 1984–85; Visiting Prof Univ of California at Berkeley, USA 1987; Visiting Lecturer Univ of Cape Town, SA 1987; Pres Soc for Libyan Studies 1982–85, Soc for the Promotion of Roman Studies 1986–89; Hon D LITT (Newcastle upon Tyne) 1984. *Publications:* The Inscriptions of Roman Tripolitania (jtly) 1951, Aphrodisias and Rome 1982, Jews and Godfearers at Aphrodisias (jtly) 1987. *Leisure interest:* walking. *Address:* Newnham College, Cambridge, CB3 9DF, UK. *Telephone:* (1223) 352033.

REYNOLDS, Margaret, DIP ED, BA; Australian politician; b 19 July 1941, Launceston, Tas; d of J. Carter; m Henry Reynolds 1963; two d one s. *Education:* Launceston High School and Univs of Tasmania and Queensland. *Career:* Teacher Australia and UK 1960–76; Lecturer James Cook Univ, N Queensland 1977–82; Councillor Townsville City Council 1979–83; N Queensland Lab Party (LP) Organizer 1982–83, mem LP Nat Platform Cttee on Aboriginal and Islander Affairs 1983–, on Status of Women 1983, on Foreign Policy 1986–87; mem Senate for Queensland 1983–99, mem Cttee for Educ and the Arts 1983–87, for Science, Tech and the Environment 1983–85, for the House 1985–87, for Finance and Govt Operations 1985–87, for Constitutional and Legal Affairs 1987, for Volatile Substance Fumes 1985, for Estimates E 1983–85, D 1985, 1986–87 (Chair F 1987), mem Jt Standing Cttee for Video Material 1985–87; Minister for Local Govt 1987–90, Minister assisting Prime Minister on Status of Women 1988–90; Vice-Pres Socialist Int Women, S Pacific 1996–; Resource Adviser UNIFEM S Pacific Region 1996–; Chair Commonwealth Human Rights Int Advisory Comm 1998–; Pres UN Asscn of Australia 1999–; mem Council for Aboriginal Reconciliation 1991–96, Commonwealth Human Rights Initiative (London/New Delhi) 1992–, Commonwealth Expert Working Group on Women and Devt 1993–95. *Publications:* The Last Bastion: Labor Women Working for Equality in the Parliaments of Australia 1995; numerous papers on women's affairs. *Leisure interests:* music, theatre, reading, swimming. *Address:* 171 St John St, Launceston, Tas 7250, Australia.

REYNOLDS, Wynetka Ann, MS, PH D; American university president and professor of biological sciences; b 3 Nov 1937, Coffeyville, KS; d of John Ethelbert and Glennie (née Beanland) King; m Thomas M. Kirschbaum; one s one d. *Education:* Kansas State Teachers' Coll and Univ of Iowa. *Career:* Asst Prof of Biology Ball State Univ, IN 1962–65; Asst Prof of Anatomy Coll of Medicine, Univ of Illinois 1965–68, Assoc Prof of Anatomy 1968–73, Research Prof of Obstetrics and Gynaecology and Prof of Anatomy 1973–, Acting Assoc Dean of Academic Affairs 1977, Assoc Vice-Chancellor and Dean of Grad Coll 1977–79; Prof of Obstetrics and Gynaecology, Prof of Anatomy and Provost, Ohio State Univ, Columbus 1979–82; Chancellor California State Univ at Long Beach 1982–90, Prof of Biology 1982–90; Chancellor City Univ of New York 1990–97; Pres Univ of Alabama 1997–; Prof California State Univ at Dominguez Hills 1982; Hon Prof of Biological Sciences San Francisco State Univ 1982; Clinical Prof of Obstetrics and Gynaecology Univ of California at Los Angeles 1985; Chair Econ Literacy Council of California 1983–89; Co-Chair Humanitas Council, Los Angeles Educ Partnership 1986–89, Fed Task Force on Women, Minorities and Handicapped in Science and Tech 1987–90; mem Bd of Dirs Regional Research Inst 1984–87, California Econ Devt Corpn 1984–90, American Council for the Arts 1986–, Gen Telephone and Electric Co (CA), Maytag Corpn, Abbott Labs, American Electric Power Co; mem Advisory Bd Congressional Black Caucus, Inst of Science, Space and Tech 1987–91; Trustee Int Life Sciences Inst, Nutritional Foundation 1987–; Southwest Museum, Los Angeles 1986–; mem Nat Council for Devt Educ 1987–, Arts in Educ Advisory Bd, Nat Educ Asscn 1989–, Nat Advisory Bd Inst of American Indian Arts 1992–, California Labour Employment and Training Corpn 1993–; AAAS and numerous other professional asscns; consultant and lecturer in field; numerous contribs to books and journals; Hon D SC (Indiana State) 1980, (Ball State) 1985, (Emporia) 1987; Hon LHD (McKen-

dree) 1984, (N Carolina) 1988, (Judaism) 1989, (Nebraska) 1992, (Colgate) 1993; Hon PH D (Fu Jen) 1987; Honoree, Women's Employment Options Conf (Pasadena) 1983. *Address:* Office of the President, University of Alabama at Birmingham, 701 20th St S, Suite 1070, Birmingham, AL 35233, USA.

REZA, (Evelyne Agnès) Yasmina; French playwright, actress and comedian; b 1 May 1959, Paris; d of the late Jean Reza and of Nora (née Heltaï) Reza; one s one d. *Education:* Lycée de St-Cloud, Paris Univ X, Nanterre, Ecole Jacques Lecoq. *Career:* Fmr actress; plays have been performed in France, UK, Switzerland, Austria, Canada, Israel, the Netherlands and Germany; Chevalier des Arts et des Lettres; Prix du Jeune Théâtre Beatrix Dussane-André Roussin de l'Acad Française 1991. *Stage appearances include:* Le malade imaginaire 1977, Antigone 1977, Un sang fort 1977, La mort de Gaspard Hauser 1978, L'An mil 1980, Le piège de Méduse 1983, Le veilleur de nuit 1986, Enorme changement de dernière minute 1989, La fausse suivante 1990; Plays directed include: Birds in the Night 1979, Marie la louve 1981; Plays written include: Conversations après un enterrement 1987 (Molière Award for Best Author, Prix des Talents nouveaux de la Soc des Auteurs et Compositeurs dramatiques, Johnson Foundation Prize), La Traversée de l'hiver 1989, La Métamorphose (adapted) 1988, Art 1994, L'Homme du hasard, Trois versions d'une vie 2000, Life X3 2000; Screenplays written include: Jusqu'à la nuit (also dir) 1984, Le goûter chez Niels 1986, A demain 1992; *Publication:* Hammerklavier 2000. *Address:* c/o Marta Andras (Marton Play), 14 rue des Sablons, 75116 Paris, France.

RHEINSBERG, Anna Rose Anette; German poet and essayist; b 24 Sept 1956, Berlin; d of Joachim and Anneliese Puscheck Rheinsberg; m 1st Matthias Hoffbauer 1975 (divorced 1979); m 2nd Mischka Krahl Rheinsberg 1980; one s. *Education:* Friedrichs Gymnasium (Kassel) and Philipps Univ (Marburg). *Career:* Mem feminist movt 1975–; writer and ed; acted in Anna experimental film, Austria 1980. *Publications:* Bella Donna 1981, Hannah 1982, Alles trutschen (2nd edn) 1989, Wolfskuss 1984, Annakonda 1985, 1986, Marthe und Ruth 1987, Fée 1987, Herzlos 1988, Kriegs/Läufe 1989, Narcisse noir 1990. *Leisure interests:* going for walks with the dog, swimming, films, researching women of the 1920s. *Address:* Wehrdaer Weg 43A, 3550 Marburg/Lahn 1, Germany. *Telephone:* (6421) 64375.

RHODES, Jeannine Marie Andrée (Jane); French opera singer; b 13 March 1929, Paris; m Roberto Benzi 1966. *Education:* Centre de la rue Blanche. *Career:* Operatic debut in La damnation de Faust in Nancy 1953; performances at the Opéra de Paris, Opéra Comique, Metropolitan Opera House (New York, USA), Théâtre de Paris and at festivals; has taken part in numerous nat and int tours, including tours of Japan, USA and Argentina; has made many recordings, including Prokofiev's L'ange de feu (Premier Grand Prix, Acad du disque français, Acad Charles Cros 1958); Chevalier de l'Ordre Nat du Mérite; Officier des Art et des Lettres. *Operas include:* La damnation de Faust 1953, Le fou, La belle Hélène (also recording, Premier Prix, Disque Lyrique), Salome, Werther, Tosca, Carmen (also film, Prize for Best Televised Film 1962) 1959, 1961–63, La voix humaine 1968, La Périchole 1969, Il était une fois l'opérette 1972, La vie parisienne 1985; *Film:* Un mari c'est un mari 1976. *Address:* 12 Villa Sainte Foy, 92200 Neuilly-sur-Seine, France.

RHODES, Zandra Lindsey, CBE, FCSD, FSIAD; British textile and fashion designer; b 19 Sept 1940, Chatham, Kent; d of Albert James and Beatrice Ellen (née Twigg) Rhodes. *Education:* Medway and Royal Colls of Art. *Career:* Began producing dresses using own prints 1966; founding partner and designer Fulham Clothes Shop, London 1967–68; freelance designer, producing own collections for British and US markets 1968–75; Founder-Dir (with Anne Knight and Ronnie Stirling) Zandra Rhodes (UK) Ltd and Zandra Rhodes (Shops) Ltd 1975, opened first shop, London 1975; designs featured in Bloomingdale's (New York), Marshall Field's (Chicago, USA), Seibu, Tokyo, and Harrods (London); licences include Wamsutta sheets and pillowcases (USA) 1976, Eve Stillman Lingerie (USA) 1977, CVP designs, interior fabrics and settings (UK) 1977, Philip Hockley decorative furs (UK) 1986, Zandra Rhodes saris (India) 1987, Littlewoods catalogues (UK) for printed T-shirts and intarsia sweaters 1988, Hilmet silk scarves and men's ties (UK) 1989, Bonnay perfume (UK) 1993, Coats Patons needlepoint (UK) 1993, Pologeorgis Furs (USA) 1995, Zandra Rhodes

II handpainted ready-to-wear collection (Hong Kong) 1995, Grattons Catalogue sheets and duvets (UK) 1996; work featured in numerous exhibitions and perm collections including Victoria and Albert Museum, London, Metropolitan Museum of Art, New York, Smithsonian Inst, Washington, DC, Museum of Applied Arts and Sciences, Sydney, Australia; retrospectives in El Paso, Texas 1984, Columbus, Ohio 1987, Tokyo 1987, 1991, Athenaeum Library, La Jolla 1996; water-colour exhibitions in New York, Los Angeles, New Orleans 1989, N Carolina 1992, f Zandra Rhodes Museum of Fashion and Textiles, UK 1996; Fellow Soc of Industrial Artists and Designers; Hon Fellow Kent Inst of Art and Design 1992; Hon DFA (Int Fine Arts Coll, Miami) 1986; Hon DD (CNAA) 1987, Hon D LITT (Westminster) 2000; Dr hc (Royal Coll of Art) 1986; numerous awards include Designer of the Year, English Fashion Trade 1972, Royal Designer for Industry 1974, Emmy Award for Best Costume Designs in Romeo and Juliet on Ice, CBS TV 1984, Alpha Award, New Orleans 1985, 1991, Woman of Distinction Award, Northwood Inst, Dallas 1986, Observer Award as top UK Textile Designer 1990, Hall of Fame Award, British Fashion Council 1995. Publications: The Art of Zandra Rhodes (autobiog) 1984, The Zandra Rhodes Collection by Brother 1988. Leisure interests: travelling, drawing, gardening, cooking. Address: 79–85 Bermondsey St, London SE1 3XF, UK. Telephone: (20) 7403-5333 (Office).

RHYS-JAMES, Shani, BA; British artist; b 2 May 1953, Australia; d of Harold Marcus Rhys-James and Jeannie James-Money; m Stephen West 1977; two s. Education: Parliament Hill Girls School (London), Loughborough Coll of Art and Cen St Martin's Coll of Art and Design (London). Career: Regular exhibitions with Martin Tinney (Cardiff) 1991–99, Stephen Lacey (London); work in art collections of Nat Museum of Wales, Newport Museum and Art Gallery, Cyfartha Castle, Merthyr Tidfyl, Usher Gallery, Arts Council of England, Gallery of Modern Art (Glasgow), Wolverhampton Art Gallery, Birmingham City Museum and Art Gallery, National Library of Wales; featured artist Carlow Festival 2000, Royal Cambrian Acad Three-Person show 2001; mem Royal Cambrian Acad 1994; awards include BBC Wales Visual Artist Award 1994, BP Nat Portrait Award, Gold Medal for Fine Art Royal Nat Eisteddfod, First Prize Hunting/Observer Prize, and others. Exhibitions include: solo: Blood Ties (Wrexham Arts Centre and touring) 1993, Facing the Self (Oriel Mostyn and touring) 1997, Stephen Lacey Gallery 2000; group: Disclosure(s) (Oriel Mostyn and touring) 1994, Reclaiming the Madonna (Usher Gallery, Lincoln and touring) 1994, In the Looking Glass (Usher Gallery and touring) 1996, Birmingham City Art Gallery Gas Hall 2000; TV: Blood Ties 1993, Painting the Dragon 2000, The Little Picture 2000, Paintings from Paradise 2000. Leisure interests: piano, films, plays, books, writing poetry, restoring our Welsh farm. Address: Dolpebyll, Llangadfan, Welshpool, Powys, SY21 0PU, UK. Telephone: (1938) 820469; Fax: (1938) 820469.

RIBNIKAR, Jara; Yugoslav writer; b 23 Aug 1912, Hradec, Czech Republic; d of Emil and Ana Hajek; m Vladislav Ribnikar 1936; one s one d. Education: Classic Gymnasium (Prague). Career: Fought with the Nat Liberation Army (Partisans) in Second World War; Ed works on arts and literature, Yugoslavia publishing house; work trans in USA, Russia, Germany, Bulgaria, Czechoslovakia, Hungary, Romania, UK, Poland; Pres Yugoslav PEN; literary awards for short story (Zagreb, Croatia) and film-script (Bosnia). Publications include: Novels: Jan Nepomuk (Serbian Writers Asscn Award), I and You and She, Copperskin, Hallucinations and others; Short stories: Life and Story (Yugoslav Award), The Power of Life and others. Address: 11000 Belgrade, Generala Zdanova 32, Yugoslavia. Telephone: (11) 334 1468.

RICARDO-CAMPBELL, Rita, PH D; American economist; b 16 March 1920, Boston, MA; d of David and Elizabeth (née Jones) Ricardo; m W. Glenn Campbell 1946; three d. Education: Simmons Coll and Harvard Univ. Career: Teaching posts at Harvard and Tufts Univs 1946–51; mem Labor Economist Wage Stabilization Bd, Washington, DC 1951–53; Economist Ways and Means Comm, House of Reps 1953, Consultant Economist House of Reps 1957–70; Visiting Prof San José State Univ, CA 1960–61; Sr Fellow Hoover Inst on War, Revolution and Peace, Stanford Univ, CA 1968–, Lecturer Medical School 1973–78; California Commr Western Interstate Comm for Higher Educ (WICHE) 1967–75, Chair 1970–71; Chair, Chief Exec round-table on containing health care costs, New York 1990; Speaker World Congress on Health Econs, Zurich, Switzerland 1990; Dir

Watkins-Johnson Co, Samaritan Medical Center Man Group, Gillette Co; mem Advisory Council SRI Int 1977–, Pres's Econ Policy Advisory Bd 1981–89, Nat Council on the Humanities 1982–88, Pres's Cttee on the Nat Medal of Science 1988–. Publications include: Drug Lag: Federal Government Decision Making 1976, Social Security: Promise and Reality 1977, Economics of Mobilization and War (jtly), The Economics and Politics of Health (2nd edn) 1985, Below-Replacement Fertility in Industrial Societies (co-ed) 1987, Issues in Contemporary Retirement (co-ed) 1988, Hostile Takeover that Failed: The Gillette Company 1997; contribs to econ publs. Leisure interests: tennis, swimming, reading. Address: Stanford University, Hoover Institution on War, Revolution and Peace, Stanford, CA 94305-6010, USA. Telephone: (415) 723-2074; Fax: (415) 723-1687.

RICCI, Christina; American actress; b 12 Feb 1980, Santa Monica, CA. Career: Began acting career in commercials. Films: Mermaids 1990, The Hard Way 1991, The Addams Family 1991, The Cemetery Club 1993, Addams Family Values 1993, Casper 1995, Now and Then 1995, Gold Diggers: The Secret of Bear Mountain 1995, That Darn Cat 1996, Last of the High Kings 1996, Bastard Out of Carolina 1996, Ice Storm 1997, Little Red Riding Hood 1997, Fear and Loathing in Las Vegas 1998, Desert Blue 1998, Buffalo 66 1998, The Opposite of Sex 1998, Small Soldiers 1998, Pecker 1999, 200 Cigarettes 1999, Sleepy Hollow 1999, The Man Who Cried 2000. Address: c/o ICM, 8942 Wilshire Blvd, Beverly Hills, CA 90211, USA.

RICCIARDI, Mirella; Kenyan photographer; b 1933; m Lorenzo Ricciardi; two c. Career: Fashion photographer for magazines including Vogue, Cosmopolitan and Brides; special Stills Photographer for films including The Mission and Out of Africa; Expedition Photographer for African Rainbow project 1989; made Frontiers of Fire film for BBC while photographing S American Indian tribal life. Publications: Vanishing Africa, Vanishing Amazon 1991.

RICCIARELLI, Katia; Italian opera singer; b 18 Jan 1946, Rovigo; m Pippo Baudo 1986. Education: Benedetto Marcello Conservatory (Venice). Career: Debut at Mantua 1969; appearances include Lyric Opera, Chicago, USA 1972, Royal Opera House, Covent Garden, London 1974, La Scala, Milan 1976, Metropolitan Opera Co, New York, USA 1975, San Francisco Opera, USA, Paris Opera, Verona Festival. Operas include: La Bohème 1969, 1974, I Due Foscari 1972, Suor Angelica 1976, Anna Bolena, Lucrezia Borgia, Imogene, Don Carlos 1989; Recordings include: I Due Foscari, Turandot, Carmen, Aida, Un Ballo in Maschera, Falstaff, Il Trovatore, La Bohème, Tosca. Address: c/o John Coast Ltd, Manfield House, 376-9 Strand, London WC2R 0LR, UK (Office).

RICE, Condoleezza, PH D; American professor of political science; b 14 Nov 1954, Birmingham, AL. Education: Univ of Denver and Univ of Notre Dame. Career: Lecturer at Stanford Univ (Calif) 1981–2001, Provost 1993–99, currently Hoover Sr Fellow and Prof of Political Science; Special Asst to Dir of Jt Chiefs of Staff 1986; Dir, then Sr Dir of Soviet and East European Affairs, Nat Security Council 1989–91; Special Asst to Pres for Nat Security Affairs 1989–91; primary foreign policy advisor to presidential cand George W. Bush 1999–; Nat Security Advisor Jan 2001–; mem Bd of Dirs Chevron Corpn, Charles Schwab Corpn, William and Flora Hewlett Foundation, and numerous other bds; Sr Fellow Inst for Int Studies, Stanford; Fellow American Acad of Arts and Sciences; Dr hc (Morehouse Coll) 1991, (Univ of AL) 1994, (Univ of Notre Dame) 1995. Publications: Uncertain Allegiance: The Soviet Union and the Czechoslovak Army 1984, The Gorbachev Era (co-author) 1986, Germany Unified and Europe Transformed (co-author) 1995; and numerous articles on Soviet and East European foreign and defence policy. Address: c/o The White House, 1600 Pennsylvania Avenue, NW, Washington, DC 20500, USA.

RICE, Dorothy P., BA; American professor emeritus and medical economist; b 11 June 1922, Brooklyn, NY; d of Gershon and Lena (née Schiff) Pechman; m John D. Rice 1943; three s. Education: Brooklyn Coll (NY), Univ of Wisconsin and George Washington Univ (Washington, DC). Career: Clerk Dept of Labor 1941–42; Economist War Production Bd 1942–44, Nat War Labor Bd 1944–45, Nat Wage Stabilization Bd 1945–47; Health Economist, US Public Health Service (USPHS) 1947–49, Public Health Analyst 1960–62, 1964–65; Social

Science Analyst, Social Security Admin 1962–64, Chief Health Insurance Research Br 1965–72, Deputy Asst Commr Office of Research and Statistics 1972–76; Dir Nat Center for Health Statistics, Hyattsville, MD 1976–82; Prof-in-Residence Dept of Social and Behavioral Sciences, Inst for Health and Ageing, Univ of California at San Francisco 1982–, Inst for Health Policy Studies 1982–94, Prof Emer 1994–; more than 200 articles and 15 books and monographs published; numerous honours and awards including Presidential Sr Exec Meritorious Award 1982, Sedgwick Memorial Award, American Public Health Asscn 1988, Presidential Award, Asscn for Health Services Research 1988. *Address:* University of California at San Francisco, Inst for Health and Ageing, Dept of Social and Behavioral Sciences, School of Nursing, San Francisco, CA 94143-0646, USA (Office); 13895 Campus Drive, Oakland, CA 94605, USA (Home). *Telephone:* (415) 476-2771 (Office); (510) 638-7150 (Home); *Fax:* (415) 502-5208 (Office); *E-mail:* rice@itsa.ucsf.edu (Office); drice39223@aol.com (Home); *Internet:* nurseweb.ucsf.edu/iha (Office).

RICH, Adrienne, AB; American writer; b 16 May 1929, Baltimore, MD; d of Arnold Rich and Helen Elizabeth Jones; m Alfred Conrad (died 1970); three s. *Education:* Radcliffe Coll (MA). *Career:* Teacher New York Poetry Center 1966–67; Visiting Lecturer Swarthmore Coll 1967–69; Adjunct Prof Columbia Univ 1967–69; Lecturer City Coll of New York 1968–70, Instructor 1970–71, Asst Prof of English 1971–72, 1974–75; Visiting Prof of Creative Literature, Brandeis Univ 1972–73; Prof of English Rutgers Univ 1976–79; Prof-at-Large Cornell Univ 1981–87; Lecturer and Visiting Prof, Scripps Coll 1983, 1984; Prof of English and Feminist Studies, Stanford Univ 1986–93; Marjorie Kovler Visiting Lecturer, Univ of Chicago 1989; mem American Acad of Arts and Letters, PEN; Guggenheim Fellow 1952, 1961; Acad of American Poets Fellowship 1993; MacArthur Fellowship 1994–99; Hon LITT D (Wheaton Coll) 1967, (Smith Coll) 1979, (Brandeis) 1987, (Wooster Coll) 1989, (Harvard, City Coll of New York 1990; Yale Series of Younger Poets Award 1951; Ridgely Torrance Memorial Award, Poetry Soc of America 1955; Shelley Memorial Award 1971; Nat Book Award 1974; Ruth Lilly Prize 1987; Brandeis Medal in Poetry 1987; Nat Poetry Asscn Award 1989; LA Times Book Award 1992; Frost Silver Medal, Poetry Soc of America 1992; The Poets' Prize 1993; Acad of American Poets Dorothea Tanning Award 1996; Lannan Foundation Lifetime Achievement Award 1999. *Publications:* A Change of World 1951, The Diamond Cutters and Other Poems 1955, Snapshots of a Daughter-in-Law 1963, Necessities of Life 1962–65, 1965–68 1969, Leaflets, Poems 1965–68, The Will to Change 1971, Diving into the Wreck 1973, Of Woman Born: Motherhood as Experience and Institution 1976, On Lies, Secrets and Silence: Selected Prose 1966–78 1979, A Wild Patience Has Taken Me This Far: Poems 1978–81 1981, The Fact of a Doorframe: Poems 1950–84 1984, Blood, Bread and Poverty: Selected Prose 1979–85 1986, Your Native Land, Your Life 1986, Time's Power: Poems 1985–88 1989, An Atlas of the Difficult World: Poems 1988–91 1991, Collected Early Poems 1950–1970 1993, What Is Found There: Notebooks on Poetry and Politics 1993, Dark Fields of the Republic: Poems 1991–95 1995, Midnight Salvage 1999, Arts of the Possible: Essays and Conversations 2001, Fox: Poems 1998–2000 2001. *Address:* c/o W. W. Norton, 500 Fifth Ave, New York, NY 10110, USA.

RICHARD, Wendy; British actress; b 20 July, Teesside. *Career:* Has appeared in numerous films and TV programmes since 1960. *Films include:* No Blade of Grass, Gumshoe, Carry on Matron, Bless This House, On the Buses, Carry on Girls; *TV includes:* Are You Being Served?, Z Cars, Dad's Army, Please Sir, On The Buses, Fenn Street Gang, Not on Your Nellie, EastEnders 1986–. *Address:* c/o David White, 2 Ormond Rd, Richmond, Surrey TW10 6TH, UK.

RICHARDS, (Dorothy) Ann Willis, BA; American former state governor; b 1 Sept 1933, Waco, TX; d of Cecil and Ona (née Warren) Willis; m David Richards 1953 (divorced 1984); two s two d. *Education:* Waco High School, Baylor Univ and Univ of Texas. *Career:* Teacher of govt and history 1955–57; Campaign Man and Asst to Sarah Weddington 1972–75; Co-Commr with responsibility for road maintenance and social services (first woman), Travis Co, Austin, TX 1977–82; cr Infant Parent Training Program and centres for rape victims and battered women; mem Pres's Advisory Comm on Women 1979; Texas State Treas for Austin 1983–91; mem State Banking Bd, TX 1982; Chair Texas Depository Bd 1983; mem various bds and cttees;

Gov of Texas (Democrat) 1991–95; Sr Adviser Verner, Liipfert, Bernhard, McPherson & Hand, Austin 1995–; fmr mem Nat Asscn for the Advancement of Colored People; Woman of the Year, Texas Women's Political Caucus 1981; mem Texas Women's Hall of Fame 1985. *Publication:* Straight From the Heart 1989. *Leisure interests:* films, basketball. *Address:* Verner, Liipfert, Bernhard, McPherson & Hand, POB 684746, Austin, TX 78768, USA.

RICHARDSON, Joanna, MA, FRSL; British writer; b London; d of the late Frederick and Charlotte (née Benjamin) Richardson. *Education:* The Downs School (Seaford, Sussex) and St Anne's Coll (Oxford). *Career:* Mem Council RSL 1961–86; Chevalier des Arts et des Lettres 1987. *Publications:* Fanny Brawne: a biography 1952, Théophile Gautier: His Life and Times 1958, Edward FitzGerald 1960, The Pre-Eminent Victorian: A Study of Tennyson 1962, The Everlasting Spell: A Study of Keats and His Friends 1963, Introduction to Victor Hugo: Choses Vues 1964, Edward Lear 1965, George IV: A Portrait 1966, Creevey and Greville 1967, Princess Mathilde 1969, Verlaine 1971, Enid Starkie 1973, Stendhal: a critical biography 1974, Victor Hugo 1976, Zola 1978, Keats and His Circle: an album of portraits 1980, The Life and Letters of John Keats 1981, Letters from Lambeth: The Correspondence of the Reynolds Family with John Freeman Milward Dovaston 1808–1815 1981, Colette 1983, Judith Gautier (Prix Goncourt de la Biographie 1989, first non-French writer to receive this award) 1987, Portrait of a Bonaparte: The Life and Times of Joseph-Napoleon Primoli 1851–1927 1987, Baudelaire 1994; Works translated and edited include: FitzGerald: Selected Works 1962 (ed), Verlaine Poems (ed and trans) 1974, Baudelaire Poems (ed and trans) 1975, Gautier, Mademoiselle de Maupin (trans) 1981; has contributed to The Times, The Times Literary Supplement, Spectator, New Statesman, New York Times Book Review, The Washington Post, French Studies, French Studies Bulletin, Modern Language Review, Keats–Shelley Memorial Bulletin, etc. *Leisure interest:* collecting antiques. *Address:* c/o Curtis Brown Group, Haymarket House, 28–29 Haymarket, London SW1Y 4SP, UK. *Telephone:* (20) 7396-6600.

RICHARDSON, Joely; British actress; b 1958, Lancs; d of the late Tony Richardson and of Vanessa Redgrave (qv); sister of Natasha Richardson (qv); m Tim Bevan (divorced 1997); one d. *Education:* Lycée Français and St Paul's Girls' School, Pinellas Park High School (FL, USA), The Thacher School (Ojai, CA) and Royal Acad of Dramatic Art (London). *Career:* Has appeared in several films; London stage debut in Steel Magnolias 1989. *Films:* Wetherby 1985, Drowning by Numbers 1988, Shining Through 1991, Rebecca's Daughters 1992, Lady Chatterley's Lover (TV film) 1993, Loch Ness 1994, Sister, My Sister 1995, 101 Dalmatians 1995, Believe Me 1995, The Hollow Reed 1996, Event Horizon 1996, Wrestling with Alligators, Under Heaven, Patriot, Maybe Baby 2000; *TV appearances include:* Body Contact, Behaving Badly 1989, Heading Home, Lady Chatterley's Lover 1993, The Tribe, Echo.

RICHARDSON, Margaret Milner (Peggy), AB, JD; American lawyer and federal official; b 14 May 1943, Waco, TX; d of James W. and Margaret Wiebusch Milner; m John L. Richardson 1967; one d. *Education:* Vassar Coll and George Washington Univ. *Career:* Called to the Bar, VA and DC 1968, US District Court, DC 1968, US Court of Appeals 1968, US Claims Court 1969, US Tax Court 1970, US Supreme Court 1971; Clerk US Claims Court, Washington, DC; mem staff Office of the Chief Counsel, Inland Revenue Service, Washington, DC 1969–77, mem Commr's Advisory Group 1988–90 (Chair 1990), Commr 1993–97; Partner Ernst & Young, Washington 1997–; mem staff specializing in tax and insurance regulation Sutherland, Asbill and Brennan, Washington, DC 1977–80, Partner 1980–93; mem Fed Tax Advisory Group Prentice Hall; helped in Clinton 1992 presidential election campaign, Team Leader Justice Dept/Civil Rights Cluster, Presidential Transition; mem ABA, Fed Bar Asscn; contribs to professional journals. *Address:* 1225 Connecticut Ave, NW, Washington, DC 20036, USA.

RICHARDSON, Miranda; British actress; b 3 March 1958, Southport; d of William Alan and Marian Georgina (née Townsend) Richardson. *Education:* St Wyburn (Southport), Southport High School for Girls and Bristol Old Vic Theatre School. *Career:* Performed at Manchester Library Theatre 1979–80, Derby Playhouse, Duke's Playhouse (Lancaster), Bristol Old Vic, Leicester Haymarket 1982–83; Best Actress Award, London Evening Standard 1985; Most Promising Artiste Award, Variety Club 1985; Golden Globe Award for Best Comedy Actress 1993. *Plays include:* Moving 1980–81, Edmund 1985, A Lie of the Mind 1987, The Changeling 1988, Mountain Language 1988, Etta Jankes 1990, Orlando 1996, The Designated Mourner 1996, Aunt Dan and Lemon 1999; *Films include:* Dance With a Stranger (City Limits Best Film Actress 1985), Underworld, Death of the Heart, Empire of the Sun, The Mad Monkey, Dr Grasler, Eat the Rich, Twisted Obsession, The Bachelor 1992, Enchanted April (Golden Globe Award for Best Musical or Comedy Film Actress) 1992, The Crying Game 1992, Damage (BAFTA Award for Best Supporting Actress 1993), Tom and Viv 1994, La Nuit et Le Moment 1994, Kansas City, Evening Star 1996, The Designated Mourner 1996, Apostle 1996, All for Love 1996, Jacob Two Two and the Hooded Fang 1998, The Big Brass Ring 1998, Sleepy Hollow 1999, Get Carter 1999; *TV appearances include:* Series: Agony, The Hard Word, Sorrell and Son, Blackadder II, III and IV, Die Kinder 1990, A Dance to the Music of Time 1998; Plays: The Master Builder, The Demon Lover, After Pilkington, Sweet As You Are (Royal TV Soc Award 1987–88), Ball-trap on the Côte Sauvage 1989, Fatherland (Golden Globe Award), Old Times 1991, The Scold's Bridle, Merlin 1997, Alice 1998, Ted and Ralph 1998. *Leisure interests:* reading, walking, softball, gardening, music, junk shops, occasional art. *Address:* c/o ICM, 76 Oxford St, London W1N 0AX, UK.

RICHARDSON, Natasha Jane; British actress; b 11 May 1963, London; d of the late Tony Richardson and of Vanessa Redgrave (qv); sister of Joely Richardson (qv); m 1st Robert Fox 1990 (divorced 1994); m 2nd Liam Neeson 1994; two s. *Education:* Lycée Français (London), St Paul's Girls' School and Cen School of Speech and Drama (London). *Career:* Film and theatre actress 1983–; Most Promising Newcomer Award 1986, Best Actress, Plays and Players Award 1986, 1990; Best Actress, London Evening Standard Film Awards 1990; Best Actress, London Theatre Critics Award 1990. *Plays include:* A Midsummer Night's Dream, Hamlet, The Seagull 1985, China 1986, High Society 1986, Anna Christie 1990, 1992, Cabaret (Tony Award) 1998, Closer 1999; *Films include:* Every Picture Tells A Story 1985, Gothic 1987, A Month in the Country 1987, Patty Hearst 1988, Fat Man and the Little Boy 1989, The Handmaid's Tale 1990, The Comfort of Strangers 1990, The Favor, the Watch and the Very Big Fish 1992, Past Midnight 1994, Widow's Peak 1994, Nell 1994, The Parent Trap 1998, Blow Dry 2000, Waking up in Reno 2000; *TV appearances include:* The Adventures of Sherlock Holmes, The Copper Beeches, In a Secret State 1985, Ghosts 1986, Hostages 1992, Suddenly Last Summer 1993, Zelda 1993, Tales from the Crypt 1996, Haven 2000. *Address:* ICM Limited, Oxford House, 76 Oxford St, London W1N 0AX, UK.

RICHARDSON, Ruth (R. M.), LL B; New Zealand politician; b 13 Dec 1950; d of Ross Pearce and Rita Joan Richardson; m Andrew Evan Wright 1975; one s one d. *Education:* Univ of Canterbury (NZ). *Career:* Fmr Legal Adviser Federated Farmers; mem House of Reps (Parl, Nat Party) for Selwyn 1981–94, Shadow Minister of Finance 1987, Minister of Finance and Minister with responsibility for Earthquake and War Damage Comm, Nat Provident Fund 1990–94; consultant Ruth Richardson (NZ) Ltd 1994–; Dir Reserve Bank of NZ 1999–. *Leisure interests:* gardening, running, swimming. *Address:* RD5, Christchurch, New Zealand. *Telephone:* (3) 347-9146.

RICHARDSON OF CALOW, Baroness (Life Peer), cr 1998, of Calow in the County of Derbyshire, **Rev Kathleen Margaret Richardson,** OBE, DIP ED; British Methodist minister; b 24 Feb 1938, Chesterfield; d of Francis William and Margaret Fountain; m Ian D. G. Richardson 1964; three d. *Education:* St Helena School (Chesterfield), Stockwell Coll (Bromley, Kent), Wesley Deaconess Coll (Ilkley, W Yorks) and Wesley House Theological Coll (Cambridge). *Career:* Teacher of Religious Educ, Chesterfield 1958–61; Wesley Deaconess Champness Hall, Rochdale 1961–64; mem Team Ministry in ecumenical project, Stevenage, Herts 1973–77; Methodist Minister, Denby Dale and Clayton W Circuit, W Yorks 1979–87; Chair W Yorks Methodist Dist 1987–95; Pres Methodist Conf 1992–93; Moderator Free Church Fed Council 1995–99; Co-Pres Churches Together in England 1995–99; Hon D LITT; Hon LL D; Hon DD. *Leisure interests:* craft design, music, literature. *Address:* House of Lords, London SW1A 0PW, UK. *Telephone:* (20) 7219-0314.

RICHES, Lucinda Jane, MA; British financier; b 26 July 1967, Dorking; d of Kenneth Riches and Margaret Blake; m Timothy Fitzroy Foreman 1993; two d. *Education:* Brasenose Coll (Oxford) and Univ of Pennsylvania (PA, USA). *Career:* With Chase Manhattan Bank (London) 1984–86; Exec Corp Finance, SG Warburg & Co Ltd (now UBS Warburg) 1986–89, joined Equity Capital Markets Dept 1989, Head of Equity Capital Markets (NY) 1992–94, Head of European Capital Markets (London) 1995–99, Jt Global Head of Equity Capital Markets (London) 1999–; Thouron Scholarship to Univ of Pennsylvania 1983–84. *Leisure interests:* outdoors, hiking, family. *Address:* 1 Finsbury Avenue, London EC2M 2PP, UK. *Telephone:* (20) 7568-2260; *Fax:* (20) 7568-4127; *E-mail:* lucinda.riches@ubsw.com.

RICHMAN, Stella; British television producer and actress; b 9 Nov 1922, London; d of Jacob and Leoni Richman; m 1st Alec Clunes 1950; m 2nd Victor Brusa 1953 (died 1965); one d one s; m 3rd Alec Hyams. *Education:* John Howard Secondary School and London Theatre Studio. *Career:* Actress Perth and Dundee Repertory cos; script-reader for TV cos including BBC; formed Script Dept for ATV 1960, Drama Producer 1963; Producer Rediffusion 1964, later Head of Series; Drama Producer London Weekend TV 1968, Man Dir London Weekend Int 1969, Controller of Programmes London Weekend TV 1970–71; Co-Founder Stella Richman Productions 1965–88; propr the White Elephant Club, the White Elephant on the River 1972–78; intermittent actress Bristol Old Vic 1990–; Fellow Royal TV Soc 1982. *TV productions include:* Love Story, The Informer, Blackmail, Half Hour Story, Jennie, Lady Randolph Churchill, Clayhanger, Just William; *Plays acted in include:* Prick Up Your Ears, The Accountant; *Publications:* White Elephant Cookery Book, Celebrity Cookery Book. *Leisure interests:* travel, growing herbs, theatre, reading biographies. *Address:* Garden Flat, 5 Hill Rd, London NW8 9QE, UK. *Telephone:* (20) 7286-5127; *E-mail:* stellarichman@aol.com.

RICKARDS, Jocelyn; Australian costume designer and painter; b 29 July 1924, Melbourne; d of Bertie and Gertrud Rickards; m Clive Donner 1971. *Education:* Merton Hall (Melbourne), Ascham and Royal Coll of Art (Sydney). *Career:* Film and theatre designer 1956–; group exhibitions include Soc of Artists, Sydney 1940–48, Redfern Gallery, London 1951, Pigeonhole Gallery, London 1977, Contemporary Art Soc, British Film Archives; Lecturer in Print Design Univ of S California 1979–80; took part in BBC TV programme on the life of Graham Greene 1992; regular contrib to Richard Ingram's The Oldie magazine. *Plays include:* West Side Story, The World of Paul Slickey, The Party, Meals on Wheels, Stealing Heaven 1988; *Films include:* Look Back in Anger, The Entertainer, From Russia with Love, The Knack, Blow Up, Morgan a Suitable Case for Treatment (Acad Award nomination) 1965, Mademoiselle (British Film Award 1966), Alfred the Great, Ryan's Daughter (Silver Medal Belgrade Film Festival) 1972, Sunday Bloody Sunday, Charlie Chan and the Curse of the Dragon Queen; *Publication:* The Painted Banquet (autobiog) 1987. *Leisure interests:* painting, reading, cooking, travel, writing. *Address:* Flat 20, Thames Reach, Rainville Rd, London W6 9HS, UK.

RIDE, Sally, PH D; American astronaut and professor of physics; b 26 May 1951, Los Angeles; d of Dale and Joyce Ride; m Steven Hawley (divorced). *Education:* Westlake High School (Los Angeles) and Stanford Univ. *Career:* Trainee Astronaut NASA 1978–79, astronaut 1979–87, on-orbit capsule communicator STS-2 mission, Johnson Space Center, NASA, Houston, on-orbit capsule communicator STS-3 mission NASA, mission specialist STS-7 1983, STS-41G 1984; Scientific Fellow Stanford Univ 1987–89; Prof of Physics, Univ of California at San Diego 1989–96; mem Presidential Comm on Space Shuttle 1986, Presidential Comm of Advisers on Science and Tech 1994–; Dir Apple Computer Inc 1988–90. *Publications:* To Space and Back (jtly) 1986, Voyager: An Adventure to the Edge of the Solar System 1992, The Third Planet: Exploring the Earth from Space 1994, The Mystery of Mars 1999. *Address:* California Space Institute, 0426, University of California at San Diego, La Jolla, CA 92093, USA. *Telephone:* (619) 534-5827 Fax: (619) 822-1277; *Fax:* (619) 822-1277.

RIDGWAY, Rozanne Le Jeanne, BA; American former diplomatist, civil servant and business executive; b 22 Aug 1935, St Paul; d of H. Clay and Ethel Rozanne (née Cote) Ridgway; m Theodore E. Deming. *Education:* Hamline Univ (St Paul, MN). *Career:* Foreign Service

1957–89, Amb for Oceans and Fisheries 1975–77, Amb to Finland 1977–80, to GDR 1982–85; Counselor Dept of State, Washington, DC 1980–81, Special Asst to Sec of State 1981, Asst Sec of State for Europe and Canada 1985–89; Pres The Atlantic Council of US 1989–93, Co-Chair 1993–96; mem Bd Dirs 3M Corpn, RJR Nabisco, Union Carbide Corpn, Bell Atlantic, Citicorp; Trustee Hamline Univ; Fellow Nat Acad of Public Admin; Hon LL D (Hamline) 1978, (George Washington) 1986, (Helsinki, Hood Coll, Albright Coll, William and Mary); Dept of State Professional Awards 1967, 1970, 1975, 1981, 1989; Joseph C. Wilson Int Relations Achievement Award 1982; Sharansky Award, Union Counsel of Soviet Jewry 1989; Grand Cross of the Order of the Lion (Finland) 1989; US Presidential Citizens' Achievement Medal 1989; Kt Commdr of the Order of Merit (FRG) 1989; Nat Fisheries Inst Person of the Year 1977. *Address:* 2695 Marcey Rd, Arlington, VA 22207, USA.

RIDLEY, Una Lynette, B SC, MA; Canadian (b Jamaican) nursing educator; b 7 April 1933, Jamaica; d of Thomas and Mabel Ridley. *Education:* Mannings High School, Kingston Public Hosp, Univ of Windsor (Canada) and Michigan State Univ (USA). *Career:* Staff Nurse Univ of the W Indies 1955–57; Nursing Sister, UK 1958–59; Staff Nurse Windsor, ON, Canada 1959–60; teacher Grace Hosp School of Nursing 1960–64; Dir Sarnia Gen Hosp School of Nursing, ON 1964–67; Devt Programmer, then First Dir St Clair Regional School of Nursing, Sarnia 1967–70; Dir Kingston Gen Hosp School of Nursing, ON 1971–73; Chair Health Services Dept, St Lawrence's Coll, Kingston 1973–76, Acting Prin Kingston 1976–77, Prin Brockville 1978–80; Dean of Nursing Univ of Saskatchewan, Canada 1980–89; Dean of Nursing Univ of Lethbridge, Canada 1989–; mem Canadian Asscn of Univ Schools of Nursing, Registered Nurses' Asscn of Ontario. *Leisure interests:* reading, cooking, travel, weaving. *Address:* University of Lethbridge, AB T1K 6E7, Canada (Office); 214 Sherwood Pl, Lethbridge, AB T1K 3M4, Canada (Home).

RIDRUEJO, Mónica, BA; Spanish broadcasting executive; b 1963, San Francisco, CA, USA; d of José Antonio Ridruejo. *Education:* Madrid, Switzerland, England and Hollyoak Coll, MA. *Career:* Mem staff Chase Manhattan Bank Chicago; credit analyst Citibank Madrid, later responsible for accounts of public sector companies and orgs; Dir of accounts The First National Bank of Chicago 1984; est Corppenta (counselling body for new audiovisual businesses) 1989; represented interests of Canal Plus France; apptd Dir-Gen RTVE (Radiotelevisión Española) 1996. *Leisure interests:* skiing, athletics, swimming, horse riding. *Address:* RTVE–Radiotelevisión Española, Casa de la Radio, Prado del Rey, 28023 Madrid, Spain.

RIEFENSTAHL, Leni; German film director, photographer and writer; b 22 Aug 1902; d of Alfred and Bertha Riefenstahl. *Education:* Kunstakademie (Berlin). *Career:* Dancer 1920s; film actress 1920s and 1930s; directed first film 1932; Gold Medal Venice Biennale 1937, 1938. *Films include:* Acted in: The White Hell of Pitz Palu 1929, The Blue Light (Silver Medal Venice Biennale, also dir) 1932, SOS Iceberg 1933; Directed: Triumph of the Will 1934, Olympische Spiele 1936, Tiefland 1945; *Publications:* The Last of the Nuba 1974, People of the Kau 1976, Coral Gardens 1978, Mein Afrika (photographs) 1982, Memoiren 1987, Wonders Under Water 1991, The Sieve of Time (autobiog) 1992, Leni Riefenstahl: A Memoir 1994. *Address:* 82343 Pöcking, Germany. *Telephone:* (89) 2780165.

RIESS-PASSER, Susanne; Austrian politician and lawyer; b 1960, Brandau. *Career:* Fmr MEP; joined Freedom Party as Press Officer 1987, succeeded Jörg Haider as Leader 2000; Vice-Chancellor and Minister for Public Affairs and Sports 2000–. *Address:* Freiheitliche Partei Österreichs, Kärntnerstr 28, 1010 Vienna, Austria. *Telephone:* (1) 512-35-35; *Fax:* (1) 513-88-58; *E-mail:* www.fpoe.at.

RIFFAULT, Hélène; French business executive; b 1 July 1921, Meudon; d of Robert and Jeanne (née Contour) Riffault. *Education:* Lycées Victor Hugo and Hélène Boucher and Ecole des Hautes Etudes Commerciales (Paris). *Career:* Worked at Comm Générale d'Organisation du Travail (CEGOS) 1940–44; opinion poll practitioner 1944–49; Dir-Gen Inst Français d'Opinion Publique (IFOP/ETMAR) 1950–79; mem Bd Gallup Int 1960–, Co-Dir Social Surveys (Gallup Poll) Ltd, London 1970–73, Pres Gallup Int 1989–; Dir-Gen Faits et Opinions

1980–89; has written research articles on public opinion in Europe published by EC Comm; Officier de l'Ordre Nat du Mérite 1975; World Asscn for Public Opinion Research (WAPOR) award winner 1994. *Publication:* Les valeurs des Français 1994. *Address:* 6 rue Paul Saunière, 75116 Paris, France. *Telephone:* (1) 45-03-06-75; *Fax:* (1) 45-04-21-06.

RIGBY, Jean Prescott, ARAM, ARCM; British opera singer (mezzo-soprano); b Fleetwood, Lancs; d of the late Thomas Boulton and of Margaret Annie Rigby; m James Hayes 1987; three s. *Education:* Elmslie Girls' School (Blackpool), Birmingham School of Music, RAM and Opera Studio. *Career:* Studied piano and viola, then singing with Patricia Clark; Prin Mezzo-Soprano, English Nat Opera 1982–90; debut Royal Opera House, Covent Garden, London 1983, Glyndebourne 1984; American debut 1993; recordings with Giuseppe Sinopoli, Ozawa, Marriner, Hickox and Davis; Hon FRAM 1989; Hon ABC (Birmingham Conservatoire) 1996; numerous prizes and scholarships at RAM including Countess of Munster, Leverhulme, Peter Stuyvesant, RSA scholarships and the Prin's Prize, Royal Overseas League and Young Artists' Competition 1981. *Operas include:* Eugene Onegin, Albert Herring, Carmen, Boris Godunov, Lucretia, Così fan tutte (also TV), Der Rosenkavalier, Return of Ulysses, The Magic Flute; videos of Xerxes, Rigoletto, Lucretia, Carmen, Albert Herring; extensive concert repertoire. *Leisure interests:* theatre, sport, British heritage. *Address:* c/o Askonas Holt, Lonsdale Chambers, 27 Chancery Lane, London WC2A 1PF, UK.

RIGG, Dame (Enid) Diana (Elizabeth), DBE; British actress; b 20 July 1938, Doncaster, Yorks; d of Louis and Beryl (née Helliwell) Rigg; m 1st Menaham Gueffen 1973 (divorced 1976); m 2nd Archibald Hugh Stirling 1982 (divorced 1993); one d. *Education:* Fulneck Girls' School (Pudsey, Yorks) and Royal Acad of Dramatic Art. *Career:* Professional debut as Natella Abashwilli in The Caucasian Chalk Circle, York Festival 1957; repertory Chesterfield and Scarborough 1958; mem Nat Theatre 1972; Chair MacRobert Arts Centre, Univ of Stirling, Chancellor Univ of Stirling 1997–; Prof of Theatre Studies, Oxford Univ 1998–; Dir United British Artists 1982–; mem Arts Council Cttee 1986, British Museum Devt Fund, Asscn for Business Sponsorship of the Arts; Assoc Artist of RSC, Stratford and Aldwych 1962–79; Vice-Pres BLISS (Baby Life Support Systems) 1984–; Dr hc (Stirling) 1988; Hon D LITT (Leeds) 1992, (Nottingham) 1996, (S Bank) 1996; Special Award for The Avengers BAFTA 2000. *Plays include:* Troilus and Cressida, Ondine, Becket, The Taming of the Shrew, The Art of Seduction, A Midsummer Night's Dream, Comedy of Errors, King Lear, Twelfth Night 1966, Macbeth 1972, 'Tis Pity She's A Whore 1972, The Misanthrope 1973, 1975, Phaedra Britannica (Award for Best Actress, Plays and Players) 1975, The Guardsman 1978, Abelard and Heloise 1970, Pygmalion 1974, Night and Day (Award for Best Actress, Plays and Players) 1978, Heartbreak House 1983, Little Eyolf 1985, Antony and Cleopatra 1985, Follies 1987, Love Letters 1990, All For Love 1991, Berlin Bertie 1992, Medea (Evening Standard and Tony Awards for Best Actress) 1992, Berlin Bertie 1993, Mother Courage and Her Children (Evening Standard Award for Best Actress 1996) 1995, Who's Afraid of Virginia Woolf (Evening Standard Award for Best Actress 1996) 1996, Phèdre 1998, Britannicus 1998; *Films include:* A Midsummer Night's Dream 1969, The Assassination Bureau 1969, On Her Majesty's Secret Service 1969, Julius Caesar 1970, The Hospital 1971, Theatre of Blood 1973, A Little Night Music 1977, The Great Muppet Caper 1981, Evil Under the Sun 1982, A Good Man in Africa 1993; *TV appearances include:* Sentimental Agent 1963, A Comedy of Errors 1964, The Avengers 1965–67, Women Beware Women 1965, Married Alive 1970, Diana (series) 1973, In This House of Brede 1975, The Serpent Son 1979, The Marquise 1980, Hedda Gabler 1981, Little Eyolf 1982, King Lear 1983, Witness for the Prosecution 1983, Bleak House 1984, Held in Trust (Host), A Hazard of Hearts 1987, Unexplained Laughter 1989, Mother Love (BAFTA Award for Best Actress 1990) 1989, Mystery! (Host) 1989, Gai-Jin 1995, Zoya 1995, The Haunting of Helen Walker 1995, Moll Flanders 1996, Samson and Delilah 1996, Rebecca (Emmy Award for Best Supporting Actress 1997) 1996; *Publications:* No Turn Unstoned 1982, So To The Land 1994. *Leisure interests:* reading, writing, cooking, travel. *Address:* c/o Duncan Heath, ICM, Oxford House, 76 Oxford St, London W1N 0AX, UK.

RIHTER, Andreja; Slovenian politician and professor of history and sociology; b 25 Aug 1957, Celje; d of Robert Konćan and Silva Weinberger; m Janez Rihter 1982; one d. *Education:* Celje Grammar School (Slovenia) and Univ of Ljubljana. *Career:* Dir Museum of Recent History 1986–; currently Minister of Culture; Pres Museums Asscn of Slovenia, Nat Corresp European Museum Forum; has organized int museum confs and meetings including Museums Asscn of Slovenia 'European Museum of the Year Award' 1999; exhibitions include 'To Live in Celje' 2000–; Founder 'Herman's Den' (only museum for children in Slovenia); awards include Bronze Shield of the City of Celje 1992, Švab Award 1993, Valvasor Award 1996, Silver Shield of the City of Celje 1999. *Publications include:* Pearl on the Savinja (jtly) 1993, Josip Pelikan, Slovene Photographer (1996), Monograph of Celje 1999. *Leisure interests:* skiing, golf, F1, tennis, arts, history. *Address:* Cankarjeva 5, 1000 Ljubljana, Slovenia. *Telephone:* (1) 478-5991; *Fax:* (1) 478-5904; *E-mail:* andreja.rihter@gov.si; *Internet:* www.sigov.si/mk.

RIIS-JØRGENSEN, Karin, LL M; Danish politician; b 7 Nov 1952, Odense; m 1978; one s. *Education:* Univ of Copenhagen. *Career:* Worked at Danish Fed of Crafts and Small Industries; assigned to Dir-Gen for Small- and Medium-Sized Enterprises, European Comm 1987–89, mem Team EC 92 lecture group; apptd to Coopers & Lybrand accountancy and consultancy firm 1989, responsible for opening offices in the Baltic countries 1991, currently Head EU Dept; adviser, mem Editorial Bd Ugebrevet Mandag Morgen weekly newsletter; MEP (European Liberal Democratic and Reformist Party) 1994–, mem Cttee on Econ and Monetary Affairs and Industrial Policy, substitute mem Cttee on the Environment, Public Health and Consumer Protection, substitute mem Del for the Baltic States; participant White House Conf on Small Businesses, Washington, DC 1986; has written articles on European issues and research studies for the European Comm. *Leisure interest:* tennis. *Address:* European Parliament, rue Wiertz, 1047 Brussels, Belgium (Office); Dalgas Blvd 46, 2000 Frederiksberg, Denmark (Home). *Telephone:* (2) 284-21-11 (Office); 31-86-98-16 (Home); *Fax:* (2) 230-69-43 (Office); 31-87-98-16 (Home).

RILEY, Bridget Louise, CH, CBE, ARCA; British artist; b 24 April 1931, London; d of John Fisher and the late Bessie Louise (née Gladstone) Riley. *Education:* Cheltenham Ladies' Coll, Goldsmiths Coll and Royal Coll of Art (London). *Career:* Solo exhibitions include Gallery One, London 1962, Hayward Gallery, London 1992, PaceWildenstein, NY 2000, Dia Center for the Arts, NY 2000–2001 and in UK, USA, Switzerland, Australia and Japan; group exhibitions in Australia, Italy, France, Netherlands, Germany, Israel, USA, Japan and Argentina, including Kunsthalle, Nuremberg and Bottrop (Germany) 1992; UK Rep Biennale des Jeunes, Paris 1965, Venice Biennale (Italy) 1968; British Council retrospective exhibition tour of Europe and UK 1970–72, USA, Australia and Japan 1978–80; Arts Council touring exhibitions 1965–78, 1980–82, 1984–85; collections of paintings, drawings and prints in UK, Ireland, Switzerland, Netherlands, Austria, Germany, Japan, Israel, USA, Australia and NZ; installed sculpture for Citibank in Canary Wharf, London 2000; Founder-mem and fmr Dir SPACE Ltd; Trustee Nat Gallery 1981–88; Hon D LITT (Manchester) 1976, (Cambridge) 1995, (Exeter) 1997; Dr hc (Ulster) 1986, (Oxford) 1993, (Cambridge) 1995, (De Montfort) 1996; prizes include AICA Critics Prize 1963, Open Section Prize, Johns Moores Liverpool Exhibition 1963, medal at Venice Biennale 1968, Tokyo Print Biennale 1971, Gold Medal, Grafikk-bienniale, Fredrikstad, Norway 1980. *Address:* c/o Karsten Schubert Ltd, 42 Brecknock Rd, London N7 0DD, UK.

RILEY, Matilda White, MA, D SC; American professor emeritus of sociology; b 19 April 1911, Boston, MA; d of Percival and Mary (née Cliff) White; m John Winchell Riley, Jr 1931; one s one d. *Education:* Radcliffe Coll (Cambridge, MA) and Bowdoin Coll (Brunswick, ME). *Career:* Research Asst Harvard Univ 1932; Vice-Pres Market Research Co of American 1938–49; Research Specialist Rutgers Univ 1950, Prof 1951–73, Dir of Sociology Lab and Chair Dept of Sociology and Anthropology 1959–73, Prof Emer 1973–; Daniel B. Fayerweather Prof of Political Econ and Sociology, Bowdoin Coll 1974–81, Prof Emer 1981–; Assoc Dir Nat Inst on Aging 1979–91, Sr Social Scientist 1991–; Staff Assoc and Dir of Aging and Soc, Russell Sage Foundation 1964–73, Staff Sociologist 1974–77; Winkelman Lecturer Univ of Michigan 1984; Selo Lecturer Univ of Northern California 1987; Distinguished Lecturer Southwestern Social Sciences Asscn 1990; Standing Lecturer State Univ of New York 1992, Duke Univ 1993; mem Comm on Middle Years Social Science Research Council 1973–77, Chair Comm on Life Course 1977–80; Chair Task Force on Health and Behavior NIH 1986–91; Sr Research Assoc Center for Social Sciences, Columbia Univ 1978–80; mem Advisory Bd, Carnegie Aging Soc Project 1985–87; mem Inst of Medicine, AAAS, Int Org for Study of Human Devt, American Philosophical Soc; Hon LHD (Rutgers) 1983; Commonwealth Award 1984; Scientific Achievement Award, Washington Acad of Sciences 1989; Distinguished Science Award 1989; est Matilda White Riley Prize, Bowdoin Coll 1987. *Publications:* Gliding and Soaring (jtly), Sociological Studies in Scale Analysis (jtly) 1954, Aging and Soc (jtly, 3 vols) 1968–72, Sociological Observation 1974, Aging From Birth to Death: interdisciplinary perspectives 1982, Sociological Traditions from Generation to Generation (jtly) 1980, Aging From Birth to Death: sociotemporal perspectives (jtly) 1982, Aging in Society (jtly) 1983, Perspectives in Behavioral Medecine: the aging dimension (co-ed) 1987, AIDS in an Aging Society (ed) 1989, The Quality of Aging (co-ed) 1989; Structural Lag (sr ed) 1994; numerous contribs to professional journals. *Address:* NIH, Nat Inst on Aging, 7201 Wisconsin Ave, Bethesda, MD 20814, USA (Office); 4701 Willard Ave, Apt 1607, Chevy Chase, MD 20814, USA (Home).

RIMINGTON, Dame Stella, DBE, MA; British civil servant; b (Stella Whitehouse) 1935, Croydon, Surrey; m John Rimington 1963 (separated); two d. *Education:* Nottingham High School for Girls and Univ of Edinburgh. *Career:* Joined MI5 (security service) 1969–, Desk Officer and later Dir of Counter-Terrorism, F2 section of F Branch until 1990, Sr Deputy Dir-Gen 1990–92, first woman and first named Dir-Gen 1992–96; Non-Exec Dir Marks and Spencer 1997–, BG PLC 1997–2000, BG Int 2000–, GKR Group (now Whitehead Mann GKR) 1997–; Chair Inst of Cancer Research 1997–; gave Dimbleby Lecture 1994; Hon Air Commodore 7006 (VR) Squadron Royal Auxiliary Air Force 1997–; Hon LL B (Nottingham) 1995; Hon DCL (Exeter) 1996. *Address:* POB 1604, London SW1P 1XB, UK.

RINSER, Luise; German writer; b 30 April 1911, Pitzling/Oberbayern; d of Joseph and Luise Rinser; m 1st Horst-Guenther Schnell 1939 (died 1943); two s; m 2nd Carl Orff 1954 (died 1982). *Education:* Univ of Munich. *Career:* Teacher 1935–39; writer 1940–; works banned 1941; imprisoned 1944–45; after World War II became literary critic, Neue Zeitung, Munich; freelance writer and Pres Volks-Hochschule Rocca di Papa, Italy 1988–; mem Akad der Künste, PEN Centre of Germany; most of her books translated into 24 languages; Hon Citizen Rocca di Papa, Italy; recipient many literary prizes. *Publications include:* Novels: Die gläsernen Ringe 1940, Mitte des Lebens 1950, Daniela 1953, Abenteuer der Tugend 1957, Ich Bin Tobias 1968, Der schwarze Esel 1974, Mirjam 1983, Silberschuld 1987, Abaelards Liebe 1991; Short stories: Ein Bündel weißer Narzissen 1956, Geschichten aus der Loewengrube 1986; Plays: Philemon, Leo und Sonja Tolstoi 1991; Essays: Schwerpunkt, Über die Hoffnung, Vom Sinn der Traurigkeit, Unterentwickeltes Land Frau, Wie, wenn wir ärmer würden 1974, Dem Tode geweiht 1974; Jr fiction: Bruder Feuer 1975, Das Squirrel, Drei Kinder und ein Mann 1988; Travel books: Wenn die Wale kämpfen 1976, Khomeini und der islamische Gottesstaat 1979, Nordkoreanisches Reise-Tagebuch 1981; Diaries: Gefängnis/Tagebuch 1946, Baustelle 1970, Grenz-Übergänge 1972, Kriegsspielzeug 1978, Winterfruehling 1982, Im Dunkeln Singen 1984, Wachsender Mond 1988; Autobiography: Den Wolf umarmen 1981, Das Geheimnis des Brunnens; Letters: Hochzeit der Widersprüche 1973, Reinheit und Ekstase: Briefe über die Liebe 1997. *Leisure interests:* politics, theology, music, psychology. *Address:* c/o 00040 Rocca di Papa, Rome, Italy.

RIPLEY, Alexandra, BA; American writer; b 8 Jan 1934, Charleston, SC; d of the late Alexander J. and Elizabeth J. Braid; m 1st Leonard Ripley 1958 (divorced); m 2nd John Graham 1981; two d. *Education:* Vassar Coll. *Career:* Chosen by the estate of Margaret Mitchell to write a sequel to Gone With The Wind. *Publications:* Who's That Lady in the President's Bed? 1972, Charleston 1981, On Leaving Charleston 1983, The Time Returns 1985, New Orleans Legacy 1987, Scarlett (sequel to Gone With The Wind) 1991, From Fields of Gold 1994, A Love Divine 1996. *Leisure interests:* gardening, reading. *Address:* c/o Janklow & Nesbit, 445 Park Ave, Floor 13, New York, NY 10022-2606, USA.

RIPLEY, Pida Sandra Ann, MA, FRSA; British business executive and charity director; b 19 Sept 1944, Tadcaster, Yorks; d of Peter Charles Russell and Elise Covington; m Sydney Ripley 1972 (died 1991). *Education:* King's Coll (London) and LSE. *Career:* Founder, Dir Chelsea Gallery, London 1969–76; Dir Inplan Designs, London 1972–76; Partner property devt co, London 1977–85; Dir garden tool products import-export co 1987–90; f WomenAid charity and devt agency 1988; apptd Dir of Devt, Royal Inst of Int Affairs 1989; Chair Bd of Govs, St Martin's School of Art 1976–82, UK Cttee of UN Devt Fund for Women 1985–90; Co-opted mem GLC Arts Cttee and Housing Bd 1970–81; mem Bd UK Cttee for UNICEF 1983–88, Nat Exec UN Asscn, Int Inst of Strategic Studies; Assoc King's Coll, Univ of London 1985; MacArthur Fellow Univ of Maryland (USA) 1986. *Leisure interests:* collecting, travel. *Address:* The Royal Institute of International Affairs, Chatham House, 10 St James's Square, London SW1Y 4LE, UK (Office); 3 Whitehall Court, Apt 145, Whitehall, London SW1A 2EL, UK (Home). *Telephone:* (20) 7930-2233 (Office); (20) 7408-0842 (Home); *Fax:* (20) 7839-3593 (Office).

RIPPON, Angela; British broadcaster and journalist; b 12 Oct 1944, Plymouth, Devon; d of John and Edna Rippon; m Christopher Dare 1967 (divorced). *Education:* Plymouth Grammar School. *Career:* Ed, Producer and Presenter, Westward TV (ITV) 1967–73; Presenter and Reporter, BBC TV Plymouth 1966–69; Reporter, BBC TV Nat News 1973–75, Newsreader 1975–81; Presenter TV-AM Feb–April 1983, LBC until 1994; Arts and Entertainment Corresp for WNEV-TV (Boston) 1984–85, 1990–94; Vice-Pres Int Club for Women in TV 1979–; Dir Nirex 1986–; Chair English Nat Ballet 2000–; Newsreader of the Year 1975, 1976, 1977; TV Personality of the Year 1977. *TV includes:* Angela Rippon Reporting (documentary), Antiques Roadshow, In the Country, Compere, Eurovision Song Contest 1976, Royal Wedding 1981, Masterteam (BBC) 1985, 1986, 1987, Come Dancing 1988–, What's My Line? 1988–, Healthcheck Holidays; *Radio includes:* Angela Rippon's Morning Report for LBC 1992, Angela Rippon's Drive Time Show, (LBC) 1993; *Publications:* Riding, In the Country, Victoria Plum (children's stories), Mark Phillips—The Man and his Horses 1982, Angela Rippon's West Country 1982, Badminton: A Celebration 1987. *Leisure interests:* cooking, gardening, riding. *Address:* Knight Ayton, 114 St Martin's Lane, London WC2N 4AZ, UK. *Telephone:* (20) 7287-4405.

RISCA, Maria Rodica, MD, PH D; Romanian research scientist; b 13 Nov 1937, Dej, Cluj Dist; d of Cotul S. and Pioras Octavia; m Mircea Risca 1962; one d one s. *Education:* Univ of Cluj-Napoca. *Career:* Gen Practitioner 1961–66; Pathologist 1969; Cancer Research Scientist Dept of Experimental Pathology, apptd Prof Dr I. Chiricuta Oncological Inst, Cluj-Napoca 1966, Prin Cancer Research Scientist 1976, Chief Experimental Pathology Dept 1989; Visiting Scientist Buffalo, NY, USA 1979. *Publications:* Laboratory Animal Biology (ed) 1992; co-author of ten books on oncology; 178 papers on experimental oncology. *Leisure interests:* art history, collecting antiques. *Address:* Prof Dr I. Chiricuta Oncological Institute, Dept of Experimental Pathology, 3400 Cluj-Napoca, Str Republicii 34-36, Romania (Office); 3400 Cluj-Napoca, Str Hatieganu 7, Romania (Home). *Telephone:* (51) 95118361; *Fax:* (51) 95118365.

RISDEN-HUNTER, Winnifred, BA; Jamaican communications consultant; m Lloyd Hunter. *Education:* Univ Coll of the W Indies and Univ of Oxford (UK). *Career:* Lecturer in English Univ of the W Indies 1965–70; Dir of Public Relations Jamaican Tourist Bd 1973–77; pvt Communications Consultant 1977–81; Press Sec Office of the Prime Minister 1982–84; Chair Task Force on the Jamaican Information Service; Exec Dir Jamaica Information Service 1984–89; Communications Consultant WRH and Assocs Ltd 1989–; Hon B LITT; Commdr of the Order of Distinction, Jamaica. *Leisure interests:* conversation, reading, writing, art, theatre. *Address:* WRH and Assocs Ltd, 22G Old Hope Rd Kingston 5, Jamaica. *Telephone:* 929-9304; *Fax:* 929-1071.

RISSEEUW-LIGTERMOET, Mickey (Marie-Louise); Netherlands international organization executive; b 8 March 1943, Rotterdam; m Henri-Marinus Risseeuw 1966. *Education:* Univ of Paris (Sorbonne), Cambridge School of Tech (UK) and Interpreters and Translators Course (The Hague). *Career:* Information Officer Town Planning and Urban Devt Dept, Municipality of Rotterdam 1963–70; Asst Dir Int Translations Centre (int co-operative network), Delft 1979–86, Dir 1986–; mem Dutch Asscn of Translators 1971–; fmr mem Council EUSIDIC (asscn for orgs involving information professionals). *Publications:* Access to Existing Sci-Tech Translations from Japanese Literature 1987; contribs to professional journals and conf papers. *Leisure interests:* music, arts, tennis, golf. *Address:* International Translations Centre, Schuttersveld 2 2611 WE Delft, Netherlands. *Telephone:* (15) 214-22-42; *Fax:* (15) 215-85-35; *E-mail:* mickeyrisseeuw@library.tudelft.nl.

RITCHIE, Marguerite Elizabeth Winifred, QC, BA, LL D; Canadian human rights campaigner; b 20 May 1919, Edmonton, AB; d of Allan Isaac and Marguerite Blanche (née Baxter) Ritchie. *Education:* Univ of Alberta and Dalhousie and McGill Univs. *Career:* Called to the Bar, AB 1944; Joined Combined Investigation Div, Fed Public Service 1944, Fed Dept of Justice 1949, Legal Adviser in Constitutional and Int Law, UN Parl Procedure and Domestic Law, Exec Asst to Ministers of Justice, apptd Sr Advisory Counsel Dept of Justice; Legal Adviser to Canadian Del, The Hague Conf on Air Law 1955; Founder and Pres Human Rights Inst of Canada 1979–; Adviser to UN Rights Cttee 1982; mem Interdepartmental Cttees on UN, Women, Int Law and others; participated in drafting of 1968 Fed Divorce Act; Vice-Chair Fed Anti-Dumping Tribunal 1972–79; First Legal Adviser Elizabeth Fry Soc (Ottawa); Lecturer in Constitutional Law Carleton Univ 1967–68; Visiting Lecturer Univ of Ottawa, Trent Univ, McGill Univ; numerous contribs to professional journals; mem Canadian Bar Asscn, Int Law Asscn, Int Comm of Jurists, Int Abolitionist Fed, Canadian Fed of Univ Women; Hon LL D (Alberta) 1975; Centennial Medal 1967; Province of Ottawa Outstanding Woman Award 1975; Gov-Gen's Award in Commemoration of the Person's Case for Lifetime of Work for Women's Equality 1997. *Leisure interests:* travel, walking, reading, planting. *Address:* 303-246 Queen St, Ottawa, ON K1P 5E4, Canada (Office); 30, 216 Metcalfe St, Ottawa, ON K2P 1R1, Canada (Home). *Telephone:* (613) 232-2920 (Office); (613) 236-5709 (Home); *Fax:* (613) 232-3735 (Office); *E-mail:* hric@pobox.mondenet.com; *Internet:* www.mondenet.com/hric.

RITTERMAN, Janet Elizabeth, PH D, M MUS, FRSA; Australian musician and music college administrator; b 1 Dec 1941, Sydney, NSW (Australia); d of Charles Eric and Laurie Helen Palmer; m Gerrard Peter Ritterman 1970. *Education:* N Sydney Girls' High School, NSW State Conservatorium of Music and Univ of Durham and King's Coll, Univ of London (UK). *Career:* Teacher Watford Grammar School for Girls, UK 1969–74; Sr Lecturer in Music Middx Polytechnic 1975–79, Goldsmiths Coll, Univ of London 1980–87; Recognized Teacher Univ of London 1984; Head of Music Dartington Coll of Arts 1987–90, Dean, Academic Affairs 1988–90, Prin 1991–93; Dir Royal Coll of Music 1993–; Visiting Prof of Music Educ, Univ of Plymouth 1993–; Chair Assoc Bd Royal Schools of Music (Publ) Ltd 1993–, The Mendelssohn and Boise Foundations 1996–98, Advisory Council, Arts Research Ltd 1997–, Fed of British Conservatoires 1998–; Vice-Pres Nat Asscn of Youth Orchestras 1993–; mem Music Panel, Arts Council of England 1992–98, Council Royal Musical Asscn 1994– (Vice-Pres 1998–), Bd English Nat Opera 1996–, Exec Cttee Inc Soc of Musicians 1996–99, Postgrad Panel, Arts and Humanities Research Bd 1998–, Steering Cttee, London Higher Educ Consortium 1999–, Arts Council of England 2000–, Dept for Educ and Employment Advisory Group, Music and Ballet Scheme 2000–; Trustee Countess of Munster Musical Trust 1993–, Prince Consort Foundation 1993–; Gov Associated Bd Royal Schools of Music 1993–, Purcell School 1996–2000, Heythrop Coll Univ of London 1996–; Fellow Royal N Coll of Music 1996, Nene Coll 1997, Univ Coll, Northampton 1997, Dartington Coll of Arts 1997; articles published in learned journals in France, Germany, Australia and UK; Hon Fellow RAM 1995, Guildhall School of Music and Drama 2000; Hon D UNIV (Univ of Cen England) 1996. *Leisure interests:* theatre, reading, country walking. *Address:* Royal College of Music, Prince Consort Rd, London SW7 2BS, UK. *Telephone:* (20) 7591-4363; *Fax:* (20) 7589-7740; *E-mail:* jritterman@rcm.ac.uk; *Internet:* www.rcm.ac.uk.

RIVERA, Chita (Conchita del Rivero); American actress, singer and dancer; b 23 Jan 1933, Washington; d of Pedro Figuerva del Rivero; m Anthony Mordente. *Education:* American School of Ballet (New York). *Career:* Performs in nightclubs and cabarets around the world.

Performances include: Call Me Madam, Guys and Dolls, Can-Can, Seventh Heaven, Mister Wonderful, West Side Story, Father's Day, Bye Bye Birdie, Threepenny Opera, Flower Drum Song, Zorba, Sweet Charity, Born Yesterday, Jacques is Alive and Well and Living in Paris, Sondheim—A Musical Tribute, Kiss Me Kate, Ivanhoe, Chicago, Bring Back Birdie, Merlin, The Rink 1984 (Tony Award 1984), Jerry's Girl's 1985, Kiss of the Spider Woman 1993 (Tony Award for Best Actress in a Musical); *TV:* Kojak and the Marcus Nelson Murders 1973, The New Dick Van Dyke Show 1973–74, Kennedy Center Tonight–Broadway to Washington!, Pippin 1982, The Mayflower Madam 1987. *Address:* c/o Gayle Nachlis, William Morris Agency, 1325 Ave of the Americas, New York, NY 10019, USA.

RIVERS, Joan, BA; American entertainer; b 8 June 1933, New York; d of Meyer C. Molinsky; m Edgar Rosenberg 1965 (deceased); one d. *Education:* Barnard Coll. *Career:* Fashion Co-ordinator Bond Clothing Stores; entertaining debut 1960, TV debut Tonight Show 1965, Las Vegas debut 1969; Columnist Chicago Tribune 1973–76; creator Husbands and Wives (CBS TV) 1976–77; originator and screenwriter The Girl Most Likely To (ABC) 1973; Nat Chair Cystic Fibrosis 1982–; mem From Second City 1961–62; Woman of the Year, Harvard Hasty Pudding Soc 1984. *TV appearances include:* Tonight Show 1983–86, Joan Rivers and Friends Salute Heidi Abromowitz 1985, The Late Show Starring Joan Rivers 1986–87, Hollywood Squares 1987–, Joan Rivers (Daytime Emmy Award 1990) 1989–, How to Murder a Millionaire (film) 1990; *Films include:* The Swimmer 1968, Rabbit Test (co-writer) 1978, Uncle Sam, The Muppets Take Manhattan 1984, Spaceballs 1987; *Theatre includes:* Broadway Bound 1988; *Recording:* What Becomes a Semi-Legend Most 1983; *Publications:* Having a Baby Can Be a Scream 1974, The Life and Hard Times of Heidi Abromowitz 1984, Enter Walking (autobiog, jtly) 1986, Still Talking (jtly) 1991. *Address:* William Morris Agency, 151 S El Camino Drive, Beverly Hills, CA 90212, USA.

RIVLIN, Alice Mitchell, MA, PH D; American economist and government official; b 4 March 1931, Philadelphia, PA; d of Allan Mitchell and Georgianna Fales; m 1st Lewis A. Rivlin 1955 (divorced 1977); two s one d; m 2nd Sidney G. Winter 1989. *Education:* Bryn Mawr Coll and Radcliffe Coll. *Career:* Mem staff Brookings Inst, Washington, DC 1957–66, 1969–75, 1983–93, Dir of Econ Studies 1983–87; Dir Congressional Budget Office 1975–83; Prof of Public Policy George Mason Univ 1992; Deputy Dir US Office of Man and Budget 1993–94, Dir 1994–96; Vice-Chair Fed Reserve Bd 1996–99; with Brookings Inst 1999–; mem American Econ Asscn, Nat Pres 1986; MacArthur Fellow 1983–88. *Publications:* The Role of the Federal Government in Financing Higher Education 1961, Microanalysis of Socioeconomic Systems (jtly) 1961, Systematic Thinking for Social Action 1971, Economic Choices (jtly) 1986, The Swedish Economy (jtly) 1987, Caring for the Disabled Elderly: Who Will Pay? 1988, Reviving the American Dream 1992. *Address:* The Brookings Institution, 1775 Massachusetts Ave NW, Washington DC 20036, USA. *Telephone:* (202) 797-6000; *Fax:* (202) 797-6004; *Internet:* www.brook.edu.

RIVOYRE, Christine Berthe Claude Denis de, L ÈS L; French journalist and writer; b 29 Nov 1921, Tarbes; d of François Denis and Madeleine (née Ballande) de Rivoyre. *Education:* Inst du Sacré Cœur (Bordeaux and Poitiers), Univs of Paris and Syracuse (USA). *Career:* Journalist on Le Monde (daily) 1950–55; Literary Dir Marie-Claire (monthly magazine) 1955–65; mem Haut Comité de la Langue Française, Conseil Supérieur des Lettres, Prix Médicis Jury; Chevalier de la Légion d'Honneur; Chevalier des Arts et des Lettres; Prix Paul Morand (Acad Française) 1984 and other awards. *Publications:* L'alouette au miroir 1956, La mandarine 1957, La tête en fleurs 1960, La glace à l'ananas 1962, Les sultans 1964, Le petit matin 1968, Le seigneur des chevaux (jtly) 1969, Fleur d'agonie 1970, Boy 1973, Le voyage à l'envers 1977, Belle alliance 1982, Reine-Mère 1985, Crépuscule taille unique 1989, Racontez-moi les flamboyants 1995, Le petit matin 1998. *Address:* Editions Grasset, 61 rue des Saints-Pères, 75006 Paris, France (Office); Dichats Ha, Onesse-Laharie, 40110 Morcenx, France (Home).

ROBA, Fatuma; Ethiopian athlete; b 18 Dec 1973, Arsi. *Career:* Police officer; marathon runner; came Second in Great North Run 1995; winner Marrakesh and Rome marathons 1996; winner Gold Medal,

Marathon (first African woman to gain medal in Olympic marathon), Olympic Games, Atlanta, GA, USA 1996; winner Boston marathon 1997, 1998, 1999 (first woman in history to win for 3 consecutive years).

ROBERTS, Barbara; American state official; b 21 Dec 1936, Corvallis, OR; m Frank Roberts 1974; two s. *Career:* Mem Multnomah Co Bd of Commrs, OR 1978; mem Oregon House of Reps 1981–85; Sec of State of Oregon 1985–91; Gov (Democrat) 1991–95.

ROBERTS, Deborah Margaret, MA; Canadian publisher and political party executive; b 2 Sept 1947, Kingston, ON; d of the late Raymond and of June Roberts; m Richard Biggs 1974; two s. *Education:* London Teachers' Coll and Univ of Western Ontario. *Career:* Owner New Image Publishing Co 1981–; Exec Sec Green Party of Canada 1994; has written some short fiction and poetry. *Leisure interests:* reading, gardening, bicycling, sewing, knitting. *Address:* c/o Green Party of Canada, Box 397, London, ON N6A 4W1, Canada.

ROBERTS, Julia; American actress; b 28 Oct 1967, Smyrna, GA; d of the late Walter and of Betty Roberts; m Lyle Lovett 1993 (divorced 1995). *Education:* Campbell High school. *Career:* Film debut in Blood Red 1986; UNICEF Goodwill Amb 1995. *Films:* Satisfaction 1988, Mystic Pizza 1988, Steel Magnolias (Golden Globe Award, Acad Award nomination) 1989, Flatliners 1990, Pretty Woman (Golden Globe Award, Acad Award nomination) 1990, Sleeping with the Enemy 1991, Dying Young 1991, Hook 1992, The Player, The Pelican Brief 1993, I Love Trouble 1994, Prêt à Porter 1994, Mary Reilly 1994, Something to Talk About 1996, Michael Collins 1996, Everyone Says I Love You 1996, My Best Friend's Wedding 1997, Conspiracy Theory 1997, Rasputin, Stepmom 1998, Notting Hill 1999, Runaway Bride 1999, Erin Brockovich (Acad Award for Best Actress) 2000, The Mexican 2001, America's Sweethearts 2001, Ocean's Eleven 2001; *TV appearances include:* Baja Oklahoma (film) 1988, In the Wild: Horsemen of Mongolia with Julia Roberts 2000. *Leisure interest:* poetry. *Address:* ICM, 8942 Wilshire Blvd, Beverly Hills, CA 90211, USA.

ROBERTS, Michèle Brigitte, MA, ALA, FRSL; British writer; b 20 May 1949, Herts; d of Reginald George Roberts and Monique Pauline (née Caulle) Joseph; m Jim Latter 1991; two step-s. *Education:* Somerville Coll (Oxford) and Univ Coll London. *Career:* British Council Librarian, Bangkok 1973–74; writer and poet 1974–; Poetry Ed Spare Rib feminist magazine 1970s, City Limits 1981–83; Visiting Fellow Univ of E Anglia 1992, Univ of Nottingham Trent 1994; Visiting Prof Univ of Nottingham Trent 1996–; Chair Literary Cttee British Council 1998–; regular reviewer and broadcaster; Hon MA (Nene) 1999; W. H. Smith Literary Award 1993. *Publications include:* Novels: A Piece of the Night 1978, The Visitation 1983, The Wild Girl 1984, The Book of Mrs Noah 1987, In the Red Kitchen 1990, Daughters of the House (shortlisted Booker Prize, W. H. Smith Literary Award 1993) 1992, Flesh and Blood 1994, Impossible Saints 1997, Fair Exchange 1999, The Looking-Glass 2000; (co-ed) Mind Readings 1996; Short Stories: During Mother's Absence 1993, The Yellow-Haired Boy 2000; Poetry: The Mirror of the Mother 1986, Psyche and the Hurricane 1991, All the Selves I Was 1995; Plays: The Journeywoman 1987, Child-Lover 1995; Film: The Heavenly Twins 1993; Essays: Food, Sex and God 1998; contribs to poetry and short story anthologies. *Leisure interests:* reading, talking with friends, cooking, gardening, looking at art. *Address:* c/o Gillon Aitken, Gillon Aitken Associates, 29 Fernshaw Rd, London SW10 0TG, UK. *Telephone:* (20) 7351-7561.

ROBERTS, Yvonne; British journalist and writer; b 1949; fmr partner John Pilger; one d; partner Stephen Scott; one c. *Education:* Univ of Warwick. *Career:* Worked for Weekend World 1970s; writer for New Statesman and New Society magazines (now New Statesman and Society). *Publications include:* Man Enough 1984, Mad About Women 1994, Every Woman Deserves an Adventure (novel) 1994.

ROBERTSON, Brenda Mary, B SC; Canadian politician; b 23 May 1929, Sussex, NB; d of John James and Clara (née Rothwell) Tubb; m Wilmont Waldon Robertson 1955; two d one s. *Education:* Mount Allison Univ. *Career:* Elected to New Brunswick Legislature (first woman) 1967, Minister of Social Services and Youth (first woman Cabinet Minister for New Brunswick) 1971–74, Minister of Health, Chair of Social Policy 1976–82, Minister of Social Program Reform,

Chair Treasury Bd 1982–84; mem Senate, Ottawa 1984–; Hon D HUM LITT (Mount St Vincent) 1974; Hon D SC S (Moncton) 1983. *Publication:* Dear Senator—Cher Senateur (jtly). *Leisure interests:* reading, gardening, bird-watching. *Address:* The Senate, Victoria Bldg, Ottawa, ON K1A 0A4, Canada. *Telephone:* (613) 998-5585; *Fax:* (613) 998-0916.

ROBILLARD, Lucienne, BA; Canadian politician; b Montréal. *Education:* Ecole Marie Médiatrice, Coll Basile Moreau and Univ of Montréal. *Career:* Worked in health and welfare 1967–86; fmr Sr Admin Centre de Services Sociaux Richelieu; Youth Leader Kibbutz, Israel 1969–72; Public Trustee and Guardian, Québec 1986–89; mem Québec Nat Asscn Sept 1989–; Minister of Cultural Affairs 1989–90, of Higher Educ and Science 1990–93, of Educ and Science 1993–94, of Health and Social Services 1994–95, of Labour 1995–96, of Citizenship and Immigration 1996–97, 1997–; Pres Treasury Board Aug 1999–; Pres Asscn des practiciens de service social (Québec) 1984–86; Pres Admin Comm on Mental Health Services 1983–86; Consultant Mental Health Dossier, Rochon Comm 1986. *Address:* East Tower, L'Esplanade Laurier, 140 O'Connor St, Ottawa, ON K1A 0R5, Canada.

ROBINA BUSTOS, Soledad, M ED; Mexican academic and informatics consultant; b 8 Jan 1953, México, DF; m Gabriel Rodríguez; one s one d. *Education:* Lycée Franco-Mexicain, Univ Nacional Autónoma de México (México, DF) and Univ Catholique de Louvain (Belgium). *Career:* Prof Univ Nacional Autónoma de México; Co-ordinator New Information Techs Research Program, Instituto Latinoamericano de Estudios Transnacionales (ILET) and Consultant to Dir of Informatics Policy, Govt of Mexico; publs on mass media and new information techs in nat and int magazines. *Leisure interests:* reading, sports, cinema. *Address:* ILET, Canadá 190, Col Parque San Andrés Coyoacán, CP 04040, México, DF, Mexico (Office); Ignacio Zaragoza 17, Col Lomas Hipódromo, Edif de México, México, DF, Mexico (Home). *Telephone:* (5) 491106 (Office); (5) 896359; *Fax:* (5) 441642 (Office).

ROBINS, Lee Nelken, MA, PH D; American professor of social science; b 29 Aug 1922, New Orleans, LA; d of Abe and Leona (née Reiman) Nelken; m Eli Robins 1946; four s. *Education:* Radcliffe Coll and Harvard Univ. *Career:* Research Assoc Inst for Urban and Regional Studies, Washington Univ Medical School, St Louis, MO 1962–63, Research Assoc Prof Dept of Psychiatry 1962–66, Research Prof of Sociology in Psychiatry 1966–68, Nat Inst of Mental Health Special Research Fellow 1968–70, Prof of Sociology in Psychiatry 1968–91, Prof Dept of Sociology 1969–91, Univ Prof of Social Science, Prof of Social Science in Psychiatry 1991; mem Inst of Medicine (NAS); Research Scientist Award 1970–90; Lifetime Achievement Award, American Public Health Asscn 1994. *Publications include:* Deviant Children Grown Up: A Sociological and Psychiatric Study of Sociopathic Personality 1966, Studying Drug Abuse 1985, Psychiatric Disorders in America 1991. *Address:* Washington University School of Medicine, Dept of Psychiatry, 4940 Children's Place, St Louis, MO 63110, USA. *Telephone:* (314) 362-2469.

ROBINSON, Ann, PH D; British organization executive; b 28 Jan 1937; d of Edwin Samual and Dora (née Thorne) James; m Michael Finlay Robinson 1961; two s. *Education:* St Anne's Coll (Oxford) and McGill Univ (Canada). *Career:* Financial journalist Beaverbrook Newspapers 1959–61; Lecturer Univs of Durham 1962–63, Bristol 1970–72, Bath 1972–75, Cardiff 1972–87, Sr Lecturer 1987–89; Cons Cand EP elections 1979; Head Policy Unit Inst of Dirs 1989–95; Dir-Gen Nat Asscn of Pension Funds Ltd 1995–2000; Dir Welsh Nat Opera 1992–94; mem Equal Opportunities Comm 1980–85, Econ and Social Cttee (EC) 1986–93 (Chair Industry Section 1990–92), Welsh Arts Council 1991–93, Royal Inst for Int Affairs Council 1991, Bd of Academic Govs Richmond Coll (London) 1992–, Bd of Govs Commonwealth Inst 1992–97, Higher Educ Funding Council for Wales 1993–97, Monopolies and Mergers Comm 1993–99, Bd Harwich Haven Authority 1999–; TV appearances on Question Time and breakfast TV. *Publications:* Parliament and Public Spending 1978, Tax Policy Making in the United Kingdom (jtly) 1984; articles in academic journals. *Leisure interests:* Alpine summer and winter sports, gardening. *Address:* Northridge House, Usk Rd, Shirenewton, Monmouthshire NP16 6RZ, UK.

ROBINSON, Ann Elisabeth, PH D, C CHEM, FRSC, FCIC; Canadian (b British) toxicologist and former civil servant; b 9 April 1933, Ilford, Essex, UK; d of Ronald Sidney and Kathleen Muriel (née Evershed) Robinson; m 1st Richard George Lingard 1960 (deceased); m 2nd Francis Edward Camps 1972 (deceased). *Education:* Queen Anne's School (Caversham) and Chelsea Coll (Univ of London). *Career:* Asst Lecturer in Pharmaceutical Chem Chelsea Coll, Univ of London 1957–59, Lecturer 1959–64; Lecturer in Forensic Medicine, London Hosp Medical Coll, Univ of London 1964–68, Sr Lecturer 1968–77, Hon Toxicologist 1977; fmr Adjunct Prof Univ of Toronto; Chief of Occupational Health Lab, Consultant in Toxicology, Ontario Ministry of Labour 1978–80, Asst Deputy Minister Occupational Health and Safety Div 1980–87, Science Policy Adviser on Occupational and Environmental Health and Safety 1987–91; fmr Gov Canadian Centre for Occupational Health and Safety; mem Inst for Risk Research, Univ of Waterloo, ON 1991–; fmr Adviser to WHO Int Programme on Chemical Safety and Consultant to WHO; Citizen-at-Large mem Toronto Bd of Health 1996–98; mem Soroptimist Int of Toronto, Pres 1985–87, 1995–96, mem Bd of Dirs Soroptimist Foundation of Canada 1996–2000; mem Nat Ballet of Canada Volunteer Cttee. *Publications:* Gradwohl's Legal Medicine (co-ed, 3rd edn) 1976, Substance Abuse in the Workforce (jtly) 1992; numerous contribs to scientific publs. *Leisure interests:* travel, photography. *Address:* 80 Quebec Ave, No 601, Toronto, ON M6P 4B7, Canada. *Telephone:* (416) 762-6488; *Fax:* (416) 762-6488; *E-mail:* aecamps@sympatico.ca.

ROBINSON, Ann (Moureen Ann), FRSA; British organization executive and former civil servant; d of William and Winifred Flatley; m Peter Crawford Robinson 1961. *Career:* Civil servant; Dir of Policy and Planning, Benefits Agency, DSS 1990–93; Chief Exec The Spastics Soc, then Scope 1993–95; Head Govt Consultancy Computer Sciences Corpn 1995–96; Dir-Gen British Retail Consortium 1997–99; Chair Gas and Electricity Consumers Council 2000–; Chair Victim Support, London 1999–. *Address:* 1 Heathfield Rd, Maidstone, ME14 2AD, UK.

ROBINSON, Anne Josephine; British journalist and broadcaster; b 26 Sept 1944. *Education:* Farnborough Hill Convent and Les Ambassadrices (Paris). *Career:* Reporter Daily Mail 1967–68, Sunday Times 1968–77; Women's Ed Daily Mirror 1979–80, Asst Ed 1980–93; columnist Daily Mirror 1983–93, Today 1993–95, The Times 1993–95, 1998–, The Sun 1995–97, The Express 1997–98; Hon Fellow John Moores Univ 1996. *Radio work includes:* Anne Robinson Show (Radio 2) 1988–93; *TV Presenting includes:* Points of View 1987–98, Watchdog 1993–, Weekend Watchdog 1997–, Going for a Song 2000–, The Weakest Link 2000– (also USA 2001–) (all BBC). *Address:* Penrose Media, 19 Victoria Grove, London W8 5RW, UK.

ROBINSON, Glynne, BA; American photographer; b 23 Feb 1934, Fredericksburg, VA; d of Frederick Hampden and Jessie (née Maguire) Robinson; two d one s. *Education:* Wells Coll and Univs of Columbia and New York. *Career:* Studied photography at The New School 1967, 1971, with Ansel Adams 1968, Paul Caponigro 1969–71; Leader photographic workshops in New York schools 1973, photostudy project New York public school 1974–75; News and Publicity Dept Riverdale Neighbourhood House 1974–76; Photographer The Reporter (Ethical Culture Schools publ) 1974–76; Guest Lecturer Univ of Maine 1979; solo exhibitions include Wells Coll 1973, New York Public Library 1973, Soho Photo Gallery, New York 1974; group exhibitions include Riverdale Neighbourhood House 1968, Guild Hall, New York 1970, Soho Photo Gallery 1973, Wells Coll 1974–75, Cosmopolitan Club, New York 1976, Metropolitan Museum of Art 1976, Carnegie House 1978; works appeared in The Lakeville Journal, The Millerton News (New York), New York Times, Washington Post, New York Daily News, Christian Science Monitor, Village Voice, San Francisco Chronicle, LA Times, Asia America Heritage, Women at Work 1977; mem American Soc of Magazine Photographers. *Publication:* Writers in Residence 1981. *Address:* 15 E 91st St, Apt 11C, New York, NY 10128, USA.

ROBINSON, Jancis Mary, MA, MW, D UNIV; British writer and broadcaster; b 22 April 1950, Carlisle; d of Thomas Edward and Ann Sheelagh Margaret (née Conacher) Robinson; m Nicholas Laurence Lander 1981; two d one s. *Education:* Carlisle and County High School for Girls and St Anne's Coll (Oxford). *Career:* Ed Wine and Spirit

1975–80; Founder and Ed Drinker's Digest (now Which? Wine Monthly) 1977–82; Ed Which? Wine Guide 1980–82; Wine Corresp Sunday Times 1980–86, Evening Standard 1987–88, Financial Times Wine Writer 1989–, Wine Spectator columnist 1989–97; freelance journalist writing on food and wine 1980–; freelance radio and TV broadcaster 1982–; writer and presenter The Wine Programme (Glenfiddich Trophy) 1983, 1985, 1987, Jancis Robinson Meets... 1987, Matters of Taste 1989, 1991, Vintners' Tales 1993, 1999 (World Food Media Gold Award, Australia), Jancis Robinson's Wine Course (James Beard Award, USA 1996) 1995, The Food Chain 1996; TV Producer for Eden Productions 1989–; judge and lecturer in field 1983–; Marqués de Cáceres Award 1985; Wine Literary Award, Wine Appreciation Guild 1995; Catalan Agric Medal (Spain) 1995; numerous Glenfiddich awards including Trophy for Food and Drink Communicators 1996, TV Personality of the Year 1999; Wine Guild's Premier Award 1996; Silver Medal, Acad of Gastronomes (Germany) 1998; Florida Winefest André Simon Wine Writer's Award 2001. *Publications:* The Great Wine Book (Glenfiddich Award) 1982, The Wine Book (2nd edn) 1983, How to Choose and Enjoy Wines 1984, Vines, Grapes and Wines (André Simon Memorial Prize, Wine Guild Award, Clicquot Book of the Year) 1986, Masterglass (2nd edn) 1987, Jancis Robinson's Adventures with Food and Wine 1987, Jancis Robinson on the Demon Drink 1988, Vintage Timecharts 1989, The Oxford Companion to Wine (ed, numerous awards) 1994, 1999, Jancis Robinson's Wine Course (Wine Book of the Year, Wine Guild, UK) 1995, Jancis Robinson's Guide to Wine Grapes 1996, Confessions of a Wine Lover 1997, The Good Nose 1999, Oxford Companion to the Wines of North America (consultant ed) 2000, World Atlas of Wine (5th edn) 2001. *Leisure interests:* family, wine, food, words. *Address:* c/o A. P. Watt, 20 John St, London WC1N 2DR, UK. *Internet:* www.jancisrobinson.com.

ROBINSON, Jeanne Annette, B SC, D ED; Jamaican foundation executive; b 25 Sept 1934, Jamaica; d of the late Lister Mair and Nettie Mair; m Edward Robinson 1957; two d. *Education:* St Andrew High, Univ of Birmingham, UK, Galudet Coll, Univ of Washington and Univ of Arkansas, USA. *Career:* Head Science Dept Immaculate Conception High School; Exec Dir Jamaica Asscn for the Deaf, Greater Houston Service for the learning impaired; Assoc Dir SCILS Foundation in Texas; Dir Jamaica Conservation and Devt Trust, Environmental Foundation of Jamaica, United Way of Jamaica; Sec, Exec Dir ICWI Group Foundation 1989; Chair Council of Voluntary Social Services; mem Int Cttee Council on Foundations; Hon Sec Workforce Devt Consortium, Jamaica Foundations and Corporate Donors; Gov Gen's Award for Voluntary Service, Rotary Award for Community Service; contribs to professional journals. *Leisure interests:* travel, reading, collectables. *Address:* ICWI Group Foundation, 2 St Lucia Ave, Kingston 5, Jamaica.

ROBINSON, Joyce Lilieth, MBE, LL D, FLA; Jamaican librarian and organization executive; b 2 July 1925, St James; d of the late F. and Lynette (née Lawson) Stewart; m Leslie Robinson 1957; one s one d. *Education:* St Simon's Coll, Northwestern Polytechnic and Univ of London. *Career:* Teacher 1945–50; Acting Dir Jamaica Library Service 1955–57, Dir 1957–76; Dir Nat Literary Programme 1976–81; Gen Man Jamaica Broadcasting Corpn 1981–82; Man Dir HEART Trust 1982; mem Jamaica Inst of Man, Bd of Man Nat Library of Jamaica, Council Inst of Jamaica; Chair Nat Council on Libraries, Archives and Documentation Services; apptd Vice-Chair UNESCO Int Advisory Cttee on Documentation, Libraries and Archives 1975; numerous papers on libraries; Hon Vice-Pres (Life) The Library Asscn of GB; Hon LL D (Dalhousie); UNESCO Literary Prize 1983; UN Decade for Women Award 1985. *Leisure interests:* interior decorating, gardening, cooking, reading. *Address:* 84 Lady Musgrave Rd, Kingston 10, Jamaica (Office); 5 Millsborough Ave, Kingston 6, Jamaica (Home). *Telephone:* 978-8772 (Office).

ROBINSON, Madeleine (pseudonym of Madeleine Svoboda); French actress; b 5 Nov 1917, Paris; d of Victor and Suzanne (née Boura) Svoboda; m 1st Gaston Barré 1940 (divorced); m 2nd Guillaume Amestoy 1947 (divorced); one d one s. *Education:* Charles-Dullin School of Dramatic Arts. *Career:* Actress Compagnie du Rideau Gris; over 120 stage, film and TV appearances; Commdr des Arts et des Lettres 1983; Chevalier de la Légion d'Honneur 1989; Prix Réjane 1939; Best French Actress Award 1951; Prix Féminin du Cinéma 1950;

Coupe Volpi, Venice, Italy 1961; Grande Médaille d'Or, Arts, Sciences, Lettres 1987. *Plays include:* Une grande fille toute simple, Un tramway nommé Désir, Qui a peur de Virginia Woolf? (Best Stage Actress Award) 1964, Le locataire 1971, Madame Marguerite 1975, Monstres sacrés 1977, Les parents terribles 1977, La villa bleue 1986, La folle de Chaillot 1994; *Films include:* Le mioche 1936, Le garçon sauvage, Giorno per giorno disperatamente, Piège pour Cendrillon, Le petit matin 1971, On peut le dire sans se fâcher 1977, J'ai épousé une ombre 1983, Hors-la-loi 1985, Camille Claudel 1988, L'ours en peluche; *TV appearances include:* Le sixième sens (series) 1974, Noix de coco 1974, La fortune des Rougon (series) 1980, Mozart 1982, Un adolescent d'autrefois 1982, Nyne 1983, Le dialogue des carmélites 1984, La sorcière de Conflens 1985, La métamorphose, Un été alsacien, Mes coquins, l'Affaire Seznec, La récréation, La rage au cœur, La star de Babelsberg; *Publication:* Les canards majuscules 1978. *Leisure interests:* collecting books, reading, yachting, swimming. *Address:* c/o Clos du Lac, 147 rue du Lac, 1815 Clarins, Switzerland.

ROBINSON, Mary Lou, BA, LL B; American federal judge; b 25 Aug 1926, Dodge City, KS; d of Gerald J. and Frances (née Pierce) Strueber; m A. J. Robinson 1949; two d one s. *Education:* Univ of Texas. *Career:* Called to the Bar, TX 1949; own practice, Amarillo 1950–55; Judge Potter Co Court, TX 1955–59, Amarillo 108th Dist Court 1961–73; Assoc Justice Court of Civil Appeals for 7th Supreme Judicial Dist of Texas 1973–77, Chief Justice 1977–79; US Dist Judge, Northern Dist of Texas 1979–; mem Nat Asscn of Women Lawyers, ABA, Texas Bar Asscn, Amarillo Bar Asscn; Woman of the Year, Texan Fed of Business and Professional Women 1973. *Address:* US District Court, 205 E 5th Ave, Rm 13248 Amarillo, TX 79101, USA.

ROBINSON, Mary Terese Winifred, MA, LL M, DCL, SC; Irish UN High Commissioner and former head of state; b 21 May 1944, Ballina, Co Mayo; d of Dr Aubrey and Tessa (née O'Donnell) Bourke; m Nicholas K. Robinson 1970; two s one d. *Education:* Mount Anville, Trinity Coll (Dublin), and Harvard Univ (USA). *Career:* Called to the Bar, King's Inn, Dublin 1967, Middle Temple, UK 1973; Sr Counsel 1980–; Reid Prof of Criminal Law, later Lecturer in European Law, Univ of Dublin Trinity Coll 1969–90; mem Seanad Éireann (Senate) 1969–89, Chair Parl Jt Cttee on EC Secondary Legislation 1973–89, Social Affairs Subcttee 1977–87, Legal Affairs Cttee 1987–89, mem Parl Jt Cttee on Marital Breakdown 1983–85; mem Dublin City Council 1979–83; Sr Counsel 1980–90; Founder, Dir Irish Centre for European Law 1988–90; Pres of Repub of Ireland 1990–97; UN High Commissioner for Human Rights 1997–; Chancellor Dublin Univ 1998–; Sec-Gen Durban World Conf against Racism 2001–; Gen Rapporteur, Council of Europe Prep Conf for Vienna World Conf on Human Rights 1993; mem EC Vedel Cttee on enlargement of the EP 1971–72, EC St Geours Cttee on Energy Efficiency 1978–79; mem New Ireland Forum 1983–84, Editorial Bd Irish Current Law Statutes Annotated 1984–90, Advisory Cttee of Interights, London 1984–90, Int Comm of Jurists, Geneva 1987–90; Co-Founder and Dir Irish Centre for European Law 1988–90; Pres Cherish (asscn for single parents) 1973–90; First Pres Women's Political Asscn; many other voluntary activities; mem Int Comm of Jurists 1987–90; mem Royal Irish Acad 1992–, American Phil Soc 1998–; Hon Bencher King's Inns, Dublin, Middle Temple, London; Hon Fellow Trinity Coll Dublin, Inst of Engineers of Ireland, Royal Coll of Physicians in Ireland, Hertford Coll Oxford, LSE, Royal Coll of Psychiatrists, London, Royal Coll of Surgeons, Ireland, Royal Coll of Obstetricians and Gynaecologists, London; Hon mem New York Bar Asscn, Bar of Tanzania; Hon Prof of Law, Univ of Manchester (UK); Hon LL D (Basle, Queen's (Belfast), Brown Univ, Cambridge, Columbia, Coventry, Dublin, Dublin City, Dublin Inst of Tech, Fordham, Harvard, Katholieke (Leuven), Kyung-Hee (Seoul), Liverpool, London, Melbourne, Adam Mickiewicz (Poznan), Montpellier, Nat Univ of Ireland, Nat Univ of Mongolia, Nat Univ of Wales, Northeastern, Rennes, Albert Schweitzer (Bern), St Andrew's, Toronto, UN Univ for Peace (Costa Rica), Uppsala, Yale); Hon D UNIV (Essex); Berkeley Medal, Univ of California; Medal of Honour, Univ of Coimbra; Medal of Honour, Ordem dos Advogados, Portugal; Gold Medal of Honour, Univ of Salamanca; Andrés Bello Medal, Univ of Chile; New Zealand Suffrage Centennial Medal; Freedom Prize, Max Schmidheiny Foundation, Switzerland; UNIFEM Award, Noel Foundation, Los Angeles; Marisa Bellisario Prize, Italy 1991; CARE Humanitarian Award (USA) 1993; Int Human Rights Award, Int

League of Human Rights, New York 1993; Liberal Int Prize for Freedom 1993; Stephen P. Duggan Award, USA 1994; Freedom of the City of Cork; Int Women's Forum Hall of Fame Award; UN Asscn of New York Global Leadership Award; Collar of Hussein Bin Ali Jordan 1997; Council of Europe North–South Prize 1997; Franklin D. Roosevelt Four Freedoms Medal 1998; Dag Hammarskjöld Medal, Sweden 1998; J. William Fulbright Prize for Int Understanding, USA 1999; Erasmus Prize, Netherlands 1999; Garrigues Walker Prize, Spain 2000; William Butler Medal, USA 2000; Int Geographical Union Medal 'Planet and Humanity' 2000; Indira Gandhi Peace Prize, India 2000; UNESCO Félix Houphouët-Boigny Peace Prize 2000. *Address:* Office of the High Commissioner for Human Rights, United Nations, Palais des Nations, 1211 Geneva 10, Switzerland. *Telephone:* (22) 9179240; *Fax:* (22) 9179012; *E-mail:* secrt.hchr.unog.ch; *Internet:* www.unhchr.ch.

ROBINSON-REGIS, Camille; Trinidad and Tobago politician. *Career:* Fmr Minister in the Office of the Prime Minister and Minister of Consumer Affairs. *Address:* Office of the Prime Minister, Central Bank Tower, Eric Williams Plaza, Independence Sq, Port of Spain, Trinidad and Tobago.

ROBLES, Marisa, FRCM; British concert harpist; b 4 May 1937, Madrid, Spain; d of Cristóbal Robles and Maria Bonilla; m 3rd David W. Bean 1985; two s one d (from previous marriages). *Education:* Madrid Royal Conservatoire of Music. *Career:* Prof of Harp, Madrid Conservatoire 1958–, Royal Coll of Music, London 1969–; Harp Tutor to Nat Youth Orchestra 1964–69; soloist with James Galway, Royal Albert Hall, London 1978; played with major orchestras including New York Philharmonic, USA 1984; Artistic Dir World Harp Festival, Cardiff, Wales 1991, World Harp Festival II 1994; tours in Europe, USA, Australia, Japan, S America, Canada; numerous recordings and appearances on TV; has published several harp pieces and arrangements. *Leisure interests:* theatre, indoor plants, nature, cooking, family. *Address:* 38 Luttrell Ave, London SW15 6PE, UK. *Telephone:* (20) 8785-2204.

ROBOZ, Zsuzsi, FRSA; British artist; b 15 Aug 1939, Budapest, Hungary; d of Imre Roboz and Edith Grosz; m A.T. (Teddy) Smith 1964. *Education:* Royal Acad of Arts (London). *Career:* Also studied with Pietro Annigoni, Florence; various commissions 1956–, including scenes back-stage at Windmill Theatre, London 1964, theatre card of ballet movts for Theatre Museum 1979, portrait of HRH Alice, Duchess of Gloucester 1981, portraits painted include Dame Ninette de Valois, Lord Olivier and Lucian Freud; rep in perm public collections at Tate Gallery (London), Nat Portrait Gallery (London), Theatre Museum (London), Museum of Fine Arts (Budapest), Graves Art Gallery (Sheffield), Bradford Museum and City Art Galleries, St Andrew's Convent (London), Barnwell Church (Northants), New Scotland Yard (London), Durham Univ, St John's Coll (Cambridge), Royal Festival Hall (London), Pablo Casals Museum (Jamaica); also rep in various pvt collections; guest of honour Spring Festival, Budapest 1984. *Art Exhibitions:* Walker Galleries (London) 1958, André Weil Gallery (Paris) 1960, 1968, O'Hana Gallery (London) 1967, 1970, 1973, Hong Kong Arts Festival 1976, Curwen Gallery (London) 1977, Victoria and Albert Museum (London) 1978, Hamilton Gallery (London) 1979, L'Horizon Gallery (Brussels) 1980, Piccadilly Festival of Arts 1981, Vigado Gallery (Budapest) 1988, Amsterdam Gallery, Lincoln Center (New York) 1989, Business Design Centre (London) 1993, Mall Galleries 1993, Roy Miles Gallery 1994, David Messum Gallery 1995, 1997, 1998; *Publications:* Women and Men's Daughters 1970, Chichester 1975, British Ballet Today 1975, British Ballet Today (with James Monahan) 1980, British Art Now (with Edward Lucie-Smith) 1993, Twentieth Century Illusions 1998. *Leisure interests:* classical music, reading, swimming. *Address:* 6 Bryanston Court, George St, London W1H 7HA, UK (Home). *Telephone:* (20) 7723-6540 (Home); *Fax:* (20) 7724-6844 (Home).

ROCHE, Adi; Irish humanitarian and peace activist; b 11 July 1955; d of Seán Roche and Christine Murphy; m Seán Dunne 1978. *Education:* Presentation Convent (Clonmel) and Eccle St Coll (Dublin). *Career:* mem sales staff Aer Lingus; resgnd to work full-time in voluntary capacity for Irish Campaign for Nuclear Disarmament; Founder, Exec Dir Chernobyl Children's Project 1995–; Co-Producer TV documentary programmes Black Wind—White Land (Dublin) 1993,

Chernobyl Legacy (BBC, London) 1995, Death's Dream Kingdom (Dublin) 1996; Irish Carer of the Year 1994–95; Humanitarian Person of the Year, Irish Jr Chamber 1994/95; Irish People of the Year Award 1994/95; European Woman Laureate 1994/95; Irish European Person of the Year 1996; Sunday Independent Person of the Year 1996; Tipperary Person of the Year 1996. *Publication:* Children of Chernobyl 1996. *Leisure interests:* walking, music, reading. *Address:* Chernobyl Children's Project, 8 Sidneyville, Bellevue Park, St Luke's, Cork, Ireland. *Telephone:* (21) 506411; *Fax:* (21) 551544; *E-mail:* adiroche@ indigo.ie; *Internet:* www.aardvark.ie/ccp/.

ROCHFORD, Patricia Anne, MA; Australian business executive; b Sydney; d of Joseph Rochford and Marie Bishop. *Education:* Univ of Sydney and New S Wales Conservatorium of Music. *Career:* Teacher 1965–70; educational psychologist 1970–77; Dir Rochford Williams Int 1982–83, Man Dir 1984–86, Chair 1986–87; Chair Rochford Int Pty Ltd 1997–; Dir State Rail Authority, NSW 1989–92; Dir Univ of NSW Foundation 1991–2001, mem Council Univ NSW 1993–98; Chair IBM Australia Ltd 1978–80, Australian Region Int Search Partnership 1984–; Trustee Cttee for the Econ Devt of Australia (CEDA) 1982–91, 1996–; mem Australian Psychological Soc 1975–, affil American Psychological Soc, Int Asscn Applied Psychology, Australian Admin Staff Coll Asscn 1979–, Council Art Gallery Soc NSW 1978–82, Sydney Int Piano Competition Friends 1983–89, Royal Flying Doctor Service Cttee 1986–94, Torch Appeal Sydney Legacy 1988–92, Variety Club 1988–93, Inst Chartered Man Consultants (foundation mem), Chief Exec Women 1989–, Sydney Tourism Advisory Bd 1995–, Council Australian Business Arts Foundation 2000–; Dir Sydney Symphony Orchestra Foundation Bd 1992–94. *Leisure interests:* ballet, opera, music, theatre, reading. *Address:* POB 2672, Sydney, NSW 2001, Australia. *Telephone:* (2) 92350422; *Fax:* (2) 92331224; *E-mail:* mail@ rochford-int.com.au.

ROCKBURNE, Dorothea; American artist; b 18 Oct 1934, Montréal, Canada; m 1951 (divorced); one d. *Education:* Black Mountain Coll (NC). *Career:* Solo exhibitions include Bykert Gallery, New York 1970, 1972, 1973, Sonnabend Gallery, Paris 1971, Galleria Toselli, Milan, Italy 1972, 1974, 1983, Lisson Gallery, London 1973, Galleria Schema, Florence, Italy 1973, 1975, John Weber Gallery, New York 1976, 1978, Texas Gallery, Houston 1979, 1980, Museum of Modern Art, New York 1980, Xavier Fourcade, New York 1980, 1985, 1986, Arts Club of Chicago 1987, André Emmerich Gallery, New York 1988, 1989, 1991, 1992, 1994, 1995, Rose Museum, Brandeis Univ 1989, 1996, Portland Museum of Art 1996, Rockefeller Foundation Center, Bellagio, Italy 1997, Lawrence Rubin, Greenberg Van Doren Fine Art, New York 2000; numerous group exhibitions; rep in collections including Whitney Museum, Museum of Modern Art, Metropolitan Museum of Art and Guggenheim Museum, New York, and Corcoran Gallery, Washington, DC; Visiting Artist Skowhegan School of Painting and Sculpture 1984; Avery Distinguished Prof Bard Coll, Annandale-on-Hudson, NY 1986; Artist-in-Residence American Acad, Rome 1991; comms include San Jose Hilton 1993, wall fresco for Sony USA headquarters, New York 1995 and Edward T. Gignoux Fed Courthouse, Portland (ME) 1996; Guggenheim Fellow 1972; Art Inst of Chicago Painting Award 1972; Nat Endowment for the Arts 1974; mem Dept of Art, American Acad of Arts and Letters 2001; Art Inst of Chicago Painting Award 1972; Creative Arts Award, Brandeis Univ 1985. *Leisure interests:* music, mathematics. *Address:* 140 Grand St, New York, NY 10013, USA. *Telephone:* (212) 226-4471; *Fax:* (212) 925-0942; *E-mail:* octgrace@aol.com (Office); *Internet:* www .dorothearockburne.com (Office).

RODDICK, Anita Lucia, OBE; British business executive; b 23 Oct 1942, Littlehampton; d of the late Henry and Gilda (née de Vita) Perelli; m Thomas Gordon Roddick 1970; two d. *Education:* Maude Allen Secondary Modern School for Girls, Newton Park Coll of Educ (Bath). *Career:* Teacher of English and History 1962; worked in Cuttings Dept, New York Herald Tribune, UN Geneva; mem staff Women's Dept, ILO Geneva; owned and managed restaurant and hotel 1962–76; opened first UK Body Shop, Brighton, Sussex 1976, first overseas Body Shop Belgium 1978; The Body Shop Int floated on Unlisted Securities Market 1984, Group Man Dir The Body Shop Int PLC until 1994, CEO 1994–98, Jt Chair 1998–; Trustee The Body Shop Foundation 1990–, New Acad of Business 1996; Patron of various orgs; mem Demos 'think-tank'; Hon Fellow Bath Coll of Higher Educ 1994; Hon D UNIV (Sussex) 1988, (Open Univ) 1995; Hon LL D (Nottingham) 1990, (New England Coll) 1991, (Victoria, Canada) 1995; Hon D SC (Portsmouth) 1994; Hon DBA, (Kingston) 1996; Veuve Clicquot Business Woman of the Year 1985; British Asscn of Industrial Eds Communicator of the Year 1988; Co NatWest Retailer of the Year Award 1989; UN 'Global 500' Environment Award 1989; Centre for World Devt Educ World Vision Award 1991; Business Leader of the Year, Nat Asscn of Women Business Owners, USA 1992; Botwinick Prize in Business Ethics 1994; Business Leadership Award, Univ of Michigan 1994; First Annual Womanpower Award, Women's Business Devt Center 1995; USA Women's Center Leadership Award 1996; American Dream Award, Hunter Coll 1996; Philanthropist of the Year, Inst of Fundraising Managers 1996. *Publication:*Body and Soul (autobiog) 1991, Business as Unusual 2000. *Leisure interests:* talking to radical thinkers, theatre, arts. *Address:* The Body Shop Int PLC, Watersmead, Littlehampton, W Sussex, BN17 6LS, UK. *Telephone:* (1903) 731500; *Fax:* (1903) 726250.

RODGER, Eleanor J. (Joey); American library organization executive. *Career:* Fmrly Head of Network System Enoch Pratt Free Library, Co-ordinator of Evaluation Fairfax Co Public Library, Research Assoc King Research, Library Consultant; Exec Dir Public Library Asscn 1986–92; Pres Urban Libraries Council 1992; childhood specialist Carroll Co Public Library. *Address:* Urban Libraries Council, Suite 1080, 1603 Orrington Ave, Evanston, IL 60201, USA. *Telephone:* (847) 866-9999.

RODGERS, Brid, BA, DIP EDUC; British politician; b 20 Feb 1935, Co Donegal; d of Thomas Stratford and Josephine Coll; m Antoin Rodgers 1960; three s three d. *Education:* St Louis Convent Grammar School (Monaghan) and Univ Coll, Dublin. *Career:* Active in Civil Rights Movt 1967–71; mem N Ireland Civil Rights Asscn 1969–71; Chair SDLP 1978–80, Gen Sec 1981–83, Leader SDLP Council Group, Craigavon Borough Council 1985–93, Chair SDLP Negotiating Team for Good Friday Agreement 1996–98; mem Irish Senate 1983–87; elected to N Ireland Exec as Mem for Upper Bann 1998–; Minister of Agric and Rural Devt, N Ireland Ass 1999–. *Leisure interests:* reading, swimming, golf. *Address:* Dundonald House, Upper Newtownards Rd, Belfast, BT4 3SB, UK. *Telephone:* (28) 3832-2140; *Fax:* (28) 3831-6996; *E-mail:* b .rodgers@sdlp.ie.

RODGERS, Joan, CBE, BA; British opera and concert singer (soprano); b 4 Nov 1956, Whitehaven, Cumbria; d of the late Thomas and of Julia Rodgers; m Paul Daniel 1988; two d. *Education:* Whitehaven Grammar School, Univ of Liverpool and Royal Northern Coll of Music (Manchester). *Career:* Professional debut as Pamina in Die Zauberflöte, Aix-en-Provence Festival, France 1982; appearances include Glynde-bourne Festival, Royal Opera House, Covent Garden (London), Zurich (Switzerland), Amsterdam (Netherlands), English Nat Opera, Maggio Musicale, Florence (Italy), Vienna, Salzburg (Austria), Madrid, Paris, Los Angeles and Chicago (USA); regular appearances at Royal Opera House, English Nat Opera, Glyndebourne, Promenade Concerts and with leading British and European cos; mostly associated with Mozart roles; recordings of major works with Chandos, EMI and Hyperion; concert appearances with Solti, Mehta, Salonen, Barenboim, Harnon-court, Andrew Davis; recipient Kathleen Ferrier Memorial Scholarship 1981; Royal Philharmonic Soc Award as Singer of the Year 1997; Evening Standard Award for Outstanding Individual Performance in Opera 1997. *Operas include:* The Marriage of Figaro, Don Giovanni, Rigoletto, Turn of the Screw, Pelléas et Mélisande, Blanche in Dialogues des Carmelites. *Leisure interests:* walking, cooking, swimming, gardening. *Address:* c/o Ingpen & Williams Ltd, 26 Wadham Rd, London SW15 2LR, UK; 5 Grange Grove, London N1 2NP, UK (Home). *Telephone:* (20) 7359-0120; *Fax:* (20) 7226-0101.

RODGERS, Mary Columbro, MA, PH D; American university chancellor and writer; b 17 April 1925, Autora, OH; d of Nicola and Nancy (née DeNicola) Columbro; m Daniel Richard Rodgers 1965; two d one s. *Education:* Notre Dame Coll, Western Reserve Univ and Ohio State Univ. *Career:* Teacher of English, Cleveland, OH 1945–62; Supervisor Ohio State Univ 1962–64; Asst Prof of English Univ of Maryland 1965–66; Assoc Prof Trinity Coll 1967–68; Prof of English, Dist of Columbia Teachers' Coll 1968–; Chancellor and Dean American Open Univ 1965–; Pres Maryland Nat Univ 1972–; Fellow Catholic Scholars;

mem Poetry Soc of America, Nat Council of English Teachers, American Educational Research Asscn; Hon DIP ED (California Nat Open) 1975; Hon D LITT (California Nat Open) 1978. *Publications include:* A Short Course in English Compositions 1976, Chapbook of Children's Literature 1977, Essays and Poems on Life and Literature 1979, Modes and Models: Four Lessons for Young Writers 1981, Open University Structures and Adult Learning 1982, English Pedagogy in the American Open University 1983, Design for Personalized Graduate Degrees in the Urban University 1984, Poet and Pedagogue in Moscow and Leningrad: a travel report 1989, Twelve Lectures in Literary Analysis 1990, Ten Lectures in Literary Production 1990, Analyzing Fact and Fiction 1991, Analyzing Poetry and Drama 1991, A Chapbook of Poetry and Drama Analysis 1992, Convent Poems 1943–61 1993, Catholic Marriage Poems 1962–79 1993, New Design Responses 1945–93 (10 vols) 1993, Catholic Widow with Children Poems 1979–93 1994, Journals: Reflections and Resolves 1984–95 (16 vols) 1995, Biographical Sourcebook: Mary Columbro Rodgers 1969–95 1995, Catholic Teacher Poems 1945–95 1995. *Address:* College Heights Estate, 3916 Commander Drive, Hyattsville, MD 20782, USA.

RODGERS, Patricia Elaine Joan, MA, D POL SC; Bahamian diplomatist; b Nassau; d of the late Dr Kenneth V. A. and Anatol C. (née Reeves) Rodgers. *Education:* School of St Helen and St Catherine (Abingdon, Oxon, UK), Univ of Aberdeen (UK), Grad Inst of Int Relations (St Augustine, Trinidad), and Univ of Geneva (Switzerland). *Career:* Counsellor and Consul, Washington, DC 1978–83; Alt Rep to OAS 1982–83; Deputy High Commr (Acting High Commr), Canada 1983–86, High Commr 1986–88; High Commr, UK (also accredited to France, Belgium and Germany) 1988–92; Perm Sec Ministry of Tourism, Nassau 1995–; mem Bahamas Del to UN Conf on Law of the Sea 1974, 1975, OAS Gen Ass 1982, Caribbean Co-ordinating Meeting (Head of Del), OAS 1983, Canada/Commonwealth Caribbean Heads of Govt Meeting 1985, Commonwealth Heads of Govt Meeting, Nassau 1985, Vancouver, Canada 1987; Adviser to Bahamas Del, Annual Gen Meetings of IBRD and IMF 1978–82; mem Commonwealth Observer Group, Gen Elections Lesotho 1993; Perm Sec, Ministry of Tourism 1995–. *Publications:* Mid-Ocean Archipelagos and International Law, A Study of the Progressive Development of International Law 1981. *Leisure interests:* folk art, interior decorating, theatre, gourmet cooking. *Address:* c/o Ministry of Tourism, POB N-3701, Market Plaza, Bay St, Nassau, Bahamas. *Telephone:* 322-7500; *Fax:* 322-4041; *E-mail:* prodgers@bahamas.com; pejrodgers@yahoo.com.

RODI, Nelly-Claire; French fashion executive; b 26 July 1943, Ponts-de-Cé; d of Gilbert and Nelly (née Bruhin) Rodi; m 2nd Jean-Michel Le Louet; two d one s. *Education:* Lycée Marcel Robby (Saint-Germain-en-Laye). *Career:* Fashion Asst Woolmark 1963–67; Dir Fashion and Publicity Int Inst for Cotton 1967–69; in charge of Image and Studio for André Courrèges (fashion designer) 1969–72; Dir Cttee of Co-ordination of Fashion Industries 1972–85; Founder, Pres Agence de Style Nelly Rodi 1985–, Nelly Rodi-Japan 1987–; Pres Inst supérieur européen de management de la mode 1989; Dir Cttee of the Devt and Promotion of Textiles and Clothing 1995–97; Chevalier de la Légion d'Honneur. *Leisure interests:* piano, collecting glass. *Address:* 28 ave de St-Ouen, 75018 Paris, France (Office); 199 rue du Général de Gaulle, 78740 Vaux-sur-Seine, France (Home); Ty var lin, 29950 Bénodet, France (Home). *Telephone:* (1) 42-93-04-06 (Office); *Fax:* (1) 45-22-79-68 (Office); *E-mail:* nr@nelly-rodi.com.

RODIN, Judith, PH D; American professor of psychology, medicine and psychiatry and university president; b 9 Sept 1944, Philadelphia, PA; d of Morris Rodin and Sally (née Winson) Seitz; m 1st Nicholas Neijelow 1978; one s; m 2nd Paul Verkuil 1994. *Education:* Univ of Pennsylvania and Columbia Univ. *Career:* Nat Science Foundation Postdoctoral Fellow, Univ of California 1971; Asst Prof of Psychology, Univ of New York 1970–72; Asst Prof Yale Univ 1972–75, Assoc Prof 1975–79, Prof of Psychology 1979–83, Dir Grad Studies 1982–89, Philip R. Allen Prof of Psychology 1984–94, Prof of Medicine and Psychiatry 1985–94, Chair Dept Psychology 1989–91, Dean Grad School of Arts and Sciences 1991–92, Provost 1992–94; Prof of Medicine and Psychiatry Univ of Pennsylvania 1994–, Prof of Psychology 1994–, Pres Univ of Pennsylvania 1994–; Chair John D. and Catherine T. MacArthur Foundation Research Network on Health-Promoting and Health-Damaging Behaviour 1983–93; Chair Council of Presidents, Univs

Research Asscn 1995–96; has served on numerous Bds of Dirs, including Int Life Sciences Inst 1993–, Aetna Life & Casualty Co 1995–; mem numerous professional cttees, including Pres Clinton's Cttee of Advisors on Science and Tech 1994–, Pennsylvania Women's Forum 1995–; Chief Ed Appetite 1979–92; mem numerous editorial bds; mem Bd of Trustees Brookings Inst 1995–; Fellow AAAS, American Acad of Arts and Sciences; Hon D HUM LITT (New Haven) 1994, (Medical Coll of Pennsylvania and Hahnemann Univ) 1995; awards and prizes include 21st Century Award, Int Alliance, Glass Ceiling Award, American Red Cross. *Publications:* Women and Weight: a normative discontent (jtly) 1985; author or co-author of nine other books on the relationship between psychological and biological processes in human health and behaviour; 100 articles in academic journals. *Leisure interests:* tennis, travel, reading. *Address:* University of Pennsylvania, Office of the President, 100 College Hall, Philadelphia, PA 19104, USA. *Telephone:* (215) 898-7221; *Fax:* (215) 898-9659.

RODRÍGUEZ, Bélgica, PH D; Venezuelan arts executive; b 25 July 1941; m Vidal Rodríguez-Lemoine 1964; two s. *Education:* Cen Univ (Caracas) and Univs of London and Paris. *Career:* Gen Co-ordinator, Ateneo 1964–71; Curator Visual Arts Fundarte 1978–84; apptd Prof of Latin-American Art, Cen Univ 1978; Dir Nat Gallery 1984–86, Museum of Modern Art of Latin America, OAS, Washington, DC 1988; apptd Pres Int Asscn of Art Critics 1987. *Publications:* A Short History of Venezuelan Sculpture 1978, Abstract Art in Venezuela: A History 1980. *Address:* International Association of Art Critics, 9 rue Berryer, 75008 Paris, France. *Telephone:* (1) 42-56-17-53.

RODRÍGUEZ, Ketty, PH D; American librarian; b Canóvanas, Puerto Rico; d of Elías Rodríguez and Rafaela Casillas; divorced 1977; one s. *Education:* Univ of Puerto Rico and Indiana Univ at Bloomington (USA). *Career:* Admin Asst to Sec-Gen of Asscn of Caribbean Univs and Research Insts 1982–84; Librarian Univ of Puerto Rico 1984–85, 1986–88; Librarian Univ of Florida 1991; Visiting Lecturer Texas Woman's Univ School of Library and Information Studies 1991–92, Asst Prof 1992; Sara Rebecca Reed Scholarship Indiana Univ 1988; Nat Hispanic Scholarship Fund Scholarship 1989. *Leisure interest:* travel in Europe and Latin America. *Address:* 2708 N Bell Ave, Denton, TX 76201, USA. *Telephone:* (817) 898-1168; *Fax:* (817) 898-3198.

RODRÍGUEZ RODRÍGUEZ, Martha; Mexican poet; b 20 Oct 1939, Chihuahua. *Education:* Studies in accountancy. *Career:* Poet; made a record 1990; numerous awards for poetry including Golden Rose Award, Ciudad Juárez 1971; Silver Medal and First Prize for poem El Campesino 1984. *Address:* Calle Colima 415, Departamento 1303, Col Condesa, México, DF 06700, Mexico. *Telephone:* (5) 2112149; *Fax:* (5) 2112149.

ROE, Marion Audrey; British politician; b 15 July 1936, London; d of William and Grace Mary (née Bocking) Keyte; m James Kenneth Roe 1958; one s two d. *Education:* Bromley and Croydon High Schools GPDST (Girls' Public Day School Trust) and English School of Languages (Vevey, Switzerland). *Career:* Elected to GLC (Cons) for Ilford N 1977, mem GLC Cons Leader's Cttee, Cons GLC Deputy Chief Whip 1982–83; MP for Broxbourne, Herts 1983–, Parl Pvt Sec to Sec of State for Transport 1986, Parl Under-Sec of State Dept of the Environment 1987–88; responsible for Pvt Mem's Bill, Prohibition of Female Circumcision Act, passed 1985; mem Social Services Select Cttee 1988–89, Select Cttee on Procedure 1990–92, Sittings of the House Select Cttee 1991–92, House of Commons Admin Cttee 1991–97; Jt Chair All-Party Fairs and Showgrounds Group 1989–92; Chair Select Cttee on Health 1992–97, mem 2000–; Sec All-Party Hospices Group 1990–92, Chair 1992–; Sec All-Party British–Canadian Parl Group 1991–97, Vice-Chair 1997–; Jt Chair All-Party Group on Breast Cancer 1997–; Vice-Chair All-Party Parl Group on Domestic Violence 1999–; mem Dept of Employment Advisory Cttee on Women's Employment 1989–92; Substitute mem UK Del to Parl Ass of the Council of Europe and WEU 1989–92; Vice-Pres Women's Nat Cancer Control Campaign 1985–87, 1988–; Gov Research into Ageing Trust 1988–97; mem Nat Health Service Confed Parl Panel 2000–; Trustee Nat Benevolent Fund for the Aged 1999–; Fellow Industry and Parl Trust, Royal Soc for the Encouragement of Arts, Manufacture and Commerce (RSA) 1990; Freeman of the City of London, Liveryman

Worshipful Co of Gardeners. *Leisure interests:* ballet, opera. *Address:* House of Commons, London SW1A 0AA, UK. *Telephone:* (20) 7219-3528.

ROE, Dame Raigh (Edith), DBE, JP; Australian executive; b 12 Dec 1922; d of Alwyn and Laura Kurts; m James Arthur Roe 1941; three s. *Education:* Perth Girls' School. *Career:* Mem Country Women's Asscn, State Pres 1967–70, Nat Pres 1969–71; World Pres Associated Country Women of the World 1977–80; World Amb WA Council 1978–; Hon Amb State of Louisiana, USA 1979–; Commr ABC 1978–83; Nat Dir Queen Elizabeth II Silver Jubilee Trust for Young Australians 1978–; Dir Airlines of WA 1981–; Australian of the Year 1977. *Address:* 76 Regency Drive, Crestwood, Thornlie, WA 6108, Australia. *Telephone:* (87) 459 8765.

ROEHM, Carolyne, BFA; American fashion designer; b 7 May 1951, Kirksville, MO; d of Kenneth Smith and Elaine (Beaty) Bresee; m 1st Axel Roehm 1978 (divorced 1981); m 2nd Henry R. Kravis 1985. *Education:* Washington Univ, St Louis. *Career:* Designed sportswear for Kellwood Co, New York; apprentice Oscar de la Renta, Rome 1975–84; Pres Carolyne Roehm Inc (fashion design house) 1984–; Pres Council of Fashion Designers of America 1989. *Leisure interests:* gardening, skiing, tennis, opera, playing the piano.

ROGELL, Irma Rose, BA; American harpsichordist; b Malden, MA; d of Mitchell Edward and Sara (née Freedman) Rose; m Bernard C. Rogell 1942 (died 1964); two s one d. *Education:* Harvard Univ. *Career:* Studied under Wanda Landowska; debut Jordan Hall, Boston 1960, Carnegie Recital Hall, New York 1961; soloist with symphony orchestras including Boston and Brazil Symphony Orchestras; tours in Europe; appeared on TV and radio; recorded works with Titanic Records; has given lectures and recitals in numerous univs and colls; faculty mem City Univ of New York 1973–78, Ethical Culture School of New York; visiting faculty mem Longy School of Music, Cambridge, MA and New England Conservatory 1988–; mem Coll of Music Soc, Piano Teachers' Congress of New York. *Leisure interests:* reading, drawing, writing poetry. *Address:* 250 Hammond Pond Parkway, Apt 715N, Chestnut Hill, MA 02467-1551, USA.

ROGERS, Judith W., BA, LL B; American judge. *Education:* Radcliffe Coll and Harvard Univ. *Career:* Law Clerk Juvenile Court of Dist of Columbia 1964–65; called to the Bar, DC 1965; Asst US Attorney, DC 1965–68; Trial Attorney San Francisco Neighbourhood Legal Assistance Foundation 1968–69; Attorney US Dept of Justice 1969–71; Gen Counsel Congressional Comm on Org of Dist of Columbia Govt 1971–72; Co-ordinator Legis Programme, Office of Deputy Mayor, DC 1972–74; Special Asst to Mayor for Legislation 1974–79; Corp Counsel 1979–83; Assoc Judge Dist of Columbia Court of Appeals 1983–88, Chief Judge 1988–94, Circuit Judge 1994; mem Dist of Columbia Law Revision Comm 1979–83, Mayor's Comm on Crime and Justice 1982, Visiting Cttee Harvard Law School 1984–90; mem Bd Dirs Wider Opportunities for Women 1972–74; Trustee Radcliffe Coll 1982–88; Fellow ABA; mem Dist of Columbia Bar Asscn; mem Exec Cttee Chief Justices Conf 1993–94; Hon LL M (Virginia) 1988, Hon LL D (DC School of Law) 1992. *Address:* District of Columbia Court of Appeals, 500 Indiana Ave, NW, 6th Floor, Washington, DC 20001, USA.

ROGERS, Mimi; American actress; b 27 Jan 1956, Coral Gables, FL; m Tom Cruise (divorced). *Films include:* Blue Skies 1983, Gung Ho, Street Smart, Someone to Watch Over Me, The Mighty Quinn, Kider in the House, Desperate Hours, The Doors, The Rapture, To Forget Palermo/The Palermo Connection, The Player, White Sands, Dark Horse, Monkey Trouble, Far From Home: The Adventures of Yellow Dog, Bulletproof Heart, Reflections in the Dark; several films for TV including Virtual Obsession 1998, Lost in Space 1998, Devil's Arithmetic 1999, Manchester Prep 1999, Common Ground 2000.

ROGERS, Su, B SC; British architect; b 22 Feb 1939, Cornwall; d of Irene and Marcus Brumwell; m 1st Richard Rogers 1960; three s; m 2nd John Millers 1985; two step-d. *Education:* Frensham Heights School, LSE and Yale Univ (USA). *Career:* Partner Team 4 Architects 1963–67, Richard and Su Rogers Architects 1967–70, Piano and Rogers Architects 1970–72, Colquhoun Miller and Partners 1986–90, John Miller and Partners 1990–; Unit Master Architectural Asscn 1972–76;

Tutor Royal Coll of Art 1975–85; Dir Royal Coll of Art Project Office 1979–86; Visiting Tutor Univ of Cambridge, Univ of Wales at Cardiff, Columbia Univ (New York, USA) Univ of Bristol, Univ of Bath, Univ Coll Dublin, Univ Coll Toronto (Canada). *Major Works include:* Pillwood House Cornwall (RIBA Regional Award 1975), Housing Albion Brownlow Shrubland Rd (Civic Trust Award 1985, Architectural Design Award 1986), Whitechappel Art Gallery (Civic Trust Award 1987, European Prize for Architecture 1988, RIBA Regional Award 1988), Queen's Building Univ of E Anglia (RIBA Nat and Regional Awards 1994), Halton Arts Centre Runcorn (Architect's Journal/Bovis Lend Lease Non Mem's Award at Royal Acad Summer Exhibition 2000), Nat Galleries of Scotland – Playfair Project (Architect's Journal/Bovis Lend Lease Non Mem's Award at Royal Acad 2000, Worshipful Co of Chartered Architects Measured Drawing Prize 2000). *Leisure interests:* exhibitions, architecture, reading, travelling, cooking. *Address:* John Miller and Partners, The Elephant House Brewery, Hawley Crescent, London, NW1 8NP; 23 Regents Park Rd, London NW1 7TL, UK. *Telephone:* (20) 7482-4686; *Fax:* (02) 7267-9907; *E-mail:* s.rogers@johnmillerandpartners.co.uk.

ROITZSCH, Ingrid; German politician; b 30 July 1940, Munich; two c. *Education:* Univ of Angers (France). *Career:* Mem Civil Cttee of Quickborn Town Council 1970–80; mem Pinneberg Dist Cttee, CDU 1971, mem State Cttees Schleswig-Holstein 1979, 1981; Ed Pinneberg daily paper, Hamburg daily paper, Die Welt 1971–80; mem Kreistag Pinneberg 1978–80; mem of Bundestag (Parl, CDU), Parl Sec CDU/CSU Group 1987, for Defence 1992–93; mem Fed Cttee CDU Women's Asscn 1981–. *Address:* Bundestag, 11011 Berlin, Germany.

ROJAS, Ixora; Venezuelan politician. *Career:* Deputy in the Congreso de la República (Parl), Pres of Congress's Tourism Cttee. *Address:* Congreso de la República, Palacio Federal Legislativo, Caracas, Venezuela. *Telephone:* (2) 481-4184; *Fax:* (2) 481-4184.

ROJAS DE MORENO DÍAZ, María Eugenia; Colombian politician; b 1934; d of the late Gen Gustavo Rojas Pinilla (Pres of Colombia 1953–57); m Samuel Moreno Díaz; two s. *Career:* Fmr mem Senate; Majority Leader Santa Fe de Bogotá City Council; Leader Alianza Nacional Popular (ANAPO) 1975–. *Address:* Alianza Nacional Popular (ANAPO), Santa Fe de Bogotá, Colombia. *Telephone:* (1) 287-7050; *Fax:* (1) 245-3138.

ROLIM RAMOS, Maria; Portuguese publishing executive; b 27 Dec 1941, Évora. *Education:* Inst des Sciences de la Communication and Inst des Sciences Politiques (Paris). *Career:* Journalist Office de Radiodiffusion-Télévision Française (ORTF), France; Paris Corresp Radiodifusão Portuguesa, EP (RDP); Producer Société Nat de Programmes—France Régions 3 (FR3) TV channel, France; Ed Edições Rolim 1976–92, Publr and Man Dir 1992–; Ed Colares Editora 1990–92, Publr and Man Dir 1992–; five prizes from Mulheres Magazine 1985–89. *Publications:* (as Loy Rolim) Medos Mudos 1975, A Oposição em Espanha 1976. *Leisure interests:* reading, travel. *Address:* Edições Rolim Lda, Apdo 3079, 1032 Lisbon Codex, Portugal (Office); Colares Editora, Apdo 2048, 2710 Colares/Sintra, Portugal (Office); Rua Fialho de Almeida 38, 2° Dto, 1000 Lisbon, Portugal (Home). *Telephone:* (1) 9290662 (Home); *Fax:* (1) 9293029 (Home).

ROLLETT, Brigitte, DR PHIL; Austrian professor of educational psychology; b 9 Oct 1934, Graz; d of Georg Gorbach; m Gerald Rollett; two d two s. *Education:* Univ of Graz. *Career:* Asst Univ of Graz 1962–65; Chair of Psychology Pädagogische Hochschule, Osnabrück, Germany 1965–71; Prof of Educational Psychology and Child Psychotherapy Gesamthochschule, Kassel, Germany 1971–75; fmr Chair of Educational Psychology Ruhr-Univ Bochum, Germany; currently Prof of Developmental and Educational Psychology, Faculty of Philosophy, Univ of Vienna; Großes Silbernes Ehrenzeichen für Verdienste um die Republik Österreich Kardinal Innitzer Stiftungspreis. *Publications include:* Lernen und Lehren. Eine Einfürung in die Pädagogische Psychologie und ihre entwicklungpsychologischen Grundlagen 1997, Der Anstrengungsvermeidungstest. Manual und Test 1997, Autismus. Ein Leitfaden für Eltern, Erzieher, Lehrer und Therapeuten (jtly) 2001. *Address:* University of Vienna, Liebiggasse 5, 1010 Vienna, Austria;

Reimersgasse 16/D5, 1190 Vienna, Austria (Home). *Telephone:* (1) 4277-47806; *Fax:* (1) 4277-47869; *E-mail:* brigitte.rollett@univie.ac.at.

ROMILLY, Jacqeline de (see de Romilly, Jacqueline).

RÖNKKÖ, Marja-Liisa, PH D; Finnish project director; b 28 Oct 1945; d of Viljo Rönkkö and Annikki Korhonen; m Tapio Lampinen 1969 (divorced 1982); one s. *Education:* Univ of Helsinki. *Career:* Curator Satakunta Museum, Pori 1971–73; Curator Helsinki City Museum 1973–78, Dir 1978–90; Dir-Gen Finnish Nat Gallery 1990–2000; Project Dir Finnish Book Inst 2000–; mem ICOM 1974–, Scandinavian Museums Asscn 1974–, Network of European Museum Orgs, Museum Cttee of the Nordic Council of Ministers; has written several books and articles on the history of art, architecture, the theatre, the city of Helsinki and on museology. *Leisure interest:* writing. *Address:* Finnish Book Institute, Museum of the Book, Puistokatu 10, 38200 Vammala, Finland. *Telephone:* (9) 1356880 (Office); (50) 3680818 (Mobile); *Fax:* (3) 5198376 (Office); *E-mail:* moronkko@vammala.fi; *Internet:* www.vammala.fi.

RONSTADT, Linda Marie; American singer; b 15 July 1946, Tucson, AZ; d of Gilbert and Ruthmary (née Copeman) Ronstadt. *Career:* First album 1967; appeared in stage version of Pirates of Penzance 1981, film version 1983; featured in La Bohème 1984; American Music Award 1978; Grammy Awards 1975, 1976, 1987, 1988 (with Emmylou Harris, qv and Dolly Parton, qv), 1989, 1990 (jtly); Emmy Award 1988, 1989; Acad of Country Music Award 1987, 1988. *Albums include:* Evergreen 1967, Home Sown, Home Grown 1969, Silk Purse 1970, Don't Cry Now 1973, Heart Like a Wheel 1974, Different Drum 1974, Prisoner in Disguise 1975, Hasten Down the Wind 1976, Simple Dreams, Blue Bayou 1977, Living in the USA 1978, Get Closer 1982, What's New 1983, Lush Life 1984, For Sentimental Reasons 1986, Trio (with Emmylou Harris and Dolly Parton, Country Music Album of the Year 1987) 1986, Canciones de Mi Padre 1987, Cry Like a Rainstorm—Howl Like the Wind 1989, All My Life 1990, Mas Canciones 1991, Frenesi 1992, Winter Light 1993, Feels Like Home 1995, We Ran 1998, Trio 2 (with Emmylou Harris and Dolly Parton) 1999, Western Wall: The Tucson Sessions (wih Emmylou Harris). *Address:* Electra Records, 75 Rockefeller Plaza, New York, NY 10019, USA.

RONTÓ, Györgyi; Hungarian biophysicist; b 13 July 1934, Budapest; d of György Rontó and Erzsébet Lanczkor; m Dr Dezso Holnapy 1961; two s. *Education:* Semmelweis Univ of Medicine (Budapest). *Career:* Prof of Biophysics Semmelweis Univ 1980–, Dir Semmelweis Univ Inst of Biophysics 1982–99; Head of Research Group for Biophysics of the Hungarian Acad of Sciences 1982–; Gen Sec Hungarian Biophysical Soc 1969–90, Vice-Pres 1990–98; Vice-Pres Asscn Int de Photobiologie 1988–92; officer European Soc for Photobiology; specialises in effects of environmental physical and chemical agents on nucleo-proteins; special interest in biological dosimetry of environmental and artificial UV radiations; Gold Ring, Semmelweis Univ 1999. *Publications:* A biofizika alapjai (An Introduction to Biophysics) (co-author) 1981 (also English and German editions), Light in Biology and Medicine (Vol 2) 1991; more than 100 articles. *Leisure interests:* arts, architecture, gardening. *Address:* 1444 Budapest, POB 263, Hungary. *Telephone:* (1) 266-6656.

ROOCROFT, Amanda; British opera singer; b 9 Feb 1966, Coppull; d of Roger and Valerie (née Metcalfe) Roocroft; m 1st Manfred Hemm 1995; one s; m 2nd David Gowland 1999; one s. *Education:* Royal N Coll of Music (Manchester). *Career:* Appearances include Wesh Nat Opera 1990, Covent Garden 1991, 1993, 1995, Glyndebourne 1991, 1994, European tour with John Eliot Gardiner 1992, Bavarian State Opera 1993, 1994, 1995, English Nat Opera 1993, BBC Promenade Concert 1993, Edinburgh Festival 1993, Glyndebourne 2000, Covent Garden 2000; regular concert engagements and recitals; Kathleen Ferrier Prize 1988; Silver Medal, Worshipful Co of Musicians 1988; Royal Philharmonic Soc/Charles Heidsieck Award 1990, Barclay Opera Award 2000. *Performances include:* Der Rosenkavalier 1990, The Magic Flute 1991, 1993, Così fan tutte 1991, I Capuleti e i Montecchi 1993, Ariodante 1993, Don Giovanni 1994, Simon Boccanegra 1995, Otello 1999; *Recordings include:* Amanda Roocroft (solo album) 1994, Mozart and his Contemporaries 1996. *Leisure interests:* theatre, cinema, reading, cooking. *Address:* c/o Ingpen & Williams Ltd, 26 Wadham Rd, London SW15 2LR, UK. *Telephone:* (20) 8874-3222; *Fax:* (20) 8877-3113.

ROOT, Jane; British television executive; b 18 May 1957, Canvey Island; d of James William and Kathleen Root. *Education:* Univ of Sussex and London Coll of Printing. *Career:* Manager Cinema of Women (film distribution co) 1981–83; freelance journalist and film critic 1981–83; Lecturer in Film Studies Univ of E Anglia 1981–84; Researcher Open the Box, Beat Productions 1983; Co-Founder The Media Show 1983; Co-Founder and Jt Man Dir Wall to Wall Television 1987–96; Head of Ind Commissioning Group, BBC 1997–98; Controller BBC2 1999–; mem Exec Cttee Edinburgh TV Festival, Chair 1995. *Publications:* Pictures of Women: Sexuality 1981, Open the Box: About Television 1983. *Leisure interests:* Travel, reading. *Address:* BBC Television Centre, Wood Lane, London W12 7RJ, UK.

ROSEANNE; American actress; b (Roseanne Barr) 3 Nov 1952, Salt Lake City, UT; d of Jerry and Helen Barr; m 1st Bill Pentland 1974 (divorced 1989); m 2nd Tom Arnold 1990 (divorced 1994); three c (from previous m); m 3rd Ben Thomas 1994; one s. *Career:* Fmrly window dresser and cocktail waitress, worked as comedienne in bars and church coffee-house, Denver, CO; Producer Take Back the Mike forum for women performers, Univ of Boulder, CO; performer at The Comedy Store, Los Angeles, CA; Consultant to New Yorker magazine 1996; Emmy award (Outstanding Leading Actress in a Comedy Series) 1993. *Films:* She Devil 1989, Freddy's Dead 1991, Look Who's Talking Too (voice), Even Cowgirls Get the Blues 1994, Blue in the Face 1995, Unzipped 1995, Meet Wally Sparks 1997; *TV appearances include:* Funny, The Tonight Show, On Location: The Roseanne Barr Show 1987, Roseanne (also exec producer, Peabody and Golden Globe Awards for Best Series, Emmy Award for Best Actress 1993) 1988–97, Saturday Night Special (exec producer), host Roseanne Show 1998–; *Publication:* My Life as a Woman 1989, My Lives 1994. *Address:* c/o Full Moon and High Tide Productions 4024 Radford Ave, Dressing Rm 916, Studio City, CA 91604, USA.

ROSENBLATT, Joan Raup, BA, PH D; American statistician; b 15 April 1926, New York; d of Robert Bruce and Clara (née Eliot) Raup; m David Rosenblatt 1950. *Education:* Barnard Coll and Univ of N Carolina. *Career:* Intern Nat Inst of Public Affairs, Washington, DC 1946–47; Statistical Analyst US Bureau of Budget 1947–48; Research Asst Univ of N Carolina 1953–54; Mathematician Nat Inst of Standards and Tech, Washington, DC 1955–, Asst Chief of Statistical Eng 1963–68, Chief of Lab 1969–78, Deputy Dir Center for Applied Maths 1978–88, Deputy Dir Center for Computing and Applied Maths 1988–93, Dir 1993–95; mem Advisory Cttee on Industrial Relations, Dept of Statistics, Ohio State Univ 1981–; mem Cttee on Applied and Theoretical Statistics, Nat Research Council 1985–88; numerous contribs to professional journals; Fellow AAAS (Sec 1987–), Inst of Mathematical Statistics, Washington Acad of Sciences, American Statistical Asscn (Vice-Pres 1981–83); mem American Asscn of Univ Women, Royal Statistical Soc, Bernoulli Soc for Probability and Mathematical Statistics, Caucus of Women Statisticians, Asscn of Women Mathematicians, Exec Women in Govt; Fed Women's Award 1971; Dept of Commerce Gold Medal 1976; Presidential Meritorious Exec Rank Award 1982. *Address:* National Institute of Standards and Technology, 100 Bureau Drive, Stop 8980, Gaithersburg, MD 20899, USA (Office); 2939 Van Vess St, NW, Washington, DC 20008, USA (Home).

ROSENSTEIN, Erna; Polish artist and writer; b 17 May 1913, Lvov; d of Maximilian and Anna (née Schrager) Rosenstein; m Artur Sandauer 1958; one s. *Education:* Acad of Fine Arts (Vienna and Cracow). *Career:* First exhibition Cracow 1939; f Group of Cracow (artists); four vols of poetry 1972, 1976, 1978, 1984; numerous prizes and awards including São Paulo Int Salon award, Brazil (jtly) 1964, Prix des Critiques d'Art 1976. *Leisure interests:* painting, theatre, poetry. *Address:* Al Kartowicza 10, 2-552 Warsaw, Poland. *Telephone:* (22) 499445.

ROSEWELL, Bridget; British economist and business executive. *Career:* Fmr Chief European Economist Wharton Econometrics, Deputy Dir of Econs Confed of British Industry; Co-Founder Business Strategies Ltd (BSL) econ consultancy group.

ROSHAN KUMARI, (see Faqir Muhommad, Roshan Kumari).

ROSINGER, Eva L. J., M SC, PH D, D ENG; Canadian scientist and international organization official; b 21 July 1941, Prague, Czechoslovakia; d of Leopold K. and Anna (née Simak) Hartl; m Herbert E. Rosinger 1969. *Education:* Tech Univ of Prague and Univ of Toronto. *Career:* Research Engineer Inst of Fine Ceramics, Karlsbad 1967–68; Fellow Dept of Eng Univ of Toronto 1968–70; Tech Information Services Tech Univ, Aachen, Germany 1970–72; Research Scientist AECL Research, Whiteshell Labs 1973–79, Section Head 1979–80, Scientific Asst to Dir of Waste Man Div 1980–84, Man Environment and Safety Assessment Br 1984–85, Exec Asst to Pres 1986–87, Dir Waste Man Concept Review 1987–90; Dir-Gen and CEO Canadian Council of Ministers of the Environment 1990–94; Deputy Dir Environment Directorate, OECD, Paris 1994–98; Prin Rosinger & Assocs 1998–; Vice-Pres Radioactive Waste Man Cttee, jt OECD-Nuclear Energy Agency, Paris 1982–85; Pres Canadian Nuclear Soc 1989–90; mem Bd on Radioactive Waste Man, US Nat Acad of Sciences 1989–90; Bd of Dirs Canadian Nuclear Asscn 1989–90, Canadian Engineer Memorial Foundation 1990–94, Asscn of Professional Engineers of Manitoba, Materials Research Soc, Women in Science and Eng, Winnipeg Symphony Orchestra 1990–94, Canadian Council for Human Resources in the Environmental Industry; mem Advisory Cttee Univ of Waterloo 1990–96, Advisory Cttee on Nuclear Safety, Atomic Control Bd 1991–94, Employment Projects for Women Inc 1992–94, Advisory Bd Inst for Technical Devt, Univ of Manitoba 1992–94; over 40 papers and articles on environment, waste, polymer science and chemical processes in nuclear industry. *Leisure interests:* cross-country skiing (qualified instructor), trekking, orienteering, photography. *Address:* 329 Lady MacDonald Crescent, Canmore, AB T1W 1H5, Canada. *E-mail:* evarosinger@expertcanmore.net.

ROSS, Diana; American singer and actress; b 26 March 1944, Detroit, MI; d of Fred and Ernestine Ross; m 1st Robert Ellis Silberstein 1971 (divorced 1976); three d; m 2nd Arne Naess 1985; one s. *Education:* High school. *Career:* Lead singer The Supremes until 1969, solo singer 1969–; numerous records with The Supremes and solo; Pres Diana Ross Enterprises Inc, Anaid Film Productions Inc, RTC Man Corpn, Chondee Inc; has made TV specials; citation from Vice-Pres Humphrey for efforts on behalf of Pres Johnson's Youth Opportunity Programme, from Mrs Martin Luther King and Rev Abernathy for contrib to Southern Christian Leadership Conf cause; Billboard, Cash Box and Record World magazine awards as world's outstanding female singer; Grammy Award 1970; Female Entertainer of the Year, Nat Asscn for the Advancement of Colored People 1970; Cue Award as Entertainer of the Year 1972; Golden Apple Award 1972; Gold Medal Award, Photoplay 1972; Antoinette Perry Award 1977; Golden Globe Award 1972; named to Rock and Roll Hall of Fame 1988. *Films include:* Lady Sings the Blues (Motion Pictures Acad Award nomination) 1972, Mahogany 1975, The Wiz 1978; *Albums include:* I'm Still Waiting 1971, Touch Me In The Morning 1973, Baby It's Me 1977, The Boss 1979, Diana 1981, Why Do Fools Fall in Love? 1981, Silk Electric 1982, Swept Away 1984, Eaten Alive 1985, Chain Reaction 1986, Red Hot Rhythm and Blues 1987, Workin' Overtime 1989, Surrender 1989, Ain't No Mountain High Enough 1989, The Forces Behind the Power 1991, The Remixes 1994, Take Me Higher 1995, Gift of Love, Voice of Love 1996, The Real Thing 1998, Every Day is a New Day 1999; *Publication:* Secrets of a Sparrow (autobiog) 1993. *Address:* c/o Motown Records, Suite 825, Eighth Ave, New York 10019, USA.

ROSS, Katharine; American actress; b 29 Jan 1943, Los Angeles, CA; m Sam Elliott. *Education:* Santa Rosa Coll. *Career:* Actress with the San Francisco Workshop; numerous film and TV appearances. *Films include:* Shenandoah, Mister Buddwing, The Singing Nun, The Graduate (Most Promising Female Newcomer, Golden Globe Award, Acad Award nomination) 1967, Hellfighters, Butch Cassidy and the Sundance Kid 1969, Fools 1970, Tell Them Willy Boy is Here 1970, They Only Kill Their Masters 1972, The Stepford Wives 1975, Voyage of the Damned 1976, The Betsy 1978, The Swarm 1978, The Legacy 1979, The Final Countdown 1980, Wrong is Right 1982, Red-Headed Stranger 1987, A Climate for Killing 1991, Home Before Dark 1996; *TV appearances include:* Films: The Longest Hundred Miles, Wanted: The Sundance Woman, Murder in Texas, Marian Rose White, Travis McGee, Secrets of a Mother and Daughter, Conagher (also co-scriptwriter); Series: The

Virginian (guest), Wagon Train (guest), The Colbys. *Address:* The Artists Agency, 1000 Santa Monica Blvd, Suite 305, Los Angeles, CA 90067.

ROSS, Rhoda Honoré, MFA; American artist; b 24 Dec 1941, Boston, MA. *Education:* Rhode Island School of Design, Skowhegan School of Painting and Sculpture and Carnegie Mellon and Yale Univs. *Career:* Teacher of Collage Lucy Moses School, New York Univ, New York; Juror Nat Asscn of Women Artists; teacher Chautaqua School of Art (NY) 1991, New York Univ 1994–; participated in Art in Embassies Program Dept of State, Havana 1991–93; group exhibitions include The Crane Colllection, Boston, MA, The Michael Ingbor Gallery, New York, Springfield Art Museum, MO, Lehman Coll Art Gallery, New York, Cape Museum of Fine Arts, Dennis, MA, Nat Asscn of Women Artists Traveling Exhibition; works in perm collections including Museum of the City of New York, the White House, Washington, DC, Juilliard School, New York, Chemical Bank, New York, Canadian Imperial Bank of Commerce, New York; portrait of retiring Pres commissioned by Lehman Coll, New York, Brooklyn Union Gas; numerous other comms; Susan B. Whedon Prize; First Prize Mademoiselle Magazine; Grumbacher Gold Medal. *Address:* 473 W End Ave, No 7B, New York, NY 10024, USA. *Telephone:* (212) 724-7253.

ROSSANT, Janet, PH D, FRS; British scientist; b 13 July 1950; d of Leslie and Doris Rossant; m Alexander Bain 1977; one d one s. *Education:* St Hugh's Coll (Oxford) and Darwin Coll (Cambridge). *Career:* Research Fellow in Zoology, Univ of Oxford 1975–77; Asst Prof Brock Univ, ON, Canada 1977–82, Assoc Prof 1982–85; Assoc Prof Univ of Toronto 1985–88, Prof Dept of Molecular and Medical Genetics 1988–; Sr Scientist Samuel Lunenfeld Research Inst, Mount Sinai Hosp, Toronto 1985–, Co-Head 1998–; Univ Prof, Univ of Toronto 2001–; Pres Soc for Developmental Biology; mem American and Canadian Socs for Cell Biology; Fellow Royal Soc of London 2000; Gibb's Prize for Zoology, Oxford 1972; Beit Memorial Fellowship 1975, E. W. R. Steacie Memorial Fellowship 1983; Howard Hughes Int Scholar 1991, MRC Distinguished Scientist 1996; McLaughlin Medal (Royal Soc of Canada) 1998; NCIC/Eli Lilly Robert L. Noble Prize 2000. *Publications:* Experimental Approaches to Mammalian Embryonic Development (co-ed) 1986; over 100 contribs to scientific journals and symposia. *Leisure interests:* cooking, running. *Address:* Mount Sinai Hospital, Samuel Lunenfeld Research Inst, 600 University Ave, Toronto, ON M5G 1X5, Canada. *Telephone:* (416) 586-8267; *Fax:* (416) 586-8588.

ROSSELLINI, Isabella; American actress and model; b 18 June 1952, Rome; d of Roberto Rossellini and Ingrid Bergman; m 1st Martin Scorsese 1979 (divorced 1982); m 2nd Jonathan Wiedemann (divorced); one d. *Education:* Acad of Fashion and Costume (Rome) and New School for Social Research (New York). *Career:* Worked briefly as costume designer for father's films; went to New York 1972; worked as journalist for Italian TV; cover-girl for Vogue 1980, Harper's Bazaar and Italian Elle; contract to model Lancôme cosmetics 1982–95; Vice-Pres Lancaster Cosmetics GPs Marketing Dept 1995–. *Films include:* A Matter of Time 1976, The Meadow, Il Papocchio, White Nights 1985, Blue Velvet 1986, Tough Guys Don't Dance 1987, Siesta 1987, Zelly and Me 1988, Cousins 1989, Adriana, Wild at Heart 1990, The Siege of Venice 1991, Death Becomes Her 1992, The Pickle, The Innocent, Fearless 1994, Wyatt Earp 1994, Immortal Beloved 1994, The Innocent 1995, The Funeral 1996, Big Night 1996, Crime of the Century 1996, Left Luggage 1998, The Imposters, The Real Blonde 1998. *Address:* c/o Pakseghian Planco, William Morris Agency, 1350 Ave of the Americas, New York, NY 110019, USA.

ROSSI, Emma; San Marino politician. *Career:* Mem Consiglio Grande e Generale (Grand and Gen Council, Parl); Substitute mem Council of Europe, mem Cttees for Relations with European Non-mem Countries and Social Affairs, Health and Family; currently Sec of State for Educ, Culture, Social Affairs and Information. *Address:* Secretariat of State for Education, Culture, Social Affairs and Information, Palazzo Begni, Contrada Omerelli, 47890, San Marino. *Telephone:* (0549) 882250; *Fax:* (0549) 882301.

ROSSI, Marie-Louise Elizabeth, MA, FRSA; British non-governmental organization executive; b 18 Feb 1956, London; d of Sir Hugh and Lady (Philomena) (née Jennings) Rossi. *Education:* St Paul's Girls' School

(London) and St Anne's Coll (Oxford). *Career:* Export Credits Specialist, Hogg Robinson Group PLC 1979–87; Risk Management Consultant, Sedgwick Group PLC 1987–90; Man Consultant, Tillinghast (Towers Perrin) 1990–93; Chief Exec London Int Insurance and Reinsurance Market Asscn (LIRMA) 1993–98, Int Underwriting Asscn of London 1998–; Dir The London Processing Centre LTD 1993–2001; mem (Cons) Westminster City Council 1986–94, Chair Educ 1989–92; Chair Bow Group 1988–89; Chair Foreign Affairs Forum of the Cons Party 1993–96, Organizing Cttee Pro-Euro Cons Party 1999; mem Inst of Export, Inst of Risk Man, London Cen Learning and Skills Council 2000–; mem Gov Council, Univ of Nottingham 2001–; Hon Citizen City of Baltimore (MD, USA) 1994. *Publication:* 1992: The Single Market in Insurance (with N. Hawkins, MP and others) 1990. *Leisure interests:* gardening, music. *Address:* International Underwriting Association of London, London Underwriting Centre, 3 Minster Court, Mincing Lane, London, EC3R 7DD, UK. *Telephone:* (20) 7617-4444; *Fax:* (20) 7617-4440; *E-mail:* ml.rossi@iua.co.uk; *Internet:* www.iua.co.uk.

RÖSSLER, Almut; German organist and conductor; b 12 June 1932, Beveringen; d of Helmut Rößler; one s. *Education:* Secondary educ in Düsseldorf, studied the organ, church music and composition in Detmold and Paris. *Career:* Has performed at numerous concerts and music festivals in Germany and abroad; numerous TV and radio appearances; conductor Johannes-Kantorei; Chevalier de l'Ordre des Palmes Académiques (France) 1981; Förderpreis für junge Künstler, Fed State of N Rhine-Westphalia 1960; Organist of the Year, Univ of Michigan, USA 1986. *Publications include:* Beiträge zur geistigen Welt Olivier Messiaens (trans to English 1986) 1984, Ur- und Erstaufführungen von Werken von Jolivet, David, Baur, Leitner, und andere (essays), Konzert für Orgel und Orchestra von Klebe 1980, Livre du Saint Sacrement von Olivier Messiaen 1986. *Leisure interests:* art, literature, travel. *Address:* c/o Martin-Luther-Platz 39, 40212 Düsseldorf, Germany.

ROSSNER, Petra; German cyclist. *Career:* Gold Medallist in 3,000m Individual Pursuit cycling event, Olympic Games, Barcelona, Spain 1992; World Champion 1992.

ROST, Andrea; Hungarian opera singer (soprano); b 1962, Budapest; d of Ferenc Rost and Erzsébet Privoda; m Miklós Harazdy 1985 (divorced); one s one d. *Education:* Ferenc Liszt Acad of Music (Budapest). *Career:* Operatic debut, Budapest 1989; First Prize, Helsinki Competition 1989; debut, La Scala as Gilda in Rigoletto 1994; debut, Metropolitan Opera (New York) as Adina 1996; took part in Superconcert with José Carreras and Plácido Domingo (Budapest) 1996; appeared as Elisabeth in Donizetti's opera (London) 1997; debut, Tokyo Opera as Violetta 1998; took part in concert in memory of Lehár with José Carreras and Plácido Domingo, Bad Ischl (Austria) 1998; has also appeared at Staatsoper, Vienna, Salzburg Festival, Opéra Bastille, Paris, Royal Opera House, Covent Garden and Chicago Opera; Ferenc Liszt Artistic Merit of Honour 1997; Nat Artistic Merit of Honour 1999. *Address:* Budaörs, Nefelejes u 27, 2040, Hungary. *Telephone:* (23) 416-583 (Home); *E-mail:* arost@elender.hu.

ROSTBØLL, Grethe Fogh, MA, PH D; Danish politician and writer; b 30 May 1941, Aarhus; d of Gustav and Ellen Marie (née Brandt) Fogh; m Torben Rostbøll 1961; four s. *Education:* Teacher Training Coll. *Career:* Co-Prin and teacher Folk High School, Ryslinge 1962–90; mem Ryslinge Local Council 1966–70; cand EP 1979; mem Legis Cttee for Folk High Schools 1985–87, Programme Cttee for Children's Daily Life 1987–88, Cttee for Further Educ 1989–90, Minister of Cultural Affairs 1990–92; Mem of City Council 1993–; MP 1995–98; newspaper critic and columnist 1987–90; Chair Soc for the Advancement of the Danish Language 1984–90; Deputy Chair Nordic Folk Acad 1985–90; Pres Fulton Foundation; Vice-Pres Sasakawa Foundation; Commdr of Danebrog. *Publications:* About Seven Gothic Tales 1980, Family and Future 1986, European Values 1994, Longing for Wings – Analysis in Isak Dinesen 1996; ed numerous journals on language and linguistics; contribs to The Personal Freedom and Myths on the Nordic Countries and the EC. *Leisure interests:* music, food, fashion. *Address:* Allegade 22F, 2000 Frederiksberg, Denmark (Home). *Telephone:* 38-21-21-21 (Office); *Fax:* 33-31-24-03 (Office); *E-mail:* GFR@frederiksberg.dk.

RØSTVIG, Maren-Sofie, PH D; Norwegian professor of English literature (retd); b 27 March 1920, Melbo; d of Olaf and Sigrid Røstvig. *Education:* Univ of Oslo and Univ of California (LA, USA). *Career:* Imprisoned by Nazi regime 1943, subsequently released; joined Resistance Movt and published underground newspaper until end of World War II 1944–45; Reader in English Literature, Univ of Oslo 1955–67, Prof 1968–87, Sr Research Fellow 1988, retd 1990; mem Norwegian Acad of Science and Letters; Mil Medal of Participation in World War II. *Publications:* The Happy Man: Studies in the Metamorphoses of a Classical Ideal 1600–1760 (two Vols) 1954–58, The Hidden Sense and Other Essays 1963, Fair Forms 1975, Configurations: A Topomorphical Approach to Renaissance Poetry 1994; contribs to learned journals and collections of scholarly essays on English literature. *Address:* 14 Urb Rosa de Piedras, Carretera de Coín, 29650 Mijas, Málaga, Spain. *Telephone:* (95) 248 6938.

ROTH, Claudia; German politician; b 15 May 1955, Ulm. *Career:* Actress Swabian State Theatre, Bühnen Dortmund and Hoffman Comic Theatre; mem political pop group Ton Steine Scherben; Parl Press Spokesperson Die Grünen 1985–; MEP 1989–99, fmr Jt Vice-Chair Green Group, also Chair; fmr mem Cttee on Youth, Culture, Educ, Media and Sport; mem Cttee on Civil Liberties and Internal Affairs, Del to the EU-Turkey Jt Parl Cttee, Del for Relations with SE Europe. *Address:* c/o Bundestag, 11011 Berlin, Germany.

ROTH, Daryl; American theatre producer; m Steven Roth. *Education:* Univ of New York. *Career:* Began career as interior designer; f Daryl Roth Theater 1996; mem Bd Lincoln Center Theater 1992–, Vineyard Theater 1994–. *Plays include:* Nick and Nora 1991, Twilight: Los Angeles 1992 1993, Three Tall Women 1994 (Pulitzer Prize), How I Learned to Drive 1998 (Pulitzer Prize), Wit 1999 (Pulitzer Prize), Snakebit, Villa Villa.

ROTH, Jane Richards, BA, LL B; American federal judge; b 16 June 1935, Philadelphia, PA; d of Robert Henry, Jr and Harriett (née Kellond) Richards; m William V. Roth, Jr 1965; one s one d. *Education:* Smith Coll and Harvard Univ. *Career:* Admin Asst Foreign Service Section of US State Dept 1956–62; called to the Bar, DE 1965, US Dist Court, DE 1966, US Court of Appeals (3rd Circuit) 1974; Assoc Richards, Layton and Finger, Wilmington 1965–73, Partner 1973–85; Judge US Dist Court of DE 1985–91, US Court of Appeals (3rd Circuit), Wilmington 1991–; Trustee History Soc of Delaware; Hon Chair Arthritis Foundation, Delaware; mem Bd of Overseers Widener Univ Law School; mem Fed Judges' Asscn, Delaware State Bar Asscn; Hon LL D (Widener) 1986, (Delaware) 1994; Arthritis Foundation Nat Voluntary Service Citation 1982. *Address:* J Caleb Boggs Federal Bldg, 844 King St, Rm 5100, Wilmington, DE 19801, USA.

ROTH-BEHRENDT, Dagmar; German politician; b 21 Feb 1953, Frankfurt/Main. *Career:* Lawyer, Berlin; Counsellor Mayor's Office, Berlin; elected MEP (SDP) 1989, mem and co-ordinator PSE (Party of European Socialists) group on Cttee on the Environment, Public Health and Consumer Protection, mem Cttee on Women's Rights 1989, substitute mem Budget Cttee; Vice-Chair Globe EU and Globe Int. *Address:* European Parliament, rue Wiertz, 1047 Brussels, Belgium. *Telephone:* (2) 284-54-53; *Fax:* (2) 284-94-53.

ROTHE, Mechtild; German politician; b 10 Aug 1947, Paderborn. *Career:* Teacher; mem SPD Fed Council and Town Council, Bad Lippspringe; elected MEP (PSE, SPD) 1984, fmr Vice-Chair Del to Cyprus, also Chair; fmr mem Cttee on Agric, Fisheries and Food 1984, mem Cttee on Research, Technological Devt and Energy. *Address:* European Parliament, rue Wiertz, 1047 Brussels, Belgium. *Telephone:* (2) 284-21-11; *Fax:* (2) 230-69-43.

ROTHE-VALLBONA, Rima Gretel (see Vallbona, Rima Gretel Rothe).

ROTHENBERG, Susan, BFA; American artist; b 20 Jan 1945, Buffalo, NY; d of Leonard Rothenberg and Adele Cohen; m George Trakas 1971 (divorced 1976); one d; m Bruce Nauman 1989. *Education:* Cornell and George Washington Univs and Corcoran Museum School. *Career:* Solo exhibitions include Willard Gallery 1976, 1977, 1979, 1981, 1983,

Akron Art Museum 1981–82, Stedelijk Museum, Amsterdam, Netherlands 1982, San Francisco Museum of Art 1983, Carnegie Inst Museum of Art, Pittsburgh 1984, Los Angeles Co Museum of Art 1983, Boston Inst of Contemporary Art 1984, Aspen Center for the Visual Arts 1984; Rooseum, Malmö, Sweden 1990; Albright Knox Art Gallery 1992; Hirshhorn Museum and Sculpture Garden 1993; St Louis Art Museum 1993; Museo de Arte Contemporáneo de Monterrey, Mexico 1996; group exhibitions include Museum of Modern Art, Whitney Museum of American Art, Venice Biennale, Italy and galleries in Germany, Denmark, Spain and Finland; rep in collections in the USA and Netherlands; Guggenheim Fellow 1980. *Address:* c/o Sperone Westwater, 142 Greene St, New York, NY 10012, USA.

ROTHENBERGER, Anneliese; German opera singer (soprano) and painter; b 19 June 1926, Salenstein, Switzerland; d of Josef Rothenberger and Sophie Häffner; m Gerd W. Dieberitz 1954 (deceased). *Education:* Real- und Musikhochschule (Mannheim). *Career:* Debut Coblenz Theatre 1947; sang with Hamburg, Munich, Germany and Vienna State Operas 1958–70; guest singer at La Scala, Milan, Italy, Metropolitan Opera, New York, USA and festivals in Salzburg (Austria), Munich and Glyndebourne (UK); TV Special 1969–; several exhibitions as painter, Germany and Switzerland; Distinguished Service Cross First Class, Great Cross. *Films:* Die Fledermaus 1955, Der Rosenkavalier; *Publication:* Melody of My Life 1973. *Leisure interests:* driving, books, painting, modelling. *Address:* Quellenhof, 8268 Salenstein am Untersee, Switzerland.

ROTHSCHILD, Hon Dame Miriam (Louisa), DBE, FRS; British biologist; b 5 Aug 1908; d of N. C. Rothschild; m Capt George Lane 1943 (divorced 1957); four d (one deceased) two s (one deceased). *Education:* At home, Chelsea Polytechnic and Bedford Coll. *Career:* World authority on fleas and intestinal worms; worked in Foreign Office 1940–42; Visiting Prof of Biology Royal Free Hosp, London; Romanes Lecturer Univ of Oxford 1985; Trustee British Museum of Natural History 1967–75; mem Zoological and Entomological Research Council, Marine Biological Asscn, Royal Entomological Soc, Soc for Promotion of Nature Reserves, American Acad of Arts and Sciences; Hon Fellow St Hugh's Coll, Oxford; Hon D SC (Oxford) 1968, (Gothenburg) 1983, (Hull) 1984, (Northwestern Univ) 1986, (Leicester) 1987, (Open Univ) 1989, (Essex) 1998, (Cambridge) 1999; Defence Medal 1940–45; Victoria Medal of Honour, Royal Horticultural Soc 1990. *Publications:* Fleas, Flukes and Cuckoos (jtly) 1952, Catalogue Rothschild Collection of Fleas (British Museum, six vols) 1953–1983, The Butterfly Gardener (jtly) 1983, Dear Lord Rothschild (biog) 1983, Atlas of Insect Tissue (jtly) 1985, Animals and Man 1986, Butterfly Cooing Like a Dove 1990, The Rothschilds' Gardens 1996, Rothschild's Reserves 1997; numerous contribs to scientific journals. *Leisure interest:* watching butterflies. *Address:* Ashton Wold, Peterborough PE8 5LZ, UK.

ROTHSTEIN, Barbara Jacobs, BA, LL B; American federal judge; b 3 Feb 1939, Brooklyn, NY; d of Solomon and Pauline Jacobs; m Ted L. Rothstein 1968; one s. *Education:* Cornell and Harvard Univs. *Career:* Called to the Bar, MA 1966, US Dist Court (W Dist) 1971, US Supreme Court 1975, US Supreme Court of Appeals (Circuit) 1977; pvt law practice, Boston 1966–68; Asst Attorney-Gen State of Washington 1968–77; Judge Superior Court, Seattle 1977–80, Fed Dist Court (W Washington), Seattle 1980–, Chief Judge 1987–94; mem Law Faculty Univ of Washington 1975–77, Hastings Inst of Trial Advocacy 1977, NW Inst of Trial Advocacy 1979–; mem ABA, American Judicature Soc, Nat Asscn of Women Judges, Washington State Bar Asscn; Matrix Table Woman of the Year Award, Women in Communications 1980. *Address:* US District Court 705, US Courthouse, 1010 Fifth Ave, Suite 215, Seattle, WA 98104-1187, USA.

ROTHWELL, Margaret Irene, CMG, BA; British diplomatist (retd); b 25 Aug 1938, Edinburgh; d of Prof Harry and Martha (née Goedecke) Rothwell. *Education:* Southampton Grammar School for Girls and Lady Margaret Hall (Oxford). *Career:* Joined Foreign Office 1961, mem staff 1966, 1972, 1980, Counsellor and Head of Training Dept 1981, Counsellor 1987; Third, then Second Sec UK Del to the Council of Europe, Strasbourg 1964; Second Sec, Pvt Sec to the Special Rep in Africa, Nairobi 1967; Second, then First Sec, Washington, DC 1968; First Sec and Head of Chancery, Helsinki 1976; Counsellor, Head of

Chancery, Jakarta, Indonesia 1984; Amb and Consul-Gen, Abidjan, Côte d'Ivoire, also accredited to Burkina Faso and Niger 1990–97, and Liberia 1992–97; Reviewer Quinquennial Review, Marshall Scholarship Comm 1998; Rep US/UK Comm on Student Travel Exchanges 1998; Volonteer British Exec Service Overseas, Rwanda 2001; Hon LL D (Southampton) 1994. *Leisure interests:* gardening, cooking, travel, tennis. *Address:* Hill House, Knapp, Ampfield, Romsey, Hants SO51 9BT, UK (Home).

ROUARD, Margo Michèle; French graphic designer; b 3 Sept 1945, Romans; d of Edmond and Odette (née Prat) Rouard; m Nicholas Snowman 1983; one s. *Education:* Lycée de Romans and Ecole Nat Supérieure des Arts Décoratifs (Paris). *Career:* Graphic Artist 1970–73; Exhibition Curator Centre de Création Industrielle, Centre Nat d'Art et de Culture Georges-Pompidou, Paris 1972–1978; Prof of Visual Communication Ecole Nat Supérieure des Arts Décoratifs 1978; in charge of Design, Parc de la Villette, Paris 1979–83; Adviser, Del of Visual Arts, Ministry of Culture 1983–85; Dir Agence Promotion Création Industrielle 1983–92; has produced exhibitions for museums in London, Amsterdam, Tokyo and Paris; Chevalier des Arts et des Lettres 1988. *Publications:* Aires de jeux 1978, 100 objets quotidiens Made in France 1987, Museum Graphics 1992; numerous exhibition catalogues including Roman Cieslewicz 1993, Jean Widmer 1995. *Leisure interests:* music, swimming, literature. *Address:* 4 rue du Parc Royal, 75003 Paris, France. *Telephone:* (1) 42-71-86-18.

ROUBIČKOVÁ, Miluše; Czech glass designer; b 20 July 1922, Prague; d of Jan and Marie Kytka; m René Roubiček 1949; two d. *Education:* Acad of Applied Arts (Prague). *Career:* Glass designer for Art Studio and Crystalex, Nový Bor 1946–70, J. and L. Lobmeyr, Kamenický Šenov 1946–47, Design Centre, Prague 1955–68, Hergiswiler Glas AG, Switzerland 1980–85; exhibitions include Expo '58, Brussels (awarded Great Prize), Expo '67, Montréal, Canada (Honour Prize), Expo '70, Osaka, Japan, Corning Museum of Glass, New York, USA 1979, Verre de Bohême 1400–1989, Musée des Arts Décoratifs, Paris 1989; mem Union of Czech Creative Artists, Glass-Forum (Nový Bor), Umělecká Beseda union; Silver Medal XI Triennale, Milan, Italy 1957; Honour Prize, I. Coburger Glaspreis 1977. *Leisure interest:* literature. *Address:* Laubova 10, 130 00 Prague 3, Vinohrady, Czech Republic. *Telephone:* (2) 6271012.

ROUDY, Yvette; French politician; b 10 April 1929, Pessac; d of Joseph Saldou and Jeanne Dicharry; m Pierre Roudy 1951. *Education:* Collège de jeunes filles (Bordeaux). *Career:* Trans with an American co 1952–63; literary translations 1964–; Sec-Gen Mouvement démocratique féminin; Founder and Ed-in-Chief, La Femme du 20ème siècle; joined Convention des institutions républicaines 1965, mem Exec Bureau; worked in PS 1971–76, Founder Training Section, mem Steering Cttee, elected Nat Sec 1979, Nat Sec for Women's Rights 1988–; MEP (PS) 1979–81; Minister in charge of Women's Rights 1981–86; Deputy to Nat Ass (Parl) for Calvados 1986–93, 1997, Sec of Nat Ass 1997–; mem Foreign Affairs Comm 1997–; Vice-Pres Socialist Int 1988–, PS Nat Sec for the Rights of Women 1988–93; Mayor of Lisieux 1989. *Publications include:* La réussite de la femme 1969, La femme en marge 1975, A cause d'elles 1985. *Leisure interests:* tennis, swimming. *Address:* Assemblée Nationale, 75355 Paris, Cedex, France; Parti Socialiste, 10 rue de Solférino, 75333 Paris, France.

ROUNTHWAITE, Ann Elizabeth, BA, LL B; Canadian judge; b 8 July 1950, Montréal, PQ; d of Francis John and Rachel Alma (née Horton) Rounthwaite; one s one d. *Education:* Neuchâtel Jr Coll, Univ of Toronto and Osgoode Hall Law School. *Career:* Called to the Bar, BC 1976; Defence Counsel specializing in Criminal Law and admin tribunals; practised at all levels in British Columbia Courts; Counsel on Royal Comms; Counsel Inquiry into W Coast Oil Ports 1977–78, into Incarceration of Female Offenders 1978, into Uranium Mining 1979–80, into Habitual Criminals 1983; Prov Court Judge of British Columbia 1986–; Consultant Law Reform Comm of Canada, Fed Ministry of Labour, British Columbia Legal Services Comm, British Columbia Justice Devt Comm; Consultant Mayor's Office, Vancouver; Co-ordinator Pollution Probe 1971–72; Founder, Dir W Coast Environment Law Asscn 1975–86; Dir Canadian Environmental Law Research Foundation 1972–75, Sudbury Environmental Law Asscn 1973, Community Planning Asscn of Canada (BC) 1977–78; Lecturer

Simon Fraser Univ 1980–86; Instructor British Columbia Continuing Legal Educ 1984–86; writer and broadcaster on TV and radio 1971–77; Officer Canadian Asscn of Prov Court Judges 1993–98 (Pres 1996–97); mem Exec and Educ Cttee British Columbia Province Judges' Asscn 1987–90; mem Advisory Panel Laskin Memorial Moot 1988–. *Publications:* Pollution Law in Canada 1975; numerous reviews and articles for newspapers and journals. *Leisure interests:* walking, reading. *Address:* 14340 57th Ave, Surrey, BC V3X 1B2, Canada.

ROUSSEAU, Jeannine Marie, BA, LL L; Canadian legal executive and judge; b 29 Aug 1941, Montréal, PQ; d of J. Rodolphe and Mary Sarah (née MacIntosh) Rousseau; m J. Maurice Tremblay 1987. *Education:* Univ of Montréal. *Career:* Called to the Bar, PQ 1966; legal practice 1966–71; Sec and Asst Sec Janin-Foundation Group, Montréal and Toronto 1971–76; Counsel and Asst Sec Northern Telecom Ltd, Montréal 1976–77; Vice-Pres, Sec and Gen Counsel Asbestos Corpn Ltd, Montréal 1977–82; Legal Counsel and Sec Montréal Stock Exchange 1982–84; Corp Sec Telemedia Corpn, Montréal 1984–87; Justice Superior Court of Québec 1987–; mem Canadian Bar Asscn, Canadian Inst for the Admin of Justice. *Address:* Palais de Justice, 1 Notre-Dame St E, Rm 7.51, Montréal, PQ H2Y 1B6, Canada. *Telephone:* (514) 393-2136; *Fax:* (514) 873-6815.

ROUSSEVA, Zlatka; Bulgarian politician; b 9 July 1954, Haskovo; d of Roussy Roussev and Smyliana Rousseva. *Education:* Klimment Ohridsky Univ (Sofia). *Career:* Lawyer, Plovdiv 1979–90; mem Narodno Sobraniye (Nat Ass, Parl) for Plovdiv 1990, 1991, Vice-Pres Democratic Party (part of UDF—United Democratic Front), UDF Parl Group. *Leisure interests:* literature, theatre. *Address:* Democratic Party, Narodno Sobraniye, 1000 Sofia, pl Narodno Sobraniye 3, Bulgaria (Office); 4000 Plovdiv, Blvd Bulgaria 98, Bulgaria (Home). *Telephone:* (2) 88-17-34 (Office); (32) 55-39-83 (Home).

ROUSSOU, Nayia, PH D; Cypriot lecturer in media and writer; b 27 April 1935, Larnaca; d of Antonios Chrysostomou and Polymnia Antoniou; m Costas Roussos 1967; one d one s. *Education:* American Acad (Larnaca), Nat Conservatory of Cyprus, Indiana Univ at Bloomington (USA) and Univ of Coventry (UK). *Career:* Editorial Asst Cyprus Broadcasting Corpn 1956–59, Gramophone Librarian 1959–69, Music Programmes Producer 1969–70, Sr TV Producer 1972–88, Head of Public and Int Relations 1988–95; column in Kypros weekly newspaper 1964–77; Lecturer in Mass Media, Advertising and Public Relations in local colls, Higher Tech Inst and Police Acad 1977–95; currently Asst Prof Intercoll, Nicosia; mem Cyprus PEN Centre 1986–, Vice-Pres 1991–; State Prize for Poetry 1985, honoured for poetry: Athens 1989, Crete 1992, Rhodes 1993. *Publications include:* (In Greek) Memories of War (poetry and essays) 1975, Children and TV Violence 1978, Mass Media: History, Aesthetics, Influence 1979, Channels of Ariadne (State Prize for Poetry) 1985, Testimony at the Borderless Line (poetry) 1988, The Executioner and Other Stories (short stories) 1988, Rage of Second June (poetry) 1992, Television and the Cultural Identity of Cyprus 2001, Television Language and National Identity in Cyprus 2001; review articles on mass culture and aggression in young people. *Leisure interests:* reading, swimming. *Address:* Intercollege, Nicosia, POB 4005, Nicosia, Cyprus (Office); 10c Euripides St, Aglandja, Nicosia, Cyprus (Home). *Telephone:* (2) 357735 (Office); (2) 422603 (Home); *Fax:* (2) 357481 (Office); *E-mail:* cybercom@intercol .edu.

ROUX, Annette; French business executive; b 4 Aug 1942, La Croix-de-Vie; d of André and Georgina (née Brochard) Beneteau; m Louis-Claude Roux 1964; one d one s. *Career:* Man Chantiers Beneteau, SA (shipbuilders) 1964–76, Pres Bd 1976–; mem French Centre for External Trade (CFCE) 1981–; mem Exec Council Conseil Nat du Patronat Français (CNPF—employers' org) 1981–83, 1996–99; in charge of NMMA (French nautical industries Fed) 1992–95, 1996–; Chevalier de la Légion d'Honneur. *Address:* Zone Industrielle des Mares, BP 66, 85270 Saint-Hilaire-de-Riez, France (Office); Le Clouzeau, Bois-de-Céné, 85710 La Garnache, France (Home). *Telephone:* (2) 51-55-53-82 (Office); *Fax:* (2) 51-55-89-10 (Office).

ROVNER, Ilana Kara Diamond, BA, JD; American federal judge; b 21 Aug 1938; d of Stanley and Ronny (née Medalje) Diamond; m Richard Nyles Rovner 1963; one s. *Education:* Bryn Mawr Coll, King's Coll

(London), Georgetown Univ and Illinois Inst of Tech. *Career:* Called to the Bar, IL 1972, US Dist Court, N Dist, IL 1972, US Court of Appeals (7th Circuit) 1977, US Supreme Court 1981, Fed Trial Bar, N Dist, IL 1982; Judicial Clerk, US Dist Court, Chicago 1972–73; Asst US Attorney, Chicago 1973–77, Deputy Chief of Public Protection 1975–76, Chief 1976–77; Deputy Gov and Legal Counsel to Gov, Chicago 1977–84; US Dist Judge (N Dist, IL), Chicago 1984–92; Dist Court Exec Cttee 1989–92; Seventh Circuit Judicial Council 1991–; US Circuit Judge (Seventh Circuit), Chicago 1992–; Trustee Bryn Mawr Coll 1983–89, Illinois Inst of Tech 1989–; mem Bd of Overseers Chicago-Kent Coll of Law 1983–, Visiting Cttee N Illinois Univ Coll of Law 1992–94, Univ of Chicago Law School 1993–96, 2000–(03), Northwestern Univ School of Law 1993–98; mem Chicago Bar Asscn, Women's Bar Asscn of Illinois, Chicago Council of Lawyers, Decalogue Soc of Lawyers, Int Asscn of Jewish Lawyers and Jurists, Seventh Circuit Bar Asscn, Nat Asscn of Women Judges, Fed Judges Asscn; mem Fed Bar Asscn, Chicago Chapter, Treas 1978–79, Sec 1979–80, Second Vice-Pres 1980–81, First Vice-Pres 1981–82, Pres 1982–83, Seventh Circuit Second Vice-Pres 1983–84, Vice-Pres 1984–85; Chicago-Kent Coll of Law Ilana Diamond Rovner Appellate Advocacy Program and Moot Court Competition instituted 1992; Hon D LITT (Rosary, Mundelein) 1989; DHL (Spertus) 1992; US Dept of Justice Special Commendation 1975, Special Achievement Award 1976; Annual Guardian Police Award 1977; Illinois Inst of Tech Professional Achievement Award 1986; Chicago Bar Asscn Defense of Prisoner Cttee Commendation 1987; Brandeis Medal for Distinguished Legal Service 1993; Valparaiso Univ School of Law First Woman 1993; Women's Bar Asscn of Illinois Myra Bradwell Award 1994; Decalogue Soc of Lawyers Merit Award 1996–97; Nat Asscn of Women Lawyers Arabella Babb Mansfield Award 1998; Women's Bar Asscn of IL and Chicago Bar Asscn Alliance for Women First Woman Award 2000; Georgetown Univ Center First Woman Award 2001. *Address:* US Court of Appeals for the Seventh Circuit, 219 S Dearborn St, Chicago, IL 60604, USA.

ROWAN, Patricia Adrienne; British journalist; d of the late Henry Matthew and Gladys Talintyre; m Ivan Settle Harris Rowan 1960; one s. *Education:* Harrow Co Grammar School for Girls. *Career:* Journalist Time and Tide 1952–56, Sunday Express 1956–57, Daily Sketch 1957–58, News Chronicle 1958–60, Granada TV 1961–62, Sunday Times 1962–66, Times Educational Supplement 1972–89, Ed 1989–97; mem Bd Nat Children's Bureau 1997–, Research Cttee Teacher Training Agency 1997–2000; Hon FRSA 1989; Hon Fellow Inst of Educ, Univ of London 1997. *Publications:* What Sort of Life? 1980, Education—the Wasted Years? (contrib) 1988. *Leisure interests:* cooking, gardening. *Address:* Park View, Nupend, Horsley, Stroud, Glos, GL6 0PY, UK. *Telephone:* (1453) 833305; *Fax:* (1453) 833305; *E-mail:* prowan@connectfree.co.uk.

ROWE, Bridget; British newspaper editor; b 16 March 1950; d of Peter and Myrtle Rowe; m James Anthony Nolan; one s. *Education:* St Michael's School (Limpsfield). *Career:* Ed Look Now 1971–76, Women's World 1976–81; Asst Ed The Sun 1981–82; launched News of the World Sunday magazine 1981–86; Ed Woman's Own 1986–90, TV Times 1990–91, Sunday Mirror 1991–92, The People 1992–96, Man Dir 1995–98; Man Dir Sunday Mirror 1995–98, Ed 1997–98; Dir of Communications National Magazines 1998–99. *Leisure interests:* equestrian sports, travel. *Address:* The People, 1 Canada Sq, Canary Wharf, London E14 5AP, UK.

ROWLAND, Beryl, MA, PH D, D LIT; Canadian writer and professor of English; b UK; m Edward Murray Rowland 1948. *Education:* Univs of Alberta, British Columbia and London (UK). *Career:* Asst Prof of English York Univ, ON 1962–68, Assoc Prof 1968–71, Prof 1971–, Distinguished Research Prof 1983–; Visiting Scholar Univ of Victoria, Toronto 1987–89, Adjunct Prof 1989–; Dir Goward House Soc 1990–; mem Asscn of Canadian Univ Teachers of English, Humanities Asscn, Int Asscn of Univ Teachers of English, English Asscn, Modern Languages Asscn, Medieval Acad of America, New Chaucer Soc; mem Consultative Cttee Epopée Animale Fable et Fabliau Soc Int; Huntingdon Fellow 1976; Hon D LITT (Mount St Vincent) 1982; Book Award, American Univ Presses 1974; Commemoration Medal for 125th Anniversary of Canadian Fed 1993. *Publications:* Cressida in Alberta (assoc ed, Alberta Golden Jubilee Drama Award 1955), Behold a Pale Horse (CBC Drama) 1956, Blind Beasts: Chaucer's Animal World 1971, Animals With Human Faces: A Guide to Animal Symbolism 1973, Chaucer and Middle English Studies in Honor of Rossell Hope Robbins (ed) 1974, Birds With Human Souls: A Guide to Bird Symbolism 1978, Companion to Chaucer Studies (ed, 2nd edn) 1979, Medieval Woman's Guide to Health: The First Gynaecological Handbook 1981, Earle Birney: Essays on Chaucerian Irony (ed) 1985, Poetry in English: The Middle Ages (ed) 1987; over 150 contribs to professional journals in Canada, USA, Japan and Europe. *Address:* 2203–2829 Arbutus Rd, Victoria, BC V8N 5X5, Canada (Home).

ROWLEY, Janet Davidson, PH B, MD; American physician; b 5 April 1925, New York; d of Hurford Henry and Ethel Mary (née Ballantyne) Davidson; m Donald A. Rowley 1948; three s. *Education:* Univ of Chicago. *Career:* Research Asst Univ of Chicago 1949–50; Prof Dept of Medicine, Franklin McLean Memorial Research Centre 1977–84, Dept of Molecular Genetics and Cell Biology 1984–; mem Nat Cancer Advisory Bd 1979–84, Nat Human Genome Research Inst 1994–97, Chair 1997–99; mem Council for Human Genome Research 1999–, Advisory Bd G & P Charitable Foundation 1999–, Selection Panel for Clinical Science Award, Doris Duke Charitable Foundation 2000–; mem NAS, Chair Section 41 1955–99; mem American Soc of Human Genetics, Pres 1993; mem American Philosophical Soc, Genetical Soc (UK), American Inst of Medicine, American Asscn of Cancer Research; Visiting lecturer at numerous univs and guest speaker for numerous orgs; Co-Founder, Co-Ed Genes, Chromosomes and Cancer; mem ed Bd numerous journals; First Kuwait Cancer Prize 1984; Prix Antoine Lacassagne Ligue Nat Française Contre le Cancer 1987; Charles Mott Prize GM Cancer Research Foundation (jtly) 1989; Woman Extraordinaire Award, Int Women's Asscns 1999; Fellow AAAS, Nominating Cttee 1998; Hon D SC (Arizona) 1989, (PA) 1989, (Knox Coll) 1981, (S California) 1992, (St Louis) 1997, (St Xavier) 1999, (Oxford, UK) 2000. *Address:* University of Chicago, 5841 S Maryland Ave 2115, Chicago, IL 60637, USA (Office); 5310 S Univ Ave Chicago, IL 60615, USA (Home).

ROWLING, J.K. (Joanne Kathleen), BA; British writer; b 31 July 1965, Chipping Sodbury; d of Peter and Anne Rowling; m (divorced); one d. *Education:* Wyedean Comprehensive School, Univ of Exeter and Moray House Teacher Training Coll. *Career:* British Book Awards Children's Book of the Year 1999; Smarties Prize. *Publications:* Harry Potter and the Philosopher's Stone 1997, Harry Potter and the Chamber of Secrets 1998, Harry Potter and the Prisoner of Azkaban 1999, Harry Potter and the Goblet of Fire 2000, Quidditch Through the Ages 2001, Fantastic Beasts and Where to Find Them 2001. *Address:* c/o Bloomsbury Publishing PLC, 38 Soho Square, London W1V 6HB, UK. *Telephone:* (20) 7494 2111; *Fax:* (20) 7434 0151; *Internet:* www.bloomsbury.com.

ROWLINSON, Elizabeth Maude, B SC, MA, PH D; British academic; b 22 May 1930, Sutton, Surrey; d of Charles and Mary (née Maude) Hunter; m Hugh Rowlinson 1953; three s. *Education:* Wallington Co School for Girls, St Hugh's Coll and Lady Margaret Hall (Oxford), Northwestern Univ (USA) and McGill Univ (Canada). *Career:* Mem Defence Research Bd of Canada 1954–56; Asst Prof and Assoc Dean of Students McGill Univ 1965–78; Dean St Hilda's Coll, Toronto, Canada 1978–91; Dean of Women and Fellow Trinity Coll, Univ of Toronto 1978–91; Assoc Chaplain McGill Univ 1993–; numerous contribs and papers on maths to professional journals; mem Canadian Maths Soc, Canadian Amateur Musicians, Art Gallery of Ontario. *Publication:* Subgroups of Finite Groups (ed). *Leisure interests:* travel, mountain-walking, music. *Address:* St Hilda's College, 44 Devonshire Place, Toronto, ON M5S 2E2, Canada (Office); 43 Eight Mile Point, RR1, Orillia, ON L3V 6H1, Canada (Home).

ROY, Arundhati; Indian writer; b 1960, Kerala; m 1st Gerard Da Cunha (divorced); m 2nd Pradeep Krishen. *Education:* Delhi School of Architecture. *Career:* Fmrly with Nat Inst of Urban Affairs; has written newspaper articles, including an article on Phoolan Devi, the so-called 'Bandit Queen'; environmental campaigner. *Publications include:* The God of Small Things (Booker Prize 1997) 1996; *Screenplay:* In Which Annie Gives It Those Ones, Electric Moon. *Address:* c/o India Ink Publishing Co Pvt Ltd, C-1, Soami Nagar, New Delhi 110 017, India.

ROYAL, HRH The Princess, Anne Elizabeth Alice Louise, LG, GCVO; British royal; b 15 Aug 1950; d of Queen Elizabeth II (qv) and Prince Philip, Duke of Edinburgh; m Capt Mark Anthony Peter Phillips 1973 (divorced 1992); two c: Peter Mark Andrew, b 15 Nov 1977, Zara Anne Elizabeth, b 15 May 1981; m 2nd Commdr Timothy Laurence, RN, MVO 1992. *Education:* Benenden School (Kent). *Career:* Col-in-Chief 14th/20th King's Hussars, Worcs and Sherwood Foresters Regt (29th/45th Foot), Royal Regina Rifles, 8th Canadian Hussars (Princess Louise's), Royal Corps of Signals, The Canadian Armed Forces Communications and Electronics Br, The Royal Australian Corps of Signals, The Royal Scots, Royal New Zealand Corps of Signals, King's Royal Hussars, Royal Logistics Corps, Royal New Zealand Nursing Corps, The Grey and Simcoe Foresters Militia; Chief Commdt WRNS; Hon Air Cdre RAF Lyneham; Pres WRNS Benevolent Trust, British Acad of Film and Television Arts, Hunters' Improvement and Light Horse Breeding Soc, Save the Children Fund (SCF), Windsor Horse Trials, The Royal School for Daughters of Officers of the Royal Navy and Royal Marines (Haslemere), British Olympic Asscn, Council for Nat Acad Awards; Patron Asscn of Wrens, Riding for the Disabled Asscn, Jersey Wildlife Preservation Fund, The Royal Corps of Signals Asscn, The Royal Corps of Signals Inst, Missions to Seamen, British Knitting and Clothing Export Council, The Army and Royal Artillery Hunter Trials, Gloucs and N Avon Fed of Young Farmers' Clubs, Royal Lymington Yacht Club, Royal Port Moresby Soc for the Prevention of Cruelty to Animals, Horse of the Year Ball, Benenden Ball, British School of Osteopathy, the Royal Tournament, Communications and Electronics Br Inst, All England Women's Lacrosse Asscn, Home Farm Trust; Vice-Patron British Show Jumping Asscn; Commdt-in-Chief St John Ambulance and Nursing Cadets, Women's Transport Service; Freeman of the City of London, of the Fishmongers' Co, Master Warden Farriers' Co, Master and Hon Liveryman, Carmen's Co, Hon Liveryman Farriers' Co; Hon Freeman Farmers' Co, Loriners' Co; Yeoman Saddlers' Co; Hon mem British Equine Veterinary Asscn, Royal Yacht Squadron, Royal Thames Yacht Club, Minchinhampton Golf Club, Lloyds of London; Hon Life mem RNVR Officers' Asscn; Life mem Royal British Legion Women's Section, Royal Naval Saddle Club; mem Island Sailing Club; Visitor Felixstowe Coll; official visits abroad to the 14th/20th King's Hussars 1969, 1975, to see work of SCF in Kenya 1971, to the 2,500th anniversary celebrations of the Iranian monarchy 1971, to 14th/20th King's Hussars and to see work of SCF, Hong Kong 1971, to SE Asia 1972, Munich, Germany 1972, Yugoslavia 1972, Ethiopia and Sudan 1973, to visit Worcs and Sherwood Foresters Regt in Berlin 1973, Germany 1974, to Canada 1974, to Australia 1975, to USA 1977, to Germany and Norway 1978, to Portugal, Germany, Thailand, Gilbert Islands, New Zealand, Australia, the Bahamas and Canada 1979, to Royal Corps of Signals in Cyprus, France, Belgium and Fiji 1980, Royal Corps of Signals in Berlin, Nepal, Worcs and Sherwood Foresters Regt and 14th/20th King's Hussars in Germany; visits to USA, Canada and tour of Africa, N Yemen and Lebanon 1982, to France, Japan, Hong Kong, Singapore, Pakistan, Australia, Netherlands and British Army of the Rhine 1983, USA, Africa, India, Bangladesh, Germany, UAE 1984; Chancellor Univ of London 1981–; has accompanied Queen Elizabeth II and the Duke of Edinburgh on several state visits; has taken part in numerous equestrian competitions including Montréal Olympics, Canada 1976, Horse of the Year Show, Wembley and Badminton Horse Trials; winner Raleigh Trophy 1971 and Silver Medal Individual European Three Day Event 1975; named Sportswoman of the Year, Sports Writers' Asscn, Daily Express, World of Sport, BBC Sports Personality 1971; Special BAFTA Award 1993. *Publication:* Riding Through My Life 1991. *Address:* Buckingham Palace, London SW1, UK.

ROYAL, Ségolène, M SC; French politician and writer; b 22 Sept 1953, Dakar, Senegal; d of Jacques and Hélène (née Dehaye) Royal; partner François Hollande; two s two d. *Education:* Lycée d'Epinal, Univ of Nancy, Inst d'Etudes Politiques de Paris and Ecole Nat d'Admin (Paris). *Career:* Rep for Social Affairs to Office of the Pres 1982–88; Adviser Admin Tribunal, Paris; mem Nat Ass (Parl, PS) for Deux-Sèvres 1988–92, 1993–, Sec Comm for Production and Exchange, mem Nat Cttee on Tourism; Adviser on environment, town planning and social affairs to Pres of Repub 1982–88; Municipal Councillor, Melle 1989–; Minister of the Environment 1992–93; Councillor-Gen, Deux-Sèvres 1992; Pres Nat Council, PS 1994–95; called to the Bar, Paris 1994; Deputy Minister of Educ 1997–2000, of Family and Childhood

2000–. *Publications:* Le printemps des grands-parents, Le ras-le-bol des bébés zappeurs 1989, Pays, Paysans, Paysages 1993, La vérité d'une femme 1996. *Address:* Ministère de la Famille et de l'Enfance, 110 rue de Grenelle, 75007 Paris, France (Office); Parti Socialiste, 10 rue de Solférino, 75333 Paris, France.

ROZES, Simone Andrée, L EN D; French lawyer and former judge; b 29 March 1920, Paris; d of Léon and Marcelle (née Cêtre) Ludwig; m Gabriel Rozes 1942; one s one d. *Education:* Lycée de Sèvres, Lycée de St-Germain-en-Laye, Univ of Paris and Ecole Libre des Sciences Politiques. *Career:* Trainee lawyer, Paris 1947–49; Surrogate Judge, Bourges 1949–50; Attaché Justice Dept 1951–58; Admin Chief Cabinet of the Minister of Justice and Keeper of the Seals 1958–62; Judge Tribunal de Grande Instance de Paris 1962, Vice-Pres 1969–73, Pres 1976–81; Dir Reformatory Educ, Ministry of Justice 1973–76; mem UN Crime Prevention and Control Cttee 1977–81; Advocate-Gen European Court of Justice 1981–82, First Advocate-Gen 1982–84; Pres Cour de Cassation (Chief Justice) 1984–88, Hon Pres 1989–; Pres Int Soc of Social Defence, fmr Pres Soc of Comparative Law; Hon Vice-Pres Int Asscn of Penal Law; Inst Frederik R. Bull; mem Bd Alliance Française; int and nat Arbitrator 1989–; Hon LL D (Edinburgh); Grand Officer de la Légion d'Honneur; Officier de l'Ordre Nat du Mérite; Médaille de l'Educ Surveillée; Médaille de l'Admin Pénitentiaire; Commdr Cross Order of Merit, Germany. *Publication:* Le juge et l'avocat (jtly) 1992. *Leisure interest:* travelling. *Address:* 2 rue Villaret de Joyeuse, 75017 Paris, France. *Telephone:* (1) 43-80-16-67; *Fax:* (1) 47-63-42-90.

ROZHKOVA, Lyubov, LL D; Russian lawyer and politician; b 13 Nov 1947, Makarovo Village, Kaluga Dist; m Boris Rozhkov 1967; one d. *Education:* All-Union Juridical Correspondence Inst (Moscow) and Leningrad (now St Petersburg) State Univ. *Career:* Asst Lecturer, later Assoc Prof, Head of Dept, then Dean Samara State Univ 1975–93; mem State Duma (Parl) of the Fed Ass of the Russian Fed, Chair Cttee on Educ, Culture and Science 1993, Consultant to Juridical Dept 1996; has written monographs on law. *Leisure interests:* reading, theatre, art, politics. *Address:* State Duma, 103265 Moscow, Okhotny Ryad Str 1, Russian Federation (Office); Moscow, Fl 560, 8-2, Koroleva Str, Russian Federation (Home). *Telephone:* (095) 292-39-96 (Office).

ROZSÍVALOVÁ, Věra, PH D, MU DR, D SC; Czech medical practitioner; b 8 Oct 1924, Prague; d of František Matyáš and Anna Matyášová; m Vladimír Rozsíval 1949; two s one d. *Education:* Charles Univ School of Medicine. *Career:* Prof Charles Univ, Hradec Králové 1968, fmr Head of Dermatology Clinic, Prof of Dermatovenerology 1990–; fmr Visiting Prof at Univs in Denmark, Germany, Austria, Hungary, Poland, Bulgaria and fmr USSR; Gold Medal of Charles Univ; univ and hosp awards for scientific activities 1968, 1974, 1987, 1988. *Publications:* Clinical Problems of Some Bullious Dermatosis (6th edn) 1991; has also written eight textbooks and more than 140 papers. *Leisure interests:* Egyptology, history of cosmetics. *Address:* M. Horákové 1101, 500 06 Hradec Králové, Czech Republic. *Telephone:* (49) 615322.

RUBENS, Bernice Ruth, BA; British writer; b 26 July 1928, Cardiff; d of Eli and Dorothy Reuben; m Rudi Nassauer 1947; two d. *Education:* Cardiff High School for Girls and Univ of Wales (Cardiff). *Career:* Author and Dir of documentary films on Third World subjects; Fellow Univ Coll, Cardiff; Hon D LIT (Wales) 1991; American Blue Ribbon for a documentary film 1972. *Publications:* Novels: Set on Edge 1960, Madame Sousatzka 1962, Mate in Three 1964, The Elected Member (Booker Prize 1970) 1968, Sunday Best 1970, Go Tell the Lemming 1972, I Sent a Letter To My Love 1974, Ponsonby Post 1976, A Five-year Sentence 1978, Spring Sonata 1979, Birds of Passage 1980, Brothers 1982, Mr Wakefield's Crusade 1985, Our Father 1987, Kingdom Come 1990, A Solitary Grief 1991, Mother Russia 1992, Autobiopsy 1993, Yesterday in the Back Lane 1995, The Waiting Game 1997, I, Dreyfus 1999, Milwaukee 2001. *Leisure interest:* playing the cello. *Address:* 111 Canfield Gardens, London NW6 3DY, UK. *Telephone:* (20) 7625-4845.

RUBERY, Eileen Doris, CB, MB, CH B, PH D; British academic, civil servant and medical expert; b 16 May 1943; d of James and Doris Sarah McDonnell; m Philip Rubery 1972; one d. *Education:* Univs of Sheffield and Cambridge. *Career:* Sr Research Student St John's Coll, Cambridge 1977–79; Hon Consultant in Radiotherapy and Oncology 1979–83; Sr

Research Fellow Girton Coll, Cambridge 1980–83; Head of Environmental and Radiation Protection Section, Dept of Health 1987–88, Head of Microbiological Safety, Food Div 1988–90, Sr Prin Medical Officer, Head of Health Promotion (Medical) Div 1991–95, Under Sec and Head of Health Aspects of Environment and Food Div 1995–97, Under Sec and Head Protection of Health Div 1996–99; Sr Research Assoc Judge Inst of Man Studies, Cambridge 1997–; Visiting Sr Fellow Girton Coll, Cambridge 1997–, Registrar of the Roll 2000–. *Publications:* Indications for Iodine Prophylaxis following a Nuclear Accident (ed) 1990, Medicine: a degree course guide (ed) 1974–83; publs on medical educ, radiation, microbiological safety of food, toxicology of food, tumour viruses and comparative risk assessment. *Leisure interests:* reading, tapestry, theatre, opera, music. *Address:* Judge Institute of Management Studies, University of Cambridge, Trumpington St, Cambridge, CB2 1AG, UK. *Telephone:* (20) 7972-5001; *Fax:* (20) 7972-1683.

RUBERY, Jill Christine, MA, PH D; British labour economist; b 4 Nov 1951, Newcastle upon Tyne; d of Austin and Gladys Rubery; m Andrew Wilson 1974; one d. *Education:* Wintringham Grammar School for Girls and Newnham Coll (Cambridge). *Career:* Research Asst in Devt Econs, Univ of Oxford 1973–75; Researcher in labour econs, women's employment and low pay, Dept of Applied Econs, Univ of Cambridge 1976–89, Fellow New Hall 1978–89; Lecturer UMIST 1989–91, apptd Sr Lecturer 1992; Co-ordinator of European Comm Network of Experts on the Situation of Women in the Labour Market 1991. *Publications:* Labour Market Structure, Industrial Organization and Low Pay 1982, Women and Recession 1988, Employers' Working Time Policies and Women's Employment 1991; numerous contribs to books and journals. *Address:* UMIST, POB 88, Sackville St, Manchester M60 1QD, UK (Office); 55 Fog Lane, Manchester M20 0AR, UK (Home). *Telephone:* (161) 236-3311 (Office); (161) 200-3406 (Home); *Fax:* (161) 200-3505 (Office).

RUBIN, Gloria Beatriz Godoy de, PH D; Paraguayan broadcasting executive, psychologist and feminist; b 26 March 1943, Asunción; m Humberto Rubin; four c. *Education:* Univ Católica 'Nuestra Señora de la Asunción', Pontificia Univ Católica do Rio de Janeiro and Univ of Asunción. *Career:* Co-Dir Radio Ñanduti (AM), Dir Radio Ñanduti (FM); Dir Editora Ñanduti Vive (est when Govt closed Radio Ñanduti 1987–89); Co-Founder, Lecturer Ñanduti Mujer group promoting women's devt and constitutional change; attended Nat Endowment for Democracy Forum for Democracy, Washington, DC 1987, other int confs on democracy and communications; mem Coordinación de Mujeres del Paraguay. *Address:* Radio Ñanduti, Avda Choferes del Chaco 1194, esq Mcal Estigarribia, Asunción, Paraguay. *Telephone:* (21) 552603; *Fax:* (21) 606074.

RUBIN, Vera Cooper, PH D; American astronomer; b 23 July 1928, Philadelphia, PA; d of Philip and Rose (née Applebaum) Cooper; m Robert J. Rubin 1948; three s one d. *Education:* Vassar Coll, Cornell Univ and Georgetown Univ. *Career:* Research Assoc to Asst Prof Georgetown Univ 1955–65; mem Staff Dept of Terrestrial Magnetism, Carnegie Inst of Washington, DC 1965–; Distinguished Visiting Astronomer Cerro Tololo Inter-American Observatory 1978; Chancellor's Distinguished Prof of Astronomy Univ of California at Berkeley 1981; Pres's Distinguished Visitor Vassar Coll 1987; B. Tinsley Visiting Prof Univ of Texas at Austin 1988; has observed at Kitt Peak Nat Observatory, Lowell, Palomar, McDonald, Las Campanas and Chile observatories; Assoc Ed Astronomical Journal 1972–77, Astrophysical Journal of Letters 1977–82; mem Council American Astronomical Soc 1977–80, Editorial Bd Science Magazine 1979–, Council Smithsonian Inst 1979–85, Space Telescope Science Inst 1990–92, Nat Science Bd 1996–2002; Pres Galaxy Comm Int Astronomical Union 1982–85; mem NAS, American Acad of Arts and Sciences, American Philosophical Soc, Pres's Cttee to select recipients of Nat Medal of Science, Pontifical Acad of Sciences; over 150 scientific papers published in specialist journals and books on the dynamics of galaxies; delivered Jansky Lecture, Nat Radio Astronomy Observatory 1994, Russel Lecture, American Astronomical Soc 1995; Hon D SC (Creighton) 1978, (Harvard) 1988, (Yale) 1990, (Williams Coll) 1993, (Michigan) 1996, (Ohio State) 1998; Hon DHL (Georgetown) 1997; Nat Medal of Science 1993; Dickson Prize for Science, Carnegie Mellon Univ 1994; Gold Medal, Royal Astronomical Soc 1996; Weizman Women and

Science Award 1996; Helen Hogg Prize, Canadian Astronomical Soc 1997. *Publications include:* Bright Galaxies, Dark Matters 1999; over 150 scientific papers on the dynamics of galaxies in specialist journals. *Leisure interests:* family, garden, hiking, travel. *Address:* Carnegie Institution of Washington, Dept of Terrestrial Magnetism, 5241 Broad Branch Rd, NW, Washington, DC 20015, USA. *Telephone:* (202) 686-4370.

RUBINA, Vija; Latvian state official and international organization executive. *Career:* Mem Latvian Women's League; Counsellor to the Dir-Gen, State Employment Service; Deputy Chair Latvian Nat Preparatory Cttee for the UN Fourth World Conf on Women (Beijing) 1995.

RUDDOCK, Joan Mary, B SC, ARCS; British politician and former antinuclear campaigner; b 28 Dec 1943; d of Ken and Eileen Anthony; m Dr Keith Ruddock 1963 (separated 1990, died 1996). *Education:* Pontypool Grammar School for Girls and Imperial Coll (London). *Career:* Worked for Shelter (nat campaign for the homeless) 1968–73; Dir Oxford Housing Aid Centre 1973–77; Special Programmes Officer with unemployed young people, Manpower Services Comm 1977–79; Organizer Citizens Advice Bureau, Reading, Berks 1979–87; Chair Campaign for Nuclear Disarmament (CND) 1981–85, Vice-Chair 1985–86; Lab MP for Deptford 1987–, mem Select Cttee on Televising House of Commons; mem British Del to Council of Europe 1988–89; Shadow Spokesperson on Transport 1989–92, on Home Affairs 1992–94, on Environmental Protection 1994–; Minister for Women 1997–98; Frank Cousins Peace Award 1984. *Publications:* The CND Story (contrib) 1983, CND Scrapbook 1987, Voices for One World (contrib) 1988. *Leisure interests:* gardening, music, contemporary dance. *Address:* House of Commons, London SW1 0AA, UK. *Telephone:* (20) 7219-4513; *Fax:* (20) 7219-6045; *E-mail:* alexanderh@parliament.uk; *Internet:* www.joanruddock.org.uk.

RUDIAKOV, Shoshana; German (b USSR) pianist and professor of music; b Riga, Latvia. *Education:* Music school (Riga) and Moscow P. I. Tchaikovsky State Conservatoire (USSR, now Russian Fed). *Career:* Soloist in concerts and recitals, and appearances on radio and TV in UK, Germany, Italy, USA, Israel, Puerto Rico, Switzerland, Belgium, Netherlands, Yugoslavia; Prof Staatliche Hochschule für Musik und Darstellende Kunst, Stuttgart 1981–. *Address:* Staatliche Hochschule für Musik und Darstellende Kunst, Urbansplatz 2, 7000 Stuttgart, Germany (Office); Libanonstr 58, 70184 Stuttgart, Germany (Home).

RUDIN, Anne Noto, B ED, MPA; American city official; b 27 Jan 1924, Passaic, NJ; m Edward Rudin 1948; three d one s. *Education:* Temple Univ and Univ of S California. *Career:* Faculty mem Temple Univ School of Nursing, PA 1946–48; mem Nursing Faculty Mount Zion Hosp, San Francisco, CA 1948–49; mem Sacramento City Council, CA 1971–83; Mayor of Sacramento City 1983–92; mem World Conf of Mayors for Peace; Pres League of Women Voters, Sacramento 1957, 1961, California Elected Women Asscn 1973–89; mem Bd of Dirs Sacramento Commerce and Trade Org 1984–89; Hon LL D (Golden Gate) 1990; Women in Govt Award, US Jaycee Women 1984; Sacramento Area Soroptimist Clubs Woman of Distinction Award 1985; Civic Contribution Award, Sacramento League of Women Voters 1989; Woman of Courage Award, Sacramento History Center 1989; Girl Scouts of America Role Model 1989; Regional Prize Award Sacramento Magazine 1993; Humanitarian Award Japanese American Citizens' League 1993; Outstanding Public Service Award American Public Admin Soc 1994; Community Service Recognition Award, Japanese American Citizens' League 1999; Sacramento Traditional Jazz Soc Hall of Fame 20000. *Leisure interests:* theatre, music, drama, language. *Address:* 1410 Birchwood Lane, Sacramento, CA 95822, USA (Home).

RUDLER, Michèle Odette Marthe, D ÈS SC; French toxicologist; b 23 April 1941, Nantes; d of Henri and Madeleine (née Barel) Rey; m Jean Rudler (divorced); two d one s. *Education:* Lycée Gabriel Guist'hau (Nantes) and Univ of Paris. *Career:* Intern Paris hosps 1966–70; Asst Faculty of Pharmacology, Univ of Paris 1964–69, Sr Lecturer Faculty of Pharmaceutical and Biological Sciences 1968; Biology and Toxicology Attaché Hôpital Fernand Widal 1970–73; Rep to Minister of Public Health 1970–72, to Gen Del on Scientific and Tech Research 1974–78, to Secr of State for War Veterans 1978–81; Sr Lecturer in Toxicology

Univ of Nancy 1976; Prof of Medico-Legal Toxicology Univ of Paris V (René Descartes) 1981–, Deputy Dir Teaching and Research Unit in Legal Medicine, the Law and Medical Deontology 1983–86, Dir 1986–; Dir Toxicology Lab Prefecture of Police, Paris 1985–, Police Scientific Lab 1987–94; Prof Laboratoire d'Ethique Médicale Necker Medical Faculty for Sick Children, Paris 1997–; Founder-mem Centre nat de prévention, d'études et de recherches en toxicomanie 1987; Expert Adviser to UN 1988–; Sec-Gen Comité nat des familles pour l'aide et le sauvetage des adolescents et jeunes toxicomanes; Pres Soc française de victimologie 1994–; mem Nat Council for the Prevention of Delinquency 1986–, Conseil nat des univs 1987–; Chevalier de la Légion d'Honneur; Chevalier de l'Ordre Nat du Mérite; Chevalier des Arts et des Lettres; Chevalier des Palmes Académiques; Officier de l'Ordre Nat du Lion, Senegal; Prix Jansen, Acad de Médecine 1977. *Address:* Laboratoire d'Ethique Médicale, 156 rue de Vaugirard, 75015 Paris, France (Office); 44 ave Niel, 75017 Paris, France (Home).

RUEHL, Mercedes, BA; American actress; b 1950, Queens, New York. *Education:* Coll of New Rochelle (NY). *Career:* Stage appearances in regional theatre productions. *Plays include:* I'm Not Rappaport, American Notes, The Marriage of Bette and Boo (Obie Award), Coming of Age in Soho, Other People's Money, Lost in Yonkers (Tony Award 1991); *Films include:* The Warriors 1979, Four Friends 1981, Heartburn 1986, Radio Days 1987, 84 Charing Cross Road 1987, The Secret of My Success 1987, Big 1988, Married to the Mob 1988, Slaves of New York 1989, Crazy People 1990, Another You, The Fisher King (Acad Award for Best Supporting Actress 1992) 1991, Lost in Yonkers 1993, Last Action Hero, Roseanna's Grave 1996; *TV appearances include:* Late Bloomer, Our Family Honor (guest), Indictment: The McMartin Trial (film), Frasier.

RUETHER, Rosemary Radford, PH D; American professor of theology; b 2 Nov 1936; d of Robert A. Radford and Rebecca C. Ord; m Herman J. Ruether 1957; one s two d. *Education:* Scripps Coll (Claremont, CA) and Claremont Grad School. *Career:* Howard Univ School of Religion 1965–76; Visiting Prof Harvard Divinity School 1972–73; Georgia Harkness Prof of Theology, Garrett Evangelical Seminary 1976; mem Grad Faculty Northwestern Univ, Evanston, IL 1976; Visiting Prof Harvard Divinity School 1972–73; Fulbright Scholar, Sweden 1984; eight hon degrees. *Publications include:* Religion and Sexism 1974, Mary, the Feminine Face of the Church 1977, Womanguides: Texts for Feminist Theology 1985, Contemporary Catholicism 1987, The Wrath of Jonah: Religious Nationalism in the Arab-Israeli Conflict 1989, Gaia and God: Ecofeminism and Earth-Healing 1992. *Leisure interests:* painting, swimming. *Address:* 1426 Hinman Ave, Evanston, IL 60201, USA.

RUGGIER, Maria; Maltese politician; b 8 Sept 1936; d of Saviour Zarb Adami and Rose Steptow; m Antoine Ruggier 1960; one d two s. *Education:* St Joseph (Paola) and Mater Admirabilis Teacher Training Coll. *Career:* Secondary school language teacher 1955–75; Art Studio Man 1975–85; mem Nationalist Party (PN) 1980–, Pres 1992; Sec USA–Malta AIUTA; Chair Welfare Comm on the Care of the Elderly, Gold Butterfly Award USA–Malta. *Leisure interests:* reading, studying foreign languages. *Address:* Markenvil, Triq Patri Delia, Balzan/Bznoy, Malta. *Telephone:* 486896; *Fax:* 245145.

RÜHMKORF, Eva, DIP; German politician; b 3 March 1935, Breslau; d of Kurt and Margot Titze; m Peter Rühmkorf 1964. *Education:* Univs of Marburg and Hamburg. *Career:* Marketing Researcher int advertising agencies 1961–68; Planning and Devt of Prison Service Reform, Dept of Justice, City of Hamburg 1968–73; Prison Gov (male juvenile delinquents) 1973–79; Head Dept of Equal Opportunities for Women, Hamburg 1979–83; apptd Under-Sec of State, Fed State of Schleswig-Holstein 1983, Minister of Educ and Cultural Affairs 1988, Minister of Fed Affairs and Deputy Prime Minister 1990–92; Deputy Chair ProFamilia 1993; Woman of the Year, Deutscher Staats-Bürgerinnen Verband 1985. *Publications:* Wer unten ist, der fällt auch tief 1977; other articles on juvenile delinquency and equal rights for women. *Leisure interests:* reading, gardening, cooking. *Address:* Oevelgönne 50, 22605 Hamburg, Germany.

RUIZ-CERUTTI, Susana, LL B; Argentine diplomatist; b 18 Nov 1940, Buenos Aires. *Education:* Nat Univ of Buenos Aires. *Career:* Lawyer; diplomatist specializing in public int law; mem or Head of Del to several arbitral proceedings and to int confs; Legal Adviser 1985–87; Vice-Minister 1987–89; Minister of Foreign Affairs 1989; Amb Extraordinary and Plenipotentiary to Switzerland and Liechtenstein 1989; Agent to Int Arbitral Tribunal on the frontier controversy between Argentina and Chile 1991–96; mem nat list of judges of the Permanent Court of Arbitration, The Hague; Insignis Crucis Pro Ecclesia et Pontifice, Holy See; Gt Cross of the Repub of Hungary; Gt Cross of the Order of Río Branco, Brazil. *Address:* Embassy of Argentina, Jubiläumsplatz 6, 3006 Berne, Switzerland; Rodriguez Peña 2087, 8°A, 1021 Buenos Aires, Argentina. *Telephone:* (1) 814-3430 (Buenos Aires).

RUKMANA, Siti Hardijanti; Indonesian business executive; b 1949; d of Gen Suharto (Pres of Indonesia) and Siti Hartinah; m Indra Rukmana Kowara. *Career:* Pres Citra Lamtoro Gung Persada (construction, pharmaceutical, telecommunications and media corpn); Chair Indonesian Social Workers' Asscn, United Pvt Radio Broadcasting Service of Indonesia, Indonesian Blood Donor Asscn, Org for Indonesian Youth. *Address:* Citra Lamtoro Gung Persada, Jakarta, Indonesia.

RULE, Jane Vance, BA; Canadian writer; b 28 March 1931, Plainfield, NJ; d of Arthur Richard and Carlotta Jane (née Hink) Rule. *Education:* Palo Alto High School (CA), Mills Coll (Oakland, CA), Univ Coll London (UK) and Stanford Univ. *Career:* Teacher of English Concord Acad, MA 1954–56; Asst Dir Int House, Univ of British Columbia, Canada 1958–59, part-time Lecturer 1959–73; subject of film Fiction and Other Truths: A Film About Jane Rule 1995; mem Writers' Union of Canada, PEN; Phi Beta Kappa; Hon D LITT (British Columbia) 1994; Order of BC; Canadian Authors' Asscn Award for Best Novel 1978; Benson and Hedges Award for Best Short Stories 1978; Literary Award, Gay Acad Union, USA 1978; Award of Merit, The Fund for Human Dignity, USA 1983; British Columbia Gay Lifetime Achievement Award 1996; Talking Book of the Year. *Publications:* Novels: The Desert of the Heart 1964, This Is Not For You 1971, Against the Season 1971, The Young in One Another's Arms 1977, Contract With the World 1980, Memory Board 1987, After the Fire 1989; Criticism: Lesbian Images 1975; Stories and essays: Theme for Diverse Instruments 1975, Outlander 1981, A Hot-Eyed Moderate 1985, Inland Passage and Other Stories 1985; numerous articles and short stories for journals and anthologies. *Leisure interests:* swimming, walking, collecting paintings. *Address:* The Fork Route 1, S19 C17, Galiano, BC V0N 1P0, Canada.

RUMBOLD, Rt Hon Dame Angela Claire Rosemary, DBE, PC; British politician; b 11 Aug 1932, Bristol; d of the late Harry and Molly Jones; m John Marix Rumbold 1958; two s one d. *Education:* Notting Hill and Ealing High School and King's Coll (London). *Career:* Founder-mem Nat Asscn for the Welfare of Children in Hospital, Nat Chair 1974–76; Councillor Royal Borough of Kingston upon Thames 1974–83, Chair Policy and Resource; Political Researcher 1975–82; Chair Educ Cttee Asscn of Metropolitan Authorities 1979–80, Council Local Educ Authorities 1979–80; Cons MP for Mitcham and Morden (fmrly Merton, Mitcham and Morden) 1982–, mem Social Services Select Cttee 1982–83; Pvt Parl Sec to Finance Sec to the Treasury 1983, to Sec of State for Transport 1983–85; Parl Under-Sec of State Dept of Employment 1985–86; Minister of State at Dept of Environment 1985–86, Dept of Educ and Science 1986–90, Home Office 1990–92; Deputy Chair Cons Party 1992–95, Vice-Chair 1995–97; mem Doctors and Dentists Review Body 1979–81; Co-Chair Women's Nat Comm 1986–90; Chair One Nation Forum 1992–94; Freeman City of London 1988. *Leisure interests:* swimming, cinema, reading, ballet. *Address:* House of Commons, London SW1A 0AA, UK. *Telephone:* (20) 7219-5218.

RUPPA, Myriam Renée Frédérique Gaëtane; French shipping executive; b 17 June 1931, Le Havre; d of René and Paulette (née Gentien) Pesnel; m Pierre Ruppa 1959. *Education:* Lycée François I (Le Havre) and Chambre de commerce britannique. *Career:* Teacher 1951–56; Asst Consignment Service, Worms CMC co, Le Havre 1956–57; Rep for Taconet ship-brokers, Rouen 1957–58; Head Consignment Service Jules Roy SA, Le Havre 1958–62, Asst Dir 1964–73, Deputy Dir 1973–75; worked for Delmas Vieljeux shipping co, Le Havre 1962–64; Man Dir United Agencies SA, Le Havre 1975–81, Pres, Dir-Gen 1981–; Pres Asscn havraise des agents consignataires de navires du Havre 1980–96, now Hon Pres ; Vice-Pres Fédération nat des agents maritimes et consignataires 1980–; Judge Tribunal de Commerce, Le Havre 1981–86; Pres Admin Council Inst portuaire d'enseignement et de recherche 1985; Admin Port autonome du Havre 1984, Sec 1989, Vice-Pres 1993; Founder, Man Uniseas 1989; Hon Norwegian Consul to Le Havre 1982–; Chevalier de l'Ordre Nat du Mérite; Officier du Mérite Maritime; Officer of Merit, Norway. *Publication:* Une femme à bord (ed) 1996. *Leisure interest:* gymnastics. *Address:* 46 ave Foch, 76600 Le Havre, France.

RUSHESHA, Oppah Charm Zvipange (née Muchinguri), B SC, MPA; Zimbabwean politician; b 14 Dec 1958, Mutare; m T. Rushesha 1990; one d. *Education:* Univ of S California and Mankato State Univ (MN, USA). *Career:* Pvt Sec to Pres of Zimbabwe 1980–81; mem House of Ass, apptd Deputy Minister of Political Affairs (External Affairs) 1989; Pres Global Parliamentarian Asscn 1990–92. *Leisure interests:* reading, sport. *Address:* ZANU PF HQ, Rotten Row, Private Bag 7762, Causeway, Harare, Zimbabwe. *Telephone:* (4) 729307; *Fax:* (4) 735638.

RUSS, Joanna, MFA; American writer and professor of English; b 22 Feb 1937, New York; d of Everett and Bertha (née Zinner) Russ. *Education:* Cornell Univ and Yale Univ School of Drama. *Career:* Prof of English Univ of Washington. *Publications include:* When It Changed (Nebula Award for Best Short Story) 1972, The Female Man 1975, The Two of Them 1978, Kittatinny: A Tale of Magic 1978, On Strike Against God 1980, The Zanzibar Cat (short stories) 1983, Souls (Hugo Gernsback Award for Best Novella) 1983, Adventures of Alyx (short stories) 1983, How to Suppress Women's Writing (non-fiction) 1983, Extra(Ordinary) People 1984, Magic Mommas, etc (essays) 1985, Other Side of the Moon (short stories) 1987. *Address:* University of Washington, Dept of English, GN-30, Seattle, WA 98195, USA.

RUSSELL, Anna; Canadian comedienne; b 27 Dec 1911; d of C. Russell-Brown and Beatrice M. Tandy. *Education:* St Felix School (Southwold) and Royal Coll of Music (London, UK). *Career:* Folk Singer BBC 1935–40, CBC 1942–46, radio interviewer 1945–46; debut as comedienne, New York, USA 1948; appearances include Broadway, New York, 1953, Mayfair Theatre, London 1976 and in USA, Canada, UK, Australia, New Zealand, S Africa. *Publications:* The Power of Being a Positive Stinker, The Anna Russell Song Book, I'm Not Making This Up, You Know (autobiog). *Leisure interest:* gardening. *Address:* 70 Anna Russell Way, Unionville, ON L3R 3X3, Canada.

RUSSELL, Francia; American ballet dancer and director; b 10 Jan 1938, Los Angeles; d of Frank and Marion (née Whitney) Russell; m Kent Stowell 1965; three s. *Education:* Univs of New York and Columbia. *Career:* Studied under George Balanchine, Vera Volkova, Felia Doubrouska, Antonia Tumkovsky and Benjamin Harkarvy; Soloist New York City Ballet 1956–62, Ballet Mistress 1965–70; Dancer USA and Jerome Robbins Ballets, New York 1962; teacher School of American Ballet 1963–64; Dir of ballet productions in USA, Europe, Asia, fmr USSR and People's Repub of China 1964–; Co-Dir Frankfurt Opera Ballet, Germany 1976–77; apptd Dir and Artistic Co-Dir Pacific NW Ballet, Seattle, WA 1977; Affiliated Prof of Dance Univ of Washington; mem Dance-USA, Ballet America; Matrix Table Women in Communications Woman of Achievement 1987. *Address:* Pacific NW Ballet, 4649 Sunnyside Ave, N Seattle, WA 98103, USA.

RUSSELL, Theresa; American actress; b 20 March 1957, San Diego, CA; d of Jerry Russell Paup and Carole Joy; m Nicolas Jack Roeg 1986; two s. *Education:* Burbank High School and the Actors' Studio (Hollywood, CA). *Career:* Began modelling at the age of 12; numerous film appearances; Nat Asscn of Theater Owners Star of Tomorrow 1986. *Films include:* The Last Tycoon 1977, Straight Time 1978, Bad Timing 1980, Eureka 1982, The Razor's Edge 1983, Insignificance 1984, Aria 1985, Black Widow 1986, Track 29 1987, Physical Evidence 1988, Impulse 1989, Cold Heaven 1990, Whore 1991, Kafka 1991, Cold Heaven 1992, The Grotesque, Woman's Guide to Adultery 1993, Thicker Than Water 1994, Trade Off 1994, Young Connecticut Yankee in King Arthur's Court 1995, Spy Within 1995, Public Enemies 1996, Proposition 1996, Grave Indiscretion 1997, Running Woman 1997,

Lucky Town 2000; *TV appearances include:* Blind Ambition (mini-series) 1979, Thicker Than Water (film). *Address:* c/o PFD, Drury House, 34-43 Russell St, London WC2B 5HA, UK. *Telephone:* (20) 7344-1000.

RUSSO, René; American actress; b 1955, CA; m Dan Gilroy; one d. *Career:* Fmr model with Eileen Ford Agency before first film role in 1989. *Films include:* Major League 1989, Mr Destiny, One Good Cop, Freejack, Lethal Weapon 3, In the Line of Fire, Outbreak, Get Shorty, Tin Cup, Ransom, Buddy, Lethal Weapon 4 1998, The Adventures of Rocky and Bullwinkle 1999, The Thomas Crown Affair 1999; *TV appearance:* Sable (series). *Address:* c/o Progressive Artists Agency, 400 S Beverly Drive, Suite 216, Beverly Hills, CA 90212, USA.

RUSSO JERVOLINO, Rosa; Italian politician; b 1936, Naples. *Education:* Univ of Rome. *Career:* Worked in Research Dept CNEL 1961–68; joined Legislative Div, Ministry of the Budget 1969; mem staff, subsequently Nat Vice-Pres Centro Italiano femminile 1969–78; mem Nat Exec Women's Movt of Christian Democrat (DC) Party 1968–78, Pres 1992–; Nat Organizer DC Family Div 1974–; mem Senate 1979–; Minister for Social Affairs 1989–92, of Educ 1992–94; Chair Parl Supervisory Comm of RAI (nat TV and radio corpn) 1985–. *Address:* Senato, Palazzio Madama, 00186 Rome, Italy.

RUTTERFORD, Janette Marie, M SC, MBA, PH D; British economist; b 16 Oct 1950, Liverpool; d of John and Janine Rutterford; m Sebastian Wakefield 1979 (divorced 1993); one s. *Education:* Royal Holloway Coll (Univ of London), St Anne's Coll (Oxford), London Business School and LSE. *Career:* Corporate Finance Exec N. M. Rothschild & Sons, London and Paris 1973–77; Asst Prof LSE 1979–86; Trend Analyst Crédit Lyonnais 1986–88; Abbey Nat Prof of Financial Man Open Univ Business School 1988–; mem various Govt and other cttees; appearances on radio and TV; European Investment Bank Prize 1988. *Publications:* Introduction to Stock Exchange Investment; numerous articles on finance and investment. *Leisure interests:* France, cooking, cycling, long-distance walking, cinema. *Address:* Open University Business School, Walton Hall, Milton Keynes MK7 6AA, UK. *Telephone:* (1908) 655812; *Fax:* (1908) 655898; *E-mail:* j.rutterford@open.ac.uk.

RŮŽIČKOVÁ, Zuzana; Czech harpsichordist; b 14 Jan 1927; d of Jaroslav and Leopolda (née Lederer) Růžička; m Viktor Kalabis 1952. *Education:* Pilsen School of Music and Acad of Performing Arts (AMU, Prague). *Career:* Interned in concentration camps including Auschwitz and Bergen–Belsen 1942–45; concert harpsichordist in Europe, Japan, Canada and the USA 1956–; music teacher Acad of Performing Arts (AMU) 1951–, Acad of Music and Dramatic Art, Bratislava 1978–82, Zurich Masterclass, Switzerland 1969–; Prof of Music AMU 1990–; Hon mem Nat Early Music Asscn, Oxford (UK) 1988; winner Arbeitsgemeinschaft der öffentlich-rechtlichen Rundfunkanstalten der Bundesrepublik Deutschland (ARD) Competition, Munich (Germany) 1956; State Prize of Czechoslovakia 1970; Nat Artist of Czechoslovakia 1989; Medal of Arts and Sciences, Hamburg (Germany) 1992. *Recordings include:* J. S. Bach, Purcell, Handel, Haydn, Scarlatti; more than 70 records. *Leisure interests:* gardening, literature. *Address:* Slezská 107, 130-00 Prague 3, Czech Republic. *Telephone:* (2) 67312104.

RYABINKINA, Yelena Lvovna; Russian ballet dancer; b 1941, Moscow; m 1st E. Martzevich 1964; m 2nd Yu Fidler 1974. *Education:* Bolshoi Theatre Ballet School; State Inst of Theatrical Art. *Career:* Dancer at Bolshoi Theatre Ballet Co 1959–; major roles in Swan Lake, Raimonda, Giselle, Don Quixote, Vanina Vanini, Persian Dance, Fountain of Bakhtchisarai; mem USSR Union of Arts; Hon RSFSR Actress. *Address:* c/o Academic Bolshoi State Theatre, Moscow, Teatralnaya 1, Russian Federation. *Telephone:* (095) 290-00-50.

RYAN, Geraldine Noreen Bernadette; Australian dance instructor; b 1930, Melbourne; d of Jeremiah and Bridget (née Thistleton) O'Shea; m Patrick N. Ryan; two s one d. *Education:* Brigidine Convent and Zerchos Business Coll (Vic). *Career:* Irish Dance adjudicator and teacher 1953–; Choreographer for Papal visit to Melbourne 1986, for O'Shea-Ryan Irish Dancers, Midosuje Festival, Japan 1990; Adjudicator World Folkdance Festival, Bavaria, Germany 1985, Majorca, Spain 1987, 1989, 1993, 1997, Europe 1991, Int Eisteddfod, SA 1993; Pilgrimage Co-ordinator Holy Land Tour 1993; Prin Geraldine O'Shea

Acad of Irish Dancing; fmr Australian Irish Dance Champion; trained and provided dancers for films Against the Wind and The Last Outlaw; Sec Melbourne Irish Festival; Founder-mem Australian Irish Dance Comm, Examiner; Life mem Australian Irish Dance Asscn 1991; mem Irish Dance Comm, Dublin; Vice-Pres An Coimisiun; numerous articles published on dance and Irish dance in Australia; Award of Excellence and Appreciation, Irish Community 1982. *Leisure interests:* piano and pipe playing, travel. *Address:* 406 Highbury Rd, Mount Waverley, Vic 3149, Australia.

RYAN, Meg; American actress; b (Margaret Hyra) 19 Nov 1961, Fairfield, CT; m Dennis Quaid 1991 (divorced); one s. *Education:* Bethel High School and New York Univ. *Career:* Fmrly appeared in TV commercials; debut in As The World Turns 1983–85; Head Prufrock Pictures. *Films include:* Rich and Famous 1981, Amityville III-D 1983, Top Gun 1986, Armed and Dangerous 1986, Innerspace 1987, DOA 1988, Promised Land 1988, The Presidio 1988, When Harry Met Sally 1989, Joe Versus the Volcano 1990, The Doors 1991, Prelude to a Kiss, Sleepless in Seattle, Flesh and Bone, Significant Other, When a Man Loves a Woman, IQ, French Kiss, Restoration, Lost Soul, Courage Under Fire 1996, Addicted to Love 1997, City of Angels 1998, You've Got Mail 1998, Hanging Up 1999, Lost Souls 1999, Proof of Life 2000; *TV appearances include:* As the World Turns, One of the Boys, Amy and the Angel, The Wild Side, Charles in Charge.

RYAN, Susan Maree, AO, MA; Australian politician and organization executive; b 10 Oct 1942, Sydney, NSW; d of A. F. Ryan; one s one d. *Education:* Brigidine Convent (Maroubra, Sydney), Univ of Sydney and ANU. *Career:* School teacher 1963; Research Officer and Tutor Canberra Coll of Advanced Educ 1971–72; Lecturer in Adult Educ ANU; Nat Exec Officer Australian Council of State School Orgs and Consultant Australian Schools Comm 1973–75; Founder-mem Women's Electoral Lobby, ACT 1972; Senator (Australian Labor Party) 1975–88; Minister Assisting the Prime Minister on the Status of Women 1983–88, Minister for Youth Affairs 1983–84, Minister for Educ 1984–87, Special Minister of State, Minister Assisting the Prime Minister on the Status of Women and the Bicentenary, Minister Assisting the Minister of Community Services and Health 1987; Publr Penguin Books, Melbourne 1987–; Exec-Dir Plastics Industry Asscn Inc, Melbourne 1989–93; Exec Dir Asscn of Superannuation Funds of Australia 1993–97; Deputy Chair NRMA Ltd 1999, mem Bd dirs 1997–, NRMA Insurance 1999–, SGIO Insurance 1998–; mem Republican Advisory Cttee 1993–. *Leisure interests:* reading, theatre, music, travel, swimming, tennis. *Address:* NRMA Ltd, 388 George St, Sydney, NSW 2000, Australia.

RYDER, Winona; American actress; b 29 Oct 1971, Winona, MN; d of Michael Horowitz and Cynthia Istas. *Education:* Petaluma Jr High School and American Conservatory Theatre (San Francisco, CA). *Career:* Spotted by talent scout while in school play; screen debut in Lucas 1986. *Films include:* Square Dance 1987, Beetlejuice 1988, 1969 1988, Heathers 1989, Great Balls of Fire! 1989, Welcome Home Rosy Carmichael 1990, Edward Scissorhands 1991, Mermaids 1991, Night on Earth 1992, Bram Stoker's Dracula, The Age of Innocence (Golden Globe Award, Acad Award nomination), Reality Bites, The House of the Spirits, Little Women (Acad Award nomination), How to Make an American Quilt 1996, The Crucible, Boys 1996, Looking for Richard, Alien Resurrection, Girl Interrupted 1999, Lost Souls 1999, Autumn in New York 1999.

RYKIEL, Sonia; French fashion designer; b (Sonia Flis) 25 May 1930, Paris; d of Alfred and Fanny (née Tesler) Flis; one s one d. *Education:* Secondary school in Neuilly-sur-Seine. *Career:* Began designing rabbit-hair sweaters which established her reputation 1962; opened own boutique, Paris 1968, New York, USA 1983; opened further boutiques specializing in men's knitwear and household linens 1976, 1981; launched first perfume '7ème Sens' 1979; launched first children's collection 1984; supervised renovation of Hotel Crillon, Paris 1982; Vice-Pres Chambre Syndicale du Prêt-à-Porter des Couturiers et des Créateurs de Mode, Paris 1982; launched Sonia Rykiel perfume 1997; Hon Prof China Textile Univ, Shanghai 1998; currently Chair Sonia Rykiel CDM; Pres Acad des Arts et du Vin Calver 1992; mem Int Asscn of Women Writers; Croix des Arts et des Lettres 1983; Officier des Arts et des Lettres 1993, Officier de la Légion d'Honneur 1996; Fashion Oscar, Fashion Group of New York 1986; Award for Design Excellence, Costume Cttee, Chicago Historial Soc. *Publications include:* Et je la voudrais nue 1979, Rykiel 1985, Célébration 1988, La collection 1989, Colette et la mode 1991, Collection terminée, collection interminable 1993, Tatiana Acacia (jtly) 1993, Les lèvres rouges 1996, Sonia Rykiel (memoirs) 1997. *Leisure interests:* travel, writing, collecting paintings and silverware. *Address:* 175 blvd Saint-Germain, 75006 Paris, France. *Telephone:* (1) 49-54-60-00; *Fax:* (1) 49-54-60-96; *Internet:* www .soniarykiel.com.

RYMER, Pamela Ann, BA, LL B; American federal judge; b 6 Jan 1941, Knoxville, TN. *Education:* Vassar Coll and Stanford Univ. *Career:* Called to the Bar, CA 1966, US Court of Appeals (9th Circuit) 1966, (10th Circuit), US Supreme Court; Assoc Lillick, McHouse and Charles, Los Angeles 1966–72, Partner 1973–75, Toy and Rymer 1975–83; Judge US Dist Court of California (Cen) 1983–89, US Court of Appeals (9th Circuit), Los Angeles 1989–; mem California Post-secondary Educ Comm 1974–, Chair 1980–84; Faculty mem Nat Judicial Coll 1986; Chair Exec Cttee 9th Circuit Judicial Conf 1990–94; mem Bd visitors of Stanford Univ Law School 1986–, Pepperdine Univ 1987; mem Educ Comm, States Task Force on State Policy and Ind Higher Educ 1987; mem Bd Dirs Constitutional Rights Foundation 1985; mem Los Angeles Olympic Games Advisory Comm; mem ABA, Asscn of Business Trial Lawyers, Stanford Law Soc, Los Angeles Co Bar Asscn; Hon LL D (Pepperdine) 1988. *Address:* US Court of Appeals, 9th Circuit, Suite 600, 125 S Grand Ave, Pasadena, CA 91105, USA.

RYSTE, Ruth Anlaug; Norwegian politician; b 24 July 1932, Bamble; d of Hans and Christine Skaugen; m Øyvind Ryste 1954. *Career:* Official, then Head of Section Bamble Insurance Office 1950–69; Sec Norwegian Inst of Tech 1970–73; Personal Sec to Minister of Consumer Affairs and Admin 1973–75; Sec Civil Servants' Asscn 1975–76; Minister of Social Affairs 1976–79; Dir Norwegian Refugee Council 1980–82, Norwegian Govt Refugee Agency 1982–87, Royal Ministry of Local Govt 1988; mem Bamble Local Bd, Norwegian Confed of TUs 1969–71, Cen Bd Norwegian Lab Party 1976–, Bd of Nat Theatre 1975–. *Address:* c/o Vassfaret 12, Oslo 3, Norway.

RYYNÄNEN, Mirja; Finnish politician; b 11 Nov 1944, Kuopio mlk. *Career:* Fmr MEP (Group of the European Liberal, Democrat and Reform Party), mem Cttee on Culture, Youth, Educ and the Media, Del for Relations with Australia and New Zealand. *Address:* c/o European Parliament, rue Wiertz, 1047 Brussels, Belgium.

S

SAAL, Agnès; French civil servant; b 1957, Tunis, Tunisia. *Education:* Inst d'études politiques de Paris and Ecole nationale d'administration (Paris). *Career:* Began career at Ministry of Culture 1983; employee Centre nat de la cinématographie 1990–97; Tech Adviser to Minister of Culture and Communication 1997–98, Deputy Dir Cabinet 1998–2001; Dir-Gen Bibliothèque nationale de France 2001–. *Address:* quai Francois Mauriac, 75706 Paris, Cedex 13, France.

SAALBACH, Astrid; Danish writer; b 29 Nov 1955, Elsinore; m Jens Kaas 1987; two s. *Education:* Nat School of Theatre (Copenhagen). *Career:* Actress at different theatres until 1985; first radio play 1982, first stage play 1986; first collection of short stories 1985, first novel 1987; awards include Statens Kunsfonds Trearige Legat, Kjell Abell Prisen, Preben Harris Rejelegat, Dramatikernes Haderspris, Nørdisk Radiospilspris, Edv Petersens Bibliotekspris, The Holberg Medal, Statens Kunstfonds Livsvarige Legat, Henri Nathansens Fodselsdags Legat. *Publications include:* Plays: Fading Colours (TV) 1980, Footmarks in the Sand 1982, The Hidden City 1985, Myung (TV) 1989, Morning and Evening 1992, Sacred Child 1996, Ashes to Ashes, Dust to Dust 1998, The Cold Heart 2001; Novels: Who She Is 2000; Short Stories: The Face of the Moon 1985. *Address:* Holsteinsgade 9, 3 tv, 2100 Copenhagen Ø, Denmark. *Telephone:* 35-38-18-83.

SAARIAHO, Kaija; Finnish composer; b 1952; m Jean-Baptiste Barrière; one s one d. *Career:* Lives in Paris; comms written for Salzburg Festival 1996; works performed at BBC Henry Wood Promenade Concerts 1995. *Works include:* Maa (ballet), Verblendungen, Lichtbogen, Stilleben, Io 1986–87, Graal Théâtre (violin concerto), Château de l'âme (vocal work); *Recordings:* Maa, Verblendungen, Lichtbogen, Io, Stilleben.

SABATINI, Gabriela; Argentine tennis player; b 16 May 1970, Buenos Aires. *Career:* Coached by Angel Gimenez; won French and Italian Jr and Orange Bowl 18s 1984; reached Semifinals French Open, won Japan Open 1985; reached Semifinals Wimbledon (UK), runner-up French Open 1986; reached Semifinals French Open, runner-up Italian Open, winner Tokyo and Brighton (UK), runner-up French Open Doubles (with Steffi Graf, qv) 1987; finalist Virginia Slims tournament (FL, USA) and US Open 1988; finalist German Open 1989; winner Virginia Slims (FL, USA) and US Open 1990; reached finals, Wimbledon 1991; winner Italian Open 1992; ranked 29th in the world 1996; announced retirement from professional tennis Oct 1996.

SADDLEMYER, (Eleanor) Ann, PH D, FRSC, FRSA; Canadian professor of drama and English and university administrator; b 28 Nov 1932, Prince Albert; d of Orrin Angus and Elsie Sarah (née Ellis) Saddlemyer. *Education:* Univ of Saskatchewan, Queen's Univ (Kingston, ON) and Bedford Coll (London). *Career:* Lecturer Univ of Victoria, BC 1956–57, Instructor 1960–62, Asst Prof 1962–65, Prof of English 1971; Prof of English Victoria Coll, Univ of Toronto, Ontario 1971–95, Dir Grad Centre for the Study of Drama, Univ of Toronto 1972–77, 1985–86, Master of Massey Coll 1988–95; Berg Prof Univ of New York, USA 1975; mem Bd of Dirs Colin Smythe Publishers, UK 1970; Co-Founder and Vice-Pres Bd of Dirs of Theatre Plus, Toronto 1972–84; Chair Int Asscn for the Study of Anglo-Irish Literature 1973–76; Founder and Pres Asscn for Canadian Theatre History 1976–77; mem Chancellor's Council Victoria Coll 1984–; Guggenheim Fellow 1965, 1977; Hon LL D (Queen's) 1977; Hon D LITT (Victoria, McGill) 1989, (Windsor) 1990, (Toronto) 1999; Prov of Ontario Distinguished Service Award 1985; British Acad Rosemary Crawshay Award for Criticism 1986; cr Ann Saddlemyer Book Prize for Theatre History 1989; YWCA Toronto Woman of the Year Award 1994.

Publications include: The World of W. B. Yeats: Essays in Perspective (jtly) 1965, In Defence of Lady Gregory, Playwright 1966, The Plays of J. M. Synge (2 vols) 1968, Theatre History in Canada (co-ed) 1980–86, Theatre Business, the Letters of the First Abbey Theatre Directors 1982, Early Stages: Theatre in Ontario 1800–1914 1990, The World's Classics J. M. Synge 1995, Later Stages: Essays on Theatre in Ontario 1800–1914 1997. *Leisure interests:* acting, music, travel, book-collecting. *Address:* 10876 Madrona Drive, Sidney, BC V8L 5N9, Canada (Home). *E-mail:* saddlemy@uvic.ca.

SADIK, Nafis, MD; Pakistani international official and physician; b 18 Aug 1929, Jaunpur, India; d of Mohammad Shoaib and Iffat Ara; m Azhar Sadik 1954; two d one s and two adopted d. *Education:* Loretto Coll (Calcutta) and Calcutta Medical Coll (India), Dow Medical Coll (Karachi) and Johns Hopkins Univ (USA). *Career:* Intern Gynaecology and Obstetrics, City Hosp, Baltimore, MD, USA 1952–54; civilian Medical Officer in charge of women's and children's wards in various Pakistani armed forces hosps 1954–63; Resident in Physiology Queen's Univ, Kingston, ON, Canada 1958; Head Health Section, Planning Comm on Health and Family Planning, Pakistan 1964; Dir of Planning and Training, Pakistan Cen Family Planning Council 1966–68, Deputy Dir-Gen 1968–70, Dir-Gen 1970–71; Tech Adviser UN Population Fund (UNFPA) 1971–72, Chief Programme Div 1973–77, Asst Exec Dir 1977–87, Exec Dir UNFPA 1987–2000; Sec-Gen Int Conf on Population and Devt 1994; Pres Soc for Int Devt 1994–; Fellow *ad eundem*, Royal Coll of Obstetricians and Gynaecologists; Hon D HUM LITT (Johns Hopkins) 1989, (Brown) 1993, (Duke) 1995; Hon LL D (Wilfrid Laurier) 1995; Hon D SC (Michigan) 1996, (Claremont) 1996; Hugh Moore Award 1976; Women's Global Leadership Award 1994; Peace Award (UNA) 1994; Order of Merit, First Class (Egypt) 1994; Prince Mahidol Award 1995; Bruno H. Schubert-Stiftung Prize 1995. *Publications:* Population: National Family Planning Programme in Pakistan 1968, Population: The UNFPA Experience (ed) 1984, Population Policies and Programmes: Lessons Learned from Two Decades of Experience 1991, Making a Difference: Twenty-five Years of UNFPA Experience 1994; contribs to professional journals. *Leisure interests:* bridge, reading, theatre, travel. *Address:* United Nations Population Fund, 220 E 42nd St, 19th Floor, New York, NY 10017, USA. *Telephone:* (212) 297-5111; *Fax:* (212) 297-4911.

SADUR, Nina Nikolayevna; Russian playwright; b 15 Oct 1950, Novosibirsk; d of Nikolai Sadur. *Education:* Moscow Inst of Culture (Novosibirsk) and Moscow Literary Inst (workshop of V Rozov). *Career:* Librarian; literary activities started late 1970s; her works were forbidden for not satisfying ideological norms; work first published in magazine Sibirskiye Ogni; author of numerous plays produced in many theatres of Russia and other countries since 1990s; mem USSR Writers' Union 1989. *Publications:* Those Who Penetrated 1990, New Amazons 1991, Irons and Diamonds 1993, German (novel) 1997, Garden (collection of stories); Plays: Strange Baba, Chardym, My brother Chichikov, Go!!!!, Wonderful Signs. *Address:* Vagrius Publishers, Kazakova place 18, 107005 Moscow, Russian Federation. *Telephone:* (095) 785-09-63.

SÁEZ, Irene, BA; Venezuelan civil servant; b 1962. *Career:* Mayor of Chacao (a dist of Caracas) 1992–98; f political group Integration, Renovation and New Hope (IRENE) 1998; Cand Presidential Elections 1998; Miss Universe 1981. *Address:* c/o Edif Atrium, 6°, Calle Sorocaima c/c Avda Venezuela, El Rosal, Caracas, Venezuela.

SAFIEVA, Gulruhsor, BA; Tajikistan politician and poet; b 17 Dec 1947; m Rajabov Negmat; one s. *Education:* Tajik State Univ. *Career:* Gen Ed Universal Culture of Tadjikistan 1987; mem Supreme Soviet and Int Comm 1989–91; apptd Chair Int Tajik Culture Fund 1987; mem Presidium Russian Culture Fund 1991; Prize Youth of Tajikistan 1976; Prize Youth of USSR 1978. *Publications include:* Selected Poems 1983, 1984, 1985, 1987, Women of Mountains 1990. *Leisure interests:* tennis, growing flowers. *Address:* 734003 Dushanbe, Gogolstr 18/3, kv 7, Tajikistan. *Telephone:* (3772) 24-56-82.

SAFONOVA, Yelena Vsevolodovna; Russian actress; b 14 June 1956, Leningrad (now St Petersburg); d of Vsevolod Safonov; m. *Education:* All-Union Inst of Cinematography and Leningrad Inst of Theatre, Music and Cinema. *Career:* Actress Mosfilm Studio 1986–. *Films:* Return of Butterfly, Winter Cherries, Winter Cherries 2, Winter Cherries 3, Sofia Kovalevskaya, Secret of the Earth, Strange Call, Confrontation, Sleuth, Continuation of the Clan, Taxi Blues, Butterflies, Music for December, The President and His Woman, All Red; Black Eyes (David di Donatello Prize for Best Role, Italy) 1988. *Address:* Taganskaya pl 31/22, Apt 167, 109004 Moscow, Russian Federation. *Telephone:* (095) 278-07-36.

SAFWAT, Khadiga M., PH D; Sudanese sociologist; b 7 July 1937, Wad Medani; d of Mohammed and Galila Fahmi (née Samara) Safwat; m Mohammed Ibrahi Mohammed 1955; one s one d. *Education:* Unity High School, Univs of Cairo and Wales (Swansea, UK). *Career:* Lecturer Univ of Eduardo Mondlane, Maputo, Mozambique 1980–83, Univ of Algiers 1983–85; mem, Exec mem, Trustee, Consultant and Resource Adviser to numerous Arab, African, E and W European orgs; Co-Founder Sudanese Writers' and Artists' Fed 1965; f Sudanese Women's Co-operative 1968; Founder and Exec Dir Middle East and African Research Centre of Wales (MERAWEC); Co-Founder Gaza Community Health Programme 1989; Co-Founder Omdurman Nat Univ 1990; mem Bd of Black Labour Int; Hon Pres Org of Democratic Sudanese, UK and Ireland 1989–; Hon Research Fellow, Dept of Geography, Univ Coll of Swansea 1986. *Publications:* The Joys of Asia 1960, A Message to Polina Lomumba 1963, The Silence Curtain, on Portuguese Africa 1964, The Pharaohs and the Neo-Pharaohs: State Formation in the Nile Valley from Pristine to Modern 1992, The Ordeal of Flight: Capital and Political Islam in Sudan 1992; numerous publs in English, Arabic, Portuguese and French. *Leisure interests:* reading, walking, travel, music. *Address:* c/o University College of Swansea, MERAWEC, Dept of Geography, Singleton Park, Swansea SA2 8PP, UK. *Telephone:* (1792) 295647 (Office); (1792) 463014 (Home); *Fax:* (1792) 205556.

SAGAN, Françoise; French writer; b (Françoise Quoirez) 21 June 1935, Cajarc; d of Pierre and Marie (née Laubard) Quoirez; m 1st Guy Schoeller 1958 (divorced); m 2nd Robert Westhoff 1962 (divorced); one s. *Education:* Couvent des Oiseaux and Couvent du Sacré Cœur (Paris). *Career:* Writer 1954–; Prize from Fondation du Prince Pierre de Monaco 1985. *Publications include:* Novels: Bonjour tristesse (Prix des Critiques) 1954, Un certain sourire 1956, Dans un mois, dans un an 1957, Aimez-vous Brahms… 1959, La chamade 1965, Le garde du cœur 1968, Un peu de soleil dans l'eau froide 1969, Des bleus à l'âme 1972, Il est des parfums (jtly) 1973, Les merveilleux nuages 1973, Un profil perdu 1974, Réponses 1975, Des yeux de soie 1976, La femme fardée 1981, Musique de scène 1981, Un orage immobile 1983, De guerre lasse 1985, Un sang d'aquarelle 1987, Sarah Bernhardt ou le rire incassable 1987, La Laisse 1989, Les faux-fuyants 1991, Répliques 1992, …Et toute ma sympathie 1993, Evasion 1993, Un chagrin de passage 1994, le miroir égaré 1996; Plays: Château en Suède 1959, Les violons parfois… 1961, La robe mauve de Valentine 1963, Bonheur, impair et passe 1964, Le cheval évanoui 1966, L'écharde 1966, Un piano dans l'herbe 1970, Zaphorie 1973, Le lit défait 1977, Pol Vandromme 1978, Il fait beau jour et nuit 1978, Le chien couchant 1980, Un orage immobile 1983, L'excès contraire 1987; Scenario for ballet: Le rendez-vous manqué (jtly); Filmscripts: Dans un mois, dans un an, Landru (with Claude Chabrol) 1963; Songs: La valse, De toute manière; *Film:* Les fougères bleues (dir) 1976. *Address:* Editions Julliard, 24 ave Marceau, 75008 Paris, France (Office); 14600 Honfleur, France (Home).

SAGARRA, Eda, MA, D PHIL, LITT D, MRIA; Irish professor of Germanic languages; b 15 Aug 1933, Dublin; d of Kevin O'Shiel and Cecil Smiddy; m Albert Sagarra i Zacarini 1961; one d. *Education:* Loreto Convent (Bray and Foxrock), Univ Coll Dublin and Univs of Freiburg

and Zurich (Switzerland) and Vienna. *Career:* Jr Lecturer, Lecturer, Univ of Manchester, UK 1958–68; Special Lecturer in German History 1968–75; Prof of German Trinity Coll, Dublin 1975–, Dean of Visiting Students 1979–86, Prof Emer 1998–; Registrar of Dublin Univ 1981–86, Pro-Chancellor 1999–; Chair Irish Research Council for the Humanities and Social Sciences 2000–; mem Council Royal Irish Acad (Sec 1993–2000), Nat Council for Educational Awards 1991–96; mem Germanistische Kommission of German Research Council 1982–90; mem Bd Inst of Germanic Studies, Univ of London 1983–87; mem Academia Europaea 1991–, Quality Review Group 1998–, Max Planck Inst; awarded Bundesverdienstkreuz by Austria and Germany, Goethe Medal 1990; Jacob and Wilhelm Grimm Prize 1995. *Publications:* Tradition and Revolution 1971, A Social History of Germany 1648–1914 1977, Theodor Fontane: Der Stechlin 1986, Das Selbstverständnis der Deutschen 1991, Der deutsche Michel 1992, Literatur und Anthropologie um 1800 (ed, jtly) 1992, Companion to German Literature 1494 to the Present (jtly) 1997, Germany in the 19th Century: History and Literature 2001; scientific bibliographies and review essays on German women writers; articles on legal, social and literary history of servants in Germany. *Leisure interests:* golf (county golfer 1969–75), ornithology, cooking, European politics. *Address:* 5066 Arts Bldg, Trinity College, Dublin 2, Ireland (Office); 30 Garville Ave, Rathgar, Dublin 6, Ireland (Home). *Telephone:* (1) 608-1373 (Office); (1) 497-5967 (Home); *Fax:* (1) 677-2694 (Office); *E-mail:* irchss@hea.ie (Office); esagarra@tcd.ie (Home).

SÄGEBRECHT, Marianne; German actress; b Aug 1945, Starnberg. *Career:* Actress in German and American film productions; creator Opera Curiosa revue 1977; stage and TV appearances. *Films:* Die Schaukel 1983, Sugarbaby 1985, Crazy Boys, Bagdad Cafe 1988, Moon Over Parador 1988, The War of the Roses 1989, Rosalie Goes Shopping 1990, La Vida Lactea, Dust Devil, Mona Must Die, Martha and I, Erotique, All Men Are Mortal, Le roi des aulnes 1996.

SAGER, Krista; German politician. *Career:* Speaker of Exec, Bündnis 90/Die Grünen (Alliance 90/The Greens). *Address:* 53332 Bornheim-Roisdorf, Im Ehrental 2–4, Germany. *Telephone:* (228) 91660; *Fax:* (228) 9166199.

SAHGAL, Nayantara, BA; Indian writer; b 10 May 1927, Allahabad; d of Ranjit Sitaram and Vijaya Lakshmi Pandit; m 1st Gautam Sahgal 1949 (divorced 1967); two d one s; m 2nd E. N. Mangat Rai 1979. *Education:* Wellesley Coll (MA, USA). *Career:* Writer-in-Residence Southern Methodist Univ, Dallas, TX, USA 1973, 1977; Adviser English Language Bd, Sahitya Akademi (Nat Acad of Letters) New Delhi; mem Indian Del to UN Gen Ass 1978; mem Nat Exec People's Union for Civil Liberties; mem Jury Commonwealth Writers' Prize 1990, Chair Eurasia Region 1991; Annie Besant Memorial Lecture (Banares Hindu Univ) 1992; Arthur Ravenscroft Memorial Lecture (Univ of Leeds) 1993; Fellow Radcliffe Inst, Harvard Univ, MA, USA 1976, Woodrow Wilson Int Center for Scholars, Washington, DC 1981–82, Nat Humanities Center, NC, USA 1983–84; Foreign Hon mem American Acad of Arts and Sciences 1990; Hon D LITT (Leeds) 1997. *Publications:* Prison and Chocolate Cake 1954, A Time to Be Happy (Book Soc Recommendation) 1958, From Fear Set Free 1962, This Time of Morning 1965, Storm in Chandigarh 1969, History of the Freedom Movement 1970, The Day in Shadow 1972, A Situation in New Delhi 1977, A Voice for Freedom 1977, Indira Gandhi's Emergence and Style 1978, Indira Gandhi: Her Road to Power 1982, Rich Like Us (Sinclair Fiction Prize 1985, Sahitya Akad Award 1987) 1985, Plans for Departure (Commonwealth Writers' Prize 1987) 1986, Mistaken Identity 1988, Relationship: Extracts from a Correspondence 1994, Point of View 1996, Before Freedom: Nehru's Letters to His Sister 1909–1947 (ed) 2000. *Leisure interests:* walking, reading, music, meditation. *Address:* 181B Rajpur Rd, Dehra Dun 248009, Uttaranchal, India. *Telephone:* (135) 734-278.

SAHLIN, Mona; Swedish politician; b 9 March 1957, Sollefteå; m Bo Sahlin; three c. *Education:* Correspondence School. *Career:* Swedish Co-operative Movt 1978–80; Sec State Employees' Union 1980–82; Govt Rep Bd of Swedish Sports Confed 1983–90; mem Riksdag (Parl, Swedish Social Democratic Lab Party—SDAP), Chair Cttee on Working Hours; mem Bd Centre for Working Life 1982–90; Minister of Lab 1990–91; Sec-Gen SDAP 1992–94; Deputy Prime Minister and

Minister with Special Responsibility for Equality Issues 1994–95; self-employed 1995–98; Minister, Ministry of Industry, Employment and Communications 1998–; Govt Rep Bd of Swedish Sports Confed 1983–90; mem Bd Centre for Working Life 1982–90. *Address:* Ministry of Industry, Employment and Communications, 103 33 Stockholm, Sweden. *Telephone:* (8) 405 39 91 (Office); (8) 718 06 28 (Home); *Fax:* (8) 405 39 99 (Office); (8) 718 48 77 (Home); *E-mail:* registrator@industry.ministry.se (Office).

SAIKALI, Nadia; Lebanese artist; b 8 Dec 1936, Beirut. *Education:* Lebanese Acad of Fine Arts, Nat School of Fine Arts (Paris) and Grande Chaumière Acad. *Career:* Prof of Painting, Acad of Fine Arts 1962–74, Inst of Fine Arts, Univ of Lebanon 1965–74; scholarship to study art of mural tapestry, Paris 1974–76; solo exhibitions in Frankfurt and Marburg, Germany 1964, Paris 1964, 1973; group exhibitions in Moscow, Belgrade, Rome, London, Belfast (UK), Brussels, USA, Germany, Tokyo, Paris Biennale 1961, 1963, Alexandria Biennale (Egypt) 1962, São Paolo Biennale (Brazil) 1965; exhibition of kinetic works 1970.

SAINT-CRIQ, Régine Edith Gabrielle Eugénie; French civil servant and politician; b 31 May 1938, Murviel-les-Béziers; d of Jean and Jeanne (née Chagrigues) Albrand; m Roland Saint-Criq 1959; three d. *Career:* Controller Postes, Télécommunications et Télédiffusion (PTT) 1962–74; Insp France Télécom 1975–81; mem Dept Office and of the Exec Cttee, Confédération française démocratique du travail (CFDT) 1980; Spokesperson for Minister Del of Trade and Artisan Industries 1981–83; Tech Adviser to Minister of Overseas Depts and Territories 1983–84, to Minister of Postal Services and Telecommunications 1984–86; Municipal Councillor for Meudon 1983–95; mem Exec Cttee PS 1989–94; Regional Councillor for Ile de France 1986–92; Rep to Ombudsman of the Repub 1986–91; Pres Asscn Parité, mem Observatoire de la Parité; Chevalier de l'Ordre Nat du Mérite. *Publication:* Vol au-dessus d'un nid de machos (jtly) 1993. *Leisure interests:* reading, cinema, theatre, opera, nature, travel, tennis. *Address:* Observatoire de la parité, 31 rue Le Peletier, 75009 Paris, France (Office); 17 rue du Val, 92190 Meudon, France (Home). *Telephone:* (5) 46-26-65-78 (Home).

SAINT-PHALLE, Niki de; French artist; b 29 Oct 1930, Neuilly-sur-Seine; m Harry Mathews 1948 (separated 1960); two d; partner Jean Tinguely since 1960. *Education:* Convent of Sacré Cœur (New York). *Career:* Numerous one-woman shows in Paris, New York (USA), London, Amsterdam, Brussels, Munich, Zurich and Geneva (Switzerland), Tokyo, etc 1961–; retrospective exhibitions at Kunstverein (Düsseldorf, Germany) 1968, Kunstverein (Hanover, Germany) 1969, Kunstmuseum (Lucerne, Switzerland) 1969, Centre Nat d'Art et de Culture Georges Pompidou (Paris, and touring) 1980; participant in group exhibitions including Paris Biennale 1963, Dada, Surrealism and Their Heritage (Museum of Modern Art, New York) 1968, The Figurative Tradition (Whitney Museum, New York) 1980; works feature in public collections including Centre Nat d'Art et de Culture Georges Pompidou, Stedelijk Musuem (Amsterdam), Whitney Museum (New York) and Moderna Museet (Stockholm); work includes painting, 'Nana' sculptures, object-reliefs and assemblages, theatre sets, films and outdoor sculptures. *Address:* c/o Gimpel Fils, 30 Davies St, London W1Y 1LG, UK; L'Auberge du Cheval-Blanc, 91840 Soisy-sur-Ecole, Essones, France (Home).

SAKS, Judith-Ann, BFA; American artist; b 20 Dec 1943, Anniston, AL; d of Julien and Lucy-Jane (née Watson) Saks; m Haskell Irvin Rosenthal 1974; one s. *Education:* Sophie Newcomb Coll (Tulane Univ of Louisiana), Univ of Houston, Rice Univ (Houston, TX), Museum of Fine Arts (Houston) and Texas Acad of Art. *Career:* Curator of Perm Student Art Collection, Univ of Houston 1968–72; artist 1967–; solo exhibitions include Scenes from the World of Judith-Ann Saks (Bertha Alice Campus, Houston, TX), With Emphasis on Animals (Houston Cen Library, TX), Paintings of the Port and City of Houston (The World Trade Club, Houston, TX), Scenes of Houston (M. D. Anderson Hosp, Houston, TX), In Celebration of Houston's 135th Birthday (Bank of the Southwest, Houston, TX), Windows of Houston (The Alley and 2131 Galleries, Houston, TX); several jt exhibitions; comms include M. D. Anderson Library (Univ of Houston, TX), Port of Houston's American Revolution Bicentennial Project (six historical oil paintings), Roberts Steamship Agency (New Orleans, LA, painting now in the Peninsular and Orient Museum, London), L. B. Johnson Manned Space Center Exhibition Hall, Univ of Houston Permanent Art Collection, etc; many TV and radio appearances. *Address:* c/o 2215 Briar Branch Drive, Houston, TX 77042, USA.

SALAMON, Julie; American journalist and film critic. *Career:* Film critic The Wall Street Journal. *Publication:* The Devil's Candy, Facing the Wind: A True Story of Tragedy and Reconciliation 2001. *Address:* The Wall Street Journal, 200 Liberty St, New York, NY 10281-1099, USA.

SALCUDEAN, Martha Eva, B SC, M ENG, PH D; Canadian (b Romanian) professor of mechanical engineering; b 26 Feb 1934, Cluj, Romania; d of Edmund and Sarolta (née Hirsch) Abel; m George Salcudean 1955; one s. *Education:* Univs of Cluj and Braşov (Romania) and Ottawa. *Career:* Mechanical Engineer Armatura, Cluj 1956–63; Sr Research Officer Heat Transfer Lab, Nat Research Inst of Metallurgy, Bucharest 1963–75; part-time Lecturer Polytechnic Inst, Bucharest 1967–75; emigrated to Canada 1976, natualized 1979; sessional Lecturer Univ of Ottawa 1976–77, Asst Prof 1977–79, Assoc Prof 1979–81, Prof 1981–85; Prof and Head Dept of Mechanical Eng, Univ of British Columbia 1985–93, Assoc Vice-Pres of Research 1993–96, Vice-Pres for Research (acting) 1995, Weyerhauser Industrial Research Chair in Computational Fluid Dynamics 1996–; mem Grant Selection Comm for Mechanical Eng (Natural Sciences and Eng Research Council of Canada), Nat Advisory Panel to Ministry of Science and Tech on Advanced Industrial Materials 1990, Governing Council Nat Research Council, Defence Science Advisory Bd (Dept of Nat Defense); Fellow Canadian Acad of Eng, Royal Soc of Canada; Gold Medal, British Columbia Science Council 1991; Killam Research Prize, Univ of British Columbia; Commemorative Medal 125th Anniversary of Canadian Confed 1993; Julian C. Smith Medal, Eng Council of Canada 1994–95; Killam Memorial Award for Eng 1998; Order of BC 1998. *Publications:* Fluid Flow and Heat Transfer 1975; over 80 papers, contribs to professional journals. *Leisure interests:* modern history, music. *Address:* University of British Columbia, Dept of Mechanical Engineering, 2324 Main Mall, Vancouver, BC V6T 1Z4, Canada (Office); 1938 Western Parkway, Vancouver, BC V6T 1W5, Canada (Home). *Telephone:* (604) 822-2732 (Office); *Fax:* (604) 822-2005 (Office); *E-mail:* msal@unixg.ubc.ca.

SALINA, Elisabeth; Swiss business executive; b 1955. *Career:* Fmr lawyer; Chair Soc Générale de Surveillance (world's largest trade inspection and testing org) 1989–98, Chair Exec Bd 1994–98, Dir 1998–2001. *Address:* c/o Société Générale de Surveillance SA, 1 place des Alpes, BP 2152, 1211 Geneva 1, Switzerland. *Telephone:* (22) 739-91-11; *Fax:* (22) 739-98-86; *Internet:* www.sgs.com.

SALLIER, Marina, D SC; Russian geologist; b 19 Oct 1934. *Education:* Leningrad State Univ (now St Petersburg). *Career:* Mem staff Inst of Geology and Precambrian Geochronology, Leningrad (now St Petersburg) 1957–90; Co-Leader Leningrad Popular Front 1988–90; Co-Chair Democratic Russia 1992; mem St Petersburg City Council 1990–93, Chair Food Comm 1990–92, Rep to Supreme Council of Russia 1992–93; Founder and Leader Free Democratic Party of Russia 1990; Founder, Pres European Future for Russia org 1996–; mem Council Transformation of Motherland org; organized competition to develop a programme for the reform of local self-govt 1994–95; mem Public Chamber of the Pres of Russia 1995–96; has published over 100 research papers and six monographs; refused to be nominated for the State Prize 1983; Govt Awards: Medal to commemorate the 250th anniversary of St Petersburg, Veteran of Labour of the USSR Medal, 900 Days: Badge for a Resident of Besieged Leningrad; numerous other awards and honours. *Leisure interests:* history, crosswords, computer games, films, theatre, records. *Address:* 127018 Moscow, ul Streletskaya 6, kv 28, Russian Federation. *Telephone:* (095) 289-40-50; *Fax:* (095) 289-4050.

SALOTE MAFILE'O PILOLEVU TUKU'AHO TUITA, Princess; Tongan royal and organization executive; b 17 Nov 1951; d of King Taufa'ahau Tupou IV and Queen Halaevalu Mata'aho; m Capt Ma'ulupekotofa Tuita 1976. *Career:* Head of Tongasat (Tongan satellite-orbit leasing agency). *Address:* The Palace, POB 6, Nuku'alofa, Tonga.

SALZMAN, Pnina; Israeli pianist; b 1923, Tel-Aviv; m Igal Weissmann 1947; one d. *Education:* Ecole Normale de Musique and Conservatoire Nat de Musique (Paris). *Career:* Gave first concert in Paris at the age of 12; has since given concerts in Israel, Japan, fmr USSR, S Africa, Australia, New Zealand, France, UK, Belgium, Denmark, Sweden, Norway, Finland, USA; has worked with Sir Malcolm Sargent, Charles Munch and Koussevitsky; over 300 concerts with Israeli orchestras and regular performances with orchestras all over the world; fmr Prof of Piano Tel-Aviv Univ. *Leisure interests:* gardening, painting, graphology. *Address:* 20 Dubnov St, Tel-Aviv, Israel. *Telephone:* (3) 261993.

SAMARAS, Zoe, BS, MA, PH D; Greek professor of French literature; b 1935, Karpathos; d of Constantinos and Maria Malaxos; m Nicholas Samaras 1960 (died 1981); one s one d (deceased). *Education:* Columbia Univ (NY, USA). *Career:* Lecturer of French Columbia Univ 1960; Lecturer City Univ of New York, USA 1965, Asst Prof of French and French Literature 1968; Prof of French Literature and Theory of Literature Aristotle Univ of Thessaloniki 1978, Chair Dept of French Literature 1978–92, Chair Grad Program of French Literature; Visiting Prof of Theory of Literature Univ of Athens 1987, 1995, 1998; Phi Beta Kappa 1959; Silver Medal of the City of Paris 1988; Officier de l'Ordre Nat du Mérite (France) 1988, Montaigne Int Award 1992. *Publications include:* The Comic Element of Montaigne's Style 1971, L'Enfant du Taygète 1974, Le Règne de Cronos 1983, Text Perspectives (in Greek) 1987, Montaigne: Espace Voyage Ecriture (ed) 1995, Approaches bachelardienne des œuvres littéraires (ed) 1996, Simulation of Theatrical Discourse (in Greek) 1996, Miltos Sahtouris (in Greek) 1997; Poetry (in Greek): For Maria 1991, Days of Dryness 1994, The Passage of Eurydice 1997; numerous contribs to professional journals. *Leisure interest:* translation of poetry and plays. *Address:* Aristotle University of Thessaloniki, Faculty of Philosophy, 54006 Thessaloniki, Greece (Office); Vassilikou 10, 54636 Thessaloniki, Greece (Home). *Telephone:* (31) 212418 (Office); *Fax:* (31) 997491 (Office); *E-mail:* zsamara@frl.auth.gr.

SAMKOVÁ, Klára, DR JUR; Czech lawyer and politician; b 23 March in Brno; d of Bohumil Samek and Eva Samková. *Education:* Charles Univ (Prague). *Career:* Lawyer Prague City Hall and Adviser to Lord Mayor 1986–90; mem staff council and advocacy office specializing in Admin Law; Founder-mem Gypsy Civil Initiative 1989; mem Fed Ass, House of Nations 1990, mem Cttee for Law and Constitution, Special Standing Cttee for Human Rights and Minorities; Vice-Chair Fed Party for Gypsies (GCI); mem various charities and social orgs. *Leisure interests:* work, modern art. *Address:* Pštrossova 25, 110 00 Prague 1, Czech Republic. *Telephone:* (2) 204267.

SAMOILOVA, Tatyana Yevgeniyevna; Russian actress; b 4 May 1934, Leningrad (now St Petersburg); d of Eugeniy V. Samoilov and Zinaida I. Levina-Samoilova; one s. *Education:* Shchukin Theatre School. *Career:* Cannes Festival Special Prize for personal creative achievements in cinematography 1990; Merited Artist of the RSFSR; Order of the Badge of Honour. *Films include:* The Mexican 1955, The Cranes Are Flying (Cannes Festival Palm Award 1958) 1957, The Unsent Letter 1960, Leon Garros Looks for a Friend 1960, Alba Regia 1961, They Went East 1964, Anna Karenina 1968, Ykaterina (A Long Way to a Short Day) 1972, Masha (Ocean) 1974, Maria (Jewels for the Dictatorship of the Proletariat) 1976. *Address:* 103104 Moscow, Spiridonyevsky per 8/11, Russian Federation. *Telephone:* (095) 202-78-18.

SAMPERMANS, Françoise Clarisse, L ÈS L; French business executive; b 10 July 1947, Paris; d of Jacques and Jeannine (née Behot) Durand; one s one d. *Education:* Univ of Paris XIII. *Career:* Information Dept Transac SA 1974–78, Chapelle Darblay 1978–81; Dir of Communications Groupe Thomson 1982–83; Deputy Dir, later Dir of Communications Alcatel CIT 1984–87; Dir of Communications Compagnie Générale d'Electricité, Alcatel NV 1987–91; Dir-Gen Générale Occidentale (Alcatel Asthom group) 1991–95; Pres Dir-Gen Groupe Express 1992–95; Vice-Pres Québecor-Europe 1996–; Pres, Dir-Gen Nouvel Economiste 1999–; Dir-Gen Marianne and L'Evènement du Jeudi 1999–; Vice-Pres Nouvelles Messageries de la Presse Parisienne; Chevalier des Arts et des Lettres. *Address:* 18 rue Charles Silvestri, 94300 Vincennes, France.

SAMSOVA, Galina; Russian ballet dancer and producer; b 1937, Stalingrad (now Volgograd); m 1st Alexander Ursuliak; m 2nd André Prokovsky. *Education:* Ballet School (Kiev). *Career:* Dancer, then Soloist Kiev Ballet 1956, Canadian Ballet 1961; performed in Europe, the Far East and USA; has danced with the Festival Ballet 1964–73 and the New London Ballet 1977–79; Prin Dancer Birmingham Royal Ballet (fmrly Sadler's Wells) 1980–; Dance Mistress Royal Ballet and Royal Ballet School; Artistic Dir Scottish Ballet 1991–97; Gold Medal for Best Dancer, Paris Festival 1963. *Ballets include:* Cendrillon (cr, Paris) 1963, Sleeping Beauty, Nutcracker Suite, Giselle, Swan Lake, Anna Karenina; *Productions:* Sequence from Paquita 1980, Swan Lake 1983, 1991, 1995, Giselle 1986, Raymonda (Act III) 1991, Sleeping Beauty 1994, Swan Lake 1995. *Address:* Scottish Ballet, 261 West Princes St, Glasgow G4 9EE, UK.

SAMUEL, Molly Irene; British martial artist; b 12 Sept 1961, Paddington; d of Peter and Bertillier Samuel; one d. *Education:* Sarah Bonnel (Stratford, London). *Career:* Middle weight Karate Champion; English Champion 1985, 1986, 1988, 1989, 1991; British Champion 1986, 1987, 1988, 1990, 1991; European Champion 1986, 1987, 1989; World Silver Medallist 1986, Bronze Medallist 1990; World Cup Champion 1987, 1989; apptd Women's Nat Karate Coach 1989; Int Sportswoman of the Year, Sunday Times 1988. *Leisure interests:* badminton, circuit training, socializing. *Address:* c/o 45 Forest St, London E7 6HP, UK.

SAMUEL, Rhian, B MUS, MA, PH D; British composer and professor of music; b 3 Feb 1944, Aberdare, Wales; d of David Hopkin Samuel and Gwenllian Forey; m Curtis A. Price; one s. *Education:* Aberdare Girls' Grammar School, Univ of Reading (UK) and Washington Univ (St Louis, USA). *Career:* Teacher of Composition, USA 1970s, Univ of Reading 1984–95, currently Prof of Music City Univ, London; Co-Ed Grove Dictionary of Women Composers 1994–; Composer-in-Residence 31st Pontino Festival, Italy 1995, Presteigne Festival 1996; commissions from the BBC, Sinfonia 21, St Louis Symphony Orchestra; Judge London Sinfonietta/Women in Music Composers' Prize 1995, Nat Eisteddfod of Wales 1996; Mendelssohn Scholarship 2000; Trustee Britten–Pears Foundation 1997–; First Prize, Greenwich Festival 1979; ASCAP/Rudolph Nissim Award 1983; Britten Award 1996; Royal Philharmonic Prize 2001. *Compositions include:* Elegy-Symphony 1981, La Belle Dame sans Merci 1982, A Song for the Divine Miss C 1986, Lovesongs and Observations 1989, The White Amaryllis 1991, Clytemnestra 1994, Scenes from an Aria 1996, Daughters' Letters 1996, Dances of the Stream 1999, Tirluniau (Landscapes) 2000. *Leisure interests:* reading, gardening, travel. *Address:* Music Dept, City University, London EC1V 0HB, UK; 47 York Terrace East, London NW1 4PT, UK (Home). *Telephone:* (20) 7040-8277 (Office); *Fax:* (20) 7040-8576 (Office); *E-mail:* r.samuel@city.ac.uk; *Internet:* www.stainer.co.uk/samuel.

SAMUELS, Blossom Yvonne, MA; Jamaican town planner; b 15 Jan 1939; d of C. V. S. Adolphus and Amy Johnson-Adolphus; m Norman Samuels 1973; two s. *Education:* Univs of Toronto and British Columbia (Canada). *Career:* Planning Officer 1967–68; Asst Regional Planner 1980; Asst Govt Town Planner 1975, Deputy Town Planner 1976–79, Town Planner since 1979; Dir Urban Devt Corpn; Chair Town and Country Planning Authority; Acting Exec-Dir Jamaica Nat Heritage Trust 2000; participant at numerous confs; publs on town planning and urban devt. *Address:* Jamaica National Heritage Trust, Maima-Seville Heritage Park, St Ann, Jamaica. *E-mail:* jnht@wtjam.net.

SAMUELSSON, Marianne; Swedish politician; b 9 Dec 1945, Alingsås; d of John Johansson and Frida Emanuelsson; m Sven Samuelsson 1967; two d one s. *Career:* Caretaker 1968–88; mem Council of Reps, Green Party of Sweden 1983–84, mem Admin Cttee 1984–87, Parl Spokesperson and mem Bd 1992; mem Vårgårda Municipal Council 1985–88, 1991; mem Riksdag (Parl) 1988–91, 1994, mem Speaker's Conf, Nordic Council, Swedish Parl 1996 Intergovernmental Conf Cttee. *Address:* Riksdagen, 100 12 Stockholm, Sweden (Office); Skjul 5505, 441 94 Alingsås, Sweden (Home). *Telephone:* (8) 786 57 75 (Office); (322) 910 65 (Home); *Fax:* (8) 786 53 75 (Office); (322) 910 65 (Home); *E-mail:* marianne.samuelsson@riksdagen.se.

SAN GIACOMO, Laura; American actress; b 11 Nov 1962, New Jersey; m Cameron Dye. *Education:* Carnegie Mellon Univ (PA). *Career:* Actress in theatre and films; film debut in Sex Lies and Videotape 1989. *Plays include:* North Shore Fish, Beirut, The Love Talker, Italian American Reconciliation; *Films:* Sex Lies and Videotape (New Generation Award, LA Film Critics' Asscn) 1989, Pretty Woman 1990, Vital Signs 1990, Quigley Down Under, Once Around, Under Suspicion, Where the Day Takes You, Nina Takes a Lover, Stuart Saves His Family, Eat Your Heart Out 1997, Suicide Kings 1997, Apocalypse 1997, With Friends Like These... 1998, Mom's on the Roof; *TV appearances include:* Miami Vice, Crime Story, Spenser: For Hire, The Equalizer, Stephen King's The Stand (mini-series), Just Shoot Me. *Address:* More Medavoy Management, 7920 W Sunset Blvd, Suite 401, Los Angeles, CA 90046, USA.

SANCHEZ BORBON, Olga; Panamanian artist; b 14 June 1921, Bocas del Tore, Panamá. *Education:* Acad of Fine Arts (Barcelona, Spain). *Career:* Apptd Prof of Ceramics Centro de Arte y Cultura, Ministry of Educ 1974; solo exhibitions include Atenee Barcelonés 1960, 1964, Inst de Cultura Hispánica (Madrid) 1965, Casa de América (Granada) 1965, Chase Manhattan Bank (Panamá) 1976, Galería Habitante (Panamá) 1982, 1986, Arte Ol (Panamá) 1988; group exhibitions include III Bienal Hispanoamericana (Barcelona) 1955, Club Int Femenino de París (Barcelona) 1960, Colective Patrocinada por el IVU (Panamá) 1964, Instituto de Estudios Hispánicas (Barcelona) 1966, Cerámica (Valencia, Spain) 1971, Mujeres Universitarias (Panamá) 1978, Expro sién Plástica Centroamericano (Panamá) 1985, Visiones del Mundo de 8 Pintoras (Panamá) 1991. *Address:* Apdo 7839, Zona 9, Panamá, Panama. *Telephone:* 270187.

SANCHEZ-VICARIO, Arantxa; Spanish tennis player; b 18 Dec 1971, Barcelona; d of Emilio and Marisa Vicario. *Career:* Coached by Juan Núñez; won first professional title at Brussels 1988; winner, French Open Women's title 1989, 1994, 1998, Int Championships of Spain 1989, 1990, Virginia Slims Tournaments Newport 1991, Washington 1991, Canadian Open 1992, Australian Open 1992, 1993, US Open 1994; named Int Tennis Fed World Champion 1994; Silver Medal (doubles), Bronze Medal (singles) Olympic Games, Barcelona 1992; runner-up, Australian Open 1995, French Open 1995, Wimbledon, UK 1995, 1996; winner Women's Doubles (with Jana Novotná qv) Australian Open 1995, Wimbledon 1995; Silver Medallist Olympic Games, Atlanta, GA, USA 1996; Bronze Medal (doubles) Olympic Games, Atlanta 1996. *Leisure interests:* soccer, water-skiing, reading. *Address:* International Management Group, 1 Erieview Plaza, Suite 1300, Cleveland, OH 4414, USA.

SANDARS, Nancy Katharine, B LITT, FBA, FSA; British archaeologist; b 29 June 1914; d of Edward Carew and Gertrude Annie (née Phipps) Sandars. *Education:* Privately, Wychwood School (Oxford), Univ of London and St Hugh's Coll (Oxford). *Career:* Archaeological Research and European travel 1949–69, Middle-Eastern travel 1957, 1958, 1962, 1966; gives confs and lectures in field; excavations in UK and Greece. *Publications:* Bronze Age Cultures in France 1957, The Epic of Gilgamesh: an English version 1960, Poems of Heaven and Hell From Ancient Mesopotamia 1971, The Sea-Peoples: Warriors of the Ancient Mediterranean 1978, Prehistoric Art in Europe (2nd edn) 1985. *Leisure interests:* walking, translating, viewing pictures. *Address:* The Manor House, Little Tew, Oxford OX7 4JF, UK.

SANDBAEK, Ulla Margrethe; Danish politician; b 1 April 1943, Viborg. *Career:* Minister, State Church; MEP (Europe of Nations Group, JuniBevaegelsen) 1989, mem Cttee on Social Affairs, Employment and the Working Environment 1989, Cttee on Devt and Co-operation, Del for Relations with Transcaucasia. *Address:* European Parliament, rue Wiertz, 1047 Brussels, Belgium. *Telephone:* (2) 284-21-11; *Fax:* (2) 230-69-43.

SANDER, Jil (Heidemarie Jiline); German fashion designer; b 1944, Wesselburen. *Education:* Studied textile eng. *Career:* Stylist on fashion magazine; designs clothes for working women; owns own co Jil Sander AG, currently Chair; first boutique opened, Hamburg 1968; boutiques in Germany, Paris, Chicago (IL) and San Francisco (CA, USA) etc 1973–2000; first collection designed 1973; launched first fragrances, Woman Pure and Man Pure 1977; introduced menswear range Jan 1997. *Leisure interests:* modern art, gardening. *Address:* Jil Sander AG, Osterfeldstr 32–34, 22529 Hamburg, Germany. *Telephone:* (40) 22529.

SANDERS, Carol, MA, DU; British professor of French; b 31 Dec 1944, Cambridge; d of the late Ronald H. Sanders and Evelyn (née Bradbury) Payn; m Peter E. Figueroa 1978; one s one d. *Education:* Univs of Cambridge, London and Toulouse and Paris (France). *Career:* Lecturer in French Univ of Reading 1969–72, Univ of the West Indies, Jamaica 1972–76; Lecturer and Dir of Language Centre, Univ of Sussex 1977–84; Reader, then Prof and Head of Dept of Modern Languages ANU 1984–88; Prof in French Univ of Surrey 1988–; mem Asscn of French Language Studies, Pres 1981–83, Soc for French Studies; Fellow Inst of Linguists 1988; Chevalier des Palmes Académiques 1983. *Publications:* Cours de Français Contemporain: Niveau Approfondi (jtly) 1986, Franc Exchange (jtly) 1991, French Today (ed) 1992, Raymond Queneau 1994; writer for BBC and France Extra language courses. *Leisure interests:* travel, reading, writing. *Address:* University of Surrey, Dept of Linguistics and Int Studies, Guildford GU2 5XH, UK. *Telephone:* (1483) 300800; *Fax:* (1483) 302605; *E-mail:* c.sanders@surrey.ac.uk.

SANDERSON, Tessa, OBE; British athlete and broadcaster; b 14 March 1956, Jamaica. *Education:* Bilston Coll of Further Educ. *Career:* Competed in six Olympic Games from Montréal, Canada 1976, through to Atlanta, GA, USA 1996; three times Commonwealth Javelin Champion including 1978; Silver Medal for Javelin European Championships 1978; Gold Medallist Javelin (Olympic record), Olympic Games, Los Angeles, CA, USA 1984, came Fourth in Javelin, Olympic Games, Barcelona, Spain 1992, competed Olympic Games, Atlanta 1996; European Cup Title 1991; Gold Medal World Cup 1992; sports newsreader for Sky News (TV) 1989–92; Bd mem English Sports Council 1998–; Patron Disabled Olympics; numerous TV appearances; Hon Fellow Wolverhampton Polytechnic; Hon B SC (Birmingham). *Publication:* My Life in Athletics (autobiog) 1985. *Leisure interest:* cardio-funk (low impact aerobic exercise workout). *Address:* c/o Derek Evans, 68 Meadowbank Rd, Kingsway, London NW9, UK. *E-mail:* tessa@tprmplus.freeserve.co.uk (Office).

SANDLER, Bernice Resnick, ED D; American association executive; b 3 March 1928, New York; d of Abraham Hyman and Ivy (née Ernst) Resnick; two d. *Education:* Brooklyn Coll (NY), City Coll of New York and Univ of Maryland. *Career:* Head Action Cttee for Fed Contract Compliance, Women's Equity Action League 1970–71, mem Educ and Legal Defense Fund 1980–, Trustee 1974–80; Educ Specialist US House of Reps, Washington, DC 1970; Dir Project on Status and Educ of Women, Asscn of American Colleges 1971–91; Ed On Campus With Women 1971–91, About Women on Campus 1991–; Sr Assoc Centre for Women Policy Studies 1991–94; Sr Scholar-in-Residence Nat Asscn for Women in Educ, Washington, DC 1994; Visiting Lecturer Univ of Maryland 1968–69; mem Advisory Bd New Jersey Project Inst for Research on Women, Rutgers Univ, NJ 1987–; mem Bd Dirs Women's Policy Studies 1972–, Exec Cttee Inst for Educational Leadership 1982–87 (mem Advisory Cttee 1987–), Equality Center 1983–, Evaluation and Training Inst (CA) 1980–; Hon LL D (Bloomfield Coll) 1973, (Hood Coll) 1974, (Rhode Island Coll) 1980, (Colby-Sawyer Coll) 1984, (Goucher Coll) 1991; Hon LHD (Plymouth State Coll) 1992, (Wittenberg) 1993; Hon LHD (Grand Valley State Coll) 1974; Athena Award (Intercollegiate Asscn Women's Studies) 1974; Elizabeth Boyer Award (Women's Equity Action League) 1976; Rockefeller Public Service Award (Princeton Univ, NJ) 1976; One of 100 Most Powerful Women (Washington Magazine, DC) 1982; Women Readers' Choice Honours (Washington Woman Magazine, DC) 1987; Woman of Distinction Award (Nat Asscn of Women in Educ) 1991; Georgina Smith Award (American Asscn of Univ Professors) 1992; Woman of Achievement (Turner Broadcasting System) 1994. *Publications:* Sexual Harassment on Campus: A Guide for Administrators, Faculty and Students (co-ed) 1996, The Chilly Classroom Climate: A Guide to Improve the Education of Women (jtly) 1996. *Address:* National Association of Women in Education, 1350 Connecticut Ave, NW, Suite 850, Washington, DC 20036, USA.

SANDOR, Anna, BA; Canadian (b Hungarian) scriptwriter; b Budapest, Hungary; d of Paul and Agnes Elizabeth (née Laszlo) Sandor; m William Gough 1981; one d. *Education:* Harbord Coll Inst (Toronto) and Univ of Windsor. *Career:* Lecturer in Writing for TV Summer Inst of Film, Ottawa; held screenwriting workshops; Co-Chair Crime Writers of Canada 1985–86; mem Asscn of Canadian TV and Radio Artists (ACTRA) Writers' Council 1985, Acad of TV Arts and Sciences, Writers' Guild of America and Canada; Prix Anik 1981, 1985, 1986, 1989; ACTRA for Best Writer Original Drama award 1986; Chris Plaque for Best Script (Columbus Film Festival) 1989; Humanitas Award 1993. *Productions:* Films: A Population of One 1980, Charlie Grant's War 1985, The Marriage Bed 1986, Mama's Going to Buy You a Mockingbird 1987–88, Martha, Ruth and Edie (jtly) 1988, Two Men 1988, Tarzan in Manhattan 1989, Stolen: One Husband 1990, Miss Rose White (Emmy nomination) 1992, A Stranger in the Family 1993, The Anissa Ayala Story 1993, Amelia Earhart: The Final Flight 1994; Series: King of Kensington 1975–80, Seeing Things (jtly) 1983–85, Running Man 1982–83, High Card 1982–83, Danger Bay 1986–88, Tarzan (exec producer) 1991. *Leisure interests:* reading, music, ballet. *Address:* c/o Steve Weiss, William Morris Agency, 151 S El Camino Drive, Beverly Hills, CA 90212, USA.

SANGARE, Oumou; Malian singer and songwriter; b 1968, Bamako; d of Aminata Diakhite; m Ousmane Haidara; one s. *Career:* Began singing aged five; first performance Stade des Omnisports, Bamako aged six; fmr mem Nat Ensemble of Mali, Djoliba percussion group 1986–89 (tour of Europe 1986); singer with own group 1989–; sings in wassoulou style; concerts and tours in Mali, W Africa, Europe, New Morning jazz club, Paris, Netherlands, Switzerland, Cen Park, New York; has been featured on BBC Radio 1, and on TV in The Late Show, BBC2; campaigns for women's rights in Mali; numerous African music and other awards, including Performance of the Year 1993. *Recordings include:* Moussolou (Women, Award for Best-Selling African Album of the Year) 1989, Ko Sira (Marriage Today, European World Music Album of the Year 1993), Worotan (Ten Kola Nuts—the traditional bride-price in Mali) 1996. *Address:* c/o World Circuit Records, 106 Cleveland St, London W1P 5DP, UK. *Telephone:* (20) 7383-4907; *Fax:* (20) 7383-4908; *E-mail:* oumou@worldcir.domon.co.uk; *Internet:* www.demon.co.uk/andys/worldcir.html.

SANGER, Ruth Ann, PH D, FRS; British medical research scientist; b 6 June 1918, Southport, Qld, Australia; d of Hubert Sanger and Katharine M. (née Cameron) Ross; m Robert Russell Race 1956 (died 1984). *Education:* Abbotsleigh (Sydney) and Univs of Sydney and London. *Career:* Mem of scientific staff, Red Cross Blood Transfusion Service, Sydney 1941–46; staff mem MRC Blood Group Unit, Lister Inst, London 1946–83, Dir 1973–83; Hon MD (Helsinki) 1990; jt recipient Karl Landsteiner Award, American Asscn of Blood Banks 1957, Philip Levine Award, American Soc of Clinical Pathologists 1970; recipient Gairdner Award (Toronto) 1972, Oliver Memorial Award 1973. *Publications:* Blood Groups in Man (jtly, six edns) 1950–75; numerous papers on blood groups in professional journals. *Address:* 22 Vicarage Rd, E Sheen, London SW14 8RU, UK. *Telephone:* (20) 8876-1508.

SANIN DE RUBIO, Noemi, LL D; Colombian diplomatist and politician; b 5 June 1949, Medellín; d of Jaime Sanin Echeverri and Noemi Posada de Sanin; m Mario Alberto Rubio; one d. *Education:* Pontificia Univ Javeriana (Bogotá). *Career:* Fmr Minister of Communications, of Foreign Affairs; fmr Amb to Venezuela, to UK 1994; law practice; Pres Corporación Colmena, Corporación Financiera Colombiana, Instituto Colombiano de Ahorro y Vivienda; mem Bd of Dirs Interamerican Savings and Loan Union, Asociación Bancaria de Colombia, Administración Postal Nacional, Instituto Nacional de Radio y Televisión, etc; mem Peace Comm; Exec of the Year, Junior Chamber 1983; Order of Zurriago 1983; Officier de l'Ordre Nat du Mérite (France) 1986; Order of Isabel la Católica (Spain); Kt Commdr of the Military Order of Venezuela; Gonzalo Jiménez de Quesada Award for services rendered to the City of Bogotá.

SANTAELLA, Irma Vidal, LL B, BA, JD; American judge; b 4 Oct 1924, New York; d of Rafael and Sixta (née Thillet) Vidal; m Mr Santaella; one s one d. *Education:* Modern Business Coll (Puerto Rico), Hunter Coll and Brooklyn Law School (New York). *Career:* Self-employed accountant 1955–61; called to the Bar, NY 1961; civil practice 1961–63,

1966–68; Deputy Commr New York City Dept of Corrections 1963–66; mem New York State Human Rights Appeal Bd 1968–73, Chair 1974–83; Justice New York State Supreme Court (Bronx Co) 1983–94; Congressional cand for Democratic Primary 1966–68, Nat Conf Del 1968, 1972, 1976, 1980; f Legion of Voters, Nat Fed of Puerto Rican Women Inc, Nat Asscn for Puerto Rican Civil Rights Inc; Chair New York Chapter of Puerto Rican Cancer Asscn 1974–; mem Bd Metropolitan Women's Bar Asscn, Planned Parenthood Inc 1968–69; Hon D JUR (Connecticut) 1990; has recieved more than 100 honours and awards including Key to Cities of San Juan (Puerto Rico) 1967 and East Chicago 1968, Annual Civic Award, Instituto de Puerto Rico 1972, Nat Puerto Rican Coalition Life Achievement Award 1990, Nat Council of Women's Life Achievement Award (Washington, DC) 1991. *Address:* Supreme Court of the State of New York, 60 Center St, New York, NY 10007, USA (Office); 853 Seventh Ave, Manhattan, NY 10019, USA (Home). *Telephone:* (212) 374-4508 (Office).

SANTANDER, Teresa, PH D; Spanish librarian; b 11 June 1925, Salamanca. *Education:* Univ of Salamanca. *Career:* Instructor in Greek Language, Instituto Nacional de Enseñanza Media 'Lucia de Medrano', Salamanca 1949–50; Asst Archives, Libraries and Museums, Univ of Salamanca 1955, Librarian 1960–74, Dir of Library and Archives 1974–90; mem of Corps of Professional Archivists, Librarians and Archaeologists 1958; Dir León Public Library and León Libraries Prov Co-ordinating Centre 1958–60; mem Centro de Estudios Salmantinos. *Publications include:* Indice de médicos españoles (jtly) 1957, La creación de la cátedra de Cirugía en la Universidad de Salamanca 1965, Cristóbal de Vega en la Universidad de Salamanca 1968, Un manuscrito desconocido de Plotino en Salamanca 1969, Hipócrates en España (16th century) 1971, La iglesia de San Nicolás y el antiguo teatro anatómico de la Universidad de Salamanca 1983, Escolares médicos en Salamanca 1984, Publicaciones periódicas salmantinas existentes en la Biblioteca Universitaria 1793–1981 1986, Un autógrafo del doctor Francisco López de Villalobos 1987, Incunables de la Biblioteca Universitaria de Salamanca 1990, Antonio Tovar: Bibliografía y recuerdos 1911–1985 1990, Fuentes para una historia de la Universidad de Salamanca 1990, Aproximación a la biblioteca de don Diego de Covarrubias 1992, El Hospital del Estudio (Asistencia y hospitalidad de la Universidad de Salamanca 1413–1810) 1993, La imprenta en el siglo XVI 1994, El Doctor Cosme de Medina y su biblioteca (1551–1591) 1999, La biblioteca de Don Diego de Covarrubias y Leyva, obispo de Ciudad Rodrigo y de Segovia, y Presidente del Consejo de Estado (1512–1577) 2000. *Address:* Calle de Zamora 44, 1°, 37002 Salamanca, Spain.

SANTIAGO, Miriam Defensor; Philippine politician; b 1946. *Career:* Fmr Judge and Head Comm on Immigration; fmrly Sec for Agrarian Reform; f People's Reform Party (PRP) 1991, Pres Cand 1992. *Address:* People's Reform Party (PRP), Metro Manila, Philippines.

SANTO, Akiko; Japanese politician; b 11 May 1942, Tokyo; d of Yoshiki and Hatsu Santo. *Education:* Bunka Gakuin Coll (Tokyo). *Career:* Film actress and singer 1953–74, appeared in over 70 films and made nine recordings; mem House of Councillors (Parl) 1974, Parl Vice-Minister for Environment, Chair Cttee on Foreign Affairs 1989; Minister of State for Science and Tech 1990–91; Vice-Pres Liberal Democratic Party (LDP) Cttee on Social Security 1991, mem Special Cttee on Global Environment 1991. *Publications include:* Ganbare, Nippon no otoktachi (Never say die, Japanese men!) 1974, Koseiha no setsuyaku: 175 no sakusens (175 highly original tactics for money saving) 1974. *Leisure interests:* music, sport. *Address:* 4-25-8 Komazawa, Setagaya, Tokyo, Japan (Home). *Telephone:* (3) 3421-0148 (Home); *Fax:* (3) 3502-8818 (Home).

SANTOS-OCAMPO, Perla, MD; Philippine executive; b 25 July 1931, Dagupan City; one s one d. *Education:* Univ of the Philippines and Case Western Reserve Univ (OH, USA). *Career:* Council mem ASEAN Paediatric Fed 1976–78; Nat Pres Philippine Paediatric Soc 1978–80, Chair Int Affairs Cttee 1978–88; Consultant to Minister of Health 1979–80; Chair Paediatrics Dept, Univ of the Philippines 1979–85; Pres Philippines Medical Asscn 1981–82; Chair Medical Asscn of the SE Asian Nations 1982–84, Sec-Gen 1984; Pres 17th Int Congress of Paediatrics 1983; Sec-Treas Int Soc of Tropical Paediatrics; Pres Int Paediatric Asscn; mem WHO Expert Advisory Panel on Maternal and

Child Health. *Publication:* Child Health in the Philippines: a situational report (jtly) 1986. *Address:* c/o International Pediatric Association, Château de Longchamp, Bois de Boulogne, 75016 Paris, France.

SARABHAI, Mrinalini; Indian dancer and choreographer; b 11 May 1918, Madras (now Chennai); d of Shri and Ammu Swaminadham; m Vikram A. Sarabhai (deceased); one s one d. *Career:* Studied dance under Sri Meenakshi Sundaram Pillai; Founder and Hon Dir Darpana Acad of Performing Arts 1949–; Chair Handicrafts and Handloom Devt Corpn of Gujarat State, Friends of Trees; mem Sangeet Natak Acad, New Delhi, Fellow 1994; Hon Consultant, Nat Centre for Performing Arts, Bombay; Pres Alliance Française; mem Exec Cttee Int Dance Council 1990–; adviser to many arts and cultural insts in India; has written various works on a dance theme; Hon D LITT (Calcutta) 1979; first Indian recipient of the French Archives internationales de la danse; first woman to receive Vishwa Gurjari Award 1984; Deshikothama Award (Vishwa Bharati Univ Shantiniketan) 1987; Fellowship Award Kerala Acad of Arts 1990; Honor Summus Award, Watumull Foundation, Honolulu, HI, USA 1991; Life-long Service Award Dynasty Culture Club 1991; Vijay Shri Award from Int Friendship Soc of India 1991; Pandit Omkarnath Thakur Award, Gujarat Govt 1991; awarded the Padma Bhushan by Pres of India 1992; Scroll of Honour from Vice-Pres of India 1995; Kerala Kalamandalam Fellowship 1995; Kalidas Samman Award 1996. *Publications include:* Staging a Sanskrit Classic – Bhasa's Vision of Vasavadatta (jtly) 1992, one novel, textbook on Bharata Natyam, a book on various classical dance-dramas, children's books and articles in newspapers and journals. *Leisure interests:* reading, watching TV, writing, dancing, social work. *Address:* Darpana Academy of Performing Arts, Usmanpura, Ahmadabad 380 013, Gujarat, India. *Telephone:* (272) 445189; *Fax:* (272) 469101.

SARANDON, Susan Abigail, BA; American actress; b 4 Oct 1946, New York; d of Philip Leslie and Lenora Marie (née Criscione) Tomalin; m Chris Sarandon 1967 (divorced 1979); one d with Franco Amurri; partner Tim Robbins; two s. *Education:* Catholic Univ of America (Washington, DC). *Career:* Actress in plays, films and on TV. *Plays include:* An Evening with Richard Nixon 1972, A Coupla White Chicks Sittin' Around Talkin' 1980, Albert's Bridge, Private Ear, Public Eye, Extremities 1982; *Films include:* Joe 1970, Lady Liberty 1971, The Rocky Horror Picture Show 1974, Lovin' Molly 1974, The Great Waldo Pepper 1975, The Front Page 1976, Dragon Fly 1976, The Last of the Cowboys (co-producer) 1977, Pretty Baby 1978, King of the Gypsies 1978, Loving Couples 1980, Atlantic City (Acad Award nomination, Canadian Cinema Genie Award for Best Foreign Actress) 1981, Tempest (Best Actress Award, Venice Film Festival) 1982, The Hunger 1983, Buddy System 1984, Compromising Positions 1985, The Witches of Eastwick 1987, Bull Durham 1988, Sweet Heart's Dance 1988, A Dry White Season 1989, The January Man 1989, Through the Wire (narrator), White Palace 1990, Thelma and Louise 1991, Light Sleeper 1991, The Player 1992, Bob Roberts 1992, Lorenzo's Oil (Acad Award nomination) 1992, The Client (Acad Award nomination) 1994, Little Women 1994, Safe Passage 1994, Dead Man Walking (Acad Award for Best Actress 1996) 1995, The Celluloid Closet, James and the Giant Peach 1996, Illuminata 1998, Twilight 1998, Stepmom 1999, Anywhere But Here 1999, The Cradle Will Rock 1999; *TV appearances include:* A World Apart (series) 1970–71, Search For Tomorrow (series), F. Scott Fitzgerald and the Last of the Belles (film) 1974, June Moon, The Haunting of Rosalind (series) 1973, The Life of Ben Franklin, Owen Marshall, AD (mini-series) 1985, Mussolini and I 1985, Women of Valor 1986. *Address:* c/o Samuel Cohen, ICM, 40 W 57th St, New York, NY 10019, USA.

SARASWATHI, S., MA, PH D; Indian social scientist; b 24 Nov 1934, Madras (now Chennai); d of A. K. Srinivasan and S. Lalitha. *Education:* Nagpur Univ and Univ of Madras. *Career:* Worked with numerous research orgs; del to numerous confs; Dir Indian Council of Social Science Research, New Delhi. *Publications:* Minorities in Madras State 1974, The Madras Panchayat System: A Historical Survey 1973, Youth in India 1988; contribs to books and journals. *Leisure interest:* music. *Address:* Indian Council of Social Science Research, 35 Ferozeshah Rd, New Delhi 110 001, India. *Telephone:* (11) 382177; *Fax:* (11) 388037.

SARNE, Tanya, BA; British fashion designer; b 15 Jan 1945, London; d of Jean-Claude Gordon and Daphne Tucar; m Michael Sarne 1969 (divorced); one s one d. *Education:* Univ of Sussex. *Career:* Worked as a model then as a teacher, then briefly in film production; travelled extensively throughout S America and Europe; returned to England and set up co importing Alpaca wool knitted garments influenced by traditional Inca designs which launched career in 1970s; introduced Scandinavian labels In Wear and Laize Adzer to UK; est successful labels Miz 1978 and Ghost 1984; British Apparel Export Award for Womenswear 1993, 1995. *Leisure interests:* cooking, tennis. *Address:* Ghost, The Chapel, 263 Kensal Rd, London W10 5DB, UK. *Telephone:* (20) 8960-3121; *Fax:* (20) 8960-8374.

SARNOFF, Lili-Charlotte (Lolo); American/Swiss artist and sculptor; b 1 Sept 1916, Frankfurt, Germany; d of the late Willy and Martha (née Koch von Hirsch) Dreyfus; m Stanley Jay Sarnoff 1948 (deceased); one s one d. *Education:* Reimann Art School (Berlin) and Univs of Berlin and Florence (Italy). *Career:* Research Asst Harvard School of Public Health 1948–54; Research Assoc Nat Heart Inst, Bethesda, MD 1954–58; Pres Rodana Research Corpn, Bethesda, MD 1958–61; Vice-Pres Catrix Corpn, Bethesda, MD 1958–61; co-inventor of electrophenic respirator; inventor of flowmeter; Sculptor and inventor of FloLite light sculptures 1968–; solo exhibitions include Gallery Two (Woodstock) 1970, Int Art Mart (Basle) 1972, Alwin Gallery (London) 1980, La Galerie de l'Hôtel de Ville (Geneva) 1982, Centre Int d'art contemporain (Paris) 1985, Pfalzgalerie (Kaiserslautern, Germany) 1985, Gallery K (Washington, DC) 1982–85, 1987–91, Int Sculpture Congress (Washington, DC) 1990; works feature in perm collections including Nat Air and Space Museum (Washington, DC), Chase Manhattan Bank (New York), Israel Museum (Jerusalem), Nat Museum of Women in the Arts (Washington, DC), Kennedy Center (Washington, DC); Founder and Pres Art Barn, Arts for the Aging Inc 1988–, Ed newsletter 1988; numerous publications 1950–90; Gold Medal, Accademia Italia delle Arti e del Lavoro 1980. *Leisure interests:* skiing, tennis, opera, ballet, gardening. *Address:* 7507 Hampden Lane, Bethesda, MD 20814, USA. *Telephone:* (301) 656-6307; *Fax:* (301) 656-3698.

SARTIN, Pierrette Anne-Marie, L PH; French writer and former administrator; b 10 Nov 1911, Guéret, Creuse; d of Elie and Marcelle (née Refeuille) Sartin; two d. *Education:* Univs of Clermont-Ferrand and Lyons. *Career:* Writer 1939–; civil servant 1946–75; Asst to Sec of State for Civil Aviation 1953; Technical Adviser Comm on Productivity and Planning 1954–63; Special Adviser on Women and Young People at Work, OECD and BIT 1965–71; Visiting Prof Univ of Laval, PQ, Canada 1968, 1980; Vice-Pres Soc des gens de lettres 1968; mem PEN-Club, Asscn Int des Critiques Littéraires; Hon LITT D (Laval) 1980; Chevalier de la Légion d'Honneur. *Publications include:* Novels: Chroniques du Temps Passé (trilogy, prizes from Société des gens de lettres): Souvenirs d'une jeune fille mal rangée 1982, Un enfer bien convenable 1983, L'or de Mathieu Gaumard 1987, Belles-mères 1991; 23 vols of poems 1939–95 (several literary prizes, including Grand Prix, Maison de Poésie for Ce Destin Accepté 1973); Essays: La promotion des femmes (prize from Académie française) 1964, La femme libérée? 1968, Aujourd'hui la femme 1974; writer of numerous informative works. *Leisure interests:* reading, cinema. *Address:* 10 rue Saint-Lazare, 75009 Paris, France; 12 Le Prieuré, 77320 La Ferté-Gaucher, France. *Telephone:* (1) 48-74-87-79 (Paris); (1) 64-04-00-81 (La Ferté-Gaucher).

SASIAIN Y AZCUNE DE CALABRESE, María Palmyra, B SC; Argentine (b Spanish) biochemist (retd); b 15 Oct 1928, San Sebastián, Spain; d of Marcos Sasiain and María Azcune; m Roque Hugo Calabrese 1961. *Education:* Coll of Mar del Plata and Univ of Córdoba. *Career:* Pharmacist and Biochemist Univ of Córdoba, Argentina 1950–52, Asst Head Quantitative Analytical Chemistry 1951, Head Lab Technician Neurology Clinic 1953; Prof Nat Coll and Business School, Mar del Plata; Biochemist Mar del Plata Hosp 1954–59, Anabol Labs 1960–62; Propr and Technician Sasiain Pharmacy, Clinical Analysis Lab 1954–86; Jt Propr Fractures and Orthopaedic Clinic SA, Mar del Plata; mem Coll of Biochemists, Argentinian Asscn of Biochemists, Argentinian Fed of Univ Women (Pres 1984–87), Int Fed of Univ Women (Council mem 1985, mem Membership Cttee 1986–89, Second Triennium Vice-Pres 1989–95); recipient Quijote 1990 (Buenos

Aires), Hipocampo (Lions Club of Mar del Plata) 1991. *Leisure interests:* music, literature. *Address:* San Luis 2342, 7600 Mar del Plata, Argentina. *Telephone:* (23) 958304; *Fax:* (23) 519298.

SASIMA SRIVIKORN, Khunying, BA, MPA; Thai business executive; b 6 Oct 1937; m Mr Chalermbhand; four c. *Education:* St Joseph's Convent (Bangkok), Guildhall School of Music and Drama (UK) and Harvard Univ (USA). *Career:* Chair Exec Bd Thailand Carpet Manufacturing Co Ltd; Pres Golden Land Property Devt Co Ltd, Baan Chang Estate Co Ltd, Krabi Estate Co Ltd, Kirikhan Estate Co Ltd; Dir American Standard Sanitaryware (Thailand) Ltd, Bangna Cen Property Co Ltd, Prosperity Industrial Estate Co Ltd, Sri Dhana Finance and Securities Ltd; Man Dir Srivikorn School; mem Nat Legis Cttee 1991, Cttee Fed of Thai Industries, Bangkok Symphony Orchestra Foundation; Pres The Youth for Youth Aid Program, Ruamchit Nomklao Foundation for Youngsters; Fourth Class of The Most Illustrious Order of Chula Chom Klao 1983; Kt Commdr (Second Class) of the Most Exalted Order of the White Elephant 1985. *Leisure interests:* bridge, singing. *Address:* c/o Golden Land Property Development Co Ltd, 18/2-3 Sukhumvit 21 (Asoke Rd), Bangkok 10110, Thailand. *Telephone:* (2) 258-0423; *Fax:* (2) 258-0426.

SASS, Barbara; Polish film director and scriptwriter; b 14 Oct 1936, Łódź. *Education:* Film school (Łódź). *Career:* Began film career as Asst Dir; Film Dir 1972–; Vice-Pres Int Women in Film Asscn. *Films include:* Bez miłości (Without Love, Gold Medal and FIPRESCI Award, Mannheim) 1980, Debiutantka (The Outsider) 1981, Krzyk (The Scream, Award, San Sebastián 1983) 1982, Dziewczęta z Nowolipek (The Girls from Novlipki Street) 1985, Rajska jabłoń (The Paradise Appletree) 1985, W klatce (Caged) 1988.

SATPATHY, Nandini, MA; Indian politician, social worker and writer; b 9 June 1931, Cuttack; d of Kalindi Charan and Ratnamani Panigrahi; m Devendra Satpathy; two s. *Education:* Ravenshaw Coll (Cuttack). *Career:* Leader of the students' movts in Orissa and Sec Girl Students' Asscn 1948–49; took part in many welfare activities, organized and became Sec of the Orissa Women's Relief Cttee; organized Orissa br, Asscn of Social and Moral Hygiene in India 1958; Assoc of numerous nat welfare, literary and other orgs; mem Rajya Sabha (Council of States, Parl) 1962–72; Deputy Minister for Information and Broadcasting 1966–69, Deputy Minister attached to Prime Minister 1969–70, Minister of State for Information and Broadcasting 1971–72; Leader Indian film del to Moscow 1966, 1968 and Tashkent 1972; Del-Gen Conf UNESCO, Paris 1972; mem Indian Del to Commemorative Session UN, New York 1970; mem Orissa Legis Ass 1972–, Chief Minister of Orissa 1972–73, 1974–76; resgnd from Congress Party 1977; rejoined Indian Nat Congress 1988, Pres Orissa State Unit of Congress Party; Chair Orissa State Planning Bd, Govt of Orissa 1995–; mem All India Janata Party Exec Cttee, Orissa Legis Ass; Chair Orissa Flood and Cyclone Relief Cttee; mem Nat Young Women's Cttee; Chair Children's Film Soc, Bombay; mem Bd of Dirs Int Centre of Films for Children and Young People, Paris 1968–; Ed Dharitri (Mother Earth) and Kalana (Assessment) magazines; recipient numerous literary prizes. *Publications:* Short Stories: Ketoti Katha, Sapatodasi. *Leisure interests:* reading, writing. *Address:* 107 Surya Nagar, Bhubaneswar 751 003, Orissa, India. *Telephone:* (674) 400506.

SATTLER, Johanna Barbara, D PHIL; German psychologist; b 29 June 1953, Heidenheim. *Education:* Ludwig-Maximilians-Univ (Munich). *Career:* Chair German section of Org for Neural Research and Science (ONRS) 1984–, Adviser ONRS Foundation, Vaduz (Liechtenstein), mem ONRS Centre, Vaduz, Chair Advisory Bd on the devt of methods of testing the diagnosis of brain hemisphere lateralization; Head first German consulting and information centre for left-handed people and converted left-handers (brain-breaking), Munich 1985–; Project Leader, mem Asscn for Left-Handed People 1985–; public speaker on left-handedness and brain hemisphere lateralization; organizer of exhibition of works of left-handed artists 1986. *Publications:* Ikonographische und psychologische Aspekte der 'Seitigkeit' in der Kunst 1983, Psychologische Probleme durch Umschulung 1985, Umschulung der Händigkeit: Ein massiver Eingriff ins menschliche Gehirn 1986, Umgeschulte Linkshänder: Links vorbeitherapiert 1987, Das linkshändige Kind bei Schuleintritt 1989, Linkshänder in der Arztpraxis 1991, Expert advice: Linkshändig? Ein Ratgeber 1991, 'Beidhänder'

sind hirngeschädigt 1993, 2001, Das linkshändige Kind in der Grundschule 1993, Der umgeschulte Linkshänder oder Der Knoten im Gehirn 1995, 2000, Übungen für Linkshänder: Schreiben und Hantieren mit links 1996, 2001, Die Psyche des Linkshändigen Kindes. Von der Seele, die mit Tieren spricht 1999, 2000, Links und Rechts in der Wahrnehmung des Menschen. Zur Geschichte der Linkshändigkeit 2000. *Leisure interests:* art, travel. *Address:* c/o ONRS, Sendlinger Str 17, 80331 Munich, Germany. *Telephone:* (89) 268614; *Internet:* www .lefthander-consulting.org.

SAUNDERS, Dame Cicely (Mary Strode), OM, DBE, FRCP, FRCS; British hospice director; b 22 June 1918; d of Gordon Saunders and Mary Christian Knight; m Marian Bohusz-Szyszko 1980 (died 1995). *Education:* St Anne's Coll (Oxford), St Thomas's Hospital Medical School and Nightingale School of Nursing. *Career:* Medical Dir St Christophers's Hospice 1967–85, Chair 1985–; f Int Hospice Movt; numerous hon doctorates and fellowships. *Address:* St Christopher's Hospice, 51-59 Lawrie Park Rd, Sydenham, London SE26 6DZ, UK.

SAUNDERS, Jennifer; British actress and writer; b 1 July 1958; m Adrian Edmondson; three d. *Education:* Univ of Manchester and Cen School of Speech and Drama (London). *Career:* French and Saunders stage shows and TV series with Dawn French (qv); featured in The Full Wax (with Ruby Wax, qv) on TV 1991; opened shop with Dawn French. *Plays include:* An Evening with French and Saunders (nat tour) 1989, Me and Mamie O'Rourke 1993; *TV appearances include:* The Comic Strip: Strike, Consuela, Five Go Mad in Dorset, Supergrass, Ken, The Yob, Suzy etc, Girls on Top, French and Saunders (5 series), Absolutely Fabulous (with Joanna Lumley, qv) (Emmy Award 1993) 1992–96, 2001 Ab Fab The Last Shout 1996, Let Them Eat Cake 1999, Mirrorball 2000; *Films include:* The Supergrass 1984, Muppet Treasure Island 1996, Maybe Baby 2000. *Address:* c/o PFD, Drury House, 34–43 Russell St, London WC2B 5HA, UK.

SAUNIER-SEÏTÉ, Alice Louise, D ÈS L; French politician and former professor of geography; b 26 April 1925, Saint-Jean-le-Centenier; d of Daniel-René and Marie-Louise (née Lascombe) Saunier; m 1st Elie-Jacques Picard 1947; two s; m 2nd Jérôme Seïté (deceased). *Education:* Lycée de Tournon, Facultés des Lettres et des Sciences de Paris and Ecole Nat des Langues Orientales Vivantes. *Career:* Asst, then Researcher CNRS 1958–63, mem Perm Section 1967–70; Lecturer in Geography, Faculté des Lettres, Rennes 1963–65, Prof 1965–69; mem Nat Cttee for Scientific Research 1963–70; Dir Coll Littéraire Universitaire, Brest 1966–68, Dean Faculté des Lettres 1968–69; Dir Inst Universitaire de Technologie, Sceaux 1970–73; Prof Univ of Paris XI (Paris-Sud) 1969–73, Vice-Pres 1970–71; Rector Acad of Reims 1973–76; Prof of Geographic Org of Space, Conservatoire Nat des Arts et Métiers 1981–94; Municipal Councillor, Manso 1971–83, Deputy Mayor 1977–83; mem Political Bureau, Parti Républicain 1978–; Councillor, Paris 1983–; Sec of State for Univs 1976–77, Minister of Univs 1978–81, of the Family and Women's Affairs 1981; Pres Fondation de la Mutuelle des Elus Locaux 1991–98; Vice-Pres Nat Movt of Local Reps 1983–90, Pres 1990–98; Dir, Treas Council Inst Océanographique (Pres 1996–98); Dir then Vice-Pres Inst de barrages-réservoirs du Bassin de la Seine; Dir Vieux Paris Comm; mem Jury Prix Mémorial, French Inst 1995–; Pres Club des Explorateurs Français; Assoc mem Inst d'Egypte, Acad of Sciences (Iceland); Commdr de la Légion d'Honneur; Commdr des Palmes Académiques; Commdr des Arts et des Lettres; Médaille d'Or de la Jeunesse et des Sports; Medal of CNRS; Medal of Société de Géographie de Paris; decorations from Burkina Faso, Cameroon, Ivory Coast, Egypt, Gabon, Greece, Indonesia, Iceland, Luxembourg, Portugal and Sweden. *Publications:* Les vallées septentrionales du Massif de l'Oetztal 1963, En première ligne 1982, Remettre l'état à sa place 1984, Une Europe à la carte 1985, Le Cardinal de Tournon, le Richelieu de François 1er 1997, Les Courtenay, destin d'une illustre famille bourguignonne 1998. *Leisure interest:* fencing. *Address:* Institut de France, 23 quai de Conti, 75006 Paris, France (Office); 5 rue Visconti, 75006 Paris, France (Home).

SAUQUILLO PÉREZ DEL ARCO, Francisca, LL B; Spanish politician and lawyer; b 31 July 1943, Madrid; m Jacobo Echenerria-Torres 1969. *Education:* Univ Complutense de Madrid. *Career:* Fmr mem ORT (political party); PSOE Cand mayoral elections 1979; Senator and Deputy Autonomous Community of Madrid until 1994;

MEP (PSE, PSOE), mem Cttee on Devt and Co-operation, Jt Parl Cttee, EU–ACP Jt Ass; mem UN Univ of Peace in Cen America, Asscn of Women for Europe, MDPL (Movt for Peace, Disarmament and Freedom), PSOE Exec and Fed Cttee 1994–2000; Co-ordinator of the Socialist Group at the Devt Comm; European Woman of the Year 1994. *Publication:* Mirada de mujer (autobiog) 2000. *Address:* European Parliament, rue Wiertz, 1047 Brussels, Belgium. *Telephone:* (2) 284-54-74; *Fax:* (2) 284-94-74; *E-mail:* fsauquillo@europarl.eu.int.

SAVAGE, Wendy Diane, BA, MB, FRCOG, MRCS; British obstetrician and gynaecologist (retd); b 12 April 1935, Thornton Heath, Surrey; d of the late William George and Anne (née Smith) Edwards; m Miguel Richard Babatunde Savage 1960 (divorced 1973); two s two d. *Education:* Croydon High School for Girls, Girton Coll (Cambridge) and London Hosp Medical Coll. *Career:* Resident Fellow Harvard Univ, USA 1963–64; Medical Officer, Nigeria 1964–67; Registrar Obstetrics and Gynaecology, Kenya 1967–69, Royal Free Hosp, London 1970–71; work in venereology, abortion and family planning, Islington 1971–73; Specialist in obstetrics, gynaecology, family planning and venereology, Gisborne, New Zealand 1973–76; Lecturer in Obstetrics and Gynaecology London Hosp Medical Coll 1976–77, Sr Lecturer 1977–; Hon Consultant Royal London Hosp (suspended 1985, exonerated and reinstated 1986); Hon Visiting Prof Middlesex Univ 1991–2001; elected mem Gen Medical Council 1989–; Pres-Elect Medical Women's Fed 1991, Pres 1992; Hon D SC 2000. *Publications:* Hysterectomy 1982, Coping With Caesarean Section and Other Difficult Births (jtly) 1983, A Savage Enquiry: who controls childbirth? 1986, Caesarean Birth in Britain (jtly) 1993; numerous scientific papers. *Leisure interests:* novels, piano, travel. *Address:* 19 Vincent Terrace, London N1 8HN, UK. *Telephone:* (20) 7837-7635; *Fax:* (20) 7278-2881; *E-mail:* marsh.gate@talk21.com.

SAVELYEVA, Lyudmila Mikhailovna; Russian actress; b 24 Jan 1942, Leningrad (now St Petersburg). *Education:* Vaganova Ballet School (Leningrad). *Career:* Soloist, Kirorskiy (Mariinskiy) Theatre 1961–65; actress; People's Artist of the RSFSR 1985. *Films include:* War and Peace 1966–67, The Sunflowers 1971, The Seagull 1971, Flight 1971, The Headless Horseman 1973, Yulia Vrevskaya 1978, The Hat 1982, The Fourth Year of War 1983, Another's Belaya and Ryaboy 1986, White Rose – Emblem of Grief, Red Rose – Emblem of Love 1989, The Mystery of Nazd 1999; *Plays include:* The Price (Miller). *Address:* 103050 Moscow, Tverskaya ul 19, kv 76, Russian Federation. *Telephone:* (095) 299-99-34.

SAVILL, Rosalind Joy, CE, BA, FSA, FRSA; British art gallery director; b 12 May 1951, Hants; d of Guy Savill and Lorna Williams; one d. *Education:* Wycombe Abbey School, Chatelard School (Montreux) and Univ of Leeds. *Career:* Museum Asst Ceramics Dept, Victoria & Albert Museum, London 1973–74; Museum Asst and Sr Asst The Wallace Collection 1974–78, Asst to Dir 1978–92, Dir 1992–; mem Arts Panel, Nat Trust 1995–; mem Art Advisory Cttee NMGW 1998–, Royal Mint Advisory Cttee; Gov Camden School for Girls 1996–; Pres French Porcelain Soc 1999–; Trustee Somerset House 1997–, Campaign for Museums 1999–; Leverhulme Scholar 1975; Getty Scholar 1985; Nat Art Collections Fund Prize 1990. *Publications:* The Wallace Collection Catalogue of Sèvres Porcelain (3 vols) 1988; articles, reviews, contribs to exhibition catalogues, etc. *Leisure interests:* music, the countryside and gardens. *Address:* The Wallace Collection, Hertford House, Manchester Square, London W1M 6BN, UK. *Telephone:* (20) 7563-9500; *Fax:* (20) 7224-2155; *E-mail:* admin@wallace-collection.com; *Internet:* www.the-wallace-collection.com.

SAVILLE, Lynn Adele, BA, MFA; American photographer; b 7 May 1950; d of Lloyd Blackstone and Eugenia Turk (née Curtis) Saville; m Philip Henry Fried 1985. *Education:* Duke Univ (Durham, NC) and Pratt Inst (Brooklyn, NY). *Career:* Freelance photographer specializing in commercial portraiture and fashion, and fine art photographer; represented by Yancey Richardson Gallery, New York and the Photographers' Gallery, London; Prof of Photography Oaxaca (Mexico), New Jersey and New School for Social Research (New York); Staff photographer Pratt Inst; Studio Asst to Bill King; solo exhibitions include Roosevelt Hotel (New York) 1978, Casa de la Cultura (Tiaxiaco, Mexico) 1980, Playhouse 21 (NB, Canada) 1985, Bertha Urdang Gallery (New York) 1987, 1989, 1990, Univ of Arkansas 1988,

Univ of Texas (Dallas) 1990, Mincher-Wilcox Gallery (San Francisco, CA) 1991, Marymount Coll (Tarrytown) 1992, Jackson Fine Art Gallery (New York) 1999, Hudson River Museum (New York) 2000, Baudoin Lebon Gallery (Paris) 2001, Yancey Richardson Gallery (New York) 2002; group exhibitions include UN Lobby of Gen Ass 1978, Foto Gallery (New York) 1983, Harkness Center for Ballet (New York) 1985, Chevron Corp Art Gallery (San Francisco) 1990; group juried exhibitions include Essex (UK) 1991, Laguna Gloria Art Museum (Austin, TX) 1991; works feature in perm collections including Brooklyn Museum, Oxford Univ Bodleian Library (UK), Prudential Insurance Co, Readers' Digest Corpn; mem American Soc of Magazine Photographers, Foundation for the Community of Artists; New York Foundation for the Arts Fellowship for Photography 1987; Lee Witkin Award for Best Photograph in Exhibition (Perkins Art Exhibition) 1982, 1989; Premio, Scanno, Italy Festival of Photography 1998; New York State Council on the Arts Award 1999. *Publications:* Horses in the Circus Ring 1989, Acquainted with the Night – Photographs by Lynn Saville (monograph) 1997; portfolio published in Swiss photographic magazine 1989; articles in Harper's magazine, 2wice Journal and other magazines. *Leisure interests:* tennis, travel, art. *Address:* 440 Riverside Drive, Apt 38, New York, NY 10027, USA. *Telephone:* (212) 932-1854; *Fax:* (212) 665-0467; *E-mail:* lynnsaville@earthlink.net.

SAVVINA, Iya Sergeyevna; Russian actress; b 2 March 1936, Voronezh. *Education:* Moscow State Univ. *Career:* Actress in cinema, and on stage with Mossovet Theatre, Moscow 1960–78, with Moscow Arts Theatre 1978–; USSR State Prize 1983; People's Artist of the USSR 1990. *Films include:* The Lady with the Lap-dog 1960, A Gentle Woman 1960, Asya's Happiness (State Prize 1990) 1967, Anna Karenina 1968, A Day in the Life of Dr Kalinnikova 1974, A Lovers' Romance 1975, An Open Book 1980, Garage 1980, Private Life 1983, Last, Last the Fascination… 1985, Mother and Son 1990, Lev Trotsky 1993; numerous stage roles in classical and contemporary works. *Address:* 123242 Moscow, Bolshaya Gruzinskaya ul 12, kv 43, Russian Federation. *Telephone:* (095) 254-97-39.

SAWALHA, Julia; British actress; b 9 Sept. *Education:* Italia Conti Acad of Theatre Arts (London). *Career:* Actress for three seasons Newcastle Playhouse; numerous TV appearances; Royal TV Soc Best Female Performance 1994–95. *Plays include:* A Midsummer Night's Dream; *TV appearances include:* Press Gang (48 episodes), Second Thoughts (six series), Absolutely Fabulous (three series), Martin Chuzzlewit, Pride and Prejudice, In the Bleak Midwinter, Faith in the Future (two series). *Address:* 71 Victoria Rd, Stroud Green, London N4 3SN, UK. *Telephone:* (20) 7272-0362.

SAWYER, Diane, BA; American journalist; b 22 Dec 1945, Glasgow, KY; d of E. P. and Jean W. (née Dunagan) Sawyer; m Mike Nichols 1988. *Education:* Wellesley Coll. *Career:* Reporter WLKY-TV, Louisville, KY 1967–70; Admin White House Press Office 1970–74; mem Nixon–Ford transition team 1974–75; Asst to Richard Nixon (fmr US Pres) 1974, 1975; Gen Reporter, later Dept of State Corresp, CBS News 1978–81, apptd Co-Anchor Morning News 1981, Co-Anchor Early Morning News 1982–84, Corresp and Co-Ed 60 Minutes 1984–89; Co-Anchor PrimeTime Live, ABC News from 1989, Turning Point from 1994, Day One 1995; awards include nine Emmy awards, Nat Headliner Awards, George Foster Peabody Award for Public Service, Robert F. Kennedy Journalism Award, Special Dupont Award, Ohio State Award, IRTS Lifetime Achievement Award. *Address:* PrimeTime Live, 147 Columbus Ave, New York, NY 10023, USA. *Telephone:* (212) 456-2060; *Fax:* (212) 456-1246.

SAX, Ursula; German sculptor; b 27 July 1935, Backnang, Baden-Württemberg; d of Hans S. and Ida (née Haller) Lehrer. *Education:* Akad der Bildenden Künste (Stuttgart) and Hochschule der Künste (Berlin). *Career:* Guest Prof Hochschule der Künste, Berlin 1985–86, 1989–90; Prof Hochschule für Bildende Künste, Braunschweig (Brunswick) 1990–, Hochschule für Bildende Künste, Dresden 1993–; exhibitions include retrospective at the Orangerie, Schloß Charlottenburg, Neuer Berliner Kunstverein 1989, Kunstverein Heilbronn 1991; sculptures, wall reliefs, fountains, etc on display include pieces for Freie Univ Berlin, Rathausplatz (Bad Friedrichshall), Berlin 1968, 1973, 1979–80, Rathaus (Kaiserslautern), German school (Brussels) 1977–80, Ministry of the Interior (Bonn) 1978, German Embassy (Cairo) 1980, Bundespost (Stuttgart) 1991, Messe (Berlin) 1992; awards include Villa-Romana-Preis 1963, Will-Grohmann-Preis 1970, Cité des Arts Award (Paris) 1979–80, Hand Hallow Foundation Award (USA) 1981. *Address:* Dresdner Str 10A, 01445 Radebeul, Germany. *Telephone:* (351) 8302150.

SAYLAN, Türkan; Turkish medical practitioner; b 13 Dec 1935, Istanbul; divorced; two s. *Education:* Kandilli Girls' School and Univ of Istanbul. *Career:* Medical practitioner 1963–; specialist in Dermato-Venereology 1968–; Assoc Prof 1972, Prof 1972; mem Medical Faculty, Dir Leprosy Study Centre, Dir Leprosy Hosp 1980–; Pres numerous non-govt orgs; Int Gandhi Award 1985; Melvin Jones Award; has written books on dermatology and numerous articles. *Leisure interests:* secularism, women's issues, leprosy, writing, modern education. *Address:* Beyazgül Sokak 67, Arnavutkoy, Istanbul, Turkey (Home). *Telephone:* (212) 5702575 (Office); *Fax:* (212) 5830086 (Office).

SAZANAMI, Yoko; Japanese economist; b 1933. *Career:* Began career as teacher, Keio 1961; Prof of Econs Keio Univ; Chair Financial Crisis Man Cttee for Deposit Insurance Corpn 1988; mem Council on Monetary System, Fiscal System Council, Econ Council to the Prime Minister. *Publication:* Measuring the Costs of Protection in Japan (co-author) 1995. *Address:* Dept of Economics, University of Keio, 2-15-45, Mita, Minato-ku, Tokyo, 108, Japan. *Telephone:* (3) 3453-4511 ext 3540; *Fax:* (3) 3453-5640.

SCACCHI, Greta; British actress; b 18 Feb 1960, Milan, Italy; one d by Vincent D'Onotrio; one s by Carlo Mantegazza. *Education:* Bristol Old Vic Drama School. *Films include:* Dead on Time 1982, Heat and Dust 1983, The Coca-Cola Kid 1985, Defence of the Realm 1987, A Man in Love 1987, Good Morning Babylon 1987, White Mischief 1988, The Second Sight 1989, La Donna dell Luna (Woman in the Moon), Schoolmates, Presumed Innocent 1990, Shattered, Fires Within 1991, Turtle Beach, The Player, Distant Shores 1991, The Three Sisters 1991, Salt on our Skin, The Browning Version, Jefferson in Paris 1994, Country Life 1995, Rasputin (Emmy Award for Best Supporting Actress 1996), Emma 1996, Bravo Randy 1996, Cosi, The Serpent's Kiss 1997, The Red Violin 1998, Cotton Mary 1998, Ladies Room 1999, The Manor 1999, Tom's Midnight Garden 2000, Looking for Anbrandi 2000, One of the Hollywood Ten 2000; *TV appearances include:* The Ebony Tower, Dr Fischer of Geneva, Waterfront (series), Camille), Rasputin (Emmy Award 1996), The Odyssey (series) 1996, Macbeth 1998; *Plays include:* Cider with Rosie, In Times Like These, Airbase, Uncle Vanya, The Guardsman.

SCALES, Prunella Margaret Rumney West, CBE; British actress; b Sutton Abinger; d of John Richardson Illingworth and Catherine Scales; m Timothy West 1963; two s. *Education:* Moira House (Eastbourne), Old Vic Theatre School (London) and Herbert Berghof Studio (New York). *Career:* In repertory Huddersfield, Salisbury, Oxford, Bristol Old Vic, etc; seasons at Stratford and Chichester; directed plays at numerous theatres including Bristol Old Vic, Arts Theatre (Cambridge), Nottingham Playhouse, W Yorks Playhouse; Pres CPRE 1997–; Hon D LITT (Bradford) 1995, (E Anglia) 1996; Freeman of City of London 1990. *Plays include:* In London: The Promise 1967, Hay Fever 1968, The Wolf 1975, Make and Break 1980, An Evening with Queen Victoria 1980, The Merchant of Venice 1981, Quartermaine's Terms 1981, When We Are Married 1986, Single Spies (double bill) 1988, School for Scandal, Long Day's Journey into Night, Some Singing Blood, Happy Days 1993, The Mother Tongue, The Editing Process 1994, The Birthday Party 2000, The Cherry Orchard 2000; *TV appearances include:* Fawlty Towers (series) 1975, 1978, Mapp and Lucia (series) 1985–86, Absurd Person Singular 1985, What the Butler Saw 1987, After Henry (series) 1988–92, A Question of Attribution 1991, Signs and Wonders 1995, Breaking the Code 1995, Lord of Misrule 1995, Dalziel & Pascoe 1996, Breaking the Code 1997, Midsomer Murders 1999, Silent Witness 2000; *Films:* An Awfully Big Adventure 1994, Stiff Upper Lips 1997, Wolf, An Ideal Husband 1999, The Ghost of Grenville Lodge 2001; *Radio work includes:* Smelling of Roses 2000, Ladies of Letters 2001; numerous readings, poetry recitals, fringe productions. *Leisure interests:* cats, canal boat, growing herbs, gardening, crosswords. *Address:* c/o Jeremy Conway, 18–21 Jermyn St, London SW1Y 6HP, UK. *Telephone:* (20) 7287-0077; *Fax:* (20) 7287-1940.

SCARDINO, Marjorie Morris, BA, JD; American business executive; b 25 Jan 1947, Flagstaff, AZ; d of Robert Weldon and Beth (née Lamb) Morris; m Albert James Scardino 1974; two s one d. *Education:* Baylor Univ, TX and Univ of San Francisco, CA. *Career:* Partner Brannen Wessels and Searcy, Savannah, GA 1976–85; Publr Georgia Gazette, Savannah, GA 1978–85; Pres The Economist Newspaper Group Inc, New York 1985–93; Worldwide Man Dir Economist Intelligence Unit New York 1992–93; Chief Exec The Economist Group, London 1993–97; Dir, Chief Exec Pearson PLC 1997–; Dir Con Agra Inc 1994–; Non-Exec Dir W H Smith; Fellow London Business School; Veuve Clicquot Businesswoman of the Year Award 1998. *Address:* Pearson PLC, 3 Burlington Gardens, London W1X 1LE, UK. *Telephone:* 20) 7411-2300; *Fax:* (20) 7411-2399.

SCHAFFER, Teresita Currie, BA; American diplomatist; b 28 Sept 1945, Washington, DC; d of Francis and Teresita Sparre Currie; m Howard B. Schaffer 1971; two s. *Education:* Bryn Mawr Coll, Inst d'Etudes Politiques (Paris) and Georgetown Univ. *Career:* Diplomatic assignments in Tel Aviv 1967–69, Islamabad 1974–77, New Delhi 1977–79; Analyst for Near East, Dept of State 1969–71, Financial Economist 1972–73, Deputy Dir Office of Pakistan–Afghanistan–Bangladesh 1979–80, Div Chief then Dir Office of Int Trade 1980–84, Dir of Egyptian Affairs 1987–89, Deputy Asst Sec of State for South Asia 1989–92; Amb to Sri Lanka 1992–95; Dir Foreign Service Inst 1995; Presidential Meritorious Service Award 1985; Presidential Distinguished Service Award 1992. *Publications:* Survey of Women in Bangladesh (Dhaka) 1985, Survey of Development Projects for Women (Dhaka) 1986. *Leisure interest:* music. *Address:* Foreign Service Institute, SA-42, 4000 Arlington Blvd, Arlington, VA 22204-1500, USA. *Telephone:* (703) 302-6703; *Fax:* (703) 302-7461; *E-mail:* teresita .schaffer@state.gov.

SCHAFFNER, Anne-Marie; French politician; b 31 May 1945, Nancy. *Career:* Deputy Mayor of Fontenay-Trésigny 1983–95; mem Gen Council Seine-et-Marne 1986, Regional Councillor Ile-de-France 1992–94, 1998–; MEP (Group Union for Europe, RPR) 1994–99, mem Cttee on Legal Affairs and Citizens' Rights, on Petitions, Del for relations with the People's Repub of China; Nat Sec RPR with responsibility for state reform. *Address:* 18 ave du Général Leclerc, BP 25, 77610 Fontenay-Trésigny, France.

SCHALL HOLBERG, Britta; Danish politician; b 25 July 1941, Naestved; d of Preben Schall Holberg. *Education:* N. Zahle's Teacher Training Coll (Copenhagen). *Career:* Owner the Hagenskov estate on Funen; fmr Deputy Mayor of Assens and Deputy Chair of Fed of Danish Social Cttees; Minister for the Interior 1982; elected mem Folketinget (Parl, Liberal Party) 1984; Chair Inter-Church Council, World Council of Churches. *Address:* Hagenskov Slot, 5631 Ebberup, Odense, Denmark.

SCHALZ-LAURENZE, Ute; German music expert and journalist; b 1 Aug 1943, Friedrichstadt/Eider; m Nicolas Schalz; two s one d. *Education:* Univs of Frankfurt and Kiel. *Career:* Freelance music journalist for newspapers, specialist music journals, radio and TV; teacher Univs of Oldenburg and Bremen; has attended int music congresses including the Int Congress on Women in Music, Bremen 1988; Organizer Cultural Section of Women in Computers conf, Bremen 1989; involved in Congress and Festival for Women, Bremen 1993; Founder-mem Neue Musik project group, Bremen. *Publication:* Zur neuen Musik und zur Probleme der Interpretation. *Leisure interests:* theatre, film, painting, women's movement. *Address:* Köpkenstr 12, 28203 Bremen 1, Germany.

SCHAPIRO, Miriam, MA, MFA; American artist; b 15 Nov 1923, Toronto, Canada; d of Theodore Schapiro and Fannie Cohen; m Paul Brach 1946; one s. *Education:* State Univ of Iowa. *Career:* Co-Founder feminist art programme, California Inst of Arts, Valencia 1971; Womanhouse, Los Angeles 1972, Heresies magazine, New York 1975 (then Assoc mem Heresies Collective); Founder mem Feminist Art Inst, New York; Lecturer Dept of Art History, Univ of Michigan 1987; solo exhibitions include Basle, Switzerland 1979, Spencer Museum of Art, Lawrence (KS) 1981, Cologne, Germany 1981, Stuttgart, Germany 1983, Bernice Steinbaum Gallery, New York 1986, 1988, 1990, 1991, 1994, Melbourne (FL) 1991, ARC Gallery, Chicago (IL) 1993, West

Virginia Univ, Morgantown (VA) 1994, James Madison Univ, Harrisonburg (VA) 1996; group exhibitions include Palais des Beaux Arts, Brussels 1979, Inst of Contemporary Art, Philadelphia (PA) 1979, Sydney Biennale, Australia 1982, American Acad of Arts and Letters, New York 1985, Museum of Modern Art, New York 1988, Nat Museum of Women in Arts, Washington (DC) 1993, Museum of Fine Arts, Boston (MA) 1994, Bronx Museum of the Arts, New York 1995, Nat Museum of American Art, Washington (DC) 1996; rep in numerous collections, books and catalogues; Fellow Nat Endowment for the Arts 1976; several residencies; Guggenheim Fellow 1987; Dr hc (Wooster Coll) 1983, (California Coll of Arts and Crafts) 1989, (Minneapolis Coll of Art and Design, Miami Univ, Oxford) 1994, (Moore Coll of Art) 1995; Skowhegan Medal for Collage 1982; Award from Women's Caucus for Art 1988. *Publications:* Women and the Creative Process 1974, Rondo: An Artist's Book 1988. *Address:* c/o Bernice Steinbaum Gallery, 3550 N Miami Ave, Miami, FL 33127, USA.

SCHARBERTH, Irmgard; German opera and concert producer; b 28 Nov 1919, Hamburg. *Education:* Univs of Hamburg and Kiel. *Career:* Opera and concert producer Hamburg Staatsoper 1957–76, Bayerische Staatsoper, Munich 1976–77, Oper Stadt Köln, Cologne 1977–85; producer Gürzenichkonzerte, Cologne until 1991. *Publications:* Die Hamburger Staatsoper in Amerika 1967, Rolf Liebermann zum sechzigsten Geburtstag 1970, Musiktheater mit Rolf Liebermann 1975, Oper in Köln 1975–85, Michael Hampe 1985, Die Gürzenichorchester Köln 1988. *Leisure interests:* opera, classical music and jazz. *Address:* c/o Am Kiekeberg 24, 22587 Hamburg, Germany.

SCHAUMAYER, Maria; Austrian banking executive; b 1932. *Career:* Fmr Dir State Oil Co; Pres Austrian Nat Bank 1990–95. *Address:* c/o Österreichische Nationalbank, Otto Wagner-Platz 3, 1090 Vienna, Austria. *Telephone:* (1) 43-60-0.

SCHELL, Maria; Austrian actress; b 15 Jan 1926, Vienna; d of Hermann Ferdinand and Margarethe (née von Noé) Schell; m 1st Horst Hächler; one s; m 2nd Veit Relin 1966 (until 1989); one d. *Education:* Studied acting in Zurich (Switzerland). *Career:* Actress in Austria, Switzerland and Germany; first film part in Steinbruch at the age of 15; Bundesverdienstkreuz 1974; other awards include Bambi-Preis (Film-Revue) 1951–52, 1954–57, French film and British Acad Prize 1957, Filmband in Gold 1977, HÖRZU Gold Camera 1983. *Plays and films include:* Es kommt ein Tag, Wenn das Herz spricht, Der träumende Mund, Solange du da bist, Die letzte Brücke (Best Actress Prize, Cannes Film Festival 1954), Die Ratten, Gervaise (Volpi Prize, Venice Biennale 1956), Rose Bernd, Die Brüder Karamasow, Ein Frauenleben, The Hanging Tree, Raubfischer in Hellas, Ich bin auch nur eine Frau, Pack den Tiger schnell am Schwanz, The Odessa File, Voyage of the Damned, Folies Bourgeoises, Superman, Just a Gigolo, 1919; *TV appearances include:* Schrei vor das Fenster 1969, Willy und Lilly 1971, Immobilien 1973, Die Kurpfuscherin, Teerosen; also TV appearances in USA. *Leisure interest:* music.

SCHEMBRI ORLAND, Lorraine, LL D; Maltese lawyer and organization executive; b 21 June 1959, St Julian's; d of Albert A. and Marceline Palmier; m George Roland Schembri Orland 1983; one s. *Education:* Convent of the Sacred Heart and Univ of Malta. *Career:* Salzburg Fellow on American Laws and Legal Insts 1985; Legal Adviser to Nat Council of Women 1982, Pres 1988–91; apptd Vice-Chair Comm for Advancement of Women 1989; Chair Action Team, Violence Against Women 1991; mem Bd Conseil Int des Femmes 1990; drafted new code on Family Law 1990; numerous contribs to professional journals. *Leisure interests:* travel, reading. *Address:* 70 Old College St, St Julian's, Malta (Office); Nampara, Old Railway Track, Attard, Malta (Home). *Telephone:* 446405 (Office); *Fax:* 446405 (Office).

SCHERRER, Jutta, PH D; French/German professor of Russian history; b 1942, Berlin; d of Werner Martyn and Charlotte (née Wuttge) Scherrer; m Klaus Scherrer 1961. *Education:* Freie Univ Berlin, Univ of Harvard (USA), Univ of Paris (Sorbonne) and Ecole des Hautes Etudes en Sciences Sociales (Paris). *Career:* Historical Researcher until 1974; Prof Univ of Paris VIII (Vincennes à St-Denis) 1975–79; Prof Univ of Bochum 1978–79; Dir of Studies Ecole des Hautes Etudes en Sciences Sociales, Paris 1980–; Visiting Prof Columbia Univ, NY, USA; awarded

Palmes Académiques, Ministry of Educ, France 1991. *Publications:* Die Petersburger religiös-philosophische Vereinigung 1973; books and contribs to newspapers and magazines on Russian culture, social history and on the USSR. *Leisure interest:* music. *Address:* Ecole des Hautes Etudes en Sciences Sociales, 54 blvd Raspail, 75006 Paris, France (Office); 1 bis rue Georges Braque, 75014 Paris, France (Home). *Telephone:* (1) 49-54-25-25 (Office); (1) 45-80-50-15 (Home); *Fax:* (1) 45-44-93-11 (Office).

SCHIERHUBER, Agnes; Austrian politician; b 31 May 1946, Reith. *Career:* MEP (EPP, Österreichische Volkspartei), mem Cttee on Agric and Rural Devt, Del for relations with Switzerland, Iceland and Norway. *Address:* European Parliament, rue Wiertz, 1047 Brussels, Belgium. *Telephone:* (2) 284-21-11; *Fax:* (2) 230-69-43.

SCHIFFER, Claudia; German former fashion model; b 25 Aug 1970, Düsseldorf. *Career:* Modelling debut with Karl Lagerfeld's Chanel couture show 1990; has appeared at int fashion shows world-wide; Model for Revlon 1992–96, Chanel until 1997; Co-propr Fashion Café, London (with Naomi Campbell, Elle MacPherson and Christy Turlington, qv) 1996–; numerous covers for magazines and journals; designs calendars; appearances on TV specials; created exercise video; has share in Fashion Café, New York; announced retirement from modelling 1998; mem US Cttee UNICEF 1995–98. *Publication:* Memories 1995; *Film:* Richie Rich, Black Out 1997, Black and White 2000. *Address:* c/o United Talent Agency, 9560 Wilshire Blvd, Beverly Hills, CA 90212, USA.

SCHIMMEL, Annemarie, D PHIL; German professor of Indo-Muslim culture; b 7 April 1922, Erfurt; d of Paul and Anna (née Ulfers) Schimmel. *Education:* Univ of Berlin. *Career:* Assoc Prof of Islamic Languages and Culture Univ of Marburg 1953; Prof of the History of Religions, Ankara 1954; Lecturer, Assoc Prof of Islamic Languages and Culture, Bonn 1961; Prof of Indo-Muslim Culture Harvard Univ, Cambridge, MA, USA 1967–92; mem American Acad of Arts and Sciences; Corresp mem Royal Netherlands Acad of Arts and Sciences; Dr hc (Sind, Seluk); Hon D LITT (Quaid-i-Azam) 1977; Hon LL D (Peshawar) 1978; Hon DD (Uppsala) 1986; Großes Bundesverdienstkreuz 1989; Hon Citizen of Islamabad; other awards include Friedrich-Rückert-Preis 1965, Johann-Heinrich-Voss-Preis (Deutsche Akad für Sprache und Dichtung) 1980, Order of Hilal-i Imtiaz 1983, Friedenspreis des Deutschen Buchhandels 1995, Presidential Award for the best book on IQBAL (Pakistan) 1998. *Publications include:* Gabriel's Wing 1963, Islamic Literature in India 1973, Classical Urdu Literature 1975, A Dance of Sparks 1977, Islam in the Indian Subcontinent 1980, Märchen aus Pakistan 1980, As Through a Veil 1982, Die orientalische Katze 1983, Calligraphy and Islamic Culture 1984, And Muhammed is His Messenger 1985, Islamic Names 1989, Muhammad Iqbal 1989, A Two-Colored Brocade 1990, Deciphering the Signs of God 1993; also publr, co-publr and trans of books on Islamic languages and culture. *Address:* Lennéstr 42, 53113 Bonn, Germany.

SCHLEICHER, Ursula; German politician; b 15 May 1933, Aschaffenburg. *Education:* Univ of Frankfurt and Hochschule für Musik (Munich). *Career:* Journalist, Munich 1963–64; Adviser on Women's Rights, CSU 1965–75; mem Bundestag (Parl) 1972–80; MEP 1979–, Vice-Pres Cttee on Environment, Public Health and Consumer Protection 1984–94, Vice-Pres EP 1994–99; Chair European Union of Women 1983–87; Vice-Pres Paneuropa Union Germany 1995–; articles on the environment, law on foodstuffs and int market in medicine. *Leisure interest:* playing the harp. *Address:* European Parliament, rue Wiertz, 1047 Brussels, Belgium. *Telephone:* (2) 284-53-05; *Fax:* (2) 284-93-05.

SCHMALZ-JACOBSEN, Cornelia; German politician; b 1934, Berlin. *Career:* Worked as journalist in radio, TV and newspapers 1962; joined Free Democratic Party (FDP) 1968; mem Munich City Council 1972–85; Senator for Youth and Family Affairs, Berlin 1985–89; Gen Sec FDP 1988–91; mem Bundestag (Parl) 1990–; Head Fed Dept for Problems of Foreigners 1991. *Address:* Postfach 140280, 513107 Bonn, Germany.

SCHMIDBAUER, Barbara; German politician; b 15 Nov 1937, Berlin. *Career:* Fmr mem Darmstadt Council; mem Exec SPD; MEP 1989–99, mem Cttee on Petitions, on Transport and Tourism, Del for relations with the mem States of ASEAN, SE Asia and the Repub of Korea, fmrly mem Cttees on External Econ Relations, Devt and Co-operation and Women's Rights. *Address:* c/o European Parliament, rue Wiertz, 1047 Brussels, Belgium.

SCHMIDT, Mia (Maria Margarete Gertrud), MA; German composer; b 5 Jan 1952, Dresden (then GDR); one d. *Education:* Univs of Munich and Tübingen, Fachhochschule (Munich) and Musikhochschule (Freiburg). *Career:* Composition studies with Milko Kelemen, Brian Ferneyhough, Klaus Huber and Messias Maiguashca; currently freelance composer and music teacher, Freiburg; performances in Amsterdam, Berlin, Paris, Rome, Tokyo, Vienna, Zürich (Switzerland), and festivals of contemporary music in Darmstadt, Erice, Frankfurt, Graz (Austria), Krefeld and Witten; Künstlerische Reife; scholarships from Rosenberg-Stiftung 1985, Heinrich-Strobel-Stiftung des Südwestfunks 1995, 1999; Forum junger Komponisten competition award, Cologne 1985, 1992; Special Prize Eighth Int Composition Competition, GEDOK, Mannheim 1985; First Prize (Chamber Music), Premio Europa competition, Rome 1985; Förderpreis für das Musikprotokoll des Steirischen Herbstes, Graz 1986; Chamber Music Prize, IRINO, Tokyo 1987; prize from first Int Kompositionswettbewerb des Schweizer Frauenmusik-Forums, Berne 1992; Johann Joseph Fux Musikpreis des Landes Steiermark 1998; Johann Joseph Fux Opernkompositionswettbewerb des Landes Steiermark 2000. *Compositions include:* Ihre Geschichte 1985, Mondwein 1985, Vollmond 1986, A Rose is a Rose 1988, Für Fanny 1990, 5 Stücke für Bläserquintett und Kontrabaß 1992, Aïda domí 1996, Requiem für Fanny Goldmann 1998, Der Fall Franza 2000. *Leisure interests:* music, theatre, cinema. *Address:* Poststr 5, 75098 Freiburg, Germany. *Telephone:* (761) 33479; *E-mail:* mia .schmidt@smx.de; *Internet:* www.miaschmidt.de.

SCHMIDT-BLEIBTREU, Ellen; German writer; b 11 June 1929, Heidelberg; d of Hans and Ellen (née Nass) Kesseler; m B. Schmidt-Bleibtreu 1956; one d one s. *Education:* Univ studies in Mainz-Germersheim. *Career:* European Rep for Arts, Letters and Music, Conseil Int des Femmes; Dr hc (Istituto Europeo di Cultura) 1989; World Culture Prize, Accad Italia 1984. *Publications include:* Poetry: Kraniche 1970, Fragmente 1973, Unter dem Windsegel 1978, Zeitzeichen 1983, Klimawechsel 1989; Prose: Ruhestörung (stories) 1975, Im Schatten der Genius 1981, 1989, Die Schillers 1986, 1989; Co-ed: Anthologie de la poésie féminine mondiale 1973, Kinder aus 14 Ländern (short stories) 1982, Deutsche Komponistinnen des 20 Jahrhunderts 1984, Begegnung über Grenzen hinweg 1993. *Address:* Pregelstr 5, 5300 Bonn 1, Germany.

SCHMIDT-DECKER, Petra; German songwriter, record producer and writer; b Berlin; d of Felix-Peter and Ingeborg (née Lohse) Schmidt-Decker. *Education:* Acting classes. *Career:* Actress on stage, TV and in films for 13 years; songwriter, then Producer of children's records; produced 150 records, including 30 records for Disney and 25 recorded biographies of composers from Vivaldi to Ravel (with Karlheinz Böhm) 1976–92; writer of TV and theatre scripts; geschäftspühreude gesellschaftesin (leading companion) of START Wort-Ton-Bild Verlags GmbH Hamburg, Germany; has worked on Jungle Book and Sesame Street productions; 18 Gold, one Double Platinum and six Platinum Discs. *Publications:* Books: Die jungen Bosse, Unternehmer Portraits 1984, Das große Buch des guten Benehmens 1985, Die Seherin 1996; Plays: In Between (TV), Casanova bevorzugt (theatre) 1998. *Leisure interests:* reading, writing, classical and modern music, dreaming, painting, learning. *Address:* Papenhuder Str 42, 22087 Hamburg-Uhlenhorst, Germany. *Telephone:* (40) 223773.

SCHMÜCKLE-MOLLARD, Christiane; French architect; b 8 Aug 1946, Chambéry; m Jörg Schmückle-von Minckwitz 1972; one c. *Education:* Acad of Fine Arts and Tech Univ of Munich (Germany). *Career:* Architect Munich 1970–79; Consultant Architect Supplies Dept, Val-de-Marne 1977–80, Chief Architectural Adviser for Town Planning and the Environment 1980–82, Architect in charge of Historical Monuments 1981, in Aude, Hérault and Lozère 1982–87, Sarthe and Mayenne 1987–, Orne and Val-de-Marne 1996–; part-time Lecturer Nat School of Architecture, Paris 1984–87; Consultant

Architect Nat Bureau of Historical Monuments and Sites 1985–87; mem Int Council of Monuments and Sites, Vice-Pres 1996–; restoration projects include Cathedrals in Mende, Laval, Montpellier and Le Mans, the Law Courts (Montpellier), Abbeys of St Vincent and L'Epau (Le Mans), Gallo-Roman ramparts of Le Mans, Croisilles Hotel (Paris), La Flèche Military Acad and Ursuline Convent bldgs at Château Gontier; mem High Comm on Historical Monuments 1986–90, Int Council of Monuments and Sites (Icomos), French Archaeological Soc. *Leisure interests:* skiing, golf. *Address:* 34 rue Guynemer, 75006 Paris, France (Office); 19 rue Ampère, 75017 Paris, France (Home).

SCHNAPPER, Dominique, D SC; French writer and sociologist; b 9 Nov 1934, Paris; m Antoine Schnapper 1958; three c. *Education:* Sorbonne, Paris. *Career:* Prof Ecole des Hautes Etudes en Sciences Sociales (Paris) 1980–; apptd Mem Conseil Constitutionnel (French Supreme Court) 2001; Prix de l'Assemblée Nat 1994. *Publications:* La communauté des citoyens 1994, La rélations a l'autre 1998, Qu'est ce que la citoyénneté? 2000. *Address:* Maison des Sciences de l'Homme, 54 blvd Raspail, 75007 Paris, France.

SCHNEEMANN, Carolee; American artist; b 12 Oct 1939, Fox Chase, PA. *Career:* Teacher Univ of Texas at Austin, Hunter Coll (NY), San Francisco Art Inst (CA), Univ of California at Los Angeles and Pratt Inst (New York); exhibitions include Emily Harvey Gallery (New York), Max Hutchinson Gallery (New York), Walter/McBean Gallery, San Francisco Museum of Modern Art 1991, Venice Biennale (Italy) 1991, San Francisco Art Inst (CA) 1992, Museum of Modern Art (New York) 1992, New Museum (New York) 1992, 1996, Whitney Museum of American Art (New York) 1993, 1995, Musée d'Art Moderne (Centre Georges Pompidou, Paris) 1995, Kunstraum (Vienna) 1995; rep in perm collections including Museum of Modern Art, Foundation Mudima (Milan, Italy), Ludwig Museum (Cologne, Germany), Collection Conz (Verona, Italy), Erotica Archives Museum (Zagreb, Croatia), San Francisco Museum of Modern Art. *Address:* 114 W 29th St, New York, NY 10001, USA.

SCHNEIDER, Cynthia P., PH D; American diplomatist and professor of art history; b 16 Aug 1953, PA. *Education:* Harvard Univ and Univ of Oxford (UK). *Career:* Asst Curator of European Paintings, Museum of Fine Arts, Boston; Asst Prof of Art History, Georgetown Univ 1984–90, Assoc Prof 1990–; Amb to Netherlands 1998–; Vice-Chair Pres's Cttee on the Arts and Humanities; fmr mem Bd of Dirs Nat Museum of Women in the Arts, Australian-American Leadership Dialogue. *Publications:* Rembrandt's Landscapes 1990, Rembrandt's Landscapes: Drawing and Prints 1990. *Address:* American Embassy, Lange Voorhout 102, 2514 EJ The Hague, Netherlands. *Telephone:* (70) 3109209; *Fax:* (70) 3614688.

SCHNEIDER-MATTHIES, Irene; German ballet dancer and choreographer; b 10 Oct 1942, Metz, France; d of Alfons and Elisabeth Schneider; m Eberhard Matthies; one s one d. *Education:* High school (Speyer) and dance in Munich, Paris and London. *Career:* Ballet dancer with Stuttgart Ballet; ballet teacher at John Cranko Acad; Ballet Dir and Choreographer in Ulm and Heidelberg; fmrly Ballet Dir Krefeld-Mönchengladbach Theatre; Ballet Dir Staatstheater Magdeburg 1993–. *Ballets include:* Du sollst nicht töten, Sommernachtstraum, Der Feuervogel, Coppelia, Der Sturm, Ancient Voices of Children, Hamlet, Drei Musketiere, Stella, Le sacre du printemps, Romeo and Juliet, The Beatles World Première, Die schöne Lau. *Leisure interests:* literature, music, painting. *Address:* Richard Wagner Str 3, 39106 Magdeburg, Germany. *Telephone:* (2166) 40465.

SCHOETTLER, Gail Sinton, PH D; American former state official; b 21 Oct 1943, Los Angeles, CA; d of James and Norma (née McLellan) Sinton; m 1st John Schoettler; m 2nd Donald L. Stevens 1990; two s one d. *Education:* Stanford Univ and Univ of California (Santa Barbara). *Career:* Gen Partner Avenales Land and Cattle Co 1965–; Exec Dir Colorado Dept of Personnel 1983–86; Treas State of Colorado 1987–95, Lt-Gov 1995–99; Chair Bd of Dirs, Denver Children's Museum 1975–85; Dir Women's Bank 1978–87; Pres Douglas Co Bd of Educ, CO 1979–87; Vice-Chair Bd of Dirs Equitable Bankshares of Colorado 1981–87; mem Bd of Trustees Univ of Northern Colorado 1981–87; mem Bd of Dirs Women Execs in State Govt 1981–89, (Chair 1988), Public Employees' Retirement Asscn 1987–95, Nat Taxpayers'

Union 1992; mem Int Women's Forum, Pres 1983–85; US Amb World Radiocomms Conf 2000; Distinguished Alumna Award (California) 1987; Big Sisters of Colorado Salute to Women Award 1987. *Leisure interests:* skiing, hiking, gardening. *Address:* 11855 E Daley Circle, Parkes, CO 80134, USA.

SCHÖNTHAN, Gaby von; German writer and actress; b 12 Sept 1926; m 1st Paul Frischauer 1957 (died 1977); m 2nd Henry C. Alter 1984. *Education:* Hochschule für Musik und Darstellende Kunst and Reinhardt Seminar (Vienna). *Career:* Actress Theater in der Josefstadt, Vienna, Staatstheater, Wiesbaden and Munich 1944–55. *Publications:* Die Geliebte des Königs 1963, So nah der Liebe 1963, Die Rosen von Malcuaison 1966, Madame Casanova 1968, Die Löwin von San Marco 1972, Das Herrenhaus 1977, Zwei ungleiche Schwestern 1979, Wie viele Stunden hat die Nacht 1982, Aunnia 1986 (translated into many languages). *Leisure interest:* poodles. *Address:* 17 Maplewood Ave, Dobbs Ferry, NY 10522, USA.

SCHOONMAKER-POWELL, Thelma; American film editor; m Michael Powell (died 1990). *Education:* New York Univ. *Career:* Collaborates with Martin Scorsese. *Films edited include:* Raging Bull (Acad Award), The Last Temptation of Christ, Goodfellas, Cape Fear.

SCHREYER, Michaele, PH D; German politician; b 9 Aug 1951, Cologne. *Education:* Univ of Cologne. *Career:* Research Asst Inst for Public Finances and Social Policy, Free Univ of Berlin 1977–82, Lecturer 1996–99; Research Asst and Adviser for Green Caucus in Fed Parl 1983–87; researcher Inst for Economic Research 1987–88; Minister for Urban Devt and Environmental Protection in the State Govt (Senate) of Berlin 1989–90, mem State Parl of Berlin 1991–99, mem Cttee on Budget and Public Finance, Spokeswoman of the Green Caucus for Public Finance (Chair Green Caucus 1998–99), mem Sub-Cttee on Public Capital and Real Estate; mem Presidency of the Berlin Parl 1991–95, various parl cttees of inquiry 1993–99, Chair Sub-Cttee on Funds for Public Housing 1995–97; European Commr for the Budget 1999–; mem Bd Berlin br of the German soc for the UN. *Address:* European Commission, 200 rue de la Loi, 1049 Brussels, Belgium. *Telephone:* (2) 296-3285; *Fax:* (2) 299-4745.

SCHROEDER, Mary Murphy, JD; American federal judge and professor of law; b 4 Dec 1940, Boulder, CO; d of Richard and Theresa (née Kahn) Murphy; m Milton R. Schroeder 1965; two d. *Education:* Swarthmore Coll (PA) and Univ of Chicago (IL). *Career:* Called to the Bar, IL 1966, DC 1966, AZ 1970; Trial Attorney Dept of Justice, Washington, DC 1965–69; Law Clerk Arizona Supreme Court 1970; mem Lewis and Roca, Phoenix, AZ 1971–75; Judge Arizona Court of Appeals 1975–79, US Court of Appeals (9th Circuit) 1979–, Chief Judge 2000–; currently Adjunct Lecturer Duke Univ; Visiting Instructor Arizona State Univ 1976, 1977, 1978; numerous contribs to professional journals; mem ABA, Fed Bar Asscn, State Bar Asscn, IL Bar Asscn, American Law Inst, American Judicature Soc, Nat Asscn of Women Judges (Pres 1998–99), AZ Asscn of Women Lawyers, Nat Asscn of Women Lawyers, Soroptimist Club of Phoenix; Max Beberman Distinguished Alumni Award, Univ High School, Urbana (IL) 1988; Arizona Women Lawyers Asscn Honoree of the Year 1997; ABA Margaret Brent Award 2001. *Address:* US Court of Appeals, 9th Circuit, 6421 Courthouse-Fed Bldg, 230 N First Ave, Phoenix, AZ 85025-0230, USA. *Telephone:* (602) 322-7320; *Fax:* (602) 322-7329.

SCHROEDER, Patricia Nell (Scott), JD; American administrator and politician; b 30 July 1940, Portland, OR; d of Lee Combs and Bernice (née Lemoin) Scott; m James White Schroeder 1962; one s one d. *Education:* Univ of Minnesota and Harvard Univ (MA). *Career:* Called to the Bar, CO 1964; Field Attorney Nat Labor Relations Bd, Denver, CO 1964–66; pvt practice 1966–72; Hearing Officer Colorado Dept of Personnel 1971–72; mem Faculty Univ of Colorado 1969–72, Community Coll, Denver 1969–70, Regis Coll, Denver CO 1970–72; mem House of Reps from First Colorado Dist 1972–96, Co-Chair Congressional Caucus for Women's Issues 1976–, mem House of Reps Armed Services Cttee, Judiciary Cttee, Post Office and Civil Service Cttee, Select Cttee on Children, Youth and Families 1991–93; Prof Woodrow Wilson School of Public and Int Affairs, Princeton Univ Jan–June 1997; Pres and CEO Asscn of American Publishers (AAP) 1997–; Leader New Century/New Solutions think-tank, Inst for Civil Soc, Newton, MA.

Publications include: Champion of the Great American Family 1989, 24 Years of House Work... and the Place is Still a Mess 1998. *Address:* Association of American Publishers Inc, 50 F St, NW, Suite 400, Washington, DC 20001, USA; 4102 Lester Court, Alex, VA 22311, USA (Home). *Telephone:* (202) 347-3375 (Office); *Fax:* (202) 347-3690 (Office); *Internet:* www.publishers.org (Office).

SCHROEDTER, Elisabeth; German politician; b 11 March 1959, Dresden. *Career:* MEP (The Green Group, GRÜNE), mem Cttee on Regional Policy, Del for relations with Ukraine, Belarus and Moldova. *Address:* European Parliament, rue Wiertz, 1047 Brussels, Belgium. *Telephone:* (2) 284-21-11; *Fax:* (2) 230-69-43.

SCHUCHARDT, Erika; German professor of education and politician; b 29 Jan 1940, Hamburg; d of Karl and Erna (née Aurisch) Schuchardt. *Career:* Prof of Educ Univ of Hanover 1986–; mem Bundestag (Parl) 1994–; First Vice-Pres German Comm for UNESCO; prizes include Buchpreis AWMM (Luxembourg) 1985. *Publications include:* Krise als Lernchance 1985, Women and Disabililty (trans to French and Spanish) 1985, Gesundheit in eigener Verantwortung 1992, Freiwilliges ökologisches Jahr: von Modellprojekt zum Bundesgesetz 1994, Jede Krise ist ein neuer Anfang (4th edn, trans to several languages, and Braille) 1994, Warum gerade ich... ? Leiden und Glauben (8th edn, Literature Prize, trans to several languages, and Braille) 1994. *Leisure interests:* literature, music, walking, skiing. *Address:* Gieselerwall 2, 38100 Brauschweig, Germany.

SCHUCHARDT, Helga; German politician; b 2 Aug 1939, Hanover; d of Robert Meyer and Liselotte (née Schulze) Wenck; m Wolfgang Schuchardt 1968. *Career:* Engineer at Deutsche Lufthansa AG 1965; FDP Senator 1965–82; mem Hamburg City Council 1970–72; mem Bundestag (Parl) 1972–83; Minister for Science and Culture, Fed State of Niedersachsen (Lower Saxony) 1990–98. *Publication:* Das liberale Gewissen (ed) 1982. *Address:* Leibnizufer 9, 30169 Hanover, Germany. *Telephone:* (511) 1201.

SCHULZE, Hadwiga, DR MED; German orthopaedic specialist; b Waltershausen. *Education:* Univs of Innsbruck (Austria), Prague and Cologne. *Career:* Sr Physician, Lecturer in Orthopaedics Occupational Therapy and Massage Educ Establishment, Acad for Public Health, Heinrich-Heine-Univ, Düsseldorf, currently Dir of Studies; has given around 80 papers at nat and int confs; more than 60 medical and scientific publs. *Leisure interests:* art, theatre, travel, ski, golf. *Address:* Alte Landstr 42, 40489 Düsseldorf, Germany. *Telephone:* (211) 400282.

SCHÜTZ, Helga; German writer; b 2 Oct 1937, Falkenhain/Goldberg; one s one d (deceased). *Education:* Secondary school (Dresden), Arbeiter und Bauernfakultät (ABF) and Hochschule für Film und Fernsehen (Potsdam). *Career:* Gardener, Dresden 1951–55; writer of novels, stories and screenplays 1964–; Heinrich Mann Preis, Akad der Künste (Berlin); Theodor Fontane Preis, Stadt Potsdam; Stadtschreiber-Preis, Stadt Mainz 1991; Literaturpreis, Brandenburg 1992. *Address:* Jägersteig 4, 14482 Potsdam, Germany. *Telephone:* (33) 78656.

SCHWAETZER, Irmgard, D SC; German politician and pharmacist; b 5 April 1942, Münster; m Udo Philipp. *Education:* Grammar School for Girls (Warburg), Univs of Passau, Münster and Bonn. *Career:* Exec posts in pharmaceutical firms in Germany and abroad 1971–80; mem FDP 1975–, Exec Cttee of North-Rhine/Westphalia 1980–, Sec-Gen 1982–84, Treas 1984–87, Vice-Chair 1988–; mem Bundestag 1980–; mem Landesvorstand Nordrhein-Westfalen 1980–; Minister of State at Fed Ministry of Foreign Affairs 1987–91, Fed Minister for Regional Planning, Building and Urban Devt 1991–94; Chair Nat Union of Liberal Women Asscn 1990–95; Regional Pres, Aachen 1997–. *Address:* The Bundestag, Reichstags gebaeurde, Scheidemannstr 2, 10557 Berlin, Germany. *Telephone:* (228) 337-3013.

SCHWAN, Gesine Marianne, DR RER POL; German professor of political science; b 22 May 1943, Berlin; d of Hans R. and Hildegard (née Olejak) Schneider; m Alexander Schwan (died 1989); one s one d. *Education:* Lycée Français de Berlin and Free Univ of Berlin. *Career:* Asst Prof Dept of Political Sciences, Free Univ of Berlin 1971–77, Prof 1977–; Fellow Woodrow Wilson Int Center for Scholars 1980–81; Bye-

Fellow Robinson Coll, Cambridge, UK 1984; Verdienstkreuz (1st class). *Publications:* Leszek Kolakowski, eine Philosophie der Freiheit nach Marx 1971, Die Gesellschaftskritik von Karl Marx 1974, Sozialdemokratie und Marxismus (jtly) 1974, Sozialismus in der Demokratie, eine Theorie konsequent sozialdemokratischen Politik 1982, Der normative Horizont moderner Politik I und II (jtly) 1985, Politik und Schuld: Die zerstörerische Macht des Schweigens 1997, Jahrbuch für Politik (co-ed) 1991–. *Leisure interests:* music, theatre, travel. *Address:* Free University of Berlin, Dept of Political Science, Ihnestr 21, 1000 Berlin 33, Germany (Office); Teutonenstr 6, 14129 Berlin, Germany (Home). *Telephone:* (30) 8382340 (Office); (30) 8038366 (Home).

SCHWANK, Inge Elisabeth, DR RER NAT; German mathematician; b 6 July 1959, Königstein-Taunus; d of Günter and Elfriede Schwank; one d. *Education:* Univ of Osnabrück. *Career:* Asst Univ of Osnabrück 1982–84; Man Forschungsinst für Mathematikdidaktik eV mathematics educ research inst 1984–, Head 1985–, Lecturer 1992–94, Prof 1994–. *Publication:* On the Analysis of Cognitive Structures in Algorithmic Thinking, The Role of Microworlds for Constructing Mathematical Concepts. *Leisure interest:* classical music. *Address:* Forschungsinstitut für Mathematikdidaktik eV, Rückertstr 56, Postfach 1847, 49008 Osnabrück, Germany. *Telephone:* (541) 49869; *Fax:* (541) 9692523; *Internet:* mathesis.informatik.uni_osnabrueck.de/pers/schwank/ schwank.html.

SCHWARTZ, Maxime; French administrator and scientist; b 1 June 1940, Blois. *Education:* Ecole Polytechnique. *Career:* Entered Inst Pasteur 1963, Deputy Dir 1985–87, Dir-Gen 1987–; also mem of the Scientific Council of the Inst Pasteur and Head of the Dept of Molecular Biology. *Address:* L'Institut Pasteur, 25–28 rue du Dr Roux, 75015 Paris, France.

SCHWARTZ, Nancy E., PH D; Canadian nutritionist; b 1 Oct 1947, Moose Jaw, SK; d of Maurice and Sally (née Fisherman) Schwartz; m Glenn R. Williams 1975; one s. *Education:* Univ of British Columbia and Ohio State Univ (USA). *Career:* Therapeutic Dietitian and Nutrition Instructor Queen Elizabeth Hosp, Montréal, PQ 1969–70; Asst, then Assoc Prof and Dir of Continuing Educ in Nutrition and Dietetics, Univ of British Columbia 1973–87; Pres Nat Inst of Nutrition; Dir Nat Center for Nutrition and Dietetics 1990–; Consultant WHO 1979, 1986; Fellow Canadian Dietetic Asscn, Soc for Nutrition Educ, Canadian Soc for Nutritional Sciences, Scientific Research Soc; author of two books and 34 papers for professional journals; Goodhost Achievement Award 1987. *Leisure interest:* travel. *Address:* 216 W Jackson Blvd, Suite 800, Chicago, IL 60606-6995, USA (Office). *Telephone:* (312) 899-0040; *Fax:* (312) 899-1739; *E-mail:* nschwar@ eatright.org.

SCHWARZENBERG, Ilse; Chilean artist; b 16 July 1913, Peulla, Chile; d of Artur and Helene (née Westphal) Strasser; m Adolf Schwarzenberg 1936; two d one s. *Education:* Escuela de Bellas Artes (Santiago). *Career:* Teacher Escuela de Cultura y Difusión Artística, Valdivia 1973–76; cr silhouette figures for Los Encantados puppet theatre, with which she toured Spain, Germany, Belgium and Latin America; paintings have been exhibited in S Chile, Viña del Mar, Buenos Aires, Saõ Paulo (Brazil), etc; Prize of Honour at Puppet Festival, Ministry of Educ, Chile 1966. *Publications:* Impresiones personales, Begegnungen in Chile. *Leisure interest:* staging plays with puppets. *Address:* c/o Diego Portales 1200, Dep 405, CP 970, Viña del Mar, Chile.

SCHWARZKOPF, Dame Elisabeth, DBE; Austrian/British (b German) opera singer; b 9 Dec 1915, Jarotschin (now Poland); d of Friedrich and Elisabeth (née Fröhlich) Schwarzkopf; m Walter Legge 1953 (died 1979). *Education:* Privately and at Hochschule für Musik (Berlin). *Career:* Debut in Parsifal at Deutsches Opernhaus, Berlin 1938; sang at inauguration of post-war Bayreuth Festival 1951; Prin Soprano at Vienna State Opera, La Scala, Milan (Italy), Royal Opera House, Covent Garden (London), San Francisco 1947– and Metropolitan Opera (New York) 1964–66; singer Salzburg Festival 1947–64; cr Anne Trulove in Stravinsky's Rake's Progress; Hon mem Accad di Santa Cecilia (Rome), Acad of Arts and Letters (Stockholm), RAM; Corresp mem Bayerische Akad der Künste; Prof (Govt of Baden-Württemberg)

1990; Hon D MUS (Cambridge and Washington) 1976; Hon D LITT (Glasgow) 1990; mem Order of Merit, Germany 1983; Commdr des Arts et des Lettres 1985; awarded Lilli Lehmann Medal (Salzburg) 1950, Großes Verdienstkreuz 1974, Order of Dannebrog (First Class), Diapason d'Or Prize 1984, Premio Viotti 1991, Médaille Mozart (UNESCO) 1991, Grosses Bundesverdienstkreuz mit Stern 1995. *Operas include:* Ariadne auf Naxos 1941, Le Nozze di Figaro, Der Rosenkavalier, Così fan Tutte, Die Meistersinger, Don Giovanni, Capriccio; Producer: Der Rosenkavalier (Brussels) 1981; *Publications include:* Walter Legge: On and Off the Record, A Memoir of Walter Legge 1982; recordings include 16 complete operas, 6 complete operettas, songs, arias and lieder. *Leisure interests:* photography, mountain-walking. *Address:* Kammersängerin, Rebhusstr 29, 8126 Zumikon, Switzerland.

SCHYGULLA, Hanna; German actress; b 25 Dec 1943, Germany. *Career:* Worked in Action Theater, Munich with Rainer Werner Fassbinder; has made nearly 40 films; Bundesverdienstkreuz Erster Klasse. *Plays include:* Mother Courage 1979; *Films include:* Die Ehe der Maria Braun (Silberner Bär, Berlinale) 1979, The Bitter Tears of Petra Von Kant, Effi Briest, Berlin Alexanderplatz, Die Dritte Generation 1979, Lili Marleen 1980, Die Fälschung 1981, La nuit de Varennes 1982, Eine Liebe in Deutschland 1983, The Story of Piera 1983, Miss Arizona 1987, The Summer of Mr Forbes, Dead Again 1991, The Merchant of Four Seasons 1998; *TV appearances include:* Acht Stunden sind kein Tag (series) 1972, Peter the Great, Barnum, Casanova. *Leisure interests:* travel, painting. *Address:* c/o Nymphenburger Str 67, 8000 Munich 2, Germany.

SCHYMAN, Gudrun, B SC C; Swedish politician; b 9 June 1948, Täby; one s one d. *Education:* Stockholm. *Career:* Office employee, Stockholm 1964–69; social worker, Stockholm 1971–76, Yrtad 1981–87; freelance documentary film-maker 1976–80; in local govt 1980–87; mem Bd Vänsterpartiet (Left Party) 1981–, Deputy Leader 1988–91, Leader 1993–; mem Social Welfare Cttee 1989–91, Comm for JAS Project 1993. *Leisure interests:* walking, swimming. *Address:* Kungsgt 8, POB 12660, 11293 Stockholm, Sweden. *Telephone:* (8) 786-46-52; *Fax:* (8) 213-353.

SCIORRA, Annabella; American actress; b 1964, New York. *Education:* HB Studio and American Acad of Dramatic Art. *Career:* Actress on stage, in films and on TV; Founder The Brass Ring Theatre Co. *Plays include:* Orpheus Descending, Bus Stop, Three Sisters, Snow Angel, Cries and Shouts, Trip Back Down, Love and Junk, Stay with Me, Those the River Keeps; *Films:* True Love 1989, Internal Affairs, Cadillac Man, Reversal of Fortune, The Hard Way, Jungle Fever, The Hand that Rocks the Cradle 1992, Whispers in the Dark, The Night We Never Met, Mr Wonderful, Romeo is Bleeding, The Cure, The Addiction, The Innocent Sleep, The Funeral, What Dreams May Come True; *TV appearances include:* The Fortunate Pilgrim (mini-series), Doing Time: Women in Prison.

SCITOVSKY, Anne A., MA; American economist; b (Anne Marie Aickelin) 17 April 1915, Ludwigshafen, Germany; d of H. W. and Gertrude M. Aickelin; m Tibor Scitovsky 1942 (divorced 1966); one d. *Education:* Barnard Coll (New York), LSE (UK) and Columbia Univ. *Career:* Economist Legis Reference Service, Library of Congress 1941–44, Bureau of Research and Statistics, Social Security Bd 1944–46; Sr Research Assoc Palo Alto Medical Research Foundation 1963–73, Chief Health Economics Dept 1973–91, Sr Staff Scientist 1992–2000; Lecturer Inst for Health Policy Studies, School of Medicine, Univ of California at San Francisco 1975–91; mem Nat Cttee on Vital Health Statistics 1975–79, Pres's Comm for the Study of Ethical Problems in Medicine and Biomedical and Behavioral Research 1979–82, Inst of Medicine Council on Health Care Tech Assessment 1986–90, Health Resources and Services Admin, AIDS Advisory Comm 1990–94; mem NAS Inst of Medicine 1980–; numerous contribs to official documents and professional journals. *Leisure interests:* reading, photography, swimming. *Address:* Research Institute, Palo Alto Medical Foundation, 795 El Carnino Real, Ames Bldg, Palo Alto, CA 94301, USA (Office); 161 Erica Way, Menlo Park, CA 94025, USA (Home). *Telephone:* (650) 326-8120 (Office); (650) 854-5767; *E-mail:* ascitovsky@aol.com (Home).

SCOFIELD, Sandra; American writer; b 1943, Wichita Falls, TX. *Career:* Creative Writing Fellowship, Nat Endowment of the Arts. *Publications:* Gringa (New American Fiction Award, American Acad and Inst of Arts and Letters First Fiction Award nomination) 1989, Beyond Deserving (American Book Award, New American Fiction Award, finalist for Nat Book Award, one of New York Times Book Review's Notable Books of the Year) 1992, Walking Dunes.

SCOTCHMER, Suzanne Andersen, PH D; American professor of economics and public policy; b 23 Jan 1950, Seattle; d of Toivo and Margaret Anderson. *Education:* Univ of Washington and Univ of California at Berkeley. *Career:* Asst and Assoc Prof of Econs, Harvard Univ 1980–86; Prof of Econs and Public Policy, Univ of Calif 1986–; Sloan Fellowship, Olin Fellowship (Yale), Hoover Nat Fellowship (Stanford); numerous articles on econs in professional journals including Econometric and Science. *Address:* Graduate School of Public Policy and Department of Economics, University of California at Berkeley, 2607 Hearst Ave, Berkeley, CA 94720, USA. *Telephone:* (510) 643-8562; *E-mail:* scotch@socrates.berkeley.edu; *Internet:* www .socrates.berkeley.edu/~scotch.

SCOTLAND OF ASTHAL, Baroness (Life Peer), cr 1997, of Asthal in the County of Oxfordshire, **Patricia Janet Scotland,** QC, LL B; British barrister; b 1956, Dominica; m Richard Mawhinney 1985; two s. *Education:* Univ of London. *Career:* Called to the Bar, Middle Temple 1977, Bencher 1997; mem Bar, Antigua, Recorder 2000; Parl Under-Sec of State, Foreign and Commonwealth Office 1999–; fmr mem Comm for Racial Equality, Gen Council Bar Race Relations Cttee; Commr Millenium Comm 1994–. *Address:* House of Lords, London SW1A 0PW, UK.

SCOTT, Hannah; British charity administrator; b Harriseahead, Staffs; d of Martin and Elizabeth Hulme; m Peter John Murray Scott 1963; one s one d. *Education:* Kidsgrove and School of Commerce (Burslem, Staffs). *Career:* Div Chair Leek Young Cons 1956–58, mem W Midlands Exec Cttee of Cons Party 1956–58, mem City of London Young Cons Policy Group 1961–62; Personal Asst to Airey Neave 1960–65; Sec and Admin The Airey Neave Trust 1987–. *Leisure interests:* tennis, fine arts, reading, walking. *Address:* Airey Neave Trust, House of Commons, London SW1 0AA, UK (Office); The Pippins, Roydon CM19 5DA, UK (Home). *Telephone:* (1279) 793219.

SCOTT, Dame Margaret, DBE; Australian ballet director (retd); b 26 April 1922, Johannesburg, South Africa; d of John and Marjorie (née Heath Bagley) Douglas Scott; m Derek Ashworth Denton 1953; two s. *Education:* Parktown Convent (Johannesburg). *Career:* Dancer Sadler's Wells Ballet 1940–43; Prin Dancer Ballet Rambert 1943–49, Australian Nat Ballet 1949–50; Mistress Ballet Rambert and John Cranko Group 1951–53; pvt teaching 1953–61; Founder, Dir Australian Ballet School 1962–90; Hon life mem Australian Ballet Foundation 1988–; Hon LL D (Melbourne) 1989; Grenn Room Lifetime Achievement Award 1998; Australian Dance Lifetime Achievement Award 1998. *Leisure interests:* music, theatre, gardening, swimming. *Address:* 816 Orrong Rd, Toorak, Melbourne, Vic 3142, Australia. *Telephone:* (3) 9827-2640.

SCOTT, Marianne Florence, OC, BA, BLS; Canadian librarian; b 4 Dec 1928, Toronto, ON; d of Merle Redvers and Florence Ethel (née Hutton) Scott. *Education:* McGill Univ (Montréal). *Career:* Asst Librarian Bank of Montréal 1952–55; Law Librarian McGill Univ 1955–73, Law Area Librarian 1973–74, Lecturer in Legal Bibliography 1964–74, Dir of Libraries 1975–84; Nat Librarian of Canada 1984–99; Co-Founder and Ed Index to Canadian Legal Periodical Literature 1963–; mem Int Asscn Law Libraries, American Asscn Law Libraries, Canadian Asscn of Law Libraries, Pres 1963–69, Exec Bd 1973–77, First Hon mem 1980–; mem Canadian Asscn Research Libraries, Pres 1978–79, Exec 1980–81, Sec-Treas 1983–84; Chair Conf of Dirs of Nat Libraries 1988–92; Hon LL D (York) 1985, (Dalhousie) 1989; Hon D LITT (Sudbury) 1990; Queen's Silver Jubilee Medal 1977. *Address:* 119 Dorothea Drive, Ottawa, ON K1V 0N4, Canada (Home).

SCOTT, Rosie Judy, MA; New Zealand/Australian writer; b 22 March 1948, Wellington; d of Dick and Elsie Scott; m Danny Vendramini 1987; two d. *Education:* Univ of Auckland and Victoria Univ (Wellington). *Career:* Numerous jobs including actress, social worker, counsellor, publr, waitress, factory and home worker; diploma in drama; now novelist, essayist and short story writer; mem Cttee of Australian Soc of Authors and PEN; active in various political campaigns; Bruce Mason Nat Times Play Award 1985. *Publications include:* Novels: Glory Days, Nights with Grace, Feral City, Lives on Fire, Movie Dreams, Faith Singer 2001; Poetry: Flesh and Blood; Short stories: Queen of Love; Play: Say Thankyou to the Lady; Non-fiction: The Red Heart 1999. *Leisure interests:* reading, walking, gardening, friendships, travelling. *Address:* 21 Darghan St, Glebe, NSW 2037, Australia. *Telephone:* (2) 9552 14 27; *Fax:* (2) 9660 61 16; *E-mail:* rosie@amaze.net.au.

SCOTT, Thérèse Striggner; Ghanaian barrister and former diplomatist. *Career:* Called to the Bar, Middle Temple, UK; fmr Chair Juvenile Courts; Judge Ghana High Court; apptd to Zimbabwean High Court 1983 (first woman in Zimbabwe); Amb to France until 1994; elected to Exec Bd of UNESCO 1991 (first African woman); Chair and Spokeswoman African Group of Ambs UNESCO; fmr mem Exec Council Ghana Medical School, Advisory Cttee Int Academy of Trial Lawyers; fmr Pres Ghana Chapter Int Fed of Women Lawyers. *Address:* c/o Ministry of Foreign Affairs, POB M53, Accra, Ghana. *Telephone:* (21) 665421.

SCOTT-BHOORASINGH, Donna, LL B; Jamaican lawyer and politician; b 6 Oct 1956, Westmoreland; d of Woodrow and Daphne Scott. *Education:* Univ of the West Indies and Norman Manley Law School. *Career:* Assoc Fairclough and Watson; Attorney; Deputy Pres of Senate 1986–98; apptd Parl Sec Ministry of Information and Culture 1989, Perm Sec 1992–94; Partner Scott-Bhoorasingh, Bonnick and Lynch. *Leisure interests:* jogging, music, word games, theatre. *Address:* c/o Ministry of Youth, Culture and Community Development, 12 Ocean Blvd, 5th Floor, POB 503, Kingston, Jamaica.

SCOTT BROWN, Denise, M ARCH, RIBA; American architect and urban planner; b 3 Oct 1931, Nkana, Zambia; d of Simon and Phyllis (née Hepker) Lakofski; m 1st Robert Scott Brown 1955 (died 1959); m 2nd Robert Charles Venturi 1967; one s. *Education:* Univ of Witwatersrand (South Africa), London Architectural Asscn and Univ of Pennsylvania. *Career:* Asst Prof Univ of Pennsylvania School of Fine Arts 1960–65; Visiting Prof Univ of California at Berkeley 1965; Assoc Prof Univ of California at Los Angeles 1965–68; Visiting Prof Yale Univ 1967–71; joined Venturi and Rauch (later Venturi, Rauch and Scott Brown, currently Venturi, Scott Brown and Assocs) 1967, Partner 1969–89, Prin 1989–; mem Visiting Cttee MIT, School of Architecture and Urban Planning 1973–83; mem Advisory Cttee Temple Univ 1980–; Policy Panellist Design Arts Program; Nat Endowment for the Arts 1981–83, Fellow Princeton Univ, Butler Coll 1983–; mem Bd of Dirs Cen Philadelphia Devt Corpn 1985–; Eero Saarinen Visiting Critic, Yale Univ 1987; Eliot Noyes Design Critic in Architecture, Harvard Univ 1989–90; mem Advisory Council Greater Philadelphia Urban Affairs Coalition 1991–, Advisory Bd Carnegie Mellon Univ Dept of Architecture 1992–, Bd of Overseers for Univ Libraries, Univ of Pennsylvania 1995–, American Planning Asscn, Architectural Asscn, London, Soc Architectural Historians and numerous others; Hon DFA (Oberlin) 1977, (Philadelphia Coll of Art) 1985, (Parsons School of Design) 1985, (Pennsylvania) 1994; Hon LHD (New Jersey) 1984, (Philadelphia Coll of Textiles and Science, Pratt Inst) 1992; Hon D ENG (Nova Scotia) 1991; Hon D Arch (Miami) 1997; Hon D LITT (Nevada) 1998; other awards include Commendation of Innovative Leadership in Architecture, Women's Way 1986, President's Medal, Architectural League of NY 1986, Chicago Architecture Award 1987, Commendatore Repub of Italy 1987, Tau Sigma Delta Gold Medal 1991, Nat Medal of Arts (US Presidential Award) 1992, Philadelphia Award 1992, The Benjamin Franklin Award (Royal Soc for the Arts) 1993, ACSA-AIA Topaz Medallion 1996, Giants of Design Award, House Beautiful Magazine 2000. *Publications:* Learning from Las Vegas (jtly) 1977, A View from the Campidoglio: Selected Essays (jtly) 1984, Urban Concepts 1990; numerous articles in professional journals. *Leisure interests:* travel, writing, teaching, lecturing. *Address:* Venturi, Scott Brown and Associates Inc, 4236 Main St, Philadelphia, PA 19127-1696, USA. *Telephone:* (215) 487-0400; *Fax:* (215) 487-2520.

SCOTT-JAMES, Anne Eleanor, (Lady Lancaster); British journalist and writer; b 5 April 1913; d of R. A. and Violet (née Brooks) Scott-James; m 1st Macdonald Hastings 1944 (died 1982); one s one d; m 2nd Sir Osbert Lancaster 1967 (died 1986). *Education:* St Paul's Girls' School and Somerville Coll (Oxford). *Career:* Mem editorial staff Vogue 1934–41; Women's Ed Picture Post 1941–45, Sunday Express 1953–57; Ed Harper's Bazaar 1945–51; Women's Adviser Beaverbrook Newspapers 1959–60; Columnist Daily Mail 1960–68; freelance journalist 1968–; mem Council Royal Horticultural Soc 1978–82. *Publications:* In the Mink 1952, Down to Earth 1971, Sissinghurst: the making of a garden 1975, The Pleasure Garden (jtly) 1977, The Cottage Garden 1981, Glyndebourne – the Gardens (jtly) 1983, The Language of the Garden: a personal anthology 1984, The Best Plants for Your Garden 1988, The British Museum Book of Flowers (jtly) 1989, Gardening Letters to My Daughter 1990, Sketches from a Life (autobiog) 1993. *Leisure interests:* reading, gardening, travel, churches, flowers. *Address:* 78 Cheyne Court, Royal Hospital Rd, London SW3 5TT, UK.

SCOTT-THOMAS, Kristin; British actress; b Redruth; m; one s one d. *Education:* Cen School of Speech and Drama (London) and Ecole Nat Des Arts et Technique de Théâtre (Paris). *Career:* Stage debut in Schnitzler's La lune déclinante sur 4 ou 5 personnages qui danse while student in Paris; has lived in France since age of 18; appearances on French, German, Australian, US and British TV. *Plays include:* La terre étrangère, Naïve hirondelles, Yes peut-être; *TV appearances include:* L'ami d'enfance de Maigret, Blockhaus, Chaméléon/La tricheuse, Sentimental Journey, The Tenth Man, Endless Game, Framed (film), Titmuss Regained, Look at it this Way, Body and Soul, La belle époque; *Films include:* Djamel et Juliette, L'agent troubé, La méridienne, Under the Cherry Moon, A Handful of Dust, Force majeure, Bille en tête, The Bachelor, Bitter Moon, Four Weddings and a Funeral (BAFTA Award), Angels and Insects (Evening Standard Film Award for Best Actress), Le Confessional, The English Patient, Richard III, Mission Impossible, Amour et Confusions, The Horse Whisperer, Random Hearts, Up at the Villa.

SCOTTER, Sheila Winifred Gordon, AM, MBE; Australian business executive; b 2 Dec 1920; d of H. G. Scotter. *Education:* St Swithun's School (Winchester, UK) and Royal Coll of England. *Career:* Fashion Buyer Myer Melb 1949–53, Georges Melb 1953–56; Promotion Dir, Marketing Div (Australia and NZ) Joseph Bancroft and Son, Wilmington, DE, USA 1956–58, Head Marketing Div (Continental Europe) 1958–62; Ed-in-Chief Vogue (Australia), Vogue Living Magazine; Dir Condé Nast Publs 1969–71; mem Bd Australia Opera 1969–72, Victoria State Opera 1980–83; Vice-Chair Victoria State Opera Foundation 1982–88; Chair The Dame Joan Hammond Award 1998–; Pres Melbourne Symphony Orchestra Notable Occasions. *Publication:* A Bedside Cookbook 1978. *Leisure interests:* theatre, music, reading, needlepoint, cooking, travel. *Address:* 7 The Biltmore, 152 Bridport St, Albert Park, Melbourne, Vic 3206, Australia.

SCOTTO, Renata; Italian opera singer (soprano); b 24 Feb 1935, Savona; m Lorenzo Anselmi. *Education:* Milan. *Career:* Joined La Scala Opera Co after debut in La Traviata at Teatro Nuovo, Milan 1953; subsequently studied under Ghirardini, Merlino and Mercedes Llopart. *Operas include:* La Sonnambula, I Puritani, L'Elisir d'Amore, Lucia di Lammermoor, Falstaff, La Bohème, Turandot, I Capuleti, Madam Butterfly, Tosca, Manon Lescaut, Otello, Der Rosenkavalier 1992, La Voix Humaine 1993, Pirata 1993. *Address:* c/o Robert Lombardo Associates, 61 W 62nd St, Suite 6F, New York, NY 10023, USA.

SCRIVENER, Christiane; French international official; b 1 Sept 1925, Mulhouse; d of Pierre and Louise (née Scheer) Fries; m Pierre Scrivener 1944; one s (deceased). *Education:* Lycée de Grenoble, Univ of Paris and Harvard Business School (USA). *Career:* Dir-Gen Asscn pour l'Organisation des Stages en France 1958, Asscn pour l'Organisation des Missions de Coopération Technique 1961, Agence pour la Coopération Technique et Économique 1969 (orgs of French tech co-operation with more than 100 countries, devt of int tech and industrial exchanges and promotion of French tech abroad); State Sec for Consumer Affairs 1976–78; mem UDF; MEP 1979–89; EC Commr for Taxation and Customs Union, Matters relating to the Overall Tax Burden—Taxes plus Social Security Contributions 1989–95; mem Bd Alliance

Française 1995–97; Mediateur Société Générale 1995–; Chair Plan Int France 1997–; Grand-croix Ordre de Leopold (Belgium); Grand-croix de Mérite (Luxembourg), Officier de Polonia Restituta (Poland); Commdr de la Légion d'Honneur 2001; Harvard Business School Alumni Achievement Award 1976; Médaille d'Or du Mérite Européen 1990. *Publications:* Le rôle et la responsabilité de la publicité à l'égard du public 1978, L'Europe, une bataille pour l'avenir 1984, L'histoire du petit Troll (children's book) 1986. *Leisure interests:* skiing, tennis, classical music. *Address:* 21 ave Robert-Schuman, 92100 Boulogne-Billancourt, France. *Telephone:* (1) 48-25-44-11; *Fax:* (1) 46-05-58-71; *E-mail:* ch.scrivener@wanadoo.fr.

SCULLY, (Marie Elizabeth) Ann; British organization executive; b 21 Nov 1943, Winchester; d of Charles Francis and Mary Elizabeth (née Godfrey) Lyons; m Michael Scully 1965 (separated 1990); two s one d. *Education:* Notre Dame High School (Sheffield) and Lanchester Coll (Coventry). *Career:* Social worker in Children's Dept, Lincs, Health Dept, Coventry, Citizens' Advice Bureau, Coventry, London and Lancs, Approved School, Formby; Parish Councillor 1975–87; Partner in three Chester firms 1980–89; apptd Chair Domestic Coal Consumers' Council 1987, Vice-Chair Nat Consumer Council 1990; mem ECSC Consultative Cttee 1990, Nat Asscn of Citizens' Advice Bureaux, Merseyside Area 1990, Chester Man Cttee 1990, Consumer Policy Cttee British Standards Inst 1992, British Inst of Man 1982; Fellow Inst of Credit Man 1986; mem Chester and N Wales Chamber of Commerce. *Leisure interest:* music. *Address:* Hockenhall House, 20 Hockenhall Lane, Tarvin, Chester CH3 8LB, UK (Home). *Telephone:* (1829) 40561; *Fax:* (1829) 40218.

SCUTT, Jocelynne Annette, MA, LLB, LL M, SJD; Australian barrister and writer; b 8 June 1947, Perth; d of Athol Everad and Marjorie Josephine (née Needham) Scutt. *Education:* Univs of New S Wales, Sydney, Michigan (USA), Western Australia and Cambridge (UK). *Career:* Sr Research Asst, Tutor and Lecturer Univ of Sydney 1969–73, Sr Tutor in Family Law 1976–77; Research Scholar USA, UK and Germany 1973–76; Sr Law Reform Officer Australian Law Reform Comm 1976–77; Research Criminologist Australian Inst of Criminology, Canberra 1978–81; Barrister and Solicitor High Court of Australia 1980, Supreme Court, ACT, Vic 1981, NT 1989, SA 1995; Barrister Supreme Court, NSW 1981, Qld 1992; Barrister, Solicitor and Proctor Supreme Court of W Australia 1990; Barrister at Law, Sydney 1981–82, Melbourne 1986–; Assoc High Court of Australia 1982–83; Dir of Research Legal and Constitutional Cttee, Victoria Parl 1983–84; Commr and Deputy Chair Law Reform Comm, Vic 1984–86; Anti-Discrimination Commr, Tasmania 1999–; has attended and spoken at numerous confs; mem Bd Social Biology Resources Centre 1988–92; Editorial Consultant Australian Journal of Law and Society 1981–; Dir Artemis Publishing, Victorian Women's Trust 1992–95; Deputy Chair Australian Archives Council 1984–90, Council for Adult Educ (also mem Bd) 1991–94; mem Australian Soc of Criminology, Women's Electoral Lobby, Feminist Book Fortnight Group Inc, Int Feminist Bookfair Organizing Group, Australian Inst of Political Science (also Dir and Deputy Chair) 1979–84, Copyright Tribunal 1994; Commonwealth Univ Scholarship 1965–69; Fellowship Southern Methodist Univ, Dallas, TX, USA 1973–74, Univ of Michigan 1973–74, 1977–78; Hon LL D (Macquarie); Dip of Jurisprudence (Sydney), Dip of Legal Studies (Cambridge); Violet Goode Bequest Gardener Postgrad Award, Girton Coll, Cambridge, UK 1974–75; German Govt Scholarship (DAAD) 1976–77; Women 1988 Australian Bicentenary Award 1988; Varuna Writers' Fellowship 1992; Centenary of Fed Award 2001. *Publications include:* The Female Offender: An Annotated Bibliography (jtly) 1975, Women and Crime (co-ed) 1981, Growing Up Feminist: The New Generation of Australian Women 1985, Poor Nation of the Pacific: Australia's Future? (ed) 1985, Different Lives: Reflections on the Women's Movement and Visions of its Future (ed) 1987, Lionel Murphy: A Radical Judge (ed) 1987, The Baby Machine: The Commercialisation of Motherhood (ed) 1988, Even in the Best of Homes: Violence in the Family (2nd edn) 1990, Women and the Law: Materials and Commentary 1990, Breaking Through: Women, Work and Careers (ed) 1992, As a Woman: Writing Women's Lives (ed) 1992, Glorious Age: Growing Older Gloriously (ed) 1993, No Fear of Flying: Women at Home and Abroad (ed) 1993, Taking a Stand: Women in Politics and Society (ed) 1994, City Women Country Women: Crossing the Boundaries (ed) 1995, Singular Women: Reclaiming Spinsterhood (ed) 1995, Living Generously: Women Mentoring Women (ed) 1996, Growing Up Feminist Too: Raising Women, Raising Consciousness 1996, The Sexual Gerrymander – Women and the Economics of Power 1994, The Incredible Woman – Power and Sexual Politics (2 vols) 1996; As Melissa Chan: Too Rich (novel) 1991, One Too Many 1993, Guilt 1995, A Modern Woman and Other Crimes (co-ed), Calling up the Devil and Associated Misdemeanours (co-ed), Spies, Lies and Watching Eyes (co-ed), Don't Go Near the Water and Additional Warnings (co-ed); Short stories: Getting Your Man, More on Getting Your Man; law reports, articles and book reviews. *Leisure interests:* politics, reading. *Address:* Owen Dixon Chambers, 205 William St, Melbourne, Vic 3000, Australia. *Telephone:* (3) 6224-4905; *Fax:* (3) 6233-5333.

SEAGROVE, Jennifer (Jenny) Ann; British actress; b 4 July 1957, Kuala Lumpur, Malaysia; d of Derek and Pauline Seagrove; m Madhav Sharma 1984 (divorced 1988); partner Bill Kenwright. *Education:* St Hilary's School (Godalming), Queen Anne's School (Caversham), Kirby Lodge (Cambridge) and Bristol Old Vic Theatre School. *Career:* Began career in repertory theatre and moved on to combine TV, theatre and films; involved in many charitable orgs. *Films include:* Moonlighting, Local Hero 1981, Nate and Hayes, A Shocking Accident (Acad Award for Best Short) 1982, Savage Islands 1983, Appointment With Death 1987, A Chorus of Disapproval 1988, The Guardian (Acad Award for Best Short Film) 1990, Miss Beatty's Children 1992, Don't Go Breaking My Heart 1997, Zoe 1999; *TV includes:* The Brack Report, The Woman in White, Hold the Dream, In Like Flynn, Killer, Lucy Walker, Magic Moments, Some Other Spring, The Betrothed, A Woman of Substance 1984, Judge John Deed; *Plays include:* Jane Eyre 1986, The Guardsman 1992, King Lear in New York 1993, Present Laughter 1993, The Miracle Worker 1994, Dead Guilty 1995–96, Hurly Burly 1997, Vertigo 1998, Brief Encounter 2000, The Odd Couple (Female Version) 2001. *Leisure interests:* animals, gardening, environment, theatre, art exhibitions, travel, poetry, scribbling. *Address:* c/o ICM, Oxford House, 76 Oxford St, London W1, UK. *Telephone:* (20) 7636-6565.

SEARCY-HEITMAN, Imke Anne; German cellist; b 5 March 1941, Lübeck; d of Hans and Annelise (née Boysen) Heitmann; m David Searcy 1966 (divorced 1968). *Education:* Staatliche Hochschule für Musik (Freiburg) and New England Conservatory (Boston, MA, USA). *Career:* Solo Cellist Bergen, Norway 1966–67, Herford 1968–73; Cellist Radio Sinfonie Orchestra, Frankfurt 1973–; First Prize New England Conservatory Competition, Boston, USA 1965. *Recordings:* Offenbach: Quatre Pièces 1980, Strauss: Drei Romanzen 1980. *Leisure interests:* gardening, cats, walking, botany, psychology. *Address:* Ringstr 19, 61389 Schmitten, Germany. *Telephone:* (6084) 3100.

SECCOMBE, Baroness (Life Peer), cr 1990, of Kineton in the County of Warwickshire, **Joan Anna Dalziel Seccombe,** DBE; British political administrator; b 3 May 1930, Birmingham; d of Robert John and Olive (née Barlow) Owen; m Henry Lawrence Seccombe 1950; two s. *Education:* St Martin's School (Solihull). *Career:* Mem Exec Nat Union of Cons and Unionist Asscns 1975–, Vice-Chair 1984–87, Chair 1987–88; Chair W Midlands Area Cons Women's Cttee 1975–78; Deputy Chair W Midlands Area Cons Council 1979–81; Chair Cons Women's Nat Cttee 1981–84, mem Women's Nat Comm 1984–90, mem Cons Party Social Affairs Forum 1985–87; Vice-Chair Cons Party with Special Responsibility for Women 1987–97; mem House of Lords 1990–, an Opposition Whip 1997–; mem W Midlands Co Council 1979–81, Chair Trading Standards Cttee 1979–81; JP (Solihull) 1968–2000, Chair of the Bench 1981–84; Gov Nuffield Hosps 1988–, mem Exec Cttee 1989, Deputy Chair 1994–, Chair Nuffield Pension Fund Trustees 1992–; mem Midlands Electricity Council 1981–90. *Leisure interests:* skiing, golf, embroidery. *Address:* Linden Cottage, The Green, Little Kineton, Warwicks CV35 0DJ, UK. *Telephone:* (1926) 640562.

SECKA, Pap Cheyassin; Gambian politician. *Career:* Fmr mem Alliance for Patriotic Reorientation and Construction (APRC); sentenced to death after military coup 1981, pardoned 1991; Sec of State for Justice and Attorney-Gen March 2000–. *Address:* Department of State for Justice, Col Muammar Ghadaffi Ave, Banjul, The Gambia. *Telephone:* 228181; *Fax:* 225352.

SEDDON, Margaret Rhea, MD; American medical practitioner and astronaut; b 8 Sept 1947, Murfreesboro, TN; d of Edward C. Seddon; m Robert L. Gibson; two s one d. *Education:* Univs of California at Berkeley and Tennessee. *Career:* Astronaut NASA Lyndon B. Johnson Space Center, Houston, TX 1979–, mem crew shuttle flights STS 51D 1985, STS 40 1991, STS 58 1993; mem American Coll of Emergency Physicians, American Medical Women's Asscn, Texas Medical Asscn. *Address:* NASA, Johnson Space Center, Astronaut Office, Houston, TX 77058, USA.

SEDOC-DAHLBERG, Betty, PH D; Suriname former university administrator and sociologist; b 21 July 1938, Paramaribo; d of Henri and Pauline (née Samson) Dahlberg; m Edwin Sedoc 1964; one s. *Education:* Algemene Middlebare School (Paramibo) and Univ of Amsterdam. *Career:* Lecturer in Sociology of Devt Agricultural Inst, Netherlands 1964–71; part-time lecturer in Dutch univ grad courses, Netherlands 1966–71; Lecturer in Sociology Tropical Inst, Netherlands 1968–71; Inst of Training, Suriname 1972–75; Planner Planning Agency and Head of Div on Human Resources, Suriname 1972–75; Dir and Lecturer Coll for Social and Economic Studies (Suriname) 1974–75; Sr Lecturer Faculty of Social and Econ Sciences, Univ of Suriname 1975–79, Dean 1975–77, Rector 1979–81, Prof of Policy and Planning for Devt in the Caribbean 1981–82; Visiting Prof Center for Latin American Studies, Univ of Florida, USA 1983–84, Researcher 1985–86, Dept of Urban Regional Planning, Coll of Architecture 1985–87, Visiting Prof Center for Latin American Studies 1987–89; Visiting Prof Univ of Netherlands Antilles 1987, 1989; Consultant Inter-American Devt Bank, Washington, DC 1990; mem World Acad of Co-operation and Devt 1987, Latin American Studies Asscn 1984, American Political Science Asscn 1984; UN Peace Medal 1981; Fulbright Award 1982–85. *Publications:* The Dutch Caribbean: prospects for democracy (ed) 1991, Women in University Administration in Suriname 1991, Human Rights in the Hemisphere (ed) 1992; articles on migration, militarization, political systems, planning, democracy and education. *Leisure interests:* piano, tennis, museums, countryside, ethnic festivals. *Address:* 5 Riverview, Leonsberg, Suriname. *Telephone:* 454131; *Fax:* 456019.

SEEMANOVÁ, Eva, MD, D SC; Czech geneticist; b 3 April 1939, Louny. *Education:* Charles Univ and Acad of Sciences Inst of Experimental Biology and Genetics (Prague). *Career:* WHO Grantee, Fellow Acad of Sciences 1962–68; Head Genetic Counselling Centre, Research Inst for Child Devt 1969–90; Assoc Prof of Medical Genetics, Charles Univ 1990, Prof 1992–, Head Dept of Clinical Genetics, Charles Univ Hosp 1991–; Pres Soc of Medical Genetics; mem Presidium Asscn of Medical Socs; Ministry of Health Prize 1971, 1980; Hálek Prize 1974; Soc of Medical Genetics Prize 1979, 1986, 1991. *Publications include:* A Study of Children of Incestuous Matings 1971, Effect of Consanguinity on Offspring 1973, Genetic Syndromes and Genetic Counselling 1987, Familial Microcephaly with Normal Intelligence, Immunodeficiency and Risk of Lymphoreticular Malignancies: A New Syndrome 1985. *Leisure interests:* general history, art history. *Address:* Rašínovo náb 66, 120 00 Prague 2, Nové Město, Czech Republic. *Telephone:* (2) 24433500 (Office); (2) 291398 (Home); *Fax:* (2) 24433520 (Office).

SEET, Ai-Mee, B SC, PH D; Singaporean politician and biochemist; b 31 March 1943, Malacca, W Malaysia; d of Ding-Ming Ling and Swee-Lin Chan; m Lip-Chai Seet 1967; one s one d. *Education:* Methodist Girls' School and High School (Malacca, Malaysia), Univ of Adelaide (Australia) and Univ of Singapore. *Career:* Tutor Dept of Biochemistry, Univ of Malaya, Kuala Lumpur 1965–76; Biochemist Dept of Pathology, Ministry of Health, Singapore 1966–73; Prin Research Fellow Singapore Inst of Standards and Industrial Research 1973–77; pvt medical lab practice 1978–88; mem Resource Panel, Govt Parl Cttee for Health and Environment 1987–88; MP for Bukit Gombak 1988–91; Minister of State for Community Devt and Educ 1988, Acting Minister for Community Devt July–Sept 1991; apptd Man Dir AM Labs Pte Ltd 1991; Sr Visiting Fellow Inst of SE Asian Studies 1991; Pres Singapore Asscn for the Deaf 1985–88; Fellow Singapore Nat Inst of Chemistry 1977; Fellow Royal Inst of Chemistry (UK) 1978, Royal Soc of Chemistry (UK) 1980, American Inst of Chemists 1982; has written 23 papers on biochemistry and clinical biochemistry; Colombo Plan Scholar 1961–65. *Leisure interests:* reading, music, singing, tennis, walking, jogging. *Address:* AM Laboratories Pte Ltd, 19 Tanglin Rd, No 05-19, Tanglin Shopping Centre, Singapore 1024, Singapore. *Telephone:* 2356955; *Fax:* 7338563.

SEGAL, Hanna Maria, MD, FRCPSYCH; British (b Polish) psychoanalyst; b 20 Aug 1918, Poland; d of Czeslav Poznanski and Izabella (née Weintraub); m Paul Segal 1944; three s. *Education:* Univ of Edinburgh and British Inst of Psychoanalysis. *Career:* Trained as psychoanalyst in London, since then practising as psychoanalyst, training and teaching at British Inst of Psychoanalysis and abroad; fmr Pres British Psychoanalytic Soc, Int Psychoanalytic Asscn; Mary Sigourney Award for Service to Psychoanalysis, American Psychoanalytic Asscn 1992. *Publications include:* Dream, Phantasy and Art 1991, Delusion and Artistic Creativity and Other Psychoanalytic Essays; numerous papers. *Leisure interests:* reading, writing, out of door sports, looking after grandchildren. *Address:* 44 Queen's Ave, London N10 3NU, UK. *Telephone:* (20) 8883-3768.

SEGAL, Lynne, PH D; Australian feminist and academic. *Career:* Fmr Lecturer in Psychology Enfield Polytechnic (now Univ of Middx); involved in grassroots socialist and feminist politics in Islington (London) in the 1970s; Prof of Psychology and Gender Studies Birkbeck Coll, London 2000–. *Publications:* Slow Motion: Changing Masculinities, Changing Men 1990, Straight Sex: The Politics of Pleasure 1994, Is the Future Female? Troubled Thoughts on Contemporary Feminism, Why Feminism?. *Address:* School of English and Humanities, Birkbeck College, Malet St, London WC1E 7HX, UK. *Telephone:* (20) 7631 6070; *E-mail:* office@eng.bbk.ac.uk.

SEGER, Martha Romagne, PH D; American civil servant and economist; b 17 Feb 1932, MI. *Education:* Univ of Michigan. *Career:* Fed Reserve Bank, Chicago, IL; Chief Economist Detroit Bank and Trust Co 1967–74; Vice-Pres for Econs and Investment Bank of Commonwealth, Detroit, MI 1971–74; Assoc Prof of Business Econs Univ of Michigan 1976–79, Prof 1983–84; Assoc Prof of Econs and Finance Oakland Univ, CA 1980; apptd Commr Finance Insts State of Michigan 1980; Gov Fed Reserve System 1984–91; mem Bd of Dirs Fluor Corpn, Kroger co 1991; consultant Martha R. Seger and Assocs Econ and Financial Consulting; mem Bd Dirs Unisource Energy Corpn 2001–. *Address:* Unisource Energy Corporation, Public Affairs, POB 711, Tucson, AZ 85702, USA. *Internet:* www.UniSourceEnergy.com.

SEHNAOUI, Mouna Bassili; Lebanese artist. *Education:* Art studies in Egypt, American Univ of Beirut and Univ of Tucson (AZ, USA). *Career:* Exhibitions in Lebanon and abroad; numerous illustrations for children's books and games; designed postage stamps.

SEIDELMAN, Susan, BA, MFA; American film director; b 11 Dec 1952, Abington, PA; d of Michael and Florence Seidelman. *Education:* Drexel Univ and New York Univ School of Film and Television. *Career:* Worked at a UHF TV station, Philadelphia; directing debut with And You Act Like One, Too (Student Acad Award, Acad of Motion Picture Arts and Sciences 1977); then dir Deficit (short film funded by American Film Inst) and Yours Truly, Andrea G. Stern (awards from Chicago, American and Athens int Film Festivals); mem Dirs' Guild of America. *Films:* Smithereens (also producer and co-writer) 1982, Desperately Seeking Susan 1985, Making Mr Right 1987, Cookie 1989, She-Devil 1989, The Dutch Master 1994, The Barefoot Executive 1995, Tales of Erotica, A Cooler Climate 1999. *Address:* c/o Michael Shedler, 350 Fifth Ave, New York, NY 10118; c/o Gary Pearl Pictures, 10956 Weyburn Ave, Suite 200, Los Angeles, CA 90024, USA.

SEIP, Anne-Lise, D PHIL; Norwegian professor emeritus of modern history; b 6 Nov 1933; d of Edvin and Birgit Thomassen; m Jens Arup Seip 1960 (died 1992); one s one d. *Education:* Univ of Oslo. *Career:* Sr Lecturer Inst of Criminology and Penal Law, Univ of Oslo 1974–75, Dept of History 1975–85, Prof of Modern History 1985–2000, Prof Emer 2000; mem Norwegian Acad of Science, Danish Acad of Science. *Publications include:* Vitenskap og virkelighet T. H. Asehehoug 1974, Eilert Sundt. Fire studier 1983, Sosialhjelpstaten blir til 1984, Veier til velferdsstaten 1994, Anehehougs Norges historie, Vol 8 1830–1870 1997; numerous articles. *Leisure interests:* books, music, gardening. *Address:* Gamle Drammensvei 144, 1363 Høvik, Norway. *Telephone:* 67-53-40-39; *E-mail:* a.l.seip@hi.uio.no.

SEIZINGER, Katja; German skier. *Career:* Gold Medal, Winter Olympics 1994; World Cup winner, Super Giant Slalom, Val d'Isère, France 1996; overall World Cup champion 1996.

ŠEKARIĆ, Jasna; Yugoslav sportswoman; b 17 Dec 1965, Belgrade. *Education:* School of Economics (Osijek). *Career:* Mem Yugoslav Shooting Team 1984–; European Champion 1986, 1991, 1992; World Champion 1987, 1990; Gold Medallist Air Pistol event, Bronze Medallist Sport Pistol event Olympic Games; World Air Pistol Record 1988, Sport Pistol Record 1991; won over 23 Gold Medals in world competitions 1986–92; Best Sportsperson in Yugoslavia 1988; World Shooter of the Year 1990. *Address:* 11070 Belgrade, Jurija Gagarina 84A, Yugoslavia.

SELBERG, Ingrid Maria, BA; American publishing executive; b 13 March 1950, Princeton, NJ; d of Atle and Helvig (née Liebermann) Selberg. *Education:* Univ of Columbia (New York). *Career:* Ed Collins Publs 1978–84; Editorial Dir Bantam (UK) 1984–85; Publr Heinemann Young Books, William Heinemann and Methuen Children's Books, London 1986–1995. *Publications:* Trees and Leaves 1977, Our Changing World 1981, Our Hidden World 1983.

SELEŠ, Monica; American (b Yugoslav) tennis player; b 2 Dec 1973, Novi Sad, Yugoslavia; d of the late Karol and Esther Seles. *Career:* Moved to USA 1986; winner Sport Goofy Singles 1984, Singles and Doubles 1985; Semi-finalist, French Open 1989; quarter-finalist, Wimbledon Championships (UK) 1990, finalist 1992; winner Lipton Int (USA), Italian Open, Lufthansa Cup (Berlin), French Open 1990, 1991, 1992, Virginia Slims Championships (Los Angeles, CA) 1990, 1991, 1992, Australian Open 1991, 1992, 1993, 1996, US Open 1991, 1992, Spanish Open (Barcelona, Spain) 1992, Canadian Open 1997, Tokyo Open 1997; named youngest No 1 ranked player in tennis history for women and men, at 17 years 3 months 9 days; runner-up US Open 1995. *Publication:* Monica: From Fear to Victory 1996. *Address:* c/o International Management Group, 1 Erieview Plaza, Cleveland, OH 44114, USA.

SELLICK, Phyllis, OBE, FRAM; British concert pianist; b 16 June 1911, Newbury Park, Essex; m Cyril Smith 1937 (died 1974); one s (deceased) one d. *Education:* Glenarm Coll (Ilford), Royal Acad of Music (London) and in Paris. *Career:* Prof Royal Coll of Music, London; Vice-Pres Inc Soc of Musicians Centenary Year 1982–83; works dedicated to her by Malcolm Arnold, Bliss, Gordon Jacob, Tippett and Vaughan Williams; Hon FRCM. *Leisure interests:* reading, Scrabble, bridge. *Address:* Beverley House, 29A Ranelagh Ave, Barnes, London SW13 0BN, UK.

SELLIER, Michèle Jeanne Henriette, MCL, DR RER POL; French civil servant; b 10 April 1941, Clermont-Ferrand; d of Robert and Christiane (née Sterckx) Lemaire; m Jean Sellier 1965; two d one s. *Education:* Lycées Jean de la Fontaine and Janson-de-Sailly and Law Faculty (Paris). *Career:* Asst Lecturer in Civil Law Univ of Paris X (Nanterre) 1969, Asst Lecturer 1969–75; Sr Lecturer Univ of Amiens 1975–83, Sr Lecturer in Civil Law and Dean of Law Faculty 1976–79; Head of Maison de la Culture, Amiens 1977–83; Town Councillor, Amiens 1977–83; Rector Acad of Reims 1983–87; Admin Insp-Gen for Nat Educ 1987–89, Insp-Gen 1989–; Head Int Centre for Pedagogy 1990–94; Expert Advisor to EU 1995–98; Under Sec for French Language Ministry of Foreign Affairs 1999–; Chevalier de la Légion d'Honneur; Chevalier de l'Ordre Nat du Mérite. *Publications:* Guide politique de Picardie (jtly) 1973, Les groupes d'action municipale 1975, Les conseillers régionaux 1983. *Leisure interests:* theatre, travel, swimming, skiing. *Address:* 244 blvd St Germain, 75007 Paris, France.

SEMENYAKA, Lyudmila Ivanova; Russian ballet dancer; b 16 Jan 1952, Leningrad (now St Petersburg); m (divorced); one s. *Education:* Leningrad Choreographic School. *Career:* Dancer with Kirov Ballet 1970–72; Prima Ballerina Bolshoi Theatre Co, Moscow 1972–96; has worked with English Nat Ballet 1990–91 and Scottish Nat Ballet; ballet teacher 1994–, with Moscow State Acad of Choreography 1999–; mem jury several int ballet competitions; performed in Europe, USA and Argentina; roles in ballets by Balanchine, Petit, Lavrovsky, Vassilyev, Boccadoro, Ben Stivenson, May Murdmaa; has partnered Mikhail Baryshnikov, Vladimir Vassilyev, Ivek Mukhamedov, Farukh Ruzimatov etc; winner Moscow Int Ballet Competition 1969, 1972, Varna 1972, Tokyo (First Prize and Gold Medal) 1976, Anna Pavlova Prize, Paris 1976, USSR State Prize 1977, USSR People's Artist 1986, Evening Standard Prize 1986. *Ballets include:* Angara, Giselle, Swan Lake, Spartak, Ivan the Terrible, Stone Flower; *Films include:* Ludmila Semenyaka Danse, The Bolshoi Ballerina, Spartak, The Story Flower, Raymonda, The Nutcracker, Fantasy on the theme of Casanova and others. *Address:* Bolshoi Theatre, Moscow, Teatralnaya pl 1, Russian Federation. *Telephone:* (095) 253-87-42 (Home); *Fax:* (095) 253-87-42 (Home); *Internet:* www.bolshoi.ru (Office).

SEMIZOROVA, Nina Lvovna; Russian ballet dancer; b 15 Oct 1956, Krivoi Rog; d of Lev Alexandrovich Semizorov and Larisa Dmitrievna Semizorova; m 1st Maris Liepa 1980; m 2nd Mark Peretokine 1988; one d. *Education:* Kiev Choreographic School. *Career:* Danced with Shevchenko Theatre of Opera and Ballet, Kiev 1975–78, with Bolshoi, Moscow 1978–; numerous int appearances; First Prize Int Ballet Competition (Moscow) 1977; Artist of Merit of Ukrainian SSR 1977, Honoured Artist of Russia 1987; Laureate of Moscow Komsomol 1987. *Ballets include:* Swan Lake, Lady Macbeth, Giselle, Don Quixote, Sleeping Beauty, La Bayadère, Spartacus, The Golden Age, Paquita, Raymonda, Les Sylphides. *Leisure interest:* reading. *Address:* 2 Zhukovskaya St, Apt 8, Moscow, Russian Federation. *Telephone:* (095) 923-40-84; *Fax:* (095) 923-40-84.

SEN, Aparna; Indian actress and film director. *Career:* Debut as actress in Sampati 1961; also Dir of several films. *Films include:* Actress: Akash Kusum, Ekhonee, Guru, Bombay Talkies, Hullabaloo, Jana Avanya; Dir: 36 Chowringhee Lane 1981, Paroma 1985, Sati (Special Jury Mention, Montréal Film Festival 1989) 1986. *Address:* Aparna Sharma, Flat 8C, Sonali Apts, 8-2A Alipur Park Rd, Kolkata 700 027, India.

SEN, Gita, PH D; Indian economist; b 30 Oct 1948, Pune; d of V. and Lakshmi Kalyanasundaram; m Chiranjib Sen 1971; one d. *Education:* Fergusson Coll (Pune), Delhi School of Econs and Stanford Univ (USA). *Career:* Asst Prof New School for Social Research, New York 1975–81; Fellow Centre for Devt Studies, Trivandrum 1981; Rama Mehta Endowment Lecturer, Radcliffe Coll, MA, USA 1988; Distinguished Mellon Professor, Vassar Coll, NY, USA 1991–92; Visiting Prof Center for Population and Devt Studies, Harvard Univ, USA 1992; Founder-mem Devt Alternatives with Women for a New Era (DAWN) 1984. *Publication:* Development, Crises and Alternative Visions: Third World Women's Perspectives 1987. *Leisure interests:* reading, swimming. *Address:* Centre for Development Studies, Aadalam Rd, Ulloor, Trivandrum, Kerala State, India; Harvard University, Harvard Center for Population and Devt Studies, 9 Bow St, Cambridge, MA 02138, USA.

SÉRAPHIM, Juliana; Lebanese artist; b Jaffa (then Palestine). *Education:* Acads of Fine Arts (Paris, Madrid and Florence). *Career:* Group exhibitions in Lebanon and Europe and at Biennales in Paris, Alexandria, São Paolo.

SERENY, Gitta; Austrian writer; b 13 March 1923, Austria; d of Gyula and Margit Sereny; m Donald Honeyman 1948; one s one d. *Education:* Vienna Realgymnasium Luithlen, Stonar House School (Sandwich, Kent) and Sorbonne (Paris). *Career:* Writer and journalist for several newspapers and periodicals including The Times, The Independent, Die Ziet, Dagens Nyheter, NY Review of Books. *Publications:* The Medallion 1957, The Case of Mary Bell 1972, Into that Darkness 1974, The Invisible Children 1984, Albert Speer, His Battle with Truth 1995, Cries Unheard 1998, German Trauma 2000. *Leisure interests:* reading, hiking. *Address:* c/o Metropolitan Books, Henry Holt and Co, 115 West 18th St, New York, NY 10011, USA.

SERGEYEVA, Tatyana Pavlovna; Russian composer; b 28 Nov 1951, Kalinin (now Tver); d of Korovkin Pavel Petrovich and Vershinskaya Yevgenya Analolyevna; m Vikharev Ivan Timofeyevich. *Education:* Moscow State Conservatory. *Career:* Concertmaster for class of symphony conducting, Moscow State Conservatory 1975–88; music teacher Little Music Studios (pvt school) 1997–; works performed in festivals of contemporary music in USA, Scotland, France, Belgium, Germany, Finland, Italy, Poland; performs as pianist, organist, clavichordist; mem Composers' Union 1982; D. Shostakovich Prize

1987. *Works include:* 3 piano concertos 1975, 1985, 2000, concerto for bass and string orchestra 1980, for trombone and orchestra 1986, for violin and keyboard instruments, sonatas for trombone and cello 1986, for cello and organ 1988, for violin and organ 1994, variations on the theme of T. Tolstaya 1991, variations for violin, organ and winds, variations on the theme of Juan Idalgo for 4 cellos, vocal cycles on lyrics of Russian poets of the 18th century and Antiquity poets, instrumental ensembles; *Repertoire includes:* Bach, Beethoven, Liszt, Mendelsohnn, Chopin, Busoni, Russian music by Bortnyansky, Tchaikovsky, Balakirev, N. Rubinstein, Arensky, N. Cherepnin, A. Rubinstein, contemporary music. *Leisure interests:* painting, exhibitions in Russia. *Address:* Novopeschanaya str 19/10, apt 165, 125252 Moscow, Russian Federation. *Telephone:* (095) 930-78-21.

SEROTA, Baroness (Life Peer), cr 1967, of Hampstead in Greater London, **Beatrice Serota,** DBE, B SC; British politician; b 15 Oct 1919; m Stanley Serota 1942; one s one d. *Education:* John Howard School and LSE. *Career:* Mem Hampstead Borough Council 1945–49, London Co Council (Brixton) 1954–65, Chair Children's Cttee 1958–65; mem GLC (Lambeth) 1964–67; Chief Whip; Minister of State for Health, Dept of Health and Social Security 1969–70; Deputy Speaker House of Lords 1985–, Prin Deputy Chair of Cttees and Chair EC Select Cttee 1986–92; Founder, Chair Comm for Local Admin 1974–82; mem Advisory Council on Child Care, Cen Training Council on Child Care 1958–68; mem Treatment Comm on Penal System 1964–68, Advisory Council on Penal Systems 1966–68, 1974–79, Chair 1976–79; mem Seebohm Cttee on Org of Local Authority Personal Social Services 1966–68, Community Relations Comm 1970–76; mem BBC Complaints Comm 1975–77, Gov BBC 1977–82; JP Inner London; Hon D LITT (Loughborough) 1983. *Leisure interests:* needlepoint, gardening, collecting shells. *Address:* The Coach House, 15 Lyndhurst Terrace, London NW3 5QA, UK.

SERREAU, Coline; French film director; d of Jean-Marie Serreau. *Career:* Acted in several stage plays including Lapin, lapin in Paris; wrote and acted in Bertuccelli's On s'est trompé d'histoire d'amour 1973; f trapeze school in Canada. *Films:* Oedipus the King (TV), Mais qu'est-ce quelles veulent (documentary) 1975, Pourquoi pas! 1976, Qu'est-ce qu'on attend pour être heureux! 1982, Trois hommes et un couffin (Three Men and a Cradle) 1985, Romuald et Juliette 1989.

SERVICE, Louisa Anne, OBE, MA; British business executive and magistrate; d of the late Henry Harold and Alice Louisa (née Weaver) Hemming; m Alistair Stanley Douglas Service 1959 (divorced 1984); one s one d. *Education:* Schools in USA, Canada and UK, Ecole des Sciences Politiques (Paris) and St Hilda's Coll (Oxford). *Career:* Export Dir Ladybird Appliances Ltd 1957–59; Dir Hemming Group of Cos 1966, Deputy Chair 1974–76; Jt Chair 1976–; Dir Glass's Information Services Ltd 1971, Deputy Chair 1976–81, Chair 1981–95; JP Inner London Courts, Juvenile, Youth and Family 1969–2001, Chair 1995–2001; Chair Exec Cttee Inner London Juvenile Courts 1977–79, Inner London Juvenile Liaison Cttee 1986–88 (mem 1980–86); JP Inner London Petty Sessional Div 1980–; mem Inner London Family Panel 1991–; mem Dept of Trade Consumer Credit Act Appeals Panel 1981–, Cttee of Magistrates 1985–88, Inner London Magistrates Court Cttee 1995–2001 (Chair Audit Cttee), Financial Intermediaries, Managers' and Brokers' Regulatory Asscn Appeals Tribunal 1989–92, Adjudication & Appeals Cttee Solicitors Complaints Bureau 1992–93; Vice-Chair Paddington Probation Hostel 1976–85; Vice-Pres Commonwealth Countries League 1999–; Hon Sec Women's India Asscn 1967–74; Chair Council Mayer-Lismann Opera Workshop 1976–91; mem Man Cttee Friends of Covent Garden 1982–; Dir Youth and Music 1988–90, Chair 1990–2001; mem Haydn/Mozart Soc 1990–92, Performing Arts Lab 1996–99; Dir Jacqueline du Pré Music Building Ltd 1995–, Chair 2001–; mem Rudolph Kempe Advisory Panel 2000–; Dir Opera Circus Ltd 2001–; mem St Hilda's Coll Oxford Devt Cttee 1995–; Trustee Kamilla Trust 1989–, Commonwealth Countries League Educ Fund 2000–; Hon Treas St Hilda's Coll Law Network 1998–. *Leisure interests:* travel, companionship. *Address:* c/o Hemming Publishing Ltd, 32 Vauxhall Bridge Rd, London SW1V 2SS, UK.

SESSAR-KARPP, Ellen E., MA; German feminist sociologist; b 5 Dec 1943, Bonn; m Klaus Sessar 1970; one s one d. *Education:* Univs of Bonn, Tübingen and Dallas (TX, USA). *Career:* Educator Montréal,

Canada and Boston, MA, USA 1970–72; Asst Prof Univ of Freiburg 1973–79; Researcher in Social Sciences and Women's Studies, teacher Univ of Hamburg 1977–; Co-Founder, Dir FrauenTechnikZentrum, Deutscher Frauenring eV (a computer centre run for and by women) 1985–; mem German UNESCO Nat Comm. *Publications:* Lernvoraussetzungen jugendlicher Inhaftierter 1981, Berufsbezogene Bildungsangebote für Frauen nach der Familienphase 1987, Erweiterte Berufschancen für Frauen durch Informationstechnische Bildung (jtly) 1992. *Address:* Deutscher Frauenring eV, Normannenweg 2, 2000 Hamburg, Germany (Office); Heidelerchenweg 67, 2000 Hamburg 65, Germany (Home). *Telephone:* (40) 2514399 (Office); (40) 6062411 (Home); *Fax:* (40) 2517730 (Office).

SETON, Lady Julia Clements, OBE; British writer and floral art judge; d of the late Frank Clements; m Sir Alexander Hay Seton 1962 (died 1963). *Education:* Isle of Wight and Zwicker Coll (Belgium). *Career:* Organized and led first Judge's School Royal Horticultural Soc; conducted classes for floral art judges in the UK; speaker in field; awarded Victoria Medal of Honour, Royal Horticultural Soc 1974. *Publications include:* Fun With Flowers, Fun Without Flowers, 101 Ideas for Flower Arrangement, Party Pieces, The Julia Clements Colour Book of Flower Arrangments, Flower Arrangements in Stately Homes, Julia Clements' Gift Book of Flower Arranging, Flowers in Praise, The Art of Arranging a Flower, My Life with Flowers 1993. *Address:* 122 Swan Court, London SW3 5RU, UK. *Telephone:* (20) 7352-9039.

SEVERINSEN, Hanne; Danish politician; b 12 June 1944, Copenhagen; d of Erik and Else Maris (née Madsen) Severinsen; m William McFetrich 1986. *Education:* Univ of Copenhagen. *Career:* Mem Venstre (Liberal Party) 1971, mem Exec Cttee 1976–85, Vice-Chair 1982–85; mem Copenhagen Town Council 1974–84; Sr Lecturer in History and Political Science; mem Bd Danish Centre for Human Rights; mem Folketinget (Parl) 1984, Chair Cttee for Research and Tech, Party Spokesperson on science, on human rights and on Higher Educ; mem Comm for Women of UN 1984–88 (Vice-Pres 1986–88); mem Council of Europe 1991, Chair 2001. *Publications:* Ny-Liberalismen—og dens Rodder; numerous articles. *Address:* Folketinget, Christiansborg Slot, 1240 Copenhagen K, Denmark; Lønborgvej 7, Hedeby, 6900 Skjern, Denmark (Home). *Telephone:* 97-35-35-33 (Home); *Fax:* 97-35-35-33 (Home).

SEYMOUR, Jane; British actress; b (Joyce Frankenberg) 15 Feb 1951, Hillingdon, Middx; d of John Benjamin and Mieke Frankenberg; m David Flynn 1981 (separated); m 4th James Keach; four s two d. *Education:* Arts Educational School (London). *Career:* Fmr Dancer with London Festival Ballet; has appeared on Broadway, on TV and in numerous films; mem Screen Actors' Guild, Actors' Equity, American Fed of TV and Radio Artists; Hon Citizen of Illinois 1977. *Films include:* Oh What a Lovely War 1968, The Only Way 1968, Young Winston 1969, Live and Let Die 1971, Sinbad and the Eye of the Tiger 1973, Somewhere in Time 1979, Oh Heavenly Dog 1979, Lassiter 1984, Head Office, Scarlet Pimpernel, Haunting Passion, Dark Mirror, Obsessed with a Married Woman, Killer on Board, The Tunnel 1988, The French Revolution, Keys to Freedom; *TV appearances include:* Films: Frankenstein, The True Story 1972, Captains and the Kings 1976, 7th Avenue 1976, The Awakening Land 1977, The Four Feathers 1977, Battlestar Galactica, Dallas Cowboy Cheerleaders 1979, Our Mutual Friend, Jamaica Inn 1982, Sun Also Rises 1984, Crossings 1986, Keys to Freedom, Angel of Death 1990, Sunstroke (also exec producer), Heidi, Praying Mantis (also co-producer), A Passion for Justice: The Hazel Brannon Smith Story (also co-exec producer); Mini-series: East of Eden 1980, The Richest Man in the World (Emmy Award) 1988, The Women He Loved 1988, Onassis, Jack the Ripper 1988, War and Remembrance 1988, 1989; Series: The Onedine Line, Dr Quinn Medicine Woman (Golden Globe Award for Best Actress in a TV Drama); *Musicals include:* Amadeus 1980–81. *Address:* c/o Metropolitan Talent Agency, 4526 Wilshire Blvd, Los Angeles, CA 90010, USA.

SEYMOUR, Lynn, CBE; Canadian ballet dancer; b 8 March 1939, Wainwright, AB; d of E. V. Springett; m 1st Colin Jones 1963 (divorced 1974); three s; m 2nd Philip Pace 1974; m 3rd Vanya Hackel 1983 (divorced 1988). *Education:* Royal Ballet School. *Career:* Graduated to Royal Ballet 1957, Soloist, then Prin Dancer 1958, Guest Artist Royal Ballet 1970–78; joined Deutsche Oper, Berlin 1966; Artistic Dir of

Ballet Bayerische Staatsoper, Munich, Germany 1979–80; Guest Artist with other cos including Alvin Ailey; London Evening Standard Drama Award 1977. *Ballets include:* The Burrow 1958, Swan Lake 1958, Giselle 1958, The Invitation 1960, The Two Pigeons 1961, Symphony 1963, Romeo and Juliet 1964, Anastasia 1966, Dances at a Gathering, The Concert, The Seven Deadly Sins, Flowers 1972, Shukumei, The Four Seasons 1975, Side Show, Rituals 1975, Manon Lescaut 1976, A Month in the Country 1976, Mayerling 1978, Manon 1978, Choreography for Rashomon 1976, The Court of Love 1977, Intimate Letters 1978, Mae and Polly, Boreas, Tattooed Lady, Wolfy, The Ballet Rambert 1987; *Publication:* Lynn: Leaps and Boundaries (autobiog, jtly) 1984. *Address:* c/o Artistes in Action, 16 Balderton St, London W1Y 1TF, UK.

SEYMOUR, Stephanie Kulp, JD; American federal judge; b 16 Oct 1940, Battle Creek, MI; d of Francis Bruce and Frances Cecelia (née Bria) Kulp; m R. Thomas Seymour 1972; four c. *Education:* Smith Coll (MA) and Harvard Univ (MA). *Career:* Called to the Bar, OK 1965; pvt practice Boston, MA 1965–66, Tulsa, OK 1966–67, 1971–79, and Houston, TX 1968–69; Assoc Doerner, Stuart, Saunders, Daniel and Anderson 1971–75, Partner 1975–79; Judge US Court of Appeals (Tenth Circuit), Tulsa, OK 1979–94, Chief Justice 1994–; Assoc Bar Examiner Oklahoma Bar Asscn 1973–79; Trustee Tulsa Co Law Library 1977–78; mem Cttee on Defender Services, US Judicial Conf 1985, 1994–, ABA. *Address:* US Court of Appeals, 4-562 US Courthouse, 333 W Fourth St, Tulsa, OK 74103, USA.

SHABBIR, Behjat, MA; Pakistani broadcasting executive; b Wazirabad; d of Mohammad Aslam; m Gilani Shabbir 1983; two s. *Education:* Govt Coll (Faisalabad), Univ of the Punjab (Lahore), Pakistan Broadcasting Acad and Nat Inst of Modern Languages. *Career:* Professional training with Deutsche Welle, Germany; staff reporter, The Muslim English newspaper 1979; Research Officer compiling study of old tribes, Nat Inst of Folk Heritage 1978; joined Pakistan Broadcasting Corpn as Programme Producer, Sr Producer 1979; Merit Scholarship 1969–76; has been awarded more than 50 First and Second Prizes in Urdu and English debates. *Publications:* Magic Bird (trans) 1989, Thoughts To Build On (trans) 1989, Here is Help (trans) 1989. *Leisure interests:* reading literature, poetry, fiction, philosophy and psychology, listening to music. *Address:* House 13, St 35, F-6/1, Islamabad, Pakistan. *Telephone:* (51) 855044.

SHAFFER, Beverly Victoria, M SC; Canadian film director and producer; b 8 May 1945, Montréal; d of Phillip and Anne (née Simack) Shaffer. *Education:* McGill Univ (Montréal) and Univ of Boston (MA, USA). *Career:* Teacher 1967–69; Assoc Producer WGBH TV, Boston 1971–75; Film Dir and Producer Nat Film Bd of Canada 1976–; many awards including Emily Award, American Film Festival 1989. *Productions:* Children of Canada (series), I'll Find a Way (Acad Award for Best Live Action Short 1978) 1977, To a Safer Place 1988, Children of Jerusalem 1996, Just a Wedding 1999. *Address:* National Film Board, POB 6100, Montréal, PQ H3C 3H5, Canada. *Telephone:* (514) 283-9509.

SHAFFER, Gail S., BA; American state official; b 1 Aug 1948, Kingston, NY; d of Robert and Marion (née Gallagher) Shaffer. *Education:* Elmira Coll (NY) and Inst d'Etudes Politiques (Paris). *Career:* Legal Asst Rahmas Law Firm 1973–76; Special Asst to Commr, New York State Environmental Conservation 1977–79; Exec Dir New York State Rural Affairs Council 1979–80; elected to New York State Ass 1980–83; apptd Sec of State by Gov of New York State 1983; fmr Supervisor Town of Blenheim, NY; mem NY State Democratic Cttee 1976, Women Execs in Govt State NY State Asscn; Exec Dir Business and Professional Women USA, Rep on Women's Business Enterprise Nat Council. *Leisure interests:* music, theatre, art, skiing. *Address:* c/o National Women's Business Council, 409 3rd St, SW, Suite 210, Washington, DC 20024, USA; Indian Trail Rd, N Blenheim, NY 12131, USA.

SHAHANI, Leticia Ramos, MA, PH D; Philippine former United Nations official, diplomatist and politician; b 30 Sept 1929, Lingayen, Pangasinan; d of Narciso Ramos; m Ranjee Shanani; two s one d. *Education:* Wellesley Coll (MA, USA), Univs of Columbia (NY, USA) and Paris. *Career:* Chair UN Comm on Status of Women 1964, Alt Rep 1969, Rep 1970–74, Rapporteur 1972; mem Del UN Gen Ass 1974–79, Alt mem 1980; Rep to Third Cttee of Gen Ass 1974–79, Chair 1978;

mem Del to UN World Conf on Int Women's Year (Mexico) 1975; Rep Preparatory Cttee for UN Conf on the Mid-Decade for Women 1978–80, Vice-Chair 1980; UN Asst Sec-Gen for Social Devt and Humanitarian Affairs 1981–86; Special Rep of UN Sec-Gen during Int Year of Disabled Persons 1981; Sec-Gen World Conf to Review and Appraise the Achievements of the UN Decade for Women 1985; Sec-Gen UN Congress on the Prevention of Crime and the Treatment of Offenders 1985; Vice-Chair Del to Philippine-Romanian Jt Trade Comm 1976, Philippine-Romanian Scientific and Technological Comm 1976; Chair Jt Philippine-Australian Trade Comm 1978, 1980, Vice-Chair 1979; Chair ASEAN-Canberra Cttee 1979; Amb to Romania and concurrently non-resident Amb to Hungary and the GDR 1975–78, Amb to Australia 1978–80; Under-Sec of Foreign Affairs 1986–87; apptd Senator 1987; Chair Nat Comm on Women, Cttee on Foreign Relations; fmr Faculty mem Univ of the Philippines, New School for Social Research (NY, USA), Int Study and Research Inst (NY); Dean Grad School, Lyceum of the Philippines 1970–72, William Quasha Prof of Int Relations 1974–75; Pres Asscn of Awardees of the Outstanding Women of the Philippines 1974–78; Commr Nat Comm on the Role of Filipino Women (Manila) 1975; mem Exec Cttee World Young Women's Christian Asscn 1975–79; Hon LL D (Centro Escolar) 1976; Hon DH (Silliman) 1983; One of Outstanding Women in the Nation's Service 1974; awarded Order of Teodor Vladimirescu (Romania) 1978; Distinguished Alumni Achievement Award (Wellesley Coll) 1987. *Publication:* The Philippines: the land and the people 1965. *Address:* Senate, Batasang Pambansa Bldg, Quezon City, Manila, Philippines.

SHAHEEN, C. Jeanne, BA, M SC; American state governor; b 28 Jan 1947, St Charles, MO; m William H. Shaheen; three c. *Education:* Univ of Shippensburg and Univ of Mississippi. *Career:* Mem NH Senate (Democrat); Gov of NH 1997–. *Address:* Office of the Governor, 107 N Main St, Room 208, Concord, NH 03301, USA.

SHAIKH, Raana; Pakistani broadcasting executive; b 1946; m Naj-muddin; two c. *Education:* Univ of Oxford (UK). *Career:* Joined Pakistan TV Corpn 1967, Man Dir 1995. *Address:* Pakistan Television Corpn Ltd, Federal TV Complex, Constitution Ave, POB 1221, Islamabad, Pakistan.

SHAKHNAZAROV, Karen Georgyevich; Russian film director and scriptwriter; b 8 July 1952, Krasnodar; s of Georgy Shakhnazarov and Anna Shakhnazarova; m Darya Igorevna Mayorova 1972; two s one d. *Education:* All-Union Inst of Cinematography. *Career:* Asst Film Dir Mosfilm Studio 1973–75; on staff Mosfilm 1976–; Chair Bd of Dirs Courier Studio at Mosfilm 1991–, Pres, Dir-Gen Mosfilm Concern 1998–; Artistic Dir VI Creative Union 1987; Boris Polevoy Prize 1982, Special Prize of the Jury (Grenoble) 1984, Silver Medal of Int Film Festival (Lodz) 1984, Comsomol Prize 1986, Brothers Vassilyev State Prize 1988, Merited Worker of Arts of Russia. *Film scripts:* Ladies Invite Partners 1981, God Souls 1980, We Are From Jazz (Int Film Festival Diplomas, London, Chicago, Belgrade 1984) 1983, Winter Evening in Gagry 1985, Courier (Int Film Festival Prize, Moscow) 1986, Town Zero 1989, Tsar-Murderer (Grand Prix, Int Film Festival, Belgrade) 1991, Dreams 1993, American Daughter 1995, Day of Full Moon (Special Prize, Karlovy Vary Film Festival) 1998. *Leisure interests:* swimming, driving. *Address:* Mosfilmovskaya str 1, 119858 Moscow, Russian Federation (Home).

SHALALA, Donna Edna, PH D; American professor of political science; b 14 Feb 1941, Cleveland, OH; d of James A. Shalala and Edna Smith. *Education:* Western Coll and Syracuse Univ. *Career:* Volunteer Peace Corps, Iran 1962–64; Asst to Dir Metropolitan Studies Program, Syracuse Univ 1965–69, Instructor and Asst to Dean, Maxwell Grad School 1969–70; Asst Prof of Political Science, Bernard Baruch Coll, City Univ, New York 1970–72; Prof of Political Science and Pres Hunter Coll 1980–88; Assoc Prof of Politics and Educ Teachers' Coll, Columbia Univ 1972–79; Asst Sec for Policy Devt and Research, Dept of Housing and Urban Devt, Washington, DC 1977–80; Prof of Political Science and Pres Hunter Coll, City Univ New York 1980–88; Dir Inst of Int Econs, Ditchley Foundation 1981–93; Prof of Political Science and Chancellor, Univ of Wisconsin, Madison, WI 1988–92; Sec of Health and Human Services 1993–; Dir Inst of Int Econs 1981–93, Ditchley Foundation 1981–93; mem Nat. Acad of Arts and Sciences,

American Soc for Public Admin; 24 hon degrees. *Publications:* Neighborhood Governance 1971, The City and the Constitution 1972, The Property Tax and the Voters 1973, The Decentralization Approach 1974. *Leisure interests:* tennis, mountain-climbing, reading, spectator sports. *Address:* Department of Health and Human Services, 200 Independence Ave, SW, Room 61F, Washington, DC 20201-0001, USA. *Telephone:* (608) 263-3288.

SHAM POO, Karin Elise Holmgrunn, LL B; Norwegian international organization official; b 18 Dec 1943, Oslo; d of Thomas and Ruth Holmgrunn; m Stanley Sham Poo 1992; one d. *Education:* Norwegian Coll of Banking. *Career:* Sec Bd of Dirs and Man Bergens Kreditbank, Oslo 1973–75, Man 1975–77; Asst Gen Man A/S Kjobmandsbanken, Oslo 1977–79; Asst Gen Man Christiania Bank, Baerum 1979–80, Deputy Gen Man 1980–82, Gen Man Marketing Div and Sr Vice-Pres 1982–85; Comptroller UNICEF, New York, USA 1985–87, Deputy Exec Dir 1987. *Address:* 12 Lynwood Rd, Scarsdale, NY 10583, USA. *Telephone:* (212) 326-7014; *Fax:* (212) 326-7758; *E-mail:* kshampoo@unicef.org.

SHANGE, Ntozake, MA; American playwright and poet; b 18 Oct 1948, Trenton, NJ; d of Paul and Eloise Williams; m David Murray 1977 (divorced); one c. *Education:* Barnard Coll and Univ of S California. *Career:* Mem Faculty, Sonoma State Univ 1973–75, Mills Coll 1975, City Coll of New York 1975, Douglass Coll 1978; performing mem Sounds in Motion Dance Co; Dir The Mighty Gents 1979; author, An Evening with Diana Ross: The Big Event 1977; Guggenheim Fellow 1981; mem Nat Acad of TV Arts and Sciences, Acad of American Poets, PEN America; recipient of numerous drama and poetry awards. *Publications:* plays: Melissa and Smith 1976, For Colored Girls Who Have Considered Suicide/When the Rainbow is Enuf (also acted in) 1976, Where the Mississippi Meets the Amazon (also acted in) 1977, From Okra to Greens 1978, Spell #7 1979, Black and White Two Dimensional Planes 1979, A Photograph: A Study in Cruelty (also dir) 1979, Boogie Woogie Landscapes 1980, Mouths 1981, A Photograph: Lovers in Motion 1981, Three Views of Mt Fuji 1987; novels: Sassafrass, Cypress and Indigo 1976, Betsey Brown 1985, The Love Space Demands 1991, I Live in Music 1994; poetry: Natural Disasters and Other Festive Occasions 1977, Nappy Edges 1978, Three Pieces 1981, A Daughter's Geography 1983, From Okra to Greens 1984; essays, short stories, non-fiction, adaptations; contribs to magazines and anthologies. *Address:* c/o St Martin's Press, 175 Fifth Ave, New York, NY 10010, USA.

SHANKAR, Anoushka; Indian sitar player; b 9 June 1981, London; d of Sukanya and Ravi Shankar. *Education:* San Dieguito Acad (San Diego, CA). *Career:* Professional debut in New Delhi 1995 at age of 13; performances since then at major concert halls in India, Europe, USA and Asia; House of Commons Shield 1998; Nat Council on Youth Leadership Award 1998; San Dieguito Acad Award Winner 1999. *Recordings include:* Anoushka 1998, Anourag 2000. *Leisure interests:* reading, theatre, ballet, travelling. *Address:* c/o Sulivan Sweetland, 28 Albion St, London W2 2AX, UK. *Telephone:* (20) 7262-0333; *Fax:* (20) 7402-5851; *E-mail:* as@sulivansweetland.co.uk; *Internet:* www.anoushkashankar.com.

SHANKS, Ann Zane; American film producer and director and photographer; b New York; d of Louis and Sadye (née Rosenthal) Kushner; m 1st Ira Zane (deceased); m 2nd Robert Horton Shanks 1959; three c. *Education:* Carnegie-Mellon (PA) and Columbia (NY) Univs. *Career:* Teacher and Moderator Special Symposia Museum of Modern Art, New York; teacher New School for Social Research; film producer and dir, photographer and writer for numerous magazines and newspapers; has exhibited photographs at Museum of Modern Art, Metropolitan Museum of Art and Jewish Museum (New York); mem American Soc of Magazine Photographers, Overseas Press Club, American Women in Film, Dirs' Guild of America; has received awards from int competitions. *Films include:* Central Park (Cine Golden Eagle Award, Cambodia Film Festival Award) 1969, Denmark... A Loving Embrace (Cine Golden Eagle Award 1973), Tivoli (San Francisco Film Festival Award, American Film Festival Award); *TV programmes include:* Producer: American Life Style (Silver Award, five Gold Medal Awards, Int TV and Film Festival, New York, two Cine Golden Eagle Awards), Mousie Baby, Drop-out Father, A Day in the Country (also Dir), The

Avant Garde in Russia 1910–1930, ABC Morning Show, Good Afternoon Detroit; Dir: Friendships, Secrets and Lies; *Publications include:* Old Is What You Get, Busted Lives... Dialogues with Kids in Jail, Garbage and Stuff.

SHANNON, Lois, BA; American business executive; b 19 Jan 1962, Charlottesville, VA; d of Edgar Finley and Eleanor Bosworth Shannon; m Thomas William Virden 1990; two s. *Education:* Duke Univ (NC) and l'Université Catholique de l'Ouest (Angers). *Career:* Man Consultant Bain & Co, Boston; Dir Business and Channel Devt in Europe, Consumer Marketing – Retail Channel Devt in the US, Apple Computer Inc; currently MD Internet Practice Russell Reynolds Assocs Inc. *Address:* Russell Reynolds Associates, Inc, London SW1, UK; 27 Shawfield St, London SW3 4BA, UK. *Telephone:* (20) 7830-8013; *E-mail:* lshannon@russellreynolds.com.

SHAPIRO, Erin Patria Margaret (see Pizzey, Erin Patria Margaret).

SHAPIRO, Norma Sondra Levy, BA, JD; American federal judge; b 27 July 1928; d of Bert and Jane (née Kotkin) Levy; m Bernard Shapiro 1949; three s. *Education:* Univs of Michigan and Pennsylvania. *Career:* Instructor in Legal Writing Univ of Pennsylvania 1951–52, Law and Psychiatry 1955–56; Law Clerk Supreme Court of Pennsylvania 1951–52; Assoc Dechert Price & Rhoads, Philadelphia 1956–58, 1967–73, Partner 1973–78, mem Policy Cttee 1976–78; US Dist Court Judge, Philadelphia 1978–; Legal Adviser Regional Council Child Psychiatry; Guest Ed Shingle 1972; mem American, Pennsylvania, Philadelphia and Fed Bar Asscns, American Law Inst, Nat Asscn of Women Judges; Fellow American Bar Foundation; Vice-Pres Jewish Publication Soc; Assoc Trustee Univ of PA Law School 1978–93; fmr Trustee Women's Law Project, Albert Einstein Medical Center 1979, Fed of Jewish Agencies 1980–83; Woman of Distinction (Golden Slipper Club) 1979; Woman of the Year (Oxford Circle Jewish Community Center) 1979; Bill of Rights Award (Fed Bar Asscn) 1991; Hannah G. Solomon Award (Nat Council of Jewish Women) 1992. *Address:* US District Courthouse, Rm 10614, US Courthouse, Independence Mall, W, Philadelphia, PA 19106, USA (Office); 417 Hidden River Rd, Penn Valley, Narbeth, PA 19072, USA (Home). *Telephone:* (215) 597-9141 (Office); (215) 839-3037 (Home).

SHARAF, Leila Abdul Hamid, MA; Jordanian (b Lebanese) politician; b Beirut, Lebanon; m Abdul Hamid Sharaf 1965 (died 1980); two s. *Education:* American Univ of Beirut (Lebanon). *Career:* Ed, Newscaster, Special Interviewer TV News Dept, Lebanon 1962–65; moved to Jordan 1965; mem Consultative Cttee on the Theatre, Ministry of Culture 1976–79; mem Nat Consultative Council (temp Parl) 1982–84, Minister of Information 1984–85, mem Senate; Pres Muslim Women's Asscn (Washington, DC, USA) 1967–72, Islamic Cultural Soc (NY, USA) 1972–76; Founder-mem and Pres Cerebral Palsy Foundation 1977–79; mem Bd of Trustees Univ of Jordan 1981–85, American Univ of Beirut 1981, The Royal Endowment for Culture and Educ, Noor Al-Hussein Foundation, Arab Org for Human Rights, Arab Thought Forum; mem Jordan Bd of Educ 1984–85. *Address:* POB 94, Jubaiha, Jordan. *Telephone:* (6) 842155; *Fax:* (6) 835414.

SHARAN RANI, MA; Indian musician and composer; b 9 April 1929, Delhi; d of Pannu Lal and Nand Rani; m Sultan S. Backliwal 1960; one d. *Education:* Delhi Univ and City Univ of Los Angeles (CA, USA), and with gurus Ustad Allauddin Khan and Ustad Ali Akbar Khan. *Career:* Plays Sarod (Indian musical instrument); numerous TV and radio appearances; concert tours to fmr USSR 1960, Mongolia 1960, Nepal 1960, 1982, USA 1961, 1986, UK 1961, 1966, 1967, 1986, 2000, France 1961, 1966, 1967, 1989, 2000, Italy 1961, Switzerland 1961, Germany 1961, 1966, Australia 1961, Fiji 1961, Iran 1966, 1967, Bangladesh 1972, Greece 1989, Czechoslovakia 1989, Belgium 1989, Morocco 2000, Poland 2000; Trustee Indraprastha Educational Trust 1975–, Chair 1985–90; mem Governing Body Indraprastha Coll for Women 1975–; Life mem Lalit Inst of Pacific Archaeology 1970–; Assoc Founder-mem Indian Musicological Soc; mem Selection Cttee Kuru-shetra Univ until 1990; mem Arts Council of Delhi State for Music, Dance, Literature and Fine Arts, All India Women's Conf; donated over 300 musical instruments to Nat Museum, Sharan Rani Gallery opened 1980; Hon D MUS; numerous awards including Padma Shri 1968, Delhi State Gov Sahitya Kala Parishad Award 1974, Sangeet Natak

Akademi Award 1986, Padma Bhushan 2000. *Recordings include:* Bhairavi/Puriya-Dhanashri, Malkanus/Mian-ki-Todi, Lalit/Kausi-Ka-nada, Nat-Bhairav/Darbari-kanada, Yaman-Kalyan/Bhairavi-Vogue, Hemant/Bhairavi, Puriya Dhanashri/Bageshree, Ahir Bhairav/Jogia/Lalit, Bilas Khani Todi/Zila-Kafi; *Publication:* The Divine Sarod (Its Antiquity, Origin and Development from 200 BC) 1992. *Leisure interests:* collecting old and rare musical instruments, manuscripts, books. *Address:* C-183 Defence Colony, New Delhi 110 024, India. *Telephone:* (11) 4633806; *Fax:* (11) 4633806.

SHARISHVILI-CHANTURIA, Irina; Georgian politician; m Georgi Chanturia (deceased); one s. *Career:* Leader Nat Democratic Party of Georgia following assassination of her husband 1994–. *Address:* Nat Democratic Party of Georgia, 380008 Tbilisi, Rustaveli 21, Georgia.

SHARMA, Archana, PH D, D SC; Indian professor of botany; b 16 Feb 1932, Poona; d of the late N. P. and R. Mookerjea; m Arun Kumar Sharma 1955. *Education:* Univ of Calcutta. *Career:* Research Fellow Univ of Calcutta 1951, Research Officer 1956, Reader in Genetics 1971, apptd Prof of Genetics 1977, currently Prof of Botany; Sec-Gen Indian Science Congress Asscn 1983–85, Gen Pres 1986–87; Pres Biological Sciences, Nat Acad of Sciences (India) 1985; Pres Indian Botanical Soc 1989; Fellow and Council mem Indian Nat Science Acad (New Delhi), Indian Acad of Sciences (Bangalore) 1976; S. S. Bhatnagar Award, Council Scientific and Industrial Research (New Delhi) 1976; awarded Padma Bhushan by Pres of India 1984, Birbal Sahni Medal, Indian Botanical Soc 1984, Fed of Chambers of Commerce Award in Life Sciences 1984, G. P. Chatterjee Award (ISCA) 1994, Ashutosh Memorial Prize (ISCA) 1999. *Publications:* author of seven books, ed of 14 books; 350 papers on genetics and genetic toxicology in int scientific journals. *Address:* Calcutta University, Dept of Botany, Centre for Advanced Study in Cell and Chromosome Research, 35 Ballygunj Circular Rd, Kolkata 700 019, India. *Telephone:* (33) 405802.

SHARMA, Prem Lata, PH D; Indian educator; b 10 May 1927, Nakodar, Punjab; d of L. C. and Mayadevi Sharma. *Education:* Univ of Delhi and Banaras Hindu Univ. *Career:* Lecturer in Music Banaras Hindu Univ 1955–57, Reader in Theory of Music and Researcher 1957–81, Prof in Musicology 1981–87, Emer Prof 1993–; Acting Prin College of Music and Fine Arts, Banaras Hindu Univ 1957–61, Head of Dept 1957–61, Dean 1957–61, 1964–66, 1969–71, Head Dept of Musicology 1966–85, Dean Faculty of Performing Arts 1979–83; Vice-Chancellor Indira Kala Sangit Vishwavidyalaya Khairagarh (MP) 1985–88; Chair UP Sangit Natak Akademi, Lucknow 1983–86; Vice-Chair Sangeet Natak Akademi, New Delhi 1994–; teacher at Summer schools in USA; has attended int confs on Sanskrit studies; Dir of reconstructed Sanskrit dramas 1973, 1975, 1978, 1981, of festivals of Dhrupad Indian music 1979, 1980, 1981, 1982; mem Exec Bd Sangeet Natak Akademi 1978–82, Advisory Cttee for Sanskrit, Sahitya Akademi (New Delhi) 1979–84, Man Soc, Nat School of Drama (New Delhi) 1978–82, Bi-Nat Cttee, American Inst of Indian Studies 1984–, Advisory and Editorial Cttee for Nātyaśāstra Project, Kalidas Akademi 1985–, Advisory Cttee for Kalā-tattva-kośa, Indira Gandhi Nat Centre for Arts (New Delhi) 1987–, Govt Review Scheme Cttee 1988–90; Fulbright Fellow 1978; Fellow UP Sangit Natak Akademi 1977–78; Fellow Sangit Natak Akademi 1992; publication prizes. *Publications include:* Rasavilāsa (Sanskrit poetics) 1952, Sahasarasa (Dhrupad song-texts) 1972, Thirty Songs from Punjab and Kashmir 1994, Bhārtīya Sangīta Kā Itihāsa 1994, Indian Music 1995; trans of works from Bengali to Hindi. *Leisure interest:* composing Sanskrit verses. *Address:* Āhnāya 209/1, Karaundi, Varanasi 221 005, India. *Telephone:* (542) 316460.

SHARMAN, Helen, OBE, B SC, PH D; British astronaut and chemist; b 30 May 1963, Sheffield. *Education:* Univ of Sheffield and Birkbeck Coll (London). *Career:* Engineer, Section Head Marconi Osram Valve 1984–87; Food Technologist Mars Confectionery Ltd 1987–89; selected to be first Briton in Space as part of Juno Space Mission of fmr USSR 1989, travelled to Mir space station 1991; awarded Freedom of the City of Sheffield 1991. *Leisure interests:* cycling, swimming, badminton, running, saxophone, piano. *Address:* c/o Fox Management, 101 Shepherd's Bush Rd, London W6 7LP, UK. *Telephone:* (20) 7602-8822; *Fax:* (20) 7603-3956.

SHARP, Anne Catherine, MFA; American artist; b 1 Nov 1943, Red Bank, NJ; d of Elmer Eugene and Ethel Violet (née Hunter) Sharp. *Education:* Pratt Inst and Brooklyn Coll (New York). *Career:* Teacher School of Visual Arts 1978–89, New York Univ 1978, State Univ of New York at Purchase 1983, Pratt Manhattan Center 1982–84, Parsons School of Design 1984–89, Univ of Alaska, Anchorage 1994–96; solo exhibitions include Pace Editions (New York), Ten/Downtown (New York), Katonah Gallery (New York) 1974, Contemporary Gallery (Dallas, TX) 1975, Art in a Public Space (New York) 1979, Eatontown History Museum (NJ) 1980, New York Public Library, Epiphany Br 1988, Books and Co (New York) 1989, Kendall Gallery (New York) 1990, Carr Gottstein Gallery (Alaska Pacific Univ, Anchorage) 1993, Int Gallery of Contemporary Art (Anchorage) 1993, Art Think Tank Gallery (New York) 1994, Stonington Gallery (Anchorage) 1994, US Geological Survey (Reston, VA) 1994; group exhibitions include Arnot Art Museum (New York) 1975, Museum of Modern Art (New York) 1975–76, California Museum of Photography 1983–89, Museum of Modern Art (Weddel, Germany) 1985, Museum of Contemporary Art (Bahia, Brazil) 1986, Museum Salon-de-Provence (France) 1987, Adirondack Lakes Center for Arts (New York) 1987, F. M. K. Gallery (Budapest) 1989, Galerie des Kulturbundes Schwarzenberg (Germany), Q Sen Do Gallery (Kobe, Japan) 1989, Anchorage Museum of History and Art (AK) 1990–91, 1995, Smithsonian Inst Nat Air and Space Museum (Washington, DC), Albright Knox Gallery (New York), The White House (Washington, DC); mem Coll Art Asscn of America, Nat Space Soc, Foundation for Community Artists; Pippin Award Our Town (New York) 1984; mem staff Anchorage Press, writer of The Art Scene: An Artist's View (photo-journalism) 1995–96. *Address:* POB 100480, Anchorage, AK 99510-0480, USA.

SHARPE-NEWTON, Geraldine, BA; American business executive; b 1945; m 1st Thomas Alan Newton 1962 (divorced 1974); m 2nd John Peter Bluff 1992; one s one d. *Education:* Univs of Illinois and Pittsburgh (PA). *Career:* Assoc Dir of Special Projects Burson Marsteller public relations co 1974–77; Vice-Pres Niki Singer public relations co, New York 1977–79; Vice-Pres of Public Relations Simon and Schuster 1979–80; Dir of Information Services CBS News 1980–83; Head of Press and Public Affairs, Ind Television News 1983–91; Strategic Dir of Communications (UK) World Wide Fund for Nature (WWF, fmrly World Wildlife Fund) 1991–94; Sr Vice-Pres of Int Public Relations Turner Broadcasting System Ltd 1994–98; Chief Exec GSN Associates 1998–; Woman of Achievement, Pittsburgh YMCA; Alberta Parker Swan Humanitarian Award. *Leisure interests:* reading, gardening, sailing, hiking, beach rock collecting, bird watching through kitchen window. *Address:* 29 Albert Mansions, Albert Bridge Rd, London SW11 4QB, UK. *Telephone:* (20) 7228-1151; (7771) 765989 (Mobile); *Fax:* (20) 7585-3910; *E-mail:* sharpenewt@aol.com.

SHAW, Fiona, CBE, BA, FRSA; Irish actress; b (Fiona Wilson) 10 July 1958, Cork; d of Denis Joseph Wilson and Mary Teresa Flynn. *Education:* Univ Coll Cork and Royal Acad of Dramatic Art. *Career:* Debut in Love's Labours Lost; joined RSC 1985; appearances at Nat Theatre, Old Vic, etc; Hon LL D (Nat Univ of Ireland) 1998; Hon D UNIV (Open Univ) 1999; Tree Prize 1982, Royal Acad of Dramatic Art (RADA); Ronson Award (RADA) 1982; Bancroft Gold Medal (RADA); BAFTA Award for Machinal 1995; Officier des Arts et des Lettres 2000. *Plays include:* The Rivals, Bloody Poetry, As You Like It, Philistines, Les Liaisons Dangereuses, Much Ado About Nothing, The Merchant of Venice, The Taming of the Shrew, Hyde Park, Electra, As You Like It 1990, The Good Person of Sichuan (Olivier Award for Best Actress, London Critics Award for Best Actress) 1990, Hedda Gabler 1991, Beckett's Footfalls 1994, Richard II (title role) 1995, The Waste Land 1996, The Prime of Miss Jean Brodie 1998, Widower's Houses 1999, Medea 2000; *Films include:* My Left Foot, Mountains of the Moon, Three Men and a Little Lady 1990, Super Mario Brothers 1992, Undercover Blues 1993, The Waste Land 1995, Persuasion 1995, Jane Eyre 1996, The Avengers 1997, The Butcher's Boy 1997, Anna Karenina 1997, The Last September 1999, The Triumph of Love 2000, Harry Potter 2000; *TV appearances include:* Gormenghast 1999, Mind Games; *Radio work includes:* Transfiguration 2000, Aiding and Abetting 2000. *Leisure interests:* opera, running. *Address:* c/o ICM, Oxford House, 76 Oxford St, London W1N 0AX, UK; Eglantine, Montenotte, Cork, Ireland.

SHAW, P(ixie) Mudge Massey; Canadian artist and sculptor; b 30 April 1944, Toronto, ON; d of Edward and Fern (née Smith) Mudge; m 1st Allen Massey 1965 (divorced 1975); one s one d; m 2nd Neil Shaw 1985. *Education:* Ontario Coll of Art. *Career:* Mem staff Faculty of Fine Arts, Ontario Coll of Art 1974–85, Pres 1981; Dir Hands on Art 1975–81; Sculptor for the blind 1980–83; cr first sculpture course for the blind, Toronto; has taken part in numerous group exhibitions. *Address:* The Studio, Titness Park Mill Lane, Ascot, Sunninghill, Berks SL5 7RU, UK; 56 MacPherson Ave, Toronto, ON M5R 1W8, Canada.

SHAW, Rose Tobias; American casting director. *Career:* Worked in radio and TV; Casting Dir for films and TV, especially mini-series 1963–. *Productions cast include:* Films, TV films, TV specials and mini-series: Equus, A Little Night Music, The Last Remake of Beau Geste, The Cat and the Canary, Wild Geese 1977, Lady Oscar, Nijinsky, A Man Called Intrepid, Sea Wolves, In Search of Eden, The Day Christ Died, Escape to Victory 1981, The Wall, The Bunker, Murder is Easy, High Road to China, Arthur the King, The Scarlet Pimpernel, Baby, Lace 1983–84, Lace 2 1984–85, 13 At Dinner, War and Remembrance, Jewel of the Nile 1986, If Tomorrow Comes 1986, The Two Mrs Grenvilles 1987, Queenie 1987, Roman Holiday 1988, The Bourne Identity 1988, Voice of the Heart 1988–89, Around the World in 80 Days 1988–89, The Last Temptation of Christ 1988–89, Bert Rigby, You're a Fool, Michelangelo 1989–90, The Skipper 1989–90, Till We Meet Again 1989–90, Voice of the Heart 1990–91, To Be The Best 1990–91. *Address:* 219 Liverpool Rd, London N1, UK.

SHEARER, Moira; British writer, former actress and ballet dancer; b 17 Jan 1926, Dunfermline; d of Harold King; m Ludovic Kennedy 1950; three d one s. *Education:* Schools in Dunfermline, Bearsden (Scotland) and Ndola (Northern Rhodesia, now Zambia) and Mayfair School. *Career:* Debut with Int Ballet 1941; joined Sadler's Wells 1942 performing all major roles, also performed with the Old Vic and The Bristol Old Vic; Dir Border TV 1977–82; mem Scottish Arts Council 1971–73, BBC Gen Advisory Council 1970–77; touring lecturer on ballet; poetry recitals Edinburgh Festival 1974, 1975. *Ballets and plays include:* Sleeping Beauty 1946, Cinderella (cr) 1948, Carmen 1950, Ballet Imperial 1950, A Midsummer Night's Dream 1954, I Am a Camera 1955, Man of Distinction 1957, The Cherry Orchard 1977, Hay Fever 1978, A Simple Man (for BBC) 1987, The Aspern Papers 1994; *Films:* The Red Shoes 1948, Tales of Hoffmann 1950, Story of Three Loves 1952, The Man Who Loved Redheads 1954, Peeping Tom 1960, Black Tights 1961; *Recordings include:* Tess of the D'Urbervilles 1977, The Ballad of Peckham Rye (BBC Radio Four) 1982, Short Stories of Dame Ninette de Valois (Acad of Sound and Vision) 1990; *Publications:* Balletmaster: A Dancer's View of George Balanchine 1986, Ellen Terry (biog) 1998.

SHEEHY, Gail Henion, BS; American writer and journalist; b 27 Nov 1937, Mamaronick, NY; d of Harold Merritt and Lillian Rainey (née Paquin) Henion; m 1st Albert F. Sheehy 1960 (divorced 1967); two d (one adopted); m 2nd Clay Felker 1984. *Education:* Univ of Vermont. *Career:* Home economists J. C. Penney & Co 1958–60; Fashion Ed Rochester Democrat & Chronicle 1961–63; Feature writer New York Herald Tribune 1963–66; Contributing Ed New York magazine 1968–77; Fellow Journalism School, Columbia Univ 1970; Political Contributing Ed Vanity Fair 1988–; has contributed to New York Times Magazine, Parade, New Republic, Washington Point; mem Advisory Bd Women's Health Initiative, NIH, Eminent Citizens' Comm, UN Int Conf on Population and Devt 1994; four Front Page Awards, Newswomen's Club of New York; Nat Magazine Award, Columbia Univ 1973; Penney-Missouri Journalism Award, Univ of Missouri 1975; Anisfield-Wolf Book Award 1986; Best Magazine Writer Award, Washington Journalism Review 1991; New York Public Library Lion 1992. *Publications include:* Lovesounds 1970, Panthermania: The Clash of Black Against Black in One American City 1971, Speed is of the Essence 1971, Hustling: Prostitution in our Wide-Open Society 1973, Passages: Predictable Crises of Adult Life (trans to 28 languages) 1976, Pathfinders 1981, Spirit of Survival 1986, Character: America's Search for Leadership 1988, Gorbachev: The Man Who Changed the World 1990, Maggie and Misha (play) 1991, The Silent Passage: Menopause 1992, New Passages 1995, Hillary's Choice 1999.

SHEFFER, Andra Lyn, BA; Canadian arts administrator; b 9 June 1951; d of Harry and Evelyn (née Widman) Sheffer; m Denis Hamel; one d. *Education:* Nepean High School (Ontario) and Carleton Univ. *Career:* Planning Officer Strategic Planning Dept, Sec of State's Office, Ottawa 1973, Film Festivals Officer 1974, Film Certification Officer 1976–78; Man Dir Toronto Festival of Festivals 1978–79; Dir Acad of Canadian Cinema and TV 1979–89; freelance Arts Administrator and Consultant 1989–91; Exec Dir Maclean Hunter TV Fund 1991–, Ind Production Fund 1991–, COGECO Program Devt Fund 1992–, Bell Broadcast and New Media Fund 1997–; Toronto Women in Film and TV Award 1991. *Publication:* Making It: The Business of Film and Television Production in Canada (co-ed) 1995. *Address:* 24 Hambly Ave, Toronto, ON M4E 2R6, Canada.

SHEILA, (pseudonym of Annie Chancel); French singer; b 16 Aug 1945, Créteil; d of André and Micheline (née Gaultier) Chancel; m Guy (Ringo) Bayle (divorced); one s. *Education:* Rue de Patay School (Paris). *Career:* Singer 1962–; numerous concerts including performances at Zénith 1985 and Olympia, Paris 1989; performer Bang Bang (film) 1967. *Recordings include:* Sheila, L'école est finie, Première surprise partie, Pendant les vacances, Chaque instant de chaque jour, Ecoute ce disque, C'est toi que j'aime, Le folklore américain, Le cinéma, Bang Bang, L'heure de la sortie, La famille, Adios amor, Dans une heure, Dalila, Petite fille de français moyen, Arlequin, La colline de Santa Maria, Oncle Jo, Julietta, Reviens je t'aime, Les rois mages, Blancs, jaunes, rouges, noirs, Mélancolie, Le couple, Tu es le soleil, On dit, Tangue Au, Vis vas, Je suis comme toi, Emmenez-moi, Vivre mieux. *Leisure interests:* skiing, water-skiing, dance, tennis. *Address:* c/o EMI Music, 43 rue Camille Desmoulin, 92130 Issy-les-Moulineaux, France; c/o Editions Ramsay, 103 blvd Murat, 75016 Paris, France.

SHEININ, Rose, LHD, PH D, FRSC, D SC; Canadian biologist; b 18 May 1930, Toronto, ON; d of Harry and Anne (née Szyber) Shuber; m Joseph Sheinin 1951; two d one s. *Education:* Univ of Toronto. *Career:* Demonstrator Dept of Biochemistry, Univ of Toronto 1951–53; Asst Prof Dept of Medical Biophysics, 1967–72, Assoc Prof 1972–78, Grad Sec 1973–75, Chair and Prof Dept of Microbiology and Parasitology 1975–82, Prof Dept of Medical Biophysics 1978–90, Prof Dept of Microbiology, 1982–90, Vice-Dean School of Grad Studies 1984–89, Sr Fellow Massey Coll 1983–90, Continuing Fellow, Sr Resident Fellow 1990–; Visiting Research Assoc, Univ of Cambridge, UK 1956–57, Nat Inst for Medical Research 1957–58; Research Assoc and Fellow Ontario Cancer Inst 1958–67; Visiting Prof Univ of Alberta 1971; Researcher Dept of Enzyme Research, CNRS, France 1982; Vice-Rector, Academic, Researcher and Prof Dept of Biology, Concordia Univ 1989–94; mem Canadian Science Del to China 1973; Assoc Ed Intervirology 1974–85; Consultant Z. L. Bochnek Labs 1983–89, Canada Packers Ltd 1985–87; mem numerous cttees and panels; external reviewer for numerous foundations; mem Scientific Council of Canada 1984–87, Nat Advisory Bd of Canadian Encyclopedia 1985; mem Canadian Asscn for Women in Science, Science for Peace, Canadian Soc for Cell Biology, American Soc for Microbiology, American Soc for Virology, Canadian Biochemical Soc; Fellow American Acad of Microbiology 1978–, Royal Soc of Canada 1981–; Josiah Macy Jr Faculty Scholar 1981–82; Archibald Byron Macallum Memorial Lecturer 1981; Hon Fellow Ryerson Polytechnic Univ (Toronto) 1993; Hon LHD (Mt St Vincent) 1985; Hon D SC (Acadia) 1987, (Guelph) 1991; Queen's Silver Jubilee Medal 1978; Inaugural Award, Canadian Asscn for Women in Science and Canadian Biochemical Soc 1985; Woman of Distinction Award, YWCA 1988. *Address:* Massey College, University of Toronto, 4 Devonshire Place, Toronto, ON M5S 2E1, Canada; 28 Inglewood Drive, Toronto, ON M4T 1G8, Canada (Home). *Telephone:* (416) 978-5014 (Office); (416) 488-8687 (Home); *Fax:* (416) 978-1759 (Office).

SHELTON, Lucy, BA, MUS M; American concert singer (soprano). *Education:* Pomona Coll (CA) and New England Conservatory of Music. *Career:* Asst Prof of Voice Eastman School of Music, Univ of Rochester, NY 1979; Visiting Prof Cleveland Inst of Music, OH 1986; appearances at Chamber Music NW, Bethlehem, Bach, Casals, Tanglewood and Aspen Music Festivals, with all major US orchestras, at BBC Promenade Concerts (London); numerous recitals and guest appearances; best known for 20th century repertoire (including premières of Carter, Knussen, Ruders, Grisey, Albert, Schwantner,

Smirnov, etc); recordings with Nonesuch Records, Vox, Vanguard, Bridge, Smithsonian Inst, Deutsche Grammophon; teacher New England Conservatory, Tanglewood Music Center; Walter W. Naumburg Prize (jtly) 1977, (solo) 1980. *Address:* New England Conservatory of Music, 290 Huntington Ave, Boston, MA 02115, USA. *Internet:* www .newenglandconservatory.edu.

SHEPHARD, Rt Hon Gillian Patricia, PC, MA; British politician; b 22 Jan 1940; d of Reginald and Bertha Watts; m Thomas Shephard 1975; two step-s. *Education:* North Walsham Girls' School and St Hilda's Coll (Oxford). *Career:* Educ Officer and School Insp 1963–75; Lecturer Extra-Mural Bd, Cambridge 1965–87; Councillor Norfolk Co Council 1977–89, Chair Social Services Cttee 1978–83, Educ Cttee 1983–85; Chair W Norfolk and Wisbech Health Authority 1981–85, Norwich Health Authority 1985–87; MP (Cons) for SW Norfolk 1987–; Parl Pvt Sec to Econ Sec to the Treasury 1988–89; Parl Under-Sec of State Dept of Social Security 1989–90; Minister of State (Treasury) 1990–92; Sec of State for Employment 1992–93, for Agric, Fisheries and Food 1993–94, for Educ 1994–95, for Educ and Employment 1995–97; Shadow Leader of House of Commons and Shadow Chancellor of Duchy of Lancaster 1997–99; Opposition Spokesman on Environment, Transport and the Regions 1998–99; Deputy Chair of Cons Party 1991–92; Co-Chair Cons Women's Nat Comm 1990–91; Vice-Pres Hansard Soc 1997–; Hon Fellow St Hilda's Coll 1991. *Publication:* Shephard's Watch 2000. *Leisure interests:* gardening, music, France. *Address:* House of Commons, London SW1A 0AA, UK.

SHEPHERD, Cybill; American actress; b 18 Feb 1950, Memphis, TN; d of William Jennings Shepherd and Patty Shobe Micci; m 1st David Ford 1978 (divorced); one d; m 2nd Bruce Oppenheim 1987; twin s. *Education:* Hunter Coll (City Univ of New York) and Univ of Southern California. *Career:* Began career as fashion model; fmr magazine cover girl; eight years of commercials for L'Oréal Préférence; film debut in The Last Picture Show 1971; Model of the Year 1968. *Plays include:* A Shot in the Dark 1977, Vanities 1981, The Muse 1999, Marine Life 2000; *Films include:* The Last Picture Show 1971, The Heartbreak Kid 1972, Daisy Miller 1974, At Long Last Love 1975, Taxi Driver 1976, Special Delivery 1976, Silver Bears 1978, The Lady Vanishes, The Return, Chances Are 1989, Texasville 1990, Alice 1990, Once Upon A Crime 1992, Married to It 1993, Criminals, Memphis (also producer and co-writer); *TV appearances include:* Series: The Yellow Rose 1983–84, Moonlighting (Emmy Award 1985) 1985–89, Cybill 1994–98; Films: A Guide for the Married Woman, Secrets of a Married Man, Seduced, The Long Hot Summer, Which Way Home, Telling Secrets, There was a Little Boy, Baby Brokers, For the Love of My Daughter, While Justice Sleeps, The Last Word; *Recordings include:* Cybill Does It... To Cole Porter 1974, Stan Getz: Mad About the Boy, Vanilla, Somewhere Down the Road.

SHEPHERD, Helen Parsons, RCA; Canadian artist; b 16 Jan 1923, St John's (NF); d of Richard Augustus and Bessie Ash Parsons; m Reginald Shepherd 1948; one s. *Education:* Bishop Spencer Coll (St John's), Memorial Univ of Newfoundland and Ontario Coll of Art (Toronto). *Career:* Co-Founder and Teacher Newfoundland Acad of Art 1949–61; various comms for Memorial Univ, Canadian Fed Govt, etc, including the portraits of HRH Prince Philip, Gov-Gen and Mrs Schreyer, the Speakers of the Newfoundland House of Ass, Mayors of St John's, etc; exhibitions at Memorial Univ 1975, 1989, Ontario and Atlantic regions 1975–76, The Gallery (Mauskopf) 1982; Hon LL D (Newfoundland) 1988; elected to Newfoundland and Labrador Arts Council Hall of Honour 1990. *Leisure interests:* swimming, reading, nature studies. *Address:* 26 Oxen Pond Rd, St John's, NF A1B 3J3, Canada; POB 195, Clarke's Beach, NF A0A 1W0, Canada (Summer). *Telephone:* (709) 722-7616.

SHERBELL, Rhoda; American painter and sculptor; b New York; d of Alexander and Syd (née Steinberg) Sherbell; m Mervin Honig 1956; one d. *Education:* Art Students' League, Brooklyn Museum Art School and privately in Italy, France and UK. *Career:* Instructor Museum of Modern Art, New York 1959, Nat Acad of Design, New York 1988–89, Art Students' League, New York 1985–90; Consultant mem Council Emily Lowe Gallery, Hofstra Univ, NY 1978, Pres 1980–81, Life mem Bd of Friends and Bd of Trustees; solo exhibitions include Country Art Gallery (Locust Valley, NY), Adelphi Coll, Brooklyn Museum of Art

(New York), Rehn Gallery (Washington, DC), Gallery of Modern Art (New York), Bergen Museum of Arts and Sciences (NJ), William Benton Museum (CT), Hofstra Museum of Art (NY), Montclair Museum of Art, Nat Museum of Sport, Jewish Museum (New York), The Smithsonian Inst (Washington, DC), Nat Acad of Design (New York), Emily Lowe Museum (NY), Heckshire Museum (NY), Gallery Emmanuel (NY); has taken part in numerous group exhibitions and is represented in perm collections; several TV and radio appearances, contribs to professional journals, magazines and newspapers; Trustee Nat Art Museum of Sports Inc 1975–, Women's Boxing Fed 1978; mem Sculpture Guild, Nat Asscn of Women Artists, Allied Artists' Soc, Audubon Artists, Professional Artists' Guild; The Art Cttee of the City of New York 1993; Grantee Ford Foundation 1964, 1967, American Acad of Arts and Letters, Nat Inst of Arts and Letters 1960; McDowell Colony Fellow 1976; Fellow Nat Sculpture Asscn; awards include Alfred G. B. Steel Memorial Award (Pennsylvania Acad of Fine Arts) 1963–64, Prize for Sculpture (Jersey City Museum) 1961, Award for Sculpture (Knickerbocker Artists) 1980, Sawyer Award (Nat Acad of Design) 1985, Gold Medal of Honor (Audubon Artists) 1985, Gold Medal (Allied Artists of America) 1989, 1990. *Address:* 64 Jane Court, Westbury, NY 11590, USA.

SHERMAN, Cindy, BA; American artist; b 1954, Glen Ridge, NJ. *Education:* State Univ Coll (Buffalo). *Career:* Solo exhibitions include Buffalo, Houston, New York, Genoa (Italy), Paris, Amsterdam (Netherlands), Tokyo; group exhibitions include Buffalo, New York, Chicago, Washington, DC, London, Paris, Venice Biennale (Italy) 1982, Documenta 7 (Kassel, Germany) 1982, etc; work in perm collections including Museum of Fine Arts (Houston), Museum Boymans-van Beuningen (Rotterdam, Netherlands), Museum of Modern Art (New York), Tate Gallery (London), Centre Nat d'Art et de Culture Georges Pompidou (Paris), Stedelijk Museum (Amsterdam), Metropolitan Museum of Art (New York), San Francisco Museum of Modern Art. *Address:* c/o Metro Pictures, 519 West 24th St, New York, NY 10011-1104, USA.

SHERRY, Ann Caroline, BA; Australian business executive; b 2 Feb 1954, Gympie, Qld; d of John Morgan and June Caroline Sherry; m Matthew Michael 1975; one s. *Education:* Somerville House (Brisbane), Univ of Qld and Qld Univ of Tech. *Career:* Sr Organiser Admin and Clerical Officers Asscn 1983–87; Deputy Dir Women's Policy Co-ordination Unit Premier and Cabinet (Vic) 1987–88; Man Women's Employment Br, Dept Lab (Vic) 1988–90; Dir and CEO Office of Pre-school and Child Care (Vic) 1990–92; Dir Primary Care Div, Dept Health and Community Services 1992–93; First Asst Sec Office Status of Women, Dept PM and Cabinet 1993–94; Chief Man Human Resources (HR) Westpac Banking Corpn 1994–95, Gen Man HR 1995–99, Group Exec 1999–; CEO Bank of Melbourne 1999–; Chair Australian Inst of Family Studies 1995–98; Chair Functional Review of Child Care 1991; mem Bd Australian Council of Trade Unions Women's Cttee 1983–86, Women's Employment Advisory Cttee 1987–88, Prahran Community Health Centre 1987–92, mem Australian Inst of Bankers 1994–; Dir Australian Council of Businesswomen 1995–98, Chair 1997–98; mem HR Cttee, Univ of Melbourne Council 1998–99; mem Council Monash Univ 1998–, Exec Cttee 2000–, Bd Monash Commercial Pty Ltd, Monash Univ 2001–; Adjunct Prof, Nat Inst for Governance, Univ of Canberra 2000–; numerous articles in journals and business magazines; lectures widely; inducted into Australian Businesswomen's Hall of Fame. *Address:* Westpac Banking Corpn, Level 27, 60 Martin Place, Sydney, NSW 2000, Australia. *Telephone:* (2) 9226 1837; *Fax:* (2) 9226 1391; *E-mail:* asherry@westpac .com.au; *Internet:* www.wizfirm.com/annsherry.

SHESTAKOVA, Tatyana Borisovna; Russian actress; b 23 Oct 1948, Leningrad (now St Petersburg); d of Boris Shestakov and Aleksandra Shestakova; m Lev Dodin 1972. *Education:* Leningrad Inst of Theatre, Music and Cinema. *Career:* Actress Leningrad Theatre for Children 1972–75, Leningrad Comedy Theatre 1975–80, Maly Drama Theatre 1980–; has also played for Moscow Arts Theatre; toured abroad 1983, 1987, 1992; USSR State Prize 1986; Merited Artist of the RSFSR 1987; Nat Triumph Prize 1992. *Plays include:* The House 1980, Uncle Vanya 1982, Brothers and Sisters 1986, The Meek One 1985, Stars of the Morning Sky 1987, The Possessed, The Cherry Orchard 1994, Roberto Zucco 1994, Claustrophobia 1994, Play Without a Name 1997; *Films*

include: Go and See, My Dearest, Anxious Dream. *Leisure interests:* music, walking, reading, cooking. *Address:* Maly Drama Theatre, 191002 St Petersburg, Rubinstein ul 18, Russian Federation. *Telephone:* (812) 113-20-08; *Fax:* (812) 113-33-66.

SHIELDS, Brooke Christa Camille, BA; American actress and model; b 31 May 1965, New York; d of Francis Shields and Teri Schmon; m 1st Andre Agassi 1997 (divorced 1999); m 2nd Chris Henchy 2001. *Career:* Began modelling in Ivory Soap commericals 1966, later model for Calvin Klein jeans and Colgate toothpaste commercials. *Films include:* Alice, Sweet Alice 1975, Pretty Baby 1977, King of the Gypsies 1978, Wanda Nevada 1978, Just You and Me Kid 1978, Blue Lagoon 1979, Endless Love 1980, Sahara 1983, Brenda Starr 1986, Backstreet Strays 1989, An American Love, Seventh Floor 1993, Running Wild 1993, Freaked 1993, Freeway 1997, Way of the Gun 2000, After Sex 2000; *Play:* Grease 1994–95; *TV appearances include:* The Tonight Show, Bob Hope specials, The Prince of Central Park (film) 1977, After the Fall, Wet Gold, The Diamond Trap 1988, Suddenly Susan 1996, Friends. *Address:* c/o Christa Inc, Suite 630, 2300 W Sahara, Box 18, Las Vegas, NV 89102, USA.

SHIELDS, Carol Ann, OC, MA; Canadian/American writer and university professor; b 2 June 1935, Oak Park, IL; d of Robert and Inez (née Sellgren) Warner; m Donald Hugh Shields 1957; four d one s. *Education:* Hanover Coll (IA) and Univ of Ottawa (ON). *Career:* Writer of novels, short stories, plays and poetry 1972–; Editorial Asst Canadian Slavonic Papers 1973–75; Lecturer Univ of Ottawa 1976–77 (Writer-in-Residence 1989), Univ of British Columbia 1978–80; Prof Univ of Manitoba 1980–2000, Emer 2000–; Writer-in-Residence, Univ of Winnipeg 1987, Chancellor 1996–2000; mem Canada Council, Royal Soc of Canada, Manitoba Writers' Guild, Writers' Union of Canada, Manitoba Asscn of Playwrights; hon degrees Univs of Ottawa, Winnipeg, BC, Toronto and Western Ontario, Queen's Univ, Hanover Coll; Canadian Authors' Asscn Award 1976; CBC Prize for Drama 1983; Nat Magazine Award 1984, 1985; Gov-Gen's Award nomination 1988; Arthur Ellis Award 1988; Marian Ensel Award 1990; Gov-Gen's Award 1993; Nat Book Critics Circle Award 1995; Pulitzer Prize for Literature 1995, 1999; Orange Prize 1998. *Publications include:* Others 1972, Intersect 1974, Small Ceremonies 1976, The Box Garden 1977, Happenstance 1980, A Fairly Conventional Woman 1982, Women Waiting 1983, Various Miracles 1985, Not Another Anniversary (jtly) 1986, Swann 1987, Face Off 1987, The Orange Fish 1989, Departures and Arrivals 1990, Happenstance 1991, The Republic of Love 1992, The Stone Diaries 1993, Various Miracles 1994, Small Ceremonies 1994, The Box Garden 1995, Larry's Party 1997, A Celibate Season (jtly) 1999, Dressing Up for the Carnival 2000, Jane Austen 2000; contribs to numerous Canadian magazines and journals. *Leisure interests:* talking, reading, theatre, France. *Address:* 237 Wellington Crescent, Winnipeg, MB R3M 0A1, Canada. *Telephone:* (204) 284-9907.

SHIELDS, Hon Margaret Kerslake, QSO, BA; New Zealand politician; b 18 Dec 1941, Wellington; d of Ernest Blake and Dorothy Bessie (née Levy) Porter; m Patrick John Shields 1960; two d. *Education:* Victoria Univ (Wellington). *Career:* Researcher Consumers' Inst and Dept of Statistics; Lab mem House of Reps (Parl) for Kapiti 1981–90; Minister of Customs and of Consumer Affairs 1984–87, of Women's Affairs, Consumer Affairs and Statistics 1987–88, 1989–90, of Customs 1988–89, Assoc Minister of Educ 1989–90; Dir UN Int Research and Training Inst for the Advancement of Women (INSTRAW) 1991–94; Vice-Pres Local Govt New Zealand; Deputy Chair Hutt Valley Dist Health Bd 2000; mem Wellington Hosp Bd 1977–80, Wellington Regional Council 1995–, Deputy Chair 1998–, Human Rights Comm Complaints Review Tribunal 1995–, Council of Vic Univ of Wellington 1996–99; Co-Founder, Pres and Nat Sec Soc for Research on Women; Co-Convenor Second UN Women's Convention 1975; Govt Del to UN Int Women's Year Conf, Mexico 1975, participated in Inter-Parl Union Conf, Seoul 1983, Keynote Speaker Inter-Parl Union Conf, Geneva 1989. *Leisure interests:* hiking, gardening, music, drama. *Address:* 23 Haunui Rd, Pukerua Bay, Porirua, New Zealand. *Telephone:* (4) 239 9949; *Fax:* (4) 239 9084.

SHIMIZU, Kayoko; Japanese politician; b 9 Nov 1935. *Education:* Univ of Tokyo. *Career:* Fmr Asst Head Liberal-Democratic Party (LDP) Women's Section, Section Man Ministry of Health and Welfare; mem

House of Councillors (Parl, Upper House) 1990, mem Cttee on Social and Labour Affairs and on Audit 1990; Dir-Gen Environment Agency; Minister of the Environment 2000–2001. *Address:* House of Councillors, 1-7-1 Nagata-cho, Tokyo 100, Japan. *Telephone:* (3) 3581-3111.

SHIMIZU, Sumiko; Japanese politician; b 1 March 1928. *Education:* High School. *Career:* Fmr Chair Japan Women's Conf; elected to House of Councillors (Parl, Upper House) 1990 as mem of Social Democratic Party of Japan (fmrly Japan Socialist Party), mem Cttee on Judicial Affairs, Special Cttee on the Environment 1990. *Address:* House of Councillors, 1-7-1 Nagata-cho, Tokyo 100, Japan. *Telephone:* (3) 3581-3111.

SHIPLEY, Rt Hon Jennifer (Jenny) Mary, PC; New Zealand politician; b 4 Feb 1952; d of Leonard and Adele Robson; m Burton Ross Shipley 1973; one s one d. *Education:* Marlborough Girls' Coll and Christchurch Teachers' Coll. *Career:* Teacher 1972–76; farmer 1973–88; joined Nat Party 1975; Child Safety Officer, Plunket 1979–81; Malvern Plunket Exec 1979–84; Tutor Lincoln Coll 1983–87; Malvern Co Councillor 1983–86; mem House of Reps (Parl, Nat Party) for Ashburton (now Rakaia) 1987–, mem Planning and Devt Cttee, Regulations Review Cttee, Educ and Science Cttee, Social Service Select Cttee 1987–90; Opposition Educ Assoc Spokesperson 1989–90, Social Welfare Spokesperson 1990; Minister of Social Welfare and Women's Affairs 1990–93, of Health and of Women's Affairs 1993–96, of State Services 1996–97, also of State Owned Enterprises, of Transport, of Accident Rehabilitation and Compensation Insurance, Minister Responsible for Radio New Zealand; Minister in Charge of NZ Security Intelligence Service 1997–; Prime Minister of NZ 1997–99; Leader of the Opposition 1999–; mem Aged People's Welfare Cttee 1983, Party Policy Co-ordinating Cttee. *Leisure interests:* family, gardening, reading, outdoor recreation. *Address:* Parliament Buildings, Private Bag, Wellington, New Zealand. *Telephone:* (4) 471-9838; *Fax:* (4) 472-2075; *E-mail:* leader@national.org.nz; *Internet:* www.national .org.nz.

SHIRLEY, Dame Stephanie (Steve), DBE, B SC, CBIM, FRSA; British business executive; b 16 Sept 1933; d of the late Arnold Buchthal and Margaret (née Schick) Brook; m Derek George Millington Shirley 1959; one s (died 1998). *Education:* Sir John Cass Coll (London) and Univ of London. *Career:* Post Office worker 1951–59; worked at CDL (subsidiary of Int Computers Ltd) 1959–62; Founder, Dir and sometime Chair Xansa (FI Group PLC) 1962–93, currently Life Pres; Dir AEA Tech 1992–2000, Tandem Computers Inc 1992–, John Lewis Partnership 1999–; mem Computer, Systems and Electronic Requirements Bd 1979–81, Electronics and Avionics Requirement Bd 1981–83, Open Tech Manpower Services Comm 1983–86, Council Industrial Soc 1984–90, Nat Council for Vocational Qualifications 1986–89, Council Duke of Edinburgh's Seventh Commonwealth Study Conf 1991–92, British–N American Cttee 1992–; Pres British Computer Soc 1989–90, Fellow 1971; Consulting Ed J. Wiley and Sons 1978–87; Trustee Help the Aged 1987–90; Patron Disablement Income Group 1989–2000; Master Information Technologists 1992; Chair Women of Influence 1993; f Kingwood Trust 1993; Founder and Chair Shirley Foundation; Foundation Fellow (Balliol Coll, Oxford Univ) 2001; Freeman City of London 1987; Master of the Worshipful Co of Information Technologists; Hon FCGI 1989; Hon Fellow Manchester Polytechnic (now Manchester Metropolitan Univ) 1989, Staffordshire Univ 1991, Sheffield Hallam Univ 1992; Hon D SC (Buckingham) 1991, (Aston) 1993, (Nottingham Trent) 1994; Hon D TECH (Loughborough) 1991, (Kingston) 1995; Hon D UNIV (Leeds Metropolitan) 1993; Hon D LIT (de Montfort) 1993; Hon DBA (W of England) 1995; Recognition of IT Achievement Award 1985; BIM Gold Medal 1991; US Nat Women's Hall of Fame 1995; IEE Mountbatten Medal 1999; has written numerous papers for professional journals and confs. *Leisure interest:* sleep. *Address:* 47 Thames House, Phyllis Court Drive, Henley-on-Thames, Oxon RG9 2NA, UK. *Telephone:* (1491) 579004; *Fax:* (1491) 574995; *E-mail:* steve.shirley@dial.pipex.com.

SHIVA, Vandana, PH D; Indian environmentalist and writer. *Career:* Researcher Indian Inst of Man (Bangalore) 1978–82; Dir Research Foundation for Science Tech and Natural Resource Policy (New Delhi); Assoc Ed The Ecologist magazine; Contributing Ed PCR Forum; mem Third World Network; Founder-mem Int Forum on Globalization;

Leader Int Campaign on Food Rights; Right Livelihood Award 1993. *Publications:* Stolen Harvest: The Hijacking of the Global Food Supply, Biopiracy: The Plunder of Nature and Knowledge, Ecofeminism (jtly), The Violence of the Green Revolution, Monocultures of the Mind, Biopolitics, Diodiversity: Social and Ecological Consequences. *Address:* A-60 Hauz Khas, New Delhi, 110 016, India. *Telephone:* (11) 6968077; *E-mail:* twn@unv.ernet.in.

SHOPE, Gertrude; South African political activist; b 15 Aug 1925, Johannesburg; d of John and Mary Moeketsi; m Mark Shope 1957; two d one s. *Education:* Woddilove Training Inst (Marandellas, Rhodesia, now Zimbabwe) and St Hilda's Coll (Ladysmith). *Career:* Teacher 1948–54; mem Occupational Therapy Dept, Coronation Hosp 1955–56; mem Johannesburg City Council 1956–66; Prov Sec Fed of SA Women 1965–66; mem staff World Fed of Trade Unions, Prague, Czechoslovakia (now Czech Repub) 1967–70; Sec Women's Section, Dar es Salaam, Tanzania 1971–72; Sec African Nat Congress (ANC) Office, Lusaka, Zambia 1973, Chief Rep 1974–76, Sec ANC Mission, Nigeria 1978–81, Leader ANC Women's Section Del End of Decade for Women Conf, Nairobi, Kenya 1981, mem ANC Nat Exec Council 1985, apptd Head of Women's Section 1987, Co-Convenor (with Albertina Nontsikelelo Sisulu, qv) ANC Women's League Task Force 1990, apptd Pres Women's League 1991. *Leisure interests:* welfare work with political prisoners, children and disabled people, women's issues. *Address:* POB 61884, Mashalltown 2107, South Africa. *Telephone:* (11) 3307288; *Fax:* (11) 3307144.

SHORE, Elizabeth Catherine, CB, FRCP, FFCM; British medical practitioner; b 19 Aug 1927, Oxford; d of Edward Murray and Rosalind Grace (née Smith) Wrong; m Peter David Shore 1948; two d two s (one deceased). *Education:* Newnham Coll (Cambridge) and St Bartholomew's Hosp (London). *Career:* Joined Medical Service St Bartholomew's Hosp 1962; Deputy Chief Medical Officer, Dept of Health 1977–84; Dean of Postgrad Medical Educ, Univ of London, NW Thames Region 1985–93; Ed Medical Woman 1992–97; Chair of Council and Chair of Professional Cttee Child Accident Prevention Trust 1986–89, Trustee 1986–90; Pres Medical Women's Fed 1990–92; mem Gen Medical Council 1989–94; Hon Sr Lecturer Charing Cross and Westminster Medical School 1993–97; Exec mem National Asscn of Women's Organizations; mem of Council Policy Studies Inst 1992–; has written numerous articles and textbook chapters on planning medical manpower, women doctors and postgrad medical educ. *Leisure interests:* modern English and American literature, gardening, cooking, tennis, rough sea swimming, European history. *Address:* 23 Dryburgh Rd, London SW15 1BN, UK.

SHORT, Rt Hon Clare, PC, BA; British politician; b 15 Feb 1946, Birmingham; d of the late Frank and Joan (née O'Loughlin) Short; m 1st 1964 (divorced 1974); one s; m 2nd Alex Lyon 1981 (died 1993). *Education:* St Paul's Grammar School for Girls, Univs of Keele and Leeds. *Career:* Mem of Lab Party 1970–, mem Lab Party Nat Exec Cttee 1988–; mem staff Home Office 1970–75; Dir All Faiths for One Race 1976–78, Youth Aid and the Unemployed Unit 1979–83; MP for Birmingham Ladywood 1983–, mem Home Affairs Select Cttee 1983–85, Chair All Party Parl Group on Race Relations 1985–86, Nat Exec Cttee (NEC) Women's Cttee 1993–97, Front Bench Spokesperson on Employment 1985–88, on Social Security 1989–91, on Environmental Protection 1992–93, on Women 1993–95, Shadow Sec of State for Transport 1995–96, for Overseas Devt 1996–97; Sec of State for Int Devt 1997–; Vice-Pres Socialist Int Women 1992–97; mem Select Cttee on Home Affairs 1983–95, NEC of Labour Party 1988–98, UNISON; Campaigner of the Year, The Spectator 1990. *Publications:* Talking Blues: A Study of Young West Indians' Views of Policing 1978, Handbook of Immigration Law 1978, Dear Clare... This Is What Women Think About Page 3 1991. *Leisure interests:* books, family, friends, swimming, dog. *Address:* House of Commons, London SW1 0AA, UK. *Telephone:* (20) 7219-4148.

SHRESTHA, Ambica, BA; Nepalese business executive; b 12 Feb 1933; two d. *Education:* In India. *Career:* Man Dir Kathmandu Travels and Tours, Nepal Trek and Natural History Expeditions; Dir Davs Enterprises Pvt Ltd; Pres Dwarika's Hotel (Pata Heritage Award, Business and Professional Women's Club 1980); Gorkha Dakchin Bahu

Award. *Address:* c/o Kathmandu Travels and Tours Ltd, POB 459, Battish Putali, Kathmandu, Nepal. *Telephone:* (1) 473724; *Fax:* (1) 223151.

SHREVE, Susan Richards, MA; American writer; b 2 May 1939, Toledo, OH; d of Robert Shreve and Helen Richards; m 1st Porter Shreve (divorced 1987); m 2nd Timothy Seldes 1987; two s two d. *Education:* Univs of Pennsylvania and Virginia. *Career:* Prof of English Literature, George Mason Univ, Fairfax, VA 1976–; Visiting Prof Columbia Univ, New York 1982–; Princeton Univ, NJ 1991, 1992, 1993; Pres PEN/Faulkner Foundation 1985–; Producer The American Voice for TV 1986–; Essayist MacNeil/Lehrer Newshour; Guggenheim Fellowship; NEIA Fellowship in Fiction. *Publications:* Novels: A Fortunate Madness 1974, A Woman Like That 1977, Children of Power 1979, Miracle Play 1981, Dreaming of Heroes 1984, Queen of Hearts 1987, A Country of Strangers 1989, Daughters of the New World 1992, The Train House 1993, The Visiting Physician 1996, Outside the Law 1997, How We Want to Live (co-ed) 1998, Plum and Jaggers 2000; Children's books: Jonah, The Whale 1997, Ghost Cats 1999, The End of Amanda, The Good 2000. *Address:* 3319 Newark St, NW, Washington, DC 20008, USA.

SHRIVER, Maria Owings, BA; American broadcaster and journalist; b 6 Nov 1955, Chicago, IL; d of Robert Sargent and Eunice Mary (née Kennedy) Shriver; m Arnold Schwarzenegger 1986; two d. *Education:* Sacred Heart Acad (Stamford, CT) and Georgetown Univ. *Career:* Began career as writer and Producer on TV news at KYW-TV, Philadelphia, PA 1977; journalist on Evening Magazine, WJZ-TV, Baltimore, MD 1978–80; Nat Corresp on PM Magazine 1981–83; W Coast Reporter for CBS Morning News, then Co-Presenter, New York 1985–86; joined NBC News 1986, Co-Presenter Sunday Today 1987–90, Main Street 1987, Yesterday, Today and Tomorrow 1989, Presenter NBC Nightly News Weekend Edition 1989–90, Cutting Edge with Maria Shriver 1990, First Person with Maria Shriver 1991; writer and presenter of many news programmes, documentaries and TV specials including The Baby Business, Men, Women, Sex and AIDS, Wall Street: Money, Greed and Power, and Fatal Addictions (Christopher Award 1990); exclusive interviews with King Hussein of Jordan, Fidel Castro, US Vice-Pres J. Danforth Quayle and Pres Corazón Aquino of the Philippines (Exceptional Merit Media Award, Nat Women's Political Caucus). *Address:* NBC, 30 Rockefeller Plaza, New York, NY 10112, USA.

SHU TING; Chinese writer; b 30 May 1952; d of Shi Mo Gang and Xiu Zhen Yong; m Zhong Yi Chen 1981; one s. *Career:* Dir Chinese Writers' Union; Vice-Chair Fujian Literature Foundation; numerous publs; many awards. *Address:* Writers' Association, Beijing, People's Republic of China; 13 Zhong Hua Rd, Gu Lang Yu, Xiamen, Fujian, People's Republic of China. *Telephone:* (592) 233762.

SHUE, Elisabeth; American actress; b 6 Oct 1963; m Davis Guggenhiem. *Education:* Wellesley Coll and Harvard Univ. *Career:* Studied with Sylvie Leigh, Showcase Theater; appeared in Broadway plays including Some Americans Abroad, Birth and After Birth. *Films:* The Karate Kid 1984, Link 1986, Adventures in Babysitting 1987, Cocktail 1988, Body Wars 1989, Back to the Future Part II 1989, Part III 1990, Soapdish 1991, The Marrying Man 1991, Twenty Bucks 1993, Heart and Souls 1993, Radio Inside 1994, Blind Justice 1994, The Underneath 1995, Leaving Las Vegas 1995, The Trigger Effect 1996, The Saint 1996, Palmetto 1997, Deconstructing Harry 1997, Cousin Bette 1997, Molly 1998; *TV:* films: Charles and Diana, Double Switch 1987, Hale the Hero 1992, Blind Justice; series: Call to Glory 1984. *Address:* c/o Creative Arts Agency, 9830 Wilshire Blvd, Beverly Hills, CA 90212, USA.

SHULMAN, Alexandra; British journalist; b 13 Nov 1957, London; d of Milton Shulman and Drusilla Beyfuss; m Paul Spike 1994; one s. *Education:* St Paul's Girls' School and Univ of Sussex. *Career:* Sec Over-21 magazine; writer and Commissioning Ed, later Features Ed Tatler 1982–87; Ed Women's Page Sunday Telegraph 1987, later Deputy Ed 7 Days current affairs photo/reportage; Features Ed Vogue 1988; Ed GQ 1990; Ed Vogue 1992–; mem Bd Condé Nast UK 1997–; Trustee Nat Portrait Gallery, London 1999–; Ed of the Year 1997. *Address:* Condé Nast Publications, Vogue House, Hanover Square, London W1R 0AD, UK. *Telephone:* (20) 7499-9080.

SHVETSOVA, Ludmila Ivanovna; Russian politician; b 24 Sept 1949, Alma-Ata; m; one s. *Education:* Kharkov Inst of Aviation, Moscow State Social Univ. *Career:* Technician, then engineer Kiev Mechanical factory; employee Antonov Aviation Construction Bureau in Kiev 1971–75; Comsomol functionary in Ukraine 1975–, Sec Cen Comsomol Cttee of Ukrainian SSR; Sec Cen Comsomol Cttee 1981–89; Chair Council of Pioneers' Org 1984–86; Head of Div, Secr of USSR Supreme Soviet 1989–92; Head Group of Gen Expertise, Higher Econ Council of USSR Supreme Soviet 1992–93; initiator and first Head State Cttee on Problems of Family and Women 1994–; mem Govt City of Moscow 1994–, First Deputy Chair 2000–, Head Complex of Social Sphere 2000–; Head Cttee of Public and Inter-regional Relations 1994–2000; Pres Women's Initiative Foundation 1997–, Asscn of Research of Women's Movt; Co-Chair Confed Women's League. *Address:* Moscow Government, Tverskaya str 13, 103032 Moscow, Russian Federation. *Telephone:* (095) 290-71-96; (095) 299-49-60.

SIAO, Josephine; Hong Kong actress; b 1947, Shanghai, China; m Clarence Chang; two d. *Education:* Seton Hall Univ (New Jersey, USA) and Regis Univ (Denver, CO, USA). *Career:* Came to Hong Kong 1949; began acting in films at the age of five, and had appeared in 200 films by the age of 21; played comedy character Lam Au Chun, known as Asia's Charlie Chaplin 1970s. *Films include:* Nobody's Child 1958, The Story of a Rebellious Child 1969, Lam Au Chun, Summer Snow (Silver Bear Award for Best Actress, Berlin Film Festival 1995), Hu Du Men.

SIBERRY, Jane, B SC; Canadian singer; b 12 Oct 1955, Toronto. *Education:* Univ of Guelph, ON. *Career:* Recorded with Windham Hill/A & M 1984–87, with Reprise/Warner 1987–96; Founder and Pres Sheeba Records 1996–; has contributed to several soundtracks including Until The End Of The World, Faraway So Close, The Crow, Songs From The Cold Seas; Casby Awards for Producer and Album of the Year. *Albums include:* Jane Siberry 1981, No Borders Here 1984, The Speckless Here 1985, The Walking 1987, Bound By The Beauty 1989, When I Was A Boy 1993, Maria 1995, Teenager 1996. *Address:* Box 291, 238 Davenport Rd, Toronto, ON M5R 1J6, Canada. *Telephone:* (416) 531-4151; *Fax:* (416) 531-7281; *E-mail:* sib@sheeba.ca.

SIBLEY, Dame Antoinette, DBE; British ballet dancer; b 27 Feb 1939, Bromley, Kent; d of Edward G. and Winifred (née Smith) Sibley; m 1st Michael Somes 1964 (divorced 1973, died 1994); m 2nd Panton Corbett 1974; one s one d. *Education:* Arts Educational School (Tring, Herts) and Royal Ballet School (fmrly Sadler's Wells Ballet School, London). *Career:* Joined Royal Ballet 1956, Soloist 1959, Prin Ballerina 1960–79; retd 1979, but returned to stage for various seasons with Royal Ballet 1981–89; danced world-wide on tour with Royal Ballet and as Guest Artist with major ballet cos; Vice-Pres Royal Acad of Dancing (now Royal Acad of Dance) 1989–91, Pres 1991–; Gov Elmhurst Ballet School; Patron Cecchetti Centre, Cecchetti Soc, Youth Ballet Workshop, Peterborough Dance Project, London Suzuki Group; Adjudicator London Evening Standard Dance Awards. *Ballets include:* The Sleeping Beauty 1958, Swan Lake 1959, Coppelia 1959, Jabez and the Devil (cr Mary) 1959, La fille mal gardée 1962, The Good-Humoured Ladies 1962, The Dream (cr Titania) 1964, Romeo and Juliet 1965, Symphonic Variations 1967, The Nutcracker 1968, Jazz Calendar (cr Friday's Child) 1968, Enigma Variations (cr Dorabella) 1968, Daphnis and Chloë 1969, Anastasia (cr Mathilde Kchessinska) 1971, Triad (cr the Girl) 1972, In The Night 1973, Manon (cr Manon) 1974, Soupirs (cr Pas de Deux) 1982, L'Invitation au Voyage 1982, Varii Capricci 1983, Fleeting Figures 1984, A Month in the Country 1989; *Films include:* The Turning Point 1978; *Publications include:* Sibley and Dowell 1976, Antoinette Sibley 1981, Reflections of a Ballerina 1985. *Leisure interests:* doing nothing, opera, cinema, reading. *Address:* c/o Royal Academy of Dance, 36 Battersea Square, London SW11 3RA, UK.

SIDIBÉ, Sy Oumou Louise; Malian politician and teacher. *Career:* Mem Transition Cttee for the Salvation of the People (CTSP); fmr Minister of Public Health, Welfare and Women's Affairs; Headmistress Les Castors school, Bamako. *Address:* Les Castors, BP 3102, Bamako, Mali. *Telephone:* 227721.

SIDIKOU, Fatoumata, LL M; Niger United Nations official; b 2 June 1949, Say; d of Trémoko Hasrani; m 1971; three s two d. *Education:* Lycée Nat (Niamey) and Univ of Abidjan (Côte d'Ivoire). *Career:* Mem staff Credit Services, Int Bank of W Africa 1973–77; mem staff UNDP 1978–83; apptd Programme Head UNFPA, Dakar, Senegal 1983. *Leisure interests:* reading, cinema. *Address:* UNDP, 19 rue Parchappe, BP 154, Dakar, Senegal. *Telephone:* 239168; *Fax:* 235500.

SIDIMUS, Joysanne; Canadian international arts organization executive and ballet mistress; b New York, USA; d of Jerome Hillel and Bessie (née Brodsky) Sidimus; m (divorced); one d. *Education:* Adelphi Acad and Barnard Coll. *Career:* Dancer New York City Ballet, USA; Soloist London Festival Ballet; Prin Dancer Nat Ballet of Canada, Pennsylvania Ballet, USA; Ballet Mistress Les Grands Ballets de Genève (Switzerland), Ballet Repertory Co (now ABT II); teacher ABT School, Dance Theater of Harlem (NY, USA), Briansky Saratoga Ballet Center, George Brown Coll, York Univ, Nat Ballet School; Founder and Exec Dir Dancer Transition Center 1985–; numerous stagings of works of Balanchine; Faculty mem N Carolina School of Arts, USA; Alt mem Canadian Advisory Cttee on Status of the Artist; Certificate of Appreciation, Canadian Olympic Asscn; Vice-Pres, Artists' Health Centre Foundation; mem Exec Cttee, Int Organization for the Transition of Professional Dancers; Dance Ontario Award 1989; Commemorative Medal for 125th Anniversary of Canadian Confed for Services to the Arts Community 1993; Canada Council for the Arts Jacqueline Lemieux Prize 1999. *Publication:* Exchanges: Life After Dance 1986. *Address:* Dancer Transition Resource Centre, 66 Gerrard St E, Suite 202, Toronto, ON M5B 1G3, Canada.

SIEPMANN, Mary Aline (see Wesley, Mary).

SIERRA GONZALEZ, Angela del Carmen; Spanish politician; b 10 Jan 1945, Tenerife. *Career:* Fmr MEP (GUE/Nordic Green Left, IU), mem Cttee on Legal Affairs and Citizens' Rights, Del for relations with the Maghreb Countries and the Arab Maghreb Union. *Address:* c/o European Parliament, rue Wiertz, 1047 Brussels, Belgium.

SIGCAU, Princess Stella, BA; South African politician; b 1937; d of Botha Sigcau (fmr Pres of Transkei); m Ronald Tshabalala 1962 (deceased); two c. *Education:* Univ of Fort Hare. *Career:* Mem Transkei Parl for Lusikisiki 1968; Minister of the Interior, Public Works and Energy, Educ and Post and Telecommunications until 1976, of Interior Affairs 1976–81, Post and Telecommunications 1981–87; Leader Transkei Nat Independence Party 1987; Prime Minister of Transkei 1987 (ousted in a coup); Del for Cape Traditional Leaders at Multiparty Negotiation Process, World Trade Centre 1994; Minister for Public Enterprises, Govt of Nat Unity 1994–99, of Public Works 1999–; Chair ANC Women's League, Transkei; mem ANC Women's League Nat Exec Council. *Leisure interests:* reading, farming. *Address:* Ministry of Public Works, Central Government Bldg, Corner Bosman and Vermeulen Sts, Pretoria 0002, South Africa. *Telephone:* (12) 3241510; *Fax:* (12) 3256380; *E-mail:* imochaliban@pwdmail.pwv.gov.za; *Internet:* www.publicworks.gov.za.

SIGURÐARDÓTTIR, Jóhanna; Icelandic politician; b 4 Oct 1942; m Thorvaldur Steiner Jóhannesson. *Education:* Commercial Coll of Iceland. *Career:* Stewardess Loftleider (Icelandic Airways) 1962–71; Clerk Kassagerd Reykjavíkur 1971–78; mem Althingi (Parl) for Reykjavík 1978–; Deputy Leader Social Democratic Party; Minister of Social Affairs 1987–94; Chair Govt Cttee on Handicapped 1979–83; mem Social Security Bd 1978–, Chair 1979–80; Chair Leadership Cttee Icelandic Air Hostesses' Union 1961, 1966, mem 1966–69; mem Reykjavík Shop and Office Workers' Union 1976–83. *Address:* c/o Ministry of Social Affairs, Hafnarhúsinu við Tryggvagötu, 150 Reykjavík, Iceland.

ŠIKLOVÁ, Jiřina, PH D; Czech sociologist; b 17 June 1935, Prague; d of Karel and Jarmila Herold; m Zdeněk Šikl 1956 (divorced); one s one d. *Education:* Charles Univ (Prague). *Career:* Asst Prof Dept of Philosophy, Charles Univ 1960–65, Dept of Sociology 1965–69, apptd Head of Social Work and Gender Studies 1990; Social Researcher in Prague Hosp 1971–88; imprisoned for dissident activities 1981–82, 1988; Women for Europe Award 1995; T. G. Masaryk Medal 1999;

Higher Medal of Czech Repub. *Publications:* History of the YMCA in Czechoslovakia 1965, Students and the New Left Movement 1968, How Much More Can Women Bear? 1975, Grey Zone and the Future of Dissent 1989, The Solidarity of the Culpable 1991, Women in Leadership 1992, What Did We Lose After 1989?, Roots of Apathy Toward Feminism 1999. *Leisure interests:* gardening, playing with grandchildren. *Address:* Klimentská 17, 110 00 Prague 1, Czech Republic. *Telephone:* (2) 2327106; *E-mail:* jirina.siklova@ecn.cz.

SILJA, Anja; German opera singer; b 17 April 1940, Berlin; m Christoph von Dohnanyi; two d one s. *Career:* Guest appearances in Vienna, New York, San Francisco and Chicago (USA), Salzburg Festivals (Austria), Stuttgart, Cologne, Budapest, Brussels, London, Tokyo, Geneva (Switzerland), Paris, Rome, Barcelona (Spain), Copenhagen, Hamburg, Frankfurt and Bayreuth. *Operas include:* Salome, Lulu, Fidelio, Elektra, Wozzeck, The Merry Widow, Carmen, Tosca, Katya Kabanová, Erwartung, The Makropoulos Case, The Girl of the Golden West, Kabale und Liebe, Rise and Fall of the City of Mahagonny, Lady Macbeth of Mtsensk; the complete Wagner repertoire. *Leisure interests:* driving, decorating, tennis, ice-skating, gardening. *Address:* Severence Hall, Cleveland, OH 44106, USA.

SILLS, Beverly; American opera singer (coloratura soprano, retd) and arts administrator; b (Belle Silverman) 25 May 1929, Brooklyn, NY; d of the late Morris Silverman and of Sonia Bahn; m Peter Bulkeley Greenough 1956; one s one d three step-c. *Career:* Studied under Estelle Liebling; debut at San Francisco Opera in Mefistofele 1953, at New York City Opera in Die Fledermaus 1955; singer with New York City Opera 1955–80 (retd as singer 1980), Gen Dir 1979–88, Pres New York City Opera Bd 1989–90; Man Dir Metropolitan Opera, New York 1991–94; Chair Lincoln Center 1994–; has appeared at most major opera houses in Europe and Latin America, including Vienna State Opera, La Scala (Milan, Italy), Royal Opera House (Covent Garden, London), and has given numerous recitals with leading orchestras throughout USA; retd 1980; Dir Warner Communications Inc, New York 1982–, American Express, Macy's; recordings for Columbia, RCA, Angel, ABC—Audio Treasury; host Live from Lincoln Center (TV series) 1998; Presidential Medal of Freedom; Chevalier des Arts et des Lettres. *Operas include:* Mefistofele 1953, Die Fledermaus 1955, The Magic Flute 1967, The Siege of Corinth 1969, 1975, Lucia di Lammermoor 1970, Julius Caesar, Roberto Devereux, The Tales of Hoffmann, Manon, La Traviata, Daughter of the Regiment, The Barber of Seville, Anna Bolena, Maria Stuarda, Norma, Lucrezia Borgia; *Publications:* Bubbles: a self-portrait 1976, Beverly (autobiog) 1987. *Address:* c/o Vincent and Farrell Associates, 481 8th Ave, Suite 740, New York, NY 10001, USA.

SILVER, Joan Micklin, BA; American film and theatre director and scriptwriter; b 24 May 1935, Omaha, NE; d of Maurice Micklin and Doris Shoshone; m Raphael Silver 1956; three d. *Education:* Sarah Lawrence Coll (Bronxville, NY). *Career:* Began career as writer for educational films; original screenplay for Limbo purchased by Universal Pictures; commissioned by Learning Corpn of America to write and direct The Immigrant Experience 1972 and wrote and directed two children's films for same co; also TV Dir. *Films include:* Hester Street (dir and screenplay), Bernice Bobs Her Hair (dir and screenplay), Between the Lines (dir), On the Yard (producer), Head Over Heels (dir and screenplay, retitled Chilly Scenes of Winter), Crossing Delancey (dir), Loverboy (dir), Big Girls Don't Cry... They Get Even (dir), A Private Matter (dir), In the Presence of Mine Enemies (dir) 1996, Fish in the Bathtub 1997, Invisible Child (dir) 1998; *Plays:* Album (dir), Maybe I'm Doing it Wrong (dir), A... My Name Is Alice (dir), A... My Name Is Still Alice (dir); *Radio:* Great Jewish Short Stories from Eastern Europe and Beyond (dir) 1995. *Address:* Silverfilm Productions Inc, 510 Park Ave, Suite 9B, New York, NY 10022-1105, USA. *Telephone:* (212) 355-0282; *Fax:* (212) 421-8254; *E-mail:* jmicksil@aol.com.

SILVERSTONE, Alicia; American actress; b 4 Oct 1976, CA. *Career:* Debut on stage in Carol's Eve, LA; star of three videos for Aerosmith including Cryin'; formed own production co First Kiss Productions. *Films:* The Crush 1993, The Babysitter 1995, True Crime 1995, Le Nouveau Monde 1995, Hideaway 1995, Clueless 1995, Excess Baggage (co-producer), Batman and Robin 1997, Free Money 1998, Love's Labor Lost 1999, Blast from the Past 1999; *TV appearances include:*

Torch Song, Shattered Dreams, The Cool and the Crazy 1994, The Wonder Years 1997. *Address:* c/o Premiere Artists Agency, Suite 510, 8899 Beverly Blvd, Los Angeles, CA 90048, USA; First Kiss Productions, c/o Columbia Pictures, 10202 Washington Blvd, Culver City, CA 90232, USA.

SIMARD, Monique; Canadian politician; b 19 Feb 1950, Montréal; m; one s. *Education:* Univ of Quebec (Montréal). *Career:* Mem staff Confed des Syndicats Nationaux (trade union Confed) 1973–91, First Vice-Pres 1981–85; host and commentator on radio and TV 1991–94; First Vice-Pres and Dir-Gen Parti Québécois 1994–96; mem Quebec Nat Ass 1996; mem Council on the Status of Women 1983–88, Consultative Council on Science and Tech 1991–94. *Address:* Hôtel du Gouvernement, Bureau 1.59, Québec, PQ G1A 1A4, Canada. *Telephone:* (514) 635-9590; *Fax:* (514) 635-0749.

SIMEÓN NEGRÍN, Rosa Elena, MD, PH D; Cuban politician and professor of veterinary medicine; b 17 June 1943, Havana; d of Juan Simeón and Juana Negrín; m Ramón Ortiz 1973; one d. *Education:* Marianao High School, Univ of Havana, Pasteur Inst (France) and Maison d'Alfort (Canada). *Career:* Chief Virology Dept, Nat Center of Scientific Research (CENIC) 1968–73, Microbiological Div 1974–76; Prof School of Veterinary Medicine 1969–73, Nat Hosp and Nat Center of Scientific Investigations 1975, Nat Inst of Veterinary Medicine 1977–78, 1981; Dir Nat Center of Agric Health (CENSA) 1985; Pres Acad of Sciences of Cuba 1985–94; Pres Nat Comm for Environment 1985–; Minister of Science, Tech and Environment 1994–; mem UN Advisory Cttee on Science and Tech for Devt 1991; many other professional appointments; has written numerous reports and articles on swine fever; Heroina del Trabajo 1992; awards and decorations from Cuba, Czechoslovakia and France. *Leisure interest:* study. *Address:* Ministry of Science, Technology and Environment, Capitolio Nacional, 10200 Havana, Cuba. *Telephone:* (7) 62-8631; *Fax:* (7) 93-8654.

SIMHA, Ethia; Israeli lawyer and political adviser; b 25 May 1929, Poland; m Aaron Simha 1956; two s two d. *Education:* Advanced School for Law and Econs (Tel-Aviv) and Hebrew Univ of Jerusalem. *Career:* Called to the Bar 1955; Chief Asst to Ed Israel Supreme Court Gazette 1955–57; pvt practice 1958–83, 1984–87; Adviser to Prime Minister on Women's Affairs 1983–84, 1987–92; Head Israel Women's Del to UN, Vienna 1983–84, 1988–92; Rep of Israel to UN Gen Ass 1989–90; Deputy Chair Comm on the Status of Women in Israel (WIZO) 1974–78, Chair Center for Information on the Rights of Women in Jerusalem and Legal Counsellor 1973–82, mem Jerusalem and Israel Exec Bd 1973–82; Int Hon Sec Int Alliance of Women (IAW) 1976–80, mem World Exec 1980–86, Rep to UN Agencies, Vienna 1982–86; mem Bd Jerusalem Bar Asscn 1979–85, World Council of the Int Asscn of Jewish Lawyers and Jurists 1980–92; Chair Cultural Cttee Jerusalem Bar Asscn; Vice-Chair Int Cttee of Israeli Bar Asscn 1987–92; Pres Jerusalem Lion's Int Club 1989–90; lecturer at numerous int seminars and workshops and numerous contribs to professional journals on women and domestic violence; Adelaida Ristory Award (Italy) 1990; Award of the Israel Inst of Public Opinion Surveys 1991. *Leisure interests:* art, literature. *Address:* Office of the Prime Minister, 3 Rehov Kaplan, Hakirya, Jerusalem 91919, Israel (Office); 12 Bartenura St, Jerusalem, Israel (Home). *Telephone:* (2) 663923.

SIMMONDS, Posy, BA; British illustrator and cartoonist; b 9 Aug 1945; d of Reginald A. C. and Betty (née Cahusac) Simmonds; m Richard Hollis 1974. *Education:* Queen Anne's School (Caversham), Ecole des Beaux Arts (Paris) and Central School of Art and Design. *Career:* Freelance illustrator 1969–; Cartoonist The Guardian 1977–87, 1988–90, 1992–, The Spectator 1988–90; exhibitions The Cartoon Gallery (fmrly The Workshop) 1974, 1976, 1979, 1981, 1982, 1984, Museum of Modern Art (Oxford) 1981, Manor House Museum and Art Gallery (Ilkley) 1985; Hon D ART (Plymouth) 1993; Cartoonist of the Year (jtly, Granada TV and What the Papers Say) 1980, British Press Awards 1981. *Publications include:* Bear Book 1969, Mrs Weber's Diary 1979, True Love 1981, Pick of Posy 1982, The Young Visitors (illustrator) 1984, Very Posy 1985, Fred 1987, Pure Posy 1987, Lulu and the Flying Babies 1988, The Chocolate Wedding 1990, Matilda, Who Told Such Dreadful Lies (illustrator) 1991, Mustn't Grumble

1993, Bouncing Buffalo 1994, F-Freezing ABC 1995; *TV documentary:* Tresoddit for Easter 1991. *Address:* c/o PFD, Drury House, 34–43 Russell St, London WC2B 5HA, UK.

SIMMONS, Adele Smith, PH D; American college and foundation administrator; b 21 June 1941, Lake Forest, IL; d of Hermon Dunlap and Ellen T. (née Thorne) Smith; m John L. Simmons; two s one d. *Education:* Radcliffe Coll and Univ of Oxford (UK). *Career:* Asst Prof Jackson Coll, Tufts Univ, Medford, MA 1969–72, Dean 1970–72; Asst Prof of History and Dean Student Affairs, Princeton Univ 1972–77; Pres Hampshire Coll, Amherst, MA 1977–89, John D. and Catherine T. MacArthur Foundation, Chicago, IL 1989; Dir Marsh & McLennan 1978, Affiliated Publs (Boston Globe) 1981, Zayre Corpn, First Chicago Corpn 1990; Adviser to UN 1993; Dir Synergos Asscn; Trustee and Chair Bd Carnegie Foundation for Advancement of Teaching 1978–86; Trustee Union of Concerned Scientists 1983, World Policy Inst 1983–86; mem American Asscn for Higher Educ, Pres's Comm on World Hunger 1978–80, on Environmental Quality 1991; Hon LHD (Lake Forest) 1976, (Amherst) 1977, (Franklin Pierce) 1978, (Massachusetts) 1982, (Alverno) 1986; Dr hc (Marlboro) 1987, (Smith Coll) 1988, (Mt Holyoake Coll) 1989, (American Univ) 1992, (Tufts) 1994. *Publications:* Exploitation from 9 to 5 (jtly) 1975, Women's History 1975, Modern Mauritius 1980; contribs to professional journals. *Address:* John D. and Catherine T. MacArthur Foundation, 140 South Dearborn St, Suite 1100, Chicago, IL 60603-5285, USA.

SIMMONS, Jean; British actress; b 31 Jan 1929, London; d of Charles and Winifred Ada (née Loveland) Simmons; m 1st Stewart Granger 1950 (divorced 1960); one d; m 2nd Richard Brooks 1960 (divorced 1977, died 1992); one d. *Education:* Orange Hill School (Burnt Oak, London). *Career:* Film Actress 1943–; stage appearances in Philadelphia, USA and on tour in A Little Night Music 1974–75; Homage Award (Cannes Film Festival) 1988; Lake Como Italian Film Award 1989; Commdr des Arts et des Lettres 1990; British Film Inst Fellowship 1994. *Films include:* Great Expectations 1946, Black Narcissus 1946, Hamlet (Acad Award nomination, Best Actress Award, Venice Film Festival) 1948, Adam and Evelyne 1949, So Long at the Fair 1950, Young Bess 1953, The Robe 1953, The Actress 1953, Guys and Dolls 1956, The Big Country 1958, Home Before Dark 1958, Elmer Gantry 1960, Spartacus 1960, The Grass is Greener 1961, All the Way Home 1963, Life at the Top 1965, Tough Night in Jericho 1967, Divorce American Style 1967, The Happy Ending (Acad Award nomination) 1969, Dominique 1979, The Dawning 1988, How to Make an American Quilt 1996; *TV appearances include:* The Dain Curse (series) 1978, The Thornbirds (Emmy Award) 1982, Down at the Hydro (series) 1982, Great Expectations 1989, People Like Us 1990, December Flower. *Address:* c/o A. Morgan Maree, Jr and Assoc, 4727 Wilshire Blvd, Suite 600, Los Angeles, CA 90010, USA.

SIMMONS, Ruth J., PH D; American university administrator. *Career:* Provost Spelman Coll 1990–1992; Vice Provost Princeton Univ 1992–1995; Pres Smith Coll (Northampton MA) 1995–; Pres-Elect Brown Univ (first black Pres of an Ivy League institution); Dir Metropolitan Life Insurance Co, Pfizer Inc, Texas Instruments, Goldman Sachs; Trustee Carnegie Corpn; mem Bd of Trustees The Clarke School for the Deaf; mem Advisory Council, Bill and Melinda Gates Millennium Scholars Foundation. *Address:* Office of the President, Brown University, Providence, RI 02912, USA. *Telephone:* (401) 863-1000.

SIMON, Carly; American singer; b 25 June 1945, New York; d of Richard Simon; m James Taylor 1972 (divorced 1983); one d one s. *Career:* Singer and composer 1971–; Best New Artist Grammy Award 1971; cr opera Romulus Hart 1993. *Recordings include:* Albums: Carly Simon 1971, Anticipation 1972, No Secrets 1973, Hotcakes 1974, Playing Possum 1975, The Best of Carly Simon 1975, Another Passenger 1976, Boys in the Trees 1978, Spy 1979, Come Upstairs 1980, Torch 1981, Hello Big Man 1983, Spoiled Girl 1985, Coming Around Again 1987, Greatest Hits Live 1988, My Romance 1990, Have You Seen Me Lately? 1990, This is my Life 1992, Letters Never Sent 1994; Singles: You're So Vain, Nobody Does It Better 1977, Let the River Run (Best Original Song Acad Award 1989) 1988, In the Wee Small Hours of the Morning (jtly) 1993, Come Upstairs (jtly) 1996,

Film Noir 1997, The Bedroom Tapes 2000; *Film:* No Nukes 1980; *TV appearances include:* Carly in Concert: My Romance 1990. *Address:* c/o Arista, 6 W 57th St, NY 10019, USA.

SIMON, Josette, OBE; British actress; d of Charles Simon and Eileen Petty; m Mark Padmore 1996. *Education:* Cen School of Speech Training and Dramatic Art. *Career:* Joined RSC; Hon MA (Leicester) 1995, several concert performances. *Plays include:* Measure for Measure 1988, After the Fall, The White Devil 1991, The Lady From the Sea 1994, The Taming of the Shrew 1995, The Maids 1997, A Midsummer Night's Dream 1999; *Films include:* Cry Freedom, Milk and Honey (Best Actress Atlantic Film Festival 1988, Paris Film Festival 1990), A Child From the South, Bitter Harvest, Bridge of Time; *TV appearances include:* Blake's 7, Henry IV, Parts 1 and 2, Bodyguards, Kavanagh QC. *Leisure interests:* cinema, gardening, travel. *Address:* c/o Conway van Gelder Ltd, 18–21 Jermyn St, London SW1Y 6HP, UK. *Telephone:* (20) 7287-0077; *Fax:* (20) 7287-1940.

SIMONE, Nina; American singer; b (Eunice Wayman) 21 Feb 1933, Tryon, NC. *Education:* Juilliard School of Music (New York). *Career:* Sang in clubs in Philadelphia; signed contract with Bethlehem Records 1959, Colpix 1960, Phillips 1965, RCA 1967; active in civil rights movt in early 1960s; has lived in Paris and the Netherlands; Dr hc (Chicago, Massachusetts, Amherst). *Recordings include:* I Loves You Porgy, Don't Let Me Be Misunderstood, I Put a Spell on You, Ain't Got No..., I Got Life, Young, Gifted and Black, Baltimore, My Baby Just Cares For Me.

SIMONETTA, PH D; Italian fashion designer; b (Duchess Colonna di Cesarò); d of Duke Giovanni Colonna di Cesarò and Countess Barbara Antonelli; m 1st Count Galeazzo Visconti di Modrone 1944; one d; m 2nd Alberto Fabiani 1952 (separated 1970 and has taken back her maiden name of Duchess Colonna di Cesarò); one s. *Career:* Opened fashion Atelier, Rome 1946; transferred fashion business to Paris 1962; Philadelphia Fashion Group Award, PA, USA 1953; Davison Paxon Award, Atlanta, GA, USA 1959; Fashion Oscar from Filene's of Boston 1960; after five consecutive years in list of world's best-dressed women is in 'Hall of Fame'; Hon citizen of Austin, New Orleans and Las Vegas, USA. *Publication:* A Snob in the Kitchen 1967.

SIMONIS, Heide, MA; German politician; b 4 July 1943, Bonn; d of Horst and Sophia (née Brück) Steinhardt; m Udo E. Simonis 1967. *Education:* Studied econs and social sciences. *Career:* German teacher Univ of Zambia 1967–69, Goethe Inst and radio and TV, Tokyo 1970–72; mem Bundestag (Parl, SPD) 1976–88; Minister of Finance, Fed State of Schleswig-Holstein 1988–93, Prime Minister 1993–; negotiator for employers in public sector pay negotiations 1992. *Leisure interests:* literature, music. *Address:* Klosterufer 2, 24582 Bordesholm, Germany.

SIMPSON, Joanne, PH D; American meteorologist; b 23 March 1923, Boston, MA; d of Russell and Virginia (née Vaughan) Gerould; m 1st Victor Starr 1944; m 2nd William Malkus 1948; two s one d; m 3rd Robert Simpson 1965. *Education:* Univ of Chicago (IL). *Career:* Instructor in Physics and Meteorology Illinois Inst of Tech 1946–49, Asst Prof 1949–51; Meteorologist Woods Hole Oceanographic Institution 1951–61; Prof of Meteorology Univ of California at Los Angeles 1961–65; Dir of Experimental Meteorology Lab Nat Oceanographic and Atmospheric Admin, Dept of Commerce, Washington, DC 1965–74; Prof of Environmental Sciences Univ of Virginia, Charlottesville 1974–76; W. W. Corcoran Prof of Environmental Sciences Univ of Virginia 1976–81; Head Severe Storms Br, Goddard Lab of Atmospheres, NASA, Greenbelt, MD 1981–88, Project Scientist for Tropical Rainfall Measuring Satellite 1986–89, Chief Scientist for Meteorology 1988–98; mem Bd on Geophysical and Environmental Data 1993–96, on Atmospheric Sciences and Climate 1991–93; Assoc Ed Geophysics and Space Physics reviews 1964–72, 1975–77; mem American Geophysical Union (Fellow 1994), Oceanography Soc, Cosmos Club, Nat Acad of Engineering 1988; over 190 papers on tropical meteorology, tropical cloud systems and modelling, tropical storms and tropical rain measurement from space in professional journals; Guggenheim Fellow 1954–55; Goddard Sr Fellow, NASA 1989–94; Fellow American Meteorological Soc, Pres 1989, Hon mem 1995; Hon mem Royal Meteorological Soc 1999–; Hon D SC (State Univ of New York) 1991; numerous awards including Meisinger Award 1962, Woman of the Year

(Los Angeles Times) 1963, Distinguished Authorship Award (Nat Oceanographic and Atmospheric Admin) 1969, Silver and Gold Medals (Dept of Commerce) 1967, 1972, Vincent J. Schaefer Award (Weather Modification Asscn) 1979, Community Headliner Award (Women in Communications) 1973, Professional Achievement Award (Univ of Chicago Alumni Asscn) 1975, Exceptional Science Achievement Award (NASA) 1982, Rossby Research Medal (American Meteorological Soc) 1983, Lifetime Achievement Award (Women in Science and Eng) 1990, Charles Franklin Brooks Award (American Meteorological Soc) 1992, NASA Nordberg Award 1994, NASA Outstanding Leadership Medal 1998. *Leisure interests:* sailing, history, ballet, reading, travel. *Address:* NASA/GSFC, Center for Earth Sciences, Greenbelt, MD 20771, USA. *Telephone:* (301) 614-6310; *Fax:* (301) 614-5484.

SIMPSON, Patricia, PH D, FRS; British research scientist. *Education:* Univ of Southampton and Univ Pierre et Marie Curie (Paris). *Career:* Ind researcher Centre de Génétique Moléculaire (CGM) (Gif sur Yvette) 1975–80; Research Dir Centre National de la Recherche Scientifique (CNRS) Strasbourg. *Address:* Institut de Génetique et de Biologie Moleculaire et Cellulaire, CRNS, Strasbourg, France.

SIMS, Monica Louie, OBE, MA, LRAM; British broadcasting executive; d of the late Albert Charles and Eva Elizabeth (née Preen) Sims. *Education:* Gloucester Girls' High School and St Hugh's Coll (Oxford). *Career:* Tutor in Drama and Literature Dept of Adult Educ, Univ of Hull 1947–50; Tutor in Educ Nat Fed of Women's Insts 1950–53; worked for BBC 1953–84, Radio Producer Sound Talks 1953–55, Ed Woman's Hour (Radio 4) 1964–67, Controller Radio 4 1978–83, Dir of Programmes 1983–84, TV Producer 1955–64, Head of Children's Programmes 1967–78; Vice-Pres British Bd of Film Classification 1985–99; Dir of Production Children's Film and TV Foundation 1985–98; Chair Careers Advisory Bd Univ of Bristol 1991–; Licentiate Guildhall School of Music and Drama; Hon D LITT (Bristol) 2000. *Leisure interests:* theatre, cinema, gardening. *Address:* 97 Gloucester Terrace, London W2 3HB, UK.

SINCLAIR, Anne Elise, L EN D; American journalist and television producer; b 15 July 1948, New York; d of Robert and Micheline (née Rosenberg) Sinclair; m 2nd Dominique Strauss-Kahn 1991; one s one d. *Education:* Nanterre and Paris. *Career:* Journalist Europe 1 radio station 1973–76; Producer and Presenter l'Homme en question, Société Nat de Programmes—France Régions 3 (FR3) 1976–78, L'invité du jeudi, Société Nat de Télévision en Couleur—Antenne 2 (A2) 1978–82, Visiteurs du jour, Télévision Française 1 (TF1) 1982; Producer and journalist TF1 1983–2001, Deputy Dir of Current Affairs 1995–, Dir e-TF1 1997–2001 (Vice-Pres), Deputy Man Dir TF1 1997–2001; Host Questions d'Actualité current political affairs programme, RTL 1994–; Sept d'or for best journalist 1986, for best discussion programme 1988; Best Political Journalist, Profession Politique magazine 1990. *TV Productions include:* Edition spéciale, Sept sur sept (Sept d'or 1985, Sept d'or for best discussion programme 1990), Questions à domicile, Le point sur la table; *Publication:* Une année particulière 1982. *Leisure interests:* opera, tennis, skiing. *Address:* TF1, 1 quai du Point du Jour, 92100 Boulogne-Billancourt, France.

SINCLAIR, Helen K., MA; Canadian banking executive; b 3 April 1951, Edmonton, AB; d of A. Richard and Sonja (née Morawetz) Sinclair; m James S. Coatsworth; one s one d. *Education:* Glendon Coll (York), Univ of Toronto and Harvard Univ (USA). *Career:* Consultant J. J. Singer Consulting Economists 1974; Supervisor Scotiabank 1975–1980, Sr Vice-Pres Planning and Legislation 1985–89; Dir Public Affairs Canadian Bankers' Asscn (CBA) 1980–85, Pres (first woman) 1989–96; Founder and CEO BankWorks Trading Inc 1996–; fmr Chair Banks Div, United Way of Greater Toronto's Campaign Cabinet; fmr Dir Canadian Payments Asscn, Star Data Inc; Dir Toronto-Dominion Bank, Stelco Inc, Superbuild Corpn, Canada Pension Plan (CPP) Investment Bd; mem Bd Govs Univ of York; mem Ontario Securities Comm Five Year Review Cttee; Hon DCL (Acadia) 1992. *Publication:* Beyond the Third Option: Trade policy in the 1990s 1996; numerous papers for confs. *Leisure interests:* tennis, hiking, cross-country skiing, golf. *Address:* BankWorks Trading Inc, 20 Adelaide St E, 8th Floor, Toronto, ON M5C 2T6, Canada (Office); 73 Weyboune Crescent,

Toronto ON M4N 2R6 Canada (Home). *Telephone:* (416) 362-2361; *Fax:* (416)640-1460; *E-mail:* helens@bankworks.com; *Internet:* www .bankworks.com.

SINCLAIR, Olga, MA; Panamanian artist; b 14 Feb 1957; d of Alfredo and Olga Avila de Sinclair; m Hans Risseau 1987; two d. *Education:* Basics of painting with father, Acad of Applied Arts (Madrid) and Univ Santa María la Antigua (Panamá). *Career:* Art studio in London 1985; Cultural Attaché to Bolivia 1987–88; living in Indonesia 1989–; solo exhibitions include Etcetera Gallery (Panama) 1975, La Paz Garden (Acapulco, Mexico) 1980, Panamerican Union (Washington, DC, USA) 1982, Instituto de Cooperación Iberoamericano (Madrid) 1985, Canning House (London) 1985, Elizabeth den Bieman de Haas Gallery (Amsterdam, Netherlands) 1989; group exhibitions include Museum of Contemporary Art (Santa Fé de Bogotá, Colombia) 1976, Homage to Joan Miró (Geneva, Switzerland) 1983, Int Art Fair (Knokke, Belgium) 1988; works feature in corp collections in Panama, Colombia, Bolivia, Spain and USA; has been featured in publs around the world; First Prize in Art Contest, Acad of Applied Arts, Madrid 1977; Hon Mention in Art Contest, First Biennial, Panama 1982. *Leisure interests:* classical music, religious affairs. *Address:* POB 4529, Jakarta 10001, Indonesia; POB 6-488, El Dorado, Panamá; Buiten de Veste 6, 2871 GE Schoonhoven, Netherlands. *Telephone:* (21) 7980820 (Indonesia); 603662 (Panamá); (1823) 2881 (Netherlands); *Fax:* (21) 5211222 (Indonesia).

SINGER, Jeanne Walsh, BA; American composer and pianist; b 4 Aug 1924, New York; d of Harold Vandervoort and Helen (née Loucks) Walsh; m Richard G. Singer 1945 (deceased); one s. *Education:* Columbia Univ, Barnard Coll (NY) and Nat Guild of Piano Teachers. *Career:* Composer, Concert Pianist 1947–; teacher of piano 1960–; mem Composers, Authors and Artists of America, League of Women Composers, Nat League of American PEN Women, Int League of Women Composers; Ed Magazine of Composers, Authors and Artists of America 1972–80; numerous TV and radio appearances; Grantee New York Arts Council; Special Award of Merit (Nat Fed of Music Clubs); First Prize Nat Competition (Composers' Guild) 1979, Grand Prize 1982; honoured at All-Singer Concert (Santa Fé de Bogotá, Colombia) 1980; First Prize (Composers' and Songwriters' Int) 1985. *Compositions include:* Summons 1975, A Cycle of Love 1976, Suite in Harpsichord Style 1976, From the Green Mountain 1977, Composers' Prayer, Nocturne for Clarinet 1980, Suite for Horn and Harp 1980, From Petrarch 1981, Come Greet the Spring 1981, Quartet for Flute, Oboe, Violin, Cello 1982, Trio for Viola, Oboe, Piano 1984, An American Vision 1985, Wry Rimes 1986, The Lost Garden 1988, To Be Brave is All 1993. *Address:* c/o 64 Stuart Place, Manhasset, NY 11030, USA.

SINGER, Maxine, PH D; American biochemist; b 15 Feb 1931, New York; d of Hyman and Henrietta (née Perlowitz) Frank; m Daniel M. Singer 1952; three d one s. *Education:* Swarthmore Coll and Yale Univ. *Career:* Research Chemist Enzymes and Cellular Biochem Section, Nat Inst of Arthritis and Metabolic Diseases, NIH, Bethesda, MD 1958–74; Chief Nucleic Acid Enzymology Section, Biochem Lab, Div of Cancer Biology and Diagnosis, Nat Cancer Inst 1974–79, Chief Biochem Lab 1979–87, Research Chemist 1987–88, Scientist Emer 1988–; Pres Carnegie Inst, Washington, DC 1988–; Visiting Scientist Dept of Genetics, Weizmann Inst of Science, Rehovot, Israel 1971–72; Dir Foundation for Advanced Educ in Sciences 1972–78, 1985–86; mem Yale Corpn 1975–90, Scientific Council Int Inst of Genetics and Biophysics (Naples, Italy) 1982–86, Bd of Dirs Johnson & Johnson; mem Editorial Bd Journal of Biology and Chemistry 1968–74, Science 1972–82; Chair Editorial Bd Proceedings of NAS 1985–88, Comm on the Future of the Smithsonian Inst 1993–95; mem Bd of Govs of Weizmann Inst, Human Genome Org 1989–, Cttee on Science, Eng and Public Policy, NAS 1989–91, Smithsonian Council 1990–94 (Chair 1992–94), Int Advisory Bd (Chulabhorn Research Inst) 1990–, Bd of Washington Trustees of Fed City Council 1996; Trustee Wesleyan Univ, Middletown, CT 1972–75, Whitehead Inst 1985–94; mem NAS, American Soc of Biological Chemists, American Soc of Microbiologists, American Chemical Soc, American Acad of Arts and Sciences, Inst of Medicine of NAS, American Philosophical Soc, New York Acad of Sciences, Pontifical Acad of Sciences; numerous papers in scientific journals, two books on molecular biology (jtly) including Why Aren't Black Holes Black?; Hon D SC (Wesleyan) 1977, (Swarthmore Coll) 1978, (Maryland) 1985, (Brandeis, City Univ of NY) 1988, (Radcliffe

Coll, Williams Coll) 1990, (Franklin and Marshall Coll) 1991, (George Washington Univ, New York Univ, Lehigh) 1992, (Dartmouth) 1993, (Yale, Harvard) 1994; awards include Dir's Award (NIH) 1977, Presidential Distinguished Exec Rank Award 1987, Wilbur Lucius Cross Medal of Honour (Yale Graduate School Asscn) 1991, Nat Medal for Science (NSF) 1992. *Leisure interests:* scuba-diving, cooking, literature. *Address:* Carnegie Institution of Washington, 1530 P St NW, Washington, DC 20005, USA (Office); 5410 39th St, NW, Washington, DC 20015, USA (Home). *Telephone:* (202) 387-6404; *Fax:* (202) 462-7395 (Office); *Internet:* www.carnegieinstitution.org.

SINHA, Tara; Indian advertising executive; b 21 June 1932, Ranchi, Bihar; d of Chiranjiv Lal and Sita Pasricha. *Career:* Account Exec D. J. Keymer and Co 1954–56; Founder, Dir Clarion Advertising Services Ltd, later Man Bombay and Calcutta Brs, Clarion-McCann Advertising Services Ltd 1956–70, Chief Commercial Exec Advertising Consultants India Ltd (subsidiary of Clarion-McCann) 1970–73, Pres and Chief Exec Clarion Advertising Services Ltd 1983–85; Asst to Area Man Communication and Planning Dept, Coca Cola Export Corpn, New Delhi 1973–78, Exec Int Public Relations Group Coca Cola Co, USA 1978–80, Man Issues Man and Programme Planning, External Affairs Div 1980–83; Pres Tara Sinha McCann-Erickson Pvt Ltd since 1985; mem Inst of Public Relations, Market Research Soc, Inst of Marketing, Communication, Advertising and Marketing Asscn (all UK); numerous contribs to professional journals 1958–. *Leisure interests:* reading, cooking. *Address:* Tara Sinha McCann-Erickson Pvt Ltd, V-15 Green Park Extension, New Delhi 110 016, India (Office); C-309 Defence Colony, New Delhi 110024, India (Home). *Telephone:* (11) 6852814 (Office); (11) 6863935 (Home); *Fax:* (11) 6853363 (Office).

SINKE, Digna; Netherlands film-maker; b 17 Oct 1949, Zonnemaire, Zeeland. *Education:* Utrecht Secondary School and Dutch Film and Television Acad (Amsterdam). *Career:* Film-maker 1972–; has made feature films, films for TV and documentaries; Chair Federatie van Kunstenaars Verenigingen. *Films include:* De Gebroeders Helle (The Brothers Helle) 1975, Een Van Gogh aan de muur (A Van Gogh on the Wall—Dutch entry for the Prix d'Italia) 1977, De Hoop van Let Vaderland (The Hope of the Fatherland, documentary) 1982, De Stille Oceaan (The Silent Pacific—selected for the Berlin Film Festival Competition) 1984, Nothing Lasts Forever (documentary) 1990, Above the Mountains 1992, Belle van Zuvlen/Madame de Charrière (main prize at Mannheim–Heidelberg Festival 1994) 1993. *Leisure interests:* walking, gardening. *Address:* Reyer Anslostraat 10, 1054 KV Amsterdam, Netherlands. *Telephone:* (20) 618-24-53; *Fax:* (20) 618-24-53.

SINT, Marjanne; Netherlands public servant; b 24 July 1949, Amsterdam; m H. G. van Noordenburg 1985. *Education:* Univ of Amsterdam and IMEDE Business School. *Career:* Mem staff Ministry of Econ Affairs 1974–77, Ministry of Culture, Health and Social Affairs 1977–79; Econ Ed Intermediair 1979–80, Chief Ed 1980–81; Publr VNU Business Publs 1981–87; Pres Dutch Labour Party (PvdA) 1987, Chair 1988; mem staff Ministry of the Interior 1991–95; Chief Exec City of Amsterdam 1995–. *Publications:* Tussen wal en schip, etnische minderheden in Nederland 1980, Economen over crisis 1982. *Leisure interests:* literature, poetry, music, modern art and architecture. *Address:* Partij van de Arbeid, Nic Witsenkade 30, 1017 ZT Amsterdam, Netherlands. *Telephone:* (20) 551-21-55.

SINYAVSKAYA, Tamara Ilyinichna; Russian opera singer (mezzo-soprano); b 6 July 1943, Moscow; m Muslim Magovaev 1974. *Education:* Moscow Music Coll and State Theatre Art Inst. *Career:* Soloist with Bolshoi Theatre 1964–; studied at La Scala, Milan, Italy 1973–74; awarded First Prize Int Singing Competition (Sofia) 1968, Grand Prix Int Singing Competition (Belgium) 1969, First Prize Int Tchaikovsky Competition (Moscow) 1970; People's Artist of RSFSR 1976; People's Artist of USSR 1982. *Operas include:* Eugene Onegin, Carmen, The Gambler, Semyon Kotko, A Life for the Tsar, Russlan and Ludmilla, The Tsar's Bride, Not Love Alone. *Address:* Bolshoi Theatre, Moscow, Teatralnaya pl 1, Russian Federation.

SIOUXSIE SIOUX; British singer and songwriter; b (Susan Dallion) 1957, Chislehurst, Kent; m Budgie. *Education:* Mottinham Secondary Modern School for Girls (Kent). *Career:* Punk rock singer 1970s; singer and songwriter with Siouxsie and the Banshees 1978–95; also singer with The Creatures (with Budgie); performer song in film Batman Returns 1992; lives in France. *Recordings include:* (With Siouxsie and the Banshees) Albums: The Scream 1978, Join Hands, Kaleidoscope 1980, Ju Ju 1981, Kiss in the Dream House 1983, Hyena, Nocturne 1984, Tinderbox 1987, Twice Upon a Time 1992, The Rapture 1995; Singles: Hong Kong Garden 1978, Playground Twist 1979, Happy House 1980, Christine 1980, Spellbound 1981, Dear Prudence 1984, Cities in Dust, The Candyman 1987, Peek-a-boo 1988, Kiss Them For Me 1991, Oh Baby 1994; (With The Creatures) Album: Feast; Single: Right Now, Mad-Eyed Screamer; (Solo) Single: Interlude (with Morrissey) 1994.

SIREN, Katri (Kaija) Anna-Maija Helena; Finnish architect; b 23 Oct 1920, Kotka; d of Gottlieb and Lydia (née Erkko) Tuominen; m Heikki Siren 1944; two s two d. *Education:* Helsinki Univ of Tech. *Career:* Pvt practice in partnership with Heikki Siren, Siren Architects Ltd 1949–; Hon FAIA; Hon mem Finnish Architects' Asscn 1992; Foreign mem Acad d'Architecture, Paris 1983; Hon Citation and Medal São Paulo Biennal, Brazil 1957, Medal São Paulo Biennal 1961; Hon Citation 'Auguste Perret' (Union Int des Architectes) 1965; Grand Silver Order of Austria (with star) 1977; Grande Médaille d'Or (Acad d'Architecture, Paris) 1980; Officer of the Order of the Finnish White Rose 1980; Architectural Prize of the State of Finland 1980; Prize of Finnish Cultural Foundation 1984; Prize of the City of Helsinki 1988. *Publications:* selected works published in Kaija and Heikki Siren, Architects 1978. *Leisure interest:* fine arts and nature. *Address:* Tiirasaarentie 35, Helsinki 20, Finland. *Telephone:* (0) 673032.

SIRIVEDHIN, Tanya, MA (ECON); Thai banker; b 19 Feb 1946, Bangkok; d of Boonma Wongsawan and Chirie Voravarn; m Anumongkoi Sirivedhin 1968; two d. *Education:* Victoria Univ of Wellington (NZ) and Univ of Wisconsin (USA). *Career:* Joined Bank of Thailand as Economist Int Finance Section, Econ Research Dept 1972, Dep Dir Int Dept 1985–92, Dir 1992–95, Dir Banking Dept 1995–96, Asst Gov 1996–98, Deputy Gov and Vice Chair, Court of Dirs 1998–. *Leisure interests:* jogging, tennis, golf, painting, reading. *Address:* POB 154, 273 Thanon Samsen, Bangkhunprom, Bangkok, Thailand. *Telephone:* (662) 283-5003; *Fax:* (662) 283-5098; *E-mail:* tsiri@bot.or.th.

SISLER, Rebecca Jean, RCA; Canadian writer and sculptor; b 16 Oct 1932, Mount Forest, ON; d of Byron Cooper and Mildred (née Ramsden) Sisler. *Education:* St Thomas Coll Inst (Ontario), Ontario Coll of Art, Royal Danish Acad of Fine Arts. *Career:* Curator Erindale Campus Art Gallery, Univ of Toronto 1986–; Cultural Attaché to Canadian Gov-Gen 1982–84; mem Nat Council Royal Canadian Acad of Arts 1977–78, Exec Dir 1978–82; sculpture comms include The Minstrels (St Thomas, ON) 1967, Cross and Candlesticks (London, ON) 1968; mem Ontario Soc of Artists; Canadian Woman Artist of the Year Medal, Ontario Soc of Artists 1982. *Publications:* The Girls: a biography of Frances Loring and Florence Wyle 1972, Passionate Spirits: a history of the Royal Canadian Acad of Arts 1880–1980 1980, Aquarelle! A History of the Canadian Soc of Painters in Water Colour 1925–1985 1986, Art for Enlightenment: A History of Art in Toronto Schools 1993; numerous essays and articles. *Leisure interests:* reading, walking, gardening, travel. *Address:* c/o Fitzhenry & Whiteside, 195 Allstate Parkway, Markham, ON L3R 4T8, Canada.

SISULU, Albertina Nontsikelelo; South African politician; b 1919, Tsomo, Transkei; m Walter Max Ulyate Sisulu 1944; five c. *Career:* Trained as a nurse, Johannesburg NE Hosp; mem Women's League, African Nat Congress (ANC) 1948, Deputy Pres 1991, mem Nat Exec Cttee of ANC 1991–; joined Fed of S African Women 1954, Pres 1984; participated in women's protest against introduction of Women's Pass; under continual banning orders (including house arrest) 1964–82; Transvaal Pres United Democratic Front (UDF) 1983–91; tried and sentenced to four years' imprisonment for furthering aims of ANC 1984, successful appeal 1987; elected to Nat Council, Women's Congress, UDF 1987; Leader UDF Del to USA and to UK July 1989; Co-Convenor (with Gertrude Shope, qv) African Nat Congress (ANC) Women's League Task Force 1990; mem Parl (ANC) 1994–; Pres World Peace Council 1993. *Address:* POB 61884, Marshalltown 2107, South Africa.

SIXSMITH, Jane; British hockey player; b 5 Sept 1967. *Career:* Over 300 int appearances, scored over 100 goals; competed in Olymic Games (Seoul) 1988, (Barcelona) 1992, (Atlanta) 1996, (Sydney) 2000; fmr Captain English Hockey Team; retd 2000; UK Hockey Player of the Year 2000. *Address:* c/o Robyn Kohl, English Hockey Association, The Stadium, Filbury Blvd, Milton Keynes MK9 1HA, UK.

SIZOVA, Alla Ivanovna; Russian ballet dancer and teacher; b 22 Sept 1939, Moscow; d of Ivan Sizov and Ekaterina Sizova; m Mikhail Serebrennikov 1965 (died 1980); one s. *Education:* Leningrad (now St Petersburg) School of Ballet. *Career:* Dancer Leningrad Kirov Theatre of Opera and Ballet 1958–88; a frequent partner of Mikhail Baryshnikov and Rudolph Nureyev; teacher A. Vagnova Choreography School 1987–91, Universal Ballet Acad 1991–; People's Artist of the RSFSR 1983; Gold Medals Youth Festival, Vienna 1959, First Int Ballet Contest, Varna, Bulgaria; Anna Pavlova Diploma (Paris) 1964; People's Artist of the RSFSR 1983. *Ballets include:* Nutcracker, Giselle, Corsair, Stone Flower, Chopiniana, Swan Lake, Sleeping Beauty, Fountain of Bakhchisarai, Romeo and Juliet, Cinderella, Don Quixote, Leningrad Symphony. *Address:* Universal Ballet School, 4301 Harewood Rd, NE, Washington, DC 20017, USA; 4301 Harewood Rd, NE, Washington, DC 20017, USA. *Telephone:* (202) 832-1087; *Fax:* (202) 526-4274.

SKÁLOVÁ, Olga; Czech ballet dancer and teacher; b 25 April 1928; d of Karel Skála and Julie Skálová; m M. D. Jaromír 1974. *Education:* Ballet School of I. V. Psota, Brno and Bolshoi Theatre (Moscow, USSR, now Russian Fed). *Career:* Solo Dancer State Theatre, Brno 1945–52, Head of Ballet Corps 1978–90; Dir of Dance Conservatory, Brno 1983–90, Prof of Dance 1990–; Prima Ballerina Nat Theatre of Prague 1952–78; featured in biographical works, on TV and radio; Laureate of Czechoslovak State Prize 1954; Meritory Artist 1958, Nat Artist 1968; State Order of Work 1983; Thalia Prize, Czech Repub 1996. *Leisure interests:* art, history, gardening. *Address:* Cacovická 53, 614 00 Brno-Husovice, Czech Republic. *Telephone:* (5) 577211.

SKÁLOVÁ, Zuzana, DS; Czech art historian and icon restorer; b 30 March 1945, Prague; d of Jaroslav Skála and Emilie Antoïnova Jelinková. *Education:* Art Acad (Prague), Univ of Amsterdam (Netherlands) and Instituto del Restauro (Rome). *Career:* Journalist Reporter Magazine 1964–68; emigrated to the Netherlands 1968; studies of Art Restoration in Italy, Greece, fmr USSR and USA; worked in Icon Dept, All Union Scientific Inst for Restoration, Moscow 1983, 1985; freelance restorer of Icons, Netherlands 1976–87; apptd Ind Consultant to Dutch Govt for Conservation of Coptic Icons in Egypt, and Head of Project, Coptic Museum, Cairo 1988; Co-ordinator Conservation Cttee ICOM 1990; lecturer in restoration; mem Icon Coptic Soc of Egypt; numerous articles and studies on icons. *Leisure interests:* history, nature, remarkable men and women. *Address:* 28 Mohammed Mazhak St, Zamelek, Cairo, Egypt. *Telephone:* (2) 3419778; *Fax:* (2) 3421202.

SKARD, Torild, MA; Norwegian international organization official; b 29 Nov 1936, Oslo; d of Sigmund and Åse Gruda Skard; m Kåre Øistein Hansen. *Education:* Univ of Oslo. *Career:* Psychologist 1965–67; Lecturer Norwegian Post Grad Teachers' Coll for Special Educ 1965–72, Inst for Social Sciences Univ of Tromsø 1972–73; mem Storting (Parl), Pres Lagting (Senate) and Vice-Pres Judiciary Cttee 1973–77; Sr Researcher Work Research Insts, Oslo 1978–84; Dir, Co-ordinator programmes relating to the status of women, UNESCO, Paris, 1984–86; Dir-Gen Multilateral Dept for Devt Co-operation, Norwegian Ministry of Devt Co-operation/Ministry of Foreign Affairs 1986–91, Asst Sec-Gen 1991–94; UNICEF Regional Dir for W and Cen Africa; Norwegian Del to UN Gen Ass 1974, UN Women's Conf (Mexico) 1975, Int Parl Union (Canberra, ACT) 1977; Leader Norwegian Nat Comm for UNESCO 1977–84, Vice-Pres Del to Gen Confs 1978, 1980, 1982, 1983; Pres UNICEF Exec Bd 1988–89. *Publications include:* Youth in Youth Clubs 1970, It is Oslo that is Remote 1974, Chosen for Parliament – a study of Women's Progress and Men's Power 1980, Everyday Life in Parliament – Personal Experiences 1981, Norwegian Local Councils – a Place for Women? (jtly) 1985, Unfinished Democracy – Women in Nordic Politics 1985; numerous contribs to professional journals. *Address:* 04 BP 443, Abidjan, Côte d'Ivoire. *Telephone:* 21-31-31; *Fax:* 22-76-07; *E-mail:* tskard@unicef.org.

SKEET, Muriel Harvey, FRSM; British World Health Organization consultant; b 12 July 1926; d of the late F. W. C. Harvey-Skeet. *Education:* Endsleigh House, Middlesex Hosp and Univ of London. *Career:* Ward Sister Middlesex Hosp 1949–60; Field Work Organizer Nuffield Provincial Hosps Trust 1961–64; Research Organizer Cttee, Florence Nightingale Cttee of GB and N Ireland 1965–70; Chief Nursing Officer and Nursing Adviser British Red Cross Soc, St John of Jerusalem and British Red Cross Soc Jt Cttee 1970–78; Research Consultant WHO (SE Asia) 1970–96; European Del and first Chair of Bd Commonwealth Nurses' Fed 1971; Health Services Adviser and Consultant WHO and other int agencies and orgs 1978–; mem numerous cttees including Hosp and Medical Services, Ex-Services War Disabled, Queen's Inst of Dist Nursing, Nat Council of Nurses; mem Royal Soc for the Promotion of Health; Leverhulme Fellowship 1974, 1977; Fellow Royal Coll of Nursing. *Publications include:* Waiting in Outpatient Departments 1965, Marriage and Nursing 1968, Home From Hospital 1970, Home Nursing 1975, Manual: Disaster Relief Work 1977, Self Care for the People of Developing Countries 1979, Notes on Nursing 1860 and 1980 1980, The Third Age 1982, Protecting the Health of the Elderly 1983, Know Your Own Body 1987, Add Life to Years 1989, Tropical Health: concise notes 1989, Better Opportunities for Disabled People 1989, Care and Safe Use of Hospital Equipment 1996, History of Nursing at the Middlesex Hospital 2000; numerous articles for professional journals. *Leisure interests:* music, opera, reading, painting. *Address:* 8 Scarsdale Court, Douglas Ave, Exmouth, Devon EX8 2AU, UK. *Telephone:* (1395) 275948.

SKIN; British singer and songwriter; b (Deborah Ann Dyer) 1968. *Education:* Teesside Polytechnic. *Career:* Singer with group Skunk Anansie; three Top Twenty hits in UK 1994–96; tour of USA 1996; Kerrang!! Best Rock Band Award 1995, Best British Live Act Award 1996. *Recordings include:* Albums: Paranoid and Sunburnt, Stoosh; Singles: Little Baby Swastikkka, Intellectualise My Blackness, I Can Dream, Charity, We Love Your Apathy, Selling Jesus; *Film:* Strange Days (cameo appearance by Skunk Anansie).

SKORIK, Irène (pseudonym of Irène Baudemont); French composer, actress and former ballet dancer; b 27 Jan 1924, Paris; d of René and Alexandra (née Skorik) Baudemont. *Education:* Lycée Racine and Conservatoire Russe de Musique (Paris). *Career:* Dancer Ballet des Champs Elysées 1945–50, Munich Opera, Germany 1951–52, London Ballet 1954, Berlin Ballet 1956, Ballets des Etoiles de Paris 1957–59, Netherlands Ballet 1959–60, London Festival Ballet 1963; Prof of Ballet American Univ (Paris) 1970–89, Conservatoire du 9ème 1983–89; guest appearances include Munich, Berlin, Rome, Zurich (Switzerland) and Strasbourg (France); numerous festival and TV appearances; debut as TV actress (Munich, Germany) 1961, as theatre actress (Paris) 1966 and in A Streetcar Named Desire (Trier, Germany) 1973; Actress in TV Films 1960–87, in Theatre 1983; Composer 1979–82; has made recordings; awarded Médaille Taglioni (London) 1948. *Ballets include:* Swan Lake, Cinderella, Bacchus and Ariane, Daphnis and Chloë, Giselle, Peer Gynt, La Sylphide (Médaille Taglioni, London) 1948; *Composition:* La Leçon de Danse (vol 1) 1979, (vol 2) 1984. *Leisure interest:* bridge. *Address:* 28 blvd des Batignolles, 75017 Paris, France. *Telephone:* (1) 45-22-46-48.

SKORYK, Larysa; (b Polish) Ukrainian politician, architect and academic; b 4 Oct 1939, Lubytsa, Poland; d of Pavlo and Olha-Stephania (née Kryna) Kuzma; m Miroslav Skoryk 1964 (divorced); one d. *Education:* Polytechnic Inst (Lvov) and Arts Inst (Kiev). *Career:* Practising architect 1960–; apptd Lecturer and Prof of Architecture Inst of Arts 1971; Human Rights activist and campaigner for Ukrainian independence; Assoc Ukrainian Observer Helsinki Union Human Rights Group 1970s; Co-Founder People's Movt of Ukraine (Rukh) 1989; elected to Ukrainian Parl from Democratic Bloc Coalition 1990; Vice-Chair Ukrainian Soc of Architects 1988; Chair Ukrainian Asscn for the Preservation of Historical Districts 1990; over 30 articles in professional journals 1964–; recipient Pres's Medal for Historic Preservation of Buildings and Monuments 1991, five other awards for architecture. *Leisure interests:* drawing, reading, philosophy, gardening. *Address:* Kiev 54, prospekt Peremohy 20, kv 196, Ukraine. *Telephone:* (044) 274-31-35; *Fax:* (044) 224-91-51.

SKURATOWICZ, Charlotte Gabrielle Butler; British ballet dancer and productions director; b 27 May 1951, Malta; d of Terence and Beryl Mary (née Trotter) Butler; m Marek Skuratowicz 1982; one d. *Education:* Arts Educational Trust (Tring and London). *Career:* Worked with Ballet de la Jeunesse Romande, Lausanne (Switzerland), Städtische Bühnen Freiburg and Tanztheater Wuppertal (Germany); joined Berlin Ballet 1974, Prin Dancer 1979–, Ballet Asst 1991–, Dir of Productions 1996–. *Leisure interests:* travel, theatre, art, cooking. *Address:* Laubenheimerstr 19, 14197 Berlin, Germany. *Telephone:* (30) 8212897; *Fax:* (30) 8212897; *E-mail:* Butler@deutscheoperberlin.de.

SKUSE, Jean Enid, AO, MBE; Australian former church official; b 1 Jan 1932; d of Rev H. Skuse. *Education:* Methodist Ladies' Coll (NSW) and Univ of New S Wales. *Career:* Accountant and Auditor, London and Sydney 1949–63; Admin Methodist Girls' Hostel, Waverley 1963–69; UN Observer for Methodist Church, USA 1969–70; mem UN Comm on Status of Women, Geneva, Switzerland 1970; Exec Sec Australian Council of Churches, NSW 1971–75, Gen Sec Australian Council of Churches 1976–88; Vice-Moderator Cen Cttee of World Council of Churches 1975–83; mem Premier of New S Wales Women's Advisory Council 1981–84; mem Nat Advisory Council Australian Broadcasting Corpn 1983–85; mem Task Force New S Wales Govt Services for Victims of Crime 1986; Nat Co-ordinator World Council of Churches Ass 1988–91; Home Care Advisory Bd NSW Govt 1992–93. *Publications:* Don't Just Stand There 1971, Racism: the Australian experience 1972, Deliver Us From Eve 1977, To See With One's Own Eyes 1982. *Leisure interests:* reading, theatre. *Address:* 25/3 Gallimore Ave, East Balmain, NSW 2041, Australia.

SLANEY, Mary Teresa Decker; American athlete; b 4 Aug 1958, Bunnvale, NJ; d of John and Jacqueline Decker; m 1st Ron Tabb (divorced 1983); m 2nd Richard Slaney 1985; one c. *Education:* Univ of Colorado. *Career:* Amateur middle- and long-distance track athlete 1969–; Winner 1,500m and 3,000m events World Championships, Helsinki 1983; American outdoor track records (up to 1990) are 10,000m 1982, 1,500m 1983, one mile 1985, 2,000m 1984, 800m 1985, 3,000m 1985, 1,000m 1988; American indoor track records (up to 1990) are 800m 1980, 1,500m 1980, one mile 1982, 1,000m 1989; Jesse Owens Int Amateur Athlete Award 1982; Sullivan Award, Amateur Athletic Union 1982; Sportswoman of the Year, Women's Sports Foundation 1982, 1983; Top Sportswoman Associated Press, Europe 1985. *Address:* c/o The Athletics Congress, POB 120, Indianapolis, IN 46206-0120, USA; 2923 Flintlock St, Eugene, OR 97401-4660, USA (Home).

SLAUGHTER, Audrey Cecelia; British writer and journalist; b 17 Jan 1930; d of Frederick George and Ethel Louise Smith; m 1st W. A. Slaughter 1950 (divorced); m 2nd Charles Vere Wintour 1979 (died 1999). *Education:* Chislehurst High School and Stand Grammar School (Manchester). *Career:* Fashion journalist until 1960; Ed Honey magazine 1960–68; Founder Petticoat 1964; columnist Evening News 1968–69; Ed Vanity Fair 1970–72; Founder, Dir and Ed Over 21 1972–79; Assoc Ed Sunday Times 1979–81, Sunday Express magazine 1981–82; Founder, Ed Working Woman 1984–86; Lifestyle Ed The Independent 1986–87; Magazine Ed of the Year 1966. *Publications:* Non-fiction: Every Man Should Have One (jtly) 1969, Getting Through... 1981, Working Woman's Handbook 1986, Your Brilliant Career 1987; Fiction: Private View 1990, Blooming 1992, Unknown Country 1994. *Leisure interests:* theatre, film, opera, gardening, painting, reading. *Address:* 613 Cross St, Barnes, London SW13 0AP, UK. *Telephone:* (20) 8876-8772; *E-mail:* wintoura@aol.com.

SLAVKOVSKÁ, Eva, PH D; Slovak politician; 17 July 1942, Bratislava; m Prof Ján Slavkovský 1965; one s one d. *Education:* Comenius Univ (Bratislava). *Career:* Teacher at elementary and secondary schools 1964–77; Researcher in History Slovak Acad of Sciences 1977–94; Minister of Educ 1994; has written 50 papers in the field of history. *Leisure interests:* history, fiction, the arts. *Address:* Ministry of Education, Hlboká 2, 813 30 Bratislava, Slovakia. *Telephone:* (7) 395-772; *Fax:* (7) 397-098.

SŁAWIŃSKA, Irena Zofia, PH D; Polish professor emeritus of drama; b 30 Aug 1913, Wilno (now Vilnius, Lithuania); d of Seweryn and Helena (née Kurnatowska) Sławińska. *Education:* Univ of St Batory

(Wilno), Univ of Paris (Sorbonne) and Nicholas Copernicus Univ of Toruń. *Career:* Manual worker and teacher 1939–45; Assoc Prof Nicholas Copernicus Univ 1945–49; Full Prof of Drama, Dept of Humanities, Catholic Univ of Lublin 1950–, currently Emer Prof; Univ teacher in Canada 1957, 1982, Brown Univ, RI, USA 1968–69, Univ of Illinois, USA 1969, Univ of Fribourg, Switzerland 1979; Yale Univ Fellowship, USA 1957–58; numerous scientific awards. *Publications:* Le théâtre dans la pensée contemporaine; over 350 studies and articles, 12 books on drama and theatre. *Leisure interests:* swimming, sailing, travel. *Address:* Catholic University of Lublin, al Racławickie 14, 20-950 Lublin, Poland (Office); Ul Chopina 29-12, 20-023 Lublin, Poland (Home). *Telephone:* (81) 30426 (Office); (81) 25195 (Home); *Fax:* (81) 30433 (Office).

SLIPMAN, Sue, OBE, BA; British organization official; b 3 Aug 1949; d of Mark and Doris (née Barham) Slipman; one s. *Education:* Stockwell Manor School, Univs of Wales, Leeds and London. *Career:* Mem Exec Nat Council for Civil Liberties 1974–75; Sec and Nat Pres Nat Union of Students 1975–78; Vice-Chair British Youth Council 1977–78; mem Advisory Council for Adult and Continuing Educ 1978–79; Area Officer Nat Union of Public Employees 1979–85; Chair Women for Social Democracy 1983–86, Advice Guidance and Counselling Lead Body 1992–, Better Regulation Task Force 1997; Vice-Chair British Youth Council 1977–78; mem Exec and Chair of Training 300 Group 1985–86; Dir Nat Council for One Parent Families 1985–95; Dir London Training and Enterprise Council 1995–96; Dir Gas Consumer's Council 1996–98; Dir for Social Responsibility, Camelot Group PLC 1998–, Bd mem, Dir Social Relations and Compliance 2000–; Dir London E Training and Enterprise Council 1990–, Social Market Foundation 1992–93; mem Exec London Voluntary Service Council 1986–; Gen Election cand (SDP/Alliance) for Hayes and Harlington 1987; Trustee Full Employment UK 1990–95; mem Sec of State for Employment's advisory group on women's issues 1992–94. *Publications:* Re-Birth of Britain (contrib) 1983, Helping Ourselves to Power: A Handbook for Women on the Skills of Public Life 1986, Helping One Parent Families to Work 1988, Maintenance: A System to Benefit Children 1989, Making Maintenance Pay 1990. *Address:* Camelot Group PLC, 20 Cockspur St, London SW1Y 5BL, UK. *Telephone:* (20) 7839-6051; *Fax:* (20) 7839-6053.

SLISKA, Lubov Konstantinovna; Russian politician and lawyer; b 15 Oct 1953, Saratov; m. *Education:* Saratov Inst of Law. *Career:* Lawyer Soyuzpechat Saratov 1977–89; on staff regional trade cttee of heavy machine construction industry workers 1992–96; Perm Rep of Govt in Regional Duma, Deputy Chair Regional Govt 1996–2000; mem State Duma Russia (Yedinstvo Movt List) 1999; Deputy Chair (Speaker) of State Duma 2000–; Order for Service to Motherland. *Leisure interests:* countryside, fishing. *Address:* State Duma, Okhotny Ryad 1, 103265 Moscow, Russian Federation. *Telephone:* (095) 292 5552; *Fax:* (095) 292 8600.

ŠLOTOVÁ, Jana, PH D; Czech radiation biophysicist and cytogeneticist; b 7 June 1937, Brno; m Mr Šloth 1959; one d. *Education:* Masaryk Univ (Brno). *Career:* Scientific worker at Inst of Biophysics, Acad of Sciences of Czechoslovakia (now Acad of Sciences of the Czech Repub) 1960–, Research Assoc 1960–66, Scientific Sec 1990–, mem Scientific Council 1990–93 (Chair 1993–97), mem Acad of Sciences Cttee for Foreign Affairs 1990–; Scientific Sec Czechoslovak Comm for IUPAB 1984–92, Czech and Slovak Comm for IUPAB 1993–95, Czech Comm for IUPAB 1996–2000; Rep of the Czech Repub to ICSU 1994–; mem European Soc of Radiation Biology 1969–, Czechoslovak Comm for UNESCO 1990–94; Visiting Scientist Inst für Genetik und Kulturpflanz, Gatersleben (Germany) 1972, 1974, 1976; has published 95 scientific papers; Acad of Sciences Award 1968, 1973, 1980, 1987. *Leisure interests:* literature, music, walking. *Address:* Institute of Biophysics, Academy of Sciences of the Czech Republic, Královopolská 135, 612 65 Brno, Czech Republic. *Telephone:* (5) 41517501; *Fax:* (5) 41211293; *E-mail:* slotova@ibp.cz; *Internet:* www.ibp.cz.

SLOVITER, Dolores Korman, LL B; American federal judge; b 5 Sept 1932, Philadelphia, PA; d of David and Tillie Korman; m Henry A. Sloviter 1969; one d. *Education:* Temple Univ (PA) and Univ of Philadelphia (PA). *Career:* Called to the Bar, PA 1957; Assoc, then Partner Dilworth, Paxson, Kalish, Kohn and Levy 1956–69; mem

Harold E. Kohn 1969–72; Assoc Prof, then Prof of Law, School of Law, Temple Univ 1972–79; Judge US Court of Appeals, Third Circuit, PA 1979–, Chief Judge 1991–98; mem hearing panel disciplinary Bd, Supreme Court, PA 1978–79, SE Region Gov's Council on Aging, PA 1976–79, Cttee of 70 1976–79; Trustee Jewish Public Soc of America 1983–89; mem ABA, American Law Inst, Fed Bar Asscn, Fed Judges' Asscn, American Judicature Soc, Order of Coif, Cttee on Rules of Practice and Procedure 1990–93; Hon LL D (The Dickinson School of Law) 1984, (Richmond) 1992, (Widener) 1994; Distinguished Fulbright Scholar (Chile) 1990; Judicial Award, PA Bar Asscn 1994. *Address:* US Court of Appeals 18614, US Courthouse, 601 Market St, Philadelphia, PA 19106, USA.

SLUTSKAYA, Irina; Russian ice-skater; b 1979. *Career:* Nat Figure Skating Champion of Russia 1996–97, 2000–2001; European Figure Skating Champion 1996, 1998, 2000, 2001; winner 3 Silver Medals, World Championships. *Address:* c/o National Olympic Committee of the Russian Federation, 103064 Moscow, Kazakova uk 18, Russian Federation.

SMELIK, Anneke M., MA; Netherlands lecturer in women's studies. *Education:* Univ of Utrecht. *Career:* Writer and lecturer on women in film and popular culture, Univ of Utrecht; Researcher in feminist film theory 1989–. *Address:* Drift 13, 3512 BR Utrecht, Netherlands (Office); Van Brammendreef 173, 3561 XJ Utrecht, Netherlands (Home). *Telephone:* (30) 62-57-88 (Home).

SMET, Miet; Belgian politician; b 5 April 1943, St Niklaas; d of Albert and Irma (née Ivens) Smet. *Career:* Councillor Dender-Durme en Schelde 1971; Press Attaché Ministry of Regional Economy 1972; Dir Inst of Political Training 1973–79; mem Nat Cttee CVP 1973–; Pres Working Party on Women and Soc 1973–83; Pres Comm for Women's Work, Ministry of Employment and Labour 1974–85; mem Chamber of Reps 1978, Sec of State for the Environment and Social Emancipation 1985–92, for Employment and Sexual Equality 1992; Minister of Employment 1993, of Labour and Equal Opportunities 1996; Rep UN Conf on Status of Women 1975, 1980, 1985. *Address:* Chambre des Représentants/Kamer van Volksvertegenwoordigers, Palais de la Nation, 2 place de la Nation, 1000 Brussels, Belgium.

SMILEY, Jane Graves, MFA, PH D; American writer and university professor; b 26 Sept 1949, Los Angeles; d of James La Verne Smiley and Frances (Graves) Nuelle; m 1st John Whiston 1970 (divorced); m 2nd William Silag 1978 (divorced); two d; m 3rd Stephen M. Mortensen 1987; one s. *Education:* Vassar Coll and Univ of Iowa. *Career:* Asst Prof Iowa State Univ at Ames 1981–84, Assoc Prof 1984–89, Prof 1989–90, Distinguished Prof 1992–; Visiting Prof Univ of Iowa 1981, 1987; Pulitzer Prize for Fiction 1992; Nat Book Critics' Circle Award 1992 and other awards and prizes. *Publications:* Barn Blind 1980, At Paradise Gate 1981, Dupliate Keys 1984, The Age of Grief 1987, The Greenlanders 1988, Ordinary Love and Goodwill 1989, A Thousand Acres 1991, Moo: A Novel 1995, The All-True Travels and Adventures of Lidie Newton 1998. *Leisure interests:* cooking, swimming, playing piano, quilting. *Address:* Iowa State University, Dept of English, 201 Ross Ames, IA 50011, USA.

SMIT-KROES, Neelie, B ECONS; Netherlands politician; b 19 July 1941; m Wouter-Jan Smit; one s. *Education:* Netherlands School of Econs and Rotterdam Univ. *Career:* Mem academic staff Netherlands School of Econs, Rotterdam Chamber of Commerce, Rotterdam Municipal Council; mem States-Gen (Parl) 1971–77, 1981–82; Sec of State for Transport and Public Works 1977–81, Minister of Transport and Public Works 1982–90; Hon D SC (Hull) 1989.

SMITH, Delia, OBE; British cookery writer and television presenter; b 18 June 1941; m Michael Wynn Jones. *Career:* Creator and presenter of several TV series on cookery; cookery writer London Evening Standard, later the Standard 1972–85; columnist Radio Times; Consultant Food Ed Sainsbury's Magazine; Dir Norwich Football Club; Fellow Royal Television Soc; Dr hc (Nottingham) 1996, (Univ of E Anglia) 1999; Special Award, Andre Simon Memorial Fund 1994. *Publications:* How to Cheat at Cooking 1971, Country Fare 1973, Recipes from Country Inns and Restaurants 1973, Family Fare (vol 1) 1973, (vol 2) 1974, Evening Standard Cook Book 1974, Country Recipes from Look East

1975, More Country Recipes from Look East 1976, Frugal Food 1976, Book of Cakes 1977, Recipes from Look East 1977, Food for Our Times 1978, Cookery Course (vol 1) 1978, (vol 2) 1979, (vol 3) 1981, The Complete Cookery Course 1982, A Feast for Lent 1983, A Feast for Advent 1983, One is Fun 1985, Food Aid Cookery Book (ed) 1986, A Journey into God 1988, Delia Smith's Christmas 1990, Delia Smith's Summer Collection 1993, Delia Smith's Winter Collection 1995, How to Cook: Book 1 1998, How to Cook: Book 2 1999. *Address:* c/o Deborah Owen Literary Agency, 78 Narrow St, Limehouse, London E14 8BP, UK. *Telephone:* (20) 7987-5119; (20) 7987-5441; *Fax:* (20) 7538-4004; *E-mail:* debowen@dial.pipex.com.

SMITH, Elizabeth Jean, MA; British broadcasting and international organization executive; b 15 Aug 1936, Ajmer, India; d of Sir Robert and Lady Hay; m Geoffrey P. Smith 1960; one d one s. *Education:* St George's School (Edinburgh) and Univ of Edinburgh. *Career:* Joined BBC Radio as Studio Man 1958, Producer, Sub-Ed Radio News 1961–70, Producer Current Affairs (Radio), later Deputy Ed of Consumer Affairs 1970–78, Producer experimental broadcasting of Parl 1975, Producer Current Affairs (TV) working on Nationwide and Tonight programmes 1978–79, Sr Asst BBC Secr 1979–81; apptd to BBC World Service as Asst Head Cen Talks and Features 1981, Head of Current Affairs 1984–87, Controller English Services 1987–94; Sec-Gen Commonwealth Broadcasting Asscn 1994–; Fellow, Radio Acad; Columnist on The Listener writing Consumer Viewpoint 1975–78; Commonwealth Bursary to study the impact of satellite TV on India 1984. *Publications:* Healing Herbs (as Elizabeth Hay) 1978, Sambo Sahib (biog of Helen Bannerman) 1980. *Address:* Commonwealth Broadcasting Association, 17 Fleet St, London EC4Y 1AA, UK (Office); 12 Highbury Terrace, London N5 1UP, UK (Home). *Telephone:* (20) 7583-5550 (Office); (20) 7226-3519 (Home); *Fax:* (20) 7583-5549 (Office); (20) 7354-0188 (Home); *E-mail:* elizabeth@cba .org.uk; *Internet:* www.cba.org.uk.

SMITH, Jean Kennedy, BA; American diplomatist and foundation executive; b 20 Feb 1928, MA; d of Joseph P. and Rose (née Fitzgerald) Kennedy; m Stephen E. Smith 1956 (died 1990); two s two d. *Education:* Manhattanville Coll (Purchase, NY). *Career:* Mem Bd Trustees Joseph P. Kennedy Jr Foundation 1964–, John F. Kennedy Center for the Performing Arts 1964– (Chair Educ Cttee 1964–74 and f center's children's programmes); fmr mem Bd Carnegie Endowment for Int Peace; f Very Special Arts (int programme for people with disabilities) 1974; Amb to Ireland 1993–98; Hon Irish Citizen; several hon degrees; Jefferson Award for Outstanding Public Service, American Inst for Public Service; Margaret Mead Humanitarian Award, Council of Cerebral Palsy Auxiliaries; Irish American of the Year Award, Irish America Magazine 1995; Rotary One Int Award, Rotary Club of Chicago 1997; Terence HE Cardinal Cooke Humanitarian Award 1997. *Publication:* Chronicles of Courage: Very Special Artists 1993. *Leisure interests:* the arts, tennis, golf, sailing, reading. *Address:* 4 Sutton Place, New York, NY 10022, USA. *Telephone:* (212) 758-3610; *Fax:* (212) 813-1871.

SMITH, Jennifer M.; Bermudan politician; b 14 Oct 1947; d of the late Eugene O. and Lilian E. Smith. *Career:* Began career as journalist; reporter Bermuda Recorder 1970–74, Ed 1974; on staff of Fame magazine, later Ed; joined ZBM Radio and TV; art teacher at Sr Training School (attached to Bermuda Prison Service) for eight years; represented Bermuda as an artist at CARIFESTA, Jamaica; last exhibition 1996; contested St George's N seat for Progressive Labour Party (PLP) in House of Ass elections 1972, 1976, 1980; mem Senate 1980–; Shadow Minister for Educ; mem House of Ass (PLP) 1989, 1993, 1998–; Leader of PLP 1996–; Prime Minister of Bermuda 1998–; Outstanding Woman in Journalism Award 1972 and several other awards. *Leisure interests:* painting, dancing, reading, working with young people, writing, collecting match-book covers and first day stamp covers. *Address:* The Cabinet Office, 105 Front St, Hamilton, HM12, Bermuda. *Telephone:* 292-5501; *Fax:* 292-0304; *E-mail:* premier@ bdagov.bm.

SMITH, Lois Irene, OC; Canadian ballet dancer and choreographer; b 8 Oct 1929, Vancouver, BC; d of William and Doris (née Newbury) Smith; m David Adams 1950 (divorced); one d. *Education:* Rosemary Daveson and Mara McBirney Schools. *Career:* Professional debut 1945;

dancer Nat Ballet Co 1951–69, first Canadian Prima Ballerina 1955–69; performances on CBC TV 1954–69; Founder Lois Smith School of Dance 1969; Chair Dance School, George Brown Coll of Applied Arts and Tech 1975–88; choreographer Canadian Nat Opera 1972–82, Alberta Ballet Co, Winnipeg Opera Co, Florida Ballet Co, USA 1975, South West Ballet Co 1977; Co-choreographer Dance Co of Ontario 1979; first and second Annual Celebration of Dance, Sechelt 1993–94; numerous guest appearances; freelance teacher, choreographer and artist 1988–95; mem Bd Prologue to the Performing Arts 1986, 1987, Encore, Encore 1986, Gibsons Landing Theatre Project 1989, Ballet of British Columbia 1991–94, Hunter Gallery, Gibsons 1991–95, Festival of the Written Arts 1992–95; Pres Sunshine Coast Dance Soc 1993–95; Dance Ontario Award for outstanding contrib to dance 1983; City of Toronto Service Medal 1985. *Leisure interests:* drawing, needlework, stained glass work. *Address:* RR 1, 216–1585 Feild Rd, Sechelt, BC V0N 3A0, Canada.

SMITH, Dame Maggie Natalie, DBE; British actress; b 28 Dec 1934, Ilford, Essex; d of Nathaniel Smith and Margaret Little; m 1st Robert Stephens 1967 (divorced 1975, died 1995); two s; m 2nd Beverley Cross 1975 (died 1998). *Education:* Oxford High School for Girls. *Career:* First appeared with Oxford Univ Dramatic Soc in Twelfth Night 1952; appeared in revue New Faces, New York, USA 1956, Share My Lettuce 1957, The Stepmother 1958; with Old Vic Co 1959–60; Actress with Nat Theatre; played 1976, 1977, 1978 and 1980 seasons, Stratford, ON, Canada; Dir United British Artists 1983–; Hon D LITT (St Andrews, Univ of Leicester) 1982, (Bath) 1986, (Cambridge) 1993; awards for stage, film and TV performances include London Evening Standard Best Actress Award 1962, 1970, 1982, 1985, Variety Club Actress of the Year 1963, Acad Award for Best Actress 1969, for Best Supporting Actress 1979, Best Actress Award, Soc of Film and Television Arts, UK 1969, Best Actress Award, Film Critics' Guild, USA 1969, Variety Club Best Stage Actress Award 1972, BAFTA Award for Best Actress 1984, 1987, 1989, Tony Award 1990; Shakespeare Prize, FVS Foundation, Hamburg 1991; BAFTA Award for Lifetime Achievement 1992. *Plays include:* The Double Dealer, As You Like It, Richard II, The Merry Wives of Windsor, What Every Woman Knows, Rhinoceros 1960, Strip the Willow 1960, The Rehearsal 1961, The Private Ear and The Public Eye 1962, Mary, Mary 1963, The Recruiting Officer 1963, Othello 1964, The Master Builder 1964, Hay Fever 1964, Much Ado About Nothing 1965, Miss Julie 1965, A Bond Honoured 1966, The Beaux' Stratagem 1970, Hedda Gabler 1970, Three Sisters, Design for Living (Los Angeles) 1971, Private Lives (London) 1972, (USA) 1974–75, Peter Pan 1973, Snap 1974, Night and Day 1979, Virginia 1981, The Way of the World 1984–85, Interpreters 1985, The Infernal Machine 1986, Coming in to Land 1987, Lettice and Lovage (London) 1987, (New York) 1990, The Importance of Being Earnest 1992, Three Tall Women 1994, Talking Heads 1996, A Delicate Balance 1997, The Lady in the Van 1999; *Films include:* The VIPs 1963, The Pumpkin Eater 1964, Young Cassidy 1965, Othello 1966, The Honey Pot 1967, Hot Millions 1968, The Prime of Miss Jean Brodie 1969, Travels with My Aunt 1972, Love and Pain and the Whole Damn Thing 1973, Murder by Death 1975, Death on the Nile 1978, California Suite 1978, Quartet 1980, Clash of the Titans 1981, Evil Under the Sun 1982, Ménage à Trois 1982, The Missionary 1982, A Private Function 1984, A Room With a View 1986, The Lonely Passion of Judith Hearn 1987, Paris by Night 1988, Hook 1991, Sister Act 1992, The Secret Garden 1993, Richard III 1995, First Wives Club 1996, Washington Square 1998, Tea with Mussolini (BAFTA Award for Best Supporting Actress) 1999, The Last September 2000; *TV appearances include:* Talking Heads: Bed Among the Lentils (RTS Award) 1989, All the King's Men 1999, David Copperfield 1999. *Leisure interest:* reading. *Address:* c/o Write on Cue, 29 Whitcomb St, London WC2H 7EP, UK. *Telephone:* (20) 7839-3040.

SMITH, Patti; American singer, songwriter and artist; b 30 Dec 1946, Chicago, IL; d of Grant and Beverly Smith; m Fred 'Sonic' Smith 1980 (deceased); two c. *Education:* Glassboro State Teachers' Coll (NJ). *Career:* Avant-garde poet, singer and artist in Manhattan, New York; performed in and co-wrote Cowboy Mouth with Sam Shepard 1971; fmr rock critic for Creem, Rock, Crawdaddy and Rolling Stone magazines; formed the Patti Smith Group 1974; nat and int tours of USA, Europe, etc, including UK tour 1996 with performances at ICA, Serpentine Gallery and Shepherd's Bush Empire, London, Royal

Concert Hall, Glasgow, Labbat's Apollo, Manchester, etc. *Recordings include:* Horses 1975, Radio Ethiopia 1976, Easter 1978, Because the Night (single), Wave 1979, Dream of Life 1988, Gone Again 1996; *Publications:* Poetry: Seventh Heaven 1971, Kodak 1972, Witt 1973, Early Work 1970–1979, Woolgathering, The Coral Sea (prose poems in memory of Robert Mapplethorpe) 1996; Prose: Babel 1978. *Address:* c/o Arista Records Inc, Arista Bldg, 6 W 57th St, New York, NY 10019, USA.

SMITH, Philippa Judith, AM, B ECONS; Australian organization and business executive; b 19 Aug 1950; d of J. O. Smith. *Education:* Sydney Church of England Grammar School and Univ of Sydney. *Career:* Mem and Sr Policy Analyst Australian Council Social Services 1974–83, Acting Sec-Gen 1982; mem Advisory Council New S Wales Women 1977–79; Commr Accident Compensation Brief New S Wales Law Reform Comm 1982–84; mem New S Wales Univ Council 1983–85; Chair Nat Advisory Council on Social Welfare 1983–85; Man Complaints Unit New S Wales Dept of Health 1984–85; Policy and Public Affairs Man Australian Consumers' Assen 1985–89; mem Nat Advisory Council on Consumer Affairs 1985–89; mem Council Australian Inst of Health 1985–87; mem NSW Medical Tribunal 1988–; Dir Corp Policy and Planning Australian Broadcasting Corpn 1989–90; mem Advisory Cttee Constitution Comm 1986–88, Econ and Trade Cttee 1986–1987, Environmental Futures Group 1991, Admin Appeals Tribunal 1991–93; Commonwealth and Tax Ombudsman 1993–97; CEO Assen of Superannuation Funds of Australia 1998–. *Leisure interests:* film, theatre, reading. *Address:* Association of Superannuation Funds of Australia, Level 19, 133 Castlereagh St, Sydney, NSW 2000, Australia.

SMITH, Zadie; British writer; b London 1975. *Education:* Univ of Cambridge. *Career:* Writer-in-Residence Inst of Contemporary Arts (ICA), London. *Publication:* White Teeth (Guardian First Book Award 2000, Whitbread First Novel Prize 2001) 2000. *Address:* c/o Random House UK Ltd, 20 Vauxhall Bridge Rd, London SW1V 2SA, UK. *Telephone:* (20) 7840-8400; *Fax:* (20) 7233-6115; *E-mail:* zsmith@ literati.net; *Internet:* www.randomhouse.co.uk.

SMITH DE BRUIN, Michelle; Irish swimmer; b 1969, Dublin; d of Brian and Patricia Smith; m Erik de Bruin 1996. *Education:* Scoil Crónáin (Rathcoole), Coláiste Chilliain (Clondalkin) and Univ of Houston (TX, USA). *Career:* European Gold Medallist 200m butterfly, 200m individual medley, Silver Medallist 400m individual medley, Vienna 1995; Gold Medallist 400m, 200m individual medley, 400m freestyle (first Gold Medals won by an Irish woman), Bronze Medallist 200m butterfly, Olympic Games, Atlanta, GA, USA 1996; holds numerous Irish swimming records; Best Overall Athlete, Olympic Games, Atlanta, GA, USA 1996; Irish Sports Personality of the Year 1996; banned from swimming for four years after being found guilty of tampering with urine sample 1998. *Publication:* Gold 1996. *Leisure interests:* clay pigeon shooting, gardening. *Address:* c/o Kathy Stapleton, Kathy Stapleton PR, 89 Windsor Drive, Monkstown, Co Dublin, Ireland. *Telephone:* (1) 2809655; *Fax:* (1) 2809655.

SNELL, Marie Letty, BA; American artist; b 15 May 1924, Detroit, MI; d of Samuel Harris and Sylvia Doris (née Cohen) Glucksman; m John Richard Snell 1948 (died 1989); two d. *Education:* Wayne State Univ and Univ of Michigan. *Career:* US Marine Corps 1944–46; teacher and Asst in English; specialized in stained glass 1975–; Art Therapist Pontiac Gen Hosp 1986; solo exhibitions include Oak Park Public Library 1980, Pontiac Art Center 1982, Southfield Civic Center 1983, 1986, COMERICA Headquarters 1983, State Capitol Bldg 1986, Michigan Tech Univ 1987, Art of Crafts Gallery (Royal Oak) 1988, Unitarian Church Birmingham 1989, AAA Headquarters 1995; group exhibitions include Pontiac Art Center 1981, 1982, 1989, Paint Creek Center for the Arts 1983, 1987–89, Port con Toronto 1982–83, Oak Park Public Library 1983–87, La Galerie du Vitrail (Chartes, France) 1985, Artsource Gallery 1986, Detroit Artists' Market 1987, 1990, Corning Museum of Glass (New York) 1987, Watertower Art Assen (Louisville) 1987, Birmingham Bloomfield Art Assen 1989, Huntington Woods Library Gallery 1989; perm exhibition at La Galerie du Vitrail (Chartres); Chair City of Oak Park Arts and Cultural Comm, Ed Michigan Glass Guild Newsletter (fmrly mem Bd of Dirs); mem Stained Glass Assen of America, Assoc Sec 1981–84; US Co-ordinator Vitraux

des USA 1985; mem Oak Park Arts and Cultural Comm 1982–, Michigan Glass Month Cttee 1984–86, Centre Int Vitrail, Women's Caucus for Art, Huntington Woods Studio Artists; fmr Treas The Artists' Gallery; recipient numerous awards in stained glass exhibitions; has written articles for professional publs. *Publication:* Crafting in Glass 1981. *Leisure interests:* mail art, reading, cryptic puzzles, computers. *Address:* 14201 Hart, Oak Park, MI 48237-1179, USA. *Telephone:* (810) 399-8224.

SNOWE, Olympia J., BA; American politician; b 21 Feb 1947, Augusta, ME; d of George John and Georgia G. Bouchles; m John McKeenan 1969. *Education:* Univ of Maine. *Career:* Mem Maine House of Reps 1973–76, Senate 1976–78; mem House of Reps, Second Dist (ME) 1979–95, mem Foreign Affairs Cttee, Jt Econ Cttee, Select Cttee on Aging; Co-Chair Congressional Caucus for Women's Issues; Deputy Republican Whip; Senator for Maine Jan 1995–; Hon LL D (Husson Coll) 1981, (Maine) 1982, (Bowdoin Coll) 1985, (Suffolk) 1994, (Colby Coll) 1996, (Bates Coll) 1998; numerous awards and distinctions. *Address:* US Senate, 250 Russell Senate Bldg, Washington, DC 20510, USA.

SNYDER, Joan, MFA; American artist; b 16 April 1940, Highland Park, NJ; d of Leon D. and Edythe A. (née Cohen) Snyder; one d. *Education:* Douglass Coll and Rutgers Univ (NJ). *Career:* Mem Faculty State Univ of New York at Stony Brook 1967–69, Yale Univ, CT 1974, Univ of California at Irvine 1975, San Francisco Art Inst 1976, Princeton Univ 1975–77; one-woman exhibitions include Paley and Lowe (New Brunswick, NJ) 1971, 1973, Michael Walls Gallery (San Francisco, CA) 1971, Parker 470 (Boston, MA) 1972, Los Angeles Inst of Contemporary Art (CA) 1976, Portland Center of Visual Arts (OR) 1976, Carl Solway Gallery (New York) 1978, 1979, 1982, 1983, Nielson Gallery (Boston) 1983, 1986, Hirshl and Adler Modern Art Museum (New York) 1985–87, 1988, Jim Rose Gallery (Chicago, IL) 1988, travelling show San Francisco Art Inst, Grand Rapids Art Museum, Renaissance Soc, Univ of Chicago, Anderson Gallery, Commonwealth Univ 1979–80; group exhibitions include Whitney Annual 1972, Whitney Biennial 1974, 1980, Corcoran Biennial 1975, 1987, Museum of Modern Art (New York); Grantee Nat Endowment of the Arts 1974; Guggenheim Fellow 1981–82.

SO CHAU, Yim-Ping, JP; Hong Kong politician; b 22 Oct 1927, Hong Kong; three c. *Education:* Ying Wa Girls' School. *Career:* Mem Legis Council (Parl); Man Dir New Island Printing Co Ltd; Chair S Dist Industrialists' Assen Ltd, Arts and Culture Assen Ltd; mem Cttee Road Safety Assen Ltd; Pres W Dist Jr Police Cell, S Dist Fight Crime Cttee; Chair Community Bldg Cttee; Second Vice-Pres S Dist Recreation and Sports Council; Chair Industry Contribution Programme 1989; Hon Pres Scout Assen of Hong Kong (S Island Dist). *Address:* Legislative Council, Government House, Hong Kong.

SOBEL, Dava; American writer; b 1948; m Arthur Klein (separated); two c. *Publications include:* Backache Relief and Arthritis: What Works (with Arthur Klein), Longitude 1996, Galileo's Daughter 2001.

SOBSKI, Jozefa Bronislawa, BA, DIP ED; Australian college principal and administrator; b 24 March 1949; d of W. Sobski. *Education:* St Patrick's School (NSW), Holy Trinity School (NSW), Birrong Girls' High School and Univ of New S Wales. *Career:* High school teacher New S Wales Dept of Educ 1973–77; mem Ministerial Cttee on Equality of the Sexes in Educ 1976–86; Professional Asst Social Devt Unit, Office of the Minister for Educ (NSW) 1978–82, Sr Adviser in Sexism 1982–84, Sr Admin Officer 1984; mem and Exec Head of New S Wales Support Group, Tech and Further Educ (TAFE) Advisory Council 1984–87, Dir Man Services Dept 1987–90, Prin Meadowbank Coll 1990–92; Dir S W Sydney Inst of TAFE 1992–97; mem Advanced Educ Council CTEC 1984–86; part-time Commonwealth Tertiary Educ Commr 1986–88; Chair TAFE Women's Policy and Planning Advisory Cttee 1993–, TAFE Equity Strategy Cttee 1994–. *Leisure interests:* film, theatre, bush walking, tennis. *Address:* 148 Ramsay St, Haberfield, NSW 2045, Australia.

SOCQUET-CLERC LAFONT, Jacqueline Raymonde, L EN D; French lawyer; b 23 Nov 1933, Paris; d of Raymond and Renée (née Renaud) Socquet-Clerc; m Hubert Lafont 1958; one d. *Education:*

Lycée Molière and Law Faculty (Paris). *Career:* Lawyer, Paris 1961–; First Vice-Pres Confed Union of Lawyers 1985–87, Pres 1988–, Hon Pres 1990–; mem European Union of Women, Nat Council of French Women; Pres Présence, Promotion of French Women; Vice-Pres Nat Union, Asscn of Professional People 1990; awarded Prix de Président, Young Lawyers Conf (Brussels) 1965; Officier de l'Ordre Nat du Mérite. *Publications:* Lois Auroux (jtly) 1984, L'entreprise en difficulté (jtly) 1988; numerous contribs to professional journals. *Leisure interests:* hunting, golf. *Address:* 36 rue de Monceau, 75008 Paris, France. *Telephone:* (1) 42-25-30-22; *Fax:* (1) 45-63-69-65.

SÖDER, Karin Anne-Marie; Swedish politician; b 30 Nov 1928, Frykerud; d of Yngve and Lilly Bergenfur; m Gunnar Söder 1952; two s one d. *Career:* Vocational Guidance Teacher 1965; Co Councillor, Stockholm 1968–73; mem Riksdag (Parl) 1971–91; Minister for Foreign Affairs 1976–78, for Health and Social Affairs 1979–82; Pres Nordic Council 1984–85, Vice-Pres 1985–86; Second Vice-Chair Centre Party 1971, Chair 1986–87; Pres Swedish Save the Children Asscn 1983–95; Vice-Chair Stockholm Int Environmental Inst 1989–93, Chair 1993–97; mem Bd Royal Inst of Tech, Stockholm 1988–97, Vice-Chair 1994–97; Chair The Letterstedt Soc 1991, Selma Lagerlöf Soc 1998; mem China Council for Int Co-operation on Environment and Devt 1992–96; mem Bd Skandia 1987–99, Werm-landsbanken 1988–92; fmr Chair Governing Bd Stockholm Int Peace Research Inst 1978–79; mem Nat Bd of Health and Welfare 1972–76, Nat Courts Admin Bd 1975–76; mem Bd Royal Dramatic Theatre 1973–76, Rädda Barnen; Hon D TECH 1995. *Leisure interests:* music, nature, mountain trekking. *Address:* Näsbydalsvägen 10, 183 37 Täby, Sweden. *Telephone:* (8) 7589492 (Home); *Fax:* (8) 7682105 (Home); *E-mail:* twosoder@gamma.telenordia.se (Home).

SODERBERG, Nancy E., BA; American government administrator; b 13 March 1958, San Turce, Puerto Rico; d of Lars Olof and Nancy (née MacGilvrey) Soderberg. *Education:* Vanderbilt Univ and Georgetown Univ. *Career:* Budget and reports analyst Bank of New England, Boston 1980–82; Research Asst Brookings Inst, Washington, DC 1982–83; Research Asst US Agency for Int Devt, Washington, DC 1983; Del Selection Asst Mondale–Ferraro Cttee, Washington, DC 1983, Foreign Policy Adviser 1984; Deputy Issues Dir, Foreign Policy, Dukakis for Pres Cttee, Boston 1988; Foreign Policy Adviser to Senator Edward Kennedy, Washington, DC 1985–88, 1989–92; Foreign Policy Dir Clinton/Gore Transition, Little Rock 1992–93; Special Asst to Pres for Nat Security Affairs, Staff Dir Nat Security Council, Washington, DC 1993–95, Deputy Asst to Pres for Nat Security Affairs 1995–2001; mem Council for Foreign Relations. *Address:* National Security Council, The White House, 1600 Pennsylvania Ave, NW, Washington, DC 20500, USA.

SÖDERSTROM, Elisabeth Anna, CBE; Swedish opera singer (soprano); b 7 May 1927, Stockholm; m Sverker Olow 1950; three s. *Education:* Studied singing under Andrejewa de Skilonz and Opera School (Stockholm). *Career:* Engaged at Royal Opera, Stockholm 1950–; appearances at Salzburg (Austria) 1955, Glyndebourne (UK) 1957, 1959, 1961, 1963, 1964, 1979, Metropolitan Opera (New York) 1959, 1960, 1962, 1963, 1983, 1984, 1986, 1987, 1999; Artistic Dir Drottningholms Slottsteater, Stockholm 1992–97; frequent concert and TV appearances in Europe and USA; toured fmr USSR 1966; mem Royal Acad of Music; Hon RAM; Hon Prof 1996; Singer of the Court (Sweden) 1959; Stelle della Solidarietà dell'Italia; Prize for Best Acting, Royal Swedish Acad 1965, 'Literis et Artibus' award 1969; Commdr of the Order of Vasa 1973; Commdr des Arts et des Lettres 1986; Ingmar Bergman Award 1988. *Operas include:* Così fan Tutte, The Marriage of Figaro, Capriccio, Intermezzo, Der Rosenkavalier; *Recordings include:* complete Rakhmaninov songs with Vladimir Ashkenazy, Janácek's operas Katya Kabanova, Jenufa and the Makropoulos Case conducted by Sir Charles Mackerras; *Publications:* I Min Tonart 1978, Sjung ut Elisabeth 1986. *Leisure interests:* sailing, literature, embroidery. *Address:* c/o Drottningholms Slottsteater, Box 27050, 10251 Stockholm, Sweden. *Telephone:* (8) 665-14-52 (Office); (8) 765-22-89 (Home); *Fax:* (8) 665-14-73.

SOFÍA, HM Queen of Spain; Spanish (b Greek) royal; b 2 Nov 1938, Greece; d of the late King Paul I of the Hellenes and Queen Frederica; m King Juan Carlos I of Spain 1962; three c: Princess Elena, b 20 Dec 1963; Princess Cristina, b 13 June 1965; Prince Felipe, b 30 Jan 1968. *Education:* In Germany, and studied Paediatrics in Greece. *Career:* Pres Nat Orchestra of Spain; active in Cáritas, the Red Cross, Asscn for the Aid of the Mentally Handicapped and other charitable orgs; has published two archaeological treatises on Attica (jtly). *Leisure interests:* archaeology, drawing, music, riding, skiing, sailing. *Address:* Palacio de la Zarzuela, Madrid, Spain. *Telephone:* (1) 2229075.

SOIN, Kanwaljit Kaur, M MED, FRACS; Singaporean orthopaedic and hand surgeon; b 4 Feb 1942, India; d of Gurnam Singh and Satwant Kaur Soin; m Amarjeet Singh 1968; three s. *Education:* Univ of Singapore. *Career:* Left India 1948; Consultant Orthopaedic and Hand Surgeon in pvt practice 1975–; mem Parl 1992–; Regional Rep Steering Cttee of Commonwealth Women Parliamentarians Group; mem Bd Centre for Asia-Pacific Women in Politics 1992, Washington Univ Int Advisory Council for Asia 1996, Legal Inquiry Panel, Bd of Dirs The Necessary Stage (non-profit theatre co); Patron Lupus Asscn; Colombo Plan Scholarship to train in Hand Surgery, Australia 1970; Univ Medals 1962, 1964, 1965, 1966; Lim Boon Keng Medal, Hoops Medal and Gibbs Medals 1966; Woman of the Year 1992. *Leisure interest:* women's issues activist. *Address:* Orthopaedic Surgery Pte Ltd, 3 Mount Elizabeth 03-01/05, Mount Elizabeth Medical Centre, Singapore 228510, Singapore. *Telephone:* 7374533; *Fax:* 7338879; *E-mail:* ksoin@pacific .net.sg.

SOKOLOGORSKY, Irène, D ÈS L; French former university president; b 3 Aug 1936; one s. *Education:* Lycée de Clermont-Ferrand. *Career:* Teacher Ecole Normale Supérieure, Fontenay-St-Cloud 1959; Prof of Slav Language and Literature, Univ of Paris VIII—Vincennes à St-Denis 1982, Univ Pres 1991; Co-Dir Study Group on Central and Eastern Europe and the Orient 1985; Ed-in-Chief Littérature russe et soviétique et des pays de l'est 1985. *Publications:* Perestroïka 89 (jtly) 1989, La littérature soviétique par lettres recommandées 1990. *Leisure interests:* dancing, skiing. *Address:* c/o University of Paris VIII—Vincennes à St-Denis, 2 rue de la Liberté, 93526 Saint-Denis, Cedex 02, France.

SOL, Ana Cristina; Salvadorean diplomatist; b 2 Nov 1945, San Salvador; d of Benjamín and María Luisa (née Midence) Sol Millet; one s one d. *Education:* Arizona State Univ (USA) and Univ of Paris (Sorbonne). *Career:* Pres Inversiones SA de CV Soc; mem Head Office Compañia general de equipos SA de CV, Empresa Cafetalara; Founder and Assoc mem Salvadorean Foundation for Econ and Social Devt; Founder, Treas Women's Cttee of the Salvadorean Popular Front 1972–76, Sec-Gen 1976; Sec-Gen Salvadorean Red Cross 1974, mem Exec Council 1974; Amb to France, concurrently to Belgium, Portugal, UNESCO and EC 1989–93, to USA 1993; mem Bd of Dirs of several cos in El Salvador. *Leisure interests:* travel, working with the Salvadorean community. *Address:* Embassy of El Salvador, 2308 California St, NW, Washington, DC 20008, USA.

SOLLIE, Solveig; Norwegian politician; b 19 April 1939, Skien; d of Sigurd and Marit Elisabeth (née Olsen) Berger; m Finn Sollie 1961; three d one s. *Career:* Mem Skien Municipal Council 1975; Chair Women's Org, Christian Democratic Party 1984–88, Vice-Chair Christian Democratic Party 1987; mem Storting (Parl) 1981–; Minister of Consumer Affairs and Govt Admin 1989–90. *Address:* c/o Ministry of Consumer Affairs and Government Administration, Akersgt 42, POB 8004 Dep, 0030 Oslo 1, Norway.

SOLOMON, Hollis, BA; American gallery owner and film producer; b 12 Feb, CT; d of Nathan Dworken and Ethel Goldman; m Horace Solomon 1954 (separated 1985); two s. *Education:* Vassar Coll and Sarah Lawrence Coll (Bronxville, NY). *Career:* Opened alternative space called 28 Greene Street 1969–72, Holly Solomon Gallery, 392 W Broadway 1975–84, Holly Solomon Gallery at 724 Fifth Avenue 1985–. *Leisure interests:* reading, TV, Scrabble. *Address:* 444 E 57 St, New York, NY 10022, USA. *Telephone:* (212) 758-1887.

SOLOMON, Susan, PH D, MS; American scientist; b 19 Jan 1956, Chicago, IL; d of Leonard Marvin and Alice (née Rutman) Solomon; m Barry Lane Sidwell 1988. *Education:* Illinois Inst of Tech and Univ of California at Berkeley. *Career:* Research Chemist Aeronomy Lab, Nat Oceanic and Atmospheric Admin, Boulder, CO 1981–88, apptd

Programme Leader Middle Atmosphere Group 1988–; Head science project Nat Ozone Expedition, Antarctica 1986, 1987; discovered link between chlorofluorocarbons (CFCs) and ozone depletion; apptd Adjunct Univ of Colorado 1982; Fellow Royal Meteorological Soc, American Meteorological Soc, American Geophysical Union (J. B. McElwane Award 1985); Gold Medal US Dept of Commerce 1985; Commonwealth Award winner 1992; Nat Medal for Science 1999. *Publications:* Aeronomy of the Middle Atmosphere (jtly) 1984; numerous scientific papers. *Address:* National Oceanic and Atmospheric Administration, Research Chemist Aeronomy Lab, Boulder, CO, USA. *Telephone:* (202) 357-9764.

SOLOVEY, Yelena Yakovlevna; Russian actress; b 24 Feb 1947; one s one d. *Education:* VGIK. *Career:* Worked in cinema 1970–83; with Lensoret Theatre, Leningrad (now St Petersburg) 1983–90; over 40 films; emigrated to USA 1991 (lives in New York); actress with Russian émigré theatre Wandering Stars; People's Artist of the USSR 1990. *Films and plays include:* King Stag 1970, The Seven Brides of Zbruyev 1971, Yegor Bulychov and Others 1973, An Old-Style Drama 1972, Vanyushin's Kids 1974, Slave of Love 1976, An Unfinished Piece for Mechanical Piano 1977, A Few Days in the Life of I. I. Oblomov 1980, Crazy Money 1982, The Fact (Cannes Prize 1981) 1982, There Was No Sorrow 1983, On the Eve 1985, Life of Klim Samgin 1988.

SOLOVYEVA, Yevgenya Fedorovna; Russian fashion designer; b 5 March 1949, Odessa; d of Mikhail Fedorovich and Vera Stepanovna Shender; m Solovuyev German Aleksandrovich; one s. *Education:* Odessa Designers' Coll. *Career:* Head Int Cruises Odessa (cultural programme); Man, Artistic Dir Defilé of Yudashkin Fashion House (Moscow), fashion shows in Europe and USA; Artistic Dir Elite Fashion Studio Jenia 1992–; Dir Boutique Jenia Couture; Dir Night Theatre Metropol Moscow; mem English Club (Moscow). *Leisure interest:* collecting toys. *Address:* 1 Khoroshevsky proyezd 14, korp 3 Apt 87, Moscow, Russian Federation. *Telephone:* (095) 212-84-06 (Office); (095) 946-09-33 (Home).

SOLTWEDEL-SCHÄFER, Irene Barbara Lilia; German politician; b 28 Jan 1955, Celle. *Career:* MEP (V, GRÜNE), mem Cttee on Econ and Monetary Affairs and Industrial Policy, Del for relations with Canada. *Address:* European Parliament, rue Wiertz, 1047 Brussels, Belgium. *Telephone:* (2) 284-21-11; *Fax:* (2) 230-69-43.

SOMERS COCKS, Anna Gwenllian, MA, FSA; British museum curator, editor and journalist; b 18 April 1950, Rome; d of John Sebastian and Marjorie Olive (née Weller) Somers Cocks; m 1st Martin Walker 1971 (divorced); m 2nd John Hardy 1978 (divorced); one s one d; m 3rd Umberto Allemandi. *Education:* Abroad and Convent of the Sacred Heart (Woldingham), St Anne's Coll (Oxford) and Courtauld Inst (London). *Career:* Asst Keeper Dept of Metal Work, Victoria and Albert Museum, London 1973–85, Dept of Ceramics 1985–87; Ed The Art Newspaper 1990–94, 1996–; Assoc Publr Umberto Allemandi Publishing Srl 1994–; fmr expert adviser to the National Heritage Lottery Fund; Chair Venice in Peril Fund 1999–; Trustee Gilbert Collection 1999–; Nat Art Collections Fund Award for Outstanding Achievement in the Arts 1992. *Publications:* Victoria and Albert Museum: the making of the collection 1980, Princely Magnificence: court jewels of the Renaissance (jtly) 1980, Renaissance Jewels, Gold Boxes and Objets de Vertu in the Thyssen Collection (jtly) 1985. *Leisure interests:* skiing, entertaining, travel, walking. *Address:* 70 South Lambeth Rd, London SW8 1RL, UK. *Telephone:* (20) 7735-3331; *Fax:* (20) 7735-3332; *E-mail:* contact@theartnewspaper.com.

SOMERVILLE, Margaret Anne Ganley, AM, DCL, FRSC; Australian professor of law; b 13 April 1942, Adelaide; d of George Patrick and Gertrude Honora (née Rowe) Ganley. *Education:* Mercedes Coll, Univ of Adelaide, Univ of Sydney and McGill Univ (Canada). *Career:* Pharmacist 1963–69; Attorney Mallesons, Sydney 1974–75; solicitor Supreme Court of New S Wales 1975; called to the Bar, PQ, Canada 1982; Consultant Law Reform Comm of Canada 1976–85; Asst Prof Faculty of Law McGill Univ 1978, Assoc Prof 1979, Prof 1984–, Assoc Prof Faculty of Medicine McGill Univ 1980, Prof 1984–85, Dir McGill Center for Medicine Ethics and Law 1986–, Gale Prof of Law McGill Univ 1989–; Chair Clinical Ethics Cttee Royal Victoria Hosp 1980–, mem Research Inst 1985–; Chair Grad Studies Cttee 1988–89; Assoc

mem Nat Advisory Cttee on AIDS, Ministry of Health and Welfare 1986–92, McGill AIDS Centre 1990–; Chair Nat Research Council of Canada Ethics Cttee 1991–95; Visiting Prof Univ of Sydney 1984, 1986, 1990; mem Editorial Bd Bioethics 1986–, Kennedy Inst Ethics Journal 1990–, Health and Human Rights 1993–, Ecosystem Health and Medicine 1993–; mem American Soc of Law Ethics and Medicine, Bd of Dirs Canadian Anti-Doping Org 1992–, Bd of Dirs Canadian Centre for Ethics in Sport 1992–; writer of numerous articles, reviews, lectures and papers; Fellow Royal Soc of Canada; Hon LL B (Sydney) 1973; DCL (McGill) 1978; Hon LL D (Windsor, ON) 1992, (Macquarie, NSW) 1993, (St Francis Xavier, NS) 1996; Distinguished Service Award, American Soc of Law and Medicine 1985; Pax Orbis ex Jure Gold Medal, Assocs of the World Peace Through Law Center 1985. *Address:* McGill Centre for Medicine Ethics and Law, 3690 Peel St, Montréal, PQ H3A 1W9, Canada (Office); 2600 Pierre Dupuy, Habitat '67 Phase 3, Apt 1025, Montréal, PQ H3C 3R6, Canada (Home).

SOMMER, Elke; German actress; b 5 Nov 1940, Berlin; d of Friedrich Schletz and Renate Schletz; m Joe Hyams (twice). *Career:* Film debut in L'Amico del Giaguaro 1958; since then has made more than 70 films; own TV show (PBS), Painting with Elke 1985; Jefferson Award; Golden Globe Award 1965; Merit of Achievement Award 1990. *Films include:* The Prize, The Victors, Love the Italian Way, Shot in the Dark, The Money Trap, The Oscar, the Venetian Affair, Deadlier than the Male, Ten Little Indians, The Prisoner of Zenda, Lily in Love, Himmelsheim, Neat and Tidy; *TV appearances include:* Probe, The Top of the Hill, Inside the Third Reich, Jenny's War, Anastasia: The Mystery of Anya, Peter the Great (mini-series), Severed Ties (own TV show, PBS), Painting with Elke 1985. *Leisure interests:* tennis, nature, riding, art. *Address:* 540 N Beverly Glen Blvd W, Los Angeles, CA 90024, USA; 91080 Marloffstein, Germany. *Telephone:* (310) 724-8990 (USA); (9131) 5366-0 (Germany); *Fax:* (310) 724-8993 (USA); (9131) 5366-99 (Germany).

SONNTAG-WOLGAST, Cornelie, D PHIL; German politician; b 29 Aug 1942, Nuremberg; m Thomas Wolgast 1969. *Education:* Hamburg and Erlangen. *Career:* Journalist for Hamburger Morgenpost; Ed and Presenter political broadcasts for Norddeutscher Rundfunk (NDR) 1975–88; mem SPD 1971–; mem Bundestag (Parl, Schleswig-Holstein party list) 1988–; Spokesperson for SPD party leader 1991–93; has written numerous articles on Women's Affairs. *Address:* Bundestag, 11011 Berlin, Germany. *Telephone:* (228) 16-3898; *Fax:* (228) 16-7775.

SONTAG, Susan, MA; American writer and film director; b 16 Jan 1933; m Philip Rieff 1950 (divorced 1958); one s. *Education:* Univ of Chicago and Harvard Univ. *Career:* Mem American Acad and Inst of Arts and Letters, PEN (Pres American Centre 1987–89); Dr hc (Columbia, Harvard) 1993; Commdr des Arts et des Lettres; Guggenheim Fellow 1966, 1975; Rockefeller Foundation Fellow 1965, 1974; recipient Ingram Merrill Foundation Award in Literature in the Field of American Letters 1976, Creative Arts Award (Brandeis Univ) 1976, Arts and Letters Award (American Acad of Arts and Letters) 1976, Nat Book Critics' Circle Prize 1978, MacArthur Fellowship 1990–95, Elmer Holmes Bobst Award 1990, Malaparte Prize 1992, Culural Achievement Award (Montblanc de la Culture) 1994, Nat Book Award for Fiction 2000, Jerusalem Prize for Literature 2001. *Films include:* Duet for Cannibals 1970, Brother Carl 1971, Promised Lands 1974, Unguided Tour 1983; *Publications:* Fiction: The Benefactor 1963, Death Kit 1967, Illness as Metaphor 1978, I, etcetera (stories) 1978, Under the Sign of Saturn 1980, The Way We Live Now (story) 1991, The Volcano Lover 1992, Alice in Bed (play) 1993, Under the Sign of Saturn (poetry) 1996, In America 2000, Women (with Annie Liebowitz, qv) 2000; Essays: Against Interpretation 1966, Styles of Radical Will 1969, On Photography 1977, Under the Sign of Saturn 1980, A Susan Sontag Reader (anthology) 1982, AIDS and Its Metaphors 1989, Where the Stress Falls 2001. *Address:* c/o The White Agency, 250 W 57th St, Suite 2114, New York, NY 10107, USA.

SOREL, Claudette Marguerite, BS; American (b French) pianist and professor of music; b Paris; d of Michel M. and Elizabeth Sorel. *Education:* Columbia Univ (NY), Curtis Inst of Music and Juilliard School of Music (New York). *Career:* Debut New York 1943, since then has appeared with major US and European orchestras, on radio and TV and at several int festivals; European concert tours 1956, 1957, 1958;

Visiting Prof Faculty of Music, Kansas Univ 1961–62; Assoc Prof of Music Ohio State Univ 1962–64; Prof of Music and Head Piano Dept State Univ of New York at Fredonia 1964–, Distinguished Univ Prof 1969–, Univ Artist 1969–, Faculty Exchange Scholar 1976–; Chair Music Panel Presidential Scholars in Arts Program 1979–; Special Ed Music Insider; mem Int Jury Van Cliburn Int Piano Competition (TX) 1966, Québec and Ontario (Canada) Music Festivals 1967, 1975; Fulbright Fellow 1951; Ford Foundation Concert Grantee 1962; Harry Rosenberg Memorial Prize 1947; Frank Damrosch Prize 1947; Young Artist Award (Nat Fed of Music Clubs) 1951; Citation for Service to American Music (Nat Fed of Music Clubs) 1966; Citation (Nat Asscn of Composers and Conductors) 1971; Freedom Medal US Senatorial Cttee 1994. *Publications include:* The 24 Magic Keys Vols I, II, III, 1974, Arensky Piano Etudes 1976, Compendium of Piano Technique (2nd edn) 1987, The Three Nocturnes of Rachmaninoff (3rd edn) 1988; Mind Your Music Manners – Off and On Stage (3rd edn) 1995, Fifteen Smorgasbord Studies for the Piano (2nd edn) 1995; Compiler: The Modern Music of Today 1947, Serge Prokofieff – His Life and Works 1947, The Ornamentations in Mozart's Music 1948; *Recording:* MacDowell Piano Concerto No 2 (with NY Philharmonic Orchestra) 1993. *Address:* c/o 333 West End Ave, New York, NY 10023, USA.

SORENSTAM, Annika; Swedish golfer; b 9 Oct 1970; m David Esch. *Education:* Univ of Arizona. *Career:* Lives in Nevada, USA; winner Australian tournament 1994; champion in USA and Europe 1995 (two wins in Europe, three in USA including US Women's Open); winner World Championship, Repub of Korea, Australian Masters 1995, Rite LPGA Classic 1998, JAL Big Apple Classic 1998, SAFECO Classic 1998; Rookie of the Year 1993; Sports Personality of the Year, Sweden 1995; Vare Trophy Award 1998. *Address:* LPGA, 100 International Golf Drive, Daytona Beach, FL 32124, USA.

SORG, Margarete; German writer and publisher; b 4 July 1937, Bochum; m; one d (Margarete Sorg-Rose, qv). *Education:* Fachhochschule (Frankfurt/Main). *Career:* Freelance writer 1978–; Publr GEDOK-Journal (magazine for the arts) 1986–95, various anthologies of poetry; organizer literary competitions, mem Jury, Germany 1986–; Pres Jury Andreas Gryphius Award for Literature and Nikolaus Lenau Award for Lyric Poetry 1993–96; Pres Literary Section of Die Künstlergilde eV 1993–96, Pres Künstlergilde Hessen 1993; Pres Kulturring HDH, Wiesbaden 1995–; Pres GEDOK Rhein-Main-Taunus cultural man co for artists 1995–; Second GEDOK Award for Lyric Poetry 1982; Art-GEDOK-Nadel for Meritorious Artistic and Cultural Activities 1995. *Publications:* Streiflichter (lyric poetry) (2nd edn) 1984; 55 publs of lyric poetry in anthologies and literary reviews; poetry has been translated into English, Polish and Arabic. *Address:* Henkellstr 3, 65187 Wiesbaden, Germany. *Telephone:* (611) 691216; *Fax:* (611) 691219.

SORG-ROSE, Margarete; German composer; b 11 April 1960, Remscheid; d of Margarete Sorg (qv). *Education:* Piano and conducting studies in Mainz, composition in Cologne with Hans Werner Henze and Krzysztof Meyer, Univs of Mainz and Tübingen. *Career:* Bachchor (choir) coach, Mainz 1985–87; Production Asst Zweites Deutsches Fernsehen (ZDF), Mainz 1987; freelance composer 1992–; works performed at nat and int concerts and festivals, including Festival Cantiere Int d'Arte Montepulciano (Italy) 1990; compositions include pieces for orchestra, choir, Lieder and chamber music; several awards and prizes. *Address:* Henkellstr 3, 65187 Wiesbaden, Germany. *Telephone:* (611) 691875; *Fax:* (611) 691219.

SORNOSA MARTINEZ, María; Spanish politician; b 15 June 1949, Manises. *Education:* Univ of Valencia. *Career:* MEP (European Socialist Party), mem Cttee on Environment, Womens Rights, Petitions; mem Del to the EU–Czech Repub Jt Parliamentary Cttee. *Publication:* Viajes, memoria parlamentaria. *Leisure interest:* reading. *Address:* PSPV, c/Blanqueries, 4, 46003 Valencia, Spain; European Parliament, rue Wiertz, 1047 Brussels, Belgium. *Telephone:* (2) 284-59-74 (Belgium); *Fax:* (2) 284-99-74 (Belgium); *E-mail:* MSornosa@europarl.eu.int.

SOROS, Susan Weber, MA; American art historian; b 1956; m George Soros 1983; two s. *Education:* Barnard Coll (Columbia Univ). *Career:* Fmrly worked in arts TV, Producer documentaries on Mark Roghko and Willem De Kooning; fmr Exec Dir Open Soc Fund (administers the Soros Foundation network); Founder, Dir Bard Graduate Center for Studies in the Decorative Arts 1991; Trustee American Fed of the Arts, New York 1995–. *Leisure interest:* horse-riding. *Address:* Bard Graduate Center for Studies in Decorative Arts, 18 W 86th St, New York, NY 10024, USA.

SORVINO, Mira, AB; American actress; b 28 Sept 1968; d of Paul and Lorraine Sorvino. *Education:* Harvard Univ. *Films include:* Amongst Friends (also assoc producer) 1993, The Second Greatest Story Ever Told 1993, Quiz Show 1994, Parallel Lives 1994, Barcelona 1994, Tarantella 1995, Sweet Nothing 1995, Mighty Aphrodite (Acad Award for Best Supporting Actress 1996) 1995, The Dutch Master 1995, Blue in the Face 1995, Beautiful Girls 1996, Norma Jean and Marilyn 1996, Jake's Women 1996, Romy and Michele's High School Reunion 1997, The Replacement Killers 1997, Mimic 1997, Summer of Sam 1999, At First Sight 1999, Joan of Arc: The Virgin Warrior 2000; *TV:* The Great Gatsby 2000. *Address:* c/o Michelle Stern, The William Morris Agency, 1325 Ave of the Americas, New York, NY 10019, USA.

SOUCHET, Dominique; French politician; b 9 July 1946, La Rochelle. *Career:* MEP (Group of Nations Group, L'autre Europe), mem Cttee on Foreign Affairs, Security and Defence Policy, on Fisheries, Del for relations with Russia. *Address:* European Parliament, rue Wiertz, 1047 Brussels, Belgium. *Telephone:* (2) 284-21-11; *Fax:* (2) 230-69-43.

SOULIOTI, Stella; Cypriot politician and lawyer; b 13 Feb 1920, Limassol; d of Panayiotis and Angeliki Cacoyannis; m Demetrios Souliotis 1949; one d. *Education:* Cyprus, Egypt, St James' Secretarial Coll (London) and Gray's Inn (London). *Career:* Joined Women's Auxiliary Air Force, Nicosia and served in Middle East 1943–46; called to the Bar, London 1951; law practice, Limassol 1952–60; Minister of Justice 1960–70, concurrently Minister of Health 1964–66; Law Commr 1971–84; Attorney-Gen 1984–88; Co-ordinator of Foreign Aid to Cyprus Refugees 1974–; Adviser to Greek Cypriot Negotiator on Cyprus Intercommunal Talks 1976–; Chair Cyprus Overseas Relief Fund 1977–82; Visiting Fellow Wolfson Coll, Cambridge 1982–83; Pres Cyprus Red Cross 1961–; Chair Cyprus Scholarship Bd 1962–, Cyprus Town and Country Planning Cttee 1967–70; Vice-Pres Cyprus Anti-Cancer Soc 1971–; Hon Vice-Pres Int Fed of Women Lawyers 1967–; Trustee Cambridge Commonwealth Scholarship Trust for Cyprus 1983–; mem Exec Bd UNESCO 1987–91; Hon LL D (Nottingham) 1972; Medal of the Order of the Kts of St Katherine, Sina Oros 1967; Gold Medal of Int Asscn of Lions Clubs for Outstanding Humanitarian Work 1975; Officer of Cedars (Lebanon) 1975; Paul Harris Fellow, Rotary Int 1988; Melvin Jones Fellow, Lions Clubs Int 1993; Second World War Veterans Medal, Russian Fed 1995. *Leisure interests:* reading, writing, music, theatre. *Address:* POB 4102, 1701 Nicosia, Cyprus (Office); Flat 71, Arethusa House, Kerkyras St, 3107 Limassol, Cyprus (Home). *Telephone:* (5) 587227; (5) 221070; *Fax:* (5) 587227; (5) 221070.

SPAAK, Antoinette; Belgian politician; b 27 June 1928, Brussels. *Career:* Fmr MEP (Group of European Liberal , Democrat and Reform Party, PRL/Front démocratique des francophones), mem Cttee on Institutional Affairs, Del for relations with the Maghreb countries and the Arab Maghreb Union. *Address:* c/o European Parliament, rue Wiertz, 1047 Brussels, Belgium.

SPACEK, Sissy (Mary Elizabeth); American actress; b 25 Dec 1949, Quitman, TX; d of Edwin A. and Virginia Spacek; m Jack Fisk 1974; one d. *Education:* Lee Strasberg Theater Inst. *Career:* Best Actress, New York and Los Angeles Film Critics, Foreign Press Asscn, Nat Soc of Film Critics 1980; Album of the Year Award, Country Music Asscn for Coal Miner's Daughter 1980. *Films include:* Prime Cut 1972, Ginger in the Morning 1972, Badlands 1974, Carrie (Best Actress, Nat Soc of Film Critics) 1976, Three Women (Best Supporting Actress, New York Film Critics) 1977, Welcome to LA 1977, Heart Beat 1980, Coal Miner's Daughter (Album of the Year Award, Country Music Asscn) 1980, Raggedy Man 1981, Missing 1982, The River 1984, Marie 1985, Violets are Blue 1986, Crimes of the Heart 1986, 'Night Mother 1986, The Plastic Nightmare 1989, JFK 1991, The Long Walk Home, Hard Promises 1992, Trading Mom 1994, The Grass Harp 1995, Streets of Laredo 1995, If These Walls Could Talk 1996, Affliction 1998, Blast From the Past 1999; *TV films:* The Girls of Huntington House 1973,

The Migrants 1973, Katherine 1975, Verna, USO Girl 1978, A Private Matter 1992, A Place for Annie 1994, The Good Old Boys 1995. *Address:* c/o Steve Tellez, 9830 Wilshire Blvd, Beverly Hills, CA 90212, USA.

SPAGNA, Ivana; Italian singer and songwriter. *Career:* Fmrly sang in rock group with her brother; now solo singer; numerous concerts in Italy and France; singles have been hits in Italy, France, Spain, UK, etc; several Gold Discs for albums. *Recordings include:* No Way Out (album), Call Me (single), Easy Lady (single); *Video:* Love at First Sight. *Leisure interest:* cats.

SPALDING, Frances, PH D, FRSL; British art historian, critic and writer; b 16 May 1950, Woldingham, Surrey; d of Hedley Stinston Crabtree and Margaret Holiday; m Julian Spalding 1974 (divorced 1991); one s. *Education:* Farringtons School (Kent) and Univ of Nottingham. *Career:* Lecturer Sheffield Polytechnic 1978–88; art historian, critic and biographer (freelance 1989–99), Univ of Newcastle upon Tyne 2000–; Hon Fellow RCA. *Publications include:* Roger Fry: Art and Life 1983, Vanessa Bell 1983, British Art Since 1900 1986, Stevie Smith: A Critical Biography 1988, A Dictionary of Twentieth Century British Painters and Sculpture 1990, Dance Till the Stars Come Down: A Biography of John Minton 1991, Duncan Grant: A Biography 1997, The Tate: A History 1998, Gwen Raverat: Friends, Family & Affections 2001. *Leisure interest:* music. *Address:* c/o Coleridge, Rogers and White, 20 Powis Mews, London W11 1JN, UK. *Telephone:* (20) 7221-3717.

SPANDORFER, Merle Sue, BS; American artist; b 4 Sept 1934, Baltimore, MD; m Lester M. Spandorfer 1956; one s one d. *Education:* Syracuse Univ (NY) and Univ of Maryland. *Career:* Mem faculty Cheltenham School of Fine Arts, PA 1969–96; Instructor of Print-making Tyler School of Art, Temple Univ, PA 1980–84; mem faculty Pratt Graphics Center, New York 1985–86; solo exhibitions include Richard Feigen Gallery (New York) 1970, Univ of Pennsylvania 1974, Philadelphia Coll of Textiles and Science (PA) 1977, Ericson Gallery (New York) 1978, 1979, Rhode Island School of Design 1980, Syracuse Univ (NY) 1981, Marian Locks Gallery (Philadelphia, PA) 1973, 1978, 1982, Temple Univ (PA) 1984, Tyler School of Art (PA) 1985, Univ City Science Center 1987, Gov's Residence 1988, Wenniger Graphics Gallery (Provincetown, MA) 1989, Mangel Gallery (Philadelphia, PA) 1992, 1997, Widener Univ Art Museum (Chester, PA) 1995; numerous group exhibitions in USA, Fundación Joan Miró (Barcelona, Spain) 1977, Carlsberg Glyptotek Museum (Copenhagen) 1980, Tiajin Fine Arts Coll (People's Repub of China) 1986, Sichuan Fine Arts Inst (Chongging, People's Repub of China) 1988, Glynn Vivian Museum (Swansea, UK) 1989, Foreign Museum (Rīga, Latvia) 1996; rep in perm collections at Metropolitan Museum of Art, Whitney Museum of American Art and Museum of Modern Art (New York), The Israel Museum, Philadelphia Museum of Art, Baltimore Museum (MD), Toyoh Bijutsu Gakko (Tokyo), Library of Congress (Washington, DC); Gov's Prize and Purchase Award (Baltimore Museum, MD); Purchase Award (Philadelphia Museum of Art); Graphics Joan Mondale (Wallingford Art Center, PA); Outstanding Art Educator (Pennsylvania Art Educ Asscn) 1981–82. *Publication:* Making Art Safely 1992. *Leisure interest:* travel. *Address:* 8012 Ellen Lane, Cheltenham, PA 19012, USA. *Telephone:* (215) 248-1017.

SPANGENBERG, Christa; German publisher; b 1928, Munich; d of Edgar J. and Minni Jung; m Berthold Spangenberg 1946 (died 1986); two s. *Education:* Music (with Carl Orff) and language studies. *Career:* Assoc Nymphenburger Verlagshandlung 1960–; Publr and owner Ellermann Verlag 1967–; hon work for Börsenverein des Deutschen Buchhandels; Lecturer Univ of Munich 1987–; Founder and Pres Int Youth Library, Munich 1992–; Bundesverdienstkreuz 1990; Kultur-preis der Bayrischen Landesstiftung 1999 and other awards. *Publications:* Elly Petersens praktisches Gartenlexikon 1964, Praktisches Balkon- und Zimmerpflanzenlexikon 1967, Grüne Uhr 1974, Garten Uhr 1980, ABC für kleine Gärtner 1991. *Leisure interests:* gardening, music. *Address:* Bäumlstr 6, 80638 Munich, Germany. *Telephone:* (89) 171423; *Fax:* (89) 171423.

SPARG, Marion Monica, BA; South African political organization official; b 13 Sept 1958, East London, SA; d of the late W. W. and of E. A. Sparg. *Education:* Rhodes Univ (Grahamstown). *Career:* Political journalist on Sunday Times, Johannesburg 1980–81; Exiled from SA, joined African Nat Congress (ANC) and underwent military training 1981; worked at ANC Dept of Information and Publicity, Zambia and Angola 1982–85; returned to SA as mem of Umkhonto We Sizwe (ANC liberation army) 1985; arrested, charged with High Treason and sentenced to 25 years in prison 1986, released in political amnesty 1991; Media Officer ANC Border Region, E London 1991–92, elected Regional Publicity Sec at conf 1991, elected to Nat Exec Cttee, ANC at Nat Conf 1991, Political Asst to Sec-Gen, ANC Head Office, Johannesburg. *Leisure interests:* videos, reading, listening to music, knitting, sewing. *Address:* African National Congress (ANC) Head-quarters, Office of the Sec-Gen, 51 Plein St, Johannesburg 2001, South Africa. *Telephone:* (11) 3307210; *Fax:* (11) 3339090.

SPARK, Dame Muriel Sarah, DBE, C LIT, FRSE; British writer; b Edinburgh; d of Bernard Camberg and Sarah Elizabeth Maud Uezzell; m S. O. Spark 1937 (divorced); one s. *Education:* James Gillespie's High School for Girls (Edinburgh) and Heriot-Watt Coll (Edinburgh). *Career:* Foreign Office 1944–45; Ed The Poetry Review 1947–49; Gen Sec Poetry Soc, London; Hon mem American Acad of Arts and Letters 1978, Scottish PEN; Hon D LITT (Strathclyde) 1971, (Edinburgh) 1989, (Aberdeen) 1995, (St Andrews) 1998, (Oxford) 1999; Hon D UNIV (Heriot-Watt) 1995; Commdr des Arts et des Lettres 1996; The Observer Story Prize 1951; Italia Prize 1962; James Tait Black Memorial Prize 1965; Ingersoll Prize (USA); T. S. Eliot Award 1992; David Cohen British Literature Prize 1997; Int PEN Gold Pen Award 1998. *Publications:* A Reassessment of Mary Wollstonecraft Shelley 1951, The Fanfarlo and Other Verse 1952, John Masefield (a critical study) 1953, The Comforters 1957, Robinson 1958, The Go-Away Bird and Other Stories 1958, Memento Mori 1959 (play 1964, BBC TV 1992), The Bachelors 1960, The Ballad of Peckham Rye 1960, The Prime of Miss Jean Brodie 1961 (play 1966, film 1969, TV 1978), Voices at Play 1961, Doctors of Philosophy (play) 1963, The Girls of Slender Means 1963, The Mandelbaum Gate 1965, Collected Stories I 1967, Collected Poems I 1967, The Public Image 1968, The Very Fine Clock (children's book) 1968, The Driver's Seat 1970 (film 1974), Not to Disturb 1971, The Hothouse by The East River 1973, The Abbess of Crewe 1974 (film 1977), The Takeover 1976, Territorial Rights 1979, Loitering with Intent 1981, Bang-Bang You're Dead (stories) 1982, Going Up to Sotheby's (poems) 1982, The Only Problem 1984, The Stories of Muriel Spark 1985, Mary Shelley 1987, A Far Cry from Kensington 1988, Symposium 1990, Curriculum Vitae (autobiog) 1992, The Essence of the Brontës 1993, The French Window and The Small Telephone (children's) 1993, Omnibus I 1993, Omnibus II 1994, The Portobello Road (stories) 1995, The Hanging Judge (stories) 1995, Reality and Dreams 1996, Harper and Wilton 1996, Omnibus III 1996, Omnibus IV 1997, Aiding and Abetting 2000. *Address:* c/o David Higham Associates Ltd, 5–8 Lower John St, Golden Square, London W1R 4HA, UK.

SPATE, Virginia, MA, PH D; British/Australian professor of fine art; d of O. H. K. Spate. *Education:* King Alfred's School (London), Cambridge High School, Univ of Melbourne and Bryn Mawr Coll (USA). *Career:* Lecturer in Art History Bath Acad of Art and Cen School of Arts, London 1966–70; Dir of Studies New Hall, King's Coll, Pembroke Coll and Jesus Coll, Cambridge 1970–78; Prof Dept of Fine Arts Univ of Sydney 1979–, Dir of Power Inst of Fine Arts 1979–94; Slade Prof of Fine Arts Cambridge Univ 1998. *Publications:* John Olsen 1962, Tom Roberts 1973, Orphism 1978, The Colour of Time. Claude Monet 1992. *Leisure interests:* paintings, reading, talking. *Address:* Dept of Art Hietory and Theory, University of Sydney, Sydney, NSW 2006, Australia.

SPEAR, Laurinda Hope, MA, FAIA; American architect; b 23 Aug 1950, Rochester, MN; d of Harold Spear; m Bernardo Fort-Brescia 1976; five s one d. *Education:* Columbia and Brown Univs. *Career:* Founding Prin Arquitectonica Int Corpn 1977–; designs low-income housing, high-rise condominiums, office towers, medical office bldgs, retail complexes and hotels; projects include The Atlantis, Miami, FL 1982, Banco de Credito del Peru, Lima 1988, Banque de Luxembourg 1993, Disney All-Star Resorts, Orlando, FL 1994, US Embassy, Lima 1994, Altamira Center, Caracas 1995, Parque Fundidora Convention Hotel, Mon-terrey, Mexico 1995, Yau Yat Tsuen Shopping Centre and Office Bldg, Hong Kong 1996, Performing Arts Centre and Urban Complex, Dijon,

France 1996, Festival Walk, Hong Kong 1998; lecturer to professional, civil and academic groups; numerous exhibitions throughout USA and Europe including Cooper-Hewitt Museum, New York 1979, Pennsylvania State Univ 1980, Paris Biennale 1982, Inst of Contemporary Art, Philadelphia 1986, Buenos Aires Biennale 1987, Inst Français d'Architecture, Paris 1988, Galerie Westersingel 8, Rotterdam, The Netherlands 1988, Architekturforum, Zurich 1989, Taipei Fine Arts Museum, Taiwan 1990, Centrum voor Architectuur en Stedebouw, Brussels 1991, Gallery MA, Tokyo 1993, Philips Arena, Atlanta 1999; mem Bd Dirs Miami Youth Museum, Beaux Arts Support Group, Miami Lowe Art Museum; Fellow AIA 1992; various architectural awards including Rome Prize in Architecture 1975, Progressive Architecture Design Award 1975, 1980, Honor Award, Virginia AIA, Center for Innovative Technology 1989, Atlanta Urban Design Comm Award for Excellence in Architecture, Rio, 1989, AIA Built Award for Excellence 1994. *Address:* 550 Brickell Ave, Suite 200, Miami, FL 33131, USA. *Telephone:* (305) 372-1812; *Fax:* (305) 372-1175; *E-mail:* 72345.516@ compuserve.com.

SPENCER, Elizabeth, MA; American writer; b 1921, Carollton, MS; d of James Luther and Mary James (née McCain) Spencer; m John Arthur Blackwood Rusher 1956 (died 1998). *Education:* Belhaven Coll (Jackson) and Vanderbilt Univ (Nashville). *Career:* Teacher 1943–44; journalist 1945–46; Writer-in-Residence Univ of N Carolina 1969, Visiting Prof 1986–92; Writer-in-Residence Hollins Coll 1973; Visiting Prof Concordia Univ, Montréal, Canada 1976–86, Adjunct Prof 1981–86; Visiting Prof Univ of NC, Chapel Hill 1986–92; Vice-Chancellor Fellowship of Southern Writers 1993–97; mem American Acad of Arts and Letters; Guggenheim Foundation Fellow 1953; Hon LITT D (Southwestern Univ) 1968, (Concordia) 1988, (Univ of the South) 1992, (Univ of NC) 1998, (Belhaven Coll) 1999; awards include Rosenthal Foundation Award (American Acad of Arts and Letters) 1952, 1957, McGraw-Hill Fiction Award 1960, Award of Merit for Short Story (American Acad of Arts and Letters) 1983, Salem Award for Literature 1992, Dos Passos Award for Fiction 1992, NC Gov's Award for Literature 1994, Fortner Award for Literature 1998, Mississippi State Library Assn Award for Non-fiction 1999 and other awards. *Publications include:* Fire in the Morning 1948, This Crooked Way 1952, The Voice at the Back Door 1956, The Light in the Piazza 1960, Knights and Dragons 1965, No Place for an Angel 1967, Ship Island and other stories 1968, The Snare 1972, The Stories of Elizabeth Spencer 1981, Marilee 1981, The Salt Line 1984, Jack of Diamonds and other stories 1988, For Lease or Sale 1989, The Night Travellers 1991, Landscapes of the Heart (memoir) 1998; short stories in magazines and collections. *Leisure interests:* movies, theatre, travel. *Address:* 402 Longleaf Drive, Chapel Hill, NC 27514, USA. *Telephone:* (919) 929-2115.

SPENCER, Metta, PH D; American/Canadian sociologist; b 29 Aug 1931 Calera, OK; d of Howard and Gladys (née Turner) Wells; m Robert L. Spencer 1951 (divorced 1962); one s. *Education:* Univ of California. *Career:* Research Assoc Harvard Univ Center for Int Affairs 1968–69, Survey Research Center, Univ of California 1969–71; apptd Prof of Sociology, Univ of Toronto 1971, now Prof Emer; Founding Pres and Dir Canadian Disarmament Information Service 1982–; Ed-in-Chief Peace Magazine 1985–; Dir Hunger Project of Canada 1981–83, Science for Peace 1983–86, Consortium for Peace Research, Educ and Devt 1985–; mem The Group of 88, Helsinki Citizens' Assn 1990–. *Publications:* Foundations of Modern Sociology 1975, Adolescent Prejudice 1975, Research in Social Movements, Conflict and Change 1991, World Security: The New Challenge 1994, Women in Post-Communism: Research on Russian and Eastern Europe 1996, Separatism, Democracy and Disintegration 1998. *Address:* 155 Marlee Ave, Apt 201, Toronto, ON M6B 4B5, Canada (Home). *E-mail:* mspencer@web.net; *Internet:* www.peacemagazine.org.

SPENCER, Dame Rosemary Jane, DCMG, BA; British diplomatist; b 1 April 1941, Newark; d of Geoffrey Roger Cole and Juliet Mary (née Warwick) Spencer. *Education:* Upper Chine School (Shanklin) and St Hilda's Coll (Oxford). *Career:* Foreign Office 1962–65; Third Sec, Nairobi 1965–67; Second Sec FCO 1967–70; Second Sec UK Del to EC and Pvt Sec to Leader of UK negotiating team 1970–71; First Sec Office of Perm Rep to EC 1972–73; First Sec, Lagos 1974–77; First Sec and Asst Head of Rhodesia Dept, FCO 1977–80; Royal Coll of Defence Studies 1980; Counsellor, Paris 1980–84; Head of EC Dept (External)

FCO 1987–89; Asst Under-Sec of State (Public Depts) 1989–92; Minister and Head of British Embassy, Berlin office 1993–96; Amb to Netherlands 1996–2001; mem Council Britain in Europe 2001, Anglo-Netherlands Soc 2001–, mem Bd Imperial Coll (London) 2001–, Council St Swithun's School 2001–; Gov Int Coll, Sherborne School 2001–. *Leisure interests:* country walks, travel, the arts. *Address:* c/o FCO Association, Old Admiralty Bldg, Room 2/110, Spring Gardens, London SW1A 2PA, UK. *Telephone:* (1722) 322769; *Fax:* (1722) 322769.

SPERO, Nancy, BFA; American artist; b 24 Aug 1926, Cleveland, OH; d of Henry and Polly Spero; m Leon Golub 1951; three s. *Education:* Chicago Art Inst, Atelier André l'Hôte and Ecole des Beaux Arts (Paris). *Career:* Solo exhibitions include Everson Museum of Art (Syracuse, NY) 1987, Rhona Hoffman Gallery (Chicago) 1988, Museum of Contemporary Art (Los Angeles) 1988, Le Grand Halle de la Villette (Paris) 1989, S. L. Simpson Gallery (Toronto, Canada) 1989, Josh Baer Gallery (New York) 1989, 1991, Haus am Walsee (Berlin) 1990, Honolulu Acad of Arts (HI), Gallery Hibell (Tokyo) 1990, Anthony Reynolds Gallery (London) 1990, Galleria Stefani Miscetti (Rome) 1991, Künstlerhaus Salzburg (Austria) 1991, Barbara Gross Galerie (Munich, Germany) 1991, Galerie Raymond Bollag (Zurich, Switzerland) 1991, Jürgen Becker Galerie (Hamburg, Germany) 1991, Museum of Modern Art (New York) 1992, The American Center (Paris) 1994, Hiroshima City Museum of Contemporary Art (Hiroshima, Japan) 1996, Miami Univ (Oxford, Ohio) 2000; joint exhibitions include: Whitney Museum of American Art (New York) 1993, Museum of Modern Art (New York) 1995; permanently installed works at sites including R. C. Harris Water Filtration Plant (Toronto) 1988, Well Woman Centre and exterior mural (Londonderry, N Ireland) 1990, Inst of Contemporary Art (Philadelphia) 1991, Von der Heydt Museum (Wuppertal, Germany) 1991, Circulo de Bellas Artes (Madrid) 1991; rep in perm collections including Art Gallery of Ontario (Toronto), Australian Nat Gallery, Centro Cultural (Mexico), Museum of Fine Arts (Hanoi), Ulmer Museum (Germany), Musée des Beaux-Arts de Montréal (Canada); CAPS Fellow New York State Council on the Arts 1976–77; Hon DFA (Chicago) 1991. *Address:* 530 La Guardia Place, New York, NY 10012, USA.

SPHEERIS, Penelope; American film director; b 1945, New Orleans. *Education:* Univ of California at Los Angeles. *Career:* Started film career as promotional video producer; TV work has included Saturday Night Live (Producer) and Roseanne (Story Ed). *Films include:* The Decline of Western Civilization (documentary), Suburbia, The Boys Next Door, Hollywood Vice Squad, Dudes, Wayne's World, The Decline of Western Civilization – Part II: The Metal Years, Real Life (producer), Wedding Band (actress), Wayne's World, The Beverly Hillbillies 1994, The Little Rascals, Black Sheep; *TV includes:* Saturday Night Live (producer), Danger Theatre (co-creator, dir, co-writer), Prison Stories: Women on the Inside (New Chicks).

SPOERRI, Helen B. Rose; Swiss artist; b 14 Dec 1937, Zurich; m E. Keck 1961; one s. *Education:* Univs of Basel, Zurich, Hamburg (Germany) and Paris. *Career:* Workshop theatre New York 1960; Lecturer Univ of Minneapolis, USA 1961; Artist-in-Residence Sydney-Wollongong, Australia 1988; painter in studio, Berlin 1983–; nat and int exhibitions include Gedok Gallery (Hamburg) 1984, Kunst Konzentriert (Hamburg) 1987, Gallery Marina Dinkler (Berlin) 1988, Swiss Inst (New York) 1988, Brisbane (Australia) 1988, Gallery E. L. Stark (New York) 1989, Gallery Zimmermann und Franken (Cologne, Germany) 1991; several catalogues of exhibitions published. *Leisure interests:* literature, music, sport, travel in Africa. *Address:* Papenkamp 6, 2000 Hamburg 52, Germany. *Telephone:* (40) 827086.

SPOTTISWOODE, Clare Mary Joan, CBE, MA, M PHIL; British business executive; b 20 March 1953, Lancs; d of Robert Spottiswoode and Charlotte Nuttall; m Oliver Richards 1977; three d one s. *Education:* Cheltenham Ladies' Coll, Clare Coll (Cambridge) and Yale Univ (USA). *Career:* Economist HM Treasury 1977–80; sole proprietor Spottiswoode Trading (import business) 1980–84; Chair and Man Dir Spottiswoode & Spottiswoode Ltd (micro-computer software house) 1984–90; also held several non-exec directorships, taught at London Business School and acted as software consultant; Dir-Gen Office of Gas Supply (OFGAS) 1993–; Sr Vice-Pres European Water 1998–;

mem Man Group PA Consulting Group 1999–; Non-Exec Dir Booker PLC; Gov Nat Inst of Econ and Social Research; mem Inst of Man Bd of Companions; Hon D SC S (Brunel) 1997. *Publications include:* Quill 1984, Abacus 1984. *Leisure interests:* children, theatre, gardening. *Address:* PA Consulting Group, 123 Buckingham Palace Rd, London SW1W 9SR, UK. *Telephone:* (20) 7730-9000; *Fax:* (20) 733- 5050; *E-mail:* info@paconsulting.com; *Internet:* www.pa-consulting.com.

SPRINGMAN, Sarah Marcella, OBE, MA, PH D; British engineer and athlete; b 26 Dec 1956, London; d of Paul Michael Eyre and Ann Marcella (née Mulloy) Springman. *Education:* Wycombe Abbey School and Cambridge Univ. *Career:* Geotechnical Engineer in Australia, UK and Fiji 1979–83; Chartered Engineer 1983; Research Asst Cambridge Univ 1983–89, Research Assoc 1989–90, Research, Asst Lecturer in soil mechanics 1990–93, Lecturer 1993–96, mem Soil Mechanics Group Magdalene Coll; Fiji and Pacific Squash Champion 1981, 82; British Triathlon Champion (ten times) and mem of Nat team 1984–93, European Champion 1985, 1986, 1988, team champion five times; Co-Chair Women's Comm, Int Triathlon Union 1990–92, Vice Pres 1992–96; Student Liaison Officer Inst of Civil Engineers 1990–96; Prof Eidgenössische Technische Hochschule, Zürich (Switzerland) 1997–; Gov Marlborough Coll 1991–94, Wycombe Abbey School 1993–96; mem ICE, GB Sports Council (UK Sports Council from 1997) 1993–2001, Swiss Council for Science and Tech 2000–; numerous articles as freelance journalist for sports magazines; Roscoe Memorial Prize (Univ of Cambridge) 1978; Cosmopolitan–Clairol Women of Achievement Award (Sports) 1991. *Leisure interests:* triathlon, sculling, multi-sports, languages for engineers, opera. *Address:* Eidgenössische Technische Hochschule—Hönggerberg, 8093 Zürich, Switzerland. *Telephone:* (1) 6332525; *Fax:* (1) 6331079; *E-mail:* springman@igt.baug.ethz.ch.

SPRINGS, Alice (pseudonym of June Browne); Australian photographer; b June 1923, Melbourne; m Helmut Newton 1948. *Career:* Fmr professional actress; professional photographer 1970–, fashion and publicity photographer 1970–76, portrait photographer 1976–; clients have included Jean-Louis David, Fashion Magazine Dépêche Mode, Elle, Marie-Claire, Vogue, Vogue Homme, Nova, Mode Int, Absolu, London Cosmoplitan; assignments for Harpers & Queen and Tatler (London), Vanity Fair (New York), Egoiste, Interview, Passion, Stern, Decoration Internationale, Photo, Les Cahiers de l'Energumène; one-woman show at Nat Portrait Gallery, London 1988–89; solo exhibitions include: Canon Gallery, Amsterdam 1978, Canon Gallery, Geneva 1980, Duc et Camroux, Paris 1980, David Heath Gallery, Atlanta 1982, Yuen Lui Gallery, Seattle 1982, Olympus Gallery, London 1983, Galerie de France, Paris 1983, Musée Cheret, Nice 1984, Musée Sainte Croix, Poitiers 1985, Documenta Gallery, Turin 1985, Centre Culturel, Orleans 1985, Centre Culturel et Artistique, Arbusson 1986, Espace Photographie de la Ville de Paris/Paris Audiovisuel 1986, Fotoform, Frankfurt Main 1987, Gerfiollet, Amsterdam 1988, Olympus Galerie, Hamburg 1988, Nat Portrait Gallery London 1988, Musée d'Art Moderne, Paris 1988, Museo Contemporáneo, Mexico City 1990, Rheinisches Landesmuseum, Bonn 1991/92, 'Arrêt sur l'image', Bordeaux 1993, Galerie im alten Rathaus am Markt, Wittlich 1993, Hochschule für Graphik und Buchkunst, Leipzig 1993, FORUM, Bremen 1993; group exhibitions include: Photokina, Cologne 1976, Photographers' Gallery, London 1979, G. Ray Hawkins, LA 1981, Grey Art Gallery, NY 1981, Paris Audiovisuel, French Photographers, Museum of Modern Art, Bratislava 1991, Teatro Circo (courtesy of Paris Audiovisuel), Braga 1992. *Catalogues include:* Alice Springs Portraits, Musée Sainte Croix, Poitiers 1985, Espace Photo, Paris 1986, Musée d'Art Moderne de la Ville de Paris 1988, Centro Cultural Arte Contemporaneo, Mexico City 1991, Rheinisches Landesmuseum, Bonn 1991/92; *Publications include:* Alice Springs Portraits 1983, 1986, 1991; *Films include:* Helmut by June (TV documentary) 1995. *Address:* Résidence Saint-Roman, Apt T1008, 7 ave Saint-Roman, Monte Carlo, Monaco.

SPURLING, (Susan) Hilary, BA; British writer and critic; b 25 Dec 1940; d of Gilbert Alexander and Emily Maureen (née Armstrong) Forrest; m John Spurling 1961; two s one d. *Education:* Somerville Coll (Oxford). *Career:* Theatre Critic The Spectator 1964–69, Literary Ed 1966–70; Book Reviewer The Observer 1969–86, Daily Telegraph 1986–; Biographer; Rose Mary Cranshaw Prize 1974; Heinemann

Award 1984; Duff Cooper Prize 1984. *Publications:* Ivy When Young: the early life of I. Compton-Burnett 1884–1919 1974, Handbook to Anthony Powell's Music of Time 1977, Secrets of A Woman's Heart: the later life of I. Compton-Burnett 1920–69 (Duff Cooper Prize and Heinemann Award) 1984, Elinor Fettiplace's Receipt Book 1986, Paul Scott: A Life 1990, Paper Spirits 1992, The Unknown Matisse: 1869–1908 1998, La Grande Thérèse 1999. *Leisure interest:* gossip and swimming. *Address:* c/o David Higham Associates, 5–8 Lower John St, Golden Square, London W1R 4HA, UK. *Telephone:* (20) 7437-7888.

SPYCHALSKA, Ewa; Polish politician and trade unionist; b 17 Aug 1946, Warsaw; d of Bronisław and Stefania Pękała-Czuma; m Zbigniew Spychalski 1974; one s one d. *Education:* Acad of Social Sciences (Warsaw). *Career:* Teacher 1969–78; employed in bldg company 1978–85; Pres Voivodship Council of Builders' Trade Union 1985–87; Sec Builders' Trade Union Fed 1987–90; Vice-Pres All-Poland Trade Unions Alliance (OPZZ) 1990–91, Pres 1991–96; Deputy to Sejm (Parl) 1991–96, Vice-Chair Democratic Left Alliance Parl Club (SLD); Amb to Belarus 1996–98; Adviser Chancellery of the Pres 1998–; awarded Silver Order of Merit 1988. *Leisure interests:* hiking, reading. *Address:* Kancelaria Prezydenta RP, ul Wiejska 10, 00 902 Warsaw, Poland (Office); ul Kopernika 36/40, 00-928 Warsaw 56, Poland (Home). *Telephone:* (22) 695 26 91 (Office).

ST AUBIN DE TERAN, Lisa Gioconda; British writer; b 2 Oct 1953, London; d of Jan Rynveld Carew and Joan Mary St Aubin; m 1st Jaime Cesar Teran Mejia 1969 (divorced 1981); one d; m 2nd George Mann Macbeth 1981 (divorced 1988, deceased); one s; m 3rd Robbie Charles Duff-Scott 1989; one d. *Education:* James Allen's Girls' School (Dulwich). *Career:* Travelled widely in France and Italy 1969–71; managed sugar plantation in Venezuelan Andes 1971–78; moved to Italy 1983; appeared in BBC TV documentary Santos to Santa Cruz in Great Railway Journeys series 1994; Vice-Pres Umbria Film Festival; Somerset Maugham Award; John Llewelyn Rhys Award; Eric Gregory Award for Poetry. *Publications:* Keepers of the House 1982, The Slow Train to Milan 1983, The Tiger 1984, The Bay of Silence 1986, Black Idol 1987, Joanna 1990, The High Place (poetry) 1985, The Marble Mountain (short stories) 1989, Off the Rails: A Memoir 1989, Venice: the Four Seasons (essays) 1992, Nocturne (novel) 1993, A Valley in Italy 1994, Distant Landscapes (novella) 1995; *Film:* screenplay of The Slow Train to Milan (jtly); *Radio:* adapted and read Off the Rails for the BBC 1995. *Leisure interests:* travel, medicinal plants, gardening, architecture, bric-a-brac, falconry, antiques, reading. *Address:* c/o Maggie Phillips, Ed Victor Ltd, 6 Bayley St, Bedford Square, London WC1B 3HB, UK. *Telephone:* (20) 7304-4100; *Fax:* (20) 7304-4111.

STADTMAN, Thressa Campbell, PH D; American biochemist; b 12 Feb 1920, Sterling, New York; d of Earl and Bessie (née Waldron) Campbell; m Earl Reece Stadtman 1943. *Education:* Cornell Univ and Univ of California at Berkeley. *Career:* Research Assoc Univ of California at Berkeley 1942–47, Harvard Medical School, Boston, MA 1949–50; Biochemist Nat Heart, Lung and Blood Inst, NIH 1950–, Section Head, Lab of Biochem 1974–; Ed-in-Chief Bio Factors 1987–; Pres Int Soc of Vitamins and Related Biofactors 1996; elected mem NAS 1981; mem American Acad of Arts and Sciences 1981–, Soc of American Microbiology Burroughs Wellcome Fund Toxicology Advisory Cttee 1994–; Helen Haye Whitney Fellow Oxford Univ, UK 1954–55; Rockefeller Foundation Grantee Univ of Munich, Germany 1959–60; has published original research papers in fields of methane biosynthesis, amino acid metabolism, vitamin B12 biochemistry and selenium biochemistry; Hillebrand Award, Chemical Soc of Washington, DC 1979; William C. Rose Award, American Soc of Biological Chemists 1988; Klaus Schwarz Medal 1988; Public Health Service Special Recognition Award 1991; L'Oréal-UNESCO Women in Science Lifetime Achievement Award 2000; Gabriel Bertrand Medal 2000, Prize 2001. *Leisure interests:* travel, gardening, skiing. *Address:* NIH, National Heart, Lung and Blood Institute, HHS Bldg 50, Rm 2120, Bethesda, MD 20892, USA (Office); 16907 Redland Rd, Derwood, MD 20855, USA (Home). *Telephone:* (301) 496-3002 (Office); (301) 896-1747 (Home); *Fax:* (301) 496-0599 (Office); *E-mail:* TCStadman@nih.gov.

STAINTON, Gwendolyn Mary; Australian arts administrator; b 11 Oct 1933, Melbourne; d of Francis Arthur and Ethel May Norris; m Alan Lenard Stainton 1953; two d one s. *Education:* Ballarat High School. *Career:* Community Arts Officer City of Mildura 1976–78; Dir Mildura Arts Centre 1978–82; Arts Admin City of Waverley 1982–89; Chair Victorian Arts Council 1984–89; Fed Pres Arts Council of Australia 1987–89; Chair Asscn for Local Arts Devt 1988; Nat Seminar Consultant Museum Asscns of Australia 1989; Exec Officer Victorian Museums Advisory Bd 1990–95; Arts Consultant 1996–. *Leisure interests:* landscape gardening, theatre, exhibitions, creative arts. *Address:* POB 37, Warburton, Vic 3799, Australia.

STALLER, Ilona (Elena Anna—La Cicciolina); Italian politician and actress; b 26 Dec 1951, Budapest; m 1st Salvatore Mercuri 1972; m 2nd Jeff Koons (divorced 1994); one s. *Education:* Studied medicine and archaeology. *Career:* Founder Partito del Sole (Sun Party—ecology party); mem Radical Party 1987–92; mem Chamber of Deputies 1987–92; radical political campaigner; has been prosecuted on numerous occasions for indecent exposure, imprisoned for obscene performances at Diva Futura, campaigner for reform of obscenity laws; fmr actress in pornagraphic films and photographic model. *Films include:* Incontro d'amore, Cuore di Cane, Came Bollente; *TV appearances include:* Proibito, Root Into Europe; *Political satire:* Vorrei fare l'amore per tre, Cicciolina Story. *Address:* Via Cassia 1818, 00123 Rome, Italy. *Telephone:* (6) 30896368; *Fax:* (6) 30896368.

STANCHEVA, Magdalina Mihailova; Bulgarian archaeologist; b 8 Sept 1924, Sofia; d of the late Mihail Georgiev and Mara Georgieva; m 1st T. Ivanov 1949 (divorced 1950); m 2nd S. Stanchev 1950 (divorced 1967). *Education:* Sofia Univ. *Career:* Asst Curator, Curator, Head of Archaeology, Scientific Researcher, then Sr Scientific Researcher, Sofia History Museum 1952–85; Part-time Asst Prof in Museology Acad of Fine Arts 1979–90, Sofia Univ 1979–, New Bulgarian Univ 1994; Pres Nat Council of Cultural Monuments; Bulgarian Del to World Heritage Cttee 1979–91; recipient Bulgarian Silver Medal of Labour, Order of Cyril and Methodius (First and Second Class), Austrian Order of Merit with Silver Cross, awarded two medals to celebrate 1,300 Years of Bulgaria. *Publications:* Bulgaria: three ancient capitals 1981, Archaeological Sites in Modern Bulgarian Towns 1982, The Bulgarian Contribution to the World Heritage (ed) 1989, Beliki Preslav 1993, Nine Bulgarian Wonders 1993, Madarskiat Konnik 1996; 150 scientific and 300 popular scientific papers. *Leisure interests:* nature, literature. *Address:* 1184 Sofia, Mladost bl 5 vh V app 55, Bulgaria. *Telephone:* (2) 74-79-37.

STANIFORTH, Francesca, BA; British textile designer; b 2 June 1958, Mark Cross, Sussex. *Education:* Brighton Polytechnic and Winchester Coll of Art. *Career:* Works commissioned in UK and Europe 1980–; f own business, Frannie 1987–; specializes in hand-painted silk designs; Allens of Duke St Award. *Address:* c/o Liberty Retail Ltd, Regent St, London W1R 6AH, UK. *Telephone:* (20) 7734-8323.

STANISZKIS, Joanna Katarzyna, BFA, RCA; Canadian tapestry artist; b Czestochowa, Poland; d of Stefan and Amelia (née Krukowska) Kiljanski; m Olgierd Staniszkis 1968; one s. *Education:* Warsaw Acad of Fine Arts and Chicago Art Inst (USA). *Career:* Head of Design Univ of British Columbia 1969–73, apptd Assoc Prof of Design, School of Home Econs 1973; Acting Head of Textiles Ontario Coll of Art 1975–76; Vice-Pres Bd of Trustees, Cartwright Street Gallery, Vancouver; solo exhibitions include Merton Gallery (Toronto) 1972, 1974, 1976, Mido Gallery (Vancouver) 1973, Equinox Gallery (Vancouver) 1978; group exhibitions include Jacques Baruch Gallery (Chicago) 1976, Int Tapestry Exhibition (Vevey, Switzerland) 1977, Łódź, (Poland) 1977, RCA Centennial Exhibition (Toronto) 1980, Canada House (London), Centre Culturel Canadien (Paris) 1980; comms for Bank of Montréal, Textile Museum (Łódź), Canadian Pacific (London), Mercantile Bank (Los Angeles, CA, USA); Saidye Bronfman Award for Excellence in Crafts 1981. *Leisure interests:* skiing, travel. *Address:* c/o 604 Stamps Landing, False Creek, Vancouver, BC V5Z 3Z1, Canada.

STAŇKOVÁ, Marie, MD; Czech professor of medicine; b 2 April 1941, Beroun; d of the late Vladimír Macourek and Marie Macourková; m Josef Staněk 1974 (died 1987); two s one d. *Education:* Charles Univ

(Prague). *Career:* Began work in Clinic for Infectious Diseases (Prague), later Sr House Officer 1968–78; Lecturer Faculty of Medicine, Charles Univ (Prague) 1978–89, Assoc Prof 1989–; mem Nat AIDS Cttee and Head Therapeutic Div, Ministry of Health 1991–; Head Czech Medical Soc for Infectious Diseases 1993–; published numerous works on meningitis, legionellosis and AIDS; awarded prize by Czechoslovak Acad of Science 1986 and by the Soc for Infectious Diseases 1988. *Leisure interests:* music, theatre, literature. *Address:* U Průhonu 17, 170 00 Prague 7, Czech Republic. *Telephone:* (2) 878658.

STANLEY, Fiona Juliet, AC, M SC, MD; Australian paediatrician; b 1 Aug 1946, Sydney; d of Neville Stanley and Muriel MacDonald; m Geoffrey R. Shellam 1973; two d. *Education:* Maroubra Junction School (Sydney), St Hilda's School (Perth), Univ of Western Australia and London School of Hygiene and Tropical Medicine. *Career:* Visiting Scientist NIH, USA 1976–77; Sr Medical Officer of Child Health, W Australia Health Dept 1977–79; Deputy Dir Nat Health and Medical Research Council, Epidemiology and Preventative Medicine Research Unit 1980–89; Dir TVW Telethon Inst for Child Health Research 1990–, concurrently Prof of Paediatrics Univ of Western Australia; researcher in epidemiology, and maternal, child and Aboriginal health; mem Prime Minister's Science, Eng and Innovation Council 1998–; Fellow Faculty of Public Health Medicine (UK), Australian Faculty of Public Health Medicine, Royal Australian Coll of Paediatrics, Royal Australian Coll of Obstetrics and Gynaecology, Acad of Social Sciences of Australia 1996; Hon D SC (Murdoch) 1998. *Publications:* The Epidemiology of Prematurity (co-ed) 1977, The Epidemiology of Cerebral Palsies (co-ed) 1984; 120 papers in scientific journals, Seminars in Neonatology (ed) 1997, The Cerebral Palsies: Epidemiology and Causal Pathways 2000. *Leisure interests:* bush walking, reading. *Address:* TVW Telethon Institute for Child Health Research, POB 855, West Perth, WA 6872, Australia (Office); 28 Stanley St, Nedlands, WA 6009, Australia (Home). *Telephone:* (8) 9489-7969 (Office); *Fax:* (8) 9489-7702 (Office); *E-mail:* fiona@ichr.uwa.edu.au.

STANLEY, Kathleen (Kay) Louise, BA; Canadian civil servant; b 24 March 1942, Ottawa; d of the late Clarence and Florence (née Barrett) Mulvagh. *Education:* Ottawa Teachers' Coll and Carleton Univ. *Career:* Teaching posts, USA 1960–81, on secondment to Ministry of Nat Defence as teacher in Germany 1971–74, 1978–80; Pres Teachers' Fed of Carleton 1969–71, 1981–85, Overseas Teachers' Asscn 1972–74, 1979–80; founding Pres Fed Privy Councillor Women's Caucus of Ottawa 1981–83, Pres Nat Privy Council Fed 1983–86; Chief of Staff to Ministry of State (Immigration) and Ministry Responsible for the Status of Women 1985–86; Sr Policy Adviser to the Sec of State and Minister Responsible for the Status of Women 1985; Co-ordinator Status of Women Canada 1986–93; Asst Deputy Solicitor Gen 1993; Asst Deputy Minister Health Programs and Services Br, Health Canada 1993–97; Asst Sec Employment Equity Div, Treas Bd Secr 1997–; mem OECD Working Party on Role of Women in the Econ 1987, Chair of Bureau 1988–91, Head of Canadian Del to OECD Conf on Improving Employment Prospects for Women in a Changing Soc: The Year Ahead, Istanbul, Turkey 1989; Alt Head of Canadian Del to UN Comm on Status of Women 1987–90, Head 1991–92; apptd Canada's Prin Del to Inter-American Comm, OAS 1990; Chair The Children's Aid Foundation 1990–93; mem Asscn of Professional Execs of the Public Service of Canada (Pres 1996–99), The Elizabeth Fry Soc of Ottawa. *Leisure interests:* travel, gardening, skiing. *Address:* Employment Equity Div, Treasury Board Secretariat, Ottawa, ON K1A 0R5, Canada (Office); 1380 Plante Drive, Ottawa, ON K1V 9G3, Canada (Home).

STANSFIELD, Lisa; British singer; b 1967, Rochdale, Lancs. *Career:* Fmr Presenter Razzamatazz children's TV programme; Three Brit Awards for Best Female Vocalist. *Recordings include:* Affection 1989, All Around the World (single) 1989, Live Together 1990, What Did I Do To You 1990, Change 1991, Real Love 1991, All Woman (single) 1991, Set Your Loving Free 1992, Time To Make You Mine (single) 1992, So Natural 1993.

STAPLETON, Maureen; American actress; b 21 June 1925, Troy, NY; d of John P. and Irene (née Walsh) Stapleton; m 1st Max Allentuck 1949 (divorced 1959); one s one d; m 2nd David Rayfiel 1963 (divorced). *Education:* Siena Coll and acting with Herbert Berghof (New York). *Career:* Mem Actors' Studio; Broadway debut in The Playboy of the

Western World 1946; Nat Inst of Arts and Letters Award 1969. *Plays include:* Antony and Cleopatra 1947, Detective Story, Bird Cage, The Rose Tattoo (Tony Award) 1951, The Emperor's Clothes, The Crucible, Richard III, The Seagull, Orpheus Descending, The Cold Wind and the Warm, The Glass Menagerie 1965, 1975, Plaza Suite 1969, Norman Is That You?, Gingerbread Lady (Tony Award) 1970, Country Girl 1972, Secret Affairs of Mildred Wild 1972, The Gin Game 1977–78, The Little Foxes 1981; *Films include:* Lonelyhearts 1958, A View from the Bridge 1962, Airport 1970, Plaza Suite 1971, Interiors 1978, The Fan 1981, On the Right Track 1981, Reds (Acad Award for Best Supporting Actress) 1981, Johnny Dangerously 1984, The Cosmic Eye (voice), Cocoon 1985, The Money Pit 1986, Heartburn, Sweet Lorraine, Nuts, Doin' Time on Planet Earth, Cocoon: The Return, Passed Away 1992, Trading Mom 1994, Addicted to Love 1997, Dead Silence 1998; *TV appearances include:* The Thorns, For Whom the Bell Tolls 1959, Among the Paths to Eden (Emmy Award) 1968; Films: Tell Me Where It Hurts 1974, Cat on a Hot Tin Roof 1976, The Gathering 1977, The Gathering Part II 1979, The Electric Grandmother, Family Secrets, Private Sessions 1985, Liberace: Behind the Music, Last Wish 1992, Miss Rose White 1992. *Address:* c/o Silvia Gold, International Creative Management, 8899 Beverly B, Los Angeles, CA 90048, USA.

STARFIELD, Barbara, MD, M PH; American professor of medicine; b 18 Dec 1932, Brooklyn, New York; d of Martin and Eva (née Illions) Starfield; m Neil A. Holtzman 1955; three s one d. *Education:* Swarthmore Coll, State Univ of New York and Johns Hopkins Univ. *Career:* Asst Teacher in Anatomy Downstate Medical Center, New York 1955–57; internship in Paediatrics Johns Hopkins Univ Hosp 1959–60, Resident 1960–62, Dir Paediatric Medical Care Clinic 1963–66; Dir Paediatric Clinical Scholars Program, Johns Hopkins Univ 1971–76; Asst Prof, then Assoc Prof of Health Policy, Johns Hopkins Univ School of Hygiene and Public Health 1967–76, Prof and Div Head 1976–94, Distinguished Univ Prof 1994–, Dir Primary Care Policy Center 1996–; mem Inst of Medicine, NAS, American Paediatric Soc, Nat Advisory Council for Health Care Policy, Research and Evaluation, US Dept of Health and Human Services 1990–95, Nat Cttee on Vital and Health Statistics 1995–; Hon Fellow Royal Coll of Gen Practitioners (UK) 2000; Dave Luckman Memorial Award 1958; Career Devt Award 1970–75; Armstrong Award (Ambulatory Pediatric Asscn) 1983; Annual Research Award (Ambulatory Paediatric Asscn) 1990; Pew Primary Care Achievement Award 1994; Martha May Eliot Award (APHA) 1994; Maurice Wood Award for Lifetime Contrib to Primary Care Research 2000. *Publications:* Effectiveness of Medical Care 1985, Primary Care: Concept, Evaluation and Policy 1992, Primary Care: Balancing Health Needs, Services and Technology 1998; over 150 scientific publications. *Address:* Johns Hopkins University School of Hygiene and Public Health, 624 N Broadway, Baltimore, MD 21205, USA. *Telephone:* (410) 955-9725; *Fax:* (410) 614-9046.

STARK, Ethel, CM, LL D, FRSA; Canadian conductor and concert violinist; b 25 Aug 1916, Montréal, PQ; d of Adolph and Laura (née Haupt) Stark. *Education:* McGill Conservatory, Curtis Inst (Philadelphia, USA), Univ of Montréal and under Fritz Reiner, Carl Flesch, Lea Luboshutz, Louis Bailly and Arthur Rodzinski. *Career:* Founder, Conductor Montréal Women's Symphony Orchestra, Montréal Women's Symphony Strings, Ethel Stark Symphonietta, New York Women's Chamber Orchestra, Canadian Chorus; guest conductor with Tokyo Asahi Philharmonic, Nippon Hoso Kyokai Orchestra, Jerusalem Symphony, Québec Symphony, Toronto Symphony, Miami Symphony, CBC Symphony; guest violinist with Curtis Symphony, Les Concerts Symphoniques, Les Petits Concerts, Montréal Symphony, Toronto Symphony; Music Tutor Catholic Univ of Washington, USA; Prof of Violin Conservatoire Prov de Musique; Hon mem Musicians' Guild of Montréal. *Address:* Toronto Symphony Orchestra, No C116, 69 Simcoe St, Toronto, ON M5J 2H5, Canada.

STAUNTON, Imelda Mary Philomena Bernadette; British actress; b 9 Jan 1956; d of Joseph Staunton and Bridie McNicholas; m Jim Carter 1983; one d. *Education:* La Sainte Union Convent (Highgate, London) and Royal Acad of Dramatic Art. *Career:* Repertory Exeter, Nottingham, York 1976–81; Screen Actors' Guild Award 1999. *Plays include:* Guys and Dolls 1982, 1996, Beggar's Opera 1985, She Stoops to Conquer, Chorus of Disapproval (Olivier Award, Best Supporting Actress) 1985, The Corn is Green 1985, Fair Maid of the West 1986, The Wizard of

Oz 1986, Comrades 1987, Uncle Vanya 1988, Into the Woods 1990, Phoenix (Olivier Award, Best Actress in a Musical) 1990, Life x 3 2000; *TV includes:* The Singing Detective 1986, Yellowbacks 1990, Sleeping Life, Roots, Up the Garden Path 1990, Antonia and Jane, David Copperfield 1999, Victoria Wood Xmas Special 2000; *Films include:* Peter's Friends 1992, Much Ado About Nothing 1993, Deadly Advice 1994, Sense and Sensibility, Twelfth Night, Remember Me 1996, Shakespeare in Love 1998, Another Life 1999, Rat 1999, Crush 2000. *Address:* c/o PFD, Drury House, 34-43 Russell St, London WC2B 5HA, UK.

STCHIN GOWA; Chinese actress; b 2 Nov 1949, Guangzhou City. *Career:* With Inner Mongolia Song and Dance Ensemble 1965–79; film actress First August Film Studio 1981–; winner Golden Rooster Award, Hundred Flowers. *Films include:* Luotuo Xiangzi (Best Actress Award, China 1982) 1981, Fleeting Time (Best Actress Award, Hong Kong) 1984, Xianghun Girl (Best Film, Berlin Film Festival) 1992. *Address:* Building 2, Rm 307, Panjiapo Hutong, Beijing 100020, People's Republic of China.

STEADMAN, Alison, OBE; British actress; b 26 Aug 1946, Liverpool; d of George Percival Steadman and the late Margorie Evans; m Mike Leigh (separated); two s. *Education:* Drama School (Loughton, Essex). *Career:* Began career in repertory theatre in Lincoln, Bolton, Liverpool, Worcester and Nottingham; TV and film actress 1971–; mem Royal Shakespeare Co 1987–8; Hon MA (Univ of E London). *Plays include:* The Prime of Miss Jean Brodie, Abigail's Party, Cat on a Hot Tin Roof 1988, The Rise and Fall of Little Voice, Maydays, Tartuffe, Joking Apart, Kafka's Dick, Marvin's Room 1993, The Plotters of Cabbage Patch Corner, When We Are Married 1996, The Provok'd Wife 1997; *Films include:* Clockwise 1983, Champions 1984, A Private Function 1985, The Adventures of Baron Munchausen, Shirley Valentine, Wilt, Life is Sweet, Blame it on the Bellboy, Topsy-Turvy 1999; *TV includes:* Z Cars, Hard Labour, Nuts in May 1976, Abigail's Party 1980, P'tang Yang Kipperbang 1983, The Caucasian Chalk Circle 1986, The Singing Detective, 1000 Nights, Selling Hitler 1991, Virtuoso, Newshounds, The Short and Curlies, Gone to Seed, Selling Hitler, Pride and Prejudice, The Wimbledon Poisoner, Karaoke, No Bananas, The Missing Postman, Let Them Eat Cake, Fat Friends. *Address:* c/o PFD, Drury House, 34-43 Russell St, London WC2B 5HA. *Fax:* (20) 7352-7356.

STEEG, Helga; German international organization official; b 8 June 1927, Bonn; d of Johann P. and Annemarie (neé Küper) Steeg. *Education:* Univs of Bonn and Lausanne (Switzerland). *Career:* Joined Ministry of Finance 1954, Deputy Head Third World Politics Dept 1970–73, Head of Foreign Trade Dept 1973; mem staff IBRD 1965–67; Exec Dir Int Energy Agency, OECD 1984–94; Lecturer Ruhr Univ, Bochum 1994–. *Address:* Klein Villip, 53343 Wachtberg, Germany.

STEEL, Danielle; American writer; b (Danielle Fernande Schüelein-Steel) 14 Aug 1950, New York; d of John Steel and Norma (née Stone) Schüelein-Steel; m 1st 1967 (divorced); one d; m 2nd Bill Toth 1977; one s; m 3rd John A. Traina, Jr; four d one s two step- s. *Education:* Lycée Français, Parsons School of Design (New York) and Univ of New York. *Career:* Vice-Pres of public relations and new business, Supergirls Ltd, Manhattan, New York 1968–71; mem staff Grey Advertising Agency, San Francisco 1973–74; published first novel 1973, then wrote poems for women's magazines; wrote first bestseller, The Promise 1979; several novels have been filmed or made into mini-series for TV. *Publications:* Going Home 1973, Passion's Promise 1977, Now and Forever 1978 (film 1983), Season of Passion 1978, The Promise 1979, Summer's End 1980, The Ring 1980, To Love Again 1981, Palomino 1981, Loving 1981, Remembrance 1981, A Perfect Stranger 1982, Once in a Lifetime 1982, Crossings 1982, Changes 1983, Thurston House 1983, Full Circle 1984, Love: Poems by Danielle Steel 1984, Having a Baby (contrib, non-fiction) 1984, Family Album 1985, Wanderlust 1986, Fine Things 1987, Kaleidoscope 1987, Zoya 1988, Star 1989, Daddy 1989, Heartbeat 1990, Message from Nam 1990, No Greater Love 1991, Jewels 1992, Mixed Blessings 1992, Vanished 1993, Accident 1994, The Gift 1994, Wings 1995, Lightning 1995, Five Days in Paris 1995, Malice 1995, Malice 1995, Silent Honor 1996, The Ghost 1997, Special Delivery 1997, His Bright Light 1998, The Ranch 1998, The Long Road Home 1998, The Klone and I 1998, Mirror Image 1998,

Bittersweet 1999, The Wedding 2000, The House on Hope Street 2000, Journey 2000, Lone Eagle 2001. *Leisure interest:* my children. *Address:* c/o Dell Publishing, 1540 Broadway, New York, NY 10036, USA (Office); POB 1637, New York, NY 10156, USA (Home).

STEENBURGEN, Mary; American actress; b 8 Feb 1953, Newport, AZ; m 1st Malcolm McDowell 1980 (divorced); one d one s; m 2nd Ted Danson 1995. *Education:* Neighborhood Playhouse. *Career:* Numerous TV and film appearances 1978–; Dr hc (Arkansas at Little Rock, Hendrix Coll, AR). *Films include:* Goin' South 1978, Ragtime 1981, A Midsummer Night's Sex Comedy 1982, Time After Time 1979, Romantic Comedy 1982, Cross Creek 1983, Melvin and Howard (Acad Award for Best Supporting Actress) 1980, One Magic Christmas 1985, Dead of Winter 1987, End of the Line 1987, Parenthood 1989, Back to the Future Part III 1989, Miss Firecracker 1989, The Long Walk Home 1990, The Butcher's Wife 1991, What's Eating Gilbert Grape 1993, Philadelphia 1993, Clifford 1994, It Runs in the Family (My Summer Story) 1994, Pontiac Moon 1994, My Family/Mi Familia, Powder, The Grass Harp, Nixon, About Sarah 1995, Trumpet of the Swan 1999; *TV appearances include:* Little Red Riding Hood, Tender Is the Night 1985, The Attic: The Hiding of Anne Frank 1988, Back to the Future (voice for cartoon series), Gulliver's Travels 1996; *Plays include:* Holiday 1987, Candida 1993. *Address:* c/o Ames Cushing, William Morris Agency Inc, 151 El Camino, Beverly Hills, CA 90212, USA.

STEGER, Debra Pauline, BA, LL M; Canadian lawyer; b 8 May 1952, Oliver; d of Frank and Doreen (née Cheveldave) Steger; m Murray Smith 1972; one s one d. *Education:* Univs of British Columbia, Victoria and Michigan (USA). *Career:* Sec to Cabinet Cttee, Govt of British Columbia 1979–80; Prof of Law Univ of Victoria 1983; Consultant to govt and research insts 1983–85; Lawyer McCarthy and McCarthy 1985–87; Int Trade Lawyer Fraser and Beatty 1987–91; Sr Adviser on Multilateral Trade Negotiations, External Affairs and Int Trade Canada 1988–94; Gen Counsel Canadian Int Trade Tribunal 1991–94; Hyman Soloway Prof of Int Business Law, Univ of Ottawa 1995–96, part-time Prof of Law; Dir Appellate Body Secr, WTO 1995–; mem Exec Bd Canadian Council on Int Law; mem Law Soc of Upper Canada, Canadian Bar Asscn, Int Bar Asscn, Canada-Japan Trade Council. *Publications:* A Concise Guide to the Canada–US Free Trade Agreement 1988, Living With Free Trade (ed) 1990, In Whose Interest? Due Process and Transparency in International Trade (ed) 1991; Trade Policy in the 1990s 1993; numerous articles in professional journals. *Leisure interests:* cycling, jogging, swimming, aerobics. *Address:* Centre William Rappard, rue de Lausanne 154, 1211 Geneva, Switzerland (Office); 10 rue du Colombier, 1202 Geneva, Switzerland (Home). *E-mail:* degra.steger@wto.org.

STEICHEN, René, D EN D; Luxembourg politician; b 27 Nov 1942, Luxembourg; m; three c. *Education:* Lycée Classique (Diekirch), Cours Supérieurs (Luxembourg), Faculties of Law, Aix-en-Provence (France) and Paris Inst d'Etudes Politiques (France). *Career:* Lawyer, Diekirch 1969–84; mem Diekirch Town Council 1969, Mayor 1974–84; Christian Social Deputy in Parl 1979; Sec of State for Agric and Viticulture 1984, of Agric, Viticulture and Rural Devt and Minister-Del for Cultural Research and Scientific Research 1989–93; Commr for Agric and Rural Devt, EC 1993–95, now Co-Chair. *Address:* c/o European Commission, 200 rue de la Loi, 1049 Brussels, Belgium; Société Européene des Satellites, Château de Betzdorf, L-6815 Betzdorf, Luxembourg.

STEINBERG, Hannah, PH D; British psychologist and professor of psychopharmacology; d of the late Dr Michael and Marie (née Wein) Steinberg. *Education:* Putney High School, Queen Anne's School (Caversham), Univ of Reading, Denton Secretarial Coll (London) and Univ Coll London. *Career:* Sec Omes Ltd 1943–44; Asst Lecturer in Pharmacology Univ Coll London 1954–55, Lecturer 1955–62, Reader in Psychopharmacology 1962–70, Prof (first in Europe) and then Head Psychopharmacology Group, Dept of Psychology 1970, currently Emer Prof of Psychopharmacology; Hon Consulting Clinical Psychologist, Medical Royal Free Hosp 1970; Visiting Prof McMaster Univ, Ontario, Canada 1971; currently Hon Research Prof School of Psychology, Middlesex Univ; Vice-Pres Collegium Internationale Neuro-Psychopharmacologicum 1968–74 (Emer Fellow 1995–), British Asscn for Psychopharmacology 1974–76 (Hon mem 1992); mem Biological

Council 1977–80; Convenor Academic Women's Achievement Group 1979–92; mem Editorial Bd, British Journal of Pharmacology 1965–72, Psychopharmacologia 1965–80, Pharmacopsychoecologia 1987–; Founder-mem European Behavioural Pharmacology Soc 1986–, European Coll of Neuro-Psychopharmacology 1986–; Special Trustee Middx Hosp 1988–92; Fellow British Psychological Soc; Chartered Psychologist. *Publications include:* Animal Behaviour and Drug Action (jtly) 1963, Scientific Basis of Drug Dependence 1968, Psychopharmacology: Sexual Disorders and Drug Abuse (jtly) 1972, Exercise Addiction (jtly) 1995, Quality and Quantity: Research Methods in Sport and Exercise Psychology (jtly) 1996; numerous articles in journals. *Address:* Middlesex University, School of Psychology, Queensway, Enfield EN3 4SF, UK. *Telephone:* (71) 388-5406; *Fax:* (71) 380-7232; *E-mail:* hannah3@mdx.ac.uk.

STEINBERG, Marcia Irene, PH D; American biochemist; b 7 March 1944, New York; d of Solomon and Sylvia (née Feldman) Steinberg; m Michael Flashner 1966 (divorced 1978); one s. *Education:* Brooklyn Coll (NY) and Univ of Michigan. *Career:* Research Scientist Brooklyn Methodist Hosp, NY 1966–67, Dept of Surgical Research Univ of Michigan, Ann Arbor 1967–68; Post-doctoral Fellow Dept of Biology, Syracuse Univ 1973–76; Post-doctoral Fellow, then Assoc Prof State Univ of New York 1976–90; apptd Programme Dir Biochem Program, Nat Science Foundation, Washington, DC 1990; Reviewer NATO Fellowship, Nat Science Foundation, San Francisco, CA 1988; contribs to professional journals; mem AAAS, American Soc of Biochem and Molecular Biology, American Heart Asscn, Asscn of Women in Science; Regents Scholar (State Univ of New York) 1960–64; Wellcome Research Travel Grant (Wellcome Foundation, Cambridge Univ, UK) 1985. *Address:* National Science Foundation, Rm 325, 1800 G St, NW, Washington, DC 20550, USA.

STEINECKERT, Gisela; German writer and journalist; b 13 May 1931, Berlin; m Wilhelm Penndorf 1973; one d. *Career:* Former social worker, office worker and ed in Berlin; writer of poetry, novels, essays, songs, prose and films 1957–; Cttee Pres Demokratisches Frauenbund 1984–90, later Hon Chair; Heinrich Heine award 1977; Nat Preis für Kunst und Literatur 1986. *Address:* Leipziger Str 41, 1080 Berlin, Germany. *Telephone:* (30) 2081948.

STEINEM, Gloria, BA; American writer, journalist and feminist activist; b 25 March, 1934, Toledo; d of Leo and Ruth (née Nuneviller) Steinem; m David Bale 2000. *Education:* Smith Coll (MA). *Career:* Chester Bowles Asian Fellow, India 1957–58; Co-Dir, Dir Ind Research Service, Cambridge, MA and New York 1959–60; Editorial Asst, contributing Ed, Ed, freelance writer various nat and New York publs 1960–; Co-Founder New York Magazine 1968, contrib 1968–72, Ms Magazine 1971 (Ed 1971–87, Columnist 1980–, Consulting Ed 1987–); feminist lecturer 1969–; active in civil rights and peace campaigns including United Farmworkers, Vietnam War Tax Protest, Cttee for the Legal Defense of Angela Davis and political campaigns of Adlai Stevenson, Robert Kennedy, Eugene McCarthy, Shirley Chisholm, George McGovern; Co-Founder and mem Bd Women's Action Alliance 1970–; Convenor, mem Nat Advisory Cttee Nat Women's Political Caucus 1971–; Co-Founder, Pres Bd Ms Foundation for Women; founding mem Coalition of Labor Union Women; contributing Corresp NBC Today show 1987–88; Woodrow Wilson Int Center for Scholars Fellow 1977; Penney-Missouri Journalism Award 1970; Ohio Gov's Award for Journalism 1972; named Woman of the Year, McCall's Magazine 1972. *Publications:* The Thousand Indias 1957, The Beach Book 1963, Outrageous Acts and Everyday Rebellions 1983, Marilyn 1986, Revolution From Within, a Book of Self-Esteem 1992, Moving Beyond Words 1994; contribs to various anthologies; *Film:* First Wives Club (cameo) 1996. *Address:* c/o Ms Magazine, 20 Exchange Place, 22nd Floor, New York, NY 10005, USA. *Telephone:* (212) 509-2092; *Fax:* (212) 425-1247.

STENIUS-KAUKONEN, Minna Majatta; Finnish politician; b 19 July 1947, Kuopio; d of Martti Stenius and Annikki Lehtinen; m Dr Erkki Kaukonen 1981. *Education:* Technical Univ (Helsinki). *Career:* Asst in Textile Tech, Tech Univ, Helsinki 1970, 1972–73; Chief of Quality Control Virke Oy 1972; Sr Eng Labour Protection Inspectorate, Home Dist 1973–75; mem Eduskunta (Parl) 1975–95; MEP 1995–99, fmr mem Cttee on Social Affairs and Employment. *Leisure interest:*

crafts. *Address:* Provastinkatu 33, 33250 Tampere, Finland (Home). *Telephone:* (31) 2120417 (Home); *Fax:* (31) 2120417 (Home); *E-mail:* stenius@sci.fi.

STEORTS, Nancy Harvey, B SC; American management consultant; b 28 Nov 1936, Syracuse, NY; d of Frederick William Harvey and Josephine Eliz Jones; one d. *Education:* Syracuse Univ. *Career:* Pres Nancy Harvey Steorts Int Inc, Chevy Chase, MD and Nancy Harvey Steorts and Assocs (int management consulting firm), Dallas, TX and Washington, DC; Pres Dallas Citizens' Council; Chair US Consumer Product Safety Comm 1981–85; Consultant to Dir of US Office of Consumer Affairs at the White House during Pres Reagan's admin; mem Nat Consumer Advisory Cttee of the Fed Reserve Bd, Nat Consumer Advisory Council of the American Nat Standards Inst; Distinguished Lecturer Strom Thurmond Inst of Govt and Public Affairs, Clemson Univ; Host, Exec Ed TV special Washington: 1989 Consumer Forecast; nat and int guest lecturer, TV presenter and contrib to magazines and other publs; Vice-Chair, Fundraiser Bush/Quayle '92, Washington, DC; mem Int Dels to NATO Conf (Mainz, Germany) 1986, People to People Trade Mission to Spain (Dir) 1987, Women Leaders' Del to China (Taiwan, Chair) 1989, Int Women's Forum Del to USSR 1989; fmr Chair Exec Women in Govt; mem Bd Govs Nat Consumer Advisory Cttee, Fed Reserve 1990–93; George P. Arents Medal for Excellence in Govt, Syracuse Univ; named in Gallagher Report as One of the Best Public Servants of 1984. *Leisure interests:* travel, the arts, music. *Address:* Nancy Harvey Steorts Assocs, 4689 S Versailles Ave, Dallas, TX 75209, USA. *Telephone:* (214) 522-9211; *Fax:* (214) 522-5929.

ŠTĚPÁNKOVÁ, Jana; Czech actress; b 6 Sept 1934, Žilina; d of Zdeněk and Elena (née Hálková) Štěpánek; m Jaroslav Dudek 1962; one s. *Education:* Acad of Performing Arts (Prague). *Career:* Actress Theater Pardubice 1953–59, Theater SKN (Prague) 1959–72, Theater Na Vinohradech (Prague) 1972–; State Prize for Radio Dramatic Art 1988, 2000. *Plays include:* Jeanne d'Arc, Mary Stuart, Bolt, Cyrano de Bergerac, As You Like It, Oedipus, Othello, The Entertainer, Richard III, El Cid; *TV includes:* Hospital on the Edge of Town 1977. *Leisure interest:* history. *Address:* Blanická 5, 120 00 Prague 2, Czech Republic. *Telephone:* (2) 22510062; *Fax:* (2) 24256373; *E-mail:* dudek1@mbox .vol.cz.

STÉPHANIE, Princess Stéphanie Marie Elisabeth; Monégasque royal, singer and designer; b 1 Feb 1965; d of Prince Rainier III and the late Princess Grace (née Kelly); m Daniel Ducruet 1995 (separated 1996); one s two d. *Career:* Several hit singles in Europe, including Comme un Ouragan (Like a Hurricane); Designer of own swimwear collection; opened boutique 1996. *Address:* Palais de Monaco, Monte Carlo, Monaco.

STEPHENSON, Helga Mary Anna, BA; Canadian film company executive. *Education:* McGill Univ (Montréal) and Univ de Fribourg (Switzerland). *Career:* Public Relations Officer Nat Arts Centre, Ottawa 1971–73; Dir of Communications Nat Touring Office, Canada Council, Ottawa 1973–74; Prof Univ of Havana 1974–75; Partner Stephenson, Ramsay, O'Donnell Ltd public relations firm 1975–79; Asst to Pres Film Consortium of Canada 1979–80; Vice-Pres Simcom Ltd 1980–82; Pres Preview Ltd public relations co 1982–86; Exec Dir Cinematheque Ontario, responsible for combining Ontario Film Inst and Festival of Festivals 1989–94, Exec Dir Festival of Festivals/Toronto Int Film Festival 1986–94; Chair Viacom Canada Ltd, Toronto 1994–99; mem Bd of Dirs Canadian Foundation for the Americas, Toronto Int Film Festival Group, Cinematheque Ontario, Entertainment Venture Corpn Advisory Council, Dirs' Guild of Canada Advisory Council; Advisor to Civitella Ranieri Foundation, New York; Women Who Make a Difference Award 1988; Toronto Women in Film and TV Outstanding Achievement Award 1993; William Kilbourn Award for Lifetime Achievement, Toronto Arts Awards 1996. *Address:* 34 Farnham Ave, Toronto, ON M4V 1H4, Canada. *Telephone:* (416) 975-5567 (Office); (416) 922-0439 (Home); *Fax:* (416) 975-8618.

STEPHENSON, Olwen Diane, MD, FRCP; Canadian pathologist; b 31 Jan 1943, Saskatoon, SK; d of James N. and Olwen E. (née Maule) Stephenson. *Education:* Univ of Saskatoon. *Career:* Internship Christchurch, NZ 1969–71; Resident Pathologist Univ Hosp, SK 1971–76;

Pathologist Regina Gen Hosp 1976–87, Pasqua Hosp, Regina 1987–; Clinical Asst Prof Univ of Saskatoon 1977–; Chief Coroner for Prov of Saskatchewan 1987–; mem Saskatchewan, Canadian and Int Asscns of Pathologists, American Acad of Forensic Scientists, Canadian Soc of Forensic Scientists. *Address:* Office of the Coroner, 1874 Scarth St, Regina, SK S4P 3V7, Canada (Office); 2507 Philip Rd, Regina, SK S4V 1Z7, Canada (Home). *Telephone:* (306) 359-2434 (Office); *Fax:* (306) 787-8084 (Office).

ŠTĚPOVÁ, Vlasta Anna Marie, C SC; Czech sociologist and politician; b 7 June 1938, Letohrad; d of Leopold Appelt and Marie (née Turková) Appeltová; m Miloš Marcel Štěp 1963; two s one d. *Education:* Prague and Bratislava Schools of Econs. *Career:* Sr Exec Inst of Trade Research 1961–83, Inst of Living Standards Research 1983–89; Assoc Inst for Philosophy and Sociology, Czechoslovak Acad of Sciences; mem Civic Forum 1989; Minister of Trade and Tourism, Czech Repub 1989–92; apptd Deputy for Southern Bohemia, Czech Nat Ass 1990; mem Civic Forum's Ministers' Club; several publs on econs. *Leisure interests:* gardening, travel, swimming, theatre, reading, architecture, classical music. *Address:* Anny Letenské 7, Prague 2, Czech Republic (Home).

STERLING, A. Mary Fackler, JD; American lawyer and federal official; b 4 Sept 1955, Pioneer, OH. *Education:* Harvard Univ, Ohio State and New York Univs. *Career:* Called to the Bar, MO 1980; Assoc Watson, Ess, Marshall and Enggs, Kansas City, MO 1980–82; Asst US Attorney, US Dept of Justice, MO 1982–85, Fed Prosecutor 1985–86; White House Fellow and Special Asst to US Attorney-Gen, US Dept of Justice, Washington, DC 1987–88; apptd Asst Sec Labor Man Standards, US Dept of Labor, Washington, DC 1989; Attorney McDowell, Rice and Smith, Kansas City, MO 1989; mem House of Dels 1986–89, numerous house cttees; Instructor US Attorney-Gen's Advocacy Inst, Washington, DC 1986, 1988, FBI Acad, Quantico, VA 1988; Guest Lecturer Law School, New York Univ 1986, 1988; mem Bd Dirs Dept of Labor Acad 1989–90, Root-Tilden Scholarship Program, New York Univ 1982–89, Urban Crime Prevention Authority (Kansas City, MO) 1980–81; Fellow Ohio State Univ 1976–77; Root-Tilden Legal Scholar, New York Univ 1977–80; Thompson Award (Ohio State Univ Alumni) 1988; One of Top Ten Coll Women in USA 1975; One of Ten Outstanding Young Working Women in America 1987; Kansas City Career Woman of the Year 1988.

STERN, Jane, MFA; American writer; b 24 Oct 1946; d of Milton Grossman and Norma Weyler; m Michael Stern 1970. *Education:* The Pratt Inst (Brooklyn, NY) and Yale Univ. *Career:* Writer on popular American culture (jtly, with Michael Stern). *Publications include:* Trucker: a portrait of the last American cowboy (jtly) 1976, Friendly Relations 1979, Horror Holiday 1981, Roadfood and Goodfood 1986, Elvis World 1987, A Taste of America 1988, Sixties People 1990, The Encyclopedia of Bad Taste 1990, American Gourmet 1991, Jane and Michael Stern's Encyclopedia of Pop Culture (jtly) 1992; numerous magazine features and articles, appearances on radio and television. *Leisure interests:* studying exotic birds, designing cowboy boots, collecting American-Indian jewellery. *Address:* 28 Wayside, West Redding, CT 06896, USA. *Fax:* (203) 938-8084.

STERN, Baroness (Life Peer), cr 1999, of Vauxhall in the London Borough of Lambeth, **Vivien Helen Stern,** CBE, BA, M LITT; British international organization executive; b 25 Sept 1941; d of Frederick and Renate (née Mills) Stern. *Education:* Kent Coll and Bristol Univ. *Career:* Lecturer in Further Educ until 1970; mem Community Relations Comm 1970–77; Dir Nat Asscn for the Care and Resettlement of Offenders 1977–96; Sec-Gen Penal Reform Int 1989–; mem Special Programmes Bd, Manpower Services Comm 1980–82, Youth Training Bd 1982–88, Gen Advisory Council, IBA 1982–87, Cttee on the Prison Disciplinary System 1984–85, Advisory Council, Policy Studies Inst 1993–96; mem Bd Asscn for the Prevention of Torture, Geneva 1993–, Eisenhower Foundation, Washington 1993–, Law Advisory Council (British Council) 1995–; Visiting Fellow Nuffield Coll, Oxford 1984–91; Sr Research Fellow Int Centre for Prison Studies, King's Coll, London 1997–; Hon Fellow LSE 1997; Hon LL D (Bristol) 1990, (Oxford Brookes) 1996; Margaret Mead Award for contrib to social justice, Int Asscn for Residential & Community Alternatives 1995. *Publications:* Bricks of Shame 1987, Imprisoned by our Prisons 1989, Deprived of their Liberty, a report for Caribbean Rights 1990, A Sin

Against the Future: Imprisonment in the World 1998, Alternatives to Prison in Developing Countries 1999. *Address:* Int Centre for Prison Studies, School of Law, King's Coll, 75-79 York Rd, London SE1 7AW, UK. *Telephone:* (20) 7582-6500; *Fax:* (20) 7735-4666.

STEVENS, Christine, PH D; Belgian diplomatist; b 1 Aug 1951, Nairobi; d of Willy Stevens and Lucy Van Den Herrewegnen; m Khalid Jehangir 1986; two d one s. *Education:* Lycée Français de Téhéran (Iran), Monastère de Berlaymont (Waterloo) and Univ Libre de Bruxelles. *Career:* Vice-Consul Belgian Consulate-Gen, Amsterdam office 1976–77; Second Sec Belgian Embassy, The Hague office, Netherlands 1977–78, Spain 1978–79; mem Belgian Del to Conf on Security and Co-operation in Europe, Madrid 1979–81, Deputy Head of Del, Brussels 1993, Paris 1994; Deputy Spokesperson Ministry of Foreign Affairs, Brussels 1981–83, Head of Maghreb Section, Dept of the Middle East, Political Dept 1991–94; First Sec Belgian Embassy, Brazil 1983–85; Counsellor Belgian Embassy, Finland 1985–86, Denmark 1986–91; Amb to Bolivia 1994; Kt of the Order of the Crown, Belgium; Orden del Merito Civil, Spain; Kt First Class of the Order of Dannebrog, Denmark. *Publication:* Parnell Square, Dublin: demeures bourgeoises du XVIIIème siècle 1976. *Leisure interests:* golf, tennis, oil painting, piano, reading. *Address:* c/o Ministry of Foreign Affairs, 2 rue des Quatre Bras, 1000 Brussels, Belgium.

STEVENS, Rosemary Anne, PH D; American professor of history and sociology of science; b 18 March 1935, UK; d of William E. and Mary A. Wallace; m 1st Robert B. Stevens 1961 (divorced 1983); one s one d; m 2nd Jack D. Barchas 1994. *Education:* Univs of Oxford and Manchester (UK) and Yale Univ (USA). *Career:* Trained in hosp admin and worked as Hosp Admin Nat Health Service, UK; moved to USA 1961, naturalized 1968; mem Faculty, Prof of Public Health, Prof in Inst of Policy Studies, Yale Univ 1962–76; Prof Dept of Health Systems Man (Chair 1977–78) and Adjunct Prof of Political Science, Tulane Univ 1976–79; Prof of History and Sociology of Science, Univ of Pennsylvania 1979–, Chair 1980–83, 1986–91, Foundation Prof in Social Sciences 1990–91, Thomas S. Gates Prof and Dean School of Arts and Sciences 1991–96; Stanley I. Sheerr Prof 1997–; Chair of Bd Center for the Advancement of Health; mem Inst of Medicine of NAS, Bd of Dirs Milbank Memorial Fund; Fellow American Acad of Arts and Sciences; Dr hc (Hahnemann Univ, Philadelphia) 1988, (Medical Coll of Pennsylvania) 1992, (Rutgers) 1995, (Northeastern Ohio Univ Coll of Medicine) 1995; Rockefeller Humanities Award 1983–84; Guggenheim Fellow 1984–85; Baxter Foundation Prize for Health Services Research 1990; James A. Hamilton Book Award 1990; Welch Medal 1990; ABMS Special Award 1990. *Publications:* Medical Practice in Modern England 1966, American Medicine and the Public Interest 1971, Foreign Trained Physicians and American Medicine 1972, Welfare Medicine in America 1974, The Alien Doctors: Foreign Medical Graduates in American Hospitals 1978, In Sickness and in Wealth: American Hospitals in the Twentieth Century 1989; various articles. *Leisure interests:* painting, piano, reading, antiques. *Address:* 324 Logan Hall, University of Pennsylvania, 249 S 36th St, Philadelphia, PA 19104, USA (Office); 1900 Rittenhouse Square, #18A, Philadelphia, PA 19103, USA (Home). *Telephone:* (215) 898-8400 (Office); *Fax:* (215) 573-2231 (Office).

STEVENSON, Juliet Anne Virginia, CBE; British actress; b 30 Oct 1956, Essex; d of Michael Guy Stevens and Virginia Ruth Marshall; partner Hugh Brody; one d one s. *Education:* Hurst Lodge School (Sunningdale, Berks), St Catherine's School (Bramley, Surrey) and Royal Acad of Dramatic Art (London). *Career:* Actress with RSC 1978–86, now Assoc Artist of RSC; performed at the Nat Theatre, Royal Court Theatre, theatres in the London West End, etc; London Evening Standard British Film Awards, Best Actress 1992; Dr hc (Georgetown, USA). *Plays include:* Other Worlds 1982, Yerma 1987, Hedda Gabler 1988, The Caucasian Chalk Circle, Burn This 1990, Death and the Maiden (Time Out Theatre Award 1991, Laurence Olivier Theatre Awards, Best Actress 1992) 1991–92, The Duchess of Malfi, Private Lies 1999, The Country 2000; *TV appearances include:* Trial by Fire, Cider with Rosie, The Politician's Wife, A Doll's House, Life Story, Antigone, The March, Maybury, Thomas and Ruth, Aimée, The Mallens; *Films include:* Drowning by Numbers, Ladder of Swords, Truly Madly Deeply, The Trial, The Secret Rapture, Emma; *Publications:* Clamorous Voices (jtly) 1988, Shall I See You Again? (jtly), Players of

Shakespeare (jtly). *Leisure interests:* gardening, cinema, theatre, piano, walking, travel, reading, talking, painting, tennis. *Address:* c/o Markham and Froggatt Ltd, Julian House, 4 Windmill St, London W1P 1HF, UK. *Telephone:* (20) 7636-4412 (Office).

STEVENSON, Olive, CBE, MA, D LITT; British professor emeritus of social work studies; b 13 Dec 1930, Croydon; d of John and Evelyn (née Dobbs) Stevenson; one s one d. *Education:* Lady Margaret Hall (Oxford) and LSE. *Career:* Child Care Officer Devon Co Council 1954–58; Lecturer in Applied Social Studies, Univ of Bristol 1958–60; Lecturer Univ of Oxford 1960–68, Reader 1970–76, Fellow St Anne's Coll 1970–; Adviser Supplementary Benefits Comm 1968–70; Prof Univ of Keele 1976–83, Univ of Liverpool 1983–84, Univ of Nottingham 1984–94, Prof of Social Work Studies 1986–94, Emer Prof 1994–; mem Royal Comm on Compensation for Personal Injury 1973–78, Social Security Advisory Cttee 1980–, Registered Homes Tribunal 1985–90, COST A5 (European) 1992–; Chair Age Concern (England) 1980–83, Council of Voluntary Service Nat Asscn 1985–88, Chair Care and Repair 1993–98, Peterborough, Cambridgeshire, Leicester City and Leicester County Area Child Protection Cttees 1997–2000; Hon D LITT (E Anglia) 1996. *Publications:* Claimant or Client? 1970, Someone Else's Child 1977, Social Service Teams 1978, Specialisation in Social Services Teams 1980, Child Abuse: aspects of interprofessional co-operation 1980, Age and Vulnerability 1989, Child Abuse: public policy and professional practice 1990, Neglected Children: Issues and Dilemmas 1998, Child Welfare in the United Kingdom (ed) 1998. *Leisure interests:* music, cookery, conversation. *Address:* 11 Rose Hall Lane, Middleton Cheney, Banbury OX17 2NQ, UK (Home). *Telephone:* (1295) 711153 (Home); *Fax:* (1295) 710683 (Home); *E-mail:* olivestevenson@hotmail.com.

STEWART, Alice, FRCP; British epidemiologist; b 1906; m; two c. *Education:* St Leonard's School (St Andrews), Girton Coll (Cambridge), Royal Free Hosp (London). *Career:* Fmr Researcher Nuffield Dept of Clinical Medicine, Oxford, later Reader of Social Medicine and Professorial Fellow, Lady Margaret Hall, Oxford; carried out research for MRC; worked at Univ of Birmingham Medical School (now retd); currently Prof of Medicine Dept of Public Health; showed that low levels of radiation are harmful to human health 1950s; frequent contrib to peer review journals; Hon degree (Bristol) 1995; Right Livelihood Award 1986; Ramazzni Award 198; British Soc of Industrial Medicine Award 1998. *Address:* Evenlode Cottage, Fawler, Oxon OX7 3AQ, UK. *Telephone:* (1993) 891667; *Fax:* (1993) 898523; *E-mail:* anstew@ waitrose.com.

STEWART, Frances Julia, MA, D PHIL; British development economist; b 4 Aug 1940; d of Nicholas Kaldor and Clarissa Goldschmidt; m Michael James Stewart 1962; two d one s. *Education:* Cambridge High School for Girls and Univ of Oxford. *Career:* Econ Asst, then Adviser UK Treasury, Dept of Econ 1961–67; Lecturer Univ of E Africa, Nairobi 1967–69; Sr Research Officer Int Devt Centre, Oxford 1970–93, apptd Dir 1993; Fellow Somerville Coll 1975–; Pres Devt Studies Asscn of UK and Ireland 1990–92; Special Adviser to UNICEF 1985–86. *Publications:* Technology and Under-Development 1977, Planning to Meet Basic Needs 1985, Adjustment With a Human Face (jtly) 1987, Adjustment and Poverty Options and Choices 1995. *Address:* Queen Elizabeth House, 21 St Giles, Oxford OX1 3LA, UK (Office); 79 S Hill Park, London NW3 2SS, UK (Home). *Telephone:* (1865) 273600 (Office); *Fax:* (1865) 273607 (Office).

STEWART, Jane, B SC; Canadian politician; b 1955, St George, ON; m; two s. *Education:* Trent Univ. *Career:* Worked in human resources depts for many cos in Canada and USA including Imperial Oil; mem House of Commons (Parl) for Brant 1993–, fmr mem Standing Cttees on Finance and on Aboriginal Affairs; Minister of Nat Revenue 1995–97, of Indian Affairs and Northern Devt 1997–99, of Human Resources Devt 1999–; Chair Nat Liberal Caucus 1994–. *Address:* Phase IV, 19th Floor, 140 Promenade du Portage, Hull, PQ, K1A 0J9, Canada.

STEWART, Martha Kostyra, BA; American caterer and writer; b 1942, Jersey City, NJ; d of Edward and Martha (née Ruszkowski) Kostyra; m Andy Stewart 1961 (divorced 1990); one s. *Education:* Barnard Coll (New York). *Career:* Former model and stockbroker, New York; became professional caterer; owner and Ed-in-Chief Martha Stewart Living

1990–; Chair, CEO Martha Stewart Living Omnimedia 1997–; lifestyle Consultant K-Mart Corpn; weekly cooking feature slot on Today Show (NBC-TV), own TV show. *Publications:* Entertaining (jtly) 1982, Weddings (jtly) 1987, Martha Stewart's Hors d'Oeuvres: The Creation and Presentation of Fabulous Finger Food 1984, Martha Stewart's Pies and Tarts 1985, Martha Stewart's Quick Cook Menus: Fifty-two Meals You Can Make in Under an Hour 1988, The Wedding Planner 1988, Martha Stewart's Gardening: Month by Month 1991, Martha Stewart's New Old House: Restoration, Renovation, Decoration 1992, Martha Stewart's Christmas 1993, Martha Stewart's Menus for Entertaining 1994, Holidays 1994, Martha Stewart Cookbook 1996. *Address:* c/o Susan Magrino Agency, 40 W 57th St, 31st Floor, New York, NY 10019, USA.

STEWART-ROBERTS, Phyllida Katharine, OBE, DL; British organization executive; b 19 Aug 1933; d of Walter Harold and Veronica (née Grissell) Bamfield; m Andrew Kerr Stewart-Roberts 1955; one s one d. *Education:* Tormead School and Royal Acad of Music. *Career:* Teacher 1954–57; mem Man Cttee Love Walk Hostel for Disabled Workers 1972–89, Vice-Chair 1980–83, Chair 1983–89, Pres 1995–; Trustee Community Service Volunteers 1984–; mem Man Cttee Habinteg Housing Asscn 1988–95; mem St John Ambulance (Sussex) 1962–, County Pres 1984–89, Supt-in-Chief 1990–93; JP Inner London 1980–95; Vice-Lord-Lieutenant of Sussex 1996–2000, Lord-Lieutenant 2000–; mem Florence Nightingale Memorial Cttee 1990–, Council Univ of Sussex 1995–2001; Vice-Pres Voluntary Aid Detachment (VAD) Asscn 1991–; Chair Jt Cttee Order of St John of Jerusalem, British Red Cross Soc 1991–; Order of St John of Jerusalem 1987, Dame of the Order of St John of Jerusalem 1993. *Leisure interests:* needlework, country pursuits. *Address:* Mount Harry Lodge, Offham, Lewes, Sussex, BN7 3QW, UK. *Telephone:* (1273) 476400; *Fax:* (1273) 487273; *E-mail:* stewartroberts@cwcom.net.

STIBOROVÁ, Věra; Czech writer; b 15 Jan 1926, Písek; m Jaroslav Putík 1954; one d. *Education:* School of Applied Arts. *Career:* Journalist Lidové Noviny daily newspaper, Prague; Journalist, translator Práce daily newspaper; collaborator with various literary magazine until 1969; works prohibited in 1969, but many published through Samizdat; labourer and sales rep 1972–89. *Published works include:* Blue Loves (Literary Award) 1963, The Minute on the Road 1968, Ikariana 1969 (published in 1991), Forget, My River 1989 (published in 1996), The Day of the Dames 1991, Come Back to Sorrento... 1992 (published in 1995); *Unpublished works:* And What About Me? (now known by title If You Make it However, You Make it Badly) 1974, We Are Musicians 1971, Hypnotics 1974, Who Can Sleep If Troia is in Flames? 1981. *Leisure interest:* literature. *Address:* Pod Marjánkou 10, 169 00 Prague 6, Czech Republic.

STIEVENARD, Gisèle; French political executive; b 11 Dec 1950, Sarcelles, Val d'Oise; d of Eugène and Titania (née Benard) Stievenard. *Career:* Sec Volantes Banking Co and Temping Agency; MP Asst 1975–80; Municipal Councillor (Paris) 13ème 1983–89, 14ème 1989; Councillor (Paris) 1984–; currently Deputy Mayor of Paris, with responsibility for Solidarity and Social Affairs and First Vice-Pres of the Co Council; mem Nat Exec Cttee PS 1983–, Chair PS, Paris 1983–87; mem Nat Ass for Paris 1986–88; Nat Del of PS for Poverty and Employment Insecurity 1987–88, Nat Sec for Humanitarian Action 1990–93, mem Nat Council PS 1993–, Faction for Econ Issues and Overall Econ situation in Econ and Social Council 1999–; Nat Rep L'Assemblée des Femmes; mem League for Human Rights. *Address:* Office of the Deputy Mayor, Hôtel de Ville, 75196 Paris, France. *Telephone:* (1) 42-76-57-71; *Fax:* (1) 42-76-65-60; *Internet:* www.paris-france.org.

STILLMAN, Elinor Hadley, JD; American lawyer; b 12 Oct 1938, Kansas City, MO; d of Hugh Gordon and Freda (née Brooks) Hadley; m Richard C. Stillman 1965 (divorced 1975). *Education:* Univ of Kansas (MO) and Yale (CT) and George Washington (DC) Univs. *Career:* Lecturer in English City Univ of New York 1963–65; Asst Ed Stanford Univ Press, CA 1967–69; Law Clerk US Dist Court, DC 1972–73; called to the Bar, DC 1973; Appellate Attorney Nat Labor Relations Bd, Washington, DC 1972–73, Supervising Appellate Attorney 1982–86, Chief Counsel to mem Bd 1986–88, 1994–, to Chair Bd 1988–94; Asst

to Solicitor-Gen US Dept of Justice, Washington, DC 1978–82; mem ABA, Order of the Coif. *Address:* National Labor Relations Board, 1099 14th St NW, Washington, DC 20005, USA.

STIMPSON, Catharine Roslyn, PH D; American professor of English and writer; b 4 June 1936, Bellingham, WA; d of Edward Keown and Catharine (née Watts) Stimpson. *Education:* Bryn Mawr Coll (PA), Cambridge Univ (UK) and Columbia Univ (NY). *Career:* Mem faculty Barnard Coll, New York 1963–80; Prof of English, Dean of Grad School and Vice-Provost of Grad Educ Rutgers Univ, NJ 1980–92, apptd Univ Prof 1991; Prof, Dean of Grad School Univ of New York 1998–; Chair Bd Scholars Ms Magazine (New York) 1981–92; Founding Ed Signs: Journal of Women in Culture and Society 1974–81; Columnist Change magazine 1992–93; Chair New York Council of Humanities 1984–87, Nat Council of Research on Women 1984–89; mem Bd Dirs Stephens Coll, Columbia, MO 1982–85, PEN 1991–, Public Broadcasting System 1994–; Dir Fellows Programme MacArthur Foundation 1994–; Hon Fellow Woodrow Wilson Foundation 1958; Fulbright Fellow 1958–60; Nat Humanities Inst Fellow 1975–76; Rockefeller Humanities Fellow 1983–84. *Publications include:* Class Notes 1979, Women in Culture and Society (Ed) 1981, Where The Meanings Are 1988. *Address:* New York University, 6 Washington Square N, New York, NY10003-6668, USA (Office); 29 Washington Square, New York, NY 10003-6668, USA (Home).

STIRBOIS, Marie-France; French politician; b 11 Nov 1944, Paris. *Career:* English teacher 1969–76; Man printing co 1976–; mem Political Office Nat Front Party 1990–; Local Councillor for Dreux 1984–, Gen Councillor Dreux-Ouest 1994–; MEP (FN) 1994–99, mem Cttee on Social Affairs and Employment, on Women's Rights, Del to the EU-Romania Jt Parl Cttee until 1999. *Address:* Mairie, 28100 Dreux, France; Conseil régional du Centre, 8 rue St Pierre-Lentin, 45041 Orléans Cedex, France.

STODDART, Anne Elizabeth, CMG, MA; British diplomatist; b 29 March 1937, Middlesbrough; d of the late James and Ann Jack (née Inglis) Stoddart. *Education:* Kirby Grammar School (Middlesbrough) and Somerville Coll (Oxford). *Career:* Entered Foreign Office 1960; British Mil Govt, Berlin 1963–67; First Sec (Economic), Ankara office 1970–73; Head of Chancery, Colombo 1974–76; FCO 1977–81; Deputy UK Perm Rep to Council of Europe, Strasbourg 1981–87; Head Import Policy Br, Dept of Trade and Industry 1987–91; Deputy Perm Rep (Econ Affairs) UK Mission to UN, Geneva, Switzerland 1991–96. *Address:* 1/63 The Avenue, Richmond, Surrey TW9 2AH, UK. *Telephone:* (20) 8948-2497.

STONE, Caroline Fleming; American artist; b 26 March 1936, New York; d of Ralph Emerson and Elizabeth (née Fleming) Stone; m Oakleigh B. Thorne 1956 (divorced 1969); two s. *Education:* Art Students' League and Pratt Graphics. *Career:* Solo exhibitions include Saginaw Art Museum (MI) 1978, Jesse Besser Museum (MI) 1979, Washington Art Asscn CT, Ella Sharp Museum (MI), San Diego Public Library (CA), Trustman Gallery, Simmons Coll (Boston, MA) 1985, Mary Ryan Gallery (New York) 1989; group exhibitions include Katonah Gallery (New York) 1986, Davidson Gallery 1990, De Cordova and Dana Museum (New York), Mary Ryan Gallery 1985, 1988, Virginia Lynch Gallery (RI) 1989; rep in perm collections including Art Inst of Chicago (IL), Mid-West Museum of American Art (IN), Museum of New Mexico, Boston Public Library, Univ of Chicago (IL), Univ of Michigan, Exxon Corpn, Chase Manhattan Bank, IBM, Mellon Bank; Pres Bd The Kitchen. *Address:* C. Stone Press, 80 Wooster St, New York, NY 10012, USA.

STONE, Sharon; American actress; b 10 March 1958, Meadville, PA; m Michael Greenburg 1984 (divorced 1987); m 2nd Phil Bronstein 1998; one adopted s. *Education:* High School in Pennsylvania and Edinboro Coll. *Career:* Fmr model; film debut in Star Dust Memories; Chevalier des Arts et des Lettres. *Films include:* Above the Law, Action Jackson, King Solomon's Mines, Allan Quatermain and the Lost City of Gold, Irreconcilable Differences, Police Academy 4: Citizens on Patrol, Deadly Blessing, Personal Choice, Total Recall, Scissors, Year of the Gun, Basic Instinct, Diary of a Hit Man, Where Sleeping Dogs Lie, Sliver, Last Action Hero (cameo), Intersection, The Specialist, The Quick and the Dead (also co-producer), Casino (Golden Globe Award

1996), Diabolique 1996, Last Dance, Sphere, The Mighty 1999, The Muse 1999, Simpatico 1999; *TV appearances include:* Bay City Blues (series), Tears in the Rain (film), War and Remembrance (mini-series), Calendar Girl Murders (film), The Vegas Strip Wars (film). *Address:* c/o Guy McElwaine, POB 7304, North Hollywood, CA 91603, USA.

STONES, (Elsie) Margaret, AM, MBE; British botanical artist; b 28 Aug 1920, Australia; d of Frederick and Agnes Kirkwood (née Flemming) Stones. *Education:* Swinbourne Tech Coll (Melbourne) and Melbourne Nat Gallery Art School. *Career:* Ind botanical artist in UK 1951–, notably at Royal Botanical Gardens (Kew), Nat History Museum, Royal Horticultural Soc; contributing artist Curtis's Botanical Magazine 1957–82; Visiting Artist Louisiana State Univ, USA 1977–86; exhibitions include Colnaghi's (London) 1967–, Melbourne Univ (Australia) 1976, Smithsonian Inst (USA) 1980, Louisiana State Museum (USA) 1985, Baskett and Day 1984, 1989, Fitzwilliam Museum (Cambridge) 1991, Royal Botanical Garden (Edinburgh) 1991, Ashmolean Museum (Oxford) 1991, Univ of Virginia (USA) 1993, Boston Athenaeum (USA) 1993, Nat Gallery of Victoria (Melbourne, Australia) 1996; drawings include 20 Australian Plants, Nat Library (Canberra) 1962–63, 250 Tasmanian endemic plants 1962–77, Basalt Plains Flora, Melbourne Univ 1975–76; Hon D SC (Louisiana) 1986, (Melbourne) 1989; awarded Eloise Payne Luquer Medal (Garden Club of America) 1987, Gold Veitch Memorial Medal, Royal Horticultural Soc 1989. *Publications:* Illustrator: The Endemic Flora of Tasmania (6 vols) 1967–78, Flora of Louisiana: water-colour drawings 1991; numerous other books. *Leisure interests:* gardening, reading. *Address:* 1 Bushwood Rd, Kew, Richmond, Surrey TW9 3BG, UK. *Telephone:* (20) 8940-6183.

STOPPARD, Miriam, (Lady Hogg), MD, MRCP; British medical practitioner, writer and broadcaster; b 12 May 1937; d of Sydney and Jenny Stern; m Tom Stoppard 1972 (divorced 1992); two s two step-s; m 2nd Sir Christopher Hogg 1997. *Education:* Newcastle Cen High School, Royal Free Hosp School of Medicine (London) and King's Coll Medical School (Durham). *Career:* House Surgeon Royal Victoria Infirmary, Newcastle 1961, House Physician 1962, Sr House Officer in Medicine 1962–63; Resident Fellow Dept of Chemical Pathology, Univ of Bristol 1963–65, Registrar in Dermatology 1965–66, Sr Registrar 1966–68; Assoc Medical Dir Syntex Pharmaceuticals Ltd 1968–71, Deputy Medical Dir 1971–74, Medical Dir 1974–76, Deputy Man Dir 1976–77, Man Dir 1977–81; writer and broadcaster; mem Heberden Soc, British Asscn of Rheumatology and Rehabilitation; Hon D SC (Durham) 2000. *TV series:* Where There's Life 1981–, Baby and Co 1984–, Woman to Woman 1985–, Miriam Stoppard's Health and Beauty Show 1988–, Dear Miriam 1989–; *Publications:* Miriam Stoppard's Book of Baby Care 1977, Miriam Stoppard's Book of Health Care 1979, The Face and Body Book 1980, Every Woman's Lifeguide 1982, Your Baby 1982, Fifty Plus Lifeguide 1982, Your Growing Child 1983, Baby Care Book 1983, Pregnancy and Birth Book 1984, Baby and Child Medical Handbook 1986, Everygirl's Lifeguide 1987, Feeding Your Family 1987, Miriam Stoppard's Health and Beauty Book 1988, Every Woman's Medical Handbook 1988, Lose 7lb in 7 Days 1990, Test Your Child 1991, The Magic of Sex 1991, Conception, Pregnancy and Birth 1993, The Menopause 1994, Questions Children Ask and How to Answer Them 1997, Sex Ed – Growing Up, Relationships and Sex 1997, Baby's Play and Learn Pack 2000; over 40 articles in medical journals. *Leisure interests:* family, gardening. *Address:* Iver Grove, Iver, Bucks, UK.

STORB, Ilse, MUS D; German professor of music (jazz); b 18 June 1929, Essen; d of Friedrich and Maria Storb. *Education:* Girls' school (Essen), Musikhochschule (Cologne) and Univs of Cologne and Paris (Sorbonne). *Career:* Secondary school teacher 1957–68; Sr Teacher Pädagogische Hochschule Ruhr, Duisburg 1968; Co-Founder Jazz Lab for music teacher training, Munich 1971; took part in Jazz Summer Workshops for Music Educators, Berklee Coll of Music, Boston, MA, USA 1980, 1981; Prof of Musicology and Jazz Research, Head Jazz Lab, Univ Duisburg Gesamthochschule 1982–; organizer int congresses on Jazz Teaching and Improvized Music 1985, 1987, 1990, 1995; Founder Ilse and her Satchmos, Jazz History Live group 1991; has given concert-lectures in Brazil, Nigeria and Tunisia; TV and radio performances; awards for Outstanding Service to Jazz Educ, Detroit (USA) 1988 and Miami (USA) 1992. *Publications:* Claude Debussy 1966, Jazz: Musik in

der Schule 1983, 1987, 1990, Louis Armstrong 1989, Dave Brubeck: Improvisationen und Kompositionen, die Idee der kulturellen Wechselbeziehungen 1990 (English trans 1994); *Recordings:* Interaction 1989, Ilse and her Satchmos 1995. *Leisure interests:* music, travel, swimming, dance. *Address:* Universität Duisburg Gesamthochschule, Lothar Str 65, 47048 Duisburg, Germany (Office); Bredeneyer Str 44, 4300 Essen 1, Germany (Home). *Telephone:* (203) 3792298 (Office); (201) 411079 (Home); *Fax:* (203) 3793333 (Office).

STOREY, Helen; British fashion designer; b 15 Aug 1959, London; d of David and Barbara Storey; m Ron Brinkers 1985; one s. *Education:* Kingston Polytechnic. *Career:* Worked with Valentino, Rome 1981–82; Head of Design Studio, Publicity Co-ordination and Licensing, Lancetti, Rome 1983; launched own label under Amalgamated Talent 1984; opened Boyd and Storey with Karen Boyd and Caroline Coates 1987–90, re opened as Helen Storey 1990; collection shown in Designer Forum in London Fashion Week 1988, also shown at The British Designer Show (London), La Mode aux Tuilleries (Paris) and La Coterie (New York) 1988; solo show, London Fashion Week 1990; first menswear collection launched, Paris 1991; Present Times solo show 1991; worked on design projects for Doctor Martens (UK), Jigsaw, Knickerbox, Wrangler, Next and the Sock Shop; nominated Young Designer of the Year Award and Best Eveningwear Designer, British Fashion Council 1989; won The British Apparel Export Award (with Karen Boyd) 1989; nominated Designer of the Year British Fashion Awards 1990; awarded Most Innovative Designer of the Year 1990; nominated Most Innovative Designer of the Year 1991. *Art exhibition:* Mental ICA 2001. *Address:* 12 Newburgh St, London W1V 1LG, UK. *Telephone:* (20) 7494-3188; *Fax:* (20) 7494-3777.

STORGAARD MADSEN, Birgit, PH D; Danish diplomatist; b 24 May 1938, Silkeborg; d of the late Bjarne and of Hanna (née Norager) Madsen; m (died 1980). *Education:* Bispebjerg Hosp (Copenhagen) and Univ of Aarhus. *Career:* Nursing Officer 1960–62; Lecturer Univ of Aarhus 1969–75; Researcher Centre for Devt Studies, Copenhagen 1971–75; freelance consultant, India and Sweden 1975–78; Consultant Ministry of Foreign Affairs, Copenhagen 1978–82, 1985–87, Head of Dept 1988–94; Counsellor Embassy of Denmark, New Delhi office 1982–85; Head Int Dept, Danish Red Cross 1987–88; Amb to Ghana 1994; Knight of the Order of the Dannebrog 1989, Knight of the Order of the Dannebrog of the First Degree 1996. *Publications:* Ujamaa – Socialism from Above 1975; various scientific articles 1975–80. *Leisure interests:* literature, sports, gardening. *Address:* c/o Ministry of Foreign Affairs, Asiatisk Plads 2, 1448 Copenhagen K, Denmark.

STOTLER, Alicemarie Huber, JD; American federal judge; b 29 May 1942, Alhambra, CA; d of James R. and Loretta M. Huber; m James A. Stotler 1971. *Education:* Univ of Southern California. *Career:* Called to the Bar, CA 1967, US Dist Court (CA) 1967, 1973, US Supreme Court 1973, 1976; Deputy Orange Co Dist Attorney's Office 1967–73; mem Stotler and Stotler 1973–76, 1983–84; Judge Orange Co Municipal Court 1976–78, Superior Court 1978–83, US Dist Court, Cen Dist, CA 1984–; mem Exec Cttee Ninth Circuit Judicial Conf, Fed State Judicial Council 1989–93; Chair US Constitution Bicentennial Cttee 1986–91; mem Standing Cttee on rules of practice and procedure US Judicial Conf 1991–, Chair 1993–; mem ABA, Ninth Circuit Judges Asscn, Nat Asscn of Women Judges, Orange Co Trial Lawyers' Asscn; Judge of the Year, Orange Co Trial Lawyers' Asscn 1978; most outstanding Judge, Orange Co business litigation Section 1990; Franklin G. West Award Orange Co Bar Asscn 1985. *Address:* Ronald Reagan Federal Bldg and Courthouse, 411 W Fourth St, Santa Ana, CA 92701, USA.

STOTT, Kathryn, ARCM; British concert pianist; b 10 Dec 1958, Nelson, Lancs; d of Desmond Stott and Elsie Cheetham; m 1st Michael Ardron 1979 (divorced 1983); m 2nd John Elliott 1983 (divorced 1997); one d. *Education:* Yehudi Menuhin School (Stoke d'Abernon, Surrey) and Royal Coll of Music (London). *Career:* Has performed with all major orchestras in the UK; gave world première of George Lloyd's Concerto No 4 1984; has performed at concerts in the Netherlands, Germany, Switzerland, Italy, Turkey, Poland, Czechoslovakia, USA, Canada, Hong Kong, Japan and Repub of China (Taiwan); has made ten appearances at Henry Wood Promenade (BBC Proms) concerts; 20 recordings including premieres of concertos by George Lloyd and Michael Nyman; Dir Fauré and the French Connection Festival,

Manchester 1995, 2000, Piano 2000; Fifth Prize, Leeds Int Piano Competition 1978; Churchill Scholarship 1979; Chevalier des Arts et des Lettres 1996. *Recordings include:* Piano Concertos (George Lloyd), Concerto (John Ireland), Concerto (Herbert Howells), The Rio Grande (Constant Lambert); Solo Albums: Fauré Vols 1 and 2, Chopin, Rachmaninov, Liszt, Debussy, Ravel, Bridge. *Leisure interests:* horse-riding, films, travel. *Address:* c/o Jane Ward, 38 Townfield, Rickmansworth, Herts WD3 2DD, UK. *Telephone:* (1923) 493903; *Fax:* (1923) 493903.

STOWE, Madeleine; American actress; b 18 Aug 1958, Los Angeles, CA; m Brian Benben; one d. *Education:* Univ of Southern California. *Career:* Began acting career at Solari Theatre, Beverly Hills. *Films include:* Stakeout 1987, Tropical Snow, Worth Winning 1989, Revenge 1990, The Two Jakes 1990, Closet Land 1991, China Moon, Unlawful Entry 1992, The Last of the Mohicans, Another Stakeout, Short Cuts 1993, Blink, Bad Girls, Twelve Monkeys 1995, The House of Mirth 1996, The Proposition 1998, Dancing About Architecture 1999, Imposter 1999, The General's Daughter 1999; *TV appearances include:* The Gangster Chronicles (series), Beulah Land (mini-series), The Nativity (film), The Deerslayer (film), Amazons (film), Blood and Orchids (film). *Address:* c/o David Schiff, UTA, 9560 Wilshire Blvd, 5th Floor, Beverly Hills, CA 90212, USA.

STRACHAN, Dame Valerie Patricia Marie, DBE, CB, BA; British civil servant; b 10 Jan 1940; d of John Jonas and Louise Nicholls; m John Strachan 1965; one s one d. *Education:* Newland High School (Hull) and Univ of Manchester. *Career:* Joined HM Customs and Excise as Graduate Trainee 1961, Prin 1966, Asst Sec 1974, Commr 1980, Deputy Chair 1987–93, Chair of Bd 1993–2000; worked at Dept of Econ Affairs, Home Office, Treasury and Cabinet Office; Head Jt Treasury/Cabinet Office Unit leading the Programme of Civil Service Man Reforms 1985–87; Leader UK Negotiating Team on Indirect Tax Affairs, Brussels, UK Rep on EC group responsible for implementation of Single European Market in Fiscal Affairs; Chair World Customs Co-operation Council; Deputy Chair Community Fund 2000–; Hon LL D (Manchester) 1995; Dr hc (Humberside); Woman of Europe Award 1992. *Leisure interest:* Scottish dancing. *Address:* Community Fund, St Vincent House, 16 Suffolk St, London SW1Y 4NL, UK. *E-mail:* val .strac@ukgateway.net.

STRAND GERHARDSEN, Tove, B ECONS; Norwegian politician; b 29 Sept 1948, Solør; m Rune Gerhardsen. *Education:* Univ of Oslo. *Career:* Town Councillor, Oslo 1971–75; Political Sec Ministry of Trade and Shipping and Ministry of Finance; Head of Div Ministry of Consumer Affairs and Govt Admin 1978; Head of Dept Nat Hosp, Oslo 1982–86; Minister of Health and Social Affairs 1986–89; Minister of Labour and Govt Admin 1990–92.

STRANGE, Baroness (Life Peer), cr 1628, **Jean Cherry Drummond,** MA; British politician and writer; b 17 Dec 1928, London; d of the late John Drummond of Megginch, 15th Baron Strange and the late Violet Margaret Florence Buchanan-Jardine; m Humphrey ap Evans (now Drummond of Megginch) 1952; three s three d. *Education:* Oxenfoord Castle School (Midlothian) and Univs of St Andrews and Cambridge. *Career:* Chair Glencarse Jr Unionists 1947–52, Megginch Farming Co 1966–, Caledonian Schools Sale 1971; mem House of Lords 1986–, mem Cons Peers Exec Cttee 1990–94, All-Party Defence Studies Group, Int Parl Union, Commonwealth Parl Asscn, Scottish Peers' Asscn, All-Party Arts and Heritage Group; Pres War Widows' Asscn of GB 1990–. *Publications:* Love From Belinda 1960, Lalage in Love 1962, Creatures Great and Small 1968, Love is Forever 1988, The Remarkable Life of Victoria Drummond Marine Engineer 1994. *Leisure interests:* family, children, conservation, arts, heritage. *Address:* House of Lords, London SW1A 0PW, UK (Office); Megginch Castle, Errol, Perthshire PH2 7SW, UK (Home).

STRATAS, Teresa, OC; Canadian opera singer; b 26 May 1938, Toronto, ON; d of Emmanuel Stratas and Argero Stratakis. *Career:* Began singing career in nightclubs in Toronto; debut at Toronto Opera Festival 1958; noted opera performances at Metropolitan Opera, New York include Berg's Lulu and Jenny in Brecht and Weill's Mahagonny; appeared as Violetta in Zeffirelli's film of La Traviata 1983; appeared in Broadway musical Rags 1986; cr role of Marie Antoinette in Ghosts of

Versailles, premièred Metropolitan Opera, NY 1992; Hon LL D (McMaster) 1986, (Toronto) 1994, (Rochester) 1998; Drama Desk Award for Leading Actress in a musical on Broadway 1986–87; Gemini Award for Best Supporting Actress (for Under the Piano) 1997. *Address:* c/o Vincent & Farrell Associates, 157 W 57th St, Suite 502, New York, NY 10019, USA; c/o Metropolitan Opera Company, Lincoln Center Plaza, New York, NY 10023, USA.

STRATHERN, Marilyn, FBA; British anthropologist; b 6 March 1941; d of Eric Charles and Joyce Florence Evans; m Andrew Jamieson Strathern 1963 (divorced 1986); two s one d. *Education:* Bromley High School and Girton Coll (Cambridge). *Career:* Asst Curator Museum of Ethnology, Cambridge 1966–68; Research Fellow ANU 1970–72, 1974–75, Sr Research Fellow 1983–83; Bye-Fellow, Sr Research Fellow, then Official Fellow Girton Coll, Cambridge 1976–83, Mistress of Girton Coll 1998–; Fellow and Lecturer Trinity Coll, Cambridge 1984–85; Visiting Prof Univ of California at Berkeley, USA 1984; Prof of Social Anthropology and Head of Dept Univ of Manchester 1985–93; William Wyse Prof of Social Anthropology and Head of Dept, Univ of Cambridge 1993–; Rivers Memorial Medal 1976. *Publications include:* Self-Decoration in Mt Hagen (jtly) 1971, Women In Between 1972, Nature, Culture and Gender (co-ed) 1980, Kinship at the Core: an anthropology of Elmdon, Essex 1981, Dealing With Inequality (ed) 1987, The Gender of Gift 1988, Partial Connections 1991, After Nature 1992, Technologies of Procreation (jtly) 1993, Shifting Contexts 1995, Property, Substance and Effect 1999. *Address:* Girton College, Cambridge, CB3 0JG, UK.

STRÁŽNICKÁ, Viera, DR JUR, PH D; Slovak lawyer and diplomatist; b 28 Dec 1942, Bratislava; m Karol Strážnický 1967; once c. *Education:* Comenius Univ (Bratislava). *Career:* Assoc Prof of Law 1986; Arbiter Czechoslovak Chamber of Commerce and Industry, Prague 1979–92; Head Dept of Int Law and Politics, Head Faculty of Law and Vice-Rector for Int Relations, Comenius Univ, Bratislava 1991–92; Judge Czechoslovak Constitutional Court until 1993, then Adviser to Pres of Slovak Constitutional Court; Amb to the Council of Europe 1994; publs on law in int trade and human rights; Gold Medal, Comenius Univ 1993. *Leisure interests:* tennis, skiing, literature, theatre. *Address:* Kempelenova č 15, 841 05 Bratislava, Slovakia. *Telephone:* (7) 725339.

STREEP, Meryl (Mary Louise), AB, MFA; American actress; b 22 June 1949, Summit, NJ; d of Harry Streep, Jr and Mary W. Streep; m Donald Gummer 1978; two d one s. *Education:* Singing studies with Estelle Liebling and studied drama at Vassar and Yale School of Drama. *Career:* Stage debut in New York in Trelawny of the Wells; acted in 27 Wagons Full of Cotton (New York), Henry V, Measure for Measure (New York Shakespeare Festival) 1976; also acted in Happy End (musical), The Taming of the Shrew, Wonderland (musical), Taken in Marriage and numerous other plays; British Acad Award 1982; Dr hc (Dartmouth) 1981, (Yale) 1983, (Lafayette) 1985; Bette Davis Lifetime Achievement Award 1998; Special Award Berlin Int Film Festival 1999. *Films include:* Julia 1976, The Deer Hunter (Best Supporting Actress Award, Nat Soc of Film Critics) 1978, Manhattan 1979, The Seduction of Joe Tynan (Best Supporting Actress Award, New York Film Critics' Circle) 1979, The Senator 1979, Kramer vs Kramer (Acad Award for Best Supporting Actress 1980, Best Supporting Actress Award, New York Film Critics' Circle) 1979, The French Lieutenant's Woman 1980, Sophie's Choice (Acad Award for Best Actress, Best Actress Award, New York Film Critics' Circle) 1982, Still of the Night 1982, Silkwood 1983, Plenty 1984, Falling in Love 1984, Out of Africa 1985, Heartburn 1985, Ironweed 1987, A Cry in the Dark (Best Actress Award, New York Critics' Circle 1988, Cannes 1989) 1988, She-Devil 1989, Hollywood and Me 1989, Postcards from the Edge 1991, Defending Your Life 1991, Death Becomes Her 1992, The House of the Spirits, The River Wild 1994, The Bridges of Madison County 1995, Before and After, Marvin's Room, One True Thing 1998, Dancing at Lughnasa 1999, Music of the Heart 1999; *TV appearances include:* The Deadliest Season, Uncommon Women, Holocaust (Emmy Award), Velveteen Rabbit, First Do No Harm 1997. *Leisure interests:* peace and anti-nuclear causes, gardening, skiing, raising family, visiting art galleries and museums. *Address:* c/o Creative Artists Agency, 9830 Wilshire Blvd, Beverly Hills, CA 90212, USA.

STREET, Picabo; American skier; b 1971, Triumph, ID. *Career:* Professional downhill skier 1994–; Silver Medallist downhill alpine skiing race, Olympic Games, Lillehammer, Norway 1994; Gold Medallist downhill race, Bronze Medallist Super Giant Slalom (first American), World Alpine Skiing Championships, Sierra Nevada, Spain 1996. *Address:* US Olympic Cttee, 1750 E Boulder St, Colorado Springs CO 80909, USA.

STREET-PORTER, Janet; British broadcasting executive; b 27 Dec 1946; m 1st Tim Street-Porter 1967 (divorced 1975); m 2nd A. M. M. Elliott 1976 (divorced 1978); m 3rd Frank Cvitanovich 1978 (divorced 1988, died 1995); m 4th David Sorkin 1996 (divorced). *Education:* Lady Margaret Grammar School and Architectural Asscn. *Career:* Columnist and fashion writer, Petticoat Magazine 1968, Daily Mail 1969–71, Evening Standard 1971–73; own show LBC Radio 1973; Presenter London Weekend Show, London Weekend TV (LWT) 1975; Presenter Saturday Night People (with Clive James and Russell Harty), The Six O'Clock Show (with Michael Aspel), Around Midnight 1976–80; devised Twentieth Century Box (LWT), Get Fresh (ITV), Bliss (Channel 4), Network 7 (Channel 4); TV Producer 1986–; Head of Youth and Entertainment Features, BBC TV 1988–94; Head, Ind Production for Entertainment 1994; Man Dir Live TV 1994–95; Dir Mirror TV 1994–95; TV presenter Design Awards, Travels with Pevsner, Coast to Coast, The Midnight Hour 1996–98, As The Crow Flies (series) 1999, Cathedral Calls 2000 (all BBC2), J'Accuse, Internet 1996 (Channel 4); Ed The Independent on Sunday 1999–2001, currently Ed-at-Large; Pres Ramblers' Asscn 1994–97, currently Vice-Pres; Fellow Royal TV Soc 1994; Hon Fellow RIBA 2001; BAFTA Award for Originality 1988; Prix Italia 1993. *TV includes:* Reportage, Rough Guide (travel series), The Full Wax, The Travel Show, On the Line, That's Showbusiness, Dance Energy, Rapido; *Publications:* The British Teapot 1977, Scandal 1981, Coast to Coast 1998, As the Crow Flies 1999. *Leisure interests:* walking, talking, modern art. *Address:* c/o Bob Storer, Harbottle & Lewis, 14 Hanover Square, London W1R 0BE, UK. *Telephone:* (20) 7629-7633; *Fax:* (20) 7667-5100.

STREISAND, Barbra Joan; American actress, singer, film director and producer; b (Barbara Jean) 24 April 1942, Brooklyn, New York; d of Emanuel and Diana (née Rosen) Streisand; m Elliot Gould 1963 (divorced 1971); one s; m 2nd James Brolin 1998. *Education:* Erasmus Hall High School. *Career:* Nightclub debut at Bon Soir 1961; appeared in off-Broadway revue Another Evening with Harry Stoones 1961; appeared at Caucus Club, Detroit and Blue Angel, New York 1961; played in musical comedy I Can Get It for You Wholesale 1962; began recording career with Columbia Records 1963; appeared in musical play Funny Girl, New York 1964, London 1966; TV programme My Name is Barbra shown in UK, Netherlands, Australia, Sweden, Bermuda and the Philippines, winning five Emmy awards; second programme Color Me Barbra also shown abroad; numerous concert and nightclub appearances; Commdr des Arts et des Lettres 1984; New York Critics' Best Supporting Actress Award 1962; Grammy awards for Best Female Pop Vocalist 1963, 1964, 1965, 1977, 1986, special Grammy Legend Award for lifetime achievement 1992; London Critics' Musical Award 1966; American Guild of Variety Artists' Entertainer of the Year Award 1970; Dorothy Arzner Award (Women in Film Crystal Awards) 1992; Nat Medal of Arts. *Films:* Funny Girl (Acad Award) 1968, Hello Dolly 1969, On a Clear Day You Can See Forever 1969, The Owl and the Pussycat 1971, What's up Doc? 1972, Up the Sandbox 1973, The Way We Were 1973, For Pete's Sake 1974, Funny Lady 1975, A Star is Born 1977, Yentl 1983 (also dir and producer), Nuts 1987, Sing 1989, Prince of Tides (also dir, co-producer) 1990, The Mirror Has Two Faces (also dir) 1996; *Recordings include:* People 1965, My Name is Barbra 1965, The Way we Were 1974, Guilty 1980, The Broadway Album (Grammy Award) 1986, Love Songs, Just For the Record 1991, People 1991, Prince of Tides (soundtrack), Places That Belong to You (single) 1992, Back to Broadway 1993, Barbra Streisand, the Concert (double album and video) 1994, The Mirror Has Two Faces (soundtrack) 1996, Higher Ground 1997. *Address:* c/o Jeff Berg, ICM, 8942 Wilshire Blvd, Beverly Hills, CA 90211, USA.

STRETTON, Virginia Valda, MS; Australian civil servant; b 14 Feb 1947, Melbourne; d of Alan and Valda Stretton; m Colin Teese 1977 (divorced). *Education:* ANU (Canberra). *Career:* Australian Public Service 1964–; Dept of Business and Consumer Affairs 1976–82; Dept of the Prime Minister and Cabinet 1980–; various posts in the Dept of Industry, Tech and Commerce 1983–88, including Exec Dir Industry Research and Devt 1986–88, Asst Sec Chemicals, Plastics and Biotech 1986; various posts in Australian Customs Service, including Nat Man Industry Assistance 1988–91, Corp Services 1991–92, Inland Revenue 1993–94, Collector of Customs (Vic) 1994–95, Regional Dir, Vic 1995–. *Leisure interests:* golf, skiing, reading, music, tennis, backgammon. *Address:* Australian Customs Service – Victoria, Customs House, POB 2809, Melbourne, Vic 3001, Australia.

STRITCH, Elaine; American singer and actress; b 2 Feb 1925, Detroit, MI; d of George J. and Mildred (née Jobe) Stritch; m John Bay 1973 (died 1982). *Education:* Sacred Heart Convent (Detroit), Drama Workshop, New School for Social Research. *Career:* Broadway debut as Pamela Brewster in Loco 1946; Hon D HUM LITT (Stritch Univ). *Plays include:* Made in Heaven 1946, Three Indelicate Ladies 1947, The Shape of Things 1947, The Little Foxes 1947, Angel in the Wings 1947, Yes M'Lord 1949, Call Me Madam 1950, Pal Joey (revival) 1952, Bus Stop 1955, The Sin of Pat Muldoon 1957, Goldilocks (musical) 1958, Sail Away (New York) 1961, (London) 1962, Who's Afraid of Virginia Woolf? 1962, 1965, Wonderful Town 1967, Private Lives 1969, Company (New York) 1970, (London) 1971, Small Craft Warnings (London) 1973, The Gingerbread Lady (London) 1977, Suite in Two Keys 1982, Dancing in the End Zone 1983, Love Letters (London) 1990, A Delicate Balance (Drama Desk Award) 1996; *TV includes:* My Sister Eileen 1962, Full Moon Over Brooklyn, Red Peppers, Two's Company (series) 1975–76, 1979, Ellen Burstyn 1986–87, Stranded 1986, Law and Order (Emmy Award) 1991–1993, Third Rock From the Sun 1997, 2000, Soul Man 1998; *Films include:* The Scarlet Hour 1956, Three Violent People 1956, A Farewell to Arms 1957, The Perfect Furlough 1958, Who Killed Teddy Bear 1965, Pigeons 1971, Providence 1977, September 1988, Cocoon: The Return 1988, Cadillac Man 1990, Out to Sea 1997, Autumn in New York 2000, Screwed 2000, Small Time Crooks 2000; *Publication:* Am I Blue?: Living With Diabetes, Dammit, Having Fun 1984. *Address:* c/o Actors' Equity, 165 W 46th St, New York, NY 10036, USA; The Blake Agency, 415 N Camden Drive, Suite 121, Beverly Hills, CA 90210, USA.

STRÖJE-WILKENS, (Zackie Birgitta) Madeleine; Swedish diplomatist; b 15 August 1942; d of Herman and Agnes (née Isaksson) Ströje; m Martin Wilkens 1970; two s one d. *Education:* Darien High School (CT, USA), Coll of Landskrona, Univ of Lund and Ministry of Foreign Affairs (Sweden). *Career:* Joined Swedish Ministry of Foreign Affairs 1967; Second Sec Swedish Mission to the UN, New York, USA 1970–73; Resident Rep UNDP, Santiago, Chile 1973–75; First Sec, Policy Div and Div for Int Devt Co-operation, Stockholm 1975–81; Asst Resident Rep UNDP, Nairobi, Kenya 1981–85; Ind Consultant to devt projects, Maseru, Lesotho 1985–88; Deputy Dir Stockholm Int Peace Research Inst 1988–91; Amb to Chile 1992. *Leisure interests:* tennis, nature, theatre, books, skiing. *Address:* c/o Ministry of Foreign Affairs, Gustav Adolfstorg 1, 103 39 Stockholm, Sweden.

STRÖKER, Elisabeth, D PHIL; German professor of philosophy; b 17 Aug 1928, Dortmund; d of Wilhelm and Luise Ströker. *Education:* Univ of Bonn. *Career:* Mem teaching staff Univ of Hamburg; Prof Tech Univ Carolo Wilhelmina zu Braunschweig 1965, Dean 1968–70; Prof of Philosophy, Dir Dept of Philosophy and Dir Husserl Archives, Univ of Cologne 1971–, Dean 1976–77; Guest Prof at univs in the USA, Canada and Europe; mem various scientific and philosophical socs; Hon D PHIL. *Publications include:* Denkwege der Chemie 1967, Philosophische Untersuchung zum Raum (2nd edn 1977, trans to English 1986), Einführung in die Wissenschaftstheorie (4th edn 1992, trans to Japanese 1978, to Turkish 1990), Wissenschaftsgeschichte als Herausforderung (trans to Japanese 1980) 1976, Theoriewandel in der Wissenschaftsgeschichte 1982, Husserlian Foundations of Science 1986 (2nd edn 1996), Phänomenologische Studien 1987, Husserls transzendentale Phänomenologie (American edn 1990) 1987, Wissenschaftsphilosophische Studien 1989, Phänomenologische Philosophie (jtly) 1989, Wissenschaftsphilosophische Studien zur Chemie 1996, Contributions to Phenomenology 2000; also numerous essays on the philosophy and history of science, philosophy of language, phenomenology, ethics, etc. *Leisure interests:* history, literature, theology. *Address:* Wüllnerstr 135, 5000 Cologne, 41, Germany.

STROSSEN, Nadine, BA, JD; American human rights lawyer; b 18 Aug 1950, Jersey City, NJ; d of Woodrow John and Sylvia Strossen; m Eli Michael Noam 1980. *Education:* Harvard Law School and Radcliffe Coll. *Career:* Assoc Attorney Sullivan and Cromwell 1978–83; Partner Harvis and Zeichner 1983–84; mem Nat Bd of Dirs, American Civil Liberties Union (ACLU) 1983–, Pres 1991–, mem Advisory Cttee on Reproductive Freedom Project 1983–, Nat Exec Cttee 1985–, Nat Gen Council 1986–91, Pres 1991–; Asst Prof of Clinical Law, Faculty of Law, Univ of New York 1984–87, Visiting Prof of Law 1987–88, Prof of Law 1989–; Adjunct Prof Grad School of Business, Univ of Columbia 1990–; mem Exec Cttee Human Rights Watch 1989–91; mem Bd of Dirs Coalition to Free Soviet Jewry 1984–, Asia Watch 1987–(Vice-Chair 1989–91), Nat Coalition Against Censorship 1988, Middle East Watch 1989–91, The Fund for Free Expression 1990–; mem Steering Cttee New York Legal Council for Soviet Jewry 1987–; Jaycees Outstanding Young People of the World Award 1986. *Publications include:* Regulating Campus Hate Speech: A Modest Proposal? 1990, Recent US and International Judicial Protection of Individuals Rights: A Comparative Legal Process Analysis and Proposed Synthesis 1990, In Defense of Pornography: Free Speech and the Fight for Women's Rights 1995; numerous articles in professional journals. *Address:* New York Law School, 57 Worth St, New York, NY 10013-2959, USA; 450 Riverside Drive, #51, New York, NY 10027, USA (Home).

STRUCHKOVA, Raisa Stepanovna; Russian ballet dancer; b 5 Oct 1925, Moscow. *Education:* Bolshoi Theatre Ballet School. *Career:* Soloist Bolshoi Theatre Ballet 1944–67; Lecturer in Classical Dancing Lunacharsky State Inst of Theatrical Art 1968, Prof 1978–; Ed-in-Chief Sovietskiy Balet (now Balet) journal 1981–96; Coach, Bolshoi Theatre 1996–; mem CPSU 1962–91; People's Artist of USSR 1958. *Ballets include:* Cinderella, Romeo and Juliet, Giselle, Sleeping Beauty, Swan Lake, Don Quixote, Copper Rider, Red Poppy, Fountain of Bakchchisarai, Flames of Paris, Gayane, Walpurgisnacht; *Films:* Crystal Slipper, Your Name. *Address:* Bolshoi Theatre, Teatralnaya pl 1, 103009 Moscow, Russian Federation. *Telephone:* (095) 915-40-57.

STRUM, Shirley Carol, PH D; American primatologist; b 11 Sept 1947, Stuttgart, Germany; d of Joseph and Ellen Strum; m David Western 1983; one s one d. *Education:* Univ of California at Berkeley. *Career:* Field Research on baboons 1972–; apptd Prof of Anthropology Univ of California at San Diego 1974; apptd Dir Uaso Ngiro Baboon Project, Kenya 1975; Research Assoc Inst of Primate Research, Kenya since 1977; Research Fellow New York Zoological Soc Wildlife Conservation Int 1982; mem Primate Specialist Group 1982–; Adviser to Govt of Kenya on conservation 1982–88; discovered social complexity of baboon soc 1976; revised evolutionary view of aggression and intelligence 1978; active in worldwide conservation; conservation experiment to translocate three groups of baboons 1984; Distinguished Prof of the Year Univ of California at San Diego 1987–88; Outstanding Contribution to Wildlife Clubs of Kenya Award 1988; many other grants and awards. *TV appearances include:* The Nature of Things (CBC) 1982, Moving Day for the Pumphouse Gang (Survival Anglia Productions, UK) 1984, Trials of Life: Friends and Rivals (BBC Natural History Unit, UK) 1991; numerous other TV programmes for French, British, Canadian, etc channels; *Publications:* Appendix, Perspective on Human Evolution (jtly) 1973, Almost Human: a journey into the world of baboons (trans into many languages) 1987; numerous articles in journals. *Address:* University of California, Dept of Anthropology, Gilman Drive, La Jolla, CA 92093-0101, USA; Wildlife Conservation International, Box 62844, Nairobi, Kenya. *Telephone:* (619) 534-4145 (California); (2) 21699 (Nairobi); *Fax:* (2) 215969 (Nairobi).

STRUNECKÁ, Anna, D SC; Czech scientist; b 24 Jan 1944, Prague; d of Václav Smutný and Anna Smutná; m Otakar Strunecký; one s one d. *Education:* Prague High School and Charles Univ (Prague). *Career:* Prof of Physiology Faculty of Sciences, Charles Univ 1980–, Head of Dept 1980–91; mem CP of Czechoslovakia 1965–91, New York Acad of Sciences; Woman of the Year (ABI, USA) 1995. *Publications:* over 300 papers in scientific journals about the role of phospholipids in pathophysiology and the detrimental effects of aluminium and fluoride in the environment; 4 textbooks on Physiology (in Czech); produced CD-ROM Colourful Relaxation 1999. *Leisure interests:* alternative medicine, healing, gardening. *Address:* Charles University, Faculty of Science, Dept of Physiology, Viničná 7, 128 00 Prague 2, Czech Republic (Office); Bulharská 38, 10 101 Prague, Czech Republic (Home). *Telephone:* (2) 21953239 (Office); *Fax:* (2) 299713 (Office); *E-mail:* astrun@mboxcesnet.cz.

STUART, Mary Alice, BA, LLD; Canadian business executive; b 5 May 1928, Toronto, ON; d of Edgar Gordon and Clayton (née Callaway) Burton; m Alexander Kyle Stuart 1949; four s. *Education:* Branksome Hall School (Toronto) and Univ of Toronto. *Career:* Chair and CEO CJRT-FM Inc 1974–95, Emer 1995–; Dir S. C. Johnson and Son Ltd (Brandtford, ON), Bank of Montréal, Nat Ballet of Canada 1979–86 (Hon Gov 1986–), Bata Shoe Foundation 1985–, Int Mozart Festival 1991; Founder, Dir Malignant Hyperthermia Asscn 1979–83, Hon Dir 1983–; Trustee Metropolitan Toronto Community Foundation 1983–90, (Vice-Chair 1986–87), Canadian Museum of Civilization, Hull, PQ 1990–; Chair Int Choral Festival 1993; mem Univ Coll Cttee Univ of Toronto 1982–, Nat Chair $100 million Breakthrough Campaign 1987–90; Hon Gov Massey and Roy Thomson Halls 1987–; Pres The Burton Charitable Foundation 1981–; mem Advisory Cttee The Nature Conservancy Council of Canada 1985–, Bd of Govs Canadian Scottish Heritage Foundation 1985, Canadiana Fund Nat Capital Comm, Ottawa 1990–92 (Hon mem 1992–); mem Order of Canada 1991, Order of Ontario 1993. *Address:* 150 Mutual St, Toronto, ON M5B 2M1, Canada (Office); 52 Binscarth Rd, Toronto, ON M4W 1V4, Canada (Home).

STUBBS, Imogen, MA; British actress; b 20 Feb 1961, Rothbury; d of the late Robin Stubbs and Heather McCracken; m Trevor Nunn 1994; one d one s. *Education:* St Paul's Girls School (London), Exeter Coll (Oxford) and Royal Acad of Dramatic Art. *Career:* Stage debut in Cabaret 1985 and The Boyfriend, Ipswich; performed with the RSC 1986–91; Gold Medal, Chicago Film Festival. *Plays:* The Rover 1986, The Two Noble Kinsmen 1987, Richard II 1987–88, Othello 1991, Heartbreak House 1992, St Joan 1994, Uncle Vanya 1996, A Streetcar Named Desire 1996, Closer 1998, Betrayal 1998; *Films:* Privileged, A Summer Story 1988, Nanou 1988, Erik the Viking 1989, True Colors 1991, A Pin for the Butterfly, Fellow Traveller, Sandra c'est la vie, Jack and Sarah, Sense and Sensibility 1995, Twelfth Night 1996; *TV appearances include:* The Browning Version, Deadline, The Rainbow, Anna Lee, After the Dance. *Leisure interests:* writing, skiing, collecting junk. *Address:* UK.

STUCKEY, Johanna Heather, MA, PH D; Canadian professor emeritus of humanities; b 5 Sept 1933, Gananoque, ON; d of William Henry Stuckey and Mary M. F. Diplock (née Smith). *Education:* Univ of Toronto and Yale Univ (USA). *Career:* Lecturer in English Univ of Maryland (USA) 1961–64; Asst, later Assoc Prof York Univ 1962–94, Vice-Chair Faculty Asscn 1973–74, mem Religious Studies Programme 1982–, mem Women's Studies Programme 1982–, Co-ordinator 1986–89, Acting Master Founders Coll 1972–73, Chair Dept of Humanities 1974–79; Adviser to Pres on Status of Women 1981–85, Chair Senate Task Force on Status of Women 1972–75; Ed Canadian WomanStudies Journal 1981–84; mem Canadian Women's Studies Asscn, Canadian Soc for Mesopotamian Studies, Soc for Mediterranean Studies, American Schools of Oriental Research, Canadian Soc for Studies in Religion; Teaching Excellence Award Ontario Confed of Univ Faculty Asscns 1984. *Publications:* A Bibliography of Petronius (jtly) 1977, Senate Task Force Report on Status of Women (ed) 1975, Equity for Women: the first decade (ed) 1985, Feminist Spirituality: Feminist Theology in Judaism, Christianity, Islam, and Feminist Goddess Worship 1998; numerous articles in professional and popular journals. *Leisure interests:* cooking, swimming, philately. *Address:* c/o Founders College, York University, 4700 Keele St, North York, ON M3J 1P3, Canada. *E-mail:* jstuckey@yorku.ca.

STUDER, Cheryl; American opera singer (soprano); b 24 Oct 1955, Midland, MI; m 2nd Ewald Schwarz; two d (one by previous marriage). *Education:* Interlochen Arts Acad, Oberlin Coll (Cleveland, OH) and Univ of Tennessee. *Career:* Studied singing with Gwendolyn Pike, at Berkshire Music Centre, at Tanglewood with Phyllis Curtin and at Hochschule für Musik, Vienna with Hans Hotter; engaged for concert series with Boston Symphony Orchestra by Seiji Ozawa 1979; opera debut as the First Lady in The Magic Flute, Munich, Germany 1980–82; with Darmstadt State Theatre, Germany 1982–84, Deutsche

Oper, Berlin 1984–86; USA debut as Micaela in Carmen, Lyric Opera of Chicago, IL 1984; debut at Bayreuth, Germany 1985, Royal Opera House, Covent Garden, UK 1987, Metropolitan Opera, New York 1988; sings wide variety of roles, especially Wagner, Verdi, Mozart and Strauss; Int Music Award 1993; Vocalist of the Year, USA 1994. *Operas include:* The Magic Flute, Carmen, Arabella 1996. *Address:* c/o International Performing Artists Inc, 125 Crowfield Drive, Knoxville, TN 37922, USA.

STURGESS, Jennifer Mary, B SC, PH D; British medical practitioner and business executive; b 26 Sept 1944, Hucknall, Notts; d of Daniel and Dorothy Joan (née McKeand) Liptrot; m Robert W. J. Sturgess 1966; two s one d. *Education:* Univs of Bristol and London (UK). *Career:* Research Asst MRC, UK 1966–67; Research Asst in Experimental Pathology Brompton Hosp, London 1967–68; Lecturer in Experimental Pathology Univ of London 1966–70; Scientist Hosp for Sick Children, Research Inst of Toronto 1970–79, Consultant Scientist 1979–87; Assoc Prof of Pathology Univ of Toronto 1973–90, Prof 1990–, Assoc Dean Faculty of Medicine 1990–92; Pres Toronto Hosp Research Inst 1993–96; Pres The Sturgess Group Inc 1996–98; Dir Warner Lambert, Parke-Davis Research Inst 1979–86; Dir Medical and Scientific Affairs Warner Lambert (Canada) Inc 1986–89, Vice-Pres Scientific Affairs Parke-Davis, Warner Lambert (Canada) Inc 1986–90, mem Exec Cttee, Consultant Medical Dir Warner Lambert (Canada) 1996–98, Vice-Pres Clinical and Medical Research Warner Lambert (Europe) 1998–2001; mem Science Council of Canada 1987–92, MRC 1990–97, Nat Advisory Council on Pharmaceutical Research 1990–91, Health Industries Sector Council 1994–; mem Bd Dirs ON Cancer Inst/Princess Margaret Hospital 1992–93; Sr Fellow Massey Coll 1992–94; Adviser WHO, Int Paediatric Asscn; Consultant NIH, USA; Scholar Medical Research Council of Canada 1974–79; Scientific Award, Canadian Asscn of Pathologists 1975. *Publications:* Electron Microscopy (ed) 1978, Perspectives in Cystic Fibrosis 1980. *Address:* 80 Hazelton Ave, Toronto, ON M5R 2E2, Canada (Home). *Telephone:* (416) 975-5194 (Office); *Fax:* (416) 975-2547 (Office); *E-mail:* sturgess@sympatico.ca.

STYLES, Margretta, ED D; American professor of nursing; b 19 March 1930, Mt Union, PA; d of Russell B. and Agnes Wilson Madden; m Douglas F. Styles 1954; two s one d. *Education:* Juniata Coll, Yale Univ and Univ of Florida. *Career:* Prof and Dean School of Nursing, Univ of Texas at San Antonio 1969–73, Wayne State Univ, Detroit 1973–77, Univ of California at San Francisco 1977–87, Prof and Livingston Chair in Nursing 1987–; Pres Int Council of Nurses 1996–, American Nurses Credentialing Center 1996–; mem Nat Comm on Nursing 1980–; Pres American Nurses' Asscn 1986–88; First Distinguished Scholar, American Nurses' Foundation; mem NAS, Inst of Medicine; Hon Recognition Award, American Nurses' Asscn. *Publications:* On Nursing: Toward a New Endowment, Project on the Regulation of Nursing, Int Council of Nurses 1985. *Leisure interest:* sky-diving. *Address:* University of California at San Francisco, School of Nursing, N 531C-D, Box 0608, San Francisco, CA 94143, USA (Office); 12 Commons Lane, Foster City, CA 94404, USA (Home). *Telephone:* (415) 476-6701 (Office); (415) 754-3870 (Home).

SU YE; Chinese writer and film editor; b 31 Aug 1949, Honjiang, Hunan Dist; d of the late Sue Linxun and Wen Zhinan; m Chen Chunnian 1980 (divorced 1991); one s. *Education:* Jiangsu Jr Coll of Theatre and Nanjing Univ. *Career:* Mem Jiangsu Song and Dance Ensemble Chorus 1970; Narrator Nanjing Film Studio 1972–79, apptd Ed 1979; Writer 1979–; mem Chinese Writers' Union 1980; First Prize for Prose (Youth Magazine) 1982, Fiction Competition (Nanjing Daily) 1983, for Literature (Nanjing Municipal) 1986, Yan Wu Literary Works Solicitation 1988, Jinling Full Moon Prose Competition 1991; Gold Cup Award, Spring Breeze Monthly 1988; Second Prize for Literature, Nanjing Municipal 1989; Creation Award, Supplement to Nanjing Daily 1989; Literary Prize, Chinese Writers' Union and China Literary Foundation 1990; Third Prize for Excellent Works, Chinese Newspapers' Supplements 1990. *Publications include:* Infatuation (Short story) 1982, Ever Hard to Forget 1986, Paper Wild Goose 1988, Ode to the Starry Sky 1991, A Visit to La She's Tea House 1990, Only the Fan-shaped Cliff 1992, Ever Hard to Forget (collected prose) 1992. *Leisure interests:* music, fine arts, film, travel. *Address:* c/o 43 Gulou Lane, Rm 701, Nanjing 210008, People's Republic of China.

SUBADIO, Haryati, PH D; Indonesian politician; b 24 June 1928. *Education:* Gemeentelijke Univ (Amsterdam). *Career:* Lecturer Univ of Indonesia 1957, Prof 1975, Dean Faculty of Letters 1975–78; Head Faculties of Art and Philosophy, Dept of Educ and Culture 1972–77, Dir-Gen Culture 1978–88; Minister of Social Affairs 1988–93. *Address:* c/o Ministry of Social Affairs, Jalan Ir H. Juanda 36, Jakarta Pusat, Indonesia. *Telephone:* (21) 341329.

SUBBULAKSHMI, Madurai Shanmugavadivu; Indian classical musician; b 16 Sept 1916, Madurai; m T. Sadasivam 1940. *Education:* Privately. *Career:* Recitals with her mother, Guru Veena Shanmugavadivu 1928–32; gave solo performances and became a leading classical Karnatic musician before age 18; acted title role in Hindi film Meera; numerous benefit performances, donated royalties from many of her records to social and religious causes; rep Karnatic music at Edinburgh Festival 1963; seven-week tour of USA 1966; concerts and performances in London, Frankfurt (Germany), Geneva (Switzerland), Cairo, Tokyo, Bangkok, Hong Kong, Manila, Singapore, Malaysia, New York and Pittsburgh (USA); Pres Madras Music Acad Conf 1968; Nat Research Prof 1995–; Producer Emer, All India Radio and Doordarshan 1979–; Life mem Int Music Council 1981; Trustee Indira Gandhi Nat Centre for Arts; Hon D LITT (Ravindra Bharati Univ) 1967, (Shri Venkateswara Univ) 1971, (Delhi) 1973, (Banaras Hindu Univ), (Madhya Pradesh) 1979, (Madras) 1987, (Tirupati) 1989, (Madurai Kamaraj) 1994; Padma Bhushan 1954; Pres's Award for Karnatic Music 1956; Ramon Magsaysay Award for Public Service (Philippines) 1974; Sangeet Natak Acad Fellowship 1974; Padma Vibhushan 1975; hon title Sangeetha Khalanidhi, Sapthagiri Sangeetha Vidwanmani 1975, Thanipperum Kalagnyar 1980, Gayaka Ratnam 1990; Melvin Jones Fellowship Award for Outstanding Humanitarian Services 1986; Indira Gandhi Award 1990; Woman of the Year Award, Int Women's Asscn 1992; Swaralaya Puraskaram–Delhi Award 1997. *Address:* 'Sivam-Subham', 11 First Main Rd, Kotturpuram, Chennai 600 085, India. *Telephone:* (44) 472288.

SUCHOCKA, Hanna, D IUR; Polish politician and lawyer; b 3 April 1946, Pleszew. *Education:* Adam Mickiewicz Univ (Poznań). *Career:* Scientific worker Dept of Constitutional Law, Adam Mickiewicz Univ, Poznań 1972–89, Catholic Univ, Lublin 1988–92, Polish Acad of Science 1990–; mem Democratic Party 1969–84; Deputy to Sejm (Parl) 1980–84, 1989–; mem Civic Parl Club 1989–91, Democratic Union Club 1991–94, Freedom Union 1994–, Deputy Chair Parl Legislative Comm 1989–92; Chair Council of Ministers (first woman Prime Minister) 1992–93; Minister of Justice and Attorney-Gen 1997–99; mem Pontifical Acad of Social Sciences 1994–; author of reports and articles for professional publs and int confs; Dr hc (Oklahoma); Max Schmidt Heine Prize 1994. *Address:* c/o Ministerstwo Sprawiedliwosci, Al Ujazdowskie 11, 00-950 Warsaw, Poland.

SUDARKASA, Niara, PH D; American university president and anthropologist; b 14 Aug 1938, Fort Lauderdale, FL; d of Alex Charlton and Rowena (née Evans) Marshall; m John L. Sudarkasa. *Education:* Fisk Univ (TN), Oberlin Coll (OH) and Columbia Univ (NY). *Career:* Asst Prof of Anthropology New York Univ 1964–67; Asst Prof Univ of Michigan, Ann Arbor 1967–70, Assoc Prof 1970–76, Prof 1976–87, Dir Center for Afro-American/African Studies 1981–84, Assoc Vice-Pres of Acad Affairs 1984–87; apptd Pres Lincoln Univ, PA 1987; mem Bd Dirs Ford Foundation Project on New Immigrants and Established Residents 1987, Pennsylvania Econ Devt Partnership 1987, The Barnes Foundation 1989; Fulbright Sr Research Scholar, Benin 1982–83; Ford Foundation Foreign Area Training Fellow 1960–63; Middle East and Africa Research Fellow 1973–74, Grantee 1983–84; Research Council for African Studies Fellow 1973–74; numerous honours and awards include Dr Niara Sudarkasa Day, Fort Lauderdale (FL) 1976, Borough of Manhattan (New York) 1987, Altanic City, Atlanta (GA) 1987; E. Luther Cunningham Award 1988; One of Top 100 Business and Professional Women (Dollars and Sense Magazine) 1988; Frederick D. Patterson Award 1988. *Publications include:* Where Women Work 1973, Women and National Development (co-ed) 1977; numerous contribs to professional journals. *Address:* Lincoln University, Office of the President, PA 19352, USA.

SUDRE, Margie (Marguerite Josette Germaine); French politician and medical practitioner; b 17 Oct 1943, Vinh, Indochina; d of Robert Demaiche and N'Guyen-Thi-Khue; m Camille Sudre 1984. *Education:* Faculty of Medicine, Marseilles. *Career:* Anaesthetist, Marseilles N Hosp 1969–73, Belledonne Clinic, Grenoble 1973–77, Jeanne d'Arc Clinic, Port, Réunion 1977–95; Chair Regional Council, Réunion 1993–; Sec of State for French-speaking Communities 1995–97; Pres Tourism Bureau Réunion 1998–; MEP (Union pour l'Europe) 1999–. *Address:* European Parliament, rue Wiertz, 1047 Brussels, Belgium.

SUHASINI; Indian actress. *Career:* Has worked in more than 50 films in four languages; numerous awards for acting and directing; Nat Award for Performance 1995. *Films include:* Nenjathai Killathe, Gopurangal Saivathillai, Lottery Ticket, Koode Vide, Adaminte Variyethu, Sindhu Bhairavi, India 1995, Vanaprastham 1999, Teergadanam 2001, Women with Vision: Crossing Boundaries (dir) 2001; *TV includes:* Dir: Penn (series – India's Best Serial, Best Directing Awards). *Address:* 172 Eldams Rd, Alwarpet, Chennai 600 018, India.

SUI, Anna; American fashion designer; b 1955, Dearborn Heights, MI; d of Paul and Grace Sui. *Education:* Parsons School of Design (New York). *Career:* First catwalk show 1991; f own design co Anna Sui 1992–; opened boutiques, Macy's, Herald Square, New York and SoHo dist, New York 1992; est reputation with 'baby-doll' collection 1993; launched new line of special-occasion gowns 1997; Perry Ellis Award for New Fasion Talent, Council of Fashion Designers of America 1992. *Address:* 113 Green St, New York, NY 10012, USA.

SUKARNOPUTRI, Megawati (see Megawati Sukarnoputri).

SUKOWA, Barbara; German actress; b 1950, Bremen; m Hans-Michael Rehberg; one s. *Education:* Max-Reinhardt-Seminar (Berlin). *Career:* Has performed at theatres in Darmstadt 1971, Bremen, Frankfurt/Main and Hamburg 1976–80, Munich 1981; Bundesfilmpreis/Filmband in Gold (for Die bleierne Zeit and Lola) 1982. *Films include:* Lola 1981, Death Game 1982, Die bleierne Zeit, Rosa Luxembourg (Palme d'Or, Cannes Film Festival) 1986, Der Rückkehr, Homo Faber, Europa, Voyager 1992; *TV appearances include:* Berlin Alexanderplatz (series). *Address:* Agentur Jovanovic, Kathi-Kobus-Str 24, 80797 Munich, Germany.

ŠULÍKOVÁ, Ol'ga Simona Petronela, MA; Slovak actress; b 12 May 1965, Bratislava; d of Ladislav and Ol'ga Margaréta Páleník; m Martin Šulík 1988. *Education:* Acad of Dramatic Arts (Bratislava). *Career:* Actress 1987–, at Theatre JGT, Zvolen 1987–89, Nat Theatre of Martin 1989–. *Films include:* Smug Citizens 1987, Baal 1988, Season's Greetings 1989, The Visit 1989, La Ronde 1990, The Raven 1991; numerous roles in theatre, TV and radio productions. *Leisure interests:* art, music, sports. *Address:* National Theatre of Martin, Martin, Slovakia (Office); Bárdošova 7, 831 01 Bratislava, Slovakia (Home). *Telephone:* (842) 32444 (Office); (7) 373617 (Home).

SULIOTIS, Elena; Greek opera singer (soprano); b 28 May 1943, Athens; d of Constantino Souliotis and Gallia Cavalengo; m Marcello Guerrini 1970; one d. *Education:* Buenos Aires (Argentina) and Milan (Italy). *Career:* Grew up in Argentina; went to Milan and was introduced to Gianandrea Gavazzeni 1962; studied singing with Mercedes Llopart; debut in Cavalleria Rusticana, Teatro San Carlo, Naples, Italy 1964; sang in Un Ballo in Maschera, Trieste 1965 and has since sung frequently throughout Italy; debut at La Scala, Milan in Nabucco 1966; USA debut in Mefistofele, Chicago, IL 1966; debut at Covent Garden, London in Macbeth 1969; has also appeared at Teatro Colón, Buenos Aires and in Rio de Janeiro, São Paulo (Brazil), México City, New York, Dallas, Philadelphia and San Antonio (USA), Montréal (Canada), Paris, Kiel and Lübeck (Germany), Tokyo, Lisbon, Athens and Madrid; has recorded Norma, Cavalleria Rusticana, Nabucco, Anna Bolena, Macbeth and arias for Decca; recipient of several prizes. *Operas include:* Manon Lescaut, La Gioconda, Macbeth, Norma, Otello, Aida, Luisa Miller, Il Trovatore, Tosca, Loreley, La Forza del Destino, etc. *Leisure interests:* country life, looking after plants and animals. *Address:* Villa il Poderino, via Incontri 38, Florence, Italy.

SULLEROT, Evelyne Annie Henriette, L ÈS L; French sociologist, journalist and writer; b 10 Oct 1924, Montrouge, Seine; d of André and Georgette (née Roustain) Pasteur; m François Sullerot 1946; three s one d. *Education:* Colls of Compiègne, Royan and Uzès, Free School of Political Sciences, Univs of Paris and Aix-en-Provence. *Career:* Teacher 1947–49; f French Family Planning Movt 1955, Sec-Gen 1955–58, then Hon Pres; Researcher Centre for Mass Communications, Tech Coll 1960–63; teacher French Press Inst 1963–68; Prof Free Univ of Brussels 1966–68; Head Faculty of Letters Univ of Paris (Nanterre) 1967; Specialist EC 1969–92, ILO 1970; mem Econ and Social Council 1974–89; Founder, Pres Retravailler (Back to Work) Centres; mem Nat Advisory Comm for Human Rights 1986–99; fmr mem French Comm UNESCO; Corresp mem Acad des sciences morales et politiques 1999; Officier de la Légion d'Honneur; Commdr de l'Ordre Nat du Mérite. *Publications:* La presse féminine 1963, La vie des femmes 1964, Demain les femmes 1965, Aspects sociaux de la radiotélévision 1966, Histoire de la presse féminine des origines à 1848 1966, Histoire et sociologie du travail féminin 1968, Le droit de regard, La femme dans le monde moderne 1970, Les françaises aux travail 1973, Les crèches et les équipements d'accueil pour la petite enfance (jtly) 1974, Histoire et mythologie de l'amour 1976, Le fait féminin 1978, L'Aman 1981, Le statut matrimonial et ses conséquences juridiques, fiscales et sociales 1984, Pour le meilleur et sans le pire 1984, L'âge de travailler 1986, L'enveloppe 1987, Quels pères? Quels fils? 1992, Alias 1996, Le grand remue-ménage, la crise de la famille 1997; numerous research papers for UNESCO, OECD, EU, ILO. *Address:* 95 blvd Saint-Michel, 75005 Paris, France.

SULLIVAN, Kathryn D., PH D; American geologist and astronaut; b 3 Oct 1951, Paterson, NJ; d of Donald P. and Barbara K. Sullivan. *Education:* Univ of California at Santa Cruz and Dalhousie Univ (Canada). *Career:* Joined NASA 1978–, Astronaut 1979–93, mission specialist flight STS-41G 1984, flight STS-31 1990; Adjunct Prof Rice Univ, Houston, TX 1985–92; mem Nat Comm on Space 1985–86, Exec Panel Chief of Naval Operations 1988–; first woman to perform extra-vehicular activity; Lieut-Commdr US Naval Reserve; mem Geology Soc of America, American Geophysicists' Union, Soc of Women Geographers, Explorers' Club, American Inst for Aeronautics and Astronautics; Trophy of Nat Air and Space Museum (Smithsonian Inst, Washington, DC); Space Flight Medal NASA 1984, 1990, 1992; Exceptional Service Medal 1985; Haley Space Flight Award 1991; Outstanding Leadership Medal 1992. *Address:* Dept Commerce NOAA, 14th and Constitution Ave NW, Washington, DC 20230, USA (Office); 2610 Key Blvd, Arlington, VA 22201, USA (Home).

SULLIVAN, Kathryn Jean, BA; Australian politician; b 8 March 1942, Brisbane; d of Andrew I. and Edna Mavis (née Sproul) Martin; m Robert Sullivan 1983. *Education:* Univ of Queensland. *Career:* Grammar school teacher 1964–66; Exec mem Trade Union for Teachers at Independent Schools 1964–66; Admin Officer Univ of Queensland 1966–74; part-time Lecturer Queensland Inst of Tech 1971–73; part-time Adult Educ Lecturer 1971–73; Life mem Queensland State Young Liberal s 1964–; mem Liberal Party State Exec (Queensland) 1974–77, 1979–81, 1982–83; mem Jt House Cttee 1974, mem and Chair of several standing and estimates cttees 1974–84, Asst Whip in Senate 1975–77, mem, then Chair Coalition Parl Policy Cttees on Rural Affairs, Tourism, Educ, Youth Affairs, Employment and Training 1976–79, (Sec 1985–88), on Immigration and Ethnic Affairs 1985–90, Chair Senate House Cttee 1981–83, mem Jt Standing Cttee on New Parl House 1981–89; Shadow Minister for Home Affairs and Admin Services 1983–84; Deputy Chair House of Reps Standing Cttee on Employment, Educ and Training 1987–90, House of Reps Cttees 1990–; Parl Opposition Del and Deputy Leader Confs on Inter-Parl Union 1990–93; Parl Sec Deputy Leader Opposition 1993–94; Deputy Opposition Whip 1994–96; mem Speakers Panel, House of Reps 1997–97; Fed Parl Sec to Minister for Foreign Affairs 1997–2000; Exec mem Amnesty Int Parl Group 1986–; Vice-Pres Australian Parl Asscn for UNICEF 1987–; mem Govt Del to Japan and China 1977, Commonwealth Del to Bangladesh, India and Sri Lanka 1978, USA Congressional Women's Del to Phnom Penh 1979, Australian Del to UN World Conf on Women (Copenhagen) 1980; Govt Rep Australian Del to 35th Gen Ass of UN 1980; Deputy Leader Parl Del to Fiji, Western Samoa, Vanuatu and Solomon Islands 1989; Trustee Queensland Children's Leukaemia Soc; Assoc Fellow Australian Inst of Man;

Vice-Pres Nat Council of Women (Queensland); Outstanding Young Australian of the Year 1976. *Leisure interests:* theatre, reading, music, gardening, sport (as spectator). *Address:* House of Representatives, Parliament House, Rm M80, Canberra, ACT 2600, Australia. *Telephone:* (62) 277-7111; *Fax:* (62) 277-8594.

SUMMER, Donna; American singer and actress; b (LaDonna Adrian Gaines) 31 Dec 1948, Boston, MA; d of Andrew and Mary Gaines; m 1st Helmut Sommer (divorced); one d; m 2nd Bruce Sudano; one s one d. *Career:* Singer 1967–; appeared in German stage production of Hair; in Europe 1967–75, appearing in Vienna Folk productions of Porgy and Bess, and German productions of The Me Nobody Knows; Best Rhythm and Blues Female Vocalist, Nat Acad of Recording Arts and Sciences 1978; Best Female Rock Vocalist, Favourite Female Pop Vocalist, American Music Awards 1979; Favourite Female Vocalist of Soul Music 1979; Ampex Golden Reel Award for single and album On the Radio 1979, album Bad Girls; Soul Artist of the Year, Rolling Stone Magazine 1979; Best Rock Performance, Best of Las Vegas Jimmy Award 1980; Grammy Award for Best Inspirational Performance 1984; several awards for best-selling records; has sold over 20 million records. *Albums:* The Wanderer, Star Collection, Love to Love You Baby, Love Trilogy, Four Seasons of Love, I Remember Yesterday, The Deep, Shut Out, Once upon a Time, Bad Girls, On the Radio, Walk Away, She Works Hard for the Money, Cats without Claws, All Systems Go 1988, Another Time and Place 1989, Endless Summer 1994, I'm a Rainbow 1996, Live & More Encore 1999. *Address:* 2401 Main St, Santa Monica, CA 90405, USA.

SUN JIA-XIU, Dora, MA; Chinese professor of drama; b 15 Jan 1915, Tientsin; d of the late Sun Feng-Zao and Sun Xuan-Wei-Zhen; m Wu Bao-Dan; two s one d. *Education:* Keen School (Tientsin), Yenching Univ, Mills Coll (CA, USA) and Mount Holyoke Coll (MA, USA). *Career:* Lecturer Dept of English S Western Associated Univ 1940–41; Prof of English Tongji Univ 1942; Prof of English Literature Wuhan Univ 1942–46; Prof of Western Drama and Dramatic Theory Nanking Drama School 1948–49; Prof of Dramatic Literature Cen Acad of Drama 1949–95, Chair Dept of Dramatic Literature 1953–56, 1978–81, Dir Shakespeare Research Centre 1980–94; mem Nat Cttee Chinese Consultative Conf 1982–92; Vice-Chair Shakespeare Soc of China; title of Nat 8 March Red Banner Pace-setter conferred (twice); Model Worker of Beijing; Advanced Worker, Cen Drama Acad. *Publications include:* Repatriation (play) 1973, Marx, Engels and Shakespearean Drama 1978, Li Ya Wang (adaptation of King Lear) 1986, On the Four Great Tragedies of Shakespeare 1988, Shakespeare Dictionary (ed) 1992, Shakespeare and Western Modern Drama 1994, Essays on Shakespeare 1995. *Leisure interests:* watching plays and good TV, reading, visiting friends and relatives. *Address:* The Central Academy of Drama, Beijing, People's Republic of China (Office); 7 Da Xiang-feng, Back Sea, Beijing 10009, People's Republic of China (Home). *Telephone:* (1) 66182368 (Home).

SUONIO, Kaarina Elisabet, MA, LL M; Finnish politician, lawyer and psychologist; b 7 Feb 1941, Helsinki; d of Karl Otto Brusiin and Ulla Helena Raassina; m 1st Reino Kalevi 1961; m 2nd Kyösti Kullervo Suonio 1967 (divorced 1977); one s one d; m 3rd Ilkka Kaarlo Tanner 1993. *Education:* Univ of Helsinki. *Career:* Psychologist Inst of Occupational Health 1963–71; Researcher Ministry of Justice 1971–75; mem Helsinki City Council 1973–; mem Eduskunta (Parl) 1975–86; Alt mem Social Democratic Party Exec 1981–84; Second Minister of Educ (Minister of Culture and Science) 1982–83, Minister of Educ 1983–86; Deputy Mayor of Tampere 1986–94; Gov Province of Häme 1994–97; Man Dir Tampere Hall Conf and Concert Centre 1997; Commdr des Arts et des Lettres. *Address:* c/o Box 16, 33101 Tampere, Finland. *Telephone:* (40) 5509701 (Home); *Fax:* (3) 2434199 (Office); (3) 6372175 (Home); *E-mail:* kaarina.suonio@tampere.talo.fi (Office); kaarina.suonio@mail.htk.fi (Home); *Internet:* www.tampere.fi/ tampere-talo (Office).

SÜRER, Nur; Turkish actress; b 21 June 1954, Bursa; d of Ahmet and Rabia Sürer; m Bülent Kayabaş 1981; one s. *Education:* Bursa Girls' High School. *Career:* Actress in 20 films 1979–; Best Actress Award Nat Film Festival (Antalya) 1982, 1989; Best Actress Award, Movie Authors 1983. *Films include:* Anya (The Mirror) 1984, Umuda Yolculuk

(Journey of Hope, Acad Award Winner) 1990, Uzlaşma 1991. *Leisure interests:* travel, reading, music, sport. *Address:* Ihlamur Yolu, 19 Mayis Apt 60/1, Teşvikiye, Istanbul, Turkey. *Telephone:* (1) 2411241.

SUSANTI, Susi; Indonesian sportswoman. *Career:* Gold Medallist Badminton (singles), Olympic Games, Barcelona, Spain 1992; Bronze Medallist Badminton (singles), Olympic Games, Atlanta, GA, USA 1996.

ŠUŠIĆ, Veselinka, MD; Yugoslav professor of physiology; b 11 May 1934, Belgrade; m 1982; one d. *Education:* Univ of Belgrade and Stanford Univ Medical School (USA). *Career:* Post-doctoral Fellow in Psychiatry, Stanford Univ Medical School, CA (USA) 1966–67; Lecturer in Physiology, then Prof and Clinical Consultant in Neurology and Psychiatry at sleep disorder centre, Univ of Belgrade Medical School; f experimental sleep laboratory; mem Serbian Acad of Science and Arts, Serbian Medical Asscn; publications on sleep and REM (rapid eye movt) sleep deprivation and its consequences; invited speaker at several congresses on sleep; October Award for Science, Belgrade 1979. *Leisure interests:* walking, reading. *Address:* 11000 Belgrade, Maglajska 34, Yugoslavia. *Telephone:* (11) 660-983; *Fax:* (11) 644-263.

SÜSSMUTH, Rita, D PHIL; German professor of education and politician; b 17 Feb 1937, Wuppertal; m Hans Süßmuth; one d. *Education:* Münster, Tübingen and Paris. *Career:* Research Asst Univs of Stuttgart and Osnabrück 1963–66; Asst Prof Pädagogische Hochschule Ruhr 1966, Prof 1971; Prof of Int Comparative Educ Ruhr-Univ Bochum 1969–82; Head Inst for Social Educ, Prof of Educ Univ of Dortmund 1980–; Dir Inst Frau und Gesellschaft, Hanover 1982–85; Adviser to Ministry of Youth, Family, Women and Health Affairs 1971–85; mem CDU 1981–, Fed Chair CDU Women's Union 1986, Vice-Chair Niedersachsen CDU 1988–, mem CDU Presidium; Minister of Youth, Family, Women and Health Affairs 1986–88; mem Bundestag (Parl) for Göttingen 1987–, Pres Bundestag 1988–98; Chair Comm for Immigration 2000–; Pres German Asscn of Adult Educ Centres 1998; mem Advisory Council, Bertelsmann Stiftung 1997–; Vice-Pres Familienbund Deutscher Katholiken 1980–85; Dr hc (Hildesheim) 1988, (Bochum) 1990, (Veliko Tarnovo, Czech Repub) 1994, (Timisoara, Romania) 1995, (Sorbonne Nouvelle) 1996, (Johns Hopkins) 1998, (Ben Gurion, Israel) 1998. *Publications:* Frauen: Der Resignation keine Chance 1985, Aids: Wege aus dem Angst 1987, Kämpfen und Bewegen: Frauenreden 1989, Wenn der Zeit der Rhythmus ändert 1991, Die planlosen Eliten (jtly) 1993, Wer nicht Kämpft, hat schon verloren 2000. *Leisure interest:* tennis. *Address:* Bundestag, Platz der Republik 1, 11011 Berlin, Germany. *Telephone:* (30) 227-77998; *Fax:* (30) 227-76998.

SUTHERLAND, Dame Joan, OM, AC, DBE, FRCM; Australian opera singer (retd); b 7 Nov 1926, Sydney; d of William McDonald and Muriel Beatrice (née Alston) Sutherland; m Richard Bonynge 1954; one s. *Education:* St Catherine's School (Waverley, Sydney). *Career:* Debut as Dido in Purcell's Dido and Aeneas, Sydney 1947; singer with Royal Opera Co, Covent Garden, London 1952–88; has sung leading soprano roles at the Vienna State Opera, La Scala (Milan, Italy), Teatro Fenice (Venice, Italy), Opéra de Paris, Glyndebourne (UK), San Francisco (CA) and Chicago (IL) Operas and Metropolitan Opera (New York, USA), the Australian Opera, Hamburg Opera (Germany), the Canadian Opera, etc; has specialized in the popular and lesser-known bel canto operatic repertoire of the 18th and 19th centuries, has made numerous recordings; retd Oct 1990; Hon Life mem Australia Opera Co 1974; Hon D MUS (Sydney) 1984 and numerous hon degrees, awards and prizes. *Operas include:* Lucia di Lammermoor, La Traviata, Andriana Lecouvreur, Les Contes D'Hoffmann, Lucrezia Borgia, Semiramide, Don Giovanni, Faust, Die Zauberflöte, Dido and Aeneas, The Merry Widow, Les Huguenots etc; *Publication:* The Joan Sutherland Album (autobiog, jtly) 1986, A Prima Donna's Progress: the Autobiography of Joan Sutherland 1997. *Leisure interests:* reading, needlepoint, gardening. *Address:* c/o Ingpen and Williams, 26 Wadham Rd, London SW15 2LR, UK.

SUTHERLAND, Sandra D., QC, B COM, LL B; Canadian lawyer and business executive; b 12 June 1944, Vancouver, BC; d of C. R. and Lucille Sutherland. *Education:* Kitsilano High School and Univ of British Columbia. *Career:* Called to the Bar, BC and admitted as

Solicitor of the Supreme Court of British Columbia 1970; Assoc Campney and Murphy 1970–73, Partner 1973–79; Partner Freeman and Co, BC 1979, Partner Goodman, Freeman, Phillips & Vineberg int law firm; apptd QC 1984; Dir Vancouver City Savings Credit Union 1974–85, Vice-Chair 1977–81, Chair 1981–83; Dir British Columbia Cen Credit Union 1976–81, Vice-Chair 1980–81; Dir Insurance Corpn of British Columbia 1977–81; Public Gov Vancouver Stock Exchange 1977–80; Dir British Columbia Hydro and Power Authority 1981–92, The Imperial Life Assurance Co of Canada 1984, Yorkshire Trust Co 1985–87, Eaton Trust Co 1986–88; Tutor Co Law Course Bar Admission 1975–80, Head 1979–80; Dir Vancouver Opera Asscn 1984–, Vice-Pres 1988; Dir Power Smart Inc 1990–92; Trustee Vancouver Opera Foundation 1987–, Chair 1988; mem Personal Property Security Cttee, Canadian Bar Asscn 1976–; Chair Solicitors' Legal Opinions Cttee 1988, Personal Property Security Act Consultative Cttee 1992–; mem Law Soc of British Columbia. *Leisure interests:* reading, swimming, gardening, bridge, opera. *Address:* 3937 W 12th Ave, Vancouver, BC V5Z 4G3, Canada.

SUTHERLAND, Dame Veronica Evelyn, DBE, MA; British diplomatist; b 25 April 1939, York; d of the late Lieut-Col Maurice G. Beckett and of Constance M. Cavenagh-Mainwaring; m Alex James Sutherland 1981. *Education:* Royal School (Bath) and Univs of London and Southampton. *Career:* Entered Diplomatic Service 1965; Second, then First Sec, Sweden 1967–70, India 1975–80; FCO 1970–75, 1978–80, Counsellor 1981, 1984–87, Asst Under-Sec of State (Personnel) 1990–95; Perm Del to UNESCO 1981–84; Amb to Côte d'Ivoire, Burkina Faso and Niger 1987–90, to Ireland 1995–99; Deputy Sec-Gen (Econ and Social) Commonwealth Secr, London 1999–2001; Pres Lucy Cavendish Coll, Cambridge Univ Oct 2001–; Chair Airey Neave Trust 2000–; Hon LL D (Trinity Coll, Dublin) 1998. *Leisure interests:* theatre, painting. *Address:* Lucy Cavendish College, Cambridge CB3 0BU, UK.

SUZMAN, Helen, B COM; South African politician (retd); b 7 Nov 1917, Germiston, Transvaal; m M. M. Suzman 1937 (died 1994); two d. *Education:* Parktown Convent and Univ of the Witwatersrand. *Career:* Asst Statistician, War Supplies Bd 1941–44; part-time Lecturer Dept of Econs and Econ History, Univ of the Witwatersrand 1944–52; MP for Houghton 1953–89; mem United Party 1953–61, Progressive Party (now Progressive Fed Party, merged with Democratic Party 1989) 1961–89; Pres S African Inst of Race Relations 1991–93; part-time mem S African Human Rights Comm 1996–98; Hon Fellow St Hugh's Coll, Oxford 1973, LSE 1975, New Hall, Cambridge 1990; 28 hon doctorates; recipient Human Rights Award, UN 1978; Medallion of Heroism (New York) 1980; American Liberties Medallion, American Jewish Cttee 1984; Moses Mendelssohn Award, Berlin Senate 1988; Hon DBE 1989; Order of Merit (Gold) 1997. *Publication:* In No Uncertain Terms (memoirs) 1993. *Leisure interests:* fishing, bridge. *Address:* 52 Second Avenue, Illovo, Sandton 2196, South Africa. *Telephone:* (11) 788-2833; *Fax:* (11) 788-2833.

SUZMAN, Janet, BA; British actress and director; b 9 Feb 1939, Johannesburg; d of Saul and Betty (née Sonnenberg) Suzman; m Trevor Nunn 1969 (divorced 1986); one s. *Education:* Kingsmead Coll, Univ of the Witwatersrand (SA) and London Acad of Music and Dramatic Art. *Career:* Moved to UK 1960; Vice-Pres Council of London Acad of Music and Dramatic Art; delivered Tanner Lectures, Brasenose Coll, Oxford 1995, The Drapers Lecture Queen Mary and Westfield Coll, Univ of London 1996, The Morell Lecture Univ of York 1999; Vice-Chair Council of London Acad of Music and Dramatic Art; Hon Assoc Artist RSC; Hon Patron the Market Theatre; Hon MA (Open Univ) 1986; Hon D LITT (Warwick) 1990, (Leicester) 1992, (Queen Mary and Westfield, London) 1997; Hon Assoc Artist RSC; Best Actress, London Evening Standard Drama Award 1973, 1976; Plays and Players Best Actress Award 1976, Barclays Award for Best Director 1997. *Plays include:* With RSC: Joan of Arc, Henry IV (part I), The Birthday Party 1963–64, The Merchant of Venice, The Balcony, She Stoops to Conquer 1966, The Relapse 1967, Much Ado About Nothing, As You Like It 1968–69, Antony and Cleopatra 1972–73, Hello and Goodbye 1973, Three Sisters 1976; With other cos: The Good Woman of Setzuan (Tyneside Theatre Co) 1976, (Royal Court Theatre) 1977, Hedda Gabler 1977, Duchess of Malfi 1978, The Greeks 1980, Cowardice 1983, Boesman and Lena 1984, Vassa 1985, Andromache 1987,

Another Time 1989–90, Hippolytus 1991, The Sisters Rosensweig 1994/95, The Retreat from Moscow 1999; *Plays directed:* Othello (Johannesburg) 1987 (TV, UK) 1988, A Dream of People 1990, The Cruel Grasp 1991, No Flies on Mr Hunter 1992, Death of a Salesman 1993, The Deep Blue Sea 1996, The Good Woman of Sharkville 1996, The Free State 1997, 2000, The Snow Palace 2000; *Films include:* A Day in the Death of Joe Egg 1970, Nicholas and Alexandra (Acad Award Nomination) 1971, Nijinsky 1978, The Priest of Love 1981, The Draughtsman's Contract 1981, E la Nave Va 1982, A Dry White Season 1988, Nuns on the Run 1990, Leon the Pig-Farmer 1992; *TV appearances include:* The Family Reunion 1967, Saint Joan 1968, The Three Sisters 1969, Macbeth 1970, Hedda Gabler 1972, Twelfth Night 1973, Antony and Cleopatra 1974, Miss Nightingale, Clayhanger (series) 1975–76, Robin Hood (CBS TV) 1983, Mountbatten: The Last Viceroy 1985, The Singing Detective (series) 1986, The Miser 1987, Revolutionary Witness 1989, Hildegard (Omnibus) 1994, The Ruth Rendell Mysteries 1996; Dir: Cripples 1989, The Amazon 1989; *Masterclass:* Shakespearian Comedy 1990; *Publications:* Acting With Shakespeare: The Comedies 1996, The Tanner Lectures on Human Values 1995, Hedda Gabler: The Play in Performance 1980, The Free State – A South African Response to the Cherry Orchard 2000, Textual Commentary on Antony and Cleopatra 2001. *Leisure interest:* pretending to write the great novel. *Address:* c/o Steve Kenis & Co, Royalty House, 72–74 Dean St, London W1D 3SG, UK. *Telephone:* (20) 7534-6001; *Fax:* (20) 7287-6328.

ŠVANKMAJEROVÁ, Eva; Czech artist; b 25 Sept 1940, Kostelec Nad Černými; d of Václav and Anna Nikolná Dvořák; m Jan Švankmajer 1960; one s one d. *Education:* School of Art and Acad of Arts (Prague). *Career:* Mem Czechoslovak Surrealist group; group exhibitions include Prague 1985, Brussels 1987, 1991, Paris 1990, Annecy, France 1991; co-creator of film sets 1967, 1983, 1987. *Address:* Černínská 5, 118 00 Prague 1, Czech Republic. *Telephone:* (2) 536793.

SVETLOVA, Marina; French ballet dancer and choreographer; b 3 May 1922, Paris; d of Max and Tamara (née Andreieff) Hartman. *Education:* Paris and New York. *Career:* Soloist Dancer Ballet Russe de Monte Carlo 1939–41; Prima Ballerina Metropolitan Opera, New York 1943–50, New York City Opera 1950–52; Guest Dancer Ballet Opera (Stockholm), Suomi Opera (Helsinki), Het Nederland Ballet (Netherlands), Cork Irish Ballet, Paris Opera Comique, London Palladium, Teatro Colón (Buenos Aires); tours in Asia, Middle East, Europe, S America and USA; Ballet Dir S Vermont Art Center 1959–64; Dir Svetlova Dance Center 1965–; Prof of Ballet Indiana Univ, Bloomington 1969–92; Choreographer Dallas Civic Opera, TX 1964–67, Fort Worth Opera, TX 1967–83, San Antonio Opera, TX 1983, Seattle Opera, WA, Houston Opera, TX, Kansas City Performing Arts Foundation, MO; mem American Guild of Music Artists, Nat Soc of Arts and Letters; numerous contribs to professional journals. *Address:* 2100 Maxwell Lane, Bloomington, IN 47401, USA.

SWADOS, Elizabeth A., BA; American composer and writer; b 5 Feb 1951, Buffalo, NY; d of Robert O. and Sylvia (née Maisel) Swados. *Education:* Bennington Coll (VT). *Career:* Composer and Music Dir Peter Brook, France, Africa, USA 1972–73; Composer-in-Residence La Mama Experimental Theater Club, New York 1977–; mem faculty Carnegie-Mellon Univ (PA) 1974, Bard Coll (NY) 1976–77, Sarah Lawrence Coll (NY) 1976–77; Creative Artists Service Program Grantee 1976; New York State Arts Council Playwriting Grantee 1977–; Guggenheim Fellow; Obie Award (Village Voice) 1972; Outer Critics' Circle Award 1977. *Compositions include:* Theatre scores: Medea 1972, Elektra 1970, Fragments of Trilogy 1974, Trojan Women 1974, The Good Women of Setzuan 1975, The Cherry Orchard 1977, As You Like It 1979, Haggadah 1980, Doonesbury (with Gary Trudeau) 1983, The Tower of Evil 1990, The Mermaid Wakes 1991; Film scores: Step By Step 1973, Sky Dance 1979, Seize the Day 1986, Family Sins 1987; *Publications include:* The Girl With the Incredible Feeling 1976, Runaways 1979, Lullaby 1980, Sky Dance 1980, The Beautiful Lady (musical) 1984, Listening Out Loud: Becoming a Composer 1988, The Four of Us 1991, The Myth Man 1994. *Address:* c/o Sam Cohn, International Creative Management, 40 W 57th St, New York, NY 10019, USA (Office); 112 Waverly Place, New York, NY 10011, USA (Home).

SWAIN, Patricia; British administrator. *Career:* Exec Sec League for the Exchange of Commonwealth Teachers. *Address:* League for the Exchange of Commonwealth Teachers, 7 Lion Yard, Tremadoc Rd, London SW4 7NF, UK. *Telephone:* (20) 7498-1101; *Fax:* (20) 7720-5403.

SWAN, Yvette Victoria Angela, B SC; Bermudan international organization executive; b 20 Aug 1945, St Thomas, Jamaica; d of Webster Wellesley and Rebecca Emily Lewis; m Malcolm Stanley Swan 1970; three s. *Education:* Ferncourt Prep School, Wolmer's High School for Girls, Paddington Technical Coll (London) and Univ of Aston (Birmingham). *Career:* Fmr mem Energy Conservation Cttee, Human Rights Comm and Women's Advisory Council; Pres Business and Professional Women's Asscn 1979–81, Chair Special Projects 1986–88, mem Fundraising Cttee 1988–89; Del to Bd Meeting, Int Fed of Business and Professional Women 1982, Chair Legis Cttee 1983, 1985, First Vice-Pres 1987–89, Int Pres 1989–93; Chair Credential Cttee, Congress 1983; awarded key to city of Tijuana (Mexico) 1988. *Leisure interests:* reading, classical music, walking. *Address:* 21 Warwick Park Rd, Warwick WK 05, Bermuda. *Telephone:* (71) 738-8323 (Office); 238-1087 (Home); *Fax:* 238-0210 (Home).

SWANK, Hilary; American actress; b 1974; m Chad Low. *Films:* Buffy the Vampire Slayer, The Next Karate Kid 1994, Sometimes They Came Back… Again 1996, Heartwood 1997, Boys Don't Cry (Acad Award for Best Actress) 1999, The Gift 2000, Affair of the Necklace 2000; *TV:* Terror in the Family 1996, Leaving LA 1997.

SWARAJ, Sushma, BA, LLB; Indian politician; b 14 Feb 1952, Ambala Cantt; m Kaushal Swaraj. *Education:* Punjab Univ. *Career:* State Pres Hindi Sahitya Sammelan 1978–82; Pres Haryana State Janata Party 1981–83; Minister in Devi Lal's Govt 1977–78, Minister for Food and Supplies 1988–89; Sec All India Bharatiya Janata Party (BJP); elected to Rajya Sabha (Council of States) 1990, to Lok Sabha (House of the People) 1996–; Minister of Information and Broadcasting March–Oct 1998, Oct 2000–; Chief Minister of Delhi Oct–Nov 1998. *Address:* Ministry of Information and Broadcasting, Shastri Bhavan, New Delhi, 110 011, India. *Telephone:* (11) 3382639; *Fax:* (11) 3383513.

SWENSON, Ruth Ann; American opera singer (coloratura soprano). *Career:* Debut San Francisco (CA) 1983, Royal Opera House, Covent Garden (London) 1996; has sung in Berlin, Geneva (Switzerland), Paris, etc. *Operas include:* Orlando, Rigoletto, Elisir d'amore, Lucia di Lammermoor, Puritani, Semele; *Recordings include:* Coloratura Arias from the Golden Age 1996, Roméo et Juliette (with Placido Domingo) 1996.

SWIFT, Jane, BA; American politician; b 1966, N Adams; m Chuck Hunt; one d. *Education:* Trinity Coll. *Career:* Elected to Mass State Senate 1991, becoming Asst Minority Leader, mem Senate Ways and Means Cttee, Educ Reform Conf Cttee; Lieut-Gov of Mass 1998–2001, Gov April 2001–; Dir Regional Airport Devt, Mass Port Authority until 1997; Dir Mass Office of Consumer Affairs and Business Regulation 1997–; mem Fed Trade Comm Advisory Cttee on Online Access and Security; mem Bd W Mass Girl Scout Council, Mass Coll of Liberal Arts. *Address:* Office of the Governor, Boston, Massachusetts, USA.

SWINTON, Tilda; British actress. *Education:* New Hall, Cambridge. *Career:* Performance art appearance sleeping in a glass case, Serpentine Gallery, London 1996; *Films include:* The Last of England, The Garden 1990, Edward II 1991, Orlando 1993, Wittgenstein 1993, Female Perversions 1996, Love is the Devil 1997, Conceiving Ada 1997, The War Zone 1998; *TV appearances include:* Your Cheating Heart 1989.

SWITZER, Barbara; British trade union official; b 26 Nov 1940, Manchester; d of Albert and Edith McMinn; m Michael Switzer 1973. *Education:* Chorlton Cen School (Manchester), Wythenshawe and Stretford Tech Colls. *Career:* Electrical Technician apprenticeship, Metropolitan Vickers 1957–62; Draughtswoman GEC, Trafford Park 1962–70, Cableform, Romiley 1970–71, Mather and Platt 1972–76; Regional Officer Manufacturing Science and Finance Union (MSF) 1976–80, Nat Officer 1980–87, Asst Gen Sec for Political and Int Solidarity Work 1976–97; Div Organizer AUEW 1976–79, Nat

Organiser 1979–83; Deputy Gen Sec Tech, Admin and Supervisory Section (TASS) of AUEW (now part of MSF) 1983–87; Vice-Chair Anti-Apartheid Movt; awarded TUC Women's Gold Badge. *Leisure interests:* gardening, music, cooking, reading. *Address:* 16 Follett Drive, Abbots Langley, Herts WD5 0LP, UK (Home), UK. *Telephone:* (1923) 674662 (Home); *Fax:* (20) 8877-1160 (Office).

SY, Oumou; Senegalese stylist and internet entrepreneur. *Career:* Opened Metissacana (1st Internet café in W Africa), Senegal 1996; Founder, CEO Internet Service Co; also fashion, house and film designer; won RFI Net Afrique Prize 2001. *Address:* 30 rue de Thiong, BP 6491, Dakar, Senegal. *Telephone:* 821-90-19; 637-77-53; *E-mail:* oumousy@metissacana.sn; *Internet:* www.metissacana.sn.

SYAL, Meera, BA; British writer and actress; b 27 June 1963, Wolverhampton; d of Surendra and Surrinder Syal; m 1989; one d. *Education:* Queen Mary's High School for Girls (Walsall) and Univ of Manchester. *Career:* Actress in one-woman comedy One Of Us after graduation, since then actress and comedienne in theatre, film and on TV; also writer of screenplays and novel; Scottish Critics Award for Most Promising Performer 1984; Woman of the Year in the Performing Arts, Cosmopolitan magazine 1994. *Plays include:* Serious Money (London and Broadway, New York) 1987, Stitch, Peer Gynt 1990; *TV appearances include:* The Real McCoy (5 series) 1990–95, My Sister Wife 1992, Absolutely Fabulous 1995, Soldier Soldier 1995; *Publications:* A Nice Arrangement (short TV film) 1991, My Sister Wife (TV film; Best TV Drama Award, Comm for Racial Equality, Awards for Best Actress and for Best Screenplay, Asian Film Acad 1993) 1992, Bhaji on the Beach (film) 1994, Anita and Me (novel; Betty Trask Award 1996) 1996. *Leisure interests:* singing in jazz quintet, netball. *Address:* c/o Rochelle Stevens, 2 Terretts Place, Islington, London N1 1QZ, UK. *Telephone:* (1973) 417762.

SYBESMA-KNOL, Neri, DR JUR, PH D; Netherlands professor of international law; b 17 Sept 1932, Helmond; d of Christiaan Knol and Wilhelmina ten Bensel; m Christiaan Sybesma 1957; two s one d. *Education:* Univs of Amsterdam and Leiden. *Career:* Prof of Int Law Free Univ of Brussels 1972–, Researcher Centre for the Study of the Law of the UN and the Specialized Agencies 1974–, Dir 1988–. *Publications:* The Status of Observers in the United Nations 1981, International Legal Aspects of the Dutch Language Union 1987, Telecommunications Satellites and International Law 1988, Compulsory Jurisdiction of the International Court of Justice 1991, In Search of Peace – The Structures of International Co-operation 1993; various articles on the UN, maritime law, law of outer space and human rights. *Leisure interest:* music. *Address:* Vrije Universiteit Brussel, Faculty of Law, Pleinlaan 2, 1050 Brussels, Belgium. *Telephone:* (2) 629-26-41; *Fax:* (2) 629-36-33.

SYDNES, Anne Kristin; Norwegian politician; b 13 May 1956, Oslo; d of Alf and Wenche Sydnes; m Jan Egeland; two d. *Education:* Univ of Oslo. *Career:* Programme Dir and Research Fellow, Fridtjof Nansen Inst 1985–97, Deputy Dir 1996–97; Vice-Pres, Int Exploration and Production, Country Risk and Human Rights, Statoil 1998–2000; Minister of Int Devt 2000–. *Publications include:* Norway's Stance in the North–South Conflict in the Oil Market: Economic Interests and Foreign Policy Orientations 1985, Naïve Newcomer or Shrewd Salesman? Norway – A Major Oil and Gas Exporter (co-ed) 1990, Norway in the Global Greenhouse (jtly) 1995, Natural Gas in Western Europe: Markets, Organisation and Politics (jtly) 1998. *Address:* Ministry of Foreign Affairs, 7 juni pl 1, POB 8114 Dep, 0032 Oslo, Norway. *Telephone:* (22) 24-39-01; *Fax:* (22) 24-95-88; *E-mail:* anne.kristin.sydnes@mfa.no.

SYKOVÁ, Eva, MD, D SC; Czech scientist; b 24 July 1944, Rožmitál; d of Karel Sýkora and Anna Sýkorová; m Josef Syka; two s. *Education:* Charles Univ (Prague). *Career:* Head of Laboratory of Cellular Neurophysiology Czechoslovak Acad of Sciences and Charles Univ, Prague 1983–; Visiting Sr Research Fellow Univ of Western Australia 1985–86, La Trobe Univ, Melbourne, Australia 1990; Visiting Prof Univ of Heidelberg, Germany 1987; Scientific Sec Czechoslovak Physiological Soc 1989–; mem Cttee Czechoslovak Neuroscience Soc 1990; has given numerous lectures and seminars abroad, and organized two int symposia in Prague 1980, 1987; Czechoslovak Acad of Sciences Award for selected publs 1978, Prize 1983; Czechoslovak Physiological

Soc Prize 1984. *Publications:* Ion-Selective Microelectrodes (ed), Ionic and Volume Changes in the Micro-environment of Nerve and Receptor Cells 1992; numerous articles in int books and journals. *Leisure interests:* literature, music, tennis. *Address:* Czech Academy of Sciences, Laboratory of Cellular Neurophysiology, Bulovka, Pavillion 11, 180 85 Prague 8, Czech Republic. *Telephone:* (2) 828486; *Fax:* (2) 828486.

SYLBERT, Anthea, MA; American costume designer and film producer; b 6 Oct 1939, New York. *Education:* Barnard Coll and Parsons School of Design (New York). *Career:* Costume designer for plays and films; Vice-Pres Special Projects (liaison), Warner Bros 1977, Vice-Pres Production 1978; Vice-Pres Production, United Artists 1980; currently ind producer, Partner Hawn/Sylbert Movie Co with Goldie Hawn (qv). *Films include:* Costume designs: Rosemary's Baby, FIST, Shampoo, The Fortune, The Heartbreak Kid, Julia (Acad Award nomination), Chinatown (Acad Award nomination); Producer: One Trick Pony, Personal Best, Jinxed, Still of the Night, Yentl, Swing Shift, Protocol, Wildcats, Overboard, My Blue Heaven, Deceived, Alone Together, Crisscross, Something to Talk About.

SYMONS OF VERNHAM DEAN, Baroness (Life Peer), cr 1996, of Vernham Dean in the County of Hampshire, **Elizabeth Conway,** MA, FRSA; British trade union executive; b 14 April 1951, Liverpool; d of Ernest Vize and Elizabeth Megan (née Jenkins) Symons; partner Philip Alan Bassett; one s. *Education:* Putney High School for Girls and Girton Coll (Cambridge). *Career:* Researcher Girton Coll, Cambridge 1972–74; Admin Trainee Dept of the Environment 1974–77; Asst Sec Inland Revenue Staff Fed 1977–78, Deputy Sec-Gen 1988–89, mem Employment Appeal Tribunal 1995; Sec-Gen Asscn of First Div Civil Servants 1989–96; Parl Under-Sec of State, FO 1997–99; Minister of State, Ministry of Defence 1999–; mem Gen Council TUC, Council Royal Inst of Public Admin 1989–97, Exec Council Campaign for Freedom of Information 1989–96, Council Hansard Soc 1992–, Advisory Council Civil Service Coll 1992–97, Council Industrial Soc 1994–97, Council Open Univ 1994–97, Equal Opportunities Comm 1995–97; Exec mem Involvement and Participation Asscn 1992–97; Trustee Inst for Public Policy Research 1993; Gov Polytechnic of N London (now Univ) 1989–94, London Business School 1993–97; Hon Assoc Nat Council of Women. *Leisure interests:* reading, gardening, friends. *Address:* Association of First Division Civil Servants, 2 Caxton St, London SW1H 0QH, UK. *Telephone:* (20) 7222-6242.

SYMS, Sylvia; British actress and director; b 6 Jan 1934, London; m Alan Edney 1957 (divorced 1989); one s one d. *Education:* Royal Acad of Dramatic Art. *Career:* Began career in the theatre and went on to work in film, TV and radio; Founder-mem and Artistic Dir Arbela Production Co; Visiting Lecturer Tulane Univ, USA 1986; mem The Actors' Centre 1986–91, Arts Council New Writing Panel, Drama Panel 1991–96, Council Royal Acad of Dramatic Art 1992–; has delivered lectures, including the Dodo White McLarty Memorial Lecture 1986, recitals and many after dinner speeches; Gerald Lawrence Shakespearean Scholarship; H M Tennants Prize; Variety Club Best Actress in Films Award 1958; Ondas Award Most Popular Foreign Actress (Spain) 1964, Manchester Evening News Best Actress Award. *Films include:* The Birthday Present 1956, Ice Cold in Alex 1953, The World of Suzie Wong 1961, Run Wild Run Free 1969, The Tamarind Seed (British Film Acad nomination) 1974, Chorus of Disapproval 1988, Shirley Valentine 1989, Shining Through 1991, Dirty Weekend 1992, Staggered 1994, Dancing 1995, Food For Love 1996, Neville's Island 1997, Mavis and the Mermaid 1999; *TV appearances include:* Love Story 1964, The Saint 1967, My Good Woman 1972–73, Nancy Astor 1982, Ruth Rendell Mysteries 1989, 1993, 1997–98, Dr Who 1989–90, May to December 1989–90, The Last Days of Margaret Thatcher 1991, Natural Lies, Mulberry, The Glass Virgin 1994, Peak Practice 1994–95, Half the Picture 1994–95, Ghost Hour 1995, Original Sin 1996–97, House of Angelo 1997–98, Heartbeat 1998, At Home With The Braithwaites 1999, 2000–01, The Jury 2001; *Plays include:* Dance of Death, Much Ado About Nothing, The Ideal Husband, Ghosts, Entertaining Mr Sloane (Best Actress Award, Manchester Evening News) 1985, Who's Afraid of Virginia Woolf? 1989, The Floating Lightbulb 1990, Antony and Cleopatra 1991, For Services Rendered 1993, Post Mortem 1993, Half the Picture 1994, Funny Money 1995–96, Ugly Rumours (The Queen and Margaret Thatcher) 1998; *Radio includes:* Little Dorrit, Danger in the Village, Post Mortems, Dead

Reckoning, Equal Terms, Point of Departure, Love's Labours Lost; *Plays and TV productions directed:* Better in my Dreams 1988, The Price 1991, Natural Lies 1991–92. *Address:* c/o Barry Brown, 6 Bridgehouse Court, 109 Blackfriars Rd, London SE1 8HW, UK. *Telephone:* (20) 7928-1229.

SZABO, Gabriela; Romanian athlete; b 14 Nov 1975, Bistrita. *Career:* Indoor European record holder and Outdoor World record holder 5000m; world's fastest at 1500m, one mile, 2000m, 3000m and 5000m 1998; Bronze Medal (1500m) Olympic Games, Sydney 2000; Silver Medal (1500m) Olympic Games, Atlanta 1996; Gold Medal (5000m) Olympic Games, Sydney 2000; European Athlete of the Year 1999, IAAF Athlete of the Year 1999.

SZABÓ, Katalin, D ECON; Hungarian economist; b 1944, Gödöllő; d of Gyula and Katalin (née Varga) Szabó; m Balázs Hámori 1971; two s. *Education:* Karl Marx Univ of Econs (Budapest). *Career:* Ed-in-Chief Közgazdasági Szemle 1986–; apptd Head of Dept of Econs Budapest Univ of Econ Sciences 1988, currently Prof; mem Econs Cttee Hungarian Acad of Sciences 1980–90; Int Social Science Award 1986. *Publications:* Terv vagy piac? (Plan or Market?) 1970, A nagyvállalati kihívás (The Challenge of the Giant Firm) 1974, A lágyuló gazdaság (The Softening Economy) 1989. *Leisure interests:* theatre, reading, poems. *Address:* 1125 Budapest, Tusnádi út 6C, Hungary. *Telephone:* (1) 558-186; *Fax:* (1) 170-796.

SZABÓ, Magda; Hungarian writer; b 5 Oct 1917, Debrecen; d of Alex Szabó and Madeleine Jablonczay; m Tibor Szobotka 1948. *Career:* Graduated as a teacher 1940; worked in secondary schools 1940–44, 1950–59; started literary career as poet and has since written novels, plays, radio dramas, essays and film scripts; works have been translated into 30 languages including English, French, German, Italian, Russian, Polish, Swedish; mem Acad of Sciences of Europe; Baumgarten Prize 1947; József Attila Prize 1959 and 1972; Kossuth Prize 1978; Getz Corpn Prize 1992. *Publications:* Children's books: Szigetkék (Island-Blue), Tündér Lala (Lala the Fairy), Abigél (Abigail); Novels: Az őz (The Fawn), Fresko (Fresco), Disznótor (Night of Pig-Killing), Pilatus (Pilate), A Danaida (The Danaid), Mózes 1.22 (Genesis 1.22), Katalin utca (Kathleen Street), A szemlélők (The Onlookers), Régimódi történet (Old-Fashioned Story), Az ajtó (The Door), The Moment 1990; Plays: Az a szép fényes nap (That Bright Beautiful Day), A meráni fiu (The Boy of Meran), A csata (The Battle) 1982, Béla Király (King Béla), A Macskák Szerdája (The Wednesday of the Cats) 1985; Neszek (Noises, poems), Ókut (Old Well, autobiog); Essays: The Logic of the Butterfly 1997, The Mondogue of Cseke. *Leisure interests:* pets, ancient books. *Address:* 1026 Budapest II, Julia u 3, Hungary. *Telephone:* (1) 565-013.

SZÁSZY, Miraka (Mira) Petricevich, DBE, JP; New Zealand campaigner for Maori rights; b 7 Aug 1921, Waihopo; d of Lawrence and Mákeretá (née Raharuhi) Petricevich; m Albert Szászy 1956 (deceased); two s. *Education:* Auckland Girls' Grammar School, Univs of Auckland and Hawaii (USA). *Career:* Teacher 1946–70; Social Worker Maori Affairs Dept 1946–48, Employment Officer 1951–52; Exec Sec Maori Women's Welfare League (MWWL) 1952–57, Vice-Pres 1971, Acting Pres 1973, Pres 1974–77; Lecturer Secretarial Teachers' Coll 1972–78; Dir Community Dept, Nga Tapuwae Coll 1979–84; retired to Far North 1985; mem First Maori Educ Foundation Trust Bd 1962–70; mem Nat Cttee on Maori Educ 1976, Social Welfare Comm 1988, Advisory Cttee resulting in establishment of Women's Ministry 1988, and Maori Women's Secr within the Ministry 1988; Pres Three Combined Tribes 1988; mem Orangi Trust, Maori Fisheries Comm 1990–, Shellfish Recovery Trust 1993–, Ngati Kuri Trust Bd 1993; Chair local Marae in Far North 1987, elected Runanga o Ngati Kuri, Aupouri, Ngaitakoto; Del to Maori Congress 1990, Taitikeran Forum 1990; many interviews in journals and on TV; Hon LL D (Victoria Univ of Wellington) 1993; Queen's Service Medal (NZ); Silver Jubilee Medal 1977. *Leisure interests:* reading, gardening. *Address:* Ngataki, RD4, Kaitaia, New Zealand. *Telephone:* (9) 409-8558.

SZATHMÁRY, Emőke Jolán Erzsébet, PH D; Canadian (b Hungarian) professor of anthropology, biochemistry and medical genetics; b 25 Jan 1944, Ungvár, Hungary; d of Károly Béla and Lenke Etelka Vilma (née Legánÿ) Szathmáry; m George Alexander Reilly 1974; one s one d. *Education:* Univ of Toronto. *Career:* Asst Prof of Anthropolgy Trent Univ, Peterborough, ON 1974–74; Asst Prof of Anthropology McMaster Univ, Hamilton, ON 1975–78, Assoc Prof 1978–83, Prof 1983–85, Chair of Anthropology 1985–89, Assoc mem Biology 1985–89; Dean Faculty of Social Science Univ of Western Ontario 1989–94, Prof Dept of Anthropology 1989–94, Hon Prof Dept of Zoology 1989–94; Provost and Vice-Pres (Academic) McMaster Univ 1994–96, Prof Depts of Biology and Anthropology 1994–96; Pres and Vice-Chancellor Univ of Manitoba 1996–, Prof Depts of Anthropology and Human Genetics 1996–; Ed Yearbook of Physical Anthropology 1987–91, American Journal of Physical Anthropology 1995–2001; Chair Pres's Cttee on the Ethics of Research on Human Subjects 1987–88; mem Exec Cttee American Asscn of Physiological Anthropologists; Pres Human Biology Council 1989–90, Pres 1990–92; Pres Canadian Asscn for Physical Anthropology 1975–77, 1977–79, Canadian Soc for Circumpolar Health; elected Fellow of the Arctic Inst of North America 1989, AAAS 1996; Hon LL D (Toronto) 2001. *Publications:* Diseases of Complex Etiology in Small Populations (jtly) 1985, Out of Asia (jtly) 1985, Prehistoric Mongoloid Dispersals (jtly) 1996; numerous articles, abstracts, reviews. *Leisure interests:* swimming, needlework, reading. *Address:* University of Manitoba, Winnipeg, MB R3T 2NZ, Canada (Office); 37 Kings Drive, Winnipeg, MB R5T 3E6, Canada (Home).

SZATMÁRI, Marianna, MD, PH D; Hungarian medical practitioner and international organization official; b 27 April 1931, Budapest; d of Tibor and Magda (née Altai) Szatmári; m Béla Takács 1956 (died 1977). *Education:* Semmelweis Medical Univ (Budapest) and Acad of Sciences (Budapest). *Career:* Internship at Tétényi uti kórház, Budapest 1955–58; Gen Practitioner 1958–79, Chief Consultant 1979–85; Head of Dept for Primary Health Care and Rehabilitation, Ministry of Health 1985–90, Deputy Head Dept of Medical Care 1989–90; Deputy Dir Dept of Int Relations, Ministry of Welfare 1990; WHO Liaison Officer for Hungary 1990; Visiting Prof Loránd Eötvös Univ, Budapest; mem Societas Internationalis Medicinae Generalis (awarded Int Hippocrates Medal 1985, Extraordinary Physician Medal 1988), Hungarian Scientific Soc of Gen Practitioners (awarded Medicus Anonimus 1977), British Royal Coll of Gen Practitioners, European Workshop on Research in Gen Practice; award for extraordinary work from the Ministry of Health 1979, Heim Medal, German Scientific Soc 1985, Purkinje Medal Tschechoslov, Purkinje Soc 1985, Int Généraliste d'Honneur 1990; Order of Merit of the Hungarian Officer's Cross 1995. *Publications:* Special Problems of General Practice 1978, Psychosomatics (jtly) 1985; 89 other publs 1958–91. *Leisure interests:* music, knitting, animals. *Address:* Ministry of Welfare, 1057 Budapest, Arany Janos ut 6–8, Hungary (Office); 1136 Budapest, Balzac ut 48/b, Hungary (Home). *Telephone:* (1) 331-7450 (Office); (1) 149-5857 (Home); *Fax:* (1) 269-1303 (Office); *E-mail:* wholohu@who.hu.

SZEKELY, Deborah; American business executive; b 3 May 1922, Brooklyn, NY; d of the late Harry and Rebecca Shainman; m 1st Edmond Bordeaux Szekely 1939 (divorced 1969); m 2nd Vincent Mazzanti 1972 (divorced 1978); one s one d. *Career:* Co-Founder Rancho La Puerta (fitness center), Mexico 1940–; f Golden Door (fitness center), CA 1958; pioneer of the fitness spa offering health, relaxation, athletic and cultural programmes; Pres Szekely Foundation for American Volunteers (now known as Szekely Family Foundation) 1982–; mem Public Relations Cttee, US Information Agency 1983–84; Pres Eureka Communities 1990–95, Founder, Chair Eureka Foundation 1996; mem Bd Center for Science in the Public Interest (Washington), Nat Council of La Raza, Partners for Livable Communities, Youth Service America, Ford's Theatre (Washington, DC); Small Businessperson of the Year for California 1976; Living Legacy Award, Women's Int Center 1990; Honoree Women Together 1990. *Publications:* Secrets of the Golden Door 1979, Golden Door Cookbook: the Greening of American Cuisine 1985, Rancho La Puerta Cookbook 1990. *Leisure interests:* gardening, collecting oriental antiques, science-

fiction, volunteerism. *Address:* Szekely Family Foundation, 3134 P St, NW, Washington, DC 20007, USA. *Telephone:* (202) 337-6332; *Fax:* (202) 342-2399.

SZLAZAK, Anita Christina, BA; Canadian civil servant (retd); b 1 Jan 1943, Fulmer, UK; d of Jan P. and Christina W. (née Matecz) Szlazak. *Education:* Univ of Toronto, Coll of Europe (Bruges, Belgium) and Harvard Graduate School of Business Admin (USA). *Career:* Econ Researcher Devt Centre, OECD, Paris 1964–67; Foreign Service Officer, Dept of External Affairs, Ottawa 1967–72, Special Adviser 1984–86; Deputy Dir-Gen Int Telecommunications, Dept of Communications, Ottawa 1972–73, Dir-Gen 1973–76; Commr Public Service Comm of Canada 1976–82; Exec Dir Canadian Govt Office for 1988 Olympic Winter Games 1982–84; Sr Policy Adviser Treasury Bd of Canada 1986–88; Special Adviser, Int Relations, Canada Mortgage and Housing Corpn 1988–90; Dir-Gen, Programme Man Canadian Parks Service, Environment Canada 1990–92; Dir-Gen Special Projects, Atmospheric Environment Service, Environment Canada 1992–94; mem Canadian Int Trade Tribunal 1995–99; fmr mem Inst of Public Admin of Canada (Nat Exec Cttee 1976–80), Int Inst of Admin Sciences, Brussels (Exec Cttee 1983–86, Vice-Pres for N America 1986–89); Queen Elizabeth II Silver Jubilee Medal 1977. *Address:* 60 Belvedere Crescent, Ottawa, ON K1M 2G4, Canada. *Telephone:* (613) 746-5695; *Fax:* (613) 746-3906; *E-mail:* aszlazak@sympatico.ca.

SZŐNYI, Erzsébet; Hungarian musician, composer and university professor; b 25 April 1924, Budapest; d of Jenő and Erzsébet (née Piszanoff) Szőnyi; m Lajos Gémes 1948; two s. *Education:* Music Acad (Budapest) and Paris Conservatoire. *Career:* Music teacher grammar school, Budapest 1945–48, Music Acad, Budapest 1948– (leading Prof 1960–81); Vice-Pres Int Soc for Music Educ 1970–74; Co-Chair Hungarian Kodály Soc 1978–, Gen adviser of methodology 1978–, Bárdos Soc 1988–; Hon Pres Hungarian Choir Asscn 1990–, Co-Chair Hungarian Musicians Forum 1995–; mem Hungarian Acad of the Arts, Chopin Soc of Warsaw, Liszt Soc of Hungary, Bd Asscn of Hungarian Composers 1999–; awards include Erkel Prize 1959, Hungarian Republic Cross 1993, Apáczai Csere János Prize 1994, Bartók–Pászthory Prize 1995, Excellent Artist Award 2000, Pro Cultura Kodály Prize 2001. *Works:* Concerto for Organ and Orchestra; Symphonic works: Musica Festiva, Divertimento 1 and 2, Prelude and Fugue, Three Ideas in Four Movements; Operas: Tragedy of Firenze, A Gay Lament, Break of Transmission, Elfrida (madrigal opera) 1987–, several children's operas; chamber music, oratorios, vocal compositions, etc; *Publications:* Methods of Musical Reading and Writing, Kodály's Principles in Practice, Travels on Five Continents, Twentieth Century Music Methods. *Leisure interests:* gardening, cooking. *Address:* 1124 Budapest XII, Ormódi-utca 13-II-9, Hungary. *Telephone:* (1) 1356-7329.

SZYMBORSKA, Wisława; Polish poet, translator and literary critic; b 2 July 1923, Prowent-Bnin nr Poznań. *Education:* Jagiellonian Univ (Cracow). *Career:* First work published 1945; mem Polish Writers' Asscn 1952–83, Gen Bd 1978–83; mem Editorial Staff Zycie Literackie (weekly) 1953–81; Gold Cross of Merit 1955, Kt's Cross, Order of Polonia Restituta; Goethe Award (Frankfurt) 1991; Herder Award 1995; Polish PEN Club Award 1996; Nobel Prize for Literature 1996. *Publications:* Poetry: Dlatego zyjemy (That's Why We're Alive) 1952, Pylania szadawane sobie (Questioning Oneself) 1954, Wołanie do Yeti (Calling Out to Yeti) 1957, Sól (Salt) 1962, Sto pociech (No End of Fun) 1967, Wybór wierszy (Selected Poems) 1967, 1973, Poezje 1970, Wszelki wypadek (Could Have) 1972, Wielka liczba (A Large Number) 1976, Ludzie na moscie (The People on the Bridge) 1986, Koniec i poczatek (The End and the Beginning) 1993, Widok z ziarnkiem piasku (View With a Grain of Sand) 1996, Poems New and Collected 1957–97 1998. *Address:* Stowarzyszenie Pisarzy Polskich, ul Kanonicza 7, 31-002 Cracow, Poland.

T

TABAKAUCORO, Adi Tamari Finau, BA; Fijian politician. *Education:* Univ of Wellington (NZ). *Career:* Training Officer Dept of Localization and Training 1969; Asst Sec Ministry of Social Welfare, Urban Devt and Housing 1971, Cen Planning Office 1975; Programme Asst, S Pacific Office, UNDP 1976; mem Nat Econ Council 1986, Great Council of Chiefs; Minister for Women's Affairs and Social Welfare 1987–92; Fellow Univ of the S Pacific. *Telephone:* 312681.

TABART, Jillian Claire, MB, BS; Australian medical practitioner and church executive; b 18 April 1941, Melbourne; m Ken Tabart 1966; two s two d. *Education:* Methodist Ladies' Coll (Melbourne) and Univ of Melbourne. *Career:* Gen practice, Vic 1967–69, Tas 1970–89; Schools Child Health Medical Officer, Govt State Health Depts 1970–89; Municipal Medical Officer for Health, Launceston 1989–; Moderator Uniting Church in Australia Synod of Tasmania 1984–85; Pres Tasmanian Council of Churches 1993–94; Exec Nat Council of Churches in Australia 1994–; Nat Pres Uniting Church in Australia 1994–97. *Leisure interests:* reading, gardening, handcrafts, people. *Address:* POB 95, St Leonards, Tas 7250, Australia. *Telephone:* (03) 391-479; *Fax:* (03) 394-204.

TABBERER, Maggie (Margaret May); Australian journalist; b 11 Dec 1936; d of A. Trigar; m (divorced); two d. *Education:* Unley Tech Coll. *Career:* Model 1957–61; Fashion Publicity Promotions, Maggie Tabberer and Assocs 1961–80; Fashion writer Sydney Daily Mirror 1965–80; Host Maggie Show Channel Seven Network 1968–70; Fashion Ed Australian Women's Weekly 1981–96; currently Dir Maggie T Licencing. *Leisure interests:* farming, cooking. *Address:* POB 166, Edgecliffe, NSW 2027, Australia.

TACHA, Deanell Reece, JD; American federal judge; b 26 Jan 1946. *Education:* Univs of Kansas and Michigan. *Career:* Special Asst to US Sec of Labor, Washington, DC 1971–72; Assoc Hogan and Hartson 1973, Thomas J. Pitner 1973–74; Assoc Prof of Law Univ of Kansas 1974–77, Prof 1977–85, Assoc Dean 1977–79, Assoc Vice-Chancellor 1979–81, Vice-Chancellor 1981–85; Judge US Court of Appeals, 10th Circuit 1985–; Dir Douglas Co Legal Aid Soc, Lawrence, KS 1974–77. *Address:* US Court of Appeals, 4830 W 15th St, Suite 100, Lawrence, KS 66049-3846, USA.

TAHEDL, Ernestine, MA; Canadian (b Austrian) artist; b 12 Oct 1940, Austria; d of Heinrich and Elisabeth (née Leutgeb) Tahedl; m Richard Ian Ogilvie 1965; one s one d. *Education:* Acad for Applied Arts (Vienna). *Career:* Came to Canada 1963; solo exhibitions include Edmonton, Calgary, Montréal and Toronto 1963–96, Wiener Sezession, Vienna 1971, Ecole des Beaux Arts, Montpellier, France 1975, 15th Int Biennial of Graphic Art, Ljubljana, Yugoslavia (now Slovenia) 1983, Int Biennial Print Exhibition, Taipei 1985, 1987, Metropolitan Museum of Fine Art, Tokyo 1985, 1987; stained glass comms include Sisters of Holy Cross, Edmonton 1964, Christkoenigs Church, Klagenfurt 1989, St Peter's Estonian Evangelical Lutheran Church of Toronto 1990–92; public and pvt collections in Vienna, San Salvador, Montpellier; Asst Prof Acad for Applied Arts, Vienna 1961–63; teacher Edmonton Art Gallery 1963–64; fmr Exec Vice-Pres and Exhibition Chair Royal Canadian Acad of Arts; mem Royal Canadian Acad of Arts 1977; mem Ontario Soc of Artists 1984–, Council 1986–88, Vice-Pres 1988–89, Pres 1996–; Royal Architectural Inst of Canada Allied Arts Medal 1966; Canadian Council Arts Award 1967; Dame, Order of the Kts of Malta 1989. *Leisure interests:* travel, music, skiing. *Address:* 79 Collard Drive, RR I, King City, ON L7B 1E4, Canada. *Telephone:* (905) 833-0686; *Fax:* (905) 833-0686.

TAHOUX, Martine, D SC S; Côte d'Ivoire geographical and ecological researcher; b 18 July 1951, Abidjan; d of Felix Touao and Juliette Siah; m Maurice Tahoux 1981; one s one d. *Education:* Univs of Abidjan and Paris (Sorbonne). *Career:* Regional Dir of SW Planning Authority 1977–81; Parl Pvt Sec Ministry of Scientific Research 1981–84, Ministry of Animal Production 1986–88; Researcher and Head of Departmental Planning, Institut d'Ecologie Tropicale 1984–. *Publications:* Ecosystèmes forestiers et effets de leur dégradation sur l'environnement 1987, Rôle des femmes dans la lutte contre la désertification 1989, Dynamiques des systèmes d'exploitation agricole et blocage foncier: quelles solutions 1991, Impacts des programmes agro-industriels sur l'espace du sud-ouest ivoirien 1992. *Leisure interests:* music, cinema, nature, charity work. *Address:* Institut d'Ecologie Tropicale, BP 109, Abidjan 08, Côte d'Ivoire (Office); BP 29, Cédex III, Abidjan-Riviera, Côte d'Ivoire (Home). *Telephone:* 431218 (Office).

TAINA, Anneli, M SC S; Finnish politician; b 21 June 1951, Imatra; m Heikki Taina 1972. *Career:* Social worker 1977–87; mem Tampere City Council 1981–, Tampere City Exec Bd 1985–87, City Planning Cttee 1985–87; mem Eduskunta (Parl, Nat Coalition Party) 1987–94, Vice-Chair Parl Cttee for Social and Health Affairs 1991–94, mem Parl Lab Cttee 1991–94, Grand Cttee 1991–94; Minister of Housing, Ministry of the Environment 1995, Minister of Defence 1995; Presidential elector 1988; apptd Chair Non-socialist Health and Social Policy Asscn 1987; Vice-Chair Women's Asscn of the Nat Coalition Party 1990–93; mem Veterans' Affairs Advisory Bd 1986–95, Council for Equality 1987–95, Council of Finnish Allergy and Asthma Asscn 1988–, Council of Finnish Diabetes Asscn 1990–, Cen Bd of Women's Asscns 1991–. *Address:* c/o Ministry of Defence, Fabianinkatu 2, POB 31, 00130 Helsinki, Finland. *Telephone:* (0) 16161; *Fax:* (0) 653254.

TAIPALE, Vappu Tuulikki, MD; Finnish psychiatrist, politician and organization executive; b 1 May 1940, Vaasa; m Ilkka Taipale; two s two d. *Education:* Univ of Helsinki. *Career:* Psychiatrist Aurora Youth Polyclinic 1970–74; Paediatric Clinic 1975–79; Asst Prof of Child Psychiatry Kuopio Univ 1980–83, Tampere Univ 1983–; First Minister of Social Affairs and Health 1982–1983, Second Minister 1983–84; Dir-Gen Nat Bd of Social Welfare 1984–90; Dir-Gen Nat Agency for Welfare and Health 1991–92, STAKES (Nat Research and Devt Centre for Welfare and Health) 1992–. *Address:* STAKES, Siltasaarenkatu 18, POB 220, 00531 Helsinki, Finland. *Telephone:* (0) 39672011; *Fax:* (0) 39672417; *E-mail:* vappu.taipale@stakes.fi. (Office); *Internet:* www .stakes.fi. (Office).

TAIT, Marion Hooper, OBE; British ballet dancer and teacher; b 7 Oct 1950, Herts; d of Charles Arnold Browel Tait and Betty Maude Hooper; m David Morse 1971. *Education:* Royal Acad of Dancing and Royal Ballet School. *Career:* Joined Royal Ballet School aged 15, graduating to Royal Ballet's touring co (later known as Sadler's Wells Royal Ballet, now Birmingham Royal Ballet) 1968; Prin Dancer 1974; danced all the classics and in ballets by Ashton, MacMillan, Bintley, Tudor, DeMille, Tetley and Bruce and other prin roles including Juliet, Elite Syncopations, Las Hermanas, The Invitation, Hobson's Choice, The Dream, The Burrow, Lizzie Borden in Fall River Legend and Hagar in Pillars of Fire; created many roles for Kenneth MacMillan and David Bintley; guest appearances world-wide; Ballet Mistress, Birmingham Royal Ballet 1995–; Dancer of Year 1994; Evening Standard Ballet Award 1994. *Leisure interest:* needlework. *Address:* Birmingham Royal Ballet, Birmingham Hippodrome, Thorp St, Birmingham B5 4AU, UK. *Telephone:* (121) 622-2555; *Fax:* (121) 622-5038.

TAIT, Sylvia Agnes Sophia, FRS; British research scientist; m James Tait 1956. *Career:* Research Asst Courtauld Inst of Biochem, Middlesex Hosp Medical School 1944–55, External Scientific Staff 1955–58, Research Assoc and Co-Dir Biophysical Endocrinology Unit, Dept of Physics as Applied to Medicine 1970–82, Hon Research Assoc and Co-Dir 1982–; Sr Scientist Worcester Foundation for Experimental Biology, USA 1958–70; R. Douglas Wright Lecture and Medallion, Melbourne, Australia 1989; Hon D SC (Hull) 1979; Int Endocrine Soc Tadeus Reichstein Award 1976; American Heart Asscn for Hypertension Research award 1977; Soc for Endocrinology Sir Henry Dale Medal 1979. *Address:* Moorlands, Main Rd, East Boldre, Brockenhurst, Hants SO42 7WT, UK. *Telephone:* (1590) 626312.

TAITTINGER, Anne-Claire; French business executive; d of Jean Taittinger and Corinne Deville; m; two s. *Education:* Inst de l'Assomption (Paris). *Career:* Fmr urban planner; fmrly held positions within several Soc du Louvre cos, Head Soc du Louvre 1997–; Dir Marengo Soc, Deville Soc. *Address:* Société du Louvre, 58 blvd Gouvion Saint-Cyr, 75858 Paris, Cedex 17, France.

TAKAHASHI, Hisako, B ECONS; Japanese civil servant and judge (retd); b 21 Sept 1927. *Education:* Univ of Tokyo. *Career:* Joined Ministry of Labour 1953, Dir Women and Young Workers' Bureau 1980; Dir Inspection Div, Saitama Labour Standards Bureau 1966; Cabinet Counsellor, Cabinet Secr 1979; Pres Japan Inst of Workers' Evolution 1993; Supreme Court Justice (first woman) 1994–97; retd 1997. *Address:* c/o Supreme Court, 4-2 Hayabusa-cho, Chiyoda-ku, Tokyo, 102-8651, Japan.

TAKAHASHI, Seiko, BA; Japanese United Nations official; b 2 Jan 1936, Tokyo; d of the late Saburo and of Utako Takahashi. *Education:* Int Christian Univ (Tokyo) and Univ of Toronto (Canada). *Career:* Worked at Ministry of Health and Welfare 1959–62, Inst of Population Problems 1962–69; mem staff United Nations Econ and Social Comm for Asia and the Pacific (UN ESCAP) 1969, apptd Deputy Exec Sec 1990. *Leisure interest:* golf. *Address:* UN ESCAP, United Nations Bldg, Rajdamnern Ave, Bangkok 10200, Thailand. *Telephone:* (2) 281-4250; *Fax:* (2) 282-9602.

TAKAHASHI, Tomoko, BA; Japanese artist; b 1966, Tokyo. *Education:* Tama Art Univ, Univ of Tokyo, Goldsmiths Coll (London, UK) and Slade School of Fine Art (London, UK). *Career:* Assoc Research Student, Goldsmiths Coll 1996–; solo exhibitions include Hales Gallery (London), The Drawing Center (New York), Entwistle (London) 1999, Grant Selwyn (LA) 1999; group exhibitions include EAST Int (Norwich) 1997, Gonzo (London) 1997, Generation Z, PS1 (New York) 1999, New Neurotic Realism, Saatchi Gallery (London) 1999; Seventh East Award 1997. *Address:* c/o Entwistle Gallery, 6 Cork St, London W1. *Telephone:* (20) 7734-6440.

TAKEDA, Kiyoko, D LITT; Japanese university professor; b 20 June 1917, Hyogoken; d of Takehira and Hiroko Takeda; m Yukio Cho 1953; one s. *Education:* Kobe Coll, Olivet Coll, Union Theological Seminary and Columbia Univ (USA), and Tokyo Univ. *Career:* Instructor in History of Thought, Int Christian Univ 1953–55, Asst Prof 1955–61, Prof 1961–83, Dean Coll of Liberal Arts 1967–69, Grad School Prof 1983–88, Dean Grad School 1970–74, Prof Emer 1988–; Lecturer Tokyo Univ 1962–72; Research Assoc Princeton Univ 1965–66, on Asian Studies Harvard Univ, USA 1966–67; Sr Assoc Fellow St Antony's Coll, Oxford, UK 1975–76; Dir Cttee on Asian Cultural Studies 1958–71, Inst of Asian Cultural Studies 1971–83; mem Pres Cttee World Council of Churches 1971–75; Hon D HUM LITT (Int Christian Univ, Tokyo). *Publications include:* Conflict in the Concept of Man in Modern Japan 1959, The Emperor System and Education 1964, The Genealogy of Apostates: The Japanese and Christianity 1973, Between Orthodoxy and Heterodoxy 1976, We and the World 1983, The Milestones for Women's Liberation in Modern Japan 1985, Liberalism in the Intellectual Climate of Japan 1987, Dual Image of the Japanese Emperor (Mainichi Newspaper Cultural Prize) 1988, Profound Insight and Tolerance – Focusing on Uchimura Kanzo 1995, The Roots of Japan's Post-war Democracy 1995, A Story of New University in Postwar Japan 2000, Uemura Masahisa in the Perspective of Intellectual History of Japan 2001; Ed: Method and Objectives of Intellectual History – Japan and the West 1961, Christianity in Modern

Japan 1964, Theory of Comparative Modernization 1970, Human Rights in Modern Japan 1970, The Archetypes of Japanese Culture 1984, A Bridge to China 2000; trans works of Reinhold Niebuhr into Japanese. *Leisure interests:* folk art, floriculture. *Address:* 1-59-6 Nishigahara, Kita-ku, Tokyo, Japan. *Telephone:* (3) 3915-0886.

TAKLA, Laila, LL B, PH D; Egyptian politician and diplomatist; m; two c. *Education:* Cairo Univ (Egypt), Univ of Southern California and New York Univ (USA). *Career:* Lecturer in Admin New York Univ, Lecturer Higher Inst of Admin, Cairo Univ; Public Admin Expert Arab League 1969; Chair Foreign Affairs Cttee, People's Ass (Parl); mem Cen Cttee, Arab Socialist Union 1971; mem Nat Specialised Councils 1972; Rep for Egypt, UN Gen Ass 1973; Vice-Pres Int Parl Union 1977; Chair Cttee on Educ; Pres Finnish-Egyptian Soc 1976; Chair Nat Cttee on Environmental Law; Chair UN Experts Group on the Advancement of Women 1976. *Publications:* Public Administration Principles and Dynamics (2 vols) 1968, 1971, 1976, The Six Hour War: An Analysis of the Arab–Israeli October War 1973, The Ombudsman: A Comparative Study 1971. *Leisure interests:* swimming, tennis, sculpture, folk arts. *Address:* Majlis ash-Sha'ab (People's Assembly), Maglis esh-Sha'ab, Cairo, Egypt.

TALAGI, Sisilia, B SC; Niuean diplomatist and civil servant; b 27 Feb 1952, Niue; one s three d. *Career:* Food technologist 1976–81, food industry trainer 1981–83; Agric Projects Man and Exports Promoter 1983–88; Dir of Agric and Fisheries 1988–94; Asst Head of External Affairs 1994–99; Sec to the Govt 1999–. *Leisure interests:* research reading, golf, watching sports. *Address:* Secretary to the Government, POB 40, Alofi, Niue (Office); POB 175 Alofi, Niue (Home). *Telephone:* (683) 4200 (Office); (683) 4227 (Home); *Fax:* (683) 4232 (Office); *E-mail:* seegov.premier@mail.gov.nu (Office).

TALLAWY, Mervat; Egyptian diplomatist and politician; b 1 Dec 1937, Menya; d of Mehani Tallawy and Soraya Abdel-Hamid; m Ali Abdel-Rahman Rahmy 1964; one d. *Education:* American Univ (Cairo), Inst for Diplomatic Studies (Cairo) and Grad Inst of Int Studies (Geneva, Switzerland). *Career:* Joined Ministry of Foreign Affairs 1963, Minister Plenipotentiary, Deputy Dir Dept of Int Orgs 1985–88, Dir of Int Econ Dept 1991, Asst Minister for Int Political and Econ Affairs 1992–93; served Geneva, New York and Caribbean countries, Vienna and Tokyo; Deputy Dir UN Inst for the Advancement of Women 1982–85; Amb to Austria and Resident Rep to IAEA, UNIDO and UN Centre for Social and Humanitarian Affairs 1988–91; Amb to Japan 1993–97; Minister of Insurance and Social Affairs 1997–99; Asst UN Sec for UNDP, Arab countries 1997; Sec-Gen Nat Council for Women 2000; Exec Sec UN Econ and Social Comm for Western Asia (ESCWA) 2001–; Rapporteur-Gen UN Conf on Adoption of Int Convention on Prevention of Illicit Drug Trafficking, Vienna 1988; mem UN Cttee on Elimination of Discrimination against Women (CEDAW), Chair 1990–92; Chair UN Comm on Status of Women 1991–93; Chair Working Group on Health, UN Int Conf for the Advancement of Women, Beijing 1995; Head Egyptian Del to Multilateral Middle East Peace Talks Working Group on Econ Regional Co-operation, Brussels 1992, Paris 1992, Rome 1993, to Steering Cttee of Multilateral Middle East Talks, Tokyo 1994; Del to UN Environment Conf, Rio de Janeiro, Brazil 1992, to UN Int Conf on Population and Devt, Cairo 1994; initiator of proposal leading to adoption of UN Declaration for the Protection of Women and Children in Time of Armed Conflicts; mem Club of Rome. *Leisure interests:* theatre, classical music, walking, reading, writing, painting, visiting new places. *Address:* UN House (ESCWA), POB 118575, Beirut, Lebanon (Office); 18 el-Mansour Mohammed St, Apt 15, Zamalek, 11211, Cairo, Egypt (Home). *Telephone:* 198-1301 (Office); (2) 735-8102 (Home); *Fax:* 198-1515 (Office); (2) 735-8102 (Home).

TALLCHIEF, Maria; American ballet dancer; b 24 Jan 1925, Fairfax, OK; d of Alexander Joseph and Ruth Mary (née Porter) Tallchief; m 1st George Balanchine 1946; m 2nd Henry D. Paschen 1956, one d. *Career:* Studied with Bronislava Nijinska; Dancer Ballet Russe de Monte-Carlo 1942–47; Dancer New York City Ballet Co 1947–65, Prima Ballerina 1947–60; Prima Ballerina American Ballet Theatre 1960; Guest Dancer Royal Danish Ballet 1961, Paris Opera 1947; f Chicago City Ballet 1979, Chicago School of Ballet; currently Artistic Dir Lyric Opera Ballet, Chicago, IL; mem Nat Soc of Arts and Letters; several hon degrees; Hon Princess Osage Indian Tribe 1953; Women's Nat Press Club Achievement Award 1953; Dance Educators of America Award 1956; Dance Magazine Award 1960; Capexio Award 1965; Univ of Oklahoma Distinguished Service Award 1972; Jane Addams Humanitarian Award, Rockford Coll 1973; Rosary Coll Bravo Award 1983; Roosevelt Univ Scholarship Asscn Leadership for Freedom Award 1986, Kennedy Center Honor 1996; inducted into Nat Women's Hall of Fame 1996, Int Women's Forum Hall of Fame 1997; Nat Medal of Arts 1999. *Address:* Lyric Opera Ballet, 20 North Wacker Drive, Suite 860, Chicago, IL 60606, USA (Office); 48 Prospect, Highland Park, IL 60035, USA (Home). *Fax:* (847) 266-8782.

TALLCHIEF, Marjorie; American ballet dancer; b 1927; d of the Chief of the Osages Indians; m George Skibine 1947 (died 1981); two s. *Education:* Beverly Hills High School (CA). *Career:* studied with Bronislava Nijinska; joined American Ballet Theatre; Prima Ballerina Ballet de Monte-Carlo 1948, American Ballet Theater 1960, Hamburg State Opera, Germany 1965–; Première Danseuse Etoile Paris Opera 1957–; created role of Medusa in Undertow; Chevalier du Nicham-Iftikar. *Ballets include:* Somnambula, Concerto Barrocco, Les Biches, Boléro, Idylle, Prisoner of the Caucasus, Annabel Lee, The Firebird, Les Noces Fantastiques, Giselle, Conte Cruel, Concerto.

TAMER, Meral, B ARCH; Turkish architect and journalist; b 19 Feb 1946, Istanbul; d of Osman Nuri and Çaziye Artun; m 1st Aydın Kayır 1967 (divorced 1969); m 2nd İsmail Tamer 1971 (divorced 1986); one d. *Education:* German School (Istanbul), Istanbul State Conservatory and Univ of Architecture (Istanbul). *Career:* Architect 1968–; apptd journalist Foreign News Dept, Cumhuriyet 1974, Consumer Affairs columnist 1983–92, Behind the News column 1985–92, Ed Econ Dept 1991; columnist for Sabah newspaper 1992; has appeared in 150 TV programmes on consumer rights; Asscn of Contemporary Journalists Prize 1984, 1986; Municipality of Fatih Prize 1989; Inst of Turkish Standards Prize 1989–91; TUSIAD (Turkish business org) Prize 1990. *Leisure interests:* classical music, piano, travel, reading. *Address:* Sabah Yayincilik Ç, Medya Plaza, Besin Ekspres Yolu, 34540 Güneşli, Istanbul, Turkey (Office); Ortaklar cad, Akıncı bayırı sok, Germi-yanoğlu apt, Mecidiyeköy, Istanbul, Turkey (Home). *Telephone:* (1) 5028184 (Office); (1) 2674904 (Home); *Fax:* (1) 5018590 (Office).

TAMMEL, Leili; Estonian opera and concert singer (mezzo-soprano); b 29 July 1943, Saaremaa; d of Karl and Liina (née Kärner) Tammel; one s. *Education:* Leningrad Conservatoire (now St Petersburg, Russian Fed) and with Vladimir Neroda. *Career:* Soloist Estonia Opera, Tallinn 1973–; Lecturer Estonian Music Acad, Tallinn 1986–; Soloist Camerata Tallinn Ensemble 1986–; has toured Italy, Germany, Portugal, Hungary, Australia, etc 1989–; has played leading roles at Opéra Comique, Paris, Komische Oper Berlin, Halle Opera and Karlsruhe State Opera, Germany, Danish Royal Opera, Copenhagen, Swedish Royal Opera, Stockholm, Finnish Nat Opera, Helsinki, Latvian Nat Opera, Rīga, Maria Theatre, St Petersburg, Bosra Festival, Syria 1987, Savonlinna Opera Festival, Finland 1987; mem jury various nat and int singing contests 1990–; specializes in works of modern Estonian composers and has performed leading roles in operas and oratorios written for her; Georg Ots Vocal Prize 1987; named People's Artist of the Repub of Estonia 1989. *Operas include:* Il Trovatore 1975, 1989, Don Carlos 1976, 1994–, Luisa Miller 1981, Carmen 1982, 1987–88, Alcina 1985, 1989, Un ballo in maschera 1985, Khovanshchina 1987, Cavalleria rusticana 1993; *Recordings include:* Recitals with Camerata Tallinn 1987, 1995, works of Kuldar Sink 1989, 1996, works of Veljo Tormis 1990; numerous film and video recordings. *Leisure interests:* reading, fine arts, nature. *Address:* Estonia Theatre, Estonia pst 4, Tallinn 0105, Estonia (Office); Estonian Music Academy, Kaarli pst 4, 0001 Tallinn, Estonia (Office). *Telephone:* (2) 6260211; *Fax:* (2) 6313680.

TAMONDONG-HELIN, Susan Daet, MA; Philippine international organization official; b 31 Jan 1957, Quezon City; d of Marceline and Concepcion (née Daet) Tamondong; m William Henry Helin 1985. *Education:* Univ of the Philippines, Univ Coll of Law (Manila), Asian Inst of Man, The American Univ (Washington, DC). *Career:* Asst Man, Social Worker Bagong Pag-Asa Foundation, Palawan Islands 1979–80; Supervising Organizational Devt Specialist Ministry of Human Settlements 1980; Resettlement Counsellor, Field Officer and Social Services Officer UNHCR, Manila, Bangkok and Mogadishu 1980–87; Project

Man Consultant Asiatrust Bank, Quezon City 1983–84; Information and Public Relations Officer, Office of the President 1983–84; Founder Tanglaw Publs 1986; Health and Family Services Co-ordinator El Centro De La Raza, Seattle, WA, USA, Area Rep American Int Intercultural Programs, Seattle, Field Dir of Girl Scouts, Seattle 1986–87; Grad Fellow The American Univ, Washington, DC 1988–90; Ed, Resettlement Specialist, Project Admin and Consultant for Asia Region (Environment and Social Issues, Tech Dept) IBRD, Washington, DC 1990–92; mem Women's Int for Peace and Justice, Filipino Asscn for Community Educ, Amnesty Int 1986–87, Soc for Int Devt, Soc for Intercultural Educ, Training and Research; articles on migration in specialist journals. *Leisure interests:* poetry, painting, music, tennis, swimming, photography. *Address:* 3022 Cedar Hill Rd, Falls Church, VA 22042, USA. *Telephone:* (703) 572-6605.

TAMZALI, Wassyla, L EN D; Algerian international organization official; b 10 July 1941. *Education:* Univ of Algiers and Inst des Sciences Politiques (Algiers). *Career:* Lawyer 1967–76; writer and feminist political journalist, Ed-in-Chief of Algerian magazine dealing with women's rights; UNESCO Official in Div of Human Rights and Peace, specializing in Women's Rights and Feminism 1979–. *Publications:* Le Cinéma Algérien et Maghrébin 1979, La Parure des Femmes Abzim 1980. *Address:* UNESCO, Division of Human Rights and Peace, 7 place de Fontenoy, 75700 Paris, France (Office); 23 blvd de Strasbourg, 75010 Paris, France (Home). *Telephone:* (1) 48-00-02-48; *Fax:* (1) 40-65-98-71.

TAN, Amy Ruth, MA, LHD; American writer; b 19 Feb 1952, Oakland, CA; d of John Yuehhan and Daisy Ching (Tu) Tan; m Lou DeMattei 1974. *Education:* San Jose State Univ (CA) and Dominican Coll (San Rafael). *Career:* Specialist in language devt Alameda Co Asscn for Mentally Retarded 1976–80; Project Dir MORE, San Francisco, CA 1980–81; freelance writer 1981–88, now full-time writer; Best American Essays Award 1991. *Publications:* The Joy Luck Club (Best Fiction Award, Commonwealth Club and Bay Area Book Reviewers) 1989, The Kitchen God's Wife 1991, The Moon Lady 1992, The Chinese Siamese Cat 1994, The Hundred Secret Senses 1996, The Bonesetter's Daughter 2000; numerous short stories and essays; *Film:* The Joy Luck Club (screenwriter, producer) 1993. *Address:* c/o Ballantine Publications Publicity, 201 E 50th St, New York, NY 10022, USA.

TAN, Anamah, LL B; Singaporean solicitor; b 6 Sept 1940, Singapore; m 1983; one s one d. *Education:* Univ of Singapore and Royal Inst of Chartered Surveyors. *Career:* Prin Partner all-women law firm, Ann Tan and Assocs; Pres Singapore Council of Women's Orgs 1996; Gen Sec ASEAN Confed of Women's Orgs 1996; Co-Chair Women and Family Violence Cttee 1996; Hon Treas Singapore Asscn of Women Lawyers 1996–; mem Bd and Dir Nat Crime Prevention Council 1995; mem Law Soc of Singapore Council 1995–97, Acad of Law Senate 1996–, Singapore Family Values Promotion Cttee 1996–, ASEAN Women's Programmes 1996–; Professional Assoc Royal Inst of Chartered Surveyors; Pingat Bintang Mars Yarakat (Nat Medal for Community Service) 1993; State Medal (Bronze) for Public Admin 1996. *Publications:* Voices and Choices (jtly, Nat Book Council Award) 1994, Family Law and You, You and the Law II. *Leisure interests:* reading, community work. *Address:* Ann Tan and Associates, 09-05 Far East Finance Bldg, 14 Robinson Rd, 048545, Singapore. *Telephone:* 2255822; *Fax:* 2241515.

TANAKA, Makiko; Japanese politician; b 14 Jan 1944; d of Kakuei Tanaka; m Naoki Tanaka; one s two d. *Education:* Germantown Friends School (USA) and Waseda Univ. *Career:* Pres transport co 1991; joined Social Democratic Party of Japan (SDPJ) 1991; Diet Mem House of Reps for Nigata 1993–; Minister of State, Dir-Gen Science and Tech Agency 1994–2001; Minister for Foreign Affairs 2001–; mem Parl Research Comm on the Constitution, Cttee on Budget, Cttee on Nat Land Devt, Advisory Council on Social Security; Dir Cttee on Health and Welfare, on Educ; Chair Special Cttee on the Aged; mem SDPJ Policy Deliberation Comm; Man Dir BSN (Broadcasting System of Niigata); Vice-Pres, Man Dir Echigo Kotsu (transportation co); mem ILBS (Int Ladies Benevolent Soc); fmr Deputy Dir-Gen LDP Int Bureau. *Publication:* Toki no Sugiyuku Mama ni (As Time Goes By)

1989. *Address:* Ministry of Foreign Affairs, 2-2-1 Kasumigaseki, Chiyoda-ku, 100-8919 Tokyo, Japan. *Telephone:* (3) 3580-3311; *Internet:* www.mofa.go.jp/index.

TANG, Raili Kaarina; Finnish painter; b 19 Dec 1950, Helsinki; d of Leo and Vilma (née Urb) Tang. *Education:* The Free Art School, Univ of Industrial Arts (Helsinki) and School of Finnish Acad of Fine Arts. *Career:* Solo exhibitions in Helsinki, Malmö and Norrköping (Sweden), Stockholm, Turku, Bonn 1980–; group exhibitions 1976–; Dukat Prize for Young Artists 1979. *Leisure interests:* jogging, dogs, art. *Address:* Lemuntie 6, 00510 Helsinki, Finland (Office); Luotsikatu 11 A3, 00160 Helsinki, Finland. *Telephone:* (0) 656450.

TANG MIN. *Career:* Pres China Nat Computer Software and Tech Service Corpn (CS&S), responsible for signing of agreement with Microsoft for jt devt of security components for the Windows operating system in China; Vice-Chair China Software Industry Asscn. *Address:* China National Computer Software & Technology Service Corporation (CS&S), 55 Xueyuan Nanlu, Haidian, Beijing, People's Republic of China.

TANKARD, Meryl; Australian choreographer; b 8 Sept 1955, Darwin; d of (Mick) Clifford and Margot Tankard. *Education:* Australian Ballet School. *Career:* Dancer with Australian Ballet Co 1975–78; Soloist, Pina Bausch Wuppertal Tanztheater (Germany) 1978–84, Guest Performer and Choreographer 1984–89; Artistic Dir Meryl Tankard Co (Canberra) 1989–92, Australian Dance Theatre (Adelaide) 1993–99, Meryl Tankard Australian Dance Theatre 1993–; numerous awards include Sidney Myer Performing Arts Award for Individual Achievement 1993, Victoria Green Room Awards 1993, 1994, Betty Pounder Award for Original Choreography 1994, 'Age' Performing Arts Award for Best Collaboration (Dance) 1995, Mobil Pegasus Award for Best Production 1997. *Major works choreographed include:* Echo Point (Australia) 1984, 1990, Travelling Light (UK and Australia) 1986–87, Two Feet (Australia, NZ, Japan and Germany) 1988–94, VX 18504 (Australia) 1989–95, Court of Flora (Australia) 1990–93, Nuti & Kikimora (Italy, Indonesia, Australia, China and Germany) 1990–94, Chants of Marriage I and II (Australia) 1991–92, Furioso (Australia and overseas) 1993–99, O Let Me Weep (Australia) 1994, Aurora (Australia) 1994–96, Orphee et Eurydice (Australia) 1995–96, Possessed (Australia, France and Germany) 1995–99, The Deep End (Australia) 1996, The Beautiful Game (UK) 2000. *Address:* POB 3129, Bellevue Hill, NSW 2023, Australia.

TANNEN, Deborah; American professor of linguistics and writer. *Career:* Prof of Linguistics Georgetown Univ, Washington, DC; writer Washington Post, New York Times, New York Magazine; appearances on major news and information TV programmes; public speaker to major corpns and civic, professional and govt orgs. *Publications include:* Talking from 9 to 5, You Just Don't Understand, That's Not What I Meant!; has also written 12 other books. *Address:* Georgetown University, Dept of Linguistics, 37th and O Sts, NW, Washington, DC 20057, USA.

TANOUE, Donna; American public administrator. *Education:* Univ of Hawaii and Univ of Georgetown. *Career:* Special Deputy Attorney-Gen Dept of Commerce and Consumer Affairs (Hawaii) 1981–83; Commr for Financial Insts (Hawaii) 1983–87; joined pvt law firm Goodsill Anderson Quinn & Stifel (Hawaii) 1987–, partner; Chair Fed Deposit Insurance Corpn (FDIC) 1998–2001. *Address:* c/o Federal Deposit Insurance Corporation, 550 17th St, NW, Washington, DC 20429, USA.

TANSLEY, Samere Christine; British/Jamaican artist; b 15 June 1944, Worcs, UK; d of Walter and Helen Marjorie Tansley; one s. *Education:* Stourbridge School of Art, Birmingham Coll of Art, Cen School of Art and Goldsmith Coll (London) and Edna Manley School of Visual Arts (Kingston). *Career:* Teacher of art UK 1965–69, Jamaica 1970–80; Lecturer Edna Manley School of Visual Arts 1977, Univ of the W Indies 1979–81; solo exhibitions in Jamaica 1975–2000, UK 1975–90, 1999, Bermuda 1997; group exhibitions in Jamaica, Trinidad, Cayman Islands and Cuba 1975–92; int exhibitions in Los Angeles, Miami, Florida and New York (USA) 1991–92; works feature in public and pvt collections in the Caribbean, UK, Canada and USA including Nat Gallery of

Jamaica; Sec Jamaica Artist and Craftsmen Guild 1977–79, Treas 1979–82; illustrator of children's books for Heinemann and Ministry of Educ 1978–83; Founder-mem Women's Media Watch 1987; Silver Medal for Painting, Jamaica Independence 1985; Rotary Club of Kingston and St Andrew Art Award 1986. *Leisure interests:* walking, swimming, gardening. *Address:* POB 344, Stony Hill, Kingston 9, Jamaica (Home). *Telephone:* 942-2203 (Home).

TAO JIE; Chinese professor of English; b 19 Sept 1936, Shanghai; d of Kangde and Mangqing (née Ho) Tao; m Cheng'en Ni 1965; one d. *Education:* No 1 Girls' School (Shanghai), Beijing Univ and State Univ of New York. *Career:* Asst Lecturer Dept of Western Languages, Beijing Univ 1958–78, Lecturer 1978–80, Assoc Prof 1980–85, mem Council 1984–, Assoc Chair Dept of English 1985–88, Prof 1985–, apptd Dir Women's Studies Center 1991; Visiting Scholar State Univ of New York 1979–81; Fulbright Visiting Scholar Univ of Virginia, USA 1986–87; Pres Soc for the Study of Women's Literature 1995–; mem Council Beijing Branch Soc of Translators 1983–, Chinese Asscn for Study of American Literature 1985–88 (Vice-Pres 1991–), Chinese Asscn of Foreign Literature 1987–. *Publications:* A Companion to English Studies (Research Award 1987) 1986, The Best of Faulkner (ed) 1990; numerous articles on American Literature for Chinese journals and magazines. *Leisure interests:* knitting, philately. *Address:* Beijing University, Dept of English, Beijing, People's Republic of China. *Telephone:* (1) 62752684; *Fax:* (1) 62751587.

TAPIA, Amalia, BA; Panamanian artist. *Education:* Nat Univ of Panama. *Career:* Solo exhibitions in Panamá include Panamanian Art Inst 1974, 1976, 1978, 1979, Etcetera Gallery 1975, 1980, Union Club 1981, Arte ol Gallery 1982, Atlapa 1985, Mery de Bernal Gallery 1987; group exhibitions include Univ of Panamá 1973, 1974, Chase Manhattan Bank Gallery, Panamá 1976, 2nd Art Biennial of Cen America, San Salvador 1977, Art Biennial of Honduras 1979, Casa de las Americas, Havana 1982, Museum of Mar del Plata, Argentina 1986, First Ceramic Contest, Art Museum of San José, Costa Rica 1991, Gran Avda Gallery, Santa Fe de Bogotá 1991, Lisbon 1991; Fellow Inst for Int Educ 1975; First Prize Second Nat Painting Contest, Cervecería Nacional 1986. *Leisure interest:* ceramics. *Address:* POB 1254, Panamá 9A, Panama.

TARJÁN, Anna, DR ING; Hungarian politician; b 27 Aug 1932, Lenti; d of József and Anna (née Keserü) Tajnafói; m László Tarján 1957; one s one d. *Education:* Univ of Forestry (Sopron). *Career:* Forestry Engineer Forestry and Timber Office, Somogy County 1957–60, Sr Officer 1960–77, Dir of Forest Econ 1989–90; Forestry Engineer Nature Conservation Advisory Bd 1977–79; Sec for Environmental Protection, Somogy County Council 1979–89; Sec-Gen Ind Smallholders' Party, mem Political Parl Cttee 1989–90, Nat Bd Political Comm 1990; elected mem Nat Ass (Parl) 1990, Parl State Sec 1990; mem Nat Asscn of Forestry; Széchenyi Commemorative Medal, Nat Environment Authority 1977; Medal for Devt of the Human Environment 1979; Pro Urbe Medal, Hungarian Asscn of Architects 1989; Order of Labour 1989 Silver. *Publications:* Environmental Values on the Coast of Lake Balaton 1984, Protected Nature Values in County Somogy 1989; 26 papers on forestry and environmental protection 1958–89. *Leisure interests:* belles-lettres, tourism. *Address:* c/o Ministry of the Environment and Regional Policy, 1394 Budapest, Fő u 44-50, POB 351, Hungary (Office); 1054 Budapest, Bank u 3, Hungary (Home). *Telephone:* (1) 201-2725 (Office); *Fax:* (1) 201-4880 (Office).

TARKOWSKA, Anna, MD; Polish scientist and educator; b 11 October 1931, Lublin; d of the late Władysław Tarkowski and Irena Tarkowska. *Education:* Medical Univs of Lublin and Poznań and Medical Research Centre (Warsaw). *Career:* Scientist Univ of Lublin 1959–; Asst then Sr Asst, Clinic of Internal Medicine 1959–68, Head of Radioisotope Dept 1969–77, apptd Head of Dept of Nuclear Medicine 1977, Assoc Prof 1977–87, Prof 1987–; has written about 190 scientific papers mainly on the application of radioisotopes in cardiology and pulmonology; Fellow Humboldt Foundation 1972–73, 1978–79, 1983; mem Cttee of Medical Physics 1984–89, Nat Consultant Group for Radiology, Nuclear Medicine and Ultrasonography 1987–91, Cttee of Applied Radiation Research, Polish Acad of Science (PAN) 1990–92; Pres Polish Soc of Nuclear Medicine 1984–90; IAEA Expert in Nuclear Medicine 1988–; Gold Cross of Merit 1979. *Leisure interests:* collecting books, tourism, swimming. *Address:* Akademia Medyczna w Lublinie, Dept of Nuclear Medicine, Ulica Jaczewskiego 8, 20-090 Lublin, Poland. *Telephone:* (81) 776391; *Fax:* (81) 775710.

TASCA, Catherine, L EN D; French politician and business executive; b 13 Dec 1941, Lyons; d of Angelo Tasca and Alice Naturel; one d. *Education:* Inst d'Etudes Politiques and Ecole Nat d'Admin (Paris). *Career:* Civil servant Ministry of Culture 1967; Dir Maison de la Culture, Grenoble 1973; Gen Man Ensemble Intercontemporain 1978; Co-Dir Théâtre de Nanterre-Amandiers 1982; mem Comm Nat de la Communication et des Libertés (CNCL) 1986; Minister-Del attached to the Minister of Culture and Communications 1988–91, Sec of State for Francophone Countries and External Cultural Relations attached to the Minister for Foreign Affairs 1992–93; Minister of Culture and Communications 2000–; Pres Admin Bd Canal + Horizons 1993–97; Deputy to Nat Ass from Yvelines 1997–, mem Socialist Party. *Address:* Ministry of Culture, 3 rue Valois, 75001 Paris, France (Office); 21 rue Saint-Amand, 75015 Paris, France (Home). *Telephone:* (1) 40-15-80-00 (Office); *Fax:* (1) 42-61-35-77 (Office).

TASS, Nadia, BA, DIP ED; Australian film director; b 30 June 1956, Greece; d of Christo Tashevski and Ekaterina Tashevska; m David Parker 1981; two s. *Education:* Univ of Melbourne, State Coll (Melbourne), Secondary Teachers' Coll (Melbourne) and Australian Nat Theatre. *Career:* Film and Theatre Dir; owner The Melbourne Film Studio; Byron Kennedy Award for Pursuit of Excellence 1986; Australian Critics' Circle Award for Best Dir 1987; Australian Hellenic Award 1987. *Films:* Malcolm (Australian Film Inst Award for Best Dir, Golden Sprocket Award for Best Film of London Film Festival) 1986, Rikki and Pete 1988, The Big Steal 1990, Pure Luck 1991, Stark 1992, Mr Reliable 1996. *Address:* Cascade Films, 117 Rouse St, Port Melbourne, Victoria, NSW 3207, Australia. *Telephone:* (613) 646 4022; *Fax:* (613) 646 6336.

TATISHVILI, Tsisana Bezhanovna; Georgian opera singer (soprano); b 30 Dec 1939, Tbilisi. *Education:* Sarandzhishvili Conservatoire (Tbilisi). *Career:* Soloist with Tbilisi State Opera 1963–; has toured in Germany, Poland, Czechoslovakia and other countries; People's Artist of Georgian SSR 1973; Paliashvili Prize 1979; People's Artist of USSR 1979. *Operas include:* Eugene Onegin, Queen of Spades, Aida, Il Trovatore, Don Giovanni, Lohengrin, Salome, Otello, Cavalleria Rusticana, Absalom and Eteri. *Address:* c/o Georgian State Opera, Tbilisi, Georgia.

TAUBIRA-DELANNON, Christiane; French politician; b 2 Feb 1952, Cayenne (Guyana). *Career:* Fmr MEP (Group of the European Radical Alliance, Energie Radicale), mem Cttee on Devt and Co-operation, Del for relations with the countries of S America. *Address:* c/o European Parliament, rue Wiertz, 1047 Brussels, Belgium.

TAUZIAT, Nathalie; French tennis player; b 17 Oct 1967, Bangui (Cen African Repub). *Career:* French women's No 1 lawn tennis player 1987–94; first player selected to play for France in Fed Cup 11 times; ranked 11th in the world 1992, 18th 1994, 24th 1995, 3rd 2000; quarter-finalist French Open 1991, Wimbledon 1992, 1997, 1999, 2001, US Open 2000; semi-finalist Masters of New York 1997, 1999, Grand Slam Cup 1998; finalist Wimbledon 1998; has won ten World Tennis Asscn Singles Titles including Futures/Limoges 1987, Québec 1993, Eastbourne 1995, Moscow 1999, Paris Indoors 2000; mem Exec Cttee Fed Française de Tennis; Tennis Consultant Eurosport TV Channel. *Publication:* Les Dessous du Tennis Féminin 2000. *Leisure interests:* films, golf. *Address:* Residence les Arcades, rue Barthes, 64600 Anglet, France; c/o BML, 8 rue de Saintonge, 75003 Paris, France. *Telephone:* (6) 08-48-03-27 (Anglet); (1) 42-77-82-18 (Paris); *Fax:* (5) 59-52-27-98.

TAVARES DA SILVA, Maria Regina, BA; Portuguese civil servant; b 11 Oct 1938; d of Eduardo da Conceicão and Maria Helena de Noura Neves Xavier Amorim; m Armando Tavares Da Silva 1967; three d. *Education:* Univs of Lisbon and Cambridge (UK). *Career:* Officer Govt Comm on the Status of Women, Pres 1986–92; Pres Cttee for Equality of Women, Council of Europe 1987, 1988, 1992, 1993, EC Advisory Cttee on Equal Opportunities 1991, Experts Group on Parity Democracy, Council of Europe 1991–92; Consultant Div for the

Advancement of Women, UN 1991; apptd Adviser Govt Comm for Equality and Women's Rights 1992; elected mem Cttee on the Elimination of Discrimination Against Women of the UN 2001–(2004); numerous contribs to professional journals 1976–; Pres of the Repub's Medal of Merit 1995. *Publications include:* Feminismo em Portugal na voz das Mulheres Escritoras do imício do séc XX 1982, A Mulher: Bibliografia Portuguesa Anotada (1518–1998) 1999. *Leisure interest:* reading. *Address:* c/o Commissão para a Igualdade e para os Direitos das Mulheres, Av da República 32, 1°, 1050-193 Lisbon, Portugal (Office); Rua Cidade de Cádiz 9, 7°, 1500-156 Lisbon, Portugal (Home). *Telephone:* (21) 7983014 (Office); (21) 7262624 (Home); *Fax:* (21) 7983098 (Office); *E-mail:* regina.tavares@mail.sitepae.pt.

TAVARES DIAS, Marina; Portuguese publishing executive and writer; b 25 May 1960. *Career:* Journalist on Portugal Hoje, Diario Popular, Diario de Lisboa 1979–; writer 1987–; Publishing Dir Ibis Editores 1990–; Julio Cezar Machado Award for Journalism 1985, 1986; Julio Castilho Award for Literature 1987. *Publications:* Lisboa Desaparecida (vol 1) 1987, (vol 2) 1990, Photographias de Lisboa 1988, Mario Sá-Carneiro – Fotobiografia 1988, Rossio, Feira da Ladra, A Lisboa de Fernando Pessoa 1990. *Leisure interests:* collecting postcards, collecting film memorabilia. *Address:* Ibis Editores, Av D. Vasco da Gama 30, 1300 Lisbon, Portugal (Office); Av Almirante Reis 29, 3 Dto, 1100 Lisbon, Portugal (Home). *Telephone:* (1) 3018337 (Office); (1) 530518 (Home).

TAVERNE, Suzanna, BA; British museum administrator; b 3 Feb 1960; d of Dick and Janice Taverne; m Marc Vlessing 1993; one s one d. *Education:* Pimlico School, Westminster School and Balliol Coll (Oxford). *Career:* Publishing adviser Corp Finance Dept, S. G. Warburg and Co 1982–90; Strategic Planning Exec Newspaper Publishing PLC 1990–92, Finance Dir (first woman mem Bd of Dirs) 1992–94; consultant to Saatchi & Saatchi PLC 1994–95; Dir of Strategy and Devt, Pearson PLC then Man Dir FT Finance, Financial Times Group 1995–98; Man Dir British Museum, London 1999–. *Address:* British Museum, Great Russell St, London WC1B 3DG, UK. *Telephone:* (20) 7323-8948; *Fax:* (20) 7323-8118; *E-mail:* info@british-museum.ac.uk; *Internet:* www.british-museum.ac.uk.

TAVERNER, Sonia; Canadian ballet dancer; b 18 May 1936, Byfleet, Surrey, UK; d of H. F. and Evelyn N. Taverner. *Education:* Elmhurst Ballet School, Royal Ballet School (London) and Ballet Arts and American Ballet Theater (New York). *Career:* Joined Royal Ballet, London 1955, and toured USA and Canada; joined Royal Winnipeg Ballet 1956, Leading Dancer 1957, Ballerina 1962–66; appeared with Royal Winnipeg Ballet, Commonwealth Arts Festival, London 1964; Prin Dancer Les Grands Ballets Canadiens 1966–74; Prin Artist with The Pennsylvania Ballet, USA 1971–72; Head of Ballet Div, Grant MacEwan Community Coll 1975–80; Dir Professional Program Devt, Alberta Ballet School 1981–82; f School of Classical Ballet, AB 1982–97; Producer own concert 'Variations' 1977; Guest Artist with Boston Ballet Co 1967, Vancouver Opera 1977, Les Grands Ballets Canadiens 1977, 1978, Alberta Ballet Co 1978, 1979, Toronto, Winnipeg and Vancouver Symphony Orchestras; Guest Teacher Les Grands Ballets Canadiens Summer School 1970, Alberta Ballet Summer School 1975, 1976, Pacific Ballet Theatre Summer School 1979, in Penticton, BC 1984–85; guest teacher with Edmonton Dance Centre 1998–; has toured extensively in N America, Jamaica and UK; mem Royal Acad of Dancing, Actors' Equity Asscn, American Guild of Musical Artists; Dame Adeline Genée Silver Medal 1954; Canada Council Exploration Grant 1977. *Ballets include:* Swan Lake, Sleeping Beauty, Giselle, Nutcracker, Raymonda and Les Sylphides. *Leisure interests:* books, cooking, gardening. *Address:* POB 2039, Stony Plain, AB T7Z 1X6, Canada.

TAWIL, Suha; Israeli political adviser; b 1963; d of Raymonda Tawil; m Yasser Arafat 1991. *Education:* Univ de Paris (Sorbonne). *Career:* Responsible for protocol during Yasser Arafat's visit to Paris 1989, later econs adviser to Yasser Arafat. *Address:* c/o Palestine National Authority (PNA), Gaza City, Israel.

TAY, Alice Erh-Soon, AO, PH D; Australian professor of jurisprudence; b 2 Feb 1934, Singapore; d of Tay Chin Wah and Tan Guek Cheng; m Eugene Kamenka 1964 (deceased). *Education:* Raffles Girls' School (Singapore), ANU and Lincoln's Inn (UK). *Career:* Called to Bar,

Singapore 1956, legal practice 1956–58; Asst Lecturer Univ of Malaya 1958–60; Postdoctoral Research Scholar Moscow State Univ 1961–64; Tutor, Sr Tutor, Lecturer, Sr Lecturer, Reader ANU 1966–75; Challis Prof of Jurisprudence Univ of Sydney 1975–; Pres Human Rights and Equal Opportunity Comm 1998–; Visiting Fellow and Prof numerous univs in USA and Canada; Fellow Acad of Social Sciences of Australia 1986; Hon LL D (Edinburgh) 1989; Titular Academician (Int Acad of Comparative Law) 1986. *Publications include:* Human Rights in Australia 1988; Law and Australian Legal Thinking in the 1980s, Australian Law and Legal Thinking between the Decades; numerous contribs to professional journals. *Leisure interest:* thinking. *Address:* 24 Batemans Rd, Gladesville, NSW 2111, Australia.

TAY, Jannie, M SC; Singaporean business executive; b 7 May 1945, Ipoh, Perak, Malaysia; m Henry Tay Yun Chwan; two d one s. *Education:* Monash Univ (Australia). *Career:* Worked in family watch-manufacturing enterprise; Lecturer Physiology Dept, Nat Univ of Singapore 1971–73; Man Dir, Co Dir The Hour Glass Ltd (mfr, wholesaler and retailer of high quality time pieces and jewellery in Singapore, Australia, Hong Kong, Indonesia, Malaysia, Switzerland, Repun of China (Taiwan) and Thailand) 1979–; co has received numerous awards including Enterprise Award 1990, Nat Productivity Award 1991, Specialty Store of the Year Award (Singapore Tourist Promotion Bd); Co-Founder East–West Foundation, Australia; Vice-Pres Singapore Retailers Asscn; Chair Women for Women Foundation (Asia Pacific) Inc (Pres Women for Women Asscn, Singapore); Deputy Pres Governing Council ASEAN Business Forum; mem Int Women's Forum, World Econ Forum; Special Volunteer Award, Community Chest of Singapore 1988. *Leisure interests:* charities, helping women's development, swimming, reading. *Address:* The Hour Glass Ltd, 302 Orchard Rd, 11-01 Tong Bldg, 0923, Singapore (Office); 4 AC Nassim Rd, 1025 Singapore (Home). *Telephone:* 787-2288 (Office); *Fax:* 732-8683 (Office).

TAYLOR, Ann (Winifred Ann), MA, B SC; British politician; b 2 July 1947, Motherwell; d of the late John and Doreen (née Bowling) Walker; m David Taylor 1966; one s one d. *Education:* Bolton School, Univs of Bradford and Sheffield. *Career:* Mem Lab Party; Councillor Holmfirth Urban Dist Council 1972–74; MP for Bolton West 1974–83, for Dewsbury 1987–; Parl Pvt Sec to Sec of State for Educ and Science 1975–76, for Defence 1976–79; Asst Govt Whip 1977–79; Opposition Spokesperson on Educ 1979–81, on Housing 1981–83, on the Home Office 1987–90, on the Environment 1990–92, on Education 1992–94, Shadow Leader of the House of Commons and Spokesperson on Citizen's Charter 1994–, Chief Whip 1998–2001; part-time tutor Open Univ; Monitoring Officer Housing Corpn 1985–87; mem Asscn of Univ Teachers; Hon Fellow Birkbeck Coll (London). *Publication:* Choosing Our Future: a practical politics of the environment 1992. *Leisure interests:* reading, walking, football. *Address:* House of Commons, London SW1A 0AA, UK (Office); Glyn Garth, Stoney Bank Rd, Thongsbridge, Huddersfield, Yorks HD7 2SL, UK (Home). *Telephone:* (20) 7219-3000.

TAYLOR, Anna Diggs, LL B; American federal judge; b 9 Dec 1932, Washington, DC; d of Virginius Douglass and Hazel (née Bramlette) Johnston; m S. Martin Taylor 1976; one s one d. *Education:* Barnard Coll and Yale Univ (CT). *Career:* Called to the Bar, DC 1957, MI 1961; Asst Prosecutor Wayne Co, MI 1961–62; Asst US Attorney E Dist of Michigan 1966, Dist Judge 1979–; Partner Zwerdling, Maurer, Diggs and Papp 1970–75; Asst Corp Counsel City of Detroit, MI 1975–79; Adjunct Prof of Labor Law Wayne State Univ, MI 1976; mem Fed Bar Asscn, Yale Law Asscn; Trustee Receiving Hosp, Detroit, Detroit Symphony, Community Foundation, Greater Detroit Health Council. *Address:* US District Court, 231 W Lafayette Blvd, 740 US Courthouse, Detroit, MI 48226, USA.

TAYLOR, Dame Elizabeth Rosemond, DBE; British film actress; b 27 Feb 1932, London; d of Francis and Sara (née Sothern) Taylor; m 1st Conrad Nicholas Hilton, Jr 1950 (divorced); m 2nd Michael Wilding 1952 (divorced); two s; m 3rd Mike Todd 1957 (died 1958); one d; m 4th Eddie Fisher 1959 (divorced); m 5th Richard Burton 1964 (divorced 1974, remarried 1975, divorced 1976); one adopted d; m 7th John Warner 1976 (divorced 1982); m 8th Larry Fortensky 1991 (divorced 1996). *Education:* Byron House, Hawthorne School and Metro-

Goldwyn-Mayer School. *Career:* Active in philanthropic and relief charitable causes internationally including Israeli War Victims Fund for the Chaim Sheba Hosp 1976, UNICEF, Variety Children's Hosps, medical clinics in Botswana; initiated Ben Gurion V–Elizabeth Taylor Fund for Children of the Negev 1982; Chair American Foundation for AIDS Research 1985–, Int Fund 1985–; Founder Elizabeth Taylor AIDS Foundation 1991–; several licensed fragrances: Elizabeth Taylor's Passion, Passion for Men, White Diamonds/Elizabeth Taylor, Elizabeth Taylor's Diamonds and Emeralds, Diamonds and Rubies, Diamonds and Sapphires, jewelry: The Elizabeth Taylor Fashion Jewelry Collection for Avon; Cecil B. De Mille Award 1984; Commdr des Arts et des Lettres 1985; Commdr de la Légion d'Honneur 1987; Onassis Foundation Award 1988; Jean Hersholt Humanitarian Acad Award (for work as AIDS advocate); Life Achievement Award, American Film Inst 1993; Lifetime Achievement Award, Screen Actors Guild 1998; BAFTA Fellowship 1999; honoured with dedication of Elizabeth Taylor Clinic, Washington 1993. *Plays include:* The Little Foxes, (New York) 1981, (Los Angeles) 1981, (London) 1982, Private Lives 1983; *Films include:* Lassie Come Home 1942, The White Cliffs of Dover 1943, Jane Eyre 1943, National Velvet 1944, Courage of Lassie 1945, Life With Father 1946, A Date With Judy 1948, Little Women 1949, Father of the Bride 1950, A Place in the Sun 1951, Ivanhoe 1952, Elephant Walk 1954, Beau Brummel 1954, Rhapsody 1954, The Last Time I Saw Paris 1955, Giant 1956, Raintree Country 1957, Cat on a Hot Tin Roof 1958, Suddenly Last Summer 1959, Butterfield 8 (Acad Award for Best Actress) 1960, Cleopatra 1962, The VIPs 1963, The Sandpiper 1965, Who's Afraid of Virginia Woolf? (Acad Award for Best Actress) 1966, The Taming of the Shrew 1967, The Comedians 1967, Reflections in a Golden Eye 1967, Doctor Faustus 1968, Boom 1968, Secret Ceremony 1968, The Only Game in Town 1969, Under Milk Wood 1971, X, Y and Zee 1971, Hammersmith is Out (Silver Bear Award, Berlin) 1972, Night Watch 1973, Ash Wednesday 1974, Identikit 1974, Blue Bird 1975, A Little Night Music 1976, The Mirror Crack'd 1981, Winter Kills 1985, The Young Toscanini 1988, The Flintstones 1994; *TV appearances include:* Return Engagement 1979, Between Friends 1983, Malice in Wonderland 1985, North and South 1985, Hotel, Poker Alice, Sweet Bird of Youth 1989; *Publications:* World Enough and Time (with Richard Burton) 1964, Elizabeth Taylor 1965, Elizabeth Taylor Takes Off – On Weight Gain, Weight Loss, Self-Esteem and Self Image 1988. *Address:* POB 55995, Sherman Oaks, CA 91413, USA.

TAYLOR, Joyce, BA, M SC; British television executive; b 14 March 1948, Glasgow; d of Lord and Lady Taylor of Gryfe; m John Huw Lloyd-Richards 1982; one s one d. *Education:* Hutchesons Girls' Grammar School and Univ of Strathclyde. *Career:* Mem Production Staff BBC 1968–70; Producer in audio-visual service, Univ of Glasgow 1977–85; Head of Programming Clyde Cablevision 1985–89; Chief Exec United Artists Programming 1989–95; Man Dir Discovery Communications Europe 1995–; Fellow Royal Television Soc; Lifetime Achievement Award (Royal Television Soc) 1998. *Leisure interests:* theatre, reading, walking. *Address:* Discovery Communications Europe, 160 Great Portland St, London W1N 5TB, UK; 75 Wood Vale, London N10 3DL, UK (Home). *Telephone:* (20) 7462-3600 (Office); (20) 8374-1063 (Home); *Fax:* (20) 7631-1558 (Office); (20) 8374-1064 (Home).

TAYLOR, Judy (Julia Marie), MBE, FRSA; British writer; b 12 Aug 1932, Murton, S Wales; adopted d of Gladys Spicer Taylor; m Richard Hough 1980 (died 1999). *Education:* St Paul's Girls' School (London). *Career:* Joined Children's Book Section, The Bodley Head publishing house 1951–67, Dir 1967–84, Deputy Man Dir 1971–80; mem UNICEF Int Arts Cttee 1968–70, 1976, 1982–83, UK UNICEF Greetings Card Cttee 1982–85; Chair Children's Book Group 1969–72, mem Council 1972–78; mem Publishers' Asscn Council 1972–78; mem Book Devt Council 1973–76; Consultant to Penguin Books on Beatrix Potter 1981–87, 1989–92; Assoc Dir Weston Woods Inst, USA 1984–; Consulting Ed Reinhardt Books 1988–93; Trustee Volunteer Reading Help 2000–. *Publications include:* Sophie and Jack 1982, My First Year: a Beatrix Potter baby book 1983, Sophie and Jack in the Snow 1984, Beatrix Potter: artist, storyteller and countrywoman 1986, Dudley and the Monster 1986, That Naughty Rabbit: Beatrix Potter and Peter Rabbit 1987, My Cat 1987, Dudley Bakes a Cake 1988, Sophie and Jack in the Rain 1989, Beatrix Potter's Letters: a selection 1989, Letters to Children from Beatrix Potter 1992, Beatrix: a Play (jtly) 1996, Sketches for Friends by Edward Ardizzone (ed) 2000. *Leisure interests:* gardening, collecting early children's books. *Address:* 31 Meadowbank, Primrose Hill Rd, London NW3 3AY, UK. *Telephone:* (20) 7722-5663; *Fax:* (20) 7722-7750; *E-mail:* taylor.hough@talk21.com.

TAYLOR, Wendy Ann, CBE, FZS, FRBS; British sculptor; b 29 July 1945, Stamford, Lincs; d of Edward P. Taylor and Lilian M. Wright; m Bruce Robertson 1982; one s. *Education:* St Martin's School of Art (London). *Career:* Solo exhibitions at Axiom Gallery, London 1970, Angela Flowers Gallery, London 1972, King's Lynn Festival and World Trade Centre, London 1974, Annely Juda Fine Art, London 1975, Oxford Gallery, Oxford 1976, Oliver Dowling Gallery, Dublin 1976, 1979, Bldg Centre Gallery 1986, Austin, Desmond and Phipps, London 1992, Nature and Eng, Osbourne Group, London 1998; participated in more than 100 group exhibitions 1964–82; work rep in collections in UK, Europe, USA; numerous major comms in towns and cities throughout UK including Globe View, Blackfriars, London 2000, Millennium Fountain, Chase Gardens, Enfield 2000; designed numerous awards; mem Fine Art Bd, Council of Acad Awards 1980–85, specialist adviser 1985–93; mem Cttee for Art and Design, Council of Nat Acad Awards, Royal Fine Art Comm 1981–99, Council Morley Coll 1984–88, Court RCA; Design Consultant New Towns Comm, Basildon 1985–88, London Borough of Barking and Dagenham 1989–93, 1997–; mem Advisory Bd London Docklands Devt Corpn 1989–98, Advisory Group of the Polytechnics and Colls Funding Council 1989–90; Trustee Leics Arts and Music Appeal 1993–; Fellow Queen Mary and Westfield Coll London, Royal Soc of British Sculptors; Walter Neurath Award 1964; Pratt Award 1965; Sainsbury Award 1966; Arts Council Award 1977; Duais Na Riochta Gold Medal, Ireland 1977. *Leisure interest:* gardening. *Address:* 73 Bow Rd, London E3 2AN, UK. *Telephone:* (20) 8981-2037; *Fax:* (20) 8980-3153.

TCHERINA, Ludmila (Tchemerzine, Monika); French actress, dancer, painter, sculptor and writer; b 10 Oct 1924, Paris; d of Prince Avenir Tchemerzine and Stéphane Finette; m 1st Edmond Audran (deceased); m 2nd Raymond Roi 1953. *Education:* Privately and studied under Yvan Clustine. *Career:* First Dancer and Choreographer Grands Ballets de Monte-Carlo (youngest ever prima ballerina) 1940–44, Ballets de Paris 1951–58; has performed in Paris, at La Scala, Milan, Italy 1954, Bolshoi Theatre, Moscow 1959, Buenos Aires 1967, Venice 1961, Brussels, Florence, Italy; Founder Compagnie de Ballet Ludmila Tcherina 1958; works have been exhibited at Sully Museum and Centre Nat d'Art et de Culture Georges-Pompidou, Paris, Universal Exhibition, Seville, Spain 1992, EP, Strasbourg, France and in many cities world-wide; Officier de la Légion d'Honneur 1980; Chevalier des Arts et des Lettres, des Palmes Académiques; Paris Gold Medal 1959; Oscar Italien de la Popularité 1959; Prix Michel Ange 1973; Prix d'Honneur Gemail 1973; Grande Médaille de Vermeil de la Ville de Paris 1978; Prix d'Interprétation, Monte-Carlo. *Ballets include:* Romeo and Juliet 1942, Giselle 1954, 1959, Le martyre de Saint Sébastien 1957, 1967, Les amants de Téruel 1959, Gala (by Salvador Dali and Maurice Béjart) 1961, 1962, La muette de Portici 1968, Anna Karénine 1975; *Films include:* The Red Shoes, The Tales of Hoffmann (Acad Award for Best Performance by a Foreign Actress 1952), Clara de Montargis, La légende de Parsifal, La nuit s'achève (Prize for Best Feminine Performance, Vichy Film Festival 1950), Oh! Rosalinda, A la mémoire d'un héros (First Prize Dance Film Festival, Buenos Aires 1952), La fille de Mata-Hari, Honeymoon, Les amants de Téruel (Cannes Film Festival French Entry 1962, New York Critics' Award), Jeanne au bûcher; *TV appearances include:* Le mandarin merveilleux, Bonaparte, Salomé, La possédée, La dame aux camélias, La passion d'Anna Karénine, La création de la Féminine (based on her career), La Reine de Saba, Portrait de Ludmila Tcherina; *Publications:* Novels: L'amour au miroir 1983, La femme à l'envers 1986. *Address:* 42 cours Albert 1er, 75008 Paris, France. *Telephone:* (1) 43-59-18-33.

TCHERKASSKY, Marianna Alexsavena; American ballet dancer; b 28 Oct 1952, Glen Cove, NY; d of Alexis and Lillian (née Oka) Tcherkassky; m Terrence S. Orr. *Education:* Washington School of Ballet and School of American Ballet. *Career:* Dancer (while still at ballet school) Bolshoi Ballet 1961, 1962, New York City Ballet 1963; Dancer Andre Eglevsky Ballet Co, American Ballet Theater 1970–, Soloist 1972–76, Prin Dancer 1976–; Guest Dancer with ballet cos in USA and Europe; several TV appearances; Ford Foundation Scholar 1967–70; First Prize Nat Soc of Arts and Letters Competition 1967. *Ballets include:*

Configuration, Grand Pas Romantique, Push Comes to Shove, The Nutcracker, Romeo and Juliet. *Address:* c/o American Ballet Theater, 890 Broadway, New York, NY 10003, USA.

TE ATAIRANGIKAAHU, Arikinui, ONZ, DBE; New Zealand head of Maori kingship; b 23 July 1931; d of King Koroki V; m Whatumoana 1952; five d two s. *Education:* Waikato School (Hamilton, NZ). *Career:* Elected Head of Maori Kingship and made Arikinui (Queen) 1966; Dr hc (Waikato) 1979; Order of St John 1986. *Leisure interest:* promoting Maori culture and tradition. *Address:* Turongo House, Turangawaewae Marae, Ngaruawahia, New Zealand.

TE KANAWA, Dame Kiri Jeanette Claire, DBE, ONZ, AO; New Zealand opera singer (soprano); b 6 March 1944, Gisborne; m Desmond Park 1967 (divorced 1997); one s one d (both adopted). *Education:* St Mary's Coll (Auckland) and London Opera Centre. *Career:* Debut at Royal Opera, Covent Garden, London 1970, Santa Fe Opera, USA 1971, Lyons Opera 1972, Metropolitan Opera, New York 1974, La Scala, Milan 1978, Salzburg Festival 1979; appeared at Australian Opera, Royal Opera House Covent Garden, Paris Opera during 1976–77 season; appeared at San Francisco Opera Co, USA, Edinburgh Festival, Helsinki Festival 1980, Last Night of the BBC Promenade Concerts, London 1992; sang at wedding of HRH the Prince of Wales and Lady Diana Spencer July 1981; appeared in '2000 Today' on 1 January 2000; Hon Fellow Somerville Coll, Oxford 1983, Wolfson Coll, Cambridge 1997; Hon LL D (Dundee) 1982; Hon D MUS (Durham) 1982, (Oxford) 1983, (Nottingham) 1992, (Waikato) 1995, (Cambridge) 1997; Hon D LITT (Warwick) 1989. *Operas include:* Boris Godunov, Parsifal, The Marriage of Figaro, Otello, Carmen, Simon Boccanegra, Carmen, Faust, Don Giovanni, The Magic Flute, La Bohème, Eugene Onegin, Così fan Tutte, Arabella, Die Fledermaus, La Traviata, Der Rosenkavalier, Manon Lescaut, Don Giovanni (film) 1979, Samson, Don Carlos, Capriccio, Vanessa 2001; *Recordings include:* Don Giovanni, Così fan Tutte, Carmen, Mozart Vespers, Mozart C Minor Mass, The Magic Flute, The Marriage of Figaro, Hansel and Gretel, La Bohème, Capriccio, French and German arias and songs, Maori songs, Strauss Songs with Orchestra; recital records; *Publication:* Land of the Long White Cloud 1989, Opera for Lovers 1997. *Leisure interests:* golf, swimming, cooking. *Address:* c/o Jules Haefliger, Impresario AG, Postfach 3320, 6002 Lucerne, Switzerland. *Telephone:* (41) 320 1915.

TEBALDI, Renata; Italian opera singer (soprano); b 1 Feb 1922, Pesaro; d of Teobaldo and Guiseppina (née Barbieri) Tebaldi. *Education:* Arrigo Boito Conservatory (Parma), Gioacchino Rossini Conservatory (Pesaro), then pupil of Carmen Melis and Giuseppe Pais. *Career:* Debut as Elena in Mefistofele, Rovigo 1944; has sung the principal soprano operatic roles in America and Europe; Chevalier de la Légion d'Honneur 1995. *Recordings include:* Cavalleria Rusticana, La Traviata, Tosca, Adriana Lecouvreur, La Giaconda, Manon Lescaut. *Address:* 1 piazza Guastalla, Milan, Italy; c/o S A Gorlinsky Ltd, 33 Dover St, London W1X 4NJ, UK. *Telephone:* (20) 7493-9158 (London).

TEETERS, Nancy Hays, MA; American economist and civil servant; b 29 July 1930, Marion, IN; d of S. Edgar and Mabel (née Drake) Hays; m Robert D. Teeters 1952; two s one d. *Education:* Public schools in Marion, IN, Oberlin Coll and Univ of Michigan. *Career:* Teaching Fellow Univ of Michigan and Univ of Maryland Overseas, Germany 1954–57; Economist Bd of Govs, Fed Reserve System 1957–62, 1963–66, mem Bd of Govs 1978–84; Economist seconded to Council of Econ Advisers 1962–63; Fiscal Analyst Office of Man and Budget, Exec Office of the Pres 1966–70; Sr Fellow Brookings Inst 1970–73; Sr Specialist Congressional Research Service, Library of Congress 1973–74; Chief Economist House Budget Cttee, House of Reps, US Congress 1973–78; Vice-Pres, Chief Economist IBM Corpn 1984–90; fmr mem Bd of Dirs IBM World Trade: Europe/Middle East/Africa Corpn; mem Bd of Dirs Prudential Securities Mutual Funds, Inland Steel Industries Inc, Forum for World Affairs, Horace H. Rackham School of Grad Studies (Univ of Michigan), Women in Man; mem Del from Fed Reserve System to People's Repub of China 1980; Hon LL D (Oberlin Coll) 1979, (Bates Coll) 1981, (Mount Holyoke) 1983, (Michigan) 1984; Comfort Starr Award (Econs), Oberlin Coll 1952; Athena Award, Alumnae Council, Univ of Michigan 1982; Industry

Achievement Award, Nat Asscn of Bank Women 1985. *Publications:* Setting National Priorities: the 1972 Budget (jtly) 1971, Setting National Priorities: the 1973 Budget (jtly) 1972, Setting National Priorities: the 1974 Budget (jtly) 1973, Long-Term Economic Forecast 1988–2000 (jtly) 1989; numerous articles on econs in professional journals. *Leisure interest:* travel. *Address:* 243 Willowbrook Ave, Stamford, CT 06902, USA. *Telephone:* (203) 969-4467; *Fax:* (203) 967-4467.

TEFERRA, Jember, M PHIL; Ethiopian development worker; b 21 May 1943, Madagascar; d of the late Geberemariam and Shiferraw (née Etsegenet) Teferra; m Workneh Hailegiorgis 1968; two s two d. *Education:* Clarendon School, Tunbridge Wells School of Nursing and Univ of Manchester (UK). *Career:* Staff Nurse, Tunbridge Wells, UK 1964–65; Pvt Nurse, London 1966; Ward Sister St Paul's Hosp, Addis Ababa 1967, Matron 1967–69; Health, Educ and Social Services Co-ordinator and Head of Dept, Ethiopian Red Cross Soc 1969–76; imprisoned 1976–81; Project Officer for Health, Norwegian Save The Children 1981–86; Liaison Officer Swedish Save The Children until 1990; Founder, Co-ordinator and Fund-Raiser Integrated Holistic Approach Urban Devt Project 1989; Trustee Ethiopian Gemini Trust until 1989; mem Royal Coll of Nurses, Ethiopian Bible Soc, British Fed of Univ Women, Int Fed of Business and Professional Women, Int Urban Assocs in Christian Org (USA); Jane Finlay Memorial Award, British Fed of Univ Women 1987; Edwina Matbetter Trust award 1987; Dorothy Lee Grant Award, Int Fed of Univ Women 1988; Tear Fund Educ Award 1988. *Leisure interests:* reading, writing, travel, theatre, cinema, swimming, horse-riding, walking. *Address:* POB 6889, Addis Ababa, Ethiopia (Office); POB 1296, Addis Ababa, Ethiopia (Home). *Telephone:* (1) 511845 (Office); (1) 750202 (Home); *Fax:* (1) 512177 (Office).

TEICHMÜLLER, Marlies, DR RER NAT; German geologist and organic petrologist; b 11 Nov 1914, Herne; d of Emil and Clara Köster; m Rolf Teichmüller 1938 (died 1983). *Education:* Lyzeum (Herne), Univs of Freiburg and Berlin, Clark Univ (Worcester, MA) and Bureau of Mines (Pittsburgh, PA, USA). *Career:* Geologist Reichsamt für Bodenforschung, Berlin 1940–45, Univ of Bonn 1945–46; worked on geological surveys of N Rhine-Westphalia, Geologisches Landesamt Nordrhein-Westfalen 1946–79, Land Geologist 1961–64, Sr Land Geologist 1964–70, Dir of Geology 1970–79; retd 1979; voluntary research worker, contrib to scientific pubs and co-ed scientific journal 1979–; Bundesverdienstkreuz 1979; other awards include Reinhardt Thiessen Medal (Krefeld) 1971, Carl Engler Medal (Berlin) 1978, Van Waterschoot van der Gracht Medal (The Hague, Netherlands) 1987, Cady Award (Boston, MA, USA). *Publications:* Textbook of Coal Petrology 1975, 1982, Inkohlung und Erdöl 1974, Inkohlung und Geothermik 1979, Coal and Coal Bearing Strata 1987, Low Temperature Metamorphism 1987; 184 publs on organic petrology and geology. *Leisure interests:* travel, walking, classical arts. *Address:* Am Hohen Haus 15, 47799 Krefeld, Germany. *Telephone:* (2151) 24790.

TEIŠERSKYTE, Dalia; Lithuanian magazine editor and business executive; b 27 Nov 1944, Raseiniai; m Anatoly Clipkov 1979; two s. *Education:* Vilnius State Univ. *Career:* Family deported to Siberia under Communist govt; later worked as wood-cutter, maid, in publishing co, as radio Corresp, Dir of art gallery and Ed of newspaper; later established own co; Chair and Vice-Pres Gabija; Pres Kaunas Businessman; mem Nat UNESCO Cttee; has published five books of poetry and numerous articles in local and other publications. *Leisure interests:* travel, nature, reading, poetry and other serious books. *Address:* Gabija, Kestucio 64, 3000 Kaunas, Lithuania (Office); Dainavos 17-3, 3000 Kaunas, Lithuania (Home). *Telephone:* (7) 226640 (Office); (7) 225616 (Home); *Fax:* (7) 201809 (Office); (7) 225616 (Home).

TEISSIER, Elizabeth (pseudonym of Elizabeth Teissier du Cros); French astrologer and writer; b 6 Jan 1938, Algiers; d of Walter and Germaine (née Lebar) Hanselmann; m André Teissier du Cros 1960; two d. *Education:* Progymnasium (Berne, Switzerland), colls in Casablanca (Morocco), Chambon-sur-Lignon and Annemasse and Univ of Paris (Sorbonne). *Career:* Fmr model for Chanel and int covergirl; fmrly actress in films and on TV; astrologer 1975–; TV astrologer in France and Germany; weekly astrology columns in Télé 7 Jours (France), Bild und Funk (Germany), L'Illustré (Switzerland) and Eeva

(Finland); most read astrologer in Europe (60 million readers per month); mem Société des gens de lettres, Société française d'astrologie (Vice-Pres), American Fed of Astrologers, Fédération belge d'astrologie, Astrological Asscn (UK). *TV appearances include:* Presenter: Astralement vôtre 1975–76, Au bonheur des astres 1978–79, La légende des ciels 1979–80, Astro-Show 1981–83; *Publications:* Ne brûlez pas la sorcière 1976, Astralement vôtre ou le triomphe d'une vocation 1980, Votre horoscope (annual) 1982–, L'astrologie, science du XXIème siècle 1988, Vos étoiles jusqu'en l'an 2000 1989, Sterne und Moleküle (jtly), Enzyklopädie Astrologie-Passion, Les étoiles de l'Elysée 1995, Ihr Horoskop 1994, 1995, Sous le signe de Mitterrand 1997, 1999–(2004), Le passage de tous les dangers 1999; books trans into English, German, Spanish, Italian, Portuguese, Dutch, Polish and Chinese. *Leisure interests:* yoga, reading. *Address:* Télé 7 Jours, 149 rue Anatole France, 92534 Levallois-Perret Cedex, France (Office); 2 chemin de Beau-Soleil, 1206 Geneva, Switzerland (Home).

TEKELİ, Çirin, PH D; Turkish writer and academic; b 28 Feb 1944, Ankara; m Ahmet Tekeli 1966. *Education:* Univs of Lausanne (Switzerland) and Istanbul. *Career:* Prof of Econ Univ of Istanbul 1968–81; active in women's movt 1981–92; Co-Founder and Dir Women's Library of Istanbul 1990; f Human Rights Org 1987; apptd Ed Eğitim ve Bilim 1988; writer and trans specializing in women's studies and political science. *Publications:* Women: Political and Social Life 1982, For Women 1988, Women in 1980s Turkey: A Woman's Perspective 1990, Women, State, Politics 1991; has translated books from French and English, and has written numerous articles. *Leisure interests:* painting, music, cinema. *Address:* Gazeteciler Sitesi, Dergiler Sok 1, Levent, 80300 Istanbul, Turkey. *Telephone:* (1) 1664330; *Fax:* (1) 1456441.

TEKELİOĞLU, Meral, MD; Turkish professor of histology and embryology; b 23 Dec 1936, Ermenek; d of Çefik and Zeynep Tekelioğlu; m Ziya Llysal 1961; one s. *Education:* Girls' school (Ankara) and Ankara Univ. *Career:* Specialist in Histology-Embryology Ankara Univ 1964–, Lecturer 1969, Prof 1975–, apptd Dir Dept of Histology-Embryology, Faculty of Medicine 1983. *Publications:* The Cell: Organelles and Inclusions (jtly, four edns) 1972–82, Medical Embryology 1984, General Medical Histology (2nd edn) 1993, Sobotta/Hammersen Histology Atlas (trans and ed, 4th edn) 1994, Human Reproduction and Embryology 1995. *Leisure interests:* prehistoric archaeology, classical music. *Address:* Ankara Univ, Faculty of Medicine, Morphology Bldg, Sihhiye, 06100 Ankara, Turkey (Office); Süslü Sok, 1/4, Tandoğan, 06580 Mebusevleri, Ankara, Turkey (Home).

TEKIN, Latife; Turkish writer; b 1 Jan 1957, Kayseri; d of Mustafa and Hatice Erdoğan; m 1st Ertuğrul Tekin (divorced); one s; m 2nd Latif Demirci; one d. *Career:* Writer of novels 1983–. *Publications include:* Dear Shameless Death 1983, Berci Kristin Garbage Tales 1984, Night Lessons 1986, Swords By Ice 1989. *Leisure interests:* music, dance. *Address:* Kirechane Gediği Sok 6, Arnavutköy, Istanbul, Turkey. *Telephone:* (1) 2636687; *Fax:* (1) 5139518.

TELEN, Ludmila Olegovna; Russian journalist; b 2 Oct 1957, Zhukovsky, Russia; d of Oleg P. and Elmira F. Telen; m Valery Vyzhutovich 1980; one s. *Education:* Moscow M. V. Lomonosov State Univ. *Career:* Journalist with Komsomolskaya Pravda newspaper 1977–85; Special Corresp for Socialisticheskaya Industria 1985–89; analyst for Narodny Deputat magazine 1990–91; Political Columnist Moscow News weekly newspaper 1991–; Presenter regular TV programme Political Kitchen 1991–. *Leisure interest:* travel. *Address:* Moscow News, 103829 Moscow, 16/2 Tverskaia, Russian Federation (Office); Moscow, Vargas ul 1, 244, Russian Federation (Home). *Telephone:* (095) 200-38-11 (Office); *Fax:* (095) 209-17-28 (Office).

TEMKOVA, Ana; Macedonian painter; b 24 Sept 1943, Kavadarci; m 1972 (divorced); one s. *Education:* Acad of Fine Arts (Belgrade, Yugoslavia) and Acad of Mosaic (Ravenna, Italy). *Career:* Freelance painter 1967–87, 1993–; Assoc Prof of Painting and Drawing Acad of Fine Arts, Skopje 1987–93; mem Macedonian Painters' Asscn 1967–, Yugoslav Painters' Asscn 1969; has taken part in over 100 group and 12 solo exhibitions in countries including Macedonia, Yugoslavia, Italy, Romania, USA, Australia, etc; Vincenco Monti Award, Italy 1969; Tuzla Portrait Award (Yugoslavia) 1967, 1971, 1979; 11 October

Award, Macedonian State Award 1978; Grand Prix, Macedonian Painters' Asscn 1996. *Leisure interest:* going to the cinema. *Address:* 20/II-3 Ognjan Prica St, Skopje, 1000, The Fmr Yugoslav Republic of Macedonia. *Telephone:* (2) 162442; *E-mail:* fikiki@on.net.mk.

TEMPLE, Nina Claire, B SC; British party official; b 21 April 1956, London; d of Landon and Barbara Temple; partner John Davies 1979 (separated); one d one s. *Education:* Camden School for Girls (London) and Imperial Coll, (London). *Career:* Gen Sec Young Communist League 1979; Head of Press and Publicity, Communist Party 1983, Sec, Organizer transformation of Communist Party into Democratic Left 1990–92, Sec Democratic Left 1992; part-time journalist and teacher 1986–89. *Leisure interests:* gardening, rambling, trips with family. *Address:* Democratic Left, 6 Cynthia St, London N1 9JF, UK. *Telephone:* (20) 7278-4443; *Fax:* (20) 7278-4425.

TEMPLE, Shirley (see Black, Shirley Temple).

TEMPLETON, Edith; British writer; b 7 April 1916, Prague; d of Louis Gideon and Irma de Szèll; m 1st W. S. Templeton 1938 (divorced); m 2nd Edmund Ronald 1956 (died 1984); one s. *Education:* Lycée in Paris and Prague Medical Univ. *Career:* Mem staff Office of Chief Surgeon, US War Office 1942–45; Conf and Law-Court Interpreter for British Forces with rank of Capt, Germany 1945–46. *Publications:* Summer in the Country 1950, Living on Yesterday 1951, The Island of Desire 1952, Surprise of Cremona (Book Soc Choice) 1954, This Charming Pastime 1955, Gordon 1966; has contributed short stories to The New Yorker 1956–91, Holiday, Atlantic Monthly, Vogue and Harper's Magazine. *Leisure interest:* travel. *Address:* 76 corso Europa, 18012 Bordighera, Italy. *Telephone:* (184) 261858.

TENNANT, Emma Christina, FRSL; British writer; b 20 Oct 1937, London; d of the late 2nd Baron Glenconner and Elizabeth Lady Glenconner; m 1st S. Yorke 1957 (divorced 1963); m 2nd A. Cockburn 1969 (divorced 1973); two d one s. *Education:* St Paul's Girls' School. *Career:* Freelance journalist until 1973, writer 1973–; founding Ed Bananas 1975–78; Gen Ed In Verse 1982–, Lives of Modern Women 1985–; Hon D LITT (Aberdeen) 1996. *Publications include:* The Colour of Rain (as Catherine Aydy) 1963, The Time of the Crack 1973, The Last of the Country House Murders 1975, Hotel de Dream 1976, Bananas Anthology (ed) 1977, Saturday Night Reader (ed) 1978, The Bad Sister 1978, Wild Nights 1979, Alice Fell 1980, Queen of Stones 1982, Woman Beware Woman 1983, Black Marina 1985, Adventures of Robina by Herself (ed) 1986, Cycle of the Sun: The House of Hospitalities 1987, A Wedding of Cousins 1988, The Magic Drum 1989, Two Women of London 1989, Sisters and Strangers 1990, Faustine 1992, Tess 1993, Pemberley 1993, An Unequal Marriage 1994, Strangers: A Family Romance 1998; Children's books: The Boggart (jtly), The Search for Treasure Island 1981, The Ghost Child 1984, Emma In Love 1996, Girlitude 1999, Burnt Diaries 1999; TV film script: Frankenstein's Baby 1990; contribs to The Guardian and other publs. *Leisure interests:* walking in Dorset, planning trips that never happen. *Address:* c/o Jonathan Cape, Random House, 20 Vauxhall Bridge Rd, London SW1V 2SA, UK. *Telephone:* (20) 7221-391.

TENNANT, Stella; British fashion model; b 17 Dec 1971, Scotland; d of Lady Emma Tennant, granddaughter of Duke of Devonshire; m David Lasnet 1999; one s. *Education:* St Leonards Girls' School (St Andrews), Marlborough Coll, Kingston Polytechnic and Winchester School of Art. *Career:* Fmr art student; has featured in fashion pages of The Face and i-D magazines, on the cover of Italian Vogue, in advertisements for The Gap, Valentino, Gianfranco Ferré, Versace; now works in London, New York and Paris and with photographers including Mario Testino, Paolo Roversi and Bruce Weber; selected by Karl Lagerfeld as new face of Chanel 1996; announced retirement from modelling 1998. *Leisure interest:* sculpture. *Address:* c/o Select Model Management, Thomas Archer House, 43 King St, London WC2E 8RJ, UK. *Telephone:* (20) 7470-5220; *Fax:* (20) 7470-5233.

TENNANT, Veronica, OC; Canadian (b British) ballet dancer; b 15 Jan 1947, London, UK; d of Harry and Doris (née Bassous) Tennant; m John Wright 1969; one d. *Education:* Nat Ballet School (Toronto, ON). *Career:* Prin Dancer Nat Ballet Co 1965–89; numerous guest appearances and world premières; Adjunct Prof Faculty of the Fine Arts, York

Univ, ON 1989; featured in numerous TV programmes and tributes; subject of TV documentries Veronica Tennant; A Dancer of Distinction 1983 and Veronica: Completing the Circle 1989; Host, creative consultant and writer Sunday Arts Entertainment CBC TV 1989–92, Producer, Arts and Entertainment Specials CBC TV ; Hon LL D (Brock) 1985; Hon D LITT (York) 1987, (Simon Fraser) 1992, (Toronto) 1992; Toronto Arts Award for the Performing Arts 1987; City of Toronto Award of Merit 1989; Canadian Club Arts and Letters Award, City of New York 1991. *Repertoire includes:* Romeo and Juliet, Cinderella, Kraanerg, Sleeping Beauty, La sylphide, Giselle, Le loup, Swan Lake, The Dream, La fille mal gardée, Etudes, Don Juan, Coppelia, Serenade, Dark Elegies, Napoli, Washington Square, All Night Wonder, Portrait of Love and Death, Liebestod, Onegin, The Merry Widow, Masada, Botticelli Pictures, Tchaikovsky Pas de Deux, Forgotten Land, Rendezvous des cœurs; *TV:* Karen Kain: Dancing in the Moment (Writer and Producer) (Int Emmy Award 1999) *Publications:* On Stage Please (also recording) 1977, The Nutcracker (also recording) 1985; has written several articles for The National Ballet Magazine and Toronto Star. *Leisure interests:* theatre, reading, textile design, writing. *Address:* CBC Toronto, POB 500, Station A, Toronto, ON M5W 1E6, Canada.

TENNANT, Victoria; British actress; b 30 Sept 1953, London; d of Cecil Tennant and Irina Baronova; m Steve Martin (divorced). *Education:* Elmhurst Ballet School and Cen School of Speech and Drama (London). *Career:* Stage and screen actress. *Films include:* The Ragman's Daughter 1978, Stranger's Kiss 1984, All of Me 1984, The Funniest Guy in the World, Best Seller 1987, Flowers in the Attic 1987, The Handmaid's Tale 1990, LA Story 1991, Whispers, The Plague, Edie and Pen (writer and producer); *TV includes:* Winds of War 1980, Dempsey, War and Remembrance 1988, Act of Will 1991, The Man from Snowy River; *Plays include:* Love Letters, Getting Married.

TENNET, Patricia Elizabeth; New Zealand politician; b Feilding; d of Maurice Tennet; m John Francis Galvin 1978; one s. *Education:* Feilding Agric High School and Victoria Univ (Wellington). *Career:* Factory Insp Labour Dept; Researcher at Arbitration Court; Sec-Gen Cen Clerical Workers' Union; mem Nat Exec NZ Labour Party; Chair Labour Women's Council, Wellington Labour Regional Council, Wellington Harbour City Conf 1984, Govt's Employment Promotion Conf 1985; mem Wellington Polytechnic Council until 1990, Wellington Business Devt Bd until 1990, Capital Discovery Place Children's Museum; elected to House of Reps (Parl) for Island Bay 1987, Opposition Labour Jr Whip, Labour Spokesperson for Employment, Assoc Spokesperson for Women, mem Parl Services Comm, numerous cttees including Finance and Expenditure Select Cttee, Procedures Cttee, Labour Environment Cttee and Labour Women's Caucus Cttee; Commemorative Medal 1990. *Leisure interests:* tramping, gardening, piano. *Address:* POB 7353, Wellington S, New Zealand.

TER-MINASSIAN, Teresa, LLB, MA; Italian international organization executive; b 7 Oct 1943, Melfi; d of Enrico and Rosa Rizzitiello; m Viguen Ter-Minassian 1968; two d one s. *Education:* Univ of Rome and Harvard Univ (USA). *Career:* Employee Cen Bank of Italy 1967–78; joined IMF 1971, Economist in Fiscal Affairs Dept 1972–74, in European Dept 1974–78, Sr Economist 1978–80, Head of Div 1980–88; Deputy Dir Fiscal Affairs Dept 1996–97 (Dir 2000–), W Hemisphere Dept 1997–2000. *Publication:* Fiscal Federalism in Theory and Practice. *Leisure interests:* reading, classical music, exercising, cooking. *Address:* Fiscal Affairs Dept, IMF, 700 19th St, NW, Washington, DC 20431, USA. *Telephone:* (202) 623-8844; *Fax:* (202) 623-4259; *E-mail:* tterminassian@imf.org.

TER VELD, Elske; Netherlands politician; b 1 Aug 1944, Groningen; d of Romke Bertus and Christina (née Stappershoef) ter Veld. *Education:* Higher Professional School, Acad for Social and Cultural Work (Groningen). *Career:* Mem PvdA (Labour Party); Press Sec for Women, Dutch Asscn of Trade Unions 1972–81; mem Advisory Comm for Emancipation of Female Employees 1975–80; Mem Second Chamber of States-Gen (Parl) 1981–89; State Sec, Ministry of Social Affairs and Employment 1989–93; leader youth training centre, Assen 1968–70; Pres Communal House for Young People, De Heerd Groningen 1970–72. *Publication:* Vrouw en Beleid 1985. *Address:* Moleneind 70, 1241 NK Kortenhoef, Netherlands.

TEREKHOVA, Margarita Borisovna; Russian actress; b 25 Aug 1942, Turinsk, Urals; d of Boris Ivanovich Terekhov and Galina Stanislavovna Tomashevich; one s one d. *Education:* Tashkent Univ and Mossoviet Studio School. *Career:* With Mossoviet Theatre 1964–83; Founder, Dir Theatre Studio, Balaganchik 1987–; film debut 1966; RSFSR Artist of Merit 1976; K. Stanislavsky Prize 1992. *Films include:* Hi! It's Me! 1966, Byelorussian Station 1971, My Life 1972, Monologue 1973, Mirror 1975, Day Train 1976, Who'll go to Truskovets? 1977, Dog in a Manger 1977, Kids, Kids, Kids 1978, D'Artagnan and Three Musketeers 1978, Let's Get Married 1983, Only for Crazy/For Mental Cases Only (San Remo Int Film Festival Prize, Bruges Int Film Festival Prize 1993) 1991, Forbidden Fruit 1993, The Way 1995, Kings of Russian Investigation (TV) 1996; *Plays include:* Dir and actress: When Five Years Elapse, The Tsars Hunt. *Leisure interest:* son's upbringing and education. *Address:* 123056 Moscow, Bolshaya Gruzinskaya ul 57, kv 92, Russian Federation. *Telephone:* (095) 254-96-95; *Fax:* (095) 299-44-37.

TERENTYEVA, Nina Nikolayevna; Russian opera singer (mezzo-soprano); b 9 Jan 1946, Kusa, Chelyabinsk Region; d of Nikolai Fedorovich Terentyev and Tatyana Vladimirovna Terentyeva; one d. *Education:* Leningrad State Conservatory (class of Olga Mshanskaya). *Career:* Soloist Kirov (now Mariinsky) Theatre 1971–77, Bolshoi 1979; leading solo mezz-soprano; participated in productions of major theatres of the world including Deutsche Opera and Staatsoper Berlin, Munich and Hamburg (Germany), Bordeaux (France), Los Angeles (USA) opera houses, Metropolitan Opera, New York 1993, La Scala, Milan (Italy) 1994, Royal Opera House, Covent Garden, London 1995; has participated at int festivals; concert repertoire comprises Russian classics; People's Artist of Russia. *Operas include:* Khovanshchina, Tsar's Bride, Sadko, Boris Godunov, Aida, Il Trovatore, Samson and Delila, Don Carlos, Cavalleria Rusticana etc. *Leisure interest:* driving. *Address:* Bolshoi Theatre, 103009 Moscow, Teatralnaya pl 1, Russian Federation (Office). *Telephone:* (095) 971-6761 (Home).

TERESHKOVA, Maj-Gen Valentina Vladimirovna; Russian politician and former cosmonaut; b 6 March 1937, Tutayev, Yaroslavl Region; d of the late Vladimir Aksyonovich Tereshkov and of Elena Fyodorovna Tereshkova; m Andriyan Nikolayev 1963 (divorced); one d. *Education:* Yaroslavl Textile Coll and Zhukovsky Air Force Eng Acad. *Career:* Fmr textile worker Krasny Perekop textile mill, Yaroslavl; fmr textile mill Sec Young Communist League; mem CPSU 1962–, Cen Cttee CPSU 1971–90; cosmonaut training 1962–; first woman in world to go into space; made 48 orbital flights of the Earth in Vostok VI spacecraft 16–19 June 1963; Deputy to USSR Supreme Soviet 1962–89; USSR People's Deputy 1989–91; Chair Soviet Women's Cttee 1968–87; mem Supreme Soviet Presidium 1974–90; Head USSR Int Cultural and Friendship Union 1988–91; Chair Russian Asscn of Int Co-operation 1992–; Pres Int Union House of Europe 1992–; Head Russian Centre for Int Scientific and Cultural Co-operation 1994–; currently Cosmonaut Instructor Gagarin Cosmonaut Centre; Pilot-Cosmonaut of USSR; Hero of Soviet Union; Order of Lenin (twice); Joliot-Curie Gold Medal, World Peace Council 1966; Order of the Nile (Egypt) 1971; Order of the Red Banner of Labour 1986. *Publication:* Valentina, First Woman in Space 1993. *Address:* Russian Association of International Co-operation, 103885 Moscow, Vozvizhenka Str 14, Russian Federation. *Telephone:* (095) 290-12-45.

TERPENING, Virginia Ann; American artist; b 17 July 1917, Lewistown, MO; d of the late Floyd Raymond and Bertha Edda (née Rodefer) Shoup; m 1st Jack D. Baltzelle 1940; one d; m 2nd Charles W. Terpening 1951. *Education:* William Woods Coll (Fulton, MO) and Washington Univ School of Fine Art (St Louis, MO). *Career:* Solo exhibitions include Culver-Stockton Coll, Canton, MO 1956, Creative Gallery, New York 1968, The Breakers, Palm Beach, FL 1976; group exhibitions include City Art Museum, St Louis 1956, 1965, Madison Gallery, New York 1960, 1964, Ligoa Duncan Gallery, New York 1964, 1978, Two Flags Festival of Art, Douglas, AZ 1975, 1978–79, Int Art Exhibition, El Centro, CA 1977, Salon des Nations, Paris 1985, UN World Conf of Women, Nairobi, Kenya 1985, William Woods Univ, Fulton, MO 1993, 1994, 1995, Harlin Museum, Des Plains, MO 1994; Lecturer on art; Chair Centennial Art Show, Lewistown 1971, Bicentennial 1976; Golden Medallion Award, Douglas 1975; mem Artist Equity Asscn Inc, Int Soc of Artists, Nat Museum Women in Art,

Animal Protection Inst; Artist Laureate Nepenthe Mondi Soc 1984; granted Key to the City of Lewistown (MO) for Lifetime Achievements 1999. *Leisure interests:* original crafts, rugs, wall-hangings. *Address:* 105 S Vine St, POB 117, Lewistown, MO 63452, USA. *Telephone:* (573) 497-2360.

TERPSTRA, Erica G.; Netherlands politician; b 26 May 1943, The Hague; divorced; two s. *Education:* Gymnasium B (The Hague) and Univ of Leiden. *Career:* Journalist; mem Second Chamber of States-Gen (Parl, VVD) 1977–94, 1998–; elected mem Provincial States of Utrecht 1987–91, mem various Parl Cttees including Devt Co-operation, Care and Policy for the Aged, Care for the Disabled, Psychiatry, Public Health, Cancer Control, Alternative Medicine, Hosp Construction, Netherlands Antilles; Sec of State for Wellbeing, Health and Sports 1997–98; Chair Standing Cttee on Social Affairs, Parl Cttee on Biotechnology; mem Bd Univ of Amsterdam, Global Cttee of Parliamentarians on Population and Devt, Global Forum of Spiritual and Parliamentarian Leaders on Human Survival; Exec mem Nat Olympic Cttee, European Olympic Cttee, Int Olympic Truce Foundation; mem Advisory Women's Cttee UNFPA, Nat Cttee for Refugees, Nat Revalidation Fund; fmr Olympic Swimmer (Rome 1960, Tokyo 1964), Silver and Bronze Medallist, Tokyo 1964; Companion of the Order of Orange (Nassau); Companion of the Order of the Dutch Lion; Holder of Cross of Honour and Lion of the House of Orange for personal services to the Royal House. *Leisure interests:* sport, reading. *Address:* Tweede Kamer, Binnenhof 1A, Postbus 20018, 2500 EA The Hague, Netherlands (Office). *Telephone:* (70) 3182893; *Fax:* (70) 3183848; *E-mail:* e.terpstra@tk.parlement.nl.

TERRON I CUSÍ, Anna; Spanish politician; b 6 Oct 1962, Barcelona; divorced; one s. *Career:* MEP (PSE), mem Cttee on Civil Liberties and Internal Affairs, Del for relations with the Mashreq countries and the Gulf States. *Address:* European Parliament, rue Wiertz, 1047 Brussels, Belgium (Office); Nicaragua 75, 08029 Barcelona, Spain (Home). *Telephone:* (2) 284-21-11 (Office); *Fax:* (2) 230-69-43.

TERRY GONZÁLEZ, Marta, PH D; Cuban former national library director; b 7 May 1931, Havana; d of Nicolas Terry and Dora González; m Luis Forte; one s. *Education:* Inst de la Habana, Centro Especial de Inglés (Havana), Univ of Havana and New York Univ (USA). *Career:* Apptd Prof of English and Library Studies at Univ of Havana 1952; Dir José Antonio Echevarría Library, Casa de las Américas 1967–87; Dir Nat Library of Cuba 1987–97; mem Perm Cttee for Latin America and the Caribbean of the Int Fed of Library Asscns and Insts (IFLA) 1981, Pres Latin American and Caribbean Regional Activities 1987, elected to Exec Bd 1991; grants awarded from Inst of Int Seminar on Freedom and Security (The American Friends Service Cttee) 1953 and UNESCO 1968; Order of Raúl García 1983; Distinction of Nat Culture 1984; Distinction of Nat Educ; Order of Rafael María de Mendive. *Publications:* La clasificación y asignación de epígrafes a las literaturas de los países del Caribe, El desarrollo del trabajo bibliotecario en Cuba, Library Situation in Cuba: A Brief Account; text books and numerous articles in books and journals. *Address:* c/o Biblioteca Nacional, Dirección Biblioteca, Calle Independencia esq a 20 de Mayo y Aranguren, Plaza de la Revolución José Martí, Havana, Cuba.

TETZNER, Ruth (Hallard); German writer; b 25 Nov 1917, Flensburg; d of Werner and Agnes (née Hach) Wodick; m Rudolf Tetzner 1948; one s. *Career:* Founder, Dir Essen Health Centre 1963–67; awards include prizes from Freier Deutscher Autorenverband 1974 and Gedok-Bonn-Lübeck 1973–90. *Publications include:* Poetry: Sdgnale 1974; Short stories: Kreuzungen 1978, Greta (5th edn) 1981, Schlangenbeschwörer-Industrie Impressionen 1985, Ein Trip ins Paradies 1986; Diaries: Neue Wege und Straßen 1956–82 1983, Inventory 1987–89. *Address:* Fehlingstr 45, 2400 Lübeck-Travemünde, Germany.

THALÉN, Ingela; Swedish politician; b 1 Oct 1943, Gothenburg; m Lars Thalén; two d one s. *Career:* Fmrly shop asst; clerk at Social Democratic Youth League, Gothenburg, Social Democratic Labour Party (SDAP), Stockholm County Council and ARE-Bolagen 1959–74; Dist Sec Gothenburg Br, SDAP 1975–78, Stockholm City Br 1979; engaged in local politics, Järfälla 1979–87, Municipal Commr and Chair Municipal Exec Bd 1983–87; mem Riksdag (Parl) 1988, 1991–;

Minister of Labour 1987–90, of Social Health and Welfare 1990–91, of Health and Social Affairs 1994–96, for Social Security 1999–; Sec Gen Social Democratic Party 1996–99. *Address:* Ministry of Health and Social Affairs, 10333 Stockholm, Sweden. *Telephone:* (8) 405-1000; *Fax:* (8) 411-1663; *E-mail:* registrator@social.ministry.se; *Internet:* www.regeringen.se.

THANE, Sarah Ann; British broadcasting executive; b 21 Sept 1951, Birmingham; d of John and Winifred Thane. *Education:* Sutton Coldfield Grammar School, Co High School (Stourbridge) and City of Birmingham Polytechnic. *Career:* Regional Officer E of England IBA 1982–87; Deputy Controller Public Affairs, IBA 1987–88, Controller Public Affairs 1989–90, Controller Public Affairs Independent Television Comm (ITC—IBA's replacement body) 1990–96, Dir of Programmes 1996–; Vice-Chair Royal TV Soc 1998–2000, Chair 2000–. *Leisure interests:* music, reading, travelling, wine, food. *Address:* ITC, 33 Foley St, London W1W 7TL, UK. *Telephone:* (20) 7255-3000; *Fax:* (20) 7306-7800; *E-mail:* sarah.thane@itc.org.uk.

THARP, Twyla; American dancer and choreographer; b 1 July 1941, Portland, IN; m 1st Peter Young (divorced); m 2nd Robert Huot (divorced); one s. *Education:* Pomona Coll, American Ballet Theater School and Barnard Coll. *Career:* Studied with Richard Thomas, Merce Cunningham, Igor Schwezoff, Louis Mattox, Paul Taylor, Margaret Craske, Erick Hawkins; with Paul Taylor Dance Co 1963–65; freelance choreographer with own modern dance troupe and various other cos, including Joffrey Ballet and American Ballet Theater 1965–87; Artistic Assoc Choreographer American Ballet Theater, New York 1988–91; Hon mem American Acad of Arts and Letters 1997; Hon Doctor of Performing Arts (Brown) 1981 and 14 other hon doctorates; two Emmy Awards; Dance Magazine Annual Award 1981; Laurence Olivier Award 1991; Doris Duke Awards for New Work 1999. *Works choreographed include:* Tank Dive 1965, Re-Moves 1966, Forevermore 1967, Generation 1968, Medley 1969, Fugue 1970, Eight Jelly Rolls 1971, The Raggedy Dances 1972, As Time Goes By 1974, Sue's Leg 1975, Push Comes to Shove 1976, Once More Frank 1976, Mud 1977, Baker's Dozen 1979, When We Were Very Young 1980, The Catherine Wheel 1981, Nine Sinatra Songs 1982, Amadeus 1984, White Nights 1985, In the Upper Room 1986, Rules of the Game 1989, Octet 1991, Cutting Up (US tour) 1993, Demeter and Persephone 1993, 1994, Waterbaby Bagatelles 1994, Americans We, Jump Start 1995, Red White and Blues 1995, How Near Heaven 1995, Mr Worldly Wise 1996; Films: Hair 1979, I'll do Anything 1992; Videos: Making Television Dance 1977, CBS Cable Confessions of a Corner Maker 1980; *Publication:* Push Comes to Shove (autobiog) 1992. *Address:* Tharp Productions, 336 Central Park West, Flat 17B, New York, NY 10025, USA. *Internet:* twylatharp.org.

THATCHER, Baroness (Life Peer), cr 1992, of Kesteven in the County of Lincolnshire, **Margaret Hilda Thatcher,** LG, OM, PC, MA, B SC, FRS; British politician and barrister; b 13 Oct 1925; d of the late Alfred Roberts and of Beatrice Ethel Stephenson; m Denis Thatcher (now Sir Denis Thatcher, BT) 1951; one s one d (twins). *Education:* Grantham High School and Somerville Coll (Oxford). *Career:* Research Chemist 1947–51; called to the Bar, Lincoln's Inn 1953; MP (Cons) for Barnet, Finchley 1959–92; Parl Sec Ministry of Pensions and Nat Insurance 1961–64; Chief Opposition Spokesperson on Educ 1969–70; Sec of State for Educ and Science 1970–74; Leader Cons Party 1975–90; Leader HM Opposition 1975–79; Prime Minister, First Lord of the Treasury and Minister for the Civil Service 1979–90; Pres No Turning Back Group 1990–; Hon Pres Bruges Group 1991–; Dir Tiger Man 1998–; mem House of Lords 1992–; Chancellor Univ of Buckingham 1992–98, William and Mary Coll, VA, USA 1993–2000; Chair Advisory Bd, Univ of London's Inst of US Studies 1994–; Hon Bencher, Lincoln's Inn 1975; Hon Master of the Bench of Gray's Inn 1983; Hon Fellow Royal Inst of Chem 1979; Freedom of Royal Borough of Kensington and Chelsea 1979, of London Borough of Barnet 1980, of Falkland Islands 1983, of the City of London 1989, of the City of Westminster 1990; mem Worshipful Co of Glovers 1983–, Int Advisory Bd British-American Chamber of Commerce 1993–; Conservative Companion of Guild of Cambridge Benefactors 1999–; Hon LL D (Univ of Buckingham) 1986; Dr hc (Rand Afrikaans Univ, SA) 1991, (Weizmann Inst of Science) 1992, (Mendeleyev Univ) 1993, (Brunel) 1996; MacArthur Foundation Fellowship 1992; Presidential Medal of

Freedom, USA 1991; Order of Good Hope, SA 1991; Hon Citizen of Gorazde 1993; Hilal-i-Imitaz 1996. *Publication:* In Defence of Freedom 1986, The Downing Street Years 1979–90 1993, The Path to Power 1995, The Collected Speeches of Margaret Thatcher 1997. *Address:* House of Lords, London SW1A 0AA, UK; POB 1466, London SW1X 9HY, UK.

THEILE, Ursel, MD; German professor of medicine; b 17 April 1938, Weiden nr Cologne. *Career:* Chief Medical Practitioner Second Medical Clinic, Univ of Mainz until 1983, currently Prof of Internal Medicine Univ of Mainz; Head Genetic Advice Centre, Fed State of Rheinland-Pfalz 1975–; Hufelandpreis 1975; Soemmering-Plakette 1983. *Publications:* Genetische Beratung (jtly) 1973, Genetik und Moral (jtly) 1985, Checkliste Genetische Beratung 1992. *Leisure interests:* playing music, modern literature, walking in the mountains, travel, geology. *Address:* Oechsnerstr 6, 55131 Mainz, Germany. *Telephone:* (6131) 51055.

THENAULT-MONDOLONI, Magdeleine Camille-Renée; French organization executive; b 19 Nov 1921, Brux; d of Roger and Armandine (née Marquet) Thenault; m Joseph Mondoloni (divorced). *Education:* Lycée de Poitiers and Acad de Soins Esthétiques. *Career:* Dir Beautician School; Pres Syndicat Nat des Insts de Beauté (union for insts of beauticians), Midi-Côte d'Azur area 1966–85; Pres, later Hon Pres Syndicat Nat des Ecoles de Soins Esthétiques (union of beautician schools) 1968; Vice-Pres Fed Française d'Esthétique-Cosmétiques 1969–79, Pres 1979, Hon Pres 1991–; Technical Counsellor on Educ to Groupe Yves Rocher 1983, to Acad de Paris 1985, 1991, to Int Forum on Make-up and Aesthetics; Technical Counsellor to Festa Cosmetics, Japan 1992–95, Hon Pres 1995–, Pres Festa Int Group 1996–; Pres Syndicat Gen de l'Industrie et du Commerce 1987–95, Int School for French Aesthetics, Tokyo and Hiroshima 1992–95, World Confed of Cosmetic Aesthetics 1995, Eidef-Forum Make-Up Paris 1996–; Vice-Pres, later Pres Consultative Cttee to Ministry of Educ 1989–91; fmr Pres Int Fed of Aestheticians. *Leisure interest:* travel. *Address:* c/o Festa International Group, 49 ave de l'Opéra, 75002 Paris, France (Office); 103 rue du Faubourg Saint-Honoré, 75008 Paris, France (Home).

THEODORESCU, Roxana, MA; Romanian art historian and museum director; b 17 May 1951, Bucharest; d of Aurelian and Ileana Ionescu; m Razvan Theodorescu 1974; one s one d. *Education:* Acad of Fine Arts (Bucharest). *Career:* Mem staff Editing Dept, Publicom Publishing House 1976–84; Head Exhibitions Dept, Romanian Artists' Union 1984–91; Head Cultural Exchanges Dept, Romanian Cultural Foundation 1991–94; Dir Nat Museum of Art of Romania 1994–. *Leisure interest:* travel. *Address:* Calea Victoriei 49–53, 70101 Bucharest, Romania (Office); Str Hatmanul Arbore No 3–7, Bucharest, Romania (Home). *Telephone:* (1) 6133030 (Office); *Fax:* (1) 3124327 (Office).

THÉOPHILE, Josette, D PHIL; French business executive; b 1946, Périgueux; one d. *Career:* Carried out psycho-social research on employees at Messier-Hispano aeronautics co 1970; joined Lesieur-Cotelle co 1971, in charge of Training and Working Conditions 1971–76; joined Centre for Man Training and Advice 1976, Dir-Gen 1978–84; joined Bull 1984, Dir of Training until 1990; Dir Potential and Training Dept RATP (Paris transport co) 1990–95, Dir of Human Resources 1995–99, Deputy Dir Gen 1999–. *Address:* RATP, 54 quai de la Rapée, 75012 Paris, France; 335 rue de Vaugirard, 75015 Paris, France.

THEORIN, Maj Britt; Swedish politician; b 22 Dec 1932; d of Herold and Märta Fagerberg; m Rolf Theorin 1957; two d two s. *Education:* Univ of Manchester (UK) and Holiroyde Coll. *Career:* Mem Stockholm City Council 1966–70; mem Riksdag (Parl, Social Democratic Party) 1971–95, mem Foreign Affairs Cttee; Del to UN 1976–94; Amb for Disarmament (Chair Swedish Disarmament Comm) 1982–91; MEP 1995–, Pres Cttee on Women's Rights and Equal Opportunities 1999–; Founder and Pres World Women Parliamentarians for Peace 1985; Pres Int Peace Bureau, Geneva, Switzerland 1992–2000, Parliamentarians for Global Action 1995, Green Cross Sweden 1994–2000; mem Bureau Nat Org of Social Democratic Women in Sweden 1971–95; Hon PH D (Gothenburg) 1991. *Publications:* UN studies on Nuclear Weapons and Military and the Environment 1989, 1990, UN expert group report on Gender and the Agenda for Peace 1994. *Leisure interests:* classical music, weaving, grandchildren. *Address:* European Parliament, 15G302, rue Wiertz, 1047 Brussels, Belgium; Upplandsgt 19B, 113 60 Stockholm, Sweden. *Telephone:* (2) 284-56-61 (Belgium); (8) 34 64 30 (Sweden); *Fax:* (2) 284-96-61 (Belgium); (8) 34 64 30 (Sweden); *E-mail:* mtheorin@europarl.eu.int.

THESMAR, Ghislaine Minella; French ballet dancer; b 18 March 1943, Beijing; d of Michel and Micheline (née Meadmore) Thesmar; m Pierre Lacotte 1968. *Education:* Walshingham House School (Bombay, India) and Conservatoire Nat Supérieur de Musique et de Danse (Paris). *Career:* Worked for numerous ballet cos including Grands Ballets du Marquis de Cuevas 1961–62, Jeunesses musicales de France, Ballets Roland Petit, Grands Ballets du Canada, Opéra de Paris, New York City Ballet; has toured fmr USSR, Europe, Japan, Brazil, Argentina, USA, etc; Co-Dir Ballets de Monte Carlo 1985–88; currently Prof and Tutor for Soloists at Opéra de Paris; Chevalier de l'Ordre Nat du Mérite; Chevalier de la Légion d'Honneur. *Ballets include:* La Sylphide (also video, USA) 1971–73, Coppélia, Giselle, La belle au bois dormant, Le lac des cygnes, La symphonie fantastique, La nuit transfigurée, La valse, Orphée, La somnambule, Palais de cristal, Prélude à l'après-midi d'un faune, Les noces, Jardins aux lilas, Le songe d'une nuit d'été 1986. *Leisure interests:* roses, cooking, dachshunds, writing book on China. *Address:* 6 rue du Port-Mahon, 75002 Paris, France.

THIBAUT, Monique, MD, PH D; French research scientist; b Nogent; d of Raymond and Marie Madeleine (née Labriet) Thibaut. *Education:* Univ of Paris. *Career:* Research Asst CNRS 1963–67, Research Deputy 1967–77, Head of Research 1977–84, Research Dir 1984–; Head Medical Mycology Research, Univ of Paris VI 1975–; Visiting Prof Fed Univ, Rio de Janeiro, Brazil 1972; mem French Soc of Allergology and Clinical Immunology, French Soc of Parisitology, French Soc of Medical Mycology, American Soc Microbiology, New York Acad of Sciences; Silver Medal Faculty of Medicine (Paris) 1964; Dexo Prize of French Soc of Allergology 1965; Catherine Hadot Prize, Nat Acad of Medicine (Paris) 1966; Laveran Prize, Science Acad (Paris) 1973. *Publications:* Mycotic Allergy Diseases 1963; numerous articles and treatises. *Leisure interests:* reading, classical music, walking. *Address:* CNRS, Laboratoire de Parasitologie et de Mycologie, 15 rue de l'Ecole de Médecine, 75270 Paris Cedex 06, France. *Telephone:* (1) 43-29-29-20.

THIRSK, (Irene) Joan, CBE, MA, PH D, FBA, FRHISTS; British historian; b 19 June 1922, London; d of William Henry and Daisy (née Frayer) Watkins; m James Wood Thirsk 1945; one s one d. *Education:* Camden School for Girls (London) and Westfield Coll (Univ of London). *Career:* War service in Auxiliary Territorial Service (ATS) Intelligence Corps 1942–45; Asst Lecturer in Sociology LSE 1950–51; Sr Research Fellow in Agrarian History, Dept of English Local History, Univ of Leicester 1951–65; Reader in Econ History, Univ of Oxford and Professorial Fellow, St Hilda's Coll 1965–83, Ford Lecturer in English History 1975; mem Royal Comm on Historical Monuments of England 1977–86, on Historical Manuscripts 1989–96; Pres British Agricultural Hist Soc 1983–86, 1995–98, British Asscn for Local History 1986–92, Kent History Fed 1990–99; Gen Ed Agrarian History of England and Wales 1975–2000; Sr Mellon Fellow, Nat Humanities Center, NC, USA 1986–87; Foreign mem American Philosophical Soc 1982–; Corresp mem Colonial Soc of Massachusetts 1983; Hon Fellow St Hilda's Coll 1983–, Queen Mary and Westfield Coll, Univ of London 1997; Hon D LITT (Leicester) 1985, (East Anglia) 1990, (Kent) 1993, (Sussex) 1994, (Southampton) 1999, (Greenwich) 2001; Hon D UNIV (Open) 1991; Dr hc (Agricultural Univ, Wageningen) 1993. *Publications:* Ed and Contrib: The Agrarian History of England and Wales, IV 1500–1640 1967, V 1640–1750 1985; English Peasant Farming 1957, Seventeenth-Century Economic Documents (jtly) 1972, The Restoration 1976, Economic Policy and Projects: The Development of a Consumer Society in Early Modern England 1978, The Rural Economy of England: Collected Essays 1984, England's Agricultural Regions and Agrarian History 1500–1750 1987, Alternative Agriculture. A History from the Black Death to the Present Day 1997, The English Rural Landscape 2000. *Leisure interests:* gardening, sewing, machine knitting. *Address:* 1 Hadlow Castle, Hadlow, Tonbridge, Kent, TN11 0EG, UK. *Telephone:* (1732) 850708; *Fax:* (1732) 850708.

THOM, Linda M., CM; Canadian sportswoman; b 30 Dec, Hamilton, ON; d of the late J. Neill and of Carissima (née Lundin-Stanhope) Malcolm; m Donald Thom 1972; one s one d. *Education:* Lisgar Collegiate Inst, Ridgemont High School, Carleton Univ and Le Cordon Bleu (Paris). *Career:* Mem Canadian Shooting Team; winner of six gold, four silver and three bronze medals in int competitions 1970–75, 1982–87; Gold Medallist in Sport Pistol event, Olympic Games (Los Angeles, USA) 1984; Chair Ontario Sports Medicine and Safety Advisory Bd 1985–88; Vice-Chair Canadian Advisory Council on Firearms 1988–91; mem Bd Dirs Ontario Trillium Foundation 1998–2001; cooking school proprietor, caterer and writer on food and restaurants 1975–83; f Soc for American Wines 1980; Sales Rep Royal Lepage 1989–; mem Shooting Fed of Canada, Canadian Fed of Chefs de Cuisine; Bachelor of Journalism; Canadian Woman Athlete of the Year 1984; Key to the City of Ottawa; Canadian Amateur Sports Hall of Fame 1986; Canada Sports Hall of Fame 1992. *Leisure interests:* Alpine Skiing, Hiking, Canoeing, Target Shooting. *Address:* 19-551 Riverdale Ave, Ottawa, ON K1S 1S3, Canada. *Telephone:* (613) 737-5775.

THOMAS, Audrey Grace, MA; Canadian (b American) writer; b 17 Nov 1935, Binghamton, New York; d of Donald Earle and Frances Waldron (née Corbett) Callahan; m Ian Thomas 1959 (divorced 1979); three d. *Education:* The Mary A. Burnham School (Northampton, MA), Smith Coll and Univ of British Colombia. *Career:* Teacher of English Language Univ of Science and Tech, Ghana 1964–66; Visiting Lecturer Univ of British Columbia 1975–76, Sr Lecturer 1981–82; Visiting Asst Prof Concordia Univ, Montréal 1978, Visiting Prof 1989–90; Visiting Prof Univ of Victoria 1978–79, 1988; Writer-in-Residence Simon Fraser Univ 1982, David Thompson Univ Centre, Nelson, BC 1984, Univ of Ottawa 1987; Visiting Prof Dartmouth Coll, Hanover, NH 1994; mem Nat Exec Writers Union of Canada; mem Canada Council Periodicals Cttee 1980–83, Editorial Collective, Women and Words Anthology 1984; mem PEN, Amnesty Int; Canada-Scotland Literary Fellow (Edinburgh) 1985–86; Dr hc (Simon Fraser Univ, Univ of BC) 1994; Ethel Wilson Award 1985; Marian Engel Award 1987; Canada-Australia Literary Prize 1990. *Publications:* Ten Green Bottles 1967, Mrs Blood 1970, Muchmeyer and Prospero on the Island 1972, Songs My Mother Taught Me 1973, Blown Figures 1975, Ladies and Escorts 1977, Latakia 1979, Two in the Bush and Other Stories 1980, Real Mothers 1981, Intertidal Life (nominated Gov Gen's Award in Fiction) 1984, Goodbye Harold, Good Luck! 1986, The Wild Blue Yonder 1990, Graven Images 1993; Radio dramas include: Once Your Submarine Cable is Gone... 1973, The Milky Way 1984, The Woman in Black Velvet 1985, Rosa 1987, Shonadithit 1988, Sanctuary 1989, A Day in the Life of Medusa 1989; writer of several articles. *Address:* R R 2, Galiano, BC V0N 1P0, Canada.

THOMAS, Betty; American director and actress; b 27 July 1949, St Louis, MO. *Education:* Univ of Ohio, Chicago Art Inst and Roosevelt Univ. *Career:* Fmr mem Second City improvisation group, Chicago; performed at the Comedy Store, LA. *Films:* Dir: Only You, The Brady Bunch Movie 1995, Private Parts, Dr Dolittle 1998, 28 Days 1999; actress: Tunnelvision, Chesty Anderson—US Navy, Loose Shoes, Used Cars, Homework, Troop Beverly Hills, Jackson County Jail; *TV:* Dir, series: Doogie Howser MD, Dream On (Emmy Award 1993), Hooperman, Mancuso FBI, Arresting Behavior, Couples; TV film: My Breast; documentary drama: The Late Shift (Dirs' Guild of America Award 1997); actress, series: Hill Street Blues (Emmy Award 1985); TV films: Outside Chance, Nashville Grab, When Your Lover Leaves, Prison for Children. *Address:* Directors Guild of America, 7920 Sunset Blvd, Los Angeles, CA 90046, USA.

THOMAS, Debi; American ice-skater; b 25 March 1967, Poughkeepsie, NY; d of McKinley and Janice Thomas; m Brian Vanden Hogen. *Education:* Stanford Univ (CA). *Career:* Figure-Skater 1976–88; US Figure-Skating Champion 1986, 1988, Women's World Figure-Skating Champion 1986, World Professional Figure-Skating Champion 1988, 1989, Bronze Medallist Olympic Games, Seoul, 1988; Ebony Magazine American Black Achievement Award; Woman Athlete of the Year 1986. *Address:* c/o IMG, 22 E 71st St, New York, NY 10021, USA.

THOMAS, Helen A., BA; American journalist; b 4 Aug 1920, Winchester, KY; d of George and Mary (née Thomas) Thomas; m Douglas B. Cornell. *Education:* Wayne Univ. *Career:* Reporter United Press Int (UPI) 1943–74, White House Bureau Chief 1974–; first woman mem Gridiron Club 1975, apptd Pres (first woman) 1992; mem Women's Nat Press Club, Pres 1959–60 (William Allen White Journalism Award); mem American Newspaper Women's Club (fmr Vice-Pres), White House Correspondents Asscn (Pres 1976); numerous hon degrees including Hon LL D (Eastern Michigan State) 1972, (Ferris State Coll) 1978, (Brown) 1986, (St Bonaventure) 1988, (Franklin Marshall) 1989, (Skidmore Coll, MO) 1992, (Susquehanna) 1993, (Sage Coll, MO) 1994, (Nothwestern) 1995, (Franklin Coll) 1995; Hon LHD (Wayne State) 1974, (Detroit) 1979; Woman of the Year Award, Ladies Home Journal 1975; Fourth Estate Award, Nat Press Club 1984; Journalism Award, Univ of Missouri 1990; Al Newharth Award 1990; Ralph McGill Award 1995; Lifetime Achievement Award, White House Corresps Asscn 1998. *Publication:* Dateline White House. *Address:* 2501 Calvert St, NW, Washington, DC 20008-2620, USA (Home).

THOMAS, Jacqueline Mauricette Christiane, D ÈS L; French linguistic researcher; b 29 Nov 1930, Paris; d of Maurice and Yvonne (née Fromenteau) Thomas; one d. *Education:* Lycée Lamartine (Paris), Univ of Paris and Ecole Nat des Langues Orientales Vivantes. *Career:* Trainee CNRS 1954, Research Asst 1958, Researcher 1962, Prin Researcher 1966, Dir of Research 1970–; Pres Gen Linguistics Section, Nat CNRS Cttee 1966–75; Dir Languages and Civilizations with Oral Traditions Lab, CNRS 1976–89; Dir of Publs Soc d'Etudes Linguistiques et Anthropologiques de France 1967–; Dir numerous linguistic seminars; mem Soc de linguistique de Paris, Soc des africanistes; Prix Volney; des Cinq Académies; Médaille d'argent du CNRS; Chevalier de l'Ordre Nat du Mérite; Chevalier des Palmes Académiques. *Publications include:* Instructions pour la notation des langues exotiques (in collection) 1956, Le parler ngbaka de Bokanga: phonologie, morphologie, syntaxe (Volney Prize 1967) 1963, Les Ngbaka de la Lobaye: le dépeuplement rural chez une population forestière de République centrafricaine 1963, La notation des langues: phonétique et phonologie 1967, Les Mimbo, génies du piégeage et le monde surnaturel des Ngbaka-mabo 1974, Encyclopédie des pygmées aka (in collection) 1981. *Leisure interest:* garden. *Address:* Lacito, 7 rue Guy Môquet, Bât 23, 94801 Villejuif, Cedex, France (Office); 6 rue de l'église, 76340 Saint-Martin-au-Bosc, France (Home). *Telephone:* (2) 35-93-45-43; *Fax:* (2) 35-93-66-80; *E-mail:* thomas.bouquiaux@wanadoo.fr.

THOMAS, Jean Olwen, CBE, SC D, FRS, C CHEM; British professor of macromolecular biochemistry; b 1 Oct 1942; d of John Robert and Lorna Prunella (née Harris) Thomas. *Education:* Llwyn-y-Bryn High School for Girls (Swansea) and Univ Coll Swansea (Univ of Wales). *Career:* Demonstrator in Biochem, Univ of Cambridge 1969–73, Lecturer 1973–87, Reader in the Biochem of Macromolecules 1987–91, Prof of Macromolecular Biochemistry 1991–, Chair Cambridge Centre for Molecular Recognition 1993–; Coll Lecturer 1969–91; Fellow New Hall, Cambridge 1969–, Tutor 1970–76, Vice-Pres 1983–87; mem EMBO, Royal Soc Council, Science and Eng Research Council, Academia Europaea, Royal Soc of Chem, Council and Scientific Advisory Cttee Imperial Cancer Research Fund 1994–, Scientific Advisory Cttee Lister Inst 1994–2000; Trustee British Museum 1994–; Gov Wellcome Trust 2000–; Beit Memorial Fellow; Hon Fellow Univ Coll of Swansea 1987, Cardiff Univ 1998; Hon D SC (Wales) 1992; awards include Ayling Prize 1964, Hinkel Research Prize 1967, K. M. Stott Research Prize (Newnham Coll, Cambridge) 1976. *Publications:* Companion to Biochemistry: Selected Topics for Further Study (jt ed and contrib, vol 1) 1974, (vol 2) 1979; numerous papers in scientific journals. *Leisure interests:* reading, music, walking. *Address:* Department of Biochemistry, Tennis Court Rd, Cambridge CB2 1QW, UK (Office); 26 Eachard Rd, Cambridge CB3 0HY, UK (Home). *Telephone:* (1223) 333670 (Office); (1223) 62620 (Home).

THOMAS, Margaret; British artist; b 26 Sept 1916, London; d of the late Francis Stewart and Grace (née Whetherly) Thomas. *Education:* Sidcup Art School, Slade School and Royal Acad Schools (London). *Career:* Solo exhibitions include Leicester Galleries, London 1949, 1951, Aitken Dotts and the Scottish Gallery, Edinburgh 1952–, Wakefield Art Gallery 1961, Canaletto Gallery, London 1961, Howard Roberts, Cardiff 1963, Minorities, Colchester 1964, Mall Galleries, London 1972, Octagon Gallery, Belfast 1973, Maltings Concert Hall Gallery, Snape, Sally Hunter Fine Art 1988, 1991, 1995, 1998, Messum Gallery 2001; works acquired by public and corp collections including Arts Council, Royal Acad, Royal Scottish Acad, Ministry of Works, Nuffield Foundation for Hospitals, Scottish Nat Orchestra, Edinburgh City Corpn, Mitsukshi Ltd (Tokyo), Lloyds of London, Ministry of Educ, HRH Prince Philip, Nat Library of Wales, portrait of Sir Kyffin Williams, RA; works featured in numerous periodicals; mem Women's Int Art Club 1940–, Royal Soc of British Arts 1947–, New English Art Club 1950–, Contemporary Portrait Soc 1970–, RWA 1971–; Hunting Group Award for oil painting of the year 1981. *Leisure interests:* antiques, gardening, vintage cars. *Address:* Ellingham Mill, nr Bungay, Suffolk NR35 2EP, UK. *Telephone:* (1508) 518656 (Ellingham Mill).

THOMAS, Mary Madeline, B SC; Canadian executive; b 23 May 1948, Shuswap Tribe, Canim Lake, BC; d of James Prentiss Charlie and Bertha Rita Isadore Frank (native Princess); m Jacob Thomas 1966 (divorced 1981); three s one d. *Education:* Prince George Catholic Coll and Coll of Higher Educ (High Wycombe, UK). *Career:* Native Child-Care Worker 1971–74; Clerk Indian Affairs Govt 1975–77; Native Community Planner in Resource Man and Econ Devt 1978–; Community Planner Canim Lake Native Govt 1978–81; Co-ordinator and Political Lobbyist for First Nations of Canada (UK) 1981–82; Community Planner in Econ Devt, Cariboo Tribal Council 1986–91; Pvt Consultant Intertribal Forestry Asscn of BC 1990–91, apptd Exec Dir 1990; Pvt Consultant First Nations Advancement for Self-Govt 1991–; Life mem Asscn of the Inst of Wood Science; Assoc mem Nat Aboriginal Forestry Asscn (Canada), Intertribal Timber Council (USA). *Publication:* Healing Journey of a Shuswap Tribal Member 1992. *Leisure interests:* native needlework, painting, drawing, writing poetry, music. *Address:* POB 216, Canim Lake, BC V0K 1J0, Canada. *Telephone:* (250) 395-7588.

THOMAS ELLIS, Alice (see Haycraft, Anna Margaret).

THOMAS-FELIX, Deborah Agnes, LL B; Trinidad and Tobago judge; b 21 Jan 1962, Trinidad; d of Charles and Bernadette Thomas; divorced; two s. *Education:* North Eastern Coll (Trinidad), Univ of the West Indies (Barbados) and Hugh Wooding Law School (Trinidad). *Career:* Attorney-at-Law, Pvt Practice 1986–90; Magistrate specializing in family-related matters, Trinidad and Tobago 1990–94; Sr Magistrate specializing in criminal matters 1994–95; Pres Family Court, specializing in all family-related matters, St Vincent and the Grenadines 1995. *Leisure interests:* reading, playing cards, gardening. *Address:* Lyric Bldg, Kingstown, Saint Vincent and the Grenadines. *Telephone:* 457-1307; *Fax:* 456-2837.

THOMPSON, Anne Elise, LL B, MA; American federal judge; b 8 July 1934, Philadelphia, PA; d of Leroy Henry and Mary Elise (née Jackson) Jenkins; m William H. Thompson 1965; one d one s. *Education:* Howard (DC) and Temple (PA) Univs. *Career:* Called to the Bar, DC 1964, NJ 1966; Staff Attorney Office of Solicitor, Dept of Labor, Chicago, IL 1964–65; Asst Deputy Public Defender Trenton, NJ 1967–70; Municipal Prosecutor Lawrence Township, Lawrenceville, NJ 1970–72; Municipal Court Judge, Trenton 1972–75; Prosecutor Mercer Co 1975–79; US Dist Judge, NJ 1979–, currently Chief Judge; Vice-Chair Mercer Co Criminal Justice Planning Cttee 1972; Del Democratic Nat Convention 1972; mem Criminal Practice Cttee, New Jersey Supreme Court 1975–79; mem ABA, Fed Bar Asscn; numerous awards include Asscn of Black Women Lawyers Award 1976, Distinguished Service Award (Nat Dist Attorneys' Asscn) 1978–79, Gene Carte Memorial Award (American Criminal Justice Asscn) 1980, John Mercer Langston Outstanding Alumnus Award (Howard Univ Law School) 1981. *Address:* US District Court, US Courthouse-4000, 402 E State St, POB 401, Trenton, NJ 08608, USA.

THOMPSON, Caroline Warner, BA; American screenwriter, film producer and director; b 23 April 1956, Washington, DC; d of Thomas Carlton, Jr and Bettie Marshall (née Warner) Thompson; m Alfred Henry Bromell 1982 (divorced 1985). *Education:* Amherst Coll, Harvard Univ. *Career:* Fmr freelance journalist. *Screenplays include:* Edward Scissorhands (also assoc producer) 1990, The Addams Family 1991, Homeward Bound: The Incredible Journey 1993, The Secret

Garden (also assoc producer) 1993, Tim Burton's The Nightmare Before Christmas 1993, Black Beauty (also dir) 1994, Buddy (also dir) 1997; *Publication:* First Born 1993. *Address:* c/o William Morris Agency Inc, 151 El Camino Drive, Beverly Hills, CA 90212-2775, USA.

THOMPSON, Dianne, BA; British business executive; b 1951, Batley, Yorkshire; m (divorced); one d. *Education:* Univ of Manchester. *Career:* Began career as Marketing Trainee Co-operative Wholesale Soc; also worked in marketing roles for ICI, Sterling Roncraft, Woolworths and Signet Retail Group until 1997; fmr Man Dir Sandvik saws and tools; Commercial Operations Dir Camelot (UK nat lottery operator) 1997–2000, Chief Exec Feb 2000–. *Address:* St Vincent House, Suffolk St, London SW1, UK.

THOMPSON, Emma; British actress and screenwriter; b 15 April 1959, London; d of the late Eric Thompson and of Phyllida Law; m Kenneth Branagh 1989 (divorced); partner Greg Wise; one d. *Education:* Camden Girls' School (London) and Newnham Coll (Cambridge). *Career:* Appeared with Cambridge Footlights; writer, producer, performer first all-woman revue, Univ of Cambridge; several Best Actress awards and Acad Award nominations. *Plays include:* The Cellar Tapes (Perrier Pick of the Fringe Award, Edinburgh Festival 1981) 1981–82, A Sense of Nonsense (revue tour) 1983, Short Vehicle 1984, Me and My Girl, Look Back in Anger 1989, King Lear (world tour) 1990, A Midsummer Night's Dream (world tour) 1990; *Films include:* The Tall Guy, Henry V 1989, Impromptu 1991, Dead Again 1991, Howards End (Acad Award, BAFTA Award, Golden Globe Best Dramatic Actress Award, Evening Standard Award) 1992, Peter's Friends 1992, Much Ado About Nothing 1993, The Remains of the Day (Evening Standard Award 1994) 1993, In the Name of the Father 1993, My Father the Hero 1994, Junior 1994, Carrington 1995, Sense and Sensibility (also wrote screenplay, Acad Award for Best Screenplay Adaptation, BAFTA Best Leading Actress Award) 1996, The Winter Guest (Venice Film Festival Panisetti award for Best Actress) 1996, Primary Colors 1997, Judas Kiss 1997, Wit 2000; *TV appearances include:* Emma Thompson Special, Channel 4 1983, Alfresco 1983–84, The Crystal Cube 1984, Carrott's Lib, Saturday Night Live, Tutti Frutti (BAFTA Award for Best Actress), Fortunes of War (BAFTA Award for Best Actress) 1986–87, Thompson 1988, Knuckle 1988, The Winslow Boy 1988, Look Back in Anger, Thames 1989, Blue Boy 1994, Ellen (Emmy Award for Outstanding Guest Actress in a Comedy Series) 1998. *Address:* c/o Hamilton Asper Ltd, Ground Floor, 24 Hanway St, London W1P 9DD, UK. *Telephone:* (20) 7636-1221; *Fax:* (20) 7636-1226.

THOMPSON, Judith Clare Francesca, BA; Canadian playwright; b 20 Sept 1954, Montréal, PQ; d of William and Mary (née Forde) Thompson; m Gregor Campbell 1983; three d one s. *Education:* Queen's Univ and Nat Theatre School (Montréal). *Career:* Numerous workshops 1980–90; Tutor in Playwriting Univ of Toronto 1983–84; mem Playwright's Unit Tarragon Theatre 1984–86; Resident Instructor and Dir Univ of New Brunswick 1989–90; Assoc Prof of Drama, Univ of Guelph 1991–; Dir The Crucible, Hedda Gabler (adapted at Shaw Festival) 1991; Screenwriter; Toronto Arts Award for Writing and Editing 1988; B'nai Brith Award for Anti-Racism (for White Sand); Gov-Gen's Literary Award (for The Other Side of the Dark) 1990. *TV includes:* Don't Talk (Chalmers Award 1988), Airwaves, Life with Billy (Best Screenplay, Golden Gate Awards, San Francisco) 1992, Turning to Stone (Prix Italia for Best Film Screenplay); *Plays include:* Lion in the Streets, White Biting Dog (Gov-Gen Literary Award), The Crackwalker, I am Yours, Sled; *Radio includes:* Tornado (Nellie Award for Best Radio Drama), Sugarcane, Stop Talking Like That. *Address:* Great North Artists' Management, Inc, 350 Dupont St, Toronto, ON M5R 1V9, Canada.

THOMPSON, Sophie; British actress; b Jan 1965, London; d of Eric Thompson and Phyllida Law (qv); m Richard Lumsden 1995; two s. *Education:* Camden School (London) and Bristol Old Vic Theatre School. *Theatre includes:* Company (Donmar Theatre, Clarence Derwent Award) 1996, Into the Woods (Donmar Theatre, Lawrence Olivier Award); *Films include:* Four Weddings and a Funeral 1993, Emma 1995, Dancing at Lughnasa 1997, Relative Values 1999, Gosford Park 2001. *Leisure interests:* glueing, gardening. *Address:* c/o Jonathan Altaras Associates, 2nd Floor, 13 Shorts Gardens, London WC2H 9AT, UK.

THOMSON, Pamela A., BA, LL B; Canadian judge; b 27 Aug 1942, Timmins, ON; d of James and Ruth (née Ashkanase) Thomson; m E. Gordon Hachborn; two s. *Education:* Queen's Univ and Univ of Toronto. *Career:* Law Practice 1968–71, 1975–81; Co-Dir Centre for Public Interest Law 1971–75; called to the Bar, ON 1968, PQ 1973; Judge Ontario Prov Court 1981–; Police Complaints Bd 1982–86; Co-ordinator Case Flow Program, Small Claims Court Br, Ontario Court of Justice 1990–; mem Canadian Asscn of Prov Court Judges, Exec Dir 1990–96, Sec-Treas 1991–96. *Publication:* Consumer Access to Justice 1976. *Address:* Ministry of the Attorney-General, 444 Yonge St, 2nd Floor, Toronto, ON M5B 2H7, Canada.

THOMSON, Shirley Lavinia, OC, PH D; Canadian museum director; b 19 Feb 1930, Wakerville, ON; d of Walter T. and Edith May (née Mackenzie) Cull. *Education:* Univs of W Ontario and of Maryland (USA) and McGill Univ. *Career:* Ed NATO Conf, Paris 1956–60; Asst Sec-Gen World Universities Service, Toronto 1960–63; Asst Sec-Gen Canadian Comm for UNESCO, Ottawa 1964–67, Sec-Gen Directorate 1985–87; Research Co-ordinator and writer Memoirs of Senator Thérèse Casgrain 1968–70; Dir at UNESCO Pavillion, Man and His World, Montréal 1978–80; Special Co-ordinator Largillière Exhibition, Museum of Fine Arts, Montréal 1981; Dir McCord Museum, Montréal 1982–85; Nat Gallery of Canada, Ottawa 1987–97; Dir Canadian Museums Asscn; Dir Canada Council 1997–; mem Council Canadian Soc for Decorative Arts; Dr hc (Ottawa) 1988, (McGill) 1989, (Mt Allison, W Ontario) 1990; Canadian Council Fellow 1977–78, Doctoral Award 1978–79; Chevalier des Arts et des Lettres (France) 1990. *Address:* 350 Albert St, POB 1047, Ottawa, ON K1P 5V8, Canada (Office); 208-404 Laurier Ave E, Ottawa, ON K1N 6R2, Canada (Home).

THORNE, Rosemary Prudence, B SC; British business executive; b 12 Feb 1952. *Education:* Univ of Warwick. *Career:* Fmrly Financial Dir and Co Sec Harrods, worked in Finance Dept at Storehouse, later Group Financial Controller Grand Metropolitan; apptd Group Finance Dir J. Sainsbury 1992; Trustee and Treas Prince's Youth Business Trust; mem 100 Group, mem Main and Technical Cttee; Fellow Chartered Inst of Man Accountants, Asscn of Corporate Treasurers. *Address:* J. Sainsbury PLC, Stamford House, Stamford St, London SE1 9LL, UK. *Telephone:* (20) 7921-6025; *Fax:* (20) 7921-6644.

THORNEWILL, Fiona; British Arctic/Antarctic explorer; b 10 July 1968, Upton, Notts; d of Ralph and Jean Cowling; m 1st Bill Shepley 1986 (died 1991); m Mike Leslie Thornewill 1996. *Education:* Rodney School (Kirklington, Notts). *Career:* Studied Hotel Man; worked as admin at RAF Newton 1986; qualified as gym instructor, owned and operated ladies gym 1989–95; recruitment consultant 1995–; trained as competitive cyclist and undertook solo journey to Far East, including ascent of Mt Kinabula 1997; dog sledge expedition to Spitzbergen 1998; first British woman (with Catharine Hartley, qv) to walk across the Antarctic to the Geographic S Pole 2000, also first British woman (with Catharine Hartley) to walk to Geographic N Pole 2001, becoming first ever woman to manhaul own sledge to both N and S Poles; Pride of Britain Award 2000; People of the Year Award 2001. *Leisure interests:* travelling – the non-tourist way, cycling, running, reading, socializing with friends and parties. *Address:* c/o Blue Peter, BBC Broadcasting House, Portland Place, London W1A 1AA, UK. *Telephone:* (115) 989-7474 (Office); (1636) 830944 (Home); *Fax:* (115) 989-7475 (Office); (1636) 830944 (Home); *E-mail:* southpole2000@talk21.com.

THORNTON, Janet Maureen, CBE, PH D, FRS; British professor of molecular biology; b 23 May 1949; d of Stanley James McLoughlin and Kathleen Barlow; m Alan Thornton 1970; one s one d. *Education:* Univ of Nottingham, King's Coll (London) and Nat Inst of Medical Research. *Career:* Tutor Open Univ 1976–83; molecular pharmacologist Nat Inst of Medical Research 1978; Science and Eng Research Council Advanced Fellow, Birkbeck Coll 1979–83, Lecturer 1983–89, Sr Lecturer 1989–90, Bernal Chair of Crystallography 1996–; Dir Biomolecular Structure and Modelling Unit, Univ Coll London 1990–, Prof of Biomolecular Structure 1990–; Head Jt Research School in Molecular Sciences, Univ Coll London and Birkbeck Coll 1996–; consultant European Bioinformatics Inst, European Molecular Biology Lab 1994–; numerous articles in scientific journals; Hans Neurath Award, Protein Soc (USA) 2000. *Leisure interests:* reading, music, gardening, walking. *Address:* Birkbeck College, University College London, Gower St, London WC1E 6BT, UK. *Telephone:* (20) 7679-7048; *Fax:* (20) 7916-8499; *E-mail:* thornton@biochem.ucl.ac.uk.

THORNTON, Kathryn C., PH D; American physicist and astronaut; b 17 Aug 1952, Montgomery, AL; d of William C. and Elsie Cordell; m Stephen T. Thornton; two d two step-s. *Education:* Auburn Univ (AL) and Univ of Virginia. *Career:* NATO Postdoctoral Fellow Max Planck Inst of Nuclear Physics, Heidelberg, Germany 1979–80; Physicist US Army Foreign Service and Tech Center, Charlottesville, VA 1980–84; Joined NASA 1984, Astronaut Lyndon B. Johnson Space Center, Houston, TX 1985–, mission specialist Space Discovery flight STS-33 1989; aboard maiden flight of Space Shuttle Endeavor 1992; mem AAAS, American Physics Soc. *Address:* NASA, Johnson Space Center, Astronaut Office, Houston, TX 77058, USA.

THORP, Rosemary, MA; British economist; b 2 Oct 1940; d of Hugh W. and Angela M. Mason; m Timothy L. Thorp 1964; two c. *Education:* Univ of Oxford. *Career:* Lecturer Univ of California at Berkeley, USA 1967–70; Research Officer Univ of Oxford 1962–67, Lecturer in Econs of Latin America 1971–, Fellow St Antony's Coll, Oxford 1979–. *Publications:* Growth and Policy in an Open Economy: Peru 1890–1977 (jtly) 1978, Latin America in the 1930s 1984, Economic Management and Economic Development in Peru and Colombia 1991. *Leisure interests:* walking, community activities, work with NGOs. *Address:* St Antony's College, Oxford OX2 6JF, UK (Office); Park Farm, Harcourt Rd, Malvern WR14 4DW, UK (Home). *Telephone:* (1865) 274486 (Office); *Fax:* (1865) 558680 (Office).

THORPE, Marjorie, PH D; Trinidad and Tobago diplomatist; b 8 July 1941, Trinidad; d of Lester and Violet Thorpe. *Education:* McGill Univ (Montréal) and Queen's Univ (ON, Canada). *Career:* Asst Lecturer Univ of the W Indies 1965, Sr Lecturer 1982, Head Dept of English 1979–85, Vice-Dean Faculty of Arts and Gen Studies 1983–84, Dean 1987–88; Perm Rep to UN 1988–92; Sr Fellowship Award Howard Univ, Washington, DC 1985; Ford Foundation Fellowship, Inst of Devt Studies, Univ of Sussex, UK 1986; frequently attends confs relating to women and devt issues. *Address:* c/o Ministry of Foreign Affairs, Knowsley Bldg, Queen's Park West, Port of Spain, Trinidad and Tobago.

THULIN, Ingrid; Swedish actress and director; b 27 Jan 1929, Sollefteå; d of Adam Thulin and Nanna Larsson; m 1st Claes Sylwander 1951; m 2nd Harry Schein 1956. *Education:* Royal Dramatic Theatre School (Stockholm). *Career:* Appeared in many modern and classical plays in Stockholm and Malmö until 1962; appeared in several films by Ingmar Bergman; has also acted in theatre and on TV in USA and Italy; numerous nat and int awards. *Films include:* When Love Comes to the Village 1950, Wild Strawberries 1957, So Close to Life 1958, The Face 1958, The Judge 1960, The Four Horsemen of the Apocalypse 1961, Winter Light 1962, The Silence 1963, La guerre est finie 1968, The Damned 1970, Cries and Whispers 1973, A Handful of Love 1974, La cage 1975, Cassandra Crossing 1976, Agnes Will Die 1977, One and One 1978, The Rehearsal, Broken Skies (writer and dir) 1983, Il Corsario 1983, La Casa Sorire 1991, Rabbit Face; *Publication:* Någon jag kände (Someone I Knew) 1993. *Address:* 00060 Sacrofano, Rome, Italy; Kevingestrand 7B, 18231 Danderyd, Sweden. *Telephone:* (06) 9084171 (Italy); (8) 755 68 98 (Sweden).

THURDIN, Görel; Swedish politician; b 26 May 1942, Västerås; m Ernst Thurdin; three s. *Education:* Univ of Umeå. *Career:* Municipal Councillor Örnsköldsvik 1979, mem Municipal Exec Bd 1983–85; Co Clerk Tax Authority 1984; elected to Riksdag (Parl) 1986, Deputy mem Parl Standing Cttee on Labour Market 1986–88, on Foreign Affairs, on Finance 1987–88, on Educ 1988–91, apptd Parl War Del 1988, Deputy mem Bd Office of Nat Debt 1988–89, Speaker's Conf 1988–91; mem Centre Party Parl Group Council 1987, Income Tax Cttee 1987–89, Research Council Del 1987–91; Minister for Physical Planning, Ministry of the Environment and Natural Resources 1991–94; elected Second Vice-Chair Centre Party 1987; Chair Cttee on Sexual Equality 1991. *Leisure interests:* skiing, walking, environmental issues.

THURMAN, Uma; American actress; b 29 April 1970, Boston, MA; d of Robert and Nena (née Schlebrugge) Thurman; m 1st Gary Oldman 1991 (divorced 1992); m 2nd Ethan Hawke 1997; one c. *Education:* Professional Children's School (New York). *Career:* Worked as model and dishwasher before film debut in Kiss Daddy Good Night 1988. *Films include:* Johnny Be Good 1988, Dangerous Liaisons 1988, The Adventures of Baron Munchhausen 1989, Where the Heart Is 1990, Henry and June 1990, Robin Hood 1991, Final Analysis 1992, Jennifer Eight 1992, Mad Dog and Glory 1993, Even Cowgirls Get the Blues 1994, Pulp Fiction (Acad Award nomination) 1994, Dylan, A Month by the Lake 1995, The Truth About Cats and Dogs 1996, Beautiful Girls 1996, Batman and Robin 1997, Addicted to Love 1997, Gattaca 1997, The Avengers 1998, Les Miserables 1998, Sweet and Lowdown 1999, Vatel 2000, The Golden Bowl 2000; *Stage appearances include:* The Misanthrope 1999. *Address:* c/o CAA, 9830 Wilshire Blvd, Beverly Hills, CA 90212, USA.

THYSSEN, Marianne L. P.; Belgian politician; b 24 July 1956, Sint-Gillis-Waas. *Career:* MEP (PPE, CVP), mem Cttee on Econ and Monetary Affairs and Industrial Policy, Del for relations with the countries of Cen America and Mexico. *Address:* European Parliament, rue Wiertz, 1047 Brussels, Belgium. *Telephone:* (2) 284-21-11; *Fax:* (2) 230-69-43.

TIDBALL, M. Elizabeth Peters, PH D; American professor of physiology; b 15 Oct 1929, Anderson, IN; d of John Winton and Beatrice (née Ryan) Peters; m Charles S. Tidball 1952. *Education:* Mount Holyoke Coll (MA) and Univ of Wisconsin. *Career:* Asst Research Prof Dept of Pharmacology, George Washington Univ, DC 1962–64, Dept of Physiology 1964–70, Research Prof 1970–71, Prof 1971–94; Prof Emer 1994–; Asst Dir M of Theological Studies, Wesley Theological seminary 1993–94; Distinguished Research Scholar, Co-Dir Tidball Center for Educ Environments 1994–; Consultant Food and Drug Admin 1966–67, Woodrow Wilson Nat Fellowship Foundation 1975–94, Nat Science Foundation 1974–91, Asscn of American Colls 1986; Nat Panellist American Council on Educ 1983–90; Trustee Mount Holyoke Coll, MA 1968–73, Vice-Chair 1972–73, Trustee Fellow 1988–; Trustee Hood Coll, MD 1972–84, 1986–, Exec Cttee 1974–84, 1989–92; Trustee Skidmore Coll 1988–, mem Exec Cttee 1993–; mem Bd Visitors Salem Coll 1986–93; mem Editorial Bd Journal of Higher Educ 1979–83, Consultant Ed 1984–; numerous contribs to professional journals; Alumnae Medal of Honor (Mount Holyoke Coll) 1971; Medal for Outstanding Achievement, Chestnut Hill Coll (PA) 1987; Outstanding Graduate, Penn Hall School 1988. *Address:* 4100 Cathedral Ave NW, Washington, DC 20016, USA.

TIELSCH, Ilse, D PHIL; Austrian (b Czechoslovakian) writer; b 20 March 1929, Czechoslovakia; d of Fritz and Marianne (née Zamanek) Felzmann; m Herr Tielsch 1950; two s two d. *Education:* Univ of Vienna. *Career:* Resident in Austria 1945–; studied journalism before becoming a writer of poetry and prose; Vice-Pres Austrian PEN-Club; Austrian Medal of Honour for Science and Art; Andreas Gryphius-Preis 1989; Anton Wildgans-Preis 1990. *Publications include:* Novels and stories: Ein Elefant in unserer Straße, Erinnerung mit Bäumen, Die Ahnenpyramide (trilogy) 1980, 1982, 1988, Heimatsuchen, Fremder Strand, Die Früchte der Tränen, Der Solitär; Poetry: In meinem Orangengarten, Anrufung des Mondes, Regenzeit, Nicht beweisbar, Zwischenbericht. *Address:* St-Michael-Gasse 68, 1210 Vienna, Austria. *Telephone:* (222) 25-26-94.

TIEMANN, Susanne, D JUR; German lawyer; b 20 April 1947, Schwandorf; d of Hermann and Anna-Maria Bamberg; m Burkhard Tiemann 1969; two d one s. *Education:* Ludwig-Maximilian Univ (Munich). *Career:* Called to the Bar and established as lawyer, Munich 1975; lawyer, Cologne 1980; Prof of Social and Admin Law Univ of Bonn, Catholic Univ of Cologne; mem Econ and Social Cttee (EC, now EU) 1987–, Chair 1992–; mem Bd German Fed of Liberal Professions 1988–; mem Exec Bd and Vice-Pres European Secr of the Liberal, Intellectual and Social Professions (SEPLIS) 1988, Pres 1989–95; Chair German Taxpayers' Asscn 1992–94; mem Bundestag 1994–; Frauen für Europa Prize 1993. *Address:* OberLänder Ufer 174, 50968 Cologne, Germany.

TILGHMAN, Shirley Marie, PH D; Canadian university president. *Education:* Queen's Univ (Kingston, ON), Temple Univ, (Philadelphia, USA). *Career:* Mem Inst for Cancer Research 1979–86; Howard A. Prior Prof of Life Sciences, Princeton Univ 1986–, Head, Inst for Integrative Genomics 1998–; Pres Princeton Univ May 2001–; Pres's Award for Distinguished Teaching 1996. *Address:* Office of the President, Princeton University, Princeton, NJ 08544, USA. *Telephone:* (609) 258-2900; *Fax:* (609) 258-3345; *E-mail:* stilghman@molbio .princeton.edu.

TILLMAN, Lynne; American writer and film-maker. *Career:* Writer of novels, short stories and essays, Dir of short and feature-length films. *Films:* Earth Angel 1974, Gestures 1978, Committed (co-dir) 1984; *Publications include:* Living With Contradictions (with drawings by Jane Dickson) 1982, Weird Fucks 1982, Madame Realism (with drawings by Kiki Smith)1984, Tagebuch einer Masochistin 1987, Haunted Houses 1987, Absence Makes The Heart 1990, Motion Sickness 1991, The Madame Realism Complex 1992, Cast in Doubt 1992, Beyond Recognition: representation, power, culture (co-ed), The Velvet Years: Warhol and the Factory 1965–1967 (text by L. Tillman, photographs by Stephen Shore) 1995; numerous articles and short stories in magazines. *Address:* c/o Serpent's Tail, 4 Blackstock Mews, London N4 2BT, UK (Office); Peter Stuyvesant Station, POB 360, New York, NY 10009, USA (Home). *Telephone:* (212) 979-1739 (Home).

TIMMS, Vera Kate, CB; British civil servant; b 8 Oct 1944; d of the late Kenneth and of Elsie (née Cussans) Timms; m Ernest Gordon 1977; one step-d. *Education:* St Hilda's Coll (Oxford). *Career:* Fmrly with Nat Econ Devt Office; Ministry of Agric, Food and Fisheries (MAFF) 1970–, Asst Pvt Sec to Minister of Agric 1974–75, Prin Pvt Sec 1980–82; mem European Secr Cabinet Office 1976–79; Asst Sec of Marketing Policy, MAFF 1982–84, Asst Sec and Head of Sugar and Oilseeds Div 1988–89, Under-Sec Arable Crops Group 1989–90, Prin Finance Officer 1995–96, Deputy Sec Agric, Crops and Commodities 1996–; Diplomatic Counsellor, Paris 1984–88; Agric Minister Office of UK Perm Rep, Brussels 1990–95; Ordre du Mérite Agricole (France) 1988. *Address:* 42 The Foreshore, London SE8 3AG, UK. *Telephone:* (20) 8691-0823.

TIMNEY, Janet Susan Patricia, MA, RCA; British textile designer; b 9 July 1950, Libya; d of Maj A. L. and the late Janet Stoba Carruthers; m 1st John Timney 1969 (divorced 1979); m 2nd Grahame Fowler 1981; three s one d. *Education:* British Forces Schools, Jarrow Grammar School, Carlisle Coll of Art, Newcastle Polytechnic, Heriot-Watt Univ and Royal Coll of Art. *Career:* Founded Timney Fowler Partnership 1979–, then Dir; Lecturer American Coll in London 1979–82, RCA 1979–80; Visiting Lecturer colls in UK 1982–; Moderator Brighton School of Art 1985–89, St Martin's School of Art 1985–90, Glasgow School of Art 1991, Middlesex Polytechnic 1992; mem Textile Cttee Design Council, Cttee for Young Designers into Industry of RSA, Scottish Devt Council Scotfree Cttee for selecting top textile designers in Scotland, Interior Designers and Decorators Asscn, Textile Inst; Fellow Chartered Soc of Designers; Roscow Award for Textiles (USA) 1989, 1990; Chartered Soc of Designers Design Medal 1991. *Address:* 388 Kings Rd, London SW3 5UZ, UK. *Telephone:* (20) 7352-2263; *Fax:* (20) 7352-0351.

TIMOFEYEVA, Nina Vladimirovna; Russian ballet dancer and teacher; b 11 June 1935, Leningrad (now St Petersburg); one d. *Education:* Leningrad Ballet School. *Career:* With Ballet Company of the Leningrad Kirov State Academic Theatre of Opera and Ballet 1953–56; Deputy to Supreme Soviet of the USSR 1966–70; mem Bolshoi Theatre 1956–88, ballet teacher 1989–; in Israel 1991–; has toured with Bolshoi Ballet in USA, Germany and other countries; People's Artist of the RSFSR 1963; People's Artist of USSR 1969; prizewinner at three int classic dance competitions; various decorations. *Ballets include:* Swan Lake, Giselle, Laurensia, Spartacus, Don Quixote, Stone Flower, Flames of Paris, Gayane, Raymonda, Sleeping Beauty, Leili and Medjnun, Legend of Love, Asel, Faust, Nutcracker, Much Ado About Nothing, Romeo and Juliet, Macbeth, Le tambour mystérieux, Baiser de la fée, Adan pas de deux; *Films:* White Nights (Dostoevsky), Phaedra (Euripides), The Way the Heart Reveals Itself, Raymonda, Classic

Duets, Spartacus, Macbeth, This Wonderful World, Improvisations, The Three Cards, Allegro, Something More About Ballet, Grand Pas, Five Corners 1988. *Leisure interests:* motor sports, music.

TIMOSHENKO, Yulia; Ukrainian politician and business executive; b 27 Nov 1960, Dniepropetrovsk; m Oleksandr Gennadyovich Timoshenko; one d. *Education:* Dniepropetrovsk State Univ. *Career:* Planning engineer Dniepropetrovsk Machine-Construction Plant 1984–89; Commercial Dir Dniepropetrovsk Youth Centre Terminal 1989–91; Dir-Gen Ukraine Petrol Corpn 1991–; Pres Union United Energy Systems of Ukraine (UES), First Deputy Chair, Bd of Dirs, Head Cttee on Budget Problems; Founder-mem political union Hromada (with Pavlo Lazarenko) 1997–; Leader Batkivshchina faction 1998–; Deputy Prime Minister of Ukraine 1999–2001; arrested on charge of corruption March 2001, released due to pressure of opposition; Higher Order of Orthodox Church Santa Barbara Great Martyr 1997. *Address:* c/o Hromada, 18 Kutuzova St, Kiev, Ukraine. *Telephone:* (44) 296-32-06; *Internet:* www.hromada.kiev.ua.

TIMSIT, Joëlle Marie-Paule Adrienne, L ÈS L; French diplomatist; b 1 May 1938, Rennes; d of Georges and Madame (née Demoire) Jaffray; m Gérard Timsit 1965. *Education:* Lycée (Fontainebleau), Lycée Marie Curie (Sceaux), Univ of Paris (Sorbonne), Inst d'Etudes Politiques de Paris and Ecole Nat d'Admin. *Career:* Attached to Cen Admin, Europe Div, Ministry of Foreign Affairs 1963–64, 1968–78, Sub-Dir 1978–82, Deputy Dir 1982–86, Dir of Political Affairs 1991; Second Sec, FRG 1964–68; Amb to GDR 1986–90; Diplomatic Adviser to then Prime Minister Edith Cresson (qv) 1991–92; Minister Plenipotentiary 1992; Amb to Sweden 1993–96; Diplomatic Adviser to Govt 1996–; Chevalier de la Légion d'Honneur; Officier de l'Ordre Nat du Mérite. *Address:* c/o Ministry of Foreign Affairs, 37 quai d'Orsay, 75007 Paris, France (Office); 52 rue du Docteur Thore, 92330 Sceaux, France (Home).

TINDALL, Gillian, MA, FRSA; British writer; b 4 May 1938; d of D. H. Tindall and U. M. D. Orange; m Richard G. Lansdown 1963; one s. *Education:* Univ of Oxford. *Career:* Freelance journalist working on The Independent, The Times and other newspapers and periodicals; JP, Inner London 1980–98; Chevalier des Arts et des Lettres 2001. *Publications:* Novels: No Name in the Street 1959, The Water and the Sound 1961, The Edge of the Paper 1963, The Youngest 1967, Someone Else 1969, Fly Away Home (Somerset Maugham Award 1972) 1971, The Traveller and His Child 1975, The Intruder 1979, Looking Forward 1983, To The City 1987, Give Them All My Love 1989, Spirit Weddings 1992; Short stories: Dance of Death 1973, The China Egg and Other Stories 1981, Journey of a Lifetime and Other Stories 1990; Non-fiction: A Handbook on Witchcraft 1965, The Born Exile (biog of George Gissing) 1974, The Fields Beneath 1977, Rosamond Lehmann: an appreciation 1985, Countries of the Mind: the meaning of places to writers 1990, City of Gold: the biography of Bombay (2nd edn) 1992, Célestine: voices from a French village 1995 (Franco-British Soc Award 1996), The Journey of Martin Nadaud 1999. *Leisure interests:* house-keeping, travel. *Address:* c/o Curtis Brown Ltd, 28/29 Haymarket, London SW1Y 4SP, UK.

TIPTON, Jennifer, BA; American lighting designer; b 11 Sept 1937, Columbus, OH; d of Samuel Ridley and Isabel (née Hanson) Tipton; m William F. Beaton 1976. *Education:* Cornell Univ (NY). *Career:* Lighting Designer for numerous theatre and ballet cos; Artistic Assoc Goodman Theater, Chicago, IL, American Repertory Theatre, Cambridge, MA; Lighting Instructor Yale Univ (CT) School of Drama; Creative Arts Award, Brandeis Univ, MA 1981; numerous prizes and hons include two Bessie Awards, Olivier Award, Joseph Jefferson Award, Drama-Logue Award, Obie Award. *Designs include:* Macbeth, Richard II, Love's Labours Lost, Horseman Pass By, Airs, Amnon V'Tamar, Bach Partita, The Little Ballet, A Ballet Behind the Bridge, The Tempest, A Midsummer Night's Dream, Dreyfus in Rehearsal, The Leaves Are Fading, Murder Among Friends, For Colored Girls Who Consider Suicide, When The Rainbow is Enuf (Drama Desk Award), The Nutcracker, The Landscape of the Body, The Cherry Orchard (Drama Desk Award, Tony Award 1977), Agamemnon, Runaways, All's Well That Ends Well, The Taming of the Shrew, Don Quixote, The Goodbye People, Drinks Before Dinner, The Pirates of Penzance, Lunch Hour, Billy Bishop Goes to War, The Sea Gull, Sophisticated Ladies, Orgasmo Adulto Escapes from the Zoo, Baby With the

Bathwater, Hurlyburly, Whoopie Goldberg, Endgame, The Ballad of Soapy Smith, Jerome Robbins' Broadway (Antoinette Perry Award 1989), Lousie 1999, Tannhäuser, Parsifal, Hänsel und Gretal, Così fan tutte, Dialogues of the Carmelites, The Trojan Women, The Iphigenia Cycle. *Address:* c/o School of Drama, Yale University, New Haven, CT 06520, USA. *Telephone:* (203) 432-1579; *E-mail:* jennifer.tipton@yale.edu.

TIRIKATENE-SULLIVAN, The Hon Tini Whetu Marama, BA, FRAI; New Zealand social worker and politician; b 9 Jan 1932, Ratana Pa, via Wanganui; d of the late Hon Sir Eruera Tirikatene and of Lady Tirikatene; m Dr Denis Sullivan; one s one d. *Education:* Rangiora High School, Victoria Univ of Wellington and ANU. *Career:* Sec NZ Labour Party's Maori Policy Cttee 1949–60, Jt Sec 1960–63, 1963–65, Exec mem 1967, Chair 1979–86; Sec Royal Tour Staff for visit of HM Queen Elizabeth II and HRH The Duke of Edinburgh 1953–54; fmr Social Worker Depts of Maori Affairs, Social Security and Child Welfare; elected mem for Southern Maori House of Reps 1967; Assoc Minister of Social Welfare 1972–74; Minister of Tourism 1972–75; Minister for the Environment 1974–75. *Leisure interests:* historical, political, social and scriptural research, tutoring Christian youth leaders. *Address:* Parliament House, Wellington, New Zealand. *Telephone:* (4) 719-999.

TISSIER, Marie-Solange Thérèse; French mining engineer; b 6 April 1955, Paris; d of Jean-Pierre and Madeleine (née Vinot) Tissier; m Michel Massoni 1990; one s. *Education:* Ecole Polytechnique (Paris) and Ecole des Mines de Paris. *Career:* Attached to Ministry of Industry Environment Div, Lorraine 1979–82, Asst Head of Dept, Gen Council on Mining 1982–84, Head of Dept 1990–, Tech Adviser Energy Office 1984–86, Head of Nuclear Dept 1986–88, Tech Adviser to Minister of Industry and Regional Planning 1988–89; Asst Dir Ecole des Mines de Paris 1989–; Chevalier de l'Ordre Nat du Mérite. *Address:* Ecole Nationale Supérieure des Mines de Paris, 60 blvd Saint-Michel, 75006 Paris, France. *Telephone:* (1) 40-51-90-33; *Fax:* (1) 40-51-92-87; *E-mail:* tissier@paris.ensmp.fr.

TITLEY, Jane, CBE; British military nursing officer; b 22 April 1940; d of Louis and Phyllis Titley. *Education:* St Bartholomew's Hosp and Sussex Maternity Hosp. *Career:* Joined Queen Alexandra's Royal Naval Nursing Service 1965; Nurse naval hosps in UK, Malta, Singapore, Naples (Italy), Gibraltar; Matron 1986; Deputy Matron-in-Chief 1988; Matron-in-Chief 1990–94; Dir of Defence Nursing Services 1992–95; Order of St John 1990; Royal Red Cross; Queen's Hon Nursing Sister 1990–94. *Leisure interests:* writing letters, contemplation, gardening, needlework. *Address:* Flat 10, 28 Pembridge Square, London W2 4DS, UK.

TIWANA, Dalip Kaur, PH D; Indian professor of Punjabi and writer; b 4 May 1935, Vill-Rabbon, Punjab; d of Kaka Singh and Chand Kaur Tiwana; m Bhupinder Singh 1972; one s. *Education:* Mohindra Coll (Patiala). *Career:* Mem Senate, Syndicate, Acad Council and Bd of Studies in Punjabi, Punjabi Univ, Patiala, Head of Dept of Foreign Languages, Head Nawab Sher Mohammad Khan Inst of Advanced Studies in Urdu, Persian, Arabic and Malerkotla, Dean Faculty of Languages, apptd Prof and Head Dept of Punjabi 1981; works translated into many languages, several adapted for TV; mem Punjab Arts Council (Chandigarh), Punjabi Bd Sahitya Acad (New Delhi), Language Advisory Cttee (Bhartiya Jnanpith); Vice-Pres Kendri Lekhak Sabha; Canadian Int Asscn of Punjabi Authors and Artists Award 1985; Shiromani Sahitkai Award, Govt of Punjab 1987, Praman Patar Award 1989; Dhaliwal Award, Punjabi Acad (Ludhiana) 1991. *Publications include:* Sadhana (Govt of Punjab Award for Short Stories 1961–62) 1961, Ehu Hamar Jeevna (Sahitya Acad Award) 1972, Panchaan Vich Parmesar (Ministry of Educ and Social Welfare Award for Children's Short Stories) 1975, Peele Patian Di Dastan (Nanak Singh Award, Govt of Punjab) 1980, Nange Pairan Da Safar (Gurmukh Singh Musafir Award for Autobiog, Govt of Punjab) 1982. *Leisure interests:* reading, philosophy, films. *Address:* Punjabi University Campus, B-13, Patiala 147 002, India. *Telephone:* (175) 782 2166.

TIZARD, Dame Catherine (Anne), GCMG, GCVO, DBE, QSO, JP, BA; New Zealand public official; b 4 April 1931, Auckland; d of Neil and Helen (née Montgomery) Maclean; m Robert James Tizard 1951 (divorced 1983); three d one s. *Education:* Matamata Coll and Univ of

Auckland. *Career:* Sr Tutor in Zoology Univ of Auckland 1963–83; mem Auckland City Council 1971–83, Auckland Regional Authority 1980–83, Mayor of Auckland 1983–90; Gov-Gen of New Zealand 1990–96; Chair NZ Worldwide Fund for Nature 1996–2000, NZ Historic Places Trust 1996–, Harrahs Sky City Trust; Hon Fellow Lucy Cavendish Coll, Cambridge, UK, and Winston Churchill Fellow 1981; Hon LL D (Auckland) 1992. *Leisure interests:* music, reading, cryptic crosswords, drama, scuba-diving. *Address:* 12A Wallace St, Herne Bay, Auckland 1, New Zealand. *Telephone:* (9) 376-2555; *Fax:* (9) 360-0656; *E-mail:* cath.tizard@etca.co.nz (Home).

TLASKALOVÁ-HOGENOVÁ, Helena, MD, PH D, D SC; Czech medical practitioner and scientific worker; b 29 Dec 1938, Prague; d of Hynek Hogen and Marie HogenovÁ; m Vlastimil Tlaskal 1964; one s one d. *Education:* Charles Univ (Prague). *Career:* Clinician Dept of Haematology, hosp in Ústí nad Labem 1962–63; Scientific worker Div of Immunology and Gnotobiology, Inst of Microbiology, Acad of Sciences of the Czech Republic, Prague 1968–92, apptd Head of Div of Immunology and Gnotobiology 1990; Czech Acad of Sciences Awards 1980, 1985, 1991. *Publications:* Advances in Mucosal Immunology (ed) 1995; has published about 150 papers in int journals. *Leisure interests:* walking, swimming, fishing. *Address:* Institute of Microbiology, Academy of Sciences of the Czech Republic, Vídeňska 1083, 142 20 Prague 4, Czech Republic. *Telephone:* (2) 475-2345; *Fax:* (2) 472-1143; *E-mail:* tlaskalo@biomed.cas.cz.

TOBACH, Ethel, PH D; American psychologist and former curator; b 7 Nov 1921, Miaskovka, fmr USSR; d of Ralph Wiener and Fanny (née Schechterman) Wiener Idels; m Charles Tobach 1947 (died 1969). *Education:* Hunter Coll and New York Univ. *Career:* Moved to USA 1923; Research Fellow American Museum of Natural History 1958–61, Assoc Curator 1964–69, Curator 1969–87; Research Fellow New York Univ 1961–64; Prof of Psychology City Univ of New York 1964–; Co-Ed Genes and Gender series 1978–96; Ed Int Journal of Comparative Psychology 1987–93; Fellow American Psychology Asscn, Int Soc of Comparative Psychology, New York Acad of Sciences, Eastern Psychology Asscn; Distinguished Science Career Award, Asscn of Women in Science 1974; Distinguished Scientific Publ Award, Asscn for Women in Psychology 1982; Kurt Lewin Award, Soc for the Psychological Study of Social Issues 1993. *Address:* American Museum of Natural History, Central Parkway at 79th St, New York, NY 10024-5192, USA.

TODOROVA, Liljana, D ÈS L; Macedonian professor of philology; b 14 Aug 1934, Čačak; m Alexandre Todorov 1959; one s one d. *Education:* St Cyril and St Methodius Univ (Skopje). *Career:* Asst Faculty of Philology, Univ of Skopje 1961, Prof of French and Comparative Literature 1978–, apptd Dean of Faculty 1995; Deputy to Yugoslav Fed Ass 1982–85; Yugoslav Amb to Guinea 1986–90; Chevalier de la Légion d'Honneur 1983; Commdr dans l'Ordre des Palmes Académiques 1983. *Publications:* Le dialogue de la littérature macédonienne entre la tradition nationale et les littératures étrangères 1976, Qui est l'auteur de 'La Napoléone' revendiquée par Charles Nodier 1978, Les slaves du sud au XIX siècle vus par Xavier Marmier 1980. *Address:* 91000 Skopje, ul Nikola Rusinski 10/I-10, Macedonia. *Telephone:* (91) 254734; *Fax:* (91) 223811.

TOENSING, Victoria, JD; American lawyer; b 16 Oct 1941, Colón, Panama; d of Philip William and Victoria (née Brady) Long; m 1st Trent David Toensing 1962 (divorced 1976); m 2nd Joseph E. diGenova 1981; two s one d. *Education:* Indiana Univ and Univ of Detroit (MI). *Career:* Called to the Bar, MI 1976, DC 1978; Law Clerk to Justice US Court of Appeals, Detroit 1975–76; Asst US Attorney, Detroit 1976–81; Chief Counsel US Senate Intelligence Cttee, Washington, DC 1981–84; Deputy Asst Attorney-Gen Criminal Div, Dept of Justice, Washington, DC 1984–88; Special Counsel Hughes, Hubbard and Reed 1988–90; Partner Cooter and Gell 1990–91; Partner, Co-Chair Manatt, Phelps and Phillips, Washington, DC 1991–95; Founding Partner diGenova & Toensing, Washington, DC 1996; Co-Chair Coalition for Women's Appointments, Justice Judiciary Task Force 1988–92; mem Bd Dirs Project on Equal Educ Rights, MI 1980–81, Nat History Intelligence Museum 1987–; mem US House of Reps Sub Cttee on Oversight and Investigations of Cttee on Educ and the Workforce 1997–98; MSNBC legal analyst 1998–99; mem ABA; Office of the US

Attorney-Gen Special Commendation Award 1980; CIA Agency Seal Medallion 1986; Award of Achievement Alpha Chi Omega 1992. *Publications include:* Bringing Sanity to the Insanity Defense 1983, Mens Rea: Insanity by Another Name 1984, Fighting Back: Winning The War Against Terrorism (jtly), Desk Book on White Collar Crime (jtly) 1991; numerous contribs to professional journals.

TOIA, Patrizia; Italian politician; b 17 March 1950, Pogliani, Milan. *Career:* Mem Partito della Democrazia Christiana (DC) early 1970s, responsible for social services Region of Lombardy 1989; MP and Head DC health portfolio 1991; mem Partito Popolare Italiano (PPI) 1994–; fmr Foreign Under-sec; Minister of European Policy 1999–2001; Minister for Relations with Parl 2001–. *Address:* Partito Popolare Italiano, Piazza del Gesù 46, 00186 Rome, Italy. *Telephone:* (6) 699591; *Fax:* (6) 6790449; *E-mail:* toia_p@posta.senato.it.

TOKODY, Ilona; Hungarian opera singer (soprano); b Szeged; d of András Tokody and Ilona Nagy. *Education:* Liszt Ferenc Music Acad (Budapest). *Career:* Won Kodály singing competition 1972, Erkel competition of Inter-konzert Agency 1973, Ostend competition operatic category 1976; joined State Opera, Budapest 1976; regular guest performer Staatsoper Wien and Deutsche Oper, Berlin; appearances in opera houses and concert halls world-wide, including Metropolitan Opera House (New York), Royal Opera House (Covent Garden, London), Vienna State Opera, San Francisco Opera (CA, USA), Teatro Colón (Buenos Aires), Liceo (Barcelona, Spain), Bavarian State Opera (Germany), San Carlo (Naples) and Rome Opera (Italy), Bolshoi (Moscow), Carnegie Hall (New York), Musikverein (Vienna), Royal Opera (Copenhagen). *Operas include:* La Forza del Destino, Don Carlo, Suor Angelica, Madam Butterfly, Il Trovatore, Aida, La Juive, La Bohème, I Pagliacci, Carmen, Falstaff, I Lombardi, Otello; *Recordings:* Suor Angelica, Nerone, La Fiamma, Brahms Requiem, Il Tabarro, Guntram, Iris. *Leisure interests:* cooking, badminton, gymnastics, table tennis, reading. *Address:* c/o Hungarian State Opera, 1062 Budapest, Andrássy ut 22, Hungary; 1121 Budapest, 27/c Mártonhegyi út, Hungary (Home). *Telephone:* (1) 312-550 (Office); *Fax:* (1) 755-696 (Office).

TOKOMBAYEVA, Aysulu Asanbekovna; Kyrgyzstan ballet dancer; b 22 Sept 1947, Frunze (now Bishkek); d of Asanbek Tokombayev and Munzia Erkinbaeva. *Education:* Vaganova Dancing School (Leningrad). *Career:* Soloist with Theatre of Kirghizia (now Kyrgyzstan) 1966–95; ballet teacher Conservatoire, Ankara, Turkey 1995–; mem CPSU 1973–91; awards include Youth Prize 1968, USSR State Prize 1976, People's Artist of Kirghizia 1976, USSR People's Artist 1981, Aitmatov Int Prize 1994. *Ballets include:* Swan Lake, Sleeping Beauty, Giselle, Bayadère, Chopiniana, Pakhita, Schelkunchik, Don Quixote, Spartacus, Lady Macbeth, Carmen; *Films:* Dance is My Life 1976, Aysulu Tokombayeva 1991. *Leisure interests:* classical music, poetry, nature. *Address:* Kyrgyz State Opera and Ballet Theatre, Bishkek, Kyrgyzstan; Usenbaev Str 37, Apt 33, 720021 Bishkek, Kyrgyzstan (Home). *Telephone:* (3312) 28-29-57 (Home).

TOLSTAYA, Tatyana Nikitchna; Russian writer; b 3 May 1951, Leningrad (now St Petersburg); d of Mikhail Lozinsky and Nikita Tolstoy; m Andrey V. Lebedev; two s. *Education:* Leningrad State Univ. *Career:* Ed of Oriental Literature Nauka Publishing, Moscow 1987–89; Lecturer, Skidmore Coll, NJ, USA. *Publications:* On the Golden Porch (short stories) 1989, Sleepwalkers in a Fog (short stories) 1992. *Address:* c/o Penguin Books Ltd, Bath Rd, Harmondsworth, Middx UB7 0DA, UK. *Telephone:* (1856) 770474 (UK); (095) 238-22-15 (Moscow); (908) 821-3007 (USA).

TOMALIN, Claire, MA, FRSL; British writer; b 20 June 1933; d of Emile Delavenay and Muriel Emily Herbert; m Nicholas Osborne Tomalin 1955 (died 1973); three d (one deceased) two s (one deceased); m 2nd Michael Frayn 1993. *Education:* Hitchin Girls' Grammar School, Dartington Hall School and Newnham Coll (Cambridge). *Career:* Worked in publishing, then journalism 1955–67; worked at London Evening Standard 1967–68; Asst Literary Ed New Statesman magazine 1968–70, Literary Ed 1974–77, Sunday Times 1979–86; writer and broadcaster 1986–; Vice-Pres English PEN 1997, Royal Literary Fund 2000; mem London Library Cttee 1997–2000, Advisory Cttee for the Arts, Humanities and Social Sciences, British Library 1997–, Council

Royal Soc of Literature 1997–2000; Trustee Nat Portrait Gallery 1992–; Whitbread First Book Prize 1974; James Tait Black Prize 1991; Hawthornden Prize 1991; NCR Book Award 1991. *Publications:* The Life and Death of Mary Wollstonecraft 1974, Shelley and his World 1980, Katherine Mansfield: A Secret Life 1986, The Invisible Woman: The Story of Nelly Ternan and Charles Dickens (NCR Prize) 1991, The Winter Wife (play) 1991, Mrs Jordan's Profession 1994, Jane Austen: A Life 1997, Maurice by Mary Shelley (ed) 1998, Several Strangers: Writing From Three Decades 1999. *Leisure interests:* walking, cooking, travel. *Address:* c/o David Godwin, 55 Monmouth St, London WC2H 9ZG, UK; 57 Gloucester Cres, London NW1 7EG, UK (Home). *Telephone:* (20) 7485-6481 (Home); *Fax:* (20) 7267-1307 (Home); *E-mail:* clairetomalin@dial.pipex.com (Office).

TOMASZKIEWICZ, Teresa, D ÈS L; Polish philology researcher; b 21 Jan 1956, Łódź; m Zbigniew Tomaszkiewicz 1982; one s one d. *Education:* Univ of Warsaw Inst of Applied Linguistics. *Career:* Apptd Lecturer and Researcher Inst of Romance Philology, Univ A. Mickiewicz, Poznań, Sr Lecturer 1987; apptd Sec-Gen Polish Soc of Modern Languages 1989. *Publications:* Temps, aspect, modalité 1989, Jouez avec nous 1990. *Leisure interests:* travel, cinema, theatre. *Address:* ul Zagłoby 7, 61177 Poznań, Poland. *Telephone:* (64) 328461.

TOMEI, Marisa; American actress; b 4 Dec 1964, Brooklyn, New York. *Education:* Univ of Boston. *Career:* Actress in plays, films and on TV. *Films inlcude:* The Flamingo Kid 1984, Playing for Keeps, Oscar, Zandalee, My Cousin Vinny (Acad Award for Best Supporting Actress 1992), Chaplin, Untamed Heart, Equinox, The Paper, Only You, The Perez Family, Four Rooms, A Brother's Kiss, Unhook the Stars 1996; *TV appearances include:* As the World Turns (series), A Different World (series), Parker Kane (film); *Plays include:* Beirut, Daughers (Theatre World Award), The Comedy of Errors, What the Butler Saw, Slavs!.

TOMLIN, Lily; American actress and entertainer; b 1939, Detroit, MI. *Education:* Wayne State Univ (MI). *Career:* Has appeared on Broadway, in concerts and films and on TV; Grammy Award 1971. *Films include:* Nashville (New York Film Critics' Award) 1975, The Late Show 1977, Moment by Moment 1978, The Incredible Shrinking Woman 1981, Nine to Five 1980, All of Me 1984, Big Business 1988, The Search for Signs of Intelligent Life in the Universe, Shadows and Fog 1992, The Player 1992, Short Cuts 1993, The Beverly Hillbillies 1993, Blue in the Face, Getting Away with Murder, The Celluloid Closet (narrator), Flirting with Disaster; *Musicals include:* Appearing Nitely (Special Tony Award) 1977, The Search for Signs of Intelligent Life in the Universe (Drama Desk Award, Outer Critics' Circle Award, Tony Award 1986) 1985; *TV appearances include:* Lily Tomlin CBS Specials 1973, 1981, 1982 (five Emmy Awards), Lily Tomlin ABC Specials 1975 (Emmy Award), Edith Ann: A Few Pieces of the Puzzle (voice, also exec producer), Edith Ann: Homeless Go Home (voice, also exec producer), And The Band Played On 1993 (nominated for best supporting actress Emmy Award 1994), Edith Ann: Animated Specials 1994; *Recordings include:* This is a Recording (Grammy Award 1971), And That's The Truth, Modern Scream, On Stage. *Address:* POB 27700, Los Angeles, CA 90027, USA.

TOMOWA-SINTOW, Anna; Austrian (b Bulgarian) opera singer; b 22 Sept 1943, Stara Zagora, Bulgaria; m Albert Sintow 1963; one d. *Education:* Nat Conservatory of Sofia. *Career:* Debut at Leipzig Opera, fmr GDR 1967; joined Deutsche Staatsoper, Berlin 1969; guest engagements at most leading European and US opera houses including La Scala (Milan, Italy), Vienna, Royal Opera House (Covent Garden, London), Paris, Bavarian State Opera (Germany) and Bolshoi (Moscow); debut in N America at Metropolitan Opera, New York 1978; has toured Japan with Scala di Milano and Berlin Philharmonic under von Karajan; regular guest at Salzburg Festival 1973–; has sung in several TV productions; title of Kammersängerin conferred. *Operas include:* Ariadne auf Naxos, Capriccio, Lohengrin, Tannhäuser, Aida, Tosca, Madam Butterfly, La Traviata, Manon Lescaut, Andrea Chenier, La Forza del Destino, Der Rosenkavalier; *Recordings include:* Lohengrin, Le Nozze di Figaro, Don Giovanni, Die Zauberflöte, Mozart's Coronation Mass, Mozart's Requiem, Brahms' German Requiem, Four Last Songs, Capriccio monologue, Missa Solemnis, Ariadne auf Naxos, Madam Butterfly, La Traviata, Tosca, Eugene

Onegin, recitals of Verdi arias and of Italian and German arias; recording and film of Verdi's Requiem with von Karajan. *Leisure interests:* nature, reading, singing.

TONGUE, Carole, BA; British consultant and politician; b 14 Oct 1955, Lausanne, Switzerland; d of Walter Archer and Muriel (née Lambert) Tongue; m Chris Pond 1990. *Education:* Brentwood Co High School (Essex) and Loughborough Univ of Tech. *Career:* Asst Ed Laboratory Practice 1977–78; Courier and Guide Sunsites Ltd 1978–79; Robert Schuman Scholarship for Research on EP 1979–80; Admin Asst Socialist Group of EP 1980–84; MEP 1984–99, Deputy Leader British Lab Group 1989–91, Socialist Policy Co-ordinator Cttee on Media, Culture, Youth and Educ, Vice-Pres Cinema Intergroup 1994–; Chair London East European Forum 1994–; Dir Centre for Alternative Industrial and Technological Systems 1992; Prin Assoc ACE Assocs Consultancy; adviser and lecturer on media, broadcasting and Europe 1999–; mem Council Charter '88 1988–, Bd Westminster Foundation for Democracy 1992–95; mem Advisory Bd European Media Forum 1996–, Bd London Film and Video Devt Agency 1999–; Pres Cities and Cinemas Asscn 1997–; numerous contribs to professional journals 1984–. *Leisure interests:* piano, cello, tennis, squash, horse-riding, theatre, opera, cinema. *Address:* 409 Liverpool Rd, London N7 8PR, Belgium (Office); 97A Ilford Lane, Ilford, Essex IG1 2RJ, UK (Home). *Telephone:* (20) 7609-0878 (Home); *Fax:* (20) 7607-4648 (Home).

TORFEH, Massoumeh, PH D; Iranian journalist and radio producer; b 14 Feb 1950, Tehran; d of Yahya and Pourandokht Kamiab; m 1972–75; one s. *Education:* City Univ (London) and LSE. *Career:* Living in UK since 1967; Journalist specializing in affairs of Iran, Afghanistan and Tajikistan 1976–; Sr Producer Persian Section, BBC World Service 1984–. *Leisure interests:* reading, jazz, swimming, travel. *Address:* 94A Kensington Church St, London W8 4BU, UK. *Telephone:* (20) 7257-2742; *Fax:* (20) 7240-4638.

TORNBERG, Eva Margareta, D SC; Swedish scientist; b 22 May 1948, Sundsvall; d of Axel and Ulla Tornberg; m Kaj Söderström 1978; one d one s. *Education:* Technical Univ of Lund. *Career:* Teaching and research Food Science Dept, Technical Univ of Lund 1971–77, Research Assoc 1977–80, Adjunct Prof in Meat Technology; Research leader Research Section Biophysics Group, Swedish Meat Research Inst, Kävlinge 1980–86, Research Dir Swedish Meat Research Inst; about 70 int scientific publs. *Leisure interests:* family life, sports, cultural events. *Address:* Swedish Meat Research Institute, POB 504, 244 24 Kävlinge, Sweden.

TÖRNUDD, Elin Maria, MS; Finnish information consultant and former library director; b 22 April 1924, Helsinki; d of Titus Fingal and Ester Törnudd. *Education:* Helsinki Univ of Tech and Carnegie Inst of Tech (USA). *Career:* Information Specialist Cen Chemical Asscn 1949–56; Sec-Gen Scandinavian Council for Applied Research 1956–68; Dir Library, Helsinki Univ of Tech 1968–91, Emer Dir 1991–; currently Sr Consultant; Chair and Vice-Chair Finnish Council for Scientific Information 1970–85; Pres UNESCO Intergovernmental Council for the Gen Information Programme 1981–88; Pres Int Asscn of Technological Univ Libraries 1990–92; several nat and int decorations. *Publications:* Scandinavian Research Guide (latest edn) 1971, Nordic Research Directory Nordres 1990. *Leisure interest:* work. *Address:* Helsinki University of Technology Library, Otaniementie 9, 02150 Espoo, Finland (Office); Harjuviita 18A4, 02110 Espoo, Finland (Home). *Telephone:* (0) 4514103 (Office); *Fax:* (0) 4514132 (Office).

TÖRŐCSIK, Mari; Hungarian actress; b 23 Nov 1935, Pély; d of Joachim and Júlia (née Rusz) Törőcsik; m Gyula Maár 1972; two d. *Education:* Acad of Drama and Film (Budapest). *Career:* Acting in films and on stage 1955–; theatre includes works by Shakespeare, Molière, Brecht, Gorky, Chekhov, Dostoevsky and others; Teacher Acad of Drama and Film; numerous awards including all the major Hungarian prizes for acting, Kossuth Prize, Pro-Art Prize, Golden Palm, Mandragora, Silver Hugo (Chicago, USA), Karlovy Vary for Best Actress and Taormina for Best Actress. *Films include:* Carousel 1955, Fleur de Fer 1957, Silence and Cry 1963, Love 1970, Déryué 1975. *Leisure interests:* village life, music. *Address:* Magyar Televízió, 1810 Budapest, Szabadság tér 17, Hungary (Office); 1016 Budapest, Bérc u 18, Hungary (Home). *Telephone:* (1) 856-333 (Home).

TORRENCE, Gwen; American athlete; b 12 June 1965, Atlanta, GA; m Manley Waller; one s. *Education:* Columbia High School and Georgia Coll. *Career:* Gold Medallist in 200m track event, Olympic Games, Barcelona, Spain 1992; Bronze Medallist in 100m track event, Silver Medallist in 200m track event, World Championships 1993; Gold Medallist in 100m track event World Championships 1995; Bronze Medallist in 100m track event, Olympic Games, Atlanta, GA, USA 1996;. *Address:* c/o US Olympic Cttee, 1750 E Boulder St, Colorado Springs, CO 80909, USA.

TORRES, Marcela; Portuguese publishing executive; b 27 Sept 1940, Tondela, Viseu; d of Flausino Torres and Fernanda C. Figueiredo; m J. A. Gomes Bento 1961 (died 1984); one s. *Education:* Univs of Porto and Lisbon. *Career:* Dir Edições Afrontamento (publishers), Porto. *Leisure interests:* reading, travel. *Address:* Edições Afrontamento Lda, Rua de Costa Cabral 859, 4200 Porto, Portugal. *Telephone:* (2) 489271; *Fax:* (2) 491777.

TORRES MARQUES, Helena de Melo; Portuguese politician; b 8 Aug 1941, Lisbon. *Career:* MEP (PSE, PS), mem Cttee on Econ and Monetary Affairs and Industrial Policy, on Women's Rights, Del for relations with the countries of S America. *Address:* European Parliament, rue Wiertz, 1047 Brussels, Belgium. *Telephone:* (2) 284-21-11; *Fax:* (2) 230-69-43.

TORRES SEGUEL, Elena; Chilean lawyer; b 29 Dec 1944, Los Angeles, Chile; three s three d. *Education:* Univs of Concepción and Chile. *Career:* Lawyer and Notary Public; Dir and Man Publishing Monte Grande; Pres Chilean Fed; Dir Asscn of Notaries; mem Paul Harris Int Rotary, fmr Pres Rotary Calican; numerous articles published in journals and has also written two short plays. *Address:* Avda Bulnes No 141, Santiago, Chile. *Telephone:* (2) 6972339; *Fax:* (2) 6711228.

TORVILL, Jayne, OBE; British figure-skater; b 7 Oct 1957, Nottingham; d of George and Betty (née Smart) Torvill; m Phil Christensen 1990. *Education:* Clifton Hall Girls Grammar School (Nottingham). *Career:* Insurance clerk 1974–80; British Pair Skating Champion (with Michael Hutchinson) 1971; with Christopher Dean for rest of professional career; British Ice Dance Champions 1978–83, 1994; European Ice Dance Champions 1981–82, 1984, 1994; World Ice Dance Champions 1981–84; Olympic Ice Dance Champions, Sarajevo, Yugoslavia 1984, Olympic Ice Dance Bronze Medal, Lillehammer, Norway 1994; World Professional Champions 1984–85, 1990, 1995–96; tours with ice dance shows including Fire and Ice, and Ukrainian Ice Spectacular; World tour 1985; tour of Russia 1992, UK (Manchester and London) with show The Best of Torvill and Dean 1992; awarded Jacques Favert Trophy and BBC Sports Personality and Team Awards 1983–84; received a record 136 perfect marks of six (as amateurs); Hon MA (Nottingham Trent) 1994. *Publications:* (with Christopher Dean) Torvill and Dean: Fire on Ice 1984, Torvill and Dean: An Autobiography 1994, Torvill and Dean: Face the Music and Dance 1995, Facing the Music 1995. *Leisure interests:* theatre, ballet, dogs. *Address:* c/o Sue Young, POB 32, Heathfield, E Sussex TN21 0BW, UK. *Telephone:* (1435) 867826; *Fax:* (1435) 867826.

TOTH, Gwendolyn Joyce, D MUS; American musician; b 28 July 1955, Cleveland, OH; d of Ernest J. and Ruth M. (née Office) Toth; m 1st Philip M. Rosenberg 1981 (divorced 1988); m 2nd Dongsok Shin 1989; one d. *Education:* Middlebury Coll (VT), Southern Methodist Univ (TX), City Univ of New York and Yale Univ (CT). *Career:* Artist-in-Residence Alabama Shakespeare Festival 1982–85; Music Dir Festivanni '85, Anniston, AL 1985, The Artek Ensemble, New York 1987, Monteverdi Music Festival 1988, St Francis of Assisi Church, New York 1989; Organist Union Temple, New York 1985; Artistic Dir Art of the Early Keyboard, New York 1986; acting Dir Maplewood Music Festival, Essex Co, NY 1988; First Prize American Guild of Organists 1977, 1979; One of 10 Top Conductors (Opera News) 1989. *Address:* 170 W 73rd St, No 3C, New York, NY 10023, USA.

TÓTHOVÁ, Katarína, JU DR, D SC; Slovakian lawyer and politician; b 6 Feb 1940, Bratislava; d of František Seemann and Magdaléna Seemannová; m Ľudovít Tóth 1961; one d. *Education:* Comenius Univ (Bratislava). *Career:* Mem teaching staff Faculty of Law, Comenius

Univ, Bratislava, later Head of Administrative Law Dept 1963–92; Minister of Justice, Legislative Council Czechoslovak Govt 1990–91; Chair Legislative Council of the Govt of the Slovak Repub 1992, 1994–98; Deputy Prime Minister, Nat Council of the Slovak Repub 1994–98; Chair Slovak Repub Govt Council for Mass Media 1995–96; mem Parl 1998–; mem Movt for Democratic Slovakia; mem bd several legal journals; has written monographs on law, environmental law, university textbooks, articles, etc; A. Hlinka Order, Gold Medal, Univ Komenského, Medal of Nat Centre of Human Rights. *Publication:* Decision-making in State Administration 1989. *Leisure interests:* culture, literature, classic and modern art. *Address:* Nr Sr, Mudronova 1, 812 80 Bratislava, Slovakia; Movement for Democratic Slovakia, Tomásikova 32/a, Bratislava, Slovakia. *Telephone:* (7) 43330144.

TOU, Noelie Victoire, MA; Burkinabè economic adviser and politician; b 25 Dec 1950; d of the late Roger Tou Baba and Catherine Kansole; one s one d. *Education:* State Univ of Kiev (USSR, now Ukraine). *Career:* Economic Counsellor 1979–85; Dir of Int Financial Relations 1985–88; Economic Adviser to Pres of Burkina Faso 1989–90, 1992; Minister of Trade and Community Supplies 1990–91; Sec-Gen and mem Council of Ministers 1991–92. *Leisure interests:* reading, swimming, cooking. *Address:* BP 7070, Ouagadougou, Burkina Faso. *Telephone:* 30145.

TOURAINE, Marisol, PH D; French politician; b 7 March 1959, Paris; d of Alain and Adriana (née Arenas) Touraine; m Michel Reveyrand 1989; two d one s. *Education:* Lycée Louis-le-Grand (Paris), Harvard Univ (USA) and Institut d'Etudes Politiques (Paris). *Career:* Rep to Councillor for Strategic Affairs, Gen Defence Secr 1984–88; Tech Adviser Office of Prime Minister Michel Rocard 1988–91; Maître des requêtes Conseil d'Etat 1991–; Deputy (PS) to Nat Ass for Indre-et-Loire 1997, Councillor Indre-et-Loire 1998–; Dir of Studies Inst d'Etudes Politiques 1985–; Nat Sec Parti Socialiste. *Address:* Permanence Parlementaire, 23 rue Nationale, BP 11, 37250 Montbazon, France; Assemblée Nationale, 75355 Paris, France.

TOURNÉ, Andrée Marie Louise Juliette, L EN D; French army officer and educationalist; b 27 Sept 1929, Cauderan; d of Roger and Paule (née Vigien-Touchard) Tourné. *Education:* Lycée Camille Julian (Bordeaux) and Univ of Bordeaux. *Career:* Lieut 1951, Specialist in Women Personnel, 4th Military Dist, Bordeaux 1952–64, Second-in-Command Ecole des Personnels Féminins, Dieppe 1964–71, Capt 1965, Maj 1973, Lieut-Col 1976, Head of Div Army Military Personnel Section 1978–83, Col 1981, Deputy Insp 1983–85, Brig 1985; Office Dir Ministry of Defence, Div of Legal and Contentious Affairs 1971–78; Auditor Inst des Hautes Etudes de Défense Nat 1978–79, Deputy Dir 1985–88; Deputy Dir Enseignement Militaire Supérieur and Centre des Hautes Etudes Militaires 1985–88; Chevalier de la Légion d'Honneur; Officier de l'Ordre Nat du Mérite. *Leisure interests:* swimming, music, reading, photography, cross-country skiing, rambling. *Address:* 170 rue Nationale, 75013 Paris, France (Home). *Telephone:* (1) 45-84-23-34 (Home).

TOUSSAINT, Rose Marie, MD; American renal transplant surgeon; b 15 June 1956, Haiti; d of Alfred Paul Marie and Justine Toussaint. *Education:* Loyola Univ (LA) and Howard Univ (DC). *Career:* Resident in Gen Surgery Howard Univ Hosp 1983–88; Liver and Kidney Transplant Fellow Univ of Pittsburgh, PA 1988–99; Research Asst NIH, Bethesda, MD 1980, 1981; Asst Prof Surgery and Transplantation Coll of Medicine, Howard Univ Hosp, Washington 1991–97; Medical Dir and Pres Horus Corpn, Burtonsville, MD 1995–; Founder, Pres Nat Transplant Foundation 1999; mem American Medical Asscn, American Coll of Surgeons, Nat Medical Asscn, All-African Physicians of N America; Best Gen Surgery Resident (Dist of Columbia Gen Hosp) 1986. *Address:* 7425 Forbes Rd, Suite 200, Lanham, Seabrook, MD 20706, USA.

TOWER, Joan Peabody, MA; American composer; b 6 Sept 1938, New Rochelle, NY. *Education:* Bennington Coll (VT) and Columbia Univ (NY). *Career:* Pianist Da Capo Chamber Players 1969–84; apptd Assoc Prof Bard Coll, New York 1972; Composer-in-Residence St Louis Symphony 1985–87; comms from Contemporary Music Soc, Jerome Foundation, Massachusetts State Arts Council, Schubert Club, Richard Stolzman, St Louis Symphony, Elmar Oliveira, NY Philharmonic, Chicago Symphony, Fromm Foundation, Nat Endowment for the Arts;

Guggenheim Fellow 1976; Nat Endowment for the Arts Fellow 1974, 1975, 1980, 1984; New York State Council for Arts Award 1980; American Acad and Inst of Arts and Letters Award in Music 1983. *Compositions include:* Amazon, Amazon II, Sequoia, Silver Ladders (Grawemeyer Award, Univ of Louisville 1990) 1985, Breakfast Rhythms, Black Topaz, Wings, Fantasy, Cello Concerto, Piano Concerto, Clarinet Concerto. *Address:* Bard College, Annandale-On-Hudson, NY 12504, USA.

TOWNSEND, Marjorie Rhodes, BEE; American aerospace engineer and business executive; b 12 March 1930, Washington, DC; d of the late Lewis Boling and Marjorie Olive (née Trees) Rhodes; m Charles Eby Townsend 1948; four s. *Education:* George Washington Univ and Univ of Maryland. *Career:* Mem staff Dept of Terrestrial Magnetism, Carnegie Inst, Washington, DC 1945, Nat Bureau of Standards 1948–51; Electronic Scientist Naval Research Lab, Washington, DC 1951–59; Research Engineer Instrumentation Br, NASA Goddard Space Flight Center 1959–65, Technical Asst Systems Div 1965–66, Project Man Small Astronomy Satellites 1966–75, Applications Explorer Missions 1975–76, Man Preliminary Systems Design Group 1976–80; patented design of Digital Telemetry System 1968; Consultant to cos including Space Communications Co, American Science and Tech Corpn 1980–83, BDM Corpn and Agusta in Tradate, Italy 1984–90; Vice-Pres Systems Devt, American Science and Tech Corpn 1983, Space America Inc 1983–84; Dir Space Systems Eng, BDM Int Inc 1990–91; apptd Dir Space Applications, BDM Eng Services Co 1991; numerous papers for specialist journals; Fellow Inst of Electrical and Electronics Engineers, Washington Acad of Sciences; Assoc Fellow American Inst of Aeronautics and Astronautics; Life mem AAAS, Soc of Women Engineers; mem Daughters of the American Revolution, MENSA; NASA Exceptional Service Medal 1971; Outstanding Leadership Medal 1980; Eye-of-the-Needle Award 1991; Kt of the Italian Repub Order 1972; Fed Woman's Award 1973; George Washington Gen Alumni Asscn Achievement Award 1976. *Leisure interests:* travel, reading, crosswords, bridge. *Address:* BDM, 409 Third St, SW, Suite 340, Washington, DC 20024, USA (Office); 3529 Tilden St, NW, Washington, DC 20008-3194, USA (Home). *Telephone:* (202) 479-5286 (Office); *Fax:* (202) 863-8405 (Office).

TOWNSEND, Sue; British writer; b 2 April 1946, Leicester; m (divorced); three c. *Career:* Started writing professionally in the early 1980s; wrote, narrated and presented Think of England (TV) 1991; Hon MA (Leicester) 1991. *Publications:* The Secret Diary of Adrian Mole Aged 13¾ (trans into 20 languages), The Growing Pains of Adrian Mole, True Confessions of Adrian Albert Mole, Margaret Hilda Roberts and Susan Lilian Townsend, Rebuilding Coventry, Ten Tiny Fingers, Nine Tiny Toes 1990, Adrian Mole: From Minor to Major 1991, The Queen and I (adapted for stage 1994) 1992, Adrian Mole: The Wilderness Years 1993, Plays 1996, Ghost Children 1997, Adrian Mole: The Cappuccino Years (televised 2001) 1999; Stage plays: Ten Tiny Fingers, Nine Tiny Toes, Groping for Words 1984, Womberang 1984, The Great Celestial Cow 1985. *Leisure interests:* canoeing, reading. *Address:* Bridge Works, Knighton Fields Rd West, Leicester LE2 6LH, UK (Office). *Telephone:* (116) 283-1176 (Office).

TOYE, Wendy, CBE; British theatrical producer, film director, choreographer, actress and dancer; b 1 May 1917, London; d of Ernest W. and Jessie Crichton (née Ramsay) Toye. *Education:* Privately, trained with Euphen MacLaren, Tamara Karsavina, Anton Dolin, Morosoff, Legat, Marie Rambert, Ninette de Valois. *Career:* First performance aged three years at Royal Albert Hall, London; first professional appearance at Old Vic 1929; Prin Dancer Royal Albert Hall 1931; British Ballet (Denmark) 1932, Coliseum 1934; Dancer Lyceum 1932; acted and produced dances, Toad of Toad Hall, Royalty 1931–32; masked dancer Ballerina, Gaiety 1933; Dancer and Choreographer Carmargo Soc of Ballet; mem Vic Wells Ballet, toured as Choreographer with Anton Dolin's Ballet 1934–35; Prin Dancer and Choreographer Markova-Dolin Ballet 1935; arranged dances and ballets for many shows and films 1935–42, including most of George Black's productions; Shakespearean season at Open Air Theatre 1939; retrospective of films Paris Film Festival 1990, Tokyo Film Festival 1991; Guest Artist with Sadler's Wells Ballet and Mme Rambert's Ballet Club; Adviser Arts Council Training Scheme 1978–; Dir Royal Theatrical Fund; Vice-Pres TACT; Pres Vic Wells Asscn; mem Grand Council,

Royal Acad of Dancing, Wavendon All Music scheme, Richard Stilgoe Award scheme, original Accreditation Bd, Nat Council of Drama Training for Acting Courses; Patron Millennium 2000 Dance, London Theatre; Hon D LITT (City) 1997; The Queen's Silver Jubilee Medal. *Productions include:* Theatre: Bless the Bride, Peter Pan (co-dir and choreographer), And So To Bed, Feu d'artifice (co-dir and choreographer), Night of Masquerade, Three's Company (choreographer) in Joyce Grenfell Requests the Pleasure, Lady at the Wheel, As You Like It, A Midsummer Night's Dream (S and Cen America) 1964, The Soldier's Tale 1967, The Great Waltz 1970, Showboat 1971, She Stoops to Conquer 1972, Stand and Deliver 1972, R Loves J 1973, Follow The Star 1974, Made in Heaven 1975, Oh Mr Porter 1977, Gingerbread Man 1981, This Thing Called Love 1982, 1983, Singing in the Rain (assoc producer) 1983, Noel and Gertie 1983, Birds of a Feather 1984, Barnum (assoc producer) 1985, Torville and Dean World Tour (assoc producer) 1985, Kiss Me Kate 1986, Laburnum Grove 1987, Miranda 1987, Get the Message 1987, Cinderella 1989, Penny Black 1990, Moll Flanders 1990, Heaven's Up 1990, Bernard Shaw and Mrs Patrick Campbell (musical) 1990, See How They Run 1992, The Kingfisher 1993, Under Their Hats 1994, The Anastasia File 1994, Der Apotheker 1995, Warts and all 1996, Sadler's Wells Finale Gala 1996, Rogues to Riches 1996; Opera: Bluebeard's Castle, The Telephone, Rusalka, La vie parisienne, Die Fledermaus, The Abduction from the Seraglio 1967, Don Pasquale (for Phoenix Opera Group) 1968, L'Italiana in Algeri 1968, 1982, Orpheus 1978, 1981, Merry Widow 1979–80, Mikado 1982, Serva Padrona and the Apothecary Operas (for Aix-en-Provence Festival) 1991; Films: The Stranger Left No Card 1952, The Twelfth Day of Christmas, Three Cases of Murder 1954, All for Mary 1955, We Joined the Navy 1962, The King's Breakfast, Girls Wanted—Istanbul; retrospective of films, Paris Film Festival 1990, Nat Film Theatre 1995; TV productions include: Chelsea at 8 and Chelsea at 9 and Orphans in the Underworld (also dir); directed Esma Divided 1957, Follow the Star 1979, Tales of the Unexpected 1981, Trial by Jury 1982, Di Ballo 1982; choreographed many revues for the BBC. *Leisure interests:* embroidery, gardening. *Address:* c/o Jean Diamond, London Management, 2 Noel St, London W1, UK (agent); 5 Wedderburn House, 95 Lower Sloane St, London SW1W 8BZ, UK (Home).

TOYNBEE, Polly; British journalist and broadcaster; b 27 Dec 1946; d of the late Philip Toynbee and of Anne Powell; m Peter Jenkins 1970 (died 1992); three d one s. *Education:* Badminton School (Bristol), Holland Park Comprehensive (London) and St Anne's Coll (Oxford). *Career:* Feature Writer on The Observer newspaper 1968–70, 1971–77; Ed The Washington Monthly, USA 1970–71; columnist on The Guardian newspaper 1977–88, 1998–; SDP Parl cand for Lewisham E 1983; Social Affairs Ed BBC 1989–95; Assoc Ed, Columnist on The Independent newspaper 1995–98; Gov LSE 1988–99; mem Dept of Health Advisory Cttee on the Ethics of Xenotransplantation 1996, Nat Screening Cttee 1996–; Catherine Pakenham Award 1976; British Press Awards 1977, 1982; Columnist of the Year 1986; BBC What the Papers Say Award 1996; Magazine Writer of the Year, PPA 1996; George Orwell Prize 1997. *Publications:* Leftovers 1966, A Working Life 1970, Lost Children 1985, Hospital 1987, The Way We Live Now 1987. *Address:* The Guardian, 119 Farringdon Rd, London EC1R 3ER, UK. *Telephone:* (20) 7278-2332.

TRAHAN, Hon Anne-Marie, LL L, BA; Canadian judge; b 27 July 1946, Montréal; d of Marcel and Emélie (née Bourbonnière) Trahan. *Education:* Univs of Caen (France) and Montréal. *Career:* Called to the Bar, Québec 1968; pvt practice Lavery, O'Brien 1968–79; Legal Officer UN, Vienna 1979–81; QC 1983; Assoc Deputy Minister for Civil Law of Justice, Govt of Canada 1986–94; Judge Superior Court of Québec for Dist of Montréal 1994–; Commr Canadian Transport Comm 1981–86, Chair Water Transport Cttee 1984–86; Canadian Rep EC Inland Transport Cttee 1985, 1986; Lecturer Univ of Montréal, McGill Univ, Québec Real Estate Asscn; numerous papers for legal periodicals; Pres Int Asscn of Young Lawyers 1977–78, Hon Pres 1979–; Vice-Chair Cttee on Admin of Justice, Int Bar Asscn 1984–86, Chair Ind Bar Asscn 1986–90, Council mem (Section on Gen Practice) 1988–92; mem Council and Canadian Del, UNIDROIT 1988–; mem and Vice-Pres Canadian Inst for Advanced Legal Studies; mem Canadian Fed of Univ Women; apptd to dispute settlement mechanism of Conf on Security and Co-operation in Europe (CSCE—one of two Canadian mems) 1993; Québec Bar Prize for Commercial Law 1967; named Great

Montréaler of the Future in the Field of Law 1983. *Leisure interests:* reading, music, opera, hiking. *Address:* Palais de Justice, 1 E Notre-Dame St, Montréal, PQ H2Y 1B6, Canada (Office); 294 Outremont Ave, Outremont, PQ H2V 3M1, Canada (Home). *Telephone:* (514) 393-2193 (Office); (514) 277-7749 (Home); *Fax:* (514) 393-2773 (Office).

TRAINER, Karin; American librarian. *Career:* Descriptive cataloguer Princeton Univ, NJ 1972, later catalogue maintenance librarian, apptd Univ Librarian 1996; Dir of Technical and Automated Services New York Univ Libraries 1978; Assoc Univ Librarian, Yale Univ, New Haven, CT 1983–96. *Address:* University of Princeton, Library, Princeton, NJ 08544, USA. *Telephone:* (609) 258-3180.

TRASHLIEVA-KOITCHEVA, Mariana, PH D, MD; Bulgarian dermatologist and paediatrician; b 20 Dec 1937, Sofia; d of Stefan and Vera Trashliev; m Konstantin Koitchev 1960; two s. *Education:* Pleven High School and Acad of Medicine (Sofia). *Career:* Gen Practitioner, Djurovo 1960–63; Head of Paediatric Dept, Dobroslavtzy 1963–67; Asst Univ Dermatology Clinic, Sofia 1967–79; apptd Asst Prof and Head of Dept of Dermatology, Pleven Medical Univ 1979; Visiting Prof Leningrad (now St Petersburg, Russian Fed), Vienna, Bordeaux (France). *Publications:* Skin Diseases: therapeutic and diagnostic guidelines for paediatrists 1977, Eruptions in Viral Diseases in Paediatric Practice 1984, Atopic Dermatitis 1984, Dermatology in Childhood 1990. *Leisure interests:* music, literature, theatre. *Address:* Academy of Medicine, Dermatology Dept, 5800 Pleven, Bulgaria (Office); 13B Tzar Simeon Str, 5800 Pleven, Bulgaria (Home). *Telephone:* (64) 22-12-7 (Office); (64) 33-88-4 (Home); *Fax:* (64) 29-15-3 (Office).

TRAUTMANN, Catherine; French politician; b 15 Jan 1951, Strasbourg. *Career:* MEP (PSE, PS) 1989–97, mem Cttee on Budgets, Del for relations with Canada; Deputy to Nat Ass (Parl) for Bas-Rhin 1997; Govt Spokesperson 1997–98; Minister of Culture and Communications 1997–2000; Pres Communauté Urbain de Strasbourg 2000–. *Address:* Mairie, Centre Administratif, 1 place de l'Etoile, 67000 Strasbourg, France. *Telephone:* (2) 284-21-11; *Fax:* (2) 230-69-43.

TREMAIN, Rose, BA, FRSL; British writer; b 2 Aug 1943, London; d of Keith Nicholas and Viola Mabel (née Dudley) Thomson; m 1st Jon Tremain 1971; one d; m 2nd Jonathan Dudley 1982 (divorced 1990). *Education:* Frances Holland School (London), Univ of Paris (Sorbonne) and Univ of E Anglia. *Career:* Full-time novelist and playwright 1971–; part-time Lecturer Dept of English and American Studies, Univ of E Anglia 1984–94; Hon D LITT (E Anglia); Dylan Thomas Short Story Prize 1984; Giles Cooper Award for Best Radio Play 1985; Angel Literary Award 1986; James Tait Black Memorial Prize 1993; Prix Femina Etranger 1994; Song Award 1996. *Publications:* Novels: Sadler's Birthday 1976, Letter to Sister Benedicta 1978, The Cupboard 1981, The Swimming Pool Season 1984, Restoration (Sunday Express Book of the Year Award) 1989, Sacred Country 1992, The Way I Found Her 1995, Music & Silence (Whitbread Novel of the Year) 1999; Short stories: The Colonel's Daughter 1982, The Garden of the Villa Mollini 1988, Evangelista's Fan 1994; Children's book: Journey to the Volcano 1985; *Radio plays include:* Who Was Emily Davison? 1996, The End of Love 1999. *Leisure interests:* yoga, gardening, walking, swimming. *Address:* 2 High House, South Ave, Thorpe St Andrew, Norwich, NR7 0EZ, UK. *Telephone:* (1603) 439682; *Fax:* (1603) 434234.

TŘEŠTÍKOVÁ, Helena; Czech film-maker; b 22 June 1949; d of Jaroslav Böhm and Duna Böhmová; m Michael Třeštík 1975; one s one d. *Education:* FAMU Film School and Charles Univ (Prague). *Career:* Dir of documentaries 1972–; active in movt of ind film-makers 1990–; Co-Founder Film and Sociology Foundation 1991; Co-Founder Man and Time Foundation 1994; awards from film festivals in Czechoslovakia 1976, 1988, 1991, Bilbao, Spain 1980, Lausanne, Switzerland (UNICEF) 1981; TV award, Prague 1991; Czech Film Award 1995. *Films include:* The Miracle 1975, A Touch of Light 1979, Marital Stories 1987, Out of Love 1988, Tell Me Something About Yourself 1992; more than 50 films and documentaries. *Leisure interests:* family, children, reading, travel. *Address:* Kostelní 14, 170 00 Prague 7, Czech Republic. *Telephone:* (2) 375976.

TREVIS, Di (Diane) Ellen; British theatre director; b 8 Nov 1947; d of the late Joseph B. and of Margaret Trevis; m Dominic Muldowney 1986; one d. *Education:* Waverley Grammar School (Birmingham) and Univ of Sussex. *Career:* Actress Citizens Co, Glasgow 1972–75, Dir 1981–83; Asst Dir Nat Theatre 1981–82, Dir 1984–87; Assoc Dir Arts Council 1983–84; Asst Dir RSC 1983–85, Dir 1985–88; Dir Royal Opera House 1991–. *Productions include:* Desperado Corner 1981, Nothing to do With Toothpaste 1982, Minnesota Moon 1982, A New Way to Pay Off Old Debts 1983, To Those Born Later 1984, The Resistible Rise of Arturo Ui 1984, 1991, Happy End 1985, The Taming of the Shrew 1985, A Matter of Life and Death 1986, The Mother 1987, Yerma 1987, School for Wives 1987, Much Ado About Nothing 1988, Gawain 1991, Elgar's Rondo 1993, Inadmissable Evidence 1993, Human Canon, Ballad of California (USA) 1996, Daughter in Law 1996, House of Bernarda Alba 1997, Love's Labour's Lost 1998, Happy Birthday Brecht 1998, Awake and Sing (USA) 1998, The Voluptuous Tango 2000, Private Jenny 2000, Death of a Salesman 2000, Remembrance of Things Past (adapted with Harold Pinter) 2001; *Publications include:* Remembrance of Things Proust 2000. *Leisure interests:* movies, Morocco, long mountain walks. *Address:* c/o National Theatre, Upper Ground, South Bank, London SE1 9PX, UK. *Telephone:* (20) 7928-2033.

TRINIDAD, Lally Laurel, BA; Philippine politician; b 5 July 1941, Manila; d of Jose B. Laurel, Jr and Remedios Lerma; m Noel F. Trinidad 1965; two s one d. *Education:* Maryknoll Coll. *Career:* Sales Rep Pan American World Airways 1962–65; Man Dir Express Tours Inc 1968–86; Consultant United Airlines 1986–87; Personal Sec to Jose B. Laurel 1984–86; elected to House of Reps (Nacionalista Party) 1987, mem numerous house Cttees on Banks and Currencies, Foreign Affairs and Agrarian Reform; Personality of the Year 1988; Pagkakaisa Award for Outstanding Achievements (Devt of Filipino Writers Inc) 1990. *Leisure interest:* promoting tourism. *Address:* House of Representatives, Quezon City, Philippines (Office); Laurel Hill, Natatas, Tanauan, Batangas, Philippines (Home).

TRINTIGNANT, Nadine; French film director, screenwriter and writer; b 11 Nov 1934, Nice; d of Jean and Lucienne (née Cornillad) Marquand; m 1st Jean-Louis Trintignant 1961 (divorced 1997); two d (one deceased) one s; m 2nd Alain Corneau 1998. *Education:* Lycée Molière, Inst Fénelon and Cours Lamartine (Paris). *Career:* Trainee LTC lab 1952; Trainee Film Ed 1953–54, Asst Film Ed 1954–58, Chief Ed and Continuity Person 1958–64; Dir TV programmes in the Le Cinéma and Les Femmes Aussi series 1965–66; writer and Dir of films and TV programmes. *Films:* Dir: Fragilité, ton nom est femme (Festival de Hyères Prize, Salonika Festival Prize, Greece) 1965, L'île bleue 2000; Writer and Dir: Mon amour, mon amour 1967, Le voleur de crimes 1969, Ça n'arrive qu'aux autres 1971, La semaine des quatre jeudis 1972, Défense de savoir 1973, Le voyage de noces 1976, Madame le Juge, L'innocent 1977, Premier voyage 1980, Portrait de Mikis Theodorakis, L'été prochain 1984, La maison de jade 1988, Fugueuses 1994, L'insoumise 1996; *TV includes:* film: Le tiroir secret 1985, Lucas 1988, Rêveuse jeunesse 1992, Les inséparables; Dir: Qui c'est ce garçon? (series) 1986, Victoire 1998, L'île bleue 2000; *Publications:* Ton chapeau au vestiaire 1998, Combien d'enfant 2000. *Leisure interests:* music, travelling. *Address:* 30 rue des Francs-Bourgeois, 75003 Paris, France. *Telephone:* (1) 42-74-47-01; *Fax:* (1) 42-74-55-03; *E-mail:* nadine.trintignant@libertysurf.fr.

TRITTON, (Elizabeth) Clare, MA; British barrister; b 18 Aug 1935, Cardiff; d of Alfonsus and Elizabeth (née Throckmorton) d'Abreu; m 1st Alan Tritton 1958 (divorced 1971); two s one d; m 2nd Andrew McLaren 1973. *Education:* Univ of Birmingham. *Career:* Barrister 1964–; called to the Bar, Inner Temple 1968; Chair Bar European Group 1982–84; Charlemagne Chambers, Brussels 1985–89; f own chambers specializing in European Law 1987; Sr Partner Throckmorton Estates 1989, now Chief Exec; non-exec mem Hansard Comm for Parl Govt; Vice-Chair Int Practice Cttee Gen Council of the Bar 1988–91; Chair Sub-Cttee on European Legislation, Hansard Comm on Legis Reform 1991–93; mem European Cttee British Invisible Exports Council 1989–93, Monopolies and Mergers Comm 1993–97; Ind mem Council Financial Intermediaries, Managers and Brokers Regulatory Asscn (FIMBRA) 1991–98; Dir Severn Trent Plc 1991–; numerous articles in professional journals. *Leisure interests:* gardening, theatre, reading, travel, walking, children. *Address:* 5 Paper Bldgs, Temple, London EC4Y 7HB, UK (Office); Coughton Court, Alcester, Warwicks B49 5JA, UK (Home). *Telephone:* (20) 7583-4555 (Office); (1789) 400777 (Home); *Fax:* (1789) 765544 (Home).

TRNKA, Monique Claude; French broadcasting executive; b 10 March 1931, Bellegarde; d of Arthur and Aline (née Philippe) Davoine; m Hervé Trnka 1954; two s. *Education:* Lycée Hélène Boucher (Paris), Inst d'Etudes Politiques (Paris) and Inst des Hautes Etudes de Défense Nat. *Career:* Man Asst Gen Admin Dept, Office de Radiodiffusion-Télévision Française (ORTF) 1960–67, Admin in Charge of Fiction Programme Production 1967–72, Head Admin Responsible for Artistic Production, First Channel 1973–75; Head Dept of External Production and Commercial Relations Télévision Française 1 (TF1) 1975–78, Deputy Dir and Sec-Gen of Programmes 1978–82, Dir of Co-Productions 1983; Dir-Gen Télé-Hachette 1983–87; Sec-Gen of Production Société Nat de Télévision en Couleur—Antenne 2 1987–90, Dir of Programming and Programmes 1990–91; Dir-Gen Fit Production 1991–; Dir responsible for Int Co-Productions Groupe Expand group 1993–; mem Bd Banque Régionale d'Escompte et de Dépôts 1983–87; Chevalier de la Légion d'Honneur; Chevalier de l'Ordre Nat du Mérite. *Publications:* L'ORTF et l'industrie électronique 1967, Télévision et démocratie moderne 1978, La grille de programme, un dialogue à trois voix 1982. *Leisure interests:* cinema, theatre, skiing. *Address:* 276 blvd Saint-Germain, 75007 Paris, France.

TROEDSSON, Ingegerd, M SC S; Swedish politician; b 5 June 1929, Vaxholm, Stockholm; d of Emil Johan and Gerd (née Wibom) Cederlöf; m Tryggve Bengt Johan Troedsson 1949; three s two d. *Education:* Saltsjöbaden School and Univ of Stockholm. *Career:* Local Govt Councillor, North Trögd 1959–70, Enköping City 1971–76; Vice-Chair Moderata Samlingspartiet (Moderate Party) 1986–91, mem Bd 1966–76, 1978–91; Vice-Chair Moderate Party Parl Group 1983–86; Vice-Chair Moderata Women's Fed 1966–76; Mem Riksdag (Parl) 1973–94; Minister for Health and Social Affairs 1976–78; mem Taxation Cttee 1975–91, Social Affairs Cttee 1974–76, 1978–91; First Deputy Speaker of Riksdag 1979–91, first woman Speaker 1991–94; mem Bd Euroc 1979–91, Svenska Dagbladet Foundation 1981–94, WASA Life 1987–91, Skandinaviska Enskilda Banken 1987–91; HM the King's Medal and Chain. *Publications:* Hög tid för ny familjepolitik 1962, Om tryggheten 1964, Aktiv Vårdpolitik 1966, Att få ta ansvar 1967, Politik för 70-talet 1969, Den Kommenderade familjen 1999, Frigör familjen 2000. *Leisure interest:* historical research. *Address:* Hakesta, 74081 Grillby, Sweden. *Telephone:* (171) 476-080; *Fax:* (171) 476-082.

TROISIER, Solange Louise, D EN MED; French politician and medical practitioner; b 19 July 1919, Paris; d of Jean and Geneviève (née Emile-Ollivier) Troisier. *Education:* Cours Victor-Hugo and Univ of Paris. *Career:* Head of Clinic Faculty of Medicine, Univ of Paris 1952–; Asst Paris Hosps 1955–; Gynaecological Surgeon, Paris 1955–; Expert at Cour de Cassation; mem Nat Ass (Parl, UDR) for Sarcelles, Gonesse, Val-d'Oise 1968–73; Vice-Pres Comm on Cultural, Family and Social Affairs 1968–69; Medical Insp-Gen Prisons Admin 1973–83; Prof of Legal and Penitentiary Medicine Centre Hospitalier Universitaire Lariboisière 1977–86; Medical Practitioner Fernand Vidal Hosp 1970–83; Pres Ordre Nat des Sages-Femmes (Midwives' Org) 1970–83; Pres Conseil Nat des Femmes Françaises 1976–, Int Council of Medical Penitentiary Services; mem High Comm of Study and Information on Alcoholism 1969–83, Council on Sexual Information, Regulation of Births and Family Educ, RPR Nat Council, Econ and Social Council; Officier de la Légion d'Honneur; Officier de l'Ordre Nat du Mérite; Croix de Guerre 1939–45. *Publication:* J'étais médecin des prisons 1985. *Address:* 15 rue des Tapisseries, 75017 Paris, France.

TROITSKAYA, Natalia Leonidovna; Russian opera singer (soprano); b 18 May 1956, Moscow. *Education:* Gnesins Music Inst. *Career:* Left USSR 1980; winner of int competitions in Toulouse, France, Vercelli, Italy and Barcelona, Spain; debut as opera singer in Theatro Liseo, Barcelona with José Carreras 1981; performances as guest singer La Scala, Milan (Italy), Royal Opera House, Covent Garden (London), Deutsche Oper Berlin, Wiener Staatsoper, Teatro Colón, Buenos Aires, Rome Opera, etc; has participated in numerous music festivals including Arena di Verona, Italy; debut in Moscow as Adrienna Lecouvrer with La Scala 1989; f fund for promotion of young singers, Moscow 1994; Gold

Rose Prize of Critics, Germany. *Operas include:* Queen of Spades, La Traviata, Aida, Andre Chenier, Il Trovatore, Don Carlow, Othello, Un Ballo in Maschera, Prince Igor. *Address:* c/o Klostergasse 37, 1170 Vienna, Austria. *Telephone:* (095) 299-2044 (Moscow).

TROLLOPE, Joanna, OBE, MA; British writer; b 9 July 1943, Glos; d of Arthur George and Rosemary (née Hodson) Trollope; m 1st David Potter 1966; two d; m 2nd Ian Curteis 1985 (divorced 2001); two step s. *Education:* Reigate County School for Girls (Surrey) and St Hugh's Coll (Oxford). *Career:* Information and Research Dept, Foreign Office 1965–67; Teacher 1967–79; Writer 1979–; occasional contrib to periodicals; Chair Advisory Cttee on Nat Reading Initiative, Dept of Nat Heritage 1996–97; mem Council Soc of Authors 1997–, Govt Advisory Body, Nat Year of Reading 1998, Campaign Bd, St Hugh's Coll, Oxford; Writer-in-Residence Victoria Magazine (USA) 1999; Vice-Pres Trollope Soc 1995–, West Country Writers' Asscn 1998–; Patron Glouc Community Foundation 1994–; Trustee Joanna Trollope Charitable Trust 1995–. *Publications:* Historical Fiction: (1st issued as Joanna Trollope, republished since 1995 under pseudonym Caroline Harvey) Eliza Stanhope 1978, Parson Harding's Daughter (Romantic Historical Novel of the Year 1980) 1979, Leaves from the Valley 1980, The City of Gems 1981, The Steps of the Sun 1983, The Taverner's Place 1986; Contemporary Fiction: The Choir 1988 (televised by BBC 1995), A Village Affair 1989 (televised by Carlton TV), A Passionate Man 1990, The Rector's Wife 1991 (televised by Talisman Film for Chnnel 4 1994), The Men and the Girls 1992, A Spanish Lover 1993, The Best of Friends 1995, Next of Kind 1996, Other People's Children 1998 (televised by BBC 1999), Marrying the Mistress 2000; Non-fiction: Britannia's Daughters: A Study of Women in the British Empire 1983, The Country Habit: An Anthology (ed) 1993; under pseudonym of Caroline Harvey: A Legacy of Love 1992, A Second Legacy 1993, A Castle in Italy 1993, The Brass Dolphin 1997. *Leisure interests:* reading, conversation, very long baths. *Address:* c/o PFD, Drury House, 34–43 Russell St, London WC2B 5HA, UK.

TROTTER, Dame Janet Olive, DBE, MA, M SC, BD; British college principal; b 29 Oct 1943, Chatham, Kent; d of Anthony G. and Joyce E. Trotter. *Education:* Tech High School for Girls (Maidstone), Derby Coll of Educ, Univ of London, Brunel Univ (Uxbridge) and Henley Man Coll. *Career:* Teacher 1965–73; Lecturer in Theology, then Head of Professional Studies King Alfred's Coll, Winchester 1973–84; Vice-Prin St Martin's Coll, Lancaster 1985–86; Prin St Paul and St Mary's Coll, Cheltenham 1986–90; Dir Cheltenham and Gloucester Coll of Higher Educ 1990–; Commr Equal Opportunities Comm 1991–93; Regional Chair South and West Health 1996–2001; delivered Hockerill Lecture criticizing the management of Christian Colls 1991; mem Royal Soc of Arts, Teacher Training Agency, Higher Educ Funding Council; Hon Fellow King Alfred's Coll, Winchester 1999, Christchurch Univ Coll, Canterbury 2001; Dr hc (Pecs, Hungary) 1997, (W of England) 2001. *Leisure interests:* reading, music, walking. *Address:* Cheltenham and Gloucester College of Higher Education, POB 220, The Park Campus, The Park, Cheltenham, Glos GL50 2QF, UK; I Tivoli Court, Tivoli Rd, Cheltenham, UK. *Telephone:* (1242) 532701; *Fax:* (1242) 532879; *E-mail:* jtrotter@chelt.ac.uk.

TROTTER, Judith; New Zealand diplomatist. *Career:* Perm Rep to OECD 1988–92; Amb to France 1988–93, to Greece 1995, later to Italy. *Address:* c/o Ministry of Foreign Affairs and Trade, Private Bag 18901, Wellington, New Zealand.

TROUBLÉ, Agnès (Agnès B); French designer; b 1941, Versailles. *Education:* Ecole des Beaux-Arts (Versailles). *Career:* Began career as Junior Ed, French edn of Elle; worked as Asst to designer Dorothée Bis; freelance designer for Limitex, Pierre d'Alby, V de V and Eversbin; opened first shop, Paris 1975, SoHo, NY 1980, and subsequently further brs in London, Amsterdam and Tokyo; launched own perfume (Le B) and also skincare and cosmetics range and maternity collection 1987. *Address:* 17 rue Dieu, 75010 Paris, France. *Telephone:* (1) 40-03-45-00.

TRUEBODY, Miriam, MA; Namibian business executive and anthropologist; b 31 July 1947, S Africa; d of Louis and Maria Martha Ferreira; m Charles Thomas Truebody 1988. *Education:* Univ of Stellenbosch (S Africa) and Indiana Univ (USA). *Career:* Teacher 1970–75; Researcher

The Rossing Foundation, Namibia 1982–83; Small Business Developer Pvt Sector Foundation 1984–90, apptd Gen Man 1990, Nat Pres Namibian Fed of Business and Professional Women 1991; mem Namibian Bd of Trade and Industry 1992; mem Namibian Network of AIDS Service Orgs 1991. *Leisure interests:* reading, music, cooking. *Address:* POB 11137, 5 Rusch St, Klein Windhoek, Namibia. *Telephone:* (61) 33397; *Fax:* (61) 228261.

TRUMPINGTON, Baroness (Life Peer), cr 1980, of Sandwich in the County of Kent, **Jean Alys Barker,** PC; British politician; b 23 Oct 1922, London; d of the late Arthur Edward and Doris (née Robson) Campbell-Harris; m William Alan Barker 1954 (died 1988); one s. *Education:* Privately. *Career:* Worked at Foreign Office, Bletchley Park 1941–45, European Cen Inland Transport Org 1945–49; Sec to Viscount Hinchingbrooke, MP 1950–52; Councillor (Cons) Cambridge City Council, Trumpington Ward 1963–73, Mayor of Cambridge 1971–72, Deputy Mayor 1972–73, Hon Councillor of the City of Cambridge 1975–; Cambridgeshire Co Councillor from Trumpington Ward 1973–75; mem House of Lords 1980–; Parl Under-Sec of State Dept of Health and Social Security 1985–87, Ministry of Agriculture, Fisheries and Food 1987–89, Minister of State 1989–92; Baroness in Waiting 1983–85, 1992–97; Extra Baroness in Waiting to the Queen 1998–; JP, Cambridge 1972–75, S Westminster 1976–82; Gen Commr of Taxes 1976–83; Del to UN Comm on the Status of Women 1979–82; Pres Asscn of Heads of Ind Schools 1980–89; Steward Folkestone Racecourse 1980–; Hon Fellow Lucy Cavendish Coll, Cambridge 1980. *Leisure interests:* antiques, golf, needlepoint. *Address:* House of Lords, London SW1, UK. *Telephone:* (20) 7219-5242; *Fax:* (20) 7219-6396.

TRYON, Valerie Ann; Canadian (b British) pianist and academic; b 5 Sept 1934, Portsmouth; d of Kenneth Montague and Winifred (née Lunan) Tryon. *Education:* Royal Acad of Music (London). *Career:* Performances in the UK include Cheltenham Festival, Royal Festival Hall, Royal Albert Hall, Royal Opera House, Covent Garden, Aldeburgh Festival; has performed throughout Canada and the USA, including Library of Congress, Washington, DC; currently pianist in Rembrandt Trio; Artist-in-Residence McMaster Univ, Hamilton, ON 1978–86, Assoc Prof 1986–; Fellow RAM 1984; RAM Dove Prize 1955; Harriet Cohen Int Music Award 1967; Franz Liszt Medal of Honour, Hungarian Ministry of Culture 1986. *Recordings include:* Liszt's Sonata for Violin and Piano, Rachmaninov and Hoddinott, Valerie Tryon plays Richard Baker's most requested pieces, These You Have Loved, Valerie Tryon Piano, The Joy of Piano, Debussy Songs (Juno Winner with Claudette Leblanc) 1994. *Leisure interests:* art, opera, nature. *Address:* McMaster University, Dept of Music, Hamilton, ON L8S 4L8, Canada (Office); 609 Tuscarora Drive, Ancaster, ON L9G 3N9, Canada (Home). *Telephone:* (416) 525-9140 (Office); (416) 648-5883 (Home); *Fax:* (416) 527-0100 (Office).

TSERENDULAM, Rentsen, PH D, D SC; Mongolian zoologist; b 12 March 1931; d of Rentsen and Gurbadam Tserendulam; m J. Togtoh; three d two s. *Education:* Mongolian State Univ. *Career:* Lecturer Agricultural Univ, Ulan Bator 1957–61; Sec-Gen, then Div Chief, Scientific Research Centre on Cattle-Breeding 1961–96; Adviser on research into Mongolian pastural cattle 1992–; awarded Gold Star 1971, Labour Red Ban Medal 1983. *Publications:* Workshop on Foddering of Agricultural Animals 1965, Nutrients of Different Sorts of Fodder 1968, Tables and Schedules of Foddering 1980, Pastural Breeding and Foddering of Herds 1980, The System of Cattle-Breeding 1982. *Leisure interests:* literature, music. *Address:* Research Institute of Animal Husbandry, Zaisan 53, 210153 Ulan Bator, Mongolia (Office); House 45, Flat 7, Enh-Taiwan St, 40000 Ulan Bator, Mongolia (Home). *Telephone:* 341015 (Office); 368981 (Home).

TSHILUILA, Josette Shaje, D SC S; Democratic Republic of the Congo anthropologist and museum executive; b 5 March 1949, Likasi, Zaire (now Democratic Republic of the Congo); m Badi-Banga N'Sampuka 1974; two d two s. *Education:* Coll Albert 1er (Kinshasa), Univ Lovanium (now Univ of Kinshasa) and Univ of Lubumbashi. *Career:* Joined Inst des Musées Nationaux du Zaïre 1973, Head Traditional Art Section 1983–86, apptd Deputy Dir-Gen 1987; Dir Kinshasa Museum 1986; mem study and art-collecting missions to Bas-Zaïre 1974, 1980, 1984, 1985, E and W Kasaï and Shaba 1975, Haut-Zaïre 1983, Angola 1983; Prof Univ of Kinshasa 1990–; Visiting Prof Univ Catholique de

Leuven, Guest Prof Univ Libre de Bruxelles 1994; Assoc mem Centre d'Anthropologie, Univ Libre de Bruxelles 1991–; apptd Pres ICOM for Cen Africa 1996; consultant Nat Environmental Action Plan (PNAE), UNESCO Inventaire des Musées du Congo-Brazzaville Project 1996; attended numerous int confs, colloquia and seminars in Kenya 1975, Belgium 1975, 1979, 1980, 1983, 1991, France 1975, 1979, 1980, 1983, 1991, Cameroon 1980, 1991, USA 1981, 1990, UK 1983, Netherlands 1989, Canada 1990, Denmark 1990, Gabon 1991; mem ICOM, Advisory Bd UNESCO Museum magazine, Cttee Man and Biosphere MAB/Zaire, Cttee of Ethics and Struggle against AIDS. *Publications:* A la mémoire des ancêtres: le grand art funéraire Kongo, contexte social, historique 1986, L'intégration de la femme au développement du Zaïre 1990, Interprétation structurale des mythes songye d'origine 1991; articles in professional journals. *Leisure interests:* reading, jogging, cooking. *Address:* Institut des Musées Nationaux du Zaïre, ave de la Montagne, BP 13933, Kinshasa 1, Democratic Republic of the Congo. *Telephone:* (12) 60263.

TSIELAVA, Ilze; Latvian economist; b 26 Nov 1949; d of Verner Kruminsh and Mirdza Vitolinja; m Arnis Tsielavs 1970 (divorced 1990); three d. *Education:* Univ of Latvia. *Career:* Economist on Exec Cttee, Ventspils City 1964–70; Head of Dept, Bank of Latvia 1973–80; Ed and writer Ogres Atmoda (Awakening of the Ogre) newspaper 1988–89; Asst to Deputy Chair of Latvian Popular Front 1989–91; Asst to Latvian Prime Minister 1991–93; mem Deputy Council Latvian Popular Front 1991–93; Adviser to Latvian Honorary Consul-Gen, India. *Leisure interests:* Christianity, politics, fine arts. *Address:* Kr Valdemāra iela 101, Rīga, Latvia; Papelu St 12, Ikshkile, 5052 Ogre Dist, Latvia. *Telephone:* (2) 379725 (Rīga); (250) 30465 (Ikshkile); *Fax:* (2) 379725 (Rīga).

TSOUDEROS, Virginia, MA; Greek politician; b 24 June 1924, Iraklion, Crete; d of Emmanuel J. and Maria (née Thiakaki) Tsouderos; m 1950 (divorced); two d one s. *Education:* Univs of Oxford (UK) and Minneapolis (USA), and Radcliffe Coll (USA). *Career:* Economist FAO and Columnist IMF 1952–67; Mem Enossi Dimokratikou Kentrou (EDIK, Union of Democratic Centre Party) 1974–78, Komma Dimokratikou Socialismou (KODISO, Democratic Socialist Party) 1979–, Nea Dimokratia (ND, New Democracy Party), Spokesperson 1990; mem Vouli (Parl) EDIK 1974–77, Independent 1978–81, of State 1985–89, 1990–, mem Foreign Affairs Cttee 1974–; Under-Sec for Foreign Affairs 1991; mem Economist Asscn, Amnesty Int; Hon Pres Family Planning Asscn; Woman of Europe for Greece 1988. *Publications include:* Talking With the Citizens 1981, Europe as Our Compass 1985, Libraries in Greece, Medical Care, Historical Archives of E. I. Tsouderos 1941–44 (Greek Acad Award) 1991. *Address:* Vouli, Parliament Bldg, Syntagma, Athens, Greece (Office); Vasileos Georgiou II 14, 10674 Athens, Greece (Home). *Telephone:* (1) 7210812 (Home).

TSUCHIYA, Suma, B ED; Japanese artist; b 12 Feb 1924, Ueno, Mie; d of Hinomatsu and Kachi Kawase; m Kimio Tsuchiya 1950 (died 1984); one c. *Education:* Mie Univ. *Career:* Pres Suma Bright Art Inst, Osaka 1968–; Lecturer Osaka Arts Coll 1982–; inventor New Bright Arts, Suma Bright Art, Cosmo Art, Bllirian Imazue Art and Brighting Bright Art; exhibitions include Salon de Mai, Grand Palais 1989, Takamatsu New Airport Lobby 1990, Expo '90 Sumitomo Pavilion 1990, GAS Pavilion 1990, Rokko Island Hospital Lobby 1991, Brilliant Art, Shizoka 1994, Civil Centre, Kadoma City 1994; mem Designers' Asscn, Artists, Architects and Industrialists Asscn, Lighting Acad Circles, Salon de Finale Asscn; recipient Japan Display Design Prize (Japan Display Design Asscn) 1978, Construction Industry Lighting Design Prize (Daiko Denko) 1979, Int Art Exhibition Prize (Salon de Finale) 1985, 1986, 1987, 1988, 17th Int Art Exhibition Award (Mainichi Newspapers) 1988, Variety Prize (Int Electric Cinema Festival, Tokyo-Montreux) 1990, Osaka Prefectual Govs Prize 1993, Int Illomi Design Award 1995; Japan Display Design Award 1996; Int Illumination Design Award (USA) 1996. *Publication:* The World of Brilliant Image Art 1988. *Leisure interest:* painting. *Address:* Suma Bright Art Institute, 2-10-14 Sugimoto, Sumiyoshi-ku, Osaka 558, Japan. *Telephone:* (6) 6698-2525; *Fax:* (6) 6698-2525; *E-mail:* sba@art-tuchiya .com; *Internet:* www.art-tuchiya.com.

TSUNG, Christine Tsai-yi, MBA; Taiwanese business executive; b 1949; m Jerome Chen. *Education:* Nat Taiwan Univ and Univ of Missouri. *Career:* Fmr Exec farm machinery co in Texas; fmr Budget Man Columbia Pictures; Consultant Kaohsiung Mass Rapid Transit System 1999; Pres and CEO China Airlines 2000–. *Address:* China Airlines, 131 Nanking E Rd, Section 3, Taipei City, Taiwan. *Telephone:* (2) 2715-1212; *Internet:* www.china-airlines.com.

TSUSHIMA, Nobuko, MD, PH D; Japanese internist and cardiologist; b 7 May 1937, Yoichi; d of Masayoshi and Matsue (née Saito) Tsushima. *Education:* Hokkaido Univ. *Career:* Intern Hiroo Tokyo Municipal Hosp 1962–63; Resident Hokkaido Univ 1963–67; mem staff Tonan Hosp, Saporo 1967–72, Chief of Internal Medicine 1972–81; Chief Physician Artificial Organs Dept, Cleveland Clinic 1976–77; apptd Chair of Internal Medicine, Nat Cardiovascular Centre, Suita 1982; cr intravital video microscopic system 1979; mem Cerebro-Vascular Disease Research Asscn, American, European and Japanese Socs of Micro-circulation, Japanese Soc of Circulation, Internal Medicine, Angiology, Diabetes Mellitus and Automatic Nervous System Disorders. *Address:* National Cardiovascular Centre, 5-7-1 Fujishirodai, Suita 565, Japan (Office); 203 D-10, 3-chome, Aoyamadai, Suita, Japan (Home).

TSUSHIMA, Yuko, BA; Japanese writer; b 30 March 1947, Tokyo; d of Shuji and Michiko Tsushima; one d. *Education:* Shirayuni Women's Coll (Tokyo). *Career:* Writer of novels; mem Japan's Writers Asscn, Literary Women's Asscn. *Publications:* Child of Fortune (Women's Literary Award) 1978, Territory of Light (Noma Award for new writers) 1979, By the River of Fire 1983, Silent Trader (Kawabata Literary Award) 1984, Driven by the Night Light (Yomiari Literary Award 1987) 1986, The Shooting Gallery 1989, Woman Running in the Mountains 1991. *Address:* The Women's Press, 34 Gt Sutton St, London EC1V 0DX, UK (Office); c/o Japan PEN-Club, Rm 265, 9-1-7 Akasaka, Minato-ku, Tokyo, Japan (Office); 6-7-10 Honkomagome, Bunkyo-ku, Tokyo 113, Japan (Home).

TU, Elsie, CBE, BA; British teacher and politician; b 2 June 1913, Newcastle upon Tyne (UK); d of the late John and Florence Hume; m Andrew H. K. Tu 1985. *Education:* Heaton Secondary School and Armstrong Coll (br of Univ of Durham). *Career:* Teacher, UK 1937–47; missionary in China 1948–51; social, educational and political work in Hong Kong 1951–; supervisor Mu Kuang English School 1954–; Hong Kong Urban Councillor 1963–95 (Vice-Chair 1986–89); Legislative Councillor 1988–95 (House Cttee Chair 1991–95); Hong Kong Affairs Adviser to People's Repub of China 1994–; Pres Hong Kong Council of Women; mem Transport Advisory Cttee 1965–82, Hong Kong Housing Authority 1973–85, Dist Bd 1981–89, Basic Law Consultative Cttee 1985–90, Asscn for the Promotion of Public Justice; Adviser and mem Int Women's Forum, Hong Kong; Dr hc (Hong Kong) 1988, (Hong Kong Polytechnic, Open Learning Inst) 1994, (Durham, Newcastle) 1996; Magsaysay Award for Public Service 1976; Outstanding Woman Award, Univ Women of Asia 1992–95. *Publication:* Autobiography 1981. *Leisure interests:* reading, writing. *Address:* Mu Kuang English School, 55 Kung Lok Rd, Kwun Tong, Hong Kong. *Telephone:* 234-56168; *Fax:* 238-95048.

TUCHMAN MATHEWS, Jessica, PH D; American research centre executive and journalist; b 1946, New York; d of Lester Reginald and Barbara (née Wertheim) Tuchman; m Colin D. Mathews 1978; two s one step-s one step-d. *Education:* The Brearley School (New York), Radcliffe Coll (MA) and California Inst of Tech. *Career:* Professional mem staff House Interior Cttee on Energy and Environment 1973–74; Issues Dir for Morris Udall's presidential campaign, Washington, DC 1975–76; Dir Office of Global Issues, mem staff Nat Security Council, The White House, Washington, DC 1977–79; mem Editorial Bd The Washington Post, Washington, DC 1980–82, columnist 1990; apptd Vice-Pres and Research Dir World Resources Inst, Washington, DC 1982; mem numerous bds, councils and cttees; Hon D SC (Claremont Grad School) 1990, (Hood Coll) 1992. *Address:* World Resources Institute, 1709 New York Ave, NW, Washington, DC 20006, USA. *Telephone:* (202) 638-6300; *Fax:* (202) 638-0036.

TUKAHIRWA, Joy Margaret, M SC; Ugandan environmental scientist; b 11 April 1955, Kabale; d of Benyamini and Dolotiya Biteete; m Eldad Tukahirwa 1985; two s one d. *Education:* Hornby High School (Kabale),

Gayaza High School (Kampala), Makerere Univ (Kampala) and Univ of E Anglia (Norwich, UK). *Career:* Researcher and writer on soil management; has attended many forums world-wide on sustainable devt; made presentation Global Women Ass, Miami, FL, USA 1991; apptd Sr Lecturer in Land Use, Resource Assessment and Bio-geography, Makerere Univ 1990; mem Cttee Uganda Women in Evangelism and Devt, UNESCO Nat Cttee, Chapel Council; Scholar-ship Award from EC 1982–83, from FAO 1990–91; Social Science Research Council Award 1989–90. *Publications:* Prospects and Sensi-tivity of Soil Resources in the Highlands of Uganda 1986, Key Issues Causing the Failure of Soil Conservation in Uganda 1989, Decision-Making In Soil Conservation Among Rural Small-Scale Farmers of a Montane Agroecosystem of SW Uganda 1990. *Leisure interests:* knitting, tennis. *Address:* Makerere University, Dept of Geography, POB 7062, Kampala, Uganda. *Telephone:* (41) 554721; *Fax:* (41) 245597.

TULVING, Ruth, RCA; Canadian (b Estonian) artist and printmaker; b 23 Dec 1930, Estonia; d of Edward and Hilda (née Martinson) Mikkelsaar; m Endel Tulving 1950; two d. *Education:* Ontario and California (USA) Colls of Art and L'Acad de la Grande Chaumière (Paris). *Career:* Teacher of painting and printmaking, Ontario Coll of Art 1965–73; solo exhibitions in Canada, USA, France, UK, Sweden, Estonia and People's Repub of China; lecture tours of People's Repub of China 1984, 1987, 1989; featured in documentary 'The Coming', Estonian TV 1994; elected mem Royal Canadian Acad of Arts 1977; Pres Ontario Soc of Artists 1983–84; mem Arts and Letters Club; awards include Nat Acad of Design Award, USA 1966. *Publication:* Ruth Tulving 1995. *Leisure interests:* opera, history. *Address:* 45 Baby Point Crescent, Toronto, ON M6S 2B7, Canada. *Telephone:* (416) 763-2777.

TUMENDEMBEREL, Sarantuya, MA; Mongolian broadcasting exec-utive and former state official; b 10 Jan 1951, Ulan Bator; d of Tumendemberel and Nordov; m Zanabazar R. 1973 (died 1988); two s. *Education:* All-Union State Inst of Cinematography and Acad of Social Sciences (Moscow). *Career:* Economist; Head of Film Production Dept, Ministry of Culture 1972–75, 1981–83; Head of Dept Mongolkino State Co 1975–81; Dir Nat Film Distribution Bd 1983–85; Dir Telekino State Org 1987–89; Deputy Mayor Ulan Bator City Council, responsible for social and cultural affairs 1989–92; apptd Dir Ulan Bator TV Org 1992. *Leisure interests:* reading, foreign languages, knitting. *Address:* POB 350, Ulan Bator 13, Mongolia. *Telephone:* 22174.

TUNG, Rosalie Lam, BA, MBA, PH D; American professor of business studies; b 2 Dec 1948; d of Andrew Yan-Fu and Pauline Wai-Kam (née Cheung) Lam; m Byron Poon-Yan Tung 1972; one d. *Education:* York Univ and Univ of British Columbia (Canada). *Career:* Lecturer Univ of British Columbia 1975; Asst Prof of Man Univ of Oregon 1977–80; Assoc Prof Univ of Pennsylvania 1981–86; Prof and Dir Int Business Center, Univ of Wisconsin 1986–90, Distinguished Prof 1988–90; Endowed Chair Prof Simon Fraser Univ 1991–; Ming and Stella Wong Chair in Int Business 1991–; Visiting Scholar UMIST, UK 1980; Visiting Prof Univ of California at Los Angeles 1981, Harvard Univ 1988; Fellow Oppenheimer Brothers Foundation 1973–74, MacMillan Foundation 1975–77; mem Acad of Int Business, Acad of Man, Int Asscn of Applied Psychology, American Arbitration Asscn; Leonore Rowe Williams Award, Univ of Pennsylvania 1990. *Publications:* Management Practices in China 1980, US–China Trade Negotiations 1982, Chinese Industrial Society After Mao 1982, Business Negotia-tions with the Japanese 1984, Key to Japan's Economic Strength: Human Power 1984, Strategic Management in the US and Japan (ed) 1987, The New Expatriates: Managing Human Resources Abroad 1988. *Leisure interest:* writing. *Address:* Simon Fraser Univ, Faculty of Business Administration, Burnaby, BC V5A 1S6, Canada. *Telephone:* (604) 291-3111; *Fax:* (604) 291-4969.

TURCO, Livia; Italian politician. *Career:* MP Democratici di Sinistra (DC) 1987–, Head Nat Comm for Equal Opportunities 1995; currently Minister of Social Solidarity. *Address:* Democratici di Sinistra, Via delle Botteghe Oscure 4, 00186 Rome, Italy. *Telephone:* (6) 67111; *Fax:* (6) 6711596.

TURECK, Rosalyn, D MUS; American concert artist, conductor and professor of music; b 14 Dec 1914, Chicago, IL; d of Samuel and Monya (née Lipson) Tureck; m George Wallingford Downs 1964. *Education:*

Juilliard School of Music (New York). *Career:* Debut at age nine, Chicago 1924; first New York appearance Carnegie Hall 1932; concert tours include USA and Canada 1937–, Europe 1947–, SA 1959, S America 1963, 1985–86, Israel 1963, Far East, India, Australia 1971, Europe, Israel, Turkey, N American Bach Festivals 1985/86, Chile 1990, Italy 1991; appearances at major int festivals; specializes in the keyboard works of J. S. Bach; conductor 1956–; Conductor-Soloist London Philharmonic 1958, New York Philharmonic 1958, Israel Philharmonic 1963, Kol Israel Orchestra 1963, Int Bach Soc Orchestra 1967, 1969, 1970, Washington Nat Symphony 1970, Madrid Chamber Orchestra 1970, Tureck Bach Players, Carnegie Hall 1981, Bach Triennial Celebration Series (solo recitals and orchestral concerts conducting Tureck Bach Players), Carnegie Hall 1984, 1985; Visiting Prof of Music, Washington Univ, MO 1963–64; Prof of Music Univ of California at San Diego 1967–72, Regents Lecturer 1966; Visiting Fellow St Hilda's Coll, Oxford, UK 1974, Hon Life Fellow 1974–; Visiting Fellow Wolfson Coll, Oxford, UK 1975–; Visiting Prof Univ of Maryland 1982–84, Yale Univ 1992; lecturer and teacher of Master Classes at numerous univs and colls of music in USA, Canada and Europe; Founder-Dir Composers of Today 1951–55, Tureck Bach Players, London 1957, New York 1981, Int Bach Soc 1966 (now Tureck Bach Inst), Int Bach Soc Orchestra 1967, Inst for Bach Studies 1968, Tureck Bach Research Foundation 1994; numerous nat and int TV appearances; holder many grants for research on J. S. Bach; Hon D MUS (Colby Coll) 1964, (Roosevelt, Wilson Coll) 1968, (Oxford) 1977, (Music and Art Inst of San Francisco) 1987; First Prize Greater Chicago Piano Playing Tournament 1928; Winner Schubert Memorial Contest, Nat Fed of Music Clubs 1935; Bundesverdienstkreuz (Germany) 1979; Musician of the Year, Music Teachers Nat Asscn 1987. *Recordings include:* The Well-tempered Clavier (Books I and II), Goldberg Variations, Six Partitas, Italian Concerto, French Overture, Introduction to Bach, A Bach Recital, A Harpsichord Recital, Goldberg Variations and Aria and Ten Variations in the Italian Style (harp-sichord), Italian Concerto, Chromatic Fantasia and Fugue, Four Duets (piano), Rosalyn Tureck Plays Bach (Live at the Teatro Colón, Buenos Aires) 1992, Live in St Petersburg (5 vols) 1995; *Films:* Fantasy and Fugue: Rosalyn Tureck plays Bach 1972, Rosalyn Tureck plays Bach on Harpsichord and Organ 1977, Joy of Bach (soloist and consultant) 1979, Bach on the Frontier of the Future 1980, Rosalyn Tureck plays Bach in Ephesus, Turkey 1985, Rosalyn Tureck plays Bach, Live at the Teatro Colón, Buenos Aires 1992, Live in St Petersburg 1995; *Publications:* An Introduction to the Performance of Bach (three vols) 1959–60, A Critical and Performance Edition of J. S. Bach's Chromatic Fantasia and Fugue; numerous articles in periodicals; Ed: Paganini, Niccolo—Per-petuum Mobile 1950, J. S. Bach—Sarabande, C Minor 1960, Scarlatti, Alessandro—Sarabande and Gavotte; Ed Tureck Bach Urtext Series, Publr Italian Concerto 1983, Lute Suite, E Minor 1984, Lute Suite C Minor 1985, Authenticity 1994. *Address:* Hotel El Paradiso, Ctra Cádiz, Km 167, Apdo 134, 29680 Marbella, Spain; Tureck Bach Institute, 215 East 68th St, New York, NY 10021, USA. *Telephone:* (952) 88 30 00 (Marbella).

TÜRKMEN-ÖZGENTÜRK, Işıl; Turkish film director and writer; b 19 Sept 1948, Gaziantep; d of Rahmi and Sabriye Türkmen; m Ali Özgentürk 1972; one d. *Education:* Univ of Gaziantep. *Career:* Took part in street theatre; newspaper journalist; writer of articles, books, film scripts and plays; Children's Literature Award, Short Story Award. *Works include:* Play: Küçük Mutluluklar Bulmalıyım; Stories: Hançer, Dünyana Masallar; Film scripts: Bekçi, Su Da Yanar, I Love You Rosa (also dir) 1991. *Leisure interest:* dreaming. *Address:* Asya Film, Gazeteci Erol Demek Sok, Erman Han, Kat 1, Beyoglu, Istanbul, Turkey (Office); Perçem Sokak No 23/15, Arca Apt, Göztepe, Kadıköy, Istanbul, Turkey (Home). *Telephone:* (1) 3590163 (Home); *Fax:* (1) 2521226 (Home).

TURLAN, Juliette Marie, D EN D; French professor emeritus of law; b 5 June 1913, Paris; d of Julien and Anna (née Marcillac) Turlan. *Education:* Univ of Paris. *Career:* Uses pseudonym Françoise Candèze; Asst Admin Dept Chausson co 1942–45; Sec to Coal Distributor, Ministry of Industry 1945–49; Asst Faculty of Law, Univ of Paris 1950; Prof Faculty of Law, Univ of Rennes 1957–67, Univ of Amiens 1967–70, Univ of Paris-West 1968, Univ of Paris II (Univ Panthéon-Assas) 1974–81, Emer Prof 1981–; Founder-Dir Law and Soc Research Inst, Univ of Paris V (René Descartes); sent to Madagascar 1960,

Senegal 1961–62, Cambodia 1963; Chevalier de la Légion d'Honneur; Chevalier de l'Ordre Nat du Mérite; Officier des Palmes Académiques. *Publications:* La commune et le corps de ville de Sens 1942; articles on the history of law and on the sociology of religion. *Leisure interests:* photography, painting. *Address:* University of Paris II (Panthéon-Assas), 12 place du Panthéon, 75231 Paris Cedex 05, France.

TURLINGTON, Christy; American fashion model; b 2 Jan 1969, Walnut Creek, CA. *Career:* Discovered at age 14; with Ford Models Inc 1985; model for Revlon, Maybelline 1993; Co-propr Fashion Café, London (with Naomi Campbell, Elle MacPherson and Claudia Schiffer, qv) 1996–; advertisement campaigns for Calvin Klein, Michael Kors, Camay Soap, Special K Cereal; est own holistic cosmetics co. *Films include:* Catwalk 1996, appeared in George Michael's video Freedom. *Address:* c/o United Talent Agency, 9560 Wilshire Blvd, Suite 500, Beverly Hills, CA 90212, USA (Office); 344 East 59th Street, New York, NY 10022, USA (Office).

TURNER, Cynthia (pseudonym of Cynthia Caruana-Turner), LRAM; Maltese concert pianist; b 12 Dec 1932; d of Edward and Alice (née Debono) Turner; m Anthony Caruana 1954; two s. *Education:* Convent of the Sacred Heart (Malta), Royal Acad of Music (London), studies in Munich (Germany), Paris and Rome. *Career:* Finalist Piano Competition, Bayreuth, Germany 1953, Munich 1954; concerts broadcast on Radio Luxembourg, BBC, Deutscher Rundfunk, Italian and Maltese TV; performes at concerts and arts festivals in Europe; conducts master classes and gives sr grade piano tuition; Chair and adjudicator in piano competitions; solo performance for HM Queen Elizabeth II 1967. *Leisure interests:* skiing, mono water-skiing, ballet, gymnastics. *Telephone:* 330578; *Fax:* 493332.

TURNER, Kathleen, MFA; American actress; b 19 June 1954, Springfield, MO; m Jay Weiss 1984; one d. *Education:* Cen School of Speech and Drama (London), SW Missouri State Univ and Univ of Maryland. *Career:* Various theatre roles including Broadway debut in Gemini 1978, and Cat on a Hot Tin Roof. *Plays include:* Gemini 1978, The Graduate 2000; *Films include:* Body Heat 1981, The Man With Two Brains 1983, Crimes of Passion 1984, Romancing the Stone 1984, Prizzi's Honour 1985, The Jewel of the Nile 1985, Peggy Sue Got Married 1986, Julia and Julia 1988, Who Framed Roger Rabbit? (voice) 1988, Switching Channels 1988, The Accidental Tourist 1989, The War of the Roses 1990, Hard Boiled (producer) 1990, V. I. Warshawski 1991, House of Cards, Undercover Blues 1993, Serial Mom 1994, Naked in New York 1994, Moonlight and Valentino 1996, A Simple Wish, The Real Blonde, The Virgin Suicides 1999, Prince of Central Park 1999, Love and Action in Chicago 1999, Baby Geniuses 1999; producer Hard Boiled 1990; *TV Series:* The Doctors 1977, Style and Substance 1996. *Address:* c/o Chris Andrews, ICM, 8942 Wilshire Blvd, Beverly Hills, CA 90211, USA.

TURNER, Tina (Annie Mae Bullock); American singer and actress; b 26 Nov 1939, Brownsville, TN; m Ike Turner 1956 (divorced 1978); four s. *Career:* Singer with Ike Turner Kings of Rhythm, Ike and Tina Turner Revue; numerous concert tours of 1966, 1983–84, Japan and Africa 1971; Grammy Awards 1972, 1985 (three), 1986; Chevalier des Arts et des Lettres. *Recordings include:* River Deep, Mountain High 1966, Proud Mary 1970, Blues Roots 1972, Nutbush City Limits 1973, The Gospel According to Ike and Tina 1974; Solo albums: Let Me Touch Your Mind 1972, Tina Turns the Country On 1974, Acid Queen 1975, Rough 1978, Private Dancer 1984, Break Every Rule 1986, Foreign Affair 1989, The Best of Proud Mary 1991, Tina's Prayer 1992, 40 Rare Recordings 1992, The Collected Recordings: Sixties to Nineties (jtly) 1994, Wildest Dreams 1996; Solo singles: Let's Stay Together, Private Dancer, What's Love Got To Do With It, We Don't Need Another Hero, Simply the Best, Steamy Windows; *Films:* Gimme Shelter 1970, Soul to Soul 1971, Tommy 1975, Mad Max Beyond The Thunderdome 1985, What's Love Got to Do with It (vocals) 1993, Last Action Hero 1993. *Address:* c/o CAA, 9830 Wilshire Blvd, Beverly Hills, CA 90212, USA.

TURNER-WARWICK, Dame Margaret Elizabeth Harvey, DBE, MA, DM, PH D, FRCP(UK), FRACP, FRCP(E), F MED SCI; British medical practitioner and organization executive; b 19 Nov 1924; d of William Harvey Moore and Maud Baden-Powell; m Richard Trevor Turner-

Warwick 1950; two d. *Education:* St Paul's Girls School, Lady Margaret Hall (Oxford) and Oxford Univ Coll Hosp. *Career:* Consultant Physician Elizabeth Garrett Anderson Hosp 1961–67, London Chest Hosp 1967–72; Consultant Physician Brompton Hosp 1965–, Prof of Medicine Cardiothoracic Inst 1972–87, Dean 1984–87, now Emer Prof; Sr Lecturer Inst of Diseases of the Chest 1961–72; Lectures: Mark Daniels 1974, Phillip Ellman 1980, Tudor Edwards 1985, Harveian 1994, Royal Coll of Physicians; Chair Royal Devon and Exeter Health Care NHS Trust 1992–95, Lettsomian Medical Soc of London 1982; Pres British Thoracic Soc 1982–85, Royal Coll of Physicians 1989–92; Chair Cen Acad Council, British Postgrad Medical Fed 1982–85, Asthma Research Council, Conf of Colls and their Faculties (UK) 1990–92, UK Co-ordinating Cttee on Cancer Research 1991–97; mem Medical Research Council Systems Bd (DHSS nomination) 1982–85, Council British Lung Foundation 1984–90, Gen Council King's Fund 1991, Council British Heart Foundation 1994–; mem Council and Vice-Pres Action on Smoking and Health (ASH) 1990–; mem Senate and Academic Council Univ of London 1983–87, mem Scolarships Cttee and Cttee of Extra-Mural Studies 1984–87; mem Nuffield Biotechnics Council 1993–, Round Table on Sustainable Devt 1995–98; Fellow Faculty of Public Health Medicine 1990, Royal Coll of Gen Practitioners 1991, Univ Coll London 1991; Hon Fellow Girton Coll (Cambridge) 1993, Green Coll (Oxford) 1993, Lady Margaret Hall (Oxford) 1991, Imperial Coll (London) 1996; Hon FACP 1988, Hon Fellow Royal Coll of Physicians and Surgeons (Canada) 1990, Hon Fellow Royal Coll of Anaesthetists 1991, Hon Fellow Royal Coll of Medicine SA 1991, Hon mem Royal Coll of Pathologists 1992, Hon FRCS 1993, Hon Fellow Royal Coll Radiologists 1994; Hon Bencher Middle Temple 1990; Hon mem Asscn of Physicians of GB and Ireland 1991, S German and Australasian Thoratic Socs; mem Alpha Omega Alpha (USA) 1987, Acad of Malaysia 1991; Hon D SC (New York) 1985, (Exeter) 1990, (London) 1990, (Hull) 1991, (Sussex) 1992, (Oxford) 1992, (Cambridge) 1993, (Leicester) 1998; Tuke Silver Medal (Univ Coll Hosp, London); Osler Memorial Medal (Univ of Oxford) 1995. *Publications include:* Immunology of the Lung 1978, Occupational Lung Disease: Research Approaches and Methods (jtly) 1981; contribs to professional books and journals. *Leisure interests:* family, gardening, country life, watercolour painting, violin playing. *Address:* Pynes House, Thorverton, Exeter EX5 5LT, UK. *Telephone:* (1392) 861173; *Fax:* (1392) 860940.

TUROFF, Carole Ruth, BA, JD; American lawyer; b 14 June 1937, Cleveland, OH; d of Sam and Edan (née Siegel) Lecht; m Jack Turoff 1961; four d. *Education:* American Int Coll and Cleveland Marshall Law School. *Career:* Called to the Bar, OH 1970; pvt practice 1970–; Special Counsel to Attorney-Gen, OH 1971–84; Real Estate Broker 1976–; journalist Cleveland Press 1974–81; Partner Gill and Turoff; Del Israeli Political Affairs Comm; Founder Women in Divorce, The Carole Turoff Legal Clinic 1987–; mem Int Platform Asscn, American Trial Lawyers Asscn, Cleveland Bar Asscn, Nat Asscn for the Advancement of Colored People, Nat Women Lawyers. *Address:* 2569 Snowberry Lane, Pepper Pike, OH 44124, USA (Home).

TUSHINGHAM, Rita; British actress; b 14 March 1942, Liverpool; d of John and Enid Tushingham; m 1st Terence Bicknell 1962 (divorced 1976); m 2nd Ousama Rawi 1981 (divorced 1996); two d. *Education:* La Sagesse Convent (Liverpool) and Liverpool Playhouse. *Career:* Has appeared in numerous plays and films and on TV; BBC Personality of the Year (Variety Club of GB) 1988. *Plays include:* The Changeling 1960, The Kitchen 1961, A Midsummer Night's Dream 1962, Twelfth Night 1962, The Knack 1962, The Giveaway 1969, Lorna and Ted 1970, Mistress of Novices 1973, My Fat Friend 1981, Children, Children 1984; *Films include:* A Taste of Honey (Most Promising Newcomer Award, British Film Acad and Variety Club of GB, New York Critics' Award and Hollywood Foreign Press Asscn Award, USA, Cannes Film Festival Award, France) 1961, The Leather Boys 1962, A Place to Go 1963, Girl with Green Eyes (Variety Club of GB Award) 1963, The Knack (Silver Goddess Award, Mexican Asscn of Film Corresps) 1964, Dr Zhivago 1965, The Trap 1966, Smashing Time 1967, Diamonds For Breakfast 1967, The Guru 1968, The Bed-Sitting Room 1970, Straight on Till Morning 1972, Situation 1972, Instant Coffee 1973, Rachel's Man 1974, Pot Luck 1977, Mysteries 1978, Incredible Mrs Chadwick 1979, The Spaghetti House Siege 1982, Flying 1984, A Judgement in Stone 1986, The Housekeeper 1987,

Resurrected 1989, Dante and Beatrice in Liverpool 1989, Hard Days Hard Nights 1990, Paper Marriage 1991, Rapture of Deceit 1992, Desert Lunch 1993, An Awfully Big Adventure 1995, The Boy from Mercury 1996; *TV appearances include:* Red Riding Hood 1973, No Strings 1974, Don't Let Them Kill Me on Wednesday 1980, Confessions of Felix Krull 1980, Seeing Red 1983, Pippi Longstocking 1984, The White Whale – The Life of Ernest Hemingway 1987, Bread 1988, Sunday Pursuit, Gütt ein Journalist (film) 1991, Hamburg Poison (film) 1992, Family Secrets (film) 1995, I've Been Eddie Mostyn 1996; *Recording:* Smashing Time. *Leisure interests:* cooking, painting, gardening. *Address:* c/o Grizelda Burgess, Noel House, 2–4 Noel St, London W1V 3RB, UK.

TUTWILER, Margaret DeBardeleben, BA; American political campaigner and civil servant; b 28 Dec 1950, Birmingham, AL; d of Temple Wilson and Margaret (née DeBardeleben) Tutwiler. *Education:* Univ of Alabama and Finch Coll (NY). *Career:* Scheduler Surrogates for Pres Ford Cttee, Washington, DC 1975–76; Exec Dir Pres Ford Cttee for Alabama 1976; Public Affairs Rep for Alabama and Mississippi, Nat Asscn of Mfrs, Washington, DC 1977–78; Dir of Scheduling, Amb George Bush Presidential Campaign, Houston, TX and Alexandria, VA 1978–80, for Vice-Presidential Cand George Bush, Reagan–Bush Gen Election Campaign, Washington, DC 1980; Special Asst to Pres, Exec Asst to Chief of Staff, White House 1981–84; Dir of Public Liaison 50th American Presidential Inaugural Cttee (White House Rep) 1984–85; Deputy Asst for Political Affairs to Pres 1984–85; Asst Sec for Public Affairs and Public Liaison, Dept of the Treasury 1985–88; Deputy to Chair Bush–Quayle Campaign 1988; Sr Adviser Transition Team, Dept of State 1988–89, Consultant 1989, Asst Sec of State and Dept Spokesperson 1989–92; Partner Fitzwater and Tutwiler Inc 1993–; Wake Forest Univ Woman of the Year Award 1986; American Center for Int Leadership Marshall Award for Outstanding Leadership 1991. *Telephone:* (202) 647-5548; *Fax:* (202) 647-5939.

TWAIN, Shania; Canadian country music singer; b (Eileen Regina Edwards) 28 Aug 1965, Windsor, Toronto; d of Gerry and Sahrn Twain; m Robert John Lange. *Career:* Fmr cabaret singer; recipient of numerous awards including Favorite New Country Artist, American Music Award 1995, Female Vocalist Award, Canadian Country Music Awards 1995, Female Artist of the Year, Country Music TV/Europe 1996. *Recordings include:* singles: From This Moment On, That Don't Impress Me Much, Man! I Feel Like a Woman, Don't Be Stupid (You Know I Love You); Albums: Shania Twain 1993, The Woman in Me 1995 (Grammy Award for Best Country Album 1996), Come on Over 1998. *Address:* Mercury Nashville, 54 Music Square E, Nashville, TN 37203, USA.

TWIGGY, (see Lawson, Lesley).

TYACKE, Sarah Jacqueline, BA, CB, FSA; British archivist; b 29 Sept 1945; d of the late Colin Walton Jeacock and Elsie Marguerite Stanton; m Nicholas Tyacke 1971; one d. *Education:* Chelmsford Co High School and Bedford Coll (London). *Career:* Asst Keeper Map Room, British Museum 1968; Deputy Map Librarian British Library 1973–85, responsible for establishing British Library preservation under Cabinet Office Efficiency Unit 1985–86, Dir of Special Collections 1986–91; Chief Exec and Keeper of Public Records, Public Record Office 1992–; Chair European Co-ordinating Bd, Int Council on Archives 1992–96; Vice-Pres Inst of Contemporary Arts 1996–2000, Royal Historical Soc 2000–; Pres Haklyt Soc 1997–; Dir Imago Mundi 1987–; Trustee Mappa Mundi 1989–; Fellow Royal Holloway (London Univ) 1999; Hon D PHIL (Guildhall) 1996. *Publications:* Copernicus and the New Astronomy (jtly) 1973, My Head is a Map: Essay and Memoirs in Honour of R. V. Tooley (jt-ed) 1973, London Map-Sellers 1660–1720 1978, Christopher Saxton and Tudor Map-making (jtly) 1980, English Map-Making 1500–1650: Historical Essays (ed) 1983, Catalogue of Maps, Charts and Plans in the Pepys Library, Magdalene College, Cambridge 1989; contribs to professional, library and cartographic journals. *Leisure interests:* travel, the sea, hill-walking, painting. *Address:* Public Record Office, Ruskin Ave, Kew, Richmond, Surrey TW9 4DU, UK. *Telephone:* (20) 8392-5220; *Fax:* (20) 8392-5221; *E-mail:* sarah .tyacke@pro.gov.uk; *Internet:* www.pro.gov.uk.

TYLER, Anne, BA; American writer; b 25 Oct 1941, Minneapolis; d of Lloyd Parry and Phyllis (née Mahon) Tyler; m Taghi M. Modarressi 1963 (died 1997); two c. *Education:* Duke and Columbia Univs. *Career:* Has written novels, and short stories for magazines. *Publications:* If Morning Ever Comes 1964, The Tin Can Tree 1965, A Slipping-Down Life 1970, The Clock Winder 1972, Celestian Navigation 1974, Searching for Caleb 1976, Earthly Possessions 1977, Morgan's Passing 1980, Dinner at the Homesick Restaurant 1982, The Accidental Tourist 1985, Breathing Lessons (Pulitzer Prize for Fiction 1989) 1988, Saint Maybe 1991, Ladder of Years 1995, A Patchwork Planet 1998, Back When We Were Grown-ups 2001. *Address:* 222 Tunbridge Rd, Baltimore, MD 21212, USA.

TYLER, Liv; American actress and film maker; b 7 Jan 1977, Portland, ME; d of Steve Tyler and Bebe Buell. *Career:* Fmrly model Eileen Ford Agency. *Film appearances include:* Silent Fall, Empire Records, Heavy, Stealing Beauty, That Thing You Do!, Inventing the Abbotts, Plunkett and Macleane 1999, Armageddon 1998, Cookie's Fortune 1999, Onegin 1999, The Little Black Book 1999, Dr T and the Women 2000. *Address:* c/o CAA, 9830 Wilshire Blvd, Beverly Hills, CA 90212, USA.

TYNG, Anne Griswold, BA, M ARCH, PH D; American architect; b 14 July 1920, Kuling, Kiangsi, People's Repub of China; d of Walworth and Ethel (née Arens) Tyng; one d. *Education:* Radcliffe Coll and Harvard Univ. *Career:* Assoc Stonorov and Kahn 1945–47, Louis I. Kahn 1947–73; pvt practice 1973–; Adjunct Assoc Prof of Architecture, Grad School of Fine Arts, Univ of Pennsylvania 1968–; Assoc Consultant Architect Philadelphia Planning Comm, Philadelphia Redevt Authority 1952–54; Visiting Critic of Architecture Pratt Inst 1969, Visiting Prof 1979–81; Visiting Critic Carnegie Mellon Univ 1970, Drexel Univ 1972–73, Cooper Union 1974–75, Univ of Texas at Austin 1976; Lecturer Architectural Inst, London, Xian Univ, People's Repub of China, Univs of Bath (UK), Hong Kong and Mexico, Baltic Summer School Parnu, Estonia 1993; works include Probability Pyramid at the Smithsonian Museum of American History 1984, Louis I. Kahn: In the Realm of Architecture (travelling exhibition) 1990–94; mem Nat Acad of Design, Nat Asscn of Architectural Historians; Fellow AIA; numerous articles in professional journals. *Address:* University of Pennsylvania, Dept of Architecture, Graduate School of Fine Arts, Philadelphia, PA 19107, USA (Office); 2511 Waverly St, Philadephia, PA 19146, USA (Home).

TYRA; American fashion model; b (Tyra Banks) 4 Dec 1973; d of Carolyn London-Johnson. *Education:* Immaculate Heart High School. *Career:* Has modelled since 1991 for Karl Lagerfeld, Yves St Laurent, Oscar De La Renta, Chanel, etc; featured on covers of German Harper's Bazaar, German Cosmopolitan, Spanish Vogue, Spanish Elle, Amica, Scene, Arena. *Film appearances include:* Higher Learning, Love Changes; *TV appearances include:* Fresh Prince of Bel Aire, NY Undercover; *Video appearances include:* Too Funky (George Michael), Black or White (Michael Jackson), Love Thing (Tina Turner). *Address:* c/o IMG Models, 13–16 Jacob's Well Mews, George St, London W1H 5PD, UK. *Telephone:* (20) 7486-8011; *Fax:* (20) 7487-3116.

TYSON, Cicely; American actress; d of William and Theodesia Tyson; m Miles Davis 1981 (divorced). *Education:* Univ of New York. *Career:* Co-Founder Dance Theatre of Harlem; mem Bd of Dirs Urban Gateways; Trustee Human Family Inst, American Film Inst; Dr hc (Atlanta, Loyola and Lincoln); awards include Vernon Price Award 1962, Emmy Award for Best Actress 1973, Capitol Press Award. *Films include:* Twelve Angry Men 1957, A Man Called Adam 1966, The Heart is a Lonely Hunter 1968, Sounder (Best Actress, Atlanta Film Festival) 1972, The Blue Bird 1976, The Concorde—Airport '79 1979, Bustin' Loose 1981, Fried Green Tomatoes at the Whistle Stop Café 1992, The Grass Harp; *TV includes:* The Autobiography of Miss Jane Pitman 1973, Roots (series) 1977, A Woman Called Moses 1978, The Marva Collins Story 1981, Heat Wave, The Women of Brewster Place 1989, Oldest Living Confederate Widow Tells All (Emmy Award 1994), A Century of Women 1994; *Plays include:* The Blacks 1961–63, Moon on a Rainbow Shawl 1962–63, Tiger, Tiger, Burning Bright, The Corn is Green. *Address:* c/o CAA, 9830 Wilshire Blvd, Beverly Hills, CA 90212, USA.

TYSON, Laura D'Andrea, PH D; American economist; b 28 June 1947, New Jersey; m Erik Tarloff; one s. *Education:* Smith Coll (Northampton, MA) and MIT. *Career:* Asst Prof Princeton Univ 1974–77; Nat Fellows Program Fellowship, Hoover Inst 1978–79; Visiting Prof Harvard Business School 1989–90; Prof Dept of Econs and Business Admin, Dir Inst of Int Studies 1978–98, Univ of California at Berkeley, Bank-America, Dean, Haas School of Business 1998–; Chair Council of Econ Advisers to Pres Clinton 1993–95, Nat Econ Adviser to Pres US Nat Econ Council 1995–97; Visiting Scholar Inst of Int Econs; Consultant IBRD 1980–86, Pres's Comm on Industrial Competitiveness 1983–84, Hambrecht & Quist 1984–86, PlanEcon 1984–86, W Govs' Asscn 1986, Council on Competitiveness 1986–89, Electronics Industry Asscn 1989, Motorola 1989–90; mem Bd of Economists Los Angeles Times, Council on Foreign Relations; numerous other professional and public appts. *Publications:* The Yugoslav Economic System and its Performance in the 1970s 1980, Economic Adjustment in Eastern Europe 1984, Who's Bashing Whom? Trade Conflict in High Technology Industries 1992; articles in professional journals. *Address:* Haas School of Business, S-545 Haas, Berkeley, CA 94720, USA.

TYZACK, Margaret Maud, OBE; British actress; b 9 Sept 1931; d of Thomas Edward Tyzack and Doris Moseley; m Alan Stephenson 1958; one s. *Education:* St Angela's Ursuline Convent and Royal Acad of Dramatic Art (London). *Career:* Numerous plays with RSC; has performed on stage in UK, USA and Canada; Royal Acad of Dramatic Art Gilbert Prize for Comedy. *Plays include:* The Lower Depths 1962, Macbeth 1962, The Ginger Man 1964, The Cherry Orchard 1969, Find Your Way Home 1970, Vivat! Vivat Regina! 1971, Titus Andronicus 1972, Julius Caesar 1972, 1973, Coriolanus 1972, 1973, Summerfolk (London and New York) 1974–75, Richard III, All's Well That Ends Well, Ghosts 1977, People Are Living There 1979, Who's Afraid of Virginia Woolf? (SWET—Soc of West End Theatres Best Actress in a Revival Award) 1981, An Inspector Calls 1983, Tom and Viv (London) 1984, (New York) 1985, Mornings at Seven 1984, Night Must Fall 1986, Lettice and Lovage (London, Variety Club of GB Best Stage Actress Award) 1987, (New York, Tony Award) 1990, The Importance of Being Earnest 1993, An Inspector Calls 1994, Indian Ink 1995, Talking Heads 1996, The Family Reunion 1999; *Films:* Ring of Spies, 2001: A Space Odyssey, The Whisperers, A Clockwork Orange, The Legacy, The King's Whore, Thacker 1992, The Chronicles of the Young Indiana Jones; *TV appearances include:* The Forsyte Saga, The First Churchills (BAFTA Actress of the Year Award) 1969, Cousin Bette 1970–71, I, Claudius 1976, Quatermass 1979, A Winter's Tale, Soldiering On. *Address:* c/o Representation Joyce Edwards, 275 Kennington Rd, London SE11 6BY, UK. *Telephone:* (20) 7735-5736; *Fax:* (20) 7820-1845.

U

UBAIDULLAYEVA, Rano, D ECON; Uzbekistan politician and economist; b 4 Nov 1936, Tashkent; d of Ahat Tashpulatov and Ibahon Tashpulatova; m A. M. Ubaidullayev 1959; two s. *Education:* Tashkent Financial and Econ Inst. *Career:* Mem staff Inst of Econs, Acad of Science of Uzbekistan 1958–; mem Congress of People's Deputies (Parl, CPSU) elected from Soviet Women's Cttee 1989–91; Deputy Minister of Lab, Repub of Uzbekistan 1993; awarded Badge of Honour 1974. *Publications:* Women's Labour in Agriculture 1969, Effectivity of Labour Resources Use 1979, The Development of Population and Problems with Working Resources in Republics of Central Asia 1986, Uzbekistan: Structural Re-organization in Economy and Employment of Women 1996. *Leisure interests:* books, friends, housekeeping. *Address:* Institute of Economics, Academy of Sciences of Uzbekistan, 700060 Tashkent, ul Borovskogo 5, Uzbekistan (Office); Ministry of Labour, 700011 Tashkent, ul Abav 6, Uzbekistan (Office); 700002 Tashkent, ul X Usmanhbolaev 24, Uzbekistan (Home). *Telephone:* (3712) 44-24-28 (Home).

UCHEAGWU, Grace Ukamaka; Nigerian nurse and nursing school principal; b 9 Jan 1948, Onitsha; d of S. N. and C. N. Ucheagwu. *Education:* Holy Child Coll (Lagos), Lagos Univ Teaching Hosp, Inst of Man and Tech (Enugu) and Enugu State Univ of Science and Tech. *Career:* Nursing at Edgware Gen Hosp and Hammersmith Hosp (London) and Mill Road Maternity Hosp (Liverpool, UK); apptd Asst Head Nurse Tutor and Prin Post Basic School of Orthopaedic Nursing, Enugu 1986. *Leisure interests:* reading, cooking, dancing, sewing, religion. *Address:* School of Orthopaedic Nursing, National Orthopaedic Hospital, PMB 01294, Enugu, Anambra State, Nigeria. *Telephone:* (42) 339885.

UCHIDA, Irene Ayako, OC, PH D; Canadian professor emeritus of paediatrics; b 8 April 1917, Vancouver, BC; d of Sentaro and Shizuko Uchida. *Education:* Univ of Toronto. *Career:* Reseach Assoc Hosp for Sick Children, Toronto 1951–59; Dir Dept of Medical Genetics, Children's Hosp of Winnipeg 1960–69; Asst Prof of Paediatrics Univ of Manitoba 1962, Assoc Prof 1967–69; Prof of Paediatrics and Pathology, Regional Cytogenetics Lab, McMaster Univ 1969–91, Emer Prof Dept of Paediatrics 1985–; Visiting Scientist Univ of London and Harwell Radiobiological Research Unit 1969; Visiting Prof Univ of Alabama, USA 1968, Univ of Western Ontario 1973; mem Science Council of Canada (Ottawa) 1970–73; Medical Research Council of Canada Grants Cttee 1970–73; Consultant Int Program in Radiation Genetics, Paris 1973; mem Task Force on Cytogenetics for Advisory Cttee on Genetic Services 1977; mem Canadian Council of Medical Geneticists 1978–, Cytogenetics Cttee 1978, Accreditation Cttee 1979, Bd mem 1980–84, Chair Cttee on Quality Control of Labs 1980–86, Emeritus Fellow 1991–; Chair Ontario Medical Asscn Laboratory Proficiency Testing Program 1978–88; mem Advisory Cttee on Genetic Services to Ontario Ministry of Health 1979–86; mem Cttee US Nat Inst of Child Health and Human Devt 1980–84; mem Int Advisory Council Eighth Int Congress of Human Genetics, Washington, DC 1989–91; published scientific papers in journals and books; Hon D SC (Western Ontario) 1996; Woman of the Century 1867–1967, Nat Council of Jewish Women 1967; one of 25 Outstanding Women Ontario Govt 1975; one of 1000 Canadian Women of Note 1867–1967, Media Club of Canada and Women's Press Club of Toronto 1983. *Leisure interests:* music, photography. *Address:* McMaster University, 1200 Main St W, Hamilton, ON L8N 3Z5, Canada (Office); 20 N Shore Blvd W, Apt 120, Burlington, ON L7T 1A1 Canada (Home). *Telephone:* (416) 521-2100 (Office); *Fax:* (416) 521-1703 (Office).

UCHIDA, Mitsuko, OBE; Japanese pianist; b 20 Dec 1948, Tokyo; d of Fujio and Yasuko Uchida. *Education:* Vienna Acad of Music and under Richard Hauser, Stefan Askenase and Wilhelm Kempff. *Career:* Recitals and concerto performances with all major London orchestras, Chicago Symphony, Boston Symphony and Cleveland Orchestras (USA), Berlin Philharmonic, etc; played and directed the cycle of 21 Mozart piano concertos with the English Chamber Orchestra, London 1985–86; performances include Wigmore Hall, London 1982, Alice Tullt Hall, New York (USA) 1987, Auditorium Theater, Chicago 1987, Metropolitan Museum of Art, Lincoln Center, New York 1989, Severance Hall, Cleveland, OH 1990, Kennedy Center Concert Hall, Washington, DC 1991; renowned for performing works of Mozart; repertoire also includes Schönberg, Schubert, Chopin and Debussy; gave US premiere of piano concerto Antiphonies by Harrison Birtwistle 1996; Co-Dir Marlboro Music Festival; First Prize Beethoven Competition, Vienna 1969; Second Prize Chopin Competition, Warsaw 1970; Second Prize Leeds Int Piano Competition 1975. *Recordings include:* Mozart Complete Piano Sonatas (Gramophone Award, Mumm Champagne Classical Music Award) and 21 Piano Concertos (Gramophone Instrumental Award 1989), Chopin Piano Sonatas, Debussy Etudes for Piano. *Leisure interest:* cycling (preferably on the flat). *Address:* c/o Van Walsum Management Ltd, 4 Addison Bridge Place, London W14 8XP, UK. *Telephone:* (20) 7371-4343; *Fax:* (20) 7371-4344; *E-mail:* c/o edesmond@vanwalsum.co.uk; *Internet:* www.vanwalsum.co.uk.

UEHLING, Barbara S., PH D; American educationalist; b 12 June 1932, Wichita, KA; d of Roy W. and Mary Elizabeth (née Hilt) Staner; m 2nd Stanley R. Johnson 1981; two s. *Education:* Wichita State Univ and Northwestern Univ. *Career:* Mem Faculty of Psychology Oglethorpe Univ, Atlanta 1959–64, Emory Univ, Atlanta, GA 1964–70; Adjunct Prof Univ of Rhode Island, Kingston 1970–71, Academic Dean Roger Williams Coll, Univ of Rhode Island, Bristol 1972–74; Dean of Arts and Science Illinois State Univ 1974–76; Provost Univ of Oklahoma 1976–78; Chancellor Univ of Missouri 1978–86, Univ of California at Santa Barbara 1987–94; apptd Exec Dir Business Higher Educ Forum 1994; Sr Visiting Fellow American Council on Educ 1986–87; mem Comm on Military–Higher Educ Relations, American Council on Higher Educ 1978–86; mem Bd Dirs Meredith Corpn 1980–, Comm on Postsecondary Educ 1990–; mem Western Asscn of Schools and Colls, Int Comm for Study of Educational Exchange; Hon LHD (Drury Coll) 1978, Hon LL D (Ohio) 1980. *Publications:* Women in Academe: steps to greater equality 1979; numerous articles on higher educ and psychology. *Leisure interests:* music, walking, theatre. *Address:* Business Higher Education Forum, 1 Dupont Circle, Suite 800, Washington, DC 20036, USA.

UGGLAS, Baroness Margaretha af, BA; Swedish politician; b 5 Jan 1939. *Education:* Harvard-Radcliffe Business Admin Program (USA) and Stockholm School of Econs. *Career:* Leader Writer Svenska Dagbladet (daily newspaper) 1968–74; mem Stockholm Co Council; mem Riksdag (Parl, Moderata Samlingspartiet—Moderate Party) 1974, Moderate Party Spokesperson on Foreign Affairs, mem Parl Standing Cttee on Foreign Affairs and Advisory Council on Foreign Affairs; Minister for Foreign Affairs 1991–94; Vice-Pres European People's Party (EPP) 1996; Observer EP; Substitute mem Council of Europe, mem Cttee on Econ Affaris and Devt; Publr Svensk Tidskrift (magazine); Chair Swedish Save the Children Fed, Stockholm 1970–76, Swedish Section European Union of Women 1981–; Robert Schuman Medal 1995. *Leisure interests:* art, walking in woods, countryside and mountains, sailing. *Address:* c/o Moderata Samlingspartiet, POB 1243, 111 82 Stockholm, Sweden.

UHLEN, Gisela; Swiss actress and writer; b 16 May 1919; d of August Uhlen; m 6th Beat Hodel 1975; two d. *Education:* Studied acting and ballet. *Career:* Has taken part in 52 films, 86 TV programmes and 210 theatre productions; formed own touring theatre Wanderbühne Gisela Uhlen 1982; Filmband in Gold (for Die Ehe der Maria Braun) 1979. *Publications:* Mein Glashaus (autobiog) 1979, Meine Droge heißt Leben 1991. *Address:* c/o Promenadengasse 8, 8001 Zurich, Switzerland. *Telephone:* (1) 2512082.

UHRMAN, Celia, PH D; American artist and poet; b 14 May 1927, New London, CT; d of the late David Aaron and Pauline (née Schwartz) Uhrman. *Education:* Brooklyn Coll (NY), Univ of Gdańsk (Poland), City Univ of New York, Brooklyn Museum Art School and Columbia Univ (New York). *Career:* Teacher, New York 1948–82; Partner Uhrman Studio 1973–83; solo exhibitions include Leffert Jr High School (Brooklyn) 1958, Connecticut Chamber of Commerce (New London) 1962, Flatbush Chamber of Commerce (New York) 1963; group exhibitions include Smithsonian Inst (Washington, DC) 1958, Springfield Museum of Fine Arts (MA) 1959, Brooklyn Museum 1959, Old Mystic Art Center (CT) 1959, Carnegie Endowment Int Center (New York) 1959, Lyman Allyn Museum (New London, CT) 1960, Palacio de la Virrelna (Barcelona, Spain) 1961, Soc of 4 Arts (Palm Beach, FL) 1964, Premier Salon Int (Charleroi, Belgium) 1968, Int Arts Guild Shows (Monte Carlo) 1969–88, Dibiux-Joan Miró Premi Int (Barcelona) 1970, Ovar Museum (Portugal) 1974; works in perm collections of Brooklyn Coll and Brooklyn Evangelical Church; Founding Fellow World Literary Acad and Int Acad of Poets 1985; Hon Life mem World Poetry Day Comm Inc, Nat Poetry Day Comm 1977–; recipient George Washington Medal of Honor 1964; Diplôme d'Honneur, Palme d'Or des Beaux Arts Exhibition (Monaco) 1969, 1972; Order of Gandhi Award of Honour, Kt of Grand Cross 1972; Gold Laurel Award, Exposition Int d'Art Contemporain (Paris) 1974. *Publications:* Poetic Ponderances 1969, A Pause for Poetry 1970, Poetic Love Fancies 1970, A Pause for Poetry for Children 1973, The Chimps are Coming 1975, Love Fancies 1987. *Leisure interests:* dancing, walking, swimming, theatre. *Address:* 1655 Flatbush Ave, Apt and Studio C-106, Brooklyn, NY 11210, USA. *Telephone:* (718) 338-0257.

UKEJE, Rose Nonyem, LL B, BL; Nigerian high court judge; b 5 Jan 1943; d of John and Jane Ekezie; m Elendu Ukeje; two s two d. *Education:* Univ of Nigeria (Nsukka) and Nigeria Law School (Lagos). *Career:* Asst Legal Draftsman Ministry of Legal Affairs, Lusaka, Zambia 1971–73; Deputy Legal Draftsman Fed Ministry of Justice, Lagos 1973–86; Judge Fed High Court of Nigeria 1986–2001, Chief Judge 2001–; mem UN Cttee on the Elimination of Discrimination Against Women 1986–90, Recorder 1988–90; Consultant Awareness Seminar at UN Convention on the Elimination of All Forms of Discrimination Against Women, Kiev, Ukraine 1989; mem Nigerian Del UN World Conf on Women, Nairobi, Kenya 1985; mem Nigerian Del Int Judicial Colloquium, Abuja 1991; mem numerous Commonwealth Confs on law and fugitives, victims of crime, white-collar crime and others; Vice-Pres Nat Assn of Women Judges, Int Dir for Nigeria Int Assn of Women Judges 1991–; has published several papers in field of law; Dip Legis Drafting; named Alumna of High Achievement, Univ of Nigeria, Nsukka 1989; Distinguished Daughter of the State Award 1989; Nigerian Women's Award 1998. *Leisure interests:* comedy films, reading, global status of women. *Address:* Federal High Court, 24 Queen's Drive, Ikoyi, PMB 40012, Falomo, Lagos, Nigeria; 16 Club Rd, Ikeyin, Lagos, Nigeria (Home). *Telephone:* (1) 2671268 (Office); (1) 2670477 (Home); *Fax:* (1) 2671261; *E-mail:* judgeukeje@hotmail.com.

ULITSKAYA, Ludmila Yevgenyevna; Russian writer; b 21 Feb 1943, Davlekanovo, Bashkiria; m Krasulin Andrei Nikolayevich; two s. *Education:* Moscow State Univ. *Career:* Head of Literary Div, Jewish Chamber Theatre 1979–89; books, stories and plays translated into 17 languages; Medici Prize for Best Translated Novel 1996; Giuseppe Acerbi Prize; Moscow Pen Club Medal. *Publications:* Novels and short stories including One Hundred Buttons (for children) 1983, Sonechka 1992, Daughter of Bukhara 1993, Medea and Her Children 1996, Merry Funerals 1998, It is Easy for Me 1999, Poor Relatives 1999, Kukotsky Casus 2000; Plays: Carmen, Jose and Death, My Grandchild Benjamin; Film scripts: Sisters Liberty, A Woman for Everybody, It is

Easy to Die 1999. *Address:* EKSMO Publishers, Narodnogo Opolcheniya str 38, 123298 Moscow, Russian Federation. *Telephone:* (095) 950-48-10.

ULLENIUS, Christina C. I., PH D; Swedish scientist; b 10 March 1943, Karlstad; d of Axel and Ingrid Ullenius; m Olof Wennerström 1965; two s. *Education:* Royal Inst of Tech (Stockholm), Chalmers Univ of Tech (Göteborg) and Univ of Oregon (USA). *Career:* Lecturer Chalmers Univ of Tech 1975–81, Head of Dept 1981–87, Vice-Dean Technical Faculty 1987–89, Pro-Vice-Chancellor and Assoc Prof 1989–95; Pres Univ of Karlstad 1995–; Visiting Scientist fmr Soviet Acad of Sciences (Moscow) 1969, Princeton Univ (USA) 1981–82; scientific publs on organometallic chemistry in int journals. *Leisure interests:* theatre, classical music, outdoor activities, sailing. *Address:* University of Karlstad, 651 88 Karlstad, Sweden (Office); Kungsgt 4, 652 24 Karlstad, Sweden (Home). *Telephone:* (54) 7001010 (Office); *Fax:* (54) 7001466 (Office); *E-mail:* christina.ullenius@kau.se; *Internet:* www.kau .se.

ULLMAN, Tracey; British actress, comedienne and singer; b 30 Dec 1959, Slough; d of the late Anthony John Ullman and of Dorin Cleaver; m Allan McKeown 1984; one s one d. *Education:* Italia Conti Stage School (London). *Career:* Numerous appearances on stage and TV in UK and USA, where she currently has her own TV show; British Acad Award for Best Light Entertainment Performance 1983; Golden Globe Award for Best Performer in Comedy, Musical or Variety Series 1988; Rudolph Valentino Cinema Lifetime Achievement Award 1992. *Stage appearances include:* Gigi, Elvis, Grease, Four in a Million (London Theatre Critics' Award 1981), The Taming of the Shrew, The Big Love; *Films include:* The Rocky Horror Picture Show, Give My Regards to Broad Street, Plenty 1985, Jumpin' Jack Flash 1986, I Love You To Death 1990, Robin Hood: Men in Tights 1993, Household Saints, Bullets over Broadway 1995, Prêt-à-Porter 1995, Everybody Says I Love You 1996, Small Town Crooks 2000; *TV appearances include:* Three of a Kind, A Kick Up the Eighties, Girls on Top, The Tracey Ullman Show (USA, series, five Emmy nominations 1987) 1987–90, The Best of the Tracey Ullman Show 1990; Tracey Takes On 1996; *Recordings:* You Broke My Heart in Seventeen Places (Gold Album), They Don't Know (also video). *Leisure interests:* hiking, riding. *Address:* c/o ICM, Oxford House, 76 Oxford St, London W1N 0AX, UK; IFA Talent Agency, 8730 W Sunset Blvd, #490, Los Angeles, CA 90069, USA. *Telephone:* (20) 7636-6565 (London); *Fax:* (20) 7323-0101 (London).

ULLMANN, Agnès, DR RER NAT; French (b Romanian) biologist; b 14 April 1927, Satu Mare, Romania; d of Eugène and Irène (née Kolb) Ullmann; m Thomas Erdos 1956. *Education:* School in Satu Mare and Arad, Univs of Cluj (Romania) and Budapest. *Career:* Lecturer, then Sr Lecturer Univ of Budapest 1949–60; Rockefeller Fellow Inst Pasteur, Paris 1960–61, Head of Lab, Head of Biochemistry of Cellular Regulations Unit 1978–, Prof 1983–; Researcher CNRS 1961, Master of Research 1968, Dir of Research 1986–; Assoc Prof Univ of Paris VII 1978; has written 120 scientific articles and co-edited three books; Chevalier de l'Ordre Nat du Mérite. *Leisure interests:* skiing, sailing, music. *Address:* Institut Pasteur, 28 rue du Docteur Roux, 75015 Paris, France (Office); 3 rue Paul Dupuy, 75016 Paris, France (Home). *Telephone:* (1) 45-68-83-85 (Office); *Fax:* (1) 40-61-30-19 (Office).

ULLMANN, Liv Johanne; Norwegian actress; b 16 Dec 1938, Tokyo, Japan; d of the late Viggo and of Janna (née Lund) Ullmann; m 1st Gappe Stang 1960 (divorced 1965); one d; m 2nd Donald Saunders 1985. *Career:* Worked in repertory co, Stavanger 1956–59; has appeared at Nat Theatre and Norwegian State Theatre, Oslo; debut on Broadway in The Doll's House 1975; work for UNICEF as Goodwill Amb 1980–; Vice-Chair Int Rescue Cttee; 12 hon doctorates; Best Actress of the Year, Nat Soc of Critics in America 1969, 1970, 1974; New York Film Critics' Award 1973, 1974; Hollywood Foreign Press Assn's Golden Globe 1973; Best Actress of the Year, Swedish TV 1973, 1974; Donatello Award (Italy) 1975; Bambi Award (Germany) 1975; Peer Gynt Award (Norway); Eleanor Roosevelt Award 1982; Roosevelt Freedom Medal 1984; Dag Hammarskjöld Award 1986; Rudolf Valentino Cinema Lifetime Achievement Award 1992; Commdr of Olav 1994. *Films include:* Pan 1965, Persona 1966, The Hour of the Wolf 1968, Shame 1968, The Passion of Anna 1969, The Night Visitor 1971, The Emigrants 1972, Cries and Whispers 1972, Pope Joan 1972, Lost

Horizon 1973, 40 Carats 1973, The New Land 1973, Zandy's Bride 1973, Scenes from a Marriage 1974, The Abdication 1974, Face to Face (Los Angeles Film Critics' Award 1976, New York Film Critics' Award 1977, Nat Bd of Review of Motion Pictures Award 1977) 1975, The Serpent's Egg 1978, Sonate d'automne 1978, Richard's Things 1980, The Wild Duck 1983, Love Streams 1983, Baby Boy 1984, Let's Hope It's a Girl 1985, Dangerous Moves 1985, Gaby Brimmer 1986, Moscow Adieu 1986, Time of Indifference 1987, La Amiga 1987, The Ox, The Long Shadow, Sophie (dir) 1993, Kristin Lavrandsdatter (also wrote screenplay), Faithless (dir) 2000; *Plays include:* Brand 1973, The Doll's House 1975, Anna Christie 1977, I Remember Mama 1979, Ghosts 1982, Old Times 1985, The Six Faces of Women (TV), Mother Courage; *Publication:* Changing (autobiog) 1976, Choices (autobiog) 1984. *Leisure interest:* reading. *Address:* c/o Robert Lantz, 888 Seventh Ave, New York, NY 10106, USA; c/o London Management, 235 Regent St, London W1, UK. *Fax:* (617) 267-9632 (New York).

ULMANN, Martine Régine, M ECON SC; French economist and civil servant; b 28 Nov 1948, Paris; d of Albert and Claudine (née Biger) Teperman; m Fabrice Ulmann 1971; one d one s one step-d. *Education:* Lycée Camille Sée (Paris) and Inst Britannique de Paris. *Career:* Economist at Radiotechnique Compélec (RTC) 1970–72; Researcher Secr-Gen of the Merchant Navy 1972–79, Head of Office on Budget, Accounting and Finances 1980–82; Sub-Dir of Gen Admin, Ministry of the Sea 1982–84, Tech Adviser in Charge of the Budget in the Minister's Cabinet 1981–84; Public Auditor Cour des Comptes (admin tribunal) 1984; External Auditor to UN 1986–88; Deputy Dir of Cabinet Minister of Overseas Depts and Territories and Govt Spokesperson 1988–90; Dir of Overseas Political, Admin and Financial Affairs at Ministry of Overseas Depts and Territories 1990–93; Govt Commr at Société néo-calédonienne d'énergie (Enercal) 1988–93; Advisor to CGEA 1993–96, Rep to CGE 1996–97; Advisor to Minister of Agric and Fisheries 1997; Dir Intervention and Regularisation Body for Sugar Markets (FIRS) 1999–; Magistrate Cour des Comptes; Chevalier du Mérite Maritime. *Address:* Firs, 120 blvd de Courcelles, 75017 Paris, France (Office); Direction des Affaires Politiques, Administratives et Financières de l'Outre-Mer, 27 rue Oudinot, 75700 Paris, France (Office).

UMBRICO, Judy Loman; Canadian harpist; b 3 Nov 1936, Goshen, IN, USA; d of Herschel and Sabra (née Waltz) Leatherman; m Joseph Umbrico 1956; three d one s. *Education:* Inst of Music. *Career:* Harpist Toronto Symphony Orchestra; Adjunct Prof Univ of Toronto; Asst Prof Harp McGill Univ; Instructor Royal Conservatory of Music, Fenelon Falls Harp School; tours in Europe, USA and Canada; numerous recordings; Grand Prix du Disque 1980. *Address:* 38 Burnside Drive, Toronto, ON M6G 2M8, Canada.

UMLAUFOVÁ, Miloslava, M SC, PH D; Czech academic and entrepreneur; b 5 April 1939, Planá; d of František and Vlasta Čížek; m Karel Umlauf 1963; one s. *Education:* Czech Technical Univ (Prague). *Career:* Teacher of Org and Man; Researcher in Man and Org, Strategic Man and Personnel Man 1990–94; Vice-Dean Civil Eng Faculty, Czech Tech Univ; Founder, Chair and Sr Consultant Triton Man Consultancy 1990–; Founder and Pres Czech Women's Business and Man Asscn 1990–; Czech Repub Successful Man Award 1994; Gold Award, Czech Woman Business and Professional Asscn 1995; Franz Kafka Award 1998. *Publications:* Critical Approach to Organization 1990, Management in Devt 1990, Organization Behaviour 1990, Through Organizational Thinking Towards Business Success 1991, Company Culture 1993, Crisis Management in Czech Republic 1995; numerous articles on economics and management in journals. *Leisure interests:* skiing, tourism, cars. *Address:* Naokraji 6, 162 00 Prague 6, Czech Republic. *Telephone:* (2) 35362104; *Fax:* (2) 20513400; *E-mail:* mila@umlaufova .cz.

UNDERHILL, Nancy Dudley Hoffman, PH D; Australian (b American) art historian; b 1 July 1938, New York; d of K. L. Hoffman; m Peter Underhill 1962; two s. *Education:* Bryn Mawr Coll (PA, USA), Courtauld Inst (London) and Univ of Melbourne. *Career:* Tutor Dept of History Univ of Queensland 1966–70, Lecturer Dept of Fine Arts 1971–74, Sr Lecturer 1975–78, Head Dept of Fine Arts 1978–94, Dir Univ Art Museum 1978–95; Chair Cultural Heritage Comm 1993–2000 (Vice-Chair Nat Cultural Heritage (moveable) Cttee

1995–); mem Visual Arts Bd of Australia 1976–80; mem Bd of Dirs Australian Gallery of Dirs 1977, Exec 1978–79, Vice-Chair 1979; Pres The Art Asscn of Australia 1980–82; mem Editorial Bd Australian and Int Art Monthly 1987–. *Publications:* Guide to Temporary Exhibition Spaces in Selected Australian Art Museums 1979, Eureka 1982, Quarante ans d'art Australien 1983, Sydney Ure Smith 1991, Making Australian Art 1911–49 1991, John Reed's Letters 2001. *Leisure interests:* music, gardening. *Address:* University of Queensland, Dept of Art History, Qld 4072, Australia. *Telephone:* (7) 3365-2211; *E-mail:* n .underhill@mailbox.uq.edu.au.

UNRUH, Trude; German politician; b 7 March 1925; m Helmut Unruh 1944 (died 1993); two s. *Career:* Fmrly worked in business as Man and Chief Sec; Founder, Chair Graue Panther (die Grauen, Grey Panther, pensioners' rights party) 1975–; Founder Graue Panther magazine 1983; Founder Graue Panther Bundesakademie für Selbstverwaltung 1984; mem Bundestag (Parl) 1987–90. *Publications:* Aufruf zur Rebellion 1984, Trümmerfrauen 1987, Tatort Pflegeheim 1989, Grau kommt, das ist die Zukunft 1990, Schluß mit dem Terror gegen Alte 1991. *Address:* Kothener Str 1–5, 42285 Wuppertal, Germany.

UOSUKAINEN, Riitta Maria, MA, L PH; Finnish politician; b 1942; m Toivo Uosukainen 1968; one s. *Education:* Univ of Helsinki. *Career:* Teacher of Finnish Language at an Upper Secondary School 1969–; MP (cons) 1983–, Speaker 1994–; Minister of Educ 1991–94; Dr hc (Finlandia Univ, USA) 1997, (Lappeenranta Inst of Tech) 1999; Speaker of the Year Award 1985. *Publication:* Fluttering Flame 1996. *Leisure interest:* literature. *Address:* Parliament of Finland, 00102 Eduskunta, Helsinki, Finland. *Telephone:* (9) 4321; *Fax:* (9) 4322705; *E-mail:* riitta.uosukainen@eduskunta.fi.

UPRIGHT, Diane Warner, MA, PH D; American art historian and art gallery director; b Cleveland, OH; d of Rodney Upright and Shirley (née Warner) Lavine. *Education:* Wellesley Coll and Univs of Pittsburgh and Michigan. *Career:* Asst Prof Univ of Virginia 1976–78; Assoc Prof Harvard Univ 1979–83; Sr Curator Fort Worth Art Museum 1984–86; Dir Jan Krugier Gallery, New York 1986–90; Sr Vice-Pres and Head Contemporary Art Dept, Christie's, New York 1990–95; Pres Diane Upright Fine Arts, New York 1995–; mem Coll Art Asscn, Art Table Inc. *Publications:* Morris Louis: The Complete Paintings 1979, Ellsworth Kelly: Works on Paper 1987; numerous contribs to art journals and catalogues. *Address:* Diane Upright Fine Arts, 188 E 76th St, New York, NY 10021, USA.

UPSHAW, Dawn, MA; American opera singer (soprano); b 17 July 1960, Nashville, TN; m Michael Nott 1986; one d. *Education:* Illinois Wesleyan Univ and Manhattan School of Music. *Career:* Joined young artists devt program at the Metropolitan Opera, New York after winning int auditions sponsored by Young Concert Artists; has performed with major orchestras, opera cos and chamber groups in the USA and Europe including the Netherlands Opera Co, Vienna and Hamburg (Germany) operas, Los Angeles Philharmonic, Rotterdam Philharmonic (Netherlands) and Chicago Symphony Orchestras, etc; has given numerous solo recitals; Awarded Jt First Prize, Naumburg Competition 1985. *Operas include:* Rigoletto, Simon Boccanegra, Khovanshchina, Carmen, La Clemenza di Tito, Dialogues of the Carmelites, The Magic Flute 1985, Death in the Family 1986, Alice in Wonderland, The Marriage of Figaro (also on TV), L'elisir d'amore 1988, Così fan Tutte 1988, Idomeneo 1988–89, Werther 1988–89, Don Giovanni 1989–90; *Recordings include:* Ariadne auf Naxos, songs by Rachmaninov, Hugo Wolf, Richard Strauss, Charles Ives and Kurt Weill, songs and pieces by Samuel Barber, John Harbison, Stravinsky and Gian-Carlo Menotti (Grammy Award for Best Classical Vocal Soloist 1990), Bach's Magnificat and Vivaldi's Gloria 1989, Lucio Silla, L'elisir d'amore. *Leisure interests:* reading, music. *Address:* c/o IMG Artists, 420 W 45th St, New York, NY 10036, USA.

URBACH, Susan (Zsuzsa), PH D; Hungarian art historian and former curator; b 9 Nov 1933, Budapest; d of László Urbach; m József Cserny (divorced); one d. *Education:* Calvinist Gymnasium (Budapest), Univs of Budapest, Munich (Germany) and London. *Career:* Curator of Early Flemish and German paintings, Museum of Fine Arts, Budapest 1966–94; several papers on art history and iconography in professional journals; awarded several Hungarian prizes. *Leisure interests:* travel, sailing. *Address:* Szépművészeti Múzeum, 1146 Budapest, Dózsa György ut 41, Hungary (Office); 1025 Budapest, Törökvész ut 128 Hungary (Home). *Telephone:* (1) 343-9756 (Office); (1) 176-0129 (Home); *Fax:* (1) 343-8298 (Office).

URBÁNKOVÁ-GALANDAUEROVÁ, Jarmila; Czech writer and translator; b 23 Feb 1911; d of Jaroslav Urbánek and Herjína (née Marešová; m Dr Max Galandauer (died 1943); one s. *Education:* Masaryk Univ (Brno). *Career:* Poems published 1926–; teacher, Brno, later mem staff Ministry of Culture, then ed and trans in Prague; freelance writer and trans 1960–; several prizes including Nat Prize (for the Logganstone) 1937, 1941, 1961, 1987. *Publications include:* The Broken Looking-glass, The Sunflower, The Logganstone, The Dogs. *Address:* c/o Vysočnská 243, 190 00 Prague 9, Czech Republic.

URBANOVÁ, Eva; Czech opera and concert singer (soprano); b 20 April 1961, Slaný. *Education:* Acad of Musical Arts. *Career:* Opera debut Plzen Josef Kajetan Tyl Theatre 1987; soloist Plzen Opera 1988–90; Chief of opera singer section Conservatory Plzen 1989; soloist Nat Theatre Prague 1990–, Metropolitan Opera New York 1996–; charity concert tours with Karel Gott, Czech Repub 1998; concert tours and opera performances in Canada, France, Italy, USA (Dvorák operas) and Hong Kong (Janácek operas); Classic Prize for propagation of Czech music in the world 1999. *Recordings:* Duets (with Karel Gott) 1998, Czech Opera Airs 1998, Czech Christmas Carols 2000. *Leisure interests:* cooking, piano. *Address:* Národní divadlo, National Theatre, Prague 1 – Ostrovní 1 110 00, Prague 1, Czech Republic. *Telephone:* (2) 24 91 03 12; *Fax:* (2) 24 91 15 24.

URBANYI-KRASNODĘBSKA, Zofia Jadwiga, MA; Polish conductor; b 18 March 1934, Bydgoszcz; d of the late F. Z. and Jadwiga Urbanyi; m Rysard Krasnodębski 1975; one s. *Education:* Frederick Chopin Acad of Music (Warsaw). *Career:* Conductor, Choirmaster, then Man Great Theatre Choir, Warsaw 1957–72; Conductor State Opera House, Wrocław 1972–80; Founder Warsaw Madrigal Ensemble 1966; Founder and Chief Conductor Choir in Wrocław 1986; Lecturer Frederick Chopin Acad of Music; Lecturer then Prof Acad of Music, Wrocław from 1980; Man Feichtinum Academic Choir; Prin Conducting Inst; has performed in Yugoslavia, Czechoslovakia, Germany, Italy, Belgium, the Netherlands, France, Belarus and Russia; has composed music for choirs, and made radio recordings; mem Gen Council of Educ in the Arts; prizes from Ministry of Culture and Fine Arts 1989, 1991. *Leisure interests:* literature, poetry, philosophy, mountains. *Address:* 51-676 Wrocław, ul M. Kasprzaka 4/1, Poland. *Telephone:* (71) 676210.

URQUHART, Jane, BA; Canadian writer; b 21 June 1949, Gerladton, ON; d of Walter Andrew and Marian (née Quinn) Carter; m Tony Urquhart 1976; one d. *Education:* Havergal Coll (Toronto) and Univ of Guelph. *Career:* Writer 1978–; Writer-in-Residence Univ of Ottawa 1990–, Memorial Univ of Newfoundland 1992–, Massey Coll, Univ of Toronto 1997–; books have been published in Canada, UK, France, USA, Germany, Spain, Italy, Sweden and Norway; mem Writer's Union

of Canada, PEN Int, League of Canadian Poets; Canada Council and Ontario Arts Council Grants; Hon LL D (Waterloo) 1997, (St Thomas) 1998, (Newfoundland) 1999, (Guelph) 1999, (Toronto) 1999; winner Govt of ON Trillium Award (with Margaret Atwood, qv) 1993, Marian Engel Award 1994. *Publications:* False Shuffles 1981, I am Waking in the Garden of His Imaginary Palace 1981, The Little Flowers of Mme de Montespan (poetry) 1984, The Whirlpool (novel, published as Niagara in France, winner Best Foreign Book Award, Paris 1992) 1986, Storm Glass (short story) 1987, Changing Heaven (Novel) 1990, Away (novel) 1993, The Underpainter (Gov-Gen's Award) 1997. *Leisure interest:* tapdancing. *Address:* c/o POB 208, Wellesley, ON N0B 2T0, Canada. *Telephone:* (519) 656-2613.

USTVOLSKAYA, Galina Ivanovna; Russian composer; b 17 June 1919, Petrograd (now St Petersburg). *Education:* Leningrad Conservatory (pupil of D. Shostakovich). *Career:* Teacher, then Prof of Composition N. Rimsky-Korsakov School of Music, Leningrad (now St Petersburg) 1947–; composer of major orchestral compositions rarely performed in USSR up to late 1980s because of ban on contemporary sacred music. *Works include:* Symphonies: 1 1955, 2 (Genuine Eternal Beauty) 1979, 3 (Jesus, Messiah, Rescue Us) 1983, 4 (Pray) 1987, 5 (Amen) 1989/90; numerous compositions for different instruments and piano pieces, including Dona nobis pacem (for piccolo, tuba and piano) 1970/71, Dies irae (for 8 double basses, percussion and piano 1972/73, Benedictus qui venit (for 4 flutes, 4 bassoons and piano) 1974/75. *Address:* 196135 St Petersburg, Gagarina kv 27, Apt 72, Russian Federation. *Telephone:* (812) 443 1512.

UTTAMCHANDANI, Sundri Assandas, MA; Indian writer; b 28 Sept 1924, Hyderabad Sind (now Pakistan); d of Doolaram Ichatanmal Narwani; m Assandas Uttamchandani 1947; two d. *Education:* Univs in Pakistan and India. *Career:* Writer 1946–; has acted on stage and in one film; Pres Sindhu Women's Org; numerous awards including Soviet Land Nehru Peace Prize, Hindi Directorate Award, Sahitya Acad Award 1986, Akhil B. B. Sabha Prize. *Publications:* two novels and eight short story collections including Bhuri, To Jineeji Tat Bardhan, Travelogue (essays); has published translations of several novels; magazine articles and works for TV and radio. *Leisure interests:* social work, reading, writing. *Address:* B-9 Floreana, Miraway Society, ST Rd, Mumbai 400 016, India. *Telephone:* (22) 4374136.

UZIELL-HAMILTON, Adrianne Pauline, FRSA; British circuit judge; b 14 May 1932; d of the late Dr Marcus and Ella Grantham; m Mario R. Uziell-Hamilton 1952 (died 1988); one d one s. *Education:* Maria Gray's Acad for Girls and privately. *Career:* Called to the Bar, Middle Temple 1965; *ad eundem* mem Inner Temple 1976–, Head of Chambers 1976–90; Recorder 1985–90; Circuit Judge, SE Circuit, London 1990–; mem Legal Aid Panel 1969–, Gen Council of the Bar 1970–74 (Exec Cttee 1973–74); Pres Mental Health Review Tribunals 1988; Gov Polytechnic of N London 1986– (now Univ of N London); has written articles on marriage contracts. *Leisure interests:* collecting ballet and theatre costume design, conversation, cooking for friends. *Address:* SE Circuit, New Cavendish House, 18 Maltravers St, London WC2R 3EU, UK.

V

VACKOVÁ, Jarmila, PH D; Slovak art historian; b 5 Oct 1930, Topolčany; d of the late Josef Vacek and Marie Vacková; one d. *Education:* Masaryk Univ (Brno) and Czech Acad of Sciences (Prague). *Career:* Curator Nat Gallery, Prague 1954–56; mem staff Inst of Theory and History of Art 1956–91; retd 1991; Assoc mem Royal Acad of Belgium 1992. *Publications:* Les monuments dans les pays Tchèques (vols 1–4, jtly) 1977–82, Primitifs flamands (jtly) 1985, La peinture néerlandaise du XVème et du XVIème siècle 1989. *Leisure interest:* sports. *Address:* Za Pohořelcem 11, 11600 Prague 6, Czech Republic. *Telephone:* (2) 355256.

VADUVA, Leontina; French (b Romanian) opera singer (soprano); b 1962, Romania; d of Maria Ciobanu; m Gheorghe Codre. *Education:* Bucharest Conservatoire. *Career:* Came to the West in 1986, subsequently gaining political asylum in France; debut in Massenet's Manon, Toulouse, France; debut Royal Opera House, Covent Garden, London as Manon 1988; appeared at Covent Garden as Gilda in Rigoletto 1989 and as Juliet in Romeo and Juliet 1995; has also sung in Paris, Munich, Hamburg, Zurich, Brussels, Barcelona, Florence, Buenos Aires, San Francisco and Tokyo; Olivier Award for Outstanding Achievement in Opera 1988; Chevalier des Arts et des Lettres 1998. *Address:* c/o Theateragentur Luisa Petrov, Glauburgstr 95, 60318 Frankfurt, Germany.

VAIZEY, Lady Marina, MA; British (b American) art critic, lecturer and writer; b 16 Jan 1938; d of Lyman and the late Ruth Stansky; m Lord Vaizey 1961 (died 1984); two s one d. *Education:* Brearley School (New York), Putney School (Vermont), Radcliffe Coll (Harvard Univ) and Girton Coll (Cambridge, UK). *Career:* Art Critic Financial Times 1970–74, Sunday Times 1974–; Dance Critic Now! 1979–81; mem Art Panel Arts Council 1973–78, Deputy Chair 1976–78; mem Paintings for Hosps 1974–; mem Advisory Cttee Dept of Environment 1975–81, mem Art Working Group on Nat Curriculum, Dept of Educ and Science 1990–91; mem Cttee Contemporary Arts Soc 1975–79, 1980–; Exec Dir Mitchell Prize for the History of Art 1976–87; mem History of Art and Complementary Studies Bd, CNAA 1978–82, Photography Bd 1979–81, Fine Arts Bd 1980–83, Cttee 20th Century Soc 1995–; Trustee Nat Museums and Galleries on Merseyside 1986–2001, Geffrye Museum (London) 1990–, Imperial War Museum 1991–; mem Fine Arts Advisory Cttee British Council 1987–, Crafts Council 1988–94, Cttee British Museum Members' Soc, Int Rescue Cttee UK 1998–; Editorial Dir Nat Art Collections Fund 1991–94 (Consultant 1994–98); Gov Camberwell Coll of Arts and Crafts 1971–82, Bath Acad of Art 1978–81, S Bank Centre 1993–; touring exhibition Painter as Photographer 1982–85; Turner Prize Judge 1997. *Publications:* 100 Masterpieces of Art 1979, Andrew Wyeth 1980, The Artist as Photographer 1982, Peter Blake 1985, Christiane Kubrick 1990, Christo 1990, Sorensen 1994, Picasso's Ladies 1998, Sutton Taylor 1999, Felim Egan 1999, Great Women Collectors (with Charlotte Gere) 1999, Art, the Critics' Choice (ed) 1999, Magdalene Odundo 2001; articles in periodicals, anthologies and catalogues. *Leisure interests:* arts, travel. *Address:* 24 Heathfield Terrace, London W4 4JE, UK. *Telephone:* (20) 8994-7994; *Fax:* (20) 8995-8057; *E-mail:* marina@vaizey.demon.co.uk.

VALADIAN, Margaret, AO, MBE, M ED, M SC S, FACE; Australian administrator; b 3 Sept 1936; d of O. Valadian. *Education:* Univs of Queensland and Hawaii and New York (USA). *Career:* Welfare Worker 1961–62; Resident Officer Dept of Territories, Papua New Guinea 1964, Dept of Native Affairs, WA 1966; Consultant Schools Comm, Canberra 1974; Dir Queensland Aboriginal/Islander Teacher AIDE Devt Programme 1976–78; Co-Dir Aboriginal Training and Cultural Inst 1978–; Deputy Chair New S Wales Bd of Adult Educ 1984–87; Visiting Prof of Rural Educ, Univ of Alaska, USA 1984. *Leisure interests:* performing arts, classical music. *Address:* POB 149, Thirroul, NSW 2515, Australia.

VALASKAKIS, Gail Guthrie, PH D; American/Canadian professor of communications studies; b 9 May 1939, Ashland, WI; d of Benedict and Miriam (née Van Buskirk) Guthrie; two c. *Education:* Univ of Wisconsin and Cornell and McGill (Canada) Univs. *Career:* Lecturer in Communication Arts Loyola Coll 1969–71, Co-ordinator Programme of Canadian Studies 1978–79; Asst Prof of Communication Studies, Concordia Univ, Montréal, Canada 1971, Assoc Prof 1979–89, Prof 1989–98, Dir MA course in Media Studies 1982–84, Chair 1983–85, Vice-Dean of Academic Planning Faculty of Arts and Sciences 1985–90, Dean Faculty of Arts and Science 1992–97, currently Special Advisor to the Rector for Aboriginal Affairs; Research Dir Aboriginal Healing Foundation; Fellow School of Community and Public Affairs 1979–83; Trustee Simone de Beauvoir Inst 1985; mem Advisory Council Asia-Pacific Project Broadcasting in Devt, Canadian Int Devt Agency (CIDA), Ryerson Int Devt Centre 1986–90, Advisory Bd Centre for Research Action in Race Relations 1984–87, Dir 1987–; Founder-mem Montréal Native Friendship Centre; Pres Canadian Communications Asscn; mem Int Soc of Intercultural Educ, Training and Research, Canadian Asscn to Support Native Peoples; has written numerous articles. *Address:* 110–173 Cooper St, Ottawa, ON K2P 0E9, Canada.

VALDÉS ZACKY, Dolores, MA; American advertising executive; b 22 Sept 1947, Mexico; d of German Valdés and Dolores Menendez; m Ralf Zacky 1978; two d. *Education:* Univ of the Americas (Mexico), Univ of London (UK) and Univ of California at Los Angeles. *Career:* Mem staff McCann–Erickson advertising agency, Mexico; moved to Los Angeles 1976; Founder, Vice-Pres and Creative Dir J. Walter Thompson Hispanic subsidiary, JWT/Hispania; Founder, Pres and CEO advertising, marketing and communications agency Valdés Zacky Assocs Inc 1987–; named One of Top Four Women in Advertising in USA, Adweek 1986; numerous Belding Awards 1987; named one of the 1989 Southern California Rising Stars, Los Angeles Times 1989. *Publication:* Hispanic Market Handbook (contrib) 1995. *Leisure interests:* downhill skiing, tennis, writing, collecting art and antiques. *Address:* c/o 1875 Century Park East, No 1000, Los Angeles, CA 90067, USA. *E-mail:* luliboss@aol.com.

VALENTE, Benita; American opera singer; b 19 Oct 1934, Delano, CA; d of Lorenzo Giuseppe and the late Severina Antonia (née Masonati) Valente; m Anthony Checchia 1959; one s. *Education:* Delano High School, Music Acad of the West (Santa Barbara, CA), Curtis Inst of Music (Philadelphia, PA) and Metropolitan Opera Studio (New York). *Career:* Concert debut in New York 1960; singer with Freiburg Opera, then Nuremberg Opera, Germany 1966; US opera debut in The Magic Flute at the Metropolitan Opera, New York 1973; has performed with major nat and int orchestras; nat and int opera performances and concert recitals include New York Town Hall 1966, Mostly Mozart Festival (New York) 1967, Rome 1968, Aspen Music Festival, Zurich (Switzerland), Strasbourg (France), Frankfurt (Germany), Netherlands, etc; teacher Aspen Music Festival; winner Metropolitan Opera, New York auditions 1960. *Operas include:* The Magic Flute, Turn of the Screw, Falstaff, Orfeo; *Recordings include:* Schubert and Brahms songs on Marlboro Festival album 1960, David del Tredici's Night Conjure-Verse 1966. *Address:* c/o Anthony Checchia, 135 S 18th St, Philadelphia, PA 19103, USA.

VALENTE, Francesca, MA; Italian executive; b 24 Oct 1943, Vicenza; d of Francesco and Cristina Valente; m Branko Gorjup 1979; one s. *Education:* Univs of Venice and Toronto (Canada). *Career:* Asst Dir Italian Cultural Inst, Toronto 1977–79, Dir 1985–91, 1993–98; Acting Dir Italian Cultural Inst, San Francisco, USA 1980–81, Vice-Dir 1982, Dir 1983–85, Dir San Francisco and Los Angeles 1990; Dir Italian Cultural Inst, Vancouver 1993–98; Project Dir Italy on Stage 1987, Italy in Canada 1990–91; Research, Planning and Sponsorship Officer, Ministry of Foreign Affairs, Rome 1991–92, Consultant 1999–; Consultant on Culture, UNESCO 1999–; translator of Italian works; critic of Canadian works; Dir The Canadian Club of Toronto 1989–91; mem Exhibition Cttee Design Exchange (Toronto) 1989–91, Advisory Bd Northrop Frye Centre (Toronto); consultant Le Fenice Theatre, Venice 1999–; Fellow Univ of Toronto 1976–77, Univ of Essex (UK) 1974, Massey Coll; Proclamation Mayor of San Francisco 1985, of Toronto 1991; Gold Medal, City of Vicenza 1988. *Leisure interests:* mountaineering, walking, tennis. *Address:* Commissione Nazionale Italiana, UNESCO, Piazza Firenze 27, 00186 Rome, Italy.

VALENTOVA, Petronela; Slovak actress; b 12 Jan 1952, Trnava; d of Rudolf and Florica (née Bodea) Dočolomanský; m Jozef Valenta 1974; one s one d. *Education:* Acad of Music and Dramatic Arts (Bratislava). *Career:* Actress Theatre of Slovak Nat Uprising, Martin 1977–; has performed in Czechoslovakia, Poland, Yugoslavia and UK. *Plays include:* Step Outside Yourself 1974, Cherry Orchard 1979, Amadeus 1981, Talisman 1981, Purgatory 1984, One Flew Over The Cuckoo's Nest 1985, Thyl Ullenspiegel 1986, The Holy Family 1987, Dangerous Liaisons 1987, Mother 1987, Dispute 1988, Baal 1988, Talents and Admirers 1989, Merry Christmas 1990, Merry-Go-Round 1991. *Leisure interests:* reading, singing, cooking. *Address:* Theatre of Slovak Nat Uprising, Martin, Slovakia (Work); Šefčenkova 5, 036 01 Martin, Slovakia (Home). *Telephone:* (842) 35841 (Home).

VALENZUELA, Luisa; Argentine writer and journalist; b 26 Nov 1938, Buenos Aires; d of Pablo F. Valenzuela and Luisa Mercedes Levinson; m Théodore Marjak 1958 (divorced); one d. *Education:* Belgrano Girls' School and Colegio Nacional Vicente Lopez (Buenos Aires). *Career:* Lived in Paris, writing for Argentinian newspapers and for the Office de Radiodiffusion-Télévision Française (ORTF) 1958–61; Asst Ed La Nación Sunday supplement, Buenos Aires 1964–69; writer, lecturer, freelance journalist in USA, Mexico, France, Spain 1970–73, Buenos Aires 1973–79; taught in Writing Div, Columbia Univ, New York, USA 1980–83; conducted writers' workshops English Dept, New York Univ and seminars in Spanish Dept 1984–89; returned to Buenos Aires 1989; Fulbright Grant 1969–70; Guggenheim Fellow 1983; Fellow New York Inst for the Humanities; mem Acad of Arts and Sciences, Puerto Rico; Dr hc (Knox Coll, IL, USA) 1991; Machado de Assis Medal, Brazilian Acad of Letters 1997. *Publications:* Novels: Hay que sonreír 1966, El Gato Eficaz 1972, Como en la guerra 1977, Cambio de armas 1982, Cola de la gartija 1983, Novela negra con argentinos 1990, Realidad nacional desde la cama 1990; Short stories: Los heréticos 1967, Aquí pasan cosas raras 1976, Libro que no muerde 1980, Donde viven las águilas 1983, Simetrías (Cuentos de Hades) 1993, Antología Personal 1998, Cuentos completos y uno más 1999, La travesía 2001, Peligrosas palabras 2001; most books trans into English. *Leisure interests:* masks, anthropology, ceremonies. *Address:* Artilleros 2130, 1428 Buenos Aires, Argentina; New York Institute for the Humanities, 26 Washington Place, New York, NY 10003, USA. *Telephone:* (11) 4781-3593 (Buenos Aires); (212) 998-2100 (New York).

VALETON, Ida, DR RER NAT; German geologist; b 26 May 1922, Hamburg; d of Friedrich and Jakobine (née Krebs) Meggendorfer; m Johannes Valeton 1952; one d one s. *Career:* Asst Prof Univ of Göttingen 1942–47, Univ of Würzburg 1948–52; Teacher Univ of Hamburg 1957–, Assoc Prof of Mineralogy and Petrology, then Prof 1966, Head of Dept and Prof 1970, Prof, Head Sediment-Petrology Lab, Geologische Paläontologie Inst, Hamburg 1952–, now retd; Exchange Prof to Bordeaux 1963/64; Guest Prof Ben Gurion Univ of the Negev (Israel) 1979, Univ of Ife (Nigeria) 1983, Univ of Dar es Salaam (Tanzania) 1988. *Publications:* Bauxites Elsevier 1972, Sedimente und Sedimentgesteine (textbook, jtly); papers in sedimentary petrology, lateritic aluminium ores, clay mineralogy, Pleistocene petrology and environmental pollution; numerous contribs to periodicals. *Address:* c/o Auf dem Heinberg 56, 2094 Brackel 2, Germany.

VALJAKKA, Taru Aura Helena; Finnish opera singer; b 16 Sept 1938, Helsinki; d of Oiva and Aili (née Kivirinta) Kumpunen; m Risto Valjakka 1960; one s one d. *Education:* Sibelius Acad (Helsinki), Mozarteum Salzburg (Austria) and Santiago de Compostella (Spain). *Career:* Guest Prof Estonian Music Acad 1966–; singer with Finnish Nat Opera 1969–89; Guest Singer Int Soc for Contemporary Music 1968–90; performances include Bolshoi Theatre (Moscow, USSR, now Russian Fed) 1982, 1984, Metropolitan (New York, USA) 1984, Teatro Colón (Buenos Aires) 1987, and appearances in Europe, N and S America, Canada, fmr USSR, Japan and People's Repub of China; Second Prize, Rio de Janeiro singing competition 1966; Sibelius Prize 1978; Pro Finlandia Medal 1989. *Recordings:* Reittersman (also film), Red Line, Lady Macbeth of Mtsensk, Peer Gynt, The Damask Drum (also film). *Leisure interest:* fashion designing. *Address:* Bulevardi 19A2, 00120 Helsinki, Finland. *Telephone:* (0) 6932995.

VALK, (Elizabeth) Lisa; American publishing executive; b 1951. *Career:* Publr People magazine 1988–92; first woman Publr Time magazine (Time Inc Magazine Co) 1992; Matrix Women in Communications Award 1992. *Address:* Time, Time-Life Bldg, Rockefeller Center New York, NY 10020-1393, USA. *Telephone:* (212) 522-1212; *Fax:* (212) 522-1863.

VALK, Marika; Estonian art historian and museum director; b 3 Aug 1954, Tallin; d of Aino and Elmar Runge; m Heinrich Valk 1981; two d. *Education:* Tallinn Technical Univ and Tartu Univ. *Career:* Researcher in Econs State Bd of Statistics 1976–79; Researcher Estonian Open Air Museum 1979–84; Dir Museum of Applied Arts, Tallinn 1984–90; Gen Dir Art Museum of Estonia, Tallinn 1991–. *Leisure interest:* collecting folk art. *Address:* Art Museum of Estonia, Kiriku plats 1, Tallinn 0001, Estonia; Raja 5A-19, Tallinn 0026, Estonia (Home). *Telephone:* (2) 449340 (Office); (2) 538484 (Home); *Fax:* (2) 442094 (Office).

VALLA, Kristin Hille; Norwegian politician; b 31 Dec 1944, Hafslo; two c. *Education:* Nat Coll for Teachers of Home Econs, Univ of Trondheim and Møre and Romsdal Dist Coll. *Career:* Primary school teacher 1968–72; secondary school teacher 1972–75; Rector Nesbyen Upper Secondary School 1975; apptd Chair Nat Council for Upper Secondary Educ 1984; Chief Co Educ Officer, Oppland County 1989; Second Vice-Chair Centre Party 1987–91; Minister of the Environment 1989–90. *Address:* c/o Ministry of the Environment, Myntgt 2, POB 8013 Dep, 0030 Oslo, Norway.

VALLBONA, Rima Gretel Rothe, BS, MA; Costa Rican/American professor of Spanish and writer; b 15 March 1931, San José, Costa Rica; d of the late Ferdinand Hermann and Emilia (née Strassburger) Rothe; m Carlos Vallbona 1956; four c. *Education:* Colegio Superior de Señoritas (San José), Univ of Costa Rica, Middlebury Coll (Vermont), Univ of Paris (Sorbonne) and Univ of Salamanca (Spain). *Career:* Faculty mem specializing in Latin American Literature Univ of St Thomas, Houston, TX 1964–, Head then Chair Spanish Dept 1966–71, Chair Modern Languages Dept 1979–81; Visiting Prof Univ of Houston 1975–76, Madrid 1980, Rice Univ and Univ of Houston 1980–83, 1995, Cullen Foundation Prof of Spanish 1989–; mem American Asscn of Teachers of Spanish and Portuguese, Asociación de Literatura Femenina Hispánica, Instituto Internacional de Literatura Iberoamericana; recipient Nat Novel Prize (Costa Rica) 1968, Jorge Luis Borges Short Story Prize (Argentina) 1977, Agripina Montes del Valle Latin American Novel Prize (Colombia) 1978, Prof Lilia Ramos Children's Poetry Prize (Uruguay) 1978, Southwest Conf of Latin American Studies Literary Prize 1982, ANCORA Award for Best Book (Costa Rica) 1982; El Lazo de Dama de la Orden del Mérito Civil (Spain) 1988. *Publications:* Literary studies: Yolanda Oreamuno 1971, La obra en prosa de Eunice Odio 1981, Vida i sucesos de la Monja Alférez 1992, La narrativa de Yolanda Oreamuno 1995; Novels: Noche en vela 1968, Las sombras que perseguimos 1983, Mundo, demonio y mujer 1991; Short stories: Polvo del camino 1973, La salamandra rosada 1979, Mujeres y agonías 1982, Baraja de soledades 1983, Cosecha de pecadores 1988, El arcángel del perdón 1990, Los infernos de la mujer y algo más... 1992, Flowering Inferno: Tales of Sinking Hearts 1992, Tormy, la gata prodigiosa de Donaldito 1997. *Leisure interests:* classical music, travel, collecting pre-Hispanic artefacts. *Address:* 3706 Lake St, Houston, TX 77098, USA. *Telephone:* (715) 528-6137; *Fax:* (713) 528-3218; *E-mail:* rvallbona@aol.com.

VÁMOS, Éva, PH D; Hungarian academic; b 22 May 1950, Budapest; d of Endre and Lilly (née Vigyázó) Vámos. *Education:* Eötvös Loránd Univ of Budapest and Tech Univ of Budapest. *Career:* Affiliated to Hungarian Museum for Science and Tech (Országos Muszaki Múzeum) 1973–, Curator 1973–78; scientific co-worker 1978–86; Head of Ind Group of History of Science, scientific sec in charge of public relations 1986–87, Sr scientific co-worker 1987–89, Head of dept 1989–91, Scientific Deputy Dir Gen 1991–93, Dir Gen 1994–; Memorial Medal 1997; Justus von Liebig Memorial Medal 2000. *Publications:* Chapters from the History of Communication 1979, History of Writing and Writing Utensils 1980–82, Creative Hungarians 1988, László József Bíró 1996. *Address:* Hungarian Museums for Science and Tech, Kaposvár u 13, 1117 Budapest, Hungary (Office); 1015 Budapest, Batthyány u 3, VI 32, Hungary (Home). *Telephone:* (1) 204-4095; (1) 204-4090 (Office); (1) 201-7317 (Home); *Fax:* (1) 204-4088 (Office); *E-mail:* vam13378@ helka.iif.hu.

VAN ALMSICK, Franziska; German swimmer; b 1978. *Career:* Olympic Silver Medallist in 200m freestyle swimming event, also Bronze Medal winner, Barcelona, Spain 1992; world records Women's 200m short-course and 100m short-course freestyle races, Beijing 1993.

VAN ALSTYNE, Thelma Selina, RCA; Canadian artist; b 26 Jan 1913, Victoria, BC; d of Alpha and Rosetta (née Cooper) Scribbans; m E. Lloyd Van Alstyne 1953 (deceased); one step-d. *Education:* Duffus School of Business, Vancouver School of Art, Doone School of Art and under Jock MacDonald. *Career:* Solo exhibitions include Pollock Gallery 1960–80, Le Fevre Gallery (Edmonton) 1981, Quan Gallery (Toronto) 1982–84, 1987; group exhibitions include Brian Robertson White Gallery (London, UK) 1967, Art Gallery of Ontario 1968, 1971, Masters Gallery (Calgary) 1994; works rep in perm collections including Canadian Council Art Bank, Oise Coll; Hadassah Auction Prizes 1972–80. *Leisure interests:* religion, gardening, travel, Tai Chi. *Address:* 81 Bramley St S, Port Hope, ON L1A 3K6, Canada. *Telephone:* (905) 885-6945.

VAN BLADEL, Leonie G. L.; Netherlands politician; b 22 June 1939, Utrecht. *Career:* Fmr MEP (PSE, PvdA), mem Cttee on Foreign Affairs, Security and Defence Policy, Del for relations with Israel. *Address:* c/o European Parliament, rue Wiertz, 1047 Brussels, Belgium. *Telephone:* (2) 284-21-11; *Fax:* (2) 230-69-43.

VAN DER VALK, Sonja, PH D; Netherlands drama critic and magazine editor; b 8 Oct 1952, Poeldijk; partner Joost Sternheim (died 1992); two d. *Education:* Univ of Utrecht. *Career:* Theatre critic 1977–, writer for Toneel Teatraal, Serpentine (women's magazine), De groene Amsterdammer (weekly); apptd Ed Toneel Theatraal 1990; teacher at theatre school, Amsterdam 1992–; Art Adviser to Amsterdamse Kunstraad 1992–. *Publications:* Theater Persona: Een Terugblik op Negen Jaar Theater Maken; articles on the theatre. *Leisure interests:* music, dance, literature, cycling, walking. *Address:* Uithoornstraat 4, II, 1070 SX Amsterdam, Netherlands. *Telephone:* (20) 6648848; *Fax:* (20) 6648848.

VAN DUYN, Mona Jane, MA; American poet; b 9 May 1921, Waterloo, IA; d of Earl and Lora (née Kramer) Van Duyn; m Jarvis Thurston 1943. *Education:* Univ of Iowa. *Career:* English Tutor Univ of Iowa 1943–46, Univ of Louisville 1946–50; Lecturer in English Univ of Washington 1950–67, Adjunct Prof of Poetry 1983, Visiting Hurst Prof 1987; US Poet Laureate (first woman) 1992–93; poetry reader 1970–; poet-in-residence numerous poetry confs; Poetry Ed and Co-Publr Perspective 1947–67; Chancellor Acad of Poets 1985–99; mem Nat Inst of Arts and Letters; Fellow Acad of American Poets 1980; Guggenheim Fellow 1972; Hon D LITT (Washington) 1971, (Cornell) 1972; numerous awards include Missouri Arts Award 1990, Bollingen Prize 1970, Nat Book Award 1971, Ruth Lilly Award 1989. *Publications:* Valentines to the Wide World 1959, A Time of Bees 1964, To See, To Take 1970, Bedtime Stories 1972, Merciful Disguises 1973, Letters From a Father and Other Poems 1983, Near Changes (Pulitzer Prize for poetry 1991)

1990, Firefall: Poems 1993, If It Be Not I: Collected Poems 1959–1982 1993. *Leisure interests:* gardening, reading. *Address:* 7505 Teasdale Ave, St Louis, MO 63130, USA.

VAN GINKEL, Blanche Lemco, RCA, FRAIC, B ARCH; Canadian architect; b 14 Dec 1923, London, UK; d of Myer and Claire Lemco; m H. P. D. Van Ginkel 1956; one s one d. *Education:* Westmount High School (Montréal), McGill Univ (Montréal) and Harvard Univ (USA). *Career:* Manager City Planning Office Regina, SK 1946; Architect Atelier le Corbusier, Paris 1948; Architect in UK 1948–51; Asst Prof of Architecture Univ of Pennsylvania, USA 1951–56; Partner van Ginkel Assocs 1957–; Visiting Prof Harvard Univ 1958, Univ of Montréal 1961–63, 1969, McGill Univ 1973–77; Prof of Architecture Univ of Toronto 1977–, Dir School of Architecture 1977–80, Dean 1980–82; Pres Asscn of Collegiate Schools of Architecture 1986–87; Hon Fellow American Inst of Architects 1995; Master of City Planning (USA); Mem Order of Canada 2000; recipient Massey Medal for Architecture 1965, Canadian Architecture Award for Excellence 1972, Queen's Silver Jubilee Medal 1977, Canadian Citizenship Citation 1991. *Film:* It Can Be Done (Grand Prix, Int Fed of Housing and Planning) 1956; *Publications:* Urban Mapping 1951; numerous articles for books and professional periodicals 1956–. *Address:* 38 Summerhill Gardens, Toronto, ON M4T 1B4, Canada. *Telephone:* (416) 964-8651; *Fax:* (416) 964-8651.

VAN HAMEL, Martine; American ballet dancer; b 16 Nov 1945, Brussels, Belgium; d of D. A. van Hamel and Manette van Hamel-Cramer. *Education:* Nat Ballet School (Canada). *Career:* Started ballet training at age four; debut aged 11 with Nat Ballet of Venezuela; joined Nat Ballet of Canada as soloist 1963; moved to New York and danced with Joffrey Ballet 1969–70; joined American Ballet Theater 1970, as Prin Ballerina danced classic roles including Swan Lake, Sleeping Beauty, Raimonda as well as contemporary works choreographed by Petipa, Balanchine, Glen Tetley, Anthony Tudor, Kenneth MacMillan, Mark Morris, Twyla Tharp, Alvin Ailey; danced with Nederlands Dans Theater III 1993–98; Artistic Dir New Amsterdam Ballet (f 1986); mem Founding Bd Kaatsbaan Int Dance Center; prizes include Gold Medal, Varna Competition 1996, Prix de Varna 1996, Dance Magazine Award, Cue Magazine Award, Award for Excellence (Washington Coll), Dance Educators of America Award. *Choreography:* Amnon V'Tamar for American Ballet Theatre 1984 and creator of works for Milwaukee Ballet, Washington Ballet, Royal Winnipeg Ballet and New Amsterdam Ballet. *Leisure interest:* singing. *Address:* c/o American Ballet Theater, 890 Broadway, New York, NY 10003, USA. *Telephone:* (212) 749-1942; *Fax:* (212) 678-0320.

VAN HEMELDONCK, Marijke Joan Hermina, MA; Belgian politician; b 23 Dec 1931, Hove; two d. *Education:* Univs of Brussels and Columbia (NY, USA). *Career:* Entered Diplomatic service 1953; Adviser to Belgian Govt 1954–82; elected MEP (SP) 1982, mem ACP–EEC Jt Ass; Vice-Pres Univ of Brussels 1989–; Pres Univ Centre for Devt 1991–. *Leisure interests:* reading, gardening, trekking. *Address:* Rond Point de l'Etoile 3, 1050 Brussels, Belgium (Office); Le Grand Orient, 48400 Barre des Cévennes, Lozère, France (Home). *Telephone:* (4) 66-45-09-63 (Home); *Fax:* (4) 66-45-20-21 (Home).

VAN HERREWEGHE, Marie Louise; Belgian university professor and organization executive; b 10 May 1923, Ledeberg. *Education:* Ghent Univ. *Career:* Scientific Asst Ghent Univ 1949–58, Scientific Org Dir 1958–68, Lecturer 1968–70, Assoc Prof 1970–71, Prof 1971–88; Sec-Gen World Asscn for Educational Research 1969–. *Address:* World Association for Educational Research, Ghent University, Henri Dunantlaan 1, 9000 Ghent, Belgium. *Telephone:* (9) 264-63-78.

VAN LANCKER, Anne E. M.; Belgian politician; b 4 March 1954. *Education:* Catholic Univ of Leuven and Free Univ of Brussels. *Career:* Scientific Researcher in Social Policy, Catholic Univ of Leuven 1978–79, Lecturer in Sociology of Labour 1979–84; Socialist Party Adviser, Belgian Parl 1984–89; Head of Cabinet, Flemish Minister of Employment 1989–94; MEP (PSE) 1994–, Vice-Chair Cttee for Women's Rights, mem Cttee for Social Affairs, Cttee for Civil Liberties 1994–. *Leisure interests:* reading, music, sport (volleyball, squash and mountaineering). *Address:* European Parliament, rue Wiertz, 1047 Brussels, Belgium. *Telephone:* (2) 284-54-94; *Fax:* (2) 284-94-94; *E-mail:* avanlancker@europarl.eu.int.

VAN LENGEN, Karen, BA, M ARCH; American architect; b 9 April 1951, Syracuse, NY; d of Robert and Carol (née Freiberger) Van Lengen. *Education:* Vassar Coll and Columbia Univ. *Career:* Assoc I. M. Pei and Partners 1976–82; Partner Heisel/Van Lengen Architects 1986–88, Karen Van Lengen Architects 1988–; Asst Adjunct Prof Columbia Univ, New York 1986–; Chair of Architecture and Environmental Design, Parsons School of Design, New York 1995–; Fulbright Fellow 1983; Fellow Asscn of American Univ Women; mem AIA, Nat Council Architectural Registration Bd; winner American Memorial Library competition, Berlin 1989. *Address:* 424 Broome St, New York, NY 10013, USA.

VAN NESS, Patricia Catheline, B MUS; American composer and violinist; b 25 June 1951, Seattle, WA; d of C. Charles and Marjorie (née Dexter) Van Ness; m 1st Wendell Ketcham 1972 (divorced 1977); m 2nd Adam Sherman 1983. *Education:* Wheaton and Gordon Colls. *Career:* Founder-mem Private Lightning 1975–82; composer numerous ballet and dance scores 1985–; mem American Women Composers; Grantee MA Cultural Council 1993; has made recordings for A & M Records with Private Lightning.

VAN PUTTEN, Maartje; Netherlands politician; b 5 July 1951, Bussum; one s one d. *Education:* Sociale Acad (Amsterdam). *Career:* Journalist 1977–79; mem staff Evert Vermeer Stichting (inst dealing with N–S issues), PvdA 1980–89; MEP (Socialist Group) 1989–99, fmr mem Cttee on the Environment, Public Health and Consumer Protection. *Publications:* Made in Heaven: Women and the International Division of Labour (jtly) 1985, The Future has Begun (film). *Address:* Koemer Visscherstraat 21, 1054 EV Amsterdam, Netherlands (Home). *Telephone:* (20) 612-81-55 (Home); *Fax:* (20) 616-45-69 (Home).

VANDERBILT, Gloria Morgan; American artist, actress and fashion designer; b 20 Feb 1924, New York; d of Reginald and Gloria (née Morgan) Vanderbilt; m 1st Pasquale di Cicco (divorced); m 2nd Leopold Stokowski 1945 (divorced 1955); two s; m 3rd Sidney Lumet 1956 (divorced); m 4th Wyatt Cooper 1963; two s (one deceased). *Education:* studied under Sanford Meisner. *Career:* Solo exhibitions include Rabun Studio (New York) 1948, Bertha Shaeffer Gallery (New York) 1954, Hammer Gallery (New York) 1966, 1968, Washington Gallery of Art 1968, Parish Museum (Southampton, NY); group exhibitions include Hoover Gallery (San Francisco) 1971; professional acting debut in The Time of Your Life, Broadway 1955; designer of stationery, fabrics, clothing and household accessories; gave name to Vanderbilt perfume; mem Actors' Equity, Screen Actors' Guild, Authors' League of America, American Fed of Arts; several awards for design. *Plays include:* Picnic 1955, Peter Pan 1958, The Green Hat; numerous TV appearances; *Publications:* Love Poems 1955, Gloria Vanderbilt Book of Collage (jtly) 1970, Woman to Woman 1979, Once Upon a Time: A True Story 1985, Black White, White Knight (jtly) 1987, Never Say Good-Bye 1989, The Memory Book of Starr Faithfull 1994.

VANNI, Carla, LL D; Italian magazine publishing executive; b 18 Feb 1936, Livorno; m Vincenzo Nisivoccia; two c. *Education:* Univ of Milan. *Career:* Joined Mondadori publrs 1959, working on fashion desk of Grazia magazine, Head Fashion Desk 1964, Jt Ed-in-Chief 1974, Ed-in-Chief 1978–, creator several supplements (Grazia Bricolage, Grazia Blu and Grazia Int, Grazia Accessori and Grazia Uomo and introduced coverage of social problems), Ed-in-Chief Grazie Casa; launched Marie Claire magazine in Italy 1987, Publ Dir Marie Claire and Cento Cose-Energy 1987–99, Donna Moderna 1995–; mem juries several nat and int literary awards and many beauty competitions; Montenapoleone d'Oro for Best Fashion Journalist 1970; Journalist of the Year, The Oner 1987; Gullace (for coverage of women's interest issues) 1995. *Address:* c/o Grazia, Via Arnoldo Mondadori, 20090 Segrate, Milan, Italy. *Telephone:* (2) 754212390; *Fax:* (2) 75422515; *E-mail:* vanni@mondadori.it.

VANSTONE, Amanda Eloise, BA, LL B; Australian politician; b 7 Dec 1952, Adelaide; m. *Education:* S Australian Inst Tech and Univ of Adelaide. *Career:* Retailer, wholesaler; pvt practice barrister and solicitor, S Australia; mem Senate for S Australia 1984–, Shadow Special Minister of State 1987, Spokesperson on the Status of Women 1987; Parl Sec to Deputy Leader of the Opposition; Minister for Employment, Educ, Training and Youth Affairs 1996–97, for Justice 1997–98, for Justice and Customs 1998–2001, for Family and Community Services 2001–; Mem assisting the Prime Minister for the Status of Women until 2001. *Address:* Senate, Parliament House, Suite M660, Canberra, ACT 2600, Australia (Office); 81 Flinders St, Adelaide 5000, SA, Australia (Home). *Telephone:* (8) 8223-1757 (Office); *Fax:* (8) 8223-1750 (Office); *E-mail:* minister.vanstone@facs .gov.au; *Internet:* www.facs.gov.au.

VAPTSAROVA, Maya Borisova, BA; Bulgarian political party official, film-maker and writer; b 7 July 1944, Bansko; d of Boris Ivanov Vaptsarov and Venera Ivanova Vaptsarova; m Evgeny Borislavov Trifonov 1976; one s. *Education:* Budapest Art Univ and Univ of New York (USA). *Career:* Director of 53 documentaries and three feature films; elected Leader All-Bulgarian Union 'Macedonia' 1989; apptd Man Publishing House 1990; Golden Ducat Award, Mannheim, Germany 1977; Igne Signai (Vatican) 1977. *Films include:* 5 + 1 1977, The Voynods 1986; *Publications include:* Poetry: Stairs 1974, Directions 1979. *Leisure interest:* mountaineering. *Address:* Sofia, 25 James Bowcher St, Bulgaria. *Telephone:* (2) 66-57-57.

VARDA, Agnès; French film writer and director; b 30 May 1928, Ixelles, Belgium; d of Eugène Jean Varda and Christiane Pasquet; m Jacques Demy 1962 (died 1990); one s one d. *Education:* Sète (Hérault), Univ of Paris (Sorbonne) and Ecole du Louvre. *Career:* Official Photographer Théâtre Nat Populaire 1951–61; reporter and photographer, film-maker 1954–; Commdr des Arts et des Lettres; Chevalier de la Légion d'Honneur. *Full-length films:* La pointe-courte 1955, Cléo de 5 à 7 (Prix Méliès 1962) 1961, Le Bonheur (Prix Louis Delluc, David Selznick Award, Silver Bear Berlin Festival 1965) 1964, Les créatures 1965, Loin du Vietnam 1967, Lions Love (Popular Univs jury 1970) 1969, Nausicaa 1970, Daguerréotypes 1975, L'une chante, l'autre pas (Grand Prix, Taormina, Sicily 1977) 1976, Mur Murs (Firenze 1981) 1980, Documenteur: An Emotion Picture 1981, Sans toit ni loi (also known as Vagabonde, Golden Lion for Best Film Venice Film Festival, Prix Méliès, Los Angeles Critics Best Foreign Film) 1985, Jane B par Agnés V 1987, Kung Fu Master 1987, Jacquot De Nantes 1992, Les cent et une nuits 1994; *Short-length films:* O saisons, O châteaux 1957, L'opéra-Mouffe 1958, Du côté de la côte 1958, Salut les cubains (Bronze Lion, Venice Festival 1964) 1963, Uncle Yanco 1967, Black Panthers (First Prize Oberhausen Black Panthers) 1968, Réponse de femmes 1975, Plaisir d'amour en Iran 1975, Ulysse (César Award 1984) 1982, Les dites Cariatides 1984, T'as de beaux escaliers... tu sais 1986, Les demoiselles ont 25 ans 1992, L'univers de Jacques Demy 1993; *Publication:* Varda par Agnès 1994. *Address:* c/o Cine-Tamaris, 86 rue Daguerre, 75014 Paris, France. *Telephone:* (1) 43-22-66-00; *Fax:* (1) 43-21-75-00.

VÁRKONYI, Ágnes R., PH D; Hungarian historian; b 9 Feb 1928, Salgótarján, Nógrád Co; d of József and Mária (née Bérczy) Várkonyi; m Kálmán Ruttkay; two d. *Education:* Eötvös Lóránd Univ of Budapest. *Career:* Asst Prof Inst for Historical Research of Hungarian Acad of Sciences 1951–83; Prof, Head of Dept of Medieval and Early Modern Hungarian History in Eötvös Lóránd Univ of Budapest 1983–98, Prof Emer 1998–; Corresp Fellow of Royal Historical Soc; several awards including Széchenyi Prize. *Publications:* 28 books and numerous articles. *Address:* Eötvös Lóránd University of Budapest, Faculty of Arts, Múzeum krt 6-8, 1088 Budapest, Hungary; 1021 Budapest, Széher út 24, Hungary (Home). *Telephone:* (1) 266-9833 (Office); *Fax:* (1) 266-7952 (Office).

VARMA, Suseela, BM, MS; Indian medical practitioner; b 26 Sept 1928, Mavelikara, Kerala State; d of Ravi Varma and Aswathy Nal. *Education:* Holy Angels Convent (Kerala State), Univ Coll of Trivandrum, Madras Medical Coll and King George's Medical Coll (Lucknow). *Career:* Specializes in spinal cord injuries and rehabilitation of physically disabled; Physician and Surgeon Madras Medical Coll, then Kasturba Gandhi Hosp, Madras 1954–55; Medical Officer Church of S India Hosp 1955–56; House Officer, then Sr House Officer in Brighton, Watford, Birmingham and Yorks (UK) 1957–60; Jr Medical Officer Nat Spinal Injuries Centre, Stoke Mandeville Hosp, UK 1961–67; Pool

Officer, Medical Officer, Sr Medical Officer, Jt Dir, Dir then Dir-Prof Rehabilitation and Artificial Limb Centre, King George Medical Coll, Lucknow 1967–86; Hon Regional Dir District Rehabilitation Scheme (jtly Govts of India and USA) 1985–86; Hon Visiting Scientist Chitra Tirunal Inst for Medical Sciences and Tech, Trivandrum) 1990; team Doctor for Int Games and Skills Contest for the Disabled (Japan) 1975, 1981; Indian Del Conf on Spinal Cord Injuries (USA) 1975; Founder-mem Int Medical Science Acad; papers in scientific periodicals; Holmes Prize, BMA 1966; Hon Mention The Rolex Award for Enterprise 1987. *Leisure interests:* reading, sketching, handicrafts. *Address:* Raveena, Pongammudu, Ulloor, Trivandrum 695011, Kerala State, India. *Telephone:* (471) 448333.

VARNAITĖ-EIDUKAITIENĖ, Regina-Marija; Lithuanian actress; b 19 May 1927, Ukmergė; d of the late Rapolas Varnas and Filomena Varnienė; m Vytautas Eidukaitis 1955 (died 1989); two d. *Education:* Ukmergė Grammar School and Inst of Theatrical Art (Moscow, then USSR). *Career:* Actress Kaunas Drama Theatre 1952–; lectures and talks to theatre audiences. *Plays include:* Baltaragis Mill 1967, Šventežeris 1970, America in Sauna 1974, Twelfth Night 1993; *Film:* A Devil's Bride (musical) 1972. *Leisure interest:* enjoying time with three grandchildren. *Address:* Baltijos G-VĖ 9-18, Kaunas 3008, Lithuania. *Telephone:* (7) 239471.

VARTAN, Sylvie; French singer and entertainer; b 15 August 1944, Iskretz, Bulgaria; d of Georges and Ilona (née Rudolf-Mayer) Vartan; m 1st Johnny Hallyday 1965 (divorced 1980); one s; m 2nd Tony Scotti 1984; one d. *Education:* Lycée Hélène-Boucher (Paris). *Career:* Singing debut in duet with Frankie Jordan (Panne d'essence); nat tours 1961–, int tours 1965–, including Paris Olympia 1961, 1962, 1963, 1964 (with The Beatles), 1967, 1968, 1970, 1972, 1996, 1999, Palais des Congrès, Paris 1975–76, 1977–78, 1983, Palais des Sports, Paris 1981, 1991, Casino de Paris 1995, Las Vegas, NV (USA) 1982, Los Angeles, CA (USA) 1983, Atlantic City, NJ (USA) 1984, Sofia, Bulgaria 1990; Chevalier des Arts et des Lettres 1985; Chevalier de l'Ordre Nat du Mérite 1987; Ordre du Cavalier de Madara (Bulgaria) 1996; Chevalier de la Légion d'Honneur 1998; Triomphe des Variétés Award 1970. *Songs include:* Tous mes copains, En écoutant la pluie, I'm Watching, Si je chante, La plus belle pour aller danser, Quand tu es là, Par amour par pitié, 2'35 de bonheur, Le Kid, Comme un garçon, La Maritza, La chasse à l'homme, Loup, Dilindam, L'heure la plus douce de ma vie, Pour lui je reviens, Mon père, J'ai un problème (with Johnny Hallyday), Toi le garçon, Bye bye Leroy Brown, La drôle de fin, Qu'est-ce qui fait pleurer les blondes?, Le temps du swing, Petit rainbow, I Don't Want the Night to End, Nicolas, Merveilleusement désenchantée, L'amour c'est comme une cigarette, Aimer, Des heures de désir, Double exposure, Virage, Femme sous influence, C'est fatal, Qui tu es, Je n'aime encore que toi, sensible; *Films:* Un clair de lune à Maubeuge 1962, D'où viens-tu Johnny? 1963, Cherchez l'idole 1964, Patate 1964, Les poneyttes 1967, Malpertuis 1971, Mon amie Sylvie 1972, L'ange noir 1994; *TV appearances include:* Show Smet 1965, Jolie poupée 1968, Doppia coppia (Italy) 1969, Sacha Sylvie Show 1969, Sylvissima 1970, Top à Sylvie Vartan 1972, Top à Sylvie et Johnny 1973, Je chante pour Swanee 1974, Sylvie 1975, Punto e basta (Italy) 1975, Dancing Star 1977, La Maritza 1990, Sylvie sa vie 1994, Irrésistiblement… Sylvie 1998, Qu'est-ce qui fait rêver Sylvie? 2000; *Publications include:* Si je chante 1981, Beauty Book 1985. *Address:* c/o Charley Marouani, 37 rue Marbeuf, 75008 Paris, France.

VARTE, Rosy; French actress; b 22 Nov 1927, Istanbul, Turkey; d of Jean and Colombe (née Sarkis) Manuelian; m Pierre Badel 1980. *Education:* Institution Saint-Joseph-du-Parchamp. *Career:* Actress; worked with the Comédie Française 1971–74; Chevalier de la Légion d'Honneur; Chevalier des Arts et des Lettres; Sept d'or Best Actress Award 1987; Ecran d'or 1990. *Plays include:* La famille Arlequin 1958, Ubu-Roi 1961, Marie Tudor 1970, Henri IV 1973, Périclès 1974, Le Pape kidnappé 1975, La Magouille 1978, Le bourgeois gentilhomme 1982, Les rustres 1982, La source bleue 1994; *Films include:* Fortuna 1961, Le Tracassin 1963, Mon oncle Benjamin 1963, La belle affaire 1972, Le bar de la Fourche 1972, T'inquiète pas ça se soigne 1980, Le braconnier de Dieu 1983, Rock and Torah, Garçon! 1983, Tango 1983, Joyeuses Pâques 1984, Monsieur de Pourceaugnac 1985; *TV appearances include:* Si jamais j'te pince 1960, La mégère apprivoisée 1964, Noëlle aux quatre vents (series) 1970, Le Cardinal de Retz 1974, La

fleur des pois 1974, La loupe du diable 1980, La Ramendeuse 1981, Novgorod 1981, Un Noël de Maigret 1983, Les cerfs-volants 1983, Maguy (series) 1985–93, Bonnes vacances 1997. *Leisure interests:* painting, cooking, walking. *Address:* 16 place Dauphine, 75001 Paris, France.

VARTIKOVA, Elena, DR RER NAT; Slovak (b Yugoslav) botanist, teacher and business executive; b 13 March 1945, Kisač, Yugoslavia; d of Jan and Maria Kollar; m Dušan Vartik 1969 (divorced 1993); one s one d. *Education:* Comenius Univ (Bratislava). *Career:* Asst Prof Botany, Comenius Univ, Bratislava 1967–79; expert in nature conservation, Ministry of Culture 1979–80; specialist in nature conservation, Slovak Union of Nature and Landscape Protectors, Bratislava 1980–93; employed as Int Coordinator, Head Office Greenway, Bratislava 1993–95, as volunteer 1995–2001; business manager, pvt co 1995–2001. *Publications include:* Atlas of Medicine Plants (jtly) 1983, Flora of Eastern Part Low Tatra Mountains 1975, Flora of Stiavnicke Urchy Mountains (jtly) 1985, Clean Up the World 1995–2000; numerous articles and reports dealing with environmental educ. *Leisure interests:* music, theatre, reading, travelling, exercise/walking, swimming, skiing. *Address:* POB 163, 814 99 Bratislava, Slovak Republic; Pribisova 19, 841 05 Bratislava 4, Slovak Republic. *Telephone:* (2) 55414674; *Fax:* (2) 55414674; *E-mail:* greenway@isternet.sk; vartikova@isternet.sk.

VÁŠÁRYOVÁ, Magdaléna; Slovak former diplomatist and actress; b 26 Aug 1948, Banská Štiavnica, Slovakia; d of Jozef and Hermína (née Schmidt) Vášary; m 1st Dušan Jamrich 1973 (divorced 1977); m 2nd Milan Lasica 1980; two d. *Education:* Comenius Univ (Bratislava). *Career:* Began acting career at the age of 15; acted in Divadlo na Korze theatre 1970–71, Nová Scéna 1971–80, Slovak Nat Theatre 1983–90; Amb to Austria 1990–92. *Films:* Markéta Lazarová 1966, Siroty, vtáčky a blázni (Orphans, Birds and Fools) 1968, Krotká (La Douce, Grand Prix, Monte Carlo) 1968, A pozdravuji vlaštovky (And Give my Greetings to the Swallows) 1972, Postřižiny 1981, Tichá radosť (Silent Joy, Best Actress Award, San Remo) 1983, Turn of the Screw (TV) 1983; *Publication:* Krátke listy jednému mestu (Short Letters to a Town) 1984. *Leisure interests:* literature, history. *Telephone:* (1) 884-21-25; *Fax:* (1) 894-12-00.

VASCONCELLOS, Josephina Alys Hermes de, MBE, FRBS; British sculptor; b 26 Oct 1904; d of the late Hippolyto and Freda (née Coleman) de Vasconcellos; m Delmar Banner 1930 (died 1983); two s. *Education:* Convent of the Sacred Heart (Southampton), Bournemouth High School, Royal Acad Schools (London) and in Paris and Florence (Italy). *Career:* Works include High Altar and Statue, Varengeville (Normandy, France) 1925, Bronze St Hubert, Nat Gallery of Brazil 1926, Music in Trees, Southampton Gallery 1933, Ducks, Glasgow Art Gallery 1946, Episcopal Crozier, Bristol Cathedral 1948, Refugees, Sheffield Art Gallery 1949, Christ, Nat War Memorial to Battle of Britain (Aldershot) 1950, Mary and Child, St Paul's Cathedral 1955, Winter, Oldham Gallery 1958, Flight Into Egypt, St Martin-in-the-Fields 1958, Winged Victory Crucifix, Clewer Church 1964, Holy Family, Liverpool Cathedral 1965, Portrait of Lord Denning 1969, Virgin and Child, Blackburn Cathedral 1974, Reunion, Bradford Univ 1977, Holy Family, St Martin-in-the-Fields 1983, Revelation XXI, Lake Artists' Exhibition (Grasmere) 1986, Mary and Babe, Carlisle Cathedral 1989, Sea Legend, Hutton in the Forest 1990, Childline to God, Carlisle Cathedral 1990, two casts in bronze of life-size Reconciliation (given to Coventry Cathedral and Hiroshima Peace Park, Japan, by Richard Branson) 1995; exhibitions include Christmas Solo Exhibition Manchester Cathedral 1991–92; Pres Guild of Lakeland Craftsmen 1971–73; Out of Nature documentary film made about her work 1949, BBC programme Viewpoint TV 1968; Hon mem Glider Pilots' Regimental Asscn; Hon D LITT (Bradford) 1977. *Publications:* Woodcut Illustrations for the Cup 1938, They Became Christians (contrib) 1966. *Leisure interest:* music. *Address:* Holehird, Patterdale Rd, Windermere, Cumbria LA23 1NR, UK.

VASILYEVA, Larisa Nikolayevna; Russian poet and writer; b 23 Nov 1935, Kharkov, Ukraine; d of Nikolai Alekseyevich and Yekaterina Vasilievna Kucherenko; m Oleg Vasiliyev 1957; one s. *Education:* Moscow Univ. *Career:* Started publishing works 1957; first collection of verse 1966; Sec Moscow Br of Russian Union of Writers; Pres Fed of Russian Women Writers 1989–, Int Publishing League Atlantida 1992–;

Moscow Komsomol Prize 1971. *Publications include:* Poetry: Fire-fly 1969, The Swan 1970, Blue Twilight 1970, Encounter 1974, A Rainbow of Snow 1974, Meadows 1975, Fire in the Window 1978, Russian Names 1980, Foliage 1980, Fireflower 1981, Selected Poetry 1981, Grove 1984, Mirror 1985, Moskovorechie 1985, Lantern 1985, Waiting For You In The Sky 1986, A Strange Virtue 1991; Stories and other prose works: Albion and the Secret of Time 1978, Novel About My Father 1983, Cloud of Fire 1988, Selected Works (2 vols) 1989, The Kremlin Wives 1992, The Kremlin Children 1996, The Wives of the Russian Crown. *Address:* 125319 Moscow, Usievicha str 8, Kv 86, Russian Federation. *Telephone:* (095) 155-7486.

VASILYEVA, Tatyana Griogoryevna; Russian actress; b 28 Feb 1947, Lenningrad (now St Petersburg); two s one d. *Education:* Studio-School of Moscow Art Theatre. *Career:* With Moscow Satire Theatre until 1984; actress Moscow Mayakovsky Theatre 1984–93; later freelance; People's Artist of Russia, Nika Prize 1992. *Films:* Hello, I'm Your Auntie, To See Paris and Die; *Plays include:* Ordinary Miracle, Pippi Long Stocking, Run, Inspector, The Threepenny Opera. *Address:* Goncharny proyezd 8/40, Apt 62, 121248 Moscow, Russian Federation.

VASQUEZ NAVA, María Elena; Mexican politician. *Career:* Comptroller-Gen (mem Cabinet) 1989–94. *Address:* c/o Office of the Comptroller-General, Avda Insurgentes Sur 1735, 10°, 01029 México, DF, Mexico. *Telephone:* (5) 5592690.

VASS, Joan, BA; American fashion designer; b 19 May 1925, New York; d of Max and Rose Kaplan; m Gene Vass 1947 (divorced); two s one d. *Education:* Vassar Coll and Univ of Wisconsin. *Career:* Pres Joan Vass Inc 1977–, Vass-Ludacer 1993–; Coty Award 1979; Distinguished Woman in Fashion award, Smithsonian Inst 1980; Prix de Cachet 1983. *Address:* Joan Vass Inc, 36 East 31st St, New York, NY 10016-6821, USA; 485 7th Ave, Rm 510 New York, NY 10018-6850.

VASSALLO, Marie Thérèse; Maltese opera and concert singer (mezzo-soprano) and singing teacher; b 4 March 1949, St Julien's; d of the late Francis X. and of Theresa (née Theuma) Vassallo; m Charles Axiak 1969; two s. *Education:* St Catherine's High School, Maria Regina Grammar School and Acad Int de Formation Musicale (Paris). *Career:* Performances include Stabat Mater (Dvořák), Paulus (Mendelssohn), Missa Requiem and Coronation Mass (Mozart), Messiah and Judas Maccabaeus (Handel), Oratorio For Our Time (Lizieschi), Stabat Mater (Pergolesi), Te Deum (Bruckner), Dido and Aeneas (Purcell), Symphony No 9 (Beethoven), Stabat Mater (Rossini), Missa Sancti Nicolai and Paukenmesse (Hadyn), Carmen (Bizet), Cavalleria Rusticana and L'Amico Fritz (Mascagni), Ipogeana and Caterina Desguanez (Pace), Il-Weghda (Camilleri), Madam Butterfly (Puccini), Le Nozze di Figaro (Mozart), Cencerentola and Il Barbiere di Siviglia (Rossini), Otello (Verdi); has premiered several works by Maltese composers; Head of Del to Democratic People's Repub of Korea 1986, 1987; currently Dir Marie Thérèse Vassallo Voice Studio; Pres Asscn of Maltese Lyrical Singers; organizer annual Melita-Rossiya Competition for lyrical singers and of concerts for Foundation for Int Studies, Univ of Malta and Malta Cultural Inst; Assoc mem Performing Rights Soc, London; twice winner of Festival del Vulcano d'Oro, winner of Festival del Grappolo d'Oro and Festival della Canzone Mediterranea, Premio Città di Valletta 1994; Award for the Promotion of Cultural Relations between Malta and Russia 1995. *Publications include:* Songs: Bit-Tlikki Tlikki 1967, Stejjer Ghal Qabel Jidlam 1979. *Leisure interests:* swimming, walking, reading, cooking. *Address:* La Paloma, 16 St Henry St, Sliema SLM 03, Malta. *Telephone:* 338923; *Fax:* 338923.

VASSILIOU, Androula, MIA; Cypriot lawyer and organization executive; b 30 Nov 1943, Paphos; d of Mr Georgiadou; m George Vassiliou 1966 (Pres of Cyprus 1988–93); two d one s. *Education:* Pancyprian Gymnasium (Nicosia) and Univ Coll London. *Career:* Called to the Bar, Middle Temple Inn of Court, London 1964; practised law in Cyprus until the election of her husband as Pres of Cyprus in 1988, specializing in corp law; Legal Adviser Standard Chartered Bank, Bank of Cyprus and others 1969–88; mem Bd of Dirs of numerous cos; Hon Pres Bureau of Women's Affairs, Ministry of Justice 1988; Gen Sec, then Hon Pres UN Asscn of Cyprus; mem Exec Cttee World Fed of UN Asscns (WFUNA), later first woman Pres 1991; Co-Founder and Pres Cyprus Asscn of Univ Women, Cttee for Restoration of Human Rights

Throughout Cyprus; Hon Pres Perm Agency on Womens' Rights in Cyprus 1988; Founder and Pres Cyprus Fund for Music and Other Fine Arts; Pres Cyprus Welfare Council; Hon Pres Cttee for Restoration of Human Rights; Patron Muscular Dystrophy Research Trust, Cyprus Family Planning Asscn, Anti-rheumatism Soc, Asscn of Friends of Cancer Patients, Asscn of Friends of Children with Speech Problems. *Leisure interests:* walking, swimming, music. *Address:* World Federation of UN Asscns (WFUNA), c/o Palais des Nations, 1211 Geneva 10, Switzerland. *Telephone:* (22) 7330730; *Fax:* (22) 7334838.

VATSYAYAN, Kapila (Malik), MA, PH D; Indian civil servant and organization executive; b 25 Dec 1928; d of Ramlal and Satyawati Malik; m S. H. Vatsyayan. *Education:* Univs of Delhi and Michigan (USA) and Banaras Hindu Univ. *Career:* Faculty of English Univ of Delhi 1949–54; Asst Educational Adviser Ministry of Educ 1954–62, Deputy Educational Adviser, Dept of Culture 1964–74, Joint Educational Adviser 1975–82, Additional Sec 1982–85; Sec Dept of Arts, Ministry of Human Resource Devt 1985–90; Joint Sec XXVI Int Congress of Orientalists, New Delhi 1962–64; Visiting Prof Univ of Colombia 1979–80, Univ of Philadelphia, USA 1981; Academic Dir Indira Gandhi Nat Centre for the Arts 1987–; Vice-Pres Indian Council for Cultural Relations, Vice-Pres India Int Centre, New Delhi; Fellow of Nat Acad of Music, Dance and Drama 1970, Manipuri Akademi of Dance, Drama and the Arts 1978, Manipur Sahitya Akademi (Imphal) 1985, Asiatic Soc of Bombay 1991; Foreign mem Russian Acad of Sciences; Hon D LITT (Banaras Hindu Univ, Rabindra Bharati Calcutta, Manipuri Univ, Mt Hollyoke Coll, USA, Rashtriya Sanskrit Vidyapeetham); awards include Campbell Memorial Gold Medal, Asiatic Soc 1980, Sarangdeva Prize of the Surasringar (Bombay) 1981, R. P. Chanda Centenary Medal, Asiatic Soc (Calcutta) 1982, Srimanta Sankardeva Award (Govt of Assam) 1990, NPI Award (Bharat Vasundhara Samman) 1994, Padma Shri (Govt of India), John D. Rockefeller III Award (Asian Cultural Council, New York). *Publications:* Classical Indian Dance in Literature and the Arts 1968, Indian Classical Dance 1972, Traditions of Indian Folk Dance 1975, Indian Theatre: the multiple traditions 1981, Painting and Dance 1982, The Square and the Circle of the Indian Art 1983, Bundi Gita Govinda 1983, Assam Gita Govinda 1985, Mewari Gita Govinda 1987. *Address:* Indira Gandhi National Centre for the Arts, Central Vista Mess, Janpath, New Delhi 110 01, India (Office); D1/23 Satya Marg, Chanakya Puri, New Delhi 110 021, India (Home). *Telephone:* (11) 3384901 (Office); (11) 4670674 (Home).

VAUGHAN, Martha, MD; American biochemist; b 4 Aug 1926, Dodgeville, WI; d of John Anthony and Luciel (née Ellingen) Vaughan; m Jack Orloff 1951 (died 1988); three s. *Education:* Univ of Chicago and Yale Univ School of Medicine. *Career:* Internship Medical Service, New Haven Hosp, Yale 1950–51; Fellow Dept of Research Medicine, Univ of Pennsylvania 1951–52; Fellow Laboratory of Cellular Physiology, Nat Heart Inst 1952–54, mem Research Staff 1954–; Chief Metabolism Dept Nat Heart and Lung Inst, Bethesda; MD 1968–74, Acting Chief Molecular Disease Br 1974–76, Chief Lab of Cellular Metabolism 1974–94, apptd Deputy Chief Pulmonary-Critical Care Medicine Br 1994; mem Editorial Bd Journal of Biology and Chemistry 1971–76, 1980–83, 1988–90; mem Editorial Advisory Bd Molecular Pharmacology 1972–80; Ed Biochemistry and Biophysics Research 1990–92; has published 200 research papers and 90 reviews in professional journals; mem Bd of Dirs Foundation for Advanced Educ in Sciences Inc (Bethesda) 1979–, Exec Cttee 1980–, Treas 1984–86, Vice-Pres 1986–88, Pres 1988–90; mem Asscn of American Physicians, American Soc of Clinical Investigation; elected to NAS 1985, American Acad of Arts and Sciences 1991; Meritorious Service Medal US Public Health Service 1974, Distinguished Service Medal 1979, Commissioned Officer award 1982. *Address:* NIH, National Heart, Lung and Blood Institute, Bldg 10, Room 5N-307, Bethesda, MD 20892, USA (Office); 11608 W Hill Drive, Rockville, MD 20892, USA (Home). *Telephone:* (301) 496-4554 (Office); *Fax:* (301) 402-1610 (Office).

VAZ DA SILVA, Helena M.; Portuguese politician; b 3 July 1939, Lisbon. *Career:* Fmr MEP (Group of the European Liberal, Democrat and Reform Party – ELDR, PSD), fmr mem Cttee on Culture, Youth, Educ and the Media, Del for relations with Israel. *Address:* c/o European Parliament, rue Wiertz, 1047 Brussels, Belgium.

VEASEY, Josephine, CBE; British opera and concert singer (retd) and vocal consultant; b 10 July 1930, London; m Ande Anderson 1952 (divorced 1969); one s one d. *Career:* Mem chorus Covent Garden Opera Co 1948–50, Soloist 1955; Prin Mezzo-Soprano, Royal Opera House, Covent Garden; has sung every major mezzo-soprano role in repertory; many foreign engagements including Salzburg Festival (Austria), La Scala, Milan (Italy), Metropolitan Opera House, New York (USA), and Paris opera; has made recordings with von Karajan, Solti, Bernstein and Colin Davis; Prof Royal Acad of Music 1982–83; Vocal Consultant, English Nat Opera 1985–94; now teaching privately; Hon RAM. *Operas include:* Der Rosenkavalier, Le Nozze di Figaro, Iphigènie, Così fan Tutte, Aida, Die Walküre, Das Rheingold, Carmen, Les Troyens, La Damnation de Faust, Beatrice and Benedict, Death of Cleopatra, Combattimento di Tancredi e Clorinda, Werther, Don Carlos, Orfeo, Norma, The Barber of Seville, Parsifal, Hamlet 1980, We Come to the River; *Concert performances include:* Requiem (Verdi), L'enfance du Christ and Romeo and Juliet (Berlioz), Petite Messe Solennelle and Stabat Mater (Rossini), Messiah (Handel). *Leisure interests:* reading, gardening. *Address:* 5 Meadow View, Whitchurch, Hants RG28 7BL, UK. *Telephone:* (1256) 896813.

VECSEI, Eva Hollo, B ARCH, FRAIC; Canadian/Hungarian architect; b 21 Aug 1930, Vienna; m André Vecsei 1952; one s one d. *Education:* School of Architecture (Univ of Tech Sciences, Budapest). *Career:* Assoc Prof School of Architecture, Univ of Budapest, designer various public bldgs in Budapest, and winner of housing competitions 1952–56; Designer/Developer, later Assoc ARCOP Architects, Montréal, PQ, Canada in charge of design of Massey Award winners: Place Bonaventure, Montréal, Life Science Bldg, Univ of Dalhousie, Halifax, City Hall and Police Station, Laval, Student Centre, McGill Univ, Montréal 1957–71; Assoc of D. Dimakopoulos, Architect, Montréal 1971–73; in pvt practice, Eva H. Vecsei, Architect 1973–84, maj projects include La Cité (7 acres redevt project) Montréal, Commercial and Financial Centre, Karachi, Pakistan; with Vecsei Architects 1984–, projects include Drama Faculty and Experimental Theatre, St Thérèse, PQ, Inter-Municipal Library and Recreational Centre, Dollard-des-Ormeaux, PQ, Coll Marie de France, new Elementary School and Gym, Montréal, Residence Montefiore, Montréal, Municipal Library, St Lambert, PQ; lecture tour People's Repub of China 1984; mem Nat Capital Comm Advisory Cttee on Design 1982–87; Juror Nat Arts Council Cttee for grants, and for several architectural competitions and Gov Gen Awards; advisor to Master of Architecture programme, McGill Univ School of Architecture 2000; Hon Fellow American Inst of Architects; Canadian Architect Award of Excellence for office bldg; Prix Orange for renovation of Passage du Musée, Montréal. *Exhibitions include:* Int Union of Woman Architects, Paris 1978; 'Travelling Canadian Exhibition', Europe; Boston – the 300th Year Anniversary: 'La Cité Linéaire'; *Publications include:* History of American Architecture 1980, Encyclopedia of Contemporary Architects 1980, 1997–98, La Bâtisseuse de la Cité 1993, Designing Women 2000. *Address:* 4417 Circle Rd, Montréal, PQ H3W 1Y6, Canada. *Telephone:* (514) 932-7100; *Fax:* (514) 932-7987; *E-mail:* vecsei@total.net.

VEGA, Suzanne; American singer and songwriter; m Mitchell Froom 1995; one d. *Recordings include:* Solitude Standing, Marlene on the Wall, Tom's Diner, Luka, Small Blue Thing, Book of Dreams 1990, Days of Open Hand 1990, Men in a War 1990, Tired of Sleeping 1990, Tom's Album 1991, Left of Centre, In Liverpool 1992, 99F° 1992, Nine Objects of Desire 1996.

VEIERØD, Tove; Norwegian politician; b 19 Sept 1940, Harstad; m Tom Veierød; two c. *Career:* Fmr secondary school teacher of English, Norwegian and Literature; State Sec Ministry of Science and Cultural Affairs 1986–88; Chief Information Officer Norsk Hydro, Harstad then Oslo 1988–90; Deputy Chair Norwegian Cultural Council and Exec Cttee Norwegian Broadcasting Corpn until Nov 1990; Minister of Health and Social Affairs Nov 1990–92; fmr Chair N Norway Arts Festival; fmr mem Troms Co Exec Bd and Co Council, N Norwegian Cultural Council. *Telephone:* (2) 34-90-90; *Fax:* (2) 34-95-75.

VEIL, Simone, DBE, L EN D; French politician; b 13 July 1927, Nice; d of André Jacob and Yvonne Steinmetz; m Antoine Veil 1946; three s. *Education:* Inst d'Etudes Politiques de Paris. *Career:* Apptd to Magistrature 1956; Titular Attaché Ministry of Justice 1957–59, various posts 1957–69; mem pvt office of Mr Pleven Lord Chancellor 1969; Sec-Gen Conseil Supérieur de la Magistrature 1970–74; mem Office de Radiodiffusion-Télévision Française (ORTF) Admin Council 1972–74; Dir Fondation de France 1972; Minister of Health 1974–76, of Health and Social Security 1977–79, Chair Information Bd on Nuclear Power 1977, Minister of Health and Family 1978, of Social Affairs, Health and Urban Devt 1993–95; MEP 1979–93, Pres of EP 1979–82, Chair of Legal Affairs Cttee 1982, 1984–93, Chair Liberal and Democratic Group 1984–93, Pres French Cttee on the Environment 1984–89; Leader Centre-Right List for European elections 1989, mem Conseil Constitutionnel 1998–; Pres Fondation pour la Mémoire de la Shoah 2001; Hon DBE, UK 1998; Dr hc (Princeton) 1975, (Weizmann Inst) 1976, (Bar Ilan, Yale, Cambridge, Edinburgh) 1980, (Georgetown, Urbino) 1981, (Yeshiva) 1982, (Free Univ of Brussels, Sussex) 1984, (Brandeis) 1989; Hon LL D (Glasgow) 1995; Chevalier de l'Ordre Nat du Mérite; Médaille pénitentiaire; Médaille de l'éduc surveillée; numerous foreign decorations including Grand Officer, Nat Order of the Lion (Senegal), Order of Merit of the Repub (Ivory Coast), Order of Isabel la Católica (Spain), Grand Cross Order of Merit (Fed Repub of Germany), Order of Rio Branco (Brazil), Blue Cross of Social Security (Spain), Grand Cross (Senegal), Commdr Wissam al' Auwit (Morocco), Order of Merit (Luxembourg), Order of the Phoenix (Greece), Grand Cordon Order of the Liberator (Venezuela); awards include Onassis Foundation Prize 1980, Charlemagne Prize 1981, 1985, Louise Weiss Foundation Prize 1981, Louise Michel Prize 1983, European Merit Prize 1983, Jabotinsky Prize (USA) 1983, Prize for Everyday Courage 1984, Special Freedom Prize 1984, Fiera di Messina 1984, Thomas Dehler Prize 1988, Klein Foundation Prize (USA) 1991, Truman Prize for Peace (Jerusalem) 1991, Giulietta Prize (Verona) 1991, Atlantida Prize (Barcelona) 1991. *Publication:* Les données psycho-sociologiques de l'adoption (jtly) 1969. *Address:* 10 rue de Rome, 75008 Paris, France (Office); 11 place Vauban, 75007 Paris, France (Home). *Telephone:* (1) 42-93-00-60 (Office); (1) 40-56-48-75 (Home); *Fax:* (1) 40-08-03-62 (Office).

VEIVERYTÈ-LIUGAILIENÈ, Sofija; Lithuanian artist; b 13 April 1926, Kaunas; d of the late Motiejus Veiverys and Bronè Veivierienè; m Boguslovas Liugaila 1944; one s one d. *Education:* Inst of Monumental and Applied Arts (Kaunas). *Career:* Teacher Inst of Monumental and Applied Arts, Kaunas 1949; Head Studio of Fresco/Mosaic, Lithuania State Art Acad, Vilnius 1968, Head Personal Painting Studio 1978, Prof 1982–; has participated in nat and int exhibitions; Honoured Art Worker 1974; Painter of the Nation 1976; Lithuania Prize 1976; Laureate of the Baltic Countries 1981; Grand Prix for Portrait, Yugoslavia Biennale 1984; Exhibition Silver Medal, Moscow 1981; Nation's Friendship Order 1986; Order of the Grand Duke Gediminas (III) of the Repub of Lithuania 1996; People's Artist of Lithuania. *Publications:* Monographs 1976, 1986, exhibition catalogues, Vilnius 1981, Bulgaria 1986, book of reproductions of her paintings 1987. *Leisure interest:* painting. *Address:* Kuosu 4-1, 2055 Vilnius, Lithuania. *Telephone:* (2) 341669.

VELHO RODRIGUES, Frances Vitória; Mozambican diplomatist; b 30 April 1952, Maputo; m Isaac Murargy; one s one d. *Education:* Geneva and Florence. *Career:* Expert Researcher in Econ Planning, Ministry of Foreign Affairs 1977–79, Dir Int Econ Relations Dept 1979–85; Amb 1980, to Belgium 1985, concurrently to the EU (fmrly EC) 1985, to Luxembourg and the Netherlands 1988, to Austria 1990, to Greece 1992; mem Standing Cttee Southern Africa Devt Co-ordination Conf 1980–85; mem Nat Exec Council UNESCO, Mozambique 1990; Distinction Roll of Honour, Ministry of Foreign Affairs 1981. *Address:* c/o Ministry of Foreign Affairs and Co-operation, Avda Julius Nyerere 4, Maputo, Mozambique (Office); Ave Marie Jeanne 19, 1640 Rhode Saint Genèse, Belgium (Home); Av dos Cronistas 12, Sommershild, Maputo, Mozambique (Home).

VELKOVA, Anna Jordanova, DIP ENG; Bulgarian business executive; b 5 April 1943, Varna; m Dragomir Velkov 1968; one d. *Education:* Higher Inst of Chemical Tech (Sofia) and Univ of Sofia. *Career:* Pres Uni Logos Ltd training co; Pres ETERNA Women in Business Club, Sofia; Bulgarian Businesswoman of 1991. *Leisure interest:* work. *Address:* ETERNA, 1000 Sofia, Vasil Levski Str 39, 5th Floor, Bulgaria. *Telephone:* (2) 89-78-26; *Fax:* (2) 87-25-48.

VELLIDIS, Katarina; Greek publisher; b 1947, Thessaloniki; d of Ioannis and Anna Vellidis; m (divorced); one d. *Education:* Univ of Geneva (Switzerland) and Univ of Paris (Sorbonne). *Career:* Pres of Bd and Man Dir I. K. Vellidis Press Org of Northern Greece (publrs of newspapers and magazines) 1980–; Pres Ioannis and Anna Vellidis Foundation; numerous awards including Silver Medal of Acad of Athens. *Address:* Tsimiski 77, 54622 Thessaloniki, Greece. *Telephone:* (31) 521621.

VENDLER, Helen Hennessy, PH D; American professor of English literature and literary critic; b 30 April 1933, Boston, MA; d of George Hennessy and Helen Conway; one s. *Education:* Emmanuel Coll (Boston, MA) and Harvard Univ. *Career:* Instructor Cornell Univ 1960–63; Lecturer Swarthmore and Haverford Colls, PA 1963–64; Asst Prof Smith Coll, Northampton, MA 1964–66; Assoc Prof Boston Univ 1966–68, Prof 1968–85; Visiting Prof Harvard Univ 1981–85, Kenan Prof 1985–, Assoc Academic Dean 1987–92, Porter Univ Prof 1990–; Sr Fellow Harvard Soc of Fellows 1981–92; Fulbright Lecturer Univ of Bordeaux 1968–69; Overseas Fellow Churchill Coll, Cambridge 1980; Parnell Fellow Magdalene Coll, Cambridge 1995, Hon Fellow 1996–; poetry critic New Yorker 1978–; mem American Acad of Arts and Sciences, Norwegian Acad, American Philosophical Soc, Educ Advisory Bd Guggenheim Foundation, Pulitzer Prize Bd 1990–99; Fulbright Fellow 1954; American Asscn of University Women (AAUW) Fellow 1959; Guggenheim Fellow 1971–72; American Council of Learned Socs Fellow 1971–72; NEH Fellow 1980, 1985, 1994; Wilson Fellow 1994; several hon degrees; Lowell Prize 1969; Explicator Prize 1969; Nat Inst of Arts and Letters Award 1975; Nat Book Critics Award 1980; Newton Arvin/Truman Capote Prize 1996. *Publications include:* Yeats's Vision and the Later Plays 1963, On Extended Wings: Wallace Stevens' Longer Poems 1969, The Poetry of George Herbert 1975, Part of Nature, Part of Us 1980, The Odes of John Keats 1983, Wallace Stevens: Words Chosen Out of Desire 1985, Harvard Book of Contemporary American Poetry 1985, The Music of What Happens 1988, The Given and the Made 1995, The Breaking of Style 1995, Soul Says 1995, Poems, Poets, Poetry 1996, The Art of Shakespeare's Sonnets 1997, Seamus Heaney 2000. *Leisure interests:* travel, music. *Address:* Harvard University, Dept of English, The Barker Center, Cambridge, MA 02138, USA (Office); 54 Trowbridge St, Apt B, Cambridge, MA 02138, USA (Home). *Telephone:* (617) 496-6028 (Office); (617) 547-9197 (Home); *Fax:* (617) 496-8737 (Office).

VENEMAN, Ann M.; American politician and lawyer. *Career:* Assoc Admin Foreign Agric Service, US Dept of Agric 1986–89, Deputy Under-Sec of Agric for Int Affairs and Commodity Programmes 1989–91, Deputy Sec of Dept 1991–93; Sec Calif Dept of Food and Agric 1995–99; partner Nossaman, Guthner, Knox and Elliott 1999–2001; Sec of Agric 2001–. *Address:* Department of Agriculture, 1400 Independence Ave, SW, Washington, DC 20250, USA. *Telephone:* (202) 720-2791; *Internet:* www.usda.gov.

VENTER, Elizabeth Hendrina (Rina), D PHIL; South African social worker and politician; b 9 Dec 1938, Krug; m H. S. Venter 1963; two s. *Education:* Carletonville Afrikaans High School. *Career:* Part-time Lecturer Univ of Pretoria 1970–73; mem South African Welfare Bd 1982–85, South African Birth Control Bd 1983–, Welfare Bd of N Transvaal 1979–82; Supervisor Adoption Services SAVF 1974–79; mem Parl 1984, for Innesdale 1989–94; Minister of Nat Health and Population Devt 1989–90, of Nat Health and Health Services 1990–94, of Welfare 1991–94. *Leisure interests:* welfare work, reading, international history. *Address:* POB 12200, Clubview 0014, South Africa. *Telephone:* (12) 6458490.

VENTURA, Isabella; Italian European Union official. *Career:* Fmr Chef de Cabinet to Vice-Pres of Comm of the EC; fmr Head Directorate B (Resources), Directorate-Gen XIX: Budgets, Comm of the EC (now European Comm of the EU); Dir-Gen (Financial Controller) Directorate-Gen XX: Financial Control. *Address:* European Commission of the EU, Rue de la Loi 200, 1049 Brussels, Belgium. *Telephone:* (2) 295-37-75; *Fax:* (2) 295-66-35.

VERBITSKAYA, Ludmila Alekseyevna; Russian philologist; b 17 June 1936; m; two d. *Career:* Lab asst, then jr researcher, docent Chair of Philology, Leningrad State Univ until 1979, Prof Chair of Phonetics 1979–85, Head Chair of Gen Linguistics 1985–, Pro-Rector on scientific work, First Pro-Rector 1989, Acting Rector 1994, Rector 1995–; Vice-Pres UNESCO Comm on Problems of Women's Educ; Rep to Exec Council of Int Asscn of Univs; mem Russian Acad of Humanitarian Sciences, Acad of Sciences of Higher School, Presidium Int Asscn of Russian Language and Literature Teachers, Presidium Conf of Rectors of European Univs; mem of Council Our Home Russia movt 1996–99; has written over 150 publs; Dr Linguistics; Hon degrees from numerous foreign univs. *Address:* St Petersburg State Univ, Universitetskaya nab 7/9, 199034 St Petersburg, Russian Federation. *Telephone:* (812) 218-51-52.

VERDIEVA, Zemfiza Nadiz Kizi, PH D; Georgian/Azerbaijani professor of English and French; b 19 Nov 1935, Tbilisi; two d. *Education:* Azerbaijan State Pedagogical Inst of Foreign Languages. *Career:* Apptd Jr Asst in English and French Azerbaijan State Pedagogical Inst of Foreign Languages 1957, apptd Lecturer 1968, Prof 1972, Chair of English until 1973, Rector 1973–95; leader Inst Glossary Dept preparing dictionaries; mem Azerbaijan Parl 1990–95, mem Women's Cttee; mem Azerbaijan Women's Soc 1973–, apptd Chair 1989; about 184 publs on women's and social issues, typological linguistics, methods of teaching foreign languages, lexicology and lexicography; numerous magazine and newspaper articles; Assoc mem Acad of Sciences of Azerbaijan. *Address:* Azerbaijan Women's Committee, 37004 Baku, Bojuk Jalce St 6, Azerbaijan.

VERDY, Violette (pseudonym of Nelly Armande Guillerm); French ballet dancer and dance teacher; b 1 Dec 1933, Pont-l'Abbé; d of Renan and Jeanne (née Chateaureynaud) Guillerm; m Colin M. A. Clark 1961. *Education:* Cours Hattemer (Paris). *Career:* Ballet debut with Ballets des Champs-Elysées, Paris; Dancer with numerous ballet cos including Ballets de Paris–Roland Petit, American Ballet Theater, La Scala Ballet (Milan, Italy), London Festival Ballet, etc; Prin Dancer New York City Ballet, USA 1957–76, Assoc Prof 1984–; Dance Dir Opéra de Paris 1977–80; Artistic Dir Boston Ballet (USA) 1980–84; Prof Indiana Univ School of Music 1996–; CORPS de Ballet Int Award (USA) 2001; GALA XV Woman of Distinction Award (Birmingham Southern Coll, USA) 2001. *Ballets and plays include:* Miss Julie, Sonatine, Malatesta. *Address:* School of Music, Indiana University, Bloomington, IN 47405-2200, USA.

VERHASSELT, Yola L. G., D ÈS SC; Belgian professor of geography; b 14 Aug 1937, Antwerp; d of Louis and Joanna (née Cornelis) Verhasselt; m Paul Van Wettere 1966 (divorced 1972). *Education:* Université Libre de Bruxelles. *Career:* Asst Lecturer Université Libre de Bruxelles 1959–61; Research Fellow Fonds Nat de la Recherche Scientifique 1961–65; Tutor Centre Universitaire d'Anvers 1966–70; Prof Geography Inst, Vrije Universiteit Brussel 1968–; Perm Sec Royal Acad of Overseas Sciences; Pres Nat Cttee of Geography, Belgian Asscn Geographic Studies; Vice-Pres Royal Geographic Soc of Belgium; Treasurer ICSU; Temporary advisor of WHO; Hon Pres Comm on Health and Devt, Int Geographic Union; writer of 4 books (3 jtly) and 93 articles published in scientific journals; awarded Prix de Géographie Maurice Rahir 1966, Lauréat d'Honneur Int Geographic Union 1996. *Leisure interests:* swimming, tennis, judo, poetry, music, theatre. *Address:* Vrije Universiteit Brussel, Geografisch Instituut, Pleinlaan 2, 1050 Brussels, Belgium. *Telephone:* (2) 629-33-81; *Fax:* (2) 539-23-53.

VERMA, Veena, MA; Indian politician; b 1 Sept 1941, Rajasthan; d of P. N. and V. Raizada; m Shrikant Verma 1967 (deceased); one s. *Education:* Rajasthan Univ. *Career:* Congress Party mem Rajya Sabha (Council of States, Upper House) 1986–, Vice-Pres Parl Cttee on Official Language, Anti-Dowry and Women's Welfare Cttee, mem Indo-German Parl Group; Pres Children's Acad; f Shrikant Verma Literary Award, Karmja All India Women's Asscn; Vice-Pres All India Women's Congress, Indian Council of World Affairs, Nehru Bal Samiti; Chair Family Counselling Centre Nehru Bal Samiti; Patron Indian Writers' Asscn, Calcutta (now Kolkata); mem Cen Social Welfare Bd; Sec Cultural Cttee, Indo-China Soc; awards include Shiromani Award 1989, Priyadarshini Award 1989, Rashtra Gaurav Award, Bhartiya Pratishtha Award, Feroz Gandhi Award for Nat Integration. *Leisure interests:* reading, music, travel, computers, gardening. *Address:* Rajya

Sabha, Parliament House, New Delhi 100 011, India (Office); 4 Safdarjung Lane, New Delhi 110 011, India (Home). *Telephone:* (11) 3793301 (Office); (11) 3010001 (Home); *Fax:* (11) 3019999 (Home).

VERMEULE, Emily Dickinson Townsend, PH D; American professor of classics and classical archaeology; b 11 Aug 1928, New York; d of Clinton Blake and Eleanor Mary (née Meneely) Townsend; m Cornelius Clarkson Vermeule 1957; one s one d. *Education:* Bryn Mawr Coll (PA), Radcliffe Coll (Cambridge, MA) and St Anne's Coll (Oxford, UK). *Career:* Instructor Bryn Mawr Coll 1956–57, Wellesley Coll 1957–58, Prof of Art and Greek 1965–70, Chair Dept of Art 1966–67; Asst Prof of Classics Boston Univ 1958–61, Assoc Prof 1961–65; Research Fellow Boston Museum of Fine Arts 1965–; Zemurray Stone-Radcliffe Prof Harvard Univ 1970–94, Emer Prof 1994–; Sather Prof Univ of California at Berkeley 1975, mem Bd Dirs Humanities Research Inst 1988–91, Bd of Govs 1988–89; Geddes-Harrower Prof of Greek Art and Archaeology, Univ of Aberdeen, UK 1980–81; James C. Loeb Visiting Prof Harvard Univ 1969, Bernhard Visiting Prof Williams Coll 1986; Dir Univ Cyprus Expedition 1971–; excavations in Greece, Turkey, Libya and Cyprus; Trustee Isabella Stewart Gardner Museum, Boston 1988–; Pres American Philological Asscn 1994–95; mem American Inst of Archaeology, American Acad of Arts and Sciences, Library of Congress, Smithsonian Council; Guggenheim Fellow 1964–65; Hon D LITT (Rutgers) 1968, (Smith Coll) 1972, (Wheaton Coll) 1973, (Trinity Coll) 1974, (Tufts) 1980, (Bates Coll) 1983, (Miami) 1986; Hon DFA (Massachusetts) 1971; Hon LL D (Regis Coll) 1971; Hon LHD (Emmanuel Coll) 1980, (Pittsburgh) 1983, (Princeton) 1989, (Bard Coll) 1993; Charles J. Goodwin Award of Merit (American Philological Asscn) 1980. *Publications:* Euripides V Electra 1959, Greece in the Bronze Age 1964, The Trojan War in Greek Art 1964, Götterkult 1974, The Mound of Darkness 1975, Death in Early Greek Art and Poetry 1978, Myceanean Pictorial Vase-Painting (jtly) 1982, A Bronze Age Potters' Quarter on Morphon Bay in Cyprus 1990; numerous articles in professional journals. *Leisure interests:* dogs, gardening. *Address:* Harvard University, Dept of Classics, 319 Boylston Hall, Cambridge, MA 02138, USA (Office); 47 Coolidge Hill Rd, Cambridge, MA 02138, USA (Home). *Telephone:* (617) 495-1734 (Office); (617) 864-1879 (Home); *Fax:* (617) 495-1769 (Office).

VERNON, Konstanze; German ballet dancer and ballet teacher; b 2 Jan 1939, Berlin; d of the late Friedrich Herzfeld and of Thea Eckstein-Vernon; m Fred G. Hoffmann 1968. *Education:* Studied dance with Tatjana Gsovsky (Berlin) and Nora Kiss (Paris). *Career:* Prima Ballerina, Bayerische Staatsoper, Munich 1963–81, currently Dir Ballet Acad; Founder Heinz-Bosl-Stiftung (for promotion of young talent in ballet) 1978; awards include Berlin Art Prize, Bayerischer Verdienstorden 1982, Culture Prize (Munich) 1990, German Dance Prize (Deutscher Berufsverband für Tanzpädagogie) 1991, Bayerischer Maximilians Orden für Kunst und Wissenschaft 1993. *Leisure interests:* painting, music, skiing. *Address:* Ballettzentrum, Wilhelmstr 19B, 80801 Munich, Germany. *Telephone:* (89) 337763.

VERRETT, Shirley; American opera singer (soprano); b 31 May 1931, New Orleans, LA; d of Leon and Elvira Verrett; m Louis Lomonaco 1963; one d. *Education:* Juilliard School of Music (New York). *Career:* Operatic debut as mezzo-soprano taking title role in Carmen, Spoleto Festival 1962; same role for debut at Bolshoi Opera, Moscow 1963, New York City Opera 1966, Florence, Italy 1968, Metropolitan Opera, New York 1968; sang at Royal Opera House, Covent Garden, London in Un Ballo in Maschera 1966, Aida 1967, Don Carlos 1968, Il Trovatore 1970; debut at San Carlo, Naples, Italy in Maria Stuarda 1969, at La Scala, Milan in Samson et Dalila 1970, at Vienna Staatsoper 1970, at Teatro Liceo, Barcelona, Spain 1971, at Paris Opera as Azucena 1972; other mezzo-soprano roles in Orfeo, Les Troyens, Bluebeard's Castle, Siege of Corinth, Norma; debut as soprano in title role of La Favorita, Dallas Civic Opera 1971; debut at San Francisco Opera in title role of L'Africaine 1972; first artist to sing roles of both Dido and Cassandra in one single full-length production of Les Troyens, Metropolitan Opera, New York 1973; other soprano roles at La Scala, Milan 1975, La Scala at Kennedy Center, Washington, DC 1976, with Opera Co of Boston 1976, etc; sang title role of Norma, Metropolitan Opera, New York 1976 (in the same season took mezzo-soprano role of Adalgisa—first singer since Grisi to sing both roles); now sings only soprano roles; debut appearance at Opéra Bastille, Paris 1990; appeared in film Maggio

Musicale 1990, as Nettie Fowler in Broadway production of Carousel 1994–95; frequent appearances with US and European opera houses, with US symphony orchestras; has appeared as soloist on Milan's Radiotelevisione Italiana (RAI); was subject of BBC TV feature Profiles in Music 1971, of documentary Black Diva 1985; Prof of Voice, School of Music, Univ of Michigan 1996–; Dr hc (Holy Cross Coll, Worcester, Massachusetts, Northeastern Univ); Commdr des Arts et des Lettres 1984. *Leisure interests:* cooking, musical biographies, collecting English and American antiques, collecting engravings of famous singers. *Address:* School of Music, University of Michigan, Ann Arbor, MI 48109, USA.

VERSACE, Donatella; Italian designer; b 1955, Reggio Calabria; d of Antonio and Francesca Versace; sister of the late Gianni Versace; m Paul Beck; one s one d. *Career:* Joined Versace 1978, fmrly overseer of advertising and public relations, accessories designer, children's collection designer, sole designer Versus and Isante lines; Creative Dir Gianni Versace Group 1997–. *Address:* c/o Keeble Cavaco and Duka Inc, 450 West 15th St, Suite 604, New York, NY 10011, USA.

VERSNEL-SCHMITZ, Machteld Maria; Netherlands politician; b 8 Sept 1940, Bilthoven; d of W. K. E. Schmitz and E. C. J. Blömer; m J. F. Versnel 1968; three s. *Education:* Univ of Utrecht. *Career:* Mem staff Univ of Utrecht Museum 1961–72; mem Democraten 66 party, mem Party Insts Bds 1966–89; mem Utrecht City Council 1970–74, 1982–86; mem Utrecht Prov Council 1978–79; mem staff Ministry of the Interior 1986–89; mem Staten-Generaal (States-Gen, Parl) 1989–; Bd mem of several cultural insts 1970–. *Leisure interests:* reading, tennis, swimming, music. *Address:* Parkstraat 41, 3501 PE Utrecht, Netherlands. *Telephone:* (30) 231-5015; *Fax:* (30) 236-9269; *E-mail:* versnelm .icns.nl.

VERTINSKAIA, Lidia Vladimirovna; Russian artist and actress; b 14 April 1923, China; d of the late Vladimir and Lidia Tsirgvava; m Alexander Vertinsky 1942 (died 1957); two d. *Education:* Privately in China and Surikov Art Inst (Moscow). *Career:* Came to Russia from Shanghai 1943; mem Russian Union of Artists 1958–; nat and int exhibitions include Prague and Bratislava, Bucharest and Budapest 1956–58, Soviet Women Artists 1963, 1967, 'The Blue Roads of Russia', Lenin's Memorial House 1979–82, Young Moscow Artists; Ed books of husband's memoirs 1989, 1990; awarded several Certificates of Approval from London Acad of Art for drawings; received other awards from Moscow Cttee for the Active Work of Peace Activists 1980, 1981, Women World Congress 1981, Moscow Women Artists World Congress 1987. *Films:* Sak Ko, Kiev Lianka; three films of fairy tales. *Leisure interests:* reading, visiting art exhibitions, theatre. *Address:* 103009 Moscow, Tverskaia ul 12, kv 283, Russian Federation. *Telephone:* (095) 209-20-33.

VERTINSKAYA, Anastasiya Aleksandrovna; Russian actress; b 19 Dec 1944, Moscow; d of Aleksander Vertinsky; one s. *Education:* Schukin Theatre School. *Career:* Actress Theatre Sovremennik 1969–80, Moscow Art Theatre 1980–90; theatre teacher in Oxford, UK, Switzerland (European Film School), France (Comédie Française); f Russian Drama troupe in Paris; Dir production Mirage or The Route of The Russian Pierrot; cinema debut 1961; Dir Benefit Fund for Actors 1996; Honoured Artist of Russia 1980; People's Artist of Russia 1988. *Films include:* Red Sails 1961, A Man-Amphibia 1962, Hamlet 1964, War and Peace 1967, Anna Karenina 1968, Do Not Grieve! 1969, A Man Before His Time 1973, The Master and Margarita 1994, Gad-Fly, Occurence with Polynin, Bremen Musicians 1999 and others; *Plays include:* You Can Only Dream about Rest 1962, Princess Turaudot 1964, Naked King 1967, Craftsmen 1967, Seagull 1968, Norodovoltsy 1968, Decembrists 1969, Bolmsheviks 1970, Twelfth Night 1969, Provincial Jokes 1970, The Cherry Orchard 1973, Echelon 1975, Do Not Part with Beloved Once 1976, Valentin and Valentina 1972, Seagull 1980, Tartuffe 1981, The Living Corpse 1982, In Private with All 1983, The Ball at the Candles 1984, Uncle Vanya 1986, Pearl Zinaida 1988, The Mirage 1989; *TV films include:* Unnamed Star 1989, Theft and others. *Address:* Benefit Fund for Actors, Office 540, Arbat str, 121002 Moscow, Russian Federation (Office); 103006 Moscow, Malaya Dmitrovka str 31/22, Apt 38, Russian Federation (Home). *Telephone:* (095) 248-30-22 (Office); *Fax:* (095) 248-30-22 (Office).

VĖSAITĖ, Birutė, PH D; Lithuanian chemist; b 19 Aug 1951; d of Stasys Vėsa and Birutė Vėsienė; m Edmundas Miliutis 1978; one s. *Education:* Polytechnic Inst (Kaunas), Univ of Vilnius, Textile Inst (Leningrad, now St Petersburg, Russian Fed), Agricultural Univ of Uppsala (Sweden) and Nat Centre for Women (Paris). *Career:* Artificial Fibre Plant, Kaunas 1979–85; Assoc Prof Lithuanian Veterinary Acad 1985–; WHO Nat Health Programme Co-ordinator 1992; Dir Kaunas Women's Employment Information Centre 1994; External Collaborator ILO programme 1995; Chair Lithuanian Social Democratic Women Union 1992–; has written numerous articles in newspapers on politics, women's issues, science, etc. *Leisure interests:* sports, gardening, cooking. *Address:* Šilalės 46-2, 3000 Kaunas, Lithuania. *Telephone:* (7) 200-392; *Fax:* (7) 200-392.

VESTAGER, Margrethe, M ECON; Danish politician; b 13 April 1968; m Thomas Jensen; two d. *Education:* Varde Gymnasium and Univ of Copenhagen. *Career:* Mem Exec Cttee Radical-Liberal Party 1989–; Parl Cand for Esbjerg 1988–92; Ed Party Newspaper 'Radikal Politik' 1990–91; Stagiaire with Radical-Liberal Party, EP 1991; Nat Chair Radical-Liberal Party 1993–97; Head of Section Ministry of Finance 1993–95; Special Adviser Agency for Financial Man and Admin Affairs 1995–97, Head of Secr 1997; Minister of Educ and Ecclesiastical Affairs March 1998–; mem Bd ID-Sparinvest A/S, Care Danmark until 1988. *Address:* Frederiksholms Kanal 21-25, 1220 Copenhagen K, Denmark.

VEYRET, Renée Marcelle Anne, L EN D; French diplomatist; b 16 Feb 1946, Grenoble; d of Marcel and Marie (née Verzeroli) Sillon; m André Veyret 1971. *Education:* Univ of Grenoble, Inst d'Etudes Politiques (Grenoble) and Inst Nat des Langues Orientales Vivantes de Paris. *Career:* Admin Asst at Cen Registry Office, Ministry of Foreign Affairs 1971–72, at Cultural, Scientific and Tech Relations Dept 1972–75, at Political (Military Aid) Dept 1975–77, at Asia-Oceania Dept 1981–84; Second Sec, Japan 1977–81; Councillor, Libya 1984–88; Consul-Gen to Osaka and Kobe, Japan 1988–92; mem staff Inspection Générale (monitoring service) 1992–95; Amb to Bangladesh 1995–99; Head Humanitarian Service Ministry of Foreign Affairs 1999–; Chevalier de l'Ordre Nat du Mérite. *Leisure interests:* music, swimming, walking. *Address:* Ministère d'Affaires Etrangères, 37 quai d'Orsay, 75007 Paris, France.

VÉZINA, Monique; Canadian politician; b July 1935, Rimouski; m; four c. *Career:* Dir and Chair Fédération des caisses populaires Desjardins du Bas Saint-Laurent; Chair Gérardin-Vaillancourt Foundation; Sec and Dir Confédération des caisses populaires Desjardins du Québec; mem Progressive Cons Party; Minister for External Relations 1984–86, of Supply and Services 1986–87, of State for Transport 1987–88, of State for Employment and Immigration 1988–93, for Sr Citizens Sept 1988–93, for External Affairs Jan–Nov 1993; mem Bd of Dirs Rimouski Chamber of Commerce, Soc immobilière du Québec; fmr Chair Comm on Secondary Educ; fmr Vice-Pres Régie de l'assurance automobile du Québec; fmr mem Superior Council of Educ; Progressive Conservative. *Address:* c/o Progressive Conservative Party of Canada, 275 Slater St, Suite 501, Ottawa, ON K1P 5H9, Canada; 408 Notre Dame E, Apt 203, Montréal, PQ H2Y 1C9, Canada.

VIALA, Michèle-Daniele, D SC; French nuclear engineer; b 17 Sept 1944, Mostaganem, Algeria; d of Louis and Renée (née Gasset) Viala; m Paul Pigny; one d one s. *Education:* Lycées (Mostaganem and Toulon), Univ of Paris VI (Paris-Jussieu), Ecole Centrale de Paris. *Career:* Technical Adviser to a chemical research co 1972–74; Research Engineer on Hydrometallurgy Atomic Energy Comm 1974–77, on reprocessing nuclear waste 1977–80, Asst Head of Radioactive Eng, Nuclear Research Centre, Fontenay-aux-Roses 1980–84, Head of Dept of Isotopic Separation, Nuclear Research Centre, Saclay 1984–90, Head of Nuclear Reprocessing Procedure Dept, Nuclear Research Centre, Marcoule 1990–94; Head Dept, Programme Man Reprocessing-Partition-Transmutation, Commissariat à l'Energie Atomique 1994–98; Dir for Safety of Waste, Inst de Protection et de Sûreté Nucléaire 1998–; Officier de la Légion d'Honneur 1999; Prix des Jeunes, French Soc of Civil Engineers 1975. *Leisure interests:* cinema, swimming, rambling. *Address:* Institut de Protection et de Sûreté Nucléaire, CEA/FAR, BP n° 6, 92265 Fontenay aux Roses, Cedex,

France (Office); 2 bis rue des Vergers, 91400 Orsay, France (Home). *Telephone:* (1) 46-54-77-01 (Office); *Fax:* (1) 46-54-79-64 (Office); *E-mail:* michele.viala@ipsn.fr.

VICKERS, Catherine Myrle; Canadian pianist; b 24 July 1952, Regina, SK; d of John Wesley and Anne Nelson (née MacColl) Vickers; partner Nicholaus A. Huber. *Education:* Albert and Connaught Schools (Regina, SK), Univ of Alberta and Staatliche Hochschule für Musik und Theater (Hanover, Germany). *Career:* First public performance as pianist at age five, first concerto performance at age eight; teacher of Music at Folkwang Hochschule, Essen, Germany 1981–; has made numerous recordings; has been granted numerous scholarships; awarded Busoni Prize and Gold Medal 1979, Prize at Sydney Int Piano Competition 1981, award winner Canada Council. *Address:* Waldsaum 72, 45134 Essen, Germany. *Telephone:* (201) 440491; *Fax:* (201) 444341.

VIDMANOVÁ-SCHMIDTOVÁ, Anežka, PH D, C SC; Czech researcher emeritus in medieval Latin literature and philology; b 22 Oct 1929, Mladá Boleslav; d of Oskar Schmidt and Anežka Schmidtová; m Dr Ladislav Vidman 1961; two d. *Education:* Charles Univ (Prague). *Career:* Teacher 1952; Asst Researcher Faculty of Greek, Roman and Latin Studies, Czech Acad of Sciences 1953–60, Master of Research 1960–83, Dir of Research 1983–90; currently retd, but collaborates with Inst of Classical Studies and Inst of History, Acad of Sciences, and with Faculty of Letters, Charles Univ; Jan Hus Medals, Ministry of Educ and Charles Univ 1965; Awards from Vyšehrad and Odeon publrs 1984; V. Dobrovsky Medal, Acad of Sciences 1999. *Publications include:* M. I. Hus Opera Omnia (vol VII) 1959, (vol VIII) 1973, (vol IX) 1988, Slovník latinských spisovatelů (Dictionary of Latin Writers) 1984, Sestra Múza (Medieval Latin Profane Poetry) 1990, Laborintus (Medieval Latin Literature of Bohemia) 1994, Listy na husovu obranu z let 1410–1412 (Letters of Jan Hus's Defence 1410–1412) (jtly) 1999. *Leisure interest:* reading. *Address:* Institute for Classical Studies, Sídlištní 210, 165 00 Prague 6-Lysolaje, Czech Republic. *Telephone:* (2) 20920216; *Fax:* (2) 22828305; *E-mail:* vidmanova@ics.cas.cz.

VIELMAN-TEJEDA, Liza María; Guatemalan anthropologist and film director; b 20 April 1955; d of Julio and Ada (née Tejeda) Vielman. *Education:* Univ del Valle de Guatemala. *Career:* Exec Sec Gibbs School, Guatemala 1975; Asst to Dean School of Social Sciences 1980–84; Team Leader Ministry of Health and Agency for Int Devt, Honduras 1981; Researcher and Consultant Instituto de Nutrición para Centroamerica y Panamá 1985–88; Consultant AID (Guatemala) 1986, 1989–90, (El Salvador) 1989; Project Manager Co-operative American Relief Everywhere (CARE), Guatemala 1989; Consultant for various int orgs 1989–90; Statistical Surveyor Specialist Consultores Agroindustrales, Guatemala 1990; apptd Scriptwriter and Dir of Documentaries for Univ del Valle de Guatemala 1990, Consultant in Anthropology 1992; writer of short stories. *Film:* The Murals of Bonampak 1984. *Leisure interests:* mountaineering, photography. *Address:* c/o Universidad del Valle de Guatemala, Apdo Postal 82, 01901 Guatemala City, Guatemala (Office); Avda Hincapié 21-77, Zona 13, Guatemala City, Guatemala (Home). *Telephone:* (2) 321078 (Home).

VIGROUX, Suzanne Marie-Thérèse Simone, D EN D; French lawyer; b 26 Feb 1931, Saint-Amans des Côts; d of Joseph and Marguerite (née Delort) Gauzit; m François Vigroux 1964; one s. *Education:* Inst Jeanne d'Arc (Rodez) and Univ of Montpellier. *Career:* Deputy Judge Court of Appeal, Orléans 1957–59; Deputy Judge, Blois, then seconded to Cen Admin, Ministry of Justice 1959–70; Deputy at Documentation and Research Service, Cour de Cassation 1970–76, Public Auditor 1979–88; Deputy to Public Prosecutor, Paris 1976–79; Pres of Chamber at Court of Appeal, Paris 1988–91; Counsellor Cour de Cassation 1991–, Hon Councillor 1998–; Pres Jury Professional Examination for Admittance to Appeal Courts; Chevalier de la Légion d'Honneur; Officier de l'Ordre Nat du Mérite; Chevalier du Mérite Agricole. *Publication:* Les conventions sur la preuve 1958. *Address:* Cour de Cassation, 5 quai de l'Horloge, 75001 Paris, France (Office); 81 rue Caulaincourt, 75018 Paris, France (Home).

VIHANOVÁ, Drahomíra; Czech film director and editor; b 31 July 1930, Moravský Krumlov. *Education:* Conservatoire (Brno), Acad of Performing Arts (Prague) and Univ of Brno. *Career:* Worked on musical programmes for Czech TV; film director and editor 1965–, at KF AS studio, Prague 1984; prohibited from filming 1969 after making first feature film, Le dimanche perdu, until 1977; has been making film documentaries 1977–; apptd Prof Acad of Performing Arts 1982; Int Festival Prizes at Marseilles (France) 1965, Dakar 1965, Tours (France) 1967, Bilbao (Spain) 1980, 1989, Cracow (Poland) 1982, 1983, 1984, Kranj (Slovenia, then Yugoslavia) 1985, Torino (Italy) 1985, San Remo (Italy) 1989, Oberhausen (Germany) 1989, Montecatini (Italy) 1989, Trilobit 1990, San Sebastian 1994, Casablanca 1994, St Etienne 1995, St Thérèse 1995, Figueira da Foz 1995, Litfond Praha 2000, Finale Plzeň 2001. *Films:* La Fugue sur les touches noires 1964, Le dimanche perdu 1969, La recherche 1980, Questions pour deux femmes 1983, Entretiens 1983, L'obsession 1986, Derrière la fenêtre 1989, Les metamorphoses de mon amie Eva 1990, Rafael Kubelík 1990, La forteresse 1994, Nouvelles du pélerinage de Pierre et de Jacques 2000. *Leisure interest:* music. *Address:* Karlín, Šaldova 6, 186 00 Prague 8, Czech Republic; Praha 8, Šaldova 6, 18600 Czech Republic. *Telephone:* (2) 24818537; *Fax:* (2) 22310692.

VIKE-FREIBERGA, Vaira, PH D, LL D, FRSC; Latvian Head of State and former professor of psychology; b 1 Dec 1937, Rīga; d of Karlis and Annemarie (née Rankis) Vikis; m Imants Freibergs 1960; one s one d. *Education:* Coll Mers-Sultan (Morocco), Univ of Toronto and McGill Univ (Canada). *Career:* Clinical Psychologist Toronto Psychiatric Hosp 1960–61; Asst Prof of Psychology Univ of Montréal 1965–72, Assoc Prof 1972–77, Prof 1977–98; Dir Latvian Inst in Riga 1998–; Pres of Latvia 1999–; mem Special Programme Panel on Human Factors, NATO Science Cttee 1979–82, Chair 1980–81; Pres Canadian Psychological Asscn 1980–81, Social Science Fed of Canada 1980–81, Acad des Lettres et des Sciences Humaines of Royal Soc of Canada; Chair Asscn of Advanced Baltic Studies (USA) 1984–86; Vice-Chair Science Council of Canada 1988–97; mem Latvian Acad of Sciences; Trustee Latvian Heritage Cultural Seminars Divreizdivi; lectures and seminars on Latvian culture in USA, Canada, Latvia and numerous other countries; Hon Prof Victoria Univ (Canada) 2000; Hon LL D (Latvia) 1991; awards include Anna Abele Prize 1979, World Asscn of Free Latvians Distinguished Contrib Prize 1989; Marcel-Vincent Prize in Social Sciences, Asscn Canadienne Française pour l'Avancement des Sciences 1992, Pierre Chauvreau Medal in the Humanities, Royal Soc of Canada 1995, Three Star Order of Latvia 1995. *Publications:* Fréquence lexicale des mots au Québec 1979, Latvian Sun Songs (jtly) 1988, Linguistics and Poetics of Latvian Folk Songs (ed) 1989, On the Amber Mountain 1989, The Chronological Sun 1999, On the Amber Mountain 1993, 1999 and over 400 articles and papers. *Leisure interests:* gardening, travel. *Address:* Chancery of the President, Pils Laukums 3, Riga, 1900, Latvia. *Telephone:* (7) 377 548; *Fax:* (7) 325 800; *Internet:* www.president.lv.

VIKOVÁ, Jindra; Czech sculptor; b 2 Feb 1946, Prague; d of Jindřich and Jaroslava Vik; m Pavel Baňka 1968; one d. *Education:* Secondary Art School, Acad of Applied Art (Prague). *Career:* Ceramic artist; has exhibited works in Czechoslovakia, Germany, Austria, Switzerland, France, Italy, Finland, Poland, Hungary, Cuba, Australia and USA; Visiting Artist and Prof, Coll of Art, Univ of Michigan, Ann Arbor, USA 1991; mem Asscn Int des Critiques d'Art 1983; First Prize for work (Faenza, Italy) 1981, Gold Medal 1984; Gold Medal (France) 1986; Grand Prix Triennial of Contemporary Porcelain (Switzerland) 1986; Hon Award (Japan) 1986; First Prize Festival of Art (Iraq) 1988. *Leisure interests:* nature, animals. *Address:* Benice 8, 10300 Prague 10, Czech Republic. *Telephone:* 759440.

VILARIÑO PINTOS, Daría, L PH; Spanish librarian (retd); b 26 Jan 1928, Santiago de Compostela; d of José Vilariño de Andrés and Daría Pintos Castro. *Career:* Mem staff state library, museum and archives depts 1957–70; Deputy Dir Univ of Santiago Library 1970–73, Dir 1973–93; mem Research Group 'Galicia hasta 1500' 1982–; Insignia de Oro de la Univ de Santiago de Compostela, Medalla de Bronce de Galicia. *Publications:* O Libro Galego onte e hoxe (jtly) 1981, Hechos de D. Berenguel de Landoria (jtly) 1983, Vasco de Aponte: Recuento de las Casas Antiguas del Reino de Galicìa, Edición crítica (jtly) 1986, Ordoño de Celanova: Vida y Milagros de San Rosendo, Edición crítica (jtly) 1990, Guía do Fondo Antigo de Monografías da Biblioteca Xeral da Use. Literaturas Hispánicas Séculos XV-XVIII (jtly) 2000; articles in

professional journals, bibliographical catalogues. *Leisure interests:* reading, travel. *Address:* Calle San Miguel No 5, 2°, 15704 Santiago de Compostela, La Coruña, Spain. *Telephone:* (81) 583658.

VILLALAZ, Anita; Panamanian actress and director. *Education:* Saint Mary's Dominican Coll (Los Angeles, CA, USA). *Career:* Has worked in theatre, TV and radio all over the Americas, including Chile, Mexico, USA, Panama, Nicaragua, Costa Rica; has worked for radio stations including WOR Radio (New York, USA) 1932, Radio Mercurio (Santiago) 1935, XEW Radio (Mexico) and Radio Panamericana, for theatre companies including Pedro Ureta Comedy Co, Enrique Barrenechea Theatre Co, Teatro Hispano (New York) and La Barraca Popular Theatre Co (Founder); worked at Channel Two TV, Panama for 21 years; has performed in works by Prokofiev, Bizet, Camus, Anouilh, Benavente and others; fmr Prof of Theatre and Drama Nat Conservatory of Music and Drama, Panama; currently pvt teacher; numerous awards including Orden de Vasco Nuñez de Balboa, Govt of Panama. *Address:* Via Argentina 10, Edif Alejandra, Apt 12, Apdo Postal 87-0485, Zona 7, Panamá, Panama. *Telephone:* 693762.

VILLALBA, Ismenia; Venezuelan politician. *Career:* Leader Unión Republicana Democrática (URD–Democratic Republican Union); Cand in Pres elections 1998. *Address:* Unión Republicana Democrática (URD), Caracas, Venezuela.

VILLAMIZAR DE HILL, Lucia Elena, M SC, PH D; Colombian medical practitioner and health educator; b 26 June 1921, Bogotá; d of Rafael Villmizar-Gallardo Romero and Mercedes Martinez-Montoya; m George Clifford Hill 1965. *Education:* Sacred Heart Coll (Bogotá), Catholic Univ of America (Washington, DC) and Univs of Columbia (New York), Javerina (Bogotá) and Barcelona (Spain). *Career:* Pres Catholic Action, Archdiocese of Bogotá 1940s; Social Worker and Health Educator; Co-Founder and Sec of Cruzda Social (Social Crusade) 1950s; Ed Juventud Femenina 1945–50; Corresp El Colombiano; Asst Dir Faculty of Nursing Javeriana Univ; Dir of Nursing San Ignacio Hosp; Co-Founder Colombian Center, Washington 1970; Researcher in Washington and Bogotá 1970–73; Dean School of Nursing, Colombian Red Cross Soc (Faculty of Nursing, Univ Colegio Mayor de Nuestra Señora del Rosario), Bogotá (now Santa Fe de Bogotá) 1974–84; Dir Dept of Educ and Training 1984; founding mem Asscn of Business and Professional Women of Colombia, Pres 1986–88; Regional mem Standing Cttee on Health, Int Fed of Business and Professional Women 1983–85, 1987–89, Pres 1989–91, Regional mem 1991–. *Publications:* National Nursing Legislation and Education in Latin American Countries 1962, Factors Influencing the Brain Drain of Professionals from Colombia 1972. *Leisure interests:* photography, producing audio-visual aids, ceramic and china painting. *Address:* Apdo Aéreo 90159, Zona 8, Santa Fe de Bogotà, Colombia. *Telephone:* (1) 2152571; *Fax:* (1) 319208.

VILLENEUVE, Jeanne Madeleine; French journalist; b 29 Jan 1949, Paris; d of Henry Villeneuve and Jacqueline Picq. *Education:* Inst d'Etudes Politiques. *Career:* Financial Analyst Banque Nat de Paris 1974–78; Chef de Service Soc Générale de Presse 1978–82, daily newspaper Libération 1982–86, weekly l'Express Feb–Sept 1986; Chief Reporter l'Evènement du Jeudi 1986–91; Asst Ed Parisien 1991–95; Ed Libération 1996–97. *Publication:* Le mythe Tapie 1988. *Address:* c/o Journal Libération, 11 rue Béranger, 75003 Paris, France.

VINE, Barbara (pseudonym of Ruth Rendell) (see Rendell of Babergh).

VINER, Monique Sylvaine, CBE, QC, MA; British judge; b 3 Oct 1926; d of the late Hugh and Eliane (née Collon) Viner; m Pieter Francis Gray 1958; three d one s. *Education:* Convent of the Sacred Heart (Roehampton, London), St Hugh's Coll (Oxford) and Gray's Inn (London). *Career:* Variety of posts including factory head, shop asst, fruit picker, tutor, and Legal Ed Asst 1947–50; called to the Bar, Gray's Inn 1950; Barrister 1951–90; QC 1979; Recorder 1985–90; Bencher 1988; Circuit Judge 1990–; mem or Chair of various Wages Councils 1952–94; mem Industrial Court 1976; Hon Fellow St Hugh's Coll, Oxford 1991. *Leisure interests:* music, reading, sailing, walking, gardening, friends, conversation, bird-watching. *Address:* South Eastern Circuit, New Cavendish Hosue, 18 Maltravers St, London WC2R 3EU,

UK (Office); Old Glebe Waldron, Heathfield, Sussex TM21 0RB, UK (Home). *Telephone:* (1435) 863865 (Home); *Fax:* (1435) 862599 (Home).

VINNIKAVA, Tamara Dzmitryyewna; Belarusian banking executive. *Career:* Fmr Chair Bd of Nat Bank of Belarus. *Address:* c/o National Bank of Belarus, 220008 Minsk, F. Skaryny 20, Belarus.

VIRKNER, Helle; Danish actress; b 15 Sept 1925; d of Morris and Ellen Lotinga; m J. O. Krag 1959; one d one s. *Education:* Royal Theatre School (Copenhagen). *Career:* Major roles in more than 50 films and TV series. *Address:* Strandparksvej 1, 3, 2900 Hellerup, Denmark.

VIRSALADZE, Eliso Konstantinovna; Georgian pianist; b 14 Sept 1942, Tbilisi. *Education:* Studied under grandmother, Prof Anastasia Virsaladze and at Tbilisi Conservatory. *Career:* Asst Prof Moscow Conservatory, USSR (now Russian Fed) 1962–; played as a soloist all over the world and on tour in Europe and USA with Leningrad Philharmonic; soloist with USSR Symphony Orchestra in UK 1983–84, Germany 1984–85; Founder Tkvarcheli Music Festival and Summer School; many other tours as soloist in Europe and Japan; gave Master Classes in Munich, Germany 1996; won First Prize at Soviet Competition of Performing Musicians, Moscow 1961; Bronze Medal at Tchaikovsky Competition 1962; Prize at Schumann Competition; Georgian State Prize 1983; USSR People's Artist 1989. *Address:* Moscow, Moscow Conservatory, Bolshaya Nikitskaya Str 13, Russian Federation. *Telephone:* (095) 268-69-12 (Home).

VISHNEVSKAYA, Galina Pavlovna; Russian opera singer (soprano); b 25 Oct 1926, Leningrad (now St Petersburg); m Mstislav Rostropovich; two d. *Career:* Studied with Vera Garina 1942–52; Leningrad Musical Theatres 1944–52; leading soloist with Bolshoi Theatre 1952–74; left USSR 1974; stripped of Citizenship 1978 (citizenship restored 1990); retd from operatic stage as Tatiana in Eugene Onegin, Paris 1982; actress Moscow Arts Theatre 1993–94; subject of Marcel Landowski's opera Galina 1996; f opera School in Moscow 1999. *Operas include:* Fidelio, Eugene Onegin (also film), Aida, Snow Maiden, Queen of Spades, Madam Butterfly, Faust, War and Peace, Marriage of Figaro, Tsar's Bride, La Traviata, Turandot, Lady Macbeth of Mtsensk; *Publication:* Galina (autobiog) 1985. *Address:* 103009 Moscow, Gazetny per 13, Apt 79, Russian Federation. *Telephone:* (095) 229-04-96 (Moscow); (1) 42-27-85-06 (Paris).

VISHNYOVA, Diana Viktorovna; Russian ballet dancer; b 13 July 1976, Leningrad (now St Petersburg). *Education:* Vaganova Acad of Russian Ballet. *Career:* Soloist Mariinsky Theatre 1995–; main roles include: Masha (Nutcracker), Kitri (Don Quixote), Aurore (Sleeping Beauty), Henriette (Raymonda), Gulnary (Corsaire); first Russian ballerina to have won Prix de Lausanne 1994; Divine Isadora prize, Benoit de la Dance prize. *Address:* c/o Mariinsky Theatre, Teatralnaya pl 1, St Petersburg, Russian Federation. *Telephone:* (812) 315-57-24.

VISSER, Anna Seraphine Catharina, LL M; Netherlands police commissioner (retd); b 18 Feb 1937, Rotterdam; d of M. J. C. and F. Th. (née Zemann) Visser. *Education:* Gymnasium Erasmianum (Rotterdam) and Univ of Utrecht. *Career:* Leader of Juvenile Police, Vlaardingen 1962–70; Head of Juvenile Police and Vice-Squad, Utrecht 1970–81, The Hague 1981–87; Head Dept of Crime Prevention and Victim Care, The Hague 1987–92, Commr 1992–97; Head Dept of Social Scientific Research 1992–96; mem working group WHO comm on the psychosocial consequences of crime 1981; mem Dutch Del to Harare Conf on Children and Apartheid 1987; Head Dutch Police Union Del to South Africa 1992. *Publications:* Helping Victims of Rape, the Utrecht Experience (jtly) 1983, Verkrachting, symptoom van machtsongelijkheid 1983, Veranderend denken over wetstoepassing bij sexuele delicten 1984, Incest en de sterke arm 1986, Macht en onmacht van de politie bij de aanpak van incest 1986, Prostitutiebeleid, de overheid kan er met goed fatsoen niet omheen 1986, Pédophilie et responabilité 1987, Oorlog tegen de kinderen 1987, Signalen van incest, de school en de politie 1988, Weerzien in Johannesburg 1991, Vakboden solidair met POPCRU 1991. *Address:* c/o Police Headquarters, Burgemeester Patijnlaan 35, 2585 BG The Hague, Netherlands.

VITRENKO, Natalia Mikhailovna, D ECON; Ukrainian politician; b 28 Dec 1958, Kiev; m; one s one d. *Education:* Kiev State Inst of Nat Econs. *Career:* Sr Economist Cen Dept of Statistics 1973–76; Sr Researcher Research Inst of Information, State Planning Comm 1979–89; Docent Kiev Inst of Nat Econs 1979–89; Sr Researcher Council on Production Forces, Ukrainian Acad of Sciences 1989–94; Ed Vybor (journal) 1993–; People's Deputy 1994–; Counsellor on Socio-econ Problems, Verkhovna Rada; mem Socialist Party of Ukraine 1991–, Progressive Socialist Party (Prohresyvna Sotsialistychna Partiya) 1998–, currently Chair; Presidium of Political Council 1993–, Acad of Construction, Acad of Econ Cybernetics 1997. *Address:* Verkhovna Rada, M. Hrushevskogo str 5, Kiev, Ukraine.

VITTI, Monica (pseudonym of Monica Luisa Ceciarelli); Italian actress; b 3 Nov 1931, Rome. *Education:* Nat Acad (Rome). *Films include:* L'Avventura 1959, La Notte 1960, L'Eclisse 1962, Dragées au poivre 1963, The Red Desert 1964, Modesty Blaise 1966, The Chastity Belt 1967, Girl With a Pistol 1969, Le Coppie 1971, La pacifiste 1971, La Tosca 1971, Teresa la larda 1973, A mezzanotte va la ronda di piacere 1975, Duck in Orange Sauce 1975, An Almost Perfect Affair 1979, Teresa the Thief 1979, The Oberwald Mystery 1981, Broadway Danny Rose 1984, Secret Scandal (also writer and dir) 1990; *Publication:* A Bed is Like a Rose 1997.

VITUKHNOVSKAYA, Alina Aleksandrovna; Russian poet; b 27 March 1973, Moscow. *Career:* Avant-garde poet; first verses published late 1980s in periodicals; arrested on charge of drugs trafficking, freed Oct 1995, arrested Nov 1997; mem Russian Writers' Union, PEN; Pushkin Scholarship, Hamburg, Germany 1998. *Publications include:* Anomaly 1993, Children's Book of the Dead 1994, Pavlov's Dog (jtly) 1996, The Last Old Woman Money-lender of Russian Literature (stories) 1996, Land of Zero 1996, Romance with Phenamine (novel). *Address:* Leningradskoye shosse 80, Apt 89, 125565 Moscow, Russian Federation. *Telephone:* (095) 452-15-31.

VIVIANI, Nancy Macdonald, MA, PH D; Australian professor of politics; b 21 Feb 1940; d of A. Wood; one s one d. *Education:* ANU. *Career:* Research Asst Dept of Econs, Research School of Pacific Studies, ANU 1964–70, Resident Fellow in Australian-Japanese Project 1976–77, Prof of Political Science, Faculty of Arts 1988–90; Consultant Australian Devt Assistance Agency 1974; Fellow Center for Int Affairs, Harvard Univ 1977–78; Dir Centre of Study of Australian–Asian Relations and Sr Lecturer, School of Modern Asian Studies 1978–82; Chief Social Devt Div, Econ and Social Comm for Asia and Pacific, UN ESCAP, Bangkok 1983–85; Reader School of Modern Asian Studies, later Prof of Int Politics, Div of Asian and Int Studies, Griffith Univ 1990–, Adjunct Prof 1998–. *Publications:* Nauru: Phosphate and Political Progress 1970, The Long Journey: Vietnamese Migration and Settlement in Australia 1984, The Indochinese in Australia 1993, Burnt Boats and Barbecues 1996. *Address:* International Politics Division, Asian and International Studies, Griffith University, Nathan, Qld 4111, Australia.

VLIEGENTHART, Margo A.; Netherlands politician; b 18 July 1958. *Career:* Mem Second Chamber of Staten Generaal (Parl, Lab); State Sec of Public Health, Welfare and Sport 2001. *Address:* c/o Ministry of Public Health, Welfare and Sport, Parnassusplein 5, POB 20350, 2500 EJ The Hague, Netherlands.

VLIES VANDER, Inge C., LL D; Netherlands civil servant and professor of constitutional law; b 30 Aug 1948. *Education:* Gymnasuim Felisenum (Velsen) and Univ of Amsterdam. *Career:* Head of Task Force on Law-making, Ministry of Finance 1983; Sr Officer Ministry of Justice 1986; Head Dept of Law-making Ministry of Health and Culture 1988; apptd Prof of Constitutional Law 1991. *Publications:* Principles of Law-making 1983, 1987, 1991, Legal Protection Against the Administration 1987, Principles of Administrative Law 1992. *Leisure interests:* music, art. *Address:* Centrale Directie Wetgeving en Juridische Zaken, Postbus 5406, 2280 HK Rijswijk, Netherlands; Prins Hendriklaan 2B, 1075 BB Amsterdam, Netherlands. *Telephone:* (20) 676-13-28; *Fax:* (20) 525-20-86.

VODŇANSKÁ, Jitka, DR RER NAT; Czech psychotherapist and politician; b 12 Nov 1944, Prague; d of Václav Schánilec and Olga Schánilcová; m Jan Vodňanský 1977 (divorced 1982); one s. *Education:* Charles Univ (Prague). *Career:* Anthropologist 1966–68; Psychotherapist Centre for Treatment of Alcoholics and Drug Addicts, Prague 1968–82; Leader Czechoslovak Soc for Music Therapy 1975; apptd Dir Centre for Family Therapy, Prague 1982; mem Opposition Dissent Movt 1977–89; Civic Democratic Alliance parl cand 1992; has written numerous articles and papers for journals on psychotherapy and music therapy. *Film:* 24 Hours in Prague. *Leisure interests:* music, dance, nature, skiing, animals, cooking, humour. *Address:* Tulipánová 2804/5, 10600 Prague 10, Czech Republic. *Telephone:* (2) 753591.

VOGT, Marthe Louise, DR MED, D PHIL, PH D, FRS; British scientist; b 1903; d of Oskar Vogt and Cécile Mugnier. *Education:* Univ of Berlin. *Career:* Research Asst Dept of Pharmacology, Univ of Berlin 1930; Research Asst and Head Chemical Div, Kaiser Wilhelm Inst für Hirnforschung, Berlin 1931–35; Rockefeller Travelling Fellow 1935–36; Research Worker Dept of Pharmacology, Univ of Cambridge 1935–40; Alfred Yarrow Research Fellow Girton Coll, Cambridge 1937–40; mem Staff Coll of Pharmaceutical Soc, London 1941–46; Lecturer, later Reader in Pharmacology, Univ of Edinburgh 1947–60; Head Pharmacology Unit, Agricultural Research Council Inst of Animal Physiology 1960–68; Visiting Assoc Prof in Pharmacology Columbia Univ, New York 1949; Visiting Prof Univ of Sydney, Australia 1965, Montréal, Canada 1968; Hon mem Physiological Soc 1974, British Pharmacological Soc 1974, Hungarian Acad of Sciences 1981, British Asscn for Psychopharmacology 1983; Foreign Hon mem American Acad of Arts and Sciences 1977; Life Fellow, Girton Coll, Cambridge 1970; numerous papers in neurological, physiological and pharmacological journals; Hon FRSM; Hon D SC (Edinburgh) 1974, (Cambridge) 1983; Schmiedeberg Plakette 1974; Royal Medal, Royal Soc 1981. *Leisure interests:* gardening, travel. *Address:* c/o Chateau La Jolla Terrace, 7544 La Jolla Blvd, La Jolla, CA 92037, USA.

VOKIC, Ljilja; Croatian politician. *Career:* Minister of Educ and Sport 1994–98. *Address:* c/o Ministry of Education and Sport, 41000 Zagrab, trg Burze 6, Croatia.

VOLCHEK, Galina Borisovna; Russian stage director and actress; b 19 Dec 1933, Moscow; d of Boris Volchek Vera Maimyna; m 1st Yevgeniy Yevstigneyev 1957 (divorced 1964); m 2nd Mark Abelev 1966 (divorced 1976); one s. *Education:* Studio-School of Moscow Art Theatre. *Career:* Co-Founder, actress and stage dir Theatre Sovremennik 1956–72, Artistic Dir 1972–; Deputy to State Duma (Parl) 1995–; roles in films by dirs Kozintsev (King Lear), Yutkevich, Danelia and others; first Soviet stage dir to work in USA; stage productions in many countries including Alley Theatre (Houston), Abbey Theatre (Ireland), Hungary, Finland, Bulgaria, Germany, Czechoslovakia; master classes in Tisch School New York Univ; USSR People's Artist, State Prize, State Orders of USSR, Hungary, Bulgaria and Russia. *Plays include:* Dir: Common Story (Goncharov), On the Bottom (Gorky), Cherry Orchard and Three Sisters (Chekhov), Ascent over Fujiyama (Aitmatov), Echelone (Roshchin), Anfissa (Andreyev), Steep Route (Ginzburg); Actress: Who's Afraid of Virginia Woolf?, The Ballad of the Sad Café (Albee), Inspector (Gogol). *Leisure interest:* designing clothes. *Address:* Chistoprudny blvd 19A, 101000 Moscow, Russian Federation (Office); Povarskaya str 26, Apt 43, Moscow, Russian Federation (Home). *Telephone:* (095) 921-25-43 (Office); *Fax:* (095) 921-66-29 (Office).

VOLK, Patricia, BFA; American writer; b 16 July 1943, New York; d of Cecil Sussman and Audrey Elayne Morgen Volk; m Andrew Blitzer 1969; one s one d. *Education:* Syracuse Univ, Acad de la Grande Chaumière (Paris), School of Visual Arts, The New School, Columbia Univ. *Career:* Art Dir Appelbaum and Curtis 1964–65, Seventeen Magazine 1967–68, Harper's Bazaar 1969; copy-writer, Assoc Creative Dir, Sr Vice-Pres Doyle Dane Bernbach Inc (DDB Needham Worldwide Inc) 1969–88; Adjunct Instructor of Fiction Yeshiva Coll 1991; mem PEN Authors Guild; Yaddo Fellow; MacDowell Fellow; Word Beat Fiction Book Award 1984; numerous other awards. *Publications include:* The Yellow Banana 1985, Stories About How Things Fall Appart and What's Left When They Do 1985, White Light 1987, All it Takes 1990, A Reader for Developing Writers 1990, Exploring Language 1992, Magazine and Feature Writing 1992, Hers

1993, Her Face in the Mirror 1994, Stuffed 2001; contribs to The New York Times Magazine, The Atlantic, Quarterly, Cosmopolitan, Family Circle, Mirabella, Playboy, 7 Days, Manhattan Inc, The New Yorker, New York Magazine, Red Book, Good Housekeeping, Allure. *Leisure interests:* fly-fishing, gardening, travel. *Address:* c/o Gloria Loomis, 133 East 35th St, New York, NY 10016, USA.

VON BONIN, Wibke Anna, PH D; German television producer and art critic; b 17 April 1936, Kiel; d of Henning Heinrich and Irmela Dorothea (née Troschke) von Bonin. *Education:* Univs of Berlin, Paris and Kiel. *Career:* Curator Staatliche Kunsthalle, Baden Baden 1965; apptd Art Ed and Exec Producer Westdeutscher Rundfunk (WDR) TV, Cologne 1966, Head Dept of Art and Architecture 1992; has produced about 30 films on art and architecture; Vice-Pres Int Asscn of Art Critics; awarded Goldene Kamara by Hör Zu 1986, Literaturpreis, Deutsche Architeckturen und Ingeneurvereine 1988. *Publications:* 100 Meisterwerke aus den großen Museen der Welt (ed, 4 vols) 1983–88; numerous articles in magazines and catalogues. *Address:* WDR, Appelhofplatz 1, 5000 Cologne 1, Germany. *Telephone:* (221) 2202955; *Fax:* (221) 2203804.

VON FIEANDT, Dorrit Margareta; Finnish ceramic artist; b 5 Nov 1927, Helsinki; d of John Rafael and Anna Elisabet (née Finnlund) Flinkenberg; m Berndt Johan von Fieandt 1950; two d one s. *Education:* High School of Applied Arts (Helsinki). *Career:* Freelance ceramic artist 1949–53, 1965–; Guest Artist Porcelain Factory ARABIA, Helsinki 1986; solo and group exhibitions in Finland 1967–87, Netherlands 1989, Australia, Sweden, Norway 1990, Helsinki 1991; mem Finnish Organization for Industrial Design and Applied Art; recipient Prize for Culture from City of Helsinki 1982. *Leisure interests:* art and ceramic history, gardening, music. *Address:* Merikatu 7A, 00140 Helsinki, Finland. *Telephone:* (0) 631229.

VON OTTER, Anne Sofie; Swedish opera and concert singer; b 9 May 1955, Stockholm. *Education:* Conservatorium (Stockholm), studied interpretation with Erik Werba (Vienna) and Geoffrey Parsons (London), and vocal studies since 1981 with Vera Rozsa. *Career:* Mem Basle Opera, Switzerland 1982–85; debut in France at Opéra de Marseille and at Aix-en-Provence Festival 1984, in Italy at Accad di Santa Cecilia, Rome 1984, Switzerland in Geneva 1985, Germany in Berlin 1985, USA in Chicago (Mozart's C minor Mass) and Philadelphia (Bach's B minor Mass) 1985, UK at Royal Opera, Covent Garden, London 1985; debut performances also at La Scala, Milan, Italy 1987, Munich, Germany 1987, Stockholm 1988, The Metropolitan Opera, New York, USA 1988, The Royal Albert Hall, London 1989; has given recitals in Lyons, France, Brussels, Geneva, Switzerland, Stockholm and London; Hon D SC (Bath) 1992. *Operas include:* Le Nozze di Figaro 1984, 1985, 1987, 1988, La Finta Giardiniera 1984, 1986, Così fan Tutte 1985, Alceste 1987, Der Rosenkavalier 1988, Faust 1989; numerous recordings for Philips, EMI and Decca, including Bluebeard's Castle (Bartok) 1996. *Address:* c/o IMG, Lovell House, 616 Chiswick High Rd, London W4 2TH, UK. *Telephone:* (20) 8233-5800; *Fax:* (20) 8233-5801.

VON RAFFLER-ENGEL, Walburga, MS, D LITT, PH D; American professor emeritus of linguistics; b 25 Sept 1920, Munich, Germany; d of Friedrich J. and Gertrud E. (née Kiefer) von Raffler; m A. Ferdinand Engel 1957 (died 1991); one s one d. *Education:* Univ of Turin (Italy) and Columbia (New York) and Indiana (Bloomington) Univs. *Career:* Came to USA 1949; worked as freelance journalist 1949–58; Lecturer Bennet Coll, Greensboro, NC 1953–55, Morris Harvey Coll, Charleston, WV 1955–57, Adelphi Univ and City Univ of NY 1957–58, New York Univ 1958–59, Univ of Florence, Italy 1959–60, Istituto Postuniversitario Organizzazione Aziendale, Turin, Italy 1960–61, Bologna Center of Johns Hopkins Univ 1964; Prof Vanderbilt Univ, Nashville, TN 1965–86 (first person to sue Vanderbilt Univ for sex discrimination 1969); Prof of Linguistics 1977–86, Dir Linguistics Program 1978–86, Prof Emer and Sr Research Assoc, Inst for Public Policy Studies 1986–; Visiting Prof Univ of Ottawa, ON 1971–72, Inst for Language Sciences, Tokyo 1976, Shanxi Univ, People's Repub of China 1985, Psychology Inst, Univ of Florence, Italy 1986–87, NATO Advanced Study Inst, Cortona, Italy 1988; Pres Kinesics Int, Inc 1988; mem American Asscn of Univ Profs, Int Linguistics Asscn, Linguistic Soc of America (Chair Golden Anniversary Film Cttee 1974), Int

Sociology Asscn, Int Asscn for Applied Linguistics, Language Origins Soc (Exec Cttee 1985–, Chair Int Congress 1987), Int Asscn for Study of Child Language (Chair Int Conf 1972, Vice-Pres 1975–78), Inst for Non-Verbal Communication Research, Tennessee Conf on Linguistics (Pres 1976), Southeastern Conf on Linguistics (Hon mem 1985), Semiotic Soc of America. *Publications include:* Il prelinguaggio infantile 1964, Language Intervention Programs 1960–74 (jtly) 1975, The Perception of Non-Verbal Behavior in the Career Interview 1983, The Perception of the Unborn Across the Cultures of the World 1994; has also written numerous articles on cross-cultural communication and edited and co-edited 12 books. *Leisure interests:* research, writing. *Address:* 116 Brighton Close, Nashville, TN 37205, USA. *Telephone:* (615) 297-6236.

VON STADE, Frederica; American opera singer (mezzo-soprano); b 1 June 1945, Somerville, NJ; m 1st Peter Elkus 1973 (divorced); two d; m 2nd Michael G. Gorman 1991. *Education:* Mannes Coll of Music (New York). *Career:* Opera debut with Metropolitan Opera, New York in Die Zauberflöte 1970; has also sung at Paris Opera, San Francisco Opera, Salzburg Festival (Austria), Royal Opera (Covent Garden, London), Spoleto Festival (Italy), Boston Opera Co, Santa Fe Opera, Houston Grand Opera (TX, USA), La Scala (Milan, Italy); also recital and concert artist; Dr hc (Yale), (Boston), (Georgetown Univ School of Medicine), (Mannes School of Music); two Grand Prix du Disc awards, Deutshe Schallplattenpreis, Premio della Critica Discografica and many other awards and prizes; Officier des Arts et des Lettres. *Recordings include:* Frederica von Stade Sings Mozart and Rossini Opera Arias, French Opera Arias, Songs of the Cat with Garrison Keillor; over 60 other recordings. *Address:* c/o Jeffrey D. Vanderveen, Columbia Artists Management Inc, 165 W 57th St, New York, NY 10019, USA.

VON TROTTA, Margarethe; German film director and actress; b 21 Feb 1942, Berlin; m Volker Schlöndorff 1971 (divorced 1991). *Career:* Has written scripts for The Sudden Wealth of the Poor People of Kombach 1971, Summer Lightning 1972, Fangschuss 1974 and Unerreichbare Nahe 1984. *Films include:* Die Verlorene Ehre der Katharina Blum (The Lost Honour of Katharina Blum) 1975, Das zweite Erwachen der Christa Klages (The Second Awakening of Christa Klages) 1978, Schwestern, oder die Balance des Glücks (Sisters, or the Balance of Happiness) 1979, Die Bleierne Zeit (The German Sisters) 1981, Heller Wahn (Friends and Husbands) 1983, Rosa Luxemburg 1985, Felix 1987, Paura e amore (Love and Fear) 1988, L'Africana 1990, Il lungo silenzio (The Long Silence) 1993, Das Versprechen (The Promise) 1995, Winterkind (TV film) 1996, Dunkle Tage (TV film) 1998. *Address:* c/o Bioskop-Film, Turkenstr 91, 80799 Munich, Germany.

VORDERMAN, Carol, MA, MBE, FRSA; British broadcaster and author; b 24 Dec 1960, Bedford; d of Anton Joseph and Edwina Jean Vorderman; m 1st Christopher Mather 1985 (divorced 1987); m 2nd Patrick John King 1990; one d one s. *Education:* Blessed Edward Jones High School (Rhyl) and Sidney Sussex Coll (Cambridge). *Career:* First woman to appear on Channel 4 1982; columnist Daily Telegraph 1996–98, Mirror 1998–; Hon Fellow Univ of Wales, Bangor; Hon MA (Bath) 2000. *TV programmes include:* Countdown 1982–, Take Nobody's Word for It 1987–89, The World Chess Championship 1993, Kremlin Stars Grand Prix Chess Tournament 1994, Tomorrow's World 1994–95, Mysteries with Carol Vorderman 1997–98, Dream House 1998–99, Carol Vorderman's Better Homes 1999–, Carol Vorderman's Better Gardens 1999–2000, Star Lives 1999–, Find a Fortune 1999–2000, Pride of Britain Awards Ceremony 2000, 2001; *Publications include:* How Mathematics Works 1996, Carol Vorderman's Guide to the Internet (co-author) 1998, Maths Made Easy 1999, Science Made Easy 2000, English Made Easy 2000. *Address:* c/o John Miles Organisation, Cadbury Camp Lane, Clapton-in-Gordano, Bristol BS20 7SB, UK. *Telephone:* (1275) 854675; *Fax:* (1275) 810186.

VORONENKOVA, Galina, D PHIL; Russian professor of journalism; b 30 Jan 1947, Kostroma Region; d of the late Fydor and of Alexandra Smirnov; m Mikhail Voronenkov; one d. *Education:* Moscow State Univ and Leipzig Univ (GDR). *Career:* Literary contrib to local newspaper, Kostroma Region 1965–67; mem staff Journalism Dept, Moscow State Univ 1974–87; teacher of Russian language, House of Soviet Science

and Culture (Berlin, GDR), Business Manager Journalists' Club (Berlin) 1987–90; reporter for Soviet Women (Germany) 1990–92; Prof Faculty of Journalism, Moscow State Univ 1992–; Dir Free Russian-German Inst for Publishing 1994–; Corresp mem Acad of Information and Communication; award from Fed Council of Russian Fed 1996. *Publications:* Bürger in der Demokratie (Russian ed) 1997, Sredstva Massovoy Informatii Germanii v 90-e Gody 1998, Neue Technologien und die Entwicklung der Medien in Russland und Deutschland (Russian ed) 1998, Russland vor den Wahlen Die Rolle der Medien bei den Wahlen–ein Deutsch-Russischer Vergleich (Russian ed) 2000. *Leisure interests:* classical music, world history, science fiction. *Address:* Mochovaya ul 9, Apt 235, 103009 Moscow, Russian Federation (Office); Fadeyva ul 6, Apt 60, 125047 Moscow, Russian Federation (Home). *Telephone:* (095) 203-26-43 (Office); (095) 251-97-76 (Home); *Fax:* (095) 203-26-43 (Office); (095) 251-97-76 (Home); *E-mail:* frdip@journ.msu.ru (Office); galine-w@dataforce.net (Home); *Internet:* www.frdip.ru (Office).

VOYNET, Dominique Marie Denise, MD; French politician and doctor; b 4 Nov 1958, Montbéliard; d of Jean and Monique (née Richard) Voynet; two d. *Education:* Lycée Courbet (Belfort) and Univ of Besançon. *Career:* Anaesthetist and intensive care specialist, Dole (Jura) public hosp 1985–89; activist in several ecological and other orgs, Belfort and Besançon 1976–; Co-Founder Les Verts ('Green' movt) 1984, Sec-Gen 2001–; Gen Sec Green Group in European Parl 1989–91, Nat Spokesperson 1991–; Municipal Councillor, Dole 1989–, Co Councillor 1998–; mem Franche-Comté Regional Council 1992–94 (resgnd); cand presidential election 1995; elected Nat Ass Deputy (Les Verts and Parti Socialiste) for Dole-Arbois 1997; Minister for Town and Country Planning and the Environment 1997–2001; Councillor-Gen, Jura 1998–. *Address:* Les Verts, 107 ave Parmentier, 75011 Paris, France. *E-mail:* secretar@verts.imaginet.fr.

VRÁNOVÁ, Gabriela; Czech actress; b 27 July 1939, Nové Mesto nad Váhom; d of the late Jaroslav Vrána and Marie Vránová; m Jiří Kepka 1968; one s. *Education:* Jamu Univ of Brno. *Career:* Actress Ostrava Theatre 1960–62, Vinohrady Theatre (Prague) 1962–; conservatoire teacher, Prague 1977–; mem Cttee Fed of Radio Authors, Capek brothers Corpn; Jaroslav Prucha Prize 1973, 1977, 1982; Czech Literature Foundation Prize 1973; Czech Radio Prize for literature and poetry interpretation 1982. *Plays include:* the works of Ibsen, Čechov, Turgeněv; *Films include:* Where the Rivers Have the Sun, Agent from Vaduk, Merchant from Byzance Treasure, Miss Rajka, Father is Looking For; numerous TV appearances. *Leisure interests:* music, literature, feuilleton writing, plastic arts. *Address:* Nad kaplickou 6, 10000 Prague 10, Czech Republic. *Telephone:* (2) 773080.

VRBOVÁ, Alena Liberta, PH D, MU DR; Czech writer and neurologist; b 3 Oct 1919, Plzeň; d of Jan Tadeáš and Albertina Vrba. *Education:* Univ of Poitiers (France) and Charles Univ (Prague). *Career:* Began writing at the age of 11; Asst Acad of Sciences, Prague 1942–44; nurse 1944–45; Neurologist State Sanitorium for Nervous Diseases (Mar Lázně) 1951–77, Chair 1963–77; mem Syndicate of Czech Writers 1941–89; Founder-mem Community of Czech Writers 1990–; mem Cttee Corporation of Culture, Svatobor 1990–; has attended numerous int confs for writers or medical specialists in Europe, USA, India, Mongolia, etc; Hon MA 1982; Rustavelli Medal 1958, Nezval Medal 1989, Franz Kafka Medal 1999. *Publications include:* Poetry: River Voyage 1942, Contention 1946, Sounds and Songs 1963, Fountain di Trevi 1963, Antigony 1969, Time-Sorcery 1988; Novels: We Are Two 1943, In Monte Rose Again 1971, Veneziana 1975, Departure Via Madras 1978, Indian Summer 1987; six collections of short stories 1964–88; two historical novel trilogies 1976–89–96; numerous scientific papers for professional journals. *Leisure interests:* golf, travel, genealogy, antiquity. *Address:* Pohořelec 3, Hradčany, 118-00 Prague 1, Czech Republic; Dm Experiment 599, 353-01 Mariánské Lázně, Czech Republic. *Telephone:* (2) 20515417.

VYRODOVA-GOTIE, Valentina Gavrilovna; Ukrainian artist and professor of painting; b 4 Oct 1934, Kiev; d of Gavril and Anna Vyrodov-Gotie; m 1st Genady Nebozhatko 1963 (until 1964); m 2nd Pavel Karev 1967; one d. *Education:* Republican Art School, Kiev State Inst of Arts. *Career:* Teacher Kiev State Inst of Arts 1959–72, Docent 1972–90, apptd Prof of Painting 1990; solo exhibition Kiev 1985; group exhibitions in Italy, Germany, Belgium, Yugoslavia, Spain, Czechoslovakia 1976–85; participated in Venice Biennale 1962, 1973, 1975; works on show in numerous Ukrainian cities; Merited Art Worker 1989. *Leisure interest:* painting. *Address:* Kiev Art Institute, Kiev, Ukraine (Office); Kiev 254114, Avtozavodsky ul, 27v, fl 7, Ukraine (Home). *Telephone:* (44) 430-74-65 (Home).

W

WAAS, Anna-Luise; German artist; b 12 Feb 1916, Allmannsdorf; d of Gustavo Caesar. *Career:* Works include linocuts, collages, wall hangings, stained glass, dolls and portraits; has painted portraits of Popes Pius XII and Paul VI. *Publication:* Steinbrüche... das Geschichtebuch der Erde (companion vol to exhibition). *Leisure interests:* mineralogy, collecting fossils. *Address:* 32545 Bad Oeynhausen, Germany.

WADA, Emi; Japanese costume designer; b 18 March 1937, Kyoto; d of Nobu Wada and Sumiko Noguchi; m Ben Wada 1957; one s. *Education:* Kyoto City Coll of Arts (now Kyoto Univ of Arts). *Career:* Exhibition Emi Wada Recreates the Momoyama Period, Kyoto 1989; mem Acad of Motion Picture Arts and Sciences, USA, Costume Designers' Guild, USA; Gold Medal, Cannes Film Festival 1987. *Costumes designed:* Theatre: Aoi Hi (Blue Fire) 1957, Image Mandala 1987, King Lear 1993; Films: Marco 1972, Ran (Acad Award for Best Costume Design) 1985, Rokumeikan 1986, Princess from the Moon 1987, Momotaro Forever 1988, Rikyu 1989, Dreams 1990, Prospero's Books 1991; Dance: Carmen 1991; TV: Silk Art by Emi Wada (Grand Prix, Montreux Int HDTV Festival) 1991; Opera: Oedipus Rex 1992; *Publication:* My Costume – Emi Wada 1989. *Leisure interest:* reading. *Address:* 3-31-3-105 Kinuta, Setagaya-ku, Tokyo 157, Japan. *Telephone:* (3) 3417-0425; *Fax:* (3) 3417-1773.

WADDINGTON, Miriam (Dworkin), MA, D LITT; Canadian poet and teacher; b 23 Dec 1917, Winnipeg, MB; d of Isaac and Mussia (née Dobrusin) Dworkin; m Patrick Donald Waddington 1939 (divorced 1965); two s. *Education:* Jr High School (Winnipeg), Lisgar Coll Inst (Ottawa) and Univs of Toronto, Pennsylvania (USA), Lakehead and York. *Career:* Psychiatric Caseworker and Counsellor until 1963; Prof of English and Canadian Literature, York Univ 1973–, Sr Scholar and Prof Emer; writer; numerous awards. *Publications include:* Driving Home 1970, A. M. Klein 1970, Collected Poems 1986, Apartment Seven (essays) 1989, Summer at Lonely Beach, The Last Landscape (Poems) 1992, Cercando Fragole in Guino: altne poésie 1993, En Guise d'Amants: Poèmes Choisis 1994. *Leisure interests:* translation from Yiddish, Yiddish literature. *Address:* 625 W 27th Ave, Vancouver, BC V5Z 4H7, Canada.

WADDINGTON, Susan, BA, M ED; British consultant and politician; b 23 Aug 1944, Norfolk; m 1966; one d one s. *Education:* Blyth Secondary School (Norwich) and Univ of Leicester. *Career:* Tutor Open Univ 1967–73; Community Project Leader 1973–80; Lecturer in Social Policy, Westhill Coll, Birmingham 1980–82; Leader Leics Co Council 1982–84; mem staff Adult Educ (NIACE) 1984–88; Asst Dir of Educ, Derbyshire and Birmingham 1988–94; MEP (Lab) for Leicester 1994–99, mem Cttees on Social Affairs, Employment and Women's Rights; Consultant on Lifelong Learning and Europe 2000–. *Address:* 5 Roundhill Rd, Leicester LE5 5RJ, UK. *E-mail:* office@sue-waddington .co.uk.

WADE, Jan Louise Murray, LL B, BA; Australian politician; b 8 July 1937; d of John and Lillian (née Knight) Noone; m Peter Wade 1978; three s one d one step-d. *Education:* Sydney High School, Firbank Girls' Grammar School and Univ of Melbourne. *Career:* Tutor Univ of Melbourne 1963–64, Univ of Monash 1968; Solicitor 1965–67; Parl Counsel 1967–79, Asst Chief Parl Counsel 1978–79, Commr for Corp Affairs 1979–85; Pres Equal Opportunity Bd 1985–88; Liberal mem Senate for Kew 1988; Shadow Minister for Consumer Affairs 1989–90; Shadow Attorney-Gen and Shadow Minister for Women's Affairs 1990–92; Minister for Fair Trading 1992–99; Minister responsible for Women's Affairs 1992–99; Attorney-Gen for Vic 1992–99; numerous

contribs to professional journals. *Leisure interests:* family, art, reading, gardening. *Address:* 400 High St, Suite 1, Kew, Vic 3101, Australia. *Telephone:* (3) 862-2999; *Fax:* (3) 862-1299.

WADE, Rebekah; British newspaper editor; b 27 May 1968; d of the late Robert and of Deborah Wade. *Education:* Appleton Hall (Cheshire) and Sorbonne (Paris, France). *Career:* Began career as Features Ed, later Assoc Ed and Deputy Ed News of the World, Ed 2000–; Deputy Ed The Sun 1998–2000; Founder-mem and Pres Women in Journalism. *Address:* 1 Virginia St, London E1 9BD, UK. *Telephone:* (20) 7782-4406.

WADE, (Sarah) Virginia, OBE, B SC; British tennis player; b 10 July 1945, Bournemouth, Hants (now Dorset); d of Canon Eustace Wade. *Education:* Univ of Sussex. *Career:* Amateur player 1962–68, professional from 1968; British Hard Court Champion 1967, 1968, 1973, 1974; US Champion 1968 (Singles), 1973, 1975 (Doubles); Italian Champion 1971; Australian Champion 1972; Wimbledon Ladies Champion, UK 1977; played Wightman Cup for GB 1965–81, Capt 1973–80; played Fed Cup for GB 1967–81, Capt 1973–81; commentator BBC 1980–; mem Cttee All-England Lawn Tennis Club 1983–91; Hon LL D (Sussex) 1985; Int Tennis Hall of Fame 1989. *Publications:* Courting Triumph (jtly) 1978, Ladies of the Court 1984. *Leisure interest:* reading. *Address:* c/o International Management Group, Pier House, Strand on the Green, London W4 3NN, UK. *Telephone:* (20) 8994-1444.

WADIA, Coomi, DIP AD; Indian musician; b 6 Aug 1933, Bombay (now Mumbai); d of Aloo and Rustom Umrigar; m Nariman Wadia 1965; one s. *Education:* J. B. Petit High School (Bombay) and Sir J. J. School of Applied Arts (Bombay). *Career:* Assoc Trinity Coll of Music, London 1950, Licentiate 1952; Conductor and Dir of Music, Paranjoti Chorus 1967–, led concert tours of Europe 1974, 1977, 1981, 1989, Japan and USA 1989, Manila 1998, Europe 2001; World Festival of Sacred Music, Bangalore 2000; Observer-Conductor Int Univ Choral Festival, Lincoln Center, New York 1972; Conductor Sister Cities Festival, Stuttgart (Germany) 1981; juried at Int Choral Competition, Brazil 1989, Nat Music Competition, Sri Lanka 1998, Miedzyzdroje (Poland) 2000; mem selection panel All-India Radio; mem Bd of Examiners Univ of Bombay; Palamkote Gold Medals for Assoc and Licentiate of Trinity Coll of Music (London); Amber Award, Ninth Int Choral Competition, Poland 1974; Two Silver Medals for Polyphony and for Folk Music, Spain 1977; Golden Olive Award from Mayor of Jaen (Spain) 1977; Golden Baton Award, Bombay Citizen's Felicitation Cttee 1982; Bombay Zoroastrian Asscn Award 1990; Rotary Club of S Bombay Award 1994. *Leisure interests:* reading, needlework, yoga, meditation. *Address:* 909 Cumballa Crest, 42 Peddar Rd, Mumbai 400 026, India. *Telephone:* (22) 3860219; *Fax:* (22) 3081568; *E-mail:* nhwadia@vsnl .com.

WADIA, Nagris, DIP AD; British visual designer and advertising executive; b 17 Jan 1935, Karachi, India (now Pakistan); d of K. F. Khambata; m V. Wadia 1961; two s. *Education:* Sir J. J. School of Applied Arts and Cen School of Arts and Crafts (London). *Career:* Visual designer at Air India; agency work in London and for Lintas, Bombay; Founder, Man Dir Inter Publicity agency 1964; Vice-Pres Press Guild of India; Founder-mem, Chair Media Monitoring Services; Pres (first woman) Advertising Agencies Asscn of India 1975–77. *Leisure interests:* reading, yoga, holistic medicine, astrology, films. *Address:* Inter Publicity Pvt Ltd, Orient House, Adi Marzban Path, Mumbai 400 038, India. *Telephone:* (22) 261673; *Fax:* (22) 2626430.

WAELSCH, Salome Gluecksohn, PH D; American (b German) geneticist; b 6 Oct 1907, Danzig, Germany (now Gdańsk, Poland); d of Ilyia and Nadia Gluecksohn; m Heinrich B. Waelsch 1943; one s one d. *Education:* Univs of Königsberg, Berlin and Freiburg. *Career:* Research Assoc in Genetics, Columbia Univ, New York 1936–55; Assoc Prof of Anatomy (Genetics), Albert Einstein Coll of Medicine, Bronx, New York 1955–58, Prof of Anatomy (Genetics) 1958–63, Chair Dept of Genetics 1963–76, Prof of Genetics 1963–89, of Molecular Genetics 1989–; mem NAS; Hon Life mem New York Acad of Sciences; Fellow American Acad of Arts and Sciences; has published more than 100 articles in the field of developmental genetics in various scientific journals. *Address:* Dept of Molecular Genetics, Albert Einstein College of Medicine, 1300 Morris Park Ave, Bronx, New York, NY 10461, USA (Office); 90 Morningside Drive, New York, NY 10027, USA (Home). *Telephone:* (718) 430-3185 (Office); *Fax:* (718) 822-0845 (Office).

WAGNER, Allison; American swimmer; b 21 July 1977. *Education:* Univ of Florida. *Career:* Eight-time USA Nat Champion; set world record in 200m Individual Medley, Short Course World Championships 1993; Silver Medallist in 200m and 400m Individual Medley events World Championships 1994; Silver Medallist in 400m Individual Medley event Olympic Games, Atlanta, GA, USA 1996; mem USS Nat Jr Team. *Leisure interests:* painting, drawing. *Address:* c/o United States Swimming Inc, One Olympic Plaza, Colorado Springs, CO 80909, USA.

WAGNER, Sue Ellen, MA; American state official; b 6 Jan 1940, Portland, ME; d of Raymond and Kathryn (née Hooper) Pooler; m Peter Wagner 1964; one s one d. *Education:* Univ of Arizona and Northwestern Univ (Evanston, IL). *Career:* Fmr teacher and journalist; mem Mayor's Advisory Cttee 1973–84, Washoe County Republican Cen Cttee 1974–84, Nevada State Republican Cen Cttee 1975–84; mem Nevada State Ass 1975–83, Legis Comm 1976–77, Senate 1980; Lieut-Gov of Nevada; mem American Asscn of Univ Women; named One of Ten Outstanding Young Women in America. *Publication:* Diary of a Candidate: On People and Things. *Address:* c/o Office of the Lieutenant-Governor, 845 Tamarack Drive, Reno, NV 89509, USA.

WAGNER-PASQUIER, Eva; German opera director; b 14 April 1945, Oberwarmensteinach; d of Wolfgang and Ellen (née Drexel) Wagner; m Yves Pasquer 1977; one s. *Education:* Musical High School (Bayreuth). *Career:* Artistic Agent Robert Schulz Agency, Munich 1967; Asst to Dir Bayreuth Festival, then Production Asst and Asst Dir working on various musical productions 1967–76; mem New Philharmonia Chorus, London 1970–72; Production Asst Wiener Staatsoper, Vienna 1972; Artistic Dir Unitel Film and Television Productions, Munich 1973–84; Dir Royal Opera, Covent Garden, London 1984–87; Dir of Programming Opéra-Bastille, Paris 1988–93; Artistic Adviser Théâtre du Châtelet 1994–; Founder-mem Fondation Orcofi pour l'Opéra et la Musique 1986–; currently Dir Royal Opera House; mem Film and Opera Comm, Cannes Film Festival 1987; Nin-On Art Award, Japan 1986. *Leisure interests:* films, tennis. *Address:* c/o Royal Opera House, Covent Garden, London WC2, UK; 140 Oakwood Court, Abbotsbury Rd, London W14 83S, UK.

WAINWRIGHT, Hilary, BA, B PHIL; British journalist and editor; b 1949, Leeds. *Education:* The Mount School (York), St Anne's Coll (Oxford) and St Anthony's Coll (Oxford). *Career:* Research Asst Sociology Dept, Durham Univ 1973–75, Research Fellow 1975–78; Social Science Council Research Fellow, Open Univ 1979–81; Asst Chief Econ Advisor and Co-ordinator Popular Planning Unit, GLC (now GLA) 1982–86; freelance writer, lecturer and journalist, The New Statesman and The Guardian 1986–88; Fellow Transnat Inst (Amsterdam) 1988–; Sr Simon Fellow Sociology Dept, Univ of Manchester 1989–90; Visiting Fellow Center for Social Theory and Comparative History, Univ of California at Los Angeles 1991; Sr Research Fellow Center for Labour Studies, Univ of Manchester 1992–; visiting posts at several univs in Japan, NZ and USA; Political Ed Red Pepper Magazine 1994–95, Ed 1995–; mem Council Charter 88; frequent TV and radio appearances on discussion programmes including Question Time (BBC), Channel 4 News, Any Questions, Today Programme (BBC Radio 4) etc. *Publications:* The Workers' Report of Vickers (co-author) 1978, Beyond the Fragments (co-author) 1980, State Intervention in Industry: A Worker's Inquiry 1981, The

Lucas Plan: A New Trades Unionism in the Making? 1982, A Taste of Power: The Politics of Local Economics (co-ed) 1986, Labour: A Tale of Two Parties 1987, After the Wall: Social Movements and Democratic Politics in the New Europe (ed) 1991, Arguments for a New Left: Answering the Free Market Right 1994; numerous essays and articles; regular articles in the Guardian. *Leisure interests:* swimming, films, fell walking, eating and drinking with friends. *Address:* 83 Thornton Rd, Manchester M14 7NT, UK. *Telephone:* (161) 225-0807.

WAITZ, Greta; Norwegian athlete; b 1953. *Career:* Winner New York Marathon 1978–80, 1982–86, 1988; World Champion in Marathon, Helsinki 1983. *Address:* c/o Norges Fri-Idrettsforbund, Karl Johansgt 2, 0154 Oslo 1, Norway.

WAKELEY, Amanda; British fashion designer; b 15 Sept 1962, Chester; d of Sir John and Lady Wakeley; m Neil David Gillon 1992. *Education:* Cheltenham Ladies' Coll. *Career:* Worked in fashion industry, New Yor 1983–85; began designing for pvt clients in UK 1986; f Amanda Wakeley (women's designer clothing) 1990, opened shop in Chelsea, London 1993, shop in Harvey Nichols, London 1996; raised funds for 'Breakthrough' in 1996, 1998 and 2000 as Co-Chair of Fashion Targets Breast Cancer Campaign; winner Glamour Category, British Fashion Awards 1992, 1993, 1996. *Leisure interests:* travel, riding, driving, skiing, water-skiing, roller-blading, music. *Address:* First Floor, 79-91 New Kings Rd, London SW6 4SQ, UK. *Telephone:* (20) 7471-8807; *Fax:* (20) 7471-8833; *Internet:* www.amandawakely.com.

WAKEM, Beverley Ann, MA; New Zealand broadcasting executive; b 27 Jan 1944, Wellington. *Education:* Victoria Univ, Kentucky Univ (USA) and Trinity Coll of Music (UK). *Career:* Mem staff New Zealand Broadcasting Corpn 1963–75; Controller of Programmes Radio New Zealand 1975–85, Dir-Gen 1984–88, Acting Chief Exec, later Chief Exec 1988–91; Pres Asia-Pacific Broadcasting Union 1992; mem Bd Australian Acad of Broadcast Arts and Sciences; mem Australia-New Zealand Foundation. *Address:* Asia-Pacific Broadcasting Union, POB 1164, Jalan Pantai Bahru, 59700 Kuala Lumpur, Malaysia.

WAKOSKI, Diane, BA; American poet; b 3 Aug 1937, Whitter CA. *Education:* Univ of California at Berkeley. *Career:* Began writing poetry, New York 1960–73; worked as a book shop clerk, a jr high school teacher and by giving poetry readings on coll campuses; Poet-in-Residence Michigan State Univ 1975–; Prof of English Michigan State Univ 1975–; Guggenheim Grant 1972; Michigan Arts Foundation Award 1989. *Publications:* Coins and Coffins 1962, Discrepancies and Apparitions 1966, The George Washington Poems 1967, Inside the Blood Factory 1968, The Magellanic Clouds 1970, The Motorcycle Betrayal Poems 1971, Smudging 1972, Dancing on the Grave of a Son of a Bitch 1973, Trilogy (reprint of first three collections) 1974, Virtuoso Literature for Two and Four Hands 1975, Waiting for the King of Spain 1976, The Man Who Shook Hands 1978, Cap of Darkness 1980, The Magician's Feastletters 1982, Norii Magellanici (collection of poems from various vols trans into Romanian) 1982, The Collected Greed 1984, The Rings of Saturn 1986, Emerald Ice: selected poems 1962–87 (William Carlos Williams Prize 1989) 1988, The Archaeology of Movies and Books: Vol I Medea The Sorceress 1991, Vol II Jason The Sailor 1993, Vol III The Emerald City of Las Vegas 1995, Vol IV Argonaut Rose 1998; Towards A New Poetry (criticism) 1980. *Leisure interests:* cooking, films, letters, gambling. *Address:* 607 Division St, East Lansing, MI 48823, USA (Home). *Telephone:* (517) 355-0308 (Office); (517) 332-3385 (Home).

WALCOTT, Clotil; Trinidad and Tobago trade union official; b 7 Sept 1925, Trinidad; three d two s. *Career:* Pres-Gen Nat Union of Domestic Employees, Trinidad and Tobago; Grand Certificate of Honour, Bank and Gen Workers Union 1984; Star Citizen Award, The People's Popular Movt 1985; Award for contribution to the devt and advancement of family/community and the soc of Trinidad and Tobago, Network of Non-Govt Orgs of Trinidad and Tobago for the Advancement of Women 1991; Partners of the Americas Citation. Publication: Fight Back Says A Woman 1980. *Leisure interest:* reading. *Address:* Wattley Circular, Mt Pleasant Rd, Arima, Trinidad and Tobago. *Telephone:* 667-5247.

WALD, Patricia McGowan, LL B; American judge; b 16 Sept 1928, Torrington, CT; d of Joseph and Margaret (née O'Keefe) McGowan; m Robert L. Wald 1952; three d two s. *Education:* Connecticut Coll for Women and Yale Univ Law School. *Career:* Law Clerk US Court of Appeals, Second Circuit 1951–52; Assoc Arnold, Fortas and Porter, Washington, DC 1952–53; mem Nat Conf on Bail and Criminal Justice 1963–64; Consultant Nat Conf on Law and Poverty 1965; mem Pres's Comm on Crime in the Dist of Columbia 1965–66, on Law Enforcement and Admin of Criminal Justice 1966–67; Attorney Dept of Justice 1967–70; Co-Dir Ford Foundation Drug Abuse Research Project 1970; Attorney Center for Law and Social Policy 1971–72, Mental Health Law Project 1972–77; Asst Attorney for Legis Affairs, Dept of Justice 1977–79; Circuit Judge US Court of Appeals, DC 1979–, Chief Judge 1986–91; First Vice-Pres American Law Inst 1993–98; mem Exec Bd CEELI (ABA) 1994–97; Judge Int Criminal Tribunal for Fmr Yugoslavia, The Hague, Netherlands 1999–; Hon LL D (George Washington Univ) 1983, (John Jay School of Criminal Justice, Mount Holyoke) 1985, (Georgetown) 1987, (Villanova, Amherst Coll, New York Law School) 1988, (Colgate) 1989; August Voelmer Award, American Soc of Criminology 1976; Woman Lawyer of the Year, Women's Bar Asscn 1984; Sandra Day O'Connor Medal of Honor (Seton Hall Law School) 1993; Margaret Brent Award for Distinguished Women in the Legal Profession 1994. *Publications:* Bail in the United States (jtly) 1964, Bail Reform: A Decade of Promise Without Fulfillment (vol 1) 1972, Pursuing Justice for the Child (contrib) 1977, Child Psychiatry and the Law (contrib) 1980, Dealing with Drug Abuse: A Report to the Ford Foundation (jtly) 1972, Law and Poverty: Report to the National Conference on Law and Poverty 1965; numerous articles in learned journals. *Address:* International Criminal Tribunal for the Former Yugoslavia, 1 Churchilliplain, 2571 JW The Hague, Netherlands (Office); 2101 Connecticut Ave, NW, Apt 38, Washington, DC 20008, USA (Home). *Telephone:* (202) 232-1158 (Home).

WALDHOLTZ, Enid Greene, BS, JD; American lawyer and politician; b 5 Oct 1958, San Rafael, CA; m Joe Waldholtz. *Education:* Univ of Utah and Brigham Young Univ. *Career:* Caseworker and Research Asst to mem House of Reps 1982; law clerk Andrew & Kurth 1982; Attorney Ray, Quinney & Nebecker 1983–90; Deputy Chief of Staff to Gov Norman H. Bangerter of Utah 1990–92; Corporate Counsel Novell Inc 1993–94; mem House of Reps (Republican), mem House Rules Cttee. *Address:* c/o House of Representatives, 414 Cannon House Office Bldg, Washington, DC 20515-4402, USA.

WALDO-BALTZER, Carolyn, OC; Canadian swimmer; b 11 Dec 1964, Montréal, PQ; d of Stuart and Sally Waldo; m Tom Baltzer 1989; one d one s. *Education:* Univ of Calgary. *Career:* Olympic Silver Medallist in Synchronized Swimming event, Los Angeles, USA 1984, Double Olympic Gold Medallist, Seoul 1988; World Cup Champion 1985, 1987; World Solo, Duet and Team Champion 1986; health and fitness consultant and TV personality; Sports Presenter CJOH TV, Ottawa, ON 1990–; Spokesperson Lupus 1989–90, Sears clothing collection 1988–92; Chair Canadian Lung Asscn 1985–86; mem Drug Awareness Programme 1987–90; Hon Deputy United Way 1990; named Canadian Female Athlete of the Year 1985, 1986, 1987, 1988. *Address:* c/o CJOH TV, 15 Merivale Rd, Ottawa, ON K2C 3G6, Canada.

WALEWSKA, Malgorzata; Polish opera singer (mezzo-soprano); b 5 July 1965, Warsaw; one d. *Education:* Acad of Music (Warsaw) and Nat Opera (Warsaw). *Career:* Has sung at Bremer Theater 1994, Staatsoper, Vienna 1996–98, Semperoper, Dresden 1999; has participated in numerous festivals in Brussels, London, Athens; winner Second Int Moniuszko Competition (Warsaw) 1992, Luciano Pavarotti Competition (Philadelphia) 1992.

WALKER, Alice Malsenior; American writer; b 9 Feb 1944, Eatonton, GA; d of Willie L. and Minnie (née Grant) Walker; m Melvyn R. Leventhal 1967 (divorced 1977); one d. *Education:* Sarah Lawrence Coll (Bronxville, NY). *Career:* Hon PH D (Russell Sage Univ) 1972; Hon DHL (Massachusetts) 1983; Lillian Smith Award 1974; Rosenthal Award, Nat Inst of Arts and Letters 1973; Guggenheim Foundation Award 1979; American Book Award 1983; Pulitzer Prize 1983. *Publications:* Once 1968, The Third Life of George Copeland 1970, In

Love and Trouble 1973, Langston Hughes, American Poet 1973, Revolutionary Petunias 1974, Meridian 1976, I Love Myself When I Am Laughing 1979, Good Night Willi Lee, I'll See You in the Morning 1979, You Can't Keep a Good Woman Down 1981, The Color Purple 1982 (film 1985), In Search of Our Mothers' Gardens 1983, Horses Make a Landscape Look More Beautiful 1984, To Hell With Dying 1988, Living By the Word 1988, The Temple of My Familiar 1989, Possessing the Secret of Joy 1992, Warrior Marks (jtly) 1993, Double Stitch: Black Women Write About Mothers and Daughters (jtly) 1993, Everyday Use 1994, Alice Walker Banned 1996, Everything We Love Can Be Saved 1997, The Same River Twice 1997. *Address:* c/o Random House, 201 E 50th St, New York, NY 10022, USA.

WALKER, Catherine, MA; French fashion designer; b Pas-de-Calais; d of Rémy Baheux and Agnes Lefèbvre; m John Walker (deceased); two d. *Education:* Univs of Lille and Aix-en-Provence. *Career:* Dir Film Dept, French Inst, London 1970, Lecture Dept, French Embassy, London 1971, The Chelsea Design Co Ltd 1978–; Founder, Sponsor Gilda's Club and Hon mem of Bd; Founder, Sponsor Haven Trust; Designer of the Year for British Couture 1990–91, British Fashion Awards 1990; Designer of the Year for Glamour Award 1991–92, British Fashion Awards 1991. *Publication:* Catherine Walker, an Autobiography by the Private Couturier to Diana, Princess of Wales 1998. *Address:* The Chelsea Design Co, 65 Sydney St, Chelsea, London SW3 6PX, UK. *Telephone:* (20) 7352-4626.

WALKER, Celine Foster; American United Nations official; b Saint Lucia; d of Ernest A. and Marie Foster; one d. *Education:* Univ of Illinois and Univ of Southern California at Los Angeles (USA). *Career:* Librarian Aerospace Corpn 1966–69, Rand Corpn 1969–72; Dir Information Services R & D Asscn, Santa Monica, CA, USA 1972–74; Chief Science and Tech Libraries, Stanford Univ, CA 1974–82; apptd Exec Sec UN Advisory Cttee for the Co-ordination of Information Sciences 1986; UN Human Rights Award (Albuquerque Chapter) 1964. *Leisure interests:* travel, reading. *Address:* UN, Palais des Nations, 1211 Geneva 10, Switzerland (Office); Borex-Soleil, 1261 Borex, Switzerland (Home). *Telephone:* (22) 7988591 (Office); *Fax:* (22) 7401269 (Office).

WALKER, Polly; British actress; b 1966, Warrington, Cheshire. *Education:* French convent, Drama Centre (London) and Ballet Rambert School. *Career:* Joined RSC, later stage and TV actress. *Plays include:* Hess is Dead, As You Like It, Hamlet; *Films include:* Lorna Doone 1990, Shogun Mayeda 1990, Les Equilibristes 1991, Enchanted April 1991, A Dangerous Man 1992, Patriot Games 1992, The Trial, Silver, Restoration, Talk of Angels, Emma, Woodlanders, Robinson Crusoe, Rosanna's Grave, Brute, The Gambler; *TV appearances include:* Kremlin Farewell 1990, The Trial 1992, Lorna Doone. *Address:* c/o Markham and Foggatt Ltd, 4 Windmill St, London W1P, UK. *Telephone:* (20) 7636-4412; *Fax:* (20) 7637-5233.

WALKER, Sarah Elizabeth Royle, CBE, LRAM, FRCM; British opera and concert singer (mezzo-soprano); b Cheltenham; d of Alan Royle Walker and Elizabeth Brownrigg; m Graham Allum 1972. *Education:* Pate's Grammar School for Girls (Cheltenham), violin and cello, then voice studies with Ruth Packer and Cuthbert Smith at Royal Coll of Music (London). *Career:* Martin Musical Trust Scholarship to begin vocal studies with Vera Rozsa 1967; operatic debuts at Kent Opera in Coronation of Poppea 1969, Glyndebourne Festival in La Calisto 1970, Scottish Opera in Les Troyens 1971, English Nat Opera in The Ring 1971; Prin singer with English Nat Opera 1972–76; debut Royal Opera House, Covent Garden in Werther 1979; debut Metropolitan Opera, New York, USA in Handel's Samson 1986; performances in Chicago and San Francisco (USA), Göttingen (Germany), Geneva (Switzerland), Vienna and Brussels; concert repertoire includes contemporary and avant-garde works by Berio, Boulez, Cage, Ligeti, Xenakis, etc; recital debut Wigmore Hall, London with regular recital partner, Roger Vignoles 1979; recital tours in Australia, N America and Europe; sang Rule Britannia at last night of BBC Henry Wood Promenade Concerts, London 1985 and 1989; Pres Cheltenham Bach Chair 1986–; Hon FGSM; Liveryman Worshipful Co of Musicians. *Recordings include:* Handel's Hercules and Julius Caesar, Stravinsky's Rake's Progress; *Videos include:* Gloriana, Julius Caesar, King Priam. *Leisure interests:* interior design, gardening, battling against incipient laziness. *Address:*

c/o Askonas Holt Ltd, Lonsdale Chambers, 27 Chancery Lane, London WC2A 1PF, UK (Agent); 152 Inchmery Rd, London SE6 1DF, UK (Home). *Telephone:* (20) 8461-5659; *Fax:* (20) 8461-5659; *E-mail:* megamezzo@sarahwalker.com (Home); *Internet:* www.sarahwalker.com (Home).

WALLACE, Helen, PH D, CMG, FBA; British professor of European Studies; b 25 June 1946, Manchester; d of the late Edward and of Joyce (née Robinson) Rushworth; m William Wallace 1968; one s one d. *Education:* Univs of Oxford, Bruges (Belgium) and Manchester. *Career:* Lecturer in European Studies UMIST 1974–78, in Public Admin, Civil Service Coll 1978–85; Head Western European Prog, Royal Inst of Int Affairs 1985–92; Prof of Contemporary European Studies and Dir Sussex European Inst, Univ of Sussex 1992–2001; Dir Robert Schuman Centre, European Univ Inst, Florence 2001–; Visiting Prof Coll of Europe (Bruges) 1976–; mem Planning Staff FCO 1979–80; mem Acad of Learned Socs for the Social Sciences 2000; Ordre Nat du Mérite (France) 1996. *Publications:* Policy-Making in the European Community (jtly) 1983, French and British Foreign Policies in Transition (jtly) 1990, The Wider Western Europe (ed) 1991, The European Community: the Challenge of Enlargement (jtly) 1992, The Council of Ministers (jtly) 1997, Participation and Policy-Making (jtly) 1997, Policy Making in the European Union (ed) 2000, Interlocking Dimensions of European Integration (ed) 2001. *Leisure interests:* gardening, walking. *Address:* Robert Schuman Centre for Advanced Studies, European University Institute, Via dei Roccettini 9, 50016 San Domenico di Fiesole, Italy. *Telephone:* (055) 4685-792; *Fax:* (0553) 4685-730; *E-mail:* helen.wallace@iue.it.

WALLACE, Joan Scott, BS, M SC, PH D; American international organization official; b 8 Nov 1930, Chicago, IL; d of William Edouard and Esther (née Fulks) Scott; m 1st John Wallace 1954 (divorced 1978); three s; m 2nd Maurice Dawkins 1979. *Education:* Bradley Univ (IL), Colombia Univ (NY) and Northwestern Univ (IL). *Career:* Child Welfare Worker, then Family Therapist 1952–67; Asst and Assoc Prof Univ of Illinois, Chicago 1967–73; Assoc Dean and Prof Howard Univ, Washington, DC 1973–76; Vice-Pres Programs, Nat Urban League, New York 1975–76; Vice-Pres Admin, Morgan State Univ 1976–77; Asst Sec Admin, US Dept of Agric 1977–81; Admin Office of Int Co-operation and Devt 1981–89; on secondment to Inter-American Inst for Co-operation on Agriculture (IICA), as Diplomatic Rep to Trinidad and Tobago 1989; Int Consultant US Partnership Int, Fort Lauderdale, FL 1993–; lecturer in field; numerous contribs to professional journals; mem American Psychological Asscn, Amercian Consortium for Int Public Admin, Caribbean Studies Soc, Caribbean Asscn of Agriculture Economists, Asscn of Political Psychologists, Int Science and Educ Council (Chair 1981–89); Hon HLD (Maryland) 1984; Hon LHD (Bowie State) 1986; Hon LL D (Alabama) 1990; Presidential Award for Meritorious Exec 1980; Nat Asscn of Female Execs Award 1989. *Leisure interest:* collecting art. *Address:* US Partnership Int, 5557 W Oakland Park Blvd, Fort Lauderdale, FL 33313-1411, USA (Office); 6010 S Falls Circle Drive, Fort Lauderdale, FL 33319-6900, USA (Home).

WALLACE, Marjorie Shiona, MBE, BA; British former journalist and organization executive; d of William Wallace and Doris Tulloch; m Count Adrzej Skarbek; three s one d. *Education:* Univ Coll London. *Career:* Worked in TV on The Frost Programme 1966–68, ITV religious programmes 1966–68, London Weekend TV current affairs 1968–69; Dir, Reporter Current Affairs, BBC TV 1969–72; Feature writer Sunday Times 1972–89, writer articles on thalidomide and schizophrenia (The Times 1985–89); Guardian Research Fellow Nuffield Coll, Oxford 1989–91; Founder and Chief Exec SANE (mental health charity) 1989–; mem Cttee of Man Inst of Psychiatry 1989–, Ethics Cttee 1991–, Schizophrenia Advisory Panel 1991–; mem Advisory Panel Sainsbury Centre 1992–; Campaigning Journalist of the Year, British Press Awards 1982, 1986; John Pringle Memorial Award 1986; Oddfellows Book Trust Prize 1987; Snowdon Special Award 1988; Medical Journalist of the Year 1988; Evian Health Award 1991. *Publications:* On Giant's Shoulders (jtly, also TV screenplay which won Int Emmy award 1979) 1976, Suffer the Children: The story of Thalidomide (jtly) 1978, The Superpoison, The Dioxin Disaster 1980, The Silent Twins (also TV screenplay) 1986, Campaign and Be

Damned 1991. *Leisure interests:* piano, poetry, music, Victorian ballads, opera, dining out. *Address:* 26 Bisham Gardens, London N6 6DD, UK. *Telephone:* (20) 8341-0435.

WALLACE, Naomi; American poet and playwright. *Career:* Plays have been performed by the RSC, Barbican, London 1996, and at other theatres in the UK and in USA. *Plays include:* War Boys, In the Heart of America, One Flea Spare, Slaughter City 1996.

WALLEY, Joan Lorraine, BA; British politician; b 23 Jan 1949; d of the late Arthur and of Mary Walley; m Jan Ostrowski 1980; two s. *Education:* Biddulph Grammar School (Staffs), Univ of Hull and Univ Coll of Swansea (Univ of Wales). *Career:* Voluntary work at St Martin in the Fields, London, then worked with single homeless people; Local Govt Officer Swansea City Planning Dept 1974–78, Wandsworth Borough Council 1978–79; mem staff Nat Asscn for the Care and Resettlement of Offenders 1979–82; mem Lambeth Borough Council, Chair Health and Consumer Services Cttee, Assoc London Authorities Public Protection Cttee 1982–85; MP (Lab) for Stoke on Trent N 1987–, Opposition Front Bench Spokesperson on the Environment 1991, Spokesperson on Transport 1991–95, mem Dept of Trade and Industry Select Cttee 1995; Pres W Midlands Home and Water Safety Council; Vice-Pres Inst of Environmental Health Officers. *Leisure interests:* walking, music, swimming, football. *Address:* House of Commons, London SW1A 0AA, UK. *Telephone:* (1782) 577900 (Stoke on Trent); *Fax:* (1782) 836462 (Stoke on Trent).

WALLIS, Diana Lynn; British artistic director; b 11 Dec 1946, Windsor; d of Dennis and Joan (née Gatcombe) Wallis. *Education:* Tonbridge Grammar School for Girls. *Career:* Mem Royal Ballet Touring Co 1965–68; Artistic Co-ordinator Nat Ballet of Canada 1984–86, Assoc Artistic Dir 1986–87, Co-Artistic Dir 1987–89; Deputy Artistic Dir English Nat Ballet 1991–94; Artistic Dir Royal Acad of Dance 1994–; Fellow Imperial Soc of Dancing Teachers. *Address:* 41 Musard Rd, London W6 8NR, UK.

WALLISER, Maria Anesini; Swiss skier; b 27 May 1963, Mosnang; d of Georges and Maria Walliser; m Guido Anesini 1991; one d. *Career:* Joined Nat Ski Team of Switzerland after leaving school; winner of World Cup 1980–90; World Champion (three times) in Downhill and Slalom 1987, in Downhill 1989; Olympic Medallist in Downhill, Slalom and Combination Sarajevo, (Yugoslavia) 1984, Calgary (Canada) 1988. *Address:* Jeninserstr 86F, 7208 Malians, Switzerland. *Telephone:* (81) 511796.

WALLSTRÖM, Margot; Swedish politician; b 28 Sept 1954, Kåge, Västerbotten Co; m Håkan Olsson; two s. *Education:* Univ of Stockholm. *Career:* Ombudsman Värmland br Social Democratic Youth League 1974–77; Accountant Alfa Savings Bank (Karlstad) 1977–79, Sr Accountant 1986–87; mem Riksdag (Parl) 1979–85; Minister of Civil Affairs with special responsibility for Consumer Affairs, Women and Youth 1988–91, Minister of Culture 1994–96, of Health and Social Affairs 1996–98; EU Commr for the Environment 1999–; CEO TV Värmland 1993–94; Chair Worldview Int Foundation until 1994, Exec Vice-Pres Worldview Global Media, Colombo (Sri Lanka) 1998–99; mem Exec Cttee Swedish Social Democratic Party 1993–; mem Bd for Alternative Nat Service Training, Swedish State Railways, Civil Aviation Admin, Nat Environmental Protection Agency, Nat Council for Cultural Affairs, State Youth Council. *Address:* European Commission, 200 rue de la Loi, 1049 Brussels, Belgium.

WALSH, Diane, MUS M; American pianist; b 16 Aug 1950, Washington, DC; d of William and Estelle (née Stokes) Walsh; m 1st Henry Forbes 1969 (divorced 1979); m 2nd Richard Polak 1982. *Education:* Juilliard School of Music (New York) and Mannes Coll. *Career:* Professional debut in Young Concert Artists series 1974; Founder Mannes Trio 1983–94; performances include Kennedy Center for Performing Arts (Washington, DC) 1976, Wigmore Hall (London) 1980, Library of Congress 1987, Miller Theatre 1994; appearances with major orchestras including San Francisco Symphony, Bavarian Radio Symphony of Munich and Berlin Radio Symphony (Germany); tours of USA and Europe; recordings with Nonesuch Records 1980–82, Book-of-the-

Month Records 1985, Music and Arts 1990, CRI 1991; Koch, Biddulph Records 1995; winner Munich Int Piano Competition 1975; Naumburg Chamber Music Award 1986.

WALSH, Julia Montgomery, BA, B COM; American investment banking executive; b 29 March 1923; d of Edward A. and Catherine (née Skurkay) Curry; m 1st John M. Montgomery 1948 (died 1957); four s; m 2nd Thomas M. Walsh 1963; five d three s. *Education:* Kent State Univ and Harvard Univ. *Career:* Dir Fulbright Programme, Ankara, Turkey; Personnel Officer American Consulate-Gen, Munich, Germany until 1955; Sr Vice-Pres and Registered Rep Ferris and Co Inc 1955–74, Vice-Chair of Bd 1974–77; Chair of Bd Julia M. Walsh and Sons Inc 1977–83, apptd Man Dir Tucker Anthony Inc (parent co of J. M. Walsh) 1984; mem Bd of Dirs Pitney Bowes Inc 1977; apptd Dir Czech Slovak-American Enterprise Fund (Presidential appointment) 1991; mem Investment Banking Advisory Cttee of American Stock Exchange, Advisory Bd First American Bank; Dir Nat Bd of the Shrine of the Immaculate Conception; Dir and mem Exec Cttee Greater Washington Bd of Trade; Trustee Dole Comm, Nat Asscn of Bank Women, Kent State Univ Foundation, Mount St Mary's Coll (MD); Hon LL D (Kent State); Oustanding Alumni, Kent State Univ 1967. *Address:* Tucker Anthony Inc, 1300 I St, NW, Suite 450 E, Washington, DC 20005, USA (Office); 5001 Millwood Lane, Washington, DC 20016, USA (Home). *Telephone:* (202) 408-4511 (Office); *Fax:* (202) 408-4535 (Office).

WALSH, (Mary) Noëlle, BA; British journalist; b 26 Dec 1954; d of Thomas and Mary (née Ferguson) Walsh; m David Heslam 1988; one s one d. *Education:* Univ of East Anglia. *Career:* Editorial Asst Public Relations Dept, St Dunstan's Org for the War-Blinded 1977–79; News Ed Cosmopolitan 1979–85; Ed London Week 1985–86; freelance writer 1986–; Deputy Ed Good Housekeeping 1986–87, Ed 1987–91; Dir The Value For Money Co Ltd 1992–. *Publications:* Hot Lips, the Ultimate Kiss and Tell Guide 1985, Ragtime to Wartime: the best of Good Housekeeping 1922–39 1986, The Home Front: the best of Good Housekeeping 1939–45 (co-ed) 1987, The Christmas Book: the best of Good Housekeeping at Christmas 1922–62 (co-ed) 1988, Food Glorious Food: eating and drinking with Good Housekeeping 1922–42 1990, Things My Mother Should Have Told Me 1991, Childhood Memories 1991, The Good Deal Directory 1992–, The Home Shopping Handbook 1995, Baby on a Budget 1995, Wonderful Wedding That Won't Cost a Fortune 1996, The Good Mail Order Guide 1996; *TV:* presenter Consumer Issues, Channel 5 1998. *Leisure interests:* history, being an agony aunt. *Address:* Pip Cottage, Filkins, nr Lechlade, Glos GL7 3JJ, UK.

WALTERS, Barbara, BA; American television broadcaster; b 25 Sept 1931, Brookline, MA; d of Lou and Dena (née Selett) Walters; m 1st Lee Guber 1963 (divorced 1976); one adopted d; m 2nd Merv Adelson 1986 (divorced 1993). *Education:* Sarah Lawrence Coll (Bronxville, NY). *Career:* Fmr writer and producer with WNBC TV, then Station WPIX and CBS TV morning broadcasts; Producer NBC TV; joined Today programme as a writer, then gen reporter, NBC TV 1961, regular panel mem 1963–74, Co-Host 1974–76; Moderator Not for Women Only (syndicated TV programme) for five years; corresp ABC News, Co-Anchor evening news programme 1976–78, Co-Host 20/20 1979–; Host Barbara Walters Specials 1976–, Ten Most Fascinating People 1994–; Co-exec producer The View (ABC), NY 1997–; contrib to Issues and Answers; retrospective of career at Museum of Broadcasting, New York 1988; Hon LHD (Ohio State, Marymount Coll, Temple, Wheaton Coll and Hofstra Univ); Broadcaster of the Year, Int Radio and TV Soc 1975; Emmy Award, Nat Acad of TV Arts and Sciences 1975, 1983; Silver Satellite Award, American Women in Radio and TV 1985; named one of the 100 Most Important Women of the Century, Good Housekeeping 1985; Pres's Award, Overseas Press Club 1988; Lowell Thomas Award for Journalism 1990, 1994; Lifetime Achievement Award, Int Women's Media Foundation 1992; several other awards. *Publications:* How to Talk with Practically Anybody about Practically Anything 1970; contribs to Good Housekeeping, Family Weekly, Reader's Digest. *Address:* 20/20, 147 Columbus Ave, 10th Floor, New York, NY 10023, USA; Barwall Productions, The Barbara Walters Specials, 825 7th Ave, Third Floor, New York, NY 10019, USA.

WALTERS, Julie Mary, OBE; British actress; b 22 Feb 1950, Birmingham; d of the late Thomas and of Mary Bridget (née O'Brien) Walters; m Grant Roffey 1998; one d. *Education:* St Paul's Prep School (Edgbaston), Holly Lodge Grammar School for Girls (Smethwick) and Manchester Polytechnic. *Career:* Trained to be a nurse; School Gov Open Univ 1990. *Plays include:* Educating Rita (Variety Club Best Newcomer Award) 1980, Having a Ball 1981, Fool for Love 1984–85, Macbeth 1985, When I Was a Girl I Used to Scream and Shout 1986–87, Frankie and Johnny in the Clair de Lune 1989, The Rose Tattoo 1991, All My Sons (Olivier Award) 2000; *Films include:* Educating Rita (Variety Club Best Actress Award 1984, British Acad Award for Best Actress 1984, Golden Globe Award 1984, Acad Award nomination) 1983, She'll be Wearing Pink Pyjamas 1984, Car Trouble 1986, Personal Services (BAFTA Award nomination) 1986, Prick Up Your Ears 1986, Buster 1987, Mack the Knife 1988, Killing Dad 1989, Stepping Out 1991, Just Like a Woman 1992, The Summer House 1992, Wide Eyed and Legless 1993, Sister My Sister 1995, Intimate Relations 1996, Titanic Town 1997, Girls Night 1997, All Forgotten 1999, Dancer 1999, Billy Elliot (Acad Award nomination) 2000; *TV appearances include:* Talent 1980, Wood and Walters (with Victoria Wood, qv) 1981, Boys from the Blackstuff (BAFTA Award nomination) 1982, Say Something Happened (BAFTA Award nomination) 1982, Victoria Wood as seen on TV (BAFTA Award nomination) 1984, 1986, 1987, Secret Diary of Adrian Mole 1985, The Birthday Party 1986, Her Big Chance 1987, Julie Walters and Friends, Me – I'm Afraid of Virginia Woolf, Intensive Care, Talking Heads 1988, GBH 1991, Julie Walters and Friends 1991, Clothes in the Wardrobe 1992, Bambino Mio 1993, Pat and Margaret 1994, Jake's Progress 1995, Little Red Riding Hood 1995, Intimate Relations 1996, Julie Walters is an Alien 1997, Dinner Ladies 1998, Jack and the Beanstalk 1998, Dinner Ladies 1999, Oliver Twist 1999; *Radio appearances include:* Dave's Back 1992, Telling Stories (book serialization); *Publication:* Baby Talk 1990. *Leisure interests:* reading, travel. *Address:* c/o ICM, Oxford House, 76 Oxford St, London W1N 0AX, UK. *Telephone:* (20) 7636-6565.

WALTERS, (Mary) Shirley; Australian politician; b 31 Aug 1925, Sydney; d of the late Sir Eric and Mary Harrison; m David John Walters 1949; two s two d. *Education:* Kambala Girls' School (Sydney). *Career:* Trained as nurse, Royal Prince Alfred Hosp, Sydney; Liberal Senator for Tasmania 1975–93, mem Jt Standing Cttee Parl Library 1976–, Standing Cttee on Social Welfare 1976–, Jt Select Cttee on Family Law 1978–80, Industrial Relations Legislation Cttee 1982, Jt Select Cttee on Video Material 1985–89, Senate Legis and Gen Purpose Standing Cttee for Community Affairs 1987, Estimate Cttee on Social Security, Community Services and Health, Veterans' Affairs 1990–, Parl Sec to Leader of Opposition 1987–89, Chair Opposition Social Policy and Health Task Force 1990; mem Industrial Relations Cttee Manpower and Labour Market Reform Task Force 1990, Industry and Structural Reform Task Force 1991–; Deputy Chair Senate Select Cttee on Community Standards Relevant to the Supply of Services Utilising Telecommunications Tech 1991–; mem Parl Liaison Cttee on AIDS 1991–93; Convenor Opposition Aged Care Tax Reform Campaign Task Force 1991; mem OECD Council of Europe Parl Symposium on Devt Co-operation, Paris 1978; mem IPU Conf, Havana 1981, Budapest 1989; Head of Opposition Del to Japan 1984; mem HRH Duke of Edinburgh's Commonwealth Study Conf 1985–89; mem Cttee Southern Region, Nat Trust of Australia. *Leisure interests:* reading, gardening, golf, fishing. *Address:* 16 Caroline St, Dynnyrne, Hobart, TAS 7005, Australia. *Telephone:* (2) 34 1409.

WALTERS, Phyllis Carole; British public relations executive; b London; one d. *Education:* Clarks Coll and Hornsey Coll of Art (London). *Career:* Founder, Prin Phyllis Walters Public Relations consultancy co 1972; Public Relations consultant for clients in retailing industry including Next, Marks and Spencer, Debenhams, Gianni Versace, Penhaligons and other nat and int cos. *Leisure interests:* sport, yoga, swimming, squash, gardening, watercolour painting. *Address:* 27 Bruton St, London W1X 7DB, UK. *Telephone:* (20) 7499-6891; *Fax:* (20) 7409-7536.

WALTON, Nancy-Bird, AO, OBE; Australian aviator; b 16 Oct 1915, Kew, NSW; d of William Raymond and Fanny Louisa (née Thornton) Bird; m John Charles Walton 1939; one s one d. *Education:* Elmswood Coll (Ashfield) and Brighton Coll (Manly). *Career:* Organizer First

Ladies' Flying Tour of Australia 1935; first woman to operate commercial flights as pilot in Far West Children's Health Scheme 1935–36; operated Charter Air Service 1937–38; studied aviation devt 1938–39; exhibition on flying (Sydney and Melbourne) 1939; Commdt W Australian Turf Club (WATC) 1940–45; aided in foundation and devt of the New S Wales Air Ambulance service 1961–; Pres Australian Women's Flying Club 1940; Founder, Pres Australian Women Pilots' Asscn 1950; Pres Women's Section, Nat Heart Foundation 1960; Hon Life mem Royal Aero Club of New S Wales, Narromine Aero Club; mem Aviation Medical Soc of Australia and New Zealand, German Women Pilots' Asscn; Hon M ENG (Sydney) 1987; Hon D SC (Newcastle); winner Ladies' Trophy South Australia Centenary Air Race (Brisbane to Adelaide) 1936; Dame of Merit, KTs of Malta, Most Excellent Order of St John of Jerusalem Hospitaliers 1977. *Publications:* Born to Fly 1961, My God! It's a Woman 1990. *Leisure interest:* public speaking. *Address:* 22 Adderstone Ave, North Sydney, NSW 2060, Australia. *Telephone:* (2) 44 3185.

WALZOG, Nancy Lee, BFA; American television producer; b 12 Feb 1963, Baltimore, MD; d of William and Barbara (née Lombardi) Walzog. *Education:* Univ of New York and Pace Univ. *Career:* Commercial Producer Nancy Walzog Film and TV Ltd 1982–84; Producer ABC Entertainment 1984; Dir TV Sales and Marketing, Int Film Exchange, New York 1984–86; apptd Vice-Pres Tapestry Int Ltd 1986; Emmy award 1987, nomination 1990; ACE award, Nat Acad of Cable TV Programming 1987; Gold award, San Francisco Int Film Festival 1987; Hugo Award, Chicago Int Film Festival 1988. *Address:* Tapestry International Ltd, 920 Broadway Suite 1501, New York, NY 10010, USA. *Telephone:* (212) 505-2288; *Fax:* (212) 505-5059; *E-mail:* nwalzog@tapestry-intl.com.

WAN SHAO-FEN, LL B; Chinese party official, economist and lawyer; b 16 Aug 1930, Nanchang; d of Wan De-Sheng and Yuan Zhi-Xiu. *Education:* Nat Chung-Cheng Univ and Zhongzheng Univ. *Career:* Joined CCP 1952; Deputy Sec Nanchang City Cttee, Chinese Communist Youth League (CCYL) 1955–66; mem Cen Cttee CCYL; Deputy Dir Labour Office, Jiangxi Prov Govt; first woman Sec CCP Cttee, Jiangxi 1985–87; mem CCP Cen Cttee 1985–; Chair Prov Women's Fed, Jiangxi 1983–85; Vice-Chair All-China Fed of TU; Vice-Dir United Front Work Dept, Cen Cttee CCP 1988–; mem CCP Cen Discipline Inspection Comm 1992–97, 8th NPC Standing Cttee 1993–98, Preliminary Working Cttee of the Preparatory Cttee of the Hong Kong Special Admin Region 1993–96; Vice-Chair Internal Affairs and Judicial Cttee of the 9th NPC 1998; NPC Deputy Tibet Autonomous Region; Nat Women's Fed award 1984. *Publications:* Learning of the Development of Children's Talents (ed) 1986, Visiting South Pacific Islands, Cultivation (poetry), Sowing (poetry). *Leisure interests:* reading, table tennis, shooting. *Address:* c/o Standing Committee of National People's Congress, Beijing, People's Republic of China.

WANAMAKER, Zoë, CBE; British/American actress; b New York, USA; d of the late Sam and of Charlotte Wanamaker; m Gawn Grainger 1994; one step-s one step-d. *Education:* Cen School of Speech and Drama (London). *Career:* Professional debut as Hermia in A Midsummer Night's Dream, Manchester 1970; repertory at Royal Lyceum 1971–72, Oxford Playhouse 1974–75, Nottingham 1975–76; has worked with RSC and Nat Theatre, and on Broadway, New York; Hon Vice-Pres Voluntary Euthanasia Soc; Hon D LITT (South Bank Univ) 1993, (American Int Univ, London) 1999. *Plays include:* Once in a Lifetime (SWET Award) 1979, Piaf 1980, Twelfth Night 1983, A Comedy of Errors 1983, Time of Your Life 1983, Mother Courage (Drama Award 1985) 1984, Loot 1986, Othello 1989, The Crucible 1990, The Last Yankee 1993, Dead Funny 1994, The Glass Menagerie 1995/96, Sylvia 1996, Electra (Olivier Award, Variety Club Award for Best Actress) 1997–98, The Old Neighbourhood 1998, Battle Royal 1999–2001, Boston Marriage 2001; *TV appearances include:* Enemies of the State, Edge of Darkness, Paradise Postponed, Poor Little Rich Girl (mini-series), Love Hurts (series) (BAFTA Award for Best Actress 1998), Prime Suspect, The Widowing of Mrs Holroyd, Dance to the Music of Time 1997, Gormenghast (series) 1999, Leprechauns 1999, David Copperfield 1999, My Family (series) 1999–, Adrian Mole: The Cappuccino Years (series) 2001; *Films include:* The Last Ten Days of Hitler, Inside the Third Reich, The Hunger 1982, The Raggedy Rawney

1987, Wilde (BAFTA Award for Best Actress) 1997, Harry Potter & the Philosopher's Stone 2001; *Radio work includes:* The Golden Bowl, Plenty Bay at Nice, A February Morning, Carol, Such Rotten Luck. *Address:* c/o Jeremy Conway, Conway van Gelder Ltd, 18–21 Jermyn St, London SW1Y 6HP, UK; c/o Peggy Thompson, 1st & 2nd Floor Offices, 296 Sandycombe Rd, Kew, Richmond, Surrey TW9 3NG, UK. *Telephone:* (20) 7287-0077; *Fax:* (20) 7287-1940.

WANG, Nina; British (b Chinese) business executive; m Teddy Wang (kidnapped 1990 and presumed dead 1999). *Career:* Chair Chinachem Group (real estate co, oversees large portfolio of offices, shopping centres, housing blocks, cinemas and industrial sites in Hong Kong); launched cartoon strip 'Nina Nina' based on herself 2001; under investigation for forgery of her husband's will 2001; named Britain's richest woman, The Mail on Sunday (UK) and S China Morning Post 2001. *Address:* Chinachem Group Headquarters, Hong Kong Special Administrative Region, People's Republic of China. *Internet:* www .chinachemgroup.com.

WANG ANYI; Chinese writer; b 6 March 1954, Nanjing; d of Wang Xiaoping and Ru Zijuan; m Li Zhang 1970. *Education:* Xiangming Middle School and Chinese RuXun Literary Coll. *Career:* Worked on farm 1970–72; mem song and dance troupe (Xu Zhou) 1972–78; joined children's publishing house Shanghai 1978; accepted as professional writer by Shanghai Writers' Asscn 1987, Vice-Pres 1988. *Publications include:* novels: 69 jie chuzhong sheng (The 1969 Junior Middle School Graduates) 1984, Huanghe gudao ren (Man at the Old Course of the Huanghe River) 1986, Huangshan zhi lian (Love on a Barren Mountain) 1986, Xiaocheng zhi lian (Love in a Small Town) 1986, Jinxiugu zhi lian (Brocade Valley) 1987, Liushui sanshi zhang 1988, Changhen ge 1995, The Ode of Eternal Hatred (Mao Dun Prize); novellas: Elapse (Chinese Novella Prize 1983), Epilogue, Xiao Baozhuang (Baotown) 1985; short stories: Liushi (Lapse of Time) 1982, The Newly Arrived Coach, Black and White, The Destination (Chinese Short Story Prize) 1982; collected stories: Wang Aiyi Story Collection, Rain, Sha, Sha, Sha, Shushu de gushi 1990; screenplay: Temptress Moon 1996. *Leisure interests:* films, watching TV, music, travel, painting. *Address:* 675 Ju Lu Rd, Shanghai 200040, People's Republic of China; Shanghai Writers Association, Shanghai, People's Republic of China. *Telephone:* (21) 377175.

WANG FULI; Chinese actress; b Nov 1949, Xuzhou, Jiangsu Prov. *Education:* Jiangsu Prov Drama Acad. *Career:* Actress Jiangsu Prov Peking Opera Troupe, then Jiangsu Prov Drama Troupe 1968–90; with China Broadcasting Art Co 1990–; winner TV Gold Eagle Award for Best Actress, Hundred-Flower Award for Best Supporting Actress, Gold Rooster Award for Best Supporting Actress, New Decade Movie Award for Best Actress. *Films:* The Legend of Tianyun Mountain 1980, Xu Mao and His Daughters 1981, Our Niu Baisui, Sunrise 1985, God of Mountains 1992, The Romance of Blacksmith Zhang, The Wooden Man's Bride 1993. *Address:* China Broadcasting Art Company, People's Republic of China.

WANG JUNXIA; Chinese athlete; b Jan 1973, Dalian, Liaoning Prov. *Career:* Set new world record for women's 10,000 m race and 1,500 m race in 1993; Gold Medallist women's 5,000 m race, Olympics Games, Atlanta 1996. *Address:* c/o State General Bureau for Physical Culture and Sports, 9 Tiyuguan Rd, Chongwen District, Beijing, People's Republic of China.

WANG KE-FEN; Chinese dance historian; b 1 April 1927, Yunyang, Sichuan; d of Wang Baifan and Liao Huiqing; m Zhang Wengang 1949; one s one d. *Education:* Advanced Teaching Coll (Wanxian Co) and Chinese Acad of Arts (Shanghai). *Career:* Choreographer and Dancer Cen Nat Song and Dance Co 1952–58; Research Fellow Chinese Nat Dance Asscn 1956–66, Dance Inst Chinese Acad of Arts 1977–; Academic Prize Arts Acad of China 1989; Award for Special Contribution, Award for Outstanding Contributions of Culture and Education Exchange. *Publications:* The History of Chinese Dance 1980, The Stories of Ancient Chinese Dancer 1983, The History of Chinese Dance: Ming Dynasty, Qing Dynasty 1984, Sui Dynasty and Tang Dynasty 1987, The History of Chinese Dance Development, Dictionary of Chinese Dance (chief ed) 1989, History of Chinese Civilization (10 vols, chief ed on dance), Sui and Tang Civilization (co-ed and contrib) 1990, Chinese Dance of the 20th Century 1991, Buddhism and Chinese

Dance 1995, The History of Chinese Dance 1996, The Chinese Contemporary History of Dance 1840–1996 1999, Chinese Music and Dance in the Tang Dynasty from Japanese History Books 2000, The Culture of the Wei Dynasty, Jin Dynasty, Northern Dynasty and Southern Dynasty (jtly) 2000. *Leisure interests:* choreography, dance, writing. *Address:* 1601-4 Bldg, Changyungong, Xi Sahuan Bei Lu, Beijing, 100044, People's Republic of China. *Telephone:* (1) 68411250.

WANG NAN; Chinese table tennis player. *Career:* Singles finalist Int Table Tennis Fed (ITTF) Pro Tour Grand Final 1997, 2000, China Open 1997, winner Lebanon Open 1997, US Open 1997, ITTF Pro Tour Grand Final 1998, China Open 1998, World Cup 1997, 1998, World Table Tennis Championships 1999; doubles winner ITTF Pro Tour Grand Final 1997, Lebanon Open 1997. *Address:* c/o International Table Tennis Federation, Avenue Mon Repos 30, 1005 Lausanne, Switzerland. *Telephone:* (21) 340-7090; *Fax:* (21) 340-7099; *Internet:* www.ittf.com.

WANG YANI; Chinese artist; b 1975; d of Wang Shiqiang. *Career:* Painter since age of three; solo exhibition Smithsonian Inst, Washington, DC 1989; workshop Children's Museum, Washington, DC 1991.

WANGCHUCK, HRH Princess (Ashi) Sonam Chhoden; Bhutanese royal; b 26 July 1953, Zurich, Switzerland; sister of The Druk Gyalpo Jigme Singhye Wangchuck, King of Bhutan; m Tsewang Jurmed Rixin 1979; two c. *Career:* Apptd Chair Royal Insurance Corpn 1975, Dunk Air Corpn 1981, Royal Civil Service Comm and Royal Monetary Authority 1982; fmrly Rep of HM, in the Ministry of Finance, Rep of HM in the Ministry of Agric; apptd Pres Nat Women's Assch 1981. *Address:* Ministry of Agriculture, Thimphu, Bhutan. *Telephone:* 2450.

WANGCHUCK DORJI, HRH Princess (Ashi) Dechen Wangmo; Bhutanese royal; sister of The Druk Gyalpo Jigme Singhye Wangchuck, King of Bhutan. *Career:* Rep of HM in the Ministry of Communications. *Address:* Ministry of Communications, Thimphu, Bhutan.

WANIEK, Danuta, D JUR; Polish politician and former professor of political science; b 26 Oct 1946, Włocławek; d of Jerzy and Juzefina Waniek; m (husband deceased); two s. *Education:* Univs of Warsaw and Vienna and Acad of Social Sciences. *Career:* Prof of Political Science until 1994; mem Inst of Political Studies, Polish Acad of Sciences (PAN) 1989–, Polish United Workers' Party (PZPR) 1967–90, Social Democracy of the Repub of Poland 1990–, Democratic Union of Women; mem Sejm (Parl, Alliance of Democratic Left) 1992–, mem Parl Cttee of Nat Defence; Chair Women's Democratic Union 1990–; Deputy Minister of Nat Defence 1994–95; Head Alexander Kwaśniewski's presidential campaign 1995; Minister of State and Head of Chancellery of the Pres of Poland 1995–97; awarded Krzyz Kasługi (Cross of Merit). *Publications:* Compromise within the Political System of Germany: Partnership or Struggle? 1988, Constitution and Political Reality 1989, Debate over 'Little Constitution' (ed) 1992, Creating New Constitutional Order in Poland (ed) 1993. *Leisure interests:* painting, music (listening and playing), opera, reading newspapers, embroidering. *Address:* Biuro Poselskie, ul Rozbrat 44A, 00-419 Warsaw, Poland. *Telephone:* (22) 6215830.

WARBURTON, Dame Anne Marion, DCVO, CMG, MA; British former diplomatist and college president; b 8 June 1927, London; d of Capt Eliot and Mary Louise (née Thompson) Warburton. *Education:* Barnard Coll, Columbia Univ (New York) and Somerville Coll (Oxford). *Career:* With Econ Co-operation Admin, London 1949–52; mem staff NATO Secr, Paris 1952–54; mem staff Lazard Bros, London 1955–57; entered Diplomatic Service 1957; Second Sec Foreign Office 1957–59; Second, then First Sec UK Mission to UN, New York 1959–62; First Sec, Bonn 1962–65, Diplomatic Service Admin Office, London 1965–67, Foreign Office, then FCO 1967–70; Counsellor UK Mission to UN, Geneva, Switzerland 1970–75; Head of Guidance and Information Policy Dept, FCO 1975–76; Amb to Denmark 1976–83, to UN at Geneva 1983–85; Equal Opportunities Commr 1986–87; Head EU investigation team into accusations of rape of Muslim women by Serbian soldiers in fmr Yugoslavia 1993; Pres Lucy Cavendish Coll, Cambridge 1985–94; mem Council Univ of E Anglia 1991–97, British Library Bd 1989–95, Cttee on Standards in Public Life (Nolan Cttee) 1994–97; Hon Fellow

Somerville Coll, Oxford 1977, Lucy Cavendish Coll, Cambridge 1994; Dr hc (Arkansas) 1994; Bundesverdienstkreuz (First Class), Germany 1965; Grand Cross, Order of Dannebrog, Denmark 1979; Order of Isabel la Católica, Spain 1988. *Leisure interests:* enjoying the arts, walking, travel. *Address:* Ansted, Thornham Magna, Eye, Suffolk IP23 8HB, UK.

WARD, Rachel; British actress; b 9 Dec 1957; m Bryan Brown; one d. *Career:* Model; professional acting debut in Three Blind Mice. *Films include:* Night School 1981, Sharky's Machine 1981, Dead Men Don't Wear Plaid 1982, The Final Terror 1984, Against All Odds 1984, Fortress 1985, The Good Wife 1987, How to Get Ahead in Advertising 1989, After Dark My Sweet 1990, Christopher Columbus 1992; *TV appearances include:* The Thorn Birds (mini-series) 1983. *Address:* c/o David Schiff, Creative Artists Agency, 9830 Wilshire Blvd, Beverly Hills, CA 90212, USA.

WARE, Helen Ruth, BA, PH D; Australian (b British) organization executive and former diplomatist; b 9 July 1944, Paddington, UK; d of Walter and Irene Batty; two s one d. *Education:* Univs of Durham and London. *Career:* Research Fellow ANU 1971–80; Field Dir Changing Africa, Family Project 1972–80; Sr Research Fellow Univ of Ibadan, Nigeria 1973–74; ind consultant 1980–81; Dir of Projects Human Rights Comm 1981–84; Dir Legal and Int Office of the Status of Women, Dept of the Prime Minister and the Cabinet 1984–85; Asst Dir-Gen Australian Int Devt Assistance Bureau 1986–88, 1991–; Amb to Angola 1988–91, concurrently High Commr to Zambia, Malawi and Namibia 1988–91; mem Exec Bd Australian Population and Immigration Council 1974–76, UNICEF 1986–88. *Publications:* Women, Development and Demography 1981, A Profile of the Italian Community in Australia 1981, Improving Statistics and Indicators on Women 1988. *Leisure interests:* conversation, reading, demography. *Address:* 26 Booth Crescent, Cook, ACT 2614, Australia.

WARK, Kirsty Anne, BA; British broadcaster; b 3 Feb 1955; d of Jamea Allan Wark and Roberta Eason Forrest; m Alan Clements 1990; one s one d. *Education:* Wellington School and Univ of Edinburgh. *Career:* Joined BBC 1976, Radio then TV producer, politics and current affairs programmes 1977–90; Co-Founder Wark, Clements & Co (ind production co) 1990; presenter The Late Show and Edinburgh Nights 1990–93, Newsnight, One Foot in the Past, Words With Wark and Building a Nation 1993–, Gen Elections, Scottish Gen Elections and Referendum and Rough Justice 1998–; The Kirsty Wark Show 1999–; Hon D LITT (Abertay) 1995; Scotland Journalist of the Year 1993; Scotland Presenter of the Year 1997; BAFTA Award; Scot of the Year 1998. *Publication:* Restless Nation 1997. *Leisure interests:* reading, tennis, beachcombing, architecture, cooking, film, music. *Address:* Wark, Clements & Co Ltd, The Production Centre, The Tollgate, 19 Marine Crescent, Glasgow G51 1HD, UK. *Telephone:* (141) 429-1750.

WARKENTIN, Juliet, BA; Canadian magazine editor; b 10 May 1961; m Andrew Lamb 1991. *Education:* Univ of Toronto and London Coll of Fashion (UK). *Career:* Fashion ed local newspaper, Canada, then mem staff Toronto Life Fashion; Ed Draper's Record, UK 1993–96, Marie Claire (UK) 1996–98; Man Dir Marketing and Internet Devt Arcadia Group PLC 1998–; Nat Magazine Award, Canada 1989; PPA Business Ed of the Year 1994. *Leisure interests:* reading magazines, food, books. *Address:* Arcadia Group plc, Colegrave House, 70 Berners St, London W1P 3AE, UK (Office); 14 Kelly St, London NW1 8PH, UK (Home). *Fax:* (20) 7261-5277 (Office).

WARNER, Deborah; British theatre director and opera director; b 12 May 1959, Oxford; d of Roger and Ruth Warner. *Education:* Sidcot School (Winscombe, Avon), St Clare's Coll (Oxford) and Cen School of Speech and Drama (London). *Career:* Founder Kick Theatre Co 1980, Artistic Dir 1980–86; Resident Dir RSC 1987–89; Assoc Dir Royal Nat Theatre 1989–98; Assoc Dir Abbey Theatre, Dublin 2000; has also staged productions at English Nat Opera, Glyndebourne Festival Opera, Royal Opera House and Opera North, and productions for Fitzroy Productions, Odeon Theatre, Paris, Salzburg Festival and Perth Int Arts Festival; Dir Fitzroy Productions; Officier des Arts et des Lettres 2000; London Evening Standard Drama Award for Direction 1988, 1998; Laurence Olivier Award for Direction 1989, 1992, New York Drama Desk Award 1997; South Bank Show Arts Award 1998.

Theatre productions include: The Good Person of Szechwan 1980, 1989, Woyzeck 1981–82, The Tempest 1983, Measure for Measure 1984, King Lear 1985, 1990, Coriolanus 1986, Titus Andronicus 1987, King John, Electra 1988, 1992, Hedda Gabler 1991, Footfalls 1994, Richard II 1995, The Waste Land 1995–99, Une Maison de Poupée 1996, Medea 1999–2000; *Opera productions include:* Wozzeck 1993, 1996, Don Giovanni 1994, 1995, The Turn of the Screw 1997, The Diary of One Who Vanished 1999; *Film productions include:* The Waste Land 1996, The Last September 2000; *TV productions include:* Richard II, Hedda Gabler, Don Giovanni. *Leisure interest:* travel. *Address:* c/o Conway van Gelder Ltd, 18–21 Jermyn St, London SW1Y 6HP, UK. *Telephone:* (20) 7287-0077; *Fax:* (20) 7287-1940.

WARNER, Lavinia; British television producer. *Career:* Ind Producer, Founder and Co-Dir (with Jane Wellesley, qv) Warner Sisters 1984. *TV productions:* Tenko, Wish Me Luck, She Play, Rides, Selling Hitler 1991. *Address:* Warner Sisters, Canalot Studios, 222 Kensal Rd, London W10 5BN, UK. *Telephone:* (20) 8960-3550.

WARNER, Marina Sarah, MA, FRSL; British writer; b 9 Nov 1946, London; d of Esmond Pelham and Emilia (née Terzulli) Warner; m 1st William Shawcross 1972; one s; m 2nd John Dewe Mathews 1981. *Education:* St Mary's Convent (Ascot) and Lady Margaret Hall (Oxford). *Career:* Writer 1971–; mem Advisory Bd Royal Mint 1986–, Inst of Contemporary Arts 1987–; Getty Scholar, Getty Centre for the History of Art and the Humanities 1987–88; Tinbergen Prof Erasmus Univ, Rotterdam, Netherlands 1990–91; Visiting Prof Univ of Ulster 1995–96, Queen Mary and Westfield Coll, Univ of London 1995–, Univ of York 1996–; Tanner Lecturer, Yale Univ (USA) 1999; Clarendon Lecturer, Oxford 2001; delivered Reith Lectures (on Managing Monsters: Six Myths of Our Time) 1994; mem Exec Cttee Charter 88 until 1997, Literature Panel Arts Council of England until 1997, Advisory Council British Library until 1997, Man Cttee Nat Council for One-Parent Families, Bd Artangel, Cttee London Library, Cttee PEN; Fellow Commonership, Trinity Coll, Cambridge 1998; Visiting Fellow, All Souls Coll Oxford 2001; Hon D LITT (Exeter) 1995, (York) 1997, (E London) 1999; Dr hc (Sheffield Hallam, York, N London, St Andrews) 1998; Fawcett Prize 1986; Commonwealth Writers Prize (Eurasia) 1989; Harvey Darton Award 1996; Mythopoetic Fantasy Award 1996; Katherine M. Briggs Award 1999; Rosemary Crawsmay Prize, British Acad 2000; Chevalier des Arts et des Lettres 2000. *Publications include:* The Dragon Empress 1972, Alone of All Her Sex: the Myth and the Cult of the Virgin Mary 1976, The Crack in the Teacup (historical essay) 1979, Queen Victoria's Sketchbook 1980, Joan of Arc: the Image of Female Heroism 1981, Monuments and Maidens: the Allegory of the Female Form 1985, The Lost Father 1988, Indigo 1992, Six Myths of Our Time – The 1994 Reith Lectures, From the Beast is the Blonde: On Fairytales and their Tellers (Harvey Darton Award 1995) 1994, The Inner Eye: Art Beyond the Visible 1996, No Go the Bogey Man: On Scaring, Lulling and Making Mock (Katherine Briggs Award 1999, British Acad Rose Mary Crawshay Prize 2000) 1998; Fiction: In a Dark Wood 1977, The Skating Party 1983, The Lost Father 1988, Indigo 1992, In the House of Crossed Desires (opera libretto) 1996, The Leto Bundle 2001; Jr fiction: The Impossible Day 1981, The Impossible Night 1981, The Impossible Bath 1982, The Impossible Rocket 1982, The Wobbly Tooth 1984, The Mermaids in the Basement (short stories) 1993, Wonder Tales (ed) 1994. *Leisure interests:* friendship, travel, reading, gardening. *Address:* c/o Rogers, Coleridge and White, 20 Powis Mews, London W11 1NJ, UK. *Telephone:* (20) 7221-3717; *Fax:* (20) 7229-9084.

WARNER, Suzanne Elizabeth, BA; British civil servant and business executive; b 12 Aug 1942; d of Charles Clifford and Elizabeth Joan (née Armstrong) Reeder; m 1st Jonathan Reeve 1967 (divorced 1980); one s; m 2nd Norman Reginald Warner 1990; one s. *Education:* Badminton School (Bristol), Univs of Sussex and Cambridge. *Career:* Mem staff Home Office Research Unit 1966–67; Personal Asst to Sec of State for Social Services, DHSS 1968–70, Prin 1970–73, Cen Policy Review Staff 1973–74, Asst Sec 1979–85, Sec 1985–88; Acting Chair Econ and Social Research Council (ESRC) 1987–88; Exec Dir Food From Britain 1988–90; Chief Exec Foundation for Educ Business Partnerships 1990–91; Personal Adviser to Deputy Chair BT (fmrly British Telecom) 1991–93; Dir of Group Govt Relations Cable & Wireless PLC 1993–96; Deputy Chair Broadcasting Standards Comm 1998–; Non-Exec Dir

Broadmoor Special Health Authority 1996–98; mem Tech Foresight Steering Group 1994–97, Acad Council Wilton Park 1995– (Chair 1999–), Scientific Policy Reserve Unit, Univ of Sussex 1998–, Court 2000–; Chair Trustees Botanic Gardens Conservation Int 1999–. *Leisure interests:* reading, films, cooking, gardening. *Address:* Broadcasting Standards Commission, 7 The Sanctuary, London SW1P 3JS, UK.

WARNOCK, Baroness (Life Peer), cr 1985, of Weeke in the City of Westminster, **(Helen) Mary Warnock,** DBE, FCP, FRSM; British philosopher and former university administrator; b 14 April 1924; d of the late Archibald Edward Wilson; m Geoffrey J. Warnock 1949 (died 1995); three d two s. *Education:* St Swithun's (Winchester) and Lady Margaret Hall (Oxford). *Career:* Tutor in Philosophy St Hugh's Coll, Oxford 1949–66, Sr Research Fellow 1976–84; Headmistress Oxford High School 1966–72; Talbot Research Fellow Lady Margaret Hall 1972–76; Mistress Girton Coll, Cambridge 1985–91; Chair Cttee of Inquiry into Special Educ 1974–78, Advisory Cttee on Animal Experiments 1979–86, Cttee of Inquiry into Human Fertilization 1982–844, Educ Cttee Girls' Day School Trust 1994–2001; mem IBA 1973–81, Royal Comm on Environmental Pollution 1979–84, Social Science Research Council 1981–85, UK Nat Comm for UNESCO 1981–85, Archbishop of Canterbury's Advisory Group on Medical Ethics 1992–; Hon Master of the Bench, Gray's Inn 1986; Hon FIC 1986; Hon Fellow Hertford Coll, Oxford 1997; Hon FBA 2000; Hon D UNIV (Open Univ) 1980, (St Andrews) 1992; Hon LL D (Manchester) 1987, (Liverpool, London) 1991; Hon D LITT (Glasgow) 1988; Dr hc (York) 1989; numerous hon degrees; RSA Albert Medal 1999. *Publications:* Ethics since 1900 1960, J.-P. Sartre 1963, Existentialist Ethics 1966, Existentialism 1970, Imagination 1976, Schools of Thought 1977, What Must We Teach? (jtly) 1977, Education: A Way Forward 1979, A Question of Life 1985, Teacher Teach Thyself (Dimbleby Lecture) 1985, Memory 1987, A Common Policy for Education 1989, Universities: Knowing Our Minds 1989, The Uses of Philosophy 1991, Imagination and Time 1994, Women Philosophers (ed) 1996, An Intelligent Person's Guide to Ethics 1998, A Memoir: People and Places 2000. *Leisure interests:* music, gardening. *Address:* 3 Church St, Great Bedwyn, Marlborough, Wilts SN8 3PE, UK (Home); House of Lords, London SW1A 0PW, UK (Office). *Telephone:* (1672) 870214.

WARREN, Minnie Mae; American trade union official; b 5 Nov 1945, Dowagiac, MI; d of Wyndell and Mollie (née Matthew) Macon; m Willie Warren 1964 (divorced 1988); three c. *Education:* Indianapolis Univ, Michigan State Univ and George Meaney Labor Inst. *Career:* Apptd Int Rep Int Union of Electronic, Electrical, Technical, Salaried, Machine and Furniture Workers, Washington, DC 1984, Social Action Chair for Indianapolis, Michigan, Wisconsin and Illinois 1988, Women's Council Chair Great Lakes Dist 1988; apptd Chair Housing Comm, Nat Asscn for the Advancement of Colored People, Michigan 1988; mem Nat Asscn of Female Execs, Coalition Labor Union Women. *Address:* c/o International Union of Electronic, Electrical, Technical, Salaried, Machine and Furniture Workers, 1126 16th St, NW, Washington, DC 20036, USA.

WARRINGTON, Elizabeth Kerr, PH D, D SC, FRS; British professor emeritus of clinical neuro-psychology; d of the late John A. V. and of Margaret L. Butler; m; one d. *Education:* Univ Coll London. *Career:* Research Fellow Inst of Neurology 1956; Sr Clinical Psychologist Nat Hosp 1960, Prin Psychologist 1962, Top Grade Clinical Psychologist 1972–82, Prof of Clinical Neuropsychology 1982–96, Emer 1996–, Consultant Neuropsychologist to Dementia Research Group 1996–; Hon Consultant Nat Hosp for Neurology and Neurosurgery 1996–; Fellow Univ Coll London; Dr hc (Bologna) 1998, (York) 1999. *Publications:* Cognitive Neuropsychology (jtly) 1990; numerous papers in professional journals. *Address:* Dementia Research Group, National Hospital for Neurology and Neurosurgery, Queen Square, London WC1N 3BG, UK. *Telephone:* (20) 7837-3611.

WARSI, Perween, MBE, DBA; British business executive; b 10 Aug 1956; m Dr Talib Warsi 1972; two s. *Career:* Founder and Owner S&A Foods 1987–, opened factory, Derby 1989, launched range of Chinese dishes with Ken Hom; fmr mem Dept of Trade and Industry Cttee on Competitiveness; Hon MBA (Nottingham Trent) 2000; Midlands Business Woman of the Year 1994; Royal Asscn for Disability and

Rehabilitation (RADAR) People of theYear Award 1995; Woman Entrepreneur of the World 1996. *Address:* S&A Foods Ltd, Sir Frances Ley Industrial Park, 37 Shaftsbury St South, Derby DE23 8YH, UK. *Telephone:* (1332) 270670.

WARWICK, Dionne; American singer; b 12 Dec 1941, E Orange, NJ; m Bill Elliott (divorced 1975); two s. *Education:* Hartt Coll of Music (Hartford, CT). *Career:* As teenager formed Gospelaires; later sang backing vocals for recording studio 1966; debut Philharmonic Hall, Lincoln Center, New York 1966; appearances at London Palladium, Olympia (Paris), Lincoln Center, etc; Co-Host Solid Gold (TV show); Host A Gift of Music (TV show) 1981; Presenter Dionne Warwick Special (TV show); appeared in Sisters in the Name of Love (TV show) 1986; Grammy Awards 1969, 1970, 1980. *Recordings include:* Albums: Valley of the Dolls and Others 1968, Promises, Promises 1975, Dionne 1979, Then Came You, Friends 1986, Reservations for Two 1987, Greatest Hits 1990, Dionne Warwick Sings Cole Porter 1990, Hidden Gems: The Best of Dionne Warwick (vol 2) 1992, Friends Can Be Lovers (with Whitney Houston) 1993, Dionne Warwick and Placido Domingo 1994, Aquarela do Brasil 1994, From the Vaults 1995, Dionne Sings Dionne 1998, I Say a Little Prayer For You 2000; Singles: I'll Never Love This Way Again, That's What Friends Are For; *Films:* The Slaves 1969, No Night, So Long, Hot! Live and Otherwise. *Address:* c/o Arista Records Inc, 6 W 57th St, New York, NY 10019, USA.

WARWICK OF UNDERCLIFFE, Baroness (Life Peer), cr 1999, of Undercliffe in the County of West Yorkshire, **Diana Warwick,** BA, FRSA; British public official and former trade union leader; b 16 July 1945; d of Jack and Olive Warwick; m Sean Young 1969. *Education:* St Joseph's Coll (Bradford) and Bedford Coll (Univ of London). *Career:* Tech Asst to Gen Sec Nat Union of Teachers (NUT) 1969–72; Asst Sec Civil and Public Services Asscn (CPSA) 1972–83; Gen Sec Asscn of Univ Teachers (AUT) 1983–92; Chief Exec Westminster Foundation for Democracy 1992–95; Chief Exec Cttee of Vice-Chancellors and Prins 1995–; Gov Commonwealth Inst 1988–; Chair Voluntary Service Overseas 1994–; mem Bd The British Council 1985–95, Exec and Council Industrial Soc 1987–, Employment Appeals Tribunal 1987–99, Gen Council TUC 1989–92, Exec and Council Inst of Employment Rights 1989, Council Duke of Edinburgh's Seventh Commonwealth Study Conf 1991–, Cttee on Standards in Public Life 1994–99, Tech Foresight Steering Group; Trustee Royal Anniversary Trust 1991–93, St Catharine's Foundation, Windsor 1996–; Hon D LITT (Bradford) 1993, (Open Univ) 1998. *Leisure interests:* reading, horse-riding, theatre, looking at pictures. *Address:* Committee of Vice-Chancellors and Principals, Woburn House, 20 Tavistock Square, London WC1H 9HQ, UK. *Telephone:* (20) 7419-5402; *Fax:* (20) 7380-0137; *E-mail:* diana .warwick@cvcp.ac.uk; *Internet:* www.cvcp.ac.uk.

WASSERSTEIN, Wendy, BA, MFA; American playwright and script-writer; b 18 Oct 1950, Brooklyn, NY; d of Morris and Lola Wasserstein; one d. *Education:* Mount Holyoke Coll and Yale School of Drama. *Career:* Playwright 1978–; Tutor Columbia and New York Univs; Contributing Ed New York Woman magazine; Dir Channel Thirteen, MacDowell Colony, British American Arts Asscn; mem Council Dramatists' Guild, Artistic Bd Playwrights' Horizons; Dr hc (Mount Holyoke). *Publications:* Uncommon Women and Others 1978, The Heidi Chronicles (Pulitzer Prize, New York Drama Critics' Circle Award, Drama Desk, Outer Critics Circle Award, Antoinette Perry Award, Susan Smith Blackburn Prize, Tony Award) 1988, When Dinah Shore Ruled the Earth, Isn't It Romantic, Any Woman Can't, Montpelier, Pa-Zazz, Miami, The Sisters Rosensweig, Old Money, Drive, She Said, Bachelor Girls (essays) 1990, The House of Husbands, An American Daughter 1996, Pamela's First Musical (children's book). *Address:* c/o Royce Carlton Inc, 866 UN Plaza, Suite 4030, New York, NY 10017-1880, USA. *Telephone:* (212) 355-7700; *Fax:* (212) 888-8659.

WATERHOUSE, (Gai) Gabriel Marie, BA; Australian racehorse trainer; b 3 Sept 1954, Sydney; d of Thomas John and Valerie Lillian Smith; m Robert Waterhouse; one s one d. *Education:* Univ of New South Wales. *Career:* Actress 1974–78; journalist; stable foreman 1978–92; racehorse trainer 1992–; Dir Gayval Investments Pty Ltd, Gai Waterhouse Racing Pty Ltd; Australian Racing Personality of the Year 1994–95; fmr NSW Sports Star of the Year; Sarah Kennedy Award for

Contrib to Racing; Silver Horseshoe Award for Best Trainer 1995; NSW Businesswoman of the Year 2000. *Publication:* Against All Odds (biog). *Leisure interests:* skiing, movies, theatre. *Address:* Gai Waterhouse Racing Pty Ltd, POB 834, Kensington, NSW 1465, Australia. *Telephone:* (2) 9662-1488 (Office); *Fax:* (2) 9662-6328 (Office).

WATERMAN, Fanny, CBE, FRCM; British concert pianist and piano teacher; b 22 March 1920; d of Myer and Mary (née Behrmann) Waterman; m Geoffrey de Keyser 1944; two s. *Education:* Allerton High School (Leeds) and Royal Coll of Music (London). *Career:* Co-Founder Leeds Int Pianoforte Competition 1961, Chair 1963–, Chair of Jury 1981–; Vice-Pres European Piano-Teachers Asscn 1975–; Trustee Edward Boyle Memorial Trust 1981–; Gov Harrogate Festival 1983; mem Int Juries, Vienna 1977, 1993, Terni (Italy) 1978, Munich 1979, 1986 and Leipzig (Germany) 1980, 1984, Calgary (Canada) 1982, Salt Lake City (USA) 1982, 1984, Viña del Mar (Chile) 1982, 1987, 1992, Maryland (USA) 1983, Cologne (Germany) 1983, 1986, Pretoria (S Africa) 1984, 1992, Santander (Spain) 1984, Rubinstein 1986, 1989, Moscow 1986, Vladigerov (Bulgaria) 1986, Lisbon 1987, 1991, CBC Toronto (Canada) 1989; Hon MA (Leeds) 1966; Hon MUS DOC (Leeds) 1992; Hon D UNIV (York) 1995. *Publications include:* Piano Tutors (series, jtly) 1967–, Fanny Waterman on Piano Playing and Performing 1983, Young Violinists Repertoire (4 vols), Music Lovers' Diary 1984–86, Christmas Carol Time 1986, Animal Magic 1989, Piano Competition: the story of Leeds (jtly) 1990, Me and My Piano: Repertoire and Duets (books 1 and 2) 1992. *Leisure interests:* travel, reading, voluntary work, cooking. *Address:* Woodgarth, Oakwood Grove, Leeds LS8 2PA, UK. *Telephone:* (113) 265-5771.

WATKINS, Winifred May, D SC, PH D, FRS, FRCPATH, F MED SCI; British research scientist; b 6 Aug 1924, London; d of Albert E. and Annie B. Watkins. *Education:* Godolphin and Latymer School (London) and Univ of London. *Career:* Research Student St Bartholomew's Hosp Medical School, London 1948–50; MRC Grantee Lister Inst of Preventative Medicine, London 1950–52, Beit Memorial Research Fellow 1952–55, mem scientific staff 1955–75, Prof of Biochem and Head Dept of Biochem 1968–75; Wellcome Travelling Fellow Univ of California at Berkeley, USA 1960–61; Reader in Biochem Univ of London 1965–68; Head of Div of Immunochemical Genetics, MRC Clinical Research Centre 1976–89; Visiting Prof Dept of Haematology, Royal Postgrad Medical School, London 1990–; Hon mem Int Soc of Blood Transfusion 1983, Japanese Biochemical Soc 1990, British Blood Transfusion Soc 1996, British Biochem Soc 2000; Foreign mem Polish Acad of Sciences (PAN) 1988, Royal Swedish Acad of Sciences 1998; Hon D SC (Utrecht) 1990; Oliver Memorial Fund Award for outstanding contribs in the field of blood transfusion 1965; Karl Landsteiner Award, American Asscn of Blood Banks (jtly) 1967; Paul Erhlich-Ludwig Darmstädter Medal and Prize (jtly) 1969; Mickle Fellowship Award, Univ of London 1970; Kenneth Goldsmith Award, British Blood Transfusion Soc 1986; Royal Medal, Royal Soc 1988; Franz-Oehleckler Medal, German Soc of Transfusion Medicine and Immunohaematology 1989; Philip Levine Award, American Soc of Chemical Pathologists (jtly) 1990; has written numerous papers on immunology, biochem and genetics in scientific journals. *Leisure interests:* reading, art, architecture. *Address:* Department of Haematology, Imperial College School of Medicine, Hammersmith Hospital, Du Cane Rd, London W12 0NN, UK. *Telephone:* (20) 8383-2171; *Fax:* (20) 8742-9335; *E-mail:* w.watkins@ic.ac.uk.

WATSON, Emily, BA; British actress; b 1967; m Jack Waters 1995. *Education:* Univ of Bristol. *Career:* Has worked with the RSC; Félix d'Or for Best European Actress of the Year, France 1996. *Films include:* Breaking the Waves (New York Soc of Film Critics Award, Nat Soc of Film Critics Award) 1996, Metroland, The Boxer, Hilary and Jackie, Angela's Ashes, The Cradle Will Rock, Trixie, The Luzhin Defense, Equilibrium; *TV appearances include:* A Summer Day's Dream, The Mill On The Floss. *Address:* c/o ICM Ltd, Oxford House, 76 Oxford St, London W1N 0AX, UK.

WATTLETON, Faye, MA; American organization executive and television presenter; b 8 July 1943, St Louis, MO; d of George and Ozie (née Garrett) Wattleton; m Franklin Gordon (divorced); one d. *Education:* Ohio State Univ, Columbia Univ (New York) and Harlem Hosp. *Career:* Instructor Miami Valley Hosp School of Nursing, Dayton,

OH 1964–66; Asst Dir Nursing Service, Dept of Health, City of Dayton 1967–69; Exec Dir Planned Parenthood Asscn of Miami Valley, Dayton 1970–78; Pres Planned Parenthood Fed of America, New York 1978–92; proposed Reproductive Rights Amendment to US Constitution 1989; Host syndicated TV show for Tribune Entertainment 1992–; Pres Center for Gender Equality, New York 1995–; mem Bd US Cttee for UNICEF, Young Pres's Org, Nat Advisory Cttee to Tufts School of Public Service; numerous awards for humanitarian works. *Publications:* How to Talk With Your Child About Sexuality 1986; has written a book on the history of birth control and abortion. *Leisure interests:* skiing, tennis. *Address:* Center for Gender Equality, 25 W 43rd St, New York, NY 10036, USA.

WATTS, Heather; American ballet dancer; b 27 Sept 1953, Long Beach, CA; d of Keith and Sheelagh (née Woodhead) Watts. *Education:* School of American Ballet (New York). *Career:* Dancer New York Ballet Co 1970–78, Soloist 1978–79, Prin Dancer 1979–95; retired 1995; Dir Summer School, New York School of Dance 1982–; Dance magazine award 1985; New York Public Library Lions of the Performing Arts award 1986. *Performances include:* Rossini Pas de Deux, Histoire du Soldat, Sonate di Scarlatti, Concerto for Two Solo Pianos, Song of the Auvergne, Ecstatic Orange, I'm Old Fashioned, The Four Seasons, Balanchine Celebration 1993; *TV appearances:* Bournonville Dances, The Magic Flute, A Choreographer's Notebook, Balanchine Celebrates Stravinsky. *Address:* New York City Ballet Inc, New York State Theatre, Lincoln Center Plaza, New York, NY 10023, USA; c/o Sharon Wagner Artists' Service, 150 W End Ave, New York, NY 10023, USA.

WATTS, Helen Josephine, CBE; British opera singer (contralto) (retd); b 7 Dec 1927, Milford Haven, Wales; d of Thomas Watts and Winifred Morgan; m Michael Mitchell 1980. *Education:* St Mary and St Anne's School (Abbot Bromley). *Career:* Singer in Glyndebourne and BBC choruses; toured fmr USSR with English Opera Group 1964; concert tours in USA 1967–85; has appeared with all major European and American orchestras; performances include Salzburg Festival (Austria), Royal Opera House (Covent Garden, London), Hong Kong Festival; major appearances include The Ring at Covent Garden, Mozart Opera at Salzburg Festival, four Promenade concerts 1974; Hon FRAM. *Recordings include:* Handel Arias, Orfeo, B Minor Mass, Beethoven's Mass in C Minor, The Dream of Gerontius, The Apostles, Götterdämmerung. *Leisure interest:* gardening. *Address:* 14 Cavendish Place, London W1M 9DJ, UK.

WAUGH, Carol-Lynn Rössel, MA; American writer, artist and photographer; b 5 Jan 1947, Staten Island, NY; d of Carl and Muriel (née Kiefer) Rössel; m Charles Waugh 1967 (divorced 2001); one s one d. *Education:* State Univ of New York at Binghamton (Harpur Coll) and Kent State Univ. *Career:* Instructor in Art History Univ of Maine 1977; freelance writer and artist 1973–; articles and lectures on teddy bears, dolls and antique toys; sculptor of original dolls 1973–; designer original teddy bears for House of Nisbet, UK 1987–, Effanbee Dolls 1989–, Ashton-Drake Galleries 1989–, Russ Berrie Ltd (USA and UK) 1991–; designer plates for Brimark Ltd 1986; numerous awards for watercolours, photography and designs; mem Soc of Children's Book Writers, Original Doll Artist Council of America, Mystery Writers of America, Maine Soc of Doll and Bear Artists. *Publications include:* Author: Petite Portraits 1982, My Friend Bear 1982, Teddy Bear Artists 1984, Contemporary Artist Dolls (jtly) 1986, The Official Guide to Antique and Modern Teddy Bears (jtly) 1990, Selling Your Dolls and Teddy Bears (jtly) 1996, Holmes for Christmas (jtly) 1996, Bear Making 101 1999, Heirloom Sewing for Teddy Bears and Dolls 2001; Co-ed: The Twelve Crimes of Christmas 1981, Big Apple Mysteries 1982, Show Business Is Murder 1983, Murder on the Menu 1984, Manhattan Mysteries 1987, Hound Dunnit 1987, The Sport of Crime, Purr-fect Crime 1989, Senior Sleuths 1989, More Holmes for the Holidays 1999 (co-ed) 1999; contribs to professional magazines. *Leisure interests:* embroidery, theology, Russian studies, acting. *Address:* 17 Morrill St, Winthrop, ME 04364, USA. *Telephone:* (207) 377-6769; *Fax:* (207) 377-4158; *E-mail:* CLWaugh@aol.com.

WAUGH, Sylvia; British writer; m; three c. *Career:* Fmr teacher; now writer of children's books. *Publications include:* The Mennyms (Guardian Children's Fiction Prize 1994, Carnegie Award nomination, trans to

Japanese, French, German, Italian, Spanish, Danish, Swedish) 1993, Mennyms in the Wilderness 1995, Mennyms Under Siege 1995, The Maker of the Mennyms.

WAX, Ruby; American writer, actress and comedienne; b 19 April 1951, Chicago, IL; d of Edward and Berta Wax; m Edward Richard Morison Bye 1988; one s one d. *Education:* Evanston Township High School, Univ of California at Berkeley and Royal Scottish Acad of Music and Drama. *Career:* Actress with Crucible Theatre 1976; with RSC 1977–82; writer for BBC TV series Not The Nine O'Clock News 1980; has written for and acted in own series and in TV specials on BBC TV including interview with the Duchess of York (qv) 1996; has also appeared in commercials; Gold Medal, Royal Scottish Acad. *TV includes:* Writer and Performer: Not the Nine O'clock News 1982–83, Girls on Top 1985–86, Don't Miss Wax 1987–88, Miami Memoirs 1987, East Meets Wax 1988, Hit and Run 1989, Class of '69 1989, The Full Wax 1990–92, Ruby Takes a Trip 1991, Ruby Wax Meets... 1996–98, Ruby 1997, 1998, 1999, Ruby's American Pie 1999, 2000; *Theatre:* Writer and Performer: Wax Acts 1992. *Leisure interests:* skiing, swimming, writing. *Address:* c/o PFD, Drury House, 34-43 Russell St, London WC2B 5HA, UK.

WAYNE, Naomi, LL B; British organisation executive; b London. *Education:* LSE and Univ of Cambridge. *Career:* Educ Officer Transport and Gen Workers' Union (TGWU), Dublin; Enforcements Officer N Ireland Equal Opportunities Comm; mem staff London Enterprise Bd 1984–87; Legal Officer Confed of Health Service Employees 1987–90; Chief Exec Terence Higgins Trust (AIDS charity) 1990–91.

WEARING, Gillian, BA; British artist; b 1963, Birmingham. *Education:* Chelsea School of Art (London) and Goldsmith's Coll (London). *Career:* First solo exhibition City Racing (London) 1993, numerous exhibitions around the world; concentrates on video and photography; solo exhibitions include: Kunsthaus Zurich (Chisenhale Gallery, London) 1997, Centre d'Art contemporain (Geneva) 1998, Serpentine Gallery (London) 2000, Fundación 'la Caixa' (Madrid) 2001, ARC (Paris) 2001; BT New Contemporaries Award 1993; Turner Prize 1997. *Publications:* Signs that say what you want them to say and not signs that say what someone else wants you to say 1997, Gillian Wearing 1999. *Address:* c/o Maureen Paley Interim Art, 21 Herald St, London E2 6JT, UK. *Telephone:* (20) 7729-4112; *Fax:* (20) 7729-4113.

WEAVER, Sigourney (Susan Alexandra), BA; American actress; b 8 Oct 1949, New York; d of Pat Weaver and Elizabeth Inglis; m James Simpson 1984; one d. *Education:* Ethel Walker School (Simsbury, CT) and Stanford and Yale Univs. *Career:* Appeared in improvisational productions before stage debut with Ingrid Bergman in The Constant Wife 1975; propr Goat Cay film production co. *Plays include:* Titanic 1976, Das Lusitania Songspiel, Better Dead Than Sorry, The Marriage of Bette and Boo, Das Lusitania Songspiel 1980, Lone Star 1980, Beyond Therapy, Hurlyburly (Tony nomination) 1984, The Merchant of Venice 1986; *Films include:* Annie Hall 1977, Madman 1978, Camp 708 1974, Alien 1979, Eyewitness/The Janitor 1981, The Year of Living Dangerously 1982, Deal of the Century 1983, Ghostbusters 1984, Une Femme ou Deux 1985, Aliens (Acad Award nomination) 1986, Half Moon Street 1986, Gorillas in the Mist (Golden Globe Best Actress Award, Acad Award nomination) 1988, Working Girl (Golden Globe Best Supporting Actress Award, Acad Award nomination) 1988, Ghostbusters 2 1989, Helmut Newton: Frames from the Edge 1990, Alien 3 (also co-producer) 1991, 1492: The Conquest of Paradise 1992, Dave 1993, Death and the Maiden 1994, Jeffrey 1995, Copycat 1996, Snow White in the Black Forest 1996, Ice Storm 1996, Alien Resurrection 1997, A Map of the World 1999, Galaxy Quest 1999, Get Bruce 1999, Company Man 1999, Airframe 1999; *TV appearances include:* The Best of Families, Somerset. *Leisure interests:* reading, walking, theatre. *Address:* c/o ICM, 8942 Wilshire Blvd, Beverly Hills, CA 90211, USA.

WEBB, Karrie; Australian golfer; b 1974, Qld; d of Robert and Evely Webb. *Career:* Professional golfer 1994–; came second in her first US golfing event, won her second US event, finished in top 20 15 times in 18 US tournaments; Winner Weetabix Women's British Open 1995, 1997, Sprint Titleholders Championship 1996, Titleholders Championship (Florida, USA) 1999, Office Depot (USA) 1999, 2000,

Australian Woman's Open 2000, Australian Women's Masters 2000, Ladies Professional Golf Asscn Takefuji Classic (Hawaii) 2000, US Women's Open 2000, etc; World Ranking no 1 1999; WEPGA Rookie of the Year 1995; ALPEGA Rookie of the Year 1996; top of US Money List 1996. *Address:* c/o International Management Group, 21 Clarence St, Sydney, NSW 2000, Australia.

WEBB, Martha Jeanne; American film producer; b 26 Oct 1947, Grinnell, IA; d of Frederick and Helen (née Potter) Webb; m Bruce Clark; two d one s. *Education:* St Cloud State Univ, Univ of Minnesota and Coll of St Catherine. *Career:* Mem staff dealing with drug abuse educ, NIH 1967–77; Account Services Doremus and Co, Minnesota 1977–79; Vice-Pres Admin, Webb Enterprises Inc, Minneapolis 1979–81; Vice-Pres Russell–Manning Productions 1981–88; Pres Clark Webb Inc 1986–91; Pres Minnesota Film Bd 1986–87, BCW Corpn 1988; numerous awards including Golden Eagle Awards, CINE Festival 1985, Gold Telly Award 1987. *Address:* c/o BCW Corpn, 420 Fifth St, Minneapolis, MN 55401, USA.

WEBB, Phyllis, OC, BA; Canadian poet; b 8 April 1927, Victoria, BC; d of Alfred and Mary (née Patton) Webb. *Education:* Univ of British Columbia and McGill Univ. *Career:* Teaching Asst Univ of British Columbia 1960; mem Public Affairs Dept, CBC 1964; Co-creator and Exec Producer Ideas (radio programme) 1967; Writer-in-Residence Univ of Alberta 1980–81; Adjunct Prof Creative Writing Dept, Univ of Victoria 1989–91; mem Amnesty Int. *Publications include:* Trio 1954, Even Your Right Eye 1956, The Sea is Also a Garden 1962, Selected Poems 1954–65 1965, Naked Poems 1965, Wilson's Bowl 1980, The Vision Tree (Gov-Gen's Award for Poetry) 1982, Talking (essays) 1982, Sunday Water 1982, Water and Light 1984, Hanging Fire 1990, Nothing But Brush Strokes (selected prose) 1995. *Address:* 128 Menhinick Drive, Salt Spring Island, BC V8K 1W7, Canada.

WEDDERBURN, Dorothy Enid, MA; British former college principal and professor of social and economic studies; b 18 Sept 1925, London; d of Frederick and Ethel Barnard. *Education:* Walthamstow High School for Girls and Girton Coll (Cambridge). *Career:* Research Officer, then Sr Research Officer Dept of Applied Econs, Univ of Cambridge 1950–65; Lecturer, then Prof and Head Dept of Social and Econ Studies Imperial Coll, Univ of London 1965–81, Prin Bedford Coll (became Royal Holloway and Bedford New Coll 1985) 1981–90, Pro-Vice-Chancellor Univ of London 1986–89, currently Sr Research Fellow Man School, Imperial Coll; Hon D LITT (Warwick) 1984; Hon D UNIV (Brunel) 1989; Hon DS (Loughborough) 1989, (City) 1991; Hon LL D (Cambridge) 1991; Hon PH D (London Guildhall) 2000. *Publications include:* White Collar Redundancy 1964, Worker Attitudes and Technology 1972, Justice for Women: the Case for Reform 2000. *Leisure interests:* politics, walking, cooking. *Address:* Imperial College of Science, Technology and Medicine, School of Management, 52-53 Prince's Gate, Exhibition Rd, London SW7 2PG, UK. *Telephone:* (20) 7589-5111; *Fax:* (20) 7023-7685.

WEEKS, Heather Marguerite, OBE, MA; British organization executive; b 27 Feb 1945, Batley, Yorks; d of Clifford and Amy Wilman; m David Weeks 1971. *Education:* Batley Girls' Grammar School, New Hall (Cambridge) and Univ of Birmingham. *Career:* Press Library Royal Inst of Int Affairs 1969–72, Deputy Meetings Sec 1976–84; Hon Sec British Atlantic Group of Young Politicians 1972–82; mem Nat Council European Movt 1972–84, Cons Group for Europe 1972–84; Founder-mem, Hon Sec and subsequently Vice-Chair Westminster for Europe 1977–84; mem Council The Bow Group 1974–78; mem Exec Cttee Westminster Community Relations Council 1976–80; Chair of Govs S Bank Adult Educ Inst 1977–80; Sec and Deputy Dir Ditchley Foundation 1984–98, Ed 1986–98; Head Meetings Dept, Royal Inst of Int Affairs 1998–. *Leisure interests:* opera, antiques, travel, cooking. *Address:* The Royal Institute of International Affairs, Chatham House, 10 St James Square, London SW1Y 4LE, UK (Office); 908 Beatty House, Dolphin Square, London SW1V 3PN, UK (Home). *Telephone:* (20) 7957-5722 (Office); *Fax:* (20) 7957-5745 (Office); *E-mail:* hweeks@riia.org.

WEEKS, Janet Healy, B SC, JD; American judge; b 19 Oct 1932, Quincy, MA; d of John and Sheila (née Jackson) Healy; m George Weeks 1959; one s one d. *Education:* Emmanuel Coll and Boston Coll. *Career:* Called

to the Bar, MA 1958, Guam 1972; Trial Attorney Dept of Justice, Washington, DC 1958–60, Trapp and Gayle, Agana, Guam 1971–73; Partner Trapp, Gayle, Teker, Weeks and Friedman, Agana, Guam 1973–75; Judge Superior Court of Guam 1975–96; Justice Supreme Court of Guam 1996; mem Guam Law Revision Comm 1981–, ABA, Nat Asscn of Women Judges, American Judges' Asscn, Fed Bar Asscn, Guam Bar Asscn. *Address:* Supreme Court of Guam, Judicial Center, Agana, GU 96910, Guam.

WEI JUN-YI; Chinese writer; b Oct 1917, Beijing; d of Wei Hang; m Yuang Shu; three c. *Education:* Qing Hua Univ (Beijing). *Career:* Apptd Ed and Pres Renmin Wenxue Chubunshe (People's Literature Publishing House) 1950; Nat Award for writing 1983. *Publication:* Mother and Son 1982. *Address:* People's Literature Publishing House, 166 Chaoyangmen Nei Dajie, Beijing 100705, People's Republic of China. *Telephone:* (10) 5138394.

WEI WEI; Chinese singer; m Michael Smith; one s. *Career:* Singer at 11th Asian Games, Beijing 1990; performed a duet with Julio Iglesias at East Asian Games, Shanghai 1993; tour of China 1995. *Recordings include:* Album: Twilight.

WEIDEMANN, Celia Jean, MS, PH D; American social scientist and development consultant; b 6 Dec 1942, Denver, CO; d of John Clement and Hazel R. (née Van Tuyl) Kirlin; m Wesley Clark Weidemann 1972; one d. *Education:* Univs of Southern California, Wisconsin and Iowa State. *Career:* Adviser UN and FAO, Nigeria 1973–77; Researcher Asia and Near East 1977–78; Asst Prof and Research Assoc New Options Program, Univ of Wisconsin 1979–81; Div Chief US AID Bd on Int Food and Agricultural Devt 1982–84; Team Leader and Consultant, Sumatra, Indonesia 1984; Dir Fed Econ Program, Mid-West Research Inst 1985–86; Consultant IBRD, Nigeria, Gambia, Pakistan, Indonesia, US AID, Kenya, Jordan, Int Center for Research on Women, Zaire, US Congress, FAO, Ghana, Int Statistical Inst, Netherlands, FINNIDA, Ford Foundation and various govts 1986–; Pres Weidemann Assocs Inc 1986–; mem Asscn for Women in Devt, American Home Econs Asscn, American Sociological Asscn. *Publications include:* Egyptian Women, Microenterprise: the invisible entrepreneurs, Planning Home Economics Curriculum for Social and Economic Development, Agricultural Extension for Women Farmers in Africa 1990; more than 25 publs 1973–. *Leisure interests:* mountain trekking, piano, organ, canoeing, photography, poetry. *Address:* 2607 N 24th St, Arlington, VA 22207, USA. *Telephone:* (703) 525-0277; *Fax:* (703) 525-6169.

WEIDINGER, Christine; American opera singer (soprano). *Career:* Fmrly with Stuttgart Opera, Germany; joined Bielefeld Opera, Germany 1979; int appearances include Barcelona (Spain), Marseilles (France), Catania (Italy), Spoleto/Charleston Festival of Two Worlds, Los Angeles Music Center Opera (USA). *Operas include:* Der Vampyr, Mary, Queen of Scots, Lucia di Lammermoor, La Sonnambula, Le Prophète, Roberto Devereux, Norma 1989, L'Africaine, I Capuleti e i Montecchi, Siege of Corinth, Beatrice di Tenda, Spanish Conquest, Tancredi 1989. *Address:* c/o Bielefelder Opernhaus, Bielefeld, Germany.

WEILER, Barbara; German politician; b 17 Sept 1946, Düsseldorf. *Career:* MEP (PSE, SPD), mem Cttee on Social Affairs and Employment, Del to the EU-Malta Jt Parl Cttee. *Address:* European Parliament, rue Wiertz, 1047 Brussels, Belgium. *Telephone:* (2) 284-21-11; *Fax:* (2) 230-69-43.

WEILER, Karen Merle Magnuson, BA, LL M; Canadian judge; b 13 June 1945, Regina, SK; d of Edgar and Rose (née Beliveau) Magnuson; m Robert David Weiler 1967; two d. *Education:* Univ of Saskatchewan and Osgoode Hall Law School (Toronto). *Career:* Called to the Bar, Toronto 1969; apptd to Bench Ontario Court of Justice 1980, Judge (Gen Div) 1989–92; Justice Ontario Court of Appeal 1992–, Fed Court Martial Appeal Court 1996–; law practice Weiler, Weiler and Maloney 1969–72; Lecturer Lakehead Univ 1970–72, Instructor in Family Law 1975–79; Solicitor Dept of Community and Social Services 1973–74; Counsel Dept of Justice and Office of the Attorney-Gen, Policy Devt Div 1974, Sr Counsel until 1980; Dir Canadian Judges Conf; mem Canadian Inst for the Admin of Justice, Women's Law Asscn, Canadian Bar Asscn, Asscn des juristes d'expression française. *Publications:* Gender Bias in the Courts (jtly), Law and Practice Under the Family

Law Reform Act (Ontario) to 1988 (jtly); publs in law journals. *Leisure interests:* tennis, swimming, cycling, golf, skiing, reading. *Address:* Ontario Court of Justice, Osgoode Hall, 130 Queen St, Toronto, ON M5H 2N5, Canada (Office); 11 Anderson Ave, Toronto, ON M5P 1H2, Canada (Home). *Telephone:* (416) 327-5000 (Office); *Fax:* (416) 327-5080 (Office).

WEINGARTEN, Hilde (Kevess), BFA; American (b German) artist; b Berlin; d of Morris and Clara Weingarten; m Arthur Kevess 1951 (died 1973); one s one d. *Education:* Art Students' League, Cooper Union School of Art, Pratt Graphics Center and Univ of New York (New York). *Career:* Solo exhibitions include Carlebach Gallery (New York) 1949, Contemporary Arts Inc (New York) 1962, 1966, Brooklyn Heights Gallery (New York) 1962, 1968, Cadman Plaza North (New York) 1971; group exhibitions include Corcoran Gallery (Washington, DC), American Acad and Inst of Arts and Letters, Philadelphia Art Alliance, Denver Art Museum, Seattle Art Museum, Fujikawa Gallery (Osaka, Japan), Palazzo Gallery (Florence) and Pompeiian Pavilion (Naples, Italy), Warwick Gallery (UK), Associated American Artists and Rizzoli Gallery (New York); rep in perm collections including Fogg Art Museum (Harvard Univ, MA), Rose Art Museum (Brandeis Univ, MA), Israel Museum (Jerusalem), Western Electric, Arwood Corpn; mem Audubon Artists, Nat Asscn of Women Artists, Painters and Sculptors Soc of New Jersey, Artists Equity Asscn of New York (Bd Dirs 1964–72, 1990–), American Soc of Contemporary Artists 1983; awards for graphics include Painters and Sculptors Soc of New Jersey 1973, 1978, 1979, 1985, American Soc of Contemporary Artists 1971, 1976, 1978–80, 1982–83, 1989, Nat Asscn of Women Artists 1975, 1980, 1989, League of Present Day Artists 1974. *Leisure interests:* reading, theatre, film, dance, piano. *Address:* 140 Cadman Plaza W, Brooklyn Heights, New York, NY 11201, USA. *Telephone:* (212) 852-8509.

WEINSHIENK, Zita Leeson, BA, JD; American federal judge; b 3 April 1933, St Paul; d of Louis and Ada (née Dubov) Leeson; m 1st Hubert Weinshienk 1956 (died 1983); three d; m 2nd James Schaffner 1986. *Education:* Univs of Colorado, Arizona and Copenhagen and Harvard Univ. *Career:* Called to the Bar, CO 1959; Probation Counsellor, Legal Advisor and Referee, Denver Juvenile Court 1959–64; Judge Denver Co Court 1964–71, Denver Dist Court 1972–79, US Dist Judge for Colorado 1979–; mem ABA, Nat Conf Fed of Trial Judges. *Address:* US District Court, US Courthouse, Rm C-550, 1929 Stout St, Denver, CO 80294, USA.

WEINSTEIN, Deborah J., BA; Canadian producer and public relations executive; b 26 Oct 1949, Prince Albert, SK; d of Saul Arnold and Florence (née Cosman) Weinstein; m Allan F. Lee Marshall 1988; one d. *Education:* Ecole Vincent D'Indy and McGill Univ. *Career:* Freelance Producer CBC Radio Network 1971–74, Producer 1976–79; Producer Radio Canada Int 1974–76; Feature Reporter Newshour, CTV TV News, Toronto 1980–81; Location Producer and Dir CTV TV Network 1981–83; Co-Founder, Pres and Partner Strategic Objectives Inc 1983–; mem Retail Council of Canada 1992 Convention Cttee, Fashion Group (Toronto), Bd of Dirs Second Harvest, Bd of Dirs Toronto Women in Film and TV Advisory Council; awards include Gold Award for Video (Asscn for Multi-Image Canada) 1986, Gold Quill of Excellence for Media Relations (Int Asscn of Business Communicators) 1987, Golden World Trophy for Total Communications Program (Int Public Relations Asscn) 1990, UN Grand Award for Public Service 1995, Golden World Award for Marketing New Product (Int Public Relations Asscn) 1996, Gold Quill Award (Int Asscn of Business Communicators) 1996. *Productions include:* Radio and TV: North American Transmission 1974–76, Stroke – A Family Portrait 1975, Nightcap (Asscn of Canadian TV and Radio Artists Award for Best Radio Program 1977) 1976–79, Thrill of a Lifetime (dir) 1981–83. *Address:* Strategic Objectives Inc, 184 Front St E, Suite 701, Toronto, ON M5A 4N3, Canada. *Telephone:* (416) 366-7735; *Fax:* (416) 366-2295.

WEINSTEIN, Diane Gilbert, BA, JD; American lawyer and judge; b 14 June 1947, Rochester, NY; d of Myron Birne and Doris Isabelle (née Robie) Gilbert; m 1st Allan Weinstein 1969; two s; m 2nd Dwight D. Sypolt 1995. *Education:* Smith Coll (Northampton), Univs of Stanford and Georgetown and Boston Univ Law School. *Career:* Called to the Bar, DC 1979; Law Clerk Dist of Columbia Co Appeals 1970–80; Assoc

Peabody, Lambert and Meyers 1980–83; Asst Gen Counsel, US Office of Man and Budget 1983–86; Deputy Gen Counsel, then Acting Gen Counsel Dept of Educ 1986–89; Counsellor to Vice-Pres J. Danforth Quayle, The White House 1989–90; Counsel to Pres's Competitiveness Council 1989–90; Judge US Claims Court 1990–; Young Lawyer's Chair Award, Boston Univ Law School 1989. *Leisure interests:* cycling, skiing. *Address:* US Federal Claims Court, 717 Madison Place, NW, Washington, DC 20005, USA (Office); 1850 Kalorama Rd, NW, Washington, DC 20009, USA (Home). *Telephone:* (202) 786-0649 (Office); (202) 633-7255 (Home).

WEINSTEIN, Paula; American film producer; b 19 Nov 1945; d of the late Hannah Weinstein; m Mark Rosenberg. *Education:* Columbia Univ. *Career:* Partner WW Productions, Warner Brothers, Vice-Pres of Production, Warner Brothers 1976–78; Theatrical Agent William Morris and Int Creative Man; Vice-Pres of Production 20th Century Fox, Sr Vice-Pres Worldwide Productions 1980; Vice-Pres, Producer Ladd Co 1981; Pres Motion Picture Div, United Artists 1983; started own production co at Columbia Pictures 1987; Consultant to Columbia Pictures 1987; Exec Consultant to MGM film co; Co-Founder Spring Creek Productions. *Films:* A Dry White Season, The Fabulous Baker Boys, The Rose and the Jackal (TV film), Fearless, Flesh and Bone, With Honors, Something to Talk About, Citizen Cohn (TV film), Truman (TV film).

WEIR, Dame Gillian Constance, DBE; British (b New Zealand) concert organist and harpsichordist; b 17 Jan 1941, Martinborough, New Zealand; d of Cecil Alexander and Clarice Mildred Foy (née Bignell) Weir; m 1st Clive Rowland Webster 1967 (divorced 1971); m 2nd Lawrence Irving Phelps 1972 (died 1999). *Education:* Wanganui Girls' Coll (NZ) and Royal Coll of Music (London). *Career:* Winner St Albans Int Organ Festival Competition 1964; debuts at Royal Festival Hall and Royal Albert Hall, London 1965; performances as organist and latterly as harpsichordist include Royal Festival Hall, Royal Albert Hall, Lincoln Center (New York) and Kennedy Center (USA), Palais des Beaux Arts (Paris), Sydney Opera House, Westminster Abbey 1965–; appeared with major British and int orchestras under leading conductors; festival performances include Edinburgh, Flanders, Aldeburgh and Bath Festivals, and BBC Promenade Concerts; adjudicator at int competitions; lecturer and tutor world-wide; Organ Consultant Birmingham Symphony Hall; many premières including first British performance of Messiaen's Méditations of 1972 and concertos by Mathias and Fricker; Presenter The King of Instruments (BBC TV series) 1989; many radio and TV appearances; Pres Inc Asscn of Organists (first woman Pres) 1981–83, 1992–, Inc Soc of Musicians 1992–93; mem Council Royal Coll of Organists (first woman) 1977–, Exec Council (first woman) 1981–85, Pres (first woman) 1994–96; mem Council Royal Philharmonic Soc 1996–; subject of South Bank Show, ITV 2000; Hon FRCO (Canada); Hon FRCM; Hon mem RAM 1989; Hon D MUS (Wellington) 1983, (Hull) 1999, (Exeter) 2001; Hon D LITT (Huddersfield) 1997; Hon D UNIV (Univ of Cen England) 2001; Int Performer of Year Award, American Guild of Organists 1981; one of Int Music Guide's Musicians of the Year 1982; Turnovsky Prize for Outstanding Achievement in the Arts (first musician to win prize) 1985; Silver Medal, Albert Schweitzer Asscn (Sweden) 1998; Evening Standard Award for Outstanding Solo Performance in 1998. *Recordings include:* Complete Organ Works of Messiaen 1994; major series of French baroque music for Argo; *Publications include:* contrib to The Messiaen Companion 1995 and articles in professional journals. *Leisure interests:* theatre, reading, opera. *Address:* c/o D. Lyster Artists Management, 25 Courthope Rd, London NW3 2LE, UK (Office). *Telephone:* (20) 7485-5932 (Office); *Fax:* (20) 7267-0179 (Office); *Internet:* www.dennylyster.free-online.co.uk (Office).

WEIR, Judith, CBE, MA; British composer; b 11 May 1954, Cambridge; d of Jack and Ishbel Weir. *Education:* N London Collegiate School and King's Coll (Cambridge). *Career:* Composer-in-Residence Southern Arts Asscn 1976–79; Cramb Fellow in Composition Univ of Glasgow 1979–82; Creative Arts Fellowship Trinity Coll, Cambridge 1983–85; Composer-in-Residence Royal Scottish Acad of Music and Drama, Glasgow 1988–91; Fairbairn Composer in asscn with City of Birmingham Orchestra 1995–98; Artistic Dir Spitalfields Festival 1995–2000; Visiting Prof in Opera Studies, Univ of Oxford 1999–; Dr hc (Aberdeen) 1995; Critics' Circle Award for most outstanding contrib to British Musical Life 1994, Lincoln Center Stoeger Prize 1997. *Compositions include:* King Harald's Saga 1979, Consolations of Scholarship 1985, A Night at the Chinese Opera 1987, Missa del Cid 1988, Heaven Ablaze in His Breast 1989, The Vanishing Bridegroom (opera) 1990, Ardnamurchan Point 1990, Ox Mountain was Covered by Trees 1990, String Quartet 1990, Music Untangled 1991–92, Heroic Strokes of the Bow 1992, Blond Eckbert 1993, Musicians Wrestle Everywhere 1994, Moon and Star 1995, Forest 1995, Natural History 1998, All the Ends of the Earth 1999, We Are Shadows 2000. *Address:* c/o Chester Music, 8–9 Frith St, London W1D 3JB, UK. *Telephone:* (20) 7434-0066; *Fax:* (20) 7287-6329.

WEIS, Heidelinde (pseudonym of Heidelinde Duna); Austrian actress; b 17 Sept 1940, Villach; m Hellmuth Duna 1960. *Education:* Max Reinhardt-Seminar (Vienna) and song and dance studies in Munich (Germany). *Career:* Actress Theater in der Josefstadt, Vienna 1958–60; guest performances in Berlin, Munich and Hamburg (Germany), Vienna, Salzburg Festival, etc; awards include Goldener Bildschirm 1972, German Record Prize (Phonoakademie Berlin) 1976, Goldene Kamera 1977. *Plays include:* Othello, Boulevard: Nächstes Jahr – gleiche Zeit, Warte, bis es dunkel ist, Gaslicht, Nie wieder Mary, Ein Glas Wasser 1977–78, Helden, Alte Zeiten 1988; *Films include:* Der Tote von Beverly Hills, Der Lügner und die Nonne, Lausbubengeschichte, Die Festung, Something for Everyone, Mädchen Hinter Gittern; *TV appearances include:* Mary Rose, Meine Frau Susanne (series) 1966, Die Marquise von Brenvillies, Die Frau in Weiss, Die Erbin, Die Fräulein, Quadrille, Die Selige Edwina Black, Heidelinde Weis Specials; *Screenplay:* Umwege nach Venedig (TV film) 1988; *Recordings include:* So sing ich 1975, So ein Narr bin ich 1977, Aber Träume hatt' ich viel 1978. *Address:* Dröschitz 37, 9231 Köstenberg, Austria.

WEISBERG, Ruth, MFA; American artist. *Education:* Univ of Michigan. *Career:* Tutor Univ of Michigan 1987, 1988, Univ of Hawaii 1988; Acting Assoc Dean School of Architecture and Fine Arts, Univ of Southern California, Chair Studio Art Dept 1986–87, currently Dean of Fine Arts; solo and jt exhibitions include Pollack Art Gallery (Toronto, ON, Canada) 1969, 1971, Municipal Art Gallery (Oslo) 1972, Univ of Alaska 1981, Jack Rutberg Fine Arts (Los Angeles, CA) 1983, 1985, 1988, 1991, 1999, Univ of Tennessee 1986, Associated American Artists (New York) 1987, 1990, Gwenda Jay Gallery (Chicago, IL) 1991, 1992, Bethel Coll (KS) 1991, Temple Univ (Rome) 1994, The Huntington Library (CA) 1999; group exhibitions include American Embassy in Ankara 1975, Malaspina Printmakers Soc (Vancouver, BC, Canada) 1975, Oslo and Tromso Art Asscn (Norway) 1982, Louisiana World Exposition (New Orleans) 1984, Sherry French Gallery (New York) 1988, Leband Gallery (Los Angeles, CA) 1991, 1998, Gwenda Jay Gallery (IL) 1997, Tryon Center for Visual Art (NC) 2001; rep in collections including Bibliothèque Nationale (Paris), Lincoln Center (New York), The Jewish Museum of New York, National Gallery (Washington, DC), American Museum of Art, Smithsonian (Washington DC, Instituto Nazionale per la Grafica (Rome), the Norwegian Nat Gallery (Oslo), Trans-America Corpn (San Francisco), Standard Oil of Indiana; Visiting Artist American Acad (Rome) 1992, 1994, 1995, San Francisco State Univ 2001; juror and curator of numerous exhibitions; Pres College Art Asscn 1990–92; mem Tamarind Inst, Los Angeles Printmaking Soc; Laureate in Painting and Printmaking, Accademia di Belle Arti (Perugia, Italy) 1962; Hon D HUM LITT (Hewbrew Union Coll) 2001; Nat Women's Caucus for Art Mid-Career Achievement Award 1987; Distinguished Artist of the Year Award (Fresno Art Museum) 1990; Sr Research Fulbright Award Italy 1992; Univ of Michigan Distinguished Art Alumni/AE Award 1992; Los Angeles Art Core Eighth Annual Award 1996; Coll Art Asscn Distinguished Teaching of Art Award 1999. *Address:* University of Southern California, School of Fine Arts, Watt Hall 104, Los Angeles, CA 90089-0292, USA (Office); 2205 Oak St, Apt C, Santa Monica, CA 90405, USA (Home). *Telephone:* (213) 740-6267 (Office); (310) 396-4451 (Home); *Fax:* (213) 740-8938 (Office); (310) 399-6451 (Home).

WEISGERBER, Antje; German actress; b 17 May 1922, Königsberg; d of Friedrich and Elisabeth (née Abt) Weisgerber; m 1st Horst Caspar (died 1952); one s (deceased) one d; m 2nd Reinhard Schilling (divorced). *Education:* Lyzeum Königsberg and Theatre School of the Preußisches Staatstheater (Berlin). *Career:* Actress at theatres including

Staatstheater and Hebbel-Theater, Berlin, Kammerspiele München, Burgtheater Wien, Schauspielhaus Düsseldorf, Schauspielhaus Hamburg, New York (USA), Edinburgh (UK), Salzburg (Austria), etc; Hersfeld-Preis 1965; Filmband in Gold 1990. *Plays include:* Faust I, Faust II, Die Jungfrau von Orleans, Minna von Barnhelm 1968, Maria Stuart; *Films include:* Zwei Welten, Das doppelte Lottchen, Rittmeister Wronski, Vor Gott und den Menschen, Du bist der Richtige, Oberarzt Dr Solm, San Salvatore, Der Mann, der sich verkaufte, Lampenfieber; *TV appearances include:* Herodes und Mariamne, Gyges und sein Ring, Die Nibelungen, Um Lucretia, Der Landarzt (series). *Leisure interests:* music, painting. *Address:* Rosenstr 6, 83700 Rottach-Egern/Obb, Germany.

WEISS, Ann, MA; American (b Italian) writer and photographer; b 17 July 1949, Modena, Italy; d of Leo and Athalie Weiss; two d. *Education:* Univs of Rochester and Pennsylvania and Drexel Univ. *Career:* Ed, consultant, writer and freelance photographer 1974–; Head Children's Dept Tredyffrin Public Library 1973–79, Jt Head Reference Dept 1979–87; apptd Consultant in Educ and Libraries, Gulf Arab States Educ and Research Center, UNESCO 1977; Photo-journalist in E Europe 1987; Co-Producer, Co-Dir and Writer Eyes From the Ashes 1989–90, Lighting Six Candles 1990; Co-Writer Zosia Story 1987–88; editorial consultant to numerous publs on puppetry; Counsellor Int Network of Children of Holocaust Survivors; Project Dir Psychiatry Documentary Inst, Pennsylvania Hosp 1989–91; mem Union of Concerned Scientists, Schizophrenia – A National Emergency (SANE), Physicians for Social Responsibility, Amnesty Int, New Jewish Agenda. *Address:* 438 Barclay Rd, Rosemont, PA 19010, USA.

WEISZ, Rachel; British actress; b 1972. *Plays:* Design for Living 1995, Suddenly Last Summer 1999, The Shape of Things 2001; *Films:* Seventeen, Chain Reaction, Stealing Beauty, Going All the Way, Amy Foster, Bent, I Want You, Land Girls, The Mummy, Sunshine, Beautiful Creatures, Enemy at the Gates, The Mummy Returns. *Address:* c/o ICM Ltd, Oxford House, 76 Oxford St, London W1N 0AX, UK. *Telephone:* (20) 7636-6565; *Fax:* (20) 7323-0101.

WELCH, Raquel; American actress; b 5 Sept 1940, Chicago, IL; d of Armand and Josepha (née Hall) Tejada; m 1st James Westley Welch 1959 (divorced); one s one d; m 2nd Patrick Curtis (divorced); m 3rd Andre Weinfeld 1980 (divorced). *Career:* Fmr model for Neiman-Marcus stores; actress in numerous film and TV films; World Concert tour 1977–78, and special appearances in Las Vegas. *Films include:* Fantastic Voyage 1966, One Million Years BC 1967, Fathom 1967, The Biggest Bundle of Them All 1968, Magic Christian 1970, Myra Breckinridge 1970, Fuzz 1972, Bluebeard 1972, Hannie Caulder 1972, Kansas City Bomber 1972, The Last of Sheila 1973, The Three Musketeers 1974, The Wild Party 1975, The Four Musketeers 1975, Mother, Jugs and Speed 1976, Crossed Swords 1978, L'animal 1979, Right to Die 1987, Scandal in a Small Town 1988, Trouble in Paradise 1989, Naked Gun 33 1/3 1993, Folle d'Elle 1998; *TV appearances include:* The Legend of Walks for Women 1982, Right to Die 1989; *Plays:* Woman of the Year 1982, Torch Song 1993; *Videos:* Raquel: Total Beauty and Fitness 1984, A Week with Raquel 1987, Raquel: Lose 10lbs in 3 Weeks 1989; *Publication:* The Raquel Welch Total Beauty and Fitness Program 1984. *Address:* Innovative Artists, 1999 Ave of the Stars, Suite 2850, Los Angeles, CA 90067, USA.

WELD, Tuesday Ker (Susan Ker Weld); American actress; b 27 Aug 1943, New York; d of Lathrop M. Weld and Aileen Ker; m 1st Claude Harz 1965 (divorced 1971); one d; m 2nd Dudley Moore 1975 (divorced); one s; m 3rd Pinchas Zukerman 1985. *Education:* Hollywood Professional School. *Career:* Fashion and catalogue model aged three; regular appearances as magazine cover-girl and in child roles on TV by age 12; appearances in numerous films, TV programmes and TV films. *Films include:* Rock Rock 1956, Serial, Rally Round the Flag Boys, The Five Pennies, The Private Lives of Adam and Eve, Return to Peyton Place, Wild in the Country, Bachelor Flat, Lord Love a Duck, Pretty Poison, I Walk the Line, A Safe Place, Play it as it Lays, Because They're Young, High Time, Sex Kittens Go to College, The Cincinnati Kid, Soldier in the Rain, Looking for Mr Goodbar, Thief, Author!, Once Upon a Time In America, Heartbreak Hotel, Falling Down, Feeling Minnesota 1996; *TV appearances include:* Cimarron Strip, Playhouse 90, Climax, Ozzie and Harriet, 77 Sunset Strip, The Millionaire, Tab

Hunter Show, Dick Powell Theatre, Adventures in Paradise, Naked City, The Greatest Show on Earth, Mr Broadway, Fugitive. *Address:* c/o Viderman Oberman & Associates, 103 W Pico Blvd, Los Angeles, CA 90015, USA.

WELDON, Fay, CBE, MA; British writer; b 22 Sept 1931, Alvechurch, Worcs; d of Frank T. and Margaret J. Birkinshaw; m 1st Ronald Weldon 1960 (divorced 1994); four s; m 2nd Nicolas Fox 1995. *Education:* Girls' High School (Christchurch, New Zealand) and Univ of St Andrews. *Career:* Chair of Judges Booker McConnell Prize 1983; fmr mem Arts Council Literary Panel; mem Video Censorship Appeals Cttee; Fellow City of Bath Coll 1999; Hon D LITT (Bath) 1989, (St Andrews) 1992; Women in Publishing Pandora Award 1997. *Publications:* Novels: The Fat Woman's Joke 1967 (USA title ...And the Wife Ran Away 1968), Down Among the Women 1972, Female Friends 1975, Remember Me 1976, Little Sisters (USA title Words of Advice) 1977, Praxis 1978, Puffball 1980, The President's Child 1982, The Life and Loves of a She-Devil (made into TV series and film) 1984, The Shrapnel Academy 1986, The Heart of the Country 1987, The Hearts and Lives of Men 1987, The Rules of Life (novella) 1987, Leader of the Band 1988, The Cloning of Joanna May (made into TV series) 1989, Darcy's Utopia 1990, Growing Rich 1992, Life Force 1992, Affliction 1994, Splitting 1995, Worst Fears 1996, Big Women 1998, Rhode Island Blues 2000; Short stories: Watching Me Watching You 1981, Polaris 1985, Moon Over Minneapolis 1991, Wicked Woman 1996, Hard Time To Be a Father 1999; Plays: Words of Advice 1974, Friends 1975, Moving House 1976, Mr Director 1977, Action Replay 1979, I Love My Love 1981, Woodworm 1981, Jane Eyre 1986, The Hole in the Top of the World 1987, The Four Alice Bakers 1999, more than 30 TV plays, dramatizations and radio plays; Jr fiction: Wolf the Mechanical Dog 1988, Party Puddle 1989, Nobody Likes Me! 1997; Essay: Godless in Eden 2000; *TV includes:* Big Women (series) 1999. *Address:* c/o Giles Gordon, Curtis Brown, 37 Queensferry St, Edinburgh EH2 4QS, UK.

WELDON, Virginia Verral, AB, MD; American professor of paediatrics and business executive; b 8 Sept 1935, Toronto, ON, Canada; d of John Edward Verral and Carolyn Edith Swif; m (divorced); two d. *Education:* Smith Coll, State Univ of New York at Buffalo and Johns Hopkins Univ School of Medicine. *Career:* Instructor in Paediatrics Johns Hopkins Hosp 1967–68; Instructor in Paediatrics School of Medicine, Washington Univ 1968–69, Asst Prof of Paediatrics 1973–79, Prof 1979–89, Asst Vice-Chancellor for Medical Affairs 1975–81, Assoc Vice-Chancellor 1981–83, Deputy Vice-Chancellor 1983–89, Vice-Pres Medical Center 1980–89; Vice-Pres Scientific Affairs Monsanto Co 1989, Vice-Pres Public Policy 1989–93, Sr Vice-Pres Public Policy 1993–98, Advisor, Dir Monsanto Co 1989–98; Dir Center for Study of American Business, Washington Univ, St Louis 1998–; mem Environmental Protection Agency Risk Assessment Man Comm 1992–97, Pres's Cttee of Advisors on Science and Tech 1994–; Trustee Calif Inst of Tech 1996–, Whitaker Foundation 1997–, Whitfield School 1997–; Fellow AAAS; numerous contribs to scientific journals; Smith Coll Medal 1984. *Leisure interest:* civic affairs. *Address:* Center for Study of American Business, Washington University, POB 1027, St Louis, MO 63188, USA (Office); 242 Carlyle Lake Drive, St Louis, MO 63141, USA (Home).

WELLESLEY, Jane; British television producer. *Career:* Co-Dir Warner Sisters (with Lavinia Warner, qv) 1984–. *TV productions:* Tenko, Wish Me Luck, She Play, Rides, Selling Hitler 1991. *Address:* Warner Sisters, Canalot Studios, 222 Kensal Rd, London W10 5BN, UK. *Telephone:* (20) 8960-3550.

WELLS, Melissa Foelsch, BS; American UN official; b 18 Nov 1932, Tallinn, Estonia; d of Kuno Georg and Miliza (née Korjus) Foelsch; m Alfred Washburn Wells 1960; two s. *Education:* Georgetown Univ. *Career:* Foreign Service Officer Dept of State, Washington, DC 1958–61, Consular Officer, Trinidad 1961–64; Econ Officer OECD, Paris 1964–66, London 1966–71; int economist 1971–73; Deputy Dir major exports projects Dept of Commerce 1973–75, commercial counsellor Brazil 1975–76; Amb to Guinea-Bissau and Cape Verde 1976–77, to Mozambique 1987–90, to Zaire 1991–93, to Repub of Estonia Dept of State 1998–; Under-Sec-Gen for Admin and Man UN, New York 1993–94; US Rep ECOSOC UN, New York 1977–79; resident Rep UNDP, Kampala, Uganda 1979–81; Dir IMPACT

programme UNDP, Geneva, Switzerland 1982–86; mem American Foreign Service Asscn. *Address:* Embassy of the USA, 15099 Tallinn, Estonia.

WENDELBURG, Norma Ruth, MUS M, PH D; American composer and pianist; b 1918, Stafford, KS; d of the late Henry and Anna (née Moeckel) Wendelburg. *Education:* Bethany Coll (Lindsborg), Univ of Michigan, Eastman School of Music (New York), Mozarteum and State Acad of Music (Vienna). *Career:* Instructor in Music, Wayne State Coll 1947–50; Asst Prof of Music Bethany Coll 1952–53, Northern Iowa Univ 1956–58, Hardin-Simmons Univ (Abilene, TX) 1958–63, Chair Grad Comm, School of Music 1960–66, Founder and Chair Annual Festival of Contemporary Music 1959–; Assoc Prof SW Texas State Univ at San Marcos 1969–72, Dallas Baptist Univ 1973–75, Friends Coll (Haviland, KS) 1977–80; Resident Fellow Huntingdon Hartford Foundation 1955–56, 1958, 1961, MacDowell Colony 1958, 1960, 1970; Guest Composer Univ of Ottawa (Canada) 1984; professional concert pianist; composer Festival of American Music, Charles Ives Centre of American Music 1990; mem Music Teachers' Nat Conf, American Music Center, American Soc of Univ Composers, American Women Composers; Fellow Nat Festival of the Performing Arts 1989; Fulbright Awards, Austria 1953–55; Meet the Composer award, New York State Council of the Arts 1979; Kans Composer of the Year, Kans Fed Music Festival 2000. *Compositions:* Suite for Violin and Piano 1965, Symphony 1967, Song Cycle for Soprano, Flutes, Piano 1974, Affirmation 1982, Interlacings 1983, Music for Two Pianos 1985, Suite No 2 for Violin and Piano 1989 (recording on CRS), Fantasy for Trumpet and Piano 1990 (recording on CRS), Sonata for Clarinet and Piano 1992 (recording on CRS), Symphonietta (recorded by St Petersburg Russian Philharmonic Orchestra 1994); composer of more than 100 works, three recordings of works in progress. *Leisure interests:* travel, photography, gardening, cooking. *Address:* 2206 N Van Buren, Hutchinson, KS 67502, USA. *Telephone:* (316) 662-5445.

WENDLING-PARDON, Charlotte; German trumpet player; b 20 June 1953; m Manfred Pardon 1982; one d. *Education:* Music studies in Saarbrücken. *Career:* Plays trumpet duets with her brother Jürgen Wendling; has performed at nat and int concerts and on radio and TV; several recordings; Fed winner young musicians' competitions 1965, 1967, 1969, 1971; Carl-Orff Prize. *Address:* Steinkopfweg 10, 66386 St Ingbert, Germany. *Telephone:* (6894) 8233.

WENIG, Mary Moers, BA, JD; American lawyer and professor of law; b New York; d of Robert and Celia (née Kauffman) Moers; m Jerome Wenig 1946; one s one d. *Education:* Vassar Coll and Columbia Univ. *Career:* Called to the Bar, NY 1952, US Court of Appeals 1954, US Dist Court 1956, CT 1977; Assoc Cahill, Gordon, Reindel and Ohl 1951–57, Greenbaum, Wolff and Ernst 1957–60, Skadden, Arps, Slate, Meagher and Flom 1960–71; Asst Prof Law Faculty, St John's Univ, New York 1971–75, Assoc Prof 1975–78; Prof Law Faculty, Univ of Bridgeport, CT 1978–82, Charles A. Dana Prof of Law 1982–92; apptd Prof Law Faculty Quinnipiac Coll, Bridgeport, CT 1992–; Consultant The Merrill Anderson Co, Stratford 1982–, Connecticut Perm Comm on the Status of Women 1978–79; mem Bd of Dirs Tax Analysts, Tax Notes, Fairfax, NY 1980–; Commr State of Connecticut Perm Comm on the Status of Women 1985–91; mem Editorial Bd Estates, Gifts and Trusts Journal 1976–, Estate Planning for the Elderly and Disabled 1987–90; mem numerous comms and task forces on the probate system and on marriage; mem Int Acad of Estates and Trust Law (mem Exec Council 1992–94); mem ABA, Asscn of American Law Schools, American Law Inst; Award for Equality, UN Asscn of USA 1987. *Publications:* Unmarried Couples and the Law (jtly) 1970, PLI Tax Handbooks (ed) 1978–86, Bittker, Fundamentals of Federal Income Taxation (co-ed) 1983. *Address:* Quinnipiac University, Law School, 275 Mount Carmel Ave, Law Library 325, Hamden, CT 06518-1940, USA (Office); 5 Lamplight Lane, Westport, CT 06880, USA (Home). *Telephone:* (203) 582-3253; *E-mail:* Mary.Moers.Wenig@quinnipiac.edu.

WENSLEY, (Penny) Penelope Anne, AO, BA; Australian diplomatist; b 18 Oct 1946, Toowoomba; m Stuart McCosker 1974; two d. *Education:* Univ of Queensland. *Career:* Diplomatic service 1968–, Paris 1969–72, Mexico City 1975–77, Wellington, NZ 1982–85, Consul Gen Hong Kong 1986–88; Head Int Orgs Div, Dept of Foreign Affairs and

Trade 1991–92, Perm Rep to UN, Geneva 1993–95, also Amb for Environment, UN 1992–95, Head N Asia Div 1996–97; Perm Rep to UN, New York 1997–; Sr Advisor Australian del to UN Conf on Environment and Devt 1992; Vice-Pres World Conf on Human Rights, Vienna 1993–; Vice-Chair UN Climate Change Convention Negotiations 1993–96; Co-ordinator W Group Negotiations on UN Conventions on Biodiversity and Desertification 1994–96; Chair Preparatory Process UN Conf for the Sustainable Devt of Small Island Developing States 1993–94; Chair Int Coral Reef Initiative Conf 1995; Vice-Chair UN Inst for Training and Research; mem WHO High Level Advisory Council on Health and the Environment; Chair UN Gen Ass (UNGA) Fifth Cttee (Admin and Budgetary) 1999; Co-Chair Preparatory Process for UNGA Special Session on HIV/AIDS 2001; Patron UN Youth Asscn of Australia; Fellow Women's Coll (Univ of Queensland); Adjunct Prof Univ of Queensland 2000; Hon PH D (Queensland). *Leisure interests:* music, theatre, reading, tennis, bush walking. *Address:* Permanent Mission of Australia to the United Nations, 150 42nd St, 33rd Floor, New York, NY 10017, USA. *Telephone:* (212) 351-6600; *Fax:* (212) 351-6610.

WERLEIGH, Claudette; Haitian politician and social worker. *Career:* Worked for Caritas (Catholic aid org) 1976–86; Minister of Social Affairs March–Aug 1990, of Foreign Affairs 1993–95, Prime Minister 1995–1996. *Address:* c/o Office of the Prime Minister, Port-au-Prince, Haiti.

WERNER, Margot; Austrian singer, dancer and actress; b 8 Dec 1937, Salzburg; m 2nd Jochen Litt 1978. *Education:* Salzburg. *Career:* With Salzburger Landestheater 1954; joined Bayerische Staatsoper, Munich, Germany 1955, Leading Dancer 1959, Soloist 1961, Prima Ballerina 1963; actress and entertainer 1973–; performances in Europe, Metropolitan Opera (New York) and Los Angeles (CA, USA), Canada and fmr USSR 1989, etc; has made numerous solo recordings and recordings with Engelbert Humperdinck; awards include Art Prize (Schwabing), Trude-Hesterberg-Ring, Gold Europa Prize, Show Star of the Year Award, Liederpfennig 1987. *Films:* Bomber und Paganini, Lieb' Vaterland magst ruhig sein, Insel der Krebse, Im Weißen Rössel, Collin, Ali Baba; *TV appearances include:* Margot-Werner-Show, Margot bei Montag, Chez Margot, Musik mit Margot, Liebt diese Erde (series); *Publication:* Traumflügel (autobiog). *Address:* Geiselgasteigstr 54, 81545 Munich 90, Germany.

WERNER, Patricia Ann, MS, PH D; Australian/American scientist and professor of botany; b 7 July 1941, Flint, MI; d of M. H. Snyder, Jr and L. B. Van Wormer; m 1st Thomas Helma 1964 (divorced 1970); m 2nd Earl Werner 1971 (divorced 1987); m 3rd David Wigston 1991. *Education:* Michigan State Univ. *Career:* Asst Prof of Botany Michigan State Univ 1973–78, Assoc Prof 1978–84, Prof of Botany and Zoology 1983–87; Visiting Fellow ANU 1982–83; Visiting Scientist Div of Land and Water Resources, CSIRO, Darwin 1982–83, Sr Prin Research Scientist Div of Wildlife and Ecology, Dir Tropical Ecosystems Research Centre 1985–90; Dir Div of Environmental Biology, NSF, Washington, DC 1990–92; apptd Prof and Head Dept of Wildlife, Univ of Florida 1993; Founder, Pres Int Soc of Plant Population Biologists 1976–91; Fellow AAAS for distinguished research 1976; Outstanding Sr Exec Service (US Govt award) 1990, 1991. *Publications:* Predictions of Fate from Rosette Size in Teasel (Distinction Science Citation Classic), The Greenhouse Effect (ed) 1989, Australian Savannas (jtly) 1990, Savanna Ecology and Management (ed) 1991; over 50 articles in scientific journals. *Leisure interests:* reading, music, walking, travel. *Address:* Dept of Wildlife, University of Florida, Gainesville, FL 32611, USA; 118 Newins-Ziegler, Gainesville, FL 32611, USA (Home). *Telephone:* (904) 392-3261 (Office).

WERNISCHOVÁ, Helena; Czech artist; b 7 Aug 1942; m Ivan Wernisch 1962 (divorced 1973); two s. *Education:* School of Ceramics (Carlsbad) and privately. *Career:* Painter, illustrator and graphic artist; solo exhibitions include Prague 1969, 1971, 1974, 1980, 1982, 1984, 1986, 1989, 1990; group exhibitions include Czechoslovakia, Berlin, Wiesbaden and Mönchengladbach (Germany), Sint Niklaas (Belgium), Arezzo and Pascara (Italy), Paris, Rīga; rep in collections in Czech Repub, Belgium, Italy, Netherlands, Slovakia, Switzerland, Sweden,

France, Germany, USA and Venezuela; illustrator of several books; winner Annual Prize, Vyšetrad Publications (Prague) 1986. *Address:* Jerevanská 8, 100 00 Prague 10, Czech Republic. *Telephone:* (2) 741946.

WERTENBAKER, Timberlake, FRSL; British playwright; m John Man; one d. *Career:* Resident Playwright, Royal Court Theatre 1984–85; Plays and Players Most Promising Playwright (for The Grace of Mary Traverse) 1985; Evening Standard Most Promising Playwright; Critics' Circle Best West End Play 1991; Writers' Guild Best West End Play; Mrs Giles Whiting Award (for gen body of work) 1989. *Films:* The Children, Do Not Disturb (BBC TV); *Plays:* Case to Answer 1980, New Anatomies 1982, Abel's Sister 1984, The Grace of Mary Traverse 1985, Our Country's Good (Olivier Play of the Year) 1988, The Love of the Nightingale (Eileen Anderson Cen Drama Award 1989) 1988, Three Birds Alighting on a Field (Susan Smith Blackburn Award 1992) 1991, The Break of Day 1996, Timberlake Wertenbaker: Plays 1996, After Darwin 1999, Filumena 1999, The Ash Girl 2000, Credible Witness 2001; *Trans:* Arianne Mnouchkine's Mephisto, Sophocles' Thebans, Euripides' Hecuba; Eduardo de Filippo's Filumena 1998, Successful Strategies, False Admissions, La Dispute (Marivaux), Leocadia (Anouilh). *Address:* c/o Casarotto Ramsay, National House, 60–66 Wardour St, London W1V 4ND, UK.

WERTMULLER, Lina; Italian film director; b (Arcangela Felice Assunta Wertmuller von Elgg) 14 Aug 1928, Rome; m Enrico Job. *Education:* Rome Theatre Acad. *Career:* Toured Europe with a puppet show after graduating; worked in theatre for ten years as actress, dir and playwright. *Films:* Dir and screenwriter: I Basilischi (The Lizards) 1963, Questa Volta parliamo di Uomini (Let's Talk About Men) 1965, Rita la zanzara (Rita the Mosquito) 1966, Non stuzzicate la zanzara (Don't Sting the Mosquito) 1967, Mimi Metallurgio Ferito nell'Onore (The Seduction of Mimi) 1972, Film d'amore e d'anarchia (Love and Anarchy) 1973, Tutto a Posto e Niente in Ordine (All Screwed Up), Travolti da un Insolito Destino nell'Azzurro Mare d'Agosto (Swept Away) 1974, Pasqualino Settebellezze (Seven Beauties) 1976, The End of the World in Our Usual Bed in a Night Full of Rain, Shimmy Lagano Tarantelle e Vino 1978, Revenge 1979, Summer Night, On a Moonlit Night, Saturday, Sunday, Monday, Ciao, Professore! *Address:* Piazza Clotilde 5, 00196 Rome. *Address:* Italy.

WESLEY, Mary (pseudonym of Mary Aline Siepmann), CBE; British writer; b 24 June 1912; d of Harold Mynors and Violet Hyacinth (née Dalby) Farmar; m 1st Baron Swinfen 1937 (divorced 1945); two s; m 2nd Eric Siepmann 1952 (died 1970); one s. *Education:* Privately and LSE. *Publications include:* Novels: Jumping the Queue 1983, The Camomile Lawn 1984 (made into TV mini-series 1992), Harnessing Peacocks 1985, The Vacillations of Poppy Carew 1986, Not That Sort of Girl 1987, Second Fiddle 1988, A Sensible Life 1990, A Dubious Legacy 1992, An Imaginative Experience 1994, Part of the Furniture 1997; Jr fiction: Speaking Terms 1968, The Sixth Seal 1968, Haphazard House 1983. *Leisure interest:* reading. *Address:* c/o Transworld Publishers, Bantam Press, 61-63 Uxbridge Rd, London W5 5SA, UK.

WEST, Stephanie Roberta, MA, D PHIL, FBA; British senior research fellow in classics and librarian; b 1 Dec 1937, Norwich; d of Robert Enoch and Ruth (née Batters) Pickard; m Martin West 1960; one s one d. *Education:* Nottingham High School for Girls and Somerville Coll (Oxford). *Career:* Mary Ewart Research Fellow, Somerville Coll, Oxford 1965–67, Lecturer in Classics, Hertford Coll, Oxford 1966–90, Sr Research Fellow and Librarian 1990–, Lecturer in Greek, Keble Coll, Oxford 1981–. *Publications:* The Ptolemaic Papyri of Homer 1967, Omero, Odissea I (Libri i–iv) 1981, A Commentary on Homer's Odyssey I (jtly) 1988. *Leisure interests:* opera, curious information. *Address:* Hertford College, Oxford OX1 3BW, UK (Office); 42 Portland Rd, Oxford OX2 7EY, UK (Home). *Telephone:* (1865) 279452 (Office); (1865) 56060 (Home); *E-mail:* stephanie.west@hertford.ox.ac.uk.

WESTHEIMER, (Karola) Ruth Siegel, MA, ED D; American (b German) psychologist and broadcaster; b Frankfurt, Germany; m Manfred Westheimer; one s one d. *Education:* Univ of Paris (Sorbonne), New School for Social Research and Columbia Univ. *Career:* Research Asst School of Public Health, Columbia Univ 1967–70; Assoc Prof Lehman Coll, New York 1979–77; Assoc Prof Brooklyn Coll; Counsellor and Presenter Sexually Speaking Station WYNY-FM

1980–; Presenter Good Sex, Dr Ruth Show, Ask Dr Ruth 1987–; film appearance in A Woman or Two 1986; TV appearance in Quantum Leap 1993. *Publications:* Dr Ruth's Guide to Good Sex 1983, First Love: A Young People's Guide to Sexual Information 1985, Dr Ruth's Guide for Married Lovers 1986, All in a Lifetime (autobiog) 1987, Dr Ruth's Guide to Erotic and Sensuous Pleasures 1991, Dr Ruth's Guide to Safer Sex 1992, Dr Ruth Talks to Kids 1993, The Art of Arousal 1993, Dr Ruth's Encyclopaedia of Sex 1994, The Value of Family: A Blueprint for the 21st Century 1996; numerous contribs to magazines. *Address:* King Features Syndicate Inc, 235 E 45th St, New York, NY 10017, USA.

WESTON, Joy; British business executive; b Staffs; d of Donald and Joyce Weston; m 1960 (divorced); one d. *Education:* Westwood Hall Girls' High School (Leek). *Career:* Area Controller Chelsea Girl (retail) 1971–74; Partner antique business 1974–77; Gen Man Peter Robinson (retail) 1977–81, Lillywhites (retail) 1981–82; Concessions Dir Hornes Menswear PLC, Operations Dir 1982–89; Commercial Dir Gatwick Airport Ltd (Div of British Airports Authority—BAA PLC) 1989–95, Operations Dir 1992–95; started own business specialising in holistic and aromatherapy treatment 1995–. *Leisure interests:* reading, walking, theatre, eating out, family. *Address:* Joy Weston Beauty Treatments for the Body and Soul, 142 Notting Hill Gate, London W11, UK (Office); 24B Thorney Crescent, Morgans Walk, London SW11 3TT, UK (Home). *Telephone:* (20) 7229-4111 (Office); (20) 7228-7114 (Home).

WESTWOOD, Vivienne, OBE; British fashion designer; b (Vivienne Swire) 1941, Tintwistle, Derbyshire; d of Gordon and Dora Swire; m 1st Derek Westwood (divorced); one s; fmr partner Malcolm McLaren; one s; m 2nd Andreas Kronthaler 1993. *Career:* Fmr primary school teacher; during 1970s worked with partner Malcolm McLaren, developing 'punk' look; has designed for the Sex Pistols, Boy George and Bananarama; created Pirate collection (adopted by Adam Ant and Bow Wow Wow) 1980; ended partnership with Malcolm McLaren 1983; moved to Italy for deal with Sergio Galeotti (partner of Giorgio Armani) 1984; launched 'Mini Crini' 1985; produced collection featuring Harris tweed suits and princess coats; Pagan 5 (latest of England Goes Pagan Collections) 1989; regular fashion shows, Paris, New York, London; launched signature fragrance Boudoir 1998; Prof of Fashion Acad of Applied Arts 1989–91, Hochschule der Künste, Berlin 1993–; Founder Vivienne Westwood Ltd; shops in UK, Japan, etc; retrospective exhibition Bordeaux Museum of Contemporary Art, France 1992; TV series Painted Ladies (Channel Four) 1996; launch of signature fragrance Boudoir 1998; Dr hc (Royal Coll of Art) 1992, (Heriot-Watt) 1995; Designer of the Year 1990, 1991; Queen's Award for Export 1998. *Address:* Westwood Studios, 9-15 Elcho St, London SW11 4AU, UK. *Telephone:* (20) 7924-4747.

WHALLEY-KILMER, Joanne; British actress; b 25 Aug 1964, Salford; m Val Kilmer 1988 (divorced 1996). *Career:* Stage career began during teens and has included season of Edward Bond plays at Royal Court Theatre, London. *Plays include:* Three Sisters, What the Butler Saw, Lulu; *Films:* Pink Floyd – the Wall 1982, Dance With a Stranger 1985, No Surrender 1986, The Good Father 1987, To Kill a Priest 1989, Willow 1988, Scandal 1989, Kill Me Again 1989, The Big Man, Navy Seals 1990, Miss Helen, Shattered, Crossing the Line, Storyville, Mother's Boys, A Good Man in Africa, Trial By Jury, The Man Who Knew Too Little, Run the Wild Fields, The Guilty, Jacqueline Kennedy Onassis: A Life 2000; *TV appearances include:* The Singing Detective, A Kind of Loving, A Quiet Life, The Gentle Touch, Bergerac, Reilly, Edge of Darkness, A Christmas Carol, Save Your Kisses, Will You Love Me Tomorrow?, Scarlett. *Address:* c/o Creative Artists Agency, 9830 Wilshire Blvd, Beverly Hills, CA 90212, USA.

WHEELER, Anne; Canadian film director, producer and writer; b 23 Sept 1946, Edmonton, AB; d of Benjamin and Nell (née Pawsey) Wheeler. *Career:* Jt propr Filmwest Assocs Ltd 1971–76; freelance producer, writer and broadcaster 1976–78; Producer, Dir and Writer NW Studio, Nat Film Bd of Canada 1978–83; Dir Wheeler-Hendren Enterprises Ltd 1983–; lecturer in field; Hon D UNIV (Athabasca) 1990; Hon D LITT (Alberta) 1990; Hon LL D (Calgary) 1991, (Lethbridge, Brock) 1993, (Winnipeg) 1994. *Films include:* Producer: Happily Unmarried (also dir, ed and cinematographer) 1976, Priory The Only Home I've Got (Best Short Documentary Genie Awards 1979, Red Ribbon Award American Film Festival 1979) 1977, A

Change of Heart (also dir, award from Alberta Motion Picture Industry Awards—AMPIA, Blue Ribbon Award American Film Festival 1986) 1983, Loyalties (also dir, Best Film, Performance and Direction, N American Indian Festival, Best Film, Dir, Performance and Script, AMPIA 1987) 1985, Cowboys Don't Cry (also writer and dir, Best Film of Festival, Best Dramatic Script and Direction, AMPIA 1988) 1987, Bye Bye Blues (also writer, dir and ed) 1989, Angel Square (also writer and dir) 1990, The Martian 1991–92 (dir), Mom P.I. (dir two episodes) 1991–92, The Diviners (dir) 1991–92, Other Women's Children (dir) 1992–93, The War Between Us 1994. *Address:* 25 2nd Ave East, 3rd Floor, Vancouver, BC V5T 1B3, Canada.

WHITAKER, Sally Maureen; British publishing executive; b 12 Feb 1939, London; d of Haddon and Mollie Whitaker. *Education:* St Paul's Girls' School and St Bartholomew's Medical Coll (London). *Career:* Account Exec Export Dept, Marks & Spencer 1966–73; Advertisement Man J. Whitaker & Sons Ltd 1973–78, Commercial Dir 1978–82, apptd Man Dir 1982, apptd Chief Exec 1991; Chair Book Trade Benevolent Soc; Hon Sec Soc of Bookmen; mem Man Cttee UKOLN. *Leisure interests:* conversation, design, well-written thrillers. *Address:* J. Whitaker and Sons Ltd, 12 Dyott St, London WC1A 1DF, UK. *Telephone:* (20) 7420-6000; *Fax:* (20) 7420-6194.

WHITAKER, Sheila, BA; British film executive; b 1 April 1936, Thornton Heath, Surrey; d of Charles and Hilda Whitaker. *Education:* Cathays High School for Girls (Cardiff), King's Norton Grammar School for Girls (Birmingham) and Univ of Warwick. *Career:* Sec and Admin in industry 1956–68; Chief Stills Officer Nat Film Archive 1968–74; Dir Tyneside Cinema, Tyneside Film Festival 1979–84; Founder, Co-Ed Writing Women 1982–84; Gen Ed Tyneside Publs 1984; Head of Programming Nat Film Theatre 1984–90; Dir London Film Festival 1987–, Free Form Arts Trust; Hon D LITT (Newcastle) 1997; Chevalier des Arts et des Lettres. *Publications:* Life and Art: The New Iranian Cinema (co-ed) 1999, An Argentine Passion: Maria Luisa Bemberg and her Films (co-ed) 2000. *Leisure interest:* reading. *Address:* 9 Buckingham Rd, London N1 4DG, UK. *Telephone:* (20) 7254-5155; *Fax:* (20) 7254-5155; *E-mail:* sheila@hellolondon.freeserve.co.uk.

WHITBREAD, Fatima, MBE; British former athlete; b 3 March 1961, Stoke Newington, London; adopted d of Margaret Whitbread; m Andrew Norman 1997; one s. *Career:* UK int debut as javelin thrower 1977; European Jr Champion 1979; European Cup Champion 1983; European Cup Silver Medallist 1985; European Champion 1986; Commonwealth Games Bronze Medallist 1982, Silver Medallist 1986; Silver Medallist, World Championships 1983; World Record Holder 1986; World Champion 1987; Bronze Medallist, Olympic Games, Los Angeles, USA 1984, Silver Medallist, Seoul, Repub of Korea 1988; Founder-mem, Pres Chafford Hundred Athletic Club, concurrently Marketing and Promotion Consultant; Marketing and Man Dir Champ International; mem Bd Eastern Region Sports Council 1992–96; Non-Exec Dir Thameside Community Health Care NHS Trust 1993–; Voluntary Service Overseas Amb 1992–93; Pres Turrock Harriers Athletic Club 1993–96; BBC and ITV Panasonic Sports Personality of the Year 1987; Sportswoman of the Year, British Sports Writers 1986, 1987; Woman Athlete of the Year, British Athletic Writers 1986, 1987. *Publication:* Fatima (autobiog) 1988. *Leisure interests:* travel, interior design, theatre. *Address:* Javel-Inn, Mill Hill, Shenfield, Brentwood, Essex CM15 8EU, UK (Office); 5 Hemley Rd, Orsett, Essex, UK (Home). *Telephone:* (1277) 213948 (Office); *Fax:* (1277) 211979 (Office); *E-mail:* champinternational@tinyworld.co.uk.

WHITBY, Joy, MA; British media executive and writer; b 27 July 1930, Helsinki, Finland; d of James and Esther Field; m Anthony Whitby 1954 (died 1975); three s. *Education:* Oxford High School and St Anne's Coll (Oxford). *Career:* Children's TV Producer, BBC 1958–68; Head of Children's Programmes London Weekend TV (LWT) 1968–70; Yorkshire TV 1976–85; Founder Grasshopper Productions Ltd 1970; Dir of Bd Channel Four 1980–84; Creator of The European Broadcasting Union (EBU) Drama Exchange for Children 1984; mem Advisory Panel for Youth, Nat Trust 1985–89, Bd Unicorn Theatre 1987–92; Trustee Int Childcare Trust 1994–97; Eleanor Farjeon Award for Services to Children's Books 1979. *TV Productions:* Creator of: Play School (BAFTA Award, Prix Jeunesse 1965) 1964, Jackanory 1965, Catweazle 1970, The Book Tower (BAFTA Award 1980, 1983, Prix

Jeunesse 1980) 1979; Independent productions: Grasshopper Island 1971, A Pattern of Roses 1983, Emma and Grandpa 1984, East of the Moon 1988, The Angel and the Soldier Boy 1989, On Christmas Eve 1992, The Mousehole Cat 1994, The Story of Arion and the Dolphin 1996, Mouse and Mole 1996; *Publications:* Grasshopper Island 1971, Emma and Grandpa (4 vols) 1984. *Leisure interests:* reading, theatre, film. *Address:* 50 Peel St, London W8 7PD, UK. *Telephone:* (20) 7229-1181; *Fax:* (20) 7229-2070; *E-mail:* joy@peelstreet.demon.co.uk; *Internet:* www.grasshopper.co.uk.

WHITELAW, Billie, CBE; British actress; b 6 June 1932, Coventry; d of Perceval and Frances Whitelaw; m 1st Peter Vaughan (divorced); m 2nd Robert Muller; one s. *Education:* Thornton Grammar School (Bradford). *Career:* With Nat Theatre 1963–65; has lectured on Beckett in numerous USA colls; Annenberg-Beckett Fellow Univ of Reading 1993; Hon D LITT (Bradford) 1981, (Birmingham, St Andrew's) 1997; Variety Club Silver Heart Award 1961; TV Actress of Year 1961, 1972; British Acad Award 1968; US Film Critics' Award 1977; Evening News Film Award for Best Actress 1977; Sony Best Radio Actress Award 1987; London Evening Standard Best Film Actress Award 1988. *Plays include:* Hotel Paradiso 1954, 1956, England our England 1962, Touch of the Poet 1962, Othello, Hobson's Choice, Play (Beckett), Trelawny of the Wells, The Dutch Courtesan, After Haggerty, Criterion 1971, Not I 1973, 1975, Footfalls 1976, Molly 1978, Happy Days 1979, The Greeks 1980, Passion Play 1981, Rockaby 1982, 1982, 1984–1986, Tales From Hollywood 1983, Who's Afraid of Virginia Woolf? 1987; *Films include:* No Love For Johnnie 1961, Charlie Bubbles 1968, Twisted Nerve 1968, The Adding Machine 1968, Start the Revolution Without Me, Eagle in a Cage 1969, Gumshoe 1971, Frenzy 1972, Night Watch 1973, The Omen 1976, Leopard in the Snow, The Water Babies 1977, An Unsuitable Job for a Woman 1981, Slayground 1983, The Chain 1984, Shadey 1985, Maurice 1986, The Dressmaker 1988, Joyriders 1989, The Krays 1990, Jane Eyre 1995, Canterbury Tales (animated film), Quills 2000; *TV appearances include:* No Trams to Lime Street, Lena Oh My Lena, Beyond the Horizon, Anna Christie, Lady of the Camelias, The Pity of it All, Love on the Dole, A World of Time, Poet Game, Sextet (8 plays), Napoleon and Love (9 plays), The Fifty Pound Note (Ten From the Twenties), The Withered Arm (Wessex Tales), The Werewolf Reunion (2 plays), Shades by Samuel Beckett, Not I, Eustace and Hilda (2 plays), The Serpent Son, Happy Days (dir by Beckett), A Tale of Two Cities, Jamaica Inn, Private Schultz, Camille, Old Girlfriends, The Picnic, The Secret Garden, Imaginary Friends, The 15 Streets, Footfalls, Rockaby, Eh Joe, Duel of Love, Lorna Doone, Murder of Quality, The Cloning of Joanna May, Firm Friends, Born to Run, Shooting the Past; *Radio plays:* The Master Builder, Hindle Wakes, Jane Eyre, The Female Messiah, Alpha Beta, Marching Song, The Cherry Orchard, Vassa, All that Fall, Embers, Becket Evening (one-woman) 1997; *Publication:* Billie Whitelaw – Who He? (memoirs) 1995. *Leisure interest:* pottering about the house. *Address:* c/o ICM, Oxford House, 76 Oxford St, London W1N 0AX, UK. *Telephone:* (20) 7636-6565; *Fax:* (20) 7323-0101.

WHITEREAD, Rachel, MA; British sculptor; b 20 April 1963, London; d of Thomas and Patricia Whiteread. *Education:* Brighton Polytechnic and Slade School of Art, Univ Coll London. *Career:* Solo exhibitions include Chisenhale Gallery, London 1990, Stedelijk Van-Abbemuseum, Eindhoven, Netherlands 1993, Museum of Contemporary Art, Chicago, IL, USA 1993, Kunsthalle Basel, Switzerland 1994–95, Inst of Contemporary Art, Philadelphia and Inst of Contemporary Art, Boston, MA, USA 1994–95, Tate Gallery, Liverpool 1996–97, Madrid 1997, The British Pavilion Venice Biennale 1997, Water Tower Project, NY 1998, Fourth Plinth Project, Trafalgar Square, London 2000, Holocaust Memorial, Judenplatz, Vienna 2000, also in Spain, France, Italy and Austria; numerous group exhibitions; Hon D LITT (Brighton Polytechnic, Univ of E London) 1998; prizes include Deutscher Akademischer Austauschdienst (DAAD, Berlin) 1992, Turner Prize 1993, Prix Eliette von Karajan 1996, Venice Biennale Award for Best Young Artist 1997. *Address:* c/o Anthony d'Offay, 29 Dering St, London W1R 9AA, UK. *Telephone:* (20) 7499-4100; *Fax:* (20) 7493-4443; *E-mail:* whiteread@schubertco.uk.

WHITFIELD, June Rosemary, CBE; British actress; b 11 Nov 1925; d of John and Bertha Whitfield; m Timothy Aitchison 1955 (died 2001); one d. *Education:* Royal Acad of Dramatic Arts (London). *Career:*

Comedy actress; performances on TV, radio, stage and screen; Freeman City of London 1982. *Plays include:* An Ideal Husband 1987, Ring Round the Moon 1988, Over My Dead Body 1989, Babes in the Wood 1990, 1991, 1992, Cinderella 1994; *Films include:* Carry on Nurse 1959, Carry on Abroad 1972, Bless This House 1972, Carry on Girls 1973, Carry on Columbus 1992, Jude the Obscure 1995; *TV includes:* Fast and Loose 1954, Beggar My Neighbour 1966, Scott on... 1969–73, Happy Ever After 1974–78, Terry and June 1979–87, Cluedo 1990, Absolutely Fabulous 1992, 1993, 1994, 2001, Common as Muck 1996, Family Money 1997, Friends 1998, The Secret 2000; *Radio includes:* Take it From Here 1953–60, The News Huddlines 1984–, series of plays as Miss Marple (Agatha Christie) 1993–2001, Like They've Never Been Gone 1998, 1999, 2001. *Address:* c/o April Young Ltd, 11 Woodlands Rd, Barnes, London SW13 0JZ, UK. *Telephone:* (20) 8876-7030; *Fax:* (20) 8878-7017.

WHITMAN, Christine Todd; American public official and former state governor; b 26 Sept 1946, New York; d of the late Webster Bray and of Eleanor Schley Todd; m John R. Whitman 1974; one d one s. *Education:* Wheaton Coll (MA). *Career:* Freeholder Bd of Freeholders, Somerset Co, NJ 1983–88; Pres Bd of Public Utilities, Newark, NJ 1988–90; fmr host, radio talk show, Station WKXW, Trenton, NJ; fmr newspaper columnist; Chair Comm for an Affordable NJ; Gov State of New Jersey 1994–2001; Head Environmental Protection Agency 2001–; Republican; Women's Award, Nat Republican Club 1994; Woman of the Year, Glamour magazine 1994; Leadership in Govt Award, Columbia Business School 1995. *Leisure interests:* cycling, horse-riding, reading. *Address:* Environmental Protection Agency, Ariel Rios Bldg, 1200 Pennsylvania Ave, NW, Washington, DC 20460, USA. *Telephone:* (202) 260-2090; *Internet:* www.epa.gov.

WHITMAN, Margaret, BA, MBA; American business executive. *Education:* Princetown Univ and Harvard Univ. *Career:* Brand Asst Procter & Gamble, Brand Man, responsible for global marketing of Playskool and Mr Potato Head brands; Gen Man Hasbro Inc Pre-school Div; Pres and CEO Florists Transworld Delivery, led launch of its Internet Strategy; Pres Stride Rite Div, Exec Vice-Pres Keds Div Stride Rite Corpn; Sr Vice-Pres Marketing in Consumer Products Div Walt Disney Co; Vice-Pres Bain & Co; Pres and CEO eBay Inc. *Address:* eBay Inc, 2125 Hamilton Ave, San Jose, CA 95125, USA. *Internet:* www.ebay.com.

WHITMAN, Marina von Neumann, MA, PH D; American economist and business executive; b 6 March 1935, New York; d of John and Mariette (née Kovesi) von Neumann; m Robert F. Whitman 1956; one s one d. *Education:* Radcliffe Coll (MA) and Columbia Univ (New York). *Career:* Lecturer in Econs Univ of Pittsburgh 1962–64, Asst Prof 1964–66, Assoc Prof 1966–71, Prof of Econs 1971–73, Distinguished Public Service Prof 1973–79; Sr Staff Economist Council of Econ Advisors 1970–71; mem Pres's Price Comm 1971–72, Pres's Council of Econ Advisors (with special responsibility for int monetary and trade problems) 1972–73; Vice-Pres, Chief Economist Gen Motors Corpn, New York 1979–85; Group Vice-Pres for Public Affairs 1985–92; Distinguished Visiting Prof of Business Admin and Public Policy, Univ of Michigan 1992–94, Prof 1994–; Dir Nat Bureau of Econ Research 1993–, Inst for Int Econs 1986–, Salzburg Seminar 1994–; mem Bd of Dirs Proctor and Gamble Co 1976–, Unocal 1993–, ALCOA 1994–, Chase Manhattan Corpn 1996–2001, J. P. Morgan Chase Corpn 2001–; mem Bd of Overseers Harvard Univ 1972–78, Bd of Trustees Princeton Univ 1980–90; mem Consultative Group on Int Econ and Monetary Affairs 1979–; mem AAAS, Phi Beta Kappa; Univ of Columbia Medal for Excellence 1973; Catalyst Award honouring outstanding women in the corporate world 1976; William F. Butler Award, New York Asscn of Business Economists 1988; more than 20 hon degrees. *Publications include:* New World, New Rules: The Changing Role of the American Corporation 1999, The Evolving Corporation: Global Imperatives and National Responses (ed) 2000; numerous other books and articles on econs. *Address:* Gerald R. Ford School of Public Policy, University of Michigan, 411 Lorch Hall, 611 Tappan St, Ann Arbor, MI 49109-1220, USA. *Telephone:* (734) 764-3490; *Fax:* (734) 763-9181; *E-mail:* marinaw@umich.edu.

WHITNEY, Phyllis Ayame; American writer; b 9 Sept 1903, Yokohama, Japan; d of Charles and Lillian (née Mandeville) Whitney; m 1st George Garner 1925; m 2nd Lovell Jahnke 1950 (died 1973).

Education: McKinley High School (Chicago, IL). *Career:* Children's Book Ed Chicago Sun 1942–46, Philadelphia Inquirer 1947–48; Instructor in writing juvenile fiction, Univ of New York 1947–58; fmrly writer of juvenile fiction, currently writes for adult market; mem Mystery Writers of America; awards include Agatha Award Malice Domestic 1990, Rita award Romance Writers of America 1990. *Publications include:* A Place for Ann 1941, Red is for Murder 1943, The Silver Inkwell 1945, Writing Juvenile Fiction 1947, Linda's Homecoming 1950, Love Me, Love Me Not 1952, Mystery of the Black Diamonds 1954, The Fire and the Gold (Jr Literary Guild) 1956, Mystery of the Green Cat (Jr Literary Guild) 1957, Mystery of the Haunted Pool (Mystery Writers' Asscn Edgar award) 1961, Seven Tears for Apollo 1963, Sea Jade 1965, Hunter's Green 1968, The Vanishing Scarecrow 1971, The Turquoise Mask 1974, The Glass Flame 1978, Vermilion 1981, Guide to Fiction Writing 1982, Rainsong 1984, Dream of Orchids 1985, Flaming Tree 1986, Silversword 1987, Feather on the Moon 1988, Rainbow in the Mist 1989, The Singing Stones 1990, The Ebony Swan 1992, Star Flight 1993, Daughter of the Stars.

WHYLIE, Marjorie Arnoldene Gregory, BA; Jamaican music educator, composer, cultural consultant and actress; b 31 Oct 1944, St Andrew; d of Halcot L. and Florrie Whylie. *Education:* St Andrew High School for Girls, Univ of the W Indies and Jamaica School of Music. *Career:* Teacher of Spanish Music, Kingston Coll 1966–74; Cultural Officer Penal Insts and Bellvue Mental Hosp 1974; Head Folk Music Research Dept, Jamaica School of Music 1975–85, Dir of Studies 1982–85, Prin (acting) 1983, Consultant, External Examiner 1989; apptd Resource Tutor Music Unit, Univ of the W Indies 1981–83, 1991; Lecturer Orientation Programs for US Peace Corps Volunteers 1988; apptd Music Dir Nat Dance Theatre Co of Jamaica 1967; Consultant to CBC 1979; Artist-in-Residence Oberlin Univ, OH, USA, Cave Arts Centre, Birmingham, UK; Visiting Lecturer Ministry of Educ, Virgin Islands, Univ of the W Indies, Cave Hill, Barbados; devised and presented several radio programmes 1976–79; compositions include 24 ballet scores, 15 choral works and 29 instrumental pieces 1968–; has appeared at numerous Jazz festivals throughout the Caribbean 1989–92; Award for Music, Univ of the W Indies 1965; Bronze Musgrave Medal 1974; Silver Medal Best Supporting Actress 1976; Centenary Medal, Inst of Jamaica 1982; Prime Minister's Medal of Appreciation 1983. *Recordings include:* Mystic Revelation of Rastafari 1973, Traditional Music of the Caribbean 1979, Heritage 1980, Rhythm Kit (cassette and notes) 1983. *Leisure interests:* anthropology, Egyptology, comparative religion, film. *Address:* 10 Milverton Crescent, Kingston 6, Jamaica. *Telephone:* 927-8183.

WIBERG, Pernilla; Swedish skier; b 1971. *Career:* Gold Medallist, Combined Event, Olympic Games, Lillehammer, Norway 1994, World Alpine Skiing Championships, Sierra Nevada, Spain 1996.

WICHTERICH, Christa, DR RER POL; German journalist and writer; b 4 March 1949, Brühl; m Uwe Hoering 1979. *Education:* Univs of Bonn, Munich and Kassel. *Career:* Lecturer Univ of Gilan, Rasht, Iran 1978–79, Jawaharlal Nehru Univ, New Delhi 1979–82; Guest Lecturer Univ of Kassel 1983, Göttingen 1984, Münster 1986, Frankfurt/Main 1991, Bochum 1994; Foreign Corresp for Africa for German newspapers and radio stations, Nairobi 1988–90; currently freelance journalist and writer; German Govt Award for Journalists working in the field of Devt Politics 1986. *Publications:* Stree Shakti, Frauen in Indien 1986, Kein Zustand dauert ewig, Afrika in den neunziger Jahren 1991, Die Erde bemuttern, Frauen und Ökologie nach dem Erdgipfel in Rio 1992, Menshen nach Maß, Bevölkerungspolitik in Nord und Süd 1994, Frauen der Welt, vom Fortschritt der Ungleichheit 1995, Wir sind das Wunder, Durch das wir Überleben, die Vierte Weltfrauenkonferenz in Peking 1996. *Leisure interests:* travel, reading, swimming. *Address:* Schloßtr 2, 53115 Bonn, Germany. *Telephone:* (228) 265032; *Fax:* (228) 265033.

WICKER-MIURIN, Fields, MA; American financial executive; b 30 July 1958, NC; d of Warren Jake and Marie P. Wicker; m Paolo Miurin 1994. *Education:* Univ of Virginia, Johns Hopkins Univ School of Advanced Int Studies and Inst d'Etudes Politiques (Paris). *Career:* Vice-Pres Philadelphia Nat Bank/Corestates 1982–89; Partner and Vice-Pres Mercer Management Consulting/Strategic Planning Assocs 1989–94; Exec Dir, Dir of Strategy and Finance, London Stock Exchange, UK

1994; Non-Exec Dir Proshare (UK) Ltd 1995; mem Bd of Trustees Johns Hopkins Univ Charitable Trust 1995. *Leisure interests:* riding, violin, good food, wine and friends. *Address:* London Stock Exchange, Old Broad St, London EC2N 1HP, UK. *Telephone:* (20) 7797-3456; *Fax:* (20) 7797-3259.

WICKI-FINK, Agnes; Swiss actress; b 14 Dec 1919, Frankfurt am Main, Germany; d of Ludwig Fink and Anna Agnes Klotz; m Bernhard Wicki 1945 (died 2000). *Education:* Dr Hoch's Konservatorium für Schauspielstudium (Frankfurt am Main). *Career:* Has appeared in Heidelberg, Leipzig, Munich, Stuttgart and Hamburg (Germany), Zurich, Vienna, Berlin, Maria Theater, Hamburg 1989–90; TV Kritikerpreis 1957; Goldene Bildschirm (twice); Großes Bundesverdienstkreu. *Address:* c/o Weisgerberstr 2, 8000 Munich 40, Germany.

WIDDECOMBE, Rt Hon Ann (Noreen), PC, MA; British politician; b 4 Oct 1947; d of the late James Murray and of Rita Widdecombe. *Education:* La Sainte Union Convent (Bath), Univ of Birmingham and Lady Margaret Hall (Oxford). *Career:* Worked in Marketing Dept Unilever 1973–75; Sr Admin Univ of London 1975–87; mem Runnymede Dist Council 1976–78; Parl Cand (Cons) for Burnley 1979, Plymouth Devonport 1983; MP for Maidstone 1987–97, Maidstone and The Weald 1997–; Parl Pvt Sec to Tristan Garel-Jones, MP 1990; Parl Under-Sec of State Dept of Social Security 1990–93, Dept of Employment 1993–94; Minister of State Dept of Employment 1994–95, Home Office 1995–97; Shadow Health Minister 1997–99, Shadow Home Sec 1999–; Founder-mem, Vice-Chair Women and Families for Defence. *Publication:* Layman's Guide to Defence 1984, Inspired and Outspoken 1999, The Clematis Tree (novel) 2000. *Leisure interests:* horse-riding, reading, research into Charles II's escape. *Address:* House of Commons, London SW1A 0AA, UK (Office); 9 Tamar House, Kennington Lane, London SE11 4XA, UK (Home); Kloor Cottage, Sutton Valence, Maidstone, Kent, UK (Home). *Telephone:* (20) 7219-3000 (Office); (20) 7735-5192 (London, Home); (1622) 843868 (Kent, Home).

WIDETZKY, Judi, BA; Israeli organization executive; b 22 May 1941, Minneapolis, MN, USA. *Education:* Oranim Teachers' Seminary, Hebrew Univ (Jerusalem) and Georgetown Univ (Washington, DC). *Career:* Fmr Admin Asst to David Ben Gurion, Leader Israeli Govt Del to UN Planning Cttee for Year of the Family, mem Israeli Govt Del to UN Comm on the Status of Women (Vienna), mem Israeli Del to Forum '85 (Nairobi, Kenya); Chair and mem Presidium World Labor Zionist Movt; mem Exec Int Council of Women (Chair Standing Cttee on Migrants and Refugees, Rep to UNHCR 1994, 1995, 1996), Int Council of Jewish Women (Chair Cttee for Aliya and Refugees, Rep to UNHCR 1994, 1995, 1996); mem Bd Devt Study Center, Rehovot, Advisory Cttee on Women's Affairs to Mayor of Jerusalem, Bd Bat Shalom (Israeli Women's Peace Network); Chair Bd of Dirs Moshe Sharett Educational Center; Co-Chair Budget and Finance Cttee, Jt Authority on Jewish-Zionist Educ; numerous papers presented at int confs and forums. *Leisure interests:* photography, music. *Address:* 9 Alharizi St, Jerusalem 91070, Israel. *Telephone:* (2) 663141; *Fax:* (2) 630830.

WIDNALL, Sheila Evans, PH D, SC D; American professor of aeronautics and astronautics and federal official; b 13 July 1938, Tacoma, WA; d of Rolland John and Genevieve Alice (née Krause) Evans; m William Soule Widnall 1960; one s one d. *Education:* MIT. *Career:* Mem staff The Boeing Co 1957, 1959, 1961, Aeronautical Research Inst of Sweden 1960; Research Staff Engineer Dept of Aeronautics and Astronautics, MIT 1961–62, Research Asst 1962–64, Asst Prof 1964–70, Assoc Prof 1970–74, Prof 1974–86, Abby Rockefeller Mauze Prof 1986–93, Assoc Provost 1992–93, Inst Prof 1998–; Dir of Univ Research US Dept of Transportation 1974–75; Sec of US Air Force 1993–98; mem Bd of Dirs Chemical Fabrics Inc 1984–, Aerospace Corpn, Draper Labs; mem Editorial Bd Science 1985–87, Pres 1987–88, Chair 1988–89; mem Bd of Trustees Carnegie Corpn 1984–92; mem Military Airlift Cttee NDTA 1985–89; mem Smithsonian Council 1986–89, Trustee Aerospace Corpn 1986–, ANSER Corpn 1988–, Boston Museum of Science 1989–; more than 60 papers published; lectures in field; mem Bd of Dirs American Acad of Arts and Sciences 1982–89, Pres-Elect 1986–87, Pres 1987–88, Chair 1988–89, Fellow 1989–; mem Bd of Dirs and Fellow American Int Acad of

Astronautics (AIAA) 1975–77; Fellow Exec Cttee American Physics Soc 1979–82, American Inst of Aeronautics and Astronautics, American Physics Soc; mem Int Acad of Astronautics, Soc of Women Engineers, Nat Acad of Eng, American Acad of Arts and Sciences; Lawrence Spery Award (AIAA) 1972; six hon degrees including Hon PH D (New England) 1975, (Lawrence Univ) 1987, (Cedar Crest Coll) 1988; Hon D SC (Princeton) 1994; Outstanding Achievement Award, Soc of Women Engineers 1975; Washburn Award, Boston Museum of Science 1987; Distinguished Service Award, Nat Acad of Eng 1993; Women in Aviation Pioneer Hall of Fame 1996; Goddard Award, Nat Space Club 1998. *Address:* Massachusetts Institute of Technology, 77 Massachusetts Ave, Bldg 33–411, Cambridge, MA 02139, USA.

WIECZOREK-ZEUL, Heidemarie; German politician; b 21 Nov 1942, Frankfurt/Main. *Education:* Johann Wolfgang Goethe-Univ (Frankfurt/Main). *Career:* Teacher 1965–78; mem SPD 1965–, Fed Chair Jungsozialisten 1974–77, mem Party Bd 1984–, mem Presidium 1986–, Chair S Hesse Area Party 1988–; Chair European Co-ordinating Office Int Youth Asscn 1977–79; MEP 1979–87; mem Bundestag (Parl) for Hesse 1987–, Fed Minister for Econ Co-operation and Devt 1998–. *Address:* Bundestag, Platz der Republik 1, 11011 Berlin, Germany (Office). *Telephone:* (30) 227-73386; *Fax:* (30) 227-76748; *E-mail:* heidemarie.wieczorek-zeul@bundestag.de.

WIED, Thekla Carola; Austrian actress; b Breslau. *Education:* Gymnasium zum Grauen Kloster (Berlin) and Folkwang-Hochschule (Essen). *Career:* Stage appearances in Essen, Saarbrücken, Braunschweig, Wiesbaden, Bochum, Gandersheim Festival, Germany, etc; has toured Germany, Switzerland and Austria; awards include Bundesfilmpreis (Gold, for Spur eines Mädchens) 1968, Bambi Prize for Best-loved Actress 1984, for Best-loved Actress in a Series 1985, Goldene Cleo for Best-loved Actress in a Series (Austria), Goldene Kamera 1985, Bambi Prize (Leipzig) 1990, Gold Romy (Austrian TV prize) 1991, Telestar Prize 1991. *TV appearances include:* Ich heirate eine Familie (Bambi Prize 1985), Wie gut, daß es Maria gibt, Kabale und Liebe, Amphytrion, Kunstfehler, Colin, Der Alte, Derrick, Auf eigene Gefahr 1993, Eine Frau in den allerbesten Jahren, Ich klage an (Bayerischer Fernsehpreis 1994) 1994. *Address:* Amsterdamer Str 3, 80805 Munich, Germany.

WIELAND, Joyce, OC; Canadian artist and film-maker; b 30 June 1931, Toronto. *Education:* Cen Tech School (Toronto, ON). *Career:* Solo exhibitions include Isaacs Gallery, Toronto 1960, 1963, 1967, 1972, 1974, 1981, 1983, 1987, Vancouver Art Gallery 1968, Museum of Modern Art, New York (USA) 1971, Cannes Film Festival, France 1976, Canadian Film Arts Centre, Hong Kong 1981, Nat Gallery of Canada 1978, Yajima Gallery, Montréal 1982; group exhibitions include Expo '67, Montréal 1967; retrospective exhibitions include Art Gallery of Ontario, Toronto 1981–82, 1987–88, Canada House, London 1988–89; retrospective Films of Joyce Wieland, Whitney Museum, New York 1973, San Francisco Art Inst 1985, Art Gallery of Ontario (touring) 1987–88, Nat Film Theatre, London 1988, Centre Nat d'Art et de Culture Georges-Pompidou, Paris 1989; selection of films screened at Ciné-Club de Saint-Charles, Univ of Paris IV (Paris-Sorbonne) 1986; Artists on Fire film documentary 1987; Artist-in-Residence Univ of Toronto 1988–89; YWCA Woman of Distinction Award 1987. *Films include:* Rat Life (Third Ind Filmmakers Festival Award, New York 1969), Diet in North America (Third Ind Filmmakers Festival Award, New York 1969), The Far Shore (three Canadian awards 1977), A and B in Ontario (Ann Arbor Film Festival Award 1986), Artists on Fire (documentary) 1987; *Publications:* True Patriot Love 1971, Joyce Wieland 1987, Joyce Wieland: Quilts, Paintings and Works of Paper 1988. *Address:* 497 Queen St E, Toronto, ON M5A 1V1, Canada; 179 John St, Toronto, ON M5T 1X4, Canada. *Telephone:* (416) 366-2986.

WIENER, Céline, D JUR; French (b Polish) civil servant; b 31 July 1936, Łódź, Poland; d of Louis and Irène (née Cukierman) Kaminski; m Emmanuel Wiener 1958; two s one d. *Education:* Lycée Racine (Paris) and Univ of Paris. *Career:* Researcher and Dir of Research CNRS, Paris 1969–84; Technical Adviser to Sec of State for the Civil Service, Paris 1984–85; Chief Insp Ministry of Nat Educ 1985–91, Head of Inspectorate 1991–; Officier de la Légion d'Honneur 1997; Commdr des Palmes Académiques 1999. *Publications:* Recherches sur le pouvoir réglementaire des ministres 1970, Le contrôle et la protection des citoyens 1973, Vers une codification de la procédure administrative 1975, L'évolution des rapports entre l'administration et les usagers 1991, Le citoyen et son administration 2000. *Address:* Ministry of National Education, 107 rue de Grenelle, 75007 Paris, France (Office); 27 rue de Vergniaud, 75013 Paris, France (Home). *Telephone:* (1) 55-55-14-33 (Office); *Fax:* (1) 55-55-10-01 (Office).

WIENER, Valerie, MA; American politician, media executive and writer; b 30 Oct 1948, Las Vegas, NV; d of Louis and Tui (née Knight) Wiener; m 1972 (divorced 1979). *Education:* Univ of Missouri, Univ of Illinois and McGeorge School of Law. *Career:* Propr and Vice-Pres Broadcast Assocs Inc 1972–86; Public Affairs Dir First Illinois Cable TV 1973–74; Ed Illinois State Register 1973–74; Producer KLVX-TV 1974–75; Account Exec KBMI 1975–79; Exec Vice-Pres and Gen-Man KXKS and KKJY Stations 1980–81; Exec Admin KSET, KVEG, KFMS and KKJY 1981–83; propr Wiener Communications Group 1988–; NV State Senator 1996–(2004), Senate Democratic Whip; mem Nat Asscn of Women Business Owners, Soc for Professional Journalists, Nat Fed of Press Women; winner 141 communications awards; Outstanding Woman Advocate for Education, Virginia Commonwealth Univ 2000; Int Community Service Award; Int New Thought Alliance Award 2001. *Publications:* Power Communications 1994, Gang Free 1995, The Nesting Syndrome 1997, Winning the War Against Youth Gangs 1999, Power Positioning 2000, Advancing Yourself Through Media Relations 2000, Advancing Yourself Through Political Positioning 2000, Advancing Yourself Through Self-Promotion 2000. *Leisure interests:* reading, community service, fitness, weightlifting (especially competition). *Address:* 1500 Foremaster Lane, Suite 2, Las Vegas, NV 89101-1103, USA; 3540 W Sahara Ave, #352, Las Vegas, NV 89102, USA. *Telephone:* (702) 871-6536; *Fax:* (702) 221-9239; *E-mail:* www .valeriewiener.com.

WIER, Patricia Ann, BA, MBA; American publishing executive; b 10 Nov 1937, AR; d of Horace and Bridget (née McMahon) Norton; m Richard A. Wier 1962; one d. *Education:* Univs of Missouri and Chicago. *Career:* Computer Programmer AT&T 1960–62; Head Programmer City of Kansas 1963–65, Playboy Enterprises, Chicago 1965–71, Man Systems and Programming 1971; Man Computer Services and Exec Dir of Man Services Encyclopaedia Britannica Inc, Chicago 1971–75, Vice-Pres of Man Services 1975–83, Planning and Devt 1983–85; Pres Compton Learning Co Div 1985–86, Chair 1987; Pres Encyclopaedia Britannica N America 1986–91; man consultant pvt practice, Chicago 1994–; mem Bd of Dirs Direct Selling Asscn 1984–93 (Chair 1987–88, Hall of Fame 1991), NICOR Inc; mem Bd of Dirs NICOR; Hon Life mem Women's Council, Univ of Missouri. *Leisure interests:* contemporary art, reading. *Address:* Patricia A. Wier Inc, 175 E Delaware Suite 8305, Chicago, IL 60611, USA (Office); 230 E Delaware Place, Chicago, IL 60611, USA (Home).

WIESE, Barbara Jean; Australian politician; b 14 Jan 1950; d of G. Wiese. *Education:* Flinders Univ. *Career:* Asst Institution for Blind and Deaf Children 1967–72; Sec Public Bldgs Dept, Public Services, S Australia 1972; Personal Asst to Chief Sec S Australian Govt 1972–78; mem S Australia Legis Chamber (Parl) 1979–, Minister of Youth Affairs 1985–89, of Tourism 1989–92, assisting Minister for the Arts 1985–89, Minister for State Services 1989, for Consumer Affairs and for Small Business 1989–92, for Transport Devt 1992–93, Shadow Minister for Transport, for Housing, Urban Devt and Local Govt 1994. *Leisure interests:* cinema, reading, music, walking. *Address:* Parliament House, Adelaide, SA 5000, Australia.

WIEST, Dianne; American actress; b 28 March 1948, Kansas City, MO. *Education:* Univ of Maryland. *Career:* Regional theatre work; performer New York Shakespeare Festival. *Plays include:* Heartbreak House, Our Town, The Art of Dining (Theatre World Award) 1983, The Dybbuk, Inherit the Wind, Ashes, Agamemnon, Frankenstein, Othello, Beyond Therapy, Not About Heroes (dir), Hunting Cockroaches 1987, Square One, In the Summer House 1993, Blue Light 1994; *Films:* It's My Turn 1980, I'm Dancing as Fast as I Can 1982, Independence Day 1982, Footloose 1984, Falling in Love 1984, The Purple Rose of Cairo 1985, Hannah and Her Sisters (Acad Award for Best Supporting Actress) 1986, Radio Days 1987, Lost Boys 1987, September 1987, Bright Lights Big City 1988, Parenthood 1989, Cookie 1989, Edward Scissorhands 1991, Little Man Tate 1991, Cops and Robbersons 1994,

The Scout 1994, Bullets Over Broadway (Acad Award for Best Supporting Actress 1994, Golden Globe, New York Film Critics, LA Film Critics and Nat Bd of Review Awards) 1994, Drunks, Birds of a Feather, The Birdcage 1996; *TV appearances include:* Zalman or the Madness of God, Out of Our Father's House, The Wall 1982, The Face of Rage 1983. *Address:* c/o Paul Wolfowitz, International Creative Management, Suite 22, 59 E 54th St, New York, NY 10022, USA.

WIGDOR, Blossom T(emkin), CM, MA, PH D; Canadian gerontologist and psychologist; b 13 June 1924, Montréal, PQ; d of Solomon and Olga (née Gilels) Temkin; m Leon Wigdor 1945; one c. *Education:* McGill Univ and Univ of Toronto. *Career:* Sr Consultant in Psychology, Queen Elizabeth Hosp, Montréal 1963–74; Dir of Psychological Services, Centre Hospitalier Côte des Neiges 1961–79, Psychiatric-Psychological Research Unit 1965–78; Assoc Prof of Psychology, McGill Univ 1972–79; Prof of Psychology and Behavioural Science, Univ of Toronto 1979–91 (Prof Emer 1991–), Dir Programme of Gerontology 1979–89, Centre for Studies of Aging 1989–90, Prof Emer of Psychology and Public Health Sciences 1991–; Chair Nat Advisory Council on Aging 1990–93, Chair and mem Bd of Dirs Canadian Memorial Services 1993–; Vice-Chair and Dir Gerontological Research Council of Ontario 1980–90; Trustee Inst for Research on Public Policy 1983–89, Ontario Psychological Foundation; Fellow Canadian Psychological Asscn, Soc of Personal Assessment, Gerontological Soc of America, American Psychological Asscn; mem Bd of Dirs Canadian Geriatrics Research Soc 1980–86, Canadian Stage Co 1993–; Hon D SC (Victoria) 1990, (Guelph) 1994; Hon LL D (St Thomas) 1995; Canadian Asscn of Gerontology award 1989. *Publications:* Canadian Gerontological Collection I 1977, Planning Your Retirement 1985, The Over Forty Society 1988. *Leisure interests:* reading, theatre, cross-country. *Address:* Inst for Human Development, Life Course and Aging, 222 College St, Suite 106, Toronto, ON M5T 3J1, Canada (Office); 21 Dale Ave, Apt 708, Toronto, ON M4W 1K3, Canada (Home).

WIGGINS, Marianne; American writer; m Salman Rushdie (divorced). *Career:* Lives in London; shortlisted for Orange award 1996. *Publications include:* John Dollar, Eveless Eden 1996; two short story collections.

WIIG, Marit; Norwegian civil servant; b 14 Oct 1949. *Education:* Oslo Commercial Coll and, Univ of Oslo and Govt School of Public Admin and Man. *Career:* Exec Officer Dept of Personnel, Ministry of Consumer Affairs and Govt Admin 1976–79, Exec Officer Govt Admin Services 1979–82, Head of Div 1982–85, Asst Dir-Gen Ministry of Consumer Affairs and Govt Admin 1985–86, Acting Dir Gen 1986–87, Advisor to the Sec Gen 1987–88, Dir Gen 1988–90; Sr Advisor World Bank, Washington 1992–94; Dir Post Office Savings Bank of Norway 1994–95; Dir Confed of Norwegian Business and Industry 1995–; numerous honorary appointments. *Address:* Confederation of Norwegian Business and Industry, Middelthunsgate 27, POB 5250 Majorstua, 0303 Oslo, Norway. *Telephone:* 22-96-51-40; *Fax:* 22-96-52-22; *E-mail:* marit.wiig@nho.no.

WILCOX, Baroness (Life Peer), cr 1995, of Plymouth in the County of Devon, **Judith Ann Wilcox,** FRSA, FBIM; British organization executive and politician; b 31 Oct 1940; d of John and Elsie Freeman; m 1st Keith Davenport 1961; one s; m 2nd Sir Malcolm George Wilcox 1986 (died 1986). *Education:* St Mary's Convent (Wantage) and Polytechnic South West. *Career:* Man family business, Devon 1969–79; Founder, Chair Chanel Foods, Cornwall 1979–84; Founder, Finance Dir Capstan Fisheries Ltd 1984–89; Chair, Man Dir Pêcheries de la Morinie, France 1989–91; Chair Morinie et Cie, France 1990–94; Chair Nat Consumer Council 1990–96; Commr Local Govt Comm 1992–95; Prime Minister's Adviser to Citizen's Charter Unit 1992–96, Chair Citizen's Charter Complaints Task Force 1993–95; mem Bd Automobile Asscn 1991–97, Cadbury Schweppes 1997, Inland Revenue 1992–95, Port of London Authority 1993–96; mem Council Royal Nat Mission to Deep Sea Fishermen, Inst of Dirs; mem Church of England Bd for Social Responsibility, BBC Gen Advisory Council, Tax Law Review Cttee; Gov Plymouth Univ, Ashridge Man Coll; Vice-Pres Girl Guides Asscn;. *Leisure interests:* sailing, 14th century calligraphy, fishing, walking. *Address:* House of Lords, London SW1A 0PW, UK. *Telephone:* (20) 7219-3000.

WILD, Hilary Frances; British business executive; b 1949; d of Bishop Eric and Frances Moyra (née Reynolds) Wild. *Education:* Casterton School, Cumbria. *Career:* Mem staff Wenn Townsend and Co, Oxford 1967–71, Ernst and Young, London 1971–75, Edward Bates and Sons Ltd 1973–79, Marine Midland Bank NA, London 1979–80, Asst Vice-Pres 1980–83, Vice-Pres 1983–85; Finance Dir City Wheels Ltd 1985–86; Chief of Finance UNICEF, New York 1986–90; Asst Dir Kleinwort Benson Ltd 1990–92, Dir 1992–94, Dir Kleinwort Benson Investment Management Ltd 1994, apptd Man-Dir Kleinwort Benson Charities 1994; FCA; Trustee Hackney Music Devt Trust; Gov Downe House School 1992–. *Leisure interests:* theatre, music, travel. *Address:* Kleinwort Benson, Investment Management Ltd, 10 Fenchurch St, London EC3M 3LB, UK. *Telephone:* (20) 7956-6122; *Fax:* (20) 7956-7126.

WILDE, Fran (Francis Helen), B SC S; New Zealand politician; b 1948, Wellington; three c. *Education:* Wellington Polytechnic and Victoria Univ of Wellington. *Career:* Elected Mem House of Reps (Parl, Labour) for Wellington Cen 1981, mem Cttees on Commerce and Energy, Official Information, Standing Orders, fmr Opposition Spokesperson on State Services, Govt Whip 1984–87, Chair Govt Admin Select Cttee 1984–87; Assoc Minister of Conservation 1987, of External Relations and Trade 1988–90; Minister for Disarmament 1988–90, for Tourism 1989–90. *Leisure interests:* theatre, music, reading, travel. *Address:* House of Representatives, POB 18041, Wellington, New Zealand. *Telephone:* (4) 719-199; *Fax:* (4) 499-0704.

WILDE, Patricia; American (b Canadian) dancer and artistic director; b 16 July 1928, Ottawa, Canada; d of John Herbert and Eileen Lucy (née Simpson) White; m George Bardyguine 1953; one s one d. *Education:* Professional Children's School, Lodges Tutoring School and under Dorothy Littlefield (New York). *Career:* Dancer American Concert Ballet 1943–44, Marquis de Cuevas Ballet Int 1944–45, Ballet Russe de Monte Carlo 1945–49; Prin Dancer Roland Petit's Ballet de Paris 1949, British Metropolitan Ballet 1949–50, New York City Ballet 1950–65; ballet teacher 1968–69; Dir School of Harkness House of Ballet 1965–66, School of Grand Theatre of Geneva, Switzerland 1969–70; Mistress American Ballet Theatre 1970–77, Dir 1977–82; Artistic Dir Pittsburgh Ballet Theatre 1982–; cr roles in many works of George Balanchine; Jury Chair First Int Munich Ballet Competition, Germany 1982; Jury mem Prix de Lausanne Int Ballet Competition, Switzerland; panellist Nat Choreographic Project 1984; several TV appearances; Dance Educators of America Award 1957; Dance Masters; Leadership in Arts 1990; Woman of the Year, Pittsburgh YWCA 1990, 1993; Culture Award 1997; History Makers 1999. *Leisure interests:* cooking, reading, horses, dogs. *Address:* Pittsburgh Ballet Theatre, 2900 Liberty Ave, Pittsburgh, PA 15201, USA. *Telephone:* (412) 281-0360; *Fax:* (412) 281-9901.

WILENSKY, Gail Roggin, BA, M ECONS, PH D; American economist and federal agency official; b 14 June 1943, Detroit, MI; d of Albert and Sophia (née Blitz) Roggin; m Robert Wilensky 1963; one s one d. *Education:* Univ of Michigan. *Career:* Economist Pres's Comm on Income Maintenance Programs and Exec Dir Maryland Council of Econ Advisors 1969–71; Sr Researcher Urban Inst, Washington, DC 1971–73; Assoc Research Scientist in public policy and public health, Univ of Michigan 1973–75, Visiting Asst Prof of Econs 1973–75; Sr Research Man Nat Center for Health Services Research 1975–83; Vice-Pres Div of Health Affairs, HOPE Project, Milwood 1983–90; apptd Head Health Care Financing Admin 1990; Deputy Asst to the Pres for Policy Devt, White House 1992–93; Chair Medicare Payment Advisory Comm 1997–; mem Physician Payment Comm 1989–90 (Chair 1995–97), Health Advisory Comm, Comptroller-Gen of US 1987–90, American Econ Asscn, Fed of Orgs of Professional Women, American Statistics Asscn, Nat Tax Asscn, Asscn of Health Services Research, Inst of Medicine, NAS; Sr Fellow Project HOPE, Bethesda 1993–; Dean Conley Award, American Coll of Healthcare Execs 1989. *Address:* 2807 Battery Place, NW, Washington, DC 20016, USA.

WILKENING, Laurel Lynn, PH D; American former university chancellor and planetary scientist; b 23 Nov 1944, Richland, WA; d of Marvin Hubert and Ruby Alma (née Barks) Wilkening; m Godfrey Theodore Sill 1974. *Education:* Reed Coll (Portland, OR) and Univ of California at San Diego. *Career:* NASA Trainee 1967–70; Asst Prof

Univ of Arizona 1973–80, Dir Lunar and Planetary Lab and Head of Planetary Sciences 1981–83, Vice-Provost and Prof of Planetary Sciences 1983–85, Vice-Pres for Research and Dean of Grad School 1985–88; Prof of Geological Sciences and Adjunct Prof of Astronomy, Provost and Vice-Pres for Academic Affairs, Univ of Washington, Seattle 1988–93; Chancellor and Prof Program in Earth System Sciences, Univ of California at Irvine 1993–98; Div Scientist NASA Headquarters, Washington, DC 1980, Chair Comm Rendezvous Science Working Group 1983–85, Co-Chair primitive bodies mission study team NASA–European Space Agency (ESA) 1984–85; Vice-Chair Nat Comm on Space, Washington, DC 1984–86, Advisory Comm on the Future of US Space Programs 1990–91; mem Panel on Int Co-operation and Competition in Space, Congressional Office of Technical Assessment 1982–83; mem American Astronomy Soc, American Geophysics Union, Int Astronomy Union, American Acad of Arts and Sciences; Trustee Reed Coll 1992–; Regents Fellow, Univ of California 1966–67; Fellow Meteoritical Soc 1978; Mortar Bd Hall of Fame (Arizona) 1983; YMCA Women on the Move Award 1984; Tucson Trade Bureau Faculty Recognition Award 1984. *Publications:* Comets (ed) 1982, Pioneering the Space Frontier 1986; numerous articles and papers for scientific journals on meteorites and their relationship to asteroids, comets and the formation of the solar system. *Leisure interests:* gardening, camping, swimming. *Address:* University of California at Irvine, Office of the Chancellor, 501 Admin, Irvine, CA 92697, USA. *Telephone:* (714) 824-5111; *Fax:* (714) 824-2087.

WILKES, Joanne; New Zealand university lecturer and writer. *Career:* Lecturer in English, Univ of Auckland; Rose Mary Crawshay Prize 2000. *Publications:* Lord Byron and Mme de Staël: Born for Opposition 2000, Geraldine Jewsbury's The Half Sisters (ed), numerous articles. *Address:* c/o Department of English, University of Auckland, Private Bag 92019, Auckland 1, New Zealand. *Telephone:* (9) 373-7999; *Fax:* (9) 373-7400; *E-mail:* j.wilkes@auckland.ac.nz; *Internet:* www2.arts .auckland.ac.nz.

WILKES, Kathleen Vaughan, PH D; British lecturer in philosophy; b 23 June 1946, Abingdon, Berks; d of the Rev John and Joan (née Alington) Wilkes. *Education:* Univs of Oxford and Princeton (USA). *Career:* Research Fellow King's Coll, Cambridge 1972–73; Lecturer Univ of Oxford, Fellow and Tutor in Philosophy St Hilda's Coll, Oxford 1973–; co-f underground univ in Czechoslovakia; Adviser to Mayor of Dubrovnik (Croatia, fmrly Yugoslavia) during siege 1991; Medal, Charles Univ, Prague 1992; Medal, Ministry of Educ, Warsaw 1993; Hon Citizen, Dubrovnik 1993. *Publications:* Physicalism 1978, Real People 1988. *Leisure interests:* travel, especially to Central and Eastern Europe and People's Republic of China. *Address:* St Hilda's College, Oxford OX4 1DY, UK. *Telephone:* (1865) 276840; *Fax:* (1865) 276816.

WILKINSON, Lisa Clare; Australian magazine editor; b 19 Dec 1958, Wollongong, NSW; d of the late Raymond William and of Beryl Jean Wilkinson; m Peter FitzSimons 1992. *Education:* Campbelltown High School (NSW). *Career:* Editorial Asst Dolly Magazine (magazine for girls) 1978, Asst Ed 1979–80, apptd Ed aged 21, youngest ever ed of nat women's magazine 1980, doubled circulation 1981–85, later Ed-in-Chief, currently Consultant; apptd Ed Cleo (women's lifestyle magazine) magazine 1985, Int Ed-in-Chief Cleo's int edns in NZ, Singapore, Malaysia and Thailand; consultant Australian Consolidated Press. *Leisure interests:* photography, classical music, interior design, architecture. *Address:* c/o Cleo, 54 Park St, Sydney, NSW 2000, Australia.

WILKOMIRSKA, Wanda; Polish violinist and professor of music; b 11 Jan 1929, Warsaw; d of Alfred and Dorota (née Temkin) Wilkomirski; m Mieczysław Rakowski 1952 (divorced 1980); two s. *Education:* Music Acad (Łódź), Liszt Acad (Budapest) and under Irena Dubiska, Ede Zathureczky and Henryk Szeryng (Paris). *Career:* First public appearance 1936, first concert 1945; concerts world-wide, including debuts in London 1952 and New York 1960; currently Prof Hochschule für Musik Heidelberg–Mannheim; many recordings under int record labels; defected whilst on tour of Fed Repub of Germany March 1982; prizes awarded at int competitions in Warsaw 1938, Geneva (Switzerland) 1946, Budapest 1949, Bach Competition, Leipzig 1950, Wieniawski Competition, Poznań 1952; State prizes 1952, 1963; Connoisseur Soc Best of the Year award, New York 1971; Officer's Cross of Polonia Restituta 1953; Order of the Banner of Labour (2nd Class) 1959, (1st

Class) 1964; Culture and Arts Prize (1st Class) 1975; Orpheus Prize, Polish Musicians' Asscn 1979. *Leisure interests:* nature, books, films, theatre, sports. *Address:* Augusta Anlage 53, 6800 Mannheim, Germany. *Telephone:* (621) 415650.

WILLARD-GALLO, Karen Elizabeth, MS, PH D; American molecular biologist; b 8 July 1953, Oak Ridge, TN; d of Harvey Bradford and Isabella Victoria (née Rallis) Willard; m James Paul Gallo 1982. *Education:* Virginia Polytechnic Inst and State Univ, Univ of Reading (UK) and Randolph-Macon Woman's Coll (Lynchburg, VA). *Career:* Teaching Asst of Microbiology and Immunology, Virginia Polytechnic Inst and State Univ 1976–78; Assoc Researcher Argonne Nat Laboratory, IL 1978–81; Post-Doctoral Fellow 1981–82; Investigator Ludwig Inst for Cancer Research, Brussels 1982–85; Guest Investigator Int Inst of Cellular and Molecular Pathology, Brussels 1986–90, Assoc mem 1990; Visiting Scientist Dept of Clinical Biochem, Rikshospitalet, Oslo 1980, 1981, Basle Inst for Immunology, Switzerland 1986; Consultant Baxter-Travenol 1986–88, Market Research Intelligence Corpn 1991; Temporary Adviser on Immunology, WHO 1987; patented method for early detection of infectious mononucleosis 1984; mem American Soc for Cell Biology, Electrophoresis Soc; Award for Teaching Excellence, Virginia Polytechnic Inst and State Univ 1977, 1978; numerous articles and abstracts published in scientific books and journals. *Leisure interest:* golf. *Address:* International Institute of Cellular and Molecular Pathology, Dept of Biochemistry, UCL 7539, Ave Hippocrate 75, 1200 Brussels, Belgium (Office); Ave Chevalier Jehan 117, 1300 Wavre, Belgium (Home). *Telephone:* (2) 764-75-76 (Office); *Fax:* (2) 763-12-43 (Office).

WILLCOCK, Elizabeth, CM; Canadian citizenship judge (retd); b 12 Oct 1927, Sherbrooke, PQ; d of Terence Gerard and Mary Irene (née Wolf) Walsh; m David Noel 1950; three s two d. *Education:* Mont Notre Dame Convent, Notre Dame Coll and Francis Robinson Duff School of Theatre. *Career:* Teacher of History and Drama 1948–49; radio broadcaster, Sherbrooke 1948–49; freelance broadcaster, Toronto 1949–50, Montréal 1950–68; Researcher and Interviewer CBC-TV, Winnipeg 1969–71; Dir of Research Cons Party of Manitoba 1972–76; Exec Dir Citizenship Council of Manitoba 1977–84; Chief of Staff Ministry of State for Multiculturalism 1984–85; Citizenship Court Judge 1985–87, Sr Citizenship Judge for Canada 1987–98; Pres Terry Fox Youth Centre, MB 1980–81, UN Asscn (Winnipeg) 1986–87, 1996–, Nat Pres of Cons Women's Caucus. *Address:* 28–126 Portsmouth Blvd, Winnipeg, MB R3P 1B6, Canada. *Telephone:* (204) 888-3945 (Home).

WILLENZ, June Adele, BS, MA; American organization executive, academic and writer; b 17 Dec 1924; m Eric Willenz 1951 (divorced 1966); two d. *Education:* Univ of Michigan and New School for Social Research (New York). *Career:* Exec Dir American Veterans' Cttee (AVC) 1965–, Ed AVC Bulletin; columnist on Stars and Stripes, Nat Tribune Newspaper; Convenor Working Group on Refugee Women, NGO Cttee on the Status of Women; Chair Standing Cttee on Women, World Veterans' Fed 1985–; Scholar-in-Residence American Univ (Washington, DC); mem Pres's Advisory Cttee on Women Veterans 1983–86 (Chair Sub-Cttee on Disabled Veterans), Pres's Cttee on Employment of Persons with Disabilities; speaker Nat Urban League, Centre for Policy Research; Del White House Confs on Youth, Aging; appearances on radio and TV; Military Women of New York City Award 1993; Presidential Cttee on Employment of People with Disabilities Award 1996; Certificate of Special Congressional Recognition 1997; City of Paris Bronze Echelon 2000. *Publications:* Dialogue on the Draft 1967, Human Rights of the Man in Uniform 1969, Women Veterans: America's Forgotten Heroines 1983; Plays: Olie and Sam 1987, Sinners Can Stand Too 1988. *Leisure interests:* reading, music, art, theatre, tennis, swimming, walking. *Address:* 6309 Bannockburn Drive, Bethesda, MD 20817, USA. *Telephone:* (301) 229-5670; *Fax:* (301) 320-6490; *E-mail:* willenzj@mindspring.com.

WILLIAMS, Betty; British peace campaigner; b 22 May 1943, Belfast; m 1st Ralph Williams 1961 (divorced); one s one d; m 2nd James T. Perkins 1982. *Education:* St Teresa's Primary School (Belfast). *Career:* Works as office receptionist; Co-Founder N Ireland Peace Movt (later renamed Community of the Peace People) 1976, Jt Leader 1976–78; Hon LL D (Yale); Hon D HUM LITT (Coll of Sienna Heights, MI)

1977; Nobel Peace Prize (with Mairead Corrigan-Maguire, qv) 1976; Carl von Ossietzky Medal for Courage, Berlin Section, Int League of Human Rights. *Leisure interest:* gardening. *Address:* POB 725, Valparaiso, FL 32580, USA.

WILLIAMS, Deniece; American soul and gospel singer; b 1951; m 2nd Brad Westering; two s by previous marriage. *Education:* Purdue Univ. *Career:* Grammy awards for Best Female Soul Gospel Vocal 1986, Best Group Gospel Performance 1986, Best Female Gospel Performance 1987. *Albums include:* This is Nicey, Hot on the Trail, I'm So Proud, Let's Hear it for the Boy, My Melody, Niecey, Special Love, Water Under the Bridge 1987, As Good as it Gets 1989, Greatest Gospel Hits 1995, Best of Deniece Williams 1996. *Address:* c/o General Talent International, 1700 Broadway, 10th Floor, New York, NY 10019, USA.

WILLIAMS, Elizabeth (see Williams, Betty).

WILLIAMS, Hilary Denise, B SC; British international organization executive; b 3 July 1949, London; d of Sydney and Joan Hamilton; m Andrew Williams 1974 (divorced); one s one d. *Education:* Mary Datchelor Girls' School and King's Coll (London). *Career:* Medical Librarian and Information Officer CIBA Foundation, London 1974–82; Admin Dept of Analytical Pharmacology, King's Coll, London 1984–86; Sec-Gen London Sports Medicine Inst, St Bartholomew's Hosp Medical Coll, London 1986–89; Exec Dir Int Diabetes Fed 1989. *Leisure interests:* travel, collecting embroidery. *Address:* International Diabetes Federation, 1 rue Defacqz, 1000 Brussels, Belgium. *Telephone:* (2) 538-55-11; *Fax:* (2) 538-51-14.

WILLIAMS, Lorraine Bernadine, LL B; Saint Lucia politician and attorney-general; b 20 May 1958, St Lucia; d of Nathalbert and Lucelta Husbands; m Basil Williams 1983; one s. *Education:* St Joseph's Convent and Advanced Level Coll (Castries) and Univ of the West Indies (Barbados). *Career:* Attorney-at-Law in pvt practice 1983–90; Magistrate, then Chief Magistrate 1990–92; Attorney-Gen and Minister of Legal Affairs and Women's Affairs 1992; Prin Del from St Lucia to Inter-American Comm on Women 1995; Degree of Excellence Award 1995. *Leisure interests:* interior decorating, reading, listening to music, chess, football. *Address:* Rodney Heights, Quarter of Gros Islet, POB 433, Castries, Saint Lucia (Home).

WILLIAMS, Maria Antoinette, B SC; Jamaican business executive; b 24 April 1951, Kingston; d of the late Wilfred and Elsie Lawrence; one s. *Education:* Univ of the W Indies. *Career:* Clerk Barclays Bank 1968–69; Accounts Clerk Air Jamaica 1969–75, Reservations Supervisor 1975–78, Man of Tariffs and Industry Affairs 1978–81, Sales Man for Jamaica and the Caribbean 1981–83, Special Asst to Dir N America 1983–84, Dir Marketing and Sales for the Caribbean 1984–85, Dir Marketing 1985–86, apptd Vice-Pres Marketing and Sales 1986. *Leisure interests:* needlework, reading, decorating, cricket, badminton, tennis. *Address:* Air Jamaica, 72 Harbour St, Kingston, Jamaica (Office); Stock Farm Rd, Golden Spring, Story Hill PO, St Andrew, Jamaica (Home).

WILLIAMS, Patricia; American professor of law and broadcaster; b 1952; one s (adopted). *Education:* Harvard Law School (MA). *Career:* Fmrly lawyer; currently Prof of Law Columbia Univ (New York); delivered Reith Lectures (first black woman), UK 1997. *Address:* Columbia University, Faculty of Law, Morningside Heights, New York, NY 10027, USA. *Telephone:* (212) 854-1754.

WILLIAMS, Serena; American tennis player; b Saginaw, Michigan; sister of Venus Williams (qv). *Career:* Finalist Roland Garros mixed doubles 1998; doubles winner (with Venus Williams) Oklahoma City 1998, French Open 1999, Hanover 1999, Wimbledon 2000; singles semi-finalist Sydney Open 1997, Chicago 1998; singles finalist Wimbledon 2000; winner US Open 1999, Paris Indoors 1999, Indian Wells 1999, LA 1999. *Address:* USTA, 70 W Red Oak Lane, White Plains, NY 10604, USA.

WILLIAMS, Venus; American tennis player; b 17 June, Lynwood, CA; sister of Serena Williams (qv). *Career:* Professional debut Bank of West Classic (Oakland, CA) 1994; Bausch & Lomb Championships 1996; winner numerous singles titles WTA Tour including Oklahoma City

1998, Lipton 1998, 1999, Hamburg 1999, Italian Open 1999, Grand Slam Cup 1998, Wimbledon 2000, 2001; four doubles titles (with Serena Williams) including French Open 1999, Hanover 1999; Tennis Magazine Most Impressive Newcomer 1997, Most Improved Player 1998. *Address:* USTA, 70 W Red Oak Lane, White Plains, NY 10604, USA.

WILLIAMS OF CROSBY, Baroness (Life Peer), cr 1993, of Stevenage in the County of Hertfordshire, **Shirley Williams,** PC, MA; British politician; b 27 July 1930, London; d of the late Sir George Catlin and Vera Brittain; m 1st Bernard Williams 1955 (divorced 1974); one d; m 2nd Richard Neustadt 1987; one step-d. *Education:* Summit School (MN, USA), St Paul's Girls' School, London, Somerville Coll (Oxford) and Columbia Univ (New York). *Career:* Gen Sec Fabian Soc 1960–64; MP (Lab) for Hitchin 1964–74, for Hertford and Stevenage 1974–79; Parl Pvt Sec to Minister of Health 1964–66; Parl Sec to Minister of Labour 1966–67; Minister of State, Dept of Educ and Science 1967–69; Minister of State, Home Office 1969–70; Opposition Spokesperson on Health and Social Security 1970–71, on Home Affairs 1971–73, on Prices and Consumer Affairs 1973–74; Sec of State for Prices and Consumer Protection 1974–76, for Educ and Science 1976–79; Paymaster-Gen 1976–79; mem Lab Party Nat Exec Cttee 1970–81; mem Council for Social Democracy 1981; left Labour Party 1981; Co-Founder SDP 1981, Pres 1982–88; MP (SDP) for Crosby 1981–83; mem Social and Lib Dem Party (Lib Dem) 1988–; Deputy Leader Lib Dem Party, House of Lords 1999–; Prof of Elective Politics John F. Kennedy School of Govt, Harvard Univ, MA, USA 1988–2000, Prof Emer 2000–; Visiting Fellow Nuffield Coll, Oxford 1967–75; Sr Research Fellow (part-time) Policy Research Inst 1979–85; Dir Turing Inst, Glasgow 1985–90, Learning by Experience Trust 1986–94, Project Liberty 1990–98; TV series Shirley Williams in Conversation 1979; BBC Radio series: Women in Parliament 1997; Trustee Twentieth Century Fund, USA; Chair European Job Creation Competition 1997; mem EU Comité des Sages 1995–96, Council Int Crisis Group 1998–; Fellow Inst of Politics, Harvard 1979–80 (mem Sr Advisory Council 1986–); Hon Fellow Somerville Coll, Oxford, Newnham Coll, Cambridge; Hon D ED (CNAA); Hon Dr of Political Econs (Louvain, Belgium, Radcliffe Coll, USA); Hon LL D (Leeds) 1979, (Southampton) 1981, (Ulster) 1997; Silver Medal, Royal Inst. *Publications:* Politics is for People 1981, A Job to Live 1985, Snakes and Ladders: a Diary of a Political Life 1996; pamphlets on EU, and econs of Cen Africa; articles and broadcasts. *Leisure interests:* riding, hill walking, music. *Address:* c/o Liberal Democrats, 4 Cowley St, London SW1P 3NB, UK; House of Lords, London SW1A 0PW, UK. *Telephone:* (20) 7219-5850; *Fax:* (20) 7219-1174; *E-mail:* williamss@parliament.uk.

WILLOUGHBY, (Helen) Lynette (Estelle), M SC; British lecturer in computing; b 18 July 1949, Yorks; d of Norman and Joan Willoughby. *Education:* Univs of Surrey and Bradford. *Career:* School teacher 1974–76; Medical Physics Technician 1977–81; tutor, women's workshop 1981–84; Univ Lecturer 1985–; mem Council Women's Eng Soc 1984–, Pres 1993–95; has given conf papers on women in eng and the electronics industry. *Leisure interests:* photography, art, archaeology, caving, walking. *Address:* 53 Gledhow Park Grove, Leeds LS7 4JW, UK. *Telephone:* (113) 262-2776; *E-mail:* l.willoughby@lmu.ac.uk.

WILSON, Ann D.; American rock singer; b 1950; d of John and Lou Wilson. *Education:* Cornish Allied Inst of Fine Arts (Seattle). *Career:* Lead singer Heart 1975–. *Recordings include:* Albums: Dreamboat Annie 1975, Little Queen 1977, Dog and Butterfly 1978, Audition 1982, Passionworks 1983, Heart 1985, Bad Animals 1987, Brigade 1990; Singles: Barracuda 1977, Straight On 1978, Even It Up 1980, This Man is Mine 1982, How Can I Refuse 1983, Almost Paradise 1984, These Dreams 1986, Nothin' at All 1986, Alone 1987, Who Will You Run To 1987, There's the Girl 1987, I Want You So Bad 1988, All I Want To Do is Make Love to You 1990, I Don't Want to Need You 1990, Stranded 1990. *Address:* 219 First Ave, N, Suite 333, Seattle, WA 98109, USA.

WILSON, Bertha, MA, LL B; Canadian former Supreme Court judge; b 18 Sept 1923, Kirkaldy, Scotland; d of Archibald Wernham and Christine Noble; m John Wilson 1945. *Education:* Univ of Aberdeen and Dalhousie Univ. *Career:* Called to the Bar, NS 1957, ON 1959; Assoc Osler, Hoskin and Harcourt 1958–68, Partner 1968–75; QC 1973; first woman Judge Canadian Court of Appeals, Ontario 1975–82, Supreme Court of Canada 1982–91, Canadian Perm Court of Arbitration 1984–90; Commr Royal Comm on Aboriginal Peoples 1991–; Chair Canadian Bar Asscns Task Force on Gender Equality in the Legal Profession 1991–; mem Bd of Dirs Canadian Centre for Philanthropy 1981–; mem Canadian Bar Asscn; Hon LL D (Dalhousie) 1980, (Queen's, Calgary) 1983, (Toronto) 1984, (Alberta) 1985, (York) 1986, (British Columbia) 1988, (Aberdeen) 1989, (Mount Allison, Carleton, Concordia, Victoria) 1991; Hon LHD (Mt St Vincent) 1984; Hon DCL (Windsor and W Ontario) 1985; Hon DHL (Chatham Coll, Pittsburg); Hon D UNIV (Ottawa) 1990. *Address:* 1403–1200 Rideau Terrace, Ottawa, ON K1M 0Z3, Canada.

WILSON, Blenda Jacqueline, MA, PH D; American university chancellor; b 28 Jan 1941, Woodbridge, NJ; d of Horace and Margaret (née Brogsdale) Wilson; m Louis Fair, Jr. *Education:* Cedar Crest Coll, Seton Hall Univ and Boston Coll. *Career:* Exec Dir Middx Co Econ Opportunities Corpn, New Brunswick 1966–69; Exec Asst to Pres, Rutgers Univ 1969–72; Sr Assoc Dean Grad School of Educ, Harvard Univ 1972–82; Vice-Pres Indiana Sector 1982–84; Exec Dir Colorado Comm on Higher Educ 1984–88; Chancellor Univ of Michigan 1988–92; Pres California State Univ at Northridge 1992–99, Nellie Mae Foundation, Braintree, MA 1999–; mem Asscn of Governing Bds, Educ Comm of the States, American Asscn of Higher Educ, Women Execs in State Govt, Int Women's Forum; Hon LHD (Cedar Crest) 1987, (Loretto Heights) 1988, (Detroit) 1989; Hon LL D (Rutgers) 1989, (E Michigan) 1990, (Cambridge Coll) 1991, (Schoolcraft Coll) 1992. *Address:* Nellie Mae Foundation, 50 Braintree Hill Park, Braintree, MA 02184-8724, USA. *Telephone:* (818) 885-1200.

WILSON, Clare Eleanor, M SC; Australian (b British) clinical psychologist; b 3 Aug 1947, Leeds; d of the late Charles Henry and Marion Joan Wilson; m Neil Murray Drew 1986; two d. *Education:* Leeds Girls' High School, City Univ (London) and Univ of Birmingham. *Career:* Lecturer in Psychology, Middx Hosp Medical School 1972–73; Psychologist Govt of Seychelles 1973–76; Sr Psychologist St Brendan's Hosp, Bermuda 1976–78; Sr Clinical Psychologist, Isle of Wight 1978–80; Head of Counselling Centre James Cook Univ of N Queensland 1980–89; Head of St Catherine's Coll, Univ of W Australia 1989–94; Manager Therapy Team Cambridge Pvt Hosp 1994–95; Manager Counselling Services, INDRAD 1995–99; Counsellor Palmeston Drug Research and Rehabilitation Centre 1995–; Deputy Head Univ Counselling Service, Curtin Univ (Perth) 1999–; mem Mental Health Tribunal Patient Review Cttee 1985–89, Parole Advisory Cttee Queensland Correctional Services Comm 1985–88. *Leisure interests:* theatre, music, running, outdoors, travel. *Address:* 36 Robinson St, Nedlands, WA 6009, Australia. *Telephone:* (9) 389-8671.

WILSON, Dierdre, MA, ED D; American dance instructor, director and choreographer; b 21 Feb 1945, La Mesa, CA; d of Joseph and Audrie (née Branin) Wilson; m Douglas Hammel 1978; two c. *Education:* Grossmont Coll, Antioch Univ and Washington State Univ. *Career:* Studied at Agnes Moorehead Actors' Workshop, Lee Strasberg Inst, Odyssey Improvisation Theatre, Theatre East Actors' Workshop, and American Conservatory Theatre; teacher numerous dance theatres; dance therapist and mental health counsellor; dance instructor and designer of Creative Arts for the Handicapped curriculum, Washington State Univ 1980, ballet instructor 1980, acting instructor 1982–83, mem Senate 1981; Founder, Dir and Admin Acad of Performing Arts, Pullman, WA 1986–; mem San Francisco Ballet; Soloist San Francisco Opera Co; consultant Washington Comm for the Humanities; mem American Guild of Musical Artists, Nat Asscn of Drama Therapists, American Asscn for Counselling Devt. *Publication:* Introduction to the Theatre for the Aged Disabled. *Address:* Academy of Performing Arts, W 106 Main, Pullman, WA 99163, USA.

WILSON, Jeanne Patricia Pauline; British writer; b 31 May 1920, London; d of Francis and the late Emily (née Williams) Staples; m Wilbert Smith-Wilson 1943; one s. *Education:* Privately. *Career:* Fmr nurse and teacher; mem jury nominating cands for Nobel Prize for Literature; mem UK Soc of Authors, Authors' Guild of America, Int PEN; Inst of Jamaica Centenary Medal 1980. *Publications:* No Justice in October, Legacy for Isabel, No Medicine for Murder, Model for Murder, Weep in the Sun, Troubled Heritage, Mulatto, The Golden Harlot, The House that Liked to Travel, Holiday with Guns, Flight from the Islands, Fettered Freedom. *Leisure interests:* swimming, theatre, reading, cooking. *Address:* 3 Vantage Point, POB 147, Red Hills PO, St Andrew, Jamaica. *Telephone:* 944-2622.

WILSON, Linda Smith, PH D; American university administrator and chemist; b 10 Nov 1936, Washington, DC; d of Fred M. and Virginia D. (née Thompson) Smith; m 1st Malcolm C. Whatley 1957 (divorced); one d; m 2nd Paul A. Wilson 1970; one step-d. *Education:* Tulane Univ and Univ of Wisconsin (Madison). *Career:* Asst Vice-Chancellor for Research Washington Univ, St Louis, MO 1968–74, Assoc Vice-Chancellor 1974–75; Assoc Vice-Chancellor for Research Univ of Illinois, Urbana 1975–85, Assoc Dean Grad Coll 1978–85; Vice-Pres for Research Univ of Michigan, Ann Arbor, MI 1985–89; Pres Radcliffe Coll, Cambridge, MA 1989–99, Pres Emer 1999; Chair Advisory Cttee Office of Science and Eng Personnel, Nat Research Council 1990–96; mem NIH Advisory Council on Research Resources 1978–82, Nat Comm on Research 1978–80, Dirs Advisory Council NSF 1980–89, Govt-Univ-Industry Research Roundtable (NAS) 1984–88, Inst of Medicine Council 1986–89, Inst of Medicine Cttee on Govt-Industry Collaboration in Research and Educ 1988–89, Advisory Comm on Science Educ 1990, Inst of Medicine Cttee on NIH Priority-Setting 1998–99; mem Bd of Dirs AAAS 1984–88, Michigan Materials Processing Inst 1985–89, Michigan Biotech Inst 1986–89, American Chemical Soc; Fellow AAAS; Overseer Museum of Science, Boston 1992–2001; Trustee Massachusetts Gen Hosp 1992–99 (Hon Trustee 1999–), Cttee on Econ Devt 1995–; Dir Citizens Financial Group 1996–99–, Inacom Corpn 1997–, ValueLine Inc 1998–2000, Myriad Genetics Inc 1999–, Internet Corpn for Assigned Names and Numbers (ICANN) 1998–; comms include studies on chem, science and research policy; hon degrees from Tulane Univ, Univ of Maryland; Distinguished Contribution to Research Admin Award, Soc of Research Admins; Distinguished Service Award, Univ of Illinois; Centennial Award for Outstanding Accomplishments, Newcomb Coll; Distinguished Service Award, Univ of Illinois; Distinguished Alumni Award, Univ of Wisconsin 1997; Endowed Chair for Dir of Radcliffe Public Policy Center 1999; Radcliffe Medal 1999; 7 book chapters, 10 journal articles, 6 maj reports, 4 commissioned studies, 12 papers on chem, science policy and research policy. *Leisure interests:* sailing, reading, music, woodland management and preservation. *Address:* POB 6, 79 Kelsey Drive, Walpole, ME 04573, USA. *Telephone:* (207) 563-6094; *Fax:* (207) 563-6794; *E-mail:* lwilson@free.midcoast.com.

WILSON, The Very Rev the Hon Lois Miriam, OC, DD, LL D, STD, DCL, D HUM LITT; Canadian ecclesiastic and senator; b 8 April 1927, Winnipeg, MB; d of Edwin Gardner Dunn Freeman and Ada Minnie Davis; m Roy Fyfe Wilson 1950; two s two d. *Education:* United Coll (now Univ of Winnipeg). *Career:* Ordained United Church of Canada 1965; Minister First Church United, Thunder Bay, ON 1965–69, Hamilton, ON 1969–78, Chalmers United Church, Kingston, ON 1978–80; Ontario Human Rights Officer 1974–75; Pres Canadian Council of Churches 1976–79; Moderator (first woman) United Church of Canada 1980–82; Dir Ecumenical Forum of Canada 1983–89; Pres World Council of Churches 1983–91; The United Church of Canada McGeachy Sr Scholar 1989–91; Vice-Pres Canadian Civil Liberties Asscn 1988–; Govt appointee to Environmental Assessment Panel reviewing nuclear waste disposal 1989–97; Senator 1998–; Canada's Special Envoy to Sudan 1999–; Chair Urban Rural Mission (Canada) 1990–95; Chancellor Lakehead Univ, Thunder Bay 1991–; Nat Pres UNIFEM 1993–95, Int Centre for Human Rights and Democratic Devt 1997–; mem Bd Amnesty Int 1978–88, Canadian Inst for Int Peace and Security 1984–89, Refugee Status Advisory Bd 1985–89, Canadian Asscn of Adult Educ 1987–90, Co-op Program in Int Devt, Univ of Toronto 1987–92, Public Review Bd, Canada 1989–, Bd of Regents (Victoria Univ) 1990–, Advisory Bd, Canadian Women's Studies Journal, York Univ, Toronto 1993–, Bd Centre for Study of Religions and Soc, Victoria Univ, BC 1993–; Monitor, El Salvador elections 1994; Keynote speaker Christian/Jewish Conf, Jerusalem 1994; 11 hon degrees in law and divinity; Pearson Peace Prize 1984; World Federalist Peace Prize 1984; Queen's Jubilee Medal; Order of Ontario 1991; Commemorative Medal of 125th Anniversary of Canadian Confed 1992. *Publications:* Like a Mighty River 1980, Turning the World Upside Down (memoir) 1989, Telling Her Story 1992, Miriam, Mary and Me 1992, Stories Seldom Told 1997, Nuclear

Waste – Exploring the Ethical Options 2000. *Leisure interests:* skiing, sailing, canoeing, reading. *Address:* The Senate, VB #807, Ottawa, ON K1A 0A4, Canada; 40 Glen Rd, Apt 310, Toronto, ON, M4W 2V1, Canada (Home). *Telephone:* (613) 992-7396 (Office); (416) 975-0395 (Home); *Fax:* (613) 9432-2269 (Office); (613) 975-0848 (Home); *E-mail:* wilsol@sen.parl.gc.ca (Office); *Internet:* www.sen.parl.gc.ca/lwilson (Office).

WILSON-BARNETT, Jenifer, BA, M SC, PH D; British professor of nursing; b 10 Aug 1944; adopted d of Edith M. Barnett and Barbara M. Wilson; m Michael Trimble 1975. *Education:* Chichester High School for Girls, St George's Hosp, Univs of Leicester and Edinburgh, and Guy's Hosp Medical School (London). *Career:* Nurse St George's Hosp 1966, Sister 1972–74; Researcher Guy's Hosp 1974–77; Lecturer in Nursing Chelsea Coll 1977, Sr Lecturer 1983, Reader and Head of Dept 1984; Prof and Head Dept of Nursing Studies, King's Coll, London 1986–, Fellow 1995, Head of Florence Nightingale School of Nursing and Midwifery 1999–; Fellow Royal Coll of Nursing 1984. *Publications:* Stress in Hospital: patients' psychological reactions to illness and health care 1979, Recovery From Illness (jtly) 1982, Patient Teaching 1983, Nursing Research: ten studies in patient care 1982, Nursing Issues and Research in Terminal Care 1988, Patient Problems: a research base for nursing care 1988, Direction in Nursing Research (jtly) 1989, Health Promotion and Nursing Research (jtly) 1993, Nursing Research in Cancer Care (jtly) 1995. *Leisure interests:* music, writing, shopping, skiing. *Address:* King's College London, Florence Nightingale School of Nursing and Midwifery, James Clerk Maxwell Building, London SE1 8WA, UK.

WILTON, Penelope; British actress; b 1947; m 1st Daniel Massey; m 2nd Ian Holm. *Career:* Has appeared in theatre, film and TV productions. *Plays include:* The Deep Blue Sea (Critics Circle Award), Screaming, Vita and Virginia, Landscape, Long Days Journey into Night, The Cherry Orchard; *TV appearances include:* The Secret Rapture, The Borrowers; *Film:* Laughterhouse (1984). *Leisure interest:* paintings. *Address:* c/o BBC, Broadcasting House, London W1A 1AA, UK. *Telephone:* (20) 7580-4468; *Fax:* (20) 7637-1630.

WILTSHIRE, Carolyn Margaret, BA; Australian civil servant and business executive; b 15 Nov 1950; d of H. and A. Brown; m Donald Wiltshire 1973; one d. *Education:* Univ of Queensland and Queensland Conservatorium of Music. *Career:* Project Officer Planning and Research, Dept of Overseas Trade, Canberra 1972–73, Dept of the Media, Sydney 1973–74; Exec Officer Recreation and Tourism Dept, Capital Territory 1974; Sr Exec Officer of Devt and Co-ordination, Australian Devt Assistance Bureau, Dept of Foreign Affairs 1975–78; Exec Sec and Prin Exec Officer, Office of Women's Affairs Nat Women's Advisory Council 1978–82; Dir Cultural Affairs Br, Dept of Home Affairs and the Environment 1982–83; apptd Asst Sec Bilateral Relations and Air Freight Br, Dept of Civil Aviation 1983; Sr Adviser on Int Aviation Policy and Prin Int Aviation Negotiator, Dept of Transport and Communications 1987–89; Man Dir Carolyn Wiltshire and Assocs Pty Ltd, Int Aviation, Tourism and Man Consultants 1989–; Del S Pacific Forum 1977; Del and Consultant ESCAP Round Table on the Participation of Women and their Emancipation Through the Application of Science and Tech to Devt 1979; Del World Conf UN Decade for Women 1980; mem Int Think-tank on Multilateral Aviation Liberalisation 1990–91. *Leisure interests:* writing poetry, music, surfing, landscaping, decorating, debating. *Address:* 24 La Perouse St, Griffith, ACT 2603, Australia.

WINBLAD, Ann, BA; American finance executive. *Education:* St Thomas Coll. *Career:* Co-Founder Open Systems Inc 1976–83; fmrly strategic planning consultant; partner Hummer Winblad Venture Partners 1989–. *Publication:* Object-Oriented Software (jtly) 1990. *Address:* Hummer Winblad Venture Partners, 2nd Floor, 2 South Park, San Francisco, CA 94107, USA.

WINDER, Anne; British broadcasting executive; b Burnham-on-Crouch, Essex; m 1985. *Education:* Ursuline Convent High School (Brentwood). *Career:* Trainee BBC Journalists Training Scheme 1968–70; Scriptwriter and Producer BBC Current Affairs 1970–74, Arts Progs and Documentaries 1974–86, Ed Kaleidoscope (BBC Radio 4) 1986, Head of Arts, Science and Features, BBC Radio and Chair

Equal Opportunities Group 1988–. *Leisure interest:* sailing. *Address:* BBC, Broadcasting House, London W1A 1AA, UK. *Telephone:* (20) 7765-4809.

WINFREY, Oprah, BA; American television presenter, actress and producer; b 29 Jan 1954, Kosciusko, MS; d of Vernon Winfrey and Vernita Lee. *Education:* Tennessee State Univ. *Career:* Worked for WVOL radio, Nashville, TN while still at school, subsequently as Reporter/Anchor, WTVF-TV, Nashville; joined WJZ-TV News, Baltimore, MD as Co-Anchor 1976, became Co-Host, People Are Talking 1978; joined WLS-TV, Chicago as Host of AM Chicago, subsequently renamed The Oprah Winfrey Show 1984–99; Founder, Propr and Producer Harpo Productions Inc 1986–; Founder, Editorial Dir The Oprah Magazines 2000–; partner Oxygen Media 2000–; numerous awards including Nat Daytime Emmy Award 1987, Broadcaster of the Year Award (Int Radio and Television Soc) 1988, Lifetime Achievement Award, Nat Acad of TV Arts and Sciences 1998. *Films include:* The Color Purple (Acad Award nomination) 1985, Native Son 1986, Throw Momma From the Train 1988, Listen Up: The Lives of Quincy Jones 1990, Beloved 1998; *TV appearances include:* Pee-wee's Playhouse Christmas Special, The Women of Brewster Place (also co-exec producer) 1989, Brewster Place (also exec producer), The Oprah Winfrey Show; *Publications:* Oprah (autobiog) 1993, In the Kitchen with Rosie 1996, Make the Connection (jtly) 1996. *Address:* Harpo Productions, 110 N Carpenter St, Chicago, IL 60607, USA.

WINGER, Debra; American actress; b 16 May 1955, Cleveland, OH; d of Robert and Ruth Winger; m Timothy Hutton 1986 (divorced 1990); one s. *Education:* California State Univ at Northridge. *Career:* Served with Israeli army 1972; professional debut in Wonder Woman TV series 1976–77. *Films include:* Thank God It's Friday 1978, French Postcards 1979, Urban Cowboy 1980, Cannery Row 1982, An Officer and a Gentleman 1982, Terms of Endearment 1983, Mike's Murder 1984, Legal Eagles 1986, Black Widow 1987, Made in Heaven 1987, Betrayed 1988, The Barber of Siberia, The Sheltering Sky 1990, Everybody Wins 1991, Leap of Faith 1992, Shadowlands 1993, A Dangerous Woman 1993, Forget Paris 1995. *Address:* c/o CAA, 9830 Wilshire Blvd, Beverly Hills, CA 90212, USA.

WINSLET, Kate; British actress; b 5 Oct 1975, Reading; d of Roger and Sally Winslet; m Jim Threapleton 1998; one d. *Education:* Theatre School (Maidenhead, Berks). *Career:* Film actress. *Films include:* A Kid in King Arthur's Court, Heavenly Creatures (Best Foreign Actress NZ Film and TV Critics' Awards, Best Actress London Film Critics' Circle Awards) 1994, Sense and Sensibility (Acad Award nomination, Best Supporting Actress Screen Actors' Guild and BAFTA Award) 1996, Jude 1996, Hamlet (Best British Actress Empire Magazine Awards) 1996, Titanic 1997 (Best European Actress, European Film Acad 1998, Film Actress of the Year, Variety Club of GB 1998), Hideous Kinky 1997, Holy Smoke 1998, Quills 1999, Enigma 2000; *TV includes:* Dark Season, Get Back, Casualty, Anglo-Saxon Attitudes; *Plays include:* What the Butler Saw. *Address:* c/o Dallas Smith, PFD, Drury House, 34-43 Russell St, London WC2B 5HA. *Telephone:* (20) 7344-1010.

WINTERS, Shelley; American actress; b 18 Aug 1922, St Louis, MO; m 1st Vittorio Gassmann (divorced); one d; m 2nd Anthony Franciosa 1957 (divorced 1960). *Education:* Wayne State Univ. *Career:* Numerous appearances on stage, in films and on TV; Emmy Award for Best Actress 1964, Monte Carlo Golden Nymph Award 1964; Int Television Award, Cannes Film Festival, France 1965. *Plays include:* A Hatful of Rain 1955, Girls of Summer 1957, The Night of the Iguana, Cages, Who's Afraid of Virginia Woolf?, Minnie's Boys, Marlon Brando: The Wild One 1996; *Films include:* A Thousand and One Nights, A Place in the Sun, Playgirl, Executive Suite, The Diary of Anne Frank (Acad Award for Best Supporting Actress 1959) 1958, Let No Man Write My Epitaph, Lolita 1962, Wives and Lovers 1963, The Balcony 1964, A House is Not a Home 1964, A Patch of Blue (Acad Award for Best Supporting Actress) 1965, Time of Indifference 1965, Alfie 1965, The Moving Target 1965, The Poseidon Adventure 1972, Cleopatra Jones 1973, Blume in Love 1974, Whoever Slew Auntie Roo 1974, Heaven Save Us From Our Friends 1975, Diamonds 1975, That Lucky Touch 1975, Next Stop Greenwich Village 1976, The Tenant 1976, Pete's Dragon 1977, The Magician 1979, King of the Gypsies 1979, The

Visitor 1980, Over the Brooklyn Bridge 1983, The Delta Force 1985, Awakenings 1990, Stepping Out 1991, The Pickle, Portrait of a Lady 1996, Gideon's Webb 1998, La Bamba 1999; *TV appearances include:* Two is the Number (Emmy Award for Best Actress) 1964, The Vamp 1972–73, Roseanne (series); *Publications include:* Shelley also Known as Shirley (autobiog), One Night Stands of a Noisy Passenger (play) 1971, Shelley II: The Middle of My Century (autobiog) 1989. *Address:* c/o Jack Gilliardi, ICM, 8942 Wilshire Blvd, Beverly Hills, CA 90211, USA.

WINTERSON, Jeanette, BA; British writer; b 27 Aug 1959, Manchester, Lancs; adopted; partner Margaret Reynolds. *Education:* Accrington Girls' High School (Lancs) and St Catherine's Coll (Oxford). *Career:* Int Fiction Prize, Letteratura Festivale (Italy) 1999. *Publications:* Fiction: Oranges Are Not The Only Fruit (Whitbread Prize) 1985, Boating for Beginners (comic book) 1985, The Passion (Llewellyn Rhys Prize) 1987, Sexing the Cherry (E. M. Forster Award) 1989, Written on the Body 1992, Art and Lies 1994, Gut Symmetries 1997, The World and Other Places (short stories) 1998, The.PowerBook 2000, The King of Capri (for children) 2001; Essays: Art Objects 1995; Screenplays: Oranges Are Not The Only Fruit (for BBC TV, BAFTA Best Drama Award, FIPA d'Argent Award, Cannes Film Festival, France, Golden Gate Award, San Francisco Int Film Festival, CA, USA) 1991, Great Moments in Aviation (for BBC TV) 1995. *Leisure interests:* opera, ballet, champagne, horses, hens. *Address:* c/o ICM, 40 W 57 St, New York, NY 10019, USA; c/o Jonathan Cape Ltd, 20 Vauxhall Bridge Rd, London SW1V 2SA, UK. *E-mail:* info@jeanettewinterson.com; *Internet:* www.jeanettewinterson.com.

WINTERTON, Ann (Jane Ann); British politician; b 6 March 1941; d of Joseph and Ellen Hodgson; m Nicholas Winterton 1960; two s one d. *Education:* Erdington Grammar School for Girls. *Career:* Mem W Midlands Cons Women's Advisory Cttee 1969–71; Cons MP for Congleton 1983–; mem Select Cttee Agric, Social Security 2000; Sec All-Party Pro-Life Group; Jt Treas All-Party Taiwan Group 1997; Jt Sec All-Party Danish Group 2000; Sec All-Party St Helena Group 2000, Indonesia Group 2001; Vice Chair All-Party Finnish Group 2001; Parl Rep Hairdressing Council. *Leisure interests:* hunting, riding, music, tennis, theatre, cinema, skiing. *Address:* House of Commons, London SW1A 0AA, UK (Office); Whitehall Farm, Newbold Astbury, Congleton, Cheshire, UK (Home). *Telephone:* (20) 7219-3585 (Office); (1260) 278866 (Home); *Fax:* (1260) 271212 (Home).

WINTHER, Eva; Swedish politician; b 3 Aug 1921, Stockholm; d of Martin and Gunhild F. (née Aschan) Fornander; m Arne Winther 1946; two d one s. *Education:* Red Cross School for Nurses. *Career:* Qualified as children's nurse 1945; mem Exec, Liberal Party 1971–81; mem Kiruna Municipal Council and Social Welfare Cttee 1967–76; mem Norrbotten Co Council 1976–78, Chair Norrbotten Constituency Asscn until 1978; mem Riksdag (Parl) 1976–82; Minister for Immigrant Affairs and Questions concerning Equality between Men and Women in Labour Ministry 1978–79; Chair Standing Cttee on Labour Market Affairs 1978, mem 1979–82; mem Halland County Council 1985–91; currently working on Questions concerning Pensioners; Kerslin Hesselgrem Medal 1992; Karl Staaff Gold Medal 1993. *Leisure interests:* art, fiction, poetry, outdoor life. *Address:* Box 10160, 43422 Kungsbacka, Sweden. *Telephone:* (300) 126 98.

WINTOUR, Anna; British journalist; b 3 Nov 1949; d of the late Charles Wintour; m David Shaffer 1984; one s one d. *Education:* Queen's Coll School (London) and N London Collegiate School. *Career:* Deputy Fashion Ed Harpers & Queen 1970–76, Harper's Bazaar, New York 1976–77; Fashion and Beauty Ed Viva 1977–78; contributing Ed for fashion and style Savvy Magazine 1980–81; Sr Ed New York Magazine 1981–83; Creative Dir US Vogue 1983–86; Ed-in-Chief Vogue 1986–87; Ed House & Garden, New York 1987–88; Ed US Vogue 1988–. *Address:* Condé Nast Bldg, 350 Madison Ave, New York, NY 10017, USA; 25 Ladbroke Square, London W11, UK.

WIRTZ, Tiny; German pianist. *Career:* Has performed with major orchestras and conductors and given concerts in Europe, America and Asia; has held int Master Classes; currently Prof, Head Piano Master Class Staatliche Hochschule für Musik, Cologne; has made several recordings and radio appearances. *Leisure interests:* modern art, literature. *Address:* Belvederestr 34, 50933 Cologne, Germany. *Telephone:* (221) 4971826; *Fax:* (221) 4971826.

WISEMAN, Debbie, B MUS; British composer and conductor; b 10 May 1963, London; d of Paul and Barbara Wiseman; m Tony Wharmby 1987. *Education:* Guildhall School of Music and Drama (London). *Career:* Studied piano and composition 1981–84; Composer and Conductor of music for film and TV productions 1989–, including The Dying of the Light, Shrinks (Best Original TV Theme Music, Silents to Satellite Awards 1991), The Good Guys (TV Theme Music of the Year, TV and Radio Industries Club Awards 1993), It Might be You, A Week in Politics, The Upper Hand, The Churchills, Children's Hospital, Tom and Viv 1994, Death of Yugoslavia (Best Commissioned Score nomination, Ivor Novello Awards 1995), Haunted 1995, Wilde 1998, Othello, Warriors (Royal TV Soc Award) 2000; nominated for the Rank Film Labs Award for Creative Originality, Women in Film and TV Awards 1994. *Address:* c/o Roz Colls, Music Matters International, Crest House, 102-104 Church Rd, Teddington, Middx TW11 8PY, UK. *Telephone:* (20) 8979-4580; *Fax:* (20) 8979-4590; *Internet:* www.debbiewiseman.co.uk.

WISTI, Helle; Danish foundation official; b (Ahlefeldt Laurvig) 4 Feb 1923, Funen; m Folmer Wisti 1955. *Career:* Mem staff Int Refugee Org, Copenhagen 1949–52; mem staff Tours and Confs Dept, Danish Inst 1953–84; Sec Foundation for Int Understanding 1984–. *Address:* c/o Foundation for International Understanding, Kultorvet 2, POB 85, 1003 Copenhagen K, Denmark.

WITHERS, Googie, AO, CBE; British actress; b 12 March 1917, Karachi, India (now Pakistan); d of the late Capt E. C. Withers and Lizette van Wageningen; m John McCallum 1948; two d one s. *Education:* Fredville Park (Kent, UK) and School of the Holy Family (London, UK). *Career:* Actress and dancer. *Plays include:* Private Lives, The Deep Blue Sea, Janus, Much Ado About Nothing 1958, Hamlet 1958, The Complaisant Lover 1962, Exit the King 1963, Getting Married 1967, The Cherry Orchard, An Ideal Husband 1972, The Circle 1976, The Importance of Being Earnest 1979, Time and the Conways 1983, The School for Scandal 1984, Ring Round the Moon 1988, The Cocktail Hour 1989–90, High Spirits 1991, 1993, On Golden Pond 1992, The Chalk Garden 1995, Lady Windermere's Fan; *Films include;* One of Our Aircraft is Missing, The Silver Fleet, It Always Rains on Sunday, Nickel Queen, White Corridors, Country Life 1994, Shine 1996; *TV appearances include:* The Public Prosecutor, Amphitryon 38, The Deep Blue Sea (Best Actress of the Year) 1954, Last Year's Confetti 1971, Within These Walls (Best Actress of the Year 1974) 1974–76, Time After Time (ACE Best Actress Award 1988) 1985, Hotel du Lac 1985, Northanger Abbey 1986, Ending Up 1989. *Leisure interests:* reading, decorating, reading, travel. *Address:* 1740 Pittwater Rd, Bay View, Sydney, NSW 2104, Australia. *Telephone:* (2) 9997-6879; *Fax:* (2) 9999-0841.

WITHROW, Mary Ellen; American politician and federal official; b 2 Oct 1930, Marion, OH; d of Clyde Welsh and Mildred (née Stump) Hinamon; m Norman David Withrow 1948; four d. *Education:* Marion Harding High School. *Career:* Dir of Safety Programs American Red Cross 1968–72; mem Elgin Local Bd of Educ, Marion 1969–72, Pres 1972; Deputy Registrar State of Ohio 1972–75; Deputy Co Auditor, Marion Co 1975–77; Treas Marion Co 1977–83, Treas State of Ohio 1983–94; US Treas, Dept of the Treasury 1994–; Chair Ohio State Bd Deposits 1983–; mem Anthony Comm on Public Finance, Democratic Nat Cttee, Exec Cttee Women's Cttee; mem Women Execs in State Govt, League of Women Voters, Fed of Democratic Women, Metropolitan Women's Center, Nat Asscn of State Treas (Pres 1992, Jesse Unruh Award 1993, Chair Long-Range Planning Comm, mem Exec Comm), Nat Asscn of State Auditors, Comptrollers and Treas (Pres 1990), Exec Council of State Govts, Int Affairs Cttee; Small Business Admin Advocate of the Year 1988; named Most Valuable State Public Official, City and State Magazine 1990; Donald L. Scantlebury Memorial Award 1992; Women of Achievement Award, YWCA of Metropolitan Columbus 1993. *Leisure interests:* reading, gardening, sewing. *Address:* Department of the Treasury, 1500 Pennsylvania Ave, NW, Rm 2134, Washington, DC 20220, USA (Office).

WITT, Katarina; German figure-skater; b 3 Dec 1965, Staaken; d of Manfred and Käte Witt. *Career:* European Champion Figure-Skater 1983–88, World Champion 1984, 1985, 1987, 1988; Gold Medallist, Olympic Games, Sarajevo, Yugoslavia 1984, Calgary, Canada 1988; subject of numerous TV programmes 1988–. *Productions include:* Carmen on Ice (Emmy Award for Outstanding Performance) 1990, The Ice Princess (TV film) 1995. *Address:* c/o Arts und Promotion Organisation GmbH, Berger Str 295, 60385 Frankfurt am Main, Germany.

WITTE, Marlys, MD; American medical practitioner and organization executive; b 9 Jan 1943, New York; m Charles L. Witte 1956; three c. *Education:* Barnard Coll (New York) and New York Univ. *Career:* Medical posts Chapel Hill, NC 1960–61, New York Univ Hosp 1964–65; mem staff St Louis City Hosp, MO 1965–69, Dir Emergency and Admitting Dept 1966–67; mem Medical and Surgery Depts Veterans' Admin Hosp, Tucson, AZ 1969–; educational posts held at various univs 1964–71; Surgeon in Lymphology 1971–; Program Dir Clinical Research Unit, Univ of Arizona 1972–80, Assoc Prof of Surgery 1972–77, Prof 1977–; Sec-Gen Int Soc of Lymphology. *Address:* University of Arizona, Int Soc of Lymphology, Dept of Surgery, Rm 4406, College of Medicine, 1501 N Campbell Ave, Tucson, AZ 85724, USA. *Telephone:* (602) 626-6118; *Fax:* (602) 626-4884.

WITTIG-TERHARDT, Margret Hildegard Theresia; German broadcasting executive; b 17 Sept 1934, Rhede; m Ejnar Wittig 1969. *Education:* Studied Law in Bonn, Freiburg, Münster and Berlin. *Career:* Lawyer, Freiburg 1962; Asst Legal Adviser Süddeutscher Rundfunk, Finance Dir and Legal Adviser Süddeutscher Rundfunk Inst of Public Law, Stuttgart 1990–; mem several admin and supervisory bds and Chair several comms. *Leisure interests:* literature, theatre, ballet, travel, sailing. *Address:* Straußweg 44, 7000 Stuttgart, 1, Germany.

WOHMANN, Gabriele; German writer; b 21 May 1932, Darmstadt; d of Paul and Luise (née Lettermann) Guyot; m Reiner Wohmann 1953. *Education:* Univ of Frankfurt/Main. *Career:* Teacher 1953–56; Writer-in-Residence Gutenberg-Museum, Mainz (Literature Prize Zweites Deutsches Fernsehen ZDF/Mainz) 1984; mem Berlin Akademie der Künste, Deutsche Akademie für Sprache und Dichtung; Hon Fellow American Asscn of Teachers of German 1994; awards include Bremen Literature Prize 1971, Bundesverdienstkreuz (First Class) 1980, Deutsches Schallplattenpreis 1981, J. H. Merck Honour (Darmstadt) 1982, Adenauerpreis 1994. *Publications include:* Novels: Jetzt und nie 1958, Abschied für länger 1965, Ernste Absicht 1970, Paulinchen war allein zu Haus 1974 (also TV play 1981), Ausflug mit der Mutter 1976, Ach wie gut, daß niemand weiß 1980, Das Glücksspiel 1981, Der Flötenton 1987, Bitte nicht sterben 1993, Das Handicap 1996; Short stories: Mit einem Messer 1958, Trinken ist das Herrlichste 1963, Gegenangriff 1972, Dorothea Wörth 1975, Alles zu seiner Zeit 1976, Streit 1978, Wir sind eine Familie 1980, Stolze Zeiten 1981, Einsamkeit 1982, Der Kirschbaum 1984, Ein russischer Sommer 1988, Kassensturz 1989, Das Salz, bitte! 1992, Die Schönste im ganzen Land 1995; Poetry: Grund zur Aufregung 1978, Komm lieber Mai 1981, Passau-Gleis 3 1984, Das könnte icht sein 1989; Radio plays: Komm Donnerstag 1964, Norwegian Wood 1967, Kurerfolg 1970, Tod in Basel 1972, Wanda Lords Gespenster 1978, Ein gehorsamer Diener 1987, Es geht mir gut, ihr Kinder 1988, Drück mir die Daumen 1991, Der Mann am Fenster 1994, Besser als Liegen ist tot sein 1996; TV plays: Große Liebe 1966, Die Witwen 1972, Heiratskandidaten 1975, Unterweg 1985, Schreiben müssen 1990. *Address:* Erbacher Str 76A, Park Rosenhöhe, 64287 Darmstadt, Germany. *Telephone:* (6151) 46801.

WOLF, Christa; German writer; b 18 March 1929, Landsberg/Warthe, fmr GDR. *Education:* In Jena and Leipzig. *Career:* Fmr mem, GDR CP, resigned 1989; Heinrich-Mann Prize 1963; Nationalpreis für Kunst und Literatur (GDR) 1964; Georg-Büchner Prize, Deutsche Akademie der Sprache und Dichtung 1980. *Publications include:* Der geteilte Himmel, Unter den Linden, Moskauer Novelle 1961, Nachdenken über Christa T. 1968, Kein Ort. Nirgends 1979, Kassandra 1983, Störfall 1987, What Remains (short story) 1990, Medea: Stimmen 1996, Hierzulande, Andernorts 2000; several collections of short stories.

WOLF, Naomi, BA; American writer and feminist; b 12 Nov 1962, San Francisco, CA; d of Leonard and Deborah Wolf; m David Shipley 1993. *Education:* Yale Univ (CT). *Career:* Rhodes Scholar 1986. *Publications include:* The Beauty Myth: How Images of Beauty Are Used Against Women 1990, Fire With Fire: The New Female Power and How It Will Change the 21st Century 1993. *Address:* c/o Royce Carlton Inc, 866, UN Plaza, New York, NY 10017, USA; c/o John Brockman Associates Inc, 2307 Broadway, New York, NY 10024, USA.

WOLF, Ulrike; German television journalist; b 8 Sept 1944, Bautzen (Saxony); two s one d. *Education:* Journalism coll (Munich). *Career:* Training with ZDF and ARD broadcasting cos; Ed Constanze magazine 1966–67; mem editorial staff Tagesschau news programme 1967–71; freelance journalist; mem staff ARD-aktuell 1977; Head of Editorial Staff NDR-Redaktion Aktuelles 1982; Co-Presenter Tagesthemen news programme, ARD 1985; Chief Ed NDR Fernsehen TV co 1987; apptd Chair Bd of Dirs Mitteldeutscher Rundfunk broadcasting co, Leipzig 1991, Dir MDR Landesfunkhaus Sachsen; Deputy Chair CDU faction, Elmsbüttel City Council; Silberne Kamera award 1987. *Address:* c/o MDR, Landesfunkhaus Sachsen, St Petersburger Str 15, 01069 Dresden, Germany. *Telephone:* (351) 846-3500.

WOLFF, Sidney Carne, BA, PH D; American astronomer; b 6 June 1941, Sioux City, IA; d of George and Ethel (née Smith) Carne; m Richard Wolff 1962. *Education:* Carleton Coll and Univ of California at Berkeley. *Career:* Research Fellow Licks Observatory, Santa Cruz 1969; Asst Astronomer Univ of Hawaii 1967–71, Assoc Astronomer 1971–76; Astronomer and Assoc Dir Inst of Astronomy, Honolulu 1976–83, Acting Dir 1983–84; Dir Kitt Peak Nat Observatory, Tucson, AZ 1984–87, Nat Optical Astronomy Observatories 1987–2000, Gemini 8-m telescopes project 1992–94; Trustee Carleton Coll 1989–; mem Astronomy Soc of the Pacific, American Astronomical Soc (Pres 1992–94), Int Astronomical Union; Hon D SC (Carleton) 1985. *Publications:* The A-Type Stars—Problems and Perspectives 1983, Exploration of the Universe (jtly) 1987, Realm of the Universe 1988, Frontiers of Astronomy 1990; numerous contribs to scientific journals. *Address:* National Optical Astronomy Observatory, 950 N Cherry Ave, POB 26732, Tucson, AZ 85719, USA.

WOLL, Erna (Ernestine); German composer and lecturer in music; b 23 March 1917; d of Karl and Ann (née Illig) Woll. *Education:* St Ingbert School (Heidelberg), Musikhochschule (Heidelberg, Munich and Cologne) and Univs of Heidelberg, Munich and Würzburg. *Career:* Choirmistress 1938–40; choirmistress and teacher, Munich, Cologne, Speyer 1941–50; teacher of music, Weißenhorn 1950–62; Lecturer in Music Pädagogische Hochschule, Augsburg and Univ of Augsburg 1962–72; Hon Prof Univs of Munich and Augsburg 1968–; freelance composer 1972–; wrote six books on teaching music 1968–84, and two books about herself 1985, 1987; numerous recordings 1966–90; awarded prizes for compositions 1961, 1963, 1972, 1974, 1975. *Compositions include:* Süßes Saitenspiel, Ballade vom Clown, Requiem für Lebende, Martin Luther: Ich glaube, Augsburger Kyrie, Sola gratia, Über die Schmerzgrenze; other songs and compositions for choir, orchestra, organ, etc. *Leisure interests:* reading theological and philosophical literature and biographies, novels and poetry. *Address:* E.-M.-Arndt-Str 32 1/2, 86167 Augsburg, Germany. *Telephone:* (821) 705292.

WOLLENBERGER, Vera Cornelia; German politician; b 4 May 1952, Sondershausen, Thuringia, fmr GDR; d of Franz and Ursula Lengsfeld; three s. *Education:* Secondary school (Berlin), Karl-Marx-Univ (Leipzig), Humboldt Univ zu Berlin and Univ of Cambridge (UK). *Career:* Scientific Assoc Akad der Wissenschaften, fmr GDR 1975–80; joined SED (Socialist Unity Party) 1975, expelled from party because of public statement against the stationing of nuclear weapons in the GDR 1983; Ed Neues Leben publishing co 1981–83; Co-Founder several peace and ecological groups 1981–87; banned from work by govt ruling 1983; worked as a piarist and translator Urania-Verlag, Leipzig; arrested and accused of conspiracy and deported to UK 1988; returned to GDR 1989; joined Die Grünen (Green Party) 1989; mem Volkskammer (People's Chamber, Parl of the fmr GDR) March–Oct 1990; after German reunification elected to Bundestag (Parl, Die Grünen) from Thuringia party list 1990, mem Defence Cttee; Aachener Friedenspreis (peace prize) 1990. *Leisure interests:* opera, gardening.

Address: Bundeshaus, Hochhaus Tulpenfeld, 5300 Bonn 1, Germany (Office); Am Amalienpark 2, 0-1100 Berlin, Germany (Home). *Telephone:* (228) 169145 (Office); *Fax:* (228) 1686701 (Office).

WONFOR, Andrea Jean, BA; British broadcasting executive; b 31 July 1944; d of George Duncan and Audrey Joan Player; m 1st Patrick Masefield 1967 (divorced 1974); m 2nd Geoffrey Wonfor 1974; two d. *Education:* Simon Langton Girls' School (Canterbury) and New Hall (Cambridge). *Career:* Trainee Granada TV 1966–67; Researcher Tyne Tees TV 1967–73, Dir/Producer 1973–76, Head Youth Dept 1976–82, Dir of Programmes 1982–87; Man Dir Zenith North Ltd 1988–90; Deputy Dir of Programmes Channel Four TV 1989, Controller Arts and Entertainment 1990–93, Deputy Dir of Programmes 1993; Dir of Programmes Granada TV 1993–94, Jt Man Dir 1994–2000, Exec Chair Granada Creative 2000–; mem Bd of Govs BFI 1989–94; Fellow Royal Television Soc 1991. *Leisure interests:* music, reading. *Address:* Fell Pasture, Ingoe, Matfen, Northumberland NE20 0SP, UK. *Telephone:* (1661) 886487.

WONG, Elizabeth, BA, DIP ED; New Zealand politician and writer; b 15 Sept 1937, Shanghai, China (now People's Repub of China); d of the late Sam and Josephine Chien; m Edwin Wong 1959; two c. *Education:* Univ of Hong Kong, New Zealand Staff Coll (Levine) and Harvard Business School (USA). *Career:* Admin Officer 1969, 1975, 1978, 1982, 1987; Admin Asst Social Welfare Dept, Hong Kong 1970, apptd Dir of Social Welfare 1987, Sec for Health and Welfare 1990, now retired; mem Legis Council; Asst Financial Sec 1973–75, 1977; Commr for Recreation and Culture 1982, Deputy Sec (Municipal Services Br) 1986; Deputy Sec for Home Affairs 1983–84; Deputy Commr Assessment Office 1984; Deputy Sec Acad for Performing Arts (Municipal Services Br) 1985–86; JP 1982; mem Soc of Authors (UK); Imperial Service Order 1989. *Publications:* Cat-Street Morality 1967, The Man Who Was 1967, The Street Musician 1968, The Village Negotiator 1982. *Leisure interests:* music, swimming. *Address:* Government Secretariat, Health and Welfare Branch, Government Offices, Lower Alberta Rd, Hong Kong, Special Administrative Region, People's Republic of China. *Telephone:* 8102550; *Fax:* 8400467.

WONG YICK MING, Rosanna; Chinese administrator and official; b 15 Aug 1952, Hong Kong. *Education:* St Stephen's Girls' School, Univ of Hong Kong, Univ of Toronto (Canada), LSE (UK), Chinese Univ of Hong Kong and Univ of California at Davis (USA). *Career:* Exec Dir Hong Kong Fed of Youth Groups; Chair Hong Kong Housing Authority, Complaints Cttee of Hong Kong Ind Comm Against Corruption, Children's Thalassaemia Foundation, Social Welfare Advisory Cttee 1988–91, Comm on Youth 1990–91, Police Complaints Cttee 1993; mem Legis Council 1985–91, Exec Council 1988–91, 1992–97, Exec Council of Hong Kong Special Admin Region July 1997–; mem Co-ordinating Cttee for Children and Youth at Risk, Exec Cttee Hong Kong Council of Social Service, Bd World Vision Hong Kong; Patron Mother's Choice, Children's Kidney Trust Fund; Hon Fellow Hong Kong Inst of Housing 1994; Hon mem Chartered Inst of Housing 1994. *Address:* Executive Council Secretariat, First Floor, Main Wing, Central Government Offices, Central, Hong Kong Special Administrative Region, People's Republic of China.

WONGWANTANEE, Lucksmee Ongkasuwan, BA, MBA; Thai finance executive; b 18 June 1940, Chiengrai; d of Him and Kao Ongkasuwan; m Pirin Wongwantanee 1974; two c. *Education:* Thammasat and Loyola Univs (USA). *Career:* Accountant Foreign Exchange Dept, Wattana Wittaya Acad 1965–71, Banque d'Indochine, Singapore and Thailand 1973–74, Bangkok Metropolitan Bank 1974–75; Pre-auditor Commercial Motor Co Ltd, Bangkok 1976, Accountant and Finance Man 1977–82, Controlling Dir 1983–88; Internal Auditor Commercial Trust Co Ltd 1980–82, Asst Man Dir 1982–83; apptd Vice-Pres Thai Financial Syndicate Ltd 1988. *Address:* Thai Financial Syndicate Ltd, 575 Yaowaraj Rd, Bangkok 10100, Thailand (Office); 20/71 Laaprao 87, Bangkapi, Bangkok 10310, Thailand (Home).

WOOD, Anne, CBE; British television producer; b 18 Dec 1937, Spennymoor, Co Durham; d of Jack and Eleanor (née Thomson) Savage; m Barrie Wood 1959; one s one d. *Education:* Alderman Wraith Grammar School and Bingley Teachers' Training Coll (W Yorks). *Career:* Teacher of English Language and Literature 1960s; f Books For

Your Children magazine; co-creator and producer TV programmes The Book Tower 1979, Ragdolly Anna; Head Children's Programmes TV AM (ITV) 1982–84; f Ragdoll Ltd (TV production co) 1984, Creative Dir 1984–; creator (with Robin Stevens) Pob, Rosie and Jim, Tots TV, Brum, Open a Door, Teletubbies (shown in 120 countries worldwide); Eleanor Farjeon Award for Services to Children's Books 1969, Ronald Politzer Award 1974; for The Book Tower: BAFTA 1979, 1982, Prix Jeunesse 1980; for Tots TV: Prix Jeunesse 1996, BAFTA 1996, 1997; Baird Medal, Royal TV Soc 1997; numerous awards for Teletubbies including Grand Prize, Winner Pre-School Educ Category, Prize Int Contest (Japan) 1997, Children's BAFTA for Best Pre-School Programme 1998, Indies Nickleodeon UK Children's Award 1999, five awards at Int Licensing Industry Merchandisers' Asscn 1999; Veuve Clicquot Business Woman of the Year Award 1999; BBC Audiocall Children's Award 2000; BAFTA Special Award for Outstanding Contrib in Children's TV and Film 2000; Fellow of the Royal TV Soc. *Address:* Ragdoll Ltd, Russell House, Ely St, Stratford-Upon-Avon CV37 6LW, UK. *Telephone:* (1789) 404100; *Fax:* (1789) 404136; *Internet:* www.ragdoll.co.uk.

WOOD, Sharon Adele; Canadian mountaineer; b 18 May 1957, Halifax, NS; d of Stanley C. and Peggy Jean (née White) Wood; m Christopher Jon Stethem 1988; two s. *Education:* High School (Vancouver). *Career:* Began rock-climbing 1973; Climbing Instructor and Mountain Guide 1975; first fully-certified female Canadian Climbing Guide 1984; climbed Mt McKinley (AK, USA), Mt Logan (Canada) 1977, Mt Aconcagua (Argentina), Mt Makalu (Himalayas); solo climbs in Peru 1985; first N American woman to conquer Everest 1986; public speaker; Hon D IUR (Calgary); Breakthrough Award (jtly), Sports Fed of Canada and Canadian Asscn for the Advancement of Women in Sports 1987; Alberta Acheivement Award; Tenzing Norgay Professional Mountaineer of the Year Award (jtly), Explorers Club of New York and American Alpine Club 1987. *Leisure interests:* climbing, skiing, cross-country ski racing. *Address:* Adventure Synamics Inc, 120 McNeil, Canmor, AB T1W 2R8, Canada. *Telephone:* (403) 678-2091; *Fax:* (403) 678-3898.

WOOD, Victoria, BA; British writer and comedienne; b 19 May 1953; d of the late Stanley and of Helen Wood; m Geoffrey Durham 1980; one d one s. *Education:* Univ of Birmingham. *Career:* Singer and performer on TV and radio 1974–78; first play Talent, at Crucible Theatre, Sheffield 1978, TV production won three Nat Drama Awards 1980; numerous tours; Hon D LITT (Lancaster) 1989, (Sunderland) 1994, (Bolton) 1995, (Birmingham) 1996; Variety Club BBC Personality of the Year 1987; Top Female Comedy Performer, British Comedy Awards 1996. *TV includes:* As writer and performer: Wood and Walters (with Julie Walters, qv) 1981–82, Victoria Wood As Seen on TV (first series—Broadcasting Press Guilds Award, BAFTA Best Light Entertainment Programme and Performance Awards) 1985, (second series—BAFTA Best Light Entertainment Programme Award) 1986, (Special—BAFTA Best Light Entertainment Programme Award) 1987, An Audience With Victoria Wood (BAFTA Best Light Entertainment Programme and Performance Awards) 1988, Victoria Wood 1989, Victoria Wood's All Day Breakfast 1994, Chunky 1995, Victoria Wood Live in Your Own Home 1995, Pat and Margaret 1995, Great Railway Journeys 1996, Dinnerladies 1998–, Still Standing 1998; *Stage appearances include:* Good Fun (writer, musical) 1980, Funny Turns 1982, Lucky Bag 1984, Victoria Wood 1987, Victoria Wood Up West 1990; *Film:* The Wind in the Willows; *Publications:* Victoria Wood Song Book 1984, Up to You, Porky 1985, Barmy 1987, Mens Sana in Thingummy Doodah 1990, Chunky 1996. *Leisure interests:* talking, walking. *Address:* c/o Phil McIntyre, 35 Soho Square, London W1V 5DG, UK. *Telephone:* (20) 7439-2270.

WOODRUFF, Judy Carline, BA; American broadcast journalist; b 20 Nov 1946, Tulsa, OK; d of William Henry and Anna Lee (née Payne) Woodruff; m Albert R. Hunt, Jr 1980; two s one d. *Education:* Meredith Coll and Duke Univ. *Career:* News Announcer, Reporter WAGA-TV, Atlanta, GA 1970–75; News Corresp NBC News, Atlanta 1975–76; White House Corresp, NBC News, Washington, DC 1977–83; Corresp MacNeil–Lehrer News Hour, PBS, Washington 1983–93; Anchor for Frontline (PBS documentary series) 1983–90; Anchor and Sr Corresp CNN (Cable News Network), Washington, DC 1993–; mem Bd of Advisors Henry Grady School of Journalism, Univ of Georgia 1979–82,

Bd of Visitors Wake Forest Univ 1982–88, Bd of Advisors Benton Fellowship in Broadcast Journalism, Univ of Chicago 1984–90; Trustee Duke Univ 1985–; Co-Chair Int Women's Media Foundation 1991– (Founder, Dir 1989–); Knight Fellow in broadcast journalism Stanford Univ 1985–; mem Nat Acad of TV Arts and Sciences, White House Corresps' Asscn; Pres's Award Nat Women's Hall of Fame 1994; Allen H. Neuharth Award for Excellence in Journalism 1995. *Publication:* This is Judy Woodruff at the White House 1982. *Address:* CNN, 820 First St, NE, 11th Floor, Washington, DC 20002, USA.

WOODS, Harriett Ruth, BA; American federal official; b 2 June 1927, Cleveland, OH; d of Armin and Ruth (née Wise) Friedman; m James B. Woods 1953; three s. *Education:* Univs of Chicago and Michigan. *Career:* Reporter 1948–51; moderator and writer KETC-TV, St Louis 1962–64; Producer KPLR-TV, St Louis, MO 1964–74; mem Council Univ City, MO 1967–74; mem Highway Comm 1974, Transport Comm, MO 1974–76; mem Senate, MO 1976–84; Lt-Gov State of Missouri 1985–89; Pres Inst for Policy Leadership, Univ of Missouri, St Louis 1989–91; Pres Nat Women's Political Caucus 1991–95; apptd Dir Fed Home Loan Mortgage Corpn 1995; Fellow Inst of Politics, J. F. Kennedy School of Govt, Harvard Univ, Ct 1988; Democrat; Hon LL D (Webster) 1988. *Address:* 1211 Connecticut Ave, NW, Washington, DC 20036, USA.

WOODWARD, Joanne Gignilliat; American actress; b 27 Feb 1930, Thomasville, GA; d of Wade Woodward and Elinor Trimmier; m Paul Newman 1958; three d. *Education:* Louisiana State Univ. *Career:* Many stage appearances; numerous awards including Foreign Press Award for Best Actress 1957, Nat Bd Review Award 1957, Best Actress Award (Soc of Film and TV Arts) 1974, Franklin D. Roosevelt Four Freedoms Medal 1991, Kennedy Center Honor 1992. *Films include:* Count Three and Pray 1955, A Kiss Before Dying 1956, The Three Faces of Eve (Acad Award for Best Actress) 1957, The Long Hot Summer 1958, Rally Round the Flag Boys 1958, The Sound and the Fury 1959, The Fugitive Kind 1959, From the Terrace 1960, Paris Blues 1961, The Stripper 1963, A New Kind of Love 1963, Signpost to Murder 1964, A Big Hand for the Little Lady 1966, A Fine Madness 1966, Rachel Rachel (Acad Award nomination) 1968, Winning 1969, WUSA 1970, They Might Be Giants 1971, The Effects of Gamma Rays on Man-in-the-Moon Marigolds 1972, The Death of a Snow Queen 1973, Summer Wishes, Winter Dreams (Acad Award nomination) 1973, The Drowning Pool 1975, The End 1978, The Shadow Box 1980, Candida (Play) 1981, Harry and Son 1984, The Glass Menagerie 1987, Mr and Mrs Bridge (Acad Award nomination) 1990, Philadelphia 1993, My Knees Were Jumping: Remembering the Kindertransports (voice) 1998; *TV appearances include:* All the Way Home, See How She Runs 1978, Streets of LA 1979, Crisis at Central High 1981, Do You Remember Love? 1985, Blind Spot 1993, Breathing Lessons 1994, James Dean: A Portrait 1996. *Address:* ICM, 40 W 57th St, New York, NY 10019, USA.

WOODWARD, Kirsten; British fashion designer; b 15 Nov 1959, London; d of Prof and J. B. Woodward. *Education:* London Coll of Fashion. *Career:* Stall at Hyper Hyper while still a student 1983; Designer Karl Lagerfeld 1984–; Founder Kirsten Woodward Hats 1985–; also designed for Lanvin, Victor Edelstein, Betty Jackson, Alistair Blair, The Emanuels, Belleville Sassoon, Katharine Hamnett. *Leisure interests:* boats, horses, geography and ancient history, anthropology, writing.

WOOLCOCK, Ann Janet, AO, MD, FRACP; Australian professor of respiratory medicine; b 11 Dec 1937, Adelaide; d of Angus and Dulcie Woolcock; m Charles Bickerton Blackburn; two s. *Education:* Univs of Adelaide and Sydney, and McGill Univ (Canada). *Career:* Research Fellow Univ of Sydney 1964, McGill Univ 1966, Asthma Foundation of New S Wales 1969, RACP 1970; Visiting MOH Repatriation Gen Hosp 1971–84; Head Dept of Respiratory Medicine Univ of Sydney 1976–, Assoc Prof of Respiratory Medicine 1976–84, Sr Lecturer 1977–86, Prof 1984–, apptd Dir Inst of Respiratory Medicine 1985–; mem Health Advisory Cttee to Minister of Health, New S Wales; mem Nat Health and Medical Research Council, Medical Research Advisory Council 1979–84; Convenor Conf on Ethics of Allocating Health Resources, New S Wales Dept of Health 1991; Sims Travelling Prof 1992; has written numerous scientific papers; Fellow American Coll of Chest Physicians; mem Thoracic Soc of Australia and NZ,

American Thoracic Soc, Int Epidemiological Soc. *Leisure interests:* skiing, Christian art, opera. *Address:* University of Sydney, Dept of Respiratory Medicine, Sydney, NSW 2006, Australia (Office); 64/10 Etham Ave, Darling Point, NSW 2027, Australia (Home). *Telephone:* (2) 692 2222 (Office); *Fax:* (2) 692 4203 (Office).

WORDEN, Katharine Cole; American sculptor; b 4 May 1925, New York; d of Philip and Katharine (née Pyle) Cole; m Frederic Worden 1944; three s two d. *Education:* Sarah Lawrence Coll (Bronxville, NY). *Career:* Occupational Therapist Los Angeles Co Gen Hosp 1953–57; teacher Watt Towers Art Center 1967–69; exhibitions include Royce Galleries, Galerie Françoise Besnard (Paris), Cooling Gallery (London), Galerie Schumacher (Munich), Weiner Gallery (New York), House of Humour and Satire (Bulgaria) 1984; rep in perm collections including Grand Palais (Paris), Dakar, Bathurst (Africa); Dir Stride Rite Corpn 1980–85; mem Bd of Govs Newport Seamen's Christian Inst 1989–; mem Bd of Dirs Boston Center for the Arts 1976–80, Child and Family Services of Newport Co 1983–90, 1991–; Trustee Newport Art Museum 1984–86, Newport Health Foundation 1986–91, Hawthorne Sea Fund 1990–93; mem Common Cause, Massachusetts Civil Liberties Union. *Address:* 24 Fort Wetherill Rd, Jamestown, RI 02835, USA.

WORTH, Irene; American actress; b 23 June 1916, NE. *Education:* Univ of California at Los Angeles. *Career:* Stage appearances in UK and USA; debut in Escape Me Never, New York 1942; debut on Broadway in The Two Mrs Carrolls 1948; worked with Peter Brook's Int Theatre Research Centre, Paris and Iran 1970, 1971; Hon CBE 1975; Hon DA (Tufts and Queens); Daily Mail Nat Television Award 1953–54; Antoinette Perry Award for distinguished achievement in the Theatre 1965; London Evening Standard Award for Noel Coward Trilogy 1966; Whitbread Anglo-American Theatre Award 1967; Variety Club of GB Award 1967; Whitbread Anglo-American Award 1967; Hon CBE 1975; New York Mayor's Award of Honor for Arts and Culture 1990. *Plays include:* The Cocktail Party 1950, 1952, 1953, 1959, Othello 1951, A Midsummer Night's Dream 1952, The Merchant of Venice 1953, A Day by the Sea 1953–54, The Queen and the Rebels 1955, A Life in the Sun 1955, Hotel Paradiso 1956, Maria Stuart 1957, 1958, The Potting Shed 1958, Toys in the Attic (Page One Award, Newspaper Guild of New York) 1960, 1962, King Lear 1962, 1964, The Physicists 1963, The Ides of March 1963, Tiny Alice (Tony Award for Best Actress) 1965, A Song at Twilight 1966, Shadows of the Evening 1966, Come into the Garden Maud 1966, Heartbreak House 1967, Oedipus 1968, Hedda Gabler 1970, The Seagull 1973, 1974, Ghosts, Hamlet 1974, Sweet Bird of Youth (Tony Award for Best Actress, Jefferson Award) 1975, Misalliance 1976, The Cherry Orchard (Obie Award for Best Actress, Drama Desk Award) 1977, Old Times 1977, After the Season 1978, Happy Days 1979, The Lady from Dubuque 1980, L'Olimpiade 1982, The Chalk Garden 1982, The Physicists 1983, The Golden Age 1984, Coriolanus 1984, 1988, The Bay at Nice 1986, The Mask of the Red Death 1987, You Never Can Tell 1987–88, Lost in Yonkers (Tony Award for Best Supporting Actress, Drama Desk and Obie Awards) 1991, Irene Worth's Portrait of Edith Wharton (recital), A Week's Worth 1995, The Gypsy and the Yellow Canary 1997, Ancestral Voices 2000; *Films include:* Orders to Kill (British Film Acad Award 1958) 1957, The Scapegoat 1958, King Lear, Nicholas and Alexandra 1971, Eye Witness 1980, Fast Forward 1985, Forbidden 1985, The Big Knife 1988, The Shell Seekers 1989, Lost in Yonkers 1993, Piece of Cake 1997, Onegin 1998, Just the Ticket 1999; *TV appearance:* Coriolanus 1984. *Address:* c/o Sam Cohn, International Creative Management, 40 W 57th St, New York, NY 10019, USA; 333 W 56th St, New York, NY 10019, USA (Home).

WOYTOWICZ-RUDNICKA, Stefania; Polish concert singer (soprano); b 8 Oct 1922, Orynin; d of Michał and Domicela Zwolakowska Woytowicz; m 1952. *Education:* State Higher School of Music. *Career:* Concerts in Europe, USA, People's Repub of China, Japan; mem Australian Broadcasting Comm tour of Singapore, Hong Kong, New Zealand, India; appearances at Festivals in Vienna, Edinburgh (UK), Warsaw, etc; Pres Gen Bd Warsaw Music Asscn; recordings with Deutsche Grammophon, RCA Victor, Supraphon, Polskie Nagrania etc; Pres Gen Bd, Warsaw Music Asscn 1977–92; First Prize, Prague Spring Int Singing Competition 1954; State Prize (2nd Class) 1964; Officer's Cross, Order of Polonia Restituta 1968; Orpheus

Prize, Polish Musicians' Assen 1967; Diploma of Ministry of Foreign Affairs 1970; Medal of 30th Anniversary of People's Poland 1974; Prize of Minister of Culture and Arts (1st Class) 1975; Prize of Union of Polish Composers 1978; Prize of daily Trybuna Ludu 1978; Solidarity Award 1983; Polskie Nagrania Gold Record for recording of Górecki's Symphony No 3 1997 (Platinum Record 1999); Karol Szymanowski Foundation Award 1998. *Address:* Al Przyjaciół 3 m 13, 00-565 Warsaw, Poland. *Telephone:* (22) 628-11-33 (Home).

WRIGHT, Anne Margaret, BA, PH D; British university rector; b 26 July 1946, Kent; d of Herbert and Florence Holden; m Martin Wright 1970; one d. *Education:* Holy Trinity Convent (Bromley, Kent) and King's Coll (London). *Career:* Lecturer Univ of Lancaster 1969–71; Lecturer, then Sr Lecturer, Prin Lecturer and Reader in Modern English Hatfield Polytechnic (now Univ of Hertfordshire) 1971–84; Registrar Council for Nat Academic Awards 1984–86; Deputy Rector Liverpool Polytechnic (now Liverpool John Moores Univ) 1986–90; Rector and Chief Exec Sunderland Polytechnic (now Univ of Sunderland) 1990–92, Chancellor and Chief Exec 1992–98; Chief Exec UFI Ltd 1998–; mem Council Northern Examining Assen 1989, Cttee for Int Co-operation in Higher Educ, British Council 1990, Everyman Theatre Bd (Liverpool), Northern Arts Bd; Dir The City of Sunderland Opportunity 1991–97, Northern Sinfonia 1991–96; Chair City of Sunderland Common Purpose 1990–97; British Acad Research Award 1979. *Publications:* Heartbreak House: a facsimile of the revised typescript (co-ed) 1981, Literature of Crisis 1910–1922 1984, Bernard Shaw's Saint Joan 1984. *Leisure interests:* theatre, arts, opera, family. *Address:* UFI Ltd, Innovation Centre, 217 Portobello St, Sheffield S1 4DR, UK.

WRIGHT, Barbara, MA, LL B, PH D, D LITT, MRIA; Irish professor of French literature; b 8 March 1935, Dublin; d of W. Edward and Rosaleen H. Robinson; m William Wright 1961 (died 1985); one s. *Education:* Alexandra Coll (Dublin), Trinity Coll (Dublin) and Newnham Coll (Cambridge, UK). *Career:* Teaching posts at Univs of Manchester 1960–61, Exeter 1963–65; mem staff Trinity Coll Dublin 1965–, Prof of French Literature 1978–, Dean Faculty of Arts (Letters) 1983–86, 1990–96; mem Academia Europaea; Sr Fellow Trinity Coll Dublin; Chevalier de l'Ordre Nat du Mérite. *Publications:* Eugène Fromentin's Dominique (critical edn) 1966, Correspondence of Eugène Fromentin and Gustave Moreau (jtly) 1972, La vie et l'œuvre d'Eugène Fromentin (jtly) 1987, Correspondence of Eugène Fromentin (2 vols) 1995, Eugène Fromentin: A Life in Art and Letters 2000; studies on Gustave Drouineau 1969, Edgar Quinet 1982, Charles Baudelaire (jtly) 1987. *Leisure interest:* music. *Address:* Dept of French, Arts Bldg, Trinity College, Dublin 2, Ireland (Office); 1 Lynton Court, Merrion Rd, Dublin 4, Ireland (Home). *Telephone:* (1) 6081575 (Office); (1) 6601276 (Home); *Fax:* (1) 6717118; *E-mail:* b.wright@tcd.ie.

WRIGHT, Faith-Dorian, BS, MA; American artist; b 9 Feb 1934, New York; d of Abraham and Molly Janoff; m Martin Wright 1958; one s one d. *Education:* Midwood High School (Brooklyn, New York), New York Univ and Pratt and Parsons School of Design (New York). *Career:* Exhibitions include Bergen Museum of Arts and Science, Paramus, NJ 1986, Benton Gallery, New York 1988–92, Henri Gallery, Washington, DC 1988–96, Aart Vark, Philadelphia 1990–91, Nat Museum of Women in the Arts, Washington, DC 1990–92, Museum of Modern Art, New York 1990, Arlene Brefese Gallery, Benton 1992–96, Barnard–Biderman and Worth Gallery, New York 1994–96; rep in perm exhibitions including Museum of Modern Art, New York, Nat Museum of Women in the Arts, Washington, DC, Brenau Coll, Gainsville, GA, Nat Postal Art Museum, Ottawa, ON (Canada), Fine Arts Acad, New Dehli and Nat Inst of Design, Ahmedabad (India), and The Israel Museum, Jerusalem; art teacher 1979–; mem Women in the Arts, Women's Caucus for the Arts. *Publication:* The Collage Handbook 1985. *Address:* 300 E 74th St, New York, NY 10021, USA. *Telephone:* (212) 517-7655.

WRIGHT, Karen Jocelyn, MA, MBA; American editor and journalist; b 15 Nov 1950, New York; d of Louis David and Carlin Wile; m 1981; two d. *Education:* Brandeis Univ, Univ of Cambridge and London Grad School of Business Studies, UK. *Career:* Founder, owner Hobson Gallery (Cambridge, UK) 1981–87; Co-Founder (with Peter Fuller) Modern Painters magazine 1987–, Ed 1990–; Co-Founder (with David Bowie, Sir Timothy Sainsbury and Bernard Jacobson) 21 Publishing

1997–; mem Assen Int des Critiques d'Art. *Publications:* The Penguin Book of Art Writing (co-ed) 1998, Colour for Kosovo (ed) 1999. *Leisure interests:* looking at art, children, reading, theatre. *Address:* 31 Storeys Way, Cambridge CB3 0DP, UK. *Telephone:* (1223) 313235; *Fax:* (1223) 461726.

WRIGHT, Mary Jean (pseudonym Gee Karlshonn); Panamanian musician, composer and conductor; b 12 Oct 1945. *Education:* Instituto Nacional de Música de Panamá, Univ of Chile, Palacio de Bellas Artes (Dominican Repub), Acad de Santa Cecilia (Rome), Univ de Rosario (Argentina) and State Univ of Florida (USA). *Career:* Teacher of Musical Educ, Panamá 1962–66; Founder, Dir children's choir of Panama 1962–66; Prof of Harmony, History and Musical Form, Conservatorio Nacional de Música de El Salvador 1975; writer of musical arrangements; Man Artistic Dept and Production Chief of DECESA (subsidiary of RCA in Cen America and Panama), El Salvador 1975–76; Dir of El Salvador Orchestra at int song festival, Caracas (Venezuela) 1979; Pres, Dir-Gen own cos, Tukan Productions (jingles), Tukan Record and Tapes and Tukan-Alba Productions, Panamá 1981–; Nat Supervisor of Music, Instituto Nacional de Cultura, Panamá, then Dir Instituto Nacional de Musica 1991; has written jingles for Cen and S American countries; composer many works for orchestra and choirs; prize-winner at Festival of Children's Song, San Salvador 1979; Panama Rep (composer, music arranger and conductor) to OTI Int Song Festival, Brazil 1973, Acapulco, Mexico 1974, El Salvador Rep to OTI Int Song Festival, Madrid (fourth prize) 1977; First Prize First Belmont Song Fes. *Publications:* The Jingle as Substantial Element in Modern Advertising 1988, Compendio de Armonía Funcional 1989, Canciones para Lectura a Primera Vista 1991; Music: Elegía a Victoriano Lorenzo 1968, Rondo Espacial 1982, Fantasía Burlesque 1984. *Address:* Tukan-Alba Productions, Panamá, Panama.

WRIGHT, Rosalind, LLB, CB; British barrister and civil servant; b 2 Nov 1942, London; d of Alfred and Felicie Kerstein; m Dr David Julian Maurice Wright 1966; three d. *Education:* St Paul's Girls' School (London) and Univ Coll, London. *Career:* Called to the Bar (Middle Temple) 1964, Bencher 2001, Practising Barrister 1964–69, Legal Asst and later Sr Legal Asst, Dept of the Dir of Public Prosecutions (DPP) 1969–81, Asst Dir 1981–83, Asst Dir and Head of Fraud Investigation Group (London) 1983–87; Head of Prosecutions, The Securities Assen 1987–92; Exec Dir and Gen Counsel, Securities and Futures Authority 1992–97; Dir Serious Fraud Office 1997–. *Leisure interests:* promoting good business ethics amongst teenagers and professionals, enjoying my family, music, theatre, art. *Address:* 10–16 Elm St, London WC1X 0BJ, UK. *Telephone:* (20) 7239-7100; *Fax:* (20) 7833-5479; *E-mail:* rosalind .wright@sfu.gsi.gov.uk; *Internet:* www.sfo.gov.uk.

WU WENYING; Chinese party official; b 1932, Changzhou. *Education:* E China Textile Eng Inst (Shanghai). *Career:* Joined CCP 1949; worked as cotton spinner in textile mill, Chagzhou 1947; held various leading posts in textile mills, Changzhou Municipal Party Cttee and City Govt; Deputy Sec Changzhou Municipality CCP 1982–83; Alt mem 12th Cen Cttee CCP 1982–85, mem 1985–87, 13th Cen Cttee 1987–92, 14th 1992; Minister of the Textile Industry 1983–93; Vice-Pres Women's Fed; apptd Chair Chinese Gen Assen of Textile Industry 1993. *Address:* c/o State Council, Beijing, People's Republic of China.

WU XI-JUN; Chinese party official; b 5 Aug 1933, Jiangsu; d of Wu Boa-on and Kuo Wan-jin. *Education:* E China Inst of Chemical Technology (Shanghai). *Career:* Sr Engineer and Pres Nanjing Research Inst of Chemical Tech 1955–83, apptd Prof 1984; Assoc Prof, then Prof E China Inst of Chemical Tech 1982; apptd Chair Scientific and Technical Comm of Jiangsu Prov 1983; Deputy NPC from 1983; Vice-Gov Jiangsu Prov 1987; Nat Scientific and Tech Awards 1981, 1983, 1984. *Publications:* Synthetic Ammonia 1976; papers on sequential methods and process optimization. *Leisure interests:* playing the guitar, music. *Address:* National People's Congress, Great Hall of the People, Beijing, People's Republic of China (Office); 68 W Beijing Rd, Nanjing 210024, People's Republic of China (Home). *Telephone:* (1) 639331 (Home).

WU YI; Chinese engineer and party official; b Nov 1938, Whuan City, Hubei Prov. *Education:* Dept of Petroleum Refining, Beijing Petroleum Inst. *Career:* Joined CCP 1962; Vice-Mayor of Beijing 1988; alt mem

13th CCP Cen Cttee 1987–92, mem 14th 1992–; Minister of Foreign Trade and Econ Co-operation 1993–; Chair Bd Dirs Foreign Trade Univ 1995–. *Address:* Ministry of Foreign Trade and Economic Co-operation, 2 Dongchangan Jie, Dongcheng Qu, Beijing 100731, People's Republic of China.

WULF-MATHIES, Monika (née Baier), B ECONS, D PHIL; German international organization official; b 17 March 1942, Wernigerode; d of Carl-Hermann and Margott (née Meisser) Baier; m Carsten Wulf-Mathies 1968. *Education:* Univs of Hamburg and Freiburg. *Career:* Br Asst Ministry of Econs 1968–71; mem staff Chancellery, later Head Dept for Social Policy 1971–76; mem SPD 1965–; mem Gewerkschaft Öffentliche Dienste, Transport und Verkehr (ÖTV—Public Services and Transport Workers' Union) 1971–, mem Man Exec Cttee 1976–95, Chair (representing around 2.3 million workers) 1982–95; EU Commr for Regional Policies 1995–99; First Vice-Pres Public Services Int 1985–89, Pres 1989–94; mem Exec Bd Deutsche Lufthansa AG 1978–95 (Deputy Chair 1988–95), VEBA 1989–95. *Leisure interests:* gardening, cross-country skiing. *Address:* European Commission, 200 rue de la Loi, 1049 Brussels, Belgium. *Telephone:* (2) 299-38-70; *Fax:* (2) 295-01-22.

WUYTS, Christiane J. J.; Belgian harpsichordist; b 16 July 1938, Antwerp; d of Jacques and Irene Crèvecoeur; m Alfons H. Wuyts 1960; one s one d. *Education:* Music studies in Ahlgrim. *Career:* Piano recitals began at age 10; began playing concertos with orchestras at age 12; recitals and concerts on organ and harpsichord in Europe 1965–81; various solo recordings 1970–; currently Prof in Harpsichord, specializing in baroque music; Croix de Chevalier, Ordre Léopold II 1989. *Recordings:* Works of J. H. Fiocco 1988, 22 Works of J. S. Bach 1989, Baroque Music of the Low Countries 1990. *Leisure interests:* literature, politics, philosophy. *Address:* Irisstreet 14, 2650 Boom, Belgium. *Telephone:* (3) 888-22-99.

WYMAN, Jane (Sarah Jane Fulks); American actress; b 4 Jan 1914, St Joseph, MO; d of R. D. Fulks and Emme Reise; m 1st Myron Futterman 1937; m 2nd Ronald Reagan 1940 (divorced 1948); one s one d; m 3rd Fred Karger (divorced). *Education:* Univ of Missouri. *Career:* Fmr radio singer and chorus girl. *Films include:* My Man Godfrey 1936, Brother Rat 1938, Lost Weekend 1945, The Yearling 1946, Johnny Belinda (Acad Award) 1948, Stage Fright 1950, The Glass Menagerie 1950, The Blue Veil 1951, Magnificent Obsession 1954, All That Heaven Allows 1956, Miracle in the Rain 1956, Holiday for Lovers 1959, Pollyanna 1960, Bon Voyage 1962, How to Commit Marriage 1969; *TV appearances include:* Jane Wyman Theater 1956–60, Amanda Fallon, Falcon Crest, The Failing of Raymond (film), The Incredible Journey of Dr Meg Laurel (film). *Address:* c/o Lorimar Productions, 3970 Overland Ave, Culver City, CA 90230, USA.

WYSE PRIEST, Mary Hartwell, BA; American artist; b 1 Jan 1901, Brantford, ON, Canada; d of Frank Henry and Rachel Thayer (née Gavet) Wyse; m A. J. Gustin Priest 1927; one s one d. *Education:* High School (Toronto, Canada) and Smith Coll (Northampton, MA). *Career:* Studied art under André L'Hôte (Paris) 1925–45, Hans Hofmann (New York) 1950; Tutor in Print-Making Virginia Art Inst 1967–75; solo exhibitions include Univ of Maine 1951, Argent Gallery (New York) 1955, 1958, 1960, 1973, 1977, 1981, (Virginia) 1969, 1971, Nantucket (MA) 1956, Florida Art Center 1956, Pen and Brush (New York) 1973, McGuffey Arts Center (VA) 1984, 1990, 1991, (New York) 1984, 1988, Bombay, India 1989, Woodstock Artists Gallery 1990; group exhibitions include Florence (Italy) 1972, Ojibway Hotel Club (ON, Canada), McGuffey Arts Center (VA) 1988, 1990, Soc of American Graphic Artists 1989, Woodstock 1990; rep in perm collections including Library of Congress (Washington, DC), Norton Gallery (Palm Beach, FL), Soc of American Graphic Artists, Hunterdon County Art Center, Carnegie Mellon Univ; participant in Nat Asscn of Women Artists tours of Puerto Rico 1987, India 1988; mem Soc of American Graphic Artists, Nat Asscn of Women Artists, Pen and Brush Soc, Washington Print Club, McGuffey Arts Center (VA); numerous awards for lithographs 1956–; Washington Watercolour Soc Award 1959; Medal of Honour, Nat Asscn of Women Artists. *Leisure interests:* recorder, piano, walking, singing. *Address:* 41 Old Farm Rd, Bellair, Charlottesville, VA 22903, USA. *Telephone:* (804) 293-4558.

X

XENAKIS, Françoise Marguerite Claude; French journalist and writer; b 27 Sept 1930, Blois; d of Robert and Suzanne (née Richard) Gargouil; m Yannis Xenakis 1953; one c. *Career:* Journalist and literary critic on Le Matin de Paris and L'Express, Paris 1987–. *Publications:* Des dimanches et des dimanches 1977, Moi, j'aime pas la mer, Le temps usé, La natte coupée, Zut, on a encore oublié Madame Freud 1985, Mouche-toi Cléopâtre 1986, Elle lui dirait dans l'île (play) 1987, La vie exemplaire de Rita Capuchon 1988, Chéri, tu viens pour la photo 1990, Attends moi (Prix des Libraires) 1993, Désolée mais ça ne se fait pas 1996. *Address:* 9 rue Chaptal, 75009 Paris, France.

XHEPA, Magarita; Albanian actress; b 2 May 1934, Lushnjë; m Xhevit Xhepa 1950; three s. *Education:* Nat Theatre (Tirana). *Career:* Film, stage and radio actress. *Plays include:* Romeo and Juliet, Fox and Grape; has appeared in plays by Shakespeare, Molière and Schiller, and in 34 films. *Leisure interests:* poetry, music. *Address:* Rruga Kongresi i Përmetit, Pll 11, Shk 4, Apt 28, Tirana, Albania. *Telephone:* (42) 25127.

XIA JUHUA; Chinese party official and acrobat; b 16 Oct 1937, Qianshan, Anhui; m 1972; two d. *Education:* Jiang Han Univ. *Career:* Acrobat since the age of six; leader, performer acrobatic troupe; performances in Japan, Brazil, Mexico, Canada, Argentina, Italy, France, Switzerland, UK, fmr USSR and USA, etc; Judge Acrobatic Contests, Paris and Monte-Carlo 1983; Deputy to 3rd–7th NPCs, mem Standing Cttee during 4th and 5th Congresses; Deputy Chief Standing Cttee of Wuhan Municipality 8th NPC; Chief Wuhan Cultural Bureau 1985–88; Chair Asscn of Chinese Acrobatic Artists; Deputy Chair Asscn of Chinese Writers and Artists; winner Golden Award in Acrobatic Contest, World Young Get-together Festival, Moscow 1957. *Leisure interests:* music, dance, films, horse-riding, gymnastics, painting. *Address:* National People's Congress, Great Hall of the People, Beijing, People's Republic of China (Office); 130 Yian Jiang Rd, Hankou, Wuhan, People's Republic of China (Home). *Telephone:* (27) 216855 (Home).

XIAO WENYAN, (pseudonym of Zhang Shi Qin); Chinese opera singer and actress; b 2 March 1922, Huainan, Jiangsu; foster d of Zhang Shao Qing and Zhang Liu Shi; m Chen Yu Hu 1938; two s one d. *Education:* Shanghai Continuation Sr Middle School. *Career:* Opera singer since 1939; performances in Shanghai and Jiangsu Provs with Beijing, Kunqu, Huiju and Bangzi Operas; developed popular tone (named after her) of Huaiju Opera; mem 3rd, 4th and 5th Nat Cttees CPPCC; Deputy 4th NPC; mem China Fed of Literary and Art Circles, Council China Asscn of Drama Artists (Deputy Chair Shanghai Br), Nat Conf of Culture and Art Circles 1979; Chair Art Cttee Shanghai People's Huaiju Opera Troupe, later Pres and Hon Pres; recordings for China Phonogram Co; numerous awards include Nat Model Artist 1956, Gold Disc (China Phonogram Co) 1989. *Operas include:* Qing Xiang Lian, Women Judge (film 1954), Story about the White Snake, Morning in the Seaport, Appointment on Lanqiao Bridge (film 1961). *Leisure interests:* Chinese calligraphy, gardening. *Address:* Lane 12, Apt 401, No 1, Wu Xing Rd, Shanghai, People's Republic of China. *Telephone:* (21) 4315348.

XIE JUN; Chinese chess player; b 30 Oct 1970, Beijing. *Career:* Nat Jr Champion 1984, 1985; Nat Women's Champion 1989; World Women's Champion 1991, 1993, 1999. *Address:* c/o State General Bureau of Physical Culture and Sports, 9 Tiyuguan Lu, Beijing, 100061, People's Republic of China.

XIE LIJUAN; Chinese medical practitioner and party official; b 11 March 1936, Shanghai; d of the late Xie Rong Sun and Shen Mei Zhen; m Jin Xinrong 1964; two d. *Education:* Shanghai Second Medical Univ. *Career:* Medical practitioner Cen Hosp of Shanghai, Lu Wan Dist 1961–78, Chief Dr 1979–82, Vice-Pres and Deputy Chief Physician 1983–84; Deputy Chair Shanghai Lu Wan Dist 1984–85; Shanghai Municipal People's Rep, Pres Shanghai TV Univ and Vice-Mayor Shanghai Municipal People's Govt 1985; Vice-Mayor of Shanghai 1988, 1993; Deputy Dir China Women Mayor Friendship Asscn 1991; mem CPPCC 1994, Vice-Chair Shanghai Cttee of CPPCC 1996; Chair Shanghai Cttee of Jiu San Soc 1996, mem Standing Cttee of China Cen Cttee of Jiu San Soc; articles published in professional journals. *Leisure interests:* classical music, ball games. *Address:* Shanghai Committee of the Chinese People's Political Consultative Conference, 860 Beijing Rd W, Shanghai 200041, People's Republic of China. *Telephone:* (21) 62553532; *Fax:* (21) 62535173.

XIE QIHUA; Chinese business executive; b 22 June 1943, Yinxian, Zhejiang. *Education:* Tsinghua Univ. *Career:* Section chief, Dept Dir, Asst Commdr, Vice-Commdr of Baoshan Iron and Steel Works project; Vice-Chair Gen Man Baogan Group 1968–; named Nat Excellent Women Entrepreneur. *Address:* Baogan Group, Baoshan, Shanghai, People's Republic of China.

XU YONGJIU; Chinese athlete; b 29 Oct 1962, Dalian, Liae Ning; m Li Gang 1988; one s. *Education:* Liae Ning Physical Training School. *Career:* Trained as long-distance runner 1977–; mem walking team 1981–87; broke World Record for Long-Distance Walking, World Championship, Morocco 1987; won 10,000m Walking race Sixth Nat Games 1987; Asst Coach 1988–90. *Leisure interests:* reading, knitting, walking. *Address:* Liae Ning Physical Training School, Wang Hu Rd, He Ping Dist, Shen Yang, Liae Ning, People's Republic of China. *Telephone:* (24) 363839.

XUXA, Xuxa Meneghel; Brazilian actress and singer; b 27 March 1963; one d (with L Szafir). *Career:* Fmr model, cover-girl on numerous magazines; film actress before becoming children's TV presenter 1985; own show on TV Globo since 1986; numerous hits with children's songs; richest businesswoman in S America. *Films include:* Super Xuxa Against Depression 1988, Princess Xuxa and the Trapalhõ 1989. *Address:* c/o Xuxa Promoçoes e Prod Artisticas Ltda, Rua Voluntários da Patria, 89–29 andar, Botafogo, RJ 22270-000, Brazil (Office); c/o Sigla—Sistema Globo de Gravaçoes Audio Visuais, Rua Assunçao 443, Botafogo, RJ 22251-030, Brazil (Office).

Y

YAAR, Ora, B ARCH, DIP ENG; Israeli architect; b 14 April 1929, Lvov, Poland (now Ukraine); d of Avraham and Sara Gerstenfeld; m Yaacov Yaar 1954; two s one d. *Education:* Israeli Inst of Tech (Haifa). *Career:* Served Israeli army 1948–50; staff mem architect's office, London 1953, Tel-Aviv 1954–58; pvt practice Yaar Architects 1958–, Dir; mem Asscn of Engineers and Architects in Israel, Architectural Cttee of Tel-Aviv Municipality, Planning and Building Bd of Ramar-Hasharon Authority 1976–80; Rokach Prize for Restoration of Old City of Jaffa 1967, for Town Planning of Kfir area, Tel-Aviv 1980; Rozen Prize for Restoration of Old City of Jerusalem 1969. *Projects include:* Rebuilding of Jaffa and Jerusalem 1960–77, Creating new areas in Kfar Sabba 1965, Tel-Aviv 1973–82 and Jerusalem 1980–91, J. Silver Inst for Biomedical Eng, Haifa 1972–75. *Address:* 4 Bustenai St, Tel-Aviv 65147, Israel (Office); 10 Hagilboa St, Tel-Aviv 65223, Israel (Home). *Telephone:* (3) 5101399 (Office); *Fax:* (3) 5101481 (Office).

YALDIZ, Marianne, D PHIL; German museum director; b 5 Oct 1944, Berlin; m Kazim Yaldiz 1976; two s. *Education:* Free Univ of Berlin. *Career:* Curator of Cen Asian Art, Museum für Indische Kunst Berlin 1974–86, Dir 1986–. *Publications:* Archäologie und Kunst Chinesisch – Zentralasiens 1987, Palast de Götter – 1500 Jahre Kunst aus Judien 1991, Treasures of Indian Art – India's Cultural Heritage 1998, Les Arts de L'Asie Centrale Bouddhique – Les Turkestans 1999, Magische Götterwelten – Werke aus dem Museum für Indische Kunst 2000. *Address:* Museum für Indische Kunst, Takustr 40, 14195 Berlin, Germany. *Telephone:* (30) 8301362; *Fax:* (30) 8301502; *E-mail:* mik@smb.spk-berlin.de.

YALOW, Rosalyn Sussman, PH D; American medical physicist and academic; b 19 July 1921, New York; d of Simon and Clara (née Zipper) Sussman; m Aaron Yalow 1943; one s one d. *Education:* Hunter Coll (New York) and Univ of Illinois. *Career:* Asst in Physics Univ of Illinois 1941–43, Instructor 1944–45; Lecturer and temp Asst Prof in Physics, Hunter Coll, New York 1946–50; Physicist and Asst Chief Radioisotope Service, Veterans' Admin Hosp, Bronx 1950–70, Chief Radioimmuno-assay Reference Lab 1969, Chief Nuclear Medicine Service 1970–80, Sr Medical Investigator 1972–92, Sr Medical Investigator Emer 1992–; Research Prof Dept of Medicine, Mount Sinai School of Medicine, New York 1968–74, Distinguished Service Prof 1974–79, Dir Solomon A. Berson Research Lab Veterans' Admin Medical Centre 1973–92; Solomon A. Berson Distinguished Prof-at-Large 1986–; Distinguished Prof-at-Large Albert Einstein Coll of Medicine, Yeshiva Univ, NY 1979–85, Prof Emer 1985–; Chair Dept of Clinical Sciences, Montefiore Hosp, Bronx 1980–85; Harvey Lecturer 1966, American Gastroenterology Asscn Memorial Lecturer 1972, Joslyn Lecturer, New England Diabetes Asscn 1972, Franklin I. Harris Memorial Lecturer 1973, First Hagedorn Memorial Lecturer, Acta Endocrinologica Congress 1973; mem NAS 1975–, American Acad of Arts and Sciences 1979–, and many other scientific orgs; Foreign Assoc French Acad of Medicine 1981–; Fellow New York Acad of Science, Radiation Research Soc, American Asscn of Physicists in Medicine; Assoc Fellow in Physics, American Coll of Radiology, American Diabetes Asscn, Endocrine Soc, Soc of Nuclear Medicine; more than 60 hon doctorates 1974–91; Nobel Prize for Physiology or Medicine for discoveries concerning peptide hormones (jtly) 1977; more than 30 other awards including Gratum Genus Humanum Gold Medal (World Fed of Nuclear Medicine and Biology) 1978, Von Hevesy Medal 1978 and Von Hevesy Nuclear Medicine Pioneer Award 1986, Sarasota Medical Award for Achievement and Excellence 1979, First Joseph Handleman Award (Jewish Acad of Arts and Sciences) 1981, Nat Medal of Science 1988. *Address:* Veterans' Administration Medical Centre, 130 W Kingsbridge Rd,

Bronx, New York, NY 10468, USA (Office); 3242 Tibbett Ave, Bronx, New York, NY 10463, USA (Home). *Telephone:* (718) 584-9000 (Office); *Fax:* (718) 562-9120 (Office).

YAMADA, Ruth Chizuko, BA; Canadian artist; b 23 March 1923, Vancouver, BC; d of John Renzo and Teruyo (née Kometani) Hagino; m Sam Isamu Yamada 1947; two d one s. *Education:* All Japan Nanga (Tokyo), Satsuki Kai Sumi-e (Kyoto, Japan), Ontario Coll of Art and Univ of Toronto. *Career:* Solo exhibitions throughout Canada; works rep in perm collections including Windsor Castle (UK), Gov's Office, Jiangsu Prov (People's Repub of China); works rep in corp collections including Sony of Canada, IBM Canada, Honda of Canada, Confed Life, Fuji Bank, Trent Univ; introduced art of Sumi-e (Brush Art) to Japanese-Canadian Cultural Centre, Chief Instructor for 19 years; Consultant Sumi-e Artists of Canada; illustrated Waves by Pearl Buck 1965; cr John Yamada Scholarship for Architectural School, Univ of Toronto 1984; mem Nanga Soc 1968–, Satsuki Kai Soc (Kyoto) 1968–, Canadian Soc of Painters in Watercolours 1980; Hon mem Sumi-e Artists of Canada; Nanga Soc Awards 1974, 1975, 1976; Award Sunrise Soc of America 1985. *Leisure interests:* skiing, golf. *Address:* 20 Glenayr Rd, Toronto, ON M5P 3B8, Canada. *Telephone:* (416) 483-5084.

YANG, Loretta; Taiwanese actress; b 16 July 1952. *Education:* Provence Univ. *Career:* Made 121 films over 11-year acting career; also artist making glass artefacts. *Films include:* Jade Love (Best Actress, Taiwan Golden Horse Award) 1985, Guie-Met (Best Actress, Asia Pacific Film Festival, Best Actress, Taiwan Golden Horse Award) 1986. *Leisure interests:* art, design, acting. *Address:* 120, 3F Fu-Shin S Rd, Taipei, Republic of China (Taiwan). *Telephone:* (2) 721-2950; *Fax:* (2) 741-5062.

YANG CHUN; Chinese politician and civil servant; b 16 Feb 1918, Beijing; d of Wan Shu Fang and Huang Rui Zhen; m Zhang Yan 1942; three s one d. *Education:* Wuhan Univ. *Career:* Fighter in war against Japanese invasion 1937–45, and for CP in civil war 1945–49; joined Agrarian Reform Movt 1949–52; Deputy Chief of Textile Industries Bureau (E China Region) 1952–54; Sec to Chinese Premier 1954–57; Pres Medical Coll of Beijing 1957–66; Vice-Chair Comm of Cultural Relations with Foreign Countries 1966–73; Head Chinese Acad of Medical Sciences 1973–76; apptd Vice-Minister Ministry of Public Health 1977; Vice-Pres Red Cross Soc of China 1978–84; mem Nat Cttee of the CPPCC 1983. *Leisure interests:* swimming, calligraphy. *Address:* Ministry of Public Health, 44 Houhai Beiyan, Beijing, People's Republic of China. *Telephone:* (10) 4033120; *Fax:* (10) 4012369.

YANG FU-QING, BA, MBA; Chinese university professor; b 6 Nov 1932, Wuxi, Jiangsu Prov. *Education:* Tsinghua Univ (Peking Univ). *Career:* Prof, Dept of Computer Science and Tech Univ of Peking 1983–, Dean 1983–99, Dean of Faculty of Information and Eng Science 1999–, Dir Inst of Software Eng Research 1999–; Dir Nat Eng Research Center for Software Eng 1997–; mem Chinese Acad of Sciences, Academic Degree Cttee of the State Council; numerous awards and prizes including Special Prize for Advancement of Science and Tech, Electronics Industry Admin 1996, First Class Prize of the Guang Hua Tech Fund from the Nat Defense Tech Ministry 1996, Science and Tech Progress Awards of He Liang and He Li Fund 1997. *Publications:* Operating System, Compiler, The Fundamental Theory of Software Engineering, Software Engineering Environment, Software Production Industrialization Technology. *Address:* Dept of Computer Science and Technology, University of Peking, 2125 Hamilton Ave, Beijing, 100871, People's Republic of China. *Telephone:* (8610) 62751782; *Fax:* (8610) 62751792; *E-mail:* yang@cs.pku.edu.cn.

YANG GUIZHEN, MD, PH D; Chinese immunologist and micro-biologist; b 25 July 1923, Anqing, Anhui; d of Futian Yang and Lanxuan Wu; m Ziran Li 1947; two s. *Education:* Beijing Univ, Beijing Furen Univ and Leningrad (now St Petersburg) Medical Coll (USSR, now Russian Fed). *Career:* Asst Lecturer Beijing Medical Coll 1947–50; Lecturer First Military Medical Coll 1950–52; Asst Prof Jilin Medical Univ 1957–63, Assoc Prof 1963–78; Prof Norman Bethune Univ of Medical Sciences, Jilin 1978–; apptd Vice-Pres Chinese Soc of Microbiology and Immunology 1983, Chinese Soc of Immunology 1989; apptd Vice-Chief Ed Chinese Journal of Immunology 1985; several awards from Ministry of Public Health and Nat Educ Cttee 1986, 1990, 1991. *Publications include:* Medical Immunology 1980, The Functions of Immunopotentiating Cells 1986, An Outline of Immuno-bioengineering 1992. *Address:* Norman Bethune University of Medical Sciences, School of Basic Medical Sciences, Dept of Immunology, Changchun, Jilin 130021, People's Republic of China. *Telephone:* (432) 645911; *Fax:* (432) 644739.

YANG JIE; Chinese television director; b 27 April 1929, Xin Yang, He Nan; d of the late Yang Bo Kai and of Wei Shu Yuan; m Wang Chong Qiou 1968; three d one s. *Education:* Pvt school. *Career:* Broadcaster, Qing Dao 1949–54; Ed Cen Broadcasting Station 1954–58; apptd TV Dir and independent Producer China Cen TV station 1958; one of Top Ten TV Dirs 1988. *Productions:* Perfumed Handkerchief 1979, In Love With a Mermaid 1981, Kindness and Emnity 1981, The Pilgrimage to the West (winner several awards) 1988, The Artist Was Named Ji Gong 1989, Historian, Writer, Ci Maqian 1988. *Leisure interests:* reading, travel. *Address:* Ministry of Radio, Film and Television, Fuxingmenwai 302, 42 Dar Yuang 6, POB 4501, Beijing, People's Republic of China. *Telephone:* (1) 3268110; *Fax:* (1) 3018830.

YANG WENYI; Chinese swimmer; b 11 Jan 1972 Shanghai; d of Yang Yuehua and Zhu Qifang. *Education:* Shanghai Sports Tech Inst and Beijing Inst of Physical Educ. *Career:* Silver Medal 50m freestyle, Olympic Games, Seoul 1988; Gold Medals in 100m backstroke, 50m freestyle, 4 x 100m freestyle and 4 x 100m medley 11th Asian Games 1990; Gold Medal in 50m freestyle event (set world record), Olympic Games, Barcelona, Spain 1992. *Leisure interests:* music, fashion. *Address:* c/o Swimming Team, 2 Tiyuguan Rd, Beijing 10006, People's Republic of China. *Telephone:* (10) 2263410.

YANOVSKAYA, Henrietta Naumovna; Russian theatre director; b 24 June 1940, Lenningrad (now St Petersburg); d of Naum Ignatyevich Yanovsky and Rosa lazarevna Yanovskaya; m Kama Mironovich Ginkas; one s. *Education:* Leningrad Inst of Radio Tech and Leningrad Inst of Theatre, Music and Cinema. *Career:* Fmr constructor of radio devices, electrician and engineer; Stage Dir in Krasnoyarsk 1970–72, Riga 1972–74, Pskov 1974–75; previously banned from theatres of Leningrad and Moscow because her work did not ideologically comply with the Communist Party strategy; founder of several amateur theatres in Russian towns; Chief Stage Dir Moscow Theatre of Young Spectators 1986–; first Soviet Stage Dir to work in Israel (The Dog's Heart); held masterclasses in Berlin, Germany, workshop Soviet Vision in Nottingham, UK and Turku, Finland; participated in Avignon Theatre Festival; Crystal Turandot Prize; Seagull Prize. *Stage Productions include:* The Taste of Honey (Leningrad, now St Petersburg) 1973, Widows' Vessel (Mossoviet theatre) 1984, Galina (Mayakovsky theatre); Moscow Theatre of Young Spectators 1986–: The Dog's Heart, Nightingale, Storm (Belgrade Int Theatre Festival Prize). *Leisure interests:* crosswords, mathematics, passions. *Address:* B. Tishinsky per 24, Apt 7, Moscow, Russian Federation (Home). *Telephone:* (095) 253-43-15 (Home); (095) 299-99-61 (Office).

YAROSHINSKAYA, Alla Aleksandrovna; Russian/Ukrainian journalist, writer and government official; b 1953, Zhitomir, Ukraine; m Aleksander Kirko; two s. *Education:* Kiev State Univ and professional courses in journalism (USA and Japan). *Career:* Journalist Radyanska Zhitomirshchina (Ukrainian newspaper) 1976–89; subjected to admin sanction for exposing Party corruption and cover-up of Chernobyl nuclear disaster; mem Helsinki Int Cttee on Human Rights 1989–; USSR People's Deputy, mem USSR Supreme Soviet; mem Cttee on Freedom of Press, Human Rights and Ecology 1989–91; Chair All-Union Cttee on Rights of Journalists and Freedom of Press 1989–91; Head Mass Media Dept, Ministry of Press and Information, Russian Fed 1991–92; Head Int Liaison of Mass Media Dept Fed Information Centre of Pres Boris Yeltsin 1992–93; Adviser to Pres 1993–; Sec Journalists' Union of Russian Fed 1992–; Pres Alla Yaroshinskaya Charity Fund to assist victims of nuclear disasters 1993–; Head Chief Dept of Mass Media, State Cttee of Press 1995–98; mem Russian br Int Green Cross Foundation 1992–; Guest Lecturer EP, Int A. Sakharov Univ (Germany), etc; All-Union Golden PEN Award 1980; Int Journalists' Prize 1985; Right Livelihood Award (Stockholm, jtly) 1992. *Publications include:* Earth is Alarmed (jtly) 1990, Chernobyl is with Us 1991, Chernobyl: Top Secret 1992, Hunt in the City (novel); numerous short stories and articles in newspapers and magazines. *Leisure interests:* chess, poetry, art, travel. *Address:* Office of the President, The Kremlin, Moscow, Russian Federation. *Telephone:* (095) 203-75-90; *Fax:* (095) 203-93-04.

YATES, Sandra Lee; Australian publishing executive; b 15 July 1947, Brisbane; d of William and Margaret Woff; one s one d (by 1st marriage); m 2nd Michael Leonard Skinner 1980. *Education:* Salisbury High School (Brisbane) and Univ of Hawaii (USA). *Career:* Advertising Sales Exec TVO 1974–77; Advertising Man Family Circle Magazines 1977–80, The Sun newspaper 1980–81; Deputy Gen Man Fairfax Magazines 1981–87, Pres (US) 1987–88, Pres 1988–89; Pres and CEO Matilda Mags (US), Founder Sassy magazine 1988–89; Assoc Publr Time Magazine (Australia) 1989, Publr 1991–; Man Dir The Demeter Group Pty Ltd 1994; Chair Saatchi and Saatchi Advertising Australia 1996–, NSW TAFE (Tech and Further Educ) Comm Bd 1997–; numerous TV and radio appearances. *Leisure interests:* cooking, reading, piano, opera. *Address:* POB 847, Double Bay, NSW 2028, Australia.

YAU, Carrie, B SC S; Chinese politician; b (Tsang Ka Lai) 4 June 1955, Hong Kong; d of Tsang Hin Yeung and Tsang Choon Kway; m Francis Yau; one s. *Education:* Maryknoll Sisters' School, Diocesan Girls' School and Univ of Hong Kong. *Career:* Joined Hong Kong Govt as an Admin Officer 1977, various posts in maj policy areas, Govt Spokeswoman, Chief Sec's Office 1994–95, Dir of Admin 1997–2000, Sec for Information Tech and Broadcasting 2000–; Chair Bd of Review (Film Censorship), Steering Cttee on Cyberport; Vice-Chair Broadcasting Authority; mem Business Advisory Cttee, Services Promotion Strategy Group. *Leisure interests:* singing, hiking, family activities. *Address:* Department of Information Technology and Broadcasting, 2/F Murray Bldg, Garden Rd, Central, Hong Kong Special Administrative Region, People's Republic of China. *Telephone:* 2189 2283; *Fax:* 2588 1421; *E-mail:* tklyau@itbb.gov.hk; *Internet:* www.info.gov.hk/itbb/.

YAVCHITZ, Geneviève Marie-Thérèse; French economist and civil servant; b 5 Aug 1947, Mulhouse; d of Pierre-Louis and Claude (née Dubrana) Garès; m Olivier Yavchitz 1971; two d one s. *Education:* Lycée de Mulhouse and Univ of Paris (Nanterre). *Career:* Economist Inst Nat de la Santé et de la Recherche Médicale 1973–76; Head Dept of Study and Finance, Ministry of Social Affairs 1981–85, Tech Adviser to Minister of Social Affairs 1985–86; Rep to Banque Centrale des Coopératives et des Mutuelles 1986–87; Del for Health to Caisse des Dépôts-Développement 1988; Cabinet Dir for Sec of State for the Disabled and the Casualties of Life 1988–89; Rep to Inter-Ministerial Del for Towns 1990; Advisor to Directeur des Services aux Collectivités locales, Caisse des Dépôts et Consignations 1996. *Address:* 27 bis rue Vauvenargues, 75018 Paris, France (Home); La Febvrerie, Morainville-Jouveaux, 27260 Cormeilles, France (Home).

YELLEN, Janet Louise, PH D; American economist and government official; b 13 Aug 1946, Brooklyn; d of Julius and Anna Ruth (née Blumenthal) Yellen; m George Arthur Akerlof 1978; one s. *Education:* Brown Univ and Yale Univ. *Career:* Asst Prof of Econs Harvard Univ 1971–76; Lecturer LSE (UK) 1978–80; Asst Prof of Econs School of Business Admin, Univ of Calif at Berkeley 1980–82, Assoc Prof 1982–85, Prof Haas School of Business 1985–; Bernard T. Rocca Jr Prof of Int Business and Trade 1992–; consultant Div of Int Finance, Bd Govs of Fed Reserve System 1974–75, economist Trade and Financial Studies section 1977–78, mem 1994–97; Assoc Ed Journal of Econ Perspectives 1987–91; Research Fellow MIT 1974; consultant Congressional Budget Office 1975–76, mem Panel of Econ Advisors 1993–; Chair Council of Econ Advisors 1997–; research affiliate, Yale Univ 1976; mem Advisory Panel on Econs Nat Science Foundation 1977–78, 1991–92; mem Brookings Panel on Econ Activity 1987–88, 1990–91, Sr

Advisor 1989–; Lecturer on Macroeconomic Theory, Yrjö Jahnsson Foundation, Helsinki 1977–78; mem Council on Foreign Relations 1976–81, American Econ Asscn; Grad Fellow Nat Science Foundation 1967–71; Guggenheim Fellow 1986–87; Hon Woodrow Wilson Fellow 1967. *Publications:* The Limits of the Market in Resource Allocation (jtly) 1977, contrib articles to professional journals. *Address:* Council of Economic Advisors, 314 Old Executive Office Bldg, 17th St and Pennsylvania Ave, NW, Washington, DC 20502, USA.

YELLEN, Linda Beverly, MFA, PH D; American film director, writer and producer; b 13 July 1949, Forest Hills, NY; d of Seymour and Bernice (née Mittelman) Yellen. *Education:* Columbia Univ, Barnard Coll, Harvard Univ and City Univ of New York. *Career:* Prin Chrysalis—Yellen Productions Inc 1982; Pres The Linda Yellen Co 1988–; mem Dirs' Guild of America, Writers' Guild of America, Acad of TV Arts and Sciences. *TV and films include:* Prospera 1969, Come Out, Come Out 1971, Looking Up 1978, Mayflower: The Pilgrims' Adventure 1979, Hard Hat and Legs 1980, Playing For Time (Emmy Award, Peabody Award, Christopher Award) 1980, The Royal Romance of Charles and Diana 1982, Prisoner Without a Name, Cell Without a Number (Peabody Award) 1983, Second Serve: The Renee Richards Story (Luminous Award) 1986, Liberace 1988, Hunt For Stolen War Treasures 1989, Everybody Wins 1989, Sweet Bird of Youth 1989, Chantilly Lace 1993, Parallel Lives 1994.

YENERSU, Isik; Turkish actress; b 19 March 1942, Caycuma; m Alpay Izbirak 1970 (divorced 1971). *Education:* Ulus Secondary School (Ankara) and State Conservatoire of Ankara. *Career:* Actress, then Dir State Theatre of Ankara 1963–, later State Theatre of Istanbul; Asst to French Dir Roger Planchon 1968–69; Asst Drama Programmes Office de Radiodiffusion-Télévision Française (ORTF) 1969–70; Asst Dir of two films; teacher Dept of Drama, State Conservatoire of Ankara; Best Actress Awards from Avni Dilligil 1978, 1987, Sanat Sevenler Dernegi 1978, Tiyatro Dergisi 1979, Sanat Kurumu 1983, Ulvi Uraz 1984, Ministry of Culture 1988. *Productions include:* Caesar and Cleopatra 1963, Wilds 1965, All My Sons 1967, This Property is Condemned 1967, The Unknown Soldier and His Wife 1968, Les Possédés 1968, Amédée 1968, Taming of the Shrew 1985, Women in Mind 1987, Two for the Seesaw 1991, Death and the Maiden 1991. *Leisure interests:* travel, animals, flowers. *Address:* Istanbul Devlet Tiyatrosu, Taksim, Istanbul, Turkey (Office); Kumrulu Sok 28/14, Deniz Apt, Cihangir, Istanbul, Turkey (Home). *Telephone:* (1) 2453380 (Office).

YEO, Diane Helen, FRSA; British charity executive; b 22 July 1945, London; d of Brian and Joan Daisy (née Packham) Pickard; m Timothy Stephen Kenneth Yeo 1970; one s one d. *Education:* Blackheath High School, London Univ and Inst Français de Presse (Paris). *Career:* BBC Radio 1968–74; Africa Educational Trust 1974–79; Girl Guides Asscn 1979–82; YWCA of GB 1982–85; Dir Inst of Charity Fundraising Managers 1985–88; Charity Commr 1989–95; currently Chief Exec Sargent Cancer Care for Children; Consultant Centre for Charity and Trust Research, S Bank Univ 1995–; mem Nat Council for Voluntary Orgs (NCVO) Advisory Council 1995–, Council and Audit Cttee, Advertising Standards Authority (ASA) 1997–; Fellow Inst of Charity Fundraising Managers; Paul Barnes Fellow, Rotary Int 2000. *Leisure interests:* piano, tennis, photography. *Address:* Sargent Cancer Care for Children, Griffin House, 161 Hammersmith Rd, London W6 8SG, UK. *Telephone:* (20) 8752-2800; *Fax:* (20) 8752-2806; *E-mail:* dianeyeo@ sargent.org.

YEOH, Michelle, BA; Malaysian actress; b (Yeoh Choo-Keng, sometimes credited as Michelle Khan, Ziqiong Yang or Chi-King Yeung), 6 Aug 1962, Ipoh, Perak; m Dickson Poon 1988 (divorced 1992). *Education:* Royal Acad of Dance (London). *Films include:* Owls vs Dumbo 1984, In the Line of Duty 2 1985, The Target 1985, Magnificent Warriors 1987, Easy Money 1987, The Heroic Trio 1993, Police Story 3 1992 (Part 2 1993), Butterfly Sword 1993, Heroic Trio 2: Executioners 1993, Seven Maidens 1993, Tai-Chi 1993, Wonder Seven 1994, The Stunt Woman 1996, The Soong Sisters 1997, Tomorrow Never Dies 1997, Moonlight Express 1999, Crouching Tiger, Hidden Dragon 2000. *Address:* c/o Ang Lee, CAA, 9830 Wilshire Blvd, Beverly Hills, CA 90212, USA.

YHAP, Laetitia Karoline, DFA; British artist; b 1 May 1941, St Albans; d of Leslie Neville Yhap and Elizabeth Kögler; m Jeffrey Camp 1962 (divorced 1980); one s. *Education:* Camberwell School of Arts and Crafts, Slade School of Fine Art and Univ Coll London. *Career:* Artist-in-Residence Chatham House Grammar School, Ramsgate 1981; mem of London Group 1971–; solo exhibitions include Piccadily Gallery (London) 1965, 1970, 1973, Serpentine Gallery (London) 1979, Hastings Museum and Art Gallery 1979, Air Gallery (London) 1984, The Business of the Beach (tour) 1988–89, Rye Art Gallery (Sussex) 1991, Riviera Gallery (Hastings) 1991, Life at the Edge, Charleston Farmhouse 1993, Bound by the Sea (retrospective), Berwick Gymnasium 1994, Maritime Counterpoint, Boundary Gallery 1996; most recent 'in monochrome' Lydd Library Gallery 1998, 'The Story So Far' Hastings Trust 1999, and others in UK and overseas; rep in public collections in UK; Leverhulme Research Award 1962–63; John Moores Prize 1974. *Leisure interests:* music, concerts, badminton. *Address:* c/o Riviera Gallery, Pelham Arcade, Hastings, Sussex TN34 3HH, UK (Gallery); 12 The Croft, Hastings, Sussex TN34 3HH, UK (Home). *Telephone:* (1424) 426222 (Gallery).

YIN CHANGMIN; Chinese scientist and party and state official; b 4 Oct 1923, Nanchang, Jiangxi Prov; d of Yin Renqing and Wu Yahui; m Bei Xiaoliang 1948; two s. *Career:* Prof Hunan Normal Univ 1979–, Vice-Pres 1973–81, Pres 1981–83, Consultant 1985–; Alt mem 12th CCP Cen Cttee 1982, mem 1986, alt mem 13th Cttee 1987–92; Vice-Chair CPPCC Prov Cttee, Hunan 1985–92; mem CCP Cttee, Hunan 1983–85; Vice-Chair Hunan Br, Asscn for Science and Tech 1980–85, Hon Chair 1985–; mem Bd Dirs Chinese Zoological Soc 1984; Chair Bd Dirs Hunan Biology Soc and Zoological Soc 1981–92, Hunan Zoological Soc 1992–; Deputy Nat Cultural and Educational Conf 1960; awards and prizes include Nat Red Banner Women's Pacesetter 1959, Model Worker of Hunan Prov 1960, First Prize for Improvement of Science and Tech, Dept of Agric and Forestry 1980, First Prize Nat Cttee of Educ. *Publications:* Field Spiders 1980, Textbook of Zoology 1983, Spiders in China: One Hundred New and Newly Recorded Species of the Araneidae and Agelenidae Family 1990, Fauna Sinica; 70 research papers. *Leisure interests:* literature, collecting postage stamps. *Address:* Dept of Biology, Hunan Normal University, Changsha, Hunan Province, People's Republic of China. *Telephone:* (731) 8883310; *Fax:* (731) 8851226.

YING, Diane; Taiwanese magazine publisher and editor; b Xian, People's Repub of China. *Education:* Univ of Iowa (USA). *Career:* Emigrated with family from mainland China to Repub of China (Taiwan) 1949; fmr reporter The Philadelphia Inquirer, USA; Repub of China (Taiwan) corresp at various times for Asian Wall Street Journal, New York Times and United Press Int; Co-Founder, Chief Ed and Publr Commonwealth Magazine financial monthly 1981–; teaches journalism at Nat Chengchi Univ; mem Nat Unification Comm. *Address:* 4th Floor, 87 Sungkiang Rd, Taipei, Taiwan.

YORK, The Duchess of, Sarah Margaret; British royal; b 15 Oct 1959; d of Maj Ronald Ivor and Susan Mary Ferguson (née Wright, now Susan Mary Barrantes); m Prince Andrew Albert Christian Edward, Duke of York 1986 (divorced); two d: Princess Beatrice Elizabeth Mary, b 1988; Princess Eugenie Victoria Helena, b 1990. *Education:* Queen's Secretarial Coll. *Career:* Worked in public relations, an art gallery and in publishing prior to marriage; currently TV presenter USA and UK. *Publications:* My Story: The Duchess of York (autobiog) 1996, A Guard Within, Bright Lights, The Royal Switch, Victoria and Albert: Life at Osborne House, Sarah Ferguson: The Royal Redhead (Taking Part Series), Dining With the Duchess: Making Everyday Meals a Special Occasion (jtly) 1999, Dieting with the Duchess: Secrets and Sensible Advice for a Great Body; For Children: Budgie: The Little Helicopter 1989, Budgie at Bendick's Point 1996, The Adventures of Budgie.

YORK, Susannah; British actress; b 9 Jan 1942, London; d of William Fletcher and Joan Bowring; m Michael Wells 1960 (divorced 1976); one s one d. *Education:* Royal Acad of Dramatic Art (London). *Career:* Actress in plays, films, TV etc. *Plays include:* Wings of a Dove, Man and Superman, Private Lives, Hedda Gabler (London and New York), Appearances (London and Paris), Peter Pan, Cinderella, The Singular Life of Albert Nobbs, Fatal Attraction, The Women, The Apple Cart, Agnes of God, The Human Voice, Multiple Choice, A Private Treason,

Lyric for a Tango, The Glass Menagerie, A Streetcar Named Desire, Noonbreak, September Tide 1993–94, The Merry Wives of Windsor 1997, Camino Real 1998, Hamlet 1998, An Ideal Husband 1998, Small Craft Warnings 1999; Dir: Revelations 1991, Salome 1992, The Eagle Has Two Heads 1994, The First Years/Beginnings 1995; *Films include:* Tunes of Glory 1960, The Greengage Summer 1961, Freud 1962, Tom Jones 1963, Act One Scene Nun 1964, Sands of the Kalahari 1965, Kaleidoscope 1966, A Man for All Seasons 1966, Sebastian 1967, The Killing of Sister George 1968, Lock up Your Daughters 1969, They Shoot Horses, Don't They? (Acad Award nomination) 1969, Country Dance 1970, Jane Eyre 1970, Zee and Co 1971, Happy Birthday Wanda June 1971, Images (Best Actress Award, Cannes Film Festival) 1972, The Maids, Gold 1974, Conduct Unbecoming 1974, That Lucky Touch 1975, Skyriders 1976, Eliza Fraser 1976, The Shout 1977, Superman 1978, The Silent Partner, Superman II 1980, Yellowbeard, Fatal Attraction 1985, Just Ask for Diamond 1988, A Summer Story 1988, The Glass Menagerie 1989, Melancholia 1989, Loophole, Golden Gate Murders, Alice, A Christmas Carol, Mio my Mio, Bluebeard, Barbablu Barbablu, Little Women, Princess 1993; *TV appearances include:* The Crucible, Fallen Angels, Second Chance, We'll Meet Again, The Other Side of Me, Macho, Trainer, Devices and Desires; Producer: The Big One 1983; *Publications:* Children's books: In Search of Unicorns, Lark's Castle. *Leisure interests:* reading, writing, gardening, travelling, riding, theatre and cinema going. *Address:* c/o PFD, Drury House, 34-43 Russell St, London WC2B 5HA, UK.

YOSHIDA, Miyako; Japanese ballet dancer; b 28 Oct 1965, Tokyo; d of Eiji and Etsuko (née Fukuda) Yoshida. *Education:* Kunitachi Ballet Studio, Matsuyama Ballet School, Tokyo and Royal Ballet School, London. *Career:* Joined Sadler's Wells Royal Ballet 1984; Principal Dancer Birmingham Royal Ballet, 1988–95, Royal Ballet, London 1995–; Prix de Lausanne 1983; Global Award 1989; Dancer of the Year Award, Dance and Dancer Magazine 1991. *Performances include:* Swan Lake, Sleeping Beauty, The Nutcracker, Giselle, Elite Syncopations, La Fille Mal Gardée, Hobson's Choice, The Dream, Don Quixote Pas de deux, Paquita, Allegri Diversi, Theme and Variations, Concerto Barnocco, Les Sylphides, Divertimento No 15, Dance Concertantes Symphony in three movements, Choreatium, Five Tangos, Pavaue Pas de deux; *Film:* Hobson's Choice. *Leisure interests:* reading, watching films, listening to music. *Address:* c/o Royal Ballet, Covent Garden, London WC2 9DD, UK.

YOSHIMOTO, Banana (Mahoko); Japanese writer; b 1964; d of Takaaki Yoshimoto. *Education:* Nihon Univ. *Career:* Worked as a waitress before becoming a writer; novels translated into English, Italian and German; winner five literary prizes. *Publications include:* Kitchen, Pineapple Pudding, Fruit Basket, Lizard.

YOSHINAGA, Sayuri; Japanese actress; b 1945; m Tado Okada. *Education:* Waseda Univ. *Career:* Film debut in Town with a Cupola 1962; has since appeared in nearly 100 films; Japan Acad Award for Best Actress 1985. *Films include:* The Sound of Waves, The Makioka Sisters, The Diary of Yumechiyo, Ohan, Heaven Station, Killing Time by the Shores of a Mysterious Sea, Joyu.

YOUNG, Baroness (Life Peer), cr 1971, of Farnworth in the County Palatine of Lancaster, **Janet Mary Young,** PC, DL, MA; British politician and university chancellor; b 23 Oct 1926, Widnes; d of John Norman Leonard and Phyllis Marguerite (née Hancock) Baker; m Geoffrey Tyndale Young 1950; three d. *Education:* Dragon School (Oxford), Headington School, St Anne's Coll (Oxford) and New Haven (CT, USA). *Career:* Councillor Oxford City Council 1957, Alderman and leader of Cons Group 1967; Baroness-in-Waiting (Govt Whip in House of Lords) 1972–73; Parl Under-Sec of State Dept of the Environment 1973–74; Minister of State Dept of Educ and Science 1979–81; Chancellor of Duchy of Lancaster and Leader of House of Lords 1981–82; Minister in charge of Civil Service Dept 1981; Minister in charge of Man and Personnel Office 1981–83; Lord Privy Seal and Leader of House of Lords 1982–83; Minister of State FCO 1983–87; a Vice-Chair Cons Party Org 1975–83, Deputy Chair 1977–79, Co-Chair Women's Nat Comm 1979–83; Chancellor Univ of Greenwich 1993–98; Dir Nat Westminster Bank PLC 1987–96, Marks and Spencer PLC 1987–97; Chair Ind Schools Jt Council 1989–92, 1994–97, Asscn of Cons Peers 1995–2000, Pres 2001–; Deputy Lieut for Oxon 1989;

Vice-Pres W India Cttee 1987–95, Pres 1995–, Vice-Pres Asscn of Dist Councils 1990–; mem Council Ditchley Foundation 1990–, Court Cranfield Univ 1991–; Trustee Dorneywood 1992–; Hon Fellow Inst of Civil Engineers, St Anne's Coll (Oxford) 1978; Hon DCL (Mt Holyoke Coll) 1982; Dr hc (Greenwich) 1998; Max Beloff Award 2000; Parliamentarian of the Year Award, The Spectator 2001; Peer of the Year Award, Channel 4 2001. *Leisure interest:* music. *Address:* House of Lords, London SW1A 0PW, UK. *Telephone:* (20) 7219-3156; *Fax:* (20) 7219-0785; *E-mail:* stevensonmm@parliament.uk.

YOUNG, Frances Margaret, OBE, PH D; British professor of theology and ecclesiastical history; b 25 Nov 1939, Frome, Somerset; d of Alfred Stanley and Mary Frances (née Marshall) Worrall; m Robert Charles Young 1964; three s. *Education:* County Grammar Schools (Birkenhead and Gloucester), Bedford Coll (London) and Girton Coll (Cambridge). *Career:* Research Fellow Clare Hall, Cambridge 1967–68; temp Lecturer Univ of Birmingham 1971–73, Lecturer Dept of Theology 1973–82, Sr Lecturer 1982–86, Edward Cadbury Prof 1986–, Head Dept of Theology 1986–95, Head of School of Philosophy and Theology 1989–93, Dean Faculty of Arts 1995–97; Pro-Vice-Chancellor Univ of Birmingham 1997–2002; Ordained Methodist Minister 1984; Hon DD (Aberdeen) 1994. *Publications include:* Sacrifice and the Death of Christ 1975, Can These Dry Bones Live? 1982, From Nicaea to Chalcedon 1983, Face to Face: A Narrative Essay in the Theology of Suffering 1985, The Art of Performance 1990, The Theology of the Pastoral Letters 1994, Biblical Exegesis and the Formation of Christian Culture 1997; numerous books and articles on the theology of the early church. *Leisure interests:* walking, cycling, camping, travel, music, poetry, literature. *Address:* Pro-Vice-Chancellor's Office, University of Birmingham, POB 363, Edgbaston, Birmingham B15 2TT, UK (Office); 142 Selly Park Rd, Birmingham B29 7LH, UK (Home). *Telephone:* (121) 414-5940 (Office); (121) 472-4841 (Home); *Fax:* (121) 414-4534 (Office); *E-mail:* f.m.young@bham.ac.uk.

YOUNG, Kirsty; British television presenter; b 1969, Glasgow; d of John and Catherine Young; m;. *Career:* Fmrly with BBC Radio Scotland; fmr newsreader Scottish TV, presenter Kirsty (own talkshow); newsreader Channel 5 News 1997–99; now with Ind TV News; presenter Talk Radio 1998–; Newsreader of the Year, TV and Radio Industries Awards 1998. *Address:* c/o Mike Hollingsworth, Venture Artistes, Cuddesdon House, Cuddesdon, Oxford OX44 9HB. *Telephone:* (7000) 402001; *Fax:* (7000) 402002; *E-mail:* venture-artistes@msn.com.

YOUNG, Lola, OBE; British professor of cultural studies. *Career:* Began career in arts devt promoting black arts and culture; Prof of Cultural Studies Univ of Middx; Project Dir Nat Museum and Archives of Black History and Culture (NMABHC); mem Bd of Resource: Council of Museums, Archives and Libraries; mem Bd Royal Nat Theatre; Chair Panel of Judges Orange Prize for Fiction 1999. *Publication:* Fear of the Dark: Race, Gender and Sexuality in Cinema 1996. *Address:* Department of Cultural Studies, Middlesex University, White Hart Lane, London N17, UK.

YOUNG, Rosie Margaret, CBE, MD, FRCP (UK), FRCP(E), FRACP; British university administrator and professor of medicine; b 23 Oct 1930, Hong Kong; d of Yeung Shun Hang and Shiu Shui Ying. *Education:* Univ of Hong Kong. *Career:* Prof of Medicine Univ of Hong Kong, Dean Faculty of Medicine 1983–85, Pro-Vice-Chancellor 1985–93; Chair Medical Council of Hong Kong 1988–96; Overseas Adviser Royal Coll of Physicians of Edinburgh 1987–96; mem Council RACP 1993–96; JP, Hong Kong 1971; has published over 100 articles in int medical journals, mostly on diabetes, CHO metabolism and endocrinology; Hon D SC (Hong Kong, Open Learning Inst of Hong Kong) 1995; Fellow Royal Coll of Physicians (Glasgow); Hon Fellow Newnham Coll, Cambridge 1988; Hon D SC Univ of Hong Kong. *Address:* Rm 413, Professorial Block, Queen Mary Hospital, Hong Kong Special Administrative Region, People's Republic of China. *Telephone:* 2855-4253; *Fax:* 2855-1143.

YOUNG, Sean; American actress; b 20 Nov 1959, Louisville, KY; d of Lee Guthrie. *Education:* Interlochen Arts Acad (MI). *Career:* Worked as a receptionist and model before film debut in Jane Austen in Manhattan 1980. *Films:* Jane Austen in Manhattan 1980, Stripes 1981, Blade Runner 1982, Young Doctors in Love 1982, Dune 1984, Baby: The

Secret of the Lost Legend 1985, No Way Out 1987, Wall Street 1987, The Boost 1988, Cousins 1989, Fire Birds, A Kiss Before Dying, Love Crimes, Once Upon a Crime, Hold Me Thrill Me Kiss Me, Forever, Fatal Instinct, Ace Ventura: Pet Detective, Even Cowgirls Get the Blues, Mirage, Dr Jekyll and Ms Hyde; *TV appearances include:* Under the Biltmore Clock, Tender Is The Night (mini-series), Blood and Orchids (film), Blue Ice (film), Witness to the Execution (film), Model by Day (film).

YOUNG, Simone; Australian conductor and musical director; b 2 March 1961. *Education:* Sydney Conservatorium of Music. *Career:* Conductor Paris Opera, Vienna Philharmonic, Berlin and Vienna Staatsoper, Cologne Opera, Royal Opera House (London), Metropolitan Opera (New York), Houston Grand Opera, Munich Philharmonic Orchestra, Maggio Musicale (Florence), ORF Radio Orchestra Vienna, NDR Hanover, NHK Symphony Orchestra (Japan), Hamburg Philharmonic Orchestra; with Opera Australia 1997–; Chief Conductor Bergen Philharmonic Orchestra 1999–; repertoire: The Little Mermaid, Aida, The Bamboo Flute, The Mikado, Falstaff, Tannhäuser, Don Carlo; Young Australian of the Year 1987. *Address:* c/o Arts Management, Station House, Rawson Place, 790 George St, Sydney, NSW 2000, Australia. *Telephone:* (2) 9699-1099; *Fax:* (2) 9699-3184; *Internet:* www.opera-australia.org.au.

YOUSRA; Egyptian actress; b (Sevine Mohammed Nessim) 1956. *Education:* English-language schools in Heliopolis (Cairo). *Career:* Film actress; has appeared in about 80 films. *Films include:* The Nightmare, The Emigrant 1994, Birds of Darkness.

YSTAD, Vigdis, D PHIL; Norwegian professor of Scandinavian literature; b 13 Jan 1942, Verdal; d of Ottar Ystad and Guri Todal; m 1st Asbjørn Liland 1962; m 2nd Daniel Haakonsen 1971; one s one d. *Education:* Univ of Trondheim and Univ of Oslo. *Career:* Lecturer Univ of Oslo 1974, Prof of Scandinavian Literature 1979–, mem Univ Bd 1990–92; Chair Council for Research in the Humanities 1985; Chair Bd Centre for Advanced Study, Norwegian Acad of Science and Letters 1992–93; Vice-Chair Nat Acad of Dramatic Art 1993–96; mem Norwegian Research Council 1979–85, Norwegian Govt Research Cttee 1982–84, Norwegian Acad of Science and Letters, Norwegian Acad for Language and Literature; mem Bd Nat Acad of Art 2000–. *Publications:* Kristofer Uppdals Lyrikk 1978, Henrik Ibsens Dikt 1991, Sigrid Undsel: Et kvinneliv–"livets endeløse gåde" 1993, Ibsens dikt og drama 1996, Contemporary Approaches to Ibsen's Drama (ed). *Address:* Centre for Ibsen Studies, Box 1116, Blindern, 0316 Oslo, Norway; Nils Tollers vei 3, 0851 Oslo, Norway (Home). *Telephone:* 22-85-91-65 (Office); 22-69-10-95 (Home); *Fax:* 22-85-91-69 (Office); *E-mail:* a.v .ystad@ibsen.uio.no.

YUAN ENFENG; Chinese folk singer; b 22 Jan 1940, Shaanxi Prov; d of Yuan Zaiming and the late Li Dexian; m Sun Shao; two d one s. *Education:* Dong Yangshi Elementary School (Xian). *Career:* Joined Cultural Troupe of Provincial Broadcasting Station 1951; Participated in over 3,000 performances, including numerous solo concerts and 1,000 radio and TV programmes; Hon Dir and Chair Folk Music Section, Shaanxi Broadcasting Station 1986–; Vice-Chair Shaanxi TV Station; appearances abroad include Romania, Bulgaria, Czechoslovakia, USSR, Japan, Thailand, Philippines and USA; mem Chinese Musicians' Asscn; mem of Bd (Shaanxi Branch) Chinese Cultural Exchange Centre; mem many other official orgs; State Actress Award 1987; May Day Labour Medal Award 1993. *Compositions include:* (jtly) Millet is Delicious and Caves are Warm, Nowhere is Better than Our North Shaanxi; 300 songs on record, cassette and CD and many song books; *TV film:* Silver Bell. *Leisure interests:* table tennis, fabric weaving. *Address:* Folk Music Section, Provincial Broadcasting and Television Station, Xian, Shaanxi, People's Republic of China. *Telephone:* (29) 7852689.

YUE JINGYU; Chinese swimmer; b March 1975, Shanghai. *Career:* Entered Chinese Women's Swimming Team 1991; broke Olympic record for women's 100m free style and won Gold Medal at 26th Olympics, Atlanta. *Publications:* My Way of Coaching. *Address:* c/o State General Bureau for Physical Culture and Sports, 9 Tiyuguan Rd, Chongwen District, Beijing, 100763, People's Republic of China.

YUK, Zoya, PH D; Belarusian economist and academic; b 20 Sept 1933, Kotelnichesky Dist, Kirov Region, Russian Fed; m (husband deceased); one d. *Education:* Moscow Inst of Nat Economy and Belarusian Polytechnic Acad. *Career:* Vice-Rector Belarusian Public Univ of Management 1993–2001, Chair-Head of Econs, Dir of the Belarusian Scientific Research Centre of Gender Problems 1999–2001; Chair-Head of Political Economy, Belarusian Tech Univ of Informatics and Radio-Electronics; mem Academic Council, Belarusian State Univ on defending cand and doctorate degree dissertations; Pres Belarusian Asscn of Women Managers; more than 100 papers and articles published; Honour Award for Excellent Achievement in Educ in USSR 1983; Honour Award for Excellent Achievement in Educ in Belarus 1995; Silver Medal of Achievements, Exhibition of Nat Economy of USSR; Diploma of the Ministry of Educ of the USSR; Diploma of the Ministry of Educ of the Repub of Belarus. *Publications include:* Monographs: Labour of a Woman and Family 1975, The Scientific-Technical Progress and Women's Labour 1982, A Woman In Working Collective 1985, A Man–A Key Basis of the Sustainable Development of Society: The Gender Approach 1999, The Family and Its Social Meaning in Common Values Education 2000, A Man in the System of Education: The Gender Approach 2000. *Leisure interests:* dancing, sport. *Address:* Minsk 220015, 28 ul Yanki Mavra, kv 28, Belarus. *Telephone:* (172) 21-33-28; *Fax:* (172) 226-12-32.

YUKAWA, Setsuko, PH D; Japanese economist; b 22 Jan 1941, Kobe; d of Yoshitake and Yaeko (née Hiramatsu) Yukawa. *Education:* Osaka Univ. *Career:* Lecturer in Econs Kyoto Sangyo Univ 1968–72, Assoc Prof 1972–80, apptd Prof 1980; Programme Officer UN, Tokyo 1983–84, Consultant 1984–87; Visiting Researcher, México (Govt of Mexico Fellow) 1974–75; mem Japanese Soc of Int Econs, Japanese Soc of Social Sciences on Latin America, Japanese Asscn for Planning Admins, Japanese Soc of Econ Policies. *Publications:* Agricultural Development in LDCs 1978, The Mexican Economy 1982, Development Planning in Mixed Economies (ed) 1988, The Political Economy of Fiscal Policy (ed) 1989, Development Planning 1990; numerous contribs to professional journals. *Address:* Kyoto Sangyo University, Kamigamo-Motoyama Kita-ku, Kyoto 603, Japan.

YUVAL-DAVIS, Nira, PH D; British/Israeli professor in gender and ethnic studies; b 22 Aug 1943, Tel-Aviv; d of Itzhak and Rivlea Yuval. *Education:* Hebrew Univ of Jerusalem and Sussex Univ (UK). *Career:* Specialist on Israel; Research Asst, teacher in Israel, USA and UK 1966–73; Lecturer in Sociology Thames Polytechnic (now Univ of Greenwich) 1974, Sr Lecturer 1978, Reader in Gender and Ethnic Studies 1989, apptd Prof 1995; Elizabeth Poppleton Visiting Fellow ANU 1989; Ginsbury Fellow LSE (UK) 1990–91; Visiting Fellow ISS, The Hague (Netherlands) 1992; mem Ichamsin publication forum on the Middle East, Women Against Fundamentalism. *Publications:* Israel and the Palestinians (co-ed) 1975, Israeli Women and Men: Division Behind the Unity 1981, Woman-Nation-State (co-ed) 1989, The Gulf War and the New World Order (co-ed) 1991, Racialized Boundaries (jtly) 1992, Refusing Holy Orders: Women and Fundamentalism in Britain (jtly) 1992, Unsettling Settler Society 1995, Gender and Nation 1996. *Leisure interests:* sun, sea, sand, national dancing, reading, soaps. *Address:* University of Greenwich, Bexley Rd, Eltham, London SE9 2HB, UK (Office); 7 Montague Rd, London E8 2HN, UK (Home). *Telephone:* (20) 8331-8934; *Fax:* (20) 8331-8905; *E-mail:* n .yuvaldavis@gre.ac.uk.

Z

ZABALETA-HINRICHSEN, Marta Raquel, B SC, MA, D PHIL; British/Argentine writer and lecturer; b 26 June 1937, Alcorta, Argentina; d of the late Roque Zabaleta and Catalina Gerlo de Zabaleta; m Ricardo A. Hinrichsen (separated); one s one d. *Education:* Univ del Litoral (Argentina), Univ de Chile and Univ of Sussex. *Career:* Lecturer Univ del Litoral 1961–62; research in Chile on Family Planning, the Chilean Peasant Movt, Agrarian Reform, women in Argentina, adult literacy and ideology 1965; Jr Fellow CELADE, Chile 1965–66; Jr Fellow ICIRA (FAO), Chile 1966–67; Lecturer, then Sr Lecturer, Univ of Concepción, Chile 1968–73, Deputy Head, Dept of Econs 1973; expelled from Chile 1973; Sr Lecturer in Spanish and Latin American Studies, Culture and Gender and Philosophy, Psychology and Sociology Univ of Middx (fmrly Middx Polytechnic) 1989–; Adviser Change UK 1980–; featured in video and film documentaries including Daughters of de Beauvoir 1989; Presidential Decree of Recognition for work as Social Scientist awarded by Govt of Argentina 1973. *Publications:* Reclaim the Earth: women speak out for life on earth (contrib) 1983, Daughters of de Beauvoir (contrib) 1989, Women in Argentina 1810–1992 1993, Change International UK 1993, An Analysis of the Speeches of Eva Perón 1994. *Leisure interests:* poetry, conversation and debate with son and daughter, letter-writing. *Address:* University of Middlesex, White Hart Lane, London N17 8HR, UK (Office); Garnon Cottage, Bower Hill, Epping, Essex CM16 7AB, UK (Home). *Telephone:* (20) 8362-5000 (Office); *Fax:* (20) 8362-6878 (Office).

ZABELINA, Aleksandra Ivanovna; Russian sportswoman; b 11 March 1931, Moscow; one s. *Education:* Inst of History of the USSR (Moscow). *Career:* Began Fencing 1953; Individual World Champion 1957, 1967, Individual Jr World Champion 1958; mem winning team World Championships (seven times); Olympic Champion (three times); mem winning team USSR Championships (six times); fencing coach 1973–; awarded Insignia of Honour, Medals of Labour Bravery. *Leisure interests:* reading, sewing, journalism. *Address:* 125083 Moscow, Novaya Basmannaya ul 3, kv 99, Russian Federation. *Telephone:* (095) 212-71-23.

ZACK, Badanna, BA, MFA, RCA; Canadian sculptor; b 22 March 1933, Montréal, PQ. *Education:* Concordia Univ. *Career:* Tutor Rutgers Univ 1966–67, Georgian Coll, Humber Coll, The Art Gallery of Ontario, Guelph Univ 1969–85, Sheridan Coll 1980–; solo exhibitions include Rutgers Univ, Gallery O (Toronto) 1973, 1975, Burnaby Art Gallery 1977, Factory 77 (Toronto) 1981, The Art Gallery of Hamilton 1983–84, travelling exhibition 1990, Univ of Toronto 1991; group exhibitions include New Jersey State Museum (USA) 1967, Harbourfront Art Gallery (Toronto) 1975, 1977, 1978, Artspace Travelling Exhibition 1978–80, Toronto Int Art Fair 1981, Juxtaposition Powerhouse (Montréal) 1982, Woodstock Livestock 1985, Sculpture Biennial (Antwerp, Belgium) 1985, Gairloch Gardens 1988, Workscene Gallery (Toronto) 1990; works held in numerous public and pvt collections; contribs to professional journals and catalogues; Canada Council Awards 1968–69, 1974–75, 1978, 1985; Ontario Arts Council awards 1975–85. *Address:* 83 Elm Grove Ave, Toronto, ON M6K 2J2, Canada.

ZADEK, Hilde; Austrian singing teacher and former opera singer; b 15 Dec 1917, Bromberg, Germany; d of Alex and Elisabeth Zadek. *Education:* Conservatories of Jerusalem (Israel) and Zurich (Switzerland). *Career:* Austrian State Opera, Vienna 1947–71; has performed at Royal Opera House, Covent Garden (London), Metropolitan Opera (New York), in Berlin, Düsseldorf and Zurich, and at Glyndebourne (UK), Salzburg, Edinburgh (UK) and Amsterdam (Netherlands) Festivals; Head of Vocal Dept, Vienna Municipal Conservatory 1964–78; has given Master Classes world-wide since 1978; Hon mem Vienna State Opera; awarded Austrian Ehrenkreuz for Arts and Sciences (First Class). *Operas include:* Aida, Tosca, Ariadne, Salome. *Leisure interests:* painting, country house. *Address:* Gustav-Tschermak-Gasse 34, 1190 Vienna, Austria.

ZAHER, Celia Ribeiro, PH D; Brazilian librarian and United Nations official; b 3 June 1931, Rio de Janeiro; d of Frederico and Maria-Eugenia (née Figueirinha) Ribeiro; m Ahmed Saad El Dine Zaher 1959; one s. *Education:* Library School (Rio de Janeiro), Faculdade Nacional de Direito and Columbia Univ (New York). *Career:* Chief Biology, Research and Trans Section, Brazilian Inst for Bibliography and Documentation 1954–64, Prof 1963–72, Dir of Bibliography Services 1966–68, Pres 1969–71; apptd Prof Fed Univ, Rio de Janeiro 1971; Divisional Dir UNESCO, Paris 1972–74, Acting Dir Documentation, Libraries and Archives Dept 1974–76, Dir 1976–77, Div of Book Promotion and Encouragement of Int Cultural Exchanges 1977–84, Dir Div on Book Promotion, Audiovisual Archives and Int Exchanges 1985–87, Deputy Asst Dir Gen Communications Sector 1984–87, Chief of Mission, México, Dominican Repub 1987–88, Sec-Gen History of Mankind Programme 1988, apptd Dir Div of Cultural Studies and Policies 1988; Dir Brazilian Nat Library 1982–84; mem Int Fed of Library Asscns; Commdr Rio Branco Order. *Leisure interests:* sailing, fishing. *Address:* UNESCO, 7 place de Fontenoy, 75700 Paris, France.

ZAHIROVIĆ, Ajša (Džemila); Bosnia and Herzegovina writer; b 21 March 1940, Sarajevo; d of Ago Zahirović and Džemila Haćam; one d. *Education:* Faculty of Law (Sarajevo). *Career:* Adviser and Chef de Cabinet Cen Cttee Bosnia and Herzegovina Communist Party 1970–78; Cultural Adviser and Chef de Cabinet Presidency of Bosnia and Herzegovina 1978–84; writer and poet 1984–; has published 11 books of poetry, works included in seven anthologies of women's poetry and over 25 int anthologies; Co-Ed Skylark int journal of poetry, India; mem World Acad of Arts and Culture, Int Women's Writing Guild (USA), Int Poets' Acad (Madras, now Chennai, India), World Poetry Research Inst Council of Dirs (Repub of Korea), Poet–India Editorial Bd; Hon D LITT World Acad of Arts and Culture 1988; has recieved 11 awards and prizes for poetry and one for humanity including Int Eminent Poet (Int Poets' Acad, Madras), Robert Frost Award (Adult Literary Arts, San Mateo, USA) 1990, Silver Crown (Accademia Int di Pontzen, Italy) 1991, Int Prize for Poetry (Int Soc of Greek Writers) 1994. *Publications include:* The Porch 1981, By The White Eye 1983, Terra Mare Amore 1983, Italy 1985, Under the Shadows 1985, Another Moment 1987, By the Edge of Road 1987, Skylark 1988, One Echo More 1989, Under the Crown (Australia Day Medallion 1991) 1991, The Poetic Voices of Women from all Meridians (ed, anthology) 1992; ed of numerous anthologies; poems trans to languages including Italian, Hindi, English, Arabic, Urdu, Turkish, German, Greek, Spanish, Japanese, Punjabi, Bengali, French, Portuguese, etc. *Leisure interests:* travel, reading, walking, friendship. *Address:* Kranjčevićeva 41/3, 71000 Sarajevo, Bosnia and Herzegovina. *Telephone:* (71) 542645; *Fax:* (71) 542645.

ZÁHLAVOVÁ, Eva, MU DR; Czech dentist; b 26 May 1935, Prague; d of Ladislav and Jarmila Salzer; m Jan Záhlava 1957; one s one d. *Education:* Charles Univ (Plzeň). *Career:* Lecturer Plzeň Dental Clinic 1960–90, Sr Lecturer 1990–; mem CP of Czechoslovakia until resignation in 1969; Pres Czech Soc of Operative Dentistry 1990–; mem Comm for Dental Materials; Dentistry Teaching Awards 1979, 1981, 1985; Stomatological Soc Award for Best Scientific Publication 1989. *Publications:* Dental Materials 1980, Operative Dentistry (jtly) 1984, Propaeduetic of Dentistry (jtly) 1987; 71 articles in scientific journals. *Leisure interests:* tennis, history of art, gardening. *Address:* Stomatol

Klinika, LL 17 Listopadu 1, 350 99 Plzeň, Czech Republic (Office); Borská 41, 320 23 Plzeň, Czech Republic (Home). *Telephone:* (19) 272019 (Home).

ZALEHA ISMAIL, Datin Paduka Hajjah, BA; Malaysian politician; b 18 May 1936, Batu Laut, Selangor; three c. *Education:* Univ of Malaya. *Career:* Fmrly mem staff Radio Malaysia 1951–68; Tutor Univ of Malaya 1965–71; Official of Dewan Bahasa dan Pustaka 1968–74; Political Sec to Minister of Welfare 1974–78, Parl Sec Ministry of Land and Regional Devt 1986–87; mem Selangor State Ass for Permatang 1978–82, mem Selangor State Cabinet 1978–82; mem House of Reps (Parl) for Tanjung Karang 1982–86, for Selayang 1986–95, for Gombak 1995–; Deputy Minister of Transport 1987–95, Minister of Nat Unity and Social Devt 1995; Pres Child Welfare Council Malaysia 1981–, Nat Council of Women's Orgs Malaysia 1989–; mem Bd ASEAN Confed of Women's Org 1981–; Officer of the Most Esteemed Order of the Defender of the Realm 1979; Commdr of the Order of the Crown of Selangor 1980. *Address:* c/o Wisma Bumiraya, 21st Floor, No 10 Jalan Raja Laut, 50562 Kuala Lumpur, Malaysia.

ZALESKI, Jean; American artist; b Birkikara, Malta; d of John and Caroline (née Micallef) Busuttil; two s one d. *Education:* Art Students' League, New School and Parsons School of Design (New York), and Moore Coll of Art (PA). *Career:* Instructor Hussian Coll of Art, PA 1970–71; Dir Naples Art Studio, Italy 1972–74; Dir Art Studio 733, New York 1974–75; Adjunct Lecturer Brooklyn Coll, New York 1974–75, Hofstra Univ 1977–82, Cooper Union 1986–; Corp Sec Women in the Arts, NY 1974–75, Exec Co-ordinator 1976–78; Painter and Print-maker; solo exhibitions include Galleria Stuciv (Florence, Italy) 1973, Adelphi Univ 1975, Women in the Arts Gallery (New York) 1975, Il Gabbiano Gallery (Naples, Italy) 1973, Alonzo Gallery (New York) 1979, 1980, Elaine Starkman Gallery (New York) 1986, Romano Gallery (NJ) 1987, 1988, Citicorp Center (New York) 1988, 1989, Z Gallery (New York) 1991, Sweet Briar Coll (VA) 1993, A/E Gallery (New York) 1995, Trinity Coll (CT) 1996, Myungsook Lee Gallery (New York) 1996, Westbeth Gallery (New York) 2000; group exhibitions include Art USA 1969, Int Art Exhibition (Cannes, France) 1969, Frick Museum (Pittsburgh) 1970, Palazzo Vecchio (Florence) 1972, Int Women's Art Festival (Milan, Italy) 1975, Allbright Knox Museum (Buffalo) 1986, Museum of the City of New York 1993, Slater Memorial Museum (CT) 1999; Invitation to White House for Top Five Women Artists 1977; Susan B. Anthony Award for Painting, Nat Org for Women 1986. *Publications:* COW-LINES (jtly) 1983, Winged Spirits 1996. *Leisure interests:* swimming, walking, music, reading. *Address:* 55 Bethune St, New York, NY 10014, USA. *Telephone:* (212) 929-4194; *E-mail:* valletta@aol.com; *Internet:* www.aboutmalta.com/grazio/zaleskiances.html.

ZALLINGER, Ursula von; Austrian foundation executive; b 16 May 1939, Munich; d of Meinhard and Maria (née Ziegler) von Zallinger; m R. W. Schmidt 1972. *Education:* Salzburg, Vienna and Munich (Germany). *Career:* Freelance mem staff Int Music Competition, ARD (radio and TV), Germany; joined Prix Jeunesse Foundation, Munich, Germany 1963, Organizational Man until 1990, Sec-Gen 1991–; Exec Dir World Alliance of TV for Children (WATCH), Munich; Trustee Int Inst of Communication (London); Corresp mem Academía Argentina de Comunicación; awarded German Order of Merit for Service to the Community 1996. *Leisure interests:* skiing, collecting paintings. *Address:* Bayerischer Rundfunk, 80300 Munich, Germany (Office); Destouchestr 14, 80803 Munich, Germany (Home). *Telephone:* (89) 59002058; *Fax:* (89) 59003058.

ZAMBELLO, Francesca; American opera and musical director; b New York. *Career:* Works directed include: San Francisco Opera: La Traviata 1983, La Voix Humaine 1986, Faust 1986, La Bohème 1988, Prince Igor; New York Metropolitan Opera: Lucia di Lammermoor 1992; Royal Opera House (Covent Garden, UK): Billy Budd 1995–96, Arianna 1995–96; English Nat Opera: Khovanshchina 1995–96; Copenhagen: Tannhäuser 1995–96; Santa Fe Opera: Modern Painters 1995–96; Nat Theatre: Lady in the Dark 1997; Shaftesbury Theatre (London): Napoleon 2000; several Olivier awards. *Address:* c/o Shaftesbury Theatre, Manager's Office, 210 Shaftesbury Ave, London WC2, UK.

ZÁMEČNÍKOVÁ, Dana; Czech artist; b 24 March 1945, Prague; d of Lubomír Zámečníc and Božena Zámečníková; m Marian Karel 1976; one d. *Education:* Czech Tech Univ (Prague) and Acad of Applied Arts (Prague). *Career:* Artist creating works out of glass; Instructor and Artist-in-Residence Pilchuer School (USA) 1983, 1985, 1989, Miasa (Japan) 1988, Sydney (Australia) 1991; exhibitions include Heller Gallery (New York), Galerie Gottschack Betz (Frankfurt, Germany), Gallery Clara-Scremini (Paris), Galerie Sanske (Zurich, Switzerland), Hokkaido Museum (Japan), American Craft Museum (New York), Museum Rihimäki (Finland), XLIII La Bienale di Venezia (Venice, Italy), Musée des Arts Décoratifs (Paris and Lausanne, Switzerland), Kunstmuseum (Düsseldorf, Germany), Yokohama Museum of Art (Japan); works rep in perm collections including Arts and Craft Museum (Prague), Corning Museum (New York), Hokkaido Museum of Modern Art, Victoria and Albert Museum (London), Toledo Museum (USA), Yokohama Museum (Japan), Musée des Arts Décoratifs (Paris and Lausanne), Victoria Museum (Melbourne, Australia), Museum Frauenau (Stuttgart, Germany); Award for Glaskunst '81 Kassel (Germany) 1981; Gold Award Kristal Nacht Project (PA, USA) 1992. *Address:* Stodůlecká 11, 158 00 Prague 5, Czech Republic. *Telephone:* (2) 551165; *Fax:* (2) 551165.

ZAMORA, Monica; Spanish ballet dancer; b 1974, Basque Country. *Career:* Began ballet aged 10; won scholarship to Royal Ballet School, UK 1990; Dancer with Birmingham Royal Ballet 1992–. *Ballets include:* Agon (Balanchine), The Cage (Robbins), Far from the Madding Crowd (Bintley), Swan Lake. *Address:* Birmingham Royal Ballet, Birmingham Hippodrome, Thorp St, Birmingham B5 4AU, UK.

ZAMORA-CHAVARRÍA, Eugenia M., LL M; Costa Rican executive; b 25 May 1957, San José. *Education:* Univ of Costa Rica and Harvard Univ. *Career:* Legal Advisor to Finance Minister 1980; Legal Asst Daremblum and Assocs 1980; Assoc Protection Officer UN High Comm, Mexico 1983–85; Ombudsman Nat Registry, Ministry of Justice and Grace 1985–86; Vice-Minister of Justice and Grace 1986–87; Chief of Cabinet and Spokesperson for Pres 1987–88; apptd Dir-Gen Inter-American Children's Inst, OAS 1988; Teaching and Research Asst Univ of Costa Rica Law School 1979–81, Prof of Roman Law 1982, Prof of Constitutional Law 1986; Research Asst Harvard Univ 1982–83; Prof of Constitutional Law Universidad Autónoma de Centro América 1985–86; Advisor Florida Int Univ 1986; Co-ordinator Inter-American System's Activities, UN Int Year of the Family 1990–94; mem American Soc of Int Law 1981–93, Bar Assoc of Costa Rica, Costa Rican Lawyers Union 1982–93; has written numerous papers on legislation and children's rights. *Address:* OAS, Avda 8 Octubre 2904, Montevideo, Uruguay; Rivera 2810, apdo 102, Montevideo, Uruguay (Home). *Telephone:* (2) 801412.

ZAMPATTI, Carla Maria, AM; Australian (b Italian) fashion designer and business executive; d of Domenico and Anna (née Caratti) Zampatti; m 1st Leo Schuman 1964; one s; m 2nd John Michael Spender 1975; two d. *Education:* In Italy and Western Australia. *Career:* Founder Zampatti Pty Ltd 1965, Founder and CEO Carla Zampatti Pty Ltd 1970–; Dir Australian Quality Council, Int Wool Secr 1993–, Australian Wool Research and Promotion Org 1993–, Business/Higher Educ Round Table 1994–, Australian Ballet School Council of Man 1995–, McDonald's Australia Ltd 1996–; Patron Alliance of Independent Girls' Schools 1996–; mem Bd of Govs Univ of W Sydney 1993, Bd of Man Australian Grad School of Man 1994– (Advisory Council 1994–); Chair Special Broadcasting Service 1999–; Qantas/Bulletin Businesswoman of the Year 1980; L'Onórificenza di Ufficiale 1981; BHP awards for excellence, Industry and Commerce Cttee 1984; Designer of the Year, Australian Fashion Awards 1994. *Leisure interests:* reading, travel, swimming, walking. *Address:* 11 Wellington St, Woollahra, NSW 2025, Australia; 437 Kent St, Sydney 2000, Australia. *Telephone:* (2) 264 8244 (Sydney); *Fax:* (2) 264 2220 (Sydney).

ZANA, Leyla; Turkish politician; b 1960. *Career:* Fmr Kurdish mem Turkish Grand Nat Ass (Parl); stripped of parliamentary immunity 1994; sentenced to 15 years' imprisonment by Turkish court for having links with PKK (Kurdistan Workers' Party) 1995; EP Sakharov Prize 1995.

ZANN, Lenore E.; Australian actress, singer and writer; b 22 Nov 1959, Sydney; d of Vincent and Janice (née Marshall) Zann; m Ralph Kerr 1987. *Education:* York Univ (Canada). *Career:* Film and theatre actress living and working in Canada; guest singer on Rita McNeil's Gold Album; mem Performing Artists for Nuclear Disarmament. *Plays include:* Two for the See-Saw, Salt Water Moon (ACTRA Best Actress Award) 1986; *Films include:* Hey Marilyné 1980, Visiting Hours 1982, Def-Con 4 1985, The Hounds of Notre Dame, Down Home. *Leisure interests:* poetry, art, music, dance, Zen Buddhism, philosophy, travel.

ZARAÏ, Rika; Israeli singer; b 19 Feb 1940, Jerusalem; d of Eliezer and Fruma (née Yosefovitch) Gozman; m Johanan Zaraï (divorced); one c. *Education:* Lemel Girls' School (Jerusalem), Hatirhon School and Conservatory of Music (Jerusalem). *Career:* Musical Dir Israeli Army variety group 1960; singer and songwriter 1963–; has toured Europe, N America and Asia; performed at l'Olympia, Paris 1986; Co-Founder Pronatura 1986; Médaille d'Argent, Ville de Paris; Médaille de Vermeil, Acad Française; several Gold Discs, France, the Netherlands, Canada. *Songs include:* Alors je chante, L'olivier, Hava Naguila, Et pourtant le temps, Sans chemise, sans pantalon, Quand je faisais mon service militaire, Balapapa, Une étoile d'or, Israël et Ismaël, Tu t'appelais Belz, Les drapeaux de la Méditerranée, Mon tour de France, Prague, Un beau jour je partirai, Viens danser avec moi, Ami, Hochana; Albums: D'amour et de paix 1999, Hava 2000; *Publications:* Ma médecine naturelle 1985, Mes secrets naturels 1988, Mes recettes saines et gourmandes 1990, Ces émotions qui guérissent, Le code secret de votre personnalité 1996. *Leisure interests:* natural medicine, reading, gardening, collecting antique furniture and books, walking. *Address:* Villa Montmorency, 2 bis ave des Tilleuls, 75016 Paris, France.

ZASLAVSKAYA, Tatiana Ivanovna, D ECON; Russian economist and sociologist; b 9 Sept 1927, Kiev, Ukraine; d of Ivan Vasilievich Karpov and Tatiana Georgievich Karpova; m Mikahil Zaslavsky; two d. *Education:* Moscow State Univ. *Career:* Sr Researcher Inst of Econs, Acad of Sciences, Moscow 1950–63; mem of Inst of Econs and Org of Industrial Production, Acad of Sciences, Novosibirsk 1963–87; Corresp mem of USSR Acad of Sciences 1968–81, mem 1981–; Dir Public Opinion Research Center, Moscow 1988–91, Head of Dept 1992–; Pres of Interdisciplinary Academic Center for Social Sciences (InterCenter), Moscow 1993–; Pres Sociological Asscn of USSR 1989–91; mem CPSU 1954–90; USSR People's Deputy 1989–91, mem Pres's Consulting Council 1991–, Comm for Labour, Prices and Social Policy; mem All-Union Agricultural Acad 1988, Council Int Fund for Survival and Devt of Humanity 1988, Acad Europea 1993–; Hon mem Polish Acad of Sciences; several hon degrees. *Publications include:* The Principle of Material Interest and Wage-Earning on Soviet Kolkhozes 1958, Contemporary Economics of Kolkhozes 1960, Labour Division on the Kolkhoz 1966, The Migration of the Rural Population in the USSR, A Voice of Reform 1989, The Second Socialist Revolution: An Alternative Strategy 1990, The Sociology of Economic Life 1991. *Leisure interests:* reading, gardening. *Address:* InterCenter, Vernadskogo prospekt 282, Moscow, Russian Federation. *Telephone:* (095) 938-21-12.

ZAVALA, Iris M., PH D; Puerto Rican professor of Hispanic literature and writer; b 27 Dec 1936, Puerto Rico; one c. *Education:* Univs of Puerto Rico and Salamanca (Spain). *Career:* Asst Prof Univ of Puerto Rico 1962–64, Visiting Prof 1978, 1981; Research Fellow El Colegio de México 1964–65, Visiting Prof 1979; Visiting Lecturer Queen's Coll, New York 1966; Asst Prof Hunter Coll, New York 1968–69; Assoc Prof State Univ of New York at Stony Brook 1969–71, Prof 1971–83, Jt Prof of Comparative Literature 1976–83; apptd Chair of Hispanic Literatures Rijksuniv te Utrecht, Netherlands 1983; Visiting Prof Univ di Calabria, Italy 1985, Univ de les Illes Balears, Mallorca, Spain 1989; mem Editorial Bd numerous journals including Third Woman 1982–, Anales de la Narrativa Española Contemporánea 1977–, Diálogos Hispánicos 1986–, La Torre 1986–, Journal of Interdisciplinary Studies 1988–; mem Soc for Spanish-Portuguese Historical Studies, American Asscn of Teachers of Spanish and Portuguese; has lectured on culture, literature and history in N and S America, E and W Europe, etc; Fellow American Philosophical Soc 1966; Guggenheim Foundation Fellowship 1966–67; Dr hc (Univ of Puerto Rico) 1996; Encomienda Lazo de Dama d la Orden de Mérito (Spain) 1988. *Publications include:* Unamuno y su teatro de conciencia (Nat Literary Prize of Puerto Rico 1964) 1963, La Revolución de 1868: historia, pensamiento, literatura

(co-ed) 1970, Ideología y política en la novela española del siglo XIX (Nat Literary Prize of Puerto Rico 1972) 1971, Escritura destada (ed) 1974, Historia social de la literatura española 1979, Que nadie muera sin amar el mar 1983, Nocturna mas no funesta (Finalist Premio Herralde) 1987, Rubén Darío bajo el signo del cisne (Nat Literary Prize 1990) 1989, Teorías de la modernidad 1991, Historia feminista de la literatura española (ed) 1992; numerous articles. *Leisure interests:* archaeology, antiques. *Address:* Rijksuniversiteit te Utrecht, Faculteit der Letteren, Kromme Nieuwegracht 29, 3512 KD Utrecht, Netherlands. *Telephone:* (30) 253-6537; *Fax:* (30) 253-6167.

ZELA, Vace; Albanian singer; b 7 April 1940; d of Hasan and Hava Zela; m Pjetër Rodiqi 1962; one d. *Education:* Lyceum of Fine Arts and Acad of Arts (Tirana). *Career:* Singer 1962–85; has taken part in numerous festivals in Albania and has represented Albania at concerts and festivals in France, Italy, Germany, Austria, Sweden, Switzerland, Norway, Greece, Yugoslavia, People's Repub of China and Egypt; has made several recordings; numerous honours and awards include Honoured Artist 1973, People's Artist 1977. *Leisure interests:* gardening, film, literature, playing the guitar. *Address:* Rruga Luigj Gurakuqi, Tirana, Pallati 15/1, Apt 4, Albania. *Telephone:* (42) 26329; *Fax:* (42) 26329.

ZELENSKAYA, Yelena Emilyevna; Russian opera singer (soprano); b Baku, Azerbaijan. *Education:* Baku State Conservatory (Azerbaijan). *Career:* Soloist Moscow Municipal Opera Theatre New Opera 1991–, Bolshoi Theatre; tours abroad 1992–; Guest-Soloist Chamber Opera, Vienna, Austria 1992–; performed in Opera Festivals in Lucerne, Savonnlinna (Finland). *Repertoire includes:* leading parts in operas Pique Dame, Eugene Onegin, in Prince Igor, Macbeth, Ball-Masquerade, Force of Destiny, Tosca, Marriage of Figaro. *Address:* Bolshoi Theatre, Teatralnaya square 1, Moscow, Russian Federation. *Telephone:* (095) 229-75-37.

ZELLER, Eva; German writer; b 25 Jan 1923, Eberswalde; d of Franz-Maria and Elisabeth (née Bertrand) Feldhaus; m Reimar Zeller 1951; one s three d. *Education:* Secondary school in Droyssig bei Zeitz, Univs of Greifswald, Marburg and Berlin. *Career:* Left GDR for FRG 1956; Guest Prof of Poetry Univ of Mainz 1987; mem Deutsche Akad für Sprache und Dichtung, Akad der Wissenschaften und der Literatur zu Mainz; awarded Droste Preis 1975, Ida-Dehmel Preis 1986, Eichendorff-Preis 1991. *Publications:* Novels: Der Sprung über den Schatten, Lampenfieber, Die Hauptfrau, Solange ich denken kann 1980, Nein und Amen 1985, Ein Stein aus Davids Hirtentasche 1992; Short stories: Die magische Rechnung, Ein Morgen Ende Mai, Der Turmbau 1975, Tod der Singschwäne; Poetry: Sage und schreibe, Fliehkraft, Auf dem Wasser gehn, Stellprobe 1989; Ed: Dreißig deutsche Jahre: zum Generationsbruch heute; also radio plays, etc. *Leisure interest:* swimming. *Address:* c/o Werderstr 17, 6900 Heidelberg 1, Germany.

ZELLWEGER, Renee, BA; American actress; b 25 April 1969, Katy, Texas. *Education:* Katy High School and Univ of Texas at Austin. *Films:* Dazed and Confused 1993, Reality Bites 1994, Love and a .45 1994, 8 Seconds 1994, The Low Life 1995, Empire Records 1995, The Whole Wide World 1996, Jerry Maguire 1996, Texas Chainsaw Massacre: The Next Generation 1997, Deceiver 1997, One True Thing 1998, A Price Above Rubies 1998, The Bachelor 1999, Me, Myself and Irene 2000, Nurse Betty (Golden Globe, Best Comedy Film Actress) 2000, Bridget Jones' Diary 2001; *TV:* Shake, Rattle and Rock Movie 1993, Murder in the Heartland 1994. *Address:* c/o United Talent Agency, 9560 Wilshire Blvd, Suite 500, Beverly Hills, CA 90212, USA.

ZEMANS, Joyce Lynn Pearl, MA; Canadian art historian and arts administrator; b 21 April 1941, Toronto; d of Harry and Cecile (née Minisman) Pearl; m Frederick H. Zemans 1960; two d one s. *Education:* Univ of Toronto and Courtauld Inst (Univ of London). *Career:* Lecturer, later Co-Chair of Art History, Chair Dept of Liberal Arts Studies Ontario Coll of Art 1966–75; Chair Dept of Visual Arts, York Univ, ON 1975–81, Assoc Prof of Art History 1975–95, Prof 1995–, Dean Faculty of Fine Arts 1985–88, Co-Dir MBA Programme in Arts and Media Man, Faculty of Admin Studies 1994–, acting Dir Graduate Programme in Art History 1994–95, Robart Chair in Canadian Studies 1995–96; Dir The Canada Council 1989–92; mem Int Council of Fine Arts Deans, Int Asscn of Art Critics, Canadian Asscn of Fine Arts Deans; mem Bd Inst for Research on Public Policy 1990–92, Laidlaw

Foundation 1992–. *Publications:* Author: Art 1976, J. W. G. Macdonald: The Inner Landscape 1981, Christopher Pratt 1985, Jock Macdonald 1986; Co-Author: Frederick Varley 1983, Kathleen Munn and Edna Taçon: New Perspectives on Modernism in Canada 1988. *Address:* Faculty of Fine Arts, York Univ, 4700 Keele St, North York, ON M3J 1P3, Canada (Office); 99 Metcalfe St, Ottawa, ON K1P 5V8, Canada (Home). *Telephone:* (613) 598-4301 (Office); *Fax:* (613) 598-4411 (Office).

ZENKER, Silvia; German pianist; b Kiel; d of Erich and Gerda (née Rohwer) Zenker. *Education:* London, Lübeck and Hamburg. *Career:* Piano duettist with Ulrike Bachmann-Arnold (qv) 1984–89, Evelinde Trenkner 1989–; nat and int concert tours 1985–, toured fmr USSR 1991–92; has performed on radio and TV; first album made 1986; First Prize in Music, Possehlstiftung, Lübeck 1984; Hanse-Kulturpreis, Stadt Lübeck 1987; First Prize Carlo Soliva Music Competition, Italy 1988. *Leisure interests:* foreign languages, travel, sports.

ŽERTOVÁ, Jiřina; Czech artist; b 13 Aug 1932, Prague; d of Josef Rejholec and Marie Rejholcová; m Bedřich Žert 1951; one s one d. *Education:* Coll of Art (Prague) and Acad of Applied Art (Prague). *Career:* Specialist in blown-glass design, incorporating other media into her works such as metal, wood and paint, movng on to paint on a layer of flat glass in the early 1990s; solo exhibitions include Museum of N Bohemia 1975, Gallery Centrum (Prague) 1981, 1984, 1987, Gallery Gottschalk-Betz (Frankfurt, Germany) 1988, Gallery Miller (New York) 1992; group exhibitions include Triennale di Milano 1957, 1960, Expo '58 (Brussels) 1958, Montréal Expo (Canada) 1967, German tour 1973, Brno 1974, New Glass Exhibition, Corning Museum (New York) 1979, Annecy (France) 1979, UK tour 1986, Musée des Arts Décoratifs (Lausanne, Switzerland) 1989, Sculptures in Glass (Liège, Belgium) 1989, Verre de Bohème (Paris) 1989, Expo du Vitrailes (Romont and Chartres, France) 1989, Int Exhibition of Glass (Kanazawa, Japan) 1989, Neues Glass in Europa (Düsseldorf, Germany) 1989, 1990, Le Verre (Rouen, France) 1991–92, Heller Gallery (New York) 1992, Bohemia Crystal (Sergovia, Spain) 1993, Vychodočeské Museum (Pardubice) 1994, 1999, Int Glass Exhibition (Venezia Aperto Vetro, Italy) 1996, Bender Art Calender 1998, Art Gallery (Ostrova, Czech Repub) 2000, Verriales (Biot, France) 2001; worked freelance in Czechoslovakia; subject of book: Glass of Jirina Zertova 2000; mem Glass Artists' Asscn of France; Silver Medal Triennale di Milano 1957; Coburger Glasspreis 1977, 1985; Prague Glass Prize 1991. *Publication:* Dictionnaire du Design et des Arts Appliqués 1997. *Leisure interests:* literature, nature. *Address:* Fragnerova 38, 160 00 Prague 6, Czech Republic (Home); Jindřišská 11, 110 00 Prague 1, Czech Republic (Office). *Telephone:* (2) 33331456; *Fax:* (2) 33331456; *E-mail:* jirina@zertova.com; *Internet:* www.zertova.com.

ZEUMER, Brigitta; German artist; b 31 May 1939, Rendsburg; d of Hans and Annemarie Rochlitz; m Axel Zeumer 1962 (divorced 1986); three s. *Education:* Univ of Hamburg. *Career:* Painter in watercolours and oils; exhibitions include Cologne 1971, Del Bello Gallery (Toronto, Canada First Prize in Watercolour category) 1988, Berlin, Hamburg, Bonn, Frankfurt, Düsseldorf, Stuttgart, Munich, UK, France, Monaco, Italy, Austria, Switzerland, Spain, Belgium, Hong Kong, USA, Japan, Canada; invited to exhibit works in the People's Repub of China in the Great Hall of the Palace (Beijing), Jiangsu Art Gallery (Nanking) and Shanghai 1991; has participated in int art fairs including Cologne, Düsseldorf, Frankfurt, Basle (Switzerland), Ghent (Belgium), Barcelona (Spain), Chicago and New York (USA); works have been reproduced as posters, postcards and calendars and in art books; Gold Medal, Ministry of Culture, People's Repub of China 1993. *Leisure interests:* music, theatre. *Address:* Große Telegraphenstr 14, 50676 Cologne, Germany. *Telephone:* (221) 213426; *Fax:* (221) 216085.

ZEZINA, Maria; Russian historian; b 26 Aug 1949, Moscow; d of Rostislav and Nina (née Bratzeva) Dadykin; m Nikolai Zezin 1972; one s. *Education:* Moscow State Univ. *Career:* Tutor and Lecturer in Sovietology, Dept of History, Moscow State Univ 1975–85, apptd Sr Lecturer 1985; part-time Lecturer Samarkand State Univ 1989, Russian Humanitarian Univ 1989–90. *Publications:* Istoria Kultury Narodov SSR (History of the Culture of the Soviet Nations, jtly) 1988, Istoria Russkoi Kultury (History of Russian Culture) 1990; numerous articles.

Leisure interests: travel, gardening, music. *Address:* 117513 Moscow, Leninskii prospekt, dom 123, k 3, kv 247, Russian Federation. *Telephone:* (095) 438-35-45.

ZHANG CAIZHEN; Chinese party official; b July 1930, Ningbo, Zhejiang Prov; m 1958; one d. *Education:* Tongji Univ (Shanghai). *Career:* Head of Art Troupe, Drama Unit, 2nd Field Army 1948–50; Sec Literature and Art Section, Propaganda Dept (SW Office) 1950–54; Sec, Head of Research, Deputy Dir of Gen Office, then Dir of Policy Research Dept, Comm for Physical Culture and Sports 1954–85, apptd Deputy Minister in Charge 1985; Vice-Pres Chinese Olympic Cttee 1986; Vice-Chair All-China Sports Fed 1986; Pres Chinese Softball Asscn 1986, Chinese Soft Tennis Asscn 1987; First Vice-Pres Asian Soft Tennis Fed 1987, Int Soft Tennis Fed 1990; Pres Strategical Research Soc of Devt of Physical Culture in China; Deputy Council Dir of Chinese Sports Science Soc; Adviser Chinese Qigong Research Soc; Medallist of Olympic Order 1993. *Publications:* The Spring of China's Sports, The Honour of China's Sports, The Spring of China's Table Tennis, China's Contemporary Sports (collective award as Assoc Ed-in-Chief, Medal of Honour in Sports 1986). *Address:* State Commission for Physical Culture and Sports, 9 Tiyuguan Rd, Beijing, People's Republic of China.

ZHANG DEDI; Chinese sculptor; b 9 Feb 1932, Jinan, Shandong Prov; d of Zhang Hui-ruo and Zhu Di-hua; m Zhang Runkai 1956; two s. *Education:* Cen Inst of Fine Arts (Beijing). *Career:* Mem staff Research Inst of Sculpture Creation, Cen Inst of Fine Arts 1955–, later Prof; exhibitions include Beijing, Shanghai, Repub of China (Taiwan), Japan, Italy; works feature in perm collections including Ravenna Dante Centre Museum of Italy, Chinese Art Gallery, Chinese Physical Culture Cttee, Soc of Artists (Beijing); has created sculptures for cities in ten Chinese provinces; mem Nat Cttee Urban Sculpture Art, Jury Cttees for Ministry of Culture; has published numerous research papers. *Sculptures include:* Little Dawa (Silver Medal Beijing Art Exhibition) 1981, Song Qingling Memorial Statue (Award for Best Work, First All-China Urban Sculpture Competition 1984) 1983, Day and Night (Silver Medal Sixth Nat Art Exhibition) 1984, Invitation From the Orient (Presidential Award, Int Sculpture Competition, Ravenna, Italy) 1985, The Ship Sailing in the Course of History (Silver Award, Int Sculpture Competition, Ravenna) 1990. *Leisure interest:* dance. *Address:* Research Institute of Sculpture Creation, Central Institute of Fine Arts, 5 Xiaowei hutong, E Dist, Beijing, People's Republic of China. *Telephone:* (10) 5075860.

ZHANG GUOYING; Chinese politician; b 1935, Dongguan Co, Guangdong Prov. *Career:* Vice-Pres All-China Women's Fed Exec Cttee 1988–; mem 12th CCP Cen Cttee 1982–87, 13th 1987–92, 14th 1992; a Deputy Sec CCP 7th Guangdong Prov Cttee 1990–; Political Commissar Unit in Tibet 1992–. *Address:* All-China Women's Federation, Beijing, People's Republic of China.

ZHANG JIE, BA; Chinese writer; b 27 April 1937, Beijing; d of Zhang Shanzhi; m Sun Youyu 1986; one d. *Education:* People's Univ (Beijing). *Career:* Deputy Ed-in-Chief Xinhua News Agency 1986–; Visiting Prof Wesleyan Univ, Middletown, CT, USA 1989–90, 1994–95; Council mem Chinese Asscn of Writers; mem Beijing Political Consultative Conf; Vice-Pres Beijing Writers' Asscn; mem Int PEN; Hon mem American Acad and Inst of Arts and Letters; Nat Awards for Short Stories, Novella and Novel (only writer to have won all three awards 1949–2000); several other awards. *Publications:* Novels: Heavy Wings (Maodun Nat Award 1985) 1981, Only One Sun 1988, My Unlettered Heart 1998; Short stories and novellas: A Child From the Forest (Nat Short Story Award) 1978, Who Lives a Better Life (Nat Short Story Award) 1979, Conditions Have Not Ripened Yet (Nat Short Story Award) 1983, The Ark 1983, The Emerald (Nat Award for Novellas) 1985, Zhang Jie's Literature 1986, As Long as Nothing Happens, Nothing Will (Malaparte Literary Prize, Italy 1989), Smaragd, Inner Fire 1992; Collections: Love Must Not Be Forgotten 1980, Zhang Jie's Collection of Short Stories and Movie Scripts 1980, On a Green Lawn 1983, A Chinese Woman in Europe 1989, You Are a Friend of My Soul 1990, Gone is the One Who Held Me Dearest in the World 1994, My Unlettered Heart (vol I) 1998; five collections of memoirs; works have been published in Germany, France, Sweden, UK, the Netherlands, Norway, USA, Brazil, fmr USSR, etc. *Leisure interest:* music. *Address:*

501, #97 Qian Men Xi Da Jie, Beijing 100031, People's Republic of China; c/o Tang Di, 20 Hemlock Drive, Sleepy Hollow, NY 10591, USA. *Telephone:* (10) 6603-8673 (Beijing); (914) 631-3761 (USA).

ZHANG JIN; Chinese aeronautical engineer. *Education:* Qinghua Univ, Beijing. *Career:* Began career in research and design of aircraft engines; Prof Beijing Univ of Aeronautics and Astronautics; advanced new method for predicting aircraft engine breakdowns; devised Jin's Method (computes dynamic performance of propeller blades); Guest Prof MIT; Guest Research Fellow Univ of California at Berkeley; participated in World Conf on Mechanics 1992; has written numerous papers on the computation of structural dynamics and mechanics of new complex materials. *Address:* Beijing University of Aeronautics and Astronautics, 37 Xueyuan Rd, Beijing 100083, People's Republic of China.

ZHANG KANG KANG; Chinese writer; b 3 July 1950, Hangzhou, Zhejiang Province; d of Zhang Bai Huai and Zhu Wei Xian; m Liu Jiamin 1983; one s. *Education:* Coll of the Humanities and Luxun Inst of Literature. *Career:* Farm labourer during Cultural Revolution 1969–77; writer 1972–; Vice-Chair Heilongjiang Br, Chinese Writers' Asscn; winner of various nat prizes for novellas and short stories. *Publications include:* The Light 1972, The Dividing Line 1975, The Thin Morning Mists (Nat Novella Prize 1980), Summer (Nat Short Story Prize 1980) 1981, Olive 1982, Cruelty, The Northern Lights 1981, The Fourth World, Sandstorm, The Red Poppy Flower 1985, The Invisible Companion 1987, The Gallery of Love, Self-selected Works of Zhang Kang Kang (5 vols), The Epidemic Disease (Fiction Month Prize 1988), Dialogue Between Men on the Globe 1990. *Leisure interests:* music, travel. *Address:* Heilongjiang Provincial Writers Association, Harbin, Heilongjiang Province, People's Republic of China.

ZHANG MING; Chinese government official; b June 1922, Hebei Prov; m Xue Weimin; two d one s. *Education:* North China Union Univ. *Career:* Fought in war following Japanese invasion 1940–45; mem staff Govt of Hebei Province 1945–49; apptd Deputy Dir of Personnel Bureau, Chinese Govt 1949; apptd Vice-Minister Ministry of Civil Affairs 1949, apptd Special Adviser 1987; apptd Deputy Dir Nat Cttee on Ageing and Vice-Pres Red Cross Soc of China 1949; elected mem CPPCC 1987. *Leisure interests:* reading, calligraphy. *Address:* 9 Xihuang-Chenggen Nanjie, Xicheng Dist, Beijing, People's Republic of China. *Telephone:* (10) 6017244.

ZHANG RUIFANG; Chinese film producer; b 1918, Beijing. *Career:* Fmr Dir Actors' Section, Shanghai Film Studio; Chair Shanghai Asscn of Film Producers 1994–; Hon mem Fed of Chinese Literary and Art Circles 1997–. *Address:* Shanghai Asscn of Film Producers, Shanghai, People's Republic of China.

ZHANG YU; Chinese actress and diplomatist; b Oct 1957, Shanghai; m Zhang Jianya. *Education:* USA. *Career:* Mem 8th NPC 1993–; Amb to Guyana 1994–99. *Films include:* Evening Rain (Hundred Flowers Best Actress Award) 1981, Love at Lushan (Golden Rooster Best Actress Award) 1981. *Address:* c/o Shanghai Film Studio, 595 Caoxi Beilu St, Shanghai City, People's Republic of China.

ZHAO BAOZHEN; Chinese diplomatist; b 1943, Tianjin. *Career:* Amb to Madagascar 1994, concurrently to the Comoros (first People's Repub of China female amb to African countries) 1995–96. *Address:* c/o Ministry of Foreign Affairs, 225 Chaoyangmennei Dajie, Dongsi, Beijing, 100701, People's Republic of China.

ZHAO DI; Chinese politician; b 1938, Weinan Co, Shaanxi Prov. *Career:* Vice-Mayor Kaifeng City; mem Standing Cttee Henan Prov CCP Cttee 1983, Deputy Sec 1984–86; a Vice-Pres All-China Women's Fed 1992–, also a Sec 1991–; alt mem CCP Cen Cttee 1985–; mem Standing Cttee of Cen Comm for Discipline Inspection. *Address:* Central Committee of the Chinese Communist Party, Zhongnanhai, Beijing, People's Republic of China.

ZHAO QING, (Ludan); Chinese dancer and choreographer; b 16 Nov 1936, Shanghai City; d of Zhao Dan and Ye Luxi; m Chen Mingyuan. *Education:* Beijing Dancing Coll. *Career:* Prin actress China Opera and Dance Drama Theatre 1959–, First Grade Dancer 1982–; Prin Dancer

Chinese Art Del to France, England, Italy, USA, USSR, Poland, Singapore, Japan, Latin America; mem 8th Nat Cttee CPPCC 1993–; mem China Dancers Asscn; Gold Medal (World Youth Festival); Excellent Performance Award 1980; First Prize Ministry of Culture for 'The Sword' (ballet) 1982. *Performances include:* The Lotus Lantern (ballet), Xiaodao Hui (ballet) 1961, Liang Zhu (ballet) 1962, The Red Silk Dance 1978, The Sword 1980, The Poetry of the Sea 1982, Children of Dragon (TV) 1983–84, Golden Dream (film) 1984–85, Luotuo Xiangzi (ballet) 1986, Luoshen (ballet) 1987, Dance of Calligraphy 1990, The Father and the Daughter (ballet) 1993. *Address:* 2 Nanhuadong St, Hufang Rd, Beijing, 100050, People's Republic of China.

ZHAO YANXIA; Chinese opera singer; b 29 April 1928, Beijing; d of the late Zhao Xiaolou; m Liu Xinyuan; one d. *Education:* Performance School (Beijing). *Career:* Actress Beijing Opera, Beijing Opera Theatre 1961–; has toured People's Repub of China. *Plays include:* Story of Susan, The Pavilion of Red Palm, The Fairy in the Blue Wave, The Story of the White Snake. *Leisure interests:* appreciating music, films, reading, cookery. *Address:* 24 Xisibai 2nd Lane, Beijing 100034, People's Republic of China. *Telephone:* (10) 66161121.

ZHAO YUFEN, PH D; Chinese academic and chemist; b 1948, Hankou, Hubei Prov. *Education:* Taiwan Univ and State Univ of New York. *Career:* Researcher State Univ of New York until 1979; mem staff Chemistry Inst, Chinese Acad of Sciences 1979–, began research on the origin of life, elected academician 1991; mem staff Nat Tsing Hua Univ 1988–, later formed theory suggesting link between phos-amino acids and the origin of life, later Dir Bio-organic Phosphorus Chemistry Lab, State Educ Comm and Vice-Pres School of Life Science and Engineering; elected academician Int Acad of Science 1995; working with Peking Univ to establish the Int Soc for Study of the Origin of Life; has attended several int confs on chem; has written numerous publications for scientific journals. *Address:* c/o School of Life Science and Engineering, Nat Tsing Hua University, 101, Sec 2, Kuang Fu Rd, Hsinchu, Republic of China (Taiwan).

ZHELYASKOVA-PANAYOTOVA, Maria, PH D; Bulgarian geologist; b 22 May 1928, Yambol; d of Dimitar Zhelyaskov and Sasha Zhelyaskova; m Georgi Panayotov 1952; two d. *Education:* Univ of Moscow. *Career:* Asst Faculty of Geology and Geography, Sofia Univ 1952–54, Lecturer 1958–65, Asst Prof 1965–72, Prof of Econ Geology 1972, apptd Head Dept of Econ Geology and Geochemistry 1969; Pres Bulgarian Geological Soc 1980–86, Carpath-Balkan Geological Asscn since 1989; apptd Vice-Pres Bulgarian Nat Geological Cttee 1980; has published over 150 articles, monographs and books; has received numerous state awards, and First Prize for Best Textbook 1986–87. *Leisure interest:* collecting dolls and miniature paintings. *Address:* Sofia University, Faculty of Geology and Geography, 1000 Sofia, 15 Tzar Osvoboditel blvd, Bulgaria; Sofia, 13B Yanko Sakuzov Blvd, Bulgaria (Home). *Telephone:* (2) 46-50-27 (Office); (2) 44-41-86 (Home); *Fax:* (2) 46-35-89 (Office).

ZHENG FENGRONG; Chinese sports administrator; b 18 May 1937, Shan Dong Prov; m Duan Qi Yan 1967; two d. *Education:* Beijing Sports Univ. *Career:* Vice-Chair Chinese Athletic Asscn 1977; Chief Dir Dept of Sports Competition Admin, SCSPC 1979; Chair Bd China Int Sports Travel Corpn 1985; Man Sino-American Exploration, Yangtze River 1986; Exec Deputy Sec-Gen All-China Sports Fed 1989–93. *Leisure interest:* tennis. *Address:* 9 Tipuguan Rd, Beijing, People's Republic of China. *Telephone:* (10) 67112325; *Fax:* (10) 67115858.

ZHENG XIAOYING; Chinese conductor and professor of music; b 27 Sept 1929, Shanghai; d of Zheng Wei and Wen Siying; m Liu Enyü 1974; one d. *Education:* Ginling Coll and Cen Conservatory of China. *Career:* Studied under L. N. Tymascheve, N. P. Anosov, G. N. Rozhdestvensky and I. B. Bain, Moscow P. I. Tchaikovsky State Conservatoire, USSR (now Russian Fed); mem Song and Dance Troupe 1949; teacher and Conductor Cen Conservatory 1950–60, 1963–; performances include Cen Conservatory Chorus and Symphony Orchestra, Radio Orchestra of USSR (Kremlin Theatre, Moscow) 1961–63, Moscow Musical Theatre 1962, Hong Kong Performing Arts Festival, Savonlinna Opera Festival (Finland), Singapore Inaugural, Macau Int Music Festival, Chinese Arts Festival; has conducted Cen

Philharmonic, China Broadcasting Orchestra, Canberra Orchestra (Australia), Hong Kong Philharmonic; Chief Conductor Cen Opera Theatre 1978–88; Founder, Musical Dir and Conductor Women's Chamber Orchestra, Capital Opera Inst 1988; lecturer in field; mem Exec Council Chinese Musicians' Asscn; has made numerous recordings; awarded Special Honour for Outstanding Women 1979, 1983, Nat First Prize for Conductors 1981, La Donna Nel Mondo 1983, French Arts and Literature Meda. *Works performed include:* Ayiguli, The Song of the Grass, The 100th Bride, La Traviata, Tosca, Madam Butterfly, Carmen, The Marriage of Figaro, The Magic Flute, Rigoletto, Turandot, Beethoven and Brahms Symphonies, works by Tchaikovsky, Debussy, Mahler, etc. *Leisure interests:* travel, sports. *Address:* Central Conservatory, Beijing, People's Republic of China (Office); 113, 2-906, Dong Zhong Jie, Beijing 100020, People's Republic of China (Home). *Telephone:* (1) 5003019 (Home).

ZHOU JIHONG; Chinese diver and coach; b 11 Jan 1965, Hubei; m Tian Bingyi 1990. *Education:* Univ of Beijing. *Career:* Gold Medal in platform diving, World Championships 1983; Gold Medallist in platform diving, Olympic Games, Los Angeles, CA, USA 1984; currently diving coach. *Leisure interests:* singing, dance. *Address:* State Physical Culture and Sports Commission, 2 Ti Yuguan Rd, Beijing, People's Republic of China. *Telephone:* (10) 7102266.

ZHU LILAN; Chinese scientist and organization official; b 18 Aug 1935, Zhejiang Province; d of Yan Boyou and Zhu Zhixian; m Fan Yaozu 1965; one s one d. *Education:* Shanghai No 3 Girls' Middle School and Odessa Univ (Ukraine, fmr USSR). *Career:* Head of Research Group Inst of Chemistry, Chinese Acad of Sciences 1961–78, Deputy Chief of Research Lab, then Dir 1981–85; Visiting Scholar Inst of Polymer Chemistry, Freiburg Univ, Germany 1978–80; Vice-Chair State Science and Tech Comm of China 1986–91, apptd Exec Vice-Chair 1991; Major Achievement Award, Chinese Acad of Sciences 1978; awarded two nat prizes of Excellent Application 1984. *Publications:* A New Staining Technique for Electron Microscopy of Poly(ester)s and Segmented Copolymers (with Ester Linkages) 1981, The Morphology of Semicrystalline Segmented Poly(etherester) Thermoplastic Elastomers Makromt 1981, Relationship Between Crystallization Rate and Tensile Behaviour of PET Films 1982, Morphotogical Studies of PET Films with Different Crystallization Rate in Drawing Process 1984. *Leisure interest:* music. *Address:* State Science and Technology Commission, Beijing, People's Republic of China (Office); 15B Fuxing Rd, Beijing 100862, People's Republic of China (Home). *Telephone:* (10) 68512648; *Fax:* (10) 6851259.

ZHU LIN; Chinese actress; b 7 April 1923, Lian Yungang, Jiangsu Province; d of Zhu Xiaofang and Zhao Shouxuan; m Diao Guangtan 1942; three s one d. *Education:* Hua Yin Teaching Coll and Wu Chang Art Training Scool. *Career:* Actress Anti-Japanese troupe 1938–49, Datong Film Studio 1948–50, China Youth Art Theatre 1950–52, Beijing People's Art Theatre 1953–; currently People's Rep, Beijing; mem Standing Cttee China Dramatists' Asscn; title Class A Actress conferred; Hon Award for promoting Chinese Drama 1988; Best Actress Award, Beijing 1989. *Films include:* Weakling, Your Name is Woman, Trials and Hardships, Profile of a Smatterer, Film Fan, Waiting, The Last Emperor (Gold Eagle Prize for Best Supporting Actress) 1989, Su Wu Graze Sheep 1996; *Plays include:* Put Down Your Whip 1937, Yan Wei Port, Sunrise, Death of An Actor, March of Triumph, Spring Cold, Beautiful Women 1947, Thunderstorm 1953, Three Sisters 1959, Cai Wenji 1959, 1962, 1978, Wu Zetian 1962–64, Death of a Salesman 1983, Jin Game 1987, Der Besuch der Alten Dame, Candied Haws on a Stick 1996, Thunderstorm 1997. *Leisure interests:* singing, music. *Address:* Room 601, Unit 2, Bldg 38, Dongzhi Menwai St, Beijing 100027, People's Republic of China. *Telephone:* (10) 64168165.

ZHU XI JUAN, BA; Chinese actress and television producer; b 17 Jan 1938; m Feng-Min Hou 1964; one s one d. *Education:* Shanghai Drama Coll. *Career:* Actress and Manager Shenzhen TV Centre. *Films include:* The Woman Army (Best Actress Award) 1962, Mountain Love 1964, The Last Anniversary 1989, A Delegate at Law (Best Actress Award) 1991; *Plays include:* Nothing Trouble 1961, Dirty Hand 1980, Goodbye Paris 1980, Break (First Prize, Guangdong Art Award) 1987. *Leisure*

interests: plants, swimming. *Address:* Shenzhen Television Co, Rm 302, Bldg 27, Tong Xing Ling, Shenzhen, Guangdong, People's Republic of China. *Telephone:* (755) 244095.

ZHUANG YONG; Chinese swimmer; b 10 Aug 1972, Shanghai; d of Zhuang Fuling and Chen Weili. *Education:* Shanghai Sports Technology Inst. *Career:* Silver Medallist in 100m freestyle swimming event, Olympic Games, Seoul 1988; Gold Medallist in 100m and 200m freestyle, 4 x 100m freestyle and 4 x 100m medley relay, 11th Asian Games 1990; winner 50m freestyle World Swimming Championships 1991; Olympic Silver Medallist in 50m freestyle event, Olympic Games, Barcelona, Spain 1992. *Leisure interests:* music, studying language, travel. *Address:* State Swimming Team, 2 Tiyuguan Rd, Beijing 100001, People's Republic of China. *Telephone:* (1) 7012266.

ZI HUAYUN; Chinese dancer and dance teacher; b 10 March 1936, Tianjin City; d of Zi Yaohua and Tong Yijun; m Wang Shouyin 1960; one s one d. *Education:* Tianjin Nankai High School, Beijing Normal Univ and Beijing Cen Drama Coll. *Career:* Dancer China Cen Dance Ensemble 1950–; Dir and Sr Fellow Dance Research Inst of Chinese Arts Acad 1987–; Chief Ed The Art of Dance; prizes include Gold Medal for Tibetan Dance (Third World Youth Festival, Berlin) 1950, Bronze Medal for Flying Apsara (Fifth World Youth Festival, Warsaw) 1955, Prize for Excellent Performance (First Nat Dancing Competition) 1984. *Publications:* Dance and I 1987, Chinese and Foreign Artists 1989, Introduction to Choreology (jtly) 1991, Treatises on Choreology (jtly), The Rise and Development of Chinese Folk Dance during the past 50 years 1992, Collection of Essays of Hua Yun 1994, Fantasy of Dance 1995, Graceful Life 1997, The Art of Dance and Theory of Dance 1998, The Chinese Dance 1999, Studying Keeps Young for Ever 2000. *Address:* Dance Research Institute, Chinese Academy of Arts, 17 Qianhai Xijie, Beijing 100009, People's Republic of China.

ZI ZHONGYUN, BA; Chinese researcher and professor of international relations; b 22 June 1930; d of Zi Yaohua and Tong Yijun; m Chen Lemin 1957; one d. *Education:* Yaohua High School, Univs of Yenching and Qinghua. *Career:* Mem Chinese People's Cttee for the Defense of World Peace 1951–72; Asst to Chinese Rep at Secr of World Council of Peace 1956–59; Head of American Affairs, Chinese People's Asscn for Friendship with Foreign Countries 1972–80; Research Fellow Chinese Inst of Int Studies 1980–85; Visiting Fellow Inst of Int Studies, Princeton Univ (USA) 1982–83; Sr Fellow Inst of American Studies, Chinese Acad of Social Sciences 1987–, Deputy Dir 1985–88, Dir 1988–92; Fellow Woodrow Wilson Center, Washington (DC) Jan–Sept 1991; Ed Journal of American Studies 1993–98; Pres Soc for Chinese Scholars of Sino-American Relations 1993–97; mem Exec Cttee Chinese Asscn for American Studies 1988–2000; concurrently mem Bd of Dirs Chinese People's Inst of Foreign Affairs; mem Standing Cttee Pacific Soc of China; Prof Johns Hopkins–Nanjing Univ Center for Chinese and American Studies; Chair Research Council Inst of Int Research Johns Hopkins–Nanjing Center; recipient Outstanding Woman of the Nation Award 1983, Outstanding Scholar of the Nation (title for life) 1992, Chinese Acad of Social Sciences Prize for Work Published 1995–98 2000. *Publications:* The Origin and Evolution of US Policy Towards China 1945–50 (prize for best work in social sciences 1979–1994, Chinese Acad of Social Sciences 1994) 1987, (added title: Tracing the Roots) 2000, Forty Years of US–Taiwan Relations 1949–89 (ed) 1992, A History of Postwar US Foreign Relations from Truman to Reagan (ed and leading author) 1994, On the Shore of the Sea of Learning (essays, jtly) 1995, Building up a Bridge of Understanding: American Studies in China 1979–93 (ed) 1996, Revelations of the Ups and Downs of the 20th Century (2 vols, ed and jt author) 2000; numerous articles and essays on the US, Sino–US relations, history, culture and intellectual and social critique; translations from French and English literature including Balzac and Willa Cather. *Leisure interest:* piano. *Address:* Chinese Academy of Social Sciences, Institute of US Studies, 3 Dong Yuan, Zhangzizhong Rd, Beijing 100007, People's Republic of China; Fangguyuan Yiqu, 1-3-404, Fangzhuang, Beijing, 100078, People's Republic of China. *Telephone:* (10) 67611414; *Fax:* (10) 64000021; *E-mail:* zizy@public3.bta.net.cn.

ZIA, Begum Khaleda; Bangladeshi politician; b 15 Aug 1945, Dinajpur Dist; d of the late Iskander Majumder and of Begum Taiyaba Majumder; m Gen Ziaur Rahman 1960 (fmr Pres of Bangladesh, assassinated 1981); two s. *Education:* Surendranath Coll (Dinajpur). *Career:* Held captive during Bangladesh's war of independence; Vice-Chair Bangladesh Nat Party (BNP) 1982–84, Chair 1984–; helped to form seven-party alliance leading to ousting of Pres Ershad from power 1990; elected Prime Minister of Bangladesh 1991–96, Minister of Information, Energy and Establishment 1991, of Defence, of the Establishment and of the Cabinet Div 1991; Chair South Asian Asscns for Regional Co-operation (SAARC) 1993–94. *Leisure interests:* reading, listening to music, gardening. *Address:* c/o BNP, 29 Minto Rd, Dhaka, Bangladesh. *Telephone:* (2) 328292.

ZIACH, Krystyna; Netherlands/Polish artist; b 13 June 1953, Poland. *Education:* Acad of Fine Arts (Cracow), Jagiellonian Univ (Poland) and Acad of Fine Arts (Enschede, Netherlands). *Career:* Has lived in the Netherlands since 1979; workshop in Perspektief, Rotterdam 1986, in Projects UK, Newcastle upon Tyne 1991; work-project, Japan 1987; solo exhibitions include Arti et Amicitiae, Amsterdam 1988, Gallery Moment, Hamburg (Germany) 1989, RAM Gallery, Rotterdam 1993, Netherlands Photography Museum Sittard 1994, Netherlands Photography Inst, Rotterdam 1996; group exhibitions include Photography Biennale, Rotterdam 1988, Photography Biennale, Vigo (Spain) 1988, Galleria d'Arte Moderna, Bologna (Italy) 1988, Musée de la Photographie, Charleroi (Belgium) 1989, Gallery Lichtbild, Bremen (Germany) 1991, Outer Space touring exhibition (UK) 1992, Museum of Fine Arts, Houston, TX (USA) 1994, Worlds in a Box touring exhibition (UK) 1994, Whitechapel Art Gallery, London 1995, Copenhagen 1996; works in perm collections including Netherlands Office for Fine Arts, Foundation of Visual Arts, Amsterdam, Museum of Fine Arts, Houston, TX, (USA), Musée de la Photographie, Charleroi, Museum Ludwig, Cologne (Germany), Maison Européenne de la Photographie, Paris, Bibliothèque Nat de France, Paris, pvt colls in the Netherlands and abroad. *Publications include:* Nude 1987, Erotim in der modernen Fotografie 1987, Krystyna Ziach – Melancholie (catalogue) 1990, Krystyna Ziach – A Garden of Illusion (catalogue) 1993; numerous exhibition catalogues. *Leisure interest:* travel. *Address:* 'S Gravesandeplein 11, No 3, 1091 BB Amsterdam, Netherlands. *Telephone:* (20) 668-16-40; *Fax:* (20) 668-16-40.

ZIDE-BOOTH, Rochelle Deena, BA; American dancer, dance teacher and choreographer; b 21 April 1938, Boston, MA; d of David Sewell and Ruth (née Sawyer) Zide; m Robert Elliot Booth 1964; two s one d. *Education:* Adelphi Univ (New York), American Ballet Center (New York) and Ballet Theater School (New York). *Career:* Soloist Ballet Russe de Monte-Carlo 1954–58; Prin Dancer Robert Joffrey Ballet 1958–62, Ballet Mistress 1973–75; Prima Ballerina New York Opera Ballet 1962–65; Artistic Dir Netherlands Dance Theatre, The Hague 1973–75; Head of Ballet Program Jacob's Pillow Dance Festival, MA 1975–79; Prof of Ballet Adelphi Univ 1975–88, apptd Prof of Performing Arts and Dance 1988; Faculty mem Alvin Ailey American Dance Center 1989; apptd Adjudicator Nat Asscn of Regional Ballet 1973, First Nat Regional Dance Festival 1990; mem American Guild of Musical Artists, American Coll Dance Festival; has written articles for professional journals; Medal for Distinguished Service to Korean Ballet 1987; Merit Award for Teaching Excellence (Adelphi) 1988; Fulbright Lectureship 1991–92; Medal from Ministry of Educ (Czech Repub) 1992. *Ballets choreographed include:* Psalms 1979, As Quiet As... 1982, Russian Suite 1982, Folksing 1983, Freeplay 1984, Screen Scenes 1984, Glory Songs 1985, Silent Woods 1986, Rococo Variations 1986, Gershwin! 1987, A Midsummer Night's Dream 1987, The Sisters of My Sister 1988, Mujerio 1989, Bagatelle 1989, Classical Symphony, or the Balanchine Variations 1991. *Leisure interests:* theatre, music, concerts, reading, travel, baseball. *Address:* Adelphi University, Woodruff Hall, Garden City, NY 11530, USA (Office); 170–16 Henley Rd, Jamaica Estates, New York, NY 11432-2741, USA (Home). *Telephone:* (718) 526-4185 (Home).

ZIERITZ, Grete von; Austrian composer; b 10 March 1899, Vienna; d of Karl Ferdinand and Vera Henrica (née Neumann) von Zieritz; one d. *Education:* Konservatorium (Graz) and in Berlin. *Career:* Schubert Grant, Columbia Phonograph Co, New York 1928; has composed works for choirs, more than 140 songs, 59 pieces of chamber music, 13 works for orchestra, concertos, etc; works performed at Berlin Festival 1984, Moscow, Dresden, etc; Mendelssohn-Staatspreis 1928; Austrian Cross of Honour for Science and Art (First Class) 1978; Bundesver-

dienstkreuz 1979. *Publication:* Grete von Zieritz: Leben und Werk 1990. *Leisure interests:* crystal, mandrakes. *Address:* Marburger Str 16/III, 10789 Berlin, Germany. *Telephone:* (30) 2182954.

ZIMMERMAN, Jo Ann, BA; American nurse and state official; b 24 Dec 1936, Van Buren Co, IA; d of Russell and Hazel (née Ward) McIntosh; m A. Tom Zimmerman 1956; three s two d. *Education:* Broadlawns School of Nursing, Drake Univ and Iowa State Univ. *Career:* Nurse Maternity Dept, Broadlawns Medical Center 1958–68; Instructor in Maternity Nursing Broadlawns School of Nursing 1968–71; Health Planner, Community Relations Assoc, Iowa Health Systems Agency 1978–82; mem Iowa House of Reps 1982–86; Lieut-Gov of Iowa 1987–91; consultant health services Zimmerman and Assocs 1991–; Operations Dir Medlink Services 1992; Founder-mem Democratic Activist Women's Network (DAWN) 1992–; mem numerous cttees and comms on health and nursing; mem American Nursing Asscn, Family Centered Childbirth Educ Asscn, American Lung Asscn, Iowa Cattlemen's Asscn. *Address:* Zimmerman and Assocs, 7630 Asworth Rd W, Des Moines, IA 50266, USA.

ZIMMERMAN, Kathleen Marie; American artist; b 24 April 1923, Floral Park, NY; d of Harold and Evelyn (née Andrade) Zimmerman; m Ralph S. Iwamoto 1963. *Education:* Art Students' League (New York) and Nat Acad of Fine Arts (New York). *Career:* Teacher Midtown School, New York 1947–52; co-illustrator of Diet for a Small Planet 1971; solo exhibitions include Westbeth Gallery (New York) 1973, 1974, St Mary's Coll (MD) 1990; group exhibitions include Nat Acad of Design (New York) 1969, 1975–78, 1980, 1982, 1984, 1986, 1988, 1990, 1991, 1993–95, 1997, 1999, 2001, Edward Dean Museum (CA) 1975, 1976, 1977, Martello Museum (FL) 1976, Anchorage Fine Arts Museum (AL) 1976, Butler Inst of American Art (OH) 1978, Int Festival of Women Artists (Copenhagen) 1980, Bergen Museum (NJ) 1983, Kenkeleba Gallery (New York) 1985, Temperance Hall Gallery (New York) 1987, Lever House (New York) 1989; rep in perm collections including Sheldon Swope Art Museum (IN), Univ of Wyoming Art Museum, Butler Inst of American Art, N Carolina Museum of Art, Erie Art Center, Nat Acad of Design (New York), Zimmerli Museum (Rutgers Univ, NJ); represented in many books about collage and watercolour 1978–94; mem American Watercolor Soc, Allied Artists of America, Nat Asscn of Women Artists, Audubon Artists, Nat Acad of Design; recipient 14 awards from Nat Asscn of Women Artists 1957–96, American Watercolor Soc Award 1976; Aubudon Artists Award 1978, 1981, 1987, 1994; Allied Artists of America 1981, 1985, 1989, 1991, 1997, 1998; New York Artists Equity 1985; awards from Nat Acad of Design 1988, 1991, 1997, 2001; awards from Nat Soc of Painters in Casein and Acrylic 1997, 1999, 2001. *Leisure interest:* gardening. *Address:* 463 W St, A1110, New York, NY 10014, USA. *Telephone:* (212) 691-0259.

ZIMMERMANN, Wilmya; Netherlands politician; b 30 July 1944, Heerland. *Education:* Sittard (Nijmegen). *Career:* Technical Asst Heerlen Hosp, later Univs of Nijmegen and Marburg/Lahn and Nuremberg, Germany 1963–; moved to Germany 1974; mem SPD 1988–; Councillor, Forchheim 1993, Leader SPD Group, responsible for Social Policy, Women, Immigration and Employment; elected MEP 1994 (Germany's only foreign MEP), mem Cttee on Civil Liberties and Internal Affairs, Del to EU-Romania Jt Parl Cttee, Del to EU-Bulgaria Jt Parl Cttee. *Address:* European Parliament, rue Wiertz, 1047 Brussels, Belgium. *Telephone:* (2) 284-21-11; *Fax:* (2) 230-69-43.

ZINGALE, Roxanne, BA; American film editor; b 11 July 1961, Cleveland, OH; d of Joseph and Mary (née Erbland) Zingale. *Education:* Univ of Arizona, Loyola Univ (Rome) and Loyola Marymount Univ (Los Angeles, CA). *Career:* Feature Film Ed, Los Angeles 1984–. *Films:* Asst Ed: The Ladies Club, Wired to Kill, Aloha Summer, That's Life 1984; Ed: Vicious Lips 1985, Journey to the Center of the Earth 1986, Cyborg 1988, Deceptions 1989; Dir and Ed: Electricity (Jack Haley Award, Samuel Arkoff Award) 1984.

ZISKIN, Laura; American film producer. *Career:* Fmr writer for game shows; mem staff Jon Peters' production co; Co-Founder Fogwood Films with Sally Field; Pres Fox 2000 co. *Films include:* Assoc Producer: A Star is Born, The Eyes of Laura Mars; Producer: Murphy's Romance, No Way Out, DOA, The Rescue, Everybody's All American, Pretty

Woman (exec producer), What About Bob?, The Doctor, Hero (also co-story-writer), To Die For. *Address:* Laura Ziskin Productions, 10202 W Washington Blvd, Culver City, CA 90232-3195, USA.

ZLOKOVIĆ, Vera; musician and arts administrator; b 30 Nov 1950, Belgrade; d of Bozidar Zloković and Marianne Elisabeth Puschner; m Stefaan de Meester 1992. *Education:* Novi Sad Arts Acad. *Career:* Studied composition, conducting and singing, specializing in early music, Vienna, Liechtenstein, Basle (Switzerland) and Thessaloniki (Greece); Founder and Art Dir Musica Antiqua professional early music ensemble, Belgrade 1977–, and Musica Antiqua Serbiana study group, specializing in eary music of the Orthodox people 1987–; groups have performed at more than 1,700 concerts, festivals, radio and TV appearances in Yugoslavia and abroad; Ed numerous TV broadcasts, including Music of Elizabethan Epoch 1980, A Musical Feast 1983, Musica Adriatica 1986, Viva Musica Antiqua 1989–90, The East Empire Light 1985, The Presence of Prayer in Music and Music in Prayer 1996; has published 31 works; mem Asscn of Serbian Music Artists; numerous festival awards, including BEMUS Award, Belgrade Music Festival BEMUS 1987. *Address:* 11000 Belgrade, Kosovska, 32, Yugoslavia. *Telephone:* (11) 344736; *Fax:* (11) 602391.

ZOBEL, Rya W., BA, LL B; American federal judge; b 18 Dec 1931, Germany. *Education:* Radcliffe Coll and Harvard Univ. *Career:* Called to the Bar, MA 1956, US Dist Court 1956, US Court of Appeals 1967; mem Hill and Barlow, Boston, MA 1967–73, Goodwin, Procter and Hoar 1973–79; US MA Dist Judge, Boston 1979–; Dir Fed Judicial Court, Washington 1995–99; mem ABA, American Bar Foundation, American Law Inst. *Address:* US District Court, 1 Courthouse Way, Boston, MA 02210-3002, USA; 294 Jerusalem Rd, Cohasset, MA 02025, USA (Home).

ZOLOTOW, Charlotte Shapiro; American publishing executive and writer; b 26 June 1915, Norfolk, VA; d of Louis J. and Ella (née Bernstein) Shapiro; m Maurice Zolotow 1938 (divorced 1969); one s one d. *Education:* Univ of Wisconsin. *Career:* Editorial Dir Junior Books Dept, Harper and Row 1938–44, Sr Ed 1962–70; Vice-Pres and Assoc Publr Harper Jr Books 1976–81; Publr Emer, Advisor to Harper-Collins Jr Books 1991–; Editorial Dir Charlotte Zolotow Books 1982–90; mem PEN, Authors' League; Harper Gold Medal Award for Editorial Excellence 1974; Irvin Kerlan Award (Univ of Minnesota) 1986. *Publications include:* Children's books: The Park Book 1944, The Storm Book 1952, Over and Over 1957, Do You Know What I'll Do? 1958, Big Brother 1960, The Three Funny Friends 1961, Mr Rabbit and the Lovely Present 1962, A Tiger Called Thomas 1963, The Quarreling Book 1963, The Sky Was Blue 1963, Someday (Outstanding Children's Book of 1964–65) 1965, When I Have a Little Girl 1965, Big Sister and Little Sister 1966, If It Weren't For You 1966, When I Have a Little Boy 1967, My Friend John 1968, The Hating Book 1969, A Father Like That 1971, Wake Up and Goodnight 1971, Hold My Hand 1972, William's Doll (Outstanding Children's Book of 1972) 1972, Janey 1973, The Summer Night 1974, My Grandson Lew (Christopher Award) 1974, The Unfriendly Book 1975, When the Wind Stops 1975, May I Visit? 1976, It's Not Fair 1976, Someone New 1978, If You Listen 1980, But Not Billy 1983, The Poodle Who Barked at the Wind 1987, A Rose, a Bridge and a Wild Black Horse 1987, Sleepy Book 1988, Something is Going to Happen, The Seashore Book 1992, Snippets 1992, This Quiet Lady 1992, The Moon was Best 1993, Peter and the Pigeons 1993, The Old Dog 1995, Who is Ben 1997; Jr fiction short stories: An Overpraised Season 1973, Early Sorrow 1986. *Leisure interests:* books, music, flowers, friends. *Address:* Harper and Row Publishers Inc, 10 E 53rd St, New York, NY 10022, USA (Office); 29 Elm Place, Hastings-on-Hudson, NY 10706, USA (Home). *Telephone:* (914) 478-2655 (Home).

ZONG PU, (pseudonym of Feng Zhong-pu); Chinese writer; b 26 July 1928, Beijing; d of Feng You-lan and Zen Zaikun; m Cai Zhong-de; one d. *Education:* Qinghua Univ. *Career:* Mem Editorial Bds Literary Gazette and World Literature magazines; Researcher Inst of Foreign Literature, Chinese Acad of Social Science 1981–88. *Publications:* The Red Beans 1957, Melody in Dreams (Nat Prize for Short Stories) 1978, Who Am I? 1979, Lu Lu 1980, The Everlasting Rock (Nat Prize for Novella) 1980, Fairy Tales from a Wind Cottage 1984, Bear Palm (short stories) 1985, Lilac Knot (Nat Prize for Essay) 1986, Retreat to the South (Vol

I of Ordeal) 1988, The Story of a Fish (Nat Prize for Children's Literature) 1988, The Discourse on an Iron Flute 1994, Tales from a Windy Cottage (short stories) 1995, Collected Works of Zong Pu (4 vols) 1996, Hiding in the East (Vol II of Ordeal); numerous essays. *Leisure interests:* music, travel, calligraphy. *Address:* Beijing University, 57 Yan Nan Yuan, Beijing 100871, People's Republic of China.

ZORE-ARMANDA, Mira, D SC; Croatian oceanographer; b 6 Jan 1930, Zagreb; d of Miro Zore and Marija Nabergoj; m Igor Armanda 1959. *Education:* Univs of Zagreb and Paris (Sorbonne). *Career:* Scientific Asst Inst of Oceanography and Fisheries, Split 1952–61, Scientific Officer 1961–67, Sr Scientific Officer 1967–74, Prin Scientific Officer 1974–90, Dir 1976–78; now retd; has published about 150 scientific and technical papers concerning hydrography and dynamics of the Adriatic Sea and the Mediterranean. *Leisure interests:* history, reading. *Address:* 21000 Split, Šetalište Ivana Meštrovića 61, Croatia. *Telephone:* (21) 358217; *E-mail:* zore@izor.hr.

ZORRILLA, China; Uruguayan actress, director and producer; b 1922; d of José Luis Zorrilla de San Martín. *Education:* Royal Acad of Dramatic Art (London). *Career:* Worked with Ars Pulchra group, Uruguayan Ind Theatre, later worked as journalist and as actress and Dir Nat Theatre of Uruguay; Co-Founder Theatre of City of Montevideo 1961; directed show Canciones para mirar, New York 1965, later in Buenos Aires; staged Jacobo Langsner's El Tobogán and Neil Simon's Plaza Suite, Montevideo 1969; has made several films in Argentina; Dir Como en casa (TV show); newscaster Radio Belgrano; noted theatrical appearances include one-woman show Hola, hola, un, dos, tres (toured Argentina, Venezuela and USA) and as Emily in Spanish-language version of William Luce's The Belle of Amherst throughout Cen and S America and in USA.

ZOUNI, Opy; Greek artist; b 4 Feb 1941, Cairo; d of John and Helen Sarpakis; m Alexander Zounis 1965; two s. *Education:* Athens School of Fine Arts. *Career:* Solo exhibitions include: Desmos 1973, Athens Gallery 1975, 1978, 1990, 1992, Lausanne Museum of Fine Art 1980, Galerie Jeanneret (Geneva) 1982, Gallery 3 1984, Peter Noser Gallery (Zurich) 1985, Trito Mati 1986, Int Cultural Centre (Antwerp) 1986, Galerie Kara (Geneva) 1989, 1991, Vellidio Cultural Centre 1989, Athens French Inst 1992, Mylos 1993, Galerie Donguy (Paris) 1994, Kreonidis Gallery 1996, Art Forum Gallery 1996, Art Athina 4/Amymoni Gallery 1996, Municipal Gallery of Patras 1998, Stiftung für Griechische Kultur (Berlin) 1999, Museum of Cycladic Art (Athens) 1999, Art Forum Gallery 2000, Anemos Gallery, Art Athina 8 2000, Miart Milan 2001; group exhibitions include: Biennials of São Paolo 1979, Alexandria 1970, Ljubljana 1979, 1983, 1985, 1987, Contemporary Graphics with Medusa in collaboration with Alexander Iolas 1982, Bradford 1984, and numerous int exhibitions. *Film:* Light – Shadow – Co-incidences? (video-art installation) 1999; *Publications:* Symmetry 2 1989, Arte e Tecnologia 1993; bilingual monograph 1997; numerous articles in books and reviews. *Address:* 22 Vrilisson St, 152 36 P Penteli, Athens, Greece. *Telephone:* 8042-950; *Fax:* 8044-264.

ZUMA, Nkosazana Dlamini, B SC; South African politician; b 1949. *Education:* Amazimtoti Training Coll, Univ of Zululand and Univ of Bristol, UK. *Career:* Research technician, Univ of Natal 1972, later medical student; Vice-Pres South African Students Organisation 1976; escaped to UK, continued studies at Univ of Bristol; mem staff Frenchay Hosp, Bristol; returned to Africa 1980, worked in Swaziland and Zambia; Minister of Health, South Africa 1990; currently Minister of Foreign Affairs. *Address:* Ministry of Foreign Affairs, Union Bldgs, East Wing, Government Ave, Pretoria, 0002, South Africa. *Telephone:* (12) 3510005; *Fax:* (12) 3510243.

ZUNGU, Sibongile; South African tribal chief; b Dec 1962; m Bhekisizwe Zungu (deceased); two c. *Career:* Became first female tribal chief following death of her husband. *Address:* Madlebe Tribe, Kwa-Zulu, Natal, South Africa.

ZUTSHI, Gita, BA; Indian athlete; b 20 Dec 1956, Patna, Bihar. *Education:* Nat Inst of Sports and Secretarial Coll (New York). *Career:* Medical Sec, New York 1986–; winner of 400m and 800m events, Quaid-i-Azam Int Meet (Pakistan) 1976; Gold Medallist in 800m, Silver Medallist in 1,500m, Asian Games (Bangkok) 1978; Silver Medallist in

800m and 1,500m, Asian Games (India) 1982; Gold Medallist in 800m, Silver Medallist 1,500m, Asian Track and Field Championship (Tokyo) 1979, 1981; Gold Medallist in 800m Colgate Games (New York) 1988, holder of indoor 1,500m world record 1988; rep India at World Cup (Montréal, Canada) 1979 and Olympics (Moscow) 1980, (Los Angeles, USA) 1984; Arjun Award 1976; Haryana State Award 1982; Padma Shri award 1984. *Address:* 111 Acharya Puri, Gurgaon, Haryana, India; POB 1669, Cathedral Station, New York, NY 10025, USA. *Telephone:* (212) 439-1102 (USA).

ZVEREVA, Natalia (Natasha); Belarusian tennis player; b 16 April 1971, Minsk; d of Marat Zverev and Nina Zvereva. *Career:* Winner doubles (with Larisa Neiland) French Open 1989, (with Gigi Fernandez, qv) 1992–1995; winner doubles (with Larisa Neiland) Wimbledon 1991, (with Gigi Fernandez) 1992–1994; winner doubles (with Pam Shriver) US Open 1991, (with Gigi Fernandez) 1992, 1995; winner mixed doubles Australian Open 1990, 1995, doubles (with Gigi Fernandez) 1993–1994; Bronze Medallist in doubles (mem of Unified Team), Olympic Games, Barcelona, Spain 1992; winner doubles (with Gigi Fernandez) Pan Pacific 1996; Most Improved Female Pro Award, Tennis magazine 1988; Most Impressive Newcomer Award, Corel WTA Tour 1988; Doubles Team of the Year Award, Corel WTA Tour (with Larisa Neiland) 1992, (with Gigi Fernandez) 1993–1995. *Leisure interests:* listening to music, watching water polo, table tennis, nightclubs, reading. *Address:* c/o International Olympic Committee, Château de Vidy, 1007 Lausanne, Switzerland.

ZWEIFEL, Françoise; Swiss international organization executive; b 6 Feb 1944, Lausanne; m Ulrich Zweifel; two d. *Education:* Lausanne. *Career:* Fmrly mem staff Lausanne City Council working in tourism and econ devt; apptd to Int Olympic Cttee to re-open Musée Olympique, Lausanne 1982, Sec-Gen Int Olympic Cttee 1985–. *Leisure interests:* sports, particularly skiing. *Address:* Comité International Olympique, Château de Vidy, 1006 Lausanne, Switzerland. *Telephone:* (21) 6216111; *Fax:* (21) 6216216; *Internet:* www.olympic.org.

ZWICK, Lis; Danish/Swedish artist; b 16 Aug 1942, Copenhagen; d of Holger Eriksen and Ragna Zwick; m Jørgen Nash 1969; one s one d. *Education:* Acad of Fine Art (Aarhus), School of Graphic Art and Design (Copenhagen) and the Bauhaus Situationist Drakabygget Wrkshop of Freedom (Sweden). *Career:* More than 50 solo exhibitions since 1963, in Scandinavia, México, Museo Nacional de Belle Artes (Havana), Paris, London, Tokyo, Munich, Hamburg, Cologne, Düsseldorf and Berlin (Germany), Reykjavík, etc; group exhibitions include Alternativ Documenta, Kassel (Germany) 1972, Centre Culturel Suèdois, Paris 1980, Salon de Tokyo, Museum of Modern Art, Tokyo 1982, Graphic Biennal, Ljubliana (then Yugoslavia), Int Exhibition of Original Drawings, Museum of Modern Art, Riijeka (Yugoslavia), FIAC, Grand Palais, Paris 1988, Ueno Municipal Art Museum, Tokyo 1989, Musée d'Art Moderne, Paris 1989, Royal Coll of Art, London 1990, Int Biennale of Graphic Art, Tallinn 1992; retrospective exhibition, Selected Works from 1963–96, Landskrona Art Hall, Sweden; works rep in perm collections including Malmö Museum, Museum of Modern Art, México, Statens Kunsfond, Denmark, Kobe Art Museum, Japan, Museo Nacional de Belle Artes, Havanna, Riksdagshuset, Stockholm, Univ of Copenhagen; appeared on Japanese TV 1988; has had two biographies written about her; Bauhaus Situationist Drakabygget Prize 1964; Artist of the Month, Danish TV 1984; Kobe Mayor Prize, Japan 1988; First Prize, Malmö City Monumental Painter; Graphic Award, Stockholm 1995. *Leisure interests:* travelling round the world, music, film, theatre, ballet, classical and modern art. *Address:* The Bauhaus Situationist Drakabygget, 286 92 Örkelljunga, Sweden. *Telephone:* (435) 802 81; *Fax:* (435) 802 58.

ZWILICH, Ellen Taaffe, D MUS; American composer; b 30 April 1939, Miami, FL; d of Edward and Ruth (née Howard) Taaffe; m Joseph Zwilich 1969 (died 1979). *Education:* Florida State Univ and Juilliard School (New York). *Career:* Violinist American Symphony, New York 1965–73; Composer-in-Residence Santa Fe Chamber Music Festival 1990, American Acad, Rome 1990; Carnegie Hall Composer's Chair 1995–; Lifetime Hon mem American Fed of Musicians; Guggenheim Fellow 1981; elected mem American Acad of Arts and Letters 1992;

Hon D MUS (Oberlin Coll) 1987, (Manhattanville Coll) 1990, (Marymount Manhattan Coll, Converse Coll) 1994, (New School, Mannes Coll) 1995; Elizabeth Sprague Coolidge Chamber Music Prize 1974; Gold Medal G. B. Viotti, Vercelli, Italy 1975; Ernst Von Dohnanyi Citation 1981; Pulitzer Prize 1983; Acad Award, American Acad of Arts and Letters 1984; Arturo Toscanini Music Critics Award 1987; Florida Artists Hall of Fame 1993; Musical America Composer of the Year 1999. *Compositions include:* Einsame Nacht 1971, Im Nebel 1972, Sonata in Three Movements 1973, String Quartet 1974, Clarino Quartet 1977, Chamber Symphony 1979, Passages 1981, String Trio 1982, Symphony No 1: Three Movements for Orchestra (Grammy nomination) 1982, Fantasy for Harpsichord 1983, Double Quartet for Strings 1984, Concerto Grosso 1985, Concerto for Piano and Orchestra 1986, Tanzspiel 1987, Symphony No 2 (Grammy nomination) 1985, Piano Trio 1987, Concerto for Trombone and Orchestra 1988, Symbolon 1988, Concerto for Bass Trombone, Strings, Timpani and Cymbals 1989, Concerto for Flute and Orchestra (Grammy nomination) 1989, Concerto for Oboe and Orchestra 1990, Quintet for Clarinet and Strings 1990, Concerto for Violin, Cello and Orchestra 1991, Concerto for Bassoon and Orchestra 1992, Symphony No 3 (Grammy nomination) 1992, Concerto for Horn and String Orchestra 1993, Fantasy for Orchestra 1993, American Concerto for Trumpet and Orchestra 1994, A Simple Magnificat 1994, Triple Concerto 1995, Jubilation 1995, Peanuts Gallery 1996, Violin Concerto 1997, String Quartet No 2 1998, Lament for Piano 1999, Upbeat! 1999, Symphony No 4 1999, Lament for Cello and Piano 2000, Millennium Fantasy for Piano and Orchestra 2000, Partita for Violin and String Orchestra 2000. *Address:* 600 W 246th St, Riverdale, NY 10471, USA.

ZWINGER, Anne Haymond, MA; American natural history writer and illustrator; b 12 March 1925, Muncie, IN; d of William T. and Helen G. Haymond; m Herman H. Zwinger 1952; three d. *Education:* Wellesley Coll, Indiana Univ (Bloomington) and Radcliffe Coll (Cambridge, MA). *Career:* Freelance natural history writer and illustrator 1969–; Outdoor Consultant for various river cos since 1975; apptd Dir American Electric Power 1977; Adjunct Prof Colorado Coll since 1980; Trustee Nature Conservancy 1984; endowed Chair Hulbert Center for Southwest Studies 1991; Dr hc (Colorado Coll) 1976, (Carleton Coll) 1984; Burroughs Medal for Natural History Writing 1976; Wellesley Coll Alumnae Award 1977. *Publications:* Beyond the Aspen Grove 1970, Land Above the Trees 1972, Run, River Run 1975, Wind in the Rock 1978, A Desert Country Near the Sea 1983, The Mysterious Lands 1987; numerous further books and articles in magazines. *Leisure interest:* reading. *Address:* c/o Frances Collin, Rodell-Collin Literary Agency, 110 W 40th St, New York, NY 10018, USA.

ZYKINA, Lyudmila Georgiyevna; Russian singer; b 10 June 1929, Cheremushki, Moscow Region. *Education:* Ippolitov-Ivanov School of Music. *Career:* Soloist with Pyatnitsky Choir 1947–51; soloist with Choir for Russian Vocal Music of Union Radio and TV Station 1951–60; soloist with Moskontsert 1960–77; Artistic Dir Ensemble Russia 1977–; Pres Moscow Regional Charity Public Foundation of Peace 1998–, Russian Acad of Folk Art; mem of Council Our Home is Russia Movt 1995–99; People's Artist of the RSFSR 1968; Lenin Prize 1970; People's Artist of the USSR 1973, Glinka Prize 1983, Kyrill and Methodius Prize 1998, Ovation Prize 1998; People's Artist of Russia, Ukraine, Azerbaijan; Hero of Socialist Labour. *Address:* Moscow, Kotelnicheskaya nab 15 Korp B, kv 64, Russian Federation. *Telephone:* (095) 245-18-13.

ZYLIS-GARA, Teresa; Polish soprano; b 23 Jan 1935, Vilnius; m; one c. *Education:* State Higher School of Music (Łódź). *Career:* Soloist Cracow Philharmonic 1954–58 and Cracow Opera 1958–59; foreign contracts in operas at Oberhausen 1961–63, Städtishce Bühnen, Dortmund 1963–65, Deutsche Oper am Rhein, Düsseldorf (all Germany) 1965–70; debuts abroad at Paris Opera 1966, San Francisco Opera (USA) 1968, Metropolitan Opera, New York 1968, Royal Opera House, Covent Garden (London) 1968, Vienna Opera 1970, Nat Theatre, Prague 1974, Nat Theatre, Budapest 1976, Great Theatre, Warsaw 1976, La Scala, Milan (Italy) 1977, Bolshoi Theatre, Moscow 1978, Teatro Colón, Buenos Aires 1981; has participated in int festivals including Glyndebourne (UK) 1965, Salzburg (Austria) 1968, Aix-en-Provence (France) 1972, Orange (France) 1975; has performed in many countries; regular performances at Metropolitan Opera, New York 1968–; also song recitals; renowned for interpretation of works by Szymanowski; Prime Minister's Prize (First Class) 1979; Knights' Cross Order of Polonia Restituta. *Address:* 16A blvd de Belgique, Monaco.

INDEX BY CAREER

Index by Career

Entrants are listed under career headings in alphabetical order. The index gives the Name, First Names, Nationality and Profession of the entrants. The index headings and the pages on which each starts, are as follows:

INDEX BY CAREER

ART

BROADCASTING AND JOURNALISM

BUSINESS AND BANKING

CIVIL AND PUBLIC SERVICE

DIPLOMACY

FASHION

FILM AND THEATRE

LAW

LITERATURE

MEDICINE

NATIONAL AND INTERNATIONAL
ORGANIZATIONS

POLITICS AND GOVERNMENT

RELIGION

SPORT AND LEISURE

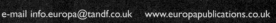

Major Titles from Europa

The European Union Encyclopedia and Directory

- The very latest information on the European Union
- Charts the Union's development from its creation, through the Treaty of Amsterdam, to present day policies and activities
- Includes an A-Z section, introductory articles, a statistical section and an extensive directory, including details of all major European Union institutes and their official bodies
- Details MEPs, their political groups and national parties, members of major committees, Directorates-General and other Commission bodies

The Environment Encyclopedia and Directory

- Provides an A-Z section of key terms relating to the environment
- A directory section organized alphabetically by country lists main governmental and non-governmental organizations, both national and international
- A series of maps show areas of pollution, rainforest and other environmental features both regionally and world-wide
- Includes an extensive bibliography of relevant periodicals
- A Who's Who section of people actively involved with environmental organizations

The Directory of University Libraries in Europe

- Extensive information on central and other university libraries of European universities and, where appropriate, details of attached institutes and research centres
- Almost 4,000 entries, with full contact details, including the names of chief librarians and other relevant staff, and further information such as size and composition of library holdings, on-line subscription details and details of libraries' own publications
- Fully indexed

The Territories of the Russian Federation

- This new reference survey provides much needed up-to-date information on the 89 constituent units of the Russian Federation
- Over 300 pages of 100 current maps, analysis, statistics and detailed information
- Provides comprehensive individual territory surveys
- Includes a chronology of Russia, an essay on the economic perspective of the Russian federative system and an introduction to the structure of the Federal Government

A Political & Economic Dictionary of Eastern Europe

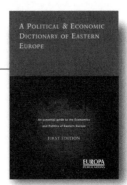

- A new dictionary written by a respected team of reference book compilers
- Over 1,000 concise entries concerning the politics and economics of central, eastern and south-eastern Europe, trans-Caucasus and the Russian Federation
- Information is provided on the countries, regions, ethnic groups, political parties, prime ministers, presidents and other prominent politicians, business organizations, geographical features, religions and border disputes
- Includes separate articles on each country, and on its economy

A Dictionary of Human Rights

By David Robertson

- Over 200 mini articles, arranged alphabetically and extensively cross-referenced
- Explanations of the terms, issues, organizations and laws occurring within the subject of human rights
- Outlines the significance of eminent thinkers, such as Locke, Cardozo and Nozick
- Contains extracts of leading documents, such as the Declaration of the Rights of Man and of the Citizen and the Convention on the Rights of the Child

Europa's Regional Surveys of the World

A unique series of regularly revised reference titles aimed at businesses, libraries, universities, government departments, embassies, newspapers and international organizations

'Europa's Regional Surveys of the World are justly renowned for their exceptionally high levels of production, content and accuracy.' Reference Reviews

South America, Central America and the Caribbean

- An incomparable source of factual and statistical information for this vast region
- Reflects the very latest political and economic developments
- Includes contributions from over 30 leading authorities on Latin American and Caribbean affairs
- Provides a systematic survey of each country
- Enlightened commentary on topical issues, such as international trade and the banana war, the environment and the drug crisis

Africa South of the Sahara

- A one-volume library of essential data on all the countries of Sub-Saharan Africa
- Over 1,200 pages of economic and demographic statistics, wide-ranging directory material and authoritative articles
- Contributions from 50 leading experts on African affairs
- Incisive analysis and the latest available information
- Includes details of international organizations active in the region

Central and South Eastern Europe

- This title is one of the two new successor volumes to Europa's award-winning Eastern Europe and the Commonwealth of Independent States
- Includes country-by-country surveys, political, economic and social information
- Detailed articles by acknowledged experts cover issues of regional importance such as integration with the West, social policy and religion, the Macedonian Question
- Coverage of regional organizations, research institutes and periodicals
- A select bibliography and a political profile section

Western Europe

- Over 660 pages of statistics, directory and analytical information
- Introductory essays on the region cover political, economic and social issues ranging from the impact of the European Union to Western Europe's environmental politics and its relations with the wider world
- Acknowledged authorities write on regional and country-specific topics
- Chronologies detailing the history of each country

Eastern Europe, Russia and Central Asia

- This title is one of the two successor volumes to the award-winning Eastern Europe and the Commonwealth of Independent States
- Includes country-by-country surveys, political, economic and social information
- Articles by acknowledged authorities covering regional issues such as the politics of energy and the environment
- Coverage of regional organizations, institutes and periodicals
- A select bibliography and a political profile section

The Middle East and North Africa

- Covers the Middle Eastern world from Algeria to Yemen
- Draws together the events of the past twelve months
- Provides comprehensive information on the United Nations and all major international organizations operating in the area
- A detailed calendar of events, expert articles, up to date statistics and directory information
- An invaluable reference source in business matters relating to the area

The Far East and Australasia

- A systematic survey of all the countries of East Asia, South Asia, South-East Asia, Australasia and the Pacific Islands
- Essential for anyone with a professional interest in this part of the world, the book keeps you up to date with current economic and political developments
- Presents over 1,400 pages of statistics, directory information and expert analysis
- Provides details of all major international organizations active in the region

The USA and Canada

- Invaluable reference guide to the political, economic and social affairs of these two powerful North American nations
- Contributions from over 30 acknowledged authorities
- Specially commissioned articles cover issues such as the USA and the United Nations, Aboriginal Peoples in North America, the Canadian Economy
- Includes wide-ranging statistics and directory information
- Provides geographical and historical introductions to each state/province, data on the economies, and a comprehensive governmental and legislative directory section

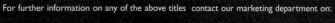

For further information on any of the above titles contact our marketing department on:

tel. + 44 (0) 20 7842 2110   fax. + 44 (0) 20 7842 2249

e-mail info.europa@tandf.co.uk   www.europapublications.co.uk

Other Titles from Europa

Political Chronologies of the World Series

- Each of the six volumes profiles the major events in the histories of the region
- Includes an individual chronology for each country
- The chronologies provide concise details of events from early history to the mid-twentieth century and present greater detail on more recent events
- Available individually or as a six-volume set

A Political Chronology of Europe
A Political Chronology of Central, South and East Asia
A Political Chronology of the Middle East
A Political Chronology of Africa
A Political Chronology of South-East Asia and Oceania
A Political Chronology of the Americas

The International Who's Who of Women

- Over 5,500 detailed biographies of the most talented and distinguished women in the world today
- Includes women from all occupations, from Heads of State to supermodels
- Over 500 new entries for this edition
- Includes an extensive index by profession
- A must for libraries and press offices

Gutteridge and Megrah's Law of Bankers' Commerical Credits

- Presents a systematic study of the law of bankers' commercial credits
- Includes a table of cases and statutes relevant to bankers' commercial credits
- Provides information on the types of credit, mechanism and operation
- Discusses the legal aspects; relationship between buyer and seller; bankers' security

A Dictionary of Modern Politics

By David Robertson

- A thorough guide to the complex terminology and ideology which surrounds the world of politics
- Over 500 definitions/mini essays
- Defines political theories, ideas and "isms"
- Explains highly specialized terms
- Invaluable for anyone concerned with politics and current affairs

The International Directory of Government

- The definitive guide to people in power world-wide
- Details over 17,500 government ministries, departments, agencies, corporations and their connected bodies and people who work within them
- Also includes an outline of the each country's legislature and governmental system
- Explains the constitutional position of the head of state
- Entries contain: name and title of principal officials, postal and e-mail address, telephone, telex and fax numbers, and an outline of each organization's activities

International Relations Research Directory

- Directory information on every major research institute concerned with international relations throughout the world
- Provides details of institutes names, address, telephone, fax and e-mail, principal officers, date of foundation, activities and publications
- Lists periodicals and journals in the field of international relations with details of name, address, telephone, fax and e-mail, editor, publisher, date of foundation, subject of coverage, frequency and circulation

Who's Who in International Affairs

- Provides up-to-date biographical information on more than 7,000 principal figures in the fields of international politics, economics, legal, medical, cultural and scientific affairs
- Fully indexed by organization and nationality, it is a useful directory of international organizations as well as an invaluable A-Z guide of leading personalities
- Each entry contains, where available, name, nationality, date of birth, family details, education, career details, publications, contact address, telephone, fax numbers, e-mail addresses and leisure interests

Profiles of People in Power: the World's Government Leaders

- Individual country sections explain the types of government; the respective roles of the head of state, the head of government and the legislature
- Lists the most recent heads of state and head of goverment, with dates of office
- Biographical profiles of the current head of state and head of government and other significant past leaders who remain an active political presence
- Photographic section of many of the world's political leaders